Stanley Gibbons
Simplified Catalogue

Stamps of the World

Stanley Gibbons Simplified Catalogue

Stamps of the World

2015 Edition

Countries **German Commands – Jasdan**

3

Stanley Gibbons Ltd
London and Ringwood

BY APPOINTMENT TO
HER MAJESTY THE QUEEN
PHILATELISTS
STANLEY GIBBONS LTD
LONDON

1914 - 2014

80th Edition
Published in Great Britain by
Stanley Gibbons Ltd
Publications Editorial, Sales Offices and Distribution Centre
7, Parkside, Christchurch Road,
Ringwood, Hampshire BH24 3SH
Telephone +44 (0) 1425 472363

British Library Cataloguing in
Publication Data.
A catalogue record for this book is available
from the British Library.

Volume 3
ISBN 10: 0-85259-931-5
ISBN 13: 978-0-85259-931-0

Boxed Set
ISBN 10: 0-85259-936-6
ISBN 13: 978-0-85259-936-5

Published as Stanley Gibbons Simplified Catalogue from 1934 to 1970,
renamed Stamps of the World in 1971, and produced in two (1982-
88), three (1989-2001), four (2002-2005) five (2006-2010) and six from
2011 volumes as Stanley Gibbons Simplified Catalogue of Stamps of
the World.

© Stanley Gibbons Ltd 2014

Item No. 2881– Set 15

Printed and bound in Wales by Stephens & George

Contents – Volume 3

Introduction

The ultimate reference work for all stamps issued around the world since the very first Penny Black of 1840, now with an improved layout.

Stamps of the World provides a comprehensive, illustrated, priced guide to postage stamps, and is the standard reference tool for every collector. It will help you to identify those elusive stamps, to value your collection, and to learn more about the background to issues. *Stamps of the World* was first published in 1934 and has been updated every year since 1950.

Included is a guide to stamp identification so that you can easily discover which country issued your stamp.

Re-designed to provide more colourful, clearer, and easy-to-navigate listings, these volumes continue to present you with a wealth of information to enhance your enjoyment of stamp collecting.

Features:

▶ Current values for every stamp in the world

▶ Easy-to-use simplified listings

▶ World-recognised Stanley Gibbons catalogue numbers

▶ A wealth of historical, geographical and currency information

▶ Indexing and cross-referencing throughout the volumes

▶ Worldwide miniature sheets listed and priced

▶ Thousands of new issues since the last edition

For this edition, prices have been thoroughly reviewed for Great Britain and the Channel Islands up to date, and all Commonwealth countries up to 1970, with further updates for Commonwealth countries which have appeared in our recently-published or forthcoming comprehensive catalogues under the titles *Brunei, Malaysia and Singapore, Falkland Islands, Western Pacific, St Helena and Dependencies, New Zealand and Canada*. Other countries with complete price updates from the following comprehensive catalogues are: *Italy and Switzerland, Russia* and *China*. New issues received from all other countries have been listed and priced. The first *Gibbons Stamp Monthly* Catalogue Supplement to this edition is September 2014.

Information for users

Scope of the Catalogue

Stamps of the World contains listings of postage stamps only. Apart from the ordinary definitive, commemorative and air-mail stamps of each country there are sections for the following, where appropriate. Noted below are the Prefixes used for each section (see Guide to Entries for further information):

▶ postage due stamps –   Prefix in listing D

▶ parcel post or postcard stamps –   Prefix P

▶ official stamps –   Prefix O

▶ express and special delivery stamps -   Prefix E

▶ frank stamps –   Prefix F

▶ charity tax stamps –   Prefix J

▶ newspaper and journal stamps –   Prefix N

▶ printed matter stamps –   Prefix P

▶ registration stamps -   Prefix R

▶ acknowledgement of receipt stamps –   Prefix AR

▶ late fee and too late stamps –   Prefix L

▶ military post stamps-   Prefix M

▶ recorded message stamps –   Prefix RM

▶ personal delivery stamps –   Prefix P

▶ concessional letter post –   Prefix CL

▶ concessional parcel post –   Prefix CP

▶ pneumatic post stamps –   Prefix PE

▶ publicity envelope stamps –   Prefix B

▶ bulk mail stamps –   Prefix BP

▶ telegraph stamps used for postage –   Prefix PT

▶ telegraph stamps (Commonwealth Countries) – Prefix T

▶ obligatory tax –   Prefix T

As this is a simplified listing, the following are NOT included:

Fiscal or revenue stamps: stamps used solely in collecting taxes or fees for non-postal purposes. For example, stamps which pay a tax on a receipt, represent the stamp duty on a contract, or frank a customs document. Common inscriptions found include: Documentary, Proprietary, Internal Revenue and Contract Note.

Local stamps: postage stamps whose validity and use are limited in area to a prescribed district, town or country, or on certain routes where there is no government postal service. They may be issued by private carriers and freight companies, municipal authorities or private individuals.

Local carriage labels and Private local issues: many labels exist ostensibly to cover the cost of ferrying mail from one of Great Britain's offshore islands to the nearest mainland post office. They are not recognised as valid for national or international mail. Examples: Calf of Man, Davaar, Herm, Lundy, Pabay, Stroma.

Telegraph stamps: stamps intended solely for the prepayment of telegraphic communication.

Bogus or "phantom" stamps: labels from mythical places or non-existent administrations. Examples in the classical period were Sedang, Counani, Clipperton Island and in modern times Thomond and Monte Bello Islands. Numerous labels have also appeared since the War from dissident groups as propaganda for their claims and without authority from the home governments. Common examples are the numerous issues for Nagaland.

Railway letter fee stamps: special stamps issued by railway companies for the conveyance of letters by rail. Example: Talyllyn Railway. Similar services are now offered by some bus companies and the labels they issue likewise do not qualify for inclusion in the catalogue.

Perfins ("perforated initials"): stamps perforated with the initials or emblems of firms as a security measure to prevent pilferage by office staff.

Labels: Slips of paper with an adhesive backing. Collectors tend to make a distinction between stamps, which have postal validity and anything else, which has not.

Cut-outs: Embossed or impressed stamps found on postal stationery, which are cut out if the stationery has been ruined and re-used as adhesives.

Further information on a wealth of terms is in *Philatelic Terms Illustrated*, published by Stanley Gibbons, details are listed under Stanley Gibbons Publications. There is also a priced listing of the postal fiscals of Great Britain in our *Commonwealth & British Empire Stamps 1840-1970* Catalogue and in Volume 1 of the *Great Britain Specialised Catalogue* (5th and later editions). A full list of our current publications is given on page xiv

Organisation of the Catalogue

The catalogue lists countries in alphabetical order with country headers on each page and extra introductory information such as philatelic historical background at the beginning of each section. The Contents list provides a detailed guide to each volume, and the Index has full cross-referencing to locate each country in each volume.

Each country lists postage stamps in order of date of issue, from earliest to most recent, followed by separate sections for categories such as postage due stamps, express stamps, official stamps, and so on (see above for a complete listing).

"Appendix" Countries

Since 1968 Stanley Gibbons has listed in an appendix stamps which are judged to be in excess of true postal needs. The appendix also contains stamps which have not fulfilled all the normal conditions for full catalogue listing. Full catalogue listing requires a stamp to be:

- ▶ issued by a legitimate postal authority
- ▶ recognised by the government concerned
- ▶ adhesive
- ▶ valid for proper postal use in the class of service for which they are inscribed
- ▶ available to the general public at face value with no artificial restrictions being imposed on their distribution (with the exception of categories such as postage dues and officials)

Only stamps issued from component parts of otherwise united territories which represent a genuine political, historical or postal division within the country concerned have a full catalogue listing. Any such issues which do not fulfil this stipulation will be recorded in the Catalogue Appendix only.

Stamps listed in the Appendix are constantly under review in light of newly acquired information about them. If we are satisfied that a stamp qualifies for proper listing in the body of the catalogue it will be moved in the next edition.

"Undesirable Issues"

The rules governing many competitive exhibitions are set by the Federation Internationale de Philatelie and stipulate a downgrading of marks for stamps classed as "undesirable issues".

This catalogue can be taken as a guide to status. All stamps in the main listings are acceptable. Stamps in the Appendix are considered, "undesirable issues" and should not be entered for competition.

Correspondence

We welcome information and suggestions but we must ask correspondents to include the cost of postage for the return of any materials, plus registration where appropriate. Letters and emails should be addressed to Lorraine Holcombe, 7 Parkside, Christchurch Road, Ringwood, Hampshire BH24 3SH, UK. lholcombe@stanleygibbons.co.uk. Where information is solicited purely for the benefit of the enquirer we regret we are seldom able to reply.

Identification of Stamps

We regret we do not give opinion on the authenticity of stamps, nor do we identify stamps or number them by our Catalogue.

Thematic Collectors

Stanley Gibbons publishes a range of thematic catalogues (see page xiv for details) and *Stamps of the World* is ideal to use with these titles, as it supplements those listings with extra information.

Type numbers

Type numbers (in bold) refer to illustrations, and are not the Stanley Gibbons Catalogue numbers.

A brief description of the stamp design subject is given below or beside the illustrations, or close by in the entry, where needed. Where a design is not illustrated, it is usually the same shape and size as a related design, unless otherwise indicated.

Watermarks

Watermarks are not covered in this catalogue. Stamps of the same issue with differing watermarks are not listed separately.

Perforations

Perforations – all stamps are perforated unless otherwise stated. No distinction is made between the various gauges of perforation but early stamp issues which exist both imperforate and perforated are usually listed separately. Where a heading states, "Imperf or perf" or "Perf. or rouletted" this does not necessarily mean that all values of the issue are found in both conditions

Se-tenant Pairs

Se-tenant Pairs – Many modern issues are printed in sheets containing different designs or face values. Such pairs, blocks, strips or sheets are described as being *"se-tenant"* and they are outside the scope of this catalogue, although reference to them may occur in instances where they form a composite design.

Miniature Sheets are now fully listed.

Guide to Entries

(A) Country of Issue

(B) Part Number – shows where to find more detailed listings in the Stanley Gibbons Comprehensive Catalogue. Part 6 refers to France and so on – see p. li for further information on the breakdown of the Catalogue.

(C) Country Information – Brief geographical and historical details for the issuing country.

(D) Currency – Details of the currency, and dates of earliest use where applicable, on the face value of the stamps. Where a Colony has the same currency as the Mother Country, see the details given in that country.

(E) Year Date – When a set of definitive stamps has been issued over several years the Year Date given is for the earliest issue, commeorative sets are listed in chronological order. As stamps of the same design or issue are usually grouped together, a list of King George VI stamps, for example, headed "1938" may include stamps issued from 1938 to the end of the reign.

(F) Stanley Gibbons Catalogue number – This is a unique number for each stamp to help the collector identify stamps in the listing. The Stanley Gibbons numbering system is universally recognized as definitive. The majority of listings are in chronological order, but where a definitive set of stamps has been re-issued with a new watermark, perforation change or imprint date, the cheapest example is given; in such cases catalogue numbers may not be in numerical order.

Where insufficient numbers have been left to provide for additional stamps to a listing, some stamps will have a suffix letter after the catalogue number. If numbers have been left for additions to a set and not used they will be left vacant.

The separate type numbers (in bold) refer to illustrations (see M).

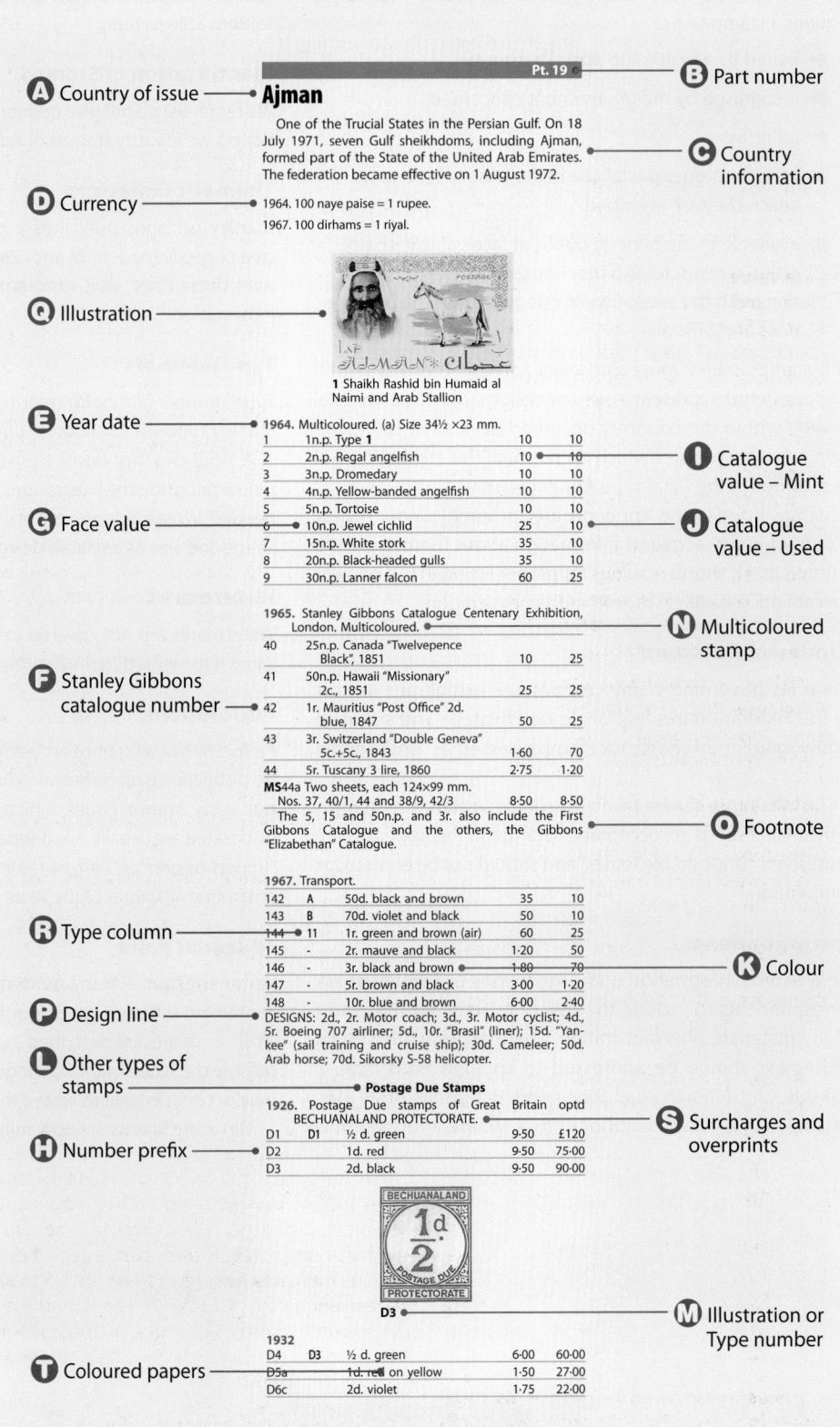

(A) Country of issue → **Ajman**

Pt. 19 (B)

(B) Part number

One of the Trucial States in the Persian Gulf. On 18 July 1971, seven Gulf sheikhdoms, including Ajman, formed part of the State of the United Arab Emirates. The federation became effective on 1 August 1972.

(C) Country information

(D) Currency
1964. 100 naye paise = 1 rupee.
1967. 100 dirhams = 1 riyal.

(Q) Illustration

1 Shaikh Rashid bin Humaid al Naimi and Arab Stallion

(E) Year date — 1964. Multicoloured. (a) Size 34½ ×23 mm.

			Mint	Used
1	1	1n.p. Type **1**	10	10
2		2n.p. Regal angelfish	10	10
3		3n.p. Dromedary	10	10
4		4n.p. Yellow-banded angelfish	10	10
5		5n.p. Tortoise	10	10
6		10n.p. Jewel cichlid	25	10
7		15n.p. White stork	35	10
8		20n.p. Black-headed gulls	35	10
9		30n.p. Lanner falcon	60	25

(I) Catalogue value – Mint

(J) Catalogue value – Used

1965. Stanley Gibbons Catalogue Centenary Exhibition, London. Multicoloured.

40	25n.p. Canada "Twelvepence Black", 1851		10	25
41	50n.p. Hawaii "Missionary" 2c., 1851		25	25
42	1r. Mauritius "Post Office" 2d. blue, 1847		50	25
43	3r. Switzerland "Double Geneva" 5c.+5c., 1843		1·60	70
44	5r. Tuscany 3 lire, 1860		2·75	1·20

(N) Multicoloured stamp

MS44a Two sheets, each 124x99 mm. Nos. 37, 40/1, 44 and 38/9, 42/3 | 8·50 | 8·50

The 5, 15 and 50n.p. and 3r. also include the First Gibbons Catalogue and the others, the Gibbons "Elizabethan" Catalogue.

(O) Footnote

1967. Transport.

142	A	50d. black and brown	35	10
143	B	70d. violet and black	50	10
144	11	1r. green and brown (air)	60	25
145	-	2r. mauve and black	1·20	50
146	-	3r. black and brown	1·80	70
147	-	5r. brown and black	3·00	1·20
148	-	10r. blue and brown	6·00	2·40

(R) Type column

(K) Colour

DESIGNS: 2d., 2r. Motor coach; 3d., 3r. Motor cyclist; 4d., 5r. Boeing 707 airliner; 5d., 10r. "Brasil" (liner); 15d. "Yankee" (sail training and cruise ship); 30d. Cameleer; 50d. Arab horse; 70d. Sikorsky S-58 helicopter.

(P) Design line

Postage Due Stamps

(L) Other types of stamps

1926. Postage Due stamps of Great Britain optd BECHUANALAND PROTECTORATE.

D1	D1	½ d. green	9·50	£120
D2		1d. red	9·50	75·00
D3		2d. black	9·50	90·00

(S) Surcharges and overprints

(H) Number prefix

D3

(M) Illustration or Type number

1932

D4	D3	½ d. green	6·00	60·00
D5a		1d. red on yellow	1·50	27·00
D6c		2d. violet	1·75	22·00

(T) Coloured papers

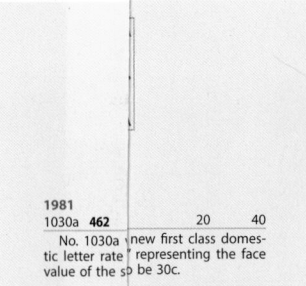

1981
1030a **462**   20   40
No. 1030a new first class domestic letter rate representing the face
value of the s be 30c.

Ⓖ **Face value** to the value of each
stamp and t was sold for at the
Post Office d. Some modern
stamps do eir values in figures
but instead tter, see for example
the entry a a 1030a/Illustration
462.

Ⓗ **Number** amps other than
definitive emoratives have a
prefix lett catalogue number.
Such stam nd at the end of the
normal list ountry. (See Scope of
the Catalo list of other types of
stamps co er with the list of the
main abb d in the Catalogue).

Other also used in the
Catalogue explained in the text:
some exa or airmail, E for East
Germany livery stamps.

Ⓘ **Catalogu** int/Unused. Prices
quoted fo amps are for lightly
hinged ex es quoted of unused
King Edw en Elizabeth II issues
are for un t.

Ⓙ **Catalogu** ed. Prices generally
refer to f used examples. For
certain iss or cancelled-to-order.

Prices

Prices pence and pounds.
Stamps w d over are shown in
whole po

Sh	
Cata	
as	
10	10 pence
1.7	£1.75
15	£15
£1	£150
£2	£2300

Prices amps are in 'fine
conditio sk more for superb
and less f lower quality. The

minimum catalogue price quoted is 10p and
is intended as a guide for catalogue users. The
lowest price for individual stamps purchased
from Stanley Gibbons is £1.

**Prices quoted are for the cheapest
variety of that particular stamp**. Differences
of watermark, perforation, or other details,
outside the scope of this catalogue, often
increase the value. Prices quoted for mint
issues are for single examples. Those in
se-tenant pairs, strips, blocks or sheets may
be worth more. Where no prices are listed it
is either because the stamps are not known
to exist in that particular condition, or,
more usually, because there is no reliable
information on which to base their value.

**All prices are subject to change without
prior notice and we cannot guarantee to
supply all stamps as priced**. Prices quoted
in advertisements are also subject to change
without prior notice. Due to differing
production schedules it is possible that new
editions of Parts 2 to 22 will show revised
prices which are not included in that year's
Stamps of the World.

Ⓚ **Colour** – Colour of stamp (if fewer than four
colours, otherwise noted as "multicoloured"–
see N below). Colour descriptions are
simple in this catalogue, and only expanded
to aid identification – see other more
comprehensive Stanley Gibbons catalogues
for more detailed colour descriptions (see
p.xxxix).

**Where stamps are printed in two or
more colours, the central portion of the
design is the first colour given, unless
otherwise stated.**

Ⓛ **Other Types of Stamps** – See Scope of
the Catalogue p.viii for a list of the types of
stamps included.

Ⓜ **Illustration or Type Number** – These
numbers are used to help identify stamps,
either in the listing, type column, design line
or footnote, usually the first value in a set.
These type numbers are in a bold type face
– **123**; when bracketed (**123**) an overprint
or a surcharge is indicated. Some type
numbers include a lower-case letter – **123a**,
this indicates they have been added to an
existing set. N Multicoloured – Nearly all
modern stamps are multicoloured; this is
indicated in the heading, with a description
of the stamp given in the listing.

Ⓝ **Footnote** – further information on
background or key facts on issues

Ⓟ **Design line** – Further details on design
variations

Ⓠ **Illustration** – Generally, the first stamp in the
set. Stamp illustrations are reduced to 60%,
with overprints and surcharges shown actual
size.

Ⓡ **Key Type** – indicates a design type (see p.
xii for further details) on which the stamp
is based. These are the bold figures found
below each illustration. The type numbers
are also given in bold in the second column
of figures alongside the stamp description
to indicate the design of each stamp. Where
an issue comprises stamps of similar design,
the corresponding type number should be
taken as indicating the general design. Where
there are blanks in the type number column
it means that the type of the corresponding
stamp is that shown by the number in the
type column of the same issue. A dash (–)
in the type column means that the stamp is
not illustrated. Where type numbers refer
to stamps of another country, e.g. where
stamps of one country are overprinted for
use in another, this is always made clear in
the text.

Ⓢ **Surcharges and Overprints** – usually
described in the headings. Any actual
wordings are shown in bold type.
Descriptions clarify words and figures used
in the overprint. Stamps with the same
overprints in different colours are not listed
separately. Numbers in brackets after the
descriptions are the catalogue numbers of
the non-overprinted stamps. The words
"inscribed" or "inscription" refer to the
wording incorporated in the design of a
stamp and not surcharges or overprints.

Ⓣ **Coloured Papers** – stamps printed on
coloured paper are shown – e.g. "brn on yell"
indicates brown printed on yellow paper. No
information on the texture of paper, e.g. laid
or wove, is provided in this catalogue.

Key-Types

Standard designs frequently occuring on the stamps of the French, German, Portuguese and Spanish colonies are illustrated below together with the descriptive names and letters by which they are referred to in the lists to avoid repetition. Please see the Guide to Entries for further information.

French Group

A "Blanc" B "Mouchon" C "Merson" D "Tablet"

INTERNATIONAL COLONIAL EXHIBITION

E F " G H

I "Faidherbe" J "Palms" K "Balay" L "Natives" M "Figure"

German Group

N "Yacht" O "Yacht"

Spanish Group

X "Alfonso XII" Y "Baby" Z "Curly Head"

Portuguese Group

P "Crown" Q "Embossed" R "Figures" S "Carlos" T "Manoel" U Ceres V "Newspaper"

Selling Your Stamps?

Summary Tip #20:
5 Different Ways to Sell your Stamps: Dealer 'runners'/ Private Treaty.

Dear Collecto

In Part 2 o Your Stamps' (Volume 2) we discussed the advanta ect sale to dealers and how with careful handling an ss of the 'strength of your collection' it is often possi ln more for your collection selling directly to dealers t ling through auction.

In Part 4 your Stamps' we'll discuss the potential advantages lvantages of selling through auction on your own a out in this article we'll deal with two lesser known but ss important aspects of selling your stamps .... the first lers 'runners'.

Before yo rt to try selling your stamps; preparation is all. Make so ch:

1. Draw up vhom you consider as a possible target to sell / ha ollection. ..... then consider –

...bu s I might – I never once sa uvertisement by those cnies to sell stamps.

2. Why hav those dealers/organisations ?

Here's so think about ... for the best part of 20 years I watched t vertisements extolling the merits of selling to this or ular dealer ... but try as I might – I never once saw æ ement by those companies to sell stamps. This was i met' days ... nowadays people trade on the internet w ner of weird and unusual trading names, sometimes e who they actually are – but in those days traditional enues' were shops, stamp fairs, auctions, approvals, nail-order lists ....

... so w h mpossible to find out how those dealers actually co eir business? The answer was simple – they sold to oth they rarely if ever sold to collectors – they were Deal s'. Now for you to part with your beloved collection t dealer that you contact does not necessarily mean that nade a mistake ... but, if that dealer writes you out a c d almost before the ink has even dried on it – (probabl u have presented the cheque at your bank) ... he or sh nearest big dealer 50 miles away being paid

a profit upon the price you sold your collection for – this is NOT in your best interest.

So what should you be looking for? You should be looking for an organisation / dealer that you can see and understand how they conduct their business. Dealers that sell to other dealers are unlikely to be paying the best price.

Private Treaty: What is it?
The idea of Private Treaty is that collectors 'place' their collection with a dealer or auction that charges a small commission to sell their collection outright. Sometimes it is claimed that the Buyer will pay the commission so that the collector pays no charges whatsoever. Historically 'Private Treaty' has acquired notoriety as an excuse for the company handling the transaction to 'buy-in' the collection for themselves. Maybe collectors and dealers should forget the concept of private treaty in favour of an open approach whereby the dealer/auction explains that they are purchasing on their own account ... or will charge a small percentage for handling/passing the collector/collection to a more appropriate buyer. In Part 4 of 'Selling your Stamps?' (Volume 4) we'll discuss consigning your stamps for sale by auction.

> **To read the rest of this series 'SELLING YOUR STAMPS?' see the relevant pages in each volume:**
>
> Summary Tip 18 – Volume 1 (opposite Key Types)
> Summary Tip 19 – Volume 2 (opposite Key Types)
> Summary Tip 20 – Volume 3 (opposite Key Types)
> Summary Tip 21 – Volume 4 (opposite Key Types)
> Summary Tip 22 – Volume 5 (opposite Key Types)
>
> **Please go to Volume 6 (opposite Key Types) to see how UPA can pay you up to 36% more for your collection.**

Happy collecting from us all,

PS. If you find this 'tip' interesting please forward it to a philatelic friend.

Andrew McGavin
Managing Director: Universal Philatelic Auctions, Omniphil & Avon Approvals, Avon Mixtures, Universal Philatelic (Ebay)

GERMAN COMMANDS
Pt. 7

100 pfennig = 1 mark.

EASTERN COMMAND

German occupation of Estonia, Latvia and Lithuania during the war of 1914–18.

1916. Stamps of Germany inscr "DEUTSCHES REICH" optd **Postgebiet Ob. Ost.**

1	24	2½pf. grey	70	2·40
2	10	3pf. brown	35	95
3	10	5pf. green	1·10	2·50
4	24	7½pf. orange	70	3·00
5	10	10pf. red	7·00	2·00
6	24	15pf. brown	4·75	6·00
7	24	15pf. violet	1·50	3·00
8	10	20pf. blue	3·50	3·00
9	10	25pf. black & red on yellow	45	1·40
10	10	40pf. black and red	4·25	9·50
11	10	50pf. black & pur on buff	3·50	4·75
12a	12	1m. red	14·00	9·50

WESTERN COMMAND

For Forces in Belgium and Northern France.

1916. Stamps of Germany surch with new values as **2 Cent, 1F. or 1F.25 Cent.**

1	10	3c. on 3pf. brown	60	1·70
2	10	5c. on 5pf. green	1·80	3·00
3	24	8c. on 7½pf. orange	1·20	3·25
4	10	10c. on 10pf. red	2·75	4·75
5	24	15c. on 15pf. brown	60	1·70
6	10	25c. on 20pf. blue	1·50	4·75
7	10	40c. on 30pf. black and orange on buff	1·50	3·00
8	10	50c. on 40pf. black and red	1·50	4·25
9	10	75c. on 60pf. purple	9·75	18·00
10	10	1f. on 80pf. black and red on red	5·00	13·00
11a	12	1f.25 on 1m. red	43·00	41·00
12	13	2f.50 on 2m. blue	37·00	35·00

GERMAN EAST AFRICA
Pt. 7

A German colony on the east coast of Africa. Placed under British mandate after the First World War.

1893. 64 pesa = 1 rupee.
1905. 100 heller = 1 rupee.

1893. Stamps of Germany surch with value in **PESA.**

1	8	2p. on 3pf. brown	55·00	65·00
2	8	3p. on 5pf. green	65·00	70·00
4	9	5p. on 10pf. red	55·00	39·00
5	9	10p. on 20pf. blue	39·00	20·00
6	9	25p. on 50pf. brown	55·00	39·00

1896. Stamps of Germany surch **Deutsch-Ostafrika** and value in" Pesa".

7	8	2p. on 3pf. brown	16·00	16·00
10	8	3p. on 5pf. green	3·25	6·25
11	9	5p. on 10pf. red	5·50	6·25
13	9	10p. on 20pf. blue	7·25	7·25
14	9	25p. on 50pf. brown	31·00	38·00

1901. "Yacht", key-type inscr "DEUTSCH-OSTAFRIKA". Currency in pesa and rupees.

15	N	2p. brown	4·00	2·20
16	N	3p. green	4·00	2·75
17	N	5p. red	4·50	3·25
18	N	10p. blue	7·25	6·75
19	N	15p. black and orange on buff	7·25	9·00
20	N	20p. black and red	10·00	20·00
21	N	25p. black and purple on buff	10·00	20·00
22	N	40p. black and red on rose	12·50	31·00
23	O	1r. red	27·00	65·00
24	O	2r. green	13·50	£110
44	O	3r. black and red	65·00	£325

1905. "Yacht" key-types inscr "DEUTSCH-OSTAFRIKA". Currency in heller.

34	N	2½h. brown	1·30	1·30
35	N	4h. green	1·30	90
36	N	7½h. red	1·60	2·00
37	N	15h. blue	3·00	2·00
38	N	20h. black and red on yellow	3·25	28·00
39	N	30h. black and red	3·50	11·00
40	N	45h. black and mauve	7·75	80·00
33	N	60h. black and red on rose	50·00	£130

For stamps issued for this territory under British auspices since 1915 see under Tanganyika in Volume 4.

GERMAN NEW GUINEA
Pt. 7

A German colony, part of the island of New Guinea.

100 pfennig = 1 mark.

1897. Stamps of Germany optd **Deutsch-Neu-Guinea.**

1a	8	3pf. brown	11·00	15·00
2	8	5pf. green	5·50	7·50
3	9	10pf. red	8·75	12·50
4	9	20pf. blue	12·00	18·00
5	9	25pf. orange	38·00	70·00
6	9	50pf. brown	44·00	65·00

1901. "Yacht" key-types inscr "DEUTSCH-NEU-GUINEA".

7	N	3pf. brown	1·60	1·60
8	N	5pf. green	9·50	1·60
9	N	10pf. red	32·00	4·50
10	N	20pf. blue	2·20	4·50
11	N	25pf. black and red on yellow	2·20	22·00
12	N	30pf. black & orange on buff	2·20	27·00
13	N	40pf. black and red	2·20	31·00
14	N	50pf. black & purple on buff	2·75	26·00
15	N	80pf. black and red on rose	5·00	37·00
16	O	1m. red	10·00	70·00
17	O	2m. blue	11·00	£100
18	O	3m. black	15·00	£200
19	O	5m. red and black	£225	£650

Australian forces occupied German New Guinea in 1914 and it was administered as a League of Nations mandate from 1920. For stamps issued since 1914 see under New Guinea.

GERMAN OCCUPATION OF ALSACE
Pt. 4

100 pfennig = 1 mark.

1940. Stamps of Germany optd **Elsa**

1	94	3pf. brown	40	75
2	94	4pf. slate	75	1·50
3	94	5pf. green	40	75
4	94	6pf. green	40	75
5	94	8pf. orange	40	75
6	94	10pf. brown	40	1·10
7	94	12pf. red	40	75
8	94	15pf. red	75	1·50
9	94	20pf. blue	75	1·50
10	94	25pf. blue	1·10	2·20
11	94	30pf. olive	1·50	2·40
12	94	40pf. mauve	1·50	2·40
13	94	50pf. black and green	2·20	3·75
14	94	60pf. black and red	2·50	4·50
15	94	80pf. black and blue	3·50	6·50
16	94	100pf. black and yellow	8·25	7·25

GERMAN OCCUPATION OF BELGIUM
Pt. 4

German occupation of E. Belgium during the war of 1914–18.

100 centimes = 1 franc.

Stamps of Germany inscr "DEUTSCHES REICH" surcharged

1914. Surch **Belgien** and value thus: **3 Centimes, 1Franc or 1Fr.25C.**

1	10	3c. on 3pf. brown	50	60
2	10	5c. on 5pf. green	50	60
3	10	10c. on 10pf. red	50	60
4	10	25c. on 20pf. blue	2·40	2·40
5	10	50c. on 40pf. black and red	6·00	6·75
6	10	75c. on 60pf. purple	2·40	3·75
7	10	1f. on 80pf. black and red on rose	5·75	5·75
8	12	1f.25 on 1m. red	46·00	46·00
9	13	2f.50 on 2m. blue	44·00	44·00

1916. Surch **Belgien** and value, thus: **2 Cent.,1F.,** or **1F.25 Cent**

10	24	2c. on 2pf. grey	35	1·70
11	10	3c. on 3pf. brown	1·10	2·40
12	10	5c. on 5pf. green	1·10	3·75
13	24	8c. on 7½pf. orange	1·10	3·25
14	10	10c. on 10pf. red	1·50	2·40
15	24	15c. on 15pf. brown	2·40	3·00
16	24	15c. on 15pf. violet	1·50	3·00
17	10	20c. on 25pf. black and red on yellow	50	2·20
18	10	25c. on 20pf. blue	1·50	2·75
19	10	40c. on 30pf. black and orange on buff	50	1·50
20	10	50c. on 40pf. black and red	1·50	3·00
21	10	75c. on 60pf. mauve	2·10	43·00
22	10	1f. on 80f. black and red on rose	4·00	10·50
23a	12	1f.25 on 1m. red	7·25	9·25
24	13	2f.50 on 2m. blue	37·00	49·00
25	15	6f.25 on 5m. red and black	£100	£100

GERMAN OCCUPATION OF DALMATIA
Pt. 3

Area formerly under Italian control which was occupied by the Germans in 1943

100 centesimi = 1 lira.

A. ZARA (Zadar)

1943. Imperial series of Italy, 1929, optd **Deutsche Besetzung Zara.**

1	98	5c. brown	80·00	£190
2	-	10c. brown	5·25	16·00
3	-	15c. green	8·00	26·00
4	99	20c. red	5·25	18·00
5	-	25c. green	5·25	18·00
6	103	30c. brown	5·25	18·00
7	-	35c. blue	£250	£600
8	-	75c. red	16·00	42·00
9	99	1l. violet	5·25	18·00
10	99	1l.25 blue	6·25	26·00
11	99	1l.75 red	19·00	70·00
12	-	2l. red	80·00	£130
13	98	2l.55 green	£250	£700
14	98	3l.70 violet	£1400	£2750
15	98	5l. red	80·00	£150
16	-	10l. violet	£1100	£2000
17	99	20l. green	£11000	£22000
18	-	25l. black	£35000	£64000
19	-	50l. violet	£27000	£43000

1943. War Propaganda stamps of Italy (Nos. 571/4) optd **Deutsche Besetzung Zara** on stamp and label.

20	103	50c. violet (Navy)	32·00	85·00
21	103	50c. violet (Army)	32·00	85·00
22	103	50c. violet (Air Force)	32·00	85·00
23	103	50c. violet (Militia)	32·00	85·00

1943. Air. Nos. 270/7 of Italy optd **Deutsche Besetzung Zara.**

26	-	25c. green	10·50	26·00
27	110	50c. brown	10·50	26·00
28	-	75c. brown	£325	£650
29	-	80c. red	32·00	90·00
30	-	1l. violet	13·00	32·00
31	113	2l. blue	37·00	85·00
32	110	5l. green	£5500	£11000
33	110	10l. red	£2000	£37000

1943. Imperial series of Italy, 1929, optd **ZARA** within pattern of bars.

46	103	50c. violet	10·50	26·00
47	-	75c. red	10·50	26·00
48	-	1l.25 blue	60·00	£170

1943. War Propaganda stamps of Italy (Nos. 563/70) optd **ZARA** within pattern of bars on stamp and label.

49	-	25c. green (Navy)	21·00	42·00
50	-	25c. green (Army)	21·00	42·00
51	-	25c. green (Air Force)	21·00	42·00
52	-	25c. green (Militia)	21·00	42·00
53	103	30c. brown (Navy)	21·00	42·00
54	103	30c. brown (Army)	21·00	42·00
55	103	30c. brown (Air Force)	21·00	42·00
56	103	30c. brown (Militia)	21·00	42·00

EXPRESS LETTER STAMPS

1943. Nos. E350/1 of Italy optd **Deutsche Besetzung Zara.**

E24	E132	1l.25 green	13·00	37·00
E25	E132	2l.50 orange	£130	£250

1943. Air. No. E370 of Italy optd **Deutsche Besetzung Zara.**

E34	E133	2l. black	29·00	65·00

1943. Nos. E350/1 of Italy optd **ZARA** within pattern of bars, twice.

E57	E132	1l.25 green	13·00	55·00
E58	E132	2l.50 orange	£150	£375

POSTAGE DUE STAMPS

1943. Italian Postage Due stamps optd **Deutsche Besetzung Zara.**

D35	D141	5c. brown	32·00	£130
D36	D141	10c. blue	32·00	£130
D37	D141	20c. red	32·00	£130
D38	D141	25c. green	£550	£1300
D39	D141	30c. red	32·00	£130
D40	D141	40c. brown	32·00	£130
D41	D141	50c. violet	32·00	£130
D42	D141	60c. olive	£550	£1300
D43	D142	1l. orange	£550	£1300
D44	D142	2l. green	£800	£1800
D45	D142	5l. violet	£550	£1300

B. GULF OF KOTOR
Italian series and German currency.

1944. Imperial series of Italy, 1929, surch **Deutsche Militar-verwaltung Kotor** and new value in lire.

1	-	0.50LIT. on 10c. brown	55·00	95·00
2	-	1LIT. on 25c. green	£130	£190
3	103	1.50LIT. on 50c. violet	55·00	95·00
4	103	3LIT. on 30c. brown	55·00	95·00
5	99	4LIT. on 20c. red	55·00	95·00
6	99	10LIT. on 20c. red	55·00	95·00

1944. Nos. 419/20 of Yugoslavia (King Petar II) surch **Boka Kotorska** and new value in Reichsmarks.

7		0,10R.M. on 3d. brown	6·25	7·50
8		0,15R.M. on 3d. brown	6·25	7·50
9		0,25R.M. on 4d. blue	9·50	12·50
10		0,50R.M. on 4d. blue	13·00	21·00

GERMAN OCCUPATION OF ESTONIA
Pt. 10

100 kopeks = 1 rouble.

2

1941. Tartu issue.

3A	2	15(k.) brown	17·00	22·00
4B	2	20(k.) green	13·50	16·00
5B	2	30(k.) blue	16·00	16·00

Originally issued for local use, the above were made available for use throughout Estonia from 29.9.41 to 30.4.42. However, not many were used since the German **OSTLAND** stamps were used from 1 December 1941.

3 "Long Hermann" Tower, Reval (Tallinn)

1941. Reconstruction Fund.

6	3	15+15(k.) sepia and brown	65	6·50
7	-	20+20(k.) purple and brown	65	6·50
8	-	30+30(k.) blue and brown	65	6·50
9	-	50+50(k.) green and brown	75	13·00
10	-	60+60(k.) red and brown	1·10	11·00
11	-	100+100(k.) slate and brown	1·60	13·00

DESIGNS—HORIZ: 20k. Stone Bridge, Tartu; 30k. Two Narva Castles; 50k. Reval of Tallinn. VERT: 60k. Tartu University; 100k. Hermann Castle, Narva.

German stamps optd **OSTLAND** (see German Occupation of Russia, Nos. 1/20) were used from 1 December 1941 until the Russian re-occupation of Estonia in 1944. Since then Russian stamps have been in use, and since 1991 Estonia have issued their own stamps.

GERMAN OCCUPATION OF LATVIA
Pt. 10

100 kopeks = 1 rouble.

1941. Russian stamps of 1936–39 optd **LATVIJA 1941. 1. VII.**

1		5k. red (No. 847a)	80	5·25
2		10k. blue (No. 727f)	80	5·25
3		15k. green (No. 847c)	32·00	95·00
4		20k. green (No. 727h)	80	5·25
5		30k. blue (No. 847d)	80	5·25
6		50k. brown on buff (No. 727m)	3·25	12·50

German stamps optd **OSTLAND** (see German Occupation of Russia, Nos. 1/20) were used from 4th November, 1941, until the Russian re-occupation of Latvia in 1944–45. Since then Russian stamps have been in use, and since 1991 Latvia have issued their own stamps.

GERMAN OCCUPATION OF LITHUANIA
Pt. 10

100 kopeks = 1 rouble.

1941. Russian stamps of 1936–40 optd **NEPRIKLAUSOMA LIETUVA 1941-VI-23.**

1		2k. green (No. 542)	32·00	£190
2		5k. red (No. 847a)	1·90	16·00
3		10k. blue (No. 727f)	1·90	16·00
4		15k. green (No. 847c)	1·90	16·00
5		20k. green (No. 727h)	1·90	16·00
6		30k. blue (No. 847d)	1·90	16·00
7		50k. brown on buff (No. 727m)	8·00	32·00
8		60k. red (No. 847f)	13·00	65·00
9		80k. blue (No. 905)	13·00	65·00

1941. Issue for Vilnius and South Lithuania. Russian stamps of 1936–39 optd **VILNIUS.**

10		5k. red (No. 847a)	1·60	5·25
11		10k. blue (No. 727f)	1·60	5·25
12		15k. green (No. 847c)	1·60	5·25
13		20k. green (No. 727h)	4·25	16·00
14		30k. blue (No. 847d)	3·75	10·50
15		50k. brown on buff (No. 727m)	4·25	10·50
16		60k. red (No. 847f)	4·25	12·50
17		80k. red and deep red (No. 772)	£275	£325
18		1r. black and red (No. 779)	£850	£750

German stamps optd **OSTLAND** (see German Occupation of Russia, Nos. 1/20) were used from 4th November, 1941, till the Russian re-occupation of Lithuania in 1944. Since then Russian stamps have been in use.

GERMAN OCCUPATION OF LORRAINE
Pt. 7

100 pfennig = 1 mark.

1940. Stamps of Germany optd **Lothringen.**

1	94	3pf. brown	80	1·30
2	94	4pf. slate	80	1·30
3	94	5pf. green	80	1·30
4	94	6pf. green	65	85
5	94	8pf. orange	80	1·30
6	94	10pf. brown	80	85
7	94	12pf. red	65	85
8	94	15pf. lake	80	1·30
9	94	20pf. blue	1·10	1·60
10	94	25pf. blue	1·10	1·60
11	94	30pf. olive	1·10	1·90
12	94	40pf. mauve	1·10	1·90
13	94	50pf. black and green	2·10	3·75
14	94	60pf. black and red	2·10	4·25
15	94	80pf. black and blue	3·25	4·75
16	94	100pf. black and yellow	4·75	8·50

GERMAN OCCUPATION OF POLAND
Pt. 5

German Occupation of Poland, 1915 - 18.

100 pfennig = 1 mark.

1915. Stamps of Germany inscr "DEUTSCHES REICH" optd **Russisch-Polen.**

1	10	3pf. brown	85	60
2	10	5pf. green	1·40	60
3	10	10pf. red	1·40	95
4	10	20pf. blue	6·00	95
5	10	40pf. black and red	7·00	4·25

1916. Stamps of Germany inscr "DEUTSCHES REICH" optd **Gen.-Gouv. Warschau.**

6	24	2½pf. grey	1·10	2·40
7	24	3pf. brown	1·10	3·25
8	10	5pf. green	1·20	4·25
9	24	7½pf. orange	1·40	2·50
10	10	10pf. red	4·25	2·50
11	24	15pf. brown	4·25	3·50
12	24	15pf. violet	1·20	2·50
13	10	20pf. blue	4·25	3·00
14	10	30pf. black & orange on buff	9·50	17·00
15	10	40pf. black and red	3·25	2·50
16	10	60pf. purple	3·50	3·25

GERMAN OCCUPATION OF ROMANIA
Pt. 3

German Occupation of Romania, 1917 - 18.

100 bani = 1 leu.

Stamps of Germany inscr "DEUTSCHES REICH".

1917. Surch **M.V.i.R.** in frame and value in "Bani".

1	24	15b. on 15pf. violet	1·20	1·50
2	10	25b. on 20pf. blue	1·20	1·50
3	10	40b. on 30pf. black and orange on buff	22·00	39·00

1917. Surch **M.V.i.R.** (not in frame) and value in "Bani".

4		10b. on 10pf. red	1·70	2·40
5	24	15b. on 15pf. violet	8·25	9·50
6	10	25b. on 20pf. blue	4·75	7·00
7	10	40b. on 30pf. black and orange on buff	1·80	2·50

1918. Surch **Rumanien** and value in "Bani".

8		5b. on 5pf. green	1·20	2·75
9		10b. on 10pf. red	1·20	2·50
10	24	15b. on 15pf. violet	35	70
11	10	25b. on 20pf. blue	1·20	2·50
12	10	40b. on 30pf. black and orange on buff	35	60

1918. Stamps of Germany inscr "DEUTSCHES REICH" optd **Gultig 9. Armee** in frame.

13		10pf. red	14·00	65·00

14	24	15pf. violet	21·00	60·00
15	10	20pf. blue	3·00	4·75
16	10	30pf. black & orange on buff	21·00	35·00

POSTAGE DUE STAMPS

1918. Postage Due stamps of Rumania optd **M.V.i.R.** in frame.

D1B	D38	5b. blue on green	18·00	21·00
D2B	D38	10b. blue on green	18·00	21·00
D3B	D38	20b. blue on green	4·75	4·75
D4B	D38	30b. blue on green	4·75	4·75
D5B	D38	50b. blue on green	4·75	4·75

GERMAN OCCUPATION OF RUSSIA
Pt. 10

100 pfennig = 1 reichsmark.

1941. Issue for Ostland. Stamps of Germany of 1941 optd **OSTLAND.**

1	173	1pf. grey	20	30
2	173	3pf. brown	20	30
3	173	4pf. slate	20	30
4	173	5pf. green	20	30
5	173	6pf. violet	20	30
6	173	8pf. red	20	30
7	173	10pf. brown	85·00	1·90
9	173	12pf. red	85	1·90
11	173	15pf. lake	20	30
12	173	16pf. green	20	30
13	173	20pf. blue	20	30
14	173	24pf. brown	20	30
15	173	25pf. blue	20	30
16	173	30pf. olive	20	30
17	173	40pf. mauve	20	30
18	173	50pf. green	20	30
19	173	60pf. brown	20	30
20	173	80pf. blue	20	30

1941. Issue for Ukraine. Stamps of Germany of 1941 optd **UKRAINE.**

21		1pf. grey	10	20
22		3pf. brown	10	20
23		4pf. slate	10	20
24		5pf. green	10	20
25		6pf. violet	10	20
26		8pf. red	10	20
27		10pf. brown	70	2·10
29		12pf. red	70	2·10
31		15pf. lake	10	20
32		16pf. green	10	30
33		20pf. blue	10	20
34		24pf. brown	10	30
35		25pf. blue	10	20
36		30pf. olive	10	20
37		40pf. mauve	10	30
38		50pf. green	10	20
39		60pf. brown	10	20
40		80pf. blue	10	30

GERMAN OCCUPATION OF ZANTE
Pt. 3

German occupation of Ionian Islands, 1943-44.

100 centesimi = 1 lira = 8 drachma.

(1)

1943. Stamps of Italian Occupation of Ionian Islands further optd with T **1.**

1	-	25c. green (postage)	32·00	60·00
2	103	50c. violet	32·00	60·00
3	110	50c. brown (air)	44·00	95·00

GERMAN POST OFFICES IN CHINA
Pt. 7

German Post Offices in China, now closed.

1898. 100 pfennig = 1 mark.
1905. 100 cents = 1 dollar.

1898. Stamps of Germany optd **China.**

7	8	3pf. brown	8·75	8·25
8	8	5pf. green	5·25	4·50
9	9	10pf. red	8·75	8·25
4	9	20pf. blue	23·00	16·00
11	9	25pf. orange	44·00	50·00
12	9	50pf. brown	23·00	20·00

1901. Stamps of Germany inscr "REICHSPOST" optd **China.**

22	10	3pf. brown	2·30	3·25
23	10	5pf. green	2·30	2·50
24	10	10pf. red	3·75	1·90
25	10	20pf. blue	5·00	2·50

26	10	25pf. black & red on yellow	15·00	25·00
27	10	30pf. black & orge on pink	15·00	20·00
28	10	40pf. black and red	15·00	14·50
29	10	50pf. black & pur on pink	15·00	14·50
30	10	80pf. black and red on pink	18·00	18·00
31	12	1m. red	43·00	55·00
32	13	2m. blue	40·00	44·00
33	14	3m. black	75·00	£100
35b	15	5m. red and black	£325	£500

1905. Stamps of Germany inscr "DEUTSCHES REICH" surch **China** and new value.

46	10	1c. on 3pf. brown	65	2·10
47	10	2c. on 5pf. green	65	2·10
48	10	4c. on 10pf. red	65	2·50
39	10	10c. on 20pf. blue	4·50	2·75
50	10	20c. on 40pf. black and red	1·50	5·75
51	10	40c. on 80pf. black and red on yellow	1·80	80·00
42	12	½d. on 1m. red	25·00	31·00
43	13	1d. on 2m. blue	25·00	35·00
44a	14	1½d. on 3m. black	25·00	75·00
55	15	2½d. on 5m. red and black	£160	£200

GERMAN POST OFFICES IN MOROCCO
Pt. 7

German Post Offices in Morocco, now closed.

100 centimos = 1 peseta.

Stamps of Germany surcharged Marocco (or Marokko) and new value.

1889. Spelt Marocco.

1	8	3c. on 3pf. brown	5·00	3·00
2	8	5c. on 5pf. green	5·00	3·50
3	9	10c. on 10pf. red	13·00	11·00
4	9	25c. on 20pf. blue	26·00	21·00
5	9	30c. on 25pf. orange	38·00	46·00
6	9	60c. on 50pf. brown	33·00	55·00

1900. Inscr "REICHSPOST" surch Marocco (3c. to 1p.) or Marocco Marocco (others).

7	10	3c. on 3pf. brown	1·80	3·25
8	10	5c. on 5pf. green	2·20	2·20
9	10	10c. on 10pf. red	2·75	2·20
10	10	25c. on 20pf. blue	4·50	4·00
11	10	30c. on 25pf. black and red on yellow	13·00	21·00
12	10	35c. on 30pf. black and orange on rose	10·00	8·75
13	10	50c. on 40pf. black and red	10·00	8·75
14	10	60c. on 50pf. black and purple on rose	20·00	42·00
15	10	1p. on 80pf. black and red on rose	22·00	33·00
16	12	1p.25 on 1m. red	44·00	65·00
17	13	2p.50 on 2m. blue	49·00	75·00
18	14	3p.75 on 3m. black	65·00	95·00
19	15	6p.25 on 5m. red and black	£250	£450

1905. Inscr "DEUTSCHES REICH" surch Marocco (3c. to 1p.) or Marocco Marocco (others).

26	10	3c. on 3pf. brown	3·75	3·50
27	10	5c. on 5pf. green	6·50	1·50
41	10	10c. on 10pf. red	9·25	1·60
29	10	25c. on 20pf. blue	26·00	4·50
30	10	30c. on 25pf. black and red on yellow	8·75	7·75
31	10	35c. on 30pf. black and orange on buff	13·00	7·75
32	10	50c. on 40pf. black and red	13·00	11·00
46	10	60c. on 50pf. black and purple on buff	33·00	24·00
34	10	1p. on 80pf. black and red on rose	29·00	26·00
35a	12	1p.25 on 1m. red	70·00	55·00
49	13	2p.50 on 2m. blue	90·00	£250
37a	14	3p.75 on 3m. black	60·00	75·00
38	15	6p.25 on 5m. red & black	£225	£275

1911. Inscr "DEUTSCHES REICH". Spelt Marokko.

51		3c. on 3pf. brown	75	1·10
52		5c. on 5pf. green	75	1·40
53		10c. on 10pf. red	75	1·50
54		25c. on 20pf. blue	90	1·90
55		30c. on 25pf. black and red on yellow	2·20	22·00
56		35c. on 30pf. black and orange on buff	2·20	12·00
57		50c. on 40pf. black and red	1·80	7·25
58		60c. on 50pf. black and purple on buff	3·50	49·00
59		1p. on 80pf. black and red on rose	2·20	33·00

60	12	1p.25 on 1m. red	6·50	90·00
61	13	2p.50 on 2m. blue	8·75	65·00
62	14	3p.75 on 3m. black	15·00	£275
63	15	6p.25 on 5m. red & black	27·00	£450

GERMAN POST OFFICES IN TURKISH EMPIRE
Pt. 7

German Post Offices in the Turkish Empire, now closed.

1884. 40 para = 1 piastre.
1908. 100 centimes = 1 franc.

1884. Stamps of Germany inscr "DEUTSCHE REICHS-POST" and "PFENNIG" without final "E" surch with new value.

1	5	10pa. on 5pf. mauve	75·00	44·00
2	6	20pa. on 10pf. red	£110	£110
3	6	1pi. on 20pf. blue	90·00	11·00
4	6	1¼pi. on 25pf. brown	£180	£375
6	6	2½pi. on 50pf. green	£140	£110

1889. Stamps of Germany inscr "REICHSPOST" surch with new value.

10	8	10pa. on 5pf. green	5·00	5·50
11	9	20pa. on 10pf. red	11·00	3·75
12	9	1pi. on 20pf. blue	7·75	3·25
14	9	1¼pi. on 25pf. orange	33·00	29·00
16	9	2½pi. on 50pf. brown	49·00	33·00

1900. Stamps of Germany inscr "REICHSPOST" surch in **PARA** or **PIASTER.**

17	10	10pa. on 5pf. green	2·40	2·75
18	10	20pa. on 10pf. red	3·75	3·25
19	10	1pi. on 20pf. blue	6·50	2·75
20	10	1¼pi. on 25pf. black and red on yellow	8·75	6·50
21	10	1½pi. on 30pf. black and orange on buff	8·75	6·50
22	10	2pi. on 40pf. black and red	8·75	6·50
23	10	2½pi. on 50pf. black and purple on buff	18·00	18·00
24	10	4pi. on 80pf. black and red on rose	20·00	19·00
25	12	5pi. on 1m. red	49·00	55·00
26	13	10pi. on 2m. blue	44·00	60·00
27	14	15pi. on 3m. black	65·00	£150
28c	15	25pi. on 5m. red and black	£250	£450

1905. Stamps of Germany inscr "DEUTSCHES REICH" surch in **Para** or **Piaster.**

38	10	1¼pi. on 25pf. black and red on yellow	13·00	11·00
45	14	15pi. on 3m. black	65·00	75·00
47	10	10pa. on 5pf. green	3·25	1·30
48	10	20pa. on 10pf. red	6·50	1·30
49	10	1pi. on 20pf. blue	8·75	1·30
51	10	1½pi. on 30pf. black and orange on buff	18·00	14·50
52	10	2pi. on 40pf. black and red	8·75	2·40
53	10	2½pi. on 50pf. black and purple on buff	13·00	24·00
54	10	4pi. on 80pf. black and red on pink	22·00	31·00
55	12	5pi. on 1m. red	49·00	44·00
56	13	10pi. on 2m. blue	49·00	65·00
58	15	25pi. on 5m. red and black	44·00	£110

1908. Stamps of Germany inscr "DEUTSCHES REICH", surch in **Centimes.**

60	10	5c. on 5pf. green	2·40	3·75
61	10	10c. on 10pf. red	3·75	6·50
62	10	25c. on 20pf. blue	9·00	33·00
63	10	50c. on 40pf. black and red	39·00	80·00
64	10	100c. on 80pf. black and red on rose	80·00	90·00

GERMAN SOUTH WEST AFRICA
Pt. 7

A German colony in S.W. Africa.

100 pfennig = 1 mark.

1897. Stamps of Germany optd. (a) **Deutsch-Sudwest-Afrika.**

1	8	3pf. brown	11·00	16·00
2	8	5pf. green	6·00	6·50
3	9	10pf. red	29·00	22·00
4	9	20pf. blue	7·75	7·75

(b) Deutsch-Sudwestafrika.

5	8	3pf. brown	5·50	29·00
6	8	5pf. green	4·50	4·50
7	9	10pf. red	4·50	5·50
8	9	20pf. blue	15·00	20·00
9	9	25pf. orange	£450	£550
10	9	50pf. brown	16·00	15·00

1901. "Yacht" key-types inscr "DEUTSCH-SUDWESTAFRIKA".

24	N	3pf. brown	1·10	4·75
25	N	5pf. green	1·10	1·90
26	N	10pf. red	1·30	2·00
27	N	20pf. blue	1·30	5·00
15	N	25pf. black and red on yellow	2·00	7·75
16	N	30pf. black & orange on buff	£100	3·75
17	N	40pf. black and red	2·40	4·50
18	N	50pf. black & purple on buff	2·75	5·25
19	N	80pf. black and red on rose	2·75	12·00
29	O	1m. red	16·00	£100
21	O	2m. blue	42·00	49·00
22	O	3m. black	44·00	65·00
32	O	5m. red and black	49·00	£450

South Africa occupied the colony in 1914 and administered the territory under a League of Nations mandate from 1920. For stamps issued from 1923 see under South West Africa in Volume 4.

Pt. 7

GERMANY

A country in Northern Central Europe. A federation of states forming the German Reich. An empire till November 1918 and then a republic until the collapse of Germany in 1945. Until 1949 under Allied Military Control when the German Federal Republic was set up for W. Germany and the German Democratic Republic for E. Germany. See also notes before No. 899.

Germany.
1872. Northern areas including Alsace and Lorraine: 30 groschen = 1 thaler.
Southern areas: 90 kreuzer = 1 gulden.
1875. Throughout Germany: 100 pfennig = 1 mark.
1923. 100 renten-pfennig = 1 rentenmark (gold currency).
1928. 100 pfennig = 1 reichsmark.

Allied Occupation.
100 pfennige = 1 Reichsmark.
21.6.48. 100 pfennige = 1 Deutsche Mark (West).
24.6.48. 100 pfennige = 1 Deutsche Mark (East).

German Federal Republic.
1949. 100 pfennig = 1 Deutsche Mark (West).
2002. 100 cents = 1 euro.

West Berlin.
1948. 100 pfennig = 1 Deutsche Mark (East).
1949. 100 pfennig = 1 Deutsche Mark (West).

German Democratic Republic (East Germany).
1949. 100 pfennig = 1 Deutsche Mark (West).
1990. 100 pfennig = 1 Deutsche Mark (West).

I. GERMANY 1871–1945

1   A

1872. Arms embossed as Type **A**.

1	1	¼g. violet	£300	£140
2	1	⅓g. green	£700	60·00
3	1	½g. red	£1400	65·00
4	1	½g. yellow	£1700	75·00
5	1	1g. red	£450	9·25
6	1	2g. blue	£2500	23·00
7	1	5g. bistre	£1300	£140
8	1	1k. green	£1000	80·00
9	1	2k. red	£900	£475
10	1	2k. yellow	55·00	£250
11	1	3k. red	£2750	20·00
12	1	7k. blue	£3500	£140
13	1	18k. bistre	£700	£600

2   B

1872

14	2	10g. grey	80·00	£250
15	-	30g. blue	£160	£4000
38d	2	2m. purple	90·00	7·50

On the 30g. the figures are in a rectangular frame.

1872. Arms embossed as Type **B**.

16	1	¼g. purple	£110	£150
17	1	⅓g. green	50·00	23·00
18	1	½g. orange	55·00	14·00
19	1	1g. red	£110	9·25
20	1	2g. blue	33·00	10·50
21	1	2½g. brown	£3000	£120
22	1	5g. olive	45·00	45·00
23	1	1k. green	50·00	50·00
24	1	2k. orange	£700	£3750
25	1	3k. red	33·00	10·50
26	1	7k. blue	45·00	£110
27	1	9k. brown	£650	£650
28	1	18k. olive	50·00	£3250

1874. Surch with bold figures over arms.

29		"2½" on 2½g. brown	55·00	65·00
30		"9" on 9k. brown	£110	£700

5   6

1875. "PFENNIGE" with final "E".

31	5	3pf. green	85·00	8·25
32	5	5pf. mauve	£140	5·75
33	5	10pf. red	60·00	2·30
34a	6	20pf. blue	£650	3·00
35	6	25pf. brown	£700	28·00
36	6	50pf. grey	£2500	18·00
37	6	50pf. green	£2750	21·00

1880. "PFENNIG" without final "E".

39a	5	3pf. green	4·50	2·30
40a	5	5pf. purple	3·25	2·30
41b	6	10pf. red	16·00	2·30
42a	6	20pf. blue	9·00	2·30
43b	6	25pf. brown	25·00	8·25
44a	6	50pf. green	22·00	2·30

8   9

1889

45	8	2pf. grey	1·30	1·30
46	8	3pf. brown	3·25	2·10
47a	8	5pf. green	2·20	2·10
48b	9	10pf. red	3·25	2·10
49	9	20pf. blue	11·00	2·10
50b	9	25pf. yellow	45·00	3·00
51b	9	50pf. brown	39·00	2·10

10 "Germania"   12 General Post Office, Berlin

13 Allegory of Union of N. and S. Germany (after Anton von Werner)   14 Unveiling of Kaiser Wilhelm I Memorial in Berlin (after W. Pape)

15 25th Anniv of German Empire Address by Wilhelm II (after W. Pape)

1899. Types **10** to **15** inscr "REICHSPOST".

52	10	2pf. grey	1·20	95
53	10	3pf. brown	1·20	1·60
54	10	5pf. green	2·20	1·40
55	10	10pf. red	3·25	1·20
56	10	20pf. blue	16·00	1·40
57a	10	25pf. black & red on yellow	22·00	6·50
58a	10	30pf. black & orge on rose	33·00	1·40
59a	10	40pf. black and red	39·00	2·30
60a	10	50pf. black & pur on rose	39·00	1·80
61a	10	80pf. black and red on rose	55·00	3·50
62	12	1m. red	£160	4·00
63	13	2m. blue	£130	10·50
64	14	3m. black	£170	70·00
65b	15	5m. red and black	£550	£600

1902. T **10** to **15** inscr "DEUTSCHES REICH".

67	10	2pf. grey	2·20	95
68	10	3pf. brown	1·10	1·50
84a	10	5pf. green	90	2·30
85	10	10pf. red	16·00	2·30
86d	10	20pf. blue	1·10	2·30
87	10	25pf. black & red on yellow	55·00	4·00
88a	10	30pf. black & orge on buff	1·10	2·30
89a	10	40pf. black and red	1·70	2·30
90a	10	50pf. black & pur on buff	1·10	2·30
91a	10	60pf. purple	2·20	2·10
92a	10	80pf. black and red on rose	1·70	3·00
93B	12	1m. red	4·00	3·50
94B	13	2m. blue	7·75	7·50
95B	14	3m. black	4·50	7·00
96B	15	5m. red and black	4·50	7·50

No. 93 has three pedestrians in front of the carriage in the right foreground and has no tram in the background. See No. 113 for redrawn design.

24 Unshaded background   26   27

28

1916. Inscr "DEUTSCHES REICH".

97	24	2pf. grey	45	5·75
98	24	2½pf. grey	35	3·00
140	10	5pf. brown	35	3·00
99a	24	7½pf. yellow	80	3·50
141	10	10pf. orange	20	3·00
100	24	15pf. brown	4·50	3·50
101	24	15pf. violet	35	3·50
102	24	15pf. purple	4·50	5·25
142	10	20pf. green	35	3·50
143a	10	30pf. blue	20	2·30
103	24	35pf. brown	45	3·50
144a	10	40pf. red	20	2·30
145a	10	50pf. purple	90	3·50
146	10	60pf. olive	20	2·30
104	10	75pf. black and green	45	3·50
147a	10	75pf. purple	90	3·00
148a	10	80pf. blue	35	3·50
113	12	1m. red	3·25	3·50
149	10	1m. green and violet	20	3·50
114	12	1m.25 green	2·20	2·75
150	10	1¼m. purple and red	20	3·00
115	12	1m.50 brown	65	2·75
151	10	2m. blue and red	90	2·30
116a	13	2m.50 red	£140	£1100
152	10	4m. red and black	20	3·50

No. 113 has one pedestrian behind the carriage in the right foreground and a tram in the background.

1919. War Wounded Fund. Surch **5 Pf. fur Kriegs=beschadigte**.

105	10	10pf.+5pf. (No. 85a)	65	6·50
106	24	15pf.+5pf. (No. 101)	65	7·00

1919. National Assembly, Weimar.

107	26	10pf. red	20	2·30
108	27	15pf. blue and brown	20	2·30
109	28	25pf. red and green	20	2·30
110	28	30pf. red and purple	20	3·50

29   30 L.V.G. Schneider Biplane

1919. Air.

111	29	10pf. orange	35	4·00
112	30	40pf. green	35	4·75

1920. Stamps of Bavaria optd **Deutsches Reich**.

117	26	5pf. green	20	2·30
118	26	10pf. orange	20	2·30
119	26	15pf. red	20	2·30
120	27	20pf. purple	20	2·30
121	27	30pf. blue	20	2·30
122	27	40pf. brown	20	2·30
123	28	50pf. red	20	3·50
124	28	60pf. green	20	2·10
125	28	75pf. purple	65	7·50
126	28	80pf. blue	55	4·00
127	29	1m. red and grey	65	4·00
128	29	1¼m. blue and bistre	65	4·00
129	29	1½m. green and grey	80	5·25
130	29	2m. violet and bistre	1·10	5·75
131	29	2½m. black and grey	20	4·75
132	30	3m. blue	4·50	14·00
133	30	4m. red	4·50	15·00
134	30	5m. yellow	4·50	14·00
135	30	10m. green	7·25	23·00
136	30	20m. black	8·25	19·00

1920. Surch with new value and stars.

137	12	1m.25 on 1m. green	55	9·25
138	12	1m.50 on 1m. brown	55	10·50
139	13	2m.50 on 2m. purple	13·50	£300

35   36 Blacksmiths   37 Miners

38 Reapers   40

41 Ploughman

1921

153	35	5pf. red	20	3·00
154	35	10pf. olive	20	3·00
155	35	15pf. blue	20	2·30
156	35	25pf. brown	20	2·30
157	35	30pf. green	20	2·30
158	35	40pf. orange	20	2·30
182	35	50pf. purple	35	2·30
160	36	60pf. red	20	2·30
184	35	75pf. blue	20	4·25
161	36	80pf. red	20	8·25
186	37	100pf. green	20	2·30
163	37	120pf. blue	20	2·30
188	38	150pf. orange	20	2·30
165	38	160pf. green	20	13·00
193	40	5m. orange	45	3·00
194	40	10m. red	45	3·50
195	41	20m. blue and green	20	4·75

1921. 1902 stamps surch.

172	10	1m.60 on 5pf. brown	20	3·50
173	10	3m. on 1¼m. purple and red	20	4·00
174	10	5m. on 75pf. purple	35	3·50
175	10	10m. on 75pf. purple	55	3·50

39 Posthorn

1921

190	39	2m. violet and pink	20	2·30
204	39	2m. purple	35	2·30
191	39	3m. red and yellow	20	2·30
205	39	3m. red	35	2·30
192	39	4m. green and light green	20	2·30
206	39	4m. green	35	2·30
207	39	5m. orange and yellow	35	3·25
208	39	5m. orange	35	2·30
209	39	6m. blue	35	2·30
210	39	8m. green	35	2·30
211	39	10m. red and pink	35	2·30
212	39	20m. violet and red	55	2·30
213	39	20m. violet	35	2·30
214	39	30m. brown and yellow	35	2·30
215	39	30m. brown	35	11·50
216	39	40m. green	35	3·50
217	39	50m. green and purple	35	3·25

47 Arms of Munich

1922. Munich Exhibition.

198	47	1¼m. red	45	3·00
199	47	2m. violet	35	3·00
200	47	3m. red	20	3·00
201	47	4m. blue	20	3·00
202	47	10m. brown on buff	90	4·00
203	47	20m. red on rose	5·50	18·00

48

1922. Air.

218	**48**	25pf. brown	65	28·00
219	**48**	40pf. orange	55	37·00
220	**48**	50pf. purple	35	13·00
221	**48**	60pf. red	80	30·00
222	**48**	80pf. green	55	30·00
223	-	1m. green	20	5·75
224	-	2m. red and grey	20	5·75
225	-	3m. blue and grey	35	7·00
226	-	5m. orange and yellow	20	5·75
227	-	10m. purple and red	20	14·00
228	-	25m. brown and yellow	20	13·00
229	-	100m. olive and red	20	10·50

The mark values are larger (21×27 mm).
See also Nos. 269/73 and 358/64.

1922. New values.

235	**40**	50m. black	35	2·30
230	**40**	100m. purple on buff	35	2·10
231	**40**	200m. red on buff	20	2·10
238	**40**	300m. green on buff	20	2·10
239	**40**	400m. brown on buff	20	2·10
240	**40**	500m. green on buff	20	2·10
241	**40**	1000m. grey	20	2·10
242	**40**	2000m. blue	45	3·00
243	**40**	3000m. brown	35	2·30
244	**40**	4000m. violet	20	2·30
245	**40**	5000m. green	45	2·30
246	**40**	100000m. red	20	2·10

50 Allegory of Charity

1922. Fund for the Old and for Children.

247	**50**	6m.+4m. blue and bistre	20	35·00
248	**50**	12m.+8m. red and lilac	20	35·00

51 Miners

1923

249	**51**	5m. orange	20	19·00
250	**38**	10m. blue	20	2·30
251	**38**	12m. red	20	2·30
252	**51**	20m. purple	20	2·30
253	**38**	25m. bistre	20	2·30
254	**51**	30m. olive	20	3·50
255	**38**	40m. green	35	2·30
256	**51**	50m. blue	55	£180

1923. Relief Fund for Sufferers in the Rhine and Ruhr Occupation Districts. Surch Rhein=Ruhr=Hilfe and premium.

257		5+100m. orange	20	14·00
259	**41**	20+1000m. blue and green	3·00	£130
258	**38**	25+500m. bistre	20	35·00

54

1923. T = Tausend (thousand).

261	**54**	100m. purple	35	2·30
262	**54**	200m. red	20	2·30
263	**54**	300m. green	20	2·30
264	**54**	400m. brown	20	8·75
265	**54**	500m. red	20	9·25
266	**54**	1000m. grey	20	2·30
312	**54**	5T. blue	20	26·00
313	**54**	50T. brown	20	2·30
314	**54**	75T. purple	20	16·00

55 Wartburg Castle

1923

267	**55**	5000m. blue	45	4·75
268	-	10,000m. olive	45	5·75

DESIGN—VERT: 10,000m. Cologne Cathedral.

1923. Air. As T 48, but larger (21×27 mm).

269		5m. orange	20	65·00
270		10m. purple	20	15·00
271		25m. brown	20	15·00
272		100m. green	20	18·00
273		200m. blue	20	55·00

1923. Surch with new value in Tausend or Millionen (marks). Perf or rouletted.

274	**35**	5T. on 40pf. orange	10	2·50
275a	**35**	8T. on 30pf. green	10	2·30
276	**38**	15T. on 40m. green	35	3·00
277	**38**	20T. on 12m. red	10	2·30
278	**38**	20T. on 25m. brown	10	3·50
279	**54**	20T. on 200m. red	35	3·50
280	**38**	25T. on 25m. brown	10	21·00
281	**38**	25T. on 10m. blue	10	2·30
282	**54**	30T. on 200m. blue	10	2·30
283	**54**	75T. on 300m. green	10	21·00
284	**54**	75T. on 400m. red	35	2·30
285	**54**	75T. on 1000m. green	35	3·00
286	**54**	100T. on 100m. purple	35	3·50
287	**54**	100T. on 400m. brown	10	2·30
288	**54**	125T. on 1000m. red	20	3·00
289	**54**	250T. on 200m. red	10	8·25
290	**54**	250T. on 300m. green	10	26·00
291	**54**	250T. on 400m. brown	10	29·00
292	**54**	250T. on 500m. pink	10	2·30
293	**54**	250T. on 500m. orange	10	29·00
306	**35**	400T. on 15pf. brown	20	7·00
307	**35**	400T. on 25pf. brown	20	7·00
308	**35**	400T. on 30pf. brown	20	7·00
309	**35**	400T. on 40pf. brown	20	7·00
294	**35**	800T. on 5pf. green	20	6·50
295	**35**	800T. on 10pf. green	20	7·50
296	**54**	800T. on 200m. red	20	£120
297	**54**	800T. on 300m. green	20	7·50
298	**54**	800T. on 400m. green	20	5·75
299	**54**	800T. on 400m. brown	20	19·00
300	**54**	800T. on 500m. green	20	£2250
301	**54**	800T. on 1000m. green	35	2·30
302	**54**	2M. on 200m. red	20	3·25
303	**54**	2M. on 300m. green	20	3·25
304	**54**	2M. on 500m. red	20	9·25
305	**54**	2M. on 5T. red	20	14·00

62

1923. Perf or rouletted.

315	**62**	500T. brown	20	4·00
316	**62**	1M. blue	20	2·50
317	**62**	2M. purple	20	30·00
318	**62**	4M. green	20	2·30
319	**62**	5M. red	20	2·30
320	**62**	10M. red	20	2·30
321	**62**	20M. blue	20	3·00
322	**62**	30M. purple	20	14·00
323	**62**	50M. green	35	3·00
324	**62**	100M. grey	20	2·30
325	**62**	200M. brown	20	2·30
326	**62**	500M. olive	20	2·30

1923. As T 62, but value in "Milliarden". Perf or roul.

327		1Md. brown	45	3·00
328		2Md. green and flesh	20	3·00
329		5Md. brown and yellow	20	2·30
330		10Md. green & light green	20	2·30
331		20Md. brown and green	20	3·00
332		50Md. blue	35	55·00

1923. Surch in Milliarden. Perf or roul.

342	**54**	1Md. on 100m. purple	35	44·00
343	**62**	5Md. on 2M. purple	35	£200
344	**62**	5Md. on 4M. green	20	35·00
345	**62**	5Md. on 10M. red	20	4·00
346	**62**	10Md. on 20M. blue	35	7·00
347	**62**	10Md. on 50M. green	20	7·00
348	**62**	10Md. on 100M. grey	20	11·50

1923. As T 62, but without value in words and tablet blank.

352		3pf. brown	55	35
353		5pf. green	55	35
354		10pf. red	55	35
355		20pf. blue	1·70	60
356		50pf. orange	4·00	1·50
357		100pf. purple	12·50	1·80

The values of this and the following issues are expressed on the basis of the gold mark.

1924. Air.

358	**48**	5pf. green	1·90	3·50
359	**48**	10pf. red	1·90	3·50

360	**48**	20pf. blue	10·00	8·25
361	**48**	50pf. orange	17·00	41·00
362	**48**	100pf. purple	45·00	90·00
363	**48**	200pf. blue	85·00	£120
364	**48**	300pf. grey	£140	£160

65

1924. Welfare Fund.

365	**65**	5+15pf. green	2·20	5·25
366		10+30pf. red	2·20	5·25
367		20+60pf. blue	10·00	13·00
368		50+1m.50 brown	33·00	£100

DESIGNS: St. Elizabeth feeding the hungry (5pf.); giving drink to the thirsty (10pf.); clothing the naked (20pf.); and caring for the sick (50pf.).

66

1924

369	**66**	3pf. brown	45	60
370	**66**	5pf. green	45	60
371	**66**	10pf. red	60	60
372	**66**	20pf. blue	2·75	60
373	**66**	30pf. red	2·75	70
374	**66**	40pf. olive	19·00	1·10
375	**66**	50pf. orange	22·00	1·80

67 Rheinstein

1924

376	**67**	1m. green	17·00	5·25
377	-	2m. blue (A)	28·00	5·25
458	-	2m. blue (B)	39·00	22·00
378	-	3m. red	33·00	9·25
379	-	5m. green	50·00	23·00

DESIGNS: 2m. Cologne. (A) inscr "Zwei Mark"; (B) inscr "ZWEI REICHSMARK"; 3m. Marienburg; 5m. Speyer Cathedral.

71 Dr. von Stephan

1924. 50th Anniv of U.P.U.

380	**71**	10pf. green	90	45
381	**71**	20pf. blue	2·20	1·20
382	-	60pf. brown	5·50	1·20
383	-	80pf. deep green	14·50	2·30

DESIGN: Nos. 382/3. Similar to Type **71** but with border changed.

73 German Eagle and Rhine

1925. Rhineland Millenary.

384	**73**	5pf. green	65	60
385	**73**	10pf. red	1·30	60
386	**73**	20pf. blue	7·25	1·60

74

1925. Munich Exhibition.

387	**74**	5pf. green	4·75	8·25
388	**74**	10pf. red	5·75	15·00

75 Arms of Prussia

1925. Welfare Fund. Arms dated "1925".

389	**75**	5pf.+5pf. yell, blk & grn	80	3·00
390		10pf.+10pf. brn, bl & red	1·70	3·00
391		20pf.+20pf. brn, grn & bl	9·50	21·00

ARMS: 10pf. Bavaria; 20pf. Saxony.
See also Nos. 413/16a, 446/50 and 451/5.

76

1926. Air.

392	**76**	5pf. green	1·70	1·80
393	**76**	10pf. red	2·75	1·80
394	**76**	15pf. purple	2·75	3·00
395	**76**	20pf. blue	2·75	3·00
396	**76**	50pf. orange	27·00	8·25
397	**76**	1m. red and black	27·00	9·25
398	**76**	2m. blue and black	27·00	35·00
399	**76**	3m. olive and black	80·00	£140

78 Goethe

1926. Portraits.

400	**78**	3pf. brown	1·70	60
402	-	5pf. green (Schiller)	1·70	60
404	-	8pf. green (Beethoven)	2·20	60
405	-	10pf. red (Frederick the Great)	2·20	60
406	-	15pf. red (Kant)	3·25	60
407	-	20pf. deep green (Beethoven)	16·00	1·80
408	**78**	25pf. blue	5·00	1·40
409	-	30pf. olive (Lessing)	9·50	95
410	-	40pf. violet (Leibniz)	17·00	95
411	-	50pf. brown (Bach)	21·00	11·50
412	-	80pf. brown (Durer)	45·00	7·50

1926. Welfare Fund. As T 75. Arms, dated "1926".

413		5pf.+5pf. multicoloured	1·50	3·50
414		10pf.+10pf. red, gold and rose	2·20	4·75
415		25pf.+25pf. blue, yell & red	17·00	29·00
416a		50pf.+50pf. multicoloured	60·00	£150

ARMS: 5pf. Wurttemberg; 10pf. Baden; 25pf. Thuringia; 50pf. Hesse.

79 Pres. von Hindenburg

1927. Welfare Fund. President's 80th Birthday.

417	**79**	8pf.+7pf. green	£110	£4750
418	**79**	15pf.+15pf. red	1·40	3·50
419	**79**	25pf.+25pf. blue	10·00	33·00
420	**79**	50pf.+50pf. brown	16·00	37·00

1927. International Labour Office Session, Berlin. Optd I.A.A. 10.–15. 10. 1927.

421	-	8pf. green (No. 404)	26·00	£100
422	-	15pf. red (No. 406)	26·00	£100
423	**78**	25pf. blue	26·00	£100

81 Pres. Ebert   **82** Pres. von Hindenburg

1928

424	**81**	3pf. brown	35	95
425	**82**	4pf. blue	1·30	1·90
426	**82**	5pf. green	55	95
427	**81**	6pf. olive	1·10	1·10
428	**81**	8pf. green	35	95
429	**81**	10pf. red	2·75	3·50
430	**81**	10pf. purple	1·40	1·20
431	**82**	12pf. orange	1·70	1·10
432	**82**	15pf. red	90	95
433	**81**	20pf. deep green	9·50	5·75
434	**81**	20pf. grey	10·00	1·20
435	**82**	25pf. blue	11·00	1·40
436	**81**	30pf. olive	7·75	1·40
437	**82**	40pf. violet	22·00	1·40
438	**81**	45pf. orange	13·50	4·75
439	**82**	50pf. brown	14·50	4·00
440	**81**	60pf. brown	17·00	4·75
441	**82**	80pf. brown	33·00	10·50
442	**82**	80pf. yellow	14·00	3·50

83 Airship LZ-127 "Graf Zeppelin"

1928. Air.
443	83	1m. red	36·00	55·00
444	83	2m. blue	60·00	75·00
445	83	4m. brown	39·00	55·00

1928. Welfare Fund. As T **75**, dated "1928".
446		5pf.+5pf. green, red & yellow	90	5·75
447		8pf.+7pf. multicoloured	80	5·75
448		15pf.+15pf. red, bl & yellow	1·10	5·75
449		25pf.+25pf. blue, red & yellow	13·50	75·00
450		50pf.+50pf. multicoloured	65·00	£140

ARMS: 5pf. Hamburg; 8pf. Mecklenburg-Schwerin; 15pf. Oldenburg; 25pf. Brunswick; 50pf. Anhalt.

1929. Welfare Fund. As T **75**, dated "1929".
451		5pf.+2pf. green, yellow & red	90	3·00
452		8pf.+4pf. yellow, red & green	1·00	3·00
453		15pf.+5pf. yellow, blk & red	1·10	2·40
454		25pf.+10pf. multicoloured	17·00	75·00
455		50pf.+40pf. yellow, red & brn	60·00	£140

ARMS: 5pf. Bremen; 8pf. Lippe; 15pf. Lubeck; 25pf. Mecklenburg-Strelitz; 50pf. Schaumburg-Lippe.

1930. Air. LZ-127 *Graf Zeppelin* 1st S. American Flight. T **83** inscr "I. SUDAMERIKA FAHRT".
456		2m. blue	£450	£600
457		4m. brown	£450	£600

1930. Evacuation of Rhineland by Allied Forces. Optd **30. JUNI 1930**.
459	81	8pf. green	2·20	1·40
460	82	15pf. red	2·75	1·40

86 Aachen

1930. International Philatelic Exhibition, Berlin.
461	86	8pf.+4pf. green	45·00	£160
462	-	15pf.+5pf. red	45·00	£160
463	-	25pf.+10pf. blue	45·00	£160
464	-	50pf.+40pf. brown	45·00	£160

MS464a 195×148 mm. Nos. 461/4 (sold at 2m.70 in the exhibition) £600 £2250

DESIGNS: 15p. Berlin; 25pf. Marienwerder; 50pf. Wurzburg.

1930. Welfare Fund.
465	86	8pf.+4pf. green	55	1·40
466	-	15pf.+5pf. red	65	1·90
467	-	25pf.+10pf. blue	11·00	35·00
468	-	50pf.+40pf. brown	33·00	£130

DESIGNS: 15pf. Berlin; 25pf. Marienwerder; 50pf. Wurzburg.

1931. Air. LZ-125 *Graf Zeppelin* Polar Flight. Optd **POLAR-FAHRT 1931**.
469	83	1m. red	£170	£160
470	83	2m. blue	£250	£300
471	83	4m. brown	£600	£1000

92 Heidelberg Castle

1931. Welfare Fund.
472	-	8pf.+4pf. green	55	1·80
473	-	15pf.+5pf. red	65	1·80
474	92	25pf.+10pf. blue	11·00	47·00
475	-	50pf.+40pf. brown	48·00	£120

DESIGNS—VERT: 8pf. The Zwinger, Dresden; 15pf. Town Hall, Breslau; 50pf. The Holstentor, Lubeck.
See also Nos. 485/9.

1932. Welfare Fund. Nos. 472/3 surch with new values.
476		6+4pf. on 8pf.+4pf. green	5·50	15·00
477		12+3pf. on 15pf.+5pf. red	7·75	18·00

94 President von Hindenburg

1932. 85th Birthday of Pres. von Hindenburg.
478	94	4pf. blue	80	95
496B	94	5pf. green	20	60
480	94	12pf. orange	6·75	95
481	94	15pf. red	4·50	15·00
503B	94	25pf. blue	65	60
483	94	40pf. violet	26·00	2·30
484	94	50pf. brown	8·50	16·00

See also Nos. 493/509 and 545/50.

1932. Welfare Fund. As T **92**.
485		4pf.+2pf. blue	70	1·80
486		6pf.+4pf. olive	90	1·80
487		12pf.+3pf. red	70	1·80
488		25pf.+10pf. blue	13·50	28·00
489		40pf.+40pf. purple	39·00	£100

CASTLES: 4pf. Wartburg; 6pf. Stolzenfels; 12pf. Nuremberg; 25pf. Lichtenstein; 40pf. Marburg.

96 Frederick the Great (after A. von Menzel)

1933. Opening of Reichstag in Potsdam.
490	96	6pf. green	85	1·40
491	96	12pf. red	1·10	1·40
492	96	25pf. blue	55·00	33·00

1933
493B	94	1pf. black	20	60
494B	94	3pf. brown	20	60
495B	94	4pf. grey	20	60
497B	94	6pf. brown	20	60
498B	94	8pf. orange	20	60
499B	94	10pf. brown	20	60
500B	94	12pf. red	20	60
501B	94	15pf. red	45	60
502B	94	20pf. blue	65	60
504B	94	30pf. green	1·10	60
505B	94	40pf. mauve	2·20	60
506B	94	50pf. black and green	4·50	60
507B	94	60pf. black and red	1·10	60
508B	94	80pf. black and blue	3·25	1·90
509B	94	100pf. black and yellow	4·50	1·80

1933. Air. LZ-127 *Graf Zeppelin* Chicago World Exhibition Flight. Optd **Chicagofahrt Weltausstellung 1933**.
510	83	1m. red	£1000	£600
511	83	2m. blue	£100	£300
512	83	4m. brown	£100	£300

99 Tannhauser

1933. Welfare Fund. Wagner's Operas.
513	99	3pf.+2pf. brown	2·50	8·75
514	-	4pf.+2pf. blue	1·70	3·50
515	-	5pf.+2pf. green	4·50	10·50
516	-	6pf.+4pf. green	1·70	3·50
517	-	8pf.+4pf. orange	2·75	5·75
518	-	12pf.+3pf. red	2·50	4·00
519a	-	20pf.+10pf. light blue	£160	£150
520	-	25pf.+15pf. blue	39·00	60·00
521	-	40pf.+35pf. mauve	£160	£200

OPERAS: 4pf. *The Flying Dutchman*; 5pf. *Rhinegold*; 6pf. *The Mastersingers*; 8pf. *The Valkyries*; 12pf. *Siegfried*; 20pf. *Tristan and Isolde*; 25pf. *Lohengrin*; 40pf. *Parsifal*.

1933. Welfare Fund. Stamps as 1924, issued together in sheets of four, each stamp optd **1923–1933**.
522	65	5+15pf. green	£130	£600
523	-	10+30pf. red	£130	£600
524	-	20+60pf. blue	£130	£600
525	-	50pf.+1.50m. brown	£130	£600

MS525a 210×148 mm. Nos. 522/5 £2000 £16000

100 Golden Eagle, Globe and Swastika
101 Count Zeppelin and Airship LZ-127 *Graf Zeppelin*

1934. Air.
526	100	5pf. green	1·70	1·40
527	100	10pf. red	1·70	1·40
528	100	15pf. blue	2·75	1·90
529	100	20pf. blue	5·00	2·50
530	100	25pf. brown	6·75	3·00
531	100	40pf. mauve	10·00	1·80
532	100	50pf. green	18·00	1·40
533	100	80pf. yellow	5·50	5·75
534	100	100pf. black	11·00	4·00
535	-	2m. grey and green	25·00	29·00
536	101	3m. grey and blue	45·00	65·00

DESIGN—As Type **101**: 2m. Otto Lilienthal and Lilienthal biplane glider.

103 Franz A. E. Luderitz

1934. German Colonizers' Jubilee.
537	103	3pf. brown and chocolate	3·25	9·25
538	-	6pf. brown and green	1·70	2·30
539	-	12pf. brown and red	2·75	2·30
540	-	25pf. brown and blue	14·00	30·00

DESIGNS: 6pf. Gustav Nachtigal; 12pf. Karl Peters; 25pf. Hermann von Wissmann.

104 "Saar Ownership"

1934. Saar Plebiscite.
541	104	6pf. green	4·25	95
542	-	12pf. red	6·75	95

DESIGN: 12pf. Eagle inscribed "Saar" in rays from a swastika-eclipsed sun.

105 Nuremberg Castle

1934. Nuremberg Congress.
543	105	6pf. green	4·25	95
544	105	12pf. red	6·75	95

1934. Hindenburg Memorial. Portrait with black borders.
545	94	3pf. brown	1·10	70
546	94	5pf. green	1·10	80
547	94	6pf. green	2·00	70
548	94	8pf. orange	3·25	70
549	94	12pf. red	3·50	70
550	94	25pf. blue	11·00	13·00

106 Blacksmith

1934. Welfare Fund.
551	-	3pf.+2pf. brown	1·30	2·30
552	106	4pf.+2pf. black	1·10	2·30
553	-	5pf.+2pf. green	9·00	11·50
554	-	6pf.+4pf. green	85	95
555	-	8pf.+4pf. red	1·30	3·00
556	-	12pf.+3pf. red	80	95
557	-	20pf.+10pf. green	26·00	33·00
558	-	25pf.+15pf. blue	26·00	33·00
559	-	40pf.+35pf. lilac	70·00	£110

DESIGNS: 3pf. Merchant; 5pf. Mason; 6pf. Miner; 8pf. Architect; 12pf. Farmer; 20pf. Scientist; 25pf. Sculptor; 40pf. Judge.

107 Friedrich von Schiller

1934. 175th Birth Anniv of Schiller.
560	107	6pf. green	4·00	95
561	107	12pf. red	6·75	95

108 "The Saar comes home"

1935. Saar Restoration.
562	108	3pf. brown	1·00	1·80
563	108	6pf. green	1·00	1·20
564	108	12pf. red	3·00	1·20
565	108	25pf. blue	12·50	13·00

109 "Steel Helmet"

1935. War Heroes' Day.
566	109	6pf. green	1·30	2·30
567	109	12pf. red	1·30	2·30

110 "Victor's Crown"

1935. Apprentices Vocational Contest.
568	110	6pf. green	1·30	2·10
569	110	12pf. red	1·70	2·10

111 Heinrich Schutz

1935. Musicians' Anniversaries.
570	111	6pf. green	80	1·20
571	-	12pf. red (Bach)	1·10	1·20
572	-	25pf. blue (Handel)	2·20	1·40

112 Allenstein Castle

1935. International Philatelic Exhibition, Konigsberg. In miniature sheets.
573	112	3pf. brown	50·00	60·00
574	-	6pf. green	50·00	60·00
575	-	12pf. red	50·00	60·00
576	-	25pf. blue	50·00	60·00

MS576a 148×105 mm. Nos. 573/6 £1200 £1100

DESIGNS: 6pf. Tannenberg Memorial; 12pf. Konigsberg Castle; 25pf. Heilsberg Castle.

113 Stephenson Locomotive *Adler*, 1835

1935. German Railway Centenary. Locomotive types inscr "1835–1935".
577	113	6pf. green	1·70	1·20
578	-	12pf. red	1·70	1·20
579	-	25pf. blue	8·25	2·75
580	-	40pf. purple	14·00	2·75

DESIGNS: 12pf. Class 03 steam train, 1930s; 25pf. Diesel train *Flying Hamburger*; 40pf. Class 05 streamlined steam locomotive No. 001, 1935.

114 Trumpeter

1935. World Jamboree of "Hitler Youth".
581	114	6pf. green	1·80	3·50
582	114	15pf. red	2·50	4·75

115 Nuremberg

1935. Nuremberg Congress.
583	115	6pf. green	1·30	80
584	115	12pf. red	3·25	80

116 East Prussia

1935. Welfare Fund. Provincial Costumes.

585	116	3pf.+2pf. brown	45	60
586	-	4pf.+3pf. blue	1·70	2·30
587	-	5pf.+3pf. green	45	1·50
588	-	6pf.+4pf. green	30	60
589	-	8pf.+4pf. brown	2·75	2·30
590	-	12pf.+6pf. red	40	60
591	-	15pf.+10pf. brown	6·75	8·75
592	-	25pf.+15pf. blue	11·50	9·25
593	-	30pf.+20pf. grey	17·00	30·00
594	-	40pf.+35pf. mauve	13·50	22·00

COSTUMES: 4pf. Silesia; 5pf. Rhineland; 6pf. Lower Saxony; 8pf. Kurmark; 12pf. Black Forest; 15pf. Hesse; 25pf. Upper Bavaria; 30pf. Friesland; 40pf. Franconia.

117 S.A. Man and Feldherrnhalle, Munich

1935. 12th Anniv of 1st Hitler Putsch.

595	117	3pf. brown	50	1·10
596	117	12pf. red	1·30	1·10

118 Skating

1935. Winter Olympic Games, Garmisch-Partenkirchen.

597	118	6pf.+4pf. green	1·10	2·10
598	-	12pf.+6pf. red	2·00	1·90
599	-	25pf.+15pf. blue	10·00	11·50

DESIGNS: 12pf. Ski jumping; 25pf. Bobsleighing.

119 Heinkel He 70 Blitz

1936. Tenth Anniv of Lufthansa Airways.

600	119	40pf. blue	9·00	4·75

120 Gottlieb Daimler

1936. Berlin Motor Show. 50th Anniv of Invention of First Motor Car.

601	120	6pf. green	85	1·50
602	120	12pf. red (Carl Benz)	1·10	1·50

121 Airship LZ-129 "Hindenburg"

1936. Air.

603	121	50pf. blue	27·00	1·20
604	121	75pf. green	29·00	1·60

122 Otto von Guericke

1936. 250th Death Anniv of Otto von Guericke (scientist).

605	122	6pf. green	45	80

123 Gymnastics

1936. Summer Olympic Games, Berlin.

606	123	3pf.+2pf. brown	50	70
607	-	4pf.+3pf. blue	45	1·20
608	-	6pf.+4pf. green	50	70
609	-	8pf.+4pf. red	4·50	2·00
610	-	12pf.+6pf. red	55	70
611	-	15pf.+10pf. red	7·75	4·75

612	-	25pf.+15pf. blue	5·00	5·75
613	-	40pf.+35pf. violet	9·25	11·50
MS613a		Two sheets, each 148×105 mm. (a) Nos. 606/8 and 613; (b)		
		Nos. 609/12	£100	£150

DESIGNS: 4pf. Diver; 6pf. Footballer; 8pf. Javelin thrower; 12pf. Olympic torchbearer; 15pf. Fencer; 25pf. Double scullers; 40pf. Show jumper.

124 Symbolical of Local Government

1936. Sixth Int Local Government Congress.

614	124	3pf. brown	65	45
615	124	5pf. green	70	45
616	124	12pf. red	1·10	95
617	124	25pf. blue	2·00	1·60

125 "Brown Ribbon" Race

1936. "Brown Ribbon of Germany". Single stamp in miniature sheet.

MS618	125	42pf. brown	14·50	21·00

126 "Leisure Time"

1936. Int Recreational Congress, Hamburg.

619	126	6pf. green	65	80
620	126	15pf. red	1·30	1·50

127 Saluting the Swastika

1936. Nuremberg Congress.

621	127	6pf. green	80	95
622	127	12pf. red	1·30	95

128 Luitpoldhain Heroes Memorial, Nuremberg

1936. Winter Relief Fund.

623	-	3pf.+2pf. brown	35	60
624	-	4pf.+3pf. black	35	70
625	128	5pf.+3pf. green	35	60
626	-	6pf.+4pf. green	35	60
627	-	8pf.+4pf. brown	1·30	2·00
628	-	12pf.+6pf. red	35	60
629	-	15pf.+10pf. brown	3·25	5·25
630	-	25pf.+15pf. blue	2·75	5·75
631	-	40pf.+35pf. mauve	4·25	10·50

DESIGNS: 3pf. Munich frontier road; 4pf. Air Ministry, Berlin; 6pf. Bridge over River Saale; 8pf. Deutschlandhalle, Berlin; 12pf. Alpine road; 15pf. Fuhrerhaus, Munich; 25pf. Bridge over River Mangfall; 40pf. German Art Museum, Munich.

129 R(eichs) L(uftschutz) B(und) = Civil Defence Union

1937. Fourth Anniv of Civil Defence Union.

632	129	3pf. brown	70	60
633	129	6pf. green	90	60
634	129	12pf. red	1·70	1·20

130 Adolf Hitler

1937. Hitler's Culture Fund and 48th birthday. Four stamps in miniature sheet (148×105 mm). Perf or Imperf.

MS635	130	6+19pf. green	27·00	19·00

1937. "Brown Ribbon of Germany". No. MS618 optd with German eagle and ornamental border surrounding, "**1. AUGUST 1937 MUNCHEN-REIM**" in red.

MS637a	125	42pf. (+108pf.) brown	90·00	£150

1937. Nuremberg Congress. Four stamps in miniature sheet, as No. MS637, but optd **REICHSPARTEITAG NURNBERG 1937** in panels of stamps.

MS638	130	6+19pf. green	£110	70·00

131 Fishing Smacks

1937. Winter Relief Fund.

639	-	3pf.+2pf. brown	30	60
640	-	4pf.+3pf. black	1·70	1·80
641	131	5pf.+3pf. green	30	60
642	-	6pf.+4pf. green	30	60
643	-	8pf.+4pf. orange	1·10	1·80
644	-	12pf.+6pf. red	35	60
645	-	15pf.+10pf. brown	2·50	5·75
646	-	25pf.+15pf. blue	5·00	5·75
647	-	40pf.+35pf. purple	9·00	11·50

DESIGNS: 3pf. *Bremen* (lifeboat), 1931; 4pf. *Burgemeister Oswald* (lightship); 6pf. *Wilhelm Gustloff* (liner); 8pf. *Padua* (barque); 12pf. *Tannenberg* (liner); 15pf. *Schwerin* (train ferry); 25pf. *Hamburg* (liner); 40pf. *Europa* (liner).

132 Hitler Youth

1938. Hitler Culture Fund. Fifth Anniv of Hitler's Leadership.

648	132	6pf.+4pf. green	1·40	3·00
649	132	12pf.+8pf. red	1·40	3·00

133 "Unity"

1938. Austrian Plebiscite.

650	133	6pf. green	1·10	95

134 Adolf Hitler

1938. Hitler's Culture Fund and 49th Birthday.

652	134	12pf.+38pf. red	2·75	4·00

See also No. 660.

135 Breslau Cathedral

1938. 16th German Sports Tournament, Breslau. Inscr as in T **135**.

653	135	3pf. brown	55	80
654	-	6pf. green	55	80
655	-	12pf. red	1·10	80
656	-	15pf. brown	1·80	1·20

DESIGNS: 6pf. Hermann Goering Stadium; 12pf. Breslau Town Hall; 15pf. Centenary Hall.

136 Airship Gondola and Airship LZ-127 *Graf Zeppelin*

1938. Air. Birth Cent of Count Zeppelin.

657	-	25pf. blue	3·75	2·30
658	136	50pf. green	5·25	2·30

DESIGN: 25pf. Count Zeppelin and airship LZ-5.

137 Horsewoman

1938. "Brown Ribbon of Germany".

659	137	42pf.+108pf. brown	31·00	70·00

1938. Nuremberg Congress and Hitler's Culture Fund. As No. 652, but inscr "Reichsparteitag 1938".

660	134	6pf.+19pf. green	3·25	6·50

138 Saarpfalz Gautheater, Saarbrucken

1938. Opening of Gautheater and Hitler's Culture Fund.

661	138	6pf.+4pf. green	1·60	3·00
662	138	12pf.+8pf. red	3·00	4·00

139 Forchtenstein Castle, Burgenland

1938. Winter Relief.

663	139	3pf.+2pf. brown	35	70
664	-	4pf.+3pf. blue	2·50	1·80
665	-	5pf.+3pf. green	35	70
666	-	6pf.+4pf. green	35	70
667	-	8pf.+4pf. red	2·50	1·80
668	-	12pf.+6pf. red	40	70
669	-	15pf.+10pf. red	5·00	7·00
670	-	25pf.+15pf. blue	4·50	7·00
671	-	40pf.+35pf. mauve	10·00	11·50

DESIGNS: 4pf. Flexenstrasse; 5pf. Zell am See; 6pf. Grossglockner; 8pf. Augstein Castle, Wachau; 12pf. Wien (Prince Eugene Statue, Vienna); 15pf. Erzberg, Steiermark; 25pf. Hall-in-Tirol; 40pf. Braunau.

140 Sudeten Miner and Wife

1938. Acquisition of Sudetenland and Hitler's Culture Fund.

672	140	6pf.+4pf. green	2·20	4·75
673	140	12pf.+8pf. red	3·25	4·75

141 Racing Cars

1939. Int Motor Show, Berlin, and Hitler's Culture Fund.

674	-	6pf.+4pf. green	4·50	5·25
675	141	12pf.+8pf. red	4·50	5·25
676	-	25pf.+10pf. blue	11·00	9·25

DESIGNS: 6pf. Early Benz and Daimler cars; 25pf. Volkswagen car.

142 Eagle and Laurel Wreath

1939. Apprentices' Vocational Contest.

677	142	6pf. green	2·20	5·75
678	142	12pf. red	3·25	5·75

143 Adolf Hitler
in Braunau

1939. Hitler's 50th Birthday and Culture Fund.
| 679 | 143 | 12pf.+38pf. red | 2·20 | 7·00 |

144
Horticultural
Exhibition
Entrance and
Arms of
Stuttgart

1939. Stuttgart Horticultural Exhibition and Hitler's Culture Fund.
| 680 | 144 | 6pf.+4pf. green | 1·70 | 4·75 |
| 681 | 144 | 15pf.+5pf. red | 2·00 | 5·75 |

145 Adolf Hitler
Speaking

1939. National Labour Day and Hitler's Culture Fund.
| 682 | 145 | 6pf.+19pf. brown | 5·50 | 7·50 |

See also No. 689.

1939. Nurburgring Races and Hitler's Culture Fund. Nos. 674/6 optd **Nurburgring-Rennen**.
683	-	6pf.+4pf. green	31·00	41·00
684	141	12pf.+8pf. red	31·00	41·00
685	-	25pf.+10pf. blue	31·00	41·00

147 *Investment* and
Jockey

1939. 70th Anniv of German Derby.
| 686 | 147 | 25pf.+50pf. blue | 23·00 | 23·00 |

148 Training
Thoroughbred Horses

1939. "Brown Ribbon of Germany" and Hitler's Culture Fund.
| 687 | 148 | 42pf.+108pf. brown | 23·00 | 37·00 |

149 *Young
Venetian Woman*
after Durer

1939. German Art Day.
| 688 | 149 | 6pf.+19pf. green | 7·75 | 15·00 |

1939. Nuremberg Congress and Hitler's Culture Fund. As T **145**, but inscr "REICHS-PARTEITAG 1939".
| 689 | | 6pf.+19pf. brown | 6·25 | 14·00 |

150 Mechanics at Work
and Play

1939. Postal Employees' and Hitler's Culture Funds. Inscr "Kameradschaftsblock der Deutschen Reichspost".
690	-	3pf.+2pf. brown	3·25	8·25
691	-	4pf.+3pf. red	3·00	8·25
692	150	5pf.+3pf. green	1·00	2·30
693	-	6pf.+4pf. green	1·10	2·30
694	-	8pf.+4pf. orange	1·10	2·30

695	-	10pf.+5pf. brown	1·10	3·00
696	-	12pf.+6pf. red	1·30	3·00
697	-	15pf.+10pf. red	1·10	3·50
698	-	16pf.+10pf. green	1·10	3·50
699	-	20pf.+10pf. blue	1·10	3·50
700	-	24pf.+10pf. olive	3·25	5·75
701	-	25pf.+15pf. blue	3·00	4·75

DESIGNS: 3pf. Postal employees' rally; 4pf. Review in Vienna; 6pf. Youths on parade; 8pf. Flag bearers; 10pf. Distributing prizes; 12pf. Motor race; 15pf. Women athletes; 16pf. Postal police; 20pf. Glider workshop; 24pf. Mail coach; 25pf. Sanatorium, Konigstein.
See also Nos. 761/6 and 876/81.

151 St. Mary's
Church, Danzig

1939. Occupation of Danzig. Inscr "DANZIG IST DEUTSCH".
| 702 | 151 | 6pf. green | 55 | 1·20 |
| 703 | - | 12pf. red (Crane Gate) | 90 | 1·30 |

1939. Stamps of Danzig surch **Deutsches Reich** and new values.
704	28	Rpf. on 3pf. brown	90	3·25
705	28	4Rpf. on 35pf. blue	90	3·50
706	28	Rpf. on 5pf. orange	90	4·00
707	28	Rpf. on 8pf. green	1·40	5·75
708	28	Rpf. on 10pf. green	2·75	5·75
709	28	12Rpf. on 7pf. green	2·00	3·25
710	28	Rpf. on 15pf. red	8·25	16·00
711	28	Rpf. on 20pf. grey	4·00	11·50
712	28	Rpf. on 25pf. red	6·25	15·00
713	28	Rpf. on 30pf. purple	2·75	6·50
714	28	Rpf. on 40pf. blue	3·25	8·25
715	28	Rpf. on 50pf. red and blue	5·00	10·00
716	42	1Rm on 1g. black & orge	19·00	80·00
717	-	2Rm on 2g. black and red (No. 206)	25·00	80·00

155 Elbogen Castle

1939. Winter Relief Fund.
718	155	3pf.+2pf. brown	30	70
719	-	4pf.+3pf. black	2·20	3·00
720	-	5pf.+3pf. green	35	80
721	-	6pf.+4pf. green	30	60
722	-	8pf.+4pf. red	2·20	2·50
723	-	12pf.+6pf. red	45	2·30
724	-	15pf.+10pf. brown	3·50	7·00
725	-	25pf.+15pf. blue	3·50	7·00
726	-	40pf.+35pf. purple	4·25	9·25

DESIGNS: 4pf. Drachenfels; 5pf. Goslar Castle; 6pf. Clocktower, Graz; 8pf. The Romer, Frankfurt; 12pf. City Hall, Klagenfurt; 15pf. Ruins of Schreckenstein Castle; 25pf. Salzburg Fortress; 40pf. Hohentwiel Castle.

156 Leipzig Library
and Gutenberg

1940. Leipzig Fair.
727	156	3pf. brown	55	70
728	-	6pf. green	55	70
729	-	12pf. red	55	70
730	-	25pf. blue	1·30	1·80

DESIGNS: 6pf. Augustusplatz; 12pf. Old Town Hall; 25pf. View of Fair.

157 Courtyard of
Chancellery, Berlin

1940. Second Berlin Philatelic Exhibition.
| 731 | 157 | 24pf.+76pf. green | 9·00 | 26·00 |

158 Hitler and
Child

1940. Hitler's 51st Birthday.
| 732 | 158 | 12pf.+38pf. red | 4·50 | 9·25 |

159
Wehrmacht
Symbol

1940. National Fete Day and Hitler's Culture Fund.
| 733 | 159 | 6pf.+4pf. green | 45 | 2·00 |

160 Horseman

1940. Hamburg Derby and Hitler's Culture Fund.
| 734 | 160 | 25pf.+100pf. blue | 6·25 | 18·00 |

161 Chariot

1940. Hitler's Culture Fund and "Brown Ribbon" Race.
| 735 | 161 | 42pf.+108pf. brown | 33·00 | 41·00 |

162 Malmedy

1940. Eupen and Malmedy reincorporated in Germany, and Hitler's Culture Fund. Inscr "Eupen-Malmedy wieder Deutsch".
| 736 | 162 | 6pf.+4pf. green | 1·30 | 4·50 |
| 737 | - | 12pf.+8pf. red | 1·30 | 4·50 |

DESIGNS: 12pf. View of Eupen.

163 Heligoland

1940. 50th Anniv of Cession of Heligoland to Germany and Hitler's Culture Fund.
| 738 | 163 | 6pf.+94pf. red and green | 8·25 | 18·00 |

164 Artushof,
Danzig

1940. Winter Relief Fund.
739	164	3pf.+2pf. brown	30	70
740	-	4pf.+3pf. blue	80	1·20
741	-	5pf.+3pf. green	30	70
742	-	6pf.+4pf. green	35	70
743	-	8pf.+4pf. orange	1·30	1·30
744	-	12pf.+6pf. red	40	70
745	-	15pf.+10pf. brown	1·40	4·00
746	-	25pf.+15pf. blue	2·20	4·00
747	-	40pf.+35pf. purple	3·50	9·25

DESIGNS: 4pf. Town Hall, Thorn; 5pf. Kaub Castle; 6pf. City Theatre, Posen; 8pf. Heidelberg Castle; 12pf. Porta Nigra, Trier; 15pf. New Theatre, Prague; 25pf. Town Hall, Bremen; 40pf. Town Hall, Munster.

165 Emil von
Behring
(bacteriologist)

1940. 50th Anniv of Development of Diphtheria Antitoxin.
| 748 | 165 | 6pf.+4pf. green | 90 | 3·25 |
| 749 | 165 | 25pf.+10pf. blue | 1·60 | 3·50 |

166 Postilion
and Globe

1941. Stamp Day.
| 750 | 166 | 6pf.+24pf. green | 1·70 | 4·75 |

167 Mussolini and Hitler

1941. Hitler's Culture Fund.
| 751 | 167 | 12pf.+38pf. red | 1·70 | 6·50 |

168 House of
Nations, Leipzig

1941. Leipzig Fair. Buildings. Inscr "REICHSMESSE LEIPZIG 1941".
752	168	3pf. brown	35	1·50
753	-	6pf. green	35	1·50
754	-	12pf. red	45	1·80
755	-	25pf. blue	1·10	2·30

DESIGNS: 6pf. Cloth Hall; 12pf. Exhibition Building; 25pf. Railway Station.

169 Dancer

1941. Vienna Fair.
756	169	3pf. brown	55	80
757	-	6pf. green	55	80
758	-	12pf. red	55	95
759	-	25pf. blue	1·40	2·30

DESIGNS: 6pf. Arms and Exhibition Building; 12pf. Allegory and Municipal Theatre; 25pf. Prince Eugene's Equestrian Monument.

170 Adolf Hitler

1941. Hitler's 52nd Birthday and Culture Fund.
| 760 | 170 | 12pf.+38pf. red | 1·70 | 4·75 |

1941. Postal Employees' and Hitler's Culture Funds. Inscr "Kameradschaftsblock der Deutschen Reichspost" as Nos. 693/4, 696 and 698/700, but premium values and colours changed.
761		6pf.+9pf. green	1·10	3·50
762		8pf.+12pf. red	1·30	2·30
763		12pf.+18pf. red	1·30	3·00
764		16pf.+24pf. blue	1·30	5·75
765		20pf.+30pf. blue	1·90	5·75
766		24pf.+36pf. violet	6·75	18·00

171 Racehorse

1941. 72nd Anniv of Hamburg Derby.
| 767 | 171 | 25pf.+100pf. blue | 4·50 | 11·50 |

172 Two Amazons

1941. "Brown Ribbon of Germany".

768	172	42pf.+108pf. brown	2·75	7·50

173 Adolf Hitler

1941

769	173	1pf. grey	20	45
770	173	3pf. brown	20	45
771	173	4pf. slate	20	45
772	173	5pf. green	20	45
773	173	6pf. violet	20	45
774	173	8pf. red	20	45
777	173	10pf. brown	55	65
776	173	12pf. red	35	70
779	173	15pf. lake	45	2·30
780	173	16pf. green	20	2·30
781	173	20pf. blue	20	60
782	173	24pf. brown	20	2·30
783	173	25pf. blue	20	70
784	173	30pf. olive	20	70
785	173	40pf. mauve	20	70
786	173	50pf. green	20	70
787	173	60pf. brown	20	70
788	173	80pf. blue	20	70

Nos. 783/8 are larger (21½x26 mm).

174 Brandenburg Gate, Berlin

1941. Berlin Grand Prix and Hitler's Culture Fund.

789	174	25pf.+50pf. blue	4·00	10·50

175 Belvedere Palace, Vienna   **176** Belvedere Gardens, Vienna

1941. Vienna Fair and Hitler's Culture Fund.

790	175	12pf.+8pf. red	1·70	5·75
791	176	15pf.+10pf. violet	1·70	5·75

177 Marburg   **178** Veldes

1941. Annexation of Northern Slovenia, and Hitler's Culture Fund.

792	177	3pf.+7pf. brown	1·30	3·50
793	178	6pf.+9pf. violet	1·30	3·50
794	-	12pf.+13pf. red	1·30	4·00
795	-	25pf.+15pf. blue	2·30	4·00

DESIGNS: 12pf. Pettau; 25pf. Triglav.

179 Mozart

1941. 150th Death Anniv of Mozart and Hitler's Culture Fund.

796	179	6pf.+4pf. purple	30	1·40

180 Philatelist

1942. Stamp Day and Hitler's Culture Fund.

797	180	6pf.+24pf. violet	80	4·50

181 Symbolical of Heroism

1942. Heroes' Remembrance Day and Hitler's Culture Fund.

798	181	12pf.+38pf. slate	2·75	2·30

182 Adolf Hitler

1942

799a	182	1m. green	65	8·25
800a	182	2m. violet	2·20	11·50
801	182	3m. red	2·20	23·00
802a	182	5m. blue	4·50	75·00

183 Adolf Hitler

1942. Hitler's 53rd Birthday and Culture Fund.

803	183	12pf.+38pf. red	2·20	9·25

184 Jockey and Three-year-old Horse

1942. Hamburg Derby and Hitler's Culture Fund.

804	184	25pf.+100pf. blue	6·75	18·00

185 Equine Trio

1942. "Brown Ribbon of Germany" and Hitler's Culture Fund.

805	185	42pf.+108pf. brown	2·20	8·25

186 Cream Jug and Loving Cup

1942. Tenth Anniv of National Goldsmiths' Institution.

806	186	6pf.+4pf. brown	40	2·30
807	186	12pf.+88pf. green	85	3·50

187 Badge of Armed S.A.

1942. S.A. Military Training Month.

808	187	6pf. violet	20	1·20

188 Peter Henlein

1942. 400th Death Anniv of Henlein (inventor of the watch).

809	188	6pf.+24pf. violet	65	2·30

189 Mounted Postilion

1942. European Postal Congress, Vienna.

810	-	3pf.+7pf. blue	45	2·30
811	-	6pf.+14pf. brown & blue	65	2·30
812	189	12pf.+38pf. brown & red	90	4·00

DESIGNS—HORIZ: 3pf. Postilion and map of Europe. VERT: 6pf. Mounted postilion and globe.

1942. Signing of European Postal Union Agreement. Nos. 810/2 optd **19.Okt.1942**.

813	-	3pf.+7pf. blue	1·10	4·00
814	-	6pf.+14pf. brown & blue	1·10	4·00
815	189	12pf.+38pf. brown & red	1·70	7·00

191 Mail Coach

1943. Stamp Day and Hitler's Culture Fund.

816	191	6pf.+24pf. brn, yell & bl	20	1·40

192 Brandenburg Gate and Torchlight Parade

1943. Tenth Anniv of Third Reich.

817	192	54pf.+96pf. red	65	3·50

193

1943. Philatelic Cancellation Premium.

818	193	3pf.+2pf. bistre	20	1·40

194 Machine Gunners

1943. Armed Forces' and Heroes' Day.

819	-	3pf.+2pf. brown	55	1·90
820	194	4pf.+3pf. brown	55	1·90
821	-	5pf.+4pf. green	55	1·90
822	-	6pf.+9pf. violet	55	1·90
823	-	8pf.+7pf. red	55	1·90
824	-	12pf.+8pf. red	55	1·90
825	-	15pf.+10pf. purple	55	1·90
826	-	20pf.+14pf. blue	55	1·90
827	-	25pf.+15pf. blue	55	1·90
828	-	30pf.+30pf. green	90	3·00
829	-	40pf.+40pf. purple	90	3·00
830	-	50pf.+50pf. green	1·30	4·75

DESIGNS: 3pf. U-boat Type VIIA (submarine); 5pf. Armed motor cyclists; 6pf. Wireless operators; 8pf. Engineers making pontoon; 12pf. Grenade thrower; 15pf. Heavy artillery; 20pf. Anti-aircraft gunners; 25pf. Junkers Ju 87B "Stuka" dive bombers; 30pf. Parachutists; 40pf. Tank; 50pf. "S-22" (motor torpedo-boat).

195 Hitler Youth

1943. Youth Dedication Day.

831	195	6pf.+4pf. green	35	2·00

196 Adolf Hitler

1943. Hitler's 54th Birthday and Culture Fund.

832	196	3pf.+7pf. black	70	2·30
833	196	6pf.+14pf. green	70	2·30
834	196	8pf.+22pf. blue	70	2·30
835	196	12pf.+38pf. red	70	2·30
836	196	24pf.+76pf. purple	1·40	5·25
837	196	40pf.+160pf. olive	1·40	5·25

197 Attestation

1943. Labour Corps.

838	197	3pf.+7pf. brown	20	1·20

839	-	5pf.+10pf. green	20	1·20
840	-	6pf.+14pf. blue	20	1·20
841	-	12pf.+18pf. red	50	2·10

DESIGNS: 5pf. Harvester sharpening scythe; 6pf. Labourer wielding sledge-hammer; 12pf. "Pick and shovel fatigue".

198 Huntsman

1943. "Brown Ribbon of Germany".

842	198	42pf.+108pf. brown	35	1·90

199 Birthplace of Peter Rosegger   **200** Peter Rosegger

1943. Birth Cent of Peter Rosegger (poet).

843	199	6pf.+4pf. green	20	1·40
844	200	12pf.+8pf. red	35	1·40

201 Racehorse

1943. Grand Prix, Vienna.

845	201	6pf.+4pf. violet	35	1·90
846	201	12pf.+88pf. red	35	1·90

202 Mother and Children

1943. Tenth Anniv of Winter Relief Fund.

847	202	12pf.+38pf. red	35	1·90

203 St George and the Dragon

1943. 11th Anniv of National Goldsmiths' Institution.

848	203	6pf.+4pf. green	30	1·20
849	203	12pf.+88pf. purple	35	1·80

204 Lubeck

1943. 800th Anniv of Lubeck.

850	204	12pf.+8pf. red	20	1·80

205

1943. 20th Anniv of Munich Rising.

851	205	24pf.+26pf. red	20	2·30

206 Dr. Robert Koch

1944. Birth Centenary of Dr. Robert Koch (bacteriologist).

852	206	12pf.+38pf. sepia	20	1·80

207 Adolf Hitler

1944. 11th Anniv of Third Reich.

853	207	54pf.+96pf. brown	35	3·50

208 Focke Wulf Fw 200 Condor over Tempelhof Airport   **209** Dornier Do-26 Flying Boat

1944. 25th Anniv of Air Mail Services.

854	208	6pf.+4pf. green	35	1·80
855	209	12pf.+8pf. purple	35	1·80
856	-	42pf.+108pf. blue	50	3·50

DESIGNS—VERT: 42pf. Junkers Ju 90B airplane seen from above.

210 Day Nursery   **211** "Mothers' Help"

1944. Tenth Anniv of "Mother and Child" Organization.

857	210	3pf.+2pf. brown	20	1·10
858	211	6pf.+4pf. green	20	1·20
859	-	12pf.+8pf. red	20	1·10
860	-	15pf.+10pf. purple	20	1·20

DESIGNS: 12pf. Child auscultation; 15pf. Mothers at convalescent home.

212 Landing Craft

1944. Armed Forces' and Heroes' Day.

861	212	3pf.+2pf. brown	50	1·80
862	-	4pf.+3pf. blue	50	1·80
863	-	5pf.+3pf. green	20	80
864	-	6pf.+4pf. violet	20	80
865	-	8pf.+4pf. red	7·75	75·00
866	-	10pf.+5pf. brown	20	80
867	-	12pf.+6pf. red	20	75
868	-	15pf.+10pf. purple	20	1·20
869	-	16pf.+10pf. green	40	1·90
870	-	20pf.+10pf. blue	50	3·90
871	-	24pf.+10pf. brown	50	3·00
872	-	25pf.+15pf. blue	1·10	5·75
873	-	30pf.+20pf. olive	1·10	5·75

DESIGNS: 4pf. Caterpillar tricar; 5pf. Parachutists; 6pf. Submarine officer; 8pf. Mortar-firing party; 10pf. Searchlight unit; 12pf. Machine gunners; 15pf. Tank; 16pf. "S-128" (motor torpedo-boat); 20pf. Arado Ar 196A seaplane; 24pf. Railway gun; 25pf. Rocket projectiles; 30pf. Alpine trooper.

213 Fulda Monument

1944. 1200th Anniv of Fulda.

874	213	12pf.+38pf. brown	20	1·40

214 Adolf Hitler

1944. Hitler's 55th Birthday.

875	214	54pf.+96pf. red	45	4·75

215 Postwoman

1944. Postal Employees' and Hitler's Culture Funds. Inscr "Kameradschaftsblock der Deutschen Reichspost".

876	215	6pf.+9pf. blue	30	1·20
877	-	8pf.+12pf. grey	30	1·20
878	-	12pf.+18pf. mauve	30	1·20
879	-	16pf.+24pf. green	30	1·20
880	-	20pf.+30pf. blue	30	2·10
881	-	24pf.+36pf. violet	55	2·10

DESIGNS—As Type 150: 8pf. Mail coach; 16pf. Motor-car race; 20pf. Postal police march; 24pf. Glider workshop. As Type 215: 12pf. The Field Post on Eastern Front.

216 Girl Worker   **217** Labourer

1944. Labour Corps.

882	216	6pf.+4pf. green	20	1·10
883	217	12pf.+8pf. red	20	1·10

218 Riflemen

1944. Seventh Innsbruck Shooting Competition.

884	218	6pf.+4pf. green	20	1·30
885	218	12pf.+8pf. red	20	1·30

219 Duke Albrecht

1944. 400th Anniv of Albert University, Konigsberg.

886	219	6pf.+4pf. green	35	1·90

220 Racehorse and Foal

1944. "Brown Ribbon of Germany".

887	220	42pf.+108pf. brown	35	3·25

221 Racehorse and Laurel Wreath

1944. Vienna Grand Prix.

888	221	6pf.+4pf. green	20	1·60
889	221	12pf.+88pf. red	20	1·60

222 Chambered Nautilus Beaker

1944. National Goldsmiths' Institution.

890	222	6pf.+4pf. green	20	1·60
891	222	12pf.+88pf. red	20	1·60

223 Posthorn

1944. Stamp Day.

892	223	6pf.+24pf. green	20	1·90

224 Eagle and Dragon

1944. 21st Anniv of Munich Rising.

893	224	12pf.+8pf. red	20	1·90

225 Adolf Hitler

1944

894	225	42pf. green	20	3·00

226 Count Anton Gunther

1945. 600th Anniv of Oldenburg.

895	226	6pf.+14pf. purple	20	1·90

227 "Home Guard"

1945. Mobilization of "Home Guard".

896	227	12pf.+8pf. red	45	4·00

228 S.S. Troopers

1945. 12th Anniv of Third Reich.

897	228	12pf.+38pf. red	17·00	80·00
898	-	12pf.+38pf. red	13·50	80·00

DESIGN: No. 898, S.A. man with torch.

For Nos. 899 onwards see section B of Allied Occupation.

MILITARY FIELDPOST STAMPS

M184 Junkers Ju 52/3m

1942. Air. No value indicated. Perf. or roul.

M804	M184	(–) blue	50	70

M185

1942. Parcel Post. Size 28×23 mm. No value indicated. Perf or roul.

M805	M185	(–) brown	40	18·00

Nos. M804/5 also exist overprinted INSELPOST in various types for use in Crete and the Aegean Islands and there are various other local fieldpost issues.

1944. Christmas Parcel Post. Size 22½×18 mm. No value indicated. Perf.

M895	(–) green	90	4·50

1944. For 2 kilo parcels. No value indicated. No. 785 optd FELDPOST 2kg.

M896	173	(–) on 40pf. mauve	90	4·75

NEWSPAPER STAMPS

N156 Newspaper Messenger and Globe

1939

N727	N156	5pf. green	85	8·25
N728	N156	10pf. brown	85	8·25

OFFICIAL STAMPS

O23

1903

O82	O23	2pf. grey	1·70	7·00
O83	O23	3pf. brown	1·70	7·00
O84	O23	5pf. green	35	80
O85	O23	10pf. red	35	80
O86	O23	20pf. blue	35	80
O87	O23	25pf. black and red on yellow	1·10	2·50
O88	O23	40pf. black and red	1·10	3·00
O89	O23	50pf. blk & pur on buff	1·10	3·00

O24

1905

O90	O24	2pf. grey	80·00	£120
O91	O24	3pf. brown	9·00	16·00
O92	O24	5pf. green	6·25	14·00
O93	O24	10pf. red	1·10	3·25
O94	O24	20pf. blue	2·20	4·75
O95	O24	25pf. black and red on yellow	45·00	80·00

O31   **O32**

1920. Numeral designs as Types O31 and O32.

O117	5pf. green	35	4·75
O118	10pf. red	1·10	2·30
O119	15pf. brown	20	3·50
O120	20pf. blue	20	3·00
O121	30pf. orange on pink	20	2·30
O122	50pf. violet on pink	45	2·30
O123	1m. red on pink	12·50	5·75

1920. Similar designs but without figures "21".

O124	5pf. brown on yellow	1·30	21·00
O125	10pf. red	20	2·50
O126	10pf. orange	90	£700
O127	15pf. purple	20	3·50
O128	20pf. blue	20	3·00
O129	30pf. orange on pink	20	3·00
O130	40pf. red	20	3·00
O131	50pf. violet on pink	20	3·00
O132	60pf. brown	45	2·30
O133	1m. red on pink	20	3·00
O134	1m.25 blue on yellow	20	5·75
O135a	2m. blue	20	2·30
O136	5m. brown on yellow	1·70	4·75

1920. Official stamps of Bavaria optd Deutsches Reich.

O137	O31	5pf. green	20	4·75
O138	O31	10pf. orange	20	2·30
O139	O31	15pf. red	20	3·00
O140	O31	20pf. purple	20	2·30
O141	O31	30pf. blue	20	2·30
O142	O31	40pf. brown	20	3·00
O143	O32	50pf. red	20	3·00
O144	O32	60pf. green	20	2·30
O145	O32	70pf. violet	2·75	4·00
O146	O32	75pf. red	45	2·10
O147	O32	80pf. blue	20	2·10
O148	O32	90pf. olive	2·20	5·25
O149	O33	1m. brown	20	3·00
O150	O33	1¼m. red	20	3·00
O151	O33	1½m. red	20	3·00
O152	O33	2½m. blue	20	3·00
O153	O33	3m. red	20	3·00
O154	O33	5m. black	12·50	41·00

1920. Municipal Service stamps of Wurttemberg optd Deutsches Reich.

O155	M5	5pf. green	5·50	15·00
O156	M5	10pf. red	3·25	7·00
O157	M5	15pf. violet	3·25	7·50
O158	M5	20pf. blue	5·50	13·00
O159	M5	50pf. purple	9·00	29·00

1920. Official stamps of Wurttemberg optd Deutsches Reich.

O160	O5	5pf. green	3·25	5·75
O161	O5	10pf. red	2·20	4·75
O162	O5	15pf. purple	2·20	4·75
O163	O5	20pf. blue	2·20	2·30
O164	O5	30pf. black and orange	2·20	5·75
O165	O5	40pf. black and red	2·20	4·75
O166	O5	50pf. purple	2·20	5·75
O167	O5	1m. black and grey	3·25	11·50

O48   **O50**

1922. Figure designs.

O247	-	3m. brown on red	20	2·30
O248	O50	10m. green on red	20	2·30

O249	O48	75pf. blue	35	11·50
O251	O50	20m. blue on red	20	2·30
O252	O50	50m. violet on red	20	2·30
O253	O50	100m. red on rose	20	2·30

1923. Postage stamps optd Dienstmarke.

O274	51	20m. purple	45	11·50
O275	51	30m. olive	20	55·00
O276	38	40m. green	45	4·75
O277	54	200m. red	20	2·30
O278	54	300m. green	20	2·30
O279	54	400m. brown	20	2·30
O280	54	500m. orange	20	2·30
O342	62	100M. grey	20	£225
O343	62	200M. brown	45	£225
O344	62	2Md. green and pink	20	£180
O345	62	5Md. brown and yellow	20	£130
O346	62	10Md. green and light green	5·50	£200
O347	62	20Md. brown and green	5·50	£225
O348	62	50Md. blue	2·75	£300

1923. Official stamps of 1920 and 1922 surch Tausend or Millionen and figure.

O312	-	5T. on 5m. brown on yellow	10	4·75
O313	-	20T. on 30pf. orange on rose (No. O129)	10	4·75
O317	O50	75T. on 50m. violet on rose	10	4·75
O314	-	100T. on 15pf. purple	10	4·75
O315	-	250T. on 10pf. red (No. O125)	10	4·75
O318	-	400T. on 15pf. purple	10	42·00
O319	-	800T. on 30pf. orge on rose (No. O129)	45	7·00
O320	O48	1M. on 75pf. blue	10	60·00
O321	-	2M. on 10pf. red (No. O125)	45	5·75
O322	O50	5M. on 100m. red on rose	10	8·75

1923. Nos. 352/7 optd Dienstmarke.

O358	64	3pf. brown	35	1·20
O359	64	5pf. green	35	1·20
O360	64	10pf. red	35	1·20
O361	64	20pf. blue	90	1·80
O362	64	50pf. orange	90	2·30
O363	64	100pf. purple	5·50	11·50

1924. Optd Dienstmarke.

O376	66	3pf. brown	55	3·50
O377	66	5pf. green	45	1·20
O378	66	10pf. red	45	1·20
O379	66	20pf. blue	45	1·20
O380	66	30pf. red	1·40	1·20
O381	66	40pf. olive	1·40	1·20
O382	66	50pf. orange	11·00	5·75
O384	72	60pf. brown	2·75	5·75
O385	72	80pf. grey	11·00	55·00

O81

1927

O424	O81	3pf. brown	50	1·20
O425	O81	4pf. blue	60	1·40
O427	O81	5pf. green	20	1·20
O428	O81	6pf. green	1·10	1·40
O429	O81	8pf. green	50	1·20
O430	O81	10pf. red	11·00	9·25
O432	O81	10pf. mauve	60	1·40
O433	O81	10pf. brown	5·50	14·00
O434	O81	12pf. orange	60	1·40
O436	O81	15pf. red	65	1·40
O437	O81	20pf. green	8·00	4·75
O438	O81	20pf. grey	2·20	1·80
O439	O81	30pf. green	1·50	1·90
O440	O81	40pf. violet	1·70	1·40
O441	O81	60pf. brown	1·70	3·00

O100

1934

O809	O100	3pf. brown	55	1·80
O527	O100	4pf. blue	45	1·40
O528	O100	5pf. green	20	1·80
O529	O100	6pf. green	20	1·40
O812	O100	6pf. violet	35	1·80
O813	O100	8pf. red	35	1·80
O531	O100	10pf. brown	45	11·50
O532	O100	12pf. red	2·75	2·30
O533	O100	15pf. red	1·60	14·00
O534	O100	20pf. blue	55	2·30
O535	O100	30pf. green	1·20	2·30

O536	O100	40pf. mauve	1·20	2·30
O537	O100	50pf. yellow	1·70	5·75
O820	O100	50pf. green	4·00	£475

SPECIAL STAMPS FOR USE BY OFFICIALS OF THE NATIONAL SOCIALIST GERMAN WORKERS' PARTY

P132 Party Badge

1938

O648	P132	1pf. black	1·40	4·75
O799	P132	3pf. brown	45	1·80
O650	P132	4pf. blue	1·40	2·30
O651	P132	5pf. green	1·20	2·30
O652	P132	5pf. green	1·20	2·30
O802	P132	6pf. violet	45	3·50
O803	P132	8pf. red	45	3·50
O804	P132	12pf. red	45	1·80
O655	P132	16pf. grey	1·70	14·00
O805	P132	16pf. blue	4·50	£120
O656	P132	24pf. green	2·75	7·50
O806	P132	24pf. brown	85	47·00
O657	P132	30pf. green	2·00	11·50
O658	P132	40pf. mauve	2·00	18·00

II. ALLIED OCCUPATION

A. Allied Military Post (British and American Zones)

The defeat of Germany in May 1945 resulted in the division of the country into four zones of occupation (British, American, French and Russian), while Berlin was placed under joint allied control. Allied Military Post Stamps came into use in the British and American zones, the French issued special stamps in their zone and in the Russian zone the first issues were made by local administrations.

The territory occupied by the Anglo-American and French Zones subsequently became the German Federal Republic (West Germany) which was set up in September 1949. By the Nine Power Agreement of 3 October 1954, the occupation of West Germany was ended and full sovereignty was granted to the German Federal Government as from 5 May 1955 (see Section III).

The territory in the Russian Zone became the German Democratic Republic (East Germany) which was set up on 7 October 1949 (see Section V).

Separate issues for the Western Sectors of Berlin came into being in 1948 (see Section IV). The Russian Zone issues inscribed "STADT BERLIN" were for use in the Russian sector of the city and Brandenburg and these were superseded first by the General Issues of the Russian Zone and then by the stamps of East Germany.

A1

1945

A16	A1	1pf. black	55	6·75
A10	A1	3pf. violet	30	85
A11	A1	4pf. grey	30	85
A3	A1	5pf. green	30	55
A4	A1	6pf. yellow	30	55
A5	A1	8pf. orange	30	55
A6	A1	10pf. brown	30	55
A7	A1	12pf. purple	40	85
A8	A1	15pf. red	30	2·10
A25	A1	16pf. green	55	19·00
A26	A1	20pf. blue	55	5·25
A27a	A1	24pf. brown	55	17·00
A9	A12	25pf. blue	40	2·20
A29	A1	30pf. olive	55	2·75
A30	A1	40pf. mauve	75	4·25
A31	A1	42pf. green	55	3·25
A32	A1	50pf. slate	55	21·00
A33	A1	60pf. plum	1·10	26·00
A34b	A1	80pf. blue	42·00	£425
A35	A1	1m. green	8·50	£700

Values 30pf. to 80pf. are size 22×25 mm and 1m. is size 25×29½ mm.
Nos. A36 etc continue in Section C.
Used prices are for cancelled-to-order.

B. American, British and Russian Zones 1946–48

From February 1946 to June 1948 these zones used the same stamps (Nos. 899/956). It had been intended that they should be used throughout all four zones but until the creation of the German Federal Republic, in September 1949, the French Zone always had its own stamps, while after the revaluation of the currency in June 1948 separate stamps were again issued for the Russian Zone.

229 Numeral

1946

899	229	1pf. black	20	4·25

900	229	2pf. black	20	30
901	229	3pf. brown	20	4·75
902	229	4pf. green	20	6·25
903	229	5pf. green	20	85
904	229	6pf. violet	20	20
905	229	8pf. red	20	30
906	229	10pf. brown	20	30
907	229	12pf. red	20	30
908	229	12pf. grey	20	30
909	229	15pf. red	20	9·50
910	229	15pf. green	20	30
911	229	16pf. green	20	30
912	229	20pf. blue	20	30
913	229	24pf. brown	20	30
914	229	25pf. blue	20	8·50
915	229	25pf. orange	20	1·60
916	229	30pf. green	20	30
917	229	40pf. purple	20	30
918	229	42pf. green	3·00	42·00
919	229	45pf. red	20	40
920	229	50pf. green	20	30
921	229	60pf. red	20	30
922	229	75pf. blue	20	30
923	229	80pf. blue	20	30
924	229	84pf. green	20	30
925	229	1m. green (24×30 mm)	20	30
MS925a		107×51 mm. Nos. 912/13 and 917 (sold at 5m.)	90·00	£300

231 1160: Leipzig obtains Charter

1947. Leipzig Spring Fair. Inscr "LEIPZIGER MESSE 1947".

926	231	12pf.+26pf. brown	1·60	6·75
927	-	60pf.+40pf. blue	1·60	6·75

DESIGN: 60pf. 1268: Foreign merchants at Leipzig Fair. See also Nos. 951/4.

233 Gardener   237 "Dove of Peace"

1947

928	233	2pf. black	20	55
929	233	6pf. violet	30	30
930	A	8pf. red	30	55
931	A	10pf. green	30	55
932	B	12pf. grey	30	30
933	233	15pf. brown	55	5·25
934	C	16pf. green	30	55
935	A	20pf. blue	30	1·60
936	C	24pf. brown	30	55
937	233	25pf. orange	30	1·60
938	B	30pf. red	55	4·25
939	A	40pf. mauve	30	55
940	C	50pf. blue	55	2·75
941	B	60pf. red	30	55
942	B	60pf. brown	30	1·10
943	B	80pf. blue	30	1·60
944	C	84pf. green	55	2·75
945	237	1m. green	40	55
946	237	2m. violet	40	1·60
947	237	3m. lake	40	26·00
948	237	5m. blue	3·75	£110

DESIGNS: A, Sower; B, Labourer; C, Bricklayer and reaper.

238 Dr. von Stephan

1947. 50th Death Anniv of Von Stephan.

949	238	24pf. brown	30	2·10
950	238	75pf. blue	30	2·10

1947. Leipzig Autumn Fair. As T 231.

951		12pf. red	65	2·75
952		75pf. blue	65	3·75

DESIGNS: 12pf. 1497: Maximilian I granting Charter; 75pf. 1365: Assessment and Collection of Ground Rents.

1948. Leipzig Spring Fair. As T 231 but dated "1948".

953		50pf. blue	65	2·10
954		84pf. green	65	3·25

DESIGNS: 50pf. 1388: At the customs barrier; 84pf. 1433: Bringing merchandise.

For similar types, dated "1948", "1949" or "1950", but with premium values, see Nos. R31/2, R51/2, R60/1 of Russian Zone and E7/8 of East Germany.

239 Weighing Goods

1948. Hanover Trade Fair.

955	239	24pf. red	40	2·10
956	239	50pf. blue	40	3·25

C. British and American Zones 1948–49

(A2)

1948. Currency Reform. (a) On Pictorial issue of 1947, Nos. 928/44. (i) Optd with Type (A2).

A36		2pf. black	65	65
A37		6pf. violet	65	65
A38		8pf. red	65	65
A39		10pf. green	65	65
A40		12pf. grey	65	65
A41		15pf. brown	11·50	21·00
A42		16pf. green	1·90	3·25
A43		20pf. blue	85	1·30
A44		24pf. brown	65	65
A45		25pf. orange	65	65
A46		30pf. red	3·75	6·25
A47		40pf. mauve	1·10	2·10
A48		50pf. blue	1·20	1·30
A49		60pf. brown	1·10	1·30
A50		60pf. red	85·00	£325
A51		80pf. blue	1·70	3·25
A52		84pf. green	6·25	8·50

(ii) Optd with multiple posthorns over whole stamp.

A53		2pf. black	1·30	1·90
A54		6pf. violet	1·30	1·90
A55		8pf. red	1·30	1·90
A56		10pf. green	65	65
A57		12pf. grey	1·50	2·10
A58		15pf. brown	65	95
A59		16pf. green	2·10	3·25
A60		20pf. blue	65	65
A61		24pf. brown	1·10	2·10
A62		25pf. orange	10·50	21·00
A63		30pf. red	65	95
A64		40pf. mauve	65	85
A65		50pf. blue	65	85
A66		60pf. brown	65	95
A67		60pf. red	3·75	5·25
A68		80pf. blue	65	1·10
A69		84pf. green	2·10	1·90

(b) On Numeral issue of 1946, Nos. 900 to 924. (i) Optd with Type A2.

A70	229	2pf. black	8·50	44·00
A71	229	8pf. red	16·00	90·00
A72	229	10pf. brown	1·30	6·75
A73	229	12pf. red	11·50	75·00
A74	229	12pf. grey	£190	£800
A75	229	15pf. red	11·50	75·00
A76	229	15pf. green	3·75	23·00
A77	229	16pf. green	60·00	£275
A78	229	24pf. brown	£110	£300
A79	229	25pf. blue	21·00	90·00
A80	229	25pf. orange	1·90	12·50
A81	229	30pf. olive	3·25	12·50
A82	229	40pf. purple	85·00	£300
A83	229	45pf. red	4·25	11·50
A84	229	50pf. green	2·75	10·50
A85	229	75pf. blue	7·50	34·00
A86	229	84pf. green	8·50	34·00

(ii) Optd with multiple posthorns over whole stamp.

A87	229	2pf. black	32·00	95·00
A88	229	8pf. red	55·00	£190
A89	229	10pf. brown	55·00	£200
A90	229	12pf. red	17·00	95·00
A91	229	12pf. grey	£400	£1500
A92	229	15pf. red	17·00	70·00
A93	229	15pf. green	2·10	11·50
A94	229	16pf. green	60·00	£225
A95	229	24pf. brown	65·00	£300
A96	229	25pf. blue	17·00	90·00
A97	229	25pf. orange	60·00	£275
A98	229	30pf. olive	2·75	9·50
A99	229	40pf. purple	85·00	£350
A100	229	45pf. red	5·25	17·00
A101	229	50pf. green	5·25	17·00
A102	229	75pf. blue	3·75	17·00
A103	229	84pf. green	5·25	18·00

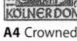

A4 Crowned Head   **A7** Cologne Cathedral

1948. 700th Anniv of Cologne Cathedral and Restoration Fund.

A104	A4	6pf.+4pf. brown	1·10	1·10
A105	-	12pf.+8pf. blue	2·10	2·75
A106	-	24pf.+16pf. red	5·75	5·25
A107	A7	50pf.+50pf. blue	10·50	13·50

DESIGNS—As Type A **4**: 12pf. The Three Wise Men; 24pf. Cologne Cathedral.

A9 The Romer, Frankfurt am Main   **A10** Frauenkirche, Munich   **A13** Holstentor Lubeck

1948. Various designs.

A108	A9	2pf. black	55	65
A109	A10	4pf. brown	55	65
A110a	A	5pf. blue	85	65
A111	A10	6pf. brown	55	1·30
A112	A10	6pf. orange	65	65
A113	A9	8pf. yellow	65	85
A114	A10	8pf. slate	55	65
A115a	A	10pf. green	65	65
A116	A9	15pf. orange	2·75	6·25
A117	A9	15pf. violet	1·50	65
A118	A9	16pf. brown	85	85
A119	A9	20pf. blue	1·30	4·25
A120	B	20pf. red	95	65
A121	B	24pf. red	65	65
A122	A	25pf. red	1·30	65
A123	B	30pf. blue	1·60	65
A124	A10	30pf. red	3·75	7·50
A125	A	40pf. mauve	2·10	65
A126	B	50pf. blue	1·60	3·25
A127	A10	50pf. green	2·10	65
A128a	A	60pf. purple	3·25	65
A129	B	80pf. mauve	3·75	65
A130	A	84pf. purple	2·30	8·50
A131	A	90pf. mauve	3·75	65
A132	A13	1Dm. green	42·00	85
A133	A13	2Dm. violet	37·00	1·10
A134	A13	3Dm. mauve	42·00	3·75
A135	A13	5Dm. blue	65·00	30·00

DESIGNS—As Type A **9/10**: A, Cologne Cathedral; B, Brandenburg Gate.

A15 Brandenburg Gate, Berlin

1948. Aid to Berlin.

A140	A15	10pf.+5pf. green	8·50	10·50
A141	A15	20pf.+10pf. red	8·50	10·50

A16 Herman Hillebrant Wedigh (after Holbein)

1949. Hanover Trade Fair.

A142	A16	10pf. green	4·25	3·75
A143	A16	20pf. red	4·25	3·25
A144	A16	30pf. blue	6·25	4·75
MS	A145 110×65 mm. Nos. A142/4 (sold at 1Dm.)		£120	£375

A17 Racing Cyclists

1949. Trans-Germany Cycle Race.

A146	A17	10pf.+5pf. green	6·25	8·50
A147	A17	20pf.+10pf. brown	17·00	23·00

A18 Goethe in Italy   **A19** Goethe

1949. Birth Bicentenary of Goethe (poet).

A148	A18	10pf.+5pf. green	5·25	5·75
A149	A19	20pf.+10pf. red	7·50	10·50
A150	-	30pf.+15pf. blue	32·00	32·00

DESIGN—VERT: 30pf. Profile portrait.

OBLIGATORY TAX STAMPS

AT14

1948. Aid for Berlin. Perf or imperf.

AT136	AT14	2pf. blue	1·10	30

The Anglo-American Zones, together with the French Zone, became the Federal German Republic (West Germany) in September 1949.

D. French Zone.

(a) General Issues, 1945–46.

F1 Arms of the Palatinate   **F2** Goethe

1945. (a) Arms.

F1	F1	1pf. green, black & yellow	30	30
F2	-	3pf. yellow, black and red	30	30
F3	-	5pf. black, yellow & brn	30	30
F4	-	8pf. red, yellow and brown	30	30
F5	F1	10pf. green, brown & yell	16·00	80·00
F6	-	12pf. yellow, black & red	30	30
F7	-	15pf. blue, black and red	30	30
F8	-	20pf. black, yellow & red	30	30
F9	-	24pf. blue, black and red	30	30
F10	-	30pf. red, yellow & black	30	30

ARMS—3, 12pf. Rhineland; 5, 20pf. Wurttemberg; 8, 30pf. Baden; 15, 24pf. Saar.

(b) Poets.

F11	2	1m. brown	4·75	25·00
F12	-	2m. blue (Schiller)	4·75	75·00
F13	-	5m. red (Heine)	5·25	95·00

(b) Baden, 1947–49.

FB1 J. P. Hebel   **FB2** Rastatt Castle

FB3 Hollental Black Forest   **FB4** Freiburg Cathedral

1947. Inscr "BADEN".

FB1	FB1	2pf. grey	30	55
FB2	-	3pf. brown	30	55
FB3	-	10pf. blue	30	55
FB4	FB1	12pf. green	30	55
FB5	-	15pf. violet	30	55
FB6	FB2	16pf. green	30	2·10
FB7	-	20pf. blue	30	55
FB8	FB2	24pf. red	30	55
FB9	-	45pf. mauve	30	1·30
FB10	FB1	60pf. orange	30	55
FB11	-	75pf. blue	30	2·75
FB12	FB3	84pf. green	30	2·75
FB13	FB4	1m. brown	40	1·10

DESIGNS—18×23 mm: 3, 15, 45pf. Badensian girl and yachts; 10, 20, 75pf. Hans Baldung Grien.

1948. Currency Reform. As 1947 issue. (a) Value in "PF".

FB14	FB1	2pf. orange	30	40
FB15	-	6pf. brown	30	40
FB16	-	10pf. brown	55	40
FB17	FB1	12pf. red	55	40
FB18	-	15pf. blue	65	85
FB19	FB2	24pf. green	75	40
FB20	-	30pf. mauve	1·50	1·60
FB21	-	50pf. blue	1·50	40

(b) New currency. Value in "D.PF" or "D.M." (="Deutschpfennig" or "Deutschmark").

FB22	-	8dpf. green	75	1·60
FB23	FB2	16dpf. violet	1·60	2·75
FB24	-	20dpf. brown	5·25	1·40
FB25	FB1	60dpf. grey	7·50	85
FB26	FB3	84dpf. red	9·50	6·25
FB27	FB4	1dm. blue	8·50	6·25

DESIGNS—As Types FB **1/2**: 6, 15pf. Badensian girl and yachts; 10pf., 20dpf. Hans Baldung Grien; 8dpf., 30pf. Black Forest girl in festive headdress; 50pf. Grand-Duchess Stephanie of Baden.

Nos. FB14/21 were sold on the new currency basis though not inscribed "D.PF.".

1948. As 1947 issue, but "PF" omitted.

FB28	FB1	2pf. orange	1·60	75
FB29	-	4pf. violet	1·10	65
FB30	-	5pf. blue	1·40	85
FB31	-	6pf. brown	34·00	19·00
FB32	-	8pf. brown	1·60	1·50
FB33	-	10pf. green	3·25	75
FB34	-	20pf. mauve	1·90	55
FB35	-	40pf. brown	80·00	£110
FB36	FB1	80pf. red	13·50	8·75
FB37	FB3	90pf. red	80·00	£110

DESIGNS—18×23 mm: 4pf., 40pf. Rastatt; 5pf., 6pf. Badensian girl and yachts; 8pf. Black Forest girl in festive headdress; 10pf., 20pf. Portrait of Hans Baldung Grien.

FB5 Cornhouse, Freiburg

1949. Freiburg Rebuilding Fund.

FB38	FB5	4pf.+16pf. violet	19·00	55·00
FB39	-	10pf.+20pf. green	19·00	55·00
FB40	-	20pf.+30pf. red	19·00	55·00
FB41	-	30pf.+50pf. blue	21·00	65·00
MS	FB41a 65×78 mm. Nos. FB38/41		80·00	£300
MS	FB41b Ditto but imperf		80·00	£300

DESIGNS—10pf. Freiburg Cathedral; 20pf. Trumpeting angel, Freiburg; 30pf. "Fischbrunnen," Freiburg.

FB6 Arms of Baden

1949. Red Cross Fund.

FB42	FB6	10pf.+20pf. green	26·00	£110
FB43	FB6	20pf.+40pf. lilac	26·00	£110
FB44	FB6	30pf.+60pf. blue	26·00	£110
FB45	FB6	40pf.+80pf. grey	26·00	£110
MS	FB45a 90×100 mm. Nos. FB42/5		£120	£1600

FB7 Seehof Hotel, Constance

1949. Engineers' Congress, Constance.

FB46	FB7	30pf. blue	27·00	90·00

FB8 Goethe

1949. Birth Bicentenary of Goethe (poet).

FB47	FB8	10pf.+5pf. green	10·50	26·00
FB48	-	20pf.+10pf. red	12·50	26·00
FB49	-	30pf.+15pf. blue	16·00	65·00

FB9 Carl Schurz and Revolutionary Scene

1949. Cent of Rastatt Insurrection.

FB50	FB9	10pf.+5pf. green	12·50	40·00
FB51	FB9	20pf.+10pf. mauve	12·50	40·00
FB52	FB9	30pf.+15pf. blue	15·00	40·00

FB10 Conradin Kreutzer

1949. Death Centenary of Conradin Kreutzer (composer).

FB53	FB10	10pf. green	4·75	16·00

FB11 1849 Mail Coach

1949. German Stamp Centenary.

FB54	FB11	10pf. green	6·75	15·00
FB55	-	20pf. brown	6·75	15·00

DESIGN: 20pf. Postal motor-coach with trailer and Douglas DC-4 airliner.

FB12 Posthorn and Globe

1949. 75th Anniv of U.P.U.

FB56	FB12	20pf. red	7·50	15·00
FB57	FB12	30pf. blue	7·50	12·50

(C) Rhineland Palatinate, 1947–49.

FR1 "Porta Nigra", Trier   **FR2** Karl Marx   **FR4** Statue of Charlemagne

1947. Inscr "RHEINLAND-PFALZ".

FR1	-	2pf. grey	30	40
FR2	-	3pf. brown	30	40
FR3	-	10pf. blue	30	40
FR4	FR1	12pf. green	30	40
FR5	FR2	15pf. violet	30	40
FR6	-	16pf. green	30	1·50
FR7	-	20pf. blue	30	40
FR8	-	24pf. red	30	40
FR9	-	30pf. mauve	20	3·25
FR10	-	45pf. mauve	20	85
FR11	-	50pf. blue	30	3·25
FR12	-	60pf. orange	30	40
FR13	-	75pf. blue	30	85
FR14	-	84pf. green	40	1·90
FR15	FR4	1m. brown	40	1·10

DESIGNS—SMALL SIZE: 2pf., 60pf. Beethoven's death mask; 3pf. Baron von Ketteler, Bishop of Mainz; 10pf. Girl vintager; 16pf. Rocks at Arnweiler; 20pf. Palatinate village house; 24pf. Worms Cathedral; 30pf., 75pf. Gutenberg (printer); 45pf., 50pf. Mainz Cathedral. LARGE SIZE—HORIZ: 84pf. Gutenfels Castle and Rhine.

1948. Currency Reform. As 1947 issue. (a) Value in "PF".

FR16	-	2pf. orange	30	40
FR17	-	6pf. brown	30	40
FR18	-	10pf. brown	55	40
FR19	FR1	12pf. red	55	40
FR20	FR2	15pf. blue	1·60	85
FR21	-	24pf. green	55	40
FR22	-	30pf. mauve	1·60	55
FR23	-	50pf. blue	2·10	55

(b) New currency. Value in "D.PF." or "D.M." (= "Deutschpfennig" or "Deutschmark").

FR24	FR1	8dpf. green	55	1·60

FR25	-	16dpf. violet	85	1·90
FR26	-	20dpf. brown	4·25	85
FR27	-	60dpf. grey	10·50	55
FR28	-	84dpf. red	6·75	8·00
FR29	FR4	1dm. blue	7·50	8·00

DESIGNS—SMALL SIZE: 6pf. Baron von Ketteler; 30pf. Mainz Cathedral; 50pf. Gutenberg (printer). Others as 1947 issue.

Nos. FR16/23 were sold on the new currency basis though not inscribed "D.PF.".

FR5 St. Martin

1948. Ludwigshafen Explosion Relief Fund.

FR30	FR5	20pf.+30pf. mauve	2·75	80·00
FR31	-	30pf.+50pf. blue	2·75	80·00

DESIGN: 30pf. St. Christopher.

1948. Inscr "RHEINLAND-PFALZ". As 1947 issue, but "PF" omitted.

FR32		2pf. orange	1·10	55
FR33		4pf. violet	1·10	55
FR34	FR2	5pf. blue	1·10	85
FR35	-	6pf. brown	37·00	21·00
FR36	FR1	8pf. red	95·00	£550
FR37	-	10pf. green	1·40	55
FR38	-	20pf. mauve	1·40	55
FR39	-	40pf. brown	5·25	5·25
FR40	FR1	80pf. red	6·25	6·75
FR41	-	90pf. red	10·50	21·00

DESIGNS—SMALL SIZE: 4pf. Rocks at Arnweiler; 40pf. Worms Cathedral. LARGE SIZE—HORIZ: 90pf. Gutenfels Castle and Rhine. Others as 1947-48 issues.

1949. Red Cross Fund. As Type FB6 of Baden, but Arms of Rhineland and inscr "RHEINLANDPFALZ".

FR42	10pf.+20pf. green	23·00	£120
FR43	20pf.+40pf. lilac	23·00	£120
FR44	30pf.+60pf. blue	23·00	£120
FR45	40pf.+80pf. grey	23·00	£120
MSFR45a	90×100 mm. Nos. FR42/5	£130	£1600

1949. Birth Bicentenary of Goethe. As Nos. FB47/9 of Baden.

FR46	10pf.+5pf. green	8·50	25·00
FR47	20pf.+10pf. mauve	8·50	25·00
FR48	30pf.+15pf. blue	16·00	60·00

1949. Centenary of German Postage Stamp. As Nos. FB54/5 of Baden.

FR49	10pf. green	11·50	26·00
FR50	20pf. brown	11·50	26·00

1949. 75th Anniv of U.P.U. As Nos. FB56/7 of Baden.

FR51	20pf. red	8·00	16·00
FR52	30pf. blue	8·00	13·50

(e) Wurttemberg

FW1 Fr. von Schiller   **FW2** Bebenhausen Monastery   **FW3** Lichtenstein Castle

1947. Inscr "WURTTEMBERG".

FW1	FW1	2pf. grey	30	85
FW2	-	3pf. brown	30	40
FW3	-	10pf. blue	30	55
FW4	FW1	12pf. green	30	40
FW5	-	15pf. violet	30	65
FW6	FW2	16pf. green	30	1·70
FW7	-	20pf. blue	30	1·70
FW8	FW2	24pf. red	30	40
FW9	-	45pf. mauve	30	1·70
FW10	FW1	60pf. orange	30	1·10
FW11	-	75pf. blue	55	1·90
FW12	FW3	84pf. green	55	1·90
FW13	-	1m. brown	55	1·90

DESIGNS—SMALL SIZE: 3pf, 15pf, 45pf. Holderlin (poet); 10pf, 20pf, 75pf. Wangen Gate. LARGE SIZE—VERT: 1m. Zwiefalten Monastery Church.

1948. Currency Reform. As 1947 issue. (a) Value in "PF".

FW14	FW1	2pf. orange	30	55
FW15	-	6pf. brown	30	40
FW16	-	10pf. brown	55	55
FW17	FW1	12pf. red	30	40
FW18	-	15pf. blue	1·10	55
FW19	FW2	24pf. green	1·60	85
FW20	-	30pf. mauve	1·60	85
FW21	-	50pf. blue	3·25	85

(b) Value in "D.PF" (= Deutsch Pfennig) or "D.M." (= Deutsch Mark).

FW22	-	8dpf. green	1·60	3·25
FW23	FW2	16dpf. violet	1·30	2·10
FW24	-	20dpf. brown	2·75	1·60
FW25	FW1	60dpf. grey	16·00	85
FW26	FW3	84dpf. red	4·25	6·25
FW27	-	1dm. blue	4·25	6·25

DESIGNS—SMALL SIZE: 6pf, 15pf. Fr. Holderlin (poet); 8 dpf, 30pf. Waldsee Castle; 50pf. Ludwig Uhland (poet). Others as 1947 issue.

Nos. FW14/21 were sold on the new currency basis though not inscribed "D.PF.".

1948. Inscr "WURTTEMBERG". As 1947 issue, but "PF" omitted.

FW28	FW1	2pf. orange	1·40	85
FW29	FW2	4pf. violet	3·25	55
FW30	-	5pf. blue	8·00	3·25
FW31	-	6pf. brown	10·50	8·00
FW32	-	8pf. red	10·50	3·25
FW33	-	10pf. green	9·50	55
FW34	-	20pf. mauve	10·50	55
FW35	FW2	40pf. brown	26·00	55·00
FW36	FW1	80pf. red	55·00	55·00
FW37	FW3	90pf. red	85·00	£140

DESIGNS—SMALL SIZE: 5pf., 6pf. Holderlin. Others as 1947 and 1948 issues.

FW4 Isny and Coat of Arms

1949. Ski Championships (Northern Combination) at Isny/Allgau.

FW38	FW4	10pf.+4pf. green	10·50	32·00
FW39	-	20pf.+6pf. lake	10·50	32·00

DESIGN: 20pf. Skier and view of Isny.

1949. Red Cross Fund. As Type FB6 of Baden, but Arms of Wurttemberg and inscr "WURTTEMBERG".

FW40	10pf.+20pf. green	42·00	£130
FW41	20pf.+40pf. lilac	42·00	£130
FW42	30pf.+60pf. blue	42·00	£130
FW43	40pf.+80pf. grey	42·00	£130
MSFW43a	90×100 mm. Nos. FW40/3	£160	£1900

1949. Birth Bicentenary of Goethe. As Nos. FB47/9 of Baden.

FW44	10pf.+5pf. green	9·50	26·00
FW45	20pf.+10pf. mauve	13·50	37·00
FW46	30pf.+15pf. blue	13·50	55·00

FW5 Gustav Werner

1949. Centenary of Christian Institution "Zum Bruderhaus".

FW47	FW5	10pf.+5pf. green	6·75	18·00
FW48	FW5	20pf.+10pf. purple	6·75	18·00

1949. German Stamp Centenary. As Nos. FB54/5 of Baden.

FW49	10pf. green	8·50	17·00
FW50	20pf. brown	8·50	17·00

1949. 75th Anniv of U.P.U. As Nos. FB56/7 of Baden.

FW51	20pf. red	6·75	14·50
FW52	30pf. blue	6·75	12·50

E. Russian Zone.

For a list of the stamps issued by the Russian Zone Provincial Administrations of Berlin (Brandenburg), Mecklenburg-Vorpommern, Saxony (Halle, Leipzig and Dresden) and Thuringia, see Stanley Gibbons Part 7 Catalogue.

In February 1946, the Provincial Issues were replaced by the General Issues, Nos. 899/956, until the revaluation of the currency in June 1948, when Nos. 928/44 were brought into use handstamped with District names and numbers as a control measure pending the introduction of the following overprinted stamps on 3rd July. There are over 1,900 different types of district handstamp.

1948. Optd Sowjetische Besatzungs Zone. (a) On Pictorial issue of 1947, Nos. 928/44.

R1	2pf. black	55	55
R2	6pf. violet	55	55
R3	8pf. red	55	55
R4	10pf. green	55	65
R5	12pf. grey	55	65
R6	15pf. brown	65	65
R7	16pf. green	55	85
R8	20pf. blue	55	55
R9	24pf. brown	55	40
R10	25pf. orange	55	40
R11	30pf. red	2·75	55
R12	40pf. mauve	55	65
R13	50pf. blue	85	2·10
R14	60pf. brown	1·60	2·10
R15	60pf. red	75·00	£180
R16	80pf. blue	3·25	4·25
R17	84pf. green	3·75	4·25

(b) On Numerical issue of 1946, Nos. 903, etc.

R18	229	5pf. green	1·10	2·10
R19	229	30pf. olive	1·70	4·25
R20	229	45pf. red	85	1·60
R21	229	75pf. blue	85	1·60
R22	229	84pf. green	1·90	4·25

Sowjetische
Besatzungs
Zone
(R1)

(c) On stamps inscr "STADT BERLIN".

R23	R1	5pf. green	55	2·10
R25	-	5pf. green	55	2·10
R26	-	8pf. orange	55	2·75
R27	-	10pf. brown	55	2·75
R28	-	12pf. red	75	21·00
R29	-	20pf. blue	55	1·30
R30	-	30pf. olive	55	9·00

DESIGNS: 6pf. Bear with spade; 8pf. Bear on shield; 10pf. Bear holding brick; 12pf. Bear carrying plank; 20pf. Bear on small shield; 30pf. Oak sapling amid ruins.

1948. Leipzig Autumn Fair. As T 231 but dated "1948".

R31	16pf.+9pf. purple	95	85
R32	50pf.+25pf. blue	95	85

DESIGNS: 16pf. 1459: The first Spring Fair; 50pf. 1469: Foreign merchants displaying cloth.

R3 Kathe Kollwitz

1948. Politicians, Artists and Scientists.

R33	R3	2pf. grey	2·10	2·10
R34	-	6pf. violet	2·10	2·10
R35	-	8pf. red	2·10	2·10
R36	-	10pf. green	2·10	1·60
R37	-	12pf. blue	5·00	1·10
R38	-	15pf. brown	1·60	3·25
R39	-	16pf. blue	4·75	3·25
R40	R3	20pf. purple	2·10	2·10
R41	-	24pf. red	5·25	2·10
R42	-	25pf. olive	2·10	2·75
R43	-	30pf. red	5·25	3·25
R44	-	40pf. purple	21·00	3·75
R45	-	50pf. green	2·10	2·75
R46	-	60pf. green	10·50	3·75
R47	-	80pf. blue	2·10	2·10
R48	-	84pf. brown	3·50	6·25
E95	-	80pf. red	17·00	12·00

PORTRAITS: 6, 40pf. Gerhart Hauptmann; 8, 50pf. Karl Marx; 10, 84pf. August Bebel; 12, 30pf. Friedrich Engels; 15, 60pf. G. F. W. Hegel; 16, 25pf. Rudolf Virchow; 24, 80pf. Ernst Thalmann.

R4

1948. Stamp Day.

R49	R4	12pf.+3pf. red	1·10	1·40

R5 Liebknecht and Rosa Luxemburg

1949. 30th Death Anniv of Karl Liebknecht and Rosa Luxemburg (revolutionaries).

R50	R5	24pf. red	1·10	1·40

1949. Leipzig Spring Fair. As T 231 but dated "1949".

R51	30pf.+15pf. red	5·00	5·75
R52	50pf.+25pf. blue	5·75	85

DESIGNS: 30pf. 1st Neubau Town Hall bazaar, 1556; 50pf. Italian merchants at Leipzig, 1536.

R6 Dove

1949. Third German Peoples' Congress.

R53	R6	24pf. red	2·10	3·00

1949. R53 Optd 3. Deutscher Volkskongreß 29.-30 Mai 1949.

R54	24pf. red	2·75	4·00

R8 Goethe

1949. Birth Bicent of Goethe. Portraits of Goethe.

R55	R8	6pf.+4pf. violet	3·25	3·75
R56	-	12pf.+8pf. brown	3·25	3·75
R57	-	24pf.+16pf. lake	2·75	3·25
R58	-	50pf.+25pf. blue	2·75	3·25
R59	-	84pf.+36pf. grey	4·75	6·25

1949. Goethe Festival Week, Weimar. Sheet 106×104 mm.

MSR59a R 9	50pf. (+Dm. 4.50) blue	£225	£650

1949. Leipzig Autumn Fair. As T 231 but dated "1949".

R60	12pf.+8pf. slate	6·25	15·00
R61	24pf.+16pf. lake	7·50	12·50

DESIGNS: 12pf. Russian merchants, 1650; 24pf. Goethe at Fair, 1765.

The Russian Zonee was incorporated in East Germany in October 1949.

III. GERMAN FEDERAL REPUBLIC

The Federal Republic was set up on 23 May 1949. Until October 1990 it comprised the territory which formerly came under the British, American and French Zones. On 3 October 1990 the former territory of East Germany (German Democratic Republic) was absorbed into the Federal Republic.

257 Constructing Parliament Building

1949. Opening of West German Parliament, Bonn.

1033	257	10pf. green	55·00	26·00
1034	257	20pf. red	60·00	31·00

258 Reproduction of T 1 of Bavaria

1949. Centenary of First German Stamps.

1035	258	10pf.+2pf. black & grn	19·00	33·00
1036	-	20pf. blue and red	44·00	49·00
1037	-	30pf. brown and blue	55·00	75·00

DESIGN: 20pf, 30pf. Reproductions of T 2 of Bavaria.

259 Dr. von Stephan, Old G.P.O., Berlin and Standehaus, Berne

1949. 75th Anniv of U.P.U.

1038	259	30pf. blue	80·00	49·00

260 St. Elisabeth of Thuringia

1949. Refugees' Relief Fund. Inscr as in T 260.

1039	260	8pf.+2pf. purple	25·00	28·00
1040	-	10pf.+5pf. green	19·00	16·00
1041	-	20pf.+10pf. red	19·00	16·00
1042	-	30pf.+15pf. blue	£110	£140

PORTRAITS: 10pf. Paracelsus von Hohenheim; 20pf. F. W. A. Froebel; 30pf. J. H. Wichern.

261 J. S. Bach's Seal

1950. Death Bicent of Bach (composer).

1043	261	10pf.+2pf. green	80·00	55·00
1044	261	20pf.+3pf. red	90·00	60·00

262 Numeral
and Posthorn

1951

1045	**262**	2pf. green	6·50	1·40
1046	**262**	4pf. brown	5·00	45
1047	**262**	5pf. purple	15·00	45
1048	**262**	6pf. orange	24·00	4·50
1049	**262**	8pf. grey	25·00	10·50
1050	**262**	10pf. green	10·00	45
1051	**262**	15pf. violet	49·00	1·40
1052	**262**	20pf. red	7·75	45
1053	**262**	25pf. plum	£120	7·75
1054	**262**	30pf. brown	65·00	90
1055	**262**	40pf. purple	£180	90
1056	**262**	50pf. grey	£225	90
1057	**262**	60pf. brown	£160	90
1058	**262**	70pf. yellow	£550	21·00
1059	**262**	80pf. red	£600	3·25
1060	**262**	90pf. green	£600	3·75

The 30pf. to 90pf. are 20×24½ mm.

264 Figures

1951. 700th Anniv of St. Mary's Church, Lubeck.

1065	**264**	10pf.+5pf. black & grn	£110	90·00
1066	**264**	20pf.+5pf. black & red	£120	£110

265 Stamps
under Magnifier

1951. National Philatelic Exn, Wuppertal.

1067	**265**	10pf.+2pf. yellow, black and green	55·00	60·00
1068	**265**	20pf.+3pf. yellow, black and red	60·00	65·00

266 St. Vincent
de Paul

1951. Humanitarian Relief Fund.

1069	**266**	4pf.+2pf. brown	11·00	12·50
1070	-	10pf.+3pf. green	16·00	10·50
1071	-	20pf.+5pf. red	16·00	10·50
1072	-	30pf.+10pf. blue	£120	£140

PORTRAITS: 10pf. F. Von Bodelschwingh; 20pf. Elsa Brandstrom; 30pf. J. H. Pestalozzi.

267 W. C.
Rontgen
(physicist)

1951. 50th Anniv of Award to Rontgen of First Nobel Prize for Physics.

1073	**267**	30pf. blue	95·00	22·00

268 *Mona Lisa*

1952. 500th Birth Anniv of Leonardo da Vinci.

1074	**268**	5pf. multicoloured	1·80	3·25

269 Martin
Luther

1952. Lutheran World Federation Assembly, Hanover.

1075	**269**	10pf. green	17·00	6·75

270 A. N. Otto
and Diagram

1952. 75th Anniv of Otto Gas Engine.

1076	**270**	30pf. blue	37·00	20·00

271 Nuremberg
Madonna

1952. Centenary of German National Museum, Nuremberg.

1077	**271**	10pf.+5pf. green	22·00	26·00

272 Trawler
Senator Schaffer
off Heligoland

1952. Rehabilitation of Heligoland.

1078	**272**	20pf. red	21·00	8·50

273 Carl Schurz

1952. Centenary of Arrival of Schurz in America.

1079	**273**	20pf. pink, black and blue	24·00	11·00

274 Boy Hikers

1952. Youth Hostels Fund. Inscr "JUGENDMARKE 1952".

1080	**274**	10pf.+2pf. green	24·00	27·00
1081	-	20pf.+3pf. red	24·00	27·00

DESIGN: 20pf. Girl hikers.

275 Elizabeth Fry

1952. Humanitarian Relief Fund.

1082	**275**	4pf.+2pf. brown	11·50	9·25
1083	-	10pf.+5pf. green	11·50	9·25
1084	-	20pf.+10pf. lake	23·00	19·00
1085	-	30pf.+10pf. blue	95·00	£120

PORTRAITS: 10pf. Dr. C. Sonnenschein; 20pf. T. Fliedner; 30pf. H. Dunant.

276 Postman, 1852

1952. Thurn and Taxis Stamp Centenary.

1086	**276**	10pf. multicoloured	10·50	3·50

277 P. Reis

1952. 75th Anniv of German Telephone Service.

1087	**277**	30pf. blue	60·00	21·00

278 Road
Accident Victim

1953. Road Safety Campaign.

1088	**278**	20pf. multicoloured	23·00	7·00

279

1953. 50th Anniv of Science Museum, Munich.

1089	**279**	10pf.+5pf. green	33·00	41·00

280 Red Cross
and Compass

1953. 125th Birth Anniv of Henri Dunant (founder of Red Cross).

1090	**280**	10pf. red and green	26·00	8·75

281 Prisoner of
War

1953. Commemorating Prisoners of War.

1091	**281**	10pf. black and grey	8·25	60

282 J. von
Liebig

1953. 150th Birth Anniv of Liebig (chemist).

1092	**282**	30pf. blue	60·00	29·00

283 "Rail
Transport"

1953. Transport Exn, Munich. Inscr as in T **283**.

1093	**283**	4pf. brown	8·25	5·75
1094	-	10pf. green	16·00	9·25
1095	-	20pf. red	22·00	11·50
1096	-	30pf. blue	60·00	29·00

DESIGNS: 10pf. "Air" (dove and aeroplanes); 20pf. "Road" (traffic lights and cars); 30pf. "Sea" (buoy and ships).

284 Gateway,
Thurn and Taxis
Palace

1953. International Philatelic Exhibition, Frankfurt am Main. Inscr "IFRABA 1953".

1097	**284**	10pf.+2pf. brown, black and green	29·00	33·00
1098	-	20pf.+3pf. grey, blue and red	29·00	33·00

DESIGN: 20pf. Telecommunications Buildings, Frankfurt am Main.

285 A. H. Francke

1953. Humanitarian Relief Fund.

1099	**285**	4pf.+2pf. brown	7·00	10·50
1100	-	10pf.+5pf. green	11·00	10·50
1101	-	20pf.+10pf. red	16·00	13·00
1102	-	30pf.+10pf. blue	70·00	85·00

PORTRAITS: 10pf. S. Kneipp; 20pf. J. C. Senckenberg; 30pf. F. Nansen.

286 Pres.
Heuss

1954. (a) Size 18½×22½ mm or 18×22 mm.

1103	**286**	2pf. green	35	35
1104	**286**	4pf. brown	35	35
1105	**286**	5pf. mauve	35	35
1106	**286**	6pf. brown	60	1·20
1107	**286**	7pf. green	35	45
1108	**286**	8pf. grey	35	95
1109	**286**	10pf. green	35	35
1110	**286**	15pf. blue	95	70
1111	**286**	20pf. red	35	35
1112	**286**	25pf. purple	1·60	80
1122a	**286**	30pf. green	60	95
1122c	**286**	40pf. blue	2·75	45
1122e	**286**	50pf. olive	1·50	45
1122f	**286**	60pf. brown	4·50	70
1122g	**286**	70pf. violet	14·00	70
1122h	**286**	80pf. orange	8·25	3·00
1122i	**286**	90pf. green	22·00	1·50

(b) Size 20×24 mm.

1113	30pf. blue	17·00	7·00
1114	40pf. purple	7·00	45
1115	50pf. slate	£225	70
1116	60pf. brown	50·00	95
1117	70pf. olive	21·00	3·00
1118	80pf. red	3·50	7·00
1119	90pf. green	17·00	3·50

(c) Size 25×30 mm.

1120	1Dm. olive	2·00	45
1121	2Dm. lavender	3·50	1·70
1122	3Dm. purple	9·25	3·50

287 P. Ehrlich and E.
von Behring

1954. Birth Centenaries of Ehrlich and Von Behring (bacteriologists).

1123	**287**	10pf. green	14·00	5·25

288 Gutenburg
and
Printing-press

1954. 500th Anniv of Gutenberg Bible.

1124	**288**	4pf. brown	1·70	95

289
Sword-pierced
Mitre

1954. 1,200th Anniv of Martyrdom of St. Boniface.

1125	**289**	20pf. red and brown	10·50	5·75

290 Kathe
Kollwitz

1954. Humanitarian Relief Fund.

1126	**290**	7pf.+3pf. brown	4·75	4·75
1127	-	10pf.+5pf. green	2·30	2·30
1128	-	20pf.+10pf. red	11·50	7·00
1129	-	40pf.+10pf. blue	42·00	50·00

PORTRAITS: 10pf. L. Werthmann; 20pf. J. F. Oberlin; 40pf. Bertha Pappenheim.

291 C. F. Gauss

1955. Death Cent of Gauss (mathematician).

1130	**291**	10pf. green	7·00	95

292 "Flight"

1955. Re-establishment of "Lufthansa" Airways.

1131	**292**	5pf. mauve and black	1·50	1·20
1132	**292**	10pf. green and black	1·90	1·70
1133	**292**	15pf. blue and black	9·25	8·25
1134	**292**	20pf. red and black	27·00	9·25

293 O. von Miller

1955. Birth Centenary of Von Miller (electrical engineer).

1135	**293**	10f. green	7·50	2·10

295 Schiller

1955. 150th Death Anniv of Schiller (poet).

1136	**295**	40pf. blue	21·00	7·50

296 Motor-coach, 1906

1955. 50th Anniv of Postal Motor Transport.

1137	**296**	20pf. black and red	16·00	6·50

297 Arms of Baden-Wurttemburg

1955. Baden-Wurttemberg Agricultural Exhibition, Stuttgart.

1138	**297**	7pf. black, brn & bistre	6·50	5·25
1139	**297**	10pf. black, grn & bistre	7·75	3·50

298 "Earth and Atom"

1955. Cosmic Research.

1140	**298**	20pf. lake	14·00	1·50

299 Refugees

1955. Tenth Anniv of Expulsion of Germans from beyond the Oder–Neisse Line.

1141	**299**	20pf. red	5·25	80

See also No. 1400.

300 Orb, Arrows and Waves

1955. Millenary of Battle of Lechfeld.

1142	**300**	20pf. purple	11·50	4·75

301 Magnifying Glass and Carrier Pigeon

1955. West European Postage Stamp Exn.

1143	**301**	10pf.+2pf. green	5·75	8·25
1144	-	20pf.+3pf. red	14·00	17·00

DESIGN: 20pf. Tweezers and posthorn.

302 Railway Signal

1955. Railway Timetable Conference.

1145	**302**	20pf. black and red	13·00	3·50

303 Stifter Monument

1955. 150th Birth Anniv of Stifter (Austrian poet).

1146	**303**	10pf. green	5·25	3·50

304 U.N. Emblem

1955. U.N. Day.

1147	**304**	10pf. green and brown	5·25	5·75

305 Amalie Sieveking

1955. Humanitarian Relief Fund.

1148	**305**	7pf.+3pf. brown	4·50	4·75
1149	-	10pf.+5pf. green	3·50	2·30
1150	-	20pf.+10pf. red	3·50	2·30
1151	-	40pf.+10pf. blue	42·00	50·00

PORTRAITS: 10pf. A. Kolping; 20pf. Dr. S. Hahnemann; 40pf. Florence Nightingale.

306

1955

1152	**306**	1pf. grey	35	60

307 Von Stephan's Signature

1955. 125th Birth Anniv of H. von Stephan.

1153	**307**	20pf. red	10·00	4·00

308 Spinet and Opening Bars of Minuet

1956. Birth Bicent of Mozart (composer).

1154	**308**	10pf. black and lilac	1·40	60

309 Heinrich Heine

1956. Death Centenary of Heine (poet).

1155	**309**	10pf. green and black	4·50	4·75

310 Old Houses and Crane

1956. Millenary of Luneburg.

1156	**310**	20pf. red	10·50	11·50

311

1956. Olympic Year.

1157	**311**	10pf. green	1·30	95

312 Boy and Dove

1956. Youth Hostels' Fund. Inscr "JUGEND".

1158	**312**	7pf.+3pf. grey, black and brown	3·00	4·75
1159	-	10pf.+5pf. grey black and green	9·25	11·50

DESIGN: 10pf. Girl playing flute and flowers.

313 Robert Schumann

1956. Death Centenary of Schumann (composer).

1160	**313**	10pf. black, red & bistre	1·00	70

314

1956. Evangelical Church Convention, Frankfurt am Main.

1161	**314**	10pf. green	5·25	5·25
1162	**314**	20pf. red	6·50	7·00

315 T. Mann (author)

1956. Thomas Mann Commemoration.

1163	**315**	20pf. red	4·75	3·25

316

1956. 800th Anniv of Maria Laach Abbey.

1164	**316**	20pf. grey and red	3·50	3·00

317 Ground Plan of Cologne Cathedral and Hand

1956. 77th Meeting of German Catholics, Cologne.

1165	**317**	10pf. green and brown	4·25	4·00

318

1956. International Police Exhibition, Essen.

1166	**318**	20pf. green, orange & blk	4·75	4·00

1956. Europa. As Nos. 1582/3 of Belgium.

1167		10pf. green	1·60	25
1168		40pf. blue	9·25	1·50

320 Midwife and Baby

1956. Humanitarian Relief Fund. Centres in black.

1169	**320**	7pf.+3pf. brown	2·30	3·50
1170	-	10pf.+5pf. green	1·70	1·20
1171	-	20pf.+10pf. red	1·70	1·20
1172	-	40pf.+10pf. blue	23·00	22·00

DESIGNS: 10pf. I. P. Semmelweis and cot; 20pf. Mother and baby in cradle; 40f. Nurse maid and children.

321 Carrier Pigeon

1956. Stamp Day.

1173	**321**	10pf. green	2·30	1·00

322 "Military Graves"

1956. War Graves Commission.

1174	**322**	10pf. green	2·30	1·00

323 Arms

1957. Return of the Saar to West Germany.

1175	**323**	10pf. brown and green	80	70

324 Children with Luggage

1957. Berlin Children's Holiday Fund.

1176	**324**	10pf.+5pf. orange and green	1·70	3·00
1177	-	20pf.+10pf. blue and orange	4·00	5·25

DESIGN: 20pf. Girl returning from holiday.

325 Heinrich Hertz

1957. Birth Cent of Hertz (physicist).
1178 **325** 10pf. black and green 2·00 95

326 Paul Gerhardt

1957. 350th Birth Anniv of Paul Gerhardt (hymn-writer).
1179 **326** 20pf. red 95 80

327 "Flora and Philately"

1957. Exhibition and Eighth Congress of Int Federation of "Constructive Philately".
1180 **327** 20pf. orange 95 80

328 Emblem of Aschaffenburg

1957. Millenary of Aschaffenburg.
1181 **328** 20pf. red and black 95 80

329 University Class

1957. 500th Anniv of Freiburg University.
1182 **329** 10pf. black, red & green 70 60

330 *Bayernstein* (freighter)

1957. German Merchant Shipping Day.
1183 **330** 15pf. black, red and blue 1·60 1·50

331 Justus Liebig University

1957. 350th Anniv of Justus Liebig University, Giessen.
1184 **331** 10pf. green 70 70

332 Albert Ballin

1957. Birth Centenary of Albert Ballin (director of Hamburg-America Shipping Line).
1185 **332** 20pf. black and red 2·00 70

333 Television Screen

1957. Publicizing West German Television Service.
1186 **333** 10pf. green and blue 70 70

334 "Europa" Tree

1957. Europa.
1187 **334** 10pf. green and blue 60 25
1188 **334** 40pf. blue 5·75 60

335 Young Miner

1957. Humanitarian Relief Fund.
1189 **335** 7pf.+3pf. black & brn 1·70 2·30
1190 - 10pf.+5pf. black & grn 1·20 1·20
1191 - 20pf.+10pf. black & red 1·70 1·20
1192 - 40pf.+10pf. black & bl 23·00 26·00
DESIGNS: 10pf. Miner drilling coal-face; 20pf. Miner with coal-cutting machine; 40pf. Operator at mine lift-shaft.

336 Water Lily

1957. Nature Protection Day.
1193 **336** 10pf. orange, yell & grn 70 60
1194 - 20pf. multicoloured 80 70
DESIGN—VERT: 20pf. European robin.

337 Carrier Pigeons

1957. International Correspondence Week.
1195 **337** 20pf. black and red 1·30 80

338 Baron von Stein

1957. Birth Bicentenary of Baron von Stein (statesman).
1196 **338** 20pf. red 2·30 95

339 Dr Leo Baeck (philosopher)

1957. First Death Anniv of Dr. Leo Baeck.
1197 **339** 20pf. red 2·30 95

340 Wurttemberg Parliament House

1957. 500th Anniv of First Wurttemberg Parliament.
1198 **340** 10pf. olive and green 1·30 80

341 Stage Coach

1957. Death Centenary of Joseph von Eichendorff (novelist).
1199 **341** 10pf. green 1·20 80

342 "Max and Moritz" (cartoon characters)

1958. 50th Death Anniv of Wilhelm Busch (writer and illustrator).
1200 **342** 10pf. olive and black 35 30
1201 - 20pf. red and black 1·20 95
DESIGN: 20pf. Wilhelm Busch.

343 "Prevent Forest Fires"

1958. Forest Fires Prevention Campaign.
1202 **343** 20pf. black and red 1·00 80

344 Rudolf Diesel and First Oil Engine

1958. Birth Centenary of Rudolf Diesel (engineer).
1203 **344** 10pf. myrtle 60 60

345 "The Fox who stole the Goose"

1958. Berlin Students' Fund. Inscr "Fur die Jugend".
1204 **345** 10pf.+5pf. red, black and green 2·30 3·00
1205 - 20pf.+10pf. brown, green and red 4·00 4·75
DESIGN: 20pf. "A hunter from the Palatinate" (horseman).

346 Giraffe and Lion

1958. Centenary of Frankfurt am Main Zoo.
1206 **346** 10pf. black and green 80 60

347 Old Munich

1958. 800th Anniv of Munich.
1207 **347** 20pf. red 80 60

348 Trier and Market Cross

1958. Millenary of Trier Market.
1208 **348** 20pf. red and black 80 60

349 Deutsche Mark (coin)

1958. Tenth Anniv of Currency Reform.
1209 **349** 20pf. black and orange 1·00 1·70

350 Emblem of Gymnastics

1958. 150th Anniv of German Gymnastics.
1210 **350** 10pf. black, green & grey 60 70

351 H. Schulze-Delitzsch

1958. 150th Birth Anniv of Schulze-Delitzsch (pioneer of German co-operative movement).
1211 **351** 10pf. green 70 60

1958. Europa. As No. 643 of Luxembourg, size 24½×30 mm.
1212 10pf. blue and green 60 35
1213 40pf. red and blue 4·75 60

352 Friedrich Raiffeisen (philanthropist)   **353** Dairymaid

1958. Humanitarian Relief and Welfare Funds.
1214 **352** 7pf.+3pf. brown, deep brown and chestnut 70 70
1215 **353** 10pf.+5pf. red, yellow and green 70 70
1216 - 20pf.+10pf. blue, green and red 70 70
1217 - 40pf.+10pf. yellow, orange and blue 8·75 10·50
DESIGNS— As Type **353**: 20pf. Vine-dresser; 40pf. Farm labourer.

354 Cardinal Nicholas of Cues (founder)

1958. 500th Anniv of Hospice of St. Nicholas.
1218 **354** 20pf. black and mauve 70 60

1959. As Type **B53** of West Berlin but without "BERLIN".
1219 7pf. green 35 30
1220 10pf. green 60 35
1221 20pf. red 60 35
1222 40pf. blue 19·00 1·40
1223 70pf. violet 5·75 1·20

355 Jakob Fugger (merchant prince)

1959. 500th Birth Anniv of Jakob Fugger.
1224 **355** 20pf. black and red 60 70

356 Adam Riese (mathematician)

1959. 400th Death Anniv of Adam Riese.
1225 **356** 10pf. black and green 60 70

357 A. von Humboldt (naturalist)

1959. Death Cent of Alexander von Humboldt.
1226 **357** 40pf. blue 2·50 2·00

358 First Hamburg Stamp of 1859

1959. International Stamp Exhibition, Hamburg, and Centenary of First Stamps of Hamburg and Lubeck.
1228 **358** 10pf.+5pf. brown & grn 35 1·20
1230 - 20pf.+10pf. brn & red 35 1·20
DESIGN: 20pf. First Lubeck stamp of 1859.

359 Buxtehude

1959. Millenary of Buxtehude.
1231 **359** 20pf. red, black and blue 60 60

360 Holy Tunic of Trier

1959. Holy Tunic of Trier Exhibition.
1232 **360** 20pf. black, buff & purple 60 60

361 Congress Emblem

1959. German Evangelical Church Day and Congress, Munich.
1233 **361** 10pf. violet, green & blk 45 45

1959. Inauguration of Beethoven Hall, Bonn. T **361a** and similar horiz designs in sheet 148×104 mm with extract from Beethoven's music notebooks.
MS1233a 10pf. green (Handell); 15pf. blue (Spohr); 20pf. red (T **361a**); 25pf. brown (Haydn); 40pf. blue (Mendelssohn) 33·00 70·00

1959. Europa. As Nos. 659/60 of Luxembourg, but size 24½×30 mm.
1234 10pf. green 45 25
1235 40pf. blue 1·90 60

362 "Feeding the Poor"

1959. Humanitarian Relief and Welfare Funds.
1236 **362** 7pf.+3pf. sepia & yellow 35 60
1237 - 10pf.+5pf. green & yell 35 60
1238 - 20pf.+10pf. red & yell 45 60
1239 - 40pf.+10pf. mult 4·75 6·50
DESIGNS: 10pf. "Clothing the Naked"; 20pf. "Bounty from Heaven" (scenes from the Brothers Grimm story *The Star Thaler*); 40pf. The Brothers Grimm.

363 "Uprooted Tree"

1960. World Refugee Year.
1240 **363** 10pf. black, purple & grn 35 35
1241 **363** 40pf. black, red and blue 3·25 3·25

364 P. Melanchthon

1960. 400th Death Anniv of Philip Melanchthon (Protestant reformer).
1242 **364** 20pf. black and red 2·00 1·70

365 Cross and Symbols of the Crucifixion

1960. Oberammergau Passion Play.
1243 **365** 10pf. grey, ochre and blue 45 45

366

1960. 37th World Eucharistic Congress, Munich.
1244 **366** 10pf. green 80 60
1245 **366** 20pf. red 1·20 1·20

367 Wrestling

1960. Olympic Year. Inscr as in T **367**.
1246 **367** 7pf. brown 35 25
1247 - 10pf. green 60 25
1248 - 20pf. red 60 25
1249 - 40pf. blue 2·00 1·90
DESIGNS: 10pf. Running; 20pf. Javelin and discus-throwing; 40pf. Chariot-racing.

368 Hildesheim Cathedral

1960. Birth Millenary of Bishops St. Bernward and St. Godehard.
1250 **368** 20pf. purple 1·20 70

368a Conference Emblem

1960. Europa.
1251 **368a** 10pf. green and olive 35 35
1252 **368a** 20pf. vermilion and red 1·20 40
1253 **368a** 40pf. light blue and blue 1·70 1·50

369 Little Red Riding Hood meeting Wolf

1960. Humanitarian Relief and Welfare Funds.
1254 **369** 7pf.+3pf. black, red and bistre 70 70
1255 - 10pf.+5pf. black, red and green 70 60
1256 - 20pf.+10pf. black, green and red 70 60
1257 - 40pf.+20pf. black, red and blue 3·50 5·75
DESIGNS: 10pf. Red Riding Hood and wolf disguised as grandmother; 20pf. Woodcutter and dead wolf; 40pf. Red Riding Hood with grandmother.

1960. First Death Anniv of Gen. George C. Marshall. Portrait as T 364.
1258 40pf. black and blue 4·00 3·25

371 *Adler*, 1835

1960. 125th Anniv of German Railway.
1259 **371** 10pf. black and bistre 45 60

372 St. George and the Dragon

1961. Pathfinders (German Boy Scouts) Commemoration.
1260 **372** 10pf. green 35 45

1961. Famous Germans. As Nos. B194, etc of West Berlin but without "BERLIN".
1261 5pf. olive 25 25
1262 7pf. brown 25 25
1263 8pf. violet 25 35
1264 10pf. green 25 35
1265a 15pf. blue 25 25

1266a 20pf. red 25 25
1267 25pf. brown 35 30
1268 30pf. sepia 35 30
1269 40pf. blue 35 30
1270 50pf. brown 45 35
1271 60pf. red 45 35
1272 70pf. green 35 35
1273 80pf. brown 60 60
1274 90pf. bistre 45 30
1275 1Dm. violet 80 35
1276 2Dm. green 4·00 80
PORTRAIT: 90pf. Franz Oppenheimer (economist).

373 Early Daimler Motor Car

1961. 75th Anniv of Daimler-Benz Patent.
1277 **373** 10pf. green and black 35 25
1278 - 20pf. red and black 45 45
DESIGN: 20pf. Early Benz motor car.

374 Nuremberg Messenger of 1700

1961. "The Letter during Five Centuries" Exhibition, Nuremberg.
1279 **374** 7pf. black and red 35 45

375 Speyer Cathedral

1961. 900th Anniv of Speyer Cathedral.
1280 **375** 20pf. red 45 70

376 Doves

1961. Europa.
1281 **376** 10pf. green 35 35
1282 **376** 40pf. blue 60 80

377 Hansel and Gretel in the Wood

1961. Humanitarian Relief and Welfare Funds. Multicoloured.
1283 7pf.+3pf. Type **377** 35 45
1284 10pf.+5pf. Hansel, Gretel and the Witch 35 45
1285 20pf.+10pf. Hansel in the Witch's cage 35 45
1286 40pf.+20pf. Hansel and Gretel reunited with their father 1·40 2·75

378 Telephone Apparatus

1961. Centenary of Philipp Reis's Telephone.
1287 **378** 10pf. green 45 60

379 Baron W. E. von Ketteler

1961. 150th Birth Anniv of Baron W. E. von Ketteler (Catholic leader).
1288 **379** 10pf. black and green 45 60

380 Drusus Stone

1962. Bimillenary of Mainz.
1289 **380** 20pf. purple 45 60

381 Apollo

1962. Child Welfare. Butterflies. Multicoloured.
1290 7pf.+3pf. Type **381** 60 80
1291 10pf.+5pf. Camberwell beauty 60 80
1292 20pf.+10pf. Small tortoiseshell 1·20 1·60
1293 40pf.+20pf. Scarce swallowtail 1·70 2·75

382 Part of "In Dulci Jubilo", from "Musae Sioniae" (M. Praetorius)

1962. "Song and Choir" (Summer Music Festivals).
1294 **382** 20pf. red and black 45 70

383 "Belief, Thanksgiving and Service"

1962. Catholics' Day.
1295 **383** 20pf. mauve 45 70

384 Open Bible

1962. 150th Anniv of Wurttembergische Bibelanstalt (Bible publishers).
1296 **384** 20pf. black and red 45 70

385 Europa "Tree"

1962. Europa.
1297 **385** 10pf. green 35 35
1298 **385** 40pf. blue 70 80

386 Snow White and the Seven Dwarfs

1962. Humanitarian Relief and Welfare Funds. Scenes from *Snow White and the Seven Dwarfs* (Brothers Grimm). Multicoloured.
1299 7pf.+3pf. The "Magic Mirror" 35 35
1300 10pf.+5pf. Type **386** 35 35
1301 20pf.+10pf. "The Poisoned Apple" 35 35
1302 40pf.+20pf. Snow White and Prince Charming 1·20 1·90

387 "Bread for the World"

1963. Freedom from Hunger.
1303 **387** 20pf. brown and black 45 70

388 Relief
Distribution

1963. CRALOG and CARE Relief Organizations.
1304 **388** 20pf. red   35   60

389 Ears of Wheat,
Cross and Globe

1963. Freedom from Hunger.
1305 **389** 20pf. black, red and grey   35   60

390 Snake's
Head Lily

1963. "Flora and Philately" Exhibition, Hamburg.
Multicoloured.
1306 10pf. Type **390**   35   35
1307 15pf. Lady's slipper orchid   35   35
1308 20pf. Columbine   35   35
1309 40pf. Sea holly   50   65

391 "Heidelberger
Catechismus"

1963. 400th Anniv of Heidelberg Catechism.
1310 **391** 20pf. black, red and
     orange   45   60

392 Cross, Sun and
Moon

1963. Consecration of Regina Martyrum Church, Berlin.
1311 **392** 10pf. multicoloured   35   45

393 Emblems of
Conference
Participating
Countries

1963. Centenary of Paris Postal Conference.
1312 **393** 40pf. blue   60   80

394 Map and
Flags

1963. Opening of Denmark–Germany Railway
("Vogelfluglinie").
1313 **394** 20pf. multicoloured   45   45

395 Red Cross
Emblem

1963. Red Cross Centenary.
1314 **395** 20pf. red, purple & yell   45   45

396 Hoopoe

1963. Child Welfare. Bird designs inscr "FUR DIE JUGEND
1963". Multicoloured.
1315 10pf.+5pf. Type **396**   70   95
1316 15pf.+5pf. Golden oriole   60   95
1317 20pf.+10pf. Northern bullfinch   60   95
1318 40pf.+20pf. River kingfisher   2·50   3·75

397 Congress
Emblem

1963. German Evangelical Church Day and Congress,
Dortmund.
1319 **397** 20pf. black and brown   45   60

398 "Co-operation"

1963. Europa.
1320 **398** 15pf. green   35   45
1321 **398** 20pf. red   35   35

399 Mother Goat
warning kids

1963. Humanitarian Relief and Welfare Funds.
1322 **399** 10pf.+5pf. mult   35   35
1323 - 15pf.+5pf. mult   35   35
1324 - 20pf.+10pf. mult   35   35
1325 - 40pf.+20pf. mult   95   1·60
DESIGNS: 15pf. Wolf entering house; 20pf. Wolf in house,
threatening kids; 40pf. Mother Goat and Kids dancing
round wolf in well. From Grimm's *Wolf and the Seven Kids*.

400 Atlantic Herring

1964. Child Welfare. Fish designs inscr "Fur die Jugend
1964". Multicoloured.
1326 10pf.+5pf. Type **400**   35   50
1327 15pf.+5pf. Redfish   35   50
1328 20pf.+10pf. Mirror carp   50   70
1329 40pf.+20pf. Atlantic cod   1·40   2·75

401 Old Town Hall,
Hanover

1964. Capitals of the Federal Lands. Multicoloured.
1330 20pf. Type **401**   35   45
1331 20pf. Hamburg   35   45
1332 20pf. Kiel   35   45
1333 20pf. Munich   35   45
1334 20pf. Wiesbaden   35   45
1335 20pf. Berlin   35   45
1336 20pf. Mainz   35   45
1337 20pf. Dusseldorf   35   45
1338 20pf. Bonn   35   45
1339 20pf. Bremen   35   45
1340 20pf. Stuttgart   35   45
1340a 20pf. Saarbrucken   35   45
DESIGNS: No. 1331, Liner *Lichtenfels* and St. Michael's
Church (775th anniv); 1332, Ferry *Kronprinz Harald*; 1333,
National Theatre; 1334, Kurhaus; 1335, Reichstag; 1336,
Gutenberg Museum; 1337, Jan Wellen's Monument and
Town Hall; 1338, Town Hall; 1339, Market Hall; 1340, Town
view; 1340a, Ludwig's Church.

402 Ottobeuren
Abbey

1964. 1200th Anniv of Benedictine Abbey, Ottobeuren.
1341 **402** 20pf. black, red and pink   35   45

1964. Re-election of Pres. Lubke. As Type **B67** of West
Berlin, inscr "DEUTSCHE BUNDESPOST" only.
1342 20pf. red   35   35
1343 40pf. blue   35   45

402b Sophie Scholl

1964. 20th Anniv of Attempt on Hitler's Life. Anti-Hitlerite
Martyrs. Each black and grey.
1343a 20pf. Type **402b**   95   1·70
1343b 20pf. Ludwig Beck   95   1·70
1343c 20pf. Dietrich Bonhoeffer   95   1·70
1343d 20pf. Alfred Delp   95   1·70
1343e 20pf. Karl Friedrich Goerdeler   95   1·70
1343f 20pf. Wilhelm Leuschner   95   1·70
1343g 20pf. Helmuth James (Von
     Moltke)   95   1·70
1343h 20pf. Claus Schenk (Von
     Stauffenberg)   95   1·70

403 Calvin

1964. World Council of Reformed Churches.
1344 **403** 20pf. black and red   35   45

404 Diagram of
Benzene
Formula

1964. Scientific Anniversaries (1st series).
1345 10pf. green, black and brown   35   35
1346 15pf. multicoloured   35   35
1347 20pf. green, black and red   35   35
DESIGNS: 10pf. Type **404** (centenary of publication of
Kekule's benzene formula); 15pf. Diagram of nuclear
reaction (25th anniv of publication of Hahn-Strassman
treatise on splitting the nucleus of the atom); 20pf. Gas
engine (centenary of Otto-Langen internal-combustion
engine).
     See also Nos. 1426/7 and 1451/3.

405 F. Lassalle

1964. Death Centenary of Ferdinand Lassalle (Socialist
founder and leader).
1348 **405** 20pf. black and blue   35   45

406 "The Sun"

1964. 80th Catholics' Day.
1349 **406** 20pf. red and blue   35   45

407 Europa
"Flower"

1964. Europa.
1350 **407** 15pf. violet and green   25   25
1351 **407** 20pf. violet and red   25   25

408 "The Sleeping
Beauty"

1964. Humanitarian Relief and Welfare Funds.
1352 **408** 10pf.+5pf. mult   35   35
1353 - 15pf.+5pf. mult   35   35
1354 - 20pf.+10pf. mult   35   35
1355 - 40pf.+20pf. mult   65   1·40
DESIGNS: 15pf., 20pf., 40pf. Various scenes from Grimm's
"The Sleeping Beauty".

409 Judo

1964. "Olympic Year".
1356 **409** 20pf. multicoloured   35   45

410 Prussian Eagle

1964. 250th Anniv of German Court of Accounts.
1357 **410** 20pf. orange and black   35   45

411 Pres.
Kennedy

1964. Pres. Kennedy Commemoration.
1358 **411** 40pf. blue   45   45

412 Castle
Gateway,
Ellwangen
(Jagst)

1964. Twelve Centuries of German Architecture. (a) Size
18½×22 mm. Plain background.
1359 - 10pf. brown   35   35
1360 - 15pf. green   35   35
1361 - 20pf. brown   40   35
1362 - 40pf. blue   40   35
1363 **412** 50pf. brown   70   35
1364 - 60pf. red   1·60   60
1365 - 70pf. green   1·90   60
1366 - 80pf. brown   1·60   50

     (b) Size 19½×24 mm. Coloured background.
1367 5pf. brown   30   15
1368 10pf. brown   30   15
1369 20pf. green   35   15
1370 30pf. green   35   15
1371 30pf. red   35   20
1372 40pf. brown   45   35
1373 50pf. blue   60   25
1374 60pf. orange   3·75   2·10
1375 70pf. green   1·60   35
1376 80pf. brown   3·00   2·10
1377 90pf. black   1·20   45
1378 1Dm. blue   1·00   35
1379 1Dm.10 brown   1·20   60
1380 1Dm.30 green   3·00   2·10
1381 2Dm. purple   3·00   95
BUILDINGS: 5pf. Berlin Gate, Stettin; 10pf. Zwinger pavilion, Dresden; 15pf. Tegel Castle, Berlin; 20pf. Monastery
Gate, Lorsch; 30pf. North Gate, Flensburg; 40pf. Trifels
Castle (Palatinate); 60pf. Treptow Portal, Neubrandenburg;
70pf. Osthofen Gate, Soest; 80pf. Ellingen Portal, Weissen-
burg (Bavaria); 90pf. Zschokk's Convent, Konigsberg; 1Dm.
Melanchthon House, Wittenberg; 1Dm.10, Trinity Hospital, Hildesheim; 1Dm.30, Tegel Castle, Berlin (diff.); 2Dm.
Burghers' Hall, Lowenberg Town Hall (Silesia).

413 Owl, Hat,
Walking-stick and
Satchel

1965. 150th Death Anniv of Matthias Claudius (poet).
1383 **413** 20pf. black and red
     on grey   35   45

414 Eurasian
Woodcock

1965. Child Welfare. Inscr "FUR DIE JUGEND 1965".
Multicoloured.
1384		10pf.+5pf. Type **414**	35	45
1385		15pf.+5pf. Common pheasant	35	45
1386		20pf.+10pf. Black grouse	35	45
1387		40pf.+20pf. Western capercaillie	45	1·40

415 Bismarck
(statesman)

1965. 150th Birth Anniv of Otto von Bismarck.
1388	**415**	20pf. black and red	35	45

416 Boeing 727-100
Airliner and Space
Capsule

1965. Int Transport Exn, Munich. Multicoloured.
1389		5pf. Traffic lights and road signs	35	45
1390		10pf. "Syncom" satellite and tracking station	35	45
1391		15pf. Old and modern postal buses	35	45
1392		20pf. Old semaphore station and modern signal tower	35	45
1393		40pf. Locomotive *Adler* (1835) and Class E.10.12 electric locomotive (1960s)	35	45
1394		60pf. Type **416**	35	45
1395		70pf. *Bremen* (liner) and *Hammonia* 19th-century steamship)	45	45

No. 1394 was also issued to mark the 10th anniv of
Lufthansa's renewed air services.

417 Bouquet

1965. 75th Anniv of "May 1st" (Labour Day).
1396	**417**	15pf. multicoloured	30	35

418 I.T.U.
Emblem

1965. Centenary of I.T.U.
1397	**418**	40pf. black and blue	45	60

419 A. Kopling

1965. Death Centenary of Adolf Kolping (miners' padre).
1398	**419**	20pf. black, red and grey	35	45

420 Rescue Vessel
"Theodor Heuss"

1965. Cent of German Sea-rescue Service.
1399	**420**	20pf. violet, black & red	35	45

1965. 20th Anniv of Influx of East German Refugees. As T
299 but inscr "ZWANZIG JAHRE VERTREIBUNG 1945
1965".
1400		20pf. purple	35	45

421 Evangelical
Church Emblem

1965. German Evangelical Church Day and Synod,
Cologne.
1401	**421**	20pf. black, turq & bl	35	45

422 Radio Tower

1965. Radio Exhibition, Stuttgart.
1402	**422**	20pf. black, blue & mve	35	45

423 Thurn and Taxis 1, 2
and 5sgr. Stamps of 1852

1965. 125th Anniv of First Postage Stamp.
1403	**423**	20pf. multicoloured	35	45

424 Europa "Sprig"

1965. Europa.
1404	**424**	15pf. green	35	35
1405	**424**	20pf. red	35	35

425 Cinderella with
Birds

1965. Humanitarian Relief Funds. Multicoloured.
1406		10pf.+5pf. Type **425**	35	35
1407		15pf.+5pf. Cinderella and birds with dress	35	35
1408		20pf.+10pf. Prince offering slipper to Cinderella	35	35
1409		40pf.+20pf. Cinderella and Prince on horse	70	1·00

426 N.
Soderblom

1966. Birth Centenary of Nathan Soderblom (Archbishop
of Uppsala).
1410	**426**	20pf. black and lilac	35	45

427 Cardinal
von Galen

1966. 20th Death Anniv of Cardinal Clemens von Galen.
1411	**427**	20pf. red, mauve & black	35	45

428
Brandenburg
Gate, Berlin

1966
1412	**428**	10pf. brown	35	25
1413	**428**	20pf. green	50	35
1414	**428**	30pf. red	50	35
1415	**428**	50pf. blue	1·90	60
1415a	**428**	100pf. blue	14·50	95

429 Roe deer

1966. Child Welfare. Multicoloured.
1416		10pf.+5pf. Type **429**	35	40
1417		20pf.+10pf. Chamois	35	40
1418		30pf.+15pf. Fallow deer	35	40
1419		50pf.+25pf. Red deer	95	1·40

430 Christ and
Fishermen
(Miracle of the
Fishes)

1966. Catholics' Day.
1420	**430**	30pf. black and salmon	35	45

431 19th-cent
Postman

1966. F.I.P. Meeting, Munich. Multicoloured.
1421		30pf.+15pf. Bavarian mail coach	60	1·00
1422		50pf.+25pf. Type **431**	80	1·00

432 G. W.
Leibniz

1966. 250th Death Anniv of Gottfried Leibniz (scientist).
1423	**432**	30pf. black and mauve	35	45

433 Europa
"Ship"

1966. Europa.
1424	**433**	20pf. multicoloured	35	45
1425	**433**	30pf. multicoloured	35	30

434 Diagram of
A.C.
Transmission
(75th Anniv)

1966. Scientific Annivs (2nd series). Multicoloured.
1426		20pf. Type **434**	30	35
1427		30pf. Diagram of electric dynamo (cent)	35	35

435 Princess and
Frog

1966. Humanitarian Relief Funds. Multicoloured.
1428		10pf.+5pf. Type **435**	30	35
1429		20pf.+10pf. Frog dining with Princess	30	35
1430		30pf.+15pf. Prince and Princess	30	35
1431		50pf.+25pf. In coach	60	1·40

Designs from Grimm's *The Frog Prince*.

436 UNICEF
Emblem

1966. Award of Nobel Peace Prize to United Nations
Children's Fund.
1432	**436**	30pf. sepia, black and red	35	45

437 W. von Siemens
(electrical engineer)

438 Common
Rabbit

1966. 150th Birth Anniv of Werner von Siemens
(electrical engineer).
1433	**437**	30pf. red	35	45

1967. Child Welfare. Multicoloured.
1434		10pf.+5pf. Type **438**	35	60
1435		20pf.+10pf. Stoat	35	60
1436		30pf.+15pf. Common hamster	70	1·20
1437		50pf.+25pf. Red fox	1·50	2·30

See also Nos. 1454/7.

439 Cogwheels

1967. Europa.
1438	**439**	20pf. multicoloured	45	45
1439	**439**	30pf. multicoloured	35	35

440 Francis of
Taxis

1967. 450th Death Anniv of Francis of Taxis.
1440	**440**	30pf. black and orange	35	45

441 Evangelical
Symbols

1967. 13th German Evangelical Churches Day.
1441	**441**	30pf. black and mauve	35	45

442 Friedrich von
Bodelschwingh
(Head of Hospital
1910–46)

1967. Cent of Bethel Hospital, Bielefeld.
1442	**442**	30pf. black and brown	35	45

443 Frau Holle at
Spinning-wheel

1967. Humanitarian Relief Funds. Multicoloured.
1443		10pf.+5pf. Type **443**	35	35
1444		20pf.+10pf. In the clouds	35	35
1445		30pf.+15pf. With shopping-basket and cockerel	35	35
1446		50pf.+25pf. Covered with soot	80	1·60

Designs from Grimm's *Frau Holle* ("Mother Carey").

1967. Re-election of Pres. Lubke. As Type **B67** of West
Berlin, but inscr "DEUTSCHE BUNDESPOST".
1447		30pf. red	35	45
1448		50pf. blue	60	60

444 Wartburg
(castle), Eisenach

1967. 450th Anniv of Luther's *Theses* and the
Reformation.
1449	**444**	30pf. red	45	60

445 Cross on South American Map

1967. "Adveniat" (Aid for Catholic Church in Latin America).

1450	**445**	30pf. multicoloured	35	45

446 Koenig's Printing Machine

1968. Scientific Anniv (3rd series). Multicoloured.

1451		10pf. Type **446**	25	25
1452		20pf. Ore Crystals	25	25
1453		30pf. Lens Refraction	35	35

ANNIVS: 10pf. 150th anniv; 20pf. Millenary of ore mining in Harz Mountains; 30pf. Centenary of Abbe-Zeiss Scientific Microscope.

1968. Child Welfare. As T **438** but inscr "1968". Multicoloured.

1454		10pf.+5pf. Wildcat	35	70
1455		20pf.+10pf. European otter	60	1·20
1456		30pf.+15pf. Eurasian badger	80	1·60
1457		50pf.+25pf. Eurasian beaver	3·00	4·00

447 Trade Symbols

1968. German Crafts and Trades.

1458	**447**	30pf. multicoloured	45	60

448 Dr. Adenauer

1968. Adenauer Commemoration (1st issue). T **448** and similar horiz designs in sheet 149×106 mm.

MS1459	10pf. brown and black; 20pf. green and black; 30pf. red and black; 50pf. blue and black	3·50	3·50

DESIGNS: 10pf. Sir Winston Churchill; 20pf. Alcide de Gasperi; 30pf. Robert Schuman.
See also No. 1469.

449 Europa "Key"

1968. Europa.

1460	**449**	20pf. yellow, brn & grn	35	45
1461	**449**	30pf. yellow, brn & red	35	35

450 Karl Marx

1968. 150th Birth Anniv of Karl Marx.

1462	**450**	30pf. red, black & grey	35	45

451 F. von Langen (horseman)

1968. Olympic Games (1972) Promotion Fund (1st series).

1463	**451**	10pf.+5pf. black & grn	45	40
1464	-	20pf.+10pf. black & grn	45	40
1465	-	30pf. black and lilac	45	40
1466	-	30pf.+15pf. black & red	80	75
1467	-	50pf.+25pf. black & bl	1·30	1·30

DESIGN: 20pf. R. Harbig (runner); 30pf. (No. 1465) Pierre de Coubertin (founder of Olympics); 30pf. (No. 1466) Helene Mayer (fencer); 50pf. Carl Diem (sports organiser).
See also Nos. 1493/6, 1524/7, 1589/92, 1621/4, **MS**1625 and 1629/32.

452 Opening Bars of *The Mastersingers*

1968. Centenary of First Performance of Richard Wagner's Opera *The Mastersingers*.

1468	**452**	30pf. multicoloured	35	45

453 Dr. Adenauer

1968. Adenauer Commemoration (2nd issue).

1469	**453**	30pf. black and orange	45	45

454 Cross, Dove and "The Universe"

1968. Catholics' Day.

1470	**454**	20pf. violet, yellow & grn	35	45

455 Northern District 1g. and Southern District 7k. stamps of 1868

1968. Cent of North German Postal Confederation and First Stamps.

1471	**455**	30pf. red, blue and black	35	45

456 Arrows

1968. Cent of German Trade Unions.

1472	**456**	30pf. multicoloured	35	45

457 Doll of 1878

1968. Humanitarian Relief Funds. Multicoloured.

1473		10pf.+5pf. Type **457**	35	35
1474		20pf.+10pf. Doll of 1850	35	35
1475		30pf.+15pf. Doll of 1870	35	35
1476		50pf.+25pf. Doll of 1885	80	1·30

458 Human Rights Emblem

1968. Human Rights Year.

1477	**458**	30pf. multicoloured	35	45

459 Pony

1969. Child Welfare.

1478	**459**	10pf.+5pf. brown, black and yellow	45	60
1479	-	20pf.+10pf. brown, black and buff	45	60
1480	-	30pf.+15pf. brown, black and red	85	1·20
1481	-	50pf.+25pf. mult	2·50	2·30

HORSES: 20pf. Draught-horse; 30pf. Saddle-horse; 50pf. Thoroughbred.

460 Junkers Ju 52/3m "Boelke"

1969. 50th Anniv of German Airmail Services. Multicoloured.

1482		20pf. Type **460**	60	35
1483		30pf. Boeing 707 airliner	95	35

461 Colonnade

1969. Europa.

1484	**461**	20pf. yellow, grn & bl	45	35
1485	**461**	30pf. yellow, red & violet	45	35

462 "The Five Continents"

1969. 50th Anniv of I.L.O.

1486	**462**	30pf. multicoloured	70	45

463 Eagle Emblems of Weimar and Federal Republics

1969. 20th Anniv of German Federal Republic.

1487	**463**	30pf. black, gold and red	1·40	70

464 "War Graves"

1969. 50th Anniv of German War Graves Commission.

1488	**464**	30pf. blue and yellow	70	45

465 Lakeside Landscape

1969. Nature Protection. Multicoloured.

1489		10pf. Type **465**	35	35
1490		20pf. Highland landscape	95	60
1491		30pf. Alpine landscape	45	35
1492		50pf. River landscape	1·40	80

466 "Running Track"

1969. Olympic Games (1972). Promotion Fund (2nd series). Multicoloured.

1493	**466**	10pf.+5pf. Type **466**	35	35
1494		20pf.+10pf. "Hockey"	60	45
1495		30pf.+15pf. "Shooting target"	80	70
1496		50pf.+25pf. "Sailing"	1·70	1·40

467 "Longing for Justice"

1969. 14th German Protestant Congress, Stuttgart.

1497	**467**	30pf. multicoloured	70	45

468 "Electromagnetic Field"

1969. German Radio Exhibition, Stuttgart.

1498	**468**	30pf. multicoloured	70	45

469 Marie Juchacz

1969. "Fifty Years of German Women's Suffrage". Sheet 102×61 mm containing T **469** and similar vert portraits of women politicians.

MS1499	10pf. olive; 20pf. green; 30pf. red	1·60	1·20

DESIGNS: 20pf. Marie-Elizabeth Luders; 30pf. Helene Weber.

470 Maltese Cross Symbol

1969. "Malteser Hilfsdienst" (welfare organization).

1500	**470**	30pf. red and black	70	45

471 Bavaria 3k. Stamp of 1867

1969. German Philatelic Federation Congress and Exn, Garmisch-Partenkirchen.

1501	**471**	30pf. red and slate	70	45

472 Map of Pipeline

1969. 350th Anniv of Bad Reichenhall–Traunstein Brine Pipeline.

1502	**472**	20pf. multicoloured	70	45

473 Rothenburg ob der Tauber

1969. Tourism.

1503	**473**	30pf. black and red	70	45

See also Nos. 1523, 1558, 1564, 1587, 1606, 1641/2, 1655/6 and 1680/2.

474 Mahatma Gandhi

1969. Birth Centenary of Mahatma Gandhi.

1504	**474**	20pf. black and green	45	45

475 Pope John XXIII

1969. Pope John XXIII Commemoration.
1505 **475** 30pf. red 60 45

476 Adler (1835)

1969. Humanitarian Relief Funds. Pewter Figurines. Multicolored. (a) Inscr. "WOHLFAHRTSMARKE".
1506 10pf.+5pf. Type **476** 30 30
1507 20pf.+10pf. Woman watering flowers (1780) 35 35
1508 30pf.+15pf. Bird salesman (1850) 45 45
1509 50pf.+25pf. Mounted dignitary (1840) 1·40 1·70

(b) Christmas. Inscr "WEIHNACHTSMARKE".
1510 10pf.+5pf. "Child Jesus in crib" (1850) 50 45

477 E. M. Arndt

1969. Birth Bicent of Ernst Arndt (writer).
1511 **477** 30pf. lake and bistre 60 45

478 "H. von Rugge"

1970. Child Welfare. Minnesinger Themes. Multicoloured.
1512 10pf.+5pf. Type **478** 60 45
1513 20pf.+10pf. "W. von Eschenbach" 95 60
1514 30pf.+15pf. "W. von Metz" 1·20 95
1515 50pf.+25pf. "W. von der Vogelweide" 2·50 2·30

479 Beethoven

1970. Birth Bicentenaries.
1516 **479** 10pf. black and blue 1·20 35
1517 - 20pf. black and olive 70 35
1518 - 30pf. black and pink 70 35
DESIGNS: 20pf. G. W. Hegel (philosopher); 30pf. F. Holderlin (poet).

480 Saar 1m. Stamp of 1947

1970. "Sabria 70" Stamp Exn, Saarbrucken.
1519 **480** 30pf. green, black and red 60 45

481 "Flaming Sun"

1970. Europa.
1520 **481** 20pf. green 45 35
1521 **481** 30pf. red 50 35

482 Von Munchhausen on Severed Horse

1970. 250th Birth Anniv of Baron H. von Munchhausen.
1522 **482** 20pf. multicoloured 60 45

1970. Tourism. As T **473**, but with view of Oberammergau.
1523 30pf. black and orange 60 45

483 Royal Palace

1970. Olympic Games (1972). Promotion Fund (3rd series).
1524 **483** 10pf.+5pf. brown 35 35
1525 - 20pf.+10pf. turquoise 70 60
1526 - 30pf.+15pf. red 95 80
1527 - 50pf.+25pf. blue 1·50 1·50
DESIGNS (Munich buildings): 20pf. Propylaea; 30pf. Glyptothek; 50pf. "Bavaria" (statue and colonnade).

484 Liner *Kungsholm IV* and Road-tunnel

1970. 75th Anniv of Kiel Canal.
1528 **484** 20pf. multicoloured 60 45

485 Nurse with Invalid

1970. Voluntary Relief Services. Multicoloured.
1529 5pf. Oxygen-lance operator 30 35
1530 10pf. Mountain rescue 35 35
1531 20pf. Type **485** 45 35
1532 30pf. Fireman with hose 1·20 35
1533 50pf. Road-accident casualty 1·20 60
1534 70pf. Rescue from drowning 1·40 1·20

486 President Heinemann

1970
1535 **486** 5pf. black 35 35
1536 **486** 10pf. brown 35 35
1537 **486** 20pf. green 35 35
1538 **486** 25pf. green 50 35
1539 **486** 30pf. brown 45 35
1540 **486** 40pf. orange 45 35
1541 **486** 50pf. blue 2·10 35
1542 **486** 60pf. blue 95 35
1543 **486** 70pf. brown 1·20 45
1544 **486** 80pf. green 1·20 45
1545 **486** 90pf. red 2·10 1·70
1546 **486** 1Dm. green 1·50 45
1547 **486** 110pf. grey 1·70 1·20
1548 **486** 120pf. brown 2·00 1·20
1549 **486** 130pf. brown 2·10 1·20
1550 **486** 140pf. green 2·20 1·40
1551 **486** 150pf. red 2·20 1·20
1552 **486** 160pf. orange 3·25 1·60
1553 **486** 170pf. orange 2·75 1·20
1554 **486** 190pf. purple 3·50 1·30
1555 **486** 2Dm. violet 3·75 60

487 Illuminated Cross

1970. Catholic Church World Mission.
1556 **487** 20pf. yellow and green 45 35

488 Stylized Cross

1970. Catholics Day and 83rd German Catholic Congress, Trier.
1557 **488** 20pf. multicoloured 45 35

1970. Tourism. As T **473**.
1558 20pf. black and green 70 45
DESIGN: 20pf. View of Cochem.

489 "Jester"

1970. Humanitarian Relief Funds. Puppets. Multicoloured. (a) Relief Funds.
1559 10pf.+5pf. Type **489** 35 35
1560 20pf.+10pf. "Buffoon" 35 45
1561 30pf.+15pf. "Clown" 60 60
1562 50pf.+25pf. "Harlequin" 1·50 1·50

(b) Christmas.
1563 10pf.+5pf. "Angel" 45 40

1970. Tourism. As T **473**, but with view of Freiburg im Breisgau.
1564 20pf. brown and green 70 45

490 A. J. Comenius (scholar)

1970. Int Education Year and 300th Death Anniv of Comenius (Jan Komensky).
1565 **490** 30pf. red and black 70 45

491 Engels as Young Man

1970. 150th Birth Anniv of Friedrich Engels.
1566 **491** 50pf. blue and red 2·10 1·20

492 German Eagle

1971. Centenary of German Unification.
1567 **492** 30pf. black, red & orange 2·10 45

493 "Ebert" Stamp of 1928 and inscr "To the German People"

1971. Birth Centenary of Friedrich Ebert (Chancellor 1918 and President 1919–25).
1568 **493** 30pf. green, black and red 2·10 45

494 "King of Blackamoors"

1971. Child Welfare. Children's Drawings. Multicoloured.
1569 10pf.+5pf. Type **494** 45 45
1570 20pf.+10pf. "Flea" 60 60
1571 30pf.+15pf. "Puss-in-Boots" 95 95
1572 50pf.+25pf. "Serpent" 1·50 1·50

495 Molecular Chain

1971. 125 Years of Chemical Fibre Research.
1573 **495** 20pf. black, red & green 45 35

496 Road-crossing Patrol

1971. New Road Traffic Regulations (1st series).
1574 **496** 10pf. black, blue and red 25 25
1575 - 20pf. black, red & green 45 35
1576 - 30pf. red, black and grey 70 35
1577 - 50pf. black, blue and red 1·20 75
ROAD SIGNS: 20pf. "Right-of-way across junction"; 30pf. "STOP"; 50pf. "Pedestrian Crossing".
See also Nos. 1579/82.

497 Luther before Charles V

1971. 450th Anniv of Diet of Worms.
1578 **497** 30pf. black and red 95 45

1971. New Traffic Regulations (2nd series). Horiz designs similar to T **496**.
1579 5pf. red, black and blue 30 30
1580 10pf. multicoloured 35 30
1581 20pf. red, black and green 60 30
1582 30pf. yellow, black and red 1·00 30
NEW HIGHWAY CODE: 5pf. Overtaking; 10pf. Warning of obstruction; 20pf. Lane discipline; 30pf. Pedestrian Crossing.

498 Europa Chain

1971. Europa.
1583 **498** 20pf. gold, green & black 40 35
1584 **498** 30pf. gold, red and black 45 35

499 Thomas a Kempis writing *The Imitation of Christ*

1971. 500th Death Anniv of Thomas a Kempis (devotional writer).
1585 **499** 30pf. black and red 80 45

500 Durer's Monogram

1971. 500th Birth Anniv of Albrecht Durer.
1586 **500** 30pf. brown & red 1·90 45

1971. Tourism. As T **473**, but with view of Nuremburg.
1587 30pf. black and red 70 45

501 Meeting Emblem

1971. Whitsun Ecumenical Meeting, Augsburg.

| 1588 | 501 | 30pf. black, orange & red | 70 | 45 |

502 Ski Jumping

1971. Olympic Games (1972). Promotion Fund (4th series). Winter Games, Sapporo.

1589	502	10pf.+5pf. black & brn	35	25
1590	-	20pf.+10pf. black & grn	70	45
1591	-	30pf.+15pf. black & red	1·30	95
1592	-	50pf.+25pf. black & bl	2·00	1·90
MS1593	112×66 mm. Nos. 1589/92		4·75	4·00

DESIGNS: 20pf. Ice dancing; 30pf. Skiing start; 50pf. Ice hockey.

503 Astronomical Calculus

1971. 400th Birth Anniv of Johann Kepler (astronomer).

| 1594 | 503 | 30pf. gold, red and black | 80 | 45 |

504 Dante

1971. 650th Death Anniv of Dante Alighieri.

| 1595 | 504 | 10pf. black | 35 | 35 |

505 Alcohol and front of Car ("Don't Drink and Drive")

1971. Accident Prevention.

1596	-	5pf. orange	35	15
1597	-	10pf. brown	35	15
1598	-	20pf. violet	45	30
1599	505	25pf. green	60	30
1600	-	30pf. red	60	30
1601	-	40pf. mauve	60	30
1602	-	50pf. blue	3·00	30
1603	-	60pf. blue	2·00	70
1603a	-	70pf. blue and green	1·70	45
1604	-	1Dm. green	3·00	35
1605	-	1Dm.50 brown	7·50	1·70

DESIGNS: 5pf. Man within flame, and spent match ("Fire Prevention"); 10pf. Fall from ladder; 20pf. Unguarded machinery ("Factory Safety"); 30pf. Falling brick and protective helmet; 40pf. Faulty electric plug; 50pf. Protruding nail in plank; 60pf., 70pf. Ball in front of car ("Child Road Safety"); 1Dm. Crate on hoist; 1Dm.50, Open manhole.

1971. Tourism. As T **473** but with view of Goslar.

| 1606 | 20pf. black and green | 70 | 60 |

506 Women churning Butter

1971. Humanitarian Relief Funds. Wooden Toys. Multicoloured. (a) Inscr. "WOHLFAHRTSMARKE".

1607	20pf.+10pf. Type **506**	35	30
1608	25pf.+10pf. Horseman on wheels	35	30
1609	30pf.+15pf. Nutcracker man	70	70
1610	60pf.+30pf. Dovecote	1·90	1·90

(b) Christmas. Inscr "WEIHNACHTSMARKE".

| 1611 | 20pf.+10pf. Angel with three candles | 80 | 60 |

507 Deaconess and Nurse

1972. Death Cent of Johann Wilhelm Lohe (founder of Deaconesses Mission, Neuendettelsau).

| 1612 | 507 | 25pf. slate, black & green | 70 | 45 |

508 Ducks crossing Road

1972. Child Welfare. Animal Protection. Multicoloured.

1613	20pf.+10pf. Type **508**	80	70
1614	25pf.+10pf. Hunter scaring deer	70	50
1615	30pf.+15pf. Child protecting bird from cat	1·40	1·40
1616	60pf.+30pf. Boy annoying mute swans	2·30	2·40

509 Senefelder's Press

1972. "175 Years of Offset Lithography".

| 1617 | 509 | 25pf. multicoloured | 70 | 45 |

510 "Communications"

1972. Europa.

| 1618 | 510 | 25pf. multicoloured | 60 | 30 |
| 1619 | 510 | 30pf. multicoloured | 65 | 35 |

511 Lucas Cranach

1972. 500th Birth Anniv of Lucas Cranach the Elder (painter).

| 1620 | 511 | 25pf. black, stone & grn | 80 | 45 |

512 Wrestling

1972. Olympic Games, Munich (5th series). Multicoloured.

1621	20pf.+10pf. Type **512**	70	60
1622	25pf.+10pf. Sailing	70	60
1623	30pf.+15pf. Gymnastics	70	60
1624	60pf.+30pf. Swimming	2·50	2·30

See also Nos. 1629/32.

513 Gymnastics Stadium

1972. Olympic Games, Munich (6th series). Sheet 148×105 mm containing T **513** and similar multicoloured designs.

| MS1625 | 25pf.+10pf. Type **513**; 30pf.+15pf. Athletics stadium; 40pf.+20pf. Tented area; 70pf.+35pf. TV tower | 6·50 | 6·50 |

514 Invalid Archer

1972. 21st Int Games for the Paralysed, Heidelberg.

| 1626 | 514 | 40pf. red, black & yellow | 95 | 45 |

515 Posthorn and Decree

1972. Cent of German Postal Museum.

| 1627 | 515 | 40pf. multicoloured | 1·30 | 45 |

516 K. Schumacher

1972. 20th Death Anniv of Kurt Schumacher (politician).

| 1628 | 516 | 40pf. black and red | 1·90 | 45 |

1972. Olympic Games, Munich (7th series). As Type **512**. Multicoloured.

1629	25pf.+5pf. Long jumping	70	70
1630	30pf.+10pf. Basketball	1·90	1·80
1631	40pf.+10pf. Throwing the discus	2·50	2·40
1632	70pf.+10pf. Canoeing	1·30	1·20
MS1633	111×66 mm. Nos. 1629/32	6·50	6·50

517 Open Book

1972. International Book Year.

| 1634 | 517 | 40pf. multicoloured | 95 | 45 |

518 Music and Signature

1972. 300th Death Anniv of Heinrich Schutz (composer).

| 1635 | 518 | 40pf. multicoloured | 1·20 | 45 |

519 Knight

1972. Humanitarian Relief Funds. Multicoloured. (a) 19th-century Faience Chessmen. Inscr "WOHLFAHRTSMARKE".

1636	25pf.+10pf. Type **519**	45	45
1637	30pf.+15pf. Rook	45	35
1638	40pf.+20pf. Queen	80	35
1639	70pf.+35pf. King	3·00	2·75

(b) Christmas. Inscr "WEIHNACHTSMARKE".

| 1640 | 30pf.+15pf. "The Three Wise Men" (horiz) | 1·20 | 80 |

1972. Tourism. As T **473**.

| 1641 | 30pf. black and green | 70 | 35 |
| 1642 | 40pf. black and orange | 80 | 35 |

VIEWS: 30pf. Heligoland; 40pf. Heidelberg.

520 Revellers

1972. 150th Anniv of Cologne Carnival.

| 1643 | 520 | 40pf. multicoloured | 1·40 | 45 |

521 H. Heine

1972. 175th Birth Anniv of Heinrich Heine (poet).

| 1644 | 521 | 40pf. black, red and pink | 1·40 | 45 |

522 "Brot fur die Welt"

1972. Freedom from Hunger Campaign.

| 1645 | 522 | 30pf. red and green | 70 | 70 |

523 Wurzburg Cathedral (seal)

1972. Catholic Synod '72.

| 1646 | 523 | 40pf. black, purple & red | 80 | 45 |

524 National Colours of France and Germany

1973. Tenth Anniv of Franco-German Treaty.

| 1647 | 524 | 40pf. multicoloured | 1·60 | 50 |

525 Osprey

1973. Youth Welfare. Birds of Prey. Multicoloured.

1648	25pf.+10pf. Type **525**	1·40	1·20
1649	30pf.+15pf. Common buzzard	1·70	1·40
1650	40pf.+20pf. Red kite	2·30	2·10
1651	70pf.+35pf. Montagu's harrier	5·00	5·25

526 Copernicus

1973. 500th Birth Anniv of Copernicus.

| 1652 | 526 | 40pf. black and red | 1·90 | 45 |

527 Radio Mast and Transmission

1973. 50th Anniv of Interpol.

| 1653 | 527 | 40pf. black, red and grey | 70 | 45 |

528 Weather Chart

1973. Cent of Int Meteorological Organization.

| 1654 | 528 | 30pf. multicoloured | 70 | 45 |

1973. Tourism. As T **473**.

| 1655 | 40pf. black and red | 1·40 | 35 |
| 1656 | 40pf. black and orange | 1·20 | 35 |

VIEWS: No. 1655, Hamburg; 1656, Rudesheim.

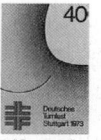

529 "Gymnast" (poster)

1973. Gymnastics Festival, Stuttgart.

| 1657 | 529 | 40pf. multicoloured | 70 | 45 |

530 Kassel (Hesse) Sign

1973. "I.B.R.A. Munchen 73" International Stamp Exhibition, Munich. F.I.P. Congress. Post-house Signs. Multicoloured.

1658		40pf.+20pf. Type **530**	1·00	1·00
1659		70pf.+35pf. Prussia	1·90	1·90

MS1660 74×105 mm. 40pf.+20pf. Wurttemberg; 70pf.+35pf. Kurpfalz (Bavaria) (sold at 2.20Dm.) 5·25 5·75

531 Europa "Posthorn"

1973. Europa.

1661	**531**	30pf. yell, myrtle & grn	70	35
1662	**531**	40pf. yellow, lake & pink	80	35

532 "R" Motif

1973. 1000th Death Anniv of Roswitha von Gandersheim (poetess).

1663	**532**	40pf. yellow, black & red	80	45

533 M. Kolbe

1973. Father Maximilian Kolbe (Concentration camp victim) Commemoration.

1664	**533**	40pf. red, brown & black	80	45

534 "Profile" (from poster)

1973. 15th German Protestant Church Conference.

1665	**534**	30pf. multicoloured	60	35

535 Environmental Conference Emblem and Waste

1973. "Protection of the Environment". Multicoloured.

1666		25pf. Type **535**	60	35
1667		30pf. Emblem and "Water"	60	35
1668		40pf. Emblem and "Noise"	1·20	35
1669		70pf. Emblem and "Air"	1·90	1·00

536 Schickard's Calculating Machine

1973. 350th Anniv of Schickard's Calculating Machine.

1670	**536**	40pf. black, red and orange	80	60

537 Otto Wels

1973. Birth Centenary of Otto Wels (Social Democratic Party leader).

1671	**537**	40pf. purple and lilac	95	45

538 Lubeck Cathedral

1973. 800th Anniv of Lubeck Cathedral.

1672	**538**	40pf. multicoloured	1·40	45

539 U.N. and German Eagle Emblems

1973. Admission of German Federal Republic to U.N. Organization.

1673	**539**	40pf. multicoloured	2·00	45

540 French Horn

1973. Humanitarian Relief Funds. Multicoloured. (a) Musical Instruments. Inscr "WOHLFAHRTSMARKE".

1674		25pf.+10pf. Type **540**	80	45
1675		30pf.+15pf. Grand piano	85	45
1676		40pf.+20pf. Violin	1·20	70
1677		70pf.+70pf. Harp	3·00	2·50

(b) Christmas. Inscr "WEIHNACHTSMARKE".

1678		30pf.+15pf. Christmas star	1·20	80

541 Radio set of 1923

1973. "50 Years of German Broadcasting".

1679	**541**	30pf. multicoloured	60	35

1974. Tourism. As Type **473**.

1680		30pf. black and green	95	35
1681		40pf. black and red	95	35
1682		40pf. black and red	95	35

VIEWS: No. 1680, Saarbrucken; 1681, Aachen; 1682, Bremen.

542 Louise Otto-Peters

1974. Women in German Politics. Each black and orange.

1683		40pf. Type **542**	95	70
1684		40pf. Helene Lange	95	70
1685		40pf. Rosa Luxemburg	95	70
1686		40pf. Gertrud Baumer	95	70

543 Drop of Blood and Emergency Light

1974. Blood Donor and Accident/Rescue Services.

1687	**543**	40pf. red and blue	1·30	45

544 *Deer in Red* (Franz Marc)

1974. German Expressionist Paintings. Multicoloured.

1688		30pf. Type **544**	70	35
1689		30pf. *Girls under Trees* (A. Macke)	95	40
1690		40pf. *Portrait in Blue* (A. von Jawiensky) (vert)	95	35
1691		50pf. *Pechstein asleep* (E. Heckel) (vert)	95	45
1692		70pf. *Still Life with Telescope* (Max Beckmann)	1·40	1·20
1693		120pf. *Old Peasant* (L. Kirchner) (vert)	2·75	2·30

545 St. Thomas teaching Pupils

1974. 700th Death Anniv of St. Thomas Aquinas.

1694	**545**	40pf. black and red	80	45

546 Disabled Persons in Outline

1974. Rehabilitation of the Handicapped.

1695	**546**	40pf. red and black	1·30	45

547 Construction (Bricklayer)

1974. Youth Welfare. Youth Activities. Multicoloured.

1696		25pf.+10pf. Type **547**	80	70
1697		30pf.+15pf. Folk dancing	1·40	1·20
1698		40pf.+20pf. Study	2·30	2·10
1699		70pf.+35pf. Research	4·25	4·25

548 "Ascending Youth" (W. Lehmbruck)

1974. Europa.

1700	**548**	30pf. black, green & sil	75	35
1701	-	40pf. black, red and lilac	80	35

DESIGN: 40pf. "Kneeling Woman" (W. Lehmbruck).

549 Immanuel Kant

1974. 250th Birth Anniv of Immanuel Kant (philosopher).

1702	**549**	90pf. red	3·00	70

550 Federal Arms and National Colours

1974. 25th Anniv of Formation of Federal Republic. Sheet 94×64 mm.

MS1703	**550**	40pf. multicoloured	2·10	2·75

551 Country Road

1974. Rambling, and Birth Centenaries of Richard Schirrman and Wilhelm Munker (founders of Youth Hostelling Assn).

1704	**551**	30pf. multicoloured	60	45

552 Friedrich Klopstock

1974. 250th Birth Anniv of Friedrich Gottlieb Klopstock (poet).

1705	**552**	40pf. black and red	80	40

553 "Crowned Cross" Symbol

1974. 125th Anniv of German Protestant Church Diaconal Association (charitable organization).

1706	**553**	40p. multicoloured	80	45

554 Goalkeeper saving Goal

1974. World Cup Football Championship. Multicoloured.

1707		30pf. Type **554**	1·20	35
1708		40pf. Mid-field melee	2·50	35

555 Hans Holbein (self-portrait)

1974. 450th Death Anniv of Hans Holbein the Elder (painter).

1709	**555**	50pf. black and red	1·20	45

556 Broken Bars of Prison Window

1974. Amnesty International Commemoration.

1710	**556**	70pf. black and blue	1·60	70

557 Man and Woman looking at the Moon

1974. Birth Bicentenary of Caspar David Friedrich (artist).

1711	**557**	50pf. multicoloured	1·50	45

558 Campion

1974. Humanitarian Relief Funds. Flowers. Multicoloured. (a) 25th Anniv of Welfare Stamps. Inscr "25 JAHRE WOHLFAHRTSMARKE".

1712		30pf.+15pf. Type **558**	45	45
1713		40pf.+20pf. Foxglove	60	45
1714		50pf.+25pf. Mallow	70	60
1715		70pf.+35pf. Campanula	2·00	2·00

(b) Christmas. Inscr "WEIHNACHTSMARKE".

1716		40pf.+20pf. Poinsettia	1·40	80

559 Early German Post-boxes

1974. Cent of Universal Postal Union.
| 1717 | **559** | 50pf. multicoloured | 1·90 | 60 |

560 Annette Kolb

1975. International Women's Year. Women Writers.
1718	30pf. Type **560**		95	45
1719	40pf. Ricarda Huch		80	45
1720	50pf. Else Lasker-Schuler		80	45
1721	70pf. Gertrud von le Fort		1·40	1·40

561 Hans Bockler (Trade Union leader)

1975. Birth Centenaries.
1722	**561**	40pf. black and green	1·00	45
1723	-	50pf. black and red	95	45
1724	-	70pf. black and blue	2·75	1·20

DESIGNS: 50pf. Matthias Erzberger (statesman); 70pf. Albert Schweitzer (medical missionary).

562 Mother and Child and Emblem

1975. 25th Anniv of Organization for the Rest and Recuperation of Mothers.
| 1725 | **562** | 50pf. multicoloured | 1·00 | 45 |

563 Detail of Ceiling Painting, Sistine Chapel

1975. 500th Birth Anniv of Michelangelo.
| 1726 | **563** | 70pf. black and blue | 2·10 | 2·00 |

564 Plan of St. Peter's, Rome within a cross

1975. "Holy Year (Year of Reconcillation)".
| 1727 | **564** | 50pf. multicoloured | 1·00 | 45 |

565 Ice Hockey

1975. World Ice Hockey Championships, Munich and Dusseldorf.
| 1728 | **565** | 50pf. multicoloured | 1·50 | 45 |

566 Class 218 Diesel Locomotive

1975. Youth Welfare. Railway Locomotives. Multicoloured.
| 1729 | 30pf.+15pf. Type **566** | | 70 | 60 |

1730	40pf.+20pf. Class 103 electric locomotive	1·00	95
1731	50pf.+25pf. Class 403 electric railcar	1·50	1·40
1732	70pf.+35pf. Transrapid Maglev train (model)	2·50	2·30

567 Concentric Group

1975. Europa. Paintings by Oskar Schlemmer. Multicoloured.
| 1733 | 40pf. Type **567** | 75 | 35 |
| 1734 | 50pf. *Bauhaus Staircase* | 1·10 | 35 |

568 Morike's Silhouette and Signature

1975. Death Cent of Eduard Morike (writer).
| 1735 | **568** | 40pf. multicoloured | 50 | 35 |

569 "Nuis" (woodcarving)

1975. 500th Anniv of Siege of Neuss.
| 1736 | **569** | 50pf. multicoloured | 1·00 | 50 |

570 Jousting Contest

1975. 500th Anniv of "Landshut Wedding" (festival).
| 1737 | **570** | 50pf. multicoloured | 1·50 | 50 |

571 Mainz Cathedral

1975. Millenary of Mainz Cathedral.
| 1738 | **571** | 40pf. multicoloured | 1·50 | 50 |

572 Telecommunication Satellite

1975. Industry and Technology.
1739	**572**	5pf. green	25	25
1740	-	10pf. mauve	25	25
1741	-	20pf. red	30	25
1742	-	30pf. lilac	35	30
1743	-	40pf. green	50	35
1744	-	50pf. mauve	60	35
1745	-	60pf. red	1·00	35
1746	-	70pf. blue	1·00	35
1747	-	80pf. green	1·10	35
1748	-	100pf. brown	1·20	35
1748a	-	110pf. purple	2·40	1·00
1749	-	120pf. blue	1·60	50
1749a	-	130pf. red	2·75	1·00
1750	-	140pf. red	1·80	60
1751	-	150pf. red	4·00	1·20
1752	-	160pf. green	2·40	1·00
1753	-	180pf. brown	3·25	1·20
1753a	-	190pf. brown	3·75	1·00
1754	-	200pf. purple	2·75	50
1754a	-	230pf. green	5·00	1·50
1754b	-	250pf. green	5·50	2·30
1754c	-	300pf. green	6·00	2·30
1755	-	500pf. black	6·75	1·80

DESIGNS: 10pf. Electric train; 20pf. Modern lighthouse; 30pf. MBB-Bolkow Bo 105C rescue helicopter; 40pf. Space laboratory; 50pf. Dish aerial; 60pf. X-ray apparatus; 70pf. Ship-building; 80pf. Farm tractor; 100pf. Lignite excavator; 110pf. Colour television camera; 120pf. Chemical plant; 130pf. Brewery plant; 140pf. Power station; 150, 190pf. Mechanical shovel; 160pf. Blast furnace; 180pf. Wheel loader; 200pf. Marine drilling platform; 230, 250pf. Frankfurt Airport; 300pf. Electromagnetic monorail; 500pf. Radio telescope.

573 Town Hall and Market, Alsfeld

1975. European Architectural Heritage Year. German Buildings. Multicoloured.
1756	50pf. Type **573**	1·20	85
1757	50pf. Plonlein corner, Siebers tower and Kobelzeller gate, Rothenburg-on-Tauber	1·20	85
1758	50pf. Town Hall ("The Steipe") Trier	1·20	85
1759	50pf. View of Xanten	1·20	85

574 Effects of Drug-taking

1975. Campaign to Fight the Abuse of Drugs and Intoxicants.
| 1760 | **574** | 40pf. multicoloured | 60 | 50 |

575 Posthouse Sign, Royal Prussian Establishment for Transport 1776

1975. Stamp Day.
| 1761 | **575** | 10pf. multicoloured | 60 | 35 |

576 Edelweiss

1975. Humanitarian Relief Funds. Alpine Flowers. Multicoloured. (a) Inscr "Wohlfartsmarke 1975".
1762	30pf.+15pf. Type **576**	60	50
1763	40pf.+20pf. Trollflower	60	50
1764	50pf.+25pf. Alpine rose	1·00	75
1765	70pf.+35pf. Pasque-flower	2·20	2·10

(b) Inscr "Weihnachtsmarke 1975".
| 1766 | 40pf.+20pf. Christmas rose | 1·70 | 1·50 |

See also Nos. 1796/9, 1839/42, 1873/6 and 1905/8.

577 Gustav Stresemann (statesman)

1975. German Nobel Peace Prize Winners. Sheet 100×70 mm containing T **577** and similar vert designs in black.
MS1767 50pf. Type **577**; 50pf. Ludwig Quidde (Reichstag deputy); 50pf. Carl von Ossietzky (journalist) | 3·00 | 2·75

578 Stylized Ski-runners

1975. Winter Olympic Games, Innsbruck.
| 1768 | **578** | 50pf. multicoloured | 1·50 | 50 |

579 Konrad Adenauer

1976. Birth Centenary of Konrad Adenauer (Chancellor 1949–63).
| 1769 | **579** | 50pf. green | 3·00 | 50 |

580 Cover Pages from Hans Sachs' Books

1976. 400th Death Anniv of Hans Sachs (poet and composer).
| 1770 | **580** | 40pf. multicoloured | 1·00 | 50 |

581 Junkers F-13 Herta

1976. 50th Anniv of Lufthansa (German civil airline).
| 1771 | **581** | 50pf. multicoloured | 1·50 | 50 |

582 Emblem and Commemorative Inscription

1976. 25th Anniv of Federal Constitutional Court.
| 1772 | **582** | 50pf. multicoloured | 1·20 | 50 |

583 Letters "E G" representing Steel Girders

1976. 25th Anniv of European Coal and Steel Community.
| 1773 | **583** | 40pf. multicoloured | 1·20 | 50 |

584 Monorail Train

1976. 75th Anniv of Wuppertal Monorailway.
| 1774 | **584** | 50pf. multicoloured | 1·20 | 50 |

585 Basketball

1976. Youth Welfare. Training for the Olympics. Multicoloured.
1775	30pf.+15pf. Type **585**	75	50
1776	40pf.+20pf. Rowing	1·30	1·00
1777	50pf.+25pf. Gymnastics	1·70	1·50
1778	70pf.+35pf. Volleyball	2·30	2·10

586 Swimming

1976. Olympic Games, Montreal. Multicoloured.
| 1779 | 40pf.+25pf. Type **586** | 1·20 | 75 |
| 1780 | 50pf.+25pf. High jumping | 1·70 | 1·20 |

MS1781 110×70 mm. 30pf.+15pf. black,
orange-red and pale yellow; 70pf. +
35pf. black, new blue and pale blue   3·00   2·50
DESIGNS: 30pf. Hockey; 50pf. High jumping; 70pf. Rowing four.

587 Girl selling
Trinkets and
Copperplate
Prints

1976. Europa. Ludwigsburg China Figures. Multicoloured.
1782   40pf. Type **587**   80   35
1783   50pf. Boy selling copperplate
prints   85   35

588 Carl
Sonnenschein

1976. Birthday Centenary of Dr. Carl Sonnenschein
(clergyman).
1784   **588**   50pf. multicoloured   1·00   50

589 Opening bars of
Hymn *Entrust
Yourself to God*

1976. 300th Birth Anniv of Paul Gerhardt (composer).
1785   **589**   40pf. multicoloured   60   35

590 Carl Maria von Weber
conducting

1976. 150th Death Anniv of Carl Maria von Weber
(composer).
1786   **590**   50pf. black and brown   1·20   50

591 Carl Schurz

1976. Bicent of American Revolution.
1787   **591**   70pf. multicoloured   1·60   60

592 Wagnerian Stage

1976. Centenary of Bayreuth Festival.
1788   **592**   50pf. multicoloured   2·00   50

593 Bronze Ritual Chariot

1976. Archaeological Heritage. Multicoloured.
1789   30pf. Type **593**   60   50
1790   40pf. Gold-ornamental bowl   85   50
1791   50pf. Silver necklet   1·20   75
1792   120pf. Roman gold goblet   2·75   2·50

594 Golden
Plover

1976. Bird Protection.
1793   **594**   50pf. multicoloured   1·70   50

595 Mythical
Creature

1976. 300th Death Anniv of J. J. C. von Grimmelshausen
(writer).
1794   **595**   40pf. multicoloured   1·70   50

596
18th-century
Posthouse Sign,
Hochst-am-
Main

1976. Stamp Day.
1795   **596**   10pf. multicoloured   50   35

1976. Humanitarian Relief Funds. Garden Flowers.
Designs similar to T **576**. Multicoloured.
1796   30pf.+15pf. Phlox   75   60
1797   40pf.+20pf. Marigolds   1·00   85
1798   50pf.+25pf. Dahlias   1·10   1·00
1799   70pf.+35pf. Pansies   1·80   1·70

597 Sophie
Schroder
("Sappho")

1976. Famous German Actresses. Multicoloured.
1800   30pf. Carolin Neuber ("Medea")   85   35
1801   40pf. Type **597**   85   35
1802   50pf. Louise Dumont ("Hedda
Gabler")   1·00   55
1803   70pf. Hermine Korner ("Macbeth")   2·00   1·60

598 "Madonna
and Child"
("Marienfenster"
window,
Frauenkirche,
Esslingen)

1976. Christmas. Sheet 71×101 mm.
MS1804 **598** 50pf.+25pf. multicoloured   1·50   1·30

599 Eltz
Castle

1977. German Castles.
1805   -   10pf. blue   25   20
1805c   -   20pf. orange   25   20
1805d   -   25pf. red   60   35
1806   -   30pf. bistre   50   25
1806c   -   35pf. red   85   50
1807   **599**   40pf. green   75   20
1807a   -   40pf. brown   85   35
1808   -   50pf. red   85   30
1808b   -   50pf. green   1·10   35
1809   -   60pf. brown   1·20   30
1809a   -   60pf. red   1·10   50
1810   -   70pf. blue   1·20   35
1810a   -   80pf. green   1·60   35
1810c   -   90pf. blue   1·90   35
1810d   -   120pf. violet   2·40   85
1811   -   190pf. red   3·00   1·20
1812   -   200pf. green   3·75   1·20

1812a   -   210pf. brown   5·00   1·80
1812b   -   230pf. green   5·00   1·80
1812c   -   280pf. blue   5·00   85
1812d   -   300pf. orange   5·75   60
DESIGNS: 10pf. Glucksburg; 20, 190pf. Pfaueninsel, Berlin;
25pf. Gemen; 30pf. Ludwigstein, Werratal; 35pf. Lichtenstein; 40pf. (1807a) Wolfsburg; 50pf. (1808) Neuschwanstein; 50pf. (1808b) Inzlingen; 60pf. (1809) Marksburg;
60pf. (1809a) Rheydt; 70pf. Mespelbrunn; 80pf. Wilhelm-
sthal; 90pf. Vischering; 120pf. Charlottenburg, Berlin;
200pf. Burresheim; 210pf. Schwanenburg; 230pf. Lichtenberg; 280pf. Ahrensburg; 300pf. Herrenhausen, Hanover.

600 Palais de l'Europe

1977. Inauguration of Palais de l'Europe (Council of
Europe buildings), Strasbourg.
1813   **600**   140pf. green and black   2·75   85

601 Book
Illustrations

1977. "Till Eulenspiegel" (popular fable).
1814   **601**   50pf. multicoloured   85   50

602 Floral
Ornament

1977. German "Nouveau" Art. Sheet 116×86 mm
containing T **602** and similar vert designs.
Multicoloured.
MS1815 30pf. Type **602**; 70pf. Woman's
head; 90pf. Chair   4·00   2·75

603 Jean Monnet

1977. Award of "Citizen of Europe" honour to Jean
Monnet (French statesman).
1816   **603**   50pf. black, grey & yell   1·00   50

604 "Flower"

1977. 25th Anniv of Federal Horticultural Show.
1817   **604**   50pf. multicoloured   1·30   50

605 Plane of
Complex
Numbers

1977. Birth Bicentenary of Carl Friedrich Gauss
(mathematician).
1818   **605**   40pf. multicoloured   2·00   50

606 *Wappen von Hamburg*
(warship)

1977. Youth Welfare. Ships. Multicoloured.
1819   30pf.+15pf. Type **606**   85   75
1820   40pf.+20pf. *Preussen* (full-rigged
sailing ship)   1·10   1·00
1821   50pf.+25pf. *Bremen* (liner)   1·50   1·30
1822   70pf.+35pf. *Sturmfels* (container
ship)   2·10   2·00

607 Head of
Barbarossa

1977. Staufer Year, Baden-Wurttemberg.
1823   **607**   40pf. multicoloured   2·00   50

608 Rhon Autobahn

1977. Europa.
1824   **608**   40pf. black and green   90   35
1825   -   50pf. black and red   1·00   35
DESIGN: 50pf. Rhine landscape.

609
Self-Portrait
(Rubens)

1977. 400th Birth Anniv of Peter Paul Rubens.
1826   **609**   30pf. black   1·30   50

610 Ulm
Cathedral

1977. 600th Anniv of Ulm Cathedral.
1827   **610**   40pf. brown, green & bl   85   50

611 Rector's Seal,
Mainz University
(500th Anniv)

1977. University Anniversaries.
1828   **611**   50pf. black and red   1·20   50
1829   -   50pf. black and red   1·20   50
1830   -   50pf. black and red   1·50   50
DESIGNS: No. 1829, Great Seal, Marburg University (450th
anniv); No. 1830, Great Seal, Tubingen University (500th
anniv).

612 *Morning*

1977. Birth Bicentenary of Phillipp Otto Runge (artist).
1831   **612**   60pf. multicoloured   1·50   60

613 Ketteler's
Coat of Arms

1977. Death Centenary of Bishop Wilhelm Emmanuel von
Ketteler.
1832 **613** 50pf. multicoloured 1·00 50

614 Fritz von
Bodelschwingh

1977. Birth Centenary of Pastor Fritz von Bodelschwingh
(pioneer of welfare work for the disabled).
1833 **614** 50pf. multicoloured 1·20 50

615 Golden Hat

1977. Archaeological Heritage. Multicoloured.
1834 30pf. Type **615** 60 50
1835 120pf. Gilt helmet 2·40 1·80
1836 200pf. Bronze centaur head 3·25 2·75

616 Operator and
Switchboard

1977. Centenary of Telephone in Germany.
1837 **616** 50pf. multicoloured 1·70 50

617
19th-century
Posthouse Sign,
Hamburg

1977. Stamp Day.
1838 **617** 10pf. multicoloured 60 35

1977. Humanitarian Relief Funds. Meadow Flowers. As T
576. Multicoloured.
1839 30pf.+15pf. Caraway 65 50
1840 40pf.+20pf. Dandelion 80 60
1841 50pf.+25pf. Red clover 1·00 75
1842 70pf.+35pf. Meadow sage 2·00 1·80

618 Travelling
Surgeon

1977. 250th Death Anniv of Dr. Johann Andreas
Eisenbarth.
1843 **618** 50pf. multicoloured 1·20 50

619 Wilhelm
Hauff

1977. 150th Death Anniv of Wilhelm Hauff (poet and
novelist).
1844 **619** 40pf. multicoloured 60 35

620 "King
presenting Gift"
(stained glass
window,
Basilica of St.
Gereon,
Cologne)

1977. Christmas. Sheet 70×105 mm.
MS1845 **620** 50pf.+25pf. multicoloured 1·50 1·30

621 Book
Cover Designs

1978. Birth Centenary of Rudolph Alexander Schroder
(writer).
1846 **621** 50pf. multicoloured 1·00 50

622 Refugees

1978. 20th Anniv of Friedland Aid Society.
1847 **622** 50pf. multicoloured 1·00 50

623 Skiing

1978. Sport Promotion Fund. Multicoloured.
1848 50pf.+25pf. Type **623** 2·20 1·80
1849 70pf.+35pf. Show jumping 4·75 4·25

624 Gerhart
Hauptmann

1978. German Winners of Nobel Prize for Literature.
Multicoloured.
1850 30pf. Type **624** 75 35
1851 50pf. Hermann Hesse 1·00 50
1852 70pf. Thomas Mann 1·20 85
MS1853 120×70 mm. Nos. 1850/2 3·25 2·20

625 Martin Buber

1978. Birth Centenary of Martin Buber (religious
philosopher).
1854 **625** 50pf. multicoloured 1·10 50

626 Museum
Tower and
Cupola

1978. 75th Anniv of German Scientific and Technical
Museum, Munich.
1855 **626** 50pf. black, yellow & red 1·10 50

627 Wilhelmine Reichart's
Balloon, Munich October
Festival, 1820

1978. Youth Welfare. Aviation History (1st series).
Multicoloured.
1856 30pf.+15pf. Type **627** 90 75
1857 40pf.+20pf. Airship LZ-1, 1900 1·10 1·00
1858 50pf.+25pf. Bleriot XI monoplane, 1909 1·50 1·30
1859 70pf.+35pf. Hans Grade's monoplane, 1909 2·00 1·80
See also Nos. 1886/9 and 1918/21.

628 Old Town Hall,
Bamberg

1978. Europa. Multicoloured.
1860 40pf. Type **628** 85 35
1861 50pf. Old Town Hall, Regensburg 1·20 35
1862 70pf. Old Town Hall, Esslingen
am Neckar 1·60 90

629 Piper and Children

1978. Pied Piper of Hamelin.
1863 **629** 50pf. multicoloured 1·20 50

630 Janusz
Korczak

1978. Birth Centenary of Janusz Korczak (educational
reformer).
1864 **630** 90pf. multicoloured 1·70 85

631 Fossil Bat

1978. Archaeological Heritage, Fossils. Multicoloured.
1865 80pf. Type **631** 2·50 2·20
1866 200pf. Horse ("eohippus")
skeleton 2·75 2·40

632 Parliament Building,
Bonn

1978. 65th Interparliamentary Union Conference, Bonn.
1867 **632** 70pf. multicoloured 1·70 60

633 Rose
Window,
Freiburg Minster

1978. 85th Conference of German Catholics, Freiburg.
1868 **633** 40pf. multicoloured 75 50

634 Silhouette

1978. Birth Bicent of Clemens Brentano (poet).
1869 **634** 30pf. multicoloured 75 50

635 Text

1978. 25th Anniv of European Convention for the
Protection of Human Rights.
1870 **635** 50pf. multicoloured 1·20 50

636 Baden
Post-house Sign

1978. Stamp Day and World Philatelic Movement.
Multicoloured.
1871 40pf. Type **636** 75 35
1872 50pf. 1850 3pf. stamp of
Saxony 75 35

1978. Humanitarian Relief Funds. Woodland Flowers. As T
576. Multicoloured.
1873 30pf.+15pf. Arum 60 50
1874 40pf.+20pf. Weasel-snout 85 75
1875 50pf.+25pf. Turk's-cap lily 1·20 1·10
1876 70pf.+35pf. Liverwort 1·60 1·50

1978. Impressionist Paintings. Multicoloured. •
1877 50pf. Type **637** 1·10 75
1878 70pf. *Horseman on the Shore
turning Left* (Max Liebermann) (vert) 1·60 1·00
1879 120pf. *Lady with a Cat* (Max
Slevogt) (vert) 2·40 2·20

638 "Christ Child"
(stained glass
window,
Frauenkirche,
Munich)

1978. Christmas. Sheet 65×93 mm.
MS1880 **638** 50pf.+25pf. multicoloured 1·20 1·20

639 Child

1979. International Year of the Child.
1881 **639** 60pf. multicoloured 1·50 50

640 Agnes
Miegel

1979. Birth Cent of Agnes Miegel (poet).
1882 **640** 60pf. multicoloured 1·10 ´50

641 Seating Plan

1979. First Direct Elections to European Parliament.
1883 **641** 50pf. multicoloured 1·50 50

642 Film

1979. 25th West German Short Film Festival.
1884 **642** 50pf. black and turquoise   1·20   50

643 Rescue Services
Emblems

1979. Rescue Services on the Road.
1885 **643** 50pf. multicoloured   1·20   50

1979. Youth Welfare. History of Aviation (2nd series). As T
627. Multicoloured.
1886 40pf.+20pf. Dornier Do-J Wal
flying boat, 1922   85   85
1887 50pf.+25pf. Heinkel He 70
Blitz, 1932   1·20   1·20
1888 60pf.+30pf. Junkers W.33
Bremen, 1928   1·50   1·50
1889 90pf.+45pf. Focke Achgelis Fa
61 helicopter, 1936   2·00   2·00

644 Handball

1979. Sport Promotion Fund. Multicoloured.
1890 60pf.+30pf. Type **644**   1·50   1·30
1891 90pf.+45pf. Canoeing   2·20   2·00

645 Telegraph
Office, 1863

1979. Europa. Multicoloured.
1892 50pf. Type **645**   1·00   35
1893 60pf. Post Office counter, 1854   1·20   35

646 Anne Frank

1979. 50th Birth Anniv of Anne Frank (concentration
camp victim and diary writer).
1894 **646** 60pf. black, grey and red   1·30   50

647 Werner von Siemens's
Electric Railway, 1879

1979. International Transport Exhibition. Hamburg.
1895 **647** 60pf. multicoloured   1·50   50

648 Hand operating Radio
Dial

1979. World Administrative Radio Conference, Geneva.
1896 **648** 60f. multicoloured   1·30   50

649 "Moses
receiving the
Tablets of the
Law" (woodcut,
Cranach the
Elder)

1979. 450th Anniv of Publication of Martin Luther's
Catechisms.
1897 **649** 50pf. black and green   1·50   50

650 Cross and
Orb

1979. Pilgrimage to Aachen.
1898 **650** 50pf. multicoloured   1·00   50

651 Hildegard von
Bingen

1979. 800th Death Anniv of Hildegard von Bingen (writer
and mystic).
1899 **651** 110pf. multicoloured   1·70   85

652 Photo-electric Effect

1979. Birth Centenaries of Nobel Prize Winners.
Multicoloured.
1900 60pf. Type **652** (Albert Einstein,
Physics, 1921)   1·20   60
1901 60pf. Splitting of uranium
nucleus (Otto Hahn, Chem-
istry, 1944)   2·40   60
1902 60pf. Diffraction pattern of
X-rays passed through crystal
(Max von Laue, Physics,
1914)   1·20   60

653 Pilot and
Helmsman

1979. 300th Anniv of First Pilotage Regulations.
1903 **653** 60pf. brown and claret   1·00   50

654 Posthouse Sign,
Altheim, Saar (German
side), 1754

1979. Stamp Day.
1904 **654** 60pf.+30pf. multicoloured   1·70   1·60

1979. Humanitarian Relief Funds. Woodland Flowers and
Fruit. As T **576**. Multicoloured.
1905 40pf.+20pf. Red beech (horiz)   75   75
1906 50pf.+25pf. English oak (horiz) 1·00   1·00
1907 60pf.+30pf. Hawthorn (horiz)   1·10   1·10
1908 90pf.+45pf. Mountain pine
(horiz)   1·80   1·70

656 Bird Garden

1979. Birth Cent of Paul Klee (artist).
1909 **656** 90pf. multicoloured   1·60   85

657 Faust and
Mephistopheles

1979. Doctor Johannes Faust.
1910 **657** 60pf. multicoloured   1·80   50

658 Lightbulb

1979. "Save Energy".
1911 **658** 40pf. multicoloured   1·00   50

659 "Nativity"
(Altenberg medieval
manuscript)

1979. Christmas.
1912 **659** 60pf.+30pf. mult   1·50   1·50

660 Iphigenia

1980. Death Centenary of Anselm Feuerbach (artist).
1913 **660** 50pf. multicoloured   1·70   50

661 Flags of NATO Members

1980. 25th Anniv of NATO Membership.
1914 **661** 100pf. multicoloured   2·75   1·20

662 Town Hall, St. Mary's
Church, and St Peter's
Cathedral

1980. 1200th Anniv of Osnabruck Town and Bishopric.
1915 **662** 60pf. multicoloured   1·20   50

663 "Gotz von
Berlichingen"
(glass picture)

1980. 500th Birth Anniv of Gotz von Berlichingen
(Frankish knight).
1916 **663** 60pf. multicoloured   1·20   50

664 Texts from 1880 and
1980 Duden Dictionaries

1980. Centenary of Konrad Duden's First Dictionary.
1917 **664** 60pf. multicoloured   1·20   50

1980. Youth Welfare. Aviation History (3rd series). As T
627. Multicoloured.
1918 40pf.+20pf. Phoenix FS 24
glider, 1957   60   60
1919 50pf.+25pf. Lockheed L.1049G
Super Constellation   1·00   1·00
1920 60pf.+30pf. Airbus Industrie
A300B2, 1972   1·30   1·30
1921 90pf.+45pf. Boeing 747-100,
1969   2·00   2·00
No. 1919 is incorrectly dated "1950".

665 Emblems of Association
Members

1980. Centenary of German Association of Welfare
Societies.
1922 **665** 60pf. blue, red and black   1·20   50

666 "Frederick I
with his sons"
(Welf Chronicle)

1980. 800th Anniv of Imperial Diet of Gelnhausen.
1923 **666** 60pf. multicoloured   1·60   50

667 Football

1980. Sport Promotion Fund. Multicoloured.
1924 50pf.+25pf. Type **667**   85   75
1925 60pf.+30pf. Dressage   1·20   1·00
1926 90pf.+45pf. Skiing   2·20   2·20

668 Albertus
Magnus (scholar)

1980. Europa. Multicoloured.
1927 50pf. Type **668**   1·20   35
1928 60pf. Gottfried Leibniz (philosopher)   1·20   35

669 Reading the
Augsburg
Confession
(engraving, G
Kohler)

1980. 450th Anniv of Augsburg Confession.
1929 **669** 50pf. black, yellow & grn   1·10   50

670 Nature Reserve

1980. Nature Conservation.
1930 **670** 40pf. multicoloured   1·60   50

671 Ear and Oscillogram
Pulses

1980. International Congress for the Training and
Education of the Hard of Hearing, Hamburg.
1931 **671** 90pf. multicoloured   1·80   60

672 First Book of Daily Bible
Readings, 1731

1980. 250th Anniv of Moravian Brethren's Book of Daily
Bible Readings.
1932 **672** 50pf. multicoloured   1·10   50

673 St. Benedict

1980. 1500th Birth Anniv of St. Benedict of Nursia
(founder of Benedictine Order).
1933 **673** 50pf. multicoloured   1·00   50

674 Helping Hand

1980. Birth Bicentenary of Friedrich Joseph Haass
(philanthropist).
1934 **674** 60pf. multicoloured   1·20   50

675 Marie von Ebner-Eschenbach

1980. 150th Birth Anniv of Marie von Ebner-Eschenbach (novelist).
1935 **675** 60pf. buff, black & orge 1·20 50

676 Rigging

1980. Birth Centenary of Johan Kinau (*Gorch Fock*) (poet).
1936 **676** 60pf. multicoloured 2·40 50

677 Positioning Keystone of South Tower Finial (engraving)

1980. Centenary of Completion of Cologne Cathedral.
1937 **677** 60pf. multicoloured 2·40 50

678 "Ceratocephalus falcatus"

1980. Humanitarian Relief Funds. Endangered Wildflowers. Multicoloured.
1938 **678** 40pf.+20pf. Type **678** 85 75
1939 50pf.+25pf. Yellow Vetchling 1·10 1·00
1940 60pf.+30pf. Corn Cockle 1·20 1·20
1941 90pf.+45pf. Tassel Hyacinth 2·00 2·00
See also Nos. 1972/5.

679 Wine-making (woodcuts)

1980. Bimillenary of Vine Growing in Central Europe.
1942 **679** 50pf. multicoloured 1·20 50

680 Posthouse Sign, Altheim, Saar, 1754 (French side)

1980. 49th International Philatelic Federation Congress, Essen.
1943 **680** 60pf.+30pf. mult 1·20 1·10

681 "Nativity" (Altomunster manuscript)

1980. Christmas.
1944 **681** 60pf.+30pf. mult 1·60 1·50

682 *Landscape with Two Fir Trees* (etching)

1980. 500th Birth Anniv of Albrecht Altdorfer (painter, engraver and architect).
1945 **682** 40pf. lt brown, blk & brn 1·00 50

683 Elly Heuss-Knapp

1981. Birth Centenary of Elly Heuss-Knapp (social reformer).
1946 **683** 60pf. multicoloured 1·20 50

684 Society accepting the Handicapped

1981. International Year of Disabled Persons.
1947 **684** 60pf. multicoloured 1·20 50

685 Old Town Houses

1981. European Campaign for Urban Renaissance.
1948 **685** 60pf. multicoloured 1·20 50

686 Telemann and Title Page of *Singet dem Herrn*

1981. 300th Birth Anniv of Georg Philipp Telemann (composer).
1949 **686** 60pf. multicoloured 1·20 50

687 Visiting a Foreign Family

1981. Integration of Guest Worker Families.
1950 **687** 50pf. multicoloured 1·30 50

688 Polluted Butterfly, Fish and Plant

1981. Preservation of the Environment.
1951 **688** 60pf. multicoloured 2·00 50

689 Patent Office Emblem and Scientific Signs

1981. Establishment of European Patent Office, Munich.
1952 **689** 60pf. grey, red and black 1·20 50

690 Scintigram showing Distribution of Radioactive Isotope

1981. Cancer Prevention through Medical Check-ups.
1953 **690** 40pf. multicoloured 1·00 50

691 Borda Circle, 1800

1981. Youth Welfare. Optical Instruments. Multicoloured.
1954 40pf.+20pf. Type **691** 85 60
1955 50pf.+25pf. Reflecting telescope, 1770 1·50 1·20
1956 60pf.+30pf. Binocular microscope, 1860 1·50 1·20
1957 90pf.+45pf. Octant, 1775 2·10 2·00

692 Rowing

1981. Sport Promotion Fund. Multicoloured.
1958 60pf.+30pf. Type **692** 1·50 1·20
1959 90pf.+45pf. Gliding 2·20 2·00

693 South German Dancers

1981. Europa. Multicoloured.
1960 50pf. Type **693** 1·10 35
1961 60pf. North German dancers 1·20 35

694 Convention Cross

1981. 19th German Protestant Convention, Hamburg.
1962 **694** 50pf. multicoloured 1·20 50

695 Group from Crucifixion Altar

1981. 450th Death Anniv of Tilman Riemenschneider (woodcarver).
1963 **695** 60pf. multicoloured 1·20 50

696 Georg von Neumayer Antarctic Research Station

1981. Polar Research.
1964 **696** 110pf. multicoloured 2·75 75

697 Solar Generator

1981. Energy Research.
1965 **697** 50pf. multicoloured 1·60 50

698 Hand holding Baby Black Coot

1981. Animal Protection.
1966 **698** 60pf. multicoloured 2·00 50

699 Arms of different Races forming Square

1981. Co-operation with Developing Countries.
1967 **699** 90pf. multicoloured 2·00 75

700 Wilhelm Raabe

1981. 150th Birth Anniv of Wilhelm Raabe (poet).
1968 **700** 50pf. light green & green 1·20 50

701 Constitutional Freedom

1981. Fundamental Concepts of Democracy. Article 20 of the Basic Law. Multicoloured.
1969 40pf. Type **701** 1·30 35
1970 50pf. Separation of Powers 1·30 35
1971 60pf. Sovereignty of the People 2·00 35

1981. Humanitarian Relief Funds. Endangered Wildflowers. As T **678**. Multicoloured.
1972 40pf.+20pf. Water nut 75 60
1973 50pf.+25pf. Floating Heart 1·00 85
1974 60pf.+30pf. Water gilly-flower 1·20 1·20
1975 90pf.+45pf. Water lobelia 2·20 2·10

702 Posthouse Scene c. 1855

1981. Stamp Day.
1976 **702** 60pf. multicoloured 2·00 50

703 "Nativity" (glass painting)

1981. Christmas.
1977 **703** 60pf.+30pf. multicoloured 1·60 1·20

704 St. Elisabeth

1981. 750th Death Anniv of St. Elisabeth of Thuringia.
1978 **704** 50pf. multicoloured 1·60 50

705 Clausewitz (after W. Wach)

1981. 150th Death Anniv of General Carl von Clausewitz (military writer).
1979 **705** 60pf. multicoloured 1·60 50

706 People forming Figure "100"

1981. Cent of Social Insurance.
1980 **706** 60pf. multicoloured 1·30 50

707 Map of Antarctica

1981. 20th Anniv of Antarctic Treaty.
1981 **707** 100pf. blue, lt blue & blk 2·20 75

708 Pot with Lid

1982. 300th Birth Anniv of Johann Friedrich Bottger (founder of Meissen China Works).
1982   **708**   60pf. multicoloured   1·30   50

709 Insulated Wall

1982. Energy Conservation.
1983   **709**   60pf. multicoloured   1·30   50

710 Silhouette (Dora Brandenburg-Polster)

1982. *The Town Band of Bremen* (German fairy tale).
1984   **710**   40pf. black and red   1·00   50

711 Goethe (after Georg Melchior Kraus)

1982. 150th Death Anniv of Johann Wolfgang von Goethe (writer).
1985   **711**   60pf. multicoloured   3·75   50

712 Robert Koch

1982. Centenary of Discovery of Tubercle Bacillus.
1986   **712**   50pf. multicoloured   4·25   50

713 Benz Patent "Motorwagen", 1886

1982. Youth Welfare. Motor Cars. Multicoloured.
1987   40pf.+20pf. Type **713**   85   75
1988   50pf.+25pf. Mercedes "Touren-wagen", 1913   1·10   1·00
1989   60pf.+30pf. Hannomag "Kom-missbrot", 1925   1·50   1·20
1990   90pf.+45pf. Opel "Olympia", 1937   2·40   2·30

714 Jogging

1982. Sport Promotion Fund. Multicoloured.
1991   60pf.+30pf. Type **714**   1·50   1·30
1992   90pf.+45pf. Disabled archers   2·20   2·10

715 "Good Helene"

1982. 150th Birth Anniv of Wilhelm Busch (writer and illustrator).
1993   **715**   50pf. black, green & yell   1·60   50

716 "Procession to Hambach Castle, 1832" (wood engraving)

1982. Europa.
1994   **716**   50pf. black, yellow & red   1·60   35
1995   -   60pf. multicoloured   2·10   35
DESIGN: 60pf. Excerpt from Treaty of Rome (instituting European Economic Community), 1957, and flags.

717 Racing Yachts

1982. Centenary of Kiel Regatta Week.
1996   **717**   60pf. multicoloured   1·60   50

718 Young Couple

1982. Centenary of Young Men's Christian Association in Germany.
1997   **718**   50pf. multicoloured   1·20   50

719 Polluted Sea

1982. "Prevent the Pollution of the Sea".
1998   **719**   120pf. multicoloured   4·25   60

720 Battered Licence Plate

1982. "Don't Drink and Drive".
1999   **720**   80pf. multicoloured   1·60   50

721 Doctor examining Leper

1982. 25th Anniv of German Lepers' Welfare Organization.
2000   **721**   80pf. multicoloured   1·60   50

722 Franck and Born

1982. Birth Centenaries of James Franck and Max Born (physicists and Nobel Prize Winners).
2001   **722**   80pf. grey, black and red   2·00   50

723 Atomic Model of Urea

1982. Death Centenary of Friedrich Wohler (chemist).
2002   **723**   50pf. multicoloured   1·50   50

724 "St. Francis preaching to the Birds" (fresco by Giotto)

1982. 87th German Catholics' Congress, Dusseldorf and 800th Birth Anniv of St. Francis of Assisi.
2003   **724**   60pf. multicoloured   1·50   50

725 Hybrid Tea Rose

1982. Humanitarian Relief Funds. Roses. Multicoloured.
2004   50pf.+20pf. Type **725**   85   75
2005   60pf.+30pf. Floribunda   1·10   1·00
2006   80pf.+40pf. Bourbon   1·70   1·60
2007   120pf.+60pf. Polyantha hybrid   2·40   2·20

726 Letters on Desk

1982. Stamp Day.
2008   **726**   80pf. multicoloured   2·20   50

727 Gregorian Calendar by Johannes Rasch, 1586

1982. 400th Anniv of Gregorian Calendar.
2009   **727**   60pf. multicoloured   1·50   50

728 Theodor Heuss

1982. Presidents of the Federal Republic. Sheet 130×100 mm containing T **728** and similar horiz designs. Multicoloured.
MS2010   80pf. Type **728**; 80pf. Heinrich Lubke; 80pf. Gustav Heinemann; 80pf. Walter Scheel; 80pf. Karl Carstens   7·25   6·75

729 "Nativity" (detail from St. Peter Altar by Master Bertram)

1982. Christmas.
2011   **729**   80pf.+40pf. mult   2·40   1·70

730 Edith Stein

1983. 40th Death Anniv (1982) of Edith Stein (philosopher).
2012   **730**   80pf. lt grey, grey & blk   2·40   75

731 White Rose and Barbed Wire

1983. Persecution and Resistance 1933–45.
2013   **731**   80pf. multicoloured   2·40   75

732 *Light Space Modulator* (Laszlo Moholy-Nagy)

1983. Birth Cent of Walter Gropius (founder of Bauhaus School of Art, Weimar). Bauhaus Art. Multicoloured.
2014   **732**   50pf. Type **732**   1·20   50
2015   60pf. *Sanctuary* (lithograph by Josef Albers)   1·70   50

2016   80pf. Skylights from Bauhaus Archives, Berlin (Walter Gropius)   2·00   55

733 Federahannes (Rottweil carnival figure)

1983. Carnival.
2017   **733**   60pf. multicoloured   1·60   50

734 Daimler-Maybach, 1885

1983. Youth Welfare. Motor Cycles. Multicoloured.
2018   50pf.+20pf. Type **734**   85   75
2019   60pf.+30pf. N.S.U., 1901   1·10   1·00
2020   80pf.+40pf. Megola "Sport", 1922   2·00   1·80
2021   120pf.+60pf. B.M.W. world record holder, 1936   3·00   2·75

735 Gymnastics (German Festival, Frankfurt am Main)

1983. Sports Promotion Fund. Multicoloured.
2022   80pf.+40pf. Type **735**   1·80   1·60
2023   120pf.+60pf. Modern pentath-lon (world championships, Warendorf)   3·00   2·75

736 Stylized Flower

1983. Fourth International Horticultural Show. Munich.
2024   **736**   60pf. multicoloured   1·60   50

737 Modern Type and Gutenberg Letters

1983. Europa. Multicoloured.
2025   60pf. Type **737**   3·00   60
2026   80pf. Resonant circuit and electric flux lines   1·80   60

738 Johannes Brahms

1983. 150th Birth Anniv of Johannes Brahms (composer).
2027   **738**   80pf. multicoloured   2·40   75

739 Kafka's Signature and Teyn Church, Prague

1983. Birth Cent of Franz Kafka (writer).
2028   **739**   80pf. multicoloured   2·40   75

740 Brewing (frontispiece of 1677 treatise)

1983. 450th Anniv of Beer Purity Law.
2029   **740**   80pf. multicoloured   2·40   75

741 Concord

1983. 300th Anniv of First German Settlers in America.
2030 **741** 80pf. multicoloured   2·75   75

742 Children crossing Road

1983. Children and Road Traffic.
2031 **742** 80pf. multicoloured   2·40   75

743 Flags forming Car

1983. 50th International Motor Show, Frankfurt-on-Main.
2032 **743** 60pf. multicoloured   1·20   50

744 Warburg (after Oberland)

1983. Birth Centenary of Otto Warburg. (physiologist and chemist).
2033 **744** 50pf. multicoloured   1·50   75

745 Wieland (after G. B. Bosio)

1983. 250th Birth Anniv of Cristoph Martin Wieland (writer).
2034 **745** 80pf. multicoloured   2·00   75

746 Rosette in National Colours

1983. Tenth Anniv of U.N. Membership.
2035 **746** 80pf. multicoloured   2·75   75

747 "Das Rauhe Haus" and Children

1983. 150th Anniv of "Das Rauhe Haus" (children's home, Hamburg).
2036 **747** 80pf. multicoloured   2·10   75

748 Surveying Maps

1983. International Geodesy and Geophysics Union General Assembly, Hamburg.
2037 **748** 120pf. multicoloured   2·75   85

749 Swiss Androsace

1983. Humanitarian Relief Funds. Endangered Alpine Flowers. Multicoloured.
2038   50pf.+20pf. Type **749**   85   75
2039   60pf.+30pf. Krain groundsel   1·10   1·00

2040   80pf.+40pf. Fleischer's willow herb   2·00   1·80
2041   120pf.+60pf. Alpine sow-thistle   3·00   2·75

750 Horseman with Posthorn

1983. Stamp Day.
2042 **750** 80pf. multicoloured   2·20   75

751 Luther (engraving by G. Konig after Cranach)

1983. 500th Birth Anniv of Martin Luther (Protestant reformer).
2043 **751** 80pf. multicoloured   3·75   75

752 Interwoven National Colours

1983. Federation, Lander and Communities Co-operation.
2044 **752** 80pf. multicoloured   2·75   75

753 Customs Stamps

1983. 150th Anniv of German Customs Union.
2045 **753** 60pf. multicoloured   2·75   50

754 Epiphany Carol Singers

1983. Christmas.
2046 **754** 80pf.+40pf. mult   2·75   2·00

755 Black Gate, Trier

1984. 2000th Anniv of Trier.
2047 **755** 80pf. multicoloured   2·75   75

756 Reis and Telephone Apparatus

1984. 150th Birth Anniv of Philipp Reis (telephone pioneer).
2048 **756** 80pf. multicoloured   2·75   75

757 Mendel and Genetic Diagram

1984. Death Cent of Gregor Mendel (geneticist).
2049 **757** 50pf. multicoloured   1·60   50

758 Town Hall

1984. 500th Anniv of Michelstadt Town Hall.
2050 **758** 60pf. multicoloured   1·60   50

759 Cloth draped on Cross

1984. 350th Anniv of Oberammergau Passion Play.
2051 **759** 60pf. multicoloured   1·60   50

760 Bee-eating Beetle

1984. Youth Welfare. Pollinating Insects. Multicoloured.
2052   50pf.+20pf. Type **760**   1·00   85
2053   60pf.+30pf. Red admiral   1·70   1·60
2054   80pf.+40pf. Honey bee   2·20   2·10
2055   120pf.+60pf. Chrysotoxum festivium (hover fly)   3·00   3·00

761 Throwing the Discus

1984. Sport Promotion Fund. Multicoloured.
2056   60pf.+30pf. Type **761**   1·70   1·20
2057   80pf.+40pf. Rhythmic gymnastics   2·20   2·00
2058   120pf.+60pf. Windsurfing   4·00   3·75

762 Parliament Emblem

1984. Second Direct Elections to European Parliament.
2059 **762** 80pf. yellow, blue and light blue   3·00   85

763 Bridge

1984. Europa. 25th Anniv of European Post and Telecommunications Conference.
2060 **763** 60pf. blue, lt blue & blk   2·00   60
2061 **763** 80pf. purple, red & black   2·00   60

764 St. Norbert (sculpture)

1984. 850th Death Anniv of St. Norbert von Xanten.
2062 **764** 80pf. green & deep green   2·00   75

765 Nursery Rhyme Illustration

1984. Death Centenary of Ludwig Richter (illustrator).
2063 **765** 60pf. black and brown   1·20   50

766 Cross and Shadow

1984. 50th Anniv of Protestant Churches' Barmen Theological Declaration.
2064 **766** 80pf. multicoloured   2·00   75

767 Letter sorting, 1800s

1984. 19th Universal Postal Union Congress, Hamburg. Sheet 138×104 mm containing T **767** and similar square designs.
MS2065 60pf. brown and black; 80pf. multicoloured; 120pf. green, black and grey   5·00   4·25
DESIGNS: 80pf. Modern automatic letter sorting machine scanning device; 120pf. Heinrich von Stephan (founder of U.P.U.).

768 Groom leading Horse (detail from tomb of Oclatius)

1984. 2000th Anniv of Neuss.
2066 **768** 80pf. multicoloured   2·00   75

769 Bessel

1984. Birth Bicentenary of Friedrich Wilhelm Bessel (astronomer and mathematician).
2067 **769** 80pf. grey, black and red   2·00   75

770 Eugenio Pacelli (Pope Pius XII)

1984. 88th German Catholics' Congress, Munich.
2068 **770** 60pf. multicoloured   1·60   50

771 Town Hall

1984. 750th Anniv of Duderstadt Town Hall.
2069 **771** 60pf. multicoloured   1·50   50

772 Medieval Document and Visual Display Unit

1984. Tenth International Archives Congress, Bonn.
2070 **772** 70pf. multicoloured   2·00   75

773 Knoop Lock

1984. Bicent of Schleswig-Holstein Canal.
2071 **773** 80pf. multicoloured   2·40   75

774 Research Centre and Storage Rings

1984. 25th Anniv of German Electron Synchrotron (physics research centre), Hamburg–Bahrenfeld.
2072 **774** 80pf. multicoloured   2·75   75

775 *Aceras anthropophorum*

1984. Humanitarian Relief Funds. Orchids. Multicoloured.
2073		50pf.+20pf. Type **775**	1·20	1·10
2074		60pf.+30pf. *Orchis ustulata*	1·20	1·10
2075		80pf.+40pf. *Limodorum abortivum*	1·80	1·70
2076		120pf.+60pf. *Dactylorhiza sambucina*	3·25	3·25

776 Taxis Posthouse, Augsburg

1984. Stamp Day.
2077	**776**	80pf. multicoloured	2·75	75

777 Burning Match

1984. Anti-smoking Campaign.
2078	**777**	60pf. multicoloured	1·70	50

778 Male and Female Symbols

1984. Equal Rights for Men and Women.
2079	**778**	80pf. black, mauve & bl	2·40	75

779 Ballot Slip

1984. For Peace and Understanding.
2080	**779**	80pf. grey, black & blue	2·00	75

780 St. Martin giving Cloak to Beggar

1984. Christmas.
2081	**780**	80pf.+40pf. mult	2·20	2·00

781 Emperor Augustus (bust), Buildings and Arms

1985. 2000th Anniv of Augsburg.
2082	**781**	80pf. multicoloured	2·40	60

782 Spener (engraving by Bartholome Kilian after Johann Georg Wagner)

1985. 350th Birth Anniv of Philipp Jakob Spener (church reformer).
2083	**782**	80pf. black and green	2·00	75

783 Grimm Brothers (engraving by Lazarus Sichling)

1985. Birth Bicentenaries of Grimm Brothers (folklorists) and Seventh International Union for German Linguistics and Literature Congress, Gottingen.
2084	**783**	80pf. black, grey and red	2·75	75

784 Romano Guardini

1985. Birth Centenary of Romano Guardini (theologian).
2085	**784**	80pf. multicoloured	2·00	75

785 Verden

1985. Millenary of Market and Coinage Rights in Verden.
2086	**785**	60pf. multicoloured	2·75	50

786 Flags and German–Danish Border

1985. 30th Anniv of Bonn–Copenhagen Declarations.
2087	**786**	80pf. multicoloured	3·00	1·00

787 Bowling

1985. Sport Promotion Fund. Multicoloured.
2088		80pf.+40pf. Type **787** (cent. of German Nine-pin Bowling Association)	2·00	1·70
2089		120pf.+60pf. Kayak (world rapid-river and slalom canoe-ing championships)	3·25	3·00

788 Kisch

1985. Birth Centenary of Egon Erwin Kisch (journalist).
2090	**788**	60pf. multicoloured	1·60	50

789 Hebel and the Margravine

1985. 225th Birth Anniv of Johann Peter Hebel (poet).
2091	**789**	80pf. multicoloured	2·00	75

790 Draisienne Bicycle, 1817

1985. Youth Welfare International Youth Year. Cycles. Multicoloured.
2092		50pf.+20pf. Type **790**	1·20	1·20
2093		60pf.+30pf. NSU Germania "ordinary", 1866	1·50	1·50
2094		80pf.+40pf. Cross-frame low bicycle, 1887	1·80	1·80
2095		120pf.+60pf. Adler tricycle, 1888	3·50	3·50

791 Handel

1985. Europa. Composers' 300th Birth Anniversaries. Multicoloured.
2096		60pf. Type **791**	2·75	60
2097		80pf. Bach	2·75	60

792 Saint George's Cathedral

1985. 750th Anniv of Limburg Cathedral.
2098	**792**	60pf. multicoloured	1·50	75

793 Capital (presbytery, "Wies" Church)

1985. 300th Birth Anniv of Dominikus Zimmermann (architect).
2099	**793**	70pf. multicoloured	1·80	75

794 Josef Kentenich

1985. Birth Centenary of Father Josef Kentenich (founder of International Schonstatt (Catholic laymen's) Movement).
2100	**794**	80pf. multicoloured	2·00	75

795 Clock and Forest

1985. Save the Forests.
2101	**795**	80pf. multicoloured	2·75	75

796 Tug of War and Scouting Emblem

1985. 30th World Scouts Conference, Munich.
2102	**796**	60pf. multicoloured	1·70	75

797 *Sunday Walk*

1985. Death Cent of Carl Spitzweg (artist).
2103	**797**	60pf. multicoloured	2·75	75

798 Horses and Postilion

1985. "Mophila 1985" Stamp Exhibition, Hamburg. Multicoloured.
2104		60pf.+20pf. Type **798**	3·25	3·00
2105		80pf.+20pf. Mail coach	3·25	3·00

Nos. 2104/5 were printed *se-tenant*, forming a composite design.

799 Stock Exchange

1985. 400th Anniv of Frankfurt Stock Exchange.
2106	**799**	80pf. black, red and grey	2·40	75

800 Flowers and Butterfly

1985. Humanitarian Relief Funds. Designs depict motifs from borders of medieval prayer book. Multicoloured.
2107		50pf.+20pf. Type **800**	1·20	1·00
2108		60pf.+30pf. Flowers, bird and butterfly	1·50	1·20
2109		80pf.+40pf. Flowers, berries and snail	1·70	1·60
2110		120pf.+60pf. Flowers, snail and butterfly	2·75	2·75

801 Fritz Reuter

1985. 175th Death Anniv of Fritz Reuter (writer).
2111	**801**	80pf. black, grey and blue	3·00	75

802 "Inauguration of First German Railway" (Heim)

1985. 150th Anniv of German Railways and Birth Bicent. of Johannes Scharrer (joint founder).
2112	**802**	80pf. multicoloured	3·00	75

803 Carpentry Joint in National Colours

1985. 40th Anniv of Integration of Refugees.
2113	**803**	80pf. multicoloured	3·00	75

804 Iron Cross and National Colours

1985. 30th Anniv of Federal Armed Forces.
2114	**804**	80pf. red, black & yellow	4·25	75

805 "Nativity" (detail, High Altar, Freiburg)

1985. Christmas. 500th Birth Anniversary of Hans Baldung Grien (artist).
2115	**805**	80pf.+40pf. mult	2·30	2·30

806 Early and Modern Cars

1986. Centenary of Motor Car.
2116	**806**	80pf. multicoloured	3·00	75

807 Town Buildings

1986. 1250th Anniv of Bad Hersfeld.
2117	**807**	60pf. multicoloured	2·00	75

808 "Self-portrait"

1986. Birth Centenary of Oskar Kokoschka (artist and writer).
2118	**808**	80pf. black, grey and red	2·00	75

809 Comet and "Giotto" Space Probe

1986. Appearance of Halley's Comet.
2119 **809** 80pf. multicoloured 3·00 85

810 Running

1986. Sport Promotion Fund. Multicoloured.
2120 80pf.+40pf. Type **810** (European Athletics Championships, Stuttgart) 2·40 2·40
2121 120pf.+55pf. Bobsleigh (World Championships, Konigsee) 3·75 3·75

811 Optician

1986. Youth Welfare. Trades (1st series). Multicoloured.
2122 50pf.+25pf. Type **811** 1·60 1·50
2123 60pf.+30pf. Bricklayer 1·80 1·70
2124 70pf.+35pf. Hairdresser 2·10 2·00
2125 80pf.+40pf. Baker 3·00 2·75
See also Nos. 2179/82.

812 Walsrode Monastery

1986. Millenary of Walsrode.
2126 **812** 60pf. multicoloured 2·00 75

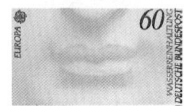

813 Ludwig and Neuschwanstein Castle

1986. Death Centenary of King Ludwig II of Bavaria.
2127 **813** 60pf. multicoloured 3·50 75

814 Mouth

1986. Europa. Details of *David* (sculpture) by Michelangelo. Multicoloured.
2128 60pf. Type **814** 1·80 60
2129 80pf. Nose 1·80 60

815 Karl Barth

1986. Birth Centenary of Karl Barth (theologian).
2130 **815** 80pf. black, red & purple 2·20 75

816 Ribbons

1986. Union of German Catholic Students' Societies 100th Assembly, Frankfurt am Main.
2131 **816** 80pf. multicoloured 2·20 75

817 Weber and Score of "Gloria"

1986. Birth Bicentenary of Carl Maria von Weber (composer).
2132 **817** 80pf. brown, black & red 3·00 75

818 "TV-Sat" and Earth

1986. Launch of German "TV-Sat" and French "TDF-1" Broadcasting Satellites.
2133 **818** 80pf. multicoloured 3·00 85

819 Doves

1986. International Peace Year.
2134 **819** 80pf. multicoloured 2·75 75

820 Liszt

1986. Death Centenary of Franz Liszt (composer).
2135 **820** 80pf. blue and orange 2·75 75

821 Reichstag, Berlin

1986. Important Buildings in West German History. Sheet 100×130 mm containing T **821** and similar horiz designs. Multicoloured.
MS2136 80pf. Type **821**; 80pf. Koenig Museum, Bonn (venue of 1948–49 Parliamentary Council); 80pf. Bundeshaus, Bonn (parliamentary building) 5·50 5·00

822 Pollution Damage of Stained Glass Window

1986. Protection of Monuments.
2137 **822** 80pf. multicoloured 3·00 75

823 Frederick the Great (after Anton Graff)

1986. Death Bicentenary of Frederick the Great.
2138 **823** 80pf. multicoloured 4·25 75

824 Congress Card

1986. Centenary of First German Skat Congress and 24th Congress, Cologne.
2139 **824** 80pf. multicoloured 3·00 75

825 Opposing Arrows

1986. 25th Anniv of Organization for Economic Co-operation and Development.
2140 **825** 80pf. multicoloured 2·20 75

826 Old University

1986. 600th Anniv of Heidelberg University.
2141 **826** 80pf. multicoloured 2·75 75

827 Fan of Stamps behind Stagecoach

1986. 50th Anniv of Stamp Day.
2142 **827** 80pf. multicoloured 2·75 75

828 Ornamental Flask, 300 A.D.

1986. Humanitarian Relief Funds. Glassware. Multicoloured.
2143 50pf.+25pf. Type **828** 1·10 1·00
2144 60pf.+30pf. Goblet with decorated stem, 1650 1·50 1·30
2145 70pf.+35pf. Imperial Eagle tankard, 1662 1·70 1·50
2146 80pf.+40pf. Engraved goblet, 1720 2·00 1·80

829 "Dance in Silence" from "Autumnal Dances"

1986. Birth Centenary of Mary Wigman (dancer).
2147 **829** 70pf. multicoloured 1·60 75

830 Cross over Map

1986. 25th Anniv of Adveniat (Advent collection for Latin America).
2148 **830** 80pf. green, blue & blk 1·60 75

831 "Adoration of the Infant Jesus" (Ortenberg altarpiece)

1986. Christmas.
2149 **831** 80pf.+40pf. mult 2·20 2·10

832 Christine Teusch (politician)

1986. Famous German Women. Inscr "Deutsche Bundespost".
2150 - 5pf. brown and grey 50 35
2151 - 10pf. brown and violet 60 35
2152 - 20pf. blue and red 1·20 60
2152a - 30pf. bistre and purple 60 50
2153 - 40pf. red and blue 1·20 35
2154 **832** 50pf. green and brown 1·20 35
2155 - 60pf. lilac and green 1·50 35
2155a - 70pf. green and red 1·80 1·00
2156 - 80pf. brown and green 1·50 35
2156a - 80pf. brown and blue 1·30 75
2157 - 100pf. grey and red 1·80 60
2157a - 100pf. bistre and lilac 1·30 75
2158 - 120pf. green and brown 2·40 1·50
2159 - 130pf. violet and blue 3·75 1·20
2160 - 140pf. ochre and blue 4·25 2·20
2161 - 150pf. blue and red 5·00 2·20
2162 - 170pf. purple and green 3·00 1·80
2163 - 180pf. purple and blue 3·75 1·80
2164 - 200pf. red and brown 3·00 1·20
2165 - 240pf. brown and green 4·25 3·00
2166 - 250pf. blue and mauve 5·75 3·00
2167 - 300pf. green and purple 3·75 1·80
2168 - 350pf. brown and black 6·00 3·75
2168a - 400pf. black and red 6·75 5·25
2168b - 450pf. ultramarine & bl 8·00 5·75
2169 - 500pf. red and green 8·00 5·00

DESIGNS: 5pf. Emma Ihrer (politician and trade unionist); 10pf. Paula Modersohn-Becker (painter); 20pf. Cilly Aussem (tennis player); 30pf. Kathe Kollwitz (artist); 40pf. Maria Sibylla Merian (artist and naturalist); 60pf. Dorothea Erxleben (first German woman Doctor of Medicine); 70pf. Elisabet Boehm (founder of Agricultural Association of Housewives); 80pf. (2156), Clara Schumann (pianist and composer); 80pf. (2156a), Rahel Varnhagen von Ense (humanist) (after Wilhelm Hensel); 100pf. (2157), Therese Giehse (actress); 100pf. (2157a), Luise Henriette of Orange (mother of King Friedrich I of Prussia) (after Gerhard von Honthorst); 120pf. Elisabeth Selbert (politician); 130pf. Lise Meitner (physicist); 140pf. Cecile Vogt (medical researcher); 150pf. Sophie Scholl (resistance member); 170pf. Hannah Arendt (sociologist); 180pf. Lotte Lehmann (opera singer); 200pf. Bertha von Suttner (novelist and pacifist); 240pf. Mathilda Franziska Anneke (women's rights activist); 250pf. Queen Louise of Prussia; 300pf. Fanny Hensel (composer) (after Eduard Magnus); 350pf. Hedwig Dransfeld (politician); 400pf. Charlotte von Stein (friend of Goethe); 450pf. Hedwig Courths-Mahler (novelist); 500pf. Alice Salomon (women's rights activist).
For similar designs inscribed "Deutschland", see Nos. 2785/95.

833 Berlin Landmarks

1987. 750th Anniv of Berlin.
2170 **833** 80pf. multicoloured 3·25 1·00

834 Staircase, Residenz Palace, Wurzburg

1987. 300th Birth Anniv of Balthasar Neumann (architect).
2171 **834** 80pf. grey, black and red 2·40 75

835 Erhard

1987. 90th Birth Anniv of Ludwig Erhard (former Chancellor).
2172 **835** 80pf. multicoloured 3·00 75

836 Abacus Beads forming Eagle

1987. Census.
2173 **836** 80pf. multicoloured 2·75 75

837 Clemenswerth Castle

1987. 250th Anniv of Clemenswerth Castle.
2174 **837** 60pf. multicoloured 2·10 75

838 Chief Winnetou (from book cover)

1987. 75th Death Anniv of Karl May (writer).
2175 **838** 80pf. multicoloured 2·30 75

839 Solar Spectrum

1987. Birth Bicentenary of Joseph von Fraunhofer (optician and physicist).
2176 **839** 80pf. multicoloured 2·10 75

840 World Sailing
Championships, Kiel

1987. Sport Promotion Fund. Multicoloured.
| 2177 | **840** | 80pf.+40pf. Type | 2·10 | 2·10 |
| 2178 | | 120pf.+55pf. World Nordic Skiing Championships, Oberstdorf | 3·25 | 3·25 |

1987. Youth Welfare. Trades (2nd series). As T **811**. Multicoloured.
2179		50pf.+25pf. Plumber	1·80	1·70
2180		60pf.+30pf. Dental technician	2·20	2·10
2181		70pf.+35pf. Butcher	2·40	2·20
2182		80pf.+40pf. Bookbinder	3·25	3·00

841 Clefs, Notes and Leaves

1987. 125th Anniv of German Choir Association.
| 2183 | **841** | 80pf. multicoloured | 2·30 | 75 |

842 Pope's Arms, Madonna and Child and Kevelaer

1987. Visit of Pope John Paul II to Kevelaer (venue for 17th Marian and 10th Mariological Congresses).
| 2184 | **842** | 80pf. multicoloured | 2·75 | 75 |

843 Dulmen's Wild Horses

1987. European Environment Year.
| 2185 | **843** | 60pf. multicoloured | 2·75 | 75 |

844 German Pavilion, International Exhibition, Barcelona, 1929 (Ludwig Mies van der Rohe)

1987. Europa. Architecture. Multicoloured.
| 2186 | | 60pf. Type **844** | 2·00 | 75 |
| 2187 | | 80pf. Kohlbrand Bridge, Hamburg (Thyssen Engineering) | 2·40 | 75 |

845 Emblem and Globe

1987. Rotary International Convention, Munich.
| 2188 | **845** | 70pf. ultram, yell & bl | 2·20 | 75 |

846 *Without Title*
(With an Early Portrait)

1987. Birth Centenary of Kurt Schwitters (artist and writer).
| 2189 | **846** | 80pf. multicoloured | 2·20 | 75 |

847 Organ Pipes and Signature

1987. 350th Birth Anniv of Dietrich Buxtehude (composer).
| 2190 | **847** | 80pf. black, stone and red | 1·60 | 75 |

848 Bengal

1987. 300th Birth Anniv of Johann Albrecht Bengel (theologian).
| 2191 | **848** | 80pf. brown, ochre & blk | 2·20 | 75 |

849 Wilhelm Kaisen

1987. Birth Centenary of Wilhelm Kaisen (Senate president and Mayor of Bremen).
| 2192 | **849** | 80pf. multicoloured | 2·20 | 75 |

850 Charlemagne, Bishop Willehad, Bremen Cathedral and City Arms (after mural)

1987. 1200th Anniv of Bremen Bishopric.
| 2193 | **850** | 80pf. multicoloured | 2·00 | 75 |

851 Target, Crossed Rifles and Wreath

1987. Seventh European Riflemen's Festival, Lippstadt.
| 2194 | **851** | 80pf. multicoloured | 2·00 | 75 |

852 4th-century Roman Bracelet

1987. Humanitarian Relief Funds. Precious Metal Work. Multicoloured.
2195		50pf.+25pf. Type **852**	1·80	1·70
2196		60pf.+30pf. 6th-century East Gothic buckle	1·80	1·70
2197		70pf.+35pf. 7th-century Merovingian disc fibula	1·80	1·70
2198		80pf.+40pf. 8th-century reliquary	2·40	2·40

853 Loading and Unloading Mail Train, 1897

1987. Stamp Day.
| 2199 | **853** | 80pf. multicoloured | 2·00 | 1·30 |

854 Corner Tower, Celle Castle

1987. Tourist Sights. Inscr "DEUTSCHE BUNDESPOST".
2200	-	5pf. blue and grey	45	35
2201	-	10pf. blue and indigo	75	25
2202	-	20pf. pink and blue	60	35
2203	**854**	30pf. brown and green	1·00	35
2204	-	33pf. green and red	75	50
2205	-	38pf. grey and blue	1·20	75
2206	-	40pf. brown, red & blue	1·00	75
2206a	-	41pf. grey and yellow	85	60
2207	-	45pf. pink and blue	75	60
2208	-	50pf. brown and blue	1·00	35
2209	-	60pf. green and black	1·20	35
2210	-	70pf. pink and blue	1·30	35
2210a	-	70pf. brown and blue	75	50
2211	-	80pf. grey and green	1·20	35
2212	-	90pf. bistre and yellow	3·50	2·40
2213	-	100pf. green and orange	3·00	50
2214	-	120pf. green and red	2·75	1·10
2215	-	140pf. bistre and yellow	3·00	1·00
2216	-	170pf. grey and yellow	3·25	1·20
2216a	-	200pf. blue and brown	3·25	1·10
2217	-	280pf. grey and blue	5·50	4·00
2218	-	300pf. pink and brown	4·25	75
2219	-	350pf. grey and blue	5·00	1·00
2220	-	400pf. red and brown	5·25	1·00
2220a	-	450pf. brown and blue	6·00	1·80
2220b	-	500pf. stone and purple	6·75	2·20
2220c	-	550pf. brown and blue	7·25	3·50
2220d	-	700pf. green and yellow	9·25	3·75

DESIGNS: 5pf. Brunswick Lion; 10pf. Frankfurt airport; 20, 70 (2210) pf. Head of Nefertiti, Berlin Museum; 33, 120pf. Schleswig Cathedral; 38, 280pf. Statue of Roland, Bremen; 40pf. Chile House, Hamburg; 41, 170pf. Russian Church, Wiesbaden; 45pf. Rastatt Castle; 50pf. Freiburg Cathedral; 60pf. "Bavaria" (bronze statue), Munich; 70pf. (2210a) Heligoland; 80pf. Zollern II Dortmund Mine Industrial Museum, Westphalia; 90, 140pf. Bronze flagon, Reinheim; 100pf. Pilgrimage Chapel, Altotting; 200pf. Magdeburg Cathedral; 300pf. Hambach Castle; 350pf. Externsteine (rock formation), Horn-Bad Meinberg; 400pf. Dresden Opera House; 450pf. New Gate, Neubrandenburg; 500pf. Cottbus State Theatre; 550pf. Suhl-Heinrichs Town Hall, Thuringia; 700pf. National Theatre, Berlin.
  The 10, 60, 80 and 100pf. also exist imperforate and self-adhesive from booklets.
  For similar designs inscribed "DEUTSCHLAND", see Nos. 2654/66.

855 Gluck and Score of *Armide*

1987. Death Bicentenary of Christoph Willibald Gluck (composer).
| 2221 | **855** | 60pf. black, grey and red | 1·60 | 60 |

856 Poster by Emil Orlik for *The Weavers*

1987. 125th Birth Anniv of Gerhart Hauptmann (playwright).
| 2222 | **856** | 80pf. lt red, black & red | 2·40 | 75 |

857 Paddy Field

1987. 25th Anniv of German Famine Aid.
| 2223 | **857** | 80pf. multicoloured | 2·40 | 75 |

858 "Birth of Christ" (13th-century Book of Psalms)

1987. Christmas.
| 2224 | **858** | 80pf.+40pf. multicoloured | 2·40 | 2·20 |

859 Jester

1988. 150th Anniv of Mainz Carnival.
| 2225 | **859** | 60pf. multicoloured | 1·70 | 75 |

860 Kaiser

1988. Birth Centenary of Jakob Kaiser (trade unionist and politician).
| 2226 | **860** | 80pf. black and grey | 1·60 | 75 |

861 Stein and Mayer

1988. Beatification of Edith Stein and Father Rupert Mayer.
| 2227 | **861** | 80pf. multicoloured | 2·00 | 75 |

862 Dr Konrad Adenauer (West German Chancellor) and Charles de Gaulle (French President)

1988. 25th Anniv of Franco-German Co-operation Treaty.
| 2228 | **862** | 80pf. purple and black | 2·75 | 1·00 |

863 "Solitude of the Green Woods" (woodcut of poem, Ludwig Richter)

1988. Birth Bicentenary of Joseph von Eichendorff (writer).
| 2229 | **863** | 60pf. multicoloured | 2·00 | 75 |

864 Raiffeisen and Ploughed Field

1988. Death Centenary of Friedrich Wilhelm Raiffeisen (philanthropist and agricultural co-operative founder).
| 2230 | **864** | 80pf. green and black | 2·75 | 75 |

865 Schopenhauer

1988. Birth Bicentenary of Arthur Schopenhauer (philosopher).
| 2231 | **865** | 80pf. brown and black | 2·40 | 75 |

866 Football (European Championship)

1988. Sport Promotion Fund. Multicoloured.
2232		60pf.+30pf. Type **866**	1·80	1·50
2233		80pf.+40pf. Tennis (Olympic Games)	3·00	2·40
2234		120pf.+55pf. Diving (Olympic Games)	3·50	3·00

867 Buddy Holly

1988. Youth Welfare. Pop Music. Multicoloured.
2235		50pf.+25pf. Type **867**	1·80	2·00
2236		60pf.+30pf. Elvis Presley	4·25	3·75
2237		70pf.+35pf. Jim Morrison	2·20	2·20
2238		80pf.+40pf. John Lennon	4·00	3·50

868 Hutten (wood engraving from *Conquestiones*)

1988. 500th Birth Anniv of Ulrich von Hutten (writer).
| 2239 | **868** | 80pf. multicoloured | 2·00 | 85 |

869 City Buildings and Jan Wellem Monument

1988. 700th Anniv of Dusseldorf.
| 2240 | **869** | 60pf. multicoloured | 2·00 | 75 |

870 Airbus Industrie A320 and Manufacturing Nations' Flag

1988. Europa. Transport and Communications. Multicoloured.

2241	60pf. Type **870**		1·60	75
2242	80pf. Diagram of Integrated Services Digital Network		1·60	75

871 University Buildings and City Landmarks

1988. 600th Anniv of Cologne University.

2243	**871**	80pf. multicoloured	2·00	75

872 Monnet

1988. Birth Centenary of Jean Monnet (statesman).

2244	**872**	80pf. multicoloured	2·00	75

873 Storm

1988. Death Centenary of Theodor Storm (writer).

2245	**873**	80pf. multicoloured	2·00	75

874 Tree supported by Stake in National Colours

1988. 25th Anniv of German Volunteer Service.

2246	**874**	80pf. multicoloured	2·00	75

875 Meersburg

1988. Millenary of Meersburg.

2247	**875**	60pf. multicoloured	1·50	75

876 Gmelin

1988. Birth Bicentenary of Leopold Gmelin (chemist).

2248	**876**	80pf. multicoloured	1·60	75

877 Vernier Caliper Rule in National Colours

1988. "Made in Germany".

2249	**877**	140pf. multicoloured	3·00	1·50

878 Bebel

1988. 75th Death Anniv of August Bebel (Social Democratic Labour Party co-founder).

2250	**878**	80pf. mauve, blue & silver	2·20	75

879 Carrier Pigeon

1988. Stamp Day.

2251	**879**	20pf. multicoloured	1·00	60

880 13th-century Rock Crystal Reliquary

1988. Humanitarian Relief Funds. Precious Metal Work. Multicoloured.

2252	50pf.+25pf. Type **880**	1·00	1·00
2253	60pf.+30pf. 14th-century bust of Charlemagne	1·50	1·50
2254	70pf.+35pf. 10th-cent. crown of Otto III	1·50	1·50
2255	80pf.+40pf. 17th-cent. jewelled flowers	2·20	2·20

881 Red Cross

1988. 125th Anniv of Red Cross.

2256	**881**	80pf. red and black	2·20	75

882 Burning Synagogue, Baden-Baden

1988. 50th Anniv of "Kristallnacht" (Nazi pogrom).

2257	**882**	80pf. purple and black	1·60	75

883 Cancelled Postage Stamps

1988. Centenary of Collection of Used Stamps for the Bethel Charity.

2258	**883**	60pf. multicoloured	1·80	75

884 Linked Arms

1988. Centenary of Samaritan Workers' (first aid) Association.

2259	**884**	80pf. multicoloured	1·80	75

885 "Adoration of the Magi" (illus from Henry the Lion's Gospel Book)

1988. Christmas.

2260	**885**	80pf.+40pf. multicoloured	2·20	2·00

886 "Bluxao I"

1989. Birth Centenary of Willi Baumeister (painter).

2261	**886**	60pf. multicoloured	1·60	75

887 Bonn

1988. 2000th Anniv of Bonn.

2262	**887**	80pf. multicoloured	2·40	1·10

888 Grass growing from Dry, Cracked Earth

1989. 30th Anniversaries of Misereor and Bread for the World (Third World relief organizations).

2263	**888**	80pf. multicoloured	1·80	75

889 "Cats in the Attic" (woodcut)

1989. Birth Cent of Gerhard Marcks (artist).

2264	**889**	60pf. black, stone and red	1·60	75

890 Table Tennis (World Championships)

1989. Sport Promotion Fund. Multicoloured.

2265	100pf.+50pf. Type **890**	3·00	2·75
2266	140pf.+60pf. Gymnastics (World Championships)	4·25	4·00

891 Elephants

1989. Youth Welfare. Circus. Multicoloured.

2267	60pf.+30pf. Type **891**	2·40	2·40
2268	70pf.+30pf. Acrobat on horseback	3·00	3·00
2269	80pf.+35pf. Clown	4·25	3·75
2270	100pf.+50pf. Caravans and Big Top	5·50	4·25

892 Posthorn and Book of Stamps

1989. "IPHLA '89" International Philatelic Literature Exhibition, Frankfurt.

2271	**892**	100pf.+50pf. mult	4·25	4·00

893 European and Members' Flags

1989. 3rd Direct Elections to European Parliament.

2272	**893**	100pf. multicoloured	3·25	1·50

894 Shipping

1989. 800th Anniv of Hamburg Harbour.

2273	**894**	60pf. multicoloured	2·20	75

895 Asam (detail of fresco, Weltenburg Abbey)

1989. 250th Death Anniv of Cosmas Damian Asam (painter and architect).

2274	**895**	60pf. multicoloured	1·20	75

896 Kites

1989. Europa. Children's Toys. Multicoloured.

2275	60pf. Type **896**	1·80	60
2276	100pf. Puppet show	2·40	60

897 Emblem, National Colours and Presidents' Signatures

1989. 40th Anniv of German Federal Republic.

2277	**897**	100pf. multicoloured	3·00	1·10

898 Council Assembly and Stars

1989. 40th Anniv of Council of Europe.

2278	**898**	100pf. blue and gold	2·75	1·20

899 Gabelsberger and Shorthand

1989. Birth Bicentenary of Franz Xaver Gabelsberger (shorthand pioneer).

2279	**899**	100pf. multicoloured	2·75	85

900 Score of *Lorelei* and Silhouette of Silcher

1989. Birth Bicentenary of Friedrich Silcher (composer).

2280	**900**	80pf. multicoloured	1·60	75

901 Saints Kilian, Totnan and Colman (from 12th-century German manuscript)

1989. 1300th Death Anniversaries of Saints Kilian, Colman and Totnan (Irish missionaries to Franconia).

2281	**901**	100pf. multicoloured	2·40	1·00

902 Age Graphs of Men and Women

1989. Centenary of National Insurance.

2282	**902**	100p. blue, red & lt blue	2·40	1·00

903 *Summer Evening* (Heinrich Vogler)

1989. Cent of Worpswede Artists' Village.

2283	**903**	60pf. multicoloured	1·30	75

904 Schneider

1989. 50th Death Anniv of Reverend Paul Schneider (concentration camp victim).

2284	**904**	100pf. blk, lt grey & grey	2·10	85

905 List (after Kriehuber) and Train

1989. Birth Bicentenary of Friedrich List (economist).

2285	**905**	170pf. black and red	3·75	1·50

906 Cathedral

1989. 750th Anniv of Frankfurt Cathedral.

2286	**906**	60pf. multicoloured	2·00	75

907 Children building House

1989. "Don't Forget the Children".

2287	**907**	100pf. multicoloured	2·10	85

908 Ammonite and Union Emblem

1989. Centenary of Mining and Power Industries Trade Union.

2288	**908**	100pf. multicoloured	2·10	85

909 18th-century Mounted Courier, Thurn and Taxis

1989. Humanitarian Relief Funds. Postal Deliveries. Multicoloured.

2289		60pf.+30pf. Type **909**	1·80	1·70
2290		80pf.+35pf. Hamburg postal messenger, 1808	2·75	2·40
2291		100pf.+50pf. Bavarian mail coach, 1900	4·00	3·75

910 Maier

1989. Birth Centenary of Reinhold Maier (politician).

2292	**910**	100pf. multicoloured	2·20	85

911 Organ Pipes

1989. 300th Anniv of Arp Schnitger Organ, St. James's Church, Hamburg.

2293	**911**	60pf. multicoloured	2·00	75

912 Angel

1989. Christmas. 16th-century Carvings by Veit Stoss, St. Lawrence's Church, Nuremberg. Multicoloured.

2294		60pf.+30pf. Type **912**	2·00	1·70
2295		100pf.+50pf. "Nativity"	2·40	2·20

913 Speyer

1990. 2000th Anniv of Speyer.

2296	**913**	60pf. multicoloured	2·00	75

914 "Courier" (Albrecht Durer)

1990. 500th Anniv of Regular European Postal Services.

2297	**914**	100pf. deep brown, light brown and brown	3·25	1·00

915 Vine forming Initial "R"

1990. 500 Years of Riesling Grape Cultivation.

2298	**915**	100pf. multicoloured	2·00	1·00

916 Old Lubeck

1990. UNESCO World Heritage Site, Old Lubeck.

2299	**916**	100pf. multicoloured	2·00	1·00

917 15th-century Seal and Grand Master's Arms

1990. 800th Anniv of Teutonic Order.

2300	**917**	100pf. multicoloured	2·40	1·00

918 Frederick II's Seal and Fair Entrance Hall

1990. 750th Anniv of Granting of Fair Privileges to Frankfurt.

2301	**918**	100pf. multicoloured	2·40	1·00

919 Maze

1990. 25th Anniv of Youth Research Science Competition.

2302	**919**	100pf. multicoloured	2·40	1·00

920 Wildlife

1990. North Sea Protection.

2303	**920**	100pf. multicoloured	3·00	1·00

921 Handball

1990. Sport Promotion Fund. Multicoloured.

2304		100pf.+50pf. Type **921**	4·00	2·40
2305		140pf.+60pf. Keep-fit	4·75	3·75

922 Widow Bolte

1990. Youth Welfare. 125th Anniv of Max and Moritz (characters from books by Wilhelm Busch). Multicoloured.

2306		60pf.+30pf. Type **922**	1·30	1·20
2307		70pf.+30pf. Max asleep	2·00	1·80
2308		80pf.+35pf. Moritz watching Max sawing through bridge	2·75	2·40
2309		100pf.+50pf. Max and Moritz	3·25	3·00

923 "1.MAI" and Factory Silhouette

1990. Centenary of Labour Day.

2310	**923**	100pf. red and black	2·00	1·00

924 Woman's Face

1990. 75th Anniv of German Association of Housewives.

2311	**924**	100pf. multicoloured	2·00	1·00

925 Collection Box

1990. 125th Anniv of German Lifeboat Institution.

2312	**925**	60pf. multicoloured	1·80	85

926 Thurn and Taxis Palace, Frankfurt

1990. Europa. Post Office Buildings. Multicoloured.

2313		60pf. Type **926**	2·20	85
2314		100pf. Postal Giro Office, Frankfurt	2·40	85

927 St Philip's Church, Protestant Church Flag and Candle Flames

1990. Centenary of Rummelsberg Diaconal Institution.

2315	**927**	100pf. multicoloured	2·00	1·00

928 Leuschner

1990. Birth Centenary of Wilhelm Leuschner (trade unionist and member of anti-Hitler Resistance).

2316	**928**	100pf. black and lilac	2·40	1·00

929 Globe

1990. 125th Anniv of I.T.U.

2317	**929**	100pf. multicoloured	2·00	1·00

930 National Colours and Students

1990. 175th Anniv of German Students' Fraternity and of their Colours (now national colours).

2318	**930**	100pf. multicoloured	2·40	1·00

931 Hands exchanging Money and Goods

1990. 30th World Congress of International Chamber of Commerce, Hamburg.

2319	**931**	80pf. multicoloured	2·00	1·20

932 Closing Sentence of Charter

1990. 40th Anniv of Expelled Germans Charter.

2320	**932**	100pf. multicoloured	2·40	85

933 Children of Different Races

1990. Tenth International Youth Philatelic Exhibition, Dusseldorf. Sheet 165×101 mm.

MS2321	**933**	6×100pf.+50pf. multicoloured	27·00	30·00

934 Claudius

1990. 250th Birth Anniv of Matthias Claudius (writer).

2322	**934**	100pf. blue, black and red	2·20	75

935 Mail Motor Wagon, 1900

1990. Humanitarian Relief Funds. Posts and Telecommunications. Multicoloured.

2323		60pf.+30pf. Type **935**	1·30	1·30
2324		80pf.+35pf. Telephone exchange, 1890	2·20	2·20
2325		100pf.+50pf. Parcel sorting office, 1900	3·25	3·25

936 "German Unity" and National Colours

1990. Reunification of Germany.

2326	**936**	50pf. black, red & yellow	1·80	60
2327	**936**	100pf. black, red & yell	2·40	85

937 Schliemann and Lion Gate, Mycenae

1990. Death Centenary of Heinrich Schliemann (archaeologist).

2328	**937**	60pf. multicoloured	2·00	75

938 Penny Black, Bavaria 1k. and West Germany 1989 100pf. Stamps

1990. Stamp Day. 150th Anniv of the Penny Black.

2329	**938**	100pf. multicoloured	2·20	75

939 National Colours spanning Breach in Wall

1990. First Anniv of Opening of Berlin Wall.

2330	50pf. Type **939**	1·80	1·10
2331	100pf. Brandenburg Gate and crowd	2·40	1·10
MS2332	146×100 mm. As Nos. 2330/1	5·00	5·00

940 Angel with Candles

1990. Christmas. Multicoloured.

2333	50pf.+20pf. Type **940**	1·20	1·20
2334	60pf.+30pf. Figure of man smoking	1·50	1·50
2335	70pf.+30pf. "Soldier" nutcrackers	2·00	2·00
2336	100pf.+50pf. Tinsel angel	3·00	3·00

941 Kathe Dorsch in "Mrs Warren's Profession"

1990. Birth Centenary of Kathe Dorsch (actress).

2337	**941** 100pf. violet and red	2·20	1·00

942 View of City

1991. 750th Anniv of Hanover.

2338	**942** 60pf. multicoloured	2·00	75

943 "Three Golden Circles with a Full Circle in Blue" (relief in wood)

1991. Birth Centenary of Erich Buchholz (artist).

2339	**943** 60pf. multicoloured	1·60	75

944 Miniature from 13th-century French Code

1991. 750th Anniv of Promulgation of Pharmaceutical Ethics in Germany.

2340	**944** 100pf. multicoloured	2·40	1·00

945 Brandenburg Gate (from Old Engravings of Berlin)

1991. Bicentenary of Brandenburg Gate.

2341	**945** 100pf. black, red and grey	2·75	75

946 Eucken

1991. Birth Centenary of Walter Eucken (economist).

2342	**946** 100pf. multicoloured	2·10	1·00

947 Globe and "25" (poster)

1991. 25th International Tourism Fair, Berlin.

2343	**947** 100pf. multicoloured	2·10	1·00

948 Two-man Bobsleigh

1991. World Bobsleigh Championships, Altenberg. Sheet 55×80 mm.

MS2344	**948** 100pf. multicoloured	1·50	1·50

949 Weightlifting (World Championships)

1991. Sport Promotion Fund. Multicoloured.

2345	70pf.+30pf. Type **949**	2·20	2·20
2346	100pf.+50pf. Cycling (world championships)	2·40	2·40
2347	140pf.+60pf. Basketball (centenary)	3·00	3·00
2348	170pf.+80pf. Wrestling (European championships)	3·75	3·75

950 Title Page of Cautio Criminalis (tract against witch trials), Langenfeld and Score of Trutz-Nachtigall

1991. 400th Birth Anniv of Friedrich Spee von Langenfeld (poet and human rights pioneer).

2349	**950** 100pf. multicoloured	2·20	75

951 Androsace

1991. Plants in Rennsteiggarten (botanical garden), Oberhof. Multicoloured.

2350	30pf. Type **951**	60	60
2351	50pf. Primula	85	85
2352	80pf. Gentian	1·50	60
2353	100pf. Cranberry	2·10	85
2354	350pf. Edelweiss	6·75	5·00

952 Werth (attr Wenzel Hollar)

1991. 400th Birth Anniv of Jan von Werth (military commander).

2355	**952** 60pf. multicoloured	1·60	75

953 Windthorst

1991. Death Centenary of Ludwig Windthorst (politician).

2356	**953** 100pf. multicoloured	2·20	75

954 Junkers F-13, 1930

1991. Historic Mail Aircraft. Multicoloured.

2357	30pf. Type **954**	60	60
2358	50pf. Hans Grade's monoplane, 1909	85	60
2359	100pf. Fokker F.III, 1922	2·40	60
2360	165pf. Airship LZ-127 Graf Zeppelin, 1928	3·75	3·50

955 Mountain Clouded Yellow

1991. Youth Welfare. Endangered Butterflies. Multicoloured.

2361	30pf.+15pf. Type **955**	60	60
2362	50pf.+25pf. Poplar admiral	75	75
2363	60pf.+30pf. Purple emperor	1·50	1·50
2364	70pf.+30pf. Violet copper	1·60	1·60
2365	80pf.+35pf. Swallowtail	2·00	2·00
2366	90pf.+45pf. Small apollo	2·40	2·40
2367	100pf.+50pf. Moorland clouded yellow	3·00	3·00
2368	140pf.+60pf. Large copper	3·75	3·75

See also Nos. 2449/53.

956 Academy Building, 1830

1991. Bicentenary of Choral Academy, Berlin.

2369	**956** 100pf. multicoloured	2·20	1·00

957 Typesetting School, 1875

1991. 125th Anniv of Lette Foundation (institute for professional training of women).

2370	**957** 100pf. multicoloured	2·20	1·00

958 Battle (detail of miniature, Schlackenwerth Codex, 1350)

1991. 750th Anniv of Battle of Legnica.

2371	**958** 100pf. multicoloured	2·40	1·50

959 Arms

1991. 700th Anniv of Granting of Charters to Six Towns of Trier.

2372	**959** 60pf. multicoloured	1·60	75

960 Speeding Train

1991. Inauguration of Inter-City Express (ICE) Railway Service.

2373	**960** 60pf. multicoloured	1·60	75

961 "ERS-1" European Remote Sensing Satellite

1991. Europa. Europe in Space. Multicoloured.

2374	60pf. Type **961**	1·80	60
2375	100pf. "Kopernikus" telecommunications satellite	2·75	60

962 Reger and Organ Pipes

1991. 75th Death Anniv of Max Reger (composer).

2376	**962** 100pf. multicoloured	2·40	75

963 Ruffs

1991. Seabirds. Multicoloured.

2390	60pf. Type **963**	1·20	75
2391	80pf. Little terns	1·80	75
2392	100pf. Brent geese	1·80	1·20
2393	140pf. White-tailed sea eagles	3·00	2·40

964 Wilhelm August Lampadius (gas pioneer)

1991. 18th World Gas Congress, Berlin. Each black and blue.

2394	60pf. Type **964**	1·20	50
2395	100pf. Gas street lamp, Berlin	1·80	75

965 Wallot (after Franz Wurbel) and Reichstag Building, Berlin

1991. 150th Birth Anniv of Paul Wallot (architect).

2396	**965** 100pf. multicoloured	2·40	75

966 Libellula depressa

1991. Dragonflies. Multicoloured.

2397	50pf. Type **966**	1·00	60
2398	60pf. Type **966**	1·80	1·00
2399	60pf. Sympetrum sanguineum	1·80	1·00
2400	60pf. Cordulegaster boltonii	1·80	1·00
2401	60pf. Aeshna viridis	1·80	1·00
2402	70pf. As No. 2399	1·80	1·20
2403	80pf. As No. 2400	1·80	1·20
2404	100pf. As No. 2401	1·80	1·20

967 Hand clutching Cloak

1991. 40th Anniv of Geneva Convention on Refugees.

2405	**967** 100pf. lilac and black	2·20	70

968 Radio Waves and Mast

1991. International Radio Exhibition, Berlin.

2406	**968** 100pf. multicoloured	2·20	70

969 Pedestrians and Traffic

1991. Road Safety Campaign.

2407	**969** 100pf. multicoloured	2·40	95

970 Lilienthal

1991. Centenary of First Heavier-than-Air Manned Flight by Otto Lilienthal and "Lilienthal '91" European Airmail Exhibition, Dresden. Sheet 57×82 mm.
MS2408 **970** 100pf.+50pf. brown, blue and red   5·00   4·50

971 August Heinrich Hoffmann von Fallersleben (lyricist) and Third Verse

1991. 50th Anniv of *Song of the Germans* (national anthem).
2409 **971** 100pf. red, black & green   2·20 70

972 Thadden-Trieglaff

1991. Birth Cent of Reinold von Thadden-Trieglaff (founder of German Protestant Convention).
2410 **972** 100pf. multicoloured   2·10 70

973 Transmission Test between Lauffen am Neckar and Frankfurt am Main

1991. Centenary of Three-phase Energy Transmission.
2411 **973** 170pf. multicoloured   3·50 1·80

974 Quill, Pen and Sword

1991. Birth Bicentenary of Theodor Korner (poet). Sheet 55×80 mm containing T **974** and similar vert designs. Multicoloured.
MS2412 60pf. Type **974**; 100pf. Korner   3·50 4·25

975 Albers in *The Winner*

1991. Birth Centenary of Hans Albers (actor).
2413 **975** 100pf. multicoloured   2·75 70

976 Harbour

1991. 275th Anniv of Rhine-Ruhr Port, Duisburg.
2414 **976** 100pf. multicoloured   2·20 70

977 Bethel Post Office

1991. Humanitarian Relief Funds. Postal Buildings. Multicoloured.
2415 30pf.+15pf. Type **977**   95 70
2416 60pf.+30pf. Budingen post station   1·50 1·40
2417 70pf.+30pf. Stralsund post office   1·80 1·70
2418 80pf.+35pf. Lauscha post office   2·40 2·10
2419 100pf.+50pf. Bonn post office   3·00 2·75
2420 140pf.+60pf. Weilburg post office   3·50 3·50

978 Postal Delivery in Spreewald Region

1991. Stamp Day.
2421 **978** 100pf. multicoloured   2·10 70

979 *Bird Monument* (detail)

1991. Birth Centenary of Max Ernst (painter).
2422 **979** 100pf. multicoloured   2·20 70

980 *Portrait of the Dancer Anita Berber*

1991. Birth Centenary of Otto Dix (painter). Multicoloured.
2423 60pf. Type **980**   1·20 70
2424 100pf. *Self-portrait in Right Profile*   2·40 85

981 "The Violinist and the Water Sprite"

1991. Sorbian Legends. Multicoloured.
2425 60pf. Type **981**   1·40 70
2426 100pf. "The Midday Woman and the Woman from Nochten"   2·10 85

982 Angel (detail of "The Annunciation")

1991. Christmas. Works by Martin Schongauer. Multicoloured.
2427 60pf.+30pf. Type **982**   1·50 1·40
2428 70pf.+30pf. Virgin Mary (detail of "The Annunciation")   1·90 1·80
2429 80pf.+35pf. Angel (detail of "Madonna in a Rose Garden")   3·75 3·25
2430 100pf.+50pf. "Nativity"   4·50 4·00

983 Leber

1991. Birth Centenary of Julius Leber (politician).
2431 **983** 100pf. multicoloured   2·10 70

984 Nelly Sachs

1991. Birth Centenary of Nelly Sachs (writer).
2432 **984** 100pf. dp violet & violet   2·20 70

985 Mozart

1991. Death Bicentenary of Wolfgang Amadeus Mozart (composer). Sheet 82×56 mm.
MS2433 **985** 100pf. lilac and brown   3·50 4·00

986 Base of William I Monument and City Silhouette

1992. 2000th Anniv of Koblenz.
2434 **986** 60pf. multicoloured   2·40 85

987 Niemoller

1992. Birth Centenary of Martin Niemoller (theologian).
2435 **987** 100pf. multicoloured   1·80 70

988 Child's Eyes

1992. 25th Anniv of Terre des Hommes (child welfare organization) in Germany.
2436 **988** 100pf. multicoloured   2·40 95

989 Arms of Baden-Wurttemberg

1992. Lander of the Federal Republic.
2437 **989** 100pf. multicoloured   2·20 1·10
See also Nos. 2448, 2465, 2470, 2474, 2479, 2506, 2526, 2527, 2534, 2539, 2556, 2567, 2580, 2584 and 2597.

990 Fencing

1992. Sport Promotion Fund. Olympic Games, Albertville and Barcelona. Multicoloured.
2438 60pf.+30pf. Type **990**   1·40 1·40
2439 80pf.+40pf. Rowing eight   1·70 1·70
2440 100pf.+50pf. Dressage   3·50 3·50
2441 170pf.+80pf. Skiing (slalom)   5·25 5·25

991 Honegger and Score of Ballet *Semiramis*

1992. Birth Centenary of Arthur Honegger (composer).
2442 **991** 100pf. black and brown   2·40 1·10

992 Zeppelin and LZ-127 *Graf Zeppelin*

1992. 75th Death Anniv of Ferdinand von Zeppelin (airship manufacturer).
2443 **992** 165pf. multicoloured   3·50 1·90

993 Kiel City and Harbour

1992. 750th Anniv of Kiel.
2444 **993** 60pf. multicoloured   1·80 85

994 Andreas Marggraf, Beet, Franz Achard and Carl Scheibler

1992. 125th Anniv of Berlin Sugar Institute.
2445 **994** 100pf. multicoloured   2·20 1·10
The stamp depicts the discoverer of beet sugar, the founder of the beet sugar industry and the founder of the Institute respectively.

995 Horses and Renz

1992. Death Centenary of Ernst Jakob Renz (circus director).
2446 **995** 100pf. multicoloured   2·20 85

996 Adenauer

1992. 25th Death Anniv of Konrad Adenauer (Chancellor, 1949–63).
2447 **996** 100pf. brn & cinnamon   2·75 85

1992. Lander of the Federal Republic. As T **989**. Multicoloured.
2448 100pf. Bavaria   2·20 1·10

1992. Youth Welfare. Endangered Moths. As T **955**. Multicoloured.
2449 60pf.+30pf. Purple tiger moth   2·10 2·10
2450 70pf.+30pf. Hawk moth   2·40 2·40
2451 80pf.+40pf. *Noctuidae* sp.   3·00 3·00
2452 100pf.+50pf. Tiger moth   3·25 3·25
2453 170pf.+80pf. *Arichanna melanaria*   3·75 3·75

997 Schall

1992. 400th Birth Anniv of Adam Schall von Bell (missionary astronomer).
2454 **997** 140pf. black, yellow & bl   3·00 1·50

998 Cathedral and St. Severus's Church

1992. 1250th Anniv of Erfurt.
2455 **998** 60pf. multicoloured   1·70 85

999 Woodcut from 1493 Edition of Columbus's Letters

1992. Europa. 500th Anniv of Discovery of America by Columbus. Multicoloured.
2456 60pf. Type **999**   1·80 70
2457 100pf. "Rene de Laudonniere and Chief Athore" (Jacques le Moyne de Morgues, 1564)   2·40 85

1000 "Consecration of St. Ludgerus" (from *Vita Liudgeri* by Altfridus)

1992. 1250th Birth Anniv of St. Ludgerus (first Bishop of Munster).
2458 **1000** 100pf. multicoloured 2·10 95

1001 Arithmetic Sum

1992. 500th Birth Anniv of Adam Riese (mathematician).
2459 **1001** 100pf. multicoloured 2·40 85

1002 Order of Merit

1992. 150th Anniv of Civil Class of Order of Merit (for scientific or artistic achievement).
2460 **1002** 100pf. multicoloured 2·10 85

1003 *Landscape with Horse* (Franz Marc)

1992. 20th-century German Paintings (1st series). Multicoloured.
2461 60pf. Type **1003** 1·20 95
2462 100pf. *Fashion Shop* (August Macke) 1·80 95
2463 170pf. *Murnau with Rainbow* (Wassily Kandinsky) 3·00 2·50
See also Nos. 2507/9, 2590/2, 2615/17 and 2704/6.

1004 Lichtenberg

1992. 250th Birth Anniv of Georg Christoph Lichtenberg (physicist and essayist).
2464 **1004** 100pf. multicoloured 2·10 95

1992. Lander of the Federal Republic. As T **989**. Multicoloured.
2465 100pf. Berlin 2·20 1·10

1005 Rainforest

1992. "Save the Tropical Rain Forest".
2466 **1005** 100pf.+50pf. multicoloured 2·75 2·75
The premium was for the benefit of environmental projects.

1006 Garden

1992. Leipzig Botanical Garden.
2467 **1006** 60pf. multicoloured 1·50 85

1007 Stylized House and Globe

1992. 17th International Home Economics Congress, Hanover.
2468 **1007** 100pf. multicoloured 2·40 95

1008 Family

1992. Family Life.
2469 **1008** 100pf. multicoloured 2·40 85

1992. Lander of the Federal Republic. As T **989**. Multicoloured.
2470 100pf. Brandenburg 2·20 1·10

1009
"Assumption of the Virgin Mary" (Rohr Monastery Church)

1992. 300th Birth Anniv of Egid Quirin Asam (sculptor).
2471 **1009** 60pf. multicoloured 1·80 85

1010 Opera House (Georg von Knobelsdorff)

1992. 250th Anniv of German State Opera House, Berlin.
2472 **1010** 80pf. multicoloured 2·00 85

1011 Masked Actors

1992. Centenary of German Amateur Theatres Federation.
2473 **1011** 100pf. multicoloured 2·40 85

1992. Lander of the Federal Republic. As T **989**. Multicoloured.
2474 100pf. Bremen 2·20 1·10

1012 Globe

1992. 500th Anniv of Martin Behaim's Terrestrial Globe.
2475 **1012** 60pf. multicoloured 1·90 85

1013 1890 Pendant and 1990 Clock

1992. 225th Anniv of Jewellery and Watch-making in Pforzheim.
2476 **1013** 100pf. multicoloured 2·00 85

1014 Bergengruen (after Hanni Fries)

1992. Birth Centenary of Werner Bergengruen (writer).
2477 **1014** 100pf. grey, blue & blk 2·00 85

1015 Neue Holzbrucke Bridge, nr Essing

1992. Inauguration of Main–Donau Canal.
2478 **1015** 100pf. multicoloured 2·00 85

1992. Lander of the Federal Republic. As T **989**. Multicoloured.
2479 100pf. Hamburg 2·20 1·10

1016 Turret Clock, 1400

1992. Humanitarian Relief Funds. Clocks. Multicoloured.
2480 60pf.+30pf. Type **1016** 1·70 1·50
2481 70pf.+30pf. Astronomical mantel clock, 1738 2·00 1·90
2482 80pf.+40pf. Flute clock, 1790 2·10 2·00
2483 100pf.+50pf. Figurine clock, 1580 2·50 2·40
2484 170pf.+80pf. Table clock, 1550 3·50 3·25

1017 Distler and Score of *We Praise Our Lord Jesus Christ*

1992. 50th Death Anniv of Hugo Distler (composer).
2485 **1017** 100pf. black and violet 2·40 85

1018 Balloon Post

1992. Stamp Day.
2486 **1018** 100pf. multicoloured 2·40 95

1019 Otto Engine, 1892, Cogwheel and Laser Beam

1992. Centenary of German Plant and Machine Builders Association.
2487 **1019** 170pf. multicoloured 2·75 1·70

1020 *Adoration of the Magi*

1992. Christmas. Carvings by Franz Maidburg, St. Anne's Church, Annaberg-Buchholz. Multicoloured.
2488 60pf.+30pf. Type **1020** 1·70 1·50
2489 100pf.+50pf. "Birth of Christ" 2·40 2·10

1021 Blucher (after Simon Meister)

1992. 250th Birth Anniv of Field Marshal Gebhard Leberecht von Blucher.
2490 **1021** 100pf. multicoloured 2·40 85

1022 Werner von Siemens

1992. Death Centenary of Werner von Siemens (electrical engineer).
2491 **1022** 100pf. brown & dp brn 2·40 85

1023 Klepper

1992. 50th Death Anniv of Jochen Klepper (writer).
2492 **1023** 100pf. multicoloured 2·40 85

1024 Star in German Colours

1992. European Single Market.
2493 **1024** 100pf. multicoloured 2·75 95

1025 Cathedral and Uberwasser Church

1993. 1200th Anniv of Munster.
2494 **1025** 60pf. multicoloured 1·50 85

1026 Newton, Sketch of Refraction of Light and Formula

1993. 350th Birth Anniv of Sir Isaac Newton (scientist).
2495 **1026** 100pf. multicoloured 2·10 85

1027 Route Map and Compass Rose

1993. 125th Anniv of North German Naval Observatory, Hamburg.
2496 **1027** 100pf. multicoloured 1·90 85

1028 Emblem and Safety Stripes

1993. European Year of Health, Hygiene and Safety in the Workplace.
2497 **1028** 100pf. blue, yell & blk 1·90 85

1029 Wires and Wall Socket forming House

1993. Centenary of German Association of Electrical Engineers.
2498 **1029** 170pf. multicoloured 2·75 1·70

1030 Ski-jumping Hill, Garmisch-Partenkirchen

1993. Sport Promotion Fund. German Olympic Venues. Multicoloured.
2499 60pf.+30pf. Type **1030** 2·40 2·10
2500 80pf.+40pf. Olympia-park, Munich 3·00 2·75
2501 100pf.+50pf. Olympic Stadium, Berlin 3·75 3·50
2502 170pf.+80pf. Olympic Harbour, Kiel 4·50 4·25

1031 Stylised Sound Vibration

1993. 250th Anniv of Leipzig Gewandhaus Orchestra.
2503 **1031** 100pf. gold and black 1·90 85

1032 Statue of St. John and Charles Bridge, Prague

1993. 600th Death Anniv of St. John of Nepomuk.
2504 **1032** 100pf. multicoloured 2·10 85

1033 Diagram explaining New Postcodes

1993. Introduction of Five-digit Postcode System.
2505 **1033** 100pf. multicoloured 2·40 85

1993. Lander of the Federal Republic. As T **989**. Multicoloured.
2506 100pf. Hesse 2·00 1·10

1993. 20th-century German Paintings (2nd series). As T **1003**. Multicoloured.
2507 100pf. multicoloured 2·00 1·20
2508 100pf. black, grey and mauve 2·00 1·20
2509 100pf. multicoloured 2·00 1·20
DESIGNS: No. 2507, *Cafe* (George Grosz); 2508. *Sea and Sun* (Otto Pankok); 2509, *Audience* (Andreas Paul Weber).

1034 Abbeys

1993. 900th Anniversaries of Maria Laach and Bursfelde Benedictine Abbeys.
2510 **1034** 80pf. multicoloured 2·10 85

1035 Alpine Longhorn Beetle

1993. Youth Welfare. Endangered Beetles. Multicoloured.
2511 80pf.+40f. Type **1035** 2·40 2·40
2512 80pf.+40pf. Rose chafer 2·40 2·40
2513 100pf.+50pf. Stag beetle 2·75 2·75
2514 100pf.+50pf. Tiger beetle 2·75 2·75
2515 200pf.+50pf. Cockchafer 4·25 4·25

1036 Plants

1993. Fifth International Horticultural Show, Stuttgart.
2516 **1036** 100pf. multicoloured 1·90 85

1037 Horse Race

1993. 125th Anniv of Hoppegarten Racecourse.
2517 **1037** 80pf. multicoloured 1·70 95

1038 *Storage Place* (Joseph Beuys)

1993. Europa. Contemporary Art. Multicoloured.
2518 80pf. Type **1038** 1·80 1·00
2519 100pf. *Homage to the Square* (Josef Albers) 1·80 1·00

1039 Church and Pupils

1993. 450th Anniv of Pforta School.
2520 **1039** 100pf. multicoloured 1·90 85

1040 Students, Flag, City Hall and Castle

1993. 125th Anniv of Coburg Association of University Student Unions.
2521 **1040** 100pf. black, grn & red 1·90 85

1041 *Hohentwiel* (lake steamer) and Flags

1993. Lake Constance European Region.
2522 **1041** 100pf. multicoloured 2·00 85

1042 "Old Market—View of St. Nicholas's Church" (detail, Ferdinand von Arnim)

1993. Millenary of Potsdam.
2523 **1042** 80pf. multicoloured 2·00 85

1043 Holderlin (after Franz Hiemer)

1993. 150th Death Anniv of Friedrich Holderlin (poet).
2524 **1043** 100pf. multicoloured 2·00 85

1044 "If People can fly to the Moon, why can't they do anything about so many Children dying?"

1993. 40th Anniv of German United Nations Children's Fund Committee.
2525 **1044** 100pf. multicoloured 1·90 85

1993. Lander of the Federal Republic. As T **989**. Multicoloured.
2526 100pf. Mecklenburg-Vorpommern 2·00 1·10

1993. Lander of the Federal Republic. As T **989**. Multicoloured.
2527 100pf. Lower Saxony 2·00 1·10

1045 Fallada (after E. O. Plauen)

1993. Birth Centenary of Hans Fallada (writer).
2528 **1045** 100pf. green, brn & red 2·10 85

1046 Harz Mountain Range

1993. Landscapes (1st series). Multicoloured.
2529 100pf. Type **1046** 2·00 1·10
2530 100pf. Rugen 2·00 1·10
2531 100pf. Hohe Rhon 2·00 1·10
See also Nos. 2585/8, 2646/9, 2709/12 and 2806/8.

1047 Stages of Manufacture

1993. 250th Death Anniv of Mathias Klotz (violin maker).
2532 **1047** 80pf. multicoloured 1·70 70

1048 George as Gotz von Berlichingen in Goethe's "Urgotz"

1993. Birth Centenary of Heinrich George (actor).
2533 **1048** 100pf. multicoloured 1·90 85

1993. Lander of the Federal Republic. As T **989**. Multicoloured.
2534 100pf. Nordrhein-Westfalen 2·00 1·10

1049 Digitalised Eye and Ear

1993. International Radio Exhibition, Berlin.
2535 **1049** 100pf. multicoloured 1·90 85

1050 Swedish Flag, Heart and Cross

1993. Birth Centenary of Birger Forell (founder of Espelkamp (town for war refugees)).
2536 **1050** 100pf. yell, ultram & bl 2·40 85

1051 "Tuledu Bridge" (engraving)

1993. Birth Centenary of Hans Leip (writer and artist).
2537 **1051** 100pf. black, red & blue 2·40 85

1052 Singing Clown

1993. "For Us Children". Sheet 49×83 mm.
MS2538 **1052** 100pf. multicoloured 2·50 2·50

1993. Lander of the Federal Republic. As T **989**. Multicoloured.
2539 100pf. Rheinland-Pfalz 2·00 1·10

1053 Postman delivering Letter

1993. Stamp Day.
2540 **1053** 100pf.+50pf. multicoloured 2·40 2·40

1054 *Swan Lake*

1993. Death Centenary of Pyotr Tchaikovsky (composer).
2541 **1054** 80pf. multicoloured 2·00 85

1055 Fohr, Schleswig-Holstein

1993. Humanitarian Relief Funds. Traditional Costumes (1st series). Multicoloured.
2542 80pf.+40pf. Type **1055** 2·10 2·10
2543 80pf.+40pf. Rugen, Mecklenburg-Vorpommern 2·10 2·10
2544 100pf.+50pf. Oberndorf, Bavaria 2·40 2·40
2545 100pf.+50pf. Schwalm, Hesse 2·40 2·40
2546 200pf.+40pf. Ernstroda, Thuringia 4·00 4·00
See also Nos. 2598/2602.

1056 St. Jadwiga (miniature, Schlackenwerther Codex)

1993. 750th Death Anniv of St. Jadwiga of Silesia.
2547 **1056** 100pf. multicoloured 2·40 85

1057 Reinhardt on Stage

1993. 50th Death Anniv of Max Reinhardt (theatrical producer).
2548 **1057** 100pf. black, brn & red 2·40 85

1058 Brandt

1993. 80th Birth Anniv of Willy Brandt (statesman).
2549 **1058** 100pf. multicoloured 3·00 1·40

1059 Monteverdi

1993. 350th Death Anniv of Claudio Monteverdi (composer).
2550 **1059** 100pf. multicoloured 2·40 85

1060 Paracelsus (after Augustin Hirschvogel)

1993. 500th Birth Anniv of Paracelsus (physician and philosopher).
2551 **1060** 100pf. ochre, brown and green 2·40 85

1061 "Adoration of the Magi"

1993. Christmas. Carvings from Altar Triptych, Blaubeuren Minster. Multicoloured.
2552 80pf.+40pf. Type **1061** 1·40 1·40
2553 100pf.+50pf. "Birth of Christ" 2·50 2·40

1062 Quayside Buildings, Town Hall and St. Cosmas's Church

1994. Millenary of Stade.
2554 **1062** 80pf. red, brown & blue 1·70 85

1063 "FAMILIE"

1994. International Year of the Family.
| 2555 | **1063** | 100pf. multicoloured | 2·10 | 1·10 |

1994. Lander of the Federal Republic. As T **989**. Multicoloured.
| 2556 | | 100pf. Saarland | 2·00 | 1·10 |

1064 Hertz and Electromagnetic Waves

1994. Death Centenary of Heinrich Hertz (physicist).
| 2557 | **1064** | 200pf. black, red and drab | 4·00 | 1·70 |

1065 Frankfurt am Main

1994. 1200th Anniv of Frankfurt am Main.
| 2558 | **1065** | 80pf. multicoloured | 1·70 | 85 |

1066 Ice Skating

1994. Sport Promotion Fund. Sporting Events and Anniversaries. Multicoloured.
2559		80pf.+40pf. Type **1066** (Winter Olympic Games, Lillehammer, Norway)	2·20	2·10
2560		100pf.+50pf. Football and trophy (World Cup Football Championship, U.S.A.)	2·50	2·40
2561		100pf.+50pf. Flame (cent of International Olympic Committee)	2·50	2·40
2562		200pf.+80pf. Skier (Winter Paralympic Games, Lillehammer)	4·25	4·00

1067 Cathedral, St. Michael's Church and Castle

1994. 1250th Anniv of Fulda.
| 2563 | **1067** | 80pf. multicoloured | 1·90 | 85 |

1068 Council Emblem

1994. Cent of Federation of German Women's Associations—German Women's Council.
| 2564 | **1068** | 100pf. black, red & yell | 2·10 | 95 |

1069 Members' Flags as Stars

1994. Fourth Direct Elections to European Parliament.
| 2565 | **1069** | 100pf. multicoloured | 2·40 | 1·10 |

1070 People holding Banner

1994. "Living Together" (integration of foreign workers in Germany).
| 2566 | **1070** | 100pf. multicoloured | 2·40 | 1·10 |

1994. Lander of the Federal Republic. As T **989**. Multicoloured.
| 2567 | | 100pf. Saxony | 2·00 | 1·10 |

1071 Johnny Head-in-the-Air

1994. Youth Welfare. Death Centenary of Heinrich Hoffmann (writer). Designs illustrating characters from *Slovenly Peter*. Multicoloured.
2568		80pf.+40pf. Type **1071**	2·40	2·40
2569		80pf.+40pf. Little Pauline	2·40	2·40
2570		100pf.+50pf. Naughty Friederich	2·50	2·50
2571		100pf.+50pf. Slovenly Peter	2·50	2·50
2572		200pf.+80pf. Fidget-Philipp	3·75	3·75

1072 Frauenkirche

1994. 500th Anniv of Frauenkirche, Munich.
| 2573 | **1072** | 100pf. multicoloured | 2·75 | 1·20 |

1073 Resistor and Formula

1994. Europa. Discoveries. Multicoloured.
| 2574 | | 80pf. Type **1073** (Ohm's Law) | 1·50 | 70 |
| 2575 | | 100pf. Radiation from black body and formula (Max Planck's Quantum Theory) | 1·90 | 70 |

1074 Pfitzner (after Emil Orlik)

1994. 125th Birth Anniv of Hans Pfitzner (composer).
| 2576 | **1074** | 100pf. deep blue, blue and red | 2·10 | 95 |

1075 Hegenbeck and Animals

1994. 150th Anniversaries. Sheet 77×108 mm containing T **1075** and similar horiz design. Multicoloured.
MS2577 100pf. Type **1075** (birth anniv of Carl Hagenbeck (circus owner and founder of first zoo without bars)); 200pf. Animals and entrance to Berlin Zoo
| | | | 5·00 | 6·00 |

1076 Spandau Castle

1994. 400th Anniv of Spandau Castle.
| 2578 | **1076** | 80pf. multicoloured | 1·80 | 85 |

1077 Village Sign showing Society Emblem

1994. Centenary of Herzogsagmuhle (Society for the Domestic Missions welfare village).
| 2579 | **1077** | 100pf. multicoloured | 1·90 | 95 |

1994. Lander of the Federal Republic. As T **989**. Multicoloured.
| 2580 | | 100pf. Saxony-Anhalt | 2·00 | 1·10 |

1078 Heart inside Square

1994. Environmental Protection.
| 2581 | **1078** | 100pf.+50pf. green and black | 2·40 | 2·40 |

1079 Friedrich II (13th-century miniature, "Book of Falcons")

1994. 800th Birth Anniv of Emperor Friedrich II.
| 2582 | **1079** | 400pf. multicoloured | 6·50 | 6·00 |

1080 "20 JULY 1944" behind Bars

1994. 50th Anniv of Attempt to Assassinate Hitler. Sheet 105×70 mm.
MS2583 **1080** 100pf. black, yellow and red
| | | | 3·00 | 3·00 |

1994. Lander of the Federal Republic. As T **989**. Multicoloured.
| 2584 | | 100pf. Schleswig-Holstein | 2·00 | 1·10 |

1994. Landscapes (2nd series). As T **1046**. Multicoloured.
2585		100pf. The Alps	1·70	1·20
2586		100pf. Erzgebirge	1·70	1·20
2587		100pf. Main valley	1·70	1·20
2588		100pf. Mecklenburg lakes	1·70	1·20

1081 Herder (after Anton Graff)

1994. 250th Birth Anniv of Johann Gottfried Herder (philosopher).
| 2589 | **1081** | 80pf. multicoloured | 1·50 | 85 |

1994. 20th-century German Paintings (3rd series). As T **1003**. Multicoloured.
2590		100pf. *Maika* (Christian Schad)	1·40	95
2591		200pf. *Dresden Landscape* (Erich Heckel)	2·75	2·40
2592		300pf. *Aleksei Javlensky and Marianne Werefkin* (Gabriele Munter)	4·25	3·75

1082 Early 20th-century Makonde Mask (Tanzania)

1994. 125th Anniv of Leipzig Ethnology Museum.
| 2593 | **1082** | 80pf. multicoloured | 1·80 | 85 |

1083 Helmholtz, Eye and Colour Triangle

1994. Death Centenary of Hermann von Helmholtz (physicist).
| 2594 | **1083** | 100pf. multicoloured | 2·10 | 85 |

1084 Richter

1994. Birth Cent of Willi Richter (President of Confederation of German Trade Unions).
| 2595 | **1084** | 100pf. brown, purple and black | 2·10 | 85 |

1085 "Flying on Dragon"

1994. "For Us Children". Sheet 106×61 mm.
MS2596 **1085** 100pf. multicoloured
| | | | 3·00 | 3·00 |

1994. Lander of the Federal Republic. As T **989**. Multicoloured.
| 2597 | | 100pf. Thuringia | 2·00 | 1·10 |

1994. Humanitarian Relief Funds. Traditional Costumes (2nd series). As T **1055**. Multicoloured.
2598		80pf.+40pf. Buckeburg	1·80	1·80
2599		80pf.+40pf. Halle an der Saale	1·80	1·80
2600		100pf.+50pf. Minden	2·40	2·40
2601		100pf.+50pf. Hoyerswerda	2·40	2·40
2602		200pf.+70pf. Betzingen	3·75	3·75

1086 St. Wolfgang with Church Model (woodcut)

1994. Death Millenary of St. Wolfgang, Bishop of Regensburg.
| 2603 | **1086** | 100pf. gold, cream and black | 1·90 | 95 |

1087 Sachs

1994. 500th Birth Anniv of Hans Sachs (mastersinger and poet).
| 2604 | **1087** | 100pf. purple and green on greyish | 1·90 | 95 |

1088 Spreewald Postman, 1900

1994. Stamp Day.
| 2605 | **1088** | 100pf. multicoloured | 1·90 | 95 |

1089 Quedlinburg

1994. Millenary of Quedlinburg.
| 2606 | **1089** | 80pf. multicoloured | 1·50 | 85 |

1090 "Adoration of the Magi"

1994. Christmas. 500th Death Anniv of Hans Memling (painter). Details of his triptych in St. John's Hospice, Bruges. Multicoloured.
| 2607 | | 80pf.+40pf. Type **1090** | 2·00 | 1·90 |
| 2608 | | 100pf.+50pf. "Nativity" | 2·50 | 2·40 |

1091 Steuben and "Surrender of Cornwallis at Yorktown" (detail, John Trumbull)

1994. Death Bicentenary of Gen. Friedrich Wilhelm von Steuben (Inspector General of Washington's Army).
| 2609 | **1091** | 100pf. multicoloured | 1·90 | 95 |

1092 Cemetery

1994. 75th Anniv of National Assn for the Preservation of German Graves Abroad.
| 2610 | **1092** | 100pf. black and red | 1·90 | 95 |

1093 Obersuhl Checkpoint, 11 November 1989

1994. Fifth Anniv of Opening of Borders between East and West Germany.
2611	**1093**	100pf. multicoloured	1·90	95

1094 Fontane (after Max Liebermann) and Lines from "Prussian Song"

1994. 175th Birth Anniv of Theodor Fontane (writer).
2612	**1094**	100pf. green, black and mauve	1·90	95

1095 Simson Fountain, Town Hall and St. Mary's and St Salvator's Churches

1995. Millenary of Gera.
2613	**1095**	80pf. multicoloured	1·80	85

1096 Emperor Friedrich III, First Page of *Libellus* and Zur Munze (venue)

1995. 500th Anniv of Diet of Worms.
2614	**1096**	100pf. black and red	1·80	95

1995. 20th-century German Paintings (4th series). As T **1003**. Multicoloured.
2615	100pf. *The Water Tower, Bremen* (Franz Radziwill)	1·80	85
2616	200pf. *Still Life with Cat* (Georg Schrimpf)	2·75	2·40
2617	300pf. *Estate in Dangast* (Karl Schmidt-Rottluff)	4·00	3·50

1097 Canoeing

1995. Sport Promotion Fund. Multicoloured.
2618	80pf.+40pf. Type **1097** (27th World Canoeing Championships, Duisburg)	1·80	1·80
2619	100pf.+50pf. Hoop exercises (10th Int Gymnastics Festival, Berlin)	1·80	1·80
2620	100pf.+50pf. Boxing (8th World Amateur Boxing Championships, Berlin)	1·80	1·80
2621	200pf.+80pf. Volleyball (centenary)	3·75	3·75

1098 Friedrich Wilhelm (after A. Romandon)

1995. 375th Birth Anniv of Friedrich Wilhelm of Brandenburg, The Great Elector.
2622	**1098**	300pf. multicoloured	4·75	3·75

1099 Deed of Donation (995) and Arms of Mecklenburg-Vorpommern

1995. Millenary of Mecklenburg.
2623	**1099**	100pf. multicoloured	1·50	95

1100 Computer Image of Terminal and Lion

1995. 250th Anniv of Carolo-Wilhelmina Technical University, Braunschweig.
2624	**1100**	100pf. multicoloured	1·50	95

1101 X-ray of Hand

1995. 150th Birth Anniv of Wilhelm Rontgen and Centenary of his Discovery of X-rays.
2625	**1101**	100pf. multicoloured	1·50	95

1102 Globe and Rainbow

1995. First Conference of Signatories to General Convention on Climate, Berlin.
2626	**1102**	100pf. multicoloured	1·50	95

1103 Old Town Hall Reliefs

1995. 750th Anniv of Regensburg.
2627	**1103**	80pf. multicoloured	1·30	85

1104 Bonhoeffer

1995. 50th Death Anniv of Dietrich Bonhoeffer (theologian).
2628	**1104**	100pf. black, bl & grey	1·50	95

1105 Symbols of Speech, Writing and Pictures

1995. Freedom of Expression.
2629	**1105**	100pf. multicoloured	1·50	95

1106 St. Clement's Church, Munster

1995. 300th Birth Anniv of Johann Conrad Schlaun (architect).
2630	**1106**	200pf. multicoloured	3·00	2·50

1107 Friedrich Schiller, Signature and Schiller Museum, Marbach

1995. Centenary of German Schiller Society.
2631	**1107**	100pf. multicoloured	1·50	95

1108 St. Vincent de Paul

1995. 150th Anniv of Vincent Conferences (charitable organization) in Germany.
2632	**1108**	100pf. multicoloured	1·50	1·10

1109 Number on Cloth and Barbed Wire

1995. 50th Anniv of Liberation of Concentration Camps. Sheet 105×70 mm.
MS2633	**1109** 100pf. grey, blue and black	2·40	2·50

1110 City Ruins

1995. 50th Anniv of End of Second World War. Sheet 104×70 mm containing T **1110** and similar square design. Multicoloured.
MS2634	100pf. Type **1110**; 100pf. Refugees	4·00	4·25

1111 Returning Soldiers ("End of War")

1995. Europa. Peace and Freedom.
2635	**1111**	100pf. black and red	1·80	1·20
2636	–	200pf. blue, yell & blk	2·50	2·40

DESIGN: 200pf. Emblem of European Community ("Moving towards Europe").

1112 Shipping Routes before and after 1895

1995. Centenary of Kiel Canal.
2637	**1112**	80pf. multicoloured	1·80	85

1113 Guglielmo Marconi and Wireless Equipment

1995. 100 Years of Radio.
2638	**1113**	100pf. multicoloured	1·90	1·30

1114 U.N. Emblem

1995. 50th Anniv of U.N.O.
2639	**1114**	100pf. lilac, gold and grey	1·50	95

1115 Munsterlander

1995. Youth Welfare. Dogs (1st series). Multicoloured.
2640	80pf.+40pf. Type **1115**	1·80	1·80
2641	80pf.+40pf. Giant schnauzer	1·80	1·80
2642	100pf.+50pf. Wire-haired dachshund	2·00	2·00
2643	100pf.+50pf. German shepherd	2·00	2·00
2644	200pf.+80pf. Keeshund	3·50	3·50

See also Nos. 2696/2700.

1116 Opening Bars of *Carmina Burana* and Characters

1995. Birth Centenary of Carl Orff (composer).
2645	**1116**	100pf. multicoloured	1·50	95

1995. Landscapes (3rd series). As T **1046**. Multicoloured.
2646	100pf. Franconian Switzerland	1·40	1·20
2647	100pf. River Havel, Berlin	1·40	1·20
2648	100pf. Oberlausitz	1·40	1·20
2649	100pf. Sauerland	1·40	1·20

1117 Lion (from 12th-century coin)

1995. 800th Death Anniv of Henry the Lion, Duke of Saxony and Bavaria.
2650	**1117**	400pf. multicoloured	4·75	4·75

1118 Kaiser Wilhelm Memorial Church

1995. Centenary of Kaiser Wilhelm Memorial Church, Berlin.
2651	**1118**	100pf. multicoloured	1·70	95

1119 Werfel and Signature

1995. 50th Death Anniv of Franz Werfel (writer).
2652	**1119**	100pf. mauve, bl & blk	1·50	95

1995. Tourist Sights. As T **854** but inscr "DEUTSCHLAND".
2654	47pf. green and black	85	70
2656	100pf. blue and black	1·20	1·20
2657	110pf. cinnamon and brown	1·30	60
2658	110pf. orange and blue	1·50	95
2659	220pf. green and black	2·40	1·20
2661	440pf. orange and blue	6·00	5·25
2663	510pf. red and blue	6·00	6·00
2665	640pf. blue and brown	8·25	4·75
2666	690pf. black and green	8·50	5·25

DESIGNS: 47pf. Berus Monument, Uberherrn; 100pf. Goethe-Schiller Monument, Weimar; 110pf. (2657) Belle-vue Castle, Berlin; 110pf. (2658) Emblem of "Expo 2000" World's Fair, Hanover; 220pf. Bruhl's Terrace, Dresden; 440pf. Town Hall, Bremen; 510pf. Holsten Gate, Lubeck; 640pf. Speyer Cathedral; 690pf. St. Michael's Church, Hamburg.

1120 Strauss

1995. 80th Birth Anniv of Franz Josef Strauss (politician).
2675	**1120**	100pf. multicoloured	1·80	1·20

1121 Postwoman

1995. Stamp Day.
2676	**1121**	200pf.+100pf. mult	4·25	4·25

1122 *Metropolis* (dir. Fritz Lang)

1995. Centenary of Motion Pictures. Sheet 100×130 mm containing T **1122** and similar horiz designs showing frames from films. Multicoloured.
MS2677 80pf. Type **1122**; 100pf. *Little Superman* (dir. Wolfgang Staudte); 200pf. *The Sky over Berlin* (dir. Wim Wenders)   7·00   8·25

1123 Eifel

1995. Humanitarian Relief Funds. Farmhouses (1st series). Multicoloured.

2678	80pf.+40pf. Type **1123**		1·70	1·50
2679	80pf.+40pf. Saxony		1·70	1·50
2680	100pf.+50pf. Lower Germany		1·90	1·80
2681	100pf.+50pf. Upper Bavaria		1·90	1·80
2682	200pf.+70pf. Mecklenburg		3·50	3·50

See also Nos. 2742/6.

1124 Schumacher

1995. Birth Centenary of Kurt Schumacher (politician).
2683 **1124** 100pf. multicoloured   1·50   95

1125 Animals gathered on Hill

1995. "For Us Children". Sheet 110×60 mm.
MS2684 **1125** 80pf. multicoloured   4·00   4·50

1126 Ranke

1995. Birth Bicentenary of Leopold von Ranke (historian).
2685 **1126** 80pf. multicoloured   1·20   85

1127 Hindemith

1995. Birth Centenary of Paul Hindemith (composer).
2686 **1127** 100pf. multicoloured   1·50   95

1128 Alfred Nobel and Will

1995. Centenary of Nobel Prize Trust Fund.
2687 **1128** 100pf. multicoloured   1·90   1·40

1129 "CARE" in American Colours

1995. 50th Anniv of CARE (Co-operative for Assistance and Remittances Overseas).
2688 **1129** 100pf. multicoloured   1·50   95

1130 Berlin Wall

1995. Commemorating Victims of Political Oppression, 1945–89.
2689 **1130** 100pf. multicoloured   1·50   95

1131 "The Annunciation"

1995. Christmas. Stained Glass Windows in Augsburg Cathedral. Multicoloured.

2690	80pf.+40pf. Type **1131**	1·80	1·70
2691	100pf.+50pf. "Nativity"	2·40	2·40

1132 Dribbling

1995. Borussia Dortmund, German Football Champions.
2692 **1132** 100pf. multicoloured   2·10   1·20

1133 Auguste von Sartorius (founder)

1996. 150th Anniv of German Institute for Children's Missionary Work.
2693 **1133** 100pf. multicoloured   1·40   1·10

1134 Bodelschwingh

1996. 50th Death Anniv of Friedrich von Bodelschwingh (theologian).
2694 **1134** 100pf. black and red   1·40   1·10

1135 Luther (after Lucas Cranach)

1996. 450th Death Anniv of Martin Luther (Protestant reformer).
2695 **1135** 100pf. multicoloured   1·50   1·30

1996. Youth Welfare. Dogs (2nd series). As T **1115**. Multicoloured.

2696	80pf.+40pf. Borzoi	1·90	1·90
2697	80pf.+40pf. Chow chow	1·90	1·90
2698	100pf.+50pf. St. Bernard	2·40	2·40
2699	100pf.+50pf. Rough collie	2·40	2·40
2700	200pf.+80pf. Briard	3·50	3·50

1136 Siebold

1996. Birth Bicentenary of Philipp Franz von Siebold (physician and Japanologist).
2701 **1136** 100pf. multicoloured   1·50   1·30

1137 Cathedral Square

1996. Millenary of Cathedral Square, Halberstadt.
2702 **1137** 80pf. multicoloured   1·10   70

1138 Galen

1996. 50th Death Anniv of Cardinal Count Clemens von Galen, Bishop of Munster.
2703 **1138** 100pf. grey, blue & gold   1·40   95

1996. 20th-century German Paintings (5th series). As T **1003**. Multicoloured.

2704	100pf. *Seated Female Nude* (Max Pechstein)	1·40	1·40
2705	200pf. *For Wilhelm Runge* (Georg Muche)	2·75	2·40
2706	300pf. *Still Life with Guitar, Book and Vase* (Helmut Kolle)	3·50	3·50

1139 Detail of Ceiling Fresco, Prince-bishop's Residence, Wurzburg

1996. 300th Birth Anniv of Giovanni Battista Tiepolo (artist).
2707 **1139** 200pf. multicoloured   2·50   2·20

1140 Post Runner

1996. "For Us Children". Sheet 83×67 mm.
MS2708 **1140** 100pf. multicoloured   2·10   2·40

1996. Landscapes (4th series). As T **1046**. Multicoloured.

2709	100pf. Eifel	1·40	1·20
2710	100pf. Holstein Switzerland	1·40	1·20
2711	100pf. Saale	1·40	1·20
2712	100pf. Spreewald	1·40	1·20

1141 *Paula Modersohn-Becker* (self-portrait)

1996. Europa. Famous Women.

2713	**1141** 80pf. multicoloured	1·40	60
2714	– 100pf. black, grey and mauve	1·50	1·20

DESIGN: 100pf. *Kathe Kollwitz* (self-portrait).

1142 Opening Lines of Document and Town (1642 engraving, Matthaeus Merian)

1996. Millenary of Granting to Freising the Right to hold Markets.
2715 **1142** 100pf. multicoloured   1·40   1·10

1143 Borchert

1996. 75th Birth Anniv of Wolfgang Borchert (writer).
2716 **1143** 100pf. multicoloured   1·40   1·10

1144 Emblem

1996. 50th Anniv of Ruhr Festival, Recklinghausen.
2717 **1144** 100pf. multicoloured   1·40   1·10

1145 Ticket and Stage Curtain

1996. 150th Anniv of German Theatre Assn.
2718 **1145** 200pf. multicoloured   2·50   1·80

1146 Leibniz and Mathematical Diagram

1996. 350th Birth Anniv of Gottfried Leibniz.
2719 **1146** 100pf. red and black   1·40   1·10

1147 Kneeling Figure and Motto forming "A"

1996. 300th Anniv of Berlin Academy of Arts.
2720 **1147** 100pf. multicoloured   1·40   1·10

1148 Carl Schuhmann (wrestling, equestrian sports and gymnastics, 1896)

1996. Sport Promotion Fund. Centenary of Modern Olympic Games. German Olympic Champions. Multicoloured.

2721	80pf.+40pf. Type **1148**	3·00	2·40
2722	100pf.+50pf. Josef Neckermann (dressage, 1964 and 1968)	3·50	2·75
2723	100pf.+50pf. Annie Hubler-Horn (ice skating, 1908)	3·50	2·75
2724	200pf.+80pf. Alfred and Gustav Flatow (gymnastics, 1896)	5·00	4·00

1149 Townscape

1996. 800th Anniv of Heidelberg.
2725 **1149** 100pf. multicoloured   1·40   1·10

1150 Children's Handprints

1996. 50th Anniv of UNICEF.
2726 **1150** 100pf. multicoloured   1·40   1·10

1151 "Wedding" (illustration by Bruno Paul)

1996. 75th Death Anniv of Ludwig Thoma (satirist).
2727 **1151** 100pf. multicoloured   1·40   1·10

1152 Beach

1996. Western Pomerania National Park. Sheet 166×111 mm containing T **1152** and similar horiz designs showing Park landscapes. Multicoloured.
MS2728 100pf. Type **1152**; 200pf.
Mudflat; 300pf. Sea inlet   8·75   8·75

1153 Map and Tropical Wildlife

1996. Environmental Protection. Preservation of Tropical Habitats.
2729 **1153** 100pf.+50pf. mult   2·10   2·40

1154 Volklingen Blast Furnace

1996. UNESCO World Heritage Sites.
2730 **1154** 100pf. multicoloured   1·40   1·10

1155 Lincke

1996. 50th Death Anniv of Paul Lincke (composer and conductor).
2731 **1155** 100pf. multicoloured   1·40   1·10

1156 Gendarmenmarkt, Berlin

1996. Images of Germany.
2732 **1156** 100pf. multicoloured   1·40   1·10

1157 "50" comprising Stamp under Magnifying Glass

1996. Stamp Day. 50th Anniv of Association of German Philatelists.
2733 **1157** 100pf. multicoloured   1·40   1·10

1158 Book

1996. Centenary of German Civil Code.
2734 **1158** 300pf. multicoloured   3·75   3·50

1159 Players

1996. Borussia Dortmund, German Football Champions.
2735 **1159** 100pf. multicoloured   1·40   1·10

1160 Bamburg Old Town

1996. UNESCO World Heritage Sites.
2736 **1160** 100pf. multicoloured   1·40   1·10

1161 Eyes

1996. "Life without Drugs".
2737 **1161** 100pf. multicoloured   1·40   1·10

1162 "Like will Cure Like" and Samuel Hahnemann (developer of principle)

1996. Bicentenary of Homeopathy.
2738 **1162** 400pf. multicoloured   4·50   4·50

1163 Bruckner and *Symphony No. III*

1996. Death Centenary of Anton Bruckner (composer).
2739 **1163** 100pf. multicoloured   1·40   1·10

1164 Mueller, Map and Plants

1996. Death Centenary of Ferdinand von Mueller (botanist).
2740 **1164** 100pf. multicoloured   1·40   1·10

1165 Score by John Cage

1996. 75th Anniv of Donaueschingen Music Festival.
2741 **1165** 100pf. blue, blk & mve   1·40   1·10

1996. Humanitarian Relief Funds. Farmhouses (2nd series). As T **1123**. Multicoloured.
2742	80pf.+40pf.	Spree Forest	1·40	1·20
2743	80pf.+40pf.	Thuringia	1·40	1·20
2744	100pf.+50pf.	Black Forest	1·70	1·70
2745	100pf.+50pf.	Westphalia	1·70	1·70
2746	200pf.+70pf.	Schleswig-Holstein	3·25	3·25

1166 Titles of Plays and Zuckmayer

1996. Birth Centenary of Carl Zuckmayer (dramatist).
2747 **1166** 100pf. multicoloured   1·40   1·10

1167 "Adoration of the Magi"

1996. Christmas. Illustrations from Henry II's *Book of Pericopes* (illuminated manuscript of readings from the Gospels). Multicoloured.
2748	80pf.+40pf.	Type **1167**	1·80	1·80
2749	100pf.+50pf.	*Nativity*	2·10	2·40

1168 Schmid

1996. Birth Centenary of Carlo Schmid (politician and writer).
2750 **1168** 100pf. multicoloured   1·40   1·10

1169 *Friends of Schubert in Afzenbrugg* (detail, L. Kupelwieser)

1997. Birth Bicentenary of Franz Schubert (composer).
2751 **1169** 100pf. multicoloured   1·40   1·10

1170 Pitch, Player and Herberger

1997. Birth Centenary of Sepp Herberger (national football team coach, 1936–64).
2752 **1170** 100pf. green, red & blk   1·40   1·10

1171 Motor Cars

1997. "More Safety for Children" (road safety campaign).
2752a	**1171**	10pf. multicoloured	45	35
2753	**1171**	100pf. multicoloured	1·40	1·10

1172 Melanchthon (after Lucas Cranach the younger)

1997. 500th Birth Anniv of Philipp Melanchthon (religious reformer).
2754 **1172** 100pf. multicoloured   1·40   1·10

1173 Revellers "Wiggling"

1997. 175th Anniv of Cologne Carnival.
2755 **1173** 100pf. multicoloured   1·40   1·10

1174 Erhard

1997. Birth Centenary of Ludwig Erhard (Chancellor, 1963–66).
2756 **1174** 100pf. black and red   1·40   1·10

1175 Aerobics

1997. Sport Promotion Fund. Fun Sports. Multicoloured.
2757	80pf.+40pf.	Type **1175**	1·70	1·90
2758	100pf.+50pf.	Inline skating	1·90	2·10
2759	100pf.+50pf.	Streetball	1·90	2·10
2760	200pf.+80pf.	Freeclimbing	3·50	4·00

1176 New Pavilion

1997. 500th Anniv of Granting of Imperial Fair Rights to Leipzig.
2761 **1176** 100pf. silver, red & blue   1·40   1·10

1177 Philharmonic, Berlin (Hans Scharoun)

1997. Post-1945 German Architecture. Sheet 137×101 mm containing T **1177** and similar square designs. Multicoloured.
MS2762 100pf. Type **1177**; 100pf. National Gallery, Berlin (Ludwig Miles van der Rohe); 100pf. St. Mary, Queen of Peace Pilgrimage Church, Neviges (Gottfried Bohm); 100pf. German Pavilion, 1967 World's Trade Fair, Montreal (Frei Otto)   6·00   6·25

1178 Straubing

1997. 1100th Anniv of Straubing.
2763 **1178** 100pf. multicoloured   1·40   1·10

1179 Stephan, Telephone and Postcards

1997. Death Centenary of Heinrich von Stephan (founder of U.P.U.).
2764 **1179** 100pf. multicoloured   1·40   1·10

1180 Augustusburg and Falkenlust Castles

1997. UNESCO World Heritage Sites.
2765 **1180** 100pf. multicoloured   1·40   1·10

1181 Diamonds

1997. 500th Anniv of Idar-Oberstein Region Gem Industry.
2766 **1181** 300pf. multicoloured   4·25   3·50

1182 St. Adalbert

1997. Death Millenary of St. Adalbert (Bishop of Prague).
2767 **1182** 100pf. lilac   1·40   1·10

1183 *The Fisherman and His Wife* (Brothers Grimm)

1997. Europa. Tales and Legends. Multicoloured.

| 2768 | 80pf. Type **1183** | 1·40 | 95 |
| 2769 | 100pf. *Rubezahl* | 1·70 | 1·20 |

1184 Knotted Ribbons

1997. 50th Anniv of Town Twinning Movement.

| 2770 | **1184** | 100pf. multicoloured | 1·40 | 1·10 |

1185 Deciduous Trees

1997. 50th Anniv of Society for the Protection of the German Forest. Sheet 105×70 mm containing T **1185** and similar square design. Multicoloured.
MS2771 100pf. Type **1185**; 200pf.
  Evergreen trees   4·75   4·75

1186 Kneipp

1997. Death Cent of Father Sebastian Kneipp (developer of naturopathic treatments).

| 2772 | **1186** | 100pf. multicoloured | 1·40 | 1·10 |

1187 United States Flag, George Marshall and Bomb Site

1997. 50th Anniv of Marshall Plan (European Recovery Program).

| 2773 | **1187** | 100pf. multicoloured | 1·40 | 1·10 |

1188 Rheno-German Heavy Horse

1997. Youth Welfare. Horses. Multicoloured.

2774	80pf.+40pf. Type **1188**	1·50	1·50
2775	80pf.+40pf. Shetland ponies	1·50	1·50
2776	100pf.+50pf. Frisian	1·80	1·80
2777	100pf.+50pf. Haflinger	1·80	1·80
2778	200pf.+80pf. Hanoverian with foal	3·75	3·75

1189 Train on Bridge

1997. Centenary of Mungsten Railway Bridge.

| 2779 | **1189** | 100pf. multicoloured | 1·40 | 1·10 |

1190 *Composition* (Fritz Winter)

1997. Tenth "Documenta" Modern Art Exhibition, Kassel. Sheet 137×97 mm containing T **1190** and similar horiz designs. Multicoloured.
MS2780 100pf. Type **1190**; 100pf.
  Mouth No. 15 (Tom Wesselmann);
  100pf. *Quathlamba* (Frank Stella);
  100pf. *"euys/Bois* (Nam June Paik)   6·50   6·50

1191 Children holding Envelopes

1997. "For Us Children". Sheet 70×105 mm.
MS2781 **1191** 100pf. multicoloured   2·40   2·40

1997. Famous Women. As T **832** but inscr "Deutschland".

2785	100pf. brown and green	1·50	1·00
2786	110pf. drab and violet	1·50	1·00
2790	220pf. ultramarine and blue	3·00	2·75
2792	300pf. brown and blue	3·50	3·00
2795	440pf. brown and violet	6·25	6·00

DESIGNS: 100pf. Elisabeth Schwarzhaupt (politician); 110pf. Marlene Dietrich (actress); 220pf. Marie-Elisabeth Luders (politician); 300pf. Maria Probst (social reformer and politician); 440pf. Gret Palucca (dancer).

Nos. 2796/2804 are vacant.

1192 Arms of Brandenburg

1997. Flood Relief Funds.

| 2805 | **1192** | 110pf.+90pf. mult | 2·75 | 2·75 |

1997. Landscapes (5th series). As T **1046**. Multicoloured.

2806	110pf. Bavarian Forest	1·50	1·40
2807	110pf. North German Moors	1·50	1·40
2808	110pf. Luneburg Heath	1·50	1·40

1193 Rudolf Diesel and First Oil Engine

1997. Centenary of Diesel Engine.

| 2809 | **1193** | 300pf. black and blue | 4·00 | 3·50 |

1194 Potato Plant and Cultivation

1997. 350th Anniv of Introduction of the Potato to Germany.

| 2810 | **1194** | 300pf. multicoloured | 4·00 | 3·50 |

1195 Biplane and Motorized Tricycle

1997. Stamp Day. Sheet 70×105 mm.
MS2811 **1195** 440pf.+220pf. multicoloured   8·25   8·50

1196 Mendelssohn-Bartholdy and Music Score

1997. 150th Death Anniv of Felix Mendelssohn-Bartholdy (composer).

| 2813 | **1196** | 110pf. green, olive & yell | 1·50 | 1·20 |

1197 Watermill, Black Forest

1997. Humanitarian Relief Funds. Mills. Multicoloured.

2814	100pf.+50pf. Type **1197**	2·75	2·75
2815	110pf.+50pf. Watermill, Hesse	3·00	3·00
2816	110pf.+50pf. Post mill, Lower Rhine	3·00	3·00
2817	110pf.+50pf. Scoop windmill, Schleswig-Holstein	3·00	3·00
2818	220pf.+80pf. Dutch windmill	4·75	4·75

1198 Emblem

1997. Saar–Lor–Lux European Region.

| 2819 | **1198** | 110pf. multicoloured | 1·70 | 1·20 |

1199 Team celebrating

1997. Bayern Munchen, German Football Champions.

| 2820 | **1199** | 110pf. multicoloured | 1·70 | 1·20 |

1200 Dehler

1997. Birth Centenary of Thomas Dehler (politician).

| 2821 | **1200** | 110pf. multicoloured | 1·40 | 1·20 |

1201 Heine (after Wilhelm Hensel)

1997. Birth Bicentenary of Heinrich Heine (journalist and poet).

| 2822 | **1201** | 110pf. multicoloured | 1·40 | 1·20 |

1202 Tree and Title of Hymn

1997. 300th Birth Anniv of Gerhard Tersteegen (religious reformer).

| 2823 | **1202** | 110pf. brown, grey and black | 1·40 | 1·20 |

1203 Emblem

1997. Cent of Deutscher Caritas Verband (Catholic charitable association).

| 2824 | **1203** | 110pf. multicoloured | 1·40 | 1·20 |

1204 Three Kings

1997. Christmas. Multicoloured.

| 2825 | 100pf.+50pf. Type **1204** | 1·90 | 1·80 |
| 2826 | 110pf.+50pf. Nativity | 2·20 | 2·20 |

The premium was for the benefit of the Federal Association of Free Welfare Work, Bonn.

1205 Monastery Plan and Church

1998. UNESCO World Heritage Site. Maulbronn Monastery.

| 2827 | **1205** | 100pf. multicoloured | 1·40 | 1·20 |

1206 Walled City

1998. 1100th Anniv of Nordlingen.

| 2828 | **1206** | 110pf. multicoloured | 1·40 | 1·20 |

1207 Glienicke Bridge, Potsdam–Berlin

1998. Bridges. (1st series).

| 2829 | **1207** | 110pf. multicoloured | 1·40 | 1·20 |

See also Nos. 2931, 2956 and 3046.

1208 Football

1998. Sport Promotion Fund. International Championships. Multicoloured.

2830	100pf.+50pf. Type **1208** (World Cup Football Championship, France)	2·40	2·40
2831	110pf.+50pf. Ski jumping (Winter Olympic Games, Nagano, Japan)	2·75	2·75
2832	110pf.+50pf. Rowing (World Rowing Championships, Cologne)	2·75	2·75
2833	300pf.+100pf. Disabled skier (Winter Paralympic Games, Nagano)	6·00	6·00

1209 Characters in Brecht's Head

1998. Birth Centenary of Bertolt Brecht (dramatist).

| 2834 | **1209** | 110pf. multicoloured | 1·40 | 1·20 |

1210 X-ray Photographs of Moon, Ionic Lattice Structure and Nerve of Goldfish and Founding Assembly

1998. 50th Anniv of Max Planck Society for the Advancement of Science.

| 2835 | **1210** | 110pf. multicoloured | 1·40 | 1·20 |

1211 Bad
Frankenhausen

1998. Millenary of First Documentary Mention of Bad
Frankenhausen.
2836 **1211** 110pf. multicoloured   1·40   1·20

1212 Signatories

1998. 350th Anniv of Peace of Westphalia (settlements
ending Thirty Years' War).
2837 **1212** 110pf. blk, grey & mve   1·70   1·20

1213 Baden-Wurttemberg (Kurt
Viertel)

1998. Federal State Parliament Buildings (1st series).
Multicoloured.
2838   110pf. Type **1213**   1·50   1·20
2839   110pf. Bavaria (designed
     Friedrich Burklein)   1·50   1·20
2840   110pf. Chamber of Deputies,
     Berlin (Friedrich Schulze)   1·50   1·20
2841   110pf. Brandenburg (Franz
     Schwechten)   1·50   1·20
   See also Nos. 2885, 2893/4, 2897, 2953, 2957, 2978,
3025, 3043, 3052, 3064 and 3071.

1214 Hildegard's
Vision of Life Cycle

1998. 900th Birth Anniv of Hildegard of Bingen (writer
and mystic).
2842 **1214** 100pf. multicoloured   1·40   1·20

1215 Marine Life

1998. "For Us Children". Sheet 110×66 mm.
MS2843 **1215** 110pf. multicoloured   2·40   2·40

1216 St. Marienstern Abbey

1998. 750th Anniv of St. Marienstern Abbey, Panschwitz-
Kuckau.
2844 **1216** 110pf. multicoloured   1·40   1·20

1217 Auditorium

1998. 250th Anniv of Bayreuth Opera House.
2845 **1217** 300pf. multicoloured   3·75   3·50

1218 Junger

1998. Ernst Junger (writer) Commemoration.
2846 **1218** 110pf. multicoloured   1·40   1·20

1219 Doves
and Tree
(German
Unification Day)

1998. Europa. National Festivals.
2847 **1219** 110pf. multicoloured   1·80   1·20

1220 Association
Manifesto

1998. 50th Anniv of German Rural Women's Association.
2848 **1220** 110pf. grn, emer & blk   1·40   1·20

1221 Opening Session
of Parliamentary
Council, 1948

1998. Parliamentary Anniversaries. Sheet 105×70 mm
containing T **1221** and similar square design.
Multicoloured.
MS2849 110pf. Type **1221**; 220pf. First
   German National Assembly, St. Paul's
   Church, Frankfurt, 1848   4·75   4·75

1222 Coast and Ocean

1998. Environmental Protection.
2850 **1222** 110pf.+50pf. mult   2·40   2·50

1223 "The Mouse"

1998. Youth Welfare. Children's Cartoons. Multicoloured.
2851   100pf.+50pf. Type **1223**   1·90   1·90
2852   100pf.+50pf. "The Sandman"   1·90   1·90
2853   110pf.+50pf. "Maja the Bee"   2·10   2·10
2854   110pf.+50pf. "Captain Bluebear"   2·10   2·10
2855   220pf.+80pf. "Pumuckl"   3·75   3·75

1224 Crowds of
People and Cross

1998. 150th Anniv of First Congress of German Catholics.
2856 **1224** 110pf. multicoloured   1·40   1·10

1225 One
Deutschmark Coin

1998. 50th Anniv of the Deutschmark.
2857 **1225** 110pf. multicoloured   2·10   1·40

1226 Harvesting Hops

1998. 1100 Years of Hop Cultivation in Germany.
2858 **1226** 110pf. multicoloured   1·40   1·20

1227 Euro Banknotes forming "EZB"

1998. Inauguration of European Central Bank, Frankfurt
am Main.
2859 **1227** 110pf. multicoloured   1·40   1·20

1228 Rock Face, Elbe
Sandstone Mountains

1998. Saxon Switzerland National Park. Sheet 105×70
mm containing T **1228** and similar square design.
Multicoloured.
MS2860 110pf. Type **1228**; 220pf. Elbe
   Sandstone Mountains   4·75   4·75

1229 Skeleton of Crocodile

1998. UNESCO World Heritage Sites. Grube Messel Fossil
Deposits.
2861 **1229** 100pf. multicoloured   1·40   1·10

1230 Coloured
Squares and
Ludolphian Number

1998. 23rd International Congress of Mathematicians,
Berlin.
2862 **1230** 110pf. multicoloured   1·40   1·20

1231 Wurzburg
Palace

1998. UNESCO World Heritage Sites. Multicoloured.
2863   110pf. Type **1231**   1·50   1·10
2864   110pf. Puning Temple,
     Chengde, China   1·50   1·10

1232 Glasses (Peter Behrens)

1998. Contemporary Design (1st series). Sheet 138×97
mm containing T **1232** and similar horiz designs.
Multicoloured.
MS2865 110pf. Type **1232**; 110pf. Tea-
   pot (Marianne Brandt); 110pf. Table
   lamp (Wilhelm Wagenfeld); 110pf.
   "Wassily" chair (Marcel Breuer)   6·50   6·50
   See also No. **MS**2922.

1233 Players, Ball and
Pitch

1998. First FC Kaiserslautern, National Football
Champions, 1998.
2866 **1233** 110pf. multicoloured   1·70   1·20

1234 Main Building

1998. 300th Anniv of Francke Charitable Institutions,
Halle.
2867 **1234** 110pf. multicoloured   1·40   1·20

1235 Hausmann
and Book Cover

1998. Birth Centenary of Manfred Hausmann (writer).
2868 **1235** 100pf. multicoloured   1·40   1·20

1236 Hands on
T-shirt

1998. Child Protection.
2869 **1236** 110pf. red and black   1·40   1·20

1237 Hen Harriers and
Chicks

1998. Humanitarian Relief Funds. Birds. Multicoloured.
2870   100pf.+50pf. Type **1237**   1·90   1·90
2871   110pf.+50pf. Great bustards   2·10   2·10
2872   110pf.+50pf. Ferruginous ducks   2·10   2·10
2873   110pf.+50pf. Aquatic warblers
     on reeds   2·10   2·10
2874   220pf.+80pf. Woodchat shrike   3·50   3·50

1238 Ear

1998. Telephone Help Lines.
2875 **1238** 110pf. black and orange   1·40   1·20

1239 *Hiorten* (sailing
packet), 1692

1998. Stamp Day.
2876 **1239** 110pf. multicoloured   1·40   1·20

1240 Ramin

1998. Birth Centenary of Gunther Ramin (choir leader and organist).
2877   **1240**   300pf. multicoloured   3·75   3·50

1241 Shepherds following Star

1998. Christmas. Multicoloured.
2878   100pf.+50pf. Type **1241**   1·90   1·80
2879   110pf.+50pf. Baby Jesus   2·00   1·80

1242 Dove

1998. 50th Anniv of Declaration of Human Rights.
2880   **1242**   110pf. multicoloured   1·40   1·20
For charity stamp for Kosovo Relief Fund in similar design see No. 2899.

1243 Conductor's Hands and Baton

1998. 450th Anniv of Saxony State Orchestra, Dresden.
2881   **1243**   300pf. multicoloured   4·00   3·50

1244 National Theatre, Schiller, Goethe, Wieland and Herder

1999. 1100th Anniv of Weimar, European City of Culture.
2882   **1244**   100pf. multicoloured   1·40   1·30

1245 Hands of Elderly Person and Child

1999. International Year of the Elderly.
2883   **1245**   110pf. multicoloured   1·50   1·30

1246 Katharina von Bora

1999. 500th Birth Anniv of Katharina von Bora (wife of Martin Luther).
2884   **1246**   110pf. multicoloured   1·50   1·30

1999. Federal State Parliament Buildings (2nd series). As T **1213**.
2885   110pf. Hesse (Richard Goerz) (former palace of Dukes of Hesse)   1·50   1·30

1247 Cycle Racing

1999. Sport Promotion Fund. Multicoloured.
2886   100pf.+50pf. Type **1247**   2·20   2·20

2887   110pf.+50pf. Horse racing   2·40   2·40
2888   110pf.+50pf. Motor racing   2·40   2·40
2889   300pf.+100pf. Motor cycle racing   4·75   4·75

1248 Cover Illustration (by Walter Trier) of *Emil and the Detectives* (novel)

1999. Birth Centenary of Erich Kastner (writer).
2890   **1248**   300pf. multicoloured   3·75   3·50

1249 Coloured Diodes

1999. 50th Anniv of Fraunhofer Society (for applied research).
2891   **1249**   110pf. multicoloured   1·50   1·30

1250 Emblem and Initials

1999. 50th Anniv of North Atlantic Treaty Organization.
2892   **1250**   110pf. multicoloured   1·50   1·30

1999. Federal State Parliament Buildings (3rd series). As T **1213**. Multicoloured.
2893   110pf. City Parliament of Hamburg   1·50   1·30
2894   110pf. Mecklenburg-Western Pomerania (Schwerin Castle, rebuilt by Georg Demmler and Friedrich Stuler)   1·50   1·30

1251 Maybach Cabriolet of 1936 and Club Emblem

1999. Centenary of German Automobile Club.
2895   **1251**   110pf. multicoloured   1·50   1·30

1252 Emblem

1999. 25th Anniv of German Cancer Relief.
2896   **1252**   110pf. multicoloured   1·50   1·30

1999. Federal State Parliament Buildings (4th series). As T **1213**.
2897   110pf. Bremen (Wassili Luckhardt)   1·50   1·30

1253 "Man, Nature, Technology"

1999. "EXPO 2000" World's Fair, Hanover (1st issue).
2898   **1253**   110pf. multicoloured   1·50   1·30
See also Nos. 2936, 2959 and 2979.

1999. Kosovo Relief Fund. As T **1242** but with inscription changed to "KOSOVO-HILFE 1999".
2899   110pf.+100pf. multicoloured   3·00   3·00

1254 Bavaria 1849 1k. and Saxony 1850 3pf. Stamps

1999. "iBRA'99" International Stamp Exhibition, Nuremberg. Sheet 140×100 mm.
MS2900 **1254** 300pf.+110pf. black, red and gold/cream   6·00   6·00

1255 Berchtesgaden National Park

1999. Europa. Parks and Gardens. Sheet 110×66 mm.
MS2901 **1255** 110pf. multicoloured   3·25   3·25

1256 Cross of St. John

1999. 900th Anniv of Order of Knights of St. John of Jerusalem.
2902   **1256**   110pf. multicoloured   1·50   1·30

1257 Flags and Children

1999. 50th Anniv of Berlin Airlift of 1948–49.
2903   **1257**   110pf. multicoloured   1·50   1·30

1258 Emblem

1999. 50th Anniv of Council of Europe.
2904   **1258**   110pf. multicoloured   1·70   1·30

1259 State Arms and Article 1

1999. 50th Anniv of German Basic Law. Sheet 110×66 mm.
MS2905 **1259** 110pf. multicoloured   2·40   3·00

1260 Politicians and New Parliament Chamber, Berlin

1999. 50th Anniv of Federal Republic of Germany. Sheet 138×97 mm containing T **1260** and similar horiz designs. Multicoloured.
MS2906 110pf. Type **1260**; 110pf. Child playing in rubble and child among flowers; 110pf. Berlin Wall and its fall; 110pf. Soldiers confronting civilians and debating chamber   6·00   6·50

1261 Lars, the Little Polar Bear

1999. Youth Welfare. Cartoon Characters. Multicoloured.
2907   100pf.+50pf. Type **1261**   2·10   2·10
2908   100pf.+50pf. Rudi the Crow   2·10   2·10
2909   110pf.+50pf. Twipsy (mascot of "Expo 2000" World's Fair, Hanover)   2·40   2·40
2910   110pf.+50pf. Mecki (hedgehog)   2·40   2·40
2911   220pf.+80pf. Tabaluga (dragon)   3·50   3·50

1262 Cross Clasp, Altar, Cathedral Spire and Time-line

1999. 1200th Anniv of Paderborn Diocese.
2912   **1262**   110pf. multicoloured   1·50   1·20

1263 House (child's painting)

1999. 50th Anniv of S.O.S. Children's Villages.
2913   **1263**   110pf. multicoloured   1·50   1·20

1264 *Ball at the Viennese Hofburg* and Score

1999. Death Centenary of Johann Strauss the younger (composer).
2914   **1264**   300pf. multicoloured   4·00   3·50

1265 Children at Desks (tapestry)

1999. 115th Anniv of Dominikus-Ringeisen Institute for Disabled People, Ursberg.
2915   **1265**   110pf. multicoloured   1·50   1·20

1266 Heinemann

1999. Birth Centenary of Gustav Heinemann (President 1969–74).
2916   **1266**   110pf. grey and red   1·50   1·20

1267 *Old Woman laughing* (Ernst Barlach)

1999. Cultural Foundation of the Federal States (1st series). Sculptures. Multicoloured.
2917   110pf. Type **1267**   1·50   1·20
2918   220pf. *Bust of a Thinker* (Wilhelm Lehmbruck)   2·50   2·40
See also Nos. 2960/1.

1268 Participating Countries and Dove

1999. Centenary of First Peace Conference, The Hague.
2919   **1268**   300pf. grey, red and blue   3·75   3·25

1269 Goethe (after J. K. Stieler)

1999. 250th Birth Anniv of Johann Wolfgang von Goethe (poet and playwright).
| 2920 | **1269** | 110pf. multicoloured | 1·50 | 1·30 |

1270 Mouse carrying Letter

1999. "For Us Children". Sheet 105×71 mm.
| MS2921 | **1270** | 110pf. multicoloured | 2·40 | 2·75 |

1271 HF1 Television Set (Herbert Hirche)

1999. Contemporary Design (2nd series). Sheet 138×97 mm containing T **1271** and similar horiz designs. Multicoloured.
| MS2922 | | 110pf. Type **1271**; 110pf. "Mono-a" cutlery (Peter Raacke); 110pf. Pearl bottles (Gunter Kupetz); 110pf. Transrapid Maglev train (Alexander Neumeister) | 6·00 | 6·50 |

1272 Player

1999. FC Bayern Munich, National Football Champions.
| 2923 | **1272** | 110pf. multicoloured | 1·50 | 1·30 |

1273 Book and Bookmark

1999. 50th Anniv of Federal Association of German Book Traders' Peace Prize.
| 2924 | **1273** | 110pf. multicoloured | 1·50 | 1·30 |

1274 Strauss and Poster from *Salome* (opera)

1999. 50th Death Anniv of Richard Strauss (composer).
| 2925 | **1274** | 300pf. multicoloured | 4·00 | 3·75 |

1275 Andromeda Galaxy

1999. Humanitarian Relief Funds. Outer Space. Multicoloured.
2926		100pf.+50pf. Type **1275**	1·90	1·90
2927		100pf.+50pf. Swan constellation	1·90	1·90
2928		110pf.+50pf. X-ray image of exploding star	2·10	2·10
2929		110pf.+50pf. Comet colliding with Jupiter	2·10	2·10
2930		300pf.+100pf. Gamma ray image of sky	5·00	5·00

1276 Goltzsch Valley Railway Bridge

1999. Bridges (2nd series).
| 2931 | **1276** | 110pf. multicoloured | 1·50 | 1·30 |

1277 "DGB"

1999. 50th Anniv of German Federation of Trade Unions.
| 2932 | **1277** | 110pf. black and bright red | 1·50 | 1·30 |

1278 Greater Horseshoe Bats

1999. Endangered Species.
| 2933 | **1278** | 100pf. multicoloured | 1·40 | 1·30 |

1279 The Annunciation

1999. Christmas. Multicoloured.
| 2934 | | 100pf.+50pf. Type **1279** | 1·90 | 1·80 |
| 2935 | | 110pf.+50pf. Nativity | 2·00 | 1·90 |

1280 Emblem and Eye

2000. "EXPO 2000" World's Fair, Hanover (2nd issue).
| 2936 | **1280** | 100pf. multicoloured | 1·40 | 1·30 |

1281 Emblem

2000. Holy Year 2000.
| 2937 | **1281** | 110pf. multicoloured | 1·50 | 1·30 |

1282 Charlemagne and Plan of Palace Chapel

2000. 1200th Anniv of Aachen Cathedral.
| 2938 | **1282** | 110pf. multicoloured | 1·50 | 1·30 |

1283 Schweitzer and Signature

2000. 125th Birth Anniv of Albert Schweitzer (missionary doctor).
| 2939 | **1283** | 110pf. multicoloured | 1·80 | 1·30 |

1284 Football

2000. Centenary of German Football Association.
| 2940 | **1284** | 110pf. multicoloured | 1·70 | 1·30 |

1285 Wehner

2000. Tenth Death Anniv of Herbert Wehner (politician).
| 2941 | **1285** | 110pf. multicoloured | 1·50 | 1·30 |

1286 Woman

2000. Prevention of Violence Against Women.
| 2942 | **1286** | 110pf. red, grey and black | 1·50 | 1·30 |

1287 "2000" in Moving Film Sequence

2000. 50th Berlin International Film Festival.
| 2943 | **1287** | 100pf. multicoloured | 1·40 | 1·30 |

1288 Boxing

2000. Sport Promotion Fund. Multicoloured.
2944		100pf.+50pf. Type **1288** (fair play)	1·90	1·90
2945		110pf.+50pf. Rhythmic gymnastics (beauty)	2·10	2·10
2946		110pf.+50pf. Running (competition)	2·10	2·10
2947		300pf.+100pf. Raised hands (culture of interaction)	4·75	4·75

1289 Gutenberg (after engraving by A. Thevet) and Letters from Gutenberg Bible

2000. 600th Birth Anniv of Johannes Gutenberg (inventor of printing press).
| 2948 | **1289** | 110pf. black and red | 1·50 | 1·30 |

1290 Jester

2000. 175th Anniv of First Dusseldorf Carnival.
| 2949 | **1290** | 110pf. multicoloured | 1·70 | 1·30 |

1291 Ebert

2000. 75th Death Anniv of Friedrich Ebert (President, 1919–25).
| 2950 | **1291** | 110pf. multicoloured | 1·50 | 1·30 |

1292 Weill at Rehearsal of *One Touch of Venus* (musical), 1943

2000. Birth Centenary of Kurt Weill (composer).
| 2951 | **1292** | 300pf. blk, stone & red | 4·00 | 3·75 |

1293 Passau

2000. Images of Germany.
| 2952 | **1293** | 110pf. multicoloured | 1·50 | 1·30 |

2000. Federal State Parliament Buildings (5th series). As T **1213**. Multicoloured.
| 2953 | | 110pf. Leine Palace, Lower Saxony | 1·50 | 1·30 |

1294 Trees

2000. Hainich National Park. Sheet 105×70 mm.
| MS2954 | **1294** | 110pf. multicoloured | 2·50 | 2·50 |

1295 Toy Windmill and "Post!"

2000
| 2955 | **1295** | 110pf. multicoloured | 1·80 | 1·70 |

1296 "Blue Wonder" Bridge, Dresden

2000. Bridges (3rd series).
| 2956 | **1296** | 100pf. multicoloured | 1·40 | 1·20 |

2000. Federal State Parliament Buildings (6th series). As T **1213**. Multicoloured.
| 2957 | | 110pf. North-Rhine/Westphalia (Fritz Eller) | 1·80 | 1·30 |

1297 City Buildings

2000. 750th Anniv of Greifswald.
| 2958 | **1297** | 110pf. multicoloured | 1·50 | 1·30 |

2000. "EXPO 2000" World's Fair, Hanover (3rd issue). As No. 2898 but self-adhesive.
| 2959 | **1253** | 110pf. multicoloured | 6·50 | 6·00 |

1298 "Expulsion from Paradise" (Leonhard Kern)

2000. Cultural Foundation of the Federal States. Sculptures. Multicoloured.
| 2960 | | 110pf. Type **1298** | 2·10 | 1·70 |
| 2961 | | 220pf. Silver table fountain (Melchior Gelb) | 2·50 | 2·40 |

1299 "Building Europe"

2000. Europa. Ordinary or self-adhesive gum.
| 2962 | **1299** | 110pf. multicoloured | 2·00 | 1·40 |

1300 Von Zinzendorf and Natives

2000. 300th Birth Anniv of Nikolaus Ludwig von Zinzendorf (leader of Moravian Brethren).
2964 **1300** 110pf. multicoloured 1·70 1·20

1301 Countryside

2000. Environmental Protection.
2965 **1301** 110pf.+50pf. mult 2·40 2·40

1302 Crowd at Music Festival

2000. Youth Welfare. "EXPO 2000" World's Fair, Hanover (4th issue). Multicoloured.
2966 100pf.+50pf. Type **1302** 2·00 2·00
2967 100pf.+50pf. Back-packers 2·00 2·00
2968 110pf.+50pf. Map of Africa and text 2·10 2·10
2969 110pf.+50pf. Eye of Buddha 2·10 2·10
2970 110pf.+50pf. Chinese cal-ligraphy 2·10 2·10
2971 300pf.+100pf. Psychedelic swirl 4·75 4·75

1303 Front Page of Issue 17, 1650, and Modern Pages of Newspaper

2000. 350th Anniv of *Einkommende Zeitungen* (first German daily newspaper).
2972 **1303** 110pf. multicoloured 1·70 1·30

1304 Emblem

2000. Centenary of Chambers of Handicrafts.
2973 **1304** 300pf. orange and black 3·75 3·50

1305 Meteorological Station

2000. Centenary of the Zugspitze Meteorological Station.
2974 **1305** 100pf. multicoloured 1·80 1·30

1306 Road Sign and Flashing Light

2000. 50th Anniv of Technisches Hilfswerk (Federal disaster relief organization).
2975 **1306** 110pf. multicoloured 1·80 1·30

1307 Bach

2000. 250th Death Anniv of Johann Sebastian Bach (composer).
2976 **1307** 110pf. multicoloured 1·80 1·30

1308 LZ-1

2000. Centenary of Inaugural Flight of LZ-1 (Zeppelin airship), 1900.
2977 **1308** 110pf. multicoloured 1·70 1·30

2000. Federal State Parliament Buildings (7th series). As T **1213**. Multicoloured.
2978 110pf. Rhineland-Palatinate, Mainz 1·70 1·30

1309 Emblem, Globe and Fingerprint

2000. "EXPO 2000" World's Fair, Hanover (5th issue).
2979 **1309** 110pf. multicoloured 1·70 1·30

1310 Wiechert

2000. 50th Death Anniv of Ernst Wiechert (writer).
2980 **1310** 110pf. multicoloured 1·70 1·30

1311 Nietzsche (Edvard Munch)

2000. Death Centenary of Friedrich Nietzsche (philosopher).
2981 **1311** 110pf. multicoloured 1·70 1·30

1312 "For You"

2000. Greetings Stamp.
2982 **1312** 100pf. multicoloured 1·40 1·30

1313 Saar River, Mettlach

2000. Images of Germany.
2983 **1313** 110pf. multicoloured 1·50 1·30

1314 Adolph Kopling

2000. 150th Anniv of Kopling Society (voluntary organization).
2984 **1314** 110pf. multicoloured 1·50 1·30

1315 Building

2000. 50th Anniv of Federal Court of Justice.
2985 **1315** 110pf. multicoloured 1·40 1·30

1316 Clown's Face

2000. "For Us Children". Sheet 55×82 mm.
MS2986 **1316** 110pf. multicoloured 2·40 2·40

1317 Nocht (founder), World Map and Microscope Images of Pathogens

2000. Centenary of Bernard Nocht Institute for Tropical Medicine.
2987 **1317** 300pf. multicoloured 4·50 4·25

1318 Town Hall, Wernigerode

2000. Tourist Sights. Showing face values in German currency and euros.
2988 **1318** 10pf. grey, orge & slate 70 35
2989 - 20pf. orange and black 70 60
2990 - 47pf. mauve and green 70 70
2991 - 50pf. brown and red 1·20 95
2992 - 80pf. green and brown 1·10 95
2993 - 100pf. blue and brown 1·80 1·70
2994 - 110pf. pur, brn & orge 1·70 1·20
2997 - 220pf. blue and brown 3·00 2·75
3000 - 300pf. brown and blue 3·50 3·25
3001 - 400pf. brown and red 4·75 4·50
3002 - 440pf. black and grey 5·00 4·75
3003 - 510pf. pink and red 6·25 6·00
3004 - 720pf. purple & mauve 8·25 8·25

DESIGNS: 20pf. Bottcherstrasse, Bremen; 47pf. Wilhelmshohe Park, Kassel; 50pf. Ceiling decoration, Kircheim Castle; 80pf. St. Reinoldi Church, Dortmund; 100pf. Schwerin Castle, Mecklenberg; 110pf. Stone bridge, Regensburg; 220pf. St. Nikolai Cathedral, Greifswald; 300pf. Town Hall Grimma; 400pf. Wartburg Castle, Eisenach; 440pf. Cologne Cathedral; 510pf. Heidelberg Castle; 720pf. Town Hall, Hildesheim.
Nos. 2988, 2993/4 also come self-adhesive.

1319 National Colours

2000. Tenth Anniv of Reunification of Germany.
3010 **1319** 110pf. black, red & yell 1·50 1·30

1320 Curd Jurgens

2000. Humanitarian Relief Funds. Actors. Multicoloured.
3011 100pf.+50pf. Type **1320** 2·10 2·10
3012 110pf.+50pf. Lilli Palmer 2·10 2·10
3013 110pf.+50pf. Heinz Ruhmann 2·40 2·40
3014 110pf.+50pf. Romy Schneider 2·40 2·40
3015 300pf.+100pf. Gert Frobe 4·75 4·75

1321 Pens, Envelope and 1999 110pf. Stamp

2000. Stamp Day.
3016 **1321** 110pf. multicoloured 1·40 1·30

1322 Grethe Weiser (actress and singer)

2000. Famous German Women.
3017 **1322** 100pf. green and brown 1·30 1·20
3018 - 110pf. red and green 1·40 1·20
3019 - 220pf. brown and green 2·50 2·40
3020 - 300pf. purple and brown 3·25 3·00
DESIGNS: 110pf. Kate Strobel (politician); 200pf. Marieluise Fleisser (writer); 300pf. Nelly Sachs (writer).

2000. Federal State Parliament Buildings (8th series). As T **1213**. Multicoloured.
3025 110pf. Saarland 1·50 1·30

1323 Book Cover

2000. 125th Birth Anniv of Rainer Maria Rilke (poet).
3026 **1323** 110pf. multicoloured 1·50 1·30

1324 Bode

2000. Birth Centenary of Arnold Bode (artist).
3027 **1324** 110pf. black and red 1·50 1·30

1325 *Birth of Christ* (Conrad von Soest)

2000. Christmas. Multicoloured.
3028 100pf.+50pf. Type **1325** 1·80 1·70
3029 110pf.+50pf. Nativity 2·00 1·80

1326 Indian Pepper (illustration from *New Book of Herbs*)

2001. 500th Birth Anniv of Leonhart Fuchs (physician and botanist).
3030 **1326** 100pf. multicoloured 1·20 1·10

1327 "VdK"

2001. 50th Anniv (2000) of Disabled War Veterans' Association.
3031 **1327** 110pf. multicoloured 1·30 1·20

1328 Prussian Eagle

2001. 300th Anniv of the Kingdom of Prussia.
3032 **1328** 110pf. multicoloured 1·30 1·20

1329 Lortzing and Music Score

2001. Birth Bicent of Albert Lortzing (composer).
3033 **1329** 110pf. multicoloured 1·30 1·20

1330 Telephone Handset and Number

2001. National Federation of Child and Youth Telephone Helplines.
3034 **1330** 110pf. yellow, red & blk 1·30 1·20

1331 Bucer

2001. 450th Death Anniv of Martin Bucer (teacher and Protestant reformer).
3035 **1331** 110pf. multicoloured 1·50 1·30

1332 Children running

2001. Sport Promotion Fund. Multicoloured.
3036 100pf.+50pf. Type **1332** 2·00 2·00
3037 110pf.+50pf. Disabled and able-bodied athletes 2·20 2·20
3038 110pf.+50pf. Adult and children skating 2·20 2·20
3039 300pf.+100pf. Men playing basketball 5·00 5·25

1333 Hand holding Quill

2001. 250th Birth Anniv of Johann Heinrich Voss (writer and translator). (a) Ordinary gum.
3040 **1333** 300pf. multicoloured 3·75 3·75

(b) Self-adhesive gum.
3040a €1.53 multicoloured 5·50 5·00

1334 Ollenhauer

2001. Birth Centenary of Erich Ollenhauer (politician).
3041 **1334** 110pf. red, black & sil 1·30 1·20

1335 Arnold

2001. Birth Centenary of Karl Arnold (politician).
3042 **1335** 110pf. black, green & red 1·30 1·20

2001. Federal State Parliament Buildings (9th series). As T **1213**. Multicoloured.
3043 110pf. Saxony 1·30 1·20

1336 Badge

2001. 50th Anniv of Federal Border Police.
3044 **1336** 110pf. multicoloured 1·30 1·20

1337 Suspension Railway

2001. Centenary of Suspension Railway, Wuppertal.
3045 **1338** 110pf.+50pf. mult 2·20 2·00

1338 Rendsberg Railway Viaduct

2001. Bridges (4th series).
3046 100pf. multicoloured 1·30 1·20

1339 "Post!"

2001
3047 **1339** 110pf. multicoloured 1·30 1·20

1340 Accordion

2001. Folk Music.
3048 **1340** 110pf. multicoloured 1·30 1·20

1341 World Map

2001. 50th Anniv of Goethe Institute.
3049 **1341** 300pf. multicoloured 3·75 3·75

1342 Glass of Water

2001. Europa. Water Resources.
3050 **1342** 110pf. multicoloured 1·80 1·30

1343 Egk

2001. Birth Centenary of Werner Egk (composer and conductor).
3051 **1343** 110pf. multicoloured 1·30 1·30

2001. Federal State Parliament Buildings (10th series). As T **1213**. Multicoloured.
3052 110pf. Saxony-Anhalt 1·30 1·30

1344 Mountain Gorilla with Young

2001. Endangered Species. Multicoloured. Ordinary or self-adhesive gum.
3053 110pf. Type **1344** 1·70 1·50
3054 110pf. Indian rhinoceros with young 1·70 1·50

1345 Pinocchio

2001. Youth Welfare. Characters from Children's Stories. Multicoloured.
3057 100pf.+50pf. Type **1345** 2·00 2·00
3058 100pf.+50pf. Pippi Longstocking 2·00 2·00
3059 100pf.+50pf. Heidi and Peter 2·20 2·20
3060 110pf.+50pf. Jim Knopf 2·20 2·20
3061 300pf.+100pf. Tom Sawyer and Huckleberry Finn 5·00 5·00

1346 St. Catherine's Monastery and Oceanographic Chart

2001. 750th Anniv of St. Catherine's Monastery and 50th Anniv of German Oceanographic Museum, Stralsund.
3062 **1346** 110pf. multicoloured 1·30 1·20

1347 Church Exterior and Plan

2001. 250th Anniv of Catholic Court Church, Dresden.
3063 **1347** 110pf. multicoloured 1·30 1·20

2001. Federal State Parliament Buildings (11th series). As T **1213**. Multicoloured.
3064 110pf. Schleswig-Holstein 1·30 1·20

1348 Church Bell Tower, Canzow

2001. Church Bell Tower, Canzow.
3065 **1348** 110pf. black, blue and mauve 1·30 1·20

1349 Hand (circulatory disease)

2001. Health Awareness Campaign. Sheet 138×110 mm containing T **1349** and similar horiz designs. Multicoloured.
MS3066 110pf. Type **1349**; 110pf. Torso (cancer); 110pf. Lower body (infectious diseases); 110pf. Man holding head (depression) 7·25 7·25

1350 Emblem

2001. Dragon Lancing Festival, Furth im Wald.
3067 **1350** 100pf. multicoloured 1·20 1·10

1351 Lime Tree, Himmelsberg

2001. Natural Heritage. Ordinary or self-adhesive gum.
3068 **1351** 110pf. multicoloured 1·30 1·20

1352 "Schoolmaster Lampel" (Wilhelm Busch) and Text

2001. Lifelong Learning.
3070 **1352** 110pf. multicoloured 1·30 1·20

1353 Felix standing on Cat

2001. "For Us Children". Sheet 110×66 mm.
MS3071 **1353** 110pf. multicoloured 1·80 1·80

2001. Federal State Parliament Buildings (12th series). As T **1213**. Multicoloured.
3072 110pf. Thuringia 1·30 1·20

1354 "Justice" (sculpture)

2001. 50th Anniv of Federal Constitutional Court.
3073 **1354** 110pf. multicoloured 1·30 1·20

1355 Members' Flags

2001. First Union Network International World Congress, Berlin.
3074 **1355** 110pf. multicoloured 1·30 1·20

1356 Museum Floor Plan

2001. Jewish Museum, Berlin.
3075 **1356** 110pf. multicoloured 1·30 1·20

1357 Marilyn Monroe

2001. Humanitarian Relief Funds. Film Industry. Multicoloured.
3076 100pf.+50pf. Type **1357** 2·00 2·00
3077 100pf.+50pf. Charlie Chaplin 2·00 2·00
3078 110pf.+50pf. Greta Garbo 2·20 2·20
3079 110pf.+50pf. Film reel 2·20 2·20
3080 300pf.+100pf. Jean Gabin 5·00 5·00
MS3080a 205×156 mm. As Nos. 3076/80 16·00 16·00

1358 Ribbon and "für Dich"

2001. Greetings Stamp.
3081 **1358** 110pf. red and black 1·30 1·20

1359 *Virgin and Child* (Alfredo Roldan)

2001. Christmas. Religious Paintings. Multicoloured.
3082 100pf.+50pf. Type **1359** 1·80 1·80
3083 110pf.+50pf. *The Shepherd's Adoration* (Jusepe de Ribera) 2·00 2·00
MS3083a 106×133 mm. Nos. 3082/3 and 3788/9 of Spain 6·00 6·00

1360 Gauss (survey barquentine)

2001. Centenary of German Antarctic Research. Sheet 135×105 mm containing T **1360** and similar horiz design. Multicoloured.

MS3084 110pf. Type **1360**; 220pf.
Polarstern (exploration ship)　　5·00　　5·00

1361 Heisenberg

2001. Birth Centenary of Werner Heisenberg (physicist).
3085　**1361**　300pf. black and blue　4·25　3·75

1362 Bautzen

2002. Millenary of Bautzen. Ordinary or self-adhesive gum.
3086　**1362**　56c. multicoloured　1·30　1·20

1363 Von Dohnanyi

2002. Birth Centenary of Hans von Dohnanyi (German resistance co-ordinator).
3087　**1363**　56c. multicoloured　1·30　1·20

1364 Graffiti

2002. "Tolerance".
3088　**1364**　56c. multicoloured　1·30　1·20

1365 " € "

2002. New Currency. Ordinary or self-adhesive gum.
3089　**1365**　56c. yellow and blue　2·00　1·80

1366 Mountains

2002. International Year of Mountains.
3091　**1366**　56c.+26c. multicoloured　1·80　1·20

No. 3091 was sold with a premium towards environmental protection.

1367 Cross-country Skier (biathlon)

2002. Winter Olympic Games, Salt Lake City, U.S.A. Multicoloured.
3092　51c.+26c. Type **1367**　2·00　2·00
3093　56c.+26c. Ice skater (speed skating)　2·20　2·20
3094　56c.+26c. Skier (ski jumping)　2·20　2·20
3095　153c.+51c. Man in helmet (luge)　5·00　5·00
MS3096 142×98 mm. As Nos. 3092/5　14·50　14·50

Nos. 3092/MS3096 were sold with a premium towards "Foundation for the Promotion of Sport in Germany".

1368 Knigge and Books

2002. 250th Birth Anniv of Adolf Freiherr Knigge (author of *Uber den Umgang mit Menschen* (book on etiquette)).
3097　**1368**　56c. multicoloured　1·50　1·30

1369 Front of Train Carriage

2002. Centenary of Berlin Subway.
3098　**1369**　56c. multicoloured　1·50　1·30

1370 Deggendorf

2002. Millenary of Deggendorf.
3099　**1370**　56c. multicoloured　1·50　1·30

1371 Mechanical Calculator (Johann Christoph Schuster)

2002. Cultural Foundation of the Federal States.
3100　**1371**　56c. multicoloured　1·50　1·30

1372 Ecksberg Pilgrimage Church

2002. 150th Anniv of Ecksberg Foundation (for people with disabilities).
3101　**1372**　56c. multicoloured　1·50　1·30

1373 Exhibits and Building

2002. Centenary of Freemason's Museum, Bayreuth.
3102　**1373**　56c. multicoloured　1·50　1·30

1374 Armorial Lions

2002. 50th Anniv of Baden-Württemberg State.
3103　**1374**　56c. black, gold and yellow　1·50　1·30

1375 "post"

2002
3104　**1375**　56c. multicoloured　1·50　1·30

1376 Emblem

2002. 50th Anniv of Federal Employment Services.
3105　**1376**　€1.53 red and black　4·00　3·75

1377 Modern Student and Elector Friedrich the Wise (founder of Wittenberg University)

2002. 500th Anniv of Martin Luther University, Halle-Wittenberg.
3106　**1377**　56c. grey, blue and mauve　1·50　1·30

1378 "KINDERGOTTESDIENST!"

2002. 150th Anniv of Children's Church Services.
3107　**1378**　56c. multicoloured　1·50　1·30

1379 "Documenta11"

2002. 11th "Documenta" Modern Art Exhibition, Kassel. Sheet 100×70 mm.
MS3108 **1379** 56c. ultramarine, lilac and blue　1·70　1·70

1380 Flags of Championship Winners and Football

2002. 20th-century World Cup Football Champions. Multicoloured.
3109　56c. Type **1380**　1·50　1·50
3110　56c. German Footballer　1·50　1·50

1381 Clown

2002. Europa. Circus. Ordinary or self-adhesive gum.
3111　**1381**　56c. black, red and green　1·50　1·30

1382 Dessau-Worlitz

2002. UNESCO World Heritage Site. Dessau-Worlitz Gardens. Ordinary or self-adhesive gum.
3113　**1382**　56c. multicoloured　1·50　1·30

1383 Thaer

2002. 250th Birth Anniv of Albrecht Daniel Thaer (agronomist).
3115　**1383**　€2.25 multicoloured　6·00　6·00

1384 Desmoulin's Whorl Snail

2002. Endangered Species. Molluscs. Multicoloured.
3116　51c. Type **1384**　1·20　1·20
3117　56c. Freshwater pearl mussel　1·30　1·30

1385 Chess Pieces

2002. Youth Welfare. Toys. Multicoloured.
3118　51c.+26c. Type **1385**　2·00　2·00
3119　51c.+26c. Wooden crane　2·00　2·00
3120　56c.+26c. Doll　2·20　2·20
3121　56c.+26c. Teddy bear　2·20　2·20
3122　153c.+51c. Electric train　5·00　5·00

1386 *Yellow Feather in Red*

2002. Birth Centenary of Ernst Wilhelm Nay (artist).
3123　**1386**　56c. multicoloured　1·50　1·30

1387 Leaves and Silhouettes

2002. 40th Anniv of "Deutsche Welthungerhilfe" (humanitarian aid organization).
3124　**1387**　51c. multicoloured　1·30　1·20

1388 *Way of Human Rights* (sculpture, Danni Karavan)

2002. 150th Anniv of National Museum of German Art and Culture, Nuremberg.
3125　**1388**　56c. multicoloured　1·50　1·30

1389 Hesse

2002. 125th Birth Anniv of Hermann Hesse (writer).
3126　**1389**　56c. blue and yellow　1·50　1·30

1390 Trees and Rocks

2002. Hochharz National Park. Sheet 110×66 mm.
MS3127 **1390** 56c. multicoloured　2·10　2·10

1391 Felder

2002. Second Death Anniv of Josef Felder (politician and journalist).
3128　**1391**　56c. multicoloured　1·50　1·30

1392 Museum Buildings

2002. UNESCO World Heritage Site. Museum Island, Berlin.
3129　**1392**　56c. black and green　1·50　1·30

1393 Firemen fighting Fire

2002. Voluntary Fire Brigades.
3130 **1393** 56c. multicoloured   1·50   1·30

1394 Building Facade

2002. 130th Anniv of Communications Museum, Berlin.
3131 **1394** 153c. multicoloured   3·75   3·50

2002. Flood Relief. As T **1222** but with "HOCHWASSERHILFE 2002" inscribed at left and new face value.
3132   56c.+44c. multicoloured   3·25   2·75

1395 Walls of Roman Bathhouse, Wurmlingen (illustration from *Die Alammannen* by Konrad Theiss)

2002. Archaeology.
3133 **1395** 51c. multicoloured   1·50   1·30

1396 Face painted on Child's Toe

2002. "For Us Children". Sheet 110×66 mm.
MS3134 **1396** 56c. multicoloured   2·10   2·00

1397 *Rotes Elisabeth-Ufer* (painting, Ernst Ludwig Kirchner)

2002
3135 **1397** 112c. multicoloured   3·00   2·50

1398 Von Kleist (miniature, Peter Friedel)

2002. 225th Birth Anniv of Heinrich von Kleist (writer).
3136 **1398** 56c. multicoloured   1·50   1·30

1399 Jochum rehearsing

2002. Birth Centenary of Eugen Jochum (conductor).
3137 **1399** 56c. multicoloured   1·50   1·30

1400 Diagram of Planets (Copernicus), Horsemen and Sphere

2002. 400th Birth Anniv of Otto von Guericke (engineer and physicist).
3138 **1400** 153c. multicoloured   4·25   3·50

1401 Angel (detail, *The Annunciation*)

2002. Christmas. Paintings by Rogier van der Weyden. Multicoloured.
3139   51c.+26c. Type **1401**   2·20   2·00
3140   56c.+26c. *The Holy Family* (detail, Miraflores alterpiece)   2·40   2·10

1402 Arrows

2002. 50th Anniv of Federal Agency for Civic Education.
3141 **1402** 56c. black, red and yellow   1·50   1·30

Deutschland 56
1403 Clock and Eye

2002. 50th Anniv of German Television.
3142 **1403** 56c. multicoloured   1·50   1·30

1404 BMW Isetta 300

2002. Cars. Multicoloured.
3144   45c.+20c. Type **1404**   2·20   2·10
3145   55c.+25c. Volkswagen Beetle   2·40   2·20
3146   55c.+25c. Mercedes Benz 300 SL   2·40   2·20
3147   55c.+25c. VEB Sachsenring Trabant P50   2·40   2·20
3148   144c.+56c. Borgward Isabella Coupe   5·50   5·25
See also Nos. 3238/42.

1405 *Halle Market Church* (Lyonel Feininger)

2002. Tourist Sights. As T **1318** but with face value in new currency.
3149 **1405** 55c. multicoloured   1·50   1·30
3150   5c. brown and green   25   25
3151   25c. olive and violet   60   55
3153   40c. multicoloured   1·00   90
3154   44c. yellow and black   1·20   1·10
3155   45c. pink and black   1·20   1·10
3156   55c. yellow and black   1·50   1·40
3157   €1 grey and black   2·40   2·00
3158   €1.44 pink and green   3·50   3·25
3159   €1.60 grey, black and orange   3·75   3·50
3160   €1.80 green and chestnut   5·00   4·00
3161   €2 red and green   5·00   4·75
3162   €2.20 blue and black   5·50   5·00
3163   €2.60 blue and red   6·00   5·75
3164   €4.10 purple and blue   9·25   8·50
DESIGNS: 5c. Erfurter Cathedral; 25c. Schloss Arolsen; 40c. J.S. Bach (statue), Leipzig; 44c. Philharmonic Hall, Berlin; 45c. Canal warehouse, Tonning; 55c. Old Opera House, Frankfurt; €1 Porta Niga (black gate), Trier; €1.44 Beethoven's birthplace, Bonn; €1.60 Bauhaus, Dessau; €1.80 Staatsgalerie, Stuttgart; €2 Bamberger Reister (statue); €2.20 Theodor Fontane monument, Neuruppin; €2.60 *Seute Dern* (four-mast barque), Maritime Museum, Bremerhaven; €4.10 Houses, Wismar.
Nos. 3151 and 3155/6 also come self-adhesive.

2002. Famous German Women. As T **1322** but with face value in new currency.
3190   45c. green and blue   1·20   1·10
3191   55c. red and black   1·30   1·10
3192   €1 purple and blue   2·40   2·30
3193   €1.44 brown and blue   3·25   3·00
DESIGNS: 45c. Annette von Droste-Hulshoff (writer); 55c. Hildegard Knef (actress); €1 Marie Juchacz (politician); €1.44 Esther von Kirchbach (writer).

1406 Town Buildings

2003. Millenary of Kronach.
3194 **1406** 45c. multicoloured   1·20   1·00

1407 Georg Elser

2003. Birth Centenary of Georg Elser (attempted assassination of Adolf Hitler).
3195 **1407** 55c. multicoloured   1·50   1·30

1408 Bridge joined by Heart

2003. 40th Anniv of German–French Co-operation Treaty.
3196 **1408** 55c. multicoloured   1·50   1·30

1409 Hand and Page

2003. Year of the Bible.
3197 **1409** 55c. multicoloured   1·50   1·30

1410 *Proun 30t* (El Lissitzky)

2003. Cultural Foundation of the Federal States.
3198 **1410** €1.44 multicoloured   3·75   3·50

1411 St. Thomas Church Choir, Leipzig

2003. Boys' Choirs. Sheet 172×77 mm containing T **1411** and similar horiz designs. Multicoloured.
MS3199 45c. Type **1411**; 55c. Dresden Church choir; 100c. St. Peter's Cathedral choir, Regensburg   5·50   5·00

1412 Rose

2003. Greetings Stamp. Ordinary or self-adhesive gum.
3200 **1412** 55c. multicoloured   1·50   1·20

1413 *Junger Argentier* (Max Beckman)

2003. Artists' Anniversaries. Multicoloured.
3202   55c. Type **1413** (53rd death anniv)   1·70   1·30
3203   €1 *Komposition* (Adolf Holzel) (150th birth anniv)   2·50   2·30

1414 Footballer

2003. Sports Promotion Fund. World Cup Football Championship (2006), Germany. Multicoloured.
3204   45c.+20c. Type **1414**   2·00   2·00
3205   55c.+25c. Boys playing football   2·20   2·20
3206   55c.+25c. Fan with arms raised   2·20   2·20
3207   55c.+25c. Young player heading ball   2·20   2·20
3208   €1.44+56c. Boy kicking ball to older man   5·00   5·00

1415 Building Facade

2003. UNESCO World Heritage Sites. Cologne Cathedral. Ordinary or self-adhesive gum.
3209 **1415** 55c. grey, red and black   1·50   1·30

1416 Flower

2003. International Horticultural Exhibition, Rostock.
3211 **1416** 45c. multicoloured   1·30   1·20

1417 Oskar von Miller (founder) and Technological Symbols

2003. Centenary of Deutsches Museum, Munich.
3212 **1417** 55c. multicoloured   1·50   1·30

1418 Cut-out Figures

2003. 50th Anniv of Deutscher Kinderschutzbund (children's organization).
3213 **1418** 55c. multicoloured   1·50   1·30

1419 Map and Representation of Radio Waves

2003. 50th Anniv of Deutsche Welle (radio station).
3214 **1419** 55c. multicoloured   1·50   1·30

1420 Aviators and Junkers W.33 Bremen

2003. 75th Anniv East–West North Atlantic Flight.
3215 **1420** 144c.+56c. multicoloured   5·50   5·00

1421 1960s Posters

2003. Europa. Poster Art.
3216 **1421** 55c. multicoloured   1·50   1·30

1422 Justus von Liebig

2003. Birth Bicentenary of Justus von Liebig (chemist).
3217 **1422** 55c. multicoloured   1·50   1·30

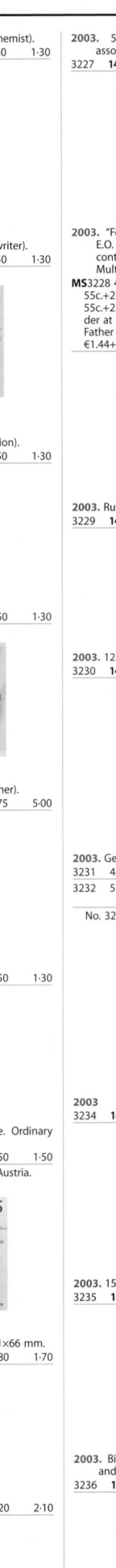

1423 Reinhold
Schneider and Text

2003. Birth Centenary of Reinhold Schneider (writer).
3218 **1423** 55c. multicoloured   1·50   1·30

1424 Eurocopter EC135 and Patrol
Vehicle

2003. Centenary of ADAC (automobile association).
3219 **1424** 55c. multicoloured   1·50   1·30

1425 Rainbow

2003. Ecumenical Church Conference, Berlin.
3220 **1425** 55c. multicoloured   1·50   1·30

1426 Hands and Text

2003. Birth Centenary of Hans Jonas (philosopher).
3221 **1426** 220c. multicoloured   5·75   5·00

1427 Hand with Face and
Feet

2003. Tenth Anniv of Postal Codes.
3222 **1427** 55c. multicoloured   1·50   1·30

1428 Bridge over Salzach
River

2003. Centenary of Oberndorf–Laufen Bridge. Ordinary
or self-adhesive gum.
3223 **1428** 55c. multicoloured   1·50   1·50
A stamp of the same design was issued by Austria.

1429 Lake, Trees and Islands

2003. Unteres Odertal National Park. Sheet 111×66 mm.
MS3225 **1429** 55c. multicoloured   1·80   1·70

1430 Protesters and Tanks

2003. 50th Anniv of Uprising in East Berlin.
3226 **1430** 55c.+25c. multicoloured   2·20   2·10

1431 Musical Notations

2003. 50th Anniv of Deutscher Musikrat (music
association). Ordinary or self-adhesive gum.
3227 **1431** €1·44 silver and blue   4·00   3·75

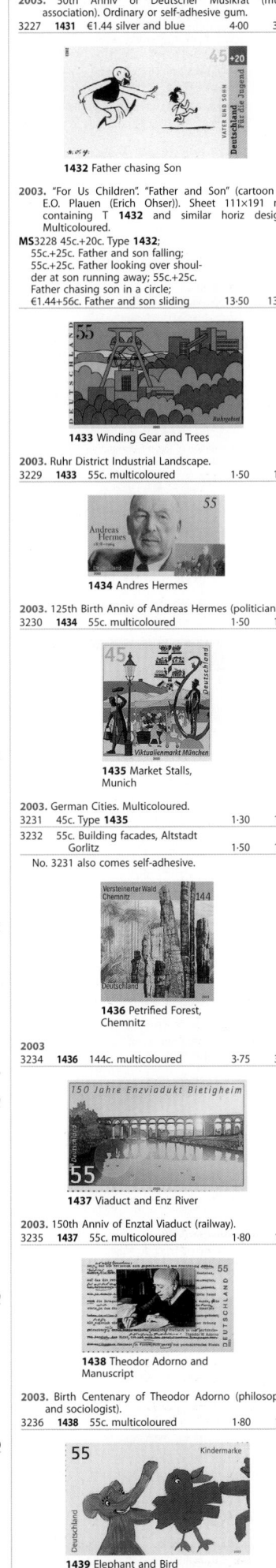

1432 Father chasing Son

2003. "For Us Children". "Father and Son" (cartoon by
E.O. Plauen (Erich Ohser)). Sheet 111×191 mm
containing T **1432** and similar horiz designs.
Multicoloured.
MS3228 45c.+20c. Type **1432**;
55c.+25c. Father and son falling;
55c.+25c. Father looking over shoulder at son running away; 55c.+25c.
Father chasing son in a circle;
€1·44+56c. Father and son sliding   13·50 13·00

1433 Winding Gear and Trees

2003. Ruhr District Industrial Landscape.
3229 **1433** 55c. multicoloured   1·50   1·30

1434 Andres Hermes

2003. 125th Birth Anniv of Andreas Hermes (politician).
3230 **1434** 55c. multicoloured   1·50   1·30

1435 Market Stalls,
Munich

2003. German Cities. Multicoloured.
3231 45c. Type **1435**   1·30   1·20
3232 55c. Building facades, Altstadt
      Gorlitz   1·50   1·30
No. 3231 also comes self-adhesive.

1436 Petrified Forest,
Chemnitz

2003
3234 **1436** 144c. multicoloured   3·75   3·50

1437 Viaduct and Enz River

2003. 150th Anniv of Enztal Viaduct (railway).
3235 **1437** 55c. multicoloured   1·80   1·40

1438 Theodor Adorno and
Manuscript

2003. Birth Centenary of Theodor Adorno (philosopher
and sociologist).
3236 **1438** 55c. multicoloured   1·80   1·40

1439 Elephant and Bird

2003. "For Us Children". Sheet 111×65 mm.
MS3237 **1439** 55c. multicoloured   2·00   1·80

2003. Cars. As T **1404**. Multicoloured.
3238 45c.+20c. Wartburg 311 Coupe   2·00   2·00
3239 55c.+25c. Ford Taunus 17 M P3   2·40   2·10
3240 55c.+25c. Porsche 356 B Coupe   2·40   2·10
3241 55c.+25c. Opel Olympia
      Rekord P1   2·40   2·10
3242 144c.+56c. Auto Union 1000 S   5·50   5·00

1440 Letter Box

2003. Post.
3243 **1440** 55c. multicoloured   1·80   1·40

1441 Lifeguards

2003. 90th Anniv of DLRG (safety organization).
3244 **1441** 144c. multicoloured   4·50   3·50

1442 Nativity Figures
(19th-century)

2003. Christmas. Multicoloured.
3245 45c.+20c. Type **1442**   2·10   1·60
3246 55c.+25c. Holy Family   2·50   2·00

1443 Dresden Opera House

2003. Birth Bicentenary of Gottfried Semper (architect).
3247 **1443** 55c. multicoloured   1·80   1·40

1444 Hands and Women

2003. Centenary of German Catholic Women's Federation.
3248 **1444** 55c. multicoloured   1·80   1·40

1445 Stars

2003. Tenth Anniv of Maastricht Treaty.
3249 **1445** 55c. blue and yellow   1·80   1·40

1446 St. Martin's Church

2004. 800th Anniv of Landshut.
3250 **1446** 45c. multicoloured   1·50   1·20

1447 Cathedral and
Images of Schleswig

2004. 1200th Anniv of Schleswig.
3251 **1447** 55c. multicoloured   1·90   1·50

1448 Clouds, Sun and
Trees

2004. Environmental Protection and Renewable Energy.
3252 **1448** 55c.+25c. multicoloured   2·75   2·20

1449 Football Players

2004. Sport Promotion Fund. Multicoloured.
3253 45c.+20c. Type **1449** (European
      Football Championship)   2·50   2·10
3254 55c.+25c. Wheelchair athlete
      (Paralympics)   2·75   2·20
3255 55c.+25c. Runner (Olympic
      Games, Greece)   2·75   2·20
3256 55c.+25c. Footballer (50th
      anniv of Germany winning
      World Cup)   2·75   2·20
3257 144c.+56c. Hands holding
      trophy (Centenary of FIFA)   6·50   5·50

1450 Paper Airplanes

2004. Post.
3258 **1450** 55c. multicoloured   1·90   1·50

1451 Buildings

2004. 1300th Anniv of Arnstadt.
3259 **1451** 55c. multicoloured   1·90   1·50

1452 Shadow of Boy,
Apple and Arrow

2004. Classic Theatre. Sheet 102×73 mm containing T
1452 and similar square design. Multicoloured.
MS3260 45c. Type **1452** (William Tell
(Friedrich von Schiller) (200th anniv)); 100c. Faust and the devil (Faust
II (Johann Wolfgang von Goethe)
(150th anniv))   5·00   4·75

1453 Joseph Schmidt

2004. Birth Centenary of Joseph Schmidt (singer).
3261 **1453** 55c. brown   1·90   1·50

1454 Paul Ehrlich (chemistry) and Emil
von Behring (medicine)

2004. 150th Birth Anniv of Nobel Prize Winners.
3262 **1454** 144c. multicoloured   4·75   3·75

1455 White Stork in Flight

2004. Endangered Species. White Stork (*Circona circona*).
3263 **1455** 55c. black, blue and red 1·90 1·50

1456 Master House, Dessau

2004. Bauhaus (design group).
3264 **1456** 55c. multicoloured 1·90 1·50

1457 Kurt Kiesinger

2004. Birth Centenary of Kurt Georg Kiesinger (politician).
3265 **1457** 55c. multicoloured 1·90 1·50

1458 Early and Modern
Light Bulbs

2004. 150th Anniv of Electric Light Bulb.
3266 **1458** 220c. multicoloured 6·75 6·50

1459 Sunflower
and Holiday
Symbols

2004. Europa. Holidays.
3267 **1459** 45c. multicoloured 1·70 1·30

1460 New
Members' Flags as
Cones

2004. Enlargement of European Union.
3268 **1460** 55c. multicoloured 1·90 1·50

1461 Reinhard
Schwarz-Schilling

2004. Birth Centenary of Reinhard Schwarz-Schilling (composer).
3269 **1461** 55c. sepia 1·90 1·50

1462 St. Boniface
under Attack

2004. 350th Anniv of Martyrdom of St. Boniface (papal envoy to Germany).
3270 **1462** 55c. multicoloured 1·90 1·50

1463 Schloss Ludwigsburg

2004. 300th Anniv of Schloss Ludwigsburg.
3271 **1463** €1.44 multicoloured 4·50 4·00

1464 Two Kittens playing
with String

2004. "For Us Children". Cats. Multicoloured.
3272 45c.+20c. Type **1464** 2·40 2·00
3273 55c.+25c. Three kittens playing
with ball 2·50 2·20
3274 55c.+25c. Mother and kitten 2·50 2·20
3275 55c.+25c. Cat washing paw 2·50 2·20
3276 €1.44+56c. Two kittens asleep 6·75 5·75

1465 Sea and
Sand

2004. Wattenmeer National Park.
3277 **1465** 55c. multicoloured 1·90 1·50

1466 National
Flags as
Heart-shaped Kite

2004. 21st-century German—Russian Youth Forum.
3278 **1466** 55c. multicoloured 1·90 1·50

1467 Greifswalder
Oie, Baltic Sea

2004. Lighthouses. Multicoloured. (a) Ordinary gum.
3279 45c. Type **1467** 1·70 1·30
3280 55c. Roter Sands 1·90 1·50

(b) Self-adhesive gum.
3281 55c. As No. 3280 (35×35 mm) 1·90 1·50

1468 *Bremen*
(passenger ship) and
New York Harbour

2004. Bremen—1929 Winner of Blue Ribbon (Europe to America speed record). Ordinary or self-adhesive gum.
3282 **1468** 55c. multicoloured 1·90 1·50

1469 Ludwig
Fuerbach

2004. Birth Bicentenary of Ludwig Fuerbach (philosopher).
3284 **1469** 144c. rosine and black 4·50 3·75

1470 Camellia

2004. Greetings Stamp. Ordinary or Self-adhesive gum.
3285 **1470** 55c. multicoloured 1·90 1·50

1471 Church
Facade

2004. Centenary of Protestant Regional Church, Speyer.
3287 **1471** 55c. multicoloured 1·90 1·50

1472 Scene from
Hansel and Gretel and
Engelbert Humperdinck

2004. 150th Birth Anniv of Engelbert Humperdinck (composer).
3288 **1472** 45c. multicoloured 1·70 1·30

1473 Ink Pot, Quill Pen,
Manuscript and Glasses

2004. Birth Bicentenary of Eduard Morike (writer).
3289 **1473** 55c. multicoloured 1·90 1·50

1474 Feet and
Hand Prints
forming Face

2004. "For Us Children".
3290 **1474** 55c. multicoloured 1·90 1·50

1475 Kaiser Wilhelm
Cathedral church, Berlin
and Egon Eiermann

2004. Birth Centenary of Egon Eiermann (architect).
3291 **1475** 100c. multicoloured 3·50 2·75

1476 Court Seal

2004. 50th Anniv of Federal Social Court.
3292 **1476** 144c. multicoloured 4·50 3·75

1477 Iceberg, Greenland

2004. Climate Zones. Multicoloured.
3293 45c.+20c. Type **1477** (arctic) 2·50 2·20
3294 55c.+25c. Mountains, Tibet
(alpine) 3·00 2·50
3295 55c.+25c. River and grazing
animals, Mecklenburg-Vor-
pommern (temperate) 3·00 2·50
3296 55c.+25c. Dunes, Sahara
(desert) 3·00 2·50
3297 144c.+56c. Rainforest, Galapagos Islands (tropics) 6·75 5·75

1478 Flying Boat
Dornier Do-X (1930)

2004. Stamp Day.
3298 **1478** 55c. ultramarine and
vermilion 2·10 1·60

1479 *Flight into
Egypt*

2004. Christmas. Paintings by Peter Paul Rubens. Multicoloured.
3299 45c.+20c. Type **1479** 2·50 2·10
3300 55c.+25c. *Adoration of the Magi* 3·00 2·40
Stamps of the same design were issued by Belgium.

1480 Snow-covered
Avenue

2004. Post.
3301 **1480** 55c. multicoloured 2·10 1·60

1481 *Das Geheimnis*

2004. Birth Centenary of Felix Nussbaum (artist).
3302 **1481** 55c. multicoloured 2·10 1·60

1482 International
Space Station

2004
3303 **1482** 55c. multicoloured 2·10 1·60

1483 City Hall

2005. 1200th Anniv of Forchheim.
3304 **1483** 45c. multicoloured 1·70 1·30

1484 Three Kings
(board painting,
Cologne (c. 1350))

2005. Art.
3305 **1484** 55c. multicoloured 2·10 1·60

1485
Sunflower

2005. Flowers. Multicoloured.

(a) Ordinary gum
3306 5c. Crocus 35 35
3306a 10c. Tulip 45 40
3307 20c. Tagetes 75 65
3307a 25c. Carnation 95 80
3308 25c. Mallow 95 80
3308a 35c. Dahlia 1·30 1·10
3308b 40c. Blue flower 1·50 1·30
3310 45c. Daisy 1·50 1·30
3310a 45c. Lily of the Valley (6.5.10) 1·90 1·60
3311 50c. Aster 1·70 1·50
3312 55c. Poppy 1·90 1·60
3313 55c. Red rose 1·90 1·60
3313a 58c. Pasque flower 1·90 1·60
3313b 60c. *Fritillaria imperialis* (5.12.13) 1·90 1·60
3314 65c. Rudbeckia 2·40 2·10
3315 70c. Pink flower 2·50 2·30
3316 75c. Balloon flower (*Platycodon
grandiflorus*) (3.1.11) 2·50 2·30
3318 90c. Narcissus 3·00 2·50
3320 95c. Type **1485** 3·00 2·50
3320b 100c. *Dicentra spectabilis* 3·25 3·00
3320b 145c. Iris 4·25 3·75
3320c 200c. *Eschscholzia californica* 7·50 6·50
3320da 240c. Gaura 7·75 6·75
3320e 390c. Lily 12·50 11·00
3320f €4.10 Ladies slipper 19·00 16·00
3321 €4.30 Larkspur 13·00 11·50
3322 €5 Gentian (7.7.11) 17·00 14·50

(b) Self-adhesive
3324 35c. Dahlia 1·30 1·10
3324a 45c. As No. 3310a (lily-of-the-
valley) (1.3.11) 1·70 1·50
3325 55c. Poppy 1·90 1·60
3326 55c. Red rose 1·90 1·60
3326a 58c. Pasque flower 1·90 1·60
3326b 60c. *Fritillaria imperialis* (5.12.13) 1·90 1·60
3327 65c. As No. 3314 2·20 2·00
3328 70c. As No. 3315 2·40 2·10
3330 90c. As No. 3318 (Narcissus) 3·25 2·75
3330a 100c. *Dicentra spectabilis*
(10.10.13) 4·00 3·50

1486 Celtic
Statue, Glauberg

2005. Archaeology.
3335 **1486** €1.44 multicoloured 5·00 4·25

1487 Championship Mascot
(⅔-size illustration)

2005. Sport Promotion Fund. Multicoloured.

3336	45c.+20c. Type **1487** (World Cup Football Championship, Germany 2006)		2·75	2·40
3337	55c.+25c. Footballers (World Cup Football Championships, Germany 2006)		3·00	2·50
3338	55c.+25c. Skier (Nordic World Ski Championships, Oberstdorf)		3·00	2·50
3339	55c.+25c. Gymnasts (International German Gymnastics Festival, Berlin)		3·00	2·50
3340	144c.+56c. Fencers (Fencing World Championships, Leipzig)		7·00	6·00

1488 Pillar

2005. 150th Anniv of Advertisement Pillars.

3341	**1488**	55c. multicoloured	2·10	1·60

1489 Cathedral Facade

2005. Centenary of Berlin Cathedral. Ordinary or self-adhesive gum.

3342	**1489**	95c. multicoloured	3·25	2·50

1490 Postman walking in Mountains

2005. Postal Service (1st series). Multicoloured.

3344	**1490**	Type **1490**	2·10	1·60
3345		55c. Postman cycling	2·10	1·60

See also Nos. 3370/1.

1491 Danish and German Flags

2005. 50th Anniv of Germany—Denmark Relations.

3346	**1491**	55c. multicoloured	2·10	1·60

A stamp of the same design was issued by Denmark.

1492 Lockheed L-1049 Super Constellation

2005. 50th Anniv of Resumption of German Air Traffic.

3347	**1492**	155c. multicoloured	5·25	4·25

1493 Aquaduct

2005. Centenary of Mittelland Canal.

3348	**1493**	45c. multicoloured	1·70	1·50

1494 Rock, Ferns and Tree

2005. National Parks. Bavarian Forest.

3349	**1494**	55c. multicoloured	2·10	1·60

1495 Silhouettes of Characters

2005. Birth Bicentenary of Hans Christian Andersen (writer). Ordinary or self-adhesive gum.

3350	**1495**	144c. light orange, orange and black	4·75	4·00

1496 Book Bindings and Signature

2005. Birth Bicentenary of Friedrich Schiller (poet). Schiller Year.

3352	**1496**	55c. multicoloured	2·10	1·60

1497 Signatories.

2005. 50th Anniv of Paris Agreements (establishing Federal Democratic Republic of Germany in Western European Union (WEU) and North Atlantic Treaty Organization (NATO).

3353	**1497**	55c. black and vermilion	2·10	1·60

1498 "Sitzende Franzi" (woodcut) (Erich Heikel)

2005. Centenary of Die Brucke (The Bridge) (group of Expressionist artists).

3354	**1498**	55c. black, vermilion and stone	2·10	1·60

1499 Wine Glass, Wine Bottle, Candle and Cup

2005. Europa. Gastronomy.

3355	**1499**	55c. chocolate, orange and rose	2·10	1·60

1500 Pope John Paul II

2005. Pope John Paul II Commemoration.

3356	**1500**	55c. multicoloured	2·10	1·60

1501 Kraftpost Omnibus

2005. Stamp Day. Centenary of Post Bus.

3357	**1501**	55c.+25c. multicoloured	3·00	2·50

1502 Greif ("Reach") (training ship)

2005. Youth Welfare. Ships. Multicoloured.

3358	45c.+20c. Type **1502**		2·75	2·40
3359	55c.+25c. Passat ("Trade Wind") (four-mast bark)		3·00	2·50
3360	55c.+25c. Rickmer Rickmers (cargo ship)		3·00	2·50
3361	55c.+25c. Grand Duchess Elizabeth (schooner)		3·00	2·50
3362	144c.+56c. Deutschland (training ship)		7·00	6·00

1503 Numbers as Map of Europe

2005. EUROSAI (European Organization of Supreme Audit Institutions) Conference, Bonn.

3363	**1503**	55c. multicoloured	2·10	1·60

1504 Cross and Globe

2005. World Youth Day.

3364	**1504**	55c. multicoloured	2·10	1·60

A stamp of the same design was issued by Vatican City.

1505 Brunsbuttel Lighthouse

2005. Lighthouses. Multicoloured. Ordinary or self-adhesive gum.

3365		45c. Type **1505**	1·70	1·50
3366		55c. Westerheversand	2·10	1·60

See also Nos. 3429/30.

1506 Albert Einstein and "E=mc²"

2005. Centenary of Special Theory of Relativity by Albert Einstein (physicist).

3368	**1506**	55c. black and scarlet	2·10	1·60

1507 New Palace, Sanssouci Park, Potsdam

2005. Prussian Schlosses. Sheet 98×70 mm.

MS3369	**1507**	220c. multicoloured	7·50	7·00

2005. Postal Service (2nd issue). As T **1490**. Multicoloured.

3370		55c. Postman with trolley	2·10	1·60
3371		55c. Postman in boat	2·10	1·60

1508 Tree and Figure

2005. Centenary of NaturFreunde Deutschlands (conservation organization).

3372	**1508**	144c. green and rose	5·25	4·50

1509 Chickens

2005. "For us Children".

3373	**1509**	55c. multicoloured	2·10	1·60

1510 City from River (15th-century woodcut)

2005. 1200th Anniv of Magdeburg.

3374	**1510**	55c. multicoloured	2·10	1·60

1511 Angel

2005. 450th Anniv of Religious Freedom.

3375	**1511**	55c. multicoloured	2·10	1·60

1512 Max Schmeling

2005. Birth Centenary of Max Schmeling (boxer).

3376	**1512**	100c. black and vermilion	2·10	1·60

1513 Church

2005. Completion of Reconstruction of Frauenkirche (Church of our Lady) Dresden (2004).

3377	**1513**	55c. multicoloured	2·10	1·60

1514 Script and Pen Nib

2005. Birth Bicentenary of Adalbert Stifter (writer).

3378	**1514**	55c. multicoloured	3·50	3·00

1515 Horse-drawn Procession

2005. 150th Anniv of Bad Tolz Leonardifahrt (festival).

3379	**1515**	45c. multicoloured	1·70	1·30

1516 Adoration of the Child Jesus

2005. Christmas. Paintings by Stefan Lochner. Multicoloured.

3380		45c.+20c. Type **1516**	2·50	2·10
3381		55c.+25c. Madonna of the Rose Bush	3·25	2·40

1517 Israeli and German Flags

2005. 40th Anniv of Diplomatic Relations with Israel.

3382	**1517**	55c. multicoloured	2·10	1·60

1518 Bertha von Suttner and Die Waffen nieder

2005. Centenary of Bertha von Suttner's Nobel Peace Prize.

3383	**1518**	55c. multicoloured	2·10	1·60

1519 "50 JAHRE BUNDES WEHR"

2005. 50th Anniv of German Federal Armed Forces.

3384	**1519**	55c. multicoloured	2·10	1·60

1520 Robert Koch and Microscope

2005. Centenary of Robert Koch's Nobel Prize for Physiology and Medicine.

3385	**1520**	55c. multicoloured	5·00	4·00

2005. Prussian Schlosses. New Palace, Sanssouci Park, Potsdam (2nd issue). Self-adhesive Stamp.

3386	**1507**	220c. multicoloured	7·50	6·50

1521 *Gonepteryx rhamni*

2005. Butterflies and Moths. Multicoloured. (a) Ordinary gum.

3387	**1521**	45c.+20c. Type **1521**	2·50	2·30
3388		55c.+25c. *Panaxia quadripunctaria*	3·00	2·40
3389		55c.+25c. *Inachis io*	3·00	2·40
3390		145c.+55c. *Brintesia circe*	6·50	5·75

(b) Self-adhesive.

3391		55c.+25c. As No. 3389	3·00	2·50

1522 Sights of Halle

2006. 1200th Anniv of Halle.

3392	**1522**	45c. multicoloured	1·70	1·30

1523 Wolfgang Mozart

2006. 250th Birth Anniv of Wolfgang Amadeus Mozart (composer).

3393	**1523**	55c. multicoloured	2·10	1·60

1524 Snow-covered Tree

2006. Winter.

3394	**1524**	55c. multicoloured	2·10	1·60

1525 Clouds over Earth

2006. Climate Protection Awareness.

3395	**1525**	55c.+25c. multicoloured	3·25	2·75

1526 Bull (detail) and Charles IV's Seal

2006. 650th Anniv of Charles IV's Golden Bull (document creating constitutional structure). (a) Ordinary or Self-adhesive gum.

3396	**1526**	145c. multicoloured	5·25	4·50

1527 German Flags

2006. Sport Promotion Fund. World Cup Football Championship, Germany. Multicoloured.

3398	**1527**	45c.+20c. Type **1527**	2·50	2·10
3399		55c.+25c. Horse and rider (World Equestrian Games, Aachen 2006)	2·75	2·30
3400		55c.+25c. Stadium lights (opening game)	2·75	2·30
3401		55c.+25c. Pitch (final)	2·75	2·30
3402		145c.+56c. Fireworks and emblem	6·50	5·50

1528 Rooftops

2006. 850th Anniv of Michaelskirche, Schwäbisch Hall.

3403	**1528**	55c. multicoloured	2·10	1·60

1529 "Fraiske Räid"

2006. 50th Anniv of Friesenrat (Frisian council).

3404	**1529**	90c. multicoloured	3·25	2·75

1530 Braille

2006. Bicentenary of Blind School, Berlin. 150th Anniv of Nikolauspflege (charitable organization).

3405	**1530**	55c. black and grey	2·10	1·60

1531 Early Town and Map

2006. 1200th Anniv of Ingolstadt.

3406	**1531**	55c. multicoloured	2·10	1·60

1532 Altes Museum, Lustgarten

2006. 225th Birth Anniv of Karl Friedrich Schinkel (architect). Ordinary or self-adhesive gum.

3407	**1532**	55c. multicoloured	2·10	1·60

1533 Self-Portrait

2006. Johannes Rau (president 1999—2004) Commemoration.

3408	**1533**	55c. multicoloured	2·10	1·60

1534 Emblem

2006. 500th Anniv of European University Viadrina Frankfurt (Oder).

3409	**1534**	55c. blue and black	2·10	1·60

1535 Blossom-covered Trees

2006. Spring.

3410	**1535**	55c. multicoloured	2·10	1·60

1536 Self-Portrait (Albrecht Dürer)

2006. Art.

3411	**1536**	145c. blue and black	5·25	4·25

2006. World Cup Football Championship, Germany. Sheet 130×180 mm containing T **1527** and similar horiz designs. Multicoloured.

MS3412	130×180 mm. Nos. 3398, 3400/2		15·00	14·00

1537 "Integration" on Jacket

2006. Europa. Integration.

3413	**1537**	55c. multicoloured	2·10	1·60

1538 Rhine Valley

2006. Upper Central Rhine Valley (Oberes Mittelrheintal). World Heritage Site. Ordinary or self-adhesive gum.

3414	**1538**	55c. multicoloured	2·10	1·60

1539 Gerd Bucerius

2006. Birth Centenary of Gerd Bucerius (politician).

3416	**1539**	85c. multicoloured	3·25	2·50

1540 Pine Marten

2006. Youth Welfare. Animals. Multicoloured.

3417		45c.+20c. Type **1540**	2·20	2·00
3418		55c.+25c. Hares	2·75	2·40
3419		55c.+25c. Red squirrel	2·75	2·40
3420		55c.+25c. Roe deer and fawn	2·75	2·40
3421		145c.+55c. Wild boar and young	6·75	5·75

1541 Stripes

2006. Birth Centenary of Stefan Andres (writer).

3422	**1541**	55c. multicoloured	2·10	1·60

1542 Brooklyn Bridge, New York

2006. Birth Bicentenary of Johan August Robling (architect).

3423	**1542**	145c. multicoloured	5·25	4·00

1543 Car Number Plates

2006. Centenary of First Number Plates.

3424	**1543**	45c. multicoloured	1·90	1·50

1544 Berghauser Castle, Burganlage

2006

3425	**1544**	55c. multicoloured	2·10	1·60

1545 Flowering Rapeseed

2006. Summer.

3426	**1545**	55c. multicoloured	2·10	1·60

1546 *Saskia van Uylenburgh*

2006. 400th Birth Anniv of Rembrandt Harmenszoon van Rijn (Rembrandt) (artist).

3427	**1546**	55c. multicoloured	2·50	2·10

2006. Lighthouses. As T **1505**. Multicoloured.

3429		45c. Neuland	1·90	1·50
3430		55c. Hohe Weg	2·10	1·60

1547 Valley

2006. Tourism. Schwarzwald. Sheet 145×70 mm.

MS3432	**1547**	55c. multicoloured	2·20	2·10

1548 Valley and Skull

2006. 150th Anniv of Discovery of Neanderthal Skull.

3433	**1548**	220c. multicoloured	7·50	6·50

1549 Cat and Envelopes

2006. For us Children

3434	**1549**	55c. multicoloured	2·10	1·60

1550 Hauptmann von Kopenick

2006. Centenary of Hauptmann von Kopenick (fraudulent identity of William Voigt) Affair.

3435	**1550**	55c. multicoloured	2·10	1·60

1551 Shipping and Trade

2006. 650th Anniv of Hanseatic league (Stadtehanse).

3436	**1551**	70c. multicoloured	2·75	2·40

1552 Fliegender Hamburger VT 877

2006. Welfare. Trains. Multicoloured. (a) Ordinary gum.

3437		45c.+20c. Type **1552**	2·50	2·30
3438		55c.+25c. Intercity Express ET 403	2·75	2·40
3439		55c.+25c. Trans Europe Express VT 11.5	2·75	2·40
3440		145c.+55c. Henschel-Wegmann-Zug 61 001	7·00	6·00

(b) Self-adhesive.

3441		55c.+25c. As No. 3438	3·00	2·50

1553 Postcard, 1896

2006. Stamp Day.

3442	**1553**	55c. multicoloured	2·10	1·60

1554 Woodland

2006. Autumn.

3443	**1554**	55c. multicoloured	2·10	1·60

1555 Hannah Arendt

2006. Birth Centenary of Hannah Arendt (political theorist and philosopher).
3444 **1555** 145c. multicoloured   5·00   4·50

1556 Eugen Bolz

2006. 125th Birth Anniv of Eugen Anton Bolz (Catholic politician).
3445 **1556** 45c. blue and yellow   1·90   1·30

1557 The Nativity

2006. Christmas. Paintings by Meister Franke. Multicoloured.
3446 45c.+20c. Type **1557**   2·20   2·00
3447 55c.+25c. Three Kings   2·75   2·40

1558 Cardinal Hoffner

2006. Birth Centenary of Cardinal Joseph Hoffner (Bishop of Munster and Archbishop of Cologne).
3448 **1558** 55c. multicoloured   2·10   1·60

2006. Seasons. Multicoloured.
3449 55c. As Type **1535**   2·10   1·60
3450 55c. As Type **1545**   2·10   1·60
3451 55c. As Type **1554**   2·10   1·60
3452 55c. As Type **1524**   2·10   1·60

1559 Werner Forbmann

2006. 50th Anniv of Werner Forbmann's (surgeon and inventor of the heart catheter) Nobel Prize for Medicine.
3453 **1559** 90c. multicoloured   3·25   3·00

1560 Street

2007. Furth Millenary. (a) Ordinary or self-adhesive gum.
3454 **1560** 45c. multicoloured   1·90   1·50

1561 Stars

2007. Germany's Presidency of European Union.
3456 **1561** 55c. black, vermilion and yellow   2·10   1·60

1562 Imperial Cathedral Facade

2007. Bamberg Diocese Millenary.
3457 **1562** 55c. rosine, blue and gold   2·10   1·60

1563 Symbols of Saarland

2007. 50th Anniv of Federal Republic of Saarland. (a) Ordinary or self-adhesive gum.
3458 **1563** 55c. multicoloured   2·10   1·60

1564 Ball and Hands

2007. Sport Promotion Fund (1st issue). World Handball Championship, Germany.
3460 **1564** 55c.+25c. multicoloured   3·25   2·75
See also Nos. 3462/4.

1565 Engine Diagram and NSU Ro80

2007. 50th Anniv of Rotary Engine designed by Felix Wankel.
3461 **1565** 145c. multicoloured   5·00   4·50

2007. Sport Promotion Fund (2nd issue). As T **1564**. Multicoloured.
3462 45c.+20c. Canoeing (world championships, Wedau Park)   2·50   2·30
3463 55c.+25c. Gymnastics (world championships, Stuttgart)   3·00   2·50
3464 145c.+55c. Swimming (world pentathlon championships, Berlin)   6·00   5·25

1566 Johann Senckenberg and Institute Building

2007. 300th Birth Anniv of Johann Christian Senckenberg (physician and health reformer).
3465 **1566** 90c. multicoloured   3·25   3·00

1567 Claus Schenk Graf von Stauffenberg and Helmuth James Graf von Moltke

2007. Birth Centenaries.
3466 **1567** 55c. vermilion and black   2·10   1·60

1568 Star of David

2007. Jewish Centre, Munich.
3467 **1568** 55c. multicoloured   2·10   1·60

1569 *Die Ausgrabung der Kreuze* (Adam Elsheimer)

2007
3468 **1569** 55c. multicoloured   2·10   1·60

1570 Signatories

2007. 50th Anniv of Treaty of Rome.
3469 **1570** 55c. multicoloured   2·10   1·60

1571 Paul Gerhardt and Score

2007. 400th Birth Anniv of Paul Gerhardt.
3470 **1571** 55c. multicoloured   2·10   1·60

1572 LZ 127 *Graf Zeppelin*

2007. Stamp Day. Sheet 105×70 mm.
MS3471 **1572** 170c.+70c. mult   8·75   7·75

1573 Writing a Letter

2007. Post. Each yellow, black and vermilion.
3472 55c. Type **1573**   2·10   1·60
3473 55c. Posting letter   2·10   1·60

1574 Pope Benedict XVI

2007. 80th Birthday of Pope Benedict XVI.
3474 **1574** 55c. multicoloured   2·10   1·60

1575 "Universalis Cosmographia"

2007. 500th Anniv of World Map drawn by Martin Waldseemüller.
3475 **1575** €2.20 multicoloured   8·00   7·00

1576 Scouts

2007. Europa. Centenary of Scouting.
3476 **1576** 45c. multicoloured   1·70   1·30

2007. 40th Anniv of Sport Promotion Fund. As T **1564**. Multicoloured.
MS3477 45c.+20c. As No. 3462; 55c.+25c. As No. 3460; 55c.+25c. As No. 3463; 145c.+55c. As No. 3464   13·00   11·50

1577 Schloss

2007. Bellevue Schloss. Ordinary or self-adhesive gum.
3478 **1577** 55c. multicoloured   2·10   1·60

1578 Schloss and Sculptures

2007. 700th Anniv of Moyland Schloss.
3480 **1578** 85c. multicoloured   3·25   2·50

1579 Early Festival Goers

2007. 175th Anniv of Hambacher Fest (democratic festival). (a) Ordinary or Self-adhesive gum.
3481 **1579** 145c. multicoloured   5·00   4·00

1580 Sawing legs from Chair

2007. 125th Birth Anniv of Valentin Ludwig Fey (Karl Valentin) (comedian and writer).
3483 **1580** 45c. multicoloured   1·90   1·50

1581 'Nichts Schonres gab's fur Tante Lotte Als Schwarze-Heidelbeer-Kompotte' (Behold Aunt Lotte's choicest snack: Blueberry compote, sweet and black)

2007. For the Young. 175th Birth Anniv of Wilhelm Busch (poet and cartoonist). Sheet 165×75 mm containing T **1581** and similar square designs showing scenes from illustrated poem Hans Huckebein–der Unglucksrabe (the unlucky raven) by Wilhelm Busch. Multicoloured.
MS3484 45c.+20c. Type **1581**; 55c.+25c. Doch Huckebein verschleudert nur Die schone Gabe der Natur (But Huckebein, unused to thrift, Just squanders nature's precious gift); 55c.+25c. Die Tante naht voll Zorn und Schrecken; Hans Huckebein verlaßt das Becken (The aunt descends in shock and wrath, Hans Huckebein deserts his bath); 145c.+55c. Und schnell betritt er, angstbeflugelt, Die Wasche, welche frisch gebugelt (And tramples, on the wings of fright, The ironed laundry, clean and white)   13·00   11·50

1582 Paul Klinger and Nadia Grey (poster for film *Hengst Maestoso Austria*)

2007. Birth Centenary of Paul Karl Heinrich Klinksik (Paul Klinger) (actor).
3485 **1582** 55c. multicoloured   2·75   2·40

2007. Lighthouses. As T **1467**. Multicoloured.
3486 45c. Bremerhaven Oberfeuer   1·90   1·50
3487 55c. Hornum   2·10   1·60

1583 House of Blackheads, Riga

2007. World Heritage Sites, Riga and Wismar. Multicoloured.
3488 65c. Type **1583**   2·20   2·00
3489 70c. City Hall and St. George's Church, Wismar   2·40   2·10
Stamps of a similar design were issued by Latvia.

1584 Banknotes and Coins from Various Currency Epochs

2007. 50th Anniv of German Bundesbank (Federal bank).
3490 **1584** 55c. multicoloured   2·20   1·60

1585 Saale River Plain

2007. 75th Anniv of Saaletalsperre Bleiloch (dam across Saale valley).
3491 **1585** 55c. multicoloured   2·20   1·60

1586 Kaiser Wilhelm Bridge

2007. Centenary of Kaiser Wilhelm Bridge, Wilhelmshaven.
3492 **1586** 145c. multicoloured   5·25   4·50

1587 Hedgehog and Hearts

2007. For us Children
3493 **1587** 55c. multicoloured   2·20   1·60

1588 Receiving a Letter

2007. Post. Multicoloured.
3494 55c. Type **1588**   2·10   1·60
3495 55c. Reading letter   2·10   1·60

1589 Symbols of Science

2007. 50th Anniv of Wissenschaftsrat (government scientific advisors).
3496 **1589** 90c. multicoloured   3·50   3·00

1590 Stylized Building

2007. Centenary of Deutscher Werkbund (artistic design group).
3497 **1590** 55c. multicoloured   2·10   1·60

1591 Section of 'Limes' and Watch Towers

2007. World Heritage Site. 'The Roman Limes' (Roman camp, castle and walls). Sheet 105×70 mm.
MS3498 **1591** 55c. multicoloured   2·10   2·00

1592 Karl Freiherr Vom Stein

2007. 250th Birth Anniv of Heinrich Friedrich Carl Freiherr Vom und Zum Stein (statesman and reformer).
3499 **1592** 145c. multicoloured   5·00   4·50

1593 Three Kings

2007. Christmas. Multicoloured.
3500 45c.+20c. Type **1593**   2·50   2·30
3501 55c.+25c. Virgin and Child   2·75   2·50

1594 St. Elizabeth feeding Invalid

2007. 800th Birth Anniv of St. Elizabeth von Thuringen.
3502 **1594** 55c. multicoloured   2·10   1·60

1595 Astrid Lindgren and Emil from Lönneberga (character from book)

2007. Birth Centenary of Astrid Lindgren (children's author).
3503 **1595** 100c. multicoloured   3·50   3·25

A stamp of the same design was issued by Sweden.

1596 Brandenburg Gate, Berlin

2007. 275th Birth Anniv of Carl Gotthard Langhans (architect). Ordinary or self-adhesive gum.
3504 **1596** 55c. multicoloured   2·10   1·60

1597 Guinea Pigs

2007. Welfare. Pets. Showing animals and young. Multicoloured. (a) Ordinary gum.
3506 45c.+20c. Type **1597**   2·50   2·30
3507 55c.+25c. Dogs   2·75   2·40
3508 55c.+25c. Horses   2·75   2·40
3509 145c.+55c. Rabbits   6·75   6·00

(b) Self-adhesive.
3510 55c.+25c. As No. 3508   3·25   3·00

1598 Liturgical Book and Gothic Wall Painting (detail), Reichenau Abbey

2008. World Heritage Site. Ordinary or self-adhesive gum.
3511 **1598** 45c. multicoloured   1·80   1·50

1599 Old Berlin Distillery

2008. 150th Birth Anniv of Heinrich Zille (artist).
3513 **1599** 55c. multicoloured   2·10   1·80

1600 '50 Jahre Bundeskartellamt'

2008. 50th Anniv of Bundeskartellamt (monopolies commission).
3514 **1600** 90c. multicoloured   3·50   3·25

1601 Cathedral Square

2008. 1100th Anniv of Eichstatt. Ordinary or self-adhesive gum.
3515 **1601** 145c. multicoloured   5·50   5·00

1602 Decorative Pot with Shell Insert

2008. 500th Birth Anniv of Wenzel Jamnitzer (goldsmith).
3517 **1602** 220c. multicoloured   8·25   7·50

1603 Der Arme Poet

2008. Birth Bicentenary of Carl Spitzweg (artist). Ordinary or self-adhesive gum.
3518 **1603** 55c. multicoloured   2·20   2·10

1604 Fish and Heart ('Herzlichen Gluckwunsch') (Congratulations)

2008. Post. Multicoloured.
3519 55c. Type **1604**   2·20   2·10
3520 55c. Cats ('Alles Gute') (All Good)   2·20   2·10

1605 Church Facade

2008. Millenary of Bochum-Stiepel Village Church.
3521 **1605** 145c. multicoloured   5·50   5·00

1606 Glider World Championships, Lusse

2008. Sports Promotion Fund. Multicoloured.
3522 45c.+20c. Type **1606**   2·40   2·20
3523 55c.+25c. European Football Championships, Austria and Switzerland   2·75   2·40
3524 55c.+25c. Chess Olympiad, Dresden   2·75   2·40
3525 145c.+55c. Olympic Games, Beijing   7·00   6·25

1607 Helmut Kautner

2008. Birth Centenary of Helmut Kautner (film director).
3526 **1607** 55c. multicoloured   2·30   2·00

1608 Gnu Herd

2008. 150th Anniv of Frankfurt Zoological Society.
3527 **1608** 65c. multicoloured   2·50   2·30

2008. 50th Anniv of Bundeskartellamt (monopolies commission) (2nd issue). Self adhesive.
3528 **1600** 90c. multicoloured   3·50   3·25

1609 Birds

2008. Centenary of State Bird Sanctuary, Seebach.
3529 **1609** 45c. multicoloured   2·10   1·60

1610 Max Planck

2008. 150th Birth Anniv of Max Planck (physicist, Nobel Prize Winner–1918).
3530 **1610** 55c. multicoloured   2·30   2·00

1611 Johann Wichern

2008. Birth Bicentenary of Johann Hinrich Wichern (theologian).
3531 **1611** 55c. multicoloured   2·30   2·00

1612 Knut (hand reared polar bear cub)

2008. Environmental Protection.
3532 **1612** 55c.+25c. multicoloured   3·25   3·00

1613 'Der Bewahrer eines einzigen Lebens hat eine ganze Welt bewahrt' ((he who saves a single life saves the whole world) (translation of Hebrew engraving on Oskar Schindler's ring, gift of farewell from rescuee on 8 May 1945))

2008. Birth Centenary of Oskar Schindler (industrialist who saved Jews during WWII).
3533 **1613** 145c. multicoloured   5·50   5·00

1614 Photograph of German Players (5 April 1908) and Parts of Original Poster

2008. Centenary of German Soccer Internationals.
3534 **1614** 170c. multicoloured   6·50   6·00

1615 Blurred Script

2008. Centenary of Christoffel Blind Mission. (Christoffel Blindoffmission) (charity founded by pastor Ernst Jakob Christoffel for sopport of the blind worldwide.
3535 **1615** 55c. multicoloured   2·30   2·00

1616 Sun and Moon ('Herzliche Grube (cordial greetings)')

2008. Greetings Stamps. Europa. The Letter (3536/8). Multicoloured. (a) Ordinary gum.
3536 55c. Type **1616**   2·30   2·00
3537 55c. Hands holding bird and flower ('Danke' (thank you))   2·30   2·00

(b) Self-adhesive.
3538 55c. As Type **1616**   2·30   2·00
3539 55c. As No. 3520   2·30   2·00
3540 55c. As No. 3519   2·30   2·00
3541 55c. As No. 3537   2·30   2·00

1617 Dornier Do J Wal

2008. Welfare. Aircraft. Multicoloured. (a) Ordinary gum.
3542 45c.+20c. Type **1617**   3·00   2·75
3543 55c.+25c. A380 Airbus   3·00   3·00
3544 55c.+25c. Junkers Ju 52   3·00   3·00
3545 145c.+55c. Messerschmitt-Bolkow-Blohm (MBB) BO 105   7·50   7·00

(b) Self-adhesive.
3546   55c.+25c. As No. 3543   3·75   3·50

1618 Faces

2008. Community Service.
3547   **1618**   55c. multicoloured   2·30   2·00

1619 Steam Locomotive, Early Station and Passengers

2008. 125th Anniv of Drachenfels Railway (Drachenfelsbahn) (rack railway line from Konigswinter to summit of Drachenfels).
3548   **1619**   45c. multicoloured   2·00   1·90

1620 Warnemunde

2008. Lighthouses. Multicoloured. (a) Ordinary gum.
3549   45c. Type **1620**   2·10   1·80
3550   55c. Amrum   2·30   2·00

(b) Self-adhesive.
3551   55c. Hornum   2·30   2·00
3552   55c. As No. 3550   2·30   2·00

1621 Man at Table (drawing by Franz Kafka)

2008. 125th Birth Anniv of Franz Kafka (Czech writer).
3553   **1621**   55c. black   2·40   2·10

1622 *Selbstportrat mit Ruckenakt* and *Morgensonne*

2008. 150th Birth Anniv of Lovis Corinth (artist).
3554   **1622**   145c. multicoloured   6·00   5·75

1623 *Gorch Fock*

2008. 50th Anniv of *Gorch Fock* (sail training ship).
3555   **1623**   55c. multicoloured   2·50   2·30

1624 Silhouette *Ringelnatz* (Ernst Moritz Engert)

2008. 125th Birth Anniv of Joachim Ringelnatz (writer and artist).
3556   **1624**   85c. blue and black   3·75   3·50

1625 Herman Schulze-Delitzsch

2008. Birth Bicentenary of Herman Schulze-Delitzsch (politician and founder of German cooperative system).
3557   **1625**   90c. multicoloured   4·00   3·75

1626 Triceratops

2008. Youth Stamp. Dinosaurs. Sheet 190×110 mm containing T **1626** and similar horiz designs. Multicoloured.
MS3558 45c.+20c. Type **1626**; 55c.+25c. Tyrannosaurus; 55c.+25c. Diplodocus; 145c.+55c. Plateosaurus   17·00   17·00

1627 Arrival of First Mail Coach in Ohrdruff

2008. Stamp Day. Philatelic Treasures.
3559   **1627**   55c. multicoloured   2·50   2·30

1628 Ronald, Gunni and Jenny the Rat riding Blue Horse

2008. For us Children
3560   **1628**   55c. multicoloured   2·50   2·30

1629 Old Bridge, Bad Sackingen–Stein/Aargau

2008. Bridges.
3561   **1629**   70c. multicoloured   3·00   2·75
A stamp of a similar design was issued by Switzerland.

1630 Livestock Market

2008. 500th Anniv of Gallimarkt (annual fair), Leer.
3562   **1630**   45c. multicoloured   2·00   1·80

1631 Disc and Two Bronze Swords

2008. Archaeology. Sky Disc of Nebra (bronze plate with apparent astronomical phenomena and religious themes).
3563   **1631**   55c. multicoloured   2·50   2·30

1632 Lorenz Werthmann

2008. 150th Birth Anniv of Lorenz Werthmann (founder and first president of the German Caritas association).
3564   **1632**   55c. multicoloured   2·50   2·30

1633 Aircraft in Flight

2008. Centenary of Hans Grade's First Powered Flight in Germany.
3565   **1633**   145c. multicoloured   6·00   5·50

2008. Winter. 450th Anniv (2005) of the 'Peace of Augsburg' (treaty marking the beginning of peaceful cohabitation of Catholics and Protestants) (3566). As Types **1484** and **1511**. Multicoloured. Self-adhesive.
3566   55c. As Type **1484**   2·50   2·30
3567   55c. As Type **1511**   2·50   2·30
See also Nos. 3305 and 3375.
Type **1634** is vacant

1635 The Nativity (Albrecht Durer)

2008. Christmas. Multicoloured.
3568   45c.+20c. Type **1635**   3·00   2·75
3569   55c.+25c. *The Nativity* (Raffaello Santi) (horiz)   3·75   3·50

1636 Association Emblem

2008. 30th Anniv of 'Heart for Children' Association (children's charity).
3570   **1636**   55c. vermilion and black   2·50   2·30

1637 'Leben'

2008. 50th Anniv of Federal Association of Life (intellectual diasablities charity).
3571   **1637**   55c. multicoloured   2·50   2·30

1638 *Nils Holgersson with Ganz* (book illustration by Wilhelm Schultz)

2008. 150th Birth Anniv of Selma Ottilia Lovisz Lagerlof (winner of Nobel Prize for Literature–1909).
3572   **1638**   100c. multicoloured   4·50   4·00

1639 Building Facade

2009. 500th Anniv of Frankenberg Hall. Multicoloured. Ordinary or self-adhesive gum.
3573   45c. Type **1639**   2·30   2·00

1640 Plates with Cereal Grains

2009. 50th Anniv of MISEREOR and Bread for the World (church charities).
3575   **1640**   55c. multicoloured   2·75   2·50

1641 Rainbow

2009. Welfare Stamps. Celestial Phenomena. Multicoloured. (a) Ordinary gum.
3576   45c.+20c. Type **1641**   3·75   3·50
3577   55c.+25c. Aurora borealis   4·00   3·75
3578   55c.+25c. Sunset   4·00   3·75
3579   145c.+55c. Lightning   9·75   9·00

(b) Self-adhesive.
3580   55c.+25c. As No. 3678   4·25   4·00

1642 Tangermunde Castle

2009. Tangermunde Castle Millennary.
3581   **1642**   90c. multicoloured   4·25   4·00

1643 Theodor Heuss

2009. 125th Birth Anniv of Theodor Heuss (politician, writer and first FDR Head of State).
3582   **1643**   145c. multicoloured   7·00   6·50

1644 Heinz Erhardt

2009. Birth Centenary of Heinz Erhardt (comedian).
3583   **1644**   55c. multicoloured   2·50   2·40

1645 Felix Mendelssohn

2009. Birth Bicentenary of Jakob Ludwig Felix Mendelssohn Bartholdy (composer).
3584   **1645**   65c. multicoloured   3·00   2·75

1646 *The Propylaea in Munich*

2009. 225th Birth Anniv of Leo von Klenze (architect).
3585   **1646**   70c. multicoloured   3·25   3·00

1647 *The Firebird*

2009. Birth Centenary of Helmut Andreas Paul (HAP) Grieshaber (artist).
3586   **1647**   165c. multicoloured   7·25   6·50

1648 Golo Mann

2009. Birth Centenary of Angelus Gottfried Thomas Mann (Golo) Mann (historian and writer).
3587 **1648** 45c. multicoloured   2·30   2·10

1649 Applying Stamp

2009. Post. Multicoloured.
3588 55c. Type **1649**   2·75   2·50
3589 55c. Post Office   2·75   2·50

1650
Stahlradwagen

2009. 175th Birth Anniv of Gottlieb Wilhelm Daimler (engineer and motor vehicle pioneer).
3590 **1650** 170c. multicoloured   8·00   7·50

1651 Hurdler

2009. Sports Promotion Fund. International Association of Athletics Federations World Championship—Berlin 2009. Multicoloured.
3591 45c.+20c. Type **1651**   3·25   3·00
3592 55c.+25c. Pole vaulter   4·00   3·75
3593 55c.+25c. Runners   4·00   3·75
3594 145c.+55c. Discus   9·75   9·00

1652 Bernhard Grzimek

2009. Birth Centenary of Bernhard Grzimek (film maker).
3595 **1652** 55c. multicoloured   2·75   2·50

1653 Planets

2009. Europa. Astronomy. 400th Anniv of Kepler's Laws.
3596 **1653** 55c. multicoloured   2·75   2·50

2009. Post. As T **1649**. Multicoloured.
3597 55c. Transport   2·75   2·50
3598 55c. Delivery   2·75   2·50

1654 Eichstatt Letter (showing first German stamps, franked 1849)

2009. Stamp Day.
3599 **1654** 55c.+25c. multicoloured   4·00   3·75

1655 Luther Memorials, Eisleben and Wittenberg

2009. World Heritage Sites.
3600 **1655** 145c. multicoloured   6·75   6·25

1656 First Exhibition Poster, Frankfurt 1909

2009. Centenary of International Aerospace Exhibition.
3601 **1656** 55c. multicoloured   2·50   2·40

1657 *Mask* (Christian Grovermann), *Emperor Agustus* (Jochen Hahnel), Hermann Monument, Teutoburg Forest and *Forest* (Thomas Serres)

2009. Bimillennary of Varus (Teutoburg Forest) Battle. Multicoloured. Ordinary or self-adhesive gum.
3602 55c. Type **1657**   2·50   2·40

1658 Illustration from *Struwwelpeter*

2009. Birth Bicentenary of Heinrich Hoffman (children's author and politician).
3604 **1658** 85c. multicoloured   4·00   3·50

1659 Eifel National Park

2009. Sheet 105×70 mm.
MS3605 **1659** 220c. multicoloured   9·75   8·75

1660 Norderney

2009. Lighthouses. Multicoloured.
3606 45c. Type **1660**   2·10   1·90
3607 55c. Dornbusch   2·50   2·40

1661 Early Campus

2009. 600th Anniv of Leipzig University. Multicoloured.
(a) Ordinary gum.
3608 55c. Type **1661**   2·50   2·40

(b) Size 38×22 mm. Self-adhesive.
3609 55c. As Type **1661**   2·50   2·40

1662 John Calvin

2009. 500th Birth Anniv of John Calvin (religious reformer).
3610 **1662** 70c. black   3·50   3·00

1663 Loading

2009. Centenary of Sassnitz to Trelleborg Ferry.
3611 **1663** 145c. multicoloured   6·75   6·25

1664 Baltic Sea Beach

2009. Youth Stamps. 50th Anniv of Unser Sandmannchen (children's television programme). Multicoloured.
3612 45c.+20c. Type **1664**   3·00   2·75
3613 55c.+25c. Flying machine   4·00   3·50
3614 55c.+25c. Harz narrow–gauge railway   4·00   3·50
3615 145c.+55c. Planet Gugel   9·25   8·50

1665 Houses and Young People

2009. Centenary of Jugendherbergen (youth hostels).
3616 **1665** 55c. multicoloured   2·50   2·40

2009. Centenary of International Aerospace Exhibition. Self-adhesive.
3616a **1656** 55c. multicoloured   2·50   2·40

1666 Early Race Cars

2009. Historic Motorsport. 115th Anniv of First Automobile Race between Paris and Rouen in France. Sheet 105×70 mm.
MS3617 **1666** 85c. multicoloured   4·25   3·75

1667 Cathedral

2009. Millenary of Mainz Cathedral (Mainzer Dom) Consecration.
3618 **1667** 90c. multicoloured   4·25   3·75

1668 Cowboy and Indian

2009. For us Children
3619 **1668** 55c. multicoloured   2·50   2·40

1669 Celebration

2009. 60th Anniv of Basic Law and 20th Anniv of Fall of Berlin Wall.
3620 **1669** 55c. multicoloured   2·50   2·40

1670 Bundestag, Reichstag Building (parliament)

2009. Government. Sheet 130×90 mm containing T **1670** and similar horiz design. Multicoloured.
MS3621 55c. Type **1670**; 90c. Bundesrat, Prussian Manor, Berlin (federal council)   7·00   6·25

1671 '20'

2009. 20th Anniv of Opening of Border between Austria and Hungary.
3622 **1671** 70c. multicoloured   3·50   3·00
   A stamp of a similar design was issued by Austria and Hungary.

1672 *Still Life with Cherries* (Georg Flegel)

2009. Art.
3623 **1672** 45c. multicoloured   2·10   1·90

1673 Crowd and Nikolai Church, Leipzig

2009. 20th Anniv of Peaceful Revolution.
3624 **1673** 55c. multicoloured   2·50   2·40

1674 Adoration of the Magi

2009. Christmas. The Hoya Missal. Multicoloured.
3625 45c.+20c. Type **1674**   3·00   2·75
3626 55c.+25c. Holy Family   4·00   3·50

1675 Badger

2009. Animal of the Year.
3627 **1675** 55c. multicoloured   2·50   2·40

1676 Marion Grafin Donhoff

2009. Birth Centenary of Marion Grafin Donhoff (political journalist).
3628 **1676** 55c. multicoloured   2·50   2·40

1677 *Die Kunste ist eine Tochter der Freiheit*

2009. Birth Bicentenary of Johann Christoph Friedrich von Schiller.
3629 **1677** 145c. black, ultramarine and brownish grey   6·75   6·25

1678 Exhibits

2010. Bicentenary of Natural History Museum, Berlin. Ordinary or self-adhesive gum.
3630 **1678** 45c. multicoloured   2·30   2·10

1679 *Malus domestica* (apple)

2010. Welfare Stamps. Fruit. Multicoloured. (a) Ordinary gum.

3632		45c.+20c. Type **1679**	3·25	3·00
3633		55c.+25c. *Citrus limon* (lemon)	4·00	3·75
3634		55c.+25c. *Fragaria ananassa* (strawberry)	4·00	3·75
3635		145c.+55c. *Vaccinium myrtillus* (bilberry)	9·75	8·75

(b) Self-adhesive.

3636		55c.+25c. As No. 3634 (strawberry)	4·00	3·75

1680 'Ruhr 2010'

2010. Ruhr–European Capital of Culture, 2010.

3637	**1680**	55c. multicoloured	2·75	2·50

1681 *Limburg an der Lahn* (George Clarkson Stanfield)

2010. 1100th Anniv of Limburg an der Lahn. Ordinary or self-adhesive gum.

3638	**1681**	145c. multicoloured	7·25	7·00

1682 St Michael's Church, Hildesheim

2010. Millenary of St Michael's Church, Hildesheim. UNESCO World Heritage Site. Ordinary or self-adhesive gum.

3640	**1682**	220c. multicoloured	11·00	10·50

1683 Disabled Athlete

2010. Sports Promotion Fund. Winter Paralympics (45c.+20c.) or Winter Olympic Games, Vancouver (55c.+25c.). Multicoloured.

3642		45c.+20c. Type **1683**	3·25	3·00
3643		55c.+25c. Skier	4·25	4·00

1684 Family playing

2010. Mensch ärgere dich nicht (board game designed by Joseph Friedrich Schmidt).

3644	**1684**	55c. multicoloured	2·75	2·50

1685 Ring

2010. 14th-century Jewish Wedding Ring found at Erfurt.

3645	**1685**	90c. multicoloured	4·75	4·50

1686 Ship

2010. Post. Greeting Stamps (1st issue). Multicoloured.

3646		55c. Type **1686**	2·75	2·50
3647		55c. Rainbow	2·75	2·50

1687 *Ariadne abandoned by Theseus*

2010. Art. Painting by Maria Anna Catharina Angelica (Angelica) Kauffmann.

3648	**1687**	260c. multicoloured	13·00	12·00

2010. Post. Greeting Stamps (2nd issue). Multicoloured.

3649		55c. Dove	2·75	2·50
3650		55c. Angel carrying heart	2·75	2·50

1688 Footballers

2010. Sports Promotion Fund. Football World Cup Championships, South Africa (55c.+25c.) or 2010 Ice Hockey World Cup, Germany (145c.+55c.). Multicoloured.

3651		55c.+25c. Type **1688**	4·25	4·00
3652		145c.+55c. Ice hockey players	10·00	9·25

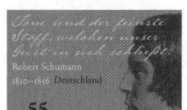

1689 Birds and Cliffs

2010. Centenary of Helgoland Ornithological Institute

(a) Sheet 105×70 mm. Ordinary gum

MS3653	**1689**	145c. multicoloured	7·25	6·75

(b) Coil stamp. Self-adhesive

3654	**1689**	145c. multicoloured	7·25	6·75

1690 Robert Schumann

2010. Birth Bicentenary of Robert Alexander Schumann (composer)

3655	**1690**	55c. multicoloured	2·75	2·50

1691 Zampino the Magical Bear

2010. Europa. Children's Books

3656	**1691**	55c. multicoloured	2·75	2·50

1692 Bee

2010. Bee Awareness Campaign

(a) Ordinary gum

3657	**1692**	55c. multicoloured	2·75	2·50

(b) Self-adhesive gum

3658	**1692**	55c. multicoloured	2·75	2·50

1693 Grey Seals

2010. Environmental Protection

3659	**1693**	55c.+25c. multicoloured	4·25	4·00

The premium was for marine conservation.

1694 Neuwerk

2010. Lighthouses. Multicoloured.

3660		45c. Type **1694**	2·20	2·10
3661		55c. Falshöft	2·75	2·50

1695 Konrad Zuse

2010. Birth Centenary of Konrad Zuse (engineer and computer pioneer)

3662	**1695**	55c. steel blue, pale blue and yellow-olive	2·75	2·50

1696 Ship and Figure holding Wine Glass (Andrea Doria)

2010. Illustrations of Songs by Udo Lindenburg (rock musician and artist). Multicoloured.

(a) Sheet stamps. Ordinary gum

3663		45c. Type **1696**	2·20	2·10
3664		55c. Train (*Sonderzug nach Pankow*)	2·75	2·50

(b) Size 38×22 mm. Booklet stamps. Self-adhesive

3665		45c. As Type **1696**	2·20	2·10
3666		55c. As No. 3664	2·75	2·50

1697 Johann Friedrich Böttger (inventor of first process) demonstrates to August the Strong (painting by Paul Kießling)

2010. 300th Anniv of Porcelain Production in Europe

3667	**1697**	55c. multicoloured	2·75	2·50

1698 Four Seater Stagecoach

2010. Historic Mail Coaches

3668	**1698**	145c. multicoloured	7·25	6·75

1699 *Germany*

2010. Youth Stamps. Multicoloured.

3669		45c.+20c. Type **1699**	3·25	3·00
3670		55c.+25c. *Imperator*	4·00	3·75
3671		55c.+25c. *Aller*	4·00	3·75
3672		145c.+55c. *Columbus*	9·75	8·75

1700 Bf 108 Taifun (D-EBEI) and Elly Beinhorn

2010. 75th Anniv of Elly Beinhorn's Long distance flight from Gliwice to Berlin, via Istanbul

3673	**1700**	55c. black and carmine	2·75	2·50

1701 Mother Teresa

2010. Birth Centenary of Agnes Gonxha Bojaxhiu (Mother Teresa) (founder of Missionaries of Charity)

3674	**1701**	70c. black and new blue	3·50	3·00

1702 Jorge Luis Borges

2010. Frankfurt Bookfair

3675	**1702**	170c. black, silver and scarlet-vermilion	8·25	7·75

2010. 300th Anniv of Porcelain Production in Europe. Self-adhesive

3676	**1697**	55c. multicoloured	2·75	2·50

1703 Bear cradling Child

2010. For Us Children

3677	**1703**	55c. multicoloured	2·75	2·50

1704 Imperial German Post to Helgoland, Norderney, Sylt (poster, 1880)

2010. Stamp Day

3678	**1704**	55c. multicoloured	2·75	2·50

1705 Merry-go-Round

2010. Bicentenary of Oktoberfest

3679	**1705**	55c. multicoloured	2·75	2·50

1706 Celebration of German Unity in Berlin

2010. 20th Anniv of Re-unification of Germany

(a) Ordinary gum

3680	**1706**	55c. multicoloured	2·75	2·50

(b) Coil stamp. Self-adhesive

3681	**1706**	55c. multicoloured	2·75	2·50

1707 Castle, Schweinspoint

2010. 150th Anniv of St John Foundation for the Disabled

3682	**1707**	90c. multicoloured	4·75	4·50

1708 Baumann'sche House (Upper German), Eppingen (1582)

2010. Half-timbered Architecture. Multicoloured.
3683   **1708**   45c. Type **1708**   2·20   2·10
3684   55c. Farmhouse (Low German), Trebel-Dunsche (1734)   2·75   2·50

1709 Ear of Corn

2010. Thanksgiving
3685   **1709**   55c. multicoloured   2·75   2·50

1710 Friedrich Loeffler and Pathogen

2010. Centenary of Friedrich Loeffler Institute
3686   **1710**   85c. multicoloured   4·50   4·25

2010. Post. Greeting Stamps (3rd issue). Self-adhesive. Multicoloured.
3686a   55c. As No. 3649   2·75   2·50
3686b   55c. As No. 3650   2·75   2·50

1711 Madonna and Child

2010. Christmas. Multicoloured.
3687   **1711**   45c.+20c. Type **1711**   3·25   3·00
3688   55c.+25c. Adoration of the Magi   4·25   4·00

The premium was for the benefit of Federal Association of Voluntary Welfare Association

1712 *Adler* Locomotive on First Journey from Nuremberg to Fürth on Bavarian Ludwig Railway

2010. 175th Anniv of German Railways
3689   **1712**   55c. multicoloured   2·75   2·50

1713 Giant Slalom

2010. Alpine Ski World Championships 2011, Garmisch-Partenkirchen
3690   **1713**   55c. multicoloured   2·75   2·50

1714 'WENN EINER DAUHN DEIHT....' and Fritz Reuter

2010. Birth Bicentenary of Fritz Reuter (writer)
3691   **1714**   100c. multicoloured   5·00   4·75

1715 Hands holding Coffeepot and Sandwich

2010. 750th Anniv of Knappschaft (providing sickness, accident, and death benefits for miners)
3692   **1715**   145c. black and carmine   7·25   6·75

1716 Glider, 1920

2011. Rhön Gliding Competitions at Wasserkuppe
3693   **1716**   45c. multicoloured   2·20   2·10

1717 *Wanderer above the Sea of Fog* (Caspar David Friedrich)

2011. German Painting

(a) Ordinary gum
3694   **1717**   55c. multicoloured   2·75   2·50

(b) Self-adhesive
3694a   **1717**   55c. multicoloured   2·75   2·50

1718 Dr. Sommer and Bello being Interviewed (*The Talking Dog*)

2011. Welfare Stamps. Multicoloured.

(a) Ordinary gum
3695   45c.+20c. Type **1718**   3·25   3·00
3696   55c.+25c. Kloebner and Mueller-Luedenscheidt in the bath (*The Bathtub*)   4·25   4·00
3697   55c.+25c. Two racegoers (*At the Racecourse*)   4·25   4·00
3698   145c.+55c. Berta and her husband eating breakfast (*The Breakfast Egg*)   10·00   9·25

(b) Self-adhesive
3699   55c.+25c. As No. 3697   4·25   4·00

1719 National Park-Edersee Keller

2011. National Parks
3700   **1719**   145c. multicoloured   7·25   6·75

1720 Franz Liszt

2011. Birth Bicentenary of Franz Liszt (pianist and composer)
3701   **1720**   55c. dull violet   2·75   2·50

2011. Post. Greeting Stamps (4th issue). Self-adhesive.
3701a   55c. As No. 3646   2·75   2·50
3701b   55c. As No. 3647   2·75   2·50

1721 Main Hall and Great Hall Pagodas, Old City, Nara Yakushi-ji

2011. World Heritage Sites. Multicoloured.

(a) Ordinary gum
3702   55c. Type **1721**   2·75   2·50
3703   75c. Regensburg Cathedral   3·75   3·75

(b) Self-adhesive
3703a   75c. Regensburg Cathedral   3·75   3·75

1722 Hanstein Castle (ruin) and Ludwigstein Castle

2011. Werratal, View of Two Castles

(a) Ordinary gum
3704   **1722**   90c. multicoloured   4·75   4·50

(b) Self-adhesive
3704a   **1722**   90c. multicoloured   4·75   4·50

1722a Droplets on Leaf (water)

2011. Post. Multicoloured.
3705   55c. Type **1722a**   2·75   2·50
3706   55c. Dunes (earth)   2·75   2·50
3707   55c. Erupting volcano (fire)   2·75   2·50
3708   55c. Clouds (air)   2·75   2·50

1723 Alsfeld Town Hall

2011. Half-timbered Architecture. Multicoloured.
3709   45c. Type **1723**   2·20   2·10
3710   55c. White Horse Inn, Hartenstein   2·75   2·50

1724 Goalkeeper

2011. Sports Promotion Fund, 2011. Women's Football World Cup (45c.+20c., 55c.+25c.), European Gymnastics Championships, Berlin (55c.+25c.) or Mönchengldbach Hockey Championship (145c.+55c.). Multicoloured.
3711   (45c. +20c.) Type **1724**   3·25   3·00
3712   (55c. +25c.) Player kicking ball   4·25   4·00
3713   (55c. +25c.) Male gymnast using bars   4·25   4·00
3714   (145c. +55c.) Player with raised stick and ball   10·00   9·25

2011. National Parks. Booklet Stamp
3715   **1724a**   145c. multicoloured   7·25   6·75

1725 Light through Tree Trunks

2011. Europa
3716   **1725**   55c. multicoloured   2·75   2·50

1726 Benz Patent-Motorwagen and Patent Details

2011. 125th Anniv of First Automobile
3717   **1726**   55c. multicoloured   2·75   2·50

1727 External and Interior of Museum

2011. 150th Anniv of Wallraff-Richartz-Museum
3718   **1727**   85c. multicoloured   4·50   4·25

1728 Chamber of Commerce Offices in Germany and DIHK Emblem

2011. 150th Anniv of Industry and Commerce Organization (DIHK)
3719   **1728**   145c. multicoloured   7·25   6·75

1729 Reich Insurance Code

2011. Centenary of Insurance Code (Reich Insurance Code (RVO))
3720   **1729**   205c. scarlet-vermilion, silver and black   10·00   9·75

1730 Train

2011. 125th Anniv of Mecklenburg Bäderbahn Steam-operated Narrow Gauge Railway ('Molli')
3721   **1730**   45c. multicoloured   2·20   2·10

1731 *Light at the end of the Tunnel*

2011. 50th Anniv of Amnesty International
3722   **1731**   55c. multicoloured   2·75   2·50

1732 The First Gymnasium in Germany (lithograph)

2011. Bicentenary of Friedrich Ludwig Jahn Turnplatz (first open air gymnasium)
3723   **1732**   165c. black and scarlet-vermilion   8·25   7·75

1733 Paddle Steamer

2011. 175th Anniv of Saxon Steamship Company

(a) Ordinary gum. Sheet 105×70 mm
MS3724   **1733**   220c. multicoloured   11·50   11·00

(b) Self-adhesive. Booklet stamp
3724a   220c. As Type **1733**   11·00   10·50

1734a Norderney

2011. Lighthouses. Booklet stamps. Multicoloured.
3724b   45c. Type **1733a**   2·20   2·10
3724c   45c. Warnemünde   2·20   2·10

1734 Till Eulenspiegel

2011. 500th Anniv of Till Eulenspiegel (folklore trickster figure)
3725   **1734**   55c. multicoloured   2·75   2·50

1735 Arngast Lighthouse

2011. Lighthouses. Multicoloured.

3726	55c. Type **1735**	3·50	3·00
3727	90c. Dahmeshöved	5·50	5·00

(b) Self-adhesive

3727a	55c. As Type **1735**	3·50	3·00

1736 Targets and 1861 Awards Ceremony

2011. 150th Anniv of German Shooting Federation

3728	**1736**	145c. multicoloured	7·25	6·75

1737 Horse Head Nebula

2011. For Us Children. Astronomy. Multicoloured.

3729	45c. +20c. Type **1737**	3·25	3·00
3730	55c. +25c. Solar System (left)	4·25	4·00
3731	55c. +25c. Solar System (right)	4·25	4·00
3732	145c. +55c. Pleiades	10·00	9·25

1738 Archaeopteryx Fossil

2011. 150th Anniv of Discovery of Archaeopteryx

3733	**1738**	55c. multicoloured	2·75	2·50

1739 Anniversary Emblem

2011. 75th Anniv of Stamp Day in Germany

3734	**1739**	55c. + 25c. multicoloured	4·25	4·00

1740 Aquarium (Marie-Helen Geißelbrecht)

2011. For Us Children

3735	**1740**	55c. multicoloured	2·75	2·50

1741 Stylized Tunnel and Shipping

2011. Centenary of St Pauli Elbe Tunnel, Hamburg

3736	**1741**	55c. black, new blue and yellow	2·75	2·50

1742 Fortified Church, Birthälmer

2011. World Heritage Site. Birthälmer Fortified Church, Transylvania (Siebenbürgen)

3737	**1742**	75c. multicoloured	3·75	3·75

1743 Thermos Flask (Reinhold Burger, 1903), Currywurst and Teabag

2011. At Home in Germany. German Designs for the Home. Multicoloured.

3738		45c. Type **1743**	2·20	2·10
3739		55c. Gramophone (Emil Berliner, 1887), tape recorder (Fritz Pfleumer, 1928) and MP3 player (Fraunhofer Institute, 1987)	2·75	2·50

1744 White Calla Flower

2011. Mourning Stamp

3740	**1744**	55c. multicoloured	2·75	2·50

1745 Museum Building c. 1880

2011. 175th Anniv of Alte Pinakothek Museum, Munich

3741	**1745**	145c. multicoloured	7·25	6·75

1746 Kaiser Wilhelm Memorial Church

2011. 50th Anniv of New Kaiser Wilhelm Memorial Church

3742	**1746**	55c. multicoloured	2·75	2·50

1747 Embroidery (Guatemala)

2011. 50th Anniv of Adveniat (Christmas charitable campaign)

3743	**1747**	55c. multicoloured	2·75	2·50

1748 St Martin (detail, stained glass window, St Martin's Church, Nettersheim)

2011. Christmas. Welfare Stamps. Multicoloured.

3744	45c. +20c. Type **1748**	3·25	3·00
3745	55c. +25c. St Nicholas (detail) (stained glass window, St Nicholas's Church, Rheurdt)	4·25	4·00

1749 Emil Wiechert

2011. 150th Birth Anniv of Emil Weichert (geophysicist and seismologist)

3746	**1749**	90c. multicoloured	4·75	4·50

1750 Winter Landscape

2012. Post. Winter

3747	**1750**	55c. multicoloured	2·50	2·30

1751 Sea Cliffs

2012. National Parks. Jasmund

(a) Sheet stamp. ordinary gum

3748	**1751**	55c. multicoloured	3·00	2·75

(b) Size 38×23 mm. Booklet stamp. Self-adhesive

3749	**1751**	55c. multicoloured	3·00	2·75

1752 Frederick II (Anton Graff)

2012. 300th Birth Anniv of Frederick II of Prussia

3750	**1752**	55c. multicoloured	3·00	2·75

1753 Ruby

2012. Welfare Stamps. Jewels. Multicoloured.

(a) Sheet stamps. Ordinary gum

3751	55c. +25c. Type **1753**	4·50	4·25
3752	90c. +40c. Emerald	7·25	6·75
3753	145c. +55c. Sapphire	11·00	10·50

(b) Self-adhesive

3754	55c. +25c. As Type **1753**	4·50	4·25

1754 Colour Spectrum

2012. 225th Birth Anniv of Joseph von Fraunhofer (pioneer of scientific methodology in the field of optics and precision engineering and entrepreneur) (1st issue)

3755	**1754**	90c. multicoloured	5·00	4·75

1755 Zwinger Palace, Dresden (designed by Matthäus Daniel Pöppelmann in collaboration with sculptor Balthasar Permoser)

2012. 350th Birth Anniv of Matthäus Daniel Pöppelmann (master builder and architect) (1st issue)

3756	**1755**	145c. multicoloured	8·00	7·50

1756 Steam Locomotive

2012. 125th Anniv of Harz Narrow-gauge Railways

(a) Ordinary gum

3757	**1756**	45c. Type **1756**	2·50	2·30

(b) Size 38×24 mm. Self-adhesive

3758	45c. As Type **1756**	2·50	2·30

1757 Athletes skiing

2012. Biathlon Championship, Ruhpolding

3759	**1757**	55c. multicoloured	3·00	2·75

1758 Lynx and Kitten

2012. Recolonization of Native Fauna

(a) Ordinary gum

3760	55c. Type **1758**	3·00	2·75
3761	55c. Moose	3·00	2·75

(b) Size 38×24 mm. Self-adhesive

3762	55c. As Type **1758**	3·00	2·75
3763	55c. As No. 3761	3·00	2·75

1759 Blue Horse (Franz Marc)

2012. Centenary of Blue Rider Group (formed by artists Wassily Kandinsky and Franz Marc (German Expressionism)

3764	**1759**	145c. multicoloured	8·00	7·50

2012. 350th Birth Anniv of Matthäus Daniel Pöppelmann (master builder and architect) (2nd issue)

3765	145c. As Type **1755** (38×24 mm)	8·00	7·50

1760 Tree and Countryside in Spring

2012. Post. Spring

(a) Ordinary gum

3766	55c. Type **1760**	3·00	2·75

(b) Size 38×24 mm. Self-adhesive

3767	55c. As Type **1760**	3·00	2·75

1761 La Madonna di San Sisto

2012. 500th Anniv of Sistine Madonna (La Madonna di San Sisto) (by Raphael). Sheet 98×134 mm

MS3768	**1761**	55c. multicoloured	3·25	3·00

1762 Trees at Dusk

2012. Mourning Stamp

3769	**1762**	55c. black	3·00	2·75

1763 Gerhard Mercator and Symbols of Cartography

2012. 500th Birth Anniv of Gerhard Mercator (Gerhard Kremer) (cartographer, surveyor and instrument maker)

3770	**1763**	220c. multicoloured	12·00	11·50

1764 Axel Springer

2012. Birth Centenary of Axel Springer (journalist)

3771	**1764**	55c. black, scarlet-vermilion and pale yellow-ochre	3·00	2·75

1765 Woman carrying Baskets on Yoke

2012. 50th Anniv of German Welthungerhilfe

3772	**1765**	55c. multicoloured	3·00	2·75

1766 Football Match

2012. Sports Promotion Fund, 2012. Euro 2012, European Football Championships, Poland and Ukraine (3773), Olympic Games, London (3774) or World Team Table Tennis Championships, Dortmund. Multicoloured.

3773		55c. +25c. Type **1766**	4·50	4·25
3774		90c. +40c. Swimmers	7·25	6·75
3775		145c. +55c. Four players and table	11·00	10·50

2012. 225th Birth Anniv of Joseph von Fraunhofer (pioneer of scientific methodology in the field of optics and precision engineering and entrepreneur) (2nd issue). Size 38×24 mm

3776		90c. As Type **1754**	3·00	2·75

1767 Crowd waving Flag

2012. German Football Enthusiasm

(a) Sheet stamp. Ordinary gum

3777	**1767**	55c. multicoloured	3·00	2·75

(b) Booklet stamp. Self-adhesive

3778	**1767**	55c. multicoloured	3·00	2·75

1768 Beach in Summer

2012. Post. Summer. Europa. Visit Germany

3779	**1768**	55c. multicoloured	3·00	2·75

No. 3780 and Type **1769** are vacant.

1770 Scene from *Frog Prince* with Rubbish Bin as Frog Prince

2012. Environmental Protection

3781	**1770**	55c. +25c. multicoloured	4·25	4·00

1771 Johann Gottlieb Fichte

2012. 250th Birth Anniv of Johann Gottlieb Fichte (philosopher)

3782	**1771**	70c. multicoloured	3·75	3·75

1772 Windeck House in Bad Münstereifel

2012. Half-timbered Architecture

3783	**1772**	165c. multicoloured	7·75	7·25

1773 Silhouette Figures from Inside Cover of Original Edition of *Children's and Household Tales*

2012. Bicentenary of Grimm Brothers' Fairy Tales (*Children's and Household Tales*)

3784	**1773**	55c. multicoloured	3·00	2·75

1774 Pfälzerhütte and Buildings

2012. Pfälzerhütte (mountain hut and inn), Liechtenstein

3785	**1774**	75c. multicoloured	4·00	3·75

1775 Mixed Choir

2012. 150th Anniv of German Choral Association

3786	**1775**	85c. multicoloured	4·50	4·25

1776 *Das Balkonzimmer* (Adolph Menzel)

2012. German Painting

3787	**1776**	260c. multicoloured	12·50	11·50

1777 Borkum Lighthouse

2012. Lighthouses. Multicoloured.

3788		45c. Type **1777**	2·40	2·20
3789		55c. Arkona	3·00	2·75

1778 Apartment Name Plates

2012. At Home in Germany. Diversity

3790	**1778**	55c. multicoloured	3·00	2·75

1779 Parkland

2012. World Heritage Site. Muskauer Park

3791	**1779**	90c. multicoloured	4·75	4·50

1780 Dog, Cat and Fish

2012. German Animal Protection Association Animal Shelters

3792	**1780**	145c. multicoloured	7·25	6·75

1781 Emperor Otto I

2012. 1100th Birth Anniv of Emperor Otto I

3793	**1781**	45c. multicoloured	2·30	2·10

1782 Symbols of Festival

2012. Bicentenary of Gäubodenfest, Straubing

3794	**1782**	55c. multicoloured	2·75	2·50

1783 Steam Locomotive S 3/6

2012. Youth Stamps. Historic Steam Locomotives. Multicoloured.

3795		55c. +25c. Type **1783**	3·25	3·00
3796		90c. +40c. PTL 2/2	7·75	7·25
3797		145c. +55c. *Leopold Friedrich*	8·50	8·00

1784 Four Car Set on Viaduct

2012. Centenary of Mittenwald Railway

3798	**1784**	75c. multicoloured	4·00	3·75

1785 Children's Imagination

2012. For Us Children

3799	**1785**	55c. multicoloured	3·50	3·00

1786 Autumn Colour

2012. Post. Autumn in Germany (1st issue)

3800	**1786**	55c. multicoloured	3·50	3·00

1787 Airmail Envelope with 1902 5pf. Stamp

2012. Stamp Day. Centenary of First Official Postal Flight in Germany

3801	**1787**	55c. multicoloured	3·50	3·00

1788 Open Book

2012. Centenary of National Library

3802	**1788**	55c. multicoloured	3·50	3·00

1789 Page 76

2012. Bicentenary of German Bible Society

3803	**1789**	85c. multicoloured	5·25	4·75

1790 Cross

2012. 50th Anniv of Second Vatican Ecumenical Council

3804	**1790**	45c. gold and black	2·75	2·25

1791 Three Castles

2012. Drei Gleichen (municipality), Thuringia

3805	**1791**	55c. pale brownish grey, grey and scarlet-vermilion	3·50	3·00

1792 Helmut Kohl

2012. Helmut Kohl - Chancellor of Germany - Honorary Citizen of Europe

3806	**1792**	55c. multicoloured		

1793 Anniversary Emblem

2012. Centenary of Domowina - Federation of Lusatian Sorbs

3807	**1793**	145c. multicoloured	8·00	7·50

1794 '3'

2012. Supplementary Stamp

(a) Sheet stamps. Ordinary gum

3808	**1794**	3c. multicoloured	75	75

(b) Size 38×22 mm. Booklet stamps. Self-adhesive

3808a	**1794**	3c. multicoloured	75	75

1795 Professors G. G. Gervinus, W. E. Albrecht, H. G. A. Ewald, F. C. Dahlmann, W. E. Weber, W. Grimm and J. Grimm

2012. 175th Anniv of Göttingen Seven (seven professors of University of Göttingen, who stoood against King Ernst August of Hanover who decreed liberal state constitution suspended)

3809	**1795**	55c. multicoloured	3·50	3·00

1796 Gerhart Hauptmann and Book Titles

2012. 150th Birth Anniv of Gerhart Hauptmann

3810	**1796**	55c. vermilion and black	3·50	3·00

1797 *Madonna and Child* (Raphael)

2012. 500th Anniv of Sistine Madonna (*La Madonna di San Sisto*) (by Raphael) (2nd issue)
3811	**1797**	55c. multicoloured	3·50	3·00

1798 Snow-covered Chapel

2012. Christmas. Welfare Stamps

(a) Ordinary gum
3812	**1798**	55c. +25c. multicoloured	4·00	4·00

(b) Self-adhesive gum
3813	**1798**	55c. +25c. multicoloured	4·00	4·00

1799 Central German Half-timbered Building, Bad Münstereifel

2012. Half-timbered Architecture
3814	**1799**	165c. multicoloured	8·25	7·75

1800 Glücksburg Schloss

2013. Prussian Schlosses. Multicoloured.

(a) Sheet stamps. Ordinary gum
3815	**1800**	45c. Type **1800**	2·75	2·25
3816		58c. Nuremberg Castle	3·50	3·00

(b) Self-adhesive
3816a		58c. Nuremberg Castle	3·50	3·00

1801 Queen Nefertiti

2013. Treasures from German Museums (1st issue). Multicoloured.
3817	**1801**	58c. Type **1801**	3·50	3·00
3818		145c. Ishtar Gate	8·00	7·50

1802 French and German Flags as Binoculars

2013. 50th Anniv of Elysée Treaty
3819	**1802**	75c. multicoloured	4·00	3·50

1803 *Die Rasenbleiche* (The Bleaching) (Max Liebermann)

2013. German Painting

(a) Ordinary gum
3820	**1803**	240c. multicoloured	13·00	12·00

(b) Self-adhesive
3821	**1803**	240c. multicoloured	13·00	12·00

1804 German Cathedral and Konzerthaus, Gendarmenmarkt, Berlin

2013. Panorama. Multicoloured.

(a) Sheet stamps. Ordinary gum
3822		58c. Type **1804**	3·75	3·25
3823		58c. Konzerthaus (right) and French Cathedral, Gendarmenmarkt	3·75	3·25

(b) Size 38×22 mm. Booklet stamps. Self-adhesive
3824		58c. As Type **1804**	3·75	3·25
3825		58c. As No. 3824	3·75	3·25

1805 Lime Tree

2013. Welfare Stamps. Flowering Trees. Multicoloured.

(a) Sheet stamps. Ordinary gum
3826		58c. +27c. Type **1805**	4·50	4·50
3827		90c. +40c. Bird Cherry	6·00	6·00
3828		145c. +55c. Horse Chestnut	8·75	8·75

(b) Self-adhesive
3829		58c. +27c. As Type **1805**	4·50	4·50

1806 Castle Hubertusburg, Wermsdorf

2013. 250th Anniv of Hubertusburg Peace Treaty (ending Seven Years War)
3830	**1806**	90c. multicoloured	4·50	4·50

1807 Tiger and Bear in Sailboat and Tiger Duck Swimming

2013. 82nd Birth Anniv of Horst Eckert (Janosch) (children's author and illustrator). Multicoloured.

(a) Sheet stamps. Ordinary gum
3831		45c. Type **1807**	2·75	2·25
3832		58c. Tiger, Tiger Duck, Bunny and Bear with presents celebrating Easter	3·75	3·25

(b) Size 38×22 mm. Booklet stamps. Self-adhesive
3833		45c. As Type **1807**	2·75	2·25
3834		58c. As No. 3832	3·75	3·25

1808 Cellist

2013. 50th Anniv of Jugend musiziert (competition for young musicians)
3835	**1808**	58c. multicoloured	3·75	3·25

2013. Treasures from German Museums (2nd issue)
3836		58c. As No. 3817	3·75	3·25

1809 Friedrich Hebbel

2013. Birth Bicentenary of Christian Friedrich (Friedrich) Hebbel (dramatist)
3837	**1809**	100c. greenish yellow and black	6·00	5·50

1810 A. H. Francke

2013. 350th Birth Anniv of August Hermann Francke (theologian and educator)
3838	**1810**	205c. multicoloured	9·00	8·50

1811 Symbols of Work of Red Cross

2013. 150th Anniv of Red Cross
3839	**1811**	58c. black and scarlet-vermilion	3·75	3·25

1812 German Sports Badge

2013. Centenary of German Sports Badge
3840	**1812**	58c. multicolored	3·75	3·25

1813 Fehmarn Bridge

2013. 50th Anniv of Fehmarn Bridge

(a) Ordinary gum
3841	**1813**	75c. multicoloured	4·00	3·50

(b) Size 38×22 mm. Booklet Stamp. Self-adhesive
3842	**1813**	75c. multicoloured	4·00	3·50

1814 Möhnetalsperre Dam

2013. Centenary of Möhnetalsperre Dam
3843	**1814**	90c. multicoloured	5·50	5·00

1815 Flag

2013. 150th Anniv of General German Workers' Association (ADAV)
3844	**1815**	145c. multicoloured	8·00	7·50

2013. Treasures from German Museums (2nd issue)
3845		145c. As No. 3818	3·75	3·25

1817 Richard Wagner

2013. Birth Bicentenary of Richard Wagner (composer)
3846	**1817**	58c. multicoloured	3·75	3·25

1818 Lloyd Paketzustellwagen, 1908

2013. Europa. Postal Transport
3847	**1818**	58c. multicoloured	3·75	3·25

1819 Mouse preparing to Sprint

2013. Sports Promotion Fund. *Sprint Mouse* (cartoon character by Uli Stein). Multicoloured.
3848	**1819**	58c. +27c. Type **1819**	3·75	3·25
3849		90c. +40c. Mouse wind surfing	7·20	6·75
3850		145c. +55c. Mouse using parallel bars	7·20	6·75

2013. Centenary of Möhnetalsperre Dam (2nd issue). Booklet Stamp
3851		90c. As Type **1814**	5·00	

No. 3852 is vacant.

1820 East German Rose Garden

2013. German Rose Show, Forst (Lausitz). Centenary of East German Rose Garden
3853	**1820**	45c. multicoloured	2·75	2·25

1821 Flügge Lighthouse

2013. Lighthouses. Multicoloured.
3854		45c. Type **1821**	2·75	2·25
3855		58c. Büsum	3·75	3·25

1822 Camouflaged People and National Flag

2013. Bundeswehr – Working for Germany
3856	**1822**	58c. multicoloured	3·25	

1823 Temple of the Sun, Bayreuth

2013. Cultural History and Architecture. Multicoloured.
3857		75c. Type **1823**	4·00	3·50
3858		150c. Hyangwonjong Pavilion, Gyeongbokgung Palace, Seoul	8·00	7·50

1824 'Dessau', Aircraft and Buildings

2013. 800th Anniv of Dessau
3859	**1824**	45c. bright orange and bright violet	2·75	2·25

1825 Lower Saxony Wadden Sea

2013. Wild Germany. Multicoloured.
3860		58c. Type **1825**	3·75	3·25
3861		58c. Berchtesgaden National Park	3·75	3·25

1826 Seascape

2013. Painting by Gerhard Richter

(a) Ordinary gum
3862	**1826**	145c. multicoloured	8·00	7·50

(b) Booklet Stamp. Self-adhesive gum

| 3863 | 1826 | 145c. multicoloured | 8·00 | 7·50 |

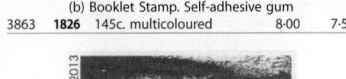

1827 Ocean and Coast

2013. Flood Relief

| 3864 | 1827 | 58c. +42c. multicoloured | 4·50 | 4·50 |

1828 Inscribed Ribbon

2013. Birth Centenary of Julius Kardinal Döpfner (Cardinal and Archbishop of Munich and Freising)

| 3865 | 1828 | 58c. multicoloured | 3·75 | 3·25 |

1829 *Carduelis carduelis* (Goldfinch)

2013. Youth Stamps. Song Birds. Multicoloured.

3866		58c. +27c. Type **1829**	4·50	4·50
3867		90c. +40c. *Pyrrhula pyrrhula* (Bullfinch)	6·75	6·75
3868		145c. +55c. *Parus caeruleus* (Bluetit)	7·25	7·25

1830 Heidelberg (left)

2013. Panorama (2nd issue). Multicoloured.

| 3869 | | 58c. Type **1828** | 3·75 | 3·25 |
| 3870 | | 58c. Heidelberg (right) | 3·75 | 3·25 |

1831 *Saxonia* (steam locomotive), 1843

2013. Stamp Day. Locomotives

| 3871 | 1831 | 58c. +27c. multicoloured | 4·50 | 4·50 |

1832 Dame, King and Knave playing Skat

2012. Bicentenary of German Card Game Skatspiel

| 3872 | 1832 | 90c. multicoloured | 5·00 | 5·00 |

No. 3873 and Type **1833** are left for Centenary of Monument, not yet received.

No. 3874 and Type **1834** are left for Birth Bicentenary of G. Buchner, not yet received.

No. 3875 and Type **1835** are left for Birth Bicentenary of L. Leichhardt, not yet received.

1836 Willy Brandt

2013. Birth Centenary of Willy Brandt (chancellor)

| 3876 | 1836 | 58c. multicoloured | 3·75 | 3·25 |

1837 Electromagnetic Rays

2013. 125th Anniv of Treatise *On Rays of Electric Force* by Heinrich Hertz

| 3877 | 1837 | 58c. multicoloured | 3·75 | 3·25 |

1838 Decorated Trees

2013. Christmas

(a) Ordinary gum

| 3878 | 1838 | 58c. multicoloured | 3·75 | 3·25 |

(b) Self-adhesive gum

| 3879 | 1838 | 58c. multicoloured | 3·75 | 3·25 |

1839 Three Kings

2013. Christmas. Welfare Stamps

(a) Ordinary gum

| 3880 | 1839 | 58c. +27c. multicoloured | 4·50 | 4·50 |

(b) Self-adhesive gum

| 3881 | 1839 | 58c. +27c. multicoloured | 4·50 | 4·50 |

1840 Professor Hirsch in her Laboratory

2013. Centenary of Award of Title of Professor to Rachel Hirsch (first woman in Prussia to be appointed professor of medicine)

| 3882 | 1840 | 145c. multicoloured | 8·00 | 7·50 |

1841 '2'

2012. Supplementary Stamp

(a) Sheet stamps. Ordinary gum

| 3883 | 1841 | 2c. multicoloured | 75 | 75 |

(b) Size 38×22 mm. Booklet stamps. Self-adhesive

| 3884 | 1841 | 2c. multicoloured | 75 | 75 |

1842 Clouds

2013. Mourning Stamp

| 3885 | 1842 | 60c. multicoloured | 3·75 | 3·25 |

1843 Salmon

2014. Reintroduction of Fish Species. Atlantic Salmon

| 3886 | 1843 | 45c. multicoloured | 2·75 | 2·25 |

1844 Lorsch Abbey

2014. World Heritage. 1250th Anniversary of Lorsch Abbey

(a) Ordinary gum

| 3887 | 1844 | 60c. multicoloured | 3·75 | 3·25 |

(b) Self-adhesive

| 3888 | 1844 | 60c. multicoloured | 3·75 | 3·25 |

1845 Fox Cubs

2014. Young Animals. Multicoloured.

(a) Ordinary gum

| 3889 | | 60c. Type **1845** | 3·75 | 3·25 |
| 3890 | | 60c. Hedgehogs | 3·75 | 3·25 |

(b) Self-adhesive

| 3891 | | 60c. As Type **1845** | 3·75 | 3·25 |
| 3892 | | 60c. As No. 3890 | 3·75 | 3·25 |

1846 Stolzenfels am Rhein Castle

2014. Stolzenfels am Rhein Castle

| 3893 | 1846 | 75c. multicoloured | 4·00 | 3·50 |

1847 Forest

2014. World Heritage. Buchenwald Forest

| 3894 | 1847 | 145c. multicoloured | 8·00 | 7·50 |

1848 Flood Plain in Lower Oder Valley

2014. Wild Germany. Multicoloured.

| 3895 | | 60c. Type **1848** | 3·75 | 3·25 |
| 3896 | | 60c. Devil's Table, Palatinate Forest | 3·75 | 3·25 |

1849 Hansel and Gretel see House in the Woods

2014. Welfare Stamps. *Hansel and Gretel*. Multicoloured.

(a) Sheet stamps. Ordinary gum

3897		60c. +30c. Type **1849**	4·50	4·50
3898		90c. +40c. In the witch's house	6·00	6·00
3899		145c. +55c. Escape	8·75	8·75

(b) Self-adhesive

| 3900 | | 58c. +27c. As Type **1849** | 4·50 | 4·50 |

IV. WEST BERLIN

The Russian Government withdrew from the four-power control of Berlin on 1 July 1948, with the Western Sectors remaining under American, British and French control. West Berlin was constituted a "Land" of the Federal Republic on 1 September 1950. The Russian Zone issues inscribed "STADT BERLIN" (which we do not list unoverprinted in this Catalogue), were not intended for use throughout Berlin, but were for the Russian sector of the city and for Brandenburg.

The first stamps to be used in the Western Sectors were Nos. A4/5 and A7 of the Anglo-American Zones, followed by Nos. A36/52, which were on sale from 24 June to 31 August 1948, and remained valid until 19 September 1948.

1948. Pictorial issue of 1947 (Nos. 928/48) optd **BERLIN**.

B21		2pf. black	3·75	3·50
B2		6pf. violet	4·50	6·75
B3		8pf. red	2·20	6·75
B4		10pf. green	2·75	2·00
B5		12pf. grey	2·20	2·00
B25		16pf. brown	13·50	2·75
B7		16pf. green	4·25	2·75
B26		20pf. blue	4·75	1·70
B9		24pf. brown	2·10	70
B10		25pf. orange	26·00	70·00
B11		30pf. red	7·50	11·50
B12		40pf. mauve	10·50	11·50
B13		50pf. blue	15·00	38·00
B14		60pf. brown	5·25	70
B15		80pf. blue	15·00	34·00
B16		84pf. green	21·00	£110
B17		1m. olive	70·00	£180

B18		2m. violet	75·00	£650
B19		3m. red	£100	£900
B20		5m. blue	£130	£950

B2 Schoneberg

1949. Inscr "DEUTSCHE POST". Berlin Views. (a) Small size.

B35	-	1pf. grey	55	55
B36	B2	4pf. brown	1·10	55
B36c	-	4pf. brown	6·25	5·75
B37	-	5pf. green	1·30	55
B38	-	6pf. purple	2·30	1·70
B39	-	8pf. orange	2·30	1·80
B40	-	10pf. green	1·10	55
B41	B3	15pf. brown	20·00	1·40
B42	-	20pf. red	6·25	55
B42b	-	20pf. red	85·00	3·50
B43	-	25pf. yellow	34·00	1·40
B44	-	30pf. blue	18·00	1·70
B45	B2	40pf. lake	26·00	1·50
B46	-	50pf. olive	26·00	55
B47	-	60pf. red	90·00	55
B48	-	80pf. blue	22·00	1·60
B49	-	90pf. green	26·00	2·10

B3 Douglas C-54 over Tempelhof Airport

(b) Large size.

B50	B3	1Dm. olive	34·00	1·70
B51	-	2Dm. purple	95·00	2·30
B52	-	3Dm. red	£375	23·00
B53	-	5Dm. blue	£180	23·00

DESIGNS—As Type B **2**: 1pf. Brandenburg Gate; 4pf. (B36c) Exhibition Building; 5, 25pf. "Tegel Schloss". 6, 50pf. Reichstag Building. 10, 30pf. "Kleistpark". 20 (B42), 80, 90pf. Technical High School; 20pf. (B42b) Olympia Stadium; 60pf. National Gallery. As Type B **3**: 2Dm. "Gendarmenmarkt"; 3Dm. Brandenburg Gate; 5Dm. "Tegel Schloss".

For similar views inscribed "DEUTSCHE POST BERLIN" see Nos. B118/19.

B4 Stephan Monument and Globe

B5 Heinrich von Stephan Monument

1949. 75th Anniv of U.P.U.

B54	B4	12pf. grey	39·00	12·50
B55	B4	16pf. green	65·00	25·00
B56	B4	24pf. orange	50·00	1·10
B57	B4	50pf. olive	£250	65·00
B58	B4	60pf. brown	£275	55·00
B59	B5	1Dm. olive	£200	£170
B60	B5	2Dm. purple	£200	£110

B6 Goethe and Scene from *Iphigenie*

1949. Birth Bicent of Goethe (poet). Portraits of Goethe and scenes from his works.

B61	B6	10pf. green	£190	90·00
B62	-	20pf. red	£200	£200
B63	-	30pf. blue	50·00	70·00

DESIGNS—Scenes from: 20pf. *Reineke Fuchs*; 30pf. *Faust*.

1949. Numeral and pictorial issues of 1946/7 surch BERLIN and bold figures.

B64	229	5pf. on 45pf. red	6·25	65
B65	C	10pf. on 24pf. brown	25·00	65
B66	B	20pf. on 80pf. blue	95·00	22·00
B67	237	1m. on 3m. lake	£225	29·00

B9 Alms Bowl and Bear

1949. Berlin Relief Fund.

| B68 | B9 | 10pf.+5pf. green | £130 | £250 |
| B69 | B9 | 20pf.+5pf. red | £160 | £250 |

B70	**B9**	30pf.+5pf. blue	£170	£300
MSB70a		111×65 mm. Nos. B68/70 (sold at 1Dm.)	£1200	£3000

B10

1950. European Recovery Programme.
B71	**B10**	20pf. red	£130	50·00

B11 Harp

1950. Restablishment of Berlin Philharmonic Orchestra.
B72	**B11**	10pf.+5pf. green	65·00	50·00
B73	-	30pf.+5pf. blue	£140	£120

DESIGN: 30pf. "Singing Angels" (after H. and J. van Eyck).

B13 G. A. Lortzing

1951. Death Cent of Lortzing (composer).
B74	**B13**	20pf. brown	75·00	75·00

B14 Freedom Bell

1951. (a) Clapper at left.
B75	**B14**	5pf. brown	3·00	11·00
B76	**B14**	10pf. green	23·00	33·00
B77	**B14**	20pf. red	12·00	29·00
B78	**B14**	30pf. blue	80·00	£100
B79	**B14**	40pf. purple	18·00	60·00

(b) Clapper at right.
B82	5pf. green	3·00	3·00
B83	10pf. green	8·75	6·00
B84	20pf. red	29·00	24·00
B85	30pf. blue	75·00	60·00
B86	40pf. red	29·00	24·00

(c) Clapper in centre.
B101	5pf. brown	1·60	1·50
B102	10pf. green	3·25	2·40
B103	20pf. red	8·75	4·75
B104	30pf. blue	16·00	15·00
B105	40pf. violet	80·00	44·00

B15 Boy Stamp Collectors

1951. Stamp Day.
B80	**B15**	10pf.+3pf. green	37·00	39·00
B81	**B15**	20pf.+2pf. red	42·00	47·00

B16 Mask of Beethoven (taken from life, 1812)

1952. 125th Death Anniv of Beethoven (composer).
B87	**B16**	30pf. blue	55·00	39·00

B17 Olympic Torch

1952. Olympic Games Festival, Berlin.
B88	**B17**	4pf. brown	1·30	3·25
B89	**B17**	10pf. green	15·00	22·00
B90	**B17**	20pf. red	23·00	34·00

B18 W. von Siemens (electrical engineer)

1952. Famous Berliners.
B91	-	4pf. brown	90	90
B92	-	5pf. blue	1·50	90
B93	-	6pf. purple	8·75	13·00
B94	-	8pf. brown	3·25	4·00
B95	-	10pf. green	4·50	90
B96	-	15pf. lilac	23·00	23·00
B97	**B18**	20pf. red	3·75	1·30
B98	-	25pf. green	70·00	10·50
B99	-	30pf. purple	25·00	13·00
B100	-	40pf. black	40·00	4·00

PORTRAITS: 4pf. Zelter (musician); 5pf. Lilienthal (aviator); 6pf. Rathenau (statesman); 8pf. Fontane (writer); 10pf. Von Menzel (artist); 15pf. Virchow (pathologist); 25pf. Schinkel (architect); 30pf. Planck (physicist); 40pf. W. von Humboldt (philologist).

B19 Church before Bombing

1953. Kaiser Wilhelm Memorial Church Reconstruction Fund.
B106	**B19**	4pf.+1pf. brown	65	24·00
B107	**B19**	10pf.+5pf. green	1·90	65·00
B108	-	20pf.+10pf. red	4·50	65·00
B109	-	30pf.+15pf. blue	25·00	£130

DESIGN: 20pf., 30pf. Church after bombing.

B20 Chainbreaker

1953. East German Uprising. Inscr "17. JUNI 1953".
B110	**B20**	20pf. black	11·50	2·40
B111	-	30pf. red	46·00	45·00

DESIGN: 30pf. Brandenburg Gate.

B21 Ernst Reuter

1954. Death of Ernst Reuter (Mayor of West Berlin).
B112	**B21**	20pf. brown	10·50	2·50

B22 Conference Buildings

1954. Four-Power Conference, Berlin.
B113	**B22**	20pf. red	11·50	6·25

B23 O. Mergenthaler and Linotype Machine

1954. Birth Cent of Mergenthaler (inventor).
B114	**B23**	10pf. green	4·75	3·75

1954. West German Presidential Election. No. B103 optd **Wahl des Bundesprasidenten in Berlin 17. Juli 1954.**
B115	**B14**	20pf. red	6·75	8·00

B25 "Germany in Bondage"

1954. Tenth Anniv of Attempt on Hitler's Life.
B116	**B25**	20pf. grey and red	7·50	6·75

B26 Prussian Postilion, 1827

1954. National Stamp Exhibition.
B117	**B26**	20pf.+10pf. mult	21·00	42·00

1954. Berlin Views. As Type **B2** but inscr "DEUTSCHE POST BERLIN".
B118	7pf. green	8·00	2·30
B119	70pf. olive	£130	28·00

DESIGNS: 7pf. Exhibition building; 70pf. Grunewald hunting lodge.

B27 Memorial Library

1954
B120	**B27**	40pf. purple	13·50	4·50

B28 Richard Strauss

1954. Fifth Death Anniv of Strauss (composer).
B121	**B28**	40pf. blue	13·50	5·00

B29 Blacksmiths forging Rail

1954. Death Cent of A. Borsig (industrialist).
B122	**B29**	20pf. brown	10·00	2·75

B30 *Berlin* (liner)

1955
B123	**B30**	10pf. green	1·70	1·10
B124	**B30**	25pf. blue	10·00	5·00

B31 Wilhelm Furtwangler (conductor)

1955. First Death Anniv of Furtwangler.
B125	**B31**	40pf. blue	26·00	26·00

B32

1955. Federal Parliament Session, Berlin.
B126	**B32**	10pf. black, yell & red	80	1·10
B127	**B32**	20pf. black, yell & red	7·50	12·50

B33 Prussian Rural Postilion, 1760

1955. Stamp Day and Philatelic Fund.
B128	**B33**	25pf.+10pf. mult	8·50	18·00

B34 St. Otto

1955. 25th Anniv of Berlin Bishopric.
B129	**B34**	7pf.+3pf. brown	1·10	3·50
B130	-	10pf.+5pf. green	2·75	5·00
B131	-	20pf.+10pf. mauve	1·70	4·00

DESIGNS: 10pf. St. Hedwig; 20pf. St. Peter.

B35 Radio Tower and Exhibition Hall

1956. Berlin Buildings and Monuments.
B133	-	1pf. grey	35	30
B133b	-	3pf. violet	35	30
B134	-	5pf. mauve	35	30
B132	**B35**	7pf. turquoise (A)	11·50	3·50
B135	-	7pf. turquoise (B)	35	30
B136	-	8pf. grey	70	55
B136a	-	8pf. red	45	55
B137	-	10pf. green	35	30
B138	-	15pf. blue	70	35
B139	-	20pf. red	70	35
B140	-	25pf. brown	70	70
B141	-	30pf. green	1·40	1·40
B142	-	40pf. blue	13·50	11·50
B143	-	50pf. green	1·40	1·40
B144	-	60pf. brown	1·40	1·40
B145	-	70pf. violet	36·00	18·00
B146	-	1Dm. green	2·75	3·00
B146a	-	3Dm. red	8·00	25·00

DESIGNS—As Type B **35** (B)—HORIZ: 1pf., 3pf. Brandenburg Gate; 5pf. P.O. Headquarters; 20pf. Free University; 40pf. Charlottenburg Castle; 60pf. Chamber of Commerce and Bourse; 70pf. Schiller Theatre. VERT: 8pf. Town Hall, Neukollin; 10pf. Kaiser Wilhelm Memorial Church; 15pf. Airlift Monument; 25pf. Lilienthal Monument; 30pf. Pfaueninsel Castle; 50pf. Reuter Power-station. LARGER (24×30 mm): 1Dm. "The Great Elector" (statue, after Schluter). (29½×25 mm): 3Dm. Congress Hall, Berlin.

7pf. (A) Type B **35**. (B) As Type **B35** but with inscription at top.

B37 Eagle and Arms of Berlin

1956. Federal Council Meeting.
B147	**B37**	10pf. black, yell & red	1·70	1·10
B148	**B37**	25pf. black, yell & red	6·25	6·25

B38

1956. Centenary of German Engineers' Union.
B149	**B38**	10pf. green	2·75	2·30
B150	**B38**	20pf. red	6·25	6·75

1956. Flood Relief Fund. As No. B77 (colour changed) surch **+10 Berlinhilfe fur die Hochwassergeschadigten DEUTSCHE BUNDESPOST-BERLIN** and bar.
B151	**B14**	20pf.+10pf. bistre	5·00	5·75

B40 P. Lincke

1956. Tenth Death Anniv of Lincke (composer).
B152	**B40**	20pf. red	3·50	4·00

B41 Wireless Transmitter

1956. Industrial Exhibition.
B153	**B41**	25pf. brown	8·50	13·50

B42 Brandenburg Postilion, 1700

1956. Stamp Day and Philatelic Fund.
B154	**B42**	25pf.+10pf. mult	4·00	5·00

B43 Spandau

1957. 725th Anniv of Spandau.
B155	**B43**	20pf. olive and brown	90	1·10

B44 Model of Hansa District

1957. International Building Exn, Berlin.
B156	**B44**	7pf. brown	55	55
B157	-	20pf. red	1·10	1·10
B158	-	40pf. blue	2·75	3·50

DESIGNS—HORIZ: 20pf. Aerial view of Exhibition; 40pf. Exhibition Congress Hall.

B45 Friedrich K. von Savigny (jurist)

1957. Portraits as Type **B45**.
B159		7pf. brown and green	35	35
B160		8pf. brown and grey	35	35
B161		10pf. brown and green	35	35
B162		15pf. sepia and blue	55	1·10
B163		20pf.+10pf. sepia and red	1·10	1·40
B164		20pf. brown and red	35	35
B165		25pf. sepia and lake	1·30	1·60
B166	**B45**	30pf. sepia and green	3·25	4·00
B167	-	40pf. sepia and blue	1·30	1·60
B168	-	50pf. sepia and olive	6·25	10·00

PORTRAITS—VERT: 7pf. T. Mommsen (historian); 8pf. H. Zille (painter); 10pf. E. Reuter (Mayor of Berlin); 15pf. F. Haber (chemist); 20pf. (No. B164), F. Schleiermacher (theologian); 20pf. (B163), L. Heck (zoologist); 25pf. Max Reinhardt (theatrical producer); 40pf. A. von Humboldt (naturalist); 50pf. C. D. Rauch (sculptor).

The premium on No. B163 was for the Berlin Zoo. No. B167 commemorates Humboldt's death centenary.

B46 Uta von Naumburg (statue)

1957. German Cultural Congress.
B169	**B46**	25pf. brown	1·40	1·70

B47 "Unity Justice and Freedom"

1957. Third Federal Parliament Assembly.
B170	**B47**	10pf. black, ochre & red	55	1·10
B171	**B47**	20pf. black, ochre & red	3·50	4·50

B48 Postilion, 1897–1925

1957. Stamp Day.
B172	**B48**	20pf. multicoloured	1·40	1·60

B49 Torch of Remembrance

1957. Seventh World War Veterans Congress.
B173	**B49**	20pf. myrtle, yell & grn	1·70	1·10

B50 Elly Heuss-Knapp (social worker)

1957. Mothers' Convalescence Fund.
B174	**B50**	20pf.+10pf. red	2·30	3·75

B51 Christ and Symbols of the Cosmos

1958. German Catholics' Day.
B175	**B51**	10pf. black and green	80	90
B176	**B51**	20pf. black and mauve	1·50	2·30

B52 Otto Suhr

1958. First Death Anniv of Burgomaster Otto Suhr.
B177	**B52**	20pf. red	1·70	2·75

See also Nos. B187 and B193.

B53 Pres. Heuss

1959
B178	**B53**	7pf. green	45	55
B179	**B53**	10pf. green	45	55
B180	**B53**	20pf. red	80	55
B181	**B53**	40pf. blue	3·50	6·75
B182	**B53**	70pf. violet	12·50	16·00

B54 Symbolic Airlift

1959. Tenth Anniv of Berlin Airlift.
B183	**B54**	25pf. black and red	90	75

B55 Brandenburg Gate, Berlin

1959. 14th World Communities Congress, Berlin.
B184	**B55**	20pf. blue, red & lt blue	1·30	70

B56 Schiller

1959. Birth Bicentenary of Schiller (poet).
B185	**B56**	20pf. brown and red	55	70

B57 Robert Koch

1960. 50th Death Anniv of Robert Koch (bacteriologist).
B186	**B57**	20pf. purple	55	70

1960. Fourth Death Anniv of Walther Schreiber (Mayor of Berlin, 1951–53). As Type **B52**.
B187		20pf. red	80	1·00

DESIGN: Portrait of Schreiber.

B58 Boy at Window

1960. Berlin Children's Holiday Fund. Inscr "FERIENPLATZE FUR BERLINER KINDER".
B188	**B58**	7pf.+3pf. dp brown, brown & light brown	35	45
B189	-	10pf.+5pf. deep green, olive and green	35	45
B190	-	20pf.+10pf. brown, red and pink	80	80
B191	-	40pf.+20pf. deep blue, blue & light blue	1·90	5·00

DESIGNS: 10pf. Girl in street; 20pf. Girl blowing on Alpine flower; 40pf. Boy on beach.

B59 Hans Boeckler

1961. Tenth Anniv of Hans Boeckler (politician).
B192	**B59**	20pf. black and red	50	55

1961. Louise Schroeder Commemoration. As Type **B52**.
B193		20pf. brown	55	55

DESIGN: Portrait of Schroeder.

B60 Durer

1961. Famous Germans.
B194		5pf. olive (Magnus)	35	35
B195		7pf. brown (St. Elizabeth of Thuringia)	35	55
B196		8pf. violet (Gutenberg)	35	55
B197		10pf. green (Type **B60**)	35	35
B198		15pf. blue (Luther)	35	55
B199		20pf. red (Bach)	35	35
B200		25pf. brown (Neumann)	35	55
B201		30pf. brown (Kant)	45	80
B202		40pf. blue (Lessing)	85	1·50
B203		50pf. brown (Goethe)	55	1·50
B204		60pf. red (Schiller)	55	1·70
B205		70pf. green (Beethoven)	80	1·70
B206		80pf. brown (Kleist)	4·50	11·50
B207		1Dm. violet (Annette von Droste-Hulshoff)	2·00	5·00
B208		2Dm. green (Hauptmann)	2·75	7·50

B61 "Five Crosses" Symbol and St. Mary's Church

1961. Tenth Evangelical Churches' Day. Crosses in violet.
B210	**B61**	10pf. green	35	35
B211	-	20pf. purple	35	35

DESIGN: 20pf. "Five Crosses" and Kaiser Wilhelm Memorial Church.

B62 Exhibition Emblem

1961. West Berlin Radio and Television Exn.
B212	**B62**	20pf. brown and red	45	55

B63 "Die Linden" (1650)

1962. "Old Berlin" series.
B213	**B63**	7pf. sepia and brown	35	35
B214	-	10pf. sepia and green	35	35
B215	-	15pf. black and blue	35	35
B216	-	20pf. sepia and brown	35	35
B217	-	25pf. sepia and olive	35	35
B218	-	40pf. black and blue	40	55
B219	-	50pf. sepia and purple	55	55
B220	-	60pf. sepia and mauve	70	70
B221	-	70pf. black and purple	70	70
B222	-	80pf. sepia and red	90	1·00
B223	-	90pf. sepia and brown	1·10	1·10
B224	-	1Dm. sepia and green	1·40	1·70

DESIGNS: 10pf. "Waisenbrucke" (Orphans' Bridge), 1783; 15pf. Mauerstrasse, 1780; 20pf. Berlin Castle, 1703; 25pf. Potsdamer Platz, 1825; 40pf. Bellevue Castle, c. 1800; 50pf. Fischer Bridge, 1830; 60pf. Halle Gate, 1880; 70pf. Parochial Church, 1780; 80pf. University, 1825; 90pf. Opera House, 1780; 1Dm. Grunewald Lake, c. 1790.

B64 Euler Gelberhund Biplane, 1912, and Boeing 707 Airliner

1962. 50th Anniv of German Airmail Transport.
B225	**B64**	60pf. black and blue	80	80

B65 Exhibition Emblem

1963. West Berlin Broadcasting Exn.
B226	**B65**	20pf. ultram, grey & bl	45	45

B66 Town Hall Schoneberg

1964. 700th Anniv of Schoneberg.
B227	**B66**	20pf. brown	45	45

B67 Pres. Lubke

1964. Re-election of Pres. Lubke.
B228	**B67**	20pf. red	35	35
B229	**B67**	40pf. blue	55	55

See also Nos. B308/9.

WEST BERLIN DESIGNS. Except where illustrated the following are the same or similar designs to German Federal Republic additonally inscr "BERLIN".

1964. Capitals of the Federal Lands. As No. 1335.
B230 20pf. multicoloured 55 55

1964. Humanitarian Relief and Welfare Funds. As Nos. 1352/5.
B231 10pf.+5pf. multicoloured 35 35
B232 15pf.+5pf. multicoloured 35 35
B233 20pf.+10pf. multicoloured 55 45
B234 40pf.+20pf. multicoloured 80 1·40

1964. Pres. Kennedy Commem. As Type 411.
B235 40pf. blue 70 80

1964. Twelve Centuries of German Architecture. (a) Size 18½×22½ mm. As Nos. 1359/66. Plain backgrounds.
B236 10pf. brown 35 35
B237 15pf. green 35 35
B238 20pf. red 35 35
B239 40pf. blue 90 1·70
B240 50pf. bistre 2·00 2·30
B241 60pf. red 1·50 1·70
B242 70pf. green 2·75 5·00
B243 80pf. brown 2·75 2·30

(b) Size 19½×24 mm. As Nos. 1367/81. Coloured backgrounds.
B244 5pf. bistre 35 35
B245 8pf. red 35 35
B246 10pf. purple 35 35
B247 20pf. green 35 35
B248 30pf. olive 35 35
B249 30pf. red 35 35
B250 40pf. bistre 80 1·10
B251 50pf. blue 65 70
B252 60pf. red 2·30 2·75
B253 70pf. bronze 1·10 1·10
B254 80pf. brown 1·50 2·75
B255 90pf. black 80 1·10
B256 1Dm. blue 80 1·10
B257 1Dm.10 brown 2·00 2·00
B258 1Dm.30 green 3·50 3·50
B259 2Dm. purple 3·50 2·75

BUILDINGS: 8pf. Palatine Castle, Kaub. Others as Nos. 1359/81 of German Federal Republic.

1965. Child Welfare. As Nos. 1384/7.
B261 10pf.+5pf. Eurasian woodcock 35 35
B262 15pf.+5pf. Common pheasant 35 35
B263 20pf.+10pf. Black grouse 35 35
B264 40pf.+20pf. Western capercaillie 70 1·10

B68 Kaiser Wilhelm Memorial Church

1965. "New Berlin". Multicoloured.
B265 10pf. Type B68 35 35
B266 15pf. Opera House (horiz) 35 35
B267 20pf. Philharmonic Hall (horiz) 35 35
B268 30pf. Jewish Community Centre (horiz) 35 35
B269 40pf. Regina Martyrum Memorial Church (horiz) 35 35
B270 50pf. Ernst-Reuter Square (horiz) 35 45
B271 60pf. Europa Centre 45 55
B272 70pf. Technical University, Charlottenburg (horiz) 70 70
B273 80pf. City Motorway 70 70
B274 90pf. Planetarium (horiz) 80 1·10
B275 1Dm. Telecommunications, Tower 85 1·40
B276 1Dm.10 University Clinic, Steglitz (horiz) 90 1·50

1965. Humanitarian Relief Funds. As Nos. 1406/9.
B277 10pf.+5pf. Type 425 35 35
B278 15pf.+5pf. Cinderella and birds with dress 35 35
B279 20pf.+10pf. Prince offering slipper to Cinderella 35 35
B280 40pf.+20pf. Cinderella and Prince on horse 65 1·10

1966. As Nos. 1412/15a.
B281 10pf. brown 35 35
B282 20pf. green 35 35
B283 30pf. red 35 35
B284 50pf. blue 80 55
B284a 100pf. blue 6·00 6·25

1966. Child Welfare. As Nos. 1416/19.
B285 10pf.+5pf. Type 429 35 35
B286 20pf.+10pf. Chamois 35 35
B287 30pf.+15pf. Fallow deer 35 45
B288 50pf.+25pf. Red deer 80 1·10

1966. Humanitarian Relief Funds. As Nos. 1428/31.
B289 10pf.+5pf. Type 435 35 35
B290 20pf.+10pf. Frog dining with Princess 35 35
B291 30pf.+15pf. Frog Prince and Princess 55 35
B292 50pf.+25pf. In coach 70 1·10
Designs from Grimm's *The Frog Prince*.

1967. Child Welfare. As Nos. 1434/7.
B293 10pf.+5pf. Common rabbit 35 35
B294 20pf.+10pf. Stoat 35 35
B295 30pf.+15pf. Common hamster 55 45
B296 50pf.+25pf. Red fox 1·40 2·00

B69 *Bust of a Young Man* (after C. Meit)

1967. Berlin Art Treasures.
B297 B69 10pf. sepia and bistre 35 35
B298 - 20pf. olive and blue 35 35
B299 - 30pf. brown and olive 35 35
B300 - 50pf. sepia and grey 55 55
B301 - 1Dm. black and blue 1·10 1·10
B302 - 1Dm.10 brn & chest 1·70 2·30

DESIGNS: 20pf. Head of *The Elector of Brandenburg* (statue by Schluter); 30pf. *St. Mark* (statue by Riemenschneider); 50pf. Head from Quadriga, Brandenburg Gate. 1Dm. *Madonna* (carving by Feuchtmayer). (22½×39 mm) 1Dm.10, *Christ and St. John* (after carving from Upper Swabia, c. 1320).

B70 Broadcasting Tower and T.V. Screen

1967. West Berlin Broadcasting Exn.
B303 B70 30pf. multicoloured 45 55

1967. Humanitarian Relief Funds. As Nos. 1443/6.
B304 10pf.+5pf. multicoloured 35 35
B305 20pf.+10pf. multicoloured 35 35
B306 30pf.+15pf. multicoloured 55 55
B307 50pf.+25pf. multicoloured 80 1·10

1967. Re-election of President Lubke. As Type B67.
B308 B67 30pf. red 35 35
B309 B67 50pf. blue 55 70

1968. Child Welfare. As Nos. 1454/7.
B310 10pf.+5pf. Wild cat 35 70
B311 20pf.+10pf. European otter 45 70
B312 30pf.+15pf. Eurasian badger 80 1·40
B313 50pf.+25pf. Eurasian beaver 2·50 3·00

B71 Former Court-house

1968. 500th Anniv of Berlin Magistrates' Court.
B314 B71 30pf. black 50 55

B72 Festival Emblems

1968. Athletics Festival, Berlin.
B315 B72 20f. red, black and grey 45 55

1968. Humanitarian Relief Funds. As Nos. 1473/6.
B316 10pf.+5pf. Doll of 1878 35 35
B317 20pf.+10pf. Doll of 1850 35 35
B318 30pf.+15pf. Doll of 1870 35 35
B319 50pf.+25pf. Doll of 1885 75 1·10

B74 The Newspaper Seller (C. W. Allers, 1889)

1969. 19th-cent Berliners. Contemporary Art.
B320 - 5pf. black 30 30
B321 B74 10pf. purple 30 30
B322 - 10pf. brown 30 30
B323 - 20pf. green 35 35
B324 - 20pf. turquoise 35 35
B325 - 30pf. brown 80 55
B326 - 30pf. brown 80 55
B327 - 50pf. blue 2·30 2·75

DESIGNS—HORIZ: 5pf. *The Cab-driver* (H. Zille, 1875). VERT: 10pf. *The Bus-driver* (C. W. Allers, 1890); 20pf. (No. B323) *The Cobblers Boy* (F. Kruger, 1839); 20pf. (No. B324) *The Cobbler* (A. von Menzel, 1833); 30pf. (No. B325) *The Borsig Forge* (P. Meyerheim, 1878); 30pf. (No. B326) *Three Berlin Ladies* (F. Kurger, 1839); 50pf. *At the Brandenburg Gate* (C. W. Allers, 1889).

1969. Child Welfare. As Nos. 1478/81.
B328 10pf.+5pf. brn, blk & yell 35 45
B329 20pf.+10pf. brown, black and buff 45 80
B330 30pf.+15pf. brn, blk & red 70 1·10
B331 50pf.+25pf. grey, yellow, black and blue 1·80 2·30

B75 Orang-Utan Family

1969. 125th Anniv of Berlin Zoo. Sheet 99×74 mm containing Type B5 and similar horiz designs.
MSB332 10pf. black and brown; 20pf. black and green; 30pf. black and purple; 50pf. black and blue (sold for 1Dm.30) 2·75 2·75
DESIGNS: 20pf. Dalmatian pelican family; 30pf. Gaur and calf; 50pf. Common zebra and foal.

B76 Postman

1969. 20th Congress of Post Office Trade Union Federation (I.P.T.T.), Berlin.
B333 B76 10pf. olive 35 35
B334 - 20pf. brown and buff 35 35
B335 - 30pf. violet and ochre 80 90
B336 - 50pf. blue and light blue 1·60 1·80
DESIGNS: 20pf. Telephonist; 30pf. Technician; 50pf. Airmail handlers.

B77 J. Joachim (violinist and director, after A. von Menzel)

1969. Anniversaries. Multicoloured.
B337 30pf. Type B77 80 70
B338 50pf. Alexander von Humboldt (after J. Stieler) 1·40 1·80
ANNIVERSARIES: 30pf. Centenary of Berlin Academy of Music; 50pf. Birth bicentenary of Humboldt.

B78 Railway Carriage (1835)

1969. Humanitarian Relief Funds. Pewter Models. Multicoloured. (a) Inscr "WOHLFAHRTSMARKE".
B339 10pf.+5pf. Type B78 35 35
B340 20pf.+10pf. Woman feeding chicken (1850) 35 35
B341 30pf.+15pf. Market stall (1850) 55 55
B342 50pf.+25pf. Mounted postilion (1860) 1·50 1·50

(b) Christmas. Inscr "WEIHNACHTSMARKE".
B343 10pf.+5pf. "The Three Kings" 55 45

B79 T. Fontane

1970. 150th Birth Anniv of Theodor Fontane (writer).
B344 B79 20pf. multicoloured 55 45

B80 Heinrich von Stretlingen

1970. Miniatures of Minnesingers. Multicoloured.
B345 10pf.+5pf. Type B80 35 35
B346 20pf.+10pf. Meinloh von Sevelingen 55 70
B347 30pf.+15pf. Burkhart von Hohenfels 80 90
B348 50pf.+25pf. Albrecht von Johannsdorf 1·80 2·20

B81 Film "Title"

1970. 20th International Film Festival, Berlin.
B349 B81 30pf. multicoloured 70 80

1970. Pres. Heinemann. As Nos. 1535/55.
B350 486 5pf. black 35 25
B351 486 8pf. brown 1·10 1·50
B352 486 10pf. brown 35 25
B353 486 15pf. bistre 35 45
B354 486 20pf. green 35 35
B355 486 25pf. green 1·40 80
B356 486 30pf. brown 1·50 70
B357 486 40pf. orange 80 35
B358 486 50pf. blue 70 30
B359 486 60pf. blue 1·40 80
B360 486 70pf. brown 1·10 90
B361 486 90pf. green 1·40 1·30
B362 486 90pf. red 2·75 3·50
B363 486 1Dm. green 1·40 1·00
B364 486 110pf. grey 1·70 1·60
B365 486 120pf. brown 1·70 1·40
B366 486 130pf. brown 2·50 2·30
B367 486 140pf. green 2·50 2·30
B368 486 150pf. red 2·50 1·70
B369 486 160pf. orange 3·50 2·75
B370 486 170pf. orange 2·50 2·40
B371 486 190pf. purple 2·75 2·75
B372 486 2Dm. violet 2·75 2·00

B82 Allegory of Folklore

1970. 20th Berlin Folklore Week.
B373 B82 30pf. multicoloured 80 80

B83 "Caspar"

1970. Humanitarian Relief Funds. Puppets. Multicoloured. (a) Relief Funds.
B374 10pf.+5pf. Type B83 35 35
B375 20pf.+10pf. "Polichinelle" 35 35
B376 30pf.+15pf. "Punch" 80 70
B377 50pf.+25pf. "Pulcinella" 1·40 1·60

(b) Christmas.
B378 10pf.+5pf. "Angel" 45 45

B84 L. von Ranke
(after painting by
J. Schrader)

1970. 175th Birth Anniv of Leopold von Ranke (historian).
B379 **B84** 30pf. multicoloured   70   55

1971. Centenary of German Unification.
B380 **492** 30pf. black, red & orange   80   80

B85 Class ET 165.8 Electric
Train, 1933

1971. Berlin Rail Transport. Multicoloured.
B381		5pf. Class T.12 steam train, 1925	35	35
B382		10pf. Electric tram, 1890	35	35
B383		20pf. Horse tram, 1880	35	35
B384		30pf. Type **B85**	65	55
B385		50pf. Electric tram, 1950	2·30	2·00
B386		1Dm. Underground train No. 2431, 1971	2·75	2·75

B86 "Fly"

1971. Child Welfare. Children's Drawings. Multicoloured.
B387		10pf.+5pf. Type **B86**	45	45
B388		20pf.+10pf. "Fish"	45	45
B389		30pf.+15pf. "Porcupine"	70	80
B390		50pf.+25pf. "Cockerel"	1·80	1·90

B87 *The
Bagpiper* (copper
engraving, Durer,
c. 1514)

1971. 500th Birth Anniv of Albrecht Durer.
B391 **B87** 10pf. black and brown   70   45

B88
Communications
Tower and Dish
Aerials

1971. West Berlin Broadcasting Exhibition.
B392 **B88** 30pf. indigo, blue & red   1·10   90

B89 Bach and part of *2nd
Brandenburg* Concerto

1971. 250th Anniv of Bach's *Brandenburg* Concertos.
B393 **B89** 30pf. multicoloured   1·00   90

B90 H. von
Helmholtz (from
painting by K.
Morell-Kramer)

1971. 150th Birth Anniv of Hermann von Helmholtz (scientist).
B394 **B90** 25pf. multicoloured   80   55

B91 "Opel"
Racing-car (1921)

1971. 50th Anniv of Avus Motor-racing Track. Sheet 100×75 mm containing horiz designs as Type **B91**. Multicoloured.
MSB395 10pf. Type **B91**; 25pf. "Auto-Union" (1936); 30pf. "Mercedes-Benz SSKL" (1931); 60pf. "Mercedes" racing with "Auto-Union" (1937)   2·30   2·00

1971. Accident Prevention. As Nos. 1596/1605.
B396		5pf. orange	35	45
B397		10pf. brown	35	35
B398		20pf. violet	35	35
B399		25pf. green	55	90
B400		30pf. red	55	70
B401		40pf. mauve	55	80
B402		50pf. blue	2·75	1·70
B403		60pf. blue	2·75	3·50
B404		70pf. blue and green	2·00	1·60
B405		100pf. green	2·75	1·70
B406		150pf. brown	8·50	10·00

B92 Dancing
Men

1971. Humanitarian Relief Funds. Wooden Toys. Multicoloured. (a) Inscr "WOHLFAHRTSMARKE".
B407		10pf.+5pf. Type **B92**	35	35
B408		25pf.+10pf. Horseman on wheels	35	35
B409		30pf.+15pf. Acrobat	80	80
B410		60pf.+30pf. Nurse and babies	1·50	1·70

(b) Christmas. Inscr "WEIHNACHTSMARKE".
B411 10pf.+5pf. Angel with two candles   55   45

B93 Microscope

1971. Birth Centenary of Material-testing Laboratory, Berlin.
B412 **B93** 30pf. multicoloured   70   55

B94 F. Gilly (after
bust by
Schadow)

1972. Birth Bicentenary of Friedrich Gilly (architect).
B413 **B94** 30pf. black and blue   80   55

B95 Boy raiding
Bird's-nest

1972. Child Welfare. Animal Protection. Multicoloured.
B414		10pf.+5pf. Type **B95**	35	35
B415		25pf.+10pf. Care of kittens	45	45
B416		30pf.+15pf. Man beating watch-dog	80	80
B417		60pf.+30pf. Animals crossing road at night	1·90	1·90

B96 *Grunewaldsee* (A. von
Riesen)

1972. Paintings of Berlin Lakes. Multicoloured.
B418		10pf. Type **B96**	35	35
B419		25pf. *Wannsee* (Max Liebermann)	75	80
B420		30pf. *Schlachtensee* (W. Leistikow)	1·40	90

B97 E. T. A.
Hoffman

1972. 150th Death Anniv of E. T. A. Hoffman (poet and musician).
B421 **B97** 60pf. black and violet   1·60   1·60

B98 Max
Liebermann
(self-portrait)

1972. 125th Birth Anniv of Max Liebermann (painter).
B422 **B98** 40pf. multicoloured   1·00   70

B99 Stamp
Printing-press

1972. Stamp Day.
B423 **B99** 20pf. blue, black & red   70   45

1972. Humanitarian Relief Funds. Multicoloured. (a) 19th-century Faience Chessmen. As Nos. 1636/40 of West Germany. Inscr "WOLFAHRTSMARKE".
B424		20pf.+10pf. Knight	45	45
B425		30pf.+15pf. Rook	70	70
B426		40pf.+20pf. Queen	1·90	1·90
B427		70pf.+35pf. King	2·75	2·75

(b) Christmas. Inscr "WEIHNACHTSMARKE".
B428 20pf.+10pf. "The Holy Family"   80   70

B100 Prince von
Hardenberg
(after Tischbein)

1972. 150th Death Anniv of Karl August von Hardenberg (statesman).
B429 **B100** 40pf. multicoloured   90   70

B101 Northern
Goshawk

1973. Youth Welfare. Birds of Prey. Multicoloured.
B430		20pf.+10pf. Type **B101**	70	70
B431		30pf.+15pf. Peregrine falcon	1·00	1·00
B432		40pf.+20pf. Northern sparrow hawk	1·50	1·50
B433		70pf.+35pf. Golden eagle	2·50	2·50

B102 Horse-bus, 1907

1973. Berlin Buses. Multicoloured.
B434		20pf. Type **B102**	55	45
B435		20pf. Trolley bus, 1933	55	45
B436		30pf. Motor bus, 1919	1·10	70
B437		30pf. Double-decker, 1970	1·60	70
B438		40pf. Double-decker, 1925	1·70	1·00
B439		40pf. "Standard" bus, 1973	1·70	1·00

B103 L. Tieck

1973. Birth Bicentenary of Ludwig Tieck (poet and writer).
B440 **B103** 40pf. multicoloured   1·00   70

B104 J. J. Quantz

1973. Death Bicentenary of Johann Quantz (composer).
B441 **B104** 40pf. black   1·10   90

B105 Radio Set,
1926

1973. "50 Years of German Broadcasting". Sheet 148×105 mm containing horiz designs as Type **B105**.
MS442 20pf. black and yellow; 30pf. black and green; 40pf. black and red; 70pf. black and blue (sold at 1.80Dm)   5·25   5·25
DESIGNS: 30pf. Hans Bredow and microphone of 1924; 40pf. Girl with TV and video tape-recorder; 70pf. TV camera.

B106
17th-century
Hurdy-Gurdy

1973. Humanitarian Relief Funds. Multicoloured. (a) Musical Instruments. Inscr "WOHLFAHRTSMARKE".
B443		20pf.+10pf. Type **B106**	55	55
B444		30pf.+15pf. 16th century drum	1·10	1·10
B445		40pf.+20pf. 18th century lute	1·40	1·40
B446		70pf.+35pf. 16th century organ	1·90	1·90

(b) Christmas. Inscr "WEIHNACHTSMARKE".
B447 20pf.+10pf. Christmas star   80   80

B107 G. W.
Knobelsdorff

1974. 275th Birth Anniv of Georg W. von Knobelsdorff (architect).
B448 **B107** 20pf. brown   65   45

B108 G. R. Kirchhoff

1974. 150th Birth Anniv of Gustav R. Kirchhoff (physicist).
B449 **B108** 30pf. green and grey   55   55

B109 A. Slaby

1974. 125th Birth Anniv of Adolf Slaby (radio pioneer).
B450 **B109** 40pf. black and red   80   70

B110 Airlift
Memorial

1974. 25th Anniv of Berlin Airlift.
B451 **B110** 90pf. multicoloured   3·25   2·30

B111 Photography

1974. Youth Welfare. Youth Activities. Multicoloured.

B452	20pf.+10pf. Type **B111**	55	70
B453	30pf.+15pf. Athletics	55	70
B454	40pf.+20pf. Music	1·40	1·50
B455	70pf.+35pf. Voluntary service (Nurse)	1·90	2·00

B112 School Seal

1974. 400th Anniv of Evangelical Grammar School, Berlin.

B456	**B112** 50pf. grey, brn & gold	1·00	70

B113 Spring Bouquet

1974. Humanitarian Relief Funds. Flowers. Multicoloured.
(a) 25th Anniv of Humanitarian Relief Stamps. Inscr "25 JAHRE WOHLFAHRTSMARKE".

B457	30pf.+15pf. Type **B113**	55	55
B458	40pf.+20pf. Autumn bouquet	1·00	1·00
B459	50pf.+25pf. Bouquet of roses	1·10	1·10
B460	70pf.+35pf. Winter bouquet	1·70	1·70

(b) Christmas. Inscr "WEIHNACHTSMARKE".

B461	30pf.+15pf. Christmas bouquet	1·10	1·30

B114 Tegel Airport

1974. Opening of Tegel Airport, Berlin.

B462	**B114** 50pf. violet, bl & grn	1·60	90

B115 *Venus* (F. E. Meyer)

1974. Berlin Porcelain Figures. Multicoloured.

B463	30pf. Type **B115**	75	70
B464	40pf. *Astronomy* (W. C. Meyer)	85	80
B465	50pf. *Justice* (J. G. Muller)	1·00	1·00

B116 Gottfried Schadow

1975. 125th Death Anniv of Gottfried Schadow (sculptor).

B466	**B116** 50pf. brown	1·10	80

B117 *Prinzess Charlotte*

1975. Berlin Pleasure Boats. Multicoloured.

B467	30pf. Type **B117**	90	45
B468	40pf. *Siegfried*	90	45
B469	50pf. *Sperber*	1·60	1·10
B470	60pf. *Vaterland*	1·60	1·10
B471	70pf. *Moby Dick*	2·10	2·00

B118 Steam Locomotive *Drache*, 1848

1975. Youth Welfare. Railway Locomotives. Multicoloured.

B472	30pf.+15pf. Type **B118**	1·10	90
B473	40pf.+20pf. Class 89 tank locomotive	1·10	1·10
B474	50pf.+25pf. Class 050 steam locomotive	2·30	1·90
B475	70pf.+35pf. Class 010 steam locomotive	3·25	3·50

B119 Ferdinand Sauerbruch (surgeon)

1975. Birth Cent of Ferdinand Sauerbruch.

B476	**B119** 50pf. dp brn, brn & pk	1·10	80

B120 Gymnastics Emblem

1975. Gymnaestrada (Gymnastic Games), Berlin.

B477	**B120** 40pf. black, gold and green	80	55

1975. Industry and Technology. As Nos. 1742/55.

B478	-	5pf. green	35	30
B479	-	10pf. purple	35	30
B480	-	20pf. red	45	35
B481	-	30pf. violet	70	35
B482	572	40pf. green	70	35
B483	-	50pf. red	1·10	55
B483a	-	60pf. red	1·30	70
B484	-	70pf. blue	1·30	40
B485	-	80pf. green	1·30	70
B486	-	100pf. brown	1·30	70
B486a	-	110pf. purple	1·90	1·70
B487	-	120pf. blue	1·70	1·40
B487a	-	130pf. red	3·25	2·00
B488	-	140pf. red	1·70	1·90
B488a	-	150pf. red	4·00	1·70
B489	-	160pf. green	3·50	1·90
B489a	-	180pf. brown	4·00	2·75
B489b	-	190pf. brown	4·00	3·50
B490	-	200pf. purple	2·30	1·10
B490a	-	230pf. purple	3·50	2·75
B490b	-	250pf. green	5·75	3·50
B490c	-	300pf. green	5·75	3·50
B491	-	500pf. black	8·00	5·75

B121 *Lovis Corinth* (self-portrait)

1975. 50th Death Anniv of Lovis Corinth (painter).

B492	**B121** 50pf. multicoloured	1·10	80

B122 Buildings in Naunynstrasse, Berlin-Kreuzberg

1975. European Architectural Heritage Year.

B493	**B122** 50pf. multicoloured	1·10	90

B123 Yellow Gentian

1975. Humanitarian Relief Funds. Alpine Flowers. Multicoloured.

B494	30pf.+15pf. Type **B123**	80	80
B495	40pf.+20pf. Arnica	80	80
B496	50pf.+25pf. Cyclamen	95	95
B497	70pf.+35pf. Blue gentian	1·60	1·60

1975. Christmas. As Type **B123**, inscr "WEIHNACHTSMARKE". Multicoloured.

B498	30pf.+15pf. Snow heather	1·10	1·10

See also Nos. B508/11, B540/3 and B557/60.

B124 Paul Lobe

1975. Birth Cent of Paul Lobe (politician).

B499	**B124** 50pf. red	1·10	80

B125 Ears of Wheat, with inscription "Grune Woche"

1976. "International Agriculture Week", Berlin.

B500	**B125** 70pf. yellow and green	1·10	1·00

B126 Putting the Shot

1976. Youth Welfare. Training for the Olympics. Multicoloured.

B501	30pf.+15pf. Type **B126**	1·10	1·10
B502	40pf.+20pf. Hockey	1·10	1·10
B503	50pf.+25pf. Handball	1·10	1·20
B504	70pf.+35pf. Swimming	2·30	2·30

B127 Hockey

1976. Women's World Hockey Championships.

B505	**B127** 30pf. green	1·00	55

B128 Treble Clef

1976. German Choristers' Festival.

B506	**B128** 40pf. multicoloured	1·10	80

B129 Fire Service Emblem

1976. 125th Anniv of Berlin Fire Service.

B507	**B129** 50pf. multicoloured	1·80	1·10

1976. Humanitarian Relief Funds. Garden Flowers. As Type **B123**. Multicoloured.

B508	30pf.+15pf. Iris	55	55
B509	40pf.+20pf. Wallflower	55	55
B510	50pf.+25pf. Dahlia	1·10	1·10
B511	70pf.+35pf. Larkspur	1·60	1·60

B130 Julius Tower, Spandau

1976. Berlin Views (1st series).

B512	-	30pf. black and blue	80	55
B513	**B130**	40pf. black and brown	1·10	55
B514	-	50pf. black and green	1·30	55

DESIGNS: 30pf. Yacht on the Havel; 50pf. Lake and Victory Column, Tiergarten park.

See also Nos. B562/4, B605/7 and B647/9.

B131 "Annunciation to the Shepherds" (window, Frauenkirche, Esslingen)

1976. Christmas. Sheet 71×101 mm.

MSB515	**B131** 30pf.+15pf. multicoloured	1·10	1·00

1977. Coil Stamps. German Castles. As Nos. 1805/12d.

B516	10pf. blue	35	25
B517	20pf. orange	35	30
B517a	25pf. red	90	55
B518	30pf. brown	40	35
B518c	35pf. red	50	45
B519	40pf. green	45	35
B519a	40pf. brown	80	45
B520	50pf. red	80	35
B520b	50pf. green	90	45
B521	60pf. brown	1·50	70
B521a	60pf. red	1·40	70
B522	70pf. blue	1·50	70
B522a	80pf. green	90	45
B522b	90pf. blue	1·40	1·10
B522c	120pf. violet	1·50	1·40
B523	190pf. red	2·00	2·00
B524	200pf. green	2·20	2·00
B524a	210pf. brown	3·00	2·30
B524b	230pf. green	3·00	2·30
B524c	280pf. blue	5·00	3·50
B524d	300pf. orange	5·00	3·50

B132 *Eugenie d'Alton* (Cristian Rauch)

1977. Birth Bicentenary of Christian Daniel Rauch (sculptor).

B525	**B132** 50pf. black	1·10	80

B133 *Eduard Gaertner* (self-portrait)

1977. Death Cent of Eduard Gaertner (artist).

B526	**B133** 40pf. black, green and deep green	80	55

B134 Bremen Kogge, 1380

1977. Youth Welfare. Ships. Multicoloured.

B527	30pf.+15pf. Type **B134**	70	70
B528	40pf.+20pf. *Helena Sloman* (steamship), 1850	80	80
B529	50pf.+25pf. *Cap Polonio* (liner), 1914	1·40	1·40
B530	70pf.+35pf. *Widar* (bulk carrier), 1971	1·70	1·70

B135 Female Figure

1977. Birth Cent of Georg Kolbe (sculptor).
B531 **B135** 30pf. green and black   80   55

B136 Crosses and Text

1977. 17th Evangelical Churches Day.
B532 **B136** 40pf. yellow, blk & grn   80   55

B137 Telephones of 1905 and 1977

1977. International Telecommunications Exhibition and Centenary of German Telephone Service.
B533 **B137** 50pf. buff, black & red   2·50   1·50

B138 Imperial German Patent Office, Berlin-Kreuzberg

1977. Centenary of German Patent Office.
B534 **B138** 60pf. black, red & grey   2·30   1·00

B139 Untitled Painting (G. Grosz)

1977. 15th European Art Exhibition.
B535 **B139** 70pf. multicoloured   1·40   1·50

B140 Picasssco Triggerfish

1977. 25th Anniv of Reopening of Berlin Aquarium. Multicoloured.
B536 20pf. Type **B140**   70   70
B537 30pf. Paddlefish   1·00   90
B538 40pf. Radiated tortoise   1·40   1·10
B539 50pf. Rhinoceros iguana   1·90   1·40

1977. Humanitarian Relief Funds. Meadow Flowers. As Type **B123**. Multicoloured.
B540 30pf.+15pf. Daisy   45   45
B541 40pf.+20pf. Marsh marigold   80   80
B542 50pf.+25pf. Sainfoin   1·10   1·10
B543 70pf.+35pf. Forget-me-not   1·70   1·70

B141 "Madonna and Child" (stained glass window, Basilica of St. Gereon, Cologne)

1977. Christmas. Sheet 70×105 mm.
MSB544 **B141** 30pf.+15pf. multicoloured   1·10   1·10

B142 Walter Kollo

1978. Birth Cent of Walter Kollo (composer).
B545 **B142** 50pf. brown and red   1·50   1·00

B143 Emblem of U.S. Chamber of Commerce

1978. 75th Anniv of U.S. Chamber of Commerce in Germany.
B546 **B143** 90pf. blue and red   1·80   1·80

1978. Youth Welfare. Aviation History (1st series). As T **627**. Multicoloured.
B547 30pf.+15pf. Montgolfier balloon, 1783   70   70
B548 40pf.+20pf. Lilienthal glider, 1891   80   80
B549 50pf.+25pf. Wright Type A biplane   1·00   80
B550 70pf.+35pf. Etrich/Rumpler Taube, 1910 1·90   1·90
See also Nos. B567/70 and B589/92.

1978. Sport Promotion Fund. As T **623**. Multicoloured.
B551 50pf.+25pf. Cycling   1·40   90
B552 70pf.+35pf. Fencing   1·80   1·60

B146 Albrecht von Graefe

1978. 150th Birth Anniv of Albrecht von Graefe (pioneer of medical eye services).
B553 **B146** 30pf. black and brown   80   55

B147 Freidrich Ludwig Jahn

1978. Birth Bicentenary of F. L. Jahn (pioneer of physical education).
B554 **B147** 50pf. red   1·10   80

B148 Swimming

1978. Third World Swimming Championships.
B555 **B148** 40pf. multicoloured   1·60   1·30

B149 The Boat (Karl Hofer)

1978. Birth Centenary of Karl Hofer (Impressionist painter).
B556 **B149** 50pf. multicoloured   1·10   90

1978. Humanitarian Relief Funds. Woodland Flowers. As Type **B123**. Multicoloured.
B557 30pf.+15pf. Solomon's seal   70   70
B558 40pf.+20pf. Wood primrose   80   80
B559 50pf.+25pf. Red helle-borine   1·10   1·10
B560 70pf.+35pf. Bugle   1·70   1·70

B150 Prussian State Library

1978. Opening of New Prussian State Library Building.
B561 **B150** 90pf. olive and red   2·00   1·60

1978. Berlin Views (2nd series). As Type **B130**.
B562 40pf. black and green   90   55
B563 50pf. black and purple   1·10   90
B564 60pf. black and brown   1·40   1·00
DESIGNS: 40pf. Belvedere; 50pf. Landwehr Canal; 60pf. Village church, Lichtenrade.

B151 "Madonna" (stained glass window, Frauenkirche, Munich)

1978. Christmas. Sheet 65×92 mm.
MSB565 **B151** 30pf.+15pf. multicoloured   1·10   1·10

B152 Congress Centre

1979. Opening of International Congress Centre, Berlin.
B566 **B152** 60pf. black, blue & red   1·60   1·00

1979. Youth Welfare. History of Aviation (2nd series). As T **627**. Multicoloured.
B567 40pf.+20pf. Vampyr glider, 1921   80   80
B568 50pf.+25pf. Junkers Ju 52/3m D-2202 "Richthofen", 1932   1·10   1·10
B569 60pf.+30pf. Messerschmitt Bf 108 D-1010, 1934   1·50   1·50
B570 90pf.+45pf. Douglas DC-3 NC-14988, 1935   2·30   2·30

B153 Relay Runners

1979. Sport Promotion Fund. Multicoloured.
B571 60pf.+30pf. Type **B153**   1·50   1·50
B572 90pf.+45pf. Archers   1·90   1·90

B154 Old and New Arms

1979. Centenary of State Printing Works, Berlin.
B573 **B154** 60pf. multicoloured   2·20   1·60

B155 Arrows and Target

1979. World Archery Championships.
B574 **B155** 50pf. multicoloured   1·10   80

B156 Television Screen

1979. International Telecommunications Exhibition, Berlin.
B575 **B156** 60pf. black, grey & red   1·60   1·10

B157 Moses Mendelssohn

1979. 250th Birth Anniv of Moses Mendelssohn (philosopher).
B576 **B157** 90pf. black   1·70   1·10

B158 Venus Slipper Orchid and Great Tropical House

1979. 300th Anniv of Berlin Botanical Gardens.
B577 **B158** 50pf. multicoloured   1·10   80

B159 Gas Lamp, Kreuzberg District

1979. 300th Anniv of Street Lighting.
B578 **B159** 10pf. green, bl & grey   55   35
B579 - 40pf. green, bis & grey   1·10   90
B580 - 50pf. green, brn & grey   1·60   1·10
B581 - 60pf. green, red & grey   1·70   1·10
DESIGNS: 40pf. Electric carbon-arc lamp, Hardenbergstrasse; 50pf. Gas Lamps, Wittenberg-platz; 60pf. Five-armed chandelier, Charlottenburg.

1979. Humanitarian Relief Funds. Woodland Flowers and Fruit. As Type **B123**, but horiz. Multicoloured.
B582 40pf.+20pf. Larch   85   70
B583 50pf.+25pf. Hazelnut   1·10   1·00
B584 60pf.+30pf. Horse chestnut   1·50   1·50
B585 90pf.+45pf. Blackthorn   1·90   1·90

B161 Advertisement Pillar

1979. 125th Anniv of Advertisement Pillars.
B586 **B161** 50pf. red and lilac   2·20   1·10

B162 "Nativity" (Altenberg medieval manuscript)

1979. Christmas.
B587 **B162** 40pf.+20pf. multicoloured   1·40   1·10

B163 Map showing Wegener's Theory of Continental Drift

1980. Birth Centenary of Alfred Wegener (explorer and geophysicist).
B588 **B163** 60pf. black, orange and blue   1·80   1·50

1980. Youth Welfare. Aviation History (3rd series). As T **627**. Multicoloured.
B589 40pf.+20pf. Vickers Viscount 810   1·00   1·00
B590 50pf.+25pf. Fokker Friendship Condor   1·50   1·50
B591 60pf.+30pf. Sud Aviation Caravelle F-BKSZ, 1955   2·00   2·00
B592 90pf.+45pf. Sikorsky S-55 helicopter OO-SHB, 1949   2·00   2·00
Nos. B589/90 are incorrectly dated.

B164 Throwing the Javelin

1980. Sport Promotion Fund. Multicoloured.
B593 50pf.+25pf. Type **B164**   1·00   1·00
B594 60pf.+30pf. Weightlifting   1·10   1·10
B595 90pf.+45pf. Water polo   1·70   1·70

B165 Cardinal Preysing

1980. 86th German Catholics Congress.
B596 **B165** 50pf. red and black 1·10 80

B166 "Operatio" (enamel medallion)

1980. 150th Anniv of Prussian Museums. Multicoloured.
B597 40pf. Type **B166** 1·10 70
B598 60pf. "Monks Reading" (oak sculpture, Ernst Barlach) 1·50 90

B167 Robert Stolz

1980. Birth Centenary of Robert Stolz (composer).
B599 **B167** 60pf. multicoloured 1·60 1·10

B168 Von Steuben

1980. 250th Birth Anniv of Friedrich Wilhelm von Steuben (American general).
B600 **B168** 40pf. multicoloured 1·60 80

B169 Orlaya grandiflora

1980. Humanitarian Relief Funds. Endangered Wild Flowers. Multicoloured.
B601 40pf.+20pf. Type **B169** 1·00 1·00
B602 50pf.+25pf. Yellow gagae 1·30 1·30
B603 60pf.+30pf. Summer pheasant's-eye 1·30 1·30
B604 90p.+45pf. Venus's looking-glass 2·20 2·20
See also Nos. B622/5.

1980. Berlin Views (3rd series). As Type **B130**.
B605 40pf. black and green 1·10 65
B606 50pf. black and brown 1·30 1·00
B607 60pf. black and blue 1·90 1·10
DESIGNS: 40pf. Lilienthal Monument; 50pf. "Grosse Neugierde"; 60pf. Grunewald Tower.

B170 "Message to the Shepherds" (Altomunster manuscript)

1980. Christmas.
B608 **B170** 40pf.+20pf. mult 1·40 1·30

B171 Von Arnim (after Strohling)

1981. Birth Bicentenary of Achim von Arnim (poet).
B609 **B171** 60pf. green 1·40 90

B172 Von Chamisso (bronze medallion, David d'Angers)

1981. Birth Bicentenary of Adelbert von Chamisso (poet and naturalist).
B610 **B172** 60pf. brown, deep brown and ochre 1·40 90

B173 Von Gontard

1981. 250th Birth Anniv of Karl Phillipp von Gontard (architect).
B611 **B173** 50pf. red, black & grey 1·40 90

B174 Kreuzberg War Memorial

1981. Birth Bicentenary of Karl Friedrich Schinkel (architect).
B612 **B174** 40pf. green and brown 1·60 1·10

B175 Theodolite, c. 1810

1981. Youth Welfare. Optical Instruments. Multicoloured.
B613 40pf.+20pf. Type **B175** 80 80
B614 50pf.+25pf. Equatorial telescope, 1820 1·10 1·10
B615 60pf.+30pf. Microscope, 1790 1·50 1·50
B616 90pf.+45pf. Sextant, 1830 2·30 2·30

B176 Group Gymnastics

1981. Sport Promotion Fund. Multicoloured.
B617 60pf.+30pf. Type **B176** 1·40 1·30
B618 90pf.+45pf. Cross-country race 2·00 1·90

B177 Cupid and Psyche

1981. 150th Birth Anniv of Reinhold Begas (sculptor).
B619 **B177** 50pf. black and blue 1·10 80

B178 Badge of Order "Pour le Merite"

1981. Prussian Exhibition, Berlin-Kreuzberg.
B620 **B178** 40pf. multicoloured 1·10 80

B179 Broadcasting House, Charlottenburg

1981. International Telecommunications Exhibition, Berlin.
B621 **B179** 60pf. multicoloured 1·80 1·10

1981. Humanitarian Relief Funds. Endangered Wild Flowers. As Type **B169**. Multicoloured.
B622 40pf.+20pf. Common bistort 1·10 1·10
B623 50pf.+25pf. Moor-king 1·30 1·10
B624 60pf.+30pf. Gladiolus palustris 1·30 1·10
B625 90pf.+45pf. Siberian iris 2·50 2·30

B180 "Three Kings" (glass painting)

1981. Christmas.
B626 **B180** 40pf.+20pf. mult 1·40 1·00

B181 Peter Beuth

1981. Birth Bicentenary of Peter Beuth (constitutional lawyer).
B627 **B181** 60pf. black and brown 1·10 1·00

B182 Dancer Nijinsky (Georg Kolbe)

1981. 20th Century Sculptures. Multicoloured.
B628 40pf. Type **B182** 80 55
B629 60pf. Mother Earth II (Ernst Barlach) 1·40 90
B630 90pf. Flora Kneeling (Richard Scheibe) 1·80 1·60

B183 Arms and View of Spandau, c. 1700

1982. 750th Anniv of Spandau.
B631 **B183** 60pf. multicoloured 1·80 1·40

B184 Daimler Steel-wheeled Car, 1889

1982. Youth Welfare Fund. Motor Cars. Multicoloured.
B632 40pf.+20pf. Type **B184** 1·00 1·00
B633 50pf.+25pf. Wanderer "Puppchen", 1911 1·10 1·10
B634 60pf.+30p. Adler limousine, 1913 1·40 1·40
B635 90pf.+45pf. DKW "F 1", 1913 2·30 2·30

B185 Sprinting

1982. Sport Promotion Fund. Multicoloured.
B636 60pf.+30pf. Type **B185** 1·40 1·10
B637 90pf.+45pf. Volleyball 2·00 1·60

B186 Harp

1982. Centenary of Berlin Philharmonic Orchestra.
B638 **B186** 60pf. grey, red & green 1·60 1·00

B187 "Emigrants reaching Prussian Frontier" (woodcut after drawing by Adolph von Menzel)

1982. 250th Anniv of Salzburg Emigrants' Arrival in Prussia.
B639 **B187** 50pf. stone, deep brown and brown 1·10 80

B188 Italian Stone Carriers (Max Pechstein)

1982. Paintings. Multicoloured.
B640 50pf. Type **B188** 1·40 1·00
B641 80pf. Two Girls Bathing (Otto Mueller) 2·00 1·60

B189 Floribunda-Grandiflora

1982. Humanitarian Relief Funds. Roses. Multicoloured.
B642 50pf.+20pf. Type **B189** 1·40 1·40
B643 60pf.+30pf. Hybrid tea 1·70 1·40
B644 80pf.+40pf. Floribunda 2·30 2·30
B645 120pf.+60pf. Miniature rose 3·75 3·75

B190 Castle Theatre, Charlottenburg

1982. 250th Birth Anniv of Carl Gotthard Langhans (architect).
B646 **B190** 80pf. red, grey and black 2·30 1·80

1982. Berlin Views (4th series). As Type **B130**.
B647 50pf. black and blue 1·50 1·00
B648 60pf. black and red 1·60 1·30
B649 80pf. black and brown 2·30 1·40
DESIGNS: 50pf. Villa Borsig; 60pf. Sts. Peter and Paul Church; 80pf. Villa von der Heydt.

B191 "Adoration of the Kings" (detail from St. Peter altar by Master Bertram)

1982. Christmas.
B650 **B191** 50pf.+20pf. mult 1·40 1·10

B192 Water Pump, Klausenerplatz

1983. Street Water Pumps. Multicoloured.
B651 50pf. Type **B192** 1·70 1·10
B652 60pf. Chamissoplatz 1·90 1·30
B653 80pf. Schloss-strasse 2·30 1·80
B654 120pf. Kuerfurstendamm 3·50 3·00

B193 Royal Prussian Telegraphy Inspectors at St. Anne's Church

1983. 150th Anniv of Berlin–Coblenz Optical-Mechanical Telegraph.
B655 **B193** 80pf. brown ..... 2·50 2·20

B194 Hildebrand & Wolfmuller, 1894

1983. Youth Welfare. Motor Cycles. Multicoloured.
B656 50pf.+20pf. Type **B194** ..... 1·10 80
B657 60pf.+30pf. Wanderer, 1908 ..... 1·70 1·50
B658 80pf.+40pf. D.K.W.-Lomos, 1922 ..... 1·90 1·60
B659 120pf.+60pf. Mars, 1925 ..... 4·25 4·00

B195 Latin-American Dancing

1983. Sport Promotion Fund. Multicoloured.
B660 80pf.+40pf. Type **B195** ..... 2·20 1·70
B661 120pf.+60pf. Ice hockey ..... 3·25 2·75

B196 *La Barbarina* (painting of Barbara Campanini)

1983. 300th Birth Anniv of Antoine Pesne (artist).
B662 **B196** 50pf. multicoloured ..... 1·40 1·00

B197 Ringelnatz (silhouette by E. M. Engert)

1983. Birth Centenary of Joachim Ringelnatz (poet and painter).
B663 **B197** 50pf. green, brn & red ..... 1·60 1·10

B198 Paul Nipkow's Picture Transmission System, 1884

1983. International Broadcasting Exn, Berlin.
B664 **B198** 80pf. multicoloured ..... 2·30 1·90

B199 Mountain Windflower

1983. Humanitarian Relief Funds. Endangered Alpine Flowers. Multicoloured.
B665 50pf.+20pf. Type **B199** 90 90
B666 60pf.+30pf. Alpine auricula ..... 1·40 1·40
B667 80pf.+40pf. Little primrose ..... 2·50 2·50
B668 120pf.+60pf. Einsele's aquilegia ..... 3·75 3·75

B200 Nigerian Yoruba Crib

1983. Christmas.
B669 **B200** 50pf.+20pf. multicoloured ..... 1·40 1·30

B201 Queen Cleopatra VII (Antikenmuseum)

1984. Art Objects in Berlin Museums. Multicoloured.
B670 30pf. Type **B201** ..... 1·40 1·10
B671 50pf. Statue of seated couple from Giza Necropolis (Egyptian Museum) ..... 1·80 1·60
B672 60pf. Goddess with pearl turban (Ethnology Museum) ..... 2·30 2·00
B673 80pf. Majolica dish (Applied Arts Museum) ..... 3·25 2·75

B202 *Trichius Fasciatus*

1984. Youth Welfare. Pollinating Insects. Multicoloured.
B674 50pf.+20pf. Type **B202** ..... 1·50 1·00
B675 60pf.+30pf. *Agrumenia carniolica* ..... 1·50 1·10
B676 80pf.+40pf. *Bombus terrestris* ..... 2·75 2·00
B677 120pf.+60pf. *Eristalis tenax* ..... 3·50 3·50

B203 Hurdling

1984. Sport Promotion Fund. Multicoloured.
B678 60pf.+30pf. Type **B203** ..... 2·30 1·60
B679 80pf.+40pf. Cycling ..... 2·75 1·60
B680 120pf.+60pf. Four-seater kayaks ..... 4·00 4·00

B204 Klausener

1984. 50th Death Anniv of Dr. Erich Klausener (chairman of Catholic Action).
B681 **B204** 80pf. green & dp green ..... 1·60 1·10

B205 "Electric Power" (K. Sutterlin)

1984. Centenary of Berlin Electricity Supply.
B682 **B205** 50pf. yell, orge & blk ..... 1·40 1·00

B206 Conference Emblem

1984. Fourth European Ministers of Culture Conference, Berlin.
B683 **B206** 60pf. multicoloured ..... 1·70 1·10

B207 Brehm and White Stork

1984. Death Centenary of Alfred Brehm (zoologist).
B684 **B207** 80pf. multicoloured ..... 2·50 1·90

B208 Heim (bust, Freidrich Tieck)

1984. 150th Death Anniv of Ernst Ludwig Heim (medical pioneer).
B685 **B208** 50pf. black and red ..... 1·60 1·10

B209 *istera cordata*

1984. Humanitarian Relief Funds. Orchids. Multicoloured.
B686 50pf.+20pf. Type **B209** ..... 2·50 1·60
B687 60pf.+30pf. *Ophrys insectifera* ..... 2·50 1·60
B688 80pf.+40pf. *Epipactis palustris* ..... 4·00 3·50
B689 120pf.+60pf. *Ophrys coriophora* ..... 6·25 5·75

B210 *Sunflowers on Grey Background*

1984. Birth Centenary of Karl Schmidt-Rottluff (artist).
B690 **B210** 60pf. multicoloured ..... 1·60 1·10

B211 St. Nicholas

1984. Christmas.
B691 **B211** 50pf.+20pf. multicoloured ..... 1·70 1·60

B212 Bettina von Arnim

1985. Birth Bicentenary of Bettina von Arnim (writer).
B692 **B212** 50pf. black, brn & red ..... 1·40 1·30

B213 Humboldt (statue, Paul Otto)

1985. 50th Death Anniv of Wilhelm von Humboldt (philologist).
B693 **B213** 80pf. black, blue & red ..... 2·20 1·90

B214 Ball in Net

1985. Sport Promotion Fund. Multicoloured.
B694 80pf.+40pf. Type **B214** (50th anniv of basketball in Germany and European championships, Stuttgart) ..... 2·00 2·00
B695 120pf.+60pf. Table tennis (60th anniv of German Table Tennis Association) ..... 3·50 3·50

B215 Stylized Flower

1985. Federal Horticultural Show, Berlin.
B696 **B215** 80pf. multicoloured ..... 1·90 1·60

B216 Bussing Bicycle, 1868

1985. Youth Welfare. International Youth Year. Bicycles. Multicoloured.
B697 50pf.+20pf. Type **B216** ..... 1·70 1·70
B698 60pf.+30pf. Child's tricycle, 1885 ..... 1·70 1·70
B699 80pf.+40pf. Jaray bicycle, 1925 ..... 2·30 2·30

B700 120pf.+60pf. Opel racing bicycle, 1925 ..... 5·00 5·00

B217 Stock Exchange, 1863–1945

1985. 300th Anniv of Berlin Stock Exchange.
B701 **B217** 50pf. multicoloured ..... 1·60 1·30

B218 Otto Klemperer

1985. Birth Centenary of Otto Klemperer (orchestral conductor).
B702 **B218** 60pf. blue ..... 1·90 1·60

B219 Association Emblem

1985. 11th International Gynaecology and Obstetrics Association Congress, Berlin.
B703 **B219** 60pf. multicoloured ..... 1·60 1·30

B220 "FE 3" Television Camera, 1935

1985. International Broadcasting Exn, Berlin.
B704 **B220** 80pf. multicoloured ..... 2·75 2·30

B221 Seal of Brandenburg-Prussia and Preamble of Edict

1985. 300th Anniv of Edict of Potsdam (admitting Huguenots to Prussia).
B705 **B221** 50pf. lilac and black ..... 1·40 1·00

B222 Flowers, Strawberries and Ladybirds

1985. Humanitarian Relief Funds. Motifs from borders of medieval prayer book. Multicoloured.
B706 50pf.+20pf. Type **B222** ..... 1·70 1·70
B707 60pf.+30pf. Flowers, bird and butterfly ..... 2·30 2·30
B708 80pf.+40pf. Flowers, bee and butterfly ..... 2·30 2·30
B709 120pf.+60pf. Flowers, berries, butterfly and snail ..... 3·50 3·50

B223 "Adoration of the Kings" (detail, Epiphany Altar)

1985. Christmas. 500th Birth Anniv of Hans Baldung Grien (artist).
B710 **B223** 50pf.+20pf. mult ..... 1·70 1·60

B224 Kurt Tucholsky

1985. 50th Death Anniv of Kurt Tucholsky (writer and journalist).
B711 **B224** 80pf. multicoloured ..... 2·30 1·60

B225 Furtwangler and Score

1986. Birth Centenary of Wilhelm Furtwangler (composer and conductor).
B712 **B225** 80pf. multicoloured   2·75   2·50

B226 Rohe and National Gallery

1986. Birth Centenary of Ludwig Mies van der Rohe (architect).
B713 **B226** 50pf. multicoloured   1·70   1·60

B227 Swimming

1986. Sport Promotion Fund. Multicoloured.
B714 80pf.+40pf. Type **B227** (European Youth Championships, Berlin)   2·75   2·75
B715 120pf.+55pf. Show-jumping (World Championships, Aachen)   3·50   3·50

B228 Glazier

1986. Youth Charity. Trades (1st series). Multicoloured.
B716 50pf.+25pf. Type **B228**   1·70   1·70
B717 60pf.+30pf. Locksmith   2·30   2·30
B718 70pf.+35pf. Tailor   2·30   2·30
B719 80pf.+40pf. Carpenter   2·75   2·75
See also Nos. B765/8.

B229 Flags

1986. 16th European Communities Day.
B720 **B229** 60pf. multicoloured   1·50   1·50

B230 Ranke

1986. Death Centenary of Leopold von Ranke (historian).
B721 **B230** 80pf. brown and grey   2·30   1·90

B231 Benn

1986. Birth Centenary of Gottfried Benn (poet).
B722 **B231** 80pf. blue   2·30   1·90

B232 Charlottenburg Gate

1986. Gateways. Multicoloured.
B723 50pf. Type **B232**   2·00   2·00
B724 60pf. Griffin Gate, Glienicke Palace   2·10   2·10
B725 80pf. Elephant Gate, Berlin Zoo   2·30   2·30

B233 "The Flute Concert" (detail, Adolph von Menzel)

1986. Death Bicentenary of Frederick the Great.
B726 **B233** 80pf. multicoloured   2·30   1·90

B234 Cantharus, 1st century A.D.

1986. Humanitarian Relief Funds. Glassware. Multicoloured.
B727 50pf.+25pf. Type **B234**   1·70   1·70
B728 60pf.+30pf. Beaker, 200 A.D.   2·30   2·30
B729 70pf.+35pf. Jug, 3rd century A.D.   2·30   2·30
B730 80pf.+40pf. Diatreta 4th century A.D.   2·50   2·50

B235 "Adoration of the Three Kings" (Ortenberg altarpiece)

1986. Christmas.
B731 **B235** 50pf.+25pf. mult   1·50   1·50

1986. Famous German Women. As Nos. 2149a/54, 2158, 2161, 2166/9a.
B732 5pf. brown and grey   55   3·25
B733 10pf. brown and violet   65   2·30
B734 20pf. blue and red   2·30   5·75
B735 40pf. red and blue   1·80   5·75
B736 50pf. green and brown   2·75   4·00
B737 60pf. lilac and green   1·70   5·00
B738 80pf. brown and green   2·00   4·00
B739 100pf. grey and red   2·75   2·30
B740 130pf. violet and blue   6·75   17·00
B741 140pf. brown and blue   3·75   13·50
B742 170pf. purple and green   5·25   19·00
B743 180pf. purple and blue   4·75   19·00
B744 240pf. brown and blue   11·00   32·00
B745 250pf. blue and mauve   11·50   28·00
B746 300pf. green and plum   8·25   23·00
B747 350pf. brown and black   12·50   50·00
B748 500pf. red and green   12·50   50·00

B236 Berlin, 1650

1987. 750th Anniv of Berlin. (a) As No. 2170.
B760 **833** 80pf. multicoloured   2·75   2·30

(b) Sheet 130×100 mm containing Type B 236 and similar horiz designs. Multicoloured.
MSB761 40pf. Type **B236**; 50pf. Charlottenburg Castle, 1830; 60pf. Turbine Hall; 80pf. Philharmonic and Chamber Music Concert Hall   5·75   5·75

B237 Louise Schroeder

1987. Birth Centenary of Louise Schroeder (Mayor of Berlin).
B762 **B237** 50pf. brown and orange on light brown   1·60   1·60

B238 German Gymnastics Festival, Berlin

1987. Sport Promotion Fund. Multicoloured.
B763 80pf.+40pf. Type **B238**   2·30   2·30
B764 120pf.+55pf. World Judo Championships, Essen   3·25   3·25

1987. Youth Welfare. Trades (2nd series). As Type **B228**. Multicoloured.
B765 50pf.+25pf. Cooper   1·70   1·70
B766 60pf.+30pf. Stonemason   1·70   1·70
B767 70pf.+35pf. Furrier   2·30   2·30
B768 80pf.+40pf. Painter/ lacquerer   2·30   2·30

B239 "Bohemian Refugees" (detail of relief, King Friedrich Wilhelm Monument, Berlin-Neukölln)

1987. 250th Anniv of Bohemian Settlement, Rixdorf.
B769 **B239** 50pf. brown and green   1·40   1·40

B240 New Buildings

1987. International Building Exhibition, Berlin.
B770 **B240** 80pf. silver, black & bl   1·90   1·70

B241 Tree in Arrow Circle

1987. 14th International Botanical Congress, Berlin.
B771 **B241** 60pf. multicoloured   1·50   1·50

B242 Compact Disc and Gramophone

1987. International Broadcasting Exhibition, Berlin. Centenary of Gramophone Record.
B772 **B242** 80pf. multicoloured   1·80   1·70

B243 5th-century Bonnet Ornament

1987. Humanitarian Relief Funds. Precious Metal Work. Multicoloured.
B773 50pf.+25pf. Type **B243**   1·10   1·10
B774 60pf.+30pf. Athene plate, 1st-century B.C.   1·70   1·70
B775 70pf.+35pf. "Armilla" armlet, 1180   2·00   2·00
B776 80pf.+40pf. Snake bracelet, 300 B.C.   2·50   2·50

1987. Tourist Sights. As Nos. 2200/19.
B777 5pf. blue and grey   45   70
B778 10pf. blue and indigo   55   55
B779 20pf. flesh and blue   55   1·10
B780 30pf. brown and green   1·50   1·50
B781 40pf. brown, red and blue   1·80   3·25
B782 50pf. ochre and blue   2·30   1·70
B783 60pf. green and black   2·30   1·70
B784 70pf. flesh and blue   2·30   4·00
B785 70pf. brown and blue   3·25   6·75
B786 80pf. grey and green   2·30   1·70
B787 100pf. green and orange   1·70   2·30
B788 120pf. green and red   3·50   5·00
B789 140pf. bistre and yellow   3·50   6·25
B790 300pf. flesh and brown   6·50   11·50
B791 350pf. brown and blue   6·50   11·50

B244 Adoration of the Magi (13th-century Book of Psalms)

1987. Christmas.
B797 **B244** 50pf.+25pf. multicoloured   1·40   1·40

B245 Heraldic Bear

1988. Berlin, European City of Culture.
B798 **B245** 80pf. multicoloured   2·75   2·75

B246 Old and New Buildings

1988. Centenary of Urania Science Museum.
B799 **B246** 50pf. multicoloured   2·00   1·90

B247 Large Pure-bred Foal (bronze)

1988. Birth Centenary of Rene Sintenis (sculptor).
B800 **B247** 60pf. multicoloured   1·40   1·40

B248 Clay-pigeon Shooting

1988. Sport Promotion Fund. Olympic Games. Multicoloured.
B801 60pf.+30pf. Type **B248**   2·20   2·20
B802 80pf.+40pf. Figure skating (pairs)   2·20   2·20
B803 120pf.+55pf. Throwing the hammer   2·75   2·75

B249 Piano, Violin and Cello

1988. Youth Welfare. Music. Multicoloured.
B804 50pf.+25pf. Type **B249**   1·70   1·70
B805 60pf.+30pf. Wind quintet   2·30   2·30
B806 70pf.+35pf. Guitar, recorder and mandolin   2·30   2·30
B807 80pf.+40pf. Children's choir   3·50   3·50

B250 Great Elector and Family in Berlin Castle Gardens

1988. 300th Death Anniv of Friedrich Wilhelm, Great Elector of Brandenburg.
B808 **B250** 50pf. multicoloured   1·60   1·60

B251 Globe

1988. International Monetary Fund and World Bank Boards of Governors Annual Meetings, Berlin.
B809 **B251** 70pf. multicoloured   1·70   1·50

B252 First Train leaving Potsdam Station

1988. 150th Anniv of Berlin–Potsdam Railway.
B810 **B252** 10pf. multicoloured   1·00   80

B253 *The Collector* (bronze statue)

1988. 50th Death Anniv of Ernst Barlach (artist).
B811   **B253**   40pf. multicoloured   1·60   1·60

B254 18th-century Breast Ornament

1988. Humanitarian Relief Funds. Precious Metal Work. Multicoloured.
B812   50pf.+25pf. Type **B254**   1·80   1·80
B813   60pf.+30pf. 16th-century lion-shaped jug   2·00   2·00
B814   70pf.+35pf. 16th-century goblet   2·50   2·50
B815   80pf.+40pf. 15th-century cope clasp   2·50   2·50

B255 "Annunciation to the Shepherds" (illus from *Henry the Lion's Gospel Book*)

1988. Christmas.
B816   **B255**   50pf.+25pf. mult   1·80   1·80

B256 Volleyball (European Championships)

1989. Sport Promotion Fund. Multicoloured.
B817   100pf.+50pf. Type **B256**   3·50   3·50
B818   140pf.+60pf. Hockey (Champions Trophy)   4·75   4·75

B257 Tigers and Tamer

1989. Youth Welfare. Circus. Multicoloured.
B819   60pf.+30pf. Type **B257**   2·30   2·30
B820   70pf.+30pf. Trapeze artistes   2·75   2·75
B821   80pf.+40pf. Sealions   4·00   4·00
B822   100pf.+50pf. Jugglers   4·75   4·75

B258 U.S. and U.K. Flags forming Airplane

1989. 40th Anniv of Berlin Airlift.
B823   **B258**   60pf. multicoloured   1·80   1·80

B259 Emblem

1989. 13th International Organization of Chief Accountants Congress.
B824   **B259**   80pf. multicoloured   1·90   1·90

B260 Reuter

1989. Birth Centenary of Ernst Reuter (politician and Mayor of Berlin).
B825   **B260**   100pf. multicoloured   2·75   2·50

B261 Satellite Radio Waves and T.V. Screen

1989. International Broadcasting Exn, Berlin.
B826   **B261**   100pf. multicoloured   2·30   2·30

B262 Plan of Berlin Zoo and Lenne

1989. Birth Bicentenary of Peter Joseph Lenne (landscape designer).
B827   **B262**   60pf. multicoloured   2·20   1·90

B263 Ossietzky and Masthead of *Die Weltbuhne*

1989. Birth Centenary of Carl von Ossietzky (journalist and peace activist).
B828   **B263**   100pf. multicoloured   2·50   2·50

B264 Former School Building

1989. 300th Anniv of Berlin Lycee Francais.
B829   **B264**   40pf. multicoloured   1·40   1·30

B265 St. Nicholas's Church, Berlin-Spandau

1989. 450th Anniv of Reformation.
B830   **B265**   60pf. multicoloured   1·40   1·30

B266 15th-century Letter Messenger

1989. Humanitarian Relief Funds. Postal Deliveries. Multicoloured.
B831   60pf.+30pf. Type **B266**   3·50   3·50
B832   80pf.+35pf. Brandenburg mail coach, 1700   4·50   4·50
B833   100pf.+50pf. 19th-century Prussian postal messengers   5·75   5·75

B267 *Journalists*

1989. Birth Centenary of Hannah Hoch (painter).
B834   **B267**   100pf. multicoloured   2·75   2·30

B268 Angel

1989. Christmas. 16th-century Carvings by Veit Stoss, St. Lawrence's Church, Nuremberg. Multicoloured.
B835   40pf.+20pf. Type **B268**   1·70   1·70
B836   60pf.+30pf. "Adoration of the Magi"   2·75   2·75

B269 Horse-drawn Passenger Vehicle

1990. 250th Anniv of Public Transport in Berlin.
B837   **B269**   60pf. multicoloured   2·75   2·30

B270 Rudorff

1990. 150th Birth Anniv of Ernst Rudorff (founder of conservation movement).
B838   **B270**   60pf. multicoloured   2·75   2·30

1990. 500th Anniv of Regular European Postal Services. As No. 2297.
B839   **914**   100pf. deep brown, light brown and brown   3·50   3·25

B271 Curtain and Theatre

1990. Cent of National Free Theatre, Berlin.
B840   **B271**   100pf. multicoloured   3·00   3·00

B272 Facade

1990. 40th Anniv of Bundeshaus, Berlin.
B841   **B272**   100pf. multicoloured   4·00   3·00

B273 Water Polo

1990. Sport Promotion Fund. Multicoloured.
B842   100pf.+50pf. Type **B273**   4·50   5·50
B843   140pf.+60pf. Wheelchair basketball   8·00   9·75

B274 Moritz filling Pipe with Gunpowder

1990. Youth Welfare. 125th Anniv of Max and Moritz (characters from books by Wilhelm Busch). Multicoloured.
B844   60pf.+30pf. Type **B274**   2·75   2·75
B845   70pf.+30pf. Max and Moritz running off   3·75   3·75
B846   80pf.+35pf. Moritz slashing sack open   4·00   4·00
B847   100pf.+50pf. Insect on Uncle Fritz's nose   4·00   4·00

B275 Poster

1990. 90th German Catholic Day.
B848   **B275**   60pf. multicoloured   2·50   2·50

B276 "Street Singer" (etching, Ludwig Knaus)

1990. Bicentenary of Barrel-organ.
B849   **B276**   100pf. multicoloured   2·75   2·75

B277 Pestle and Mortar and Diagram of Aspirin Molecule

1990. Centenary of German Pharmaceutical Society.
B850   **B277**   100pf. multicoloured   5·75   4·50

B278 Diesterweg

1990. Birth Bicentenary of Adolph Diesterweg (educationist).
B851   **B278**   60pf. multicoloured   4·00   4·25

B279 Travelling Post Office, 1900

1990. Humanitarian Relief Funds. Posts and Telecommunications. Multicoloured.
B852   60pf.+30pf. Type **B279**   3·00   3·00
B853   80pf.+35pf. Installing telephone lines, 1900   4·00   4·00
B854   100pf.+50pf. Electric parcels van, 1930   5·75   5·75

With the absorption of East Germany into the Federal Republic of Germany on 3 October 1990, separate issues for West Berlin ceased.

GERMAN DEMOCRATIC REPUBLIC (East Germany)

The German Democratic Republic was set up in October 1949 and comprised the former Russian Zone. Its stamps were used in East Berlin.

On 3 October 1990 the territory was absorbed into the German Federal Republic.

E1 Pigeon and Globe

1949. 75th Anniv of U.P.U.
E1   **E1**   50pf. blue and deep blue   15·00   12·50

E2 Postal Workers and Globe

1949. Postal Workers' Congress.
E2   **E2**   12pf. blue   11·50   13·50
E3   **E2**   30pf. red   18·00   23·00

E3 Type **1** of Bavaria and Magnifying Glass

1949. Stamp Day.
E4   **E3**   12pf.+3pf. black   9·00   7·50

E4 Skier

1950. First Winter Sports Meeting, Schierke.
E5   **E4**   12pf. violet   9·00   5·25
E6   -   24pf. blue   11·50   8·50
DESIGN: 24pf. Girl skater.

1950. Leipzig Spring Fair. As T **231** but dated "1950".
E7   24pf.+12pf. purple   12·50   12·50
E8   30pf.+14pf. red   15·00   15·00
DESIGNS: 24pf. First Dresden China Fair, 1710; 30pf. First Sample Fair, 1894.

E5 Globe and Sun

1950. 60th Anniv of Labour Day.

E9	E5	30pf. red	24·00	19·00

E6 Wilhelm
Pieck

E7 Wilhelm Pieck

1950

E68	E6	5pf. green	13·00	5·00
E10	E6	12pf. blue	34·00	2·75
E70	E6	24pf. brown	34·00	2·00
E12	E7	1Dm. green	43·00	4·90
E13	E7	2Dm. red	26·00	5·75
E14	E7	5Dm. blue	11·50	2·10

For 1 and 2Dm. with different portrait of president, see Nos. E320/1 (1953).

E8 Shepherd
Playing Pipes

1950. Death Bicentenary of J. S. Bach (composer).

E15	E8	12pf.+4pf. green	9·00	6·25
E16	-	24pf.+6pf. olive	9·00	6·25
E17	-	30pf.+8pf. red	17·00	13·50
E18	-	50pf.+16pf. blue	26·00	21·00

DESIGNS: 24pf. Girl playing hand-organ; 30pf. Bach; 50pf. Three singers.

E9 Dove, Globe and
Stamp

1950. Philatelic Exhibition (DEBRIA), Leipzig.

E19	E9	84pf.+41pf. red	60·00	14·50

E10 L. Euler

1950. 250th Anniv of Academy of Science, Berlin.

E20	E10	1pf. grey	6·00	2·40
E21	-	5pf. green	8·50	6·00
E22	-	6pf. violet	17·00	6·00
E23	-	8pf. brown	23·00	13·00
E24	-	10pf. green	21·00	13·00
E25	-	12pf. blue	18·00	5·00
E26	-	16pf. blue	24·00	23·00
E27	-	20pf. purple	22·00	18·00
E28	-	24pf. red	24·00	5·00
E29	-	50pf. blue	37·00	24·00

PORTRAITS: 5pf. A. von Humboldt; 6pf. T. Mommsen; 8pf. W. von Humboldt; 10pf. H. von Helmholtz; 12pf. M. Planck; 16pf. J. Grimm; 20pf. W. Nernst; 24pf. G. W. Leibniz; 50pf. A. von Harnack.

1950. German Stamp Exhibition, "DEBRIA". Sheet 92×52 mm.

MSE29a	Nos. E4 and E19	£200	£200

E11 Miner

1950. 750th Anniv of Mansfeld Copper Mines.

E30	E11	12pf. blue	8·50	9·75
E31	-	24pf. red	13·50	10·50

DESIGN: 24pf. Copper smelting.

E12 Ballot Box

1950. East German Elections.

E32	E12	24pf. brown	20·00	6·00

E13 Hand, Dove
and Burning
Buildings

1950. Peace Propaganda. Inscr "ERKAMPFT DEN FRIEDEN".

E33	-	6pf. blue	5·50	4·25
E34	E13	8pf. brown	5·50	2·40
E35	-	12pf. blue	7·25	5·50
E36	-	24pf. red	7·50	3·75

DESIGNS (all include hand and dove): 6pf. Tank; 12pf. Atom bomb explosion; 24pf. Rows of gravestones.

E14 Tobogganing

1951. Second Winter Sports Meeting, Oberhof.

E37	E14	12pf. blue	12·00	9·75
E38	-	24f. red (ski jumper)	16·00	12·00

E15

1951. Leipzig Spring Fair.

E39	E15	24pf. red	23·00	14·50
E40	E15	50pf. blue	23·00	14·50

E16 Presidents Pieck and
Bierut

1951. Visit of Polish President to Berlin.

E41	E16	24pf. red	27·00	22·00
E42	E16	50pf. blue	27·00	22·00

E17 Mao Tse-tung

E18 Chinese Land Reform

1951. Friendship with China.

E43	E17	12pf. green	£120	30·00
E44	E18	24pf. red	£140	37·00
E45	E17	50pf. blue	£120	37·00

E19 Youth
Hoisting Flag

1951. Third World Youth Festival. Inscr as in Type **E19**. On coloured papers.

E46	E19	12pf. brown	17·00	8·50
E47	-	24pf. green and red	17·00	5·00
E48	E19	30pf. buff and green	20·00	9·25
E49	-	50pf. red and blue	20·00	9·25

DESIGN: 24pf., 50pf. Three girls dancing.

E20 Symbols
of
Agriculture
&
Industry

1951. Five Year Plan.

E50	E20	24pf. multicoloured	6·75	3·00

E21 K.
Liebknecht

1951. 80th Birth Anniv of Liebknecht (revolutionary).

E51	E21	24pf. slate and red	7·50	3·00

E22 Instructing
Young Collectors

1951. Stamp Day.

E52	E22	12pf. blue	9·50	3·75

E23 P. Bykow and E. Wirth

1951. German–Soviet Friendship.

E53	E23	12pf. blue	6·75	5·00
E54	-	24pf. red	8·00	6·50

DESIGN: 24pf. Stalin and Pres. Pieck.

E24 Skier

1952. Third Winter Sports Meeting. Oberhof.

E55	E24	12pf. green	8·75	5·00
E56	-	24pf. blue	9·50	6·00

DESIGN: 24pf. Ski jumper.

E25 Beethoven

1952. 125th Death Anniv of Beethoven (composer).

E57		12pf. blue and light blue	3·25	1·20
E58	E25	24pf. brown and grey	4·75	1·80

DESIGN: 12pf. Full face portrait.

E26 President
Gottwald

1952. Czechoslovak–German Friendship.

E59	E26	24pf. blue	5·25	3·00

E27 Bricklayers

1952. National Reconstruction Fund.

E60	-	12pf.+3pf. violet	3·25	1·00
E61	E27	24pf.+6pf. red	2·75	1·20
E62	-	30pf.+10pf. green	3·25	1·30
E63	-	50pf.+10pf. blue	4·00	2·40

DESIGNS: 12pf. Workers clearing debris; 30pf. Carpenters; 50pf. Architect and workmen.

E28 Cyclists

1952. Fifth Warsaw–Berlin–Prague Cycle Race.

E64	E28	12pf. blue	6·00	3·00

E29 Handel

1952. Handel Festival, Halle.

E65	E29	6pf. brown	4·25	1·80
E66	-	8pf. red	5·00	3·00
E67	-	50pf. blue	5·00	3·75

COMPOSERS: 8pf. Lortzing; 50pf. Weber.

E31 Victor Hugo

1952. Cultural Anniversaries.

E73	E31	12pf. brown	5·00	6·00
E74	-	20pf. green	5·00	6·00
E75	-	24pf. red	5·00	6·00
E76	-	35pf. blue	7·25	7·50

PORTRAITS: 20pf. Leonardo da Vinci; 24pf. N. Gogol; 35pf. Avicenna.

E32 Machinery,
Dove and Globe

1952. Leipzig Autumn Fair.

E77	E32	24pf. red	4·50	2·40
E78	E32	35pf. blue	4·50	3·00

E33 F. L. Jahn

1952. Death Centenary of Jahn (patriot).

E79	E33	12pf. blue	2·75	2·40

E34 University
Building

1952. 450th Anniv of Halle-Wittenberg University.

E80	E34	24pf. green	2·75	1·50

E35 Dove,
Stamp and Flags

1952. Stamp Day.

E81	E35	24pf. brown	3·50	1·60

E36 Dove, Globe
and St.
Stephen's
Cathedral,
Vienna

1952. Vienna Peace Congress.

E97	E36	24pf. red	2·75	2·75
E98	E36	35pf. blue	2·75	5·00

E37 President Pieck

1953. President's Birthday.

E320	E37	1Dm. olive	3·50	2·30
E321	E37	2Dm. brown	6·75	2·30

E38 Karl Marx

1953. 70th Death Anniv of Marx.

E102	-	6pf. red and green	2·00	1·00
E103	-	10pf. brown and green	5·75	1·20
E104	-	12pf. red and green	1·70	1·00
E105	-	16pf. blue and red	4·50	3·00
E106	-	20pf. brown and yellow	2·00	1·30
E107	**E38**	24pf. brown and red	4·50	1·20
E108	-	35pf. yellow and purple	4·50	4·25
E109	-	48pf. brown and green	2·75	1·20
E110	-	60pf. red and brown	5·75	4·25
E111	-	84pf. brown and blue	4·50	3·00
MSE111a		Two sheets, each 148×104 mm. (a) the six vert, and (b) the four horiz designs Set of 2 sheets	2·00	5·25

DESIGNS—VERT: 6pf. Flag and foundry; 12pf. Flag and Spassky Tower, Kremlin; 20pf. Marx reading from *Das Kapital*; 35pf. Marx addressing meeting; 48pf. Marx and Engels. HORIZ: 10pf. Marx, Engels and *Communist Manifesto*; 16pf. Marching crowd; 60pf. Flag and workers; 84pf. Marx in medallion and Stalin Avenue, Berlin.

In each case the flag shows heads of Marx, Engels, Lenin and Stalin.

E39 Gorky

1953. 85th Birth Anniv of Maksim Gorky (writer).

E112	**E39**	35pf. brown	80	75

E40 Cyclists

1953. Sixth International Cycle Race.

E113	**E40**	24pf. green	3·50	3·00
E114	-	35pf. blue	1·70	1·80
E115	-	60pf. brown	2·30	2·40

DESIGNS—VERT: 35pf. Cyclists and countryside; 60pf. Cyclists in town.

E41 H. Von Kleist

1953. 700th Anniv of Frankfurt-on-Oder.

E116	**E41**	16pf. brown	2·30	2·75
E117	-	20pf. green	1·70	2·75
E118	-	24pf. red	2·30	2·75
E119	-	35pf. blue	2·30	4·00

DESIGNS—HORIZ: 20pf. St. Mary's Church; 24pf. Frankfurt from R. Oder; 35pf. Frankfurt Town Hall and coat of arms.

E42 Miner

1953. Five Year Plan. (a) Design in minute dots.

E120	**E42**	1pf. black	2·30	80
E121	-	5pf. green	2·75	1·60
E122	-	6pf. violet	2·75	1·40
E123	-	8pf. brown	4·00	1·60
E124	-	10pf. blue	2·75	1·40
E125	-	12pf. blue	4·00	1·50
E126	-	15pf. violet	4·50	2·50
E127	-	16pf. violet	9·00	3·50
E128	-	20pf. green	6·75	3·50
E129	-	24pf. red	17·00	1·70
E130	-	25pf. green	9·00	4·50
E131	-	30pf. red	11·50	6·00
E132	-	35pf. blue	23·00	6·25
E133	-	40pf. red	19·00	5·75
E134	-	48pf. mauve	19·00	5·00
E135	-	60pf. blue	19·00	7·25
E136	-	80pf. turquoise	19·00	6·75
E137	-	84pf. brown	19·00	20·00

(b) Design in lines.

E153	**E42**	1pf. black	1·10	25
E310A	-	5pf. green	55	30
E155	-	6pf. violet	5·00	55
E156	-	8pf. brown	5·25	45

E311B	-	10pf. blue	35	35
E312A	-	10pf. green	80	55
E159	-	12pf. turquoise	5·00	45
E160	-	15pf. lilac	23·00	80
E313B	-	15pf. violet	45	35
E162	-	16pf. violet	5·75	1·10
E163	-	20pf. green	£100	1·10
E314A	-	12pf. red	55	30
E165	-	24pf. red	9·00	45
E315A	-	25pf. green	55	35
E316B	-	30pf. red	45	35
E168	-	35pf. blue	6·25	1·40
E169	-	40pf. red	13·50	1·40
E317B	-	40pf. mauve	45	35
E171	-	48pf. mauve	13·50	2·00
E318B	-	50pf. blue	50	35
E173	-	60pf. blue	23·00	2·30
E319B	-	70pf. brown	50	35
E175	-	80pf. turquoise	5·75	2·30
E176	-	84pf. brown	23·00	2·30

DESIGNS—VERT: 5pf. Woman turning wheel; 6pf. Workmen shaking hands; 8pf. Students; 10pf. grn Engineers; 10pf. bl and 12pf. Agricultural and industrial workers; 15pf. mve Tele-typist; 15pf. vio and 16pf. Foundry worker; 20pf. grn Workers' health centre, Elster; 20pf. red and 24pf. Stalin Avenue, Berlin; 25pf. Locomotive construction workers; 30pf. Folk dancers; 35pf. Stadium; 40pf. red, Scientist; 40pf. mve, 48pf. Zwinger, Dresden; 50pf., 60pf. Launching ship; 80pf. Farm workers; 70pf., 84pf. Workman and family.

E43 Mechanical Grab

1953. Leipzig Autumn Fair.

E138	**E43**	24pf. brown	3·50	3·00
E139	-	35pf. green	4·25	3·50

DESIGN: 35pf. Potato-harvester.

E44 G. W. von Knobelsdorff and Opera House, Berlin

1953. German Architects.

E140	**E44**	24pf. mauve	2·30	1·40
E141	-	35pf. slate	2·75	2·30

DESIGN: 35pf. B. Neumann and Wurzburg Palace.

E45 Lucas Cranach

1953. 400th Death Anniv of Cranach (painter).

E142	**E45**	24pf. brown	4·00	1·70

E46 Nurse and Patient

1953. Red Cross.

E143	**E46**	24pf. red and brown	3·50	2·30

E47 Postman delivering Letters

1953. Stamp Day.

E144	**E47**	24pf. blue	4·50	1·10

E48 Lion

1953. 75th Anniv of Leipzig Zoo.

E145	**E48**	24pf. brown	3·00	1·10

E49 Muntzer and Peasants

1953. German Patriots.

E146	**E49**	12pf. brown	2·00	90
E147	-	16pf. brown	2·00	90
E148	-	20pf. red	2·00	55
E149	-	24pf. blue	2·00	55
E150	-	35pf. green	3·50	2·30
E151	-	48pf. sepia	3·50	1·80

DESIGNS: 16pf. Baron vom Stein and scroll; 20pf. Von Schill and cavalry; 24pf. Blucher and infantry; 35pf. Students marching; 48pf. Barricade, 1848 Revolution.

E50 Franz Schubert

1953. 125th Death Anniv of Schubert.

E152	**E50**	48pf. brown	4·00	2·30

E52 G. E. Lessing (writer)

1954. 225th Birth Anniv of Lessing.

E177	**E52**	20pf. green	3·50	1·40

E53 Conference Table and Crowd

1954. Four-Power Conference, Berlin.

E178	**E53**	12pf. blue	2·50	1·40

E54 Stalin

1954. First Death Anniv of Stalin.

E179	**E54**	20pf. brown, orange and grey	4·25	1·50

E55 Racing Cyclists

1954. Seventh International Cycle Race.

E180	**E55**	12pf. brown	2·30	1·10
E181	-	24pf. brown	2·75	1·70

DESIGN: 24pf. Cyclists racing through countryside.

E56 Folk Dancing

1954. Second German Youth Assembly.

E182	**E56**	12pf. green	1·70	1·40
E183	-	24pf. red	1·70	1·40

DESIGN: 24pf. Young people and flag.

E57 F. Reuter

1954. 80th Death Anniv of Reuter (author).

E184	**E57**	24pf. brown	2·50	1·60

E58 Dam and Forest

1954. Flood Relief Fund.

E185	**E58**	24pf.+6pf. green	1·40	1·10

E59 E. Thalmann

1954. Tenth Death Anniv of Thalmann (politician).

E186	**E59**	24pf. brown, bl & orge	1·90	1·30

E60 Exhibition Buildings

1954. Leipzig Autumn Fair.

E187	**E60**	24pf. red	1·30	1·10
E188	**E60**	35pf. blue	1·40	45

1954. (a) Nos. E155, etc surch in figures.

E189		5pf. on 6pf. violet	1·50	45
E190		5pf. on 8pf. brown	2·00	45
E191		10pf. on 12pf. turquoise	1·70	45
E192		15pf. on 16pf. lilac	1·50	45
E194		20pf. on 24pf. red	2·75	70
E195		40pf. on 48pf. mauve	4·50	1·10
E196		50pf. on 60pf. blue	4·50	1·10
E197		70pf. on 84pf. brown	12·00	1·10

(b) No. E129 similarly surch.

E193a		20pf. on 24pf. red	1·60	70

E62 President Pieck

1954. Fifth Anniv of German Democratic Republic.

E198	**E62**	20pf. brown	4·00	1·80
E199	**E62**	35pf. blue	4·00	2·00

E63 Stamp of 1953

1954. Stamp Day.

E200	**E63**	20pf. mauve	2·50	1·10
MSE200b		60×80 mm. No. E200 imperf (sold at Dm.30)	65·00	65·00

E64 Russian Pavilion

1955. Leipzig Spring Fair.

E201	**E64**	20pf. purple	1·70	1·40
E202	-	35pf. blue (Chinese Pavilion)	2·30	2·30

1955. Flood Relief Fund. Surch in figures.

E203	**E58**	20+5pf. on 24pf.+6pf. green	1·40	80

E66 "Women of All Nations"

1955. 45th Anniv of International Women's Day.

E204	**E66**	10pf. green	1·60	70
E205	**E66**	20pf. red	1·60	70

E67 Parade of Workers

1955. International Conference of Municipal Workers, Vienna.

| E206 | **E67** | 10pf. black and red | 1·40 | 1·40 |

E68 Monument to Fascist Victims, Brandenburg

1955. International Liberation Day.

E207	**E68**	10pf. blue	1·30	1·40
E208	**E68**	20pf. mauve	1·60	1·80
MSE208a	73×99 mm. Nos. E207/8		23·00	36·00

E69 Monument to Russian Soldiers, Treptow

1955. Tenth Anniv of Liberation.

| E209 | **E69** | 20pf. mauve | 2·50 | 1·70 |

E70 Schiller (poet)

1955. 150th Death Anniv of Schiller.

E210	**E70**	5pf. green	4·00	3·50
E211	-	10pf. blue	80	55
E212	-	20pf. brown	80	55
MSE212a	73×100 mm. Nos. E210/12 (+15pf.)		27·00	38·00

PORTRAITS OF SCHILLER: 10pf. Full-face; 20pf. Facing left.

E71 Cyclists

1955. Eighth International Cycle Race.

| E213 | **E71** | 10pf. turquoise | 1·10 | 90 |
| E214 | **E71** | 20pf. red | 1·40 | 1·10 |

E72 Karl Liebknecht

1955. German Labour Leaders.

E215	**E72**	5pf. green	45	35
E216	-	10pf. blue	70	35
E217	-	15pf. violet	9·00	6·00
E218	-	20pf. red	70	35
E219	-	25pf. blue	70	35
E220	-	40pf. red	3·50	35
E221	-	60pf. brown	70	35

PORTRAITS: 10pf. A. Bebel; 15pf. F. Mehring; 20pf. E. Thalmann; 25pf. Clara Zetkin; 40pf. Wilhelm Liebknecht; 60pf. Rosa Luxemburg.

E73 Pottery

1955. Leipzig Autumn Fair.

| E222 | | 10pf. blue | 1·50 | 80 |
| E223 | **E73** | 20pf. green | 1·50 | 80 |

DESIGN: 10pf. Camera and microscope.

E74 Workers and Charter

1955. Tenth Anniv of Land Reform.

E224	**E74**	5pf. green	8·00	6·75
E225	-	10pf. blue	1·10	55
E226	-	20pf. red	1·10	55

DESIGNS—VERT: 10pf. Bricklayers at work. HORIZ: 20pf. Combine-harvesters.

E75 "Solidarity"

1955. Tenth Anniv of People's Solidarity Movement.

| E227 | **E75** | 10pf. blue | 1·00 | 80 |

E76 Engels Speaking

1955. 135th Birth Anniv of Engels.

E228	**E76**	5pf. blue and yellow	45	25
E229	-	10pf. violet and yellow	90	25
E230	-	15pf. green and yellow	90	25
E231	-	20pf. brown and orange	1·80	25
E232	-	30pf. brown and grey	11·00	11·50
E233	-	70pf. green and red	4·50	45
MSE233a	148×105 mm. Nos. E228/33		85·00	£130

DESIGNS: 10pf. Engels and Marx; 15pf. Engels and newspaper; 20pf. Portrait facing right; 30pf. Portrait facing left; 70pf. 1848 Revolution scene.

E77 Magdeburg Cathedral

1955. Historic Buildings.

E234	**E77**	5pf. sepia	1·10	55
E235	-	10pf. green	1·10	55
E236	-	15pf. purple	1·10	55
E237	-	20pf. red	1·10	1·10
E238	-	30pf. brown	14·00	17·00
E239	-	40pf. blue	2·30	1·40

DESIGNS: 10pf. State Opera House, Berlin; 15pf. Old Town Hall, Leipzig; 20pf. Town Hall, Berlin; 30pf. Erfurt Cathedral; 40pf. Zwinger, Dresden.

E78 Georg Agricola

1955. 400th Death Anniv of Agricola (scholar).

| E240 | **E78** | 10pf. brown | 1·00 | 80 |

E79 *Portrait of a Young Man* (Durer)

1955. Dresden Gallery Paintings. (1st series).

E241	**E79**	5pf. brown	90	30
E242	-	10pf. brown	90	30
E243	-	15pf. purple	34·00	32·00
E244	-	20pf. sepia	90	30
E245	-	40pf. green	90	55
E246	-	70pf. blue	2·30	1·10

PAINTINGS: 10pf. *The Chocolate Girl* (Liotard); 15pf. *Portrait of a Boy* (Pinturicchio); 20pf. *Self-portrait with Saskia* (Rembrandt); 40pf. *Maiden with Letter* (Vermeer); 70pf. *Sistine Madonna* (Raphael).

See also Nos. E325/30 and E427/31.

E80 Mozart

1956. Birth Bicent of Mozart (composer).

| E247 | **E80** | 10pf. green | 17·00 | 13·50 |
| E248 | - | 20pf. brown | 5·75 | 2·75 |

PORTRAIT: 20pf. Facing left.

E81 Ilyushin II-14P DDR-ABA

1956. Establishment of East German Lufthansa Airways.

E249		5pf. multicoloured	19·00	13·50
E250	**E81**	10pf. green	1·10	55
E251	-	15pf. blue	1·10	55
E252	-	20pf. red	1·10	55

DESIGNS: 5pf. Lufthansa flag; 15pf. View of Ilyushin II-14P DDR-ABF airplane from below; 20pf. Ilyushin II-14P DDR-ABA airplane facing left.

E82 Heinrich Heine (poet)

1956. Death Centenary of Heine.

| E253 | **E82** | 10pf. green | 16·00 | 8·50 |
| E254 | - | 20pf. red | 3·50 | 90 |

PORTRAIT: 20pf. Full-face.

E83 Mobile Cranes

1956. Leipzig Spring Fair.

| E255 | **E83** | 20pf. red | 1·40 | 80 |
| E256 | **E83** | 35pf. blue | 2·00 | 1·30 |

E84 E. Thalmann

1956. 70th Birth Anniv of Thalmann (communist leader).

| E257 | **E84** | 20pf. black, brn & red | 90 | 55 |
| **MS**E257a | 73×100 mm. No. E257 | | 13·50 | 36·00 |

E85 Hand, Laurels and Cycle Wheel

1956. Ninth International Cycle Race.

| E258 | **E85** | 10pf. green | 1·10 | 50 |
| E259 | - | 20pf. red | 1·10 | 50 |

DESIGN: 20pf. Arms of Warsaw, Berlin and Prague and cycle wheel.

E86 New Buildings, Old Market-place

1956. 750th Anniv of Dresden.

E260	**E86**	10pf. green	55	25
E261	-	20pf. red	55	25
E262	-	40pf. violet	2·75	3·00

DESIGNS: 20pf. Elbe Bridge; 40pf. Technical High School.

E87 Workman

1956. Tenth Anniv of Industrial Reforms.

| E263 | **E87** | 20pf. red | 70 | 35 |

E88 Robert Schumann

1956. Death Centenary of Schumann (composer). (a) Type **88** (wrong music).

| E264 | **E88** | 10pf. green | 3·00 | 2·00 |
| E265 | **E88** | 20pf. red | 1·10 | 25 |

E88a Robert Schumann

(b) Type **E88a** (correct music).

| E266 | **E88a** | 10pf. green | 6·75 | 2·75 |
| E267 | **E88a** | 20pf. red | 4·00 | 55 |

E89 Footballers

1956. Second Sports Festival, Leipzig.

E268	**E89**	5pf. green	45	35
E269	-	10pf. blue	45	35
E270	-	15pf. purple	3·25	2·50
E271	-	20pf. red	45	35

DESIGNS: 10pf. Javelin thrower; 15pf. Hurdlers; 20pf. Gymnast.

E90 T. Mann (author)

1956. First Death Anniv of Thomas Mann.

| E272 | **E90** | 20pf. black | 1·80 | 80 |

E91 J. B. Cisinski

1956. Birth Centenary of Cisinski (poet).

| E273 | **E91** | 50pf. brown | 1·50 | 80 |

E92 Lace

1956. Leipzig Autumn Fair.

| E274 | **E92** | 10pf. green and black | 70 | 55 |
| E275 | - | 20pf. pink and black (Sailing dinghy) | 70 | 55 |

E93 Buchenwald Memorial

1956. Concentration Camp Memorials Fund.

| E276 | **E93** | 20pf.+80pf. red | 1·60 | 5·75 |

For similar stamp see No. E390.

E94 Torch and
Olympic Rings

1956. Olympic Games.
E277	**E94**	20pf. brown	80	55
E278	-	35pf. slate	1·10	80

DESIGN: 35pf. Greek athlete.

E95

1956. 500th Anniv of Greifswald University.
E279	**E95**	20pf. red	90	55

E96 Postal
Carrier, 1450

1956. Stamp Day.
E280	**E96**	20pf. red	90	55

E97 E. Abbe

1956. 110th Anniv of Zeiss Factory, Jena.
E281	**E97**	10pf. green	45	25
E282	-	20pf. brown	45	25
E283	-	25pf. blue	70	45

DESIGNS—HORIZ: 20pf. Factory buildings; 25pf. Carl Zeiss.

E98 "Negro"

1956. Human Rights Day.
E284		5pf. green on olive	1·80	1·60
E285	**E98**	10pf. brown on pink	35	35
E286	-	25pf. blue on lavender	35	35

DESIGNS: 5pf. "Chinese"; 25pf. "European".

E99 Indian Elephants

1956. Berlin Zoological Gardens. Centres in grey.
E287	**E99**	5pf. black	35	25
E288	-	10pf. green	35	25
E289	-	15pf. purple	6·25	4·50
E290	-	20pf. red	35	25
E291	-	25pf. brown	40	25
E292	-	30pf. blue	45	25

DESIGNS: 10pf. Greater flamingos; 15pf. Black rhinoceros; 20pf. Mouflon; 25pf. European bison; 30pf. Polar bear.

1956. Egyptian Relief Fund. No. E237 surch HELFT AGYPTEN +10.
E293	20pf.+10pf. red	1·00	55

1956. Hungarian Socialists' Relief Fund. No. E237 surch HELFT DEM SOZIALISTISCHEN UNGARN +10.
E294	20pf.+10pf. red	1·00	55

E103 *Frieden* (freighter)

1957. Leipzig Spring Fair.
E295	**E103**	20pf. red	45	25
E296	-	25pf. blue	45	25

DESIGN: 25pf. Class E251 electric locomotive.

E104 Silver Thistle

1957. Nature Protection Week.
E297	**E104**	5pf. brown	35	25
E298	-	10pf. green	3·50	3·25
E299	-	20pf. brown	35	25

DESIGNS: 10pf. Green lizard; 20pf. Lady's slipper orchid.

E105 Friedrich
Froebel
and Children

1957. 175th Birth Anniv of Froebel (educator).
E300		10pf. black and green	1·80	1·40
E301	**E105**	20pf. black and brown	35	25

DESIGN: 10pf. Children at play.

E106 Ravensbruck
Memorial

1957. Concentration Camp Memorials Fund.
E302	**E106**	5pf.+5pf. green	45	35
E303	-	20pf.+10pf. red	55	60

DESIGN—HORIZ: 20pf. Memorial and environs.
For similar stamp to No. E303 see No. E453.

E107 Cycle Race
Route

1957. Tenth International Cycle Race.
E304	**E107**	5pf. orange	55	45

E108 Miner

1957. Coal Mining Industry.
E305	-	10pf. green	35	30
E306	-	20pf. brown	35	30
E307	**E108**	25pf. blue	3·50	2·00

DESIGNS (39×21 mm): 10pf. Mechanical shovel and coal trucks; 20pf. Gantry.

E109 Henri Dunant and
Globe

1957. Int Red Cross Day. Cross in red.
E308	**E109**	10pf. brown and green	35	35
E309	-	25pf. brown and blue	35	35

DESIGN: 25pf. H. Dunant wearing hat, and globe.

E110
Joachim
Jungius
(botanist)

1957. Scientists' Anniversaries.
E322	**E110**	5pf. brown	2·30	1·70
E323	-	10pf. green	35	30
E324	-	20pf. brown	35	30

PORTRAITS: 10pf. L. Euler (mathematician); 20pf. H. Hertz (physicist).

1957. Dresden Gallery Paintings (2nd series). As Type E79.
E325	5pf. sepia	45	35
E326	10pf. green	45	35
E327	15pf. brown	45	35

E328	20pf. red	45	35
E329	25pf. purple	45	35
E330	40pf. grey	6·75	3·00

PAINTINGS—VERT: 5pf. *The Holy Family* (Mantegna); 10pf. *The Dancer, Barbarina Campani* (Carriera); 15pf. *Portrait of Morette* (Holbein the Younger); 20pf. *The Tribute Money* (Titian); 25pf. *Saskia with a Red Flower* (Rembrandt); 40pf. *A Young Standard-bearer* (Piazetta).

E111 Clara Zetkin
and Flower

1957. Birth Cent of Clara Zetkin (patriot).
E331	**E111**	10pf. green and red	1·00	45

E112 Bertolt
Brecht
(dramatist)

1957. First Death Anniv of Bertolt Brecht.
E332	**E112**	10pf. green	45	35
E333	**E112**	25pf. blue	85	35

E113 Congress
Emblem

1957. Fourth World Trade Unions Congress.
E334	**E113**	20pf. black and red	90	45

E114 Fair
Emblem

1957. Leipzig Autumn Fair.
E335	**E114**	20pf. red	40	35
E336	**E114**	25pf. blue	45	35

E115 Savings
Bank Book

1957. Savings Week.
E337	**E115**	10pf. black and green on grey	1·10	90
E338	**E115**	20pf. black and mauve on grey	45	45

E116 Postrider of
1563

1957. Stamp Day.
E339	**E116**	5pf. blue on brown	80	35

E117
Revolutionary's
Rifle and Red
Flag

1957. 40th Anniv of Russian Revolution.
E340	**E117**	10pf. green and red	35	35
E341	**E117**	25pf. blue and red	35	35

E118 Artificial
Satellite

1957. International Geophysical Year.
E342	**E118**	10pf. green	55	40
E343	-	20pf. red	80	25
E344	-	25pf. blue	3·00	2·00

DESIGNS: 20pf. Stratosphere balloon; 25pf. Ship using echo-sounder.

E119 Professor
Ramin

1957. "National Prize" Composers.
E345	**E119**	10pf. black and green	1·50	1·40
E346	-	20pf. black and orange	35	25

PORTRAIT: 20pf. Professor Abendroth.

E120 Ernst
Thalmann

1957. National Memorials Fund. East German War Victims. Portraits in grey.
E347	**E120**	20pf.+10pf. mauve	35	25
E348	-	25pf.+15pf. blue	35	25
E349	-	40pf.+20pf. violet	55	70
MSE349a		140×95 mm. Nos. E347/9 (+20pf.)	70·00	£150

PORTRAITS: 25pf. R. Breitscheid; 40pf. Father P. Schneider.
For other stamps as Type E **120** see Nos. E374/8, E448/52, E485/7, E496/500, E540/4 and E588/92.

E121   **E122**

1957. Air.
E350	**E121**	5pf. black and grey	4·00	25
E351	**E121**	20pf. black and red	35	25
E352	**E121**	35pf. black and violet	35	25
E353	**E121**	50pf. black and brown	45	25
E354	**E122**	1Dm. olive and yellow	1·60	25
E355	**E122**	3Dm. brown & yellow	2·50	70
E356	**E122**	5Dm. blue and yellow	5·75	1·00

E123 Fair Emblem

1958. Leipzig Spring Fair.
E357	**E123**	20pf. red	45	25
E358	**E123**	25pf. blue	55	35

E124 Transmitting Aerial
and Posthorn

1958. Communist Postal Conf, Moscow.
E359	**E124**	5pf. black and grey	1·10	90
E360	-	20pf. red	55	25

DESIGN—HORIZ: 20pf. Aerial as in 5pf. but posthorn above figures of value.

E125 *Zille at play*

1958. Birth Cent of Heinrich Zille (painter).
E361	**E125**	10pf. drab and green	3·75	2·00
E362	-	20pf. drab and red	90	35

DESIGN—VERT: 20pf. Self-portrait of Zille.

E126 Max Planck

1958. Birth Cent of Max Planck (physicist).
E363		10pf. olive	1·70	1·60
E364	**E126**	20pf. mauve	55	35

DESIGN—VERT: 10pf. "h" (symbol of Planck's Constant).

E127 Breeding Cow

1958. Sixth Markkleeberg Agricultural Exn. Inscr "6 Landwirtschaftsausstellung der DDR in Markkleeberg".
E365	**E127**	5pf. grey	3·50	2·00
E366	-	10pf. green	55	35
E367	-	20pf. red	55	35

DESIGNS (39×22½ mm): 10pf. Chaff-cutter; 20pf. Beet-harvester.

E128 Charles Darwin

1958. Centenary of Darwin's Theory of Evolution and Bicentenary of Linnaeus's Plant Classification System. Portraits in black.
E368	**E128**	10pf. green	2·00	1·70
E369	-	20pf. red	35	30

PORTRAIT—HORIZ: 20pf. Linnaeus (Carl von Linne) inscr "200 JAHRE SYSTEMA NATURAE".

E129 Congress Emblem

1958. Fifth German Socialist Unity Party Congress.
E370	**E129**	10pf. red	55	45

E130 The Seven Towers of Rostock, Liner and Freighters

1958. Rostock Port Reconstruction.
E371	-	10pf. green	35	25
E372	**E130**	20pf. orange	1·10	45
E373	-	25pf. blue	1·60	1·70

DESIGNS: 10pf. *Freundschaft* (freighter) at quayside; 25pf. *Frieden* (freighter) in Rostock harbour.

1958. "Resistance Fighters". As Type **E120**. Portraits in grey.
E374	5pf.+5pf. brown	45	1·10
E375	10pf.+5pf. green	45	1·10
E376	15pf.+10pf. violet	45	4·50
E377	20pf.+10pf. brown	45	1·10
E378	20pf.+15pf. black	1·40	17·00

PORTRAITS—VERT: 5pf. A. Kuntz; 10pf. R. Arndt; 15pf. Dr. K. Adams; 20pf. R. Renner; 25pf. W. Stoecker.

E131 Mare and Foal

1958. "Grand Prix of the D.D.R." Horse Show.
E379	**E131**	5pf. sepia	3·50	3·75
E380	-	10pf. green	35	35
E381	-	20pf. brown	35	35

DESIGNS: 10pf. Horse-trotting; 20pf. Racing horses.

E132 J. A. Komensky ("Comenius")

1958. Komensky Commem. Centres in black.
E382	**E132**	10pf. green	2·30	1·60
E383	-	20pf. brown	35	30

DESIGN: 20pf. Komensky with pupils (from an old engraving).

E133 Camp Bugler

1958. Tenth Anniv of East German "Pioneer" Organization.
E384	**E133**	10pf.+5pf. green	50	35
E385	-	20pf.+10pf. red	55	35

DESIGN—VERT: 20pf. Young Pioneer saluting.

E134 University Seal

1958. 400th Anniv of Friedrich Schiller University, Jena.
E386	**E134**	5pf. black and grey	2·00	1·60
E387	-	20pf. grey and red	45	30

DESIGN: 20pf. University building.

E135 Model with Hamster-lined Coat, and Leipzig Central Railway Station

1958. Leipzig Autumn Fair.
E388	**E135**	10pf. brown and green	40	30
E389	-	25pf. black and blue	45	35

DESIGN: 25pf. Model with Karakul fur coat, and Leipzig Old Town Hall.

1958. Concentration Camp Memorials Fund. As Type **E93** but additionally inscr "14. SEPTEMBER 1958" in black.
E390	20pf.+20pf. red	90	80

E136 Soldier climbing Wall

1958. First Summer Military Games, Leipzig.
E391	**E136**	10pf. brown and green	2·30	1·50
E392	-	20pf. yellow and brown	45	35
E393	-	25pf. red and blue	45	35

DESIGNS: 20pf. Games emblem; 25pf. Marching athletes with banner.

E137 Warding off the Atomic Bomb

1958. Campaign Against Atomic Warfare.
E394	**E137**	20pf. red	45	25
E395	-	25pf. blue	70	35

E138 17th-century Mail Cart

1958. Stamp Day.
E396	**E138**	10pf. green	2·75	1·70
E397	-	20pf. red	55	25

DESIGN: 20pf. Modern postal sorting train and Baade-Bonin 152 jetliner.

E139 Revolutionary and Soldier

1958. 40th Anniv of November Revolution.
E398	**E139**	20pf. purple and red	12·50	22·00

E140 Brandenburg Gate, Berlin

1958. Brandenburg Gate Commemoration.
E399	**E140**	20pf. red	55	25
E400	**E140**	25pf. blue	3·75	2·30

E141 "Girl's Head" (bas-relief)

1958. Antique Art Treasures.
E401	**E141**	10pf. black and green	2·00	1·60
E402	-	20pf. black and red	45	25

DESIGN: 20pf. "Large Head" (from *Pergamon* frieze). See also Nos. E475/8.

E142 Negro and European Youths

1958. Tenth Anniv of Declaration of Human Rights.
E403	**E142**	10pf. black and green	35	30
E404	-	25pf. black and blue	2·75	1·60

DESIGN: 25pf. Chinese and European girls.

E143 O. Nuschke

1958. First Death Anniv of Vice-Premier Otto Nuschke.
E405	**E143**	20pf. red	45	40

E144 *The Red Flag* (Party Newspaper)

1958. 40th Anniv of German Communist Party.
E406	**E144**	20pf. red	55	45

E145 Pres. Pieck

1959. Pres. Pieck's 83rd Birthday.
E407	**E145**	20pf. red	70	35

For 20pf. black see No. E517.

E146 Rosa Luxemburg (revolutionary)

1959. 40th Death Anniv of Rosa Luxemburg and Karl Liebknecht. Centres in black.
E408	**E146**	10pf. green	3·00	1·80
E409	-	20pf. red	35	25

DESIGN—HORIZ: 20pf. Liebknecht-(revolutionary).

E147 Concert Hall, Leipzig

1959. 150th Birth Anniv of Felix Mendelssohn-Bartholdy (composer).
E410	**E147**	10pf. green on green	80	80
E411	-	25pf. blue on white	2·30	4·00

DESIGN—HORIZ: 25pf. Opening theme of Symphony in A Major (*The Italian*).

E148 "Schwarze Pumpe" plant

1959. Leipzig Spring Fair. Inscr as in Type **E148**.
E412	**E148**	20pf. red	45	25
E413	-	25pf. blue	55	30

DESIGN—HORIZ: 25pf. Various cameras.

E149 Boy holding Book for Girl

1959. Fifth Anniv of "Youth Consecration".
E414	**E149**	10pf. black on green	2·30	1·50
E415	-	20pf. black on salmon	35	25

DESIGN: 20pf. Girl holding book for boy.

E150 Handel's Statue, Oboe and Arms of Halle

1959. Death Bicentenary of Handel. Centre in black.
E416	**E150**	10pf. green	2·50	1·60
E417	-	20pf. red	35	30

DESIGN: 20pf. Portrait of Handel (after oil painting by Thomas Hudson).

E151 A. von Humboldt and Jungle Scene

1959. Death Centenary of Alexander von Humboldt (naturalist).
E418	**E151**	10pf. green	2·00	1·60
E419	-	20pf. red	45	25

DESIGN: 20pf. As Type **E151** but with view of sleigh in forest.

E152 Posthorn

1959. Socialist Countries' Postal Ministers Conference, Berlin.
E420	**E152**	20pf. black, yell & red	45	25
E421	**E152**	25pf. black, yell & bl	1·10	1·10

E153 Grey Heron

1959. Nature Preservation.
E422	**E153**	5pf. lilac, black & blue	35	25
E423	-	10pf. brn, sep & turq	35	25
E424	-	20pf. multicoloured	35	25
E425	-	25pf. multicoloured	35	25
E426	-	40pf. yell, blk & grey	8·50	5·00

DESIGNS: 10pf. Eurasian bittern; 20pf. Lily of the valley and *Inachis io* (butterfly); 25pf. Eurasian beaver; 40pf. *Apis mellifera* (bee) and willow catkin.

1959. Dresden Gallery Paintings as Type **E79** (3rd series).
E427	5pf. olive	35	25
E428	10pf. green	35	25
E429	20pf. orange	35	25
E430	25pf. brown	55	35
E431	40pf. red	8·00	4·00

PAINTINGS—VERT: 5pf. *The Vestal Virgin* (Kauffman); 10pf. *The Needlewoman* (Metsu); 20pf. *Mlle. Lavergne reading a letter* (Liotard); 25pf. *Old woman with a brazier* (Rubens); 40pf. *Young man in black coat* (Hals).

E154 Great Cormoran

1959. "Birds of the Homeland". Centres and inscriptions in black.

E432	E154	5pf. yellow	35	25
E433	-	10pf. green	35	25
E434	-	15pf. violet	7·50	4·00
E435	-	20pf. pink	35	25
E436	-	25pf. blue	35	25
E437	-	40pf. red	35	25

BIRDS: 10pf. Black Stork; 15pf. Eagle Owl; 20pf. Black Grouse; 25pf. Hoopoe; 40pf. Peregrine Falcon.

E155

1959. Seventh World Youth Festival, Vienna.

E438	E155	20pf. red	45	35
E439	-	25pf. blue	1·40	1·10

DESIGN—HORIZ: 25pf. White girl embracing negro girl.

E156 Hoop Exercises

1959. Third German Gymnastic and Sports Festival, Leipzig.

E440	E156	5pf.+5pf. brown	35	25
E441	-	10pf.+5pf. green	35	25
E442	-	20pf.+10pf. red	35	25
E443	-	25pf.+10pf. blue	35	25
E444	-	40pf.+20pf. purple	2·50	1·10

DESIGNS: 10pf. High jumping; 20pf. Vaulting; 25pf. Club exercises; 40pf. Fireworks over Leipzig Stadium.

E157 Modern Leipzig Building

1959. Leipzig Autumn Fair.

E445	E157	20pf. grey and red	55	45

See also Nos. E483/4.

E158 Glass Tea-set

1959. 75 Years of Jena Glassware.

E446	E158	10pf. turquoise	30	25
E447	-	25pf. blue	2·75	1·70

DESIGN—VERT: 25pf. Laboratory retorts.

1959. Ravensbruck Concentration Camp Victims. As Type **E120**. Portraits in black.

E448		5pf.+5pf. brown	35	30
E449	-	10pf.+5pf. green	35	30
E450	-	15pf.+10pf. violet	35	30
E451	-	20pf.+10pf. mauve	35	30
E452	-	25pf.+15pf. blue	1·50	1·50

PORTRAITS: 5pf. T. Klose; 10pf. K. Niederkirchner; 15pf. C. Eisenblatter; 20pf. O. Benario-Prestes; 25pf. M. Grollmuss.

1959. Concentration Camp Memorials Fund. As No. E303 but inscr "12. SEPTEMBER 1959" in black.

E453		20pf.+10pf. red	80	45

E159 "Russian Pennant on the Moon"

1959. Landing of Russian Rocket on the Moon.

E454	E159	20pf. red	90	55

E160 E. German Flag and Combine-harvester

1959. Tenth Anniv of German Democratic Republic. Designs as Type **E160** showing E. German flag in black, red and yellow. Inscriptions in black and red on coloured paper.

E455	E160	5pf. buff	25	25
E456	-	10pf. grey	25	25
E457	-	15pf. pale yellow	25	25
E458	-	20pf. lilac	25	25
E459	-	25pf. pale olive	25	25
E460	-	40pf. yellow	25	25
E461	-	50pf. salmon	25	25
E462	-	60pf. turquoise	25	25
E463	-	70pf. pale green	25	25
E464	-	1Dm. brown	55	65

DESIGNS—East German flag and: 10pf. "Fritz Heckert" convalescent home; 15pf. Zwinger Palace, Dresden; 20pf. Steel worker; 25pf. Industrial chemist; 40pf. Leipzig Stadium; 50pf. Woman tractor-driver; 60pf. Ilyushin Il-14M airplane; 70pf. Shipbuilding; 1Dm. East Germany's first atomic reactor.

E161 J. R. Becher

1959. First Death Anniv of Becher (poet).

E465	E161	20pf. slate and red	1·80	35

E162 Schiller

1959. Birth Bicentenary of Schiller (poet).

E466	-	10pf. green on green	2·20	1·60
E467	E162	20pf. lake on pink	80	25

DESIGN: 10pf. Schiller's house, Weimar.

E163 18th-century Courier and Milestone

1959. Stamp Day.

E468	E163	10pf. green	1·90	1·50
E469	-	20pf. lake	35	25

DESIGN: 20pf. Postwoman on motor cycle.

E164 Eurasian Red Squirrels

1959. Forest Animals.

E470	E164	5pf. red, brown & grey	55	25
E471	-	10pf. lt brn, brn & grn	70	25
E472	-	20pf. multicoloured	70	25
E473	-	25pf. multicoloured	80	35
E474	-	40pf. yellow, brown and blue	15·00	5·00

ANIMALS: 10pf. Brown hares; 20pf. Roe deer; 25pf. Red deer; 40pf. Lynx.

1959. Antique Art Treasures (2nd series). As Type **E141**.

E475		5pf. black and yellow	45	25
E476		10pf. black and green	45	25
E477		20pf. black and red	45	25
E478		25pf. black and blue	1·80	1·10

DESIGNS: 5pf. Attic goddess (about 580 B.C.); 10pf. Princess of Tell el-Amarna (about 1360 B.C.); 20pf. Bronze horse of Toprak-Kale, Armenia (7th-century B.C.). HORIZ: (49×22 mm): 25pf. Altar of Zeus, Pergamon (about 160 B.C.).

E165 Boxing

1960. Olympic Games. As Type **E165** inscr "OLYMPISCHE SOMMERSPIELE 1960" or "WINTERSPIELE" etc (20pf.). Centres and inscriptions in bistre.

E479	E165	5pf. brown	6·75	3·50
E480	-	10pf. green	35	25
E481	-	20pf. red	35	25
E482	-	25pf. blue	35	25

DESIGNS: 10pf. Running; 20pf. Ski jumping; 25pf. Sailing.

1960. Leipzig Spring Fair. As Type **E157** but inscr "LEIPZIGER FRUHJAHRSMESSE 1960".

E483		20pf. grey and red	30	25
E484		25pf. grey and blue	35	25

DESIGNS: 20pf. Northern Entrance, Technical Fair; 25pf. Ring Fair Building.

1960. Sachsenhausen Concentration Camp Victims (1st issue). As Type **E120**. Portraits in black.

E485		5pf.+5pf. drab	35	30
E486		10pf.+5pf. myrtle	35	30
E487		20pf.+10pf. purple	35	30

PORTRAITS: 5pf. L. Erdmann; 10pf. E. Schneller; 20pf. L. Horn.

See also Nos. E496/500.

E166 Purple Foxglove

1960. Medicinal Flowers. Background in pale drab.

E488	E166	5pf. red and green	35	25
E489	-	10pf. olive and green	35	25
E490	-	15pf. red and green	35	25
E491	-	20pf. violet & turq	35	25
E492	-	40pf. red, green & brn	7·50	3·50

FLOWERS: 10pf. Camomile; 15pf. Peppermint; 20pf. Poppy; 40pf. Wild Rose.

E167 Lenin

1960. 90th Birth Anniv of Lenin.

E493	E167	20pf. red	55	35

1960. Re-opening of Rostock Port. No. E371 optd Inbetriebnahme des Hochsee-hafens 1. Mai 1960.

E494		10pf. green	90	55

E169 Russian Soldier and Liberated Prisoner

1960. 15th Anniv of Liberation.

E495	E169	20pf. red	55	45

1960. Sachsenhausen Concentration Camp Victims (2nd issue). As Type **E120**. Portraits in black.

E496		10pf.+5pf. green	35	25
E497		15pf.+5pf. violet	1·10	80
E498		20pf.+10pf. lake	35	25
E499		25pf.+10pf. blue	35	35
E500		40pf.+20pf. brown	2·50	3·50

PORTRAITS: 10pf. M. Lademann; 15pf. L. Breunig; 20pf. M. Thesen; 25pf. G. Sandtner; 40pf. H. Rothbarth.

E170 Model and Plan of *Fritz Heckert* (Liner)

1960. Launching of Cruise Liner *Fritz Heckert*.

E501	E170	5pf. slate, red & yell	35	25
E502	-	10pf.+5pf. black, red and yellow	35	25
E503	-	20pf.+10pf. black, red and blue	35	25
E504	-	25pf. black, yellow and blue	6·25	6·75

E171 Lenin Statue, Eisleben

1960. Lenin-Thalmann Statues.

E505	E171	10pf. green	35	35
E506	-	20pf. red	35	35

DESIGN: 20pf. Thalmann statue, Pushkin, U.S.S.R.

E172 Masked Dancer (statuette)

1960. 250th Anniv of Porcelain Industry, Meissen. Centres and inscriptions in blue. Figures in colours given.

E507	E172	5pf. orange	35	25
E508	-	10pf. green	35	25
E509	-	15pf. purple	5·00	5·00
E510	-	20pf. red	35	25
E511	-	25pf. olive	35	25

DESIGNS: 10pf. Dish inscr with swords and years "1710 1960"; 15pf. Otter; 20pf. Potter; 25pf. Coffee-pot.

E173 Racing Cyclist

1960. World Cycling Championships.

E512	E173	20pf.+10pf. multicoloured	35	35
E513	-	25pf.+10pf. brown, drab and blue	2·00	4·00

DESIGN (38½×21 mm): 25pf. Racing cyclists on track.

E174 Opera House, Leipzig

1960. Leipzig Autumn Fair.

E514	E174	20pf. grey and red	45	25
E515	-	25pf. brown and blue	45	45

DESIGN: 25pf. Export goods.

E175 Sachsenhausen Memorial

1960. Concentration Camp Memorials Fund.

E516	E175	20pf.+10pf. red	55	45

1960. President Pieck Mourning issue.

E517	E145	20pf. black	70	45

MSE517a 88×108 mm. No. E517.
| | Imperf | | 2·00 | 3·25 |

E176 18th-century Rook

1960. 14th Chess Olympiad, Leipzig. German Chessmen.

E518	E176	10pf.+5pf. green	35	25
E519	-	20pf.+10pf. purple	35	25
E520	-	25pf.+10pf. blue	1·40	4·00

DESIGNS: 20pf. 18th-century knight; 25pf. 14th-century knight.

E177 Mail Vans

1960. Stamp Day.

E521	**E177**	20pf. yell, blk & mve	35	30
E522	-	25pf. mauve, blk & bl	4·25	2·30

DESIGN: 25pf. 19th-century railway mail coach.

E178 Medal of 1518 showing Hans Burgkmair (painter)

1960. 400th Anniv of Dresden Art Collections.

E523	**E178**	20pf. ochre, green and buff	35	30
E524	-	25pf. black and blue	2·30	2·75

DESIGN: 25pf. "Dancing Peasants" (after Durer).

E179 Count N. von Gneisenau

1960. Birth Bicent of Count N. von Gneisenau.

E525	**E179**	20pf. black and red	35	30
E526	-	25pf. blue	1·90	1·90

DESIGN: 25pf. Similar portrait but vert.

E180 R. Virchow

1960. 250th Anniv of Berlin Charity and 150th Anniv of Humboldt University, Berlin. Centres in black.

E527	**E180**	5pf. ochre	35	25
E528	-	10pf. green	35	25
E529	-	20pf. brown	35	25
E530	-	25pf. blue	35	25
E531	-	40pf. red	3·50	2·20

DESIGNS—As Type E 180 (Berlin Charity); 10pf. Robert Koch; 40pf. W. Griesinger. (Humboldt University); 20pf. University building and statues of William and Alexander von Humboldt; 25pf. Plaque with profiles of Von Humboldt brothers.

E181 Scientist with Notebook

1960. Chemical Workers' Day.

E532	**E181**	5pf. grey and red	25	20
E533	-	10pf. green and orange	25	20
E534	-	20pf. red and blue	25	20
E535	-	25pf. blue and yellow	2·50	3·25

DESIGNS: 10pf. Chemical worker with fertiliser; 20pf. Girl worker with jar, and Trabant car; 25pf. Laboratory assistant and synthetic dress.

E182 *Young Socialists' Express* (double-deck train)

1960. 125th Anniv of German Railways.

E536	**E182**	10pf. black and green	35	35
E537	-	20pf. black and mauve	35	35
E538	-	25pf. black and blue	6·75	6·75

DESIGNS—As Type E 182: 25pf. Stephenson locomotive *Adler* (1835) and Class V180 diesel locomotive. (43×25½ mm): 20pf. Sassnitz Harbour station and train ferry *Sassnitz*.

E183 President Pieck

1961. 85th Birth Anniv of President Pieck.

E539	**E183**	20pf. red and black	55	45

1961. Concentration Camp Victims. As Type **E120**. Portraits in black.

E540		5pf.+5pf. green	25	25
E541		10pf.+5pf. green	25	25
E542		15pf.+5pf. violet	1·80	3·25
E543		20pf.+10pf. red	25	25
E544		25pf.+10pf. blue	25	25

PORTRAITS: 5pf. W. Kube; 10pf. H. Gunther; 15pf. Elvira Eisenschneider; 20pf. Hertha Lindner; 25pf. H. Tschape.

E184 High-voltage Switchgear

1961. Leipzig Spring Fair. Inscr as in Type **E184**.

E545	**E184**	10pf. slate and green	45	30
E546	-	25pf. slate and blue	55	35

DESIGN: 25pf. Ilyushin Il-12 over Fair Press Centre.

E185 Lilienstein Saxony

1961. Landscapes and Historical Buildings.

E547		5pf. grey	25	25
E548		10pf. green	25	25
E549	**E185**	20pf. brown	25	35
E550	-	20pf. red	25	25
E551	-	25pf. blue	25	35

DESIGNS—VERT: 5pf. Ruins of Rudelsburg; 10pf. Wartburg; 20pf. (No. E550), Town Hall, Wernigerode. HORIZ: 25pf. Brocken, Oberharz.

E186 *Ros* (Trawler)

1961. Deep Sea Fishing Industry.

E552	**E186**	10pf. green	25	20
E553	-	20pf. purple	25	20
E554	-	25pf. blue	25	20
E555	-	40pf. violet	3·25	2·50

DESIGNS: 20pf. Hauling nets; 25pf. *Robert Koch* (trawler); 40pf. Processing Atlantic cod.

E187 Cosmonaut in Capsule

1961. First Manned Space Flight. Inscr "12.4.1961".

E556		10pf. red and green	1·70	1·10
E557	**E187**	20pf. blue	1·70	1·10
E558	-	25pf. blue	6·25	6·75

DESIGNS: 10pf. Space rocket leaving globe; 25pf. Capsule's parachute descent.

E188 Marx, Engels, Lenin and Demonstrators

1961. 15th Anniv of German Socialist Unity Party.

E559	**E188**	20pf. red	70	45

E189 Common Zebra

1961. Centenary of Dresden Zoo.

E560	**E189**	10pf. black and green	6·75	6·75
E561	-	20pf. black and mauve	1·10	55

DESIGN: 20pf. Eastern black-and-white colobus.

E190 Pioneers playing Volleyball

1961. Pioneers Meeting, Erfurt. Multicoloured.

E562		10pf.+5pf. Type E 190	25	20
E563		20pf.+10pf. Folk dancing	25	20
E564		25pf.+10pf. Model airplane construction	4·25	3·50

E191 High Jump

1961. Third European Women's Gymnastic Championships, Leipzig.

E565	**E191**	10pf. green	25	20
E566	-	20pf. mauve	25	20
E567	-	25pf. blue	6·75	6·25

DESIGNS—VERT: 20pf. Gymnast. HORIZ: 25pf. Exercise on parallel bars.

E192 Salt Miners and Castle

1961. Halle (Saale) Millenary.

E568	**E192**	10pf. black, yell & grn	3·75	2·00
E569	-	20pf. black, yell & red	25	25

DESIGN: 20pf. Scientist and Five Towers of Halle.

E193 Canadian Canoe

1961. World Canoeing Championships.

E570		5pf. blue and grey	4·25	3·75
E571	**E 193**	10pf. green and grey	25	20
E572	-	20pf. purple and grey	25	20

DESIGNS: 5pf. Folding canoe; 20pf. Canadian two-seater canoe.

E194 Line-casting

1961. World Angling Championships.

E573	**E194**	10pf. green and blue	3·50	3·25
E574	-	20pf. lake and blue	55	25

DESIGN: 20pf. River-fishing.

E195 Old Weigh-house, Leipzig

1961. Leipzig Autumn Fair.

E575	**E195**	10pf. olive and green	25	20
E576	-	25pf. blue & ultram	1·50	45

DESIGN: 25pf. Old Stock Exchange, Leipzig.
See also Nos. E612/14.

E196 Walter Ulbricht

1961. Type **E196** or larger, 24×29 mm (Dm. values).

E577	5pf. blue	35	35
E578	10pf. red	45	55
E579	15pf. purple	80	25
E580	20pf. red	65	50
E581	25pf. turquoise	45	25
E582	30pf. red	25	25
E582a	35pf. green	80	55
E583	40pf. violet	25	25
E584	50pf. blue	35	25
E584a	60pf. green	45	35
E585	70pf. brown	45	25
E585a	80pf. blue	70	55
E586	1Dm. green	1·10	80

E587	2Dm. brown	2·30	80

See also Nos. E805/6, E1197/8 and E1255.

1961. Concentration Camps Memorials Fund. As Type E 120. Portraits in grey and black.

E588	5pf.+5pf. green	25	35
E589	10pf.+5pf. green	25	35
E590	20pf.+10pf. mauve	25	35
E591	25pf.+10pf. blue	25	35
E592	40pf.+20pf. lake	2·75	7·50

PORTRAITS: 5pf. C. Schonhaar; 10pf. H. Baum; 20pf. Liselotte Herrmann. HORIZ: (41×32½ mm): 25pf. Sophie and Hans Scholl; 40pf. Hilde and Hans Coppi.

E197 Dahlia

1961. International Horticultural Exn.

E593	-	10pf. red, yellow & grn	45	35
E594	**E197**	20pf. red, yellow & brn	45	35
E595	-	40pf. red, yellow & bl	11·50	12·50

FLOWERS: 10pf. Tulip. 40pf. Rose.

E198 Liszt and Berlioz (after Von Kaulbach and Prinzhofer)

1961. 150th Birth Anniv of Liszt (composer).

E596	**E198**	5pf. black	35	25
E597	-	10pf. green	2·75	3·25
E598	-	20pf. red	35	25
E599	-	25pf. blue	3·50	35

DESIGNS: 10pf. Young hand of Liszt (from French sculpture, Liszt Museum, Budapest); 20pf. Liszt (after Rietschel); 25pf. Liszt and Chopin (after Bartolini and Bovy).

E199 TV Camera and Screen

1961. Stamp Day.

E600	**E199**	10pf. black and green	2·30	3·75
E601	-	20pf. black and red	25	35

DESIGNS: 20pf. Studio microphone and radio tuning-scale.

E200 G. S. Titov with Young Pioneers

1961. Second Russian Manned Space Flight.

E602	**E200**	5pf. violet and red	35	25
E603	-	10pf. green and red	35	25
E604	-	15pf. mauve and blue	11·50	12·50
E605	-	20pf. red and blue	35	25
E606	-	25pf. blue and red	35	25
E607	-	40pf. blue and red	2·00	70

DESIGNS—HORIZ: 15pf. Titov in space-suit; 20pf. Titov receiving Karl Marx Order from Ulbricht; 25pf. "Vostok 2" rocket in flight; 40pf. Titov and Ulbricht in Berlin. VERT: 10pf. Titov in Leipzig.

E201 *Formica ruta* (Ant)

1962. Fauna Protection Campaign (1st series).

E608	**E201**	5pf. yellow, brn & blk	5·00	8·50
E609	-	10pf. brown and green	25	20
E610	-	20pf. brown and red	25	20
E611	-	40pf. yellow, blk & vio	80	55

DESIGNS: 10pf. Weasels; 20pf. Eurasian common shrews; 40pf. Common long-eared bat.
See also Nos. E699/703.

1962. Leipzig Spring Fair. As Type **E195**.

E612		10pf. sepia and green	25	25
E613	-	20pf. black and red	45	25
E614	-	25pf. purple and blue	1·10	1·10

BUILDINGS: 10pf. Zum Kaffeebaum; 20pf. Gobliser Schlosschen; 25pf. Romanus-Haus.

E203 Pilot and Mikoyan
Gurevich MiG-17 Jet
Fighters

1962. Sixth Anniv of East German People's Army.

E615	**E203**	5pf. blue	35	25
E616	-	10pf. green	35	25
E617	-	20pf. red	35	25
E618	-	25pf. blue	35	50
E619	-	40pf. brown	2·75	2·00

DESIGNS: 10pf. Soldier and armoured car; 20pf. Factory guard; 25pf. Sailor and Habich I class minesweeper; 40pf. Tank and driver.

E204 Danielle
Casanova

1962. Concentration Camps Memorial Fund. Camp Victims.

E620	**E204**	5pf.+5pf. black	25	20
E621	-	10pf.+5pf. green	25	20
E622	-	20pf.+10pf. purple	25	20
E623	-	25pf.+10pf. blue	35	25
E624	-	40pf.+20pf. purple	2·30	3·25

PORTRAITS: 10pf. Julius Fucik; 20pf. Johanna J. Schaft; 25pf. Pawel Finder; 40pf. Soja A. Kosmodemjanskaja.

E205 Racing Cyclists and
Prague Castle

1962. 15th Int Peace Cycle Race. Multicoloured.

E625		10pf. Type E **205**	25	20
E626		20pf.+10pf. Cyclists and Palace of Culture and Science, Warsaw	25	25
E627		25pf. Cyclist and Town Hall, East Berlin	1·90	1·90

E206 Johann Fichte

1962. Birth Bicent of Fichte (philosopher).

E628	-	10pf. green and black	3·25	2·75
E629	**E206**	20pf. red and black	35	35

DESIGN: 10pf. Fichte's birthplace, Ramenau.

E207 Cross of
Lidice

1962. 20th Anniv of Destruction of Lidice.

E630	-	20pf. red and black	35	25
E631	**E207**	25pf. blue and black	1·40	1·80

E208 Dimitrov
at Leipzig

1962. 80th Birth Anniv of G. Dimitrov (Bulgarian statesman).

E632	**E208**	5pf. black & turquoise	80	55
E633	-	20pf. black and red	35	25

DESIGN: 20pf. Dimitrov as Premier of Bulgaria.

E209 Maize-planting
machine

1962. Tenth D.D.R. Agricultural Exhibition, Markkleeberg. Multicoloured.

E634		10pf. Type E **209**	25	20

E635		20pf. Milking shed	25	20
E636		40pf. Combine-harvester	2·30	2·10

E210 Frieden
(freighter)

1962. Fifth Baltic Sea Week, Rostock.

E637	-	10pf. turquoise & blue	25	20
E638	-	20pf. red and yellow	25	20
E639	**E210**	25pf. bistre and blue	3·00	2·75

DESIGNS—HORIZ: 10pf. Map of Baltic Sea inscr "Meer des Friedens" ("Sea of Peace"). VERT: 20pf. Hochhaus, Rostock.

E211/E212 Brandenburg Gate,
Berlin and Youth of Three Races

E213-E214 Folk Dancers and Youth of
Three Nations

1962. World Youth Festival Games, Helsinki. Multicoloured.

E640		5pf. Type E **211**	2·75	3·50
E641		5pf. Type E **212**	2·75	3·50
E642		10pf.+5pf. Type E **213**	45	30
E643		15pf.+5pf. Type E **214**	45	30
E644		20pf. Dove	2·75	3·50
E645		20pf. National Theatre, Helsinki	2·75	3·50

Nos. 640/11 and 644/5 were issued together as a *se-tenant* block of four and Nos. 642/3 in horizontal pairs, both forming composite designs.

E217 Free-style
Swimming

1962. Tenth European Swimming Championships, Leipzig. Design in blue: value colours given.

E646	**E217**	5pf. orange	25	20
E647	-	10pf. blue	25	20
E648	-	20pf.+10pf. mauve	25	20
E649	-	25pf. blue	25	20
E650	-	40pf. violet	1·70	1·70
E651	-	70pf. brown	25	20

DESIGNS: 10pf. Back stroke; 20pf. High diving; 25pf. Butterfly stroke; 40pf. Breast stroke; 70pf. Water-polo.

On Nos. E649/51 the value, etc, appears at the foot of the design.

E218 Municipal
Store, Leipzig

1962. Leipzig Autumn Fair.

E652	**E218**	10pf. black and green	25	25
E653	-	20pf. black and red	45	30
E654	-	25pf. black and blue	1·20	1·10

DESIGNS: 20pf. Madler Arcade, Leipzig; 25pf. Leipzig Airport and Ilyushin Il-14M airplane.

E219 "Transport and
Communications"

1962. Tenth Anniv of "Friedrich List" Transport High School, Dresden.

E655	**E219**	5pf. black and blue	50	30

E219a P. Popovich
and A. Nikolaev

1962. "Vostok 3" and "Vostok 4" Space Flights. Sheet 89×108 mm.

MSE655a	**E219a**	70pf. green, blue and yellow	4·00	6·75

E220 Rene Blieck

1962. Concentration Camp Victims. Memorials Fund.

E656	**E220**	5pf.+5pf. blue	25	20
E657	-	10pf.+5pf. green	25	20
E658	-	15pf.+5pf. violet	25	20
E659	-	20pf.+10pf. purple	30	25
E660	-	40pf.+30pf. brown	2·50	3·75

PORTRAITS—As Type E **220**: 10pf. Dr. A. Klahr; 15pf. J. Diaz; 20pf. J. Alpari. HORIZ: (39×21 mm): 70pf. Seven Cervi brothers.

E221 Television Screen
and Call-sign

1962. Stamp Day and Tenth Anniv of German Television.

E661	**E221**	20pf. purple and green	25	25
E662	-	40pf. purple & mauve	2·30	2·75

DESIGN: 40pf. Children with stamp album (inscr "TAG DER BRIEFMARKE 1962").

E222 G. Hauptmann

1962. Birth Centenary of Gerhart Hauptmann (author).

E663	**E222**	20pf. black and red	60	30

E222a Gagarin
and "Vostok 1"

1962. Five Years of Russian Space Flights. Sheet 127×108 mm. Multicoloured.

MSE663a		5pf. Dogs "Belka" and "Strelka", 10pf. Type E **222a**; 15pf. "Sputniks 1, 2 and 3"; 20pf. Titov and "Vostok 2"; 25pf. "Luniks 1 and 2"; 30pf. Nikolaev and Popovich; 40pf. Interplanetary station and spacecraft; 50pf. "Lunik 3"	46·00	70·00

E223 Pierre de
Coubertin

1963. Birth Centenary of Pierre de Coubertin (reviver of Olympic Games).

E664	**E223**	20pf. red and grey	25	25
E665	-	25pf. blue and ochre	2·30	3·50

DESIGN: 25pf. Stadium.

E224 Party Flag

1963. Sixth Socialists Unity Party Day.

E666	**E224**	10pf. red, black & yell	45	30

E225 Insecticide Sprayer

1963. Malaria Eradication.

E667	**E225**	20pf. black, red & orge	25	25
E668	-	25pf. multicoloured	25	25
E669	-	50pf. multicoloured	1·70	1·90

DESIGNS: 25pf. Rod of Aesculapius; 50pf. Mosquito. Map is common to all values.

E226 Red Fox (Silver Fox
race)

1963. International Fur Auctions, Leipzig.

E670	**E226**	20pf. blue and red	25	25
E671	-	25pf. indigo and blue	2·00	3·25

DESIGN: 25pf. Karakul lamb.

E227 Barthels
Hof, Leipzig
(1748-1872)

1963. Leipzig Spring Fair.

E672	**E227**	10pf. black and yellow	25	25
E673	-	20pf. black and brown	45	35
E674	-	25pf. black and blue	1·70	1·80

LEIPZIG BUILDINGS: 20pf. New Town Hall; 25pf. Clocktower, Karl-Marx Square.

E227a Laboratory
Worker and Apparatus

1963. "Chemistry for Freedom and Socialism". Sheet 105×74 mm with Type **E227a** and similar horiz design. Imperf. No gum.

MS	E674a	50pf. blue and black (E **227a**); 70pf. blue and grey (oil refinery)	5·75	30·00

E228 J. G. Seume (poet)
and Scene from *Syracuse
Walk* (Birth Bicent)

1963. Cultural Anniversaries. Design and portrait in black.

E675	**E228**	5pf. yellow	25	25
E676	-	10pf. turquoise	25	25
E677	-	20pf. orange	25	25
E678	-	25pf. blue	2·30	2·75

DESIGNS: 10pf. F. Hebbel (poet) and scene from *Mary Magdalene* (150th birth anniv); 20pf. G. Buchner (poet) and scene from *Woyzeck* (150th birth anniv); 25pf. R. Wagner (composer) and scene from *The Flying Dutchman* (150th birth anniv).

E229 Nurse bandaging
Patient

1963. Centenary of Red Cross.

E679	**E229**	10pf. multicoloured	1·60	1·60
E680	-	20pf. black, grey and red	25	25

DESIGN: 20pf. Barkas type "B 1000" ambulance.

E230 W. Bohne
(runner)

1963. Concentration Camps Memorial Fund. Sportsmen Victims (1st series). Designs in black.

E681	**E230**	5pf.+5pf. yellow	25	35
E682	-	10pf.+5pf. green	25	35
E683	-	15pf.+5pf. mauve	25	35
E684	-	20pf.+10pf. pink	25	35
E685	-	25pf.+10pf. blue	2·75	8·00

SPORTSMEN: 10pf. W. Seelenbinder (wrestler); 15pf. A. Richter (cyclist); 20pf. H. Steyer (footballer); 25pf. K. Schlosser (mountaineer).

See also Nos. E704/8.

E231
Gymnastics

1963. Fourth East German Gymnastics and Sports Festival, Leipzig. Inscr in black.

E686	**E231**	10pf.+5pf. yellow and green	25	20
E687	-	20pf.+10pf. violet and red	30	35
E688	-	25pf.+10pf. green and blue	4·50	4·25

DESIGNS: 20pf. Dederon kerchief exercises; 25pf. Relay-racing.

E232 E. Pottier
(lyricist) and
Opening Bars of the
Internationale

1963. 75th Anniv of *Internationale* (song).

E689	**E232**	20pf. black and red	25	25
E690	-	25pf. black and blue	1·60	1·80

DESIGN: 25pf. As 20pf. but portrait of P.-C. Degeyter.

E233 V. Tereshkova and "Vostok 6"
E234 V. Bykovsky and "Vostok 5"

1963. Second "Team" Manned Space Flights.

E691	**E233**	20pf. black, grey & bl	1·10	35
E692	**E234**	20pf. black, grey & bl	1·10	35

Nos. E691/2 were printed together, *se-tenant*, forming a composite design.

E235 Motor
Cyclist
competing in
"Motocross",
Apolda

1963. World Motor Cycle Racing Championships.

E693	**E235**	10pf. emerald & green	4·50	5·00
E694	-	20pf. red and pink	35	35
E695	-	25pf. blue & light blue	35	35

DESIGNS—HORIZ (39×22 mm): 20pf. Motor cyclist; 25pf. Two motor cyclists cornering.

E236 Treblinka
Memorial

1963. Erection of Treblinka Memorial, Poland.

E696	**E236**	20pf. blue and red	45	35

E237/E238 Transport

1963. Leipzig Autumn Fair.

E697	**E237**	10pf. multicoloured	1·00	25
E698	**E238**	10pf. multicoloured	1·00	25

Nos. E697/8 were printed together, *se-tenant*, forming a composite design.

1963. Fauna Protection Campaign (2nd series). As Type **E201.** Fauna in natural colours, background colours given.

E699	-	10pf. green	25	20
E700	-	20pf. red	25	20
E701	-	30pf. red	25	20
E702	-	50pf. blue	4·50	4·50
E703	-	70pf. brown	80	80

DESIGNS: 10pf. Stag-beetle; 20pf. Salamander; 30pf. European pond tortoise; 50pf. Green toad; 70pf. West European hedgehogs.

1963. Concentration Camps Memorial Fund. Sportsmen Victims (2nd series). As Type **E230.** Designs in black.

E704	-	5pf.+5pf. yellow	25	25
E705	-	10pf.+5pf. green	25	25
E706	-	15pf.+5pf. violet	25	25
E707	-	20pf. 10pf. red	25	25
E708	-	40pf.+20pf. blue	3·50	5·00

SPORTSMEN: 5pf. H. Tops (Gymnast); 10pf. Kate Tucholla (hockey-player); 15pf. R. Seiffert (swimmer); 20pf. E. Grube (athlete); 40pf. K. Biedermann (canoeist).

E239 N. von Gneisenau and G. L.
von Blucher

1963. 150th Anniv of German War of Liberation.

E709	**E239**	5pf. black, buff & yell	25	20
E710	-	10pf. black, buff & grn	25	20
E711	-	20pf. blk, buff & orge	25	20
E712	-	25pf. black, buff & bl	25	20
E713	-	40pf. black, buff & red	3·25	1·80

DESIGNS: 10pf. "Cossacks and (German) Soldiers in Berlin" (Ludwig Wolf); 20pf. E. M. Arndt and Baron vom Stein; 25pf. Lutzow corps in battle order (detail from painting by Hans Kohlschein); 40pf. G. von Scharnhorst and Prince Kutuzov.

E240 V.
Tereshkova

1963. Visit of Soviet Cosmonauts to East Berlin.

E714	**E240**	10pf. green and blue	25	20
E715	-	20pf. black, red & buff	25	20
E716	-	20pf. green, red & buff	25	20
E717	-	25pf. orange and blue	5·75	3·50

DESIGNS—SQUARE: No. E717, Tereshkova in capsule. VERT: (24×32 mm). No. E715, Tereshkova with bouquet; No. E716, Gagarin (visit to Berlin).

E241 Synagogue
aflame

1963. 25th Anniv of "Kristallnacht" (Nazi pogrom).

E718	**E241**	10pf. multicoloured	45	45

E242 Letter-sorting Machine

1963. Stamp Day. Multicoloured.

E719	10pf. Type **E242**		2·50	2·75
E720	20pf. Fork-lift truck loading mail train		25	25

E243 Ski Jumper
commencing Run

1963. Winter Olympic Games, Innsbruck, 1964. Rings in different colours; skier in black.

E721	**E243**	5pf. yellow	25	20
E722	-	10pf. green	25	20
E723	-	20pf.+10pf. red	25	20
E724	-	25pf. blue	3·00	3·25

DESIGNS: Ski jumper—10pf. Taking-off; 20pf. In mid-air; 25pf. Landing.

E244 *Vanessa
atalanta*

1964. Butterflies. Butterflies in natural colours; inscr in black.

E725	**E244**	10pf. olive	55	25
E726	-	15pf. lilac	55	25
E727	-	20pf. orange	55	25
E728	-	25pf. blue	55	25
E729	-	40pf. blue	7·50	3·50

BUTTERFLIES: 15pf. *Parnassius phoebus*; 20pf. *Papilio machaon*; 25pf. *Colius croceus*; 40pf. *Nymphalis polychloros*.

E245 Shakespeare (b. 1564)

1964. Cultural Anniversaries.

E730		20pf. blue and pink	35	25
E731		25pf. purple and blue	35	25
E732	**E245**	40pf. blue and lilac	1·80	1·60

DESIGNS: 20pf. Quadriga, Brandenburg Gate (J. G. Schadow, sculptor, b. 1764); 25pf. Portal keystone, German Historical Museum (A. Schluter, sculptor, b. 1664).

E246
"Elektrotecknik"
Hall

1964. Leipzig Spring Fair.

E733	**E246**	10pf. black and green	3·50	45
E734	-	20pf. black and red	3·50	45

DESIGN: 20pf. Braunigkes Hof, c. 1700.

E247 A. Saefkow

1964. Concentration Camp Victims. Memorials Fund.

E735	**E247**	5pf.+5pf. brown & bl	35	20
E736	-	10pf.+5pf. brn & ol	35	20
E737	-	15pf.+5pf. brn & vio	35	20
E738	-	20pf.+5pf. olive and red	35	25
E739	-	25pf.+10pf. blue & ol	55	35
E740	-	40pf.+10pf. ol & brn	1·70	2·30

PORTRAITS—As Type E **247**: 10pf. F. Jacob; 15pf. B. Bastlein; 20pf. H. Schulze-Boysen; 25pf. Dr. A. Kuckhoff. (49×27½ mm): 40pf. Dr. A. and Mildred Harnack.

E248 Mr.
Khrushchev with
East German
Officials

1964. Mr. Khrushchev's 70th Birthday.

E741	**E248**	25pf. blue	35	25
E742	-	40pf. black and purple	4·00	3·00

DESIGN: 40pf. Mr. Khrushchev with cosmonauts Tereshkova and Gagarin.

E249 Boys and Girls

1964. German Youth Meeting, Berlin. Multicoloured.

E743	10pf. Type **E249**		25	20
E744	20pf. Young gymnasts		25	20
E745	25pf. Youth with accordion and girl with flowers		2·30	1·30

E250 Flax, Krumel
and Struppi, the
dog

1964. Children's Day. Multicoloured.

E746	5pf. Type **E250**		35	20
E747	10pf. Master Nadelohr		35	20
E748	15pf. Pittiplatsch		35	20
E749	20pf. Sandmannschen (sand-man)		35	20
E750	40pf. Bummi (teddy bear) and Schnatterinchen (duckling)		2·30	2·50

The designs show characters from children's T.V. programmes.

E251 Governess and
Child (with portrait of
Jenny Marx)

1964. East German Women's Congress. Multicoloured.

E751	20pf. Type **E251**		45	20
E752	25pf. Switchboard technicians		1·50	1·30
E753	70pf. Farm girls		45	20

E252 Cycling

1964. Olympic Games, Tokyo. Multicoloured. (a) 1st Series. As Type **E252**.

E754	5pf. Type **E252**		35	35
E755	10pf. Volleyball		35	35
E756	20pf. Judo		35	35
E757	25pf. Diving		35	35
E758	40pf.+20pf. Running		35	35
E759	70pf. Horse-jumping		2·40	2·40

E253 Diving

(b) 2nd Series. As Type **E253**

E760	10pf. Type **E253**		3·50	4·00
E761	10pf.+5pf. Horse-jumping		3·50	4·00
E762	10pf. Volleyball		3·50	4·00
E763	10pf. Cycling		3·50	4·00
E764	10pf.+5pf. Running		3·50	4·00
E765	10pf. Judo		3·50	4·00

Nos. E760/5 were printed together in *se-tenant* blocks of six (3×2) within sheets of 60 (6×10), and with an overall pattern of the five Olympic "rings" in each block.

E254 Young Artists

1964. Fifth Young Pioneers' Meeting, East Berlin. Multicoloured.

E766	10pf.+5pf. Type **E254**		2·30	60
E767	20pf.+10pf. Planting tree		2·30	60
E768	25pf.+10pf. Playing with ball		5·75	6·00

E255 Leningrad
Memorial

1964. Victims of Leningrad Siege Commem.

E769	**E255**	25pf. black, yellow and blue	1·40	35

E256 F. Joliot-Curie

1964. "World Peace".

E770	**E256**	20pf. sepia and red	35	25
E771	-	25pf. black and blue	35	25
E772	-	50pf. black and lilac	1·80	1·30

PORTRAITS (Campaigners for "World Peace"): 25pf. B. von Suttner; 50pf. C. von Ossietzky.

E257 Ancient Glazier's Shop

1964. Leipzig Autumn Fair. Multicoloured.

E773	10pf. Type **E257**	85	25
E774	15pf. Jena glass factory	85	25

E258 I.W.M.A. Cachet

1964. Centenary of "First International".

E775	**E258**	20pf. black and red	25	20
E776	**E258**	25pf. black and blue	95	95

E259 "Rostock Port" Stamp of 1958

1964. National Stamp Exn, East Berlin.

E777	**E259**	10pf.+5pf. green and orange	35	25
E778	-	20pf.+10pf. blue and purple	45	35
E779	-	50pf. brown and grey	2·75	2·10

DESIGNS: 20pf., 12pf. "Peace" stamp of 1950; 50pf., 5pf. "Dresden Paintings" stamp of 1955.

E260 Modern Buildings and Flag ("Reconstruction")

1964. 15th Anniv of German Democratic Republic. Multicoloured.

E780	10pf. Type **E260**	45	35
E781	10pf. Surveyor and conveyor ("Coal")	45	35
E782	10pf. Scientist and chemical works ("Chemical Industry")	45	35
E783	10pf. Guard and chemical works ("Chemical Industry")	45	35
E784	10pf. Milkmaid and dairy pen ("Agriculture")	45	35
E785	10pf. Furnaceman and mills ("Steel")	45	35
E786	10pf. Student with microscope, and lecture hall ("Education")	45	35
E787	10pf. Operator and lathe ("Engineering")	45	35
E788	10pf. Scientist and planetarium ("Optics")	45	35
E789	10pf. Girl with cloth, and loom ("Textiles")	45	35
E790	10pf. Docker and ship at quayside ("Shipping")	45	35
E791	10pf. Leipzig buildings and "businessmen" formed of Fair emblem ("Exports")	45	35
E792	10pf. Building worker and flats ("New Construction")	45	35
E793	10pf. Sculptor modelling and Dresden gateway ("Culture")	45	35
E794	10pf. Girl skier and holiday resort ("Recreation")	45	35
MSE794a	210×285 mm. Nos. E780/94	75·00	£110

E261 Monchgut (Rugen) Costume

1964. Provincial Costumes (1st series). Multicoloured.

E795	5pf. Type **E261**	12·50	8·25
E796	5pf. Monchgut (male)	12·50	8·25
E797	10pf. Spreewald (female)	1·10	60
E798	10pf. Spreewald (male)	1·10	60
E799	20pf. Thuringen (female)	1·10	60
E800	20pf. Thuringen (male)	1·10	60

See Nos. E932/7 and E1073/6.

E261a Observation of Sun's Activity

1964. Quiet Sun Year. Three sheets, each 108×90 mm incorporating stamp as Type **E261a**. Multicoloured.

MSE801 (a) 25pf. Rocket over part of Earth. (b) 40pf. Type **E261a**. (c) 70pf. Earth and rocket routes	14·50	24·00

E262 Dr. Schweitzer and Lambarene River

1965. 90th Birthday of Dr. Albert Schweitzer.

E802	**E262**	10pf. yellow, blk & grn	55	20
E803	-	20pf. yellow, blk & red	55	20
E804	-	25pf. yellow, blk & bl	4·50	3·00

DESIGNS: 20pf. Schweitzer and "nuclear disarmament" marchers; 25pf. Schweitzer and part of a Bach organ prelude.

1965. As Nos. E586/7 but values expressed in "MDN" (Deutschen Notenbank Marks) instead of "DM".

E805	1MDN. green	70	1·20
E806	2MDN. brown	80	1·80

E263 A. Bebel

1965. 125th Birth Anniv of August Bebel (founder of Social Democratic Party).

E807	**E263**	20pf. yellow, brn & red	55	25

See also Nos. E814/15, E839, E842 and E871.

E264 Fair Medal (obverse)

1965. Leipzig Spring Fair and 800th Anniv of Leipzig Fair.

E808	**E264**	10pf. gold and mauve	35	20
E809	-	15pf. gold and mauve	35	20
E810	-	25pf. multicoloured	80	35

DESIGNS: 15pf. Fair medal (reverse); 25pf. Chemical Works.

E265 Giraffe

1965. Tenth Anniv of East Berlin Zoo.

E811	**E265**	10pf. grey and green	25	20
E812	-	25pf. grey and blue	35	25
E813	-	30pf. grey and sepia	3·00	2·10

ANIMALS—HORIZ: 25pf. Iguana; 30pf. Black wildebeest.

1965. 120th Birth Anniv of W. C. Rontgen (physicist). As Type **E263** but portrait of Rontgen.

E814	10pf. yellow, brown and green	70	25

1985. 700th Birth Anniv of Dante. As Type **E263** but portrait of Dante.

E815	50pf. yellow, brown & lemon	2·50	35

E266 Belyaev and Leonov

1965. Space Flight of "Voskhod 2".

E816	**E266**	10pf. red	45	25
E817	-	25pf. blue	3·00	2·40

DESIGN: 25pf. Leonov in space.

E267 Boxing Gloves

1965. European Boxing Championships, Berlin.

E818	**E267**	10pf.+5pf. mult	25	20
E819	-	20pf. gold, black and red	1·20	1·20

DESIGN: 20pf. Boxing glove.

E268 Dimitrov denouncing Fascism

1965. 20th Anniv of Liberation. Multicoloured.

E820	5pf.+5pf. Type **E268**	35	25
E821	10pf.+5pf. Distributing *Communist Manifesto*	35	25
E822	15pf.+5pf. Soldiers of International Brigade fighting in Spain	35	25
E823	20pf.+10pf. "Freedom for Ernst Thalmann" demonstration	35	25
E824	25pf.+10pf. Founding of "Free Germany" National Committee (Moscow)	35	25
E825	40pf. Ulbricht and Weinert distributing *Manifesto* on Eastern Front	35	25
E826	50pf. Liberation of concentration camps	35	25
E827	60pf. Hoisting Red Flag on Reichstag	4·00	4·00
E828	70pf. Bilateral demonstration of Communist and Socialist parties	35	25

E269 Transmitter Aerial and Globe

1965. 20th Anniv of East German Broadcasting Service.

E829	**E269**	20pf. black, red and cerise	45	20
E830	-	40pf. black and blue	2·00	95

DESIGN: 40pf. Radio workers.

E270 I.T.U. Emblem and Radio Circuit Diagram

1965. Centenary of I.T.U.

E831	**E270**	20pf. black, yell & ol	55	20
E832	-	25pf. black, mve & vio	3·00	70

DESIGN: 25pf. I.T.U. emblem and switch diagram.

E271 F.D.G.B. Emblem

1965. 20th Anniv of Free German (F.D.G.B.) and World Trade Unions.

E833	**E271**	20pf. gold and red	55	25
E834	-	25pf. black, bl & gold	1·70	70

DESIGN—HORIZ (39×21½ mm): 25pf. Workers of "two hemispheres" (inscr "20 JAHRE WELTGEWERKSCHAFTS-BUND").

E272 Industrial Machine

1965. 800th Anniv of Karl-Marx-Stadt (formerly Chemnitz).

E835	**E272**	10pf. green and gold	35	20
E836	-	20pf. red and gold	35	20
E837	-	25pf. blue and gold	1·60	70

DESIGNS: 20pf. Red Tower, Chemnitz; 25pf. Town Hall, Chemnitz.

E273 Marx and Lenin

1965. Socialist Countries' Postal Ministers Conference, Peking.

E838	**E273**	20pf. black, yell & red	80	30

1965. 90th Birth Anniv of Dr. Wilhelm Kulz (politician). As Type **E263** but portrait of Kulz.

E839	25pf. yellow, brown and blue	1·30	30

E274 Congress Emblem

1965. World Peace Congress, Helsinki.

E840	**E274**	10pf.+5pf. green and blue	35	20
E841	**E274**	20pf.+5pf. blue and red	70	50

1965. 75th Birth Anniv of Erich Weinert (poet). As Type **E263**, but portrait of Weinert.

E842	40pf. yellow, brown and red	70	30

1965. "Help for Vietnam". Surch **Hilfe fur VIETNAM +10**.

E843	**E260**	10pf.+10pf. mult	55	30

E276 Rebuilt Weigh-house and Modern Buildings, Katharinenstrasse

1965. 800th Anniv of Leipzig.

E844	**E276**	10pf. purple, bl & gold	25	20
E845	-	25pf. orge, sep & gold	25	20
E846	-	40pf. multicoloured	35	20
E847	-	70pf. blue and gold	2·75	1·30

DESIGNS: 25pf. Old Town Hall; 40pf. Opera House and new G.P.O.; 70pf. "Stadt Leipzig" Hotel.

E277 "Praktica" and "Praktisix" Cameras

1965. Leipzig Autumn Fair.

E848	**E277**	10pf. blk, gold & grn	45	25
E849	-	15pf. multicoloured	45	25
E850	-	25pf. multicoloured	1·00	35

DESIGNS: 15pf. Clavichord and electric guitar; 25pf. "Zeiss" microscope.

1965. Leipzig Philatelic Exhibition, "INTERMESS III". Nos. E844/7 in two miniature sheets each 137×99 mm.
MSE851 (a) Nos. E844 and E847. (b)
Nos. E845/6 (sold for 1 MDN.75)   7·25   9·50

E278 Show Jumping

1965. World Modern Pentathlon Championships, Leipzig. Multicoloured.
E852	10pf. Type E **278**	35	20
E853	10pf. Swimming	35	20
E854	10pf. Running	3·50	3·50
E855	10pf.+5pf. Fencing	35	20
E856	10pf.+5pf. Pistol-shooting	35	20

E279 E. Leonov

1965. Soviet Cosmonauts Visit to East Germany.
E857	**E279** 20pf. blue, silver & red	80	85
E858	- 20pf. blue, silver & red	80	85
E859	- 25pf. multicoloured	80	85

DESIGNS—As Type E **275**. No. E858, Belyaev. HORIZ (48×29 mm): No. E859, "Voskhod 2" and Leonov in space.

E280 Memorial at Putten, Netherlands

1965. Putten War Victims Commem.
E860	**E280** 25pf. black, yell & bl	90	30

E281 Stoking Furnace (from old engraving)

1965. Bicent of Mining School, Freiberg. Multicoloured.
E861	10pf. Type E **281**	35	25
E862	15pf. Mining ore (old engraving)	90	1·20
E863	20pf. Ore	35	25
E864	25pf. Sulphur	35	25

E282 Red Kite

1965. Birds of Prey. Multicoloured.
E865	5pf. Type E **282**	25	20
E866	10pf. Lammergeier	25	20
E867	20pf. Common Buzzard	35	20
E868	25pf. Common Kestrel	35	20
E869	40pf. Northern Goshawk	55	25
E870	70pf. Golden Eagle	5·00	3·25

1965. 150th Birth Anniv of A. von Menzel (painter). As Type E **263** but portrait of Menzel.
E871	10pf. yellow, brown and red	1·00	30

E283 Otto Grotewohl

1965. Grotewohl Commemoration.
E872	**E283** 20f. black	1·00	30

E284 Extract from Newsletter

1966. 50th Anniv of Spartacus Group Conference. Miniature sheet 138×98 mm. Type **E284** and similar horiz design.
MSE873 20pf. black and red (Type E **284**); 50pf. black and red (Karl Liebknecht and Rosa Luxemburg)   2·75   7·00

E285 Ladies' Single-seater

1966. World Tobogganing Championships, Friedrichroda.
E874	**E285** 10pf. green and olive	25	20
E875	- 20pf. blue and red	25	20
E876	- 25pf. indigo and blue	1·70	1·20

DESIGNS: 20pf. Men's double-seater; 25pf. Men's single seater.

E286 Electronic Punch-card Computer

1966. Leipzig Spring Fair. Multicoloured.
E877	10pf. Type **E286**	35	25
E878	15pf. Drilling and milling plant	1·30	35

E287 Soldier and National Gallery, Berlin

1966. Tenth Anniv of National People's Army.
E879	**E287** 5pf. black, olive & yell	35	20
E880	- 10pf. black, ol & yell	35	20
E881	- 20pf. black, ol & yell	35	20
E882	- 25pf. black, ol & yell	1·60	1·20

DESIGNS: Soldier and—10pf. Brandenburg Gate; 20pf. Industrial plant; 25pf. Combine-harvester.

E288 J. A. Smoler (Sorb patriot and savant)

1966. 150th Birth Anniv of Jan Smoler.
E883	**E288** 20pf. black, red & blue	25	20
E884	- 25pf. black, red & blue	80	70

DESIGN: 25pf. House of the Sorbs, Bautzen.

E289 "Good Knowledge" Badge

1966. 20th Anniv of "Freie Deutsche Jugend" (Socialist Youth Movement).
E885	**E289** 20pf. multicoloured	80	30

E290 "Luna 9" on Moon

1966. Moon Landing of "Luna 9".
E886	**E290** 20pf. multicoloured	2·75	60

E291 Road Signs

1966. Road Safety.
E887	**E291** 10pf. red, bl & ultram	25	20
E888	- 15pf. black, yell & grn	25	20
E889	- 25pf. black, blue & bis	25	20
E890	- 50pf. black, yell & red	1·50	1·00

DESIGNS: 15pf. Child on scooter crossing in front of car; 25pf. Cyclist and hand-signal; 50pf. Motor cyclist, glass of beer and ambulance.

E292 Marx and Lenin Banner

1966. 20th Anniv of Socialist Unity Party (S.E.D.).
E891	5pf. multicoloured	25	20
E892	**E292** 10pf. yellow, blk & red	25	20
E893	- 15pf. black and green	25	20
E894	- 20pf. black and red	35	20
E895	- 25pf. black, yell & red	2·30	1·80

DESIGNS—VERT: 5pf. Party badge and demonstrators; 15pf. Marx, Engels and manifesto; 20pf. Pieck and Grotewohl. HORIZ: 25pf. Workers greeting Ulbricht.

E293 W.H.O. Building

1966. Inaug of W.H.O. Headquarters, Geneva.
E896	**E293** 20pf. multicoloured	55	45

E294 Spreewald

1966. National Parks. Multicoloured.
E897	10pf. Type E **294**	25	20
E898	15pf. Konigsstuhl (Isle of Rugen)	25	20
E899	20pf. Sachsische Schweiz	25	20
E900	25pf. Westdarss	35	20
E901	30pf. Teufelsmauer	35	25
E902	50pf. Feldberg Lakes	2·50	1·50

E295 Lace "Flower"

1966. Plauen Lace. Floral Patterns as Type **E295**.
E903	**E295** 10pf. myrtle and green	25	20
E904	- 20pf. indigo and blue	25	20
E905	- 25pf. red and rose	35	25
E906	- 50pf. violet and lilac	3·25	1·80

E296 Lily of the Valley

1966. Int Horticultural Show, Erfurt. Multicoloured.
E907	20pf. Type **E296**	25	20
E908	25pf. Rhododendrons	35	25
E909	40pf. Dahlias	45	35
E910	50pf. Cyclamen	5·50	5·25

E297 Parachutist on Target

1966. Eighth World Parachute Jumping Championships, Leipzig.
E911	**E297** 10pf. blue, black & bis	25	20
E912	- 15pf. multicoloured	80	80

E913	- 20pf. black, bistre & bl	25	20

DESIGNS: 15pf. Group descent; 20pf. Free fall.

E298 Hans Kahle and Music of *The Thalmann Column*

1966. 30th Anniv of International Brigade in Spain. Multicoloured.
E914	5pf. Type **E298**	35	25
E915	10pf.+5pf. W. Bredel and open-air class	35	25
E916	15pf. H. Beimler and Madrid street-fighting	35	25
E917	20pf.+10pf. H. Rau and march-past after Battle of Brunete	35	25
E918	25pf.+10pf. H. Marchwitza and soldiers	35	25
E919	40pf.+10pf. A. Becker and Ebro battle	1·90	1·80

E299 Canoeing

1966. World Canoeing Championships, Berlin. Multicoloured.
E920	10pf.+5pf. Type **E299**	35	25
E921	15pf. Kayak doubles	1·60	1·40

E300 Television Set

1966. Leipzig Autumn Fair. Multicoloured.
E922	10pf. Type **E300**	90	25
E923	15pf. Electric typewriter	2·00	35

E301 Oradour Memorial

1966. Oradour-sur-Glane War Victims Commem.
E924	**E301** 25pf. black, blue & red	55	35

E302 "Blood Donors"

1966. International Health Co-operation.
E925	**E302** 5pf. red and green	35	25
E926	- 20pf.+10pf. red and violet	55	25
E927	- 40pf. red and blue	2·50	85

DESIGNS—HORIZ: 20pf. I.C.Y. emblem. VERT: 40pf. Health symbol.

E303 Weightlifting ("snatch")

1966. World and European Weightlifting Championships, Berlin.
E928	**E303** 15pf. black and brown	2·00	2·10
E929	- 20pf.+5pf. black and blue	55	25

DESIGN: 20pf. Weightlifting ("jerk").

E304 Congress Hall

1966. Sixth Int Journalists' Congress, Berlin.
E930	**E304** 10pf. multicoloured	70	60
E931	- 20pf. yellow and blue	25	20

DESIGN—VERT: 20pf. Emblem of Int Organization of journalists.

1966. Provincial Costumes (2nd series). As Type **E261**. Multicoloured.

E932	5pf. Altenburg (female)	55	30
E933	10pf. Altenburg (male)	55	30
E934	10pf. Mecklenburg (female)	55	30
E935	15pf. Mecklenburg (male)	55	30
E936	20pf. Magdeburger Borde (female)	2·75	2·50
E937	30pf. Magdeburger Borde (male)	2·75	2·50

E305 "Vietnam is Invincible"

1966. Aid for Vietnam.

E938	**E305** 20pf.+5pf. black and pink	55	35

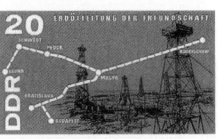

E306 Oil Rigs and Pipeline Map

1966. Inaug of Int "Friendship" Oil Pipeline.

E939	**E306** 20pf. black and red	30	25
E940	— 25pf. black and blue	1·30	60

DESIGN: 25pf. "Walter Ulbricht" Oil Works, Leuna and pipeline map.

E307 Black Phantom Tetra

1966. Aquarium Fish. Multicoloured.

E941	5pf. Type **E307**	25	20
E942	10pf. Cardinal tetra	25	20
E943	15pf. Rio Grande cichlid	3·50	3·00
E944	20pf. Blue gularis	25	20
E945	25pf. Ramirez's dwarf cichlid	35	25
E946	40pf. Honey gourami	45	30

E308 "Horse" (detail from Ishtar Gate)

1966. Babylonian Art Treasures, Vorderasiatisches Museum, Berlin. Multicoloured.

E947	10pf. Type **E308**	25	20
E948	20pf. Mythological animal, Ishtar Gate	25	20
E949	25pf. Lion facing right (vert)	25	20
E950	50pf. Lion facing left (vert)	90	1·70

E309 The Wartburg from the East

1966. 900th Anniv of Wartburg Castle.

E951	**E309** 10pf.+5pf. slate	35	25
E952	— 20pf. green	35	25
E953	— 25pf. purple	80	55

DESIGNS: 20pf. Castle bailiwick; 25pf. Residence.

E310 Gentiana pneumonanthe

1966. Protected Plants (1st series). Multicoloured.

E954	10pf. Type **E310**	25	20
E955	20pf. Cephalanthera rubra	35	25
E956	25pf. Arnica montana	1·90	1·30

See also Nos. E1177/82 and E1284/9.

E311 Son leaves Home

1966. Fairy Tales (1st series). The Wishing Table. Multicoloured.

E957	5pf. Type **E311**	35	45
E958	10pf. Setting the table	1·10	1·10
E959	20pf. The thieving inn-keeper	1·10	1·10
E960	25pf. The magic donkey	1·10	1·10
E961	30pf. The cudgel in the sack	1·10	1·10
E962	50pf. Return of the son	1·10	1·10

See also Nos. E1045/50, E1147/52, E1171/6, E1266/71, E1437/42, E1525/30, E1623/8, E1711/16, E1811/13, E1902/7, E1996/2001 and E2092/7.

E312 Worlitz Castle

1967. Principal East German Buildings. (1st series). Multicoloured.

E964	5pf. Type **E312**	25	20
E965	10pf. Stralsund Town Hall (vert)	25	20
E966	15pf. Chorin Monastery (vert)	35	20
E967	20pf. Ribbeck House, Berlin	35	20
E968	25pf. Moritzburg, Zeitz (vert)	35	20
E969	40pf. Old Town Hall, Potsdam (vert)	1·80	1·30

See also Nos. E1100/3 and E1155/60.

E313 Rifle-shooting

1967. World Biathlon Championships, Altenburg.

E970	**E313** 10pf. blue, drab & mve	20	15
E971	— 20pf. olive, blue & grn	20	15
E972	— 25pf. green, blue & ol	1·00	70

DESIGNS: 20pf. Shooting on skis; 25pf. Riflemen racing on skis.

E314 "Multilock" Loom

1967. Leipzig Spring Fair.

E973	**E314** 10pf. green, grey & pur	25	20
E974	— 15pf. bistre & blue	1·10	35

DESIGN: 15pf. Zeiss tracking telescope.

E315 Mother and Child

1967. 20th Anniv of German Democratic Women's Federation.

E975	**E315** 20pf. grey, red and purple	35	25
E976	— 25pf. brown, turquoise and brown	90	1·10

DESIGN: 25pf. Professional woman.

E316 Industrial Control Desk

1967. Socialist Party Rally. Multicoloured.(a) 1st series.

E977	10pf. Type **E316**	35	25
E978	20pf. Ulbricht meeting workers	35	25
E979	25pf. Servicemen guarding industrial plants	35	25
E980	40pf. Agricultural workers and harvesters	80	1·20

Each with inset portraits of Marx, Engels and Lenin.

(b) 2nd series. As Type **E316** but vert.

E981	5pf. Agricultural worker	25	20
E982	10pf. Teacher and pupil	25	25

E983	15pf. Socialist family	55	55
E984	20pf. Servicemen	25	25

Each with inset portraits as above.

E317 Portrait of a Girl (after F. Hodler)

1967. Dresden Gallery Paintings (1st series). Multicoloured.

E985	20pf. Type **E317**	25	20
E986	25pf. Peter at the Zoo (H. Hakenbeck)	25	20
E987	30pf. Venetian Episode (R. Bergander)	25	20
E988	40pf. Tahitian Women (Gauguin) (horiz)	25	20
E989	50pf. The Grandchild (J. Scholtz)	2·50	2·10
E990	70pf. Cairn in the Snow (C. D. Friedrich) (horiz)	45	35

See also Nos. E1114/19 and E1249/54.

E318 Barn Owl

1967. Protected Birds. Multicoloured.

E991	5pf. Type **E318**	25	20
E992	10pf. Common Crane	25	20
E993	20pf. Peregrine Falcon	25	20
E994	25pf. Northern bullfinches	25	20
E995	30pf. River kingfisher	5·25	3·50
E996	40pf. European roller	45	20

E319 Cycle Wheels

1967. 20th Warsaw–Berlin–Prague Cycle Race.

E997	**E319** 10pf. violet, black and yellow	25	20
E998	— 25pf. red and blue	70	60

DESIGN: 25pf. Racing cyclists.

E320 "Tom Cat"

1967. Int Children's Day. Multicoloured.

E999	5pf. Type **E320**	25	20
E1000	10pf. "Snow White"	25	20
E1001	15pf. "Fire Brigade"	25	20
E1002	20pf. "Cockerel"	25	20
E1003	25pf. "Vase of Flowers"	25	20
E1004	30pf. "Children Playing with Ball"	1·50	1·20

E321 Girl with Grapes (Gerard Dou)

1967. Paintings Missing from German National Galleries (after World War II).

E1005	**E 321** 5pf. blue	25	20
E1006	— 10pf. brown	25	20
E1007	— 20pf. green	25	20
E1008	— 25pf. purple	25	20
E1009	— 40pf. olive	25	20
E1010	— 50pf. sepia	2·20	1·80

DESIGNS—VERT: 25pf. Portrait of W Schroeder-Devrient (after K. Begas); 40pf. Young Girl in Straw Hat (after S. Bray); 50pf. The Four Evangelists (after Jordaens). HORIZ: 5pf. Three Horsemen (after Rubens); 20pf. Spring Idyll (after H. Thoma).

E322 Exhibition Emblem

1967. 15th Agricultural Exn, Markkleeberg.

E1011	**E322** 20pf. red, green and yellow	45	35

E323 Marie Curie (Birth Cent)

1967. Birth Anniversaries.

E1012	— 5pf. brown	35	20
E1013	**E323** 10pf. blue	35	20
E1014	— 20pf. red	35	20
E1015	— 25pf. sepia	35	20
E1016	— 40pf. green	1·10	85

PORTRAITS: 5pf. G. Herwegh (poet—150th); 20pf. Kathe Kollwitz (artist—cent); 25pf. J. J. Winckelmann (archaeologist—250th); 40pf. T. Storm (poet—150th).

E324 Jack of Diamonds

1967. German Playing-cards. Multicoloured.

E1017	5pf. Type **E324**	25	20
E1018	10pf. Jack of Hearts	25	20
E1019	20pf. Jack of Spades	25	20
E1020	25pf. Jack of Clubs	7·25	4·00

E325 Mare and Filly

1967. Thoroughbred Horse Meeting, Berlin. Multicoloured.

E1021	5pf. Type **E325**	30	20
E1022	10pf. Stallion	30	20
E1023	20pf. Horse-racing	35	25
E1024	50pf. Two fillies (vert)	4·25	3·00

E326 Kitchen Equipment

1967. Leipzig Autumn Fair. Multicoloured.

E1025	10pf. Type **E326**	55	25
E1026	15pf. Fur coat and "Interpelz" brand-mark	1·40	60

E327 Max Reichpietsch and Friedrich der Grosse (battleship), 1914–18

1967. 50th Anniv of Revolutionary Sailors' Movement. Multicoloured.

E1027	10pf. Type **E327**	25	20
E1028	15pf. Albin Kobis and Prinzregent Luitpold (battleship), 1914–18	1·70	85
E1029	20pf. Sailors' demonstration and Seydlitz (battle cruiser), 1914–18	55	20

E328 Kragujevac Memorial

1967. Victims of Kragujevac (Yugoslavia) Massacre.

E1030	**E328**	25pf. black, yellow and red	1·00	45

E329 Worker and Dam ("Electrification")

1967. 50th Anniv of October Revolution.

E1031	-	5pf. black, orange and red	25	20
E1032	**E 329**	10pf. black, red and bistre	25	20
E1033	-	15pf. black, red and grey	25	20
E1034	-	20pf. black, red and orange	45	20
E1035	-	40pf. black, red and orange	3·50	3·00
MSE1036	127×83 mm. Nos. E1034/5. Imperf (sold for 85pf.)		2·00	5·25

DESIGNS: 5pf. Worker and newspaper headline "Hands off Soviet Russia!"; 15pf. Treptow Memorial ("Victory over Fascism"); 20pf. German and Soviet soldiers ("Friendship"); 40pf. Lenin and *Aurora* (Russian cruiser). Each with hammer and sickle.

E330 Martin Luther (from engraving by Lucas Cranach the Elder)

1967. 450th Anniv of Reformation.

E1037	**E330**	20pf. black & mauve	25	20
E1038	-	25pf. black and blue	25	20
E1039	-	40pf. black and bistre	3·00	1·40

DESIGNS—HORIZ: 25pf. Luther's house, Wittenberg. VERT: 40pf. Castle church, Wittenberg.

E331 Young Workers

1967. Tenth "Masters of Tomorrow" Fair, Leipzig.

E1040	**E331**	20pf. black, gold and blue	70	60
E1041	-	20pf. black, gold and blue	70	60
E1042	-	25pf. multicoloured	70	60

DESIGNS—VERT: No. E1041, Young man and woman. HORIZ: (51×29 mm): No. E1042, Presentation of awards.

E332 Goethe's House, Weimar

1967. Cultural Places.

E1043	**E332**	20pf. blk, brn & grey	35	20
E1044	-	25pf. olive, brn & yell	2·20	85

DESIGN: 25pf. Schiller's House, Weimar.

E333 Queen and Courtiers

1967. Fairy Tales (2nd series). *King Thrushbeard.* Designs showing different scenes.

E1045	**E333**	5pf. multicoloured	35	35
E1046	-	10pf. multicoloured	35	35
E1047	-	15pf. multicoloured	1·40	1·40
E1048	-	20pf. multicoloured	1·40	1·40

E1049	-	25pf. multicoloured	35	35
E1050	-	30pf. multicoloured	35	35

E334 Peasants and Modern Farm Buildings

1967. 15th Anniv of Agricultural Co-operatives.

E1052	**E334**	10pf. sepia, green and olive	45	25

E335 Nutcracker and Two "Smokers"

1967. Popular Art of the Erzgebirge. Multicoloured.

E1053		10pf. Type **E335**	90	60
E1054		20pf. "Angel" and miner with candles (carved figures)	25	20

E336 Ice Skating

1968. Winter Olympic Games, Grenoble.

E1055	**E336**	5pf. blue, red and light blue	25	20
E1056	-	10pf.+5pf. blue, red and turquoise	25	20
E1057	-	15pf. multicoloured	25	20
E1058	-	20pf. ultramarine, red and blue	25	20
E1059	-	25pf. multicoloured	25	20
E1060	-	30pf. ultramarine, red and blue	4·50	1·90

DESIGNS: 10pf. Tobogganing; 15pf. Slalom; 20pf. Ice hockey; 25pf. Figure skating (pairs); 30pf. Cross-country skiing.

E337 Actinometer

1968. 75th Anniv of Potsdam Meteorological Observatory and World Meteorological Day (23 March).

E1061	**E337**	10pf. blk, red & pur	55	55
E1062	-	20pf. multicoloured	55	55
E1063	-	25pf. blk, yell & grn	55	55

DESIGNS—VERT: 25pf. Cornfield by day and night. HORIZ—(50×28 mm): 20pf. Satellite picture of clouds.

E338 "Venus 4"

1968. Soviet Space Achievements. Multicoloured.

E1064		20pf. Type E **338**	25	20
E1065		25pf. Coupled satellites "Cosmos 186" and "188"	1·50	85

E339 "Illegal Struggle" (man, wife and child)

1968. Stained-glass Windows, Sachsenhausen National Memorial Museum. Multicoloured.

E1066		10pf. Type **E339**	25	20
E1067		20pf. "Liberation"	25	20
E1068		25pf. "Partisans' Struggle"	70	45

E340 Type DE1 Diesel-electric Locomotive (built for Brazil)

1968. Leipzig Spring Fair. Multicoloured.

E1069		10pf. Type **E340**	45	30
E1070		15pf. Deep sea trawler	1·30	60

E341 Gorky

1968. Birth Cent of Maxim Gorky (writer).

E1071	**E341**	20pf. purple and red	45	30
E1072	-	25pf. purple and red	90	55

DESIGN: 25pf. Fulmar (from "Song of the Stormy Petrel"—poem).

1968. Provincial Costumes (3rd series). As Type **E261**. Multicoloured.

E1073		10pf. Hoyerswerda (female)	25	20
E1074		20pf. Schleife (female)	25	20
E1075		40pf. Crostwitz (female)	35	25
E1076		50pf. Spreewald (female)	3·75	1·50

E342 Common Pheasants

1968. Small Game. Multicoloured.

E1077		10pf. Type **E342**	25	25
E1078		15pf. Grey Partridges	25	25
E1079		20pf. Mallards	25	25
E1080		25pf. Greylag Geese	25	25
E1081		30pf. Wood Pigeon	25	25
E1082		40pf. Brown hares	4·00	7·00

E343 Karl Marx

1968. 150th Birth Anniv of Karl Marx.

E1083	-	10pf. black and green	35	35
E1084	**E343**	20pf. black, yell & red	35	35
E1085	-	25pf. blk, brn & yell	35	35
MSE1086	126×86 mm. Nos. E1083/5. Imperf		2·00	5·25

DESIGNS: 10pf. Title-page of "Communist Manifesto"; 25pf. Title-page of "Das Kapital".

E344 *Fritz Heckert* (after E. Hering)

1968. Seventh Confederation of Free German Trade Unions Congress. Multicoloured.

E1087		10pf. Type **E344**	25	25
E1088		20pf. Young workers and new tenements	35	35

E345 Hammer and Anvil ("The right to work")

1968. Human Rights Year.

E1089	**E345**	5pf. mauve & purple	25	20
E1090	-	10pf. bistre & brown	25	20
E1091	-	25pf. blue & turq	1·00	70

DESIGNS: 10pf. Tree and Globe ("The right to live"); 25pf. Dove and Sun ("The right to peace").

E346 Vietnamese Mother and Child

1968. Aid for Vietnam.

E1092	**E346**	10pf.+5pf. mult	35	25

E347 Angling (World Angling Championships, Gustrow)

1968. Sporting Events.

E1093	**E347**	20pf. blue, grn & red	25	20
E1094	-	20pf. blue, turq & grn	25	20
E1095	-	20pf. purple, red & bl	1·10	95

DESIGNS: No. E1094, Sculling (European Women's Rowing Championships, Berlin); No. E1095, High jumping (2nd European Youth Athletic Competitions).

E348 Brandenburg Gate and Torch

1968. German Youth Sports Day. Multicoloured.

E1096		10pf. Type **E348**	25	20
E1097		25pf. Stadium plan and torch	1·30	85

E349 Festival Emblem

1968. Peace Festival, Sofia.

E1098	**E349**	20pf.+5pf. mult	45	25
E1099	**E349**	25pf. multicoloured	1·00	65

1968. Principal East German Buildings (2nd series). As Type **E312**. Multicoloured.

E1100		10pf. Town Hall, Wernigerode	25	20
E1101		20pf. Moritzburg Castle, Dresden	25	20
E1102		25pf. Town Hall, Greifswald	25	20
E1103		30pf. New Palace, Potsdam	1·00	1·30

DESIGN SIZES—VERT: 10pf., 25pf. (24×29 mm). HORIZ: 20pf., 30pf. (51½×29½ mm).

E350 Walter Ulbricht

1968. 75th Birthday of Walter Ulbricht (Chairman of Council of State).

E1104	**E350**	20pf. black, red and orange	55	30

E351 Ancient Rostock

1968. 750th Anniv of Rostock. Multicoloured.

E1105		20pf. Type **E351**	25	20
E1106		25pf. Rostock, 1968	75	65

E352 Dr K. Landsteiner (physician and pathologist, birth cent)

1968. Celebrities' Annivs. (1st series).

E1107	**E352**	10pf. grey	25	20
E1108	-	15pf. black	25	20
E1109	-	20pf. brown	25	20
E1110	-	25pf. blue	25	20
E1111	-	40pf. red	1·10	85

DESIGNS: 15pf. Dr. E. Lasker (chess master, birth cent); 20pf. Hans Eisler (composer, 70th birth anniv); 25pf. Ignaz Semmelweis (physician, 150th birth anniv); 40pf. Max von Pettenkofer (hygienist, 150th birth anniv).
See also Nos. E1161/4 and E1256/61.

E353 Zlin
Z-226 Trener 6
DM-WKM
looping

1968. Aerobatics World Championships, Magdeburg. Multicoloured.

E1112	10pf. Type E353	25	20
E1113	25pf. Stunt flying	75	60

E354 At the Seaside
(Womacka)

1968. Dresden Gallery Paintings (2nd series). Multicoloured.

E1114	10pf. Type E354	25	20
E1115	15pf. Peasants Mowing Mountain Meadow (Egger-Lienz)	25	20
E1116	20pf. Portrait of a Farmer's Wife (Liebl) (vert)	25	20
E1117	40pf. Portrait of my Daughter (Venturelli) (vert)	55	25
E1118	50pf. High-School Girl (Michaelis) (vert)	55	25
E1119	70pf. Girl with Guitar (Castelli) (vert)	2·75	1·80

E355 Model Trains

1968. Leipzig Autumn Fair.

E1120	**E355** 10pf. multicoloured	45	35

E356 Spremberg Dam

1968. East German Post-War Dams. Multicoloured.

E1121	5pf. Type E356	25	20
E1122	10pf. Pohl Dam (vert)	25	20
E1123	15pf. Ohra Valley Dam (vert)	70	70
E1124	20pf. Rappbode Dam	35	35

E357 Sprinting

1968. Olympic Games, Mexico. Multicoloured.

E1125	5pf. Type E357	25	20
E1126	10pf.+5pf. Pole-vaulting (vert)	25	20
E1127	20pf.+10pf. Football (vert)	25	20
E1128	25pf. Gymnastics (vert)	25	20
E1129	40pf. Water-polo (vert)	35	25
E1130	70pf. Sculling	2·00	1·90

E358 Breendonk
Memorial, Belgium

1968. Breendonk War Victims Commem.

E1131	**E358** 25pf. multicoloured	55	25

E359 Cicindela
campestris

1968. "Useful Beetles". Multicoloured.

E1132	10pf. Type E359	25	20
E1133	15pf. Cychrus caraboides	25	20
E1134	20pf. Adalia bipunctata	25	20
E1135	25pf. Carabus arvensis ("arcensis")	2·75	2·50
E1136	30pf. Hister bipustulatus	35	25
E1137	40pf. Clerus mutillarius ("Pseudoclerops mutillarius")	35	25

E360 Lenin and Letter to Spartacus Group

1968. 50th Anniv of German November Revolution.

E1138	**E 360** 10pf. black, red and yellow	25	20
E1139	– 20pf. black, red and yellow	25	20
E1140	– 25pf. black, red and yellow	70	65

DESIGNS: 20pf. Revolutionaries and title of Spartacus newspaper Die Rote Fahne; 25pf. Karl Liebknecht and Rose Luxemburg.

E361 Lailio-cattleya alba rubra
("Maggie Raphaela")

1968. Orchids. Multicoloured.

E1141	5pf. Type E361	25	20
E1142	10pf. Paphiopedilum albertianum	25	20
E1143	15pf. Cattleya fabia	25	20
E1144	20pf. Cattleya aclaniae	25	20
E1145	40pf. Sobralia macrantha	35	25
E1146	50pf. Dendrobium alpha	2·75	1·90

E362 Trying on the
Boots

1968. Fairy Tales (3rd series). Puss in Boots. As Type E362. Designs showing different scenes.

E1147	5pf. multicoloured	25	25
E1148	10pf. multicoloured	25	25
E1149	15pf. multicoloured	1·40	1·40
E1150	20pf. multicoloured	1·40	1·40
E1151	25pf. multicoloured	25	25
E1152	30pf. multicoloured	25	25

E363 Young
Pioneers

1968. 20th Anniv of Ernst Thalmann's "Young Pioneers." Multicoloured.

E1153	10pf. Type E363	25	20
E1154	15pf. Young pioneers (diff)	95	45

1969. Principal East German Buildings (3rd series). As Type E312. Multicoloured.

E1155	5pf. Town Hall, Tangermunde (vert)	25	20
E1156	10pf. State Opera House, Berlin	25	20
E1157	20pf. Rampart Pavilion, Dresden Castle (vert)	25	20
E1158	25pf. Patrician's House, Luckau (vert)	1·40	95
E1159	30pf. Dornburg Castle	25	20
E1160	40pf. "Zum Stockfisch" Inn, Erfurt (vert)	35	25

1969. Celebrities' Anniversaries. (2nd series). As Type E352.

E1161	10pf. olive	25	20
E1162	20pf. brown	25	20
E1163	25pf. blue	1·10	60

E1164	40pf. brown	25	20

DESIGNS: 10pf. M. A. Nexo (Danish poet—birth cent.); 20pf. O. Nagel (painter—75th birth anniv); 25pf. A. von Humboldt (naturalist—bicent. of birth); 40pf. T. Fontane (writer—150th birth anniv).

E364 Pedestrian
Crossing

1969. Road Safety. Multicoloured.

E1165	5pf. Type E364	25	20
E1166	10pf. Traffic lights	25	20
E1167	20pf. Class 103 electric locomotive and railway crossing sign	25	20
E1168	25pf. Motor-vehicle overtaking	75	60

E365 "E-512"
Combine- harvester

1969. Leipzig Spring Fair. Multicoloured.

E1169	10pf. Type E365	25	20
E1170	15pf. "Planeta-Varianii" lithograph printing-press	35	30

E366 Jorinde and
Joringel

1969. Fairy Tales (4th series). Jorinde and Joringel. As Type E366, showing different scenes.

E1171	5pf. multicoloured	25	35
E1172	10pf. multicoloured	25	35
E1173	15pf. multicoloured	70	85
E1174	20pf. multicoloured	70	85
E1175	25pf. multicoloured	25	35
E1176	30pf. multicoloured	25	35

E367 Spring
Snowflake

1969. Protected Plants (2nd series). Multicoloured.

E1177	5pf. Type E367	25	20
E1178	10pf. Yellow pheasant's-eye (Adonis vernalis)	25	20
E1179	15pf. Globe flower (Trollius europaeus)	25	20
E1180	20pf. Martagon lily (Lilium martagon)	25	20
E1181	25pf. Sea holly (Eryngium maritmum)	3·75	2·40
E1182	30pf. Dactylorchis latifolia	45	25

See also Nos. E1284/9.

E368 Plantation of
Young Conifers

1969. Forest Fires Prevention. Multicoloured.

E1183	5pf. Type E368	35	25
E1184	10pf. Lumber, and resin extraction	35	25
E1185	20pf. Forest stream	35	25
E1186	25pf. Woodland camp	2·50	1·40

E369 Symbols
of the Societies

1969. 50th Anniv of League of Red Cross Societies. Multicoloured.

E1187	10pf. Type E369	35	25
E1188	15pf. Similar design with symbols in oblong	1·70	70

E370 Erythrite
(Schneeberg)

1969. East German Minerals. Multicoloured.

E1189	5pf. Type E370	25	20
E1190	10pf. Fluorite (Halsbrucke)	25	20
E1191	15pf. Galena (Neudorf)	25	20
E1192	20pf. Smoky Quartz (Lichtenberg)	25	20
E1193	25pf. Calcite (Niederrabenstein)	1·10	95
E1194	50pf. Silver (Freiberg)	35	25

E371 Women and Symbols

1969. Second D.D.R. Women's Congress.

E1195	**E371** 20pf. red and blue	25	20
E1196	– 25pf. blue and red	1·30	55

DESIGN: 25pf. Woman and Symbols (different).

1969. As Nos. E586/7 (Ulbricht), but with face values expressed in "M" (Mark).

E1197	1M. green	55	1·80
E1198	2M. brown	70	2·00

E372 Badge of
D.D.R.
Philatelists'
Association

1969. 20th Anniv of D.D.R. Stamp Exhibition, Magdeburg (1st issue).

E1199	**E372** 10pf. gold, blue and red	45	25

See also Nos. E1233/4.

E373 Armed
Volunteers

1969. Aid for Vietnam.

E1200	**E373** 10pf.+5pf. multicoloured	45	25

E374
"Development
of Youth"

1969. Int Peace Meeting, East Berlin. Multicoloured.

E1201	10pf. Type E374	85	1·20
E1202	20pf.+5pf. Berlin landmarks (50×28 mm)	85	1·20
E1203	25pf. "Workers of the World"	85	1·20

E375 Inaugural Ceremony

1969. Fifth Gymnastics and Athletic Meeting, Leipzig. Multicoloured.

E1204	5pf. Type E375	25	20
E1205	10pf.+5pf. Gymnastics	25	20
E1206	15pf. Athletes' parade	25	20
E1207	20pf.+5pf. "Sport" Art Exhibition	25	20
E1208	25pf. Athletic events	2·20	85
E1209	30pf. Presentation of colours	25	20

E376 Pierre de
Coubertin (from bust
by W. Forster)

1969. 75th Anniv of Pierre de Coubertin's Revival of
Olympic Games' Movement.
| E1210 | **E376** | 10pf. sepia, black & bl | 25 | 20 |
| E1211 | - | 25pf. sepia, blk & red | 1·10 | 1·10 |
DESIGN: 25pf. Coubertin monument, Olympia.

E377 Knight

1969. World Sports Championships. Multicoloured.
E1212	**E377**	20pf. gold, red & pur	35	25
E1213	-	20pf. multicoloured	35	25
E1214	-	20pf. multicoloured	35	25
DESIGNS AND EVENTS: No. E1212, 16th World Students'
Team Chess Championship, Dresden; No. E1213, Cycle
Wheel (World Covered Court Cycling Championships, Er-
furt); No. E1214, Ball and net (2nd World Volleyball Cup).

E378 Fair
Display
Samples

1969. Leipzig Autumn Fair.
| E1215 | **E378** | 10pf. multicoloured | 35 | 35 |

E379 Rostock

1969. 20th Anniv of German Democratic Republic. (1st
issue). Multicoloured.
E1216	10pf. Type **E379**	25	20
E1217	10pf. Neubrandenburg	25	20
E1218	10pf. Potsdam	25	20
E1219	10pf. Eisenhuttenstadt	25	20
E1220	10pf. Hoyerswerda	25	20
E1221	10pf. Magdeburg	25	20
E1222	10pf. Halle-Neustadt	25	20
E1223	10pf. Suhl	25	20
E1224	10pf. Dresden	25	20
E1225	10pf. Leipzig	25	20
E1226	10pf. Karl-Marx Stadt	25	20
E1227	10pf. East Berlin	25	20
MSE1228 88×110 mm. 1m. East Berlin
and D.D.R. emblem (30×52 mm) | 2·75 | 5·50 |

E380 Flags and Rejoicing Crowd (image scaled to 59% of
original size)

1969. 20th Anniv of German Democratic Republic (2nd
issue). Sheet 110×154 mm.
MSE1229 **E380** 1m. multicoloured | 3·00 | 5·00 |

E381 T.V. Tower,
East Berlin

1969. 20th Anniv of German Democratic Republic (3rd
issue). Completion of East Berlin T.V. Tower. Type
E381 and similar vert designs. Multicoloured.
| E1230 | 10pf. Type **E381** | 25 | 20 |
| E1231 | 20pf. "Globe" of Tower on T.V.
screen | 35 | 25 |
MSE1232 96×115 mm. 1m. T.V. Tower
and receiver | 2·10 | 6·00 |
The design of No. MSE1232 is larger, 21½×60½ mm.

E382 O. von Guericke Memorial, Cathedral
and Hotel International, Magdeburg

1969. 20th Anniv of D.D.R. Stamp Exhibition, Magdeburg
(2nd issue). Multicoloured.
| E1233 | 20pf. Type **E382** | 25 | 20 |
| E1234 | 40pf.+10pf. Von Guericke's
vacuum experiment | 1·60 | 1·00 |

E383 Ryvangen
Memorial

1969. War Victims' Memorial, Ryvangen (Copenhagen).
| E1235 | **E383** | 25pf. multicoloured | 1·00 | 25 |

E384 U.F.I. Emblem

1969. 36th Int Fairs Union (U.F.I.) Congress, Leipzig.
| E1236 | **E384** | 10pf. multicoloured | 25 | 25 |
| E1237 | **E384** | 15pf. multicoloured | 2·20 | 50 |

E385 I.L.O.
Emblem

1969. 50th Anniv of I.L.O.
| E1238 | **E385** | 20pf. silver and green | 25 | 20 |
| E1239 | **E385** | 25pf. silver & mauve | 2·20 | 50 |

E386 University
Seal and
Building

1969. 550th Anniv of Rostock University. Multicoloured.
| E1240 | 10pf. Type **E386** | 35 | 20 |
| E1241 | 15pf. Steam-turbine rotor and
curve (University emblem) | 1·80 | 40 |

E387
"Horseman"
Pastry-mould

1969. Lausitz Folk Art.
E1242	**E387**	10pf. brn, blk & flesh	1·50	1·50
E1243	-	20pf.+5pf. mult	50	50
E1244	-	50pf. multicoloured	2·40	2·40

DESIGNS: 20pf. Plate; 50pf. Pastry in form of Negro couple.

E388 Antonov An-24B

1969. Interflug Aircraft. Multicoloured.
E1245	20pf. Type **E388**	25	20
E1246	25pf. Ilyushin Il-18	1·70	1·50
E1247	30pf. Tupolev Tu-134	25	25
E1248	50pf. Mil Mi-8 helicopter
DM-SPA	35	25

E389 Siberian Teacher
(Svechnikov)

1969. Dresden Gallery Paintings (3rd series).
Multicoloured.
E1249	5pf. Type **E389**	25	20
E1250	10pf. Steel-worker (Serov)	25	20
E1251	20pf. Still Life (Aslamasjan)	25	20
E1252	20pf. A Warm Day (Romas)	1·50	1·50
E1253	40pf. Springtime Again
(Kabatchek)	35	25
E1254	50pf. Man by the River (Ma-
kovsky)	35	25

1970. Coil Stamp. As Nos. E577 etc, but value expressed
in "M".
| E1255 | **E196** | 1m. olive | 1·20 | 4·25 |

1970. Celebrities Annivs. (3rd series). As Type **E352**.
E1256	5pf. blue	35	20
E1257	10pf. brown	35	20
E1258	15pf. blue	35	20
E1259	20pf. purple	50	20
E1260	25pf. blue	3·00	1·00
E1261	40pf. red	60	25
DESIGNS: 5pf. E. Barlach (sculptor and playwright; birth
cent); 10pf. J. Gutenberg (printer; 500th death anniv)
(1968); 15pf. K. Tucholsky (author; 80th birth anniv); 20pf.
Beethoven (birth bicent); 25pf. F. Holderlin (poet; birth bicent); 40 pf G. W. F. Hegel (philosopher; birth bicent).

E390 Red fox

1970. Int Fur Auction, Leipzig. Multicoloured.
E1262	10pf. Rabbit	25	20
E1263	20pf. Type **E390**	25	20
E1264	25pf. European mink	4·00	3·75
E1265	40pf. Common hamster	50	25

E391 "Little Brother
and Little Sister"

1970. Fairy Tales (5th series). Little Brother and Little Sister.
E1266	**E 391**	5pf. multicoloured	35	50
E1267	-	10pf. multicoloured	35	50
E1268	-	15pf. multicoloured	85	1·00
E1269	-	20pf. multicoloured	85	1·00
E1270	-	25pf. multicoloured	35	50
E1271	-	30pf. multicoloured	35	50
DESIGNS: 10pf. to 30pf. showing different scenes.

E392 Telephone and
Electrical Switchgear

1970. Leipzig Spring Fair. Multicoloured.
| E1272 | 10pf. Type E **392** | 25 | 20 |
| E1273 | 15pf. High-voltage transformer
(vert) | 75 | 35 |

E393 Horseman's
Gravestone (A.D. 700)

1970. Archaeological Discoveries.
E1274	**E393**	10pf. olive, blk & grn	35	25
E1275	-	20pf. black, yell & red	35	25
E1276	-	25pf. grn, blk & yell	1·20	1·70
E1277	-	40pf. chestnut, black and
brown	35	25
DESIGNS: 20pf. Helmet (A.D. 500); 25pf. Bronze basin
(1000 B.C.); 40pf. Clay drum (2500 B.C.).

E394 Lenin and "Iskra" (= the Spark)
press

1970. Birth Centenary of Lenin. Multicoloured.
| E1278 | 10pf. Type **E394** | 25 | 20 |
| E1279 | 20pf. Lenin and Clara Zetkin | 25 | 20 |
| E1280 | 25pf. Lenin and State and
Revolution (book) | 2·75 | 2·20 |
| E1281 | 40pf. Lenin Monument,
Eisleben | 25 | 20 |
| E1282 | 70pf. Lenin Square, East Berlin | 50 | 25 |
MSE1283 118×84 mm. 1m. Lenin (vert) | 2·75 | 6·00 |

1970. Protected Plants (3rd series). Vert designs as Type
E367. Multicoloured.
| E1284 | 10pf. Sea kale (Crambe
maritima) | 25 | 20 |
| E1285 | 20pf. Pasque flower (Pulsatilla
vulgaris) | 25 | 20 |
| E1286 | 25pf. Fringed gentian (Gentiana
ciliata) | 2·40 | 2·75 |
| E1287 | 30pf. Military orchid (Orchis
militaris) | 25 | 25 |
| E1288 | 40pf. Labrador tea (Ledum
palustre) | 35 | 25 |
| E1289 | 70pf. Round-leaved wintergreen
(Pyrola rotundifolia) | 50 | 35 |

E395 Capture of
the Reichstag, 1945

1970. 25th Anniv of "Liberation from Fascism".
Multicoloured.
| E1290 | 10pf. Type **E395** | 35 | 20 |
| E1291 | 20pf. Newspaper headline,
Kremlin and State Building,
East Berlin | 35 | 20 |
| E1292 | 25pf. C.M.E.A. Building, Moscow
and flags | 1·80 | 1·00 |
MSE1293 135×105 mm. 70pf. Buchen-
wald Monument (horiz) | 2·40 | 5·00 |

E396 Shortwave
Aerial

1970. 25th Anniv of D.D.R. Broadcasting Service.
Multicoloured.
| E1294 | 10pf. Type **E396** | 85 | 85 |
| E1295 | 15pf. Radio Station, East Berlin
(horiz) (50×28 mm) | 1·20 | 1·20 |

E397 Globe and
Ear of Corn

1970. Fifth World Corn and Bread Congress, Dresden.
Multicoloured.
| E1296 | 20pf. Type **E397** | 1·20 | 1·20 |
| E1297 | 25pf. Palace of Culture and ear
of corn | 1·20 | 1·20 |

E398 Fritz Heckert Medal

1970. 25th Annivs of German Confederation of Trade Unions and World Trade Union Federation ("Federation Syndicale Mondiale"). Multicoloured.

E1298		20pf. Type **E398**	25	20
E1299		25pf. F.S.M. Emblem	85	75

E399 Gods Amon, Shu and Tefnut

1970. Sudanese Archaeological Excavations by Humboldt University Expedition. Multicoloured.

E1300		10pf. Type **E399**	25	20
E1301		15pf. King Arnekhamani	25	20
E1302		20pf. Cattle frieze	25	20
E1303		25pf. Prince Arka	1·50	1·00
E1304		30pf. God Arensnuphis (vert)	25	20
E1305		40pf. War elephants and prisoners	25	20
E1306		50pf. God Apedemak	25	20

The above designs reproduce carvings unearthed at the Lions' Temple, Musawwarat, Sudan.

E400 Road Patrol

1970. 25th Anniv of "Deutsche Volkspolizei" (police force). Multicoloured.

E1307		5pf. Type **E400**	35	25
E1308		10pf. Policewoman with children	35	25
E1309		15pf. Radio patrol car	35	25
E1310		20pf. Railway policeman and Class SVT18.16 diesel-hydraulic locomotive	35	25
E1311		25pf. River police in patrol boat	3·00	60

E401 D.K.B. Emblem

1970. 25th Anniv of "Deutscher Kulturbund" (cultural assn).

E1312	**E401**	10pf. brown, silver and blue	3·25	3·75
E1313	-	25pf. brown, gold and blue	3·25	3·75

DESIGN: 25pf. Johannes Becher medal.

E402 Arms of D.D.R. and Poland

1970. 20th Anniv of Gorlitz Agreement on Oder–Neisse Border.

E1314	**E402**	20pf. multicoloured	50	30

E403 Vaulting

1970. Third Children and Young People's Sports Days. Multicoloured.

E1315		10pf. Type **E403**	25	20
E1316		20pf.+5pf. Hurdling	60	25

E404 Boy Pioneer with Neckerchief

1970. Sixth Young Pioneers Meeting. Cottbus. Multicoloured.

E1317		10pf.+5pf. Type **E404**	35	50
E1318		25pf.+5pf. Girl pioneer with neckerchief	35	50

Nos. E1317/18 were issued together, *se-tenant*, forming a composite design.

E405 Cecilienhof Castle

1970. 25th Anniv of Potsdam Agreement.

E1319	**E405**	10pf. yellow, red and black	35	45
E1320	-	20pf. black, red and yellow	35	45
E1321	-	25pf. black and red	35	45

DESIGNS—VERT: 20pf. "Potsdam Agreement" in four languages. HORIZ (77×28 mm): 25pf. Conference delegates around the table.

E406 Pocket-watch and Wristwatch

1970. Leipzig Autumn Fair.

E1322	**E406**	10pf. multicoloured	50	25

E407 T. Neubauer and M. Poser

1970. "Anti-Fascist Resistance".

E1323	**E407**	20pf. purple, red & bl	25	25
E1324	-	25pf. olive and red	35	35

DESIGN—VERT: 25pf. "Motherland"—detail from Soviet War Memorial, Treptow, Berlin.

E408 Pres. Ho-Chi-Minh

1970. Aid for Vietnam and Ho-Chi-Minh Commemoration.

E1325	**E408**	20pf.+5pf. black, red and pink	60	25

E409 Compass and Map

1970. World "Orienteering" Championships. East Germany. Multicoloured.

E1326		10pf. Type E **409**	25	20
E1327		25pf. Runner and three map sections	1·70	50

E410 *Forester* Scharf's Birthday (Nagel)

1970. *The Art of Otto Nagel, Kathe Kollwitz and Ernst Barlach.*

E1328	**E410**	10pf. multicoloured	25	20
E1329	-	20pf. multicoloured	25	20
E1330	-	25pf. brown & mauve	1·50	1·60
E1331	-	30pf. black and pink	25	20
E1332	-	40pf. black and yellow	25	20
E1333	-	50pf. black and yellow	35	25

DESIGNS: 20pf. *Portrait of a Young Girl* (Nagel); 25pf. *No More War* (Kollwitz); 30pf. *Mother and Child* (Kollwitz); 40pf. Sculptured head from Gustrow Cenotaph (Barlach); 50pf. *The Flute-player* (Barlach).

E411 "The Little Trumpeter" (Weineck Memorial, Halle)

1970. Second National Youth Stamp Exhibition, Karl-Marx-Stadt. Multicoloured.

E1334		10pf. Type **E411**	25	50
E1335		15pf.+5pf. East German 25pf. stamp of 1959	25	50

E412 Flags Emblem

1970. "Comrades-in-Arms". Warsaw Pact Military Manoeuvres.

E1336	**E412**	10pf. multicoloured	25	25
E1337	**E412**	20pf. multicoloured	35	35

E413 Musk Ox

1970. Animals in East Berlin "Tierpark" (Zoo). Multicoloured.

E1338		10pf. Type **E413**	50	25
E1339		15pf. Whale-headed Stork	50	25
E1340		20pf. Addax	85	50
E1341		25pf. Sun bear	7·25	7·25

E414 U.N. Emblem and Headquarters, New York

1970. 25th Anniv of United Nations.

E1342	**E414**	20pf. multicoloured	75	35

E415 Engels

1970. 150th Birth Anniv of Friedrich Engels.

E1343	**E415**	10pf. black, grey and orange	35	20
E1344	-	20pf. blk, grn & orge	35	20
E1345	-	25pf. blk, red & orge	1·80	1·00

DESIGNS: 20pf. Engels, Marx and *Communist Manifesto*; 25pf. Engels and *Anti-Duhring*.

E416 *Epiphyllum hybr*

1970. Cacti Cultivation in D.D.R. Multicoloured.

E1346		5pf. Type **E416**	25	20
E1347		10pf. *Astrophytum myriostigma*	25	20
E1348		15pf. *Echinocereus salm-dyckianus*	25	20
E1349		20pf. *Selenicereus grandiflorus*	25	20
E1350		25pf. *Hamatoc setispinus*	2·40	2·20
E1351		30pf. *Mamillaria boolii*	30	20

1970. Birth Bicentenary of Beethoven. As No. E1259, but colour and face value changed, in sheet 81×55 mm.

MSE1352		1m. green	2·40	3·00

E417 Dancer's Mask, Bismarck Archipelago

1971. Exhibits from the Ethnological Museum, Leipzig.

E1353	**E417**	10pf. multicoloured	25	20
E1354	-	20pf. brown & orange	25	20
E1355	-	25pf. multicoloured	1·10	85
E1356	-	40pf. brown and red	35	20

DESIGNS: 20pf. Bronze head, Benin; 25pf. Tea-pot, Thailand; 40pf. Zapotec earthenware Jaguar-god, Mexico.

E418 "Venus 5"

1971. Soviet Space Research. Multicoloured.

E1357		20pf. Type **E418**	35	50
E1358		20pf. Orbital space station	35	50
E1359		20pf. "Luna 10" and "Luna 16"	75	85
E1360		20pf. Various "Soyuz" spacecraft	75	85
E1361		20pf. "Proton 1" satellite and "Vostok" rocket	75	85
E1362		20pf. "Molniya 1" communications satellite	75	85
E1363		20pf. Gagarin and "Vostok 1"	35	50
E1364		20pf. Leonov in space	35	50

E419 K. Liebknecht

1971. Birth Centenaries of Karl Liebknecht and Rosa Luxemburg (revolutionaries).

E1365	**E419**	20pf. mauve, gold and black	60	60
E1366	-	25pf. mauve, gold and black	60	60

DESIGN: 25pf. Rosa Luxemburg.

E420 J. R. Becher (poet)

1971. Celebrities' Birth Anniversaries.

E1367	**E420**	5pf. brown	25	20
E1368	-	10pf. blue	25	20
E1369	-	15pf. black	25	20
E1370	-	20pf. purple	25	20
E1371	-	25pf. green	1·00	85
E1372	-	50pf. blue	35	25

DESIGNS: 5pf. (80th birth anniv); 10pf. H. Mann (writer—birth cent); 15pf. J. Heartfield (artist—80th birth anniv); 20pf. W. Bredel (70th birth anniv); 25pf. F. Mehring (politician—125th birth anniv); 50pf. J. Kepler (astronomer—400th birth anniv).

See also Nos. E1427 and E1451/5.

E421 Soldier and Army Badge

1971. 15th Anniv of National People's Army.

E1373	**E421**	20pf. multicoloured	50	30

E422 "Sket" Mobile Ore-crusher

1971. Leipzig Spring Fair. Multicoloured.

E1374	10pf. Type **E422**	25	20
E1375	15pf. Dredger "Takraf"	25	20

E423 Proclamation of the Commune

1971. Centenary of Paris Commune.

E1376	**E423** 10pf. black, brown and red	35	25
E1377	– 20pf. black, brown and red	35	25
E1378	– 25pf. black, brown and red	80	75
E1379	– 30pf. black, grey and red	35	25

DESIGNS: 20pf. Women at the Place Blanche barricade; 25pf. Cover of *L'Internationale*; 30pf. Title page of Karl Marx's *The Civil War in France*.

E424 "Lunokhod 1" on Moon's Surface

1971. Moon Mission of "Lunokhod 1".

E1380	**E424** 20pf. turquoise, blue and red	85	50

E425 St. Mary's Church

1971. Berlin Buildings. Multicoloured.

E1381	10pf. Type **E425**	25	20
E1382	15pf. Kopenick Castle (horiz)	25	20
E1383	20pf. Old Library (horiz)	25	20
E1384	25pf. Ermeler House	4·00	3·50
E1385	50pf. New Guardhouse (horiz)	35	25
E1386	70pf. National Gallery (horiz)	50	25

E426 "The Discus-thrower"

1971. 20th Anniv of D.D.R. National Olympics Committee.

E1387	**E426** 20pf. multicoloured	1·10	35

E427 Handclasp and XXV Emblem

1971. 25th Anniv of Socialist Unity Party.

E1388	**E427** 20pf. black, red and gold	50	25

E428 Schleife Costume

1971. Sorbian Dance Costumes. Multicoloured.

E1389	10pf. Type **E428**	25	25
E1390	20pf. Hoyerswerda	25	25
E1391	25pf. Cottbus	1·00	1·20
E1392	40pf. Kamenz	35	35

For 10pf. and 20pf. in smaller size, see Nos. E1443/4.

E429 Self-portrait, c. 1500

1971. 500th Birth Anniv of Albrecht Durer. Paintings. Multicoloured.

E1393	10pf. Type **E429**	35	25
E1394	40pf. *The Three Peasants*	35	25
E1395	70pf. *Philipp Melanchthon*	2·40	1·20

E430 Construction Worker

1971. Eighth S.E.D. Party Conference.

E1396	**E430** 5pf. multicoloured	25	20
E1397	– 10pf. multicoloured	25	20
E1398	– 20pf. multicoloured	25	20
E1400	– 20pf. gold, red and mauve	50	25
E1399	– 25pf. multicoloured	55	50

DESIGNS: 10pf. Technician; 20pf. (No. E1398) Farm girl; 20pf. (No. E1400) Conference emblem (smaller, 23×29 mm); 25pf. Soldier.

E432 "Internees"

1971. 20th Anniv of International Resistance Federation (F.I.R.). Lithographs from Fritz Cremer's *Buchenwaldzyklus*.

E1401	**E432** 20pf. black & yellow	75	85
E1402	– 25pf. black and blue	75	85

DESIGN: 25pf. *Attack on Guard*.

E433 Cherry stone with 180 Carved Heads

1971. Art Treasures of Dresden's Green Vaults. Multicoloured.

E1403	5pf. Type **E433**	25	20
E1404	10pf. Insignia of the Golden Fleece, c. 1730	25	20
E1405	15pf. Nuremberg jug, c. 1530	25	20
E1406	20pf. Mounted Moorish drummer figurine, c. 1720	25	20
E1407	25pf. Writing-case, 1562	1·00	1·10
E1408	30pf. St. George medallion, c. 1570	25	20

E434 Mongolian Arms

1971. 50th Anniv of Mongolian People's Republic.

E1409	**E434** 20pf. multicoloured	50	35

E435 Child's Face

1971. 25th Anniv of UNICEF.

E1410	**E435** 20pf. multicoloured	50	30

E436 Servicemen

1971. Tenth Anniv of Berlin Wall. Multicoloured.

E1411	20pf. Type **E436**	1·00	35
E1412	35pf. Brandenburg Gate	2·30	1·60

E437 *Ivan Franko* (liner)

1971. East German Shipbuilding Industry.

E1413	**E437** 10pf. brown	25	20
E1414	– 15pf. blue and brown	25	20
E1415	– 20pf. green	25	20
E1416	– 25pf. blue	1·60	1·50
E1417	– 40pf. brown	25	20
E1418	– 50pf. blue	25	20

DESIGNS: 15pf. *Irkutsk* (freighter); 20pf. *Rostock* freighter, 1966; 25pf. *Junge Welt* (fish-factory ship); 40pf. *Hansel* (container ship); 50pf. *Akademik Kurchatov* (research ship).

E438 Vietnamese Woman and Child

1971. Aid for Vietnam.

E1419	**E438** 10pf.+5pf. mult	50	30

E439 MAG-Butadien Plant

1971. Leipzig Autumn Fair.

E1420	**E439** 10pf. vio, mve & grn	25	20
E1421	– 25pf. violet, grn & bl	40	35

DESIGN: 25pf. SKL reactor plant.

E440 Upraised Arms (motif by J. Heartfield)

1971. Racial Equality Year.

E1422	**E440** 35pf. black, sil & bl	50	30

E441 Tupolev Tu-134 Mail Plane at Airport

1971. Philatelists' Day.

E1423	**E441** 10pf.+5pf. blue, red and green	35	25
E1424	– 25pf. red, green & bl	65	60

DESIGN: 25pf. Milestone and Zurner's measuring cart.

E442 Wiltz Memorial, Luxembourg

1971. Monuments. Multicoloured.

E1425	25pf. Type **E442**	35	25
E1426	35pf. Karl Marx monument, Karl-Marx-Stadt	60	25

1971. 150th Birth Anniv of R. Virchow (physician). As Type **E420**.

E1427	40pf. plum	60	25

E443 German Violin

1971. Musical Instruments in Markneukirchen Museum. Multicoloured.

E1428	10pf. North African "darbuka"	25	20
E1429	15pf. Mongolian "morin chuur"	25	20
E1430	20pf. Type **E443**	25	20
E1431	25pf. Italian mandolin	25	20
E1432	40pf. Bohemian bagpipes	25	25
E1433	50pf. Sudanese "kasso"	1·50	1·50

E444 "Dahlta O 10 A" Theodolite

1971. 125th Anniv of Carl Zeiss Optical Works, Jena.

E1434	**E444** 10pf. black, red & bl	75	75
E1435	– 20pf. black, red & bl	75	75
E1436	– 25pf. blue, yellow and ultramarine	75	75

DESIGNS—VERT: 20pf. "Ergaval" microscope. HORIZ (52×29 mm) 25pf. Planetarium.

E445 Donkey and Windmill

1971. Fairy Tales (6th series). As Type **E445**. *The Town Musicians of Bremen*.

E1437	5pf. multicoloured	30	30
E1438	10pf. multicoloured	30	30
E1439	15pf. multicoloured	85	1·20
E1440	20pf. multicoloured	85	1·20
E1441	25pf. multicoloured	30	30
E1442	30pf. multicoloured	30	30

1971. Sorbian Dance Costumes. As Nos. E1389/90 but smaller, size 23×28 mm.

E1443	**E428** 10pf. multicoloured	35	25
E1444	– 20pf. multicoloured	85	60

E446 Tobogganing

1971. Winter Olympic Games, Sapporo, Japan (1972).

E1445	**E446** 5pf. black, green and mauve	25	20
E1446	– 10pf.+5pf. blk, bl & mve	25	20
E1447	– 15pf.+5pf. black, grn & bl	25	20
E1448	– 20pf. black, mauve & violet	25	20
E1449	– 25pf. black, violet & mauve	2·10	1·70
E1450	– 70pf. black, blue and violet	35	25

DESIGNS: 10pf. Figure skating; 15pf. Speed skating; 20pf. Cross-country skiing; 25pf. Biathlon; 70pf. Ski jumping.

1972. German Celebrities. As Type **E420**.

E1451	10pf. green	25	20
E1452	20pf. mauve	25	20
E1453	25pf. blue	25	20
E1454	35pf. brown	25	20
E1455	50pf. lilac	1·60	1·80

CELEBRITIES: 10pf. J. Tralow (writer); 20pf. L. Frank (writer); 25pf. K. A. Kocor (composer); 35pf. H. Schliemann (archaeologist); 50pf. Caroline Neuber (actress).

E447 Gypsum from Eisleben

1972. Minerals. Multicoloured.

E1456	5pf. Type **E447**	35	25
E1457	10pf. Zinnwaldite, Zinnwald	35	25
E1458	20pf. Malachite, Ullersreuth	35	25
E1459	25pf. Amethyst, Wiesenbad	35	25
E1460	35pf. Halite, Merkers	35	25
E1461	50pf. Proustite, Schneeberg	1·60	1·60

E448 Vietnamese Woman

1972. Aid for Vietnam.

E1462	**E448** 10pf.+5pf. mult	50	25

E449 Soviet Exhibition Hall

1972. Leipzig Spring Fair. Multicoloured.

E1463	10pf. Type **E449**	25	20
E1464	25pf. East German and Soviet flags	35	35

E450 Anemometer of 1896 and Koppen's Chart of 1876

1972. International Meteorologists Meeting, Leipzig. Three sheets, each 85×57 mm. Multicoloured.

MSE1465	20pf. Type **E450**; 35pf. Weather station and clouds; 70pf. Satellite and weather map	3·25	4·00

E451 W.H.O. Emblem

1972. World Health Day.

E1466	**E451** 35pf. ultramarine, silver and blue	50	30

E452 Kamov Ka-26 Helicopter

1972. East German Aircraft. Multicoloured.

E1467	5pf. Type **E452**	25	25
E1468	10pf. Letov Z-37 Cmelak crop-sprayer DM-SMC	25	25
E1469	35pf. Ilyushin Il-62M	35	25
E1470	1m. Ilyushin Il-62M	1·80	1·80

E453 Wrestling

1972. Olympic Games, Munich. Multicoloured.

E1471	5pf. Type **E453**	25	20
E1472	10pf.+5pf. High-diving	25	20
E1473	20pf. Pole-vaulting	25	20
E1474	25pf.+10pf. Rowing	25	25
E1475	35pf. Handball	35	25
E1476	70pf. Gymnastics	4·00	2·75

E454 Soviet and East German Flags

1972. 25th Anniv of German–Soviet Friendship Society. Multicoloured.

E1477	10pf. Type **E454**	1·60	1·20
E1478	20pf. Brezhnev (U.S.S.R.) and Honecker (D.D.R.)	1·60	1·20

E455 Steel Workers

1972. Trade Unions Federation Congress.

E1479	**E455** 10pf. pur, orge & brn	50	30
E1480	– 35pf. blue and brown	50	30

DESIGN: 35pf. Students.

E456 "Karneol" Rose

1972. International Rose Exhibition. German Species. Multicoloured.

E1481	5pf. Type **E456**	25	20
E1482	10pf. "Berger's Rose"	25	20
E1497	10pf. "Berger's Rose"	25	25
E1483	15pf. "Charme"	2·10	2·10
E1484	20pf. "Izetka Spreeathen"	25	20
E1485	25pf. "Kopernicker Sommer"	25	20
E1498	25pf. "Kopernicker Sommer"	1·70	75
E1486	35pf. "Professor Knoll"	25	20
E1499	35pf. "Professor Knoll"	1·70	75

Nos. E1497/9 are smaller, size 24×28 mm.

E457 *Portrait of Young Man*

1972. 500th Birth Anniv of Lucas Cranach the Elder. Multicoloured.

E1487	5pf. Type **E457**	25	25
E1488	20pf. *Mother and Child*	25	25
E1489	25pf. *Margarete Luther*	35	35
E1490	70pf. *Nymph* (horiz)	3·00	4·25

E458 Compass and Motor Cyclist

1972. Sports and Technical Sciences Association. Multicoloured.

E1491	5pf. Type **E458**	25	25
E1492	10pf. Light airplane and parachute	25	25
E1493	20pf. Target and obstacle race	25	25
E1494	25pf. Radio set and Morse key	1·00	1·00
E1495	35pf. *Wilhelm Pieck* (brigantine) and propeller	25	25

E459 Young Worker Reading (J. Damme)

1972. Int Book Year.

E1496	**E459** 50pf. multicoloured	85	50

E460 Overhead Projector

1972. Leipzig Autumn Fair.

E1500	**E460** 10pf. black and red	25	25
E1501	– 25pf. black and green	35	35

DESIGN—HORIZ: 25pf. Slide projector.

E461 G. Dimitrov

1972. 90th Birth Anniv of Georgi Dimitrov (Bulgarian statesman).

E1502	**E461** 20pf. black and red	60	35

E462 Catching Birds (Egyptian relief painting, c. 2400 B.C.)

1972. "Interartes" Stamp Exhibition, East Berlin. Multicoloured.

E1503	10pf. Type **E462**	25	20
E1504	15pf.+5pf. *Persian Spearman* (glazed tile, c. 500 B.C.)	1·20	1·10
E1505	20pf. *Anatolian tapestry c. 1400 B.C*	25	20
E1506	35pf.+5pf. *The Grapesellers* (Max Lingner, 1949) (horiz)	25	20

E463 Red Cross Team and Patient

1972. East German Red Cross.

E1507	**E463** 10pf. ultramarine, blue and red	50	35
E1508	– 15pf. ultramarine, blue and red	50	35
E1509	– 35pf. red, blue and ultramarine	50	35

DESIGNS—VERT: 15pf. Sea-rescue launch. HORIZ (50½×28 mm): 35pf. World map on cross, and transport.

E464 Terrestrial Globe (J. Praetorius, 1568)

1972. Terrestrial and Celestial Globes. Multicoloured.

E1510	5pf. Arab celestial globe, 1279	25	25
E1511	10pf. Type **E464**	25	25
E1512	15pf. Globe clock (J. Reinhold and G. Roll, 1586)	3·25	3·25
E1513	20pf. Globe clock (J. Burgi, 1590)	25	25
E1514	25pf. Armillary sphere (J. Moeller, 1687)	25	25
E1515	35pf. Heraldic celestial globe, 1690	35	35

E465 Monument

1972. German–Polish Resistance Memorial, Berlin, Inauguration.

E1516	**E465** 25pf. multicoloured	60	30

E466 Educating Juveniles

1972. Juvenile Inventions Exhibition. Multicoloured.

E1517	10pf. Type **E466**	35	35
E1518	25pf. Youths with welding machine	35	35

E467 "Mauz and Hoppel" (Cat and Hare)

1972. Children's T.V. Characters. Multicoloured.

E1519	5pf. Type **E467**	30	35
E1520	10pf. "Fuchs and Elster" (Fox and Magpie)	30	35
E1521	15pf. "Herr Uhn" (Eagle Owl)	1·10	1·20
E1522	20pf. "Frau Igel and Borstel" (Hedgehogs)	1·10	1·20
E1523	25pf. "Schuffel and Pieps" (Dog and Mouse)	30	35
E1524	35pf. "Paulchen" (Paul from the children's library)	30	35

E468 "The Snow Queen"

1972. Fairy Tales (7th series). As Type **E468**. *The Snow Queen* (Hans Christian Andersen).

E1525	5pf. multicoloured	30	40
E1526	10pf. multicoloured	85	1·20
E1527	15pf. multicoloured	30	40
E1528	20pf. multicoloured	30	40
E1529	25pf. multicoloured	85	1·20
E1530	35pf. multicoloured	30	40

E469 H. Heine

1972. 175th Birth Anniv of Heinrich Heine (poet). Sheet 60×86 mm.

MSE1531	**E469** 1m. black, red and green	2·40	2·40

E470 Arms of U.S.S.R.

1972. 50th Anniv of U.S.S.R.

E1532	**E470** 20pf. multicoloured	60	30

E471 Leninplatz, East Berlin

1973. (a) Size 29×24 mm.

E1533	– 5pf. green	35	35

E1534	-	10pf. green	60	35
E1535	-	15pf. mauve	60	35
E1536	**E471**	20pf. mauve	1·20	45
E1537	-	25pf. green	1·50	35
E1538	-	30pf. orange	60	35
E1539	-	35pf. blue	1·20	50
E1540	-	40pf. violet	75	35
E1541	-	50pf. blue	85	35
E1542	-	60pf. purple	1·20	35
E1543	-	70pf. brown	1·10	35
E1544	-	80pf. blue	1·50	35
E1545	-	1m. green	1·80	35
E1546	-	2m. red	2·50	35
E1546a	-	3m. mauve	4·25	1·20

(b) Size 22×18 mm.

E2197		5pf. green	25	20
E1548		10pf. green	60	45
E2198		10pf. green	35	20
E2199		15pf. mauve	60	35
E2200	**E471**	20pf. mauve	75	25
E1549a		25pf. green	60	35
E2202	-	30pf. orange	75	60
E2203	-	35pf. blue	75	50
E2204	-	40pf. violet	1·50	60
E2205	-	50pf. blue	85	50
E2206	-	60pf. purple	1·10	55
E2207	-	70pf. brown	1·10	75
E2208	-	80pf. blue	1·30	85
E2209	-	1m. green	1·50	1·00
E2210	-	2m. red	2·75	1·50
E2211	-	3m. mauve	4·25	1·80

DESIGNS: 5pf. Eastern white pelican and Alfred Brehm House, Tierpark, Berlin; 10pf. (Nos. E1534, E1548) Neptune Fountain and Rathausstrasse, Berlin; 15pf. Apartment Blocks, Fishers' Island, Berlin; 25pf. TV Tower, Alexander Square, Berlin; 30 pf, Workers' Memorial, Halle; 35pf. Karl-Marx-Stadt; 40pf. Brandenburg Gate Berlin; 50pf. New Guardhouse, Berlin; 60pf. Crown Gate and Zwinger, Dresden; 70pf. Old Town Hall, Leipzig; 80pf. Rostock-Warnemunde; 1m. Soviet War Memorial, Treptow; 2, 3m. Arms of East Germany.

E472 M. da Caravaggio

1973. Cultural Anniversaries.

E1551	**E472**	5pf. brown	1·10	1·10
E1552	-	10pf. green	25	20
E1553	-	20pf. purple	25	20
E1554	-	25pf. blue	25	20
E1555	-	35pf. red	25	20

PORTRAITS AND ANNIVERSARIES: 5pf. (painter, 400th birth anniv); 10pf. Friedrich Wolf (dramatist, 85th birth anniv); 20pf. Max Reger (composer, birth cent.); 25pf. Max Reinhardt (impressario, birth cent.); 35pf. Johannes Dieckmann (politician, 80th birth anniv).

E473 "Lebachia speciosa"

1973. Fossils in Palaeontological Collection, Berlin Natural History Museum. Multicoloured.

E1556	10pf. Type **E473**	25	20
E1557	15pf. "Spheronopteris hollandica"	25	20
E1558	20pf. "Pterodactylus kochi"	25	20
E1559	25pf. "Botryopteris"	25	20
E1560	35pf. "Archaeopteryx lithographica"	25	20
E1561	70pf. "Odontopleura ovata"	2·20	2·10

E474 Copernicus

1973. 500th Birth Anniv of Copernicus.

E1562	**E474**	70pf. multicoloured	1·20	60

E475 National Flags

1973. Tenth World Youth Festival, Berlin (1st issue). Multicoloured.

E1563	10pf.+5pf. Type **E475**	25	25
E1564	25pf.+5pf. Youths and peace dove	35	35

See also Nos. E1592/6.

E476 Bobsleigh Course

1973. 15th World Bobsleigh Championships, Oberhof.

E1565	**E476**	35pf. multicoloured	60	50

E477 Combine Harvester

1973. Leipzig Spring Fair. Multicoloured.

E1566	10pf. Type E **477**	25	25
E1567	25pf. Automatic lathe	50	50

E478 Firecrests

1973. Songbirds. Multicoloured.

E1568	5pf. Type **E478**	25	25
E1569	10pf. White-winged crossbill	25	25
E1570	15pf. Bohemian waxwing	25	25
E1571	20pf. Bluethroats	25	25
E1572	25pf. Eurasian goldfinch	25	25
E1573	35pf. Golden oriole	25	25
E1574	40pf. Grey wagtail	25	25
E1575	60pf. Wallcreeper	3·75	3·75

E479 Class 211 Electric Locomotive No. 200-3

1973. Railway Rolling Stock. Multicoloured.

E1576	5pf. Type **E479**	35	25
E1577	10pf. Refrigerator wagon	35	25
E1578	20pf. Long-distance passenger carriage	35	25
E1579	25pf. Tank wagon	35	25
E1580	35pf. Double-deck carriage	35	25
E1581	85pf. Passenger carriage	3·00	3·00

E480 *King Lear* (directed by W. Langhoff)

1973. Famous Theatrical Productions. Multicoloured.

E1582	10pf. Type **E480**	25	20
E1583	25pf. *A Midsummer Night's Dream* (opera) (Benjamin Britten) (directed by Walter Felsenstein)	25	20
E1584	35pf. *Mother Courage* (directed by Berthold Brecht)	1·10	1·00

E481 H. Matern

1973. 80th Birth Anniv of Hermann Matern (politician).

E1585	**E481**	40pf. red	60	35

E482 Goethe and House

1973. Cultural Celebrities and Houses in Weimar. Multicoloured.

E1586	10pf. Type **E482**	25	20
E1587	15pf. C. M. Wieland (writer)	25	20
E1588	20pf. F. Schiller (writer)	25	20
E1589	25pf. J. G. Herder (writer)	25	20
E1590	35pf. Lucas Cranach the Elder (painter)	25	20
E1591	50pf. Franz Liszt (composer)	3·00	2·00

E483 Firework Display

1973. World Festival of Youth and Students, East Berlin (2nd issue). Multicoloured.

E1592	5pf. Type **E483**	25	20
E1593	15pf. Students ("Int Solidarity")	25	20
E1594	20pf. Young workers ("Economic Integration")	25	20
E1595	30pf. Students ("Aid for Young Nations")	1·60	75
E1596	35pf. Youth and Students' Emblems	25	20
MSE1597	86×107 mm. 50pf. Emblem and Brandenburg Gate (26.7)	1·70	1·20

E484 W. Ulbricht

1973. Death of Walter Ulbricht.

E1598	**E484**	20pf. black	85	50

E485 Power Network

1973. Tenth Anniv of "Peace" United Energy Supply System.

E1599	**E485**	35pf. orge, pur & bl	60	50

E486 "Leisure Activities"

1973. Leipzig Autumn Fair. Multicoloured.

E1600	10pf. Type **E486**	25	20
E1601	25pf. Yacht, guitar and power drill	50	35

E487 Militiaman and Emblem

1973. 20th Anniv of Workers Militia. Multicoloured.

E1602	10pf. Type **E487**	25	20
E1603	20pf. Militia guard	50	30
MSE1604	61×87 mm. 50pf. Militiamen (vert)	1·60	1·60

E488 Red Flag encircling Globe

1973. 15th Anniv of "Problems of Peace and Socialism".

E1605	**E488**	20pf. red and gold	75	35

E489 Langenstein-Zwieberge Memorial

1973. Langenstein-Zwieberge Monument.

E1606	**E489**	25pf. multicoloured	75	35

E490 U.N. H.Q. and Emblems

1973. Admission of German Democratic Republic to United Nations Organization.

E1607	**E490**	35pf. multicoloured	80	35

E491 *Young Couple* (G. Glombitza)

1973. Philatelists' Day and Third Young Philatelists' Stamp Exhibition, Halle.

E1608	**E491**	20pf.+5pf. mult	50	30

E492 Congress Emblem

1973. Eighth World Trade Union Congress, Varna, Bulgaria.

E1609	**E492**	35pf. multicoloured	60	50

E493 Vietnamese Child

1973. "Solidarity with Vietnam".

E1610	**E493**	10pf.+5pf. mult	50	30

E494 Launching Rocket

1973. Soviet Science and Technology Days. Multicoloured.

E1611	10pf. Type **E494**	25	20
E1612	20pf. Soviet map and emblem (horiz)	25	20
E1613	25pf. Oil refinery	1·20	1·10

E495 L. Corvalan

1973. Solidarity with the Chilean People. Multicoloured.

| E1614 | 10pf.+5pf. Type **E495** | 30 | 30 |
| E1615 | 25pf.+5pf. Pres. Allende | 60 | 60 |

E496 *Child with Doll*
(C. L. Vogel)

1973. Paintings by Old Masters. Multicoloured.

E1616	10pf. Type **E496**	25	25
E1617	15pf. *Madonna with Rose* (Parmigianino)	25	25
E1618	20pf. *Woman with Fair Hair* (Rubens)	25	25
E1619	25pf. *Lady in White* (Titian)	25	25
E1620	35pf. *Archimedes* (D. Fetti)	25	25
E1621	70pf. *Flower Arrangement* (Jan D. de Heem)	3·50	2·40

E497 *Flame Emblem*

1973. 25th Anniv of Declaration of Human Rights.

| E1622 | **E497** 35pf. multicoloured | 75 | 50 |

E498 "Catching the Pike"

1973. Fairy Tales (8th series). As Type **E498**. *At the Bidding of the Pike.*

E1623	5pf. multicoloured	30	35
E1624	10pf. multicoloured	1·20	1·80
E1625	15pf. multicoloured	30	35
E1626	20pf. multicoloured	30	35
E1627	25pf. multicoloured	1·20	1·80
E1628	35pf. multicoloured	30	35

E499 *E. Hoernle*

1974. Socialist Personalities.

E1629	**E499** 10pf. grey	35	25
E1630	- 10pf. lilac	35	25
E1631	- 10pf. blue	35	25
E1632	- 10pf. brown	35	25
E1633	- 10pf. green	35	25
E1634	- 10pf. brown	35	25
E1635	- 10pf. blue	35	25
E1636	- 10pf. brown	35	25

PERSONALITIES: No. E1630, Etkar Andre; E1631, Paul Merker; E1632, Hermann Duncker; E1633, Fritz Heckert; E1634, Otto Grotewohl; E1635, Wilhelm Florin; E1636, Georg Handke.
See also Nos. E1682/4.

E500 *Pablo Neruda*

1974. Pablo Neruda (Chilean poet) Commem.

| E1637 | **E500** 20pf. multicoloured | 60 | 35 |

E501 "Comecon" Emblem

1974. 25th Anniv of Council for Mutual Economic Aid.

| E1638 | **E501** 20pf. multicoloured | 60 | 30 |

E502 *Echinopsis multiplex*

1974. Cacti. Multicoloured.

E1639	5pf. Type **E502**	25	25
E1640	10pf. *Lobivia haageana*	25	25
E1641	15pf. *Parodia sanguiniflora*	3·00	3·00
E1642	20pf. *Gymnocal monvillei*	25	25
E1643	25pf. *Neoporteria rapifera*	25	25
E1644	35pf. *Notocactus concinnus*	35	35

E503 *Handball Players*

1974. Eighth Men's World Indoor Handball Championships.

E1645	**E503** 5pf. multicoloured	50	50
E1646	- 10pf. multicoloured	50	50
E1647	- 35pf. multicoloured	50	50

Nos. E1645/7 were issued together, se-tenant, forming a composite design of a handball match.

E504 *High-tension Testing Plant*

1974. Leipzig Spring Fair. Multicoloured.

| E1648 | 10pf. Type **E504** | 25 | 20 |
| E1649 | 25pf. "Robotron" computer (horiz) | 50 | 35 |

E505 *Rhodophyllus sinuatus*

1974. Poisonous Fungi. Multicoloured.

E1650	5pf. Type **E505**	25	20
E1651	10pf. *Boletus satanas*	25	20
E1652	15pf. *Amanita pantherina*	25	20
E1653	20pf. *Amanita muscaria*	25	20
E1654	25pf. *Gyromitra esculenta*	25	20
E1655	30pf. *Inocybe patouillardii*	35	25
E1656	35pf. *Amanita phalloides*	35	25
E1657	40pf. *Clitocybe dealbata*	2·30	2·10

E506 *Gustav Kirchhoff*

1974. Celebrities' Birth Anniversaries.

E1658	**E506** 5pf. black and grey	25	20
E1659	- 10pf. ultram & bl	25	20
E1660	- 20pf. red and pink	25	25
E1661	- 25pf. green & turq	25	25
E1662	- 35pf. choc & brn	1·00	1·00

PORTRAITS AND ANNIVERSARIES: 5pf. (physicist, 150th); 10pf. Immanuel Kant (philosopher, 250th); 20pf. Elm Welk (writer, 90th); 25pf. Johann Herder (author, 230th); 35pf. Lion Feuchtwanger (novelist, 90th).

E507 Globe and "PEACE"

1974. 25th Anniv of First World Peace Congress.

| E1663 | **E507** 35pf. multicoloured | 60 | 50 |

E508 *Tractor Driver*

1974. 25th Anniv of German Democratic Republic. Multicoloured.

E1664	10pf. Type **E508**	25	20
E1665	20pf. Students	25	20
E1666	25pf. Woman worker	25	25
E1667	35pf. East German family	1·30	1·20

E509 *Buk Lighthouse, 1878*

1974. Lighthouses (1st series). Multicoloured.

E1668	10pf. Type **E509**	25	20
E1669	15pf. Warnemunde lighthouse, 1898	25	20
E1670	20pf. Darsser Ort lighthouse, 1848	25	20
E1671	35pf. Arkona lighthouse in 1827 and 1902	25	20
E1672	40pf. Greifswalder Oie lighthouse, 1855	1·70	1·50

See also Nos. E1760/4.

E510 *Man and Woman looking at the Moon*

1974. Birth Bicentenary of Caspar Friedrich (painter). Multicoloured.

E1673	10pf. Type **E510**	25	20
E1674	20pf. *The Stages of Life* (seaside scene)	25	20
E1675	25pf. *Heath near Dresden*	2·40	2·40
E1676	35pf. *Trees in the Elbe Valley*	35	25
MSE1677	80×55 mm. **E511** 70pf. sepia	2·00	2·50

E512 *Lace Pattern*

1974. Plauen Lace.

E1678	**E512** 10pf. black and violet	25	20
E1679	- 20pf. brown, black and bistre	25	20
E1680	- 25pf. black, blue and turquoise	1·80	1·60
E1681	- 35pf. black, mauve and pink	25	25

DESIGNS: Nos. E1679/81, Lace patterns similar to Type **E512.**

1974. Socialist Personalities. As Type **E499.**

E1682	10pf. blue	35	25
E1683	10pf. violet	35	25
E1684	10pf. brown	35	25

DESIGNS: No. E1682, R. Breitscheid; No. E1683, K. Burger; No. E1684, C. Moltmann.

E513 Show Jumping

1974. International Horse-breeders' Congress, Berlin. Multicoloured.

E1685	10pf. Type **E513**	25	20
E1686	20pf. Horse & trap (horiz)	25	20
E1687	25pf. Haflinger draught horses (horiz)	2·20	2·75
E1688	35pf. Horse-racing (horiz)	35	25

E514 Crane lifting Diesel Locomotive

1974. Leipzig Autumn Fair. Multicoloured.

| E1689 | 10pf. Type **E514** | 35 | 25 |
| E1690 | 25pf. Agricultural machine | 50 | 35 |

E515 "The Porcelain Shop"

1974. "Mon Plaisir". Exhibits in Dolls' Village, Castle Museum, Arnstadt. Multicoloured.

E1691	5pf. Type **E515**	25	20
E1692	10pf. "Fairground Crier"	25	20
E1693	15pf. "Wine-tasting in Cellar"	25	20
E1694	20pf. "Cooper and Apprentice"	25	20
E1695	25pf. "Bagpiper playing for Dancing Bear"	2·00	2·10
E1696	35pf. "Butcher's Wife and Crone"	25	25

E516 Ardeatine Caves Memorial, Rome

1974. International War Memorials.

| E1697 | **E516** 35pf. black, grn & red | 50 | 50 |
| E1698 | - 35pf. black, bl & red | 50 | 50 |

DESIGN: No. E1698, Resistance Memorial, Chateaubriant, France.

E517 Arms of East Germany and Family

1974. 25th Anniv of German Democratic Republic. Sheet 90×108 mm.

| MSE1699 | **E517** 1m. multicoloured | 2·40 | 2·40 |

E518 *James Watt (paddle-steamer) and Modern Freighter*

1974. Centenary of U.P.U. Multicoloured.

E1700	10pf. Type **E518**	25 20
E1701	20pf. Steam and diesel railway locomotives	25 20
E1702	25pf. Early airliner and Tupolev Tu-134	25 20
E1703	35pf. Early mail coach and modern truck	1·50 1·20

E519 *The Revolutionaries* (E. Rossdeutscher)

1974. "DDR 74" Stamp Exhibition. Sculptures in Karl-Marx-Stadt. Each black, bistre and green.

E1704	10pf.+5pf. Type **E519**	35 35
E1705	20pf. *The Dialectics*	35 35
E1706	25pf. *The Party*	35 35

E520 *The Sun shines for all* (G. Milosch)

1974. Children's Paintings. Multicoloured.

E1707	20pf. Type **E520**	50 50
E1708	20pf. *My Friend Sascha* (B. Ozminski)	50 50
E1709	20pf. *Carsten the Best Swimmer* (M. Kluge)	50 50
E1710	20pf. *Me and the Blackboard* (P. Westphal)	50 50

E521 "The Woodchopper"

1974. Fairy Tales (9th series). *Twittering To and Fro* by A. Tolstoi.

E1711	**E521** 10pf. multicoloured	25 25
E1712	15pf. multicoloured	1·30 1·30
E1713	20pf. multicoloured	25 25
E1714	30pf. multicoloured	25 25
E1715	35pf. multicoloured	1·30 1·30
E1716	40pf. multicoloured	25 25

DESIGNS: Nos. E1712/16, Scenes from *Twittering To and Fro* fairy tale, similar to Type **E521**.

E522 *Still Life* (R. Paris)

1974. Paintings from Berlin Museums. Multicoloured.

E1717	10pf. Type **E522**	25 20
E1718	15pf. *Girl in Meditation* (W. Lachnit) (vert)	25 20
E1719	20pf. *Fisherman's House* (H. Hakenbeck) (vert)	25 20
E1720	35pf. *Girl in Red* (R. Bergander)	35 20
E1721	70pf. *Parents* (W. Sitte) (vert)	2·40 2·10

E523 Banded Jasper

1974. Gem-stones in Freiberg Mining Academy Collection. Multicoloured.

E1722	10pf. Type **E523**	25 20
E1723	15pf. Smoky quartz	25 20
E1724	20pf. Topaz	25 20
E1725	25pf. Amethyst	25 20
E1726	35pf. Aquamarine	35 20
E1727	70pf. Agate	2·40 2·10

E524 Martha Arendsee

1975. 90th Birth Anniv of Martha Arendsee (Socialist).

E1728	**E524** 10pf. red	50 30

E525 Peasants doing Forced Labour

1975. 450th Anniv of Peasants' War.

E1729	**E525** 5pf. black, green and grey	50 50
E1730	– 10pf. black, brown and grey	50 50
E1731	– 20pf. black, blue and grey	50 50
E1732	– 25pf. black, yellow and grey	85 85
E1733	– 35pf. black, lilac and grey	85 85
E1734	– 50pf. black, grey and light grey	50 50

DESIGNS: 10pf. "Paying Tithe"; 20pf. Thomas Muntzer (leader); 25pf. "Armed Peasants"; 35pf. "Liberty" flag; 50pf. Peasants on trial.

E526 Women and Emblem

1975. International Women's Year.

E1735	**E526** 10pf. multicoloured	35 35
E1736	– 20pf. multicoloured	35 35
E1737	– 25pf. multicoloured	35 35

DESIGNS: 20pf., 25pf. Similar to Type E **526**.

E527 Pentakta "A-100" (microfilm camera)

1975. Leipzig Spring Fair. Multicoloured.

E1738	10pf. Type **E527**	30 25
E1739	25pf. "SKET" (cement works)	45 35

E528 Hans Otto (actor) (1900–33)

1975. Celebrities' Birth Anniversaries.

E1740	**E528** 5pf. blue	25 20
E1741	– 10pf. red	25 20
E1742	– 20pf. green	25 20
E1743	– 25pf. brown	25 20
E1744	– 35pf. blue	1·20 95

PORTRAITS AND ANNIVERSARIES: 10pf. Thomas Mann, author (1875–1955); 20pf. Dr. A. Schweitzer (1875–1965); 25pf. Michelangelo (1475–1564); 35pf. Andre-Marie Ampere, scientist (1775–1836).

E529 Blue and Yellow Macaws

1975. Zoo Animals. Multicoloured.

E1745	5pf. Type **E529**	35 25
E1746	10pf. Orang-utan	35 25
E1747	15pf. Ibex	35 25
E1748	20pf. Indian rhinoceros (horiz)	35 25
E1749	25pf. Pygmy hippopotamus (horiz)	35 25
E1750	30pf. Grey seals (horiz)	35 25

E1751	35pf. Tiger (horiz)	35 25
E1752	50pf. Common zebra	2·30 2·40

E530 Soldiers, "Industry" and "Agriculture"

1975. 20th Anniv of Warsaw Treaty.

E1753	**E530** 20pf. multicoloured	1·60 50

E531 Soviet Memorial, Berlin-Treptow

1975. 30th Anniv of Liberation. Multicoloured.

E1754	10pf. Type **E531**	25 20
E1755	20pf. Detail of Buchenwald memorial	25 20
E1756	25pf. Woman voluntary worker	25 20
E1757	55pf. "Socialist economic integration"	1·00 1·00
MSE1758	109×90 mm. 50pf. Soldier planting Red flag on Reichstag. Imperf	1·60 1·80

E532 Ribbons with "Komsomol" and "F.D.J." Badges

1975. Third Youth Friendship Festival, Halle.

E1759	**E532** 10pf. mult	60 30

1975. Lighthouses (2nd series). As Type **E509**. Multicoloured.

E1760	5pf. Trimmendorf lighthouse	35 25
E1761	10pf. Gellen lighthouse	35 25
E1762	20pf. Sassnitz lighthouse	35 25
E1763	25pf. Dornbusch lighthouse	35 25
E1764	35pf. Peenemunde lighthouse	1·40 1·20

E533 Wilhelm Leibknecht and August Bebel

1975. Centenary of Marx's "Programmkritik" and Gotha Unity Congress.

E1765	**E533** 10pf. deep brown, brown and red	35 35
E1766	– 20pf. multicoloured	35 35
E1767	– 25pf. deep brown, brown and red	35 35

DESIGNS: 20pf. Tivoli (meeting place at Gotha) and title-page of Minutes of Unity Congress; 25pf. Karl Marx and Friedrich Engels.

E534 Dove and "Scientific Co-operation between Socialist Countries"

E1768	**E534** 20pf. multicoloured	50 30

1975. 25th Anniv of Eisenhuettenstadt.

E535 Construction Workers

1975. 30th Anniv of Free-German Trade Union Association.

E1769	**E535** 20pf. multicoloured	50 30

E536 Automatic Clock, 1585

1975. Ancient Clocks. Multicoloured.

E1770	5pf. Type **E536**	25 20
E1771	10pf. Astronomical Mantlepiece clock, 1560	25 20
E1772	15pf. Automatic clock, 1600	2·10 2·10
E1773	20pf. Mantlepiece Clock, 1720	25 20
E1774	25pf. Mantlepiece Clock, 1700	25 20
E1775	35pf. Astronomical Clock, 1738	25 25

E537 Jacob and Wilhelm Grimm's German Dictionary

1975. 275th Anniv of Academy of Science.

E1776	**E537** 10pf. black, grn & red	25 20
E1777	– 20pf. black and blue	25 20
E1778	– 25pf. blk, yell & grn	25 20
E1779	– 35pf. multicoloured	1·30 1·30

DESIGNS: 20pf. Karl Schwarzschildt observatory, Tautenberg; 25pf. Electron microscope and chemical plant; 35pf. Intercosmic satellite.

E538 Runner with Torch

1975. Fifth National Youth Sports Day.

E1780	**E538** 10pf. black and pink	25 20
E1781	– 20pf. black and yellow	25 20
E1782	– 25pf. black and blue	25 20
E1783	– 35pf. black and green	1·30 1·30

DESIGNS: 20pf. Hurdling; 25pf. Swimming; 35pf. Gymnastics.

E539 Map of Europe

1975. European Security and Co-operation Conference, Helsinki.

E1784	**E539** 20pf. multicoloured	60 35

E540 Asters

1975. Flowers. Multicoloured.

E1785	5pf. Type **E540**	25 20
E1786	10pf. Pelargoniums	25 20

E1787	20pf. Gerberas	25	20
E1788	25pf. Carnation	25	20
E1789	35pf. Chrysanthemum	35	25
E1790	70pf. Pansies	3·50	3·00

E541
"Medimorph"
(Anaesthetizing
machine)

1975. Leipzig Autumn Fair. Multicoloured.

E1791	10pf. Type **E541**	30	20
E1792	25pf. Zschopau "TS-250" motor-cycle (horiz)	60	35

E542 School Crossing

1975. Road Safety. Multicoloured.

E1793	10pf. Type **E542**	25	20
E1794	15pf. Policewoman controlling traffic	2·00	1·30
E1795	20pf. Policeman assisting motorist	25	20
E1796	25pf. Car having check-up	25	20
E1797	35pf. Road safety instruction	25	20

E543 Launch of
"Soyuz"

1975. "Apollo"–"Soyuz" Space Link. Multicoloured.

E1798	10pf. Type **E543**	25	20
E1799	20pf. Spaceships in linking manoeuvre	25	20
E1800	70pf. The completed link (88×33 mm)	2·40	2·20

E544 Clenched
Fist and Red Star

1975. "International Solidarity".

E1801	**E544** 10pf.+5pf. black, red and olive	50	30

E545 *Weimar in 1650* (Merian)

1975. Millenary of Weimar.

E1802	**E545** 10pf. brown, light green and green	25	20
E1803	- 20pf. multicoloured	25	20
E1804	- 35pf. multicoloured	75	65

DESIGNS:—VERT: 20pf. Buchenwald memorial. HORIZ: 35pf. Weimar buildings (975–1975).

E546 Vienna
Memorial (F.
Cremer)

1975. Austrian Patriots Monument, Vienna.

E1805	**E546** 35pf. multicoloured	60	30

E547 Louis Braille

1975. International Braille Year. Multicoloured.

E1806	20pf. Type **E547**	25	20
E1807	35pf. Hands reading braille	25	20
E1808	50pf. An eye-ball, eye shade and safety goggles	2·00	1·80

E548 Post Office
Gate, Wurzen

1975. National Philatelists' Day. Multicoloured.

E1809	10pf.+5pf. Type **E548**	65	65
E1810	20pf. Post Office, Barenfels	25	25

E549 Hans Christian Andersen and scene from
The Emperor's New Clothes

1975. Fairy Tales (10th series). *The Emperor's New Clothes.*

E1811	**E549** 20pf. multicoloured	60	60
E1812	- 35pf. multicoloured	1·00	1·00
E1813	- 50pf. multicoloured	60	60

DESIGNS: 35, 50pf. Different scenes.

E550 Tobogganing

1975. Winter Olympic Games, Innsbruck (1976). Multicoloured.

E1814	5pf. Type **E550**	25	20
E1815	10pf.+5pf. Bobsleigh track	25	20
E1816	20pf. Speed-skating rink	25	20
E1817	25pf.+5pf. Ski-jump	35	25
E1818	35pf. Skating-rink	35	25
E1819	70pf. Skiing	2·75	2·30
MSE1820	80×55 mm. 1m. Innsbruk (33×28 mm)	3·00	2·40

E551 W. Pieck

1975. Birth Cent of President Pieck (statesman).

E1821	**E551** 10pf. brown & blue	35	25

1976. Members of German Workers' Movement. As Type **E551**.

E1822	10pf. brown and red	30	25
E1823	10pf. brown and green	30	25
E1824	10pf. brown and orange	30	25
E1825	10pf. brown and violet	30	25

PORTRAITS: No. E1822, Ernst Thalmann; E1823, Georg Schumann; E1824, Wilhelm Koenen; E1825, John Schehr.

E552 Organ,
Rotha

1976. Gottfried Silbermann (organ builder) Commemoration. Multicoloured.

E1826	10pf. Type **E552**	25	20
E1827	20pf. Organ, Freiberg	25	20
E1828	35pf. Organ, Fraureuth	25	20
E1829	50pf. Organ, Dresden	1·80	1·20

E553 Richard
Sorge

1976. Dr. Richard Sorge (Soviet agent) Commemoration. Sheet 82×65 mm.

MSE1830	**E553** 1m. black and pale olive-grey	2·75	2·75

E554 Servicemen and Emblem

1976. 20th Anniv of National Forces (N.V.A.). Multicoloured.

E1831	10pf. Type **E554**	30	20
E1832	20pf. N.V.A. equipment	50	35

E555 Telephone
and Inscription

1976. Centenary of Telephone.

E1833	**E555** 20pf. blue	50	30

E556 Block of
Flats, Leipzig

1976. Leipzig Spring Fair. Multicoloured.

E1834	10pf. Type **E556**	30	25
E1835	25pf. "Prometey" (deep sea trawler) (horiz)	60	35

E557 Palace of the Republic, Berlin

1976. Opening of Palace of Republic, Berlin.

E1836	**E557** 10pf. multicoloured	1·10	30

E558 Telecommunications
Satellite Tracking Radar

1976. "Intersputnik".

E1837	**E558** 20pf. multicoloured	50	25

E559 Marx, Engels,
Lenin and Socialist
Party Emblem

1976. Ninth East German Socialist Party Congress.

E1838	**E559** 10pf. red, gold and deep red	30	30
E1839	- 20pf. multicoloured	35	30
MSE1840	110×91 mm. **E557** 1m. multicoloured	2·10	2·10

DESIGN—HORIZ: 20pf. Industrial site, housing complex and emblem.

E560 Cycling

1976. Olympic Games, Montreal. Multicoloured.

E1841	5pf. Type **E560**	25	20
E1842	10pf.+5pf. Modern swimming pool	25	20
E1843	20pf. Modern sports hall	25	20
E1844	25pf. Regatta course	25	20
E1845	35pf.+10pf. Rifle-range	35	25
E1846	70pf. Athletics	3·00	2·75
MSE1847	81×55 mm. 1m. Modern sports stadium (33×28 mm)	2·30	2·30

E561 Intertwined Ribbon
and Emblem

1976. Tenth Youth Parliament Conference, Berlin. Multicoloured.

E1848	10pf. Type **E561**	25	25
E1849	20pf. Members of Youth Parliament and stylised industrial plant	35	35

E562 *Himantoglossum
bircinum*

1976. Flowers. Multicoloured.

E1850	10pf. Type **E562**	25	20
E1851	20pf. *Dactylorhiza incarnata*	25	20
E1852	25pf. *Anacamptis pyramidalis*	25	20
E1853	35pf. *Dactylorhiza sambucina*	35	25
E1854	40pf. *Orchis coriophora*	35	25
E1855	50pf. *Cypripedium calceolus*	3·50	2·40

E563 Shetland Pony (H. Drake)

1976. Statuettes from Berlin Museums.

E1856	**E563** 10pf. black and blue	25	20
E1857	- 20pf. black & brown	25	20
E1858	- 25pf. black & orange	25	20
E1859	- 35pf. black and green	25	20
E1860	- 50pf. black and pink	2·40	2·10

STATUETTES—VERT: 20pf. *Tanzpause* (W. Arnold); 25pf. *Am Strand* (L. Englehardt); 35pf. Herman Duncker (W. Howard); 50pf. *Das Gesprach* (G. Weidanz).

E564 Marx, Engels,
Lenin and Red Flag

1976. European Communist Parties' Conference.

E1861	**E564** 20pf. blue, deep red and red	60	30

E565 State Carriage, 1790

1976. 19th-century Horse-drawn Vehicles. Multicoloured.

E1862	10pf. Type **E565**	25	20
E1863	20pf. Russian trap, 1800	25	20
E1864	25pf. Carriage, 1840	25	20
E1865	35pf. State carriage, 1860	30	20
E1866	40pf. Stagecoach, 1850	35	25
E1867	50pf. Carriage, 1889	3·75	3·50

E566 Gera, c. 1652

1976. National Philatelists' Day, Gera. Multicoloured.

E1868	10pf.+5pf. Type **E566**	30	30
E1869	20pf. Gera buildings	30	30

E567 Boxer

1976. Domestic Dogs. Multicoloured.

E1870	5pf. Type **E567**	25	25
E1871	10pf. Airedale Terrier	25	25
E1872	20pf. Alsatian	25	25
E1873	25pf. Collie	25	25
E1874	35pf. Schnauzer	25	25
E1875	70pf. Great Dane	3·25	3·25

E568 Oil Refinery

1976. Autumn Fair, Leipzig. Multicoloured.

E1876	10pf. Type **E568**	25	20
E1877	25pf. Library, Leipzig	50	30

E569 Templin Lake Railway Bridge

1976. East German Bridges. Multicoloured.

E1878	10pf. Type **E569**	25	25
E1879	15pf. Adlergestell Railway Bridge, Berlin	25	25
E1880	20pf. River Elbe Railway Bridge, Rosslau	25	25
E1881	25pf. Goltzschtal Viaduct	25	25
E1882	35pf. Elbe River Bridge, Magdeburg	25	25
E1883	50pf. Grosser Dreesch Bridge, Schwerin	2·40	2·40

E570 Memorial Figures

1976. Patriots' Memorial, Budapest.

E1884	**E570** 35pf. multicoloured	60	50

E571 Brass Jug, c. 1500

1976. Exhibits from Applied Arts Museum, Kopenick Castle, Berlin. Multicoloured.

E1885	10pf. Type **E571**	25	25
E1886	20pf. Faience covered vase, c. 1710	25	25
E1887	25pf. Porcelain "fruit-seller" table centre, c. 1768	25	25
E1888	35pf. Silver "basket-carrier" statuette, c. 1700	25	25
E1889	70pf. Coloured glass vase, c. 1900	2·75	2·75

E572 Berlin T.V. Tower

1976. "Sozphilex 77" Stamp Exhibition. East Berlin (1st issue).

E1890	**E572** 10pf.+5pf. blue, black and red	50	30

See also Nos. E1962/3.

E573 Spade-tailed Guppy

1976. Aquarium Fish – Guppies. Multicoloured.

E1891	10pf. Type **E573**	25	20
E1892	15pf. Lyre-tailed	25	20
E1893	20pf. Flag-tailed	25	20
E1894	25pf. Sword-tailed	25	20
E1895	35pf. Delta	25	20
E1896	70pf. Round-tailed	3·00	2·75

E574 Clay Pots c. 3000 B.C.

1976. Archaeological Discoveries in D.D.R. Multicoloured.

E1897	10pf. Type **E574**	25	20
E1898	20pf. Bronze cult vessel on wheels, c. 1300 B.C.	25	20
E1899	25pf. Roman gold aureus of Tetricus I, A.D. 270–273	25	20
E1900	35pf. Viking cross-shaped pendant, 10th century A.D.	25	20
E1901	70pf. Roman glass beaker, 3rd century A.D.	2·75	2·75

E575 The Miller and the King

1976. Fairy Tales (11th series). *Rumpelstiltskin.*

E1902	**E575** 5pf. multicoloured	30	30
E1903	- 10pf. multicoloured	85	85
E1904	- 15pf. multicoloured	30	30
E1905	- 20pf. multicoloured	30	30
E1906	- 25pf. multicoloured	85	85
E1907	- 30pf. multicoloured	30	30

DESIGNS: 10pf. to 30pf. Scenes from the fairy tale.

E576 *The Air* (R. Carriera)

1976. Paintings by Old Masters from the National Art Collection, Dresden. Multicoloured.

E1908	10pf. Type **E576**	25	20
E1909	15pf. *Madonna and Child* (Murillo)	25	20
E1910	20pf. *Viola Player* (B. Strozzi)	25	20
E1911	25pf. *Ariadne Forsaken* (A. Kauffman)	25	20
E1912	35pf. *Old Man in Black Cap* (B. Nazzari)	25	20
E1913	70pf. *Officer reading a Letter* (G. Terborch)	3·00	2·20

E577 Arnold Zweig (author)

1977. German Celebrities.

E1914	**E577** 10pf. black and pink	25	20
E1915	- 20pf. black and grey	25	20
E1916	- 35pf. black and green	25	20
E1917	- 40pf. black and blue	1·20	1·20

DESIGNS: 20pf. Otto von Guericke (scientist); 35pf. Albrecht D. Thaer (agriculturalist); 40pf. Gustav Hertz (physicist).

E578 Spring near Plaue, Thuringia

1977. Natural Phenomena. Multicoloured.

E1918	10pf. Type **E578**	25	20
E1919	20pf. Rock face near Jonsdorf	25	20
E1920	25pf. Oaks near Reuterstadt Stavenhagen	25	20
E1921	35pf. Rocky ledge near Saalburg	25	20
E1922	50pf. Erratic boulder near Furstenwalde/Spree	2·00	2·00

E579 Book Fair Building

1977. Leipzig Spring Fair. Multicoloured.

E1923	10pf. Type **E579**	25	20
E1924	25pf. Aluminium casting machine	35	30

E580 Senftenberg Costume, Zly Komorrow

1977. Sorbian Historical Costumes. Multicoloured.

E1925	10pf. Type **E580**	25	20
E1926	20pf. Bautzen, Budysin	25	20
E1927	25pf. Klitten, Kletno	25	20
E1928	35pf. Nochten, Wochozy	25	20
E1929	70pf. Muskau, Muzakow	3·25	2·40

E581 Carl Friedrich Gauss

1977. Birth Bicentenary of Carl Friedrich Gauss (mathematician).

E1930	**E581** 20pf. black and blue	85	35

E582 Start of Race

1977. 30th International Peace Cycle Race. Multicoloured.

E1931	10pf. Type **E582**	35	35
E1932	20pf. Spurt	35	35
E1933	35pf. Race finish	35	35

E583 Three Flags

1977. Ninth Congress of Free German Trade Unions Association.

E1934	**E583** 20pf. multicoloured	50	30

E584 VKM Channel Converter and Filters

1977. World Telecommunications Day.

E1935	**E584** 20pf. black, blue and red	50	30

E585 Shooting

1977. 25th Anniv of Sports and Technical Sciences Association.

E1936	**E585** 10pf. black, grn & red	25	25
E1937	- 20pf. black, bl & mve	25	25
E1938	- 35pf. black, pk & grn	1·20	1·20

DESIGNS: 20pf. Skin diving; 25pf. Radio-controlled model boat.

E586 Accordion, 1900

1977. Old Musical Instruments from Vogtland. Multicoloured.

E1939	10pf. Type **E586**	25	20
E1940	20pf. Treble viola da gamba, 1747	25	20
E1941	25pf. Oboe, 1785, Clarinet, 1830, Flute, 1817	25	20
E1942	35pf. Concert zither, 1891	25	20
E1943	70pf. Trumpet, 1860	3·25	3·00

E587 *Bathsheba at the Fountain*

1977. 400th Birth Anniv of Peter Paul Rubens. Dresden Gallery Paintings. Multicoloured.

E1944	10pf. Type **E587**	25	20
E1945	15pf. *Mercury and Argus* (horiz)	25	20
E1946	20pf. *The Drunk Hercules*	25	20
E1947	25pf. *Diana's Return from Hunting* (horiz)	25	20
E1948	35pf. *The Old Woman with the Brazier*	35	25
E1949	50pf. *Leda with the Swan* (horiz)	4·25	3·25

E588 Soviet and East German Flags

1977. 30th Anniv of German-Soviet Friendship Society. Sheet 80×55 mm.

MSE1950	**E588** 50pf. multicoloured	1·60	1·50

E589 Tractor and Plough

1977. Modern Agricultural Techniques. Multicoloured.

E1951	10pf. Type **E589**	25	20
E1952	20pf. Fertilizer spreader on truck	25	20
E1953	25pf. Potato digger and loader	25	20
E1954	35pf. High pressure collecting press	25	20
E1955	50pf. Milking machine	2·75	2·40

E590 High Jump

1977. Sixth Gymnastics and Athletic Meeting and 6th Children and Young People's Sports Days, Leipzig. Multicoloured.

E1956	5pf. Type **E590**	25	20
E1957	10pf.+5pf. Running	25	20
E1958	20pf. Hurdling	25	20
E1959	25pf.+5pf. Gymnastics	25	20

E1960	35pf. Dancing	25	20
E1961	40pf. Torch bearer and flags	2·40	2·40

E591 *Bread for Everybody* (Wolfram Schubert)

1977. "Sozphilex 77" Stamp Exhibition, East Berlin (2nd issue). Multicoloured.

E1962	10pf. Type **E591**	35	25
E1963	25pf. ... *when Communists are Dreaming* (Walter Womacka)	75	60
MSE1964	Two sheets, each 77×110 mm. (a) No. E1962 ×4; (b) No. E1963 ×4 Set of 2 sheets	5·00	4·50
MSE1965	85×54 mm. 50pf.+20pf. *World Youth Song* (Lothar Zitzmann) (horiz)	2·10	2·10

E592 "Konsument" Department Store, Leipzig

1977. Leipzig Autumn Fair. Multicoloured.

E1966	10pf. Type **E592**	35	20
E1967	25pf. Carved bowl and Thuringian blown-glass vases	50	35

E593 Bust of Dzerzhinsky and Young Pioneers

1977. Birth Centenary of Feliks E. Dzerzhinsky (founder of Soviet Cheka). Sheet 127×69 mm containing Type **E593** and similar vert design. Multicoloured.

MSE1968	20pf. Type **E593**; 35pf. Portrait	2·30	2·30

E594 Steam Locomotive *Muldenthal*, 1861

1977. Transport Museum, Dresden. Multicoloured.

E1969	5pf. Type **E594**	35	25
E1970	10pf. Dresden tram, 1896	35	25
E1971	20pf. Hans Grade's monoplane, 1909	35	25
E1972	35pf. Phanomobil tricar, 1924	35	25
E1973	35pf. River Elbe passenger steamer, 1837	3·75	3·00

E595 *Aurora* (cruiser)

1977. 60th Anniv of October Revolution. Multicoloured.

E1974	10pf. Type **E595**	50	25
E1975	25pf. Assault on Winter Palace	75	60
MSE1976	55×86 mm. 1m. Lenin (vert)	3·00	2·40

E596 Soviet Memorial

1977. Soviet Memorial, Berlin-Schoenholz.

E1977	**E596** 35pf. multicoloured	60	30

E597 Flaming Torch

1977. "Solidarity".

E1978	**E597** 10pf.+5pf. multicoloured	50	30

E598 Ernst Meyer

1977. Socialist Personalities.

E1979	**E598** 10pf. brown	25	25
E1980	- 10pf. red	25	25
E1981	- 10pf. blue	25	25

PERSONALITIES: No. E1980, A. Frolich; No. E1981, G. Eisler.

E599 H. von Kleist

1977. Birth Bicentenary of Heinrich von Kleist (poet). Sheet 82×54 mm.

MSE1982	**E599** 1m. black and red	3·75	3·00

E600 Rocket pointing Right

1977. 20th "Masters of Tomorrow" Fair, Leipzig.

E1983	**E600** 10pf. red, silver and black	25	25
E1984	- 20pf. blue, gold and black	35	35

DESIGN: 20pf. Rocket pointing left.

E601 Mouflon

1977. Hunting. Multicoloured.

E1985	10pf. Type **E601**	25	20
E1986	15pf. Red deer	3·00	3·00
E1987	20pf. Shooting common pheasant	25	20
E1988	25pf. Red fox and mallard	35	25
E1989	35pf. Tractor driver with roe deer fawn	35	25
E1990	70pf. Wild boars	50	25

E602 Firemen with Scaling Ladders

1977. Fire Brigade. Multicoloured.

E1991	10pf. Type **E602**	25	20
E1992	20pf. Children visiting fire brigade (vert)	25	20
E1993	25pf. Fire engines in countryside	25	20
E1994	35pf. Artificial respiration (vert)	25	20
E1995	50pf. Fire-fighting tug	3·00	2·75

E603 Traveller and King

1977. Fairy Tales (12th series). *Six World Travellers* (Brothers Grimm).

E1996	**E603** 5pf. multicoloured	25	25
E1997	- 10pf. multicoloured	1·20	1·20
E1998	- 20pf. multicoloured	25	25
E1999	- 25pf. multicoloured	25	25
E2000	- 35pf. multicoloured	1·20	1·20
E2001	- 60pf. multicoloured	25	25

DESIGNS: 10pf. to 60pf. Scenes from the fairy tale.

E604 Rosehips

1978. Medicinal Plants. Multicoloured.

E2002	10pf. Type **E604**	25	20
E2003	15pf. Birch leaves	25	20
E2004	20pf. Camomile flowers	25	20
E2005	25pf. Coltsfoot	25	20
E2006	35pf. Lime flowers	25	20
E2007	50pf. Elder flowers	3·25	3·00

E605 Amilcar Cabral

1978. Amilcar Cabral (nationalist leader of Guinea-Bissau) Commemoration.

E2008	**E605** 20pf. multicoloured	60	50

E606 Town Hall, Suhl-Heinrichs

1978. Half-timbered Buildings. Multicoloured.

E2009	10pf. Type **E606**	25	20
E2010	20pf. Farmhouse, Niederoderwitz	25	20
E2011	25pf. Farmhouse, Strassen	25	20
E2012	35pf. House, Quedlinburg	25	20
E2013	40pf. House, Eisenach	3·00	2·75

E607 Post Office Van, 1921

1978. Postal Transport. Multicoloured.

E2014	10pf. Type **E607**	25	25
E2015	20pf. Postal truck, 1978	60	60
E2016	25pf. Railway mail coach, 1896	75	75
E2017	35pf. Railway mail coach, 1978	1·00	1·00

E608 Ear-pendant, 11th century

1978. Slavonic Treasures. Multicoloured.

E2018	10pf. Type **E608**	25	20
E2019	20pf. Ear-ring, 10th century	25	20
E2020	25pf. Bronze tag, 10th century	25	20
E2021	35pf. Bronze horse, 12th century	35	25
E2022	70pf. Arabian coin, 8th century	2·40	2·40

E609 "Royal House" Market Square, Leipzig

1978. Leipzig Spring Fair.

E2023	**E609** 10pf. yell, blk & red	30	20
E2024	- 25pf. green, blk & red	60	50

DESIGN: 25pf. Universal measuring instrument, UMK 10/1318.

E610 "M-100" Meteorological Rocket

1978. "Interkosmos" Space Programme. Multicoloured.

E2025	10pf. Type **E610**	25	25
E2026	20pf. "Interkosmos 1" satellite	25	25
E2027	35pf. "Meteor" satellite with Fourier spectrometer	1·50	1·50
MSE2028	90×109 mm. 1m. "MKF-6" multispectral camera	3·75	3·00

E611 Samuel Heinicke (founder)

1978. Bicentenary of First National Deaf and Dumb Educational Institution.

E2029	20pf. Type **E611**	25	25
E2030	25pf. Child learning alphabet	1·00	1·00

E612 Radio-range Tower, Dequede, and Television Transmission Van

1978. World Telecommunications Day. Multicoloured.

E2031	10pf. Type **E612**	35	25
E2032	20pf. Equipment in Berlin television tower and Dresden television tower	45	45

E613 Saxon miner in Gala Uniform

1978. 19th-Century Gala Uniforms of Mining and Metallurgical Industries. Multicoloured.

E2033	10pf. Type **E613**	25	20
E2034	20pf. Freiberg foundry worker	25	20
E2035	25pf. School of Mining academician	25	20
E2036	35pf. Chief Inspector of Mines	1·80	1·50

E614 Lion Cub

1978. Centenary of Leipzig Zoo. Multicoloured.

E2037	10pf. Type **E614**	35	25
E2038	20pf. Leopard cub	35	25
E2039	35pf. Tiger cub	35	25
E2040	50pf. Snow leopard cub	2·00	1·90

E615 Loading Container

1978. Container Goods Traffic. Multicoloured.

E2041	10pf. Type **E615**	25	20
E2042	20pf. Placing container on truck	25	20
E2043	35pf. Diesel locomotive and container wagons	25	20
E2044	70pf. Placing containers on "Boltenhagen"	2·75	2·30

E616 Clay Ox
(Egyptian Museum,
Leipzig)

1978. Ancient African Works of Art in Egyptian Museums at Leipzig and Berlin. Multicoloured.

E2045	5pf. Type **E616**	25	20
E2046	10pf. Clay head of woman (Leipzig)	25	20
E2047	20pf. Gold bangle (Berlin) (horiz)	25	20
E2048	25pf. Gold ring plate (Berlin)	25	20
E2049	35pf. Gold signet-ring plate (Berlin)	25	20
E2050	40pf. Necklace (Berlin) (horiz)	2·00	1·80

E617 Justus von Liebig
(agricultural chemist, 175th
birth anniv)

1978. Celebrities' Birth Anniversaries.

E2051	**E617** 5pf. black and ochre	25	20
E2052	- 10pf. black and blue	25	20
E2053	- 15pf. black and green	25	20
E2054	- 20pf. black and green	25	20
E2055	- 25pf. black and red	25	20
E2056	- 35pf. black and green	25	20
E2057	- 70pf. black and drab	2·20	2·00

DESIGNS: 10pf. Joseph Dietzgen (writer, 150th); 15pf. Alfred Doblin (novelist, 100th); 20pf. Hans Loch (politician, 80th); 25pf. Theodor Brugsch (scientist, 100th); 35pf. Freidrich Ludwig Jahn (gymnast, 200th); 70pf. Albrecht von Graefe (ophthalmatician, 150th).

E618 Cottbus, 1730

1978. Fifth National Youth Stamp Exhibition, Cottbus. Multicoloured.

E2058	10pf.+5pf. Type **E618**	35	35
E2059	20pf. Modern Cottbus	35	35

E619 Havana Buildings and
Festival Emblem

1978. 11th World Youth and Students' Festival, Havana. Multicoloured.

E2060	20pf. Type **E619**	50	50
E2061	35pf. Festival emblem and East Berlin buildings	50	50

E620 *Trooper
with Halberd*
(Hans
Schaufelein)

1978. Drawings in Berlin State Museum. Sheet 110×98 mm containing Type **E620** and similar vert designs, each brownish black and stone.

MSE2062 10pf. Type **B620**; 20pf. *Woman reading a Letter* (Jean Antoine Watteau); 25pf. *Seated Boy* (Gabriel Metsu); 30pf. *Young Man cutting a Loaf* (Cornelis Saftleven); 35pf. *St. Anthony in a Landscape* (Matthias Grunewald); 50pf. *Man seated in an Armchair* (Abraham van Diepenbeeck)	4·50 4·50

E621 "Multicar 25"
Truck

1978. Leipzig Autumn Fair. Multicoloured.

E2063	10pf. Type **E621**	30	25
E2064	25pf. "Three Kings" Fair building, Petersstrasse	60	50

E622 "Soyuz" Spaceship and
Emblems

1978. Soviet–East German Space Flight (1st issue).

E2065	**E622** 20pf. multicoloured	60	35

See also Nos. E2069/**MS**2073.

E623 Mauthausen Memorial

1978. War Victims' Memorial, Mauthausen, Austria.

E2066	**E623** 35pf. multicoloured	60	45

E624 W.M.S. Unit on the
March

1978. 25th Anniv of Workers' Militia Squads.

E2067	20pf. Type **E624**	60	50
E2068	35pf. Members of Red Army, National People's Army and W.M.S.	60	50

E625 "Soyuz", "MKF
6M" Camera and Space
Station

1978. Soviet–East German Space Flight (2nd issue). Multicoloured.

E2069	5pf. Type **E625**	25	20
E2070	10pf. Albert Einstein and "Soyuz"	25	20
E2071	20pf. Sigmund Jahn (first East German cosmonaut) (vert)	25	20
E2072	35pf. "Salyut", "Soyuz" and Lilienthal monoplane glider	1·40	1·20
MSE2073	110×90 mm. 1m. Space station and cosmonauts Valeri Bykovski and Jahn (54×32 mm)	3·00	3·00

E626 Human
Pyramid

1978. The Circus. Multicoloured.

E2074	5pf. Type **E626**	50	85
E2075	10pf. Elephant on tricycle	85	1·20
E2076	20pf. Performing horse	1·50	2·20
E2077	35pf. Polar bear kissing girl	2·40	4·25

E627 African
behind Barbed
Wire

1978. International Anti-Apartheid Year.

E2078	**E627** 20pf. multicoloured	60	30

E628 Construction of
Natural Gas Pipe Line

1978. Construction of "Friendship Line" (Drushba-Trasse) by East German Youth.

E2079	**E628** 20pf. multicoloured	60	30

E629 "Parides
hahneli" (*Papilio
hahneli*)

1978. 250th Anniv of Dresden Scientific Museums. Multicoloured.

E2080	10pf. Type **E629**	25	20
E2081	20pf. *Agama lehmanni*	25	20
E2082	25pf. Agate	25	20
E2083	35pf. *Palaeobatrachus diluvianus*	25	20
E2084	40pf. Mantlepiece clock, c. 1720	35	25
E2085	50pf. Table telescope, c. 1750	3·00	2·75

E630 Wheel-lock Gun, 1630

1978. Sporting Guns from Suhl. Multicoloured.

E2086	5pf. Type **E630**	25	25
E2087	10pf. Double-barrelled gun, 1978	25	25
E2088	20pf. Spring-cock gun, 1780	35	35
E2089	25pf. Superimposed double-barrelled gun, 1978	50	50
E2090	35pf. Percussion gun, 1850	75	75
E2091	70pf. Three-barrelled gun, 1978	1·50	1·50

E631 Old Woman
and Youth

1978. Fairy Tales. *Rapunzel*. Multicoloured.

E2092	10pf. Type **E631**	30	30
E2093	15pf. Old Woman climbing tower on Rapunzel's hair	1·30	1·30
E2094	20pf. Prince calling to Rapunzel	30	30
E2095	25pf. Prince climbing through window	30	30
E2096	35pf. Old woman about to cut Rapunzel's hair	1·30	1·30
E2097	50pf. "Happy ever after"	30	30

E632 Chaffinches

1979. Songbirds. Multicoloured.

E2098	5pf. Type **E632**	35	25
E2099	10pf. Eurasian nuthatch	35	25
E2100	20pf. European robin	35	25
E2101	25pf. Common rosefinch	35	25
E2102	35pf. Blue tit	35	25
E2103	50pf. Linnet	3·50	2·50

E633 Chabo

1979. Poultry. Multicoloured.

E2104	10pf. Type **E633**	25	20
E2105	15pf. Crows head	25	20
E2106	20pf. Porcelain-colour Feather-footed dwarf	25	20
E2107	25pf. Saxonian	25	20
E2108	35pf. Phoenix	25	20
E2109	50pf. Striped Italian	3·00	2·40

E634 Telephone Exchanges in 1900
and 1979

1979. Telephone and Telegraphs Communications. Multicoloured.

E2110	20pf. Type **E634**	25	20
E2111	35pf. Transmitting telegrams in 1800 and 1979	1·10	1·00

E635 Albert
Einstein

1979. Birth Centenary of Albert Einstein (physicist). Sheet 55×86 mm.

MSE2112	**E635** 1m. light brown, deep brown and brown	3·25	3·00

E636 Max Klinger
Exhibition House,
Leipzig

1979. Leipzig Spring Fair. Multicoloured.

E2113	10pf. Type **E636**	30	30
E2114	25pf. Horizontal drill and milling machine	50	35

E637 Otto Hahn (physicist,
centenary)

1979. Celebrities' Birth Anniversaries.

E2115	**E637** 5pf. black and pink	25	20
E2116	- 10pf. black and blue	25	20
E2117	- 20pf. black and yellow	25	20
E2118	- 25pf. black and green	25	20
E2119	- 35pf. black and blue	25	20
E2120	- 70pf. black and pink	3·00	2·20

DESIGNS: 10pf. Max von Laue (physicist, centenary); 20pf. Arthur Scheunert (physiologist, centenary); 25pf. Friedrich August Kekule (chemist, 150th); 35pf. Georg Forster (explorer and writer, 225th); 70pf. Gotth Ephraim Lessing (playwright and essayist, 250th).

E638 *Radebeul* (container ship),
Sturmvogel (tug) and Shipping Route
Map

1979. World Navigation Day.

E2121	**E638** 20pf. multicoloured	60	35

E639 Horch "8",
1911

1979. Zwickau Motor Industry. Multicoloured.

E2122	20pf. Type **E639**	50	50
E2123	35pf. Trabant "601 S de luxe", 1978	85	85

E640 MXA Electric Train

1979. East German Locomotives and Wagons. Multicoloured.

E2124	5pf. Type **E640**	35	25
E2125	10pf. Self-discharging wagon	35	25

| E2126 | 20pf. Diesel locomotive No. 110836.4 | 35 | 25 |
| E2127 | 35pf. Railway car transporter | 1·30 | 1·10 |

E641 Durga (18th century)

1979. Indian Miniatures. Multicoloured.

E2128	20pf. Type E641	25	20
E2129	35pf. Mahavira (15th/16th century)	25	20
E2130	50pf. Todi Ragini (17th century)	35	25
E2131	70pf. Asavari Ragini (17th century)	3·50	3·25

E642 Children Playing

1979. International Year of the Child. Multicoloured.

| E2132 | 10pf. Type E642 | 25 | 25 |
| E2133 | 20pf. Overseas aid for children | 60 | 60 |

E643 Construction Work on Leipziger Strasse Complex

1979. "Berlin Project" of Free German Youth Organization. Multicoloured.

| E2134 | 10pf. Type E643 | 25 | 20 |
| E2135 | 20pf. Berlin-Marzahn building site | 50 | 50 |

E644 Torchlight Procession of Free German Youth, 1949

1979. National Youth Festival. Multicoloured.

| E2136 | 10pf.+5pf. Type E644 | 35 | 35 |
| E2137 | 20pf. Youth rally | 35 | 35 |

E645 Exhibition Symbol

1979. "agra 79" Agricultural Exhibition, Markkleeberg.

| E2138 | E645 | 10pf. multicoloured | 60 | 30 |

E646 Rostock (train ferry), 1977

1979. 70th Anniv of Sassnitz–Trelleborg Railway Ferry. Multicoloured.

| E2139 | 20pf. Type E646 | 50 | 50 |
| E2140 | 35pf. Rugen (train ferry) | 50 | 50 |

E647 Hospital Classroom

1979. Rehabilitation. Multicoloured.

| E2141 | 10pf. Type E647 | 25 | 20 |

| E2142 | 35pf. Wheelchair-bound factory worker | 75 | 70 |

E648 Cycling

1979. Seventh Children's and Young People's Sports Day, Berlin. Multicoloured.

| E2143 | 10pf. Type E648 | 25 | 20 |
| E2144 | 20pf. Roller-skating | 75 | 60 |

E649 Dahlia "Rubens"

1979. "iga" International Garden Exhibition, Erfurt. Dahlias. Multicoloured.

E2145	10pf. Type E649	25	20
E2146	20pf. "Rosalie"	25	20
E2147	25pf. "Corinna"	25	20
E2148	35pf. "Enzett-Dolli"	25	20
E2149	50pf. "Enzett-Carola"	35	25
E2150	70pf. "Don Lorenzo"	3·75	3·50

E650 Goose-thief Fountain, Dresden

1979. National Stamp Exhibition, Dresden. Multicoloured.

E2151	10pf.+5pf. Type E650	75	60
E2152	20pf. Dandelion fountain, Dresden	25	20
MSE2153	86×55 mm. 1m. Dresden buildings (horiz)	3·00	2·75

E651 World Map and Russian Alphabet

1979. Fourth International Congress of Russian Language and Literature Teachers, Berlin.

| E2154 | E651 | 20pf. multicoloured | 50 | 30 |

E652 Italian Lira de Gamba, 1592

1979. Musical Instruments in Leipzig Museum. Multicoloured.

E2155	20pf. Type E652	25	20
E2156	25pf. French serpent, 17th/18th century	25	20
E2157	40pf. French barrel-lyre, 1750	35	25
E2158	85pf. German tenor flugelhorn, 1850	3·50	2·75

E653 Horseracing

1979. 30th International Congress on Horse-breeding in Socialist Countries, Berlin. Multicoloured.

| E2159 | 10pf. Type E653 | 25 | 20 |
| E2160 | 25pf. Dressage (pas de deux) | 1·20 | 1·10 |

E654 Mittelbau-Dora Memorial

1979. Mittelbau-Dora Memorial, Nordhausen.

| E2161 | E654 | 35pf. black and violet | 75 | 50 |

E655 Teddy Bear

1979. Leipzig Autumn Fair. Multicoloured.

| E2162 | 10pf. Type E655 | 25 | 20 |
| E2163 | 25pf. Grosser Blumenberg building, Richard Wagner Square | 45 | 25 |

E656 Philipp Dengel

1979. Socialist Personalities.

E2164	E656	10pf. black, green and deep green	30	25
E2165	-	10pf. black, bl & ind	30	25
E2166	-	10pf. blk, stone & bis	30	25
E2167	-	10pf. black, red & brn	30	25

DESIGNS: No. E2165, Otto Buchwitz; No. E2166, Bernard Koenen; No. E2167, Heinrich Rau.

E657 Building Worker and Flats

1979. 30th Anniv of German Democratic Republic. Multicoloured.

E2168	5pf. Type E657	25	20
E2169	10pf. Boy and girl	25	20
E2170	15pf. Soldiers	75	50
E2171	20pf. Miner and Soviet soldier	25	20
MSE2172	90×110 mm. 1m. Family and flats (29×51 mm)	2·40	2·20

E658 Girl applying Lipstick (1966/7)

1979. Meissen Porcelain. Multicoloured.

E2173	5pf. Type E658	20	20
E2174	10pf. "Altozier" coffee pot (18th cent)	25	25
E2175	15pf. "Gosser Ausschnitt" coffee pot (1973/4)	35	35
E2176	20pf. Vase with lid (18th century)	50	50
E2177	25pf. Parrot with cherry (18th century)	60	60
E2178	35pf. Harlequin with tankard (18th century)	1·00	1·00
E2179	50pf. Flower girl (18th century)	1·30	1·30
E2180	70pf. Sake bottle (18th century)	1·80	1·80

E659 Vietnamese Soldier, Mother and Child

1979. "Invincible Vietnam".

| E2181 | E659 | 10pf.+5pf. black and red | 60 | 45 |

E660 Rag-doll, 1800

1979. Dolls. Multicoloured.

E2182	10pf. Type E660	25	25
E2183	15pf. Ceramic doll, 1960	1·50	1·50
E2184	20pf. Wooden doll, 1780	25	25
E2185	35pf. Straw puppet, 1900	25	25
E2186	50pf. Jointed doll, 1800	1·50	1·50
E2187	70pf. Tumbler-doll, 1820	25	25

E661 Balance on Ice (Johanna Starke)

1980. Winter Olympic Games, Lake Placid. Multicoloured.

E2188	10pf. Bobsleigh Start (Gunter Rechn) (horiz)	25	25
E2189	20pf. Type E661	25	25
E2190	25pf.+10pf. Ski jumpers (plastic sculpture, Gunter Schultz)	25	25
E2191	35pf. Speed Skaters at the Start (Axel Wunsch)	1·80	1·80
MSE2192	79×55 mm. 1m. Skiing Girls (Lothar Zitmann) (29×24 mm)	3·00	2·75

E662 Stille Musik Rock Garden, Grosssedlitz

1980. Baroque Gardens. Multicoloured.

E2193	10pf. Type E662	25	20
E2194	20pf. Belvedere Orangery, Weimar	25	20
E2195	50pf. Flower garden, Dornburg Castle	35	20
E2196	70pf. Park, Rheinsberg Castle	2·20	2·20

E663 Cable-laying Machine and Dish Aerial

1980. Post Office Activities. Multicoloured.

| E2212 | 10pf. Type E663 | 25 | 20 |
| E2213 | 20pf. T.V. Tower, Berlin, and television | 35 | 30 |

E664 Johann Wolfgang Dobereiner (chemist, bicent)

1980. Celebrities' Birth Anniversaries.

E2214	E664	5pf. black and bistre	25	20
E2215	-	10pf. black and red	25	20
E2216	-	20pf. black and green	25	20
E2217	-	25pf. black and blue	25	20
E2218	-	35pf. black and blue	25	20
E2219	-	70pf. black and red	2·00	1·60

DESIGNS: 10pf. Frederic Joliot-Curie (physicist, and chemist, 80th anniv); 20pf. Johann Friedrich Naumann (zoologist, bicent); 25pf. Alfred Wegener (explorer and geophysicist, cent); 35pf. Carl von Clausewitz (Prussian general, bicent); 70pf. Helene Weigel (actress, 80th anniv).

E665 Karl Marx University, Leipzig

1980. Leipzig Spring Fair. Multicoloured.

E2220	10pf. Type **E665**	25	20
E2221	25pf. "ZT 303" tractor	50	35

E666 Werner Eggerath

1980. 80th Birth Anniv of Werner Eggerath (socialist).

E2222	**E666** 10pf. brown and red	60	50

E667 Cosmonauts and "Interkosmos" Emblem

1980. "Interkosmos" Programme. Sheet 109×89 mm.

MSE2223	**E667** 1m. multicoloured	3·00	2·75

E668 On the Horizontal Beam (sculpture, Erich Wurzer)

1980. Olympic Games, Moscow (1st issue). Multicoloured.

E2224	10pf. Type **E668**	35	25
E2225	20pf.+5pf. *Runners before the Winning Post* (Lothar Zitzmann)	35	25
E2226	50pf. *Coxless Four* (Wilfred Falkenthal)	2·00	1·70

See also Nos. E2247/9.

E669 Flags of Member States

1980. 25th Anniv of Warsaw Pact.

E2227	**E669** 20pf. multicoloured	75	30

E670 Co-operative Society Building (W. Gropius)

1980. Bauhaus Architecture. Multicoloured.

E2228	5pf. Type **E670**	35	25
E2229	10pf. Socialists' Memorial Place (M. v. d. Rhode) (horiz)	35	25
E2230	15pf. Monument to the Fallen of March 1922 (W. Gropius)	35	25
E2231	20pf. Steel Building 1926 (G. Muche and R. Paulick) (horiz)	35	25
E2232	50pf. Trade Union school (H. Meyer)	50	30
E2233	70pf. Bauhaus building (W. Gropius) (horiz)	3·00	2·75

E671 Rostock Buildings

1980. 18th Workers' Festival, Rostock. Multicoloured.

E2234	10pf. Type **E671**	30	25
E2235	20pf. Costumed dancers	50	35

E672 Radar Complex, Berlin-Schoenefeld Airport

1980. "Aerosozphilex 1980" International Airmail Exhibition, Berlin. Multicoloured.

E2236	20pf. Type **E672**	50	50
E2237	25pf. Ilyushin Il-62M at Schonefeld Airport	50	50
E2238	35pf. PZL-106A Kruk crop-spraying airplane	75	75
E2239	70pf. Antonov An-2 aerial photography biplane and multispectrum camera	1·50	1·50
MSE2240	64×95 mm. 1m.+10pf. Ilyushin Il-62M jetliner and globe	3·00	3·00

E673 Okapi

1980. Endangered Animals. Multicoloured.

E2241	5pf. Type **E673**	25	20
E2242	10pf. Lesser pandas	25	20
E2243	15pf. Maned wolf	25	20
E2244	20pf. Arabian oryx	25	20
E2245	25pf. White-eared pheasant	25	20
E2246	35pf. Musk oxen	2·50	2·00

1980. Olympic Games, Moscow (2nd issue). As Type **E668**. Multicoloured.

E2247	10pf. *Judo* (Erhard Schmidt)	25	20
E2248	20pf.+10pf. *Swimmer* (Willi Sitte) (vert)	25	20
E2249	50pf. *Spurt* (sculpture, Siegfried Schreiber)	2·10	1·60
MSE2250	79×55 mm. 1m. *Spinnakers* (Karl Raetsch) (29×24 mm)	3·50	3·00

E674 Suhl, 1700

1980. Sixth National Youth Stamp Exhibition, Suhl. Multicoloured.

E2251	10pf.+5pf. Type **E674**	50	50
E2252	20pf. Modern Suhl	50	50

E675 Huntley Microscope

1980. Carl Zeiss Optical Museum, Jena. Multicoloured.

E2253	20pf. Type **E675**	50	50
E2254	25pf. Magny microscope, 1751	50	50
E2255	35pf. Amici microscope, 1845	85	85
E2256	70pf. Zeiss microscope, 1873	1·40	1·40

E676 Majdanek Memorial

1980. War Victims' Memorial, Majdanek, Poland.

E2257	**E676** 35pf. multicoloured	75	50

E677 Information Centre, Leipzig

1980. Leipzig Autumn Fair. Multicoloured.

E2258	10pf. Type **E677**	30	25
E2259	25pf. Carpet-knitting machine	75	35

E678 Palace of Republic, Berlin

1980. 67th Interparliamentary Conference, Berlin.

E2260	**E678** 20pf. multicoloured	1·10	35

E679 *Laughing Boy with Flute*

1980. 400th Anniv of Frans Hals (artist). Multicoloured.

E2261	10pf. Type **E679**	25	20
E2262	20pf. *Portrait of Young Man in Drab Coat*	25	20
E2263	25pf. *The Mulatto*	25	20
E2264	35pf. *Portrait of Young Man in Black Coat*	1·50	1·30
MSE2265	80×55 mm. 1m. brown (Self-portrait) (29×23 mm)	3·00	2·50

E680 Clenched Fist and Star

1980. "Solidarity".

E2266	**E680** 10pf.+5pf. turq & red	60	30

E681 *Leccinum versipelle* ("Leccinum testaceo scabrum")

1980. Edible Mushrooms. Multicoloured.

E2267	5pf. Type **E681**	25	20
E2268	10pf. *Boletus miniatoporus* ("Boletus erythropus")	25	20
E2269	15pf. *Agaricus campestris* ("Agaricus campester")	25	20
E2270	20pf. *Xerocomus badius*	25	20
E2271	35pf. *Boletus edulis*	35	25
E2272	70pf. *Cantharellus cibarius*	2·75	2·50

E682 Gravimetry

1980. Geophysics. Multicoloured.

E2273	20pf. Type **E682**	50	30
E2274	25pf. Bore-hole measuring	60	50
E2275	35pf. Seismic prospecting	75	75
E2276	50pf. Seismology	1·20	1·20

E683 Radebeul–Radeburg Steam Locomotive

1980. Narrow-gauge Railways (1st series). Multicoloured.

E2277	20pf. Type **E683**	50	50
E2278	20pf. Bad Doberan–Ostseebad Kuhlungsborn steam locomotive	50	50
E2279	25pf. Radebeul–Radeburg passenger carriage	50	50
E2280	35pf. Bad Doberan–Ostseebad Kuhlungsborn passenger carriage	50	50

See also Nos. E2342/5, E2509/12 and E2576/9.

E684 Toy Steam Locomotive, 1850

1980. Historical Toys. Multicoloured.

E2281	10pf. Type **E684**	35	35
E2282	20pf. Aeroplane, 1914	1·50	1·50
E2283	25pf. Steam-roller, 1920	35	35
E2284	35pf. Sailing ship, 1825	35	35
E2285	40pf. Car, 1900	1·50	1·50
E2286	50pf. Balloon, 1920	35	35

E685 Mozart

1981. 225th Birth Anniv of Wolfgang Amadeus Mozart (composer). Sheet 55×80 mm.

MSE2287	**E685** 1m. black, carmine-rose and stone	3·50	3·00

E686 *Malus pumila*

1981. Rare Plants in Berlin Arboretum. Multicoloured.

E2288	5pf. Type **E686**	25	20
E2289	10pf. *Halesia carolina* (horiz)	25	20
E2290	20pf. *Colutea arborescens*	25	20
E2291	25pf. *Paulownia tomentosa*	25	20
E2292	35pf. *Lonicera periclymenum* (horiz)	35	25
E2293	50pf. *Calycanthus floridus*	3·00	2·75

E687 Heinrich von Stephan

1981. 150th Birth Anniv of Heinrich von Stephan (founder of U.P.U.).

E2294	**E687** 10pf. black and yellow	60	35

E688 Soldiers on Parade

1981. 25th Anniv of National People's Army. Multicoloured.

E2295	10pf. Type **E688**	35	25
E2296	20pf. Marching soldiers	50	25

E689 Marx and Lenin

1981. Tenth East German Socialist Party Congress (1st series).

E2297	**E689** 10pf. multicoloured	60	25

See Nos. E2309/**MS**2313.

E690 Counter Clerks

1981. Post Office Training. Multicoloured.

E2298	5pf. Type **E690**	25	20
E2299	10pf. Telephone engineers	25	20
E2300	15pf. Radio communications	25	20

E2301 20pf. Rosa Luxemburg Engineering School, Leipzig | 35 | 25
E2302 25pf. Freidrich List Communications School, Dresden | 1·70 | 1·30

E691 Erich
Baron

1981. Socialist Personalities.
E2303 **E691** 10pf. black and green | 30 | 25
E2304 - 10pf. black and yellow | 30 | 25
E2305 - 10pf. black and blue | 30 | 25
E2306 - 10pf. black and brown | 30 | 25
DESIGNS: No. E2304, Conrad Blenkle; E2305, Arthur Ewert; E2306, Walter Stoecker.

E692 Hotel
Merkur Leipzig

1981. Leipzig Spring Fair. Multicoloured.
E2307 10pf. Type **E692** | 30 | 20
E2308 25pf. Open-cast mining machine | 60 | 35

E693 *Ernst Thalmann*
(Willi Sitte)

1981. Tenth East German Socialist Party Congress (2nd series). Multicoloured.
E2309 10pf. Type **E693** | 25 | 20
E2310 20pf. *Brigadier* (Bernhard Heisig) | 25 | 20
E2311 25pf. *Festival Day* (Rudolf Bergander) | 1·20 | 1·10
E2312 35pf. *Comrades in Arms* (Paul Michaelis) | 25 | 20
MSE2313 108×82 mm. 1m. *When Communists are Dreaming* (Walter Womacka) | 2·40 | 2·10

E694 Sports Centre

1981. Sports Centre, Berlin. Sheet 110×90 mm.
MSE2314 **E694** 1m. multicoloured | 3·25 | 3·00

E695 Plugs
and Socket

1981. Conservation of Energy.
E2315 **E695** 10pf. black & orange | 35 | 30

E696 Heinrich Barkhausen

1981. Celebrities' Birth Anniversaries.
E2316 **E696** 10pf. black and blue | 25 | 20
E2317 - 20pf. black and red | 25 | 20
E2318 - 25pf. black and brown | 3·25 | 2·40
E2319 - 35pf. black and violet | 35 | 25
E2320 - 50pf. black and green | 50 | 25

E2321 - 70pf. black and brown | 75 | 30
DESIGNS: 10pf. Type E **696** (physicist, birth centenary); 20pf. Johannes R. Becher (writer, 90th birth anniv.); 25pf. Richard Dedekind (mathematician, 150th birth anniv); 35pf. Georg Philipp Telemann (composer, 300th anniv); 50pf. Adelbert V. Chamisso (poet and naturalist, bicentenary); 70pf. Wilhelm Raabe (novelist, 150th birth anniv).

E697 Free German Youth
Members and Banner

1981. 11th Free German Youth Parliament. Multicoloured.
E2322 10pf. Type **E697** | 35 | 35
E2323 20pf. Free German Youth members instructing foreign students | 35 | 35

E698 Worlitz
Park

1981. Landscaped Parks. Multicoloured.
E2324 5pf. Type **E698** | 25 | 20
E2325 10pf. Tiefurt Park, Weimar | 25 | 20
E2326 15pf. Marxwalde | 25 | 20
E2327 20pf. Branitz Park | 25 | 20
E2328 25pf. Treptow Park, Berlin | 2·40 | 2·20
E2329 35pf. Wiesenburg Park | 35 | 25

E699 Children at Play and
Sport

1981. Eighth Children's and Young People's Sports Days, Berlin. Multicoloured.
E2330 10pf.+5pf. Type **E699** | 85 | 60
E2331 20pf. Artistic gymnastics | 35 | 30

E700 Berlin Theatre

1981. Birth Bicentenary of Karl Friedrich Schinkel (architect).
E2332 **E700** 10pf. stone and black | 1·30 | 25
E2333 - 25pf. stone and black | 3·00 | 1·30
DESIGN: 25pf. Old Museum, Berlin.

E701 Throwing the Javelin
from a Wheel chair

1981. International Year of Disabled Persons. Multicoloured.
E2334 5pf. Type **E701** | 35 | 25
E2335 15pf. Disabled people in art gallery | 35 | 25

E702 House,
Zaulsdorf

1981. Half-timbered Buildings. Multicoloured.
E2336 10pf. Type **E702** | 25 | 20
E2337 20pf. "Sugar-loaf" cottage, Gross Zicker (horiz) | 25 | 20
E2338 25pf. Farmhouse, Weckersdorf | 25 | 20
E2339 35pf. House, Pillgram (horiz) | 35 | 25
E2340 50pf. House, Eschenbach | 50 | 30
E2341 70pf. House, Ludersdorf (horiz) | 4·25 | 3·25

1981. Narrow-Gauge Railways (2nd series). As Type E683. Multicoloured.
E2342 5pf. black and red | 35 | 25
E2343 5pf. black and red | 35 | 25
E2344 15pf. multicoloured | 35 | 25
E2345 20pf. multicoloured | 35 | 25

DESIGNS: Nos. E2342, Freital–Kurort Kipsdorf steam locomotive; E2343, Putbus–Gohren steam locomotive; E2344, Freital–Kurort Kipsdorf luggage van; E2345, Putbus–Gohren passenger carriage.

E703 Chemical
Works

1981. Leipzig Autumn Fair. Multicoloured.
E2346 10pf. Type **E703** | 30 | 20
E2347 25pf. New Draper's Hall (horiz) | 60 | 50

E704 Ebers
Papyrus (Leipzig
University
Library)

1981. Precious Books from East German Libraries. Multicoloured.
E2348 20pf. Type **E704** | 25 | 20
E2349 35pf. Maya manuscript (Dresden Library) | 25 | 20
E2350 50pf. Miniature from *Les six visions Messire Francoys Petrarque*"(Berlin State Library) | 2·20 | 2·20

E705 Sassnitz
Memorial

1981. Resistance Fighters' Memorial, Sassnitz.
E2351 **E705** 35pf. multicoloured | 75 | 50

E706 Henbane and
Incense Burner

1981. Early Medical Equipment in the Karl-Sudhoff Institute, Leipzig. Multicoloured.
E2352 10pf. Type **E706** | 25 | 20
E2353 20pf. Dental instruments | 25 | 20
E2354 25pf. Forceps | 25 | 20
E2355 35pf. Bladder knife and hernia shears | 35 | 25
E2356 50pf. Speculum and gynaecological forceps (vert) | 3·75 | 3·75
E2357 85pf. Triploid elevators (vert) | 75 | 50

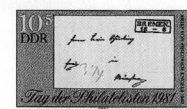

E707 Letter from Friedrich
Engels, 1840

1981. Stamp Day. Multicoloured.
E2358 10pf.+5pf. Type **E707** | 1·20 | 85
E2359 20pf. Postcard from Karl Marx, 1878 | 35 | 25

E708 African
breaking Chains

1981. "Solidarity".
E2360 **E708** 10pf.+5pf. mult | 50 | 25

E709 Tug

1981. Inland Shipping. Multicoloured.
E2361 10pf. Type **E709** | 25 | 20
E2362 20pf. Tug and barges | 25 | 20
E2363 25pf. Diesel-electric paddle-ferry, River Elbe | 25 | 20
E2364 35pf. Ice-breaker in the Oder estuary | 35 | 25
E2365 50pf. *Schonewalde* (motor barge) | 50 | 25
E2366 85pf. Dredger | 4·00 | 3·75

E710 Windmill,
Dabel

1981. Windmills. Multicoloured.
E2367 10pf. Type **E710** | 25 | 20
E2368 20pf. Pahrenz | 25 | 20
E2369 25pf. Dresden-Gohlis | 25 | 20
E2370 70pf. Ballstadt | 2·40 | 2·20

E711 Snake, 1850

1981. Historical Toys. Multicoloured.
E2371 10pf. Type **E711** | 35 | 35
E2372 20pf. Teddy bear, 1910 | 35 | 35
E2373 25pf. Goldfish, 1935 | 1·50 | 1·50
E2374 35pf. Hobby-horse, 1850 | 1·50 | 1·50
E2375 40pf. Pull-along duck, 1800 | 35 | 35
E2376 70pf. Clockwork frog, 1930 | 35 | 35

E712 Coffee Pot,
1715

1982. 300th Birth Anniv of Johann Friedrich Bottger (founder of Meissen China Works). Multicoloured.
E2377 10pf. Type **E712** | 25 | 25
E2378 20pf. Vase decorated with flowers, 1715 | 50 | 50
E2379 25pf. *Oberon* (figurine), 1969 | 75 | 75
E2380 35pf. Vase *Day and Night*, 1979 | 1·00 | 1·00
MSE2381 89×110 mm. 50pf. Portrait medal; 50pf. Bottger's seal | 4·00 | 3·00

E713 Post Office, Bad Liebenstein

1982. Post Office Building. Multicoloured.
E2382 20pf. Type **E713** | 25 | 20
E2383 25pf. Telecommunications Centre, Berlin | 25 | 20
E2384 35pf. Head Post Office, Erfurt | 35 | 25
E2385 50pf. Head Post Office, Dresden 6 | 2·40 | 2·10

E714 Alpine
Marmot

1982. International Fur Auction, Leipzig. Multicoloured.
E2386 10pf. Type **E714** | 25 | 20
E2387 20pf. Polecat | 25 | 20
E2388 25pf. European mink | 35 | 25
E2389 35pf. Beech marten | 1·80 | 1·60

E715 Silhouette of Goethe

1982. Johann Wolfgang von Goethe and Friedrich von Schiller (writers) Commemoration. Sheet 110×90 mm containing Type **E715** and similar vert design. Multicoloured.

MSE2390 50pf. Type **E715** (150th death anniv); 50pf. Silhouette of Schiller (175th death (1980) and 225th birth (1984) annivs) 4·00 3·50

E716 West Entrance to Fairground

1982. Leipzig Spring Fair. Multicoloured.

E2391	10pf. Type **E716**	25	20
E2392	25pf. Seamless steel tube plant, Riesa Zeithain	50	35

E717 Dr. Robert Koch

1982. Centenary of Discovery of Tubercle Bacillus. Sheet 80×55 mm.

MSE2393 **E717** 1m. multicoloured 3·00 2·75

E718 Max Fechner

1982. Socialist Personalities.

E2394	**E718**	10pf. brown	25	20
E2395	-	10pf. green	25	20
E2396	-	10pf. lilac	25	20
E2397	-	10pf. blue	25	20
E2398	-	10pf. green	25	20

DESIGNS: No. E2395, Ottomar Geschke; E2396, Helmut Lehmann; E2397, Herbert Warnke; E2398, Otto Winzer.

E719 Meadow Saffron

1982. Poisonous Plants. Multicoloured.

E2399	10pf. Type **E719**	25	25
E2400	15pf. Bog arum	25	25
E2401	20pf. Labrador tea	25	25
E2402	25pf. Bryony	25	25
E2403	35pf. Monkshood	35	25
E2404	50pf. Henbane	2·00	2·00

E720 Decorative Initial "I"

1982. International "Art of the Book" Exhibition, Leipzig.

E2405	**E720**	15pf. multicoloured	60	60
E2406	-	35pf. brn, red & blk	60	60

DESIGN: 35pf. Exhibition emblem.

E721 Mother with Child (W. Womacka)

1982. Tenth Free German Trade Unions Association Congress, Berlin.

E2407	**E721**	10pf. black, red and yellow	25	20
E2408	-	20pf. multicoloured	25	20
E2409	-	25pf. multicoloured	90	80

DESIGNS—HORIZ: 20pf. "Discussion by Collective of Innovators" (Willi Neubert). VERT: 25pf. "Young Couple" (Karl-Heinz Jakob).

E722 Osprey

1982. Protected Birds. Multicoloured.

E2410	10pf. Type **E722**	35	25
E2411	20pf. White-tailed sea eagle (horiz)	35	25
E2412	25pf. Little owl	35	25
E2413	35pf. Eagle owl	2·20	1·80

E723 Old and Modern Buildings

1982. 19th Workers' Festival, Neubrandenburg. Multicoloured.

E2414	10pf. Type **E723**	30	30
E2415	20pf. Couple in traditional costume	60	50

E724 Memorial Medal

1982. Birth Centenary of Georgi Dimitrov (Bulgarian statesman). Sheet 80×55 mm.

MSE2416 **E724** 1m. multicoloured 3·75 3·75

E725 Frieden (freighter)

1982. Ocean-going Ships. Multicoloured.

E2417	5pf. Type **E725**	25	20
E2418	10pf. Fichtelberg (roll on roll off freighter)	25	20
E2419	15pf. "Brocken (heavy cargo carrier)	25	20
E2420	20pf. Weimar (container ship)	25	20
E2421	25pf. Vorwarts (freighter)	25	20
E2422	35pf. Berlin (container ship)	2·10	1·80

E726 Members' Activities

1982. 30th Anniv of Sports and Science Association.

E2423	**E726**	20pf. multicoloured	60	30

E727 Bird Wedding

1982. Sorbian Folk Customs. Multicoloured.

E2424	10pf. Type **E727**	25	20
E2425	20pf. Shrove Tuesday procession	35	25
E2426	25pf. Egg rolling	50	50
E2427	35pf. Painted Easter eggs	85	85

E2428	40pf. St. John's Day riders	1·00	1·00
E2429	50pf. Distribution of Christmas gifts to hard-working children	1·20	1·20

E728 Schwerin, 1640

1982. Seventh National Youth Stamp Exhibition, Schwerin. Multicoloured.

E2430	10pf.+5pf. Type **E728**	50	50
E2431	20pf. Modern Schwerin	50	50

E729 Flag and Pioneers

1982. Seventh Pioneers Meeting, Dresden. Multicoloured.

E2432	10pf.+5pf. Type **E729**	75	75
E2433	20pf. Trumpet and drum	25	25

E730 Stormy Sea (Ludolf Backhuysen)

1982. Paintings in Schwerin State Museum. Multicoloured.

E2434	5pf. Type **E730**	25	20
E2435	10pf. Music making at Home (Frans van Mieris) (vert)	25	20
E2436	20pf. The Watchman (Carel Fabritius) (vert)	25	20
E2437	25pf. Company of Peasants (Adriaen Brouwer)	35	25
E2438	35pf. Breakfast Table with Ham (Willem Claesz Heda)	35	25
E2439	70pf. River Landscape (Jan van Goyen)	2·75	2·50

E731 Karl-Marx-Stadt

1982. 13th Socialist Countries' Postal Ministers Conference, Karl-Marx-Stadt.

E2440	**E731**	10pf. multicoloured	75	50

E732 Stentzlers Hof

1982. Leipzig Autumn Fair. Multicoloured.

E2441	10pf. Type **E732**	25	20
E2442	25pf. Amber box, ring and pendant	45	35

E733 Auschwitz-Birkenau Memorial

1982. War Victims' Memorial, Auschwitz-Birkenau.

E2443	**E733**	35pf. blue, blk & red	60	50

E734 Federation Badge

1982. Ninth International Federation of Resistance Fighters Congress, Berlin.

E2444	**E734**	10pf. multicoloured	60	35

E735 Anemone hupehensis

1982. Autumn Flowers. Multicoloured.

E2445	5pf. Type **E735**	25	20
E2446	10pf. French marigolds	25	20
E2447	15pf. Gazania	25	20
E2448	20pf. Sunflower	25	20
E2449	25pf. Annual chrysanthemum	35	25
E2450	35pf. Cosmea	3·00	2·30

E736 Palestinian Family

1982. Solidarity with Palestinian People.

E2451	**E736**	10pf.+5pf. mult	60	35

E737 "B 1000" Ambulance

1982. IFA Vehicles. Multicoloured.

E2452	5pf. Type **E737**	25	20
E2453	10pf. Road cleaner	25	20
E2454	20pf. "LD 3000" omnibus	25	20
E2455	25pf. "LD 3000" lorry	35	25
E2456	35pf. "W 50" lorry	35	25
E2457	85pf. "W 50" milk tanker	3·50	2·75

E738 Fair Emblem

1982. 25th "Masters of Tomorrow" Fair, Leipzig.

E2458	**E738**	20pf. multicoloured	50	30

E739 Aircraft and Envelope

1982. Air.

E2459	**E739**	5pf. black and blue	25	25
E2460	**E739**	15pf. black and mauve	25	50
E2461	**E739**	20pf. black and orange	35	25
E2462	**E739**	25pf. black and bistre	60	50
E2463	**E739**	30pf. black and green	35	25
E2464	**E739**	40pf. black and green	50	25
E2465	**E739**	1m. black and blue	1·50	75
E2466	**E739**	3m. black and brown	4·25	2·40
E2467	**E739**	5m. black and red	6·00	2·20

E740 Seal of Eisleben, 1500

1982. 500th Birth Anniv of Martin Luther (Protestant reformer).

E2471	10pf. Type **E740**	30	25
E2472	20pf. Luther as Junker Jog, 1521	35	25
E2473	35pf. Seal of Wittenberg, 1500	60	25
E2474	85pf. Luther (after Cranach)	5·00	3·00

See also No. **MS**2548.

E741 Carpenter

1982. Mechanical Toys. Multicoloured.

E2475	10pf. Type **E741**		30	30
E2476	20pf. Shoemaker		1·70	1·70
E2477	25pf. Baker		30	30
E2478	35pf. Cooper		30	30
E2479	40pf. Tanner		1·70	1·70
E2480	70pf. Wheelwright		30	30

E742 Johannes Brahms

1983. 150th Birth Anniv of Johannes Brahms (composer). Sheet 55×80 mm.

MSE2481 **E742** 1m.15, green, brown and sepia		4·25	3·50

E743 Franz Dahlem

1983. Socialist Personalities.

E2482	**E743**	10pf. brown	25	20
E2483	-	10pf. green	25	20
E2484	-	10pf. green	25	20
E2485	-	10pf. lilac	25	20
E2486	-	10pf. blue	25	20

DESIGN: No. E2483, Karl Maron; E2484, Josef Miller; E2485, Fred Oelssner; E2486, Siegfried Radel.

E744 Telephone Handset and Push-buttons

1983. World Communications Year.

E2487	**E744**	5pf. brown, black and deep brown	25	20
E2488	-	10pf. blue, turquoise and deep blue	25	20
E2489	-	20pf. green, deep green and black	25	20
E2490	-	35pf. multicoloured	1·80	1·30

DESIGNS: 10pf. Aerials and tankers (Rugen Radio); 20pf. Ilyushin Il-62, container ship, letter and parcel; 35pf. Optical fibre cables.

E745 Otto Nuschke

1983. Birth Cent of Otto Nuschke (politician).

E2491 **E745** 20pf. light brown, black and brown		50	35

E746 Stolberg Town Hall

1983. Historic Town Halls. Multicoloured.

E2492	10pf. Type **E746**		25	20
E2493	20pf. Gera (vert)		25	20
E2494	25pf. Possneck (vert)		25	20
E2495	35pf. Berlin		2·00	1·70

E747 Petershof

1983. Leipzig Spring Fair. Multicoloured.

E2496	10pf. Type **E747**		30	25
E2497	25pf. Robotron micro- electronic calculator		50	35

E748 Paul Robeson

1983. 85th Birth Anniv of Paul Robeson (singer).

E2498	**E748** 20pf. multicoloured	50	35

E749 Harnack, Schulze-Boysen and Sieg

1983. 40th Death Annivs of Arvid Harnack, Harro Schulze-Boysen and John Sieg (Resistance workers). Sheet 80×55 mm.

MSE2499 **E749** 85pf. black and green		2·20	2·20

E750 Karl Marx and Newspaper Mastheads

1983. Death Cent of Karl Marx. Multicoloured.

E2500	10pf. Type **E750**	25	25
E2501	20pf. Marx, Lyons silk weavers and title page of *Deutsche-Franzosische Jahrbucher*	25	25
E2502	35pf. arx, Engels and "*Communist Manifesto*"	35	25
E2503	50pf. Marx and German, Russian and French versions of *Das Kapital*	35	30
E2504	70pf. Marx and part of letter to Wilhelm Bracke containing commentary on German Workers' Party Programme	60	35
E2505	85pf. Globe and banner portraying Marx, Engels, Lenin	3·75	3·75
MSE2506	81×56 mm. 1m.15 Karl Marx (26×32 mm)	3·75	3·25

E751 "Athene"

1983. Sculptures in State Museum, Berlin.

E2507	**E751**	10pf. brown, light brown and blue	30	20
E2508	-	20pf. brown, light brown and green	60	35

DESIGN: 20pf. "Amazon".

E752 Chancery Hourglass with Wallmount, 1674

1983. Hourglasses and Sundials. Multicoloured.

E2513	5pf. Type **E752**		25	20
E2514	10pf. Chancery hour-glass, 1700		25	20
E2515	20pf. Horizontal table sundial, 1611		25	20
E2516	30pf. Equatorial sundial, 1750		35	25
E2517	60pf. Equatorial sundial, 1760		60	35
E2518	85pf. "Noon Gun" table sundial, 1800		3·50	3·00

E753 *Coryphantha elephantidens*

1983. Cultivated Cacti. Multicoloured.

E2519	5pf. Type **E753**		25	20
E2520	10pf. *Thelocactus schwarzii*		25	20
E2521	20pf. *Leuchtenbergia principis*		25	20
E2522	25pf. *Submatucana madisoniorum*		30	25
E2523	35pf. *Oroya peruviana*		35	25
E2524	50pf. *Copiapoa cinerea*		2·40	2·20

E754 Thimo and Wilhelm

1983. Founders of Naumberg Cathedral. Statues in the West Choir. Multicoloured.

E2525	20pf. Type **E754**		60	60
E2526	25pf. Gepa and Gerburg		75	75
E2527	35pf. Hermann and Reglindis		85	85
E2528	85pf. Eckehard and Uta		2·10	2·10

E755 *Glasewaldt and Zinna defending the Barricade, Berlin, 1848 (Theodor Hosemann)*

1983. "Junior Sozphilex 1983" Stamp Exhibition, Berlin.

E2529	**E755**	10pf.+5pf. brown, black and red	1·00	85
E2530	-	20pf. multicoloured	35	25

DESIGN—HORIZ: 20pf. *Instruction at Polytechnic* (Harald Metzkes).

E756 Simon Bolivar and Alexander von Humboldt

1983. Birth Bicentenary of Simon Bolivar.

E2531	**E756**	35pf. black, brown and deep brown	85	50

E757 Exercise with Balls

1983. Seventh Gymnastics and Sports Festival and Ninth Children and Young People's Sports Days, Leipzig. Multicoloured.

E2532	10pf.+5pf. Type **E757**		85	60
E2533	20pf. Volleyball		30	30

E758 Arms of Cottbus

1983. Town Arms (1st series).

E2534	**E758**	50pf. multicoloured	1·10	1·10
E2535	-	50pf. multicoloured	1·10	1·10
E2536	-	50pf. red, black and silver	1·10	1·10
E2537	-	50pf. multicoloured	1·10	1·10
E2538	-	50pf. black, red and silver	1·10	1·10

DESIGNS: No. E2535, Dresden; E2536, Erfurt; E2537, Frankfurt-on-Oder. (21×39 mm); No. E2538, Berlin.
See also Nos. E2569/73 and E2644/8.

E759 Central Fair Palace

1983. Leipzig Autumn Fair. Multicoloured.

E2539	10pf. Type **E759**		30	20
E2540	25pf. Microchip		75	35

E760 Militiaman

1983. 30th Anniv of Workers' Militia. Sheet 63×86 mm.

MSE2541 **E760** 1m. multicoloured		3·25	2·75

E761 Euler, Formula and Model

1983. Death Bicentenary of Leonhard Euler (mathematician).

E2542	**E761** 20pf. blue and black	75	45

E762 Sanssouci Castle

1983. Public Palaces and Gardens of Potsdam-Sanssouci. Multicoloured.

E2543	10pf. Type **E762**		25	20
E2544	20pf. Chinese tea house		35	25
E2545	40pf. Charlottenhof Palace		60	35
E2546	50pf. Film museum (former stables)		3·75	3·50

E763 *Mother Homeland* (Yevgeni Vuzhetich)

1983. Volograd War Memorial.

E2547	**E763** 35pf. blue, blk & grn	80	45

E764 "D.M.L." (Dr. Martin Luther)

1983. 500th Birth Anniv of Martin Luther (Protestant reformer) (2nd issue). Sheet 108×83 mm.

MSE2548 **E764** 1m. multicoloured		4·25	3·75

E765 Learning to Read and Write

1983. "Solidarity with Nicaragua".

E2549	**E765** 10pf.+5pf. mult	50	30

E766 Cockerel

1983. Thuringian Glass. Multicoloured.

E2550	10pf.	Type **E766**	35	25
E2551	20pf.	Beaker	35	25
E2552	25pf.	Vase	35	25
E2553	70pf.	Goblet	2·75	2·50

E767 Luge

1983. Winter Olmpic Games, Sarajevo (1984).

E2554	**E767**	10pf.+5pf. multicoloured	25	20
E2555	-	20pf.+10pf. multicoloured	25	20
E2556	-	25pf. multicoloured	25	20
E2557	-	35pf. multicoloured	2·20	1·80
MSE2558	83×57 mm. 85pf. blue and silver		2·75	2·40

DESIGNS: 20pf. Cross-country skiing and ski jumping; 25pf. Cross-country skiing; 35pf. Biathlion; 85pf. Olympic Centre, Sarajevo.

E768 Dove and Greeting in German and English

1983. New Year. Sheet 93×83 mm containing Type **E768** and similar horiz designs, each showing dove and greeting in named languages. Multicoloured.

MSE2559	10pf. Type **E768**; 20pf. German and Russian; 25pf. French and German; 35pf. Spanish and German	2·75	2·40

E769 Dr. Otto Schott (chemist)

1984. Centenary of Jena Glass.

E2560	**E769**	20pf. multicoloured	60	35

E770 Friedrich Ebert

1984. Socialist Personalities.

E2561	**E770**	10pf. black	30	25
E2562	-	10pf. green	30	25
E2563	-	10pf. black	30	25

DESIGNS: No. E2562, Fritz Grosse; E2563, Albert Norden.

E771 Mendelssohn

1984. 175th Birth Anniv of Felix Mendelssohn Bartholdy (composer). Sheet 82×57 mm.

MSE2564	**E771** 85pf. multicoloured	1·70	1·70

E772 Milestones, Muhlau and Oederan

1984. Postal Milestones. Multicoloured.

E2565	10pf.	Type **E772**	25	20
E2566	20pf.	Milestones, Johanngeorgenstadt and Schonbrunn	50	35
E2567	35pf.	Distance column, Freiberg	60	55
E2568	85pf.	Distance column, Pegau	1·20	1·20

1984. Town Arms (2nd series). As Type **E758**.

E2569	50pf.	multicoloured	75	65
E2570	50pf.	red, black and silver	75	65
E2571	50pf.	multicoloured	75	65
E2572	50pf.	multicoloured	75	65
E2573	50pf.	multicoloured	90	85

DESIGNS: No. E2569, Gera; E2570, Halle; E2571, Karl-Marx-Stadt; E2572, Leipzig; E2573, Magdeburg.

E773 Old Town Hall, Leipzig

1984. Leipzig Spring Fair. Multicoloured.

E2574	10pf.	Type **E773**	30	25
E2575	25pf.	Body stamping press	50	35

1984. Narrow-gauge Railways (4th series). As Type **E683**.

E2576	30pf.	grey, black and red	35	35
E2577	40pf.	grey, black and red	50	50
E2578	60pf.	multicoloured	60	60
E2579	80pf.	multicoloured	1·00	1·00

DESIGNS: 30pf. Cranzahl–Kurort Oberwiesenthal steam locomotive; 40pf. Selketalbahn steam locomotive; 60pf. Selketalbahn passenger carriage; 80pf. Cranzahl–Kurort Oberwiesenthal passenger carriage.

E774 Town Hall, Rostock

1984. Seventh International Society for Preservation of Monuments General Assembly, Rostock and Dresden. Multicoloured.

E2580	10pf.	Type **E774**	25	20
E2581	15pf.	Albrecht Castle, Meissen	25	25
E2582	40pf.	Gateway, Rostock (vert)	75	50
E2583	85pf.	Stables, Dresden	1·80	1·60

E775 Telephone, Letter, Pencil and Headquarters

1984. 25th Meeting of Posts and Telecommunications Commission of Council of Mutual Economic Aid, Cracow.

E2584	**E775**	70pf. multicoloured	1·10	50

E776 Cast Iron Bowl

1984. Cast Iron from Lauchhammer. Multicoloured.

E2585	20pf.	Type **E776**	35	30
E2586	85pf.	"Climber" (Fritz Cremer)	1·30	1·30

E777 String Puppet

1984. Puppets. Multicoloured.

E2587	50pf.	Type **E777**	85	85
E2588	80pf.	Hand puppet	1·50	1·50

E778 Marchers with Flags

1984. National Youth Festival, Berlin. Multicoloured.

E2589	10pf.+5pf.	Type **E778**	30	25
E2590	20pf.	Young construction workers	35	30

E779 Gera Buildings

1984. 20th Workers' Festival, Gera. Multicoloured.

E2591	10pf.	Type **E779**	30	25
E2592	20pf.	Couple in traditional costume	35	35

E780 Salt Carrier

1984. National Stamp Exhibition, Halle. Multicoloured.

E2593	10pf.+5pf.	Type **E780**	30	25
E2594	20pf.	Citizen of Halle with his bride	50	35

E781 Bakers' Seal, Berlin

1984. Historical Seals of 1442. Multicoloured.

E2595	5pf.	Type **E781**	50	25
E2596	10pf.	Wool weavers, Berlin	85	50
E2597	20pf.	Wool weavers, Colln on Spree	1·60	60
E2598	35pf.	Shoemakers, Colln on Spree	2·75	2·40

E782 New Flats and Restored Terrace

1984. 35th Anniv of German Democratic Republic (1st issue). Multicoloured.

E2599	10pf.	Type **E782**	30	20
E2600	20pf.	Surface mining	50	50
MSE2601	80×55 mm. 1m. Privy Council building		1·80	1·80

See also Nos. E2604/**MS**E2607 and E2069/**MS**E2613.

E783 Frege House, Katherine Street

1984. Leipzig Autumn Fair. Multicoloured.

E2602	20pf.	Type **E783**	30	25
E2603	25pf.	Crystal jar from Olbernhau	50	35

E784 East Ironworks

1984. 35th Anniv of German Democratic Republic (2nd issue). Multicoloured.

E2604	10pf.	Type **E784**	25	25
E2605	20pf.	Soldiers, Mil Mi-8 helicopter, tank and warship	35	35
E2606	25pf.	Petro-chemical complex, Schwedt	50	45
MSE2607	110×90 mm. 1m. bright carmine (Family and new flats) (51×29 mm)		2·00	2·00

E785 Members of the Resistance (Arno Wittig)

1984. Resistance Memorial, Georg-Schumann Building, Technical University of Dresden.

E2608	**E785**	35pf. multicoloured	1·10	50

E786 Construction Workers

1984. 35th Anniv of German Democratic Republic (3rd issue). Multicoloured.

E2609	10pf.	Type **E786**	25	20
E2610	20pf.	Soldiers	35	25
E2611	25pf.	Industrial workers	50	45
E2612	35pf.	Agricultural workers	60	55
MSE2613	108×88 mm. 1m. Dove and national arms (vert)		1·70	1·70

E787 Magdeburg, 1551

1984. Eighth National Youth Exhibition, Magdeburg. Multicoloured.

E2614	10pf.+5pf.	Type **E787**	30	30
E2615	20pf.	Modern Magdeburg	30	30

E788 "Spring"

1984. Statuettes by Balthasar Permoser in Green Vault, Dresden. Multicoloured.

E2616	10pf.	Type **E788**	25	25
E2617	20pf.	"Summer"	35	35
E2618	35pf.	"Autumn"	60	60
E2619	70pf.	"Winter"	1·20	1·20
MSE2620	144×115 mm. No. E 2617×8		3·75	3·75

E789 Entwined Cable and Red Star

1984. "Solidarity".

E2621	**E789**	10pf.+5pf. mult	60	45

E790 Falkenstein Castle

1984. Castles (1st series). Multicoloured.

E2622	10pf.	Type **E790**	25	25
E2623	20pf.	Kriebstein Castle	35	30
E2624	35pf.	Ranis Castle	75	75

E791 Queen and Princess

1984. Fairy Tales. *Dead Tsar's Daughter and the Seven Warriors* by Pushkin. Multicoloured.

E2626	5pf. Type **E791**	45	35
E2627	10pf. Princess and dog outside cottage	45	35
E2628	15pf. Princess and seven warriors	4·25	2·50
E2629	20pf. Princess holding poisoned apple	4·25	2·50
E2630	35pf. Princess awakened by Prince	45	35
E2631	50pf. Prince and Princess on horse	45	35

E792 Anton Ackermann

1985. Socialist Personalities.

E2632	**E792** 10pf. black	25	25
E2633	- 10pf. brown	25	25
E2634	- 10pf. purple	25	25

DESIGNS: No. E2633, Alfred Kurella; E2634, Otto Schon.

E793 Luge

1985. 24th World Luge Championships, Oberhof.

E2635	**E793** 10pf. multicoloured	50	35

E794 Letter-box, 1850

1984. Letter-boxes.

E2636	**E794** 10pf. brown and black	25	25
E2637	- 20pf. black, brown and red	25	25
E2638	- 35pf. multicoloured	50	50
E2639	- 50pf. brown, black and grey	75	75

DESIGNS: 20pf. Letter-box, 1860; 35pf. Letter-box, 1900; 50pf. Letter-box, 1920.

E795 Semper Opera House, 1985

1985. Re-opening of Semper Opera House, Dresden. Sheet 57×80 mm.

MSE2640	**E795** 85pf. brown, grey and red	1·60	1·60

E796 Bach Statue, Leipzig

1985. Leipzig Spring Fair. Multicoloured.

E2641	Type **E796** 10pf.	30	25
E2642	25pf. Meissen porcelain pot	50	35

E797 Johann Sebastian Bach

1985. 300th Birth Annivs of Bach and Handel and 400th Birth Anniv of Schutz (composers). Sheet 90×114 mm containing Type **E797** and similar vert designs, together with *se-tenant* horiz labels.

MSE2643	10pf. blue and bistre; 20pf. purple and bistre; 85pf. green and bistre	3·50	3·50

DESIGNS: 20pf. Georg Friedrich Handel; 85pf. Heinrich Schutz.

1985. Town Arms (3rd series). As Type **E758**. Multicoloured.

E2644	50pf. Neubrandenburg	75	70
E2645	50pf. Potsdam	75	70
E2646	50pf. Rostock	75	70
E2647	50pf. Schwerin	75	70
E2648	50pf. Suhl	85	80

E798 Liberation Monument

1985. Liberation Monument, Seelow Heights.

E2649	**E798** 35pf. multicoloured	75	50

E799 Egon Erwin Kisch

1985. Birth Centenary of Egon Erwin Kisch (journalist).

E2650	**E799** 35pf. multicoloured	75	60

E800 Sigmund Jahn and Valeri Bykovski

1985. 40th Anniv of Defeat of Fascism. Multicoloured.

E2651	10pf. Type **E800**	25	25
E2652	20pf. Adolf Hennecke as miner	35	35
E2653	25pf. Agricultural workers reading paper	45	45
E2654	50pf. Laboratory technicians	85	1·00
MSE2655	55×81 mm. 1m. Soviet war memorial, Berlin-Treptow (22×40 mm)	1·80	1·80

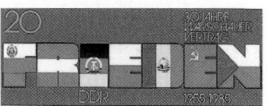

E801 Flags forming "Frieden" (Peace)

1985. 30th Anniv of Warsaw Pact.

E2656	**E801** 20pf. multicoloured	60	35

E802 Emblem and Berlin Buildings

1985. 12th Free German Youth Parliament, Berlin. Multicoloured.

E2657	10pf.+5pf. Type **E802**	35	25
E2658	20pf. Flags, Ernst Thalmann and emblem	35	25

E803 "Solidarity" and Dove on Globe

1985. "Solidarity".

E2659	**E803** 10pf.+5pf. multicoloured	50	30

E804 Olympic Flag

1985. 90th International Olympic Committee Meeting, Berlin.

E2660	**E804** 35pf. multicoloured	1·30	1·00

E805 "40" and Emblem

1985. 40th Anniv of Free German Trade Unions Federation.

E2661	**E805** 20pf. multicoloured	50	35

E806 Harpy Eagle

1985. Protected Animals. Multicoloured.

E2662	5pf. Type **E806**	25	20
E2663	10pf. Red-breasted geese (horiz)	25	20
E2664	20pf. Spectacled bear (horiz)	35	35
E2665	50pf. Bantengs (horiz)	75	60
E2666	85pf. Sunda gavial (horiz)	1·60	1·60

E807 Support Steam-engine, Gera, 1833

1985. Steam Engines. Multicoloured.

E2667	10pf. Type **E807**	30	25
E2668	85pf. Balance steam-engine, Frieberg, 1848	1·50	1·30

E808 Students reading

1985. 12th World Youth and Students' Festival, Moscow. Multicoloured.

E2669	20pf.+5pf. Type **E808**	35	35
E2670	50pf. Students with raised arms	60	60

E809 Diver at Turning Post

1985. Second World Orienteering Diving Championship, Neuglobsow. Multicoloured.

E2671	10pf. Type **E809**	25	25
E2672	70pf. Divers	1·20	1·20

E810 Bose House, Saint Thomas Churchyard

1985. Leipzig Autumn Fair. Multicoloured.

E2673	10pf. Type **E810**	30	25
E2674	25pf. J. Scherzer Bach-trumpet	60	35

E811 Passenger Mail Coach (relief, Hermann Steinemann)

1985. "Sozphilex '85" Stamp Exhibition, Berlin. Multicoloured.

E2675	5pf. Type **E811**	25	25
E2676	20pf.+5pf. Team of horses	35	35

Nos. E2675/6 were printed together, *se-tenant*, forming a composite design.

E812 Electrification of Railway

1985. Railways. Multicoloured.

E2677	20pf. Signal box	35	25
E2678	25pf. Andreas Schubert (engineer), his steam locomotive *Saxonia*, 1838, and electric locomotive Type BR250	50	35
E2679	50pf. Type **E812**	1·00	85
E2680	85pf. Leipzig Central Station	1·60	1·60

E813 Gertrauden Bridge

1985. Berlin Bridges. Multicoloured.

E2681	10pf. Type **E813**	25	25
E2682	20pf. Jungfern Bridge	35	35
E2683	35pf. Weidendammer Bridge	60	60
E2684	70pf. Marx-Engels Bridge	1·00	1·00
MSE2685	107×128 mm. No. E2673×8	4·50	4·50

1985. Castles (2nd series). As Type **E790**. Multicoloured.

E2686	10pf. Hohnstein Castle	25	25
E2687	20pf. Rochsburg	30	30
E2688	35pf. Schwarzenberg Castle	50	50
E2689	80pf. Stein Castle	1·50	1·50

E814 Humboldt University

1985. Anniversaries. Multicoloured.

E2690	20pf. Type **E814** (175th anniv of Humboldt University, Berlin)	35	35
E2691	85pf. New and old Charite buildings (275th anniv of Berlin Charite (training clinic))	1·50	1·50

E815 Cecilienhof Castle and U.N. Emblem

1985. 40th Anniv of U.N.O.

E2692	**E815** 85pf. multicoloured	1·50	75

E816 Elephants on Balls

1985. Circus. Multicoloured.

E2693	10pf. Type **E816**	50	50
E2694	20pf. Trapeze artiste	75	75
E2695	35pf. Acrobats on monocycles	1·50	1·50
E2696	50pf. Tigers and trainer	2·20	2·20

E817 Grimm Brothers

1985. Birth Bicentenaries of Jacob and Wilhelm Grimm (folklorists). Multicoloured.

E2697	5pf. Type **E817**	30	30
E2698	10pf. *The Valiant Tailor*	30	30
E2699	20pf. *Lucky John*	90	1·30
E2700	25pf. *Puss in Boots*	90	1·30
E2701	35pf. *The Seven Ravens*	30	30
E2702	85pf. *The Sweet Pap*	30	30

E818 Water Pump, Berlin, 1900

1986. Water Supply.

E2703	**E818** 10pf. green and red	25	20
E2704	– 35pf. deep brown, brown and green	50	45
E2705	– 50pf. purple & green	85	80
E2706	– 70pf. blue and brown	1·10	1·00

DESIGNS: 35pf. Water tower, Berlin-Altglienicke, 1906; 50pf. Waterworks, Berlin-Friedrichshagen, 1893; 70pf. Rappbode dam, 1959.

E819 Saxon Postilion

1986. Postal Uniforms of 1850. Multicoloured.

E2707A	10pf. Type **E819**	30	25
E2708A	20pf. Prussian postman	50	35
E2709A	85pf. Prussian postal official	1·70	1·60
E2710A	1m. Postal official from Mecklenburg region	2·20	2·20

E820 Flag

1986. 40th Anniv of Free German Youth.

E2711	**E820** 20pf. yellow, bl & blk	60	50

E821 Flag

1986. 30th Anniv of National People's Army.

E2712	**E821** 20pf. multicoloured	1·00	75

E822 Exhibition Hall

1986. Leipzig Spring Fair. Multicoloured.

E2713	35pf. Type **E822**	50	35
E2714	50pf. *Atlantik 488* (factory trawler)	85	60

E823 Yuri Gagarin and "Vostok"

1986. 25th Anniv of Manned Space Flight. Multicoloured.

E2715	40pf. Type **E823** (first man in space)	50	60

E2716	50pf. Cosmonauts Valeri Bykovski and Sigmund Jahn, space station and "Interkosmos" emblem	60	75
E2717	70pf. Space probe "Venera", orbit around Venus and spectrometer	85	1·00
E2718	85pf. Reconnaissance camera MKF-6, photo, "Soyuz 22" spaceship, airplane and research ship	1·10	1·20

E824 Marx, Engels and Lenin

1986. 11th Socialist Unity Party of Germany Day.

E2719	**E824** 10pf. black, red and silver	25	25
E2720	– 20pf. red, black and silver	35	35
E2721	– 50pf. multicoloured	75	75
E2722	– 85pf. black, red and silver	1·50	1·50
MSE2723	80×55 mm. 1m. multicoloured	1·70	1·70

DESIGNS: 20pf. Ernst Thalmann (birth centenary); 50pf. Wilhelm Pieck and Otto Grotewohl, April 1946; 85pf. Family; 1m. Construction worker holding symbolic key.

E825 Memorial

1986. Opening of Ernst Thalmann Park, Berlin.

E2724	**E825** 20pf. multicoloured	60	50

E826 Horse Tram, Dresden, 1886

1986. Trams. Multicoloured.

E2725	10pf. Type **E826**	25	25
E2726	20pf. Leipzig, 1896	35	35
E2727	40pf. Berlin, 1919	85	85
E2728	70pf. Halle, 1928	1·80	1·50

E827 Orang-utan

1986. 125th Anniv of Dresden Zoo. Multicoloured.

E2729	10pf. Type **E827**	35	25
E2730	20pf. Eastern black-and-white colobus	60	50
E2731	50pf. Mandrill	1·20	1·20
E2732	70pf. Ring-tailed lemurs	1·60	1·60

E828 City Seal, 1253

1986. 750th Anniv of Berlin (1st issue).

E2733	**E828** 10pf. deep brown, bistre and brown	35	25
E2734	– 20pf. olive, grn & brn	75	35
E2735	– 50pf. blk, brn & red	1·50	1·00
E2736	– 70pf. green & brown	2·50	1·90
MSE2737	54×80 mm. 1m. green	2·20	2·20

DESIGNS—HORIZ: 20pf. City map, 1648; 50pf. Oldest City arms. VERT: 70pf. St. Nicolas's Church, 1832; 1m. Cabinet building tower.
See also Nos. E2780/**MSE**2784 and **MSE**2828.

E829 Couple, Tractor and House

1986. 21st Workers' Festival, Magdeburg. Multicoloured.

E2738	20pf. Type **E829**	35	35
E2739	50pf. Port and town of Magdeburg	50	50

E830 Berlin, 1652

1986. Ninth Youth Stamp Exhibition, Berlin. Multicoloured.

E2740	10pf.+5pf. Type **E830**	25	25
E2741	20pf. Historic and modern Berlin buildings	35	35

E831 Schwerin Castle

1986. Castles (3rd series). Multicoloured.

E2742	10pf. Type **E831**	25	20
E2743	35pf. Gustrow castle	35	25
E2744	85pf. Rheinsberg castle	1·30	1·30
E2745	1m. Ludwigslust castle	1·80	1·80

E832 Soldiers and Girl before Brandenburg Gate

1986. 25th Anniv of Berlin Wall.

E2746	**E832** 20pf. multicoloured	1·00	60

E833 Doves flying from Emblem

1986. International Peace Year.

E2747	**E833** 35pf. multicoloured	85	60

E834 Ring-Messehaus

1986. Leipzig Autumn Fair. Sheet 82×57 mm containing Type E834 and similar vert design.

MSE2748	25pf. Type **E834**; 85pf. Merchants displaying cloth	2·00	2·00

E835 Rostock, 1637

1986. Coins.

E2749	**E835** 10pf. black, silver and red	25	20
E2750	– 35pf. black, silver and blue	50	50
E2751	– 50pf. multicoloured	75	75
E2752	– 85pf. black, silver and blue	1·20	1·20
E2753	– 1m. black, silver and red	1·70	1·70

DESIGNS: 35pf. Nordhausen, 1660; 50pf. Erfurt, 1633; 85pf. Magdeburg, 1638; 1m. Stralsund, 1622.

E836 Man with Rifle

1986. 44th World Sports Shooting Championships, Suhl.

E2754	**E836** 20pf. black, green and grey	35	25
E2755	– 70pf. black, red and grey	1·20	1·10
E2756	– 85pf. black, blue and grey	1·50	1·30

DESIGNS: 70pf. Woman with pistol; 85pf. Man with double-barrelled shotgun.

E837 Guard and Boundary Post

1986. 40th Anniv of Border Guards.

E2757	**E837** 20pf. multicoloured	60	50

E838 Hemispheres and Red Banner

1986. 11th World Trade Unions Congress, Berlin.

E2758	**E838** 70pf. multicoloured	1·50	1·20

E839 German Members Memorial, Friedrichshain

1986. 50th Anniv of Formation of International Brigades in Spain.

E2759	**E839** 20pf. brown, black and red	60	45

E840 Memorial

1986. 25th Anniv of Sachsenhausen Memorial.

E2760	**E840** 35pf. black, grn & bl	75	50

E841 Double-deck Train Ferry Loading Ramps

1986. Opening of Mukran–Klaipeda Railway Ferry Service. Multicoloured.

E2761	50pf. Type **E841**	60	60
E2762	50pf. "Mukran" (train ferry)	60	60

Nos. E2761/2 were printed together, *se-tenant*, forming a composite design.

E842 "Help for Developing Countries"

1986. "Solidarity".

E2763	**E842** 10pf.+5pf. multicoloured	50	45

E843 Weber (after F. Jugel)

1986. Birth Bicentenary of Carl Maria von Weber (composer). Sheet 82×57 mm.

MSE2764	**E843** 85pf. multicoloured	1·80	1·70

E844 Indira Gandhi

1986. Second Death Anniv of Indira Gandhi (Indian Prime Minister).
E2765 **E844** 10pf. stone & brown   50   35

E845 Candle Holder, 1778

1986. Candle Holders from the Erzgebirge. Multicoloured.
E2766 10pf. Type **E845**   30   30
E2767 20pf. Candle holder, 1796   30   30
E2768 25pf. Candle holder, 1810   85   85
E2769 35pf. Candle holder, 1821   85   85
E2770 40pf. Candle holder, 1830   30   30
E2771 85pf. Candle holder, 1925   30   30

E846 Ronald Statue, Stendal

1987. Statues of Roland (1st series).
E2772 10pf. lt brown, brown & yell   25   20
E2773 20pf. lt brown, brown & bl   35   25
E2774 35pf. lt brown, brown & orge   60   60
E2775 40pf. lt brown, brown & grn   90   90
DESIGNS: Statues at—10pf. Type **E846**; 20pf. Halle; 35pf. Brandenburg; 50pf. Quedlinburg.
   See also Nos. E2984/7.

E847 Post Office, Freiberg

1987. Post Offices.
E2776 **E847** 10pf. black, red and blue   25   25
E2777 - 20pf. multicoloured   35   35
E2778 - 70pf. multicoloured   85   85
E2779 - 1m.20 mult   1·80   1·80
DESIGNS: 20pf. Perleberg; 70pf. Weimar; 1m.20, Kirschau.

1987. 750th Anniv of Berlin (2nd issue). As Type **E828**.
E2780 20pf. brown and green   30   30
E2781 35pf. green and red   55   55
E2782 70pf. blue and red   1·10   1·10
E2783 85pf. olive and green   1·60   1·60
MSE2784 Four sheets, 75×108 mm (a) or 107×75 mm (others). (a) 10pf. As No. E2780; (b) 10pf. ×4, As No. E2781; (c) 20pf. ×4, As No. E2782; (d) 20pf. ×4, As No. E2783   6·50   7·25
DESIGNS—VERT: 20pf. Ephraim Palace. HORIZ: 35pf. New buildings, Alt Marzahn; 70pf. Marx-Engels Forum; 85pf. Friedrichstadtpalast.

E848 Woman with Flower in Hair

1987. 40th Anniv and 12th Congress (Berlin) of German Democratic Women's Federation.
E2785 **E848** 10pf. blue, red & sil   50   50

E849 Fair Hall 20

1987. Leipzig Spring Fair. Multicoloured.
E2786 35pf. Type **E849**   55   55
E2787 50pf. *Traders at Weighbridge, 1804* (Christian Geissler)   1·00   1·00

E850 Clara Zetkin

1987. Socialist Personalities. Multicoloured.
E2788 **E850** 10pf. purple   35   25
E2789 - 10pf. black   35   25
E2790 - 10pf. black   35   25
E2791 - 10pf. green   35   25
DESIGNS: No. E2789, Fritz Gabler; E2790, Walter Vesper; E2791, Robert Siewert.

E851 Construction Industry

1987. 11th Federation of Free German Trade Unions Congress, Berlin. Multicoloured.
E2792 20pf. Type **E851**   30   30
E2793 50pf. Communications industry   75   75

E852 Flag, World Map and Doves

1987. Tenth German Red Cross Congress, Dresden.
E2794 **E852** 35pf. multicoloured   75   50

E853 Museum and Karl August Lingner (founder) (after Robert Sterl)

1987. 75th Anniv of German Hygiene Museum, Dresden.
E2795 **E853** 85pf. multicoloured   1·30   1·20

E854 Old and New Farming Methods

1987. 35th Anniv of Agricultural Co-operatives.
E2796 **E854** 20pf. multicoloured   60   50

E855 Ludwig Uhland (poet)

1987. Birth Anniversaries. Multicoloured.
E2797 10pf. Type **E855** (bicent)   25   25
E2798 20pf. Arnold Zweig (writer, centenary)   35   35
E2799 35pf. Gerhart Hauptmann (writer, 125th anniv)   60   60
E2800 50pf. Gustav Hertz (physicist, centenary)   1·00   1·00

E856 Bream

1987. Freshwater Fish. Multicoloured.
E2801 5pf. Type **E856**   30   20
E2802 10pf. Brown trout   35   35
E2803 20pf. Wels   35   25
E2804 35pf. European grayling   60   60
E2805 50pf. Barbel   85   60
E2806 70pf. Northern pike   1·20   1·20

E857 Woman holding Baby

1987. "Solidarity" Anti-Apartheid Campaign.
E2807 **E857** 10pf.+5pf. multicoloured   50   35

E858 Horse-drawn Hand-pumped Fire Engine, 1756

1987. Fire Engines. Multicoloured.
E2808 10pf. Type **E858**   25   25
E2809 25pf. Steam engine, 1903   35   35
E2810 40pf. Model "LF 15", 1919   75   75
E2811 70pf. Model "LF 16-TS 8", 1971   1·20   1·20

E859 Ludwig Lazarus Zamenhof (inventor)

1987. Centenary of Esperanto (invented language). Sheet 55×80 mm.
MSE2812 **E859** 85pf. multicoloured   1·50   2·00

E860 Otters

1987. Endangered Animals. European Otter. Multicoloured.
E2813 10pf. Type **E860**   25   20
E2814 25pf. Otter swimming   45   35
E2815 35pf. Otter   60   50
E2816 60pf. Otter's head   1·50   1·40

E861 Tug-of-War

1987. Eighth Gymnastics and Sports Festival and 11th Children and Young People's Sports Days, Leipzig. Multicoloured.
E2817 5pf. Type **E861**   25   20
E2818 10pf. Handball   25   20
E2819 20pf.+5pf. Long jumping   35   30
E2820 35pf. Table tennis   50   45
E2821 40pf. Bowling   75   60
E2822 70pf. Running   1·60   1·60

E862 Association Activities

1987. 35th Anniv of Association of Sports and Technical Sciences.
E2823 **E862** 10pf. multicoloured   50   30

E863 Head Post Office, Berlin, 1760

1987. Stamp Day. Multicoloured.
E2824 10pf.+5pf. Type **E863**   30   30
E2825 20pf. Wartenberg Palace   30   30

E864 Market Scene

1987. Leipzig Autumn Fair. Sheet 80×58 mm containing Type **E864** and similar vert design showing *Market Scene* by Christian Geissler.
MSE2826 40pf. multicoloured; 50pf. multicoloured   2·00   2·00

E865 Memorial Statue (Jozsef Somogyi)

1987. War Victims' Memorial, Budapest.
E2827 **E865** 35pf. multicoloured   60   35

E866 Memorial, Ernst Thalmann Park

1987. 750th Anniv of Berlin (3rd issue). Sheet 80×55 mm.
MSE2828 **E866** 1m.35 black, stone and red   2·40   2·40

E867 Weidendamm Bridge (Arno Mohr)

1987. Tenth Art Exhibition, Dresden. Multicoloured.
E2829 10pf. Type **E867**   25   25
E2830 50pf. *They only wanted to learn Reading and Writing (Nicaragua)* (Willi Sitte)   80   80
E2831 70pf. *Big Mourning Man* (Wieland Forster)   1·00   1·00
E2832 1m. Vase (Gerd Lucke) (horiz)   1·90   1·90

E868 Red Flag, Smolny Building (Leningrad), *Aurora* and Lenin

1987. 70th Anniv of Russian Revolution. Multicoloured.
E2833 10pf. Type **E868**   30   20
E2834 20pf. Moscow Kremlin towers   35   25

E869 Youth using Personal Computer

1987. 39th "Masters of Tomorrow" Fair, Leipzig. Multicoloured.
E2835 10pf. Type **E869**   30   20
E2836 20pf. "ZIM 10-S" robot-welder   35   25

E870 Annaberg, 1810

1987. Christmas Pyramids from Erzgebirge. Multicoloured.
E2837 10pf. Type **E870**   35   35
E2838 20pf. Freiberg, 1830   85   85
E2839 25pf. Neustadtel, 1870   35   35
E2840 35pf. Schneeberg, 1870   35   35
E2841 40pf. Lossnitz, 1880   85   85
E2842 85pf. Seiffen, 1910   35   35

E871 Ski Jumping

1988. Winter Olympic Games, Calgary. Multicoloured.
E2843	5pf. Type **E871**	35	25
E2844	10pf. Speed skating	35	25
E2845	20pf.+10pf. Four-man bobsleigh	60	50
E2846	35pf. Biathlon	75	75
MSE2847	80×55 mm. 1m.20 Two-man and single luge (horiz)	2·40	2·10

E872 Berlin-Buch Post Office

1988. Postal Buildings. Multicoloured.
E2848	15pf. Type **E872**	45	25
E2849	20pf. Postal museum	55	25
E2850	50pf. Berlin-Marzahn general post office	1·20	1·00

E873 Brecht

1988. 90th Birth Anniv of Bertholt Brecht (writer). Sheet 58×82 mm.
MSE2851	**E873** 70pf. grey, black and red	1·60	1·60

E874 *Tillandsia macrochlamys*

1988. Bromeliads. Multicoloured.
E2852	10pf. Type **E874**	25	20
E2853	25pf. *Tillandsia bulbosa*	35	35
E2854	40pf. *Tillandsia kalmbacheri*	60	60
E2855	70pf. *Guzmania blassii*	1·20	1·20

E875 Madler-passage Entrance

1988. Leipzig Spring Fair. 75th Anniv of Madler-passage (fair building). Each brown, orange and pink.
E2856	20pf. Type **E875**	30	25
E2857	70pf. "Faust and Mephistopheles" (bronze statue, Matthieu Molitor)	1·20	1·00

E876 Eichendorff

1988. Birth Bicentenary of Joseph von Eichendorff (writer). Sheet 82×55 mm.
MSE2858	**E876** 70pf. olive, drab and blue	2·00	1·70

E877 Saddler, Muhlhausen, 1565

1988. Historic Seals. Multicoloured.
E2859	10pf. Type **E877**	25	25
E2860	25pf. Butcher, Dresden, 1564	35	35

E2861	35pf. Smith, Nauen, 16th-century	50	50
E2862	50pf. Clothier, Frankfurt on Oder, 16th-century	65	65

E878 Georg Forster Antarctic Research Station

1988. 12th Anniv of Georg Forster Antarctic Research Station.
E2863	**E878** 35pf. multicoloured	75	50

E879 Wismar

1988. Northern Towns of the Democratic Republic.
E2864	5pf. black, green & turquoise	25	20
E2865	10pf. black, ochre and brown	25	20
E2866	25pf. black, lightt blue & blue	45	30
E2867	60pf. black, pink and red	85	75
E2868	90pf. black, lt green & green	1·20	1·10
E2869	1m.20 black, brown and red	1·60	1·50
DESIGNS: 5pf. Type E **879**.; 10pf. Anklam; 25pf. Ribnitz-Damgarten; 60pf. Stralsund; 90pf. Bergen; 1m.20, Greifswald.

E880 Hutten

1988. 500th Birth Anniv of Ulrich von Hutten (humanist). Sheet 54×80 mm.
MSE2870	**E880** 70pf. black, yellow and ochre	1·70	1·60

E881 Chorin and Neuzelle Monasteries, Industrial and Agricultural Symbols

1988. 22nd Workers' Arts Festival, Frankfurt-on-Oder. Multicoloured.
E2871	20pf. Type **E881**	35	35
E2872	50pf. Buildings of Frankfurt	75	75

E882 Cosmonauts Sigmund Jahn and Valery Bykovski

1988. Tenth Anniv of U.S.S.R.–East German Manned Space Flight (1st issue). Multicoloured.
E2873	5pf. Type **E882**	30	25
E2874	10pf. "MKS-M" multi-channel spectrometer	30	25
E2875	20pf. "Mir"–"Soyuz" space complex	35	35
See also Nos. E2894/6.

E883 Erfurt, 1520

1988. Tenth Youth Stamp Exhibition, Erfurt and Karl-Marx-Stadt. Multicoloured.
E2876	10pf.+5pf. Type **E883**	25	25
E2877	20pf.+5pf. Chemnitz, 1620	35	35
E2878	25pf. Modern view of Erfurt	35	35
E2879	50pf. Modern view of Karl-Marx-Stadt (formerly Chemnitz)	85	85

E884 Swearing-in Ceremony

1988. 35th Anniv of Workers' Militia Squads. Multicoloured.
E2880	5pf. Type **E884**	35	25
E2881	10pf. Tribute to Ernst Thalmann	35	25
E2882	15pf. Parade	45	45
E2883	20pf. Arms distribution	35	25

E885 Balloons and Doves over Karl-Marx-Stadt

1988. Eighth Pioneers Meeting, Karl-Marx-Stadt. Multicoloured.
E2884	10pf. Type **E885**	30	30
E2885	10pf.+5pf. Doves, balloons and Pioneers	30	30

E886 Swimming

1988. Olympic Games, Seoul. Multicoloured.
E2886	5pf. Type **E886**	25	25
E2887	10pf. Handball	25	25
E2888	20pf.+10pf. Hurdling	50	50
E2889	25pf. Rowing	50	50
E2890	35pf. Boxing	75	75
E2891	50pf.+20pf. Cycling	1·10	1·10
MSE2892	55×80 mm. 85pf. Relay race	3·00	3·00

E887 Examining Fair Goods, 1810

1988. Leipzig Autumn Fair and 175th Anniv of Battle of Leipzig. Sheet 110×90 mm containing Type **E887** and similar vert designs. Multicoloured.
MSE2893	5pf. Type **E887**; 15pf. Battle of Leipzig Monument; 100pf. Fair, 1820	2·75	2·75

1988. Tenth Anniv of U.S.S.R.–East German Manned space Flight (2nd issue). As Nos. E2873/5 but values changed. Multicoloured.
E2894	10pf. Type **E882**	35	35
E2895	20pf. As No. E2874	50	50
E2896	35pf. As No. E2875	85	85

E888 Buchenwald Memorial (Fritz Cremer)

1988. War Memorials.
E2897	**E888** 10pf. green, black and brown	35	30
E2898	- 35pf. multicoloured	60	50
DESIGN: 35pf. Resistance Monument, Lake Como, Italy (Gianni Colombo).

E889 'Adolph Friedrich' at Stralsund: Captain C. Leplow (E. Laschke)

1988. 500th Anniv of Stralsund Shipping Company. Captains' Paintings. Multicoloured.
E2899	5pf. Type **E889**	35	25
E2900	10pf. 'Gartenlaube' of Stralsund: Captain J. F. Kruger (A. Luschky)	35	25
E2901	70pf. *Brigantina 'Auguste Mathilde' of Stralsund: Captain I. C. Grunwaldt* (Johnsen-Seby Bergen)	1·20	1·20
E2902	1m.20 *Brig 'Hoffnung' of Cologne-on-Rhine: Captain G. A. Luther* (anon)	1·80	1·80

E890 Medical Scene and African Child

1988. "Solidarity".
E2903	**E890** 10pf.+5pf. multicoloured	1·20	1·20

E891 Magdeburg Drawbridge

1988. Drawbridges and Ship Lifts. Multicoloured.
E2904	5pf. Type **E891**	25	20
E2905	10pf. Lift, Magdeburg–Rothensee Canal	25	25
E2906	35pf. Lift, Niederfinow	55	55
E2907	70pf. Bridge and lock, Altfriesack	1·00	1·00
E2908	90pf. Drawbridge, Rugendamm	1·20	1·20

E892 Menorah

1988. 50th Anniv of *Kristallnacht* (Nazi pogrom).
E2909	**E892** 35pf. purple, yellow and black	75	50

E893 *In the Boat*

1988. Birth Centenary of Max Lingner (artist). Multicoloured.
E2910	5pf. Type **E893**	35	25
E2911	10pf. *Mademoiselle Yvonne*	35	25
E2912	20pf. *Free, Strong and Happy*	50	30
E2913	85pf. *New Harvest*	1·60	1·50

E894 Lace (Regine Wengler)

1988. Bobbin Lace from Erzgebirge. Pieces by lacemakers named. Each black, brown and yellow.
E2914	20pf. Type **E894**	35	35
E2915	25pf. Wally Tilp	85	85
E2916	35pf. Elisabeth Mehnert-Pfabe	35	35
E2917	40pf. Ute Siewert	35	35
E2918	80pf. Regine Siebdraht	85	85
E2919	85pf. Elise Schubert	35	35

E895 W.H.O. Emblem

1988. 40th Anniv of W.H.O.
E2920	**E895** 85pf. silver, bl & grey	1·50	75

E896 Dr. Wolf

1988. Birth Centenary of Dr. Freidrich Wolf (writer). Sheet 87×59 mm.
MSE2921	**E896** 110pf. grey, black and vermilion	1·80	1·80

E897 Members' Flags

1989. 40th Anniv of Council of Mutual Economic Aid.
E2922	**E897**	20pf. multicoloured	50	35

E898 Edith Baumann

1989. Socialist Personalities.
E2923	**E898**	10pf. brown	30	20
E2924	-	10pf. green	30	20
E2925	-	10pf. brown	30	20
E2926	-	10pf. blue	30	20

DESIGNS: No. E2924, Otto Meier; E2925, Alfred Oelssner; E2926, Fritz Selbmann.

E899 Philipp Reis Telephone, 1861

1989. Telephones. Multicoloured.
E2927	10pf. Type **E899**	25	25
E2928	20pf. Siemens & Halske wall telephone, 1882	35	35
E2929	50pf. "OB 03" wall telephone, 1903	75	75
E2930	85pf. "OB 05" desk telephone, 1905	1·20	1·20

E900 Johann Beckmann (technologist, 250th anniv)

1989. Birth Anniversaries. Multicoloured.
E2931	10pf. Type **E900**	30	20
E2932	10pf. Rudolf Mauersberger and church choir (musician, cent)	30	20
E2933	10pf. Carl von Ossietzky and masthead of *Die Weltbuhne* (journalist and peace activist, centenary)	30	20
E2934	10pf. Ludwig Renn and International Brigades flag (writer, centenary)	30	20
E2935	10pf. Adam Scharrer and cover of *Stateless People* (novelist, centenary)	30	20

E901 Handelshof Fair Building

1989. Leipzig Spring Fair. Multicoloured.
E2936	70pf. Type **E901** (80th anniv)	1·20	1·00
E2937	85pf. Naschmarkt bake-house and bread shop, 1690	1·50	1·30

E902 Muntzer (after Christoph van Stichen and Romeyn de Hooghe)

1989. 500th Birth Anniv of Thomas Muntzer (religious reformer) (1st issue). Sheet 86×66 mm.
MSE2938	**E902** 110pf. black and buff	2·00	2·00

See also Nos. E2967/**MS**2972.

E903 Friedrich List (economist and promoter of railway system)

1989. 150th Anniv of Leipzig–Dresden Railway (first German long-distance service).
E2939	**E903** 15pf. brown, pale brown and green	50	35
E2940	- 20pf. black, green and red	50	25
E2941	- 50pf. black, brown and deep brown	1·00	1·00

DESIGNS: 20pf. Dresdner Station, Leipzig, 1839; 50pf. Leipziger Station, Dresden, 1839.

E904 Tea Caddy

1989. Meissen Porcelain. 250th Anniv of Onion Design. Each brown, blue and ultramarine.
E2942A	10pf. Type **E904**	35	25
E2943A	20pf. Vase	35	30
E2944A	35pf. Bread board	75	75
E2945A	70pf. Coffee pot	1·30	1·30

E905 Renaissance Initial "I"

1989. Seventh International Typography Exhibition, Leipzig.
E2946	**E905** 20pf. multicoloured	35	25
E2947	- 50pf. black, yellow and green	75	75
E2948	- 1m.35 red, black and grey	2·10	2·10

DESIGNS: 50pf. Art Nouveau initial "B"; 1m.35, Modern initial "A"s.

E906 Chollima Statue, Pyongyang

1989. 13th World Youth and Students' Festival, Pyongyang (E2949) and Free German Youth Whitsun Festival, Berlin (E2950). Multicoloured.
E2949	20pf. Type **E906**	50	50
E2950	20pf.+5pf. Berlin buildings	50	50

E907 *Princess Louise*

1989. 225th Birth Anniv of Johann Gottfried Schadow (sculptor). Details of *Princesses*. Multicoloured.
E2951	50pf. Type **E907**	1·00	75
E2952	85pf. *Princess Friederike*	1·70	1·50

E908 JENEVAL Interference Microscope

1989. Centenary of Carl Zeiss Foundation, Jena. Multicoloured.
E2953	50pf. Type **E908**	65	65
E2954	85pf. "ZKM 01-250 C" bi-coordinate measuring instrument	1·20	1·20

E909 Front Page of Address

1989. Bicentenary of Inaugural Address to Jena University by Friedrich Schiller (writer and philosopher). Each brown, black & grey.
E2955	25pf. Type **E909**	35	35
E2956	85pf. Part of address	1·10	1·10

E910 A. E. Brehm

1989. 160th Birth Anniv of Alfred Edmund Brehm and 125th Death Anniv of Christian Ludwig Brehm (naturalists). Sheet 110×80 mm containing Type **E910** and similar vert design. Multicoloured.
MSE2957	50pf. Type **E910**; 85pf. C. L. Brehm	2·40	13·00

E911 Storming the Bastille

1989. Bicent of French Revolution. Multicoloured.
E2958	5pf. Type **E911**	25	20
E2959	20pf. Sans-culottes	25	25
E2960	90pf. Invading the Tuileries	1·50	1·50

E912 Haflingers

1989. 40th International Horse Breeding in Socialist States Congress, Berlin. Multicoloured.
E2961	10pf. Type **E912**	25	25
E2962	20pf. English thoroughbreds (racehorses)	25	25
E2963	70pf. Heavy horses (plough team)	1·00	1·00
E2964	110pf. Thoroughbreds (dressage)	1·60	1·60

E913 Till Eulenspiegel Fountain

1989. National Stamp Exn, Magdeburg. Fountains by Heinrich Apel. Multicoloured.
E2965	20pf. Type **E913**	30	25
E2966	70pf.+5pf. Devil's fountain	1·20	1·20

E914 "Annunciation to the Peasants"

1989. 500th Birth Anniv of Thomas Muntzer (Protestant reformer) (2nd issue). Details of *Early Bourgeois Revolution in Germany* by Werner Tubke. Multicoloured.
E2967	5pf. Type **E914**	25	20
E2968	10pf. "Fountain of Life"	25	25
E2969	20pf. "Muntzer in the Battle"	35	30
E2970	50pf. "Lutheran Cat Battle"	85	85
E2971	85pf. "Justice, Jester"	1·60	1·60
MSE2972	99×142 mm. No. E2609/4	1·80	1·80

E915 New Fair Building

1989. Leipzig Autumn Fair. Sheet 105×75 mm containing Type **E915** and similar horiz design. Multicoloured.
MSE2973	50pf. Type **E915**; 85pf. New fair building (different)	2·30	2·30

E916 African Children

1989. "Solidarity".
E2974	**E916** 10pf.+5pf. multicoloured	35	35

E917 "Mother Group" (Fritz Cremer)

1989. 30th Anniv of Ravensbruck War Victims' Memorial.
E2975	**E917** 35pf. multicoloured	60	50

E918 "Adriana"

1989. Epiphyllums. Multicoloured.
E2976	10pf. Type **E918**	25	20
E2977	35pf. "Fire Magic"	60	50
E2978	50pf. "Franzisko"	1·00	85

E919 Dove, Flag and Schoolchildren

1989. 40th Anniv of German Democratic Republic. Multicoloured.
E2979	5pf. Type **E919**	35	25
E2980	10pf. Combine harvester and agricultural workers	35	25
E2981	20pf. Political activists working together	50	45
E2982	25pf. Industrial workers	75	65
MSE2983	113×93 mm. 135pf. Construction workers (54×32 mm)	6·00	5·00

1989. Statues of Roland (2nd series). As Type **E846**. Multicoloured.
E2984	5pf. Zerbst	25	20
E2985	10pf. Halberstadt	25	20
E2986	20pf. Buch-Altmark	35	30
E2987	50pf. Perleberg	85	85

E920 Nehru

1989. Birth Centenary of Jawaharlal Nehru (Indian statesman).
E2988 **E920** 35pf. brown and black 60 60

E921
Schneeberg, 1860

1989. Chandeliers from the Erzgebirge. Multicoloured.
E2989 10pf. Type **E921** 35 35
E2990 20pf. Schwarzenberg, 1850 85 85
E2991 25pf. Annaberg, 1880 35 35
E2992 35pf. Seiffen, 1900 35 35
E2993 50pf. Seiffen, 1930 85 85
E2994 70pf. Annaberg, 1925 35 35

E922 Bee on Apple Blossom

1990. The Honey Bee. Multicoloured.
E2995 5pf. Type **E922** 25 20
E2996 10pf. Bee on heather 25 20
E2997 20pf. Bee on rape 35 35
E2998 50pf. Bee on clover 1·20 1·20

E923 *Courier* (Albrecht Durer)

1990. 500th Anniv of Regular European Postal Services.
E2999 **E923** 35pf. chocolate, light brown and brown 75 75

E924 Erich Weinert

1990. Socialist Personalities.
E3000 **E924** 10pf. blue 45 35
E3001 - 10pf. brown 45 35
DESIGN: No. E3001, Bruno Leuschner.

E925
19th-century Sign, Blankenburg

1990. Posthouse Signs. Multicoloured.
E3002A 10pf. Type **E925** 30 20
E3003A 20pf. Royal Saxony sign (19th century) 35 25
E3004A 50pf. German Empire sign (1870s) 1·00 1·00
E3005A 110pf. German Empire auxiliary station sign (1900s) 2·20 2·20

E926 Bebel

1990. 150th Birth Anniv of August Bebel (politician).
E3006 **E926** 20pf. black, grey and red 75 60

E927 Drawings by Leonardo da Vinci

1990. "Lilienthal '91" European Airmail Exhibition. Historic Flying Machine Designs. Multicoloured.
E3007 20pf. Type **E927** 35 25
E3008 35pf.+5pf. Melchior Bauer's man-powered airplane design, 1764 75 75
E3009 50pf. Albrecht Berblinger's man-powered flying machine, 1811 1·00 1·00
E3010 90pf. Otto Lilienthal's design for a monoplane glider 1·70 1·70

E928 St. Nicholas's Church, Leipzig, and Demonstrators

1990. "We Are The People".
E3011 **E928** 35pf.+15pf. multicoloured 1·30 1·10

E929 Warrior's Head

1990. Museum of German History, Berlin. Stone Reliefs by Andreas Schluter.
E3012 **E929** 40pf. yell, grn & blk 1·00 1·00
E3013 - 70pf. multicoloured 1·30 1·30
DESIGN: 70pf. Warrior's head (different).

E930 Fair Seal, 1268

1990. Leipzig Spring Fair and 825th Anniv of Leipzig. Multicoloured.
E3014 70pf. Type **E930** 2·10 1·10
E3015 85pf. Fair seal, 1497 2·20 1·50

E931 Kurt Tucholsky (writer, centenary)

1990. Birth Anniversaries.
E3016 **E931** 10pf. black, green and deep green 50 50
E3017 - 10pf. black, brown and red 50 50
DESIGN: No. E3017, Friedrich Adolph Wilhelm Diesterweg (educationist, bicent).

E932 *Solidarity of Labour* (Walter Crane)

1990. Centenary of Labour Day.
E3018 **E932** 10pf. grey, black and red 60 60
E3019 - 20pf. red, grey and black 1·20 1·20
DESIGN: 20pf. Red carnation.

E933 Dicraeosaurus

1990. Centenary of Natural Science Museum, Berlin. Dinosaur Skeletons. Multicoloured.
E3020 10pf. Type **E933** 25 20
E3021 25pf. Kentrurosaurus 45 35
E3022 35pf. Dysalotosaurus 50 50
E3023 50pf. Brachiosaurus (vert) 75 75
E3024 85pf. Skull of brachiosaurus (vert) 1·60 1·60

E934 Penny Black

1990. 150th Anniv of the Penny Black.
E3025 **E934** 20pf. black, mauve and magenta 60 60
E3026 - 35pf.+15pf. red, lilac and black 1·10 1·10
E3027 - 110pf. multicoloured 3·00 3·00
DESIGNS: 35pf. Saxony 1850 3pf. stamp; 110pf. First East Germany stamp, 1949.

E935 Edward Hughes and 1855 Printing Telegraph

1990. 125th Anniv of I.T.U. Multicoloured.
E3028 10pf. Type **E935** 30 30
E3029 20pf. Distribution rods from Berlin-Kopenick post office 50 50
E3030 25pf. Transmitting tower and radio control desk 55 55
E3031 50pf. "Molniya" communications satellite and globe 1·20 1·20
MSE3032 82×56 mm. 70pf. Philipp Reis (telephone pioneer) 3·00 3·00

E936 Pope John Paul II

1990. Pope's 70th Birthday.
E3033 **E936** 35pf. multicoloured 1·20 1·10

E937 Halle (18th-century)

1990. 11th National Youth Stamp Exhibition, Halle. Multicoloured.
E3034 10pf.+5pf. Type **E937** 50 50
E3035 20pf. Modern Halle 50 50

E938 Rules of Order of Teutonic Knights, 1264

1990. Exhibits in German State Library, Berlin. Multicoloured.
E3036 20pf. Type **E938** 60 35
E3037 25pf. World map from *Rudimentum Novitiorum*, 1475 85 45
E3038 50pf. *Chosrou and Schirin* by Nizami (18th century Persian manuscript) 1·70 1·10
E3039 110pf. Book cover from Amalia musical library 3·25 2·75

WEST GERMAN CURRENCY

On 1 July 1990 the Ostmark was abolished and replaced by the West German Deutsche Mark.

E939 Albrechts Castle and Cathedral, Meissen

1990. Tourist Sights.
E3040 **E939** 10pf. blue 45 30
E3041 - 30pf. green 50 35
E3042 - 50pf. green 75 60
E3043 - 60pf. brown 1·00 1·00
E3044 - 70pf. brown 1·00 1·00
E3045 - 80pf. red 1·20 1·50
E3046 - 100pf. red 1·60 1·20
E3047 - 200pf. violet 2·75 2·40
E3048 - 500pf. green 7·00 5·75

DESIGNS: 30pf. Goethe-Schiller Monument, Weimar; 50pf. Brandenburg Gate, Berlin; 60pf. Kyffhauser Monument; 70pf. Semper Opera House, Dresden; 80pf. Sanssouci Palace, Potsdam; 100pf. Wartburg Castle, Eisenach; 200pf. Magdeburg Cathedral; 500pf. Schwerin Castle.

E940 Different Alphabets

1990. International Literacy Year.
E3049 **E940** 30pf.+5pf. on 10pf.+5pf. multicoloured 1·50 1·70
No. E3049 was not issued without surcharge.

E941 Letter-carrier (from playing card) and Messenger, 1486

1990. 500th Anniv of Regular European Postal Services.
E3050 **E941** 30pf. blk, brn & grn 60 60
E3051 - 50pf. black, red and blue 85 85
E3052 - 70pf. black, brown and red 1·10 1·50
E3053 - 100pf. black, grn & bl 1·80 1·80
DESIGNS: 50pf. *Courier* (Albrecht Durer) and post rider, 1590; 70pf. Open wagon, 1595, and mail carriage, 1750; 100pf. Travelling post office vans, 1842 and 1900.

E942 Louis Lewandowski (choir conductor)

1990. Reconstruction of New Synagogue, Berlin. Multicoloured.
E3054 30pf. Type **E942** 50 50
E3055 50pf.+15pf. New Synagogue 1·00 1·00

E943 Schliemann and Two-handled Vessel

1990. Death Cent of Heinrich Schliemann (archaeologist). Multicoloured.
E3056 30pf. Type **E943** 50 50
E3057 50pf. Schliemann and double pot (horiz) 1·00 1·00

E944 Dresden

1990. 41st International Astronautics Federation Congress, Dresden.
E3058 **E944** 30pf. black and grey 35 35
E3059 - 50pf. multicoloured 75 75
E3060 - 70pf. dp bl, grn & bl 1·20 1·50
E3061 - 100pf. multicoloured 1·70 1·70
DESIGNS: 50pf. Earth; 70pf. Moon; 100pf. Mars.

On 3 October 1990 the territory of the Democratic Republic was absorbed into the Federal Republic of Germany, whose stamps have been used since then.

OFFICIAL STAMPS

EO58
(Cross-piece projects to left)

1954. (a) Design in minute dots.
EO185 **EO58** 5pf. green 45
EO186 **EO58** 6pf. violet 2·30
EO187 **EO58** 8pf. brown 45
EO188 **EO58** 10pf. turquoise 45
EO189 **EO58** 12pf. blue 45

EO190	EO58	15pf. violet		45
EO191	EO58	16pf. violet		1·70
EO192	EO58	20pf. olive		45
EO193	EO58	24pf. red		80
EO194	EO58	25pf. turquoise		80
EO195	EO58	30pf. red		70
EO196	EO58	40pf. red		45
EO197	EO58	48pf. lilac		6·75
EO198	EO58	50pf. lilac		1·00
EO199	EO58	60pf. blue		1·10
EO200	EO58	70pf. brown		1·00
EO201	EO58	84pf. brown		11·50

EO59
(Cross-piece projects to right)

(b) Design in lines.

EO202	EO59	5pf. green		70
EO203	EO59	10pf. turquoise		55
EO204	EO59	12pf. turquoise		55
EO205	EO59	15pf. violet		55
EO207	EO59	25pf. green		2·50
EO210	EO59	50pf. lilac		1·10
EO211	EO59	70pf. brown		1·40
EO298	EO59	20pf. olive	70	35
EO299	EO59	30pf. red	£130	2·75
EO300	EO59	40pf. red	1·10	35

EO84

1956. For internal use.

EO257	EO84	5pf. black	4·00	35
EO258	EO84	10pf. black	1·40	35
EO259	EO84	20pf. black	80	45
EO260	EO84	40pf. black	5·75	55
EO261	EO84	70pf. black	£200	70

Nos. EO257/61 were not on sale to the public in unused condition, although specimens of all values are available on the market. The used prices are for cancelled-to-order, with segments across the corners of the stamps. Postally used are worth more.

OFFICIAL CENTRAL COURIER SERVICE STAMPS

These were for use on special postal services for confidential mail between Government officials and state-owned enterprises.

EO95

1956. With or without control figures.

EO303	EO95	10pf. black & purple	80	1·70
EO304	EO95	20pf. black & purple	2·30	1·70
EO305	EO95	40pf. black & purple	80	3·50
EO306	EO95	70pf. black & purple	4·00	75·00

EO123

1958. With various control figures. (a) With one bar (thick or thin) each side of figure.

EO357	EO123	(10pf.) red & yell	55·00	7·50
EO373	EO123	(10pf.) brown & bl	28·00	9·00
EO375	EO123	(10pf.) violet and orange	34·00	11·50
EO377	EO123	(10pf.) red and green	12·50	13·50

(b) With two bars (thick or thin) each side of figure.

EO358	(20pf.) red & yell		55·00	4·50
EO374	(20pf.) brown & bl		70·00	5·75
EO376	(20pf.) violet and orange		90·00	9·00
EO378	(20pf.) red and green		17·00	6·25

Used prices for Nos. EO357/EO378 are for postally used copies.

EO149

1959. With various control figures. (a) With one bar each side of figure.

EO414	EO149	(10pf.) red, violet and green	13·50	9·00
EO416	EO149	(10pf.) black & bl	17·00	85·00
EO418	EO149	(10pf.) black, brown and blue	55·00	95·00

(b) With two bars each side of figure.

EO415	(20pf.) blue, brown and yellow		20·00	8·00
EO417	(20pf.) green, blue and red		17·00	11·50
EO419	(20pf.) violet, black and brown		40·00	8·00

REGISTRATION STAMPS
SELF=SERVICE POST OFFICE

These registration labels embody a face value to cover the registration fee and have franking value to this extent. They are issued in pairs from automatic machines together with a certificate of posting against a 50pf. coin. The stamps are serially numbered in pairs and inscribed with the name of the town of issue.

The procedure is to affix one label to the letter (already franked with stamps for carriage of the letter) and complete page 1 of the certificate of posting which is then placed in the box provided together with the letter. The duplicate label is affixed to the second page of the certificate and retained for production as evidence in the event of a claim. They are not obtainable over the post office counter.

Unused prices are for pairs.

ER318

1967
ER992	ER318	50pf. red and black		4·75

ER319

1968
ER993	ER319	50pf. red		2·30

ER345

1968. For Parcel Post.
ER1089	ER345	50pf. black		8·00

Pt. 6

GHADAMES

A caravan halting place in the Libyan desert, under French administration from 1943 until 1951 when the area reverted to Libya. From 1943 to 1948 stamps of Fezzan were used.

100 centimes = 1 franc.

1 Cross of Agadem

1949. Cross of Agadem.

1	1	4f. chestnut & brn (postage)	8·00	20·00
2	1	5f. green and blue	8·00	20·00
3	1	8f. chestnut and brown	7·75	27·00
4	1	10f. blue and black	7·75	27·00
5	1	12f. mauve and purple	9·75	50·00
6	1	15f. chestnut and brown	10·50	45·00
7	1	20f. green and brown	11·00	45·00
8	1	25f. blue and brown	11·00	45·00
9	1	50f. cerise and purple (air)	11·00	45·00
10	1	100f. purple and brown	11·00	45·00

Pt. 1

GHANA

Formerly the British Colony of Gold Coast. Attained Dominion status on 6 March 1957, and became a republic within the British Commonwealth in 1960.

1957. 12 pence = 1 shilling; 20 shillings = 1 pound.
1965. 100 pesewas = 1 cedi.
1967. 100 new pesewas = 1 cedi.
1972. 100 pesewas = 1 cedi = 0.8 (1967) new cedi.

CANCELLED REMAINDERS. In 1961 remainders of some issues of 1957 to 1960 were put on the market cancelled-to-order in such a way as to be indistinguishable from genuine postally used copies. Our used quotations which are indicated by an asterisk are, therefore, for cancelled-to-order copies.

29 Dr. Kwame Nkrumah, Palm-nut Vulture and Map of Africa

1957. Independence Commemoration.
166	29	2d. red*	10	10
167	29	2½d. green*	10	15
168	29	4d. brown*	10	15
169	29	1s.3d. blue*	15	15

1957. Queen Elizabeth stamps of 1952 of Gold Coast optd **GHANA INDEPENDENCE 6TH. MARCH, 1957.**
170	½d. brown and red*		10	10
171	1d. blue*		10	10
172	1½d. green*		10	10
173	2d. brown		30	30
174	2½d. red		1·00	1·25
175	3d. mauve*		30	10
176	4d. blue		6·50	11·00
177	6d. black and orange*		10	10
178	1s. black and red*		10	10
179	2s. olive and red*		60	10
180	5s. purple and black*		2·50	10
181	10s. black and olive*		2·75	70

31 Viking Ship

1957. Inauguration of Black Star Shipping Line.
182	31	2½d. green	40	20
183	-	1s.3d. blue	50	1·25
184	-	5s. purple	80	3·00

DESIGNS—HORIZ: 1s.3d. Galleon; 5s. M.V. *Volta River.*

34 Ambassador Hotel, Accra

1958. First Anniv of Independence. Flag and Coat of Arms in National colours.
185	34	½d. black and red	10	40
186	-	2½d. black, red and yellow	10	10
187	-	1s.3d. black and blue	30	10
188	-	2s. yellow and black	45	50

DESIGNS—HORIZ: 2½d. State Opening of Parliament; 1s.3d. National Monument. VERT: 2s. Ghana Coat of Arms.

38 Map showing the Independent African States

1958. First Conference of Independent African States, Accra. Star in black and yellow.
189	38	2½d. red and yellow	10	10
190	38	3d. green and brown	10	10
191	-	1s. blue, yellow and orange	20	10
192	-	2s.6d. red and purple	40	65

DESIGN—VERT: 1s., 2s.6d. Map of Africa and flaming torch.

40 Palm-nut Vulture over Globe
41 Bristol Britannia

1958. Inauguration of Ghana Airways. Inscr as in T **40/41.**
193	40	2½d. black, bistre and red	35	10
194	41	1s.3d. multicoloured	55	20
195	-	2s. multicoloured	65	55
196	-	2s.6d. black and bistre	65	95

DESIGNS—(As Type **41**): 2s. Boeing Stratocruiser and yellow-nosed albatross. (As Type **40**): 2s.6d. Palm-nut vulture and Vickers VC-10 aircraft.

1958. Prime Minister's Visit to United States and Canada. Optd **PRIME MINISTER'S VISIT, U.S.A. AND CANADA.**
197	29	2d. red	10	40
198	29	2½d. green	10	30
199	29	4d. brown	10	50
200	29	1s.3d. blue	15	25

45

1958. United Nations Day.
201	45	2½d. brown, green and black	10	10
202	45	1s.3d. brown, blue and black	15	10
203	45	2s.6d. brown, violet black	15	35

46 Dr. Nkrumah and Lincoln Statue, Washington

1959. 150th Birth Anniv of Abraham Lincoln.
204	46	2½d. pink and purple	10	10
205	46	1s.3d. light blue and blue	10	10
206	46	2s.6d. yellow and olive	15	35
MS206a	102×77 mm. Nos. 204/6. Imperf		65	2·25

48 Kente Cloth and Traditional Symbols

1959. Independence. Inscr "SECOND ANNIVERSARY OF INDEPENDENCE."
207	48	½d. multicoloured	10	30
208	-	2½d. multicoloured	10	10
209	-	1s.3d. multicoloured	10	10
210	-	2s. multicoloured	30	1·40

DESIGNS—HORIZ: 2½d. Talking drums and elephant-horn blower; 2s. Map of Africa, Ghana flag and palms. VERT: 1s.3d. "Symbols of Greeting".

52 Globe and Flags

1959. Africa Freedom Day.
211	52	2½d. multicoloured	15	10
212	52	8½d. multicoloured	15	20

54 Nkrumah Statue, Accra   **55** Ghana Timber

65a Red-fronted Gazelle

1959. Multicoloured.
213	½d. "God's Omnipotence" (postage)		10	10
214	1d. Type **54**		10	10
215	1½d. Type **55**		10	10
216	2d. Volta river		10	10
217	2½d. Cocoa bean		1·50	10
218	3d. "God's Omnipotence"		10	10
219	4d. Diamond and mine		4·00	65
220	6d. Red-crowned bishop (bird)		2·25	10
221	11d. Golden-spider lily		25	10
222	1s. Shell ginger		25	10
226	1s.3d. Pennant-winged nightjar (air)		1·75	10
227	2s. Crowned cranes		1·50	10
223	2s.6d. Giant blue turaco		1·75	15
224	5s. Tiger orchid		2·00	65

225		10s. Jewel cichlid	75	70
225a		£1 Type **65a**	2·50	4·75

SIZES—HORIZ (As Type **54**): ½d. (As Type **55**): 2d., 2½d., 3d., 4d., 6d., 1s.3d., 2s.6d. (As Type **65a**): 10s. VERT (As Type **55**): 11d., 1s., 2s., 5s.
The 3d. is a different symbolic design from the ½d.

68 Gold Cup and West African Map

1959. West African Football Competition, 1959. Multicoloured.

228		½d. Type **68***	10	10
229		1d. Footballers (vert)*	10	10
230		3d. Goalkeeper saving ball*	10	10
231		8d. Forward attacking goal*	40	15
232		2s.6d. "Kwame Nkrumah" Gold Cup (vert)*	50	15

73 Duke of Edinburgh and Arms of Ghana

1959. Visit of the Duke of Edinburgh.

233	**73**	3d. black and mauve	30	10

74 Ghana Flag and Talking Drums

1959. U.N. Trusteeship Council. Multicoloured.

234		3d. Type **74***	10	10
235		6d. Ghana flag and U.N. emblem (vert)*	10	10
236		1s.3d. As 6d. but emblem above flag (vert)*	20	15
237		2s.6d. "Totem pole" (vert)*	25	15

78 Eagles in Flight

1960. Third Anniv of Independence. Multicoloured.

238		½d. Type **78***	10	10
239		3d. Fireworks*	10	10
240		1s.3d. "Third Anniversary"*	30	10
241		2s. "Ship of State"*	30	15

82 Flags and Map forming letter "A"

1960. African Freedom Day. Multicoloured.

242		3d. Type **82***	10	10
243		6d. Letter "f"*	20	10
244		1s. Letter "d"*	20	10

85 Dr. Nkrumah

1960. Republic Day. Inscr "REPUBLIC DAY 1ST JULY 1960". Multicoloured.

245		3d. Type **85**	10	10
246		1s.3d. Ghana flag	30	10
247		2s. Torch of Freedom	20	20
248		10s. Ghana arms (horiz)	50	80

MS248a 102×77 mm. Nos. 245/8. Imperf — 40 · 1·50

90 Athlete

1960. Olympic Games.

249	-	3d. multicoloured	10	10
250	-	6d. multicoloured	15	10
251	**90**	1s.3d. multicoloured	25	15
252	**90**	2s.6d. multicoloured	35	1·10

DESIGN—VERT: 3d., 6d. Olympic torch.

91 President Nkrumah

1960. Founder's Day. Inscribed as in T **91**.

253	**91**	3d. multicoloured	10	10
254	-	6d. multicoloured	10	15
255	-	1s.3d. multicoloured	20	30

DESIGNS—VERT: 6d. President Nkrumah within star; 1s.3d. Map of Africa and column.

94 U.N. Emblem and Ghana Flag

1960. Human Rights Day.

256	**94**	3d. multicoloured	10	10
257	-	6d. yellow, black and blue	15	15
258	-	1s.3d. multicoloured	25	55

DESIGNS: U.N. Emblem with torch (6d.) or within laurel (1s.3d.).

97 Talking Drums

1961. Africa Freedom Day. Inscr "15th APRIL 1961".

259	**97**	3d. multicoloured	10	10
260	-	6d. red, black and green	20	10
261	-	2s. multicoloured	50	45

DESIGNS—VERT: 6d. Map of Africa. HORIZ: 2s. Flags and map.

100 Eagle on Column

1961. First Anniv of Republic. Multicoloured.

262	**100**	3d. Type **100**	10	10
263		1s.3d. "Flower"	10	10
264		2s. Ghana flags	20	1·25

103 Dove with Olive Branch

1961. Belgrade Conference.

265	**103**	3d. green	10	10
266	-	1s.3d. blue	15	10
267	-	5s. purple	40	1·00

DESIGNS—HORIZ: 1s.3d. World map, chain and olive branch; 5s. Rostrum, Conference room.

106 President Nkrumah and Globe

1961. Founder's Day. Multicoloured.

268		3d. Type **106**	10	10
269		1s.3d. President in Kente cloth (vert)	20	10
270		5s. President in national costume (vert)	65	2·50

MS270a Three sheets, 106×86 mm (3d.) or 86×106 mm (others), each with Nos. 268/70 in block of four. Imperf Set of three sheets — 2·75 · 14·00

109 Queen Elizabeth II and African Map

1961. Royal Visit.

271	**109**	3d. multicoloured	15	10
272	**109**	1s.3d. multicoloured	30	20
273	**109**	5s. multicoloured	65	4·00

MS273a 106×84 mm. No. 273 in block of 4. Imperf — 2·25 · 8·00

110 Ships in Tema Harbour

1962. Opening of Tema Harbour. Multicoloured.

274		3d. Type **110** (postage)	15	10
275		1s.3d. Douglas DC-8 aircraft and ships at Tema (air)	65	15
276		2s.6d. As No. 275	80	2·50

112 Africa and Peace Dove

1962. First Anniv of Casablanca Conference.

277	**112**	3d. multicoloured (postage)	10	10
278	**112**	1s.3d. multicoloured (air)	20	15
279	**112**	2s.6d. multicoloured	30	2·00

113 Compass over Africa

1962. Africa Freedom Day.

280	**113**	3d. sepia, turquoise & pur	10	10
281	**113**	6d. sepia, turquoise & brn	10	15
282	**113**	1s.3d. sepia, turq & red	15	15

115 Atomic Bomb-burst "Skull"

1962. The Accra Assembly.

283	-	3d. black and lake	10	10
284	**115**	6d. black and red	25	35
285	-	1s.3d. turquoise	30	50

DESIGNS: 3d. Ghana Star over "five continents"; 1s.3d. Dove of Peace.

117 Patrice Lumumba

1962. First Death Anniv of Lumumba.

286	**117**	3d. black and yellow	10	10
287	**117**	6d. black, green and slate	10	30
288	**117**	1s.3d. black, pink and green	15	35

118 Star over Two Columns

1962. Second Anniv of Republic. Inscribed "1st JULY 1962". Multicoloured.

289		3d. Type **118**	10	10
290		6d. Flaming torch	20	20
291		1s.3d. Eagle trailing flag (horiz)	40	40

121 President Nkrumah

1962. Founder's Day.

292	**121**	1d. multicoloured	10	10
293	-	3d. multicoloured	10	10
294	-	1s.3d. black and blue	30	15
295	-	2s. multicoloured	30	1·75

DESIGNS: 3d. Nkrumah medallion; 1s.3d. President and Ghana Star; 2s. Laying "Ghana" brick.

125 Campaign Emblem

1962. Malaria Eradication.

296	**125**	1d. red	10	10
297	**125**	4d. green	20	1·25
298	**125**	6d. bistre	20	30
299	**125**	1s.3d. violet	25	90

MS299a 90×115 mm. Nos. 296/9. Imperf — 75 · 1·50

126 Campaign Emblem

1963. Freedom from Hunger.

300	**126**	1d. multicoloured	15	25
301	-	4d. sepia, yellow and orange	75	1·75
302	-	1s.3d. ochre, black and green	1·60	1·25

DESIGNS—HORIZ: 4d. Emblem in hands; 1s.3d. World map and emblem.

129 Map of Africa

1963. Africa Freedom Day.

303	**129**	1d. gold and red	10	10
304	-	4d. red, black and yellow	10	10
305	-	1s.3d. multicoloured	20	10
306	-	2s.6d. multicoloured	35	1·25

DESIGNS—HORIZ: 4d. Carved stool. VERT: 1s.3d. Map and bowl of fire; 2s.6d. Topi (antelope) and flag.

133 Red Cross

1963. Centenary of Red Cross. Multicoloured.

307		1d. Type **133**	50	15
308		1½d. Centenary emblem (horiz)	75	2·25
309		4d. Nurses and child (horiz)	1·25	20
310		1s.3d. Emblem, globe and laurel	1·75	2·00
MS310a 102×127 mm. Nos. 307/10. Imperf			2·75	12·00

137 "3rd Anniversary"

1963. Third Anniv of Republic. Multicoloured.

311		1d. Type **137**	10	10
312		4d. Three Ghanian flags	30	10
313		1s.3d. Map, flag and star (vert)	70	15
314		2s.6d. Flag and torch (vert)	70	2·50

141 President Nkrumah and Ghana Flag

1963. Founder's Day.

315	**141**	1d. multicoloured	10	10
316	-	4d. multicoloured	15	10
317	-	1s.3d. multicoloured	30	10
318	-	5s. yellow and mauve	65	90

DESIGNS—VERT: 4d. Type **141** but with larger flag behind President Nkrumah. HORIZ: 1s.3d. President Nkrumah and fireworks; 5s. Native symbol of wisdom.

145 Rameses II, Abu Simbel

1963. Preservation of Nubian Monuments. Multicoloured.

319		1d. Type **145**	15	10
320		1½d. Rock paintings (horiz)	20	65
321		2d. Queen Nefertari (horiz)	20	10
322		4d. Sphinx, Sebua	35	15
323		1s.3d. Rock Temple, Abu Simbel (horiz)	80	90

150 Class 248 Steam Locomotive and Diesel-electric Locomotive No. 1401

1963. 60th Anniv of Ghana Railway.

324	**150**	1d. multicoloured	10	10
325	**150**	4d. multicoloured	40	10
326	**150**	1s.3d. multicoloured	45	40
327	**150**	2s.6d. multicoloured	75	1·90

151 Eleanor Roosevelt and "Flame of Freedom"

1963. Fifth Anniv of Declaration of Human Rights. Multicoloured.

328		1d. Type **151**	10	10
329		4d. Type **151**	10	30
330		6d. Eleanor Roosevelt	10	10
331		1s.3d. Eleanor Roosevelt and emblems (horiz)	15	15

154 Sun and Globe Emblem

1964. International Quiet Sun Years.

332	**154**	3d. multicoloured	15	10
333	**154**	6d. multicoloured	25	10
334	**154**	1s.3d. multicoloured	25	15
MS334a 90×90 mm. No. 334 in block of 4. Imperf			75	2·50

155 Harvesting Corn on State Farm

1964. Fourth Anniv of Republic.

335	**155**	3d. olive, brown and yellow	10	10
336	-	6d. green, brown & turq	10	10
337	-	1s.3d. red, brn & salmon	10	10
338	-	5s. multicoloured	40	1·60
MS338a 126×100 mm. Nos. 335/8. Imperf			85	2·00

DESIGNS: 6d. Oil refinery, Tema; 1s.3d. "Communal Labour"; 5s. Procession headed by flag.

159 Globe and Dove

1964. First Anniv of African Unity Charter.

339	**159**	3d. multicoloured	10	10
340	-	6d. green and red	10	10
341	-	1s.3d. multicoloured	15	10
342	-	5s. multicoloured	45	70

DESIGNS—VERT: 6d. Map of Africa and quill pen; 5s. Planting flower. HORIZ: 1s.3d. Hitched rope on map of Africa.

163 President Nkrumah and Hibiscus Flowers

1964. Founder's Day.

343	**163**	3d. multicoloured	10	10
344	**163**	6d. multicoloured	15	10
345	**163**	1s.3d. multicoloured	25	10
346	**163**	2s.6d. multicoloured	40	1·00
MS346a 90×122 mm. No. 346 in block of 4. Imperf			70	2·50

164 Hurdling

1964. Olympic Games, Tokyo. Multicoloured.

347		1d. Type **164**	10	10
348		2½d. Running	10	1·50
349		3d. Boxing (vert)	10	10
350		4d. Long-jumping (vert)	10	10
351		6d. Football (vert)	15	10

352		1s.3d. Athlete holding Olympic Torch (vert)	20	10
353		5s. Olympic "Rings" and flags	55	3·25
MS353a 128×102 mm. Nos. 351/3. Imperf			75	2·50

171 G. Washington Carver (botanist) and Plant

1964. UNESCO Week.

354	**171**	6d. blue and green	15	10
355	-	1s.3d. purple and blue	30	10
356	**171**	5s. sepia and red	50	4·25
MS356a 127×77 mm. Nos. 354/6. Imperf			75	2·00

DESIGN: 1s.3d. Albert Einstein (scientist) and Atomic symbol.

173 African Elephant

1964. Multicoloured

357		1d. Type **173**	40	50
358		1½d. Secretary bird (horiz)	50	2·25
359		2½d. Purple wreath (flower)	15	2·25
360		3d. Grey parrot	50	50
361		4d. Blue-naped mousebird (horiz)	50	70
362		6d. African tulip tree (horiz)	15	30
363		1s.3d. Violet starling (horiz)	60	85
364		2s.6d. Hippopotamus (horiz)	60	5·00
MS364a Two sheets. (a) 150×86 mm. Nos. 357/9. (b) 150×110 mm. Nos. 360/4. Imperf Set of 2 sheets			3·00	14·00

181 I.C.Y. Emblem

1965. International Co-operation Year.

365	**181**	1d. multicoloured	35	70
366	**181**	4d. multicoloured	1·00	2·00
367	**181**	6d. multicoloured	1·00	70
368	**181**	1s.3d. multicoloured	1·25	2·75
MS368a 100×100 mm. No. 368 in block of 4. Imperf			2·75	5·00

182 I.T.U. Emblem and Symbols

1965. Centenary of I.T.U.

369	**182**	1d. multicoloured	15	15
370	**182**	6d. multicoloured	30	15
371	**182**	1s.3d. multicoloured	55	25
372	**182**	5s. multicoloured	1·25	3·25
MS372a 132×115 mm. Nos. 369/72. Imperf			7·50	10·00

183 Lincoln's Home

1965. Death Centenary of Abraham Lincoln.

373	**183**	6d. multicoloured	10	10
374	-	1s.3d. black, red and blue	15	15
375	-	2s. black, brown and yellow	15	35
376	-	5s. black and red	30	1·75
MS376a 115×115 mm. Nos. 373/6. Imperf			75	3·50

DESIGNS: 1s.3d. Lincoln's inaugural address; 2s. Abraham Lincoln; 5s. Adaption of U.S. 90c. Lincoln stamp of 1869.

187 Obverse (President Nkrumah) and Reverse of 5p. Coin

1965. Introduction of Decimal Currency. Multicoloured designs showing coins expressed in the same denominations as on the stamps.

377		5p. Type **187**	20	10
378		10p. As Type **187**	25	10
379		25p. Size 63×39 mm	55	1·00
380		50p. Size 71×43½ mm	1·00	2·75

1965. Nos. 214/27 surch **Ghana New Currency 19th July. 1965**. and value. Multicoloured.

381	**54**	1p. on 1d. (postage)	10	10
382	-	2p. on 2d.	10	10
383	-	3p. on 3d. (No. 218a)	1·00	6·50
384	-	4p. on 4d.	5·00	45
385	-	6p. on 6d.	50	10
386	-	11p. on 11d.	25	10
387	-	12p. on 1s.	25	10
392	-	15p. on 1s.3d. (air)	2·50	70
393	-	24p. on 2s.	2·50	30
388	-	30p. on 2s.6d.	4·75	11·00
389	-	60p. on 5s.	4·50	70
390	-	1c.20 on 10s.	75	2·25
391	**65a**	2c.40 on £1	1·00	6·50

189 "OAU" and Flag

1965. O.A.U. Summit Conf, Accra. Multicoloured.

394	**189**	1p. Type **189**	20	30
395	-	2p. "OAU" heads and flag	20	30
396	-	5p. OAU emblem and flag	30	30
397	-	6p. African map and flag (horiz) (37½×27½ mm)	30	10
398	-	15p. "Sunburst" and flag (horiz) (37½×27½ mm)	40	30
399	-	24p. "O.A.U." on map, and flag (horiz) (37½×27½ mm)	55	65

195 Goalkeeper saving Ball

1965. African Soccer Cup Competition. Multicoloured.

400	**195**	6p. Type **195**	25	10
401	-	15p. Player with ball (vert)	40	30
402	-	24p. Player, ball and Soccer Cup	45	70

198 President Kennedy and Grave Memorial

1965. Second Death Anniv of President Kennedy.

403	**198**	6p. multicoloured	15	10
404	-	15p. violet, red and green	20	35
405	-	24p. black and purple	20	60
406	-	30p. purple and black	25	1·25
MS407 114½×114 mm. Nos. 403/6. Imperf			2·50	6·50

DESIGNS: 15p. President Kennedy and Eternal Flame; 24p. President Kennedy and Memorial Inscription; 30p. President Kennedy.

202 Section of Dam and Generators

1966. Volta River Project.

408	**202**	6p. multicoloured	15	10
409	-	15p. multicoloured	20	15
410	-	24p. multicoloured	25	20
411	-	30p. black and blue	35	1·00

DESIGNS: 15p. Dam and Lake Volta; 24p. Word "GHANA" as Dam; 30p. "Fertility".

1965. "Black Stars" Victory in African Soccer Cup Competition. Optd **Black Stars Retain Africa Cup 21st Nov. 1965.**

412	**195**	6p. multicoloured	50	15
413	-	15p. multicoloured	70	30
414	-	24p. multicoloured	75	70

207 W.H.O. Building and Ghana Flag

1966. Inaug of W.H.O. Headquarters, Geneva. Multicoloured.

415	6p. Type **207**	1·00	10
416	15p. Type **207**	1·75	65
417	24p. W.H.O. Building and emblem	1·90	2·00
418	30p. W.H.O. Building and emblem	2·00	5·50
MS419	120×101 mm. Nos. 415/18. Imperf	24·00	22·00

209 Atlantic Herring

1966. Freedom from Hunger. Multicoloured.

420	6p. Type **209**	25	10
421	15p. Turbot	45	15
422	24p. Spadefish	45	35
423	30p. Red snapper	50	1·50
424	60p. Blue-finned tuna	70	5·50
MS425	126×109 mm. No. 423 in block of 4. Imperf	10·00	13·00

214 African "Links" and Ghana Flag

1966. Third Anniv of African Charter. Multicoloured.

426	6p. Type **214**	15	10
427	15p. Flags as "quill" and diamond (horiz)	35	55
428	24p. Ship's wheel, map and cocoa bean (horiz)	40	70

217 Player heading Ball, and Jules Rimet Cup

1966. World Cup Football Championship. Multicoloured.

429	5p. Type **217**	70	20
430	15p. Goalkeeper clearing ball	1·50	30
431	24p. Player and Jules Rimet Cup (replica)	1·75	50
432	30p. Players and Jules Rimet Cup (replica)	2·00	1·75
433	60p. Players with ball	3·00	10·00
MS434	120×102 mm. No. 433 in block of 4. Imperf	24·00	26·00

222 UNESCO Emblem

1966. 20th Anniv of UNESCO.

435	**222**	5p. multicoloured	1·00	25
436	**222**	15p. multicoloured	2·25	40
437	**222**	24p. multicoloured	2·75	1·25
438	**222**	30p. multicoloured	3·00	3·50
439	**222**	60p. multicoloured	3·75	13·00
MS440	140×115 mm. Nos. 435/9. Imperf	25·00	28·00

223 Fair Emblem and Crates

1967. Ghana Trade Fair, Accra. Multicoloured.

441	5p. Type **223**	10	10
442	15p. Fair emblem and world map	15	20
443	24p. Shipping and flags	25	30
444	36p. Fair emblem and hand-held hoist	40	2·75

1967. New Currency. Nos. 216/26 and 393 surch with new value.

445	1½n.p. on 2d. (postage)	2·00	12·00
446	3½n.p. on 4d.	8·50	4·50
447	5n.p. on 6d.	5·50	2·25
448	9n.p. on 11d.	30	1·00
449	10n.p. on 1s.	30	2·25
453	12½n.p. on 1s.3d. (air)	4·00	6·00
454	20n.p. on 24p. on 2s.	6·00	9·50
450	25n.p. on 2s.6d.	3·50	10·00
451	1n.c. on 10s.	2·50	16·00
452	2n.c. on £1	5·00	24·00

229 Ghana Eagle and Flag

1967. First Anniv of 24 February Revolution.

455	**229**	1n.p. multicoloured	10	90
456	**229**	4n.p. multicoloured	10	10
457	**229**	12½n.p. multicoloured	35	60
458	**229**	25n.p. multicoloured	65	3·50
MS459	89×108 mm. Nos. 455/8. Perf or imperf	5·00	12·00

230 Maize **232** The Ghana Mace

1967. Multicoloured.

460	1n.p. Type **230**	10	10
461	1½n.p. Forest kingfisher	1·00	2·75
462	2n.p. Type **232**	10	10
463	2½n.p. Commelina	35	10
464	3n.p. West African lungfish	20	40
465	4n.p. Rufous-crowned roller	1·50	10
466	6n.p. Akosombo Dam	15	2·25
467	8n.p. Adomi Bridge	15	1·00
468	9n.p. Chameleon	75	10
469	10n.p. Tema Harbour	15	10
470	20n.p. Bush hare (blue)	20	10
471	50n.p. Black-winged stilt	12·00	4·00
472	1n.c. Wooden stool	2·00	1·00
473	2n.c. Frangipani	2·00	3·50
474	2n.c.50 Seat of State	2·25	12·00

SIZES—VERT (As Type **230**): 4n.p. (As Type **232**): 1½n.p.; 2½n.p., 20n.p., 2n.c., 2n.c.50. HORIZ (as Type **230**): 8n.p. (As Type **232**): 3n.p., 6n.p., 9n.p., 10n.p., 50n.p., 1n.c.

245 Kumasi Fort

1967. Castles and Forts.

475	**245**	4n.p. multicoloured	25	10
476	-	12½n.p. multicoloured	60	1·00
477	-	20n.p. multicoloured	75	3·00
478	-	25n.p. multicoloured	75	3·75

DESIGNS: 12½n.p. Christiansborg Castle and British galleon; 20n.p. Elmina Castle and Portuguese galleon; 25n.p. Cape Coast Castle and Spanish galleon.

249 "Luna 10"

1967. "Peaceful Use of Outer Space". Multicoloured.

479	4n.p. Type **249**	10	10
480	10n.p. "Orbiter 1"	10	60
481	12½n.p. Man in Space	20	90
MS482	140×90 mm. Nos. 479/81. Imperf	1·75	4·75

252 Scouts and Campfire

1967. 50th Anniv of Ghanaian Scout Movement. Multicoloured.

483	4n.p. Type **252**	20	10
484	10n.p. Scout on march	40	50
485	12½n.p. Lord Baden-Powell	50	1·75
MS486	167×95 mm. Nos. 483/5. Imperf	4·00	10·00

255 U.N. Headquarters Building

1967. United Nations Day (24 October).

487	**255**	4n.p. multicoloured	10	10
488	**255**	10n.p. multicoloured	10	15
489	-	50n.p. multicoloured	20	70
490	-	2n.c.50 multicoloured	55	4·00
MS491	76×75 mm. No. 490. Imperf	1·75	9·50

DESIGN: 50n.p., 2n.c.50, General view of U.N. H.Q., Manhattan.

257 Leopard

1967. International Tourist Year. Multicoloured.

492	4n.p. Type **257**	1·00	20
493	12½n.p. *Papilio demodocus* (butterfly)	2·25	1·50
494	20n.p. Carmine bee eater	2·50	3·75
495	50n.p. Waterbuck	2·50	9·00
MS496	126×126 mm. Nos. 492/5. Imperf	18·00	23·00

261 Revolutionaries entering Accra

1968. Second Anniv of February Revolution. Multicoloured.

497	4n.p. Type **261**	10	10
498	12½n.p. Marching troops	20	20
499	20n.p. Cheering people	30	40
500	40n.p. Victory celebrations	50	3·25

265 Microscope and Cocoa Beans

1968. Cocoa Research.

501	**265**	4n.p. multicoloured	10	1·25
502	-	4n.p. multicoloured	10	10
503	**265**	10n.p. multicoloured	15	30
504	-	25n.p. multicoloured	60	1·75
MS505	102×102 mm. Nos. 501/4. Imperf	2·25	5·50

DESIGNS: 4n.p. and 25n.p. Microscope and cocoa tree, beans and pods.

267 Kotoka and Flowers

1968. First Death Anniv of Lt.-Gen. E. K. Kotoka. Multicoloured.

506	4n.p. Type **267**	10	10
507	12½n.p. Kotoka and wreath	20	30
508	20n.p. Kotoka in civilian clothes	35	75
509	40n.p. Lt.-Gen. Kotoka	50	3·00

271 Tobacco

1968. Flora and Fauna. Multicoloured.

510	4n.p. Type **271**	15	10
511	5n.p. North African crested porcupine	15	1·25
512	12½n.p. Rubber	30	75
513	20n.p. *Cymothoe sangaris* (butterfly)	1·00	2·75
514	40n.p. *Charaxes ameliae* (butterfly)	1·25	5·00
MS515	88×114 mm. Nos. 510 and 512/14. Imperf	2·50	9·00

276 Surgeons, Flag and W.H.O. Emblem

1968. 20th Anniv of W.H.O.

516	**276**	4n.p. multicoloured	20	10
517	**276**	12½n.p. multicoloured	40	40
518	**276**	20n.p. multicoloured	60	1·25
519	**276**	40n.p. multicoloured	1·00	3·75
MS520	132×110 mm. Nos. 516/19. Imperf	2·75	7·00

277 Hurdling

1969. Olympic Games, Mexico (1968). Multicoloured.

521	4n.p. Type **277**	10	10
522	12½n.p. Boxing	20	30
523	20n.p. Torch, Olympic Rings and flags	40	75
524	40n.p. Football	70	3·25
MS525	89×114 mm. Nos. 521/4. Imperf	3·50	8·00

281 U.N. Building

1969. United Nations Day. Multicoloured.

526	4n.p. Type **281**	10	10
527	12½n.p. Native stool, staff and U.N. emblem	15	25
528	20n.p. U.N. building and emblem over Ghanian Flag	20	45
529	40n.p. U.N. emblem encircled by flags	40	2·75
MS530	127×117 mm. Nos. 526/9. Imperf	75	3·50

285 Dr. J. B. Danquah

1969. Human Rights Year. Multicoloured.

531	4n.p. Type **285**	10	10

532	12½n.p. Dr. Martin Luther King		20	35
533	20n.p. As 12½n.p.		35	75
534	40n.p. Type **285**		50	3·00
MS535	116×50 mm. Nos. 531/4. Imperf		80	4·25

287 Constituent Assembly
Building

1969. Third Anniv of Revolution. Multicoloured.

536	4n.p. Type **287**		10	10
537	12½n.p. Arms of Ghana		10	15
538	20n.p. Type **287**		15	20
539	40n.p. As 12½n.p.		20	75
MS540	114×89 mm. Nos. 536/9. Imperf		70	3·00

1969. New Constitution. Nos. 460/74 optd **NEW CONSTITUTION 1969.**

541	**230**	1n.p. multicoloured	10	2·25
542	-	1½n.p. multicoloured	4·00	7·00
543	**232**	2n.p. multicoloured	10	4·00
544	-	2½n.p. multicoloured	10	2·50
545	-	3n.p. multicoloured	1·00	2·75
546	-	4n.p. multicoloured	3·00	1·25
547	-	6n.p. multicoloured	15	3·00
548	-	8n.p. multicoloured	15	4·75
549	-	9n.p. multicoloured	15	3·75
550	-	10n.p. multicoloured	2·00	3·75
551	-	20n.p. multicoloured	2·50	2·25
552	-	50n.p. multicoloured	7·00	8·50
553	-	1n.c. multicoloured	1·50	9·50
554	-	2n.c. multicoloured	1·50	9·50
555	-	2n.c.50 multicoloured	1·50	10·00

On Nos. 541, 545, 547/50 and 552/3 the opt is horiz. The rest are vert.

290 Map of
Africa and Flags

1969. Inauguration of Second Republic. Multicoloured.

556	4n.p. Type **290**		10	10
557	12½n.p. Figure "2", branch and Ghanaian colours		20	10
558	20n.p. Hands receiving egg		35	35
559	40n.p. Type **290**		60	1·50

293 I.L.O. Emblem and
Cogwheels

1970. 50th Anniv of I.L.O.

560	**293**	4n.p. multicoloured	10	10
561	**293**	12½n.p. multicoloured	20	55
562	**293**	20n.p. multicoloured	30	1·25
MS563	117×89 mm. Nos. 560/2. Imperf		70	3·00

294 Red Cross and
Globe

1970. 50th Anniv of League of Red Cross Societies. Multicoloured.

564	4n.p. Type **294**		20	10
565	12½n.p. Henri Dunant and Red Cross emblem (horiz)		25	25
566	20n.p. Patient receiving medicine (horiz)		30	85
567	40n.p. Patient having arm bandaged (horiz)		35	3·25
MS568	114×89 mm. Nos. 564/7. Imperf		1·50	6·00

298 General Kotoka,
Vickers VC-10 and
Airport

1970. Inauguration of Kotoka Airport. Multicoloured.

569	4n.p. Type **298**		15	10
570	12½n.p. Control tower and tail of Vickers VC-10		25	15
571	20n.p. Aerial view of airport		40	30
572	40n.p. Airport and flags		75	80

302 Lunar
Module landing
on Moon

1970. Moon Landing. Multicoloured.

573	4n.p. Type **302**		25	10
574	12½n.p. Astronaut's first step onto the Moon		30	60
575	20n.p. Astronaut with equipment on Moon (horiz)		40	1·40
576	40n.p. Astronauts (horiz)		45	3·25
MS577	142×142 mm. Nos. 573/6. Imperf		2·00	12·00

306 Adult Education

1970. International Education Year. Multicoloured.

578	4n.p. Type **306**		10	10
579	12½n.p. International education		20	20
580	20n.p. "Ntesie" and I.E.Y. symbols		35	30
581	40n.p. Nursery schools		60	1·40

310 Saluting
March-Past

1970. First Anniv of Second Republic. Multicoloured.

582	4n.p. Type **310**		20	10
583	12½n.p. Busia Declaration		15	15
584	20n.p. Doves symbol		25	30
585	40n.p. Opening of Parliament		50	1·00

314 Crinum ornatum

1970. Flora and Fauna. Multicoloured.

586	4n.p. Type **314**		1·75	25
587	12½n.p. Lioness		1·25	85
588	20n.p. Anselia africana (flower)		1·25	1·50
589	40n.p. African elephant		2·00	6·00

315 Kuduo Brass Casket

1970. Monuments and Archaeological Sites in Ghana. Multicoloured.

590	4n.p. Type **315**		15	10
591	12½n.p. Akan traditional house		30	20
592	20n.p. Larabanga Mosque		35	55
593	40n.p. Funerary clay head		50	2·50
MS594	89×71 mm. Nos. 590, 592 and 12½n.p. Basilica of Pompeii, 40n.p. Pistrinum of Pompeii. Imperf		3·50	9·50

316 Trade Fair Building

1971. International Trade Fair, Accra. Multicoloured.

595	4n.p. Type **316**		10	10
596	12½n.p. Cosmetic and pharmaceutical goods		60	20
597	20n.p. Vehicles		65	25
598	40n.p. Construction equipment		95	95

599	50n.p. Transport and packing case (vert)		1·10	1·10

317 Christ on the Cross

1971. Easter. Multicoloured.

600	4n.p. Type **317**		20	10
601	12½n.p. Christ and Disciples		40	70
602	20n.p. Christ blessing Disciples		50	1·40

318 Corn Cob

1971. Freedom from Hunger Campaign.

603	**318**	4n.p. multicoloured	10	10
604	**318**	12½n.p. multicoloured	35	90
605	**318**	20n.p. multicoloured	40	2·00

Remainder stocks of the above stamps were optd on the occasion of the death of Lord Boyd Orr and further surch 12½, 20 and 60n.p.

It is understood that 8070 sets from the agency were overprinted locally and returned to New York. Limited remainders of these stamps (only 330 of 60n.p.) were sold at the G.P.O. We do not list these as they were not freely on sale in Ghana.

319 Guides Emblem and
Ghana Flag

1971. Golden Jubilee of Ghana Girl Guides. Each design includes Guides emblem. Multicoloured.

606	4n.p. Type **319**		20	10
607	12½n.p. Mrs E. Ofuatey-Kodjoe (founder) and guides with flags		40	40
608	20n.p. Guides laying stones		50	70
609	40n.p. Camp-fire and tent		90	1·40
610	50n.p. Signallers		1·00	2·00
MS611	133×105 mm. Nos. 606/610. Imperf		7·50	12·00
MS611	133×105 mm. Nos. 606/610. Imperf		7·50	12·00

320 Child-care Centre

1971. Y.W.C.A. World Council Meeting, Accra. Multicoloured.

612	4n.p. Type **320**		10	10
613	12½n.p. Council meeting		10	15
614	20n.p. School typing class		15	30
615	40n.p. Building Fund Day		30	1·00
MS616	84×83 mm. Nos. 612/15. Imperf		70	2·00

321 Firework Display

1971. Christmas. Multicoloured.

617	4n.p. Type **321**		10	70
618	3n.p. African Nativity		15	80
619	6n.p. The Flight into Egypt		15	80

322 Weighing
Baby

1971. 25th Anniv of UNICEF. Multicoloured.

620	5n.p. Type **322**		10	10
621	15n.p. Mother and child (horiz)		20	30
622	30n.p. Nurse		30	70
623	50n.p. Young boy (horiz)		50	2·25
MS624	111×120 mm. Nos. 620/3. Imperf		1·25	6·00

323 Unity Symbol and
Trade Fair Emblem

1972. All African Trade Fair. Multicoloured.

625	5n.p. Type **323**		10	10
626	15n.p. Horn of Plenty		15	30
627	30n.p. Fireworks on map of Africa		20	70
628	60n.p. "Participating Nations"		25	2·00
629	1n.c. As No. 628		40	2·50

On 24 June 1972, on the occasion of the Belgian International Philatelic Exhibition, Nos. 625/9 were issued optd **BELGICA72**. Only very limited supplies were sent to Ghana (we understand not more than 900 sets), and for this reason we do not list them.

324 Books for the Blind

1972. International Book Year. Multicoloured.

630	5p. Type **324**		30	10
631	15p. Children's books		65	50
632	30p. Books for recreation		1·25	1·25
633	50p. Books for students		1·75	3·00
634	1c. Book and flame of knowledge (vert)		2·25	5·00
MS635	99×106 mm. Nos. 630/4. Imperf		7·00	11·00

325 Hypoxis urceolata

1972. Flora and Fauna. Multicoloured.

636	5p. Type **325**		25	10
637	15p. Mona monkey		40	40
638	30p. Crinum ornatum		2·75	3·25
639	1c. De Winton's tree squirrel		1·50	6·75

326 Football

1972. Olympic Games, Munich. Multicoloured.

640	5p. Type **326**		20	10
641	15p. Running		30	20
642	30p. Boxing		50	65
643	50p. Long-jumping		60	2·25
644	1c. High-jumping		1·10	3·50
MS645	86×43 mm. 40p. as No. 642 se-tenant with 60p. as No. 640		2·00	6·50

327 Senior Scout and Cub

1972. 65th Anniv of Boy Scouts. Multicoloured.

646	5p. Type **327**		25	10
647	15p. Scout and tent		40	30
648	30p. Sea scouts		60	80
649	50p. Leader with cubs		75	1·50
650	1c. Training school		1·00	2·75
MS651	110×110 mm. 40p. as 30p.; 60p. as 1c.		2·25	4·75

328 *The Holy Night*
(Correggio)

1972. Christmas. Multicoloured.
652	1p.	Type **328**	10	10
653	3p.	*Adoration of the Kings* (Holbein the Elder)	10	10
654	15p.	*Madonna of the Passion* (School of Ricco)	30	30
655	30p.	*King Melchior*	60	70
656	60p.	*King Gaspar, Mary and Jesus*	80	2·00
657	1c.	*King Balthasar*	1·00	3·25
MS658	139×90 mm. Nos. 655/7. Imperf		4·00	9·00

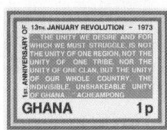

329 Extract from Speech

1973. First Anniv of 13 January Revolution. Multicoloured.
659	1p.	Type **329**	10	10
660	3p.	Market scene	10	10
661	5p.	Selling bananas (vert)	10	10
662	15p.	Farmer with hoe and produce (vert)	20	25
663	30p.	Market traders	30	40
664	1c.	Farmer cutting palm-nuts	70	1·40
MS665	90×55 mm. 40p. as 1c. and 60p. Miners		70	2·25

330 Under 5's Clinic

1973. 25th Anniv of W.H.O. Multicoloured.
666	5p.	Type **330**	10	10
667	15p.	Radiography	15	25
668	30p.	Immunisation	25	40
669	50p.	Starving child	25	80
670	1c.	W.H.O. H.Q., Geneva	25	1·75

1973. World Scouting Conference, Nairobi/Addis Ababa. Nos. 646/50 optd **1st WORLD SCOUTING CONFERENCE IN AFRICA.**
671	**327**	5p. multicoloured	10	15
672	-	15p. multicoloured	30	60
673	-	30p. multicoloured	40	1·40
674	-	50p. multicoloured	55	2·00
675	-	1c. multicoloured	70	3·00
MS676	110×110 mm. 40p. as 30p.; 60p. as 1c.		1·75	6·50

332 Poultry Farming

1973. Tenth Anniv of World Food Programme. Multicoloured.
677	5p.	Type **332**	10	10
678	15p.	Mechanisation	15	15
679	50p.	Cocoa harvest	40	90
680	1c.	F.A.O. H.Q., Rome	60	1·90
MS681	92×104 mm. 40p. as 15p.; 60p. as 1c.		60	2·25

333 "Green Alert"

1973. 50th Anniv of Interpol. Multicoloured.
682	5p.	Type **333**	25	10
683	30p.	"Red Alert"	70	80
684	50p.	"Blue Alert"	1·00	1·75
685	1c.	"Black Alert"	1·75	4·00

334 Handshake

1973. Tenth Anniv of O.A.U. Multicoloured.
686	5p.	Type **334**	10	10
687	30p.	Africa Hall, Addis Ababa	15	30
688	50p.	O.A.U. emblem	20	1·00
689	1c.	"X" in colours of Ghana flag	35	1·50

335 Weather Balloon

1973. Centenary of I.M.O./W.M.O. Multicoloured.
690	5p.	Type **335**	10	10
691	15p.	Satellite "Tiros"	15	20
692	30p.	Computer weather map	30	65
693	1c.	Radar screen	60	2·25
MS694	120×95 mm. 40p. as 15p.; 60p. as 30p.		1·25	3·25

336 Epiphany Scene

1973. Christmas. Multicoloured.
695	1p.	Type **336**	10	10
696	3p.	Madonna and Child	10	10
697	30p.	*Madonna and Child* (Murillo)	30	75
698	50p.	*Adoration of the Magi* (Tiepolo)	45	1·00
MS699	77×103 mm. Nos. 695/8. Imperf		1·25	3·00

337 *Christ carrying the Cross* (Thomas de Kolozsvar)

1974. Easter.
700	**337**	5p. multicoloured	10	10
701	-	30p. blue, silver and brown	15	35
702	-	50p. red, silver and brown	25	60
703	-	1c. green, silver and brown	35	1·25
MS704	111×106 mm. 15p. as No. 700; 20p. as No. 701; 25p. as No. 702. Imperf		80	1·75

DESIGNS (from 15th-century English carved alabaster): 30p. *The Betrayal*; 50p. *The Deposition*; 1c. *The Risen Christ and Mary Magdalene.*

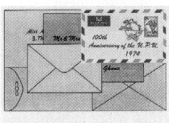

338 Letters

1974. Centenary of U.P.U. Multicoloured.
705	5p.	Type **338**	10	10
706	9p.	U.P.U. Monument and H.Q.	10	15
707	50p.	Airmail letter	35	1·00
708	1c.	U.P.U. Monument and Ghana stamp	60	1·75
MS709	108×90 mm. 20p. as No. 705; 30p. as No. 706; 40p. as No. 707; 60p. as No. 708		75	1·60

1974. "Internaba 1974" Stamp Exhibition. As Nos. 705/8 additionally inscr "INTERNABA 1974".
710	5p.	multicoloured	10	10
711	9p.	multicoloured	10	15
712	50p.	multicoloured	30	1·00
713	1c.	multicoloured	45	1·75
MS714	108×90 mm. 20p. as No. 710; 30p. as No. 711; 40p. as No. 712; 60p. as No. 713		1·50	4·00

339 Footballers

1974. World Cup Football Championship.
715	**339**	5p. multicoloured	10	10
716	-	30p. multicoloured	20	60
717	-	50p. multicoloured	25	85
718	-	1c. multicoloured	30	1·50
MS719	148×94 mm. 25, 40, 55 and 60p. as Nos. 715/18		1·00	3·25

DESIGNS: As Type **339** showing footballers in action.

340 Roundabout

1974. Change to Driving on the Right.
720	**340**	5p. green, red and black	10	10
721	-	15p. purple, red and black	20	35
722	-	30p. multicoloured	30	40
723	-	50p. multicoloured	40	85
724	-	1c. multicoloured	75	1·75

DESIGNS—HORIZ: 15p. Warning triangle sign. VERT: 30p. Highway arrow and slogan; 50p. Warning hands; 1c. Car on symbolic hands.

1974. West Germany's Victory in World Cup. Nos. 715/18 optd **WEST GERMANY WINNERS.**
725		5p. multicoloured	10	10
726		30p. multicoloured	20	40
727		50p. multicoloured	35	55
728		1c. multicoloured	45	1·25
MS729	148×94 mm. 25, 40, 55 and 60p. as Nos. 725/8		1·40	2·50

342 "Planned Family"

1974. World Population Year. Multicoloured.
730	5p.	Type **342**	10	10
731	30p.	Family planning clinic	25	35
732	50p.	Immunization	35	60
733	1c.	Population census enumeration	60	1·40

343 Angel

1974. Christmas. Multicoloured.
734	5p.	Type **343**	10	10
735	7p.	The Magi (diamond 47×47 mm)	10	10
736	9p.	The Nativity	10	10
737	1c.	The Annunciation	60	1·40
MS738	128×128 mm. 15p. Type **343**; 30p. as 7p.; 45p. as 9p.; 60p. as 1c. Imperf		80	2·50

1975. "Apollo"–"Soyuz" Space Link. Nos. 715/18 optd **APOLLO SOYUZ JULY 15, 1975.**
739	**339**	5p. multicoloured	10	10
740	-	30p. multicoloured	20	25
741	-	50p. multicoloured	30	55
742	-	1c. multicoloured	55	80
MS743	148×94 mm. 25, 40, 55 and 60p. as Nos. 739/42		1·00	2·00

345 Tractor Driver

1975. International Women's Year. Multicoloured.
744	7p.	Type **345**	45	10
745	30p.	Motor mechanic	1·00	35
746	60p.	Factory workers	1·10	40
747	1c.	Cocoa research	1·40	40
MS748	136×110 mm. 15, 40, 65 and 80p. as Nos. 744/7. Imperf		1·50	4·00

346 Angel

1975. Christmas.
749	**346**	2p. multicoloured	10	10
750	-	5p. yellow and green	10	10
751	-	7p. yellow and green	10	10
752	-	30p. yellow and green	20	20
753	-	1c. yellow and green	50	1·00
MS754	98×87 mm. 15, 65 and 80p. as Nos. 750/3. Imperf		90	3·00

DESIGNS: 5p. Angle with harp; 7p. Angel with lute; 30p. Angel with violin; 1c. Angel with trumpet.

347 Map Reading

1976. 14th World Scout Jamboree, Norway. Multicoloured.
755	7p.	Type **347**	20	10
756	30p.	Sailing	55	70
757	60p.	Hiking	60	2·00
758	1c.	Life-saving	70	2·50
MS759	133×99 mm. 15, 40, 65 and 80p. as Nos. 755/8		1·50	4·50

348 Bottles (litre)

1976. Metrication Publicity. Multicoloured.
760	7p.	Type **348**	15	10
761	30p.	Scales (kilogramme)	20	40
762	60p.	Tape measure and bale of cloth (metre)	40	1·00
763	1c.	Ice, thermometer and kettle (temperature)	60	1·75

349 Fair Site

1976. International Trade Fair, Accra.
764	**349**	7p. multicoloured	10	10
765	-	30p. multicoloured	15	20
766	-	60p. multicoloured	25	60
767	-	1c. multicoloured	40	1·00

DESIGNS: As Type **349** showing different views of the Fair.

1976. Interphil Stamp Exhibition. Nos. 755/8 optd **'INTERPHIL '76 BICENTENNIAL EXHIBITION.**
768	**347**	7p. multicoloured	15	15
769	-	30p. multicoloured	35	50
770	-	60p. multicoloured	55	75
771	-	1c. multicoloured	80	1·25
MS772	133×99 mm. 15, 40, 65 and 80p. as Nos. 768/71		1·00	2·00

351 Shot-put

1976. Olympic Games, Montreal. Multicoloured.
773	7p.	Type **351**	15	10
774	30p.	Football	30	25
775	60p.	Women's 1500 m	45	50
776	1c.	Boxing	60	80
MS777	103×135 mm. 15, 40, 65 and 80p. as Nos. 773/6		1·50	1·50

352 Supreme Court

1976. Centenary of Supreme Court.
778	352	8p. multicoloured	10	10
779	-	30p. multicoloured	20	25
780	-	60p. multicoloured	35	50
781	-	1c. multicoloured	60	1·00

DESIGNS: As Type **352** showing different views of the Court Buildings.

353 Examination for River Blindness

1976. Prevention of Blindness. Multicoloured.
782	7p. Type **353**	65	10
783	30p. Entomologist	1·75	1·40
784	60p. Normal vision	2·75	2·75
785	1c. Blackfly eradication	4·25	4·50

354 Fireworks Party, Christmas Eve

1976. Christmas. Multicoloured.
786	6p. Type **354**	15	10
787	8p. Children and gifts	15	10
788	30p. Christmas feast	35	30
789	1c. As 8p.	75	1·75
MS790	122×98 mm. 15, 40, 65 and 80p. as Nos. 786/9. Imperf	1·10	4·00

355 "Gallows Frame" Telephone and Alexander Graham Bell

1976. Centenary of Telephone. Multicoloured.
791	8p. Type **355**	15	10
792	30p. Bell and 1895 telephone	30	30
793	60p. Bell and 1929 telephone	45	70
794	1c. Bell and 1976 telephone	1·00	1·25
MS795	125×92 mm. 15, 40, 65 and 80p. as Nos. 791/4	1·00	1·40

1977. Olympic Winners. Nos. 773/6 optd **WINNERS** and country name.
796	351	7p. multicoloured	15	15
797	-	30p. multicoloured	20	40
798	-	60p. multicoloured	35	85
799	-	1c. multicoloured	40	1·50
MS800	103×135 mm. 15, 40, 65 and 80p. as Nos. 796/9		2·25	2·50

OPTD: 7p., 30p. **EAST GERMANY**; 60p. **U.S.S.R.**; 1c. **U.S.A.**

357 Dipo Dancers and Drum Ensemble

1977. Second World Black and African Festival of Arts and Culture, Nigeria. Multicoloured.
801	8p. Type **357**	15	15
802	30p. Arts and crafts	25	60
803	60p. Acon music and dancing priests	35	1·25
804	1c. African huts	40	2·00
MS805	164×120 mm. 15, 40, 65 and 80p. as Nos. 801/4	1·00	1·50

1977. Prince Charles`s Visit to Ghana. Nos. 791/94 optd **PRINCE CHARLES VISITS GHANA 17th TO 25th MARCH, 1977.**
806	8p. Type **355**	50	55
807	30p. 1895 telephone	1·25	1·00
808	60p. 1929 telephone	1·50	2·00
809	1c. 1976 telephone	2·00	2·50
MS810	125×92 mm. 15, 40, 65 and 80p. as Nos. 806/9	6·50	9·00

359 Olive Colobus Monkey

1977. Wildlife. Multicoloured.
811	8p. Type **359**	45	15
812	20p. Temminck's giant squirrel	70	80
813	30p. Hunting dog	75	1·25
814	60p. African manatee (sea cow)	1·25	2·75
MS815	140×101 mm. 15, 40, 65 and 80p. as Nos. 811/14	3·00	4·00

360 *Le Chapeau de Paille* (Rubens—400th Birth Anniv)

1977. Painters' Anniversaries. Multicoloured.
816	8p. Type **360**	25	10
817	30p. *Isabella of Portugal* (Titian—500th birth anniv)	40	40
818	60p. *Duke and Duchess of Cumberland* (Gainsborough—250th birth anniv)	55	65
819	1c. *Rubens and Isabella Brandt*	75	1·25
MS820	99×149 mm. 15, 40, 65 and 80p. as Nos. 816/19	1·50	1·25

361 The Magi, Madonna and Child

1977. Christmas. Multicoloured.
821	1p. Type **361**	10	10
822	2p. Choir, St. Andrew's Anglican Church, Abossey Okai	10	10
823	6p. Methodist Church, Wesley, Accra	10	10
824	8p. Madonna and Child	10	10
825	30p. Holy Spirit Cathedral, Accra	30	50
826	1c. Ebenezer Presbyterian Church, Accra	1·00	1·60
MS827	122×97 mm. 15, 40, 65 and 80p. as Nos. 822/3 and 825/6. Imperf	1·25	3·75

1978. Referendum. Nos. 821/26 optd **REFERENDUM 1978 VOTE EARLY.**
828	1p. Type **361**	10	10
829	2p. Choir, St. Andrew's Anglican Church, Abossey Okai	10	10
830	6p. Methodist Church, Wesley, Accra	10	10
831	8p. Madonna and Child	10	10
832	30p. Holy Spirit Cathedral, Accra	30	50
833	1c. Ebenezer Presbyterian Church, Accra	1·00	1·50
MS834	122×97 mm. 15, 40, 65 and 80p. as Nos. 829/30 and 832/3	27·00	17·00

363 Cutting Bananas

1978. Operation "Feed Yourself". Multicoloured.
835	2p. Type **363**	10	10
836	8p. Home produce	15	10
837	30p. Market	35	35
838	60p. Fishing	70	60
839	1c. Mechanisation	1·25	1·25

364 Wright Flyer III

1978. 75th Anniv of Powered Flight.
840	364	8p. black, brown and ochre	20	10
841	-	30p. black, brown and green	30	30
842	-	60p. black, brown and red	40	60
843	-	1c. black, brown and blue	2·75	1·10
MS844		167×100 mm. 15, 40, 65 and 80p. as Nos. 840/3	2·00	1·40

DESIGNS: 30p. Handley Page H.P.42; 60p. de Havilland Comet 1; 1c. Concorde.

1978. "CAPEX 1978" International Stamp Exhibition, Toronto. Nos. 840/3 optd **"CAPEX 78 JUNE 9-18 1978".**
845	364	8p. black, brown and ochre	15	15
846	-	30p. black, brown and green	25	25
847	-	60p. black, brown and red	50	50
848	-	1c. black, brown and blue	1·10	80
MS849		167×100 mm. 15, 40, 65 and 80p. as Nos. 845/8	1·25	1·60

366 Players and African Cup Emblem

1978. Football Championships. Multicoloured.
850	8p. Type **366**	20	15
851	30p. Players and African Cup emblem (different)	25	30
852	60p. Players and World Cup emblem	40	60
853	1c. Goalkeeper and World Cup emblem	55	1·00
MS854	111×105 mm. 15, 40, 65 and 80p. as Nos. 850/3	1·10	1·25

367 The Betrayal

1978. Easter. Drawings by Durer.
855	367	11p. black and mauve	10	10
856	-	39p. black and flesh	25	30
857	-	60p. black and yellow	35	45
858	-	1c. black and green	40	65

DESIGNS: 39p.*The Crucifixion*; 60p.*The Deposition*; 1c. *The Resurrection*.

1978. Football Victories of Ghana and Argentina. Nos. 850/3 and MS854 optd **"GHANA WINNERS"** (8, 30p.) or **"ARGENTINA WINS"** (others).
859	366	8p. multicoloured	45	15
860	-	30p. multicoloured	45	30
861	-	60p. multicoloured	70	45
862	-	1c. multicoloured	80	75
MS863		111×105 mm. 15, 40, 65 and 80p. as Nos. 859/62 but all optd	1·00	1·10

369 *Bauhinia purpurea*

370 Mail Van

1978. Flowers. Multicoloured.
864	11p. Type **369**	15	10
865	39p. *Cassia fistula*	20	55
866	60p. *Plumeria acutifolia*	20	70
867	1c. *Jacaranda mimosifolia*	20	1·00

1978. 75th Anniv of Ghana Railways. Multicoloured.
868	11p. Type **370**	20	10
869	39p. Pay and bank car	20	65
870	60p. Steam locomotive No. 1 "Amanful", 1922	20	1·00
871	1c. Diesel-electric locomotive No. 1651, 1960	20	1·40

371 "Orbiter" Spacecraft

1979. "Pioneer" Venus Space Project. Multicoloured.
872	11p. Type **371**	15	10
873	39p. "Multiprobe" space craft	15	30
874	60p. "Orbiter" and "Multiprobe" spacecraft in Venus orbit	20	45
875	3c. Radar chart of Venus	30	1·40
MS876	135×94 mm. 15, 40, 65p. and 2c. as Nos. 872/5. Imperf	1·10	1·25

372 O Come All Ye Faithful

1979. Christmas. Lines and Scenes from Christmas Carols. Multicoloured.
877	8p. Type **372**	10	10
878	10p. *O Little Town of Bethlehem*	10	10
879	15p. *We Three Kings of Orient Are*	10	10
880	20p. *"I Saw Three Ships come Sailing By*	10	10
881	2c. *"Away In a Manger*	30	80
882	4c. *Ding Dong Merrily on High*	50	1·40
MS883	110×95 mm. 25, 65p., 1 and 2c. as Nos. 877, 879 and 881/2	75	1·00

373 Dr. J. B. Danquah (lawyer and nationalist)

1980. Famous Ghanaians. Multicoloured.
884	20p. Type **373**	10	10
885	65p. John Mensah Sarbah (nationalist)	10	10
886	80p. Dr J. E. K. Aggrey (educationalist)	15	20
887	2c. Dr. Kwame Nkrumah (nationalist)	20	30
888	4c. G. E. (Paa) Grant (lawyer)	40	80

374 Tribesman ringing Clack Bells

1980. Death Centenary of Sir Rowland Hill (1979). Multicoloured.
889	20p. Type **374**	15	15
890	65p. As 50p.	15	20
891	2c. As 1c.	25	75
892	4c. Chieftain with ivory and gold staff	30	1·50
893	25p. Type **374**	15	40
894	50p. Chieftain with Golden Elephant staff	15	40
895	1c. Signalling with drums	20	85
896	5c. As 4c.	35	3·00
MS897	115×86 mm. Nos. 893/6	75	1·00

375 Children in Classroom

1980. International Year of the Child (1979). Multicoloured.
898	20p. Type **375**	15	15
899	65p. Playing football	25	45
900	2c. Playing in a boat	40	1·00
901	4c. Mother and child	60	1·75
MS902	156×94 mm. 25, 50p., 1 and 3c. as Nos. 898/901	75	1·75

1980. "London 1980" International Stamp Exhibition. Nos. 889/96 optd "LONDON 1980" 6th - 14th May 1980.
903	**374**	20p. multicoloured	15	15
907	-	25p. multicoloured	1·25	2·75
908	-	50p. multicoloured	1·50	3·00
904	-	65p. multicoloured	15	50
909	-	1c. multicoloured	2·25	3·50
905	-	2c. multicoloured	25	1·25
906	-	4c. multicoloured	35	2·25
910	-	5c. multicoloured	4·00	6·00
MS911	115×86 mm. Nos. 907/10		1·00	2·00

1980. Papal Visit. Nos. 898/901 optd "PAPAL VISIT" 8th - 9th May 1980.
912	**375**	20p. multicoloured	55	35
913	-	65p. multicoloured	1·00	60
914	-	2c. multicoloured	1·75	1·40
915	-	4c. multicoloured	2·50	2·50
MS916	156×94 mm. 25, 50p., 1 and 3c. as Nos. 912/15		9·00	6·50

378 Parliament House

1980. Third Republic Commemoration. Multicoloured.
917	20p. Type **378**	10	10
918	65p. Supreme Court	20	25
919	2c. The Castle	40	70
MS920	72×113 mm. 25p., 1 and 3c. as Nos. 917/19	60	1·10

379 Boeing 737 Airliner and Map of West Africa

1980. Fifth Anniv of Economic Community of West African States. Multicoloured.
921	20p. Type **379**	10	10
922	65p. Antenna and map	15	20
923	80p. Cog-wheels and map	20	25
924	2c. Corn and map	35	50

380 "O.A.U."

1980. First Organization of African Unity Economic Summit Conference, Nigeria.
925	**380**	20p. multicoloured	10	10
926	-	65p. multicoloured	15	20
927	-	80p. deep red, red and black	15	25
928	-	2c. multicoloured	20	65

DESIGNS: 65p. Maps of Africa and Ghana and banner; 80p. Map of Africa; 2c. Map of Africa, banner and Ghanaian flag.

381 *The Adoration of the Magi*

1980. Christmas. Paintings by Fra Angelico. Multicoloured.
929	15p. Type **381**	10	10
930	20p. *The Virgin and Child, enthroned with Four Angels*	10	10
931	2c. *The Virgin and Child enthroned with Eight Angels*	35	80
932	4c. *The Annunciation*	60	1·60
MS933	77×112 mm. 25, 50p., 1 and 3c. as Nos. 929/32	75	1·25

382 "Health"

1980. 75th Anniv of Rotary International. Multicoloured.
934	20p. Type **382**	10	10
935	65p. Rotary emblem and motto with maps of World and Ghana	15	30
936	2c. Rotary emblem, globe and outstretched hands	35	85
937	4c. "Eradication of Hunger"	60	1·50
MS938	121×93 mm. 25, 50p., 1 and 3c. as Nos. 934/7	1·10	2·00

383 Narina's Trogon ("Narina Trogon")

1981. Birds. Multicoloured.
939	20p. Type **383**	70	15
940	65p. White-crowned robin chat	1·00	50
941	2c. Swallow-tailed bee eater	1·25	1·75
942	4c. Rose-ringed parakeet	1·50	3·25
MS943	89×121 mm. 25, 50p., 1 and 3c. as Nos. 939/42	4·00	3·00

384 Pope John Paul II, Archbishop of Canterbury and President Limann during Papal Visit

1981. First Anniv of Papal Visit.
944	**384**	20p. multicoloured	25	15
945	**384**	65p. multicoloured	45	55
946	**384**	80p. multicoloured	60	70
947	**384**	2c. multicoloured	1·10	2·00

385 Royal Yacht *Britannia*

1981. Royal Wedding. Multicoloured.
948	20p. Prince Charles and Lady Diana Spencer	10	10
952	65p. As 20p.	15	25
949	80p. Prince Charles on visit to Ghana	15	20
953	1c. As 80p.	25	35
955	2c. Type **385**	1·00	1·50
954	3c. Type **385**	70	1·10
950	4c. Type **385**	50	80
956	5c. As 20p.	1·00	2·75
MS951	95×85 mm. 7c. St. Paul's Cathedral	70	1·25

386 Earth Satellite Station

1981. Commissioning of Earth Satellite Station. Multicoloured.
957	20p. Type **386**	10	10
958	65p. Satellites beaming signals to Earth	15	15
959	80p. Satellite	15	20
960	4c. Satellite orbiting Earth	1·00	1·50
MS961	112×100 mm. 25p., 50p., 1c. and 3c. as Nos. 957/60	70	1·40

387 Pounding Fufu

1981. World Food Day. Multicoloured.
962	20p. Type **387**	10	10
963	65p. Plucking cocoa	25	35
964	80p. Preparing banku	35	45
965	2c. Garri processing	75	2·25
MS966	131×99 mm. 25p., 50p., 1c. and 3c. as Nos. 962/5	1·00	1·50

388 *The Betrothal of St. Catherine of Alexandria* (Lucas Cranach)

1981. Christmas. Details from Paintings. Multicoloured.
967	15p. Type **388**	15	10
968	20p. *Angelic Musicians play for Mary and Child* (Aachener Altares)	15	10
969	65p. *Child Jesus embracing his Mother* (Gabriel Metsu)	20	15
970	80p. *Madonna and Child* (Fra Filippo Lippi)	20	20
971	2c. *The Madonna with Infant Jesus* (Barnaba da Modena)	40	70
972	4c. *The Immaculate Conception* (Murillo)	45	1·10
MS973	82×102 mm. 6c. *Madonna and Child with Angels* (Hans Memling)	1·00	2·25

389 Blind Person

1982. International Year for Disabled Persons. Multicoloured.
974	20p. Type **389**	25	10
975	65p. Disabled person with crutches	35	35
976	80p. Blind child reading braille	1·00	45
977	4c. Disabled people helping one another	1·75	2·25
MS978	109×85 mm. 6c. Group of disabled people	2·75	3·00

390 African Clawless Otter

1982. Flora and Fauna. Multicoloured.
979	20p. Type **390**	20	15
980	65p. Bushbuck	30	30
981	80p. Aardvark	30	40
982	1c. Scarlet bell tree	30	50
983	2c. Glory-lilies	50	1·25
984	4c. Blue-pea	80	2·25
MS985	76×100 mm. 5c. Chimpanzee	1·25	5·00

391 *Precis westermanni*

1982. Butterflies. Multicoloured.
986	20p. Type **391**	60	15
987	65p. *Papilio menestheus*	1·00	1·00
988	2c. *Antanartia delius*	1·50	3·50
989	4c. *Charaxes castor*	2·25	4·75
MS990	98×123 mm. 25p., 50p., 1c. and 3c. as Nos. 986/9	5·00	11·00

392 Scouts planting Tree

1982. 75th Anniv of Boy Scout Movement. Multicoloured.
991	20p. Type **392**	25	15
992	65p. Scouts cooking on campfire	45	45
993	80p. Sea Scouts sailing	50	55
994	3c. Scouts observing African elephant	1·25	2·50
MS995	101×71 mm. 5c. Lord Baden-Powell (vert)	1·50	5·00

393 Initial Stages of Construction

1982. Kpong Hydro-Electric Project. Multicoloured.
996	20p. Type **393**	65	10
997	65p. Truck removing rubble	1·25	45
998	80p. Hydro-electric turbines	2·00	65
999	2c. Aerial view of completed plant	2·75	1·60

394 Footballers

1982. World Cup Football Championship, Spain.
1000	**394**	20p. multicoloured	25	10
1005	**394**	30p. multicoloured	65	50
1001	-	65p. multicoloured	70	35
1002	-	80p. multicoloured (Heading)	80	45
1006	-	80p. multicoloured (Three footballers)	85	75
1007	-	1c. multicoloured	95	90
1008	-	3c. multicoloured	1·40	1·60
1003	-	4c. multicoloured	1·10	1·00
MS1004	110×90 mm. 6c. multicoloured		2·75	2·50

DESIGNS: 65p. to 6c. Scenes showing footballers.

395 The Fight against Tuberculosis

1982. Centenary of Robert Koch's Discovery of Tubercle Bacillus. Multicoloured.
1009	20p. Type **395**	70	20
1010	65p. Robert Koch	1·60	1·25
1011	80p. Robert Koch in Africa	2·00	1·75
1012	1c. Centenary of discovery of Tuberculosis	2·25	2·75
1013	2c. Robert Koch and Nobel Prize, 1905	3·25	4·00

396 The Shepherds worship Jesus

1982. Christmas. Multicoloured.
1014	15p. Type **396**	10	10
1015	20p. Mary, Joseph and baby Jesus	10	10
1016	65p. The Three Kings sight star	20	30
1017	4c. Winged Angel	70	1·75
MS1018	90×110 mm. 6c. The Three Kings with Jesus	1·00	1·75

397 Ghana and Commonwealth Flags with Coat of Arms

1983. Commonwealth Day. Multicoloured.

1019	20p. Type **397**	25	15
1020	55p. Satellite view of Ghana	45	65
1021	80p. Minerals of Ghana	1·00	1·25
1022	3c. African fish eagle	1·50	4·25

1983. Italy's Victory in World Cup Football Championship (1982). Nos. 1000/8 optd **WINNER ITALY 3–1**.

1023	20p. multicoloured	15	10
1028	30p. multicoloured	85	1·00
1024	65p. multicoloured	25	15
1025	80p. multicoloured	25	20
1029	80p. multicoloured	1·40	1·60
1030	1c. multicoloured	1·75	2·00
1031	3c. multicoloured	2·25	4·00
1026	4c. multicoloured	1·40	1·75
MS1027	110×90 mm. 6c. multicoloured	1·75	1·50

1983. No. 470 surch **C1**.

1031a	1c. on 20n.p. Bush hare (blue)	40	40

399 Short-finned Pilot Whale

1983. Coastal Marine Mammals. Multicoloured.

1032	1c. Type **399**	25	90
1033	1c.40 Risso's dolphin	30	1·00
1034	2c.30 False killer whale	35	1·00
1035	3c. Spinner dolphin	40	1·25
1036	5c. Atlantic hump-backed dolphin	40	1·60
MS1037	117×76 mm. 6c. As 4c.	1·25	1·00

400 Banded Jewelfish

1983

1038	**400** 5p. multicoloured	40	30
1039	- 10p. multicoloured	40	30
1040	- 20p. multicoloured	40	30
1041	- 50p. green, orange blk	40	45
1042	- 1c. orange, blue and black	50	20
1043	- 2c. multicoloured	50	30
1044	- 3c. multicoloured	1·25	30
1045	- 4c. multicoloured	70	40
1046	- 5c. multicoloured	50	40
1047	- 10c. multicoloured	1·50	1·50

DESIGNS—HORIZ: 10p. Banded jewelfish (different); 2c. Jet airliner. VERT: 20p. *Haemanthus rupestris*; 50p. Mounted warrior; 1c. Scorpion; 3c. White-collared mangabey; 4c. Demidoff's galago; 5c. *Kaemferia nigerica*; 10c. Grey-backed camaroptera.

401 Communication Devices

1983. World Communications Year. Multicoloured.

1048	1c. Type **401**	15	25
1049	1c.40 Satellite dish aerial	20	30
1050	2c.30 Cable and *Long Lines* (cable ship)	35	55
1051	3c. Switchboard operators	40	65
1052	5c. Aircraft cockpit and air traffic controllers	55	85
MS1053	95×70 mm. 6c. Space satellite	30	50

402 Children receiving Presents

1983. Christmas. Multicoloured.

1054	70p. Type **402**	15	10
1055	1c. Nativity and Star of Bethlehem (vert)	15	10
1056	1c.40 Children celebrating (vert)	20	55
1057	2c.30 Family praying together (vert)	25	1·00
1058	3c. Dancing to bongo drum	35	1·25
MS1059	70×90 mm. 6c. As 2c.30	30	1·00

403 Soldiers with Rifles

1983. Namibia Day.

1060	**403** 50p. green and black	10	10
1061	- 1c. multicoloured	10	10
1062	- 1c.40 blue, lt blue blk	15	15
1063	- 2c.30 multicoloured	20	25
1064	- 3c. multicoloured	25	30

DESIGNS: 1c. Soldiers supported by tank; 1c.40, Machete cutting chains; 2c.30, Peasant woman; 3c. Soldiers and artillery support.

1984. (a) Nos. 948/50, 952 and 954 surch.

1065	1c. on 20p. Prince Charles and Lady Diana Spencer	2·50	3·00
1066	9c. on 65p. Prince Charles and Lady Diana Spencer	3·00	4·00
1067	9c. on 80p. Prince Charles on visit to Ghana	3·00	4·00
1068	20c. on 3c. Type **385**	3·50	6·00
1069	20c. on 4c. Type **385**	3·50	6·00
MS1070	95×85 mm. 60c. on 7c. St. Paul's Cathedral	1·00	3·00

(b) Nos. 991/2 and 994 surch.

1071	10c. on 20p. Type **392**	40	45
1072	19c. on 65p. Scouts cooking on campfire	80	85
1073	30c. on 3c. Scouts observing African elephant	2·00	2·00
MS1074	101×71 mm. 60c. on 5c. Lord Baden-Powell	1·00	3·50

(c) Nos. 1000/3, 1005/6 and 1008 surch.

1075	**394** 1c. on 20p. multicoloured	30	50
1076	- 9c. on 65p. multicoloured	70	70
1077	- 9c. on 3c. multicoloured	70	70
1078	**394** 10c. on 30p. multicoloured	70	70
1079	- 10c. on 80p. multicoloured	70	70
1080	- 20c. on 80p. multicoloured	2·00	2·00
1081	- 20c. on 4c. multicoloured	2·00	2·00
MS1082	110×90 mm. 60c. on 6c. multicoloured	1·00	2·25

(d) Nos. 1019/22 surch.

1083	1c. on 20p. Type **397**	10	10
1084	9c. on 55p. Satellite view of Ghana	50	45
1085	30c. on 80p. Minerals of Ghana	2·25	1·75
1086	30c. on 3c. African fish eagle	3·25	3·50

(e) Nos. 1023/6, 1028/9 and 1031 surch.

1087	**394** 1c. on 20p. multicoloured	20	50
1088	- 9c. on 65p. multicoloured	55	60
1089	- 9c. on 3c. multicoloured	55	60
1090	**394** 10c. on 30p. multicoloured	55	60
1091	- 10c. on 80p. multicoloured	55	60
1092	- 20c. on 80p. multicoloured	90	1·00
1093	- 20c. on 4c. multicoloured	90	1·00
MS1094	110×90 mm. 60c. on 6c. multicoloured	1·00	2·00

1984. Universal Postal Union Congress, Hamburg. Nos. 1035/6 surch **19th U.P.U. CONGRESS - HAMBURG,** emblem and new value.

1095	10c. on 3c. Spinner dolphin	40	45
1096	50c. on 5c. Atlantic hump-backed dolphin	2·10	2·25
MS1097	117×76 mm. 60c. on 6c. as No. 1096	2·00	3·00

407 Cross and Crown of Thorns

1984. Easter. Multicoloured.

1098	1c. Type **407**	10	10
1099	1c.40 Christ praying	10	10
1100	2c.30 The Resurrection	10	10
1101	3c. Palm Sunday	10	15
1102	50c. Christ on the road to Emmaus	1·10	2·25
MS1103	102×86 mm. 60c. Type **407**	1·00	2·50

408 Women's 400 Metre Race

1984. Olympic Games, Los Angeles. Multicoloured.

1104	1c. Type **408**	10	10
1105	1c.40 Boxing	15	10
1106	2c.30 Hockey	20	15
1107	3c. Men's 400 metre hurdles race	20	15
1108	50c. Rhythmic gymnastics	1·75	3·50
MS1109	103×78 mm. 70c. Football	2·00	3·50

No. 1108 is inscribed "RYTHMIC" in error.

409 *Amorphophallus johnsonii*

1984. Flowers. Multicoloured.

1110	1c. Type **409**	10	10
1111	1c.40 *Pancratium trianthum*	10	10
1112	2c.30 *Eulophia cucullata*	10	15
1113	3c. *Amorphophallus abyssinicus*	10	15
1114	50c. *Chlorophytum togoense*	1·10	5·00
MS1115	70×96 mm. 60c. Type **409**	1·25	3·50

410 Young Bongo

1984. Endangered Antelopes. Multicoloured.

1116	1c. Type **410**	25	20
1117	2c.30 Bongo bucks fighting	35	55
1118	3c. Bongo family	40	70
1119	20c. Bongo herd in high grass	1·00	3·50
MS1120	Two sheets, each 100×71 mm. (a) 70c. Head of Kob; (b) 70c. Head of Bush buck Set of 2 sheets	10·00	13·00

411 Dipo Girl

1984. Ghanaian Culture. Multicoloured.

1121	1c. Type **411**	10	25
1122	1c.40 Adowa dancer	10	25
1123	2c.30 Agbadza dancer	10	25
1124	3c. Damba dancer	10	25
1125	50c. Dipo dancer	90	3·50
MS1126	70×84 mm. 70c. Mandolin player	1·50	3·00

412 The Three Wise Men bringing Gifts

1984. Christmas. Multicoloured.

1127	70p. Type **412**	10	10
1128	1c. Choir of angels	10	10
1129	1c.40 Mary and shepherds at manger	10	10
1130	2c.30 The flight into Egypt	10	10
1131	3c. Simeon blessing Jesus	10	15
1132	50c. Holy Family and angels	90	3·00
MS1133	70×90 mm. 70c. Type **412**	1·50	2·75

1984. Olympic Winners. Nos. 1104/8 optd.

1134	1c. Type **408** (optd **VALERIE BRISCO-HOOKS U.S.A.**)	10	10
1135	1c.40 Boxing (optd **U.S. WINNERS**)	10	10
1136	2c.30 Hockey (optd **PAKISTAN (FIELD HOCKEY)**)	10	10
1137	3c. Men's 400 metre hurdles race (optd **EDWIN MOSES U.S.A.**)	10	10
1138	50c. Rhythmic gymnastics (optd **LAURI FUNG CANADA**)	1·10	1·60
MS1139	103×78 mm. 70c. Football (optd **FRANCE**)	1·75	2·50

414 The Queen Mother attending Church Service

1985. Life and Times of Queen Elizabeth the Queen Mother. Multicoloured.

1140	5c. Type **414**	10	15
1141	12c. At Ascot Races	25	30
1142	100c. At Clarence House on her 84th birthday	1·75	2·50
MS1143	56×84 mm. 110c. With Prince Charles at Garter ceremony	1·75	3·00

Stamps as Nos. 1140/2 but with face values of 8c., 20c. and 70c. exist from additional sheetlets with changed background colours.

415 Moslems going to Mosque

1985. Islamic Festival of Id-el-Fitr. Multicoloured.

1144	5c. Type **415**	25	20
1145	8c. Moslems at prayer	35	30
1146	12c. Pilgrims visiting the Dome of the Rock	55	45
1147	18c. Preaching the Koran	70	60
1148	50c. Banda Nkwanta Mosque, Accra, and map of Ghana	1·75	1·60

416 Youths clearing Refuse ("Make Ghana Clean")

1985. International Youth Year. Multicoloured.

1149	5c. Type **416**	10	10
1150	8c. Planting sapling ("Make Ghana Green")	15	15
1151	12c. Youth carrying bananas ("Feed Ghana")	20	25
1152	100c. Open-air class ("Educate Ghana")	65	2·25
MS1153	103×78 mm. 110c. as 8c.	1·25	3·00

417 Honda "Interceptor", 1984

1985. Centenary of the Motorcycle. Multicoloured.

1154	5c. Type **417**	30	20
1155	8c. DKW, 1938	40	30
1156	12c. BMW "R 32", 1923	60	45
1157	100c. NSU, 1900	2·50	6·25
MS1158	78×108 mm. 110c. Zündapp, 1973 (vert)	2·75	4·25

418 Fork-tailed Flycatcher

1985. Birth Bicentenary of John J. Audubon (ornithologist). Designs showing original paintings. Multicoloured.

1159	5c. Type **418**	1·25	50
1160	8c. Barred owl	2·25	1·50
1161	12c. Black-throated mango	2·00	4·00
1162	100c. White-crowned pigeon	4·00	7·00
MS1163	85×115 mm. 110c. Downy Woodpecker	6·50	3·50

No. 1159 is inscribed "York-tailed fly catcher" in error.

419 United Nations Building, New York

1985. 40th Anniv of U.N.O. Multicoloured.

1164	5c. Type **419**	10	10
1165	8c. Flags of member nations and U.N. Building	10	15
1166	12c. Dove with olive branch	10	25
1167	18c. General Assembly	15	35
1168	100c. Flags of Ghana and United Nations	90	1·75
MS1169	90×70 mm. 110c. United Nations (New York) 1955 4c. 10th anniv stamp	75	1·75

420 Coffee

1985. 20th Anniv of United Nations Conference on Trade and Development. Designs showing export products. Multicoloured.

1170	5c. Type **420**	10	10
1171	8c. Cocoa	15	15
1172	12c. Timber	25	25
1173	18c. Bauxite	1·25	90
1174	100c. Gold	6·50	8·50
MS1175	104×74 mm. 110c. Agricultural produce and plate of food	1·25	2·50

421 Growth Monitoring

1985. UNICEF Child Survival Campaign. Multicoloured.

1176	5c. Type **421**	30	10
1177	8c. Oral rehydration therapy	50	30
1178	12c. Breast-feeding	70	40
1179	100c. Immunization	2·50	4·50
MS1180	99×69 mm. 110c. Campaign logo	1·75	2·25

422 Airline Stewardess and Boys with Stamp Album

1986. "Ameripex" International Stamp Exhibition, Chicago. Multicoloured.

1181	5c. Type **422**	15	15

1182	25c. Globe and Douglas DC-10 airplane	60	45
1183	100c. Ghana Airways stewardess (vert)	2·25	3·00
MS1184	90×70 mm. 150c. Stamp collecting class	1·50	2·50

423 Kejetia Roundabout, Kumasi

1986. "Inter-Tourism '86" Conference. Multicoloured.

1185	5c. Type **423**	10	10
1186	15c. Fort St. Jago, Elmina	30	30
1187	25c. Tribal warriors	45	45
1188	100c. Chief holding audience	1·75	3·25
MS1189	110×70 mm. 150c. African elephants	3·75	6·00

424 Tackling

1987. World Cup Football Championship, Mexico (1986). Multicoloured.

1190	5c. Type **424**	20	10
1191	15c. Player taking control of ball	30	15
1192	25c. Player kicking ball	50	25
1193	100c. Player with ball	1·50	1·25
MS1194	90×70 mm. 150c. Player kicking ball (different)	1·50	2·00

425 Fertility Doll

1987. Ghanaian Fertility Dolls. Designs showing different dolls.

1195	**425** 5c. multicoloured	10	10
1196	- 15c. multicoloured	15	15
1197	- 25c. multicoloured	25	25
1198	- 100c. multicoloured	90	2·00
MS1199	90×70 mm. **425** 150c. multicoloured	1·50	2·00

426 Children of Different Races, Peace Doves and Sun

1987. International Peace Year (1986). Multicoloured.

1200	5c. Type **426**	15	10
1201	25c. Plough, peace dove and rising sun	75	25
1202	100c. Peace dove, olive branch and globe (vert)	2·50	3·00
MS1203	90×70 mm. 150c. Dove perched on plough (vert)	1·75	2·25

427 Lumber and House under Construction

1987. "Gifex '87" International Forestry Exposition, Accra. Multicoloured.

1204	5c. Type **427**	10	10
1205	15c. Planks and furniture	15	15
1206	25c. Felled trees	25	25
1207	200c. Logs and wood carvings	1·60	2·25

1987. Appearance of Halley's Comet (1986). As T **151a** of Gambia. Multicoloured.

1208	5c. Mikhail Lomonosov (scientist) and Chamber of Curiosities, St. Petersburg	20	10
1209	25c. Lunar probe "Surveyor 3", 1966	70	30

1210	200c. Wedgwood plaques for Isaac Newton, 1790 and "Apollo 11" Moon landing, 1968	3·25	2·25
MS1211	100×70 mm. 250c. Halley's Comet	5·00	2·75

428 Demonstrator and Arms breaking Shackles

1987. Solidarity with the People of Southern Africa. Multicoloured.

1212	5c. Type **428**	10	10
1213	15c. Miner and gold bars	40	15
1214	25c. Xhosa warriors	30	25
1215	100c. Nelson Mandela and shackles	1·25	3·00
MS1216	70×90 mm. 150c. Nelson Mandela	1·50	2·00

429 Aerophones

1987. Musical Instruments. Multicoloured.

1217	5c. Type **429**	10	10
1218	15c. Xylophone	25	15
1219	25c. Chordophones	35	25
1220	100c. Membranophones	1·10	1·25
MS1221	90×70 mm. 200c. Idiophones	1·90	2·25

430 Woman filling Water Pot at Pump

1987. Int Year of Shelter for the Homeless. Multicoloured.

1222	5c. Type **430**	10	10
1223	15c. Building house from breeze blocks	15	15
1224	25c. Modern village with stream	20	25
1225	100c. Modern houses with verandahs	75	1·25

431 Ga Women preparing Kpokpoi for Homowo Festival

1988. Ghana Festivals. Multicoloured.

1226	5c. Type **431**	10	10
1227	15c. Efute hunters with deer, Aboakyir festival	15	15
1228	25c. Fanti chief dancing at Odwira festival	25	25
1229	100c. Chief in palanquin, Yam festival	65	1·25

432 Port Installation

1988. Fifth Anniv (1987) of 31 December Revolution. Multicoloured.

1230	5c. Type **432**	1·25	40
1231	15c. Repairing railway line	12·00	2·50
1232	25c. Planting cocoa	1·75	55
1233	100c. Miners with ore truck	13·00	14·00

433 Nurse giving Injection

1988. UNICEF Global Immunization Campaign. Multicoloured.

1234	5c. Type **433**	20	10
1235	15c. Girl receiving injection	25	20
1236	25c. Schoolgirl crippled by polio	35	50
1237	100c. Nurse giving oral vaccine to baby	60	2·25

434 Fishing

1988. Tenth Anniv of International Fund for Agricultural Development. Multicoloured.

1238	5c. Type **434**	85	30
1239	15c. Women harvesting crops	1·40	40
1240	25c. Cattle	1·75	50
1241	100c. Village granaries	4·00	8·50

435 Akwadjan Men

1988. Tribal Costumes. Multicoloured.

1242	5c. Type **435**	15	10
1243	25c. Banaa man	35	20
1244	250c. Agwasen woman	1·50	2·00

1988. Nos. 460, 464/6, 469/70, 474, 1031a, 1038/42, 1044 and 1046 surch.

1245	-	20c. on 50p. green, orange and black (No. 1041)	2·00	30
1246	-	20c. on 1c. orange, blue and black (No. 1042)	3·00	30
1247	-	50c. on 10n.p. mult (No. 469)	2·00	2·00
1248	-	50c. on 20n.p. deep blue and blue (No. 470) (surch **C50**)	15·00	10·00
1249	-	50c. on 20n.p. deep blue and blue (No. 470) (surch **C50.00**)	15·00	10·00
1250	-	50c. on 10p. mult (No. 1039)	1·00	2·00
1251	-	50c. on 1c. on 20n.p. deep blue and blue (No. 1031a) (surch **C50**)	10·00	5·00
1252	-	50c. on 1c. on 20n.p. deep blue and blue (No. 1031a) (surch **C50.00**)	10·00	10·00
1254	-	50c. on 1c. orange, blue and black (No. 1042)	6·00	30
1254m	-	50c. on 2n.c.50 multicoloured	5·00	15
1255	230	60c. on 1n.p. mult	6·00	60
1256	-	60c. on 4n.p. mult (No. 465)	6·00	1·00
1257	-	60c. on 3c. mult (No. 1044)	1·50	45
1258	400	80c. on 5p. multicoloured	1·00	45
1259	-	80c. on 5c. mult (No. 1046)	15·00	10·00
1260	-	100c. on 3n.p. mult (No. 464)	15·00	12·00
1261	-	100c. on 20n.p. deep blue and blue (No. 470)	10·00	10·00
1262	-	100c. on 20p. mult (No. 1040)	1·00	1·00
1263	-	100c. on 3c. mult (No. 1044)	2·00	2·00
1264	-	200c. on 6n.p. mult (No. 466)	8·00	10·00

440 Boxing

1988. Olympic Games, Seoul. Multicoloured.

1265	20c. Type **440**	15	15
1266	60c. Athletics	35	40
1267	80c. Discus-throwing	40	60
1268	100c. Javelin-throwing	50	1·00
1269	350c. Weightlifting	1·10	3·00
MS1270	75×105 mm. As 80c.	4·00	3·00

441 Nutrition Lecture

1988. 125th Anniv of Int Red Cross. Multicoloured.

1271	20c. Type **441**	40	15
1272	50c. Red Cross volunteer with blind woman	90	90
1273	60c. Distributing flood relief supplies	1·00	1·00
1274	200c. Giving first aid	2·50	3·25

442 Tropical Forest

1988. Christmas. Multicoloured.

1275	20c. Type **442**	15	10
1276	60c. Christ Child (vert)	35	35
1277	80c. Virgin and Child with Star (vert)	50	60
1278	100c. Three Wise Men following Star	60	70
1279	350c. Symbolic Crucifixion (vert)	2·00	2·50
MS1280	100×70 mm. 500c. Virgin and Child (vert)	2·00	2·75

443 "African Solidarity"

1989. 25th Anniv (1988) of Organization of African Unity. Multicoloured.

1281	20c. Type **443**	10	10
1282	50c. O.A.U. Headquarters Addis Ababa	15	20
1283	60c. Emperor Haile Selassie and Ethiopian flag (horiz)	30	25
1284	200c. Kwame Nkrumah (former Ghanaian President) and flag (horiz)	60	85

444 Amor

1989. 500th Birth Anniv of Titian (artist). Multicoloured.

1285	20c. Type **444**	25	15
1286	60c. The Appeal	45	30
1287	80c. Bacchus and Ariadne (detail)	50	40
1288	100c. Portrait of a Musician	60	75
1289	350c. Philip II seated	1·10	3·50
MS1290	77×115 mm. 500c. Portrait of a Gentleman	2·50	2·75

1989. Olympic Medal Winners, Seoul. Nos. 1251/5 optd.

1291	20c. Type **436** (optd **A. ZUE-LOW DDR 60 KG**)	50	10
1292	60c. (optd **G. BORDIN ITALY MARATHON**)	65	25
1293	80c. Discus-throwing (optd **J. SCHULT DDR**)	70	30
1294	100c. Javelin-throwing (optd **T. KORJUS FINLAND**)	70	35
1295	350c. Weightlifting (optd **B. GUIDIKOV BULGARIA 75 KG**)	1·75	1·10
MS1296	75×105 mm. 500c. As 80c. (optd **GOLD J. SCHULT DDR SILVER R. OUBARTAS USSR BRONZE R. DANNEBERG W. GERMANY** on sheet margin)	2·40	2·10

1989. Various stamps surch. (a) Nos. 949/50 and 952/4.

1297	80c. on 65p. Prince Charles and Lady Diana Spencer	90	90
1298	100c. on 80p. Prince Charles on visit to Ghana	1·00	1·25
1299	100c. on 1c. Prince Charles on visit to Ghana	1·00	1·25
1300	300c. on 3c. Type **385**	2·50	3·00
1301	500c. on 4c. Type **385**	3·50	4·75

(b) Nos. 1048/51 and **MS**1053.

1302	60c. on 1c. Type **401**	1·10	50
1303	80c. on 1c.40 Satellite dish aerial	1·25	65
1304	200c. on 2c.30 Cable and cable-laying ship	3·00	3·00
1305	300c. on 3c. Switchboard operators	3·25	4·00
MS1306	95×70 mm. 500c. on 6c. Space satellite	5·50	7·00

(c) Nos. 1104/7 and **MS**1109.

1307	60c. on 1c. Type **408**	30	30
1308	80c. on 1c.40 Boxing	40	40
1309	200c. on 2c.30 Hockey	1·25	1·60
1310	300c. on 3c. Men's 400 metre hurdles race	1·40	1·75
MS1311	103×78 mm. 600c. on 70c. Football	3·00	4·50

(d) Nos. 1134/7 and **MS**1139.

1312	60c. on 1c. Type **408** (optd **VALERIE BRISCO-HOOKS U.S.A.**)	1·75	1·25
1313	80c. on 1c.40 Boxing (optd **U.S. WINNERS**)	2·00	1·50
1314	200c. on 2c.30 Field hockey (optd **PAKISTAN (FIELD HOCKEY)**)	5·50	5·50
1315	300c. on 3c. Men's 400 metre hurdles race (optd **EDWIN MOSES U.S.A.**)	5·50	6·50
MS1316	103×78 mm. 600c. on 70c. Football (optd **FRANCE**)	7·00	8·00

(e) Nos. 1140/2. and **MS**1143.

1317	80c. on 5c. Type **414**	35	40
1318	250c. on 12c. At Ascot Races	1·10	1·75
1319	300c. on 100c. At Clarence House on her 84th birthday	1·25	1·75
MS1320	56×84 mm. 500c. on 110c. With Prince Charles at Garter Ceremony	3·50	4·75

(f) Nos. 1159/61 and **MS**1163.

1321	80c. on 5c. Type **418**	2·50	1·00
1322	100c. on 8c. Barred owl	3·75	2·50
1323	300c. on 12c. Black-throated mango	4·25	4·75
MS1324	85×115 mm. 500c. on 110c. Downy Woodpecker	9·50	9·50

(g) Nos. 1190/2 and **MS**1194.

1325	60c. on 5c. Type **424**	45	45
1326	200c. on 15c. Player taking control of ball	1·50	2·00
1327	300c. on 25c. Player kicking ball	2·00	2·75
MS1328	90×70 mm. 600c. on 150c. Player kicking ball (different)	7·50	8·50

(h) As Nos. 1190/2 and **MS**1194 but with unissued opt WINNERS Argentina 3 W.Germany 2.

1329	60c. on 5c. Type **424**	1·00	40
1330	200c. on 15c. Player taking control of ball	2·00	2·50
1331	300c. on 25c. Player kicking ball	2·50	3·00
MS1332	90×70 mm. 600c. on 150c. Player kicking ball (different)	4·00	5·00

(i) Nos. 1208/10.

1333	60c. on 5c. Mikhail Lomonosov (scientist) and Chamber of Curiosities, St. Petersburg	1·10	60
1334	80c. on 25c. Lunar probe "Surveyor 3", 1966	1·50	85
1335	500c. on 200c. Wedgwood plaques for Isaac Newton, 1790, and "Apollo 11" Moon landing, 1968	4·25	6·00
MS1336	100×70 mm. 750c. on 250c. Halley's Comet	5·00	6·00

(j) As Nos. 1208/10 and **MS**1211 optd **HALLEYS COMET 1985 - OFFICIAL - 1996** and emblem.

1337	60c. on 5c. Mikhail Lomonosov (scientist) and Chamber of Curiosities, St. Petersburg	75	55
1338	80c. on 25c. Lunar probe "Surveyor 3", 1966	85	65
1339	500c. on 200c. Wedgwood plaques for Isaac Newton, 1790, and "Apollo 11" Moon landing, 1968	3·50	6·00
MS1340	100×70 mm. 750c. on 250c. Halley's Comet	6·50	8·00

448 French Royal Standard and Field Gun

1989. "Philexfrance 89" International Stamp Exhibition, Paris. Multicoloured.

1341	20c. Type **448**	60	25
1342	60c. Regimental standard, 1789, and French infantry-man	1·25	90
1343	80c. Revolutionary standard, 1789, and pistol	1·50	1·00
1344	350c. Tricolour, 1794, and musket	3·75	5·50
MS1345	77×106 mm. 600c. Street plan of Paris, 1789 (horiz)	3·00	3·50

1989. Japanese Art. Portraits. As T **177a** of Gambia. Multicoloured.

1346	20c. Minamoto-no-Yoritomo (Fujiwara-no-Takanobu) (vert)	35	30
1347	50c. Takami Senseki (Watanabe Kazan) (vert)	50	30
1348	60c. Ikkyu Sojun (study) (Boku-sai) (vert)	55	35
1349	75c. Nakamura Kuranosuka (Ogata Korin) (vert)	60	40
1350	125c. Portrait of a Lady (Kyoto branch, Kano School) (vert)	85	75
1351	150c. Portrait of Zemmui (anon, 12th-century) (vert)	85	80
1352	200c. Ono no Komachi the Poet-ess (Hokusai) (vert)	1·00	1·25
1353	500c. Kobo Daisi as a Child (anon) (vert)	1·75	3·00
MS1354	Two sheets, each 102×77 mm. (a) 500c. Kodai-no-Kimi (attr Fujiwara-no-Nobuzane) (vert). (b) 500c. Emperor Hanazono (Fujiwara-no-Goshin) Set of 2 sheets	8·50	8·50

449 Storming the Bastille

1989. Bicentenary of French Revolution. Multicoloured.

1355	20c. Type **449**	55	20
1356	60c. Declaration of Human Rights	1·00	50
1357	80c. Storming the Bastille (horiz)	1·25	75
1358	200c. Revolution monument (horiz)	2·25	2·50
1359	350c. Tree of Liberty (horiz)	3·00	4·25

450 Collybia fusipes

1989. Fungi (1st series). Multicoloured.

1360	20c. Type **450**	25	25
1361	50c. Coprinus comatus	40	40
1362	60c. Xerocomus subtomentosus	40	45
1363	80c. Lepista nuda	55	55
1364	150c. Suillus placidus	80	95
1365	200c. Lepista nuda (different)	1·00	1·25
1366	300c. Marasmius oreades	1·50	1·75
1367	500c. Agaricus campestris	2·25	3·25
MS1368	Two sheets, each 110×80 mm. (a) 600c. "Boletus rhodoxanthus". (b) 600c. "Amanita rubescens" Set of 2 sheets	7·50	8·00

See also Nos. 1489/96.

451 "The Course of True Love ..."

1989. 425th Birth Anniv of Shakespeare. Verses and scenes from A Midsummer Night's Dream. Multicoloured.

1369	40c. Type **451**	75	65
1370	40c. "Love looks not with the eye but with the mind"	75	65
1371	40c. "Nature here shows art"	75	65
1372	40c. "Things growing are not ripe till their season"	75	65
1373	40c. "He is defiled that draws a sword on thee"	75	65
1374	40c. "It is not enough to speak, but to speak true"	75	65
1375	40c. "Thou art as wise as thou are beautiful"	75	65
1376	40c. Wildcat in wood (face value at left)	75	65
1377	40c. Man	75	65
1378	40c. Woman with flower	75	65
1379	40c. King and queen	75	65
1380	40c. Bottom	75	65
1381	40c. Wildcat in wood (face value at right)	75	65
1382	40c. Woman	75	65
1383	40c. Leopard	75	65
1384	40c. Tree trunk and man	75	65
1385	40c. Meadow flowers	75	65
1386	40c. Mauve flowers	75	65
1387	40c. Plants	75	65
1388	40c. Lion	75	65
1389	40c. Fern and flowers	75	65

Nos. 1369/89 were printed together, forming a composite design.

451a Bronze Mannikin

1989. Birds. Multicoloured.

1390	20c. Type **451a**	30	10
1391	50c. African pied wagtail	45	30
1392	60c. African pygmy kingfisher (inscr "Halcyon malimbicus")	1·25	1·75
1392a	60c. African pygmy kingfisher (inscr "Ispidina picta")	3·00	3·00
1393	80c. Blue-breasted kingfisher (inscr "Ispidina picta")	1·75	2·25
1393a	80c. Blue-breasted kingfisher (inscr "Halcyon malimbicus")	3·00	3·00
1394	150c. Striped kingfisher (vert)	1·10	1·25
1395	200c. Shikra (vert)	1·25	1·40
1396	300c. Grey parrot (vert)	1·50	1·75
1397	500c. Black kite (vert)	2·50	3·25
MS1398	Two sheets. (a) 128×83 mm. 600c. Cinnamon-breasted rock bunting and barn swallow (horiz). (b) 83×128 mm. 600c. Senegal puff-back flycatcher Set of 2 sheets	14·00	14·00

452 Command Module "Columbia" orbiting Moon

1989. 20th Anniv of First Manned Landing on Moon. Multicoloured.

1399	20c. Type **452**	30	15
1400	80c. Neil Armstrong's footprint on Moon	50	60
1401	200c. Edwin Aldrin on Moon	1·25	1·75
1402	300c. "Apollo 11" capsule on parachutes	1·60	2·00
MS1403	Two sheets, each 100×72 mm. (a) 500c. Launch of "Apollo 11". (b) 500c. Earth seen from Moon Set of 2 sheets	5·50	7·00

453 Desertification of Pasture

1989. World Environment Day. Multicoloured.

1404	20c. Type **453**	50	15
1405	60c. Wildlife fleeing bush fire	90	80
1406	400c. Industrial pollution	2·75	3·50
1407	500c. Erosion	3·00	3·75

454 Bebearia arcadius

1990. Butterflies. Multicoloured.

1408	20c. Type **454**	55	20
1409	60c. *Charaxes laodice*	70	40
1410	80c. *Euryphura porphyrion*	80	45
1411	100c. *Neptis nicomedes*	90	50
1412	150c. *Citrinophila erastus*	1·25	90
1413	200c. *Aethiopana honorius*	1·50	1·40
1414	300c. *Precis westermanni*	1·75	2·00
1415	500c. *Cymothoe hypatha*	2·25	3·00

MS1416 Two sheets, each 104×72 mm.
(a) 600c. *Telipna acraea*. (b) 600c.
Pentila abraxas Set of 2 sheets 9·00 10·00

455 Great Ribbed Cockle

1990. Seashells. Multicoloured.

1417	20c. Type **455**	60	25
1418	60c. Elephant's snout	75	40
1419	80c. Garter cone	85	80
1420	200c. Tankerville's ancilla	2·25	2·50
1421	350c. Coronate prickly-winkle	3·00	4·00

456 Nehru welcoming President Nkrumah of Ghana

1990. Birth Centenary of Jawaharlal Nehru (Indian statesman). Multicoloured.

1422	20c. Type **456**	60	25
1423	60c. Nehru addressing Bandung Conference, 1955	75	30
1424	80c. Nehru with garland and flowers (vert)	80	55
1425	200c. Nehru releasing pigeon (vert)	1·25	1·50
1426	350c. Nehru (vert)	1·75	2·75

457 Wyon Medal, 1838

1990. 150th Anniv of the Penny Black.

1427	**457**	20c. black and violet	40	20
1428	-	60c. black and violet	80	30
1429	-	80c. black and violet	1·00	35
1430	-	200c. black and green	1·50	1·25
1431	-	350c. black and green	2·00	2·50
1432	-	400c. black and red	2·50	3·00

MS1433 Two sheets, each 112×83 mm. (a) 600c. brown and black; (b) 600c. brown, buff and black Set of 2 sheets 6·50 8·00

DESIGNS: 60, 600c. (**MS**1433b) Bath mail coach, 1840; 80c. Leeds mail coach, 1840; 200c. Proof of Queen's head engraved by Heath, 1840; 350c. Master die, 1840; 400c. London mail coach, 1840; 600c. (**MS**1433a) Printing the Penny Black.

458 Anniversary Emblem

1990. Tenth Anniv (1989) of 4 June Revolution. Multicoloured.

1434	20c. Type **458**	15	15
1435	60c. Foodstuffs	20	20
1436	80c. Cocoa	25	30
1437	200c. Mining	2·25	2·00
1438	350c. Scales of Justice and sword	1·75	2·50

459 Map of Africa and Satellite Network

1990. 25th Anniv of Intelsat Satellite System. Multicoloured.

1439	20c. Type **459**	25	25
1440	60c. Map of Americas	40	30
1441	80c. Map of Asia and Pacific	45	35
1442	200c. Map of South America and Africa	1·10	1·25
1443	350c. Map of Indian Ocean and Pacific	1·50	2·25

460 Housewife using Telephone

1990. Second Anniv of Introduction of International Direct Dialling Service. Multicoloured.

1444	20c. Type **460**	25	20
1445	60c. Businessman using telephone	35	35
1446	80c. Man using phonecard telephone	40	40
1447	200c. Public telephones for internal and IDD services	90	1·00
1448	350c. Satellite station	1·50	2·00

461 Blue Flycatcher

1990. African Tropical Rain Forest. Multicoloured.

1449	40c. Type **461**	90	90
1450	40c. Boomslang (snake)	90	90
1451	40c. Superb sunbird	90	90
1452	40c. Bateleur	90	90
1453	40c. Yellow-casqued hornbill	90	90
1454	40c. *Salamis temora* (butterfly)	90	90
1455	40c. Potto	90	90
1456	40c. Leopard	90	90
1457	40c. Bongo	90	90
1458	40c. Grey parrot	90	90
1459	40c. Okapi	90	90
1460	40c. Gorilla	90	90
1461	40c. Flap-necked chameleon	90	90
1462	40c. West African dwarf crocodile	90	90
1463	40c. Python	90	90
1464	40c. Giant ground pangolin	90	90
1465	40c. *Pseudacraea boisduvali* (butterfly)	90	90
1466	40c. North African crested porcupine	90	90
1467	40c. Rosy-columned aerangis (orchid)	90	90
1468	40c. *Cymothoe sangaris* (butterfly)	90	90

MS1469 100×75 mm. 600c. Head of leopard (vert) 4·50 5·00

Nos. 1449/68 were printed together, *se-tenant*, forming a composite design.

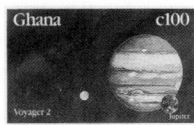

462 Jupiter

1990. Space Flight of "Voyager 2". Multicoloured.

1470	100c. Type **462**	85	85
1471	100c. Neptune and Triton	85	85
1472	100c. Ariel, moon of Uranus	85	85
1473	100c. Saturn from Mimas	85	85
1474	100c. Saturn	85	85
1475	100c. Rings of Saturn	85	85
1476	100c. Neptune	85	85
1477	100c. Uranus from Miranda	85	85
1478	100c. Volcano on Io	85	85

MS1479 Two sheets. (a) 111×81 mm. 600c. "Voyager 2" spacecraft (vert). (b) 80×111 mm. 600c. Lift off of "Voyager 2" (vert) Set of 2 sheets 4·75 6·00

463 *Eulophia guineensis*

1990. Orchids. Multicoloured.

1480	20c. Type **463**	45	45
1481	40c. *Eurychone roth-schildiana*	60	60
1482	60c. *Bulbophyllum barbigerum*	80	80
1483	80c. *Polystachya galeata*	1·10	1·10
1484	200c. *Diaphananthe kamerunensis*	2·00	1·75
1485	300c. *Podangis dactyloceras*	2·25	2·00
1486	400c. *Ancistrochilus rothschildianus*	2·50	2·00
1487	500c. *Rangaeris muscicola*	2·75	2·00

MS1488 Two sheets, each 101×70 mm. (a) 600c. *Bolusiella imbricata*. (b) *Diaphananthe rotila* Set of 2 sheets 14·00 14·00

464 *Coprinus atramentarius*

1990. Fungi (2nd series). Multicoloured.

1489	20c. Type **464**	70	45
1490	50c. *Marasmius oreades*	90	65
1491	60c. *Oudemansiella radicata*	1·00	70
1492	80c. *Boletus edulis* (Cep)	1·25	90
1493	150c. *Hebeloma crustu-liniforme*	2·00	1·50
1494	200c. *Coprinus micaceus*	2·25	2·00
1495	300c. *Macrolepiota procera* ("*Lepiota procera*")	2·50	2·50
1496	500c. *Amanita phalloides*	2·75	3·00

MS1497 Two sheets, each 104×82 mm. (a) Nos. 1489, 1491/2 and 1496. (b) Nos. 1490 and 1493/5 Set of 2 sheets 8·00 9·00

465 Italian and Swedish Players chasing Ball

1990. World Cup Football Championship, Italy. Multicoloured.

1498	20c. Type **465**	30	20
1499	50c. Egyptian player penetrating Irish defence	40	30
1500	60c. Cameroon players celebrating	45	30
1501	80c. Romanian player beating challenge	60	40
1502	100c. Russian goalkeeper Dassayev	70	65
1503	150c. Roger Milla of Cameroon (vert)	1·10	1·10
1504	400c. South Korean player challenging opponent	1·75	2·50
1505	600c. Klinsman of West Germany celebrating	2·25	3·50

MS1506 Two sheets, each 88×98 mm. (a) 800c. United Arab Emirates player watching ball. (b) 800c. Colombian player Set of 2 sheets 5·50 6·50

1990. 350th Death Anniv of Rubens. As T **195c** of Gambia, but vert. Multicoloured.

1507	20c. *Duke of Mantua*	50	20
1508	50c. *Jan Brant*	70	30
1509	60c. *Portraits of a Young Man*	75	30
1510	80c. *Michel Ophovius*	85	40
1511	100c. *Caspar Gevaerts*	95	65
1512	200c. *Head of Warrior* (detail)	1·75	1·75
1513	300c. *Study of a Bearded Man*	2·25	2·75
1514	400c. *Paracelsus*	2·50	3·75

MS1515 Two sheets, each 71×100 mm. (a) 600c. *Warrior with two Pages* (detail). (b) 600c. *Archduke Ferdinand* (detail) Set of 2 sheets 8·00 9·00

466 Manganese Ore

1991. Minerals. Multicoloured.

1516	20c. Type **466**	75	30
1517	60c. Iron ore	1·00	60
1518	80c. Bauxite ore	1·25	75
1519	200c. Gold ore	2·50	2·25
1520	350c. Diamond	3·50	4·50

MS1521 70×90 mm. 600c. Uncut and cut diamonds 9·50 10·00

467 Dance Drums

1991. Tribal Drums. Multicoloured.

1522	20c. Type **467**	50	20
1523	60c. Message drums	1·00	40
1524	80c. War drums	1·25	50
1525	200c. Dance drums (different)	2·25	2·50
1526	350c. Ceremonial drums	2·75	4·50

MS1527 70×90 mm. 600c. Drum with carrying strap 7·50 8·50

468 *Amorphophallus dracontioides*

1991. Flowers (1st series). Multicoloured.

1528	20c. Type **468**	85	25
1529	60c. *Anchomanes difformis*	1·25	50
1530	80c. *Kaemferia nigerica*	1·50	70
1531	200c. *Aframomum sceptrum*	2·50	3·00
1532	350c. *Amorphophallus flavovirens*	2·75	4·00

MS1533 70×90 mm. 600c. *Amorphophallus flavovirens* (different) 6·00 6·50

1991. Flowers (2nd series). As T **468** but inscr "GHANA" in capitals. Multicoloured.

1534	20c. *Urginea indica*	55	25
1535	60c. *Hymencallis littoralis*	90	50
1536	80c. *Crinum jagus*	1·75	80
1537	200c. *Dipcadi tacazzeanum*	2·25	3·00
1538	350c. *Haemanthus rupestris*	2·75	4·00

MS1539 70×90 mm. 600c. *Urginea indica* (different) 6·00 6·50

469 Transport and Telecommunication Symbols

1991. 40th Anniv of United Nations Development Programme. Multicoloured.

1540	20c. Type **469**	55	20
1541	60c. Agricultural research	80	40
1542	80c. Literacy	90	55
1543	200c. Advances in agricultural crop growth	1·75	2·00
1544	350c. Industrial symbols	2·75	4·00

470 Drawing of Scout from First Handbook

1991. 50th Death Anniv of Lord Baden-Powell.

1545	**470**	20c. black and buff	90	20
1546	-	50c. grey, blue and black	1·10	40
1547	-	60c. multicoloured	1·10	45
1548	-	80c. black and buff	1·40	55
1549	-	100c. multicoloured	1·60	75
1550	-	200c. multicoloured	2·00	2·00
1551	-	500c. multicoloured	2·50	4·00
1552	-	600c. multicoloured	2·75	5·50

MS1553 Two sheets. (a) 104×75 mm. 800c. multicoloured. (b) 74×105 mm. 800c. multicoloured Set of 2 sheets 8·00 11·00

DESIGNS—VERT: 50c. Lord Baden-Powell; 80c. Handbook illustrations by Norman Rockwell; 500c. Scout at prayer. HORIZ: 60c. Hands holding Boy Scout emblem; 100c. Mafeking Siege 1d. Goodyear stamp and African runner; 200c. Scouts with Blitz victim, London, 1944; 600c. Mafeking Siege 1d. Goodyear stamp; 800c. (**MS**1553a) Scout camp; 800c. (**MS**1553b) Envelope from Mafeking Siege.

471 Women sorting Fish

1991. Chorkor Smoker (fish smoking process). Multicoloured.

1554	20c. Type **471**	35	20
1555	60c. Cleaning the ovens	65	40
1556	80c. Washing fish	75	55
1557	200c. Laying fish on pallets	1·40	1·75
1558	350c. Stacking pallets over ovens	2·00	2·75

472 African Hind

1991. Fish. Multicoloured.

1559	20c. Type **472**	25	25
1560	50c. Shrew squeaker	40	40
1561	80c. West African triggerfish	55	55
1562	100c. Stonehead	70	70
1563	200c. Lesser pipefish	1·50	1·50
1564	300c. Aba	1·60	1·60
1565	400c. Jewel cichlid	1·75	1·75
1566	500c. Smooth hammerhead	1·90	1·90
MS1567	Two sheets, each 108×81 mm. (a) 800c. Bayad. (b) 800c. Eastern flying gurnard Set of 2 sheets	7·50	8·00

1991. Death Centenary (1990) of Vincent van Gogh (artist). As T **200b** of Gambia. Multicoloured.

1568	20c. Reaper with Sickle	35	25
1569	50c. The Thresher	55	40
1570	60c. The Sheaf-Binder	60	50
1571	80c. The Sheep-Shearers	70	65
1572	100c. Peasant Woman cutting Straw	85	80
1573	200c. The Sower	1·60	1·75
1574	500c. The Plough and the Harrow (horiz)	2·25	2·50
1575	600c. The Woodcutter	2·25	2·50
MS1576	Two sheets, each 117×80 mm. (a) 800c. Evening: The Watch (horiz). (b) 800c. Evening: The End of the Day (horiz). Imperf Set of 2 sheets	10·00	11·00

473 Gamal Nasser (Egypt) and Conference Hall

1991. Tenth Non-Aligned Ministers' Conference, Accra. Statesmen. Multicoloured.

1577	20c. Type **473**	50	30
1578	60c. Josip Tito (Yugoslavia)	55	45
1579	80c. Pandit Nehru (India)	4·75	1·75
1580	200c. Kwame Nkrumah (Ghana)	1·75	2·25
1581	350c. Achmad Sukarno (Indonesia)	1·90	3·50

474 Green-winged Pytila

1991. Birds. As T **474**. Multicoloured.

1582-	80c.×16, 100c.×32		
1629		22·00	25·00
MS1630	Three sheets, each 107×86 mm. (a) 800c. Marabou stork. (b) 800c. African fish eagle. (c) 800c. Saddle-bill stork Set of 3 sheets	12·00	13·00

Nos. 1582/1629 were issued together, se-tenant, as three sheetlets of 16 forming composite designs. The 80c. values show Green-winged pytila, Orange-cheeked waxbill, African paradise flycatcher, Great blue turaco ("Blue plantain-eater"), Red bishop, Splendid glossy starling, Red-faced lovebird, African palm swift, Narina's trogon ("Narina Trogon"), Tawny eagle, Bateleur, Hoopoe, Secretary bird, African white-backed vulture, White-necked bald crow ("Bare-headed rockfowl"), Abyssinian ground hornbill, and the 100c. African open-bill stork, African spoonbill, Pink-backed pelican, Little bittern, Purple swamphen ("King reed-hen"), Saddle-bill stork, Glossy ibis, White-faced whistling duck, Black-headed heron, Hammerkop, African darter, Woolly-necked stork, Yellow-billed stork, Black-winged stilt, Goliath heron, African jacana ("Lily trotter"), Shikra, Abyssinian roller, Carmine bee eater, Pin-tailed whydah, Purple glossy starling, Yellow-mantled whydah, Pel's fishing owl, Crested touraco, Red-cheeked cordon-bleu, Olive-bellied sunbird, Red-billed hornbill, Red-billed quelea, South African crowned crane, Indian blue quail ("Blue Quail"), Egyptian vulture and Helmeted guineafowl.

475 Nularda (beetle)

1991. Insects. Multicoloured.

1631	20c. Type **475**	70	20
1632	50c. Zonocrus (grasshopper)	85	30
1633	60c. Gryllotalpa africana (mole cricket)	95	30
1634	80c. Weevil	1·10	60
1635	100c. Coenagrion (dragonfly)	1·40	90
1636	150c. Sahlbergella (fly)	1·75	2·25
1637	200c. Anthia (ant)	2·00	2·50
1638	350c. Megacephala (beetle)	2·50	2·75
MS1639	106×79 mm. 600c. Lacetus (lacewing)	10·00	11·00

476 Boti Falls

1991. Multicoloured

1639a	20c. Oil palm fruit	1·00	10
1640	50c. Type **476**	1·00	10
1641	60c. Larabanga Mosque (horiz)	1·00	10
1642	80c. Fort Sebastian, Shama (horiz)	1·00	10
1643	100c. Cape Coast Castle (horiz)	2·25	30
1644	200c. White-toothed cowrie (horiz)	10·00	75
1645	400c. True achatina (horiz)	10·00	1·25

1991. Christmas. Religious Paintings. As T **200c** of Gambia. Multicoloured.

1646	20c. Adoration of the Magi (Bosch)	55	20
1647	50c. The Annunciation (Campin)	75	30
1648	60c. Virgin and Child (detail) (Bouts)	80	30
1649	80c. Presentation in the Temple (Memling)	1·00	50
1650	100c. Virgin and Child enthroned with Angel and Donor (Memling)	1·25	65
1651	200c. Virgin and Child with Saints and Donor (Van Eyck)	2·00	2·00
1652	400c. St. Luke painting the Virgin (Van der Weyden)	3·00	3·75
1653	700c. Virgin and Child (Bouts)	4·25	6·00
MS1654	Two sheets, each 103×128 mm. (a) 800c. Virgin and Child standing in a Niche (Van der Weyden). (b) 800c. The Annunciation (Memling) Set of 2 sheets	7·50	9·00

477 Women collecting Water from Bore Hole

1992. Decade of Revolutionary Progress. Multicoloured.

1655	20c. Type **477**	15	10
1656	50c. Miners	40	15
1657	60c. Wood carver	30	15
1658	80c. Forestry	30	20
1659	200c. Cacao tree	60	75
1660	350c. Village electrification	1·00	1·75

478 Mount Fuji and Flying Fish

1992. "Phila Nippon '91" International Stamp Exhibition, Tokyo. Multicoloured.

1661	20c. Type **478**	65	30
1662	60c. Itsukushima Jingu Shrine	80	40
1663	80c. Geisha	1·00	50
1664	100c. Samurai house	2·25	1·75
1665	200c. Bonsai tree	2·75	3·00
1666	400c. Olympic Sports Hall	2·75	3·00
1667	500c. Great Buddha (statue)	2·75	3·00
1668	600c. Nagoya Castle	3·00	3·50
MS1669	Two sheets, each 109×80 mm. (a) 800c. Takamatsu Castle. (b) 800c. Heian Shrine Set of 2 sheets	13·00	14·00

479 East and West Germans celebrating

1992. Reunification of Germany. Multicoloured.

1670	20c. Type **479**	30	20
1671	60c. Signing Reunification Treaty	40	40
1672	80c. Chariot on Brandenburg Gate and fireworks	45	45
1673	1000c. Germans with unified currency	8·00	10·00
MS1674	Three sheets. (a) 109×78 mm. 400c. Doves and Brandenburg Gate; 400c. Chancellor Kohl and Prime Minister De Maizière. (b) 125×87 mm. 800c. Chancellor Kohl and members of last German Democratic Republic administration. (c) 130×92 mm. 300c. President Gorbachev (vert); 300c. Chancellor Kohl (vert); 300c. Map of Western Germany (face value in black) (vert); 300c. Map of Eastern Germany (face value in white) (vert) Set of 3 sheets	13·00	13·00

480 Steam Side-tank Locomotive, 1903

1992. Ghanaian Railways. Multicoloured.

1675	20c. Type **480**	60	30
1676	50c. AIA-AIA diesel locomotive	85	40
1677	60c. First class coach, 1931	85	45
1678	80c. Railway inspection coach No. 2212	90	70
1679	100c. Steam locomotive No. 401 on Kumasi turntable	1·25	90
1680	200c. Cocoa wagon, 1921	1·75	1·75
1681	500c. Steam locomotive No. 223 "Prince of Wales"	2·75	3·50
1682	600c. Cattle wagon	2·75	3·50
MS1683	Two sheets. (a) 106×76 mm. 800c. Beyer-Garratt steam locomotive No. 301, 1943. (b) 76×106 mm. 800c. German-built steam locomotive Set of 2 sheets	9·00	10·00

1992. Olympic Games, Albertville and Barcelona. Past Medal Winners. As T **203** of Gambia. Multicoloured.

1684	20c. E. Blay (Ghana) (boxing) and windmill	50	20
1685	60c. M. Ahey (Ghana) (athletics) and Catalan coat of arms	70	35
1686	80c. T. Wilson (U.S.A.) (70 m ski jump) and grapes	90	50
1687	100c. Four-man bobsleighing (East Germany) and passport	1·25	75
1688	200c. G. Louganis (U.S.A.) (platform diving) and decorative vase	2·00	1·50
1689	300c. L. Visser (Netherlands) (5000 m speed skating) and wine bottle cork	2·25	2·25
1690	350c. J. Passler (Italy) (biathlon) and lily	2·25	2·50
1691	400c. M. Retton (U.S.A.) (gymnastics) and silhouette of castle	2·50	2·75
1692	500c. J. Hingsen (West Germany) (decathlon) and gold and silver coins	2·50	2·75
1693	600c. R. Neubert (West Germany) (heptathlon) and leather work	2·50	3·00
MS1694	Two sheets. (a) 112×82 mm. 800c. Silhouette of windmill. (b) 82×112 mm. 800c. Silhouette of folk dancer (vert) Set of 2 sheets	13·00	14·00

481 Angides lugubris

1992. Reptiles. Multicoloured.

1695	20c. Type **481**	35	20
1696	50c. Kinixys erosa (tortoise)	50	30
1697	60c. Agama agama (lizard)	50	30
1698	80c. Chameleo gracilis (chameleon)	60	40
1699	100c. Naja melanleuca (snake)	70	50
1700	200c. Crocodylus niloticus (crocodile)	1·25	1·10
1701	400c. Chelonia mydas (turtle)	2·00	2·50
1702	500c. Varanus exanthematicus (lizard)	2·25	2·75
MS1703	94×66 mm. 600c. Tortoise and snake	3·00	4·00

1992. Easter. Religious Paintings. As T **204a** of Gambia but vert designs. Multicoloured.

1704	20c. The Four Apostles (detail) (Dürer)	50	20
1705	50c. The Last Judgement (detail) (Rubens)	70	30
1706	60c. The Four Apostles (different detail) (Dürer)	70	30
1707	80c. The Last Judgement (different detail) (Rubens)	85	40
1708	100c. Crucifixion (Rubens)	1·00	50
1709	200c. The Last Judgement (different detail) (Rubens)	2·00	1·75
1710	500c. Christum Videre (Rubens)	3·25	4·00
1711	600c. The Last Judgement (different detail) (Rubens)	3·50	5·00
MS1712	Two sheets. (a) 69×100 mm. 800c. Last Communion of St. Francis of Assisi (detail) (Rubens) (vert). (b) 100×69 mm. 800c. Scourging the Money Changers from the Temple (detail) (El Greco) Set of 2 sheets	9·50	10·00

481a Two Men at Table (Velazquez)

1992. "Granada '92" International Stamp Exhibition, Spain. Spanish Paintings. Multicoloured.

1713	20c. Type **481a**	45	20
1714	60c. Christ in the House of Mary and Martha (detail) (Velazquez)	70	30
1715	80c. The Supper at Emmaus (Velazquez)	80	40
1716	100c. Three Musicians (Velazquez)	1·00	50
1717	200c. Old Woman cooking Eggs (Velazquez) (vert)	1·75	1·10
1718	400c. Old Woman cooking Eggs (detail) (Velazquez) (vert)	2·75	3·00
1719	500c. The Surrender of Breda (detail) (Velazquez) (vert)	3·00	3·25
1720	700c. The Surrender of Breda (different detail) (Velazquez) (vert)	3·50	5·00
MS1721	Two sheets. (a) 95×120 mm. 900c. The Waterseller of Seville (Velazquez) (86×111 mm). (b) 120×95 mm. 900c. They still Say that Fish is Expensive (Joaquin Sorolla y Bastida) (111×86 mm). Imperf Set of 2 sheets	10·00	11·00

482 Danaus chrysippus

1992. "Genova '92" International Thematic Stamp Exhibition. Butterflies. Multicoloured.

1722	20c. Type **482**	50	30
1723	60c. Papilio dardanus	80	45
1724	80c. Cynthia cardui	90	60
1725	100c. Meneris tulbaghia	1·00	75
1726	200c. Salamis temora	1·50	1·60
1727	400c. Charaxes jasius	2·00	2·50
1728	500c. Precis oenone	2·25	2·50
1729	700c. Precis sophia	2·50	2·75
MS1730	Two sheets, each 100×70 mm. (a) 900c. Papilio demodocus. (b) 900c. Precis octavia Set of 2 sheets	7·50	8·50

1992. Prehistoric Animals. As T **207a** of Gambia. Multicoloured.

1731	20c. Iguanodon	35	25
1732	50c. Anchisaurus	50	35
1733	60c. Heterodontosaurus	55	35
1734	80c. Ouranosaurus	60	45
1735	100c. Anatosaurus	75	55
1736	200c. Elaphrosaurus	1·25	1·50
1737	500c. Coelophysis	2·25	2·75

1738	600c. Rhamphorynchus	2·50	3·00

MS1739 Two sheets, each 100×70 mm. (a) 1500c. As 200c. (b) 1500c. As 500c. Set of 2 sheets — 9·00 10·00

483 Martin Pinzon and "Pinta"

1992. World Columbian Stamp "Expo '92", Chicago. 500th Anniv of Discovery of America by Columbus. Multicoloured.

1740	200c. Type 483	1·10	1·10
1741	200c. Vicente Pinzon and *Nina*	1·10	1·10
1742	200c. Columbus and Father Marchena at La Rabida	1·10	1·10
1743	200c. Columbus in his cabin	1·10	1·10
1744	200c. Fleet sights land	1·10	1·10
1745	200c. Columbus on Samana Cay	1·10	1·10
1746	200c. Wreck of *Santa Maria*	1·10	1·10
1747	200c. Amerindians at Spanish Court	1·10	1·10

MS1748 122×86 mm. 500c. Columbus and *Santa Maria* — 3·75 4·25

484 Olive-grey Ancilla

1992. Shells. Multicoloured.

1749	20c. Type 484	20	20
1750	20c. Radula cerith	20	20
1751	60c. Rugose donex	30	30
1752	60c. Horned murex	30	30
1753	80c. Concave ear moon	40	40
1754	80c. Triple twella	40	40
1755	200c. Pila africana	90	1·00
1756	200c. Rat cowrie	90	1·00
1757	350c. Thais hiatula	1·60	1·90
1758	350c. West African helmet	1·60	1·90

MS1759 Two sheets, each 87×117 mm. (a) 600c. Fanel moon (*Natica fanel*). (b) 600c. Giant hairy melongena (*Pugilina moria*) Set of 2 sheets — 6·00 7·00

485 Presentation in the Temple (Master of the Braunschweiti)

1992. Christmas. Religious Paintings. Multicoloured.

1760	20c. Type 485	50	20
1761	50c. *Presentation in the Temple* (detail) (Master of St. Severin)	80	30
1762	60c. *The Visitation* (Sebastiano del Piombo)	90	30
1763	80c. *The Visitation* (detail) (Giotto)	1·00	40
1764	100c. *The Circumcision* (detail) (Studio of Bellini)	1·25	50
1765	200c. *The Circumcision* (Studio of Garofalo)	2·25	1·60
1766	500c. *The Visitation* (Studio of Van der Weyden)	3·25	3·50
1767	800c. *The Visitation* (detail) (Studio of Van der Weyden)	3·75	6·50

MS1768 Two sheets, each 77×102 mm. (a) 900c. *Presentation in the Temple* (Bartolo di Fredi). (b) 900c. *The Visitation* (larger detail) (Giotto) Set of 2 sheets — 7·50 9·00

486 Calappa rubroguttata

1993. Crabs. Multicoloured.

1769	20c. Type 486	40	20

1770	60c. *Cardisoma amatum*	70	25
1771	80c. *Maia squinado*	80	30
1772	400c. *Ocypoda cursor*	1·75	2·00
1773	800c. *Grapus grapus*	2·50	3·25

MS1774 127×97 mm. Nos. 1769/73 — 6·50 6·50

487 Clerodendrum thomsoniae

1993. Flowers. Multicoloured.

1775	20c. Type 487	20	15
1776	20c. Lagerstroemia flos-reginae	20	15
1777	60c. Cassia fistula	35	25
1778	60c. Spathodea campanulata	35	25
1779	80c. Hildegardia barteri	40	25
1780	80c. Mellitea ferrugenea	40	25
1781	200c. Petrea volubilis	60	85
1782	200c. Ipomoea asarifolia	60	85
1783	350c. Bryphyllum pinnatum	90	1·25
1784	350c. Ritchiea reflexa	90	1·25

MS1785 Two sheets, each 86×125 mm. (a) 50c. As No. 1777; 100c. As No. 1783; 150c. As No. 1782; 300c. As No. 1779. (b) 50c. As No. 1778; 100c. As No. 1776; 150c. As No. 1780; 300c. As No. 1784 Set of 2 sheets — 4·50 5·00

488 Zeppelin LZ-3 entering Floating Hangar, Lake Constance

1993. Anniversaries and Events. Multicoloured.

1786	20c. Type 488	85	30
1787	100c. Launch of European "Ariane 4" rocket (vert)	1·25	75
1788	200c. Leopard	2·00	1·75
1789	300c. Colosseum and fruit	2·25	2·50
1790	400c. Mozart (vert)	3·75	3·25
1791	600c. Launch of Japanese "H-1" rocket (vert)	3·75	4·25
1792	800c. Zeppelin LZ-10 *Schwaben*	3·75	5·00

MS1793 Four sheets. (a) 106×76 mm. 900c. Count Ferdinand von Zeppelin (vert). (b) 76×106 mm. 900c. Launch of American space shuttle (vert). (c) 106×76 mm. 900c. Bongo. (d) 99×69 mm. 900c. Cherubino from *The Marriage of Figaro* (vert) Set of 4 sheets — 18·00 18·00

ANNIVERSARIES AND EVENTS: Nos. 1786, 1792, MS1793a, 75th death anniv of Count Ferdinand von Zeppelin; 1787, 1791, MS1793b, International Space Year; 1788, MS1793c, Earth Summit '92, Rio; 1789, International Conference on Nutrition, Rome; 1790, MS1793d, Death bicentenary of Mozart.

1993. Bicentenary of the Louvre, Paris. As T 209b of Gambia. Multicoloured.

1794	200c. *Carnival Minuet* (left detail) (Giovanni Domenico Tiepolo)	90	1·00
1795	200c. *Carnival Minuet* (centre detail) (Giovanni Domenico Tiepolo)	90	1·00
1796	200c. *Carnival Minuet* (right detail) (Giovanni Domenico Tiepolo)	90	1·00
1797	200c. *The Tooth Puller* (left detail) (Giovanni Domenico Tiepolo)	90	1·00
1798	200c. *The Tooth Puller* (right detail) (Giovanni Domenico Tiepolo)	90	1·00
1799	200c. *Rebecca at the Well* (Giovanni Battista Tiepolo)	90	1·00
1800	200c. *Presenting Christ to the People* (left detail) (Giovanni Battista Tiepolo)	90	1·00
1801	200c. *Presenting Christ to the People* (right detail) (Giovanni Battista Tiepolo)	90	1·00

MS1802 100×70 mm. 700c. *Chancellor Seguier* (Charles le Brun) (85×52 mm) — 2·75 3·25

489 Energy Foods

1993. Int Conference on Nutrition, Rome. Multicoloured.

1803	20c. Type 489	30	15
1804	60c. Body-building foods	50	20
1805	80c. Protective foods	55	25

1806	200c. Disease prevention equipment	1·75	1·25
1807	400c. Quality control and preservation of fish products	2·25	3·00

490 Kwame Nkrumah Mausoleum

1993. Proclamation of Fourth Republic. Multicoloured.

1808	50c. Type 490	20	15
1809	100c. Kwame Nkrumah Conference Centre	35	25
1810	200c. Book of Constitution (vert)	80	80
1811	350c. Independence Square (vert)	1·60	2·00
1812	400c. Christiansborg Castle (vert)	1·75	2·00

491 Resurrection Egg

1993. Easter. Faberge Eggs. Multicoloured.

1813	50c. Type 491	40	15
1814	80c. Imperial Red Cross egg with Resurrection triptych	65	25
1815	100c. Imperial Uspensky Cathedral egg	75	25
1816	150c. Imperial Red Cross egg with portraits	1·10	65
1817	200c. Orange Tree egg	1·25	1·25
1818	250c. Rabbit egg	1·25	1·50
1819	400c. Imperial Coronation egg	2·00	2·50
1820	900c. Silver-gilt enamel Easter egg	3·25	5·00

MS1821 Two sheet. (a) 73×100 mm. 1000c. Renaissance egg. (b) 100×73 mm. 1000c. Egg charms (horiz) Set of 2 sheets — 8·00 9·00

491a Mercedes Benz "300 SLR", Mille Migla, 1955

1993. Centenaries of Henry Ford's First Petrol Engine (Nos. 1823/4) and Karl Benz's First Four-wheeled Car (others). Multicoloured.

1822	150c. Type 491a	75	50
1823	400c. Ford "Depot Wagon", 1920	1·50	1·75
1824	600c. Ford "Mach 1 Mustang", 1970	2·00	2·75
1825	800c. Mercedes Benz racing car, Monaco Grand Prix, 1937	3·00	4·50

MS1826 Two sheets, each 110×80 mm. (a) 1000c. Mercedes Benz "Type 196" racing car, 1955 (85½×28½ mm). (b) 1000c. Ford "Super T", 1910 (85½×28½ mm) Set of 2 sheets — 7·75 8·25

491b Airship *Graf Zeppelin* over Alps

1993. Aviation Anniversaries. Multicoloured.

1827	50c. Type 491b	50	30
1828	150c. Airship LZ-7 *Deutschland* (horiz)	85	55
1829	400c. Avro Vulcan jet bomber (horiz)	1·75	1·75
1830	400c. U.S. Mail Ford Trimotor (horiz)	1·75	1·75
1831	600c. Nieuport 27 biplane	2·25	2·25
1832	600c. Loading mail on *Graf Zeppelin*	2·25	2·25
1833	800c. Airship LZ-10 *Schwaben*	3·50	4·00

MS1834 Three sheets, each 111×80 mm. (a) 1000c. LZ-127 "Graf Zeppelin". (b) 1000c. S.E.5A, 1918. (c) 1000c. Early airmail flight by Walter Edwards between Portland and Vancouver (57×42½ mm) Set of 3 sheets — 15·00 15·00

ANNIVERSARIES: Nos. 1827/28, 1833, MS1834a, 125th birth anniv of Hugo Eckener (airship commander); 1829, 1831, MS1834b, 75th anniv of Royal Air Force; 1830, 1832, MS1834c, Bicentenary of first airmail flight.

492 African Buffalo

1993. Wild Animals. Multicoloured.

1835	20c. Type 492	35	15
1836	50c. Giant forest hog	50	20
1837	60c. Potto	55	25
1838	80c. Bay duiker	75	30
1839	100c. Royal antelope	85	35
1840	200c. Serval	1·40	1·10
1841	500c. Golden cat	2·25	3·00
1842	800c. "Megaloglossus woermanni" (bat)	3·50	4·75

MS1843 Two sheets, each 68×98 mm. (a) 900c. Dormouse. (b) 900c. White-collared mangabey Set of 2 sheets — 8·50 9·00

1993. 40th Anniv of Coronation. Nos. 1549/53 optd **40TH ANNIVERSARY OF CORONATION H.M. ELIZABETH II.**

1844	100c. multicoloured	1·25	30
1845	200c. multicoloured	2·00	1·00
1846	500c. multicoloured	4·00	4·00
1847	600c. multicoloured	4·00	4·50

MS1848 Two sheets. (a) 104×75 mm. 800c. multicoloured. (b) 74×105 mm. 800c. multicoloured Set of 2 sheets — 12·00 12·00

1993. 35th Anniv of Rotary International and 60th Anniv of Ghana Red Cross Society (1992). Nos. 1562 and 1564/6 optd **35 YEARS OF ROTARY INTERNATIONAL GHANA 1958** (Nos. 1849, 1852, MS1853a) or **GHANA RED CROSS SOCIETY FOUNDED 1932** and cross (others).

1849	100c. Stonehead	1·25	30
1850	300c. Aba	3·00	3·00
1851	400c. Jewel cichlid	3·25	3·50
1852	500c. Smooth hammershark	3·75	4·25

MS1853 Two sheets, each 108×81 mm. (a) 800c. Bayad. (b) 800c. Eastern flying gurnard Set of 2 sheets — 10·00 11·00

496 Cantharellus cibarius

1993. Mushrooms. Multicoloured.

1854	20c. Type 496	40	25
1855	50c. Russula cyanoxantha	50	30
1856	60c. Clitocybe rivulosa	55	30
1857	80c. Cortinarius elatior	60	35
1858	80c. Mycena galericulata	60	35
1859	200c. Tricholoma gambosum	1·00	1·00
1860	200c. Boletus edulis	1·00	1·00
1861	200c. Lepista saeva	1·00	1·00
1862	250c. Gyroporus castaneus	1·10	1·10
1863	300c. Boletus chrysenteron	1·25	1·25
1864	350c. Nolanea sericea	1·40	1·40
1865	350c. Hygrophorus punicea ("Hygrophorus puiceus")	1·40	1·40
1866	500c. Gomphidius glutinosus	1·60	1·75
1867	600c. Russula olivacea	1·75	2·00
1868	1000c. Russula aurata	2·25	2·75

MS1869 Two sheets, each 85×130 mm. (a) 50c. As No. 1856; 100c. As No. 1858; 150c. As No. 1860; 1000c. As No. 1864. (b) 100c. As Type 496; 150c. As No. 1857; 300c. As No. 1859; 600c. As No. 1865 Set of 2 sheets — 9·50 11·00

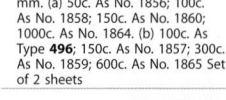

497 The Actor (Picasso)

1993. Anniversaries and Events. Multicoloured.

1870	20c. Type 497	75	50
1871	20c. Early astronomical equipment	1·50	50
1872	80c. *Portrait of Allan Stein* (Picasso)	85	50
1873	200c. Modern telescope	2·75	1·50
1874	200c. Tattoo (Lesek Sobocki)	1·50	1·50

1875	600c. *Prison* (Sasza Blonder)	2·75	3·50
1876	800c. *Seated Male Nude* (Picasso)	3·50	4·00

MS1877 Four sheets. (a) 75×105 mm. 900c. *Guernica* (Picasso). (b) 75×105 mm. 1000c. *Bajika o Czlowieku Szczesliwym* (detail) (Antoni Mickalak) (horiz). (c) 105×75 mm. 1000c. Copernicus (face value at top left). (d) 105×75 mm. 1000c. Copernicus (face value at centre top) Set of 4 sheets ... 16·00   16·00

ANNIVERSARIES AND EVENTS: Nos. 1870, 1872, 1876, **MS**1877a, 20th death anniv of Picasso (artist); 1871, 1873, **MS**1877c/d, 450th death anniv of Copernicus (astronomer); 1874/5, **MS**1877b, "Polska '93" International Stamp Exhibition, Poznan.

498 Abedi Pele (Ghana)

1993. World Cup Football Championship, U.S.A. (1st issue). Multicoloured.

1878	50c. Type **498**	80	35
1879	80c. Pedro Troglio (Argentina)	90	40
1880	100c. Fernando Alvez (Uruguay)	1·00	40
1881	200c. Franco Baresi (Italy)	2·00	1·25
1882	250c. Gomez (Colombia) and Katanec (Yugoslavia)	2·00	2·75
1883	600c. Diego Maradona (Argentina)	3·50	3·50
1884	800c. Hasek (Czechoslovakia) and Wynalda (U.S.A.)	3·50	4·25
1885	1000c. Lothar Matthaeus (Germany)	4·25	5·00

MS1886 Two sheets, each 70×100 mm. (a) 1200c. Rabie Yassein (Egypt) and Ruud Gullit (Netherlands). (b) 1200c. Giuseppe Giannini (Italy) Set of 2 sheets ... 9·00   12·00

See also Nos. 2037/43.

499 Common Turkey

1993. Domestic Animals. Multicoloured.

1887	50c. Type **499**	60	25
1888	100c. Goats	80	40
1889	150c. Muscovy ducks	1·25	75
1890	200c. Donkeys	1·50	1·00
1891	250c. Red junglefowl cock	1·50	1·25
1892	300c. Pigs	1·60	1·40
1893	400c. Helmeted guineafowl	1·90	1·75
1894	600c. Dog	2·75	3·00
1895	800c. Red junglefowl hen	3·25	3·75
1896	1000c. Sheep	3·75	4·25

MS1897 Two sheets, each 133×106 mm. (a) 100c. As No. 1888; 250c. No. 1894; 300c. No. 1892; 500c. No. 1896. (b) 100c. No. 1893; 250c. As No. 1891; 350c. No. 1895; 500c. Type **499** Set of 2 sheets ... 15·00   15·00

1993. Christmas. Religious Paintings. As T **221b** of Gambia. Black, yellow and red (Nos. 1898, 1900/1, 1905 and **MS**1906a) or multicoloured (others).

1898	50c. *Adoration of the Magi* (Dürer)	60	20
1899	100c. *The Virgin and Child with St. John and an Angel* (Botticelli)	80	25
1900	150c. *Mary as Queen of Heaven* (Dürer)	1·00	45
1901	200c. *Saint Anne* (Dürer)	1·25	65
1902	250c. *The Madonna of the Magnificat* (Botticelli)	1·40	75
1903	400c. *The Madonna of the Goldfinch* (Botticelli)	2·25	2·50
1904	600c. *The Virgin and Child with the young St. John the Baptist* (Botticelli)	3·00	3·75
1905	1000c. *Adoration of the Shepherds* (Dürer)	4·25	6·50

MS1906 Two sheets, each 102×128 mm. (a) 1000c. *Madonna in a Circle* (detail) (Botticelli). (b) 1000c. *Mystic Nativity* (detail) (Botticelli) (horiz) Set of 2 sheets ... 9·50   12·00

500 Doll

1994. Traditional Crafts. Multicoloured.

1907	50c. Type **500**	40	30
1908	50c. Pot with "head" lid	40	30
1909	200c. Bead necklace	1·00	1·00
1910	200c. Snake charmers (statuette)	1·00	1·00
1911	250c. Hoe	1·00	1·00
1912	250c. Scabbard	1·00	1·00
1913	600c. Pipe	1·75	2·50
1914	600c. Deer (carving)	1·75	2·50
1915	1000c. Mask	2·50	3·50
1916	1000c. Doll (different)	2·50	3·50

MS1917 Two sheets, each 95×128 mm. (a) 100c. As Type **500**; 250c. As No. 1909; 350c. As No. 1911; 500c. As No. 1913. (b) 100c. As No. 1908; 250c. As No. 1910; 350c. As No. 1912; 500c. As No. 1914 Set of 2 sheets ... 6·00   7·50

1994. "Hong Kong '94" International Stamp Exhibition (1st issue). As T **222a** of Gambia. Multicoloured.

1918	200c. Hong Kong 1986 50c. "Expo '86" stamp and tram	1·00	1·25
1919	200c. Ghana 1992 20c. Railways stamp and tram	1·00	1·25

Nos. 1918/19 were printed together, se-tenant, forming a complete design. See also Nos. 1920/25.

1994. "Hong Kong '94" International Stamp Exhibition (2nd issue). Imperial Palace Clocks. As T **222b** of Gambia. Multicoloured.

1920	100c. Windmill clock	1·10	1·10
1921	100c. Horse clock	1·10	1·10
1922	100c. Balloon clock	1·10	1·10
1923	100c. Zodiac clock	1·10	1·10
1924	100c. Shar-pei dog clock	1·10	1·10
1925	100c. Cat clock	1·10	1·10

501 Mickey Mouse in *Steamboat Willie*, 1928

1994. 65th Anniv (1993) of Mickey Mouse (Walt Disney cartoon character) (1993). Scenes from various cartoon films.

1926	50c. Type **501**	60	15
1927	100c. *The Band Concert*, 1935	80	20
1928	150c. *Moose Hunters*, 1937	1·10	45
1929	200c. *Brave Little Tailor*, 1938	1·25	60
1930	250c. *Fantasia*, 1940	1·40	80
1931	400c. *The Nifty Nineties*, 1941	2·25	2·75
1932	600c. *Canine Caddy*, 1941	2·75	3·25
1933	1000c. *Mickey's Christmas Carol*, 1983	3·50	4·25

MS1934 Two sheets, each 127×102 mm. (a) 1200c. *Mickey's Elephant*, 1936. (b) 1200c. *Mickey's Amateurs*, 1937 Set of 2 sheets ... 8·00   9·50

No. 1929 is inscribed "TAYLOR" in error. The dates on Nos. 1927 and 1932 are incorrectly shown as "1937" and "1944".

501a Boy Hiker

1994. Easter. Hummel Figurines. Multicoloured.

1935	50c. Type **501a**	35	15
1936	100c. Girl with basket behind back	45	20
1937	150c. Boy with rabbits	65	35
1938	200c. Boy holding basket	75	50
1939	250c. Girl with chicks	80	70
1940	400c. Girl with lamb	1·75	2·00
1941	600c. Girl waving red handkerchief with lamb	2·00	2·25
1942	1000c. Girl with basket and posy	2·75	3·25

MS1943 Two sheets, each 93×126 mm. (a) 50c. As No. 1935; 150c. As No. 1942; 500c. As No. 1936; 1200c. As No. 1938. (b) 200c. As No. 1940; 300c. As No. 1939; 500c. As No. 1941; 1000c. As No. 1937 Set of 2 sheets ... 7·50   8·00

502 Diana Monkey with Young

1994. Wildlife. Multicoloured.

1944	50c. Type **502**	40	15
1945	100c. Bushbuck (horiz)	40	20
1946	150c. Spotted hyena (horiz)	55	35
1947	200c. Diana monkey on branch facing left	75	50
1948	500c. Diana monkey on branch facing right	1·25	1·50
1949	800c. Head of Diana monkey	1·75	2·00
1950	1000c. Aardvark (horiz)	2·00	2·50

MS1951 Two sheets, each 106×76 mm. (a) 2000c. Leopard. (b) 2000c. Waterbuck Set of 2 sheets ... 10·00   11·00

Designs of Nos. 1944 and 1947/9 include the W.W.F. Panda emblem.

503 Norwegian Forest Cat

1994. Cats. Multicoloured.

1952	200c. Type **503**	50	50
1953	200c. Blue longhair	50	50
1954	200c. Red self longhair	50	50
1955	200c. Black longhair	50	50
1956	200c. Chinchilla	50	50
1957	200c. Dilute calico longhair	50	50
1958	200c. Blue tabby and white longhair	50	50
1959	200c. Ruby Somali	50	50
1960	200c. Blue smoke longhair	50	50
1961	200c. Calico longhair	50	50
1962	200c. Brown tabby longhair	50	50
1963	200c. Balinese	50	50
1964	200c. Sorrel Abyssinian	50	50
1965	200c. Silver classic tabby	50	50
1966	200c. Chocolate-point Siamese	50	50
1967	200c. Brown tortie Burmese	50	50
1968	200c. Exotic shorthair	50	50
1969	200c. Havana brown	50	50
1970	200c. Devon rex	50	50
1971	200c. Black Manx	50	50
1972	200c. British blue shorthair	50	50
1973	200c. Calico American wirehair	50	50
1974	200c. Spotted oriental Siamese	50	50
1975	200c. Red classic tabby	50	50

MS1976 Two sheets, each 102×89 mm. (a) 2000c. Brown mackerel tabby Scottish fold. (b) 2000c. Seal-point colourpoint Set of 2 sheets ... 8·50   9·00

No. 1957 is inscribed "Dilut" in error.

504 Red-billed Paradise Flycatcher

1994. Birds. Multicoloured.

1977	200c. Type **504**	60	60
1978	200c. Many-coloured bush shrike	60	60
1979	200c. Broad-tailed paradise whydah	60	60
1980	200c. White-crowned robin chat	60	60
1981	200c. Violet turaco ("Violet plantain-eater")	60	60
1982	200c. Village weaver	60	60
1983	200c. Red-crowned bishop	60	60
1984	200c. Common shoveler	60	60
1985	200c. Spur-winged goose	60	60
1986	200c. African crake	60	60
1987	200c. Purple swamphen ("King reed-hen")	60	60
1988	200c. White-crested tiger bittern	60	60
1989	200c. Oriole warbler ("Moho")	60	60
1990	200c. Superb sunbird	60	60
1991	200c. Blue-breasted kingfisher	60	60
1992	200c. African blue cuckoo shrike	60	60
1993	200c. Great blue turaco ("Blue plantain-eater")	60	60
1994	200c. Greater flamingo	60	60
1995	200c. African jacana ("Lily-trotter")	60	60
1996	200c. Black-crowned night heron	60	60
1997	200c. Black-winged stilt	60	60
1998	200c. White-spotted crake	60	60
1999	200c. African pygmy goose	60	60
2000	200c. African pitta	60	60

MS2001 Two sheets, each 113×83 mm. (a) 2000c. African spoonbill. (b) 2000c. Goliath heron Set of 2 sheets ... 8·50   9·50

505 Women at Stand-pipe

1994. First Anniv of Fourth Republic. Multicoloured.

2002	50c. Type **505**	25	15
2003	100c. Presenting certificate to farmers	35	20
2004	200c. Village electricity supply	50	35
2005	600c. Bridge	1·75	2·00
2006	800c. National Theatre	1·75	2·25
2007	1000c. Lighting perpetual flame	2·00	2·75

1994. 25th Anniv of First Manned Moon Landing. As T **326** of Antigua showing scientists. Multicoloured.

2008	300c. Sigmund Jahn	1·00	1·00
2009	300c. Ulf Merbold	1·00	1·00
2010	300c. Hans Wilhelm Schegal	1·00	1·00
2011	300c. Ulrich Walter	1·00	1·00
2012	300c. Reinhard Furrer	1·00	1·00
2013	300c. Ernst Messerschmid	1·00	1·00
2014	300c. Mamoru Mohri	1·00	1·00
2015	300c. Klaus-Dietrich Flade	1·00	1·00
2016	300c. Chaiki Naito-Mukai	1·00	1·00

MS2017 130×118 mm. 2000c. Poster for *Frau im Mond* (film) by Fritz Lang ... 6·50   7·00

1994. Centenary of International Olympic Committee. Gold Medal Winners. As T **227b** of Gambia, but vert. Multicoloured.

2018	300c. Dieter Modenburg (Germany) (high jump), 1984	70	75
2019	400c. Ruth Fuchs (Germany) (javelin), 1972 and 1976	90	1·00

MS2020 77×106 mm. 1500c. Jans Weissflog (Germany) (ski jump), 1994 ... 3·75   4·00

1994. 50th Anniv of D-Day. As T **331** of Antigua. Multicoloured.

2021	60c. H.M.S. *Roberts* (monitor)	1·50	60
2022	100c. H.M.S. *Warspite* (battleship)	1·75	1·10
2023	200c. U.S.S. *Augusta* (cruiser)	2·25	2·75

MS2024 107×76 mm. 1500c. U.S.S. *Nevada* (battleship) firing salvo ... 6·50   6·50

1994. "Philakorea '94" International Stamp Exn, Seoul. As T **227d** of Gambia. Multicoloured.

2025	20c. Ch'unghak-dong village elder in traditional costume, (24½×38 mm)	20	15
2026	150c. Stone Pagoda, Pun-hwangsa (24½×38 mm)	50	40
2027	250c. Character with eggs	50	60
2028	250c. Character with pair of birds on house	50	60
2029	250c. Character with cock	50	60
2030	250c. Character with dragon and pagoda	50	60
2031	250c. Character with orange flowers	50	60
2032	250c. Character with parrot and pagoda	50	60
2033	250c. Character with plant	50	60
2034	250c. Character with fish	50	60
2035	300c. Traditional country house, Andong (24½×34 mm)	60	65

MS2036 100×70 mm. 1500c. Temple judges deliberating (42½×28½ mm) ... 4·50   5·50

506 Dennis Bergkamp (Netherlands)

1994. World Cup Football Championship, U.S.A. (2nd issue). Multicoloured.

2037	200c. Type **506**	65	80
2038	200c. Lothar Matthaus (Germany)	65	80
2039	200c. Giuseppe Signori (Italy)	65	80
2040	200c. Carlos Valderama (Colombia)	65	80

2041	200c. Jorge Campos (Mexico)	65	80
2042	200c. Tony Meola (U.S.A.)	65	80

MS2043 Two sheets, each 100×70 mm. (a) 1200c. Giants' Stadium, New Jersey (vert). (b) 1200c. Citrus Bowl, Orlando (vert) Set of 2 sheets — 4·75 / 6·50

507 Common ("Crowned") Duiker

1994. Duikers (antelopes). Multicoloured.

2044	50c. Type **507**	35	15
2045	100c. Red-flanked duiker	45	25
2046	200c. Yellow-backed duiker	70	40
2047	400c. Ogilby's duiker	1·10	1·25
2048	600c. Bay duiker	1·40	2·00
2049	800c. Jentink's duiker	1·50	2·25

MS2050 Two sheets, each 106×76 mm. (a) 2000c. Red forest duiker. (b) 2000c. Black duiker Set of 2 sheets — 8·00 / 9·00

1994. Christmas. Religious Paintings. As T **231a** of Gambia. Multicoloured.

2051	100c. *Madonna of the Annunciation* (Simone Martini)	60	15
2052	200c. *Madonna and Child* (Niccolo di Pietro Gerini)	90	20
2053	250c. *Virgin and Child on the Throne with Angels and Saints* (Raffaello Botticini)	1·10	60
2054	300c. *Madonna and Child with Saints* (Antonio Fiorentino)	1·40	1·10
2055	400c. *Adoration of the Magi* (Bartolo di Fredi)	1·50	1·50
2056	500c. *The Annunciation* (Cima da Congeliano)	1·75	2·00
2057	600c. *Virgin and Child with the Young St. John the Baptist* (workshop of Botticelli)	2·25	2·75
2058	1000c. *The Holy Family* (Giorgione)	2·75	3·75

MS2059 Two sheets, each 135×95 mm. (a) 2000c. *Adoration of the Kings* (detail showing Holy Family) (Giorgione). (b) 2000c. *Adoration of the Kings* (detail showing King and attendants) (Giorgione) Set of 2 sheets — 8·50 / 9·00

508 Northern Region Dancer

1994. Panafest '94 (2nd Pan-African Historical Theatre Festival). Multicoloured.

2060	50c. Type **508**	20	15
2061	100c. Traditional artefacts	35	25
2062	200c. Chief with courtiers	65	60
2063	400c. Woman in ceremonial costume	1·25	1·25
2064	600c. Cape Coast Castle	2·00	2·50
2065	800c. Clay figurines	2·25	3·25

509 Red Cross Stretcher-bearers

1994. 75th Anniv of Red Cross. Multicoloured.

2066	50c. Type **509**	80	15
2067	200c. Worker with children	1·75	75
2068	600c. Workers erecting tents	2·75	4·00

MS2069 147×99 mm. Nos. 2066/7 and 1000c. as 600c. — 6·00 / 6·00

510 Fertility Doll

1994. Fertility Dolls.

2070	**510** 50c. multicoloured	40	10
2071	– 100c. multicoloured	60	15
2072	– 150c. multicoloured	80	30
2073	– 200c. multicoloured	90	30

2074	– 400c. multicoloured	1·50	1·50
2075	– 600c. multicoloured	1·75	2·00
2076	– 800c. multicoloured	2·00	2·50
2077	– 1000c. multicoloured	2·25	2·75

MS2078 147×99 mm. Nos. 2071, 2074/5 and 250c. as 1000c. — 5·00 / 5·50

DESIGNS: 100c. to 1000c. Different dolls.

511 Ghanaian Family

1994. International Year of the Family. Multicoloured.

2079	50c. Type **511**	35	15
2080	100c. Teaching carpentry	55	15
2081	200c. Child care	90	25
2082	400c. Care for the elderly	1·40	1·40
2083	600c. Learning pottery	1·75	2·00
2084	1000c. Adult education students	2·25	2·75

512 Control Tower and Emblem

1995. 50th Anniv of I.C.A.O. Mult. (a) Inscr "50th Anniversary Of Ghana Civil Aviation Authority".

2085	100c. Type **512**	2·00	
2086	400c. Communications equipment	3·00	
2087	1000c. Airliner taking off	4·50	

(b) Inscr "50th Anniversary Of The International Civil Aviation Organisation (I.C.A.O.)".

2088	100c. Type **512**	65	20
2089	400c. Communications equipment	1·40	1·40
2090	1000c. Airliner taking off	2·50	3·25

513 Pluto, Donald Duck and Chip n' Dale around Table

1995. 60th Anniv of Donald Duck. Walt Disney Cartoon Characters at Birthday Party. Multicoloured.

2091	40c. Type **513**	25	15
2092	50c. Mickey Mouse and pup with banner	25	15
2093	60c. Daisy Duck with balloons	25	20
2094	100c. Goofy making cake	35	25
2095	150c. Goofy on roller blades delivering cake	45	40
2096	250c. Donald pinning donkey tail on Goofy	60	60
2097	400c. Ludwig von Drake singing to Pluto	90	90
2098	500c. Grandma Duck giving cake to puppies	1·00	1·00
2099	1000c. Mickey and Minnie Mouse at piano	1·75	2·00
2100	1500c. Pluto with bone and ball	2·50	3·25

MS2101 Two sheets. (a) 117×95 mm. 2000c. Donald blowing out birthday candles (vert). (b) 95×117 mm. 2000c. Donald wearing party hat (vert) Set of 2 sheets — 9·00 / 9·00

514 Fort Appolonia, Beyin

1995. Forts and Castles of Ghana. Multicoloured.

2102	50c. Type **514**	30	10
2103	200c. Fort Patience, Apam	60	25
2104	250c. Fort Amsterdam, Kormantin	65	45
2105	300c. Fort St. Jago, Elmina	75	70
2106	400c. Fort William, Anomabo	90	90
2107	600c. Kumasi Fort	1·50	2·00

MS2108 Two sheets, each 102×72 mm. (a) 800c. Elmina Castle (vert). (b) 1000c. Fort St. Antonio, Axim Set of 2 sheets — 4·75 / 5·50

515 Cochem Castle, Germany

1995. Castles of the World. Multicoloured.

2109	150c. Type **515**	40	30
2110	500c. Windsor Castle, England	70	70
2111	500c. Osaka Castle, Japan	70	70
2112	500c. Vaj Dahunyad Castle, Hungary	70	70
2113	500c. Karlstejn Castle, Czech Republic	70	70
2114	500c. Kronborg Castle, Denmark	70	70
2115	500c. Alcazar of Segovia, Spain	70	70
2116	500c. Chambourd Castle, France	70	70
2117	500c. Linderhof Castle, Germany	70	70
2118	500c. Red Fort, Delhi, India	70	70
2119	600c. Hohenzollern Castle, Germany	80	80
2120	800c. Uwajima Castle, Japan	1·00	1·00
2121	1000c. Hohenschwangau Castle, Germany	1·10	1·10

MS2122 Two sheets, each 102×72 mm. (a) 2500c. Neuschwanstein Castle, Germany. (b) 2500c. Himeji Castle, Japan Set of 2 sheets — 9·00 / 9·00

516 European Pochard ("Eurasian Pochard")

1995. Ducks. Multicoloured.

2123	200c. Type **516**	80	35
2124	400c. African pygmy goose	90	90
2125	400c. Southern pochard	90	90
2126	400c. Cape teal	90	90
2127	400c. Ruddy shelduck	90	90
2128	400c. Fulvous whistling duck	90	90
2129	400c. White-faced whistling duck	90	90
2130	400c. Ferruginous duck ("Ferruginous White-eye")	90	90
2131	400c. Hottentot teal	90	90
2132	400c. African black duck	90	90
2133	400c. African yellow-bill ("Yellow-billed Duck")	90	90
2134	400c. Bahama pintail ("White-checked Pintail Duck")	90	90
2135	400c. Hartlaub's duck	90	90
2136	500c. Maccoa duck	1·00	1·10
2137	800c. Cape shoveler	1·50	1·75
2138	1000c. Red-crested pochard	1·90	2·25

MS2139 Two sheets, each 104×74 mm. (a) 2500c. Roseate tern. (b) 2500c. Northern shoveler Set of 2 sheets — 8·50 / 9·00

Nos. 2124/35 were printed together, *se-tenant*, forming a composite design.
No. 2128 is inscribed "Wistling" in error.

517 Cycling

1995. Olympic Games, Atlanta (1996) (1st issue). Multicoloured.

2140	300c. Type **517**	1·10	1·00
2141	300c. Archery	1·10	1·00
2142	300c. Diving	1·10	1·00
2143	300c. Swimming	1·10	1·00
2144	300c. Women's gymnastics	1·10	1·00
2145	300c. Fencing	1·10	1·00
2146	300c. Boxing	1·10	1·00
2147	300c. Men's gymnastics	1·10	1·00
2148	300c. Javelin	1·10	1·00
2149	300c. Tennis	1·10	1·00
2150	300c. Football	1·10	1·00
2151	300c. Equestrian	1·10	1·00
2152	500c. Carl Lewis (U.S.A.)	1·25	1·10
2153	800c. Eric Liddell (Great Britain)	1·40	1·60
2154	900c. Jesse Owens (U.S.A.)	1·40	1·60
2155	1000c. Jim Thorpe (U.S.A.)	1·40	1·60

MS2156 Two sheets, each 70×100 mm. (a) 1200c. Pierre de Coubertin (founder of International Olympic Committee). (b) 1200c. John Akii Bua (Uganda) Set of 2 sheets — 3·50 / 4·00

Nos. 2140/51 were printed together, *se-tenant*, forming a composite design.
See also Nos. 2334/55.

518 *Amorphophallus flavovirens*

518a *Cymothoe beckeri* (butterfly)

1995. Flowers and Butterflies. Multicoloured.

2156c	200c. Type **518**	50	20
2157	300c. Eurasian Goldfinch (*Carduelis chloris*)	1·50	20
2157a	400c. Type **518a**	3·00	20
2157b	500c. *Graphium policenes* (butterfly)	3·00	20
2157c	500c. *Tympanotonus fuscatus* (shell)	20·00	20
2157d	500c. *Synodontis ocellifer* (fish)	1·00	20
2158	550c. Atumpan drums	1·00	20
2158a	800c. *Cyrestis camillus* (butterfly)	20·00	65
2158b	800c. Bananas	2·00	15
2158c	1000c. African Long-tailed Hawk	10·00	80
2158d	1000c. *Boletus edulis* (mushroom)	3·00	20
2158e	1000c. *Gomphidius glutinosus* (mushroom)	2·00	20
2159	1100c. Kente cloth	20·00	1·00
2159a	1500c. *Bebearia arcadius* (butterfly)	3·00	30
2159b	1500c. Martial Eagle (*Polematus bellicosus*)	4·00	30
2160	2000c. Swordfish	4·00	1·75
2160b	2000c. *Euphaedra francina* (butterfly)	10·00	80
2160c	2000c. *Ipomoea asarifolia* (flower)	20·00	40
2161	2500c. Kestrel (*Falco tinnunculus*)	3·00	40
2161a	3000c. Guinean Finger-fish	10·00	3·00
2161b	4000c. *Lagerstroemia flos-reginae* (flower)	5·00	40
2162	5000c. Purple Heron	6·00	5·00
2162b	6000c. *Spathodea campanulata* (flower)	5·00	1·50

No. 2157b is inscribed 'Graphium policene'.

519 Ghanaian Scouts

1995. 18th World Scout Jamboree, Netherlands.

2163	**519** 400c. multicoloured	90	1·00
2164	– 800c. multicoloured	1·25	1·40
2165	– 1000c. multicoloured	1·25	1·40

MS2166 70×100 mm. 1200c. multicoloured — 1·90 / 2·25

DESIGNS: 800c. to 1200c. Ghanaian scouts (different).

1995. 50th Anniv of End of Second World War in Europe. As T **237a** of Gambia. Multicoloured.

2167	400c. Winston Churchill	75	75
2168	400c. Gen. Dwight D. Eisenhower	75	75
2169	400c. Air Marshal Sir Arthur Tedder	75	75
2170	400c. Field-Marshal Sir Bernard Montgomery	75	75
2171	400c. Gen. Omar Bradley	75	75
2172	400c. Gen. Charles de Gaulle	75	75
2173	400c. French resistance fighters	75	75
2174	400c. Gen. George S. Patton	75	75

MS2175 104×74 mm. 1200c. "GIVE ME FIVE YEARS & YOU WILL NOT RECOGNISE GERMANY AGAIN" quote by Adolf Hitler in English and German (42×57 mm) — 2·75 / 3·00

520 Trygve Lie (1946–52) and United Nations Building

1995. 50th Anniv of United Nations. Secretary-Generals. Multicoloured.

2176	200c. Type **520**	30	55
2177	300c. Dag Hammarskjold (1953–61)	40	65
2178	400c. U. Thant (1961–71)	50	70
2179	500c. Kurt Waldheim (1972–81)	60	75

2180	600c. *Javier Perez de Cuellar* (1982–91)	70	90
2181	800c. *Boutrous Boutrous-Ghali* (1992)	80	1·00
MS2182	104×74 mm. 1200c. U.N. flag (horiz)	1·90	2·50

521 Preserving Fish

1995. 50th Anniv of F.A.O. Multicoloured.

2183	200c. Type **521**	70	15
2184	300c. Fishermen with fish traps	85	40
2185	400c. Ox-drawn plough	95	80
2186	600c. Harvesting bananas	1·25	1·75
2187	800c. Planting saplings	1·50	2·50
MS2188	100×70 mm. 2000c. Canoe and cattle	3·00	3·50

522 National Flag and Rotary Emblem

1995. 90th Anniv of Rotary International. Multicoloured.

2189	600c. Type **522**	1·00	1·25
MS2190	94×65 mm. 1200c. Ghanaian Rotary banner (vert)	1·90	2·25

1995. 95th Birthday of Queen Elizabeth the Queen Mother. As T **239a** of Gambia. Multicoloured.

2191	600c. brown, light brown and black	1·25	1·75
2192	600c. multicoloured	1·25	1·75
2193	600c. multicoloured	1·25	1·75
2194	600c. multicoloured	1·25	1·75
MS2195	102×127 mm. 2500c. multicoloured	3·00	4·50

DESIGNS: No. 2191, Queen Elizabeth the Queen Mother (pastel drawing); 2192, Wearing light blue hat and floral dress; 2193, At desk (oil painting); 2194, Wearing red hat and dress; **MS**2195, Wearing pale blue hat and jacket.

1995. 50th Anniv of End of Second World War in the Pacific. Medals. As T **229b** of Gambia. Multicoloured.

2196	500c. Navy Cross and Purple Heart, U.S.A.	1·00	85
2197	500c. Air Force Cross and Distinguished Flying Cross, Great Britain	1·00	85
2198	500c. Navy and Marine Corps Medal and Distinguished Service Cross, U.S.A.	1·00	85
2199	500c. Distinguished Service Medal and Distinguished Conduct Medal, Great Britain	1·00	85
2200	500c. Military Medal and Military Cross, Great Britain	1·00	85
2201	500c. Distinguished Service Cross and Distinguished Service Order, Great Britain	1·00	85
MS2202	108×76 mm. 1200c. Congressional Medal of Honor, U.S.A.	2·50	2·50

523 Seismosaurus

1995. "Singapore '95" International Stamp Exhibition. Prehistoric Animals. Multicoloured.

2203	400c. Type **523**	65	65
2204	400c. Supersaurus	65	65
2205	400c. Ultrasaurus	65	65
2206	400c. Saurolophus	65	65
2207	400c. Lambeosaurus	65	65
2208	400c. Parasaurolophus	65	65
2209	400c. Triceratops	65	65
2210	400c. Styracosaurus	65	65
2211	400c. Pachyrhinosaurus	65	65
2212	400c. Peteinosaurus	65	65
2213	400c. Quetzalcoatlus	65	65
2214	400c. Eudimorphodon	65	65
2215	400c. Allosaurus	65	65
2216	400c. Daspletosaurus	65	65
2217	400c. Tarbosaurus bataar	65	65
2218	400c. Velociraptor mongoliensis	65	65
2219	400c. Herrerasaurus	65	65
2220	400c. Coelophysis	65	65
MS2221	Two sheets, each 106×76 mm. (a) 2500c. Tyrannosaurus rex (horiz). (b) 2500c. Albertosaurus (horiz) Set of 2 sheets	8·00	8·50

Nos. 2203/11 and 2212/20 respectively were printed together, *se-tenant*, forming composite designs.

524 Arms of Otumfuo Opoku Ware II

1995. Silver Jubilee of Otumfuo Opoku Ware II (King of Ashanti). Multicoloured.

2222	50c. Type **524**	30	10
2223	100c. Silver casket	45	10
2224	200c. Golden stool	70	20
2225	400c. Busummuru sword bearer	1·10	75
2226	600c. Otumfuo Opoku Ware II	1·75	1·75
2227	800c. Otumfuo Opoku Ware II under umbrella	2·00	2·25
2228	1000c. Mponponsuo sword bearer	2·25	2·75

525 Nelson Mandela (1993 Peace)

1995. Centenary of Nobel Prize Trust Fund. Past Prize Winners. Multicoloured.

2229	400c. Type **525**	80	80
2230	400c. Albert Schweitzer (1952 Peace)	80	80
2231	400c. Wole Soyinka (1986 Literature)	80	80
2232	400c. Emil Fischer (1902 Chemistry)	80	80
2233	400c. Rudolf Mossbauer (1961 Physics)	80	80
2234	400c. Archbishop Desmond Tutu (1984 Peace)	80	80
2235	400c. Max Born (1954 Physics)	80	80
2236	400c. Max Planck (1918 Physics)	80	80
2237	400c. Hermann Hesse (1946 Literature)	80	80
MS2238	104×75 mm. 1200c. Paul Ehrlich (1908 Medicine) and medal	1·75	2·00

1995. Christmas. Religious Paintings. As T **245a** of Gambia. Multicoloured.

2239	50c. *The Child Jesus and the Young St. John* (Murillo)	25	10
2240	80c. *Rest on the Flight into Egypt* (Memling)	30	10
2241	300c. *Holy Family* (Van Dyck)	75	35
2242	600c. *Enthroned Madonna and Child* (Uccello)	1·10	1·40
2243	800c. *Madonna and Child* (Van Eyck)	1·25	1·75
2244	1000c. *Head of Christ* (Rembrandt)	1·40	2·00
MS2245	Two sheets, each 101×127 mm. (a) 2500c. *The Holy Family* (Pulzone). (b) 2500c. *Madonna and Child with Two Saints* (Montagna) Set of 2 sheets	7·75	8·50

526 Ernemann Camera (1903)

1995. Centenary of Cinema. Multicoloured.

2246	400c. Type **526**	1·25	1·00
2247	400c. Charlie Chaplin	1·25	1·00
2248	400c. Rudolph Valentino	1·25	1·00
2249	400c. Will Rogers	1·25	1·00
2250	400c. Greta Garbo	1·25	1·00
2251	400c. Jackie Cooper	1·25	1·00
2252	400c. Bette Davis	1·25	1·00
2253	400c. John Barrymore	1·25	1·00
2254	400c. Shirley Temple	1·25	1·00
MS2255	106×76 mm. 2500c. Laurel and Hardy	5·50	5·50

No. 2246 is inscribed "ERNMANN" in error.

527 John Lennon

1995. John Lennon (musician) Commemoration. Multicoloured.

2256	400c. Type **527**	1·10	1·10
2257	400c. Full face portrait (green background)	1·10	1·10
2258	400c. With guitar	1·10	1·10
2259	400c. Wearing glasses and caftan	1·10	1·10
2260	400c. Full face portrait (red background)	1·10	1·10
2261	400c. Wearing headphones	1·10	1·10
2262	400c. Wearing purple T-shirt	1·10	1·10
2263	400c. Full face portrait (blue background)	1·10	1·10
2264	400c. Facing right	1·10	1·10
2265	400c. As No. 2263, but smaller (24×39 mm)	1·10	1·10
MS2266	102×73 mm. 2000c. John Lennon playing guitar	6·00	6·50

528 Louis Pasteur in Laboratory

1995. Death Centenary of Louis Pasteur (scientist). Multicoloured.

2267	600c. Type **528**	1·60	1·60
2268	600c. Pasteur injecting rabid dog	1·60	1·60
2269	600c. Pasteur and microscope slide	1·60	1·60
2270	600c. Laboratory equipment and birds	1·60	1·60
2271	600c. Yeast vats	1·60	1·60

529 Rat Musicians

1996. Chinese New Year ("Year of the Rat").

2272	**529**	250c. brown, violet and red	70	70
2273	-	250c. brown, violet and red	70	70
2274	-	250c. brown, violet and red	70	70
2275	-	250c. brown, violet and red	70	70
MS2276		142×60 mm. As Nos. 2272/5, but face values and "GHANA" in red instead of white	2·50	2·50
MS2277		106×75 mm. 1000c. red and orange	2·50	2·50

DESIGNS:—VERT: No. 2273, Rats carrying banners; 2274, Rats carrying palanquin; 2275, Rats with offerings. HORIZ: No. **MS**2277, Four rats carrying palanquin.

1996. 125th Anniv of Metropolitan Museum of Art, New York. As T **251** of Gambia. Multicoloured.

2278	400c. *Portrait of a Man* (Van der Goes)	85	85
2279	400c. *Paradise* (detail) (Di Paolo)	85	85
2280	400c. *Portrait of a Young Man* (Messina)	85	85
2281	400c. *"Tommaso Portinari* (detail) (Memling)	85	85
2282	400c. *Maria Portinari* (detail) (Memling)	85	85
2283	400c. *Portrait of a Lady* (detail) (Ghirlandaio)	85	85
2284	400c. *St. Christopher and the Infant Christ* (Ghirlandaio)	85	85
2285	400c. *Francesco D'Este* (detail) (Weyden)	85	85
2286	400c. *The Interrupted Sleep* (Boucher)	85	85
2287	400c. *Diana and Cupid* (detail) (Batoni)	85	85
2288	400c. *Boy blowing Bubbles* (Chardin)	85	85

2289	400c. *Ancient Rome* (detail) (Pannini)	85	85
2290	400c. *Modern Rome* (detail) (Pannini)	85	85
2291	400c. *The Calmady Children* (Lawrence)	85	85
2292	400c. *The Triumph of Marius* (detail) (Tiepolo)	85	85
2293	400c. *Garden at Vaucresson* (detail) (Vuillard)	85	85
MS2294	Two sheets, each 95×70 mm. (a) 2500c. *The Epiphany* (detail) (Giotto) (80×56 mm). (b) 2500c. *The Calling of Matthew* (detail) (Hemessen) (80×56 mm) Set of 2 sheets	12·00	13·00

530 Toco Toucan

1996. Wildlife of the Rainforest. Multicoloured.

2295	400c. Type **530**	1·00	1·00
2296	400c. Two-toed sloth	1·00	1·00
2297	400c. Orang-utan	1·00	1·00
2298	400c. Crested hawk eagle	1·00	1·00
2299	400c. Tiger	1·00	1·00
2300	400c. Painted stork	1·00	1·00
2301	400c. Green-winged macaw	1·00	1·00
2302	400c. Common squirrel-monkey	1·00	1·00
2303	400c. Crab-eating macaque	1·00	1·00
2304	400c. *Cithaerias menander* and *Ithomiidae* (butterflies)	1·00	1·00
2305	400c. *Coryptophanes cristatus* and *Gekkonidae* (lizards)	1·00	1·00
2306	400c. Boa constrictor	1·00	1·00
2307	400c. Hoatzin	1·00	1·00
2308	400c. Western tarsier	1·00	1·00
2309	400c. Golden Lion tamarin	1·00	1·00
2310	400c. *Pteropus gouldii* (bat)	1·00	1·00
2311	400c. Guianan cock of the rock	1·00	1·00
2312	400c. Resplendent quetzal	1·00	1·00
2313	400c. Tree frog and poison-arrow frog	1·00	1·00
2314	400c. Ring-tailed lemur	1·00	1·00
2315	400c. Iguana	1·00	1·00
2316	400c. *Heliconius burneyi* (butterfly)	1·00	1·00
2317	400c. Vervain hummingbird	1·00	1·00
2318	400c. Verreauv's sifaka	1·00	1·00
MS2319	Two sheets, each 74×104 mm. (a) 3000c. Raggiana bird of paradise. (b) 3000c. King vulture Set of 2 sheets	16·00	15·00

531 Pagoda of Kaiyan Si Temple, Fujian

1996. "CHINA '96" Ninth Asian International Stamp Exhibition. Pagodas. Multicoloured.

2320	400c. Type **531**	1·10	1·10
2321	400c. Kaiyuan Si Temple, Hebei	1·10	1·10
2322	400c. Fogong Si Temple, Shanxi	1·10	1·10
2323	400c. Xiangshan, Beijing	1·10	1·10
MS2324	Two sheets. (a) 100×70 mm. 1000c. Baima Si Temple, Henan. (b) 143×98 mm. 1000c. Gold statue (38×50 mm) Set of 2 sheets	4·50	5·00

1996. 70th Birthday of Queen Elizabeth II. As T **255a** of Gambia showing different photographs. Multicoloured.

2325	1000c. Queen Elizabeth II	2·00	2·00
2326	1000c. In blue hat and coat	2·00	2·00
2327	1000c. Wearing straw hat and carrying bouquet	2·00	2·00
MS2328	125×103 mm. 2500c. In open carriage at Trooping the Colour (horiz)	5·50	5·50

532 Serafim Todorow (Bulgaria)

1996. 50th Anniv of International Amateur Boxing Association. Multicoloured.

2329	300c. Type 532	65	55
2330	400c. Oscar de la Hoya (U.S.A.)	80	70
2331	400c. Ariel Hernandez (Cuba)	1·50	1·75
2332	1500c. Arnoldo Mesa (Cuba)	2·50	3·00
MS2333	80×110 mm. 3000c. Tadahiro Sasaki (Japan)	4·75	5·50

GHANA C300

533 Ancient Greek Wrestlers

1996. Olympic Games, Atlanta (2nd issue). Previous Medal Winners. Multicoloured.

2334	300c. Type 533	75	55
2335	400c. Aileen Riggin, 1920 (U.S.A.)	85	85
2336	400c. Pat McCormick, 1952 (U.S.A.)	85	85
2337	400c. Dawn Fraser, 1956 (Australia)	85	85
2338	400c. Chris von Saltza, 1960 (U.S.A.)	85	85
2339	400c. Anita Lonsbrough, 1960 (Great Britain)	85	85
2340	400c. Debbie Meyer, 1968 (U.S.A.)	85	85
2341	400c. Shane Gould, 1972 (Australia)	85	85
2342	400c. Petra Thuemer, 1976 (Germany)	85	85
2343	400c. Marjorie Gestring, 1936 (U.S.A.)	85	85
2344	400c. Abedi Pele (Ghana) (vert)	85	85
2345	400c. Quico Navarez (Spain) (vert)	85	85
2346	400c. Heino Hanson (Denmark) (vert)	85	85
2347	400c. Mostafa Ismail (Egypt) (vert)	85	85
2348	400c. Anthony Yeboah (Ghana) (vert)	85	85
2349	400c. Jurgen Klinsmann (Germany) (vert)	85	85
2350	400c. Cobi Jones (U.S.A.) (vert)	85	85
2351	400c. Franco Baresi (Italy) (vert)	85	85
2352	400c. Igor Dobrovolski (Russia) (vert)	85	85
2353	500c. Wilma Rudolph (U.S.A.) (track and field, 1960)	1·00	1·00
2354	600c. Olympic Stadium, 1960, and Roman landmarks	1·25	1·40
2355	800c. Ladies Kayak pairs, 1960 (Soviet Union)	1·50	1·75
MS2356	Two sheets, each 110×80 mm. (a) 2000c. Tracy Caulkins (U.S.A.) (200m freestyle, 1984). (b) 2000c. Kornelia Ender (Germany) (200m freestyle, 1976) Set of 2 sheets	8·50	8·50

Nos. 2335/43 (swimming and diving), and 2344/52 (football) respectively were printed together, se-tenant, with the backgrounds forming composite designs.

GHANA C100

534 E. W. Agyare (35 years service with Ghana Broadcasting)

1996. Local Broadcasting.

2357	534	100c. multicoloured	40	40

1996. 50th Anniv of UNICEF. As T 258a of Gambia. Multicoloured.

2358	400c. Ghanaian child	35	35
2359	500c. Mother and child	45	45
2360	600c. Mother and child drinking	55	70
MS2361	74×104 mm. 1000c. Young child	1·40	1·60

Ghana C400

534a St. Stephen's Gate and *Jasminum mesyni*

1996. 3000th Anniv of Jerusalem. Multicoloured.

2362	400c. Type 534a	60	40
2363	600c. The Citadel, Tower of David and *Nerium oleander*	80	80
2364	800c. Chapel of the Ascension and *Romulea bulbocodium*	1·00	1·10
MS2365	65×80 mm. 2000c. Russian Orthodox Church of St. Mary Magdalene (48×30 mm)	2·75	3·00

1996. Centenary of Radio. Entertainers. As T 259a of Gambia. Multicoloured.

2366	500c. Frank Sinatra	45	35
2367	600c. Judy Garland	60	70
2368	600c. Bing Crosby	60	70
2369	800c. Martin and Lewis	80	90
MS2370	81×110 mm. 2000c. Edgar Bergen and Charlie McCarthy	2·00	2·75

1996. 50th Anniv of UNESCO. As T 273a of Gambia. Multicoloured.

2371	400c. The Citadel, Haiti (vert)	50	25
2372	800c. Ait-Ben-Hadou (fortified village), Morocco (vert)	90	1·00
2373	1000c. Spissky Hrad, Slovakia	1·25	1·40
MS2374	106×76 mm. 2000c. Cape Coast Castle, Ghana	2·25	2·75

Ghana Musical Instruments c500

535 Fiddles

1996. Musical Instruments. Multicoloured.

2375	500c. Type 535	90	90
2376	500c. Proverbial drum	90	90
2377	500c. Double clapless bell and castanet	90	90
2378	500c. Gourd rattle	90	90
2379	500c. Horns	90	90

GHANA c60 ARIEL, FLOUNDER AND SEBASTIAN

536 Ariel, Flounder and Sebastian

1996. Disney Friends. Disney Cartoon Characters. Multicoloured.

2380	60c. Type 536	30	30
2381	60c. Pinocchio and Jiminy Cricket	30	30
2382	60c. Cogsworth and Lumiere	30	30
2383	60c. Copper and Tod	30	30
2384	60c. Pocahontas, Meeko and Flit	30	30
2385	60c. Bambi, Flower and Thumper	30	30
2386	60c. As No. 2381	50	50
2387	200c. Type 536	50	50
2388	200c. As No. 2383	50	50
2389	300c. As No. 2385	60	60
2390	350c. As No. 2382	60	60
2391	450c. As No. 2384	65	65
2392	600c. Aladdin and Abu	70	70
2393	700c. Penny and Rufus	75	75
2394	800c. Mowgli and Baloo	80	80
MS2395	Two sheets. (a) 98×124 mm. 3000c. Winnie the Pooh (vert). (b) 133×108 mm. 3000c. Simba and Timon Set of 2 sheets	6·00	6·50

1996. 20th Anniv of Rocky (film). Sheet 143×182 mm, containing vert design as T 266 of Gambia. Multicoloured.

MS2396	2000c.×3 Sylvester Stallone in *Rocky II*	5·50	6·50

GHANA C500

537 Herd Boy and Ox

1997. Chinese New Year ("Year of the Ox"). "The Herd Boy and Weaver". Each brown, silver and black.

2397	500c. Type 537	70	70
2398	500c. Ox and weaver in lake	70	70
2399	500c. Weaver at work	70	70
2400	500c. Herd boy with dying Ox	70	70
2401	500c. Weaver flying out of window	70	70
2402	500c. Herd boy carrying children	70	70
2403	500c. Family separated by "river"	70	70
2404	500c. Petitioning the emperor	70	70
2405	500c. Family reunited	70	70

GHANA 120th Anniversary of the Birth of Dr Hideyo Noguchi
Tomb of Dr. Noguchi c1000

538 The Tomb of Dr. Hideyo Noguchi

1997. 120th Birth Anniv of Dr. Hideyo Noguchi (bacteriologist). Multicoloured.

2406	1000c. Type 538	1·25	1·40
2407	1000c. Dr. Hideyo Noguchi	1·25	1·40
2408	1000c. Birthplace of Dr. Noguchi at Sanjogarta	1·25	1·40
2409	1000c. Noguchi Institute, Legon	1·25	1·40
2410	1000c. Noguchi Gardens, Accra	1·25	1·40
MS2411	Two sheets, each 67×97 mm. (a) 3000c. Dr. Noguchi in his laboratory. (b) 3000c. Statue of Dr. Noguchi Set of 2 sheets	5·50	8·00

HAIR-DO c1000 Dipo GHANA

539 Dipo Hairstyle

1997. Ghanaian Women's Hairstyle. Multicoloured.

2412	1000c. Type 539	75	75
2413	1000c. Oduku with flowers	75	75
2414	1000c. Dansinkran	75	75
2415	1000c. Mbobom	75	75
2416	1000c. Oduku with hair pins	75	75
2417	1000c. African corn row	75	75
2418	1000c. Chinese raster	75	75
2419	1000c. Chinese raster with top knot	75	75
2420	1000c. Corn row	75	75
2421	1000c. Mbakaa	75	75

GHANA C200 40TH Independence Anniversary GHANA 1957-1997

540 Independence Anniversary Emblem

1997. 40th Anniv of Independence. Multicoloured.

2422	200c. Type 540	35	25
2423	200c. President J. J. Rawlings (vert)	1·75	1·50
2424	550c. Dr. Kwane Nkrumah (first President) (vert)	75	80
2425	600c. Children in class	1·25	1·50
2426	1100c. Akosombo Dam	1·75	2·00
MS2427	Two sheets. (a) 70×100 mm. 2000c. Dr. Nkrumah proclaiming independence (vert). (b) 101×141 mm. 3000c. United Nations Secretary-General Kofi Annan (37×50 mm) Set of 2 sheets	5·50	6·50

No. 2425 is inscribed "Acheivement" in error.

1997. Tenth Anniv of Chernobyl Nuclear Disaster. As T 276b of Gambia. Multicoloured.

2428	800c. Child's face and UNESCO emblem	1·50	1·40
2429	1000c. As No. 2428, but inscribed "CHABAD'S CHILDREN OF CHERNOBYL" at foot	1·75	1·60

DENG XIAOPING (1904-1997) C300 GHANA

541 Deng Xiaoping

1997. Deng Xiaoping (Chinese statesman) Commemoration. Different portraits. Multicoloured.

2430	300c. Type 541	45	55
2431	500c. Looking thoughtful	60	75
2432	600c. Wearing glasses	70	80
2433	600c. Delivering speech	70	75
2434	800c. As No. 2432	90	1·00
2435	800c. As No. 2433	90	1·00
2436	1000c. Type 541	1·10	1·25
2437	1000c. As No. 2431	1·10	1·25
MS2438	Two sheets, each 101×70 mm. (a) 3000c. Deng Xiaoping making speech (47×34 mm). (b) 4000c. Deng Xiaoping with hand raised (47×34 mm) Set of 2 sheets	5·50	7·00

1997. 50th Death Anniv of Paul Harris (founder of Rotary International). As T 276c of Gambia. Multicoloured.

2439	2000c. Paul Harris and Egyptian patient receiving polio vaccination	2·50	2·75
MS2440	78×107 mm. 3000c. Paul Harris with Rotary and PolioPlus emblems	2·75	3·00

1997. Golden Wedding of Queen Elizabeth and Prince Philip. As T 276d of Gambia. Multicoloured.

2441	800c. Queen Elizabeth II	1·00	1·00
2442	800c. Royal coat of arms	1·00	1·00
2443	800c. Queen Elizabeth and Prince Philip waving	1·00	1·00
2444	800c. Queen Elizabeth and Prince Philip on official visit	1·00	1·00
2445	800c. Queen in Irish State Coach	1·00	1·00
2446	800c. Prince Philip in 1947	1·00	1·00
MS2447	100×71 mm. 3000c. Princess Elizabeth in 1947	3·50	3·50

1997. "Pacific '97" International Stamp Exhibition, San Francisco. Death Centenary of Heinrich von Stephan (founder of the U.P.U.). As T 276e of Gambia.

2448	1000c. blue	1·00	1·10
2449	1000c. brown	1·00	1·10
2450	1000c. red	1·00	1·10
MS2451	82×119 mm. 3000c. green	2·50	3·00

DESIGNS: No. 2448, Early motor car; 2449, Von Stephan and Mercury; 2450, Blanchard's balloon flight, 1784; MS2451, African messenger.

Nihonbashi Bridge and Edobashi Bridge
Ghana c600

541a Nihonbashi Bridge and Edobashi Bridge

1997. Birth Bicentenary of Hiroshige (Japanese painter). One Hundred Famous Views of Edo. Multicoloured.

2452	600c. Type 541a	70	70
2453	600c. View of Nihonbashi Tori 1-chome	70	70
2454	600c. Open Garden at Fukagawa Hachiman Shrine	70	70
2455	600c. Inari Bridge and Minato Shrine, Teppozu	70	70
2456	600c. Bamboo Yards, Kyobashi Bridge	70	70
2457	600c. Hall of Thirty-Three Bays, Fukagawa	70	70
MS2458	Two sheets, each 102×127 mm. (a) 3000c. Sumiyoshi Festival, Tsukudajima. (b) 3000c. Teppozu and Tsukjji Honganji Temple Set of 2 sheets	5·50	6·50

GHANA c600 JACKIE GLEASON

542 Jackie Gleason

1997. Famous Comedians. Multicoloured.

2459	600c. Type 542	85	75
2460	600c. Danny Kaye	85	75
2461	600c. John Cleese	85	75
2462	600c. Lucille Ball	85	75
2463	600c. Jerry Lewis	85	75
2464	600c. Sidney James	85	75
2465	600c. Louis Defuenes	85	75
2466	600c. Mae West	85	75
2467	600c. Bob Hope	85	75
MS2468	Two sheets. (a) 83×113 mm. 3000c. Groucho Marx. (b) 76×106 mm. 2000c. Professor Ajax Bukana in front of curtain; 2000c. Professor Ajax Bukana (different) (both 28×42 mm) Set of 2 sheets	4·50	5·00

543 *Gelerina calyptrata*

1997. Fungi of the World. Multicoloured.

2469	200c. Type **543**	40	30
2470	300c. *Lepiota ignivolvata*	50	40
2471	400c. *Omphalotus olearius*	60	50
2472	550c. *Amanita phalloides*	70	70
2473	600c. *Entoloma conferendum*	70	70
2474	800c. *Entoloma nitidum*	80	80
2475	800c. *Coprinus picaceus*	80	80
2476	800c. *Stropharia aurantiaca*	80	80
2477	800c. *Cortinarius splendens*	80	80
2478	800c. *Gomphidius roseus*	80	80
2479	800c. *Russula sardonia*	80	80
2480	800c. *Geastrum schmidelia*	80	80

MS2481 Two sheets, each 73×103 mm.
(a) 3000c. *Craterellus cornucopioides.*
(b) 3000c. *Mycena crocata* Set of
2 sheets   5·50   6·00

1997. World Football Championship, France (1998). As T 283a of Gambia. Multicoloured.

2482	200c. Azteca Stadium, Mexico	35	30
2483	300c. The Rose Bowl, U.S.A.	45	40
2484	400c. Stadio Giuseppe Meazza, Italy	60	50
2485	500c. Olympiastadion, Germany	65	55
2486	600c. Patrick Kluivert, Netherlands	70	70
2487	600c. Roy Keane, Republic of Ireland	70	70
2488	600c. Abedi Ayew Pele, Ghana	70	70
2489	600c. Peter Schmeichel, Denmark	70	70
2490	600c. Roberto di Matteo, Italy	70	70
2491	600c. Bebeto, Brazil	70	70
2492	600c. Steve McManaman, England	70	70
2493	600c. George Oppon Weah, Liberia	70	70
2494	1100c. Maracana Stadium, Brazil	1·10	1·25
2495	2000c. Bernabeu Stadium, Spain	1·75	2·00

MS2496 Two sheets. (a) 127×102 mm.
3000c. David Seaman, England. (b)
102×127 mm. 3000c. Juninho, Brazil
Set of 2 sheets   6·00   7·00

544 African Pygmy Angelfish

1997. Marine Life. Multicoloured.

2497	400c. Type **544**	60	50
2498	500c. Violet-crested turaco	60	60
2499	500c. Pied avocet	60	60
2500	500c. Bottle-nosed dolphin	60	60
2501	500c. Bottle-nosed dolphin and long-toed lapwing	60	60
2502	500c. Longfinned spadefish	60	60
2503	500c. Imperial angelfish and manta	60	60
2504	500c. Racoon butterflyfish and African pompano	60	60
2505	500c. Silvertip shark	60	60
2506	500c. Longfin banner fish	60	60
2507	500c. Longfin banner fish and manta	60	60
2508	500c. Rust parrotfish	60	60
2509	500c. Coral trout	60	60
2510	600c. Angelfish	70	70
2511	800c. Broomtail wrasse	85	85
2512	1000c. Indian butterflyfish	1·00	1·10

MS2513 Two sheets, each 106×76 mm.
(a) 3000c. King angelfish. (b) 3000c.
Crown butterflyfish Set of 2 sheets   6·00   7·00

Nos. 2498/2509 were printed together, *se-tenant*, with the backgrounds forming a composite design.

545 Ghanaian Players holding Trophy

1997. J.V.C. Under-17 World Soccer Champions (1995). Multicoloured.

2514	200c.+50c. Type **545**	40	50
2515	550c.+50c. Ghana football team (horiz)	75	85
2516	800c.+50c. Abu Iddrisu	90	1·10
2517	1000c.+50c. Emmanuel Bentil (captain)	1·10	1·50
2518	1500c.+50c. Basiru Gambo	1·60	2·00

546 *Eurychone rothschildiana*

1997. Flowers of the World. Multicoloured.

2519	200c. Type **546**	45	30
2520	550c. *Bulbophyllum lepidum*	80	60
2521	800c. *Ansellia africana*	90	90
2522	800c. *Strophanthus preusii* (vert)	90	90
2523	800c. *Ancistrochilus rothschild-lanus* (vert)	90	90
2524	800c. *Mussaenda arcuata* (vert)	90	90
2525	800c. *Microcoelia guyoniane* (vert)	90	90
2526	800c. *Gloriosa simplex* (vert)	90	90
2527	800c. *Brachycorythis kalbreyeri* (vert)	90	90
2528	800c. *Aframomum sceptrum* (vert)	90	90
2529	800c. *Thunbergia alata* (vert)	90	90
2530	800c. *Clerodendrum thomsoniae* (vert)	90	90
2531	1100c. *Combbretum grandi-florum*	1·50	1·75

MS2532 Two sheets, each 82×77 mm.
(a) 3000c. *Kigelia africana* (vert). (b)
3000c. *Spathodea campanulata* (vert)
Set of 2 sheets   5·50   6·00

Nos. 2522/30 were printed together, *se-tenant*, with the backgrounds forming a composite design.

547 Eurasian Goldfinch

1997. Birds of Africa. Multicoloured.

2533	200c. Type **547**	60	40
2534	300c. Cape puff-back flycatcher ("Cape Batis")	70	40
2535	400c. Double-toothed barbet ("Bearded Barbet")	75	50
2536	500c. African white-necked raven ("White-necked Raven")	80	60
2537	600c. Purple grenadier	90	90
2538	800c. Black bustard	1·00	1·00
2539	800c. Northern lapwing	1·00	1·00
2540	800c. Lichtenstein's sandgrouse ("Sandgrouse")	1·00	1·00
2541	800c. Red-crested turaco	1·00	1·00
2542	800c. White-browed coucal	1·00	1·00
2543	800c. Lilac-breasted roller	1·00	1·00
2544	800c. Golden pipit	1·00	1·00
2545	800c. Burchell's gonolek ("Crimson-breasted Gonolek")	1·00	1·00
2546	800c. Blackcap	1·00	1·00
2547	1000c. Zebra waxbill	1·25	1·50

MS2548 Two sheets, each 106×75
mm. (a) 3000c. Shaft-tailed whydah.
(b) 3000c. Yellow-tufted malachite
sunbird Set of 2 sheets   7·00   7·00

548 Havana Cat

1997. Cats and Dogs. Multicoloured.

2549	20c. Type **548**	25	25
2550	50c. Singapura cat	25	25
2551	80c. Papillon	30	30
2552	100c. Sphinx cat	30	30
2553	150c. British white cat	35	30
2554	200c. Bulldog	40	30
2555	300c. Snowshoe cat	45	40
2556	400c. Shetland sheepdog	60	50
2557	500c. Schnauzer	60	55
2558	600c. Persian cat	70	70
2559	800c. Shih tzu	90	90
2560	1000c. Russian wolfhound	1·00	1·00
2561	1000c. Birman cat	1·00	1·00

2562	1000c. Basset hound	1·00	1·00
2563	1000c. Silver tabby cat	1·00	1·00
2564	1000c. Afghan	1·00	1·00
2565	1000c. Burmilla cat	1·00	1·00
2566	1000c. Abyssinian cat	1·00	1·00
2567	1000c. Border terrier	1·00	1·00
2568	1000c. Scottish fold cat	1·00	1·00
2569	1000c. Boston terrier	1·00	1·00
2570	1000c. Oriental cat	1·00	1·00
2571	1000c. Keeshond	1·00	1·00
2572	2000c. Chow Chow	1·75	2·00

MS2573 Two sheets, each 73×100 mm.
(a) 3000c. Alaskan malamute. (b)
3000c. Ragdoll cat Set of 2 sheets   7·50   7·50

COLOR LANDSCAPE
HUANG BINHONG (1865-1965)

GHANA C200

549 *Landscape (Huang Binhong)*

1997. Return of Hong Kong to China.

2574	**549**	200c. multicoloured	30	30
2575	-	300c. multicoloured	35	35
2576	-	400c. multicoloured	40	40
2577	-	500c. multicoloured	50	50
2578	-	600c. multicoloured	60	60
2579	-	800c. multicoloured	70	70
2580	-	1000c. multicoloured	90	95
2581	-	2000c. multicoloured	1·60	1·75

MS2582 138×105 mm. (a) 2000c.
multicoloured (farm). (b) 2000c.
multicoloured (mountains) (each
50×37 mm). P 14×13½   3·00   3·50

MS2583 150×125 mm. (a) 1000c.×2
multicoloured (Lin Tse-Hue). (b)
1000c.×2 multicoloured (Gwen Tian-
Pei) (each 63×31 mm)   3·00   3·50

DESIGNS: Nos. 2575/81 and **MS**2582, Landscape paintings
by Huang Binhong; **MS**2583, Historical scenes.

1997. Christmas. Paintings. As T 284a of Gambia. Multicoloured.

2584	200c. *Cupid* (Botticelli)	30	10
2585	550c. *Zephyr and Chloris* (Botticelli)	65	25
2586	800c. *Triumphant Cupid* (Caravaggio)	90	65
2587	1100c. *The Seven Works of Mercy* (Caravaggio)	1·40	1·60
2588	1500c. *The Toilet of Venus* (Diego Velazquez)	1·60	2·00
2589	2000c. *Freeing of St. Peter* (Raphael)	1·75	2·25

MS2590 Two sheets. (a) 95×105 mm.
5000c. *The Cavalcanti Annunciation*
(Donatello). (b) 105×95 mm. 5000c.
Ancient Egyptian painting of Isis and
Nephthys Set of 2 sheets   8·00   8·50

550 Diana, Princess of Wales

1997. Diana, Princess of Wales Commemoration. Multicoloured (except Nos. 2591, 2596, 2602).

2591	1200c. Type **550** (red)	70	90
2592	1200c. Wearing blue suit and holding flowers	70	90
2593	1200c. Looking right	70	90
2594	1200c. Sitting crossed-legged	70	90
2595	1200c. With Prince William	70	90
2596	1200c. Wearing spotted scarf (blue and black)	70	90
2597	1200c. Wearing pink shirt	70	90
2598	1200c. Wearing red dress	70	90
2599	1200c. Carrying bouquet	70	90
2600	1200c. Wearing sunglasses	70	90
2601	1200c. With children	70	90
2602	1200c. Wearing hat (brown and black)	70	90

MS2603 Two sheets. (a) 100×70 mm.
3000c. Diana, Princess of Wales. (b)
70×100 mm. 3000c. Diana, Princess
of Wales (violet and black) Set of
2 sheets   3·75   5·00

551 Horse

1998. Animals of the Chinese Lunar Calendar. Multicoloured.

2604	400c. Type **551**	30	30
2605	400c. Monkey	30	30
2606	400c. Ram	30	30
2607	400c. Cock	30	30
2608	400c. Dog	30	30
2609	400c. Ox	30	30
2610	400c. Rabbit	30	30
2611	400c. Pig	30	30
2612	400c. Snake	30	30
2613	400c. Dragon	30	30
2614	400c. Tiger	30	30
2615	400c. Rat	30	30

552 Mortie and Ferdie (January)

1998. A Year in the Life of Mickey Mouse and Friends. Walt Disney cartoon characters. Multicoloured.

2616	1000c. Type **552**	1·40	1·40
2617	1000c. Minnie on Valentine's Day (February)	1·40	1·40
2618	1000c. Goofy with kite (March)	1·40	1·40
2619	1000c. Mickey, Minnie and Pluto in rain (April)	1·40	1·40
2620	1000c. Minnie with flowers (May)	1·40	1·40
2621	1000c. Daisy watering garden (June)	1·40	1·40
2622	1000c. Donald at Independance Day celebrations (July)	1·40	1·40
2623	1000c. Donald and Daisy on the beach (August)	1·40	1·40
2624	1000c. Morty and Ferdie returning to school (September)	1·40	1·40
2625	1000c. Hewey, Dewey and Louie at Hallowe'en (October)	1·40	1·40
2626	1000c. Mickey on Thanksgiving Day (November)	1·40	1·40
2627	1000c. Mickey and Minnie at Christmas (December)	1·40	1·40

MS2628 Four sheets, each 132×107
mm. (a) 5000c. Mickey bottle feeding
calf (Spring) (horiz). (b) 5000c. Minnie camping (Summer). (c) 5000c.
Goofy sweeping leaves (Autumn). (d)
5000c. Daisy and Nephews on ice
(Winter) (horiz) Set of 4 sheets   19·00   19·00

553 Union Pacific SD60M diesel Locomotive No. 6331, U.S.A.

1998. Trains of the World. Multicoloured.

2629	300c. Type **553**	20	15
2630	500c. ETR 450 high-speed train, Italy	40	25
2631	800c. X200 high-speed train, Sweden	60	60
2632	800c. SPS steam locomotive, Pakistan	60	60
2633	800c. Class WP steam locomotive, India	60	60
2634	800c. Class QJ steam locomotive, China	60	60
2635	800c. Type 12 steam locomotive, Belgium	60	60
2636	800c. Class P8 steam locomotive, Germany	60	60
2637	800c. Class "Castle" steam locomotive, Great Britain	60	60
2638	800c. Tank locomotive, Austria	60	60
2639	800c. Class P36 steam locomotive, Russia	60	60

2640	800c. Steam locomotive *William Mason*, U.S.A.	60	60
2641	800c. AVE high-speed train, Spain	60	60
2642	800c. Diesel locomotive No. 1602, Luxembourg	60	60
2643	800c. "Hikari" express train, Japan	60	60
2644	800c. Santa Fe Railroad GM F7 *Warbonnet* diesel locomotive, U.S.A.	60	60
2645	800c. Class E1500 diesel locomotive, Morocco	60	60
2646	800c. Class "Deltic" diesel locomotive, Great Britain	60	60
2647	800c. XPT high-speed train, Australia	60	60
2648	800c. Channel Tunnel shuttle train, France and Great Britain	60	60
2649	800c. Class 201 diesel locomotive, Ireland	60	60
2650	1000c. TGV Duplex high-speed train, France	70	70
2651	2000c. Class EL diesel locomotive, Australia	1·40	1·60
2652	3000c. Eurostar high-speed train, Great Britain	1·60	1·90

MS2653 Two sheets, each 106×76 mm. (a) 5500c. Class "Duchess" steam locomotive heading the *Irish Mail*, Great Britain (56×42 mm). (b) 5500c. TGV express train, France (56×42 mm) Set of 2 sheets   7·00   8·50

554 Maya Angelou

1998. Great Writers of the 20th Century. Multicoloured.
2654	350c. Type **554**	40	40
2655	350c. Alex Haley	40	40
2656	350c. Charles Johnson	40	40
2657	350c. Richard Wright	40	40
2658	350c. Toni Cade Bambara	40	40
2659	350c. Henri Louis Gates Jr	40	40

555 Breguet Br 14 B2, France

1998. History of Aviation. Multicoloured.
2660	800c. Type **555**	1·00	1·00
2661	800c. Curtiss BF2C-1 Goshawk, U.S.A.	1·00	1·00
2662	800c. Supermarine Spitfire Mk IX, Great Britain	1·00	1·00
2663	800c. Fiat G.50, Italy	1·00	1·00
2664	800c. Douglas B-18A, U.S.A.	1·00	1·00
2665	800c. Boeing FB-5, U.S.A.	1·00	1·00
2666	800c. Bristol F2B "Brisfit", Great Britain	1·00	1·00
2667	800c. Hawker Fury 1, Great Britain	1·00	1·00
2668	800c. Fiat CR-42, Italy	1·00	1·00
2669	800c. Messerschmitt Bf 109 E-7, Germany	1·00	1·00
2670	800c. Lockheed PV-2 Harpoon, U.S.A.	1·00	1·00
2671	800c. Airspeed Oxford Mk 1, Great Britain	1·00	1·00
2672	800c. Junkers Ju 87D-1, Germany	1·00	1·00
2673	800c. Yakovlev Yak-9D, U.S.S.R.	1·00	1·00
2674	800c. North American P-51D Mustang, U.S.A.	1·00	1·00
2675	800c. Douglas A-206 Havoc, U.S.A.	1·00	1·00
2676	800c. Supermarine Attacker F1, Great Britain	1·00	1·00
2677	800c. Mikoyan Gurevich MiG-15, U.S.S.R.	1·00	1·00

MS2678 Two sheets, each 106×76 mm. (a) 3000c. Supermarine Spitfires Mk 1 and Mk XIV, Great Britain (58×43 mm). (b) 3000c. Mitsubishi AGM8 Reisen, Japan (58×43 mm) Set of 2 sheets   8·50   8·50

556 *Empress of Ireland* (liner)

1998. Famous Ships. Multicoloured.
2679	800c. Type **556**	1·00	1·00
2680	800c. *Transylvania* (liner)	1·00	1·00
2681	800c. *Mauretania I* (liner)	1·00	1·00
2682	800c. *Reliance* (liner)	1·00	1·00
2683	800c. *Aquitania* (liner)	1·00	1·00
2684	800c. *Lapland* (liner)	1·00	1·00
2685	800c. *Cap Polonio* (liner)	1·00	1·00
2686	800c. *France I*, 1910 (liner)	1·00	1·00
2687	800c. *Imperator* (liner)	1·00	1·00
2688	800c. H.M.S. *Rodney* (battleship)	1·00	1·00
2689	800c. U.S.S. *Alabama* (battleship)	1·00	1·00
2690	800c. H.M.S. *Nelson* (battleship)	1·00	1·00
2691	800c. *Ormonde* (camouflaged liner)	1·00	1·00
2692	800c. U.S.S. *Radford* (destroyer)	1·00	1·00
2693	800c. *Empress of Russia* (camouflaged liner)	1·00	1·00
2694	800c. Type XIV U-boat	1·00	1·00
2695	800c. Japanese Type A midget submarine	1·00	1·00
2696	800c. *Brin* (Italian submarine)	1·00	1·00

MS2697 Two sheets, each 100×75 mm. (a) 5500c. "Titanic" (liner) (43×57 mm). (b) 5500c. *Amistad* (slave schooner) (43×57 mm) Set of 2 sheets   8·00   9·00

No. 2681 is inscribed "MAURITANIA" in error.

1998. "Israel 98" International Stamp Exhibition, Tel-Aviv. Nos. 2362/4 optd with Emblem.
2698	400c. St. Stephen's Gate and "Jasminum mesnyi"	65	50
2699	600c. The Citadel, Tower of David and "Nerium oleander"	75	75
2700	800c. Chapel of the Ascension and "Romulea bulbocodium"	1·00	1·00

MS2701 65×80 mm. 2000c. Russian Orthodox Church of St. Mary Magdalene (48×30 mm)   2·25   2·25

No. MS2701 is additionally overprinted **ISRAEL 98 – WORLD STAMP EXHIBITION TEL-AVIV 13–21 MAY 1998** on the sheet margin.

558 *Renanthera imschootiana*

1998. Orchids of the World. Multicoloured.
2702	800c. Type **558**	70	70
2703	800c. *Arachnis flos-aeris*	70	70
2704	800c. *Restrepia lansbergi*	70	70
2705	800c. *Paphiopedilum tonsum*	70	70
2706	800c. *Phalaenopsis ebauche*	70	70
2707	800c. *Pleione limprichti*	70	70
2708	800c. *Phragmipedium schroderae*	70	70
2709	800c. *Zygopetalum clayii*	70	70
2710	800c. *Vanda coerulea*	70	70
2711	800c. *Odontonia boussole*	70	70
2712	800c. *Disa uniflora*	70	70
2713	800c. *Dendrobium bigibbum*	70	70

MS2714 Two sheets, each 98×68 mm. (a) 5500c. *Cypripedium calceolus*. (b) 5500c. *Sobralia candida* Set of 2 sheets   9·00   10·00

559 Elvis Presley

1998. 30th Anniv of Elvis Presley's "68 Special" Television Programme. Multicoloured.
2715	800c. Type **559**	85	85
2716	800c. Elvis in white suit	85	85
2717	800c. In leather jacket, holding microphone	85	85
2718	800c. Wearing light blue jacket	85	85
2719	800c. Elvis with silhouetted figures in background	85	85
2720	800c. Elvis with guitar and microphone	85	85

560 Crest of Accra Metropolitan Assembly and Surf Boats

1998. Centenary of Accra Metropolitan Assembly. Multicoloured.
2721	200c. Type **560**	30	10
2722	550c. King Tackie Tawiah I	45	20
2723	800c. Achimota School	80	35
2724	1100c. Korle Bu Hospital	1·25	1·25
2725	1500c. Christianborg Castle	1·40	2·00

561 Tetteh Quarshie (cocoa industry pioneer)

1998. 50th Anniv of Ghana Cocoa Board. Multicoloured.
2726	200c. Type **561**	30	10
2727	550c. Ripe hybrid cocoa pods	55	20
2728	800c. Opening cocoa pods	85	45
2729	1100c. Fermenting cocoa beans	1·25	1·40
2730	1500c. Loading freighter with cocoa	1·50	2·25

562 Bamboo

1998. Oriental Flowers. Multicoloured.
2731	2000c. Type **562**	1·00	1·00
2732	2000c. Cherry blossom	1·00	1·00
2733	2000c. Yellow chrysanthemum	1·00	1·00
2734	2000c. Orchid	1·00	1·00
2735	2000c. Green peony	1·00	1·00
2736	2000c. Red peony	1·00	1·00
2737	2000c. Pink peony	1·00	1·00
2738	2000c. White peony	1·00	1·00

MS2739 Two sheets, each 109×85 mm. (a) 5500c. Cherry blossom (horiz). (b) 5500c. Peonies (horiz) Set of 2 sheets   7·00   7·50

563 Two Dolphins

1998. International Year of the Ocean. Multicoloured.
2740	500c. Type **563**	60	60
2741	500c. Dolphin	60	60
2742	500c. Seagull	60	60
2743	500c. Least tern	60	60
2744	500c. Emperor angelfish	60	60
2745	500c. White ear (juvenile)	60	60
2746	500c. Blue shark and diver	60	60
2747	500c. Parrotfish	60	60
2748	500c. Dottyback	60	60
2749	500c. Blue-spotted stingray	60	60
2750	500c. Masked butterflyfish	60	60
2751	500c. Jackknife-fish	60	60
2752	500c. Octopus	60	60
2753	500c. Lionfish	60	60
2754	500c. Seadragon	60	60
2755	500c. Rock cod	60	60

MS2756 Two sheets. (a) 63×98 mm. 3000c. Great white shark. (b) 98×63 mm. 3000c. Devil ray Set of 2 sheets   7·00   7·50

Nos. 2740/55 were printed together, *se-tenant*, with the backgrounds forming a composite design.
No. 2745 is inscribed "Whit Ear" in error.

1998. Millennium Series. Famous People of the Twentieth Century. Inventors. As T 289a of Gambia. Multicoloured.
2757	1000c. Thomas Edison	70	70
2758	1000c. Peephole kinetoscope (Edison) (53×38 mm)	70	70
2759	1000c. Tesla coil (53×38 mm)	70	70
2760	1000c. Nikola Tesla	70	70
2761	1000c. Gottlieb Daimler	70	70
2762	1000c. Motorcycle (Daimler) (53×38 mm)	70	70
2763	1000c. Early transmitter circuit (Marconi) and dish aerial (53×38 mm)	70	70

2764	1000c. Guglielmo Marconi	70	70
2765	1000c. Orville and Wilbur Wright	70	70
2766	1000c. *Flyer I* (Wright Brothers) (53×38 mm)	70	70
2767	1000c. Neon lights and signs (Claude) (53×38 mm)	70	70
2768	1000c. Georges Claude	70	70
2769	1000c. Alexander Graham Bell	70	70
2770	1000c. Early telephone transmitter (Bell) (53×38 mm)	70	70
2771	1000c. Uses of lasers (Townes) (53×38 mm)	70	70
2772	1000c. Charles Townes	70	70

MS2773 Two sheets, each 76×106 mm. (a) 5500c. Paul Ehrlich. (b) 5500c. Robert Goddard Set of 2 sheets   7·50   8·00

564 British Colourpoint with Tree Decoration

1998. Christmas. Cats and Dogs. Multicoloured.
2774	500c. Type **564**	55	15
2775	600c. American shorthair kitten with basket	65	20
2776	800c. Peke-faced Persian on piano keys	80	30
2777	1000c. German spitz dog in box	1·00	60
2778	2000c. British shorthair Blue with antlers	1·75	2·25
2779	3000c. Persian in sleigh	2·00	2·75

MS2780 Two sheets, each 76×106 mm. (a) 5500c. English pointer puppy. (b) 5500c. Manx cat with decoration Set of 2 sheets   8·00   8·50

1999. 25th Death Anniv of Pablo Picasso (painter). As T 293a of Gambia. Multicoloured.
2781	1000c. *Composition with Butterfly*	85	95
2782	1000c. *Mandolin and Clarinet* (vert)	85	95
2783	2000c. *Woman throwing a Stone*	1·75	2·00

MS2784 101×127 mm. 5500c. *Tomato Plant* (vert)   4·25   4·75

564a Lampredi

1999. Birth Centenary of Enzo Ferrari (car manufacturer). Multicoloured.
2785	2000c. Type **564a**	1·40	1·40
2786	2000c. 250 GT Cabriolet	1·40	1·40
2787	2000c. 121 LM	1·40	1·40

MS2788 100×70 mm. 3000c. 365 GTS/4 Spyder (91×34 mm)   3·00   3·50

1999. 19th World Scout Jamboree, Chile. As T 291b of Gambia. Multicoloured (except No. MS2792).
2789	2000c. Scout salute	1·25	1·50
2790	2000c. Scout with backpack	1·25	1·50
2791	2000c. Bowline knot	1·25	1·50

MS2792 55×70 mm. 5500c. Lord Baden-Powell (bistre and black)   2·75   3·25

1999. 50th Death Anniv of Mahatma Gandhi. As T 292 of Gambia. Multicoloured.
2793	2000c. Gandhi, 1931	1·90	1·90
2794	2000c. On Salt March, 1930 (53×38 mm)	1·90	1·90
2795	2000c. Collecting natural salt, 1930 (53×38 mm)	1·90	1·90
2796	2000c. After graduating from high school, 1887	1·90	1·90

MS2797 60×79 mm. 5500c. Mahatma Gandhi seated, 1931   7·50   7·00

1999. 80th Anniv of Royal Air Force. As T 292 of Gambia. Multicoloured.
2798	2000c. C-130 Hercules on tarmac	1·50	1·50
2799	2000c. HC2 Chinook helicopter	1·50	1·50
2800	2000c. C-130 Hercules W2 taking off	1·50	1·50
2801	2000c. Panavia Tornado F3	1·50	1·50

MS2802 Two sheets, each 90×70 mm. (a) 5500c. Chipmunk and EF-2000 Euro-fighter. (b) 5500c. Bristol F2B fighter and merlin (bird) Set of 2 sheets   7·50   7·50

1999. First Death Anniv of Diana, Princess of Wales. As T 293a of Gambia.
| 2803 | 1000c. multicoloured | 1·00 | 1·00 |

565 Farmer working

1999. Chinese New Year ("Year of the Rabbit"). "Farmer and the Hare" (Han Fei Tzu). Multicoloured.

2804	1400c. Type **565**	1·25	1·25
2805	1400c. Farmer watching hare hit tree	1·25	1·25
2806	1400c. Farmer with dead hare	1·25	1·25
2807	1400c. Farmer asleep under tree	1·25	1·25

566 Shirley Temple praying

1999. 70th Birthday of Shirley Temple (actress). Showing film scenes from *Curly Top*. Multicoloured.

2808	1000c. Type **566**	60	70
2809	1000c. Man looking at painting	60	70
2810	1000c. With butler	60	70
2811	1000c. As old woman in rocking chair	60	70
2812	1000c. With mother (horiz)	60	70
2813	1000c. Wearing brown coat and bowler hat (horiz)	60	70
2814	1000c. With cuddly toys (horiz)	60	70
2815	1000c. Pulling father's tie (horiz)	60	70
2816	1000c. With family (horiz)	60	70
2817	1000c. Watching parents (horiz)	60	70
MS2818	106×76 mm. 5000c. Shirley Temple on piano	3·75	4·50

567 Corythosaurus

1999. Prehistoric Animals. Multicoloured.

2819	400c. Type **567**	60	30
2820	600c. Struthiomimus	70	40
2821	800c. Pterodactylus	75	80
2822	800c. Scelidosaurus	75	80
2823	800c. Pteranodon	75	80
2824	800c. Plateosaurus	75	80
2825	800c. Ornithosuchus	75	80
2826	800c. Kentrosaurus	75	80
2827	800c. Hypsognathus	75	80
2828	800c. Erythrosuchus	75	80
2829	800c. Stegoceras	75	80
2830	800c. Ankylosaurus	75	80
2831	800c. Anatosaurus	75	80
2832	800c. Diplodocus	75	80
2833	800c. Monoclonius	75	80
2834	800c. Tyrannosaurus	75	80
2835	800c. Camptosaurus	75	80
2836	800c. Ornitholestes	75	80
2837	800c. Archaeopteryx	75	80
2838	800c. Allosaurus	75	80
2839	1000c. Lambeosaurus	80	85
2840	2000c. Hesperosaurus	1·40	1·75

MS2841 Two sheets, each 85×110 mm. (a) 5000c. Dimorphodon (vert). (b) 5000c. Apatosaurus Set of 2 sheets   8·50   9·00

Nos. 2821/9 and 2830/8 respectively were printed together, *se-tenant*, with the backgrounds forming composite designs.

568 Badgers

1999. Endangered Species. Multicoloured.

2842	200c. Type **568**	40	20
2843	400c. Azure-winged magpie	75	40
2844	600c. White stork	75	35
2845	800c. Red fox	75	40
2846	1000c. European bee eater ("*Merops apiaster*")	1·00	1·00

2847	1000c. Hoopoe (*Upupa epops*)	1·00	1·00
2848	1000c. Red deer	1·00	1·00
2849	1000c. Short-toed eagle (*Cycaetus gallicus*)	1·00	1·00
2850	1000c. Lacerta oceliata (lizard)	1·00	1·00
2851	1000c. Lynx	1·00	1·00
2852	1000c. Pine martin	1·00	1·00
2853	1000c. Tawny owl (*Strix aluco*)	1·00	1·00
2854	1000c. Wild boar	1·00	1·00
2855	1000c. Northern goshawk (*Accipiter gentilis*)	1·00	1·00
2856	1000c. Garden dormouse	1·00	1·00
2857	1000c. Stag beetles	1·00	1·00
2858	2000c. Cinereous vulture (vert)	2·00	2·25
2859	3000c. Jay (vert)	2·25	3·00

MS2860 Two sheets, each 85×110 mm. (a) 5000c. Imperial eagle ("Iberian Imperial Eagle"). (b) 5000c. Wolf cub (vert) Set of 2 sheets   10·00   9·00

Nos. 2846/51 and 2852/7 respectively were printed together, *se-tenant*, with the backgrounds forming composite designs.

569 California Sister Butterfly

1999. "Australia '99" International Stamp Exhibition, Melbourne. Butterflies. Multicoloured.

2861	300c. Type **569**	30	15
2862	500c. Red-splashed sulphur	40	20
2863	600c. Checked white	50	25
2864	800c. Blue emperor	60	30
2865	1000c. Red admiral (vert)	70	75
2866	1000c. Buckeye (vert)	70	75
2867	1000c. Desert chequered skipper (vert)	70	75
2868	1000c. Orange sulphur (vert)	70	75
2869	1000c. Tiger swallowtail (vert)	70	75
2870	1000c. Orange-bordered blue (vert)	70	75
2871	1000c. Gulf fritillary ("vanillae") (vert)	70	75
2872	1000c. Monarch (vert)	70	75
2873	1000c. Small tortoiseshell (vert)	70	75
2874	1000c. Brimstone (vert)	70	75
2875	1000c. Camberwell beauty (vert)	70	75
2876	1000c. Marbled white (vert)	70	75
2877	1000c. Purple Emperor (vert)	70	75
2878	1000c. Clouded yellow (vert)	70	75
2879	1000c. Ladoga camilla (vert)	70	75
2880	1000c. Marsh fritillary (vert)	70	75

MS2881 Two sheets, each 106×76 mm. (a) 5000c. Homerus swallowtail (vert). (b) 5000c. Blue copper Set of 2 sheets   7·00   7·00

Nos. 2865/72 and 2873/80 respectively were printed together, *se-tenant*, with the backgrounds forming composite designs.

No. 2862 is inscribed "Red-splashed Sulfer" and No. 2864 "Blue Emperorl", both in error.

571 ICE 2 (Germany), 1966

1999. Railways of the World. Multicoloured.

2883	400c. Type **571**	40	20
2884	500c. M41 No. 2112 (Hungary), 1982	50	20
2885	600c. DVR No. 2526 (Finland), 1963	60	30
2886	1000c. Class AVE 100 (Spain), 1992	80	40
2887	1300c. Conrail EMD SD80 No. 4110 (U.S.A.), 1993	90	90
2888	1300c. Columbus and Greenville EMD SDP35 No. 701 (U.S.A.), 1964–6	90	90
2889	1300c. Providence and Worcester MLW M420 (U.S.A.), 1973–77	90	90
2890	1300c. Missouri Pacific C36-7 No. 9044 (U.S.A.), 1978–85	90	90
2891	1300c. Virginia and Maryland ALCO C-420 No. 203 (U.S.A.), 1963–68	90	90
2892	1300c. Reading EMD GP30 No. 3615 (U.S.A.), 1961–63	90	90
2893	1300c. Illinois Terminal EMD GP7 No. 1506 (U.S.A.), 1949/54	90	90
2894	1300c. Canadian Pacific EMD SD 38-2 (Canada), 1972–79	90	90
2895	1300c. EMD SD 60M 500 No. 6058 (U.S.A.), 1989–96	90	90
2896	1300c. GE U25C No. 2808 (U.S.A.), 1963–65	90	90
2897	1300c. EMD GP 28 (U.S.A.), 1961–63	90	90

2898	1300c. EMD SD 9 No. 162 (U.S.A.), 1954–59	90	90

MS2899 Two sheets. (a) 85×110 mm. 5000c. Swiss Federal Class RE 6/6 No. 11630, 1972. (b) 110×85 mm. 5000c. AGP44 (U.S.A.), 1990–91 Set of 2 sheets   7·50   8·00

1999. "iBRA '99" International Stamp Exhibition, Nuremberg. Multicoloured. As T **298a** of Gambia.

2900	500c. *Schomberg* (sailing ship) and Hanover 1850 1 ggr. stamp	50	25
2901	800c. Class P8 railway locomotive and Hamburg 1859 ½s.	70	40
2902	1000c. *Schomberg* (sailing ship) and Lubeck 1859 ½s.	85	70
2903	2000c. Class P8 railway locomotive and Heligoland 1867 ½s.	1·40	1·75

MS2904 134×106 mm. 5000c. Germany 3pf. stamp on 1912 Bork-Bruck flown cover (vert)   3·25   3·50

1999. 150th Death Anniv of Katsushika Hokusai (Japanese artist). Multicoloured as T **298b** of Gambia, but horiz.

2905	1300c. *Girl picking Plum Blossoms*	80	85
2906	1300c. *Surveying a Region*	80	85
2907	1300c. *Sumo Wrestler* (bending down)	80	85
2908	1300c. *Sumo Wrestler* (dancing)	80	85
2909	1300c. *Landscape with Seaside Village*	80	85
2910	1300c. *Courtiers crossing a Bridge*	80	85
2911	1300c. *Climbing the Mountain*	80	85
2912	1300c. *Nakahara in Sagami Province*	80	85
2913	1300c. *Sumo Wrestlers*	80	85
2914	1300c. *An Oiran and Maid by a Fence*	80	85
2915	1300c. *Fujiwara Yoshitaka*	80	85

MS2916 Two sheets, each 100×70 mm. (a) 5000c. *Palanquin Bearers on a Steep Hill* (vert). (b) 5000c. *Three Ladies by a Well* (vert) Set of 2 sheets   6·50   7·00

1999. Tenth Anniv of United Nations Rights of the Child Convention. Vert designs as T **298c** of Gambia. Multicoloured.

2917	3000c. Boy smiling and U.N. Headquarters Building	1·75	2·25
2918	3000c. Dove and Earth	1·75	2·25
2919	3000c. Mother and baby	1·75	2·25

MS2920 110×85 mm. 5000c. Boy and UNICEF emblem   3·25   4·00

Nos. 2917/19 were printed together, se-tenant, forming a composite design.

1999. "PhilexFrance '99" International Stamp Exhibition, France. Railway Locomotives. Two sheets, each 106×76 mm, containing horiz designs as T **299d** of Gambia. Multicoloured.

MS2921 Two sheets. (a) 5000c. Western Railway suburban tank locomotive. (b) 5000c. National Railways Class 232-U1 Set of 2 sheets   7·50   7·50

1999. 250th Birth Anniv of Johann von Goethe (German writer). As T **298d** of Gambia. Multicoloured.

2922	2000c. Wagner entreats Faust in his study	1·25	1·50
2923	2000c. Von Goethe and Von Schiller	1·25	1·50
2924	2000c. Mephistopheles disguised as the Fool	1·25	1·50

MS2925 106×71 mm. 5000c. Faust attended by Spirits   3·25   3·75

1999. 30th Anniv of First Manned Landing on Moon. T **298e** of Gambia. Multicoloured.

2926	1300c. Command module	1·40	1·40
2927	1300c. Lunar module ascending	1·40	1·40
2928	1300c. Giant moon rock	1·40	1·40
2929	1300c. Lunar module's aerials and Earth from Moon	1·40	1·40
2930	1300c. Neil Armstrong	1·40	1·40
2931	1300c. "One small step" (alighting on lunar surface)	1·40	1·40

MS2932 71×106 mm. 5000c. Earth from Moon   3·50   4·00

Nos. 2926/31 were printed together, se-tenant, forming a composite design. No. 2927 is inscribed "LUNAR MODULE ASCENSION" in error.

572 Gate of Understanding, Macao

1999. "China '99" World Philatelic Exhibition, Beijing. Return of Macao to China.

2933	**572** 1000c. multicoloured	1·25	1·50

1999. "Queen Elizabeth the Queen Mother's Century". As T **304a** of Gambia.

2934	2000c. black and gold	1·75	1·75
2935	2000c. black and gold	1·75	1·75
2936	2000c. multicoloured	1·75	1·75
2937	2000c. multicoloured	1·75	1·75

MS2938 153×157 mm. 5000c. multicoloured   4·25   4·75

DESIGNS: No. 2934, Lady Elizabeth Bowes-Lyon with her brother, David, 1904; 2935, Queen Mother in Rhodesia, 1957; 2936, Queen Mother seated, 1970; 2937, Queen Mother holding bouquet, 1992. (37×50 mm)—**MS**2938, Queen Mother in garden, 1970.

573 Dr. Ephraim Apu

1999. Birth Centenary of Dr. Ephraim Apu (traditional musicologist). Multicoloured.

2939	200c. Type **573**	30	15
2940	800c. Playing Odurugya flute	1·00	90
2941	1100c. Indigenious flutes	1·40	2·00

574 Grandma Alice and Village

1999. 25th Anniv of S.O.S. in Ghana (200, 1100c.) and 50th Anniv of S.O.S. Kinderdorf International (children's villages) (others). Multicoloured.

2942	200c. Type **574**	40	15
2943	550c. Kindergarten	1·00	50
2944	800c. Hermann Gneiner (founder) and Asiakwa S.O.S. building	1·40	1·25
2945	1100c. Preparing food	1·75	2·50

575 Fish inside Cloud

1999. Save the Ozone Layer Campaign. Multicoloured.

2946	200c. Type **575**	35	15
2947	550c. African looking at diagram of ozone layer	65	30
2948	800c. Earth weeping	1·00	75
2949	1100c. Africans shielding Earth	1·40	1·60
2950	1500c. CFC and no-CFC appliances	1·75	2·50

576 Peace Doves flying from Ghana

1999. New Millennium. Multicoloured.

2951	300c. Type **576**	40	20
2952	700c. Kwame Nkrumah (first President) speaking (horiz)	90	80
2953	1200c. Clock tower, University of Ghana	1·75	2·25

577 Liu-Yi meets Daughter of the Dragon King

2000. Chinese New Year ("Year of the Dragon"). Vert designs showing scenes from *Daughter of the Dragon King*. Each design brown and silver.

2954	1600c. Type **577**	90	1·00
2955	1600c. Liu-Yi and Fairy Soldier	90	1·00

2956	1600c. Liu-Yi and the Dragon King	90	1·00
2957	1600c. Liu-Yi, Dragon King and Red Dragon	90	1·00
2958	1600c. Red Dragon and Dragon of Jing River fighting	90	1·00
2959	1600c. Dragon King with his daughter and brother	90	1·00
2960	1700c. Dragon King's brother inviting Liu-Yi to marry his niece	90	1·00
2961	1700c. Liu-Yi bidding farewell to Dragon King	90	1·00
2962	1700c. Liu-Yi with gifts from Dragon King	90	1·00
2963	1700c. Liu-Yi with third wife	90	1·00
2964	1700c. Liu-Yi with third wife and son	90	1·00
2965	1700c. Liu-Yi realises that third wife is Daughter of the Dragon King	90	1·00

578 Black-faced Impala

2000. African Wildlife. Multicoloured.

2966	300c. Type **578**	40	15
2967	500c. Cheetah	55	25
2968	1000c. Wildebeest	75	50
2969	1100c. Chimpanzee (vert)	1·00	1·00
2970	1100c. Boomslang tree snake (vert)	1·00	1·00
2971	1100c. Ruppell's griffon ("Vulture") (vert)	1·00	1·00
2972	1100c. Leopard (vert)	1·00	1·00
2973	1100c. African rhinoceros (vert)	1·00	1·00
2974	1100c. Zebra (vert)	1·00	1·00
2975	1100c. South African crowned crane ("Crowned Crane") (vert)	1·00	1·00
2976	1100c. Female lesser Kudu (vert)	1·00	1·00
2977	1200c. Rufous-crowned roller ("Purple Roller") (vert)	7·00	7·00
2978	1200c. Eastern white pelican ("Pelicans") (vert)	1·00	1·00
2979	1200c. Cattle egret ("Egrets") (vert)	1·00	1·00
2980	1200c. Zebra waxbill ("Orange-breasted Waxbill") (vert)	1·00	1·00
2981	1200c. Giraffe (vert)	1·00	1·00
2982	1200c. African buffalo (vert)	1·00	1·00
2983	1200c. Elephant (vert)	1·00	1·00
2984	1200c. African lion (vert)	1·00	1·00
2985	3000c. Hippopotamus	2·50	3·25
MS2986	Two sheets, each 76×106 mm. (a) 7000c. Ostrich. (b) 7000c. Young waterbuck Set of 2 sheets	9·00	9·00

Nos. 2969/76 and 2977/84 were each printed together, *se-tenant*, with the backgrounds forming composite designs.

579 Cape Coast Castle

2000. Tourism. Multicoloured.

2987	300c. Type **579**	1·00	1·40
2988	300c. Banda Nkwanta Mosque, Accra	1·00	1·40
2989	300c. Elephants	1·00	1·40
2990	1100c. Tribal chief	1·00	1·40
2991	1200c. Ghanaians with antelope	1·00	1·40
2992	1800c. Tribal chiefs	1·25	1·75

580 Banded ("Zebra") Duiker

2000. Fauna and Flora. Multicoloured.

2993	500c. Type **580**	55	20
2994	600c. Leopard	70	35
2995	1600c. Large spotted genet	1·00	1·00
2996	1600c. Tree pangolin	1·00	1·00
2997	1600c. Bongo	1·00	1·00
2998	1600c. Elephant	1·00	1·00
2999	1600c. Flap-necked chameleon	1·00	1·00
3000	1600c. West African dwarf crocodile	1·00	1·00
3001	1600c. Lowe's monkey	1·00	1·00
3002	1600c. Diana monkey	1·00	1·00
3003	1600c. Potto	1·00	1·00
3004	1600c. Moustached monkey	1·00	1·00
3005	1600c. Thomas's galago	1·00	1·00
3006	1600c. Chimpanzee	1·00	1·00

3007	1600c. Grey parrot	1·00	1·00
3008	1600c. Hoopoe	1·00	1·00
3009	1600c. European roller	1·00	1·00
3010	1600c. European bee-eater	1·00	1·00
3011	1600c. Blue-breasted kingfisher	1·00	1·00
3012	1600c. White-throated bee eater	1·00	1·00
3013	2000c. Bushbuck	1·25	1·50
3014	3000c. African wood owl	2·75	3·00
MS3015	Two sheets. (a) 100×70 mm. 6000c. Hippopotamus (vert). (b) 70×100 mm. 6000c. Great blue turaco (vert) Set of 2 sheets	11·00	11·00

Nos. 2995/3000, 3001/6 and 3007/12 were each printed together, *se-tenant*, with the backgrounds forming composite designs.

No. 2995 is inscribed "BLOTHED GENET" in error.

581 Suillus luteus

2000. African Mushrooms. Multicoloured.

3016	1500c. Type **581**	1·00	1·10
3017	1500c. Laccaria amethystina	1·00	1·10
3018	1500c. Coriolus versicolor	1·00	1·10
3019	1500c. Armillaria mellea	1·00	1·10
3020	1500c. Lepiota rhacodes	1·00	1·10
3021	1500c. Russula queletil	1·00	1·10
3022	2000c. Amanita vaginata	1·10	1·25
3023	2000c. Lycoperdon perlatum	1·10	1·25
3024	2000c. Schizophyllum commune	1·10	1·25
3025	2000c. Cantharellus cinereus	1·10	1·25
3026	2000c. Coprinus disseminatus	1·10	1·25
3027	2000c. Russula cyanoxantaha	1·10	1·25
MS3028	Two sheets, each 53×81 mm. (a) 5000c. Aleuria aurantia (vert). (b) 5000c. Tylopilus felleus (vert) Set of 2 sheets	8·50	9·00

582 Cooking Demonstration

2000. 19th International Home Economics Congress, Accra. Multicoloured.

3029	300c. Type **582**	30	15
3030	700c. Student with home economics text book (vert)	70	45
3031	1200c. Mrs. Alberta Ollennu, Ms. Patience Adow and Association logo	1·10	1·40
3032	1800c. Congress logo (vert)	1·60	2·50

2000. 18th Birthday of Prince William. At T **312b** of Gambia. Multicoloured.

3033	2000c. In skiing gear	2·00	2·00
3034	2000c. In Eton uniform	2·00	2·00
3035	2000c. With Prince Harry	2·00	2·00
3036	2000c. Prince William (Royal Artillery cap in background)	2·00	2·00
MS3037	100×80 mm. 8000c. Prince William in blue jumper (37×50 mm)	6·00	6·50

582a "Mercury"

2000. "EXPO 2000" World Stamp Exhibition, Anaheim. Manned Spacecraft. Multicoloured.

3038	2000c. Type **582a**	1·40	1·50
3039	2000c. "Gemini"	1·40	1·50
3040	2000c. "Apollo"	1·40	1·50
3041	2000c. "Vostok"	1·40	1·50
3042	2000c. "Voskhod 2"	1·40	1·50
3043	2000c. "Soyuz"	1·40	1·50
MS3044	75×115 mm. 2000c. Space Shuttle *Challenger* mission emblem (vert)	2·00	2·50

Nos. 3038/43 were printed together, *se-tenant*, with the backgrounds forming a composite design.

582b "Apollo 18"

2000. 25th Anniv of "Apollo"–"Soyuz" Joint Project. Multicoloured.

3045	4000c. Type **582b**	2·25	2·50
3046	4000c. "Apollo 18" and "Soyuz 19" docking	2·25	2·50
3047	4000c. "Soyuz 19"	2·25	2·50
MS3048	105×75 mm. 8000c. "Soyuz 19" and Earth	4·75	5·50

Nos. 3045/7 were printed together, *se-tenant*, with the backgrounds forming a composite design.

582c Wetherby, 1985

2000. 50th Anniv of Berlin Film Festival. Multicoloured.

3049	2000c. Type **582c**	1·25	1·40
3050	2000c. Die Frau und der Fremde, 1985	1·25	1·40
3051	2000c. Hong Gaoliang, 1988	1·25	1·40
3052	2000c. Skrivanci na Nitich, 1990	1·25	1·40
3053	2000c. Music Box, 1990	1·25	1·40
3054	2000c. Terma, 1987	1·25	1·40
MS3055	95×103 mm. 6000c. Justice est Faite, 1951	5·50	6·00

582d Marc Seguin

2000. 175th Anniv of Stockton and Darlington Line (first public railway). Multicoloured.

3056	4000c. Type **582d**	2·50	2·50
3057	4000c. Blenkinsop's locomotive	2·50	2·50
3058	4000c. Pumping station at Dawlish	2·50	2·50

2000. Election of Albert Einstein (mathematical physicist) as *Time Magazine* "Man of the Century". Sheet 120×90 mm, containing vert portrait as T **312d** of Gambia.

MS3059	8000c. multicoloured	5·00	5·00

582e LZ-129 Hindenburg, 1936

2000. Centenary of First Zeppelin Flight. Multicoloured.

3060	1600c. Type **582e**	1·60	1·60
3061	1600c. LZ-9 Ersatz Deutschland, 1911	1·60	1·60
3062	1600c. LZ-4, 1908	1·60	1·60
MS3063	96×65 mm. 5000c. LZ-11 Viktoria Luise, 1912	4·25	4·75

Nos. 3060/2 were printed together, *se-tenant*, with the backgrounds forming a composite design.

582f Gymnast on Parallel Bars, Athens (1896)

2000. Olympic Games, Sydney. Multicoloured.

3064	1300c. Type **582f**	1·10	1·25
3065	1300c. Long jumping	1·10	1·25
3066	1300c. Olympic Stadium, Los Angeles (1984)	1·10	1·25
3067	1300c. Ancient Greek chariot racing	1·10	1·25

583 African Shorthair Cat

2000. Domestic Cats and Dogs. Multicoloured.

3068	1100c. Type **583**	80	60
3069	1200c. Russian blue cat	80	60
3070	1600c. Weimaraner (horiz)	1·10	1·10
3071	1800c. Keeshond (horiz)	1·10	1·10

3072	1800c. Fox terrier (horiz)	1·10	1·10
3073	1800c. Saluki (horiz)	1·10	1·10
3074	1800c. Dalmatian (horiz)	1·10	1·10
3075	1800c. English setter (horiz)	1·10	1·10
3076	1800c. Basenji	1·10	1·10
3077	1800c. Silver Persian (horiz)	1·10	1·10
3078	1800c. Creampoint Himalayan (horiz)	1·10	1·10
3079	1800c. British tortoiseshell shorthair (horiz)	1·10	1·10
3080	1800c. American shorthair tabby (horiz)	1·10	1·10
3081	1800c. Black Persian (horiz)	1·10	1·10
3082	1800c. Turkish van (horiz)	1·10	1·10
3083	2000c. Basset hound	1·40	1·75
MS3084	Two sheets, each 110×85 mm. (a) 8000c. Lilac Persian cat. (b) 8000c. Cocker spaniel Set of 2 sheets	9·00	10·00

584 Xu Xian, White Lady and Xiao Qing

2001. Chinese New Year ("Year of the Snake"). Showing scenes from *Tale of the White Snake* (traditional Chinese story). Each red and silver.

3085	2500c. Type **584**	1·50	1·50
3086	2500c. White Lady and Xu Xian in pharmacy	1·50	1·50
3087	2500c. Xu Xian with monk Fa Hai	1·50	1·50
3088	2500c. Xu Xian and White Lady drinking wine	1·50	1·50
3089	2500c. Xu Xian having heart attack	1·50	1·50
3090	2500c. White Lady attacked by stork	1·50	1·50
3091	2500c. White Lady, Xiao Qing with swords confront Fa Hai	1·50	1·50
3092	2500c. Xiao Qing and Xu Xian on staircase	1·50	1·50
3093	2500c. Fa Hai entrapping White Lady beneath pagoda	1·50	1·50
3094	2500c. Xiao Qing, Xu Xian praying at pagoda	1·50	1·50
3095	2500c. Xiao Qing attacking Fa Hai	1·50	1·50
3096	2500c. Fa Hai turned into crab	1·50	1·50

585 Walter Gropius (architect)

2001. Twentieth Century Achievements in Architecture, Art and Medicine. Multicoloured.

3097	2500c. Type **585**	1·50	1·50
3098	2500c. Aldo Rossi	1·50	1·50
3099	2500c. Le Corbusier	1·50	1·50
3100	2500c. Antonio Gaudi	1·50	1·50
3101	2500c. Paolo Soleri	1·50	1·50
3102	2500c. Mies van der Rohe	1·50	1·50
3103	2500c. Wassily Kandinsky	1·50	1·50
3104	2500c. Henry Moore	1·50	1·50
3105	2500c. Marc Chagall	1·50	1·50
3106	2500c. Norman Rockwell	1·50	1·50
3107	2500c. Antonio Lopez Garcia	1·50	1·50
3108	2500c. Frida Kahlo	1·50	1·50
MS3109	Three sheets, each 93×64 mm. (a) 14000c. "FRANK LLOYD WRIGHT". (b) 14000c. "Picasso". (c) 14000c. Double helix structure of DNA molecule Set of 3 sheets	22·00	24·00

586 James Cagney

2001. Hollywood Legends. James Cagney and Edward G. Robinson. Designs showing different portraits.

3110	**586**	4000c. green and black	1·75	2·00
3111	–	4000c. green and black	1·75	2·00
3112	–	4000c. blue and black	1·75	2·00
3113	–	4000c. brown and black	1·75	2·00
3114	–	4000c. mauve and black	1·75	2·00
3115	–	4000c. orange and black	1·75	2·00
3116	–	4000c. green and black	1·75	2·00

3117	-	4000c. lilac, purple and black	1·75	2·00
3118	-	4000c. purple and black	1·75	2·00
3119	-	4000c. brown and black	1·75	2·00
3120	-	4000c. brown and black	1·75	2·00
3121	-	4000c. blue and black	1·75	2·00

Nos. 3110/15 (Cagney) and 3116/21 (Robinson) were each printed together, *se-tenant*, showing a photograph of the actor.

586a Margie Hendrix (shoulder at bottom right)

2001. Famous Girl Pop Groups. The Cookies (Nos. 3122/4), The Ronettes (Nos. 3125/7) and The Supremes (Nos. 3128/30). Multicoloured.

3122	2700c. Type **586a**	1·50	1·75
3123	2700c. Ethel McCrea (with straight hair)	1·50	1·75
3124	2700c. Pat Lyles's head (background at bottom right)	1·50	1·75
3125	2700c. Estelle Bennett (inscr and value clear of portrait)	1·50	1·75
3126	2700c. Veronica Bennett (inscr and value touch portrait)	1·50	1·75
3127	2700c. Nedra Talley (inscr touches, value clear of portrait)	1·50	1·75
3128	2700c. Florence Ballard (left earring)	1·50	1·75
3129	2700c. Mary Wilson (two earrings)	1·50	1·75
3130	2700c. Diana Ross (right earring)	1·50	1·75

Each group forms a horizontal strip with different background colour: The Cookies cobalt, The Ronettes blue and The Supremes yellow and red.

587 Edward "Kid" Ory (trombonist)

2001. Famous American Jazz Musicians. Multicoloured.

3131	4000c. Type **587**	1·75	2·00
3132	4000c. Earl "Fatha" Hines (pianist)	1·75	2·00
3133	4000c. Lil Hardin-Armstrong (pianist)	1·75	2·00
3134	4000c. John Philip Sousa (composer)	1·75	2·00
3135	4000c. James P. Johnson (pianist)	1·75	2·00
3136	4000c. Johnny St. Cyr (banjo/guitar player)	1·75	2·00
3137	4000c. Scott Joplin (composer)	1·75	2·00
3138	4000c. Clarence Williams (pianist)	1·75	2·00
3139	4000c. Sidney Bechet (clarinetist/saxophonist)	1·75	2·00
3140	4000c. Willie "The Lion" Smith (pianist)	1·75	2·00
3141	4000c. Ferdinand "Jelly Roll" Morton (composer)	1·75	2·00
3142	4000c. Coleman "Bean" Hawkins (saxophonist)	1·75	2·00

MS3143 Two sheets, each 60×77 mm. (a) 14000c. Louis "Satchmo" Armstrong (cornet player). (b) 14000c. Joe "King" Oliver (cornet player) Set of 2 sheets ... 11·00 13·00

588 Cranes (Kano Eisen'in Michinobu)

2001. "Philanippon '01" International Stamp Exhibition, Tokyo. Japanese Paintings. Multicoloured.

3144	500c. Type **588**	30	20
3145	800c. *Flowers and Trees in Chen Chun's Style* (Tsubaki Chinzan)	40	25
3146	1200c. *Poetry Contest of 42 Matches* (unsigned)	60	40
3147	2000c. *Cranes* (different detail) (Kano Eisen'in Michinobu)	1·00	75
3148	3000c. *Coming-of-Age Rite* (vert)	1·25	1·25
3149	3000c. *West Wing* (vert)	1·25	1·25
3150	3000c. *Akuta River* (vert)	1·25	1·25

3151	3000c. *Eastbound Trip: Mt. Utsu* (vert)	1·25	1·25
3152	3000c. *Eastbound Trip: Mt. Fuji* (vert)	1·25	1·25
3153	3000c. *Eastbound Trip: Black-headed Gulls* (vert)	1·25	1·25
3154	3000c. *Crossing Kawachi* (vert)	1·25	1·25
3155	3000c. *By Well Wall* (vert)	1·25	1·25
3156	4000c. *Excursion through South Gate* (vert)	1·40	1·40
3157	4000c. *Excursion through East Gate* (vert)	1·40	1·40
3158	4000c. *Excursion through North Gate* (vert)	1·40	1·40
3159	4000c. *Excursion through West Gate* (vert)	1·40	1·40
3160	4000c. *Sakyamuni entering Nirvana* (vert)	1·40	1·40
3161	4000c. *Animals* (vert)	1·40	1·40
3162	5000c. *Poetry Contest of 42 Matches* (different detail) (unsigned)	1·60	1·75
3163	12000c. *Plum Trees* (Tani Buncho)	3·50	4·50

MS3164 Four sheets, each 100×76 mm. (a) 14000c. *Cranes* (Kano Eisen'in Michinobu) ("GHANA" and value in red). (b) 14000c. *Cranes* (Kano Eisen'in Michinobu) ("GHANA" in yellow). (c) 14000c. *Coming-of-Age Rite* (Sumiyoshi Jokei). (d) 14000c. *Musashino Plain* (unknown artist) Set of 4 sheets ... 24·00 26·00

Nos. 3148/55 (*The Tales of Ise*) (Sumiyoshi Jokei) and 3156/63 (*The Story of Sakyamuni*).

589 Child with Polio and Emblem

2001. 40th Anniv of Rotary in Ghana. Each including the Rotary International symbol. Multicoloured.

3165	300c. Type **589**	50	20
3166	1100c. Boy getting clean water from tap	1·00	1·25
3167	1200c. Paul Harris (founder of Rotary International)	1·00	1·25
3168	1800c. Man giving blood	1·50	2·25

590 Bentley S-Series Convertible (1950)

2001. "Belgica 2001" International Stamp Exhibition, Brussels. Twentieth-century classic Cars. Multicoloured.

3169	2000c. Type **590**	1·00	1·00
3170	3000c. Chrysler Town and Country (1948)	1·25	1·25
3171	4000c. B.M.W. 507 (1956–59)	1·40	1·40
3172	4000c. Bentley English Tourer (1934)	1·40	1·40
3173	4000c. Morris Minor (1948)	1·40	1·40
3174	4000c. Daimler SP-250 Dart (1954)	1·40	1·40
3175	4000c. DeSoto Custom Convertible (1950)	1·40	1·40
3176	4000c. Ford Thunderbird (1955–60)	1·40	1·40
3177	4000c. Porsche 356B (1959–63)	1·40	1·40
3178	4000c. Rolls-Royce Silver Cloud (1962)	1·40	1·40
3179	4000c. Austin Healey Sprite Mk 1 (1958)	1·40	1·40
3180	4000c. Mercedes 300SL (1954–57)	1·40	1·40
3181	4000c. Citroen 2cv (1949)	1·40	1·40
3182	4000c. Cadillac Series-62 (1949)	1·40	1·40
3183	5000c. Lotus Elite (1957)	1·50	1·60
3184	6000c. Corvette Sting Ray (1966)	1·75	1·90

MS3185 Two sheets, each 102×74 mm. (a) 14000c. Mercedes-Benz (1933) (85×28 mm). (b) 14000c. Triumph TR2 (1953–55) (85×28 mm) Set of 2 sheets ... 9·50 11·00

No. 3172 is inscribed "Bentler" and No. 3181 "Citroen", both in error.

590a Princess Victoria as a Young Girl

2001. Death Centenary of Queen Victoria. Multicoloured.

3186	5000c. Type **590a**	2·00	2·25
3187	5000c. Albert Edward, Prince of Wales	2·00	2·25
3188	5000c. Queen Victoria and Prince of Wales	2·00	2·25
3189	5000c. Queen Victoria and Prince Albert on Wedding Day	2·00	2·25

MS3190 66×96 mm. 12000c. Princess Victoria (The Princess Royal) ... 5·00 6·00

MS3190 is inscr Princess Victoria in error.

590b Mao in Uniform acknowledging Crowd

2001. 25th Death Anniv of Mao Tse-tung (Chinese leader). Multicoloured.

3191	7000c. Type **590b**	1·75	2·25
3192	7000c. Head and shoulders portrait	1·75	2·25
3193	7000c. Mao in overcoat acknowledging crowd	1·75	2·25

MS3194 116×102 mm. 12000c. Mao as a young man ... 4·00 5·00

590c Zaandam

2001. 75th Death Anniv Claude-Oscar Monet. (French painter). Multicoloured.

3195	5000c. Type **590c**	2·50	2·75
3196	5000c. *On the Seine at Bennecourt*	2·50	2·75
3197	5000c. *The Studio-boat*	2·50	2·75
3198	5000c. *Houses on the Waterfront, Zaandam*	2·50	2·75

MS3199 139×110 mm. 15000c. *Madame Gaudibert* (vert) ... 6·50 7·50

590d Queen Elizabeth in pink hat

2001. 75th Birthday of Queen Elizabeth II. Multicoloured.

3200	4000c. Type **590d**	1·75	1·75
3201	4000c. Queen Elizabeth in white hat with flowers	1·75	1·75
3202	4000c. In red "trilby"	1·75	1·75
3203	4000c. Wearing tiara	1·75	1·75
3204	4000c. In matching blue and pink hat and coat	1·75	1·75
3205	4000c. Queen Elizabeth in uniform for Trooping the Colour	1·75	1·75

MS3206 85×135 mm. 15000c. Queen Elizabeth with Duke of Edinburgh (horiz) ... 6·50 7·00

590e Giuseppe Verdi

2001. Death Centenary of Giuseppe Verdi (Italian composer). Multicoloured.

3207	5000c. Type **590e**	3·00	3·00
3208	5000c. Musical scores for *Aida* and *Rigoletto*	3·00	3·00
3209	5000c. Inn at Le Roncole (Verdi's birthplace)	3·00	3·00
3210	5000c. Map of Italy	3·00	3·00

MS3211 76×106 mm. 13000c. Giuseppe Verdi ... 7·00 8·00

Nos. 3207/11 were printed together, *se-tenant*, with the backgrounds forming a composite design.

590f Jane Avril leaving the Moulin Rouge

2001. Death Centenary of Henri de Toulouse-Lautrec (French painter). Multicoloured.

3212	6700c. Type **590f**	2·50	3·00
3213	6700c. *Jane Avril dancing*	2·50	3·00
3214	6700c. *Jane Avril entering the Moulin Rouge*	2·50	3·00

591 Killer Whale

2001. Whales and Dolphins. Multicoloured.

3215	1000c. Type **591**	80	45
3216	3000c. Narwhal	1·40	1·40
3217	4000c. Humpback whale	1·50	1·50
3218	4000c. Fin whale	1·50	1·50
3219	4000c. Bowhead whale	1·50	1·50
3220	4000c. Grey whale	1·50	1·50
3221	4000c. Narwhal	1·50	1·50
3222	4000c. White whale ("Beluga")	1·50	1·50
3223	4000c. Head of blue whale	1·50	1·50
3224	4000c. Killer whale	1·50	1·50
3225	4000c. Northern bottlenose dolphin	1·50	1·50
3226	4000c. Sperm whale	1·50	1·50
3227	4000c. Southern right whale	1·50	1·50
3228	4000c. Pygmy right whale	1·50	1·50
3229	5000c. White whale ("Beluga")	1·75	1·90
3230	6000c. Bowhead whale	2·00	2·25

MS3231 Two sheets, each 100×85 mm. (a) 14000c. Blue whale adult and calf. (b) 14000c. Head of sperm whale Set of 2 sheets ... 11·00 12·00

Nos. 3217/22 and 3223/8 were each printed together, *se-tenant*, the backgrounds forming composite designs.

592 Paphiopedilum hennisianum

2001. African Orchids. Multicoloured.

3232	1100c. Type **592**	70	40
3233	1200c. *Vuylstekeara cambria Plush*	70	40
3234	1800c. *Cymbidium Ormoulu*	95	70
3235	2000c. *Phalaenopsis Barbara Moler*	1·00	70
3236	4500c. *Odontocidium Tigersun*	1·60	1·60
3237	4500c. *Miltonia Emotion*	1·60	1·60
3238	4500c. *Odontonia sappho Excul*	1·60	1·60
3239	4500c. *Cymbidium Bulbarrow*	1·60	1·60
3240	4500c. *Dendrobium nobile*	1·60	1·60
3241	4500c. *Paphiopedilum insigne*	1·60	1·60
3242	4500c. *Cattleya capra*	1·60	1·60
3243	4500c. *Odontoglossum rossii*	1·60	1·60
3244	4500c. *Epidendrum pseudepidendrum*	1·60	1·60
3245	4500c. *Encyclia cochleata*	1·60	1·60
3246	4500c. *Cymbidium Baldoyle Melbury*	1·60	1·60
3247	4500c. *Phalaenopsis asean*	1·60	1·60

MS3248 Two sheets, each 68×98 mm. (a) 15000c. *Calanthe vestita*. (b) 15000c. *Angraecum eburneum* Set of 2 sheets ... 12·00 13·00

593 50th Anniversary Logo

2001. 50th Anniv of Kwame Nkrumah University of Science and Technology, Kumasi. Multicoloured.

3249	300c. Type **593**	30	15
3250	700c. Main entrance	50	35
3251	1100c. Milking cows	80	80
3252	1200c. Students in pharmacy department	80	80
3253	1800c. Halls of residence	1·10	1·40
MS3254	120×100 mm. As Nos. 3250/3, but each with a face value of 4000c.	6·50	7·50

594 Bamboo Orchestra

2001. Musical Instruments. Multicoloured.

3255	4000c. Type **594**	1·50	1·50
3256	4000c. Women playing mensuon (wind instruments)	1·50	1·50
3257	4000c. Fontomfrom (drums)	1·50	1·50
3258	4000c. Pati	1·50	1·50

595 George Olah (Chemistry Prize, 1994)

2002. Centenary of Nobel Prizes. Chemistry Prize Winners (except Nos. **MS**3277d/e). Multicoloured.

3259	4000c. Type **595**	1·40	1·40
3260	4000c. Kary Mullis (1993)	1·40	1·40
3261	4000c. Sir Harold Kroto (1996)	1·40	1·40
3262	4000c. Richard Ernst (1991)	1·40	1·40
3263	4000c. Ahmed Zewail (1999)	1·40	1·40
3264	4000c. Paul Crutzen (1995)	1·40	1·40
3265	4000c. John Walker (1997)	1·40	1·40
3266	4000c. Jens Skou (1997)	1·40	1·40
3267	4000c. Alan MacDiarmid (2000)	1·40	1·40
3268	4000c. Thomas Cech (1989)	1·40	1·40
3269	4000c. John Pople (1998)	1·40	1·40
3270	4000c. Rudolph Marcus (1992)	1·40	1·40
3271	4000c. Walter Kohn (1998)	1·40	1·40
3272	4000c. Frank Rowland (1995)	1·40	1·40
3273	4000c. Mario Molina (1995)	1·40	1·40
3274	4000c. Hideki Shirakawa (2000)	1·40	1·40
3275	4000c. Paul Boyer (1997)	1·40	1·40
3276	4000c. Richard Smalley (1996)	1·40	1·40
MS3277	Five sheets, each 100×77 mm. (a) 15000c. Svante Arrhenius (1903). (b) 15000c. Alfred Werner (1913). (c) 15000c. Peter Debye (1936). (d) 15000c. Wole Soyinka (Literature, 1986). (e) 15000c. Nelson Mandela (Peace, 1993) Set of 5 sheets	23·00	25·00

596 Queen Elizabeth at the Races

2002. Golden Jubilee. Multicoloured.

3278	6500c. Type **596**	2·75	3·00
3279	6500c. Queen Elizabeth on horseback	2·75	3·00
3280	6500c. Queen Elizabeth inspecting horses	2·75	3·00
3281	6500c. Queen Elizabeth in carriage with Duke of Edinburgh, Ascot races	2·75	3·00
MS3282	76×108 mm. 15000c. Princess Elizabeth with Duke of Edinburgh	7·50	8·00

597 Conference Logo

2002. Fifth International Copyright Conference, Accra. Multicoloured.

3283	300c. Type **597**	35	15
3284	700c. Girl reading (horiz)	60	35
3285	1100c. Spider on web (horiz)	1·00	1·25

3286	1200c. Woven cloth in shape of Ghana (horiz)	1·00	1·25
3287	1800c. Woman playing drum (horiz)	1·50	2·25

598 Jay Jay Okacha (Nigeria)

2002. World Cup Football Championship, Japan and Korea. Multicoloured.

3288	100c. Type **598**	15	15
3289	150c. South African player	20	15
3290	300c. Pele (Brazil)	30	20
3291	400c. Roger Milla (Cameroun)	35	20
3292	500c. Bobby Charlton (England)	45	25
3293	800c. Michel Platini (France)	50	30
3294	1000c. Franz Beckenbauer (West Germany)	60	35
3295	1500c. Ulsan Munsu Stadium, Korea (horiz)	80	65
3296	2000c. German player	90	75
3297	3000c. Brazilian player	1·25	1·25
3298	4000c. South Korean player	1·40	1·40
3299	5000c. Yokohama International Stadium, Japan (horiz)	1·50	1·60
3300	6000c. Italian player	1·75	2·00
3301	11000c. Publicity poster, Brazil, 1950	3·00	3·75
3302	12000c. Publicity poster, Italy, 1934	3·25	3·75
MS3303	Two sheets. (a) 77×107 mm. 15000c. Geoff Hurst (England), 1966 (43×58 mm). (b) 107×77 mm. 15000c. Gordon Banks (England), 1970 (58×43 mm) Set of 2 sheets	11·00	13·00

599 Girl on Pony

2002. Chinese New Year ("Year of the Horse"). Multicoloured.

3304	4000c. Type **599**	1·50	1·75
3305	4000c. Girl and caparisoned pony	1·50	1·75
3306	4000c. Girl with whip and pony	1·50	1·75
3307	4000c. Girl on hobby horse	1·50	1·75

2002. No. 2159a surch **c 1000.**

3308	1000c. on 1100c. Kente cloth	4·50	3·50

2002. No. 2458e surch **c2,500.**

3309	2500c. on 800c. *Cyrestis camillus* (butterfly)	7·00	7·00

602 Crown Prince Willem-Alexander and Princess Maxima of the Netherlands

2002. "Amphilex 2002" International Stamp Exhibition, Amsterdam. Visit of Crown Prince and Princess of the Netherlands. Multicoloured.

3310	6000c. Type **602**	1·50	1·60
3311	6000c. Royal couple on wedding day	1·50	1·60
3312	6000c. Standing by windmill	1·50	1·60
3313	6000c. Serenaded by accordionist on wedding day	1·50	1·60
3314	6000c. Meeting crowds	1·50	1·60
3315	6000c. Kissing on wedding day	1·50	1·60

603 Trying to retrieve a Ball caught in a Tree

2002. Japanese Paintings by Katsukawa Shunsho. Multicoloured.

MS3316	170×123 mm. 9000c. Type **603**; 9000c. *Listening to a Cuckoo in the Bedroom*; 9000c. *Holding a Cage filled with Fireflies for a Woman to read a Book*	8·00	9·00
MS3317	170×123 mm. 9000c. *Mother and Child taking a Tub-bath while Woman holds a Revolving Lantern*; 9000c. *Strips of Paper with Wishes and Poems are Tied on a Bamboo*; 9000c.*Women enjoying the Cool Air on a Boat*	8·00	9·00
MS3318	170×123 mm. 9000c. *Celebrating Feast of the Chrysanthemum*; 9000c. *Looking out for Coloured Leaves*; 9000c. *Mother reading Picture Book while sitting at a Foot-warmer*	8·00	9·00
MS3319	Four sheets, each 95×105 mm. (a) 15000c. *Three Women decorating a Gate with Twigs of Holly on the Day before the Setting-in of the Spring.* (b) 15000c. *Woman looking at flowering plant in pot.* (c) 15000c. *Woman at writing desk.* (d) 15000c. *Woman pulling down blind* Set of 4 sheets	17·00	19·00

Nos. **MS**3316/19a show details of paintings on silk *Activities of Women in the Twelve Months.*

Nos. **MS**3319b/d show details from triptych *Snow, Moonlight and Flowers.*

604 Scout hiking

2002. 20th World Scout Jamboree, Thailand. Multicoloured.

MS3320	109×90 mm. 6500c. Type **604**; 6500c. Scout hiking (standing on horizon); 6500c. Campfire and tent; 6500c. Scout tying knot	8·00	8·50
MS3321	99×71 mm. 15000c. Ghanian scout (vert)	4·25	4·50

605 Mt. Tateyama, Japan

2002. International Year of Mountains. Multicoloured.

MS3322	105×90 mm. 6000c. Type **605**; 6000c. Mt. Shivling, India; 6000c. Wong Leng, Hong Kong; 6000c. Mt. Blanc, France	6·00	7·00
MS3323	100×72 mm. 15000c. Mt. Fuji, Japan	4·50	5·00

606 Lindbergh and Ryan NYP Special *Spirit of St. Louis*

2002. 75th Anniv of First Solo Trans-Atlantic Flight. Multicoloured.

MS3324	171×129 mm. 8500c. Type **606**; 8500c. Charles and Anne Lindbergh in *Spirit of St. Louis*	8·50	9·00
MS3325	114×81 mm. 15000c. Charles Lindbergh (vert)	5·00	5·50

607 Variable Sunbird

2002. Year of Eco Tourism. Multicoloured.

MS3326	116×125 mm. 4000c. Type **607**; 4000c. Leopard; 4000c. Kob (antelope); 4000c. African buffalo; 4000c. Chimpanzee; 4000c. Lesser bushbaby	10·00	11·00
MS3327	81×97 mm. 12000c. African elephant	7·00	7·00

2002. Queen Elizabeth the Queen Mother Commemoration. Nos. 2191/5 (95th Birthday) surch **C3000.**

3328	3000c. on 600c. brown, light brown and black	1·75	1·75
3329	3000c. on 600c. multicoloured	1·75	1·75
3330	3000c. on 600c. multicoloured	1·75	1·75
3331	3000c. on 600c. multicoloured	1·75	1·75
MS3332	102×127 mm. 20000c. on 2500c. multicoloured	8·00	8·50

The sheetlet and miniature sheet margins have black borders and are overprinted **IN MEMORIAM 1900–2002.**

609 Ice Skaters

2002. Winter Olympic Games, Salt Lake City. Multicoloured.

3333	7000c. Type **609**	3·50	3·50
3334	7000c. Skier in aerials competition	3·50	3·50
MS3335	88×119 mm. Nos. 3333/4	7·00	7·00

610 US Flag as Statue of Liberty with Ghana Flag

2002. "United We Stand". Support for Victims of 11 September 2001 Terrorist Attacks.

3336	**610**	7000c. multicoloured	2·50	3·25

611 Malachite Kingfisher

2002. Birds, Butterflies, Insects and Moths. Multicoloured.

MS3337	160×93 mm. 4500c. Type **611**; 4500c. Brown snake eagle ("Brown Harrier-eagle"); 4500c. Heuglin's masked weaver; 4500c. Egyptian plover; 4500c. Swallow-tailed bee eater; 4500c. Black-faced fire-finch	13·00	13·00
MS3338	160×93 mm. 4500c. *Iolaus menas*; 4500c. *Neptis melicerta*; 4500c. *Cymothoe lucas*; 4500c. *Euphaedra francina*; 4500c. Lilac nymph; 4500c. Mocker swallowtail	13·00	13·00
MS3339	160×93 mm. 4500c. *Phymateus viridipes* (bush-hopper); 4500c. *Tomatares citrinus* (ant-lion); 4500c. *Amegilla acraensis* (digger-bee); 4500c. *Mesotopus tarandus* (stag-beetle); 4500c. *Pseudocreobotra wahlbergi* (mantis); 4500c. *Phosphorus jansoni* (longhorn beetle)	11·00	11·00
MS3340	160×93 mm. 4500c. *Phiala cunina*; 4500c. *Mazuca strigicincta*; 4500c. Steindachner's emperor moth; 4500c. *Amphicallia pactolicus*; 4500c. Verdant sphinx moth; 4500c. Oleander hawk-moth	11·00	11·00
MS3341	Four sheets, each 83×86 mm. (a) 15000c. Rufous fishing owl. (b) 15000c. Giant blue swallowtail. (c) 15000c. *Pseudocreobotra wahlbergi* (mantis nymph). (d) 15000c. African moon-moth Set of 4 sheets	26·00	27·00

612 Casting of Net

2002. Edina Bakatue Festival. Multicoloured.

3342	1000c. Type **612**	70	30
3343	2000c. Chief in palanquin	1·10	90
3344	2500c. Canoe in regatta	1·25	1·25
3345	3000c. Fishermen in festival boat	1·40	1·60
3346	4000c. Opening ritual	1·50	1·90
3347	5000c. Parade of priestesses	1·75	2·25
MS3348	160×90 mm. 4000c. As No. 3347; 4000c. As No. 3343; 4000c. As No. 3344; 4000c. As No. 3345; 4000c. As No. 3346; 4000c. Type **612**	9·50	11·00

613 Home
Economics

2002. 25th Anniv of Japan Overseas Co-operation
Volunteers in Ghana. Multicoloured.

3349	1000c. Type **613**	70	65
3350	1000c. Public health admin-istration	70	65
3351	2000c. Education in science and mathematics	1·10	1·10
3352	2500c. Computer technology	1·25	1·50
3353	3000c. Judo coaching	1·40	1·75

MS3354 172×120 mm. 4000c. As No.
3351; 4000c. As No. 3350; 4000c. As
No. 3353; 4000c. As No. 3352; 4000c.
Type **613**   8·50   9·50

Stamps from No. **MS**3354 have the white descriptive
inscriptions omitted.

614 Kofi Annan
with Pres. Kufuor at
Nobel Prize Award
Ceremony

2002. Kofi Annan (United Nations Secretary-General).
Multicoloured.

3355	1000c. Type **614**	55	30
3356	2000c. Kofi Annan holding Cita-tion and Nobel Peace Medal	90	80
3357	2500c. Kofi Annan	1·00	1·25
3358	3000c. In academic procession, Kwame Nkrumah University, Kumasi	1·25	1·75

615 Charlie
Chaplin

2003. 25th Death Anniv of Charlie Chaplin (actor and
director). Multicoloured.

MS3359 151×126 mm. 6500c. Type
615; 6500c. Wearing dark jacket;
6500c. Wearing pinstriped dungarees; 6500c. Holding Honorary
Academy Award, 1972   11·00   11·00

616 Marlene
Dietrich

2003. Tenth Death Anniv (2002) of Marlene Dietrich
(actress and singer). Sheets containing T **616** and
similar vert designs showing different portraits.

MS3360 127×178 mm. 4500c.×6
multicoloured   8·00   9·00

MS3361 76×101 mm. 15000c. Holding
cigarette   4·50   5·00

617 Popeye alongside
Canal

2003. "Popeye the Sailorman tours Amsterdam".
Multicoloured.

MS3362 173×202 mm. 4500c. Type
617; 4500c. Outside Anne Frank's
House; 4500c. At Restaurant Row;
4500c. Downtown, carrying Olive
Oyl; 4500c. At Central Station; 4500c.
With telescope, by windmill   7·50   8·50

MS3363 136×93 mm. 15000c. Eating
spinach (50×75 mm)   4·00   4·50

618 *Under the
Pagoda Tree* (Liu
Kui Ling)

2003. Chinese New Year ("Year of the Ram").
MS3364 **618** 141×115 mm. 5000c.×4
multicoloured   7·00   8·00

619 Nana Yaa
Asantewaa (Asante
warrior)

2003. Women Achievers. Multicoloured.

3365	1000c. Type **619**	55	30
3366	2000c. Justice Annie Jiagge (judge)	90	70
3367	2500c. Dr. Esther Ocloo (industrialist)	1·10	1·25
3368	3000c. Dr. Efua T. Sutherland (playwright)	1·25	1·60
3369	5000c. Rebecca Dedei Aryeetay (womens rights activist)	1·75	2·25

620 Children
holding Drawings
("tomorrow's
leaders")

2003. 60th Anniv of British Council in Ghana.
Multicoloured.

3370	1000c. Type **620**	55	30
3371	2000c. Women holding Africa-woman newspapers	90	70
3372	2500c. Singers on stage ("part-ners in culture")	1·10	1·25
3373	3000c. People reading in library ("window on the world")	1·25	1·60
3374	5000c. Footballers and coach ("leadership through sport")	1·75	2·25

621 Queen
Elizabeth II
wearing Diadem

2003. 50th Anniv of Coronation. Multicoloured.
MS3375 156×94 mm. 10000c. Type
621; 10000c. Queen wearing blue
dress and hat; 10000c. Wearing
Garter robes   10·00   11·00

MS3376 76×106 mm. 20000c. Wearing
Garter robes (different)   9·00   9·50

---

622 Ryan NYP Special *Spirit
of St. Louis* (first non-stop
solo transatlantic crossing,
1927)

2003. Centenary of Powered Flight. Multicoloured.
MS3377 185×116 mm. 7000c. Type
622; 7000c. Lockheed Vega V *Winnie
Mae* (first solo round-the-world
flight, 1933); 7000c. Heinkel He
178 (first turbo-jet aircraft, 1939);
7000c. Bell XS-1 rocket airplane (first
manned supersonic flight, 1947)   9·00   10·00

MS3378 106×76 mm. 20000c. Dr.
Robert Goddard and first liquid-
fuelled rocket   7·50   8·00

623 Romain
Maes (1935)

2003. Centenary of Tour de France Cycle Race. Designs
showing past winners. Multicoloured.

MS3379 7000c. Type **623**; 7000c.
Sylvere Maes (1936); 7000c. Roger
Lapebie (1937); 7000c. Gino Bartali
(1938)   10·00   10·00

MS3380 107×75 mm. 20000c. Henri
Pelissier (1923)   8·00   8·00

624 Cadillac Sixty Special (1941)

2003. Centenary of General Motors Cadillac.
Multicoloured.

MS3381 126×176 mm. 7000c. Type
624; 7000c. Eldorado (1953); 7000c.
Eldorado Brougham (1957); 7000c.
Eldorado Convertible (1959)   9·00   10·00

MS3382 90×125 mm. 20000c. Early
Cadillac   6·50   7·00

625 Corvette (1962)

2003. 50th Anniv of General Motors Chevrolet Corvette.
Multicoloured.

MS3383 126×152 mm. 7000c. Type
625; 7000c. Corvette Stingray (1963);
7000c. Corvette Stingray (1964);
7000c. Corvette (1968)   9·00   10·00

MS3384 126×89 mm. 20000c. Corvette
Stingray (1966)   6·50   7·00

626 *Preparation for
Christmas* (Kwame Owusu
Aduomi)

2003. Christmas. Children's Paintings. Multicoloured.

3385	2000c. Type **626**	1·25	35
3386	4000c. *Typical Christmas Present* (Thomas Kyeremateng) (vert)	1·75	2·00
3387	4500c. *Making Merry at Christ-mas* (Samuel Baffoe Maison)	1·75	2·00
3388	5000c. *Christmas is Here* (Patrick Annan)	2·00	2·25

---

627 Female
Mandrill

2004. Chinese New Year ("Year of the Monkey").
Multicoloured.

MS3389 137×172 mm. 5000c. Type
627; 5000c. Mueller's gibbon; 5000c.
Red howler monkey   4·50   5·00

628 Richie Jen

2004. Chinese Actors and Singers. Multicoloured.

MS3390 176×126 mm. 5000c. Type
628; 5000c. Richie Jen wearing
black; 5000c.Wearing gold helmet;
5000c. With moustache; 5000c. In
Elixir of Love (wearing brown hat);
5000c. Wearing red jacket   5·50   6·50

MS3391 176×126 mm. 5000c. Ray Lui
(wearing jacket and tie); 5000c. With
shaven head; 5000c. Wearing hood;
5000c. Wearing spotted shirt; 5000c.
Wearing pigtail; 5000c. As Xiang Yu
in *The Great Emperor's Concubine*   5·50   6·50

MS3392 176×126 mm. 5000c. Jiang
Wen (with head tilted left); 5000c.
With copper pot on head; 5000c.
Looking to left; 5000c. Wearing
brown jacket; 5000c. Wearing black
T-shirt; 5000c. Wearing blue T-shirt   5·50   6·50

No. **MS**3390 shows Richie Jen (singer and actor),
MS3391 Ray Lui (actor) and **MS**3392 Jiang Wen (actor).

629 Edwene Asa

2004. Kente Designs. Multicoloured.

3393	2000c. Type **629**	60	30
3394	4000c. Fatia Fata Nkruma	1·25	1·00
3395	4500c. Asam Takra	1·25	1·25
3396	5000c. Toku Akra Ntoma	1·40	1·50
3397	6000c. Sika Futuro	1·50	2·00

630 Exodus from Notsie

2004. Festival of Hogbetsotso. Multicoloured.

3398	2000c. Type **630**	55	30
3399	4000c. Misego Dance	1·10	1·00
3400	4500c. Royal stools carried in procession	1·25	1·25
3401	5000c. Man pouring libation	1·40	1·50
3402	6000c. King carried aloft	1·50	2·00

MS3403 190×145 mm. 3000c. Two
men pouring libation; 3000c. Togbe
Adeladza II, Paramount Chief of
Anlo; 3000c. Display of traditional
symbols of wealth; 3000c. Exodus
from Notsie; 3000c. Procession of
the royalty; 3000c. Royalty at Durbar;
3000c. Ewe cultural dance; 3000c.
Woman with symbols of bountiful
harvest; 3000c. Royal stools carried
in procession (different)   7·50   8·50

631 Girl Scout

2004. 25th Death Anniv of Norman Rockwell (artist).
Multicoloured.

MS3404 180×116 mm. 7000c. Type
631; 7000c. Cub scout (with tartan
neckerchief); 7000c. Boy scout;
7000c. Cub scout (with yellow and
mauve neckerchief)   7·00   8·00

MS3405 87×94 mm. 20000c. "Good
Friends"   4·75   5·50
No. MS3404 shows details from Boy Scout calendar of
1971.

632 *Portrait of Anne of
Austria as Minerva (Simon
Vouet)*

2004. 300th Anniv of St. Petersburg. "Treasures of the
Hermitage". Multicoloured.
3406   2000c. Type **632**   60   35
3407   3000c. *Lasciviousness* (Pompeo
       Girolamo Batoni)   80   55
3408   10000c. *Allegory of Faith*
       (Moretto da Brescia)   2·50   3·50
MS3409 162×142 mm. 6500c. *Allegory
of the Arts* (Bernardo Strozzi); 6500c.
Vulcan's Forge (Luca Giordano);
6500c. *Daedalus and Icarus* (detail)
(Charles Lebrun); 6500c. *The Infant
Hercules Strangling Serpents in His
Cradle* (Sir Joshua Reynolds)   7·00   8·00
MS3410 Two sheets. (a) 55×78 mm.
20000c. *Cupid Undoing Venus's Belt*
(Sir Joshua Reynolds). (b) 78×55
mm. 20000c. *Perseus Liberating
Andromeda* (Rubens). Both Imperf.
Set of 2 sheets   9·50   10·00

633 *Jacqueline in a Black
Scarf*

2004. 30th Death Anniv of Pablo Picasso (artist) (2003).
Multicoloured.
MS3411 154×154 mm. 6500c. Type
633; 6500c. *Portrait of Olga*; 6500c.
Woman in White (Sara Murphy);
6500c. *Portrait of Dora Maar*   7·50   8·00
MS3412 45×68 mm. 16000c. *Portrait of
the Artist's Sister, Lola*. Imperf   4·75   5·00

634 *Head of a Peasant
Woman*

2004. Death Centenary of James Whistler (artist) (2003).
Multicoloured.
3413   2000c. Type **634**   60   30
3414   4000c. *The Master Smith of
       Lyme Regis*   1·00   1·00
3415   5000c. *The Little Rose of Lyme
       Regis*   1·25   1·40
3416   6000c. *Arrangement in Grey: Por-
       trait of a Painter (Self-portrait)* 1·40   1·75
MS3417 128×130 mm. 7500c. *Rose
and Silver: La Princesse du pays de la
porcelaine*; 7500c. *Variations in Flesh
Colour and Green, The Balcony*; 7500c.
*Caprice in Purple and Gold: The
Golden Screen* (detail); 7500c."*Purple
and Rose: The Lange Lijzen of the
Six Marks*"   8·00   9·00
MS3418 82×102 mm. 20000c. *Harmony
in Green and Rose: The Music Room*
(horiz)   4·75   5·00

634a *Polio Vaccination and
Rotary Emblems*

2004. Centenary of Rotary International (2005) (1st issue).
Designs showing Rotary emblem. Multicoloured.
3418a 2000c. Type **634a**   75   35

3418b 4000c. *Anopheles* mosquito
       and Ghana flag ("Rotarians
       Against Malaria") (vert)   1·25   1·00
3418c 4500c. Paul Harris (founder)
       (vert)   1·25   1·40
3418d 5000c. Jonathan B. Majiya-
       gbe (President 2003–4) and
       Ghana flag (vert)   1·40   1·75
3418e 6000c. "100 Years", emblem and
       Ghana flag (vert)   1·60   2·00
See also MS3527.

635 *Jacques Rogge and
Olympic Flame*

2004. Olympic Games, Athens. Multicoloured.
3419   500c. Type **635**   30   15
3420   800c. Abedi Ayew Pele
       (footballer)   45   20
3421   7000c. Margaret Simpson   1·75   2·00
3422   10000c. Athletes in ancient
       Greek art – 384 meter
       diaulos (horiz)   2·25   2·75

636 *Fleet Admiral
Ernest King, US
Navy*

2004. 60th Anniv of D-Day Landings. Multicoloured.
MS3423 155×108 mm. 8000c. Type
636; 8000c. General William Lee,
US Airborne; 8000c. Lt Commander
John Bulkeley, US Naval Reserve;
8000c. Admiral Sir Bertram Ramsey,
Royal Navy   8·50   9·00
MS3424 105×77 mm. 20000c. Rear
Admiral Alan Kirk, US Navy (horiz)   5·00   5·50

2004. European Football Championship 2004, Portugal.
Multicoloured designs as T **407** of Dominica.
MS3425 147×85 mm. 7500c. Gerd
Müller; 7500c. Presentation of
the European Cup; 7500c. Franz
Beckenbauer; 7500c. Heysel Stadium,
Brussels   7·00   8·00
MS3426 97×85 mm. 20000c. Germany,
1972 (50×38 mm)   4·75   5·00

2004. 25th Anniv of the Pontificate of Pope John Paul II.
Sheet 163×152 mm containing horiz designs as T
408 of Dominica. Multicoloured.
MS3427 6000c. Pope in Ghana, 1980;
6000c. Pope receiving gift, Ghana,
1982; 6000c. Pope in 1991; 6000c.
Pope giving blessing, 2000; 6000c.
Pope giving blessing to children,
2001   12·00   12·00

637 *Martin Luther King*

2004. United Nations International Year of Peace. Sheet
137×77 mm containing T **637** and similar horiz
designs showing Martin Luther King. Multicoloured.
MS3428 10000c. Type **637**; 10000c.
Making speech; 10000c. Martin
Luther King (looking to left)   6·00   7·00

638 *Deng Xiaoping*

2004. Birth Centenary of Deng Xiaoping (Chinese leader).
Sheet 98×68 mm.
MS3429 20000c. multicoloured   4·00   4·50

639 *Zebra Bullhead Shark*

2004. Sharks. Multicoloured.
MS3430 137×108 mm. 7500c. Type
639; 7500c. Swellshark; 7500c. Port
Jackson shark; 7500c. Leopard shark 9·50   10·00
MS3431 95×65 mm. 20000c. California
horn shark   6·50   7·00

640 *Lion Cubs*

2004. Lions. Multicoloured.
3432   5000c. Type **640**   1·25   1·50
3433   5000c. Lions standing in water 1·25   1·50
3434   5000c. Male lion   1·25   1·50
3435   5000c. Lioness with cubs   1·25   1·50
MS3436 155×125 mm. Nos. 3432/5,
each×2   7·50   8·50

641 *Boletus badius*

2004. Mushrooms. Multicoloured.
3437   500c. Type **641**   50   15
3438   3000c. *Clitocybe nebularis* 1·10   85
3439   5000c. *Amanita muscaria*   1·60   1·75
3440   8000c. *Russula vesca*   2·25   2·75
MS3441 115×135 mm. 7500c. *Boletus
parasiticus* (vert); 7500c. *Cortinarius
armillatus* (vert); 7500c. *Gymnopilus
spectabilis* (vert); 7500c. *Cortinarius
flexipes* (vert)   12·00   12·00
MS3442 67×95 mm. 20000c. *Chloros-
plenium aeruginosum* (vert)   8·00   8·00

642 *Serval*

2004. Animals. Multicoloured.
3443   1000c. Type **642**   40   30
3444   1200c. Sable antelope   45   30
3445   2000c. Cheetah   80   90
3446   3000c. Bohor reedbuck   1·25   1·50
MS3447 115×135 mm. 7500c. White
rhinoceros; 7500c. Leopard; 7500c.
Burchell's zebra; 7500c. Red river
hog (all horiz)   12·00   12·00
MS3448 97×66 mm. 20000c. Hippo-
potamus (horiz)   8·00   8·00

643 *Oncidium desertorum*

2004. Orchids. Multicoloured.
3449   800c. Type **643**   50   20
3450   3500c. *Oncidum variegatum*   1·50   1·10
3451   4000c. *Anguloa uniflora* (vert) 1·50 1·25
3452   10000c. *Oncidium gardneri*
       (vert)   3·00   3·75
MS3453 115×135 mm. 7500c. *Vanda
rothschildiana*; 7500c. *Laelia cattleya*;
7500c. *Laelia anceps*; 7500c. *Odon-
tioda dalmar*   12·00   12·00
MS3454 65×95 mm. 20000c. *Renan-
thera bella* (vert)   8·00   8·00

643a
*Migrating to
Freedom*

2005. Akwantukese Festival of New Juaben Area.
Multicoloured.
3454a 2000c. State Emblem of Yiadom
       and Hwedie   60   30
3454b 4000c. Type **643a**   1·00   85
3454c 4500c. Crossing Suhyien River 1·10   1·10
3454d 5000c. Chief at State Durbar 1·25   1·40
3454e 6000c. Sacrificing at the cave 1·40   1·75
MS3454f 140×115 mm. 4000c. As No.
3454c.; 4000c. Palace guards; 4000c.
As No. 3454a; 4000c. As No. 3454d;
4000c. Pouring libation; 4000c.
Parading the Royal Treasury   6·50   7·50

2005. Centenary of FIFA (Federation Internationale
de Football Association). As T **413** of Dominica.
Multicoloured.
MS3455 192×95 mm. 7500c. Roberto
Di Matteo (Italy); 7500c. Marcel
Desailly (France); 7500c. Osei Kufuor
(Germany); 7500c. Eusebio (Portugal) 8·00   9·00
MS3456 107×85 mm. 20000c. Johan
Cruyff (Holland)   5·00   5·50

644 *Talgo Train, Spain*

2005. Bicentenary of Steam Locomotives (2004).
Multicoloured.
3457- 5000c.×6 Type **644**; VIA
3462   Turbotrain, Canada; Southern
       Pacific steam locomotive No.
       4449; Union Pacific City of
       Portland; Shinkansen train,
       Japan; Deltic diesel-electric
       locomotive, Britain   10·00   11·00
3463- 5000c.×6 Stanier Class steam
3468   locomotive; Central Pacific
       steam locomotive Jupiter;
       RSC3 Class 9401 locomotive,
       Robe River; BTS trains,
       Bangkok; Streamlined
       tank locomotive; ETR450
       locomotive   10·00   11·00
3469- 5000c.×6 Mogul steam
3474   locomotive; Milwaukee
       Railroad steam locomotive;
       Shinkansen train at station;
       Steam locomotive 2101,
       Reading; HST Inter-City 125
       train; Daylight steam train 10·00   11·00
3475- 8000c.×4 Baldwin locomotive;
3478   Atchison Topeka & Santa
       Fe "American" steam train;
       Baldwin locomotive No.
       44; Baldwin 3 three-spot
       locomotive   10·00   11·00
MS3479 Four sheets, each 100×70 mm.
(a) 20000c. LMS 5305 steam train.
(b) 20000c. City train in station, Chicago. (c) 20000c. Santa Fe train. (d)
20000c. Empire Builder train, USA   22·00   24·00

644a *"A royal entry"*

2005. Panafest '05. Multicoloured.
3479a 2000c. Type **644a**   1·00   50
3479b 2000c. "a symbol of hope" (vert) 1·00 50
3479c 4000c. "Let's hold hands
       together" (horiz)   1·75   1·00
3479d 4500c. Clarion call for Black
       Unity (horiz)   1·75   1·40
3479e 5000c. "bite not one another"
       (horiz)   2·00   1·75
3479f 5000c. "back to your roots"
       (vert)   2·00   1·75
3479g 6000c. "changing oneself" (vert) 2·25 2·25
Nos. 3479a and 3479c/d are pictorial designs, other
stamps are symbolic.

645 *Setra State Transport
Coach*

2005. Early Vehicles. Multicoloured.
3480   2000c. Type **645**   1·00   50
3481   4000c. Albium double-decker
       bus   1·75   1·00
3482   4500c. Bedford Mummy truck
       with trailer   1·75   1·40
3483   5000c. Mail carrier, 1925   2·00   2·75
3484   6000c. Morris truck   2·25   2·25

646 AIDS Ribbon and Map of Ghana

2006. "HIV/AIDS is Preventable TB is Curable" Campaign. Multicoloured.

3485	2000c. Type **646**	80	80
3486	2000c. Crowd with placards (horiz)	80	80
3487	2000c. AIDS victims	80	80
3488	3000c. Profile of tuberculosis patient and AIDS ribbon	1·00	1·00
3489	4000c. Hands holding map of Africa ("TOGETHER WE FIGHT THE HIV/AIDS AND TB MENACE")	1·10	1·10
3490	4500c. Crumbling bricks in man's outline ("HIV/AIDS DESTROYS THE BODY DEFENCE SYSTEM")	1·25	1·25
3491	4500c. Nurses and patients enclosed in hand	1·25	1·25
3492	5000c. Globe enclosed in heart	1·40	1·40
3493	5000c. Emaciated man carrying "TB" and "HIV/AIDS" on yoke	1·40	1·40
3494	6000c. Hands holding "HIV/AIDS PREVENT IT" and "TUBERCULOSIS CURE IT" placards	1·60	1·60

647 Elvis Presley

2006. 70th Birth Anniv of Elvis Presley (2005). Designs showing portraits. Multicoloured.

3495-3501	3500c. Type **647**×9 Background colours given: violet (×3); green; yellow and red; green; red and yellow; yellow; emerald and blue	6·50	7·00
3502-3505	8000c.×4 Elvis Presley wearing striped jacket background colours given: mauve; grey; bistre; blue	8·00	7·00
3506-3509	8000c.×4 Elvis Presley wearing black background tint given: mauve; grey; deep grey; blue	7·50	8·00

648 Carlos Arroyo, Detroit Pistons

2006. US National Basketball Association Players. Multicoloured.

3510	3500c. Detroit Pistons emblem	75	80
3511	3500c. Type **648**	75	80
3512	3500c. Carlos Boozer, Utah Jazz	75	80
3513	3500c. Utah Jazz emblem	75	80
3514	3500c. San Antonio Spurs emblem	75	80
3515	3500c. Manu Ginobili, San Antonio Spurs	75	80
3516	3500c. Atlanta Hawks emblem	75	80
3517	3500c. Al Harrington, Atlanta Hawks	75	80
3518	3500c. Los Angeles Clippers emblem	75	80
3519	3500c. Corey Maggette, Los Angeles Clippers	75	80
3520	3500c. Houston Rockets emblem	75	80
3521	3500c. David Wesley, Houston Rockets	75	80

649 Emblem of Ghana Atomic Energy Commission (40th anniv)

2006. International Year of Physics (2005). Multicoloured.

3522	2000c. Type **649**	65	30
3523	4000c. Ghana Research Reactor	1·00	75
3524	4500c. Albert Einstein (physicist) (50th death anniv)	1·25	1·10
3525	5000c. Prof. Francis K. Allotey (Ghanaian physicist)	1·25	1·25
3526	6000c. Electricity experiment in a physics laboratory	1·40	1·60

650 Women getting Water from Standpipe

2006. Centenary of Rotary International (2005) (2nd issue). Multicoloured.

MS3527	150×88 mm. 10000c.×3 Type **650**; 10000c. Building low-cost shelter; 10000c. Girl guides planting ("Preserve Planet Earth Program")	8·00	9·00

651 Pope John Paul II ("Self Help through Rotary Village Corps")

2006. Pope John Paul II Commemoration.

3528	**651** 12000c. multicoloured	3·75	3·75

2006. 75th Anniv of First World Cup Football Championship, Uruguay (2005). As T **420** of Dominica showing scenes from World Cup, France, 1938. Multicoloured.

3529	8000c. Italian team, 1938	1·40	1·50
3530	8000c. Final between Italy and Hungary	1·40	1·50
3531	8000c. Stade Olympique de Colombes	1·40	1·50
3532	8000c. Silvio Piola (Italy)	1·40	1·50
MS3533	116×90 mm. 20000c. Group photograph of winning Italian team, 1938	3·75	5·00

652 Jules Verne

2006. Death Centenary of Jules Verne (writer) (2005). Multicoloured.

3534	8000c. Type **652**	2·00	2·00
3535	8000c. Hot-air balloon and book illustration from *Five Weeks in a Balloon*	2·00	2·00
3536	8000c. Montgolfier balloon over Paris, 1783	2·00	2·00
3537	8000c. Modern hot air balloon	2·00	2·00
MS3538	100×70 mm. 20000c. Airship LZ-129 *Hindenburg* (1937)	6·00	6·00

653 Friedrich von Schiller

2006. Death Bicentenary (2005) of Friedrich von Schiller (poet and dramatist). Multicoloured.

3539	11000c. Type **653**	2·50	2·75
3540	11000c. Friedrich von Schiller and birthplace, Marbach	2·50	2·75
3541	11000c. Johannes Brahms (composer)	2·50	2·75
MS3542	60×53 mm. 20000c. Friedrich von Schiller and Johannes Brahms. Imperf	5·50	6·00

2006. Bicentenary of the Battle of Trafalgar (2005). As T **423** of Dominica. Multicoloured.

3543	2000c. Sir John Jervis, first Earl of St. Vincent and First Lord of the Admiralty, 1801–06 (vert)	1·00	45
3544	3000c. Ship with broken mast ("Chase and Race in the Summer of 1805") (vert)	1·25	1·00
3545	5000c. HMS *Goliath* firing on *Guerrier*	2·50	2·75

3546	10000c. Death of Admiral Lord Nelson	4·00	5·50
MS3547	100×71 mm. 20000c. Nelson's flagships HMS *Agamemnon*, *Vanguard*, *Elephant* and *Captain*	11·00	10·00

654 Ghana Black Stars Team

2006. World Cup Football Championship, Germany. Ghana's Qualification for World Cup. Multicoloured.

3548	2000c. Stephen Appiah in action (vert)	50	50
3549	2000c. Type **654**	50	50
3550	4000c. Exchanging of pennants	95	95
3551	4000c. Five victorious Ghana players ("THE JOY OF SUCCESS")	95	95
3552-3559	4000c.×8 Asamoah Gyan; Sammy Adjei; Matthew Amoah; John Mensah; Emmanuel Pappoe; Mark Daniel Edusei; Abubakari Yakubu; Godwin Attram (all 42×28 mm)	6·00	6·50
3560-3567	4000c.×8 Stephen Appiah; Issah Ahmed; John Paintsil; Laryea Kingston; Michael Essien; Sule Ali Muntari; Joe Tex Frimpong; Ratomir Dujkovic (Ghana coach) (all 42×28 mm)	6·00	6·50
3568	4500c. Franz Beckenbauer (Germany) and World Cup Stadium, Hanover	1·00	1·10
3569	4500c. Michael Essien in action	1·00	1·10
3570	5000c. Ghana team ("THE VICTORY SQUAD")	1·10	1·25
3571	5000c. Ghana v. Burkina Faso World Cup qualifying match	1·10	1·25
3572	6000c. Ghana v. South Africa World Cup qualifying match	1·25	1·40
3573	6000c. Team parading with Ghana flag T-shirts	1·25	1·40

2006. Various stamps surch. (a) Nos. 1944 and 1947/9 surch **2000c.**

3574	2000c. on 50c. Type **502**	15·00	5·00
3575	2000c. on 200c. Diana monkey on branch facing left	15·00	5·00
3576	2000c. on 500c. Diana monkey on branch facing right	15·00	5·00
3577	2000c. on 800c. Head of Diana monkey	15·00	5·00

(b) Nos. 2044/9 surch **3000c.**

3578	3000c. on 50c. Type **507**	1·00	80
3579	3000c. on 100c. Red-flanked duiker	1·00	80
3580	3000c. on 200c. Yellow-backed duiker	1·00	80
3581	3000c. on 400c. Ogilby's duiker	1·00	80
3582	3000c. on 600c. Bay duiker	1·00	80
3583	3000c. on 800c. Jentink's duiker	1·00	80

(c) Nos. 2066/8 surch **4000c.**

3584	4000c. on 50c. Type **509**	1·50	1·00
3585	4000c. on 200c. Worker with children	1·50	1·00
3586	4000c. on 600c. Workers erecting tents	1·50	1·00

(d) Nos. 2070/7 (showing different fertility dolls, background colours given) surch **5000c.**

3587	5000c. on 50c. multicoloured (green)	2·00	1·50
3588	5000c. on 100c. multicoloured (yellow)	2·00	1·50
3589	5000c. on 150c. multicoloured (blue)	2·00	1·50
3590	5000c. on 200c. multicoloured (claret)	2·00	1·50
3591	5000c. on 400c. multicoloured (brown)	2·00	1·50
3592	5000c. on 600c. multicoloured (yellow)	2·00	1·50
3593	5000c. on 800c. multicoloured (yellow)	2·00	1·50
3594	5000c. on 1000c. multicoloured (blue)	2·00	1·50

(e) Nos. 2085/7 surch as T **659**.

3595	4500c. on 100c. Type **512**	1·75	1·25
3596	4500c. on 400c. Communications equipment	1·75	1·25
3597	4500c. on 1000c. Airliner taking off	1·75	1·25

(f) Nos. 2088/90 surch **6000c.**

3598	6000c. on 100c. Type **512**	2·50	2·00
3599	6000c. on 400c. Communications equipment	2·50	2·00
3600	6000c. on 1000c. Airliner taking off	2·50	2·00

(g) Nos. 2183/7 surch **2000c.**

3601	2000c. on 200c. Type **521**	75	35

3602	2000c. on 300c. Fishermen with fish traps	75	35
3603	2000c. on 400c. Ox-drawn plough	75	35
3604	2000c. on 600c. Harvesting bananas	75	35
3605	2000c. on 800c. Planting saplings	75	35

662 Queen Elizabeth II

2007. 80th Birthday (2006) of Queen Elizabeth II. Multicoloured.

3606	6000c. Type **662**	2·00	2·00
3607	6000c. Wearing purple hat	2·00	2·00
3608	6000c. Wearing pale green	2·00	2·00
3609	6000c. Wearing yellow and pale green	2·00	2·00
MS3610	120×120 mm. 25000c. Wearing tiara	8·00	8·50

663 Soyuz 19

2007. Space Anniversaries. Multicoloured. (a) 30th Anniv (2005) of Apollo-Soyuz Test Project.

MS3611	100×150 mm. 6500c.×6 Type **663**; Apollo/Soyuz emblem; Tom Stafford (Apollo Commander) and Apollo-Soyuz linkup; Aleksei Leonov (Soyuz Commander); Deke Slayton (astronaut); Vance Brand (astronaut) and Valeri Kubasov (flight engineer)	12·00	12·00

(b) 20th Anniv (2006) of Giotto Comet Probe

MS3612	150×100 mm. 6500c.×6 *Giotto* Comet Probe in space; *Giotto* and Halley's Comet above Earth's surface; *Giotto* on ground; *Giotto* and Halley's Comet; *Giotto* and diagram of structure; *Giotto* (all vert)	12·00	12·00

(c) 20th Anniv of Luna 9

MS3613	150×100 mm. 10000c.×4 Luna 9 soft lander approaching Moon; Luna 9 soft lander in space; Luna 9 flight apparatus and Moon; Luna 9 (all vert)	12·00	12·00
MS3614	Three sheets, each 100×70 mm. (a) 20000c. Handshake in space, Apollo-Soyuz, 1975. (b) 20000c. Apollo 11 astronaut Buzz Aldrin, 1969 (vert). (c) 20000c. Viking 1 on Mars, 1976	20·00	20·00

The stamps within **MS**3611 form a composite background design showing Apollo-Soyuz crew and emblem. The two left-hand stamps within **MS**3613 have a composite background of the Moon.

664 Marilyn Monroe

2007. 80th Birth Anniv of Marilyn Monroe (actress). Multicoloured.

3615	9000c. Type **664**	1·90	2·00
3616	9000c. Wearing dressing gown	1·90	2·00
3617	9000c. Wearing purple dress with single crossover strap	1·90	2·00
3618	9000c. Wearing red jacket with silver collar	1·90	2·00
MS3619	100×70 mm. 20000c. With eyes closed and head on pillow	7·00	7·50

665 Scout saluting

2007. Centenary of World Scouting. Multicoloured.
3620	12000c. Type **665**		3·00	3·25
3621	12000c. Scout blowing trumpet		3·00	3·25
3622	12000c. Scout carrying sick man		3·00	3·25
MS3623 80×110 mm. 20000c. Scout saluting (horiz)			9·00	9·50

666 50 Logo

2007. 50th Anniv of Independence (1st issue).
3624	**666**	4000c. multicoloured	1·25	1·00

See also Nos. 3625/30, 3631/41 and 3642/52.

667 Sika ne Barima

2007. 50th Anniv of Independence (2nd issue). Kente Designs. Multicoloured.
3625	4000c. Type **667**		1·10	95
3626	7300c. Edwene Si So		1·75	2·00
3627	7500c. Dakoro Yesere		1·75	2·00
3628	9000c. Nkatoa Sa		2·25	2·50
3629	9000c. Agyenegyne Nsu		2·25	2·50
3630	10000c. Edwene Asa		2·50	2·75

668 Cocoa Beverages and Spread

2007. 50th Anniv of Independence (3rd issue). Cocoa of Ghana. Multicoloured.
3631	4000c. Type **668**		1·25	95
3632	6000c. Finished cocoa products		1·50	1·75
3633	6000c. Cocoa pods (wrongly inscr 'Cocoa Beverages & Spread')		1·50	1·75
3634	6000c. Assorted chocolates		1·50	1·75
3635	6000c. Worker in cocoa processing plant		1·50	1·75
3636	6000c. Cocoa pebbles		1·50	1·75
3637	6000c. Packaging of cocoa products		1·50	1·75
3638	7300c. As No. 3636		1·75	2·00
3639	7500c. As No. 3634		1·75	2·00
3640	9000c. As No. 3635		2·25	2·50
3641	10000c. As No. 3632		2·50	2·75

669 The Bamboo Groves

2007. 50th Anniv of Independence (4th issue). Aburi Botanical Gardens. Multicoloured.
3642	4000c. Type **669**		1·25	95
3643	6000c. Royal Palm Walkway		1·50	1·75
3644	6000c. School of Horticulture		1·50	1·75
3645	6000c. The Silk Cotton Tree (oldest tree in gardens)		1·50	1·75
3646	6000c. The Famous Ficus Tree		1·50	1·75
3647	6000c. As Type **669**		1·50	1·75
3648	6000c. The Sanatorium		1·50	1·75
3649	7300c. As No. 3644		1·75	2·00
3650	7500c. As No. 3645 but vert		1·75	2·00
3651	9000c. As No. 3643		2·25	2·50
3652	10000c. As No. 3646		2·50	2·75

670 Chartreux

2007. Cats. Multicoloured.
3653	6000c. Type **670**		1·50	1·50

3654	7000c. Blue mitted Ragdoll		1·75	2·00
3655	8000c. Blue lynx point Birman (horiz)		2·25	2·50
3656	9000c. Norwegian Forest Cat		2·25	2·50
MS3657 72×100 mm. 20000c. Cinnamon point Siamese			8·50	9·00

671 American Bulldog

2007. Dogs. Multicoloured.
3658	7500c. Type **671**		1·75	2·00
3659	7500c. Old English Sheepdog		1·75	2·00
3660	7500c. Chinese Shar-pei		1·75	2·00
3661	7500c. Boston Terrier		1·75	2·00

No. **MS**3662 is left for a miniature sheet not yet received.

672 Red-billed Hornbill

2007. Birds of Africa. Multicoloured.
MS3663 133×110 mm. 7500c.×4 Type **672**; Bearded barbet; Hoopoe; Pygmy kingfisher ... 9·50 10·00
MS3664 70×101 mm. 20000c. Grey crowned-crane (vert) ... 8·50 9·00
The stamps within **MS**3663 form a composite background design.

673 *Epipactis atrorubens*

2007. Orchids. Multicoloured.
3665	7500c. Type **673**		1·75	2·00
3666	7500c. *Galeandra bicarinata*		1·75	2·00
3667	7500c. *Platanthera tipuloides*		1·75	2·00
3668	7500c. *Platanthera ciliaris*		1·75	2·00
MS3669 96×66 mm. 20000c. *Spathoglottis plicata*			8·00	8·50

674 Philip Gbeho (composer of national anthem)

2007. 50th Anniv of Independence (5th issue). Important Personalities. Multicoloured.
3670	4000c. Type **674**		90	90
3671	4000c. Sir Arko Korsah (first Ghanaian Chief Justice, 1957)		90	90
3672	4000c. Amon Kotei (designer of national coat of arms)		90	90
3673	4500c. Hon. F. K. Buah (educationist and historian)		95	95
3674	6000c. Prof. Albert Abu Boahene (historian and politician)		1·25	1·25
3675	7300c. Leticia Obeng (aquatic biologist and international civil servant)		1·60	1·60
3676	7500c. His Eminence Peter Cardinal Appiah Turkson (first Ghanaian cardinal)		1·60	1·60
3677	9000c. Susanna Alhassan (first woman minister, 1960)		1·90	1·90

675 War Dress of Northern Ghana

2007. 50th Anniv of Independence (6th issue). Costumes. Multicoloured.
3678	4000c. Type **675**		90	80
3679	7300c. Woman in traditional wear		1·75	2·00
3680	7500c. Traditional mourning wear		1·75	2·00
3681	9000c. Traditional smock (batakari)		2·00	2·50
3682	10000c. Costume of the Wulomo		2·25	2·75

676 Gold Ore

2007. 50th Anniv of Independence (7th issue). Minerals of Ghana. Multicoloured.
3683	4000c. Type **676**		1·75	1·00
3684	7300c. Melting gold ore		3·00	2·50
3685	7500c. Woman holding gold bar		3·00	2·50
3686	9000c. Entrance of Obuasi Gold Mines (horiz)		4·00	3·75
3687	10000c. Gold plated chair		4·00	3·75

677 SIC Emblem

2007. SIC State Insurance. Multicoloured.
3688	40Gp. Type **677**		80	80
3689	73Gp. The Pioneering Executive		1·25	1·25
3690	75Gp. New office building		1·60	1·60
3691	90Gp. Boy ('Focused On You')		1·90	2·25
3692	GHc1 3X CIMG award (vert)		2·00	2·50

678 GCB Emblems

2007. GCB Commercial Bank. Multicoloured.
3693	40Gp. Type **678**		80	80
3694	73Gp. Palm-nut vulture and world map ('Fast int money transfer')		1·50	1·25
3695	75Gp. GCB Tower (vert)		1·60	1·60
3696	90Gp. Palm-nut vulture and emblems ('GCB Xpress money transfer') (vert)		2·25	2·50

679 ADB Emblem

2007. Agricultural Development Bank. Multicoloured.
3697	40Gp. Type **679**		80	80
3698	75Gp. Man working abroad and woman at home ('Home link account') (vert)		1·60	1·60
3699	90Gp. Young farmers and produce ('Young farmers programme') (vert)		1·90	2·00
3700	GHc1 Farmer with vehicle ('Gold Drive motor loan') (vert)		2·00	2·50

680 Aircraft on Ground

2007. Antrak Air. Multicoloured.
3701	40Gp. Type **680**		1·50	1·00
3702	73Gp. Aircraft in flight		2·50	2·00

Values in Ghana pesewas.

681 Independence Arch

2007. 50th Anniv of Independence (12th issue). Monuments. Multicoloured.
3703	20Gp. Type **681**		40	40

3704	40Gp. Independence Square		80	80
3705	73Gp. Supreme Court Building		1·25	1·40
3706	75Gp. National Theatre		1·25	1·40
3707	90Gp. International Conference Centre		1·90	2·25

682 Dr. Kwame Nkrumah, 1957–66

2007. 50th Anniv of Independence (13th issue). Heads of State of the Republic of Ghana. Multicoloured.
3708	60Gp. Type **682**		1·25	1·25
3709	60Gp. Lt. General J. A. Ankrah, 1966–7		1·25	1·25
3710	60Gp. General A. A. Afrifa, 1967–72		1·25	1·25
3711	60Gp. Dr. Kofi Abrefa Busia, 1969–72		1·25	1·25
3712	60Gp. General I. K. Acheampong, 1972–8		1·25	1·25
3713	60Gp. Lt. General W. A. Akuffo, 1978–9		1·25	1·25
3714	60Gp. Dr. Hilla Limann, 1979–81		1·25	1·25
3715	60Gp. Flt Lt. J. J. Rawlings, 1981–2000		1·25	1·25
3716	60Gp. President J. A. Kufuor, 2001–		1·25	1·25
MS3717 110×80 mm. GHc1 Swearing in with State Sword of Dr. Kwame Nkrumah (1957) and Pres. Kufuor (2001)			2·00	2·00

683 Pope Benedict XVI

2007. 80th Birthday of Pope Benedict XVI.
3718	**683**	4000c. multicoloured	1·50	1·25

684 Kenyans in Traditional Dress

2007. 24th UPU Congress, Nairobi. Multicoloured.
3719	40Gp. Type **684**		1·00	80
3720	73Gp. Akwaaba and Karibu traditional dress (vert)		1·25	1·40
3721	75Gp. UPU emblem in opened box		1·25	1·40
3722	90Gp. UPU emblem, clasped hands and map of Africa (vert)		1·90	2·00
MS3723 192×132 mm. GHc3×3 UPU emblem (left section) and map segments; UPU emblem (right section) and map segments; Map showing Kenya and Nairobi			6·00	6·00

685 Queen Elizabeth II

2008. Diamond Wedding of Queen Elizabeth II and Prince Philip (2007). Multicoloured.
3724	60Gp. Type **685** (inscr in emerald)		1·75	1·75
3725	60Gp. Queen Elizabeth and Prince Philip in Garter robes (inscr in emerald)		1·75	1·75
3726	60Gp. As No. 3720 (inscr in orange)		1·75	1·75
3727	60Gp. Type **684** (inscr in orange)		1·75	1·75
3728	60Gp. Type **684** (inscr in blue)		1·75	1·75
3729	60Gp. As No. 3720 (inscr in blue)		1·75	1·75

686 Lotus (*Lotus and Mandarin Ducks*)

2008. 50th Death Anniv of Qi Baishi (2007). Multicoloured.
MS3730 90Gp.×4 Type **686**; Boats on river (*River Landcape with Boats*); Mandarin ducks (*Lotus and Mandarin Ducks*); Trees and river (*River Land-scape with Boats*) ... 7·50 8·50
MS3731 60×125 mm. GHc3 *Peony in a Dragon Vase* (30×80 mm) ... 5·00 5·50

686a "Love for all, hatred for none"

2008. Khilafat Ahmadiyya Centenary. Multicoloured.
3731a	40Gp. Type **686a**	1·00	80
3731b	73Gp. Ti Ahmadiyya Senior High School, Kumasi	1·25	1·40
3731c	90Gp. Wheat grown in Ghana	1·90	2·00
3731d	GHc1 Ahmadiyya Mushim Hospital, Daboase	2·00	2·00

687 Boxing

2008. Olympic Games, Beijing. Multicoloured.
3732	40Gp. Type **687**	90	1·00
3733	40Gp. Relay	90	1·00
3734	40Gp. Athletics	90	1·00
3735	40Gp. Football	90	1·00

688 Pres. George Bush

2008. Visit of US President George Bush to Ghana. Sheet 127×89 mm containing T **688** and similar vert design. Multicoloured.
MS3736 GHc1.25 Type **688**; GHc1.25 Pres. John Agyekum Kufuor of Ghana ... 2·75 3·25
The stamps and margins of No. **MS**3736 form a composite design showing Presidents Bush and Kufuor at a joint press conference at Osu Castle, Accra, Ghana on 20 February 2008.

689a

2008. Various earlier issues surch by Buck Press in new currency as T **689a** and similar
3736a	10Gp. on 20c. Type **442** (No. 1275) (16.6.10)	4·00	2·00
3736b	GHc0.20 on 800c. *Cyrestis Camillus* (Butterfly) (No. 2158a) (1.2.09)	2·00	1·00
3736c	GHc0.30 on 18c Preaching the Koran (No. 1147) (13.5.10)	—	—
3736d	GHc0.75 on 1100c. Kente cloth (No. 2159)	2·00	1·00
3736e	GHc0.75 on 2500c. on 800c. *Cyrestis Camillus* (butterfly)	—	—
3736f	GHc1 on 70p. Type **402** (No. 1054) (4.12.08)	4·00	2·00
3736h	GHc1 on 5c. Type **435** (No. 1244)	4·00	2·00
3736i	GHc1 on 20c. Type **442** (No. 1275) (10.11.09)	4·00	2·00
3736j	GHc1 on 60c. Christ Child (No. 1276) (16.9.09)		
3736k	GHc1 on 80c. Virgin and Child with Star (No. 1277)		
3736l	GHc1 on 250c. Agwasen woman (No. 1244) (10.11.09)	2·00	1·00
3736m	GHc1.20 on 550c. + 50c. Ghana football team (No. 2515) (12.11.09)		

3736n	GHc1.20 on 800c. + 50c. Abu Iddnsu (No. 2516) (27.10.09)	—	—
3736o	GHc1.20 on 800c. Bananas (No. 2158b) (2.12.09)	4·00	2·00
3736p	GHc1.20 on 1100c. Milking cows (No. 3251) (29.1.10)	—	—
3736q	GHc1.30 on 60c. Larabanya mosque (No. 1641b) (24.8.09)	—	—
3736s	GHc1.30 on 1800c. Students in pharmacy department (No. 3252) (11.11.09)	—	—

689 Medical Block, Korle Bu Teaching Hospital

2009. Korle Bu Teaching Hospital, Accra. Multicoloured.
3737	GHc1 Type **689**	2·25	2·25
3738	GHc1.10 Cardiothoracic Centre	2·25	2·50
3739	GHc1.10 The New Adminstration Block	2·25	2·50
3740	GHc1.20 Professor Frimpong Boateng (first heart surgeon) (vert)	2·25	2·50

690 Tomatoes

2009. Vegetables of Ghana. Multicoloured.
3741	GHc1 Type **690**	2·25	2·25
3742	GHc1.20 Tomatoes and garden eggs	2·50	2·50
3743	GHc1.30 Garden eggs (scarlet eggplant *Solanum aethiopicum*)	2·50	2·50

691 Aggrey Fynn

2009. Footballers of the 1960s. Multicoloured.
3744	GHc1 Type **691**	2·00	2·00
3745	GHc1 Baba Yara	2·00	2·00
3746	GHc1 Edward Acquah	2·00	2·00
3747	GHc1 Nana Gyamfi II	2·00	2·00
3748	GHc1 Robert Mensah (goalkeeper)	2·00	2·00

692 Administration Block, Tweneboa School

2009. Tweneboa Kodua School, Abuakwa. Multicoloured.
3749	GHc1 Type **692**	2·00	2·00
3750	GHc1.10 Girls Dormitory	2·10	2·10
3751	GHc1.20 Students at ICT Centre	2·25	2·25
3752	GHc1.30 Students playing volleyball	2·50	2·50

693 Arms of Ghana

2009. Personalised Stamps.
3753	**693**	GHc1 blackish-brown and lavender	2·00	2·00

694 Red Peony

2009. China 2009 World Stamp Exhibition, Luoyang. Peonies.
3754	**694**	GHc1 multicoloured	2·00	2·00

694a "At Afro Asian Solidarity Conference"

2009. Birth Centenary of Dr. Kwame Nkrumah. Multicoloured.
3755	GHc1 Type **694a**	2·25	2·25
3756	GHc1.10 "Projector of African Unity" (*horiz*)	2·25	2·25
3757	GHc1.20 "At Balmoral Castle"	2·50	2·50
3758	GHc1.30 "Signing the Charter of African Unity" (Addis Ababa)	2·50	2·50
3759	GHc1.40 With Chairman Mao	2·75	2·75
MS3760	122 × 105 mm. Nos. 3755/9	11·50	11·50

694b Signing of Akosombo Dam Agreement

2009. Dr. Kwame Nkrumah and Volta River Authority. Multicoloured.
MS3761 75Gp.×8 Type **694b**; Switching on power after commissioning; Akosombo Dam; Tema Thermal power plant; Switching on Akosombo Generating Station; Takoradi Thermal Station; Staff working on a retrofit; Kpong Dam ... 10·00 10·00

694c Symbols of Friendship and Unity

2010. 50 Years of Friendly Relations with China. Multicoloured.
3762	GHc1 Type **694c**	2·25	2·25
3763	GHc1 National Theatre	2·25	2·25
3764	GHc1.30 Dr. Nkrumah and Premier Zhou En Lai	2·50	2·50
3765	GHc1.40 The Great Wall of China	2·75	2·75

695 Prince William

2011. Royal Wedding. Multicoloured.
MS3766 150×100 mm. GHc3.50 Type **695**×2; GHc3.50 Miss Catherine Middleton×2 ... 12·00 12·00
MS3767 100×141 mm. GHc3.50 Prince William and Miss Catherine Middleton×4 ... 12·00 12·00
MS3768 75×100 mm. GHc12 Engagement photograph of Prince William and Miss Catherine Middleton ... 10·50 10·50
MS3769 101×70 mm. GHc12 As stamp within **MS**3767 ... 10·50 10·50

695a "Michael Essien shows Sportsmanship"

2011. Football World Cup (1st series). "The Black Stars". Multicoloured.
3770	GHc1 Type **695a**	2·25	2·00
3771	GHc1 The Black Stars team	2·25	2·00
3772	GHc1.20 Richard Kingson (goalkeeper)	2·25	2·50
3773	GHc1.40 Asamoah Gyan	2·75	2·75
MS3774 50Gp. x 8 Stephan Appiah; Agyeman Badu; Supporters; Sulley Muntari; Samuel Inkoom; Anthony Annan; Kwadwo Asamoah; Milovan Rajevac ... 7·25 7·25

695b Dominic Adiyiah

2011. Football World Cup (2nd series). "The Black Satellites". Multicoloured.
3775	GHc1 Type **695b**	2·25	2·00
3776	GHc1 Andre Dede Ayew	2·25	2·00
3777	GHc1.20 Coach Sellas Tetteh with Brazilian coach	2·25	2·50
3778	GHc1.40 Players celebrating	2·75	2·75
MS3779 50Gp. x 8 Dominic Adiyiah and Ransford Osei; Dominic Adiyiah; Before penalty shoot-out; "Kangaroo dance"; Daniel Adjei (goalkeeper); "Coach Tetteh our greatest hero"; Team with Cup; "Oh yes, the cup goes to Ghana" ... 7·25 7·25

695c Pawpaw

2012. Fruit. Multicoloured.
3780	10Gp. Type **695c**	10	10
3781	25Gp. Pineapple	25	30
3782	27Gp. Orange	25	30
3783	GHc1 Shallot plants	1·00	1·00
3784	GHc1.10 Tomatoes	1·00	1·00
3785	GHc1.20 Shallots	1·10	1·25
3786	GHc1.30 Carrots	1·25	1·40
3787	GHc1.40 Mangoes	1·25	1·40
3788	GHc3 Avocados	2·75	3·00
3789	GHc5 Coconuts	4·50	4·75

696 *Acraea hypoleuca*

2012. Unique Butterflies of Africa. Multicoloured.
MS3790 100×160 mm. GHc2×6 Type **696**; *Desmolycaena mazoensis*; *Aphnaeus erikssoni*; *Lycaena gigantea*; *Mimacraea marshalli*; *Iolaus alienus* ... 9·75 9·75
MS3791 100×70 mm. GHC3 *Durbania pallida* (female); GHC3 *Durbania pallida* (male) ... 4·75 4·75

697 Cape Parrot (*Poicephalus robustus*)

2012. Parrots of Africa. Multicoloured.
MS3792 75×110 mm. GHc5 Senegal parrot (*Poicephalus senegalus*) ... 2·50 2·50
MS3973 180×100 mm. GHc2×6 Type **697**; Red-bellied parrot (*Poicephalus rufiventris*); Meyer's parrot (*Poicephalus meyeri*); Ruppell's parrot (*Poicephalus rueppellii*); African grey parrot (*Psittacus erithacus*); Brown-headed parrot (*Poicephalus cryptoxanthus*) ... 9·75 9·75

698 Dollar Bill recovered from RMS *Titanic*

2012. Centenary of the Sinking of RMS *Titanic*. Multicoloured.
MS3794 180×120 mm. GHc2×4 Type **698**; Captain Edward J. Smith; RMS *Titanic*; Spoons recovered from RMS *Titanic* ... 6·50 6·50
MS3795 100×100 mm. GHc5 RMS *Titanic* (horiz) ... 4·00 4·00

699 Hoopoe (*Upupa epops*)

2012. Birds of Africa. Multicoloured.
MS3796 141×100 mm. GHc2×4 Type
699; Long-tailed glossy starling
(*Lamprotornis caudatus*); Northern
carmine bee-eater (*Merops rubicus*);
Double-collared sunbird (*Cinnyris
chalybeus*)   6·50   6·50
MS3797 100×71 mm. GHc5 Ostrich
(*Struthio camelus*) (38×50 mm)   4·00   4·00

700 *Emancipation of
the Negroes* (Thomas
Nast) (from *Harper's
Weekly*)

2012. 150th Anniv of Pres. Lincoln's Emancipation
Proclamation. Multicoloured.
MS3798 145×90 mm. GHc2×4 Type
700; Abraham Lincoln standing
(photo by Thomas Le Mere, 1863);
Watercolour of a man reading
newspaper headline "Emancipation
Proclamation" (Henry L. Stephens),
1863; First Reading of the Emancipa-
tion Proclamation of President Lincoln
(Francis B. Carpenter), 1864   6·50   6·50
MS3799 70×110 mm. GHc3 Abraham
Lincoln sitting (photo by Alexander
Gardner), 1861; GHc3 Extract from
Proclamation Declaration (both
horiz)   4·75   4·75

701 LZ 129 *Hindenburg*

2012. 75th Anniv of the *Hindenburg* Disaster.
Multicoloured.
MS3800 140×200 mm. GHc2 Type
701×4   6·50   6·50
MS3801 70×101 mm. GHc5 LZ 129
Hindenburg in searchlights (30×50
mm)   4·00   4·00

702 Female Bohor
Reedbucks

2012. Endangered Species. Bohor Reedbuck (*Redunca
redunca*). Multicoloured.
3802   GHc1.50 Type **702**   1·25   1·25
3803   GHc1.50 Two young males   1·25   1·25
3804   GHc1.50 Male and female   1·25   1·25
3805   GHc1.50 Male feeding at
        water's edge   1·25   1·25
MS3806 112×164 mm. Nos. 3802/5,
        each ×2   9·00   9·00

703 Basketball

2012. Olympic Games, London. Multicoloured.
MS3807 GHc1.50 Type **703**   1·25   1·25
MS3808 GHc1.50 Table tennis   1·25   1·25
MS3809 GHc1.50 Synchronized
        swimming   1·25   1·25
MS3810 GHc1.50 Cycling   1·25   1·25

704 Mandrill
(*Mandrillus sphinx*)

2012. Primates. Multicoloured.
MS3811 GHc2×5 Type **704**; Chimpanzee (*Pan troglodytes*); Gorilla
(*Gorilla gorilla*); Orangutan (*Pongo
pygmaeus*); Vervet (*Chlorocebus
pygerythrus*)   4·75   4·75

705 Pres. Barack Obama

2012. Visit of US Pres. Barack Obama to Pres. John Atta-
Mills, Osu Castle, Accra, 11 July 2009. Multicoloured.
MS3812 GHc3 Type **705**; GHc3 Pres.
Atta-Mills of Ghana   2·75   2·75

POSTAGE DUE STAMPS

1958. Postage Due stamps of Gold Coast optd **GHANA**
and bar.
D9   **D1**   1d. black   10   30
D10   **D1**   2d. black   10   30
D11   **D1**   3d. black   10   30
D12   **D1**   6d. black   15   65
D13   **D1**   1s. black   20   1·50

D3

1958
D14   **D3**   1d. red   10   30
D15   **D3**   2d. green   10   30
D16   **D3**   3d. orange   10   30
D17   **D3**   6d. blue   10   50
D18   **D3**   1s. violet   15   2·00

1965. Surch Ghana New Currency 19th July. 1965. and
value.
D19   1p. on 1d.   10   75
D20   2p. on 2d.   10   2·00
D21   3p. on 3d.   10   2·00
D22   6p. on 6d.   10   3·25
D23   12p. on 1s.   15   3·50

1968. Nos. D20/2 additionally surch.
D24   1½n.p. on 2p. on 2d.   6·50   4·25
D25   2½n.p. on 3p. on 3d.   1·25   5·00
D26   5n.p. on 6p. on 6d.   2·75

1970. Inscr in new currency.
D27   1n.p. red   2·25   6·50
D28   1½n.p. green   2·75   7·50
D29   2½n.p. orange   3·25   9·00
D30   5n.p. blue   3·50   9·00
D31   10n.p. violet   6·00   11·00

1980. Currency described as "p".
D32   2p. orange   1·00   4·25
D33   3p. brown   1·00   4·25

Pt. 1

GIBRALTAR

A British colony at the W. entrance to the Mediterranean.

1886. 12 pence = 1 shilling; 20 shillings = 1 pound.
1971. 100 (new) pence = 1 pound.

1886. Stamps of Bermuda (Queen Victoria) optd
GIBRALTAR.
1   **9**   ½d. green   21·00   11·00
2   **9**   1d. red   85·00   5·50
3   **9**   2d. purple   £140   85·00
4   **9**   2½d. blue   £200   3·25
5   **9**   4d. orange   £190   £110
6   **9**   6d. lilac   £300   £225
7   **9**   1s. brown   £450   £375

2

1886. Various frames.
39   **2**   ½d. green   14·00   1·75
40   **2**   1d. red   14·00   50
10   **2**   2d. purple   30·00   32·00
42   **2**   2½d. blue   42·00   50
12   **2**   4d. orange   85·00   85·00
13   **2**   6d. lilac   £140   £140
14   **2**   1s. brown   £250   £200

1889. Surch with new value in **CENTIMOS**.
15   5c. on ½d. green   9·50   32·00
16   10c. on 1d. red   14·00   18·00
17   25c. on 2d. purple   4·75   11·00
18   25c. on 2½d. blue   28·00   2·25
19   40c. on 4d. orange   55·00   75·00
20   50c. on 6d. lilac   55·00   80·00
21   75c. on 1s. brown   55·00   65·00

7

1889
22   **7**   5c. green   6·00   80
23   **7**   10c. red   4·50   50
24   **7**   20c. green and brown 45·00   24·00
25   **7**   20c. green   15·00   £100
26   **7**   25c. blue   25·00   70
27   **7**   40c. orange   3·75   4·50
28   **7**   50c. lilac   3·25   2·00
29   **7**   75c. green   32·00   32·00
30   **7**   1p. brown   75·00   20·00
31   **7**   1p. brown and blue   4·75   8·50
32   **7**   2p. black and red   11·00   30·00
33   **7**   5p. grey   42·00   £100

1898. As 1886.
41   **2**   2d. purple and blue   27·00   2·00
43   **2**   4d. brown and green   18·00   4·75
44   **2**   6d. violet and red   45·00   24·00
45   **2**   1s. brown and red   42·00   11·00

1903
66   **8**   ½d. green   13·00   1·75
57c   **8**   1d. purple on red   8·00   85
58a   **8**   2d. green and red   10·00   14·00
49   **8**   2½d. purple and black
               on blue   8·00   60
60a   **8**   6d. purple and violet 32·00   21·00
61a   **8**   1s. black and red   55·00   23·00
62a   **9**   2s. green and blue   £110   £150
53   **9**   4s. purple and green £140   £225
54   **9**   8s. purple and black
               on blue   £160   £200
55   **9**   £1 purple and black
               on red   £600   £750

8   **9**

1907
67   1d. red   5·50   60
68   2d. grey   8·50   11·00
69   2½d. blue   7·00   1·60
70   6d. purple   £140   £375
71   1s. black on green   23·00   21·00
72   **9**   2s. purple and blue
               on blue   60·00   48·00
73   **9**   4s. black and red   £160   £180
74   **9**   8s. purple and green £225   £225

1912. As T **8/9**, but portrait of King George V. (3d. A.
Inscr "3 PENCE". B. Inscr "THREE PENCE").
89   ½d. green   1·50   1·50
90   1d. red   1·75   1·00
91   1½d. chestnut   2·00   55
93   2d. grey   1·25   1·25
79   2½d. blue   10·00   2·50
95a   3d. blue (A)   2·50   1·50
95b   3d. blue (B)   7·50   2·00
97a   6d. purple   1·60   3·50
81   1s. black on green   15·00   3·25
102a 1s. olive and black   14·00   21·00
82   2s. purple and blue on blue   28·00   4·00
103   2s. brown and black   10·00   40·00
104   2s.6d. green and black   10·00   28·00

---

83   4s. black and red   38·00   55·00
105   5s. red and black   17·00   75·00
84   8s. purple and green   £100   £130
106   10s. blue and black   32·00   80·00
85   £1 purple and black on red   £140   £275
107   £1 orange and black   £190   £300
108   £5 violet and black   £1600   £6000

1918. Optd **WAR TAX**.
86   ½d. green (No. 89)   1·00   1·75

13 The Rock of Gibraltar

1931
110   **13**   1d. red   2·50   2·50
111   **13**   1½d. brown   1·75   2·25
112   **13**   2d. grey   8·50   1·75
113   **13**   3d. blue   8·50   3·00

1935. Silver Jubilee. As T **10a** of Gambia.
114   2d. blue and black   1·60   2·50
115   3d. brown and blue   3·75   5·00
116   6d. green and blue   13·00   19·00
117   1s. grey and purple   16·00   24·00

1937. Coronation. As T **10b** of Gambia.
118   ½d. green   25   50
119   2d. grey   2·75   3·25
120   3d. blue   2·75   3·25

14 King   **15** Rock of Gibraltar
George VI

1938. King George VI.
121   **14**   ½d. green   10   40
122   **14**   1d. brown   28·00   2·25
122b **14**   1d. brown   1·00   60
123   **15**   1½d. red   35·00   1·00
123b **-**   1½d. violet   50   1·50
124a **-**   2d. grey   7·00   35
124c **-**   2d. red   1·50   60
125b **-**   3d. blue   3·50   30
125c **-**   5d. orange   1·50   1·25
126b **-**   6d. red and violet   9·00   1·75
127b **-**   1s. black and green 3·25   4·25
128b **-**   2s. black and brown 11·00   6·50
129b **-**   2s. black and red   38·00   17·00
130a **-**   10s. black and blue 42·00   25·00
131   **14**   £1 orange   42·00   55·00
DESIGNS—HORIZ: 2d. The Rock (North side); 3d., 5d. Europa Point; 6d. Moorish. Castle; 1s. South-port Gate; 2s.
Eliott Memorial; 5s. Government House; 10s. Catalan Bay.

1946. Victory. As T **11a** of Gambia.
132   ½d. green   10   1·50
133   3d. blue   50   1·25

1948. Silver Wedding. As T **11b/11c** of Gambia.
134   ½d. green   1·50   3·00
135   £1 orange   60·00   80·00

1949. U.P.U. As T **11d/11g** of Gambia.
136   2d. red   1·00   1·25
137   3d. blue   2·00   1·50
138   6d. purple   1·25   2·00
139   1s. green   1·00   4·00

1950. Inauguration of Legislative Council. Optd **NEW
CONSTITUTION 1950.**
140   2d. red (No. 124c)   30   1·50
141   3d. blue (No. 125b)   65   1·00
142   6d. red and violet (No. 126b) 75   2·00
143   1s. black and green (No. 127b) 75   2·00

1953. Coronation. As T **11h** of Gambia.
144   ½d. black and green   60   2·00

24 Cargo and Passenger
Wharves

1953
145   **24**   ½d. blue and green   15   30
146   **-**   1d. green   1·50   1·00
147   **-**   1½d. black   1·00   2·25
148   **-**   2d. brown   2·50   1·00
149   **-**   2½d. red   4·75   1·25
150   **-**   3d. blue   4·75   10
151   **-**   4d. blue   7·00   1·50
152   **-**   5d. purple   1·75   1·50
153   **-**   6d. black and blue   7·00   2·00

154	-	1s. blue and brown	1·25	1·75
155a		2s. orange and violet	32·00	7·50
156	-	5s. brown	40·00	16·00
157	-	10s. brown and blue	45·00	42·00
158	-	£1 red and yellow	55·00	50·00

DESIGNS—HORIZ: 1d. South view from Straits; 1½d. Gibraltar Fish Canneries; 2d. Southport Gate; 2½d. Sailing in the Bay; 3d. Liner; 4d. Coaling wharf; 5d. English Electric Canberra at Gibraltar Airport; 6d. Europa Point; 1s. Straits from Buena Vista; 2s. Rosia Bay and Straits; 5s. Main entrance, Government House. VERT: 10s. Tower of Homage, Moorish Castle; £1 Arms of Gibraltar.

1954. Royal Visit. As No. 150, but inscr "ROYAL VISIT 1954".

159		3d. blue	1·00	20

38 Gibraltar Candytuft   **40** St. George's Hall

1960

160	**38**	½d. purple and green	15	50
161	-	1d. black and green	20	10
162	-	2d. blue and brown	1·00	20
163a	-	2½d. black and blue	1·50	30
164	-	3d. blue and orange	1·75	10
199	-	4d. brown and turquoise	30	2·75
166	-	6d. brown and green	1·00	70
167	-	7d. blue and red	2·50	1·75
168	-	9d. blue and turquoise	1·00	1·00
169	-	1s. brown and green	1·50	70
170	-	2s. brown and blue	20·00	3·25
171	-	5s. blue and green	8·00	8·00
172	-	10s. yellow and green	27·00	23·00
173	**40**	£1 black and brown	21·00	23·00

DESIGNS (As Type **38**):—HORIZ: 1d. Moorish Castle; 2d. St George's Hall; 3d. The Rock by moonlight; 4d. Catalan Bay; 1s. Barbary ape; 2s. Barbary Partridge; 5s. Blue Rock Thrush; 2½d. The keys; 6d. Map of Gibraltar; 7d. Hawker Siddeley Comet 4 over airport; 9d. American War Memorial; 10s. Rock lily.

1963. Freedom from Hunger. As T **21a** of Gambia.

174	**40**	9d. sepia	3·00	1·75

1963. Centenary of Red Cross. As T **21b** of Gambia.

175		1d. red and black	1·00	2·00
176		9d. red and blue	2·50	4·75

1964. 400th Birth Anniv of Shakespeare. As T **35a** of Gambia.

177		7d. bistre	60	20

1964. New Constitution. Nos. 164 and 166 optd **NEW CONSTITUTION 1964.**

178		3d. blue and orange	20	10
179		6d. sepia and green	20	60

52a I.T.U. Emblem

1965. Centenary of I.T.U.

180	**52a**	4d. green and yellow	2·00	50
181	**52a**	2s. green and blue	5·50	3·50

52b I.C.Y. Emblem

1965. I.C.Y.

182	**52b**	½d. green and lavender	20	2·75
183	**52b**	4d. purple and turquoise	80	50

The value of the ½d. stamp is shown as "1/2".

52c Sir Winston Churchill and St. Paul's Cathedral in Wartime

1966. Churchill Commemoration.

184	**52c**	½d. blue	20	2·25
185	**52c**	1d. green	30	10
186	**52c**	4d. brown	1·50	80
187	**52c**	9d. violet	1·25	2·50

52d Footballer's legs, ball and Jules Rimet Cup

1966. World Cup Football Championship.

188	**52d**	2½d. multicoloured	75	1·75
189	**52d**	6d. multicoloured	1·00	50

53 Red Seabream

1966. European Sea Angling Championships. Gibraltar.

190	**53**	4d. red, blue and black	30	10
191	-	7d. red, green and black	60	70
192	-	1s. brown, green and black	50	30

DESIGNS—HORIZ: 7d. Red scorpionfish. VERT: 1s. Stone bass.

54 W.H.O. Building

1966. Inauguration of W.H.O. Headquarters, Geneva.

193	**54**	6d. black, green and blue	3·00	1·50
194	**54**	9d. black, purple and ochre	3·50	3·75

56 "Our Lady of Europa"

1966. Centenary of Re-enthronement of "Our Lady of Europa".

195	**56**	2s. blue and black	30	80

56a "Education"

56b "Science"

56c "Culture"

1966. 20th Anniv of UNESCO.

196	**56a**	2d. multicoloured	60	10
197	**56b**	7d. yellow, violet and olive	2·25	10
198	**56c**	5s. black, purple & orge	4·50	3·00

57 H.M.S. *Victory*

1967. Multicoloured

200		½d. Type **57**	10	20
201		1d. *Arab* (early steamer)	10	10
202		2d. H.M.S. *Carmania* (merchant cruiser)	15	10
203		2½d. *Mons Calpe* (ferry)	40	30
204		3d. *Canberra* (liner)	20	10
205		4d. H.M.S. *Hood* (battle cruiser)	60	10
205a		5d. *Mirror* (cable ship)	2·00	55
206		6d. *Xebec* (sailing vessel)	30	50
207		7d. *Amerigo Vespucci* (Italian cadet ship)	30	1·50
208		9d. *Raffaello* (liner)	30	1·75
209		1s. *Royal Katherine* (galleon)	30	35
210		2s. Fairey Swordfish over H.M.S. *Ark Royal* (aircraft carrier, 1937)	4·50	2·75
211		5s. H.M.S. *Dreadnought* (nuclear submarine)	3·50	7·00
212		10s. *Neuralia* (liner)	12·00	21·00
213		£1 *Mary Celeste* (sailing vessel)	12·00	21·00

58 Aerial Ropeway

1967. International Tourist Year. Multicoloured.

214	**58**	7d. Type **58**	15	10
215		9d. Shark fishing (horiz)	15	10
216		1s. Skin-diving (horiz)	20	15

DESIGNS—HORIZ: 7d. Red scorpionfish. VERT: 1s. Stone bass.

59 Mary, Joseph and Child Jesus

1967. Christmas. Multicoloured.

217	**59**	2d. Type **59**	15	10
218		6d. Church window (vert)	15	10

61 General Eliott and Route Map

1967. 250th Birth Anniv of General Eliott. Multicoloured.

219	**61**	4d. Type **61**	15	10
220		9d. Heathfield Tower and Monument, Sussex	15	10
221		1s. General Eliott (vert)	15	10
222		2s. Eliott directing rescue operations (55×21 mm)	25	50

65 Lord Baden-Powell

1968. 60th Anniv of Gibraltar Scout Association.

223	**65**	4d. buff and violet	15	10
224	-	7d. ochre and green	20	20
225	-	9d. blue, orange and black	20	30
226	-	1s. yellow and green	20	30

DESIGNS: 7d. Scout flag over the Rock; 9d. Tent, Scouts and salute; 1s. Scout badges.

66 Nurse and W.H.O. Emblem

1968. 20th Anniv of W.H.O. Multicoloured.

227	**66**	2d. Type **66**	10	15
228		4d. Doctor and W.H.O. emblem	10	10

68 King John signing Magna Carta

1968. Human Rights Year.

229	**68**	1s. orange, brown and gold	15	10
230	-	2s. myrtle and gold	15	40

DESIGN: 2s. "Freedom" and Rock of Gibraltar.

70 Shepherd, Lamb and Star

1968. Christmas. Multicoloured.

231	**70**	4d. Type **70**	10	10
232		9d. Mary holding Holy Child	15	20

72 Parliament Houses

1969. Commonwealth Parliamentary Association Conference.

233	**72**	4d. green and gold	10	10
234		9d. violet and gold	10	10
235	-	2s. red, gold and blue	15	20

DESIGNS—HORIZ: 9d. Parliamentary emblem and outline of "The Rock". VERT: 2s. Clock Tower, Westminster (Big Ben) and Arms of Gibraltar.

75 Silhouette of Rock and Queen Elizabeth II

1969. New Constitution.

236	**75**	½d. gold and orange	10	10
237	**75**	5d. silver and green	20	10
238	**75**	7d. silver and purple	20	10
239	**75**	5s. silver and blue	65	1·10

77 Soldier and Cap Badge, Royal Anglian Regiment, 1969

1969. Military Uniforms (1st series). Multicoloured.

240		1d. Royal Artillery Officer, 1758, and modern cap badge	15	10
241		6d. Type **77**	20	15
242		9d. Royal Engineers' Artificer, 1786, and modern cap badge	30	15
243		2s. Private, Fox's Marines, 1704, and modern Royal Marines' cap badge	75	70

See also Nos. 248/51, 290/3, 300/303, 313/16, 331/4, 340/3 and 363/6.

80 *Madonna of the Chair* (detail, Raphael)

1969. Christmas. Multicoloured.

244		5d. Type **80**	10	35
245		7d. *Virgin and Child* (detail, Morales)	20	35
246		1s. *The Virgin of the Rocks* (detail, Leonardo da Vinci)	20	40

83 Europa Point

1970. Europa Point.
| 247 | **83** | 2s. multicoloured | 45 | 50 |

1970. Military Uniforms (2nd series). As T **77**. Multicoloured.
248		2d. Royal Scots Officer (1839) and cap badge	25	10
249		5d. South Wales Borderers Private (1763) and cap badge	35	10
250		7d. Queen's Royal Regiment Private (1742) and cap badge	35	10
251		2s. Royal Irish Rangers piper (1969) and cap badge	1·00	90

88 No. 191a and Rock of Gibraltar

1970. "Philympia 70" Stamp Exhibition, London.
| 252 | **88** | 1s. red and green | 15 | 10 |
| 253 | - | 2s. blue and mauve | 25 | 65 |

DESIGN: 2s. Stamp and Moorish Castle.
The stamps shown in the designs are well-known varieties with values omitted.

90 The Virgin and Mary (stained-glass window Gabriel Loire)

1970. Christmas.
| 254 | **90** | 2s. multicoloured | 30 | 1·00 |

91 Saluting Battery, Rosia

92 Saluting Battery, Rosia, Modern View

1971. Decimal Currency.
255	**91**	½p. multicoloured	20	30
256	**92**	½p. multicoloured	20	30
257	-	1p. multicoloured	80	30
258	-	1p. multicoloured	80	30
259	-	1½p. multicoloured	20	70
260	-	1½p. multicoloured	20	70
317	-	2p. multicoloured	1·25	2·50
318	-	2p. multicoloured	1·25	2·50
263a	-	2½p. multicoloured	40	1·40
264	-	2½p. multicoloured	20	70
265	-	3p. multicoloured	20	20
266	-	3p. multicoloured	20	20
319	-	4p. multicoloured	1·40	2·75
320	-	4p. multicoloured	1·40	2·75
269	-	5p. multicoloured	35	65
270	-	5p. multicoloured	35	65
271	-	7p. multicoloured	65	65
272	-	7p. multicoloured	65	65
273	-	8p. multicoloured	70	80
274	-	8p. multicoloured	70	80
275	-	9p. multicoloured	70	80
276	-	9p. multicoloured	70	80
277	-	10p. multicoloured	80	80
278	-	10p. multicoloured	80	80
279	-	12½p. multicoloured	1·00	1·75
280	-	12½p. multicoloured	1·00	1·75
281	-	25p. multicoloured	1·10	1·75
282	-	25p. multicoloured	1·10	1·75
283	-	50p. multicoloured	1·50	2·75
284	-	50p. multicoloured	1·50	2·75
285	-	£1 multicoloured	2·25	4·25
286	-	£1 multicoloured	2·25	4·25

DESIGNS: The two versions of each value show the same Gibraltar view taken from an early 19th-century print (first design) or modern photograph (second design): HORIZ: 1p. Prince George of Cambridge Quarters and Trinity Church; 1½p. The Wellington Bust, Alameda Gardens; 2p. Gibraltar from the North Bastion; 2½p. Catalan Bay; 3p. Convent Garden; 4p. The Exchange and Spanish Chapel; 5p. Commercial Square and Library; 7p. South Barracks and Rosia Magazine; 8p. Moorish Mosque and Castle; 9p. Europa Pass Road; 10p. South Barracks from Rosia Bay; 12½p. Southport Gates; 25p. Trooping the Colour, The Alameda. VERT: 50p. Europa Pass Gorge; £1 Prince Edward's Gate.

93

1971. Coil Stamps.
287	**93**	½p. orange	15	30
288	**93**	1p. blue	15	30
289	**93**	2p. green	50	1·10

1971. Military Uniforms (3rd series). As T **77**. Multicoloured.
290		1p. The Black Watch (1845)	35	30
291		2p. Royal Regimental of Fusiliers (1971)	55	30
292		4p. King's Own Royal Border Regiment (1704)	75	50
293		10p. Devonshire and Dorset Regiment (1801)	2·75	3·00

94 Regimental Arms

1971. Presentation of Colours to the Gibraltar Regiment.
| 294 | **94** | 3p. black, gold and red | 55 | 30 |

95 Nativity Scene

1971. Christmas. Multicoloured.
| 295 | **95** | 3p. Type **95** | 40 | 60 |
| 296 | | 5p. Mary and Joseph going to Bethlehem | 40 | 65 |

96 Soldier Artificer, 1773

1972. Bicentenary of Royal Engineers in Gibraltar. Multicoloured.
297		1p. Type **96**	50	60
298		3p. Modern tunneller	60	80
299		5p. Old and new uniforms and badge (horiz)	70	90

1972. Military Uniforms (4th series). As T **77**. Multicoloured.
300		1p. The Duke of Cornwall's Light Infantry, 1704	50	20
301		3p. King's Royal Rifle Corps, 1830	1·25	40
302		7p. 37th North Hampshire, Officer, 1825	2·00	70
303		10p. Royal Navy, 1972	2·25	1·50

97 "Our Lady of Europa"

1972. Christmas.
| 304 | **97** | 3p. multicoloured | 10 | 20 |
| 305 | **97** | 5p. multicoloured | 10 | 35 |

98 Keys of Gibraltar and "Narcissus niveus"

1972. Royal Silver Wedding.
| 306 | **98** | 5p. red | 25 | 20 |
| 307 | **98** | 7p. green | 25 | 20 |

99 Flags of Member Nations and E.E.C. Symbol

1973. Britain's Entry into E.E.C.
| 308 | **99** | 5p. multicoloured | 40 | 50 |
| 309 | **99** | 10p. multicoloured | 60 | 1·00 |

100 Skull

1973. 125th Anniv of Gibraltar Skull Discovery. Multicoloured.
310		4p. Type **100**	1·25	60
311		6p. Prehistoric man	1·50	1·25
312		10p. Prehistoric family	2·00	2·50

No. 312 is size 40×26 mm.

1973. Military Uniforms (5th series). As T **77**. Multicoloured.
313		1p. King's Own Scottish Borderers, 1770	50	50
314		4p. Royal Welsh Fusiliers, 1800	1·25	80
315		6p. Royal Northumberland Fusiliers, 1736	1·75	1·75
316		10p. Grenadier Guards, 1898	2·50	4·00

101 Nativity (Danckerts)

1973. Christmas.
| 321 | **101** | 4p. violet and red | 30 | 15 |
| 322 | **101** | 6p. mauve and blue | 40 | 1·10 |

101a Princess Anne and Captain Mark Phillips

1973. Royal Wedding.
| 323 | **101a** | 6p. multicoloured | 10 | 10 |
| 324 | **101a** | 14p. multicoloured | 20 | 20 |

102 Victorian Pillar-box

1974. Centenary of U.P.U. Multicoloured.
325		2p. Type **102**	15	30
326		6p. Pillar-box of George VI	20	35
327		14p. Pillar-box of Elizabeth II	30	80

Nos. 325/7 also come self-adhesive from booklet panes.

1974. Military Uniforms (6th series). As T **77**. Multicoloured.
331		4p. East Lancashire Regiment, 1742	50	50
332		6p. Somerset Light Infantry, 1833	70	70
333		10p. Royal Sussex Regiment, 1790	1·00	1·40
334		16p. R.A.F. officer, 1974	2·25	4·00

103 Madonna with the Green Cushion (Solario)

1974. Christmas. Multicoloured.
| 335 | | 4p. Type **103** | 40 | 30 |
| 336 | | 6p. Madonna of the Meadow (Bellini) | 60 | 95 |

104 Churchill and Houses of Parliament

1974. Birth Centenary of Sir Winston Churchill. Multicoloured.
337	**104**	6p. black, purple and lavender	25	15
338	-	20p. black, brown and lavender	35	45
MS339		114×93 mm. Nos. 337/8	4·50	6·50

DESIGN: 20p. Churchill and "King George V" (battleship).

1975. Military Uniforms (7th series). As T **77**. Multicoloured.
340		4p. East Surrey Regiment, 1846	35	20
341		6p. Highland Light Infantry, 1777	50	40
342		10p. Coldstream Guards, 1704	70	70
343		20p. Gibraltar Regiment, 1974	1·25	2·50

105 Girl Guides' Badge

1975. 50th Anniversary of Gibraltar Girl Guides.
346	**105**	5p. gold, blue and violet	25	55
347	**105**	7p. gold, brown and light brown	35	60
348	-	15p. silver, black and brown	50	1·25

No. 348 is as Type **105** but shows a different badge.

106 Child at Prayer

1975. Christmas. Multicoloured.
349		6p. Type **106**	40	60
350		6p. Angel with lute	40	60
351		6p. Child singing carols	40	60
352		6p. Three children	40	60
353		6p. Girl at prayer	40	60
354		6p. Boy and lamb	40	60

107 Bruges Madonna

1975. 500th Birth Anniv of Michelangelo. Multicoloured.
355		6p. Type **107**	20	25
356		9p. Taddei Madonna	20	40
357		15p. Pieta	30	1·10

Nos. 355/7 also come self-adhesive from booklet panes.

108 Bicentennial
Emblem and Arms
of Gibraltar

1976. Bicentenary of American Revolution.
361	**108**	25p. multicoloured	50	50
MS362	85×133 mm. No. 361×4		2·75	4·50

1976. Military Uniforms (8th series). As T **77**.
Multicoloured.
363	1p. Suffolk Regiment, 1795	20	20
364	6p. Northamptonshire Regiment, 1779	40	30
365	12p. Lancashire Fusiliers, 1793	50	60
366	25p. Ordnance Corps, 1896	60	1·40

109 The Holy
Family

1976. Christmas. Multicoloured.
367	6p. Type **109**	25	15
368	9p. Madonna and Child	35	25
369	12p. St. Bernard	50	60
370	20p. Archangel Michael	85	1·40
Nos. 367/70 show different stained-glass windows from
St. Joseph's Church, Gibraltar.

110 Queen Elizabeth
II, Royal Arms and
Gibraltar Arms

1977. Silver Jubilee. Multicoloured.
371	**110**	6p. red	15	20
372	**110**	£1 blue	1·10	2·00
MS373	124×115 mm. Nos. 371/2		1·25	1·50

111 Toothed Orchid

1977. Birds, Flowers, Fish and Butterflies. Multicoloured.
374	½p. Type **111**	60	2·50
375	1p. Red mullet (horiz)	15	70
376	2p. *Maculinea arion* (butterfly) (horiz)	30	1·75
377	2½p. Sardinian warbler	1·75	2·75
378	3p. Giant squill	20	10
379	4p. Grey wrasse (horiz)	30	10
380	5p. *Vanessa atalanta* (butterfly) (horiz)	50	1·00
381	6p. Black kite	2·25	55
382	9p. Shrubby scorpion-vetch	70	70
383	10p. John dory (fish) (horiz)	40	20
384	12p. *Colias crocea* (butterfly) (horiz)	1·00	35
384b	15p. Winged asparagus pea	1·50	55
385	20p. Audouin's gull	2·00	3·25
386	25p. Barbary nut (iris)	1·25	2·00
387	50p. Swordfish (horiz)	2·00	2·50
388	£1 *Papilio machaon* (butterfly) (horiz)	4·25	5·00
389	£2 Hoopoe	9·00	12·00
389a	£5 Arms of Gibraltar	10·00	12·00

112 "Our Lady of Europa" Stamp

1977. "Amphilex '77" Stamp Exhibition, Amsterdam.
Multicoloured.
390	6p. Type **112**	10	20
391	12p. "Europa Point" stamp	15	30
392	25p. "E.E.C. Entry" stamp	20	50

113 *The
Annunciation*
(Rubens)

1977. Christmas and 400th Birth Anniv of Rubens.
Multicoloured.
393	3p. Type **113**	10	10
394	9p. *The Adoration of the Magi*	25	25
395	12p. *The Adoration of the Magi* (horiz)	30	50
396	15p. *The Holy Family under the Apple Tree*	30	55
MS397	110×200 mm. Nos. 393/6	2·75	4·00

114 Aerial View of Gibraltar

1978. Gibraltar from Space. Multicoloured.
398	12p. Type **114**	25	50
MS399	148×108 mm. 25p. Aerial view of Straits of Gibraltar	80	80

115 Holyroodhouse

1978. 25th Anniv of Coronation. Multicoloured.

(a) From sheets
400	6p. Type **115**	20	15
401	9p. St. James's Palace	25	15
402	12p. Sandringham	30	30
403	18p. Balmoral	40	85

(b) From booklets
406	25p. Windsor Castle	1·00	2·00
Nos. 402/3 also exist as self-adhesive stamps from
booklet panes, No. 406 only coming in this form.

116 Short S.25 Sunderland,
1938–58

1978. 60th Anniv of Royal Air Force. Multicoloured.
407	3p. Type **116**	15	10
408	9p. Caudron G-3, 1918	35	40
409	12p. Avro Shackleton M.R.2, 1953–66	40	55
410	16p. Hawker Hunter F.6, 1954–77	45	1·00
411	18p. Hawker Siddeley H.S.801 Nimrod M.R.1, 1969–78	50	1·10

117 *Madonna with
Animals*

1978. Christmas. Paintings by Durer. Multicoloured.
412	5p. Type **117**	20	10
413	9p. *The Nativity*	25	15
414	12p. *Madonna of the Goldfinch*	30	40
415	15p. *Adoration of the Magi*	35	1·00

118 Sir Rowland Hill and 1d.
Stamp of 1886

1979. Death Centenary of Sir Rowland Hill.
416	**118**	3p. multicoloured	10	10
417	-	9p. multicoloured	15	15
418	-	12p. multicoloured	15	20
419	-	25p. black, purple yellow	25	50
DESIGNS: 9p. 1971 1p. coil stamp; 12p. 1840 Post Office
Regulations; 25p. "G" cancellation.

119 Posthorn, Dish Antenna and
Early Telephone

1979. Europa. Communications.
420	**119**	3p. green and pale green	15	10
421	**119**	9p. brown and ochre	30	90
422	**119**	12p. blue and violet	35	1·25

120 African Child

1979. Christmas. International Year of the Child.
Multicoloured.
423	12p. Type **120**	25	30
424	12p. Asian child	25	30
425	12p. Polynesian child	25	30
426	12p. American Indian child	25	30
427	12p. Nativity and children of different races	25	30
428	12p. European child	25	30

121 Early Policeman

1980. 150th Anniv of Gibraltar Police Force.
Multicoloured.
429	3p. Type **121**	20	10
430	6p. Policemen of 1895, early 1900s and 1980	20	15
431	12p. Police officer and police ambulance	25	20
432	37p. Policewoman and police motor-cyclist	55	1·25

122 Peter Amigo
(Archbishop)

1980. Europa. Personalities. Multicoloured.
433	12p. Type **122**	20	30
434	12p. Gustavo Bacarisas (artist)	20	30
435	12p. John Mackintosh (philanthropist)	20	30

123 Queen Elizabeth the
Queen Mother

1980. 80th Birthday of The Queen Mother.
436	**123**	15p. multicoloured	30	30

124 *Horatio
Nelson* (J. F.
Rigaud)

1980. 175th Death Anniv of Nelson. Paintings.
Multicoloured.
437	3p. Type **124**	15	10
438	9p. *H.M.S. Victory* (horiz)	25	25
439	15p. *Horatio Nelson* (Sir William Beechey)	35	35
440	40p. *'H.M.S. Victory' being towed into Gibraltar* (Clarkson Stanfield) (horiz)	80	1·00
MS441	159×99 mm. No. 439	1·00	1·50

125 Three Kings

1980. Christmas.
442	**125**	15p. brown and yellow	25	35
443	-	15p. brown and yellow	25	35
DESIGN: No. 443, Nativity scene.

126 Hercules
creating the
Mediterranean

1981. Europa. Multicoloured.
444	9p. Type **126**	20	15
445	15p. Hercules and Pillars of Hercules	25	35

127 Dining-room

1981. 450th Anniv of The Convent (Governor's
Residence). Multicoloured.
446	4p. Type **127**	10	10
447	14p. King's Chapel	15	15
448	15p. The Convent	15	15
449	55p. Cloister	60	80

128 Prince Charles and Lady
Diana Spencer

1981. Royal Wedding.
450	**128**	£1 multicoloured	1·25	1·25

129

1981
451	**129**	1p. black	50	60
452	**129**	4p. blue	50	50
453	**129**	15p. green	30	40

130 Paper Airplane

1981. 50th Anniv of Gibraltar Airmail Service.
Multicoloured.
454	14p. Type **130**	15	15
455	15p. Airmail letters, post box and aircraft tail fin	15	15
456	55p. Jet airliner circling globe	60	80

131 Carol Singers

1981. Christmas. Children's Drawings. Multicoloured.
457	15p. Type **131**		30	15
458	55p. Postbox (vert)		1·00	85

132 I.Y.D.P. Emblem and Stylized Faces

1981. International Year for Disabled Persons.
459	**132**	14p. multicoloured	30	30

133 Douglas DC-3

1982. Aircraft. Multicoloured.
460	1p. Type **133**		25	2·00
461	2p. Vickers Viking 1B		30	2·00
462	3p. Airspeed A.S.57 Ambassador G-ALZN		30	1·75
463	4p. Vickers 953 Viscount 800		40	20
464	5p. Boeing 727-100		90	60
465	10p. Vickers Vanguard		1·75	50
466	14p. Short Solent 2		1·75	4·00
467	15p. Fokker F.27 Friendship		2·75	4·00
468	17p. Boeing 737		1·00	75
469	20p. B.A.C. One Eleven 500G-AWYV		1·00	65
470	25p. Lockheed Constellation		4·00	5·00
471	50p. de Havilland Comet 4B		4·00	2·25
472	£1 Saro Windhover G-ABJP *General Godley*		5·50	2·25
473	£2 Hawker Siddeley Trident 2E		6·50	5·00
474	£5 de Havilland DH.89A Dragon Rapide		8·00	14·00

134 Crest, H.M.S. *Opossum*

1982. Naval Crests (1st series). Multicoloured.
475	½p. Type **134**		10	30
476	15½p. H.M.S. *Norfolk*		40	55
477	17p. H.M.S. *Fearless*		40	60
478	60p. H.M.S. *Rooke*		85	2·75

See also Nos. 493/6, 510/13, 522/5, 541/4, 565/8, 592/5, 616/19 and 651/4.

135 Hawker Hurricane Mk I and Supermarine Spitfires at Gibraltar

1982. Europa. Operation Torch. Multicoloured.
479	14p. Type **135**		25	70
480	17p. General Giraud, General Eisenhower and Gibraltar		35	80

136 Gibraltar Chamber of Commerce Centenary

1982. Anniversaries. Multicoloured.
481	½p. Type **136**		10	65
482	15½p. British Forces Postal Service centenary		45	30
483	60p. 75th anniv of Gibraltar Scout Association		1·25	2·00

137 Printed Circuit forming Map of World

1982. International Direct Dialling.
484	**137**	17p. black, blue and orange	35	35

138 Gibraltar illuminated at Night and Holly

1982. Christmas. Multicoloured.
485	14p. Type **138**		50	30
486	17p. Gibraltar illuminated at night and mistletoe		50	35

139 Yacht Marina

1983. Commonwealth Day. Multicoloured.
487	4p. Type **139**		10	10
488	14p. Scouts and Guides Commonwealth Day Parade		20	15
489	17p. Flag of Gibraltar (vert)		25	20
490	60p. Queen Elizabeth II (from photo by Tim Graham) (vert)		70	1·00

140 St. George's Hall Gallery

1983. Europa.
491	**140**	16p. black and brown	35	50
492	-	19p. black and blue	40	75

DESIGN: 19p. Water catchment slope.

1983. Naval Crests (2nd series). As T **134**. Multicoloured.
493	4p. H.M.S. *Faulknor*		30	10
494	14p. H.M.S. *Renown*		70	35
495	17p. H.M.S. *Ark Royal*		75	40
496	60p. H.M.S. *Sheffield*		1·75	1·50

141 Landport Gate, 1729

1983. Fortress Gibraltar in the 18th Century. Multicoloured.
497	4p. Type **141**		15	10
498	17p. Koehler Gun, 1782		35	30
499	77p. King's Bastion, 1779		1·00	1·25
MS500	97×145 mm. Nos. 497/9		2·25	1·50

142 *Adoration of the Magi* (Raphael)

1983. Christmas. 500th Birth Anniv of Raphael. Multicoloured.
501	4p. Type **142**		25	10
502	17p. *Madonna of Foligno* (vert)		70	35
503	60p. *Sistine Madonna* (vert)		1·75	1·40

143 1932 2d. Stamp and Globe

1984. Europa, Posts and Telecommunications. Multicoloured.
504	17p. Type **143**		45	50
505	23p. Circuit board and globe		55	1·00

144 Hockey

1984. Sports. Multicoloured.
506	20p. Type **144**		70	80
507	21p. Basketball		70	80
508	26p. Rowing		70	1·25
509	29p. Football		70	1·50

1984. Naval Crests (3rd series). As T **134**. Multicoloured.
510	20p. H.M.S. *Active*		1·75	2·25
511	21p. H.M.S. *Foxhound*		1·75	2·50
512	26p. H.M.S. *Valiant*		2·00	2·50
513	29p. H.M.S. *Hood*		2·50	2·75

145 Mississippi River Boat Float

1984. Christmas. Epiphany Floats. Multicoloured.
514	20p. Type **145**		30	30
515	80p. Roman Temple float		1·40	2·75

146 Musical Symbols, and Score from Beethoven's 9th (Choral) Symphony

1985. Europa. European Music Year. Multicoloured.
516	**146**	20p. multicoloured	30	30
517	-	29p. multicoloured	40	1·50

DESIGN: The 29p. is as T **146**, but shows different symbols.

147 Globe and Stop Polio Campaign Logo

1985. Stop Polio Campaign.
518	26p. multicoloured (Type **147**)		90	1·40
519	26p. multicoloured ("ST" visible)		90	1·40
520	26p. multicoloured ("STO" visible)		90	1·40
521	26p. multicoloured ("STOP" visible)		90	1·40

Each design differs in the position of the logo across the centre of the globe. On No. 518 only the letter "S" is fully visible, on No. 519 "ST", on No. 520 "STO" and on No. 521 "STOP". Other features of the design also differ, so that the word "Year" moves towards the top of the stamp and on No. 521 the upper logo is omitted.

1985. Naval Crests (4th series). As T **134**. Multicoloured.
522	4p. H.M.S. *Duncan*		70	10
523	9p. H.M.S. *Fury*		1·25	50
524	21p. H.M.S. *Firedrake*		2·50	2·00
525	80p. H.M.S. *Malaya*		4·50	6·00

148 I.Y.Y. Logo

1985. International Youth Year. Multicoloured.
526	4p. Type **148**		35	10
527	20p. Hands passing diamond		1·40	1·10
528	80p. 75th anniv logo of Girl Guide Movement		3·25	3·75

149 St. Joseph

1985. Christmas. Centenary of St. Joseph's Parish Church. Multicoloured.
529	4p. Type **149**		65	1·00
530	4p. St. Joseph's Parish Church		65	1·00
531	80p. Nativity crib		4·50	5·50

150 *Papilio machaon* (butterfly) and The Convent

1986. Europa. Nature and the Environment. Multicoloured.
532	22p. Type **150**		1·00	50
533	29p. Herring gull and Europa Point		1·50	4·25

151 1887 Queen Victoria 6d. Stamp

1986. Centenary of First Gibraltar Postage Stamps. Designs showing stamps. Multicoloured.
534	4p. Type **151**		30	10
535	22p. 1903 Edward VII 2½d.		1·00	1·00
536	32p. 1912 George V 1d.		1·50	2·00
537	36p. 1938 George VI £1		1·60	2·50
538	44p. 1953 Coronation ½d. (29×46 mm)		2·00	3·00
MS539	102×73 mm. 29p. 1886 "GIBRALTAR" overprinted on Bermuda 1d.		3·25	3·75

152 Queen Elizabeth II in Robes of Order of the Bath

1986. 60th Birthday of Queen Elizabeth II.
540	**152**	£1 multicoloured	1·75	3·00

1986. Naval Crests (5th series). As T **134**. Multicoloured.
541	22p. H.M.S. *Lightning*		1·75	1·00
542	29p. H.M.S. *Hermione*		2·00	1·75
543	32p. H.M.S. *Laforey*		2·25	3·25
544	44p. H.M.S. *Nelson*		2·75	5·50

153 Prince Andrew and Miss Sarah Ferguson

1986. Royal Wedding. Sheet 115×85 mm.
MS545	**153**	44p. multicoloured	1·40	2·25

154 Three Kings and Cathedral of St. Mary the Crowned

1986. Christmas. International Peace Year. Multicoloured.
546	18p. Type **154**		1·00	50
547	32p. St. Andrew's Church		1·50	3·00

155 Neptune House

1987. Europa. Architecture. Multicoloured.
563	22p. Type **155**	1·25	50
564	29p. Ocean Heights	2·00	4·25

1987. Naval Crests (6th series). As T **134**. Multicoloured.
565	18p. H.M.S. *Wishart*	1·60	75
566	22p. H.M.S. *Charybdis*	1·75	1·10
567	32p. H.M.S. *Antelope*	2·50	3·50
568	44p. H.M.S. *Eagle*	3·00	4·50

156 13-inch Mortar, 1783

1987. Guns. Multicoloured.
569	1p. Type **156**	20	70
570	2p. 6-inch coastal gun, 1909	30	70
571	3p. 8-inch howitzer, 1783	40	1·00
572	4p. Bofors "L40/70" AA gun, 1951	40	10
573	5p. 100 ton rifled muzzle-loader, 1882	40	70
574	10p. 5.25 inch heavy AA gun, 1953	40	70
575	18p. 25-pounder gun-how, 1943	65	1·00
576	19p. 64-pounder rifled muzzle-loader, 1873	70	1·25
577	22p. 12-pounder gun, 1758	70	50
578	50p. 10-inch rifled muzzle-loader, 1870	1·40	3·00
579	£1 Russian 24-pounder gun, 1854	2·50	2·50
580	£3 9.2 inch "Mk 10" coastal gun, 1935	3·00	12·00
581	£5 24-pounder gun, 1779	5·00	14·00

157 Victoria Stadium

1987. Bicentenary of Royal Engineers' Royal Warrant. Multicoloured.
582	18p. Type **157**	1·25	65
583	32p. Freedom of Gibraltar scroll and casket	1·75	3·25
584	44p. Royal Engineers' badge	2·50	4·50

158 The Three Kings

1987. Christmas. Multicoloured.
585	4p. Type **158**	20	10
586	22p. The Holy Family	1·00	1·00
587	44p. The Shepherds	1·90	3·50

159 *Canberra* (liner) passing Gibraltar

1988. Europa. Transport and Communications. Multicoloured.
588	22p. Type **159**	1·50	2·25
589	22p. *Gibline I* (ferry), dish aerial and Boeing 737 airliner	1·50	2·25
590	32p. Horse-drawn carriage and modern coach	2·00	2·75
591	32p. Car, telephone and Rock of Gibraltar	2·00	2·75

1988. Naval Crests (7th series). As T **134**.
592	18p. multicoloured	1·50	65
593	22p. black, brown and gold	2·00	1·25
594	32p. multicoloured	2·25	3·50
595	44p. multicoloured	3·00	4·75

DESIGNS: 18p. H.M.S. *Clyde*; 22p. H.M.S. *Foresight*; 32p. H.M.S. *Severn*; 44p. H.M.S. *Rodney*.

160 European Bee Eater

1988. Birds. Multicoloured.
596	4p. Type **160**	75	20
597	22p. Atlantic puffin	1·75	90
598	32p. Western honey buzzard ("Honey Buzzard")	2·25	2·50
599	44p. Blue rock thrush	2·75	4·00

161 *Zebu* (brigantine)

1988. Operation Raleigh. Multicoloured.
600	19p. Type **161**	65	60
601	22p. Miniature of Sir Walter Raleigh and logo	75	70
602	32p. *Sir Walter Raleigh* (expedition ship) and world map	1·10	2·00
MS603	135×86 mm. 22p. As No. 601; 44p. *Sir Walter Raleigh* (expedition ship) passing Gibraltar	4·50	5·50

162 *Snowman* (Rebecca Falero)

1988. Christmas. Children's Paintings. Multicoloured.
604	4p. Type **162**	15	10
605	22p. *The Nativity* (Dennis Penalver)	55	60
606	44p. *Father Christmas* (Gavin Key) (23×31 mm)	1·00	2·40

163 Soft Toys and Toy Train

1989. Europa. Children's Toys. Multicoloured.
607	25p. Type **163**	1·25	75
608	32p. Soft toys, toy boat and doll's house	1·75	2·75

164 Port Sergeant with Keys

1989. 50th Anniv of Gibraltar Regiment. Multicoloured.
609	4p. Type **164**	50	10
610	22p. Regimental badge and colours	1·40	1·10
611	32p. Drum major	1·90	3·50
MS612	124×83 mm. 22p. As No. 610; 44p. Former Gibraltar Defence Force badge	4·75	5·50

165 Nurse and Baby

1989. 125th Anniv of International Red Cross.
613	165	25p. black, red and brown	1·00	60
614	–	32p. black, red and brown	1·25	1·75
615	–	44p. black, red and brown	1·50	3·50

DESIGNS: 32p. Famine victims; 44p. Accident victims.

1989. Naval Crests (8th series). As T **134**.
616	22p. multicoloured	1·50	75

617	25p. black and gold	1·50	1·50
618	32p. gold, black and red	2·00	3·25
619	44p. multicoloured	3·00	5·50

DESIGNS: 22p. H.M.S. *Blankney*; 25p. H.M.S. *Deptford*; 32p. H.M.S. *Exmoor*; 44p. H.M.S. *Stork*.

166 One Penny Coin

1989. New Coinage. T **166** and similar vert designs in two miniature sheets.
MS620	72×94 mm. 4p. bronze, black and red (Type **166**); 4p. bronze, black and brown (two pence); 4p. silver, black and yellow (ten pence); 4p. silver, black and green (five pence)	1·25	2·25
MS621	100×95 mm. 22p. silver, black and green (fifty pence); 22p. gold, black and blue (five pounds); 22p. gold, black and brown (two pounds); 22p. gold, black and green (one pound); 22p. gold, black and violet (obverse of coin series); 22p. silver, black and blue (twenty pence)	5·50	7·50

167 Father Christmas in Sleigh

1989. Christmas. Multicoloured.
622	4p. Type **167**	20	10
623	22p. Shepherds and sheep	90	70
624	32p. The Nativity	1·40	1·75
625	44p. The Three Wise Men	2·25	4·00

168 General Post Office Entrance

1990. Europa. Post Office Buildings. Multicoloured.
626	22p. Type **168**	1·25	1·75
627	22p. Interior of General Post Office	1·25	1·75
628	32p. Interior of South District Post Office	1·50	2·50
629	32p. South District Post Office	1·50	2·50

169 19th-century Firemen

1990. 125th Anniv of Gibraltar Fire Service. Multicoloured.
630	4p. Type **169**	1·00	15
631	20p. Early fire engine (horiz)	2·50	1·10
632	42p. Modern fire engine (horiz)	3·00	3·75
633	44p. Modern fireman in breathing apparatus	3·00	3·75

170 Henry Corbould (artist) and Penny Black

1990. 150th Anniv of the Penny Black. Multicoloured.
634	19p. Type **170**	1·10	90
635	22p. Bath Royal Mail coach	1·25	1·00
636	32p. Sir Rowland Hill and Penny Black	2·50	4·50
MS637	145×95 mm. 44p. Penny Black with Maltese Cross cancellation	4·75	6·00

1990. Naval Crests (9th series). As T **134**. Multicoloured.
638	22p. H.M.S. *Calpe*	1·75	70

639	25p. H.M.S. *Gallant*	1·90	1·75
640	32p. H.M.S. *Wrestler*	2·50	3·25
641	44p. H.M.S. *Greyhound*	3·00	6·50

171 Model of Europort Development

1990. Development Projects. Multicoloured.
642	22p. Type **171**	75	80
643	23p. Construction of building material factory	75	1·50
644	25p. Land reclamation	95	1·50

172 Candle and Holly

1990. Christmas. Multicoloured.
645	4p. Type **172**	15	10
646	22p. Father Christmas	75	65
647	42p. Christmas tree	1·50	2·50
648	44p. Nativity crib	1·50	2·50

173 Space Laboratory and Spaceplane (Columbus Development Programme)

1991. Europa. Europe in Space. Multicoloured.
649	25p. Type **173**	75	75
650	32p. "ERS-1" earth resources remote sensing satellite	1·00	2·25

1991. Naval Crests (10th series). As T **134**.
651	4p. black, blue and gold	60	10
652	21p. multicoloured	1·75	1·25
653	22p. multicoloured	1·75	1·25
654	62p. multicoloured	3·75	7·00

DESIGNS: 4p. H.M.S. *Hesperus*; 21p. H.M.S. *Forester*; 22p. H.M.S. *Furious*; 62p. H.M.S. *Scylla*.

174 Shag

1991. Endangered Species. Birds. Multicoloured.
655	13p. Type **174**	1·40	1·60
656	13p. Barbary partridge	1·40	1·60
657	13p. Egyptian vulture	1·40	1·60
658	13p. Black stork	1·40	1·60

1991. No. 580 surch **£1.05**.
659	£1.05 on £3 9.2-inch "Mk.10" coastal gun, 1935	3·50	1·60

176 *North View of Gibraltar* (Gustavo Bacarisas)

1991. Local Paintings. Multicoloured.
660	22p. Type **176**	85	50
661	26p. *Parson's Lodge* (Elena Mifsud)	1·00	1·00
662	32p. *Governor's Parade* (Jacobo Azagury)	1·50	2·25
663	42p. *Waterport Wharf* (Rudesindo Mannia) (vert)	2·25	4·50

177 *Once in Royal David's City*

1991. Christmas. Carols. Multicoloured.

664	4p. Type **177**	40	10
665	24p. *Silent Night*	1·75	70
666	25p. *Angels We Have Heard on High*	1·75	1·25
667	49p. *O Come All Ye Faithful*	2·50	6·00

178 *Danaus chrysippus*

1991. "Phila Nippon '91" International Stamp Exhibition, Tokyo. Sheet 116×91 mm.

MS668	**178** £1.05, multicoloured	3·25	4·50

179 Columbus and *Santa Maria*

1992. Europa. 500th Anniv of Discovery of America by Columbus. Multicoloured.

669	24p. Type **179**	1·25	2·00
670	24p. Map of Old World and *Nina*	1·25	2·00
671	34p. Map of New World and *Pinta*	1·50	2·50
672	34p. Map of Old World and look-out	1·50	2·50

Nos. 669/70 and 671/2 were issued together, *se-tenant*, each pair forming a composite design.

179a Gibraltar from North

1992. 40th Anniv of Queen Elizabeth II's Accession. Multicoloured.

673	4p. Type **179a**	15	10
674	20p. H.M.S. "Arrow" (frigate) and Gibraltar from south	60	60
675	24p. Southport Gates	75	80
676	44p. Three portraits of Queen Elizabeth	1·25	1·60
677	54p. Queen Elizabeth II	1·60	1·90

180 Compass Rose, Sail, and Atlantic Map

1992. Round the World Yacht Rally. Multicoloured designs, each incorporating compass rose and sail.

678	21p. Type **180**	75	80
679	24p. Map of Indonesian Archipelago (horiz)	95	1·40
680	25p. Map of India Ocean (horiz)	95	1·75
MS681	108×72 mm. 21p. Type **180**; 49p. Map of Mediterranean and Red Sea	2·50	3·50

181 Holy Trinity Cathedral

1992. 150th Anniv of Anglican Diocese of Gibraltar-in-Europe. Multicoloured.

682	4p. Type **181**	20	10
683	24p. Diocesan crest and map (horiz)	1·00	65
684	44p. Construction of Cathedral and Sir George Don (horiz)	1·75	3·00
685	54p. Bishop Tomlinson	2·00	3·50

182 Sacred Heart of Jesus Church

1992. Christmas. Churches. Multicoloured.

686	4p. Type **182**	35	10
687	24p. Cathedral of St. Mary the Crowned	1·50	55
688	34p. St. Andrew's Church of Scotland	2·00	2·50
689	49p. St. Joseph's Church	2·50	5·50

183 "Drama and Music"

1993. Europa. Contemporary Art. Multicoloured.

690	24p. Type **183**	1·50	2·00
691	24p. "Sculpture, Art and Pottery"	1·50	2·00
692	34p. "Architecture"	2·00	2·75
693	34p. "Printing and Photography"	2·00	2·75

184 H.M.S. *Hood* (battle cruiser)

1993. Second World War Warships (1st series). Sheet 120×79 mm, containing T 184 and similar horiz designs. Multicoloured.

MS694	24p. Type **184**; 24p. H.M.S. *Ark Royal* (aircraft carrier, 1937); 24p. H.M.A.S. *Waterhen* (destroyer); 24p. U.S.S. *Gleaves* (destroyer)	11·00	11·00

See also Nos. **MS724**, **MS748**, **MS779** and **MS809**.

185 Landport Gate

1993. Architectural Heritage. Multicoloured.

695	1p. Type **185**	30	1·25
696	2p. St. Mary the Crowned Church (horiz)	50	1·25
697	3p. Parsons Lodge Battery (horiz)	50	1·50
698	4p. Moorish Castle (horiz)	65	1·25
699	5p. General Post Office	65	30
699a	6p. House of Assembly	2·00	1·25
699b	7p. Bleak House (horiz)	2·00	1·25
699c	8p. General Eliott Memorial	2·00	1·25
699d	9p. Supreme Court Building (horiz)	2·00	1·25
700	10p. South Barracks (horiz)	50	60
700a	20p. The Convent (horiz)	3·00	1·25
701	21p. American War Memorial	1·00	80
702	24p. Garrison Library (horiz)	1·10	80
703	25p. Southport Gates	1·10	80
704	26p. Casemates Gate (horiz)	1·10	80
704a	30p. St. Bernard's Hospital	4·00	1·25
704b	40p. City Hall (horiz)	4·00	2·00
705	50p. Central Police Station (horiz)	2·50	2·25
706	£1 Prince Edward's Gate	2·25	2·75
706a	£2 Church of the Sacred Heart of Jesus	8·50	8·00
707	£3 Lighthouse, Europa Point	11·00	11·00
708	£5 Coat of Arms and fortress keys	10·00	15·00

186 £sd and Decimal British Coins (25th anniv of decimal currency)

1993. Anniversaries. Multicoloured.

709	21p. Type **186**	1·00	65
710	24p. R.A.F. crest with Handley Page 0/400 and Panavia Tornado F Mk 3 (75th anniv)	1·75	75
711	34p. Garrison Library badge and building (bicent)	1·60	2·25
712	49p. Sir Winston Churchill and air raid (50th anniv of visit)	4·00	5·00

187 Mice decorating Christmas Tree

1993. Christmas. Multicoloured.

713	5p. Type **187**	25	10
714	24p. Mice pulling cracker	1·10	70
715	44p. Mice singing carols	2·25	3·00
716	49p. Mice building snowman	2·75	3·75

188 Exploding Atom (Lord Penney)

1994. Europa. Scientific Discoveries. Multicoloured.

717	24p. Type **188**	1·00	1·50
718	24p. Polonium and radium experiment (Marie Curie)	1·00	1·50
719	34p. First oil engine (Rudolph Diesel)	1·25	2·00
720	34p. Early telescope (Galileo)	1·25	2·00

189 World Cup and Map of U.S.A.

1994. World Cup Football Championship, U.S.A. Multicoloured.

721	26p. Type **189**	80	55
722	39p. Players and pitch in shape of U.S.A	1·25	2·00
723	49p. Player's legs (vert)	1·60	2·75

1994. Second World War Warships (2nd series). Sheet 112×72 mm, containing horiz designs as T 184. Multicoloured.

MS724	5p. H.M.S. *Penelope* (cruiser); 25p. H.M.S. *Warspite* (battleship); 44p. U.S.S. *McLanahan* (destroyer); 49p. *Isaac Sweers* (Dutch destroyer)	10·00	11·00

190 Pekingese

1994. "Philakorea '94" International Stamp Exhibition, Seoul. Sheet 102×76 mm.

MS725	**190** £1.05, multicoloured	2·50	4·00

191 Golden Star Coral

1994. Marine Life. Multicoloured.

726	21p. Type **191**	75	45
727	24p. Star fish	90	55
728	34p. Gorgonian sea-fan	1·50	2·25
729	49p. Peacock wrasse ("Turkish wrasse")	2·00	3·50

192 Throwing the Discus and Centenary Emblem

1994. Centenary of Int Olympic Committee. Multicoloured.

730	49p. Type **192**	1·75	2·25
731	54p. Javelin throwing and emblem	1·75	2·50

193 Great Tit

1994. Christmas. Songbirds. Multicoloured.

732	5p. Type **193**	80	10
733	24p. European robin (horiz)	2·25	70
734	34p. Blue tit (horiz)	2·50	1·50
735	54p. Eurasian goldfinch ("Goldfinch")	3·25	5·50

194 Austrian Flag, Hand and Star

1995. Expansion of European Union. Multicoloured.

736	24p. Type **194**	60	55
737	26p. Finnish flag, hand and star	60	60
738	34p. Swedish flag, hand and star	90	1·50
739	49p. Flags of new members and European Union emblem	1·60	3·25

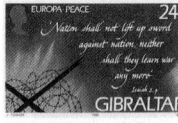

195 Barbed Wire and Quote from Isaiah Ch 2.4

1995. Europa. Peace and Freedom. Multicoloured.

740	24p. Type **195**	1·40	1·60
741	24p. Rainbow and hands releasing peace dove	1·40	1·60
742	34p. Shackles on wall and quote from Isaiah ch 61.1	1·60	2·25
743	34p. Hands and sea birds	1·60	2·25

196 Fairey Swordfish, I Class Destroyer and Rock of Gibraltar

1995. 50th Anniv of End of Second World War. Sheet 101×66 mm.

MS744	**196** £1.05, multicoloured	3·25	4·25

197 Yachting

1995. Island Games '95. Multicoloured.

745	24p. Type **197**	70	60
746	44p. Athlete on starting blocks	1·60	2·50
747	49p. Swimmer at start of race	1·60	2·50

1995. Second World War Warships (3rd series). Sheet 133×85 mm, containing horiz designs as T 184. Multicoloured.

MS748	5p. H.M.S. *Calpe* (destroyer); 24p. H.M.S. *Victorious* (aircraft carrier); 44p. U.S.S. *Weehawken* (attack transport); 49p. *Savorgan de Brazza* (French destroyer)	10·00	11·00

198 Bee Orchid

1995. "Singapore '95" International Stamp Exhibition. Orchids. Multicoloured.

749	22p. Type **198**	1·40	1·60
750	23p. Brown bee orchid	1·40	1·60
751	24p. Pyramidal orchid	1·40	1·60
752	25p. Mirror orchid	1·40	1·60
753	26p. Sawfly orchid	1·40	1·60

199 Handshake and United Nations Emblem

1995. 50th Anniv of United Nations. Multicoloured.

754	34p. Type **199**	1·50	1·10
755	49p. Peace dove and U.N. emblem	1·75	3·00

200 Marilyn Monroe

1995. Centenary of Cinema. T **200** and similar horiz designs showing film stars. Multicoloured.

MS756 Two sheets, each 116×80 mm. (a) 5p. Type **200**; 25p. Romy Schneider; 28p. Yves Montand; 38p. Audrey Hepburn. (b) 24p. Ingrid Bergman; 24p. Vittorio de Sica; 24p. Marlene Dietrich; 24p. Laurence Olivier Set of 2 sheets 4·50 5·50

201 Father Christmas

1995. Christmas. Multicoloured.

757	5p. Type **201**	40	10
758	24p. Toys in sack	1·25	55
759	34p. Reindeer	1·75	1·25
760	54p. Sleigh over houses	3·00	4·50

202 Shih Tzu

1996. Puppies. Multicoloured.

761	5p. Type **202**	40	85
762	21p. Dalmatians	75	95
763	24p. Cocker spaniels	80	1·10
764	25p. West Highland white terriers	80	1·10
765	34p. Labrador	90	1·25
766	35p. Boxer	90	1·25

No. 762 is inscr "Dalmation" in error.

203 Princess Anne

1996. Europa. Famous Women.

767	**203**	24p. black and yellow	1·60	1·60
768	-	24p. black and green	1·60	1·60
769	-	34p. black and red	2·00	2·25
770	-	34p. black and purple	2·25	2·25

DETAILS: Nos. 768, Princess Diana; 769, Queen Elizabeth II; 770, Queen Elizabeth the Queen Mother.

204 West German Player, 1980

1996. European Football Championship, England. Players from previous winning teams. Multicoloured.

771	21p. Type **204**	55	45
772	24p. French player, 1984	65	55
773	34p. Dutch player, 1988	95	1·10
774	£1.20 Danish player, 1992	2·50	4·75
MS775	135×91 mm. As Nos. 771/4	5·50	7·50

205 Ancient Greek Athletes

1996. Centenary of Modern Olympic Games.

776	**205**	34p. black, purple & orge	95	90
777	-	49p. black and brown	1·40	1·75
778	-	£1.05 multicoloured	3·00	4·50

DESIGNS: 49p. Start of early race; £1.05, Start of modern race.

1996. Second World War Warships (4th series). Sheet 118×84 mm, containing horiz designs as T **184**. Multicoloured.

MS779 5p. H.M.S. *Starling* (sloop); 25p. H.M.S. *Royalist* (cruiser); 49p. U.S.S. *Philadelphia* (cruiser); 54p. H.M.C.S. *Prescott* (corvette) 7·50 8·50

206 Asian Children

1996. 50th Anniv of UNICEF.

780	**206**	21p. multicoloured	60	80
781	-	24p. multicoloured	70	90
782	-	49p. multicoloured	1·25	2·00
783	-	54p. multicoloured	1·40	2·25

DESIGNS: 24p. to 54p. Children from different continents.

207 Red Kites in Flight

1996. Endangered Species. Red Kite. Multicoloured.

784	34p. Type **207**	1·60	1·90
785	34p. Red kite on ground	1·60	1·90
786	34p. On rock	1·60	1·90
787	34p. Pair at nest	1·60	1·90

208 Christmas Pudding

1996. Christmas. Designs created from "Lego" Blocks. Multicoloured.

788	5p. Type **208**	15	15
789	21p. Snowman face	70	45
790	24p. Present	80	55
791	34p. Father Christmas face	1·10	1·25
792	54p. Candle	1·50	2·75

209 *Mary Celeste* passing Gibraltar

1997. Europa. Tales and Legends. *The Mary Celeste.* Multicoloured.

793	28p. Type **209**	1·40	1·40
794	28p. Boarding the *Mary Celeste*	1·40	1·40
795	30p. Crew leaving *Mary Celeste*	1·40	1·60
796	30p. *Mary Celeste* found by *Dei Gratia*	1·40	1·60

210 American Shorthair Silver Tabby

1997. Kittens. Multicoloured.

797	5p. Type **210**	40	1·00
798	24p. Rumpy Manx red tabby	75	1·25
799	26p. Blue point birmans	75	1·25
800	28p. Red self longhair	80	1·25
801	30p. British shorthair tortoise-shell and white	80	1·25
802	35p. British bicolour shorthairs	90	1·40

MS803 132×80 mm. Nos. 797/802 with "HONG KONG '97" International Stamp Exhibition logo at bottom left 5·50 8·00

211 *Anthocharis belia euphenoides*

1997. Butterflies. Multicoloured.

804	23p. Type **211**	70	50
805	26p. *Charaxes jasius*	85	60
806	30p. *Vanessa cardui*	95	90
807	£1.20 *Iphiclides podalirius*	3·25	5·00
MS808	135×90 mm. Nos. 804/7	5·25	6·50

1997. Second World War Warships (5th series). Sheet 117×82 mm, containing horiz designs as T **184**. Multicoloured.

MS809 24p. H.M.S. *Enterprise* (cruiser); 26p. H.M.S. *Cleopatra* (cruiser); 38p. U.S.S. *Iowa* (battleship); 50p. *Orkan* (Polish destroyer) 4·00 5·00

212 Queen Elizabeth and Prince Philip at Carriage-driving Trials

1997. Golden Wedding of Queen Elizabeth and Prince Philip. Multicoloured.

810	£1.20 Type **212**	4·75	5·50
811	£1.40 Queen Elizabeth in Trooping the Colour uniform	4·75	5·50

213 Christian Dior Evening Dress

1997. Christian Dior Spring/Summer '97 Collection. Multicoloured.

812	30p. Type **213**	80	1·25
813	35p. Tunic top and skirt	1·00	1·60
814	50p. Ballgown	1·00	1·75
815	62p. Two-piece suit	1·25	2·25
MS816	110×90 mm. £1.20, Ballgown (different)	2·25	3·50

214 *Our Lady and St. Bernard* (St. Joseph's Parish Church)

1997. Christmas. Stained Glass Windows. Multicoloured.

817	5p. Type **214**	25	10
818	26p. *The Epiphany* (Our Lady of Sorrows Church)	1·00	60
819	38p. *St. Joseph* (Our Lady of Sorrows Church)	1·25	95
820	50p. *The Holy Family* (St. Joseph's Parish Church)	1·50	2·25
821	62p. *The Miraculous Medal* (St. Joseph's Parish Church)	1·75	3·25

215 Sir Joshua Hassan

1997. Sir Joshua Hassan (former Chief Minister) Commemoration.

822	**215** 26p. black	1·50	75

216 Wales v Brazil (1958)

1998. World Football Championship, France (1998). Multicoloured.

823	5p. Type **216**	25	10
824	26p. Northern Ireland v France (1958)	1·00	60
825	38p. Scotland v Holland (1978)	1·25	90
826	£1.20 England v West Germany (1966)	2·25	4·75
MS827	153×96 mm. Nos. 823/6	4·25	6·00

1998. Diana, Princess of Wales Commemoration. Sheet 145×70 mm, containing vert designs as T **177** of Ascension. Multicoloured.

MS828 26p. Wearing jacket with white fur collar, 1988; 26p. Wearing pink checked suit and hat; 38p. Wearing black jacket, 1995; 38p. Wearing blue jacket with gold embroidery, 1987 (sold at £1.28+20p. charity premium) 2·25 3·75

216b Saunders Roe (Saro) London (flying boat)

1998. 80th Anniv of Royal Air Force. Multicoloured.

829	24p. Type **216b**	70	55
830	26p. Fairey Fox	75	60
831	38p. Handley Page Halifax GR.VI	95	1·25
832	50p. Hawker Siddeley Buccaneer S.2B	1·25	2·50
MS833	110×77 mm. 24p. Sopwith Strutter; 26p. Bristol M.IB; 38p. Supermarine Spitfire XII; 50p. Avro York 685 York	3·50	4·50

217 Miss Gibraltar saluting

1998. Europa. Festivals. National Day. Multicoloured.

834	26p. Type **217**	1·10	1·25
835	26p. In black bodice and long red skirt	1·10	1·25
836	38p. In black bodice and short red skirt, with Gibraltar flag	1·40	1·60
837	38p. In Genoese-style costume	1·40	1·60

218 Striped Dolphin

1998. International Year of the Ocean. Sheet 155×64 mm, containing T **218** and similar multicoloured designs.

MS838 5p. Type **218**; 5p. Common dolphin (vert); 26p. Killer whale (vert); £1.20, Blue whale (vert) 5·50 6·50

219 Nileus (dog) with Hat and Telescope

1998. Bicentenary of Battle of the Nile. Multicoloured.

839	12p. Type **219**		1·00	1·25
840	26p. Rear-Admiral Sir Horatio Nelson		1·00	80
841	28p. Frances Nisbet, Lady Nelson		1·75	2·00
842	35p. H.M.S. *Vanguard* (ship of the line)		1·75	2·25
843	50p. Battle of the Nile (47×29 mm)		1·75	3·25

220 *Love comforts like Sunshine after Rain* (William Shakespeare)

1998. Famous Quotations. Multicoloured.

844	26p. Type **220**		90	1·00
845	26p. *The price of greatness is responsibility* (Sir Winston Churchill)		90	1·00
846	38p. *Hate the sin, love the sinner* (Mahatma Gandhi)		1·10	1·50
847	38p. *Imagination is more important than knowledge* (Albert Einstein)		1·10	1·50

221 The Nativity

1998. Christmas. Multicoloured.

848	5p. Type **221**		35	10
849	26p. Star and stable		1·25	70
850	30p. King with gold		1·40	75
851	35p. King with myrrh		1·40	1·25
852	50p. King with frankincense		1·75	3·25

222 Barbary Macaque

1999. Europa. Parks and Gardens. Upper Rock Nature Reserve. Multicoloured.

853	30p. Type **222**		1·75	1·50
854	30p. Dartford warbler		2·00	1·50
855	42p. Dusky grouper		2·00	2·50
856	42p. River kingfisher ("Common Kingfisher")		2·25	2·50

223 Queen Elizabeth II

1999

(a) Ordinary gum

857	**223**	1p. purple	10	70
858	**223**	2p. brown	10	70
859	**223**	4p. blue	20	60
860	**223**	5p. green	20	30
861	**223**	10p. orange	40	30
862	**223**	12p. red	45	40
863	**223**	20p. green	1·00	45
864	**223**	28p. mauve	1·25	60
865	**223**	30p. orange	1·50	65
866	**223**	40p. grey	2·00	85
867	**223**	42p. green	2·00	90
868	**223**	50p. bistre	2·00	1·25
869	**223**	£1 black	3·50	2·75
869a	**223**	£1.20 red	4·50	4·00
869b	**223**	£1.40 blue	4·50	4·25
870	**223**	£3 blue	8·50	11·00

(b) Self-adhesive.

871		(1st) orange	1·00	60

Nos. 868/71 are larger, 22×28 mm.
No. 871 was initially sold at 26p.

224 Roman Marine and Galley

1999. Maritime Heritage. Multicoloured.

872	5p. Type **224**		25	10
873	30p. Arab sailor, medieval galley house and dhow		95	65
874	42p. Marine officer and British ship of the line (1779–83)		1·50	1·50
875	£1.20 Naval rating, Queen Alexandra Dry Dock and H.M.S. *Berwick* (cruiser) (1904)		3·25	4·25
MS876	116×76 mm. Nos. 872/5		6·00	7·00

225 John Lennon (musician)

1999. 30th Wedding Anniv of John Lennon and Yoko Ono. Designs showing John Lennon.

877	–	20p. multicoloured	1·00	55
878	**225**	30p. black and blue	1·25	90
879	–	40p. multicoloured	1·50	1·90
MS880	Two sheets, each 62×100 mm. (a) £1 black and blue. (b) £1 multicoloured Set of 2 sheets		8·50	8·50

DESIGNS 20p. With flower over left eye; 40p. Wearing orange glasses; £1 (No. **MS**880a), Holding marriage certificate; £1 (No. **MS**880b), Standing on aircraft steps.

226 Postal Van at Dockside, 1930s

1999. 125th Anniv of U.P.U. Multicoloured.

881	5p. Type **226**		25	25
882	30p. Space shuttle and station		75	1·25

227 Eurofighter EF-2000 Typhoon

1999. "Wings of Prey" (1st series). Birds of Prey and R.A.F. Fighter Aircraft. Multicoloured.

883	30p. Type **227**		1·25	1·40
884	30p. Panavia Tornado F.Mk3		1·25	1·40
885	30p. BAe Harrier II GR7		1·25	1·40
886	42p. Lesser kestrel		1·40	1·60
887	42p. Peregrine falcon		1·40	1·60
888	42p. Common kestrel ("Kestrel")		1·40	1·60
MS889	Two sheets, each 105×86 mm. (a) Nos. 883/5. (b) Nos. 886/8 Set of 2 sheets		8·00	8·50

See also Nos. 943/8 and 982/7.

228 Prince Edward and Sophie Rhys-Jones

1999. Royal Wedding. Multicoloured.

890	30p. Type **228**		1·25	65
891	42p. Prince Edward and Sophie Rhys-Jones holding hands (vert)		1·60	1·00
892	54p. In carriage on wedding day		2·00	2·50
893	66p. On Chapel steps after wedding (vert)		2·50	3·00

229 Football

1999. Local Sporting Centenaries. Multicoloured.

894	30p. Type **229**		75	65
895	42p. Rowing		1·00	90
896	£1.20 Cricket		3·25	4·25

230 "Seasons Greetings"

1999. Christmas. Multicoloured.

897	5p. Type **230**		15	10
898	5p. "Happy Christmas"		15	10
899	30p. "Happy Millennium"		80	80
900	30p. "Happy Christmas" and Santa with reindeer		80	80
901	42p. Santa Claus in chimney		1·25	1·75
902	54p. Santa Claus leaving presents		1·40	2·50

231 People travelling with Environmentally-friendly Jet-packs (Colin Grech)

2000. "Stampin' the Future" (children's stamp design competition). Multicoloured.

903	30p. Type **231**		1·50	1·60
904	42p. *Robotic Postman* (Kim Barea)		1·50	1·60
905	54p. *Living on the Moon* (Stephan Williamson-Fa)		1·50	1·60
906	66p. *Jet-powered Cars* (Michael Podesta)		1·50	1·60

232 Dutch Football Player and Flag, 1988

2000. European Football Championship, Belgium and Netherlands. Multicoloured.

907	30p. Type **232**		85	90
908	30p. French player and flag, 1984		85	90
909	42p. German player scoring and flag, 1996		1·10	1·40
910	42p. Danish player and flag, 1992		1·10	1·40
MS911	Two sheets, each 115×85 mm. (a) 54p.×4, English player and flag. (b) Nos. 907/10 Set of 2 sheets		11·00	12·00

233 Fountain of Stars

2000. Europa. Multicoloured.

912	30p. Type **233**		1·00	80
913	40p. Exchanging star		1·25	1·40
914	42p. Stars and airplane		1·25	1·40
915	54p. Stars and end of rainbow		1·75	2·75

234 3000 m Waterfall between Gibraltar and North African Coast, 5 Million B.C.

2000. New Millennium. History of Gibraltar. Multicoloured (except Nos. 926/30).

916	5p. Type **234**		30	50
917	5p. Sabre-tooth tiger, 2 million B.C.		30	50
918	5p. Neanderthal hunting goat, and skull, 30,000 B.C.		30	50
919	5p. Phoenician traders and galley, 700 B.C.		30	50
920	5p. Roman warship, 100 B.C.		30	50

921	5p. Tarik-Ibn-Zayad, ape and Moorish Castle, 711 A.D.		30	50
922	5p. Coat of arms, 1502		30	50
923	5p. Admiral George Rooke and Union Jack, 1704		30	50
924	30p. General Eliott at The Great Siege, 1779–83		1·00	1·25
925	30p. H.M.S. *Victory*, 1805		1·00	1·25
926	30p. Queen Alexandra in horse-drawn carriage, 1903 (brown, silver and black)		1·00	1·25
927	30p. 100 ton gun, 1870s (grey, silver and black)		1·00	1·25
928	30p. Evacuees, 1940 (purple, silver and black)		1·00	1·25
929	30p. Tank and anti-aircraft gun, 1940s (brown, silver and black)		1·00	1·25
930	30p. Queen Elizabeth II in Gibraltar, 1954 (grey, silver and black)		1·00	1·25
931	30p. Aerial view of office district, 2000		1·00	1·25

235 Princess Diana holding Prince William, 1982

2000. 18th Birthday of Prince William. Multicoloured.

932	30p. Type **235**		90	65
933	42p. Prince William as a toddler		1·25	90
934	54p. Prince William with Prince Charles		1·50	2·00
935	66p. Prince William at 18		1·75	2·75
MS936	115×75 mm. Nos. 932/5		5·00	6·00

236 Lady Elizabeth Bowes-Lyon signing Book

2000. Queen Elizabeth the Queen Mother's 100th Birthday.

937	**236**	30p. black and blue	90	65
938	–	42p. black and brown	1·25	90
939	–	54p. multicoloured	1·50	2·00
940	–	66p. multicoloured	1·75	2·75
MS941	115×75 mm. Nos. 937/40		4·75	6·00

DESIGNS: 42p. Duke and Duchess of York; 54p. Queen Mother with bouquet; 66p. Queen Mother in orange coat and hat.

237 Moorish Castle

2000

942	**237**	£5 black, silver and gold	13·00	14·00

The Queen's head on this stamp is printed in optically variable ink, which changes colour from gold to green when viewed from different angles.

2000. "Wings of Prey" (2nd series). Birds of Prey and R.A.F. Second World War Aircraft. As T 227. Multicoloured.

943	30p. Supermarine Spitfire Mk IIA *Gibraltar*		1·75	1·75
944	30p. Hawker Hurricane Mk IIC		1·75	1·75
945	30p. Avro Lancaster BI-III *City of Lincoln*		1·75	1·75
946	42p. Merlin (male)		2·00	2·00
947	42p. Merlin (female)		2·00	2·00
948	42p. Bonelli's eagle		2·00	2·00
MS949	Two sheets, each 105×85 mm. (a) Nos. 943/5. (b) Nos. 946/8 Set of 2 sheets		10·00	10·00

238 Infant Jesus

2000. Christmas. Multicoloured.

950	5p. Type **238**		25	15
951	30p. Virgin Mary with infant Jesus		85	65
952	30p. Journey to Bethlehem		85	65
953	40p. Mary and Joseph with innkeeper		1·10	1·00
954	42p. The Nativity		1·10	1·25
955	54p. Visit of the Wise Men		1·60	2·25

239 Wedding of Queen Victoria and Prince Albert

2001. Death Centenary of Queen Victoria.

956	239	30p. blue, violet and black	1·00	65
957	-	42p. myrtle, green & black	1·40	1·00
958	-	54p. purple, red and black	2·00	2·50
959	-	66p. brown, gold & black	2·25	3·25

DESIGNS: 42p. Victoria as Empress of India; 54p. Queen Victoria in carriage; 66p. Queen Victoria standing by chair.

240 Grass Snake

2001. Snakes. Multicoloured.

960	5p. Type **240**	25	40
961	5p. Ladder snake	25	40
962	5p. Montpellier snake	25	40
963	5p. Viperine snake	85	1·00
964	30p. Southern smooth snake	85	1·00
965	30p. False smooth snake	85	1·00
966	66p. Horseshoe whip snake (30×62 mm)	1·75	2·50
MS967	155×87 mm. Nos. 960/6	7·00	7·50

No. **MS967** also commemorates the Chinese New Year "Year of the Snake".

No. 962 and **MS967** are inscribed "MONTPELIER" in error.

241 Long-snouted Seahorse

2001. Europa. Water and Nature. Multicoloured.

968	30p. Type **241**	1·75	80
969	40p. Snapdragon	2·25	1·25
970	42p. Herring gull ("Yellow-legged Gull")	3·25	1·75
971	54p. Goldfish	2·75	5·00

242 Queen Elizabeth II as a Baby

2001. 75th Birthday of Queen Elizabeth II.

972	242	30p. black and mauve	85	75
973	-	30p. black and violet	85	75
974	-	42p. black and red	1·25	1·50
975	-	42p. black and violet	1·25	1·50
976	-	54p. multicoloured	1·60	2·25
MS977		101×89 mm. £2 multicoloured	5·50	6·50

DESIGNS—HORIZ: No. 973, Queen Elizabeth as teenager; 974, On wedding day, 1947; 975, After Coronation, 1953; 976, Queen Elizabeth in blue hat. VERT: (35×49 mm)—No. **MS977**, Queen Elizabeth II, 2001 (photo by Fiona Hanson).

No. **MS977** marks a successful attempt on the record for the fastest produced stamp issue. The miniature sheet was on sale in Gibraltar 10 hours and 24 minutes after the artwork was approved at Buckingham Palace.

243 Battle of Trafalgar, 1805

2001. Bicentenary of The Gibraltar Chronicle (newspaper). Each black.

978	30p. Type **243**	1·50	65
979	42p. Invention of the telephone, 1876	1·25	90
980	54p. Winston Churchill (Victory in Second World War, 1945)	2·50	2·50

981	66p. Footprint on Moon (Moon landing, 1969)	2·50	3·75

2001. "Wings of Prey" (3rd series). Birds of Prey and Modern Military Aircraft. As T **227**. Multicoloured.

982	40p. Royal Navy Sea Harrier FA MK.2	1·25	1·50
983	40p. Western marsh harrier ("Marsh Harrier")	1·25	1·50
984	40p. R.A.F. Hawk T MK.1	1·25	1·50
985	40p. Northern sparrowhawk ("Sparrowhawk")	1·25	1·50
986	40p. R.A.F. SEPECAT Jaguar GR1B	1·25	1·50
987	40p. Northern hobby ("Hobby")	1·25	1·50
MS988	Two sheets, each 103×84 mm. (a) Nos. 982, 984 and 986. (b) Nos. 983, 985 and 987 Set of 2 sheets	6·50	7·00

244 Snoopy as Father Christmas with Woodstock

2001. Christmas. Peanuts (cartoon characters by Charles Schulz). Multicoloured.

989	5p. Type **244**	25	15
990	30p. Charlie Brown and Snoopy with Christmas tree	85	65
991	40p. Snoopy asleep in wreath	1·10	1·00
992	42p. Snoopy with plate of biscuits	1·25	1·25
993	54p. Snoopy asleep on kennel	1·75	2·50
MS994	140×85 mm. Nos. 989/93	4·75	5·50

245 One Cent Coin

2002. Introduction of Euro Currency by European Union. Coins. Sheet 165×105 mm, containing T **245** and similar square designs showing coins. Multicoloured.

MS995	5p. Type **245**; 12p. 2 cents; 30p. 5 cents; 35p. 10 cents; 40p. 20 cents; 42p. 50 cents; 54p. 1 Euro; 66p. 2 Euros.	7·00	7·50

2002. Golden Jubilee. As T **219** of Falkland Islands.

996	30p. black, red and gold	1·25	1·40
997	30p. agate, red and gold	1·25	1·40
998	30p. multicoloured	1·25	1·40
999	30p. multicoloured	1·25	1·40
1000	75p. multicoloured	2·25	3·00
MS1001	162×95 mm. Nos. 996/1000	7·00	8·00

DESIGNS—HORIZ: No. 996, Princess Elizabeth and Princess Margaret making radio broadcast, 1940; 997, Princess Elizabeth in Girl Guide uniform, 1942; 998, Queen Elizabeth in evening dress, 1961; 999, Queen Elizabeth in Chelsea, 1993. VERT: (38×51 mm): No 1000, Queen Elizabeth after Annigoni.

246 Joshua Grimaldi

2002. Europa. Circus. Famous Clowns. Multicoloured.

1002	30p. Type **246**	90	65
1003	40p. Karl Wettach ("Grock")	1·25	1·25
1004	42p. Nicolai Polakovs ("Coco")	1·25	1·25
1005	54p. Charlie Cairoli	1·75	2·50

247 Bobby Moore holding Jules Rimet Trophy, 1966

2002. World Cup Football Championship, Japan and Korea (2002). England's Victory, 1966. Multicoloured.

1006	30p. Type **247**	80	65
1007	42p. Kissing Trophy	1·25	90
1008	54p. Bobby Moore with Queen Elizabeth II	1·50	2·00
1009	66p. Bobby Moore in action	1·75	2·75
MS1010	135×90 mm. Nos. 1006/9	5·50	6·00

---

248 Barbary Macaque

2002. Wildlife. Multicoloured.

1011	30p. Type **248**	90	80
1012	30p. Red fox (horiz)	90	80
1013	40p. White-toothed shrew (horiz)	1·25	85
1014	£1 Rabbit	2·75	3·50
MS1015	125×100 mm. Nos. 1011/14	6·00	7·00

249 Gibraltar from the North

2002. Views of the Rock of Gibraltar. Multicoloured.

1016	30p. Type **249**	1·25	1·25
1017	30p. View from the south	1·25	1·25
1018	£1 View from the east (50×40 mm)	2·75	3·50
1019	£1 View from the west (50×40 mm)	2·75	3·50

Nos. 1016/19 were printed together, *se-tenant*, with powdered particles of the Rock sintered to their surface using thermography.

250 Princess Diana holding Prince Harry

2002. 18th Birthday of Prince Harry. Multicoloured.

1020	30p. Type **250**	90	65
1021	42p. Prince Harry waving	1·25	90
1022	54p. Prince Harry skiing	1·50	1·60
1023	66p. Wearing dark suit	1·90	2·75
MS1024	115×75 mm. Nos. 1020/3	5·50	6·50

251 Crib, Cathedral of St. Mary the Crowned

2002. Christmas. Cribs from Gibraltar Cathedrals and Churches. Multicoloured.

1025	5p. Type **251**	35	10
1026	30p. St. Joseph's Parish Church	1·25	65
1027	40p. St. Theresa's Parish Church	1·50	85
1028	42p. Our Lady of Sorrows Church	1·50	90
1029	52p. St. Bernard's Church	1·75	2·50
1030	54p. Cathedral of the Holy Trinity	1·75	2·50

252 Archbishop of Canterbury crowning Queen Elizabeth II

2003. 50th Anniv of the Coronation. Each black, grey and purple.

1031	30p. Type **252**	90	85
1032	30p. Queen Elizabeth II in Coronation robes	90	85
1033	40p. Queen Elizabeth holding the Orb and Sceptre	1·40	85
1034	£1 Queen Elizabeth in Coronation Coach	3·00	3·50
MS1035	116×76 mm. Nos. 1031/4	5·50	6·50

---

253 Young Prince William with Princess Diana

2003. 21st Birthday of Prince William of Wales. Each black, grey and violet.

1036	30p. Type **253**	1·50	1·00
1037	30p. Prince William at Eton College	1·50	1·00
1038	40p. Prince William	2·00	1·00
1039	£1 Prince William in Operation Raleigh sweatshirt	3·75	4·50
MS1040	115×75 mm. Nos. 1036/9	7·00	7·50

254 Drama Festival Poster

2003. Europa. Poster Art. Multicoloured.

1041	30p. Type **254**	80	65
1042	40p. Spring Festival poster	1·00	1·00
1043	42p. Art Festival poster	1·00	1·00
1044	54p. Dance festival poster	1·50	2·50

255 Wright Brothers' *Flyer I*, 1903

2003. Centenary of Powered Flight. Aircraft.

1045	255	30p. multicoloured	90	65
1046	-	40p. black and brown	1·25	1·25
1047	-	40p. black and blue	1·25	1·25
1048	-	42p. black and blue	1·25	1·25
1049	-	44p. multicoloured	1·40	1·40
1050	-	66p. multicoloured	2·00	3·25
MS1051		140×110 mm. Nos. 1045/50	7·75	8·25

DESIGNS—HORIZ: (37×28 mm) 40p. (No. 1046) Charles Lindbergh and *Spirit of St. Louis* (first Transatlantic solo flight, 1927); 40p. (No. 1047) Boeing 314 *Yankee Clipper* flying boat (first Transatlantic scheduled air service, 1939). (77×28 mm)—42p. Saunders Roe (Saro) A21 Windhover (first scheduled air service between Gibraltar and Tangier, 1931); 44p. Aerospatiale/BAe Concorde (first supersonic airliner, 1976). VERT (37×58 mm)—66p. Space shuttle *Columbia* (first shuttle flight in Space orbit, 1981).

256 Flag of St. George

2003. 1700th Death Anniv of St. George. Multicoloured.

1052	30p. Type **256**	1·00	65
1053	40p. Cross of Military Constantinian Order of St. George	1·25	95
1054	£1.20 "St. George and the Dragon" (stained glass window, St. Joseph's Church, Gibraltar) (32×63 mm)	3·50	4·50
MS1055	150×100 mm. Nos. 1052/4	5·25	6·00

257 Big Ben, Swift and Rock of Gibraltar

2003

1056	257	(£3) multicoloured†	8·00	8·50

No. 1056 is inscribed "UK express" and was initially sold at £3.

†The Queen's head on this stamp is printed in optically variable ink which changes colour from gold to green when viewed from different angles.

258 Wood Blewit
(*Lepista nuda*)

2003. Mushrooms of Gibraltar. Multicoloured.
1057	30p.	Type **258**	1·00	1·00
1058	30p.	Blue-green funnel-cap (*Clitocybe odora*)	1·00	1·00
1059	30p.	Sulphur tuft (*Hypholoma fasciculare*)	1·00	1·00
1060	£1·20	Field mushrooms (*Agaricus campestris*)	3·50	4·25
MS1061	105×90 mm. Nos. 1057/60		6·00	7·00

259 Daisy (Latvia), Cornflower (Estonia) and Rue (Lithuania)

2003. Enlargement of the European Union (2004). Designs showing the national flowers of new member countries. Multicoloured.
1062	30p.	Type **259**	1·25	80
1063	40p.	Rose (Cyprus) and Maltese Centaury (Malta)	1·50	1·25
1064	42p.	Tulip (Hungary), Carnation (Slovenia) and Dog Rose (Slovakia)	1·50	1·25
1065	54p.	Corn Poppy (Poland) and Scented Thyme (Czech Republic)	2·00	3·25

260 Baby Jesus Crib Figure, Our Lady of Sorrows Church

2003. Christmas. Multicoloured.
1066	5p.	Type **260**	20	10
1067	30p.	Children making Crib	90	65
1068	40p.	Three Kings Cavalcade	1·25	1·00
1069	42p.	Children's provisions for Santa and reindeer	1·25	1·00
1070	54p.	Cathedral of St. Mary the Crowned lit for Christmas Eve Midnight Mass	1·75	3·00
MS1071	100×80 mm. £1 Cartoon characters from Peanuts carol singing around Christmas tree (50×40 mm)		4·25	5·00

261 Street Cafe

2004. Europa. Holidays. Multicoloured.
1072	40p.	Type **261**	1·25	1·40
1073	40p.	St. Michael's Cave	1·25	1·40
1074	54p.	Dolphins	1·75	2·25
1075	54p.	Harbourside restaurant	1·75	2·25

262 Arms

2004. 300th Anniv of British Gibraltar (1st series). Multicoloured.
1076	8p.	Type **262**	65	65
MS1077	144×114 mm. 30p. Royal Katarine flying Red Ensign, 1704; 30p. Landing party, 1704; 30p. Soldiers of 1704; 30p. Arms of Gibraltar on military uniform; 30p. Royal Gibraltar police helmet and red phone box; 30p. Post Office arms and red pillar box; 30p. Graduates and University of Cambridge examination certificate; 30p. Crowd waving Union Jacks and Gibraltar flags; £1·20 Union Jack		12·00	13·00

See also MS1095.

263 Queen Elizabeth holding Bouquet

2004. 50th Anniv of Visit of Queen Elizabeth II.
1078	**263**	38p. multicoloured	1·10	85
1079	-	40p. black and yellow	1·10	85
1080	-	47p. multicoloured	1·25	1·25
1081	-	£1 black	2·75	4·00
MS1082	95×110 mm. £1·50 black		3·75	4·50

DESIGNS: 38p. Type **263**; 40p. Queen Elizabeth holding out keys; 47p. Queen and Duke of Edinburgh in car; £1 Queen, Prince Charles and Princess Anne with members of British armed forces; £1·50 Queen waving with Duke of Edinburgh.

264 Scoring a Goal

2004. European Football Championships 2004, Portugal. Multicoloured.
1083	30p.	Type **264**	90	65
1084	40p.	Two defenders blocking a goal attempt	1·25	1·25
1085	40p.	Overhead kick	1·25	1·25
1086	£1	Player performing header	2·75	4·00
MS1087	Two sheets. (a) 102×77 mm. £1·50 Player celebrating with arms in air (51×39 mm) (b) 105×105 mm (circular). Nos. 1083/6		8·00	8·50

265 Landing at St. Aubin, 1944

2004. 60th Anniv of D-Day Landings. Each black, brown and red.
1088	38p.	Type **265**	1·25	85
1089	40p.	Cruiser tank Mk VIII Cromwell	1·40	1·40
1090	47p.	Handley Page Halifax plane	1·60	1·60
1091	£1	HMS *Belfast*	3·00	4·00
MS1092	170×100 mm. Nos. 1088/91		6·00	7·00

266 Union Jack Flag

2004. 300th Anniv of British Gibraltar (2nd series). Elton John Tercentenary Concert. Circular sheet 105×105 mm.
MS1093	**266**	£1·20 multicoloured	3·00	3·25

Stamp in No. MS1093 is similar in design to the £1·20 stamp in No. MS1077.

267 Mallow-leaved Bindweed

2004. Wild Flowers. Multicoloured.
1094	1p.	Type **267**	15	35
1095	2p.	Gibraltar sea lavender	25	35
1095b	3p.	Gibraltar restharrow	30	40
1096	5p.	Gibraltar chickweed	30	30
1097	(7p.)	Romulea	45	20
1098	10p.	Common centaury	60	30
1099	(12p.)	Pyramidal orchid	75	75
1099b	15p.	Paper-white narcissus	75	50
1100	(28p.)	Friars cowl	1·25	60
1101	(38p.)	Corn poppy	1·40	85
1102	40p.	Giant Tangier fennel	1·40	65
1103	(47p.)	Snapdragon	1·75	1·10
1104	50p.	Common gladiolus	1·75	1·50
1104b	53p.	Gibraltar campion	2·00	1·60
1105	£1	Yellow horned poppy	3·50	3·50
1105b	£1·60	Sea daffodil	4·75	4·75
1106	£3	Gibraltar candytuft	9·50	10·00

Nos. 1097 and 1099/103 are inscribed "G", "G1", "S", "UK", "E" and "U" and were initially sold for 7p., 12p., 28p., 38p., 40p. and 47p. respectively.

268 Father Christmas

2004. Christmas. Decorations. Multicoloured.
1107	7p.	Type **268**	30	20
1108	28p.	Cherub	1·25	60
1109	38p.	Red star	1·40	80
1110	40p.	Gold conical tree	1·40	85
1111	47p.	Red bauble	1·60	1·25
1112	53p.	Gold star	1·90	3·50

269 Ferrari F2003 GA

2004. Ferrari. Multicoloured.
1113	5p.	Type **269**	35	40
1114	5p.	F2004	35	40
1115	30p.	F2001	1·00	1·00
1116	30p.	F2002	1·00	1·00
1117	75p.	F399	2·50	3·00
1118	75p.	F1-2000	2·50	3·00
MS1119	161×116 mm. Nos. 1113/18		7·00	7·50

270 Soldier guarding Nelson's Body

2005. Bicentenary of the Battle of Trafalgar. Multicoloured.
1120	38p.	Type **270**	1·75	75
1121	40p.	HMS *Entreprenante*	1·75	85
1122	47p.	Admiral Nelson (vert)	2·00	1·50
1123	£1·60	HMS *Victory*	5·50	7·50
MS1124	120×80 mm. £2 HMS *Victory* (44×44 mm)		12·00	12·00

Nos. 1120/4 contain traces of powdered wood from HMS *Victory*.

271 Spinach Pie

2005. Europa. Gastronomy. Multicoloured.
1125	47p.	Type **271**	1·75	2·00
1126	47p.	Grilled sea-bass	1·75	2·00
1127	47p.	Veal "Birds"	1·75	2·00
1128	47p.	Sherry trifle	1·75	2·00

272 Churchill giving Victory Salute

2005. 60th Anniv of VE Day. Multicoloured.
1129	38p.	Type **272**	1·40	90
1130	40p.	Family with Union Jack flags	1·40	90
1131	47p.	VE Day celebrations	1·60	1·50
1132	£1	Returning Gibraltar people on dockside	3·75	4·75
MS1133	150×100 mm. Nos. 1129/32		7·25	7·50

273 *Circassia*

2005. Cruise Ships (1st series). Multicoloured.
1134	38p.	Type **273**	1·40	90

1135	40p.	*Nevasa*	1·40	90
1136	47p.	*Black Prince*	1·60	1·50
1137	£1	*Arcadia*	3·75	4·75
MS1138	150×85 mm. Nos. 1134/7		7·25	7·50

See also Nos. 1180/MS1184 and 1207/MS1211.

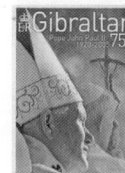

274 Early and Modern Police Officers

2005. Anniversaries. Multicoloured.
1139	38p.	Type **274** (175th anniv of Royal Gibraltar Police)	2·00	1·00
1140	47p.	Skull, plate and ceramic horses (75th anniv of Gibraltar Museum)	1·50	1·00
1141	£1	Charter of Justice (175th anniv)	3·75	5·00

The back of Nos. 1139/41 is printed with a brief description of the subject of the stamp.

275 Pope John Paul II

2005. Pope John Paul II Commemoration.
1142	**275**	75p. multicoloured	2·50	2·75

276 Map of Europe and 1979 Europa 12p. Stamp

2005. 50th Anniv of Europa Stamps.
1143	**276**	£5 multicoloured	14·00	16·00

277 Death of Nelson (William Devis)

2005. Bicentenary of the Battle of Trafalgar and Death of Admiral Lord Nelson. Multicoloured.
MS1144	120×80 mm. £1 Type **277**		3·25	4·00
MS1145	170×75 mm. £1 As Type **277**, but 50×31 mm together with £1 stamp from Isle of Man No. MS1264		6·50	7·00

No. MS1145 was also issued by Isle of Man.

278 Two Angels

2005. Christmas. Angels. Multicoloured.
1146	7p.	Type **278**	25	20
1147	38p.	Angel with children by Christmas tree	1·25	80
1148	40p.	Angel with toys	1·25	80
1149	47p.	Angel with hymn book and top of Christmas tree	1·75	1·40
1150	53p.	Angel with basket of fruit	2·00	2·75
MS1151	168×86 mm. Nos. 1146/50		6·00	7·00

279 Giant Devil Ray

2006. Endangered Species. Giant Devil Ray (*Mobula mobular*). Multicoloured.
1152	38p.	Type **279**	1·25	1·75
1153	40p.	Giant devil ray and trail of bubbles	1·40	1·75
1154	47p.	Two giant devil rays	1·75	2·00
1155	£1	Upperside of giant devil ray	3·75	4·00

280 Queen Elizabeth II

2006. 80th Birthday of Queen Elizabeth II. Each showing 1950s and more recent photograph. Multicoloured.

1156	38p. Type **280**	2·00	2·00
1157	40p. In evening dress, c. 1955 and wearing purple hat	2·00	2·00
1158	47p. Smelling carnation, c. 1955 and wearing yellow hat	2·25	2·25
1159	£1 Princess Elizabeth, c. 1950 and Queen wearing red and black hat	3·75	4·25
MS1160	Two sheets, each 142×82 mm. (a) Nos. 1156 and 1159. (b) Nos. 1157/8	8·00	9·00

281 Uruguay

2006. World Cup Football Championship, Germany. Showing children with flags painted on faces. Multicoloured.

1161	38p. Type **281**	1·25	1·40
1162	38p. Italy	1·25	1·40
1163	38p. Germany	1·25	1·40
1164	38p. Brazil	1·25	1·40
1165	38p. England	1·25	1·40
1166	38p. Argentina	1·25	1·40
1167	38p. France	1·25	1·40

282 Children making Model Building

2006. Europa. Integration. Multicoloured.

1168	47p. Type **282**	1·50	1·50
1169	47p. Boy and girl	1·50	1·50
1170	47p. Children playing football	1·50	1·50
1171	47p. Children playing music	1·50	1·50

283 Cornwallis

2006. Bicentenary of the Gibraltar Packet Agency. Designs showing packet ships of the 1800s. Multicoloured.

1172	8p. Type **283**	60	35
1173	40p. Meteor	2·00	1·00
1174	42p. Carteret	2·00	1·00
1175	68p. Prince Regent	3·00	5·00

284 Saunders Roe (Saro) A21 Windhover Flying Boat, 1931

2006. 75th Anniv of Gibraltar Airmail Service. Multicoloured.

1176	8p. Type **284**	60	30
1177	40p. Vickers Vanguard, 1959	2·00	90
1178	49p. Vickers Viscount	2·75	1·50
1179	£1.60 Boeing 737	6·50	8·50

285 Coral

2006. Cruise Ships (2nd series). Multicoloured.

1180	40p. Type **285**	1·60	1·25
1181	42p. Legend of the Seas	1·75	1·40
1182	66p. Saga Ruby	2·75	3·50
1183	78p. Costa Concordia	3·25	5·00
MS1184	100×80 mm. Nos. 1180/83	8·50	10·00

286 St. Nicholas and Christmas Tree

2006. Christmas. St. Nicholas. Multicoloured.

1185	8p. Type **286**	40	15
1186	40p. St. Nicholas (in red) carrying presents	1·50	80
1187	42p. St. Nicholas giving present to young girl	1·60	85
1188	49p. St. Nicholas (in green) carrying sack of toys	2·00	1·75
1189	55p. St. Nicholas (in white) carrying sack and small Christmas tree	2·25	3·75
MS1190	165×80 mm. Nos. 1185/8	7·00	7·50

287 Navigational Instruments

2006. 500th Death Anniv of Christopher Columbus. Multicoloured.

1191	40p. Type **287**	1·50	1·25
1192	42p. Columbus writing report of voyage, 1492	1·50	1·25
1193	66p. Santa Maria	2·50	3·00
1194	78p. Columbus and Arawak chief	3·00	4·00
MS1195	95×74 mm. £1.60 Columbus' fleet, 1492 (47×47 mm)	5·75	6·50

288 Engagement, 1947

2007. Diamond Wedding of Queen Elizabeth II and Prince Philip. Multicoloured.

1196	40p. Type **288**	1·50	1·25
1197	42p. Wedding photograph, 1947	1·60	1·40
1198	66p. Silver Wedding anniversary, 1972	2·40	2·75
1199	78p. Ruby Anniversary, 1987	2·75	3·50
MS1200	105×105 mm. £1.60 Wedding photograph with bridesmaids and pageboys, 1947 (diamond shape, 84×83 mm)	5·75	6·50

289 Flag of Belgium

2007. 50th Anniv of the Treaty of Rome. Sheet 137×100 mm containing T **289** and similar horiz designs showing national flags. Multicoloured.

MS1201	40p.×6 Type **289**; Germany; France; Italy; Luxembourg; Netherlands	6·00	7·00

290 Princess Diana

2007. Tenth Death Anniv of Princess Diana. Multicoloured.

1202	8p. Type **290**	40	25
1203	40p. Seen full-face, eyes looking sideways	1·40	1·40
1204	42p. In half profile, smiling	1·40	1·40
1205	£1.60 Seen full-face, smiling	5·50	7·00
MS1206	165×92 mm. Nos. 1202/5	8·00	9·00

2007. Cruise Ships (3rd series). As T **285**. Multicoloured.

1207	40p. Oriana	1·50	1·25
1208	42p. Oceana	1·60	1·40
1209	66p. Queen Elizabeth 2	2·75	3·25
1210	78p. Queen Mary 2	3·00	4·75
MS1211	168×67 mm. Nos. 1207/10	8·00	9·50

291 Gibraltar Scout, 1908

2007. Europa. Centenary of World Scouting. Multicoloured.

1212	8p. Type **291**	40	30
1213	40p. Scout, 1950s	1·40	1·25
1214	42p. Sea scout, 1980s	1·50	1·40
1215	£1 Modern scout	3·50	5·00

292 Postcard from Fez, 1907

2007. Gibraltar Postal Anniversaries. Multicoloured.

1216	8p. Type **292** (Cent of Gibraltar relinquishing control of British Postal Service in Morocco)	55	30
1217	40p. Gibraltar date stamp of Packet Agency, 1857 (150th anniv of Gibraltar Post Office)	2·00	1·25
1218	42p. Letter with British postage stamps cancelled 'G' (150th anniv of the introduction of British postage stamps in Gibraltar)	2·00	1·40
1219	£1 Earliest known letter from Morocco via Gibraltar (150th anniv of first British Postal Agency in Morocco)	4·50	5·50

Nos. 1216/19 have information about the anniversaries commemorated printed on the reverse (gummed) side of the stamps.

293 Bear and Cub feeding on Dolphin

2007. Prehistoric Wildlife of Gibraltar. Multicoloured.

1220	8p. Type **293**	40	40
1221	40p. Eagle owl	1·50	1·50
1222	42p. Great auk and eagle	1·60	1·50
1223	55p. Red deer and boar	1·75	2·50
1224	78p. Wolf and vulture feeding on wild horse	2·75	4·50
MS1225	154×100 mm. £2 Ibex	7·00	8·50

294 Stork ('New baby')

2007. You Stamps. Multicoloured.

1226	(8p.) Type **294**	40	40
1227	(8p.) Lion, sheep and dog wearing party hats ('Let's celebrate')	40	40
1228	(8p.) Crab finding heart written in beach sand ('With love')	40	40
1229	(8p.) Heart enclosed in wedding ring ('Commitment')	40	40
1230	(8p.) Dolphins and Rock of Gibraltar ('Greetings from Gibraltar')	40	40
1231	(40p.) As Type **294**	1·40	1·40
1232	(40p.) As No. 1227	1·40	1·40
1233	(40p.) As No. 1228	1·40	1·40
1234	(40p.) As No. 1229	1·40	1·40
1235	(40p.) As No. 1230	1·40	1·40

Nos. 1226/30 are inscr 'G' and sold for 8p. each. Nos. 1231/5 are inscr 'E' and sold for 40p. each.

295 Rock of Gibraltar

2007. Panoramic Views of Gibraltar. Multicoloured.

1236	40p. Type **295**	1·40	1·25
1237	42p. Beach and Rock of Gibraltar	1·60	1·40
1238	55p. Rock of Gibraltar at sunset	2·00	2·50
1239	78p. Town and Rock of Gibraltar	3·25	4·00
MS1240	114×67 mm. £1.70 Gibraltar Trinity Lighthouse (52×20 mm)	6·50	6·50

No. 1236 is inscr 'sepac'.

296 Joseph

2007. Christmas. Porcelain Figurines. Multicoloured.

1241	8p. Type **296**	25	25
1242	8p. Baby Jesus	25	25
1243	40p. Mary	1·25	80
1244	42p. King Melchoir	1·40	90
1245	49p. King Balthasar	1·60	1·60
1246	55p. King Gaspar	1·75	3·00
MS1247	124×105 mm. Nos. 1241/6	6·50	7·00

Nos. 1241/6 have biblical quotations printed on the reverse (gummed) side of the stamps.

297 Woodchat Shrike

2008. Birds of the Rock. Multicoloured.

1248	1p. Type **297**	10	10
1249	2p. Balearic Shearwater (Puffinus mauretanicus)	15	15
1250	5p. Eagle Owl (Bubo bubo)	20	15
1251	(8p.) European Bee-eater (Merops apiaster)	40	35
1252	10p. Razorbill (Alca torda)	50	45
1252a	10p. Black Stork (Ciconia nigra) (16.9.09)	75	80
1253	(30p.) Egyptian Vulture (Neophron percnopterus)	90	85
1253a	(30p.) Red-necked Nightjar (Caprimulgus ruficollis) (16.4.12)	90	85
1254	(40p.) Blue Rock Thrush (Monticola solitarius)	1·25	1·10
1254a	(42p.) Little Owl (Athene noctua) (16.4.12)	1·40	1·25
1255	(42p.) Hoopoe (Upupa epops)	1·40	1·25
1256	(49p.) Bonelli's Eagle (Hieraaëtus fasciatus)	1·50	1·25
1257	50p. Greater Flamingo (Phoenicopterus roseus)	1·50	1·25
1258	55p. Mediterranean Shag (Phalacrocorax aristotelis desmarestii)	1·60	1·50
1258a	59p. Barbary Partridge (Alectoris barbara) (20.10.10)	2·00	1·90
1258b	76p. Ortolan Bunting (Emberiza hortulana) (20.10.10)	2·50	2·50
1259	£1 Honey Buzzard (Pernis apivorus) (34×47 mm)	3·00	3·00
1259a	£2 Northern Gannett (Morus bassanus) (35×48 mm) (16.9.09)	6·00	6·50
1259b	£2 Pallid Swift (Apus pallidus) (20.10.10)	6·50	7·00
1259c	£3 Osprey (Pandion haliaetus) (35×38 mm) (16.9.09)	9·25	9·50
1259d	£3.44 Spotted Flycatcher (Muscicapa striata) (16.4.12)	10·50	11·00
1260	£5 Lesser Kestrel (Falco naumanni) (34×47 mm)	12·00	13·00

Nos. 1251 and 1253/6 are inscribed 'S', 'G', 'E', 'U' and 'UK' and were sold for 8p, 30p, 40p, 42p and 49p respectively.

298 Short 184 and Saro London

2008. 90th Anniv of the Royal Air Force. Multicoloured.
1261	40p. Type **298**	2·00	2·00
1262	40p. Spitfire IV and Hurricane IIc	2·00	2·00
1263	42p. Beaufighter II and Lancaster TS III	2·00	2·00
1264	42p. Hunter Mk.6 and Shackleton MR2	2·00	2·00
1265	49p. Vulcan and Mosquito	2·50	2·50
1266	49p. Tornado GR4 and Jaguar GR3	2·50	2·50
MS1267	107×75 mm. £2 Felixstowe F.3 of No. 265 Squadron on antisubmarine patrol, Gibraltar, 1918	9·50	9·50

299 HMS *La Minerve*

2008. 250th Birth Anniv of Admiral Lord Nelson. Multicoloured.
1268	40p. Type **299**	2·00	2·00
1269	40p. HMS *Agamemnon*	2·00	2·00
1270	42p. HMS *Vanguard*	2·00	2·00
1271	42p. HMS *Captain*	2·00	2·00
1272	49p. HMS *Victory*	2·50	2·50
1273	49p. HMS *Amphion*	2·50	2·50
MS1274	120×80 mm. £2 Birthplace at Burnham Thorpe, Norfolk (horiz)	7·00	8·00

300 Sir Winston Churchill

2008. Europa. Writing Letters. Multicoloured.
1275	10p. Type **300**	75	50
1276	42p. Lord Nelson	1·75	1·25
1277	44p. President John F. Kennedy	1·75	1·50
1278	£1 Mahatma Ghandi	5·50	6·00

301 Christ the Redeemer Statue, Rio de Janeiro, Brazil

2008. The New Seven Wonders of the World. Multicoloured.
1279	8p. Type **301**	35	35
1280	8p. Colosseum, Rome, Italy	35	35
1281	38p. Petra, Jordan	1·50	1·50
1282	38p. The Great Wall of China	1·50	1·50
1283	40p. Machu Picchu, Peru	1·50	1·50
1284	40p. Chichen Itza	1·50	1·50
1285	66p. Taj Mahal, India	3·25	3·25

2008. Cruise Ships (4th series). As T **285**. Multicoloured.
1286	40p. *Century*	1·75	1·25
1287	42p. *Grand Princess*	1·75	1·25
1288	66p. *Queen Victoria*	2·75	3·00
1289	78p. *Costa Mediterranea*	3·75	4·50
MS1290	168×66 mm. Nos. 1286/9	9·00	9·00

302 *Launch of Apollo 11*

2008. 50th Anniv of NASA (US National Aeronautics and Space Administration). Sheet 144×98 mm containing T **302** and similar square designs. Multicoloured.
MS1291	10p. Type **302**; 17p. The Earth seen from the Moon; 42p. Lunar module; £2 US flag on the Moon	8·50	8·50

303 Gibraltar Volunteer Corps, World War I

2008. Royal Gibraltar Regiment. Multicoloured.
1292	10p. Type **303**	45	45
1293	10p. Gibraltar Defence Force, World War II	45	45
1294	10p. Buena Vista Barracks (National Service)	45	45
1295	42p. Thomson's Battery 1958–91 (Gibraltar Regiment)	1·40	1·40
1296	42p. Infantry Company 1958–99 (Gibraltar Regiment)	1·40	1·40
1297	44p. Air Defence Troop 1958–91 (Gibraltar Regiment)	1·40	1·40
1298	44p. 'Guarding the Rock' (Royal Gibraltar Regiment)	1·40	1·40
1299	51p. Training African Peacekeepers (Royal Gibraltar Regiment)	1·90	2·00
1300	51p. Operations in Iraq (Royal Gibraltar Regiment)	1·90	2·00
1301	£2 Operations in Afghanistan (Royal Gibraltar Regiment)	7·00	8·00

304 *When Santa got stuck in a Chimney*

2008. Christmas. Christmas Songs and Carols. Multicoloured.
1302	10p. Type **304**	45	20
1303	42p. Rudolph the Red-nosed Reindeer	1·50	1·25
1304	44p. Oh Christmas Tree	1·50	1·25
1305	51p. Away in a Manger	1·90	1·90
1306	59p. Jingle Bells	2·25	2·75

305 Catherine of Aragon

2009. 500th Anniv of the Coronation of King Henry VIII. Multicoloured.
1307	10p. Type **305**	45	45
1308	10p. Anne Boleyn	45	45
1309	42p. Jane Seymour	1·75	1·50
1310	42p. Anne of Cleves	1·75	1·50
1311	44p. Catherine Howard	1·75	1·50
1312	44p. Katherine Parr	1·75	1·50
1313	51p. King Henry VIII	2·25	2·75
1314	51p. *Mary Rose* (galleon)	2·25	2·75
MS1315	120×80 mm. £2 King Henry VIII and Hampton Court Palace	7·50	8·00

306 Virgin and Child (shrine of Our Lady of Europe at Europa Point, Gibraltar)

2009. 700th Anniv of Our Lady of Europe.
1316	**306** 61p. multicoloured	3·50	3·50

Stamps of a similar design were issued by Vatican City.

307 Short S27

2009. Centenary of Naval Aviation. Multicoloured.
1317	42p. Type **307**	1·90	1·90
1318	42p. Morane-Saulnier Type L and Zeppelin LZ 37	1·90	1·90
1319	42p. Short Type 184 seaplane	1·90	1·90
1320	42p. SS Type Non Rigid Airship	1·90	1·90
1321	42p. Caudron Gill	1·90	1·90
1322	42p. Avro 504	1·90	1·90
MS1323	120×80 mm. £2 Short Type 184 seaplane hoisted over stern of First World War seaplane carrier and Hawker Siddeley Sea Harrier on ramp of modern Invincible Class CVS aircraft carrier	8·00	8·00

The stamp within No. **MS**1323 has text printed on the back describing the aircraft and ships depicted on the miniature sheet.

308 Peter Phillips

2009. Queen Elizabeth II's Grandchildren. Multicoloured.
1324	42p. Type **308**	1·50	1·50
1325	42p. Zara Phillips	1·50	1·50
1326	42p. Prince William of Wales	1·50	1·50
1327	42p. Prince Henry of Wales	1·50	1·50
1328	42p. Princess Beatrice of York	1·50	1·50
1329	42p. Princess Eugenie of York	1·50	1·50
1330	42p. Lady Louise Windsor	1·50	1·50
1331	42p. Viscount Severn	1·50	1·50

309 Aristotle (early Greek philosopher and scientist)

2009. Europa. International Year of Astronomy. Multicoloured.
1332	10p. Type **309**	40	30
1333	42p. Galileo Galilei (astronomer, mathematician and philosopher)	1·75	1·25
1334	44p. Nicolaus Copernicus (astronomer)	2·25	1·50
1335	£1.50 Sir Isaac Newton (scientist and mathematician)	4·50	6·00

310 Road to the Frontier

2009. Old Views of Gibraltar (1st series). Showing scenes from postcards. Multicoloured.
1336	10p. Type **310**	40	30
1337	42p. Catalan Bay village	1·60	1·25
1338	42p. The Rock of Gibraltar	1·60	1·25
1339	51p. The Moorish Castle	2·00	1·90
1340	59p. South Barracks	2·25	2·75
MS1341	163×79 mm. 10p. Garrison Library; 42p. The Piazza; 44p. The Piazza – Casemates; £1 Main Street	6·75	7·50

310a Charles Darwin, *Zoology of the Beagle* and *Voyages of the Adventure and Beagle*

2009. Birth Bicentenary of Charles Darwin (naturalist and evolutionary theorist). Multicoloured.
1341a	10p. Type **310a**	45	30
1341b	42p. Charles Darwin and *The Descent of Man*	1·50	1·25
1341c	44p. Charles Darwin and *Animals and Plants under Domestication*	1·50	1·40
1341d	£2 Charles Darwin and *On the Origin of Species*	7·00	7·50
MS1341e	126×86 mm. £2.42 Charles Darwin, The Mount, Shrewsbury (his birthplace) and *On the Origin of Species*	9·50	9·50

311 Santa Tree Decoration

2009. Christmas. Multicoloured.
1342	10p. Type **311**	45	30
1343	42p. Angel	1·50	1·25
1344	44p. Teddy bear	1·50	1·40
1345	51p. Filigree Christmas tree	1·90	1·60
1346	£2 Bells and baubles	6·75	7·50

312 '100 Ton' Gun, Napier of Magdala Battery, Gibraltar, 1880

2010. '100 Ton' Guns. Multicoloured.
MS1347	118×102 mm. 75p.×4 Type **312**; '100 ton' gun, Napier of Magdala Battery, Gibraltar, 2010; '100 ton' gun, Fort Rinella, Malta, 2010; '100 ton' gun, Fort Rinella, Malta, 1882	10·00	11·00

A miniature sheet containing the same designs was issued by Malta.

313 Hawker Hurricane

2010. 70th Anniv of the Battle of Britain. Multicoloured.
1348	50p. Type **313**	2·00	2·00
1349	50p. Miles Master	2·00	2·00
1350	50p. Bristol Blenheim	2·00	2·00
1351	50p. Boulton Paul Defiant	2·00	2·00
1352	50p. Gloster Gladiator	2·00	2·00
1353	50p. Supermarine Spitfire	2·00	2·00
MS1354	110×70 mm. £2 Douglas Bader (vert)	7·50	7·50

314 King George V, Queen Mary and Family

2010. Centenary of Accession of King George V. Multicoloured.
1355	10p. Type **314**	50	30
1356	42p. King George V with his stamp collection	1·75	1·25
1357	44p. King George V on horseback inspecting soldiers	1·75	1·40
1358	£2 King George V in navy uniform and gun battery	8·00	9·00

315 Charlie and the Chocolate Factory

2010. Europa. Children's Books. Multicoloured.
1359	10p. Type **315**	45	30
1360	42p. Matilda	1·75	1·25
1361	44p. The Twits	1·75	1·40
1362	£1.50 The BFG	4·75	5·50

316 Emblem

2010. 'Miss Gibraltar 2009 (Kaiane Aldorino) is Miss World. Sheet 140×84 mm
MS1363 **316** £2 gold and black   6·50   7·50

317 Second Tower, San Marino

2010. Gibraltar and San Marino. Multicoloured.
MS1364 137×105 mm. 75p.×4 Type **317**; Moorish Castle, Gibraltar; Mount Titano, San Marino; The Rock of Gibraltar   10·00   11·00
A miniature sheet containing the same designs was issued by San Marino.

318 Elise Deroche (inscr 'Baroness Raymonde de Laroche') flying Voisin Biplane, 8 March 1910

2010. Aviation Centenaries. Multicoloured.
1365   10p. Type **318** (first woman with pilot's licence)   50   30
1366   42p. DELAG's Zeppelin LZ7 (first fare paying passengers), 21 June 1910   1·50   1·25
1367   49p. Hubert Latham sets altitude record at 4,541 ft in *Antoinette VII*, 7 July 1910   2·00   1·75
1368   £2 Clément-Bayard No. 2 (first airship flight across English Channel, 16 October 1910)   6·75   7·50
MS1369 163×75 mm. 10p. Henri Fabre flies *Le Canard*, 28 March 1910; 42p. Supermarine S.6B Schneider Trophy winner, 1931; 49p. Short Sunderland, 204 Squadron, Gibraltar, 1941; £2 Saunders-ROE Princess, 22 August 1952 (centenary of seaplanes)   11·00   12·00

319 Rainbow Uniform

2010. Centenary of Girlguiding. Multicoloured.
1370   10p. Type **319**   50   30
1371   42p. Brownie   1·60   1·25
1372   44p. Guide   1·60   1·40
1373   £2 Senior   6·75   7·50

320 Emblem

2010. Commonwealth Games, Delhi. Sheet 90×103 mm
MS1374 **320** £2 multicoloured   7·50   7·50

321 Interior of Cathedral of St. Mary the Crowned

2010. Centenary of Diocese of Gibraltar. Sheet 114×80 mm
MS1375 **321** £2 multicoloured   6·50   7·00

322 Christmas Stocking, Wrapped Presents and Decorations

2010. Christmas. Multicoloured.
1376   10p. Type **322**   45   30
1377   42p. Christmas stockings hanging from mantelpiece   1·50   1·25
1378   44p. Santa's sleigh flying over snowy landscape   1·60   1·40
1379   51p. Three snowmen as musicians with accordion, fiddle and cymbals   1·75   2·25

323 Prince William and Miss Catherine Middleton

2011. Royal Engagement. Sheet 90×97 mm
MS1380 **323** £2 multicoloured   6·50   6·50

324 World War I ('Reflection')

2011. Royal British Legion. Multicoloured.
1381   50p. Type **324**   1·75   1·75
1382   50p. World War II ('Hope')   1·75   1·75
1383   50p. Northern Ireland ('Selflessness')   1·75   1·75
1384   50p. The Falklands ('Comradeship')   1·75   1·75
1385   50p. The Gulf War ('Welfare')   1·75   1·75
1386   50p. The Balkans ('Service')   1·75   1·75
1387   50p. Iraq ('Representation')   1·75   1·75
1388   50p. Afghanistan ('Remembrance')   1·75   1·75
MS1389 120×80 mm. £2 Statue and poppies   6·50   6·50

325 Queen Elizabeth II (photo by Yousuf Karsh), 1985

2011. Queen Elizabeth II and Prince Philip. 'Lifetime of Service'. Multicoloured.
1390   10p. Type **325**   45   30
1391   42p. Queen Elizabeth II and Prince Philip arriving at Ascot racecourse, 1973   1·50   1·25
1392   44p. Queen Elizabeth II and Prince Philip, 2010   1·60   1·40
1393   51p. Queen Elizabeth II and Prince Philip (photo by Donald McKague), 1959   1·75   2·25
1394   55p. Queen Elizabeth II and Prnce Philip during Silver Jubilee celebrations, 1977   1·90   2·40
1395   £2 Prince Philip (photo by Yousuf Karsh), 1985   6·50   6·50
MS1396 175×164 mm. Nos. 1390/5   13·50   13·50
MS1397 110×70 mm. £3 Princess Eliizabeth and Duke of Edinburgh on wedding day, 1947   13·50   13·50

326 The Alps

2011. Europa. Year of Forests. Multicoloured.
1398   10p. Type **326**   45   30
1399   42p. The Amazon   1·50   1·25
1400   44p. Yosemite National Park, California   1·60   1·40
1401   £1.50 Plitvice National Park, Croatia   4·75   4·25

327 1886 Gibraltar overprint on Bermuda Queen Victoria 1s. Stamp

2011. 125th Anniv of Gibraltar Stamps. Multicoloured.
1402   10p. Type **327**   45   30
1403   42p. 1903 King Edward VII £1 stamp   1·50   1·25
1404   44p. 1925 King George V £5 stamp   1·60   1·40
1405   55p. 1938 King George VI £1 stamp   1·75   1·75
1406   £1.50 1953 Coronation ½d. stamp   4·75   4·25

328 Prince William and Miss Catherine Middleton

2011. Royal Wedding. Sheet 90×97 mm
MS1407 **328** £3 multicoloured   13·50   13·50

329 Asian Elephant (*Elephas maximus*)

2011. Endangered Animals (1st series). Multicoloured.
1408   42p. Type **329**   1·50   1·25
1409   42p. Bengal Tiger (*Panthera tigris tigris*)   1·50   1·25
1410   42p. Black Rhinoceros (*Diceros bicornis*)   1·50   1·25
1411   42p. Giant Panda (*Ailuropoda melanoleuca*)   1·50   1·25
1412   42p. Polar Bear (*Ursus maritimus*)   1·50   1·25
1413   42p. Sumatran Orangutan (*Pongo abelii*)   1·50   1·25
MS1414 161×105 mm. Nos. 1408/13   8·00   8·00

330 Barbary Macaque

2011. Barbary Macaque (*Macaca sylvanus*). Multicoloured.
1415   10p. Type **330**   45   30
1416   42p. Barbary macaque, peak of Rock of Gibraltar in background   1·50   1·25
1417   44p. Barbary macaque in tree at water's edge   1·60   1·40
1418   51p. Barbary macaque, cliffs in background   1·75   2·25
1419   59p. Barbary macaque sitting on rock   2·00   2·50
1420   £1.50 Two adult macaques and baby   4·75   4·25

331 Supermarine Spitfire K5054 modified to Mk I Standard

2011. 75th Anniv of the Supermarine Spitfire. Multicoloured.
1421   10p. Type **331**   45   30
1422   42p. First flight of the Supermarine Spitfire, March 5th 1936   1·50   1·25
1423   49p. Ground testing before the first flight   1·75   2·25
1424   £2 Supermarine Spitfire Prototype K5054 under construction   6·50   7·00
MS1425 129×85 mm. £2 RAF 92 Squadron Spitfire Mk 1B   6·50   6·50

332 Invading Muslim Army approaching Gibraltar

2011. 1300th Anniv of Landing of Tariq ibn Ziyad at Gibraltar and Islamic Conquest of Spain. Multicoloured.
1426   42p. Type **332**   1·50   1·25
1427   44p. Landing of Tariq ibn Ziyad's army at Gibraltar, 711AD   1·60   1·40
1428   66p. Tariq ibn Ziyad and his army in Gibraltar   1·75   2·25
1429   £2 Battle between Tariq ibn Ziyad and the Visigothic King Roderick   6·50   7·00

333 Nativity (Giorgione (Giorgio Barbarelli da Castelfranco))

2011. Christmas. Nativity Art. Multicoloured.
1430   10p. Type **333**   45   30
1431   42p. Nativity (Lorenzo Lotto)   1·50   1·25
1432   44p. Nativity (Charles Le Brun)   1·60   1·40
1433   51p. Nativity (Agnolo di Cosimo)   1·75   2·25
1434   £2 Nativity (Gerard van Honthorst)   6·50   7·00

334 Grand Master Viktor Bologan vs GM Pia Cramling Move 49

2012. Tenth Anniv of the Gibraltar International Chess Festival. Chessboards from Games in Progress. Multicoloured.
1435   2p. Type **334**   20   10
1436   30p. GM Michael Adams vs GM Natalia Zhukova Move 52   1·10   90
1437   75p. GM Fabiano Caruana vs GM Viktor Korchnoi Move 46   2·75   3·25
1438   £2 GM Vassily Ivanchuk vs GM Nigel Short Move 63   6·50   6·50

335 Fitting of *Titanic* completed, 31st March 1912

2012. Centenary of the Sinking of the *Titanic*. Multicoloured.
1439   10p. Type **335**   45   30
1440   42p. *Titanic* sets sail on her maiden voyage, 10 April 1912   1·50   1·25
1441   44p. Iceberg strikes starboard bow, 14 April 1912, 23.40 hrs   1·60   1·40

1442	54p. First lifeboats lowered, 15 April 1912, 00.45 hrs	1·90	2·40
1443	66p. Stern rises and Titanic starts sinking, 15 April 1912, 02.10 hrs	2·00	2·25

336 Queen Elizabeth II

2012. Diamond Jubilee. Multicoloured.

1444	10p. Type **336**	45	30
1445	42p. Queen Elizabeth II wearing tiara, c. 2005	1·50	1·25
1446	44p. Queen Elizabeth II wearing flowered hat, c. 1970	1·60	1·40
1447	51p. Queen Elizabeth II, c. 1970	1·75	2·25
1448	55p. Princess Elizabeth, c, 1942	1·90	2·40
1449	£2 Queen Elizabeth II wearing Garter robes, c. 1980	6·50	6·50
MS1450	174×165 mm. Nos. 1444/9	13·75	13·75
MS1451	111×71 mm. £3 Portrait of Queen Elizabeth II, c. 1953	9·75	9·75

337 Westland WS-61 Sea King Helicopter, 22 Squadron

2012. Royal Air Force Squadrons (1st series). Multicoloured.

1452	10p. Type **337**	45	30
1453	42p. Gloster Javelin FAW 7 Mk IV, 89 Squadron	1·50	1·25
1454	76p. Panavia Tornado, 111 Squadron	2·75	2·50
1455	£2 Bristol Type 156 Beaufighter, 248 Squadron	6·50	6·50
MS1456	129×102 mm. Squadron blazer badges: 10p. No. 22 Squadron; 42p. No. 89 Squadron; 76p. No. 111 Squadron; £2 No. 248 Squadron (all 36×36 mm)	11·25	11·25

338 Musical Instruments

2012. International Jazz Festival

1457	**338** 75p. multicoloured	2·50	2·50

339 Aerial View of Gibraltar

2012. Europa. Visit Gibraltar. Multicoloured.

1458	10p. Type **339**	45	30
1459	42p. Tower of Homage (built 711AD), Moorish Castle, Upper Rock Nature Reserve	1·50	1·25
1460	44p. Aerial view of Gibraltar (different)	1·60	1·40
1461	51p. St. Michael's Cave, Upper Rock Nature Reserve	1·75	2·25
1462	54p. Trinity Lighthouse, Europa Point	1·90	2·40
1463	66p. Eliott's Column, Alameda Botanical Gardens	2·00	2·25

340 Countess of Wessex

2012. Royal Visit, June 2012. Multicoloured.

MS1464	£1×3 Type **340**; Earl and Countess of Wessex unveiling plaque at new airport terminal building; Earl of Wessex	9·00	9·50

341 Charles Dickens and *David Copperfield*

2012. Birth Bicentenary of Charles Dickens (writer). Multicoloured.

1465	10p. Type **341**	45	30
1466	42p. Charles Dickens and *Oliver Twist*	1·40	1·25
1467	44p. Charles Dickens and *A Tale of Two Cities*	1·60	1·40
1468	£2 Charles Dickens and *A Christmas Carol*	6·00	6·50
MS1469	129×89 mm. £2 Charles Dickens	6·00	6·50

2012. Old Views of Gibraltar (2nd series). Scenes from Postcards. Multicoloured.

1470	10p. The Old Moorish Castle	45	30
1471	30p. Grand Casemates Square, awaiting the Arrival of King George V and Queen Mary	90	85
1472	61p. Landing Pier	1·90	2·40
1473	78p. Waterport	2·50	2·50
1474	£1.75 Alameda Gardens	5·25	5·50
MS1475	165×80 mm. 10p. Sand Hill Road, arrival of Troops to be inspected by King George V; 42p. South Port Gates; 50p. Victoria Monument; £1 Hargraves Barracks	6·00	6·50

2012. Endangered Animals (2nd series). Multicoloured.

1476	42p. Arabian Oryx (*Oryx leucoryx*)	1·50	1·25
1477	42p. Asian One-horned Rhinoceros (*Rhinoceros unicornis*)	1·50	1·25
1478	42p. European Wolf (*Canis lupus lupus*)	1·50	1·25
1479	42p. Iberian Lynx (*Lynx pardinus*)	1·50	1·25
1480	42p. Snow Leopard (*Panthera uncia*)	1·50	1·25
1481	42p. Western Lowland Gorilla (*Gorilla gorilla gorilla*)	1·50	1·25
MS1482	160×105 mm. Nos. 1476/81	8·00	8·00

342 Santa Claus and Gifts

2012. Christmas. Santa Claus. Multicoloured.

1483	10p. Type **342**	45	30
1484	42p. Santa carrying lamp and sack of toys	1·50	1·25
1485	44p. Snowman and Christmas tree	1·60	1·40
1486	51p. Santa in sleigh	1·75	2·25
1487	£2 Santa ringing bell, reindeer and elf	6·00	6·50

343 Snake's Head

2013. Chinese New Year (Year of the Snake). Multicoloured.

1488	42p. Type **343**	1·50	1·25
1489	£1 Snake	3·00	3·25

Nos. 1488/9 were printed together, *se-tenant*, as horizontal pairs.

344 Coronation Photograph

2013. 60th Anniv of Coronation. Multicoloured.

1490	10p. Type **344**	45	30

1491	42p. Coronation photograph (wearing crown)	1·50	1·25
1492	44p. Coronation photograph (wearing diadem)	1·60	1·40
1493	£1.50 Queen Elizabeth II leaving golden State Coach on Coronation Day	4·50	5·00
MS1494	96×96 mm. £3 Portrait of Queen Elizabeth II wearing crown and silver-grey dress, c. 1952	9·00	9·50

2013. Royal Air Force Squadrons (2nd series). Multicoloured.

1495	10p. VS Spitfire 5C, 43 Squadron	45	30
1496	42p. Hawker Hurricane, 87 Squadron	1·50	1·25
1497	76p. Consolidated PBY Catalina IV A, 210 Squadron	2·25	2·25
1498	£2 Avro Shackleton MR2, 224 Squadron	6·00	6·50
MS1499	128×102 mm. Squadron badges: 10p. No. 43 Squadron; 42p. No. 87 Squadron; 76p. No. 210 Squadron; £2 No. 224 Squadron	9·00	9·00

2013. Old Views of Gibraltar (3rd series). Scenes from Postcards. Multicoloured.

1500	10p. Moorish Castle and Landport	45	30
1501	30p. Casemates Square	90	85
1502	61p. The Rock from Victoria Gardens	1·90	2·25
1503	78p. Main Street	2·50	2·50
1504	£1.75 Casemates Barracks	5·00	5·50
MS1505	163×79 mm. 10p. The Rock from North Front Camp; 42p. Rosia Bay; 50p. Kingsway Walk, Alameda Gardens; £1 Spanish water sellers drawing water from Rain Water Fountain, Gunner's Parade	6·00	6·50

345 Books

2013. Gibraltar International Literary Festival. Multicoloured.

1506	10p. Type **345**	45	30
1507	42p. Braille	1·50	1·25
1508	£2 e-book reader and open book	6·00	6·50

2013. Tel Aviv 2013 Multinational Stamp Exhibition, Israel. Sheet 149×106 mm

MS1508a	As No. 1338 but 'sepac' inscr omitted	1·60	1·40

346 Arms of Gibraltar Football Association

2013. Gibraltar, 54th Member of UEFA

1509	**346** 54p. multicoloured	1·90	2·40

347 1970 Replica of 1911 Dennis 2 Ton Mail Van used on London Contract Services LE304

2013. Europa. Postal Vehicles. Multicoloured.

1510	10p. Type **347**	45	30
1511	42p. Horse-drawn mail cart, 1897-1920s	1·40	1·25
1512	44p. Rover Motor Cycle Combination DU 5660, 1914	1·60	1·40
1513	£1.75 Electromobile 1-ton battery-electric van YX7649, 1928	5·25	5·50

348 Union Flag

2013. 300th Anniv of the Treaty of Utrecht (gave Gibraltar to Great Britain). Multicoloured.

1514	10p. Type **348**	45	30

1515	42p. "for ever, without any exception or impediment whatsoever"	1·50	1·25

350 Cargo and Passenger Wharves

2013. 60th Anniv of Gibraltar Queen Elizabeth II Definitive Stamps

1516	**350** 2p. indigo and grey-green	20	10
1517	- 10p. bluish green	45	30
1518	- 16p. black	45	40
1519	- 20p. deep olive-brown	60	55
1520	- 22p. carmine	60½	55
1521	- 30p. light blue	90	85
1522	- 42p. maroon	1·40	1·25
1523	- 44p. ultramarine	1·60	1·40
1524	- 50p. black and pale blue	1·75	2·25
1525	- 58p. pale blue and red-brown	1·90	2·40
1526	- 60p. orange and reddish violet	1·90	2·40
1527	- £2 deep brown	6·00	6·50
1528	- £3 reddish brown and ultramarine	9·00	9·50
1529	- £5 scarlet and orange-yellow	14·00	14·00

351 Duke and Duchess of Cambridge with Prince George

2013. Birth of Prince George of Cambridge

1530	**351** £2 multicoloured	6·00	6·50

2013. Endangered Animals (3rd series). Multicoloured.

1531	42p. African Penguin (*Spheniscus demersus*)	1·40	1·25
1532	42p. Atlantic Bluefin Tuna (*Thunnus thynnus*)	1·40	1·25
1533	42p. Asiatic Cheetah (*Acinonyx jubatus venaticus*)	1·40	1·25
1534	42p. Chinese Alligator (*Alligator sinensis*)	1·40	1·25
1535	42p. Red-crowned Crane (*Grus japonensis*)	1·40	1·25
1536	42p. Leatherback Sea Turtle (*Dermochelys coriacea*)	1·40	1·25
MS1537	160×105 mm. Nos. 1531/6	8·00	8·00

No. 1532 was inscr 'sepac'.

352 'MERRY CHRISTMAS'

2013. Christmas. Multicoloured.

1538	12p. Type **352**	45	40
1539	50p. Rocking horse, teddy and wrapped parcels around Christmas tree	1·75	2·25
1540	54p. Santa in sleigh	1·90	2·40
1541	64p. Wrapped present	2·00	2·25
1542	£2.50 Christmas baubles	7·50	8·00
MS1543	140×92 mm. Nos. 1538/42	13·00	14·50

353 Flag of Governor of Gibraltar and Keys

2013. Ceremony of the Keys

1544	**353** £1 multicoloured	3·00	3·25

(354)

2013. Nos. 1250 and 1254a surch as T **354**, No. 1254a in silver
1545		14p. on (42p.) Little Owl *(Athene noctua)*	45	40
1546		28p. on 5p. Eagle Owl *(Bubo bubo)*	90	85

355 Queen Elizabeth II

2014. Queen Elizabeth II
1547	**355**	2p. chestnut	20	10
1548		4p. maroon	20	10
1549		6p. violet	20	10
1550		8p. grey-black	25	10
1551		10p. dull blue-green	30	10
1552		(12p.) deep turquoise-blue and new blue	35	30
1553		14p. carmine-red	40	35
1554		20p. bronze-green	60	55
1555		28p. deep reddish violet	85	80
1556		40p. sepia	1·25	1·10
1557		50p. turquoise-green	1·75	2·25
1558		54p. rose-red	1·90	2·40
1559		64p. bistre	2·00	2·25
1560		70p. chalky blue	2·25	2·25
1561		£2 emerald	6·00	6·50
1562		£2.50 deep magenta	7·50	8·00

Nos. 1547/62 depict the inset portrait of Queen Elizabeth II from the 1953-59 definitives, Nos. 145/58.
No. 1552 was inscr 'G' and originally sold for 12p.

356 Horse's Head

2014. Chinese New Year. Year of the Horse. Multicoloured.
1563	50p. Type **356**	1·75	2·25
1564	£1 Horse	3·00	3·25

357 Poster of Lord Kitchener ('Your Country Wants You')

2014. Centenary of World War I. Multicoloured.
1565	12p. Type **357**	35	30
1566	40p. Joining up	1·25	1·10
1567	50p. Leaving family	1·75	2·25
1568	64p. Kit	2·00	2·25
1569	68p. Training	2·00	2·25
1570	£1 Embarkation	3·00	3·25

2014. Old Views of Gibraltar (4th series). Multicoloured.
1571	12p. Waterport Wharf	35	30
1572	40p. Eliott's Monument	1·25	1·10
1573	50p. Entrance to the Town	1·75	2·25
1574	64p. Sandpits	2·00	2·25
1575	70p. Alameda Gardens	2·25	2·25
MS1576	163×79 mm. 12p. Waterport Street (Main Street); 40p. The Wharfs; 50p. The Market; £1 The Cascade	6·00	6·50

358 Red Arrows Jet (BAE Hawk T1)

2014. 50th Anniv of the Red Arrows. Multicoloured.
1577	50p. Type **358**	1·75	2·25
1578	54p. Two Red Arrows	1·90	2·40
1579	64p. Red Arrow (front view)	2·00	2·25
1580	70p. Red Arrow (rear view)	2·25	2·25
1581	£2 Red Arrow (flying to upper right)	6·00	6·50

POSTAGE DUE STAMPS

D1

1956
D1	**D1**	1d. green	1·50	4·25
D2	**D1**	2d. brown	1·50	2·75
D3	**D1**	4d. blue	1·75	5·00

1971. As Nos. D1/3, but inscr in decimal currency.
D4	½p. green	25	80
D5	1p. brown	25	70
D6	2p. blue	25	1·00

D2

1976
D7	**D2**	1p. orange	15	60
D8	**D2**	3p. blue	15	75
D9	**D2**	5p. red	20	75
D10	**D2**	7p. violet	20	75
D11	**D2**	10p. green	25	75
D12	**D2**	20p. green	45	1·00

D3 Gibraltar Coat of Arms

1984
D13	**D3**	1p. black	25	60
D14	**D3**	3p. red	40	60
D15	**D3**	5p. red	45	60
D16	**D3**	10p. blue	60	60
D17	**D3**	25p. mauve	1·25	1·00
D18	**D3**	50p. orange	1·50	1·75
D19	**D3**	£1 green	2·50	3·25

D4 Water Port Gates

1996. Gibraltar Landmarks.
D20	**D4**	1p. black, emerald and green	20	75
D21	-	10p. black and grey	70	70
D22	-	25p. black, brown and chestnut	1·50	1·25
D23	-	50p. black and lilac	2·25	2·25
D24	-	£1 black, brown and chestnut	3·50	3·75
D25	-	£2 black and black	5·50	6·50

DESIGNS: 10p. Naval Dockyard; 25p. Military Hospital; 50p. Governor's Cottage; £1 Swans on the Laguna; £2 Catalan Bay.

D5 Greenfinch

2002. Gibraltar Finches. Type D **5** Multicoloured.
D26	5p. Type D **5**	10	10
D27	10p. Serin	20	15
D28	20p. Siskin	40	45
D29	50p. Linnet	1·00	1·10
D30	£1 Chaffinch	2·00	2·10
D31	£2 Goldfinch	4·00	4·25

Pt. 1

GILBERT AND ELLICE ISLANDS

A British colony in the South Pacific.

1911. 12 pence = 1 shilling; 20 shillings = 1 pound.
1966. 100 cents = $1 Australian.

1911. Stamps of Fiji (King Edward VII) optd **GILBERT & ELLICE PROTECTORATE.**
1	**23**	½d. green	5·50	50·00
2	**23**	1d. red	50·00	28·00
3	**23**	2d. grey	18·00	15·00
4	**23**	2½d. blue	18·00	50·00
5	**23**	5d. purple and green	65·00	95·00
6	**23**	6d. purple	25·00	50·00
7	**23**	1s. black on green	26·00	70·00

2 Pandanus Pine

1911
8	**2**	½d. green	4·75	23·00
9	**2**	1d. red	2·00	11·00
10	**2**	2d. grey	1·50	7·00
11	**2**	2½d. blue	11·00	15·00

3

1912
27	**3**	½d. green	3·50	3·25
13	**3**	1d. red	2·25	13·00
28	**3**	1d. violet	4·50	7·50
29	**3**	1½d. red	6·00	3·25
30	**3**	2d. grey	7·00	42·00
15	**3**	2½d. blue	1·75	11·00
16	**3**	3d. purple on yellow	2·50	10·00
17	**3**	4d. black and red on yellow	75	4·50
18	**3**	5d. purple and green	1·75	5·50
19	**3**	6d. purple	1·25	6·50
20	**3**	1s. black on green	1·25	4·00
21	**3**	2s. purple and blue on blue	14·00	30·00
22	**3**	2s.6d. black and red on blue	19·00	25·00
23	**3**	5s. green and red on yellow	32·00	65·00
35	**3**	10s. green and red on green	£160	£375
24	**3**	£1 purple and black on red	£550	£1500

1918. Optd **WAR TAX.**
26	1d. red	50	6·50

1935. Silver Jubilee. As T **10a** of Gambia.
36	1d. blue and black	2·25	16·00
37	1½d. blue and red	1·75	4·00
38	3d. brown and blue	6·50	25·00
39	1s. grey and purple	26·00	20·00

1937. Coronation. As T **10b** of Gambia.
40	1d. violet	35	65
41	1½d. red	35	65
42	3d. blue	40	70

6 Great Frigate Bird   **7** Pandanus Pine

1939
43	**6**	½d. blue and green	60	1·00
44	**7**	1d. green and purple	30	1·50
45	-	1½d. black and red	30	1·25
46	-	2d. brown and black	1·25	1·00
47	-	2½d. black and green	1·00	1·00
48	-	3d. black and blue	60	1·00
49	-	5d. blue and brown	7·00	2·75
50	-	6d. green and violet	70	60
51a	-	1s. black and turquoise	18·00	5·00
52	-	2s. blue and red	10·00	10·00
53	-	2s.6d. blue and green	10·00	11·00
54	-	5s. red and blue	13·00	16·00

DESIGNS: 1½d. Canoe crossing reef; 2d. Canoe and boat-house; 2½d. Native house; 3d. Seascape; 5d. Ellice Is. canoe; 6d. Coconut palms; 1s. Jetty, Ocean Is.; 2s. H.M.C.S. "Nimanoa"; 2s.6d. Gilbert Is. canoe; 5s. Coat of arms.

1946. Victory. As T **11a** of Gambia.
55	1d. purple	15	65
56	3d. blue	15	65

1949. Silver Wedding. As T **11b/11c** of Gambia.
57	1d. violet	50	1·50
58	£1 red	16·00	24·00

1949. U.P.U. As T **11d/11g** of Gambia.
59	1d. purple	50	2·50
60	2d. black	2·25	4·00
61	3d. blue	65	4·00
62	1s. blue	65	2·50

1953. Coronation. As T **11h** of Gambia.
63	2d. black and grey	1·50	2·25

18 Great Frigate Bird

1956. As 1939 issue but with portrait of Queen Elizabeth II as in T **18** and colours changed.
64	**18**	½d. black and blue	65	1·25
65	**7**	1d. olive and violet	60	1·25
85	-	2d. green and purple	1·00	1·25
67	-	2½d. black and green	50	60
68	-	3d. black and red	50	60
69	-	5d. blue and orange	9·00	3·25
70	-	6d. brown and black	55	2·75
71	-	1s. black and olive	4·25	60
72	-	2s. blue and sepia	6·00	4·00
73	-	2s.6d. red and blue	7·00	4·00
74	-	5s. blue and green	7·00	5·00
75	-	10s. black & turq (as 1½d.)	35·00	8·50

19 Loading Phosphate from Cantilever

1960. Diamond Jubilee of Phosphate Discovery at Ocean Is. Inscr "1900 1960".
76	**19**	2d. green and red	1·00	85
77	-	2½d. black and olive	1·00	85
78	-	1s. black and turquoise	1·00	85

DESIGNS: 2½d. Phosphate rock; 1s. Phosphate mining.

1963. Freedom from Hunger. As T **20a** of Gambia.
79	10d. blue	75	30

1963. Red Cross Cent. As T **20b** of Gambia.
80	2d. red and black	50	1·00
81	10d. red and blue	75	2·50

23 Reef Heron in Flight

1964. First Air Service.
82	-	3d. blue, black and light blue	70	30
83	**23**	1s. light blue, black and blue	1·10	30
84	-	3s.7d. green, black & emerald	1·60	1·50

DESIGNS—VERT: 3d. de Havilland Heron 2 and route map; 3s.7d. de Havilland Heron 2 over Tarawa lagoon.

1965. Cent of I.T.U. As T **44** of Gibraltar.
87	3d. orange and green	15	10
88	2s.6d. turquoise and purple	45	20

26 Gilbertese Women's Dance

1965. Multicoloured
89	½d. Maneaba and Gilbertese man blowing Bu shell (vert)	10	10
90	1d. Ellice Islanders Reef fishing by flare (vert)	10	10
91	2d. Gilbertese girl weaving head-garland (vert)	10	10
92	3d. Gilbertese woman performing Ruoia (vert)	10	10
93	4d. Gilbertese man performing Kamei (vert)	15	10
94	5d. Gilbertese girl drawing water (vert)	20	10
95	6d. Ellice Islander performing a Fatele (vert)	20	10
96	7d. Ellice youths performing spear dance (vert)	25	10
97	1s. Gilbertese girl tending Ikaroa Babai plant (vert)	75	10
98	1s.6d. Ellice Islanders dancing a Fatele (vert)	1·00	1·00
99	2s. Ellice Islanders pounding Pulaka (vert)	1·00	1·40
100	3s.7d. Type **26**	1·75	65
101	5s. Gilbertese boys playing a stick game	1·75	80
102	10s. Ellice youths beating the box for the Fatele	2·75	1·00
103	£1 Coat of arms	3·50	1·75

1965. I.C.Y. As T **45** of Gibraltar.
104	½d. purple and turquoise	10	10
105	3s.7d. green and lavender	50	20

1966. Churchill Commem. As T **46** of Gibraltar.
106	½d. blue	10	10
107	3d. green	20	10
108	3s. brown	40	35
109	3s.7d. violet	45	35

1966. Decimal Currency. Nos. 89/103 surch.
110	1c. on 1d.	10	10

111	2c. on 2d.		10	10
112	3c. on 3d.		10	10
113	4c. on ½d.		10	10
114	5c. on 6d.		15	10
115	6c. on 4d.		15	10
116	8c. on 5d.		15	10
117	10c. on 1s.		15	10
118	15c. on 7d.		60	1·00
119	20c. on 1s.6d.		30	25
120	25c. on 2s.		30	20
121	35c. on 3s.7d.		1·00	20
122	50c. on 5s.		55	35
123	$1 on 10s.		55	40
124	$2 on £1		2·50	3·25

1966. World Cup Football Championship. As T **47** of Gibraltar.

125	3c. multicoloured		20	10
126	35c. multicoloured		80	20

1966. Inauguration of W.H.O. Headquarters, Geneva. As T **54** of Gibraltar.

127	3c. black, green and blue		20	10
128	12c. black, purple and ochre		45	40

1966. 20th Anniv of UNESCO. As T **56a/56c** of Gibraltar.

129	5c. multicoloured		25	90
130	10c. yellow, violet and olive		35	15
131	20c. black, purple and orange		60	90

41 H.M.S. *Royalist*

1967. 75th Anniv of Protectorate.

132	**41**	3c. red, blue and green	30	50
133	-	10c. multicoloured	15	15
134	-	35c. sepia, yellow and green	30	50

DESIGNS: 10c. Trading post; 35c. Island family.

1968. Decimal Currency. As Nos. 89/103, but with values inscr in decimal currency.

135	1c. multicoloured (as 1d.)		10	15
136	2c. multicoloured (as 2d.)		15	10
137	3c. multicoloured (as 3d.)		15	10
138	4c. multicoloured (as ½d.)		15	10
139	5c. multicoloured (as 6d.)		15	10
140	6c. multicoloured (as 4d.)		20	10
141	8c. multicoloured (as 5d.)		20	10
142	10c. multicoloured (as 1s.)		20	10
143	15c. multicoloured (as 7d.)		50	20
144	20c. multicoloured (as 1s.6d.)		65	15
145	25c. multicoloured (as 2s.)		1·25	20
146	**26**	35c. multicoloured	1·50	20
147	-	50c. multicoloured (as 5s.)	1·50	2·50
148	-	$1 multicoloured (as 10s.)	1·50	3·75
149	-	$2 multicoloured (as £1)	5·50	6·00

45 Map of Tarawa Atoll

1968. 25th Anniversary of Battle of Tarawa.

150	3c. Type **45**		20	30
151	10c. Marines landing		20	20
152	15c. Beach-head assault		20	35
153	35c. Raising U.S. and British flags		25	50

46 Young Pupil against Outline of Abemama Island

1969. End of Inaugural Year of South Pacific University.

154	**46**	3c. multicoloured	10	25
155	-	10c. multicoloured	10	10
156	-	35c. black, brown and green	15	30

DESIGNS: 10c. Boy and girl students and Tarawa atoll; 35c. University graduate and South Pacific islands.

47 "Virgin and Child" in Pacific Setting

1969. Christmas.

157		2c. multicoloured	15	20
158	**47**	10c. multicoloured	15	10

DESIGN: 2c. as Type **47**. but with grass foreground instead of sand.

48 "Kiss of Life"

1970. Centenary of British Red Cross.

159	**48**	10c. multicoloured	20	10
160	-	15c. multicoloured	30	45
161	-	35c. multicoloured	60	90

Nos. 160/1 are as Type **48**, but arranged differently.

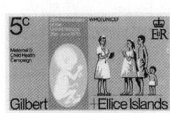

49 Foetus and Patients

1970. 25th Anniversary of U.N.

162	**49**	5c. multicoloured	15	30
163	-	10c. black, grey and red	15	15
164	-	15c. multicoloured	20	30
165	-	35c. blue, green and black	30	45

DESIGNS: 10c. Nurse and surgical instruments; 15c. X-ray plate and technician; 35c. U.N. emblem and map.

53 Map of Gilbert Islands

1970. Centenary of Landing in Gilbert islands by London Missionary Society.

166	**53**	2c. multicoloured	15	90
167	-	10c. black and green	25	15
168	-	25c. brown and blue	20	20
169	-	35c. blue, black and red	50	70

DESIGNS—VERT: 10c. Sailing-ship "John Williams III"; 25c. Rev. S. J. Whitmee. HORIZ: 35c. M.V. "John Williams VII".

57 Child with Halo (T. Collis)

1970. Christmas. Sketches. Multicoloured.

170	2c. Type **57**		10	60
171	10c. Sanctuary, Tarawa Cathedral (Mrs A. Burroughs)		10	10
172	35c. Three Ships inside Star (Mrs. C. Barnett)		20	20

60 Casting Nets

1971. Local Scenes. Multicoloured.

173	1c. Cutting toddy (vert)		10	10
174	2c. Lagoon fishing		15	30
175	3c. Cleaning pandanus leaves		15	15
176	4c. Type **60**		20	25
177	5c. Gilbertese canoe		45	15
178	6c. De-husking coconuts (vert)		30	45
179	8c. Weaving pandanus fronds (vert)		35	15
180	10c. Weaving a basket (vert)		40	15
181	15c. Tiger shark and fishermen (vert)		3·25	1·50
182	20c. Beating rolled pandanus leaf		1·50	90

183	25c. Loading copra		2·00	1·00
184	35c. Fishing at night		2·00	50
185	75c. Local handicrafts (vert)		75	1·50
186	$1 Weaving coconut screens (vert)		1·10	1·25
187	$2 Coat of arms (vert)		1·75	8·00

61 House of Representatives

1971. New Constitution. Multicoloured.

188	3c. Type **61**		10	20
189	10c. Maneaba Betio (Assembly hut)		20	10

62 Pacific Nativity Scene

1971. Christmas.

190	**62**	3c. black, yellow and blue	10	20
191	-	10c. black, gold and blue	10	10
192	-	35c. black, gold and red	25	35

DESIGNS: 10c. Star and palm leaves; 35c. Outrigger canoe and star.

63 Emblem and Young Boys

1971. 25th Anniv of UNICEF. Multicoloured.

193	**63**	3c. Type **63**	10	90
194	-	10c. Young boy	15	25
195	-	35c. Young boy's face	45	90

Nos. 193/5 include the UNICEF emblem within each design.

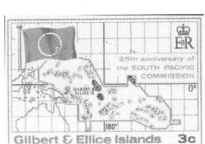

64 Flag and Map of South Pacific

1972. 25th Anniv of South Pacific Commission. Multicoloured.

196	3c. Type **64**		10	80
197	10c. Flag and native boats		15	20
198	35c. Flags of member nations		15	95

65 Alveopora

1972. Coral. Multicoloured.

199	3c. Type **65**		25	45
200	10c. "Euphyllia"		30	15
201	15c. "Melithea"		40	35
202	35c. "Spongodes"		80	60

66 Star of Peace

1972. Christmas. Multicoloured.

208	3c. Type **66**		10	10
209	10c. "The Nativity"		10	10
210	35c. Baby in "manger" (horiz)		30	30

1972. Royal Silver Wedding. As T **98** of Gibraltar, but with Floral Headdresses in background.

211	3c. brown		10	20
212	35c. brown		25	15

68 Funafuti ("The Land of Bananas")

1973. Legends of Island Names (1st series). Multicoloured.

213	3c. Type **68**		20	60
214	10c. Butaritari ("The Smell of the Sea")		20	20
215	25c. Tarawa ("The Centre of the World")		35	55
216	35c. Abemama ("The Land of the Moon")		35	65

See also Nos. 252/5.

69 Dancer

1973. Christmas. Multicoloured.

217	3c. Type **69**		10	25
218	10c. Canoe and lagoon		10	10
219	35c. Lagoon at evening		30	15
220	50c. Map of Christmas Island		40	1·60

1973. Royal Wedding. As T **101a** of Gibraltar. Multicoloured, background colours given.

221	3c. green		10	15
222	35c. blue		20	15

70 Meteorological Observation

1973. Centenary of I.M.O./W.M.O. Multicoloured.

223	3c. Type **70**		30	30
224	10c. Island observing-station		30	20
225	35c. Wind-finding radar		40	25
226	50c. World weather watch stations		50	1·25

71 Te Mataaua Crest

1974. Canoe Crests. Multicoloured.

227	3c. Type **71**		10	25
228	10c. "Te Nimta-wawa"		15	10
229	35c. "Tara-tara-venei-na"		25	10
230	50c. "Te Bou-uoua"		35	1·60
MS231	154×130 mm. Nos. 227/30		2·25	5·50

72 £1 Stamp of 1924 and Te Koroba (canoe)

1974. Centenary of U.P.U.

232	**72**	4c. multicoloured	20	40
233	-	10c. multicoloured	20	15
234	-	25c. multicoloured	25	30
235	-	35c. multicoloured	30	50

DESIGNS: 10c. 5s. stamp of 1939 and sailing vessel "Kiakia"; 25c. $2 stamp of 1971 and B.A.C. One Eleven airplane; 35c. U.P.U. emblem.

73 Toy Canoe

1974. Christmas. Multicoloured.

236	4c. Type **73**		10	30
237	10c. Toy windmill		15	15
238	25c. Coconut "ball"		20	40
239	35c. Canoes and constellation Pleiades		25	55

74 North Front Entrance, Blenheim Palace

1974. Birth Cent of Sir Winston Churchill. Multicoloured.

240		4c. Type **74**	10	40
241		10c. Churchill painting	10	15
242		35c. Churchill's statue, London	25	50

75 Barometer Crab

1975. Crabs. Multicoloured.

243		4c. Type **75**	40	1·25
244		10c. "Ranina ranina"	40	25
245		25c. Pelagic swimmming crab	65	90
246		35c. Ghost crab	75	1·75

76 Eyed Cowrie

1975. Cowrie Shells. Multicoloured.

247		4c. Type **76**	45	1·25
248		10c. Sieve cowrie	60	30
249		25c. Mole cowrie	80	1·50
250		35c. All-red map cowrie	1·00	2·50
MS251		146×137 mm. Nos. 247/50	14·00	17·00

1975. Legends of Island Names (2nd series). As T **68**. Multicoloured.

252		4c. Beru ("The Bud")	10	50
253		10c. Onotoa ("Six Giants")	10	15
254		25c. Abaiang ("Land to the North")	20	40
255		35c. Marakei ("Fish-trap floating on eaves")	30	55

77 "Christ is Born"

1975. Christmas. Multicoloured.

256		4c. Type **77**	15	80
257		10c. Protestant Chapel, Tarawa	20	35
258		25c. Catholic Church, Ocean Island	35	1·00
259		35c. Fishermen and star	40	1·75

POSTAGE DUE STAMPS

D1

1940

D1	**D1**	1d. green	13·00	25·00
D2	**D1**	2d. red	14·00	25·00
D3	**D1**	3d. brown	18·00	26·00
D4	**D1**	4d. blue	20·00	35·00
D5	**D1**	5d. olive	25·00	35·00
D6	**D1**	6d. purple	25·00	35·00
D7	**D1**	1s. violet	27·00	48·00
D8	**D1**	1s.6d. green	55·00	90·00

Pt. 1

GILBERT ISLANDS

On 1 January 1976 the Gilbert Islands and Tuvalu (Ellice) Islands became separate Crown Colonies. The Gilbert Islands became independent on 12 July 1979, under the name of Kiribati.

100 cents = $1.

1 Charts of Gilbert Islands and Tuvalu (formerly Ellice) Islands

1976. Separation of the Islands. Multicoloured.

1		4c. Type **1**	45	1·00
2		35c. Maps of Tarawa and Funafuti	80	1·50

1976. Nos. 173/87 of Gilbert and Ellice Islands optd **THE GILBERT ISLANDS**.

3		1c. Cutting toddy	25	1·00
5		2c. Lagoon fishing	50	30
12		3c. Cleaning pandanus leaves	40	2·50
7		4c. Type **60**	30	1·25
13		5c. Gilbertese canoe	50	1·00
14		6c. De-husking coconuts	50	1·00
15		8c. Weaving pandanus fronds	50	1·25
16		10c. Weaving a basket	50	1·25
17		15c. Tiger shark	2·75	1·50
18		20c. Beating a pandanus leaf	1·00	2·50
19		25c. Loading copra	1·50	1·50
20		35c. Fishing at night	2·00	1·75
21		50c. Local handicrafts	1·50	2·25
22		$1 Weaving coconut screens	2·75	8·00

3 Teraaka (training ship)

1976. Multicoloured.

23		1c. Type **3**	40	70
24		3c. Tautunu (inter-island freighter)	60	80
25		4c. Moorish idol (fish)	30	70
26		5c. Hibiscus	30	30
27		6c. Reef heron	1·50	90
28		7c. Catholic Cathedral, Tarawa	20	30
29		8c. Frangipani	20	30
30		10c. Maneaba, Bikenibeu	20	30
31		12c. Betio Harbour	35	45
32		15c. Evening scene	40	45
33		20c. Marakei Atoll	25	35
34		35c. G.I.P.C. Chapel, Tangintebu	25	40
35		40c. Flamboyant tree	40	45
36		50c. "Hypolimnas bolina", (butterfly)	1·25	1·75
37		$1 Tabakea (Tarawa Lagoon ferry)	75	2·50
38		$2 National flag	75	2·50

4 Church

1976. Christmas. Children's Drawings. Multicoloured.

39		5c. Type **4**	20	15
40		15c. Feasting (vert)	30	15
41		20c. Maneaba (vert)	30	35
42		35c. Dancing	30	45

5 Porcupine Fish Helmet

1976. Artefacts. Multicoloured.

43		5c. Type **5**	20	15
44		15c. Shark's teeth dagger	30	35
45		20c. Fighting gauntlet	30	40
46		35c. Coconut body armour	45	55
MS47		140×130 mm. Nos. 43/6	4·00	12·00

---

6 The Queen in Coronation Robes

1977. Silver Jubilee. Multicoloured.

48		8c. Prince Charles' visit, 1970	10	10
49		20c. Prince Philip's visit, 1959	15	15
50		40c. Type **6**	20	35

7 Commodore Bryon and H.M.S. Dolphin

1977. Explorers. Multicoloured.

51		5c. Type **7**	45	1·50
52		15c. Capt. Fanning and Betsey	55	2·75
53		20c. Admiral Bellingshausen and Vostok	55	2·75
54		35c. Capt. Wilkes and U.S.S. Vincennes	65	4·00

8 H.M.S. Resolution and H.M.S. Discovery

1977. Christmas and Bicentenary of Capt. Cook's Discovery of Christmas Is. Multicoloured.

55		8c. Type **8**	30	15
56		15c. Logbook entry (horiz)	30	15
57		20c. Captain Cook	40	20
58		40c. Landing party (horiz)	40	60
MS59		140×140 mm. Nos. 55/8	2·75	9·00

9 Scout Emblem and Island Scene

1977. 50th Anniv of Scouting in the Gilbert Is. Multicoloured.

60		8c. Type **9**	30	15
61		15c. Patrol meeting (horiz)	40	20
62		20c. Scout making mat (horiz)	40	20
63		40c. Canoeing	45	55

10 Taurus (The Bull)

1978. The Night Sky over the Gilbert Islands.

64	**10**	10c. black and blue	45	35
65	-	20c. black and red	50	50
66	-	25c. black and green	50	55
67	-	45c. black and orange	75	90

DESIGNS: 20c. Canis Major (the Great Dog); 25c. Scorpio (the Scorpion); 45c. Orion (the Giant Warrior).

11 Unicorn of Scotland

1978. 25th Anniv of Coronation.

68	**11**	45c. green, violet and silver	25	40
69	-	45c. multicoloured	25	40
70	-	45c. green, violet and silver	25	40

DESIGNS: No. 69, Queen Elizabeth II. No. 70, Great Frigate Bird.

12 Birds in Flight to Tarawa

1978. 25th Anniv of Return of George V School to Tarawa. Multicoloured.

71		10c. Type **12**	10	10
72		20c. Tarawa, Abemama and school badge	20	20
73		25c. Rejoicing islanders	20	20
74		45c. King George V School on Tarawa and Abemama	35	35

13 "Te Kaue ni Maie"

1978. Christmas. Kaue (traditional head decorations). Multicoloured.

75		10c. Type **13**	10	10
76		20c. "Te Itera"	15	15
77		25c. "Te Bau"	20	20
78		45c. "Te Tai"	25	30
MS79		149×99 mm. Nos. 75/8	90	4·50

14 H.M.S. Endeavour

1979. Bicent of Captain Cook's Voyages, 1768–79.

80	**14**	10c. multicoloured	20	15
81	-	20c. multicoloured	25	30
82	-	25c. black, lilac and green	25	45
83	-	45c. multicoloured	25	80

DESIGNS: 20c. Green Turtle; 25c. Quadrant; 45c. Flaxman/Wedgwood medallion.

For later issues see **KIRIBATI**.

Pt. 1

GOLD COAST

A British colony on the W. coast of Africa. For later issues after independence in 1957 see under Ghana.

12 pence = 1 shilling; 20 shillings = 1 pound.

1

1875

4	**1**	½d. yellow	90·00	35·00
11a	**1**	½d. green	4·50	1·25
5	**1**	1d. blue	35·00	6·50
12	**1**	1d. red	4·75	50
6	**1**	2d. green	£130	9·00
13b	**1**	2d. grey	15·00	50
14	**1**	2½d. blue and orange	12·00	70
15a	**1**	3d. olive	24·00	10·00
16	**1**	4d. mauve	24·00	3·75
17	**1**	6d. orange	24·00	5·50
18a	**1**	1s. mauve	14·00	2·75
19a	**1**	2s. brown	60·00	15·00

1889. Surch **ONE PENNY**. and bar.

20		1d. on 6d. orange	£150	55·00

4

1889

26	**4**	½d. mauve and green	6·50	1·50

No.	Type	Description		
27	4	1d. mauve and red	7·00	50
27b	4	2d. mauve and red	50·00	£160
28	4	2½d. mauve and blue	9·50	10·00
29	4	3d. mauve and orange	9·50	3·75
30	4	6d. mauve and violet	12·00	3·50
31	4	1s. green and black	18·00	38·00
32	4	2s. green and red	30·00	38·00
22	4	5s. mauve and blue	70·00	25·00
33	4	5s. green and mauve	90·00	50·00
23	4	10s. mauve and red	£120	16·00
34	4	10s. green and brown	£190	60·00
24	4	20s. green and red	£3250	
25	4	20s. mauve and black on red	£160	35·00

1901. Surch ONE PENNY. and bar.

35		1d. on 2½d. mauve and blue	9·00	6·50
36		1d. on 6d. mauve and violet	9·00	4·50

1902. As T 4, but with portrait of King Edward VII.

38		½d. purple and green	1·50	40
39		1d. purple and red	1·50	15
51		2d. purple and red	12·00	2·00
41		2½d. purple and blue	4·50	9·00
42		3d. purple and orange	6·00	2·75
43		6d. purple and violet	6·50	3·00
44		1s. green and black	21·00	4·25
45		2s. green and red	22·00	32·00
57		2s.6d. green and yellow	35·00	£130
46		5s. green and mauve	60·00	£120
47		10s. green and brown	80·00	£160
48		20s. purple and black on red	£180	£225

1907. As last.

59		½d. green	12·00	30
60		1d. red	17·00	40
61		2d. grey	3·00	40
62		2½d. blue	18·00	4·75
63		3d. purple on yellow	8·50	55
64a		6d. purple	7·00	60
65		1s. black and green	24·00	50
66		2s. purple and blue on blue	8·50	16·00
67		2s.6d. black and red on blue	42·00	95·00
68		5s. green and red on yellow	65·00	£225

8

1908

70	8	1d. red	8·00	10

1913. As T 4 and T 8 (1d.) but portraits of King George V.

86		½d. green	1·25	50
72		1d. red	1·75	10
87		1d. brown	1·00	10
88		1½d. red	2·00	10
89		2d. grey	2·25	30
76		2½d. blue	14·00	2·25
90		2½d. orange	2·50	13·00
77b		3d. purple on yellow	1·75	40
91		3d. blue	1·75	1·50
78		6d. purple	12·00	2·25
79e		1s. black on green	2·25	50
96		2s. purple and blue on blue	4·00	30
81		2s.6d. black and red on blue	13·00	13·00
98		5s. green and red on yellow	24·00	85·00
83a		10s. green and red on green	38·00	£100
100a		15s. purple and green	£140	£550
84		20s. purple and black on red	£170	£120
102		£2 green and orange	£550	£1600

1918. Surch WAR TAX ONE PENNY.

85		1d. on red (No. 72)	4·00	1·00

13 King George V and Christiansborg Castle

1928

103	13	½d. green	1·25	40
104	13	1d. brown	1·00	10
105	13	1½d. red	3·75	1·50
106	13	2d. grey	3·75	20
107	13	2½d. orange	4·00	3·50
108	13	3d. blue	3·75	40
109	13	6d. black and purple	4·50	40
110	13	1s. black and orange	6·00	1·50
111	13	2s. black and violet	32·00	6·50
112b	13	5s. red and olive	60·00	50·00

1935. Silver Jubilee. As T 10a of Gambia.

113		1d. blue and black	60	50
114		3d. brown and blue	3·00	6·50
115		6d. green and blue	18·00	30·00
116		1s. grey and purple	5·00	40·00

1937. Coronation. As T 10b of Gambia.

117		1d. brown	1·75	2·50
118		2d. grey	2·25	6·00
119		3d. blue	3·75	2·75

14

15 King George VI and Christiansborg Castle, Accra

1938

120a	14	½d. green	40	50
121a	14	1d. brown	40	10
122a	14	1½d. red	40	50
123a	14	2d. slate	40	10
124a	14	3d. blue	40	35
125a	14	4d. mauve	80	1·25
126a	14	6d. purple	80	20
127a	14	9d. orange	55	55
128a	15	1s. black and olive	1·50	65
129	15	1s.3d. brown and blue	2·00	50
130a	15	2s. blue and violet	6·00	21·00
131a	15	5s. olive and red	12·00	24·00
132	15	10s. black and violet	12·00	32·00

1946. Victory. As T 11a of Gambia.

133a		2d. violet	10	10
134a		4d. mauve	1·50	3·25

16 Northern Territories Mounted Constabulary

1948

135	16	½d. green	20	60
136	-	1d. blue	15	15
137	-	1½d. red	1·50	1·50
138	-	2d. brown	55	10
139	-	2½d. brown and red	2·00	5·50
140	-	3d. blue	4·00	1·75
141	-	4d. mauve	4·75	5·00
142	-	6d. black and orange	1·00	30
143	-	1s. black and red	3·25	30
144	-	2s. olive and red	11·00	4·75
145	-	5s. purple and black	42·00	14·00
146	-	10s. black and olive	21·00	15·00

DESIGNS—HORIZ: 1d. Christiansborg Castle; 1½d. Emblem of Joint Provincial Council; 2½d. Map showing position of Gold Coast; 3d. Nsuba manganese mine; 4d. Lake Bosumtwi; 1s. Breaking cocoa pods; 2s. Gold Coast Regt. trooping the Colour; 5s. Surfboats. VERT: 2d. Talking drums; 6d. Cocoa farmer; 10s. Forest.

1948. Silver Wedding. As T 11b/11c of Gambia.

147		1½d. red	30	70
148		10s. olive	35·00	45·00

1949. U.P.U. As T 11d/11g of Gambia.

149		2d. brown	25	20
150		2½d. orange	1·50	6·50
151		3d. blue	35	1·75
152		1s. green	35	30

1952. As 1948 but portrait of Queen Elizabeth II. Designs as for corresponding values except where stated.

153		½d. brown and red (as 2½d.)	20	20
154		1d. blue	40	10
155		1½d. green	30	1·50
156		2d. brown	40	10
157		2½d. red (as ½d.)	45	1·50
158		3d. mauve	1·25	10
159		4d. blue	50	30
160		6d. black and orange	10	15
161		1s. black and red	2·25	15
162		2s. olive and red	16·00	85
163		5s. purple and black	28·00	7·50
164		10s. black and olive	26·00	12·00

1953. Coronation. As T 11h of Gambia.

165		2d. black and brown	1·50	10

POSTAGE DUE STAMPS

D1

1923

D1	D1	½d. black	17·00	£120
D2	D1	1d. black	75	1·25
D3	D1	2d. black	13·00	2·25
D6	D1	3d. black	4·50	30·00
D7	D1	6d. black	1·75	17·00
D8	D1	1s. black	1·75	70·00

For later issues see **GHANA**.

Pt. 1

GREAT BRITAIN

Consisting of England, Wales, Scotland and Northern Ireland, lying to the N.W. of the European continent.

1840. 12 pence = 1 shilling;
    20 shillings = 1 pound sterling.
1971. 100 (new) pence = 1 pound sterling.

1

1840. Letters in lower corners. Imperf.

2	1	1d. black	£12500	£375
5	1	2d. blue	£45000	£900

3

1841. Imperf.

8	1	1d. brown	£600	30·00
14	3	2d. blue	£6250	85·00

In T **3** there are white lines below "POSTAGE" and above "TWO PENCE".

12   10

1847. Imperf.

59	12	6d. purple	£18000	£1000
57	10	10d. brown	£11000	£1500
54	10	1s. green	£22000	£1000

1854. Perf.

29	1	1d. brown	£225	22·00
34	3	2d. blue	£2850	70·00
40	1	1d. red	50·00	12·00

14   18   19

1855. No letters in corners.

66a	14	4d. red	£1700	£140
70	18	6d. lilac	£1350	£120
72	19	1s. green	£3000	£325

6

1858. Letters in four corners.

48	7	½d. red	£115	25·00
43	8	1d. red	25·00	2·75
52	8	1½d. red	£600	75·00
45	6	2d. blue	£350	14·00

21   22   23

24   25

1862. Small white letters in corners.

76	21	3d. red	£2500	£325
82	22	4d. red	£2000	£125
84	23	6d. lilac	£2200	£125
87	24	9d. bistre	£3750	£425
90	25	1s. green	£3000	£275

30   32

1865. Designs as 1862 and T 30 and T 32, but large white letters in corners.

103	21	3d. red	£525	60·00
94	22	4d. red	£575	75·00
97	23	6d. lilac (with hyphen)	£1100	£120
109	23	6d. lilac (without hyphen)	£675	90·00
111	24	9d. straw	£2300	£300
112	30	10d. brown	£3500	£400
117	25	1s. green	£800	45·00
118	32	2s. blue	£3800	£200
121	32	2s. brown	£28000	£4200

35

38

1867

126	35	5s. red	£11000	£675
128	-	10s. green	£60000	£3200
129	-	£1 brown	£90000	£4500
137	38	£5 orange	£14000	£4750

The 10s. and £1 are as Type **35**, but have different frames.

34

1872. Large white letters in corners.

122b	34	6d. brown	£700	60·00
125	34	6d. grey	£1850	£275

41   46

1873. Large coloured letters in corners.

141	41	2½d. mauve	£525	80·00
157	41	2½d. blue	£425	35·00
143	22	3d. red	£450	75·00
152	22	4d. red	£3000	£500
153	22	4d. green	£1400	£300
160	22	4d. brown	£425	£300
161	34	6d. grey	£450	75·00
156	46	8d. orange	£1800	£350
150	25	1s. green	£625	£150
163	25	1s. brown	£700	£160

The 3d., 4d. and 1s. are as 1862, and the 6d. as Type **34**, but all with large coloured letters.

52   53

1880. Various frames.

164	52	½d. green	55·00	20·00
187	52	½d. blue	32·00	10·00
166	53	1d. brown	35·00	15·00
167	-	1½d. red	£250	55·00

168	-	2d. red	£320	£110
169	-	5d. blue	£725	£150

57

1881

174	57	1d. lilac	2·75	1·70

1883. Types, as **1873**, surch **3d.** or **6d.**

159	21	3d. on 3d. lilac	£625	£150
162	34	6d. on 6d. lilac	£375	£150

58

61

1883

178	58	2s.6d. lilac	£600	£160
180	-	5s. red	£1100	£250
183	-	10s. blue	£2250	£525
185	61	£1 brown	£32000	£2800
212	61	£1 green	£4000	£800

The 5s. and 10s. are similar to Type **58**, but have different frames.

 62   63

1883. Various frames.

188	62	1½d. purple	£125	45·00
189	63	2d. purple	£230	80·00
190	63	2½d. purple	95·00	20·00
191	62	3d. purple	£280	£100
192	62	4d. green	£580	£210
193	62	5d. green	£580	£210
194	63	6d. green	£625	£240
195	63	9d. green	£1250	£480
196	62	1s. green	£1600	£325

71   72   73
74   75   76
77   78   79
80   81   82

1887

197	71	½d. red	1·75	1·20
213	71	½d. green*	2·00	2·25
198	72	1½d. purple and green	18·00	8·00
200	73	2d. green and red	34·00	13·00
201	74	2½d. purple on blue	25·00	3·50
202	75	3d. purple on yellow	25·00	3·50
205	76	4d. green and brown	40·00	15·00
206	77	4½d. green and red	11·00	45·00
207a	78	5d. purple and blue	42·00	13·00
208	79	6d. purple on red	40·00	12·00
209	80	9d. purple and blue	75·00	45·00
210	81	10d. purple and red	60·00	42·00
211	82	1s. green	£275	75·00
214	82	1s. green and red	65·00	£140

*No. 213, in blue, has had the colour changed after issue.

 83   90

1902. Designs not shown are as **1887** (2s.6d. to £1 as **1883**) but with portrait of King Edward VII.

217	83	½d. green	2·00	1·50
219	83	1d. red	2·00	1·50
221	-	1½d. purple and green	48·00	24·00
291	-	2d. green and red	28·00	22·00
231	83	2½d. blue	20·00	12·00
234	-	3d. purple on yellow	45·00	20·00
238	-	4d. green and brown	40·00	20·00
240	-	4d. orange	20·00	20·00
294	-	5d. purple and blue	30·00	22·00
245	83	6d. purple	45·00	22·00
249	90	7d. grey	45·00	22·00
307	-	9d. purple and blue	60·00	60·00
311	-	10d. purple and red	80·00	60·00
314	-	1s. green and red	60·00	35·00
260	-	2s.6d. purple	£280	£150
263	-	5s. red	£350	£220
265	-	10s. blue	£450	£220
266	-	£1 green	£2000	£500

 98 (Hair heavy)   99 (Lion unshaded)

1911

325	98	½d. green	8·00	1·50
327	99	1d. red	4·50	2·50

 101 (Hair light)   102 (Lion shaded)

1912

344	101	½d. green	7·00	3·00
341	102	1d. red	5·00	2·00

104   105   106

107   108

109

1912. Lined background.

418	105	½d. green	1·00	1·00
419	104	1d. red	1·00	1·00
420	105	1½d. brown	1·00	1·00
421	106	2d. orange	2·50	2·50
422	104	2½d. blue	5·00	3·00
376	106	3d. violet	9·00	3·00
424	106	4d. green	12·00	2·50
381	107	5d. brown	5·00	5·00
426a	107	6d. purple	3·00	1·50
387	107	7d. green	20·00	10·00
390	107	8d. black on yellow	32·00	11·00
392	108	9d. agate	15·00	6·00
427	108	9d. green	12·00	3·50
394	108	10d. blue	22·00	20·00
395	108	1s. brown	20·00	4·00
450	109	2s.6d. brown	80·00	40·00
451	109	5s. red	£175	85·00
452	109	10s. blue	£350	80·00
403	109	£1 green	£3500	£1250

112

1924. British Empire Exhibition. Dated "1924".

430	112	1d. red	10·00	11·00
431	112	1½d. brown	15·00	15·00

1925. Dated "1925".

432		1d. red	15·00	30·00
433		1½d. brown	40·00	70·00

 113   114   115

116 St. George and the Dragon

1929. Ninth U.P.U. Congress, London.

434	113	½d. green	2·25	2·25
435	114	1d. red	2·25	2·25
436	114	1½d. brown	2·25	1·75
437	115	2½d. blue	10·00	10·00
438	116	£1 black	£750	£550

 118   119   120

 121   122

1934. Solid background.

439	118	½d. green	50	50
440	119	1d. red	50	50
441	118	1½d. brown	50	50
442	120	2d. orange	75	75
443	119	2½d. blue	1·50	1·25
444	120	3d. violet	1·50	1·25
445	120	4d. green	2·00	1·25
446	121	5d. brown	6·50	2·75
447	122	9d. olive	12·00	2·25
448	122	10d. blue	15·00	10·00
449	122	1s. brown	15·00	1·25

123

1935. Silver Jubilee.

453	123	½d. green	1·00	1·00
454	123	1d. red	1·50	2·00
455	123	1½d. brown	1·00	1·00
456	123	2½d. blue	5·00	6·50

Emblems at right differ.

124 King Edward VIII

1936

457	124	½d. green	30	30
458	124	1d. red	60	50
459	124	1½d. brown	30	30
460	124	2½d. blue	30	85

126 King George VI and Queen Elizabeth

1937. Coronation.

461	126	1½d. brown	30	30

 128   129   130

1937

462	128	½d. green	30	25
503	128	½d. orange	30	30
463	128	1d. red	30	25
504	128	1d. blue	30	30
464	128	1½d. brown	30	25
505	128	1½d. green	65	60
465	128	2d. orange	1·20	50
506	128	2d. brown	75	40
466	128	2½d. blue	40	25
507	128	2½d. red	60	40
490	128	3d. violet	2·50	1·00
468	129	4d. green	60	75
508	129	4d. blue	2·00	1·75
469	129	5d. brown	3·50	85
470	129	6d. purple	1·50	60
471	130	7d. green	5·00	60
472	130	8d. red	7·50	80
473	130	9d. green	6·50	80
474	130	10d. blue	7·00	80
474a	130	11d. purple	3·00	2·75
475	130	1s. brown	9·00	75

131 King George VI

1939

476	131	2s.6d. brown	95·00	8·00
476a	131	2s.6d. green	15·00	1·50
477	131	5s. red	20·00	2·00
478a	-	10s. blue	45·00	5·00
478b	-	£1 brown	45·00	5·00

The 10s. and £1 values have the portrait in the centre in an ornamental frame.

134 Queen Victoria and King George VI

1940. Centenary of First Adhesive Postage Stamps.

479	134	½d. green	30	75
480	134	1d. red	1·00	75
481	134	1½d. brown	50	1·50
482	134	2d. orange	1·00	75
483	134	2½d. blue	2·25	50
484	134	3d. violet	3·00	3·50

135 Symbols of Peace and Reconstruction

1946. Victory Commemoration.

491	135	2½d. blue	20	20
492	-	3d. violet	20	50

DESIGN—HORIZ: 3d. Symbols of Peace and Reconstruction.

137 King George VI and Queen Elizabeth   138 King George VI and Queen Elizabeth

1948. Royal Silver Wedding.

493	137	2½d. blue	35	20
494	138	£1 blue	40·00	40·00

139 Globe and Laurel Wreath

140 "Speed"

1948. Olympic Games. Inscr "OLYMPIC GAMES 1948".

495	**139**	2½d. blue	50	10
496	**140**	3d. violet	50	50
497	-	6d. purple	3·25	75
498	-	1s. brown	4·50	2·00

DESIGNS: 6d. Olympic symbol; 1s. Winged Victory.

143 Two Hemispheres

144 U.P.U. Monument, Berne

1949. 75th Anniv of U.P.U. Inscr as in T **143/144**.

499	**143**	2½d. blue	25	10
500	**144**	3d. violet	25	50
501	-	6d. purple	50	75
502	-	1s. brown	1·00	1·25

DESIGNS: 6d. Goddess Concordia, globe and points of compass; 1s. Posthorn and globe.

147 H.M.S. *Victory*

1951

509	**147**	2s.6d. green	7·50	1·00
510	-	5s. red	35·00	1·00
511	-	10s. blue	15·00	7·50
512	-	£1 brown	45·00	18·00

DESIGNS: 5s. White Cliffs of Dover; 10s. St. George and Dragon; £1 Royal Coat of Arms.

152 Festival Symbol

1951. Festival of Britain.

513		2½d. red	20	15
514	**152**	4d. blue	30	35

DESIGN: 2½d. Britannia, cornucopia and Mercury.

154   155   157

158   159 Queen Elizabeth II and National Emblems

1952

570	**154**	½d. orange	10	10
571	**154**	1d. blue	10	10
517	**154**	1½d. green	10	20
573	**154**	2d. brown	10	10
519	**155**	2½d. red	15	15
575	**155**	3d. lilac	10	20
576a	**155**	4d. blue	15	15
577	**155**	4½d. brown	10	25
616c	**157**	5d. brown	55	35
617	**157**	6d. purple	55	30
617a	**157**	7d. green	55	50
617b	**158**	8d. mauve	70	45
582	**158**	9d. green	60	40
617d	**158**	10d. blue	70	60
553	**158**	11d. plum	50	1·10
617e	**159**	1s. brown	70	35
585	**159**	1s.3d. green	60	30
618a	**159**	1s.6d. blue	2·00	2·00

The 4d., 4½d. and 1s.3d. values are printed with colour tones reversed.

Stamps with either one or two vertical black lines on the back were issued in 1957 in connection with the Post Office automatic facing machine experiments in the Southampton area. Later the lines were replaced by almost invisible phosphor bands on the face, in the above and later issues. They are listed in the Stanley Gibbons British Commonwealth Catalogue.

For stamps as T **157**, but with face values in decimal currency, see Nos. 2031/3.

161   163

1953. Coronation. Portraits of Queen Elizabeth II.

532	**161**	2½d. red	20	25
533	-	4d. blue	1·10	1·90
534	**163**	1s.3d. green	5·00	3·00
535	-	1s.6d. blue	10·00	4·75

DESIGNS: 4d. Coronation and National Emblems; 1s.6d. Crowns and Sceptres dated "2 JUNE 1953".

166 Carrickfergus Castle

1955

595a	**166**	2s.6d. brown	35	40
760	-	5s. red	70	75
597a	-	10s. blue	4·50	4·50
762	-	£1 black	4·50	4·50

CASTLES: 5s. Caernarvon; 10s. Edinburgh; £1 Windsor.

170 Scout Badge and "Rolling Hitch"

171 "Scouts coming to Britain"

1957. World Scout Jubilee Jamboree.

557	**170**	2½d. red	50	50
558	**171**	4d. blue	75	1·50
559	-	1s.3d. green	5·50	4·50

DESIGN: 1s.3d. Globe within a compass.

1957. Inter-Parliamentary Union Conference. As No. 576a but inscr "46th PARLIAMENTARY CONFERENCE".

560		4d. blue	1·00	1·00

176 Welsh Dragon

1958. Sixth British Empire and Commonwealth Games, Cardiff. Inscr as in T **176**.

567	**176**	3d. lilac	20	20
568	-	6d. mauve	40	45
569	-	1s.3d. green	2·25	2·50

DESIGNS: 6d. Flag and Games emblem; 1s.3d. Welsh Dragon.

180 Postboy of 1660   181 Posthorn of 1660

1960. Tercentenary of Establishment of General Letter Office.

619	**180**	3d. lilac	50	50
620	**181**	1s.3d. green	3·75	4·25

182 Conference Emblem

1960. First Anniv of European Postal and Telecommunications Conference.

621	**182**	6d. green and purple	2·00	50
622	**182**	1s.6d. brown and blue	9·50	5·00

184 "Growth of Savings"

1961. Centenary of Post Office Savings Bank. Inscr "POST OFFICE SAVINGS BANK".

623A	-	2½d. black and red	25	25
624A	**184**	3d. brown and violet	20	20
625A	-	1s.6d. red and blue	2·50	2·25

DESIGNS—VERT: 2½d. Thrift plant. HORIZ: 1s.6d. Thrift plant.

186 C.E.P.T. Emblem   187 Doves and Emblem

1961. Europa.

626	**186**	2d. orange, pink and brown	15	10
627	**187**	4d. buff, mauve and blue	15	15
628	-	10d. turquoise, green bl	15	50

DESIGN: 10d. As 4d. but arranged differently.

189 Hammer Beam Roof, Westminster Hall

1961. Seventh Commonwealth Parliamentary Conference.

629	**189**	6d. purple and gold	25	25
630	-	1s.3d. green and blue	2·50	2·75

DESIGN—VERT: 1s.3d. Palace of Westminster.

191 "Units of Productivity"

1962. National Productivity Year.

631	**191**	2½d. green and red	20	20
632	-	3d. blue and violet	50	25
633	-	1s.3d. red, blue and green	1·50	1·70

DESIGNS: 3d. Arrows over map; 1s.3d. Arrows in formation.

194 Campaign Emblem and Family

1963. Freedom from Hunger.

634	**194**	2½d. red and pink	25	10
635	-	1s.3d. brown and yellow	1·90	1·90

DESIGN: 1s.3d. Children of Three Races.

196 "Paris Conference"

1963. Centenary of Paris Postal Conference.

636	**196**	6d. green and mauve	50	50

197 Posy of Flowers

1963. National Nature Week. Multicoloured.

637		3d. Type **197**	15	15
638		4½d. Woodland life	35	35

199 Westland Widgeon III (Rescue at Sea)

1963. Ninth International Lifeboat Conference, Edinburgh. Multicoloured.

639		2½d. Type **199**	25	25
640		4d. 19th-century lifeboat	50	50
641		1s.6d. Lifeboatmen	3·00	3·25

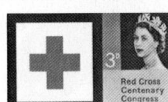

202 Red Cross

1963. Red Cross Centenary Congress.

642	**202**	3d. red and lilac	25	25
643	-	1s.3d. red, blue and grey	3·00	3·00
644	-	1s.6d. red, blue and bistre	3·00	3·00

DESIGNS: Nos. 643/4 are as Type **202** but differently arranged.

205 Commonwealth Cable

1963. COMPAC (Trans-Pacific Telephone Cable) Opening.

645	**205**	1s.6d. blue and black	2·75	2·50

206 Puck and Bottom ("*A Midsummer Night's Dream*")

210 Hamlet contemplating Yorick's Skull ("*Hamlet*") and Queen Elizabeth II

1964. Shakespeare Festival.

646	**206**	3d. multicoloured	15	15
647	-	6d. multicoloured	30	30
648	-	1s.3d. multicoloured	75	1·00
649	-	1s.6d. multicoloured	1·00	85
650	**210**	2s.6d. slate-purple	2·75	2·75

DESIGNS—As Type **206**: 6d. Feste (*Twelfth Night*); 1s.3d. Balcony scene (*Romeo and Juliet*); 1s.6d. "Eve of Agincourt" (*Henry V*).

211 Flats near Richmond Park

1964. 20th Int Geographical Congress, London. Multicoloured.

651		2½d. Type **211**	10	10
652		4d. Shipbuilding yards, Belfast	30	30
653		8d. Beddgelert Forest Park, Snowdonia	75	85
654		1s.6d. Nuclear reactor, Dounreay	3·50	3·50

The designs represent "Urban development", "Industrial activity", "Forestry" and "Technological development" respectively.

215 Spring Gentian

1964. Tenth Int Botanical Congress, Edinburgh. Multicoloured.

655		3d. Type **215**	25	25
656		6d. Dog rose	50	50
657		9d. Honeysuckle	1·70	2·25
658		1s.3d. Fringed water lily	2·50	2·50

219 Forth Road Bridge

1964. Opening of Forth Road Bridge.

659	**219**	3d. black, blue and violet	10	10
660	-	6d. lilac, blue and red	40	40

DESIGN: 6d. Forth Road and Railway Bridges.

221 Sir Winston Churchill

1965. Churchill Commemoration.

661	**221**	4d. black and drab	15	10
662	-	1s.3d. black and grey	45	40

The 1s.3d. shows a closer view of Churchill's head.

222 Simon de Montfort's Seal

1965. 700th Anniv of Simon de Montfort's Parliament.

663	222	6d. olive	20	20
664	-	2s.6d. black, grey and drab	80	1·50

DESIGN—(58½×21½ mm): 2s.6d. Parliament buildings (after engraving by Hollar, 1647).

224 Bandsmen and Banner

1965. Centenary of Salvation Army. Multicoloured.

665		3d. Type **224**	25	25
666		1s.6d. Three Salvationists	1·00	1·50

226 Lister's Carbolic Spray

1965. Centenary of Joseph Lister's Discovery of Antiseptic Surgery.

667	226	4d. blue, brown and grey	25	15
668	-	1s. black, purple and blue	1·00	1·10

DESIGN: 1s. Lister and chemical symbols.

228 Trinidad Carnival Dancers

1965. Commonwealth Arts Festival.

669	228	6d. black and orange	20	20
670	-	1s.6d. black and violet	80	1·10

DESIGN: 1s.6d. Canadian folk-dancers.

230 Flight of Supermarine Spitfires

234 Supermarine Spitfire attacking Junkers Ju 878 "Stuka"

1965. 25th Anniv of Battle of Britain. Inscr "Battle of Britain 1940".

671	230	4d. olive and black	25	25
672	-	4d. olive and black	25	25
673	-	4d. multicoloured	25	25
674	-	4d. olive and black	25	25
675	234	4d. olive and black	25	25
676	-	4d. multicoloured	25	25
677	-	9d. violet, orange and purple	1·70	1·70
678	-	1s.3d. grey, black and blue	1·70	1·70

DESIGNS: No. 672, Pilot in Hawker Hurricane Mk I; 673, Wingtips of Supermarine Spitfire and Messerschmitt BF 109; 674, Supermarine Spitfires attacking Heinkel HE 111H bomber; 676, Hawker Hurricanes Mk 1 over wreck of Dornier DO-17Z bomber; 9d. Anti-aircraft artillery in action; 1s.3d. Air battle over St. Paul's Cathedral.

239 Tower and "Nash" Terrace, Regent's Park

1965. Opening of Post Office Tower.

679		3d. yellow, blue and green	15	15
680	239	1s.3d. green and blue	45	45

DESIGN—VERT: 3d. Tower and Georgian build-ings.

240 U.N. Emblem

1965. 20th Anniv of U.N.O. and International Co-operation Year.

681	240	3d. black, orange and blue	25	20
682	-	1s.6d. black, purple blue	1·00	80

DESIGN: 1s.6d. I.C.Y. Emblem.

242 Telecommunications Network

1965. Centenary of I.T.U. Multicoloured.

683		9d. Type **242**	50	40
684		1s.6d. Radio waves and switchboard	1·50	1·20

244 Robert Burns (after Skirving chalk drawing)

1966. Burns Commemoration.

685	244	4d. black, indigo and blue	20	15
686	-	1s.3d. black, blue orange	65	70

DESIGN: 1s.3d. Robert Burns (after Nasmyth portrait).

246 Westminster Abbey

1966. 900th Anniv of Westminster Abbey.

687	246	3d. black, brown and blue	20	20
688	-	2s.6d. black	80	80

DESIGN: 2s.6d. Fan vaulting, Henry VII Chapel.

248 View near Hassocks, Sussex

1966. Landscapes.

689	248	4d. black, green and blue	10	15
690	-	6d. black, green and blue	15	20
691	-	1s.3d. black, yellow & bl	25	35
692	-	1s.6d. black, orange & blue	40	35

VIEWS: 6d. Antrim, Northern Ireland; 1s.3d. Harlech Castle, Wales; 1s.6d. Cairngorm Mountains, Scotland.

253 Goalmouth Melee

1966. World Cup Football Championship. Multicoloured.

693		4d. Players with ball (*vert*)	10	25
694		6d. Type **253**	15	25
695		1s.3d. Goalkeeper saving goal	50	1·00

255 Black-headed Gull

1966. British Birds. Multicoloured.

696		4d. Type **255**	20	20
697		4d. Blue tit	20	20
698		4d. European robin	20	20
699		4d. Blackbird	20	20

1966. England's World Cup Football Victory. As No. 693 but inscr "ENGLAND WINNERS".

700		4d. multicoloured	30	30

260 Jodrell Bank Radio Telescope

1966. British Technology.

701p	260	4d. black and lemon	10	10
702p	-	6d. red, blue and orange	15	25
703p	-	1s.3d. multicoloured	35	40
704	-	1s.6d. multicoloured	50	60

DESIGN: 6d. British motor-cars; 1s.3d. SRN 6 Hovercraft; 1s.6d. Windscale reactor.

264

265

1966. 900th Anniv of Battle of Hastings. Multicoloured.

705		4d. Type **264**	10	10
706		4d. Type **265**	10	10
707		4d. "Yellow" horse	10	10
708		4d. "Blue" horse	10	10
709		4d. "Purple" horse	10	10
710		4d. "Grey" horse	10	10
711		6d. Norman horsemen	10	10
712		1s.3d. Norman horsemen attacking Harold's troops (59×22½ mm)	20	75

272 King of the Orient

1966. Christmas. Multicoloured.

713		3d. Type **272**	10	25
714		1s.6d. Snowman	30	50

274 Sea Freight

1967. European Free Trade Assn (EFTA).

715		9d. Type **274**	25	20
716p		1s.6d. Armstrong Whitworth A.W.650 Argosy (Air freight)	25	40

276 Hawthorn and Bramble

1967. British Wild Flowers. Multicoloured.

717p		4d. Type **276**	10	15
718p		4d. Larger bindweed and viper's bugloss	10	15
719p		4d. Ox-eye daisy, coltsfoot and buttercup	10	15
720p		4d. Bluebell, red campion and wood anemone	10	15
721p		9d. Dog violet	15	25
722p		1s.9d. Primroses	20	30

282

1967

723	282	½d. brown	30	75
724	282	1d. olive	20	10
726	282	2d. brown	20	15
729	282	3d. violet	30	10
731	282	4d. sepia	30	30
733	282	4d. red	20	10
735	282	5d. blue	20	20
736	282	6d. purple	50	40
737	282	7d. green	1·00	1·00
738	282	8d. red	50	1·25
739	282	8d. turquoise	1·00	1·50
740	282	9d. green	1·00	1·50
741	282	10d. drab	1·00	1·00
742	282	1s. violet	45	45
743	282	1s.6d. blue and indigo	50	50
744	282	1s.9d. orange and black	1·00	1·00

For decimal issue, see Nos. X841 etc.

284 *Mares and Foals in a Landscape* (George Stubbs)

1967. British Paintings.

748		4d. multicoloured	10	10
749	284	9d. multicoloured	15	15
750		1s.6d. multicoloured	35	35

PAINTINGS—VERT: 4d. *Master Lambton* (Sir Thomas Lawrence). HORIZ: 1s.6d. *Children Coming Out of School* (L. S. Lowry).

286 *"Gipsy Moth IV"*

1967. Sir Francis Chichester's World Voyage.

751	286	1s.9d. multicoloured	20	20

287 Radar Screen

1967. British Discovery and Invention. Multicoloured.

752		4d. Type **287**	10	10
753		1s. *"Penicillium notatum"*	20	20
754		1s.6d. Vickers VC-10 jet engines and Gloster Whittle E28/39	25	25
755		1s.9d. Television equipment	30	30

292 *Madonna and Child* (Murillo)

1967. Christmas.

756		3d. multicoloured	10	15
757	292	4d. multicoloured	10	15
758		1s.6d. multicoloured	15	15

PAINTINGS—VERT: 3d. *The Adoration of the Shepherds* (School of Seville). HORIZ: 1s.6d. *The Adoration of the Shepherds* (Louis le Nain).

294 *Tarr Steps, Exmoor*

1968. British Bridges. Multicoloured.

763		4d. Type **294**	10	10
764		9d. Aberfeldy Bridge	15	15
765		1s.6d. Menai Bridge	25	25
766		1s.9d. M4 viaduct	30	30

298 "T U C" and Trades Unionists

1968. British Annivs. Events described on stamps.

767	298	4d. multicoloured	10	10
768	-	9d. violet, grey and black	15	15
769	-	1s. multicoloured	15	15
770	-	1s.9d. ochre and brown	35	35

DESIGNS: 9d. Mrs. Emmeline Pankhurst (statue); 1s. Sopwith Camel and English Electric Lightning fighters; 1s.9d. Captain Cook's *Endeavour* and signature.

302 *Queen Elizabeth I* (unknown artist)

1968. British Paintings.

771	302	4d. multicoloured	10	10
772	-	1s. multicoloured	10	20
773	-	1s.6d. multicoloured	20	25
774	-	1s.9d. multicoloured	25	40

PAINTINGS—VERT: 1s. "Pinkie" (Lawrence); 1s.6d. "Ruins of St. Mary Le Port" (Piper). HORIZ: 1s.9d. "The Hay Wain" (Constable).

306 Boy and Girl with Rocking Horse

1968. Christmas. Multicoloured.
775	4d. Type **306**	10	15
776	9d. Girl with doll's house (vert)	15	25
777	1s.6d. Boy with train set (vert)	15	50

310 Elizabethan Galleon

1969. British Ships. Multicoloured.
778	5d. *Queen Elizabeth 2*	10	15
779	5d. Type **310**	10	25
780	9d. East Indiaman	10	25
781	9d. *Cutty Sark*	10	25
782	1s. *Great Britain*	40	35
783	1s. *Mauretania I*	40	35

Nos. 778 and 782/3 are 58×23 mm.

315 Concorde in Flight

1969. First Flight of Concorde.
784	**315** 4d. multicoloured	25	25
785	– 9d. multicoloured	55	75
786	– 1s.6d. indigo, grey and blue	75	1·00

DESIGNS: 9d. Plan and elevation views; 1s.6d. Concorde's nose and tail.

318 Queen Elizabeth II

1969
787	**318** 2s.6d. brown	35	30
788	**318** 5s. lake	1·80	60
789	**318** 10s. blue	6·00	7·00
790	**318** £1 black	3·25	1·50

For decimal issues see Nos. 829/31b.
No. 790 has an italic "£". For larger version with roman "£" see No. 831b.

319 Page from *Daily Mail*, and Vickers FB-27 Vimy Biplane

1969. Anniversary Events described on stamps.
791	**319** 5d. multicoloured	10	15
792	– 9d. multicoloured	15	25
793	– 1s. claret, red and blue	15	25
794	– 1s.6d. multicoloured	15	30
795	– 1s.9d. turquoise, yell & sepia	40	40

DESIGNS: 9d. Europa and C.E.P.T. emblems; 1s. I.L.O. emblem; 1s.6d. Flags of N.A.T.O. countries; 1s.9d. Vickers FB-27 Vimy G-EAOU and globe showing flight route.

324 Durham Cathedral

1969. British Architecture (Cathedrals). Multicoloured.
796	5d. Type **324**	10	10
797	5d. York Minster	10	10
798	5d. St. Giles' Cathedral, Edinburgh	10	10
799	5d. Canterbury Cathedral	10	10
800	9d. St. Paul's Cathedral	25	30
801	1s.6d. Liverpool Metropolitan Cathedral	25	35

332 Queen Eleanor's Gate, Caernarvon Castle

1969. Investiture of H.R.H. The Prince of Wales.
802	– 5d. multicoloured	10	15
803	– 5d. multicoloured	10	15
804	**332** 5d. multicoloured	10	15
805	– 9d. multicoloured	15	30
806	– 1s. black and gold	15	30

DESIGNS: No. 802, The King's Gate, Caernarvon Castle; No. 803, The Eagle Tower, Caernarvon Castle; No. 805, Celtic Cross, Margam Abbey; No. 806, H.R.H. The Prince of Wales.

335 Mahatma Gandhi

1969. Gandhi Centenary Year.
807	**335** 1s.6d. multicoloured	40	30

336 National Giro "G" Symbol

1969. Post Office Technology Commemoration.
808	**336** 5d. multicoloured	10	10
809	– 9d. green, blue and black	20	25
810	– 1s. green, lavender & black	20	25
811	– 1s.6d. purple, blue & black	50	50

DESIGNS: 9d. International subscriber dialling (Telecommunications); 1s. Pulse code modulations (Telecommunications); 1s 6d. Automatic sorting (Postal Mechanisation).

340 Herald Angel

1969. Christmas. Multicoloured.
812	4d. Type **340**	10	10
813	5d. The Three Shepherds	15	15
814	1s.6d. The Three Kings	20	20

343 Fife Harling

1970. British Rural Architecture. Multicoloured.
815	5d. Type **343**	10	10
816	5d. Cotswold limestone	20	20
817	1s. Welsh stucco	25	25
818	1s.6d. Ulster thatch	30	40

The 1s. and 1s.6d. are larger (38×27 mm).

347 Signing the Declaration of Arbroath

1970. Anniversaries. Events described on stamps. Multicoloured.
819	5d. Type **347**	10	10
820	9d. Florence Nightingale attending patients	15	15
821	1s. Signing of International Co-operative Alliance	20	25
822	1s.6d. Pilgrims and *Mayflower*	20	30
823	1s.9d. Sir William and Sir John Herschel, Francis Baily and Telescope	25	30

352 Mr Pickwick and Sam (*Pickwick Papers*)

1970. Literary Annivs. Death Cent of Charles Dickens (novelist) (824/7) and Birth Bicent of William Wordsworth (poet) (828). Mult.
824	5d. Type **352**	10	25
825	5d. Mr. and Mrs. Micawber (*David Copperfield*)	10	25
826	5d. David Copperfield and Betsy Trotwood (*David Copperfield*)	10	25
827	5d. "Oliver asking for more" (*Oliver Twist*)	10	25
828	1s.6d. *Grasmere* (from engraving by J. Farrington, R.A.)	25	50

357 Queen Elizabeth II

1970. Decimal Currency. Designs as T **318** but inscr in decimal currency as T **357**.
829	**357** 10p. red	50	75
830	**357** 20p. green	60	25
831	**357** 50p. blue	1·50	40
831b	**357** £1 black	3·50	80

On No. 831b the "£" is in roman type.

360 Cyclists

1970. Ninth British Commonwealth Games. Multicoloured.
832	5d. Runners	25	25
833	1s.6d. Swimmers	50	50
834	1s.9d. Type **360**	50	50

361 1d. Black (1840)

1970. "Philympia 70" Stamp Exhibition. Multicoloured.
835	5d. Type **361**	25	10
836	9d.1s. green (1847)	25	30
837	1s.6d. 4d. red (1855)	25	45

364 Shepherds and Apparition of the Angel

1970. Christmas. Multicoloured.
838	4d. Type **364**	15	10
839	5d. Mary, Joseph, and Christ in the manger	15	15
840	1s.6d. The Wise Men bearing gifts	25	30

367 **913** **1915**

1916

1971. Decimal currency. As Nos. 723, etc. but new colours and with decimal figures of value as in T **367**.

(a) Full perforations at sides. Ordinary gum
X841	½p. turquoise-blue	10	10
X844	1p. crimson	10	15
X848	1½p. black	20	30
X849	2p. green	15	20
X851	2½p. pink	20	15
X929	2½p. red	25	40
X856	3p. blue	15	20
X857	3p. magenta	35	45
X858	3½p. olive	25	30
X931	3½p. brown	60	70
X861	4p. brown	40	50
X933	4p. blue	20	25
X865	4½p. blue	25	30
X866	5p. violet	20	20
X932	4p. greenish blue	35	50
X868	5½p. violet	40	50
X870	6p. green	25	40
X936	6p. olive	30	40
X872	6½p. blue	25	20
X875	7p. brown	25	30
X937	7p. red	1·40	1·50
X877	7½p. brown	30	40
X878	8p. red	30	30
X881	8½p. green	30	30
X882	9p. orange and black	45	55
X883	9p. violet	35	30
X885	10p. deep orange	35	45
X888	10p. pale orange	35	25
X890	10½p. yellow	40	55
X891	10½p. blue	45	75
X892	11p. pink	40	40
X942	11½p. brown	65	75
X893	11½p. grey	40	35
X895	12p. pale green	45	45
X896	12p. bright green	45	45
X898	12½p. green	45	40
X944	13p. olive	65	75
X900	13p. brown	40	40
X945	13½p. brown	70	80
X946	14p. pale blue	50	50
X903	14p. deep blue	45	50
X947	15p. blue	60	60
X949	16p. olive	55	55
X950	16½p. brown	90	1·00
X951	17p. green	60	75
X909	17p. pale blue	60	60
X910	17p. dark blue	80	85
X954	18p. violet	70	80
X912	18p. olive	70	80
X913	18p. green	60	60
X956	19p. red	80	60
X957	19½p. olive	2·00	2·00
X958	20p. purple	1·00	1·10
X959	20p. turquoise	75	70
X960	20p. black	1·00	1·00
X961	20½p. blue	1·40	1·40
X962	22p. blue	90	90
X963	22p. green	90	90
X964	22p. red	90	80
X965	23p. pink	1·25	1·10
X967	24p. violet	1·40	1·50
X968	24p. red	2·00	2·00
X969	24p. brown	80	80
X970	25p. purple	1·00	1·00
X917a	25p. red	7·50	7·50
X971	26p. red	1·10	80
X972	26p. grey	1·50	1·25
X973	27p. brown	1·25	1·25
X974	27p. violet	1·50	1·25
X975	28p. violet	1·25	1·25
X976	28p. brown	1·40	1·25
X977	28p. grey	1·40	1·25
X978	29p. brown	1·75	1·75
X979	29p. mauve	1·75	1·75
X980	30p. olive	1·25	1·25
X981	31p. purple	1·25	1·25
X983	32p. blue	1·90	1·75
X1057	33p. green	1·50	1·50
X985	34p. brown	1·75	1·75
X986	34p. grey	2·00	2·00
X987	34p. mauve	1·75	1·75
X988	35p. sepia	1·60	1·60
X989	35p. yellow	1·60	1·60
X990	37p. red	2·00	1·75
X1022	39p. mauve	1·75	1·75
X992	50p. brown	1·75	70
X1023	75p. black	3·00	1·50

(b) As T **367**. One elliptical perforation hole at each side. Ordinary gum
Y1667	1p. crimson	25	25
Y1668	2p. green	25	25
Y1669	4p. blue	25	30
Y1670	5p. brown	25	25
Y1671	6p. olive	25	35

Y1672	7p. grey	2·50	2·50
Y1673	7p. magenta	75	80
Y1674	8p. yellow	35	35
Y1675	9p. orange	15	20
Y1676	10p. orange	35	35
Y1677	12p. blue	1·00	1·25
Y1678	14p. red	50	55
Y1679	15p. magenta	60	65
Y1680	16p. pink	60	65
Y1681	17p. brown	60	65
Y1682	19p. brown	40	45
Y1684	20p. turquoise	90	90
Y1685	20p. bright green	50	50
Y1773	20p. light green	3·00	3·00
Y1688	22p. grey	70	70
Y1774	22p. brown	2·50	2·50
Y1690	25p. red	1·10	1·10
Y1691	26p. brown	90	90
Y1692	26p. gold	1·10	1·10
Y1693	29p. grey	1·25	1·25
Y1694	30p. grey	1·10	1·10
Y1695	31p. mauve	1·20	1·20
Y1696	33p. green	1·50	1·50
Y1697	34p. olive	4·00	3·00
Y1698	35p. yellow	1·50	1·50
Y1700	35p. olive	1·10	1·10
Y1701	35p. olive	50	55
Y1702	36p. blue	1·50	1·50
Y1703	37p. mauve	1·40	1·40
Y1704	37p. black	1·50	1·50
Y1705	37p. olive	90	90
Y1706	38p. red	1·50	1·50
Y1707	38p. blue	2·00	2·00
Y1708	39p. magenta	1·50	1·50
Y1709	39p. grey	1·20	1·20
Y1710	40p. pale blue	1·40	1·40
Y1711	40p. turquoise	1·40	1·40
Y1712	41p. grey	1·75	1·75
Y1714	41p. red	1·40	1·40
Y1715	42p. grey	1·40	1·40
Y1716	43p. brown	1·75	1·75
Y1718	43p. brown	1·40	1·40
Y1719	44p. brown	5·00	5·00
Y1720	44p. blue	1·10	1·10
Y1721	45p. mauve	1·50	1·50
Y1722	46p. yellow	1·00	1·00
Y1723	47p. turquoise	1·75	1·75
Y1724	48p. mauve	1·00	1·00
Y1725	49p. brown	1·50	1·50
Y1726	50p. brown	1·75	1·75
Y1727	50p. brown	1·00	1·00
Y1728	54p. brown	1·10	1·10
Y1729	56p. olive	1·25	1·25
Y1730	60p. green	1·40	1·40
Y1731	62p. red	1·40	1·40
Y1732	63p. green	2·00	2·00
Y1733	64p. turquoise	2·25	2·25
Y1734	65p. blue	2·10	2·10
Y1735	67p. mauve	1·50	1·50
Y1736	68p. brown	2·10	2·10
Y1737	72p. red	1·50	1·50
Y1738	78p. green	1·50	1·50
Y1739	81p. turquoise	1·50	1·50
Y1740	88p. magenta	2·00	2·00
Y1741	90p. blue	2·25	2·25
Y1742	97p. violet	3·00	3·00
Y1743	£1 violet	2·50	2·50
Y1744	£1 magenta	2·00	2·00
Y1745	£1.46 blue	4·00	4·00
Y1746	£1.50 red	4·00	4·00
Y1747	£2 blue	5·50	5·50
Y1748	£3 mauve	8·00	8·00
Y1803	£5 brown	15·50	5·00
Y1749	£5 blue	14·00	14·00

(c) As T **367**. One elliptical perforation hole at each side. Self-adhesive

U2920	1p. crimson	10	10
U2921	2p. green	10	10
U2922	5p. brown	10	10
U2923	10p. orange	20	20
U2924	20p. green	40	40
2297	42p. grey	3·50	3·50
U2925	50p. grey	1·00	1·00
2298	68p. brown	4·25	4·25
U2926	68p. turquoise	2·00	2·00
U2927	76p. red	2·00	2·00
U2929	87p. brown	2·00	2·00
U2912	£1 magenta	3·50	2·25
U2932	£1 brown	2·25	2·25
U2933	£1.10 olive	3·25	3·25
U2934	£1.28 brown	2·75	2·75
U2913	£1.50 red	3·25	3·25
U2935	£1.65 olive	3·50	3·50
U2937	£1.90 mauve	3·75	3·75
U2914	£2 blue	4·25	4·25
U2915	£3 mauve	6·25	6·25
U2916	£5 blue	10·50	10·50

(d) As T **913**. No Value Indicated. Ordinary gum

1670		2nd bright blue	90	90
1515		2nd deep blue	1·50	1·00
1447		1st black	1·75	1·00
1671		1st orange	1·00	1·00
1668		1st gold	1·00	1·00
1669		E blue	1·25	1·25

(e) As Types **1915/16**. No Value Indicated Large Figures. Ordinary gum

2650	**1915**	2nd blue	1·00	70
2651	**1915**	1st gold	1·25	80
2652	**1916**	2nd Large blue	1·50	1·00
2653	**1916**	1st Large gold	2·00	1·00

(f) No Value Indicated. Self-adhesive

2039	2nd blue	1·20	1·00
2040	1st orange	1·50	1·50
2295	1st gold	1·50	1·00
U3273	1st blue	2·00	1·20
U2968b	1st red	1·50	1·10
U2959	2nd Large blue	2·00	90
U2960	1st Large gold	3·00	1·10
U3276	1st Large blue	2·50	2·50
U2960a	1st Large red	1·75	1·75
U2981	Recorded Signed for 1st red and yellow	3·50	2·25
U2982	Recorded Signed for 1st Large red and yellow	4·00	2·75
U2985	Special delivery up to 100g blue and silver	10·00	10·00
U2986	Special delivery up to 500g blue and silver	11·00	11·00

368 *A Mountain Road* (T. P. Flanagan)

1971. "Ulster '71" Festival. Paintings. Multicoloured.

881	3p. Type **368**	25	25
882	7½p. *Deer's Meadow* (Tom Carr)	50	50
883	9p. *Slieve na brock* (Colin Middleton)	50	50

371 John Keats (150th Death Anniv)

1971. Literary Anniversaries.

884	**371**	3p. black, gold and blue	25	10
885		5p. black, gold and green	45	50
886	-	7½p. black, gold and brown	45	45

DESIGNS AND ANNIVERSARIES: 5p. Thomas Gray (death bicentenary); 7½p. Sir Walter Scott (birth bicentenary).

374 Servicemen and Nurse of 1921

1971. British Anniversaries Events described on stamps. Multicoloured.

887	3p. Type **374**	25	25
888	7½p. Roman centurion	50	50
889	9p. Rugby football, 1871	50	50

377 Physical Sciences Building, University College of Wales, Aberystwyth

1971. British Architecture. Modern University Buildings.

890	**377**	3p. multicoloured	10	10
891	-	5p. multicoloured	25	20
892	-	7½p. ochre, black and brown	45	55
893	-	9p. multicoloured	75	80

DESIGNS: 5p. Faraday Building, Southampton University; 7½p. Engineering Department, Leicester University; 9p. Hexagon Restaurant, Essex University.

381 "Dream of the Wise Men"

1971. Christmas. Multicoloured.

894	2½p. Type **381**	10	10
895	3p. "Adoration of the Magi"	10	10
896	7½p. "Ride of the Magi"	55	75

384 Sir James Clark Ross

1972. British Polar Explorers. Multicoloured.

897	3p. Type **384**	10	10
898	5p. Sir Martin Frobisher	15	15
899	7½p. Henry Hudson	45	50
900	9p. Capt. Robert Scott	70	85

See also Nos. 923/7.

388 Statuette of Tutankhamun

1972. General Anniversaries. Multicoloured.

901	3p. Type **388**	25	25
902	7½p. 19th-century Coastguard	50	50
903	9p. Ralph Vaughan Williams (composer) and score	50	50

ANNIVERSARIES: 3p. 50th anniversary of discovery of Tutankhamun's tomb; 7½p. 150th anniversary of Formation of H.M. Coastguard; 9p. Birth centenary.

391 St. Andrew's Greensted-juxta-Ongar, Essex

1972. British Architecture. Village Churches. Multicoloured.

904	3p. Type **391**	10	10
905	4p. All Saints, Earls Barton, Northants	10	20
906	5p. St. Andrew's, Letheringsett, Norfolk	15	20
907	7½p. St. Andrew's, Helpringham, Lincs	50	75
908	9p. St. Mary the Virgin, Huish Episcopi, Somerset	50	80

396 Microphones, 1924–69

1972. Broadcasting Anniversaries Multicoloured.

909	3p. Type **396**	10	10
910	5p. Horn loudspeaker	10	20
911	7½p. T.V. camera, 1972	45	50
912	9p. Oscillator and spark transmitter, 1897	50	50

ANNIVERSARIES: Nos. 909/11, 50th anniversary of daily broadcasting by the B.B.C.; No. 912, 75th anniversary of Marconi and Kemp's radio experiments.

400 Angel holding Trumpet

1972. Christmas. Multicoloured.

913	2½p. Type **400**	10	10
914	3p. Angel playing lute	10	10
915	7½p. Angel playing harp	50	45

403 Queen Elizabeth and Duke of Edinburgh

1972. Royal Silver Wedding.

916	**403**	3p. black, blue and silver	40	40
917	**403**	20p. black, purple & silver	1·20	1·20

404 "Europe"

1973. Britain's Entry into European Communities.

919	**404**	3p. multicoloured	25	25
920	**404**	5p. mult (blue jigsaw)	25	50
921	**404**	5p. mult (green jigsaw)	25	50

405 Oak Tree

1973. Tree Planting Year. British Trees (1st issue).

922	**405**	9p. multicoloured	35	40

See also No. 949.

1973. British Explorers. As T **384**. Multicoloured.

923	3p. David Livingstone	40	25
924	3p. H. M. Stanley	40	25
925	5p. Sir Francis Drake	40	50
926	7½p. Sir Walter Raleigh	40	50
927	9p. Charles Sturt	40	75

411 W. G. Grace

1973. County Cricket 1873–1973. Designs as T **411** showing caricatures of W. G. Grace by Harry Furniss.

928	**411**	3p. black, brown and gold	25	25
929	-	7½p. black, green and gold	75	75
930	-	9p. black, blue and gold	1·25	1·00

414 *Self-portrait* (Reynolds)

1973. British Paintings. 250th Birth Anniv of Sir Joshua Reynolds, and 150th Death Anniv of Sir Henry Raeburn. Multicoloured.

931	3p. Type **414**	10	10
932	3p. *Self-portrait* (Raeburn)	30	30
933	7½p. *Nelly O' Brien* (Reynolds)	30	30
934	9p. *Rev. R. Walker (The Skater)* (Raeburn)	60	60

418 Court Masque Costumes

1973. 400th Birth Anniv of Inigo Jones (architect and designer). Multicoloured.

935	3p. Type **418**	10	25
936	3p. St. Paul's Church, Covent Garden	10	25
937	5p. Prince's Lodging, New-market	35	50
938	5p. Court Masque stage scene	35	50

422 Palace of Westminster, seen from Whitehall

1973. 19th Commonwealth Parliamentary Conference.

939	**422** 8p. black, grey and stone	45	50
940	- 10p. gold and black	45	40

DESIGN: 10p. Palace of Westminster, seen from Millbank.

424 Princess Anne and Capt. Mark Phillips

1973. Royal Wedding.

941	**424** 3½p. violet and silver	25	25
942	**424** 20p. brown and silver	1·00	75

425 "Good King Wenceslas looked out."

1973. Christmas. Multicoloured.

943	3p. Type **425**	20	25
944	3p. King and page at window	20	25
945	3p. Leaving the palace	20	25
946	3p. Struggling against the wind	20	25
947	3p. Delivering gifts	20	25
948	3½p. King, page and peasant	20	25

431 Horse Chestnut

1974. British Trees (2nd issue).

949	**431** 10p. multicoloured	40	35

432 First Motor Fire-engine, 1904

1974. Bicentenary of Fire Prevention (Metropolis) Act. Multicoloured.

950	3½p. Type **432**	25	10
951	5½p. Prize-winning fire-engine, 1863	25	30
952	8p. First steam fire-engine, 1830	50	50
953	10p. Fire-engine. 1766	50	50

436 P.&O. Packet *Peninsular*, 1888

1974. Cent of Universal Postal Union. Multicoloured.

954	3½p. Type **436**	25	10
955	5½p. Farman H.F.III biplane, 1911	25	30
956	8p. Airmail—blue van and postbox, 1930	25	35
957	10p. Imperial Airways Short S.21 flying boat *Maia*, 1937	50	40

440 Robert the Bruce

1974. Medieval Warriors. Multicoloured.

958	4½p. Type **440**	25	10
959	5½p. Owain Glyndwr	25	35
960	8p. Henry the Fifth	50	50
961	10p. The Black Prince	50	50

444 Churchill in Royal Yacht Squadron Uniform

1974. Birth Centenary of Sir Winston Churchill.

962	**444** 4½p. silver, blue and green	20	15
963	- 5½p. silver, brown and grey	35	35
964	- 8p. silver, red and pink	60	50
965	- 10p. silver, brown and stone	60	50

DESIGNS: 5½p. Prime Minister, 1940; 8p. Secretary for War and Air, 1919; 10p. War correspondent, South Africa, 1899.

448 "Adoration of the Magi" (York Minster, *c.* 1355)

1974. Christmas. Church Roof Bosses. Multicoloured.

966	3½p. Type **448**	10	10
967	4½p. "The Nativity" (St. Helen's Church, Norwich, *c.* 1480)	10	10
968	8p. "Virgin and Child" (Ottery St. Mary Church, *c.* 1350)	25	50
969	10p. "Virgin and Child" (Worces-ter Cathedral, *c.* 1224)	50	50

452 Invalid in Wheelchair

1975. Health and Handicap Funds.

970	**452** 4½p.+1½p. blue and azure	25	25

453 Peace–Burial at Sea

1975. Birth Bicentenary of J. M. W. Turner (painter). Multicoloured.

971	4½p. Type **453**	25	25
972	5½p. Snowstorm–Steamer off a Harbour's Mouth	25	25
973	8p. The Arsenal, Venice	25	50
974	10p. St. Laurent	50	50

457 Charlotte Square, Edinburgh

1975. European Architectural Heritage Year. Multicoloured.

975	7p. Type **457**	15	15
976	7p. The Rows, Chester	15	15
977	8p. Royal Observatory, Greenwich	40	30
978	10p. St. George's Chapel, Windsor	40	30
979	12p. National Theatre, London	40	35

462 Sailing Dinghies

1975. Sailing. Multicoloured.

980	7p. Type **462**	25	20
981	8p. Racing keel yachts	35	40
982	10p. Cruising yachts	35	45
983	12p. Multihulls	50	50

466 Stephenson's *Locomotion*, 1825

1975. 150th Anniv of Public Railways. Multicoloured.

984	7p. Type **466**	25	25
985	8p. *Abbotsford*, 1876	50	50
986	10p. *Caerphilly Castle*, 1923	50	50
987	12p. High Speed Train, 1975	40	50

470 Palace of Westminster

1975. 62nd Inter-Parliamentary Union Conference.

988	**470** 12p. multicoloured	50	40

471 Emma and Mr. Woodhouse (*Emma*)

1975. Birth Bicentenary of Jane Austen (novelist). Multicoloured.

989	8½p. Type **471**	25	20
990	10p. Catherine Morland (*North-anger Abbey*)	45	45
991	11p. Mr. Darcy (*Pride and Prejudice*)	45	45
992	13p. Mary and Henry Crawford (*Mansfield Park*)	50	50

475 Angels with Harp and Lute

1975. Christmas. Multicoloured.

993	6½p. Type **475**	25	25
994	8½p. Angel with mandolin	25	40
995	11p. Angel with horn	50	45
996	13p. Angel with trumpet	50	45

479 Housewife

1976. Centenary of Telephone. Multicoloured.

997	8½p. Type **479**	25	20
998	10p. Policeman	40	40
999	11p. District nurse	50	50
1000	13p. Industrialist	60	60

483 Hewing Coal (Thomas Hepburn)

1976. Social Reformers. Multicoloured.

1001	8½p. Type **483**	25	20
1002	10p. Machinery (Robert Owen)	40	40
1003	11p. Chimney cleaning (Lord Shaftesbury)	50	50
1004	13p. Hands clutching prison bars (Elizabeth Fry)	60	60

487 Benjamin Franklin (bust by Jean-Jacques Caffieri)

1976. Bicentenary of American Revolution.

1005	**487** 11p. multicoloured	50	50

488 "Elizabeth of Glamis"

1976. Centenary of Royal National Rose Society. Multicoloured.

1006	8½p. Type **488**	15	10
1007	10p. "Grandpa Dickson"	40	40
1008	11p. *Rosa Mundi*	50	50
1009	13p. "Sweet Briar"	65	65

492 Archdruid

1976. British Cultural Traditions. Multicoloured.

1010	8½p. Type **492**	25	20
1011	10p. Morris dancing	40	40
1012	11p. Scots piper	45	45
1013	13p. Welsh harpist	60	60

The 8½p. and 13p. commemorate the 800th Anniv of the Royal National Eisteddfod.

496 Woodcut from *The Canterbury Tales*

1976. 500th Anniv of British Printing. Multicoloured.

1014	8½p. Type **496**	25	20
1015	10p. Extract from *The Tretyse of Love*	40	40
1016	11p. Woodcut from *The Game and Play of Chesse* by William Caxton	45	45
1017	13p. Early printing press	60	60

500 Virgin and Child

1976. Christmas. English Medieval Embroidery. Multicoloured.

1018	6½p. Type **500**	25	25
1019	8½p. Angel with crown	35	25
1020	11p. Angel appearing to Shepherds	40	45
1021	13p. The Three Kings	45	50

504 Lawn Tennis

1977. Racket Sports. Multicoloured.

1022	8½p. Type **504**	25	20
1023	10p. Table tennis	40	40
1024	11p. Squash	45	40
1025	13p. Badminton	45	50

508

1977

1026	**508**	£1 green and olive	3·00	25
1026b	**508**	£1.30 brown and blue	5·50	6·00
1026c	**508**	£1.33 mauve and black	7·50	8·00
1026d	**508**	£1.41 brown and blue	8·50	8·50
1026e	**508**	£1.50 olive and black	6·00	5·00
1026f	**508**	£1.60 brown and blue	6·50	7·00
1027	**508**	£2 green and brown	9·00	50
1028	**508**	£5 pink and blue	22·00	3·00

509 Steroids—Conformational Analysis

1977. Centenary of Royal Insitute of Chemistry. Multicoloured.

1029	8½p. Type **509**		25	20
1030	10p. Vitamin C—synthesis		45	45
1031	11p. Starch—chromatography		45	45
1032	13p. Salt—crystallography		45	45

513

1977. Silver Jubilee. Multicoloured.

1033	8½p. Type **513**	25	25
1034	9p. Type **513**	25	25
1035	10p. "Leaf" initials	25	25
1036	11p. "Star" initials	50	50
1037	13p. "Oak" initials	50	50

517 "Gathering of Nations"

1977. Commonwealth Heads of Government Meeting, London.

1038	**517**	13p. multicoloured	50	50

518 West European Hedgehog

1977. British Wildlife. Multicoloured.

1039	9p. Type **518**	25	20
1040	9p. Brown hare	25	20
1041	9p. Eurasian red squirrel	25	20
1042	9p. European otter	25	20
1043	9p. Eurasian badger	25	20

523 "Three French Hens, Two Turtle Doves and a Partridge in a Pear Tree"

1977. Christmas. *The Twelve Days of Christmas.* Multicoloured.

1044	7p. Type **523**	20	15
1045	7p. "Six Geese a-laying, Five Gold Rings, Four Colly Birds"	20	15
1046	7p. "Eight Maids a-milking, Seven Swans a-Swimming"	20	15
1047	7p. "Ten Pipers piping, Nine Drummers drumming"	20	15

1048	7p. "Twelve Lords a-leaping, Eleven Ladies dancing"	20	15
1049	9p. "A Partridge in a Pear Tree"	35	30

529 Oil—North Sea Production Platform

1978. Energy Resources. Multicoloured.

1050	9p. Type **529**	25	25
1051	10½p. Coal—modern pithead	25	25
1052	11p. Natural gas–flame rising from sea	50	50
1053	13p. Electricity–nuclear power station and uranium atom	50	50

533 The Tower of London

1978. British Architecture. Historic Buildings. Multicoloured.

1054	9p. Type **533**	25	20
1055	10½p. Holyrood House	25	40
1056	11p. Caernarvon Castle	60	40
1057	13p. Hampton Court Palace	60	40
MS1058	121×89 mm. Nos. 1054/7	1·50	1·75

537 State Coach

1978. 25th Anniv of Queen's Coronation.

1059	**537**	9p. gold and blue	35	25
1060	-	10½p. gold and red	45	45
1061	-	11p. gold and green	45	45
1062	-	13p. gold and violet	50	50

DESIGNS: 10½p. St. Edward's Crown; 11p. The Sovereign's Orb; 13p. Imperial State Crown.

541 Shire Horse

1978. Horses. Multicoloured.

1063	9p. Type **541**	20	10
1064	10½p. Shetland pony	35	40
1065	11p. Welsh pony	35	45
1066	13p. Thoroughbred	45	50

545 "Pennyfarthing" and 1884 Safety Bicycle

1978. Centenaries of Cyclists' Touring Club and British Cycling Federation. Multicoloured.

1067	9p. Type **545**	25	20
1068	10½p. 1920 Touring bicycles	35	40
1069	11p. Modern small-wheeled bicycles	40	40
1070	13p. 1978 Road-racers	50	50

549 Singing Carols round the Christmas Tree

1978. Christmas. Carol-singing. Multicoloured.

1071	7p. Type **549**	25	25
1072	9p. The Waits	25	25
1073	11p. 18th-century carol singers	50	50
1074	13p. *The Boar's Head Carol*	50	50

553 Old English Sheepdog

1979. Dogs. Multicoloured.

1075	9p. Type **553**	25	20
1076	10½p. Welsh springer spaniel	40	40
1077	11p. West Highland terrier	40	40
1078	13p. Irish setter	40	50

557 Primrose

1979. Spring Wild Flowers. Multicoloured.

1079	9p. Type **557**	25	20
1080	10½p. Daffodil	25	45
1081	11p. Bluebell	50	45
1082	13p. Snowdrop	50	40

561 Hands placing National Flags into Ballot Boxes

1979. First Direct Elections to European Assembly.

1083	**561**	9p. multicoloured	25	20
1084	-	10½p. multicoloured	35	35
1085	-	11p. multicoloured	40	40
1086	-	13p. multicoloured	45	40

DESIGNS: Nos. 1084/6 differ from Type **561** in the position of the hands and flags.

565 "Saddling `Mahmoud' for the Derby, 1936" (Sir Alfred Munnings)

1979. Horse-racing Paintings. Bicentenary of the Derby (9p). Multicoloured.

1087	9p. Type **565**	25	25
1088	10½p. *The Liverpool Great National Steeple Chase, 1839* (aquatint, F. C. Turner)	25	25
1089	11p. *The First Spring Meeting, Newmarket, 1793* (J. N. Sartorius)	50	50
1090	13p. *Racing at Dorsett Ferry, Windsor, 1684* (Francis Barlow)	50	50

569 *The Tale of Peter Rabbit* (Beatrix Potter)

1979. International Year of the Child. Multicoloured.

1091	9p. Type **569**	30	25
1092	10½p. *The Wind in the Willows* (Kenneth Grahame)	35	35
1093	11p. *Winnie-the-Pooh* (A. A. Milne)	40	40
1094	13p. *Alice's Adventures in Wonderland* (Lewis Carroll)	60	60

573 Sir Rowland Hill

1979. Death Cent of Sir Rowland Hill. Multicoloured.

1095	10p. Type **573**	25	20

1096	11½p. Postman, c. 1839	25	35
1097	13p. London postman, c. 1839	50	45
1098	15p. Woman and young girl with letters, 1840	75	50
MS1099	82×121 mm. Nos. 1095/8	1·30	1·50

577 Policeman on the Beat

1979. 150th Anniv of Metropolitan Police. Multicoloured.

1100	10p. Type **577**	30	20
1101	11½p. Policeman directing traffic	35	35
1102	13p. Mounted policewoman	40	55
1103	15p. River patrol boat	60	55

581 The Three Kings

1979. Christmas. Multicoloured.

1104	8p. Type **581**	25	20
1105	10p. Angel appearing to the Shepherds	25	25
1106	11½p. The Nativity	25	35
1107	13p. Mary and Joseph travelling to Bethlehem	50	50
1108	15p. The Annunciation	50	50

586 River Kingfisher ("Kingfisher")

1980. Cent of Wild Bird Protection Act. Multicoloured.

1109	10p. Type **586**	20	10
1110	11½p. White-throated dipper ("Dipper")	40	35
1111	13p. Moorhen	50	55
1112	15p. Yellow wagtails	50	55

590 *Rocket* approaching Moorish Arch, Liverpool

1980. 150th Anniv of Liverpool and Manchester Railway. Multicoloured.

1113	12p. Type **590**	20	15
1114	12p. First and Second Class carriages passing through Olive Mount cutting	20	15
1115	12p. Third Class carriage and sheep truck crossing Chat Moss	20	15
1116	12p. Horsebox and carriage truck near Bridgewater Canal	20	15
1117	12p. Truck and mail coach at Manchester	20	15

595 Montage of London Buildings

1980. "London 1980" International Stamp Exn.

1118	**595**	50p. brown	1·50	1·50
MS1119	90×123 mm. No. 1118 (sold at 75p.)	1·50	1·80

596 Buckingham Palace

1980. London Landmarks. Multicoloured.

1120	10½p. Type **596**	25	10
1121	12p. The Albert Memorial	25	15
1122	13½p. Royal Opera House	40	50
1123	15p. Hampton Court	50	75
1124	17½p. Kensington Palace	75	75

601 Charlotte Bronte (*Jane Eyre*)

1980. Famous Authoresses. Multicoloured.

1125	12p. Type **601**	35	20
1126	13½p. George Eliot (*The Mill on the Floss*)	40	45
1127	15p. Emily Bronte (*Wuthering Heights*)	40	45
1128	17½p. Elizabeth Gaskell (*North and South*)	50	50

605 Queen Elizabeth the Queen Mother

1980. 80th Birthday of The Queen Mother.

1129	**605**	12p. multicoloured	30	50

606 Sir Henry Wood

1980. British Conductors. Multicoloured.

1130	12p. Type **606**	30	10
1131	13½p. Sir Thomas Beecham	45	40
1132	15p. Sir Malcolm Sargent	50	55
1133	17½p. Sir John Barbirolli	50	55

610 Running

1980. Sport Centenaries. Multicoloured.

1134	12p. Type **610**	25	20
1135	13½p. Rugby	50	50
1136	15p. Boxing	50	45
1137	17½p. Cricket	50	50

CENTENARIES: 12p. Amateur Athletics Association; 13½p. Welsh Rugby Union; 15p. Amateur Boxing Association; 17½p. First England–Australia Test Match.

614 Christmas Tree

1980. Christmas. Multicoloured.

1138	10p. Type **614**	20	10
1139	12p. Candles	20	20
1140	13½p. Mistletoe and apples	40	40
1141	15p. Crown, chains and bell	55	50
1142	17½p. Holly wreath	55	50

619 St. Valentine's Day

1981. Folklore. Multicoloured.

1143	14p. Type **619**	25	25
1144	18p. Morris dancers	50	50
1145	22p. Lammastide	75	80
1146	25p. Medieval mummers	1·00	1·10

623 Blind Man with Guide Dog

1981. Int Year of Disabled Persons. Multicoloured.

1147	14p. Type **623**	50	25
1148	18p. Hands spelling "Deaf" in sign language	50	50
1149	22p. Disabled man in wheel-chair	75	85
1150	25p. Disabled artist painting with foot	1·00	1·00

627 *Aglais urticae*

1981. Butterflies. Multicoloured.

1151	14p. Type **627**	25	20
1152	18p. *Maculinea arion*	75	70
1153	22p. *Inachis io*	70	85
1154	25p. *Carterocephalus palaemon*	75	85

631 Glenfinnan, Scotland

1981. 50th Anniv of National Trust for Scotland. British Landscapes. Multicoloured.

1155	14p. Type **631**	15	25
1156	18p. Derwentwater, England	45	50
1157	20p. Stackpole Head, Wales	70	75
1158	22p. Giant's Causeway, Northern Ireland	75	1·00
1159	25p. St. Kilda, Scotland	90	1·00

636 Prince Charles and Lady Diana Spencer

1981. Royal Wedding.

1160	**636**	14p. multicoloured	75	25
1161	**636**	25p. multicoloured	1·50	1·50

637 "Expeditions"

1981. 25th Anniv of Duke of Edinburgh Award Scheme. Multicoloured.

1162	14p. Type **637**	25	20
1163	18p. "Skills"	45	50
1164	22p. "Service"	80	80
1165	25p. "Recreation"	90	1·00

641 Cockle-dredging from *Linsey II*

1981. Fishing Industry. Multicoloured.

1166	14p. Type **641**	25	25
1167	18p. Hauling in trawl net	50	50
1168	22p. Lobster potting	85	85
1169	25p. Hoisting seine net	85	85

645 Father Christmas

1981. Christmas. Children's Pictures. Multicoloured.

1170	11½p. Type **645**	25	20
1171	14p. Jesus Christ	35	20
1172	18p. Flying angel	50	60
1173	22p. Joseph and Mary arriving at Bethlehem	75	75
1174	25p. Three Kings approaching Bethlehem	85	85

650 Charles Darwin and Giant Tortoises

1982. Death Cent of Charles Darwin. Multicoloured.

1175	15½p. Type **650**	50	20
1176	19½p. Darwin and Marine iguanas	50	60
1177	26p. Darwin and cactus ground finch and large ground finch	75	85
1178	29p. Darwin and prehistoric skulls	95	90

654 Boys' Brigade

1982. Youth Organizations. Multicoloured.

1179	15½p. Type **654**	25	15
1180	19½p. Girls' Brigade	50	50
1181	26p. Boy Scout Movement	85	85
1182	29p. Girl Guide Movement	1·00	1·10

658 Ballerina

1982. Europa. British Theatre. Multicoloured.

1183	15½p. Type **658**	25	15
1184	19½p. Harlequin	50	50
1185	26p. Hamlet	85	1·00
1186	29p. Opera singer	1·00	1·00

662 Henry VIII and *Mary Rose*

1982. Maritime Heritage. Multicoloured.

1187	15½p. Type **662**	35	25
1188	19½p. Admiral Blake and *Triumph*	50	50
1189	24p. Lord Nelson and H.M.S. *Victory*	75	85
1190	26p. Lord Fisher and H.M.S. *Dreadnought*	75	85
1191	29p. Viscount Cunningham and H.M.S. *Warspite*	1·00	1·00

667 "Strawberry Thief" (William Morris)

1982. British Textiles. Multicoloured.

1192	15½p. Type **667**	25	25
1193	19½p. Untitled (Steiner and Co.)	75	75
1194	26p. "Cherry Orchard" (Paul Nash)	75	1·00
1195	29p. "Chevron" (Andrew Foster)	1·00	1·25

671 Development of Communications

1982. Information Technology. Multicoloured.

1196	15½p. Type **671**	50	25
1197	26p. Modern technological aids	75	1·00

673 Austin "Seven" and "Metro"

1982. British Motor Industry. Multicoloured.

1198	15½p. Type **673**	50	25
1199	19½p. Ford "Model T" and "Escort"	75	75
1200	26p. Jaguar "SS1" and "XJ6"	75	75
1201	29p. Rolls-Royce "Silver Ghost" and "Silver Spirit"	1·00	1·00

677 *While Shepherds Watche*

1982. Christmas. Carols. Multicoloured.

1202	12½p. Type **677**	30	30
1203	15½p. *The Holly and the Ivy*	50	30
1204	19½p. *I saw Three Ships*	65	75
1205	26p. *We Three Kings*	75	90
1206	29p. *Good King Wenceslas*	1·00	1·00

682 Atlantic Salmon

1983. British River Fish. Multicoloured.

1207	15½p. Type **682**	30	35
1208	19½p. Northern pike	60	60
1209	26p. Brown trout	75	85
1210	29p. Eurasian perch	1·00	1·10

686 Tropical Island

1983. Commonwealth Day. Geographical Regions. Multicoloured.

1211	15½p. Type **686**	40	30
1212	19½p. Desert	75	75
1213	26p. Temperate farmland	75	75
1214	29p. Mountain range	1·00	1·00

690 Humber Bridge

1983. Europa. Engineering Achievements. Multicoloured.

1215	16p. Type **690**	50	40
1216	20½p. Thames Flood Barrier	1·00	1·00
1217	28p. *Iolair* (oilfield emergency support vessel)	1·00	1·00

693 Musketeer and Pikeman, The Royal Scots (1633)

1983. British Army Uniforms. Multicoloured.

1218	16p. Type **693**	50	30
1219	20½p. Fusilier and Ensign, The Royal Welch Fusiliers (mid-18th century)	50	60
1220	26p. Riflemen, 95th Rifles (The Royal Green Jackets) (1805)	75	90
1221	28p. Sergeant (khaki service uniform) and Guardsman (full dress), The Irish Guards (1900)	75	90
1222	31p. Paratroopers, The Parachute Regiment (1983)	75	85

698 20th-century Garden, Sissinghurst

1983. British Gardens. Multicoloured.

1223	16p. Type **698**	50	30
1224	20½p. 19th-century garden, Biddulph Grange	50	55
1225	28p. 18th-century garden, Blenheim	75	1·00
1226	31p. 17th-century garden, Pitmedden	1·00	1·00

702 Merry-go-round

1983. British Fairs. Multicoloured.

1227	16p. Type **702**	35	35
1228	20½p. Big wheel, helter-skelter and performing animals	75	75
1229	28p. Side shows	75	1·00
1230	31p. Early produce fair	1·00	1·00

706 "Christmas Post" (pillar-box)

1983. Christmas. Multicoloured.

1231	12½p. Type **706**	30	30
1232	16p. "The Three Kings" (chimney pots)	50	35
1233	20½p. "World at Peace" (dove and blackbird)	75	1·00
1234	28p. "Light of Christmas" (street lamp)	75	1·00
1235	31p. "Christmas Dove" (hedge sculpture)	1·25	1·25

711 Arms of College of Arms

1984. 500th Anniv of College of Arms. Multicoloured.

1236	16p. Type **711**	50	30
1237	20½p. Arms of King Richard III (founder)	50	65
1238	28p. Arms of Earl Marshal of England	1·00	1·10
1239	31p. Arms of City of London	1·25	1·25

715 Highland Cow

1984. Cattle. Multicoloured.

1240	16p. Type **715**	35	30
1241	20½p. Chillingham wild bull	60	60
1242	26p. Hereford bull	80	80
1243	28p. Welsh black bull	90	90
1244	31p. Irish moiled cow	1·00	1·20

720 Garden Festival Hall, Liverpool

1984. Urban Renewal. Multicoloured.

1245	16p. Type **720**	30	35
1246	20½p. Milburngate Centre, Durham	50	60
1247	28p. Bush House, Bristol	1·25	1·25
1248	31p. Commercial Street development, Perth	1·25	1·25

725 Abduction of Europa

1984. 25th Anniv of C.E.P.T. (Europa) (Nos. 1249, 1251), and Second Election to European Parliament (others).

1249	-	16p. grey, blue and gold	60	50
1250	**725**	16p. grey, black, and gold	60	50
1251	-	20½p. red, purple and gold	70	40
1252	**725**	20½p. red, pur, blk gold	70	40

DESIGN: Nos. 1249 and 1251, Bridge (C.E.P.T. 25th anniv logo).

726 Lancaster House

1984. London Economic Summit Conference.

1253	**726**	31p. multicoloured	1·25	1·25

727 View of Earth from "Apollo 11"

1984. Centenary of Greenwich Meridian. Multicoloured.

1254	16p. Type **727**	50	35
1255	20½p. Navigational chart of the English Channel	75	80
1256	28p. Greenwich Observatory	1·00	1·00
1257	31p. Sir George Airey's Transit Telescope	1·00	1·10

731 Bath Mail Coach leaving London, 1784

1984. Bicentenary of First Mail Coach Run, Bath and Bristol to London. Multicoloured.

1258	16p. Type **731**	40	35
1259	16p. Attack on Exeter Mail, 1816	40	35
1260	16p. Norwich Mail in thunderstorm, 1827	40	35
1261	16p. Holyhead and Liverpool Mails leaving London, 1828	40	35
1262	16p. Edinburgh Mail snowbound, 1831	40	35

736 Nigerian Clinic

1984. 50th Anniv of British Council. Multicoloured.

1263	17p. Type **736**	50	35
1264	22p. Violinist and Acropolis, Athens	85	1·00
1265	31p. Building project, Sri Lanka	85	1·00
1266	34p. British Council library, Middle East	1·00	1·00

740 The Holy Family

1984. Christmas. Multicoloured.

1267	13p. Type **740**	30	30
1268	17p. Arrival in Bethlehem	50	50
1269	22p. Shepherd and Lamb	75	75
1270	31p. Virgin and Child	1·00	1·00
1271	34p. Offering of Frankincense	1·00	1·00

745 Flying Scotsman

1985. Famous Trains. Multicoloured.

1272	17p. Type **745**	75	35
1273	22p. Golden Arrow	75	1·00
1274	29p. Cheltenham Flyer	1·00	1·25
1275	31p. Royal Scot	1·25	1·50
1276	34p. Cornish Riviera	2·50	2·50

750 Bombus terrestris (bee)

1985. Insects. Multicoloured.

1277	17p. Type **750**	40	35
1278	22p. Coccinella septempunctata (ladybird)	60	60
1279	29p. Decticus verrucivorus (bush-cricket)	85	90
1280	31p. Lucanus cervus (stag beetle)	1·00	1·00
1281	34p. Anax imperator (dragonfly)	1·00	90

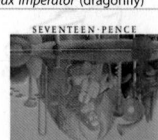

755 Water Music (George Frideric Handel)

1985. Europa. European Music Year. British Composers. Multicoloured.

1282	17p. Type **755**	55	40
1283	22p. The Planets Suite (Gustav Holst)	75	90
1284	31p. The First Cuckoo (Frederick Delius)	1·50	1·25
1285	34p. Sea Pictures (Edward Elgar)	1·50	1·25

759 R.N.L.I. Lifeboat and Signal Flags

1985. Safety at Sea. Multicoloured.

1286	17p. Type **759**	40	40
1287	22p. Beachy Head Lighthouse and chart	60	75
1288	31p. "Marecs A" communications satellite and dish aerials	1·00	1·00
1289	34p. Buoys	1·50	1·25

763 Datapost Motorcyclist, City of London

1985. 350 Years of Royal Mail Public Postal Service. Multicoloured.

1290	17p. Type **763**	50	40
1291	22p. Rural postbus	75	70
1292	31p. Parcel delivery in winter	1·00	1·00
1293	34p. Town letter delivery	1·50	1·50

767 King Arthur and Merlin

1985. Arthurian Legends. Multicoloured.

1294	17p. Type **767**	50	40
1295	22p. Lady of the Lake	75	75
1296	31p. Queen Guinevere and Sir Lancelot	1·25	1·25
1297	34p. Sir Galahad	1·25	1·25

771 Peter Sellers (from photo by Bill Brandt)

1985. British Film Year. Multicoloured.

1298	17p. Type **771**	45	40
1299	22p. David Niven (from photo by Cornell Lucas)	60	75
1300	29p. Charlie Chaplin (from photo by Lord Snowdon)	1·00	1·25
1301	31p. Vivien Leigh (from photo by Angus McBean)	1·10	1·50
1302	34p. Alfred Hitchcock (from photo by Howard Coster)	1·40	1·50

776 Principal Boy

1985. Christmas. Pantomime Characters. Multicoloured.

1303	12p. Type **776**	50	30
1304	17p. Genie	50	40
1305	22p. Dame	75	1·10
1306	31p. Good fairy	1·25	1·40
1307	34p. Pantomime cat	1·25	1·40

781 Light Bulb and North Sea Oil Drilling Rig (Energy)

1986. Industry Year. Multicoloured.

1308	17p. Type **781**	75	40
1309	22p. Thermometer and pharmaceutical laboratory (Health)	50	75
1310	31p. Garden hoe and steelworks (Steel)	1·25	1·40
1311	34p. Loaf of bread and cornfield (Agriculture)	1·25	1·40

785 Dr. Edmond Halley as Comet

1986. Appearance of Halley's Comet. Multicoloured.

1312	17p. Type **785**	50	40
1313	22p. "Giotto" spacecraft approaching comet	75	75
1314	31p. "Twice in a lifetime"	1·25	1·25
1315	34p. Comet orbiting sun and planets	1·25	1·40

789 Queen Elizabeth II in 1928, 1942 and 1952

1986. 60th Birthday of Queen Elizabeth II. Multicoloured.

1316	17p. Type **789**	60	50

1317	17p.	Queen Elizabeth II in 1958, 1973 and 1982	60	50
1318	34p.	Type **789**	1·25	1·25
1319	34p.	As No. 1317	1·25	1·25

791 Barn Owl

1986. Europa. Nature Conservation. Endangered Species. Multicoloured.

1320	17p.	Type **791**	40	45
1321	22p.	Pine marten	80	1·00
1322	31p.	Wild cat	1·50	1·25
1323	34p.	Natterjack toad	1·65	1·40

795 Peasants working in Fields

1986. 900th Anniv of Domesday Book. Multicoloured.

1324	17p.	Type **795**	40	45
1325	22p.	Freemen working at town trades	85	85
1326	31p.	Knight and retainers	1·25	1·40
1327	34p.	Lord at banquet	1·25	1·40

799 Athletics

1986. 13th Commonwealth Games. Edinburgh, and World Hockey Cup for Men, London. Multicoloured.

1328	17p.	Type **799**	40	45
1329	22p.	Rowing	55	75
1330	29p.	Weightlifting	75	1·00
1331	31p.	Rifle shooting	1·50	1·75
1332	34p.	Hockey	1·75	1·75

804 Prince Andrew and Miss Sarah Ferguson (from photo by Gene Nocon)

1986. Royal Wedding.

1333	**804**	12p. multicoloured	50	45
1334	-	17p. multicoloured	1·00	1·25

DESIGN: 17p. As Type **804** but with naval motif at foot.

806 Stylized Cross on Ballot Paper

1986. 32nd Commonwealth Parliamentary Association Conference.

1335	**806**	34p. multicoloured	1·25	1·25

807 Lord Dowding and Hawker Hurricane Mk I

1986. History of the Royal Air Force. Multicoloured.

1336	17p.	Type **807**	50	45
1337	22p.	Lord Tedder and Hawker Typhoon IB	75	95
1338	29p.	Lord Trenchard and de Havilland DH9A	1·25	1·25
1339	31p.	Sir Arthur Harris and Avro Type 683 Lancaster	1·75	1·60

1340	34p.	Lord Portal and de Havilland DH98 Mosquito	1·75	1·90

Nos. 1336/40 were issued to celebrate 50th anniv of the first R.A.F. Commands.

812 The Glastonbury Thorn

1986. Christmas. Folk Customs. Multicoloured.

1341	12p.	Type **812**	50	50
1342	13p.	Type **812**	30	40
1343	18p.	The Tanad Valley Plygain	50	50
1344	22p.	The Hebrides Tribute	1·00	1·00
1345	31p.	The Dewsbury Church Knell	1·25	1·00
1346	34p.	The Hereford Boy Bishop	1·25	1·10

817 North American Blanket Flower

1987. Flower Photographs by Alfred Lammer. Multicoloured.

1347	18p.	Type **817**	40	40
1348	22p.	Globe thistle	70	85
1349	31p.	"Echeveria"	1·10	1·25
1350	34p.	Autumn crocus	1·10	1·25

821 *Principia Mathematica*

1987. 300th Anniv of "Principia Mathematica" by Sir Isaac Newton. Multicoloured.

1351	18p.	Type **821**	50	40
1352	22p.	*Motion of Bodies in Ellipses*	75	75
1353	31p.	*Optick Treatise*	1·25	1·50
1354	34p.	*The System of the World*	1·25	1·25

825 Willis Faber Dumas Building, Ipswich

1987. Europa. British Architects in Europe.

1355	18p.	Type **825**	50	40
1356	22p.	Pompidou Centre, Paris	75	75
1357	31p.	Staatsgalerie, Stuttgart	1·25	1·25
1358	34p.	European Investment Bank, Luxembourg	1·25	1·25

829 Brigade Members with Ashford Litter, 1887

1987. Centenary of St. John Ambulance Brigade. Multicoloured.

1359	18p.	Type **829**	40	45
1360	22p.	Bandaging blitz victim, 1940	60	75
1361	31p.	Volunteer with fainting girl, 1965	1·25	1·25
1362	34p.	Transport of transplant organ by Air Wing, 1987	1·25	1·25

833 Arms of the Lord Lyon, King of Arms

1987. 300th Anniv of Revival of Order of the Thistle. Multicoloured.

1363	18p.	Type **833**	50	40
1364	22p.	Scottish heraldic banner of Prince Charles	75	90
1365	31p.	Arms of Royal Scottish Academy of Painting. Sculpture and Architecture	1·40	1·40
1366	34p.	Arms of Royal Society of Edinburgh	1·50	1·40

837 Crystal Palace, *Monarch of the Glen* (Landseer) and Grace Darling

1987. 150th Anniv of Queen Victoria's Accession. Multicoloured.

1367	18p.	Type **837**	50	45
1368	22p.	*Great Eastern, Beeton's Book of Household Management* and Prince Albert	80	75
1369	31p.	Albert Memorial, ballot box and Disraeli	1·25	1·50
1370	34p.	Diamond Jubilee emblem, newspaper placard for Relief of Mafeking and morse key	1·35	1·60

841 Pot by Bernard Leach

1987. Studio Pottery. Multicoloured.

1371	18p.	Type **841**	50	40
1372	26p.	Pot by Elizabeth Fritsch	70	75
1373	31p.	Pot by Lucie Rie	1·25	1·25
1374	34p.	Pot by Hans Coper	1·40	1·50

845 Decorating the Christmas Tree

1987. Christmas. Multicoloured.

1375	13p.	Type **845**	30	30
1376	18p.	Waiting for Father Christmas	40	40
1377	26p.	Sleeping child and Father Christmas in sleigh	80	1·00
1378	31p.	Child reading	1·10	1·25
1379	34p.	Child playing recorder and snowman	1·25	1·50

850 Short-spined Seascorpion ("Bull-rout") (Jonathan Couch)

1988. Bicentenary of Linnean Society. Archive Illustrations. Multicoloured.

1380	18p.	Type **850**	55	35
1381	26p.	Yellow Waterlily (Major Joshua Swatkin)	85	1·00
1382	31p.	Tundra swan ("Bewick's Swan") (Edward Lear)	1·10	1·25
1383	34p.	*Morchella esculenta* (James Sowerby)	1·25	1·40

854 Revd. William Morgan (Bible translator, 1588)

1988. 400th Anniversary of Welsh Bible. Multicoloured.

1384	18p.	Type **854**	40	40
1385	26p.	William Salesbury (New Testament translator, 1567)	70	95
1386	31p.	Bishop Richard Davies (New Testament translator, 1567)	1·25	1·25

1387	34p.	Bishop Richard Parry (editor of Revised Welsh Bible, 1620)	1·40	1·25

858 Gymnastics (Centenary of British Amateur Gymnastics Association)

1988. Sports Organizations. Multicoloured.

1388	18p.	Type **858**	40	40
1389	26p.	Downhill skiing (Ski Club of Great Britain)	70	80
1390	31p.	Tennis (centenary of Lawn Tennis Association)	1·10	1·25
1391	34p.	Football (centenary of Football League)	1·25	1·25

862 *Mallard* and Mailbags on Pick-up Arms

1988. Europa. Transport and Mail Services in 1930s. Multicoloured.

1392	18p.	Type **862**	50	35
1393	26p.	Loading transatlantic mail on liner *Queen Elizabeth*	1·00	1·00
1394	31p.	Glasgow tram No. 1173 and pillar box	1·25	1·25
1395	34p.	Imperial Airways Handley Page H.P.45 G-AAXD *Horatius* and airmail van	1·60	1·50

866 Early Settler and Sailing Clipper

1988. Bicentenary of Australian Settlement. Multicoloured.

1396	18p.	Type **866**	40	50
1397	18p.	Queen Elizabeth II with British and Australian Parliament Buildings	40	50
1398	34p.	W. G. Grace (cricketer) and tennis racquet	1·00	1·25
1399	34p.	Shakespeare, John Lennon (entertainer) and Sydney Opera House	1·00	1·25

Stamps in similar designs were also issued by Australia.

870 Spanish Galeasse off The Lizard

1988. 400th Anniv of Spanish Armada. Multicoloured.

1400	18p.	Type **870**	45	50
1401	18p.	English Fleet leaving Plymouth	45	50
1402	18p.	Engagement off Isle of Wight	45	50
1403	18p.	Attack of English fire-ships, Calais	45	50
1404	18p.	Armada in storm, North Sea	45	50

Nos. 1400/4 were printed together, *se-tenant*, forming a composite design.

875 *The Owl and the Pussy-cat*

1988. Death Centenary of Edward Lear (artist and author).

1405	**875**	19p. black, cream and red	65	40
1406	-	27p. black, cream yellow	1·00	1·00
1407	-	32p. black, cream green	1·25	1·40
1408	-	35p. black, cream and blue	1·40	1·40
MS1409	122×90 mm. Nos. 1405/8 (sold at £1.35)		7·00	8·50

DESIGNS: 27p. *Edward Lear as a Bird* (self-portrait); 32p. *Cat* (from alphabet book); 35p. *There was a Young Lady whose Bonnet ...* (limerick).

The premium on No. **MS**1409 was used to support the "Stamp World London 90" International Stamp Exhibition.

879 Carrickfergus Castle

1988

1410	**879**	£1 green	4·25	60
1411	-	£1.50 red	4·50	1·25
1412	-	£2 blue	8·00	60
1413	-	£5 brown	21·00	5·50

DESIGNS: £1.50, Caernarfon Castle; £2, Edinburgh Castle; £5, Windsor Castle.

For similar designs, but with silhouette of Queen's head, see Nos. 1611/14.

883 Journey to Bethlehem

1988. Christmas. Christmas Cards. Multicoloured.

1414	14p. Type **883**	45	25
1415	19p. Shepherds and Star	50	25
1416	27p. Three Wise Men	90	1·00
1417	32p. Nativity	1·10	1·25
1418	35p. The Annunciation	1·40	1·25

888 Atlantic Puffin

1989. Centenary of Royal Society for the Protection of Birds. Multicoloured.

1419	19p. Type **888**	25	40
1420	27p. Pied avocet ("Avocet")	1·25	1·25
1421	32p. Oystercatcher	1·25	1·25
1422	35p. Northern gannet ("Gannet")	1·25	1·25

892 Rose

1989. Greetings Stamps. Multicoloured.

1423	19p. Type **892**	3·00	3·00
1424	19p. Cupid	3·00	3·00
1425	19p. Yachts	3·00	3·00
1426	19p. Fruit	3·00	3·00
1427	19p. Teddy bear	3·00	3·00

897 Fruit and Vegetables

1989. Food and Farming Year. Multicoloured.

1428	19p. Type **897**	45	50
1429	27p. Meat products	90	85
1430	32p. Dairy produce	1·25	1·40
1431	35p. Cereal products	1·40	1·50

901 Mortar Board

1989. Anniversaries. Multicoloured.

1432	19p. Type **901** (150th anniv of Public Education in England)	60	60
1433	19p. Cross on Ballot paper (3rd Direct Elections to European Parliament)	60	60

1434	35p. Posthorn (26th Postal, Telegraph and Telephone International Congress, Brighton)	1·00	1·00
1435	35p. Globe (Inter-Parliamentary Union Centenary Conference, London)	1·00	1·00

905 Toy Train and Aeroplanes

1989. Europa. Games and Toys. Multicoloured.

1436	19p. Type **905**	65	50
1437	27p. Building bricks	95	1·00
1438	32p. Dice and board games	1·40	1·25
1439	35p. Toy robot, boat and doll's house	1·50	1·25

909 Ironbridge, Shropshire

1989. Industrial Archaeology. Multicoloured.

1440	19p. Type **909**	60	50
1441	27p. Tin Mine, St. Agnes Head, Cornwall	1·00	1·10
1442	32p. Cotton Mills, New Lanark, Strathclyde	1·10	1·25
1443	35p. Pontcysyllte Aqueduct, Clwyd	1·25	1·50

MS1444 122×90 mm. 19p., 27p., 32p. and 35p. each multicoloured (horiz) (sold at £1.40) — 6·00 | 6·50

The premium on **MS**1444 was used to support "Stamp World London 90" International Stamp Exhibition.

915 Snowflake (×10)

1989. 150th Anniv of Royal Microscopical Society. Multicoloured.

1453	19p. Type **915**	45	45
1454	27p. *Calliphora erythrocephala* (fly) (×5)	95	1·00
1455	32p. Blood cells (×500)	1·10	1·25
1456	35p. Microchip (×600)	1·25	1·25

919 Royal Mail Coach

1989. Lord Mayor's Show, London. Multicoloured.

1457	20p. Type **919**	45	50
1458	20p. Escort of Blues and Royals	45	50
1459	20p. Lord Mayor's Coach	45	50
1460	20p. Coach team passing St. Paul's	45	50
1461	20p. Blues and Royals drum horse	45	50

This issue commemorates the 800th anniv of the installation of the first Lord Mayor of London.

924 14th-century Peasants from Stained-glass Window

1989. Christmas. 800th Anniv of Ely Cathedral.

1462	**924**	15p. gold, silver and blue	40	50
1463	-	15p.+1p. gold, silver and blue	50	40
1464	-	20p.+1p. gold, silver and red	65	80

1465	-	34p.+1p. gold, silver and green	1·25	1·75
1466	-	37p.+1p. gold, silver and green	1·40	1·90

DESIGNS: 15p.+1p. Arches and roundels, West Front; 20p.+1p. Octagon Tower; 34p.+1p. Arcade from West Transept; 37p.+1p. Triple arch from West Front.

929 Queen Victoria and Queen Elizabeth II

1990. 150th Anniv of the Penny Black.

1467	**929**	15p. blue	80	80
1469	**929**	20p. black and cream	1·00	1·00
1471	**929**	29p. mauve	1·75	1·75
1473	**929**	34p. grey	2·00	2·00
1474	**929**	37p. red	2·25	2·25

For this design with "1st" face value see No. 2133.

930 Kitten

1990. 150th Anniv of Royal Society for Prevention of Cruelty to Animals. Multicoloured.

1479	20p. Type **930**	75	50
1480	29p. Rabbit	1·25	1·25
1481	34p. Duckling	1·25	1·50
1482	37p. Puppy	1·50	1·50

934 Teddy Bear

1990. Greetings Stamps. "Smiles". Multicoloured (except No. 1492).

1483	20p. Type **934**	2·25	2·40
1484	20p. Dennis the Menace	2·25	2·40
1485	20p. Punch	2·25	2·40
1486	20p. Cheshire Cat	2·25	2·40
1487	20p. The Man in the Moon	2·25	2·40
1488	20p. The Laughing Policeman	2·25	2·40
1489	20p. Clown	2·25	2·40
1490	20p. Mona Lisa	2·25	2·40
1491	20p. Queen of Hearts	2·25	2·40
1492	20p. Stan Laurel (comedian) (gold and black)	2·25	2·40

See also Nos. 1550/9.

944 Alexandra Palace ("Stamp World London 90" Exhibition)

1990. Europa (Nos. 1493 and 1495) and "Glasgow 1990 European City of Culture" (Nos. 1494 and 1496). Multicoloured.

1493	20p. Type **944**	50	40
1494	20p. Glasgow School of Art	50	40
1495	29p. British Philatelic Bureau, Edinburgh	1·25	1·75
1496	37p. Templeton Carpet Factory, Glasgow	1·50	1·75

948 Export Achievement Award

1990. 25th Anniv of Queen's Awards for Export and Technology. Multicoloured.

1497	20p. Type **948**	50	60
1498	20p. Technological Achievement Award	50	60
1499	37p. Type **948**	1·25	1·25
1500	37p. As No. 1498	1·25	1·25

1990. "Stamp World London 90" International Stamp Exhibition, London. Sheet 122×90 mm, containing No. 1469.

MS1501 **929** 20p. black and cream (sold at £1) — 5·50 | 5·50

The premium on No. **MS**1501 was used to support the "Stamp World London 90" International Stamp Exhibition.

950 Cycad and Sir Joseph Banks Building

1990. 150th Anniv of Kew Gardens. Multicoloured.

1502	20p. Type **950**	55	40
1503	29p. Stone pine and Princess of Wales Conservatory	75	1·00
1504	34p. Willow tree and Palm House	1·25	1·60
1505	37p. Cedar tree and Pagoda	1·50	1·50

954 Thomas Hardy and Clyffe Clump, Dorset

1990. 150th Anniv of Thomas Hardy (author).

1506	**954**	20p. multicoloured	80	75

955 Queen Elizabeth the Queen Mother

1990. 90th Birthday of Queen Elizabeth the Queen Mother. Multicoloured.

1507	20p. Type **955**	95	60
1508	29p. Queen Elizabeth	1·40	1·50
1509	34p. Elizabeth, Duchess of York	2·00	2·50
1510	37p. Lady Elizabeth Bowes-Lyon	2·25	2·50

959 Victoria Cross

1990. Gallantry Awards. Multicoloured.

1517	20p. Type **959**	80	75
1518	20p. George Cross	80	75
1519	20p. Distinguished Service Cross and Distinguished Service Medal (horiz)	80	75
1520	20p. Military Cross and Military Medal (horiz)	80	75
1521	20p. Distinguished Flying Cross and Distinguished Flying Medal (horiz)	80	75

964 Armagh Observatory, Jodrell Bank Radio Telescope and La Palma Telescope

1990. Astronomy. Multicoloured.

1522	22p. Type **964**	65	50
1523	26p. Newton's moon and tides diagram with early telescopes	1·00	1·10
1524	31p. Greenwich Old Observatory and early astronomical equipment	1·25	1·40
1525	37p. Stonehenge, gyroscope and navigating by stars	1·50	1·40

Nos. 1522/5 commemorate the Centenary of the British Astronomical Association and the Bicentenary of the Armagh Observatory.

968 Building a Snowman

1990. Christmas. Multicoloured.

1526	17p. Type **968**	50	40
1527	22p. Fetching the Christmas tree	70	50
1528	26p. Carol singing	70	1·10
1529	31p. Tobogganing	1·25	1·25
1530	37p. Ice-skating	1·25	1·50

973 *King Charles Spaniel*

1991. Dogs. Paintings by George Stubbs. Multicoloured.

1531	22p. Type **973**	50	50
1532	26p. *A Pointer*	75	1·25
1533	31p. *Two Hounds in a Landscape*	1·00	1·25
1534	33p. *A Rough Dog*	1·25	1·25
1535	37p. *Fino and Tiny*	1·25	1·25

978 Song Thrush's Nest

1991. Greetings Stamps. "Good Luck". Multicoloured.

1536	(1st) Type **978**	1·25	1·00
1537	(1st) Shooting star and rainbow	1·25	1·00
1538	(1st) Black-billed magpies and charm bracelet	1·25	1·00
1539	(1st) Black cat	1·25	1·00
1540	(1st) River kingfisher with key	1·25	1·00
1541	(1st) Mallard and frog	1·25	1·00
1542	(1st) Four-leaf clover in boot and match box	1·25	1·00
1543	(1st) Pot of gold at end of rainbow	1·25	1·00
1544	(1st) Heart-shaped butterflies	1·25	1·00
1545	(1st) Wishing well and sixpence	1·25	1·00

The background of the stamps forms a composite design.

Nos. 1536/45 were sold at the current rate.

988 Michael Faraday. (inventor of electric motor) (birth bicentenary)

1991. Scientific Achievements. Multicoloured.

1546	22p. Type **988**	60	60
1547	22p. Charles Babbage (computer science pioneer) (birth bicentenary)	60	60
1548	31p. Radar sweep of East Anglia (50th anniv of operational radar network)	1·20	1·50
1549	37p. Gloster Whittle E28/39 airplane over East Anglia (50th anniv of first flight of Sir Frank Whittle's jet engine)	1·40	1·75

992 Teddy Bear

1991. Greetings Stamps. "Smiles". As Nos. 1483/92, but inscr "1st" as in T **992**. Multicoloured (except No. 1559).

1550	(1st) Type **992**	1·25	1·00
1551	(1st) Dennis the Menace	1·25	1·00
1552	(1st) Punch	1·25	1·00
1553	(1st) Cheshire Cat	1·25	1·00
1554	(1st) The Man in the Moon	1·25	1·00
1555	(1st) The Laughing Policeman	1·25	1·00
1556	(1st) Clown	1·25	1·00
1557	(1st) Mona Lisa	1·25	1·00
1558	(1st) Queen of Hearts	1·25	1·00
1559	(1st) Stan Laurel (comedian) (gold and black)	1·25	1·00

Nos. 1550/9 were sold at the current rate.

993 Man looking at Space   **994**

1991. Europa. Europe in Space. Multicoloured.

1560	22p. Type **993**	60	60
1561	22p. Type **994**	60	60
1562	37p. Space looking at Man (Queen's head on left)	1·25	1·25
1563	37p. Similar to No. 1562 (Queen's head on right)	1·25	1·25

Stamps of the same value were printed together in horizontal pairs, each pair forming a composite design.

997 Fencing

1991. World Student Games, Sheffield (Nos. 1564/6) and World Cup Rugby Championship (No. 1567).

1564	22p. Type **997**	60	50
1565	26p. Hurdling	1·00	1·00
1566	31p. Diving	1·25	1·25
1567	37p. Rugby	1·50	1·50

1001 "Silver Jubilee"

1991. Ninth World Congress of Roses, Belfast. Multicoloured.

1568	22p. Type **1001**	50	50
1569	26p. "Mme Alfred Carrière"	75	1·25
1570	31p. "*Rosa moyesii*"	1·00	1·25
1571	33p. "Harvest Fayre"	1·25	1·50
1572	37p. "Mutabilis"	1·50	1·50

1006 Iguanodon

1991. 150th Anniv of Dinosaurs' Identification by Owen. Multicoloured.

1573	22p. Type **1006**	60	50
1574	26p. Stegosaurus	1·10	1·25
1575	31p. Tyrannosaurus	1·25	1·25
1576	33p. Protoceratops	1·50	1·50
1577	37p. Triceratops	1·60	1·50

1011 Map of 1816

1991. Bicentenary of Ordnance Survey. Maps of Hamstreet, Kent.

1578	**1011** 24p. black, mauve and cream	60	50
1579	- 28p. multicoloured	1·00	95
1580	- 33p. multicoloured	1·25	1·40
1581	- 39p. multicoloured	1·50	1·40

DESIGNS: 28p. Map of 1906; 33p. Map of 1959; 39p. Map of 1991.

1015 Adoration of the Magi

1991. Christmas. Illuminated Letters from *Acts of Mary and Jesus* Manuscript in Bodleian Library, Oxford. Multicoloured.

1582	18p. Type **1015**	75	35
1583	24p. Mary and Baby Jesus in the Stable	90	45
1584	28p. The Holy Family and Angel	95	1·25
1585	33p. The Annunciation	1·10	1·50
1586	39p. The Flight into Egypt	1·25	1·75

1020 Fallow Deer in Scottish Forest

1992. The Four Seasons. Wintertime. Multicoloured.

1587	18p. Type **1020**	55	40
1588	24p. Hare on North Yorkshire moors	75	50
1589	28p. Fox in the Fens	1·00	1·25
1590	33p. Redwing and Home Counties village	1·25	1·50
1591	39p. Welsh mountain sheep in Snowdonia	1·40	1·75

1025 Flower Spray

1992. Greetings Stamps. "Memories". Multicoloured.

1592	(1st) Type **1025**	1·25	1·00
1593	(1st) Double locket	1·25	1·00
1594	(1st) Key	1·25	1·00
1595	(1st) Model car and cigarette cards	1·25	1·00
1596	(1st) Compass and map	1·25	1·00
1597	(1st) Pocket watch	1·25	1·00
1598	(1st) 1854 1d. Red stamp and pen	1·25	1·00
1599	(1st) Pearl necklace	1·25	1·00
1600	(1st) Marbles	1·25	1·00
1601	(1st) Bucket, spade and starfish	1·25	1·00

Nos. 1592/1601 were issued together, *se-tenant*, the backgrounds forming a composite design.

1035 Queen Elizabeth in Coronation Robes and Parliamentary Emblem

1992. 40th Anniv of Accession. Multicoloured.

1602	24p. Type **1035**	90	90
1603	24p. Queen Elizabeth in Garter Robes and Archiepiscopal Arms	90	90
1604	24p. Queen Elizabeth with baby Prince Andrew and Royal Arms	90	90
1605	24p. Queen Elizabeth at Trooping the Colour	90	90
1606	24p. Queen Elizabeth and Commonwealth emblem	90	90

1040 Tennyson in 1888 and *The Beguiling of Merlin* (Sir Edward Burne-Jones)

1992. Death Centenary of Alfred, Lord Tennyson (poet). Multicoloured.

1607	24p. Type **1040**	60	50
1608	28p. Tennyson in 1856 and *April Love* (Arthur Hughes)	85	85
1609	33p. Tennyson in 1864 and *I am Sick of the Shadows* (John Waterhouse)	1·40	1·60
1610	39p. Tennyson as a young man and *Mariana* (Dante Gabriel Rossetti)	1·50	1·60

1044 Carrickfergus Castle

1992. Designs as Nos. 1410/13, but showing Queen's head in silhouette as T **1044**.

1611	**1044** £1 green and gold	5·50	1·00
1612	- £1.50 purple and gold	6·00	1·20
1613	- £2 blue and gold	8·00	1·20
1613a	**1044** £3 violet and gold	19·00	3·00
1614	- £5 brown and gold	18·00	3·00

The Queen's head on these stamps is printed in optically variable ink which changes colour from gold to green when viewed from different angles.

1045 British Olympic Association Logo (Olympic Games, Barcelona)

1992. Europa. International Events. Multicoloured.

1615	24p. Type **1045**	50	50
1616	24p. British Paralympic Association symbol (Paralympics '92, Barcelona)	50	50
1617	24p. "*Santa Maria*" (500th anniv of discovery of America by Columbus)	1·00	75
1618	39p. "*Kaisei*" (Japanese cadet brigantine) (Grand Regatta Columbus, 1992)	1·40	1·50
1619	39p. British Pavilion, "EXPO '92", Seville	1·40	1·50

1050 Pikeman

1992. 350th Anniv of the Civil War. Multicoloured.

1620	24p. Type **1050**	60	50
1621	28p. Drummer	85	85
1622	33p. Musketeer	1·40	1·50
1623	39p. Standard Bearer	1·50	1·75

1054 The Yeomen of the Guard

1992. 150th Birth Anniv of Sir Arthur Sullivan (composer). Gilbert and Sullivan Operas. Multicoloured.

1624	18p. Type **1054**	50	40
1625	24p. *The Gondoliers*	80	60
1626	28p. *The Mikado*	95	1·00
1627	33p. *The Pirates of Penzance*	1·50	1·60
1628	39p. *Iolanthe*	1·60	1·60

1059 "Acid Rain Kills"

1992. Protection of the Environment. Children's Paintings. Multicoloured.

1629	24p. Type **1059**	70	60
1630	28p. "Ozone Layer"	1·10	1·25
1631	33p. "Greenhouse Effect"	1·25	1·50
1632	39p. "Bird of Hope"	1·40	1·50

1063 European Star

1992. Single European Market.

1633	**1063** 24p. multicoloured	1·00	1·00

1064 "Angel Gabriel", St. James's, Pangbourne

1992. Christmas. Stained Glass Windows. Multicoloured.

1634	18p. Type **1064**	50	30
1635	24p. "Madonna and Child", St. Mary's, Bibury	75	60
1636	28p. "King with Gold", Our Lady and St. Peter, Leatherhead	1·00	1·10
1637	33p. "Shepherds", All Saints, Porthcawl	1·25	1·50
1638	39p. "Kings with Frankincense and Myrrh", Our Lady and St. Peter, Leatherhead	1·25	1·50

1069 Mute Swan Cob and St. Catherine's Chapel, Abbotsbury

1993. 600th Anniv of Abbotsbury Swannery. Multicoloured.

1639	18p. Type **1069**	1·25	70
1640	24p. Cygnet and decoy	1·10	70
1641	28p. Swans and cygnet	1·40	2·25
1642	33p. Eggs in nest and Tithe Barn, Abbotsbury	1·75	2·50
1643	39p. Young swan and the Fleet	1·90	2·50

1074 Long John Silver and Parrot (*Treasure Island*)

1993. Greetings Stamps. "Gift Giving". Gold, cream and black (No. 1645) or multicoloured (others).

1644	(1st) Type **1074**	1·25	1·00
1645	(1st) Tweedledum and Tweedledee (*Alice Through the Looking Glass*)	1·25	1·00
1646	(1st) William (*William* books)	1·25	1·00
1647	(1st) Mole and Toad (*The Wind in the Willows*)	1·25	1·00
1648	(1st) Teacher and Wilfrid (*The Bash Street Kids*)	1·25	1·00
1649	(1st) Peter Rabbit and Mrs. Rabbit (*The Tale of Peter Rabbit*)	1·25	1·00
1650	(1st) Snowman (*The Snowman*) and Father Christmas (*Father Christmas*)	1·25	1·00
1651	(1st) The Big Friendly Giant and Sophie (*The BFG*)	1·25	1·00
1652	(1st) Bill Badger and Rupert Bear	1·25	1·00
1653	(1st) Aladdin and the Genie	1·25	1·00

1084 Decorated Enamel Dial

1993. 300th Birth Anniv of John Harrison (inventor of the marine chronometer). Details of "H4" Clock. Multicoloured.

1654	24p. Type **1084**	60	60
1655	28p. Escapement, remontoire and fusee	1·00	1·25
1656	33p. Balance, spring and temperature compensator	1·40	1·25
1657	39p. Back of movement	1·50	1·50

1088 "Britannia"

1993

1658	**1088**	£10 multicoloured	40·00	12·00

1089 *Dendrobium hellwigianum*

1993. 14th World Orchid Conference, Glasgow. Multicoloured.

1659	18p. Type **1089**	45	40
1660	24p. *Paphiopedilum Maudiae* "Magnificum"	75	60
1661	28p. *Cymbidium lowianum*	1·00	1·25
1662	33p. *Vanda Rothschildiana*	1·25	1·50
1663	39p. *Dendrobium vexillarius var albiviride*	1·60	1·50

1094 *Family Group* (bronze sculpture) (Henry Moore)

1993. Europa. Contemporary Art. Multicoloured.

1767	24p. Type **1094**	60	60
1768	28p. *Kew Gardens* (lithograph) (Edward Bawden)	90	1·00
1769	33p. *St. Francis and the Birds* (Stanley Spencer)	1·25	1·40
1770	39p. *Still Life: Odyssey I* (Ben Nicholson)	1·75	1·75

1098 Emperor Claudius (from gold coin)

1993. Roman Britain. Multicoloured.

1771	24p. Type **1098**	60	50
1772	28p. Emperor Hadrian (bronze head)	90	1·00
1773	33p. Goddess Roma (from gemstone)	1·30	1·50
1774	39p. Christ (Hinton St. Mary mosaic)	1·50	1·60

1102 *Midland Maid* and other Narrow Boats, Grand Junction Canal

1993. Inland Waterways. Multicoloured.

1775	24p. Type **1102**	50	50
1776	28p. *Yorkshire Lass* and other Humber keels, Stainforth and Keadby Canal	1·00	1·00
1777	33p. *Valley Princess* and other horse-drawn barges, Brecknock and Abergavenny Canal	1·25	1·25
1778	39p. Steam barges, including *Pride of Scotland*, and fishing boats, Crinan Canal	1·50	1·40

Nos. 1775/8 commemorate the bicentenary of the Acts of Parliament authorizing the canals depicted.

1106 Horse Chestnut

1993. The Four Seasons. Autumn. Fruits and Leaves. Multicoloured.

1779	18p. Type **1106**	50	30
1780	24p. Blackberry	75	50
1781	28p. Hazel	1·10	1·25
1782	33p. Rowan	1·40	1·50
1783	39p. Pear	1·50	1·50

1111 *The Reigate Squire*

1993. Sherlock Holmes. Centenary of the Publication of "The Final Problem". Multicoloured.

1784	24p. Type **1111**	50	60
1785	24p. *The Hound of the Baskervilles*	50	60
1786	24p. *The Six Napoleons*	50	60
1787	24p. *The Greek Interpreter*	50	60
1788	24p. *The Final Problem*	50	60

1116

1993. Self-adhesive.

1976	**1116**	(2nd) blue	2·75	2·50
1789	**1116**	(1st) red	1·25	1·40

Nos. 1976/7 were sold at the current rates.

1117 Bob Cratchit and Tiny Tim

1993. Christmas. 150th Anniv of Publication of *A Christmas Carol* by Charles Dickens. Multicoloured.

1790	19p. Type **1117**	60	40
1791	25p. Mr. and Mrs. Fezziwig	90	60
1792	30p. Scrooge	1·25	1·50
1793	35p. The prize turkey	1·40	1·60
1794	41p. Mr. Scrooge's nephew	1·40	1·60

1122 Class 5 No. 44957 and Class B1 No. 61342 on West Highland Line

1994. The Age of Steam. Railway Photographs by Colin Gifford.

1795	**1122**	19p. green, grey black	55	45
1796	-	25p. lilac, grey and black	90	95
1797	-	30p. brown, grey and black	1·40	1·50
1798	-	35p. purple, grey & black	1·75	1·80
1799	-	41p. blue, grey and black	1·80	1·90

DESIGNS: 25p. Class A1 No. 60149 "Amadis" at Kings Cross; 30p. Class 4 No. 43000 on turntable at Blyth North; 35p. Class No. 42455 near Wigan Central; 41p. Class "Castle" No. 7002 "Devizes Castle" on bridge crossing Worcester and Birmingham Canal.

1127 Dan Dare and the Mekon

1994. Greetings Stamps. "Messages". Multicoloured.

1800	(1st) Type **1127**	1·25	1·00
1801	(1st) The Three Bears	1·25	1·00
1802	(1st) Rupert Bear	1·25	1·00
1803	(1st) Alice (*Alice in Wonderland*)	1·25	1·00
1804	(1st) Noggin and The Ice Dragon	1·25	1·00
1805	(1st) Peter Rabbit posting a letter	1·25	1·00
1806	(1st) Red Riding Hood and wolf	1·25	1·00
1807	(1st) Orlando the Marmalade Cat	1·25	1·00
1808	(1st) Biggles	1·25	1·00
1809	(1st) Paddington Bear on station	1·25	1·00

1137 Castell Y Waun (Chirk Castle), Clwyd, Wales

1994. 25th Anniv of Investiture of the Prince of Wales. Paintings by Prince Charles. Multicoloured.

1810	19p. Type **1137**	55	40
1811	25p. Ben Arkle, Sutherland, Scotland	1·00	60
1812	30p. Mourne Mountains, County Down, Northern Ireland	1·10	1·50
1813	35p. Dersingham, Norfolk, England	1·40	1·75
1814	41p. Dolwyddelan, Gwynedd, Wales	1·50	1·75

1142 Bather at Blackpool

1994. Centenary of Picture Postcards. Multicoloured.

1815	19p. Type **1142**	60	40
1816	25p. "Where's my Little Lad?"	90	60
1817	30p. "Wish You were Here!"	1·10	1·50
1818	35p. Punch and Judy show	1·40	1·75
1819	41p. "The Tower Crane" machine	1·50	1·75

1147 British Lion and French Cockerel over Tunnel

1994. Opening of Channel Tunnel. Multicoloured.

1820	25p. Type **1147**	75	60
1821	25p. Symbolic hands over train	75	60
1822	41p. Type **1147**	1·00	1·00
1823	41p. As No. 1821	1·00	1·00

1149 Groundcrew replacing Smoke Canisters on Douglas Boston of 88 Sqn

1994. 50th Anniv of D-Day. Multicoloured.

1824	25p. Type **1149**	60	60
1825	25p. H.M.S. "Warspite" (battleship) shelling enemy positions	60	60
1826	25p. Commandos landing on Gold Beach	60	60
1827	25p. Infantry regrouping on Sword Beach	60	60
1828	25p. Tank and infantry advancing, Ouistreham	60	60

1154 The Old Course, St. Andrews

1994. Scottish Golf Courses. Multicoloured.

1829	19p. Type **1154**	50	40
1830	25p. The 18th Hole, Muirfield	75	60
1831	30p. The 15th Hole ("Luckyslap"), Carnoustie	1·10	1·40
1832	35p. The 8th Hole ("The Postage Stamp"), Royal Troon	1·25	1·40
1833	41p. The 9th Hole, Turnberry	1·40	1·40

Nos. 1829/33 commemorate the 250th anniversary of golf's first set of rules produced by the Honourable Company of Edinburgh Golfers.

1159 Royal Welsh Show, Llanelwedd

1994. The Four Seasons. Summertime. Multicoloured.

1834	19p. Type **1159**	50	40
1835	25p. All England Tennis Championships, Wimbledon	75	60
1836	30p. Cowes Week	1·10	1·25
1837	35p. Test Match, Lord's	1·25	1·60
1838	41p. Braemar Gathering	1·40	1·60

1164 Ultrasonic Imaging

1994. Europa. Medical Discoveries. Multicoloured.

1839	25p. Type **1164**	75	60
1840	30p. Scanning electron microscopy	1·00	1·25
1841	35p. Magnetic resonance imaging	1·50	1·75
1842	41p. Computed tomography	1·75	1·75

1168 Mary and Joseph

1994. Christmas. Children's Nativity Plays. Multicoloured.

1843	19p. Type **1168**	50	40
1844	25p. Three Wise Men	75	60
1845	30p. Mary with doll	1·00	1·50
1846	35p. Shepherds	1·25	1·50
1847	41p. Angels	1·50	1·75

1173 Sophie (black cat)

1995. Cats. Multicoloured.

1848	19p. Type **1173**	75	40
1849	25p. Puskas (Siamese) and Tigger (tabby)	75	60
1850	30p. Chloe (ginger cat)	1·00	1·50
1851	35p. Kikko (tortoiseshell) and Rosie (Abyssinian)	1·25	1·50
1852	41p. Fred (black and white cat)	1·50	1·50

1178 Dandelions

1995. The Four Seasons. Springtime. Plant Sculptures by Andy Goldsworthy. Multicoloured.

1853	19p. Type **1178**	75	40
1854	25p. Sweet chestnut leaves	75	60
1855	30p. Garlic leaves	1·00	1·50
1856	35p. Hazel leaves	1·25	1·50
1857	41p. Spring grass	1·50	1·75

1183 *La Danse a la Campagne* (Renoir)

1995. Greetings Stamps. "Greetings in Art".

1858	**1183** (1st) multicoloured	1·25	1·00
1859	- (1st) multicoloured	1·25	1·00
1860	- (1st) multicoloured	1·25	1·00
1861	- (1st) multicoloured	1·25	1·00
1862	- (1st) multicoloured	1·25	1·00
1863	- (1st) multicoloured	1·25	1·00
1864	- (1st) brown and silver	1·25	1·00
1865	- (1st) multicoloured	1·25	1·00
1866	- (1st) multicoloured	1·25	1·00
1867	- (1st) black, yellow and silver	1·25	1·00

DESIGNS: No. 1859, *Troilus and Criseyde* (Peter Brookes); 1860, *The Kiss* (Rodin); 1861, *Girls on the Town* (Beryl Cook); 1862, *Jazz* (Andrew Mockett); 1863, *Girls performing a Kathak Dance* (Aurangzeb period); 1864, *Alice Keppel with her Daughter* (Alice Hughes); 1865, *Children Playing* (L. S. Lowry); 1866, *Circus Clowns* (Emily Firmin and Justin Mitchell); 1867, Decoration from *All the Love Poems of Shakespeare* (Eric Gill).

1193 Fireplace Decoration, Attingham Park, Shropshire

1995. Centenary of The National Trust. Multicoloured.

1868	19p. Type **1193**	60	40
1869	25p. Oak seedling	80	60
1870	30p. Carved table leg, Attingham Park	1·00	1·50
1871	35p. St. David's Head, Dyfed, Wales	1·25	1·50
1872	41p. Elizabethan window, Little Moreton Hall, Cheshire	1·40	1·75

1198 British Troops and French Civilians celebrating

1995. Europa. Peace and Freedom.

1873	**1198** 19p. silver, brown and black	70	50
1874	- 19p. multicoloured	70	50
1875	- 25p. silver, blue and black	1·00	1·00
1876	- 25p. multicoloured	1·00	1·00
1877	- 30p. multicoloured	1·25	2·25

DESIGNS: No. 1874, Symbolic hands and Red Cross; 1875, St. Paul's Cathedral and searchlights; 1876, Symbolic hand releasing peace dove; 1877, Symbolic hands.
Nos. 1873 and 1875 commemorate the 50th anniversary of the end of the Second World War, No. 1874 the 125th anniversary of the British Red Cross Society and Nos. 1876/7 the 50th anniversary of the United Nations.
Nos. 1876/7 include the "EUROPA" emblem.

1203 *The Time Machine*

1995. Science Fiction. Novels by H. G. Wells. Multicoloured.

1878	25p. Type **1203**	75	60
1879	30p. *The First Men in the Moon*	1·25	1·50
1880	35p. *The War of the Worlds*	1·25	1·60
1881	41p. *The Shape of Things to Come*	1·50	1·60

Nos. 1878/81 commemorate the centenary of publication of Wells's *The Time Machine*.

1207 The Swan, 1595

1995. Reconstruction of Shakespeare's Globe Theatre. Multicoloured.

1882	25p. Type **1207**	60	60
1883	25p. The Rose, 1592	60	60
1884	25p. The Globe, 1599	60	60
1885	25p. The Hope, 1613	60	60
1886	25p. The Globe, 1614	60	60

Nos. 1882/6 were printed together, *se-tenant*, forming a composite design.

1212 Sir Rowland Hill and Uniform Penny Postage Petition

1995. Pioneers of Communications.

1887	**1212** 19p. silver, red and black	75	40
1888	- 25p. silver, brown and black	1·00	60
1889	- 41p. silver, green and black	1·50	1·75
1890	- 60p. silver, blue and black	1·75	2·25

DESIGNS: 25p. Hill and Penny Black; 41p. Guglielmo Marconi and early wireless; 60p. Marconi and sinking of *Titanic* (liner).
Nos. 1887/8 mark the birth bicentenary of Sir Rowland Hill and Nos. 1889/90 the centenary of the first radio transmissions.

1216 Harold Wagstaff

1995. Centenary of Rugby League. Multicoloured.

1891	19p. Type **1216**	75	40
1892	25p. Gus Risman	75	60
1893	30p. Jim Sullivan	1·00	1·50
1894	35p. Billy Batten	1·00	1·50
1895	41p. Brian Bevan	1·50	1·60

1221 European Robin in Mouth of Pillar Box

1995. Christmas. Christmas Robins. Multicoloured.

1896	19p. Type **1221**	60	40
1897	25p. European robin on railings and holly	85	60
1898	30p. European robin on snow-covered milk bottles	1·25	1·50
1899	41p. European robin on road sign	1·60	1·75
1900	60p. European robin on door knob and Christmas wreath	1·75	1·90

1226 Opening Lines of *To a Mouse* and Fieldmouse

1996. Death Bicent of Robert Burns (Scottish poet).

1901	**1226** 19p. cream, brown and black	75	40
1902	- 25p. multicoloured	1·00	60
1903	- 41p. multicoloured	1·50	2·00
1904	- 60p. multicoloured	1·75	2·50

DESIGNS: 25p. *O my Luve's like a red, red rose* and wild rose; 41p. *Scots, wha hae wi Wallace bled* and Sir William Wallace; 60p. *Auld Lang Syne* and highland dancers.

1230 "MORE! LOVE" (Mel Calman)

1996. Greetings Stamps. Cartoons.

1905	**1230** (1st) black and mauve	1·25	75
1906	- (1st) black and green	1·25	75
1907	- (1st) black and blue	1·25	75
1908	- (1st) black and violet	1·25	75
1909	- (1st) black and red	1·25	75
1910	- (1st) black and blue	1·25	75
1911	- (1st) black and red	1·25	75
1912	- (1st) black and violet	1·25	75
1913	- (1st) black and green	1·25	75
1914	- (1st) black and mauve	1·25	75

DESIGNS: No. 1906, "Sincerely" (Charles Barsotti); 1907, "Do you have something for the HUMAN CONDITION?" (Mel Calman); 1908, "MENTAL FLOSS" (Leo Cullum); 1909, "4.55 P.M." (Charles Barsotti); 1910, "Dear lottery prize winner" (Larry); 1911, "I'm writing to you because …" (Mel Calman); 1912, "FETCH THIS, FETCH THAT" (Charles Barsotti); 1913, "My day starts before I'm ready for it" (Mel Calman); 1914, "THE CHEQUE IN THE POST" (Jack Ziegler).
Nos. 1905/14 were sold at the current rate.

1240 Muscovy Duck

1996. 50th Anniv of the Wildfowl and Wetlands Trust. Bird paintings by C. F. Tunnicliffe. Multicoloured.

1915	19p. Type **1240**	70	40
1916	25p. Lapwing	90	60
1917	30p. White-fronted Goose	1·00	1·25
1918	35p. Bittern	1·10	1·50
1919	41p. Whooper Swan	1·50	1·60

1245 The Odeon, Harrogate

1996. Centenary of Cinema.

1920	**1245** 19p. multicoloured	50	40
1921	- 25p. multicoloured	70	60
1922	- 30p. multicoloured	1·00	1·75
1923	- 35p. black, red and silver	1·25	2·00
1924	- 41p. multicoloured	2·00	2·25

DESIGNS: 25p. Laurence Olivier and Vivien Leigh in *Lady Hamilton* (film); 30p. Old cinema ticket; 35p. Pathe News still; 41p. Cinema sign, The Odeon, Manchester.

1250 Dixie Dean

1996. European Football Championship. Multicoloured.

1925	19p. Type **1250**	50	40
1926	25p. Bobby Moore	75	60
1927	35p. Duncan Edwards	1·25	1·75
1928	41p. Billy Wright	1·50	1·75
1929	60p. Danny Blanchflower	1·75	2·00

1255 Athlete on Starting Blocks

1996. Olympic and Paralympic Games, Atlanta. Multicoloured.

1930	26p. Type **1255**	60	60
1931	26p. Throwing the javelin	60	60
1932	26p. Basketball	60	60
1933	26p. Swimming	60	60
1934	26p. Athlete celebrating and Olympic Rings	60	60

1260 Prof. Dorothy Hodgkin (scientist)

1996. Europa. Famous Women.

1935	**1260** 20p. green, grey and black	60	50
1936	- 26p. mauve, grey & black	75	60
1937	- 31p. bronze, grey and black	1·10	1·10
1938	- 37p. silver, grey and black	1·25	1·40
1939	- 43p. gold, grey and black	1·50	1·50

DESIGNS: 26p. Dame Margot Fonteyn (ballerina); 31p. Dame Elisabeth Frink (sculptress); 37p. Dame Daphne du Maurier (novelist); 43p. Dame Marea Hartman (sports administrator).
Nos. 1936/7 include the "EUROPA" emblem.

1265 *Muffin the Mule*

1996. 50th Anniv of Children's Television. Multicoloured.

1940	20p. Type **1265**	55	30
1941	26p. *Sooty*	80	40
1942	31p. *Stingray*	1·00	1·50
1943	37p. *The Clangers*	1·40	1·75
1944	43p. *Dangermouse*	1·60	2·00

1270 *Triumph TR3*

1996. Classic Sports Cars. Multicoloured.

1945	20p. Type **1270**	55	40
1946	26p. MG TD	1·10	50
1947	37p. Austin-Healey 100	1·40	1·90
1948	43p. Jaguar XK120	1·60	1·90
1949	63p. Morgan Plus 4	1·75	2·00

1275 *The Three Kings*

1996. Christmas. Multicoloured.

1950	(2nd.) Type **1275**	1·00	60
1951	(1st) The Annunciation	1·25	70
1952	31p. The Journey to Bethlehem	1·25	1·75
1953	43p. The Nativity	1·25	1·75
1954	63p. The Shepherds	1·50	2·00

1280 *Gentiana acaulis* (Georg Ehret)

1997. Greeting Stamps. 19th-century Flower Paintings. Multicoloured.

1955	(1st) Type **1280**	1·25	1·00
1956	(1st) *Magnolia grandiflora* (Ehret)	1·25	1·00
1957	(1st) *Camellia japonica* (Alfred Chandler)	1·25	1·00
1958	(1st) *Tulipa* (Ehret)	1·25	1·00
1959	(1st) "*Fuchsia*" *Princess of Wales* (Augusta Withers)	1·25	1·00
1960	(1st) *Tulipa gesneriana* (Ehret)	1·25	1·00
1961	(1st) *Guzmania splendens* (Charlotte Sowerby)	1·25	1·00
1962	(1st) *Iris latifolia* (Ehret)	1·25	1·00
1963	(1st) *Hippeastrum rutilum* (Pierre-Joseph Redoute)	1·25	1·00
1964	(1st) *Passiflora coerulea* (Ehret)	1·25	1·00

1290 *King Henry VIII*

1997. 450th Death Anniv of King Henry VIII. Multicoloured.

1965	26p. Type **1290**	60	60
1966	26p. "Catherine of Aragon"	60	60
1967	26p. "Anne Boleyn"	60	60
1968	26p. "Jane Seymour"	60	60
1969	26p. "Anne of Cleves"	60	60
1970	26p. "Catherine Howard"	60	60
1971	26p. "Catherine Parr"	60	60

1297 *St. Columba in Boat*

1997. Religious Anniversaries. Multicoloured.

1972	26p. Type **1297**	75	60
1973	37p. St. Columba on Iona	1·10	1·50
1974	43p. St. Augustine with King Ethelbert	1·50	1·50
1975	63p. St. Augustine with Model of Cathedral	2·00	2·10

Nos. 1972/3 commemorate the 1400th death anniversary of St. Columba and Nos. 1974/5 the 1400th anniversary of the arrival of St. Augustine of Canterbury in Kent.

Dracula
1303 *Dracula*

1997. Europa. Tales and Legends. Horror Stories. Multicoloured.

1980	26p. Type **1303**	1·00	60
1981	31p. *Frankenstein*	1·10	1·50
1982	37p. *Dr. Jekyll and Mr. Hyde*	1·30	1·75
1983	43p. *The Hound of the Baskervilles*	2·00	1·95

Nos. 1980/3 commemorate the birth bicentenary of Mary Shelley (creator of Frankenstein) with the 26p. and 31p. values incorporating the "EUROPA" emblem.

1307 *Reginald Mitchell and Supermarine Spitfire Mk IIA*

1997. British Aircraft Designers. Multicoloured.

1984	20p. Type **1307**	75	50
1985	26p. Roy Chadwick and Avro Type 683 Lancaster Mk I	1·10	1·25
1986	37p. Ronald Bishop and de Havilland DH.98 Mosquito B Mk XVI	1·40	1·25
1987	43p. George Carter and Gloster Meteor T.Mk7	1·50	1·60
1988	63p. Sir Sidney Camm and Hawker Hunter FGA Mk 9	2·00	2·00

1312 *Carriage Horse and Coachman*

1997. "All the Queen's Horses". 50th Anniv of the British Horse Society. Multicoloured.

1989	20p. Type **1312**	80	45
1990	26p. Lifeguards horse and trooper	1·10	1·50
1991	43p. Blues and Royals drum horse and drummer	1·50	1·50
1992	63p. Duke of Edinburgh's horse and groom	2·00	2·00

1316 *Haroldswick, Shetland*

1997. Sub-Post Offices. Multicoloured.

1997	20p. Type **1316**	75	50
1998	26p. Painswick, Gloucestershire	1·00	1·00
1999	43p. Beddgelert, Gwynedd	1·50	1·50
2000	63p. Ballyroney, County Down	2·25	2·25

Nos. 1997/2000 were issued on the occasion of the Centenary of The National Federation of Sub-Postmasters.

Enid Blyton's Noddy
1320 *Noddy*

1997. Birth Centenary of Enid Blyton (children's author). Multicoloured.

2001	20p. Type **1320**	50	45
2002	26p. *Famous Five*	1·00	1·25
2003	37p. *Secret Seven*	1·25	1·25
2004	43p. *Faraway Tree*	1·50	2·00
2005	63p. *Malory Towers*	1·75	2·00

1325 Children and Father Christmas pulling Cracker

1997. Christmas. 150th Anniv of the Christmas Cracker. Multicoloured.

2006	(2nd.) Type **1325**	1·00	40
2007	(1st) Father Christmas with traditional cracker	1·25	60
2008	31p. Father Christmas riding cracker	1·00	1·50
2009	43p. Father Christmas on snowball	1·25	1·75
2010	63p. Father Christmas and chimney	1·60	2·00

1330 Wedding Photograph, 1947

1997. Royal Golden Wedding.

2011	**1330**	20p. gold, brown and black	85	45
2012	-	26p. multicoloured	1·10	70
2013	**1330**	43p. gold, green and black	1·90	2·25
2014	-	63p. multicoloured	2·50	3·00

DESIGNS: 26p. and 63p. Queen Elizabeth II and Prince Philip, 1997.

1332 Common Dormouse

1998. Endangered Species. Multicoloured.

2015	20p. Type **1332**	60	40
2016	26p. Lady's slipper orchid	75	40
2017	31p. Song thrush	1·00	2·00
2018	37p. Shining ram's-horn snail	1·25	1·25
2019	43p. Mole cricket	1·40	1·75
2020	63p. Devil's bolete	1·90	2·25

1338 Diana, Princess of Wales (photo by Lord Snowdon)

1998. Diana, Princess of Wales Commemoration. Multicoloured.

2021	26p. Type **1338**	50	50
2022	26p. At British Lung Foundation Function, April 1997 (photo by John Stillwell)	50	50
2023	26p. Wearing tiara, 1991 (photo by Lord Snowdon)	50	50
2024	26p. On visit to Birmingham, October 1995 (photo by Tim Graham) (checked suit)	50	50
2025	26p. In evening dress, 1987 (photo by Terence Donovan)	50	50

1343 Lion of England and Griffin of Edward III

1998. 650th Anniv of the Order of the Garter. The Queen's Beasts. Multicoloured.

2026	26p. Type **1343**	90	90
2027	26p. Falcon of Plantagenet and Bull of Clarence	90	90
2028	26p. Lion of Mortimer and Yale of Beaufort	90	90
2029	26p. Greyhound of Richmond and Dragon of Wales	90	90
2030	26p. Unicorn of Scotland and Horse of Hanover	90	90

1348

1998. As Type **157** (Wilding definitive of 1952–54) but with face values in decimal currency as Type **1348**.

2031	**1348**	20p. green	70	75
2032	**1348**	26p. brown	90	95
2033	**1348**	37p. purple	2·75	2·75

See also Nos. 2295/8 and 2378/9.

1349 St. John's Point Lighthouse, County Down

1998. 300th Anniv of the First Lighthouse and Final Year of Manned Lighthouses. Multicoloured.

2034	20p. Type **1349**	50	40
2035	26p. Smalls Lighthouse, Pembrokeshire	75	50
2036	37p. Needles Rock Lighthouse, Isle of Wight, c. 1900	1·10	1·50
2037	43p. Bell Rock Lighthouse, Arbroath, mid-19th century	1·50	1·75
2038	63p. Eddystone Lighthouse, Plymouth, 1698	2·10	2·50

1354 Tommy Cooper

1998. Comedians. Multicoloured.

2041	20p. Type **1354**	50	50
2042	26p. Eric Morecambe	75	85
2043	37p. Joyce Grenfell	1·25	1·25
2044	43p. Les Dawson	1·50	1·50
2045	63p. Peter Cook	1·75	2·10

1359 Hands forming Heart

1998. 50th Anniv of the National Health Service. Multicoloured.

2046	20p. Type **1359**	50	50
2047	26p. Adult and child holding hands	90	90
2048	43p. Hands forming cradle	1·50	1·50
2049	63p. Hand taking pulse	2·10	2·10

1363 *The Hobbit* (J. R. R. Tolkien)

1998. Famous Children's Fantasy Novels. Multicoloured.

2050	20p. Type **1363**	50	50
2051	26p. *The Lion, The Witch and the Wardrobe* (C. S. Lewis)	90	90
2052	37p. *The Phoenix and the Carpet* (E. Nesbit)	1·25	1·50
2053	43p. *The Borrowers* (Mary Norton)	1·50	1·50
2054	63p. *Through the Looking Glass* (Lewis Carroll)	2·10	2·00

Nos. 2050/4 commemorate the birth centenary of C. S. Lewis and the death centenary of Lewis Carroll.

1368 Woman in Yellow Feathered Costume

1998. Europa. Festivals. Notting Hill Carnival. Multicoloured.

2055	20p. Type **1368**	75	45
2056	26p. Woman in blue costume and headdress	95	55
2057	43p. Group of children in white and gold robes	1·50	2·00
2058	63p. Child in "Tree" costume	2·00	2·75

The 20p. and 26p. incorporate the "EUROPA" emblem.

1372 Sir Malcolm Campbell's *Bluebird*, 1925

1998. British Land Speed Record Holders. Multicoloured.

2059	20p. Type **1372**	50	40
2060	26p. Sir Henry Segrave's *Sunbeam*, 1926	75	50
2061	30p. John G. Parry Thomas's *Babs*, 1926	1·25	1·50
2062	43p. John R. Cobb's *Railton Mobil Special*, 1947	1·50	1·60
2063	63p. Donald Campbell's *Bluebird CN7*, 1964	2·00	2·40

Nos. 2059/63 commemorate the 50th death anniversary of Sir Malcolm Campbell.

1377 Angel with Hands raised in Blessing

1998. Christmas. Angels. Multicoloured.

2064	20p. Type **1377**	50	50
2065	26p. Angel praying	75	60
2066	30p. Angel plaing flute	1·25	1·50
2067	43p. Angel playing lute	1·50	1·60
2068	63p. Angel praying (different)	2·00	2·25

1382 Greenwich Meridian and Clock (John Harrison's chronometer)

1999. Millennium Series. The Inventors' Tale. Multicoloured.

2069	20p. Type **1382**	75	70
2070	26p. Industrial worker and blast furnace (James Watt's discovery of steam power)	95	1·00
2071	43p. Early photos of leaves (Henry Fox-Talbot's photographic experiments)	1·50	1·60
2072	63p. Computer inside human head (Alan Turing's work on computers)	2·25	2·40

1386 Airliner hugging Globe (International air travel)

1999. Millennium Series. The Travellers' Tale.

2073	**1386** 20p. multicoloured	75	70
2074	– 26p. multicoloured	95	1·00
2075	– 43p. black, stone and bronze	1·50	1·60
2076	– 63p. multicoloured	2·25	2·40

DESIGNS: 26p. Women on bicycle (development of the bicycle); 43p. Victorian railway station (growth of public transport); 63p. Captain Cook and Maori (Captain James Cook's voyages).

1390

1999. (a) Self-adhesive.

2077	**1390** (1st) grey (face value) (Queen's head in colourless relief)	3·00	2·50

(b) Ordinary gum.

2078	(1st) black	3·00	2·50

1391 Vaccinating Child (pattern in cow markings) (Jenner's development of smallpox vaccine)

1999. Millennium Series. The Patients' Tale. Multicoloured.

2080	20p. Type **1391**	75	70
2081	26p. Patient on trolley (nursing care)	95	1·00
2082	43p. Penicillin mould (Fleming's discovery of penicillin)	1·50	1·60
2083	63p. Sculpture of test-tube baby (development of in-vitro fertilization)	2·25	2·40

1395 Dove and Norman Settler (medieval migration to Scotland)

1999. Millennium Series. The Settlers' Tale. Multicoloured.

2084	20p. Type **1395**	75	70
2085	26p. Pilgrim Fathers and Red Indian (17th-century migration to America)	95	1·00
2086	43p. Sailing ship and aspects of settlement (19th-century migration to Australia)	2·00	1·75
2087	63p. Hummingbird and superimposed stylized face (20th-century migration to Great Britain)	3·00	3·00

1399 Woven Threads (woollen industry)

1999. Millennium Series. The Workers' Tale. Multicoloured.

2088	19p. Type **1399**	75	70
2089	26p. Salts Mill, Saltaire (cotton industry)	95	1·00
2090	44p. Hull on slipway (ship-building)	1·75	1·60
2091	64p. Lloyd's Building (City of London finance centre)	2·25	2·40

1403 Freddie Mercury (lead singer of pop group Queen) ("Popular Music")

1999. Millennium Series. The Entertainers' Tale. Multicoloured.

2092	19p. Type **1403**	75	70
2093	26p. Bobby Moore with World Cup, 1966 ("Sport")	95	1·00
2094	44p. Dalek from "Dr. Who" (science-fiction series) ("Television")	1·50	1·60
2095	64p. Charlie Chaplin (film star) ("Cinema")	2·25	2·40

1407 Prince Edward and Miss Sophie Rhys-Jones (from photo by John Swannell)

1999. Royal Wedding. Multicoloured.

2096	26p. Type **1407**	85	85
2097	64p. Couple in profile	2·50	2·50

1409 Suffragette behind Prison Window (Equal Rights for Women)

1999. Millennium Series. The Citizens' Tale. Multicoloured.

2098	19p. Type **1409**	75	70
2099	26p. Water tap (Right to Health)	95	1·00
2100	44p. Generations of school children (Right to Education)	1·75	1·60
2101	64p. "MAGNA CARTA" (Human Rights)	2·50	2·40

1413 Molecular Structures (DNA Decoding)

1999. Millennium Series. The Scientists' Tale. Multicoloured.

2102	19p. Type **1413**	75	70
2103	26p. Large ground finch and fossilized skeleton (Darwin's Theory of Evolution)	1·50	1·00
2104	44p. Rotation of polarized light by magnetism (Faraday's work on electricity)	1·50	1·60
2105	64p. Saturn (development of astronomical telescopes)	2·25	2·40

1999. Solar Eclipse. Sheet 89×101 mm.

MS2106	No. 2105×4 (sold at £2.56)	22·00	22·00

1417 Upland Landscape (Strip Farming)

1999. Millennium Series. The Farmers' Tale. Multicoloured.

2107	19p. Type **1417**	75	70
2108	26p. Horse-drawn plough (Mechanical Farming)	95	1·00
2109	44p. Man peeling potato (food imports)	2·00	1·60
2110	64p. Aerial view of combine harvester (Satellite Agriculture)	2·50	2·40

1421 Robert the Bruce (Battle of Bannockburn, 1314)

1999. The Millennium Series. The Soldiers' Tale.

2111	**1421**	19p. black, stone and silver	75	70
2112	–	26p. multicoloured	95	1·00
2113	–	44p. grey, black and silver	2·00	1·60
2114	–	64p. multicoloured	2·50	2·40

DESIGNS: 26p. Cavalier and horse (English Civil War); 44p. War Graves Cemetery, The Somme (World Wars); 64p. Soldiers with boy (Peace-keeping).

1425 Hark the herald angels sing and Hymnbook (John Wesley)

1999. Millennium Series. The Christians' Tale. Multicoloured.

2115	19p. Type **1425**	75	70
2116	26p. King James I and Bible (Authorised version of Bible)	95	1·00
2117	44p. St. Andrews Cathedral, Fife ("Pilgrimage")	1·50	1·60
2118	64p. Nativity ("First Christmas")	2·25	2·40

1429 *World of the Stage* (Allen Jones)

1999. The Millennium Series. The Artists' Tale. Multicoloured.

2119	19p. Type **1429**	75	70
2120	26p. *World of Music* (Bridget Riley)	95	1·00
2121	44p. *World of Literature* (Lisa Milroy)	1·50	1·60
2122	64p. *New Worlds* (Sir Howard Hodgkin)	2·25	2·40

1433 Clock Face and Map of North America **1434** Clock Face and Map of Asia

1435 Clock Face and Map of Middle East **1436** Clock Face and Map of Europe

1999. Millennium Series. "Millennium Timekeeper". Sheet 120×89 mm.

MS2123	64p. Type **1433**; 64p. Type **1434**; 64p. Type **1435**; 64p. Type **1436**	26·00	26·00

No. **MS**2123 also exists overprinted **EARLS COURT, LONDON 22–28 MAY 2000 THE STAMP SHOW 2000** from Exhibition Premium Passes, costing £10, available from 1 March 2000.

1437 Queen Elizabeth II

2000. New Millennium.

2124	**1437** (1st) brown	1·00	1·00

1438 Barn Owl (World Owl Trust, Muncaster)

2000. Millennium Projects (1st series). "Above and Beyond".

2125	19p. Type **1438**	1·25	70
2126	26p. Night sky (National Space Science Centre, Leicester)	95	1·00
2126a	(1st) As No. 2126	5·25	4·50
2127	44p. River Goyt and textile mills (Torrs Walkway, New Mills)	1·75	1·75
2128	64p. Northern gannets (Seabird Centre, North Berwick)	2·75	2·75

1442 Millennium Beacon (Beacons across The Land)

2000. Millennium Projects (2nd series). "Fire and Light". Multicoloured.

2129	19p. Type **1442**	75	70
2130	26p. Garratt steam locomotive No. 143 pulling train (Rheilffordd Eryri, Welsh Highland Railway)	1·25	1·00
2131	44p. Lightning (Dynamic Earth Centre, Edinburgh)	1·50	1·50
2132	64p. Multicoloured lights (Lighting Croydon's Skyline)	2·25	2·50

2000. As T **929** but with "1st" face value.

2133	(1st) black and cream	2·00	2·00

1447 Beach Pebbles
(Turning the Tide,
Durham Coast)

2000. Millennium Projects (3rd series). "Water and Coast".

2134	19p. Type **1447**		75	70
2135	26p. Frog's legs and water lilies (National Pondlife Centre, Merseyside)		1·25	1·00
2136	44p. Cliff Boardwalk (Parc Arfordirol, Llanelli Coast)		1·50	1·50
2137	64p. Reflections in water (Portsmouth Harbour Development)		2·25	2·50

1451 Reed Beds, River
Braid (ECOS, Ballymena)

2000. Millennium Projects (4th series). "Life and Earth".

2138	(2nd.) Type **1451**		1·00	70
2139	(1st) South American leaf-cutter ants ("Web of Life" Exhibition, London Zoo)		1·25	1·00
2140	44p. Solar sensors (Earth Centre, Doncaster)		1·50	1·50
2141	64p. Hydroponic leaves (Project SUZY, Teesside)		2·25	1·50

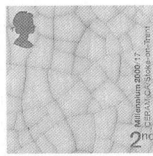

1455 Pottery Glaze
(Ceramica Museum,
Stoke-on-Trent)

2000. Millennium Projects (5th series). "Art and Craft".

2142	(2nd.) Type **1455**		1·00	70
2143	(1st) Bankside Galleries (Tate Modern, London)		1·25	1·00
2144	45p. Road marking (Cycle Network Artworks)		1·50	1·50
2145	65p. People of Salford (Lowry Centre, Salford)		2·25	2·50

2000. "Stamp Show 2000" International Stamp Exhibition, London. Jeffrey Matthews Colour Palette. Sheet 124×70 mm, containing stamps as T **367**.

MS2146	4p. blue; 5p. brown; 6p. green; 10p. orange; 31p. mauve; 39p. mauve; 64p. green; £1 violet		30·00	30·00

1459a (image scaled to 40% of original size)

2000. "Stamp Show 2000" International Stamp Exhibition, London. "Her Majesty's Stamps". Sheet 121×89 mm.

MS2147	**1459a** (1st) brown (Type **1437**) ×4; £1 green (as Type **163**)		21·00	21·00

The £1 value is an adaptation of the 1953 Coronation 1s.3d. stamp originally designed by Edmund Dulac.

1460 Children playing
(Millennium Greens
Project)

2000. Millennium Projects (6th series). "People and Places". Multicoloured.

2148	(2nd.) Type **1460**		1·00	70
2149	(1st) Millennium Bridge, Gateshead		1·25	1·00

2150	45p. Daisies (Mile End Park, London)		1·50	1·50
2151	65p. African Hut and Thatched Cottage ("On the Meridian Line" Project)		2·25	2·50

1464 Raising the Stone
(Strangford Stone,
Killyleagh)

2000. Millennium Projects (7th series). "Stone and Soil".

2152	**1464** (2nd.) blk, grey & silver		1·00	70
2153	- (1st) multicoloured		1·25	1·00
2154	- 45p. multicoloured		1·50	1·75
2155	- 65p. multicoloured		2·50	2·50

DESIGNS: No. 2153, Horse's Hooves (Trans Pennine Trail, Derbyshire); 2154 Cyclist (Kingdom of Fife Cycle Ways, Scotland); 2155, Bluebell Wood (Groundwork's "Changing Places" Project).

1468 Tree Roots ("Yews
for the Millennium"
Project)

2000. Millennium Projects (8th series). "Tree and Leaf". Multicoloured.

2156	(2nd.) Type **1468**		1·00	70
2157	(1st) Sunflower ("Eden" Project, St. Austell)		1·25	1·00
2158	45p. Sycamore seeds (Millennium Seed Bank, Wakehurst Place, Surrey)		1·50	1·60
2159	65p. Forest, Doire Dach ("Forest for Scotland")		2·50	2·50

1472 Queen
Elizabeth the
Queen Mother

1472a Royal Family on Queen Mother's 99th Birthday
(image scaled to 40% of original size)

2000. Queen Elizabeth the Queen Mother's 100th Birthday. Multicoloured.

2160	27p. Type **1472**		2·50	2·75
MS2161	121×89 mm. **1427a** multicoloured		11·00	11·00

1473 Head of *Gigantiops
destructor* (Ant)
(Wildscreen at Bristol)

2000. Millennium Projects (9th series). "Mind and Matter". Multicoloured.

2162	(2nd.) Type **1473**		1·00	70
2163	(1st) Gathering water lilies on Broads (Norfolk and Norwich Project)		1·25	1·00
2164	45p. X-ray of hand holding computer mouse (Millennium Point, Birmingham)		1·50	1·75
2165	65p. Tartan wool holder (Scottish Cultural Resources Access Network)		2·25	2·50

1477 Acrobatic
Performers (Millennium
Dome)

2000. Millennium Projects (10th series). "Body and Bone".

2166	**1477** (2nd.) black, blue & silver		1·00	70
2167	- (1st) multicoloured		1·25	1·00
2168	- 45p. multicoloured		1·50	1·50
2169	- 65p. multicoloured		2·25	2·50

DESIGNS: No. 2167, Football players (Hampden Park, Glasgow); 2168, Bather (Bath Spa Project); 2169, Hen's egg under magnification (Centre for Life, Newcastle).

1481 Virgin and Child
Stained Glass Window,
St. Edmundsbury
Cathedral (Suffolk
Cathedral Millennium
Project)

2000. Millennium Projects (11th series). "Spirit and Faith". Multicoloured.

2170	(2nd.) Type **1481**		1·00	70
2171	(1st) Floodlit church of St. Peter and St. Paul, Overstowey (Church Floodlighting Trust)		1·25	1·00
2172	45p. 12th-cent Latin Gradual (St. Patrick Centre, Downpatrick)		1·50	1·50
2173	65p. Chapter House ceiling, York Minster (York Millennium Mystery Plays)		2·25	2·50

1485 Church Bells
(Ringing in the
Millennium)

2000. Millennium Projects (12th series). "Sound and Vision". Multicoloured.

2174	(2nd.) Type **1485**		1·00	70
2175	(1st) Eye (Year of the Artist)		1·25	1·00
2176	45p. Top of harp (Canolfan Mileniwm, Cardiff)		1·50	1·50
2177	65p. Silhouetted figure within latticework (TS2K Creative Enterprise Centres, London)		2·25	2·50

1489 "Flower" ("Nurture
Children")

2001. New Millennium. Rights of the Child, Face Paintings. Multicoloured.

2178	(2nd.) Type **1489**		1·00	75
2179	(1st) "Tiger" ("Listen to Children")		1·25	1·10
2180	45p. "Owl" ("Teach Children")		1·60	1·75
2181	65p. "Butterfly" ("Ensure Children's Freedom")		2·40	2·50

1493 "Love"

2001. "Occasions" Greetings Stamps. Multicoloured.

2182	(1st) Type **1493**		1·30	1·30
2183	(1st) "THANKS"		1·30	1·30
2184	(1st) "abc" "New Baby"		1·30	1·30
2185	(1st) "WELCOME"		1·30	1·30
2186	(1st) "Cheers"		1·30	1·30

The silver-grey backgrounds are printed in Iriodin ink which gives a shiny effect.

1498 Dog and Owner
on Bench

2001. Cats and Dogs. Self-adhesive.

2187	**1498** (1st) black, grey & silver		1·25	1·00
2188	- (1st) black, grey & silver		1·25	1·00
2189	- (1st) black, grey & silver		1·25	1·00
2190	- (1st) black, grey & silver		1·25	1·00
2191	- (1st) black, grey & silver		1·25	1·00
2192	- (1st) black, grey & silver		1·25	1·00
2193	- (1st) black, grey & silver		1·25	1·00
2194	- (1st) black, grey & silver		1·25	1·00
2195	- (1st) black, grey & silver		1·25	1·00
2196	- (1st) black, grey & silver		1·25	1·00

DESIGNS: No. 2188 Dog in bath; 2189, Boxer at dog show; 2190, Cat in handbag; 2191, Cat on gate; 2192, Dog in car; 2193, Cat at window; 2194, Dog behind fence; 2195, Cat watching bird; 2196, Cat in washbasin.

1508 "RAIN"

2001. The Weather. Multicoloured.

2197	19p. Type **1508**		70	75
2198	27p. "FAIR"		85	1·00
2199	45p. "STORMY"		1·50	1·50
2200	65p. "VERY DRY"		2·40	2·50
MS2201	105×105 mm. Nos. 2197/2200		18·00	18·00

The violet on the 27p. and miniature sheet is printed in thermochromic ink, which changes from violet to blue when exposed to heat.

1512 *Vanguard* Class
Submarine, 1992

2001. Centenary of Royal Navy Submarine Service. Multicoloured. (a) Ordinary gum.

2202	(2nd) Type **1512**		1·00	75
2203	(1st) *Swiftsure* Class Submarine, 1973		1·25	90
2204	45p. *Unity* Class Submarine, 1939		1·75	1·60
2205	65p. "Holland" Type Submarine, 1901		2·40	2·50
MS2206	92×97 mm. (a) (1st) White Ensign; (b) (1st) Union Jack; (c) (1st) Jolly Roger flown by H.M.S. *Proteus* (submarine); (d) (1st) Flag of Chief of Defence Staff		9·00	9·00

(b) Self-adhesive.

2207	(1st) *Swiftsure* Class Submarine, 1973		50·00	40·00
2208	(1st) White Ensign		15·00	15·00
2209	(1st) Jolly Roger Flown by H.M.S. *Proteus* (submarine)		15·00	15·00

1520 Leyland X2 Open-top,
London General B Type,
Leyland Titan TD1 and AEC
Regent 1

1521 AEC Regent 1,
Daimler COG5, Utility Guy
Arab Mk II and AEC Regent
III RT Type

1522 AEC Regent III RT
Type, Bristol KSW5G
Open-top, AEC Routemaster
and Bristol Lodekka FSF6G

1523 Bristol Lodekka FSF6G, Leyland Titan PD3/4, Leyland Atlantean PDR1/1 and Daimler Fleetline CRG6LX-33

1524 Daimler Fleetline CRG6LX-33, MCW Metrobus DR102/43, Leyland Olympian ONLXB/1R and Dennis Trident

2001. 150th Anniv of First Double-decker Bus.

2210	**1520**	(1st) multicoloured	1·25	1·00
2211	**1521**	(1st) multicoloured	1·25	1·00
2212	**1522**	(1st) multicoloured	1·25	1·00
2213	**1523**	(1st) multicoloured	1·25	1·00
2214	**1524**	(1st) multicoloured	1·25	1·00
MS2215	120×105 mm. Nos. 2210/14		10·50	12·50

In No. **MS**2215 the illustrations of the AEC Regent III RT Type and the Daimler Fleetline CRG6LX-33 appear twice.

1525 Toque Hat by Pip Hackett

2001. Fashion Hats. Multicoloured.

2216	(1st) Type **1525**	1·25	90
2217	(E) Butterfly hat by Dai Rees	1·50	1·25
2218	45p. Top hat by Stephen Jones	1·60	1·60
2219	65p. Spiral hat by Philip Treacy	2·50	2·50

1529 Common Frog

2001. Europa. Pond Life. Multicoloured.

2220	(1st) Type **1529**	1·25	1·00
2221	(E) Great diving beetle	1·50	1·25
2222	45p. Three-spined stickleback	1·50	1·50
2223	65p. Southern hawker dragonfly	2·00	2·25

The 1st and E values incorporate the "EUROPA" emblem.

1533 Policeman

2001. Punch and Judy Show Puppets. Multicoloured. (a) Ordinary Gum.

2224	(1st) Type **1533**	1·25	1·00
2225	(1st) Clown	1·25	1·00
2226	(1st) Mr. Punch	1·25	1·00
2227	(1st) Judy	1·25	1·00
2228	(1st) Beadle	1·25	1·00
2229	(1st) Crocodile	1·25	1·00
	(b) Self-adhesive.		
2230	(1st) Mr. Punch	17·00	17·00
2231	(1st) Judy	17·00	17·00

1539 Carbon 60 Molecule (Chemistry)

2001. Centenary of Nobel Prizes.

2232	**1539**	(2nd) black, silver and grey	1·00	80
2233	-	(1st) multicoloured	1·50	1·00

2234	-	(E) black, silver and green	1·50	1·50
2235	-	40p. multicoloured	2·00	1·50
2236	-	45p. multicoloured	3·00	2·00
2237	-	65p. black and silver	5·00	2·50

DESIGNS: No. 2233, Globe (Economic Sciences); 2234, Embossed Dove (Peace); 2235, Crosses (Physiology or Medicine); 2236, Poem "The Addressing of Cats" by T. S. Eliot in Open Book (Literature); 2237, Hologram of Boron Molecule (Physics).

The grey on No. 2232 is printed in thermochromic ink which temporarily changes to pale grey when exposed to heat.

The centre of No. 2235 is coated with a eucalyptus scent.

1545 Robins with Snowman

2001. Christmas. Robins. Self-adhesive. Multicoloured.

2238	(2nd) Type **1545**	1·00	1·00
2239	(1st) Robins on bird table	1·25	1·00
2240	(E) Robins skating on bird bath	1·50	1·50
2241	45p. Robins with Christmas pudding	2·00	2·00
2242	65p. Robins in paper chain nest	3·00	3·00

1550 How the Whale got his Throat

2002. Centenary of Publication of Rudyard Kipling's *Just So Stories*. Multicoloured. Self-adhesive.

2243	(1st) Type **1550**	1·25	1·00
2244	(1st) *How the Camel got his Hump*	1·25	1·00
2245	(1st) *How the Rhinoceros got his Skin*	1·25	1·00
2246	(1st) *How the Leopard got his Spots*	1·25	1·00
2247	(1st) *The Elephant's Child*	1·25	1·00
2248	(1st) *The Sing-Song of Old Man Kangaroo*	1·25	1·00
2249	(1st) *The Beginning of the Armadillos*	1·25	1·00
2250	(1st) *The Crab that played with the Sea*	1·25	1·00
2251	(1st) *The Cat that walked by Himself*	1·25	1·00
2252	(1st) *The Butterfly that stamped*	1·25	1·00

1560 Queen Elizabeth II, 1952 (Dorothy Wilding)

2002. Golden Jubilee. Studio portraits of Queen Elizabeth II by photographers named. Multicoloured.

2253	(2nd) Type **1560**	1·00	80
2254	(1st) Queen Elizabeth II, 1968 (Cecil Beaton)	1·25	90
2255	(E) Queen Elizabeth II, 1978 (Lord Snowdon)	1·50	1·50
2256	45p. Queen Elizabeth II, 1984 (Yousef Karsh)	1·75	2·00
2257	65p. Queen Elizabeth II, 1996 (Tim Graham)	2·75	3·00

1566

2002. As T **154/5** (Wilding definitive of 1952–54), but with service indicator as T **1566**.

2258	**1566**	(2nd) red	1·20	1·00
2259	-	(1st) green	1·25	1·25

1567 Rabbits ("a new baby")

2002. "Occasions". Greetings Stamps. Multicoloured.

2260	(1st) Type **1567**	1·50	1·10
2261	(1st) "LOVE"	1·50	1·10
2262	(1st) Aircraft sky-writing "hello"	1·50	1·10
2263	(1st) Bear pulling potted topiary tree (Moving Home)	1·50	1·10
2264	(1st) Flowers ("best wishes")	1·50	1·10

No. 2262 also comes self-adhesive.

1572 Studland Bay, Dorset

2002. British Coastlines. Multicoloured.

2265	27p. Type **1572**	80	70
2266	27p. Luskentyre, South Harris	80	70
2267	27p. Cliffs, Dover, Kent	80	70
2268	27p. Padstow Harbour, Cornwall	80	70
2269	27p. Broadstairs, Kent	80	70
2270	27p. St. Abbs Head, Scottish Borders	80	70
2271	27p. Dunster Beach, Somerset	80	70
2272	27p. Newquay Beach, Cornwall	80	70
2273	27p. Portrush, County Antrim	80	70
2274	27p. Sand-spit, Conwy	80	70

1582 Slack Wire Act

2002. Circus. Multicoloured.

2275	(2nd) Type **1582**	1·00	80
2276	(1st) Lion tamer	1·25	1·00
2277	(E) Trick tri-cyclists	1·50	1·25
2278	45p. Krazy kar	1·75	1·50
2279	65p. Equestrienne	2·75	2·25

1587 Queen Elizabeth the Queen Mother

2002. Queen Elizabeth the Queen Mother Commemoration. As Nos. 1507/10 with changed face values and showing both the Queen's head and frame in black.

2280	**1587**	(1st) multicoloured	1·25	85
2281	**1587**	(E) black and blue	1·50	1·10
2282	**1587**	45p. multicoloured	1·50	1·50
2283	**1587**	65p. black, stone and brown	2·00	2·25

1588 Airbus A340-600 (2002)

2002. 50th Anniv of Passenger Jet Aviation. Airliners. Multicoloured.

2284	(2nd) Type **1588**	1·00	70
2285	(1st) Concorde (1976)	1·25	1·00
2286	(E) Trident (1964)	1·50	1·50
2287	45p. Vickers VC-10 (1964)	2·00	2·00
2288	65p. de Havilland DH.106 Comet (1952)	3·00	3·00
MS2289	120×105 mm. Nos. 2284/8	12·00	11·00

No. 2285 also comes self-adhesive.

1593 Crowned Lion with Shield of St. George **1594** Top Left Quarter of English Flag, and Football

1595 Top Right Quarter of English Flag, and Football

1596 Bottom Left Quarter of English Flag, and Football

1597 Bottom Right Quarter of English Flag, and Football

2002. World Cup Football Championship, Japan and Korea (2002).

2291	**1593**	(1st) blue, red and silver	2·50	2·50
MS2292	145×74 mm. No. 2291; **1594** (1st) multicoloured; **1595** (1st) multicoloured, **1596** (1st) multicoloured; **1597** (1st) multicoloured		7·50	6·50
	(b) Self-adhesive.			
2293	**1594**	(1st) multicoloured	6·00	6·00
2294	**1595**	(1st) multicoloured	6·00	6·00

1598 Swimming

2002. 17th Commonwealth Games, Manchester. Multicoloured.

2299	(2nd) Type **1598**	1·00	80
2300	(1st) Running	1·25	1·00
2301	(E) Cycling	1·50	1·25
2302	47p. Long jumping	1·50	1·50
2303	68p. Wheelchair racing	2·00	2·25

1603 Tinkerbell

2002. 150th Anniv of Great Ormond Street Children's Hospital. Peter Pan by Sir James Barrie. Multicoloured.

2304	(2nd) Type **1063**	1·00	80
2305	(1st) Wendy, John and Michael Darling in front of Big Ben	1·25	1·00
2306	(E) Crocodile and alarm clock	1·50	1·25
2307	47p. Captain Hook	1·50	1·50
2308	68p. Peter Pan	2·00	2·25

1608 Millennium Bridge, 2001

2002. Bridges of London. Multicoloured.

2309	(2nd) Type **1608**	1·00	80
2310	(1st) Tower Bridge, 1894	1·25	80
2311	(E) Westminster Bridge, 1864	2·00	1·50
2312	47p. "Blackfriars Bridge, c 1800" (William Marlow)	2·50	2·00
2313	68p. "London Bridge, c 1670" (Wenceslaus Hollar)	3·50	3·00

No. 2310 also comes self-adhesive.

1613 Galaxies and Nebula (image scaled to 40% of original size)

2002. Astronomy. Sheet 120×89 mm. Multicoloured.
MS2315 **1613** (1st) Planetary nebula in Aquila; (1st) Seyfert 2 galaxy in Pegasus; (1st) Planetary nebula in Norma; (1st) Seyfert 2 galaxy in Circinus .... 6·00　6·00

1614 Green Pillar Box, 1857

2002. 150th Anniv of the First Pillar Box.
2316	(2nd) Type **1614**	1·00	80
2317	(1st) Horizontal Aperture Box, 1874	1·25	1·00
2318	(E) Air Mail Box, 1934	1·75	1·75
2319	47p. Double Aperture Box, 1939	2·00	2·50
2320	68p. Modern Style Box, 1980	2·50	3·00

1619 Blue Spruce Star

2002. Christmas. Self-adhesive.
2321	(2nd) Type **1619**	1·00	80
2322	(1st) Holly	1·25	80
2323	(E) Ivy	1·50	1·50
2324	47p. Mistletoe	2·00	1·75
2325	68p. Pine cone	3·00	2·75

2002. 50th Anniv of Wilding Definitives (1st issue). Sheet 124×70 mm, containing designs as T 154/5 and 157/60 (1952–54 issue), but with values in decimal currency as T 1348 or with service indicator as T 1566, printed on cream.
MS2326 1p. red; 2p. blue; 5p. brown; (2nd) red; (1st) green; 33p. brown; 37p. mauve; 47p. brown; 50p. green .... 10·00　10·00
See also No. MS2367.

1624 Barn Owl landing

1625 Barn Owl with folded Wings and Legs down

1626 Barn Owl with extended Wings and Legs down

1627 Barn Owl in Flight with Wings lowered

1628 Barn Owl in Flight with Wings raised

1629 Kestrel with Wings folded

1630 Kestrel with Wings fully extended upwards

1631 Kestrel with Wings horizontal

1632 Kestrel with Wings partly extended downwards

1633 Kestrel with Wings fully extended downwards

2003. Birds of Prey.
2327	**1624**	(1st) multicoloured	1·25	1·00
2328	**1625**	(1st) multicoloured	1·25	1·00
2329	**1626**	(1st) multicoloured	1·25	1·00
2330	**1627**	(1st) multicoloured	1·25	1·00
2331	**1628**	(1st) multicoloured	1·25	1·00
2332	**1629**	(1st) multicoloured	1·25	1·00
2333	**1630**	(1st) multicoloured	1·25	1·00
2334	**1631**	(1st) multicoloured	1·25	1·00
2335	**1632**	(1st) multicoloured	1·25	1·00
2336	**1633**	(1st) multicoloured	1·25	1·00

1634 "Gold star, See me, Playtime"

2003. "Occasions" Greetings Stamps.
2337	**1634**	(1st) yellow and blue	1·25	1·00
2338	-	(1st) red and blue	1·25	1·00
2339	-	(1st) purple and green	1·25	1·00
2340	-	(1st) green and red	1·25	1·00
2341	-	(1st) blue and yellow	1·25	1·00
2342	-	(1st) blue and purple	1·25	1·00

DESIGNS: No. 2338, "I U, XXXX, S.W.A.L.K."; 2239, "Angel, Poppet, Little terror"; 2340, "Yes, No, Maybe"; 2341, "Oops!, Sorry, Will try harder"; 2342, "I did it!, You did it!, We did it!".

1640 Completing the Genome Jigsaw

2003. 50th Anniv of Discovery of DNA. Multicoloured.
2343	(2nd) Type **1640**	1·00	80
2344	(1st) Ape with Moustache and Scientist	1·25	1·00
2345	(E) DNA Snakes and Ladders	1·50	1·25
2346	47p. "Animal Scientists"	1·50	1·50
2347	68p. Genome Crystal Ball	2·00	2·25

1645 Strawberry

2003. Fruit and Vegetables. Self-adhesive.
2348	(1st) Type **1645**	1·25	1·00
2349	(1st) Potato	1·25	1·00
2350	(1st) Apple	1·25	1·00
2351	(1st) Red pepper	1·25	1·00
2352	(1st) Pear	1·25	1·00
2353	(1st) Orange	1·25	1·00
2354	(1st) Tomato	1·25	1·00
2355	(1st) Lemon	1·25	1·00
2356	(1st) Cabbage	1·25	1·00
2357	(1st) Aubergine	1·25	1·00

Nos. 2348/57 are accompanied by a similar-sized pane of self-adhesive labels showing ears, eyes, mouths, hats etc which are intended for the adornment of fruit and vegetables depicted.

1655

2003. Overseas Stamps. Self-adhesive.
2357a	-	(Worldwide postcard) black, red and blue	1·50	1·50
2357b	**1655**	(Europe) deep blue, new blue and rosine	1·25	1·25
2358	**1655**	(Europe) blue and red	1·90	1·90
2358a	**1655**	(Worldwide) red and blue	2·00	2·00
2359	**1655**	(Worldwide) deep mauve, new blue and rosine	3·25	3·25

Nos. 2358/9 were intended to pay postage on mail up to 40 grams to either Europe (52p.) or foreign destinations outside Europe (£1.12). No. 2357a was intended to pay postcard rate to foreign destination (43p.).

1656 Amy Johnson (pilot) and de Havilland DH.60G Gipsy Moth *Jason*

2003. Extreme Endeavours. (British Explorers).
2360	(2nd) Type **1656**	1·00	80
2361	(1st) Members of 1953 Everest team	1·25	1·00
2362	(E) Freya Stark (traveller and writer) and desert	1·50	1·50
2363	42p. Ernest Shackleton (Antarctic explorer) and wreck of *Endurance*	1·75	1·75
2364	47p. Francis Chichester (yachtsman) and *Gipsy Moth IV*	2·00	2·00
2365	68p. Robert Falcon Scott (Antarctic explorer) and Norwegian Expedition at the Pole	2·50	2·50

No. 2361 also comes self-adhesive.

2003. 50th Anniv of Wilding Definitives (2nd issue). Sheet 124×70 mm, containing designs as Nos. 519, 575, 617b and 585 (1952–54 issue), but with values in decimal currency as T 1348 or with service indicator as T 1566, printed on cream.
MS2367 4p. lilac; 8p. blue; (1st) purple; 20p. green; 28p. green; 34p. purple; (1st) chestnut; 42p. blue; 68p. blue .... 10·50　11·25

1662 Guardsmen in Coronation Procession

2003. 50th Anniv of Coronation.
2368	**1662**	(1st) multicoloured	1·25	1·00
2369	-	(1st) black and gold	1·25	1·00
2370	-	(1st) multicoloured	1·25	1·00
2371	-	(1st) black and gold	1·25	1·00
2372	-	(1st) multicoloured	1·25	1·00
2373	-	(1st) multicoloured	1·25	1·00
2374	-	(1st) multicoloured	1·25	1·00
2375	-	(1st) black and gold	1·25	1·00
2376	-	(1st) black and gold	1·25	1·00
2377	-	(1st) multicoloured	1·25	1·00

DESIGNS: No. 2369, East End children reading Coronation party poster; 2370, Queen Elizabeth II in Coronation Chair with Bishops of Durham and Bath & Wells; 2371, Children in Plymouth working on Royal Montage; 2372, Queen Elizabeth II in Coronation Robes (photograph by Cecil Beaton); 2373, Childrens Race at East End Street Party; 2374, Coronation Coach passing through Marble Arch; 2375, Children in Fancy Dress; 2376, Coronation Coach outside Buckingham Palace; 2377, Children eating at London street party.

No. 2372 does not show a silhouette of the Queens head in gold as do the other nine designs.

2003. 50th Anniv of Coronation. Designs as Nos. 585, 534 (Wilding definitive of 1952) and 163 (Coronation commemorative of 1953), but with values in decimal currency as T 1348.
2378	47p. brown	5·00	4·00
2379	68p. blue	5·00	4·00
2380	£1 green	50·00	45·00

1672 Prince William in September 2001 (Brendan Beirne)

2003. 21st Birthday of Prince William of Wales.
2381	**1672**	28p. multicoloured	1·00	80
2382	-	(E) mauve, black and green	2·25	1·50
2383	-	47p. multicoloured	2·75	2·00
2384	-	68p. deep green, black and green	4·00	2·50

DESIGNS: No. 2382, Prince William in September 2000 (Tim Graham); 2383, Prince William in September 2001 (Camera Press); 2384, Prince William in September 2001 (Tim Graham).

1676 Loch Assynt, Sutherland

2003. A British Journey: Scotland. Multicoloured.
2385	(2nd) Type **1676**	1·00	90
2386	(1st) Ben More, Isle of Mull	1·25	1·00
2387	(E) Rothiemurchus, Cairngorms	1·25	1·25
2388	42p. Dalveen Pass, Lowther Hills	1·25	1·50
2389	47p. Glenfinnan Viaduct, Lochaber	1·50	2·00
2390	68p. Papa Little, Shetland Islands	2·00	2·50

No. 2386 also comes self-adhesive.

1682 The Station (Andrew Davidson)

2003. British Pub Signs. Multicoloured.
2392	(1st) Type **1682**	1·25	70
2393	(E) *Black Swan* (Stanley Chew)	2·00	2·00
2394	42p. *The Cross Keys* (George Mackenney)	1·50	1·50
2395	47p. *The Mayflower* (Ralph Ellis)	1·75	2·00
2396	68p. "The Barley Sheaf" (Joy Cooper)	2·00	2·25

1687 Meccano Constructor Biplane, c. 1931

2003. Classic Transport Toys. Multicoloured.
2397	(1st) Type **1687**	1·25	70
2398	(E) Wells-Brimtoy Clockwork Double-decker Omnibus, c. 1938	1·50	1·25
2399	42p. Hornby M1 Clockwork Locomotive and Tender, c. 1948	1·50	1·50
2400	47p. Dinky Toys Ford Zephyr, c. 1956	1·75	1·75
2401	68p. Mettoy Friction Drive Space Ship Eagle, c. 1960	2·50	2·50
MS2402	115×105 mm. Nos. 2397/401	8·00	8·25

No. 2397 also comes self-adhesive.

1692 Coffin of Denytenamun, Egyptian, c. 900BC

2003. 250th Anniv of the British Museum. Multicoloured.
2404	(2nd) Type **1692**	1·00	70
2405	(1st) Alexander the Great, Greek, c. 200BC	1·25	90
2406	(E) Sutton Hoo Helmet, Anglo-Saxon, c. AD600	1·50	1·25
2407	42p. Sculpture of Parvati, South Indian, c. AD1550	1·50	1·50
2408	47p. Mask of Xiuhtecuhtli, Mixtec-Aztec, c. AD1500	2·00	2·00
2409	68p. Hoa Hakananai'a, Easter Island, c. AD1000	2·75	2·75

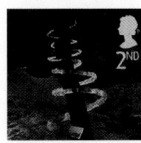
1698 Ice Spiral

2003. Christmas. Ice Sculptures by Andy Goldsworthy. Multicoloured.

2410	(2nd)	Type **1698**	1·00	70
2411	(1st)	Icicle Star	1·25	90
2412	(E)	Wall of Ice Blocks	1·50	90
2413	53p.	Ice Ball	2·00	2·00
2414	68p.	Ice Hole	2·50	2·50
2415	£1.12	Snow Pyramids	3·00	3·00

1704 (image scaled to 42% of original size)

2003. England's Victory in Rugby World Cup Championship, Australia. Sheet 115×85 mm. Multicoloured.

MS2416	**1704**	(1st) England flags and fans; (1st) England team standing in circle before match; 68p. World Cup trophy; 68p. Victorious England players after match	14·00	14·00

1705 Dolgoch, Rheilffordd Talyllyn Railway, Gwynedd

2004. Classic Locomotives. Multicoloured.

2417	20p.	Type **1705**	65	65
2418	28p.	CR Class 439, Bo'ness and Kinneil Railway, West Lothian	90	90
2419	(E)	GCR Class 8K, Leicestershire	1·50	1·20
2420	42p.	GWR Manor Class *Bradley Manor*, Severn Valley Railway, Worcestershire	1·50	1·50
2421	47p.	SR West Country class *Blackmoor Vale*, Bluebell Railway, East Sussex	2·00	2·00
2422	68p.	(1710 BR Standard class, Keighley & Worth Valley Railway, Yorkshire	3·00	3·50
MS2423	190×67 mm. Nos. 2417/22		25·00	25·00

1711 Postman

2004. Occasions.

2424	**1711**	(1st) mauve and black	1·25	1·00
2425	-	(1st) magenta and black	1·25	1·00
2426	-	(1st) lemon and black	1·25	1·00
2427	-	(1st) green and black	1·25	1·00
2428	-	(1st) blue and black	1·25	1·00

DESIGNS: No. 2425, Face; 2426, Duck; 2427, Baby; 2428, Aircraft.

1716 Map showing Middle Earth

2004. 50th Anniv of Publication of *The Fellowship of the Ring* and *The Two Towers* by J. R. R. Tolkien. Multicoloured.

2429	(1st)	Type **1716**	1·25	1·00
2430	(1st)	Forest of Lothlorien in Spring	1·25	1·00
2431	(1st)	Dust-jacket for *The Fellowship of the Ring*	1·25	1·00
2432	(1st)	Rivendell	1·25	1·00
2433	(1st)	The Hall at Bag End	1·25	1·00
2434	(1st)	Orthanc	1·25	1·00
2435	(1st)	Doors of Durin	1·25	1·00
2436	(1st)	Barad-dur	1·25	1·00

2437	(1st)	Minas Tirth	1·25	1·00
2438	(1st)	Fangorn Forest	1·25	1·00

1726 Ely Island, Lower Lough Erne

2004. A British Journey: Northern Ireland. Multicoloured.

2439	(2nd)	Type **1726**	1·00	75
2440	(1st)	Giant's Causeway, Antrim Coast	1·25	90
2441	(E)	Slemish, Antrim Mountains	1·50	1·20
2442	42p.	Banns Road, Mourne Mountains	1·30	1·30
2443	47p.	Glenelly Valley, Sperrins	1·50	1·50
2444	68p.	Islandmore, Strangford Lough	2·20	2·20

No. 2440 also comes self-adhesive.

1732 Lace 1 (trial proof) 1968 (Sir Terry Frost)

2004. Centenary of the Entente Cordiale. Contemporary Paintings.

2446	**1732**	28p. grey, black and red	1·00	85
2447	-	57p. multicoloured	2·25	2·00

DESIGN: No. 1733, *Coccinelle* (Sonia Delaunay) Stamps in similar designs were issued by France.

1734 RMS Queen Mary 2, 2004 (Edward D. Walker)

2004. Ocean Liners. Multicoloured.

2448	(1st)	Type **1734**	1·25	90
2449	(E)	SS Canberra 1961 (David Cobb)	1·50	1·30
2450	42p.	RMS Queen Mary 1936 (Charles Pears)	1·30	1·30
2451	47p.	RMS Mauretania, 1907 (Thomas Henry)	1·50	1·50
2452	57p.	SS City of New York, 1888 (Raphael Monleaon y Torres)	1·80	1·80
2453	68p.	PS Great Western, 1838 (Joseph Walter)	2·20	2·20
MS2454	114×104 mm. Nos. 2448/53		20·00	18·00

No. 2448 also comes self-adhesive.
Nos. 2448/55 commemorate the introduction to service of the *Queen Mary 2*.

1740 Dianthus Allwoodii Group

2004. Bicentenary of the Royal Horticultural Society (1st issue). Multicoloured.

2456	(2nd)	Type **1740**	1·00	80
2457	(1st)	Dahlia "Garden Princess"	1·25	1·00
2458	(E)	Clematis "Arabella"	1·50	1·30
2459	42p.	Miltonia "French Lake"	2·00	2·00
2460	47p.	Lilium "Lemon Pixie"	2·50	2·50
2461	68p.	Delphinium "Clifford Sky"	3·50	3·50
MS2462	115×105 mm. Nos. 2456/61		14·00	14·00

1746 Barmouth Bridge

2004. A British Journey: Wales. Multicoloured. (a) Ordinary gum.

2466	(2nd)	Type **1746**	1·00	80
2467	(1st)	Hyddgen, Plynlimon	1·25	1·00
2468	40p.	Brecon Beacons	1·75	1·50
2469	43p.	Pen-pych, Rhondda Valley	2·00	2·00

2470	47p.	Rhewl, Dee Valley	2·50	3·00
2471	68p.	Marloes Sands	3·50	4·00

(b) Self-adhesive.

2472	(1st)	Hyddgen, Plynlimon	8·00	8·00

The (1st) and 40p. values include the "EUROPA" emblem.

1752 Sir Rowland Hill Award

2004. 250th Anniv of the Royal Society of Arts.

2473	**1752**	(1st) multicoloured	1·25	95
2474	-	40p. multicoloured	1·30	1·30
2475	-	43p. multicoloured	1·40	1·40
2476	-	47p. multicoloured	1·50	1·50
2477	-	57p. silver, vermilion and black	2·20	2·20
2478	-	68p. silver, vermilion and black	3·00	3·00

DESIGNS: No. 2474, William Shipley (Founder of Royal Society of Arts); 2475, "RSA" as Typewriter Keys and Shorthand; 2476 Chimney Sweep; 2477, "Gill Typeface"; 2478, "Zero Waste".

1758 Pine Marten

2004. Woodland Animals. Multicoloured.

2479	(1st)	Type **1758**	1·25	1·00
2480	(1st)	Roe deer	1·25	1·00
2481	(1st)	Badger	1·25	1·00
2482	(1st)	Yellow-necked mouse	1·25	1·00
2483	(1st)	Wild cat	1·25	1·00
2484	(1st)	Red squirrel	1·25	1·00
2485	(1st)	Stoat	1·25	1·00
2486	(1st)	Natterer's bat	1·25	1·00
2487	(1st)	Mole	1·25	1·00
2488	(1st)	Fox	1·25	1·00

1768 Pte. McNamara, 5th Dragoon Guards, Heavy Brigade Charge, Battle of Balaklava

2004. 150th Anniv of the Crimean War. Multicoloured.

2489	(2nd)	Type **1768**	1·00	80
2490	(1st)	Piper Muir, 42nd Regt of Foot, Amphibious Assault on Kerch	1·25	1·00
2491	40p.	Sgt. Maj. Edwards, Scots Fusilier Guards, Gallant Action, Battle of Inkerman	2·00	2·00
2492	57p.	Sgt. Powell, 1st Regt of Foot Guards, Battles of Alma and Inkerman	2·50	2·50
2493	68p.	Sgt. Maj. Poole, Royal Sappers and Miners, Defensive Line, Battle of Inkerman	2·75	3·00
2494	£1.12	Sgt. Glasgow, Royal Artillery, Gun Battery besieged Sevastopol	4·50	5·00

Nos. 2489/94 show "Crimean Heroes" photographs taken in 1856.

1774 Father Christmas on Snowy Roof

2004. Christmas. Multicoloured. (a) Self-adhesive.

2495	(2nd)	Type **1774**	1·00	80
2496	(1st)	Celebrating the sunrise	1·25	1·00
2497	40p.	On roof in gale	1·30	1·00
2498	57p.	With umbrella in rain	1·80	1·80
2499	68p.	On edge of roof with torch	2·20	2·20
2500	£1.12	Sheltering behind chimney	3·75	3·75

(b) Ordinary gum.

MS2501	115×105 mm. As Nos. 2495/500		12·00	13·00

1780 British Saddleback Pigs

2005. Farm Animals. Multicoloured.

2502	(1st)	Type **1780**	1·25	1·00
2503	(1st)	Khaki Campbell ducks	1·25	1·00
2504	(1st)	Suffolk horses	1·25	1·00
2505	(1st)	Dairy Shorthorn cattle	1·25	1·00
2506	(1st)	Border collie dog	1·25	1·00
2507	(1st)	Light Sussex chicks	1·25	1·00
2508	(1st)	Suffolk sheep	1·25	1·00
2509	(1st)	Bagot goat	1·25	1·00
2510	(1st)	Norfolk black turkeys	1·25	1·00
2511	(1st)	Embden geese	1·25	1·00

1790 Old Harry Rocks, Studland Bay

2005. A British Journey: South West England. Multicoloured.

2512	(2nd)	Type **1790**	1·00	80
2513	(1st)	Wheal Coates, St. Agnes	1·25	90
2514	40p.	Start Point, Start Bay	1·50	1·75
2515	43p.	Horton Down, Wiltshire	1·75	2·00
2516	57p.	Chiselcombe, Exmoor	2·50	2·50
2517	68p.	St. James's Stone, Lundy	3·50	3·00

1796 "Mr Rochester"

2005. 150th Death Anniv of Charlotte Bronte. Illustrations of scenes from *Jane Eyre* by Paula Rego.

2518	**1796**	(2nd) multicoloured	1·00	80
2519	-	(1st) multicoloured	1·25	1·00
2520	-	40p. multicoloured	1·50	1·50
2521	-	57p. silver, grey and black	3·00	2·50
2522	-	68p. multicoloured	3·75	3·00
2523	-	£1.12 silver, grey and black	4·50	3·50
MS2524	114×105 mm. Nos. 2518/23		12·00	11·00

DESIGNS: No. 1797, "Come to Me"; 1798, "In the Comfort of her Bonnet"; 1799, "La Ligne des Rats"; 1800, "Refectory"; 1801, "Inspection".

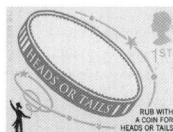
1802 Spinning Coin

2005. Centenary of the Magic Circle. Multicoloured.

2525	(1st)	Type **1802**	1·25	80
2526	40p.	Rabbit out of Hat Trick	1·00	90
2527	47p.	Knotted Scarf Trick	2·50	2·75
2528	68p.	Card Trick	3·00	3·00
2529	£1.12	Pyramid under Fez Trick	3·50	3·50

2005. 50th Anniv of First Castles Definitives. Sheet 127×73 mm, containing horiz designs as Nos. 595a/597a and 762 (Castles definitive of 1955–58) but with values in decimal currency.

MS2530	50p. black; 50p. black; £1 vermilion; **168** £1 blue		10·00	10·00

1807 (image scaled to 58% of original size)

2005. Royal Wedding. Sheet 85×115 mm. Multicoloured.
MS2531 1807 30p.×2 Prince Charles
and Mrs Camilla Parker Bowles
laughing; 68p.×2 Prince Charles and
Mrs Camilla Parker Bowles smiling
into camera .... 8·00 .... 9·00

1808 Hadrian's Wall,
England

2005. World Heritage Sites. Multicoloured.
2532	(2nd) Type **1808**	1·00	80
2533	(2nd) silver, Uluru-Kata Tjuta National Park, Australia	1·00	80
2534	(1st) Stonehenge, England	1·25	90
2535	(1st) Wet Tropics of Queensland, Australia	1·25	90
2536	47p. Blenheim Palace, England	1·00	1·00
2537	47p. Greater Blue Mountains Area, Australia	1·00	1·00
2538	68p. Heart of Neolithic Orkney, Scotland	1·50	1·40
2539	68p. Purnululu National Park, Australia	1·50	1·40

Stamps in these designs were issued by Australia.

1816 Ensign of the
Scots Guards, 2002

2005. Trooping the Colour. Multicoloured.
2540	(2nd) Type **1816**	1·00	80
2541	(1st) Queen taking the salute as Colonel-in-Chief of the Grenadier Guards, 1983	1·25	1·00
2542	42p. Trumpeter of the Household Cavalry, 2004	1·00	1·20
2543	60p. Welsh Guardsman, 1990s	2·00	2·00
2544	68p. Queen riding side-saddle, 1972	2·50	2·50
2545	£1.12 Queen and Duke of Edinburgh in carriage, 2004	3·50	3·50
MS2546	115×105 mm. Nos. 2540/5	11·00	11·00

1822 (image scaled to 42% of original size)

2005. 60th Anniv of End of the Second World War. Sheet 115×105 mm containing design as No. 1875 (1995 Peace and Freedom) but with service indicator and No. 1663b×5.
MS2547 1822 (1st) gold ×5; (1st) silver, blue and black .... 7·50 .... 7·00

1823 Norton F.1, Road
Version of Race Winner
(1991)

2005. Motorcycles. Multicoloured.
2548	(1st) Type **1823**	1·25	1·00
2549	40p. BSA Rocket 3, Early Three Cylinder "Superbike" (1969)	90	1·00
2550	42p. Vincent Black Shadow, Fastest Standard Motorcycle (1949)	1·25	1·00
2551	47p. Triumph Speed Twin, Two Cylinder Innovation (1938)	1·75	2·00
2552	60p. Brough Superior, Bespoke Luxury Motorcycle (1930)	2·50	2·50
2553	68p. Royal Enfield, Small Engined Motor Bicycle (1914)1	3·00	3·00

1829 (image scaled to 42% of original size)

2005. London's Successful Bid for Olympic Games, 2012. Sheet 115×105 mm containing designs as Nos. 1930/4, but with service indicator. Multicoloured.
MS2554 1829 (1st) Athlete celebrating×2; (1st) Throwing the javelin; (1st) Swimming; (1st) Athlete on starting blocks; (1st) Basketball .... 6·50 .... 6·50

Stamps from **MS2554** are all inscribed "London 2012–Host City" and have imprint date "2005". The design as No. 1934 omits the Olympic rings.

1830 African Woman
eating Rice

2005. Europa. Gastronomy. Changing Tastes in Britain. Multicoloured.
2555	(2nd) Type **1830**	1·00	80
2556	(1st) Indian Woman drinking tea	1·25	1·00
2557	42p. Boy eating sushi	1·30	1·40
2558	47p. Woman eating pasta	1·50	1·60
2559	60p. Woman eating chips	2·00	1·90
2560	68p. Teenage boy eating apple	2·50	2·20

1836 Inspector Morse

2005. 50th Anniv of Independent Television. Classic ITV Programmes. Multicoloured.
2561	(2nd) Type **1836**	1·00	1·00
2562	(1st) Emmerdale	1·25	1·00
2563	42p. Rising Damp	1·30	1·40
2564	47p. The Avengers	1·40	1·50
2565	60p. The South Bank Show	2·00	1·90
2566	68p. Who Wants to be a Millionaire	2·20	2·20

1842
Guzmania
splendens
(Charlotte
Sowerby)

2005. Similar Designs as Nos. 1550, 1896, 1961, **MS**2206 and 2261/2, but smaller, 20×23 mm and inscribed "1st" as T **1842**. Self-adhesive.
2567	(1st) multicoloured	2·00	2·00
2568	(1st) multicoloured	2·00	2·00
2569	(1st) multicoloured	2·00	2·00
2570	(1st) multicoloured	2·00	2·00
2571	(1st) multicoloured	2·00	2·00
2572	(1st) multicoloured	2·00	2·00

See also No. 2693.

THE ASHES ENGLAND WINNERS 2005

1843 Cricket Scenes (image scaled to 42% of original size)

2005. England's Ashes Victory. Sheet 115×90 mm. Multicoloured.
MS2573 1843 (1st) England team with Ashes trophy; (1st) Kevin Pieterson, Michael Vaughan and Andrew Flintoff on opening day of First Test, Lords; 68p. Michael Vaughan, Third Test, Old Trafford; 68p. Second Test cricket, Edgbaston .... 7·50 .... 7·50

1844 Entrepreante with dismasted British
Belle Isle

2005. Bicentenary of the Battle of Trafalgar (1st issue). Scenes from Panorama of the Battle of Trafalgar by William Heath. Multicoloured.
2574	(1st) Type **1844**	1·25	1·00
2575	(1st) Nelson wounded on Deck of HMS Victory	1·25	1·00
2576	42p. British Cutter Entrepreante attempting to rescue Crew of burning French Achille	1·00	1·10
2577	42p. Cutter and HMS Pickle (schooner)	1·00	1·10
2578	68p. British Fleet attacking in Two Columns	1·25	1·50
2579	68p. Franco/Spanish Fleet putting to Sea from Cadiz	1·25	1·50
MS2580	190×68 mm. Nos. 2574/9	10·00	11·00

Nos. 2574/5, 2576/7 and 2578/9 were each printed together, se-tenant, each pair forming a composite design.

2005. Bicentenary of the Battle of Trafalgar (2nd issue). As No. 2208. (2001 White Ensign from Submarine Centenary).
2581	**1516** (1st) multicoloured	5·00	5·00

1850 Black Madonna
and Child from Haiti

2005. Christmas. Madonna and Child Paintings. Multicoloured. (a) Self-adhesive.
2582	(2nd) Type **1850**	1·00	80
2583	(1st) "Madonna and Child" (Marianne Stokes)	1·25	1·00
2584	42p. "The Virgin Mary with the Infant Christ"	1·30	1·40
2585	60p. Choctaw Virgin Mother and Child (Fr. John Giuliani)	1·80	1·90
2586	68p. "Madonna and the Infant Jesus" (from India)	2·00	2·20
2587	£1.12 "Come let us adore Him" (Dianne Tchumut)	3·40	3·60

(b) Ordinary gum.
MS2588	115×102 mm. As Nos. 2582/7	10·50	11·00

1856 The Tale of Mr.
Jeremy Fisher (Beatrix
Potter)

2006. Animal Tales. Multicoloured.
2589	(2nd) Type **1856**	90	75
2590	(2nd) Kipper (Mick Inkpen)	90	75

2591	(1st) The Enormous Crocodile (Roald Dahl)	1·25	1·00
2592	(1st) More About Paddington (Michael Bond)	1·25	1·00
2593	42p. Comic Adventures of Boots (Satoshi Kitamura)	90	1·10
2594	42p. Alice's Adventures in Wonderland (Lewis Carroll)	90	1·10
2595	68p. The Very Hungry Caterpillar (Eric Carle)	1·25	1·60
2596	68p. Maisy's ABC (Lucy Cousins)	1·25	1·60

1864 Carding Mill
Valley, Shropshire

2006. A British Journey: England. Multicoloured.
2597	(1st) Type **1864**	1·25	1·00
2598	(1st) Beachy Head, Sussex	1·25	1·00
2599	(1st) St. Paul's Cathedral, London	1·25	1·00
2600	(1st) Brancaster, Norfolk	1·25	1·00
2601	(1st) Derwent Edge, Peak District	1·25	1·00
2602	(1st) Robin Hood's Bay, Yorkshire	1·25	1·00
2603	(1st) Buttermere, Lake District	1·25	1·00
2604	(1st) Chipping Campden, Cotswolds	1·25	1·00
2605	(1st) 1872 St. Boniface Down, Isle of Wight	1·25	1·00
2606	(1st) Chamberlain Square, Birmingham	1·25	1·00

1874 Royal Albert Bridge

2006. Birth Bicentenary of Isambard Kingdom Brunel (engineer) (1st issue).
2607	(1st) Type **1874**	1·25	80
2608	40p. Box Tunnel	1·10	1·10
2609	42p. Paddington Station	1·10	1·10
2610	47p. Great Eastern (paddle steamer)	1·50	1·50
2611	60p. Clifton Suspension Bridge design	2·00	1·75
2612	68p. Maidenhead Bridge	2·50	2·25
MS2613	190×65 mm. Nos. 2607/12	8·50	8·50

1880 Sabre-tooth Cat

2006. Ice Age Animals.
2615	**1880** (1st) black and silver	1·25	1·00
2616	- 42p. black and silver	1·00	1·00
2617	- 47p. black and silver	2·00	2·00
2618	- 68p. black and silver	2·25	2·25
2619	- £1.12 black and silver	3·25	3·25

DESIGN: 42p.Giant deer; 47p. Woolly rhino; 68p Woolly mammoth; £1.12, Cave bear.

1885 On Britannia, 1972

2006. 80th Birthday of Queen Elizabeth II.
2620	**1885** (2nd) black, green and grey	1·00	1·00
2621	- (2nd) black, green and grey	1·00	1·00
2622	- (1st) black, green and grey	1·25	1·10
2623	- (1st) black, green and grey	1·50	1·10
2624	- 44p. black, green and grey	1·00	1·25
2625	- 44p. black, green and grey	1·00	1·25
2626	- 72p. black, green and grey	1·50	2·00
2627	- 72p. black, green and grey	1·50	2·00

DESIGNS: No. 2621, At Royal Windsor Horse Show, 1985; 2622, At Heathrow Airport, 2001; 2623, As Young Princess Elizabeth with Duchess of York, 1931; 2624, At State Banquet, Ottawa, 1951; 2625, Queen in 1960; 2626, As Princess Elizabeth, 1940;2627, With Duke of Edinburgh, 1951.

1893 England (1966)

2006. World Cup Football Championship, Germany. World Cup Winners. Multicoloured.

2628	(1st) Type **1893**	1·25	1·00
2629	42p. Italy (1934, 1938, 1982)	1·25	1·10
2630	44p. Argentina (1978, 1986)	1·25	1·25
2631	50p. Germany (1954, 1974, 1990)	2·00	2·00
2632	64p. France (1998)	3·00	3·00
2633	72p. Brazil (1958, 1962, 1970, 1994, 2002)	3·50	3·50

1899 30 St. Mary Axe, London

2006. Modern Architecture. Multicoloured.

2634	(1st) Type **1899**	1·25	1·00
2635	42p. Maggie's Centre, Dundee	1·10	1·10
2636	44p. Selfridges, Birmingham	1·25	1·25
2637	50p. Downland Gridshell, Chichester	2·00	2·00
2638	64p. An Turas, Isle of Tiree	3·00	3·00
2639	72p. The Deep, Hull	3·50	3·50

1905 Sir Winston Churchill (Walter Sickert)

2006. 150th Anniv of National Portrait Gallery, London. Multicoloured.

2640	(1st) Type **1905**	1·25	1·00
2641	(1st) Sir Joshua Reynolds (self-portrait)	1·25	1·00
2642	(1st) T. S. Eliot (Patrick Heron)	1·25	1·00
2643	(1st) Emmeline Pankhurst (Georgina Agnes Brackenbury)	1·25	1·00
2644	(1st) Virginia Woolf (photo by George Charles Beresford)	1·25	1·00
2645	(1st) Bust of Sir Walter Scott (Sir Francis Leggatt Chantry)	1·25	1·00
2646	(1st) Mary Seacole (Albert Charles Challen)	1·25	1·00
2647	(1st) William Shakespeare (attrib to John Taylor)	1·25	1·00
2648	(1st) Dame Cicely Saunders (Catherine Goodman)	1·25	1·00
2649	(1st) Charles Darwin (John Collier)	1·25	1·00

1917 (image scaled to 38% of original size)

2006. 70th Anniv of the Year of Three Kings. Sheet 127×72 mm containing No. Y1728. Multicoloured.

MS2658 **1917** £3 mauve   10·00   10·00

1918 Corporal Agansing Rai

2006. 150th Anniv of the Victoria Cross (1st issue). Multicoloured.

2659	(1st) Type **1918**	1·25	1·10
2660	(1st) Boy Seaman Jack Cornwell	1·25	1·10
2661	64p. Midshipman Charles Lucas	1·25	1·50
2662	64p. Captain Noel Chavasse	1·25	1·50
2663	72p. Captain Albert Ball	2·00	2·25
2664	72p. Captain Charles Upham	2·00	2·25

MS2665 190×67 mm. Nos. 2659/64 and 2666   16·00   16·00

1924 Sitar Player and Dancer

2006. Europa. Integration. Sounds of Britain.

2667	(1st) Type **1924**	1·25	1·00
2668	42p. Reggae bass guitarist and African drummer	1·25	1·25
2669	50p. Fiddler and harpist	1·25	1·50
2670	72p. Sax Player and Blues guitarist	1·75	1·75
2671	£1.19 Maraca player and Salsa dancers	2·50	3·00

The 1st class and 50p. values include the "EUROPA" emblem.

1929 "New Baby" (Alison Carmichael)

2006. "Smiler"s. (2nd series). Occasions. Self-adhesive.

2672	**1929** (1st) yellow	1·40	1·20
2673	- (1st) multicoloured	1·40	1·20
2674	- (1st) vermilion, rosine and yellow	1·40	1·20
2675	- (1st) multicoloured	1·40	1·20
2676	- (1st) multicoloured	1·40	1·20
2677	- (1st) multicoloured	1·40	1·20

DESIGNS: No. 2673, Best Wishes" (Alan Kitching); 2674, "THANK YOU" (Alan Kitching); 2675, Balloons (Ivan Chermayeff); 2676, Firework (Kam Tang); 2677, Champagne, Flowers and Butterflies (Olaf Hajek).

1935 Snowman

2006. Christmas. Multicoloured. (a) Self-adhesive.

2678	(2nd) Type **1935**	1·00	90
2680	(2nd Large) Snowman	1·50	1·25
2679	(1st) Father Christmas	1·25	1·00
2681	(1st Large) Father Christmas	2·00	1·40
2682	72p. Reindeer	3·25	3·25
2683	£1.19 Christmas Tree	6·00	4·50

(b) Ordinary gum.

MS2684 115×102 mm. As Nos. 2678/83   12·00   12·00

1941 (image scaled to 39% of original size)

2006. "Lest We Forget" (1st issue). 90th Anniv of the Battle of the Somme. Sheet 124×71 mm containing new stamp and designs as Nos. EN15, W107, S118 and NI101.

MS2685 **1941** (1st) Poppies on barbed wire stems; 72p.×4 As Nos. EN15, W107, S118 and NI101.   9·00   9·00

1942 "with the beatles"

1948 Beatles Memorabilia (image scaled to 42% of original size)

2007. The Beatles. Album Covers. (a) Self-adhesive.

2686	(1st) Type **1942**	1·25	1·00
2687	(1st) "Sgt Pepper's Lonely Hearts Club Band"	1·25	1·00
2688	64p. "Help!"	1·50	1·50
2689	64p. "Abbey Road"	1·50	1·50
2690	72p. "Revolver"	1·80	1·80
2691	72p. "Let It Be"	1·80	1·80

Nos. 2686/91 commemorate the 50th anniversary of the first meeting of Paul McCartney and John Lennon.

(b) Ordinary gum.

MS2692 115×89 mm. **1948** (1st) Guitar; (1st) Yellow Submarine lunch-box and key-rings; (1st) Record "Love Me Do"; (1st) Beatles badges   5·00   5·00

2007. "Smilers" (3rd series). As No. 2569. Self-adhesive. One elliptical perf hole at each side

2693   (1st) multicoloured   10·00   10·00

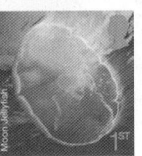

1949 Moon Jellyfish

2007. Sea Life. Multicoloured.

2699	(1st) Type **1949**	1·25	1·00
2700	(1st) Beadlet anemone	1·25	1·00
2701	(1st) Common starfish	1·25	1·00
2702	(1st) Bass	1·25	1·00
2703	(1st) Thornback ray	1·25	1·00
2704	(1st) Lesser octopus	1·25	1·00
2705	(1st) Common mussels	1·25	1·00
2706	(1st) Grey seal	1·25	1·00
2707	(1st) Shore crab	1·25	1·00
2708	(1st) Common sun star	1·25	1·00

1959 Saturn Nebula C55

2007. 50th Anniv of The Sky at Night (TV programme). Nebulae. Multicoloured. Self-adhesive.

2709	(1st) Type **1959**	1·25	90
2710	(1st) Eskimo Nebula C39	1·25	90
2711	50p. Cat's Eye Nebula C6	1·20	1·20
2712	50p. Helix Nebula C63	1·20	1·20
2713	72p. Flaming Star Nebula C31	1·70	1·70
2714	72p. The Spindle C53	1·70	1·70

1965 Iron Bridge (Thomas Telford)

2007. World of Invention (1st series). Multicoloured. Self-adhesive.

2715	(1st) Type **1965**	1·25	90
2716	(1st) Steam locomotive and railway tracks	1·25	90
2717	64p. Map of British Isles and Australia (telephone)	1·25	1·25
2718	64p. Camera and television (John Logie Baird)	1·25	1·25
2719	72p. Globe as web (email and internet)	2·00	2·25
2720	72p. Couple with suitcases on Moon (space travel)	2·00	2·25

2007. World of Invention (2nd series). Multicoloured.

2721	(1st) Type **1965**	1·25	90
2722	(1st) Steam locomotive and railway tracks	1·25	90
2723	64p. Map of British Isles and Australia (telephone)	2·50	2·50
2724	64p. Camera and television (John Logie Baird)	2·50	2·50
2725	72p. Globe as web (email and internet)	4·50	4·50
2726	72p. Couple with suitcases on Moon (space travel)	4·50	4·50

MS2727 115×104 mm. Nos. 2721/6   15·00   15·00

1971 William Wilberforce and Anti-slavery Poster

2007. Bicentenary of the Abolition of the Slave Trade. Multicoloured.

2728	(1st) Type **1971**	1·25	90
2729	(1st) Olaudah Equiano and map of slave trade routes	1·25	90
2730	50p. Granville Sharp and slave ship	1·20	1·20
2731	50p. Thomas Clarkson and diagram of slave ship	1·20	1·20
2732	72p. Hannah More and title page of "The Sorrows of Yamba"	1·80	1·80
2733	72p. Ignatius Sancho and trade/business card	1·80	1·80

1977 Ice Cream Cone

2007. "Beside the Seaside". Multicoloured.

2734	(1st) Type **1977**	1·25	90
2735	46p. Sandcastle	1·10	1·10
2736	48p. Carousel horse	1·30	1·30
2737	54p. Beach huts	1·40	1·40
2738	69p. Deckchairs	1·80	1·80
2739	78p. Beach donkeys	2·00	2·00

1983 (image scaled to 43% of original size)

2007. New Wembley Stadium, London. Sheet 112×113 mm containing design as Type **1593** but with "WORLD CUP 2002" inscription omitted, and Nos. EN6 and EN15, each×2.

MS2740 **1983** (1st) As Type **1593**; (2nd) No. EN6×2; 78p. No. EN15×2   8·00   8·00

The design as Type **1593** omits the "WORLD CUP 2002" inscription at the left of the stamp.

1984 Arnold Machin   **1985** 1967 4d. Machin

1986 (image scaled to 38% of original size)

2007. 40th Anniv of the First Machin Definitives. Sheet 127×73 mm containing new stamps and Nos. Y1725 and Y1725b.

2741	**1984** (1st) multicoloured	4·50	4·50
2742	**1985** (1st) multicoloured	4·50	4·50

MS2743	**1986** Nos. 2741/2, Y1725 and Y1725b	12·00	12·00

1987 Stirling Moss in Vanwall 2.5L, 1957

2007. Grand Prix. Racing Cars. Multicoloured.

2744	(1st) Type **1987**	1·25	90
2745	(1st) Graham Hill in BRM P57, 1962	1·25	90
2746	54p. Jim Clark in Lotus 26 Climax, 1963	1·50	1·50
2747	54p. Jackie Stewart in Tyrrell 006/2, 1973	1·50	1·50
2748	78p. James Hunt in McLaren M23, 1976	2·00	2·00
2749	78p. Nigel Mansell in Williams FW11, 1986	2·00	2·00

Nos. 2744/9 commemorate the 50th anniv of Stirling Moss victory in the British Grand Prix and the centenary of the opening of the Brooklands race track.

1993 Harry Potter and the Philosopher's Stone

2000 Crests of Hogwarts School and its Four Houses (image scaled to 39% of original size)

2007. Publication of Final Book in the Harry Potter Series. (a) Book Covers. Multicoloured.

2750	(1st) Type **1993**	1·25	90
2751	(1st) Harry Potter and the Chamber of Secrets	1·25	90
2752	(1st) Harry Potter and the Prisoner of Azkaban	1·25	90
2753	(1st) Harry Potter and the Goblet of Fire	1·25	90
2754	(1st) Harry Potter and the Order of the Phoenix	1·25	90
2755	(1st) Harry Potter and the Half-Blood Prince	1·25	90
2756	(1st) Harry Potter and the Deathly Hallows	1·25	90

(b) Crests of Hogwarts School and its Four Houses. Multicoloured.

MS2757	123×70 mm. **2000** (1st) Gryffindor; (1st) Hufflepuff; (1st) Hogwarts; (1st) Ravenclaw; (1st) Slytherin	6·00	6·00

2001 Scout and Camp Fire

2007. Europa. Centenary of Scouting and 21st World Scout Jamboree, Chelmsford, Essex. Multicoloured.

2758	(1st) Type **2001**	1·25	90
2759	46p. Scouts rock climbing	1·20	1·20
2760	48p. Scout planting tree	1·20	1·20
2761	54p. Adult volunteer teaching scout archery	1·40	1·40
2762	69p. Scouts learning gliding	1·80	1·80
2763	78p. Scouts from many nations	2·00	2·00

The 1st class and 48p. values include the 'EUROPA' emblem.

2007 White-tailed Eagle

2007. Action for Species

2764	(1st) Type **2007**	1·25	90

2765	(1st) Bearded tit	1·25	90
2766	(1st) Red kite	1·25	90
2767	(1st) Cirl Bunting	1·25	90
2768	(1st) Marsh harrier	1·25	90
2769	(1st) Avocet	1·25	90
2770	(1st) Bittern	1·25	90
2771	(1st) Dartford warbler	1·25	90
2772	(1st) Corncrake	1·25	90
2773	(1st) Peregrine falcon	1·25	90

See also Nos. 2831/40.

2017 NCO, Royal Military Police, 1999

2007. Military Uniforms (1st series). British Army Uniforms.

2774	(1st) Type **2017**	1·25	90
2775	(1st) Tank Commander, 5th Royal Tank Regiment, 1944	1·25	90
2776	(1st) Observer, Royal Field Artillery, 1917	1·25	90
2777	78p. Rifleman, 95th Rifles, 1813	2·00	2·00
2778	78p. Grenadier, Royal Regiment of Foot of Ireland, 1704	2·00	2·00
2779	78p. Trooper, Earl of Oxford's Horse, 1661	2·00	2·00

2023 Leaving St. Paul's Cathedral after Thanksgiving Service, 2006

2029 Photographs of the Royal Family

2007. Diamond Wedding of Queen Elizabeth II and Duke of Edinburgh. (a) Ordinary gum.

2780		**2023** (1st) brown and black	1·25	90
2781	–	(1st) brown and black	1·25	90
2782	–	54p. brown and black	1·40	1·40
2783	–	54p. brown and black	1·40	1·40
2784	–	78p. brown and black	2·00	2·00
2785	–	78p. brown and black	2·00	2·00

DESIGNS: No. 2781 Inspecting King's Troop Royal Horse Artillery, Regents Park, 1997; No. 2782 At Garter Ceremony, Windsor, 1980; No. 2783 At Royal Ascot, 1969; No. 2784 At Premiere of The Guns of Navarone, 1961; No. 2785 At Clydebank.

(b) Self-adhesive.

MS2786	115×89 mm. (1st) Royal family, Balmoral, 1972; (1st) Queen and Prince Philip, Buckingham Palace, 2007; 69p. Royal family, Windsor Castle, 1965; 78p. Princess Elizabeth, Prince Philip, Prince Charles and Princess Anne, Clarence House, 1951	6·00	6·00

2030 Madonna and Child

2007. Christmas (1st issue). Paintings of the Madonna and Child. Self-adhesive.

2787	(2nd) Type **2030**	1·00	80
2788	(1st) The Madonna of Humility (Lippo di Dalmasio), c 1390–1400	1·25	90

2032 Angel playing Trumpet ('PEACE') (William Dyce), c 1827

2007. Christmas (2nd issue). Angels. (a) Self-adhesive.

2789	(2nd) Type **2032**	1·00	80
2791	(2nd Large) Angel playing Trumpet ('PEACE')	1·50	1·00
2790	(1st) Angel playing Lute ('GOODWILL')	1·25	90
2792	(1st Large) Angel playing Lute ('GOODWILL')	2·00	2·00
2793	78p. Angel playing Flute ('JOY')	2·00	2·00
2794	£1.24 Angel playing Tambourine ('GLORY')	3·50	3·50

(b) Ordinary gum.

MS2795	115×102 mm. As Nos. 2789/94	10·00	10·00

2038 (image scaled to 39% of original size)

2007. Lest We Forget

MS2796	(1st) Soldiers in poppy flower; 78p.×4 As Nos. EN16, NI106, S119 and W108	10·00	10·00

2039 Casino Royale

2008. Birth Centenary of Ian Fleming (author of James Bond books). Book Covers. Multicoloured.

2797	(1st) Type **2039**	1·25	90
2798	(1st) Dr. No	1·25	90
2799	54p. Goldfinger	1·40	1·40
2800	54p. Diamonds are Forever	1·40	1·40
2801	78p. For Your Eyes Only	2·00	2·00
2802	78p. From Russia with Love	2·00	2·00
MS2803	189×68 mm. Nos. 2797/802	9·00	9·00

2008. As Nos. MS2206.

2805	(1st) multicoloured	4·25	4·25

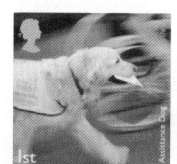

2045 Assistance Dog carrying Letter (Labrador 'Rowan')

2008. Working Dogs. Multicoloured.

2806	(1st) Type **2045**	1·25	90
2807	46p. Mountain rescue dog (Cross-bred 'Merrick')	1·20	1·20
2808	48p. Police dog (German Shepherd 'Max')	1·20	1·20
2809	54p. Customs dog (Springer Spaniel 'Max')	1·40	1·40
2810	69p. Sheepdog (Border Collie 'Bob')	1·80	1·80
2811	78p. Guide dog (Labrador 'Warwick')	2·00	2·00

The 1st value includes the 'EUROPA' emblem.

2051 Henry IV (1399–1413)

2057 The Age of Lancaster and York (image scaled to 39% of original size)

2008. Kings and Queens (1st issue). Houses of Lancaster and York. Multicoloured.

2812	(1st) Type **2051**	1·25	90
2813	(1st) Henry V (1413–1422)	1·25	90
2814	54p. Henry VI (1422–1461 & 1470–1)	1·40	1·40
2815	54p. Edward IV (1461–1470 & 1471–1473)	1·40	1·40
2816	69p. Edward V (1483)	1·80	1·80
2817	69p. Richard III (1483-1485)	1·80	1·80
MS2818	123×70 mm. **2057** (1st) Owain Glyn Dwr ('Parliament'), 1404; (1st) Henry V's triumph at Battle of Agincourt, 1415; 78p. Yorkish victory at Battle of Tewkesbury, 1471; 78p. William Caxton, first English printer, 1477	7·00	7·00

2008. 'Smilers' (4th series). As Nos. 2567/8, 2570 and 2675/7. Self-adhesive. One elliptical perf hole at each side

2819	(1st) multicoloured	2·50	2·50
2820	(1st) multicoloured	2·50	2·50
2821	(1st) multicoloured	2·50	2·50
2822	(1st) multicoloured	2·50	2·50
2823	(1st) multicoloured	2·50	2·50
2824	(1st) multicoloured	2·50	2·50

2058 Lifeboat, Barra

2008. Rescue at Sea. Multicoloured.

2825	(1st) Type **2058**	1·25	90
2826	46p. Lifeboat approaching Dinghy, Appledore	1·20	1·20
2827	48p. Helicopter Winchman, Portland	1·20	1·20
2828	54p. Inshore lifeboat, St Ives	1·40	1·40
2829	69p. Westland Seaking Rescue Helicopter, Lee-on-Solent	1·80	1·80
2830	78p. Launch of Lifeboat, Dinbych-y-Pysgod, Tenby	2·00	2·00

2064 Lysandra bellargus (Adonis blue)

2008. Action for Species. Multicoloured.

2831	(1st) Type **2064**	1·25	90
2832	(1st) Coenagrion mercuriale (southern damselfly)	1·25	90
2833	(1st) Formica rufibarbis (red-barbed ant)	1·25	90
2834	(1st) Pareulype berberata (barberry carpet moth)	1·25	90
2835	(1st) Lucanus cervus (stag beetle)	1·25	90
2836	(1st) Cryptocephalus coryli (hazel pot beetle)	1·25	90
2837	(1st) Gryllus campestris (field cricket)	1·25	90
2838	(1st) Hesperia comma (silver-spotted skipper)	1·25	90
2839	(1st) Pseudepipona herrichii (Purbeck mason wasp)	1·25	90
2840	(1st) Gnorimus nobilis (noble chafer)	1·25	90

2074 Lichfield Cathedral

2080 St. Paul's Cathedral (Illustration reduced. Actual size 115×89 mm) (image scaled to 42% of original size)

2008. Cathedrals. Multicoloured.

2841	(1st) Type **2074**	1·25	90
2842	48p. Belfast Cathedral	1·20	1·20
2843	50p. Gloucester Cathedral	1·30	1·30
2844	56p. St. David's Cathedral	1·40	1·40
2845	72p. Westminster Cathedral	1·80	1·80

2846	81p. St. Magnus Cathedral, Kirkwall, Orkney	2·00	2·00

MS2847 115×89 mm. (1st) mult; (1st) mult; 81p. mult; 81p. mult ... 7·00 7·00

No. **MS**2847 commemorates the 300th anniversary of St. Paul's Cathedral.

2008. Beside the Seaside. Self-adhesive

2848	**1977** (1st) multicoloured	4·50	4·50

2081 Carry on Sergeant

2008. Posters for Carry On and Hammer Horror Films. Multicoloured.

2849	(1st) Type **2081**	1·25	90
2850	48p. Dracula	1·20	1·20
2851	50p. Carry on Cleo	1·30	1·30
2852	56p. The Curse of Frankenstein	1·40	1·40
2853	72p. Carry on Screaming	1·80	1·80
2854	81p. The Mummy	2·00	2·00

Nos. 2849/54 commemorate the 50th anniversary of Dracula and the first Carry On film (Carry on Sergeant).

2087 Red Arrows, Dartmouth Regatta Airshow, 2006

2008. Air Displays. Multicoloured.

2855	(1st) Type **2087**	1·25	90
2856	48p. RAF Falcons Parachute Team, Biggin Hill, 2006	1·20	1·20
2857	50p. Spectator watching Red Arrows, Farnborough, 2006	1·30	1·30
2858	56p. Prototype Avro Vulcan Bombers and Avro 707s, Farnborough, 1953	1·40	1·40
2859	72p. Parachutist Robert Wyndham on Wing of Avro 504, 1933	1·80	1·80
2860	81p. Air Race rounding the Beacon, Hendon, c. 1912	2·00	2·00

2093 Landmarks of Beijing and London (image scaled to 42% of original size)

2008. Handover of Olympic Flag from Beijing to London. Sheet 115×76 mm.. Multicoloured.

MS2861 (1st) National Stadium, Beijing; (1st) London Eye; (1st) Tower of London; (1st) Corner Tower of the Forbidden City, Beijing ... 7·00 7·00

The Olympic rings overprinted on **MS**2861 are in silk-screen varnish.

2094 Drum Major, RAF Central Band, 2007

2008. Military Uniforms (2nd series). RAF Uniforms. Multicoloured.

2862	(1st) Type **2094**	1·25	90
2863	(1st) Helicopter Rescue Winch- man, 1984	1·25	90
2864	(1st) Hawker Hunter Pilot, 1951	1·25	90
2865	81p. Lancaster Air Gunner, 1944	2·00	2·00
2866	81p. WAAF Plotter, 1940	2·00	2·00
2867	81p. Pilot, 1918	2·00	2·00

2100 Millicent Garrett Fawcett (suffragist)

2008. Women of Distinction. Multicoloured.

2870	(1st) Type **2100**	1·25	90
2871	48p. Elizabeth Garrett Anderson (physician – women's health)	1·20	1·20
2872	50p. Marie Stopes (family plan- ning pioneer)	1·30	1·30
2873	56p. Eleanor Rathbone (family allowance campaigner)	1·40	1·40
2874	72p. Claudia Jones (civil rights activist)	1·80	1·80
2875	81p. Barbara Castle (politician – Equal Pay Act)	2·00	2·00

2106 Ugly Sisters from Cinderella

2008. Christmas. Multicoloured. (a) Self-adhesive.

2876	(2nd) Type **2106**	1·00	60
2878	(2nd Large) Ugly Sisters from Cinderella	1·50	1·10
2877	(1st) Genie from Aladdin	1·25	90
2879	(1st Large) Genie from Aladdin	1·30	1·30
2880	50p. Captain Hook from Peter Pan	2·00	1·50
2881	81p. Wicked Queen from Snow White	2·00	2·00

(b) Ordinary gum.

MS2882 114×102 mm. As Nos. 2876/81 ... 8·00 8·00

2112 Poppies on Barbed Wire Stem

2115 (image scaled to 39% of original size)

2008. Lest We Forget. Multicoloured.

2883	(1st) Type **2112**	1·25	90
2884	(1st) Soldiers in poppy flower	1·25	90
2885	(1st) Poppy flower	1·25	90

MS2886 124×70 mm. **2115** No. 2885 and as Nos. EN18, NI107, S120 and W109 ... 10·00 10·00

2116 Supermarine Spitfire (R. J. Mitchell)

2009. British Design Classics (1st series). Multicoloured.

2887	(1st) Type **2116**	1·25	90
2888	(1st) Mini skirt (Mary Quant)	1·25	90
2889	(1st) Mini (Sir Alec Issigonis)	1·25	90
2890	(1st) Anglepoise lamp (George Carwardine)	1·25	90
2891	(1st) Concorde (Aerospatiale- BAC)	1·25	90
2892	(1st) K2 Telephone Kiosk (Sir Giles Gilbert Scott)	1·25	90
2893	(1st) Polypropylene chair (Robin Day)	1·25	90
2894	(1st) Penguin Books (Edward Young)	1·25	90
2895	(1st) London underground map (Harry Beck)	1·25	90
2896	(1st) Routemaster bus (design team led by AAM Durrant)	1·25	90

See also Nos. 2897 and 2911/12.

2126 Charles Darwin

2132 Fauna and Map of the Galapagos Islands (image scaled to 42% of original size)

2009. Birth Bicentenary of Charles Darwin (naturalist and evolutionary theorist) (1st issue). Multicoloured. (a) Self-adhesive.

2898	(1st) Type **2126**	1·25	90
2899	48p. Marine Iguana	1·20	1·20
2900	50p. Finches	1·30	1·30
2901	56p. Atoll	1·40	1·40
2902	72p. Bee Orchid	1·80	1·80
2903	81p. Orang-utan	2·00	2·00

(b) Ordinary gum.

MS2904 115×89 mm. (1st) Flightless cormorant; (1st) Giant tortoise and cactus finch; (1st) Marine iguana; 81p. Floreana mockingbird ... 8·00 8·00

See also Nos. 2905/10.

2009. Birth Bicentenary of Charles Darwin (naturalist) (2nd issue). Multicoloured.

2905	(1st) Type **2126**	4·50	4·50
2906	48p. As No. 2899	5·00	5·00
2907	50p. As No. 2900	5·50	5·50
2908	56p. As No. 2901	6·00	6·00
2909	72p. As No. 2902	6·50	6·50
2910	81p. As No. 2903	7·00	7·00

2009. British Design Classics (3rd series). Designs as Nos. 2892 and 2896. Multicoloured. Self-adhesive.

2911	(1st) K2 Telephone Kiosk (Sir Giles Gilbert Scott)	4·25	4·25
2912	(1st) Routemaster Bus (design team led by AAM Durrant)	4·25	4·25
2913	(1st) Mini (Sir Alex Issigonis)	3·25	2·50
2914	(1st) Concorde (Aerospatiale- BAC)	3·25	2·50
2915	(1st) Mini skirt (Mary Quant)	3·25	2·50
2915b	(1st) Supermarine Spitfire (R. J. Mitchell)	2·50	2·50

2133 Matthew Boulton and Factory (Manufacturing)

2009. Pioneers of the Industrial Revolution. Multicoloured.

2916	(1st) Type **2133**	1·25	90
2917	(1st) James Watt and Boulton & Watt Condensing Engine (steam engineering)	1·25	90
2918	50p. Richard Arkwright and Spinning Machine (textiles)	1·30	1·30
2919	50p. Josiah Wedgwood and Black Basalt Teapot and Vase (ceramics)	1·30	1·30
2920	56p. George Stephenson and Locomotion (railways)	1·40	1·40
2921	56p. Henry Maudslay and Table Engine (machine making)	1·40	1·40
2922	72p. James Brindley and Bridgewater Canal Aqueduct	1·80	1·80
2923	72p. John McAdam (road building)	1·80	1·80

2141 Henry VII (1485–1509)

2147 The Age of the Tudors (image scaled to 39% of original size)

2009. Kings and Queens (2nd issue). The House of Tudor. Multicoloured.

2924	(1st) Type **2141**	1·25	90
2925	(1st) Henry VIII (1509–47)	1·25	90
2926	62p. Edward VI (1547–53)	1·60	1·60
2927	62p. Lady Jane Grey (1553)	1·60	1·60
2928	81p. Mary I (1553–8)	2·10	2·10
2929	81p. Elizabeth I (1558–1603)	2·10	2·10

MS2930 123×70 mm. **2147** (1st) Mary Rose (galleon), 1510; (1st) Field of Cloth of Gold Royal Conference, 1520; 90p. Royal Exchange (centre of commerce), 1565; 90p. Francis Drake (circumnavigation), 1580 ... 7·00 7·00

2148 Allium sphaerocephalon (round-headed leek)

2158 Royal Botanic Gardens, Kew (image scaled to 42% of original size)

2009. 'Action for Species' (3rd series). Plants. Multicolored.

2931	(1st) Type **2148**	1·25	90
2932	(1st) Luronium natans (floating water-plantain)	1·25	90
2933	(1st) Cypripedium calceolus (lady's slipper orchid)	1·25	90
2934	(1st) Polygala amarella (dwarf milkwort)	1·25	90
2935	(1st) Saxifraga hirculus (marsh saxifrage)	1·25	90
2936	(1st) Stachys germanica (downy woundwort)	1·25	90
2937	(1st) Euphorbia serrulata (up- right spurge)	1·25	90
2938	(1st) Pyrus cordata (Plymouth pear)	1·25	90
2939	(1st) Polygonum maritimum (Sea knotgrass)	1·25	90
2940	(1st) Dianthus armeria (Deptford pink)	1·25	90

(b) 250th Anniv of Royal Botanic Gardens, Kew. Multicoloured.

MS2941 115×89 mm. **2158** (1st) Palm House, Kew Gardens; (1st) Millen-nium Seed Bank, Wakehurst Place; 90p. Pagoda, Kew Gardens; 90p. Sackler Crossing, Kew Gardens ... 7·00 7·00

2009. 50th Anniv of NAFAS (National Association of Flower Arrangement Societies). Designs as Nos. 1958 and 1962 (1997 Greeting Stamps 19th-century Flower Paintings). Self-adhesive.

2942	(1st) multicoloured	4·00	4·00
2943	(1st) multicoloured	4·00	4·00

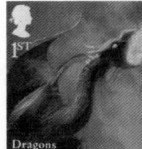

2159 Dragon

2009. Mythical Creatures. Multicoloured.

2944	(1st) Type **2159**	1·25	90
2945	(1st) Unicorn	1·25	90
2946	62p. Giant	1·60	1·60
2947	62p. Pixie	1·60	1·60
2948	90p. Mermaid	2·25	2·25
2949	90p. Fairy	2·25	2·25

2165 George V Type B Wall Letter Box, 1933–6

2169 Post Boxes (Illustration reduced. Actual size 145×74 mm) (image scaled to 33% of original size)

2009. Post Boxes. Multicoloured.

2950	(1st) Type **2165**	1·50	1·50
2951	56p. Edward VII Ludlow Letter Box, 1901–10	2·00	2·00
2952	81p. Victorian Lamp Letter Box, 1896	2·50	2·50
2953	90p. Elizabeth II Type A Wall Letter Box, 1962–3	2·75	2·75
MS2954	As Type **2169** Nos. 2950/3	8·50	8·50

2009. 'Treasures of the Archive' (1st series). As Type **929** (1990 150th anniv of the Penny Black). One elliptical perf hole at each side

2955	**929**	20p. brownish-black and grey-brown	2·75	2·75
2956	**929**	(1st) brownish-black and grey-brown	2·75	2·75

2170 Firefighting

2009. Fire and Rescue Service. Multicoloured.

2958	(1st) Type **2170**	1·25	90
2959	54p. Chemical fire	1·40	1·40
2960	56p. Emergency rescue	1·40	1·40
2961	62p. Flood rescue	1·60	1·60
2962	81p. Search and Rescue	2·00	2·00
2963	90p. Fire safety	2·25	2·25

2176 Flight Deck Officer, 2009

2009. Military Uniforms (3rd series). Royal Navy Uniforms. Multicoloured.

2964	(1st) Type **2176**	1·25	90
2965	(1st) Captain, 1941	1·25	90
2966	(1st) Second Officer WRNS, 1918	1·25	90
2967	90p. Able Seaman, 1880	2·25	2·25
2968	90p. Royal Marine, 1805	2·25	2·25
2969	90p. Admiral, 1795	2·25	2·25

2009. Royal Navy Uniforms. As No. 2209 (Jolly Roger flag from 2001 Submarine Centenary).

2970	(1st) multicoloured	5·00	5·00

2182 Fred Perry 1909–95 (lawn tennis champion)

2009. Eminent Britons. Multicoloured.

2971	(1st) Type **2182**	1·25	90
2972	(1st) Henry Purcell 1659–95 (composer and musician)	1·25	90
2973	(1st) Sir Matt Busby 1909–94 (footballer and football manager)	1·25	90
2974	(1st) William Gladstone 1809–98 (statesman and Prime Minister)	1·25	90
2975	(1st) Mary Wollstonecraft 1759–97 (pioneering feminist)	1·25	90

2976	(1st) Sir Arthur Conan Doyle 1859–1930 (writer and creator of Sherlock Holmes)	1·25	90
2977	(1st) Donald Campbell 1921–67 (water speed record broken 1959)	1·25	90
2978	(1st) Judy Fryd 1909–2000 (campaigner and founder of MENCAP)	1·25	90
2979	(1st) Samuel Johnson 1709–84 (lexicographer, critic and poet)	1·25	90
2980	(1st) Sir Martin Ryle 1918–84 (radio survey of the Universe 1959)	1·25	90

2192 Canoe Slalom

2009. Olympic and Paralympic Games, London (2012) (1st issue). Multicoloured

2981	(1st) Type **2192**	1·25	90
2982	(1st) Paralympic Games Archery	1·25	90
2983	(1st) Athletics: Track	1·25	90
2984	(1st) Diving	1·25	90
2985	(1st) Paralympic Games Boccia	1·25	90
2986	(1st) Judo	1·25	90
2987	(1st) Paralympic Games Dressage	1·25	90
2988	(1st) Badminton	1·25	90
2989	(1st) Weightlifting	1·25	90
2990	(1st) Basketball	1·25	90

2202 Angel playing Lute (William Morris), Church of St. James, Staveley, Kendal, Cumbria

2009. Christmas. Stained Glass Windows. Multicoloured.
(a) Self-adhesive.

2991	(2nd) Type **2202**	1·00	60
2993	(2nd Large) Angel playing Lute (William Morris), Church of St. James, Staveley, Kendal, Cumbria	1·50	1·10
2992	(1st) Madonna and Child (Henry Holiday), Church of Ormesby St. Michael, Great Yarmouth, Norfolk	1·25	85
2994	(1st Large) Madonna and Child (Henry Holiday), Church of Ormesby St. Michael, Ormesby, Great Yarmouth, Norfolk	1·40	1·40
2995	56p. Joseph (Henry Holiday), Parish Church of St. Michael, Minehead, Somerset	2·00	1·25
2996	90p. Wise Man (Sir Edward Burne-Jones), Church of St. Mary the Virgin, Rye, East Sussex	2·25	2·25
2997	£1.35 Shepherd (Henry Holiday), St. Mary's Church, Upavon, Wiltshire	3·50	3·50

(b) Ordinary gum.

MS2998	115×102 mm. As Nos. 2991/7	12·00	11·00

2209 The Division Bell (Pink Floyd)

2010. Classic Album Covers (1st issue). Self-adhesive.

2999	(1st) Type **2209**	1·25	90
3000	(1st) A Rush of Blood to the Head (Coldplay)	1·25	90
3001	(1st) Parklife (Blur)	1·25	90
3002	(1st) Power Corruption and Lies (New Order)	1·25	90
3003	(1st) Let It Bleed (Rolling Stones)	1·25	90
3004	(1st) London Calling (The Clash)	1·25	90
3005	(1st) Tubular Bells (Mike Oldfield)	1·25	90
3006	(1st) IV (Led Zeppelin)	1·25	90
3007	(1st) Screamadelica (Primal Scream)	1·25	90
3008	(1st) The Rise and Fall of Ziggy Stardust and the Spiders from Mars (David Bowie)	1·25	90

The right-hand edges of Nos. 2999/3008 are all cut around to show the vinyl disc protruding from the open edge of the album cover.

2010. Classic Album Covers (2nd issue). Multicoloured.

3009	(1st) As No. 3003	2·40	2·40
3010	(1st) As No. 3006	2·40	2·40
3011	(1st) As No. 3008	2·40	2·40
3012	(1st) As No. 3002	2·40	2·40
3013	(1st) As No. 3007	2·40	2·40
3014	(1st) As No. 2999	2·40	2·40
3015	(1st) As No. 3005	2·40	2·40
3016	(1st) As No. 3004	2·40	2·40
3017	(1st) As No. 3001	2·40	2·40
3018	(1st) As No 3000	2·40	2·40
MS3019	223×189 mm. Nos. 3009/18	30·00	30·00

The right-hand edges of Nos. 3009/18 and the miniature sheet **MS**3019 are all cut around in an imperforate section to show the vinyl disc protruding from the open edge of the album cover.

A miniature sheet containing No. 3014×10 (The Division Bell (Pink Floyd)) was issued on 6 March 2010 and sold for £4.75 per sheet.

2010. Olympic and Paralympic Games, London (2012) (2nd issue). As Nos. 2982 and 2986. Multicoloured. Self-adhesive.

3020	(1st) As No. 2986	4·00	4·00
3021	(1st) As No. 2982	4·00	4·00
3022	(1st) As No. 2983	4·00	4·00
3023	(1st) As No. 2990	4·00	4·00

2219 (image scaled to 39% of original size)

2010. Business and Consumer Smilers. Sheet 124×71 mm. Multicoloured.

MS3024 (1st) Propellor driven airplane (Andrew Davidson); (1st) Vintage sports roadster (Andrew Davidson); (1st) Recreation of crown seal (Neil Oliver); (1st) Steam locomotive (Andrew Davidson); (1st) Birthday cake (Annabel Wright); (1st) Ocean liner (Andrew Davidson); (1st) As Type **2112**; (1st) Birthday present (Annabel Wright); (Europe up to 20 grams) Bird carrying envelope (Lucy Davey); (Worldwide up to 20 grams) 'Hello' in plane vapour trail (Lucy Davey)   15·00   15·00

2220 Girlguiding UK (image scaled to 25% of original size)

2010. Centenary of Girlguiding. Sheet 190×67 mm. Multicoloured.

MS3025 (1st) Rainbows; 56p. Brownies; 81p. Guides; 90p. Senior Section members   8·00   7·00

2221 Sir Robert Boyle (chemistry)

2010. 350th Anniv of the Royal Society.. Multicoloured.

3026	(1st) Type **2221**	1·25	90
3027	(1st) Sir Isaac Newton (optics)	1·25	90
3028	(1st) Benjamin Franklin (electricity)	1·25	90
3029	(1st) Edward Jenner (pioneer of smallpox vaccination)	1·25	90
3030	(1st) Charles Babbage (computing)	1·25	90
3031	(1st) Alfred Russel Wallace (theory of evolution)	1·25	90
3032	(1st) Joseph Lister (antiseptic surgery)	1·25	90
3033	(1st) Ernest Rutherford (atomic structure)	1·25	90
3034	(1st) Dorothy Hodgkin (crystallography)	1·25	90
3035	(1st) Sir Nicholas Shackleton (earth sciences)	1·25	90

2231 'Pixie' (mastiff cross)

2010. 150th Anniv of Battersea Dogs and Cats Home.. Multicoloured.

3036	(1st) Type **2231**	1·25	90
3037	(1st) 'Button'	1·25	90
3038	(1st) 'Herbie' (mongrel)	1·25	90
3039	(1st) 'Mr. Tumnus'	1·25	90
3040	(1st) 'Tafka' (border collie)	1·25	90
3041	(1st) 'Boris' (bulldog cross)	1·25	90
3042	(1st) 'Casey' (lurcher)	1·25	90
3043	(1st) 'Tigger'	1·25	90
3044	(1st) 'Leonard' (Jack Russell cross)	1·25	90
3045	(1st) 'Tia' (terrier cross)	1·25	90

2241 James I (1406–37)

2248 The Age of the Stewarts (image scaled to 39% of original size)

2010. Kings and Queens (3rd series). House of Stewart.. Multicoloured.

3046	(1st) Type **2241**	1·25	90
3047	(1st) James II (1437–60)	1·25	90
3048	(1st) James III (1460–88)	1·25	90
3049	62p. James IV (1488–1513)	1·60	1·60
3050	62p. James V (1513–42)	1·60	1·60
3051	81p. Mary (1542–67)	2·00	2·00
3052	81p. James VI (1567–1625)	2·00	2·00
MS3053	123×70 mm. **2248** (1st) Foundation of the University of St. Andrews, 1413; (1st) Foundation of the College of Surgeons, Edinburgh, 1505; 81p. Foundation of Court of Session, 1532; 81p. John Knox (Reformation, 1559)	6·50	6·50

2249 Humpback Whale (Megaptera novaeangliae)

2010. 'Action for Species' (4th series). Mammals. Multicoloured.

3054	(1st) Type **2249**	1·25	1·00
3055	(1st) Wildcat (Felis silvestris)	1·25	1·00
3056	(1st) Brown Long-eared Bat (Plecotus auritus)	1·25	1·00
3057	(1st) Polecat (Mustela putorius)	1·25	1·00
3058	(1st) Sperm Whale (Physeter macrocephalus)	1·25	1·00
3059	(1st) Water Vole (Arvicola terrestris)	1·25	1·00
3060	(1st) Greater Horseshoe Bat (Rhinolophus ferrumequinum)	1·25	1·00
3061	(1st) Otter (Lutra lutra)	1·25	1·00
3062	(1st) Dormouse (Muscardinus avellanarius)	1·25	1·00
3063	(1st) Hedgehog (Erinaceus europaeus)	1·25	1·00

2260 King George V and Queen Elizabeth II (1st); Two portraits of King George V (£1) (image scaled to 34% of original size)

2010. London 2010 Festival of Stamps and Centenary of Accession of King George V. Sheet 141×74 mm.
MS3065 (1st) rosine; £1 blackish brown, grey-brown and silver   4·50   4·50

A miniature sheet as No. **MS**3065 but inscr 'BUSINESS DESIGN CENTRE, LONDON 8–15 MAY 2010' along the top right margin was only available at London 2010 Festival of Stamps.

2261 King George V and Queen Elizabeth II

2267 (image scaled to 43% of original size)

2010. London 2010 Festival of Stamps and Centenary of Accession of King George V (2nd issue).

3066	2261	(1st) rosine	1·25	1·00
3067	–	(1st) multicoloured	1·25	1·00
3068	–	(1st) multicoloured	1·25	1·00
3069	–	£1 blackish brown, grey-brown and silver	2·50	2·50
3070	–	£1 multicoloured	2·50	2·50
3071	–	£1 multicoloured	2·50	2·50

MS3072 Nos. 3067/8 and 3070/1 (8 May)   7·50   7·50

DESIGNS: Nos. 3067, 1924 British Empire Exhibition 1½d. brown stamp; 3068, 1924 British Empire Exhibition 1d. scarlet stamp; 3069, Two Portraits of King George V; 3070, 1913 £1 Green 'Sea Horses' design stamp; 3071, 1913 10s. Blue 'Sea Horses' design stamp.

No. 3066 was issued as a sheet stamp on 6 May 2010.
Nos. 3066/71 all come from £11.15 stamp booklet, No. DX50, issued on 8 May 2010.
Nos. 3066 and 3069 also come from miniature sheet **MS**3065, issued on 8 May 2010.
Nos. 3067/8 and 3070/1 also come from **MS**3072, issued on 8 May 2010.

2268 (Illustration reduced. Actual size 104×94 mm) (image scaled to 46% of original size)

2010. London 2010 Festival of Stamps. Jeffery Matthews Colour Palette. Sheet, 104×95 mm, containing stamps as T **367** with a label
MS3073 **2268** 1p. reddish purple; 2p. deep grey-green; 5p. reddish-brown; 9p. bright orange; 10p. orange; 20p. light green; 60p. emerald; 67p. bright mauve; 88p. bright magenta; 97p. bluish violet; £1.46 turquoise-blue   11·50   11·50

2269 Winston Churchill

2010. 'Britain Alone' (1st issue). Each pale stone, pale bistre and black.

3074	(1st) Type **2269**		1·25	1·00
3075	(1st) Land girl		1·25	1·00
3076	60p. Home Guard		1·50	1·50
3077	60p. Evacuees		1·50	1·50
3078	67p. Air Raid Wardens		1·70	1·70
3079	67p. Woman working in Factory		1·70	1·70
3080	97p. Royal Broadcast by Princess Elizabeth and Princess Margaret		2·40	2·40
3081	97p. Fire Service		2·40	2·40

2277 Evacuation of British Soldiers from Dunkirk

2281 Evacuation of British Troops from Dunkirk, 1940 (image scaled to 42% of original size)

2010. 'Britain Alone' (2nd issue). Each pale stone, pale bistre and black.

3082	(1st) Type **2277**	2·00	2·00
3083	60p. Vessels from Upper Thames Patrol in 'Operation Little Ships'	3·00	3·00
3084	88p. Rescued soldiers on board Royal Navy destroyer, Dover	4·00	4·00
3085	97p. Steamship and other boat loaded with troops.	4·00	4·00

MS3086 Nos. 3082/5   7·50   7·50

2282 James I (1603–25)

2010. Kings and Queens (4th series). House of Stuart. Multicoloured.

3087		(1st) Type **2282**	1·25	1·00
3088	-	(1st) Charles I (1625–49)	1·25	1·00
3089	-	60p. Charles II (1660–85)	1·50	1·50
3090	-	60p. James II (1685–8)	1·50	1·50
3091	-	67p. William III (1689–1702)	1·70	1·70
3092	-	67p. Mary II (1689–94)	1·70	1·70
3093	-	88p. Anne (1702–14)	2·25	2·25

MS3094 123×70 mm. **2289** (1st) William Harvey (discovery of blood circulation, 1628); 60p. Civil War Battle of Naseby, 1645; 88p. John Milton (*Paradise Lost*, 1667); 97p. Castle Howard (John Vanbrugh, 1712)   7·50   7·50

2010. Mammals. Nos. 3061 and 3063. Self-adhesive

3095	**2256**	(1st) multicoloured	3·25	3·25
3096	**2258**	(1st) multicoloured	3·25	3·25

2290 Paralympic Games: Rowing

2010. Olympic and Paralympic Games, London (2012) (3rd issue). Multicoloured.

3097		(1st) Type **2290**	1·25	1·00
3098	-	(1st) Shooting	1·25	1·00
3099	-	(1st) Modern pentathlon	1·25	1·00
3100	-	(1st) Taekwondo	1·25	1·00
3101	-	(1st) Cycling	1·25	1·00
3102	-	(1st) Paralympic Games: Table Tennis	1·25	1·00
3103	-	(1st) Hockey	1·25	1·00
3104	-	(1st) Football	1·25	1·00
3105	-	(1st) Paralympic Games: Goalball	1·25	1·00
3106	-	(1st) Boxing	1·25	1·00

2010. Olympic and Paralympic Games, London (2012) (4th issue). Self-adhesive

3107	(1st) As No. 3097		3·25	3·25
3108	(1st) As No. 3102		3·25	3·25
3108a	(1st) As No. 3104		3·25	3·25
3108b	(1st) As No. 3101		3·25	3·25

2300 LMS Coronation Class Locomotive, Euston Station, 1938

2010. Great British Railways. Each gold, bluish grey and black.

3109	(1st) Type **2300**	1·25	1·00
3110	(1st) BR Class 9F Locomotive Evening Star, Midsomer Norton, 1962	1·25	1·00
3111	67p. GWR King Class Locomotive *King William IV*, near Teignmouth, 1935	1·70	1·70
3112	67p. LNER Class A1 Locomotive Royal Lancer, 1929	1·70	1·70
3113	97p. SR King Arthur Class Locomotive Sir Mador de la Porte, Bournemouth Central Station, 1935–9	2·50	2·50
3114	97p. LMS NCC Class WT No. 2, Larne Harbour, c. 1947	2·50	2·50

2306 Heart-regulating Beta Blockers (Sir James Black, 1962)

2010. Medical Breakthroughs. Multicoloured.

3115	(1st) Type **2306**	1·25	1·00
3116	58p. Antibiotic Properties of Penicillin (Sir Alexander Fleming, 1928)	1·50	1·50
3117	60p. Total Hip Replacement Operation (Sir John Charnley, 1962)	1·50	1·50
3118	67p. Artificial Lens Implant Surgery (Sir Harold Ridley, 1949)	1·70	1·70
3119	88p. Malaria Parasite transmitted by Mosquitoes (proved by Sir Ronald Ross, 1897)	2·25	2·25
3120	97p. Computed Tomography Scanner (Sir Godfrey Hounsfield, 1971)	2·50	2·50

2312

2010. Europa. Children's Books. *Winnie the Pooh* by A. A. Milne. Book Illustrations by E. H. Shepard. Each yellow-brown, pale stone and black.

3121	(1st) Type **2312**	1·25	1·00
3122	58p. Winnie the Pooh and Piglet (*The House at Pooh Corner*)	1·40	1·40
3123	60p. Winnie the Pooh and Rabbit (*Winnie the Pooh*)	1·50	1·50
3124	67p. Winnie the Pooh and Eeyore (*Winnie the Pooh*)	1·70	1·70
3125	88p. Winnie the Pooh and Friends (*Winnie the Pooh*)	2·25	2·25
3126	97p. Winnie the Pooh and Tigger (*The House at Pooh Corner*)	2·40	2·40

MS3127 115×89 mm. (1st) Winnie the Pooh and Christopher Robin (from *Now we are Six*); 60p. Christopher Robin reads to Winnie the Pooh (from *Winnie the Pooh*); 88p. Winnie the Pooh and Christopher Robin sailing in umbrella (from *Winnie the Pooh*); 97p. Christopher Robin (putting on wellingtons) and Pooh (from *Winnie the Pooh*)   7·50   7·50

2319 Wallace and Gromit Carol singing

2010. Christmas with Wallace and Gromit. Multicoloured.

(a) Self-adhesive

3128	(2nd) Type **2319**		1·00	75
3129	(1st) Gromit posting Christmas Cards		1·25	1·00
3130	(2nd Large) Wallace and Gromit Carol singing		1·50	1·50
3131	60p. Wallace and Gromit decorating Christmas Tree		1·50	1·50
3132	(1st Large) Gromit posting Christmas Cards		2·00	2·00
3133	97p. Gromit carrying Christmas Pudding		2·40	2·40
3134	£1.46 Gromit wearing Oversized Sweater		3·50	3·50

(b) Ordinary gum
MS3135 115×102 mm. Nos. 3128/34   12·00   12·00

2326 Joe 90

2011. 'F.A.B. The Genius of Gerry Anderson' (producer of TV programmes). Multicoloured.

(a) Ordinary gum

3136	(1st) Type **2326**		1·25	1·00
3137	(1st) *Captain Scarlet*		1·25	1·00
3138	(1st) Thunderbird 2 (*Thunderbirds*)		1·25	1·00
3139	97p. *Stingray*		2·40	2·40
3140	97p. *Fireball XL5*		2·40	2·40
3141	97p. *Supercar*		2·40	2·40

(b) Microlenticular Cartor and Outer Aspect Ltd, New Zealand
MS3142 116×89 mm. **2332** 41p., 60p., 88p., 97p. multicoloured   8·00   8·00

(c) Self-adhesive

3143	(1st) multicoloured	2·00	2·00

2333 (image scaled to 27% of original size)

2011. Classic Locomotives (1st series). Multicoloured.
MS3144 **2333** (1st) BR Dean Goods No. 2532; 60p. Peckett R2 *Thor*; 88p. Lancashire and Yorkshire Railway 1093 No. 1100; 97p. BR WD No. 90662   7·50   7·50

2334 Oliver

2011. Musicals. Multicoloured.

3145	(1st) Type **2334**	1·25	1·00
3146	(1st) *Blood Brothers*	1·25	1·00
3147	(1st) *We Will Rock You*	1·25	1·00
3148	(1st) *Spamalot*	1·25	1·00
3149	97p. *Rocky Horror Show*	2·40	2·40
3150	97p. *Me and My Girl*	2·40	2·40
3151	97p. *Return to the Forbidden Planet*	2·40	2·40
3152	97p. *Billy Elliot*	2·40	2·40

2011. 50th Anniv of the British Heart Foundation. Self-adhesive

3153	**2306**	(1st) multicoloured	3·00	3·00

2342 Rincewind (Terry Pratchett's Discworld)

2011. Magical Realms. Multicoloured.

3154	(1st) Type **2342**	1·25	1·00
3155	(1st) Nanny Ogg (Terry Pratchett's Discworld)	1·25	1·00
3156	(1st) Michael Gambon as Dumbledore (J. K. Rowling's Harry Potter)	1·25	1·00
3157	(1st) Ralph Fiennes as Lord Voldemort (J. K. Rowling's Harry Potter)	1·25	1·00
3158	60p. Merlin (Arthurian Legend)	1·50	1·50
3159	60p. Morgan Le Fay (Arthurian Legend)	1·50	1·50
3160	97p. Aslan (C. S. Lewis's Narnia)	2·40	2·40
3161	97p. Tilda Swinton as The White Witch (C. S. Lewis's Narnia)	2·40	2·40

2350 African Elephant

2360 Wildlife of the Amazon Rainforest (image scaled to 42% of original size)

2011. 50th Anniv of the WWF. Multicoloured.

3162	(1st) Type **2350**	1·25	1·00
3163	(1st) Mountain Gorilla	1·25	1·00
3164	(1st) Siberian Tiger	1·25	1·00
3165	(1st) Polar Bear	1·25	1·00
3166	(1st) Amur Leopard	1·25	1·00
3167	(1st) Iberian Lynx	1·25	1·00
3168	(1st) Red Panda	1·25	1·00
3169	(1st) Black Rhinoceros	1·25	1·00
3170	(1st) African Wild Dog	1·25	1·00
3171	(1st) Golden Lion Tamarin	1·25	1·00

MS3172 115×89 mm. **2360** (1st) Spider monkey; 60p. Hyacinth macaw; 88p. Poison dart frog; 97p. Jaguar   7·50   7·50

2361 David Tennant as *Hamlet*, 2008

2367 The Four Theatres of the Royal Shakespeare Company, Stratford-upon-Avon (Illustration reduced. Actual size 116×89 mm) (image scaled to 42% of original size)

2011. 50th Anniv of the Royal Shakespeare Company. Multicoloured.

3173	(1st) Type **2361**	1·25	1·00
3174	66p. Antony Sher as Prospero, *The Tempest*, 2009	1·70	1·70
3175	68p. Chuk Iwuji as *Henry VI*, 2006	1·70	1·70
3176	76p. Paul Schofield as *King Lear*, 1962	1·90	1·90
3177	£1 Sara Kestelman as Titania, *A Midsummer Night's Dream*, 1970	2·50	2·50
3178	£1.10 Ian McKellen and Francesca Annis as *Romeo and Juliet*, 1976	2·75	2·75

MS3179 115×89 mm. **2367** (1st) Janet Suzman as Ophelia, *Hamlet*, 1965, Royal Shakespeare Theatre; 68p. Patrick Stewart in *Antony and Cleopatra*, 2006, Swan Theatre; 76p. Geoffrey Streatfeild in *Henry V*, 2007, The Courtyard Theatre; £1 Judy Dench as Lady Macbeth, 1976, The Other Place   7·50   7·50

2368 Prince William and Miss Catherine Middleton (Illustration reduced. Actual size 116×89 mm) (image scaled to 42% of original size)

2011. Royal Wedding. Official Engagement Portraits by Mario Testino. Sheet 115×89 mm. Multicoloured.

MS3180 **2368** (1st)×2 Prince William and Miss Catherine Middleton embracing; £1.10×2 Formal portrait of Prince William and Miss Catherine Middleton in Council Chamber, St. James's Palace   8·50   8·50

2369 Cray (fabric print by William Morris), 1884

2011. 150th Anniv of Morris and Company (designers and manufacturers of textiles, wallpaper and furniture) (1st issue). Multicoloured.

3181	(1st) Type **2369**	1·25	1·00
3182	(1st) Cherries (detail from panel by Philip Webb), 1867	1·25	1·00
3183	76p. Seaweed (wallpaper pattern by John Henry Dearle), 1901	1·90	1·90
3184	76p. Peony (ceramic tile design by Kate Faulkner), 1877	1·90	1·90
3185	£1.10 Acanthus (tile by William Morris and William De Morgan), 1876	2·75	2·75
3186	£1.10 The Merchant's Daughter (detail of stained glass window by Edward Burne-Jones), 1864	2·75	2·75

2011. 150th Anniv of Morris and Company (2nd issue)

3186a	**2202** (2nd) multicoloured	3·00	3·00

2375 Thomas the Tank Engine

2381 Book Illustrations by John T. Kenny (76p.) or C. Reginald Dalby (others) (Illustration reduced. Actual size 116×89 mm) (image scaled to 42% of original size)

2011. Thomas the Tank Engine. Multicoloured.

(a) Ordinary gum

3187	(1st) Type **2375**	1·25	1·00
3188	66p. James the Red Engine	1·70	1·70
3189	68p. Percy the Small Engine	1·70	1·70
3190	76p. Daisy (diesel railcar)	1·90	1·90
3191	£1 Toby the Tram Engine	2·50	2·50
3192	£1.10 Gordon the Big Engine	2·75	2·75

MS3193 115×89 mm. **2381** (1st) "Goodbye, Bertie," called Thomas (from *Tank Engine Thomas Again*); 68p. James was more dirty than hurt (from *Toby the Tram Engine*); 76p. "Yes, Sir," Percy shivered miserably (from *The Eight Famous Engines*); £1 They told Henry, "We shall leave you there for always" (from *The Three Railway Engines*)   7·50   7·50

(b) Self-adhesive

3194	(1st) "Goodbye, Bertie," called Thomas (from *Tank Engine Thomas Again*)	3·00	3·00

Nos. 3187/92 show scenes from TV series *Thomas and Friends*, and Nos. **MS**3193/4 book illustrations from The Railway Series.

2383 Paralympic Games: Sailing

2011. Olympic and Paralympic Games, London (2012) (5th issue). Multicoloured.

3195	(1st) Type **2383**	1·25	1·00
3196	(1st) Athletics: Field	1·25	1·00
3197	(1st) Volleyball	1·25	1·00
3198	(1st) Wheelchair Rugby	1·25	1·00
3199	(1st) Wrestling	1·25	1·00
3200	(1st) Wheelchair Tennis	1·25	1·00
3201	(1st) Fencing	1·25	1·00
3202	(1st) Gymnastics	1·25	1·00
3203	(1st) Triathlon	1·25	1·00
3204	(1st) Handball	1·25	1·00

MS3204a 210×300 mm. Nos. 2981/90, 3097/106 and 3195/204   38·00   14·00

2011. Olympic and Paralympic Games (2012) (6th issue). Multicoloured.

3205	(1st) As No. 3198	3·25	3·25
3206	(1st) As No. 3195	3·25	3·25
3206a	(1st) As No. 3202	3·25	3·25
3206b	(1st) As No. 3201	3·25	3·25

2393 The Sovereign's Sceptre with Cross

2011. Crown Jewels. Multicoloured.

3207	(1st) Type **2393**	1·25	1·00
3208	(1st) St. Edward's Crown	1·25	1·00
3209	68p. Rod and Sceptre with Doves	1·70	1·70
3210	68p. Queen Mary's Crown	1·70	1·70
3211	76p. The Sovereign's Orb	1·90	1·90
3212	76p. Jewelled Sword of Offering	1·90	1·90
3213	£1.10 Imperial State Crown	2·75	2·75
3214	£1.10 Coronation Spoon	2·75	2·75

2401 BR Dean Goods No. 2532

2011. Classic Locomotives of England. Booklet stamp. Design as 1st class stamp within **MS**3144.

3215	**2401** (1st) black and gold	3·00	3·00

2402 Pilot Gustav Hamel receiving Mailbag

2406 First United Kingdom Aerial Post, 9 September 1911 (Illustration reduced. Actual size 146×74 mm) (image scaled to 33% of original size)

2011. Centenary of First United Kingdom Aerial Post (1st issue). Multicoloured.

3216	(1st) Type **2402**	1·25	1·10
3217	68p. Gustav Hamel in Cockpit	1·70	1·70
3218	£1 Pilot Clement Greswell and Blériot Monoplane	2·50	2·50
3219	£1.10 Delivery of First Airmail to Postmaster General st Windsor	2·75	2·75

MS3220 146×74 mm. **2406** Nos. 3216/19   7·50   7·50

2407 Windsor Castle

2011. Centenary of First United Kingdom Aerial Post (2nd issue)

3221	**2407** 50p. black on cream	4·00	4·00

2408 (Illustration reduced. Actual size 124×71 mm) (image scaled to 39% of original size)

2011. Birth Centenary of Arnold Machin

MS3222	**2408** (1st) gold×10	11·00	11·00

2409 George I (1714-27)

2415 The Age of the Hanoverians (Illustration reduced. Actual size 123×70 mm) (image scaled to 39% of original size)

2011. Kings and Queens (5th issue). House of Hanover. Multicoloured.

3223	(1st) Type **2409**	1·25	1·10
3224	(1st) George II (1727-60)	1·25	1·10
3225	76p. George III (1760-1820)	1·90	1·90
3226	76p. George IV (1820-30)	1·90	1·90
3227	£1.10 William IV (1830-7)	2·75	2·75
3228	£1.10 Victoria (1837-1901)	2·75	2·75

MS3229 123×70 mm. **2415** (1st) Robert Walpole (first Prime Minister), 1721; 68p. Ceiling by Robert Adam, Kedleston Hall, 1763; 76p. Penny Black (uniform postage), 1840; £1 Queen Victoria (Diamond Jubilee), 1897   7·50   7·50

2416 Angel of the North

2011. UK A-Z (1st series). Multicoloured.

3230	(1st) Type **2416**	1·25	1·00
3231	(1st) Blackpool Tower	1·25	1·00
3232	(1st) Carrick-a-Rede, Co. Antrim	1·25	1·00
3233	(1st) Downing Street	1·25	1·00
3234	(1st) Edinburgh Castle	1·25	1·00
3235	(1st) Forth Railway Bridge	1·25	1·00
3236	(1st) Glastonbury Tor	1·25	1·00
3237	(1st) Harlech Castle	1·25	1·00
3238	(1st) Ironbridge	1·25	1·00
3239	(1st) Jodrell Bank	1·25	1·00
3240	(1st) Kursaal, Southend, Essex	1·25	1·00
3241	(1st) Lindisfarne Priory	1·25	1·00

2428 Joseph visited by the Angel (Matthew 1:21)

2011. Christmas. 400th Anniv of the King James Bible. Multicoloured.

(a) Self-adhesive

3242	(2nd) Type **2428**	1·00	75
3243	(1st) Madonna and Child (Matthew 1:23)	1·25	1·00
3244	(2nd Large) Joseph visited by the Angel (Matthew 1:21)	1·50	1·25
3245	(1st Large) Madonna and Child (Matthew 1:23)	2·00	1·50
3246	68p. Baby Jesus in the Manger (Luke 2:7)	1·70	1·70
3247	£1.10 Shepherds visited by the Angel (Luke 2:10)	2·75	2·75
3248	£1.65 Wise Men and Star (Matthew 2:10)	4·00	4·00

(b) Ordinary gum

MS3249	116×102 mm. As Nos. 3242/8	13·00	13·00

2435 Paralympic Games Emblem **2436** Olympic Games Emblem

2012. Olympic and Paralympic Games (7th issue). Self-adhesive

3250	**2435**	(1st) Type **2435**	1·75	1·25
3251	**2436**	(1st) Type **2436**	1·75	1·25
3252	**2435**	(Worldwide up to 20g) As Type **2435**	3·75	3·75
3253	**2436**	(Worldwide up to 20g) As Type **2436**	3·75	3·75

2437 Charlie and the Chocolate Factory

2012. Roald Dahl's Children's Stories (1st issue). Book Illustrations by Quentin Blake. Multicoloured.

3254	(1st) Type **2437**	1·25	1·00
3255	66p. Fantastic Mr. Fox	1·70	1·70
3256	68p. James and the Giant Peach	1·70	1·70
3257	76p. Matilda	1·90	1·90
3258	£1 The Twits	2·50	2·50
3259	£1.10 The Witches	2·75	2·75

2443 The BFG carrying Sophie in his Hand

2447 Roald Dahl's The BFG (Illustration reduced. Actual size 114×89 mm) (image scaled to 42% of original size)

2012. Roald Dahl's Children's Stories (2nd issue). Book Illustrations by Quentin Blake. Multicoloured.

3260	(1st) Type **2443**	1·25	1·25
3261	68p. The BFG wakes up the Giants	1·70	1·70
3262	76p. Sophie sat on Buckingham Palace Window-sill	1·90	1·90
3263	£1 The BFG and Sophie at Writing Desk	2·50	2·50
MS3264	115×89 mm. **2447** Nos. 3260/3	6·75	6·75

2448 Edward VII (1901-10)

2453 The Age of the Windsors (Illustration reduced. Actual size 123×70 mm) (image scaled to 39% of original size)

2012. Kings and Queens (6th issue). House of Windsor. Multicoloured.

3265	(1st) Type **2448**	1·25	1·00
3266	68p. George V (1910-36)	1·70	1·70
3267	76p. Edward VIII (1936)	1·90	1·90
3268	£1 George VI (1936-52)	2·50	2·50
3269	£1.10 Elizabeth II (1952-)	2·75	2·75
MS3270	123×70 mm. **2453** (1st) Scott Expedition to South Pole, 1912; 68p. Queen Elizabeth the Queen Mother and King George VI in bomb damaged street, c. 1940; 76p. England's winning World Cup football team, 1966; £1 Channel Tunnel, 1996	7·50	7·50

2454 Diamond Jubilee (image scaled to 33% of original size)

2012. Diamond Jubilee (2nd issue). Multicoloured.

MS3272	146×74 mm. **2454** (1st)×6 Portrait from photograph by Dorothy Wilding; 1960 £1 Banknote portrait by Robert Austin; 1971 £5 Banknote portrait by Harry Eccleston; 1953 Coinage portrait by Mary Gillick; 1971 decimal coin portrait by Arnold Machin; As No. U3271	9·00	9·00

The 1st class slate-blue machin stamp from **MS3272** has an iridescent overprint reading "DIAMOND JUBILEE"

2455 Coventry Cathedral, 1962 (Sir Basil Spence, architect)

2012. Britons of Distinction. Multicoloured.

3273	(1st) Type **2455**	1·25	1·10
3274	(1st) Frederick Delius (1862-1934, composer)	1·25	1·10
3275	(1st) Orange Tree Embroidery (Mary 'May' Morris 1862-1938, designer and textile artist)	1·25	1·10
3276	(1st) Odette Hallowes (1912-95, SOE agent in occupied France)	1·25	1·10
3277	(1st) Steam Engine, 1712 (Thomas Newcomen, inventor of atmospheric steam engine)	1·25	1·10
3278	(1st) Kathleen Ferrier (1912-53, contralto)	1·25	1·10
3279	(1st) Interior of Palace of Westminster (Augustus Pugin 1812-52, Gothic revival architect and designer)	1·25	1·10
3280	(1st) Montagu Rhodes James (1862-1936 scholar and author)	1·25	1·10
3281	(1st) Bombe Code Breaking Machine (Alan Turing 1912-54, mathematician and World War II code breaker)	1·25	1·10
3282	(1st) Joan Mary Fry (1862-1955 relief worker and social reformer)	1·25	1·10

2465 (Illustration reduced. Actual size 180×74 mm) (image scaled to 27% of original size)

2012. Classic Locomotives (2nd series). Scotland. Sheet 180×74 mm. Multicoloured.

MS3283	**2465** (1st) BR Class D34 Nos. 62471 Glen Falloch and 62496 Glen Loy at Ardlui, 9 May 1959; 68p. BR Class D40 No. 62276 Andrew Bain at Macduff, July 1950; £1 Andrew Barclay No. 807 Bon Accord propelling wagons along Miller Street, Aberdeen, June 1962; £1.10 BR Class 4P No. 54767 Clan Mackinnon pulling fish train, Kyle of Lochalsh, October 1948	8·00	8·00

2466 The Dandy and Desperate Dan

2012. Comics. Multicoloured.

3284	(1st) Type **2466**	1·25	1·10
3285	(1st) The Beano and Dennis the Menace	1·25	1·10
3286	(1st) Eagle and Dan Dare	1·25	1·10
3287	(1st) The Topper and Beryl the Peril	1·25	1·10
3288	(1st) Tiger and Roy of the Rovers	1·25	1·10
3289	(1st) Bunty and the Four Marys	1·25	1·10
3290	(1st) Buster and Cartoon Character Buster	1·25	1·10
3291	(1st) Valiant and the Steel Claw	1·25	1·10
3292	(1st) Twinkle and Nurse Nancy	1·25	1·10
3293	(1st) 2000 AD and Judge Dredd	1·25	1·10

2476 Manchester Town Hall

2012. UK A-Z (2nd series). Multicoloured.

3294	(1st) Type **2476**	1·25	1·10
3295	(1st) Narrow Water Castle, Co. Down	1·25	1·10
3296	(1st) Old Bailey, London	1·25	1·10
3297	(1st) Portmeirion, Wales	1·25	1·10
3298	(1st) The Queen's College, Oxford	1·25	1·10
3299	(1st) Roman Baths, Bath	1·25	1·10
3300	(1st) Stirling Castle, Scotland	1·25	1·10
3301	(1st) Tyne Bridge, Newcastle	1·25	1·10
3302	(1st) Urquhart Castle, Scotland	1·25	1·10
3303	(1st) Victoria and Albert Museum, London	1·25	1·10
3304	(1st) White Cliffs of Dover	1·25	1·10
3305	(1st) Station X, Bletchley Park, Buckinghamshire	1·25	1·10
3306	(1st) York Minster	1·25	1·10
3307	(1st) London Zoo	1·25	1·10
MS3308	297×210 mm. Nos. 3230/41 and 3294/307	40·00	40·00

2490 Skirt Suit by Hardy Amies, late 1940s

2012. Great British Fashion. Multicoloured.

3309	(1st) Type **2490**	1·25	1·25
3310	(1st) Outfit by Norman Hartnell, 1950s	1·25	1·25
3311	(1st) Jacket designed by John Pearce for Granny Takes a Trip Boutique, 1960s	1·25	1·25
3312	(1st) Print by Celia Birtwell for Outfit by Ossie Clark, late 1960s	1·25	1·25
3313	(1st) Suit designed for Ringo Starr by Tommy Nutter	1·25	1·25
3314	(1st) Outfit by Jean Muir, late 1970s/early 1980s	1·25	1·25
3315	(1st) 'Royal' Dress by Zandra Rhodes, 1981	1·25	1·25
3316	(1st) Harlequin dress by Vivienne Westwood, 1993	1·25	1·25
3317	(1st) Suit by Paul Smith, 2003	1·25	1·25
3318	(1st) 'Black Raven' by Alexander McQueen, 2009	1·25	1·25

2500 Queen Elizabeth II at Golden Jubilee Thanksgiving Service, St. Paul's Cathedral, London, 2002

2012. Diamond Jubilee (3rd issue). Multicoloured.

(a) Sheet stamps. Ordinary gum. Photo

A3319	(1st) Type **2500**	1·25	1·10
A3320	(1st) Queen Elizabeth II Trooping the Colour, 1967	1·25	1·10
A3321	77p. Queen Elizabeth II inspecting 2nd Battalion Royal Welsh, Tidworth, 1 March 2007	1·90	1·90
A3322	77p. First Christmas Television Broadcast, 1957	1·90	1·90
A3323	87p. Silver Jubilee Walkabout, 1977	2·25	2·25
A3324	87p. Queen Elizabeth II in Garter Ceremony Procession, 1997	2·25	2·25
A3325	£1.28 Queen Elizabeth II addressing the UN General Assembly, 1957	3·25	3·25
A3326	£1.28 Queen Elizabeth II at Commonwealth Games, Brisbane, Australia, 1982	3·25	3·25

(c) Self-adhesive booklet stamp. Photo

3327	(1st) As Type **2500**	3·00	3·00

2012. Diamond Jubilee (4th issue). As Nos. U3272/4 (3328) or as Type 159 but redrawn with 1st value indicator

3329	(1st) light brown	2·25	2·25

2508 Mr. Bumble (Oliver Twist)

2514 Scenes from Nicholas Nickleby, Bleak House, Little Dorrit and A Tale of Two Cities (image scaled to 28% of original size)

2012. Birth Bicentenary of Charles Dickens. Illustrations from Character Sketches from Charles Dickens, c. 1890 by Joseph Clayton Clarke ('Kyd') (3330/5) or Book Illustrations by Hablot Knight Browne ('Phiz') (MS3336). Multicoloured.

3330	(1st) As Type **2508**	1·00	1·00
3331	(1st) Mr. Pickwick (The Pickwick Papers)	1·25	1·10
3332	77p. The Marchioness (The Old Curiosity Shop)	1·90	1·90
3333	87p. Mrs. Gamp (Martin Chuzzlewit)	2·25	2·25
3334	£1.28 Captain Cuttle (Dombey and Son)	3·25	3·25
3335	£1.90 Mr. Micawber (David Copperfield)	4·75	4·75
MS3336	190×67 mm. **2514** (1st)×4 Nicholas Nickleby caning headmaster Wackford Squeers (Nicholas Nickleby); Mrs. Bagnet is charmed with Mr. Bucket (Bleak House); Amy Dorrit introduces Maggy to Arthur Clennam (Little Dorrit); Charles Darnay arrested by French revolutionaries (A Tale of Two Cities)	6·00	6·00

2012. Olympic and Paralympic Games (8th issue). Designs as Nos. 3250/3 but ordinary gum

3337	**2436**	(1st) black and orange-red	3·00	3·00
3338	**2435**	(1st) black and orange-red	3·00	3·00
3339	**2436**	(-) black, bright scarlet and greenish blue	5·00	5·00
3340	**2435**	(-) black, bright scarlet and greenish blue	5·00	5·00

2515 Sports and London Landmarks (image scaled to 25% of original size)

2012. Welcome to London, Olympic Games. Sheet 192×75 mm. Multicoloured.
MS3341 **2515** (1st) Fencer and Tower Bridge; (1st) Athletes in race and Olympic Stadium; £1.28 Diver and Tate Modern; £1.28 Cyclist and London Eye   9·50   9·50

2516 Helen Glover and Heather Stanning (rowing, women's pairs)

2012. British Gold Medal Winners at London Olympic Games. Multicoloured.
3342	(1st) Type **2516**	1·50	1·50
3343	(1st) Bradley Wiggins (cycling: road, men's time trial)	1·50	1·50
3344	(1st) Tim Baillie and Etienne Stott (canoe slalom: men's canoe double (C2)	1·50	1·50
3345	(1st) Peter Wilson (shooting: shotgun men's double trap)	1·50	1·50
3346	(1st) Philip Hindes, Chris Hoy and Jason Kenny (cycling: track men's team sprint)	1·50	1·50
3347	(1st) Katherine Grainger and Anna Watkins (rowing women's double sculls)	1·50	1·50
3348	(1st) Steven Burke, Ed Clancy, Peter Kennaugh and Geraint Thomas (cycling: track men's team pursuit)	1·50	1·50
3349	(1st) Victoria Pendleton (cycling: track women's keirin)	1·50	1·50
3350	(1st) Alex Gregory, Tom James, Pete Reed and Andrew Triggs Hodge (rowing men's fours)	1·50	1·50
3351	(1st) Katherine Copeland and Sophie Hosking (rowing: lightweight women's double sculls)	1·50	1·50
3352	(1st) Dani King, Joanna Rowsell and Laura Trott (cycling: track women's team pursuit)	4·00	4·00
3353	(1st) Jessica Ennis (athletics: combined women's heptathlon)	4·00	4·00
3354	(1st) Greg Rutherford (athletics: field men's long jump)	1·50	1·50
3355	(1st) Mo Farah (athletics: track men's 10,000m)	1·50	1·50
3356	(1st) Ben Ainslie (sailing: Finn men's heavyweight dinghy)	1·50	1·50
3357	(1st) Andy Murray (tennis men's singles)	1·50	1·50
3358	(1st) Scott Brash, Peter Charles, Ben Maher and Nick Skelton (equestrian: jumping team)	1·50	1·50
3359	(1st) Jason Kenny (cycling: track men's sprint)	1·50	1·50
3360	(1st) Alistair Brownlee (men's triathlon)	1·50	1·50
3361	(1st) Laura Bechtolsheimer, Charlotte Dujardin and Carl Hester (equestrian: dressage team)	1·50	1·50
3362	(1st) Laura Trott (cycling: track women's omnium)	1·50	1·50
3363	(1st) Chris Hoy (cycling: track men's keirin)	1·50	1·50
3364	(1st) Charlotte Dujardin (equestrian: dressage individual)	1·50	1·50
3365	(1st) Nicola Adams (boxing women's fly weight)	1·50	1·50
3366	(1st) Jade Jones (taekwondo women's under 57kg)	1·50	1·50
3367	(1st) Ed McKeever (canoe sprint: men's kayak single (K1) 200m)	1·50	1·50
3368	(1st) Mo Farah (athletics: track men's 5000m)	1·50	1·50
3369	(1st) Luke Campbell (boxing men's bantam weight)	1·50	1·50
3370	(1st) Anthony Joshua (boxing men's super heavy weight)	1·50	1·50

2545 Paralympic Sports and London Landmarks (image scaled to 25% of original size)

2012. Welcome to London, Paralympic Games. Sheet 193×75 mm. Multicoloured.
MS3371 **2545** (1st) Athlete wearing running blades and Olympic Stadium; (1st) Wheelchair basketball player and Palace of Westminster; £1.28 Powerlifter, Millennium Bridge and St. Paul's Cathedral; £1.28 Cyclist and London Eye   9·50   9·50

2546 Sarah Storey (cycling: track women's C5 pursuit)

2012. British Gold Medal Winners at London Paralympic Games. Multicoloured.
3372	(1st) Type **2546**	2·00	2·00
3373	(1st) Jonathan Fox (swimming: men's 100m backstroke, S7)	2·00	2·00
3374	(1st) Mark Colbourne (cycling: track men's C1 pursuit)	2·00	2·00
3375	(1st) Hannah Cockroft (athletics: track women's 100m, T34)	2·00	2·00
3376	(1st) Neil Fachie and Barney Storey (cycling: men's B 1km time trial)	2·00	2·00
3377	(1st) Richard Whitehead (athletics: track men's 200m, T42)	2·00	2·00
3378	(1st) Natasha Baker (equestrian: individual championship test, grade II)	2·00	2·00
3379	(1st) Sarah Storey (cycling: track – women's C4-5 500m time trial)	2·00	2·00
3380	(1st) Ellie Simmonds (swimming: women's 400m freestyle, S6)	2·00	2·00
3381	(1st) Pamela Relph, Naomi Riches, James Roe, David Smith and Lily van den Broecke (rowing: mixed coxed four, LTAmix4+)	2·00	2·00
3382	(1st) Aled Davies (athletics: field men's discus, F42)	2·00	2·00
3383	(1st) Anthony Kappes and Craig MacLean (cycling: track men's B sprint)	2·00	2·00
3384	(1st) Jessica-Jane Applegate (swimming: women's 200m freestyle, S14)	2·00	2·00
3385	(1st) Sophie Christiansen (equestrian: individual championship test, grade 1a)	2·00	2·00
3386	(1st) David Weir (athletics: track men's 5000m, T54)	2·00	2·00
3387	(1st) Natasha Baker (equestrian: individual freestyle test, grade II)	2·00	2·00
3388	(1st) Ellie Simmonds (swimming: women's 200m individual medley, SM6)	2·00	2·00
3389	(1st) Mickey Bushell (athletics: track men's 100m, T53)	2·00	2·00
3390	(1st) Danielle Brown (archery: women's individual compound, open)	2·00	2·00
3391	(1st) Heather Frederiksen (swimming: women's 100m backstroke, S8)	2·00	2·00
3392	(1st) Sophie Christiansen (equestrian: individual freestyle test, grade 1a)	2·00	2·00
3393	(1st) David Weir (athletics: track men's 1500m, T54)	2·00	2·00
3394	(1st) Sarah Storey (cycling: road women's C5 time trial)	2·00	2·00
3395	(1st) Ollie Hynd (swimming: men's 200m individual medley, SM8)	2·00	2·00
3396	(1st) Sophie Christiansen, Deb Criddle, Lee Pearson and Sophie Wells (equestrian team, open)	2·00	2·00
3397	(1st) Helena Lucas (sailing: single-person keelboat, 2.4mR)	2·00	2·00
3398	(1st) Sarah Storey (cycling: road women's C4-5 road race)	2·00	2·00
3399	(1st) Josef Craig (swimming: men's 400m freestyle, S7)	2·00	2·00
3400	(1st) Hannah Cockroft (athletics: track women's 200m, T34)	2·00	2·00
3401	(1st) David Weir (athletics: track men's 800m, T54)	2·00	2·00
3402	(1st) Jonnie Peacock (athletics: track men's 100m, T44)	2·00	2·00
3403	(1st) Josie Pearson (athletics: field women's discus, F51/52/53)	2·00	2·00
3404	(1st) David Stone (cycling: road mixed T1-2 road race)	2·00	2·00
3405	(1st) David Weir (athletics: road men's marathon, T54)	2·00	2·00

2580 Scenes from Olympic and Paralympic Games (image scaled to 25% of original size)

2012. Memories of London 2012 Olympic and Paralympic Games. Sheet 192×75 mm. Multicoloured.
MS3406 (1st) Procession of athletes, Paralympic Games; (1st) Games makers and Olympic Stadium; £1.28 Opening ceremony of Paralympic Games; £1.28 Olympic Games closing ceremony and handover to Rio   9·50   9·50

2581 BR Class D34 Nos. 62471 *Glen Falloch* and 62496 *Glen Loy* at Ardlui, 9 May 1959

2012. Classic Locomotives of Scotland. Booklet stamp. Design as 1st class stamp within MS3283. Multicoloured.
3407	**2581** (1st) multicoloured	2·50	2·50

2582 Sun and Particles ejected from Solar Surface seen from SOHO Observatory

2012. Space Science. Multicoloured.
3408	(1st) Type **2582**	1·25	1·10
3409	(1st) Venus with Clouds in Southern Hemisphere seen from Venus Express	1·25	1·10
3410	77p. Ice in Martian Impact Crater seen from Mars Express	1·90	1·90
3411	77p. Surface of Asteroid Lutetia seen from Rosetta Probe	1·90	1·90
3412	£1.28 Saturn and its Rings seen from Cassini Satellite	3·25	3·25
3413	£1.28 Titan (Saturn's largest moon) seen from Huygens Probe	3·25	3·25

2588 Poppies on Barbed Wire Stems

2012. "Lest We Forget" (4th issue). Multicoloured.
3414	**2588** (1st) silver, black, new blue, greenish yellow and bright magenta	1·50	1·50

2589 Reindeer with Decorated Antlers

2012. Christmas. Illustrations by Axel Scheffler. Multicoloured.

(a) Self-adhesive
3415	(2nd) Type **2589**	1·00	90
3416	(1st) Santa with Robin	1·10	1·10
3417	(2nd Large) Reindeer with Decorated Antlers	1·50	1·50
3418	87p. Snowman and Penguin	2·25	2·25
3419	(1st Large) Santa with Robin	2·25	2·25
3420	£1.28 Robin with Star Decoration in Beak	3·25	3·25
3421	£1.90 Cat and Mouse decorating Christmas Tree	4·75	4·75

(b) Ordinary gum
MS3422 115×102 mm. As Nos. 3415/21   14·00   14·00

2596 Steam Locomotive on Metropolitan Railway, 1863

2602 Classic London Underground Posters (image scaled to 26% of original size)

2013. 150th Anniv of the London Underground. Multicoloured.

(a) Ordinary gum
3423	(2nd) Type **2596**	90	90
3424	(2nd) Navvies excavating 'Deep Cut' Tube Tunnel, 1898	90	90
3425	(1st) Commuters in Carriage, 1911	1·10	1·10
3426	(1st) Boston Manor Art Deco Station, 1934	1·10	1·10
3427	£1.28 Train on Deep Cut Line, 1938	2·50	2·50
3428	£1.28 Canary Wharf Station, 1999	2·50	2·50

MS3429 184×74 mm. **2602** (1st) Golders Green, 1908, By Underground to fresh air (Maxwell Armfield), 1915 and Summer Sales (Mary Koop), 1925; 77p. For the Zoo (Charles Paine), 1921, Power (Edward McKnight-Kauffer), 1931 and The Seen (James Fitton), 1948; 87p. A train every 90 seconds (Abram Games), 1937, Thanks to the Underground (Zero (Hans Schleger)), 1935 and Cut travelling time, Victoria Line (Tom Eckersley), 1969; £1.28 The London Transport Collection (Tom Eckersley), 1975, London Zoo (Abram Games), 1976 and The Tate Gallery by Tube (David Booth), 1987   7·00   7·00

(b) Self-adhesive
3430	(1st) Boston Manor Art Deco Station, 1934	1·10	1·10

2603 Elinor and Marianne Dashwood (*Sense and Sensibility*)

2013. Bicentenary of the Publication of Jane Austen's *Pride and Prejudice*. Multicoloured.
3431	(1st) Type **2603**	1·10	1·10
3432	(1st) Elizabeth Bennet and Portrait of Mr. Darcy (*Pride and Prejudice*)	1·10	1·10
3433	77p. Fanny Price (*Mansfield Park*)	1·75	1·75
3434	77p. Emma Woodhouse and Mr. Knightley (*Emma*)	1·75	1·75
3435	£1.28 Catherine Morland (*Northanger Abbey*)	2·50	2·50
3436	£1.28 Anne Elliot and Captain Wentworth (*Persuasion*)	2·50	2·50

2609 The Eleventh Doctor (Matt Smith, from 2010)   **2620** TARDIS

2621 Dr. Who 1963-2013 (image scaled to 42% of original size)

2013. 50th Anniv of *Doctor Who* (TV programme) (1st issue). Multicoloured.

(a) Ordinary gum
3437	(1st) Type **2609**	1·10	1·10
3438	(1st) The Tenth Doctor (David Tennant, 2005-10)	1·10	1·10
3439	(1st) The Ninth Doctor (Christopher Eccleston, 2005)	1·10	1·10
3440	(1st) The Eighth Doctor (Paul McGann, 1996)	1·10	1·10

No.	Description	Mint	Used
3441	(1st) The Seventh Doctor (Sylvester McCoy, 1987-9)	1·10	1·10
3442	(1st) The Sixth Doctor (Colin Baker, 1984-6)	1·10	1·10
3443	(1st) The Fifth Doctor (Peter Davison, 1982-4)	1·10	1·10
3444	(1st) The Fourth Doctor (Tom Baker, 1974-81)	1·10	1·10
3445	(1st) The Third Doctor (Jon Pertwee, 1970-4)	1·10	1·10
3446	(1st) The Second Doctor (Patrick Troughton, 1966-9)	1·10	1·10
3447	(1st) The First Doctor (William Hartnell, 1963-6)	1·10	1·10

(b) Self-adhesive

3448	(1st) As Type 2609	1·10	1·10
3449	(1st) Type 2620	1·10	1·10
3450	(1st) The First Doctor (William Hartnell, 1963-6)	1·10	1·10

MS3451 115×89 mm. 2621 (2nd) Dalek; (2nd) The Ood; (2nd) Weeping Angel; (2nd) Cyberman; (1st) TARDIS 5·25 5·25

2013. 50th Anniv of *Doctor Who* (TV programme) (2nd issue). As No. 3449 but ordinary gum. Multicoloured.

| 3452 | 2620 (1st) multicoloured | 1·40 | 1·40 |

2622 Norman Parkinson (1913-90, portrait and fashion photographer)

2013. Great Britons. Multicoloured.

3453	(1st) Type 2622	1·25	1·10
3454	(1st) Vivien Leigh (1913-67, actress)	1·25	1·10
3455	(1st) Peter Cushing (1913-94, actor)	1·25	1·10
3456	(1st) David Lloyd George (1863-1945, Prime Minister 1916-22)	1·25	1·10
3457	(1st) Elizabeth David (1913-92, cookery writer)	1·25	1·10
3458	(1st) John Archer (1863-1932, politician and civil rights campaigner)	1·25	1·10
3459	(1st) Benjamin Britten (1913-76, composer and pianist)	1·25	1·10
3460	(1st) Mary Leakey (1913-96, archaeologist and anthropologist)	1·25	1·10
3461	(1st) Bill Shankly (1913-81, football player and manager)	1·25	1·10
3462	(1st) Richard Dimbleby (1913-65, journalist and broadcaster)	1·25	1·10

2632 Jimmy Greaves (England)

2013. Football Heroes (1st issue). Multicoloured.

(a) Ordinary paper

3463	(1st) Type 2632	1·25	1·10
3464	(1st) John Charles (Wales)	1·25	1·10
3465	(1st) Gordon Banks (England)	1·25	1·10
3466	(1st) George Best (Northern Ireland)	1·25	1·10
3467	(1st) John Barnes (England)	1·25	1·10
3468	(1st) Kevin Keegan (England)	1·25	1·10
3469	(1st) Denis Law (Scotland)	1·25	1·10
3470	(1st) Bobby Moore (England)	1·25	1·10
3471	(1st) Bryan Robson (England)	1·25	1·10
3472	(1st) Dave Mackay (Scotland)	1·25	1·10
3473	(1st) Bobby Charlton (England)	1·25	1·10
MS3474	192×74 mm. Nos. 3463/73	13·00	13·00

(b) Self-adhesive

3475	(1st) George Best (Northern Ireland)	1·50	1·50
3476	(1st) Bobby Moore (England)	1·50	1·50
3477	(1st) John Charles (Wales) (20.2.14)	1·50	1·50
3478	(1st) Dave Mackay (Scotland) (20.2.14)	1·50	1·50

Nos. 3463/85 commemorate the 150th anniversary of the Football Association and the 140th Anniversary of the Scottish Football Association.

2013. Football Heroes (2nd issue). Multicoloured.

3479	(1st) As Type 2632	1·50	1·50
3480	(1st) As No. 3464	1·50	1·50
3481	(1st) As No. 3468	1·50	1·50
3482	(1st) As No. 3469	1·50	1·50
3483	(1st) As No. 3470	1·50	1·50
3484	(1st) As No. 3465	1·50	1·50
3485	(1st) As No. 3466	1·50	1·50
3486	(1st) As No. 3467	1·50	1·50
3487	(1st) As No. 3471	1·50	1·50
3488	(1st) As No. 3472	1·50	1·50
3489	(1st) As No. 3473	1·50	1·50

No. 3490 is vacant.

2646 Preliminary Oil Sketch for *The Coronation of Queen Elizabeth II* (Terence Cuneo), 1953

2013. 60th Anniv of the Coronation. Six Decades of Royal Portraits. Multicoloured.

3491	(2nd) Type 2646	1·00	90
3492	(1st) Queen Elizabeth II in Garter Robes (Nicky Philipps), 2012	1·25	1·10
3493	78p. Portrait by Andrew Festing, 1999	1·75	1·75
3494	88p. Portrait by Pietro Annigoni, 1955	2·00	2·00
3495	£1.28 Portrait by Sergei Pavlenko, 2000	2·75	2·50
3496	£1.88 *Her Majesty Queen Elizabeth II* (Richard Stone), 1992	3·75	3·75

2652 UTA W No. 103

2653 (image scaled to 27% of original size)

2013. Classic Locomotives (3rd series). Northern Ireland. Multicoloured.

(a) Self-adhesive

| 3497 | (1st) Type 2652 | 1·25 | 1·10 |

(b) Ordinary gum. Sheet 180×74 mm

MS3498 2653 (1st) As Type 2652; 78p. UTA SG3 No. 35; 88p. Peckett No. 2; £1.28 CDRJC Class 5 No. 4 7·00 7·00

2654 Comma (*Polygonia c-album*)

2013. Butterflies. Multicoloured.

(a) Ordinary paper

3499	(1st) Type 2654	1·25	1·10
3500	(1st) Orange-tip (*Anthocharis cardamines*)	1·25	1·10
3501	(1st) Orange-tip (*Anthocharis cardamines*)	1·25	1·10
3502	(1st) Chalkhill Blue (*Polyommatus coridon*)	1·25	1·10
3503	(1st) Swallowtail (*Papilio machaon*)	1·25	1·10
3504	(1st) Purple Emperor (*Apatura iris*)	1·25	1·10
3505	(1st) Purple Emperor (*Apatura iris*)	1·25	1·10
3506	(1st) Brimstone (*Gonepteryx rhamni*)	1·25	1·10
3507	(1st) Red Admiral (*Vanessa atalanta*)	1·25	1·10
3508	(1st) Marbled White (*Melanargia galathea*)	1·25	1·10

(b) Self-adhesive

| 3509 | (1st) As No. 3502 | 1·25 | 1·10 |
| 3510 | (1st) As Type 2654 | 1·25 | 1·10 |

2664 Andy Murray's Wimbledon Victory (image scaled to 25% of original size)

2013. Andy Murray, Men's Singles Champion, Wimbledon. Sheet 192×75 mm. Multicoloured.

MS3511 2664 (1st) Andy Murray kissing Wimbledon Trophy; (1st) Andy Murray serving; £1.28 In action; £1.28 Holding Trophy 7·50 7·50

2665 Jaguar E-Type, 1961

2671 The Workhorses (image scaled to 27% of original size)

2013. British Auto Legends. Multicoloured.

3512	(1st) Type 2665	1·25	1·10
3513	(1st) Rolls-Royce Silver Shadow, 1965	1·25	1·10
3514	(1st) Aston Martin DB5, 1963	1·25	1·10
3515	£1.28 MG MGB, 1962	2·75	2·50
3516	£1.28 Morgan Plus 8, 1968	2·75	2·50
3517	£1.28 Lotus Esprit, 1976	2·75	2·50

MS3518 180×74 mm. 2671 (1st)×4 Morris Minor Royal Mail van (1953-71); Austin FX4 (1958-97) London taxi; Ford Anglia 105E (1959-67) police car; Coastguard Land Rover Defender 110 (from 1990) (all 40×30 mm) 12·00 12·00

2672 East Indiaman *Atlas*, 1813

2013. Merchant Navy (1st issue). Multicoloured.

3519	(1st) Type 2672	1·25	1·10
3520	(1st) Royal Mail Ship *Britannia*, 1840	1·25	1·10
3521	(1st) Tea Clipper *Cutty Sark*, 1870	1·25	1·10
3522	£1.28 Cargo Liner *Clan Matheson*, 1919	2·75	2·50
3523	£1.28 Royal Mail Ship *Queen Elizabeth*, 1940	2·75	2·50
3524	£1.28 Bulk Carrier *Lord Hinton*, 1986	2·75	2·50

2678 Destroyer HMS *Vanoc* escorting Atlantic Convoy

2682 Second World War Atlantic and Arctic Convoys (image scaled to 42% of original size)

2013. Merchant Navy (2nd issue). Multicoloured.

3525	(1st) Type 2678	1·40	1·40
3526	(1st) Merchant Ship passing the Naval Control Base in the Thames Estuary	1·40	1·40
3527	(1st) Sailors clearing Ice from the Decks of HMS *King George V* in Arctic Waters	1·40	1·40
3528	(1st) Naval Convoy of 24 Merchant Ships in the North Sea	1·40	1·40

MS3529 2682 115×89 mm. Nos. 3525/8 5·50 5·50

2683 Royal Mail Van

2013. Royal Mail Transport: By Land and Sea. Self-adhesive booklet stamps. Multicoloured.

| 3530 | (1st) Type 2683 | 1·25 | 1·10 |
| 3531 | (1st) Royal Mail Ship *Britannia*, 1840 (As No. 3520) | 1·25 | 1·10 |

2684 Polacanthus

2013. Dinosaurs. Multicoloured.

3532	(1st) Type 2684	1·25	1·10
3533	(1st) Ichthyosaurus	1·25	1·10
3534	(1st) Iguanodon	1·25	1·10
3535	(1st) Ornithocheirus	1·25	1·10
3536	(1st) Baryonyx	1·25	1·10
3537	(1st) Dimorphodon	1·25	1·10
3538	(1st) Hypsilophodon	1·25	1·10
3539	(1st) Hypsilophodon	1·25	1·10
3540	(1st) Megalosaurus	1·25	1·10
3541	(1st) Plesiosaurus	1·25	1·10

2694 *Madonna and Child* (Francesco Granacci)

2013. Christmas. Madonna and Child Paintings. Multicoloured.

(a) Self-adhesive

3542	(2nd) Type 2694	1·00	90
3543	(1st) Virgin and Child with the Young St. John the Baptist (detail) (Antoniazzo Romano)	1·25	1·10
3544	(2nd Large) Madonna and Child (Francesco Granacci)	1·50	1·50
3545	88p. St. Roch Praying to the Virgin for an End to the Plague (detail) (Jacques-Louis David)	2·00	2·00
3546	(1st Large) Virgin and Child with the Young St. John the Baptist (detail) (Antoniazzo Romano)	2·00	2·00
3547	£1.28 La Vierge au Lys (William-Adolphe Bouguereau)	2·75	2·50
3548	£1.88 Theotokos, Mother of God (Fadi Mikhail)	3·75	3·75

(b) Ordinary gum

MS3549 146×74 mm. As Nos. 3542/8 14·00 14·00

2701 Angels (Rosie Hargreaves)

2013. Children's Christmas. Multicoloured.

| 3550 | (2nd) Angels (Rosie Hargreaves) | 1·00 | 90 |
| 3551 | (1st) Santa (Molly Robson) | 1·25 | 1·10 |

2703 Andy Pandy

2014. Classic Children's TV. Multicoloured.

3552	(1st) Type 2703	1·25	1·10
3553	(1st) Ivor the Engine	1·25	1·10
3554	(1st) Dougal (*The Magic Roundabout*)	1·25	1·10
3555	(1st) Windy Miller (*Camberwick Green*)	1·25	1·10
3556	(1st) Mr. Benn	1·25	1·10
3557	(1st) Great Uncle Bulgaria (*The Wombles*)	1·25	1·10
3558	(1st) Bagpuss	1·25	1·10
3559	(1st) Paddington Bear	1·25	1·10
3560	(1st) Postman Pat	1·25	1·10
3561	(1st) Bob the Builder	1·25	1·10
3562	(1st) Peppa Pig	1·25	1·10
3563	(1st) Shaun the Sheep	1·25	1·10

2715 Riding for the Disabled Association

2014. Working Horses. Multicoloured.

3564	(1st) Type **2715**	1·25	1·10
3565	(1st) The King's Troop Ceremonial Horses	1·25	1·10
3566	88p. Dray Horses	2·00	2·00
3567	88p. Royal Mews Carriage Horses	2·00	2·00
3568	£1.28 Police Horses	2·75	2·50
3569	£1.28 Forestry Horse	2·75	2·50

2721 BR Dean Goods No. 2532

2729 (image scaled to 27% of original size)

2014. Classic Locomotives (4th and 5th series). Wales (**MS**3578) and United Kingdom (booklet). Multicoloured.

3570	(1st) Type **2721**	1·50	1·50
3571	(1st) BR D34 Nos. 62471 & 62496	1·50	1·50
3572	(1st) UTA W No. 103	1·50	1·50
3573	(1st) LMS No. 7720	1·50	1·50
3574	60p. Peckett R2 *Thor*	1·50	1·50
3575	68p. BR D40 No. 62276	1·75	1·75
3576	78p. UTA SG3 No. 35	2·00	2·00
3577	78p. Hunslet No. 589 *Blanche*	2·00	2·00

MS3578 180×74 mm. **2729** No. 3573; No. 3577; 88p. W&LLR No. 822 *The Earl*; £1.28 BR 5600 No. 5652 | 7·50 | 7·50 |

2730 Roy Plomley (1914-85, broadcaster and writer)

2014. Remarkable Lives. Multicoloured.

3579	(1st) Type **2730**	1·25	1·10
3580	(1st) Barbara Ward (1914-81, economist and broadcaster)	1·25	1·10
3581	(1st) Joe Mercer (1914-90, football player and manager)	1·25	1·10
3582	(1st) Kenneth More (1914-82, stage and screen actor)	1·25	1·10
3583	(1st) Dylan Thomas (1914-53, poet and writer)	1·25	1·10
3584	(1st) Sir Alec Guinness (1914-2000, stage and screen actor)	1·25	1·10
3585	(1st) Noorunissa Inayat Khan (1914-44, SOE agent in occupied France)	1·25	1·10
3586	(1st) Max Perutz (1914-2002, molecular biologist and Nobel laureate)	1·25	1·10
3587	(1st) Joan Littlewood (1914-2002, theatre director and writer)	1·25	1·10
3588	(1st) Abram Games (1914-96, graphic designer)	1·25	1·10

2740 Buckingham Palace, 2014

2014. Buckingham Palace, London (1st issue). Multicoloured.

(a) Ordinary gum

3589	(1st) Type **2740**	1·25	1·10
3590	(1st) Buckingham Palace, c. 1862	1·25	1·10
3591	(1st) Buckingham Palace, 1846	1·25	1·10
3592	(1st) Buckingham House, 1819	1·25	1·10
3593	(1st) Buckingham House, 1714	1·25	1·10
3594	(1st) Buckingham House, c. 1700	1·25	1·10

(b) Self-adhesive

3595	(1st) The Grand Staircase	1·50	1·50
3596	(1st) The Throne Room	1·50	1·50

2748 The Blue Drawing Room

2749 The Green Drawing Room

2014. Buckingham Palace, London (2nd issue). Multicoloured.

3597	(1st) The Throne Room	1·50	1·50
3598	(1st) The Grand Staircase	1·50	1·50
3599	(1st) Type **2748**	1·50	1·50
3600	(1st) Type **2749**	1·50	1·50

MS3601 146×74 mm. **2750** Nos. 3597/600 | 5·50 | 5·50 |

2751 *A Matter of Life and Death* (1946)

2757 Films by GPO Film Unit (image scaled to 42% of original size)

2014. Great British Films. Multicoloured.

3602	(1st) Type **2751**	1·25	1·10
3603	(1st) *Lawrence of Arabia* (1962)	1·25	1·10
3604	(1st) *2001 A Space Odyssey* (1968)	1·25	1·10
3605	£1.28 *Chariots of Fire* (1981)	2·75	2·50
3606	£1.28 *Secrets & Lies* (1996)	2·75	2·50
3607	£1.28 *Bend It Like Beckham* (2002)	2·75	2·50

MS3608 115×89 mm. **2757** (1st)×4 *Night Mail* (1936) directed by Harry Watt and Basil Wright; *Love on the Wing* (1938) directed by Norman McLaren; *A Colour Box* (1935) directed by Len Lye; *Spare Time* (1939) directed by Humphrey Jennings | 5·50 | 5·50 |

2758 Herring

2014. Sustainable Fish (Nos. 3609/13) and Threatened Fish (Nos. 3614/18). Multicoloured.

3609	(1st) Type **2758**	1·25	1·10
3610	(1st) Red Gurnard	1·25	1·10
3611	(1st) Dab	1·25	1·10
3612	(1st) Pouting	1·25	1·10
3613	(1st) Cornish Sardine	1·25	1·10
3614	(1st) Common Skate	1·25	1·10
3615	(1st) Spiny Dogfish	1·25	1·10
3616	(1st) Wolffish	1·25	1·10
3617	(1st) Sturgeon	1·25	1·10
3618	(1st) Conger Eel	1·25	1·10

REGIONAL ISSUES I. CHANNEL ISLANDS

Islands in the English Channel off N.W. coast of France. Occupied by German forces from June 1940 to May 1945, when separate issueds for both islands were made.

C1 Gathering Vraic (seaweed)

1948. Third Anniversary of Liberation.

C1	**C1**	1d. red	25	30
C2		2½d. blue	25	30

DESIGN: 2½d. Islanders gathering vraic.

II. GUERNSEY

2   **3**

1958

6	**2**	2½d. red	35	40
7p	**3**	3d. lilac	15	20
9	**3**	4d. blue	10	20
10	**3**	4d. sepia	10	15
11	**3**	4d. red	20	25
12	**3**	5d. blue	20	30

For War Occupation issues and issues of independent postal administration from 1967 see **GUERNSEY**.

III. ISLE OF MAN

1   **2**

1958

1	**1**	2½d. red	50	1·25
2	**2**	3d. lilac	50	20
3p	**2**	4d. blue	20	30
5	**2**	4d. sepia	25	30
6	**2**	4d. red	45	75
7	**2**	5d. blue	45	75

3

1971. Decimal Currency.

8	**3**	2½p. red	20	15
9	**3**	3p. blue	20	15
10	**3**	5p. violet	80	80
11	**3**	7½p. brown	90	90

For issues of independent postal administration from 1973 see **ISLE OF MAN**.

IV. JERSEY

8   **9**

1958

9	**8**	2½d. red	30	45
10p	**9**	3d. lilac	15	15
11p	**9**	4d. blue	15	25
12	**9**	4d. sepia	15	25
13	**9**	4d. red	15	25
14	**9**	5d. blue	15	50

For War Occupation issues and issues of independent postal administration from 1969 see **JERSEY**.

V. ENGLAND

EN1 Three Lions

2001

EN1	**EN 1**	(2nd) green and silver	1·00	1·00
EN2	-	(1st) brown and silver	1·25	1·00
EN3	-	(E) green and silver	2·25	2·25
EN4	-	65p. lilac and silver	3·00	3·00
EN5	-	68p. lilac and silver	3·00	3·00

DESIGNS: No. EN2, Crowned Lion with Shield of St. George; EN3, Oak Tree; EN4/5, Tudor Rose.

Nos EN1/3 were initially sold at 19p., 27p. and 36p., the latter representing the basic European airmail rate.

2003. As Nos. EN1/3 and EN5, and new values, but with white borders.

(b) Litho Enschedé or Cartor (1st) or Cartor (others)

EN29	**EN 1**	(2nd) greenish yellow, bright magenta, new blue and black (1.2013)	1·00	1·00
EN30	**EN 2**	(1st) greenish yellow, bright magenta, new blue and black (20.9.07)	1·25	1·25
EN31	**EN 3**	68p. silver, greenish yellow, bright magenta, new blue and black (29.3.11)	1·50	1·50
EN32		87p. silver, greenish yellow, bright magenta, new blue and black (25.4.12)	2·25	2·25
EN33		88p. silver, greenish yellow, bright magenta, new blue and black (27.3.13)	2·00	2·00
EN34		97p. silver, greenish yellow, bright magenta, new blue and black (26.3.14)	2·25	2·25
EN41	**EN 4**	£1.10 silver, greenish yellow, bright magenta, new blue and black (29.3.11)	2·75	2·75
EN42		£1.28 silver, greenish yellow, bright magenta, new blue and black (25.4.12)	2·75	2·75

EN 5 (image scaled to 39% of original size)

2007. Celebrating England. Sheet 123×70 mm.
MSEN50 (1st) No. EN7; (1st) St. George's flag; 78p. St. George; 78p. Houses of Parliament, London | 9·00 | 9·00 |

EN 6 St. George's Flag

2013. England Flag

EN51	**EN6**	(1st) multicoloured	2·00	2·00

VI. NORTHERN IRELAND

N1   **N2**   **N3**

1958

NI1	**N1**	3d. lilac	15	10
NI2	**N1**	4d. blue	15	15
NI8	**N1**	4d. sepia	15	15
NI9	**N1**	4d. red	20	20
NI10	**N1**	5d. blue	20	20
NI3	**N 2**	6d. purple	30	30
NI4	**N 2**	9d. green	30	70
NI5	**N 3**	1s.3d. green	30	70
NI6	**N 3**	1s.6d. blue	30	70

N4

1971

NI12	**N4**	2½p. mauve	70	60
NI14	**N4**	3p. blue	20	15
NI15	**N4**	3½p. grey	20	25
NI17	**N4**	4½p. blue	30	25
NI18	**N4**	5p. violet	1·00	1·00
NI19	**N4**	5½p. violet	20	20
NI21	**N4**	6½p. blue	20	20
NI22	**N4**	7p. brown	35	25
NI23	**N4**	7½p. brown	1·75	1·75
NI24	**N4**	8p. red	35	35
NI25	**N4**	8½p. green	35	40
NI26	**N4**	9p. violet	40	40
NI27	**N4**	10p. brown	40	50
NI29	**N4**	10½p. blue	40	50
NI30	**N4**	11p. red	60	60
NI34	**N4**	11½p. drab	85	85
NI31	**N4**	12p. green	50	50
NI36	**N4**	12½p. green	60	60
NI37	**N4**	13p. brown	80	50
NI32	**N4**	13½p. brown	60	70
NI38	**N4**	14p. blue	75	75
NI33	**N4**	15p. blue	60	70
NI41	**N4**	15½p. violet	80	80
NI42	**N4**	16p. brown	1·25	1·25
NI43	**N4**	17p. blue	90	95
NI45	**N4**	18p. violet	1·00	1·00

NI46	N4	18p. grey	1·00	90
NI47	N4	18p. green	1·00	95
NI49	N4	19p. red	1·00	1·00
NI69	N4	19p. bistre	90	80
NI50	N4	19½p. grey	1·50	1·75
NI51	N4	20p. black	1·00	80
NI52	N4	20½p. blue	4·50	4·25
NI53	N4	22p. blue	1·10	1·10
NI79	N4	20p. green	1·95	80
NI54	N4	22p. green	1·10	1·10
NI55	N4	22p. red	1·25	90
NI56	N4	23p. green	1·25	1·10
NI57	N4	24p. red	1·25	1·25
NI58	N4	24p. brown	1·10	90
NI72	N4	25p. red	75	75
NI60	N4	26p. red	1·25	1·25
NI61	N4	26p. drab	1·75	1·75
NI81	N4	26p. brown	1·25	1·00
NI62	N4	28p. blue	1·50	1·50
NI63	N4	28p. grey	1·50	1·50
NI74	N4	30p. grey	1·25	1·25
NI64	N4	31p. purple	1·75	2·00
NI65	N4	32p. blue	1·75	1·75
NI66	N4	34p. grey	1·75	1·75
NI67	N4	37p. red	2·00	2·50
NI82	N4	37p. mauve	2·50	2·50
NI83	N4	38p. blue	8·00	8·00
NI68	N4	39p. mauve	2·00	2·25
NI84	N4	40p. blue	2·75	2·75
NI76	N4	41p. brown	1·50	1·75
NI85	N4	63p. green	5·00	5·00
NI86	N4	64p. green	9·00	9·00
NI87	N4	65p. blue	3·50	3·50

2000. As Type N **4** but with "1st" face value.

NI88		(1st) bright red	3·00	3·00

N6 Basalt Columns, Giant's Causeway

2001

NI89	N6	(2nd) multicoloured	1·00	75
NI90	–	(1st) black, blue & yellow	1·25	1·20
NI91	–	(E) black, blue & orange	1·60	1·60
NI92	–	65p. black, mauve & yell	3·00	3·00
NI93	–	68p. black, mauve and yellow	3·25	3·25

DESIGNS: NI90, Aerial view of patchwork fields; NI91, Linen pattern; NI92/3, Vase pattern from Belleck.

Nos. NI89, NI90 and NI91 were initially sold at 19p., 27p. and 36p., the latter representing the basic European airmail rate.

2003. As Nos. NI89/91 and NI93, and new values, but with white borders.

(a) Litho Walsall (NI98), De La Rue or Enschedé (NI95), Cartor (NI101, NI104/5, NI112) or De La Rue (others)

NI94	N6	(2nd) black, new blue, bright magenta and greenish yellow	1·00	1·00
NI95	N7	(1st) black, new blue and greenish yellow	1·25	1·00
NI96	N8	(E) black and new blue	2·50	2·50
NI97		40p. black and new blue (11.5.04)	1·75	1·75
NI98		42p. black, new blue and orange-yellow (5.4.05)	1·75	1·75
NI99		44p. black, new blue and greenish yellow (28.3.06)	1·00	1·00
NI100	N9	68p. black, bright magenta* and greenish yellow	2·75	2·75
NI101	N8	68p. greenish yellow, bright magenta, new blue and black (29.3.11)	1·50	1·50
NI102	N9	72p. black, greyish black, bright magenta and greenish yellow (28.3.06)	2·50	2·50
NI103	N8	87p. greenish yellow, bright magenta, new blue and black (25.4.12)	2·00	2·00
NI104		88p. greenish yellow, bright magenta, new blue and black (27.3.13)	2·00	2·00
NI105		97p. greenish yellow, bright magenta, new blue and black (26.3.14)	2·25	2·25
NI112		£1.10 greenish yellow, bright magenta, new blue and black (29.3.11)	2·50	2·50
NI113		£1.28 greenish yellow, bright magenta, new blue and black (25.4.12)	2·50	2·50

CELEBRATING NORTHERN IRELAND

N10 (image scaled to 39% of original size)

2008. Celebrating Northern Ireland. Sheet 123×70 mm.

MSNI152		(1st) Carrickfergus Castle; (1st) Giant's Causeway; 78p. St. Patrick; 78p. Queen's Bridge and 'Angel of Thanksgiving' sculpture, Belfast	6·00	6·00

THE 50TH ANNIVERSARY OF THE COUNTRY DEFINITIVES
1958 - 2008

N 11 (image scaled to 39% of original size)

2008. 50th Anniv of the Country Definitives. Sheet 124×70 mm, containing designs as Nos. NI1, NI3, NI5, S1, S3, S5, W1, W3 and W5 (regional definitives of 1958) but inscribed 1st and printed on pale cream.

MSNI153		As No. W1; As No. S1; As No. W5; As No. S5; As No. NI1; As No. W3; As No. S3; As No. NI3; As No. NI5	8·25	8·25

See also Nos. NI112/14.

2008. 50th Anniv of the Country Definitives (2nd issue). As Nos. NI1, NI3 and NI5 (definitives of 1958) but inscribed 1st.

NI154	N1	(1st) lilac	2·50	2·50
NI155	N3	(1st) green	2·50	2·50
NI156	N2	(1st) claret	2·50	2·50

VII. SCOTLAND

S1   **S2**   **S3**

1958

S7	S1	3d. lilac	10	15
S8	S1	4d. blue	10	15
S9	S1	4d. sepia	10	10
S10	S1	4d. red	10	10
S11	S1	5d. blue	20	10
S3	S2	6d. purple	20	15
S4	S2	9d. green	35	40
S5	S3	1s.3d. green	40	40
S6	S3	1s.6d. blue	45	50

S4

1971. Decimal Currency.

S14	S4	2½p. mauve	25	20
S16	S4	3p. blue	15	15
S17	S4	3½p. grey	20	25
S19	S4	4½p. blue	30	25
S20	S4	5p. violet	1·00	1·25
S21	S4	5½p. violet	20	20
S23	S4	6½p. blue	20	20
S24	S4	7p. brown	30	30
S25	S4	7½p. brown	1·25	1·25
S26	S4	8p. red	45	40
S27	S4	8½p. green	40	40
S28	S4	9p. violet	40	40
S30	S4	10p. brown	40	50
S31	S4	10½p. blue	45	50
S32	S4	11p. red	50	50
S36	S4	11½p. drab	80	80
S33	S4	12p. green	50	50
S38	S4	12½p. green	60	70
S39	S4	13p. brown	85	75
S34	S4	13½p. brown	70	80
S54	S4	14p. blue	60	70
S35	S4	15p. blue	60	70
S41	S4	15½p. violet	80	80
S42	S4	16p. drab	80	85
S58	S4	17p. blue	1·00	1·10
S44	S4	18p. violet	80	80
S59	S4	18p. grey	1·10	85
S60	S4	18p. red	1·00	1·00
S62	S4	19p. red	70	70
S81	S4	19p. bistre	80	70

S45	S4	19½p. grey	1·75	1·75
S64	S4	20p. black	95	95
S90	S4	20p. green	1·00	90
S46	S4	20½p. blue	3·50	3·50
S47	S4	22p. blue	1·00	1·00
S65	S4	22p. green	1·25	1·50
S66	S4	22p. red	1·25	90
S67	S4	23p. green	1·25	1·10
S69	S4	24p. red	1·25	1·25
S70	S4	24p. brown	6·00	6·00
S84	S4	25p. red	1·10	1·00
S49	S4	26p. red	1·25	1·25
S73	S4	26p. drab	1·25	1·25
S91	S4	26p. brown	1·20	1·20
S74	S4	28p. blue	1·25	1·25
S75	S4	28p. grey	1·25	1·50
S86	S4	30p. grey	1·25	1·25
S76	S4	31p. purple	2·25	2·25
S77	S4	32p. blue	1·75	2·00
S78	S4	34p. grey	1·75	1·75
S79	S4	37p. red	2·00	2·25
S80	S4	39p. mauve	2·00	2·25
S92	S4	37p. mauve	1·50	1·50
S88	S4	41p. brown	1·75	2·00
S93	S4	63p. green	4·00	4·00

S5 Scottish Flag

1999

S94	S5	(2nd) blue, deep blue and silver	1·00	75
S95	–	(1st) multicoloured	1·25	1·00
S96	–	(E) lilac, deep lilac and silver	2·00	2·00
S97	–	64p. multicoloured	9·00	9·00
S98	–	65p. multicoloured	3·00	3·25
S99	–	68p. multicoloured	3·25	3·25

DESIGNS: No. S95, Scottish Lion; S96, Thistle; S97/9, Tartan.

Nos. S94, S95 and S96 were initially sold at 19p., 26p. and 30p., the latter representing the basic European airmail rate.

2000. As Type S **4** but with "1st" face value.

S108		(1st) bright red	3·00	3·25

2003. As Nos. S94/6 and S99, and new values, but with white borders.

(a) Photo Walsall or De La Rue (42p.) or De La Rue (others)

S109	S5	(2nd) new blue, blue and silver	1·00	60
S110	–	(1st) multicoloured	1·25	85
S111	–	(E) lilac, deep lilac and silver	2·50	2·50
S112	–	40p. lilac, deep lilac and silver	1·75	1·75
S113	–	42p. lilac, deep lilac and silver	1·75	1·75
S114	–	44p. lilac, deep lilac and silver	1·50	1·50
S115	–	48p. lilac, deep lilac and silver	90	90
S116	–	50p. lilac, deep lilac and silver	80	75
S117	–	56p. lilac, deep lilac and silver	1·25	1·25
S118	–	60p. lilac, deep lilac and silver	1·40	1·40
S119	–	68p. bright magenta, greenish yellow, new blue, grey-black and silver	2·00	2·00
S120	–	72p. bright magenta, greenish yellow, new blue, grey-black and silver	1·75	1·75
S121	–	78p. bright magenta, greenish yellow, new blue, grey-black and silver	1·50	1·50
S122	–	81p. bright magenta, greenish yellow, new blue, grey-black and silver	1·40	1·30
S123	–	90p. bright magenta, greenish yellow, new blue, grey-black and silver	2·00	2·00
S124	–	97p. bright magenta, greenish yellow, new blue, grey-black and silver	2·25	2·25

(b) Litho Enschede or Cartor (1st) or Cartor (others)

S130	S5	(2nd) silver, greenish yellow, bright magenta, new blue and black (27.6.12)	1·00	1·00
S131	S6	(1st) silver, greenish yellow, bright magenta, new blue and black (20.9.07)	7·50	7·50

S132	S7	68p. silver, greenish yellow, bright magenta, new blue and black (29.3.11)	1·50	1·50
S133		87p. silver, greenish yellow, bright magenta, new blue and black (25.4.12)	2·00	2·00
S134		88p. silver, greenish yellow, bright magenta, new blue and black (27.3.13)	2·00	2·00
S135		97p. silver, greenish yellow, bright magenta, new blue and black (26.3.14)	2·25	2·25
S142	S8	£1.10 silver, greenish yellow, bright magenta, new blue and black (29.3.11)	2·50	2·50
S143		£1.28 silver, greenish yellow, bright magenta, new blue and black (25.4.12)	2·50	2·50

2004. Scottish Parliament. Sheet 123×70 mm containing Nos. S109, S110×2 and S112×2.

MSS152		(2nd) deep blue; blue and silver; (1st)×2 yellow; deep red, red and silver; 40p.×2 lilac, deep lilac and silver	6·00	6·00

CELEBRATING SCOTLAND

S10 (image scaled to 39% of original size)

2006. Celebrating Scotland. Sheet 124×71 mm.

MSS153		(1st) As No. S110; (1st) Scottish Flag; 72p. St. Andrew; 72p. Edinburgh Castle	6·00	6·00

2008. 50th Anniv of the Country Definitives. As Nos. S1, S3 and S5 (definitives of 1958) but inscribed 1st.

S134	S1	(1st) lilac	2·50	2·50
S135	S3	(1st) green	2·50	2·50
S136	S2	(1st) claret	2·50	2·50

ROBERT BURNS 250TH ANNIVERSARY

A Man's a Man for a' that

S11 (image scaled to 33% of original size)

2009. 250th Birth Anniv of Robert Burns (Scottish poet). Sheet 145×74 mm.

MSS157		(2nd) No. S109; (1st) 'A Man's a Man for a' that' and Burns ploughing (detail) (James Sargent Storer) (34×34 mm); (1st) No. S110; (1st) Portrait of Burns (Alexander Nasmyth) (34×34 mm); 50p. No. S116; 81p. S120	8·00	8·00

S 12 Saltire

2013. Scotland Flag

S158	S12	(1st) multicoloured	2·00	2·00

VIII. WALES

W1   **W2**   **W3**

1958

W1	W1	3d. lilac	15	15
W8	W1	4d. blue	10	15
W9	W1	4d. sepia	15	15
W10	W1	4d. red	15	15
W11	W1	5d. blue	15	15
W3	W2	6d. purple	35	30
W4	W2	9d. green	40	35
W5	W3	1s.3d. green	40	40
W6	W3	1s.6d. blue	40	40

W4

1971. Decimal Currency.

W13	W4	2½p. mauve	20	20
W14	W4	3p. blue	25	20
W16	W4	3½p. grey	20	30
W18	W4	4½p. blue	30	30
W19	W4	5p. violet	1·25	1·25
W20	W4	5½p. violet	25	30
W22	W4	6½p. blue	20	20
W23	W4	7p. brown	25	25
W24	W4	7½p. brown	1·75	1·75
W25	W4	8p. red	30	35
W26	W4	8½p. green	30	35
W27	W4	9p. violet	40	40
W29	W4	10p. brown	40	40
W30	W4	10½p. blue	45	45
W31	W4	11p. red	45	45
W35	W4	11½p. drab	90	80
W32	W4	12p. green	50	50
W37	W4	12½p. green	70	70
W38	W4	13p. brown	60	60
W33	W4	13½p. brown	70	80
W40	W4	14p. blue	75	75
W34	W4	15p. blue	70	80
W42	W4	15½p. violet	75	75
W43	W4	16p. drab	1·75	1·75
W44	W4	17p. blue	70	80
W46	W4	18p. violet	1·00	95
W47	W4	18p. grey	95	90
W48	W4	18p. green	75	75
W50	W4	19p. red	1·00	80
W70	W4	19p. bistre	80	70
W51	W4	19½p. grey	1·75	2·00
W52	W4	20p. black	90	90
W72	W4	20p. green	1·75	2·00
W53	W4	20½p. blue	3·75	3·75
W54	W4	22p. blue	1·10	1·10
W55	W4	22p. green	95	1·10
W56	W4	22p. red	1·00	1·10
W57	W4	23p. green	1·00	1·10
W58	W4	24p. red	1·25	1·25
W59	W4	24p. brown	75	75
W73	W4	25p. red	1·25	1·00
W61	W4	26p. red	1·10	1·10
W62	W4	26p. drab	1·75	1·75
W74	W4	26p. brown	2·00	2·25
W63	W4	28p. blue	1·50	1·50
W64	W4	28p. grey	1·50	1·50
W75	W4	30p. grey	1·25	1·25
W65	W4	31p. purple	1·75	1·75
W66	W4	32p. blue	1·75	1·75
W67	W4	34p. grey	1·75	1·75
W68	W4	37p. red	2·25	2·25
W76	W4	37p. mauve	2·75	3·00
W69	W4	39p. mauve	2·25	2·25
W77	W4	41p. brown	2·00	2·00
W78	W4	63p. green	4·50	4·75

W5 Without "p"

1997

W79	W5	20p. green	1·00	1·00
W80	W5	26p. brown	1·25	1·25
W81	W5	37p. mauve	3·25	3·25
W82	W5	63p. green	3·00	3·00

W6 Leek

1999

W83	W6	(2nd) brown, orange and black	1·00	50
W84	-	(1st) multicoloured	1·25	1·00
W85	-	(E) multicoloured	1·90	1·90
W86	-	64p. multicoloured	9·00	9·00
W87	-	65p. multicoloured	3·25	3·25
W88	-	68p. multicoloured	3·25	3·25

DESIGNS: No. W84, Welsh Dragon; W85, Daffodil; W86/8, Prince of Wales Feathers.

Nos. W83, W84 and W85 were initially sold at 19p., 26p. and 30p., the latter representing the basic European airmail rate.

2000. As Type W **5** but with "1af/st" face value.

W97		(1st) bright red	3·00	2·75

2003. As Nos. W83, W84/5 and W88, and new values, but with white borders.

(b) Litho Enschedé or Cartor (1st) or Cartor (others)

W121	W6	(2nd) greenish yellow, bright magenta, new blue and black (1.2013)	1·00	1·00
W122	W7	(1st) greenish yellow, bright magenta, new blue and black (20.9.07)	1·25	1·25
W123	W8	68p. greenish yellow, bright magenta, new blue and black (29.3.11)	1·50	1·50
W124		87p. greenish yellow, bright magenta, new blue and black (25.4.12)	2·00	2·00
W125		88p. greenish yellow, bright magenta, new blue and black (27.3.13)	2·00	2·00
W126		97p. greenish yellow, bright magenta, new blue and black (26.3.14)	2·25	2·25
W133	W 9	£1.10 gold, silver, greenish yellow, bright magenta, new blue and black (29.3.11)	2·50	2·50
W134		£1.28 gold, silver, greenish yellow, bright magenta, new blue and black (25.4.12)	2·50	2·50

2006. Opening of New Welsh Assembly Building, Cardiff. Sheet 123×70 mm.

MSW143	Nos. W98, W99×2 and W106×2	5·00	5·00

2008. 50th Anniv of the Country Definitives. As Nos. W1, W3 and W5 (definitives of 1958) but inscribed 1st.

W144	W 1	(1st) lilac	4·25	4·25
W145	W 3	(1st) green	1·50	1·50
W146	W 2	(1st) claret	2·00	2·00

W11 (image scaled to 39% of original size)

2009. Celebrating Wales. Sheet 123×70 mm.

MSW147	(1st) Red dragon; (1st) No. W120; 81p. St. David; 81p. National Assembly for Wales, Cardiff	6·00	6·00

W 12 Red Dragon

2013. Wales Flag

W148	W12	(1st) multicoloured	2·00	2·00

OFFICIAL STAMPS
for Government Departments)

ADMIRALTY
Overprinted ADMIRALTY OFFICIAL

1903. Stamps of King Edward VII.

O101	83	½d. turquoise	27·00	13·00
O102	-	1d. red	16·00	6·50
O103	-	1½d. purple and green	£300	£140
O104	-	2d. green and red	£325	£150
O105	83	2½d. blue	£450	£140
O106	83	3d. purple on yellow	£400	£150

ARMY Overprinted ARMY OFFICIAL

1896. Stamps of Queen Victoria.

O41	71	½d. red	6·00	2·75
O42	71	½d. green	6·00	12·00
O43	57	1d. lilac	6·00	5·00
O44	74	2½d. purple on blue	45·00	30·00
O45	79	6d. purple on red	£100	50·00

1902. Stamps of King Edward VII.

O48	83	½d. turquoise	5·50	2·25
O49	83	1d. red	5·50	2·25
O50	83	6d. purple	£160	75·00

BOARD OF EDUCATION
Overprinted BOARD OF EDUCATION

1902. Stamps of Queen Victoria.

O81	78	5d. purple on blue	£4500	£1200
O82	82	1s. green and red	£10000	£5500

1902. Stamps of King Edward VII.

O83	83	½d. turquoise	£160	38·00
O84	83	1d. red	£160	38·00
O85	83	2½d. blue	£4700	£400
O86	-	5d. purple and blue	£32500	£9500
O87	-	1s. green and red	£185000	

GOVERNMENT PARCELS
Overprinted GOVT. PARCELS

1883. Stamps of Queen Victoria.

O61	62	1½d. purple	£375	90·00
O62	-	6d. green (No. 194)	£3000	£1200
O63	-	9d. green (No. 195)	£2500	£1000
O64	25	1s. brown (No. 163)	£1600	£275

1887. Stamps of Queen Victoria.

O69	57	1d. lilac	90·00	25·00
O65	72	1½d. purple and green	£140	20·00
O70	73	2d. green and red	£225	40·00
O71	77	4½d. green and red	£350	£250
O66	79	6d. purple on red	£250	70·00
O67	80	9d. purple and blue	£375	90·00
O68	82	1s. green	£650	£250
O72	82	1s. green and red	£600	£250

1902. Stamps of King Edward VII.

O74	83	1d. red	55·00	13·00
O75	-	2d. green and red	£200	40·00
O76	83	6d. purple	£250	40·00
O77	-	9d. purple and blue	£600	£160
O78	-	1s. green and red	£1300	£275

INLAND REVENUE
Overprinted I.R. OFFICIAL

1882. Stamps of Queen Victoria.

O1	52	½d. green	£130	50·00
O5	52	½d. blue	85·00	29·00
O3	57	1d. lilac	7·50	5·00
O6	-	2½d. purple (No. 190)	£500	£180
O4	34	6d. grey (No. 161)	£575	£135
O7	-	1s. green (No. 196)	£6000	£1800
O9	-	5s. red (No. 181)	£9500	£2400
O10	-	10s. blue (No. 183)	£11000	£3500
O11	61	£1 brown	£75000	£30000

1888

O13	71	½d. red	12·00	5·00
O17	71	½d. green	18·00	12·00
O14	74	2½d. purple on blue	£150	20·00
O18	79	6d. purple on red	£450	£110
O15	89	1s. green	£900	£325
O19	89	1s. green and red	£4200	£1800
O16	61	£1 green	£12000	£2500

1902. Stamps of King Edward VII.

O20	83	½d. turquoise	30·00	3·25
O21	83	1d. red	20·00	2·25
O22	83	2½d. blue	£900	£250
O23	83	6d. purple	£425000	£190000
O24	-	1s. green and red	£3500	£700
O25	-	5s. red	£40000	£10000
O26	-	10s. blue	£95000	£45000
O27	-	£1 green	£60000	£24000

OFFICE OF WORKS
Overprinted O.W. OFFICIAL

1896. Stamps of Queen Victoria.

O31	71	½d. red	£300	£130
O32	71	½d. green	£425	£190
O33	57	1d. lilac	£475	£130
O34	78	5d. purple and blue	£3500	£1200
O35	81	10d. purple and red	£6750	£2000

1902. Stamps of King Edward VII.

O36	83	½d. turquoise	£550	£160
O37	-	1d. red	£550	£160
O38	-	2d. green and red	£1900	£400
O39	83	2½d. blue	£3250	£600
O40	-	10d. purple and red	£45000	£6750

ROYAL HOUSEHOLD
Overprinted R.H. OFFICIAL

1902. Stamps of King Edward VII.

O91	83	½d. turquoise	£375	£200
O92	83	1d. red	£325	£175

POSTAGE DUE STAMPS

D1

1914

D1	D1	½d. green	50	25
D56	D1	½d. orange	15	1·25
D2	D1	1d. red	50	25
D57	D1	1d. blue	15	50
D3	D1	1½d. brown	48·00	20·00
D58	D1	1½d. green	2·50	2·50
D69	D1	2d. black	75	1·00
D15	D1	4d. green	15·00	4·25
D60	D1	3d. violet	30	30
D61	D1	4d. blue	30	30
D62	D1	5d. brown	45	60
D63	D1	6d. purple	50	30
D76	D1	8d. red	50	50
D17	D1	1s. blue	8·50	50
D64	D1	1s. brown	90	30
D65	D1	2s.6d. purple on yellow	3·00	50
D66	D1	5s. red on yellow	8·25	1·00
D67	D1	10s. blue on yellow	11·50	5·75
D68	D1	£1 black on yellow	45·00	8·25

On the 2s.6d. to £1 the inscription reads "TO PAY".

D4

1970. Decimal Currency.

D77	-	½p. blue	15	2·50
D78	-	1p. purple	15	15
D79	-	2p. green	20	15
D80	-	3p. blue	20	15
D81	-	4p. brown	25	15
D82	-	5p. violet	25	15
D83	-	7p. brown	35	1·00
D84	D4	10p. red	30	30
D85	D4	11p. green	50	1·00
D86	D4	20p. brown	60	25
D87	D4	50p. blue	2·00	1·00
D88	D4	£1 black	4·00	1·00
D89	D4	£5 yellow and black	36·00	1·50

DESIGN: ½p. to 7p. similar to Type D **4**, but with "TO PAY" reading vertically upwards at the left.

D5

1982

D90	D5	1p. red	10	30
D91	D5	2p. blue	30	30
D92	D5	3p. mauve	15	30
D93	D5	4p. blue	15	25
D94	D5	5p. brown	20	25
D95	-	10p. brown	30	40
D96	-	20p. green	50	60
D97	-	25p. blue	80	90
D98	-	50p. black	1·75	1·75
D99	-	£1 red	3·25	1·25
D100	-	£2 blue	7·00	4·25
D101	-	£5 orange	14·00	2·25

DESIGNS: 10p. to £5, as Type D **5** but with "TO PAY" horizontal.

D7

1994

D102	D7	1p. red, yellow and black	10	75
D103	D7	2p. mauve, purple blk	10	75
D104	D7	5p. yellow, brown blk	15	50
D105	D7	10p. yellow, green blk	30	75
D106	D7	20p. green, violet blk	75	1·50
D107	D7	25p. mauve, red black	1·50	2·00
D108	D7	£1 violet, mauve black	7·00	10·00
D109	D7	£1.20 blue, green blk	8·00	12·00
D110	D7	£5 dp green, green blk	30·00	20·00

Pt. 6

GREAT COMORO

A French island north west of Madagascar. From 1914 to 1950 the stamps of Madagascar were used. In 1950 it became part of the Comoro Islands.

100 centimes = 1 franc.

1897. "Tablet" key-type inscr "GRANDE COMORE" in red or blue.

1	D	1c. black on blue	1·10	1·50
2	D	2c. brown on buff	1·00	1·60
3	D	4c. brown on grey	2·20	2·20
4	D	5c. green on light green	2·75	1·10
5	D	10c. black on lilac	7·00	5·50
14	D	10c. red	17·00	26·00
6	D	15c. blue	22·00	18·00
15	D	15c. grey	12·00	32·00
7	D	20c. red on green	15·00	21·00
16	D	25c. blue	15·00	31·00
8	D	25c. black on pink	11·00	11·50
9	D	30c. brown on drab	17·00	29·00
17	D	35c. black on yellow	25·00	23·00
10	D	40c. red on yellow	22·00	28·00
18	D	45c. black on green	75·00	95·00
11	D	50c. red on pink	28·00	41·00
19	D	50c. brown on blue	55·00	65·00
12	D	75c. brown on blue	42·00	65·00
13	D	1f. green	26·00	55·00

1912. Surch.

20A	05 on 2c. brown on buff	1·10	45
21A	05 on 4c. brown on grey	1·40	75
22A	05 on 15c. blue	1·50	90
23A	05 on 20c. red on green	65	4·50
24A	05 on 25c. black on pink	75	75
25A	05 on 30c. brown on drab	1·30	1·50
26A	10 on 40c. red on yellow	1·50	2·30
27A	10 on 45c. black on green	1·20	1·80
28A	10 on 50c. red on pink	75	90
29A	10 on 75c. brown on orange	2·20	6·50

Pt. 3

GREECE

A country in the S.E. of Europe, under Turkish rule till 1830, when it became a kingdom. A republic was established from 1924 to 1935 when the monarchy was restored. The country was under German occupation from April 1941 to October 1944. The monarchy was once again abolished during 1973 and a republic set up.

1861. 100 lepta = 1 drachma.
2002. 100 cents = 1 euro.

1 Hermes

1861. Imperf or perf.

62	1	1l. brown	11·00	5·25
17	1	2l. buff	12·50	35·00
55	1	5l. green	16·00	2·10
19b	1	10l. orange on blue	£550	80·00
56	1	10l. orange	16·00	2·10
20	1	20l. blue	£275	16·00
59	1	20l. red	2·30	16·00
60	1	30l. blue	£150	7·25
53	1	30l. brown	55·00	8·25
28	1	40l. mauve on blue	£250	26·00
37	1	40l. orange on green	£600	80·00
43d	1	40l. bistre on blue	33·00	47·00
43f	1	40l. green on blue	70·00	65·00
50	1	40l. buff	22·00	65·00
61	1	40l. mauve	43·00	7·25
52	1	60l. green on green	27·00	80·00
54	1	60l. green	£450	47·00
22	1	80l. red	90·00	50·00

2

1886. Imperf.

73	2	1l. brown	3·00	2·10
86	2	2l. buff	1·10	1·30
87b	2	5l. green	2·40	1·60
76	2	10l. orange	15·00	2·10
89c	2	20l. red	33·00	1·00
90d	2	25l. blue	65·00	1·00
91	2	25l. purple	11·00	2·10
79	2	40l. purple	90·00	21·00
93	2	40l. blue	7·50	2·10
80	2	50l. green	11·00	4·75
81	2	1d. grey	£110	3·75

1886. Perf.

100	1l. brown	2·20	1·00
96	2l. buff	1·10	8·25
102	5l. green	8·75	1·00
103b	10l. orange	38·00	2·10
104a	20l. red	43·00	1·60
105d	25l. blue	£100	8·25
106a	25l. purple	11·00	2·10
107	40l. purple	£120	31·00
108	40l. blue	13·00	3·25
83	50l. green	16·00	5·75
84	1d. grey	£160	6·25

3 Wrestlers

4 Discus thrower

5 Vase depicting Pallas Athene

6 Quadriga of Chariot driving

1896. First International Olympic Games. Perf.

110	3	1l. yellow	2·20	1·80
111	3	2l. red	2·75	2·10
112	4	5l. mauve	11·00	3·25
113	4	10l. grey	11·00	4·50
114	5	20l. brown	24·00	4·75
115	6	25l. red	30·00	6·00
116	5	40l. violet	13·00	7·25
117	6	60l. black	41·00	21·00
118	-	1d. blue	£100	20·00
119	-	2d. olive	£300	80·00
120	-	5d. green	£550	£450
121	-	10d. brown	£600	£500

DESIGNS—As Type **6**—HORIZ: 1d. Acropolis and Stadium; 10d. Acropolis with Parthenon. VERT: 2d. "Hermes" (after statue by Praxiteles); 5d. "Victory" (after statue by Paeonius).

1900. Surch. Imperf.

122	2	20l. on 25l. blue	3·25	1·00
130	1	30l. on 40l. purple	6·50	6·25
131	1	40l. on 2l. buff	8·75	8·25
132	1	50l. on 40l. buff	6·50	6·25
123	2	1d. on 40l. purple	16·00	6·25
124	2	2d. on 40l. purple	£475	
133	1	3d. on 10l. orange	55·00	50·00
134	1	5d. on 40l. purple on blue	£140	£160

1900. Surch. Perf.

125	2	20l. on 25l. blue	3·25	1·00
135	1	30l. on 40l. purple	11·00	10·50
136	1	40l. on 2l. buff	16·00	16·00
137	1	50l. on 40l. buff	11·00	10·50
126	2	1d. on 40l. purple	22·00	10·50
127a	2	2d. on 40l. purple	11·00	12·50
138	1	3d. on 10l. orange	60·00	60·00
139	1	5d. on 40l. purple on blue	£160	£170

1900. Surch AM and value.

140	2	25l. on 40l. purple (No. 79)	5·50	10·50
142	2	25l. on 40l. purple (No. 107)	11·00	16·00
141	2	50l. on 25l. blue (No. 90d)	27·00	26·00
143	2	50l. on 25l. blue (No. 105)	55·00	65·00
144	1	1d. on 40l. brown on blue (No. 43d)	£110	£160
146	1	1d. on 40l. brown on blue (Perf)	£150	£170
145	1	2d. on 5l. blue (No. 55)	16·00	26·00
147	1	2d. on 5l. green (No. 102)	22·00	37·00

1900. Olympic Games stamps surch AM and value.

148	-	5l. on 1d. blue	22·00	31·00
149	5	25l. on 40l. violet	£110	85·00
150	-	50l. on 2d. olive	£100	75·00
151	-	1d. on 5d. green	£350	£225
152	-	2d. on 10d. brown	75·00	£120

15

16 Hermes after the "Mercury" of Giovanni da Bologna

17

1901

167A	15	1l. brown	65	20
168A	15	2l. grey	75	20
169A	15	3l. orange	85	30
170A	16	5l. green	75	30
171A	16	10l. red	1·10	30
172A	16	20l. mauve	1·10	30
173A	16	25l. blue	2·00	30
160	15	30l. purple	13·00	1·60
175B	15	40l. brown	1·60	30
176A	15	50l. lake	20·00	1·00
163	17	1d. black	40·00	2·10
164	17	2d. bronze	11·00	8·25
165	17	3d. silver	15·00	10·50
166	17	5d. gold	17·00	10·50

19 Head of Hermes

1902

178	19	5l. orange	2·30	1·00
179	19	25l. green	35·00	2·40
180	19	50l. blue	35·00	2·40
181	19	1d. red	35·00	10·00
182	19	2d. brown	65·00	44·00

20 Athlete throwing Discus

21 Jumper

23 Atlas offering the Apples of Hesperides to Hercules

1906. Olympic Games. Dated "1906".

183	20	1l. brown	55	30
184	20	2l. black	60	30
185	21	3l. orange	70	30
186	21	5l. green	1·20	50
187	-	10l. red	3·25	50
188	23	20l. red	5·50	50
189	-	25l. blue	5·75	65
190	-	30l. purple	6·50	3·25
191	-	40l. brown	6·50	3·25
192	23	50l. purple	15·00	3·25
193	-	1d. red	75·00	19·00
194	-	2d. red	£130	41·00
195	-	3d. yellow	£150	£140
196	-	5d. blue	£200	£150

DESIGNS—As Type **20**: 10l. Victory; 20l. Wrestlers; 40l. "Daemon" or God of the Games. As Type **23**: 25l. Hercules and Antaeus; 1d., 2d., 3d. Race, Ancient Greeks; 5d. Olympic Offerings.

29 Head of Hermes

30 Iris

31 Hermes

32 Hermes and Arcas

1911. Roul.

213	29	1l. green	20	20
214	30	2l. red	20	20
215	29	3l. red	20	20
216	31	5l. green	20	20
217	29	10l. red	20	20
218	30	15l. blue	55	30
219	30	20l. lilac	65	20
220	30	25l. blue	6·50	65
221	31	30l. red	85	30
222	30	40l. blue	2·75	65
223	31	50l. purple	5·50	20
224	31	80l. purple	7·50	1·40
225	32	1d. red	8·75	50
226	32	2d. red	8·75	65
209		3d. red (20¼×25¼ mm)	33·00	1·30
227	32	3d. red (20×26½ mm)	14·00	65
210		5d. blue (20¼×25¼ mm)	35·00	5·75
228		5d. blue (20×26½ mm)	17·00	75
211b		10d. blue (20¼×25¼ mm)	80·00	50·00
229		10d. blue (20×26½ mm)	17·00	1·00
212	-	25d. blue	65·00	27·00
230	-	25d. slate	17·00	2·30

The 25d. is as Type **29** but larger (24×31 mm).

(34) "Greek Administration"

1912. Optd with T 34.

232B	29	1l. green	55	50
233A	30	2l. red	65	65
234A	29	3l. red	65	65
249B	31	5l. green	55	50
236A	29	10l. red	1·60	1·60
231	15	20l. mauve	65	65
237A	30	20l. lilac	2·75	2·10
238A	30	25l. blue	2·75	2·50
239A	31	30l. red	3·25	2·50
240B	30	40l. blue	2·75	4·25
241B	31	50l. purple	3·25	3·25
242A	32	1d. blue	14·00	2·50
243A	32	2d. red	60·00	31·00
244B	32	3d. red	33·00	31·00
245A	32	5d. green	27·00	31·00
246B	32	10d. blue	49·00	70·00
251B	-	25d. blue (No. 212)	2·20	2·10

35 Vision of Constantine over Athens and Salamis

36 Victorious Eagle over Mt. Olympus

1913. Occupation of Macedonia, Epirus and the Aegean Islands. Rouletted.

252A	35	1l. brown	55	50
253A	36	2l. red	55	50
254A	36	3l. orange	55	50
255A	35	5l. green	1·30	75
256A	35	10l. red	9·75	50
257A	35	20l. violet	27·00	5·25
258A	35	25l. blue	3·25	1·00
259A	35	30l. green	85·00	3·25
260A	36	40l. blue	15·00	5·25
261A	36	50l. blue	5·50	3·25
262A	36	1d. purple	27·00	5·25
263A	36	2d. brown	60·00	8·25
264A	36	3d. blue	£250	42·00
265A	35	5d. grey	£250	48·00
266A	36	10d. red	£275	£375
267A	35	25d. black	£275	£375

37 Hoisting the Greek Flag at Suda Bay, 1 May 1913

1913. Union of Crete with Greece.

268	37	25l. black and blue	12·00	5·25

(38)

1916. Stamps of 1911 optd with T 38.

269	29	1l. green	35	20
270	30	2l. red	35	30
271	29	3l. red	55	50
272	31	5l. green	80	40
273	29	10l. red	1·60	30

274	30	20l. lilac	2·10	30
275	30	25l. blue	1·60	30
277	30	40l. blue	19·00	6·00
278	31	50l. purple	65·00	3·00
280	31	30l. red	2·40	1·20
281	32	1d. blue	60·00	5·75
282	32	2d. red	34·00	5·00
283	32	3d. red	20·00	3·75
284	32	5d. blue	80·00	12·50
285	32	10d. blue	31·00	21·00

39 Iris

1917. Perf or imperf.

286A	39	1l. green	35	30
287A	39	5l. green	35	30
288A	39	10l. red	75	30
289A	39	25l. blue	75	30
290A	39	50l. purple	6·50	2·30
291A	39	1d. blue	4·25	1·00
292A	39	2d. red	5·50	1·70
293A	39	3d. red	22·00	4·25
294A	39	5d. blue	8·75	5·25
295A	39	10d. blue	75·00	21·00
296A	39	25d. grey	£130	£150

ΕΠΑΝΑΣΤΑΣΙΣ
1922
ΛΕΠΤΑ **10**

(46) "Revolution, 1922"

1923. Revolution of 1922. Stamps of 1913, surch as T 46.

340	36	5l. on 3l. orange	70	70
341	35	10l. on 20l. violet	3·00	2·50
342	36	10l. on 25l. blue	1·60	1·60
343	35	10l. on 30l. green	1·90	1·60
344	36	10l. on 40l. blue	2·75	2·40
345	35	50l. on 50l. blue	90	90
346	36	2d. on 2d. brown	£120	£110
347	36	3d. on 3d. blue	8·75	8·25
348	35	5d. on 5d. grey	8·75	8·25
349	36	10d. on 1d. purple	20·00	19·00
350	36	10d. on 10d. red	£1900	

1923. Stamps of 1916 surch as T 46.

351	39	5l. on 10l. red	65	65
352	39	50l. on 50l. purple	70	70
353	39	1d. on 1d. blue	70	70
354	39	2d. on 2d. red	80	80
355	39	3d. on 3d. red	3·75	3·75
356	39	5d. on 5d. blue	5·00	3·75
357	39	25d. on 25d. blue	55·00	55·00

1923. Cretan stamps of 1900 surch as T 46.

358	1	5l. on 1l. brown	75·00	
359	3	10l. on 10l. red	65	65
361	3	10l. on 25l. blue	70	70
362	1	50l. on 50l. lilac	80	1·30
363	1	50l. on 50l. blue	16·00	18·00
364	4	50l. on 1d. violet	7·50	8·25
365		50l. on 5d. (No. 19)	70·00	

1923. Cretan stamps of 1905 surch as T 46.

366		10l. on 20l. (No. 24)	£250	£225
367		10l. on 25l. (No. 25)	70	70
368		50l. on 50l. (No. 26)	70	70
369	16	50l. on 1d. (No. 27)	6·00	7·75
370	-	3d. on 3d. (No. 28)	28·00	26·00
371	-	5d. on 5d. (No. 29)	19·00	21·00

1923. Cretan stamps of 1907/8 surch as T 46.

372	21	10l. on 10l. red	70	70
373	19	10l. on 25l. black and blue	2·75	2·50
374	19	50l. on 1d. (No. 31)	8·25	7·75

No. 372 is as Crete No. 36 but without "HELLAS" optd. No. 377 is the optd stamp.

1923. Optd stamps of Crete surch as T 46.

375	1	5l. on 1l. brown (No. 32)	70	70
376	-	5l. on 5l. green (No. 34)	70	70
377	21	10l. on 10l. red (No. 36)	70	70
378	-	10l. on 20l. (No. 37)	70	70
379	-	10l. on 25l. (No. 30)	70	70
381	-	50l. on 50l. (No. 39)	1·10	1·00
382	16	50l. on 1d. (No. 40)	9·25	10·50
384	-	3d. on 3d. (No. 42)	28·00	34·00
385	-	5d. on 5d. (No. 43)	£550	£425

1923. Postage Due stamps of Crete of 1900 surch as T 38.

386	D 8	5l. on 5l. red	70	70
387	D 8	5l. on 10l. red	70	70
388	D 8	10l. on 20l. red	24·00	18·00
389	D 8	10l. on 40l. red	75	1·00

390	D 8	50l. on 50l. red	75	1·00
391	D 8	50l. on 1d. red	1·00	1·60
392	D 8	50l. on 1d. on 1d. red	19·00	21·00
393	D 8	2d. on 2d. red	1·60	2·50

1923. Postage Due stamps of Crete of 1908 with opt, surch as T 46.

397		5l. on 5l. red	65	65
398		5l. on 10l. red	65	65
399		10l. on 20l. red	75	75
400		50l. on 50l. red	90	90
401		50l. on 1d. red	8·25	9·00
402		2d. on 2d. red	15·00	16·00

47 Lord Byron

1924. Byron Centenary.

403	47	80l. blue	1·00	30
404	-	2d. black and violet	3·50	95

DESIGN—HORIZ: (45×30 mm): 2d. Byron at Missolonghi.

49 Grave of Marco Botzaris

1926. Centenary of Fall of Missolonghi. Roul.

405	49	25l. mauve	2·20	65

50 Savoia Marchetti S-55C Flying Boat over Fortress

1926. Air. Each showing Savoia Marchetti S-55C flying boat. Multicoloured.

406		2d. Type **50**	5·50	3·75
407		3d. Acropolis	43·00	13·00
408		5d. Map of Greece and Mediterranean	6·00	2·10
409		10d. Colonnade	43·00	16·00

51 Corinth Canal   **52** Dodecanese Costume   **53** Temple of Theseus, Athens

54 Acropolis

1927

410	51	5l. green	20	10
411	52	10l. red	55	10
412	-	20l. violet	75	10
413	-	25l. green	75	10
414	-	40l. green	1·10	10
415	51	50l. violet	3·25	10
416	51	80l. black and blue	2·20	30
417	53	1d. brown and blue	3·25	20
418b	-	2d. black and green	4·25	20
419d	-	3d. black and violet	11·00	35
419e	-	4d. brown	49·00	1·00
420	-	5d. black and orange	43·00	1·30
421	-	10d. black and red	£150	6·50
422	-	15d. black and green	£225	12·50
423a	54	25d. black and green	£150	16·00

DESIGNS—As Type **52**: 20l. Macedonian costume; 25l. Monastery of Simon Peter, Athos; 40l. White Tower, Salonika. As Type **53**: 2d. Acropolis; 3d. Cruiser *Averoff*; 4d. Mistra Cathedral. As Type **54**: 5, 15d. The Academy of Sciences, Athens; 10d. Temple of Theseus.

55 General Favier and Acropolis

1927. Centenary of Liberation of Athens.

424	55	1d. red	80	35
425	55	3d. blue	9·75	70
426	55	6d. green	44·00	14·00

56 Navarino Bay and Pylos   **58** Sir Edward Codrington

1927. Centenary of Battle of Navarino.

427	56	1d.50 green	5·25	45
428	-	4d. blue	24·00	1·70
429	58	5d. black and brown (A)	13·50	4·75
430	58	5d. black and brown (B)	95·00	13·00
431	-	5d. black and blue	85·00	11·00
432	-	5d. black and red	49·00	10·00

DESIGNS: 4d. Battle of Navarino; 5d. (No. 429) "Sir Codrington" (A); 5d. (No. 430) "Sir Edward Codrington" (B); 5d. (No. 431) De Rigny; 5d. (No. 432) Van der Heyden.

59 Righas Ferreo

1930. Centenary of Independence.

433	59	10l. brown	20	10
434	-	20l. black	20	15
435	-	40l. green	25	20
436	-	50l. red	35	30
437	-	50l. blue	35	30
438	-	1d. red	50	30
439	-	1d. orange	50	30
440	-	1d.50 blue	90	20
441	-	1d.50 red	85	25
442	-	2d. orange	1·00	30
443	-	3d. brown	1·90	65
444	-	4d. blue	7·00	70
445	-	5d. purple	3·50	1·40
446	-	10d. black	21·00	7·00
447	-	15d. green	35·00	11·00
448	-	20d. blue	70·00	14·00
449	-	25d. black	65·00	22·00
450	-	50d. brown	£120	60·00

DESIGNS as Type **59**: 20l. Patriarch Gregory V; 40l. A. Ypsilanti; 50l. (No. 436) L. Bouboulina; 50l. (437), Ath. Diakos; 1d. (438), Th. Colocotroni; 1d. (439), C. Kanaris; 1d.50, (440), Karaiskakes; 1d.50 (441), M. Botzaris; 2d. A. Miaoulis; 3d. L. Kondouriotis; 5d. Capo d'Istria; 10d. P. Mavromichalis; 15d. Solomos; 20d. Corais. (27½×40 mm): 4d. Map of Greece. (27×44 mm): 50d. Sortie from Missolonghi. (43×28½ mm): 25d. Declaration of Independence.

64 Monastery of Arkadi, Crete, and Abbott Gabriel

1930

451	64	8d. violet	70·00	1·30

1932. Stamps of 1927 surch.

452	-	1d.50. on 5d. black and blue (No. 431)	5·50	20
453	-	1d.50. on 5d. black and red (No. 432)	5·50	20
454	55	2d. on 3d. blue	6·00	35
455	58	2d. on 5d. black and brown (No. 429)	9·25	20
456	-	2d. on 5d. black and brown (No. 430)	23·00	20
457	55	4d. on 6d. green	6·00	1·00

66 Airship LZ-127 *Graf Zeppelin* and Acropolis

1933. Air.

458	66	30d. red	55·00	24·00
459	66	100d. blue	£160	50·00
460	66	120d. brown	£160	50·00

67 Swinging the Propeller   **68** "Flight"

1933. Air. Aeroespresso Company issue.

461	67	50l. orange and green	70	50
462	-	1d. orange and blue	1·10	65
463	-	3d. brown and purple	1·70	1·00
464	68	5d. blue and orange	23·00	8·25
465	-	10d. black and red	2·40	2·50
466	-	20d. green and black	42·00	12·50
467	-	50d. blue and brown	£140	80·00

DESIGNS—HORIZ: 1d. Temple of Neptune, Corinth; 3d. Marina Fiat MF.5 flying boat over Hermoupolis; 10d. Map of Italy–Greece–Rhodes–Turkey air routes. VERT: 20d. Hermes and Marina Fiat MF.5 flying boat; 50d. Woman and Marina Fiat MF.5 flying boat.

71 Greece

1933. Air. Government issue.

468	71	50l. green	1·10	65
469	71	1d. red	2·40	75
470	-	2d. violet	3·00	1·40
471	-	5d. blue	21·00	6·25
472	-	10d. red	27·00	10·50
473	71	25d. blue	90·00	26·00
474	-	50d. brown	£130	65·00

DESIGNS—VERT: 2, 10d. Ikarian Islands. HORIZ: 5, 50d. Junkers G.24 airplane and Acropolis.

74 Admiral Kondouriotis and Cruiser *Averoff*   **75** "Greece"

1933

475	74	50d. blue and black	£160	4·25
476	75	75d. purple and black	£350	£190
477	-	100d. green and brown	£1600	38·00

DESIGN—VERT: 100d. Statue (Youth of Marathon).

78 Athens Stadium, Entrance

1934

479	78	8d. blue	£225	2·10

79 Sun Chariot

1935. Air. Mythological designs.

488a	79	1d. red	55	30
488b	-	2d. blue	55	30
488c	-	5d. mauve	55	40
488d	-	7d. blue	55	40
484	-	10d. brown	9·75	4·25
488e	-	10d. orange	7·50	7·25
485	-	25d. red	11·00	10·50
486	-	30d. green	2·40	3·25
487	-	50d. mauve	11·00	16·00
488	-	100d. brown	3·25	9·50

DESIGNS—HORIZ: 2d. Iris; 30d. Triptolemus; 100d. Phrixus and Helle. VERT: 5d. Daedalus and Icarus; 7d. Minerva; 10d. Hermes; 25d. Zeus and Ganymede; 50d. Bellerophon on Pegasus.

(81)   **(82)**

1935. Restoration of Greek Monarchy. Surch with T **81** (489/91) or T **82** (492/3).

489	D20	50l. on 40l. blue	55	30
490	D20	3d. on 3d. red	2·20	1·30
492	-	5d. on 100d. green and brown (No. 477)	4·25	1·60
493	75	15d. on 75d. pur & blk	22·00	6·75

83 King Constantine

1936. Re-interment of King Constantine and Queen Sophia.

494	83	3d. brown and black	1·10	30
495	83	8d. blue and black	2·75	1·80

85 Pallas Athene (Minerva)

1937. Cent of Athens University.

496	85	3d. brown	1·10	50

86 Bull-leaping

89 King George II

89a Statue of King Constantine

1937

497	86	5l. blue and brown	10	10
498	-	10l. brown and blue	10	10
499	-	20l. green and black	10	10
500	-	40l. black and green	10	10
501	-	50l. black and brown	10	10
502	-	80l. brown and violet	10	10
503	89	1d. green	35	10
515	89a	1d.50 green	75	30
504	-	2d. blue	20	20
505	89	3d. brown	55	20
506	-	5d. red	20	20
507	-	6d. olive	35	25
508	-	7d. brown	1·80	1·60
509	89	8d. blue	1·80	50
510	-	10d. brown	35	25
511	-	15d. green	45	30
512	-	25d. blue	35	30
516	89a	30d. red	5·25	4·25
513	89	100d. red	31·00	14·00

DESIGNS—(Size as Type **89a**). VERT: 10l. Court Lady of Tiryns; 20l. Zeus and Thunderbolt; 80l. Venus of Milo; 25d. "Glory" of Psara. HORIZ: 40l. Amphictyonic Coin; 50l. Chairing Diagoras of Rhodes; 2d. Battle of Salamis; 5d. Panathenaic chariot; 6d. Alexander the Great at Battle of Issus; 7d. St. Paul on Mt. Areopagus; 10d. Temple of St. Demetrius, Salonica; 15d. Leo III (the Isaurian) destroying Saracens.

93 Prince Paul and Princess Frederika Louise

1938. Royal Wedding.

517	93	1d. green	25	25
518	93	3d. brown	70	25
519	93	8d. blue	2·00	1·40

94 Arms of Greece, Rumania, Turkey and Yugoslavia

1938. Balkan Entente.

520	94	6d. blue	16·00	2·40

1938. Air. Postage Due stamp optd with Junkers G.24 airplane. Perf or rouletted.

521	D 20	50l. brown	20	30

96 Arms of Ionian Islands   **97** Corfu Bay and Citadel

1939. 75th Anniv of Cession of Ionian Islands.

523	96	1d. blue	1·90	50
524	97	4d. green	7·50	2·50
525	-	20d. orange	45·00	24·00
526	-	20d. blue	45·00	24·00
527	-	20d. red	45·00	24·00

DESIGN—HORIZ: 20d. As Type **1** of Ionian Is. but with portraits of George I of Greece and Queen Victoria.

99 Javelin Thrower

1939. Tenth Pan-Balkan Games, Athens.

528		50l. green	45	35
529	99	3d. red	1·50	40
530	-	6d. brown on orange	8·75	3·25
531	-	8d. blue on grey	9·00	4·25

DESIGNS: 50l. Runner; 6d. Discus-thrower; 8d. Jumper.

100 Arms of Greece, Rumania, Turkey and Yugoslavia

1940. Balkan Entente.

532	100	6d. blue	27·00	2·10
533	100	8d. slate	24·00	2·40

101 Greek Youth Badge

1940. Fourth Anniv of Greek Youth Organization. (a) Postage.

534	101	3d. blue, red and silver	2·20	1·00
535	-	5d. black and blue	13·50	5·50
536	-	10d. black and orange	16·00	11·50
537	-	15d. black and green	£120	70·00
538	-	20d. black and red	90·00	41·00
539	-	25d. black and blue	90·00	50·00
540	-	30d. black and purple	90·00	50·00
541	-	50d. black and red	£150	60·00
542	-	75d. gold, brown and blue	£150	60·00
543	101	100d. blue, red and silver	£200	95·00

DESIGNS—VERT: 5d. Boy member; 10d. Girl member; 20d. Javelin thrower; 20d. Youths in column formation; 25d. Standard bearer and buglers; 30d. Three youths in uniform; 50d. Youths on parade; 75d. Coat of arms.

103 Meteora Monasteries

(b) Air.

544	103	2d. black and orange	3·25	80
545	-	4d. black and green	19·00	3·50
546	-	6d. black and red	24·00	6·25
547	-	8d. black and blue	50·00	10·50
548	-	16d. black and violet	80·00	24·00
549	-	32d. black and orange	£140	60·00
550	-	45d. black and green	£160	65·00
551	-	55d. black and red	£160	65·00
552	-	65d. black and blue	£160	65·00
553	-	100d. black and violet	£190	75·00

DESIGNS (views and aircraft): 4d. Simon Peter Monastery, Mt. Athos; 6, 16d. Isle of Santorin; 8d. Church at Pantanassa; 32d. Ponticonissi, Corfu; 45d. Acropolis; 55d. Erechtheum; 65d. Temple of Nike; 100d. Temple of Zeus.

1941. Postage Due stamps optd with Junkers G.24 airplane, No. 556 also surch. Perf (558/60), perf or rouletted (556/7).

556	D 20	1d. on 2d. red	25	30
557	D 20	5d. blue	20	30
558	D 20	10d. green	20	30
559	D 20	25d. red	1·40	3·00
560	D 20	50d. orange	1·50	3·25

105 "Boreas" (North Wind)

1942. Air. Winds. (Symbolic designs).

561	105	2d. emerald and green	25	50
562	-	5d. orange and red	35	50
563	-	10d. red and brown	45	50
567	-	10d. red and orange	20	30
564	-	20d. ultramarine and blue	90	1·00
565	-	25d. orange & light orange	55	1·00
568	-	25d. green and grey	20	30
566	-	50d. black and grey	2·30	2·10
569	-	50d. violet and blue	20	30
570	105	100d. black and grey	35	30
571	-	200d. red and pink	35	30
572	-	400d. green and blue	35	30

DESIGNS: 5d. "Notos" (South); 10d. "Apiliotis" (East); 20d. "Lips" (South-west); 25d. "Zephyr" (West); 50d. "Kekias" (North-east); 200d. "Evros" (South-east); 400d. "Skiron" (North-west).

106 Windmills on Mykonos Is.

1942

573	106	2d. brown	10	20
574	-	5d. green	10	20
575	-	10d. blue	10	20
576	-	15d. purple	10	20
577	-	25d. orange	10	20
578	-	50d. blue	10	20
579	-	75d. red	10	20
580	-	100d. black	10	20
581	-	200d. blue	10	20
582	-	500d. brown	10	20
583	-	1000d. brown	20	20
584	-	2000d. blue	20	20
585	-	5000d. red	20	20
586	-	15,000d. purple	20	20
587	-	25,000d. green	20	20
588	-	500,000d. blue	40	50
589	106	2,000,000d. green	55	1·30
590	-	5,000,000d. red	20	20

DESIGNS: 5d., 5,000,000d. Burzi Fortress, Nauplion; 10d., 500,000d. Katokhi on Aspropotamos River; 15d. Heraklion, Crete; 25d. Houses on Hydra Is; 50d. Meteora Monastery; 75d. Edessa; 100d., 200d. Monastery on Mt. Athos; 500d., 5000d. Konitza Bridge; 1000d., 15,000d. Ekatontapiliani Church; 2000d., 25,000d. Kerkyra (Corfu) Is.

110 Child

1943. Children's Welfare Fund.

592	110	25d.+25d. green	40	35
593	-	100d.+50d. purple	40	35
594	-	200d.+100d. brown	45	40

DESIGN: 100d. Mother and child; 200d. Madonna and child.

(112)

1944. Children's Convalescent Camp Fund. Surch as T **112**.

595	106	50,000d.+450,000d. on 2d. brown	1·00	1·00
596	-	50,000d.+450,000d. on 5d. green (No. 574)	1·00	1·00
597	-	50,000d.+450,000d. on 10d. blue (No. 575)	1·00	1·00
598	-	50,000d.+450,000d. on 15d. purple (No. 576)	1·00	1·00
599	-	50,000d.+450,000d. on 25d. orange (No. 577)	1·00	1·00

(b) Air.

600	-	50,000d.+450,000d. on 10d. red (No. 567)	1·00	1·00
601	-	50,000d.+450,000d. on 25d. green (No. 568)	1·00	1·00
602	-	50,000d.+450,000d. on 50d. blue (No. 569)	1·00	1·00
603	106	50,000d.+450,000d. on 100d. black	1·00	1·00
604	-	50,000d.+450,000d. on 200d. claret (No. 571)	1·00	1·00

ΔΡΑΧΜΑΙ ΝΕΑΙ

(113) (Trans "New drachmas")

1944. Optd as T **113**. (a) Postage.

605	-	50l. black and brown (No. 501)	30	30
606	-	2d. blue (No. 504)	30	30
607	-	5d. red (No. 506)	30	30
608	-	6d. olive (No. 507)	30	30

92 "Glory" of Psara

1945

609	92	1d. purple	40	20
610	92	3d. red	40	20
611	92	5d. blue	40	20
612	92	10d. brown	45	20
613	92	20d. violet	80	20
614	92	50d. green	1·70	50
615	92	100d. blue	17·00	10·50
616	92	200d. green	12·00	2·50

For 25d. in Type **92** but larger, see No. 512.

114 "OXI" = No

1945. Resistance to Italian Ultimatum.

617	114	20d. orange	40	25
618	114	40d. blue	45	30

115 President Roosevelt

1945. Roosevelt Mourning Issue. Black borders.

619	115	30d. brown	50	20
620	115	60d. grey	50	20
621	115	200d. violet	50	20

(116)

1946. Surch as T **116**.

622	-	10d. on 10d. (No. 567)	35	20
623	-	10d. on 2000d. (No. 584)	35	20
624	-	20d. on 500d. (No. 569)	35	20
625	-	20d. on 500d. (No. 582)	35	20
626	-	20d. on 1000d. (No. 583)	35	20
627	-	30d. on 5d. (No. 574)	35	20
628	-	50d. on 50d. (No. 578)	35	20
629	-	50d. on 25,000d. (No. 587)	55	20
630	-	100d. on 10d. (No. 575)	1·90	20
631	106	100d. on 2,000,000d.	1·20	20
632	-	130d. on 20l. (No. 499)	1·10	30
633	-	250d. on 20l. (No. 499)	1·10	30

634	-	300d. on 80l. (No. 502)	1·10	40
635	-	450d. on 75d. (No. 579)	2·30	45
636	-	500d. on 5,000,000d. (No. 590)	4·25	75
637	-	1000d. on 500,000d. (No. 588)	18·00	1·60
638	-	2000d. on 5,000d. (No. 585)	60·00	6·50
639	-	5000d. on 15,000d. (No. 586)	£250	43·00

117 E. Venizelos

1946. Tenth Anniv of Death of Venizelos (statesman).

| 640 | 117 | 130d. green | 55 | 30 |
| 641 | 117 | 300d. brown | 55 | 30 |

1946. Restoration of Monarchy. Surch with value in circle and date 1-9-1946.

642	89	50d. on 1d. green	80	20
643	89	250d. on 3d. brown	1·60	25
644	89	600d. on 8d. blue	14·00	1·60
645	89	3000d. on 100d. red	30·00	1·30

119 Women carrying Munitions, Pindos Mountains

1946. Victory. War Scenes.

646	-	50d. green	45	20
647	-	100d. blue	65	20
648	119	250d. green	90	20
649	-	500d. brown	1·40	30
650	-	600d. brown	1·60	80
651	-	1000d. violet	7·50	40
652	-	2000d. blue	41·00	3·00
653	-	5000d. red	50·00	1·90
682	-	1000d. green	7·75	65

DESIGNS—HORIZ: 50d. Convoy; 500d. Infantry column; 1000d. Supermarine Spitfire Mk IIB and pilot; 1000d. (No. 682) Battle of Crete; 2000d. Torpedo boat *Hyacinth* towing submarine "Perla". VERT: 100d. Torpedoing of Cruiser *Helle*; 600d. Badge, Alpine troops and map of Italy; 5000d. War Memorial at El Alamein.

121 Panayiotis Tsaldaris

1946. Tenth Death Anniv of P. Tsaldaris (statesman).

| 654 | 121 | 250d. brown and pink | 6·50 | 1·00 |
| 655 | 121 | 600d. blue | 6·50 | 1·60 |

1947. King George II Mourning issue. Surch with value in circle in corner and black border.

656	89	50d. on 1d. green	1·40	25
657	89	250d. on 3d. brown	2·40	25
658	89	600d. on 8d. blue	7·00	95

124 Castelrosso Fortress
126 Apollo (T 1 of Dodecanese Is.)

1947. Restoration of Dodecanese Is. to Greece.

659	124	20d. blue	45	10
660	-	30d. pink and black	45	10
661	-	50d. blue	45	10
662	-	100d. green and olive	45	10
663	-	200d. orange	1·60	10
664	-	250d. grey	1·40	10
665	-	300d. orange	1·80	10
666	-	400d. blue	2·40	10
667	126	450d. blue	3·00	10
668	-	450d. blue	2·40	10
669	126	500d. red	2·20	10
670	-	600d. purple	3·00	25
671	-	700d. mauve	4·00	20
672	-	700d. green	33·00	20
673	-	800d. green and violet	5·25	20
674	-	1000d. olive	3·25	30
675	126	1300d. red	27·00	20
676	124	1500d. brown	£140	40
677	-	1600d. blue	9·75	20
678	-	2000d. red and brown	75·00	30
679	-	2600d. green	16·00	1·20
680	-	5000d. violet	75·00	75
681	-	10,000d. blue	£130	85

DESIGNS—HORIZ: 100, 400d. St. John's Convent, Patmos. VERT: 30, 1600, 2000d. Dodecanese vase; 50, 300d. Woman in national costume; 200, 250d. E. Xanthos; 450 (No. 668), 800d. Casos Is. and 19th-century frigate; 600, 700 (2), 5000d. Statue of Hippocrates; 1000, 2600, 10,000d. Colossus of Rhodes.

129 Column of Women and Children

1949. Abduction of Greek Children to neighbouring Countries.

683	129	450d. violet	9·25	1·00
684	-	1000d. brown	17·00	65
685	-	1800d. green	12·00	65

DESIGNS—VERT: 1000d. Captive children and map of Greece; 1800d. Hand menacing woman and child.

130 Maps and Flags

1950. Battle of Crete.

| 686 | 130 | 1000d. blue | 21·00 | 50 |

131 "Youth of Marathon"

1950. 75th Anniv of U.P.U. Inscr "1874–1949" in white figures at top.

| 687 | 131 | 1000d. green on buff | 3·25 | 50 |

133 St. Paul
134 St. Paul

1951. 19th Cent of St. Paul's Travels in Greece.

688	-	700d. purple	4·00	50
689	133	1600d. blue	22·00	3·00
690	134	2600d. green	30·00	3·75
691	-	10,000d. brown	£250	95·00

DESIGNS—As Type 134: 700d. Sword and altar (horiz); 10,000d. St. Paul preaching to Athenians (vert).

135 "Industry"

1951. Reconstruction Issue.

692	135	700d. orange	4·25	30
693	-	800d. green	8·50	35
694	-	1300d. brown	13·00	35
695	-	1600d. olive	38·00	40
696	-	2600d. violet	£110	2·10
697	-	5000d. purple	£120	45

DESIGNS—VERT: 800d. Fish and trident; 1300d. Workmen and column; 1600d. Ceres and tractors; 2600d. Women and loom; 5000d. Map and stars ("Electrification").

136 Blessing before Battle

1952. Air. Anti-Communist Campaign.

698	136	1000d. blue	1·40	30
699	-	1,700d. turquoise	9·25	1·00
700	-	2,700d. brown	20·00	3·50
701	-	7,000d. green	60·00	14·50

DESIGNS—VERT: 1,700d. "Victory" over mountains; 2,700d. Infantry attack; 7,000d. "Victory" and soldiers.

137 King Paul
138 "Spirit of Greece"

1952. 50th Birthday of King Paul.

702	137	200d. green	1·90	30
703	137	1,000d. red	6·50	35
704	138	1,400d. blue	26·00	1·40
705	137	10,000d. purple	75·00	12·50

139 "Oranges"

1953. National Products.

706	139	500d. orange and red	1·90	20
707	-	700d. yellow and brown	2·40	20
708	-	1,000d. green and blue	5·00	20
709	-	1,300d. buff and purple	9·25	30
710	-	2,000d. green and brown	27·00	40
711	-	2,600d. bistre and violet	35·00	1·20
712	-	5,000d. green and brown	49·00	65

DESIGNS—VERT: 700d. "Tobacco" (tobacco plant); 1,300d. "Wine" (wineglass and vase); 2,000d. "Figs" (basket of figs); 2,600d. "Dried Fruit" (grapes and currant bread); 5,000d. "Grapes" (male figure holding grapes). HORIZ: 1,000d. "Olive Oil" (Pallas Athene and olive branch).

140 Bust of Pericles
141 Alexander the Great

1954. Ancient Greek Art. Sculptures, etc.

713	140	100d. brown	55	15
714	-	200d. black	55	15
715	-	300d. violet	1·10	15
716	-	500d. green	1·60	15
717	-	600d. red	1·90	15
718	141	1,000d. black and blue	2·75	15
719	-	1,200d. olive	3·00	15
720	-	2,000d. brown	12·00	20
721	-	2,400d. blue	12·00	35
722	-	2,500d. green	18·00	30
723	-	4,000d. red	38·00	40
724	-	20,000d. purple	£275	1·30

DESIGNS—As Type 140: VERT: 200d. Mycenaean ox-head vase; 1,200d. Head of charioteer of Delphi; 2,000d. Vase of Dipylon; 2,500d. Man carrying calf; 20,000d. Two pitcher bearers. HORIZ: 2,400d. Hunting wild boar. As Type 141: VERT: 300d. Bust of Homer; 500d. Zeus of Istiaca; 600d. Youth's head; 4,000d. Dish depicting voyage of Dionysius.

See also Nos. 733a/41.

143 Athlete Bearing Torch

1954. Air. 5th Anniv of N.A.T.O. Inscr "NATO".

725	143	1,200d. orange	5·00	35
726	-	2,400d. green	55·00	3·00
727	-	4,000d. blue	90·00	4·00

DESIGNS—VERT: 2,400d. Amphictyonic coin; 4,000d. Pallas Athene.

144 Extracts from "Hansard" (Parliamentary Debates)

1954. "Enosis" (Union of Cyprus with Greece).

728	144	1.20d. black and yellow	4·25	40
729	144	2d. black and salmon	23·00	4·25
730	144	2d. black and blue	23·00	4·25
731	144	2.40d. black and lavender	23·00	3·00
732	144	2.50d. black and pink	23·00	3·00
733	144	4d. black and lemon	70·00	4·75

On No. 728 the text is in Greek, on Nos. 730/1 in French and on the remainder in English.

1955. As Nos. 713/24 but new colours and values.

733a	140	10l. green	40	15
734	-	20l. myrtle (No. 714)	55	15
734a	-	20l. purple (No. 714)	45	15
735	140	30l. brown	80	20
736	-	50l. lake (No. 716)	1·40	20
736a	-	50l. green (No. 716)	80	10
736b	-	70l. orange (No. 719)	55	10
737	-	1d. green (No. 717)	2·40	15
737a	-	1d. brown (No. 717)	3·00	10
737b	-	1d.50 blue (No. 724)	27·00	20
738	141	2d. black and brown	14·00	15
738a	141	2d.50 black and mauve	24·00	20
739	-	3d. orange (No. 721)	11·00	20
739a	-	3d. blue (No. 722)	3·50	35
740	-	3d.50 red (No. 715)	22·00	65
741	-	4d. blue (No. 723)	95·00	40

145 Samian Coin Depicting Pythagoras

1955. Pythagorean Congress.

742	145	2d. green	5·25	40
743	-	3d.50 black	15·00	3·00
744	145	5d. purple	70·00	2·10
745	-	6d. blue	55·00	39·00

DESIGNS—VERT: 3d.50, Representation of Pythagoras theorem. HORIZ: 6d. Map of Samos.

146 Rotary Emblem and Globe

1956. 50th Anniv of Rotary International.

| 746 | 146 | 2d. blue | 21·00 | 70 |

147 King George I

1956. Royal Family.

747	-	10l. violet	20	10
748	-	20l. purple	20	10
749	147	30l. brown	20	10
750	-	50l. brown	55	10
751	-	70l. blue	85	20
752	-	1d. blue	1·10	20
753	-	1d.50 grey	4·50	20
754	-	2d. black	5·50	20
755	-	3d. brown	4·25	10
756	-	3d.50 brown	16·00	30
757	-	4d. green	16·00	30
758	-	5d. red	11·00	30
759	-	7d.50 blue	11·00	2·00
760	-	10d. blue	65·00	80

PORTRAITS—HORIZ: 10l. King Alexander; 5d. King Paul and Queen Frederika; 10d. King and Queen and Crown Prince Constantine. VERT: 20l. Crown Prince Constantine; 50l. Queen Olga; 70l. King Otto; 1d. Queen Amalia; 1d.50, King Constantine; 2d. King Paul; 3d. King George II; 3d.50, Queen Sophia; 4d. Queen Frederika; 7d.50, King Paul.
See also Nos. 764/77.

148 Dionysios Solomos

1957. Death Centenary of D. Solomos (national poet).

761		2d. yellow and brown	6·50	40
762	**148**	3d.50 grey and blue	2·50	2·50
763	-	5d. bistre and green	11·50	10·50

DESIGNS—HORIZ: 2d. Solomos and K. Mantzaros (composer); 5d. Zante landscape and Solomos.

1957. As Nos. 747/60. Colours changed.

764		10l. red	20	15
765		20l. orange	20	15
766	**147**	30l. black	20	15
767	-	50l. green	40	15
768	-	70l. purple	85	15
769	-	1d. red	1·50	15
770	-	1d.50 green	2·75	15
771	-	2d. red	5·75	15
772	-	3d. blue	6·75	20
773	-	3d.50 purple	13·50	20
774	-	4d. brown	16·00	20
775	-	5d. blue	14·50	20
776	-	7d.50 yellow	3·25	1·50
777	-	10d. green	85·00	80

149 *Argo* (5th Century B.C.)

1958. Greek Merchant Marine Commemoration. Ship designs.

778		50l. multicoloured	40	10
779		1d. ochre, black and blue	45	20
780		1d.50 red, black and blue	1·90	1·20
781		2d. multicoloured	55	30
782		3d.50 black, red and blue	2·75	1·50
783	**149**	5d. multicoloured	14·00	11·50

SHIPS: 50l. *Michael Carras* (tanker); 1d. *Queen Frederika* (liner); 1d.50, Full-rigged sailing ship, 1821; 2d. Byzantine galley; 3d.50, 6th-century B.C. galley.

150 The Piraeus (Port of Athens)

1958. Air. Greek Ports.

784	**150**	10d. multicoloured	22·00	20
785	-	15d. multicoloured	2·40	30
786	-	20d. multicoloured	22·00	20
787	-	25d. multicoloured	3·00	65
788	-	30d. multicoloured	1·90	70
789	-	50d. blue, black and brown	7·50	70
790	-	100d. blue, black & brown	60·00	2·75

PORTS: 15d. Salonika; 20d. Patras; 25d. Hermoupolis (Syra); 30d. Volos (Thessaly); 50d. Kavalla; 100d. Heraklion (Crete).

151 "Narcissus" and Flower

1958. International Congress for Protection of Nature, Athens. Mythological and Floral designs. Multicoloured.

791		20l. Type **151**	20	15
792		30l. "Daphne and Apollo"	20	15
793		50l. "Venus and Adonis" (Venus and hibiscus)	25	15
794		70l. "Pan and the Nymph" (Pan and pine cones)	35	20

795		1d. Crocus (21½×26 mm)	35	25
796		2d. Iris (22×32 mm)	75	50
797		3d.50 Tulip (22×32 mm)	70	45
798		5d. Cyclamen (22×32 mm)	6·50	6·75

152 Jupiter's Head and Eagle (Olympia 4th-century B.C. coin)

1959. Ancient Greek Coins. Designs as T **152** showing both sides of each coin. Inscriptions in black.

799	**152**	10l. green and brown	40	10
800	-	20l. grey and blue	40	10
801	-	50l. grey and purple	45	10
802	-	70l. grey and blue	55	20
803	-	1d. drab and red	2·00	10
804	-	1d.50 grey and ochre	2·50	10
805	-	2d.50 drab and mauve	3·50	10
806	-	4d.50 grey and green	8·50	50
807	-	6d. blue and olive	31·00	20
808	-	8d.50 drab and red	8·25	1·80

COINS—HORIZ: 20l. Athene's head and owl (Athens 5th cent. B.C.); 50l. Nymph Arethusa and chariot (Syracuse 5th cent. B.C.); 70l. Hercules and Jupiter (Alexander the Great 4th cent. B.C.); 1d.50, Griffin and squares (Abdera, Thrace 5th cent. B.C.); 2d.50, Apollo and lyre (Chalcidice, Macedonia 4th cent. B.C.). VERT: 1d. Helios and rose (Rhodes 4th cent. B.C.); 4d.50, Apollo and labyrinth (Crete 3rd cent. B.C.); 6d. Venus and Apollo (Paphos, Cyprus 4th cent. B.C.); 8d.50, Ram's heads and incised squares (Delphi 5th cent. B.C.).

See also Nos. 909/17.

153 Amphitheatre, Delphi

1959. Ancient Greek Theatre.

809		20l. multicoloured	40	15
810		50l. brown and olive	40	20
811		1d. multicoloured	45	25
812		2d.50 brown and blue	85	40
813	**153**	3d.50 multicoloured	17·00	16·00
814	-	4d.50 brown and black	2·00	90
815	-	6d. brown, grey and black	2·40	1·20

DESIGNS—VERT: 20l. Ancient theatre audience (after a Pharsala Thessaly vase of 580 B.C.); 50l. Clay mask of 3rd century B.C.); 1d. Flute, drum and lyre; 2d.50, Actor (3rd century statuette); 6d. Performance of a satirical play (after a mixing-bowl of 410 B.C.). HORIZ: 4d.50, Performance of Euripides' *Andromeda* (after a vase of 4th century B.C.).

154 "Victory" and Greek Soldiers through the Ages

1959. Tenth Anniv of Greek Anti-Communist Victory.

816	**154**	2d.50 blue, black & brn	6·50	45

155 "The Good Samaritan"

1959. Red Cross Commem. Cross in red.

817	-	20l. multicoloured	20	20
818	-	50l. grey, red and blue	35	20
819	-	70l. black, brown, bis & bl	50	40
820	-	2d.50 blk, brn, grey & red	85	60
821	-	3d. multicoloured	10·50	10·00
822	-	4d.50 orange and red	2·00	1·30
823	**155**	6d. multicoloured	2·20	1·00

DESIGNS—HORIZ: 20l. Hippocrates Tree, Cos. VERT: 50l. Bust of Aesculapius; 70l. St. Basil (after mosaic in Hosios Loukas Monastery, Boeotia); 2d.50, Achilles and Patroclus (from vase of 6th cent B.C.); 3d. (32×47½ mm) Red Cross, globe, infirm people and nurses; 4d.50, J. H. Dunant.

156 Imre Nagy (formerly Prime Minister of Hungary)

1959. Third Anniv of Hungarian Revolt.

824	**156**	4d.50 sepia, brown & red	2·00	2·00
825	**156**	6d. black, blue & ultram	2·00	2·00

157 Kostes Palamas

1960. Birth Cent of Palamas (poet).

826	**157**	2d.50 multicoloured	8·25	50

158 Brig in Storm

1960. World Refugee Year. Multicoloured.

827		2d.50 Type **158**	70	20
828		4d.50 Brig in calm waters	2·00	95

159 Scout emulating St. George

1960. 50th Anniv of Greek Boy Scout Movement. Multicoloured.

829		20l. Type **159**	25	20
830		30l. Ephebi Oath and Scout Promise	25	20
831		40l. Fire rescue work (horiz)	25	20
832		50l. Planting tree (horiz)	25	20
833		70l. Map reading (horiz)	35	20
834		1d. Scouts on beach (horiz)	75	30
835		2d.50 Crown Prince Constantine in uniform	2·20	85
836		6d. Greek Scout Flag and Medal (horiz)	3·25	2·40

160 Sprinting

1960. Olympic Games.

837	-	20l. brown, black and blue	25	20
838	-	50l. brown and black	35	25
839	-	70l. brown, black & green	35	25
840	-	80l. multicoloured	35	25
841	-	1d. multicoloured	50	35
842	-	1d.50 brown, blk & orge	55	40
843	-	2d.50 brown, black & bl	1·40	65
844	**160**	4d.50 multicoloured	1·60	1·00
845	-	5d. multicoloured	3·50	1·40
846	-	6d. brown, black & violet	3·50	1·40
847	-	12d.50 multicoloured	21·00	17·00

DESIGNS—VERT: 20l. "Armistice" (official holding plaque); 70l. Athlete taking oath; 2d.50, Discus-throwing; 5d. Javelin-throwing. HORIZ: 50l. Olympic flame; 80l. Cutting branches from crown-bearing olive tree; 1d. Entrance of chief athletes; 1d.50 Long jumping; 6d. Crowning the victor; 12d.50, Quadriga or chariot-driving (entrance of the victor).

1960. First Anniv of European Postal and Telecommunications Conf. As T **371a** of Italy.

848		4d.50 blue	11·00	2·50

162 Crown Prince Constantine and *Nirefs*

1961. Victory of Crown Prince Constantine in Dragon-class Yacht Race, Olympic Games.

849	**162**	2d.50 multicoloured	1·20	50

163 Kastoria

1961. Tourist Publicity Issue.

850	**163**	10l. blue	15	10
851	-	20l. plum	15	10
852	-	50l. blue	15	10
853	-	70l. purple	20	10
854	-	80l. blue	60	20
855	-	1d. brown	80	10
856	-	1d.50 green	1·40	10
857	-	2d.50 red	3·75	10
858	-	3d.50 violet	1·90	50
859	-	4d. green	13·50	10
860	-	4d.50 blue	1·60	15
861	-	5d. lake	13·50	15
862	-	6d. myrtle	3·25	15
863	-	7d.50 black	80	20
864	-	8d. blue	7·00	20
865	-	8d.50 orange	8·25	50
866	-	12d.50 sepia	2·75	95

DESIGNS—HORIZ: 20l. The Meteora (Monasteries); 50l. Hydra; 70l. Acropolis, Athens; 80l. Mykonos. 1d. Salonika; 1d.50, Olympia; 2d.50, Knossos; 3d.50, Rhodes; 4d. Epidavros; 4d.50, Sounion; 5d. Temple of Zeus, Athens; 7d.50, Yannina; 12d.50, Delos. VERT: 6d. Delphi; 8d. Mount Athos; 8d.50, Santorini (Thira).

164 Lilies Vase of Knossos

1961. Minoan Art.

867	**164**	20l. multicoloured	50	15
868	-	50l. multicoloured	50	15
869	-	1d. multicoloured	70	20
870	-	1d.50 multicoloured	1·60	20
871	-	2d.50 multicoloured	8·25	20
872	-	4d.50 multicoloured	3·25	2·30
873	-	6d. multicoloured	15·00	1·60
874	-	10d. multicoloured	15·00	9·50

DESIGNS—VERT: 1d.50, Knossos rhyton-bearer; 4d.50, Part of Hagia trias sarcophagus. HORIZ: 50l. Partridges and fig-pecker (Knossos frieze); 1d. Kamares fruit dish; 2d.50, Ladies of Knossos Palace (painting); 6d. Knossos dancer (painting); 10d. Kamares prochus and pithos with spout.

165 Reactor Building

1961. Inauguration of "Democritus" Nuclear Research Centre, Aghia Paraskevi.

875	**165**	2d.50 purple and mauve	80	35
876	-	4d.50 blue and grey	1·60	95

DESIGN: 4d.50, Democritus and atomic symbol.

166 Doves

1961. Europa.

877	**166**	2d.50 red and pink	40	35
878	**166**	4d.50 ultramarine & blue	1·00	70

167 Emperor Nicephorus Phocas

1961. Millenary of Liberation of Crete from the Saracens.

879	167	2d.50 multicoloured	1·10	60

168 "Hermes" 1l. Stamp of 1861

1961. Centenary of First Greek Postage Stamps. "Hermes" stamps of 1861. Multicoloured.

880		20l. Type **168**	25	15
881		50l. "2l."	25	15
882		1d.50 "5l."	35	20
883		2d.50 "10l."	35	20
884		4d.50 "20l."	75	30
885		6d. "40l."	1·20	65
886		10d. "80l."	3·00	2·10

169 Ptolemais Steam Plant

1962. Electrification Project. Multicoloured.

887		20l. Tauropos dam (vert)	20	20
888		50l. Ladhon River hydro-electric plant (vert)	25	20
889		1d. Type **169**	35	20
890		1d.50 Louros River dam	40	20
891		2d.50 Aliverion steam plant	1·30	20
892		4d.50 Salonika hydro-electric sub-station	1·50	1·10
893		6d. Agra River power station	4·50	3·50

170 Zappion Building

1962. N.A.T.O. Ministers' Conference, Athens.

894	170	2d.50 multicoloured	40	20
895	-	3d. sepia, brown and buff	40	20
896	-	4d.50 black and blue	60	40
897	-	6d. black and red	60	40

DESIGNS—VERT: 3d. Ancient Greek warrior with shield; 4d.50, Soldier kneeling (after Marathon tomb); 6d. (21×37 mm), Soldier (statue in Temple of Aphea, Aegina).

171 Europa "Tree"

1962. Europa.

898	171	2d.50 red and black	1·10	35
899	171	4d.50 blue and black	3·00	1·20

172 "Protection"

1962. Greek Farmers' Social Insurance Scheme.

900	172	1d.50 black, brown & red	50	20
901	172	2d.50 black, brown & grn	70	20

173 Demeter, Goddess of Corn

1963. Freedom from Hunger. Multicoloured.

902		2d.50 Type **173**	50	20
903		4d.50 Wheat ears and globe	1·10	60

174 Kings of the Greek Dynasty

1963. Cent of Greek Royal Dynasty.

904	174	50l. red	25	10
905	174	1d.50 green	75	15
906	174	2d.50 brown	1·50	15
907	174	4d.50 blue	3·00	80
908	174	6d. violet	4·00	40

1963. Ancient Greek Coins. As Nos. 799/808 but colours changed and some designs rearranged. Inscr in black; coins in black and drab or grey; background colours given.

909		50l. blue (As No. 801)	20	15
910		80l. purple (As 802)	25	20
911		1d. green (As 803)	40	15
912		1d.50 red (As 804)	1·50	15
913		3d. olive (As 799)	1·00	15
914		3d.50 red (As 800)	1·00	35
915		4d.50 brown (As 806)	1·00	20
916		6d. turquoise (As 807)	1·00	20
917		8d.50 blue (As 808)	2·20	90

175 Athens at Dawn (after watercolour by Lord Baden-Powell)

1963. 11th World Scout Jamboree, Marathon.

918	**175**	1d. multicoloured	35	20
919	-	1d.50 orange, black & bl	35	20
920	-	2d.50 multicoloured	1·50	20
921	-	3d. black, brown & green	90	65
922	-	4d.50 multicoloured	1·70	85

DESIGNS—HORIZ: 3d. A. Lefkadites (founder of Greek Scout Movement) and Lord Baden-Powell. VERT: 1d.50, Jamboree Badge; 2d.50, Crown Prince Constantine, Chief Scout of Greece; 4d.50, Scout bugling with Atlantic trumpet triton shell.

176 Delphi

1963. Red Cross Centenary.

923		1d. Type **176**	65	35
924		2d. Centenary emblem	25	15
925		2d.50 Queen Olga	35	20
926		4d.50 Henri Dunant	1·20	85

177 "Co-operation"

1963. Europa.

927	177	2d.50 green	4·25	50
928	177	4d.50 purple	8·25	3·25

178 Great Lavra Church

1963. Millenary of Mt. Athos Monastic Community. Multicoloured.

929		30l. Vatopediou Monastery (horiz)	40	10
930		80l. Dionysion Monastery (horiz)	40	10
931		1d. Protaton Church, Karyae	45	10
932		2d. Stavronikita Monastery (horiz)	1·60	10
933		2d.50 Cover of Nicephorus Phocas Gospel, Great Lavra Church (horiz)	3·50	10
934		3d.50 St. Athanasius the Anthonite (fresco) (horiz)	1·60	95
935		4d.50 11th-century papyrus, Iviron Monastery (horiz)	1·40	45
936		6d. Type **178**	1·60	40

179 King Paul

1964. Death of Paul I.

937	179	30l. brown	20	10
938	179	50l. violet	25	10
939	179	1d. green	1·10	10
940	179	1d.50 orange	50	10
941	179	2d. blue	85	10
942	179	2d.50 sepia	85	10
943	179	3d.50 purple	1·40	20
944	179	4d. blue	2·20	20
945	179	4d.50 blue	2·40	95
946	179	6d. red	3·75	20

180 Gold Coin

1964. Byzantine Art Exn, Athens. Multicoloured.

947		1d. Type **180**	20	10
948		1d.50 *Two Saints*	20	15
949		2d. *Archangel Michael*	20	15
950		2d.50 *Young Lady*	40	15
951		4d.50 *Angel*	1·50	90

DESIGN origins: 1d. reign of Emperor Basil II (976–1025); 1d.50, from Harbaville's 10th cent ivory triptych (Louvre); 2d. 14th cent Constantinople icon (Byzantine Museum, Athens); 2d.50, from 14th cent fresco "The Birth of the Holy Virgin" by Panselinos (Protaton Church, Mt. Athos); 4d.50, from 11th cent mosaic (Daphne Church, Athens).

181 Trident of Paxi

1964. Centenary of Union of Ionian Islands with Greece. Inscr "1864–1964".

952	**181**	20l. grey, slate and green	20	10
953	-	30l. multicoloured	20	10
954	-	1d. lt brn, brn & red-brn	20	10
955	-	2d. multicoloured	20	10
956	-	2d.50 pale green, deep green and green	50	10
957	-	4d.50 multicoloured	1·30	90
958	-	6d. multicoloured	1·20	40

DESIGNS: 30l. Venus of Cythera; 1d. Ulysses of Ithaca; 2d. St. George of Levkas; 2d.50, Zakynthos of Zante; 4d.50, Cephalus of Cephalonia; 6d. War galley emblem of Corfu.

182 Greek Child

1964. 50th Anniv of National Institution of Social Welfare (P.I.K.P.A.).

959	182	2d.50 multicoloured	1·10	40

183 Europa "Flower"

1964. Europa.

960	183	2d.50 red and green	3·25	80
961	183	4d.50 brown and drab	5·50	1·30

184 King Constantine II and Queen Anne-Marie

1964. Royal Wedding.

962	**184**	1d.50 green	35	15
963	**184**	2d.50 red	25	15
964	**184**	4d.50 blue	70	35

185 Peleus and Atlanta (amphora)

1964. Olympic Games, Tokyo. Multicoloured.

965		10l. Type **185**	15	10
966		1d. Running (bowl) (horiz)	20	10
967		2d. Jumping (pot) (horiz)	20	10
968		2d.50 Throwing the discus	40	10
969		4d.50 Chariot-racing (sculpture) (horiz)	1·00	60
970		6d. Boxing (vase) (horiz)	45	25
971		10d. Apollo (part of frieze, Zeus Temple, Olympia)	1·00	50

186 *Christ stripping off His garments*

1965. 350th Death Anniv of El Greco. Multicoloured.

972		50l. Type **186**	25	20
973		1d. *Angels' Concert*	25	20
974		1d.50 El Greco's signature (horiz)	25	20
975		2d.50 Self-portrait	25	20
976		4d.50 *Storm-lashed Toledo*	60	45

187 Aesculapius Theatre, Epidavros

1965. Greek Artistic Festivals. Multicoloured.

977		1d.50 Type **187**	40	30
978		4d.50 Herod Atticus Theatre, Athens	70	35

188 ITU Emblem and Symbols

1965. Centenary of I.T.U.

979	188	2d.50 red, blue and grey	65	20

189 *New Member making Affirmation (after Tsokos)*

1965. 150th Anniv of "Philiki Hetaeria" ("Friends' Society"). Multicoloured.

980		1d.50 Type **189**	20	10
981		4d.50 Society flag	60	30

190 AHEPA Emblem

1965. American Hellenic Educational Progressive Assn (AHEPA) Congress, Athens.

982	190	6d. black, olive and blue	65	35

191 Venizelos as Revolutionary

1965. Birth Cent of E. Venizelos (statesman).

983	191	1d.50 green	35	20
984	-	2d. blue	55	45
985	-	2d.50 brown	25	20

DESIGNS: 2d. Venizelos signing Treaty of Sevres (1920); 2d.50, Venizelos.

192 Games' Flag

1965. Balkan Games, Athens. Multicoloured.

986	192	1d. Type **192**	20	20
987		2d. Victor's medal (vert)	20	20
988		6d. Karaiskakis Stadium, Athens	45	30

193 Symbols of the Planets

1965. Int Astronautic Conference Athens. Multicoloured.

989	193	50l. Type **193**	20	20
990		2d.50 Astronaut in space	20	20
991		6d. Rocket and space-ship	45	30

194 Europa "Sprig"

1965. Europa.

992	194	2d.50 blue, black and grey	1·90	35
993	194	4d.50 green, black & olive	2·20	70

195 Hipparchus (astronomer) and Astrolabe

1965. Opening of Evghenides Planetarium, Athens.

994	195	2d.50 black, red and green	65	20

196 Carpenter Ants

1965. 50th Anniv of P.O. Savings Bank. Multicoloured.

995		10l. Type **196**	20	20
996		2d.50 Savings Bank and book	50	20

197 St. Andrew's Church, Patras

1965. Restoration of St. Andrew's Head to Greece. Multicoloured.

997		1d. Type **197**	20	20
998		5d. St. Andrew, after 11th-cent mosaic, Hosios Loukas Monastry, Boeotia	40	20

198 T. Brysakes

1966. Modern Greek Painters. Multicoloured.

999		80l. Type **198**	20	15
1000		1d. N. Lytras	20	15
1001		2d.50 C. Volonakes	20	15
1002		4d. N. Gyses	35	20
1003		5d. G. Jacobides	35	20

199 Greek 25d. Banknote of 1867

1966. 125th Anniv of Greek National Bank.

1004	-	1d.50 green	25	10
1005	-	2d.50 brown	25	10
1006	-	4d. blue	35	15
1007	199	6d. black	55	30

DESIGNS—VERT: (23×33½ mm): 1d.50, J.-G. Eynard; 2d.50, G. Stavros (founders). HORIZ: (As Type **199**): 4d. National Bank Headquarters, Athens.

200 Geannares (revolutionary leader)

1966. Centenary of Cretan Revolt. Multicoloured.

1008	200	2d. Type **200**	25	15
1009		2d.50 Explosion of gunpowder machine, Arkadi Monastery (horiz)	25	15
1010		4d.50 Map of Crete (horiz)	40	30

201 "Movement of Water" (Decade of World Hydrology)

1966. U.N.O. Events.

1011	201	1d. blue, brown and black	25	15
1012	-	3d. multicoloured	25	15
1013	-	3d. black, blue and red	40	30

DESIGNS—VERT: 3d. U.N.E.S.C.O. emblem (20th anniv); 5d. W.H.O. Building (inauguration of H.Q., Geneva).

202 Tragedian's Mask of 4th Century, B.C.

1966. 2,500th Anniv of Greek Theatre.

1014	202	1d. multicoloured	20	15
1015	-	1d.50 black, red & brn	20	15
1016	-	2d.50 black, grn & lt grn	20	15

1017	-	4d.50 multicoloured	50	30

DESIGNS—HORIZ: 1d.50, Dionysus in a Thespian ship-chariot (vase painting, 500–480 B.C.); 2d.50, Theatre of Dionysus, Athens. VERT: 4d.50, Dionysus dancing (after vase painting by Kleophredes, c. 500 B.C.).

203 Boeing 707 Jetliner crossing Atlantic Ocean

1966. Inauguration of Greek Airways Transatlantic Flights.

1018	203	6d. indigo, blue & lt blue	60	35

204 Tending Plants

1966. Greek Tobacco. Multicoloured.

1019		1d. Type **204**	25	15
1020		5d. Sorting leaf	70	40

205 Europa "Ship"

1966. Europa.

1021	205	1d.50 black, olive & grn	1·10	35
1022	205	4d.50 deep brown, brown and light brown	3·00	65

206 Horseman (embroidery)

1966. Greek "Popular" Art. Multicoloured.

1023		10l. Knitting-needle boxes (vert)	20	10
1024		30l. Type **206**	20	10
1025		50l. Cretan lyre (vert)	20	10
1026		1d. "Massa" (Musical instrument) (vert)	20	10
1027		1d.50 "Cross and Angels" (bas-relief after Melios) (vert)	20	10
1028		2d. "Sts. Constantine and Helen" (icon) (vert)	1·20	10
1029		2d.50 Carved altar-screen, St. Nicholas' Church, Galaxidion (vert)	25	10
1030		3d. 19th-century ship of Skyros (embroidery)	25	10
1031		4d. "Psiki" (wedding procession) (embroidery)	1·10	10
1032		4d.50 Distaff (vert)	50	25
1033		5d. Earrings and necklace (vert)	90	10
1034		20d. Detail of handwoven cloth	2·75	60

207 Princess Alexia

1966. Princess Alexia's First Birthday.

1035	207	2d. green	30	15
1036	-	2d.50 brown	35	15
1037	-	3d.50 blue	65	30

PORTRAITS: 2d.50, Royal Family; 3d.50, Queen Anne-Marie with Princess Alexia.

208 "Woodcutter" (after D. Filippotes)

1967. Greek Sculpture. Multicoloured.

1038		20l. *Night* (I. Cossos) (vert)	15	10
1039		50l. *Penelope* (L. Drossos) (vert)	15	10
1040		80l. *Shepherd* (G. Phitalis) (vert)	15	10

1041		2d. *Woman's Torso* (K. Demetriades) (vert)	35	10
1042		2d.50 *Kolokotronis* (L. Sochos) (vert)	25	10
1043		3d. *Girl Sleeping* (I. Halepas)	90	35
1044		10d. Type **208**	60	30

209 Olympic Rings ("Olympic Day")

1967. Sports Events. Multicoloured.

1045		1d. Type **209**	25	10
1046		1d.50 Marathon Cup, first Olympics (1896)	25	10
1047		2d.50 Hurdling	35	15
1048		5d. "The Discus-thrower" after C. Demetriades	65	45
1049		6d. Ancient Olympic stadium	1·00	30

The 2d.50, commemorates the European Athletics Cup, 1967. 5d. (vert), The European Highest Award Championships, 1968. 6d. The Inaug of "International Academy" buildings, Olympia.

210 Cogwheels

1967. Europa.

1050	210	2d.50 multicoloured	1·40	30
1051	210	4d.50 multicoloured	3·50	1·00

211 *Lonchi* (destroyer) and Sailor

1967. Nautical Week. Multicoloured.

1052		20l. Type **211**	25	15
1053		1d. "Eugene Eugenides" (cadet ship) (vert)	25	15
1054		2d.50 Merchant Marine Academy, Aspropyrgos, Attica	25	15
1055		3d. "Averoff" (cruiser) and Naval School, Poros	80	50
1056		6d. "Australis" (liner) and figurehead	60	35

212 The Plaka, Athens

1967. International Tourist Year. Multicoloured.

1057		2d.50 Island of Skopelos (horiz)	20	10
1058		4d.50 Apollo's Temple, Bassai, Peleponnese (horiz)	1·00	30
1059		6d. Type **212**	80	20

213 Soldier and Phoenix

1967. National Revolution of April 21st (1967).

1060	213	2d.50 multicoloured	15	10
1061	213	3d. multicoloured	20	15
1062	213	4d.50 multicoloured	65	45

214 Industrial Skyline

1967. First Convention of U.N. Industrial Development Organisation, Athens.

1063	214	4d.50 ultramarine, black and blue	65	40

215 "Seaside Scene" (A. Pelaletos)

1967. Children's Drawings. Multicoloured.

1064	20l. Type **215**	20	10
1065	1d.50 "Steamer and Island" (L. Tsirikas)	20	10
1066	3d.50 "Country Cottage" (K. Ambeliotis)	60	50
1067	6d. "The Church on the Hill" (N. Frangos)	50	20

216 Throwing the Javelin

1968. Sports Events, 1968. Multicoloured.

1068	50l. Type **216**	25	10
1069	1d. Long jumping	25	10
1070	1d.50 "Apollo's Head", Temple of Zeus (vert)	25	10
1071	2d.50 Olympic scene on Attic vase (vert)	40	10
1072	4d. Olympic rings (Olympic Day)	50	30
1073	4d.50 "Throwing the Discus", sculpture by Demetriades (European Athletic Championships, 1969) (vert)	1·20	60
1074	6d. Long-distance running (vert)	60	20

The 50l., 1d. and 6d. represent the Balkan Games, and the 1d.50 and 2d.50, the Olympic Academy Meeting.

217 F.I.A. and E.L.P.A. Emblems

1968. General Assembly of International Automobile Federation (F.I.A.), Athens.

1075	217	5d. blue and brown	1·10	40

218 Europa "Key"

1968. Europa.

1076	218	2d.50 multicoloured	1·90	40
1077	218	4d.50 multicoloured	3·00	1·20

219 Athene defeats Alkyoneus (from frieze, Altar of Zeus, Pergamos)

1968. "Hellenic Fight for Civilization" Exhibition, Athens. Multicoloured.

1078	10l. Type **219**	20	10
1079	20l. Athene attired for battle (bronze from Piraeus) (vert) (24×37 mm)	20	10
1080	50l. Alexander the Great (from sarcophagus of Alexander of Sidon) (24×37 mm)	25	10
1081	1d.50 Emperors Constantine and Justinian making offerings to the Holy Mother (Byzantine mosaic)	30	20
1082	2d.50 Emperor Constantine Paleologos (lithograph by D. Tsokos) (vert) (24×37 mm)	30	15
1083	3d. "Greece in Missolonghi" (painting by Delacroix) (vert) (28×40 mm)	30	10
1084	4d.50 "Evzone" (Greek soldier, painting by G. B. Scott) (vert) (28×40 mm)	55	40
1085	6d. "Victory of Samothrace" (statue) (vert) (28×40 mm)	60	45

220 The Unknown Priest and Teacher (Rhodes monument)

1968. 20th Anniv of Dodecanese Union with Greece. Multicoloured.

1086	2d. Type **220**	50	10
1087	5d. Greek flag on map (vert)	1·50	75

221 Congress Emblem

1968. 19th Biennial Congress of Greek Orthodox Archdiocese of North and South America.

1088	221	6d. multicoloured	1·00	40

222 GAPA Emblem

1968. Regional Congress of Greek-American Progressive Association (GAPA).

1089	222	6d. multicoloured	1·00	40

223 Hand of Aesculapius (fragment of bas-relief from Asclepios' Temple, Epidaurus)

1968. Fifth European Cardiological Congress. Athens.

1090	223	4d.50 black, yell & lake	1·90	1·00

224 Panathenaic Stadium

1968. Olympic Games, Mexico. Multicoloured.

1091	2d.50 Type **224**	50	20
1092	5d. Ancient Olympia	90	25
1093	10d. One of Pindar's odes	2·10	90

The 10d. is 28×40 mm.

225 P.Z.L.P 24 ramming Savoia Marchetti S.M.79–11 Sparviero Bomber

1968. Royal Hellenic Air Force. Multicoloured

1094	2d.50 Type **225**	35	10
1095	3d.50 Mediterranean Flight in Breguet 19 bomber, 1928	50	20
1096	8d. Farman H.F.III biplane and Lockheed F-104G Super Starfighter (vert)	1·10	70

226 Goddess "Hygeia"

1968. 20th Anniv of World Health Organization.

1097	226	5d. multicoloured	1·20	40

227 St. Zeno, the Letter-carrier

1969. Greek Post Office Festival.

1098	227	2d.50 multicoloured	80	40

228 Workers' Festival Parade (detail from Minoan vase)

1969. 50th Anniv of I.L.O. Multicoloured.

1099	1d.50 "Hephaestus and Cyclops" (detail from ancient bas-relief)	40	10
1100	10d. Type **228**	1·30	75

229 Yacht Harbour, Vouliagmeni

1969. Tourism. Multicoloured.

1101	1d. Type **229**	35	10
1102	5d. "Chorus of Elders" (Ancient drama) (vert)	1·30	80
1103	6d. View of Astypalia	45	20

230 Ancient Coin of Kamarina

1969. 20th Anniv of N.A.T.O. Multicoloured.

1104	2d.50 Type **230**	45	20
1105	4d.50 "Going into Battle" (from Corinthian vase) (horiz)	1·20	90

231 Colonnade

1969. Europa.

1106	231	2d.50 multicoloured	4·25	30
1107	231	4d.50 multicoloured	7·50	1·60

232 Gold Medal

1969. Ninth European Athletic Championships, Athens. Multicoloured.

1108	20l. Type **232**	20	15
1109	3d. Pole-vaulting, and ancient pentathlon contest	35	20
1110	5d. Relay-racing, and Olympic race c. 525 B.C. (horiz)	45	20
1111	8d. Throwing the discus, modern and c. 480 B.C.	2·10	95

233 19th-century Brig and Steam-ship (I. Poulakas)

1969. Navy Week and Merchant Marine Year. Multicoloured.

1112	80l. Type **233**	20	10

1113	2d. "Olympic Garland" (tanker) (horiz)	20	10
1114	2d.50 "Themistodes and Karteria, War of Independence, 1821" (anon) (41×29 mm)	35	10
1115	4d.50 "Velos" (modern destroyer) (horiz)	1·30	45
1116	6d. "The Battle of Salamis" (K. Volonakis) (41×29 mm)	1·80	85

234 Raising the Flag on Mt. Grammos

1969. 20th Anniv of Communists' Defeat on Mounts Grammos and Vitsi.

1117	234	2d.50 multicoloured	1·10	40

235 Athena Promachos

1969. 25th Anniv of Liberation. Multicoloured.

1118	4d. Type **235**	35	10
1119	5d. "Resistance" (21×37 mm)	1·80	80
1120	6d. Map of Eastern Mediterranean theatre	50	10

236 Demetrius Karatasios (statue by G. Demetriades)

1969. Heroes of Macedonia's Fight for Freedom. Multicoloured.

1121	1d.50 Type **236**	20	10
1122	2d.50 Emmanuel Pappas (statue by N. Perantinos)	20	10
1123	3d.50 Pavlos Melas (from painting by P. Mathiopoulos)	25	25
1124	4d.50 Capetan Kotas	1·00	75

237 Dolphin Mosaic, Delos (110 B.C.)

1970. Greek Mosaics. Multicoloured.

1125	20l. "Angel of the Annunciation", Daphne (11th-century) (vert) (23×34 mm)	20	10
1126	1d. Type **237**	20	10
1127	1d.50 "The Holy Ghost", Hosios Loukas Monastery (11th-century) (vert) (23×34 mm)	25	20
1128	2d. "Hunter", Pella (4th-century B.C.) (vert) (23×34 mm)	55	10
1129	5d. "Bird", St. George's Church, Salonika (5th-century) (vert) (23×34 mm)	65	20
1130	6d. "Christ", Nea Moni Church, Khios (5th-century)	1·40	1·00

238 Overwhelming the Cretan Bull (sculpture)

1970. "The Labours of Hercules".

1131	238	20l. multicoloured	20	10
1132	-	30l. multicoloured	20	10
1133	-	1d. black, blue and slate	45	10
1134	-	1d.50 brn, grn & ochre	45	10
1135	-	2d. multicoloured	2·75	60
1136	-	2d.50 brown, red & buff	40	10
1137	-	3d. multicoloured	2·75	10
1138	-	4d.50 multicoloured	40	20

1139	-	5d. multicoloured	55	15
1140	-	6d. multicoloured	55	15
1141	-	20d. multicoloured	2·30	70

DESIGNS—HORIZ: 30l. Hercules and Cerberus (from decorated pitcher); 1d.50, The Lernean Hydra (from stamnos); 2d. Hercules and Geryon (from amphora); 4d.50, Combat with the River-god Achelous (from pitcher); 5d. Overwhelming the Nemean Lion (from amphora); 6d. The Stymphalian Birds (from vase); 20d. Wrestling with Antaeus (from bowl). VERT: 1d. Golden Apples of the Hesperides (sculpture); 2d.50, The Erymanthine Boar (from amphora); 3d. The Centaur Nessus (from vase).

239 "Flaming Sun"

1970. Europa.

1142	239	2d.50 yellow and red	3·25	65
1143	-	3d. blue and light blue	3·25	70
1144	239	4d.50 yellow and blue	10·50	2·40

DESIGN—VERT: 3d. "Owl" and CEPT emblem.

240 Satellite and Dish Aerial

1970. Satellite Earth Telecommunications Station, Thermopylae.

1145	240	2d.50 multicoloured	55	25
1146	240	4d.50 multicoloured	1·50	1·00

241 Saints Cyril and Methodius with Emperor Michael III, (from 12th-cent wall-painting)

1970. Saints Cyril and Methodius Commemoration. Multicoloured.

1147	50l.	Saints Demetrius, Cyril and Methodius (mosaic) (21×37 mm)	20	15
1148	2d.	St. Cyril (Russian miniature) (25×32 mm)	85	65
1149	5d.	Type 241	55	20
1150	10d.	St. Methodius (Russian miniature) (25×32 mm)	90	65

Nos. 1148 and 1150 were issued together, se-tenant, forming a composite design.

242 Cephalonian Fir

1970. Nature Conservation Year. Multicoloured.

1151	80l.	Type 242	45	40
1152	2d.50	"Jankaea heldreichii" (plant) (23×34 mm)	1·70	30
1153	6d.	Rock Partridge (horiz)	2·75	50
1154	8d.	Wild goat	3·75	3·00

243 "Cultural Links"

1970. American–Hellenic Education Progressive Association Congress, Athens.

1155	243	6d. multicoloured	1·50	40

244 New U.P.U. Headquarters Building, Berne (Opening)

1970. Anniversaries. Multicoloured.

1156	50l.	Type 244	15	10

245 "The Nativity"

1970. Christmas. Scenes from "The Mosaic of the Nativity", Hosios Loukas Monastery. Multicoloured.

1161	2d.	"The Shepherds" (vert)	30	20
1162	4d.50	"The Magi" (vert)	55	35
1163	6d.	Type 245	1·30	90

246 Death of Bishop of Salona in Battle, Alamana (lithograph)

1971. 150th Anniv of War of Independence (1st issue). The Church. Multicoloured.

1164	50l.	Warriors taking the oath (medal) (vert)	20	20
1165	2d.	Patriarch Gregory V (statue by Phitalis) (vert)	25	20
1166	4d.	Type 246	35	20
1167	10d.	Bishop Germanos blessing the Standard (Vryzakis)	1·60	1·10

See also Nos. 1168/73, 1178/80, 1181/6 and 1187/89.

1971. 150th Anniv of War of Independence (2nd issue). The War at Sea. As T 246. Multicoloured.

1168	20l.	Leonidas (warship) (37×24 mm)	25	20
1169	1d.	Pericles (warship) (37×24 mm)	35	20
1170	1d.50	Terpsichore (warship) (from painting by Roux) (37×24 mm)	35	20
1171	2d.50	Karteria (warship) (from painting by Hastings) (37×24 mm)	35	20
1172	3d.	Battle of Samos (contemporary painting) (40×28 mm)	95	40
1173	6d.	Turkish Frigate ablaze, Battle of Yeronda (Michalis) (40×28 mm)	2·00	95

247 Spyridon Louis winning Marathon, Athens, 1896

1971. 75th Anniv of Olympic Games Revival. Multicoloured.

1174	3d.	Type 247	80	20
1175	8d.	P. de Coubertin and Memorial, Olympia (vert)	2·20	1·10

248 Europa Chain

1971. Europa.

1176	248	2d.50 yellow, grn & blk	3·25	40
1177	248	5d. yellow, orange & blk	9·75	1·90

1971. 150th Anniv of War of Independence (3rd issue). "Teaching the People". As T 246. Multicoloured.

1178	50l.	Eugenius Voulgaris (vert)	25	10
1179	2d.50	Dr. Adamantios Korais (vert)	25	20
1180	15d.	The Secret School (N. Ghyzis) (horiz)	1·90	1·20

SIZES: 50l., 2d.50, 23×34 mm. 15d. as Type 246.

1971. 150th Anniv of War of Independence (4th issue). The War on Land. As T 246. Multicoloured.

1181	50l.	Battle of Corinth (Krazeisen) (vert)	35	20
1182	1d.	Sacrifice of Kapsalia (Vryzakis) (vert)	35	20
1183	2d.	Suliot Women in Battle (Deneuville) (horiz)	35	20
1184	5d.	Battle of Athens (Zographos) (vert)	40	20
1185	6d.50	Battle of Maniaki (lithograph) (horiz)	60	20

1186	9d.	Death of Markos Botsaris at Karpenisi (Vryzakis) (horiz)	1·40	95

SIZES: 50l., 1d., 5d.25×40 mm. 2d.40×25 mm. 6d.50, 9d. as Type 246.

249 Kaltetsi Monastery and Seal of Peloponnesian Senate

1971. 150th Anniv of War of Independence (5th issue). Government.

1187	249	2d. black, green & brown	40	20
1188	-	2d.50 black, lt blue & bl	40	20
1189	-	20d. black, yellow & brn	2·50	1·70

DESIGNS: 2d.50, National Assembly Memorial, Epidavros, and Seal of Provincial Administration; 20d. Signature and seal of John Capodistria, first President of Greece.

250 Hosios Loukas Monastery, Boeotia

1972. Greek Monasteries and Churches. Multicoloured.

1190	50l.	Type 250	15	10
1191	1d.	Daphni Church, Attica	15	10
1192	2d.	St. John the Divine, Patmos	20	10
1193	2d.50	Panaghia Koumbelidiki Church, Kastoria	20	10
1194	4d.50	Panaghia ton Chalkeon, Saloniki	30	20
1195	6d.50	Panaghia Paregoritissa Church, Arta	30	20
1196	8d.50	St. Paul's Monastery, Mount Athos	1·80	1·50

251 Cretan Costume

1972. Greek Costumes (1st series). Multicoloured.

1197	50l.	Type 251	15	10
1198	1d.	Pindus bride	15	10
1199	2d.	Warrior-chief Missolonghi	15	10
1200	2d.50	Sarakatsana woman, Attica	15	10
1201	3d.	Nisiros woman	20	10
1202	4d.50	Megara woman	25	10
1203	6d.50	Trikeri (rural)	35	10
1204	10d.	Pylaia woman, Macedonia	4·00	1·40

See also Nos. 1232/48 and 1282/96.

252 Flag and Map

1972. Fifth Anniv of 1967 Revolution. Multicoloured.

1205	2d.50	Commemorative medal (horiz)	20	10
1206	4d.50	Type 252	45	25
1207	5d.	Facets of modern development	60	40

253 "Communications"

1972. Europa.

1208	253	3d. multicoloured	1·40	35
1209	253	4d.50 multicoloured	3·50	1·50

254 Acropolis, Athens

1972. 20th Anniv of Acropolis Motor Rally. Multicoloured.

1210	4d.50	Type 254	90	65
1211	5d.	Emblem and map	90	65

255 Gaia delivering Erecthonius to Athene

1972. Greek Mythology. Museum Pieces (1st series).

1212	255	1d.50 black and green	25	10
1213	-	2d. black and blue	25	20
1214	-	2d.50 black and brown	25	20
1215	-	5d. black and brown	90	50

DESIGNS: 2d. "Uranus" (altar piece); 2d.50, "The Gods repulsing the Giants"; 5d. "Zeus".
See also Nos. 1252/5 and 1271/4.

256 "Young Athlete" (statue)

1972. Olympic Games, Munich. Ancient Olympics. Multicoloured.

1216	50l.	Type 256	25	15
1217	1d.50	"Wrestlers" (bas-relief) (horiz)	25	15
1218	3d.50	"Female athlete" (statuette)	55	15
1219	4d.50	"Ballgame" (bas-relief) (horiz)	75	20
1220	10d.	"Runners" (amphora) (horiz)	2·10	90

257 Young Stamp Collector

1972. Stamp Day.

1221	257	2d.50 multicoloured	20	20

258 "The Birth of Christ"

1972. Christmas. Multicoloured.

1222	2d.50	"Pilgrimage of the Magi"	25	20
1223	4d.50	Type 258	25	20

Nos. 1222/3 were issued together, se-tenant, forming a composite design.

259 University Buildings

1973. Cent of Nat Polytechnic University, Athens.

1224	259	2d.50 multicoloured	40	20

260 "Spring" (wall fresco)

1973. Archaeological Discoveries, Island of Thera. Multicoloured.

1225	10l.	Type 260	20	15
1226	20l.	"Barley" jug	20	15
1227	30l.	"Blue Apes" fresco (horiz)	20	15
1228	1d.50	"Bird" (jug)	20	15

1229	2d.50 "Swallows" (detail, "Spring" fresco) (horiz)	20	20
1230	5d. "Wild Goats" fresco (horiz)	20	20
1231	6d.50 "Wrestlers" (detail, fresco) (horiz)	1·10	95

1973. Greek Regional Costumes (2nd series). As Type **251**. Multicoloured.

1232	10l. Peloponnese	10	10
1233	20l. Central Greece	10	10
1234	30l. Locris (Livanates)	10	10
1235	50l. Skyros (male)	10	10
1236	1d. Spetsai	10	10
1237	1d.50 Almyros	10	10
1238	2d.50 Macedonia (Roumlouki)	10	10
1239	3d.50 Salamis	20	10
1240	4d.50 Epirus (Souli)	20	10
1241	5d. Lefkas (Santa Maura)	35	10
1242	6d.50 Skyros (female)	45	10
1243	8d.50 Corinth	60	20
1244	10d. Corfu (Garitsa)	60	10
1245	15d. Epirus	70	10
1246	20d. Thessaly (Karagouniko)	1·90	10
1247	30p. Macedonia (Episkopi)	2·40	10
1248	50d. Thrace (Makra Gefyra)	5·75	3·75

261 Europa "Posthorn"

1973. Europa.

1249	**261**	2d.50 blue and light blue	70	20
1250	**261**	3d. red, orange and lake	1·20	25
1251	**261**	4d.50 brown, bronze and green	3·00	95

262 "Olympus" (from photograph by Boissonnas)

1973. Greek Mythology (2nd series).

1252	**262**	1d. black and grey	35	25
1253	-	2d. multicoloured	35	25
1254	-	2d.50 black, grey & brn	35	25
1255	-	4d.50 multicoloured	65	45

DESIGNS: 2d. "Zeus in combat with Typhoeus" (amphora); 2d.50, "Zeus at Battle of Giants" (altar relief); 4d.50, The "Punishment of Atlas and Prometheus" (vase).

263 Dr. G. Papanicolaou

1973. Honouring Dr. George Papanicolaou (cancer specialist).

1256	**263**	2d.50 multicoloured	15	10
1257	**263**	6d.50 multicoloured	45	35

264 Our Lady of the Annunciation

1973. 150th Anniv of Discovery of Miraculous Icon of our Lady of the Annunciation, Tinos.

1258	**264**	2d.50 multicoloured	40	30

265 "Triptolemus in a Chariot" (vase)

1973. European Transport Ministers Conference, Athens.

1259	**265**	4d.50 multicoloured	45	35

266 Child examining Stamp

1973. Stamp Day.

1260	**266**	2d.50 multicoloured	25	20

267 G. Averof

1973. National Benefactors (1st series).

1261	**267**	1d.50 brown	15	10
1262	-	2d. red	15	10
1263	-	2d.50 green	15	10
1264	-	4d. lilac	25	15
1265	-	6d.50 black	55	35

DESIGNS: 2d. A. Arsakis; 2d.50, C. Zappas; 4d. A. Syngros; 6d.50, I. Varvakis.
See also Nos. 1315/18.

268 "Lord Byron in Suliot costume" (by Thomas Phillips)

1974. 150th Death Anniv of Lord Byron. Multicoloured.

1266	**268**	2d.50 Type **268**	20	15
1267		4d.50 Byron taking the Oath at Grave of Markos Botsaris (lithograph)	25	20

269 Harpist of Keros

1974. Europa. Ancient Greek Sculptures. Multicoloured.

1268	**269**	3d. Type **269**	65	15
1269	-	4d.50 Athenian Maiden	1·00	25
1270	-	6d.50 Charioteer of Delphi (bronze)	3·00	90

270 "Theocracy of Zeus" (vase)

1974. Greek Mythology (3rd series).

1271	**270**	1d.50 black and orange	15	10
1272	-	2d. brown, red & orange	15	10
1273	-	2d.50 black, brn & orge	15	10
1274	-	10d. brown, red & orange	45	30

DESIGNS—HORIZ: 2d. "Athena's Birth" (vase); 2d.50, "Artemis, Apollo and Lito" (vase). VERT: 10d. "Hermes" (vase).

271 U.P.U. Emblem within Mycenaean Vase Design

1974. Centenary of U.P.U. Multicoloured.

1275	**271**	2d. Type **271**	15	10
1276	-	4d.50 Hermes (horiz)	15	10
1277	-	6d.50 Woman reading letter	45	35

272 Crete 1d. Stamp of 1905

1974. Stamp Day.

1278	**272**	2d.50 black, red & violet	20	20

273 Joseph

1974. Christmas. Multicoloured.

1279		2d. Type **273**	20	15
1280		4d.50 Virgin and Child on donkey	20	15
1281		8d.50 Jacob	20	15

Nos. 1279/81 were issued together, se-tenant, forming a composite design.

1974. Greek Costumes (3rd series). As T **251**. Multicoloured.

1282	20l. Megara	10	10
1283	30l. Salamis	10	10
1284	50l. Edipsos	10	10
1285	1d. Kymi	10	10
1286	1d.50 Sterea Hellas	10	10
1287	2d. Desfina	10	10
1288	3d. Epirus	10	10
1289	3d.50 Naousa	10	10
1290	4d. Hasia	10	10
1291	4d.50 Thasos	10	10
1292	5d. Skopelos	10	10
1293	6d.50 Epirus	10	10
1294	10d. Pelion	35	10
1295	25d. Kerkyra	90	10
1296	30d. Boeotia (Tanagra)	2·30	1·80

274 Secret Assembly, Vostitsa

1975. 150th Death Anniv of Girgorios Dikeos Papaflessas (Soldier).

1297	**274**	4d. black, brown & stone	10	10
1298	-	7d. multicoloured	15	10
1299	-	11d. multicoloured	45	35

DESIGNS—VERT: 7d. Papaflessas in uniform. HORIZ: 11d. Aghioi Apostoli (chapel), Kalamala.

275 Roses in Vase

1975. Europa. Multicoloured.

1300	**275**	4d. Type **275**	70	20
1301		7d. Erotokritos and Aretussa	1·40	45
1302		11d. Girl and sheep	4·00	1·20

276 Mansion, Kastoria

1975. National Architecture.

1303	**276**	10l. black and blue	15	15
1304	-	40l. black and red	20	15
1305	-	4d. black and brown	20	15
1306	-	6d. black and blue	20	15
1307	-	11d. black and orange	40	30

DESIGNS: 40l. House, Arnea, Halkidiki; 4d. House, Veria; 6d. Mansion, Siatista; 11d. Mansion, Amelakia, Thessaly.

277 Neolithic Goddess

1975. International Women's Year.

1308	**277**	1d.50 brown, deep mauve and mauve	15	10
1309	-	8d.50 black, red and ochre	15	10
1310	-	11d. black, dp blue & bl	45	35

DESIGNS: 8d.50, Confrontation between Antigone and Creon; 11d. Women "Looking to the Future".

278 Alexandros Papanastasiou (founder) and University Buildings

1975. 50th Anniv of Thessaloniki University.

1311	**278**	1d.50 sepia and brown	15	10
1312	-	4d. multicoloured	15	10
1313	-	11d. multicoloured	45	35

DESIGNS: 4d. Original University building; 11d. Plan of University city.

279 Greek 100d. Stamp of 1933

1975. Stamp Day.

1314	**279**	11d. brown, cream & grn	45	35

280 Evangelos Zappas and Zappeion Building

1975. National Benefactors (2nd series).

1315	**280**	1d. black, grey and green	15	10
1316	-	4d. black, grey and brown	15	10
1317	-	6d. black, brown & orge	20	10
1318	-	11d. black, grey and red	45	35

DESIGNS: 4d. Georgios Rizaris and Rizarios Ecclesiastical School; 6d. Michael Tositsas and Metsovion Technical University; 11d. Nicolaos Zosimas and Zosimea Academy.

281 Pontos Lyre

1975. Musical Instruments. Multicoloured.

1319	10l. Type **281**	10	10
1320	20l. Musicians (Byzantine mural)	10	10
1321	1d. Cretan lyre	10	10
1322	1d.50 Tambourine	10	10
1323	4d. Cithern-player (from amphora) (horiz)	10	10
1324	6d. Bagpipes	10	10
1325	7d. Lute	10	10
1326	10d. Barrel-organ	10	10
1327	11d. Pipes and zournades	35	10
1328	20d. "Praise God" (Byzantine mural) (horiz)	50	10
1329	25d. Drums	55	10
1330	30d. Kanonaki (horiz)	1·80	1·00

282 Early telephone

1976. Telephone Centenary. Multicoloured.

1331	7d. Type **282**	30	20
1332	11d. Modern telephone and globe	30	20

Nos. 1331/2 were issued together, *se-tenant*, forming a composite design.

283 Battle of Missolonghi

1976. 150th Anniv of Fall of Missolonghi.

1333	**283**	4d. multicoloured	25	20

284 Florina Jug

1976. Europa. Multicoloured.

1334	7d. Type **284**	55	25
1335	8d.50 Plate with birds design (25×30 mm)	55	25
1336	11d. Egina pitcher	2·40	85

285 Lion attacking Bull

1976. Ancient Sealing-stones. Multicoloured.

1337	2d. Type **285**	15	10
1338	4d.50 Water birds	15	10
1339	7d. Wounded bull	15	10
1340	8d.50 Head of Silenus (27×40 mm)	20	15
1341	11d. Cow feeding calf (40×27 mm)	40	25

286 Long-jumping

1976. Olympic Games, Montreal. Multicoloured.

1342	50l. Type **286**	15	10
1343	2d. Handball	15	10
1344	3d.50 Wrestling	15	10
1345	4d. Swimming	20	10
1346	11d. Athens and Montreal stadiums (52×37 mm)	25	20
1347	25d. The Olympic flame	1·50	1·10

287 Lemnos

1976. Tourist Publicity. Multicoloured.

1348	30d. Type **287**	45	10
1349	50d. Lesbos (horiz)	1·00	10
1350	75d. Chios (horiz)	1·30	15
1351	100d. Samos (horiz)	2·40	1·50

288 The Magi speaking to the Jews

1976. Christmas. Illustrations from manuscripts at Esfigmenou Monastery. Multicoloured.

1352	4d. Type **288**	20	15
1353	7d. The Adoration of the Magi	35	25

289 Lascaris Book of Grammar, 1476

1976. 500th Anniv of Printing of First Greek Book.

1354	**289**	4d. multicoloured	25	20

290 Heinrich Schliemann

1976. Centenary of Schliemann's Excavation of the Royal Graves, Mycenae. Multicoloured.

1355	2d. Type **290**	20	10
1356	4d. Gold bracelet (horiz)	20	10
1357	5d. Silver and gold brooch	20	15
1358	7d. Gold diadem (horiz)	35	15
1359	11d. Gold mask	80	50

291 "Patients visiting Aesculapius" (relief)

1977. International Rheumatism Year.

1360	**291**	50l. black, stone and red	15	10
1361	-	1d. black, orange and red	15	10
1362	-	1d.50 black, stone and red	15	10
1363	-	2d. black, orange and red	15	10
1364	-	20d. black, stone and red	40	25

DESIGNS—(22×27 mm): 1d. Ancient clinic; 1d.50, "Aesculapius curing a young man" (relief); 2d. Hercules and nurse. (23×34 mm): 20d. "Cured patient offering model of leg" (relief).

292 Fortresses of Mani

1977. Europa. Multicoloured.

1365	5d. Type **292**	90	15
1366	7d. Santorin (vert)	1·00	20
1367	15d. Lassithi Plain, Crete	3·50	60

293 Emblem and Transport

1977. 45th European Conference of Ministers of Transport.

1368	**293**	7d. multicoloured	25	20

294 Alexandria Lighthouse (Roman coin)

1977. "The Civilizing Influence of Alexander the Great". Multicoloured.

1369	50l. Type **294**	20	10
1370	1d. "Placing the Works of Homer in Achilles' tomb" (fresco, Raphael)	20	10
1371	1d.50 Descending to sea bed in special ship (Flemish miniature)	20	10
1372	3d. In search of the water of life (Hindu plate)	25	10
1373	7d. Alexander the Great on horseback (Coptic carpet)	25	10
1374	11d. Listening to oracle (Byzantine manuscript)	40	10

1375	30d. Death of Alexander the Great (Persian miniature)	85	45

295 Wreath in Front of University

1977. Restoration of Democracy.

1376	**295**	4d. blue, green and black	15	10
1377	-	7d. multicoloured	20	10
1378	-	20d. multicoloured	55	35

DESIGNS—HORIZ: (26×22 mm) 7d. Demonstrators at University. VERT: (22×26 mm) 20d. Hand with olive branch, University and flags.

296 Archbishop Makarios

1977. Archbishop Makarios Commemoration.

1379	**296**	4d. black and grey	20	15
1380	-	7d. black, brown & stone	25	25

DESIGN: 7d. Makarios and map of Cyprus.

297 Melas Building, Athens (former post office)

1977. 19th-century Hellenic Architecture.

1381	**297**	50l. black, stone and red	15	10
1382	-	1d. black, stone & green	15	10
1383	-	1d.50 black, stone & bl	15	10
1384	-	2d. black, stone & green	20	10
1385	-	5d. black, stone & yellow	20	10
1386	-	50d. black, stone & orge	75	50

DESIGNS: 1d. Institution for the Blind, Thessalonika; 1d.50, Town Hall of Hermoupolis, Syros; 2d. Branch Office of National Bank, Piraeus; 5d. Ilissia (Palace of Duchess of Plakentia), Athens; 50d. Municipal Theatre, Patras.

298 The Battle of Navarino

1977. 150th Anniv of Battle of Navarino.

1387	**298**	4d. yellow, black & brn	20	15
1388	-	7d. multicoloured	25	20

DESIGN: 7d. Admirals Van der Heyden, Sir Edward Codrington and Comte de Rigny.

299 Parthenon and Industrial Complex

1977. Environmental Protection. Multicoloured.

1389	3d. Type **299**	20	10
1390	4d. Birds and fish (horiz)	20	10
1391	7d. Living and dead trees (horiz)	20	10
1392	30d. Head of Erechtheum caryatid and chimneys	65	50

300 Map of Greece and Ships

1977. "Greeks Abroad". Multicoloured.

1393	4d. Type **300**	15	10
1394	5d. Globe and Greek flag	15	10
1395	7d. Globe and swallows	15	10
1396	11d. Envelope with flags	20	15
1397	13d. Map of the World	50	35

301 The Port of Kalamata (C. Parthenis)

1977. Greek Paintings. Multicoloured.

1398	1d.50 Type **301**	20	10
1399	2d.50 Arsanas (S. Papaloucas) (vert)	20	10
1400	4d. Santorin (C. Maleas)	20	10
1401	7d. The Engagement (N. Gyzis)	20	10
1402	11d. The Straw Hat (N. Lytras) (vert)	20	10
1403	15d. Spring (G. Iacovidis)	40	30

302 Ebenus cretica

1978. Greek Flora. Multicoloured.

1404	1d.50 Type **302**	15	10
1405	2d.50 Fritillaria rhodokanakis	15	10
1406	3d. Campanula oreadum	15	10
1407	4d. Lilium heldreichii	15	10
1408	7d. Viola delphinantha	20	15
1409	25d. Paeonia rhodia	60	45

303 Horse Postman and Pre-stamp Cancel

1978. 150th Anniv of Postal Service. Multicoloured.

1410	4d. Type **303**	15	10
1411	5d. "Maximilianos" (passenger steamer) and Greek "Hermes" stamp	15	10
1412	7d. Steam mail train and 1896 Olympic Games stamp	20	10
1413	30d. Postmen on motor cycles and 1972 "Stamp Day" commemorative	60	45
MS1414	101×92 mm. Nos. 1410/13 (sold at 60d.)	1·40	1·20

304 Lighting the Olympic Flame

1978. 80th International Olympic Committee Session, Athens. Multicoloured.

1415	7d. Type **304**	80	35
1416	13d. Start of 100 m race	1·40	85

305 St. Sophia, Salonika

1978. Europa. Multicoloured.

1417	4d. Type **305**	1·10	30
1418	7d. Lysicrates' Monument, Athens	2·20	75

306 Bust of Aristotle

1978. 2300th Death Anniv of Aristotle. Multicoloured.

1419	2d. Type **306**	20	15
1420	4d. The School of Athens (detail Raphael)	20	10
1421	7d. Map of Chalkidiki and statue plinth	35	20

| 1422 | 20d. *Aristotle the Wise* (Byzantine fresco) (21×37 mm) | 55 | 35 |

307 Rotary Emblem (50th anniv)

1978. Anniversaries and Events. Multicoloured.

1423	1d. Type **307**	25	20
1424	1d.50 Surgery (11th Greek Surgery Congress) (vert)	25	20
1425	2d.50 Ugo Foscolo (poet, birth bicentenary)	25	20
1426	5d. Bronze head (25th anniv of European Convention on Human Rights)	25	20
1427	7d. Hand with reins (Conference of Ministers of Culture of Council of Europe countries) (vert)	25	20
1428	13d. *Wright Flyer I* with Daedalus and Icarus (75th anniv of first powered flight) (vert)	55	40

308 The Poor Woman with Five Children

1978. *The Twelve Months* (Greek fairy tale). Multicoloured.

1429	2d. Type **308**	15	10
1430	3d. The poor woman and the twelve months	15	10
1431	4d. The poor woman and the gold coins	20	15
1432	20d. The poor woman with her children and the rich woman with the snakes	40	30

309 Grafted Plant and Circulation Diagram

1978. Transplants. Multicoloured.

| 1433 | 4d. Type **309** | 20 | 10 |
| 1434 | 10d. "Miracle of Sts. Cosmas and Damian" (Alonso de Sedano) | 35 | 20 |

310 "Virgin and Child"

1978. Christmas. Icons from Stavronikita Monastery, Mount Athos. Multicoloured.

| 1435 | 4d. Type **310** | 20 | 10 |
| 1436 | 7d. "The Baptism of Christ" | 25 | 20 |

311 First Academy, Nauplion, and Cadet

1978. 150th Anniv of Military Academy. Multicoloured.

1437	1d.50 Type **311**	15	10
1438	2d. Academy coat of arms (vert)	15	10
1439	10d. Modern Academy, Athens, and cadet	40	30

312 *Antipliarchos Laskos* (destroyer)

1978. Greek Naval Ships. Multicoloured.

1440	50l. Type **312**	15	10
1441	1d. *Andromeda* (motor torpedo-boat)	15	10
1442	2d.50 *Papanicolis* (submarine)	15	10

1443	4d. *Psara* (cruiser)	15	10
1444	5d. *Madonna of Hydra* (armed sailing caique)	20	10
1445	7d. Byzantine dromon	20	15
1446	50d. Athenian trireme	75	45

313 Map of Greece

1978. The Greek State.

1447	**313**	7d. multicoloured	15	10
1448	**313**	11d. multicoloured	20	10
1449	**313**	13d. multicoloured	40	30

314 Kitsos Tsavellas

1979. "The Struggle of the Souliots".

1450	**314**	1d.50 lt brn, blk & brn	15	10
1451	-	3d. multicoloured	15	10
1452	-	10d. multicoloured	20	15
1453	-	20d. ochre, black and brown	35	25

DESIGNS—HORIZ: 3d. Souli Castle; 10d. Fighting Souliots. VERT: 20d. The dance of Zalongo.

315 Figurine found at Amorgos

1979. Art of the Aegean.

| 1454 | **315** | 20d. multicoloured | 45 | 35 |

316 Cretan Postmen

1979. Europa. Multicoloured.

| 1455 | 4d. Type **316** | 80 | 15 |
| 1456 | 7d. Mounted postman | 80 | 25 |

Nos. 1454/5 were issued in *se-tenant* pairs, forming a composite design.

317 Nicolas Skoufas

1979. Anniversaries and Events. Multicoloured.

1457	1d.50 Type **317** (founder of Friendly Society, birth bicentenary)	25	20
1458	2d. Steam and diesel locomotives (75th anniv of railway) (horiz)	25	20
1459	3d. Basketball (European Basketball Championship)	25	20
1460	4d. Fossil moonfish *Mene psarianos* (7th International Congress of Mediterranean Neogene) (horiz)	25	20
1461	10d. Greek church (Balkan Tourist Year)	25	20
1462	20d. Victory of Paeonius and flags (50th anniv of Balkan Sports)	40	35

318 Flags of Member States forming Ear of Wheat

1979. Signing of Treaty, Accession of Greece to European Community. Multicoloured.

| 1463 | 7d. Type **318** | 20 | 15 |
| 1464 | 30d. European Parliament (horiz) | 50 | 35 |

319 "Girl with Dove" (classic statue)

1979. International Year of the Child. Multicoloured.

1465	5d. Type **319**	15	10
1466	8d. Girl with doves	20	15
1467	20d. "Mother and Children" (detail, Iacovides)	35	25

320 Head of Philip of Macedonia

1979. Archaeological Discoveries from Vergina. Multicoloured.

1468	6d. Type **320**	15	10
1469	8d. Gold Wreath	15	10
1470	10d. Copper vessel	20	10
1471	14d. Golden casket (horiz)	25	10
1472	18d. Silver ewer	25	10
1473	20d. Gold quiver	25	15
1474	30d. Iron cuirass	75	50

321 Purple Heron

1979. Endangered Birds. Multicoloured.

1475	6d. Type **321**	15	15
1476	8d. Audouin's gull	15	15
1477	10d. Eleonora's falcon (horiz)	15	15
1478	14d. River kingfisher (horiz)	15	15
1479	20d. Eastern white pelican	35	15
1480	25d. White-tailed sea eagle	1·20	80

322 Agricultural Bank of Greece (50th anniv)

1979. Anniversaries and Events.

1481	**322**	3d. black, yellow & olive	20	20
1482	-	4d. multicoloured	20	20
1483	-	6d. multicoloured	25	20
1484	-	8d. multicoloured	25	20
1485	-	10d. multicoloured	25	20
1486	-	12d. multicoloured	25	20
1487	-	14d. multicoloured	25	20
1488	-	18d. multicoloured	40	25
1489	-	25d. multicoloured	75	50

DESIGNS—HORIZ: 10d. Ionic capital and map of Balkans ("Balkanfila '79" Stamp Exhibition); 25d. Parliamentary Meeting (104th anniv of Greek Parliament). VERT: 4d. Cosmas the Aetolian (monk and martyr) (death bicent.); 6d. Basil the Great (1600th death anniv); 8d. Magnifying glass and map of Balkan countries ("Balkanfila '79" Stamp Exhibition); 12d. Aristotelis Valaoritis (poet) (death centenary); 14d. Golfer (World Golfing Championship); 18d. Bust of Hippocrates (International Hippocratic Foundation, Kos).

323 Parnassos

1979. Landscapes. Multicoloured.

1490	50l. Type **323**	20	10
1491	1d. Tempi (horiz)	20	10
1492	2d. Milos	20	10
1493	4d. Vikos Gorge	20	10
1494	5d. Misolonghi (horiz)	20	10
1495	6d. Louros Aqueduct	20	10
1496	7d. Samothraki	20	10
1497	8d. Sithonia, Chalkidike (horiz)	20	10
1498	10d. Samaria Gorge	20	10
1499	12d. Sifnos	20	10
1500	14d. Kymi (horiz)	25	10
1501	18d. Ios	45	10
1502	20d. Thasos	50	10
1503	30d. Paros (horiz)	85	10
1504	50d. Cephalonia	1·60	70

324 Gate of Galerius

1980. First Hellenic Nephrology Congress, Thessalonika.

| 1505 | **324** | 8d. blue, black and red | 30 | 20 |

325 Aegosthena Castle

1980. Castles, Caves and Bridges. Multicoloured.

1506	4d. Type **325**	15	10
1507	6d. Byzantine castle, Thessalonika (horiz)	15	10
1508	8d. Perama cave, Ioannina	15	10
1509	10d. Dyros cave, Mani	15	10
1510	14d. Arta bridge (horiz)	25	15
1511	20d. Kalogiros bridge, Epirus (horiz)	40	20

326 Aristarchus' Theorem and Temple of Hera

1980. 2300th Birth Anniv of Aristarchus of Samos (astronomer).

| 1512 | **326** | 10d. pink, black & brown | 20 | 15 |
| 1513 | - | 20d. multicoloured | 50 | 30 |

DESIGN: 20d. Heliocentric system.

327 George Seferis (writer)

1980. Europa.

| 1514 | **327** | 8d. brown, blue & black | 1·10 | 15 |
| 1515 | - | 14d. brn, blk and cream | 1·60 | 50 |

DESIGN: 14d. Maria Callas (opera singer).

328 Open Book

1980. Energy Conservation. Multicoloured.

| 1516 | 8d. Type **328** | 20 | 10 |
| 1517 | 20d. Lightbulb and candle (vert) | 50 | 35 |

329 Fire-fighting

1980. Anniversaries and Events. Multicoloured.

1518	4d. Type **329** (50th anniv of fire brigade)		25	20
1519	6d. St. Demetrius (mosaic) (1700th birth anniv) (vert)		25	20
1520	8d. Revolutionaries (Theriso revolution, 75th anniv)		25	20
1521	10d. Ancient vase and olive branch (World Olive Oil Year) (vert)		25	20
1522	14d. International press emblem (15th International Journalists Federation Congress) (vert)		25	20
1523	20d. Constantinos Ikonomos (cleric and scholar), (birth bicent.) (vert)		40	30

330 Olympia and Coin of Elia

1980. Olympic Games, Moscow. Designs showing Greek stadia. Multicoloured.

1524	8d. Type **330**		20	10
1525	14d. Delphi and Delphic coin		55	40
1526	18d. Epidaurus and coin of Olympia		20	15
1527	20d. Rhodes and coin of Kos		35	15
1528	50d. Panathenaic stadium and First Olympic Games medal		1·20	65

331 Asbestos

1980. Minerals. Multicoloured.

1529	6d. Type **331**		15	10
1530	8d. Gypsum (vert)		15	10
1531	10d. Copper		15	10
1532	14d. Barite (vert)		50	30
1533	18d. Chromite		15	10
1534	20d. Mixed sulphides (vert)		35	15
1535	30d. Bauxite (vert)		60	40

332 Dassault Mirage III Jet Fighter

1980. Anniversaries and Events. Multicoloured.

1536	6d. Breakdown truck (20th anniv of Automobile and Touring Club of Greece road assistance service) (horiz)		25	20
1537	8d. Type **332** (50th anniv of Air Force)		25	20
1538	12d. Piper PA-18 Super Cub light airplane outside hangar (50th anniv of Thessalonika Flying Club) (horiz)		25	20
1539	20d. Harbour scene (50th anniv of Piraeus Port Organization)		40	30
1540	25d. Association for Macedonian Studies Headquarters (40th anniv)		55	35

333 Left Detail of Poulakis' Painting

1980. Christmas. Details from *He is Happy Thanks to You* by T. Poulakis (in St. John's Monastery, Pataros). Multicoloured.

1541	6d. Type **333**		20	20
1542	14d. Virgin and Child (centre)		25	20
1543	20d. Right detail		30	25

Nos. 1541/3 were issued together, *se-tenant*, forming a composite design.

334 Fresh and Canned Vegetables

1981. Exports. Multicoloured.

1544	9d. Type **334**		15	10
1545	17d. Fruit		20	15
1546	20d. Cotton		25	20
1547	25d. Marble		50	30

335 "Kira Maria" (Alexandrian folk dance)

1981. Europa. Multicoloured.

1548	12d. Type **335**		80	10
1549	17d. "Sousta" (Cretan dance)		1·50	40

336 Olympic Stadium, Kalogreza

1981. European Athletic Championships, Athens (1982) (1st issue).

1550	**336**	12d. blue, black & lt blue	30	10
1551	-	17d. multicoloured	55	30

DESIGN: 17d. Athletes converging on Greece. See also Nos. 1586/8.

337 Human Figure showing Kidneys

1981. Anniversaries and Events.

1552	**337**	2d. multicoloured	25	20
1553	-	3d. multicoloured	25	20
1554	-	6d. multicoloured	25	20
1555	-	9d. yellow, black & brn	25	20
1556	-	12d. multicoloured	25	20
1557	-	21d. multicoloured	40	30
1558	-	40d. red, blue & dp blue	65	50

DESIGNS AND EVENTS—VERT: 2d. Type **337** (8th World Nephrology Conference, Athens); 3d. Parachutist, glider, Potez 25 biplane and boy with model glider (50th anniv of Greek National Air Club); 6d. Meteora Monasteries, Thessaly, and Konitsa Bridge, Epirus (International Historical Symposium, Volos, and centenary of incorporation of Thessaly and Epirus into Greece); 12d. Oil rig (first Greek oil production); 40d. Heart (15th World Cardiovascular Surgery Conference Athens). HORIZ: 9d. Bowl with "eye" decoration (50th anniv of Greek Ophthalmological Society); 21d. Globes, plant and coin (Foundation in Athens of World Association for International Relations).

338 Variable Scallops

1981. Shells, Fish and Butterflies. Multicoloured.

1559	4d. Type **338**		20	10
1560	5d. Painted comber (fish)		20	10
1561	12d. Mediterranean parrotfishes		20	10
1562	15d. Dentex (fish)		20	10
1563	17d. Apollo (butterfly)		60	50
1564	50d. Pale clouded yellow (butterfly)		1·40	95

339 Aegean Island Bell Tower

1981. Bell Towers and Altar Screens. Multicoloured.

1565	4d. Type **339**		20	10
1566	6d. Altar gate, St. Paraskevi Church, Metsovo		20	10
1567	8d. Altar gate, Pelion (horiz)		20	10
1568	12d. Bell tower, Saints Constantine and Helen Church, Halkiades, Epirus		20	10
1569	17d. Altar screen, St. Nicholas Church, Velvendos (horiz)		20	15
1570	30d. Icon of St. Jacob and stand, Alexandroupolis Church Museum		45	20
1571	40d. Upper section of altar gate, St. Nicholas Church, Makrinitsa		85	70

340 Town Scene

1981. Anniversaries and Events. Multicoloured.

1572	3d. Type **340** (Council of Europe Urban Renaissance campaign)		25	20
1573	9d. St. Simeon, Archbishop of Thessalonika (Canonization by Greek Orthodox Church) (vert)		25	20
1574	15d. Child Jesus (detail from Byzantine icon) (Breast feeding campaign) (vert)		40	30
1575	17d. Gina Bachauer (pianist, 5th death anniv) (vert)		45	30
1576	21d. Constantine Broumidis (artist, 175th birth anniv) (vert)		45	30
1577	50d. "Phoenix" banknotes 1831 (first banknotes, 150th anniv)		85	70

341 Old Parliament Building (museum)

1982. Anniversaries and Events. Multicoloured.

1578	2d. Type **341** (centenary of Historical and Ethnological Society)		25	20
1579	9d. Angelos Sikelianos (poet, 31st death anniv) (vert)		25	20
1580	15d. Harilaos Tricoupis (politician, 150th birth anniv) (vert)		25	20
1581	21d. Mermaid (History of Aegean Islands Exhibition) (vert)		40	30
1582	30d. Airbus Industrie A300 jetliner and emblem (25th anniv of Olympic Airways)		55	40
1583	50d. Skull of Petralona man and Petralona cave (3rd European Congress of Anthropology, Petralona)		80	60

342 "Flight from Missolonghi"

1982. Europa. Multicoloured.

1584	21d. Bust of Miltiades and shield (Battle of Marathon)		3·50	35
1585	30d. Type **342**		5·75	95

343 Pole-vaulter and Wreath

1982. European Athletic Championships (2nd issue). Multicoloured.

1586	21d. Type **343**		25	15
1587	25d. Women runners (vert)		40	15
1588	40d. Athletes at start of race, shot putter, high jumper and hurdler		85	65

344 Lectionary Heading

1982. Byzantine Book Illustrations. Multicoloured.

1589	4d. Type **344**		20	10
1590	6d. Initial letter E (vert)		20	10
1591	12d. Initial letter T (vert)		25	10
1592	15d. Canon-table of Gospel readings (vert)		25	15
1593	80d. Heading from zoology book		1·30	80

345 *Karaiskakis' Camp in Piraeus* (detail, von Krazeisen)

1982. Birth Bicentenary of Georges Karaiskakis (revolutionary leader).

1594	**345**	12d. green, black & blue	35	15
1595	-	50d. multicoloured	95	70

DESIGN: 50d. Karaiskakis meditating.

346 Cypriot "Disappearances" Demonstration

1982. Amnesty International Year of the "Disappearances". Multicoloured.

1596	15d. Type **346**		25	20
1597	75d. Victims, barbed wire and candle		1·40	1·00

347 Demonstration in Athens, 25 March 1942–44 (P. Zachariou.)

1982. National Resistance, 1941–44. Multicoloured.

1598	1d. Type **347**		20	10
1599	2d. "Kalavryta's Sacrifice" (S. Vasillou)		20	10
1600	5d. "Resistance in Thrace" (A. Tassos) (vert)		20	10
1601	9d. "The Onset of the Struggle in Crete" (P. Gravalos) (vert)		35	10
1602	12d. Resistance Fighters (vert)		25	10
1603	21d. "Gorgopotamos" (A. Tassos) (vert)		55	30
1604	30d. "Kaisariani, Athens" (G. Sikeliotis)		55	30
1605	50d. "The Struggle in Northern Greece" (V. Katraki)		1·50	95

MS1606 Two sheets (a) 90×81 mm. Nos. 1598/9 and 1604/5; (b) 81×90 mm. Nos. 1600/3 | 6·00 | 3·75

348 Mary and Jesus

1982. Christmas. Early Christian Bas-reliefs. Multicoloured.

1607	9d. Type **348**		20	15
1608	21d. Jesus in manger		50	35

349 Figurehead from Tsamados's *Ares* (brig)

1983. 25th Anniv of International Maritime Organization. Ships' Figureheads. Multicoloured.

1609	11d. Type **349**		20	10
1610	15d. Miaoulis's "Ares" (full-rigged ship) (vert)		20	10
1611	18d. Topsail schooner from Sphakia (vert)		40	15
1612	25d. Bouboulina's "Spetses" (full-rigged ship) (vert)		55	30
1613	40d. Babas's "Epameinondas" (brig) (vert)		80	40
1614	50d. "Carteria" (steamer)		1·50	1·00

350 Letter and Map of Greece showing Postcode Districts

1983. Inauguration of Postcode. Multicoloured.
1615	15d. Type 350	20	15
1616	25d. Hermes' head within posthorn	65	35

351 Archimedes

1983. Europa. Multicoloured.
1617	25d. Acropolis, Athens (49×34 mm)	2·75	50
1618	80d. Type 351	6·00	1·60

352 Rowing

1983. Sports. Multicoloured.
1619	15d. Type 352	20	10
1620	18d. Water skiing (vert)	35	10
1621	27d. Windsurfing (vert)	90	65
1622	50d. Ski lift (vert)	70	40
1623	80d. Skiing	2·10	1·30

353 Marinos Antypas (farmers' leader)

1983. Personalities. Multicoloured.
1624	**353** 6d. multicoloured	20	10
1625	- 9d. multicoloured	20	10
1626	- 15d. multicoloured	20	10
1627	- 20d. multicoloured	35	10
1628	- 27d. multicoloured	45	15
1629	- 32d. multicoloured	65	35
1630	- 40d. yellow, brown & blk	85	35
1631	- 50d. multicoloured	1·10	85

DESIGNS: 9d. Nicholas Plastiras (soldier and statesman); 15d. George Papandreou (statesman); 20d. Constantin Cavafy (poet); 27d. Nikos Kazantzakis (writer); 32d. Manolis Calomiris (composer); 40d. George Papanicolaou (medical researcher); 50d. Despina Achladioti, "Matron of Rho" (patriot).

354 Democritus

1983. First Int Democritus Congress, Xanthe.
1632	**354** 50d. multicoloured	90	50

355 Poster by V. Katraki

1983. Tenth Anniv of Polytechnic School Uprising. Multicoloured.
1633	15d. Type 355	20	10
1634	30d. Students leaving Polytechnic	55	35

356 The Deification of Homer

1983. Homeric Odes. Multicoloured.
1635	**356** 2d. sepia and brown	20	10
1636	- 3d. brown, lt orge & orge	20	10
1637	- 4d. yellow, brn & dp brn	20	10
1638	- 5d. multicoloured	20	10
1639	- 6d. orange and brown	20	10
1640	- 10d. lt orge, brn & orge	20	10
1641	- 14d. orge, lt orge & brn	20	10
1642	- 15d. lt orge, orge & brn	25	10
1643	- 20d. bistre, black & brn	25	10
1644	- 27d. brown, pale orange and orange	40	15
1645	- 30d. brown, pale orange and orange	50	10
1646	- 32d. orge, brn & lt orge	60	15
1647	- 50d. brn, lt orge & orge	85	10
1648	- 75d. brown, orange & red	1·20	10
1649	- 100d. sepia, green & brn	2·75	95

DESIGN—HORIZ: 3d. Abduction of Helen by Paris (pot); 4d. Wooden horse; 5d. Achilles throwing dice with Ajax (jar); 14d. Battle between Ajax and Hector (dish); 15d. Priam requesting body of Hector (pot); 27d. Ulysses escaping from Polyphemus's cave; 32d. Ulysses and Sirens; 50d. Ulysses slaying suitors; 75d. Heroes of Iliad (cup). VERT: 6d. Achilles; 10d. Hector receiving arms from his parents (vase); 20d. Binding of Polyphemus; 30d. Ulysses meeting Nausica; 100d. Homer (bust).

357 Horse's Head, Chariot of Seline

1984. Parthenon Marbles. Multicoloured.
1650	14d. Type 357	75	15
1651	15d. Dionysus	45	15
1652	20d. Hestia, Dione and Aphrodite	65	35
1653	27d. Ilissus	90	35
1654	32d. Lapith and Centaur	1·90	1·00

MS1655 105×81 mm. 15d. Horseman (left); 21d. Horeman (right); 27d. Heroes (left); 32d. Heroes (right) ... 8·75 7·25

358 Bridge

1984. Europa. 25th Anniv of C.E.P.T.
1656	**358** 15d. multicoloured	80	25
1657	**358** 27d. multicoloured	2·20	1·30

359 Ancient Stadium, Olympia

1984. Olympic Games, Los Angeles. Multicoloured.
1658	14d. Type 359	25	20
1659	15d. Athletes preparing for training	35	10
1660	20d. Flute player, discus thrower and long jumper	55	25
1661	32d. Athletes training	1·00	60
1662	80d. K. Vikelas and Panathenaic Stadium	3·00	1·50

360 Tank on Map of Cyprus

1984. Tenth Anniv of Turkish Invasion of Cyprus. Multicoloured.
1663	20d. Type 360	35	20
1664	32d. Hand grasping barbed wire and map of Cyprus	80	65

361 Pelion Steam Train

1984. Railway Centenary. Multicoloured.
1665	15d. Type 361	85	30
1666	20d. Steam goods train on Papadia Bridge (vert)	2·20	1·00
1667	30d. Piraeus-Peloponnese steam train	1·00	60
1668	50d. Cogwheel railway, Kalavryta (vert)	2·50	1·10

362 Athens 5th Cent B.C. Silver Coin on Plan of City

1984. 150th Anniv of Athens as Capital. Multicoloured.
1669	15d. Type 362	50	20
1670	100d. Symbols of ancient Athens and skyline of modern Athens	1·80	1·10

363 "10" enclosing Arms

1984. Tenth Anniv of Revolution.
1671	**363** 95d. multicoloured	1·70	60

364 "Annunciation"

1984. Christmas. Multicoloured.
1672	14d. Type 364	70	40
1673	20d. "Nativity"	80	50
1674	25d. "Presentation in the Temple"	80	50
1675	32d. "Baptism of Christ"	1·10	80

Nos. 1672/5 show scenes from Hagion Panton icon by Athanasios Tountas.

365 Running

1985. 16th European Indoor Athletics Championships, New Phaleron. Multicoloured.
1676	12d. Type 365	20	20
1677	15d. Putting the shot	25	15
1678	20d. Sports stadium (37×24 mm)	50	25
1679	25d. Hurdling	70	20
1680	80d. High jumping	1·40	85

366 Catacomb Niche

1985. Catacombs of Melos. Multicoloured.
1681	15d. Type 366	25	15
1682	20d. Martyrs' altars and niches central passageway	40	20
1683	100d. Niches	1·60	1·20

367 Apollo and Marsyas

1985. Europa. Multicoloured.
1684	27d. Type 367	80	70

1685	80d. Dimitris Mitropoulos and Nikos Skalkotas (composers)	1·90	90

368 Coin (315 B.C.) and "Salonika" (relief)

1985. 2300th Anniv of Salonika. Multicoloured.
1686	1d. Type 368	20	15
1687	5d. Saints Demetrius and Methodius (mosaics) (49×34 mm)	50	20
1688	15d. Galerius's Arch (detail) (Roman period)	40	15
1689	20d. Salonika's eastern walls (Byzantine period)	50	15
1690	32d. Upper City, Salonika	50	15
1691	50d. Greek army liberating Salonika, 1912	85	15
1692	80d. Soldier's legs and Salonika (German occupation 1941–44)	1·80	35
1693	95d. Contemporary views of Salonika (60th anniv of Aristotelian University and International Trade Fair) (49×34 mm)	3·00	1·60

369 Urn on Map of Cyprus

1985. 25th Anniv of Republic of Cyprus.
1694	**369** 32d. multicoloured	70	45

370 "Democracy crowning the City" (relief)

1985. Athens, "Cultural Capital of Europe".
1695	**370** 15d. multicoloured	25	10
1696	- 20d. black, grey and blue	35	20
1697	- 32d. multicoloured	75	25
1698	- 80d. multicoloured	2·20	1·30

DESIGNS—HORIZ: 20d. Tritons and dolphins (mosaic floor, Roman baths, Hieratis); 80d. Capodistrian University, Athens. VERT: 32d. Angel (fresco, Pentelis Cave).

371 Children of different Races

1985. International Youth Year (1st issue) (15, 25d.) and 40th Anniv of United Nations Organization (27, 100d.). Multicoloured.
1699	15d. Type 371	20	10
1700	25d. Doves and youths	40	20
1701	27d. Interior of U.N. General Assembly	75	20
1702	100d. U.N. Building, New York, and U.N. emblem	1·60	1·20

See also No. MS1703.

372 Girl with Flower Crown

1985. International Youth Year (2nd issue). "Piraeus '85" Stamp Exhibition. Sheet 87×62 mm.
MS1703	**372** 100d. multicoloured	2·50	2·50

373 Folk Dance

1985. Pontic Culture. Multicoloured.
1704	12d. Type 373	25	20

1705	15d. Monastery of Our Lady of Soumela	25	20
1706	27d. Women's costumes (vert)	65	25
1707	32d. Trapezus High School	70	25
1708	80d. Sinope Castle	1·30	95

374 Hestia

1986. Gods of Olympus.

1709	374	5d. orange, black & brn	10	15
1710	-	18d. orange, black & brn	20	15
1711	-	27d. orange, black & bl	35	15
1712	-	32d. orange, black & red	45	25
1713	-	35d. orange, black & brn	45	25
1714	-	40d. orange, black & red	60	20
1715	-	50d. orange, black & grey	75	25
1716	-	110d. orange, blk & brn	95	25
1717	-	150d. orange, blk & grey	1·40	25
1718	-	200d. orange, black & bl	1·60	35
1719	-	300d. orange, black & bl	2·20	90
1720	-	500d. orange, black & bl	5·50	2·50

DESIGNS: 18d. Hermes; 27d. Aphrodite; 32d. Ares; 35d. Athene; 40d. Hephaestus; 50d. Artemis; 110d. Apollo; 150d. Demeter; 200d. Poseidon; 300d. Hera; 500d. Zeus.

375 "Ephebos of Antikythera"

1986. Sports Events and Anniversaries.

1721	375	18d. green, black & grey	50	20
1722	-	27d. yellow, black & red	1·20	55
1723	-	32d. multicoloured	1·70	80
1724	-	35d. green, black & bis	2·40	1·00
1725	-	40d. multicoloured	1·70	95
1726	-	50d. multicoloured	1·70	50
1727	-	110d. multicoloured	6·50	2·10

DESIGNS—VERT: 18d. Type **375** (1st World Junior Athletics Championships); 32d. Footballers (Pan-European Junior Football Finals); 35d. "Wrestlers" (sculpture) (Pan-European Freestyle and Greco-Roman Wrestling Championships); 50d. Cyclists (6th International Round Europe Cycling Meet.). HORIZ: 27d. "Diadoumenos" (sculpture by Polycleitus) (1st World Junior Athletics Championships); 40d. Volleyball players (Men's World Volleyball Championships); 110d. "Victory" (unadopted design by Nikephoros Lytras for first Olympic Games commemoratives, 1896) (90th anniv of modern Olympic Games).

376 Fastening Seat Belt

1986. European Road Safety Year. Multicoloured.

1728	18d. Type **376**	40	10
1729	27d. Motorcyclist in traffic	1·00	70
1730	110d. Child strapped in back seat of car and speed limit signs	2·75	1·60

377 Intelpost

1986. New Postal Services. Multicoloured.

1731	18d. Type **377**	45	20
1732	110d. "Express Mail" banner around globe	1·80	1·60

378 Sapling between Hands and burning Forest

1986. Europa.

1733	378	35d. green, black & orge	4·50	2·40
1734	-	110d. blue, black & grn	4·50	2·50

DESIGN: 110d. Dalmatian pelicans on Prespa Lake.

379 Victims' Memorial and Workers

1986. Centenary of Chicago May Day Strike.

1735	379	40d. multicoloured	90	50

380 Swearing-in of Venizelos Government

1986. 50th Death Anniv of Eleftherios Venizelos (politician) (18d.) and Sixth International Crete Conference, Hania (110d.). Multicoloured.

1736	18d. Type **380**	45	25
1737	110d. Hania harbour	1·80	1·30

381 Dove and Sun

1986. International Peace Year. Multicoloured.

1738	18d. Type **381**	35	25
1739	35d. Dove holding olive branch with flags as leaves	65	50
1740	110d. Dove with olive branch flying out of globe (horiz)	1·70	1·30

382 "Madonna and Child"

1986. Christmas. Designs showing icons. Multicoloured.

1741	22d. Type **382**	25	10
1742	46d. "Adoration of the Magi" (24×32 mm)	90	65
1743	130d. "Christ enthroned with St. John the Evangelist"	2·00	1·00

383 The Fox and the Grapes

1987. Aesop's Fables. Multicoloured.

1744A	2d. Type **383**	35	15
1745A	5d. The North Wind and the Sun	35	15
1746A	10d. The Stag at the Spring and the Lion	55	15
1747A	22d. Zeus and the Snake	1·10	15
1748A	32d. The Crow and the Fox	1·50	30
1749A	40d. The Woodcutter and Hermes	2·40	85
1750A	46d. The Ass in a Lion's Skin and the Fox	3·25	85
1751A	130d. The Hare and the Tortoise	6·75	1·30

384 Composition (Archilleas Apergis)

1987. Europa. Sculptures. Multicoloured.

1752A	40d. Type **384**	4·50	2·10
1753a	130d. Delphic Light (Gerassimos Sklavos)	4·50	2·10

385 Player shooting Goal and Indoor Court

1987. 25th European Men's Basketball Championships, Athens. Multicoloured.

1754	22d. Type **385**	80	50
1755	25d. Emblem and spectators (32×24 mm)	45	20
1756	130d. Players	2·30	1·50

MS1757 113×63 mm. 40d. Players; 60d. Players around goal; 100d. Player shooting goal (each 28×40 mm) 8·25 7·25

386 Banner and Students

1987. 150th Annivs of Athens University (3, 23d.) and National Metsovio Polytechnic Institute (others). Multicoloured.

1758	3d. Type **386**	25	15
1759	23d. Medal and owl	40	15
1760	40d. Building facade, measuring instruments and computer terminal (vert)	70	50
1761	60d. Students outside building (vert)	1·30	1·00

387 Ionic and Corinthian Capitals, Temple of Apollo, Phigaleia-Bassae

1987. Classical Architecture Capitals. Multicoloured.

1762	2d. Type **387**	15	10
1763	26d. Doric capital, Parthenon	50	25
1764	40d. Ionic capital, The Erechtheum	70	40
1765	60d. Corinthian capital, The Tholos, Epidaurus	2·00	1·30

388 Hands holding Cup Aloft

1987. Greek Victory in European Basketball Championship.

1766	388	40d. multicoloured	1·10	95

389 Diploma Engraving (Yiannis Kephalinos)

1987. 150th Anniv of Fine Arts High School (1767) and 60th Anniv of Panteios Political Science High School (1768). Multicoloured.

1767	26d. Type **389**	45	15
1768	60d. School campus (horiz)	1·20	95

390 Angel and Christmas Tree (left half)

1987. Christmas.

1769	26d. Type **390**	65	45
1770	26d. Angel and Christmas tree (right half)	65	45

Nos. 1769/70 were printed together, se-tenant, forming a composite design.

391 Eleni Papadaki in *Hecuba* (Euripides) and Philippi Amphitheatre

1987. Greek Theatre. Multicoloured.

1771	2d. Type **391**	20	10
1772	4d. Christopher Nezer in *The Wasps* (Aristophanes) and Dodona amphitheatre	20	10
1773	7d. Emilios Veakis in *Oedipus Rex* (Sophocles) and Delphi amphitheatre	20	10
1774	26d. Marika Kotopouli in *The Shepherdess's Love* (Dimitris Koromilas)	60	40
1775	40d. Katina Paxinou in *Abraham's Sacrifice* (Vitzentzos Cornaros)	1·00	40
1776	50d. Kyveli in *Countess Valeraina's Secret* (Gregory Xenopoulos)	1·10	65
1777	60d. Karolos Koun and stage set	2·00	70
1778	100d. Dimitris Rontiris teaching National Theatre dancers an ancient dance	3·25	50

392 *Codonellina* sp. (polyzoan)

1988. Marine Life. Multicoloured.

1779A	30d. Type **392**	1·30	40
1780A	40d. *Diaperoecia major* (polyzoan (clump-forming animals))	1·30	40
1781A	50d. *Artemia* (marine animal)	1·50	40
1782A	60d. *Posidonia oceanica* (plant) and Marmora sea-bream	3·75	1·50
1783A	100d. *Padina pavonica* (plant)	7·00	2·30

393 Ancient Olympia

1988. Olympic Games, Seoul. Multicoloured.

1784A	4d. Type **393**	60	20
1785A	20d. Ancient athletes in Gymnasium	1·20	20
1786A	30d. Modern Olympics centenary emblem	3·00	95
1787A	60d. Ancient athletes training	5·25	3·25
1788A	170d. Runner with Olympic flame	9·75	2·50

394 Satellite and Fax Machine

1988. Europa. Transport and Communications. Multicoloured.

1789B	60d. Type **394**	6·00	1·90
1790B	150d. Modern express and commuter trains	12·00	2·30

395 Katarraktis Falls

1988. European Campaign for Rural Areas. Waterfalls. Multicoloured.

1791A	10d. Type **395**	2·75	40
1792A	60d. Edessa waterfalls	7·00	3·25
1793A	100d. River Edessaios cascades	8·75	2·50

396 Emblems

1988. 20th European Postal Workers Trade Unions Congress.

| 1794A | **396** | 60d. multicoloured | 9·75 | 3·00 |

397 *Mytilene Harbour, Lesbos* (painting by Theophilos)

1988. Prefecture Capitals (1st series). Multicoloured.

1795B	2d. Type **397**	15	10
1796B	3d. Alexandroupolis lighthouse, Evros (vert)	15	10
1797B	4d. St. Nicholas's bell-tower, Kozani (vert)	20	10
1798B	5d. Workmen's centre, Hermoupolis, Cyclades (vert)	20	10
1799B	7d. Sparta Town Hall, Lakonia	20	10
1800B	8d. Pegasus, Leukas	30	10
1801B	10d. Castle of the Knights, Rhodes, Dodecanese (vert)	30	10
1802B	20d. Acropolis, Athens (vert)	35	15
1803B	25d. Aqueduct, Kavala	40	15
1804B	30d. Castle and statue of Athanasios Diakos, Lamia, Phthiotis (vert)	50	15
1805B	50d. Preveza Cathedral bell-tower and clock (vert)	1·20	20
1806B	60d. Esplanade, Corfu	1·60	45
1807B	70d. Aghios Nicholaos, Lassithi	3·00	25
1808B	100d. Six Springheads, Poligiros, Khalkidiki	5·50	30
1809B	200d. Church of Paul the Apostle, Corinth, Corinthia	6·50	65

See also Nos. 1848/62, 1911/22 and 1955/64.

398 Eleftherios Venizelos, Map and Flag

1988. 75th Annivs. of Union of Crete and Greece (30d.) and Liberation of Epirus and Macedonia (70d.). Multicoloured.

| 1810A | 30d. Type **398** | 1·10 | 35 |
| 1811A | 70d. Flags, map and "Liberty" | 2·20 | 1·20 |

399 *Adoration of the Magi* (El Greco)

1988. Christmas. Multicoloured.

| 1812 | 30d. Type **399** | 1·40 | 50 |
| 1813 | 70d. *The Annunciation* (Kostas Parthenis) (horiz) | 1·90 | 1·20 |

400 Map of E.E.C. and Castle of Knights, Rhodes

1988. European Economic Community. Meeting of Heads of State, Rhodes. Multicoloured.

| 1814A | 60d. Type **400** | 2·75 | 1·60 |
| 1815A | 100d. Members' flags and coin | 3·25 | 1·00 |

401 Ancient Olympia and High Jumper

1989. Centenary (1996) of Modern Olympic Games (1st issue). Multicoloured.

1816A	30d. Type **401**	70	35
1817A	60d. Wrestlers and Delphi	1·70	1·20
1818A	70d. Acropolis, Athens, and swimmers	2·20	1·50
1819A	170d. Stadium and Golden Olympics emblem	4·25	2·10

See also Nos. 1863/7, **MS**1995 and 1998/2001.

402 Flags

1989. International Anniversaries. Multicoloured.

1820A	30d. Type **402** (5th anniv of Six-nation Initiative for Peace and Disarmament)	1·10	50
1821A	50d. Flag and "Liberty" (bicentenary of French Revolution)	1·40	80
1822A	60d. Flag and ballot box (third direct European Parliament elections)	3·00	1·60
1823A	70d. Coins (cent of Interparliamentary Union)	3·75	1·60
1824A	200d. Flag (40th anniv of Council of Europe)	7·25	1·80

403 Whistling Bird

1989. Europa. Children's Toys. Multicoloured.

| 1825B | 60d. Type **403** | 5·00 | 2·50 |
| 1826B | 170d. Butterfly | 5·00 | 2·50 |

404 Magnifying Glass and Bird

1989. "Balkanfila XII" International Stamp Exhibition, Salonica. Multicoloured.

1827	60d. Type **404**	1·00	45
1828	70d. Eye looking through magnifying glass	1·10	75
MS1829	86×61 mm. 200d. Stamp collectors (42×30 mm)	4·25	4·25

405 Dog Roses

1989. Wild Flowers. Multicoloured.

1830	8d. Type **405**	25	15
1831	10d. Common myrtle	25	15
1832	20d. Common poppies	45	20
1833	30d. Anemones	60	25
1834	60d. Dandelions and chicory	90	40
1835	70d. Mallow	1·40	40
1836	200d. Thistles	3·25	1·70

406 Brown Bear

1990. Endangered Animals. Multicoloured.

1837	40d. Type **406**	80	20
1838	70d. Loggerhead turtle	80	50
1839	90d. Mediterranean monk seal	1·60	60
1840	100d. Lynx	3·00	1·30

407 Gregoris Lambrakis

1990. Politicians' Death Anniversaries. Multicoloured.

| 1841 | 40d. Type **407** (27th anniv) | 70 | 50 |
| 1842 | 40d. Pavlos Bakoyiannis (first anniv) | 70 | 50 |

408 Clasped Hands, Roses and Flag

1990. National Reconciliation. Multicoloured.

1843	40d. Type **408**	55	15
1844	70d. Dove with banner	1·00	50
1845	100d. Map and hands holding roses	1·50	1·30

409 Old Central Post Office Interior

1990. Europa. Post Offices Buildings. Multicoloured.

| 1846 | 70d. Type **409** | 4·00 | 1·60 |
| 1847 | 210d. Exterior of modern post office | 4·00 | 1·60 |

410 *Animal Fair* (D. Gioldassi) (Karditsa)

1990. Prefecture Capitals (2nd series). Multicoloured.

1848B	2d. Type **410**	20	10
1849B	5d. Fort, Trikala (horiz)	20	10
1850B	8d. Street, Veroia (Imathia)	20	10
1851B	10d. Monument to Fallen Heroes, Missolonghi (Aetolia) (horiz)	25	10
1852B	15d. Harbour, Chios (horiz)	25	10
1853B	20d. Street, Tripolis (Arcadia) (horiz)	35	10
1854B	25d. "City and Town Hall" (woodcut, A. Tassos) (Volos, Magnesia) (horiz)	60	30
1855B	40d. Town Hall, Kalamata (Messenia) (horiz)	60	30
1856B	50d. Market, Pyrgos (Elia) (horiz)	75	30
1857B	70d. Lake and island, Yannina (horiz)	85	50
1858B	80d. Harbour sculpture, Rethymnon	1·50	35
1859B	90d. Argostolion (Cephalonia) (horiz)	1·50	50
1860B	100d. Citadel and islet, Nauplion (Argolis) (horiz)	1·60	35
1861B	200d. Lighthouse, Patras (Akhaia)	3·50	45
1862B	250d. Street, Florina (horiz)	5·75	45

411 Yachting

1990. Centenary (1996) of Modern Olympic Games (2nd issue). Multicoloured.

1863	20d. Type **411**	60	20
1864	50d. Wrestling	85	35
1865	80d. Running	1·20	90
1866	100d. Handball	1·70	80
1867	250d. Football	5·00	1·50

412 Schliemann and Lion Gate, Mycenae

1990. Death Cent of Heinrich Schliemann (archaeologist).

| 1868 | **412** | 80d. multicoloured | 8·50 | 4·25 |

413 "Woman knitting" (lithograph, Vasso Katraki)

1990. 50th Anniv of Greek–Italian War. Multicoloured.

1869	50d. Type **413**	80	40
1870	80d. "Virgin Mary protecting Army" (lithograph, George Gounaropoulou)	1·10	80
1871	100d. "Women's War Work" (lithograph, Kosta Grammatopoulou)	1·30	95

414 Hermes

1990. Stamp Day. Sheet 87×62 mm.

| **MS**1872 | **414** | 300d. multicoloured | 15·00 | 15·00 |

415 Calliope, Euterpe and Erato

1991. The Nine Muses. Multicoloured.

1873	50d. Type **415**	85	40
1874	80d. Terpsichore, Polyhymnia and Melpomene	1·60	90
1875	250d. Thalia, Clio and Urania	4·25	1·20

416 Battle Scene (Ioannis Anousakis)

1991. 50th Anniv of Battle for Crete. Multicoloured.

| 1876 | 60d. Type **416** | 2·20 | 75 |
| 1877 | 300d. Map and flags of allied nations (32×24 mm) | 5·00 | 2·10 |

417 Icarus pushing Satellite

1991. Europa. Europe in Space. Multicoloured.

| 1878 | 80d. Type **417** | 4·00 | 2·40 |
| 1879 | 300d. Chariot of the Sun | 5·25 | 3·50 |

418 Swimming

1991. 11th Mediterranean Games, Athens. Multicoloured.

1880	10d. Type **418**	35	20
1881	60d. Basketball	80	35
1882	90d. Gymnastics	1·50	35
1883	130d. Weightlifting	2·10	65
1884	300d. Throwing the hammer	4·75	2·50

419 Pillar of Democracy

1991. 2500th Anniv of Birth of Democracy.

| 1885 | **419** | 100d. black, stone & blue | 1·70 | 90 |

420 Europa and Zeus as Bull (from Attic vase)

1991. Greek Presidency of European Postal and Telecommunications Conference. Sheet 81×62 mm.

| **MS**1886 | 300d. multicoloured | 19·00 | 19·00 |

421 Pres Konstantinos Karamanlis signing Treaty of Athens

1991. Tenth Anniv of Greek Admission to European Community. Multicoloured.

1887	50d. Type **421**	80	35
1888	80d. Map of Europe and Pres. Karamanlis	1·40	65

422 Emblem and Speed Skaters

1991. Winter Olympic Games, Albertville. Multicoloured.

1889	80d. Type **422**	1·90	1·00
1890	300d. Slalom skier	3·75	1·60

423 Throwing the Javelin

1992. Olympic Games, Barcelona. Multicoloured.

1891	10d. Type **423**	40	20
1892	60d. Show jumping	1·40	45
1893	90d. Runner (37×24 mm)	2·10	95
1894	120d. Gymnastics	3·50	75
1895	340d. Runners' heads forming Olympic rings (37×24 mm)	6·50	1·90

424 Couple beneath Umbrella

1992. Health. Multicoloured.

1896	60d. Type **424** (anti-AIDS campaign)	65	25
1897	80d. Doctor examining child (1st European Gastroenterology Week)	1·20	40
1898	90d. Crab killing flower on healthy plant (anti-cancer campaign)	1·40	50
1899	120d. Hephaestus's forge (from 6th-century B.C. urn) (European Year of Social Security, Hygiene and Health in the Workplace)	1·60	1·00
1900	280d. Alexandros Onassis Cardiosurgical Centre	5·50	2·10

425 Santa Maria, Map and Columbus

1992. Europa. 500th Anniv of Discovery of America by Columbus. Multicoloured.

1901	90d. Type **425**	4·00	2·10
1902	340d. Chios in late 15th century	5·25	3·25

426 Proetus, Bellerophon and Pegasus

1992. European Transport Ministers' Conference, Athens. Sheet 85×59 mm.

MS1903	**426** 300d. multicoloured	11·00	11·00

427 Head of Hercules with Lion Skin (relief)

1992. Macedonia. Multicoloured.

1904	10d. Type **427**	35	10
1905	20d. Map of Macedonia and bust of Aristotle (horiz)	45	10
1906	60d. Alexander the Great at Battle of Issus (mural) (horiz)	1·00	15
1907	80d. Tomb of Philip II at Vergina, and Manolis Andronikos (archaeologist)	1·50	50
1908	90d. Deer hunt (mosaic, Pella)	2·20	50
1909	120d. Macedonian coin	3·00	1·00
1910	340d. 4th-century Church. Philippi, and Apostle Paul	8·75	3·25

428 Piraeus

1992. Prefecture Capitals (3rd series). Multicoloured.

1911B	10d. Type **428**	15	10
1912B	20d. Amphissa (Phocis)	20	10
1913B	30d. The Heraion, Samos	25	10
1914B	40d. Canea	40	10
1915B	50d. Zakynthos	55	20
1916B	60d. Karpenisi (Evrytania)	65	20
1917B	70d. Cave, Kilkis (vert)	80	20
1918B	80d. Door of Town Hall Xanthi (vert)	1·60	20
1919B	90d. Macedonian Struggle Museum, Thessaloniki	1·90	30
1920B	120d. Tsanakleous School, Komotini (Rhodope)	2·75	50
1921B	340d. Spring, Drama	6·00	1·30
1922B	400d. Pinios Bridge, Larissa	7·75	2·10

429 Column, Map, Flags and European Community Emblem

1992. Single European Market.

1923	**429** 90d. multicoloured	1·20	1·00

430 Headstone (4th century B.C.)

1993. 2400th Anniv of Rhodes. Multicoloured.

1924	60d. Type **430**	1·10	40
1925	90d. "Aphrodite bathing" (statue)	1·90	90
1926	120d. "St. Irene" (from St. Catherine's church)	1·40	80
1927	250d. St. Paul's Gate, Naillac Mole	5·50	2·10

431 Georgakis Olympios at Sekkou Monastery, 1821

1993. Historical Events. Multicoloured.

1928	10d. Type **431** (War of Independence)	45	10
1929	30d. Theodore Kolokotronis (War of Independence)	60	20
1930	60d. Pavlos Melas (military hero)	1·00	35
1931	90d. "Glory crowns the Casualties" (Balkan Wars, 1912–13)	2·30	90

1932	120d. Soldiers of Sacred Company, El Alamein, 1942 (horiz)	3·75	1·00
1933	150d. Sacred Company on Aegean Islands, 1943–45 (horiz)	4·25	1·40
1934	200d. Victims' Monument, Kalavryta (destruction of village, 1943)	8·25	2·40

432 The Benefits of Transportation (Konstantinus Parthenis) (left half)

1993. Europa. Contemporary Art. Multicoloured.

1935	90d. Type **432**	3·50	2·10
1936	350d. The Benefits of Transportation (right half)	5·25	3·75

Nos. 1935/6 were issued together, se-tenant, forming a composite design.

433 Athens Concert Hall

1993. Modern Athens. Multicoloured.

1937	30d. Type **433**	1·10	20
1938	60d. Iliou Melathron (former house of Heinrich Schliemann (archaeologist), now Numismatic Museum)	1·60	30
1939	90d. National Library	1·90	50
1940	200d. Athens Eye Hospital	5·25	1·80

434 Presidency Emblem and Map

1993. Greek Presidency (1994) of European Union (1st issue). Sheet 84×60 mm.

MS1941	**434** 400d. multicoloured	7·50	7·50

See also Nos. 1953/4.

435 "Hermes leading Selene's Chariot" (Boeotian vase)

1994. Second Pan-European Transport Conf.

1942	**435** 200d. multicoloured	3·50	1·60

436 "Last Supper" (icon by Michael Damaskinou, St. Catherine's Church, Heraklion, Crete)

1994. Easter. Multicoloured.

1943	30d. Type **436**	55	20
1944	60d. "Crucifixion" (detail of wall painting, Great Meteoron)	80	20
1945	90d. "Burial of Christ" (icon, Church of the Presentation of the Lord, Patmos) (horiz)	1·10	40
1946	150d. "Resurrection" (detail, illuminated manuscript from Mt. Athos) (horiz)	2·75	1·00

437 Thales of Miletus (philosopher)

1994. Europa. Discoveries. Multicoloured.

1947	90d. Type **437**	3·25	2·10

438 Demetrios Vikelas (first president, after G. Roilos)

1994. Sports Events and Anniversary. Multicoloured.

1949	60d. Type **438** (centenary of International Olympic Committee)	1·00	25
1950	90d. Modern footballer and ancient relief (World Cup Football Championship, U.S.A.) (horiz)	1·10	70
1951	120d. Ball, net and laurel (World Volleyball Championship, Piraeus and Salonika)	3·25	70
MS1952	68×70 mm. 400d. Modern footballers, Statue of Liberty and ancient relief (World Cup) (41×51 mm)	8·25	8·25

1948	350d. Konstantinos Karatheodoris (mathematician) and equations	5·50	3·25

439 "Greece" driving E.U. Chariot

1994. Greek Presidency of European Union. Multicoloured.

1953	90d. Type **439**	1·40	85
1954	120d. Doric columns and E.U. flag	2·20	95

440 Parigoritissas Byzantine Church, Arta

1994. Prefecture Capitals (4th series). Multicoloured.

1955B	10d. Tsalopoulou mansion house, Katerini (Pieria) (vert)	15	10
1956B	20d. Type **440**	15	10
1957B	30d. Bridge and tower, Levadia (Boeotia) (vert)	35	10
1958B	40d. Koumbelidikis church Kastoria	45	10
1959B	50d. Outdoor theatre, Grevena	60	20
1960B	60d. Waterfall, Edessa (Pella)	70	20
1961B	80d. Red House, Chalkida (Euboea)	1·10	25
1962B	90d. Government House, Serres	1·80	35
1963B	120d. Town Hall, Heraklion	1·80	65
1964B	150d. Church of our Lady of the Annunciation, Igoumenitsa (Thesprotia) (vert)	2·75	65

441 Declaration of Constitution (detail, Carl Haupt)

1994. 150th Anniv of Constitution. Multicoloured.

1965	60d. Type **441**	55	20
1966	150d. Ioannis Makrygiannis, Andreas Metaxas and Dimitrios Kallergis (from Neos Aristophanes (magazine)	1·40	50
1967	200d. The Night of 3rd September 1843 (anon) (horiz)	3·75	1·00
1968	340d. Article 107 of 1844 Constitution and Parliament Seal (horiz)	6·50	2·10

442 Mercouri and Demonstrators (fighter for Democracy)

1995. Melina Mercouri (actress and Minister of Culture) Commemoration. Multicoloured.

1969	60d. Type **442**	80	20

1970	90d. Mercouri and Acropolis (politician)	90	50
1971	100d. Mercouri in three roles (actress)	2·75	95
1972	340d. Mercouri with flowers (vert)	7·50	2·10

443 Prisoners behind Barbed Wire

1995. Europa. Peace and Freedom. Multicoloured.

| 1973 | 90d. Type **443** | 3·00 | 2·50 |
| 1974 | 340d. Doves flying from crushed barbed wire | 5·25 | 2·50 |

Nos. 1973/4 were issued together, *se-tenant*, forming a composite design.

444 Emblem

1995. Anniversaries and Events. Multicoloured.

1975	10d. Type **444** (5th World Junior Basketball Championship)	55	10
1976	70d. Agriculture University, Athens (75th anniv) (horiz)	1·10	15
1977	90d. Delphi (50th anniv of U.N.O.)	1·40	30
1978	100d. Greek flag and returning soldier (50th anniv of end of Second World War)	1·60	50
1979	120d. "Peace" (statue by Kifissodotos) (50th anniv of U.N.O.)	1·60	70
1980	150d. Dolphins (European Nature Conservation Year) (horiz)	2·75	90
1981	200d. Old telephone and modern key-pad (cent of telephone in Greece)	4·25	1·00
1982	300d. Owl sitting on ball (29th European Basketball Championship)	8·75	1·90

445 "The First Vision of the Apocalypse" (icon, Thomas Bathas)

1995. 1900th Anniv of the Apocalypse of St. John. Multicoloured.

1983	80d. Type **445**	1·90	40
1984	110d. St. John dictating to Prochoros in front of the Cave of the Apocalypse (miniature from the Four Gospels, Codex 81 of library of Patmos Monastery)	1·90	85
1985	300d. Trumpet of the First Angel (gilded Gospel cover) (horiz)	5·00	2·10

446 Goddess Athene with Argonauts

1995. Jason and the Argonauts. Multicoloured.

1986	80d. Type **446**	80	35
1987	120d. Phineas (blind seer), god Hermes and the Voreadae pursuing Harpies	1·60	50
1988	150d. Medea, Nike and Jason taming bull	1·60	70
1989	200d. Jason and Medea killing snake and taking the Golden Fleece	3·00	1·00
1990	300d. Jason presenting Golden Fleece to Pelias	6·00	1·70

447 Psyttaleia

1995. Lighthouses. Multicoloured.

1991	80d. Type **447**	1·10	50
1992	120d. Sapienza	1·60	75
1993	150d. Kastri, Othonoi	3·25	2·40
1994	500d. Zourva, Hydra	6·50	3·25

448 1l. Stamp

1996. Centenary of Modern Olympic Games (3rd issue). Reproduction of Olympic Games issue of 1896. Three sheets each 88×88 mm, containing designs as T **448**. Inscriptions in brown, backgrounds flesh; colour of reproductions listed below.

| MS1995 | 3 sheets (a) 80d. ochre (Type **448**); 120d. pink (2l.); 150d. brown (5l.); 650d. olive (10d.). (b) 80d. red (25l.); 120d. black (60l.); 150d. blue (1d.); 650d. reddish brown (10d.). (c) 80d. brown (20l.); 120d. lilac (40l.); 150l. brown (2d.); 650d. green (5d.) | | |
| | Set of 3 sheets | 45·00 | 45·00 |

449 Sappho (poet)

1996. Europa. Famous women.

| 1996 | **449** | 120d. multicoloured | 4·25 | 3·25 |
| 1997 | — | 430d. brown, black & bl | 7·50 | 5·25 |

DESIGN: 430d. Amalia Fleming.

450 Running

1996. Centenary of Modern Olympic Games (4th issue). Multicoloured.

1998	10d. Type **450**	2·20	35
1999	80d. Throwing the discus	1·60	70
2000	120d. Weightlifting	2·75	1·00
2001	200d. Wrestling (horiz)	5·50	2·40

451 Hippocrates

1996. First Int Medical Olympiad, Athens.

| 2002 | **451** | 80d. brown, pink & black | 2·75 | 1·30 |
| 2003 | — | 120d. brown, green & blk | 3·25 | 1·80 |

DESIGN: 120d. Galen.

452 Mytilene

1996. Castles (1st series). Multicoloured.

2004B	10d. Type **452**	20	10
2005B	20d. Lindos	25	10
2006B	30d. Rethymnon	35	15
2007B	70d. Assos Cephalonia	60	20
2008B	80d. Castle of the Serbs	1·10	50
2009B	120d. Monemvasia	1·90	65
2010B	200d. Didimotihon	3·50	1·00
2011B	430d. Vonitsas	7·50	1·50
2012B	1000d. Nikopolis	15·00	5·75

See also Nos. 2069/78.

453 Puppets

1996. Shadow Puppets. Multicoloured.

2013	80d. Type **453**	1·60	70
2014	100d. Men courting woman	1·10	80
2015	120d. Soldiers	2·40	1·00
2016	200d. Men fighting dragon	4·25	1·60

454 Inscription on Wine Jug (720 B.C.)

1996. The Greek Language. Multicoloured.

2017	80d. Type **454**	80	65
2018	120d. Homer's "Iliad" (papyrus scroll, 436–45)	1·60	75
2019	150d. Psalm (6th century)	2·20	1·00
2020	350d. Dionysios Solomos (writer) and verse of poem (1824)	9·00	3·25

455 Papandreou, Cap, Degree and Books

1997. Andreas Papandreou (Prime Minister, 1981–89 and 1993–96) Commemoration. Multicoloured.

2021	80d. Type **455** (Doctorate in Economics, Harvard University, 1943)	1·10	50
2022	120d. Return from exile, 1974, and smoking pipe	1·60	75
2023	150d. Parliament building and Papandreou	2·75	95
2024	500d. State flag, dove and Papandreou wearing glasses	7·00	3·50

456 St Dimitrios (patron saint) (fresco, Aghios Nikolaos Orphanos Church)

1997. Thessaloniki, Cultural Capital of Europe. Multicoloured.

2025	80d. Type **456**	80	35
2026	100d. Hippocratic Hospital (horiz)	1·90	65
2027	120d. Marble statue pedestal (2nd century) and circular relief of woman's head	1·90	80
2028	150d. Mosaic (detail) in cupola of Rotunda	2·75	85
2029	300d. 14th-century chalice (horiz)	7·00	2·40

457 Trikomo

1997. Macedonian Bridges. Multicoloured.

2030	80d. Type **457**	1·10	40
2031	120d. Portitsa	1·40	65
2032	150d. Ziakas	2·75	95
2033	350d. Kastro	5·50	2·50

458 Prometheus the Fire-stealer

1997. Europa. Tales and Legends. Multicoloured.

| 2034 | 120d. Type **458** | 3·25 | 2·40 |
| 2035 | 430d. Knights (Digenes Akritas) | 5·00 | 2·50 |

459 Running

1997. Sixth World Athletics Championships, Athens. Multicoloured.

2036	20d. Type **459**	45	25
2037	100d. "Nike" (statue)	1·20	60
2038	140d. High jumping	2·20	85
2039	170d. Hurdling	2·75	1·50
2040	500d. Stadium, Athens	8·25	3·00

460 Alexandros Panagoulis (resistance leader)

1997. Anniversaries. Multicoloured.

2041	20d. Type **460** (20th death anniv (1996))	60	50
2042	30d. Grigorios Xenopoulos (writer, 130th birth anniv)	60	50
2043	40d. Odysseas Elytis (poet, first death anniv) (horiz)	60	50
2044	50d. Panayiotis Kanellopoulos (Prime Minister, 1945 and 1967, tenth death anniv (1996))	1·20	50
2045	100d. Harilaos Trikoupis (Prime Minister 1881–85, death centenary (1996)) (horiz)	2·50	95
2046	170d. Maria Callas (opera singer, 20th death anniv) (horiz)	4·00	1·50
2047	200d. Rigas Velestinlis-Feraios (revolutionary writer, death bicent (1998))	5·00	1·90

461 Vassilis Avlonitis

1997. Greek Actors. Multicoloured.

2048	20d. Type **461**	60	45
2049	30d. Vassilis Argyropoulos	60	45
2050	50d. Georgia Vassileiadou	60	45
2051	70d. Lambros Constantaras	60	45
2052	100d. Vassilis Logothetidis	1·70	1·40
2053	140d. Dionysis Papagiannopoulos	2·10	1·70
2054	170d. Nikos Stavrides	2·30	1·90
2055	200d. Mimis Fotopoulos	7·50	6·00

462 "Greece", Greek Flag and Colossus of Rhodes

1998. 50th Anniv of Incorporation of Dodecanese Islands into Greece. Multicoloured.

2056	100d. German commander signing surrender to British and Greek military authorities at Simi, 1945	1·70	1·40
2057	140d. Type **462**	2·10	1·70
2058	170d. Greek and British military representatives at transfer ceremony, Rhodes, 1947	2·30	1·90
2059	500d. Raising Greek flag, Kasos, 1947	7·00	5·50

463 Aghia Sofia Hospital, Athens

1998. Anniversaries and Events. Multicoloured.

2060	20d. Type **463** (cent of Aghia Sofia Children's Hospital)	10	10
2061	100d. St. Xenophon's Monastery (millenary) (vert)	1·20	95
2062	140d. Woman in traditional costume (4th International Thracian Congress, Nea Orestiada) (vert)	1·70	1·40

2063	150d. Parthenon and congress emblem (International Cardiography Research Congress, Rhodes)		1·70	1·40
2064	170d. Sculpture of man and young boy (Cardiography Congress) (vert)		2·30	1·90
2065	500d. Emblem (50th anniv of Council of Europe) (vert)		8·25	6·50

464 Ancient Theatre, Epidavros

1998. Europa. National Festivals. Multicoloured.

2066	140d. Type **464**	1·70	1·40
2067	500d. Festival in Herod Atticus Theatre, Athens	8·25	6·50

465 Players

1998. World Basketball Championship, Athens. Sheet 70×68 mm. containing T 465.

MS2068	**465** 300d. multicoloured	4·00	3·25

466 Ierapetra, Crete

1998. Castles (2nd series). Multicoloured.

2069	30d. Type **466**	10	10
2070	50d. Corfu	35	30
2071	70d. Limnos	45	35
2072	100d. Argolis	60	45
2073	150d. Iraklion, Crete	1·00	85
2074	170d. Naupaktos (vert)	1·20	95
2075	200d. Ioannina (vert)	1·30	1·00
2076	400d. Platamona	2·50	2·00
2077	550d. Karitainas (vert)	3·75	3·00
2078	600d. Fragkokastello, Crete	4·00	3·25

467 *Church of St. George of the Greeks* (18th-century copperplate)

1998. 500th Anniv of Greek Orthodox Community in Venice. Multicoloured.

2079	30d. Type **467**	25	20
2080	40d. *Christ Pantocrator* (icon) (vert)	60	45
2081	140d. Illuminated script of hymn *Epi Soi hairei* by Georgios Klontzas (vert)	1·70	1·40
2082	230d. *St. George of the Greeks* (illuminated manuscript, 1640)	3·00	2·30

468 Homer (poet)

1998. Ancient Greek Writers.

2083	**468**	20d. brown and gold	25	20
2084	-	100d. brown and gold	1·70	1·40
2085	-	140d. red and gold	2·30	1·90
2086	-	200d. black and gold	3·50	2·75
2087	-	250d. brown and gold	4·00	3·25

DESIGNS: No. 2084, Sophocles (poet); 2085, Thucydides (historian); 2086, Plato (philosopher); 2087, Demosthenes (orator).

469 Ancient Trireme and Circulation of Mediterranean Sea Currents

1999. International Year of the Ocean. Multicoloured.

2088	40d. Type **469**	25	20
2089	100d. Galleon (detail of icon *Thou art Great, O Lord* by I. Kornaros)	1·20	95
2090	200d. *Aigaio* (oceanographic vessel), astrolabe and seismic sounding of seabed	2·30	1·90
2091	500d. Apollo on ship (3rd-century B.C. silver tetradrachmon coin of Antigonus Dosonos)	4·75	3·75

470 Karamanlis

1999. First Death Anniv of Konstantinos Karamanlis (Prime Minister 1955–63 and 1974; President 1980–85 and 1990–95). Multicoloured.

2092	100d. Type **470**	95	75
2093	170d. Karamanlis and jubilant crowd, 1974	1·40	1·10
2094	200d. Karamanlis and Council of Europe emblem, 1979	1·70	1·40
2095	500d. Karamanlis and Greek flag (vert)	4·00	3·25

471 Mt. Olympus and Flowers

1999. Europa. Parks and Gardens. Multicoloured.

2096	170d. Type **471**	1·40	1·10
2097	550d. Mt. Olympus and flowers (different)	5·00	4·00

Nos. 2096/7 were issued together, *se-tenant*, forming a composite design.

472 Ancient Greek and Japanese Noh Theatre Masks

1999. Centenary of Diplomatic Relations between Greece and Japan.

2098	**472** 120d. multicoloured	1·20	95

473 Temple of Hylates Apollo, Kourion

1999. Cyprus–Greece Joint Issue. 4000 Years of Greek Culture. Multicoloured.

2099	120d. Type **473**	95	75
2100	120d. Mycenaean pot depicting warriors (Athens)	95	75
2101	120d. Mycenaean crater depicting horse (Nicosia)	95	75
2102	120d. Temple of Apollo, Delphi	95	75

474 Trains

1999. 5th Anniv of Community Support Programme. Multicoloured.

2103	20d. Type **474** (modernization of railways)	25	20
2104	120d. Bridge over River Antirrio	95	75
2105	140d. Compact disk, delivery lorries and conveyor belt (modernization of Post Office)	1·20	95

2106	250d. Athens underground train	1·70	1·40
2107	500d. Control tower, Eleftherios Venizelos airport, Athens and Boeing 747	4·00	3·25

475 Agusta-Bell 201A Helicopter and Commandos in Inflatable Boat

1999. Armed Forces. Multicoloured.

2108	20d. Type **475**	25	20
2109	30d. Missile corvette	30	25
2110	40d. Lockheed Martin F-16 Fighting Falcons	35	30
2111	50d. Canadair CL-215 aircraft dispersing water on forest fire	45	35
2112	70d. Destroyer	60	45
2113	120d. Forces distributing aid in Bosnia	1·20	95
2114	170d. Dassault Mirage 2000 jet fighter above Aegean	1·70	1·40
2115	250d. Helicopters, tanks and soldiers on joint exercise	2·30	1·90
2116	600d. Submarine *Okeanos*	4·75	3·75

476 Birth of Christ

2000. Birth Bimillenary of Jesus Christ. Icons. Multicoloured.

2117	20d. Type **476**	25	20
2118	50d. Discussion between men of different denominations	60	45
2119	120d. Angels praising God	95	75
2120	170d. Epiphany (horiz)	1·70	1·40
2121	200d. Communion (35×35 mm)	2·10	1·70
2122	500d. Heavenly beings above priests and worshippers (27×57 mm)	4·00	3·25

477 "Building Europe"

2000. Europa.

2123	**477** 170d. multicoloured	3·50	2·75

478 Ilissos (steamship)

2000. Ships. Multicoloured.

2124	10d. Type **478**	35	30
2125	120d. *Adrias* (destroyer)	80	65
2126	170d. *Ia II* (steamship)	1·70	1·40
2127	400d. *Vas Olga* (destroyer)	4·75	3·75

479 Rainbow over Village (Spyros Dalakos)

2000. "Stampin' the Future". Winning Entries in Children's International Painting Competition. Multicoloured.

2128	130d. Type **479**	80	65
2129	180d. Robots (Moshovaki-Chaiger Ornella)	1·20	95
2130	200d. Cars and house (Zisis Zariotis)	2·10	1·70
2131	620d. Children astride rocket (Athina Limioudi)	5·25	4·25

480 Torch and Flag

2000. Olympic Games, Sydney. Multicoloured.

2132	200d. Type **480**	1·70	1·40
2133	650d. Torch, flag and Sydney Opera House	5·25	4·25

481 Emblem and Olympic Rings

2000. Olympic Games, Athens (2004) (1st issue).

2134	**481**	10d. multicoloured	25	20
2135	**481**	50d. multicoloured	60	45
2136	**481**	130d. multicoloured	80	65
2137	**481**	180d. multicoloured	1·70	1·40
2138	**481**	200d. multicoloured	2·30	1·90
2139	**481**	650d. multicoloured	4·75	3·75

See also Nos. **MS**2169, 2191/**MS**2196, 2207/10, **MS**2211, 2216/21, **MS**2222, 2234/8, **MS**2239, 2246/51, 2252/**MS**2258, 2259/63, 2264/**MS**2270, **MS**2271, **MS**2272, 2275/**MS**2279, **MS**2285 and 2286/**MS**2288.

482 Create 1901 1d. Stamp

2000. Centenary of First Create Stamp. Sheet 104×73 mm containing T 482 and similar vert designs. Multicoloured.

MS2140	200d. Type **482**; 650d. Create 1901 6d. stamp	17·00	16·00

483 Orpheus Christ (sculpture)

2000. Birth Bimillenary of Jesus Christ. Multicoloured.

2141	20d. Type **483**	10	10
2142	30d. The Good Shepherd (sculpture)	25	20
2143	40d. Christ Pantocrator (mosaic, Holy Monastery of Sina)	35	30
2144	100d. Anapeson in the Protato of Mount Athos (fresco, Manuel Panselinos) (horiz)	60	45
2145	130d. Christ (icon)	80	65
2146	150d. Christ (icon)	95	75
2147	180d. Christ Pantocrator (Encaustic icon)	1·20	95
2148	1000d. Christ Pantocrator (Byzantine coin) (horiz)	8·75	7·00

484 Mother and Child holding Money Box

2001. Anniversaries and Events. Multicoloured.

2149	20d. Type **484** (centenary of Post Office Savings Bank)	25	20
2150	130d. Euro currency and emblem (centenary of Post Office Savings Bank) (horiz)	1·20	95
2151	140d. Refugees (50th anniv of United Nations High Commissioner for Refugees) (horiz)	1·50	1·20
2152	180d. Emblem and crowd (75th anniv of Thessalonika International Trade Fair)	1·70	1·40

2153	200d. University facade (75th anniv of Aristotle University, Thessalonika) (horiz)	2·00	1·60
2154	500d. Academy building (75th anniv of Academy of Athens) (horiz)	4·00	3·25
2155	700d. Ioannis Zigdis (politician, third death anniv)	7·00	5·50

485 Dried Earth

2001. Europa. Water Resources. Multicoloured.

2156	180d. Type **485**	2·30	1·90
2157	650d. Pool of water and droplet	5·75	4·75

486 Little Egret

2001. Flora and Fauna. Multicoloured.

2158	20d. Type **486**	10	10
2159	50d. White storks	35	30
2160	100d. Bearded vulture	70	55
2161	140d. Orchid (vert)	95	75
2162	150d. Dalmatian pelican (vert)	1·00	85
2163	200d. Lily, Plastina Lake, Karditsa	1·40	1·10
2164	700d. Egyptian vulture	4·75	3·75
2165	850d. Black vulture	11·50	9·25

487 Emblem

2001. New Name of Hellenic Post.

2166	**487** 140d. blue and yellow	95	75
2167	**487** 200d. blue	1·40	1·10

488 *The Annunciation* (13th century muniture Athens)

2001. 1700th Anniv of Christianity in Armenia.

MS2168	**488** 850d. multicoloured	8·75	7·00

489 Figures of Swimmers from Amphora

2001. Olympic Games, Athens (2004). Sheet 80×70 mm.

MS2169	**489** 1200d. multicoloured	11·50	9·25

490 Kamakaki, Salamina

2002. Traditional Dances. Multicoloured.

2170	2c. Type **490**	10	10
2171	3c. Prikia (bride's dowry)	10	10
2172	5c. Zagorissios, Epirus (vert)	10	10
2173	10c. Balos, Aegean Islands	25	20
2174	15c. Synkathistos, Thrace	35	30
2175	20c. Tsakonikos, Peloponnese (vert)	45	35
2176	30c. Pyrrichios (Sera) (Pontian Greek)	70	55
2177	35c. Fourles, Kythnos (vert)	80	65
2178	40c. Apokriatos, Skyros	95	75
2179	45c. Kotsari (Pontian Greek)	1·00	85
2180	50c. Pentozalis, Crete (vert)	1·20	95
2181	55c. Karagouna, Thessaly	1·30	1·00
2182	60c. Hassapiko, Smyrneikos	1·40	1·10
2183	65c. Zalistos, Naoussa	1·50	1·20
2184	85c. Pogonissios, Epirus	2·00	1·60
2185	€1 Kalamtianos, Peloponnese	2·30	1·90

2186	€2 Maleviziotis, Crete	4·75	3·75
2187	€2.15 Tsamikos, Roumeli	5·00	4·00
2188	€2.60 Zeibekikos (vert)	6·00	4·75
2189	€3 Nyfiatikos, Corfou	7·00	5·50
2190	€4 Paschaliatikos	9·25	7·50

491 Runners (vase painting)

2002. Olympics Games, Athens (2004) (3rd issue). Multicoloured.

2191	41c. Type **491**	1·20	95
2192	59c. Charioteer (8th-century bronze statuette) (vert)	1·70	1·40
2193	80c. Javelin thrower (vase painting)	2·00	1·60
2194	€2.05 Doryphoros ("Spear Bearer") (statue, Polycleitos) (vert)	4·75	3·75
2195	€2.35 Weightlifter (vase painting)	5·75	4·75
MS2196	121×80 mm. €5 "Crypt of the ancient Olympic stadium, Olympia" (49×29 mm)	13·00	12·00

492 Performing Elephant

2002. Europa. Circus. Multicoloured.

2197	60c. Type **492**	2·30	1·90
2198	€2.60 Equestrian acrobat	8·25	6·50

493 Navy Scout

2002. Scouts. Multicoloured.

2199	45c. Type **493**	1·00	85
2200	60c. Scout and World Conference emblem	1·40	1·10
2201	70c. Air scout and Cub scouts planting tree	1·60	1·30
2202	€2.15 Scouts, mountains and map	5·25	4·25

494 Fragment of 5th-century B.C. Tablet, Acropolis, Athens

2002. The Greek Language. Multicoloured.

2203	45c. Type **494**	1·00	85
2204	60c. 13th-century B.C. Linear B script tablet, Glay	1·40	1·10
2205	90c. Manuscript and General Makrygiannis (writer)	2·10	1·70
2206	€2.15 Manuscript and page from 11th-century Byzantine manuscript, Mount Athos	5·00	4·00

495 Man wearing Olive Wreath holding Two Ears of Corn

2002. Olympics Games, Athens (2004) (4th issue). Multicoloured.

2207	45c. Type **495**	1·00	85
2208	60c. Man wearing wreath and chewing ear of corn	1·40	1·10
2209	€2.15 Man beside column wearing wreath and chewing ear of corn	5·00	4·00
2210	€2.60 Man beside tilted column holding wreath	6·00	4·75

496 Facade

2002. Olympics Games, Athens (2004) (5th issue). Early Stadia. Sheet 120×75 mm.

MS2211	**496** €6 multicoloured	14·00	11·00

497 Chrysostomos Papadopoulos (1923–38)

2002. Archbishops of Athens. Multicoloured.

2212	10c. Type **497**	25	20
2213	45c. Chrysanthos Philippides (1938–41)	1·20	95
2214	€2.15 Damaskinos Papandreou (1941–49)	5·75	4·75
2215	€2.60 Seraphem Tikas (1974–98)	9·25	7·50

498 Discus

2003. Olympic Games, Athens (2004) (6th issue). Multicoloured.

2216	2c. Type **498**	10	10
2217	5c. Hammer	10	10
2218	47c. Javelin	1·20	95
2219	65c. Pole-vault	1·50	1·20
2220	€2.17 High hurdles	5·00	4·00
2221	€2.85 Weights (weightlifting)	6·75	5·25

499 Athena (Girl Mascot)

2003. Olympic Games, Athens (2004) (7th issue). Sheet 128×82 mm containing T **499** and similar horiz design. Multicoloured.

MS2222	€2.50 Type **499**; €2.85 Phevos (boy mascot)	14·00	13·00

500 Globe

2003. Greetings Stamps. Sheet 123×124 containing T **500** and similar square designs. Multicoloured.

MS2223	47c. (a) Type **500** (corporate); 47c. (b) 2004 Olympics emblem (sponsor); 47c. (c) Man wearing wreath (Greece); 47c. (d) Roses (wedding); 47c. (e) Grid and skyline (corporate); 47c. (f) Stylized train (children); 47c. (g) Couple (social occasion); 65c. (h) Statue head (Greece); 65c. (i) Acropolis (Greece)	16·00	15·00

501 Swallow and European Stars

2003. Greek Presidency of the European Union. Multicoloured.

2224	47c. Type **501**	1·20	95
2225	65c. White Tower, Thessaloniki formed from letters	1·70	1·40
2226	€2.17 Swallows (fresco, Thera)	5·25	4·25
2227	€2.85 Stars and flags of member countries as jigsaw puzzle	7·00	5·50

502 Stylized Figure

2003. Europa. Poster Art. Multicoloured.

2228	65c. Type **502**	1·70	1·40
2229	€2.85 House with flag pole and veranda	7·00	5·50

503 Apple floating in Space and Trees

2003. Environmental Protection. Multicoloured.

2230	15c. Type **503**	35	30
2231	47c. Apple floating in water	1·20	95
2232	65c. Wreath above waves	1·60	1·30
2233	€2.85 Planet above apple tree	6·75	5·50

504 High Jump

2003. Olympic Games, Athens (2004) (8th issue). Multicoloured.

2234	5c. Type **504**	10	10
2235	47c. Wrestlers	1·20	95
2236	65c. Runners	1·50	1·20
2237	80c. Cyclists (vert)	1·90	1·50
2238	€4 Windsurfer (vert)	9·25	7·50

505 Athena (Girl Mascot)

2003. Olympic Games, Athens (2004) (9th issue). Sheet 128×80 mm containing T **505** and similar horiz design. Multicoloured.

MS2239	€2.50 Type **505**; €2.85 Phevos (boy mascot)	14·00	13·00

506 Stair Maker

2003. Traditional Trades and Crafts. Multicoloured.

2240	3c. Type **506**	10	10
2241	10c. Shoemaker	25	20
2242	50c. Smith	1·20	1·10
2243	€1 Type setter	2·50	2·20
2244	€1.40 Sponge diver	3·50	3·25
2245	€4 Hand weaver	10·00	9·00
MS2245a	115×149 mm. Nos. 2240/5	16·00	16·00

507 Weightlifting

2003. Olympic Games 2004, Athens (10th issue). Athletes. Multicoloured.

2246	20c. Type **507**	55	50
2247	30c. Throwing javelin	80	75
2248	40c. Charioteers	1·10	95
2249	47c. Soldier carrying spear and shield	1·30	1·20
2250	€2 Running	5·25	5·00
2251	€2.85 Throwing discus	7·50	7·00

508 Volos

2004. Olympic Games 2004, Athens (11th issue). Cities. Multicoloured.

2252	1c. Type **508**	10	10
2253	2c. Patra	10	10
2254	5c. Herakleio, Crete	10	10
2255	47c. Athens	1·20	1·20
2256	€1.40 Thessalonika	3·50	3·25
2257	€4 Athens	10·00	9·25
MS2258	120×135 mm. Nos. 2252/7	12·50	12·00

509 Spiros Louis

2004. Olympic Games 2004, Athens (12th issue). Greek Olympic Champions. Multicoloured.

2259	3c. Type **509** (marathon, 1896)	10	10
2260	10c. Aristides Konstantinides (cycling, 1896)	25	25
2261	€2 Ioannis Fokianos (modern Olympic pioneer)	5·00	4·75
2262	€2.17 Ioannis Mitropoulos (gymnast, 1896)	5·50	5·00
2263	€3.60 Konstantinos Tsiklitiras (long jump, 1912)	9·25	8·50

510 Swimming

2004. Olympic Games 2004, Athens (13th issue). Sport Disciplines. Multicoloured.

2264	5c. Type **510**	10	10
2265	10c. Hands applying rosin	25	25
2266	20c. Canoeing	45	40
2267	47c. Relay race	1·10	1·00
2268	€2 Gymnastics floor exercise (vert)	5·00	4·75
2269	€5 Gymnastics ring exercise (vert)	12·50	12·00
MS2270	162×140 mm. Nos. 2264/9	17·00	17·00

511 Woman holding Torch

2004. Olympic Games 2004, Athens (14th issue). Greetings Stamps. Sheet 90×75 mm containing T **511** and similar square design.

MS2271	47c. multicoloured	6·75	6·75

512 Dove and Olympic Rings

2004. Olympic Games 2004, Athens (15th issue). Sheet 128×81 mm containing T **512** and similar horiz design. Multicoloured.

MS2272	47c. Type **512**; €2.50 Dove and children	6·75	6·75

513 Yacht

2004. Europa. Holidays. Multicoloured.

2273	65c. Type **513**	1·40	1·30
2274	€2.85 Hot air balloon	6·00	5·50

514 Obverse and Reverse of 3 Drachma Coin (480–450 BC)

2004. Olympic Games, Athens 2004 (16th issue). Ancient Coins. Multicoloured.

2275	47c. Type **514**	1·20	1·10
2276	65c. Philip of Macedonia gold stater	1·60	1·50
2277	€2 Obverse and reverse of 2 drachma coin (460 BC)	4·75	4·50
2278	€2.17 Obverse and reverse of 4 drachma coin	5·25	5·00
MS2279	140×120 mm. Nos. 2275/8	12·00	11·00

515 Championship Trophy

2004. Greece—European Football Champions, 2004. Multicoloured.

2280	47c. Type **515**	1·20	1·10
2281	65c. Team members	1·60	1·50
2282	€1 Team members with raised arms	2·40	2·20
2283	€2.88 Outstretched hands and trophy	7·00	6·50
MS2284	160×135 mm. Nos. 2280/3	11·00	11·00

516 Sea

2004. Olympic Games, Athens 2004 (17th issue). Modern Art. Three sheets containing T **516** and similar multicoloured designs.

MS2285 (a) 120×80 mm. 50c. Type **516**; €2.50 Rainbow. (b) 120×80 mm. €1 Multicoloured paint brush and glass; €2 Roller making Greek flag. (c) 135×163 mm. As Nos. **MS**2285a/b

		27·00	27·00

517 Temple of Heaven, Beijing

2004. Olympic Games, Athens 2004 (18th issue). Athens 2004—Beijing 2008. Multicoloured.

2286	50c. Type **517**	1·20	1·10
2287	65c. Parthenon, Athens	1·60	1·50
MS2288	90×120 mm. Nos. 2286/7	11·00	11·00

518 Athena and Phevos holding Athens 2004 Emblem

2004. Olymphilex 2004, International Olympic Stamp and Memorabilia Exhibition. Sheet 81×70 mm.

MS2289	**518** €6 multicoloured	13·50	13·50

519 Thomas Bimis and Nikos Siranidis

2004. Greek Olympic Medal Winners. Multicoloured.

2290	65c. Type **519** (gold) (synchronised diving)	1·50	1·40
2292	65c. Ilias Iliadis (gold) (judo)	1·50	1·40
2293	65c. Emilia Tsoulfa and Sofia Bekatorou (gold) (women's sailing)	1·50	1·40
2294	65c. Pyrros Dimas (bronze) (weight lifting)	1·50	1·40
2295	65c. Dimosthenis Tabacos (gold) (gymnastics)	1·50	1·40
2296	65c. Anastasia Kelesidou (silver) (discus)	1·50	1·40
2297	65c. Vasilis Polymeros and Nikos Skiathitis (bronze) (rowing)	1·50	1·40
2298	65c. Athanasia Tzoumeleka (gold) (20km.walk)	1·50	1·40
2299	65c. Chrysopigi Devezi (silver) (triple jump)	1·50	1·40
2300	65c. Fani Chalkia (gold) (400m. hurdles)	1·50	1·40
2301	65c. Nikos Kaklamanakis (silver) (sailing)	1·50	1·40
2302	65c. Artiom Kiourgian (bronze) (Greco-roman wrestling)	1·50	1·40
2303	65c. Women's water polo team (silver)	1·50	1·40
2304	65c. Mirela Maniani (bronze) (women's javelin)	1·50	1·40
2305	65c. Elisavet Mystakidou (silver) (women's Taekwondo)	1·50	1·40
2306	65c. Alexandros Nikolaidis (silver) (men's Taekwondo)	1·50	1·40

No. 2291 was later withdrawn from circulation when the athlete, Leonidas Sampanis, was stripped of his medal after failing a drug test.

520 Horse Riders

2004. Paralympics. Multicoloured.

2307	20c. Type **520**	50	50
2308	49c. Disabled runner	1·30	1·20
2309	€2 Wheelchair basket ball players	5·00	4·75
2310	€2.24 Wheelchair archer	6·00	5·50

521 Santorini

2004. Tourism. Greek Islands. Multicoloured.

2311	2c. Type **521**	15	10
2312	3c. Karpathos	15	10
2313	5c. Crete – Vai	15	10
2314	10c. Mykonos	25	25
2315	49c. Chania	1·30	1·20
2316	50c. Kastelorizo	1·30	1·20
2317	€1 Astypalaia	2·50	2·40
2318	€2 Serifos	5·00	4·75
2319	€2.24 Milos	5·75	5·50
2320	€4 Skiathos	10·00	9·50

522 Necklace (730 BC)

2005. Jewellery. Multicoloured.

2321	1c. Type **522**	15	10
2322	15c. Snake-shaped bracelet (2nd—3rd century BC) (vert)	40	35
2323	30c. Necklace with bulls head pendant (5th century)	75	70
2324	49c. Central part of crown (2nd century)	1·30	1·20
2325	€4 Earring (8th century BC) (vert)	10·00	9·50

523 Formula Diagram and "$E=mc^2$" (75th anniv of State Laboratory)

2005. Anniversaries and Events. Multicoloured.

2326	1c. Type **523**	15	10
2327	4c. Sugar cubes and stop sign (41st European Association for Diabetes Meeting) (horiz)	15	10
2328	5c. Electrocardiogram chart and heart (54th European Society for Cardiovascular Surgery Congress) (horiz)	15	10
2329	40c. I. Kondilakis (first president) (90th anniv of ESIA (journalists' union of Athens)	1·00	95
2330	49c. Emblem (2005—Year of Economic Competitiveness)	1·30	1·20
2331	€1.40 Woman examining breast (25th anniv of Senologic Hellenic Society)	3·50	3·25
2332	€3.50 Angel (painting, Alekos Kontopoylos) (birth centenary) (horiz)	9·25	8·75

524 Gladiolus illyricus

2005. Flowers. Multicoloured.

2333	20c. Type **524**	50	50
2334	40c. Crocus sieberi	1·00	95
2335	49c. Narcissus tazetta	1·30	1·20
2336	€1.40 Rhododendron luteum	3·50	3·25
2337	€3 Tulipa boetica	7·75	7·25

525 Agiorgitiko Peloponnese

2005. Wine. Grape varieties. Multicoloured.

2338	20c. Type **525**	50	50
2339	49c. White grapes on cloth (Assyrtiko Santorini)	1·30	1·20
2340	65c. Black grapes and coin (Xinomavro Macedonia)	1·70	1·60
2341	€2.24 White grapes and barrel (Robola Kefalonia)	5·75	5·50
2342	€2.40 Black grapes (Moschofilero Peloponnese)	6·25	5·75

526 Dakos

2005. Europa. Gastronomy. Multicoloured.

2343	65c. Type **526**	1·70	1·60
2344	€2.35 Rusk, tomato, herbs, oil and feta cheese	6·00	5·75

Nos. 2343/4 were issued together, se-tenant, forming a composite design.

527 Blackboard

2005. Greetings Stamps. Multicoloured.

2345	49c. Type **527**	1·30	1·20
2346	49c. Envelopes	1·30	1·20
2347	49c. Girl reading	1·30	1·20
2348	49c. Globe and stamp	1·30	1·20
2349	49c. Grid	1·30	1·20
2350	49c. Flowers	1·30	1·20
2351	49c. Figures	1·30	1·20
2352	65c. Church	1·70	1·60

528 Rocket and Mountaineers (Fokion Dimitriadis)

2005. Caricatures. Multicoloured.

2353	15c. Type **528**	40	35
2354	20c. Woman and man (Archelaus)	60	55
2355	30c. Stick figure (Themos Annios)	75	70
2356	50c. Man tying woman's shoe (Dimitris Galanis)	1·30	1·20
2357	65c. Chef icing globe with atomic rocket (Kostas Mitropoulis)	1·70	1·60
2358	€4 Stylized couple (vase painting) (Asteas)	10·00	9·50

529 Two Players, Referee and Ball

2005. Greece—European Basketball Champions, 2005 (Eurobasket 2005, Belgrade). Multicoloured.

2359	30c. Type **529**	75	70
2360	50c. Trophy	1·30	1·20
2361	65c. Team members	1·70	1·60
2362	€3.55 Holding trophy aloft	9·00	8·50
MS2363	165×138 mm. Nos. 2359/62	11·50	11·50

530 Mini Cooper

2005. Cars. Multicoloured.

2364	1c. Type **530**	15	10
2365	30c. Fiat 500	75	70
2366	50c. Citroen 2CV	1·30	1·20
2367	€2.25 Volkswagen Beetle	5·75	5·50
2368	€2.85 Ford Model T	7·50	7·00

531 Ethnikos Sports Club Emblem

2005. Sports Clubs. Multicoloured.

2369	30c. Type **531**	75	70
2370	50c. Panionios Football Club	1·30	1·20
2371	50c. Iraklis Football Club	1·30	1·20
2372	50c. Panathinakos Football Club	1·30	1·20
2373	65c. PAOK Football Club	1·70	1·60
2374	65c. Panellinios Sports Club	1·70	1·60
2375	€4 Omilos Ereton Athletics Club	10·00	9·50

532 Virgin and Child (*Hodeghetria*)

2005. Christmas. Icons. Multicoloured.

2376	1c. Type **532**	25	25
2377	20c. *Kardiotissa*	50	50
2378	70c. *Glykophiloussa*	1·80	1·70
2379	€3.20 Virgin, Child and symbols of the Passion	8·25	7·75

533 Building Facade

2006. 50th Anniv of Europa Stamps. Sheet 105×81 mm containing T **533** and similar horiz design.

MS2380	€1.50 Type **533**; €2.50 As No. 1617	13·00	12·00

534 "Ancient Drama" (Dionisis Fotopoulos)

2006. Patras—European Capital of Culture—2006. Multicoloured.

2381	1c. Type **534**	15	10
2382	15c. "Travelling" (Dimitris Milionis)	25	25
2383	20c. "Child and Art" (Rania Kapeliari)	50	50
2384	50c. "Carnival" (Charis Pressas)	1·30	1·20
2385	65c. Patras—2006 emblem (vert)	1·70	1·60
2386	€2.25 "Poetry and Music" (Kelly Mendrinou)	5·50	5·25
2387	€2.30 Icon (vert)	5·75	5·50

535 Kouros of Anavissos (National Archaeological Museum)

2006. Museum Exhibits. Multicoloured.

2388	5c. Type **535**	15	10
2389	20c. Marble seated figure (Museum of Cycladic Art, Athens)	50	50
2390	50c. Spiral (29×30 mm)	1·30	1·20
2391	50c. Parthenon pediment (Acropolis Museum) (horiz)	1·70	1·60
2392	€1.40 Antinopolis (painting) (Benaki Museum, Athens)	3·50	3·25
2393	€2.25 *Concert of the Angels* (Domenicos Theotokopoulos) (National Art Gallery) (horiz)	5·75	5·50

536 As Type 21

2006. Centenary of Intercalated Olympic Games, Athens. T **536** and similar horiz designs showing 1906 stamps "Second Olympic Games Issue, Athens". Multicoloured.

MS2394	Two sheets, each 105×81 mm. (a) 20c. Type **536**; 30c. As Type **25**; 50c. As Type **22**; €2. As Type **26**; (b) 50c. As Type **23**; 65c. As Type **27**; 85c. As Type **28**; €1. As Type **24**	13·50	13·50

537 Moon and Multicoloured Twisted Strands

2006. Europa. Integration. Multicoloured.

2395	65c. Type **537**	1·50	1·40
2396	€3 Green twisted strands and sun	7·00	6·50

538 Book and Archive Building (90th anniv of state archives)

2006. Anniversaries and Events. Multicoloured.

2397	15c. Type **538**	40	35
2398	20c. European stars (25th anniv of membership of EU)	50	50
2399	50c. Circle of squares (Eurovision Song Contest, Athens)	1·30	1·20
2400	65c. Olive tree (2006—Year of Olive Oil and Olives)	1·70	1·60
2401	€1.40 Tinia (god)	3·50	3·25
2402	€3 Council chamber (Greece's participation in UN Security Council 2005—2006)	7·00	6·50

539 Lesvos

2006. Tourism. Greek Islands. Multicoloured.

2403	1c. Type **539**	15	10
2404	3c. Hydra	15	10
2405	10c. Sifnos	15	10
2406	20c. Lefkada	20	20
2407	40c. Samothrace	1·00	95
2408	50c. Syros	1·30	1·20
2409	65c. Rhodes (30×30 mm)	1·70	1·60
2410	85c. Cephalonia	2·20	2·00
2411	€2.25 Corfu	5·00	4·75
2412	€5 Naxos	11·50	11·00

540 *Olympias* (trireme)

2006. Ancient Technology. Multicoloured.

2413	3c. Type **540**	15	10
2414	5c. 1st-century odometer (Heron of Alexandria)	15	10
2415	50c. 3rd-century piston water pump (Ktesibius) (vert)	1·30	1·20
2416	65c. The Antikythera mechanism, 80 B.C. (vert)	1·70	1·60
2417	€3.80 1st-century automatic temple gates (Heron of Alexandria) (vert)	9·50	9·00

541 Team members (left)

2006. Greece—World Basketball Championship Silver Medallists. Sheet 105×81 mm containing T **541** and similar horiz designs. Multicoloured.

MS2418	50c. Medal; €2 Type **541**; €3 Team members (right)	12·50	12·50

The stamps and margins of **MS**2417 form a composite design.

542 Apollon Kalamarias

2007. Sports Clubs. Multicoloured.

2419	2c. Type **542**	15	10
2420	3c. Atromitos Athinon	15	10
2421	52c. Aris Thessalonikis	1·30	1·20
2422	€2.27 Ethnikos Peiraio	5·75	5·50
2423	€3.20 Apollon Smirnis	8·25	7·75

543 Bleuette (doll, 1905)

2007. Children's Toys. Multicoloured.

2424	5c. Type **543**	10	10
2425	15c. Wooden aircraft (1940—5)	35	35
2426	30c. Paper Mache head dolls (1925—30)	70	65
2427	40c. Wheeled horses and cat (1920—60)	95	90
2428	52c. Clockwork cat, wheeled duck and dominoes (1930—60)	1·30	1·20
2429	72c. Parachutist (c 1950) (vert)	1·80	1·70
2430	€2.27 Airplane carousel (c. 1950) (vert)	6·75	6·25
2431	€4 Puppet show of the Resistance (1941—5) (vert)	9·50	9·00

544 Faces

2007. Greetings Stamps. Multicoloured.

2432	52c. Type **544**	1·30	1·20
2433	52c. Crescents	1·30	1·20
2434	52c. Artemis	1·30	1·20
2435	52c. Earth from space	1·30	1·20
2436	52c. Globe	1·30	1·20
2437	65c. Parthenon	1·60	1·50
2438	65c. Kore Phrasikleia	1·60	1·50
MS2439	118×122 mm. Nos. 2432/8	12·00	11·00

545 Costis Palamas (poet and critic) (engraving by Giannis Gourzis)

2007. Anniversaries and Events. Multicoloured.

2440	2c. Type **545**	10	10
2441	10c. Poseidon and head with gold mask (Year of Greece in China) (horiz)	20	20
2442	20c. Emblem (1st Symposium of Seven Wise Men in Cardiovascular Surgery, Athens and Delphi)	45	40
2443	52c. Figures with arms raised (2nd UNI Postal Global Union World Conference, Athens) (horiz)	1·20	1·20
2444	65c. Rainbow and stars (50th anniv of Treaty of Rome)	1·50	1·40
2445	85c. Georgios Kotzias (30th death anniv)	1·90	1·80
2446	€1 Rigas Velestinlis (revolutionary) (engraving by Giannis Gourzis) (250th birth anniv)	2·20	2·10
2447	€2.27 Light bulb as air balloon (2007—year of innovation)	5·00	4·75
2448	€3 Blind justice (125th anniv of Legal Council of State) (horiz)	6·75	6·25

546 Scorpio

2007. Western Zodiac. Multicoloured.

2449	2c. Type **546**	10	10
2450	3c. Cancer	10	10
2451	5c. Capricorn	10	10
2452	10c. Taurus	20	20
2453	20c. Sagittarius (*vert*)	45	40
2454	40c. Leo (*vert*)	90	85
2455	52c. Virgo (*vert*)	1·20	1·20
2456	65c. Aries	1·50	1·40
2457	85c. Aquarius	1·90	1·80
2458	€1 Libra	2·20	2·10
2459	€2.27 Pisces	5·00	4·75
2460	€2.80 Gemini	6·25	5·75

547 Emblem and Part of Dove

2007. Europa. Centenary of Scouting. Multicoloured.

2461	65c. Type **547**	1·50	1·40
2462	€3.15 Part of Dove and scouts	7·00	6·50

Nos. 2461/2 were issued together, *se-tenant*, forming a composite design.

548 Asclepius (statue) (Ampuria Museum, Spain)

2007. Asclepius (demigod of medicine). Sheet 120×76 mm containing T **548** and similar vert design. Multicoloured.

MS2463	€2.50×2, Type **548**; Asclepius (head) (National Archaeological Museum)	11·00	11·00

549 Basilica of San Clemente, Rome

2007. Anniversaries and Events. Multicoloured.

2464	2c. Type **549** (150th anniv of excavation and discovery of St Cyril's grave)	10	10

2465	3c. Emblem (50th anniv of University of Macedonia)	10	10
2466	€4 Konstantinos Tsatsos (politician and writer) (president 1975–1980) (50th death anniv) (vert)	10·50	9·75

550 Ergotelis Sports Club

2007. Sports Clubs. Multicoloured.

2467	2c. Type **550**	10	10
2468	4c. OFI Football Club	10	10
2469	54c. Olympiacos Club of Fans of Piraeus (umbrella organization)	1·30	1·20
2470	€2.29 Doxa Dramas Sports Club	5·75	5·25
2471	€5 Mytilini Nautical Club	12·00	11·00

551 Aphrodite (Greek)

2007. Statues. Multicoloured.

2472	54c. Type **551**	1·40	1·30
2473	€2.40 Anahit (Armenian)	6·00	5·50

Stamps of the same design were issued by Armenia.

552 Chios

2008. Islands. Multicoloured.

2474	2c. Type **552**	10	10
2475	5c. Amorgos	10	10
2476	10c. Nissiros	25	20
2477	20c. Paxi	50	45
2478	40c. Leros	95	90
2479	54c. Kalymnos	1·30	1·20
2480	67c. Kos	1·70	1·60
2481	€1 Simi	2·40	2·20
2482	€2.29 Zakynthos	5·50	5·25
2483	€4 Inousses	9·50	9·00

553 Discus Thrower

2008. Olympic Games, Beijing. Multicoloured.

2494	3c. Type **553**	15	15
2495	35c. Lighting Olympic flame	95	90
2496	67c. Cyclist (horiz)	1·90	1·80
2497	67c. Torch relay	1·90	1·80

554 Heart

2008. Personal Stamps. Multicoloured.

2498	54c. Type **554**	1·60	1·50
2499	54c. Kites	1·60	1·50
2500	54c. Digital symbols	1·60	1·50
2501	54c. Letter	1·60	1·50
2502	67c. Flag	2·00	1·90
2503	67c. Pillar and capitol	2·00	1·90
MS2504	120×122 mm. Nos. 2498/503	9·50	9·00

555 Ink bottle, Pen and Letters

2008. Europa. The Letter. Multicoloured.

2505	67c. Type **555**	1·90	1·80

2506	€3.17 Letter, script and pen	8·25	7·75

Nos. 2505/6 were issued together, se-tenant, forming a composite design.

556 Emblem

2008. Anniversaries. Multicoloured.

2507	3c. Type **556** (180th anniv of Hellenic Post)	15	15
2508	5c. Symbols of Greece (180th anniv of Hellenic Post)	15	15
2509	10c. Ioannis Kapodistrias (180th anniv of his election as first head of state of newly-liberated Greece)	25	25
2510	57c. Dimitris Rodopoulos (M. Karagatsis) (writer) (birth centenary)	1·60	1·50
2511	70c. Fish (International Year of Planet Earth)	2·00	1·90
2512	€1.85 '50' (50th anniv of National Hellenic Research Foundation)	5·50	5·00
2513	€3 Emblem (centenary of National Council of Women)	8·25	7·75

557 Feta Cheese

2008. Traditional Products. Multicoloured.

2514	3c. Type **557**	15	15
2515	5c. Mastic gum from Chios	15	15
2516	20c. Olive oil (horiz)	55	50
2517	57c. Ouzo spirit	1·60	1·50
2518	€1 Pistachio nuts from Aigina	3·00	2·75
2519	€4 Honey	11·00	10·00

558 Diagoras Rhodos Sports Club

2008. Sports Clubs. Multicoloured.

2520	40c. Type **558**	1·40	1·30
2521	57c. AEK Football Club	1·90	1·80
2522	70c. Asteras Tripolis Football Club	2·30	2·20
2523	€2 Panserraikos Football Club	6·25	6·00
2524	€3 Keriraikos Sports Club	8·75	8·25

559 Alexander the Great and the Mermaid

2008. Fairy Tales. Multicoloured.

2525	10c. Type **559**	25	20
2526	57c. Little Red Riding Hood	1·60	1·50
2527	€1 The Fairies	3·00	2·75
2528	€1.85 The Girl and the Matches	5·50	5·00
2529	€3 Arion and the Lyre	8·75	8·50

560 Manos Katrakis

2009. Actors. Multicoloured.

2530	1c. Type **560**	10	10
2531	20c. Dinos Iliopoulos	55	50
2532	35c. Elli Lambeti	95	90
2533	40c. Alekos Alexandrakis	95	90
2534	50c. Aliki Vougiouklaki	1·20	1·10
2535	57c. Jenny Karezi	1·60	1·50
2536	€1 Dimitris Horn	3·00	3·75
2537	€2.42 Nikos Kourkoulos	5·75	5·25
2538	€3.50 Thanos Kotsopoulos	9·75	9·25
MS2539	153×148 mm. Nos. 2530/8	24·00	23·00

561 Sivitanidios School

2009. Anniversaries and Events. Multicoloured.

2540	5c. Type **561** (80th anniv)	15	10
2541	10c. Emblem (70th anniv of University of Piraeus) (vert)	25	15
2542	20c. Exhibits (180th anniv of National Archaeological Museum)	30	20
2543	50c. Dove carrying envelope (Greek presidency of UPU Postal Operations Council)	1·30	1·10
2544	57c. Braille (birth bicentenary of Louis Braille (inventor of Braille writing for the blind))	1·70	1·50
2545	70c. € (thenth anniv of Euro)	2·50	2·30
2546	€2.42 Lord Byron (engraving) (Philhellenism and International Solidarity Day) (vert)	5·75	5·25
2547	€3 Buildings (National Real Estate Registry)	9·00	8·50
MS2548	80×121 mm. €1×2, Polar ice; Water (Preserve Polar Regions and Glaciers) (30×30 mm (circular))	6·00	6·00

562 Pulsar (model)

2009. Europa. Astronomy. Multicoloured. (a) Ordinary gum

2549	70c. Type **562**	2·00	1·70
2550	€3.20 Aristarchos telescope	9·00	8·50

Nos. 2549/50 were printed, se-tenant, each pair forming a composite design.

(b) Self-adhesive gum

2551	70c. As Type **562**	2·00	1·70
2552	€3.20 As No. 2550	9·00	8·50

563 Acropolis

2009. Greek Monuments of World Cultural Heritage. Multicoloured.

2553	57c. Type **563**	1·60	1·30
2554	57c. Meteora	1·60	1·30
2555	70c. Delphi	1·90	1·70
2556	70c. Mycenae	1·90	1·70
2557	€2 Mystras	5·25	4·75
2558	€3 Delos	8·75	8·25
MS2559	146×136 mm. Nos. 2553/8	21·00	21·00

564 Lighthouse, Didmi Islet, Gaidouronisi

2009. Lighthouses. Multicoloured.

2560	1c. Type **564**	25	15
2561	57c. Tourlitis, Andros	1·60	1·40
2562	70c. Chania	2·30	2·00
2563	€1 Korakas, Paros (horiz)	3·25	3·00
2564	€4.20 Strongyli, Kastellorizo (horiz)	11·50	11·00
MS2565	150×133 mm. Nos. 2560/4	21·00	21·00

565 Minotaur

2009. Myths and Legends. Multicoloured.

2566	1c. Type **565**	25	20
2567	5c. Triton	40	30
2568	57c. Sirens	1·60	1·40
2569	70c. Dioskouroi	2·30	2·10
2570	€5 Pegasus	15·00	14·50

566 Adult and Child's Hands

2009. Rights of the Child. Multicoloured.

2571	20c. Type **566**	55	45
2572	58c. Small girl leaning against wall (horiz)	1·90	1·70
2573	72c. Adults and chiildren's hands linked in circle (horiz)	2·30	2·10
2574	€1 Silhouette of child at window	3·25	3·00
2575	€4 Child's profile against dark background	11·00	10·50

567 2009 European Basketball Championship Gold Medal (men's under-20 team)

2009. Basketball. Three sheets, each 105×81 mm containing T **567** and similar horiz designs showing medals won by Greek athletes in 2009. Multicoloured.

MS2576	€2 Type **567**	6·00	6·00
MS2577	€2 World Championship silver medal (men's under-19 team)	6·00	6·00
MS2578	€2 European Championship bronze medal (men's team)	6·00	6·00

568 Stuffed Head (Giannis Gaitis)

2010. Modern Greek Art. Multicoloured.

2579	1c. Type **568**	20	10
2580	5c. Orpheus, Hermes and Eurydice (Nikos Engonopoulos)	30	20
2581	50c. Erotic (Yannis Moralis)	1·50	1·20
2582	58c. Sailor at Table (Yannis Tsarouchis)	1·90	1·60
2583	€2.43 Wattle Fences (Nikos Hadjikyriakos-Ghika)	6·00	5·50
2584	€3 The Drawing (Diamantis Diamantopoulos)	9·25	8·75
MS2585	148×135 mm. Nos. 2579/84	19·00	10·00

569 Man at Window (solar energy)

2010. Renewable Energy Development. Multicoloured.

2586	1c. Type **569**	15	15
2587	40c. Waterfall, turbine and goat (hydropower)	1·30	1·20
2588	58c. Wind turbine and woman with wind tossed hair (wind power) (horiz)	1·80	1·60
2589	72c. Man holding ear of corn and bicycle (self sufficiency)	2·75	2·40
2590	€2.43 Yacht (wave power)	6·50	6·00
2591	€2.50 Plants (bio energy)	7·00	6·50

570 Book as Air Balloon, Boy and Staircase

2010. Europa. Multicoloured.

2592	72c. Type **570**	2·00	1·80
2593	€3.22 Staircase as bookmark, book as house and girl	9·00	8·50

Nos. 2592/3 were issued in horizontal se-tenant pairs, each pair forming a composite design.

571 Peplos Kore

2010. New Acropolis Museum. Multicoloured.

2594	5c. Type **571**	10	10
2595	58c. Parthenon Gallery	1·30	1·10
2596	72c. Parthenon frieze (detail)	1·90	1·70
2597	€1 Entrance to museum building	2·40	2·10
2598	€4 Dog (statue)	3·00	2·75
MS2599	136×147 mm. Nos. 2594/8	17·00	17·00

572 Athenian and Persian Warriors

2010. 2500th Anniv of Battle of Marathon

2600	50c. bronze, black and gold	1·20	1·00
2601	58c. multicoloured	1·60	1·30
2602	72c. deep lilac, gold and black	2·40	2·10
2603	€3 multicoloured	7·75	7·00

Designs:- 50c. Type **572**; 58c. Phalanx of soldiers; 72c. Two warriors (different); €3 Bronze helmet

573 Vasilis Tsitsanis (songwriter and bouzouki player)

2010. Greek Popular Music. Multicoloured.

2604	10c. Type **573**	10	10
2605	20c. Giorgos Zampetas (bouzouki musician)	15	10
2606	58c. Stylianos (Stelios) Kazantz-idis (singer)	1·20	1·00
2607	72c. Grigoris Bithikotsis (folk singer and songwriter)	1·90	1·70
2608	€1 Vicky Moscholiou (singer)	2·75	2·50
2609	€4.80 Sotiria Bellou (singer and performer of rebetiko style music)	10·00	9·00
MS2610	135×147 mm. Nos. 2604/9	16·00	16·00

574 Limnos

2010. Islands. Multicoloured.

(a) Sheet stamps

2611	2c. Type **574**	15	10
2612	5c. Paros	15	10
2613	20c. Ithaki	40	30
2614	40c. Tinos	60	50
2615	50c. Skyros	95	85
2616	(58c.) Paper boat and green square (29×29 mm)	1·20	1·00
2617	(72c.) Stairway and red circle (29×29 mm)	1·90	1·70
2618	€1 Evia–Chalkida	2·50	2·20
2619	€2 Samos	4·50	4·00
2620	€4 Kassos	9·00	8·00

(b) Coil Stamps

2621	2c. As Type **574**	15	10
2622	5c. As No. 2612	15	10
2623	20c. As No. 2613	40	30
2624	40c. As No. 2614	60	50
2625	50c. As No. 2615	95	85
2626	(58c.) As No. 2616	1·20	1·00
2627	(72c.) As No. 2617	1·90	1·70
2628	€1 As No. 2618	2·50	2·20
2629	€2 As No. 2619	4·50	4·00
2630	€4 As No. 2620	9·00	8·00

Nos. 2616 and 2626 were for use on inland mail and Nos. 2617 and 2627 were for use on overseas mail.

575 Municipal Theatre, Piraeus

2010. Architecture. Multicoloured.

2631	20c. Type **575**	15	10
2632	58c. Benaki Museum	2·40	2·10
2633	€2.43 National Theatre	6·75	6·25
2634	€2.50 National Gallery, Nafplio	7·75	7·25

576 Doves, Stars and Holly

2010. Christmas. Multicoloured.

(a) Sheet stamps. Ordinary gum

2635	50c. Type **576**	1·40	1·20
2636	58c. Angel blowing horn	2·10	1·90
2637	€1 Sailing ship	3·25	2·75
2638	€3.50 Decorated tree, holly and two birds	9·25	8·75

(b) Self-adhesive

MS2639	100×150 mm. 50c. As Type **576**; 58c. As No. 2636; €1 As No. 2637; €3.50 As No. 2638	16·00	16·00

577 Aigaion V (coloured wood engraving)

2011. Greek Engravers of 20th Century

2640	3c. multicoloured	20	10
2641	30c. black and bright scarlet (horiz)	90	75
2642	60c. black, scarlet-vermilion and bright scarlet	1·90	1·70
2643	€1 black and bright scarlet (horiz)	3·00	2·50
2644	€4 black and bright scarlet	11·00	10·00

Designs:-3c. Type **577**; 30c. *To Pagoni* (peacock) (wood engraving); 60c. *Maria* (woman) (wood engraving); €1 *Plastikes Rimes* (still life) (wood engraving); €4 *Mikros Kavalaris* (horseman) (stone engraving)

578 Clasped Arms (European Year of Volunteering)

2011. Anniversaries

2645	3c. multicoloured	20	10
2646	10c. multicoloured (vert)	45	35
2647	20c. black and crimson (vert)	75	65
2648	60c. multicoloured (vert)	2·10	1·90
2649	€1.50 multicoloured	4·25	4·00
2650	€3 black and bright yellow-green (vert)	8·25	8·00

Designs:-3c. Type **578**; 10c. Pediment, frieze and Ionic column (85th anniv of Academy of Athens); 20c. Alexandros Papadiamantis (writer) (death centenary); 60c. Aircraft over Crete (70th anniv of Battle of Crete); €1.50 Globe and OECD emblem (50th anniv of Organisation for Economic Co-operation and Development (OECD)); €3 Spyridon-Filiskos Samaras (composer) (150th birth anniv)

579 Stylised Figures (volunteer programme)

2011. Special Olympics, Athens. Multicoloured.

2651	2c. Type **579**	15	10
2652	4c. Figure and buildings (Athens host city)	20	10
2653	60c. Games emblem (vert)	2·10	1·90
2654	75c. Apollon, games mascot (vert)	2·50	2·20
2655	€4.20 Emblems and games colours as band at foot of stamp	12·00	11·00

580 Ship, 15th century BC

2011. Greek Ships. Multicoloured.

2657	1c. Type **580**	15	10
2658	20c. Hellenic Polyreme, 4th-2nd century BC (horiz)	1·10	95
2659	60c. Triakontoros, 15th-4th century BC (horiz)	3·50	3·00
2660	75c. Hellenic Trireme, 7th-4th century BC (horiz)	4·25	3·75
2661	€2.47 Macedonian Hexareme, 4th-3rd century BC (horiz)	4·75	4·00
2662	€2.50 Byzantine Dromon, 5th-11th century AD	5·25	4·50
MS2663	175×117 mm. Nos. 2657/62	20·00	20·00

581 Heron, Deer and Wasp

2011. Europa. Forests. Multicoloured.

(a) Sheet stamps

2664	75c. Type **581**	3·75	3·25
2665	€3.25 Tree boles and leaves	8·25	7·00

(b) Booklet stamps

2666	75c. AsType **581**	3·75	3·25
2667	€3.25 Tree boles and leaves	7·00	7·00

Nos. 2664/5 were printed, *se-tenant*, forming a composite design.

582 Stylized Waves

2011. Tourism. Visit Greece Campaign. Multicoloured.

(a) Sheet stamps

2668	1c. Type **582**	15	10
2669	3c. Mask	20	15
2670	60c. Paper boat	2·10	1·90
2671	75c. Stylized column capitals	2·50	2·20
2672	€4 Cliff-top houses	11·75	10·00

(b) Booklet stamp. Self-adhesive

2673	75c. Stylized column capitals	2·50	2·20

583 School Book Cover from 1954

2011. Primary School Reading Books. Multicoloured.

(a) Ordinary gum

2674	2c. Type **583**	15	10
2675	20c. Children seated on picnic rug reading	1·10	95
2676	60c. Older girl helping younger boy to read	3·50	3·00
2677	75c. Children working in garden	4·25	3·75
2678	€1 Children picking flowers	5·00	3·50
2679	€3.50 Boys marching under banner	7·00	6·50
MS2680	145×155mm. Nos. 2674/9	19·00	19·00

(b) Size 30×31 mm. Personal stamp

2681	60c. As No. 2676	3·50	3·00

(c) Booklet stamp

2682	60c. As No. 2676	3·50	3·00

MS2656 175×100 mm. 60c. As No. 2653 plus stamp size label   2·10   1·90

584 Paris (As Type 1)

2011. 150th Anniv of First Greek Stamp

2683	**584**	15c. chocolate, deep green and sage green	95	80
2684	**584**	50c. dull orange, bright carmine and magenta	2·75	2·50
2685	**584**	60c. deep green, vermilion and dull rose	3·50	3·00
2686	**584**	75c. dull orange, indigo and new blue	4·25	3·75
2687	**584**	€1 deep dull blue, brown and dull orange	5·00	4·50
2688	**584**	€2 deep magenta, dull orange and yellow-brown	6·50	6·00
2689	**584**	€5 orange-vermilion, myrtle-green and dull green	8·50	8·00

585 Vassilis Diamantopoulos

2011. Actors. Multicoloured.

2690	1c. Type **585**	15	10
2691	5c. Rena Vlachopoulou	35	30
2692	50c. Orestis Makris	2·75	2·50
2693	60c. Thanasis Veggos	3·50	3·00
2694	€2.47 Mary Aroni	4·75	£425
2695	€2.50 Sapfo Notara	5·25	4·50
MS2696	135×147mm. Nos. 2690/5	15·00	15·00

586 Medal and Flag (Greek Women's Water Polo Team)

2011. Greek Gold Medal Winners, World Swimming Championships, Shanghai. Multicoloured.

MS2697	€3 Type **586**	9·50	9·00
MS2698	€3 Spyros Gianniotis	9·50	9·00

587 Palinurus elephas

2012. Riches of Greek Seas. Marine Fauna. Multicoloured.

(a) Sheet stamps

2699	2c. Type **587**	20	10
2700	3c. Octopus vulgaris	40	30
2701	5c. Anemonia viridis	50	40
2702	20c. Caretta caretta	80	75
2703	35c. Epinephelus marginatus	1·00	1·25
2704	50c. Dentex dentex	1·50	1·30
2705	(60c.) Hippocampus guttulatus	2·00	1·75
2706	€1 Aurelia aurita	3·50	3·25
2707	(€2.47) Dasyatis pastinaca	6·75	6·50
2708	€3 Charcharias taurus	7·50	7·00

(b) Coil Stamps

2709	2c. As Type **587**	20	10
2710	3c. As No. 2700	40	30
2711	5c. As No. 2701	50	40
2712	20c. As No. 2702	80	75
2713	35c. As No. 2703	1·00	1·25
2714	50c. As No. 2704	1·50	1·30
2715	(60c.) As No. 2705	2·00	1·75
2716	€1 As No. 2706	3·50	3·25
2717	(€2.47) As No. 2707	6·75	6·50
2718	€3 As No. 2708	7·50	7·00

588 Hippocampus guttulatus

2012. Personal Stamp

2719	**588**	(€1) multicoloured	3·50	3·25

589 Football

2012. Children's Games. Multicoloured.

(a) Ordinary gum

2720	2c. Type **589**	30	20
2721	10c. Scooter (vert)	70	50
2722	35c. Skipping rope	1·00	1·25
2723	(60c.) Marbles (vert)	2·00	1·75
2724	€2 Spinning tops	6·00	6·00
2725	€3 Hop scotch	7·25	6·75

(b) Booket stamp. Self-adhesive

| 2726 | (60c.) As No. 2723 | 1·75 | |

(c) Miniature Sheet. Self-adhesive

| MS2727 | As Nos. 2720/5 | 18·00 | 18·00 |

590 Sun and Island

2012. Europa. Visit Greece. Multicoloured.

(a) Sheet stamps

2728	75c. Type **590**	2·75	2·40
2729	€3.25 Sun setting over island	7·50	7·00

(b) Booklet stamps

2730	75c. As Type **590**	2·75	2·40
2731	€3.25 As No. 2729	7·50	7·00

591 Rock Climbing, Tzoumerka, Epirus

2012. Tourism. Visit Greece Campaign. Multicoloured.

(a) Sheet stamps

2732	1c. Type **591**	20	10
2733	10c. Rope bridge over Evinos River	70	50
2734	62c. Couple hiking, Samaria Gorge	2·25	2·00
2735	78c. Canoeing, Acheron River, Epirus	2·80	2·50
2736	€2 Hiking in valley, Rodori, Thrace	6·00	6·00
2737	€2.50 Hiking in fields, Xanthi, Thrace	6·75	6·50

(b) Booklet stamps. Self-adhesive

2738	62c. As No. 2734	2·25	2·00
2739	78c. As No. 2735	2·80	2·50

592 Emblem

2012. Olympic Games, London 2012. Multicoloured.

2740	78c. Type **592**	2·80	2·50
2741	€1.78 Athletes	5·75	5·50

593 Dimitris Chondrokoukis (High Jump)

2012. Greek Olympic Gold Medal Winners. Multicoloured.

MS2742	€2.50 Type **593**	18·00	18·00
MS2743	€2.50 Vlassis Maras (Gymnastics)	18·00	18·00

594 Brig Paron, 1821

2012. Greek Ships. Multicoloured.

2744	1c. Type **594**	20	10
2745	15c. Galliot, 17th century	75	60
2746	62c. Corvette, 18th century	2·25	2·00
2747	78c. Ionian - Cretan Galley, 16th century	2·80	2·50
2748	€2 Sakoleva, 19th century	6·00	6·00
2749	€2.50 Latinadiko in Shipyard, 18th century	6·75	6·50
MS2750	175×117 mm. Nos. 2744/9	18·00	18·00

595 Battle of Deskati

2012. Centenary of Liberation of Thessaloniki. Multicoloured.

2751	40c. Type **595**	1·25	1·20
2752	62c. Greek Army entering Thessaloniki (50×26 mm)	2·25	2·00
2753	85c. Armoured Cruiser G.Averof	3·00	2·75
2754	€2.50 Battle of Sarantaporos	6·75	6·50

596 Bauble and Triangle

2012. Christmas. Multicoloured.

(a) Sheet stamps. Ordinary gum

2755	10c. Type **596**	70	50
2756	62c. Tree-shaped bauble	2·25	2·00
2757	78c. Stocking-shaped bauble	2·80	2·50
2758	€3 Parcel	7·25	6·75

(c) Booklet stamp

2759	62c. As No. 2756	2·25	2·00
2760	78c. As No. 2757	2·80	2·50

597 Women of Epirus in Struggle

2013. National Historical Events. Centenary of Liberation of Ioannina. Paintings by Kenan Messare. Multicoloured.

2761	3c. Type **597**	40	30
2762	55c. Campaign	1·70	1·50
2763	62c. Shell Blast	2·25	2·00

598 Symbols

2013. 2400th Anniv of Plato's Academy. Multicoloured.

| MS2764 | €1 Type **598**; €2 'N' | 8·00 | 8·00 |

599 Taxidi sta Kithira (Voyage to Cythera, 1984)

2013. Greek Cinema. Multicoloured.

2765	20c. Type **599**	80	75
2766	30c. Elektra (Electra, 1962)	90	80
2767	62c. O Thiassos (The Travelling Players, 1975)	2·25	2·00
2768	€2.80 O Drakos (The Ogre of Athens, 1956)	7·00	6·75

600 Post Van

2013. Europa. Postal Transport. Multicoloured.

(a) Sheet stamps

2769	78c. Type **600**	2·80	2·50
2770	€3.28 Post bicycle	7·50	7·00

(b) Booklet stamps

2771	78c. As Type **600**	2·80	2·50
2772	€3.28 As No. 2770	7·50	7·00

601 Yachts

2013. Tourism. Visit Greece Campaign. Sailing. Multicoloured.

(a) Sheet stamps

2773	5c. Type **601**	50	40
2774	30c. Three yachts in line	90	80
2775	47c. Two yachts tacking	1·40	1·30
2776	(62c.) Yacht in full sail	2·25	2·00
2777	(78c.) Three yachts	2·80	2·50
2778	€3 Yacht with yellow sail	7·25	6·75

(b) Booklet stamp. Self-adhesive

2779	(62c.) As No. 2776	2·25	2·00
2780	(78c.) As No. 2778	2·80	2·50

CHARITY TAX STAMPS

C38 Dying Soldier, Widow and Child

1914. Roul.

C269	**C38**	2l. red	65	40
C270	**C38**	5l. blue	75	50

C39 Red Cross, Nurses, Wounded and Bearers

1915. Red Cross. Roul.

| C271 | **C39** | (5l.) red and blue | 21·00 | 2·40 |

C40 Greek Women's Patriotic League Badge

1915. Greek Women's Patriotic League.

| C272 | **C40** | (5l.) red and blue | 1·40 | 1·30 |

(C42)

1917. Surch as Type **C42**.

C297	**15**	1 on 1l. brown	1·10	4·25
C303	**15**	1 on 3l. orange	35	65
C299	**15**	5 on 1l. brown	2·20	2·10
C300	**15**	5 on 20l. mauve	35	2·50
C307	**36**	5 on 25l. blue	20	50
C308	**36**	5 on 40l. blue	20	30
C304	**15**	5 on 40l. brown	60	1·60
C305	**15**	5 on 50l. lake	55	1·60
C309	**35**	5 on 50l. blue	22·00	31·00
C301	**15**	10 on 30l. purple	65	2·10
C302	**15**	30 on 30l. purple	1·10	2·30
C306	**17**	5 on 1d. black	1·10	4·25

(C44)

1917. Fiscal stamps surch as Type **C44**. Roul.

C310	**C43**	1l. on 10l. blue	1·10	2·10
C328	**C43**	1l. on 50l. purple	1·10	2·10
C311	**C43**	1l. on 80l. blue	1·10	2·10
C329	**C43**	5l. on 10l. blue	1·10	2·10
C330	**C43**	5l. on 10l. purple	1·10	2·10
C312	**C43**	5l. on 60l. blue	8·75	10·50
C313	**C43**	5l. on 80l. blue	4·25	3·25
C331	**C43**	10l. on 50l. purple	12·00	19·00
C326	**C43**	10l. on 70l. blue	11·00	26·00
C315	**C43**	10l. on 90l. blue	22·00	50·00
C316	**C43**	20l. on 20l. blue	£8000	£7000
C317	**C43**	20l. on 30l. blue	11·00	12·50
C318	**C43**	20l. on 40l. blue	27·00	31·00
C319	**C43**	20l. on 50l. blue	13·00	16·00
C320	**C43**	20l. on 60l. blue	£550	
C321	**C43**	20l. on 80l. blue	£130	
C322	**C43**	20l. on 90l. blue	7·50	12·50
C333	**C43**	20l. on 2d. blue	15·00	26·00

(C46)

1917. Fiscal stamps surch as Type **C46**. Roul.

C334	1l. on 10l. blue	1·60	1·60
C341	5l. on 10l. purple & red	13·00	18·00
C335	5l. on 50l. blue	70·00	£120
C338	10l. on 50l. blue	15·00	12·50
C339	20l. on 50l. blue	35·00	29·00
C340	30l. on 50l. blue	26·00	21·00

C48 Wounded Soldier

1918. Red Cross. Roul.

| C342 | **C48** | 5l. red, blue and yellow | 11·00 | 1·60 |

1918. Optd **P.I.P.** in Greek.

| C343 | 5l. red, blue and yellow | 16·00 | 1·60 |

C49

1922. Greek Women's Patriotic League. Surch as in Type **C49**.

C344	**C49**	5l. on 10l. red and blue	£375	16·00
C345	**C49**	5l. on 20l. red and blue	£120	80·00
C346	**C49**	5l. on 50l. red and blue	£375	£275
C347	**C49**	5l. on 1d. red and blue	11·00	75·00

Nos. C344/7 were not issued without surcharge.

1924. Red Cross. As Type **C48** but wounded soldier and family.

| C406 | 10l. red, blue and yellow | 80 | 50 |

C77 St. Demetrius

1934. Salonika Int Exn Fund.

C478	C77	20l. brown	65	20

C78 Allegory of Health

1934. Postal Staff Anti-tuberculosis Fund.

C480	C78	10l. orange and green	25	20
C481	C78	20l. orange and blue	55	30
C482	C78	50l. orange and green	4·50	3·75

1935. As Type C78 but with country inscription at top.

C494	10l. orange and green	65	50
C495	20l. orange and blue	1·10	80
C496	50l. orange and green	2·75	2·50
C497	50l. orange and brown	75	45

ΠΡΟΝΟΙΑ (C85)

1937. Nos. D273 and 415 optd with Type C85.

C498	D20	10l. red	1·90	30
C500	51	50l. violet	1·10	30

Λ.50 ΠΡΟΝΟΙΑ (C95)

1938. Surch with Type C95.

C521	D20	50l. on 5l. green	7·50	1·00
C522	D20	50l. on 20l. slate	7·50	1·00
C523	52	50l. on 20l. violet	1·10	85

C96 Queens Olga and Sophia

1939

C524	C96	10l. red	20	10
C525	C96	50l. green	35	15
C526	C96	1d. blue	55	30

ΠΡΟΣΤΑΣΙΑ ΦΥΜΑΤΙΚΩΝ ΤΤΤ (C104)

1940. Postal staff Anti-tuberculosis Fund. Optd with Type C104.

C554	50l. green	45	30

Κ.Π. λεπτῶν 50 (C105)

1941. Social Funds. No. 410 surch with Type C105.

C561	51	50l. on 5l. green	45	35

1941. Postal Staff Anti-tuberculosis Fund. Surch 50 and bars.

C562	C78	50l. on 10l.	2·10	9·50
C563	-	50l. on 10l. (No. C494)	40	20

ΔΡ.1 (C107)

1942. Sample Fair, Salonika. No. C478 surch with Type C107.

C573	C77	1d. on 20l. brown	45	10

ΦΥΜ· Τ.Τ.Τ. 10 = ΔΡ. (C109)

1942. Postal Staff Anti-tuberculosis Fund. Nos. 410 and 413 surch with Type C109.

C591	51	10d. on 5l. green	35	25
C592	51	10l. on 25l. green	35	25

ΦΥΜ· Τ.Τ.Τ. (C111)

1944. Postal Staff Anti-tuberculosis Fund. No. 580 optd with Type C111.

C599	100d. black	25	25

ΦΥΜ· Τ.Τ.Τ. ΔΡ. 5000 (C112)

1944. Postal Staff Anti-tuberculosis Fund. No. 579 surch with Type C112.

C600	5000d. on 75d. red	25	40

ΥΠΕΡ ΤΩΝ ΦΥΜΑΤΙΚΩΝ Τ.Τ.Τ. ΔΡΧ. 25.000 (C113)

1944. Postal Staff Anti-tuberculosis Fund. Surch as Type C113.

C619	-	1d. on 40l. (No. 500)	25	15
C620	-	2d. on 40l. (No. 500)	25	15
C605	106	25,000d. on 2d.	60	70

ΠΡΟΝΟΙΑ ΠΡΟΣΩΠΙΚΟΥ Τ.Τ.Τ. ΔΡΑΧΜΑΙ 50 (C117)

1946. Postal Staff Anti-tuberculosis Fund. Surch as Type C117.

C640	C117	20d. on 5l.	1·60	65
C641	C117	20d. on 40l. (No. 500)	65	20

1946. Red Cross. Surch as Type C117.

C642	C96	50d. on 50l.	70	20

1946. Social Funds. Surch as Type C117.

C643	50d. on 1d. (No. C526)	55	20

ΔΡ. — 50 (C123)

1947. Postal Staff Anti-tuberculosis Fund. Additionally surch with T C123.

C660	50l. on 50d. (C554)	4·50	50
C659	50d. on 50l. (C525)	70·00	

1948. Church Restoration Fund.

C682	C127	50d. brown	35	25

1950. Postal Staff Anti-tuberculosis Fund. Surch with Type C117.

C686	50d. on 10l. (No. 498)	2·50	20

ΠΡΟΝΟΙΑ ΤΑΧ.ΥΠΑΛΛΗΛΩΝ ΔΡΑΧΜΑΙ 50 (C136)

1951. Postal Staff Welfare Fund. Surch with Type C136.

C698	86	50d. on 5l. blue & brown	3·00	40

1951. Postal Staff Anti-tuberculosis Fund. Surch with Cross of Lorraine and 50.

C699	89	50d. on 3d. brown	1·60	20

ΠΡΟΣΘΕΤΟΝ ΔΡ. 100 (C139)

1952. State Welfare Fund. No. 509 surch with Type C139.

C706	100d. on 8d. blue	1·80	20

C140 Argostoli, Cephalonia

1953. Ionian Is. Earthquake Fund.

C713	-	300d. slate	3·25	15
C714	C 140	500d. brown & yellow	3·50	90

DESIGN: 300d. Church of Faneromeni, Zante.

C148 Zeus (Macedonian Coin of Philip II)

1956. Macedonian Cultural Fund.

C761	C148	50l. red	1·90	60
C762	-	1d. blue (Aristotle)	6·25	1·50

POSTAGE DUE STAMPS

D2

1875

D73A	D2	1l. green and black	1·90	2·10
D74A	D2	2l. green and black	2·40	2·10
D75A	D2	5l. green and black	2·40	2·10
D88	D2	10l. green and black	1·30	1·30
D89	D2	20l. green and black	2·75	2·50
D78A	D2	40l. green and black	18·00	18·00
D91	D2	60l. green and black	9·75	9·50
D80A	D2	70l. green and black	18·00	18·00
D81A	D2	80l. green and black	22·00	21·00
D82A	D2	90l. green and black	18·00	18·00
D95	D2	100l. green and black	16·00	12·50
D96	D2	200l. green and black	£250	£255
D83A	D2	1d. green and black	18·00	18·00
D84A	D2	2d. green and black	27·00	26·00

D20

1902

D183	D20	1l. brown	55	35
D184	D20	2l. grey	55	35
D185	D20	3l. orange	55	35
D186	D20	5l. green	55	35
D273	D20	10l. red	35	30
D188	D20	20l. mauve	55	35
D275	D20	25l. blue	35	30
D190	D20	30l. purple	65	35
D191	D20	40l. brown	80	50
D451	D20	50l. brown	45	40
D193	D20	1d. black	1·60	85
D194	D20	2d. bronze	2·40	3·25
D195	D20	3d. silver	3·75	7·25
D196	D20	5d. gold	6·00	22·00

1912. Optd with T 34.

D252A	D20	1l. brown	65	65
D253A	D20	2l. grey	65	65
D254A	D20	3l. orange	35	30
D255A	D20	5l. green	35	30
D256A	D20	10l. red	1·40	1·40
D257D	D20	20l. mauve	85	85
D258A	D20	30l. purple	4·25	4·25
D259D	D20	40l. brown	85	85
D260D	D20	50l. brown	85	85
D261D	D20	1d. black	11·00	10·50
D262D	D20	2d. bronze	14·00	13·50
D263D	D20	3d. silver	24·00	23·00
D264D	D20	5d. gold	38·00	37·00

1913. Perf or roul.

D269	D20	1l. green	10	10
D270	D20	2l. red	10	10
D271	D20	3l. red	10	10
D274	D20	20l. slate	35	30
D276	D20	30l. red	35	30
D277	D20	40l. blue	35	30
D279	D20	80l. purple	55	50
D452	D20	1d. blue	45	40
D453	D20	2d. red	45	40
D282	D20	3d. red	12·00	8·25
D455	D20	5d. blue	45	40
D456	D20	10d. green	45	1·00
D595	D20	10d. orange	35	3·00
D457	D20	15d. brown	45	1·60
D458	D20	25d. red	1·10	2·50
D596	D20	25d. blue	35	3·00
D480	D20	50d. orange	85	5·25
D481	D20	100d. green	85	5·25
D597	D20	100d. brown	35	3·00
D598	D20	200d. violet	35	3·00

1942. Surch 50.

D564	50l. on 30l. red	6·50	13·00

GREEK WAR ISSUES, 1912-1913

For provisional issues used in territories occupied by Greece during the Balkan War, see Stanley Gibbons Part 3 (Balkans) Catalogue

Pt. 3

GREEK OCCUPATION OF ALBANIA

100 lepta = 1 drachma.

Stamps of Greece optd with T 1.

ΕΛΛΗΝΙΚΗ ΔΙΟΙΚΗΣΙΣ (1)

1940. Stamps of 1937.

1	86	5l. blue and brown	15	30
2	-	10l. brown & blue (No. 498)	15	30
3	-	20l. green & blk (No. 499)	20	50
4	-	40l. black & grn (No. 500)	20	50
5	-	50l. black & brn (No. 501)	20	50
6	-	80l. brown & vio (No. 502)	20	50
7	89	1d. green	30	1·30
8	-	2d. blue (No. 504)	35	1·30
9	89	3d. brown	45	1·30
10	-	5d. red (No. 506)	65	2·00
11	-	6d. olive (No. 507)	1·00	2·40
12	-	7d. brown (No. 508)	1·00	2·40
13	89	8d. blue	1·00	2·40
14	-	10d. brown (No. 510)	1·60	3·00
15	-	15d. green (No. 511)	1·60	5·00
16	-	25d. blue (No. 512)	4·00	9·00
17	89a	30d. red	7·50	19·00

1940. Charity Tax Stamps of 1939.

18	C96	10l. red on rose	15	40
19	C96	50l. green on green	25	85
20	C96	1d. blue on blue	65	1·90

1940. Nos. 534/53 (Youth Organization).

36	103	2d. black and orange (air)	55	1·00
26	101	3d. blue, red & sil (postage)	55	1·00
37	-	4d. black and green	2·75	4·25
27	-	5d. black and blue	2·75	2·10
38	-	6d. black and red	3·75	5·25
39	-	8d. black and blue	5·50	8·25
28	-	10d. black and orange	3·75	5·25
29	-	15d. black and green	13·00	18·00
40	-	16d. black and violet	11·00	16·00
30	-	20d. black and red	11·00	18·00
31	-	25d. black and blue	11·00	18·00
32	-	30d. black and violet	11·00	18·00
41	-	32d. black and orange	12·00	19·00
42	-	45d. black and green	12·00	19·00
33	-	50d. black and red	11·00	18·00
43	-	55d. black and red	12·00	19·00
44	-	65d. black and blue	12·00	19·00
34	-	75d. gold, blue and brown	14·00	18·00
35	101	100d. blue, red and silver	15·00	24·00
45	-	100d. black and violet	22·00	16·00

POSTAGE DUE STAMPS

1940. Postage Due stamps of 1913.

D21	D20	2d. red	35	95
D22	D20	5d. blue	80	1·90
D23	D20	10d. green	50	1·60
D24	D20	15d. brown	80	1·90

1940. Postage Due stamp surch also.

D25	50l. on 25d. red	35	95

Pt. 11

GREENLAND

A Danish possession N.E. of Canada. On 5 June 1963, Greenland became an integral part of the Danish Kingdom.

100 ore = 1 krone.

 1 Christian X   **2** Polar Bear

1938

1	1	1ore green	40	40
2	1	5ore red	2·30	1·50

3	1	7ore green	3·25	3·75
4	1	10ore violet	95	75
5	1	15ore red	95	75
5a	1	1·50ore red	2·30	1·50
6	2	30ore blue	6·25	7·50
6a	2	40ore blue	60·00	8·75
7	2	1k. brown	5·75	8·75

3 Harp Seal **4** King Christian X **5** Eskimo Kayak

1945

8	3	1ore violet and black	38·00	44·00
9	3	5ore buff and violet	38·00	44·00
10	3	7ore black and green	38·00	44·00
11	4	10ore olive and purple	38·00	44·00
12	4	15ore blue and red	38·00	44·00
13	-	30ore brown and blue	38·00	44·00
14	-	1k. grey and brown	38·00	44·00
15	5	2k. green and brown	38·00	44·00
16	5	5k. brown and purple	38·00	44·00

DESIGNS—HORIZ: As Type **5**: 30ore Dog team; 1k. Polar bear; 5k. Eider.

1945. Liberation of Denmark. Nos. 8/16 optd **DANMARK BEFRIET 5 MAJ 1945**.

17	3	1ore violet and black	£130	75·00
18	3	5ore buff and violet	£130	75·00
19	3	7ore black and green	£130	75·00
20	4	10ore olive and purple	£150	£130
21	4	15ore blue and red	£150	£130
22	-	30ore brown and blue	£150	£130
23	-	1k. grey and brown	£150	£130
24	5	2k. green and brown	£150	£130
25	-	5k. brown and purple	£150	£130

7 King Frederik IX **8** Polar Ship *Gustav Holm*

1950

26	7	1ore green	25	20
27	7	5ore red	40	30
28	7	10ore green	45	40
29a	7	15ore violet	65	50
30	7	25ore red	3·25	1·30
31	7	30ore blue	38·00	2·50
32	7	30ore red	65	40
33	8	50ore blue	80·00	14·00
34	8	1k. brown	19·00	3·25
35	8	2k. red	10·00	3·25
36	8	5k. grey	2·75	1·90

1956. Nos. 6a and 7 surch **60 ore**.

37	2	60ore on 40ore blue	10·00	1·90
38	2	60ore on 1k. brown	95·00	9·50

10 "The Boy and the Fox"

1957. Greenland Legends.

39	10	50ore red	1·80	1·30
40	-	60ore blue	3·75	1·30
41	-	80ore brown	1·90	1·50
42	-	90ore blue	4·00	3·75

DESIGNS: 60ore "Mother of the Sea"; 80ore "The Girl and the Eagle"; 90ore "Great Northern Diver and Raven".

1958. Royal Tuberculosis Relief Fund. No. 33 surch with Cross of Lorraine and **30+10**.

43	8	30ore+10ore on 50ore blue	5·00	1·50

12 Hans Egede (after J. Horner)

1958. Death Bicent of Hans Egede (missionary).

44	12	30ore red	11·50	1·50

1959. Greenland Fund. Surch **Gronlandsfonden 30+10** and bars.

45	7	30ore+10ore on 25ore red	5·75	5·00

The note below No. 413 of Denmark also applies here.

14 Knud Rasmussen (founder of Thule)

1960. 50th Anniv of Thule Settlement.

46	14	30ore red	1·90	90

15 Drum Dance

1961

47	15	35ore green	1·30	75

16 Northern Lights **17** Frederik IX **18** Polar Bear

1963

48	16	1ore green	20	15
49	16	5ore red	25	20
50	16	10ore green	40	30
51	16	12ore green	45	40
52	16	15ore purple	1·00	90
53	17	20ore blue	5·00	3·75
54	17	25ore brown	50	45
54a	17	30ore green	45	40
55	17	35ore red	45	40
56	17	40ore grey	50	45
57	17	50ore blue	10·00	8·75
57a	17	50ore red	55	50
57b	17	60ore red	65	55
58	17	80ore orange	1·10	1·00
59	17	1k. brown	75	50
60	18	2k. red	4·00	75
61	18	5k. blue	3·25	1·50
62	18	10k. green	4·50	1·00

18a Prof. Niels Bohr

1963. 50th Anniv of Bohr's Atomic Theory.

63	18a	35ore red	45	40
64	18a	60ore blue	5·00	4·50

19 S. Kleinschmidt

1964. 150th Birth Anniv of S. Kleinschmidt (philologist).

65	19	35ore brown	1·00	90

20a Princess Margrethe and Prince Henri de Monpezat

1967. Royal Wedding.

66	20a	50ore red	4·50	4·00

21a "The Children in the Round Tower" (legend)

1968. Child Welfare.

67	21a	60ore+10ore red	1·30	1·10

22 King Frederik IX and Map of Greenland

1969. King Frederik's 70th Birthday.

68	22	60ore red	1·90	1·50

24 Musk Ox

1969

69	-	1k. blue	90	75
70	-	2k. green	1·00	90
71	-	5k. blue	2·50	1·30
72	-	10k. brown	4·50	2·75
73	24	25k. olive	10·00	3·75

DESIGN—HORIZ: 1k. Bowhead whale and coastline; 2k. Narwhal; 5k. Polar bear; 10k. Walruses.

25 Celebrations at Jakobshavn

1970. 25th Anniv of Denmark's Liberation.

74	25	60ore red	2·50	2·40

26 Egede and Gertrud Rask aboard the *Haabet*

1971. 250th Anniv of Hans Egede's Arrival in Greenland.

75	26	60ore red	1·90	1·50
76	-	60ore+10ore red	2·50	2·10

DESIGN: No. 76, Hans Egede and Gertrud Rask meeting Greenlanders.

The premium on No. 76 was for the Greenland Church Building Fund.

27 Mail Kayaks

1971. Greenland Mail Transport.

77	27	50ore green	40	30
78	-	70ore red	45	40
79	-	80ore black	50	45
80	-	90ore blue	55	50
81	-	1k. red	65	55
82	-	1k.30 blue	75	70
83	-	1k.50 green	1·30	90
84	-	2k. blue	90	80

DESIGNS: 70 ore Umiak (women's boat); 80 ore Consolidated PBY-5A Catalina amphibian; 90 ore Mail dogsledge; 1k. *Kununhuak* (coaster) and *Dlik* (tug); 1k.30 *Sokongen* (schooner); 1k.50 *Karen* (sailing longboat); 2k. Sikorsky S-61N helicopter DY-HAF.

28 King Frederik IX and Royal Yacht *Dannebrog*

1972. King Frederik IX's and Queen Ingrid's Fund.

85	28	60ore+10ore red	1·30	1·10

29 Queen Margrethe

1973

86	29	10ore green	40	30
87	29	60ore brown	50	45
88	29	90ore brown	65	65
88a	29	100ore red	50	40
89	29	120ore blue	90	75
89a	29	130ore blue	75	65

For values inscribed "KALAALLIT NUNAAT" at top, see Nos. 99/104.

30 Heimaey Eruption

1973. Aid for Victims of Heimaey (Iceland) Eruption.

90	30	70ore+20ore blue and red	1·80	1·60

31 *Carl Egede* (trawler) and Kayaks

1974. Bicentenary of Royal Greenland Trade Department.

91	31	1k. brown	75	65
92	-	2k. brown	90	75

DESIGN—VERT: 2k. Trade Department Headquarters, Trangraven, Copenhagen.

32 Gyr Falcon and Radio Aerial

1975. 50th Anniv of Greenland's Telecommunications Service.

93	32	90ore red	65	55

33 Sirius Sledge Patrol

1975. 25th Anniv of Sirius Sledge Patrol.

94	33	1k.20 brown	75	70

34 Arm-wrestling (after H. Egede)

1976. Greenland Sports Publicity.

95	34	100ore+20ore brown and green on stone	65	65

35 Inuit Carved Mask

1977. Eskimo Mask.

96	35	9k. grey	3·50	3·25

36 Bronlund and Disko Bay, Jakobshavn

1977. Birth Cent of Jorgen Bronlund (explorer).

97	36	1k. brown	50	45

37 Cape York Meteorite and "Ulo" (woman's knife)

1978. Centenary of Commission for Scientific Researches in Greenland.

98	37	1k.20 brown	65	50

38 Queen Margrethe

1978

99	38	5ore red	40	25
100	38	80ore brown	40	25
101	38	120ore brown	55	50
102	38	130ore red	65	50
103	38	160ore blue	80	75
104	38	180ore green	90	80

39 Sun rising over Mountains

1978. 25th Anniv of Constitution.
105	**39**	1k.50 blue	65	55

40 Foundation Ceremony

1978. 250th Anniv of Godthab.
106	**40**	2k.50 brown	1·30	90

41 Tupilak (imaginary animal)

1978. Folk Art.
107	**41**	6k. red	2·30	2·00
108	-	7k. green	2·50	2·30
109	-	8k. blue	3·00	2·50

DESIGNS: 7k. Soapstone figure (Simon Kristoffersen; 8k. *Eskimo Family* (driftwood sculpture by Johannas Kreutzamann).

42 Helmsman

1979. Internal Autonomy.
110	**42**	1k.10 brown	65	50

43 Rasmussen with Eskimos

1979. Birth Centenary of Knud Rasmussen (polar explorer).
111	**43**	1k.30+20ore red	90	75

45 Eskimo Child

1979. International Year of the Child.
112	**45**	2k. green	90	75

47 Queen Margrethe and Map of Greenland

1980
113	**47**	50ore violet	40	30
114	**47**	80ore brown	50	45
115	**47**	1k.30 red	55	50
116	**47**	1k.50 blue	75	65
117	**47**	1k.60 blue	80	70
118	**47**	1k.80 red	90	75
119	**47**	2k.30 green	95	80
120	**47**	2k.50 red	1·00	90
121	**47**	2k.80 brown	1·80	1·00
122	**47**	3k. red	2·00	1·10
122a	**47**	3k.20 red	1·90	1·10
123	**47**	3k.80 black	1·80	1·60
124	**47**	4k.10 blue	2·30	2·10
124a	**47**	4k.40 blue	2·50	2·40

48 Eskimos and Rasmus Berthelsen in Library

1980. 150th Anniv of Greenland Public Libraries.
125	**48**	2k. brown on yellow	90	75

49 *Reindeer Sledge and the Larva* (drawing, Jens Kreutzmann)

1980. Greenland Art.
126	**49**	1k.60 red	75	65
127	-	2k.70 violet	1·10	1·00
128	-	3k. black	1·30	1·00

DESIGNS: 2k.70 *Harpooning Walrus* (printing by Jakob Danielsen); 3k. *Foot Race between Quloqutsuk and Aqigssia* (woodcut by Aron from Kangeq).

50 Mikkelsen and Eskimo

1980. Birth Centenary of Ejnar Mikkelsen (Inspector of East Greenland).
129	**50**	4k. green	1·60	1·50

52 Atlantic Cod

1981
130	**52**	25k. brown and blue	10·00	7·50

53 Stone Tent Ring, Wolf and King Eiders

1981. Peary Land Expeditions.
131	**53**	1k.60+20ore brown	1·00	90

54 Reindeer and Hunter (Saqqaq culture, 2000 B.C.)

1981. Greenland Prehistory.
132	**54**	3k.50 blue	1·50	1·30
133	-	5k. brown	1·90	1·80

DESIGN: 5k. Hunters dragging walrus (Tunit-Dorset culture, 50 B.C.).

55 Shrimps

1982
134	**55**	10k. blue and red	4·00	3·25

57 *Eric the Red discovering Greenland, 982*

1982. Millenary of Greenland (1st issue).
135	**57**	2k.+40ore brown	1·40	1·30

See also Nos. 136/7, 140/2, 145/7 and 152/3.

58 Eskimos hunting Bowhead Whale (1000–1100)

1982. Millenary of Greenland (2nd issue).
136	**58**	2k. red	75	65
137	-	2k.70 blue	1·30	1·00

DESIGN: 2k.70, Bishop Joen Smyrill's staff and house at Gardar (1100–1200).

59 Atlantic Salmon

1983
138	**59**	50k. black and blue	20·00	15·00

60 Blind Person, Armband, Cassette and White Stick

1983. Welfare of the Blind.
139	**60**	2k.50+40ore red	1·90	1·80

61 Eskimos and Northerners bartering (1200–1300)

1983. Millenary of Greenland (3rd issue).
140	**61**	2k.50 brown	1·00	90
141	-	3k.50 brown	1·40	1·30
142	-	4k.50 blue	2·00	1·90

DESIGNS: 3k.50, Mummy of Eskimo boy (1300–1400); 4k.50, Hans Pothorst's expedition to America (1400–1500).

62 Herrnhut Bandsmen

1983. 250th Anniv of Herrnhut Moravian Brethren Settlement.
143	**62**	2k.50 brown	1·30	1·10

63 *Polar Bear killing Seal Hunter*

1984. 50th Death Anniv of Karale Andreassen (writer and artist).
144	**63**	3k.70 black	1·60	1·50

64 Bowhead Whales and Glass Beads (trading goods) (1500–1600)

1984. Millenary of Greenland (4th issue).
145	**64**	2k.70 brown	1·80	1·60
146	-	3k.70 blue	1·90	1·80
147	-	5k.50 brown	2·00	1·90

DESIGNS: 3k.70 Greenlanders in European dress and apostle spoons (1600–1700); 5k.50, Hans Egede's mission station, Godthab, and key (1700–1800).

65 Prince Henrik of Denmark

1984. Prince Henrik's 50th Birthday.
148	**65**	2k.70 brown	2·10	2·00

66 Danish Grenadier, 1734

1984. 250th Anniv of Christianshab.
149	**66**	3k.70 brown	1·80	1·50

67 Lund

1984. 36th Death Anniv of Henrik Lund (composer).
150	**67**	5k. green	3·25	2·75

68 Spotted Wolffish

1984
151	**68**	10k. black and blue	6·25	5·00

69 *Hvalfisken* (brig) (1800–1900)

1985. Millenary of Greenland (5th issue).
152	**69**	2k.80 purple	1·90	1·50
153	-	6k. black	2·50	2·10

DESIGN: 6k. Communications satellite and globe (1900–2000).

70 Queen Ingrid and *Chrysanthemum frutescens* "Sofiero"

1985. 50th Anniv of Queen Ingrid's Arrival in Denmark.
154	**70**	2k.80 multicoloured	1·50	1·30

71 Nesting Birds and I.Y.Y. Emblem

1985. International Youth Year.
155	**71**	3k.80 multicoloured	1·50	1·40

72 *Hare Hunt*

1985. 130th Birth Anniv of Gerhard Kleist (artist).
156	**72**	9k. green	4·00	3·50

73 Greenland Halibut

1985
157	**73**	10k. brown and blue	4·50	3·75

74 Post Office Flags

1986. Postal Independence.
158	**74**	2k.80 red	1·30	1·10

75 Towing Man on Bladder (traditional sport)

1986. Greenland Athletic Federation.
159	**75**	2k.80+50ore mult	1·90	1·80

76 Needle Case and Combs

1986. Local Craft Artefacts.
160	**76**	2k.80 brown and red	1·80	1·50
161	-	3k. violet and red	1·30	1·10
162	-	3k.80 black and blue	1·50	1·40
163	-	3k.80 purple and mauve	1·90	1·80
164	-	5k. brown and green	2·30	1·90
165	-	6k.50 brown and green	3·25	3·00
166	-	10k. brown and purple	4·50	4·00

DESIGNS: 3k. Tubs; 3k.80, (No. 162) Ulos (knives for working sealskins); 3k.80, (No. 163) Eye masks; 5k. Harpoon heads; 6k.50, Lard lamps; 10k. Masks.

77 Daily Life in Thule (collage by Aninaaq)

1986. Art from Thule.
167 **77** 2k.80 brown — 1·30 1·10

78 Capelin

1986
168 **78** 10k. brown and green — 5·00 4·75

79 Fulmar and Iceberg

1987. "Hafnia 87" International Stamp Exhibition, Copenhagen (1st issue). Sheet 95×70 mm containing T **79** and similar vert designs showing coastal view of Greenland from sketch by Jens Lorentzen. Multicoloured.
MS169 2k.80 Type **79**; 3k.80 Uummannaq Mountain and ice floes; 6k.50 Fulmars swimming and steamer in bay (sold at 19k.50) — 10·00 10·00
See also No. MS193.

80 Ammassalik Fjord (Peter Rosing)

1987. Greenland Art.
170 **80** 2k.80 brown — 1·30 1·10

81 Father and Son on Ice-floe

1987. Fishing, Sealing and Whaling Industries Year.
171 **81** 3k.80 multicoloured — 1·50 1·40

83 Rock Ptarmigans

1987. Birds. Multicoloured.
172 **83** 3k. Gyr falcons — 1·90 1·80
173 3k.20 Long-tailed ducks — 1·50 1·40
174 4k. Snow geese — 1·90 1·80
175 4k.10 Common ravens — 2·50 2·40
176 4k.40 Snow buntings — 2·50 2·40
177 5k. Type **83** — 2·50 2·40
178 5k.50 White-tailed sea eagles — 3·75 3·50
179 5k.50 Black guillemots — 2·75 2·75
180 6k.50 Brunnich's guillemots — 3·50 3·25
181 7k. Great northern divers — 3·75 3·50
182 7k.50 Long-tailed skuas — 3·75 3·50
183 10k. Snowy owl — 5·00 4·50

84 Uummannaq Mountain

1987. "Hafnia 87" International Stamp Exhibition, Copenhagen (2nd issue). Sheet 94×68 mm.
MS193 **84** 2k.80 blue and red (sold at 4k.) — 3·50 3·50

85 Telefax, Sledge and de Havilland / Canada DHC-7 Dash Seven

1988. 50 Years of Greenland Postal Administration.
194 **85** 3k.+50ore multicoloured — 3·25 3·00

87 National Flag

1989. Tenth Anniv of Internal Autonomy. Multicoloured.
195 3k.20 Type **87** — 1·90 1·80
196 4k.40 National arms — 3·25 3·00

88 Cotton Grass

1989. Flowers. Multicoloured.
197 **88** 4k. Bellflower (vert) — 1·50 1·40
198 4k. Hairy lousewort (vert) — 1·90 1·80
199 5k. Type **88** — 2·10 2·00
200 5k.50 Labrador tea — 2·30 2·10
201 6k.50 Arctic white heather — 3·25 3·00
202 7k.25 Purple saxifrage — 3·75 3·50
203 10k. Arctic poppy (vert) — 4·75 4·50

89 Queen Margrethe

1990
210 **89** 25ore green — 40 25
211 **89** 1k. brown — 50 45
213 **89** 4k.25 red — 1·90 1·80
214 **89** 6k.50 blue — 3·00 2·75
215 **89** 7k. violet — 3·25 3·00
218 **89** 4k. red — 1·90 1·80

90 Chained Sledge Dog and nesting Eiders

1990. Greenland Environmental Foundation.
225 **90** 400ore+50ore mult — 5·00 4·75

91 Frederik Lynge

1990. Augo and Frederik Lynge (Greenland Members of Danish Folketing).
226 **91** 10k. red and blue — 5·00 4·50
227 25k. purple and blue — 11·50 9·50
DESIGN: 25k. Augo Lynge.

92 Ringed Seal (Phoca hispida)

1991. Marine Mammals. Multicoloured.
228 4k. Type **92** — 1·60 1·50
229 4k. Harp seals (Pagophilus groenlandicus) — 1·60 1·50
230 7k.25 Hooded seals (Cystophora cristata) — 3·25 3·00
231 7k.25 Walrus (Odobenus rosmarus) — 3·25 3·00

232 8k.50 Bearded seal (Erignatus barbatus) — 3·75 3·50
233 8k.50 Common seal (Phoca vitulina) — 3·75 3·50
MS234 142×86 mm. Nos. 228/33 — 21·00 20·00

93 Dogs and Fisherman

1991. 250th Anniv of Ilulissat (Jakobshavn).
235 **93** 4k. multicoloured — 1·90 1·80

94 Iceberg and Summer Flowers

1991. Nordic Countries' Postal Co-operation. Tourism. Multicoloured.
236 4k. Type **94** — 1·90 1·80
237 8k.50 Ski party and dog sled in winter — 4·50 4·25

95 Birds

1991. 75th Anniv of Blue Cross (health education organization).
238 **95** 4k.+50ore multicoloured — 11·50 10·00

96 Jonathan Petersen (composer, 110th anniv)

1991. Birth Anniversaries.
239 **96** 10k. black and blue — 3·75 3·50
240 50k. brown and blue — 19·00 18·00
DESIGN: 50k. Hans Lynge (writer and artist, 85th anniv).

97 Arms and Paamiut

1992. Bicentenary of Paamiut (Fredrikshaab).
241 **97** 7k.25 brown and blue — 4·50 4·25

98 Royal Couple in 1992 and in Official Wedding Photograph

1992. Silver Wedding of Queen Margrethe and Prince Henrik.
242 **98** 4k. multicoloured — 2·50 2·40

99 Moller and Drawing of Godthab Church

1992. 150th Birth Anniv of Lars Moller (editor and printer).
243 **99** 100k. red and blue — 31·00 30·00

100 Rainbow and Landscape

1992. Neriuffik Cancer Research Organization.
244 **100** 4k.+50ore multicoloured — 4·50 4·00

101 Mother and Child with Father Christmas

1992. Christmas.
245 **101** 4k. multicoloured — 2·50 2·40

102 Flame and Laurel Wreath framed by Dance Drum

1993. Int Year of Indigenous Peoples.
246 **102** 4k. multicoloured — 2·30 2·10

103 Flat Crab

1993. Crabs.
247 **103** 4k. red, yellow and green — 1·50 1·40
248 7k.25 brown and blue — 4·75 4·50
249 8k.50 multicoloured — 5·00 4·75
DESIGNS: 7k.25, Sand crab; 8k.50, Stone crabs.

104 Ummannaq Church

1993. Nordic Countries' Postal Co-operation. Churches. Multicoloured.
250 4k. Type **104** — 1·90 1·80
251 8k.50 Hvalso church ruins — 3·75 3·50

105 Children in Tent

1993. Anniversaries.
252 **105** 4k.+50ore multicoloured — 3·50 3·25
253 4k.+50ore red and violet — 3·50 3·25
MS254 140×80 mm. Nos. 252/3 each ×2 — 21·00 20·00
DESIGNS: No. 252 Type **105** (50th anniv of scouts in Greenland); 253, Birds, crosses and landscape (70th anniv of Red Cross in Greenland).

106 Corpuscles and "AIDS"

1993. Anti-AIDS Campaign.
255 **106** 4k. multicoloured — 1·90 1·80

107 Wolf

1993. Animals. Multicoloured.

256	4k. Polar bear	1·90	1·80
257	5k. Type **107**	2·50	2·40
258	5k.50 Ermine	2·75	2·50
259	7k.25 Arctic lemmings	3·75	3·50
260	7k.25 Wolverine	3·25	3·00
261	7k.50 Musk ox	3·50	3·25
262	8k.50 Arctic fox	3·75	3·50
263	9k. Mountain hare	4·00	3·75
264	10k. Reindeer	4·50	4·25

108 Dog Sled

1993. Christmas.

265	**108**	4k. multicoloured	2·50	2·40

109 Skiers

1994. Winter Olympic Games, Lillehammer, Norway.

266	**109**	4k.+50ore multicoloured	3·25	3·00
MS267	140×80 mm. No. 266 ×4	18·00	16·00

110 Transmission Line

1994. Inauguration of Buksefjorden Hydroelectric Power Station.

268	**110**	4k. multicoloured	1·90	1·80

111 First Church

1994. Centenary of Ammassalik.

269	**111**	7k.25 blue, brown & grn	3·25	3·00

112 *Danmark* (sail/steam barque)

1994. Europa. Discoveries. *Danmark* Expedition to Northeast Coast, 1906–08. Multicoloured.

270	4k. Type **112**	1·90	1·80
271	7k.25 *Danmark* and dogs following ELG Mobil car	3·50	3·25

113 *Ceres* (William Moen)

1994. Figureheads from Greenlandic Ships (1st series). Multicoloured.

272	4k. Type **113**	1·90	1·80
273	8k.50 "Nordlyset" (Johan Heldt)	3·75	3·50

See also Nos. 287/8 and 306/7.

114 Christmas Visiting

1994. Christmas. Multicoloured.

274	4k. Type **114**	1·90	1·80
275	5k. Santa Claus outside igloo	3·25	3·00

115 *Listera cordata*

1995. Arctic Orchids (1st series). Multicoloured.

276	4k. Type **115**	1·90	1·80
277	7k.25 *Leucorchis albida*	3·25	3·00

See also Nos. 293/5.

116 Teacher and Student

1995. 150th Anniv of Nuuk Training College.

278	**116**	4k. multicoloured	1·90	1·80

116a U.N. Emblem and "50"

1995. 50th Anniv of United Nations.

279	**116a**	blue, green and red	3·25	3·00

117 Iceberg and Meadow

1995. Nordic Countries' Postal Co-operation. Tourism.

280	4k. Type **117**	2·30	2·10
281	8k.50 Mountains and valleys	4·50	4·25

118 Airmail Envelope

1995. Europa. Peace and Freedom. Multicoloured.

282	4k. Type **118**	2·50	2·40
283	8k.50 Doves and seascape	4·50	4·25

119 King Christian X

1995. 50th Anniv of Liberation. Three sheets each 140×80 mm, containing reproductions of 1945 "American Series", surcharged in red. Multicoloured.

MS284	(a) 5k. on 10ore Type **119**; 5k. on 15ore Type **119**; (b) 1k. on 1ore Seal; 5k. on 5ore Seal; 7k. on 7ore Seal; (c) 4k. on 30ore Dog team; 4k. on 1k. Polar bear; 4k. on 2k. Eskimo kayak; 4k. on 5k. Eider Set of 3 sheets	26·00	31·00

120 Children with Flag

1995. Tenth Anniv of National Flag.

285	**120**	4k.+50ore multicoloured	3·25	3·00
MS286	80×140 mm. No. 285 ×4	15·00	14·00

The premium was for the benefit of the Greenland Flag Society.

1995. Figureheads from Greenlandic Ships (2nd series). As T **113**. Multicoloured.

287	4k. *Hvalfisken* (H. J. Moen) (vert)	1·60	1·50
288	8k.50 *Tjalfe*	4·00	3·75

121 Boy running with Lamps

1995. Christmas. Multicoloured.

289	4k. Type **121**	1·90	1·80
290	5k. Boy running with lamp and moon	2·50	2·40

1995. Nos. 210 and 213 surch.

291	**89**	4k.25 on 25ore green	2·50	2·40
292	**89**	4k.50 on 1k. brown	3·25	3·00

1996. Arctic Orchids (2nd series). As T **115**. Multicoloured.

293	4k.25 Early coral-root	1·50	1·40
294	4k.50 Round-leaved orchid	1·90	1·80
295	7k.50 Northern green orchid	3·25	3·00

124 Killer Whale

1996. Whales (1st series). Each black, red and blue.

296	25ore Type **124**	45	40
297	50ore Humpback whale	50	45
298	1k. Beluga	65	55
299	4k.50 Sperm whale	1·90	1·80
300	6k.50 Bowhead whale	3·25	3·00
301	9k.50 Minke whale	4·50	4·25
MS302	140×80 mm. Nos. 296/301	10·50	10·50

See also Nos. 318/22.

125 Arnarulunnguaq (Eskimo traveller)

1996. Europa. Famous Women.

303	**125**	4k.50 blue	3·25	3·00

126 Man in Wheelchair at Sea Shore

1996. Greenland Society of Handicapped and Disabled.

304	**126**	4k.25+50ore mult	2·50	2·40
MS305	140×81 mm. No. 304×4	10·00	9·75

1996. Figureheads from Greenlandic Ships (3rd series). As T **113**. Multicoloured.

306	15k. *Blaa Hejren*	5·75	5·25
307	20k. *Gertrud Rask* (horiz)	7·00	6·50

127 Child and Angels

1996. Christmas. Multicoloured.

308	4k.25 Type **127**	1·90	1·80
309	4k.50 Star and children	1·90	1·80

128 Arctic Fritillary

1997. Butterflies. Multicoloured.

310	4k. Type **128**	1·30	1·10
311	3k. Northern clouded yellow	1·90	1·80
312	4k.75 Arctic blue	2·30	2·10
313	8k. Small copper	3·75	3·50

129 Queen Margrethe in Greenlandic Costume

1997. Silver Jubilee of Queen Margrethe.

314	**129**	4k.50 multicoloured	1·90	1·80

130 Globe and Musicians

1997. Opening of Katuaq Cultural Centre, Nuuk.

315	**130**	4k.50+50ore mult	2·50	2·40
MS316	140×82 mm. No. 315 ×4	10·50	10·00

131 Bear of the Sea inhaling Umiak (boat)

1997. Europa. Tales and Legends.

317	**131**	4k.75 blue	3·25	3·00

1997. Whales (2nd series). As T **124**. Multicoloured.

318	5k. Blue whale	1·90	1·80
319	5k.75 Fin whale	3·00	2·75
320	6k. Sei whale	3·25	3·00
321	8k. Narwhal	3·75	3·50
MS322	140×81 mm. Nos. 318/21	12·00	11·50

132 Dancing Children and Church

1997. Bicentenary of Nanortalik.

323	**132**	4k.50 multicoloured	2·50	2·40

133 Drum Dancer

1997. Greenland Art (1st series). 20th Death Anniv of Aage Gitz-Johansen. Multicoloured.

324	10k. Type **133**	4·00	3·75
325	16k. *Ammassalik Woman*	5·75	5·50

See also Nos. 342/3 and 353/4.

134 Boy with Huskies

1997. Christmas. Multicoloured.

326	4k.50 Type **134**	1·90	1·80
327	4k.75 Family on sledge and father disentangling traces	1·90	1·80

135 Common Porpoise

1998. International Year of the Ocean. Cetaceans. Multicoloured.

328	2k. Type **135**	1·10	1·00
329	3k. White-beaked dolphin	1·40	1·30
330	4k.50 Long-finned pilot whale (*Globicephala melaena*)	1·90	1·80
331	4k.50 Northern bottle-nosed whale (*Hyperoodon ampullatus*)	1·90	1·80
332	4k.75 Atlantic white-sided dolphin (*Lagenorhynchus acutus*)	2·00	1·90
333	4k.75 Black right whale (*Eubalaena glacialis*)	2·00	1·90
MS334	141×81 mm. Nos. 328/33	10·50	10·00

136 Augo and Frederik Lynge (first Greenland members of Danish Parliament)

1998. New Order, 1950 (redefinition of Greenland's status).

335	136	4k.50 blue, lilac and red	2·00	1·90

137 Kathrine Chemnitz

1998. 20th Death Anniv of Kathrine Chemnitz (founder) and 50th Anniv of Women's Society of Greenland.

336	137	4k.50+50ore mult	2·75	2·50
MS337		80×140 mm. No. 336 ×4	11·00	10·50

138 "Children's Faces" (Class 4B, Atuarfik Ukaliusaq School)

1998. Europa. National Festivals. Children's Day. Multicoloured.

338	138	4k.75 Type **138**	2·40	2·30
339		10k. "Children playing" (Class 5A, Edvard Kruse-p Atuarfia School)	4·50	4·00

139 Gertrud Rask (sailing coaster)

1998. Nordic Countries' Postal Co-operation. Sailing Ships. Multicoloured.

340		4k.50 Type **139**	2·75	2·50
341		4k.75 Hans Egede (sailing coaster)	2·75	2·50

140 Breastfeeding Older Brother

1998. Greenland Art (2nd series). Tenth Death Anniv of Hans Lynge (artist). Multicoloured.

342		11k. Type **140**	4·00	3·75
343		25k. Refuelling	9·50	8·75

141 Jacket and Slippers on Line

1998. Christmas. Multicoloured.

344		4k.50 Type **141**	2·00	1·90
345		4k.75 Hat and slippers on line	2·40	2·30

142 Owl with Chicks

1999. Endangered Species. The Snowy Owl. Multicoloured.

346		1k. Type **142**	70	65
347		4k.75 Owl in flight	2·00	1·90
348		5k.50 Male and female owls	2·40	2·30
349		5k.75 Owl on rock	2·75	2·50

143 Ammassalik Pincushion

1999. Greenland National Museum and Archives.

350	143	4k.50+50ore black, blue and red	2·00	1·90
MS351		80×141 mm. No. 350 ×4	8·00	7·50

144 Polar Bear

1999. Europa. Parks and Gardens.

352	144	6k. multicoloured	2·75	2·50

145 The Man from Aluk

1999. Greenland Art (3rd series). Paintings by Peter Rosing. Multicoloured.

353		7k. Type **145**	2·75	2·50
354		20k. Homecoming	7·50	7·00

146 Viking Longship

1999. Greenland Vikings (1st series).

355	146	4k.50 green and blue	2·00	1·90
356	-	4k.75 green and blue	2·00	1·90
357	-	5k.75 brown and blue	2·75	2·50
358	-	8k. brown and blue	3·50	3·25
MS359		140×80 mm. Nos. 355/8	9·50	9·00

DESIGNS: 4k.75, Man collecting driftwood; 5k.75, Arrowhead and coins; 8k. Tjodhilde's Church, Brottal.
See also Nos. 363/7 and 390/4.

147 Writing Letter

1999. Christmas. Multicoloured.

360		4k.50 Type **147**	1·90	1·80
361		4k.75 Candles and clasped hands	2·00	1·90

148 Ice Cap

1999. New Millennium.

362	148	5k.75 multicoloured	2·75	2·50

2000. Greenland Vikings (2nd series). As T **146**.

363		25ore brown and blue	45	40
364		3k. brown and blue	1·10	1·00
365		5k.50 blue	2·00	1·90
366		21k. blue	7·50	7·00
MS367		140×81 mm. Nos. 363/6	11·00	10·50

DESIGNS: 25ore Walruses; 3k. Story teller and model of great northern diver; 5k.50, Dog chasing reindeer; 21k. Viking with gyr falcon, polar bear, walrus tusks and straps and bag of ship's tar (trading goods).

149 Huskies pulling Sledge

2000. 50th Anniv of Sirius (naval sledge patrol).

368	149	10k. multicoloured	3·75	3·50

150 Queen Margrethe II (from photograph by Rigmor Mydtskov)

2000

372	150	25ore blue and black	35	30
373	150	50ore blue and brown	70	65
374	150	4k.50 blue and red	1·80	1·60

375	150	4k.75 blue & ultramarine	1·90	1·80
378	150	8k. blue and bistre	2·75	2·50
379	150	10k. blue and green	3·75	3·50
380	150	12k. blue and purple	4·50	4·25

151 "Building Europe"

2000. Europa.

381	151	4k.75 multicoloured	3·50	3·25

152 Wooden Map

2000. Cultural Heritage (1st series). Multicoloured.

382		4k.50 Type **152**	1·90	1·80
383		4k.75 Sealskin	2·00	1·90

See also Nos. 395/6, 408/9 and 428/9.

153 Drum Dance

2000. "Hafnia 01" International Stamp Exhibition, Copenhagen.

384	153	4k.50+1k. multicoloured	2·30	2·10
MS385		80×141 mm. No. 384 ×4	9·50	9·00

154 Candles and Stars

2000. Christmas. Multicoloured.

386		4k.50 Type **154**	1·90	1·80
387		4k.75 Winter landscape and star	2·00	1·90

155 Gymnast and Map

2001. Arctic Winter Games, Nunavut.

388	155	4k. 50+50 multicoloured	2·00	1·90
MS389		81×140 mm. No. 388 ×4	8·50	8·25

2001. Greenland Vikings (3rd series). As T **146**.

390		1k. red and blue	55	50
391		4k.50 ultramarine and blue	1·80	1·60
392		5k. ultramarine and blue	2·00	1·90
393		10k. red and blue	3·75	3·50
MS394		141×81 mm. Nos. 390/3	8·50	8·25

DESIGNS: 1k. Fisherman and seals; 4k.50, Mouse sitting on food; 5k. Man with packhorses; 10k. Stone wall and common raven.

2001. Cultural Heritage (2nd series). As T **152**. Multicoloured.

395		4k.50 Preserving trout	1·60	1·50
396		4k.75 Fishing spear	1·80	1·60

156 Krill

2001. Europa. Water Resources.

397	156	15k. multicoloured	6·75	6·25

157 Rock Ptarmigan and Berries

2001. Christmas. Multicoloured.

398		4k.50 Type **157**	1·60	1·50
399		4k.75 Doves flying	1·80	1·60

158 Northern Lights

2001. Essays by Harry Nielsen for First Greenland Stamps. Each black and brown.

400		5k.75 Type **158**	2·40	2·30
401		8k. Seal	3·50	3·25
402		21k. Polar bear	7·75	7·25
MS403		142×80 mm. Nos. 400/2	13·50	13·00

159 Detail of Stone and Man

2002. Nordic Countries' Postal Co-operation. Modern Art. Multicoloured.

404		1k. Type **159** (sculpture project, Aka Hoegh and others)	70	65
405		31k. Snow Sculpture (Nuuk Snow Festival, 2001)	11·50	10·50

160 Banner, Igloo Builders and Polar Bears

2002. "Children are People Too" (child welfare project).

406	160	4k.50+50ore multicoloured	2·00	1·90
MS407		81×140 mm. No. 406×4	8·50	8·25

2002. Cultural Heritage (3rd series). As T **152**. Multicoloured.

408		4k.50 Drum, Thule	1·60	1·50
409		4k.75 Inuit carved mask	1·80	1·60

161 Nordlyset (sailing barque)

2002. Ships (1st series). Multicoloured.

410		2k. Type **161**	1·10	1·00
411		4k. Hvidbjornen (steam/sailing barque)	2·00	1·90
412		6k. Staerkodder (sloop)	3·50	3·25
413		16k. Haabet (crayer)	6·75	6·25

See also Nos. 438/41, 462/5 and 477/80.

162 Clown, Child and Snow Scene

2002. Europa. Circus.

414	162	11k. multicoloured	4·75	4·50

163 Man carrying Gifts and Children on Sledge

2002. Christmas. (a) Ordinary gum.

415		4k.50 Type **163**	1·90	1·80
416		4k.75 Mother with child and carol singers	2·20	2·00

(b) Self-adhesive gum.

417		4k.50 No. 414	1·90	1·80
418		4k.75 No. 416	2·20	2·00

Nos. 417/18 form a composite design.

164 Cliffs and Greenland Shark (*Somniosus microcephalus*)

2002. Centenary of International Council for the Exploration of the Sea. Multicoloured.

419	7k. Type **164**		3·50	3·25
420	19k. Deepwater redfish (*Sebates mentella*)		8·00	7·50
MS421	185×60 mm. Nos. 419/20		12·00	11·50

Stamps of a similar design were issued by Denmark and Faroe Islands.

165 Puppies

2003. Sled Dogs. Each black.

422	4k.50 Type **165**		1·90	1·80
423	4k.75 Adult		2·00	1·90
424	6k. Adult wearing harness		2·75	2·50

166 Tents and mountains

2003. Centenary of the Danish Literary Expedition to Greenland.

425	**166**	15k. agate, green and blue	5·75	5·25
426	-	21k. blue (28×22 mm)	7·75	7·25
MS427	166×61 mm Nos. 424/5 plus label		14·00	14·00

DESIGN: 21k. Knud Ramussen Stamps of a similar design were issued by Denmark.

2003. Cultural Heritage (4th series). As T **152**. Multicoloured.

428	25ore Comb, East Greenland		25	20
429	1k. Water bucket, East Greenland		40	30

167 Silamiut Theatre Poster

2003. Europa. Poster Art.

430	**167**	5k.50 multicoloured	2·75	2·50

168 Narwhals and Cliffs

2003. 50th Anniv of Qaanaaq (settlement).

431	**168**	15k. multicoloured	6·00	5·75

169 Children around Christmas Tree

2003. Christmas. (a) Ordinary gum.

432	5k. Type **169**		1·90	1·80
433	5k.50 Family entering church		2·00	1·90

Nos. 434/5 were issued together, *se-tenant*, forming a composite design.

(b) Self-adhesive gum.

434	5k. Type **169**		1·90	1·80
435	5k.50 No. 433		2·00	1·90

170 Santa Claus inside Bauble

2003. Santa Claus of Greenland.

436	**170**	5k.+50ore multicoloured	2·20	2·00
MS437	81×140 mm. No. 436×4		9·00	8·75

2003. Ships (2nd series). As T **161**. Multicoloured.

438	6k.75 *Emma* (galleass)		2·75	2·50
439	7k.75 *Gamle Fox* (screw-propelled schooner)		3·50	3·25
440	8k.75 *Godthaab* (screw-propelled barquentine)		4·00	3·75
441	26k. *Sonja* (whaling steamer)		10·00	9·50

171 Moon Man

2004. Nordic Mythology. Multicoloured.

442	5k.50 Type **171**		2·20	2·00
443	6k.50 Northern lights		2·40	2·30
MS444	106×70 mm. Nos. 442/3		5·00	5·00

Stamps of a similar theme were issued by Aland Island, Denmark, Faroe Islands, Finland, Iceland, Norway and Sweden.

172 Route Map

2004. 50th Anniv of First Scheduled Flight from Denmark to Greenland.

445	**172**	8k.75 multicoloured	3·50	3·25

173 National Arms

2004. 25th Anniv of Home Rule.

446	**173**	11k. multicoloured	4·75	4·50

174 Rowing Boat attempting Landing on Island

2004. 150th Birth Anniv of Otto Sverdrup (polar explorer).

447	**174**	17k.50 purple and buff	6·75	6·25
MS448	165×60 mm. No. 447 plus 2 labels		7·00	7·00

No. **MS448** was issued with two stamp-sized labels showing designs of Canada and Norway stamps. Stamps of similar designs were issued by Norway and Canada.

175 Children

2004. 80th Anniv of Society of Greenlandic Children.

449	**175**	5k.+50ore. Multicoloured.	2·20	2·00
MS450	140×80 mm. No. 449×4		9·50	8·75

176 Prince Frederik and Mary Donaldson

2004. Marriage of Crown Prince Frederik and Mary Elizabeth Donaldson. Multicoloured.

451	5k. Type **176**		2·00	1·90
452	5k.50 As No. 451 but with design reversed		2·20	2·00
MS453	130×65 mm. Nos. 451/2		4·75	4·50

Stamps of similar design were issued by Denmark and Faroe Islands.

177 *Angelica archangelica*

2004. Edible Plants (1st series). Multicoloured.

454	5k. Type **177**		1·90	1·80
455	5k.50 *Thymus praecox*		2·00	1·90
456	17k. *Empetrum hermaphroditum*		6·75	6·25

See also Nos. 484/6.

178 Family and Decorated Tree

2004. Christmas. (a) Ordinary gum.

457	5k. Type **178**		2·30	2·10
458	5k.50 Family entering church		2·40	2·30

(b) Self-adhesive gum.

459	5k. Type **178**		2·30	2·10
460	5k.50 No. 458		2·40	2·30

179 Girls wearing Traditional Dress

2004. Europa. Holidays.

461	**179**	6k.50 multicoloured	3·00	2·75

2004. Ships (3rd series). As T **161**. Multicoloured.

462	6k.50 *Constance* (brig)		2·75	2·50
463	8k.75 *Disko* (passenger ship)		3·50	3·25
464	14k. *Julius Thomsen* (polar ship)		5·75	5·25
465	21k.75 *Misigssut* (tuberculosis hospital ship)		9·00	8·50

180 *Leccinum*

2005. Fungi. Multicoloured. (a) Ordinary gum.

466	5k.25 Type **180**		2·20	2·10
467	6k. *Russula subrubens*		2·75	2·50
468	7k. *Amanita groenlandica*		3·00	2·75

(b) Self-adhesive gum

469	5k.25 As No. 466		2·20	2·10
470	6k. As No. 467		2·75	2·50
471	7k. As No. 468		3·00	2·75

181 Child's Face

2005. 60th Anniv of Save the Children Fund (charitable organization).

472	**181**	5k.25+50ore multicoloured	2·50	2·40
MS473	140×80 mm. No. 472×4 multicoloured		10·50	10·00

182 Ilulissat Fiord

2005. World Heritage Site. Ilulissat Fiord.

474	**182**	6k. multicoloured	2·75	2·50

183 Mountains and Church Steeple

2005. Centenary of Church Law.

475	**183**	9k.25 multicoloured	4·00	3·75

184 Musk Ox Meat

2005. Europa. Gastronomy.

476	**184**	11k.75 multicoloured	5·00	4·75

2005. Ships (4th series). As T **161**. Multicoloured.

477	5k.25 *Dannebrog* (royal yacht)		2·20	2·10
478	6k. *Kista Artica* (polar ship)		2·50	2·40
479	18k.50 *Sarpik Ittuk* (passenger ship)		8·00	7·50
480	23k. *Triton* (naval rescue and helicopter carrier)		10·00	9·25

185 Maps

2005. Completion of Geological Mapping of Greenland.

481	**185**	7k.25 multicoloured	3·25	3·00

186 Limestone Columns

2005. Ikka Fjord Conservation Area.

482	**186**	9k.25 multicoloured	4·00	3·75

187 *Limnognathia Maersk*

2005. Discovery of Limnognathia Maerski (micrognathozoa).

483	**187**	10k. multicoloured	4·25	4·00

2005. Edible Plants (2nd series). As T **177**. Multicoloured.

484	75e. *Ligusticum scoticum*		50	45
485	6k.50 *Rhodiola rosea*		3·00	2·75
486	8k.25 *Oxyrias digna*		3·75	3·50

188 Boy and Decoration

2005. Christmas. (a) Ordinary gum.

487	5k.25 Type **188**		2·20	2·10
488	6k. Girl		2·50	2·40

(b) Self-adhesive gum.

489	5k.25 Type **188**		2·20	2·10
490	6k. As. No. 488		2·50	2·40

189 Robert Peary

2005. Robert E. Peary (arctic explorer) Commemoration.

491	**189**	27k.50 multicoloured	12·00	11·50
MS492	167×60 mm **189** 27k.50 multicoloured		12·50	12·00

190 10ore Parcel Post Stamp

2005. Centenary of Parcel Post (1st issue).

| 493 | 190 | 50k. blue | 22·00 | 21·00 |

See also No. 495 and **MS**531.

191 Church

2006. 250th Anniv of Sisimiut.

| 493a | 191 | 9k.75 multicoloured | 4·25 | 4·00 |

192 Doves

2006. 50th Anniv of Norden (postal organization).

| 494 | 192 | 19k.50 multicoloured | 8·75 | 8·25 |

193 5ore Parcel Post Stamp

2006. Centenary of Parcel Post (2nd issue).

| 495 | 193 | 25k. brown | 11·00 | 10·50 |

194 2004 6k.50 Stamp (Type 179)

2006. 50th Anniv of Europa Stamps.

| 496 | 194 | 26k.50 multicoloured | 11·50 | 11·00 |

195 Crown Prince Frederick and Crown Princess Mary

2006. Children in Greenland.

| 497 | 195 | 5k.50+50 multicoloured | 3·00 | 2·75 |

The premium was for children's charities.

196 Mother of the Sea

2006. Nordic Mythology. Multicoloured.

498	196	7k.50 Type 196	3·25	3·00
499		13k.50 Mistress of the Wind	5·50	5·25
MS500		105×70 mm. Nos. 498/9	9·25	9·00

Stamps of a similar theme were issued by Aland Islands, Denmark, Faröe Islands, Finland, Iceland, Norway and Sweden.

2006. Fungi. As T 180. Multicoloured. (a) Ordinary Gum.

501		5k.50 Rozites caperatus	3·00	2·75
502		7k. Lactarius dryadophilus	3·25	3·00
503		10k. Calvatia cretacea	4·75	4·50

(b) Self-adhesive.

| 504 | | 5k.50 As No. 501 | 3·00 | 2·75 |
| 505 | | 7k. As No. 502 | 3·25 | 3·00 |

197 Ram

2006. Centenary of Sheep Farming in Greenland.

| 506 | 197 | 7k.50 multicoloured | 4·00 | 3·75 |

198 Alfred Wegener

2006. Alfred Wegener (arctic explorer) Commemoration.

| 507 | 198 | 20k.75 blue and brown | 10·50 | 9·75 |
| **MS**508 | | 166×60 mm. 198 20k.75 blue and brown | 11·00 | 10·50 |

199 Vaedderen (research ship)

2006. Galathea 3—Danish Research Expedition.

| 509 | 199 | 9k.75 multicoloured | 4·75 | 4·50 |

200 Fossilized Tree, Kap Kobenhavn Formation, North East Greenland

2006. Scientific Sites in Greenland.

510		50ore. Type 200	50	45
511		8k. Rock excavation, Isua (world's oldest mountain)	4·00	3·75
512		15k.50 Qeqertarsuaq Arctic Research Station (centenary)	8·00	7·50

201 Angel and Score

2006. Christmas. Multicoloured. Ordinary or self-adhesive gum.

| 513 | | 5k.50 Type 201 | 2·50 | 2·40 |
| 514 | | 7k. Candle and score | 3·25 | 3·00 |

202 Water and Power Lines

2007. 10th Anniv of West Nordic Council. Hydropower.

| 517 | 202 | 5k. multicoloured | 3·00 | 2·75 |

203 Children holding Heart-shaped Balloons

2007. Amnesty Kalaallit Nunat (United Nations Children's Convention in Greenland).

| 518 | 203 | 5k.75 +50ore multicoloured | 3·25 | 3·00 |

204 Scouts building Cairn

2007. Europa. Scouting. Multicoloured. Ordinary or self-adhesive gum.

| 519 | | 5k.75 Type 204 | 3·00 | 2·75 |
| 520 | | 7k.50 Building fire and tent | 3·50 | 3·25 |

205 Ice Core Drilling

2007. International Polar Year. Multicoloured.

523		7k.50 Type 205	3·50	3·25
524		8k. Three generations (urbanization of Greenland)	4·00	3·75
MS525		105×70 mm. Nos. 523/4	8·00	7·50

206 Crown Prince Frederik, Crown Princess Mary and Prince Christian

2007

| 526 | 206 | 14k.25 multicoloured | 7·25 | 6·75 |

207 Sled Dogs (Jens Rosing)

2007. Greenlandic Artists (1st series). Multicoloured.

527		3k. Type 207	1·60	1·50
528		8k.50 Bear and people (Anne-Birthe Hove) (50×43 mm)	4·00	3·75
529		10k.50 Face (Linda Riber Sørensen) (50×43 mm)	5·50	5·25

See also Nos. 542/44.

208 20ore Parcel Post Stamp

2007. Centenary of Parcel Post (3rd issue).

| 530 | 208 | 100k. red | 40·00 | 38·00 |
| **MS**531 | | 200×110 mm. 25k. As No. 495; 50k. As No. 492; 100k. As No. 530 | 70·00 | 65·00 |

209 Tubbiap Queqertaa (Tobias Island) (new island)

2007. Science. Multicoloured.

532		75ore Type 209	50	45
533		2k. Soapstone lamp	1·30	1·20
534		10k.25 Cyanobacteria (green algae (earliest form of life)) (identified by Minik Rosing)	4·75	4·50

210 Landscape

2007. SEPAC (small European mail services).

| 535 | 210 | 6k.50 multicoloured | 3·25 | 3·00 |

211 Pourquoi-Pas?

2007. Birth Centenary of Paul-Emile Victor. Jean-Baptiste Charcot (arctic explorer) Commemoration. Multicoloured.

536	211	5k.75 multicoloured	3·00	2·75
537	-	7k.50 blue and brown (29×35 mm)	3·50	3·25
MS537a		165×60 mm. As Nos. 536/7	7·25	6·75

DESIGNS: 5k.75 Type 211; 7k.50 Paul-Emile Victor. No. **MS**537a also contains a stamp size label showing Jean-Baptiste Charcot. Stamps of a similar design were issued by France.

212 Angel and Snowflakes

2007. Christmas. Multicoloured. Ordinary or self-adhesive gum.

| 538 | | 5k.75 Type 212 | 3·00 | 2·75 |
| 539 | | 7k.50 Stars and snowflakes | 3·50 | 3·25 |

213 Landscape and Figure (Ina Rosing)

2008. Greenlandic Artists (2nd series). Multicoloured.

542		5k.50 Type 213	2·40	2·30
543		14k.25 Polar bear (Buuti Pedersen)	6·00	5·75
544		30k.50 Abstract (Aka Hoegh)	13·00	12·50

214 Face and Envelope

2008. Europa. Letter Writing. Multicoloured. Ordinary or self-adhesive gum.

| 545 | | 5k.75 Type 214 | 2·75 | 2·50 |
| 546 | | 7k.50 Female face and envelope | 3·50 | 3·25 |

215 The Rocks

2008. Nordic Mythology. Multicoloured.

549		7k. Type 215	3·25	3·00
550		8k. The Bear of the Lake	3·75	3·50
MS551		105×70 mm. Nos. 549/50	7·25	6·75

Stamps of a similar theme were issued by Aland Islands, Denmark, Faröe Islands, Finland, Iceland, Norway and Sweden.

216 Halkieria evangelista

2008. Fossils. Multicoloured.

552		1k. Type 216	50	50
553		20k.50 Ichthyostega stensioei	9·25	8·75
554		25k. Eudimorphodon	11·50	11·00

217 Lungs

2008. National Campaign against Tuberculosis.

| 555 | 217 | 5k.75+50ore multicoloured | 3·00 | 2·75 |

218 Prince Joachim and Marie Cavallier

2008. Marriage of Prince Joachim and Marie Cavallier.

| 556 | 218 | 10k.25 multicoloured | 4·75 | 4·50 |

219 Reindeer

2008. Christmas. Multicoloured. (a) Ordinary gum.
557   5k.75 Type **219**   2·75   2·50
558   7k.50 Decorated tree and
         village   3·50   3·25

(b) Self-adhesive.
559   5k.75 As Type **219**   2·75   2·50
560   7k.50 As No. 558   3·50   3·25

220 Scientists and
Equipment

2008. Science. Anniversaries. Multicoloured.
561   6k.50 Type **220** (50th anniv of
         International Geophysi-
         cal Year)   3·00   3·00
562   10k.50 French Research Station,
         Scoresbysund (75th anniv)   4·75   4·50
563   28k. Danish Arctic Station,
         Nuuk (125th anniv)   13·00   12·00
MS564 166×60 mm. Nos. 561/3   20·00   19·00

221 *Sofia* (expedition ship), 1883

2008. Alfred Erik Nordenskjold's Expeditions to
Greenland, 1870–1883. Multicoloured.
565   8k.50 Type **221**   4·25   4·00
566   16k.25 A. E. Nordenskjold
         (28×33 mm)   8·00   7·50
MS567 166×60 mm. Nos. 565/6   12·00   11·50
Stamps of a similar design were issued by Finland.

222 *Schizoneura carcinoides*

2009. Fossils. Multicoloured.
568   2k. Type **222**   1·10   1·00
569   11k.50 *Scaphites rosenkrantzi* 3·50   3·50
570   22k. *Mallotus villosus*   11·00   10·00
Stamps of a similar design were issued by Finland.

223 Ice Crystal of Humans and
Animals

2009. Preserve Polar Regions and Glaciers.
571   **223**   5k. multicoloured   2·50   2·40

224 Ursa Major
and Aurora
Borealis

2009. Europa. Astronomy. Multicoloured. Ordinary gum.
572   6k.25 Type **224**   3·00   3·00
573   8k. Ursa Major showing bear
         outline   4·00   3·75

(b) Self-adhesive.
574   6k.25 As Type **224**   3·00   3·00
575   8k. As No. 573   4·00   3·75

225 Enclosed Heart

2009. Neriuffit Kattuffiat (Greenlandic Cancer Society).
576   **225**   6.25k+50ore scarlet-
         vermilion and black   3·50   3·25
No. 576 the premium was for the benefit of cancer
support.

226 Prince Henri

2009. 75th Birth Anniv of Prince Henri.
577   **226**   8k. multicoloured   4·50   4·25

227 Polar Bears (Ivalo Abelsen)

2009. Greenlandic Artists. Multicoloured.
578   6k. Type **227**   3·50   3·25
579   18k. *Window to the World* (fish)
         (Camilla Nielsen)   9·75   9·25
580   33k. *Gletscher* (Naja Abelsen) 18·00   17·00

228 Mountains and Colours

2009. Self-Governance.
581   **228**   6k.25 multicoloured   3·50   3·25

229 Matthew Henson and Polar
Map

2009. Centenary of Matthew Henson's (first Afro-
American to the North Pole) Participation in Polar
Expedition.
582   **229**   9k. multicoloured   5·00   4·75

230 Scenes from *First Steps* (comic
created by Nuka Godtfredsen)

2009. Greenlandic Comics.
583   **230**   15k.50 multicoloured   8·50   8·00
MS584 130×80 mm. As Type **230** 8·75   8·25

231 Flowers, Lake and
Mountain

2009. SEPAC (small European mail services).
585   **231**   7k. multicoloured   3·75   3·50

232 Cryolite

2009. Science. Multicoloured.
586   1k. Type **232**   80   75
587   15k.50 *Himantolophus groen-
         landicus*   8·50   8·00

233 Family

2009. Christmas. Multicoloured. (a) Ordinary gum.
590   6k.25 Type **233**   3·50   3·25
591   8k. Baby and star   4·50   4·25

(b) Self-adhesive.
592   6k.25 As Type **233**   3·50   3·25
593   8k. As No. 591   4·50   4·25

234 Family

2009. Centenary of The North Star Mission Station, Thule.
594   **234**   15k.25 black and indigo 8·50   8·00

235 Otto
Nordenskjold

2009. Otto Nordenskjold's Expeditions of 1900 and 1909.
595   **235**   30k. deep olive-brown
                     and black   16·00   15·00
MS596 166×60 mm. As Type **235** 17·00   16·00

236 *Polar Bear* (Maria Paninguak
Kjaerulff)

2010. Greenlandic Artists (4th series). Multicoloured.
597   6k.50 Type **236**   3·50   3·50
598   7k.50 *Sun* (Miki Jacobsen) (vert) 4·25   4·00
599   50k. *Razorbills* (Bolatta Sili-
         Hoegh)   27·00   26·00

237 Figure

2010. 25th Anniv of Silamiut Theatre Group.
600   **237**   7k.+50ore multicoloured 4·00   3·75
The premium was for the benefit of the theatre group.

238 Boy reading

2010. Europa. Children's Books. Multicoloured. (a)
Ordinary gum.
601   8k.50 Type **238**   4·75   4·50
602   9k.50 Children reading   5·25   5·00

(b) Self-adhesive.
603   8k.50 As Type **238**   4·75   4·50
604   9k.50 As No. 602   5·25   5·00

239 Aircraft Tailfin
and Helicopter

2010. 50th Anniv of Air Greenland Airline.
605   **239**   16k.50 multicoloured   10·00   9·50

588   23k.50 Greenlandic gold   13·00   12·50
MS589 165×60 mm. Nos. 586/8   23·00   22·00

240 Women

2010. Centenary of Women's Day.
606   **240**   12k.50 multicoloured   7·50   7·25

241 Waves

2010. Life at the Coast. Paintings by Aka Hoegh.
Multicoloured.
607   7k. Type **241**   4·25   4·00
608   8k.50 Port   5·00   4·75
MS609 111×70 mm. Nos. 607/8   10·00   9·50
Stamps of a similar theme were issued by Denmark,
Aland Islands, Farõe Islands, Finland, Iceland, Norway and
Sweden.

242 Queen Margrethe

2010. 70th Birth Anniv of Queen Margrethe.
610   **242**   35k. multicoloured   21·00   20·00

243 Flag and Ice
Floes

2010. 25th Anniv of Erfalasorput, National Flag.
611   **243**   7k. multicoloured   4·25   4·00

244 Scenes from *Boas & Co*
(comic created by Robert Holmene)

2010. Greenlandic Comics
612   **244**   23k.50 multicoloured   15·00   14·50
MS613 140×80 mm. As Type **244** 16·00   15·00

245 Hans Sakæus

2010. British Expedition, led by John Ross, to North
Greenland, 1818. Each blackish lilac, indigo and pale
green.
614   25ore Type **245**   70   65
615   32k. *Isabella* and *Alexander*
         (58×34 mm)   20·00   19·00
MS616 166×60 mm. Nos. 614/15   21·00   20·00

246 Frederik VII's
Copper Mine

2010. Mining in Greenland. Multicoloured.
617   50ore Type **246**   90   90
618   26k.50 Ivittuut Cryolite Mine   17·00   16·00

247 Knud
Rasmussen (polar
researcher and
station founder)

2010. Centenary of Thule Trading Station
619	**247**	25k. black and deep ultramarine	16·00	15·00

248 Children and
Rear of Santa

2010. Childhood Christmas. Multicoloured.

(a) Sheet stamps. Ordinary gum
620	7k. Type **248**	4·25	4·00
621	8k.50 Father as Santa	5·25	5·00

(b) Booklet stamps. Self-adhesive
622	7k. As Type **248**	4·25	4·00
623	8k.50 As No. 621	5·25	5·00

249 Kayak Post

2011. Communications in Greenland. Multicoloured.
624	2k. Type **249**	1·40	1·30
625	7k.50 Page from first edition of *Atuagagdliutit* newspaper (150th anniv)	4·75	4·50
626	46k.50 Route of Greenland Connect submarine cable	29·00	28·00
MS627	140×80 mm Nos. 624/6	37·00	36·00

250 Emblem

2011. 15th Anniv of KIMIK (artist association)
628	**250**	7k.50 +50ö multicoloured	5·00	4·75

251 Mountain
Birch in Snow

2011. Europa. Forests. Multicoloured.

(a) Sheet stamps
629	9k. Type **251**	5·75	5·50
630	10k. Scots pine tree	6·25	6·00

(b) Booklet stamps
631	9k. As Type **651**	5·75	5·50
632	10k. As No. 630	6·25	6·00

252 Flowers and Fruit,
Greenland Mountain Ash
(*Sorbus Groenlandica*)

2011. Herbs. Multicoloured.
633	13k.50 Type **252**	8·50	8·25
634	25k. Cranberries (*Vaccinium vitis*)	16·00	15·00

253 Queen Margrethe II

2011. Queen Margrethe II
635	**253**	50öre deep dull purple	3·25	3·00
636		1k. deep bluish green	6·25	6·00

Nos. 637/44 are now vacant.
It is reported that these stamps were withdrawn on 26 May 2011, due to poor printing process.

254 Strait Jacket (Julie Edel
Hardenberg)

2011. Greenlandic Artists (5th series). Multicoloured.
645	3k. Type **254**	2·10	2·00
646	7k. Key and figures (Naja Rosing-Asvid)	4·25	4·25
647	34k. Multicoloured landscape (Anne-Lise Løvstrøm)	21·00	20·00

255 Consolidated PBY Catalina Flying
Boat (1958-1965)

2011. Civil Aviation History (1st series). Each indigo and deep carmine.
648	8k. Type **255**	5·00	4·75
649	17k.50 de Havilland Canada DHC-3 Otter (1960-1965)	11·00	10·50

256 Scenes from Kaassassuk (comic
created by Christian Fleischer Rex)

2011. Greenlandic Comics
650	**256**	20k. multicoloured	12·50	12·00
MS651	165×60 mm. As Type **256**		13·00	12·50

257 Naomi Uemura and Nunatak
Uemura Peak (named after Naomi
Uemura, lying two miles west of
Greenland inland icecap)

2011. Naomi Uemura's North to South Expedition across Greenland
652	**257**	36k.50 deep blue and blackish brown	23·00	22·00
MS653	166×61 mm. 36k.50 As Type **257**		24·00	23·00

258 Glacial Ice Slice

2011. SEPAC (small European mail services)
654	**258**	8k. multicoloured	5·00	4·75

259 Shaft Tower,
Josva Mine

2011. Mining in Greenland. Multicoloured.
655	75ore. Type **259**	70	65
656	28k. Workers with truck, Qaarsuaruk	17·00	17·00

260 Star in
Window and
Strawberry Girls

2011. Christmas. Multicoloured.

(a) Sheet stamps. Ordinary gum
657	7k.50 Type **260**	4·50	4·25
658	9k. Strawberry Girls and Disco Bay dog sled (horiz)	5·75	5·50

(b) Booklet stamps. Self-adhesive
659	7k.50 As Type **260**	4·50	4·25
660	9k. As No. 658 (horiz)	5·75	5·50

261 Queen Margrethe II

2012. 40th Anniv of Accession of Queen Margrethe II
661	**261**	26k.50 multicoloured	15·00	15·00
MS662	105×70 mm 26k.50 As Type **261**		15·00	15·00

262 Inuit Family

2012. Nakuusa (collaboration between Greenland's Home Rule (Naalakkersuisut) and Unicef Danmark)
663	**262**	8k. +50öre multicoloured	4·75	4·50

263 Spirit (Jessie Kleeman)

2012. Greenlandic Artists (6th series). Multicoloured.
664	8k.50 Type **263**	4·50	4·25
665	9k.50 Ice floe (Frederik 'Kunngi' Kristensen)	5·25	5·00
666	38.50 Map of Denmark with Greenlandic names (Inuk Silis Høegh and Asmund Havsteen-Mikkelsen)	5·50	5·00
MS667	130×160 mm. As No. 666	21·00	19·50

2012. Herbs. Multicoloured.
668	14k.50 Northern bilberry (*Vaccinium uliginsum*)	7·50	7·00
669	18k.50 Labrador tea (*Ledum groenlandicum*) (*Rhododendron groenlandicum*)	13·50	12·50

264 Dog Sled and Campus

2012. 50th Anniv of Knud Rasmussen Folk High School
670	**264**	21k. multicoloured	13·75	12·00

265 Ice Floe and
Seals

2012. Life at the Coast. Multicoloured.
671	8k. Type **265**	4·75	4·50
672	9k.50 Whale's tail	5·75	5·50
MS673	111×70 mm. Nos. 671/2	10·00	10·00

266 Eqalussuit
Mine

2012. Mining in Greenland. Multicoloured.
674	25ore. Type **266**	50	50
675	14k.50 Amisoq graphite mine and product	7·50	7·00

267 Field of Crops

2012. Agriculture in Greenland. Multicoloured.
676	75öre Type **267**	2·50	2·20
677	49k. Cattle	21·00	21·00

268 Northern Lights

2012. Europa. Visit Greenland. Multicoloured.

(a) Sheet stamps
678	9k.50 Type **268**	5·75	5·50
679	10k.50 Ship and ice floes	6·25	6·00

(b) Booklet stamps
680	9k.50 As Type **268**	5·25	5·00
681	10k.50 As No. 679	5·75	5·50

269 Queen
Margrethe II

2012. Queen Margrethe II
682	**269**	50öre bright carmine and new blue	1·00	90
683		1k. green and new blue	2·20	2·00

2012. Civil Aviation History (2nd series). Multicoloured.
684	7k.50 Douglas Dc-4/DC-6B	4·50	4·25
685	28k. Sikrorsky S61N	15·00	15·00
686	36k. Bell 206 Jet Ranger	19·00	18·00

270 Inuit Girls
with Christmas
Trees

2012. Christmas. Multicoloured.

(a) Sheet stamps. Ordinary gum
687	8k. Type **270**	4·00	3·75
688	9k.50 Inuit girls as baubles (horiz)	5·25	5·00

(b) Booklet stamps. Self-adhesive
689	8k. As Type **270**	4·00	3·75
690	9k.50 As No.667 (horiz)	5·25	5·00

271 Suersaq

2012. Hans Hendrick (Suersaq) (explorer) Commemoration
691	**271**	29k.50 black and deep magenta	15·50	14·00
MS692	165×60 mm. 29k.50 As Type **271** black and deep magenta		17·00	17·00

272 Sculpture (Isle Hessner)

2013. Greenlandic Artists (7th series). Multicoloured.
693		50ö Type **272**	2·50	2·20
694		2k. Key and figures (Naja Rosing-Asvid)	5·50	5·00
695		40k.50 Multicoloured landscape (Anne-Lise Løvstrøm)	17·00	16·00

273 Children in Row Boat

2013. Nakuusa (collaboration between Greenland's Home Rule (Naalakkersuisut) and Unicef Danmark).
696	**273**	9k. +50öre multicoloured	4·50	4·25

274 Sledge Postal Delivery

2013. Europa. Postal Transport. Multicoloured.

(a) Sheet stamps
697		10k.50 Type **274**	6·25	6·00
698		11k.50 Ship and ice floes	6·50	6·25

(b) Booklet stamps
699		10k.50 Type **274**	6·25	6·00
700		11k.50 Ship and ice floes	6·50	6·25

275 Coal Mining in Qullissat

2013. Mining in Greenland. Multicoloured.
701		38k. Type **275**	50	50
702		14k.50 e Marble Quarry in Maarmorilik	7·50	7·00

2013. Herbs. Multicoloured.
703		14k.50 Northern bilberry (*Vaccinium uliginsum*)	7·50	7·00
704		18k.50 Labrador tea (*Ledum groenlandicum*) (*Rhododendron groenlandicum*)	13·50	12·50

276 Uummannaq

2013. 25th Anniv of Erfalasorput, National Flag.
705	**276**	9k. multicoloured	5·75	5·50

277 Musk Ox

2013. SEPAC (small European mail services). Pearls of Europe - Animal Life
706	**277**	11k.50 multicoloured	6·25	6·00

278 Hump-backed Whale

2013. 25th Anniv of Erfalasorput, National Flag.
707	**278**	16k. multicoloured	8·00	7·75

279 Polar Bear

2013. Endangered Species. Animals from Arctic to Desert
708	**279**	36k.50 deep blue and blackish brown	20·50	20·50
MS709		166×61 mm. 19k.50 As Type **279**	20·50	20·50

280 Sheep

2013. Agriculture in Greenland. Multicoloured.
710		20k. Type **280**	13·75	12·00
711		29k.50 Field and machinery	15·75	15·50

281 Polar Bear

2013. 75th Anniv of Greenland Post
712	**281**	20k. black and scarlet-vermilion	13·75	12·00
MS713		115×70 mm. 20k. As Type **281**	15·00	15·00

282 Sorting Fish

2013. 50th Anniv of Nordafar Fishery Operation at Føroyingahavn
714	**282**	22k.50 multicoloured	14·25	14·00
MS715		165×60 mm. 22k.50 As Type **282**	15·00	15·00

2013. Civil Aviation History (3rd series). Multicoloured.
716		1k. Sikorsky helicopter S58ET	2·20	2·00
717		28k. de Havilland Canada DHC-6 Twin Otter	15·00	15·00

283 Polar Bear and Decorations

2013. Christmas. Multicoloured.

(a) Sheet stamps. Ordinary gum
718		9k. Type **283**	5·75	5·50
719		10k.50 Polar bear amongst white decorations	6·25	6·00

2013. Queen Margrethe II
722	**269**	10k. deep blue and new blue	6·25	6·00

284 Carl Petersen

2013. Birth Bicentenary of John Carl Christian Petersen
723	**284**	31k.50 multicoloured	17·00	16·50
MS724		165×60 mm. 31k.50 As Type **284**	18·00	18·00

PARCEL POST STAMPS

P1 Arms of Greenland

1905			
P4A	**P1**	1ore green	47·00	55·00
P5A	**P1**	2ore yellow	£275	95·00
P6A	**P1**	5ore brown	£130	£130
P7A	**P1**	10ore blue	42·00	60·00
P8A	**P1**	15ore violet	£250	£225
P9A	**P1**	20ore red	6·75	9·50
P13	**P1**	70ore violet	29·00	£140
P14	**P1**	1k. yellow	29·00	80·00
P12A	**P1**	3k. brown	95·00	£180

Prices for used stamps are for rubber stamp cancellations applied in Copenhagen, the various Greenland cancellations being worth much more. Stamps with numeral cancellations have been used as saving stamps.

Pt. 1

GRENADA

One of the Windward Is., Br. W. Indies. Ministerial Government was introduced on 1 January 1960. Achieved Associated Statehood on 3 March 1967 and Independence on 7 February 1974.

1861. 12 pence = 1 shilling; 20 shillings = 1 pound.
1949. 100 cents = 1 West Indian dollar.

1

1861				
14	1	1d. green	85·00	8·00
6	1	6d. red	£600	13·00

5

1875. Surch **POSTAGE** and value in words.
21	5	½d. mauve	17·00	6·50
22	5	2½d. lake	75·00	8·50
23	5	4d. blue	£140	8·00
13	5	1s. mauve	£700	12·00

1883. Revenue stamp surch crown and value (in green) optd **POSTAGE**.
27		1d. orange	£400	60·00

1883. Revenue stamp as last but optd **POSTAGE** diagonally on each half.
29		Half of 1d. orange	£275	£110

13

1883				
30	13	½d. green	2·50	1·00
31	13	1d. red	90·00	3·25
32	13	2½d. blue	10·00	1·00
33	13	4d. grey	12·00	2·00
34	13	6d. mauve	3·75	4·25
35	13	8d. brown	10·00	13·00
36	13	1s. violet	£160	55·00

1886. Revenue stamps as No. 27 but surch **POSTAGE** and value in words or figures.
43	5	½d. on 2s. orange	17·00	30·00
37	5	1d. on 1½d. orange	60·00	50·00
39	5	1d. on 4d. orange	£170	90·00
38	5	1d. on 1s. orange	50·00	45·00
41	5	4d. on 2s. orange	48·00	21·00

1887. As T **13**, but inscr "GRENADA POSTAGE & REVENUE" at top.
40	13	1d. red	4·25	1·75

1890. Revenue stamp as No. 27 but surch **POSTAGE AND REVENUE 1d.**
45	5	1d. on 2s. orange	75·00	70·00

1891. Surch **POSTAGE AND REVENUE 1d.**
46	13	1d. on 8d. brown	11·00	18·00

1891. Surch **2½d.**
47		2½d. on 8d. brown	20·00	11·00

21

1895				
48	21	½d. mauve and green	3·50	1·75
49	21	1d. mauve and red	4·75	75
50	21	2d. mauve and brown	40·00	29·00
51	21	2½d. mauve and blue	10·00	1·50
52	21	3d. mauve and orange	6·50	16·00
53	21	6d. mauve and green	20·00	65·00
54	21	8d. mauve and black	12·00	50·00
55	21	1s. green and orange	21·00	65·00

23 Flagship of Columbus (Columbus named Grenada "La Concepcion")

1898. 400th Anniv of Discovery of Grenada by Columbus.
56	**23**	2½d. blue	22·00	6·00

1902. As T **21**, but portrait of King Edward VII.
57		½d. purple and green	4·25	1·25
58		1d. purple and red	8·00	30
59		2d. purple and brown	4·75	10·00
60		2½d. purple and blue	6·00	2·75
61		3d. purple and orange	6·00	9·00
62		6d. purple and mauve	5·00	17·00
63		1s. green and orange	9·50	40·00
64		2s. green and blue	35·00	65·00
65		5s. green and red	45·00	85·00
66		10s. green and purple	£160	£300

26 Badge of the Colony

1906				
77	26	½d. green	4·50	30
78	26	1d. red	8·50	10
79	26	2d. orange	4·25	3·00
80	26	2½d. blue	6·00	1·50
84	26	3d. purple on yellow	6·50	1·75
85	26	6d. purple	20·00	10·00
86	26	1s. black on green	7·00	4·50
87	26	2s. blue and purple on blue	35·00	14·00
88	26	5s. green and red on yellow	80·00	95·00
83	26	10s. green and red on green	£160	£300

28

1913				
112	28	½d. green	1·25	30
113	28	1d. red	80	75
114	28	1d. brown	1·50	30
115	28	1½d. red	1·75	1·00
116	28	2d. orange	1·25	30
117	28	2d. grey	2·50	2·75
118	28	2½d. grey	1·00	9·00
94	28	2½d. blue	1·75	1·25
96	28	3d. purple on yellow	65	85
121	28	3d. blue	1·25	11·00
123	28	4d. black and red on yellow	1·00	3·75
124	28	5d. purple and green	1·50	4·25
97	28	6d. purple	1·50	9·00
126	28	6d. black and red	2·25	2·50
127	28	9d. purple and black	2·25	9·50
98a	28	1s. black on green	1·25	7·50
129	28	1s. brown	3·00	9·00
99	28	2s. purple and blue on blue	6·50	12·00
131	28	2s.6d. black & red on blue	10·00	24·00
132	28	3s. green and violet	11·00	27·00
133	28	5s. green and red on yellow	12·00	35·00
101	28	10s. green and red on green	70·00	£120

1916. Optd **WAR TAX.**
111		1d. red	30	20

31 Grand Anse Beach   **32** Badge of the Colony

1934				
135	31	½d. green	15	1·25

136a	32	1d. black and brown	60	35
137a	–	1½d. black and red	1·25	40
138	32	2d. black and orange	1·00	75
139	–	2½d. blue	50	50
140	32	3d. black and olive	1·00	2·75
141	32	6d. black and purple	3·00	1·75
142	32	1s. black and brown	3·25	4·00
143	32	2s.6d. black and blue	8·00	28·00
144	32	5s. black and violet	48·00	50·00

DESIGNS—VERT: 1½d. Grand Etang; 2½d. St. George's.

1935. Silver Jubilee. As T 10a of Gambia.

145	½d. black and green	1·00	1·25
146	1d. blue and grey	1·25	1·75
147	1½d. blue and red	1·25	3·75
148	1s. grey and purple	17·00	40·00

1937. Coronation. As T 10b of Gambia.

149	1d. violet	40	1·75
150	1½d. red	40	50
151	2½d. blue	80	1·25

35 King George VI

1937

152a	35	¼d. brown	65	3·00

40 Badge of the Colony

1938. As 1934, but with portrait of King George VI.

153a	31	½d. green	60	1·25
154a	32	1d. black and brown	1·50	50
155	–	1½d. black and red	50	2·00
156	32	2d. black and orange	40	50
157	–	2½d. blue	30	30
158ab	32	3d. black and olive	40	80
159a	32	6d. black and purple	2·25	50
160a	32	1s. black and brown	5·00	2·50
161	32	2s. black and blue	40·00	2·50
162a	32	5s. black and violet	6·00	8·00
163f	40	10s. blue and red	35·00	42·00

1946. Victory. As T 11a of Gambia.

164	1½d. red	10	50
165	3½d. blue	10	1·00

1948. Silver Wedding. As T 11b/11c of Gambia.

166	1½d. red	15	10
167	10s. grey	24·00	20·00

1949. U.P.U. As T 11d/11g of Gambia.

168	5c. blue	15	10
169	6c. olive	1·50	2·50
170	12c. mauve	15	30
171	24c. brown	15	40

41 King George VI   **42** Badge of the Colony

1951

172	41	½c. black and brown	15	1·60
173	41	1c. black and green	15	25
174	41	2c. black and brown	15	50
175	41	3c. black and red	15	10
176	41	4c. black and orange	35	40
177	41	5c. black and violet	20	10
178	41	6c. black and olive	30	60
179	41	7c. black and blue	1·75	10
180	41	12c. black and purple	2·25	30
181	42	25c. black and brown	2·50	80
182	42	50c. black and blue	7·00	40
183	42	$1.50 black and orange	9·50	8·00
184	52	$2.50 slate and red	16·00	5·50

No. 184 is larger, 24½×30½ mm.

43a Arms of University   **43b** Princess Alice

1951. Inauguration of B.W.I. University College.

185	43a	3c. black and red	45	1·25
186	43b	6c. black and olive	45	50

1951. New Constitution. Nos. 175/7 and 180 optd NEW CONSTITUTION 1951.

187	41	3c. black and red	40	70
188	41	4c. black and orange	45	70
189	41	5c. black and violet	50	90
190	41	12c. black and purple	60	1·25

1953. Coronation. As T 11h of Gambia.

191	3c. black and red	30	10

1953. As T 41, but with portrait of Queen Elizabeth II, and T 42, but Royal Cypher changed.

192		½c. black and brown	10	1·00
193		1c. black and green	10	10
194	41	2c. black and brown	30	10
195		3c. black and red	20	10
196		4c. black and orange	20	10
197		5c. black and violet	20	10
198		6c. black and olive	2·25	1·25
199		7c. black and blue	2·75	10
219	41	12c. black and purple	1·25	70
201	42	25c. black and brown	1·50	20
202	42	50c. black and blue	5·50	1·00
203	42	$1.50 black and orange	14·00	14·00
204	42	$2.50 slate and red	38·00	11·00

No. 204 is larger, 24½×30½ mm.

47a Federation Map

1958. British Caribbean Federation.

205	47a	3c. green	60	10
206	47a	6c. blue	75	90
207	47a	12c. red	90	10

48 Queen Victoria, Queen Elizabeth II, Mail Van and Post Office, St. George's

1961. Grenada Stamp Centenary.

208	48	3c. red and black	25	10
209	–	8c. blue and orange	55	25
210	–	25c. lake and blue	55	25

DESIGNS (incorporating Queen Victoria and Queen Elizabeth II): 8c. Flagship of Columbus; 25c. "Solent I" (paddle-steamer) and Douglas DC-3 aircraft.

1963. Freedom from Hunger. As T 21a of Gambia.

211	8c. green	30	15

1963. Centenary of Red Cross. As T 21b of Gambia.

212	3c. red and black	20	15
213	25c. red and blue	40	15

1965. Centenary of I.T.U. As T 45 of Gibraltar.

221	2c. orange and olive	10	10
222	50c. yellow and red	25	20

1965. I.C.Y. As T 46 of Gibraltar.

223	1c. purple and turquoise	10	15
224	25c. green and lavender	45	15

1966. Churchill Commem. As T 47 of Gibraltar.

225	1c. blue	10	30
226	3c. green	30	20
227	25c. brown	65	10
228	35c. violet	70	15

49 Queen Elizabeth II and Duke of Edinburgh

1966. Royal Visit.

229	49	3c. black and blue	40	15
230	49	35c. black and mauve	1·40	15

52 Hillsborough, Carriacou

1966. Multicoloured.

231	52	1c. Type 52	20	1·25
232		2c. Bougainvillea	20	10
233		3c. Flamboyant plant	1·00	1·00
234		5c. Levera Beach	1·25	10
235		6c. Carenage, St. George's	1·00	10
236		8c. Annandale Falls	1·00	10
237		10c. Cocoa pods	1·25	10
238		12c. Inner Harbour	30	1·25
239		15c. Nutmeg	30	1·25
240		25c. St. George's	30	10
241		35c. Grand Anse beach	30	10
242		50c. Bananas	1·25	2·00
243		$1 Badge of the Colony (vert) (25×39 mm)	7·50	3·75
244		$2 Queen Elizabeth II (vert) (25×39 mm)	5·50	13·00
245		$3 Map of Grenada (vert) (25×39 mm)	4·75	19·00

1966. World Cup Football Championship. As T 48 of Gibraltar.

246	5c. multicoloured	10	10
247	50c. multicoloured	40	90

1966. Inauguration of W.H.O. Headquarters, Geneva. As T 54 of Gibraltar.

248	8c. black, green and blue	20	10
249	25c. black, purple and ochre	45	20

1966. 20th Anniv of UNESCO. As T 56a/56c of Gibraltar.

250	2c. multicoloured	10	10
251	15c. yellow, violet and orange	15	10
252	50c. black, purple and orange	50	90

1967. Statehood. Nos. 232/3, 236 and 240 optd ASSOCIATED STATEHOOD 1967.

253	2c. multicoloured	10	20
254	3c. multicoloured	10	15
255	8c. multicoloured	15	10
256	25c. multicoloured	15	15

1967. World Fair, Montreal. Nos. 232, 237, 239 and 243/4 surch or optd expo67 MONTREAL CANADA and emblem.

257	1c. on 15c. multicoloured	10	20
258	2c. multicoloured	10	20
259	3c. on 10c. multicoloured	10	20
260	$1 multicoloured	30	25
261	$2 multicoloured	45	30

1967. Nos. 231/45 optd ASSOCIATED STATEHOOD.

262	52	1c. multicoloured	10	10
263	–	2c. multicoloured	10	10
264	–	3c. multicoloured	10	10
265	–	5c. multicoloured	10	10
266	–	6c. multicoloured	10	10
267	–	8c. multicoloured	10	10
268	–	10c. multicoloured	10	10
269	–	12c. multicoloured	10	10
270	–	15c. multicoloured	15	10
271	–	25c. multicoloured	20	10
272	–	35c. multicoloured	55	10
273	–	50c. multicoloured	1·00	20
274	–	$1 multicoloured	1·50	60
275	–	$2 multicoloured	1·25	3·75
276	–	$3 multicoloured	4·00	5·50

70 Kennedy and Local Flower

1968. 50th Birth Anniv of Pres. Kennedy. Multicoloured.

277	1c. Type 70	10	25
278	15c. Type 70	15	10
279	25c. Kennedy and strelitzia	20	10
280	35c. Kennedy and roses	25	10
281	50c. As 25c.	30	20
282	$1 As 35c.	40	60

73 Scout Bugler

1968. World Scout Jamboree, Idaho. Multicoloured.

283	1c. Type 73	10	10
284	2c. Scouts camping	10	10
285	3c. Lord Baden-Powell	10	10
286	35c. Type 73	25	10
287	50c. As 2c.	35	20
288	$1 As 3c.	50	55

76 Near Antibes

1968. Paintings by Sir Winston Churchill. Multicoloured.

289	10c. Type 76	10	10
290	12c. The Mediterranean	15	10
291	15c. St. Jean, Cap Ferratt	15	10
292	25c. Type 76	20	10
293	35c. As No. 291	25	10
294	50c. Sir Winston painting	35	25

1968. No. 275 surch $5.

295	$5 on $2 multicoloured	1·25	2·25

1968. "Children Need Milk". Surch CHILDREN NEED MILK and value. (a) Nos. 244/5.

296	2c.+3c. on $2 multicoloured	10	10
297	3c.+3c. on $3 multicoloured	10	10

(b) Nos. 243/4.

298	1c.+3c. on $1 multicoloured	10	40
299	2c.+3c. on $2 multicoloured	21·00	60·00

83 Edith McGuire (U.S.A.)

1968. Olympic Games, Mexico.

300	83	1c. brown, black and blue	70	1·00
301	–	2c. multicoloured	70	1·00
302	–	3c. scarlet, brown and green	70	1·00
303	83	10c. multicoloured	80	1·10
304	–	50c. multicoloured	80	1·10
305	–	60c. red, brown and orange	80	1·10

DESIGNS: 2c., 50c. Arthur Wint (Jamaica); 3c., 60c. Ferreira da Silva (Brazil).

86 Hibiscus

1968. Multicoloured

306	1c. Type 86	10	10
307	2c. Strelitzia	10	10
308	3c. Bougainvillea	10	10
309	5c. Rock hind (horiz)	10	10
310	6c. Sailfish	10	10
311	8c. Red snapper (horiz)	10	60
312	10c. Marine toad (horiz)	10	10
313	12c. Turtle	15	10
314	15c. Tree boa (horiz)	1·00	60
314a	15c. Thunbergia	1·50	2·50
315	25c. Greater Trinidadian murine opossum	30	10
316	35c. Nine-banded armadillo (horiz)	35	10
317	50c. Mona monkey	45	25
317a	75c. Yacht in St. George's Harbour (horiz)	16·00	8·50
318	$1 Bananaquit	3·00	2·00
319	$2 Brown pelican	8·00	16·00
320	$3 Magnificent frigate bird	4·50	9·00
321	$5 Bare-eyed thrush	13·00	27·00

Nos. 318/21 are larger, 25½×48 mm.

102 Kidney Transplant

1968. 20th Anniv of W.H.O. Multicoloured.

322	5c. Type 102	20	10
323	25c. Heart transplant	30	10
324	35c. Lung transplant	30	10
325	50c. Eye transplant	40	50

106 *The Adoration of the Kings* (Veronese)

1968. Christmas.
326	**106**	5c. multicoloured	10	10
327	-	15c. multicoloured	10	10
328	-	35c. multicoloured	10	10
329	-	$1 multicoloured	30	40

DESIGNS: 15c. *"Madonna and Child with Saints John and Catherine* (Titian); 35c. *The Adoration of the Kings* (Botticelli); $1 *A Warrior Adoring* (Catena).

1969. Caribbean Free Trade Area Exhibition. Nos. 300/5 surch **VISIT CARIFTA EXPO '69 April 5-30** and value.
330	**83**	5c. on 1c.	15	30
331	-	8c. on 2c.	15	30
332	-	25c. on 3c.	15	30
333	**83**	35c. on 10c.	15	30
334	-	$1 on 50c.	20	40
335	-	$2 on 60c.	35	60

111 Dame Hylda Bynoe (Governor) and Island Scene

1969. Carifta Expo '69. Multicoloured.
336	**111**	5c. Type **111**	10	10
337	-	15c. Premier E. M. Gairy and island scene	10	10
338	-	50c. Type **111**	10	30
339	-	60c. Emblems of 1958 and 1967 World's Fairs	10	65

114 Dame Hylda Bynoe

1969. Human Rights Year. Multicoloured.
340	**114**	5c. Type **114**	10	10
341	-	25c. Dr. Martin Luther King	15	10
342	-	35c. As 5c.	15	10
343	-	$1 *Balshazzar's Feast* (Rembrandt) (horiz)	30	45

117 Batsman and Wicket-keeper

1969. Cricket.
344	**117**	3c. yellow, brown and blue	60	1·00
345	-	10c. multicoloured	60	40
346	-	25c. brown, ochre & green	75	85
347	-	35c. multicoloured	85	90

DESIGNS: 10c. Batsman playing defensive stroke; 25c. Batsman sweeping ball; 35c. Batsman playing on-drive.

129 Astronaut handling Moon Rock

1969. First Man on the Moon. Multicoloured.
348	-	½c. As Type **129** but larger (56×35 mm)	10	40
349	-	1c. Moon rocket and moon	10	40
350	-	2c. Module landing	10	40
351	-	3c. Declaration left on the moon	10	40
352	-	8c. Module leaving rocket	15	40
353	-	25c. Rocket lifting-off (vert)	35	40
354	-	35c. Spacecraft in orbit (vert)	35	40
355	-	50c. Capsule with parachutes (vert)	45	30

| 356 | - | $1 Type **129** | 60 | 1·25 |

MS357 115×90 mm. Nos. 351 and 356. Imperf   1·00   3·00

130 Gandhi

1969. Birth Cent of Mahatma Gandhi. Multicoloured.
358	-	6c. Type **130**	45	30
359	-	15c. Gandhi standing	60	10
360	-	25c. Gandhi walking	70	10
361	-	$1 Head of Gandhi	1·00	65

MS362 155×122 mm. Nos. 358/61. Imperf   2·25   3·50

1969. Christmas. Nos. 326/9 optd **1969** and surch (No. 363).
363	-	2c. on 15c. multicoloured	10	2·25
364	**106**	5c. multicoloured	10	15
365	-	35c. multicoloured	20	10
366	-	$1 multicoloured	80	2·25

135 "Blackbeard" (Edward Teach)

1970. Pirates.
367	**135**	15c. black	60	10
368	-	25c. green	80	10
369	-	50c. lilac	1·25	40
370	-	$1 carmine	1·75	1·50

DESIGNS: 25c. Anne Bonney; 50c. Jean Lafitte; $1 Mary Read.

1970. No. 348 surch **5c.**
| 371 | - | 5c. on ½c. multicoloured | 10 | 10 |

141/2 *The Last Supper* (detail, Del Sarto)

1970. Easter. Paintings.
372	**141**	5c. multicoloured	15	40
373	**142**	5c. multicoloured	15	40
374	-	15c. multicoloured	20	40
375	-	15c. multicoloured	20	40
376	-	25c. multicoloured	20	40
377	-	25c. multicoloured	20	40
378	-	60c. multicoloured	20	60
379	-	60c. multicoloured	20	60

MS380 120×140 mm. Nos. 376/9   1·00   2·00

DESIGNS: 15c. *Christ crowned with Thorns* (detail, Van Dyck); 25c. *The Passion of Christ* (detail, Memling); 60c. *Christ in the Tomb* (detail, Rubens).

Each value was issued in sheets containing the two stamps *se-tenant*. Each design is spread over two stamps as in Types **141/2**.

149 Girl with Kittens in Pram

1970. Birth Bicentenary of Wordsworth. "Children and Pets". Multicoloured.
381	-	5c. Type **149**	15	15
382	-	15c. Girl with puppy and kitten	25	15
383	-	30c. Boy with fishing-rod and cat	30	40
384	-	60c. Boys and girls with cats and dogs	40	2·00

MS385 Two sheets, each 114×126 mm. Nos. 381, 383 and Nos. 382, 384. Imperf   1·00   2·00

---

153 Parliament of India

1970. Seventh Regional Conference of Commonwealth Parliamentary Association. Parliament Buildings. Multicoloured.
386	-	5c. Type **153**	10	10
387	-	25c. Great Britain	10	10
388	-	50c. Canada	20	15
389	-	60c. Grenada	20	15

MS390 126×90 mm. Nos. 386/9   50   1·00

157 Tower of the Sun

1970. World Fair, Osaka. Multicoloured.
391	-	1c. Type **157**	10	65
392	-	2c. Livelihood and Industry Pavilion (horiz)	10	65
393	-	3c. Flower painting, 1634	10	65
394	-	10c. *Adam and Eve* (Tintoretto) (horiz)	15	10
395	-	25c. Organization For Economic Co-operation and Development (O.E.C.D.) Pavilion (horiz)	35	10
396	-	50c. San Francisco Pavilion	40	1·60

MS397 121×91 mm. $1 Japanese Pavilion (56×34 mm)   55   1·50

164 Roosevelt and "Raising U.S. Flag on Iwo Jima"

1970. 25th Anniv of Ending of World War II. Multicoloured.
398	-	½c. Type **164**	10	2·50
399	-	5c. Zhukov and "Fall of Berlin"	80	65
400	-	15c. Churchill and "Evacuation at Dunkirk"	3·00	1·50
401	-	25c. De Gaulle and "Liberation of Paris"	1·50	60
402	-	50c. Eisenhower and "D-Day Landing"	1·75	2·00
403	-	60c. Montgomery and "Battle of Alamein"	3·25	5·00

MS404 163×113 mm. Nos. 398, 400, 402/3   3·50   8·00

1970. "Philympia 1970" Stamp Exhibition, London. Nos. 353/6 optd **PHILYMPIA LONDON 1970**.
405	-	5c. multicoloured	10	10
406	-	35c. multicoloured	10	10
407	-	50c. multicoloured	15	15
408	**129**	$1 multicoloured	20	30

170 U.P.U. Headquarters Building and Transport

1970. New U.P.U. Headquarters Building. Multicoloured.
409	-	15c. Type **170**	1·50	40
410	-	25c. As Type **170**, but modern transport	1·50	40
411	-	50c. Sir Rowland Hill and U.P.U. Building (vert)	35	60
412	-	$1 Abraham Lincoln and U.P.U. Building (vert)	45	3·00

MS413 79×85 mm. Nos. 411/12   1·00   3·50

---

171 *The Madonna of the Goldfinch* (Tiepolo)

1970. Christmas. Multicoloured.
414	-	½c. Type **171**	10	35
415	-	½c. *The Virgin and Child with St. Peter and St. Paul* (Bouts)	10	35
416	-	½c. *The Virgin and Child* (Bellini)	10	35
417	-	2c. *The Madonna of the Basket* (Correggio)	10	35
418	-	3c. Type **171**	10	35
419	-	35c. As No. 415	50	10
420	-	50c. As 2c.	60	40
421	-	$1 As No. 416	70	1·60

MS422 102×87 mm. Nos. 420/1   1·00   3·00

172 19th-Century Nursing

1970. Cent of British Red Cross. Multicoloured.
423	-	5c. Type **172**	30	10
424	-	15c. Military ambulance, 1918	70	10
425	-	25c. First-aid post, 1941	70	10
426	-	60c. Red Cross transport, 1970	1·60	1·90

MS427 113×82 mm. Nos. 423/6   3·00   1·75

173 John Dewey and Art Lesson

1971. Int Education Year. Multicoloured.
428	-	5c. Type **173**	10	10
429	-	10c. Jean-Jacques Rousseau and "Alphabetization"	15	10
430	-	50c. Maimonides and laboratory	4·00	25
431	-	$1 Bertrand Russell and mathematics class	95	40

MS432 90×98 mm. Nos. 430/1   1·00   2·00

174 Jennifer Hosten and Outline of Grenada

1971. Winner of "Miss World" Competition (1970).
433	**174**	5c. multicoloured	10	10
434	**174**	10c. multicoloured	10	10
435	**174**	15c. multicoloured	15	10
436	**174**	25c. multicoloured	15	10
437	**174**	35c. multicoloured	15	10
438	**174**	50c. multicoloured	35	55

MS439 92×89 mm. **174** 50c. multicoloured. Printed on silk. Imperf   75   1·75

175 French and Canadian Scouts

1971. 13th World Scout Jamboree, Asagiri, Japan. Multicoloured.
440	-	5c. Type **175**	15	10
441	-	35c. German and American scouts	30	25
442	-	50c. Australian and Japanese scouts	30	50
443	-	75c. Grenada and British scouts	35	1·00

MS444 101×114 mm. Nos. 442/3   1·25   2·50

176 Napoleon reviewing the Guard (E. Detaille)

1971. 150th Death Anniv of Napoleon Bonaparte. Paintings. Multicoloured.
445	5c. Type **176**	15	15
446	15c. Napoleon before Madrid (Vernet)	20	15
447	35c. Napoleon crossing Mt. St. Bernard (David)	25	15
448	$2 Napoleon in his Study (David)	50	1·50
MS449	101×76 mm. No. 447. Imperf	1·25	1·60

177 1d. Stamp of 1861 and Badge of Grenada

1971. 110th Anniv of the Postal Service. Multicoloured.
450	5c. Type **177**	25	50
451	15c. 6d. stamp of 1861 and Queen Elizabeth II	30	15
452	35c. 1d. and 6d. stamps of 1861 and badge of Grenada	50	20
453	50c. Scroll and 1d. stamp of 1861	60	2·25
MS454	96×114 mm. Nos. 452/3	1·00	1·00

178 Apollo Splashdown

1971. Apollo Moon Exploration Series. Multicoloured.
455	1c. Type **178**	10	50
456	2c. Recovery of "Apollo 13"	10	50
457	3c. Separation of Lunar Module from "Apollo 14"	10	50
458	10c. Shepard and Mitchell taking samples of moon rock	25	10
459	25c. Moon Buggy	75	20
460	$1 "Apollo 15" blast-off (vert)	2·00	3·75
MS461	77×108 mm. 50c. as $1	1·40	1·50

179 67th Regt. of Foot, 1787

1971. Military Uniforms. Multicoloured.
462	½c. Type **179**	10	30
463	1c. 45th Regt. of Foot, 1792	10	30
464	2c. 29th Regt. of Foot, 1794	10	30
465	10c. 9th Regt. of Foot, 1801	45	10
466	25c. 2nd Regt. of Foot, 1815	85	20
467	$1 70th Regt. of Foot, 1764	2·50	2·25
MS468	108×99 mm. Nos. 466/7	2·25	2·75

180 The Adoration of the Kings (Memling)

1972. Christmas (1971). Multicoloured.
469	15c. Type **180**	15	10

470	25c. Madonna and Child (Michelangelo)	20	10
471	35c. Madonna and Child (Murillo)	25	10
472	50c. The Virgin with the Apple (Memling)	30	2·00
MS473	105×80 mm. $1 The Adoration of the Kings (Mostaert)	75	1·25

1972. Winter Olympic Games, Sapporo, Japan. Nos. 462/4 surch **WINTER OLYMPICS FEB.3-13,1972 SAPPORO,JAPAN**, Olympic rings and premium. Nos. 476/7 additionally optd **AIR MAIL.**
474	$2 on 2c. mult (postage)	50	90
MS475	108×99 mm. Nos. 466/7	1·00	1·25
476	35c. on ½c. multicoloured (air)	15	25
477	50c. on 1c. multicoloured	15	35

1972. General Election. Nos. 307/8, 310 and 315 optd **VOTE FEB. 28 1972.**
478	2c. multicoloured	25	80
479	3c. multicoloured	25	80
480	6c. multicoloured	25	80
481	25c. multicoloured	60	30

183 King Arthur

1972. UNICEF. Multicoloured.
482	½c. Type **183**	10	20
483	1c. Robin Hood	10	20
484	2c. Robinson Crusoe (vert)	10	20
485	25c. Type **183**	10	10
486	50c. As 1c.	25	40
487	75c. As 2c.	30	1·10
488	$1 Mary and her little lamb (vert)	45	1·25
MS489	65×98 mm. No. 488	55	80

1972. "Interpex" Stamp Exbn, New York. Nos. 433/8 optd **INTERPEX 1972.**
490	5c. multicoloured	10	10
491	10c. multicoloured	10	10
492	15c. multicoloured	10	10
493	25c. multicoloured	10	10
494	35c. multicoloured	15	15
495	50c. multicoloured	25	30
MS496	92×89 mm. **174** 50c. multicoloured. Printed on silk. Imperf	6·00	11·00

1972. Nos. 306/8 and 433 surch **12c.**
497	–	12c. on 1c. multicoloured	40	70
498	–	12c. on 2c. multicoloured	40	70
499	–	12c. on 3c. multicoloured	40	70
500	**174**	12c. on 5c. multicoloured	40	70

1972. Air. Optd **AIR MAIL** or surch in addition.
501	–	5c. mult (No. 309)	10	20
518	**175**	5c. multicoloured	1·10	20
502	–	8c. mult (No. 311)	15	10
503	–	10c. mult (No. 312)	15	10
504	–	15c. mult (No. 314a)	30	10
505	–	25c. mult (No. 315)	35	20
506	–	30c. on 1c. mult (No. 306)	40	25
507	–	35c. mult (No. 316)	40	25
519	–	35c. mult (No. 441)	2·50	30
508	–	40c. on 2c. mult (No. 307)	50	25
509	–	45c. on 3c. mult (No. 308)	55	35
510	–	50c. mult (No. 317)	55	35
520	–	50c. mult (No. 442)	2·50	45
511	–	60c. on 5c. mult (No. 309)	60	40
512	–	70c. on 6c. mult (No. 310)	70	75
521	–	75c. mult (No. 443)	3·50	1·50
513	–	$1 multicoloured (No. 318)	8·00	1·00
514	–	$1.35 on 8c. mult (No. 311)	4·50	2·25
515	–	$2 multicoloured (No. 319)	11·00	11·00
516	–	$3 multicoloured (No. 320)	11·00	12·00
517	–	$5 multicoloured (No. 321)	13·00	20·00

187 Yachting

1972. Olympic Games, Munich. Multicoloured.
522	½c. Type **187** (postage)	10	10

523	1c. Show-jumping	10	10
524	2c. Running (vert)	10	10
525	35c. As 2c.	30	10
526	50c. As 1c.	40	40
527	25c. Boxing (air)	25	10
528	$1 As 25c.	65	85
MS529	82×85 mm. 60c. as 25c. and 70c. as 1c.	1·00	1·40

1972. Royal Silver Wedding. As T **98** of Gibraltar, but with Badge of Grenada and Nutmegs in background.
530	8c. brown	10	10
531	$1 blue	45	55

189 Boy Scout Saluting

1972. 65th Anniv of Boy Scouts. Multicoloured.
532	½c. Type **189** (postage)	10	10
533	1c. Scouts knotting ropes	10	10
534	2c. Scouts shaking hands	10	10
535	3c. Lord Baden-Powell	10	10
536	75c. As 2c.	60	2·75
537	$1 As 3c.	65	2·75
538	25c. Type **189** (air)	30	20
539	35c. As 1c.	35	20
MS540	87×88 mm. 60c. as 3c. and 70c. as 2c.	1·50	1·50

190 Madonna and Child

1972. Christmas. Multicoloured.
541	1c. Type **190**	10	25
542	3c. The Three Kings	10	25
543	5c. The Nativity	10	10
544	25c. Type **190**	15	10
545	35c. As 3c.	15	10
546	$1 As 5c.	40	1·00
MS547	102×76 mm. 60c. Type **190** and 70c. as 3c.	60	80

191 Greater Flamingos

1973. National Zoo. Multicoloured.
548	25c. Type **191**	70	35
549	35c. Brazilian tapir	40	35
550	60c. Blue and yellow macaws	1·25	2·00
551	70c. Ocelot	70	2·25

192 Class II Racing Yacht

1973. Yachting. Multicoloured.
552	25c. Type **192**	25	10
553	35c. Harbour, St. George's	30	10
554	60c. Yacht "Bloodhound"	45	65
555	70c. St. George's	50	75

193 Helios (Greek god) and Earth orbiting the Sun

1973. Centenary of I.M.O./W.M.O. Greek Gods. Multicoloured.
556	½c. Type **193**	10	10
557	1c. Poseidon and "Normad" storm detector	10	10
558	2c. Zeus and radarscope	10	10
559	3c. Iris and weather balloon	10	10
560	35c. Hermes and "ATS-3" satellite	20	10

561	50c. Zephyrus and diagram of pressure zones	25	30
562	75c. Demeter and space photo	25	60
563	$1 Selene and rainfall diagram	25	1·00
MS564	123×92 mm. $2 Computer weather map (42×31 mm.)	1·00	1·25

194 Racing Class Yachts

1973. Carriacou Regatta. Multicoloured.
565	½c. Type **194**	10	10
566	1c. Cruising Class yacht	10	10
567	2c. Open-decked sloops	10	10
568	35c. Mermaid (sloop)	30	10
569	50c. St. George's Harbour	35	25
570	75c. Map of Carriacou	40	55
571	$1 Boat-building	55	70
MS572	109×88 mm. $2 End of race	1·00	1·75

195 Ignatius Semmelweis (obstetrician)

1973. 25th Anniv of W.H.O. Multicoloured.
573	½c. Type **195**	10	35
574	1c. Louis Pasteur	10	35
575	2c. Edward Jenner	10	35
576	3c. Sigmund Freud	10	35
577	25c. Emil von Behring (bacteriologist)	65	10
578	35c. Carl Jung	75	20
579	50c. Charles Calmette (bacteriologist)	1·10	1·00
580	$1 William Harvey	1·40	2·50
MS581	105×80 mm. $2 Marie Curie	1·25	1·60

196 Princess Anne and Capt. Mark Phillips

1973. Royal Wedding.
582	**196**	25c. multicoloured	10	10
583	**196**	$2 multicoloured	30	45
MS584	79×100 mm. 75c. and $1 as Nos. 582/3	40	30

197 "Virgin and Child" (Maratti)

1973. Christmas. Multicoloured.
585	½c. Type **197**	10	10
586	1c. Madonna and Child (Crivelli)	10	10
587	2c. Virgin and Child with two Angels (Verrocchio)	10	10
588	3c. Adoration of the Shepherds (Roberti)	10	10
589	25c. The Holy Family with the Infant Baptist (Baroccio)	15	10
590	35c. The Holy Family (Bronzino)	15	10
591	75c. Mystic Nativity (Botticelli)	20	20
592	$1 Adoration of the Kings (Geertgen)	25	30
MS593	89×89 mm. $2 Adoration of the Kings (Mostaert) (30×45 mm.)	1·00	1·10

1974. Independence. Nos. 306/9, 311/13, 315/16 and 317a/21 optd **INDEPENDENCE 7TH FEB. 1974.**
594	**86**	1c. multicoloured	10	75
595	–	2c. multicoloured	15	75
596	–	3c. multicoloured	15	75
597	–	5c. multicoloured	20	20
598	–	8c. multicoloured	30	10
599	–	10c. multicoloured	35	15
600	–	12c. multicoloured	35	15
601	–	25c. multicoloured	60	25
602	–	35c. multicoloured	75	25

603	-	75c. multicoloured	3·00	1·75
604	-	$1 multicoloured	4·50	2·00
605	-	$2 multicoloured	7·50	8·50
606	-	$3 multicoloured	8·00	9·50
607	-	$5 multicoloured	13·00	20·00

199 Creative Arts Theatre, Jamaica Campus

1974. 25th Anniv of University of West Indies. Multicoloured.

608	10c. Type **199**	10	10
609	25c. Marryshow House	10	10
610	50c. Chapel, Jamaica Campus (vert)	20	10
611	$1 University arms (vert)	30	30
MS612	69×86 mm. $2 as No. 611	50	1·00

200 Nutmeg Pods and Scarlet Mace

1974. Independence. Multicoloured.

613	3c. Type **200**	10	10
614	8c. Map of Grenada	30	10
615	25c. Prime Minister Eric Gairy	15	10
616	35c. Grand Anse Beach and flag	80	10
617	$1 Coat of arms	35	40
MS618	91×125 mm. $2 as $1	55	1·00

201 Footballers (West Germany v. Chile)

1974. World Cup Football Championship, West Germany. Multicoloured.

619	½c. Type **201**	10	10
620	1c. East Germany v. Australia	10	10
621	2c. Yugoslavia v. Brazil	10	10
622	10c. Scotland v. Zaire	10	10
623	25c. Netherlands v. Uruguay	15	10
624	50c. Sweden v. Bulgaria	20	10
625	75c. Italy v. Haiti	35	15
626	$1 Poland v. Argentina	50	25
MS627	114×76 mm. $2 Country flags	1·00	1·75

202 Early U.S. Mail-trains and Concorde

1974. Centenary of U.P.U. Multicoloured.

628	½c. Type **202**	30	10
629	1c. "Caesar" (snow) (1839) and Westland Wessex HU Mk 5 helicopter	30	10
630	2c. Airmail transport	30	10
631	8c. Pigeon post (1480) and telephone dial	30	10
632	15c. 18th-century bellman and tracking antenna	30	10
633	25c. Messenger (1450) and satellite	35	10
634	35c. French pillar-box (1850) and mail-boat	50	10
635	$1 18th-century German postman and British Advanced Passenger Train	1·50	85
MS636	105×66 mm. $2 St. Gotthard mail-coach (1735)	1·00	1·75

203 Sir Winston Churchill

1974. Birth Centenary of Sir Winston Churchill.

637	**203**	35c. multicoloured	15	10
638	**203**	$2 multicoloured	45	1·00
MS639	126×96 mm. 75c. as 35c. and $1 as $2		75	75

204 *Madonna and Child of the Eucharist* (Botticelli)

1974. Christmas. *Madonna and Child* paintings by named artists. Multicoloured.

640	½c. Type **204**	10	10
641	1c. Niccolo di Pietro	10	10
642	2c. Van der Weyden	10	10
643	3c. Bastiani	10	10
644	10c. Giovanni	10	10
645	25c. Van der Weyden	20	10
646	50c. Botticelli	25	20
647	$1 Mantegna	35	50
MS648	117×96 mm. $2 as 1c.	60	1·00

205 Yachts, Point Saline

1975. . Multicoloured..

649	½c. Type **205**	10	85
650	1c. Yacht Club race	10	10
651	2c. Carenage taxi	10	10
652	3c. Large working boats	10	10
653a	5c. Deep-water dock	10	15
654	6c. Cocoa beans in drying trays	10	10
655	8c. Nutmegs	1·25	10
656	10c. Rum distillery, River Antoine Estate, c. 1785	10	10
657	12c. Cocoa tree	30	10
658	15c. Fishermen at Fontenoy	10	10
659	20c. Parliament Building	15	15
660	25c. Fort George cannons	20	15
661	35c. Pearls Airport	20	15
662	50c. General Post Office	15	30
663	75c. Carib's Leap, Sauteurs Bay	45	50
664	$1 Carenage, St. George's	50	70
665	$2 St. George's Harbour by night	50	1·50
666	$3 Grand Anse Beach	55	2·00
667	$5 Canoe Bay and Black Bay	65	3·00
668	$10 Sugar-loaf Island	1·25	6·50

Nos. 663/8 are size 45×28 mm.

206 Sailfish

1975. Big Game Fishing. Multicoloured.

669	½c. Type **206**	10	10
670	1c. Blue marlin	10	10
671	2c. White marlin	10	10
672	10c. Yellow-finned tuna	10	10
673	25c. Wahoo	35	10
674	50c. Dolphin (fish)	50	15
675	70c. Giant grouper	60	20
676	$1 Great barracuda	80	35
MS677	107×80 mm. $2 Short-finned mako	1·25	1·25

207 Granadilla Barbadine

1975. Flowers. Multicoloured.

678	½c. Type **207**	10	10
679	1c. Bleeding Heart (Easter Lily)	10	10
680	2c. Poinsettia	10	10
681	3c. Cocoa flower	10	10
682	10c. Gladioli	10	10
683	25c. Redhead/Yellowhead	20	10
684	50c. Plumbago	30	15
685	$1 Orange flower	50	25
MS686	102×82 mm. $2 Barbados gooseberry	1·10	1·25

208 Dove, Grenada Flag and U.N. Emblem

1975. Grenada's Admission to the U.N. (1974). Multicoloured.

687	½c. Type **208**	10	10
688	1c. Grenada and U.N. flags	10	10
689	2c. Grenada coat of arms	10	10
690	35c. U.N. emblem over map of Grenada	15	10
691	50c. U.N. buildings and flags	20	15
692	$2 U.N. emblem and scroll	45	45
MS693	122×91 mm. 75c. Type **208** and $1 as 2c.	65	90

CANCELLED REMAINDERS*. Some of the following issues have been remaindered, cancelled to order, at a fraction of their face value. For all practical purposes these are indistinguishable from genuine postally used copies. Our used quotations, which are indicated by an asterisk, are the same for cancelled-to-order or postally used copies.

209 Paul Revere's Midnight Ride

1975. Bicentenary of American Revolution (1st issue). Multicoloured.

694	½c. Type **209** (postage)	10	10
695	1c. Crispus Attucks	10	10
696	2c. Patrick Henry	10	10
697	3c. Franklin visits Washington	10	10
698	5c. Rebel troops	10	10
699	10c. John Paul Jones	10	10
700	40c. *John Hancock* (Copley) (vert) (air)	25	10
701	50c. *Benjamin Franklin* (Roslin) (vert)	40	15
702	75c. *John Adams* (Copley) (vert)	55	15
703	$1 *Lafayette* (Casanova) (vert)	60	20
MS704	Two sheets, each 131×102 mm: $2 Grenada arms and U.S. seal; $2 Grenada and U.S. flags	1·00	60

Stamps from No. MS704 are horiz and larger: 47½×35 mm.

See also Nos. 785/92.

210 *Blood of the Redeemer* (G. Bellini)

1975. Easter. Multicoloured.

705	½c. Type **210**	10	10
706	1c. *Pieta* (Bellini)	10	10
707	2c. *The Entombment* (Van der Weyden)	10	10
708	3c. *Pieta* (Bellini)	10	10
709	35c. *Pieta* (Bellini)	20	10
710	50c. *The Dead Christ* (Bellini)	25	10
711	$1 *The Dead Christ supported by Angels* (Procaccini)	30	10
MS712	117×100 mm. $2 *Pieta* (Botticelli)	75	30

211 Wildlife Study

1975. 14th World Scout Jamboree, Norway. Multicoloured.

713	½c. Type **211**	10	10
714	1c. Sailing	10	10

715	2c. Map-reading	10	10
716	35c. First-aid	30	10
717	40c. Physical training	30	10
718	75c. Mountaineering	40	10
719	$2 Sing-song	70	20
MS720	106×80 mm. $1 Boat-building	1·00	30

212 Leafy Jewel Box

1975. Sea Shells. Multicoloured.

721	½c. Type **212**	10	10
722	1c. Emerald nerite	10	10
723	2c. Yellow American cockle	10	10
724	25c. Common purple janthina	85	10
725	50c. Atlantic turkey wing	1·75	15
726	75c. West Indian fighting conch	2·25	20
727	$1 Noble wentletrap	2·25	20
MS728	102×76 mm. $2 Music volute	2·00	80

213 *Lycorea ceres*

1975. Butterflies. Multicoloured.

729	½c. Type **213**	10	10
730	1c. *Adelpha cytherea*	10	10
731	2c. *Atlides polybe*	10	10
732	35c. *Anteos maerula*	80	10
733	45c. *Parides neophilus*	85	10
734	75c. *Nymula orestes*	1·25	15
735	$2 *Euptychia cephus*	1·75	20
MS736	108×83 mm. $1 *Papilio astyalus* (sub-species "lycophron")	1·25	40

214 Rowing

1975. Pan-American Games, Mexico City. Multicoloured.

737	½c. Type **214**	10	10
738	1c. Swimming	10	10
739	2c. Show-jumping	10	10
740	35c. Gymnastics	15	10
741	45c. Football	15	10
742	75c. Boxing	25	15
743	$2 Cycling	65	20
MS744	106×81 mm. $1 Yachting	1·00	40

215 *The Boy David* (Michelangelo)

1975. 500th Birth Anniv of Michelangelo. Multicoloured.

745	½c. Type **215**	10	10
746	1c. *Young Man* (detail)	10	10
747	2c. *Moses*	10	10
748	40c. *Prophet Zachariah*	30	10
749	50c. *St. John the Baptist*	30	15
750	75c. *Judith and Holofernes*	40	20
751	$2 "Doni Madonna" (detail from *Holy Family*)	70	25
MS752	104×89 mm. $1 *Madonna* (head from Pieta)	1·00	30

216 Madonna and Child (Filippino Lippi)

1975. Christmas. *Virgin and Child* paintings by artists named. Multicoloured.

753	½c. Type **216**	10	10
754	1c. Mantegna	10	10
755	2c. Luis de Morales	10	10
756	35c. G. M. Morandi	15	10
757	50c. Antonello da Messina	15	10
758	75c. Durer	20	10
759	$1 Velasquez	25	10
MS760	125×95 mm. $2 Bellini	1·00	30

217 Bananaquit

1976. Flora and Fauna. Multicoloured.

761	½c. Type **217**	10	10
762	1c. Brazilian agouti	10	10
763	2c. Hawksbill turtle (horiz)	10	10
764	5c. Dwarf poinciana	10	10
765	35c. Black-finned tuna ("Albacore") (horiz)	90	10
766	40c. Cardinal's guard	95	10
767	$2 Nine-banded armadillo (horiz)	2·50	30
MS768	82×89 mm. $1 Belted kingfisher	7·50	90

218 Carnival Time

1976. Tourism. Multicoloured.

769	½c. Type **218**	10	10
770	1c. Scuba diving	10	10
771	2c. Liner "Southward" at St. George's	10	10
772	35c. Game fishing	65	10
773	50c. St. George's Golf Course	2·25	20
774	75c. Tennis	2·50	25
775	$1 Ancient rock carvings at Mount Rich	2·75	25
MS776	100×73 mm. $2 Small boat sailing	1·75	60

219 Pieta (Master of Okolicsno)

1976. Easter. Paintings by artists named. Multicoloured.

777	½c. Type **219**	10	10
778	1c. Correggio	10	10
779	2c. Van der Weyden	10	10
780	3c. Durer	10	10
781	35c. Master of the Holy Spirit	15	10
782	75c. Raphael	30	15
783	$1 Raphael	35	20
MS784	108×86 mm. $2 Crespi	1·00	60

220 Sharpshooters

1976. Bicentenary of American Revolution (2nd issue). Multicoloured.

785	½c. Type **220**	10	10

786	1c. Defending the Liberty Pole	10	10
787	2c. Loading muskets	10	10
788	35c. The Fight for Liberty	30	10
789	50c. Peace Treaty, 1783	35	10
790	$1 Drummers	50	20
791	$3 Gunboat	90	30
MS792	93×79 mm. 75c. as 35c. and $2 as 50c.	75	60

221 Nature Study

1976. 50th Anniv of Girl Guides in Grenada. Multicoloured.

793	½c. Type **221**	10	10
794	1c. Campfire cooking	10	10
795	2c. First aid	10	10
796	50c. Camping	50	10
797	75c. Home economics	65	15
798	$2 First aid	90	25
MS799	111×85 mm. $1 Painting	1·00	70

222 Volleyball

1976. Olympic Games, Montreal. Multicoloured.

800	½c. Type **222**	10	10
801	1c. Cycling	10	10
802	2c. Rowing	10	10
803	35c. Judo	30	10
804	45c. Hockey	60	10
805	75c. Gymnastics	60	20
806	$1 High jump	60	20
MS807	106×81 mm. $3 Equestrian event	1·00	80

223 Cha-U-Kao at the Moulin Rouge

1976. 75th Death Anniv of Toulouse-Lautrec. Multicoloured.

808	½c. Type **223**	10	10
809	1c. Quadrille of the Moulin Rouge	10	10
810	2c. Profile of a Woman	10	10
811	3c. Salon in the Rue des Moulins	10	10
812	40c. The Laundryman	65	10
813	50c. Marcelle Lender dancing the Bolero	75	10
814	$2 Signor Boileau at the Cafe	1·75	25
MS815	152×125 mm. $1 Woman with Boa	2·50	70

223a Map of the Caribbean

1976. West Indian Victory in World Cricket Cup.

816	35c. Type **223a**	1·00	35
817	$1 The Prudential Cup	1·50	5·00

224 Piper Apache 235

1976. Airplanes. Multicoloured.

818	½c. Type **224**	10	10
819	1c. Beech 50 Twin Bonanza	10	10
820	2c. de Havilland Twin Otter 100	10	10
821	40c. Britten Norman Islander	60	10
822	50c. de Havilland Heron 2	65	10
823	$2 Hawker Siddeley H.S.748	2·00	50

MS824	75×83 mm. $3 B.A.C. One Eleven 500	1·50	80

225 Satellite Assembly

1976. Viking and Helios Space Missions. Multicoloured.

825	½c. Type **225**	10	10
826	1c. Helios satellite	10	10
827	2c. Helios encapsulation	10	10
828	15c. Systems test	10	10
829	45c. Viking lander (horiz)	20	10
830	75c. Lander on Mars	30	15
831	$2 Viking encapsulation	60	25
MS832	110×85 mm. $3 Orbiter and lander	1·00	75

226 S.S. Geestland

1976. Ships. Multicoloured.

833	½c. Type **226**	10	10
834	1c. M.V. Federal Palm	10	10
835	2c. H.M.S Blake	10	10
836	25c. M.V. Vistafjord	45	10
837	75c. S.S. Canberra	80	15
838	$1 S.S. Regina	90	20
839	$5 S.S."Arandora Star"	1·75	40
MS840	91×78 mm. $2 "Santa Maria"	1·60	4·00

227 San Barnaba Altarpiece (Botticelli)

1976. Christmas. Multicoloured.

841	½c. Type **227**	10	10
842	1c. Annunciation (Botticelli)	10	10
843	2c. Madonna of Chancellor Rolin (Jan van Eyck)	10	10
844	35c. Annunciation (Fra Filippo Lippi)	15	10
845	50c. Madonna of the Magnificat (Botticelli)	20	10
846	75c. Madonna of the Pomegranate (Botticelli)	30	15
847	$3 Madonna with St. Cosmas and other Saints (Botticelli)	70	25
MS848	71×57 mm. $2 Gypsy Madonna (Titian)	1·00	60

228 Alexander Graham Bell and Telephones

1976. Centenary of First Telephone. Multicoloured.

849	½c. Type **228**	10	10
850	1c. Telephone users within globe	10	10
851	2c. Telephone satellite	10	10
852	18c. Telephone viewer and console	20	10
853	40c. Satellite and tracking stations	25	10
854	$1 Satellite transmitting to ships	35	15
855	$2 Dish aerial and modern telephone	55	25
MS856	107×80 mm. $5 Globe encircled by flags	1·25	75

229 Coronation Scene

1977. Silver Jubilee. Multicoloured.(a) Perf.

857	½c. Type **229**	10	10
858	1c. Sceptre and orb	10	10
859	35c. The Queen on horseback	10	10
860	$2 Spoon and ampulla	25	15
861	$2.50 The Queen and Prince Philip	25	15
MS862	103×79 mm. $5 Royal Visit to Grenada	75	60

(b) Roul. Self-adhesive.

863	35c. As $2.50	15	25
864	50c. As $2	25	1·00
865	$1 As 1c.	50	1·40
866	$3 As 35c.	1·25	2·75

230 Water Skiing

1977. Easter Water Parade. Multicoloured.

867	½c. Type **230**	10	10
868	1c. Speedboat race	10	10
869	2c. Row boat race	10	10
870	22c. Swimming	20	10
871	35c. Work boat race	30	10
872	75c. Water polo	50	15
873	$2 Game fishing	1·00	25
MS874	115×85 mm. $3 Yacht race	1·25	75

231 Meeting Place, Grand Anse Beach

1977. Seventh Meeting of Organization of American States.

875	**231** 35c. multicoloured	10	10
876	**231** $1 multicoloured	25	60
877	**231** $2 multicoloured	40	1·75

232 Rafting

1977. Caribbean Scout Jamboree, Jamaica. Multicoloured.

878	½c. Type **232**	10	10
879	1c. Tug-of-war	10	10
880	2c. Sea Scouts regatta	10	10
881	18c. Camp fire	20	10
882	40c. Field kitchen	25	10
883	$1 Scouts with sea scouts	55	15
884	$2 Hiking and map reading	75	25
MS885	107×85 mm. $3 Semaphore	1·50	80

233 Angel and Shepherd

1977. Christmas. Ceiling Panels from Church of St. Martin, Zillis. Multicoloured.

886	½c. Type **233**	10	10
887	1c. St. Joseph	10	10
888	2c. Virgin and Child fleeing to Egypt	10	10
889	22c. Angel	10	10
890	35c. Magus on horseback	10	10
891	75c. Three horses	15	15
892	$2 Virgin and Child	40	25
MS893	85×112 mm. $3 Magus offering gift	1·00	70

1977. Royal Visit. Nos. 857/61 optd **Royal Visit W.I. 1977.**

894	½c. Type **229**	10	10
895	1c. Sceptre and Orb	10	10
896	35c. Queen on horseback	10	10
897	$2 Spoon and ampulla	30	40
898	$2.50 The Queen and Prince Philip	35	45
MS899	103×79 mm. $5 Royal visit to Grenada	70	80

235 Christjaan
Eijkman (Medicine)

1978. Nobel Prize Winners. Multicoloured.

900	½c. Type **235**	10	10
901	1c. Sir Winston Churchill (Literature)	30	10
902	2c. Woodrow Wilson (Peace)	10	10
903	35c. Frederic Passy (Peace)	15	10
904	$1 Albert Einstein (Physics)	1·00	20
905	$3 Carl Bosch (Chemistry)	1·75	35
MS906	114×99 mm. $2 Alfred Nobel	70	60

236 Count von Zeppelin and
First Zeppelin Airship LZ-1

1978. 75th Anniv of First Zeppelin Flight and 50th Anniv of Lindbergh's Transatlantic Flight. Multicoloured.

907	½c. Type **236**	10	10
908	1c. Lindbergh with *Spirit of St. Louis*	10	10
909	2c. Airship *Deutschland*	10	10
910	22c. Lindbergh's arrival in France	40	10
911	75c. Lindbergh and *Spirit of St. Louis* in flight	70	10
912	$1 *Graf Zeppelin* over Alps	70	15
913	$3 *Graf Zeppelin* over White House	1·40	25
MS914	103×85 mm. Lindbergh in cockpit; $2 Count von Zeppelin and airship LZ-5	1·00	60

237 Rocket
Launching

1978. Space Shuttle. Multicoloured.

915	½c. Type **237**	10	10
916	1c. Booster jettison	10	10
917	2c. External tank jettison	10	10
918	18c. Space Shuttle in orbit	30	10
919	75c. Satellite placement	65	10
920	$2 Landing approach	1·40	20
MS921	103×85 mm. $3 Shuttle after landing	1·10	60

238 Black-headed
Gull

1978. Wild Birds of Grenada. Multicoloured.

922	½c. Type **238**	10	10
923	1c. Wilson's storm petrel ("Wilsons Petrel")	10	10
924	2c. Killdeer plover ("Killdeer")	10	10
925	50c. White-necked jacobin	1·25	10
926	75c. Blue-faced booby	1·50	15
927	$1 Broad-winged hawk	2·00	20
928	$2 Red-necked pigeon	2·50	30
MS929	103×94 mm. $3 Scarlet ibis	4·50	1·00

239 *The Landing
of Marie de Medici
at Marseilles*

1978. 400th Birth Anniv of Peter Paul Rubens. Multicoloured.

930	5c. Type **239**	10	10
931	15c. *Rubens and Isabella Brandt*	10	10
932	18c. *Marchesa Brigida Spindola-Doria*	10	10
933	25c. *Ludovicus Nonninus*	10	10
934	45c. *Helene Fourment and her Children*	15	10
935	75c. *Clara Serena Rubens*	25	10
936	$3 *Le Chapeau de Paille*	60	20
MS937	65×100 mm. $5 *Self Portrait*	1·00	60

240 Ludwig van
Beethoven

1978. 150th Death Anniv of Beethoven. Multicoloured.

938	5c. Type **240**	10	10
939	15c. Woman violinist (horiz)	15	10
940	18c. Musical instruments (horiz)	20	10
941	22c. Piano (horiz)	20	10
942	50c. Violins	40	10
943	75c. Piano and sonata score	50	15
944	$3 Beethoven's portrait and home (horiz)	1·25	25
MS945	83×62 mm. $2 Beethoven and score	1·10	60

241 King Edward's
Chair

1978. 25th Anniv of Coronation. Multicoloured. (a) Perf.

946	35c. Type **241**	10	10
947	$2 Queen with regalia	30	35
948	$2.50 St. Edward's Crown	30	40
MS949	102×76 mm. $5 Queen and Prince Philip	80	80

(b) Roul×imperf. Self-adhesive.

950	25c. Queen Elizabeth II taking salute, Trooping the Colour	15	15
951	35c. Queen at Maundy Thursday ceremony	15	25
952	$5 Queen and Prince Philip at Opening of Parliament	1·50	2·50

243 Goalkeeper
reaching for Ball

1978. World Cup Football Championship, Argentina.

953	**243**	40c. multicoloured	10	10
954	–	60c. multicoloured	15	20
955	–	90c. multicoloured	25	30
956	–	$2 multicoloured	60	60
MS957	130×97 mm. $2.70, multicoloured		1·10	1·10

DESIGNS: 60c. to $2.70, Designs similar to Type **243** with goalkeeper reaching for ball.

244 Aerial Phenomena,
Germany, 1561 and U.S.A.,
1952

1978. U.F.O. Research. Multicoloured.

958	5c. Type **244**	15	10
959	35c. Various aerial phenomena, 1950	35	25
960	$3 U.F.O.s, 1965	2·00	1·75
MS961	112×89 mm. $2 Sir Eric Gairy and U.F.O. research laboratory	1·25	1·25

245 *Wright Flyer III,* 1902

1978. 75th Anniv of Powered Flight. Multicoloured.

962	5c. Type **245**	10	10
963	15c. Wright Flyer I, 1903	10	10
964	18c. Wright Type A	10	10
965	22c. Wright Flyer I from above	15	10
966	50c. Orville Wright and Wright Type A	20	20
967	75c. Wright Type A, Pau, France, 1908	25	25
968	$3 Wilbur Wright and Wright glider No. IV	80	70
MS969	114×85 mm. $2 Wright glider No. III	1·00	75

246 Cook and Hawaiian
Feast

1978. 250th Birth Anniv of Captain James Cook and Bicentenary of Discovery of Hawaii. Multicoloured.

970	18c. Type **246**	60	20
971	35c. Cook and Hawaiian dance	75	25
972	75c. Cook and Honolulu harbour	1·25	1·00
973	$3 Cook's statue and H.M.S. "Resolution"	1·75	5·50
MS974	116×88 mm. $4 Cook and death scene	3·00	1·50

247 *Paumgartner
Altarpiece* (detail)

1978. Christmas. Paintings by Durer. Multicoloured.

975	40c. Type **247**	20	15
976	60c. *The Adoration of the Magi*	25	20
977	90c. *Virgin and Child*	30	20
978	$2 *Virgin and Child with St. Anne* (detail)	55	55
MS979	113×83 mm. $4 *Madonna and Child*	1·10	1·50

248 National
Convention and
Cultural Centre
(interior)

1979. Fifth Anniv of Independence.

980	5c. Type **248**	10	10
981	18c. National Convention and Cultural Centre (exterior)	10	10
982	22c. Easter Water Parade, 1978	10	10
983	35c. Sir Eric M. Gairy (Prime Minister)	10	10
984	$3 The Cross, Fort Frederick	45	60

249 *Acalypha
hispida*

1979. Flowers. Multicoloured.

985	18c. Type **249**	10	10
986	50c. *Hibiscus rosa sinensis*	20	15
987	$1 *Thunbergia grandiflora*	30	25
988	$3 *Nerium oleander*	80	1·10
MS989	115×90 mm. $2 *Lagerstroemia speciosa*	75	1·00

250 Birds in Flight

1979. 30th Anniv of Declaration of Human Rights. Multicoloured.

990	15c. Type **250**	10	10
991	$2 Bird in Flight	55	65

251 Children
playing Cricket

1979. Int Year of the Child (1st issue). Multicoloured.

992	18c. Type **251**	1·50	1·00
993	22c. Children playing baseball	40	30
994	$5 Children playing in a tree	3·25	7·00
MS995	114×92 mm. $4 Children with model spaceship	1·25	2·25

See also Nos. 1006/7 and 1025/34.

252 *Around the World in 80
Days*

1979. 150th Birth Anniv of Jules Verne. Multicoloured.

996	18c. Type **252**	35	20
997	35c. *20,000 Leagues under the Sea*	50	20
998	75c. *From the Earth to the Moon*	60	50
999	$3 *Master of the World*	1·40	2·00
MS1000	110×85 mm. $4 *Clipper of the Clouds*	1·25	1·25

253 Mail Runner, Africa
(early 19th-century)

1979. Death Cent of Sir Rowland Hill. Multicoloured.

1001	20c. Type **253**	10	10
1002	40c. Pony Express, America (mid 19th-century)	10	10
1003	$1 Pigeon post	15	25
1004	$3 Mail coach, Europe (18–19th century)	40	80
MS1005	127×100 mm. $5 Sir Rowland Hill and 1891 1d. on 8d.×4	75	1·10

254 "The Pistol of
Peace" (vaccination
gun), Map of
Grenada and
Children

1979. International Year of the Child (2nd issue). "Grenada—First Nation 100% Immunized".

| 1006 | **254** | 5c. multicoloured | 25 | 75 |
| 1007 | **254** | $1 multicoloured | 75 | 2·50 |

255 Reef Shark

1979. Marine Wildlife. Multicoloured.

1008	40c. Type **255**	40	30
1009	45c. Spotted eagle ray	40	30
1010	50c. Many-toothed conger	45	40
1011	60c. Golden olive (shell)	70	85
1012	70c. West Indian murex (shell)	85	1·00
1013	75c. Giant tun (shell)	90	1·10
1014	90c. Brown booby	2·25	2·25
1015	$1 Magnificent frigate bird	2·25	2·25
MS1016	109×78 mm. $2.50, Sooty tern	2·50	2·00

256 The Flight into Egypt

1979. Christmas. Tapestries. Multicoloured.

1017	6c. Type **256**	10	10
1018	25c. The Flight into Egypt (detail)	10	10
1019	30c. Angel (vert)	10	10
1020	40c. (Doge Marino Grimani) (detail) (vert)	10	10
1021	90c. The Annunciation to the Shepherds (vert)	15	15
1022	$1 The Flight into Egypt (Rome) (vert)	15	15
1023	$2 The Virgin in Glory (vert)	25	40
MS1024	111×148 mm. $4 Doge Marino Grimani (vert)	70	1·00

257 Mickey Mouse playing Baseball

1979. International Year of the Child (3rd issue). Disney cartoon characters. Multicoloured.

1025	½c. Type **257**	10	10
1026	1c. Donald Duck high-jumping	10	10
1027	2c. Goofy playing basketbal	10	10
1028	3c. Goofy hurdling	10	10
1029	4c. Donald Duck playing golf	10	10
1030	5c. Mickey Mouse playing cricket	10	10
1031	10c. Mickey Mouse playing football	10	10
1032	$2 Mickey Mouse playing tennis	1·50	3·50
1033	$2.50 Minnie Mouse riding horse	1·50	3·50
MS1034	125×100 mm. $3 Goofy in riding gear	1·50	1·50

258 Paul Harris (founder)

1980. 75th Anniv of Rotary International. Multicoloured.

1035	6c. Type **258**	10	10
1036	30c. "Health"	10	15
1037	90c. "Hunger"	15	30
1038	$2 "Humanity"	40	80
MS1039	104×89 mm. $4 Rotary International emblem	1·00	1·60

1980. First Anniv of Revolution (1st issue). Nos. 651/2, 654/7, 659/60 and 662/8 optd **PEOPLE'S REVOLUTION 13 MARCH 1979.**

1040	2c. Carenage taxi	10	65
1041	3c. Large working boats	10	65
1042	6c. Cocoa beans in drying trays	15	20
1043	8c. Nutmegs	15	10
1044	10c. Rum distillery, River Antoine Estate, c. 1785	15	10
1045	12c. Cocoa tree	15	10
1046	20c. Parliament Building	20	15
1047	25c. Fort George cannons	50	30
1048	50c. General Post Office	45	30
1049	75c. Carib's Leap, Sauteurs Bay	70	60
1050	$1 Carenage, St. George's	80	80
1051	$2 St. George's Harbour by night	1·50	2·25
1052	$3 Grand Anse Beach	1·75	3·50
1053	$5 Canoe Bay and Black Bay	2·25	6·00
1054	$10 Sugar-loaf Island	3·50	9·00

See also Nos. 1069/72.

260 Boxing

1980. Olympic Games, Moscow. Multicoloured.

1055	25c. Type **260**	10	10
1056	40c. Cycling	15	15
1057	90c. Show-jumping	20	30
1058	$2 Running	40	1·00
MS1059	128×95 mm. $4 Sailing	1·00	1·40

261 Tropical Kingbird

1980. Wild Birds. Multicoloured.

1060	20c. Type **261**	85	20
1061	40c. Rufous-breasted hermit	1·25	25
1062	$1 Troupial	1·75	1·75
1063	$2 Ruddy quail dove	2·25	4·00
MS1064	85×114 mm. $3 Prarie warbler	3·75	1·75

1980. "London 1980" International Stamp Exhibition. Nos. 1001/4 optd **LONDON 1980.**

1065	20c. Type **253**	15	15
1066	40c. Pony Express, America	20	15
1067	$1 Pigeon post	30	30
1068	$3 Mail coach, Europe	85	90

263 Free Hot Lunch at Schools

1980. First Anniv of Revolution (2nd issue). Multicoloured.

1069	10c. Type **263**	10	10
1070	40c. "From tree to can" (agro-industry)	15	15
1071	$1 National Health care	30	30
1072	$2 New housing projects	50	70
MS1073	110×85 mm. $5 Prime Minister Maurice Bishop (vert)	75	85

264 Jamb Statues, West Portal, Chartres Cathedral

1980. Famous Works of Art. Multicoloured.

1074	8c. Type **264**	10	10
1075	10c. Les Demoiselles d' Avignon (painting, Picasso)	10	10
1076	40c. Winged Victory of Samothrace (statue)	15	15
1077	50c. The Night Watch (painting, Rembrandt)	15	15
1078	$1 Portrait of Edward VI as a Child (painting, Holbein the Younger)	25	25
1079	$3 Portrait head of Queen Nefertiti (carving)	70	70
MS1080	101×101 mm. $4 Weier Haws (detail of painting by Durer) (vert)	75	75

265 Carib Canoes

1980. Shipping. Multicoloured.

1081A	½c. Type **265**	10	40
1082A	1c. Boat building	10	40
1083A	2c. Small working boat	15	40
1084A	4c. Columbus's Santa Maria	40	40
1085A	5c. West Indiaman barque, c. 1840	40	30
1086A	6c. Orinoco (paddle-steamer), c. 1851	40	40
1087A	10c. Working schooner	50	10
1088A	12c. Trimaran at Grand Anse anchorage	1·00	55
1089A	15c. Spice Island cruising yacht "Petite Amie"	50	10
1090A	20c. Fishing pirogue	1·00	20
1091A	25c. Harbour police launch	2·00	50
1092A	30c. Grand Anse speedboat	1·50	30
1093A	40c. Seimstrand (freighter)	2·00	35
1094B	50c. Ariadne (cadet schooner)	50	50
1095A	90c. Geestide (freighter)	1·75	50
1096A	$1 Cunard Countess (liner)	3·00	80
1097A	$3 Rum-runner	2·50	4·25
1098A	$5 Statendam (liner) off St. George's	3·50	7·50
1099B	$10 Coastguard patrol boat	4·25	8·50

Nos. 1081/99 come with and without date imprint.

1980. Christmas. Scenes from Walt Disney's Snow White and the Seven Dwarfs. As T **257**. Multicoloured.

1100	½c. Snow White at well	10	10
1101	1c. The Wicked Queen	10	10
1102	2c. Snow White singing to animals	10	10
1103	3c. Snow White doing housework for Dwarfs	10	10
1104	4c. The Seven Dwarfs	10	10
1105	5c. Snow White with Dwarfs	10	10
1106	10c. Witch offering Snow White apple	10	10
1107	$2.50 Snow White with Prince and Dwarfs	3·25	1·75
1108	$3 Snow White and Prince	3·75	2·00
MS1109	127×102 mm. $4 Snow White sleeping (vert)	4·25	1·50

1981. 50th Anniv of Walt Disney's Pluto (cartoon character). As T **257**. Multicoloured.

| 1110 | $2 Pluto with birthday cake | 1·00 | 1·00 |
| **MS**1111 | 127×102 mm. $4 Pluto in scene from film "Pueblo Pluto" | 1·25 | 1·00 |

266 Revolution and Grenada Flags

1981. Festival of the Revolution. Multicoloured.

1112	5c. Type **266**	40	10
1113	10c. Teacher, pupil, book and pencil ("education")	15	10
1114	15c. Food processing plant ("industry")	15	10
1115	25c. Selection of fruits and farm scene ("agriculture")	20	10
1116	40c. Crawfish and boat ("fishing")	35	15
1117	90c. "Cunard Countess" arriving at St. George's Harbour ("shipping")	1·00	30
1118	$1 Straw-work ("native handi-crafts")	75	40
1119	$3 Map of Caribbean with expanded view of Grenada	2·50	1·75

1981. Easter. Walt Disney cartoon characters. As T **257**. Multicoloured.

1120	35c. Mickey Mouse and Goofy	30	15
1121	40c. Donald Duck, Chip and Daisy Duck	30	15
1122	$2 Minnie Mouse	75	1·00
1123	$2.50 Pluto and Mickey Mouse	75	1·10
MS1124	127×101 mm. $4 Goofy	1·75	1·50

267 Woman-Flower

1981. Birth Centenary of Picasso. Multicoloured.

1125	25c. Type **267**	15	10
1126	30c. Portrait of Madame	15	10
1127	90c. Cavalier with Pipe	25	30
1128	$4 Large Heads	70	1·00
MS1129	128×103 mm. $5 Woman on the Banks of the Seine (after Courbet). Imperf	2·00	1·40

268 Prince Charles playing Polo

1981. Royal Wedding (1st issue). Multicoloured.

1130	50c. As 30c.	10	10
1131	$2 As 40c.	35	50
1132	$4 Type **268**	50	75
MS1133	98×94 mm. $5 Glass Coach	75	75
1134	30c. Prince Charles and Lady Diana Spencer	20	20
1135	40c. Holyrood House	30	30

269 Lady Diana Spencer

1981. Royal Wedding (2nd issue). Multicoloured. Self-adhesive.

1136	$1 Type **269**	30	65
1137	$2 Prince Charles	30	65
1138	$5 Prince Charles and Lady Diana Spencer	1·00	1·75

270 The Bath (Mary Cassatt)

1981. "Decade for Women". Paintings. Multicoloured.

1139	15c. Type **270**	10	10
1140	40c. Mademoiselle Charlotte du Val d'Ognes (Constance Marie Charpentier)	20	10
1141	60c. Self-portrait (Mary Beale)	30	20
1142	$3 Woman in White Stockings (Suzanne Valadon)	1·25	1·00
MS1143	101×77 mm. $5 The Artist hesitating between the Arts of Music and Painting (Angelica Kauffman) (horiz)	1·75	2·00

1981. Christmas. As T **257** showing scenes from Walt Disney's cartoon film Cinderella.

1144	½c. multicoloured	10	10
1145	1c. multicoloured	10	10
1146	2c. multicoloured	10	10
1147	3c. multicoloured	10	10
1148	4c. multicoloured	10	10
1149	5c. multicoloured	10	10
1150	10c. multicoloured	15	10
1151	$2.50 multicoloured	3·50	2·50
1152	$3 multicoloured	3·50	2·75
MS1153	127×103 mm. $5 multicoloured	5·50	3·25

271 Landing

1981. Space Shuttle Project. Multicoloured.

1154	30c. Type **271**	20	15
1155	60c. Working in space	40	30
1156	70c. Lift off	45	35
1157	$3 Separation	1·10	1·25
MS1158	117×89 mm. $5 In orbit	1·75	1·25

272 West German Footballer and Flag

1981. World Cup Football Championship, Spain (1982). Multicoloured.

1159	25c.+10c. Type **272**	55	30
1160	40c.+20c. Argentinian footballer and flag	65	40
1161	50c.+25c. Brazilian footballer and flag	70	50
1162	$1+50c. English footballer and flag	95	95
MS1163	141×128 mm. $5+50c. Spanish orange mascot and Jules Rimet Trophy (vert)	2·75	2·00

273 General Post Office, St. George's

1981. Cent of U.P.U. Membership. Multicoloured.

1164	25c. Type **273**	20	15
1165	30c. 1861 1d. stamp	30	20
1166	90c. New U.P.U. Headquarters Building 25c. commemorative	70	50
1167	$4 1961 Stamp Centenary 25c. commemorative	1·25	2·25
MS1168	137×87 mm. $5 1974 Centenary of U.P.U. ½c. commemorative	3·25	4·00

274 Artist without Hands

1982. International Year for the Disabled (1981). Multicoloured.

1169	30c. Type **274**	20	10
1170	40c. Computer operator without hands	20	10
1171	70c. Blind schoolteacher teaching braille	50	15
1172	$3 Midget playing drums	1·10	80
MS1173	101×72 mm. $4 Auto mechanic confined to wheelchair	3·25	3·25

275 Tending Vegetable Patch

1982. 75th Anniv of Boy Scout Movement and 125th Birth Anniv of Lord Baden-Powell. Multicoloured.

1174	70c. Type **275**	50	45
1175	90c. Map-reading	55	55
1176	$1 Bee-keeping	65	65
1177	$4 Hospital reading	1·75	2·75
MS1178	100×71 mm. $5 Presentation of trophies	1·25	1·25

276 *Dryas julia*

1982. Butterflies. Multicoloured.

1179	10c. Type **276**	75	30
1180	60c. *Phoebis agarithe*	2·00	1·50
1181	$1 *Anartia amathea*	2·50	2·00
1182	$3 *Battus polydamas*	3·75	7·00
MS1183	111×85 mm. $5 *Junonia evarete*	6·00	2·25

277 *Saying Grace*

1982. Norman Rockwell (painter) Commemoration. Multicoloured.

1184	15c. Type **277**	40	10
1185	30c. "Nothing Up His Sleeve" (inscr "Card Tricks")	65	15
1186	60c. *Pharmacist*	85	25
1187	70c. *Hobo* (inscr "Pals")	90	35

278 Kensington Palace

1982. 21st Birthday of Princess of Wales. Multicoloured.

1188	50c. Type **278**	90	1·00
1189	60c. Type **278**	1·50	50
1190	$1 Prince and Princess of Wales	1·50	1·75
1191	$2 As $1	2·75	1·50
1192	$3 Princess of Wales	2·75	2·75
1193	$4 As $3	3·00	2·50
MS1194	103×75 mm. $5 Princess Diana (different)	3·00	1·50

279 Mary McLeod Bethune appointed Director of Negro Affairs, 1942

1982. Birth Centenary of Franklin D. Roosevelt. Multicoloured.

1195	10c. Type **279**	10	10
1196	60c. Huddie Ledbetter "Leadbelly" in concert (Works Progress administration)	30	20
1197	$1.10 Signing bill No. 8802, 1941 (Fair Employment committee)	40	25
1198	$3 Farm Security administration	55	60
MS1199	100×70 mm. $5 William Hastie, first Negro Judicial appointee	1·25	1·25

1982. Birth of Prince William of Wales. Nos. 1188/93 optd **ROYAL BABY 21.6.82**.

1200	50c. Type **278**	60	1·00
1201	60c. Type **278**	35	35
1202	$1 Prince and Princess of Wales	1·00	1·25
1203	$2 As $1	1·00	1·00
1204	$3 Princess of Wales	1·90	2·25
1205	$4 As $3	1·90	1·90
MS1206	103×75 mm. $5 Princess Diana (different)	2·00	1·25

280 Apostle and Tormentor

1982. Easter. Details from Painting *The Way to Calvary* by Raphael. Multicoloured.

1207	40c. Type **280**	25	10
1208	70c. Captain of the guards (vert)	30	15
1209	$1.10 Christ and apostle (vert)	35	25
1210	$4 Mourners (vert)	70	1·25
MS1211	102×126 mm. $5 Christ falls beneath the cross (vert)	1·50	1·50

281 *Orient Express*

1982. Famous Trains of the World. Multicoloured.

1212	30c. Type **281**	50	35
1213	60c. *Trans-Siberian Express*	60	70
1214	70c. *Fleche d'Or*	70	80
1215	90c. *Flying Scotsman*	85	1·00

1216	$1 German Federal Railways steam locomotive	1·00	1·25
1217	$3 German National Railways Class 05 steam locomotive	2·25	4·00
MS1218	109×81 mm. $5 *20th Century Limited*	2·00	2·00

282 Footballers

1982. World Cup Football Championship Winners.

1219	**282** 60c. multicoloured	35	35
1220	**282** $4 multicoloured	2·00	2·00
MS1221	93×119 mm. $5 multicoloured	2·50	2·25

1982. Christmas. Scenes from Walt Disney's cartoon film *Robin Hood*. As T **257**, but horiz.

1222	½c. multicoloured	10	10
1223	1c. multicoloured	10	10
1224	2c. multicoloured	10	10
1225	3c. multicoloured	10	10
1226	4c. multicoloured	10	10
1227	5c. multicoloured	10	10
1228	10c. multicoloured	10	10
1229	$2.50 multicoloured	3·00	3·50
1230	$3 multicoloured	3·00	3·50
MS1231	121×96 mm. $5 multicoloured	6·50	4·00

283 Killer Whale

1983. Save the Whales. Multicoloured.

1232	15c. Type **283**	1·00	30
1233	40c. Sperm whale	2·25	90
1234	70c. Blue whale	2·75	2·75
1235	$3 Common dolphin	3·50	6·50
MS1236	84×74 mm. $5 Humpback whales	6·50	4·00

284 *Construction of Ark*

1983. 500th Birth Anniv of Raphael. Multicoloured.

1237	25c. Type **284**	20	10
1238	30c. *Jacob's Vision*	20	10
1239	90c. *Joseph interprets the Dreams of his Brothers*	30	30
1240	$4 *Joseph interprets Pharaoh's dreams*	1·10	1·40
MS1241	128×100 mm. $5 *Creation of the Animals*	1·25	1·75

285 Dentistry at Health Centre

1983. Commonwealth Day. Multicoloured.

1242	10c. Type **285**	10	10
1243	70c. Airport runway construction	35	35
1244	$1.10 Tourism	40	55
1245	$3 Boat-building	80	1·40

286 Maritime Communications via Satellite

1983. World Communications Year. Multicoloured.

1246	30c. Type **286**	15	15
1247	40c. Rural telephone installation	20	15
1248	60c. Satellite weather map	60	1·00
1249	$4 Airport control room	60	1·10
MS1250	111×85 mm. $5 Communications satellite	1·25	1·25

287 Franklin Sport Sedan, 1928

1983. 75th Anniv of Model "T" Ford Car. Multicoloured.

1251	6c. Type **287**	15	20
1252	10c. Delage "D8", 1933	20	10
1253	40c. Alvis, 1938	35	25
1254	60c. Invicta "S-type" tourer, 1931	45	45
1255	70c. Alfa-Romeo "1750 Gran Sport", 1930	55	55
1256	90c. Isotta Fraschini, 1930	60	75
1257	$1 Bugatti "Royale Type 41"	70	75
1258	$2 BMW "328", 1938	1·10	1·75
1259	$3 Marmon "V16", 1931	1·25	2·50
1260	$4 Lincoln "K8" saloon, 1932	1·40	3·00
MS1261	114×90 mm. $5 Cougar "TR 7", 1972	1·50	2·00

288 Airship N.1 *Norge*

1983. Bicentenary of Manned Flight. Multicoloured.

1262	30c. Type **288**	60	30
1263	60c. Gloster VI seaplane	1·00	1·00
1264	$1.10 Curtiss NC-4 flying boat	3·50	4·50
1265	$4 Dornier Do 18 flying boat *Aeolus*	1·60	1·75
MS1266	114×85 mm. $5 Modern hot-air balloon (vert)	1·50	1·50

289 Morty

1983. Christmas. Multicoloured.

1267	½c. Type **289**	10	10
1268	1c. Ludwig von Drake	10	10
1269	2c. Gyro Gearloose	10	10
1270	3c. Pluto and Figaro	10	10
1271	4c. Morty and Ferdie	10	10
1272	5c. Mickey Mouse and Goofy	10	10
1273	10c. Chip n'Dale	10	10
1274	$2.50 Mickey and Minnie Mouse	2·25	3·50
1275	$3 Donald and Grandma Duck	2·25	3·50
MS1276	127×102 mm. $5 Goofy with Christmas tree	4·50	4·50

Nos. 1267/75 show Disney cartoon characters in scenes from *It's beginning to look a lot like Christmas* (song).

290 Daisy Duck on Pommel Horse

1984. Olympic Games. Los Angeles. Multicoloured. A. Inscr "1984 LOS ANGELES".

1277A	½c. Type **290**	10	10
1278A	1c. Mickey Mouse boxing	10	10
1279A	2c. Daisy Duck in archery event	10	10
1280A	3c. Clarabelle Cow on uneven bars	10	10
1281A	4c. Mickey and Minnie Mouse in hurdles race	10	10
1282A	5c. Donald Duck with Chip'n'Dale weightlifting	10	10
1283A	$1 Little Hiawatha in single kayak	2·50	2·25
1284A	$2 The Tortoise and the Hare in marathon	3·00	3·75
1285A	$3 Mickey Mouse polevaulting	3·50	4·00
MS1286A	127×101 mm. $5 Donald Duck in medley relay (vert)	5·50	3·50

B. Inscr "1984 OLYMPICS LOS ANGELES" and Olympic Emblem.

1227B	½c. Type **290**	10	10
1278B	1c. Mickey Mouse boxing	10	10
1279B	2c. Daisy Duck in archery event	10	10
1280B	3c. Clarabelle Cow on uneven bars	10	10

1281B	4c. Mickey and Minnie Mouse in hurdles race	10	10
1282B	5c. Donald Duck with Chip'n'Dale weightlifting	10	10
1283B	$1 Little Hiawatha in single kayak	2·50	2·25
1284B	$2 The Tortoise and the Hare in marathon	3·00	3·75
1285B	$3 Mickey Mouse polevaulting	3·50	4·00
MS1286B	127×100 mm. $5 Donald Duck in medley relay (vert)	6·50	5·50

291 William I

1984. English Monarchs. Multicoloured.

1287	$4 Type **291**	1·75	2·50
1288	$4 William II	1·75	2·50
1289	$4 Henry I	1·75	2·50
1290	$4 Stephen	1·75	2·50
1291	$4 Henry II	1·75	2·50
1292	$4 Richard I	1·75	2·50
1293	$4 John	1·75	2·50
1294	$4 "Henry III"	1·75	2·50
1295	$4 Edward I	1·75	2·50
1296	$4 Edward II	1·75	2·50
1297	$4 Edward III	1·75	2·50
1298	$4 Richard II	1·75	2·50
1299	$4 Henry IV	1·75	2·50
1300	$4 Henry V	1·75	2·50
1301	$4 Henry VI	1·75	2·50
1302	$4 Edward IV	1·75	2·50
1303	$4 Edward V	1·75	2·50
1304	$4 Richard III	1·75	2·50
1305	$4 Henry VII	1·75	2·50
1306	$4 Henry VIII	1·75	2·50
1307	$4 Edward VI	1·75	2·50
1308	$4 Jane Grey	1·75	2·50
1309	$4 Mary I	1·75	2·50
1310	$4 Elizabeth I	1·75	2·50
1311	$4 James I	1·75	2·50
1312	$4 Charles I	1·75	2·50
1313	$4 Charles II	1·75	2·50
1314	$4 James II	1·75	2·50
1315	$4 William III	1·75	2·50
1316	$4 Mary II	1·75	2·50
1317	$4 Anne	1·75	2·50
1318	$4 George I	1·75	2·50
1319	$4 George II	1·75	2·50
1320	$4 George III	1·75	2·50
1321	$4 George IV	1·75	2·50
1322	$4 William IV	1·75	2·50
1323	$4 Victoria	1·75	2·50
1324	$4 Edward VII	1·75	2·50
1325	$4 George V	1·75	2·50
1326	$4 Edward VIII	1·75	2·50
1327	$4 George VI	1·75	2·50
1328	$4 Elizabeth II	1·75	2·50

Although inscribed "Henry III" the portrait on No. 1294 is actually of Edward II.

292 Lantana

1984. Flowers. Multicoloured.

1329	25c. Type **292**	20	15
1330	30c. Plumbago	25	15
1331	90c. Spider lily	60	35
1332	$4 Giant alocasia	1·50	2·75
MS1333	108×90 mm. $5 Orange trumpet vine	1·00	1·50

293 Blue Parrotfish

1984. Coral Reef Fishes. Multicoloured.

1334	10c. Type **293**	1·40	45
1335	30c. Flame-backed angelfish	2·75	1·10
1336	70c. Painted wrasse	4·00	3·25
1337	90c. Rosy razorfish	4·75	3·50
MS1338	81×85 mm. $5 Spanish hogfish	6·50	4·75

1984. Universal Postal Union Congress, Hamburg. Nos. 1331/2 optd **19TH U.P.U CONGRESS HAMBURG.**

1339	90c. Spider lily	60	65

1340	$4 Giant alocasia	2·00	2·50
MS1341	108×90 mm. $5 Orange trumpet vine	1·50	2·50

295 Freighter

1984. Ships. Multicoloured.

1342	40c. Type **295**	1·25	55
1343	70c. Queen Elizabeth 2	1·50	1·50
1344	90c. Sailing boats	1·60	2·00
1345	$4 Amerikanis	3·50	8·00
MS1346	107×80 mm. $5 Spanish galleon	5·50	7·00

296 The Night (detail) (Correggio)

1984. 450th Death Anniv of Correggio (painter). Multicoloured.

1347	10c. Type **296**	45	15
1348	30c. The Virgin adoring the Child	80	50
1349	40c. The Mystical Marriage of St. Catherine with St. Sebastian	2·00	1·75
1350	$4 The Madonna and the Fruit Basket	4·50	5·50
MS1351	54×73 mm. $5 The Madonna at the Spring	4·25	3·00

297 L'Absinthe (Degas)

1984. 150th Birth Anniv of Edgar Degas (painter). Multicoloured.

1352	25c. Type **297**	80	30
1353	70c. Pouting (horiz)	1·50	1·25
1354	$1.10 The Millinery Shop	2·00	2·00
1355	$3 The Bellelli Family (horiz)	3·75	4·25
MS1356	84×54 mm. $5 The Cotton Market	4·25	3·00

298 Train on Puffing Billy Line, Victoria

1984. "Ausipex" International Stamp Exhibition, Melbourne. Multicoloured.

1357	$1.10 Type **298**	2·25	1·75
1358	$4 Yacht Australia II (winner of America's Cup)	4·00	4·75
MS1359	107×76 mm. $5 Melbourne tram	4·25	4·00

299 George Stephenson's Locomotion (1825)

1984. Railway Locomotives. Multicoloured.

1360	30c. Type **299**	80	35
1361	40c. Braithwaite and Ericsson's Novelty (1829)	95	40
1362	60c. William Norris's Washington Farmer (1836)	1·00	75
1363	70c. French Crampton type (1859)	1·00	1·00
1364	90c. Dutch State Railways (1873)	1·10	1·50
1365	$1.10 Champion, U.S.A. (1882)	1·10	2·00
1366	$2 Webb Compound type (1893)	1·40	3·25
1367	$4 Berlin No. 74 (1900)	2·00	5·50

MS1368	Two sheets, each 100×70 mm. (a) $5 Crampton Phoenix (1863); (b) $5 Mikado type, Japan (1897) Set of 2 sheets	6·00	6·50

1984. Opening of Point Saline International Airport (1st issue). Nos. 1247 and 1249 optd **OPENING OF POINT SALINE INT'L AIRPORT.**

1369	40c. Rural telephone installation	30	30
1370	$3 Airport control room	2·00	2·00
MS1371	111×85 mm. $5 Communications satellite	3·50	3·25

See also Nos. 1399/6.

301 Donald Duck as Father Christmas looking into Mirror

1984. Christmas. Walt Disney cartoon characters. Multicoloured.

1372	45c. Type **301**	1·25	40
1373	60c. Donald Duck filling stocking with presents	1·50	55
1374	90c. As Father Christmas pulling a sleigh	2·00	1·10
1375	$2 As Father Christmas decorating Christmas tree	3·50	3·50
1376	$4 Donald Duck and nephews singing carols	5·00	5·50
MS1377	127×102 mm. $5 Father Christmas in sleigh	7·00	8·00

1985. Birth Bicentenary of John J. Audubon (ornithologist) (1st issue). As T **418** of Ghana. Multicoloured.

1378	50c. Clapper rail (vert)	2·00	75
1379	70c. Hooded warbler (vert)	2·25	1·50
1380	90c. Common flicker (vert)	2·75	1·75
1381	$4 Bohemian waxwing (vert)	5·50	8·00
MS1382	82×112 mm. $5 Merlin ("Pigeon Hawk")	9·00	4·50

See also Nos. 1480/4.

302 Honda "XL500R"

1985. Centenary of the Motor Cycle. Multicoloured.

1383	25c. Type **302**	1·00	50
1384	50c. Suzuki "GS1100ES"	1·50	1·00
1385	90c. Kawasaki "KZ700"	2·00	2·25
1386	$4 BMW "K100"	6·00	6·50
MS1387	109×81 mm. $5 Yamaha "500CC V Four"	7·50	5·00

303 "Explorer"

1985. 75th Anniv of Girl Guide Movement. Designs showing work for Guide badges. Multicoloured.

1388	25c. Type **303**	55	30
1389	60c. "Cook"	90	65
1390	90c. "Musician"	1·50	1·10
1391	$3 "Home nurse"	3·00	4·50
MS1392	97×70 mm. $5 Flags of Girl Guides and Grenada	2·50	2·50

304 Hawker Siddeley H.S.748 on Inaugural Flight from Barbados

1985. Opening of Point Saline International Airport (1984) (2nd issue). Multicoloured.

1393	70c. Type **304**	2·50	1·00
1394	$1 Lockheed TriStar 500 on inaugural flight from New York	3·25	1·50
1395	$4 Lockheed TriStar 500 on inaugural flight to Miami	6·50	8·00
MS1396	101×72 mm. $5 Point Saline Airport terminal and Hawker Siddeley H.S.748 on tarmac	7·00	3·75

305 Douglas DC-8-61

1985. 40th Anniv of International Civil Aviation Organization. Multicoloured.

1397	10c. Type **305**	40	20
1398	50c. Lockheed Starliner (inscr "Super Constellation")	1·00	75
1399	60c. Vickers 952 Cargoliner	1·25	85
1400	$4 De Havilland Twin Otter 200/300	4·50	6·00
MS1401	102×64 mm. $5 Hawker Siddeley H.S.748 turboprop	3·00	3·00

306 Model Boat Racing

1985. Water Sports. Multicoloured.

1402	10c. Type **306**	25	10
1403	50c. Scuba diving, Carriacou	55	35
1404	$1.10 Windsurfers on Grand Anse Beach	85	1·25
1405	$4 Windsurfing	1·50	6·00
MS1406	107×77 mm. $5 Beach scene	2·25	2·75

307 Bird of Paradise (flower)

1985. Native Flowers. Multicoloured.

1407	½c. Type **307**	50	60
1408	1c. Passion flower	50	60
1409	2c. Oleander	50	60
1410a	4c. Bromeliad	1·00	60
1411a	5c. Anthurium	1·00	40
1412a	6c. Bougainvillea	1·00	50
1413a	10c. Hibiscus	1·00	30
1414a	15c. Ginger	1·75	30
1415a	25c. Poinsettia	1·75	30
1417a	40c. Angel's trumpet	1·75	50
1420a	70c. Chenille plant	2·00	1·50
1420b	75c. Cordia	2·00	2·00
1422a	$1.10 Ixora	3·25	2·75
1423a	$3 Shrimp plant	4·50	6·50
1424a	$5 Plumbago	4·50	7·00
1425a	$10 Lantana camara	5·00	10·00
1425b	$20 Peregrina	8·50	16·00
1425d	30c. Mexican creeper	30	60
1425e	50c. Amaryllis	40	1·00
1425f	60c. Prickly pear	50	1·50
1425g	$1 Periwinkle	50	1·50

308 The Queen Mother at Royal Opera House, London

1985. Life and Times of Queen Elizabeth the Queen Mother. Multicoloured.

1426	$1 Type **308**	40	60
1427	$1.50 The Queen Mother playing snooker at London Press Club (horiz)	55	85
1428	$2.50 At Epsom Races, 1960	95	1·50
MS1429	56×85 mm. $5 With Prince of Wales on 80th Birthday	1·75	3·00

Stamps as Nos. 1426/8 but with face values of 90c., $1 and $3 exist from additional sheetlets with changed background colours.

309 Youth Gardening (Horticulture)

1985. International Youth Year. Multicoloured.

1430	25c. Type **309**	25	20
1431	50c. Young people on beach (Leisure)	35	40
1432	$1.10 Girls in classroom (Education)	60	1·10
1433	$3 Nurse and young patient (Health Care)	1·50	2·50
MS1434 111×80 mm. $5 Children of different races		1·50	3·00

309a Crumhorn

1985. 300th Birth Anniv of Johann Sebastian Bach (composer).

1435	**309a** 25c. multicoloured	80	20
1436	– 70c. multicoloured	1·25	85
1437	– $1 multicoloured	1·75	1·25
1438	– $3 multicoloured	2·50	5·00
MS1439 104×74 mm. $5 black, grey and cinnamon		3·50	3·75

DESIGNS: 70c. Oboe d'amore; $1 Violin; $3 Harpsichord; $5 Johann Sebastian Bach.

310 Cub Scouts Camping

1985. Fourth Caribbean Cuboree. Multicoloured.

1440	10c. Type **310**	30	15
1441	50c. Cub scouts swimming ("Physical Fitness")	65	40
1442	$1 Stamp collecting	1·50	80
1443	$4 Birdwatching	3·50	3·00
MS1444 103×75 mm. $5 Cub scouts saluting leader (vert)		3·25	3·75

310a Flags of Great Britain and Grenada

1985. Royal Visit. Multicoloured.

1445	50c. Type **310a**	1·50	60
1446	$1 Queen Elizabeth II (vert)	1·00	1·25
1447	$4 Royal Yacht Britannia	3·00	5·50
MS1448 111×85 mm. $5 Map of Grenada		1·75	3·25

1985. 150th Birth Anniv of Mark Twain (author). As T **145a** of Gambia. Design showing Walt Disney cartoon characters in scenes from *The Prince and the Pauper.* Multicoloured.

1449	25c. Mortie as Tom meeting the Prince (Ferdie)	60	20
1450	50c. Tom and the Prince exchanging clothes	80	50
1451	$1.10 The Prince with John Cantry	1·75	1·75
1452	$1.50 The Prince knights Mike Hendon (Goofy)	2·25	2·75
1453	$2 Tom and the Whipping Boy	2·50	3·00
MS1454 124×100 mm. $5 The Prince, Tom and Mike Hendon		6·00	6·00

1985. Birth Bicentenaries of Grimm Brothers (folklorists). As T **145b** of Gambia, showing Walt Disney cartoon characters in scenes from *The Fisherman and his Wife.* Multicoloured.

1455	30c. The Fisherman (Goofy) catching enchanted fish	85	30
1456	60c. The Fisherman scolded by his Wife (Clarabelle)	1·25	80
1457	70c. The Fisherman's Wife with dream cottage	1·40	95
1458	$1 The Fisherman's Wife as King	2·25	1·50
1459	$3 The Fisherman and Wife in their original shack	3·75	4·50
MS1460 126×100 mm. $5 The Fisherman in boat		6·00	6·00

311 Red-spotted Hawkfish

1985. Marine Life. Multicoloured.

1461	25c. Type **311**	1·50	55
1462	50c. Spot-finned butterflyfish	2·25	1·10
1463	$1.10 Fire coral and orange sponges	3·75	3·25
1464	$3 Pillar coral	6·00	7·50
MS1465 127×100 mm. $5 Bigeye		3·75	4·50

311a Mary McLeod Bethune (educationist) and 1975 International Women's Year 10c.

1985. 40th Anniv of U.N.O. Designs showing United Nations (New York) stamps. Mult.

1466	50c. Type **311a**	30	30
1467	$2 Maimonides (physician) and 1966 W.H.O. 5c.	2·50	3·50
1468	$2.50 Alexander Graham Bell (telephone inventor) and 1956 I.T.U. 3c.	2·00	4·00
MS1469 110×85 mm. $5 Dag Hammarskjold (Secretary-General) (vert)		1·25	2·00

312 *Adoration of the Shepherds* (Mantegna)

1985. Christmas. Religious Paintings. Multicoloured.

1470	25c. Type **312**	20	15
1471	60c. *Journey of the Magi* (Sassetta)	30	40
1472	90c. *Madonna and Child enthroned with Saints* (Raphael)	35	70
1473	$4 *Nativity* (Monaco)	1·00	4·25
MS1474 107×81 mm. $5 *Madonna and Child enthroned with Saints* (Gaddi)		1·50	2·50

312a Columbus Monument, 1893

1986. Centenary of Statue of Liberty (1st issue). Multicoloured.

1475	5c. Type **312a**	15	20
1476	25c. Columbus Monument, 1986	30	30
1477	40c. Mounted police, Central Park, 1895 (horiz)	1·75	1·10
1478	40c. Mounted police, 1986 (horiz)	5·00	8·00
MS1479 104×76 mm. $5 Statue of Liberty (vert)		3·25	2·75

See also Nos. 1644/52.

312b Snowy Egret

1986. Birth Bicentenary of John J. Audubon (ornithologist) (2nd issue). Multicoloured.

1480	50c. Type **312b**	2·00	80
1481	90c. Greater flamingo	2·75	2·00
1482	$1.10 Canada goose	2·75	2·50
1483	$3 Smew	4·50	6·00
MS1484 103×72 mm. $5 Brent goose (horiz)		13·00	13·00

1986. Visit of President Reagan. Nos. 1418 and 1424 optd **VISIT OF PRES REAGAN 20 FEB. 1986.**

1485	50c. Amaryllis	50	50
1486	$5 Plumbago	3·00	5·00

314 Methodist Church, St. George's

1986. Bicentenary of Methodist Church in Grenada. Multicoloured.

1487	60c. Type **314**	70	1·00
MS1488 102×73 mm. $5 St. Georges		1·00	3·00

315 Player with Ball

1986. World Cup Football Championship, Mexico. Multicoloured.

1489	50c. Type **315**	60	55
1490	70c. Player heading ball	80	80
1491	90c. Player controlling ball	1·00	90
1492	$4 Player controlling ball with right foot	4·00	6·00
MS1493 103×71 mm. $5 Player tackling		3·75	5·00

1986. Appearance of Halley's Comet (1st issue). As T **151a** of Gambia. Multicoloured.

1494	5c. Clyde Tombaugh (astronomer) and Dudley Observatory, New York	40	40
1495	20c. N.A.S.A. – U.S.A.F. "X-24B" Space Shuttle prototype, 1973	50	30
1496	40c. German comet medal, 1618	70	45
1497	$4 Destruction of Sodom and Gomorrah, 1949 B.C.	3·50	4·50
MS1498 102×70 mm. $5 Halley's Comet over Grenada		6·50	7·00

See also Nos. 1533/7 and 1980/4.

1986. 60th Birthday of Queen Elizabeth II. As T **151b** of Gambia.

1499	2c. black and yellow	10	15
1500	$1.50 multicoloured	80	80
1501	$4 multicoloured	1·60	2·50
MS1502 120×85 mm. $5 black and brown		1·75	3·25

DESIGNS: 2c. Princess Elizabeth in 1951; $1.50, Queen presenting trophy at polo match, Windsor, 1965; $4 at Epsom, Derby Day, 1977; $5 King George VI and family, 1939.

315a Goofy as Pitcher

1986. "Ameripex" International Stamp Exhibition, Chicago. Designs showing Walt Disney cartoon characters playing baseball. Multicoloured.

1503	1c. Type **315a**	10	10
1504	2c. Goofy as catcher	10	10
1505	3c. Mickey Mouse striking ball and Donald Duck as catcher	10	10
1506	4c. Huey forcing out Dewey	10	10
1507	5c. Chip n'Dale chasing flyball	10	10
1508	6c. Mickey Mouse, Donald Duck and Clarabelle in argument	10	10
1509	$2 Minnie Mouse and Donald Duck reading baseball rules	1·75	2·75
1510	$3 Ludwig von Drake as umpire with Goofy and Pete colliding	2·25	3·25
MS1511 Two sheets, each 126×101 mm. (a) $5 Donald Duck striking ball. (b) $5 Minnie and Mickey Mouse running between bases Set of 2 sheets		11·00	13·00

1986. Royal Wedding. As T **153b** of Gambia. Multicoloured.

1512	2c. Prince Andrew and Miss Sarah Ferguson	10	30
1513	$1.10 Prince Andrew	70	80
1514	$4 Prince Andrew with H.M.S. "Brazen's" Westland Lynx helicopter	3·50	3·50
MS1515 88×88 mm. $5 Prince Andrew and Miss Sarah Ferguson (different)		4·50	5·00

316 Brown-lined Latirus

1986. Sea Shells. Multicoloured.

1516	25c. Type **316**	45	25
1517	60c. Lamellose wentletrap	75	90
1518	70c. Turkey wing	85	1·00
1519	$4 Rooster tail conch	2·00	5·00
MS1520 110×75 mm. $5 Angular triton		2·75	6·00

317 *Lepiota roseolamellata*

1986. Mushrooms. Multicoloured.

1521	10c. Type **317**	60	40
1522	60c. *Lentinus bertieri*	1·75	1·75
1523	$1 *Lentinus retinervis*	2·50	2·50
1524	$4 *Eccilia cystiophorus*	5·75	7·50
MS1525 127×100 mm. $5 *Cystolepiota eriophora*		10·00	13·00

1986. World Cup Football Championship Winners, Mexico. Nos. 1489/92 optd **WINNERS Argentina 3 W. Germany 2.**

1526	50c. Type **315**	75	60
1527	70c. Player heading ball	85	70
1528	90c. Player controlling ball	1·00	1·00
1529	$4 Player controlling ball with right foot	4·00	5·00
MS1530 101×71 mm. $5 Player tackling		3·00	4·50

318 Dove on Rifles and Mahatma Gandhi (Disarmament Week)

1986. International Events. Multicoloured.

1531	60c. Type **318**	75	50
1532	$4 Hands passing olive branch and Martin Luther King (International Peace Year) (horiz)	1·25	3·00

1986. Appearance of Halley's Comet (2nd issue). Nos. 1494/7 optd with T **447a** of Ghana.

1533	5c. Clyde Tombaugh (astronomer) and Dudley Observatory, New York	60	60
1534	20c. N.A.S.A. – U.S.A.F. "X-24B" Space Shuttle prototype, 1973	85	60
1535	40c. German comet medal, 1618	1·25	70
1536	$4 Destruction of Sodom and Gomorrah, 1949 B.C.	5·00	7·00
MS1537 102×70 mm. $5 Halley's Comet over Grenada		3·50	4·25

318a Mickey Mouse asleep in Armchair

1986. Christmas. Multicoloured.

1538	30c. Type **318a**	45	25
1539	45c. Young Mickey Mouse with Father Christmas	55	30
1540	60c. Donald Duck with toy telephone (horiz)	70	50
1541	70c. Pluto with pushcart (horiz)	80	70
1542	$1.10 Daisy Duck with doll (horiz)	1·25	1·25
1543	$2 Goofy as Father Christmas	2·00	2·25
1544	$2.50 Goofy singing carols at piano	2·25	3·00

1545	$3 Mickey Mouse, Donald Duck and nephew riding toy train (horiz)	2·50	3·50

MS1546 Two sheets, each 127×101 mm. (a) $5 Donald Duck, Goofy and Mickey Mouse delivering presents (vert). (b) $5 Father Christmas playing toy piano Set of 2 sheets ... 10·00 13·00

319 Cockerel and Hen

1986. Fauna and Flora. Multicoloured.

1547	10c. Type **319**	20	10
1548	30c. Fish-eating bat	35	20
1549	60c. Goat	55	45
1550	70c. Cow	60	50
1551	$1 Anthurium	1·50	1·25
1552	$1.10 Royal poinciana	1·50	1·25
1553	$2 Frangipani	2·50	3·25
1554	$4 Orchid	8·50	9·50

MS1555 Two sheets, each 104×73 mm. (a) $5 Grenada landscape. (b) $5 Horse Set of 2 sheets ... 12·00 13·00

320 Maserati "Biturbo" (1984)

1986. Centenary of Motoring. Multicoloured.

1556	10c. Type **320**	25	25
1557	30c. AC "Cobra" (1960)	40	40
1558	60c. Corvette (1963)	50	60
1559	70c. Dusenberg "SJ7" (1932)	60	70
1560	90c. Porsche (1957)	70	1·00
1561	$1 Stoewer (1930)	75	1·25
1562	$2 Volkswagen "Beetle" (1957)	1·25	2·00
1563	$3 Mercedes "600 Limo" (1963)	1·50	2·50

MS1564 Two sheets, each 106×77 mm. (a) $5 Stutz (1914). (b) $5 Packard (1941) Set of 2 sheets ... 5·50 7·00

321 Pole Vaulting

1986. Olympic Games, Seoul, South Korea (1988). Multicoloured.

1565	10c.+5c. Type **321**	10	40
1566	50c.+20c. Gymnastics	35	60
1567	70c.+30c. Putting the shot	50	95
1568	$2+$1 High jumping	1·50	2·50

MS1569 80×100 mm. $3+$1 Swimming ... 1·50 3·25

The premiums on Nos. 1565/9 were to support the participation of the Grenada team.

321a Painting by Chagall

1986. Birth Centenary of Marc Chagall (artist). Designs showing various paintings.

1570-1609	**321a** $1.40 × 40 multicoloured	24·00	26·00

MS1610 Ten sheets, each 110×95 mm. $5×10 multicoloured (each 104×89 mm). Imperf Set of 10 sheets ... 24·00 26·00

321b Columbia, 1958

1987. America's Cup Yachting Championship. Multicoloured.

1611	10c. Type **321b**	25	20
1612	60c. Resolute, 1920	55	60
1613	$1.10 Endeavor, 1934	75	1·25
1614	$4 Rainbow, 1934	1·25	3·50

MS1615 113×84 mm. $5 Weatherly, 1962 ... 2·25 4·00

322 Virgin Mary and Outline Map of Grenada

1987. 500th Anniv (1992) of Discovery of America by Christopher Columbus (1st issue). Multicoloured.

1616	10c. Type **322**	30	20
1617	30c. Santa Maria, Pinta and Nina (horiz)	80	35
1618	50c. Columbus and outline map of Grenada	90	45
1619	60c. Christopher Columbus	90	55
1620	90c. King Ferdinand and Queen Isabella of Spain (horiz)	90	80
1621	$1.10 Map of Antilles by Columbus	1·25	1·00
1622	$2 Caribs with sailing raft (horiz)	1·40	2·50
1623	$3 Columbus in the New World, 1493 (contemporary drawing)	1·60	2·50

MS1624 Two sheets, each 104×72 mm. (a) $5 Route map and Colombus' signature. (b) $5 Columbus carrying Christ Child Set of 2 sheets ... 5·00 7·50

See also Nos. 2051/5, 2091/9, 2222/30, 2389/95 and 2423/4.

322a Cornu's First Helicopter, 1907

1987. Milestones of Transportation. Multicoloured.

1625	10c. Type **322a**	1·50	65
1626	15c. Monitor and Merrimack (first battle between ironclad warships), 1862	1·50	65
1627	30c. LZ1 (first Zeppelin), 1900	1·60	80
1628	50c. Sirius (first transatlantic paddle-steamer crossing), 1838	1·75	85
1629	60c. Steam locomotive on Trans-Siberian Railway (longest line)	2·00	1·00
1630	70c. U.S.S Enterprise (largest aircraft carrier), 1960	2·00	1·25
1631	90c. Blanchard and Jeffries' balloon (first balloon across English Channel), 1785	2·00	1·40
1632	$1.50 U.S.S. Holland I (first steam-powered submarine), 1900	2·75	2·50
1633	$2 Oceanic I (first luxury liner), 1871	3·50	3·00
1634	$3 Lamborghini "Countach" (fastest commercial car), 1984	3·50	3·50

323 Black Grouper

1987. "Capex '87" International Stamp Exhibition, Toronto. Game Fish. Multicoloured.

1635	10c. Type **323**	45	15
1636	30c. Blue marlin (horiz)	50	15
1637	60c. White marlin (horiz)	70	55
1638	70c. Bigeye threshershark (horiz)	80	70
1639	$1 Bonefish (horiz)	1·00	1·00
1640	$1.10 Wahoo (horiz)	1·10	1·25
1641	$2 Sailfish (horiz)	1·40	2·50
1642	$4 Albacore (horiz)	2·25	3·75

MS1643 Two sheets, each 100×70 mm. (a) $5 Yellow-finned tuna. (b) $5 Great barracuda (horiz) Set of 2 sheets ... 8·00 11·00

323a Computer Projections on Statue and Base

1987. Centenary of Statue of Liberty (2nd issue). Multicoloured.

1644	10c. Type **323a**	15	15
1645	25c. Statue and fireworks	20	15
1646	50c. Statue and fireworks (different)	35	35
1647	60c. Statue and boats (vert)	45	45
1648	70c. Computer projection of top of Statue	50	50
1649	$1 Rear view of Statue and fireworks (vert)	80	80
1650	$1.10 Aerial view of Statue (vert)	95	1·25
1651	$2 Statue and flotilla (vert)	2·00	2·25
1652	$4 "Queen Elizabeth 2" in New York Harbour (vert)	3·50	4·00

324 Alice and the Rabbit Hole

1987. 50th Anniv of First Full-Length Disney Cartoon Film. Nos. 1653/1706 show scenes from various films and No. **MS**1707 depict scenes from *Alice in Wonderland*, *Cinderella*, *Peter Pan*, *Pinocchio*, *Sleeping Beauty* and *Snow White and the Seven Dwarfs*.

1653-1706	30c. x 43 multicoloured	18·00	19·00

MS1707 Six sheets, each 127×102 mm. $5×6 multicoloured Set of 6 sheets ... 30·00 30·00

325 Isaac Newton holding Apple (Law of Gravity)

1987. Great Scientific Discoveries. Multicoloured.

1708	50c. Type **325**	85	85
1709	$1.10 John Jacob Berzelius and symbols of chemical elements	1·75	1·75
1710	$2 Robert Boyle (law of Pressure and Volume)	2·50	3·25
1711	$3 James Watt and drawing of steam engine	5·50	5·00

MS1712 105×75 mm. $5 "Voyager" (experimental aircraft) and Wright glider No. IV ... 3·00 4·00

No. 1711 is inscribed "RUDOLF DIESEL" and No. MS1712 "Flyer I", both in error.

326 Wade Boggs (Boston Red Sox)

1987. All-star Baseball Game, Oakland, California. Sheet 114×82 mm, containing T **326** and similar horiz design. Multicoloured.

MS1713 $1 Type **326**; $1 Eric Davis (Cincinnati Reds) ... 1·00 1·75

1987. 60th Anniv of International Social Security Association. Nos. 1413, 1418 and 1423 optd **INTERNATIONAL SOCIAL SECURITY ASSOCIATION** and emblem.

1714	10c. Hibiscus	10	15
1715	50c. Amaryllis	25	35
1716	$3 Shrimp plant	1·40	2·50

327a Independence Hall, Philadelphia

1987. Bicentenary of U.S. Constitution. Multicoloured.

1717	15c. Type **327a**	10	10
1718	50c. Benjamin Franklin (Pennsylvania delegate) (horiz)	25	35

1719	60c. State Seal, Massachusetts (horiz)	25	35
1720	$4 Robert Morris (Pennsylvania delegate)	1·75	2·75

MS1721 105×75 mm. $5 James Madison (Virginia delegate) ... 1·50 3·50

328 Goofy in *The Shadow*

1987. "Hafnia '87" International Stamp Exhibition. Walt Disney cartoon characters in scenes from Hans Christian Andersen's fairy tales. Multicoloured.

1722	25c. Type **328**	50	30
1723	30c. Mother Stork and brood in "The Storks"	50	30
1724	50c. King Richard, Robin Hood and Little John (from Robin Hood) in "The Emperor's New Clothes"	75	55
1725	60c. Goofy and Pluto in "The Tinderbox"	75	55
1726	70c. Daisy and Donald Duck in "The Shepherdess and the Chimney Sweep"	80	70
1727	$1.50 Mickey and Minnie Mouse in "The Little Mermaid"	1·60	1·75
1728	$3 Clarabelle and Goofy in "The Princess and the Pea"	2·50	3·50
1729	$4 Minnie Mouse and Pegleg Pete in "The Marsh King's Daughter"	2·50	3·50

MS1730 Two sheets, each 127×102 mm. (a) $5 Goofy in "The Flying Trunk". (b) $5 Goofy as "The Sandman" Set of 2 sheets ... 12·00 14·00

329 The Annunciation (Fra Angelico)

1987. Christmas. Religious Paintings. Multicoloured.

1731	15c. Type **329**	55	10
1732	30c. The Annunciation (attr. Hubert van Eyck)	90	30
1733	60c. The Adoration of the Magi (Januarius Zick)	1·75	1·40
1734	$4 The Flight into Egypt (Gerard David)	5·50	7·00

MS1735 99×75 mm. $5 The Circumcision (Giovanni Bellini studio) ... 7·00 8·00

330 T. Albert Marryshow

1988. Birth Centenary of T. Albert Marryshow (nationalist).

1736	**330** 25c. brown, lt brn & red	30	30

330a Wedding Photograph, 1947

1988. Royal Ruby Wedding. Multicoloured.

1737	**330a** 15c. brown, black & bl	45	10
1738	- 50c. multicoloured	80	50
1739	- $1 brown and black	1·40	2·00
1740	- $4 multicoloured	4·00	4·00

MS1741 76×100 mm. $5 multicoloured ... 2·25 3·25

DESIGNS: 50c. Queen Elizabeth II with Prince Charles and Princess Anne, c. 1955; $1 Queen with Princess Anne, c. 1957; $4 Queen Elizabeth (from photo by Tim Graham), 1980; $5 Princess Elizabeth in wedding dress, 1947.

331 Goofy and Daisy Duck lighting Olympic Torch, Olympia

1988. Olympic Games, Seoul. Designs showing Walt Disney cartoon characters. Multicoloured.

1742	1c. Type **331**	10	10
1743	2c. Donald and Daisy Duck carrying Olympic torch	10	10
1744	3c. Donald Duck, Goofy and Mickey Mouse carrying flags of U.S., Korea and Spain	10	10
1745	4c. Donald Duck releasing doves	10	10
1746	5c. Mickey Mouse flying with rocket belt	10	10
1747	10c. Morty and Ferdie carrying banner with Olympic motto	10	10
1748	$6 Donald Duck, Minnie Mouse and Hodori the Tiger (mascot of Seoul Games)	6·00	5·50
1749	$7 Pluto, Hodori and old post office, Seoul	6·00	5·50

MS1750 Two sheets, each 127×101 mm. (a) $5 Mickey Mouse taking athlete's oath. (b) $5 Donald and Daisy Duck as athletes at Closing Ceremony Set of 2 sheets   8·50   10·00

1988. Stamp Exhibitions. Nos. 1631/4 optd.

1751	90c. Blanchard and Jeffries' balloon, 1785 (optd **OLYM-PHILEX '88**, Seoul)	1·25	90
1752	$1.50 U.S.S "Holland I", 1900 (optd **INDEPENDENCE 40**, Israel)	1·75	1·50
1753	$2 "Oceanic I", 1871 (optd **FINLANDIA 88**, Helsinki)	2·25	2·25
1754	$3 Lamborghini "Countach", 1984 (optd **PRAGA 88**, Prague)	2·75	2·75

332 Scout fishing from Boat

1988. World Scout Jamboree, Australia. Multicoloured.

1755	20c. Type **332**	40	15
1756	70c. Scouts hiking through forest (horiz)	80	80
1757	90c. Practising first aid (horiz)	1·00	90
1758	$3 Shooting rapids in inflatable canoe	2·75	3·50

MS1759 114×80 mm. $5 Scout with koala   2·10   3·00

333 *Santa Maria de Guia* (Columbus), 1498 and Map of Rotary District

1988. Rotary District 405 Conference, St. George's. Multicoloured.

1760	$2 Type **333**	1·00	1·25

MS1761 133×90 mm. $10 Rotary emblem (horiz)   4·25   6·00

334 Roseate Tern

1988. Birds. Multicoloured.

1762	10c. Type **334**	80	30
1763	25c. Laughing gull	1·00	30

1764	50c. Osprey	1·60	70
1765	60c. Rose-breasted grosbeak	1·60	70
1766	90c. American purple gallinule ("Purple Gallinule")	1·60	90
1767	$1.10 White-tailed tropic bird	1·60	1·00
1768	$3 Blue-faced booby	2·25	2·75
1769	$4 Common shoveler	2·25	3·00

MS1770 Two sheets, each 100×71 mm. (a) $5 Belted kingfisher. (b) $5 Grenada flycatcher ("Rusty-tailed Flycatcher") Set of 2 sheets   7·00   9·00

335 Vauxhall Type "OE 30/98", 1925

1988. Cars. Multicoloured.

1771	$2 Type **335**	1·25	1·25
1772	$2 Wills "Sainte Claire", 1926	1·25	1·25
1773	$2 Bucciali, 1928	1·25	1·25
1774	$2 Irving Napier "Golden Arrow", 1929	1·25	1·25
1775	$2 Studebaker "President", 1930	1·25	1·25
1776	$2 Thomas "Flyer", 1907	1·25	1·25
1777	$2 Isotta-Franschini "Tipo J", 1908	1·25	1·25
1778	$2 Fiat 10/14HP, 1910	1·25	1·25
1779	$2 Mercer "Type 35 Raceabout", 1911	1·25	1·25
1780	$2 Marmon "Model 34 Cloverleaf", 1917	1·25	1·25
1781	$2 Tatra "Type 77", 1934	1·25	1·25
1782	$2 Rolls-Royce "Phantom III", 1938	1·25	1·25
1783	$2 Studebaker "Champion Starlight", 1947	1·25	1·25
1784	$2 Porsche "Gmund", 1948	1·25	1·25
1785	$2 Tucker, 1948	1·25	1·25
1786	$2 Peerless "V-16", 1931	1·25	1·25
1787	$2 Minerva "AL", 1931	1·25	1·25
1788	$2 Reo "Royale", 1953	1·25	1·25
1789	$2 Pierce Arrow "Silver Arrow", 1933	1·25	1·25
1790	$2 Hupmobile "Aerodynamic", 1934	1·25	1·25
1791	$2 Peugeot "404", 1965	1·25	1·25
1792	$2 Ford "Capri", 1969	1·25	1·25
1793	$2 Ferrari "312T", 1975	1·25	1·25
1794	$2 Lotus "T-79", 1978	1·25	1·25
1795	$2 Williams-Cosworth "FW07", 1979	1·25	1·25
1796	$2 H.R.G. "1500 Sports", 1948	1·25	1·25
1797	$2 Crosley "Hotshot", 1949	1·25	1·25
1798	$2 Volvo "PV444", 1955	1·25	1·25
1799	$2 Maserati "Tipo 61", 1960	1·25	1·25
1800	$2 Saab "96", 1963	1·25	1·25

1988. 500th Birth Anniv of Titian (artist). As T **166a** of Gambia. Multicoloured.

1801	10c. *Lavinia Vecellio*	10	10
1802	20c. *Portrait of a Man*	10	10
1803	25c. *Andrea de Franceschi*	10	15
1804	90c. *Head of a Soldier*	40	45
1805	$1 *Man with a Flute*	45	50
1806	$2 *Lucrezia and Tarquinius*	80	1·00
1807	$3 *Duke of Mantua with Dog*	1·25	1·60
1808	$4 *La Bella di Tiziano*	1·60	2·00

MS1809 Two sheets, each 110×95 mm. (a) $5 *Allegory of Alfonso D'Avalos* (detail). (b) $5 *Fall of Man* (detail) (horiz) Set of 2 sheets   4·25   5·50

336 "Graf Zeppelin" over Chicago World's Fair, 1933

1988. Airships. Multicoloured.

1810	10c. Type **336**	50	20
1811	15c. LZ-1 over Lake Constance, 1901 (horiz)	60	25
1812	25c. *Washington* (balloon) and *George Washington Curtis* (balloon barge), 1862	70	30
1813	45c. *Hindenburg* and Maybach "Zeppelin" car (horiz)	80	40

1814	50c. Goodyear Aerospace airship in Statue of Liberty Centenary Race, 1986	80	40
1815	60c. *Hindenburg* over Statue of Liberty, 1937 (horiz)	90	50
1816	90c. Heinkel biplane docking experiment with *Hindenburg*, 1936 (horiz)	1·40	80
1817	$2 *Hindenburg* over Olympic Stadium, Berlin, 1936	2·00	2·00
1818	$3 *Hindenburg* over Christ of the Andes Monument, 1937	2·50	2·50
1819	$4 *Hindenburg* and *Bremen* (liner), 1936 (horiz)	2·75	2·75

MS1820 Two sheets. (a) 75×95 mm. $5 LZ-127 *Graf Zeppelin*, 1930 (horiz). (b) 95×75 mm. $5 LZ-129 *Hindenburg*, 1935 (horiz) Set of 2 sheets   4·75   5·50

337 Tasmanian Wolf, Mickey Mouse and Pluto

1988. "Sydpex '88". National Stamp Exhibition, Sydney and 60th Birthday of Mickey Mouse. Multicoloured.

1821	1c. Type **337**	10	10
1822	2c. Mickey Mouse feeding wallabies	10	10
1823	3c. Mickey Mouse and Goofy with kangaroo	10	10
1824	4c. Mickey and Minnie Mouse riding emus	10	10
1825	5c. Mickey and Minnie Mouse with wombat	10	10
1826	10c. Mickey Mouse and Donald Duck watching platypus	10	10
1827	$5 Mickey Mouse and Goofy photographing blue-winged kookaburra	5·50	5·50
1828	$6 Mickey Mouse and Koala on map of Australia	5·50	5·50

MS1829 Two sheets, each 127×102 mm. (a) $5 Mickey Mouse with birthday cake. (b) $5 Mickey and Minnie Mouse with rainbow lories Set of 2 sheets   12·00   13·00

338 Pineapple

1988. Tenth Anniv of International Fund for Agricultural Development. Multicoloured.

1830	25c. Type **338**	35	15
1831	75c. Bananas	70	60
1832	$3 Mace and nutmeg (horiz)	2·50	2·75

339 Lignum Vitae

1988. Flowering Trees and Shrubs. Multicoloured.

1833	15c. Type **339**	15	15
1834	25c. Saman	20	15
1835	35c. Red frangipani	25	20
1836	45c. Flowering maple	30	25
1837	60c. Yellow poui	40	40
1838	$1 Wild chestnut	45	70
1839	$3 Mountain immortelle	1·10	1·75
1840	$4 Queen of flowers	1·25	2·00

MS1841 Two sheets, each 117×88 mm. (a) $5 Flamboyant. (b) $5 Orchid tree Set of 2 sheets   4·25   5·50

340 Mickey Mantle (New York Yankees)

1988. Major League Baseball Players (1st series). Designs showing portraits or league emblems.

1840-	30c.×81 multicoloured		
1922		11·50	14·00

340a Donald Duck's Nephew on Mantelpiece

1988. Christmas. "Mickey's Christmas Eve". Designs showing Walt Disney cartoon characters. Multicoloured.

1923	$1 Type **340a**	65	65
1924	$1 Goofy with string of popcorn	65	65
1925	$1 Chip'n'Dale decorating Christmas tree	65	65
1926	$1 Father Christmas in sleigh	65	65
1927	$1 Donald's nephew with stocking	65	65
1928	$1 Donald's nephew unpacking decorations	65	65
1929	$1 Donald Duck with present	65	65
1930	$1 Mickey Mouse with present	65	65

MS1931 Two sheets, each 127×102 mm. (a) $5 Ferdie leaving drink for Father Christmas. (b) $5 Mordie and Ferdie asleep Set of 2 sheets   7·00   8·50

341 Tina Turner

1988. Entertainers. Multicoloured.

1932	10c. Type **341**	30	20
1933	25c. Lionel Ritchie	30	20
1934	45c. Whitney Houston	45	30
1935	60c. Joan Armatrading	60	45
1936	75c. Madonna	90	60
1937	$1 Elton John	1·00	80
1938	$3 Bruce Springsteen	2·00	2·75
1939	$4 Bob Marley	4·00	4·50

MS1940 115×155 mm. 55c.×2 Yoko Minamino; $1×2 Yoko Minamino (different)   1·90   2·75

No. 1935 is incorrectly inscribed "JOAN AMMERTRAD-ING".

342 Atlantic Railway No. 2, 1889, Canada

1989. North American Railway Locomotives. Multicoloured.

1941	$2 Type **342**	1·25	1·25
1942	$2 Virginia & Truckee Railroad "J. W Bowker" type, 1875, U.S.A.	1·25	1·25
1943	$2 Philadelphia & Reading Railway "Ariel", 1872, U.S.A.	1·25	1·25
1944	$2 Chicago & Rock Island Railroad "America" type, 1867, U.S.A.	1·25	1·25
1945	$2 Lehigh Valley Railroad Consolidation No. 63, 1866, U.S.A.	1·25	1·25
1946	$2 Great Western Railway "Scotia", 1860, Canada	1·25	1·25
1947	$2 Grand Trunk Railway Class "Birkenhead", 1854, Canada	1·25	1·25
1948	$2 Camden & Amboy Railroad "Monster", 1837, U.S.A.	1·25	1·25
1949	$2 Baltimore & Ohio Railroad Class "Grasshopper", 1834, U.S.A.	1·25	1·25
1950	$2 Peter Cooper's "Tom Thumb", 1829, Baltimore & Ohio Railroad, U.S.A.	1·25	1·25
1951	$2 United Railways of Yucatan "Yucatan", 1925, Mexico	1·25	1·25
1952	$2 Canadian National Railways Class T2, 1924	1·25	1·25
1953	$2 St. Louis–San Francisco Railroad Class "Light Mikado", 1919, U.S.A.	1·25	1·25

1954	$2 Atlantic Coast Line Railroad Class "Light Pacific", 1919, U.S.A.	1·25	1·25
1955	$2 Edaville Railroad No. 7, 1913, U.S.A.	1·25	1·25
1956	$2 Denver & Rio Grande Western Railroad Class K 27, 1903, U.S.A.	1·25	1·25
1957	$2 Pennsylvania Railroad Class E-2 No. 7002, 1902, U.S.A.	1·25	1·25
1958	$2 Pennsylvania Railroad Class H6, 1899, U.S.A.	1·25	1·25
1959	$2 John Jarvis's "De Witt Clinton", 1831, Mohawk Hudson Railroad, U.S.A.	1·25	1·25
1960	$2 St. Clair Tunnel Company No. 598, 1891, Canada	1·25	1·25
1961	$2 Chesapeake & Ohio Railroad Class M-I steam turbine electric locomotive No. 500, 1947, U.S.A.	1·25	1·25
1962	$2 Rutland Railroad steam locomotive No. 93, 1946, U.S.A.	1·25	1·25
1963	$2 Pennsylvania Railroad Class T1, 1942, U.S.A.	1·25	1·25
1964	$2 Chesapeake & Ohio Railroad Class H-8, 1942, U.S.A.	1·25	1·25
1965	$2 Atchison, Topeka & Santa Fe Railway Model FT diesel, 1941, U.S.A.	1·25	1·25
1966	$2 Gulf, Mobile & Ohio Railroad Models S-I and S-2 diesels, 1940, U.S.A.	1·25	1·25
1967	$2 New York, New Haven & Hartford Railroad Class 15, 1937, U.S.A.	1·25	1·25
1968	$2 Seaboard Air Line Railroad Class R, 1936, U.S.A.	1·25	1·25
1969	$2 Newfoundland Railway Class R-2, 1930	1·25	1·25
1970	$2 Canadian National Railway diesel No. 9000, 1928	1·25	1·25

343 Women's Long Jump (Jackie Joyner-Kersee, U.S.A.)

1989. Olympic Gold Medal Winners, Seoul (1988). Multicoloured.

1971	10c. Type **343**	30	20
1972	25c. Women's Singles Tennis (Steffi Graf, West Germany)	75	35
1973	45c. Men's 1500 m (Peter Rono, Kenya)	80	40
1974	75c. Men's 1000 m single kayak (Greg Barton, U.S.A.)	90	60
1975	$1 Women's team foil (Italy)	1·10	75
1976	$2 Women's 100 m freestyle swimming (Kristin Otto, East Germany)	2·25	2·25
1977	$3 Men's still rings gymnastics (Holger Behrendt, East Germany)	2·50	2·75
1978	$4 Synchronized swimming pair (Japan)	2·75	3·00
MS1979	Two sheets, each 76×100 mm. (a) $6 Olympic flame. (b) $6 Runner with Olympic torch Set of 2 sheets	8·50	9·50

344 Nebulae

1989. Appearance of Halley's Comet (1986) (3rd issue).

1980	**344**	25c.+5c. multicoloured	70	80
1981	-	75c.+5c. black & green	1·10	1·40
1982	-	90c.+5c. multicoloured	1·25	1·60
1983	-	$2+5c. multicoloured	1·75	2·50
MS1984		111×78 mm. $5+5c. multicoloured. Imperf	4·75	5·50

DESIGNS: 75c.+5c. Marine astronomical experiments; 90c.+5c. Moon's surface; $2+5c. Edmond Halley, Sir Isaac Newton and his book "Principia". (102×69 mm)—$5+5c. 17th-century warships and astrological signs.

1989. Japanese Art. Paintings by Hiroshige. As T **177a** of Gambia. Multicoloured.

1985	10c. "Shinagawa on Edo Bay"	30	20
1986	25c. "ine Trees on the Road to Totsuka"	40	30
1987	60c. Kanagawa on Edo Bay	60	50
1988	75c. Crossing Banyu River to Hiratsuka	65	55
1989	$1 Windy Shore at Odawara	70	70
1990	$2 Snow-Covered Post Station of Mishima	1·10	1·75
1991	$3 Full Moon at Fuchu	1·25	2·00
1992	$4 Crossing the Stream at Okitsu	1·75	2·50

MS1993	Two sheets, each 102×76 mm. (a) $5 Mountain Pass at Nissaka. (b) $5 Mt Uzu at Okabe Set of 2 sheets	4·25	5·50

345 Great Blue Heron

1989. Birds. Multicoloured.

1994	5c. Type **345**	50	70
1995	10c. Green-backed heron ("Green Heron")	60	40
1996	15c. Ruddy turnstone	70	50
1997	25c. Blue-winged teal	80	20
1998	35c. Little ringed plover ("Ring-necked Plover") (vert)	1·00	20
1999	45c. Green-throated carib ("Emerald-throated Hummingbird") (vert)	1·10	30
2000	50c. Rufous-breasted hermit ("Hairy Hermit") (vert)	1·25	45
2001	60c. Lesser Antillean bullfinch (vert)	1·50	65
2002	75c. Brown pelican (vert)	1·50	80
2003	$1 Black-crowned night heron (vert)	2·00	1·00
2004	$3 American kestrel ("Sparrow Hawk") (vert)	4·75	4·00
2005	$5 Barn swallow (vert)	5·00	5·50
2006	$10 Red-billed tropic bird (vert)	8·00	9·50
2007	$20 Barn owl (vert)	15·00	20·00

345a Scotland Player

1989. World Cup Football Championship, Italy (1990) (1st issue). Multicoloured.

2008	10c. Type **345a**	40	20
2009	25c. England and Brazil players	50	30
2010	60c. Paolo Rossi (Italy)	75	55
2011	75c. Jairzinho (Brazil)	90	70
2012	$1 Sweden striker	1·10	90
2013	$2 Pele (Brazil)	1·75	2·00
2014	$3 Mario Kempes (Argentina)	2·25	2·75
2015	$4 Pat Jennings (Northern Ireland)	2·50	3·00
MS2016	Two sheets. (a) 70×93 mm. $6 Players jumping for ball. (b) 82×71 mm. $6 Goalkeeper Set of 2 sheets	7·00	10·00

See also Nos. 2174/8 and **MS**2179.

346 Xebec and Sugar Cane

1989. "Philexfrance '89" International Stamp Exhibition, Paris. Designs showing French sailing vessels and plantation crops. Multicoloured.

2017	25c. Type **346**	1·25	30
2018	75c. Lugger and cotton	1·75	85
2019	$1 Full-rigged ship and cocoa	2·00	1·10
2020	$4 Ketch and coffee	3·75	5·50
MS2021	114×70 mm. $6"View of Fort and Town of St. George, 1779 (105×63 mm). Imperf	6·50	8·00

347 Alan Shepard and "Freedom 7" Spacecraft, 1961 (first American in Space)

1989. 20th Anniv of First Manned Landing on Moon. Multicoloured.

2022	15c. Type **347**	70	40
2023	35c. "Friendship 7" spacecraft, 1962 (first manned earth orbit)	90	55
2024	45c. "Apollo 8" orbiting Moon, 1968 (first manned lunar orbit)	1·00	65
2025	70c. "Apollo 15" lunar rover, 1972	1·50	85
2026	$1 "Apollo 11" emblem and lunar module "Eagle" on Moon, 1969	1·75	1·10

2027	$2 "Gemini 8" and "Agena" rocket, 1966 (first space docking)	3·00	3·25
2028	$3 Edward White in space, 1965 (first U.S. space walk)	3·00	3·25
2029	$4 "Apollo 7" emblem	3·75	3·50
MS2030	Two sheets, each 101×71 mm. (a) $5 Moon and track of "Apollo 11", 1969. (b) $5 Armstrong and Aldrin raising U.S. flag on Moon, 1969 Set of 2 sheets	13·00	10·00

348 Hygrocybe occidentalis

1989. Fungi. Multicoloured.

2031	15c. Type **348**	50	40
2032	40c. Marasmius haematocephalus	65	55
2033	50c. Hygrocybe hypohaemacta	75	65
2034	70c. Lepiota pseudoignicolor	1·00	90
2035	90c. Cookeina tricholoma	1·25	1·25
2036	$1.10 Leucopaxillus gracillimus	1·25	1·50
2037	$2.25 Hygrocybe nigrescens	2·00	3·00
2038	$4 Clathrus crispus	2·75	4·00
MS2039	Two sheets, each 57×70 mm. (a) $6 Mycena holoporphyra. (b) $6 Xeromphalina tenuipes Set of 2 sheets	12·00	13·00

349 Y.W.C.A. Logo and Grenada Scenery

1989. Centenary of Young Women's Christian Association. Multicoloured.

2040	50c. Type **349**	45	45
2041	75c. Y.W.C.A. logo and town (horiz)	80	80

350 Historis odius

1989. Butterflies. Multicoloured.

2042	6c. Type **350**	30	30
2043	30c. Marpesia petreus	55	55
2044	40c. Danaus gilippus	60	60
2045	60c. Dione juno	80	80
2046	$1.10 Agraulis vanillae	1·25	1·25
2047	$1.25 Danaus plexippus	1·50	1·50
2048	$4 Papilio androgeus	3·25	3·25
2049	$5 Dryas julia	3·25	3·25
MS2050	Two sheets, each 87×115 mm. (a) $6 Anartia jatrophae. (b) $6 Strymon simaethis Set of 2 sheets	9·50	11·00

351 Amerindian Hieroglyph

1989. 500th Anniv (1992) of Discovery of America by Columbus (2nd issue). Designs showing different hieroglyphs.

2051	**351**	45c. brown, black & blue	1·00	50
2052	-	60c. brown, black & grn	1·10	60
2053	-	$1 brown, black and violet	1·75	1·00
2054	-	$4 dp brown, black & brn	4·25	4·25
MS2055		74×86 mm. $6 brown, black and red	4·00	5·50

352 Amos leaving Home

1989. "World Stamp Expo '89" International Stamp Exhibition, Washington. Designs showing Walt Disney cartoon characters in scenes from "Ben and Me". Multicoloured.

2056	1c. Type **352**	10	10
2057	2c. Meeting of Benjamin Franklin and Amos	10	10
2058	3c. The Franklin stove	10	10
2059	4c. Ben and Amos with bi-focals	10	10
2060	5c. Amos on page of "Pennsylvania Gazette"	10	10
2061	6c. Ben working printing press	10	10
2062	10c. Conducting experiment with electricity	10	10
2063	$5 Ben disembarking in England	5·00	5·50
2064	$6 Ben with Document of Agreement	5·50	6·00
MS2065	Two sheets, each 127×101 mm. (a) $6 Benjamin Franklin teaching (vert). (b) $6 Signatories of Declaration of Independence Set of 2 sheets	8·00	10·00

352a Christ in the House of Mary and Martha

1990. Christmas. Paintings by Rubens. Multicoloured.

2066	20c. Type **352a**	50	25
2067	35c. The Circumcision	65	40
2068	60c. Trinity adored by Duke of Mantua and Family	1·00	65
2069	$2 Holy Family with St. Francis	2·75	2·75
2070	$3 The Ildefonso Altarpiece	3·25	3·50
2071	$4 Madonna and Child with Garland and Putti	3·75	4·00
MS2072	Two sheets, each 70×95 mm. (a) $5 Adoration of the Magi. (b) $5 Virgin and Child adored by Angels Set of 2 sheets	7·50	9·00

353 Alexander Graham Bell and Early Telephone System (150th anniv of invention)

1990. Anniversaries. Multicoloured.

2073	10c. Type **353**	30	20
2074	25c. George Washington and Capitol (bicentenary of presidential inauguration)	30	20
2075	35c. Shakespeare and birthplace, Stratford (425th birth anniv)	1·75	30
2076	75c. Nehru and Gandhi (birth cent of Nehru)	5·50	2·00
2077	$1 Dr. Hugo Eckener, Ferdinand von Zeppelin and airship Graf Zeppelin (80th anniv of first passenger Zeppelin)	2·25	1·50
2078	$2 Charlie Chaplin (birth cent)	6·00	3·25
2079	$3 Container ship in Hamburg Harbour (800th anniv)	3·00	3·75
2080	$4 Friedrich Ebert (first President) and Heidelberg gate (70th anniv of German Republic)	3·00	4·25
MS2081	Two sheets, each 100×72 mm. (a) $6 13th-century ships in Hamburg Harbour (vert) (800th anniv). (b) $6 Concorde (20th anniv of first test flight) Set of 2 sheets	10·00	12·00

No. 2080 is inscribed "40th Anniversary of German Republic" in error.

354
Odontoglossum triumphans

1990. "EXPO '90" International Garden and Greenery Exhibition, Osaka. Caribbean Orchids. Multicoloured.

2082	1c. Type **354**	10	30
2083	25c. *Oncidium splendidum*	50	20
2084	60c. *Laelia anceps*	90	60
2085	75c. *Cattleya trianaei*	1·00	75
2086	$1 *Odontoglossum rossii*	1·25	1·00
2087	$2 *Brassia gireoudiana*	2·25	2·00
2088	$3 *Cattleya dowiana*	2·75	3·00
2089	$4 *Sobralia macrantha*	3·00	3·50

MS2090 Two sheets, each 97×68 mm. (a) $6 *Oncidium lanceanum*. (b) $6 *Laelia rubescens* Set of 2 sheets   8·50   9·50

354a *Marpesia petreus*

1990. 500th Anniv (1992) of Discovery of America by Columbus (3rd issue). New World Natural History—Butterflies. Multicoloured.

2091	15c. Type **354a**	75	20
2092	25c. "Junonia evarete"	90	25
2093	75c. "Siproeta stelenes"	1·60	70
2094	90c. "Historis odius"	1·75	85
2095	$1 "Mestra cana"	1·75	90
2096	$2 "Biblis hyperia"	2·75	2·75
2097	$3 "Dryas julia"	3·25	3·75
2098	$4 "Anartia amathea"	3·25	4·00

MS2099 Two sheets, each 101×69 mm. (a) $6 "Pseudolycaena marsyas". (b) $6 "Phoebis philea" Set of 2 sheets   14·00   15·00

354b Caribbean Monk Seal

1990. Local Fauna. Multicoloured.

2100	10c. Type **354b**	60	30
2101	15c. Little brown bat	70	30
2102	45c. Brown rat	80	50
2103	60c. Common rabbit	90	60
2104	$1 Water opossum	1·40	95
2105	$2 White-nosed ichneumon	2·00	2·00
2106	$3 Little big-eared bat (vert)	2·50	3·00
2107	$4 Mouse opossum	3·00	3·00

MS2108 Two sheets, each 107×80 mm. (a) $6 Common rabbit (different). (b) $6 Water opossum (different) Set of 2 sheets   8·50   11·00

354c British Tanks during Operation Battleaxe, 1941

1990. 50th Anniv of Second World War. Multicoloured.

2109	25c. Type **354c**	60	30
2110	35c. Allied tank in southern France, 1944	70	40
2111	45c. U.S. forces landing on Guadalcanal, 1942	75	45
2112	50c. U.S. attack in New Guinea, 1943	75	50
2113	60c. Hoisting U.S. flag on Leyte, Phillippines, 1944	90	60
2114	75c. U.S. tanks entering Cologne, 1945	95	75
2115	$1 Anzio offensive, 1944	1·25	95
2116	$2 Battle of the Bismarck Sea, 1943	2·50	2·25
2117	$3 U.S.S. *Langley* and U.S.S. *Ticonderoga* (aircraft carriers), 1944	3·00	3·50
2118	$4 Focke Wulf Fw 190A fighter attacking Salerno landing, 1943	3·25	3·75

MS2119 111×83 mm. $6 German "U-30" submarine, 1939   3·75   4·50

1990. "Stamp World London '90" International Stamp Exhibition (1st issue). As T **193** of Gambia, but horiz showing Walt Disney cartoon characters and British trains.

2120	5c. Mickey Mouse driving S.R. "King Arthur" class locomotive, 1925	50	20
2121	10c. Mickey and Minnie Mouse with "Puffing Billy", 1813	50	20
2122	20c. Mickey Mouse with Pluto pulling Durham colliery wagon, 1765	75	20
2123	45c. Mickey Mouse timing L.N.E.R. locomotive No. 2509 "Silver Link", 1935	1·00	25
2124	$1 Mickey Mouse and Donald Duck with locomotive No. 60149 "Amadis", 1948	2·25	1·00
2125	$2 Goofy and Mickey Mouse with Liverpool & Manchester Railway locomotive, 1830	3·00	2·75
2126	$4 Goofy and Donald Duck with Great Northern locomotive No. 1, 1870	3·50	4·25
2127	$5 Mickey Mouse and Gyro the Mechanic with Advanced Passenger Train, 1972	3·50	4·25

MS2128 Two sheets, each 127×101 mm. (a) $6 Minnie Mouse, Donald and Daisy Duck in Trevithick's Catch-Me-Who-Can, 1808 (horiz). (b) $6 Donald Duck and Locomotion, 1825 Set of 2 sheets   14·00   15·00

No. 2126 is inscribed "Flying Scotsman" in error.
See also No. **MS**2146.

355 U.S. Paratroop Drop over Grenada

1990. 50th Anniv of United States Airborne Forces.

2129	75c. Type **355**	1·75	1·25

MS2130 Two sheets, each 115×87 mm. (a) $2.50, Paratrooper landing. (b) $6 Paratroop uniforms of 1940 and 1990 Set of 2 sheets   6·00   7·50

1990. 90th Birthday of Queen Elizabeth the Queen Mother. As T **194** of Gambia showing photographs from the 1960s. Multicoloured.

2131	$2 Queen Mother in coat and hat	1·75	1·75
2132	$2 Queen Mother in evening dress	1·75	1·75
2133	$2 Queen Mother in Garter robes	1·75	1·75

MS2134 90×75 mm. $6 Queen Mother (as No. 2131)   3·50   4·00

1990. Olympic Games, Barcelona (1992) (1st issue). As T **195a** of Gambia. Multicoloured.

2135	10c. Men's steeplechase	30	20
2136	15c. Dressage	45	30
2137	45c. Men's 200 m. butterfly swimming	50	45
2138	50c. Men's hockey	1·75	60
2139	65c. Women's beam gymnastics	60	60
2140	75c. "Flying Dutchman" class sailing	1·00	80
2141	$1 Freestyle wrestling	1·75	1·75
2142	$3 Men's springboard diving	2·25	2·75
2143	$4 Women's 1000 m. sprint cycling	4·25	4·25
2144	$5 Men's basketball	5·00	5·00

MS2145 Two sheets, each 101×70 mm. (a) $8 Equestrian three-day event. (b) $8 Men's 10000 metres Set of 2 sheets   11·00   12·00

See also Nos. 2414/22.

356 Map of North America and Logo

1990. "Stamp World London 90" International Stamp Exhibition (2nd issue). Sheet 97×75 mm.
MS2146 **356** $6 mauve   4·25   5·50

357 Yellow Goatfish

1990. Coral Reef Fish. Multicoloured.

2147	10c. Type **357**	30	30
2148	25c. Black margate	45	35
2149	65c. Blue-headed wrasse	85	75
2150	75c. Puddingwife	95	85
2151	$1 Four-eyed butterflyfish	1·10	95
2152	$2 Honey damselfish	2·00	2·00

2153	$3 Queen angelfish	2·50	2·50
2154	$5 Cherub angelfish	3·00	3·50

MS2155 Two sheets, each 103×72 mm. (a) $6 Smooth trunkfish. (b) $6 Sergeant major Set of 2 sheets   8·50   9·50

358 Tropical Mockingbird

1990. Birds. Multicoloured.

2156	15c. Type **358**	30	30
2157	25c. Grey kingbird	35	35
2158	65c. Bare-eyed thrush	75	75
2159	75c. Antillean crested hummingbird	85	85
2160	$1 House wren	1·00	1·00
2161	$2 Purple martin	1·75	1·75
2162	$4 Lesser Antillian tanager ("Hooded Tanager")	2·50	2·50
2163	$5 Scaly-breasted ground dove	3·00	3·00

MS2164 Two sheets, each 101×72 mm. (a) $6 Fork-tailed flycatcher. (b) $6 Smooth-billed ani Set of 2 sheets   13·00   14·00

359 Coral Crab

1990. Crustaceans. Multicoloured.

2165	5c. Type **359**	20	30
2166	10c. Smoothtail spiny lobster	20	30
2167	15c. Flamestreaked box crab	20	30
2168	25c. Spotted swimming crab	30	25
2169	75c. Sally lightfoot rock crab	70	60
2170	$1 Spotted spiny lobster	90	80
2171	$3 Longarm spiny lobster	2·00	2·50
2172	$20 Caribbean spiny lobster	13·00	18·00

MS2173 Two sheets, 106×75 mm. (a) $6 Copper lobster. (b) $6 Spanish lobster Set of 2 sheets   8·00   9·00

360 Cameroon Player

1990. World Cup Football Championship, Italy (2nd issue). Multicoloured.

2174	10c. Type **360**	20	15
2175	25c. Michel (Spain)	25	15
2176	$1 Brehme (West Germany)	85	85
2177	$5 Nevin (Scotland)	3·00	4·00

MS2178 Two sheets, each 95×90 mm. (a) $6 Giannini (Italy). (b) $6 Perdomo (Uruguay) Set of 2 sheets   8·00   11·00

1990. World Cup Football Championship, Italy (1990) (3rd issue). No. **MS**2016a optd **1990 W GERMANY 1 ARGENTINA 0.**
MS2179 70×93 mm. $6 Players jumping for ball   6·50   8·50

1990. Christmas. Paintings by Raphael. As T **195b** of Gambia. Multicoloured.

2180	10c. The Ansidei Madonna	20	10
2181	15c. The Sistine Madonna	20	10
2182	$1 The Madonna of the Baldacchino	1·50	70
2183	$2 The Large Holy Family (detail)	2·50	2·75
2184	$5 Madonna in the Meadow	4·00	6·00

MS2185 Two sheets, each 71×101 mm. (a) $6 Madonna of the Diadem (detail). (b) $6 The Madonna of the Veil (detail) Set of 2 sheets   14·00   15·00

1991. 350th Death Anniv of Rubens. As T **195c** of Gambia. Multicoloured.

2186	5c. The Brazen Serpent (detail)	40	20
2187	10c. The Garden of Love	40	15
2188	25c. Head of Cyrus (detail)	60	20
2189	75c. Tournament in Front of a Castle	1·50	60
2190	$1 The Brazen Serpent (different detail)	1·75	75
2191	$2 Judgement of Paris (detail)	2·25	2·25
2192	$4 The Brazen Serpent	3·25	4·25
2193	$5 The Karmesse (detail)	3·50	4·25

MS2194 Two sheets, each 101×70 mm. (a) $6 Anger of Neptune (detail). (b) $6 The Prodigal son (detail) Set of 2 sheets   14·00   15·00

362 "The Sorcerer's Apprentice"

1991. 50th Anniv of *Fantasia* (cartoon film). Multicoloured.

2195	5c. Type **362**	65	20
2196	10c. Dancing mushrooms ("The Nutcracker Suite")	65	20
2197	20c. Pterodactyls ("The Rite of Spring")	1·00	20
2198	45c. Centaurs ("The Pastoral Symphony")	1·75	40
2199	$1 Bacchus and Jacchus ("The Pastoral Symphony")	2·75	1·25
2200	$2 Dancing ostrich ("Dance of the Hours")	3·75	3·25
2201	$4 Elephant ballet ("Dance of the Hours")	4·75	5·50
2202	$5 Diana ("The Pastoral Symphony")	4·75	5·50

MS2203 Two sheets, each 122×102 mm. (a) $6 Mickey Mouse as the Sorcerer's Apprentice. (b) $6 Mickey Mouse with Leopold Stokowski (conductor) Set of 2 sheets   14·00   15·00

MS2204 176×213 mm. $12 Mickey Mouse as the Sorcerer's Apprentice (vert)   14·00   15·00

363 *Adelpha iphicla*

1991. Butterflies. Multicoloured.

2205	5c. Type **363**	60	60
2206	10c. *Nymphalidae claudina*	60	50
2207	15c. *Brassolidae polyxena*	70	30
2208	20c. Zebra Longwing	80	30
2209	25c. *Marpesia corinna*	80	25
2210	30c. *Morpho hecuba*	80	30
2211	45c. *Morpho rhetenor*	1·10	45
2212	50c. *Dismorphia spio*	1·25	55
2213	60c. *Prepona omphale*	1·25	65
2214	70c. *Morpho anaxibia*	1·50	75
2215	75c. *Marpesia iole*	1·50	80
2216	$1 *Amarynthis meneria*	1·75	1·00
2217	$2 *Morpho cisseis*	2·50	2·50
2218	$3 *Danaidae plexippus*	3·00	3·50
2219	$4 *Morpho achilleana*	3·50	4·50
2220	$5 *Calliona argenissa*	4·50	4·75

MS2221 Four sheets, each 118×80 mm. (a) $6 *Anteos clorinde*. (b) $6 *Haetera piera*. (c) $6 *Papilio cresphontes*. (d) $6 *Prepona pheridames* Set of 4 sheets   17·00   19·00

363a Vitus Bering in Bering Sea, 1728–9

1991. 500th Anniv (1992) of Discovery of America by Columbus. History of Exploration. Multicoloured.

2222	5c. Type **363a**	70	60
2223	10c. De Bougainville off Pacific island, 1766–69	70	50
2224	25c. Polynesian canoe	45	30
2225	50c. De Mendana off Solomon Islands, 1567–69	1·40	60
2226	$1 Darwin's H.M.S. *Beagle*, 1831–35	2·50	1·25
2227	$2 Cook's H.M.S. *Endeavour*, 1768–71	4·00	3·25
2228	$4 William Schouten in LeMaire Strait, 1615–17	4·00	4·50
2229	$5 Tasman off New Zealand, 1642–44	4·00	4·50

MS2230 Two sheets, each 116×77 mm. (a) $6 *Santa Maria* sinking. (b) $6 Bow of *Santa Maria* (vert) Set of 2 sheets   10·00   11·00

1991. "Phila Nippon '91" International Stamp Exhibition, Tokyo. Horiz designs as T **198c** of Gambia showing Walt Disney cartoon characters at Japanese festivals. Multicoloured.

2231	5c. Minnie Mouse and Daisy Duck at Dolls festival	40	20
2232	10c. Morty and Ferdie with Boys' Day display	40	20
2233	20c. Mickey and Minnie Mouse at Star festival	70	20
2234	45c. Minnie and Daisy folk-dancing	1·25	35

2235	$1 Huey, Dewey and Louie wearing Eboshi headdresses	2·00	85
2236	$2 Mickey and Goofy pulling decorated car at Gion festival	3·50	3·50
2237	$4 Minnie and Daisy preparing rice broth, Seven Plants festival	4·25	4·75
2238	$5 Huey and Dewey with straw boat at Lanterns festival	4·25	4·75
MS2239	Three sheets, each 127×101 mm. (a) $6 Minnie Mouse in kimono. (b) $6 Mickey taking photo (horiz). (c) $6 Goofy behind fair stall (horiz) Set of 3 sheets	14·00	15·00

1991. Death Centenary (1990) of Vincent van Gogh (artist). As T **200b** of Gambia. Multicoloured.

2240	20c. Blossoming Almond Branch in Glass (vert)	50	25
2241	25c. La Mousme sitting (vert)	50	25
2242	30c. Still Life with Red Cabbages and Onions	55	30
2243	40c. Japonaiserie: Flowering Plum Tree (vert)	70	40
2244	45c. Japonaiserie: Bridge in the Rain (vert)	70	40
2245	60c. Still Life with Basket of Apples	1·00	60
2246	75c. Italian Woman (vert)	1·10	70
2247	$1 The Painter on his Way to Work (vert)	1·60	1·00
2248	$2 Portrait of Pere Tanguy (vert)	2·50	2·25
2249	$3 Still Life with Plaster Statuette, a Rose and Two Novels (vert)	3·25	3·25
2250	$4 Still Life: Bottle, Lemons and Oranges	3·50	3·75
2251	$5 Orchard with Blossoming Apricot Trees	3·50	3·75
MS2252	Five sheets. (a) 76×102 mm. $6 Roubine du Roi Canal with Washerwoman (73×99 mm). (b) 102×76 mm. $6 Farmhouse in a Wheatfield (99×73 mm). (c) 102×76 mm. $6 The Gleize Bridge over the Vigueirat Canal (99×73 mm). (d) 102×76 mm. $6 Rocks with Oak Tree (99×73 mm). (e) 76×102 mm. $6 Japonaiserie: Oiran (73×99 mm). Imperf. Set of 5 sheets	24·00	26·00

364 Psilocybe cubensis

1991. Fungi. Multicoloured.

2253	15c. Type **364**	70	30
2254	25c. Leptonia caeruleocapitata	80	30
2255	65c. Cystolepiota eriophora	1·40	85
2256	75c. Chlorophyllum molybdites	1·40	1·00
2257	$1 Xerocomus hypoxanthus	1·60	1·25
2258	$2 Volvariella cubensis	2·50	2·75
2259	$4 Xerocomus coccolobae	3·25	4·00
2260	$5 Pluteus chrysophlebius	3·25	4·00
MS2261	Two sheets, each 100×70 mm. (a) $6 Psathyrella tuberculata. (b) $6 Hygrocybe miniata Set of 2 sheets	14·00	14·00

365 Johannes Kepler (astronomer)

1991. Exploration of Mars. Designs showing astronomers, spacecraft and Martian landscapes. Multicoloured.

2262- 2297	75c.×9, $1.25×9, $2×9, $7×9	48·00	48·00
MS2298	Three sheets, each 112×92 mm. (a) $6 Projected spacecraft. (b) $6 Mars and part of spacecraft. (c) $6 Phobos satellite over Mars Set of 3 sheets	13·00	14·00

1991. 65th Birthday of Queen Elizabeth II. As T **198a** of Gambia. Multicoloured.

2299	15c. Royal Family on balcony after Trooping the Colour, 1985	60	15
2300	40c. Queen and Prince Philip at Peterborough, 1988	75	35
2301	$2 Queen and Queen Mother at Windsor, 1986	2·50	1·75
2302	$4 Queen and Prince Philip on visit to United Arab Emirates	3·50	3·50
MS2303	68×90 mm. $5 Separate photographs of the Queen and Prince Philip	4·00	4·50

1991. Tenth Wedding Anniv of the Prince and Princess of Wales. As T **198b** of Gambia. Multicoloured.

2304	10c. Prince and Princess in July 1985	60	10

2305	50c. Separate photographs of Prince, Princess and sons	1·25	45
2306	$1 Prince Henry at Trooping the Colour and Prince William in Majorca	1·50	1·00
2307	$5 Separate photographs of Prince Charles and Princess Diana	4·25	4·50
MS2308	68×90 mm. $5 Prince, Princess and sons on holiday in Majorca	6·50	5·50

366 Anglican High School Pupils

1991. 75th Anniv of Anglican High School (10, 25c.) and 40th Anniv of University of the West Indies (45, 50c.). Multicoloured.

2309	10c. Type **366**	40	20
2310	25c. Artist's impression of new Anglican High School	70	20
2311	45c. Marryshow House, Grenada	95	20
2312	50c. University Administrative Building, Barbados	1·00	1·00

367 George Stephenson's First Locomotive, 1814 (Great Britain)

1991. Great Railways of the World. Multicoloured.

2313	75c. Type **367**	75	75
2314	75c. George Stephenson	75	75
2315	75c. Killingworth locomotive, 1816 (Great Britain)	75	75
2316	75c. George Stephenson's Locomotion, 1825 (Great Britain)	75	75
2317	75c. Locomotion in Darlington, 1825 (Great Britain)	75	75
2318	75c. Opening of Stockton & Darlington Railway, 1825	75	75
2319	75c. Timothy Hackworth's Royal George, 1827 (Great Britain)	75	75
2320	75c. Northumbrian T831 (Great Britain)	75	75
2321	75c. Planet, 1830 (Great Britain)	75	75
2322	$1 Old Ironsides, 1832 (U.S.A.)	90	90
2323	$1 Wilberforce, 1832 (Great Britain)	90	90
2324	$1 Adler, 1835 (Germany)	90	90
2325	$1 North Star, 1837 (Great Britain)	90	90
2326	$1 London & Birmingham Railway No. 1, 1838 (Great Britain)	90	90
2327	$1 Stephenson's Austria, 1838 (Austria)	90	90
2328	$1 Baltimore & Ohio Railroad No. 378 Muddigger, 1840 (U.S.A.)	90	90
2329	$1 Baltimore & Ohio Railroad Norris, 1840 (U.S.A.)	90	90
2330	$1 Centaur, 1840 (Great Britain)	90	90
2331	$2 Lion, 1841 (Great Britain)	1·50	1·50
2332	$2 Beuth, 1843 (Germany)	1·50	1·50
2333	$2 Derwent, 1845 (Great Britain)	1·50	1·50
2334	$2 Bets, 1846 (Hungary)	1·50	1·50
2335	$2 Opening of Budapest to Vac railway, 1846 (Hungary)	1·50	1·50
2336	$2 Carriages, Stockton & Darlington Railway, 1846 (Great Britain)	1·50	1·50
2337	$2 "Long Boiler" type, 1847 (France)	1·50	1·50
2338	$2 Baldwin locomotive, 1850 (U.S.A.)	1·50	1·50
2339	$2 Steam locomotive, 1850 (Germany)	1·50	1·50
MS2340	Two sheets, each 116×86 mm. (a) $6 Part of Stephenson's Locomotion, 1825 (Great Britain). (b) $6 Train on Liverpool & Manchester Railway, 1833 (Great Britain) Set of 2 sheets	14·00	15·00

368 Barbu

1991. Marine Life of the Sandflats. Multicoloured.

2341	50c. Type **368**	80	80
2342	50c. Beau Gregory	80	80
2343	50c. Porcupinefish	80	80
2344	50c. Queen or pink conch and conchfish	80	80
2345	50c. Hermit crab	80	80

2346	50c. Bluestripe lizardfish	80	80
2347	50c. Spot-finned mojarra	80	80
2348	50c. Southern stingray	80	80
2349	50c. Long-spined sea urchin and slippery dick	80	80
2350	50c. Peacock flounder	80	80
2351	50c. West Indian sea star	80	80
2352	50c. Spotted goatfish	80	80
2353	50c. Netted olive and West Indian sea egg	80	80
2354	50c. Pearly razorfish	80	80
2355	50c. Spotted jawfish and yellow-headed jawfish	80	80
MS2356	105×76 mm. $6 Short-nosed batfish	10·00	11·00

Nos. 2341/55 were printed together, *se-tenant*, forming a composite design.

1991. Christmas. Religious Paintings by Albrecht Durer. As T **200c** of Gambia. Multicoloured.

2357	10c. "doration of the Magi (detail)	60	10
2358	35c. Madonna with the Siskin (detail)	90	25
2359	50c. Feast of the Rose Garlands (detail)	1·25	45
2360	75c. Virgin with the Pear (detail)	1·75	80
2361	$1 Virgin in Half-length (detail)	2·25	1·00
2362	$2 Madonna and Child (detail)	3·25	3·25
2363	$4 Virgin and Child with St. Anne (detail)	3·75	5·00
2364	$5 Virgin and Child (detail)	3·75	5·00
MS2365	Two sheets, each 102×127 mm. (a) $6 Virgin with a Multitude of Animals (detail). (b) $6 The Nativity (detail). Set of 2 sheets	13·00	14·00

369 Goofy windsurfing

1992. Thrill Sports. Walt Disney cartoon characters. Multicoloured.

2366	5c. Type **369**	40	30
2367	10c. Mickey Mouse skateboarding	50	30
2368	20c. Daisy Duck gliding	80	30
2369	45c. Mickey's nephews stunt kite flying	1·25	30
2370	$1 Donald Duck mountain biking	2·00	1·10
2371	$2 Donald and Chipmunk parachuting	2·75	2·75
2372	$4 Mickey go-karting	4·00	4·75
2373	$5 Minnie water skiing	4·00	4·75
MS2374	Four sheets, each 128×102 mm. (a) $6 Mickey bungee jumping (vert). (b) $6 Mickey and Minnie river rafting. (c) $6 Donald's nephews playing roller hockey. (d) $6 Mickey hang-gliding Set of 4 sheets	16·00	17·00

1992. 40th Anniv of Queen Elizabeth II's Accession. As T **202a** of Gambia. Multicoloured.

2375	10c. Waterfall	65	20
2376	50c. Street in St. George's	75	40
2377	$1 Colonial-style houses, St. George's	1·40	80
2378	$5 St. George's from the sea	4·25	4·50
MS2379	Two sheets, each 75×96 mm. (a) $6 Village on hillside. (b) $6 Yacht at anchor off village Set of 2 sheets	11·00	11·00

1992. "Granada '92" International Stamp Exhibition, Spain. Spanish Paintings. As T **481a** of Ghana. Multicoloured.

2380	10c. "The Corpus Christi Procession in Seville" (Manuel Cabral y Aguado) (horiz)	40	20
2381	35c. "The Mancorbo Channel" (Carlos de Haes)	55	20
2382	50c. "Amalia de Llano y Dotres, Countess of Vilches" (Federico de Madrazo y Kuntz)	75	40
2383	75c. "Conchita Serrano y Dominguez, Countess of Santovenia" (Eduardo Rosales Gallina)	1·00	70
2384	$1 "Queen Maria Isabel de Braganza" (Bernardo Lopez Piquer)	1·40	85
2385	$2 "The Presentation of Don John of Austria to Charles V" (detail) (Gallina)	2·25	2·25
2386	$4 "The Presentation of Don John of Austria to Charles V" (different detail) (Gallina)	3·50	4·25
2387	$5 "The Testament of Isabella the Catholic" (Gallina) (horiz)	3·50	4·25
MS2388	Two sheets, each 120×95 mm. (a) $6 "The Horse Corral in the Old Madrid Bullring" (Manuel Castellano) (111×85 mm). (b) $6 "Meeting of Poets in Antonio Maríá Esquivel's Studio" (Antonia Maríá Esquivel y Suárez de Urbina) (111×85 mm). Imperf Set of 2 sheets	9·50	10·00

370 Green-winged Macaw

1992. 500th Anniv of Discovery of America by Columbus (5th issue). World Columbian Stamp "Expo '92", Chicago. Multicoloured.

2389	10c. Type **370**	1·00	40
2390	25c. Santa Maria	1·10	40
2391	35c. Christopher Columbus	1·10	40
2392	50c. 15th-century sandglass	1·10	55
2393	75c. Queen Isabella	1·25	80
2394	$4 Cantino map of 1502 (detail)	6·00	8·50
MS2395	Two sheets, each 80×108 mm. (a) $6 Map of Genoa (detail). (b) $6 Detail of 15th-century map by Thomas Bly Set of 2 sheets	11·00	12·00

370a Ruby-throated Hummingbird

1992. "Genova '92" International Thematic Stamp Exhibition. Hummingbirds. Multicoloured.

2396	10c. Type **370a**	70	25
2397	25c. Vervain hummingbird	90	25
2398	35c. Blue-headed hummingbird	95	25
2399	50c. Cuban emerald	1·25	60
2400	75c. Antillean mango	1·60	75
2401	$2 Purple-throated carib	2·50	2·50
2402	$4 Puerto Rican emerald	3·50	4·25
2403	$5 Green-throated carib	3·50	4·25
MS2404	Two sheets, each 109×80 mm. (a) $6 Young Antillean Crested Hummingbird. (b) $6 Rufous-breasted Hermit Set of 2 sheets	14·00	14·00

371 Gracie Fields

1992. 50th Anniv of United Service Organization (forces' entertainment programme). Multicoloured.

2405	15c. Type **371**	30	20
2406	25c. Jack Benny	30	20
2407	35c. Jinx Falkenburg	30	25
2408	50c. Francis Langford	45	40
2409	75c. Joe E. Brown	80	70
2410	$1 Phil Silvers	1·25	80
2411	$2 Danny Kaye	2·25	2·25
2412	$5 Frank Sinatra	6·50	6·50
MS2413	Two sheets, each 107×80 mm. (a) $6 Bob Hope. (b) $6 Anna May Wong Set of 2 sheets	8·00	9·00

372 Badminton

1992. Olympic Games, Barcelona (2nd issue). Multicoloured.

2414	10c. Type **372**	50	30
2415	25c. Women's long jump	50	20
2416	35c. Women's 100 m	50	30
2417	50c. 1000 m cycling sprint	1·00	50
2418	75c. Decathlon (horiz)	1·00	80
2419	$2 Judo (horiz)	2·00	2·25
2420	$4 Women's gymnastics—asymmetrical bars	3·25	3·75
2421	$5 Men's javelin	3·25	3·75
MS2422	Two sheets, each 100×70 mm. (a) $6 Men's gymnastics – vault. (b) $6 Men's gymnastics – floor exercise Set of 2 sheets	8·00	9·00

GRENADA $1

372a Columbus meeting Amerindians

1992. 500th Anniv of Discovery of America by Columbus (6th issue). Organization of East Caribbean States. Multicoloured.

2423	$1 Type **372a**	70	70
2424	$2 Ships approaching island	1·40	1·60

372b The Blue Comet Locomotive, Boucher (1933)

1992. Toy Trains from American Manufacturers. Multicoloured.

2425	10c. Type **372b**	50	20
2426	35c. No. 2220 switching locomotive, Voltamp (1906)	60	25
2427	40c. No. 221 tunnel locomotive, Knapp (1905)	60	30
2428	75c. Grand Canyon locomotive, American Flyer (1931)	90	55
2429	$1 Streamliner tin locomotive, Hafner (1930s)	1·25	80
2430	$2 No. 237 switching locomotive, Elektoy (1911)	2·25	2·25
2431	$4 Parlor car, Ives (1928)	3·75	4·25
2432	$5 Improved President's Special locomotive, American Flyer (1927)	3·75	4·25
MS2433	Two sheets, each 133×103 mm. (a) $6 No. 1122 locomotive, Ives (1921) (38½×50 mm). (b) $6 No. 3239 locomotive, Ives (1912) (50×38½ mm) Set of 2 sheets	9·00	10·00

1992. Postage Stamp Mega Event, New York. Sheet 100×70 mm, containing multicoloured design as T **207a** of Gambia.

MS2434	$6 Guggenheim Museum	3·75	4·50

373 Matador (yacht), Newport News Regatta

1992. World Regattas. Multicoloured.

2435	15c. Type **373**	20	20
2436	25c. Awesome, Antigua	25	25
2437	35c. Mistress Quickly, Bermuda	30	30
2438	50c. Emeraude, St. Tropez	50	50
2439	$1 Diva G, German Admirals Cup	80	80
2440	$2 Lady Be, French Admirals Cup	1·50	1·75
2441	$4 Midnight Sun, Admirals Cup	2·75	3·50
2442	$5 "CARAT", Sardinia Cup	2·75	3·50
MS2443	Two sheets, each 113×85 mm. (a) $6 Yachts, Grenada Regatta (horiz). (b) $6 Fastnet Race, 1979 (horiz) Set of 2 sheets	9·00	11·00

1992. Christmas. Religious Paintings. As T **207b** of Gambia. Multicoloured.

2444	10c. Adoration of the Magi (detail) (Fra Filippo Lippi)	45	15
2445	15c. Madonna adoring Child in a Wood (Lippi)	55	20
2446	25c. Adoration of the Magi (detail) (Botticelli)	70	20
2447	35c. The Epiphany—Adoration of the Magi (detail) (Hieronymus Bosch)	75	20
2448	50c. Adoration of the Magi (detail) (Giovanni de Paolo)	1·00	45
2449	75c. Adoration of the Magi (Gentile da Fabriano)	1·50	60
2450	90c. Adoration of the Magi (detail) (Juan Batista Maino)	1·75	70
2451	$1 "Adoration of the Child (Master of Liesborn)	1·75	90
2452	$2 Adoration of the Kings (Master of Liesborn)	2·75	2·75
2453	$3 Adoration of the Three Wise Men (Pedro Berruguete)	3·00	3·50
2454	$4 Adoration of the Child (Lippi)	3·75	4·50
2455	$5 Adoration of the Child (Correggio)	4·75	4·50

MS2456	Three sheets, each 72×97 mm. (a) $6 Adoration of the Magi (detail) (Andrea Mantegna). (b) $6 Adoration of the Magi (detail) (Hans Memling). (c) $6 Adoration of the Shepherds (La Tour) Set of 3 sheets	16·00	17·00

No. 2447 is inscribed "Hieronymous" in error.

374 Cher

1992. Gold Record Award Winners. Multicoloured.

2457	90c. Type **374**	1·25	1·25
2458	90c. Michael Jackson	1·25	1·25
2459	90c. Elvis Presley	1·25	1·25
2460	90c. Dolly Parton	1·25	1·25
2461	90c. Johnny Mathis	1·25	1·25
2462	90c. Madonna	1·25	1·25
2463	90c. Nat King Cole	1·25	1·25
2464	90c. Janis Joplin	1·25	1·25
MS2465	Two sheets, each 100×70 mm. (a) $3 Chuck Berry; $3 James Brown. (b) $3 Frank Sinatra; $3 Perry Como Set of 2 sheets	12·00	12·00

Nos. 2457/64 were printed together, se-tenant, with a composite background design.

375 Grenada Dove

1992. Anniversaries and Events. Multicoloured.

2466	10c. Type **375**	1·00	65
2467	25c. Airship LZ-1 on maiden flight, 1900 (horiz)	1·00	30
2468	50c. ENDOSAT (robot plane) project (horiz)	1·25	55
2469	75c. Konrad Adenauer (German statesman) and industrial skyline (horiz)	1·25	70
2470	$1.50 Golden lion tamarin (horiz)	2·75	2·00
2471	$2 Mountain gorilla (horiz)	3·50	2·75
2472	$2 Outline of man and heart (horiz)	3·25	2·75
2473	$3 Wolfgang Amadeus Mozart	4·50	4·50
2474	$4 "Voyager 2" and Neptune (horiz)	4·50	4·50
2475	$4 Adenauer with flag and map of West Germany (horiz)	4·50	4·50
2476	$5 Count von Zeppelin and "Graf Zeppelin" (horiz)	4·50	4·75
2477	$6 Admiral Richard Byrd (polar explorer) (horiz)	4·50	4·75
MS2478	Five sheets. (a) 110×80 mm. $6 Count von Zeppelin (horiz). (b) 110×80 mm. $6 Space shuttle recovering "Intelsat 6" satellite. (c) 110×80 mm. $6 Konrad Adenauer (horiz). (d) 95×70 mm. $6 Spotted Little Owl (horiz). (e) 100×70 mm. $6 Papageno costume from "The Magic Flute" Set of 5 sheets	25·00	26·00

ANNIVERSARIES AND EVENTS: No. 2466, National bird; 2467, 2476, MS2478a, 75th death anniv of Count Ferdinand von Zeppelin; 2468, 2475, MS2478b, International Space Year; 2469, 2475, MS2478c, 25th death anniv of Konrad Adenauer; 2470/1, MS2478d, Earth Summit '92, Rio; 2472, United Nations World Health Organization Projects; 2473, MS2478e, Death bicentenary of Mozart; 2477, 75th anniv of International Association of Lions Clubs.

376 Care Bear on Beach

1992. Ecology.

2479	75c. Type **376**	1·00	60
MS2480	71×101 mm. $2 Care Bear and butterfly (vert)	2·75	2·75

377 Samoyed and St. Basil's Cathedral, Moscow

1993. Dogs of the World. Multicoloured.

2481	10c. Type **377**	80	40
2482	15c. Chow and Ling Yin Monastery, China	1·00	40
2483	25c. Boxer and Tower of London	1·25	30
2484	90c. Basenji and Yamma Mosque, Niger	1·75	75
2485	$1 Golden labrador and Parliament Building, Ottawa	1·75	80
2486	$3 St. Bernard and Parsenn, Switzerland	3·00	3·00
2487	$4 Rhodesian ridgeback and Melrose House, South Africa	3·25	3·50
2488	$5 Afghan hound and Mazar-i-Sharif, Afghanistan	3·25	3·50
MS2489	Two sheets, each 100×70 mm. (a) $6 Australian cattle dog. (b) $6 Alaskan malamute Set of 2 sheets	11·00	10·00

No. MS2489a is inscribed "Australiian" in error.

1993. Bicentenary of the Louvre, Paris. Paintings by Jean-Antoine Watteau. As T **209b** of Gambia. Multicoloured.

2490	$1 The Faux-pas	95	95
2491	$1 Portrait of a Gentleman	95	95
2492	$1 Young Lady with Archlute	95	95
2493	$1 Young Man Dancing	95	95
2494	$1 Autumn, Pamona and a Cherub	95	95
2495	$1 Judgement of Paris	95	95
2496	$1 Pierrot (detail)	95	95
2497	$1 Pierrot (different detail)	95	95
MS2498	100×70 mm. $6 The Embarkation for Cythère (85×52 mm).	4·75	5·50

378 Baha'i Shrine, Haifa

1993. Centenary of Baha'i Faith.

2499	**378**	75c. multicoloured	1·75	1·00

379 Citheronia magnifica

1993. Moths. Multicoloured.

2500	10c. Type **379**	25	25
2501	35c. Automeris metali	40	25
2502	45c. Thysania zenobia	50	30
2503	75c. Agrius cingulatus	70	55
2504	$1 Composia fidelissima	80	65
2505	$2 Synchlora xysteraria	1·50	1·75
2506	$4 Eumorpha labruscae	2·00	2·75
2507	$5 Ascalapha odorata	2·00	2·75
MS2508	Two sheets, each 100×70 mm. (a) $6 Epimecis detexta (vert). (b) $6 Xylophanes titana (vert) Set of 2 sheets	7·50	8·50

380 Heliconia

1993. Flowers. Multicoloured.

2509	10c. Type **380**	30	25
2510	35c. Pansy	50	25
2511	45c. Water lily	60	30
2512	75c. Bougainvillea	80	55
2513	$1 Calla lily	90	65
2514	$2 California poppy	1·50	1·75
2515	$4 Red ginger	2·25	3·25
2516	$5 Anthurium	2·25	3·25
MS2517	Two sheets, each 70×100 mm. (a) $6 Christmas rose (horiz). (b) $6 Moth orchid (horiz) Set of 2 sheets	7·50	8·50

1993. 40th Anniv of Coronation. As T **215a** of Gambia.

2518	35c. multicoloured	70	75
2519	70c. multicoloured	80	85
2520	$1 brown and black	85	90
2521	$5 multicoloured	2·25	2·50
MS2522	70×100 mm. $6 multicoloured	6·00	6·50

DESIGNS: 35c. Queen Elizabeth II at Coronation (photograph by Cecil Beaton); 70c. Sceptres; $1 Queen Elizabeth receiving sceptre from Archbishop of Canterbury; $5 Queen and Prince Philip with their children, 1960s. (28½×42½ mm)—$6 "Queen Elizabeth II, 1965" (detail) (Peter Greenham).

381 Woman with Loaves (Picasso)

1993. Anniversaries and Events. Each brown, deep brown and black (Nos. 2527, 2535, MS2536d) or multicoloured (others).

2523	25c. Type **381**	40	20
2524	35c. 16th-century telescope	45	20
2525	35c. Public Library building	45	20
2526	35c. Gaetan Boucher (speed skating, 1984)	45	20
2527	50c. Willy Brandt with Senator Edward Kennedy (horiz)	55	30
2528	75c. Carnival float (horiz)	70	40
2529	90c. "Weeping Woman" (Picasso)	85	45
2530	$1 Marii Prohaska (Tyrus Czyzewski)	1·00	50
2531	$3 Marysia et Burek a Geylan (S. Wirkiewicz)	2·50	2·50
2532	$4 Woman seated in Airchair (Picasso)	3·00	3·00
2533	$4 Astronaut on Moon	3·00	3·00
2534	$5 Norbert Schramm (figure skating, 1984)	3·00	3·00
2535	$5 Willy Brandt and Kurt Waldheim (horiz)	3·00	3·00
MS2536	Five sheets. (a) 76×107 mm. $5 Copernicus. (b) 75×105 mm. $6 Three Women at the Spring (detail) (Picasso). (c) 76×105 mm. $6 Women's Super G skiing medal winners, 1988 (horiz). (d) 105×75 mm. $6 Newspaper headline, 1974. (e) 105×76 mm. $6 Parting (detail) (Witold Wojtkiewicz) Set of 5 sheets	18·00	20·00

ANNIVERSARIES AND EVENTS: Nos. 2523, 2529, 2532, MS2536b, 20th death anniv of Picasso (artist); 2524, 2533, MS2536a, 450th death anniv of Copernicus (astronomer); 2525, Centenary (1992) of Grenada Public Library; 2526, 2534, MS2536c, Winter Olympic Games '94, Lillehammer; 2527, 2535, MS2536d, 80th birth anniv (1992) of Willy Brandt (German politician); 2528, Grenada Carnival; 2530/1, MS2536e, "Polska '93" International Stamp Exhibition, Poznan.

382 Yellow-green Vireo ("Red-eyed Vireo")

1993. Songbirds. Multicoloured.

2537	15c. Type **382**	60	60
2538	25c. Fork-tailed flycatcher ("Scissor-tailed Flycatcher")	65	65
2539	35c. Palm chat	75	75
2540	35c. Chaffinch	75	75
2541	45c. Yellow wagtail	80	80
2542	45c. Painted bunting	80	80
2543	50c. Short-tailed pygmy tyrant ("Short-tailed Pygmy Flycatcher")	80	80
2544	65c. Orange-breasted bunting ("Rainbow Bunting")	90	90
2545	75c. Red crossbill	90	90
2546	90c. Kauai akialoa	90	90
2547	$1 Yellow-throated longclaw ("Yellow-throated Wagtail")	1·00	1·00
2548	$4 Barn swallow	2·50	2·50
MS2549	Two sheets, each 105×86 mm. (a) $6 Song thrush. (b) $6 White-crested laughing thrush Set of 2 sheets	7·00	8·00

Nos. 2537/48 were printed together, se-tenant, with the backgrounds forming a composite design.

383 Atlantic Grey Cowrie and Atlantic Yellow Cowrie

1993. Seashells. Multicoloured.

2550	15c. Type **383**	55	55
2551	15c. Candy-stick tellin and sunrise tellin	55	55
2552	25c. Caribbean vase	60	60
2553	35c. Lightning venus and royal comb venus	70	70
2554	35c. Crown cone	70	70

2555	45c. Reticulated cowrie-helmet	80	80
2556	50c. Barbados mitre and variegated turret shell	80	80
2557	50c. Common egg cockle and Atlantic strawberry cockle	80	80
2558	75c. Measled cowrie	90	90
2559	75c. Rooster-tail conch	90	90
2560	$1 Lion's-paw scallop and Antillean scallop	1·00	1·00
2561	$4 Dog-head triton	2·25	2·25

MS2562 Two sheets, each 76×106 mm. (a) $6 Dyson's keyhole limpet. (b) $6 Virgin nerite and Emerald nerite Set of 2 sheets — 11·00 11·00

Nos. 2550/61 were printed together, *se-tenant*, with the backgrounds forming a composite design.

1993. Asian International Stamp Exhibitions. As T 219a of Gambia. Multicoloured. (a) "Indopex '93", Surabaya, Indonesia.

2563	35c. Megalithic carving, Sumba Island	35	25
2564	45c. Entrance to Gao Gajah, Bali	45	30
2565	$1.50 Statue of kris holder	1·00	1·00
2566	$1.50 Hanuman protecting Sita	1·00	1·00
2567	$1.50 Sendi of Visu mounted on Garuda	1·00	1·00
2568	$1.50 Wahana (votif figure)	1·00	1·00
2569	$1.50 Hanuman (different)	1·00	1·00
2570	$1.50 Singa (symbolic lion)	1·00	1·00
2571	$2 Loving-mother Bridge, Taroko Gorge National Park	1·40	1·50
2572	$4 Head of Kala over temple gateway, Northern Bali	2·50	2·75

MS2573 104×134 mm. $6 Slow loris — 3·75 4·25

(b) "Taipei '93", Taiwan.

2574	35c. Fire-breathing dragon, New Year's Fair, Chongqing	35	25
2575	45c. Stone elephant, Ming Tomb, Nanjing	45	30
2576	$1.50 Ornamental Cock (Han Meilin)	1·00	1·00
2577	$1.50 He's even afraid of Cows (Meilin)	1·00	1·00
2578	$1.50 On a Moonlit Night (Meilin)	1·00	1·00
2579	$1.50 Eyes that see in the Dark (Meilin)	1·00	1·00
2580	$1.50 He's well behaved (Meilin)	1·00	1·00
2581	$1.50 He doesn't Bite (Meilin)	1·00	1·00
2582	$2 Marble peifang, Ming 13 Tombs, Beijing	1·40	1·50
2583	$4 Stone pillar, Nanjing	2·50	3·00

MS2584 104×134 mm. $6 Orang-utan, Mt. Lesuser National Park — 3·75 4·25

(c) "Bangkok 1993", Thailand.

2585	35c. Nora Nair, Prasad Phra Thepidon, Wat Phra Kaew	35	25
2586	45c. Stucco deities at Library of Wat Phra Singh	45	30
2587	$1.50 Wooden carved horses	1·00	1·00
2588	$1.50 Wheel of the law	1·00	1·00
2589	$1.50 Lanna bronze elephant	1·00	1·00
2590	$1.50 Kendi in the form of elephant	1·00	1·00
2591	$1.50 Bronze duck	1·00	1·00
2592	$1.50 Horseman	1·00	1·00
2593	$2 Naga snake, Chiang Mai's Temple	1·40	1·50
2594	$4 Stucco figures, Wat Chang Lom	2·50	2·75

MS2595 134×104 mm. $6 Elephant calf (horiz) — 3·75 4·25

No. 2590 is incorrectly inscribed "Kendi in the form of an Elphant".

1993. World Cup Football Championship, U.S.A. (1994) (1st issue). As T 221a of Gambia. Multicoloured.

2596	10c. Nikolai Larionov (Russia)	35	30
2597	25c. Andrea Carnevale (Italy)	60	25
2598	35c. Enzo Schifo (Belgium) and Soon-Ho Choi (South Korea)	70	25
2599	45c. Gary Lineker (England)	1·00	30
2600	$1 Diego Maradona (Argentina)	1·25	80
2601	$2 Lothar Mattaeus (Germany)	1·50	2·00
2602	$4 Jan Karas (Poland) and Julio Cesar Silva (Brazil)	2·00	3·25
2603	$5 Claudio Caniggia (Argentina)	2·00	3·25

MS2604 Two sheets, each 75×104 mm. (a) $6 Wlodzimierz (Poland). (b) $6 José Basualdo (Argentina) Set of 2 sheets — 7·00 8·00

See also Nos. 2743/9.

384 James K. Spensley

1993. Centenary of Italian Football. Past and present Genoa players. Each blue, red and black.

2605	$3 Type 384	2·50	2·50
2606	$3 Renzo de Vecchi	2·50	2·50
2607	$3 Giovanni de Pra'	2·50	2·50
2608	$3 Luigi Burlando	2·50	2·50
2609	$3 Felice Levratto	2·50	2·50
2610	$3 Guglielmo Stabile	2·50	2·50
2611	$3 Vittorio Sardeli	2·50	2·50
2612	$3 Juan Carlos Verdeal	2·50	2·50
2613	$3 Fosco Becattini	2·50	2·50
2614	$3 Julio Cesar Abadie	2·50	2·50
2615	$3 Luigi Meroni	2·50	2·50
2616	$3 Roberto Pruzzo	2·50	2·50

MS2617 Two sheets. (a) 100×75 mm. $15 Genoa Football Club badge (29×45 mm). (b) 129×106 mm. $15 Genoa team of 1991–92 (48×35 mm) Set of 2 sheets — 22·00 22·00

385 The Band Concert, 1935

1993. 65th Anniv of Mickey Mouse. Scenes from Walt Disney cartoon films. Multicoloured.

2618	25c. Type 385	1·00	20
2619	35c. "Mickey's Circus", 1936	1·25	20
2620	50c. "Magician Mickey", 1937	1·50	35
2621	75c. "Moose Hunters", 1937	1·75	60
2622	$1 "Mickey's Amateurs", 1937	2·00	80
2623	$2 "Tugboat Mickey", 1940	2·75	2·50
2624	$4 "Orphan's Benefit", 1941	3·75	4·50
2625	$5 "Mickey's Christmas Carol", 1983	3·75	4·50

MS2626 Two sheets, each 127×102 mm. (a) $6 "Mickey's Birthday Party", 1942. (b) $6 "Mickey's Trailer", 1938 (vert) Set of 2 sheets — 11·00 11·00

No. 2624 is inscribed "Oprhan's Benefit" in error.

1993. Christmas. Religious Paintings. As T 221b of Gambia. Black, yellow and red (Nos. 2627/8, 2632 and 2634, MS2635a) or multicoloured (others).

2627	10c. The Nativity (Durer)	25	15
2628	25c. The Annunciation (Durer)	35	15
2629	35c. The Litta Madonna (Da Vinci)	40	20
2630	60c. The Virgin and Child with St. John the Baptist and St. Anne (Da Vinci)	50	40
2631	90c. The Madonna with the Carnation (Da Vinci)	65	65
2632	$1 Adoration of the Magi (Durer)	75	75
2633	$4 The Benois Madonna (Da Vinci)	2·50	3·25
2634	$5 The Virgin Mary in the Sun (Durer)	2·50	3·25

MS2635 Two sheets, each 102×128 mm. (a) $6 The Holy Family with Three Hares (detail) (Dürer). (b) $6 Adoration of the Magi (detail) (Da Vinci) Set of 2 sheets — 8·00 9·00

Nos. 2629/31, 2633 and MS2635b are inscribed "LEONARDO DI VINCI" in error.

386 Blanchard's Balloon over Walnut St. Prison

1993. Aviation Anniversaries. Multicoloured.

2636	35c. Airship Graf Zeppelin over Vienna at night	35	20
2637	45c. Type 386	20	25
2638	50c. Lysander	50	35
2639	75c. Graf Zeppelin over Pyramids	75	55
2640	$2 Blanchard waving hat from balloon (vert)	90	95
2641	$3 Hawker Typhoon	2·00	2·50
2642	$5 Graf Zeppelin over Rio de Janeiro	3·25	3·75

MS2643 Three sheets, each 106×77 mm. (a) $6 Graf Zeppelin. (b) $6 Blanchard's balloon (vert). (c) $6 Hawker Hurricane Set of 3 sheets — 10·50 11·00

ANNIVERSARIES: Nos. 2636, 2639, 2642, MS2643a, 125th birth anniv of Hugo Eckener (airship commander); 2637, 2640, MS2643b, Bicentenary of first airmail flight; 2638, 2641, MS2643c, 75th anniv of Royal Air Force.

387 Mercedes Benz "370 S" Cabriolet, 1932

1993. Centenaries of Henry Ford's First Petrol Engine (Nos. 2645/6, MS2648b) and Karl Benz's First Four-wheeled Car (others). Multicoloured.

2644	35c. Type 387	55	20
2645	45c. Ford "Mustang", 1966	65	30
2646	$3 Ford "Model A" Phaeton, 1930	3·25	3·75
2647	$4 Mercedes Benz "300 Sl" Gullwing	3·50	4·00

MS2648 Two sheets, each 76×106 mm. (a) $6 Mercedes Benz "290", 1934. (b) $6 Ford "Model A", 1903 Set of 2 sheets — 8·00 9·00

1993. Famous Paintings by Rembrandt and Matisse. As T 221c of Gambia. Multicoloured.

2649	15c. Self-portrait, 1900 (Matisse)	40	20
2650	35c. Self-portrait, 1629 (Rembrandt)	45	20
2651	45c. Self-portrait, 1918 (Matisse)	50	25
2652	50c. Self-portrait, 1640 (Rembrandt)	60	35
2653	75c. Self-portrait, 1652 (Rembrandt)	75	55
2654	$2 Self-portrait, 1906 (Matisse)	1·60	1·75
2655	$4 Self-portrait, 1900 (different) (Matisse)	2·75	4·00
2656	$5 Self-portrait, 1625–31 (Rembrandt)	3·00	4·00

MS2657 Two sheets. (a) 100×125 mm. $6 The Painter in his Studio (detail) (Matisse). P 13½×14. (b) 125×100 mm. $6 The Sampling Officials of the Drapers' Guild (detail) (Rembrandt) (horiz).Set of 2 sheets — 7·00 8·00

388 Fishermen with Blue Marlin

1994. 25th Anniv of Spice Island Billfish Tournament. Multicoloured.

2658	15c. Type 388	50	30
2659	25c. Sailfish with angler	55	30
2660	35c. Yellow-finned tuna with angler	65	30
2661	50c. White marlin with angler	75	60
2662	75c. Catching a sailfish	85	1·00

389 National Flag and Ketch in Bay

1994. 25th Anniv of Independence.

2663	35c. Type 389	75	40

MS2664 76×106 mm. $6 Map of Grenada — 5·50 6·00

1994. "Hong Kong '94" International Stamp Exhibition (1st issue). As T 222a of Gambia. Multicoloured.

2665	40c. Hong Kong 1971 Scouting 50c. stamp and "Hong Kong Post Office, 1846" (left detail) (M. Bruce)	50	65
2666	40c. Grenada 1988 Rotary $2 and "Hong Kong Post Office, 1846" (right detail) (M. Bruce)	50	65

Nos. 2665/6 were printed together, *se-tenant*, with the centre part of each pair forming the complete painting. See also Nos. 2667/72.

1994. "Hong Kong '94" International Stamp Exhibition (2nd issue). Qing Dynasty Porcelain. As T 222b of Gambia. Multicoloured.

2667	45c. Vase with dragon decoration	65	65
2668	45c. Hat stand with brown base	65	65
2669	45c. Gourd-shaped vase	65	65
2670	45c. Rotating vase with openwork	65	65
2671	45c. Candlestick with dogs	65	65
2672	45c. Hat stand with orange base	65	65

390 Hygrocybe acutoconica

1994. Fungi. Multicoloured.

2673	35c. Type 390	50	30
2674	45c. Leucopaxillus gracillimus	55	30
2675	50c. Leptonia caeruleocapitata	55	30
2676	75c. Leucocoprinus birnbaumii	70	50
2677	$1 Marasmius atrorubens	85	75
2678	$2 Boletellus cubensis	1·40	1·50
2679	$4 Chlorophyllum molybdites	2·25	2·75
2680	$5 Psilocybe cubensis	2·25	2·75

MS2681 Two sheets, each 100×70 mm. (a) $6 Mycena pura. (b) $6 Pyrrhoglossum lilaceipes Set of 2 sheets — 9·00 9·00

391 Quetzalcoatlus

1994. Prehistoric Animals. Multicoloured.

2682	75c. Type 391	70	65
2683	75c. Pteranodon ingens	70	65
2684	75c. Tropeognathus	70	65
2685	75c. Phobetor	70	65
2686	75c. Alamosaurus	70	65
2687	75c. Triceratops	70	65
2688	75c. Tyrannosaurus rex	70	65
2689	75c. Head of Tyrannosaurus rex	70	65
2690	75c. Lambeosaurus	70	65
2691	75c. Spinosaurus	70	65
2692	75c. Parasaurolophus	70	65
2693	75c. Hadrosaurus	70	65
2694	75c. Germanodactylus	70	65
2695	75c. Dimorphodon	70	65
2696	75c. Ramphorynchus	70	65
2697	75c. Apatosaurus	70	65
2698	75c. Pterodactylus	70	65
2699	75c. Stegosaurus	70	65
2700	75c. Brathiosaurus	70	65
2701	75c. Allosaurus	70	65
2702	75c. Plesiosaurus	70	65
2703	75c. Ceratosaurus	70	65
2704	75c. Compsognathus	70	65
2705	75c. Elaphosaurus	70	65

MS2706 Two sheets. (a) 100×70 mm. $6 Pteranodon ingens (different). (b) 70×100 mm. $6 Head of Plateosaurus (vert) Set of 2 sheets — 9·00 9·00

Nos. 2682/93 and 2694/2705 respectively were printed together, *se-tenant*, forming composite designs.

1994. 25th Anniv of First Manned Moon Landing. Space Shuttle "Challenger". As T 227a of Gambia. Multicoloured.

2707	$2 Space shuttle "Challenger"	1·50	1·40
2708	$2 Judith Resnick (astronaut)	1·50	1·40
2709	$2 Aircraft in memorial fly past	1·50	1·40
2710	$2 Dick Scobee (astronaut)	1·50	1·40
2711	$2 Mission logo	1·50	1·40
2712	$2 Michael Smith (astronaut)	1·50	1·40

MS2713 107×76 mm. $6 "Challenger" crew — 3·75 4·50

1994. Centenary of International Olympic Committee. Gold Medal Winners. As T 227b of Gambia. Multicoloured.

2714	50c. Heike Dreschler (Germany) (long jump), 1992	50	30
2715	$1.50 Nadia Comaneci (Rumania) (gymnastics), 1976 and 1980	1·60	1·75

MS2716 107×76 mm. $6 Dan Jansen (U.S.A.) (1000 metre speed skating), 1994 — 3·75 4·25

391a Grenadian Family

1994. International Year of the Family.

2717	391a $1 multicoloured	1·00	1·00

1994. 50th Anniv of D-Day. As T 227c of Gambia. Multicoloured.

2718	40c. Sherman amphibious tank leaving landing craft	1·00	30
2719	$2 Tank on Churchill "Ark" bridging vehicle	2·75	2·00
2720	$3 Churchill "Bobbin" tank laying roadway	3·00	2·50

MS2721 107×76 mm. $6 Churchill AVRE with fascine — 3·75 4·00

1994. "Philakorea '94" International Stamp Exhibition, Seoul. As T 227d of Gambia. Multicoloured.

2722	40c. Wonson Park (horiz)	30	25
2723	$1 Pusan (horiz)	55	60
2724	$1 Lady in a Hooded Cloak (left detail) (Sin Yunbok)	55	60
2725	$1 Lady in a Hooded Cloak (right detail)	55	60

2726	$1 *Kiaseng House* (left detail) (Sin Yunbok)	55	60
2727	$1 *Kiaseng House* (right detail) (Sin Yunbok)	55	60
2728	$1 *Amorous Youth on a Picnic* (left detail) (Sin Yunbok)	55	60
2729	$1 *Amorous Youth on a Picnic* (right detail) (Sin Yunbok)	55	60
2730	$1 *Chasing a Cat* (left detail) (Sin Yunbok)	55	60
2731	$1 *Chasing a Cat* (right detail) (Sin Yunbok)	55	60
2732	$4 Korean orchestra, National Theatre, Seoul (horiz)	2·00	2·50
MS2733	70×102 mm. $6 *Roof Tiling* (detail) (Kim Hongdo)	3·25	3·50

Nos. 2724/31 were printed together, *se-tenant*, forming composite designs of each painting.

392 *Brassavola cuculatta*

1994. Orchids. Multicoloured.
2734	15c. Type **392**	30	20
2735	25c. *Comparettia falcata*	40	20
2736	45c. *Epidendrum ciliare*	50	30
2737	75c. *Epidendrum cochleatum*	70	50
2738	$1 *Ionopsis utricularioides*	80	70
2739	$2 *Onicidium ceboletta*	1·25	1·40
2740	$4 *Onicidium luridium*	2·25	2·50
2741	$5 *Rodriquezia secunda*	2·25	2·50
MS2742	Two sheets, each 100×70 mm. (a) $6 *Ionopsis utricularioides* (different). (b) $6 *Onicidium luridium* (different) Set of 2 sheets	8·00	8·50

No. **MS**2742b is inscribed "Onicium luridum" in error.

393 Tony Meola (U.S.A.)

1994. World Cup Football Championship, U.S.A. (2nd issue). Multicoloured.
2743	75c. Type **393**	65	80
2744	75c. Steve Mark (Grenada)	65	80
2745	75c. Gianluigi Lentini (Italy)	65	80
2746	75c. Belloumi (Algeria)	65	80
2747	75c. Nunoz (Spain)	65	80
2748	75c. Lothar Matthaus (Germany)	65	80
MS2749	Two sheets. (a) 99×70 mm. $6 World Cup Championship poster, 1930. (b) 70×114 mm. $6 Steve Mark (Grenada) (different) Set of 2 sheets	7·50	8·00

393a Sir Shridath Ramphal

1994. First Recipients of Order of the Caribbean Community. Multicoloured.
2750	15c. Type **393a**	10	10
2751	65c. William Demas	40	40
2752	$2 Derek Walcott	1·75	1·75

394 Yellow-tailed Snapper

1994. Fish. Multicoloured.
2753	15c. Type **394**	40	20
2754	20c. Blue tang	40	20
2755	25c. Porkfish (vert)	40	20
2756	75c. Four-eyed butterflyfish	75	50
2757	85c. Reid's seahorse (vert)	85	70
2758	$2 Spotted moray (vert)	1·50	1·60
2759	$4 Royal gramma ("Fairy basslet")	2·50	2·75
2760	$5 Queen triggerfish (vert)	2·50	2·75
MS2761	Two sheets, each 106×76 mm. (a) $6 Queen angelfish. (b) $6 Long-spined squirrelfish Set of 2 sheets	7·50	8·00

395 Mickey Mouse bathing Pluto

1994. Chinese New Year ("Year of the Dog"). Walt Disney cartoon characters. Multicoloured.
2762	2c. Type **395**	15	10
2763	3c. Dog taking mouthwash	15	10
2764	4c. Dog with curlers in tail	15	10
2765	5c. Brushing dog's eyelashes	15	10
2766	10c. Giving dog manicure	25	10
2767	15c. Mickey spraying Pluto with flea powder	40	15
2768	20c. Dogs on display	40	20
2769	$4 Judge checking Pluto's teeth	4·50	4·75
2770	$5 Pluto wearing "1st Prize" rosette	4·50	4·75
MS2771	Three sheets, each 127×102 mm. (a) $6 King Charles Spaniel rubbing against judge's leg. (b) $6 Pluto holding rosette. (c) $6 Pluto with No. 13 on coat Set of 3 sheets	11·00	12·00

396 *Anartia amathea*

1994. Butterflies. Multicoloured.
2772A	10c. Type **396**	40	30
2773A	15c. *Marpesia petreus*	50	30
2774B	25c. *Hylephila phylaeus*	80	25
2775B	35c. *Junonia evarete*	85	30
2776A	45c. *Pseudolycaena marsyas*	75	30
2777A	50c. *Heliconius charitonius*	75	30
2778A	75c. *Hypolimnas misippus*	1·00	55
2778cB	90c. *Purgus oilcus*	1·50	75
2779A	$1 *Cepheuptychia cephus*	1·25	70
2779cB	$1.50 *Allosmaitia piplea*	80	85
2780A	$2 *Historis odius*	2·50	1·60
2781A	$3 *Phoebis philea*	3·75	4·00
2782A	$4 *Urbanus proteus*	4·50	5·00
2783A	$5 *Battus polydamas*	4·50	5·00
2784A	$10 *Philaethria dido*	8·50	10·00
2785A	$20 *Hamadryas arethusa*	12·00	17·00

1994. Christmas. Religious Paintings by Francisco de Zurbaran. As T **231a** of Gambia. Multicoloured.
2786	10c. *The Virgin and Child with St. John* (1658)	20	15
2787	15c. *The Circumcision*	30	20
2788	25c. *Adoration of St. Joseph*	30	20
2789	35c. *Adoration of the Magi*	30	20
2790	75c. *The Portiuncula*	60	45
2791	$1 *The Virgin and Child with St. John* (1662)	75	60
2792	$2 *The Virgin and Child with St. John* (1658/64)	1·25	1·75
2793	$4 *The Flight into Egypt*	2·25	3·25
MS2794	Two sheets. (a) 74×86 mm. $6 *Our Lady of Ransom and Two Mercedarians* (detail). (b) 114×100 mm. $6 *Adoration of the Shepherds* (detail) (horiz) Set of 2 sheets	7·50	8·00

397 Grenada Dove on Nest

1995. Birds. Multicoloured.
2795	25c. Type **397**	1·25	50
2796	35c. Pair of Grenada doves at nest	1·25	50
2797	45c. Cuban tody (vert)	1·40	50
2798	75c. Grenada dove on branch (vert)	1·60	1·50
2799	75c. Painted bunting	1·60	1·50
2800	$1 Grenada dove in flight (vert)	1·75	1·60
2801	$1 Red-legged honeycreeper	1·75	1·60
2802	$5 Green jay	3·50	4·25
MS2803	Two sheets, each 101×71 mm. (a) $6 Chaffinch. (b) $6 Chestnut-sided shrike vireo Set of 2 sheets	7·50	8·00

Nos. 2795/6, 2798 and 2800 also show the W.W.F. Panda emblem.

397a Junior Murray (West Indies)

1995. Centenary of First English Cricket Tour to the West Indies. Multicoloured.
2804	25c. Type **397a**	65	30
2805	35c. Richie Richardson (West Indies)	70	30
2806	$2 Alec Stewart (England) and Wisden Trophy (horiz)	2·00	2·25
MS2807	75×95 mm. $3 West Indian team, 1994	2·50	2·50

398 Hooded Merganser

1995. Water Birds of the World. Multicoloured.
2808	25c. Type **398**	30	30
2809	35c. Green-winged teal	35	30
2810	75c. King eider	70	75
2811	75c. Common shoveler	70	75
2812	75c. Long-tailed duck	70	75
2813	75c. Chiloe wigeon	70	75
2814	75c. Red-breasted merganser	70	75
2815	75c. Falcated teal	70	75
2816	75c. Vericolor teal	70	75
2817	75c. Smew	70	75
2818	75c. Red-crested pochard	70	75
2819	75c. Pintail	70	75
2820	75c. Barrow's goldeneye	70	75
2821	75c. Stellar's eider	70	75
2822	$1 Harlequin duck	75	75
2823	$3 European wigeon	1·75	2·00
MS2824	Two sheets, each 74×104 mm. (a) $5 Common shelduck ("European Wigeon"). (b) $6 Egyptian goose Set of 2 sheets	6·50	7·50

Nos. 2810/21 were printed together, *se-tenant*, forming a composite design.
No. 2811 is inscribed "Shobeler" in error.

399 Pig Priest, China

1995. Chinese New Year ("Year of the Pig"). Ornaments. Multicoloured.
2825	50c. Type **399**	45	55
2826	75c. Porcelain pig, Scotland	55	65
2827	$1 Seated porcelain pig, Italy	60	75
MS2828	107×77 mm. $2 Jade pig, China	1·25	1·40

400 Yellow-tailed Damselfish

1995. Marine Life. Multicoloured.
2829	$1 Type **400**	75	75
2830	$1 Blue-headed wrasse	75	75
2831	$1 Balloonfish	75	75
2832	$1 Shy hamlet	75	75
2833	$1 Orange tube coral	75	75
2834	$1 Rock beauty	75	75
2835	$1 Creole wrasse	75	75
2836	$1 Queen angelfish	75	75
2837	$1 Trumpetfish	75	75
2838	$1 Barred hamlet	75	75
2839	$1 Tube sponge	75	75
2840	$1 Porcupine fish	75	75
2841	$1 Firecoral	75	75
2842	$1 Royal gramma ("Fairy basslet")	75	75
2843	$1 Sea anemone	75	75
MS2844	Two sheets, each 106×76 mm. (a) $5 Seahorse. (b) $6 Elkhorn coral Set of 2 sheets	4·75	5·50

Nos. 2829/34 and 2835/43 respectively were printed together, *se-tenant*, forming composite designs.

401 National Flags

1995. Grenada-Taiwan (Republic of China) Friendship. Multicoloured.
2845	75c. Type **401**	1·25	75
2846	$1 Prime Minister Brathwaite and President Lee Teng-hui	1·25	80
MS2847	76×106 mm. Nos. 2845/6	2·50	1·75

402 Cocker Spaniel

1995. Domestic Animals. Multicoloured.
2848	10c. Type **402**	50	30
2849	15c. Pinto (horse)	60	30
2850	25c. Rottweiler	70	20
2851	35c. German shepherd	75	20
2852	45c. Persian (cat)	80	25
2853	50c. Snowshoe (cat)	80	30
2854	75c. Percheron (horse)	1·25	60
2855	$1 Scottish fold (cat)	1·25	70
2856	$2 Arabian (horse)	2·00	2·00
2857	$3 Andalusian (horse)	2·25	2·50
2858	$4 C.P. Shorthair (cat)	2·50	3·00
2859	$5 Chihuahua	3·00	3·25
MS2860	Three sheets, each 100×71 mm. (a) $5 Manx (cat). (b) $5 Donkey. (c) $6 Shar Pei Set of 3 sheets	8·00	9·50

1995. Centenary (1992) of Sierra Club (environmental protection society). Endangered Species. As T **224a** of Gambia. Multicoloured.
2861	$1 Head of margay at night	80	80
2862	$1 Margay sitting	80	80
2863	$1 Head of margay in daylight	80	80
2864	$1 Head of Andean condor	80	80
2865	$1 Andean condor facing right	80	80
2866	$1 Andean condor facing left	80	80
2867	$1 White-faced saki on branch	80	80
2868	$1 White-faced saki showing mane	80	80
2869	$1 Patagonia landscape	80	80
2870	$1 Lesser rheas feeding (horiz)	80	80
2871	$1 Pair of lesser rheas (horiz)	80	80
2872	$1 Lesser rhea (horiz)	80	80
2873	$1 Sunset over snow-covered mountains, Patagonia (horiz)	80	80
2874	$1 Volcanic eruption, Patagonia (horiz)	80	80
2875	$1 White-faced Saki (horiz)	80	80
2876	$1 Common caracara on branch (horiz)	80	80
2877	$1 Pair of common caracaras at nest (horiz)	80	80
2878	$1 Common caracara facing left (horiz)	80	80

403 Grenadian Scout

1995. 18th World Scout Jamboree, Netherlands. Multicoloured.
2879	75c. Type **403**	45	50
2880	$1 Scout abseiling	55	60
2881	$2 Scout saluting and national flag	85	1·00
MS2882	107×77 mm. $6 Scout in canoe	3·00	3·50

1995. 50th Anniv of End of Second World War in Europe. Fighter Aircraft. As T **237a** of Gambia. Multicoloured.
2883	$2 Lavochkin La-7 (fighter)	1·90	1·50
2884	$2 Hawker Hurricane	1·90	1·50
2885	$2 North American P-51D Mustang	1·90	1·50
2886	$2 Messerschmitt Bf 109	1·90	1·50
2887	$2 Bristol Type 152 Beaufighter	1·90	1·50
2888	$2 Messerschmitt Me 262	1·90	1·50
2889	$2 Republic P-47 Thunderbolt	1·90	1·50
2890	$2 Hawker Tempest	1·90	1·50
MS2891	106×76 mm. $6 Nose of Republic P-47 Thunderbolt	4·00	4·25

404 "Swords into
Ploughshares"

1995. 50th Anniv of United Nations. Multicoloured.
2892	75c. Type **404**	40	50
2893	$1 Globe and dove	50	60
2894	$2 U.N. Building, New York	85	1·10
MS2895	101×71 mm. $6 Anniversary logo (horiz)	2·50	3·00

405 Woman with
Baskets

1995. 50th Anniv of F.A.O. Multicoloured.
2896	75c. Type **405**	40	50
2897	$1 Boy with basket on head	50	60
2898	$2 Men harvesting bananas	85	90
MS2899	72×102 mm. $6 F.A.O. logo	2·50	3·00

406 National Flag
and Rotary Logo

1995. 90th Anniv of Rotary International. Multicoloured.
2900	$5 Type **406**	2·10	2·40
MS2901	76×106 mm. $6 Paul Harris (founder) and logo	2·75	3·25

1995. 95th Birthday of Queen Elizabeth the Queen Mother. As T **239a** of Gambia.
2902	$1.50 brown, lt brown & blk	1·75	1·60
2903	$1.50 multicoloured	1·75	1·60
2904	$1.50 multicoloured	1·75	1·60
2905	$1.50 multicoloured	1·75	1·60
MS2906	127×102 mm. $6 multicoloured	6·50	6·50

DESIGNS: No. 2902, Queen Elizabeth the Queen Mother (pastel drawing); 2903, Holding rose; 2904, At desk (oil painting); 2905, In blue hat and white coat; **MS**2906, Wearing floral hat.

1995. 50th Anniv of End of Second World War in the Pacific. As T **239b** of Gambia. Multicoloured.
2907	$2 Dogfight over the Marianas	2·00	1·75
2908	$2 U.S. dive-bomber and burning aircraft carrier, Battle of Midway	2·00	1·75
2909	$2 U.S. aircraft attacking Japanese transport, Battle of the Bismarck Sea	2·00	1·75
2910	$2 *Mushashi* (Japanese battleship) on fire in Leyte Gulf	2·00	1·75
2911	$2 U.S. aircraft taking off from Henderson Field	2·00	1·75
2912	$2 Battleships at Guadalcanal	2·00	1·75
MS2913	108×77 mm. $6 U.S. bomber	3·75	4·00

407 Tian Bingyi
(China)
(badminton)

1995. Olympic Games, Atlanta (1996) (1st issue). Multicoloured.
2914	75c. Type **407**	80	80
2915	75c. Waldemar Leigien (Poland) and Frank Wieneke (West Germany) (judo)	80	80
2916	75c. Nelli Kim (U.S.S.R.) (gymnastics)	80	80
2917	75c. Alessandro Andri (Italy) (shot put)	80	80
2918	$2 Jackie Joyner (U.S.A.) (heptathlon)	1·75	1·75

2919	$2 Mitsuo Tsukahara (Japan) (gymnastics)	1·75	1·75
2920	$2 Flo Hyman (U.S.A.) and Zhang Rung Fang (China) (volleyball)	1·75	1·75
2921	$2 Steffi Graf (West Germany) (tennis)	1·75	1·75
MS2922	Two sheets, each 72×102 mm. (a) $6 Wilma Rudolph (U.S.A.) (athletics). (b) $6 Soling class yacht Set of 2 sheets	7·00	8·00

No. **MS**2922b is inscribed "Sailing" in error.
See also Nos. 3102/24.

408 Junior Murray
(West Indies)

1995. Anniversaries and Events. Multicoloured.
2923	25c. Type **408** (centenary of first English cricket tour to the West Indies)	1·50	60
2924	75c. Nutmeg (opening of Grenada Spice Factory)	90	75
2925	$1 Sendall Tunnel (centenary (1994))	1·10	1·25
2926	$1 Caribbean Development Bank building (25th anniv)	1·10	1·25

409 Ajamu

1995. Local Entertainers. Multicoloured.
2927	35c. Type **409**	50	50
2928	35c. Mighty Sparrow	50	50
2929	50c. Mighty Sparrow in evening dress	60	60
2930	75c. Ajamu (different)	75	75

410 Elvis Presley
and Signature

1995. Entertainment Legends. Multicoloured.
2931	75c. Type **410**	65	65
2932	75c. Marilyn Monroe	65	65

411 Elvis Presley

1995. 60th Birth Anniv of Elvis Presley (singer). Multicoloured.
2933	$1 Type **411**	70	70
2934	$1 With beard	70	70
2935	$1 With long hair and microphone	70	70
2936	$1 Wearing white shirt	70	70
2937	$1 Wearing pink shirt and purple jacket	70	70
2938	$1 With short hair and microphone	70	70
2939	$1 Wearing magenta shirt	70	70
2940	$1 Wearing orange shirt	70	70
2941	$1 Wearing purple shirt	70	70

412 Film Reel and Oscar
Statuette

1995. Centenary of Cinema. Multicoloured.
2942	$1 Type **412**	90	85
2943	$1 "HOLLYWOOD" sign	90	85
2944	$1 Charlie Chaplin	90	85
2945	$1 Shirley Temple	90	85
2946	$1 Spencer Tracy and Katherine Hepburn	90	85
2947	$1 Marilyn Monroe	90	85
2948	$1 John Wayne	90	85
2949	$1 Marlon Brando	90	85
2950	$1 Tom Cruise	90	85
MS2951	107×77 mm. $5 Orson Welles (horiz)	5·50	5·50

Nos. 2942/50 were printed together, *se-tenant*, forming a composite design.

413 "B1 Level Vista Dome"
Electric Locomotive, Japan

1995. Trains of the World (1st series). Multicoloured.
2952	$1 Type **413**	1·00	90
2953	$1 Rolios Rail Class 25NC steam locomotive, South Africa	1·00	90
2954	$1 Class 460 electric locomotive, Switzerland	1·00	90
2955	$1 Central Railway diesel locomotive No. 605, Peru	1·00	90
2956	$1 X2000 tilt body train, Sweden	1·00	90
2957	$1 Via Rail Toronto to Vancouver observation car, Canada	1·00	90
2958	$1 Intercity 125 diesel locomotive, Great Britain	1·00	90
2959	$1 *The Flying Scotsman* steam locomotive, Great Britain	1·00	90
2960	$1 *Indian Pacific* diesel locomotive, Australia	1·00	90
2961	$1 ETR 450 electric train, Italy	1·00	90
2962	$1 Isparta to Bozanonu Line steam locomotive, Turkey	1·00	90
2963	$1 TGV train, France	1·00	90
2964	$1 ICE train, Germany	1·00	90
2965	$1 Nishi Line electric locomotive, Japan	1·00	90
2966	$1 *Hikari* train, Japan	1·00	90
2967	$1 Central Pacific Jupiter steam locomotive, U.S.A.	1·00	90
2968	$1 Amtrak Type 900 electric locomotive, U.S.A.	1·00	90
2969	$1 *Sir Nigel Gresley* steam locomotive, Great Britain	1·00	90
MS2970	Two sheets, each 106×76 mm. (a) $5 Diesel hydraulic train, Korea. (b) $6 Peking–Ulan Bator express, Mongolia Set of 2 sheets	7·00	8·00

See also Nos. 3167/83.

414 Teresa Teng

1995. Teresa Teng (Chinese actress) Commem. Different portraits. Multicoloured unless otherwise indicated.
2971	35c. Type **414**	45	60
2972	35c. As a child (brown, ochre and yellow)	45	60
2973	35c. Wearing feather boa (black, grey and yellow)	45	60
2974	35c. With motor scooter	45	60
2975	35c. Holding microphone	45	60
2976	35c. In white sweater	45	60
2977	35c. Playing flute	45	60
2978	35c. With hand to hair (black, grey and yellow)	45	60
2979	35c. Wearing gold decorated dress	45	60
2980	35c. With fan	45	60
2981	35c. As South-sea islander	45	60
2982	35c. With hands clasped	45	60
2983	35c. In kimono	45	60

2984	35c. Holding bow tie	45	60
2985	35c. Wearing black blouse	45	60
2986	35c. Resting on chair arm	45	60
2987	75c. In army uniform	60	65
2988	75c. In navy uniform	60	65
2989	75c. In air force uniform	60	65
2990	75c. Singing with hand out stretched (black, grey and yellow)	60	65
2991	75c. Singing with flowers in hair	60	65
2992	75c. Singing in blue floral dress	60	65
2993	75c. With pink scarf	60	65
2994	75c. In fringed dress	60	65
2995	75c. In pale green sweater	60	65
2996	75c. With hands to face	60	65

Nos. 2987/96 are larger, 34×46 mm.

415 Mickey Mouse
fighting Big Pete

1995. Mickey's Pirate Adventure. Walt Disney cartoon characters. Multicoloured.
2997	15c. Type **415**	40	45
2998	25c. Mickey with treasure chest	45	20
2999	35c. Minnie Mouse trying on plunder	50	20
3000	75c. Goofy with telescope and Mickey swimming with barrel	75	40
3001	$3 Big Pete	2·25	2·25
3002	$5 Mickey with monkey, seagull and handkerchief	2·75	3·25
MS3003	Two sheets, each 108×103 mm. (a) $6 Sea rat pirate. (b) $6 Minnie being thrown overboard by pirates Set of 2 sheets	8·00	8·50

416 Albert
Michelson (1907
Physics)

1995. Centenary of Nobel Trust Fund. Multicoloured.
3004	$1 Type **416**	95	85
3005	$1 Ralph Bunche (1950 Peace)	95	85
3006	$1 Edwin Neher (1991 Medicine)	95	85
3007	$1 Klaus Vonklitzing (1985 Physics)	95	85
3008	$1 Johann Deisenhofer (1988 Chemistry)	95	85
3009	$1 Max Delbruck (1969 Medicine)	95	85
3010	$1 J. Georg Bednorz (1987 Physics)	95	85
3011	$1 Feodor Lynen (1964 Medicine)	95	85
3012	$1 Walther Bothe (1954 Physics)	95	85
3013	$1 James Franck (1925 Physics)	95	85
3014	$1 Gustav Hertz (1925 Physics)	95	85
3015	$1 Friedrich Bergius (1931 Chemistry)	95	85
3016	$1 Otto Loewi (1936 Medicine)	95	85
3017	$1 Fritz Lipmann (1953 Medicine)	95	85
3018	$1 Otto Meyerhof (1922 Medicine)	95	85
3019	$1 Paul Heyse (1910 Literature)	95	85
3020	$1 Jane Addams (1931 Peace)	95	85
3021	$1 Carl Braun (1909 Physics)	95	85
3022	$1 Hans Dehmelt (1989 Physics)	95	85
3023	$1 Heinrich Boll (1972 Literature)	95	85
3024	$1 Georges Kohler (1984 Medicine)	95	85
3025	$1 Wolfgang Pauli (1945 Physics)	95	85
3026	$1 Sir Bernard Katz (1970 Medicine)	95	85
3027	$1 Ernest Ruska (1986 Physics)	95	85
3028	$1 William Golding (1983 Literature)	95	85
3029	$1 Hartmut Michel (1988 Chemistry)	95	85
3030	$1 Hans Bethe (1967 Physics)	95	85

MS3031 Three sheets, each 105×76 mm. (a) $6 Theodore Roosevelt (1906 Peace). (b) $6 Woodrow Wilson (1919 Peace). (c) $6 Sir Winston Churchill (1953 Literature) Set of 3 sheets   13·00   13·00

Nos. 3004/12, 3013/21 and 3022/30 respectively were printed together, *se-tenant*, forming composite designs. No. 3015 is inscribed "Freidrich" in error.

1995. Christmas. Religious Paintings. As T **245a** of Gambia. Multicoloured.

3032	15c. *The Madonna* (Bartolommeo Montagna)	20	10
3033	25c. *Sacred Conversation Piece* (Bonifacio dei Pitati)	20	10
3034	35c. *Nativity* (Van Loo)	25	10
3035	75c. *Madonna of the Fountain* (Van Eyck)	45	40
3036	$2 *The Apparition of the Virgin to St. Philip Neri* (Giovanni Tiepolo)	1·25	1·50
3037	$5 *The Holy Family* (Ribera)	2·50	3·50

MS3038 Two sheets. (a) 127×101 mm. $6 *Madonna and Child* (detail) (Van Dyck). (b) 101×127 mm. $6 *The Vision of St. Anthony* (detail) (Van Dyck) Set of 2 sheets   7·50   8·50

417 Pres. Ronald Reagan at Fort George

1995. 12th Anniv of Liberation of Grenada (1st issue). Multicoloured.

3039	75c. Type **417**	85	85
3040	75c. Pres. Reagan with U.S. and Grenadian flags	85	85
3041	75c. St. George's	85	85

MS3042 Two sheets, each 70×100 mm. (a) $5 Pres. Reagan and beach. (b) $6 Pres. Reagan and waterfall Set of 2 sheets   8·00   8·00

Nos. 3039/41 were printed together, *se-tenant*, forming a composite design.
See also Nos. 3043/51.

418 Pres. Ronald Reagan

1995. 12th Anniv of Liberation of Grenada (2nd issue). Designs showing Pres. Ronald Reagan. Multicoloured.

3043	$1 With wife	95	85
3044	$1 Type **418**	95	85
3045	$1 With microphones	95	85
3046	$1 Wearing stetson	95	85
3047	$1 In front of U.S. flag	95	85
3048	$1 In front of Brandenburg Gate, Berlin	95	85
3049	$1 Saluting by helicopter	95	85
3050	$1 On horseback	95	85
3051	$1 Addressing troops	95	85

419 Pope John Paul II and Statue of Liberty

1995. Papal Visit to New York. Multicoloured.

3052	$1 Type **419**	1·10	85
3053	$1 Pope John Paul II and cathedral	1·10	85

MS3054 105×76 mm. $6 Pope John Paul II   3·50   4·00

420 Rat asleep

1996. Chinese New Year ("Year of the Rat").

3055	**420** 75c. buff, green and brown	70	70
3056	- 75c. orange, red and violet	70	70
3057	- 75c. buff, red and green	70	70

MS3058 95×58 mm. Nos. 3055/7   1·75   2·00
MS3059 76×106 mm. $1 multicoloured   1·00   1·25

DESIGNS—VERT: No. 3056, Rat eating; 3057, Rat asleep (T **420** reversed). HORIZ: No. **MS**3059, Two rats.

421 *Young Woman* (Dürer)

1996. Famous Drawings and Paintings by Dürer and Rubens. Multicoloured.

3060	15c. Type **421**	40	20
3061	25c. *Four Horsemen of the Apocalypse* (Dürer)	45	20
3062	35c. *Assumption and Coronation of the Virgin* (Dürer)	50	20
3063	75c. *Mulay Ahmed* (Rubens)	80	50
3064	$1 *Anthony van Dyck aged 15* (Rubens)	90	60
3065	$2 *Head of a Young Monk* (Rubens)	1·75	1·75
3066	$3 *A Scholar inspired by Nature* (Rubens)	2·00	2·25
3067	$5 *Hanns Dürer* (Dürer)	3·00	3·50

MS3068 Two sheets, each 102×127 mm. (a) $5 *Martyrdom of St. Ursula* (detail) (Rubens). (b) $6 *The Death of the Virgin* (detail) (Dürer) Set of 2 sheets   10·00   10·00

422 Goofy Tap-dancing

1996. Famous Dances. Walt Disney cartoon characters Dancing. Multicoloured.

3069	35c. Type **422**	70	20
3070	45c. Donald Duck doing Mexican hat dance (horiz)	80	25
3071	75c. Daisy Duck as hula dancer	1·25	55
3072	90c. Mickey and Minnie Mouse doing the tango (horiz)	1·25	90
3073	$1 Donald and Daisy doing the jitterbug	1·40	85
3074	$2 Mickey and Minnie performing Ukrainian folk dance (horiz)	2·25	2·50
3075	$3 Goofy and Pluto as ballet dancers (horiz)	2·50	2·75
3076	$4 Mickey and Minnie line-dancing	2·50	2·75

MS3077 Two sheets, each 133×109 mm. (a) $5 Minnie doing the can-can (horiz). (b) $6 Scrooge McDuck doing the Scottish sword dance Set of 2 sheets   6·50   7·50

1996. 70th Birthday of Queen Elizabeth II. As T **255a** of Gambia showing different photographs. Multicoloured.

3078	35c. As Type **255a** of Gambia	60	25
3079	75c. Wearing white hat	1·00	55
3080	$4 With bouquet	3·00	3·50

MS3081 103×125 mm. $6 Queen and Prince Philip   5·00   5·50

423 Ferrari "125 F1"

1996. Ferrari Racing Cars. Multicoloured.

3082	$1.50 Type **423**	1·50	1·50
3083	$1.50 "Tipo 625"	1·50	1·50
3084	$1.50 "P4"	1·50	1·50
3085	$1.50 "312P"	1·50	1·50
3086	$1.50 "312" Formula 1	1·50	1·50
3087	$1.50 "312B"	1·50	1·50

MS3088 100×71 mm. $6 "F333 SP" (84×28 mm)   4·00   4·00

1996. 50th Anniv of UNICEF. As T **258a** of Gambia. Multicoloured.

3089	35c. Child writing in book (horiz)	20	25
3090	$2 Child planting seedling (horiz)	1·00	1·25
3091	$3 Children and UNICEF emblem (horiz)	1·50	2·00

MS3092 75×106 mm. $5 Young boy   2·50   3·00

424 Lions' Gate, Jerusalem

1996. 3000th Anniv of Jerusalem. Multicoloured.

3093	75c. Type **424**	75	45
3094	$2 New Gate	1·60	1·40
3095	$3 Dung Gate	2·00	2·00

MS3096 114×74 mm. $5 The Old City (horiz)   3·75   3·50

1996. Centenary of Radio. Entertainers. As T **259a** of Gambia. Multicoloured.

3097	35c. Jack Benny	35	25
3098	75c. Gertrude Berg	55	45
3099	$1 Eddie Cantor	65	60
3100	$2 Groucho Marx	1·25	1·50

MS3101 70×100 mm. $6 George Burns and Gracie Allen (horiz)   3·75   3·75

425 Olympic Stadium, Athens, 1896

1996. Olympic Games, Atlanta (2nd issue). Previous Medal Winners. Multicoloured.

3102	35c. Gold medal of 1896 (vert)	50	25
3103	75c. Type **425**	75	45
3104	$1 Boughera el Quafi (France) (Gold, 1928)	80	80
3105	$1 Gustav Jansson (Sweden) (Bronze, 1952)	80	80
3106	$1 Spiridon Louis (Greece) (Gold, 1896)	80	80
3107	$1 Basil Heatley (Great Britain) (Silver, 1964)	80	80
3108	$1 Emil Zatopek (Czechoslovakia) (Gold, 1952)	80	80
3109	$1 Frank Shorter (U.S.A.) (Gold, 1972)	80	80
3110	$1 Alain Minoun O'Kacha (France) (Gold, 1956)	80	80
3111	$1 Kokichi Tsu Uraya (Japan) (Bronze, 1964)	80	80
3112	$1 Delfo Cabrera (Argentina) (Gold, 1948)	80	80
3113	$1 Harald Sakata (U.S.A.) (Silver—light heavyweight, 1948)	80	80
3114	$1 Tom Kono (U.S.A.) (Gold—middleweight, 1952 and 1956)	80	80
3115	$1 Naim Suleymanoglu (Turkey) (Gold—featherweight, 1988)	80	80
3116	$1 Lee Hyung Kun (South Korea) (Gold—light heavyweight, 1988)	80	80
3117	$1 Vassily Alexeyev (U.S.S.R.) (Gold—super heavyweight, 1972 and 1976)	80	80
3118	$1 Chen Weiqiang (China) (Gold—featherweight, 1984)	80	80
3119	$1 Ye Huanming (China) (Gold—featherweight, 1988)	80	80
3120	$1 Manfred Nerlinger (Germany) (Silver—super heavyweight, 1988)	80	80
3121	$1 Joseph Depietro (U.S.A.) (Gold—bantamweight, 1948)	80	80
3122	$2 Ancient Greek runners	1·75	1·90
3123	$3 Spiridon Louis (Greece) (Gold—marathon, 1896)	2·25	2·50

MS3124 Two sheets, each 75×105 mm. (a) $5 Manfred Nerlinger (Germany) (Silver – super heavyweight weightlifting, 1988) (vert). (b) $6 Thomas Hicks (U.S.A.) (Gold – marathon, 1904) (vert) Set of 2 sheets   9·00   9·50

Nos. 3104/12 (marathon runners) and 3113/21 (weightlifters) respectively were printed together, *se-tenant*, with the backgrounds forming composite designs.

426 Mercedes-Benz, 1929

1996. Classic Cars. Multicoloured.

3125	35c. Type **426**	35	25
3126	50c. Bugatti Type 35, 1927	45	30
3127	75c. J. Dusenberg, 1935	65	45
3128	$1 Mercer, 1914	70	70
3129	$1 Type 57C Atalante, 1939	70	70
3130	$1 Cannstatt-Daimler, 1900	70	70
3131	$1 Delage, 1925	70	70
3132	$1 Coventry Daimler, 1899	70	70
3133	$1 Vauxhall, 1900	70	70
3134	$1 T-15 Hispano-Suza, 1912	70	70
3135	$2 Alfa Romeo, 1929	1·50	1·60
3136	$3 Rolls Royce, 1910	1·90	2·25

MS3137 Two sheets, each 66×96 mm. (a) $6 L-Head Mercer, 1915 (56×42 mm). (b) $6 Mercedes, 1937 (56×42 mm) Set of 2 sheets   8·00   9·00

427 *Gorch Fock* (cadet barque), Germany, 1916

1996. Ships. Multicoloured.

3138	$1 Type **427**	90	90
3139	$1 *Henry B. Hyde*, U.S.A., 1886	90	90
3140	$1 *Resolution* (galleon), Great Britain, 1652	90	90
3141	$1 U.S.S. *Constitution* (frigate), U.S.A., 1797	90	90
3142	$1 *Nippon Maru* (cadet ship), Japan, 1930	90	90
3143	$1 *Preussen* (full-rigged sailing ship), Germany, 1902	90	90
3144	$1 *Taeping* (clipper), Great Britain, 1852	90	90
3145	$1 "*Chariot of Fame*" (clipper), U.S.A., 1853	90	90
3146	$1 *Star of India* (clipper), U.S.A., 1861	90	90
3147	$1 H.M.S. *Bounty*	90	90
3148	$1 *Bismark* (German battleship)	90	90
3149	$1 *Chuii Apoo* and two junks	90	90
3150	$1 *Lubeck* (German frigate)	90	90
3151	$1 Dutch galleon	90	90
3152	$1 *Augsburg* (German frigate)	90	90
3153	$1 *Henri Grace a Dieu* (British galleon)	90	90
3154	$1 H.M.S. *Prince of Wales* (battleship)	90	90
3155	$1 *Santa Anna* (Spanish carrack)	90	90

MS3156 Two sheets, each 104×74 mm. (a) $5 H.M.S. *Victory* (ship of the line), Great Britain, 1805. (b) $6 *Cutty Sark* (clipper), Great Britain, 1869 Set of 2 sheets   8·00   8·00

No. 3151 is inscribed "BARBARY CORSAIR" and No. 3153 is stated to be French, both in error.

428 Jacqueline Kennedy

1996. Jacqueline Kennedy Onassis Commemoration. Multicoloured.

3157	$1 Type **428**	80	80
3158	$1 Wearing mauve blouse	80	80
3159	$1 In evening dress (inscr at right)	80	80
3160	$1 In evening dress (inscr at left)	80	80
3161	$1 Wearing pink dress	80	80
3162	$1 Wearing blue dress with collar embroidered	80	80
3163	$1 Wearing white jacket and brooch	80	80
3164	$1 In yellow jacket and green shirt	80	80
3165	$1 Wearing black jacket	80	80

MS3166 76×106 mm. $6 Jacqueline Kennedy Onassis (different)   3·50   4·25

429 Class C51 Locomotive of Imperial Train, Japan

1996. Trains of the World (2nd series). Multicoloured.

3167	35c. Type **429**	60	25
3168	75c. *Rheingold* express, Germany	80	45
3169	$1 Atlantic Coast Line locomotive No. 153, 1894, U.S.A.	80	80
3170	$1 Smith Compound No. 1619, Great Britain	80	80
3171	$1 Trans-Siberian Soviet Railways	80	80
3172	$1 Palatinate Railway Krauss locomotive, 1898, Germany	80	80
3173	$1 Paris, Lyons and Mediterranean line, France	80	80
3174	$1 Diesel-electric 0341 locomotive, Italy	80	80
3175	$1 Class C62 locomotive, Japan	80	80
3176	$1 Shantung Railways locomotive, China	80	80
3177	$1 Class C57 locomotive, Japan	80	80
3178	$1 Diesel express train, Japan	80	80
3179	$1 Shanghai–Nanking Railway locomotive, China	80	80
3180	$1 Class D51 locomotive, Japan	80	80
3181	$2 *Pioneer*, 1851, U.S.A.	1·60	1·75
3182	$3 *France*, France	2·00	2·50
MS3183	Two sheets, each 105×73 mm. (a) $5 Baden State Railways locomotive, Germany. (b) $6 Class C11 locomotive, Japan Set of 2 sheets	8·00	9·00

430 Winter Jasmine

1996. Flowers. Multicoloured.

3184	$1 Type **430**	80	80
3185	$1 Chrysanthemum	80	80
3186	$1 Lilac	80	80
3187	$1 Japanese iris	80	80
3188	$1 Hibiscus	80	80
3189	$1 Sacred lotus	80	80
3190	$1 Apple blossom	80	80
3191	$1 Gladiolus	80	80
3192	$1 Japanese quince	80	80
3193	$1 Canterbury bell (vert)	80	80
3194	$1 Rose (vert)	80	80
3195	$1 Nasturtium (vert)	80	80
3196	$1 Daffodil (vert)	80	80
3197	$1 Tulip (vert)	80	80
3198	$1 Snapdragon (vert)	80	80
3199	$1 Zinnia (vert)	80	80
3200	$1 Sweetpea (vert)	80	80
3201	$1 Pansy (vert)	80	80
MS3202	Two sheets. (a) 104×74 mm. $5 Aster. (b) 74×104 mm. $6 Peony (vert) Set of 2 sheets	8·00	9·00

Nos. 3184/92 and 3193/3201 respectively were printed together, *se-tenant*, with the backgrounds forming a composite design.

431 Zeppelin L-31 (Germany)

1996. Airships. Multicoloured.

3203	30c. Type **431**	50	50
3204	30c. Zeppelin L-35 (Germany)	50	50
3205	50c. Zeppelin L-30 (Germany)	65	50
3206	75c. Zeppelin L-2 10 (Germany)	90	55
3207	$1·50 Zeppelin L-21 (Germany)	1·40	1·60
3208	$1·50 Zodiac Type 13 Spiess (France)	1·40	1·60
3209	$1·50 N1 *Norge* (Roald Amundsen)	1·40	1·60
3210	$1·50 LZ-127 *Graf Zeppelin* (Germany)	1·40	1·60
3211	$1·50 LZ-129 *Hindenburg* (Germany)	1·40	1·60
3212	$1·50 Zeppelin NT (Germany)	1·40	1·60
3213	$3 Zeppelin L-3 (Germany)	2·25	2·75
3214	$3 Beardmore No. 24 (Great Britain)	2·25	2·75
MS3215	Two sheets, each 104×74 mm. (a) $6 Zeppelin ZT (Germany). (b) $6 Zeppelin L-13 (Germany) Set of 2 sheets	11·00	10·00

432 Horned Guan

1996. West Indian Birds. Multicoloured.

3216	$1·50 Type **432**	1·60	1·60
3217	$1·50 St. Lucia amazon ("St. Lucia Parrot")	1·60	1·60
3218	$1·50 Highland guan ("Black Penelopina")	1·60	1·60
3219	$1·50 Grenada dove	1·60	1·60
3220	$1·50 St. Vincent amazon ("St. Vincent Parrot")	1·60	1·60
3221	$1·50 White-breasted trembler	1·60	1·60
MS3222	Two sheets, each 100×70 mm. (a) $5 Semper's warbler. (b) $6 Yellow warbler ("Barbados Yellow Warbler") Set of 2 sheets	8·75	8·75

The inscriptions on Nos. **MS**3222a and **MS**3222b are transposed in error.

Nos. 3216/21 were printed together, *se-tenant*, with the backgrounds forming a composite design.

433 Blue Whale

1996. Whales and Turtles. Multicoloured.

3223	$1·50 Type **433**	1·60	1·60
3224	$1·50 Humpback whale	1·60	1·60
3225	$1·50 Right whale	1·60	1·60
3226	$1·50 Hawksbill turtle	1·60	1·60
3227	$1·50 Leatherback turtle	1·60	1·60
3228	$1·50 Green turtle	1·60	1·60

434 Killer Whale

1996. Marine Life. Multicoloured.

3229	$1 Type **434**	80	80
3230	$1 Dolphin	80	80
3231	$1 Two dolphins	80	80
3232	$1 Sea lion and regal angelfish	80	80
3233	$1 Dolphins and hawksbill turtle	80	80
3234	$1 Three hawksbill turtles	80	80
3235	$1 Regal angelfish and pennant coralfish	80	80
3236	$1 Pennant coralfish	80	80
3237	$1 Sea lion and squirrelfish	80	80
3238	$1 Brown pelican	80	80
3239	$1 Killer whale (different)	80	80
3240	$1 Whale	80	80
3241	$1 Dolphins and sea lion	80	80
3242	$1 Shortfin pilot whale, blue-ringed octopus and sea lion	80	80
3243	$1 Hammerhead sharks and sea lion	80	80
3244	$1 Blue-striped grunts	80	80
3245	$1 Stingray and Van Gogh fusilier	80	80
3246	$1 Van Gogh fusilier, ribbon moray and percoid fish	80	80
MS3247	Two sheets, each 106×76 mm. (a) $6 Pair of sea lions (horiz). (b) $6 Pair of dolphins (horiz) Set of 2 sheets	8·00	9·00

Nos. 3229/37 and 3238/46 respectively were printed together, *se-tenant*, with the backgrounds forming a composite design.

1996. Christmas. Religious Paintings. As T **245a** of Gambia. Multicoloured.

3248	25c. *The Visitation* (Tintoretto)	40	20
3249	35c. *Virgin with the Child* (Palma Vecchio)	50	25
3250	50c. *The Adoration of the Magi* (Botticelli)	60	30
3251	75c. *The Annunciation* (Titian)	80	45
3252	$1 *The Flight into Egypt* (Tintoretto)	1·00	65
3253	$3 *The Holy Family with the Infant Saint John* (Andrea del Sarto)	2·25	3·25
MS3254	Two sheets, each 106×76 mm. (a) $6 *Adoration of the Magi* (Paolo Schiavo). (b) $6 *Madonna and Child with Saints* (Vincenzo Ponna) Set of 2 sheets	9·00	9·50

No. 3250 is inscr "Botticeli" in error.

1996. 20th Anniv of *Rocky* (film). Sheet 143×182 mm, containing vert design as T **266** of Gambia. Multicoloured.

MS3255	$2×3, Sylvester Stallone in *Rocky V*	3·50	4·00

435 Ox

1997. Chinese New Year ("Year of the Ox"). Sheet 150×75 mm, containing T **435** and similar triangular designs. Multicoloured. Self-adhesive on silver foil.

MS3256	$2 Type **435** ("GRENADA" in black); $2 Ox ("GRENADA" in pink); $2 Ox ("GRENADA" in blue)	4·25	4·50

436 Mickey at Tram Stop

1997. "HONG KONG '97" International Stamp Exhibition. Mickey in Hong Kong. Disney cartoon characters. Multicoloured.

3257	35c. Type **436**	80	90
3258	50c. Mickey and Donald fishing at Victoria Harbour	80	90
3259	75c. Donald and Mickey parachuting	1·00	1·10
3260	90c. Mickey and Minnie visiting Bank of China	1·00	1·10
3261	$1 Mickey with pet parrot	1·25	1·40
3262	$1 Mickey drinking Kung-fu Tea	1·25	1·40
3263	$1 Mickey, Minnie and Goofy shopping at Chinese Wet Market	1·25	1·40
3264	$1 Mickey, Minnie and Goofy with grasshoppers	1·25	1·40
3265	$1 Mickey and Goofy with lanterns	1·25	1·40
3266	$1 Mickey and Minnie practising Tai-chi	1·25	1·40
3267	$2 Goofy delivering bottled gas	1·40	1·60
3268	$3 Mickey, Minnie and Donald at "Jumbo" floating restaurant	1·60	1·75
MS3269	Four sheets, each 132×108 mm. (a) $3 Mickey and skyscrapers (vert). (b) $4 Mickey and Minnie dancing (vert). (c) $5 Mickey pulling rickshaw (vert). (d) $6 Mickey with noodles (vert) Set of 4 sheets	15·00	16·00

1997. 50th Anniv of UNESCO. As T **273a** of Gambia. Multicoloured.

3270	35c. Temple, Kyoto, Japan	50	25
3271	75c. Timbered houses, Quedlinburg, Germany	70	45
3272	90c. View from walls, Dubrovnik, Croatia	80	55
3273	$1 Ruins at Delphi, Greece	80	80
3274	$1 Bryggen Wharf, Bergen, Norway (vert)	80	80
3275	$1 Old city, Berne, Switzerland (vert)	80	80
3276	$1 Warsaw, Poland (vert)	80	80
3277	$1 Fortress walls, Luxembourg (vert)	80	80
3278	$1 Interior of Drottningholm Palace, Sweden (vert)	80	80
3279	$1 Petajavesi Church, Finland (vert)	80	80
3280	$1 Vilnius, Lithuania (vert)	80	80
3281	$1 Jelling Church, Denmark (vert)	80	80
3282	$1 Entrance to caves, Desert of Taklamakan, China (vert)	80	80
3283	$1 House, Desert of Taklamakan, China (vert)	80	80
3284	$1 Monument, Desert of Taklamakan, China (vert)	80	80
3285	$1 Palace of Cielos Purpuras, Wudang, China (vert)	80	80
3286	$1 House, Wudang, China (vert)	80	80
3287	$1 Stone Guardian, The Great Wall, China (vert)	80	80
3288	$1 Ming Dynasty statue, Wudang, China (vert)	80	80
3289	$1 The Great Wall, China (vert)	80	80
3290	$1·50 Segovia Cathedral, Spain	1·10	1·25
3291	$1·50 Wurtzburg, Germany	1·10	1·25
3292	$1·50 Plitvice Lakes, Croatia	1·10	1·25
3293	$1·50 Batalha Monastery, Portugal	1·10	1·25
3294	$1·50 River Seine, Paris, France	1·10	1·25
3295	$2 Tomar, Portugal	1·40	1·60
3296	$3 Palace of Chaillot, Paris, France	1·90	2·25

MS3297	Three sheets, each 127×102 mm. (a) $6 Popocatepetl Monastery, Mexico. (b) $6 Woodland path, Shirakami-Sanchi, Japan. (c) $6 Interior of the Hieronymites' Monastery, Portugal Set of 3 sheets	12·00	14·00

437 Devon Rex

1997. Cats and Dogs. Multicoloured.

3298	35c. Type **437**	50	25
3299	75c. King Charles spaniel	70	45
3300	90c. Japanese bobtail	80	50
3301	$1 Afghan hound	80	80
3302	$1 Turkish van	80	80
3303	$1 Ragdoll	80	80
3304	$1 Siberian	80	80
3305	$1 Egyptian mau	80	80
3306	$1 American shorthair	80	80
3307	$1 Benegal	80	80
3308	$1 Asian longhair	80	80
3309	$1 Somali	80	80
3310	$1 Turkish angora	80	80
3311	$1 Lhasa apso	80	80
3312	$1 Rough collie	80	80
3313	$1 Norwich terrier	80	80
3314	$1 American cocker spaniel	80	80
3315	$1 Chinese crested dog	80	80
3316	$1 Old English sheepdog	80	80
3317	$1 Standard poodle	80	80
3318	$1 German shepherd	80	80
3319	$1 German shorthair pointer	80	80
3320	$2 Cornish rex	1·60	1·75
3321	$3 Pekingese	2·00	2·50
MS3322	Two sheets, each 106×76 mm. (a) $6 Singapura. (b) $6 Bernese mountain dog Set of 2 sheets	8·50	9·00

438 Dunkleosteus

1997. Dinosaurs. Multicoloured.

3323	35c. Type **438**	70	30
3324	75c. Tyrannosaurus rex	1·25	55
3325	$1·50 Sordes	1·40	1·60
3326	$1·50 Dimorphodon	1·40	1·60
3327	$1·50 Diplodocus	1·40	1·60
3328	$1·50 Allosaurus	1·40	1·60
3329	$1·50 Pentaceratops	1·40	1·60
3330	$1·50 Protoceratops	1·40	1·60
3331	$2 Askeptosaurus (vert)	1·40	1·60
3332	$3 Triceratops (vert)	2·00	2·50
MS3333	Two sheets, each 103×74 mm. (a) $6 Tristychius (vert). (b) $6 Maiasaura (vert) Set of 2 sheets	9·00	9·50

Nos. 3325/30 were printed together, *se-tenant*, with the backgrounds forming a composite design.

439 Porcelain Crab

1997. Marine Life. Multicoloured.

3334	45c. Type **439**	55	30
3335	75c. Humpback whale	1·25	60
3336	90c. Hermit crab	80	50
3337	$1 Great white shark	1·40	1·60
3338	$1·50 Octopus (vert)	1·40	1·60
3339	$1·50 Lei triggerfish (vert)	1·40	1·60
3340	$1·50 Lionfish (vert)	1·40	1·60
3341	$1·50 Harlequin wrasse (vert)	1·40	1·60
3342	$1·50 Clown fish (vert)	1·40	1·60
3343	$1·50 Moray eel (vert)	1·40	1·60
3344	$2 Green sea turtle	2·25	2·50
3345	$4 Whale shark	2·50	2·75
MS3346	Two sheets, each 106×76 mm. (a) $6 Pacific barracudas. (b) $6 Scalloped hammerhead shark Set of 2 sheets	8·50	9·00

Nos. 3338/43 were printed together, *se-tenant*, with the backgrounds forming a composite design.

1997. 300th Anniv of Mother Goose Nursery Rhymes. Sheet 72×102 mm, containing multicoloured design as T **276a** of Gambia.

MS3347	$5 Boy holding umbrella ("Rain") (vert)	3·50	4·00

1997. Tenth Anniv of Chernobyl Nuclear Disaster. As T **276a** of Gambia. Multicoloured.

3348	$2 As Type **276b** of Gambia	1·40	1·60
3349	$2 As No. 3348, but inscribed "CHABAD'S CHILDREN OF CHERNOBYL" at foot	1·40	1·60

1997. 50th Death Anniv of Paul Harris (founder of Rotary International). As T **276c** of Gambia. Multicoloured.

3350	$3 Paul Harris and vocational training programme, Philippines	1·75	2·00
MS3351	78×107 mm. $6 Hands holding globe and doves	3·25	3·75

1997. Golden Wedding of Queen Elizabeth and Prince Philip. As T **276d** of Gambia. Multicoloured.

3352	$1 Queen Elizabeth and Prince Philip waving	85	85
3353	$1 Royal coat of arms	85	85
3354	$1 Queen Elizabeth with Prince Philip in naval uniform	85	85
3355	$1 Queen Elizabeth and Prince Philip at Buckingham Palace	85	85
3356	$1 Windsor Castle	85	85
3357	$1 Prince Philip	85	85
MS3358	100×70 mm. $6 Queen Elizabeth with Prince Philip in naval uniform (different)	4·75	5·50

1997. "Pacific '97" International Stamp Exhibition, San Francisco (1st issue). Death Centenary of Heinrich von Stephan (founder of the U.P.U.). As T **276e** of Gambia.

3359	$2 green and black	1·25	1·40
3360	$2 brown	1·25	1·40
3361	$2 blue	1·25	1·40
MS3362	82×119 mm. $6 violet and black	3·50	4·25

DESIGNS: No. 3359, Postman on motorcycle; 3360, Von Stephan and Mercury; 3361, Postman on skis, Rocky Mountains, 1900s; MS3362, Von Stephan and Chinese letter carrier.

See also Nos. 3392/3409.

1997. Birth Bicentenary of Hiroshige (Japanese painter). As T **541a** of Ghana. Multicoloured.

3363	$1·50 Nihon Embankment, Yoshiwara	1·10	1·25
3364	$1·50 Asakusa Ricefields and Torinomachi Festival	1·10	1·25
3365	$1·50 Senju Great Bridge	1·10	1·25
3366	$1·50 Dawn inside the Yoshiwara	1·10	1·25
3367	$1·50 Tile Kilns and Hasiba Ferry, Sumida River	1·10	1·25
3368	$1·50 View from Massaki of Suijin Shrine, Uchigawa Inlet and Sekiya	1·10	1·25
MS3369	Two sheets, each 102×127 mm. (a) $6 Kinryuzan Temple, Asakusa. (b) $6 Night view of Saruwakamachi Set of 2 sheets	8·50	9·00

1997. 175th Anniv of Brothers Grimm's Third Collection of Fairy Tales. Snow White. As T **277a** of Gambia. Multicoloured.

3370	$2 Queen looking in mirror	1·50	1·75
3371	$2 Snow White and the Seven Dwarfs	1·50	1·75
3372	$2 Snow White and Prince	1·50	1·75
MS3373	124×96 mm. $6 Witch with apple	4·00	4·50

440 One-man Luge

1997. Winter Olympic Games, Nagano, Japan. Multicoloured.

3374	45c. Type **440**	50	30
3375	75c. Men's speed skating	75	45
3376	$1 One-man luge (different)	85	85
3377	$1 Ski jumping (blue ski suit)	85	85
3378	$1 Downhill skiing	85	85
3379	$1 Speed skating	85	85
3380	$1 Two-man bobsleigh	85	85
3381	$1 Women's figure skating	85	85
3382	$1 Alpine combined	85	85
3383	$1 Ice hockey	85	85
3384	$1 Ski jumping (yellow ski suit)	85	85
3385	$2 Men's figure skating	1·60	1·75
3386	$3 Slalom	2·00	2·50
MS3387	Two sheets, each 96×69 mm. (a) $6 Four-man bobsleigh. (b) $6 Downhill skiing (vert) Set of 2 sheets	8·50	9·00

441 Bank of China

1997. Return of Hong Kong to China. Multicoloured.

3388	90c. Type **441**	65	50
3389	$1 Skyscrapers	75	55
3390	$1.75 "Hong Kong '97" on modern buildings (63×32 mm)	1·40	1·60
3391	$2 Deng Xiaoping and Hong Kong (63×32 mm)	1·60	1·75

442 Minnie Mouse dancing the Hula

1997. "Pacific '97" International Stamp Exhibition, San Francisco (2nd issue). Centenary of the Cinema. Minnie Mouse in Hawaiian Holiday. Multicoloured.

3392	50c. Type **442** (Frame 1)	60	70
3393	50c. Frame 2	60	70
3394	50c. Frame 3	60	70
3395	50c. Frame 4	60	70
3396	50c. Frame 5	60	70
3397	50c. Frame 6	60	70
3398	50c. Frame 7	60	70
3399	50c. Frame 8	60	70
3400	50c. Frame 9	60	70
3401	50c. Frame 10	60	70
3402	50c. Frame 11	60	70
3403	50c. Frame 12	60	70
3404	50c. Frame 13	60	70
3405	50c. Frame 14	60	70
3406	50c. Frame 15	60	70
3407	50c. Frame 16	60	70
3408	50c. Frame 17	60	70
MS3409	110×130 mm. $6 Frame 18	7·00	7·50

443 Hercules lifting Rock

1997. Hercules (cartoon film) (1st series). Multicoloured.

3410	$1 Type **443**	80	1·00
3411	$1 Pegasus	80	1·00
3412	$1 Megara	80	1·00
3413	$1 Philoktetes	80	1·00
3414	$1 Nessus	80	1·00
3415	$1 Hydra	80	1·00
3416	$1 Pain and Panic	80	1·00
3417	$1 Hades	80	1·00
MS3418	Two sheets. (a) 131×104 mm. $6 Hercules as a boy. (b) 104×131 mm. $6 The Muses Set of 2 sheets	9·00	11·00

See also Nos. 3561/85.

1997. World Cup Football Championship, France (1998). As T **283a** of Gambia. Multicoloured (except Nos. 3422/3 and 3428).

3419	15c. West German and Italian Players, 1982 (vert)	35	20
3420	75c. Italian player holding World Cup, 1982 (vert)	70	45
3421	90c. West German and Italian players wearing "20" shirts, 1982 (vert)	75	50
3422	$1 Uruguay team, 1950 (brown)	75	75
3423	$1 Brazilian team, 1958 (brown)	75	75
3424	$1 West German team, 1974	75	75
3425	$1 Argentine team, 1986	75	75
3426	$1 Italian team, 1982	75	75
3427	$1 West German team, 1990	75	75
3428	$1 Italian team, 1934 (brown)	75	75
3429	$1 Brazilian team, 1970	75	75
3430	$1 Seaman, England	75	75
3431	$1 Klinsmann, Germany	75	75
3432	$1 Berger, Czech Republic	75	75
3433	$1 McCoist, Scotland	75	75
3434	$1 Gascoigne, England	75	75
3435	$1 Djorkaeff, France	75	75
3436	$1 Sammer, Germany	75	75
3437	$1 Futre, Portugal	75	75
3438	$2 Italian player beating goal keeper, 1982 (vert)	1·40	1·60
3439	$3 Goal-mouth melee, 1982 (vert)	1·90	2·25
3440	$4 Two West German players tackling Italian player (vert)	2·50	2·75
MS3441	Two sheets. (a) 102×127 mm. $6 Beckenbauer holding World Cup, Germany (vert). (b) 127×102 mm. $6 Moore, England Set of 2 sheets	9·00	10·00

444 Peacock

1997. Butterflies and Moths. Multicoloured.

3442	45c. Type **444**	70	30
3443	75c. Orange flambeau	90	45
3444	90c. Eastern tailed blue	90	50
3445	$1 Brimstone	90	90
3446	$1 Mocker swallowtail	90	90
3447	$1 American painted lady	90	90
3448	$1 Tiger swallowtail	90	90
3449	$1 Long wing	90	90
3450	$1 Sunset moth	90	90
3451	$1 Australian Blue Mountain swallowtail	90	90
3452	$1 Bird wing	90	90
3453	$2 Black and red	1·50	1·60
3454	$3 Large white	1·90	2·25
3455	$4 Oriental swallowtail	2·50	2·75
MS3456	Two sheets, each 76×106 mm. (a) $5 Monarch. (b) $5 Blue morpho Set of 2 sheets	10·00	10·00

445 Paphiopedilum urbanianum

1997. Orchids of the World. Multicoloured.

3457	20c. Type **445**	45	20
3458	35c. Trichoceros parviflorus	60	25
3459	45c. Euanthe sanderiana (vert)	65	30
3460	75c. Oncidium macranthum (vert)	75	45
3461	90c. Psychopsis kramerianum (vert)	80	55
3462	$1 Oncidium hastatum (vert)	85	60
3463	$2 Broughtonia sanguinea (vert)	1·40	1·50
3464	$2 Anguloa virginalis (vert)	1·40	1·50
3465	$2 Dendrobium bigibbum (vert)	1·40	1·50
3466	$2 Lucasiana (vert)	1·40	1·50
3467	$2 Cymbidium (vert)	1·40	1·50
3468	$2 Cymbidium and vase (vert)	1·40	1·50
3469	$2 Odontoglossum crispum (vert)	1·40	1·50
3470	$2 Cattleya brabantiae (vert)	1·40	1·50
3471	$2 Cattleya bicolor (vert)	1·40	1·50
3472	$2 Trichopilia suavia (vert)	1·40	1·50
3473	$2 Encyclia mariae (vert)	1·40	1·50
3474	$2 Angraecum leonis (vert)	1·40	1·50
3475	$3 Masdevallia saltatix (vert)	1·90	2·75
3476	$4 Cattleya luteola	2·50	2·75
MS3477	Two sheets. (a) 76×106 mm. $6 Laelia milleri. (b) 106×76 mm. $6 Oncidium onustum Set of 2 sheets	9·00	10·00

Nos. 3463/8 and 3469/74 respectively were printed together, se-tenant, with the backgrounds forming composite designs.

446 Boletus erythropus

1997. Fungi of the World. Multicoloured.

3478	35c. Type **446**	60	25
3479	75c. Armilariella mellea	70	45
3480	90c. Amanita flavorubens	80	50
3481	$1 Indigo milky	85	55
3482	$1·50 Agaricus solidipes	1·25	1·40
3483	$1·50 Salmon waxy cap	1·25	1·40
3484	$1·50 Fused maramius	1·25	1·40
3485	$1·50 Shellfish-scented russula	1·25	1·40
3486	$1·50 Red-capped scaber stalk	1·25	1·40
3487	$1·50 Calocybe gambosum	1·25	1·40
3488	$1·50 Boletus parasiticus	1·25	1·40
3489	$1·50 Frostis bolete	1·25	1·40
3490	$1·50 Amanita myscara flavilolvata	1·25	1·40
3491	$1·50 Volvariella volvacea	1·25	1·40
3492	$1·50 Stuntz's blue legs	1·25	1·40
3493	$1·50 Orange-latex milky	1·25	1·40
3494	$2 Tylopilus balloui	1·40	1·90
3495	$4 Boletus parasiticus	2·50	2·75
MS3496	Two sheets, each 97×67 mm. (a) $6 Agaricus argenteus. (b) $6 Omphalotus illudens Set of 2 sheets	8·50	9·50

447 Princess Diana with Landmine Victims

1997. Diana, Princess of Wales Commemoration. Multicoloured.

3497	$1·50 Type **447**	1·25	1·25
3498	$1·50 With sick child	1·25	1·25
3499	$1·50 With young boy on crutches	1·25	1·25
3500	$1·50 With leper	1·25	1·25
3501	$1·50 Holding baby	1·25	1·25
3502	$1·50 Walking through minefield	1·25	1·25
MS3503	76×106 mm. $5 With Mother Teresa	3·75	3·75

448 Angel (Matthias Grunewald)

1997. Christmas. Religious Paintings. Multicoloured.

3504	35c. Type **448**	45	25
3505	50c. St. Demetrius (icon)	60	30
3506	75c. Three-panelled reliquary	75	45
3507	$1 Angel of the Annunciation (Jan van Eyck)	85	55
3508	$3 The Annunciation (Simone Martini)	2·25	2·50
3509	$4 St. Michael (icon)	2·50	3·00
MS3510	Two sheets. (a) 104×114 mm. $6 The Coronation of the Virgin (Fra Angelico). (b) 114×104 mm. $6 The Annunciation (Titian) (horiz) Set of 2 sheets	9·00	10·00

1998. Chinese New Year ("Year of the Tiger"). Sheet 150×75 mm, containing triangular designs as T **435** showing tigers. Multicoloured. Self-adhesive on silver foil.

MS3511	$1·50, "GRENADA" in pink; $1·50, "GRENADA" in gold; $1·50, "GRENADA" in bronze	3·75	4·00

No. MS3511 also exists on gold foil.

449 Black-tailed Damselfish

1998. Fish. Multicoloured.

3512	65c. Type **449**	55	40
3513	90c. Yellow sweetlips	75	50
3514	$1 Common squirrelfish	80	55
3515	$1·50 Blue tang	1·10	1·25
3516	$1·50 Porkfish	1·10	1·25
3517	$1·50 Banded butterflyfish	1·10	1·25
3518	$1·50 Thread-finned butterflyfish	1·10	1·25
3519	$1·50 Hooded butterflyfish ("Red-headed")	1·10	1·25
3520	$1·50 Emperor angelfish	1·10	1·25
3521	$1·50 Duboulay's angelfish ("Scribbled Anglefish")	1·10	1·25
3522	$1·50 Lemon-peel angelfish	1·10	1·25
3523	$1·50 Bandit angelfish	1·10	1·25
3524	$1·50 Bicoloured angelfish ("Biclor Cherub")	1·10	1·25
3525	$1·50 Palette surgeonfish ("Regal Tang")	1·10	1·25
3526	$1·50 Yellow tang	1·10	1·25
3527	$2 Powder-blue surgeonfish	1·40	1·60
MS3528	Two sheets, each 110×80 mm. (a) $6 Two-banded anemonefish. (b) $6 Forceps butterflyfish ("Long-nosed Butterflyfish")	9·00	10·00

Nos. 3515/20 and 3521/6 respectively were printed together, se-tenant, with the backgrounds forming composite designs.

450 Sophronitis grandiflora

1998. Flowers of the World. Multicoloured.

3529	$1·50 Type **450**	1·10	1·10
3530	$1·50 Phalaenopsis amboinensis	1·10	1·10
3531	$1·50 Zygopetalum intermedium	1·10	1·10

3532	$1.50 Paphiopedilum purpuratum	1·10	1·10
3533	$1.50 Miltonia regnellii	1·10	1·10
3534	$1.50 Dendrobium parishii	1·10	1·10
3535	$1.50 Arachnis clarkei	1·10	1·10
3536	$1.50 Cymbidium eburneum	1·10	1·10
3537	$1.50 Dendrobium chrysotoxum	1·10	1·10
3538	$1.50 Paphiopedilum insigne	1·10	1·10
3539	$1.50 Paphiopedilum venustum	1·10	1·10
3540	$1.50 Renanthera imschootiana	1·10	1·10

MS3541 Two sheets, each 104×72 mm. (a) $6 Pleione maculata. (b) $6 Lycaste aromatica Set of 2 sheets 8·00 9·00

451 Dhow

1998. Famous Ships. Multicoloured.

3542	$1 Type **451**	80	80
3543	$1 Galleon	80	80
3544	$1 Felucca	80	80
3545	$1 Schooner	80	80
3546	$1 Aircraft carrier	80	80
3547	$1 Knau	80	80
3548	$1 Destroyer	80	80
3549	$1 Viking longship	80	80
3550	$1 Queen Elizabeth 2 (liner)	80	80
3551	$1 Brig	80	80
3552	$1 Clipper	80	80
3553	$1 Caique	80	80
3554	$1 Mississippi riverboat	80	80
3555	$1 Luxury liner	80	80
3556	$1 Mayflower (Pilgrim Fathers)	80	80
3557	$1 Frigate	80	80
3558	$1 Janggolan	80	80
3559	$1 Junk	80	80

MS3560 Two sheets, each 100×75 mm. (a) $6 Nuclear submarine (58×43 mm). (b) $6 "Lusitania" (liner) (86×29 mm) Set of 2 sheets 9·00 9·50

Nos. 3542/50 and 3551/9 respectively were printed together, se-tenant, forming composite background designs.

1998. Hercules (cartoon film) (2nd series). As T **443** showing Disney cartoon characters. Multicoloured.

3561- 10c.×8 Hercules and giant
3568 statue; Hercules, Pegasus and Philoktetes; Hercules and Philoktetes with shield and arrows; Hercules swinging from blades; Nessus carrying off Megara; Hercules fighting Nessus; Hercules fighting giant lion; Hercules and Pegasus leaving prints on pavement 4·00

3569- $1×8 Baby Hercules with Zeus
3576 and Alcmene; Baby Hercules with Hades; Hades in the Underworld; Baby Hercules and young Pegasus; Baby Hercules with Pain and Panic; Baby Hercules with mortal parents; Hercules towing hay waggon; Hercules receiving gold medallion 4·00

3577- $1×8 Hercules and Megara;
3584 Megara and Hades; Hercules training with Philoktetes; Hercules confronting Hades; Giant destroying city; Zeus; Hercules saving Megara by lifting pillar; Hercules diving into sea 4·00

MS3585 Six sheets, each 127×102 mm. (a) $6 Hades. (b) $6 Baby Pegasus. (c) $6 Hercules with sword. (d) $6 Hades on fire. (e) $6 Zeus and Hercules (horiz). (f) $6 Hercules and Megara riding Pegasus (horiz) Set of 6 sheets 27·00 30·00

452 Arctic Skua

1998. Seabirds. Multicoloured.

3586	90c. Type **452**	1·00	60
3587	$1 Fulmar ("Northern Fulmar") (horiz)	1·00	1·00
3588	$1 Black-legged kittiwake (horiz)	1·00	1·00
3589	$1 Pintado petrel ("Cape Petrel") (horiz)	1·00	1·00
3590	$1 Mediterranean gull (horiz)	1·00	1·00
3591	$1 Brandt's cormorant (horiz)	1·00	1·00
3592	$1 Greater shearwater (horiz)	1·00	1·00
3593	$1 Black-footed albatross (horiz)	1·00	1·00
3594	$1 Red-necked phalarope (horiz)	1·00	1·00

3595	$1 Black skimmer (horiz)	1·00	1·00
3596	$1.10 Humboldt penguin	1·10	1·10
3597	$2 Herring gull	1·75	1·75
3598	$3 Red knot	2·25	2·50

MS3599 Two sheets, each 100×70 mm. (a) $5 Black-browed albatross. (b) $5 King penguin Set of 2 sheets 8·50 9·00

Nos. 3587/95 were printed together, se-tenant, with the backgrounds forming a composite design.

453 Supermarine Spitfire Mk I

1998. History of the Supermarine Spitfire (aircraft). Designs showing different versions. Multicoloured.

3600	$1.50 Type **453**	1·10	1·10
3601	$1.50 Mark VIII	1·10	1·10
3602	$1.50 Mark III	1·10	1·10
3603	$1.50 Mark XVI	1·10	1·10
3604	$1.50 Mark V	1·10	1·10
3605	$1.50 Mark XIX	1·10	1·10
3606	$1.50 Mark IX	1·10	1·10
3607	$1.50 Mark XIV	1·10	1·10
3608	$1.50 Mark XII	1·10	1·10
3609	$1.50 Mark XI	1·10	1·10
3610	$1.50 H.F. Mark VIII	1·10	1·10
3611	$1.50 Mark VB	1·10	1·10

MS3612 Two sheets, each 80×106 mm. (a) $6 Mark IA. (b) $6 Mark IX (different) (both 56×41 mm) Set of 2 sheets 8·50 9·50

454 Walrus

1998. International Year of the Ocean. Multicoloured.

3613	75c. Type **454**	65	65
3614	75c. Jackass penguins ("African Black-footed Penguin")	65	65
3615	75c. Jackass penguin ("African Black-footed Penguin")	65	65
3616	75c. California sealion	65	65
3617	75c. Green turtle	65	65
3618	75c. Redfin anthias	65	65
3619	75c. Sperm whale	65	65
3620	75c. French angelfish and Australian sealion	65	65
3621	75c. Jellyfish	65	65
3622	75c. Sawfish	65	65
3623	75c. Cuckoo wrasse	65	65
3624	75c. Garibaldi	65	65
3625	75c. Spinecheek anemonefish	65	65
3626	75c. Leafy seadragon	65	65
3627	75c. Blue-spotted goatfish	65	65
3628	75c. Two-spot gobies	65	65

MS3629 Two sheets, each 98×68 mm. (a) $5 Atlantic spotted dolphins. (b) $6 Octopus Set of 2 sheets 7·50 8·50

Nos. 3613/28 were printed together, se-tenant, with the backgrounds forming a composite design.

454a Flags of Grenada and CARICOM

1998. 25th Anniv of Caribbean Community.

3630	**454a** $1 multicoloured	1·00	1·00

454b Stylized Americas

1998. 50th Anniv of Organization of American States.

3631	**454b** $1 multicoloured	1·00	1·00

1998. 25th Death Anniv of Pablo Picasso (painter). As T **291a** of Gambia. Multicoloured.

3632	45c. The Bathers (vert)	45	25
3633	$2 Luncheon on the Grass	1·50	1·50
3634	$3 The Swimmer	2·00	2·25

MS3635 102×127 mm. $5 Tomato Plant (vert) 3·50 3·75

1998. Birth Centenary of Enzo Ferrari (car manufacturer). As T **564a** of Ghana. Multicoloured.

3636	$2 250 GT Berlinetta Lusso	1·50	1·50
3637	$2 250 GTO	1·50	1·50
3638	$2 250 GT Boano/Ellena cabriolet	1·50	1·50

MS3639 104×70 mm. $5 246 GTS Dino (91×34 mm) 4·00 4·50

454c Scout Saluting

1998. 19th World Scout Jamboree, Chile. Multicoloured.

3640	$2 Type **454c**	1·50	1·25
3641	$3 International scout flag	2·50	2·50
3642	$4 Applying first aid	2·50	2·75

MS3643 106×76 mm. $6 International scout flag 5·00 5·50

454d Mahatma Gandhi

1998. 50th Death Anniv of Mahatma Gandhi.

3644	**454d** $1 black, grey and mauve	1·75	1·50

MS3645 70×100 mm. $6 multicoloured 6·00 6·00
DESIGN: $6, Gandhi and spinning wheel.

1998. 80th Anniv of Royal Air Force. As T **292a** of Gambia. Multicoloured.

3646	$2 Supermarine Spitfire Mk IIa	1·50	1·50
3647	$2 Supermarine Spitfire Mk IXb from above	1·50	1·50
3648	$2 Supermarine Spitfire Mk IXb from side	1·50	1·50
3649	$2 Hawker Hurricane Mk IIC of Battle of Britain Memorial Flight	1·50	1·50
3650	$2 EF-2000 Eurofighter above clouds	1·50	1·50
3651	$2 Nimrod MR2P (maritime reconnaissance)	1·50	1·50
3652	$2 EF-2000 Eurofighter at low level	1·50	1·50
3653	$2 C-47 Dakota (transport)	1·50	1·50

MS3654 Four sheets, each 93×70 mm. (a) $6 Bristol F2B fighter and head of falcon. (b) $6 Bristol F2B fighter and northern goshawk (bird). (c) $6 Jet Provost (trainer) and EF-2000 Eurofighter. (d) $6 VC10 (transport) and EF-2000 Eurofighter Set of 4 sheets 18·00 19·00

455 Knights in Combat

1998. Birth Bicentenary of Eugene Delacroix (painter). Multicoloured.

3655	$1 Type **455**	80	80
3656	$1 Murder of Bishop of Liege	80	80
3657	$1 Still Life	80	80
3658	$1 Battle of Nancy	80	80
3659	$1 Shipwreck of Don Juan	80	80
3660	$1 The Death of Ophelia	80	80
3661	$1 Attila the Hun	80	80
3662	$1 Arab Entertainers	80	80

MS3663 100×92 mm. $5 The Capture of Constantinople 4·00 4·50

1998. First Death Anniv of Diana, Princess of Wales. As T **293a** of Gambia. Multicoloured.

3664	$1 Diana, Princess of Wales	1·00	1·00

456 Arthur Ashe

1998. Famous Tennis Players. Multicoloured.

3665	45c. Type **456**	50	25
3666	75c. Martina Hingis	60	40
3667	90c. Chris Evert	70	40
3668	$1 Steffi Graf	80	70
3669	$1.50 A. Sanchez Vicario	1·00	1·25
3670	$2 Monica Seles	1·40	1·60
3671	$3 Martina Navratilova	1·75	2·25

MS3672 81×108 mm. $6 Martina Hingis (different) 5·50 6·00

457 Dove of Peace with Stars and Streamers

1998. Grenada's Participation in U.N. Peacekeeping Operations, Beirut, 1982–4.

3673	**457** $1 multicoloured	1·00	1·00

458 The Angel's parting from Tobias (Jean Bilevelt)

1998. Christmas. Religious Paintings. Multicoloured.

3674	35c. Type **458**	40	20
3675	45c. Allegory of Faith (Moretto Da Brescia)	50	25
3676	90c. Crucifixion (Ugolino Di Tedice)	85	70
3677	$1 The Triumphal Entry into Jerusalem (Master of the Thuison Altarpiece)	1·00	1·25

459 Antillean Euphonia ("Blue-hooded Euphonia")

1998. Christmas. Birds. Multicoloured.

3678	45c. Type **459**	65	25
3679	75c. Red-billed whistling duck ("Black-bellied Whistling Duck")	85	40
3680	90c. Caribbean martin ("Purple Martin")	1·00	50
3681	$1 Imperial amazon ("Imperial Parrot")	1·25	80
3682	$2 Adelaide's warbler	1·75	1·75
3683	$3 Greater flamingo ("Roseate Flamingo")	2·00	2·75

MS3684 Two sheets, each 97×84 mm. (a) $5 Green-throated carib. (b) $6 Purple-throated carib and Canada 1898 Imperial Penny Postage 2c. stamp (37×60 mm) Set of 2 sheets 10·00 11·00

1999. Chinese New Year ("Year of the Rabbit"). Sheet 150×75 mm, containing triangular designs as T **435** showing rabbits. Multicoloured. Self-adhesive on silver foil.

MS3685 $1 "GRENADA" in green; $1 "GRENADA" in orange; $1 "GRENADA" in pink 3·00 3·25

1999. Millennium Series. Famous People of the Twentieth Century. Great Thinkers of the Past and Present. Designs as T **289a** of Gambia. Multicoloured.

3686	$1 Martin Luther King Jr (civil rights leader)	1·25	1·25
3687	$1 Socrates (Greek philosopher) (56×41 mm)	1·25	1·25
3688	$1 Sir Thomas More (English scholar) (56×41 mm)	1·25	1·25
3689	$1 Chaim Weizmann (first President of Israel)	1·25	1·25
3690	$1 Alexander Solzhenitsyn (Russian writer)	1·25	1·25
3691	$1 Galileo Galilei (Italian astronomer) (56×41 mm)	1·25	1·25
3692	$1 Michael Servetus (Spanish theologian) (56×41 mm)	1·25	1·25
3693	$1 Salman Rushdie (British novelist)	1·25	1·25

MS3694 106×76 mm. $6 Mother Teresa (founder of Missionaries of Charity) 6·00 6·00

No. 3692 is inscribed "MICHAEL SERVENTUS" in error.

460 Robert H. Goddard (rocket scientist)

1999. Space Exploration. Multicoloured.

3695	$1.50 Type **460**	1·40	1·40
3696	$1.50 Wernher von Braun (rocket scientist)	1·40	1·40
3697	$1.50 Yuri A. Gagarin (first cosmonaut to orbit Earth, 1961)	1·40	1·40
3698	$1.50 "Freedom 7" (first American manned Space flight, 1961)	1·40	1·40
3699	$1.50 Aleksei Leonov (first Russian to walk in Space, 1965)	1·40	1·40
3700	$1.50 Neil Armstrong and Edwin Aldrin (first astronauts on Moon, 1969)	1·40	1·40
3701	$1.50 "Mariner 9" (first spacecraft to orbit Mars, 1971)	1·40	1·40
3702	$1.50 "Voyager 1" (Jupiter probe, 1979)	1·40	1·40
3703	$1.50 Bruce McCandless (first astronaut to work in Space unattached, 1984)	1·40	1·40
3704	$1.50 "Giotto" probe (study of Halley's Comet, 1986)	1·40	1·40
3705	$1.50 Space Shuttle "Atlantis" (launch of "Galileo" probe, 1989)	1·40	1·40
3706	$1.50 "Magellan" (Venus probe, 1990)	1·40	1·40

MS3707 Two sheets, each 60×76 mm. (a) $6 John Glenn (first American to orbit Earth, 1962). (b) $6 Neil Armstrong (first astronaut to walk on Moon, 1969) Set of 2 sheets   9·00   10·00

Nos. 3695/3700 and 3701/6 were respectively printed together, se-tenant, with the backgrounds forming composite designs.

461 Goofy as Best Man

1999. 70th Birthday of Mickey Mouse. Mickey's Dream Wedding. Walt Disney cartoon characters. Multicoloured.

3708	$1 Type **461**	80	80
3709	$1 Mickey as groom	80	80
3710	$1 Minnie as bride	80	80
3711	$1 Daisy Duck as bridesmaid	80	80
3712	$1 Donald Duck	80	80
3713	$1 Pluto in love	80	80
3714	$1 Huey, Duey and Louie	80	80
3715	$1 Lady (Pekingese)	80	80

MS3716 Two sheets. (a) 102×127 mm. $6 Mickey's nephew eating cake. (b) 127×102 mm. $6 Mickey and Minnie in carriage (horiz) Set of 2 sheets   10·00   11·00

Nos. 3708/15 were printed together, se-tenant, with the backgrounds forming a composite design.

462 Grand Trunk Western, U.S.A.

1999. Trains of the World. Multicoloured.

3717	25c. Type **462**	60	25
3718	35c. Louisville & Nashville, U.S.A.	65	25
3719	45c. Gulf, Mobile and Ohio, U.S.A.	70	25
3720	75c. Missouri Pacific, U.S.A.	90	35
3721	90c. "RTG" National Railway, France	90	45
3722	$1 Florida East Coast, U.S.A.	1·00	45
3723	$1.50 Rio Grande, U.S.A.	1·25	1·25
3724	$1.50 Erie Lackawanna, U.S.A.	1·25	1·25
3725	$1.50 New York Central, U.S.A.	1·25	1·25
3726	$1.50 Pennsylvania, U.S.A.	1·25	1·25
3727	$1.50 Milwaukee Road, U.S.A.	1·25	1·25
3728	$1.50 Illinois Central, U.S.A.	1·25	1·25
3729	$1.50 Burlington Route, U.S.A.	1·25	1·25
3730	$1.50 Texas Special, Missouri, Kansas and Texas, U.S.A.	1·25	1·25

3731	$1.50 City of Los Angeles, U.S.A.	1·25	1·25
3732	$1.50 Northwestern, U.S.A.	1·25	1·25
3733	$1.50 Canadian National	1·25	1·25
3734	$1.50 Rock Island, U.S.A.	1·25	1·25
3735	$1.50 TGV, French National Railways	1·25	1·25
3736	$1.50 HST, British Railways	1·25	1·25
3737	$1.50 TEE, Trans Europe Express	1·25	1·25
3738	$1.50 Ancona Express, Italy	1·25	1·25
3739	$1.50 XPT, Australia	1·25	1·25
3740	$1.50 APT-P, British Railways	1·25	1·25
3741	$1.50 Western Pacific, U.S.A.	1·25	1·25
3742	$1.50 Union Pacific, U.S.A.	1·25	1·25
3743	$1.50 Chesapeake and Ohio, U.S.A.	1·25	1·25
3744	$1.50 Southern Pacific, U.S.A.	1·25	1·25
3745	$1.50 Baltimore and Ohio, U.S.A.	1·25	1·25
3746	$1.50 Wabash, U.S.A.	1·25	1·25
3747	$3 Kansas City Southern, U.S.A.	2·25	2·50
3748	$4 New Haven, U.S.A.	2·50	3·00

MS3749 Four sheets, each 98×68 mm. (a) $6 Eld 4, Netherlands. (b) $6 "Hikari" express train, Japan. (c) $6 Santa Fe, U.S.A. (d) $6 Inter City express, Germany Set of 4 sheets   18·00   18·00

Nos. 3723/8, 3729/34, 3735/40 and 3741/6 respectively were printed together, se-tenant, with the backgrounds forming composite designs.

463 Papilio blumei (butterfly)

1999. "Australia '99" World Stamp Exhibition, Melbourne. Wildlife. Multicoloured.

3750	75c. Type **463**	70	70
3751	75c. Great egret ("Egret")	70	70
3752	75c. Kumarahou (flower)	70	70
3753	75c. Javan rhinoceros	70	70
3754	75c. Grey-backed white-eye ("Silver-eye") (bird)	70	70
3755	75c. Kiore (rodent)	70	70
3756	75c. Cyclorana novaehollandiae (frog)	70	70
3757	75c. Caterpillar	70	70
3758	75c. Pacific black duck ("Grey Duck")	70	70
3759	75c. Honey blue-eye (fish)	70	70
3760	75c. Krefft's turtle	70	70
3761	75c. Archer fish	70	70
3762	75c. Binturong (vert)	70	70
3763	75c. Two Indian elephants (vert)	70	70
3764	75c. Indian elephant (vert)	70	70
3765	75c. Chestnut-capped laughing thrush (Garkulax mitratus) (vert)	70	70
3766	75c. Vanda hookeriana (orchid) (vert)	70	70
3767	75c. Grey heron ("Heron") (vert)	70	70
3768	75c. Fur seal (vert)	70	70
3769	75c. Black-faced cormorant ("Shag") (bird) (vert)	70	70
3770	75c. Round batfish (vert)	70	70
3771	75c. Loggerhead turtle (vert)	70	70
3772	75c. Three harlequin sweetlips (vert)	70	70
3773	75c. Two harlequin sweetlips (vert)	70	70
3774	$1 Orang-utan	80	80
3775	$2 Dourocouli (monkey)	1·50	1·50
3776	$3 Black caiman (alligator)	1·75	1·90
3777	$4 Panther ("Black Leopard") (vert)	2·00	2·25

MS3778 Two sheets. (a) 110×85 mm. $6 Impala. (b) 85×110 mm. $6 Ring-tailed lemur Set of 2 sheets   8·00   9·00

Nos. 3750/61 and 3762/73 respectively were printed together, se-tenant, with the backgrounds forming composite designs.

Nos. 3753 and 3775 were inscribed "JAUAN RHINOCEROS" and "DOUROCOULI" in error.

1999. "iBRA '99" International Stamp Exhibition, Nuremberg. Horiz designs as T **298a** of Gambia. Multicoloured.

3779	75c. Railway locomotive, 1893, and Prussia 1860 ½sgr. stamp	75	45
3780	90c. Humboldt (sailing ship) and Mecklenburg-Schwerin 1856 4×½s.	1·00	55
3781	$1 Railway locomotive, 1893, and Saxony 1850 3pf.	1·10	85
3782	$2 Humboldt (sailing ship) and Mecklenburg-Strelitz 1864 ½sgr.	1·75	2·40

MS3783 121×104 mm. $6 Saxony 1850 3pf. with Leipzig postmark   5·50   6·00

1999. 150th Death Anniv of Katsushika Hokusai (Japanese artist). As T **298b** of Gambia. Multicoloured.

3784	$1.50 The Actor Ichikawa Danjuro Danjuro as Tomoe Gozen	1·10	1·10
3785	$1.50 Washing Clothes (drawing)	1·10	1·10

3786	$1.50 The Prostitute of Eguchi	1·10	1·10
3787	$1.50 Sudden Shower from a Fine Sky	1·10	1·10
3788	$1.50 Hanging Clothes out to dry (drawing)	1·10	1·10
3789	$1.50 Shimada	1·10	1·10
3790	$1.50 Head of Old Man	1·10	1·10
3791	$1.50 Piebald Horse (drawing)	1·10	1·10
3792	$1.50 Girl making Cord for binding Hats	1·10	1·10
3793	$1.50 Li Po admiring Waterfall of Lo-shan	1·10	1·10
3794	$1.50 Bay Horse (drawing)	1·10	1·10
3795	$1.50 Potted Dwarf Pine with Basin	1·10	1·10

MS3796 Two sheets, each 72×102 mm. (a) $6 The Guardian God Fudo Myoo and his Attendants. (b) $6 Women on the Beach at Enoshima Set of 2 sheets   8·00   9·00

No. 3788 is inscribed "DRAWINFS" in error.

1999. Tenth Anniv of United Nations Rights of the Child Convention. As T **298c** of Gambia. Multicoloured.

3797	$3 Eskimo girl and Russian boy	1·75	2·00
3798	$3 American girl	1·75	2·00
3799	$3 African boy and Indian girl	1·75	2·00

MS3800 110×85 mm. $6 Young boy   4·50   5·00

Nos. 3797/9 were printed together, se-tenant, forming a composite design.

1999. "PhilexFrance '99" International Stamp Exhibition, Paris. Railway Locomotives. Two sheets containing horiz designs as T **299d** of Gambia. Multicoloured.

MS3801 (a) 106×76 mm. $6 Paris, Lyons and Mediterranean Railway Compound Pacific. (b) 106×81 mm. $6 French heavy freight locomotive Set of 2 sheets   10·00   11·00

1999. 250th Birth Anniv of Johann von Goethe (German poet and dramatist). Multicoloured designs as T **298d** of Gambia.

3802	$3 mauve, purple and black	1·75	1·90
3803	$3 blue, lilac and black	1·75	1·90
3804	$3 violet, deep violet and black	1·75	1·90

MS3805 76×106 mm. $6 orange, brown and black   5·50   6·00

DESIGNS—HORIZ: No. 3802, Faust contemplating Moon; 3803, Goethe and Friedrich von Schiller (dramatist); 3804, Faust talking with Wagner. VERT: No. **MS**3805, Margaret (from "Faust").

1999. 30th Anniv of First Manned Landing on Moon. Horiz designs as T **298e** of Gambia. Multicoloured.

3806	$1.50 The Moon	1·25	1·25
3807	$1.50 Edward White on first space walk	1·25	1·25
3808	$1.50 Edwin "Buzz" Aldrin	1·25	1·25
3809	$1.50 The Earth	1·25	1·25
3810	$1.50 Michael Collins	1·25	1·25
3811	$1.50 Neil Armstrong	1·25	1·25
3812	$1.50 Footprint on the Moon	1·25	1·25
3813	$1.50 V2 rocket	1·25	1·25
3814	$1.50 Command module "Columbia"	1·25	1·25
3815	$1.50 Lunar Rover	1·25	1·25
3816	$1.50 Lunar module "Eagle"	1·25	1·25
3817	$1.50 Command module re-entering Earth's atmosphere	1·25	1·25

MS3818 Two sheets. (a) 110×85 mm. $6 Neil Armstrong with American flag. (b) 85×111 mm. $6 Launch of "Apollo 11" (vert) Set of 2 sheets   10·00   10·00

464 Astronaut with Letter

1999. 125th Anniv of Universal Postal Union. Space Mail. Multicoloured.

3819	$2 Type **464**	1·75	1·75
3820	$2 Supply spaceship "Progress"	1·75	1·75
3821	$2 Postmark of space station "MIR"	1·75	1·75
3822	$2 Buran shuttle and "MIR"	1·75	1·75

MS3823 104×75 mm. $6 Space station "MIR"   6·00   7·00

465 Carry On Doctor

1999. 50th Anniv of the Variety Club of Great Britain. Scenes from "Carry On" Films. Multicoloured.

3824	$1 Carry On Dick	90	90
3825	$1 Type **465**	90	90
3826	$1 Carry On England	90	90

3827	$1 Carry On Matron	90	90
3828	$1 Carry On Round The Bend	90	90
3829	$1 Carry On Up The Jungle	90	90
3830	$1 Carry On Loving	90	90
3831	$1 Carry On Up The Khyber	90	90

MS3832 110×86 mm. $6 Actors from Carry On films   5·50   6·00

1999. Royal Wedding. As T **298** of Gambia. Multicoloured.

3833	$3 Prince Edward	2·40	2·50
3834	$3 Sophie and Prince Edward	2·40	2·50
3835	$3 Sophie Rhys-Jones	2·40	2·50

MS3836 78×108 mm. $6 Prince Edward and Sophie Rhys-Jones   6·00   6·50

466 "U.S.S. Enterprise NCC-1701" (from original series)

1999. Spacecraft of "Star Trek". Multicoloured.

3837	$1.50 Type **466**	1·10	1·10
3838	$1.50 Klingon battle cruiser (blue and orange planets in background) (Voyager series)	1·10	1·10
3839	$1.50 "U.S.S. Enterprise" 1701 (green planet in background) (Next Generation series)	1·10	1·10
3840	$1.50 Warbird "Voyager" (below blue planet)	1·10	1·10
3841	$1.50 "U.S.S. Romulan" (in front of orange planet) (original series)	1·10	1·10
3842	$1.50 "U.S.S. Enterprise" 1701 (pink planet in background) (original series)	1·10	1·10
3843	$1.50 "Borg Cube" (Next Generation series)	1·10	1·10
3844	$1.50 "U.S.S. Enterprise NCC" 1701 (in front of multicoloured flames)	1·10	1·10
3845	$1.50 Klingon "Bird of Prey" (original series)	1·10	1·10

1999. "Queen Elizabeth the Queen Mother's Century". As T **304a** of Gambia.

3846	$2 black and gold	1·75	1·75
3847	$2 multicoloured	1·75	1·75
3848	$2 black and gold	1·75	1·75
3849	$2 multicoloured	1·75	1·75

MS3850 154×157 mm. $6 multicoloured   5·50   6·00

DESIGNS: No. 3846, Queen Mother with Prince Charles, 1948; 3847, Queen Mother in pink outfit, 1970; 3848, Queen Mother in Australia, 1958; 3849, Queen Mother waving. (37×50 mm)—**MS**3850, Queen Mother in Coronation robes, 1953.

No. **MS**3850 also shows the Royal Arms embossed in gold, and inscr "Good Health and Happiness to Her Majesty The Queen Mother on her 101st Birthday".

467 George Gershwin

1999. American Entertainers. Multicoloured.

3851	$1 Type **467**	80	80
3852	$1 Florence Mills	80	80
3853	$1 Sam Beckett	80	80
3854	$1 Bessie Smith	80	80
3855	$1 Billie Holiday	80	80
3856	$1 Bert Williams	80	80
3857	$1 Cole Porter	80	80
3858	$1 Sofie Tucker	80	80
3859	$1 Lon Chaney	80	80
3860	$1 Buster Keaton	80	80
3861	$1 Norma Shearer	80	80
3862	$1 James Cagney	80	80
3863	$1 Hedda Hopper	80	80
3864	$1 Jean Harlow	80	80
3865	$1 Marlene Dietrich	80	80
3866	$1 Ramon Novarro	80	80

MS3867 Two sheets, each 76×86 mm. (a) $6 Clark Gable. (b) $6 Louis Armstrong Set of 2 sheets   8·50   9·00

Nos. 3885/8 and 3859/66 respectively were printed together, se-tenant, with the backgrounds forming composite designs.

468 Ouranosaurus

1999. Prehistoric Animals. Multicoloured.

3868	35c. Type **468**	50	30
3869	45c. Struthiomimus (vert)	55	30
3870	75c. Parasaurolophus (vert)	75	50
3871	$1 Archaeopteryx	90	90
3872	$1 Brachiosaurus	90	90
3873	$1 Dilophosaurus	90	90
3874	$1 Dimetrodon	90	90
3875	$1 Psittacosaurus	90	90
3876	$1 Acrocanthosaurus	90	90
3877	$1 Stenonychosaurus	90	90
3878	$1 Dryosaurus	90	90
3879	$1 Campsognathus	90	90
3880	$1 Agathaumas	90	90
3881	$1 Camarasaurus	90	90
3882	$1 Quetzalcoatlus	90	90
3883	$1 Alioramus	90	90
3884	$1 Camptosaurus	90	90
3885	$1 Albertosaurus	90	90
3886	$1 Anatosaurus	90	90
3887	$1 Spinosaurus	90	90
3888	$1 Centrosaurus	90	90
3889	$2 Triceratops	1·60	1·60
3890	$3 Stegoceras	2·00	2·25
3891	$4 Stegosaurus	2·25	2·50

MS3892 Two sheets, each 85×110 mm. (a) $6 Velociraptor (vert). (b) $6 Tyrannosaurus (vert) Set of 2 sheets 8·50 9·00

Nos. 3871/9 and 3880/8 were printed together, *se-tenant*, with the backgrounds forming a composite design. No. 3871 is inscribed "ARCHEOPTERYX" in error.

469 Christmas Rose

1999. Christmas. Multicoloured.

3893	20c. Type **469**	30	15
3894	75c. Tulip	60	40
3895	90c. Pear	70	50
3896	$1 Hibiscus	80	60
3897	$4 Lily	2·75	4·00

MS3898 106×91 mm. $6 "The Nativity" (Botticelli) (horiz) 5·50 6·00

1999. Faces of the Millennium: Diana, Princess of Wales. Vert designs as T **307** of Gambia showing collage of miniature flower photographs. Multicoloured.

3899	$1 Top of head (face value at left)	90	90
3900	$1 Top of head (face value at right)	90	90
3901	$1 Ear (face value at left)	90	90
3902	$1 Eye and temple (face value at right)	90	90
3903	$1 Cheek (face value at left)	90	90
3904	$1 Cheek (face value at right)	90	90
3905	$1 Blue background (face value at left)	90	90
3906	$1 Chin (face value at right)	90	90

Nos. 3899/906 were printed together, *se-tenant*, and when viewed as a whole, form a portrait of Diana, Princess of Wales.

470 Green Dragon

2000. Chinese New Year ("Year of the Dragon"). Multicoloured.

3907	$2 Type **470**	1·75	1·75
3908	$2 Dragon ("GRENADA" in red)	1·75	1·75
3909	$2 Dragon ("GRENADA" in violet)	1·75	1·75

471 Roseate Spoonbill

2000. Birds of Grenada. Multicoloured.

3910	75c. Type **471**	1·10	45
3911	90c. Scarlet ibis	1·10	55
3912	$1 Adelaide's warbler	1·10	1·10
3913	$1 Hispaniolan trogon	1·10	1·10
3914	$1 Sun conure ("Sun Parakeet")	1·10	1·10
3915	$1 Black-necked stilt	1·10	1·10
3916	$1 Sora crake ("Sora")	1·10	1·10
3917	$1 Fulvous whistling duck ("Fulvous Tree Duck")	1·10	1·10
3918	$1 Blue-headed parrot	1·10	1·10
3919	$1 Tropical mockingbird	1·10	1·10
3920	$1 Antillean euphonia ("Blue-hooded Euphonia")	1·10	1·10
3921	$1 Troupial	1·10	1·10
3922	$1 Brown-throated conure ("Caribbean Parakeet")	1·10	1·10
3923	$1 Forest thrush	1·10	1·10
3924	$1 Lesser Antillean tanager ("Hooded Tanager")	1·10	1·10
3925	$1 Stripe-headed tanager	1·10	1·10
3926	$1 Ringed kingfisher	1·10	1·10
3927	$1 Zenaida dove	1·10	1·10
3928	$1.50 Sparkling violetear	1·75	2·00
3929	$2 Northern jacana	2·00	2·25

MS3930 Two sheets, each 70×97 mm. (a) $6 Cedar waxwing (37×50 mm). (b) $6 Antillean siskin (50×37 mm) Set of 2 sheets 17·00 17·00

Nos. 3912/19 and 3920/7 were each printed together, *se-tenant*, with the backgrounds forming composite designs.

No. 3912 is inscribed "Ade; aode's Warbler" and No. 3919 "Tropical Mockinbird", both in error.

471a Jan Vermeer (Dutch painter) (died 1675)

2000. New Millennium. People and Events of Seventeenth Century (1650–1700). Multicoloured.

3931	50c. Type **471a**	60	60
3932	50c. Antoni van Leeuwenhoek (discovered micro-organisms, 1674)	60	60
3933	50c. Salem Witch Trials, Massachusetts, 1692	60	60
3934	50c. Sir Isaac Newton and reflecting telescope, 1668	60	60
3935	50c. Voltaire (French writer and historian) (born 1694)	60	60
3936	50c. Ivan V and Peter I (joint rulers of Russia, 1682)	60	60
3937	50c. Shun Zhi, first Chinese Emperor of Qing Dynasty (died 1662)	60	60
3938	50c. Christian Huggens and Saturn, 1655	60	60
3939	50c. Microscopic mite (Robert Hooke's experiments in cytology, 1665)	60	60
3940	50c. "Verdant Peaks" (Wang Shih-rnin), 1672	60	60
3941	50c. Rene Descartes (French philosopher) (died 1650)	60	60
3942	50c. Completion of Canal du Midi, 1681	60	60
3943	50c. William of Orange and Bill of Rights, 1688	60	60
3944	50c. William III on horseback (end of King William's War), 1697	60	60
3945	50c. Cassini (French astronomer) and images of Mars, 1666	60	60
3946	50c. Sir Isaac Newton and apples (law of gravity, 1666) (59×39 mm)	60	60
3947	50c. Jupiter's Moons (Olaus Roemer) (Danish astronomer) (discovered finite speed of light, 1676)	60	60

No. 3936 is dated "1694" in error.

2000. 400th Birth Anniv of Sir Anthony Van Dyck (Flemish painter). As T 312a of Gambia. Multicoloured.

3948	$1 King Charles I on Horseback	90	90
3949	$1 St. Martin dividing his Cloak	90	90
3950	$1 Gio. Paolo Babli on Horseback	90	90
3951	$1 Marchese Anton Giulio Brignole-Sale on Horseback	90	90
3952	$1 Study of a Horse	90	90
3953	$1 Oriental on Horseback	90	90
3954	$1 Young Woman resting Head on Hand	90	90
3955	$1 Self-portrait, 1613–14	90	90
3956	$1 Woman looking Upwards	90	90
3957	$1 Head of an Old Man, c. 1621	90	90
3958	$1 Head of a Boy	90	90
3959	$1 Head of an Old Man, 1616–18	90	90
3960	$1.50 Portrait of a Man	1·25	1·25
3961	$1.50 Portrait of a Man aged Seventy	1·25	1·25
3962	$1.50 Portrait of a Woman	1·25	1·25
3963	$1.50 Elderly Man	1·25	1·25
3964	$1.50 Portrait of a Young Man	1·25	1·25
3965	$1.50 Man with a Glove	1·25	1·25
3966	$1.50 St. John the Baptist	1·25	1·25
3967	$1.50 St. Anthony of Padua and the Ass of Rimini	1·25	1·25
3968	$1.50 The Stoning of St. Stephen	1·25	1·25
3969	$1.50 The Martyrdom of St. Sebastian	1·25	1·25
3970	$1.50 St. Sebastian bound for Martyrdom	1·25	1·25
3971	$1.50 St. Jerome	1·25	1·25
3972	$1.50 Portrait of Anthony Van Dyck, 1614–15	1·25	1·25
3973	$1.50 Self-portrait (after Rubens)	1·25	1·25
3974	$1.50 Isabella Brant	1·25	1·25
3975	$1.50 The Penitent Apostle Peter	1·25	1·25
3976	$1.50 Head of a Robber (used by Rubens in his *Coup de Lance*)	1·25	1·25
3977	$1.50 "Heads of the Apostles" (detail from Ruben's "Feast at the House of Simon the Pharisee")	1·25	1·25

MS3978 Six sheets. (a) 103×127 mm. $5 Prince Thomas-Francis of Savoy on Horseback. (b) 102×127 mm. $5 Emperor Theodosius refused Entry in Milan Cathedral (horiz). (c) 102×127 mm. $5 King Charles I on Horseback. (d) 127×102 mm. $6 St. Jerome in the Wilderness. (e) 102×127 mm. $6 St. Martin (horiz). (f) 127×102 mm. $6 Detail of Portrait of a Man and His Wife (horiz) Set of 6 sheets 27·00 29·00

No. MS3978b is inscribed "Emperor Theoddosius" in error.

472 Clitcybe geotropa

2000. Fungi. Multicoloured.

3979	35c. Type **472**	50	20
3980	45c. Psalliota augusta	55	25
3981	$1 Amanita rubescens	90	55
3982	$1.50 Pholiota spectabilis	1·10	1·25
3983	$1.50 Mycena polygramma	1·10	1·25
3984	$1.50 Collybia iocephala	1·10	1·25
3985	$1.50 Corinus comatus	1·10	1·25
3986	$1.50 Amanita muscaria sp.	1·10	1·25
3987	$1.50 Boletus aereus	1·10	1·25
3988	$1.50 Ungulina marginata	1·10	1·25
3989	$1.50 Pleurotus ostreatus	1·10	1·25
3990	$1.50 Flammula penetrans	1·10	1·25
3991	$1.50 Morchella crassipes	1·10	1·25
3992	$1.50 Lepiota procera	1·10	1·25
3993	$1.50 Tricholoma aurantium	1·10	1·25
3994	$4 Boletus satanas	3·00	3·25

MS3995 Two sheets. (a) 82×112 mm. $6 Daedala quercina. (b) 112×82 mm. $6 Lepiota acutesquamosa Set of 2 sheets 12·00 13·00

Nos. 3982/7 and 3988/93 were each printed together, *se-tenant*, with the backgrounds forming composite designs.

No. 3986 is inscribed "Aminita muscaria" in error.

2000. 18th Birthday of Prince William. As T 312b of Gambia. Multicoloured.

3996	$1.50 Prince William wearing blue and white tie	1·25	1·25
3997	$1.50 With Prince of Wales	1·25	1·25
3998	$1.50 Prince William waving	1·25	1·25
3999	$1.50 In skiing gear	1·25	1·25

MS4000 100×80 mm. $6 Prince William (37×50 mm) 5·00 5·50

2000. "EXPO 2000" World Stamp Exhibition, Anaheim, U.S.A. Spacecraft. As T 582a of Ghana. Multicoloured.

4001	$1.50 "Lunik 4"	1·40	1·40
4002	$1.50 "Clementine"	1·40	1·40
4003	$1.50 "Luna 12"	1·40	1·40
4004	$1.50 "Luna 16"	1·40	1·40
4005	$1.50 Lunar Module *Eagle* from "Apollo 11"	1·40	1·40
4006	$1.50 "Ranger 7"	1·40	1·40

MS4007 117×84 mm. $6 "Apollo 13" 6·00 6·50

Nos. 4001/6 were printed together, *se-tenant*, with the backgrounds forming a composite design.

2000. 25th Anniv of "Apollo–Soyuz" Joint Project. As T 582b of Ghana. Multicoloured.

4008	$3 Russian "A-2" rocket	2·50	2·50
4009	$3 "Soyuz 19"	2·50	2·50
4010	$3 "Apollo 18" command module docked with "Soyuz 19"	2·50	2·50

MS4011 88×70 mm. $6 Valeri Kubasov ("Soyuz" engineer) and Thomas Stafford ("Apollo" commander) (horiz) 5·50 6·00

2000. 50th Anniv of Berlin Film Festival. As T 582c of Ghana. Multicoloured.

4012	$1.50 *Alphaville*, 1965	1·10	1·10
4013	$1.50 Rod Steiger, 1964	1·10	1·10
4014	$1.50 *Os Fuzis*, 1964	1·10	1·10
4015	$1.50 Jean-Pierre Leaud, 1966	1·10	1·10
4016	$1.50 *Cul-de-sac*, 1966	1·10	1·10
4017	$1.50 *Ikiru*, 1961	1·10	1·10

MS4018 97×103 mm. $6 *His Yen*, 1993 4·75 5·00

No. 4012 is inscribed "ALPHAVILLE" and No. 4016 "CUL-DELSAC", both in error.

2000. 175th Anniv of Stockton and Darlington Line (first public railway). As T 582d of Ghana. Multicoloured.

4019	$3 As Type 582d of Ghana	3·75	3·75
4020	$3 Robert Stephenson's John Bull locomotive, 1831	3·75	3·75

2000. 250th Death Anniv of Johann Sebastian Bach (German composer). Sheet 77×89 mm, containing vert portrait (24×40 mm) as T 312c of Gambia.

MS4021 $6 multicoloured 6·00 6·50

2000. Election of Albert Einstein (mathematical physicist) as *Time Magazine* "Man of the Century". Sheet 117×91 mm, containing vert portrait as T 312d of Gambia.

MS4022 $6 multicoloured 7·50 7·50

2000. Centenary of First Zeppelin Flight. As T 582e of Ghana, each incorporating a different portrait of Count Ferdinand von Zeppelin. Multicoloured.

4023	$3 LZ-130 *Graf Zeppelin II*	2·75	2·75
4024	$3 LZ-2, 1906	2·75	2·75
4025	$3 LZ-127 *Graf Zeppelin*, 1928	2·75	2·75

MS4026 119×76 mm. $6 LZ-129 *Hindenburg*, 1936 (50×37 mm) 7·50 7·50

2000. Olympic Games, Sydney. As T 582f of Ghana. Multicoloured.

4027	$2 Archibald Hahn (athletics), St. Louis (1904)	2·25	2·25
4028	$2 Showjumping	2·25	2·25
4029	$2 Sports Palace, Rome (1960) and Italian flag	2·25	2·25
4030	$2 Ancient Greek chariot racing	2·25	2·25

472a Junior Murray

2000. West Indies Cricket Tour and 100th Test Match at Lord's. Multicoloured.

4031	90c. Type **472a**	1·50	75
4032	$5 Rawl Lewis	6·50	7·00

MS4033 120×105 mm. $6 Lord's Cricket Ground (horiz) 7·50 7·50

473 Brassolaelio cattleya

2000. Orchids. Multicoloured.

4034	75c. Type **473**	1·10	45
4035	90c. Maxilbara	1·10	50
4036	$1 Isochilius	1·10	55
4037	$1.50 Lycaste	1·50	1·50
4038	$1.50 Cochleanthes	1·50	1·50
4039	$1.50 Brassocattleya	1·50	1·50
4040	$1.50 Brassolaelio cattleya	1·50	1·50
4041	$1.50 Iwanagaara	1·50	1·50
4042	$1.50 Sophrocattleya	1·50	1·50
4043	$1.50 Laeliocattleya	1·50	1·50
4044	$1.50 Saphrocattleya	1·50	1·50
4045	$1.50 Epidendrum	1·50	1·50
4046	$1.50 Cattleya	1·50	1·50
4047	$1.50 Ionopsis	1·50	1·50
4048	$1.50 Brassoepidendrum	1·50	1·50
4049	$2 Oncidium	2·00	2·50

MS4050 Two sheets, each 73×103 mm. (a) $6 Brassocattleya. (b) $6 Vanilla Set of 2 sheets 18·00 18·00

474 Sir Donald Bradman playing a Stroke

2000. Famous Cricketers. Six sheets, each 290×165 mm, containing T **474** and similar vert designs. Multicoloured.

MS4051 (a) $1×8, Type **474** and similar shots in sequence. (b) $1×8, Sequence of Shane Warne bowling. (c) $2×4, Sir Garfield Sobers bowling (two different) or batting (two different). (d) $2×4, Different shots of Sir Jack Hobbs batting. (e) $2×4, Different shots of Sir Viv Richards batting. (f) $2×5, Bradman, Sobers, Hobbs, Warne and Richards Set of 6 sheets   50·00   50·00

475 Maine Coon

2000. Cats and Dogs. Multicoloured.

4052	75c. Type **475**	1·10	45
4053	90c. Selkirk rex cat	1·10	50
4054	$1.50 Spotted tabby British shorthair (horiz)	1·50	1·50
4055	$1.50 Burmilla (horiz)	1·50	1·50
4056	$1.50 British blue shorthair (horiz)	1·50	1·50
4057	$1.50 Siamese (horiz)	1·50	1·50
4058	$1.50 Japanese bobtail (horiz)	1·50	1·50
4059	$1.50 Oriental shorthair (horiz)	1·50	1·50
4060	$1.50 Labrador retriever (horiz)	1·50	1·50
4061	$1.50 Standard poodle (horiz)	1·50	1·50
4062	$1.50 Boxer (horiz)	1·50	1·50
4063	$1.50 Rough-coated jack russell terrier (horiz)	1·50	1·50
4064	$1.50 Tibetan terrier (horiz)	1·50	1·50
4065	$1.50 Welsh corgi (horiz)	1·50	1·50
4066	$2 Shetland sheepdog	2·00	2·25
4067	$3 Central Asian sheepdog	2·75	3·25

MS4068 Two sheets, each 106×76 mm. (a) $6 Scottish fold cat. (b) $6 Irish red and white setter (horiz) Set of 2 sheets   18·00   18·00

Nos. 4054/9 (cats) and 4060/5 (dogs) were each printed together, *se-tenant*, with the backgrounds forming composite designs.

476 *Marpesia eleuchea bahamaensis*

2000. Butterflies. Multicoloured.

4069	45c. Type **476**	80	25
4070	75c. *Pterourus palamedes*	1·10	45
4071	90c. *Dryas julia framptonii*	1·10	55
4072	$1 *Hypna clytemnestra iphegenia*	1·25	60
4073	$1.50 *Danaus plexippus*	1·50	1·50
4074	$1.50 *Anartia amathea*	1·50	1·50
4075	$1.50 *Colobura dirce*	1·50	1·50
4076	$1.50 *Parides gundiachianus*	1·50	1·50
4077	$1.50 *Spiroeta stelenes*	1·50	1·50
4078	$1.50 *Hammadryas feronia*	1·50	1·50
4079	$1.50 *Merchantis isthmia*	1·50	1·50
4080	$1.50 *Colias eurytheme*	1·50	1·50
4081	$1.50 *Papilio troilus*	1·50	1·50
4082	$1.50 *Junonia coenia*	1·50	1·50
4083	$1.50 *Doxocopa laure*	1·50	1·50
4084	$1.50 *Pierella hyalinus*	1·50	1·50

MS4085 Two sheets, each 95×68 mm. (a) $6 *Danaus gilippus*. (b) $6 *Agraulis vanilae insularis* Set of 2 sheets   14·00   15·00

Nos. 4073/8 and 4079/84 were each printed together, *se-tenant*, with the backgrounds forming composite designs.

477 Grenada National Cricket Stadium

2000. New National Cricket Stadium. Multicoloured.

4086	$2 Type **477**	3·00	2·50

MS4087 102×79 mm. $1 West Indies and New Zealand Test teams; $1 Cricket match in progress   2·75   3·00

478 Vanderhaeghe (Belgian player)

2000. "Euro 2000" Football Championship. Multicoloured.

4088	$1.50 Type **478**	1·10	1·10
4089	$1.50 Belgian team	1·10	1·10
4090	$1.50 Ronny Gaspercic (Belgian player)	1·10	1·10
4091	$1.50 Lorenzo Staelens (Belgian player)	1·10	1·10
4092	$1.50 Koning Boudewijn Stadium	1·10	1·10
4093	$1.50 Strupar and Mpenza (Belgian player and coach)	1·10	1·10
4094	$1.50 Sergi Barjuan (Spanish player)	1·10	1·10
4095	$1.50 Spanish team	1·10	1·10
4096	$1.50 Luis Enrique (Spanish player)	1·10	1·10
4097	$1.50 Hierro (Spanish player)	1·10	1·10
4098	$1.50 De Kuip Stadium, Rotterdam	1·10	1·10
4099	$1.50 Raul Gonzales (Spanish player)	1·10	1·10
4100	$1.50 Dejan Savicevic (Yugoslav player)	1·10	1·10
4101	$1.50 Yugoslav team	1·10	1·10
4102	$1.50 Predrag Migatovic (Yugoslav player)	1·10	1·10
4103	$1.50 Savo Milosevic (Yugoslav player)	1·10	1·10
4104	$1.50 Jan Breydel Stadium, Bruges	1·10	1·10
4105	$1.50 Darko Kovacevic (Yugoslav player)	1·10	1·10

MS4106 Three sheets, each 145×95 mm. (a) $6 Robert Waseige (Belgian trainer) (vert). (b) $6 José Antonio Camacho (Spanish trainer) (vert). (c) $6 Vujadin Boskov (Yugoslav trainer) (vert) Set of 3 sheets   13·00   14·00

479 Porkfish

2000. Tropical Fish. Multicoloured.

4107	45c. Type **479**	70	25
4108	75c. Short bigeye	90	40
4109	90c. Red snapper	1·00	50
4110	$1 Creole wrasse	1·00	80
4111	$1 Hawksbill turtle	1·00	1·00
4112	$1 Foureye butterflyfish	1·00	1·00
4113	$1 Porcupinefish	1·00	1·00
4114	$1 Yellowtail damselfish	1·00	1·00
4115	$1 Adult French angelfish	1·00	1·00
4116	$1 Yellow goatfish	1·00	1·00
4117	$1 Blue-striped grunt	1·00	1·00
4118	$1 Spanish grunt	1·00	1·00
4119	$1 Queen triggerfish	1·00	1·00
4120	$1 Juvenile French angelfish	1·00	1·00
4121	$1 Beaugregory	1·00	1·00
4122	$1 Queen angelfish	1·00	1·00
4123	$1 Sergeant major	1·00	1·00
4124	$1 Bank butterflyfish	1·00	1·00
4125	$1 Spanish hogfish	1·00	1·00
4126	$1 Porkfish (different)	1·00	1·00
4127	$1 Banded butterflyfish	1·00	1·00
4128	$1 Longsnout seahorse	1·00	1·00
4129	$2 Indigo hamlet	2·00	2·25
4130	$3 Blue tang	2·75	3·25

MS4131 Two sheets, each 102×73 mm. (a) $6 Blue tang (different). (b) $6 Queen angelfish (different) Set of 2 sheets   12·00   13·00

Nos. 4111/19 and 4120/8 were each printed together, *se-tenant*, with the backgrounds forming composite designs.

No. 4126 is inscribed "Poskfish" in error.

480 500 Mondial Sports Car, 1953

2000. Ferrari Cars. Multicoloured.

4144	20c. Type **480**	40	25
4145	45c. 166 Inter saloon, 1948	55	25
4146	75c. 340 MM sports car, 1953	85	35
4147	90c. 500 Superfast saloon, 1964	1·00	45
4148	$1 166 MM sports car, 1948	1·10	55
4149	$1.50 250 S saloon, 1952	1·50	1·50
4150	$2 250 California convertible, 1957	2·00	2·25
4151	$3 365 California convertible, 1966	2·50	3·25

481 Marmon Model 34, 1921

2000. Classic Cars. Multicoloured.

4152	45c. Type **481**	45	25
4153	75c. Buick D44, 1917	75	40
4154	90c. Hudson Runabout Landau, 1918	80	50
4155	$1 Chevrolet Royal Mail, 1915	90	55
4156	$1.50 Rolls Royce, 1929	1·10	1·10
4157	$1.50 Graham Convertible, 1932	1·10	1·10
4158	$1.50 Mercedes-Benz 540K, 1937	1·10	1·10
4159	$1.50 Jaguar Mk V, 1948	1·10	1·10
4160	$1.50 Lagonda Drophead Coupe, 1939	1·10	1·10
4161	$1.50 Alfa Romeo Gran Sport, 1930	1·10	1·10
4162	$1.50 Cadillac V63, 1925	1·10	1·10
4163	$1.50 Plymouth, 1939	1·10	1·10
4164	$1.50 Franklin Club Sedan, 1934	1·10	1·10
4165	$1.50 Fiat Ardita, 1933	1·10	1·10
4166	$1.50 Essex Speedabout, 1929	1·10	1·10
4167	$1.50 Stutz Bearcat, 1932	1·10	1·10
4168	$2 Kissel Speedster, 1925	1·60	1·75
4169	$3 Ford Model T, 1915	2·00	2·25

MS4170 Two sheets, each 94×67 mm. (a) $6 Dodge Tourer, 1915. (b) $6 Chrysler, 1924 Set of 2 sheets   10·00   11·00

482 Borsig Standard Locomotive, 1863

2000. German Railway Locomotives. Multicoloured.

4171	$1.50 Type **482**	1·60	1·60
4172	$1.50 German Federal Railway Austerity Class 52, 1940s	1·60	1·60
4173	$1.50 Stephenson locomotive *Adler* without tender, 1835	1·60	1·60
4174	$1.50 Crampton locomotive *Bardenia*, 1863	1·60	1·60
4175	$1.50 *Drache*, 1848	1·60	1·60
4176	$1.50 Stephenson locomotive *Adler* with tender, 1835	1·60	1·60
4177	$1.50 German Federal Railway Class 10, 1956	1·60	1·60
4178	$1.50 German Federal Railway Class E10 electric locomotive, 1957	1·60	1·60
4179	$1.50 German Federal Railway Class 23, 1953	1·60	1·60

2000. Monarchs of the Millenium. As T **314a** of Gambia.

4132	$1.50 multicoloured	2·00	2·00
4133	$1.50 multicoloured	2·00	2·00
4134	$1.50 lilac, stone and brown	2·00	2·00
4135	$1.50 lilac, stone and brown	2·00	2·00

MS4136 116×136 mm. $6 multicoloured   6·00   6·50

DESIGNS: No. 4132, King George III of Great Britain; 4133, King George IV of Great Britain; 4134, Duchess Charlotte of Luxembourg; 4135, Duke Jean of Luxembourg; **MS**4136 King Charles VIII of France.

2000. Popes of the Millennium. As T **314b** of Gambia. Multicoloured (except **MS**4143).

4137	$1.50 Stephen VIII	2·00	2·00
4138	$1.50 Theodore	2·00	2·00
4139	$1.50 Theodore II	2·00	2·00
4140	$1.50 Valentine	2·00	2·00
4141	$1.50 Vitalian	2·00	2·00
4142	$1.50 Zacharias	2·00	2·00

MS4143 116×136 mm. $6 Sylvester II (grey, black and stone)   6·50   6·50

483 Thai State Railway Diesel-electric Locomotive

2000. Modern Railway Locomotives of the World. Multicoloured.

4184	$1.50 Type **483**	1·60	1·60
4185	$1.50 Danish diesel-electric express locomotive	1·60	1·60
4186	$1.50 French-built Turbo train	1·60	1·60
4187	$1.50 Spanish Railways diesel unit	1·60	1·60
4188	$1.50 Spanish Railways diesel locomotive for "Virgen del Rosario"	1·60	1·60
4189	$1.50 Malayan Railways Class 22 diesel-electric locomotive	1·60	1·60
4190	$1.50 British Railways Class 87 electric locomotive	1·60	1·60
4191	$1.50 Iraqi Railway diesel-electric locomotive	1·60	1·60
4192	$1.50 Austrian Railways electric locomotive	1·60	1·60
4193	$1.50 South Australia Railways diesel locomotive	1·60	1·60
4194	$1.50 Black Mesa and Lake Powell Railroad electric locomotive	1·60	1·60
4195	$1.50 Yugoslav Railways diesel-electric unit	1·60	1·60

MS4196 Four sheets, each 96×66 mm. (a) $6 Netherlands Railway Inter-city electric train. (b) $6 Swiss Railways Suburban electric unit. (c) $6 T.E.E. diesel locomotive for "Parsifal". (d) $6 New Zealand Railways "Silver Fern" diesel railcar unit Set of 4 sheets   22·00   24·00

4180	$1.50 German Federal Railway tank locomotive, 1950s	1·60	1·60
4181	$1.50 East German State Railway rebuilt Class 01 Pacific, 1950s	1·60	1·60
4182	$1.50 East German State Railway diesel railcar on Berlin–Schonefeld service, 1950s	1·60	1·60

MS4183 Two sheets, each 80×72 mm. (a) $6 Borsig locomotive of Berlin and Anhalt Railway, 1841. (b) $6 German Federal Railway V.200 diesel-hydraulic locomotive, 1952 Set of 2 sheets   12·00   13·00

484 Girl at Skylight

2000. Nursery Rhymes. Multicoloured.

4197	$1.50 Type **484**	1·10	1·10
4198	$1.50 Woman and rainbow	1·10	1·10
4199	$1.50 Cow and rainbow	1·10	1·10
4200	$1.50 Boy in nightshirt	1·10	1·10
4201	$1.50 Old Woman with baby	1·10	1·10
4202	$1.50 Boy on show	1·10	1·10
4203	$1.50 Bird in tree and crook	1·10	1·10
4204	$1.50 Little Bo-Peep	1·10	1·10
4205	$1.50 Sheep	1·10	1·10
4206	$1.50 Goose and fence	1·10	1·10
4207	$1.50 Goose and Little Bo-Peep	1·10	1·10
4208	$1.50 Dog	1·10	1·10
4209	$1.50 Sheep and cottage	1·10	1·10
4210	$1.50 Sun and lane	1·10	1·10
4211	$1.50 Cow and haystack	1·10	1·10
4212	$1.50 Two geese	1·10	1·10
4213	$1.50 Dog and Boy Blue's leg	1·10	1·10
4214	$1.50 Little Boy Blue asleep	1·10	1·10
4215	$1.50 Dove and tower	1·10	1·10
4216	$1.50 Cow jumping over moon	1·10	1·10
4217	$1.50 Spoon	1·10	1·10
4218	$1.50 Dog laughing	1·10	1·10
4219	$1.50 Cat playing fiddle	1·10	1·10
4220	$1.50 Dish	1·10	1·10

MS4221 Four sheets, each 106×77 mm. (a) $6 Old Woman and shoe (horiz). (b) $6 Little Bo-Peep (horiz). (c) $6 Little Boy Blue asleep (horiz). (d) $6 Cow jumping over moon (horiz) Set of 4 sheets   20·00   20·00

Nos. 4197/202 (Old Woman that lived in a Shoe), 4203/8 (Little Bo-Peep), 4209/14 (Little Boy Blue) and 4215/20 (The Cat and the Fiddle) were each printed together, *se-tenant*, with the backgrounds forming composite designs.

485 Heidi walking with
Governess

2000. Shirley Temple in Heidi. Showing scenes from the film. Multicoloured.

4222	$1.50 Type **485**	1·10	1·10
4223	$1.50 Heidi with grandfather	1·10	1·10
4224	$1.50 Heidi with Peter the Goat Boy	1·10	1·10
4225	$1.50 Heidi with doves	1·10	1·10
4226	$1.50 Heidi with grandfather tying knot	1·10	1·10
4227	$1.50 Heidi and governess sitting on bench	1·10	1·10
4228	$1.50 Heidi in bed	1·10	1·10
4229	$1.50 Heidi with Klara Sesemann	1·10	1·10
4230	$1.50 Heidi with Andrews the butler	1·10	1·10
4231	$1.50 Heidi unwrapping Christmas presents with the Sesemanns	1·10	1·10
MS4232	105×75 mm. $6 Heidi sitting on log	4·75	5·00

Grenada $6

486 Betty Boop sitting in
Sports Car, Hollywood

2000. Betty Boop (cartoon character). Twelve sheets containing vert designs as T 486 showing geographical locations. Multicoloured.

MS4233 (a) 110×90 mm. $6 Type **486**. (b) 110×90 mm. $6 Riding horse, Argentina. (c) 110×90 mm. $6 Sitting on camel, Turkey. (d) 110×90 mm. $6 As flamenco dancer, Spain. (e) 110×90 mm. $6 Drinking champagne, France. (f) 110×90 mm. $6 Fishing, South Pacific. (g) 110×90 mm. $6 As belly dancer, Eygpt. (h) 90×110 mm. $6 With guardsman outside Buckingham Palace, London. (i) 90×110 mm. $6 In floral hat, Switzerland. (j) 90×110 mm. $6 In kimono, Japan. (k) 90×110 mm. $6 As Statue of Liberty, New York. (l) 90×110 mm. $6 Wearing lei, Hawaii

Set of 12 sheets 45·00 50·00

2000. Scenes from The Three Stooges (American T.V. comedy series). As T 310 of Gambia. Multicoloured.

4234	$1 Moe pointing bottle at Curly Joe	80	80
4235	$1 Eating straw with horse	80	80
4236	$1 Larry holding flowers	80	80
4237	$1 Reading letter	80	80
4238	$1 Looking in saucepan	80	80
4239	$1 Holding wads of notes	80	80
4240	$1 Moe in breastplate (guard behind in purple and green)	80	80
4241	$1 Indoors with horse	80	80
4242	$1 Larry in breastplate (guard behind in lilac and yellow)	80	80
4243	$1 Western bar brawl	80	80
4244	$1 As "DELIGATES"	80	80
4245	$1 In Victorian dress (two as women)	80	80
4246	$1 Moe pointing gun	80	80
4247	$1 Holding certificate	80	80
4248	$1 Moe using secateurs near Curly's nose	80	80
4249	$1 Larry (picture at right)	80	80
4250	$1 Moe in front of picture	80	80
4251	$1 Curly	80	80

MS4252 Twelve sheets. (a) 108×87 mm. $5 Curly in green shirt holding Moe's arm (vert). (b) 108×87 mm. $5 In evening dress with girl. (c) 108×87 mm. $5 Moe with Larry holding woman's hand (vert). (d) 91×137 mm. $5 With secretary from He Cooked His Goose (vert). (e) 108×87 mm. $5 As No. 4243. (f) 108×89 mm. $5 Having heads banged together by cowboy. (g) 97×118 mm. $5 Putting Larry in a jet engine (vert). (h) 98×125 mm. $5 Curly Joe with cigar (vert). (i) 107×88 mm. $5 Listening to jet engine. (j) 107×88 mm. $5 Swinging propeller. (k) 130×100 mm. $6 Larry and Moe in breastplates. (l) 130×100 mm. $6 Curly with hand in mangle Set of 12 sheets 40·00 45·00

GRENADA $1

487 Kane jumping over
Opponent

2000. World Wrestling Federation. Kane. Multicoloured.

4253	$1 Type **487**	80	80
4254	$1 Kneeling by injured opponent	80	80
4255	$1 Jumping	80	80
4256	$1 Kane (red background)	80	80
4257	$1 Kane (blue and yellow background)	80	80
4258	$1 Holding lifting opponent in black tunic	80	80
4259	$1 With arms folded	80	80
4260	$1 Lifting opponent in black and white trousers	80	80
4261	$1 Lifting opponent No. 59	80	80

MS4262 Two sheets, each 77×118 mm. (a) $5 With black glove on right hand. (b) $5 Lifting opponent Set of 2 sheets 7·50 8·50

2000. "Espana 2000" International Stamp Exhibition, Madrid. Paintings from the Prado Museum. As T 326a of Gambia. Multicoloured.

4263	$1.50 King Ferdinand and priest from The Virgin of the Catholic Monarchs (anon)	1·10	1·10
4264	$1.50 Virgin and Child from The Virgin of the Catholic Monarchs	1·10	1·10
4265	$1.50 Queen Isabella and priest from The Virgin of the Catholic Monarchs	1·10	1·10
4266	$1.50 The Flagellation (Alejo Fernandez)	1·10	1·10
4267	$1.50 The Virgin and Souls in Purgatory (Pedro Machuca)	1·10	1·10
4268	$1.50 The Holy Trinity (El Greco)	1·10	1·10
4269	$1.50 The Saviour's Blessing (Francisco de Zurbaran)	1·10	1·10
4270	$1.50 St. John the Baptist (Francesco Solimena)	1·10	1·10
4271	$1.50 Noli Me Tangere (Correggio)	1·10	1·10
4272	$1.50 St. Casilda (Francisco de Zurbaran)	1·10	1·10
4273	$1.50 Nicolas Omazur (Murillo)	1·10	1·10
4274	$1.50 Juan Martinez Montanes (Velazquez)	1·10	1·10
4275	$1.50 Playing at Giants (Goya)	1·10	1·10
4276	$1.50 The Holy Family with Oak Tree (Raphael and Giulio Romano)	1·10	1·10
4277	$1.50 Don Gaspar Melchor de Jovellanos (Goya)	1·10	1·10
4278	$1.50 Courtier from Joseph in Pharaoh's Palace (Jacopo Amiconi)	1·10	1·10
4279	$1.50 Pharaoh and Joseph from Joseph in Pharaoh's Palace	1·10	1·10
4280	$1.50 Servant with hat from Joseph in Pharaoh's Palace	1·10	1·10

MS4281 Three sheets. (a) 90×110 mm. $6 The Virgin of the Catholic Monarchs (anon). (b) 90×110 mm. $6 St. Anne, the Virgin, St. Elizabeth, St. John and the Christ Child (Fernando Yanez de la Almedina). (c) 110×90 mm. $6 Joseph in Pharaoh's Palace (Jacopo Amiconi) (horiz) Set of 3 sheets 13·00 14·00

GRENADA 25¢

488
American
Purple
Gallinule

2000. Birds of the Caribbean. Multicoloured.

4282	25c. Type **488**	60	15
4283	40c. Limpkin	80	40
4284	50c. Black-necked stilt	90	40
4285	60c. Painted bunting	1·00	45
4286	75c. Yellow-breasted flycatcher warbler ("Yellow-breasted Warbler")	1·25	55
4287	$1 Blackburnian warbler	1·50	75
4288	$1.25 Blue grosbeak	1·75	75
4289	$1.50 Black and white warbler	2·00	1·75
4290	$1.60 Himalayan whistling thrush ("Blue Whistling Thrush")	2·25	2·25
4291	$3 Common yellowthroat	3·75	4·25
4292	$4 Indigo bunting	4·25	5·00
4293	$5 Catbird	4·50	5·00
4294	$10 Bananaquit	8·00	9·00
4295	$20 Blue-grey gnatcatcher	14·00	18·00

Grenada $1.50

489 Messerschmitt Bf 109E
under Attack

2000. 60th Anniv of Battle of Britain. Multicoloured.

4296	$1.50 Type **489**	1·75	1·75
4297	$1.50 Supermarine Spitfire Mk XI	1·75	1·75
4298	$1.50 V1 flying bomb	1·75	1·75
4299	$1.50 U-Boat under attack	1·75	1·75
4300	$1.50 Anti-aircraft gun	1·75	1·75
4301	$1.50 Bedford army ambulance	1·75	1·75
4302	$1.50 Messerschmitt Bf 109E	1·75	1·75
4303	$1.50 German pilot parachuting	1·75	1·75
4304	$1.50 Hawker Hurricane MkI	1·75	1·75
4305	$1.50 British airfield under attack	1·75	1·75
4306	$1.50 Heinkel He 111H on fire	1·75	1·75
4307	$1.50 R.A.F. emblem on Supermarine Spitfire Mk XI	1·75	1·75

MS4308 Two sheets, each 99×71 mm. (a) $6 Supermarine Spitfire Mk IX. (b) $6 Hawker Hurricane Mk 1s on tarmac Set of 2 sheets 16·00 16·00

No. 4304 is inscribed "Hanker Hurricane HK1" and No. MS4308 "HK1", both in error.

2000. Queen Elizabeth the Queen Mother's 100th Birthday. As T 318 of Gambia. Multicoloured.

4309	$1.50 Queen Mother in grey hat	1·50	1·50

2000. Faces of the Millennium: Queen Elizabeth the Queen Mother's 100th Birthday. As T 307a of Gambia showing collage of miniature flower photographs. Multicoloured.

4310	$1 Top of head (face value at left)	1·10	1·10
4311	$1 Top of head (face value at right)	1·10	1·10
4312	$1 Eye and temple (face value at left)	1·10	1·10
4313	$1 Temple (face value at right)	1·10	1·10
4314	$1 Cheek (face value at left)	1·10	1·10
4315	$1 Cheek (face value at right)	1·10	1·10
4316	$1 Chin (face value at left)	1·10	1·10
4317	$1 Neck (face value at right)	1·10	1·10

Nos. 4310/17 were printed together, se-tenant, in sheetlets of 8 with the stamps arranged in two vertical columns separated by a gutter also containing miniature photographs. When viewed as a whole the sheetlet forms a portrait of the Queen Mother.

Grenada

490 Brassavola
nodosa

2000. Caribbean Flowers. Multicoloured.

4318	25c. Type **490**	45	20
4319	35c. Laelia anceps (horiz)	55	20
4320	75c. Plumeria rubra (horiz)	90	35
4321	$1 Bougainvillea glabra (horiz)	1·00	90
4322	$1 Allamanda cathartica	1·00	90
4323	$1.50 Cassia alata	1·25	1·25
4324	$1.50 Anthurium andreanum	1·25	1·25
4325	$1.50 Ipomea crassicaulis	1·25	1·25
4326	$1.50 Laelia anceps	1·25	1·25
4327	$1.50 Galeandra baueri	1·25	1·25
4328	$1.50 Hibiscus rosa-sinensis	1·25	1·25
4329	$1.50 Alpinia purpurata	1·25	1·25
4330	$1.50 Strelitzia reginae	1·25	1·25
4331	$1.50 Psychlis atropurpurea	1·25	1·25
4332	$1.50 Cattleya velutina	1·25	1·25
4333	$1.50 Caularthron bicornutum	1·25	1·25
4334	$1.50 Cattleya warneri	1·25	1·25
4335	$1.50 Mandevilla splendens	1·25	1·25
4336	$1.50 Tithonia rotundifolia	1·25	1·25
4337	$1.50 Lagerstromia speciosa	1·25	1·25
4338	$1.50 Columnea argentea	1·25	1·25
4339	$1.50 Brunfelsia calycina	1·25	1·25
4340	$1.50 Portlandia albiflora	1·25	1·25
4341	$1.50 Pachira insignis	1·25	1·25
4342	$1.50 Jatropha integerrima	1·25	1·25
4343	£1.50 Jacaranda filicifolia	1·25	1·25
4344	$1.50 Cordia sebestena	1·25	1·25
4345	$1.50 Allamanda cathartica	1·25	1·25
4346	$1.50 Samanea saman	1·25	1·25
4347	$2 Lisianthus nigrescens (horiz)	1·60	2·00
4348	$2 Aspasia epidendroides	1·60	2·00
4349	$3 Oncidium splendidum	2·00	2·50

MS4350 Four sheets. (a) 68×97 mm. $6 Anthurium scherzerianum (horiz). (b) 68×97 mm. $6 Ipomea learii (horiz). (c) 94×61 mm. $6 Fuchsia (horiz). (d) 94×61 mm. $6 Heliconia psittaconia Set of 4 sheets 20·00 22·00

Nos. 4323/8, 4329/34, 4335/40 and 4341/6 were each printed together, se-tenant, each forming a composite floral design.

No. 4320 is inscribed "Plumieria", 4341 "Pachira insigis", 4343 "Jacarancla filicifolia" and 4345 "Corclia filicifolia", all in error.

Grenada 15¢

491 Angel in Red

2000. Christmas. Holy Year. Multicoloured.

4351	15c. Type **491**	20	10
4352	25c. Angel praying	25	15
4353	50c. Type **491**	45	25
4354	$2 As 25c	1·75	2·00
4355	$2 Type **491**	1·75	2·00
4356	$5 As 25c	3·50	4·25

MS4357 110×120 mm. $6 Holy Child (horiz) 4·50 5·50

2001. Chinese New Year. ("Year of the Snake"). As T 470. Multicoloured.

4358	$2 Blue and yellow snake	1·75	2·00
4359	$2 Green snake (inverted triangle)	1·75	2·00
4360	$2 Red snake	1·75	2·00

GRENADA $6

491a Lucy and Desi with
Friends

2001. Scenes from I Love Lucy (American T.V. comedy series). Eight sheets, each containing multicoloured design as T 491a.

MS4361 (a) 80×112 mm. $6 Type **491a**. (b) 80×110 mm. $6 Lucy and Desi dancing. (c) 88×127 mm. $6 Lucy in checked jacket. (d) 92×124 mm. $6 Lucy in checked jacket dancing with Desi. (e) 98×120 mm. $6 Desi laughing with William Frawley. (f) 118×92 mm. $6 Lucy leaning on mantelpiece. (g) 118×100 mm. $6 Lucy sitting at desk. (h) 92×124 mm. $6 William Frawley and Desi at desk (horiz) Set of 8 sheets 32·00 35·00

2001. Bicentenary of Rijksmuseum, Amsterdam. Dutch Paintings. As T 330a of Gambia. Multicoloured.

4362	$1.50 "Syndics of Amsterdam Goldsmiths' Guild" (Thomas de Keyser)	1·10	1·10
4363	$1.50 "Gentleman" (De Keyser)	1·10	1·10
4364	$1.50 "Eva Wtewael" (Joachim Wtewael)	1·10	1·10
4365	$1.50 "Ferry Boat" (Esaias van de Velde)	1·10	1·10
4366	$1.50 "Tares among the Wheat" (Abraham Bloemaert)	1·10	1·10
4367	$1.50 "Princess Henrietta Marie Stuart" (Bartholomeus van der Heist)	1·10	1·10
4368	$1.50 "William I, Prince of Orange" (Adriaen Key)	1·10	1·10
4369	$1.50 "Schimmelpenninck Family" (Pierre-Paul Prud'hon)	1·10	1·10
4370	$1.50 "Johan Rudolf Thorbecke" (Jan Neuman)	1·10	1·10
4371	$1.50 "St. Sebastian" (Wtewael)	1·10	1·10
4372	$1.50 "St. Sebastian" (Hendrick ter Brugghen)	1·10	1·10
4373	$1.50 "Man with a Ring" (Werner van der Valckert)	1·10	1·10
4374	$1.50 "Abraham Casteleyn and his Wife, Margarieta van Bancken" (Jan de Bray)	1·10	1·10
4375	$1.50 Piper and singer from "Concert" (Ter Brugghen)	1·10	1·10
4376	$1.50 "Procuress" (Dirck van Baburen)	1·10	1·10
4377	$1.50 "Woman seated at Virginal" (Vermeer)	1·10	1·10
4378	$1.50 "Elegant Couples courting" (Willem Buytewech)	1·10	1·10
4379	$1.50 "Young Flute player" (Judith Leyster)	1·10	1·10
4380	$1.50 "Merry Fiddler" (Gerard van Honthorst)	1·10	1·10

4381	$1.50 "Merry Drinker" (Frans Hals)	1·10	1·10
4382	$1.50 "Granida and Daifilo" (Van Honthorst)	1·10	1·10
4383	$1.50 "Vertumnus and Pomona" (Paulus Moreelse)	1·10	1·10
4384	$1.50 Piper from "Concert" (Ter Brugghen)	1·10	1·10
4385	$1.50 "Young Student at his Desk" (Pieter Codde)	1·10	1·10
MS4386	Four sheets. (a) 119×88 mm. $6 "Winter Landscape with Skaters" (Hendrick Avercamp) (horiz). (b) 119×88 mm. $6 "Denial of St. Peter" (Rembrandt) (horiz). (c) 98×118 mm. $6 "Portuguese Synagogue, Amsterdam" (Emanuel de Witte). (d) 98×118 mm. $6 "The Raampoortje" (Wouter van Troostwijk) (horiz) Set of 4 sheets	18·00	20·00

No. 4381 is inscribed "Frans Hal" in error.

2001. Characters from "Pokemon" (children's cartoon series). As T **332a** of Gambia. Multicoloured.

4387	$1.50 "Rattata No. 19"	1·10	1·10
4388	$1.50 "Sandshrew No. 27"	1·10	1·10
4389	$1.50 "Wartortle No. 08"	1·10	1·10
4390	$1.50 "Primeape No. 57"	1·10	1·10
4391	$1.50 "Golduck No. 55"	1·10	1·10
4392	$1.50 "Persian No. 53"	1·10	1·10
MS4393	74×115 mm. $6 "Jolteon No. 135"	4·50	5·00

492 African Pygmy Goose

2001. "Hong Kong 2001" International Stamp Exhibition. Ducks of the World. Multicoloured.

4394	$1.25 Type **492**	1·50	1·50
4395	$1.25 Versicolor teal ("Silver Teal")	1·50	1·50
4396	$1.25 Marbled teal	1·50	1·50
4397	$1.25 Garganey	1·50	1·50
4398	$1.25 Wandering whistling duck	1·50	1·50
4399	$1.25 Northern shoveler	1·50	1·50
4400	$1.25 Flying steamer duck ("Flightless Steamer Duck")	1·50	1·50
4401	$1.25 Radjah shelduck	1·50	1·50
4402	$1.25 Cape teal	1·50	1·50
4403	$1.25 Hartlaub's duck	1·50	1·50
4404	$1.25 Ruddy shelduck	1·50	1·50
4405	$1.25 Bahama pintail ("White-cheeked Pintail")	1·50	1·50
4406	$1.25 Fulvous whistling duck (vert)	1·50	1·50
4407	$1.25 African black duck (vert)	1·50	1·50
4408	$1.25 Madagascar pochard ("Madagascan White-eye") (vert)	1·50	1·50
4409	$1.25 African pygmy goose ("Pygmy Goose") (vert)	1·50	1·50
4410	$1.25 Wood duck (female) (vert)	1·50	1·50
4411	$1.25 Wood duck (male) (vert)	1·50	1·50
MS4412	Three sheets, each 100×70 mm. (a) $6 Flying steamer duck. (b) $6 Flightless steamer duck. (c) $6 Australian shelduck (vert) Set of 3 sheets	18·00	18·00

493 Daily Life in Edo (Miyagawa Choshum)

2001. "Philanippon '01" International Stamp Exhibition, Tokyo. Japanese Paintings. Multicoloured.

4413	75c. Type **493**	70	35
4414	90c. "Twelve Famous Places in Japan" (Kano Isen'in Naganobu)	80	40
4415	$1 "After the Rain" (Kawai Gyokudo)	90	55
4416	$1.25 "Ryogoku Bridge" (Kano Kyuei)	1·10	65
4417	$2 "Courtesan of Fukagawa" (Katsukawa Shun'ei)	1·60	1·75
4418	$2 "Yugao Chapter" (85×28 mm)	1·60	1·75
4419	$2 "Suetsumuhana Chapter" (85×28 mm)	1·60	1·75
4420	$2 "Wakamurasaki Chapter" (85×28 mm)	1·60	1·75
4421	$2 "Momiji-no-ga Chapter" (85×28 mm)	1·60	1·75
4422	$2 Praying in the woods (vert)	1·60	1·75
4423	$2 Lady with servants (vert)	1·60	1·75
4424	$2 Fire by river (vert)	1·60	1·75
4425	$2 Pagoda by river (vert)	1·60	1·75
4426	$3 "Bear Killing" (unsigned)	2·25	2·50

MS4427	Two sheets. (a) 93×81 mm. $6 "Pomegranates and a Small Bird" (Onishi Keisai). (b) 97×76 mm. $6 from "Bodhisattva: Never Despise" (Enryaku-ji) (vert). Nos. 4418/21 depict "Tale of Genji" Set of 2 sheets	9·50	11·50

Nos. 4418/21 depict "Tale of Genji" (Kano Ryusetsu Hidenobu), and Nos. 4422/5 illustrates "The Lotus Sutra—Tactfulness" (Hompo-ji).

2001. Death Centenary of Queen Victoria. As T **590a** of Ghana. Multicoloured.

4428	$3 Princess Victoria as a young girl	2·00	2·25
4429	$3 Young Queen Victoria wearing crown	2·00	2·25
4430	$3 In old age	2·00	2·25
MS4431	77×107 mm. $6 Queen Victoria on throne	5·00	5·50

2001. 25th Death Anniv of Mao Tse-tung (Chinese leader). As T **590b** of Ghana. Multicoloured.

4432	$2 Mao Tse-tung in 1936	1·60	1·75
4433	$2 In 1919	1·60	1·75
4434	$2 In 1945	1·60	1·75
MS4435	133×126 mm. $3 Mao Tse-tung encouraging troops in 1938	2·00	2·25

2001. 75th Death Anniv of Claude-Oscar Monet (French painter). As T **590c** of Ghana. Multicoloured.

4436	$2 Boats in Winter Quarters, Etretat	1·60	1·75
4437	$2 Regatta at Sainte Adresse	1·60	1·75
4438	$2 Bridge at Bougival	1·60	1·75
4439	$2 Beach at Sainte Adresse	1·60	1·75
MS4440	136×111 mm. $6 Monet's Garden at Vetheuil (vert)	5·00	5·50

2001. 75th Birthday of Queen Elizabeth II. As T **590d** of Ghana. Multicoloured.

4441	$2 Queen in straw boater	1·90	1·90
4442	$2 Queen in red hat	1·90	1·90
4443	$2 Wearing multicoloured pastel hat	1·90	1·90
4444	$2 Wearing mauve turban-style hat	1·90	1·90
MS4445	76×100 mm. $6 Queen wearing mauve hat and coat (37×50 mm)	5·50	6·00

2001. Death Centenary of Giuseppe Verdi (Italian composer). As T **590e** of Ghana. Multicoloured.

4446	$2 Character from Ernani (opera)	3·00	2·25
4447	$2 Score from Ernani	3·00	2·25
4448	$2 Verdi as a young man	3·00	2·25
4449	$2 La Scala Opera House, Milan	3·00	2·25
MS4450	76×106 mm. $6 Verdi in old age	9·50	9·00

2001. Death Centenary of Henri de Toulouse-Lautrec (French painter). As T **590f** of Ghana. Multicoloured.

4451	$2 Alone	1·60	1·75
4452	$2 Two Half-naked Women	1·60	1·75
4453	$2 The Toilette	1·60	1·75
4454	$2 Justine Dieuhl	1·60	1·75
MS4455	66×84 mm. $6 Mademoiselle Dihau at the Piano	4·75	5·00

494 Woman on Beach

2001. United Nations Women's Human Rights Campaign. Multicoloured.

4456	90c. Type **494**	70	60
4457	$1 "Caribbean Woman II"	80	80

495 Marlene Dietrich smoking

2001. Birth Centenary of Marlene Dietrich (actress and singer).

4458	**495**	$2 multicoloured	1·60	1·75
4459	-	$2 black, purple and red	1·60	1·75
4460	-	$2 black, purple and red	1·60	1·75
4461	-	$2 black, purple and red	1·60	1·75

DESIGNS Nos. 4459, Marlene Dietrich on stage with microphone; 4460, Wearing feather boa; 4461, Sitting in armchair.

496 Phoenician Merchant Ship

2001. "Belgica 2001" International Stamp Exhibition, Brussels. Sailing Ships. Multicoloured.

4462	45c. Type **496**	70	25
4463	75c. Portuguese caravel	90	55
4464	90c. Marblehead schooner	1·00	70
4465	$1 Mala pansi	1·00	1·00
4466	$1 English cog	1·00	1·00
4467	$1 Roman merchantman	1·00	1·00
4468	$1 Greek war galley	1·00	1·00
4469	$1 Greek merchantman	1·00	1·00
4470	$1 Oseberg Viking longship	1·00	1·00
4471	$1 Egyptian sailing craft	1·00	1·00
4472	$1 Egyptian galley	1·00	1·00
4473	$1 16th-century galleass	1·00	1·00
4474	$1 Norman ship	1·00	1·00
4475	$1 English carrack	1·00	1·00
4476	$1 Mediterranean carrack	1·00	1·00
4477	$1 Spanish galleon	1·00	1·00
4478	$1 Elizabethan Grumster	1·00	1·00
4479	$1 British East Indiaman	1·00	1·00
4480	$1 Clipper	1·00	1·00
4481	$1 British ship of the line	1·00	1·00
4482	$1 British gun boat	1·00	1·00
4483	$1 English hoy	1·00	1·00
4484	$1 Gloucester fishing schooner	1·00	1·00
4485	$1 Sloop-rigged yacht	1·00	1·00
4486	$1 Chinese junk	1·00	1·00
4487	$1 Sambuk	1·00	1·00
4488	$1 Baltimore clipper schooner	1·00	1·00
4489	$1 Schooner-rigged yacht	1·00	1·00
4490	$1 American clipper	1·00	1·00
4491	$1 American frigate	1·00	1·00
4492	$1 Sail/steam mail packet	1·00	1·00
4493	$1 American corvette	1·50	1·75
4494	$2 Racing schooner	2·00	2·25
MS4495	Two sheets, each 60×44 mm. (a) $6 Suhaili (yacht), 1968. (b) $6 Gulf Streamer (trimaran) and Polynesian outrigger Set of 2 sheets	11·00	12·00

No. 4481 is inscribed "BRITISH GUN SHIP", 4482 "BRITISH FLAGSHIP" and 4484 "GLOUSTER", all in error.

497 Montauk Point Lighthouse, New York

2001. Lighthouses. Multicoloured.

4496	25c. Type **497**	1·25	45
4497	50c. Alcatraz lighthouse, San Francisco	1·75	70
4498	$1 Barnegat lighthouse, New Jersey	2·00	1·25
4499	$1.50 Point Amour lighthouse, Canada	2·25	2·25
4500	$1.50 Inubo-Saki lighthouse, Japan	2·25	2·25
4501	$1.50 Belle-Ile lighthouse, France	2·25	2·25
4502	$1.50 Faerder lighthouse, Norway	2·25	2·25
4503	$1.50 Cape Agulhas lighthouse, South Africa	2·25	2·25
4504	$1.50 Minicoy lighthouse, India	2·25	2·25
4505	$1.50 Admiralty lighthouse, Washington	2·25	2·25
4506	$1.50 Hooper's Strait lighthouse, Maryland	2·25	2·25
4507	$1.50 Hunting Island lighthouse, South Carolina	2·25	2·25
4508	$1.50 Key West Lighthouse Museum, Florida	2·25	2·25
4509	$1.50 Old Point Loma lighthouse, California	2·25	2·25
4510	$1.50 Old Makinac Point lighthouse, Michigan	2·25	2·25
4511	$1.50 Keri lighthouse, Estonia	2·25	2·25
4512	$1.50 Anholt lighthouse, Denmark	2·25	2·25
4513	$1.50 Porer lighthouse, Croatia	2·25	2·25
4514	$1.50 Laotieshan lighthouse, China	2·25	2·25
4515	$1.50 Sapienza Methoni lighthouse, Greece	2·25	2·25
4516	$1.50 Arkona lighthouse, Germany	2·25	2·25
4517	$2 St. Augustine lighthouse, Florida	2·50	2·75
MS4518	Four sheets, each 70×98 mm. (a) $6 Kvitsoy lighthouse, Norway. (b) $6 Mahota Pagoda lighthouse, China. (c) $6 Boston lighthouse, Massachusetts. (d) $6 Pellworm lighthouse, Germany.	30·00	30·00

Nos. 4503 and 4515 are inscribed "Africca" or "Sapientza", both in error.

497a Anatoly Karpov

2001. First e-World Chess Championship. Sheet 88×103 mm.

MS4518a	**497a** $20 multicoloured	32·00	32·00

498 Commerson's Dolphin

2001. Whales and Dolphins. Multicoloured.

4519	25c. Type **498**	65	25
4520	50c. Pacific white-sided dolphin	1·00	40
4521	$1.50 Risso's dolphin	2·00	2·00
4522	$1.50 Fraser's dolphin	2·00	2·00
4523	$1.50 Dall's porpoise	2·00	2·00
4524	$1.50 Right whale	2·00	2·00
4525	$1.50 Grey whale	2·00	2·00
4526	$1.50 Minke whale	2·00	2·00
4527	$1.50 Common dolphin	2·00	2·00
4528	$1.50 Antillean beaked whale	2·00	2·00
4529	$1.50 Killer whale's tail and divers	2·00	2·00
4530	$1.50 Bryde's whale	2·00	2·00
4531	$1.50 Cuvier's beaked whale	2·00	2·00
4532	$1.50 Sei whale	2·00	2·00
4533	$1.50 Harbour porpoise	2·00	2·00
4534	$1.50 Beluga	2·00	2·00
4535	$1.50 White-beaked dolphin	2·00	2·00
4536	$1.50 Narwhal	2·00	2·00
4537	$1.50 Bowhead whale	2·00	2·00
4538	$1.50 Fin whale	2·00	2·00
4539	$2 Northern bottlenosed whale	2·25	2·50
4540	$3 Baird's beaked whale	2·75	3·25
MS4541	Four sheets, each 75×52 mm. (a) $6 Humpback whale and calf. (b) $6 Sperm whale calf. (c) $6 Blue whale with calf. (d) $6 Southern right whale	29·00	29·00

Nos. 4521/6, 4527/32 and 4533/8 were printed together, se-tenant, with the backgrounds forming composite designs.

499 World Cup Publicity Poster, Brazil, 1950

2001. World Cup Football Championship, Japan and Korea (2002). Multicoloured.

4542	$1.50 Type **499**	1·40	1·40
4543	$1.50 West German players, Switzerland, 1954	1·40	1·40
4544	$1.50 Just Fontaine (France), Sweden, 1958	1·40	1·40
4545	$1.50 Garrincha (Brazil), Chile, 1962	1·40	1·40
4546	$1.50 Bobby Moore (England), England, 1966	1·40	1·40
4547	$1.50 Pele (Brazil), Mexico, 1970	1·40	1·40
4548	$1.50 Osvaldo Ardiles (Argentina), Argentina, 1978	1·40	1·40
4549	$1.50 Lakhdar Belloumi (Algeria), Spain, 1982	1·40	1·40
4550	$1.50 Diego Maradona (Argentina), Mexico, 1986	1·40	1·40
4551	$1.50 Lothar Matthaus and Rudi Voller (West Germany), Italy, 1990	1·40	1·40
4552	$1.50 Seo Jung Won (South Korea), U.S.A., 1994	1·40	1·40
4553	$1.50 Ronaldo (Brazil), France, 1998	1·40	1·40
MS4554	Two sheets, each 88×75 mm. (a) $6 Detail of Jules Rimet Trophy, Uruguay, 1930. (b) $6 Detail of World Cup Trophy, Japan–Korea, 2002	11·00	12·00

500 Arsenal Football Stadium, Highbury

2001. British Football Clubs (1st series). Multicoloured.

4555	$1.50 Type **500**	1·10	1·10
4556	$1.50 Players celebrating European Cup Winners' Cup success, 1994	1·10	1·10
4557	$1.50 Players celebrating Premiership success, 1998	1·10	1·10
4558	$1.50 Entrance to Highbury	1·10	1·10
4559	$1.50 Dressing room	1·10	1·10
4560	$1.50 Arsenal defenders with trophies and shield, 1998	1·10	1·10
4561	$1.50 Aston Villa emblem at Villa Park	1·10	1·10
4562	$1.50 Villa Park stands at night	1·10	1·10
4563	$1.50 Stands and boxes	1·10	1·10
4564	$1.50 Trinity Road Stand, Villa Park	1·10	1·10
4565	$1.50 Holte End Stand, Villa Park	1·10	1·10
4566	$1.50 Aston Villa supporters	1·10	1·10
4567	$1.50 Reebok Stadium, Bolton (empty)	1·10	1·10
4568	$1.50 Players celebrating Division 1 play-off success, 2001	1·10	1·10
4569	$1.50 Fan holding banner	1·10	1·10
4570	$1.50 Fans celebrating promotion	1·10	1·10
4571	$1.50 Team with Division 1 Cup, 2001	1·10	1·10
4572	$1.50 Reebok Stadium during match	1·10	1·10
4573	$1.50 Everton squad, 2001–02	1·10	1·10
4574	$1.50 Manager Duncan Ferguson, 2000	1·10	1·10
4575	$1.50 Statue of Dixie Dean (former player)	1·10	1·10
4576	$1.50 Everton supporters watching match	1·10	1·10
4577	$1.50 Goodison Park Stadium	1·10	1·10
4578	$1.50 Everton squad, League champions, 1969–70	1·10	1·10
4579	$1.50 Ipswich Town players and Division 1 Cup, 2000	1·10	1·10
4580	$1.50 Ipswich Town squad, 2001–02	1·10	1·10
4581	$1.50 Manager George Burley shaking hands with David Sheepshanks (chairman)	1·10	1·10
4582	$1.50 Pablo Counago running	1·10	1·10
4583	$1.50 Matt Holland (captain), 2001	1·10	1·10
4584	$1.50 George Burley with Manager of the Year Award, 2001	1·10	1·10
4585	$1.50 Anfield Stadium, Liverpool	1·10	1·10
4586	$1.50 Players celebrating Worthington Cup victory, 2000–01	1·10	1·10
4587	$1.50 Players celebrating F.A. Cup victory, 2000–01	1·10	1·10
4588	$1.50 Supporters watching match	1·10	1·10
4589	$1.50 Victorious U.E.F.A. Cup Team, 2000–01	1·10	1·10
4590	$1.50 Players, manager and fans, Treble victory parade, 2001	1·10	1·10
4591	$1.50 Billy Meredith, Denis Law and Bobby Charlton (former players)	1·10	1·10
4592	$1.50 Treble Trophies, 1998–9	1·10	1·10
4593	$1.50 Different views of Old Trafford before 1950s	1·10	1·10
4594	$1.50 Different views of Old Trafford since 1974	1·10	1·10
4595	$1.50 Players celebrating third successive Premiership title, 2000–01	1·10	1·10
4596	$1.50 George Best, Bryan Robson and David Beckham (players)	1·10	1·10
4597	$1.50 Exterior of Ibrox Stadium, Glasgow	1·10	1·10
4598	$1.50 Rangers' European Cup winning team, 1972	1·10	1·10
4599	$1.50 Scottish F.A. and Premier League trophies, 2000	1·10	1·10
4600	$1.50 Ibrox Stadium from the air	1·10	1·10
4601	$1.50 Match in progress at Ibrox Stadium	1·10	1·10
4602	$1.50 Scottish flag and emblem celebrating ninth consecutive league victory, 1997	1·10	1·10

501 Father Christmas and House

2001. Christmas. Father Christmas. Multicoloured.

4603	15c. Type **501**	50	20
4604	50c. Father Christmas with snowman and fir trees	75	30
4605	$1 Father Christmas ice-skating	1·50	75
4606	$4 Father Christmas with children	5·00	6·00
MS4607	107×76 mm. $6 Father Christmas eating mince pie	6·00	6·50

GRENADA $1.50

502 Princess Diana wearing Blue Dress and Tiara

2001. 40th Birth Anniv of Diana, Princess of Wales. Multicoloured.

4608	$1.50 Type **502**	1·75	1·75
4609	$1.50 Wearing white evening dress	1·75	1·75
4610	$1.50 In red dress and tiara	1·75	1·75
MS4611	80×102 mm. $6 Wearing pearl choker	6·00	7·00

GRENADA $1.50

503 John F. Kennedy

2001. Presidents John F. Kennedy and Ronald Reagan Commemoration. Multicoloured.

4612	$1.50 Type **503**	1·50	1·75
4613	$1.50 John Kennedy and Empire State Building	1·50	1·75
4614	$1.50 John Kennedy with aircraft	1·50	1·75
4615	$1.50 Ronald Reagan in *Hellcats of the Navy* (film)	1·50	1·75
4616	$1.50 Wearing dark suit and red tie	1·50	1·75
4617	$1.50 Ronald Reagan with American flag	1·50	1·75
MS4618	Two sheets. (a) 67×83 mm. $6 John F. Kennedy. (b) 78×105 mm. $6 Ronald Reagan on telephone	13·00	14·00

2001. Centenary of Nobel Prizes. Prize Winners of 1901 (Nos. 4619/22 and 4629/30) and 1921 (others). As T 595 of Ghana. Multicoloured.

4619	75c. Emil von Behring (Medicine)	1·00	45
4620	90c. Wilhelm Rontgen (Physics)	1·00	50
4621	$1 Jacobus van't Hoff (Chemistry)	1·25	75
4622	$1 Frederic Passy (Peace)	1·50	1·25
4623	$1.50 Albert Einstein as a young man (horiz)	2·00	2·00
4624	$1.50 Smoking a pipe (horiz)	2·00	2·00
4625	$1.50 Wearing grey (horiz)	2·00	2·00
4626	$1.50 In pink jumper (horiz)	2·00	2·00
4627	$1.50 Wearing black jacket (horiz)	2·00	2·00
4628	$1.50 In blue jumper (horiz)	2·00	2·00
4629	$2 Jean-Henri Dunant (Peace)	2·00	2·25
4630	$3 Rene Sully-Prudhomme (Literature)	2·50	3·00
MS4631	65×87 mm. $6 Albert Einstein wearing Panama hat	8·00	8·00

GRENADA $1.50

504 Brown Horse with Pale Mane

2001. Chinese New Year ("Year of the Horse"). Tang Dynasty Ceramic Horses. Multicoloured.

4632	$1.50 Type **504**	1·75	1·75
4633	$1.50 Purple dappled horse	1·75	1·75
4634	$1.50 Blue horse	1·75	1·75
4635	$1.50 Brown horse with short mane	1·75	1·75
MS4636	100×70 mm. $4 Brown horse with flowers on bridle	4·50	4·75

505 Ruby

2001. Precious Stones and Minerals. Multicoloured.

4637	$1.50 Type **505**	2·50	2·50
4638	$1.50 Sardonyx	2·50	2·50
4639	$1.50 Sapphire	2·50	2·50
4640	$1.50 Opal	2·50	2·50
4641	$1.50 Topaz	2·50	2·50
4642	$1.50 Turquoise	2·50	2·50
4643	$1.50 Garnet	2·50	2·50
4644	$1.50 Amethyst	2·50	2·50
4645	$1.50 Aquamarine	2·50	2·50
4646	$1.50 Diamond	2·50	2·50
4647	$1.50 Emerald	2·50	2·50
4648	$1.50 Pearl	2·50	2·50
4649	$1.50 Ruby (horiz)	2·50	2·50
4650	$1.50 Diamond (horiz)	2·50	2·50
4651	$1.50 Sapphire (horiz)	2·50	2·50
4652	$1.50 Opal (horiz)	2·50	2·50
4653	$1.50 Turquoise (horiz)	2·50	2·50
4654	$1.50 Jade (horiz)	2·50	2·50
MS4655	Three sheets. (a) 82×76 mm. $6 Uraninite (horiz). (b) 92×56 mm. $6 Calcite (horiz). (c) $6 68×78 mm. $6 Quartz	27·00	27·00

Nos. 4637/42 (polished gem stones), 4643/8 (polished gem stones) and 4649/54 (raw stones).

506 U.S. Flag as Statue of Liberty with Grenada Flag

2002. "United We Stand". Support for Victims of 11 September 2001 Terrorist Attacks.

4656	**506** $2 multicoloured	1·75	2·00

507 Queen Elizabeth with Prince Philip

2002. Golden Jubilee. Multicoloured.

4657	$2 Type **507**	2·75	2·75
4658	$2 Queen Elizabeth in open carriage	2·75	2·75
4659	$2 Queen Elizabeth in evening dress	2·75	2·75
4660	$2 Queen Elizabeth on bridge	2·75	2·75
MS4661	76×109 mm. $6 Queen Elizabeth in Grenadier uniform	7·50	8·00

508 Dale Earnhardt and Car, 1980, within "1"

2002. Dale Earnhardt (stock car driver) Commemoration. Designs each within figures commemorating his seven Winston Cup victories. Multicoloured.

4662	$2 Type **508**	1·75	1·75
4663	$2 With Winston Cup and car, 1986	1·75	1·75
4664	$2 With Winston Cup, 1987	1·75	1·75
4665	$2 With Winston Cup, 1990	1·75	1·75
4666	$2 With Winston Cup, 1991	1·75	1·75
4667	$2 With Winston Cup, 1993	1·75	1·75
4668	$2 With Winston Cup, 1994	1·75	1·75

GRENADA $1

509 Cannon on C.S.S. *Teaser* (gunboat)

2002. Naval Campaigns of the American Civil War.

4669	**509**	$1 deep brown, brown and black	1·50	1·50
4670	-	$1 deep brown, brown and black	1·50	1·50
4671	-	$1 deep brown, brown and black	1·50	1·50
4672	-	$1 deep brown, brown and black	1·50	1·50
4673	-	$1 deep brown, brown and black	1·50	1·50
4674	-	$1 deep brown, brown and black	1·50	1·50
4675	-	$1.25 brown, ochre and black	1·75	1·75
4676	-	$1.25 brown, ochre and black	1·75	1·75
4677	-	$1.25 brown, ochre and black	1·75	1·75
4678	-	$1.25 brown, ochre and black	1·75	1·75
4679	-	$1.25 brown, ochre and black	1·75	1·75
4680	-	$1.25 brown, ochre and black	1·75	1·75
4681	-	$1.50 deep brown, brown and black	2·00	2·00
4682	-	$1.50 deep brown, brown and black	2·00	2·00
4683	-	$1.50 deep brown, brown and black	2·00	2·00
4684	-	$1.50 deep brown, brown and black	2·00	2·00
4685	-	$1.50 deep brown, brown and black	2·00	2·00
4686	-	$1.50 deep brown, brown and black	2·00	2·00
4687	-	$1.50 brown, yellow and black	2·00	2·00
4688	-	$1.50 brown, yellow and black	2·00	2·00
4689	-	$1.50 brown, yellow and black	2·00	2·00
4690	-	$1.50 brown, yellow and black	2·00	2·00
4691	-	$1.50 brown, yellow and black	2·00	2·00
4692	-	$1.50 brown, yellow and black	2·00	2·00
MS4693		Four sheets, each 72×94 mm. (a) $6 blue, violet and black. (b) $6 violet, blue and black. (c) $6 deep blue, blue and black. (d) $6 deep blue, blue and black	35·00	38·00

DESIGNS: No. 4669, Type **509**; 4670, U.S. gunboats on James River, 1862; 4671, U.S.S. *Tyler* (river gunboat); 4672, U.S.S. *Maratanza* (steam gunboat); 4673, U.S.S. *Metacomet* (steam gunboat); 4674, U.S.S. *Rattler* (river gunboat); 4675, C.S.S. *Tennessee* (ironclad); 4676, U.S.S. *Hartford* (Federal flagship) engaging the *Tennessee*; 4677, U.S.S. *Chickasaw* (river monitor); 4678, U.S.S. *Ossipee* (steam sloop); 4679, Battle of Mobile Bay; 4680, U.S.S. *Chickasaw* in action at Mobile Bay; 4681, C.S.S. *Alabama* (commerce raider); 4682, U.S.S. *Kearsarge* engaging the *Alabama*; 4683, U.S.S. *Hatteras* (paddle gunboat); 4684, C.S.S. *Alabama* attacking merchant ships; 4685, C.S.S. *Sumte* (cruiser); 4686, U.S.S. *Kearsarge* (steam sloop); 4687, C.S.S. *H.L. Hunley* (submarine); 4688, U.S.S. *Cumberland* (frigate); 4689, C.S.S. *Old Dominion* (blockade runner); 4890, U.S.S. *Housatonic* (steam sloop); 4691, U.S.S. *Hartford*; 4692, U.S.S. *Essex* (river gunboat); **MS**4693a U.S.S. *Monitor* (monitor); **MS**4693b Captain Semmes of C.S.S. *Alabama*; **MS**4693c C.S.S. *Tennessee*; **MS**4693d C.S.S. *Florida* (steam corvette).

Grenada $1

510 Mickey Mouse

2002. Birth Centenary (2001) of Walt Disney. Mickey Mouse. Multicoloured.

4694	$1 Type **510**	1·25	1·25
4695	$1 In "The Nifty Nineties", 1941	1·25	1·25
4696	$1 In "Magician Mickey", 1937	1·25	1·25
4697	$1 In "Steamboat Willie", 1928	1·25	1·25
4698	$1 In "Fantasia", 1940	1·25	1·25
4699	$1 In "Mickey Mouse Club", 1955	1·25	1·25
4700	$1 In "Cactus Kid", 1930	1·25	1·25
4701	$1 In "The Prince and the Pauper", 1990	1·25	1·25

4702	$1 In "Brave Little Tailor", 1938	1·25	1·25
4703	$1 In "Canine Caddy", 1941	1·25	1·25

511 Chiune
Sugihara

2002. Chiune Sugihara (Japanese Consul-general in Lithuania who rescued Jews, 1939–40) Commemoration.

4704	**511**	$2 multicoloured	2·25	2·25

512 Mawensi Peak,
Kilimanjaro, Kenya

2002. International Year of Mountains. Multicoloured.

4705	$2 Type **512**	2·00	2·00
4706	$2 Mt. Stanley, Uganda	2·00	2·00
4707	$2 Mt. Taweche, Nepal	2·00	2·00
4708	$2 Mt. San Exupery, Argentina	2·00	2·00
MS4709	100×70 mm. $6 Mt. Aso, Japan	6·00	7·00

No. 4708 is inscribed "Exuprey" in error.

513 Church and Bunting

2002. Year of Eco Tourism. Multicoloured.

4710	$1 Type **513**	1·75	1·75
4711	$1 Little ringed plover	1·75	1·75
4712	$1 Relaxing on the patio	1·75	1·75
4713	$1 Scuba diver and grouper	1·75	1·75
4714	$1 Two red snappers	1·75	1·75
4715	$1 Four yachts	1·75	1·75
MS4716	75×75 mm. $6 Purple martin over Grenada	9·00	9·00

514 Downhill Skiing

2002. Winter Olympic Games, Salt Lake City. Multicoloured.

4717	$2 Type **514**	2·00	2·00
4718	$2 Slalom skiing	2·00	2·00
MS4719	82×102 mm. Nos. 4717/18	3·75	4·00

515 Scout in Canoe

2002. 20th World Scout Jamboree, Thailand. Multicoloured.

4720	$2 Type **515**	2·25	2·25
4721	$2 Paddling canoe	2·25	2·25
4722	$2 Scout blowing bugle	2·25	2·25
4723	$2 Scout saluting	2·25	2·25
MS4724	100×74 mm. $6 Thai scout saluting	6·50	7·00

Nos. 4720/3 were printed together, se-tenant, with the backgrounds forming a composite design.

516 Heidi Klum
(model)

2002. APS Stampshow 2002, Atlantic City, U.S.A. Designs showing Heidi Klum. Multicoloured.

4725	$1.50 Type **516**	1·40	1·40
4726	$1.50 Wearing chain earrings	1·40	1·40
4727	$1.50 Close-up of face	1·40	1·40

517 Army Bear

2002. Centenary of the Teddy Bear (1st issue). Multicoloured.

4728	$2 Type **517**	1·60	1·60
4729	$2 Navy bear	1·60	1·60
4730	$2 Air Force bear	1·60	1·60
4731	$2 Marines bear	1·60	1·60
4732	$2 Basketball bear (38×50 mm)	1·60	1·60
4733	$2 Judo bear (38×50 mm)	1·60	1·60
4734	$2 Golf bear (38×50 mm)	1·60	1·60
4735	$2 Baseball bear (38×50 mm)	1·60	1·60
4736	$5 Bear with red hat and pink bow	3·25	3·50
4737	$5 Bear with clogs	3·25	3·50
4738	$5 Bear with black hat and scarf	3·25	3·50
4739	$5 Bear with cheeses	3·25	3·50

Nos. 4728/31 (armed forces bears), 4732/5 (sports bears) and 4736/9 (Dutch bears).
See also Nos. 4851/MS4852.

518 "Mareep No. 179"

2002. Pokémon (children's cartoon series). Multicoloured.

4740	$1.50 Type **518**	1·10	1·10
4741	$1.50 "Sunkern No. 191"	1·10	1·10
4742	$1.50 "Teddiursa No. 216"	1·10	1·10
4743	$1.50 "Swinub No. 220"	1·10	1·10
4744	$1.50 "Murkrow No. 198"	1·10	1·10
4745	$1.50 "Snubbull No. 209"	1·10	1·10
MS4746	66×91 mm. $6 "Togepi No. 175"	4·50	5·00

518a Elvis Presley
wearing Stetson

2002. 25th Death Anniv of Elvis Presley.

4747	**518a**	$1 multicoloured	1·75	1·50

518b Axel, Zeeland

2002. "Amphilex '02" International Stamp Exhibition, Amsterdam (1st issue). Dutch Women's Traditional Costumes. Sheet, 120×140 mm, containing vert designs, each 37×51 mm. Multicoloured.

MS4748	$3 Type **518b**; $3 Eerde, Noord-Brabant; $3 Volendam, Noord-Holland	8·50	9·00

518c Jacobus
van't Hoff
(Chemistry, 1901)

2002. "Amphilex '02" International Stamp Exhibition, Amsterdam (2nd issue). (a) Dutch Nobel Prize Winners. Sheet 150×100 mm.

MS4749	$1.50 Type **518c** (black and green); $1.50 Peace Prize medal (black and blue); $1.50 Pieter Zeeman (Physics, 1902) (black and mauve); $1.50 Johannes van der Waals (Physics, 1910) (black and cinnamon); $1.50 Tobias Asser (Peace, 1911) (black and lilac); $1.50 Heike Kamerlingh Onnes (Physics, 1913) (black and green)	8·50	9·00

(b) Dutch Lighthouses. Sheet 128×148 mm. Multicoloured.

MS4750	$1.50 Schiermonnikoog; $1.50 Texel; $1.50 Egmond; $1.50 Scheveningen; $1.50 Schouwen; $1.50 Hellevoetsluis	11·00	11·00

519 Molly Middleton and Father

2002. Shirley Temple in Our Little Girl. Showing scenes from film. Multicoloured.

4751	$1.50 Type **519**	1·10	1·10
4752	$1.50 Family picnic	1·10	1·10
4753	$1.50 Molly with Sniff (dog), talking to park keeper	1·10	1·10
4754	$1.50 Molly with parents and another man	1·10	1·10
4755	$1.50 Molly and Sniff on see-saw	1·10	1·10
4756	$1.50 Molly with Sniff in pink bonnet	1·10	1·10
4757	$2 Molly with mother (vert)	1·60	1·60
4758	$2 Molly watching clown (vert)	1·60	1·60
4759	$2 Molly at prayer (vert)	1·60	1·60
4760	$2 Leaning on father's knee (vert)	1·60	1·60
MS4761	105×76 mm. $6 Molly wearing pink dress	4·50	5·00

520 World Trade Center

2002. First Anniv of 11 September 2001 Attacks. Sheet 140×98 mm.

MS4762	**520**	$6 multicoloured	5·50	6·00

521 Popeye at Santa
Croce Basilica, Florence

2002. "Popeye" (cartoon character). Multicoloured.

4763	$1.50 Type **521**	1·10	1·10
4764	$1.50 With Brutus at Eiffel Tower, Paris	1·10	1·10
4765	$1.50 On steps of Parthenon, Athens	1·10	1·10
4766	$1.50 With Olive Oyl near Rialto Bridge, Venice	1·10	1·10
4767	$1.50 Near Big Ben, London	1·10	1·10
4768	$1.50 In front of traditional wooden building, Norway	1·10	1·10
4769	$2 Sweet Pea on footballer's back (29×44 mm)	1·60	1·60
4770	$2 Jeep (dog) tugging footballer's shorts (29×44 mm)	1·60	1·60
4771	$2 Popeye in football kit (29×44 mm)	1·60	1·60
4772	$2 Brutus being kicked by Popeye (29×44 mm)	1·60	1·60
MS4773	Three sheets. (a) $6 Brutus heading ball (44×29 mm). (b) $6 Popeye celebrating with footballers (44×29 mm). (c) $6 Popeye and Leaning Tower of Pisa (50×78 mm)	13·00	14·00

Nos. 4769/72 were issued together, se-tenant, with the backgrounds forming a composite design.

522 Common
Morpho

2002. Flora and Fauna. Multicoloured.

4774	$1.50 Type **522**	2·00	2·00
4775	$1.50 Blue night butterfly	2·00	2·00
4776	$1.50 Small flambeau	2·00	2·00
4777	$1.50 Grecian shoemaker	2·00	2·00
4778	$1.50 Orange-barred sulphur	2·00	2·00
4779	$1.50 Cramer's mesene	2·00	2·00
4780	$1.50 Honey bee	2·00	2·00
4781	$1.50 Dragonfly	2·00	2·00
4782	$1.50 Milkweed bug	2·00	2·00
4783	$1.50 Bumble bee	2·00	2·00
4784	$1.50 Migratory grasshopper	2·00	2·00
4785	$1.50 Monarch caterpillar	2·00	2·00
4786	$1.50 Boletus crocipodius	2·00	2·00
4787	$1.50 Boletus edulis	2·00	2·00
4788	$1.50 Flammulina velutipes	2·00	2·00
4789	$1.50 Amanita phalloides	2·00	2·00
4790	$1.50 Tricholoma aurantium	2·00	2·00
4791	$1.50 Amanita muscaria	2·00	2·00
4792	$1.50 Blue whale and calf	2·00	2·00
4793	$1.50 Pygmy sperm whale	2·00	2·00
4794	$1.50 Humpback whale	2·00	2·00
4795	$1.50 Killer whale	2·00	2·00
4796	$1.50 Bowhead whale	2·00	2·00
4797	$1.50 Grey whale	2·00	2·00
MS4798	Four sheets, each 105×76 mm. (a) $6 Figure of eight butterfly. (b) $6 Hercules beetle. (c) $6 Sharp-scaled parasol (fungus). (d) $6 Blue whale	29·00	30·00

Nos. 4780/5 (butterflies), 4775/80 (insects), 4781/6 (fungi) and 4787/92 (whales) were each printed together, se-tenant, with the backgrounds forming composite designs.
Nos. 4792/7 and 4791 are inscribed "Flammula" or "Aminita", both in error.

523 Norman
Wisdom

2002. Sir Norman Wisdom (comedian and actor).

4799	**523**	$1.50 multicoloured	2·00	2·00

523a Madonna and Child,
Four Angels and St. Francis
(Cimabue)

2002. Christmas. Religious Paintings. Multicoloured.

4800	15c. Type **523a**	45	15
4801	25c. "Madonna and Child and Two Angels" (Cimabue) (vert)	55	15
4802	50c. "Madonna Enthroned" (detail) (Cimabue) (vert)	85	25
4803	$1 "Madonna Enthroned" (Cimabue) (vert)	1·50	85
4804	$4 "Madonna and Child, Four Angels and St. Francis" (Cimabue) (vert)	5·00	6·00
MS4805	72×98 mm. $6 "Nativity" (Perugino) (vert)	7·00	7·50

524 Astrolabe

2002. 550th Birth Anniv of Amerigo Vespucci (explorer). Sheets containing T **524** and similar multicoloured designs.

MS4806	Two sheets. (a) 98×147 mm. $3 Type **524**; $3 Amerigo Vespucci; $3 Caravel (b) 138×90 mm. $3 Map of South America and caravel (horiz); $3 Compass and caravels (horiz); $3 Map of Africa and Europe (horiz) Set of 2 sheets	22·00	23·00

MS4807 Two sheets. (a) 78×85 mm. $6 Compass rose (28×42 mm). (b) 85×78 mm. $6 Globe and scroll (28×42 mm) Set of 2 sheets   16·00   17·00

525 Arsenal Stadium

2002. Arsenal Football Club -- FA Community Shield Winners. Sheet 125×125 mm containing T **525** and similar horiz designs. Multicoloured.
MS4808 $1.50 Type **525**; $1.50 Footballers celebrating after winning goal; $1.50 Winning team with FA Shield; $1.50 Arsenal 2002/3 squad with trophies; $1.50 Gilberto with FA Shield; $1.50 Arsenal FC, Stadium and new crest   7·50   8·00

2002. British Football Clubs. Eight sheets, each 125×125 mm, containing horiz designs as T **525**. Multicoloured.
MS4809 Arsenal 2001/2 $1.50 Team with FA Cup, Millennium Stadium, Cardiff; $1.50 Winning team with Championship banners; $1.50 Premiership Trophy winning team; $1.50 Winning team with Premiership trophy on rostrum; $1.50 Players celebrating FA Cup winning goal; $1.50 Arsene Wenger (Manager) and Tony Adams (captain) with trophies   7·50   8·00
MS4810 Celtic $1.50 Celtic Park Stadium; $1.50 Martin O'Neill with SPL Trophy; $1.50 Henrik Larsson; $1.50 Celtic squad of 2002/3; $1.50 Celtic scoring goal; $1.50 Celtic Park   7·50   8·00
MS4811 Chelsea $1.50 Crowd watching floodlit match; $1.50 Cup Winners' Cup winning team with trophy, 1988; $1.50 Chelsea supporters at match; $1.50 "The Shed End" at Stamford Bridge ground; $1.50 Stamford Bridge stadium; $1.50 Winning team with FA Cup, 2000   7·50   8·00
MS4812 Liverpool $1.50 Anfield's Centenary stand seen from main stand; $1.50 First team squad, 2002/3; $1.50 Gerard Houllier and Phil Thompson; $1.50 Milan Baros; $1.50 Vladimir Smicer and Danny Murphy; $1.50 The Kop seen from Anfield Road end   7·50   8·00
MS4813 Manchester City $1.50 Maine Road stadium (from above); $1.50 Fans with Division One Champions flags; $1.50 Kevin Keegan (manager) with Division 1 trophy; $1.50 Winning Division 1 with trophy; $1.50 Winning team with medals; $1.50 Maine Road stadium (from stands)   7·50   8·00
MS4814 Manchester United $1.50 David Beckham; $1.50 First team squad, 2002/3; $1.50 Old Trafford stadium (aerial view); $1.50 Players after Ole Gunnar Solskjaer's 100th goal; $1.50 Manchester United fans; $1.50 North stand, Old Trafford   7·50   8·00
MS4815 Norwich City $1.50 Players at The Nest (NCFC ground 1908–35); $1.50 Norwich City players,1971/2; $1.50 With Milk Cup trophy, 1985; $1.50 Carrow Road stadium; $1.50 Winning UEFA Cup,1993; $1.50, Match of 1958/9   7·50   8·00
MS4816 Tottenham Hotspur $1.50 Fans watching match; $1.50 Spurs v. Fulham match, 2001; $1.50 Spurs v. Liverpool match, 2002; $1.50 Winning UEFA Cup team, 1972; $1.50 Players celebrating win against Chelsea, 2002; $1.50 Club Shield and White Hart Lane stadium   7·50   8·00

526 Johan Mjallby (Sweden)

2002. World Cup Football Championship, Japan and Korea. Miniature sheets containing T **526** and similar vert designs. Multicoloured.
MS4817 165×82 mm. $1.50 Type **526**; $1.50 Magnus Hedman (Sweden); $1.50 Fredrik Ljungberg (Sweden); $1.50 Khalilou Fadiga (Senegal); $1.50 El Hadji Diouf (Senegal); Papa Bouba Diop (Senegal)   6·50   7·00

MS4818 165×82 mm. $1.50 Roberto Carlos (Brazil); $1.50 Juninho Paulista (Brazil); $1.50 Ronaldinho (Brazil); $1.50 Johan Walem (Belgium); $1.50 Marc Wilmots (Belgium); $1.50 Bart Goor (Belgium)   6·50   7·00
MS4819 Four sheets, each 82×82 mm. (a) $3 Henrik Larsson (Sweden); $3 Niclas Alexandersson (Sweden). (b) $3 Khalilou Fadiga (Senegal); $3 Bruno Metsou (coach, Senegal). (c) $3 Luiz Felipe Scolari (coach, Brazil); $3 Ronaldo (Brazil). (d) $3 Wesley Sonck (Belgium); $3 Robert Waseige (coach, Belgium) Set of 4 sheets   16·00   18·00

527 Foundation Logo and US Flag

2002. National Law Enforcement and Firefighters Children's Foundation. Sheet 75×115 mm.
MS4820 **527** $6 multicoloured   8·50   8·50

528 Princess Diana wearing Bow Tie

2002. Fifth Death Anniv of Diana, Princess of Wales. Two sheets containing T **528** and similar vert designs. Multicoloured.
MS4821 137×120 mm. $2 Type **528**; $2 Wearing blue dress; $2 Wearing red and white jacket and hat; $2 Wearing pink dress   7·50   8·00
MS4822 70×100 mm. $6 Wearing headset   6·00   6·50

529 Pres Reagan on the DMZ in Korea, 1983

2002. Presidents Ronald Reagan and John F. Kennedy. Four sheets containing T **529** and similar multicoloured designs.
MS4823 175×117 mm. $1.50 Type **529**; $1.50 Pres Reagan with Prime Minister Margaret Thatcher; $1.50 Speaking at the Berlin Wall, 1987; $1.50 Signing INF Treaty with Soviet Secretary General Gorbachev; $1.50 With Egyptian President Sadat, 1981; $1.50 At home with horse Set of 4 sheets   8·00   9·00
MS4824 175×117 mm. $1.50 Pres Kennedy meeting with Cabinet; $1.50 Signing a bill into law; $1.50 Meeting Civil Rights leaders; $1.50 With astronaut John Glenn; $1.50 On the campaign trail; $1.50 With Jacqueline Kennedy arriving in Dallas, 1963   8·00   9·00
MS4825 Two sheets, each 82×115 mm. (a) $6 Pres. Reagan making speech. (b) Pres. Kennedy making speech (vert) Set of 2 sheets   11·00   12·00

531 Ram

2003. Chinese New Year ("Year of the Ram").
MS4827 130×123 mm. **531** $1.25×4, multicoloured   5·00   5·50

532 Toy Airplane

2003. Learning Resources (1st series). M Gears Childrens' Construction Sets. Sheet 222×152 mm containing T **532** and similar horiz designs showing toys. Multicoloured.
MS4828 $2 Type **532**; $2 Dune buggy; $2 Robot; $2 Racing car   6·50   7·50
See also MS4853.

533 David Brown

2003. Columbia Space Shuttle Commemoration. Sheet 184×145 mm, containing T **533** and similar vert designs showing crew members. Multicoloured.
MS4829 $1 Type **533**; $1 Commander Rick Husband; $1 Laurel Clark; $1 Kalpana Chawla; $1 Payload Commander Michael Anderson; $1 Pilot William McCool; $1 Ilan Ramon   8·00   8·50

534 Grenada Dove and "CC" Emblem

2003. 30th Anniv of CARICOM.
4830   **534** $1 multicoloured   2·00   1·50

535 "A Harlot in Repose"

2003. Japanese Art. Paintings of Women by Taiso Yoshitoshi. Multicoloured.
4831   75c. Type **535**   1·00   55
4832 $1 A 'Shakuni' or Geisha, who serves Wine or Sake   1·25   85
4833 $1.25 A 'Joro', or Low Ranking Prostitute, having a Snack   1·40   1·10
4834 $3 A Geisha known as a 'Geiko' or Entertainer relaxing   3·00   4·00
MS4835 175×135 mm. $2 Enjoying a Cool Evening Breeze in a Pleasure Boat; $2 A Fukagawa Waitress carrying a Wooden Table laden with Food; $2 A Spoiled Unmarried Woman pretending to be displeased with an Admirer; $2 A Coy Young Girl biting her Sleeve pretending to be Embarrassed   7·50   8·00
MS4836 66×132 mm. $6 A Geisha about to Board a Party-Boat (detail)   6·00   6·50

536 St. Catherine Altarpiece (detail of St. Dorothy, St. Agnes and St. Cunigonde)

2003. 450th Death Anniv of Lucas Cranach the Elder (artist). Multicoloured.
4837   50c. Type **536**   65   30
4838   75c. The St. Catherine Altarpiece (detail of St. Margaret) (vert)   90   55
4839 $1.25 The St. Catherine Altarpiece (detail of St. Barbara) (vert)   1·25   1·10
4840 $3 The St. Catherine Altarpiece (detail of young girl) (vert)   2·75   4·00
MS4841 158×191 mm. $2 Lot and his Daughters (detail); $2 David and Bathsheba (detail); $2 The Agony in the Garden (detail); $2 The Adoration of the Magi   7·50   8·00
MS4842 120×100 mm. $6 Samson and Delilah (detail) (vert)   6·00   6·50

537 Jardin Aux Tournesols

2003. 85th Death Anniv of Gustav Klimt (artist). Multicoloured.
4843   15c. Type **537**   30   25
4844   25c. L'allee Aux Poulets   40   25
4845   75c. Allee Dans Le Parc Du Schloss Kammer   1·00   55
4846 $1 Portrait de Johanna Staude   1·25   80
4847 $1.25 Portrait de Friederike Maria Beer   1·50   1·25
4848 $3 Portrait de Mada Primavesi   2·75   4·00
MS4849 180×105 mm. $2 "La Jeune Fille"; $2 "Les Amies"; $2 "Le Berceau"; $2 La Vie et la Mort   7·50   8·00
MS4850 81×102 mm. $6 "Portrait de Margaret Stonborough-Wittgenstein". Imperf   6·00   6·50

538 Embroidery Teddy Bear

2003. Centenary of the Teddy Bear (2nd issue). Embroidered Fabric Teddy Bears. Self-adhesive. Imperf.
4851   **538** $15 ochre, silver and rose-red   8·50   10·00
MS4852 126×157 mm. No. 4851×4   28·00   35·00

539 Children reading Books

2003. Learning Resources (2nd series). Reading Rods. Sheet 222×156 mm containing T **539** and similar horiz designs. Multicoloured.
MS4853 $2 Type **539**; $2 Girl playing with reading rods; $2 Children writing; $2 Teacher and children with book   7·50   8·00

530 Magnifying Glass and Globe

2002. 50th Anniv of International Federation of Stamp Dealers' Associations. P 14.
4826   **530** $2 multicoloured   2·25   2·25

540 Silvere
Maes (1939)

2003. Centenary of Tour de France Cycle Race. Designs showing past winners. Multicoloured.

MS4854 160×100 mm. $2 Type **540**; $2 Jean Lazarides (1946); $2 Jean Robic (1947); $2 Gino Bartali (1948)	8·50	9·00
MS4855 160×100 mm. $2 Fausto Coppi (1949); $2 Ferdinand Kubler (1950); $2 Hugo Koblet (1951); $2 Fausto Coppi (1952)	8·50	9·00
MS4856 160×100 mm. $2 Roger Walkowiak (1956); $2 Jacques Anquetil (1957); $2 Charly Gaul (1958); $2 Federico Bahamontes (1959)	8·50	9·00
MS4857 Three sheets, each 100×70 mm. (a) $6 Fausto Coppi (1949). (b) $6 Ferdinand Kubler (1950). (c) $6 Jacques Anquetil (1964) Set of 3 sheets	17·00	18·00

541 Louis Bleriot and *Bleriot XI* (first powered flight across English Channel, 1909)

2003. Centenary of Powered Flight. Multicoloured.

MS4858 128×150 mm. $2 Type **541**; $2 Johnnie Johnson (World War II Ace pilot) and aircraft; $2 Wright Brothers and *Flyer I* (first powered flight, 1903); $2 Jacqueline Cochran and aircraft (first woman to break sound barrier)	11·00	11·00
MS4859 119×119 mm. $2 Alcock and Brown and Vickers FB-27 *Vimy* (first non-stop transatlantic flight, 1919); $2 Amelia Earhart and aircraft; $2 Chuck Yeager and Bell XS-1 rocket airplane (first manned supersonic flight, 1947); $2 Charles Lindbergh and Ryan NYP Special *Spirit of St. Louis* (first solo non-stop transatlantic flight, 1927)	11·00	11·00

542 Queen Elizabeth II flanked by Bishops

2003. 50th Anniv of Coronation. Multicoloured.

4860	$2 Type **542**	2·25	2·25
4861	$2 Holy Communion	2·25	2·25
4863	$2 Enthronement of Queen	2·25	2·25
4864	$2 Queen and Duke of Edinburgh	2·25	2·25
4865	$2 Queen leaving Westminster Abbey in Coronation Coach	2·25	2·25
4866	$2 Queen and family on Palace balcony	2·25	2·25
4867	$2 Westminster Abbey	2·25	2·25
MS4868 106×76 mm. $6 Queen in Coronation Coach		7·50	8·00

No. 4867 is inscr "Floodlit Mall" in error.

543 Levera Pond

2003. International Year of Freshwater. Multicoloured.

MS4869 150×88 mm. $2 Type **543**; $2 Concord Falls; $2 Lake Antoine	6·50	7·00
MS4870 100×70 mm. $6 Lake Grand Etang	6·50	7·00

544 Clive Andrews

2003. Centenary of Circus Clowns. Multicoloured.

MS4871 119×194 mm. $2 Type **544**; $2 Bell Bozo; $2 Bumpsy; $2 Anne Fratellini	6·50	7·50
MS4872 146×218 mm. $2 Stag (acrobat); $2 Olga and Regina Kolpensky with white poodles; $2 Brad Byers; $2 Tiger	6·50	7·50

No. **MS**4871 shows clowns and is cut in the shape of a clown. No. **MS**4872 shows other circus performers and is cut in the shape of a circus elephant.

545 Aerial View of Campus

2003. St. George's University School of Medicine. Multicoloured.

4873	75c. Type **545**	1·00	60
4874	$1 University buildings	1·25	1·25

546 General Sir Mike Jackson and Tank

2003. Operation "Iraqi Freedom". Showing commanders of British armed forces in Iraq (**MS**4875) or British aircraft, tanks and ships (**MS**4876). Multicoloured.

MS4875 186×130 mm. $1 Type **546**; $1 Air Vice-Marshal Glenn Torpy and RAF Jaguar fighter; $1 Air Marshal Brian Burridge and RAF Harrier GR7 fighter; $1 Major General Tony Milton and warship; $1 Major General Peter Wall and soldiers; $1 Major General Barney White-Spunner ; $1 Admiral Sir Alan West and aircraft carrier; $1 Air Chief Marshal Peter Squire and surveillance aircraft	11·00	11·00
MS4876 186×130 mm. $1 Royal Marine Gazelle helicopter; $1 Royal Marine hovercraft; $1 RAF Jaguar fighter; $1 HMS *Liverpool*; $1 RAF Harrier GR7; $1 Challenger 2 tank; $1 RAF Chinook helicopter; $1 RAF Tornado F3	11·00	11·00

547 Prince William with Bouquet

2003. 21st Birthday of Prince William of Wales. Multicoloured.

MS4877 79×145 mm. $3 Type **547**; $3 Wearing blue T-shirt; $3 In close-up, looking down	9·00	9·50
MS4878 105×76 mm. $6 Prince William (horiz)	6·50	7·00

548 Yellow Allamanda

2003. Birds, Fish and Flowers of the Caribbean. Multicoloured.

4879	25c. Type **548**	50	20
4880	50c. Queen of the Night (flower)	75	20
4881	75c. Anthurium	1·00	45
4882	$1 Smallmouthed grunt (fish)	1·40	1·40
4883	$1 Spotfinned butterflyfish	1·40	1·40
4884	$1 Gold coney (fish)	1·40	1·40
4885	$1.25 Osprey	2·00	2·00
4886	$1.25 Red-eyed vireo (bird)	2·00	2·00
4887	$1.25 Northern oriole	2·00	2·00
4888	$3 Oleander	3·75	4·00
4889	$3 Night sergeant (fish)	3·75	4·00
4890	$3 Bahama pintail (duck)	3·75	4·00

MS4891 105×85 mm. $2 Blue passion flower; $2 Chinese hibiscus; $2 Poinsettia; $2 Bird of Paradise (flower)	9·00	9·50
MS4892 105×85 mm. $2 Spot-finned hogfish ("Cuban Hogfish"); $2 Blueheaded wrasse; $2 Black-capped basslet ("Black Cap Gramma"); $2 Cherub angelfish ("Cherubfish")	9·00	9·50
MS4893 105×85 mm. $2 Slaty-capped shrike vireo; $2 Common flicker ("Northern Flicker"); $2 Blackburnian warbler; $2 Common tody flycatcher	11·00	11·00
MS4894 Three sheets, each 96×66 mm. (a) $6 Shrimp plant. (b) $6 Banded butterflyfish. (c) $6 Blue grosbeak (vert) Set of 3 sheets	17·00	18·00

549 Spinosaurus

2003. Prehistoric Animals. Multicoloured.

MS4895 178×117 mm. $2 Type **549**; $2 Herrerasaurus; $2 Protarchaeopteryx; $2 Sinosauropteryx	9·00	9·50
MS4896 178×117 mm. $2 Allosaurus; $2 Crylophosaurus; $2 Eoraptor; $2 Caudipteryx	9·00	9·50
MS4897 Two sheets, each 98×68 mm. (a) $6 Triceratops (vert). (b) $6 Archaeopteryx (vert) Set of 2 sheets	13·00	14·00

550 *Madonna and Child* (detail) (Giotto) from Church of Ognissanti

2003. Christmas. Multicoloured.

4898	35c. Type **550**	55	20
4899	75c. *The Ognissanti Madonna* (detail) (Giotto)	1·00	50
4900	$1 *Madonna of the Angels* (detail) (Giotto)	1·25	80
4901	$4 *Madonna and Child* (Giotto) from Florentine Church of San Giorgio alla Costa	4·50	5·50
MS4902 74×95 mm. $6 *Holy Family with John the Baptist and St. Elizabeth* (Nicolas Poussin) (horiz)		6·50	7·00

551 *At the Palmist's* (Jean-Baptiste Le Prince)

2003. 300th Anniv of St. Petersburg. "Treasures of the Hermitage". Multicoloured.

4903	45c. Type **551**	60	25
4904	$1 *A Visit to Grandmother* (Louis Le Nain) (horiz)	1·25	70
4905	$1.50 *Musicale* (Dirck Hals) (horiz)	1·75	1·50
4906	$3 *A Young Woman in the Morning* (Frans van Mieris the Elder)	3·25	3·75
MS4907 118×181 mm. $2 *Louis, Grand Dauphin de France* (Louis Tocqué); $2 *Count P. A. Stroganov as a Child* (Jean-Baptiste Greuze); $2 *A Boy with a Book* (Jean- Baptiste Perroneau); $2 *A Girl with a Doll* (Jean-Baptiste Greuze)		7·50	8·00
MS4908 (a) 78×65 mm. $6 "The Lute Player" (Caravaggio). Imperf. (b) 67×77 mm. $6 "The Spoiled Child" (Jean-Baptiste Greuze). Imperf		11·00	12·00

552 *The Spring Tonic* 1936

2003. 25th Death Anniv of Norman Rockwell. Multicoloured.

MS4909 149×179 mm. $2 Type **552**; $2 *The Facts of Life*; $2 *The Proper Gratuity*; $2 *The Runaway*	7·50	8·00
MS4910 91×99 mm. $6 *Boy with Carriage* (detail) (horiz)	5·50	6·00

553 *Claude Drawing*

2003. 30th Death Anniv of Pablo Picasso (artist). Multicoloured.

MS4911 132×168 mm. $2 Type **553**; $2 *Claude and Paloma at Play* (detail); $2 *Paloma at Three Years Old*; $2 *Paloma with an Orange*	8·00	8·50
MS4912 72×99 mm. $6 *Paloma in Blue*. Imperf	6·50	7·00

554 Brown and White Monkey

2004. Chinese New Year ("Year of the Monkey"). Multicoloured.

MS4913 116×141 mm. $1.50 Type **554**; $1.50 Proboscis monkey; $1.50 Light brown monkey; $1.50 Grey monkey	6·00	6·50

555 *Lissy* (sail training ship) on River Weser

2004. Opening of Weser Tunnel, Germany. Sheet 113×82 mm.

MS4914 **555** $6 multicoloured	7·00	7·50

556 Chinese Lady

2004. Hong Kong 2004 International Stamp Exhibition. Paintings by Pu Hsin-yu. Multicoloured.

MS4915 156×112 mm. $1.50 Type **556**; $1.50 Two monkeys in tree; $1.50 Mountain landscape with temple and waterfall; $1.50 Bird in tree with red flower; $1.50 Man sat by gnarled tree; $1.50 Man in red	8·00	8·50
MS4916 107×105 mm. $3 Branch; $3 Bearded man	5·50	6·00

557 Muffy

2004. Arthur the Aardvark and Friends. Multicoloured.

MS4917 165×134 mm. $1.50 Type **557**;
$1.50 Francine; $1.50 Brain with pot-
ted plants; $1.50 D.W. as astronaut in
space; $1.50 Sue Ellen with insects
in jam jars; $1.50 Arthur with model
of solar system ..... 6·50 7·00

MS4918 150×184 mm. $2 Arthur as
Robin Hood; $2 Arthur as Rumpel-
stiltskin; $2 Arthur with sword; $2
Arthur as King Arthur ..... 6·50 7·00

MS4919 150×184 mm. $1.50 Arthur
holding bunch of flowers; $1.50 D.W.
holding valentines card; $1.50 Binky
holding box of chocolates; $1.50
Muffy holding out box of chocolates;
$1.50 D.W. as Cupid; $1.50 Francine
and hearts ..... 6·50 7·00

MS4920 150×183 mm. $2 Arthur as
Robinson Crusoe; $2 Arthur and
map of Treasure Island; $2 Arthur
as Tom Sawyer; $2 Arthur swinging
on rope ..... 6·50 7·00

558 Concorde, French Flag
and Concorde at Take-off

2004. Last Flight of Concorde (2003). Multicoloured.

MS4921 88×129 mm. $3 Type **558**; $3
Concorde, French flag and spectators
at perimeter fence; $3 Concorde,
French flag and control panel (first
flight, Toulouse, Fran, 1969) ..... 14·00 14·00

MS4922 88×129 mm. $3 Concorde,
Union Jack, Singapore flag and roof
of building; $3 Concorde, Union
Jack, Singapore flag and skyscraper;
$3 Concorde, Union Jack, Singapore
flag and street (London to Singapore
flights, 1977) ..... 14·00 14·00

MS4923 88×129 mm. $3 Concorde and
dome of US Capitol; $3 Concorde,
Capitol building and top of statue;
$3 Concorde, Capitol and plinth of
statue (last flight, Paris to Washington, 2003) ..... 14·00 14·00

559 Lord Killanin
(President of Olympic
Committee, 1972—80)

2004. Olympic Games, Athens, Greece. Multicoloured.

4924 75c. Type **559** ..... 1·00 45
4925 $1 Athletes running 10,000
metre race (horiz) ..... 1·10 70
4926 $1.25 Commemorative plaque
(detail) ..... 1·25 1·25
4927 $3 "The Wreath of Olive"
(Greek art) ..... 3·00 3·75

560 American Horse

2004. American Indians. Multicoloured.

4928- 75c.×12 Type **560**; Blue Bird;
4939 Crow King; Crow Man; Gall;
Good Horse; Goose; John
Grass; Rain-in-the-Face; Red
Cloud; Sitting Bull; Wild
Horse ..... 7·25 7·50

4940- $1.25×6 Retern of the Blackfoot
4945 War Party (F. Remington);
Ridden Down (F. Remington);
Smoke Signal (F. Remington);
Buffalo Hunt (C.Rssell);
Scouts (C. Russell); Piegans
(C. Russell) ..... 6·00 6·25

561 Marilyn
Monroe

2004. Marilyn Monroe Commemoration. Multicoloured.

4948 50c. Type **561** 70 70
MS4949 127×116 mm. $2 Wearing
one-shoulder red top; $2 Wearing
strapless orange top; $2 Wearing
white top; $2 Wearing off-shoulder
pink top ..... 6·00 7·00

562 Deng Xiaoping

2004. Deng Xiaoping (Chinese politician)
Commemoration. Sheet 99×68 mm.

MS4950 **562** $6 multicoloured ..... 5·00 6·00

563 Pres. George W. Bush

2004. Military Operations in Iraq. Sheet 127×118
mm containing T **563** and similar horiz designs.
Multicoloured.

MS4951 $2 Type **563**; $2 Paul Bremer;
$2 Col. James Hickey; $2 Soldier and
Iraqi civilians ..... 8·50 9·00

564 Jan Svehlik
(Czech Republic
footballer)

2004. European Football Championships 2004, Portugal.
T **564** and similar multicoloured designs.

MS4952 147×84 mm. $2 Type **564**;
$2 Franz Beckenbauer (German
footballer); $2 Karol Dobias (Czech
Republic footballer); $2 Crvena
Zvezda football ground ..... 6·50 7·00

MS4953 98×84 mm. $6 Czech Republic
football team, 1976 (50×37 mm) ..... 5·00 6·00

565 Pope John Paul II

2004. 25th Anniv of the Pontificate of Pope John Paul
II. Sheet 163×154 mm containing T **565** and similar
horiz designs. Multicoloured.

MS4954 $2 Type **565**; $2 With Mikhail
Gorbachev; $2 With arms stretched
overhead; $2 Meeting with Polish
deportees; $2 With Patriarchate of
the Russian Orthodox Church ..... 12·00 12·00

2004. 60th Anniv of D-Day Landings. As T **404** of
Dominica. Multicoloured.

4955 45c. Don Sheppard, Royal
Engineers ..... 1·10 40
4956 $1 Air Chief Marshall Sir Arthur
Tedder ..... 2·25 1·00
4957 $1.50 Douglas Kay, 13th/18th
Royal Hussars ..... 2·75 2·00
4958 $3 Gen. Sir Bernard Mont-
gomery ..... 4·50 5·00

MS4959 176×107 mm. $2 Germans
detect Allied invasion; $2 Germans
prepare to engage Allied invasion
fleet; $2 British Paratrooper at
Merville Battery; $2 Paratroopers and
captured Merville Battery ..... 11·00 12·00

MS4960 176×107 mm. $2 HMS Belfast
fires on German shore batteries;
$2 Allies pound German coastal
defences; $2 Air strikes over Utah
Beach. $2 Allied troops in landing
craft approaching Omaha Beach ..... 11·00 12·00

MS4961 Two sheets, each 100×70 mm.
(a) $6 PLUTO (Pipe Line Under The
Ocean). (b) $6 Fake Landing Craft ..... 16·00 17·00

566 GN Stirling
Single

2004. Bicentenary of Steam Locomotives. Multicoloured.

4962- $1×9 Type **566**; Beyer Peacock
4970 Mogul; Prussian GB; George
Stephenson (engineer);
James Nasmyth; James
Nasmyth's steam hammer;
Raven Z Class; Sir Vincent
Raven; Bronze statue of
Thomas Cook ..... 8·50 9·00

4971- $1×9 SR Schools class; Indian
4979 Railways SGS class; Borsig
tram, Paraguay; Richard
Trevithick; Herbert Garratt;
Isambard Kingdom Brunel;
Replica of Trevithick's
Coalbrookdale engine;
Rhodesian 20th class Garratt;
Brunel's Royal Saltash Bridge ..... 8·50 9·00

4980- $1×9 SR Lord Nelson; South
4988 African 16CR class Pacific;
Florisdorf Fireless, Austria;
GWR 57XX class; GWR Castle
class; GWR Saint class; GWR
Star Class; GWR 28XX class;
GWR 51XX class (all horiz) ..... 8·50 9·00

MS4989 Three sheets, each 96×66 mm.
(a) $6 California Zephyr (horiz). (b)
$6 Steam locomotive, Cumbres and
Toltec Railway (horiz). (c) $6 Indian
Pacific locomotive (horiz) ..... 23·00 24·00

567 Elvis Presley

2004. 50th Anniv of Elvis Presley's First Record.
Multicoloured.

4990- $1.50×6 Type **567**; Playing
4995 guitar with overhead
microphone (grey back-
ground); Playing guitar
with overhead microphone
(stone background); Playing
guitar and singing; Portrait
photograph; Playing guitar
with overhead microphone
(grey background) ..... 7·00 7·50

568 Princess Juliana in 1947 and
Palace at Soestdijk

2004. Queen Juliana of the Netherlands Commemoration.

4996 **568** $2 multicoloured ..... 2·00 2·00

569 Meriwether Lewis

2004. Bicentenary of Lewis and Clark's Expedition to the
American West and Pacific North West. T **569** and
similar vert designs. Multicoloured.

MS4997 154×180 mm. $3 Type **569**; $3
Sacagawea; $3 William Clark ..... 6·50 7·00

2004. United Nations International Year of Peace. As T
409 of Dominica. Multicoloured.

MS4998 137×77 mm. $3 Jody Williams
(Nobel Peace winner, 1997);
$3 International Campaign to Ban
Landmines; $3 Princess Diana ..... 7·50 8·00

570 Delta II Rocket at blast off

2004. The Mars Exploration Rover Mission. Multicoloured.

MS4999 170×127 mm. $1.50×6 Type
570; Entering Mars atmosphere;
Parachute descent; Landing on the
surface; Rover leaving lander; Rover
on Mars surface ..... 9·00 9·50

571 Queen Mary 2 and Queen Elizabeth II (image scaled
to 48% of original size)

2004. Ocean Liners. Multicoloured.

MS5000 125×208 mm. $2 Type **571**;
$2 Queen Elizabeth II and couple at
dining table; $2 Queen Mary and
passengers embarking; $2 Queen
Elizabeth and couple on deck ..... 12·00 12·00

MS5001 125×203 mm. $2 Titanic;
$2 Normandie; $2 Mauritania; $2
Lusitania ..... 12·00 12·00

MS5002 115×85 mm. $6 Queen Mary 2 ..... 9·00 9·00

2004. Centenary of FIFA (Federation Internationale
de Football Association). As T **413** of Dominica.
Multicoloured.

MS5003 192×96 mm. $2 Gabriel Batis-
tuta, Argentina; $2 Cafu, Brazil; $2
Michel Platini; $2 Gianluca Vialli, Italy ..... 6·00 7·00

MS5004 118×87 mm. $6 Oliver Kahn,
Germany ..... 5·00 6·00

572 Pau Gasol,
Memphis Grizzlies

2004. US National Basketball Association Players (1st
series). Multicoloured.

5005 75c. Type **572** ..... 1·25 90
5006 75c. Allen Iverson, Philadelphia
76ers ..... 1·25 90
5007 75c. Stephon Marbury ..... 1·25 90
See also Nos. 5028/30.

573 President Reagan with
Mother Teresa, 1985

2004. Ronald Reagan (US President 1981–9)
Commemoration. Multicoloured.

MS5008 170×117 mm. $2 Type **573**;
$2 With Gen. Colin Powell, 1988; $2
With Queen Elizabeth II, 1981; $2
With Canadian Prime Minister Brian
Mulroney ..... 9·00 9·00

574 Babe Ruth

2004. Centenary of Baseball World Series. T **574** and similar vert designs showing George Herman "Babe" Ruth. Multicoloured.

MS5009 125×115 mm. $2 Type **574**; $2 Looking sideways to left; $2 Standing by helicopter; $2 Wearing stripes ... 5·50 ... 6·50

MS5010 112×113 mm. $2 Wearing blue cap, facing right; $2 Wearing blue cap, facing left; $2 Wearing stripes and cap; $2 Looking sideways to left, wearing blue cap ... 5·50 ... 6·50

575 *Merry Christmas* (1920)

2004. Christmas. 25th Death Anniv of Norman Rockwell (artist). Multicoloured.

5011	35c. Type **575**	55	20
5012	75c. *Yuletide Merriment* (1931)	1·00	45
5013	$1 *Dressing Up* (1916)	1·25	75
5014	$4 *Christmas* (1927)	4·50	5·50

MS5015 70×100 mm. $6 *The London Coach* (1925) (cover for Saturday Evening Post) ... 6·50 ... 7·00

576 *Chrysanthemums, Cocks and Hens*

2005. Chinese New Year ("Year of the Rooster"). Paintings by Qi Baishi. Multicoloured.

MS5016 140×108 mm. $1×4 Type **576**×4 ... 4·00 ... 4·25

MS5017 70×100 mm. $4 *Taro Leaves and Double Hens* ... 4·00 ... 4·25

577 *Turkey Vulture*

2005. Birds of Prey. Multicoloured.

MS5018 160×140 mm. $1.50 Type **577**; $1.50 American bald eagle; $1.50 Peregrine Falcon; $1.50 Prairie Falcon; $1.50 Northern goshawk; $1.50 Cooper's hawk ... 13·00 ... 13·00

MS5019 82×102 mm. $6 Californian condor (horiz) ... 10·00 ... 10·00

578 *Cheetah*

2005. Wild Cats. Multicoloured.

MS5020 115×177 mm. $1.50 Type **578**; $1.50 Lion; $1.50 White tiger; $1.50 Leopard; $1.50 Bobcat; $1.50 Bengal tiger ... 12·00 ... 12·00

MS5021 97×72 mm. $6 Jaguar ... 8·00 ... 8·50

579 *Heraclides machaonides*

2005. Butterflies. Multicoloured.

MS5022 177×133 mm. $1.50 Type **579**; $1.50 *Limenitis archippus*; $1.50 *Cithaerias merolina*; $1.50 *Troides hypolitus*; $1.50 *Ornithoptera goliath procus*; $1.50 *Ornithoptera priamus alberio* ... 12·00 ... 12·00

MS5023 107×89 mm. $6 *Papilio demoleus malayanus* ... 9·00 ... 9·00

580 *Majungatholus*

2005. Dinosaurs. Multicoloured.

MS2026 225×110 mm. $2 Pteranodon; $2 Dimorphodon; $2 Pterodactylus; $2 Ramphorhyncus ... 6·00 ... 6·50

MS2027 Three sheets, each 95×95 mm. (a) $6 Spinosaurus. (b) $6 Pliosaur. (c) $6 Tapejara Imperator ... 13·00 ... 14·00

MS5024 155×115 mm. $2 Type **580**; $2 Diplodocus; $2 Willo; $2 Velociraptor ... 10·00 ... 10·00

MS5025 225×110 mm. $2 Archelon; $2 Ammonite; $2 Plesiosaur; $2 Xiphactinus ... 10·00 ... 10·00

2005. US National Basketball Association Players (2nd series). As T **572**. Multicoloured.

5028	75c. Zydrunas Ilgauskas	1·25	1·25
5029	75c. Dwyane Wade	1·25	1·25
5030	$3 Tracy McGrady	4·25	4·50

581 *Deities overseeing the Transplanting of Rice* (Japanese, artist unknown)

2005. International Year of Rice (2004). Multicoloured.

MS5031 137×92 mm. $3 Type **581**; $3 *The Taoist God overseeing the Rice Planting by the San Chay People of Vietnam* (artist unknown); $3 *Scene of Women transplanting Rice in Late Spring Rain* (Hiroshige) ... 6·50 ... 7·00

582 Cathedral of Immaculate Conception

2005. Hurricane Ivan—the Aftermath. Sheet 130×90 mm containing T **582** and similar horiz designs showing hurricane damage. Multicoloured.

MS5032 $2 Type **582**; $2 Anglican Church; $2 York House (House of Parliament); $2 Springs Sub-office ... 7·00 ... 8·00

583 *Elvis Presley* (1955)

2005. 70th Birth Anniv of Elvis Presley. Multicoloured.

5033- $1.50×6 Type **583**; On outdoor
5038 stage, Tupelo (1957); In room, playing guitar (1959); Performing in Memphis Charities Benefit Show (1961); On stage in "68 Special" Show (1968); With guitar on Fall Tour (1970) ... 7·00 ... 7·50

5039- $1.50×6 In *Jailhouse Rock*, hold-
5044 ing door (1957); Playing guitar in *Girl Happy* (1964); On saddle in *Tickle Me* (1965); Playing guitar in *Speedway* (1968); Playing piano in *The Trouble with Girls* (1969); On studio stage in *That's the Way It Is* (1970) ... 7·00 ... 7·50

584 *Tenement Gentleman, 1947*

2005. Ozu Yasujiro (film director) Commemoration. Sheet 145×175 mm containing T **584** and similar vert designs. Multicoloured.

MS5045 $2 Type **584**; $2 *Tokyo Story*, 1953; $2 *A Hen in the Wind*, 1948; $2 *Floating Weeds*, 1959 ... 7·00 ... 8·00

585 *King William I* (1815—40)

2005. Silver Jubilee of Queen Beatrix of the Netherlands. T **585** and similar vert designs showing Dutch royalty. Multicoloured.

MS5046 170×235 mm. $2×8 Type **585**; William II (1840—9); William III (1849—90); Wilhelmina (1890—1948); Juliana (1948—80); Queen Beatrix; Crown Prince Willem-Alexander; Princess Catharina-Amalia ... 15·00 ... 17·00

The stamps within the two horizontal rows of four making up **MS**5046 have composite background designs.

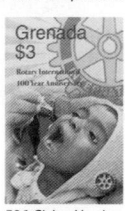

586 Giving Vaccine to Boy

2005. Centenary of Rotary International. Multicoloured.

MS5047 135×105 mm. $3 Type **586**; $3 David Edwards (Governor of District 7030) and his wife Donna; $3 Paul Harris (founder) ... 9·00 ... 9·50

MS5048 97×67 mm. $6 Richard King (President 2001—2) and two girls ... 6·50 ... 7·00

The first two designs in **MS**5047 have a composite background design showing the Rotary emblem.

587 "21 Curves" Supply Line from Rangoon to China

2005. 60th Anniv of the End of World War II. "The Route to Victory". Multicoloured.

5049	$2 Type **587**	2·50	2·50
5050	$2 British troops in jungle, Burma	2·50	2·50
5051	$2 Troops at Magwe airstrip	2·50	2·50
5052	$2 Allied troops escorting prisoners	2·50	2·50
5053	$2 Allied troops parachuting behind enemy lines	2·50	2·50
5054	$2 Allied troops firing	2·50	2·50
5055	$2 German troops moving through buildings	2·50	2·50
5056	$2 Aerial view of bridge still under German control	2·50	2·50

MS5057 Two sheets, each 106×97 mm. (a) $6 Troops discussing next move. (b) $6 Allied troops in ruined buildings ... 14·00 ... 14·00

Nos. 5049/52 depict the Burma Campaign, December 1941 to August 1945, and Nos. 5053/6 Operation Market Garden, Dutch/German border, 17 September 1944.

588 Troops wading Ashore from Landing Craft, D-Day

2005. 60th Anniv of Victory in Europe Day. Multicoloured.

5058	$2 Type **588**	2·75	2·75
5059	$2 Allied soldiers	2·75	2·75
5060	$2 Surrendering German troops	2·75	2·75
5061	$2 Crowd waving US flags on VE Day	2·75	2·75

MS5062 96×66 mm. $6 Fall of Berlin to armies of Soviet Union ... 8·00 ... 8·00

589 Airstrikes over Pacific Islands

2005. 60th Anniv of Victory in Japan Day. Multicoloured.

5063	$2 Type **589**	2·75	2·75
5064	$2 Allied forces storming beach	2·75	2·75
5065	$2 Gen. McArthur going ashore, Philippines	2·75	2·75
5066	$2 Surrender of Japanese armies	2·75	2·75

MS5067 95×65 mm. $6 Victory celebrations ... 8·00 ... 8·00

590 Rainbow over Victoria Falls, Africa

2005. EXPO 2005 World Exposition, Aichi, Japan. Multicoloured.

5068	$1.50 Type **590**	2·50	2·50
5069	$1.50 Bald eagle	2·50	2·50
5070	$1.50 Caribbean coral reef	2·50	2·50
5071	$1.50 Mother with new baby	2·50	2·50
5072	$1.50 Neil Armstrong, first man on Moon	2·50	2·50
5073	$1.50 Bee pollinating flower	2·50	2·50

591 Albert Einstein and Galaxy

2005. 50th Death Anniv of Albert Einstein (physicist). Multicoloured.

MS5074 154×90 mm. $2 Type **591**; $2 Einstein and "E=mc²"; $2 Einstein (facing sideways); $2 Einstein as young man ... 11·00 ... 11·00

MS5075 100×70 mm. $6 Einstein smoking and "E=mc²" ... 8·00 ... 8·00

592 *Tell's Memorial Statue* (Richard Kissling), Altdorf, Switzerland

2005. Death Bicentenary of Friedrich von Schiller (poet and dramatist). Multicoloured.

5076	$3 Type **592**	3·00	3·50
5077	$3 Scene from modern *William Tell* DVD film	3·00	3·50
5078	$3 William Tell play by Natural Theatre Company of UK, 1997–8	3·00	3·50

MS5079 96×67 mm. $6 Scene from *William Tell* (horiz) ... 6·00 ... 7·00

593 Admiral Lord Nelson

2005. Bicentenary of the Battle of Trafalgar. Multicoloured.

5080	$2 Type **593**	3·00	3·00
5081	$2 Napoleon Bonaparte	3·00	3·00

5082	$2 HMS *Victory*	3·00	3·00
5083	$2 *The Nelson Touch*	3·00	3·00

MS5084 100×78 mm. $6 *After the Battle of the Nile* (illustration by Thomas Rowlandson) (horiz) — 9·00 9·50

594 "How 'bout a Trade, Dad? My Broccoli, for your Chocolate Cake"

2005. Dennis the Menace (American cartoon character created by Hank Ketcham). Multicoloured.

5085	$2 Type **594**	1·60	1·60
5086	$2 "It's not a Good Idea to Scratch your Nose while you're Finger-Painting, Joey"	1·60	1·60
5087	$2 "I'll bet you were the Top of your Class at Grandpa School"	1·60	1·60
5088	$2 "Boy, I'm Glad I don't have to Clean his Sandbox"	1·60	1·60
5089	$2 "Grandpa got a New Knee Last Year, but it Still Sits like the Old One"	1·60	1·60
5090	$2 "Joey an' Me don't have any Money, but Here's a Brick for the New Church Building"	1·60	1·60
5091	$2 "Good News, Mrs. Wilson! Our Club elected you Vice President in Charge of Cookies!"	1·60	1·60
5092	$2 "I Think the Boy's a 'Born' Realtor. He's been Instrumental in the Sale of Half the Houses in This Neighborhood"	1·60	1·60

595 Private Johnson Beharry VC

2005. Award of Victoria Cross to Private Johnson Beharry. Sheet 70×87 mm.

MS5093 **595** $5 multicoloured — 6·00 6·00

596 Jules Verne

2005. Death Centenary of Jules Verne (writer). Multicoloured.

MS5094 110×120 mm. $3 Type **596**; $3 Oval portrait; $3 Jules Verne holding cigar — 9·50 9·50

MS5095 100×100 mm. $6 Rocket approaching Moon (*From the Earth to the Moon*) — 7·00 7·00

597 Hans Christian Andersen

2005. Birth Bicentenary of Hans Christian Andersen (writer). Multicoloured.

MS5096 150×90 mm. $3 Type **597**; $3 Andersen (looking left); $3 Seated — 7·00 8·00

MS5097 70×100 mm. $6 Tombstone — 5·50 6·00

598 Purple-throated Carib

2005. Purple throated Carib.

5098	**598** 10c. multicoloured	10	10

599 Tel Aviv

2005. TAIPEI 2005 International Stamp Exhibition. Multicoloured.

MS5111 85×115 mm. $2 Type **599**; $2 Empire State Building, New York; $2 Taipei; $2 Eiffel Tower, Paris — 8·00 8·00

600 Pope John Paul II with Lech Walesa (Polish trade unionist)

2005. Pope John Paul II Commemoration.

5112	**600** $4 multicoloured	6·00	6·00

601 Prince Charles and Mrs. Camilla Parker-Bowles

2005. Royal Wedding. Designs showing Prince Charles and Mrs. Camilla Parker-Bowles. Multicoloured.

5113	$2 Type **601**	2·50	2·50
5114	$2 Holding book (vert)	2·50	2·50
5115	$2 Holding posy (vert)	2·50	2·50

602 *The Nativity* (detail) (Correggio)

2005. Christmas. Multicoloured.

5116	25c. Type **602**	40	10
5117	75c. *Virgin and Child* (detail) (Lorenzo Lotto)	1·00	50
5118	$1 *The Holy Family* (detail) (Lorenzo Lotto)	1·25	75
5119	$5 *Madonna and Child with the Saints* (detail) (Lorenzo Lotto)	6·00	7·00

MS5120 70×100 mm. $6 *Allegory of Music* (Filippo Lippi) — 6·50 7·00

603 Stadium

2005. Centenary of Chelsea Football Club. Multicoloured.

5123	$1.50 Type **603**	1·10	1·25
5124	$1.50 "1905 2005" and emblem	1·10	1·25
5125	$1.50 Petr Cech, Hernan Crespo and John Terry	1·10	1·25
5126	$1.50 Chelsea team with Premier League trophy	1·10	1·25
5127	$1.50 Fans with "Chelsea FC" banner	1·10	1·25
5128	$1.50 Team with "Champions 2004–2005" banner	1·10	1·25
5129	$1.50 Chelsea players	1·10	1·25
5130	$1.50 Jose Mourinho (manager)	1·10	1·25
5131	$1.50 Emblem and stadium	1·10	1·25

5132	$1.50 Team with FA Charity Shield	1·10	1·25

604 Victory Parade

2005. Liverpool FC Champions of Europe. Multicoloured.

5133	$1.50 Type **604**	1·10	1·25
5134	$1.50 Steven Gerrard and Rafael Benitez (manager) with UEFA Champions League Cup	1·10	1·25
5135	$1.50 Entrance to Liverpool FC ground	1·10	1·25
5136	$1.50 Aerial view of Anfield stadium	1·10	1·25
5137	$1.50 Club banner	1·10	1·25
5138	$1.50 Triumphant team waving to crowd	1·10	1·25
5139	$1.50 Fans with flags	1·10	1·25
5140	$1.50 Match in progress at Anfield stadium	1·10	1·25
5141	$1.50 Victorious team on pitch at end of match	1·10	1·25
5142	$1.50 Victory parade with "Liverpool" banners	1·10	1·25

605 *The Two Hounds* (Hui-Tsung)

2005. Chinese New Year ("Year of the Dog").

5121	**605** $1 multicoloured	1·25	1·25

MS5122 100×70 mm. **605** $4 multicoloured (50×37 mm) — 3·00 3·25

606 Pope Benedict XVI

2006. Election of Pope Benedict XVI.

5143	**606** $2 multicoloured	3·25	3·25

2006. 80th Birthday of Queen Elizabeth II. As T **432** of Dominica. Multicoloured.

5144	$3 Queen Elizabeth II (looking left)	3·75	3·75
5145	$3 Princess Elizabeth as teenager	3·75	3·75
5146	$3 Painting of Queen Elizabeth II	3·75	3·75
5147	$3 Queen Elizabeth II (full face)	3·75	3·75

MS5148 120×120 mm. $6 Wearing pearls and dark blue dress — 7·50 7·50

607 USA Team

2006. World Cup Football Championship, Germany (1st issue). Designs showing national teams. Multicoloured.

5149- $1.50×32 Type **607**; Brazil; Iran;
5180 Netherlands; Czech Republic; Ghana; Serbia & Montenegro; Sweden; Spain; Australia; Ivory Coast; Portugal; Angola; South Korea; Mexico; Poland; Costa Rica; Switzerland; France; England; Croatia; Italy; Ecuador; Japan; Argentina; Trinidad & Tobago; Paraguay; Saudi Arabia; Germany; Ukraine; Tunisia; Togo — 27·00 29·00

2006. 80th Birth Anniv of Marilyn Monroe (actress). As T **452** of Gambia. Multicoloured.

5181	$3 Marilyn Monroe	2·00	2·25

2006. Winter Olympic Games, Turin. As T **431** of Dominica but vert. Multicoloured.

5182	75c. Poster for Winter Olympic Games, Lake Placid, 1980	85	80
5183	75c. Poster for Olympic Games, Turin, 2006	85	80
5184	90c. Italy 2006 Winter Olympic €1 Olympic flame stamp (horiz)	1·00	90

5185	90c. Switzerland 1948 Winter Olympics 30c.+10c. ski-runner stamp	1·00	90
5186	$2 Poster for Winter Olympic Games, St. Moritz, 1948	2·25	2·50
5187	$3 Switzerland 1948 Winter Olympics 20c.+10c. ice hockey stamp	2·75	3·25

2006. Washington 2006 International Stamp Exhibition. As T **453** of Gambia. Multicoloured.

5188	$3 Rosa Parks	2·50	3·00

608 Stylized Brazil Player (2002) and Trophy

2006. World Cup Football Championship, Germany (2nd issue). Each showing cartoon player in colours of winning team and World Cup trophy. Multicoloured.

5189	75c. Type **608**	75	50
5190	90c. Germany (1990)	90	65
5191	$3 France (1998)	2·50	3·00

609 World Cup Trophy

2006. World Cup Football Championship, Germany (3rd issue). Self-adhesive. Imperf.

5192	**609** $6 multicoloured	5·00	6·00

2006. 400th Birth Anniv of Rembrandt Harmenszoon van Rijn (artist). As T **458** of Gambia showing paintings. Multicoloured.

5193	50c. *The Little Jewish Bride* (detail)	60	40
5194	$1 *Young Man in Velvet Cap* (detail)	1·00	80
5195	$1.50 *Old Woman Sleeping* (detail)	1·40	1·10
5196	$3 *Woman Reading* (detail)	2·50	2·50
5197	$3 *Young Woman with Flowers in her Hair* (detail)	2·50	2·50
5198	$3 *Portrait of a Seated Woman* (detail)	2·50	2·50
5199	$3 *Alijdt Adriaensor* (detail)	2·50	2·50
5200	$3 *Amalia van Solms* (detail)	2·50	2·50
5201	$6 *Portrait of a Seated Man* (detail) (69×99 mm)	4·75	5·50

MS5202 70×100 mm. $6 *Portrait of a Scholar* (detail). Imperf — 5·50 6·00

610 *Graf Zeppelin D-LZ-127*

2006. 50th Death Anniv of Ludwig Durr (Zeppelin engineer). Multicoloured.

5203	$4 Type **610**	4·00	4·25
5204	$4 *Graf Zeppelin LT*	4·00	4·25
5205	$4 *Graf Zeppelin L26*	4·00	4·25

611 Scene from *The Magic Flute*

2006. 250th Birth Anniv of Wolfgang Amadeus Mozart (composer). Sheet 100×70 mm.

MS5206 **611** $6 multicoloured — 9·00 9·00

612 Girls! Girls! Girls!

2006. 50th Anniv of Elvis Presley's Film Debut. Sheet 190×127 mm containing T **612** and similar vert designs showing film posters. Multicoloured.

5207	$3 Type **612**	3·00	3·00
5208	$3 *Jailhouse Rock*	3·00	3·00
5209	$3 *Paradise–Hawaiian Style*	3·00	3·00
5210	$3 *It Happened at the World's Fair*	3·00	3·00

613 Halley's Comet

2006. Space Anniversaries. Multicoloured. (a) 20th Anniv of Giotto Comet Probe.

MS5211 150×100 mm. $2×6 Type **613**; Ariane V14 rocket; Halley's Comet (going into distance); Halley's Comet (blue and black background); Giotto Probe Launcher; Halley's Comet and Milky Way ... 13·00 ... 14·00

The two central stamps in No. **MS**5211 form a composite design showing Ariane V14 rocket on Giotto Probe Launcher.

(b) 50th Anniv of "Sputnik 1".

MS5212 150×100 mm. $2×4 Sergei Korolev; "Sputnik 1" orbiting Earth; Inside "Sputnik 1"; "Sputnik 1" capsule ... 9·00 ... 9·50

(c) 30th Anniv (2005) of "Apollo"/"Soyuz" Test Project.

MS5213 150×100 mm. $2×4 "Apollo" rocket; Apollo CM with adapter; "Soyuz" spacecraft at Baykonur Cosmodrome; "Soyuz" (all vert) ... 9·00 ... 9·50

MS5214 Three sheets, each 100×70 mm. (a) $6 Impactor and flyby spacecraft (Comet Tempel I Deep Impact Mission, 2005). (b) $6 Stardust encounters Comet Wild 2, 2004. (c) $6 Space Shuttle "Discovery", 2005 ... 17·00 ... 18·00

614 *Santa Maria* sinking, December 25 1492

2006. 500th Death Anniv of Christopher Columbus. Multicoloured.

5215	$1.50 Type **614**	2·00	1·25
5216	$2 *Santa Maria* replica (vert)	2·50	2·00
5217	$3 Christopher Columbus ashore in New World (vert)	3·25	3·50
5218	$4 Columbus and sailing ship (vert)	4·00	4·50

MS5219 100×70 mm. $6 Columbus's fleet setting sail again, 1493 (horiz) ... 6·00 ... 6·50

615 *Nymphalis antiopa* (Mourning Cloak)

2006. Butterflies. Multicoloured.

5220	10c. Type **615**	35	25
5221	25c. *Libytheana bachmanii* (snout butterfly)	60	20
5222	$1 *Tithorea pinthias*	1·50	80
5223	$2 *Hypolimnas misippus* (Diadem)	2·50	2·00
5224	$4 *Megisto rubricata* (red satyr)	4·00	4·25
5225	$5 *Taygetis chrysogone*	4·50	4·75
5226	$10 *Pierella hortona*	8·50	11·00
5227	$20 *Morpho aega*	15·00	19·00

615a Princess Maxima

2006. Princess Maxima of the Netherlands. Sheet 150×190 mm containing T **615a** and similar vert designs. Multicoloured.

5236	$1.50 Type **615a**	1·60	1·60
5237	$1.50 Princess Maxima (half-length portrait)	1·60	1·60

616 Shepherd

2006. Christmas. Showing details from painting *The Adoration of the Shepherds* by Rubens. Multicoloured.

5238	25c. Type **616**	40	15
5239	50c. Virgin Mary	65	30
5240	75c. Shepherd (wearing cloak)	95	45
5241	$1 Baby Jesus	1·25	65
5242	$2 As Type **616**	2·25	2·50
5243	$2 As No. 5229	2·25	2·50
5244	$2 As No. 5230	2·25	2·50
5245	$2 As No. 5231	2·25	2·50

617 Betty Boop

2006. Betty Boop. Multicoloured.

MS5246 180×128 mm. $1.50×6 Type **617**; Standing, leaning forward, with hands on knees; Seated, with right leg outstretched; Standing with hands clasped; Standing with arms outstretched; Standing with arms and left leg raised ... 6·50 ... 7·00

MS5247 132×108 mm. $2×4 Standing with hands clasped; Standing with arms outstretched; Standing with arms and left leg raised; With microphone ... 6·00 ... 6·50

MS5248 100×72 mm. $3×2 Looking over shoulder (head); Seated (body) (both horiz) ... 4·00 ... 4·25

MS5249 76×106 mm. $3×2 Seated in chair, holding mirror; Wearing Hawaiian style grass skirt, lei and decorated straw hat ... 4·00 ... 4·25

The two rows of stamps within **MS**5246 each have "BETTY BOOP" printed across them, forming a composite design.

618 Three Players

2007. Arsenal Football Club's New Emirates Stadium, Islington, London. Multicoloured.

MS5250 210×166 mm. $1×5 Type **618**; Match in Emirates Stadium; Terraces of stadium; Entrance to stadium; Four players. $2×5 Arsenal team; Outside of stadium; Arsenal fans; Match in stadium; Stadium at sunset ... 3·00 ... 3·00

619 Soviet Premier Krushchev at Simferopol Space Control Centre

2007. 90th Birth Anniv of John F. Kennedy (US President 1960–3). Multicoloured.

5251	$2 Type **619**	2·25	2·25
5252	$2 Pres. Kennedy meeting Premier Krushchev	2·25	2·25
5253	$2 Pres. Kennedy pressures Premier Krushchev	2·25	2·25
5254	$2 Premier Krushchev and Pres. Kennedy in US Ambassador's residence, Vienna, 3 June 1961	2·25	2·25
5255	$2 Premier Krushchev and Cuban President Fidel Castro	2·25	2·25
5256	$2 Pres. Kennedy on television, 22 October 1962	2·25	2·25
5257	$2 Completed SA-2 missile site	2·25	2·25
5258	$2 Pres. Kennedy and Premier Krushchev shaking hands in Vienna	2·25	2·25

620 French Test Pilot Andre Turcat

2007. Concorde. Multicoloured.

5259	$2 Type **620**	3·00	3·00
5260	$2 British test pilot Brian Trubshaw	3·00	3·00

621 Hand giving Salute

2007. Centenary of Scouting. Multicoloured. Background colours given (Nos. 5261/4).

5261	**621**	$3 blue	3·25	3·25
5262	**621**	$3 orange	3·25	3·25
5263	**621**	$3 magenta	3·25	3·25
5264	**621**	$3 green	3·25	3·25

MS5265 110×81 mm. $6 Hand giving salute and "21ST WORLD SCOUT JAMBOREE" ... 6·00 ... 6·50

622 "The Pig carries the Fortune to the Door" (paper cutting)

2007. Chinese New Year ("Year of the Pig").

MS5266 112×85 mm. [$1] Type **622** (black inscr); $1 As Type **622** (white inscr); $2 As Type **622** (white inscr); $2 As Type **622** (yellow inscr) ... 6·00 ... 6·50

The colours refer to the "TRADITIONAL CHINESE NEW YEAR PAPER CUTTING" inscription at the top of the stamps.

623 Pope Benedict XVI

2007. 80th Birthday of Pope Benedict XVI.

5267	**623**	$1 multicoloured	1·60	1·25

2007. World Cup Cricket, West Indies. As T **448** of Dominica. Multicoloured.

5268	$1 Outline map and flag of Grenada	1·60	80
5269	$2 Rawl Lewis	3·00	2·50
5270	$3 Queen's Park Stadium (horiz)	3·75	4·00

MS5271 117×90 mm. $6 World Cup Cricket emblem ... 6·00 ... 6·50

624 Diana, Princess of Wales

2007. Tenth Death Anniv of Diana, Princess of Wales. Multicoloured.

5272	$2 Type **624**	2·25	2·25
5273	$2 Wearing turquoise and white jacket and hat	2·25	2·25
5274	$2 Wearing white sleeveless evening dress	2·25	2·25
5275	$2 Wearing green and white jacket and hat	2·25	2·25

MS5276 Two sheets, each 100×70 mm. (a) $6 Wearing green and white dress and white headscarf. (b) $6 Wearing red dress with halter neck (horiz) ... 11·00 ... 12·00

625 Princess Elizabeth and Prince Philip, c. 1947

2007. Diamond Wedding of Queen Elizabeth II and Duke of Edinburgh. Multicoloured.

5277	$2 Type **625**	2·50	2·50
5278	$2 Queen Elizabeth II, c. 2007	2·50	2·50

MS5279 70×100 mm. $6 Queen Elizabeth and Prince Philip, c. 2007 ... 6·00 ... 6·50

626 Emperor Penguin

2007. International Polar Year. Penguins. Multicoloured.

MS5280 150×115 mm. $2×6 Type **626**; Three penguins on the ice; Adult penguin (with head bent); Chick on snow with adult; Chick with wings outstretched; Chick standing on adult's feet ... 15·00 ... 15·00

MS5281 70×100 mm. $6 Penguin skiing (horiz) ... 6·00 ... 6·50

The stamps and margins of No. **MS**5280 form a composite design showing Emperor penguins in Antarctica.

2007. Halley's Comet, 1986. As T **473** of Gambia. Frame colours given for Nos. 5282/5. Multicoloured.

5282	$2 orange	2·25	2·25
5283	$2 blue	2·25	2·25
5284	$2 violet	2·25	2·25
5285	$2 red	2·25	2·25

MS5286 100×70 mm. $6 Emblem, Halley's Comet and 'RETURNS 2062' ... 6·00 ... 6·50

627 George Washington, 1789–97

2007. Presidents of the United States of America. Multicoloured.

MS5287 Three sheets, each 168×115 mm. (a) 1c. Type **627**; 2c. John Adams, 1797–1801; 3c. Thomas Jefferson, 1801–9; 4c. James Madison, 1809–17; 5c. James Monroe, 1817–25; 6c. John Adams, 1825–9; 7c. Andrew Jackson, 1829–37; 8c. Martin Van Buren, 1837–41; 9c. William H. Harrison, 1841; 10c. John Tyler, 1841–5; 11c. James K. Polk, 1845–9; 12c. Zachary Taylor, 1849–50; 13c. Millard Fillmore, 1850–3; 14c. Franklin Pierce, 1853–7; $4 US Arms and flag. (b) 15c. James Buchanan, 1857–61; 16c. Abraham Lincoln, 1861–5; 17c. Andrew Johnson, 1865–9; 18c. Ulysses S. Grant, 1869–77; 19c. Rutherford Hayes, 1877–81; 20c. James Garfield, 1881; 21c. Chester Arthur, 1881–5; 22c. Grover Cleveland, 1885–9; 23c. Benjamin Harrison, 1889–93; 24c. Grover Cleveland, 1893–7; 25c. William McKinley, 1897–1901; 26c. Theodore Roosevelt, 1901–9; 27c. William Taft, 1909–13; 28c. Woodrow Wilson, 1913–21; $2 Capitol, Washington. (c) 29c. Warren G. Harding, 1921–3; 30c. Calvin Coolidge, 1923–9; 31c. Herbert Hoover, 1929–33; 32c. Franklin D. Roosevelt, 1933–45; 33c. Harry S. Truman, 1945–53; 34c. Dwight D. Eisenhower, 1953–61; 35c. John F. Kennedy, 1961–3; 36c. Lyndon B. Johnson, 1963–9; 37c. Richard Nixon, 1969–74; 38c. Gerald R. Ford, 1974–7; 39c. Jimmy Carter, 1977–81; 40c. Ronald Reagan, 1981–9; 41c. George H. W. Bush, 1989–93; 42c. William Clinton, 1993–2001; 43c. George W. Bush, 2001– ... 16·00 ... 16·00

628 Clymene Dolphin

2007. Endangered Species. Clymene Dolphin (Stenella clymene). Multicoloured.

5288	$1.20 Type **628**	1·25	1·40
5289	$1.20 Two dolphins	1·25	1·40
5290	$1.20 Dolphin leaping out of water	1·25	1·40
5291	$1.20 Two dolphins swimming side by side	1·25	1·40
MS5292	115×168 mm. Nos. 5288/91, each ×2	8·00	8·00

2007. Holocaust Remembrance. As T **479** of Gambia. Multicoloured.

5293- 5300	$1.40×8 Erasmo Lara-Pena, Dominican Republic; Diego Cordovez, Ecuador; Carmen M. Gallardo Hernandez, El Salvador; Lino Sima Ekua Avomo, Equatorial Guinea; Tina Intelmann, Estonia; Dawit Yohannes, Ethiopia; Isikia Rabiei Savua, Fiji; Lars Wide, Chef de Cabinet, 60th UN GA	8·00	8·00
5301- 5308	$1.40×8 Angus Friday, Grenada; Alfredo Lopes Cabral, Guinea-Bissau; Samuel Rudolph Insanally, Guyana; Leo Merares, Haiti; Ivan Romero-Martinez, Honduras; Gabor Brodi, Hungary; Hjalmar W. Hannesson, Iceland; Dan Gillerman, Israel	8·00	8·00
5309- 5316	$1.40×8 Colin Beck, Solomon Islands; Dumisani S. Kumalo, South Africa; Juan Antonio Yanez-Barnuevo, Spain; Anders Liden, Sweden; Peter Maurer, Switzerland; K. Laxanachantorn Laohaphan, Thailand; Jose Luis Guterres, Timor-Leste; Fekitamoeloa 'Utoikamanu, Tonga	8·00	8·00
5317- 5324	$1.40×8 Srgian Kerim, President, 62nd UN GA; Andrei Dapkiunas, Belarus; Jean-Marie Ehouzou, Benin; Milos Prica, Bosnia & Herzegovina; Samuel O. Outlule, Botswana; Francis K. Butagira, Uganda; Valeriy P. Kuchinsky, Ukraine; Jean Ping, President 59th UN Gen Assem	8·00	8·00

629 Corporal Bryan Budd

2007. 150th Anniv of the First Presentation of the Victoria Cross. Designs showing recipients. Multicoloured.

5325	$1.50 Type **629**	2·50	2·00
5326	$1.50 Brigadier General James Forbes-Robinson	2·50	2·00
5327	$1.50 Private Johnson Beharry	2·50	2·00
5328	$1.50 Sergeant William J. Gordon	2·50	2·00
5329	$1.50 Private Henry Tandey	2·50	2·00
5330	$1.50 Private Jorgen Christian Jensen	2·50	2·00
MS5331	100×70 mm. $6 Seaman Jack Mantel	6·50	7·00

630 Hostage Rescue Helicopter S-65/RH 53D

2007. Centenary of First Helicopter Flight. Multicoloured.

5332	$2 Type **630**	3·00	2·25
5333	$2 Autogyro ('do-it-yourself flying')	3·00	2·25
5334	$2 Multi-role military helicopter BK 117	3·00	2·25
5335	$2 Anti-ship missile helicopter AS-61	3·00	2·25
MS5336	100×70 mm. $6 AH 64 Apache tank destroyer helicopter	8·00	8·00

631 Susan Bristol (Bernard Vidal)

2007. Sheet 105×122 mm.

MS5337	**631** $6 multicoloured	4·50	5·00

632 St. George's University

2007. 30th Anniv of St. George's University, Grenada. Sheet 100×70 mm.

MS5338	**632** $6 multicoloured	5·00	5·50

633 Christ Child in Crib

2007. Christmas. Multicoloured.

5339	25c. Type **633**	35	15
5340	50c. Choir of angels	65	35
5341	75c. Praying angels	95	70
5342	$1 Flying cherub	1·25	1·40

Nos. 5339/42 all show details from painting *Nativity with the Annunciation to theShepherds* by follower of Jan Joest.

634 Rat

2007. Chinese New Year ('Year of the Rat').

5343	**634** $2 multicoloured	2·25	2·50

635 Shane Warne bowling, First Test, Bangalore, India, October 2004

2007. 'Shane Warne Collection'. Six sheets each 180×236 mm containing multicoloured designs as T **635**.

MS5344	(a) $2×8 'The Power' Shane Warne bowling; (b) $2×6 'The Mastery' Shane Warne celebrates Australia's 1999 World Cup victory; (c) $2×8 'The Artistry' Paintings of Shane Warne bowling by Phillip Howe; (d) $2×6 'The Legendary' Final Test Match, Trent Bridge, London, 2005 Ashes series; (e) $2×8 'The Revolutionary' Match scenes; (f) $2×8 'The King of Spin' Shane Warne bowling frame by frame	70·00	70·00

2007. Breast Cancer Research. Sheet 100×70 mm containing design as T **481** of Gambia. Multicoloured.

MS5345	Roman Goddess Diana reaching for arrow	5·50	6·00

Similar designs were issued by the USA (in 1998), Belize (2006) and Gambia (2007).

636 Elvis Presley

2008. Elvis Presley Commemoration. Multicoloured.

5346	$1.50 Type **636**	1·75	1·75
5347	$1.50 Wearing white jumpsuit	1·75	1·75
5348	$1.50 Wearing green	1·75	1·75
5349	$1.50 In profile, wearing leather jacket, playing guitar	1·75	1·75
5350	$1.50 Singing, with guitar and microphone	1·75	1·75
5351	$1.50 Playing guitar and singing	1·75	1·75

637 Muhammad Ali

2008. Muhammad Ali (world heavyweight boxing champion, 1964, 1974-8). Multicoloured.

5352	$2 Type **637**	1·75	1·75
5353	$2 Speaking	1·75	1·75
5354	$2 Hitting punch ball in gym	1·75	1·75
5355	$2 Boxing	1·75	1·75
5356	$2 Facing right, towel over back of head (vert)	1·75	1·75
5357	$2 Facing left, towel over back of head (vert)	1·75	1·75
5358	$2 With fist raised (vert)	1·75	1·75
5359	$2 With towel over shoulder (vert)	1·75	1·75
MS5360	Two sheets, each 100×70 mm. (a) $6 Muhammad Ali and audience (vert). (b) $6 Wearing boxing gloves and helmet (vert)	10·50	10·50

2008. 50th Death Anniv of Qi Baishi (2007). As T **475** of Gambia. Multicoloured.

5361	$1 *Magnolias and Bees*	1·00	1·00
5362	$1 *Mother Hen, Chicks and Banana Leaves*	1·00	1·00
5363	$1 *Fish, Crabs and Watergrass*	1·00	1·00
5364	$1 *Cross Returning to Wintry Trees*	1·00	1·00
MS5365	60×125 mm. $4 *Morning Glories*	3·50	3·75

638 Greece 1896 40l. Stamp for First International Olympic Games

2008. Olympic Games, Beijing. Multicoloured.

5366	$3 Type **638**	2·75	2·75
5367	$3 Poster for Olympic Games, Athens, 1896	2·75	2·75
5368	$3 Germany 1936 Summer Olympics 25pf.+15pf. double scullers stamp	2·75	2·75
5369	$3 Poster for Olympic Games, Berlin, 1936	2·75	2·75

639 Oolong Tea (*Camellia sinensis* (L.) Kuntze)

2008. Taipei 2008 International Stamp Exhibition. Flora of Taiwan. Multicoloured.

5370	$1 Type **639**	1·10	1·10
5371	$1 Pink lotus (*Nelumbo nucifera*)	1·10	1·10
5372	$1 Japanese maple (*Acer palmatum*)	1·10	1·10
5373	$1 Bitter melon (*Momordica charantia*)	1·10	1·10
5374	$1 Rice field (*Oryza sativa*)	1·10	1·10
5375	$1 Lychee (*Litchi chinensis* Sonn.)	1·10	1·10
MS5376	Shitou Forest, Taiwan (37×50 mm)	4·50	5·00

640 Aerial View of City of David and Walls of Old City of Jerusalem (image scaled to 48% of original size)

2008. Israel 2008 World Stamp Championship, Tel-Aviv. Sheet 100×110 mm. Imperf.

MS5377	**640** $6 multicoloured	7·50	7·50

641 Trevor Ariza

2008. Los Angeles Lakers—NBA Western Conference Champions. Multicoloured.

5378	$1 Type **641**	75	75
5379	$1 Jordan Farmar	75	75
5380	$1 Derek Fisher	75	75
5381	$1 Pau Gasol	75	75
5382	$1 Kobe Bryant	75	75
5383	$1 Lamar Odom	75	75
5384	$1 Vladimir Radmanovic	75	75
5385	$1 Sasha Vujacic	75	75
5386	$1 Luke Walton	75	65

642 Tortoiseshell

2008. Cats of the World. Multicoloured.

5387	$1.40 Type **642**	1·40	1·40
5388	$1.40 Korat	1·40	1·40
5389	$1.40 Turkish van	1·40	1·40
5390	$1.40 Manx	1·40	1·40
MS5391	100×70 mm. $6 British blue shorthair	5·00	5·50

643 Pope Benedict XVI

2008. First Visit of Pope Benedict XVI to the United States. Sheet 176×127 mm containing T **643** and similar vert designs.

MS5392	multicoloured	9·50	9·50

The four stamps within **MS**5392 are as Type **643** but all have slightly different backgrounds of the church ceiling showing through the stamp borders.

644 Elvis Presley

2008. Elvis Presley Commemoration. Multicoloured.

5393	$2 Type **644**	1·75	1·75
5394	$2 Wearing red shirt and dark grey tie	1·75	1·75
5395	$2 With guitar held over shoulder	1·75	1·75
5396	$2 In close-up	1·75	1·75

647 Karol Wojtyla as a Boy

2008. Pope John Paul II Commemoration. Sheet 133×167 containing T **647** and similar vert designs. Multicoloured.

MS5399 Type **647**; As Cardinal (wearing red skullcap); Wearing biretta (black and blue photo); At his Coronation; With hands raised, giving blessing; Wearing white skullcap   13·00   13·00

648 *Panaeolus papilionaceus*

2009. Mushrooms of the World. Multicoloured.

5400	25c. Type **648**	50	15
5401	50c. *Panaeolus cyanescens*	80	30
5402	75c. *Panaeolus sphinctrinus*	1·25	65
5403	90c. *Panaeolus fimicola*	1·40	75
5404	$1 *Copelandia cyanescens*	1·60	95
5405	$4 *Psilocybe cubensis*	4·50	5·50

MS5406 140×100 mm. $2.50×4 *Panaleus subbalteatus*; *Alboleptonia earlei*; *Porphyrellus portoricensis*; *Psilocybe caerulescens*   13·00   13·00

649 Pres. Barack Obama

2009. Inauguration of President Barack Obama. Sheet 133×94 mm. Multicoloured.

MS5407 Type **649**×4 multicoloured   8·50   9·50

650 International Space Station

2009. 50 Years of Space Exploration. T **650** and similar multicoloured designs. Multicoloured.

MS5408 150×100 mm. $2×6 Type **650**; NASA's new concept for a lunar truck; The Milky Way over Ontario; M16 and the Eagle Nebula; Expedition 16; Dextre robot at work on the Space Station   13·00   13·00

MS5409 150×100 mm. $2×6 304 angstrom wavelength of extreme UV light; Buzz Aldrin on the Moon; Overhead crane lifting Space Shuttle *Atlantis* inside Kennedy's Vehicle Assembly Building; Inside Victoria Crater for extended exploration; Saturn's rings (Cassini Mission); Installation of main engines in *Atlantis*, Kennedy Space Centre   13·00   13·00

MS5410 130×100 mm. $2.50×4 Kennedy Space Centre reveals space shuttle *Atlantis*; ISS from *Discovery*; Saturn Aurora; Kibo Japanese Pressurized Module and Kibo Japanese logistics module (all vert)   12·00   12·00

MS5411 130×100 mm. $2.50×4 Canadarm 2 or space station robotic arm; Shuttle Atlantis-Hubble Space Telescope service mission; Cat's Eye Nebula; NASA's Orion crew capsule (all vert)   12·00   12·00

651 White Crowned Pigeon (*Patagioenas*)

2009. Birds of the Caribbean. Multicoloured.

5412	$1 Type **651**	1·50	70
5413	$2 Blue winged warbler (*Vermivora pinus*)	2·50	1·75
5414	$4 Bananaquit (*Coereba flaveola*)	4·25	4·50
5415	$5 Monk parakeet (*Myiopsitta monachus*)	4·75	5·00

MS5416 109×100 mm. $3×3 Yellow crowned amazon (*Amazona ochrocephala*); Yellow bellied sap sucker (*Sphyrapicus varius*); Jamaican mango (*Anthracothorax mango*)   9·00   9·50

MS5417 171×121 mm. $3×3 Ringed kingfisher (*Megaceryle torquata*); Tree swallow (*Tachycineta bicolor*); Black and white warbler (*Mniotilta varia.tif*)   9·00   9·50

The stamps and margins of No. MS5417 form a composite design showing birds on branches.

652 Ox

2009. Chinese New Year. Year of the Ox. Sheet 190×90 mm.

MS5418 $2.50 Type **652**×4 multicoloured   7·00   7·50

653 Marilyn Monroe

2009. Marilyn Monroe Commemoration. Sheet 100×140 mm. Multicoloured.

MS5419 Type **653**; Looking over shoulder (facing left); Facing right; Looking over shoulder (facing camera)   7·00   7·50

654 Anthony C. George flag designer) and Grenada National Flag

2009. 35th Anniv of Independence. Multicoloured.

5420	**654** 10c. multicoloured	25	20
5421	**654** 25c. multicoloured	50	15
5422	**654** 50c. multicoloured	75	30
5423	**654** 75c. multicoloured	1·10	1·10

MS5424 100×70 mm. $6 Anthony C. George and Grenada flag flying from flagstaff (30×40 mm)   5·50   6·00

655 Peony Design on Vase

2009. China 2009 World Stamp Exhibition, Luoyang (1st issue). Peonies. Multicoloured.

5425	75c. Type **655**	1·00	1·00

MS5426 70×100 mm. $5 Pink peony (43×43 mm)   3·75   4·25

656 Pole Vault

2009. China 2009 World Stamp Exhibition (2nd issue). Sports of the Summer Games. Sheet 90×130 mm containing T **656** and similar horiz designs. Multicoloured.

MS5427 Type **656**; Hurdles; Relay; High jump   4·50   4·75

657 Orion Upper Stages and Werner von Braun

2009. 40th Anniv of the First Moon Landing. Sheet 150×100 mm containing T **657** and similar horiz designs. Multicoloured.

MS5428 Type **657**; Apollo 11 crew; Lunar orbiter; Ranger 7; Pres. John F. Kennedy, lunar module and Moon; Orion LM on Moon   12·00   12·00

658 Haydn's Birthplace, Rohrau, Austria

2009. Birth Bicentenary of Franz Joseph Haydn (composer). Sheet 164×94 mm containing T **658** and similar vert designs. Multicoloured.

MS5429 Type **658**; Johann Peter Salomon (impresario to Haydn); Austro-Hungarian Haydn Orchestra; Wolfgang Amadeus Mozart; Haydn Haus (home 1766–78), Eisenstadt, Austria; Young Ludwig van Beethoven (Haydn's student)   16·00   16·00

659 Elvis Presley

2009. 40th Anniv of Song Suspicious Minds by Elvis Presley. Sheet 160×130 mm containing T **659** and similar vert designs. Multicoloured.

MS5430 Type **659**; Full length, facing left; Full length, facing right with hand raised; Half length with guitar, facing right   7·50   8·00

660 Golden Retriever Puppy

2009. 125th Anniv of the American Kennel Club. Two sheets, each 100×120 mm containing T **660** and similar horiz designs. Multicoloured. Litho.

MS5431 Type **660**; Golden retriever (pumpkin and squashes to right); Golden retriever sitting on sofa; Two golden retriever puppies in basket   12·00   12·00

MS5432 Beagle sitting on worktop; Head of beagle; Beagle (standing); Beagle (in front of autumn leaves and logpile)   12·00   12·00

661 Pope Benedict XVI and Bethlehem

2009. Visit of Pope Benedict XVI to Bethlehem. Sheet 150×100 mm containing vert designs showing portrait of Pope Benedict XVI as in Type **661** and different views of Bethlehem. Multicoloured.

MS5433 $1.50 Type **661**; $2 As Type **661**; $2.50 As Type **661**; $3 As Type **661**   11·00   11·00

662 Charles Darwin and Finch

2009. Birth Bicentenary of Charles Darwin (evolutionary theorist). Sheet 145×160 mm containing vert designs showing portrait as T **662** and fauna.

MS5434 $2.50 x 4 Type **662**; Charles Darwin and fox; Charles Darwin and dissected tortoise; Charles Darwin and tortoise   8·50   9·00

2009. Birth Bicentenary of Abraham Lincoln (US President 1861-5). Sheet 142x182 mm containing T **663** and similar vert designs. Multicoloured.

MS5435 $3.50x3 Type **663**; Pre. Lincoln with Maj. John A. McClernand; Pres. Lincoln with Gen George B. McClellan   8·00   8·50

664 Chengdu J-5 Airplane

2009. Centenary of Chinese Aviation and Aeropex 2009, Beijing. Showing aircrafts. Multicoloured.

MS5436 145×95 mm. $2×4 Type **664**; J-6; J-7G; J-7   8·50   9·00

MS5437 120×79 mm. $6 Chengdu FC-1 Xiaolong (50×38 mm)   5·50   6·00

664a Rat

2010. Chinese Lunar Calendar. Multicoloured.

MS5437a 60c.×12 Type **664a**; Ox; Tiger; Rabbit; Dragon; Snake; Horse; Ram; Monkey; Cock; Dog; Pig   7·25   8·00

664b Head of Tiger (left)

2010. Chinese New Year. Year of the Tiger. Multicoloured.

MS5437b $5 Type **664b**; $5 Head of tiger (right)   7·00   7·50

The stamps and margins of MS5437b form a composite design showing a tiger's head.

665 Elvis Presley as Young Boy

2010. 75th Birth Anniv of Elvis Presley. Illustrations by Joe Petruccio. Sheet 180×120 mm containing T **665** and similar vert designs. Multicoloured.

MS5438 Type **665**; Singing, with mouth wide open; Singing, looking down; Smiling   8·00   8·50

666 Fish wearing Santa Hats

2010. Christmas. Multicoloured.

5439	$1 Type **666**	1·10	80
5440	$2 Christmas tree branches decorated with lights and nuts and fruit	2·00	1·40
5441	$4 Christmas bells in window	3·75	4·25
5442	$5 Outline map of Grenada, baubles and stars	4·25	4·50

667 *Brassia caudata*

2010. Orchids of the Caribbean. Multicoloured.

5443	$1.20 Type **667**	2·00	1·75
5444	$1.80 *Epidendrum imatophyllum*	2·50	2·25
5445	$3 *Ionopsis utriculoides*	4·75	4·75
5446	$5 *Habenaria bractescens*	6·50	7·50

MS5447 130×100 mm. $2.75×4 *Vanilla pompona*; *Caularthron bicornutum*; *Epidendrum nocturnum*; *Aspasia variegata*   12·00   12·00

MS5448 100×70 mm. $3×2 *Epidendrum hartii*; *Brassavola cucullata*   7·50   7·50

2010. Ferrari Cars. As Type **528** of Gambia. Multicoloured.

5449	$1.25 Engine of F355 Berlinetta, 1994	1·40	1·40
5450	$1.25 F355 Berlinetta, 1994	1·40	1·40
5451	$1.25 Steering wheel of F310 B, 1997	1·40	1·40
5452	$1.25 F 310 B, 1997	1·40	1·40
5453	$1.25 Engine of 355 F1 Berlinetta, 1997	1·40	1·40
5454	$1.25 355 F1 Berlinetta, 1997	1·40	1·40
5455	$1.25 Engine of F1-89, 1989	1·40	1·40
5456	$1.25 F1-89, 1989	1·40	1·40

668 Diana, Princess of Wales

2010. Diana, Princess of Wales Commemoration. Multicoloured.

MS5457 $2.75×4 Type **668**; Wearing black jacket with striped lapels and carrying bouquet×2; As Type **668** but dark shadow at bottom left 9·50 10·00

MS5458 $2.75×4 Wearing black and white check jacket and black hat×2; Wearing blue hat×2 9·50 10·00

669 Pres. John F. Kennedy

2010. 50th Anniv of Election of Pres. John F. Kennedy. Multicoloured..

MS5459 $2.75×4 Type **669**; Pres. Kennedy walking (colonnade at right); Pres. Kennedy (head and shoulders, colour photo); In front of microphone 9·00 9·50

670 Apache Woven Basket

2010. Native American Art. Multicoloured.

MS5460 118×107 mm. $2×6 Type **670**; Sioux beaded moccasins; Iroquois cornhusk mask; Tlingit totem pole; Inuit hunter doll; Hopi pottery 9·00 10·00

MS5461 70×100 mm. $6 Navajo woven rug 4·25 4·75

671 Guides with Camera

2010. Centenary of Girlguiding. Multicoloured.

MS5462 150×100 mm. $2.75×4 Type **671**; Two guides with cameras; Two guides making film; Four guides with camera 9·00 9·50

MS5463 70×100 mm. $6 Guide with camera (vert) 4·50 5·00

672 South Africa v. Mexico

2010. World Cup Football Championship, South Africa. Multicoloured.

MS5464 130×156 mm. $1.50×6 First Round Group A: Type **672**; Uruguay v. France; Uruguay v. South Africa; France v. Mexico; Mexico v. Uruguay; France v. South Africa 9·00 9·00

MS5465 130×156 mm. $1.50×6 First Round Group B: Korea REP v. Greece; Argentina v. Nigeria; Argentina v. Nigeria; Nigeria v. Korea REP; Greece v. Argentina 9·00 9·00

MS5465 130×156 mm. $1.50×6 First Round Group C: England v. United States; Algeria v. Slovenia; United States v. Slovenia; England v. Algeria; Slovenia v. England; Algeria v. United States 9·00 9·00

MS5467 130×156 mm. $1.50×6 First Round Group D: Serbia v. Ghana; Germany v. Australia; Germany v. Serbia; Ghana v. Australia; Ghana v. Germany; Australia v. Serbia 9·00 9·00

MS5468 86×91 mm. $3.50×2 Soccer City Stadium, Johannesburg; Moses Mabhida Stadium, Durban 7·00 7·00

MS5469 86×91 mm. $3.50×2 Nelson Mandela Bay Stadium, Port Elizabeth; Cape Town Stadium 7·00 7·00

673 Carl Edwards

2010. NASCAR (US National Association for Stock Car Auto Racing) Carl Edwards. Multicoloured.

MS5470 $2.75×4 Type **673**; On podium with arms raised in triumph; Wearing helmet; Wearing cap 8·00 9·00

674 Frédéric Chopin (drawing by Franz Xaver Winterhalter)

2010. Birth Bicentenary of Frédéric Chopin (composer and pianist). Multicoloured.

MS5471 144×93 mm. $2.50×4 Type **674**; George Sand; Frédéric Chopin (seated); Chopin's birthplace 11·00 11·00

MS5472 100×70 mm. $6 Frédéric Chopin (seated) and music 7·00 7·00

675 Louis Appia and First Geneva Convention

2010. Death Centenary of Henri Dunant (founder of Red Cross). Multicoloured.

MS5473 150×100 mm. $2.50×4 Type **675**; Gustave Moynier; Théodore Maunoir; Henri Dufour 9·50 9·50

MS5474 70×100 mm. $6 First Geneva Convention signed 22 August 1894 5·50 6·00

676 Abraham Lincoln

2010. Birth Bicentenary (2009) of Abraham Lincoln (US President 18615). Multicoloured.

5475	$2 Type **676**	1·50	1·50
5476	$2 Standing, three-quarter length portrait (sepia photo)	1·50	1·50
5477	$2 With son (sepia photo)	1·50	1·50
5478	$2 Seated (black/white photo)	1·50	1·50
5479	$2 Head and shoulders portrait (black/white photo)	1·50	1·50
5480	$2 Half length portrait (black/white photo)	1·50	1·50

677 Scout saluting

2010. Centenary of Boy Scouts of America. Multicoloured.

MS5481 164×125 mm. $2.75×4 Type **677**×2; Scout carrying young child×2 9·00 9·00

MS5482 164×125 mm. $2.75×4 Boy scout helping disabled woman with shopping×2; Boy scout singing×2 9·00 9·00

678 Pres. Obama greeting Mexican President Calderón

2010. President Barack Obama. Multicoloured.

MS5483 130×135 mm. $2.75×4 Type **678**; Pres. Felipe Calderón; Pres. Barack Obama; Presidents Obama and Calderón 9·00 9·00

MS5484 120×130 mm. Nuclear Security Summit, Washington: $2.75×4 Pres. Barack Obama speaking; Pres. Obama (speaking) and Vice President Joseph Biden; Pres. Obama; Pres. Obama and speaking to woman 9·00 9·00

679 Pope John Paul II

2011. 90th Birth Anniv of Pope John Paul II. Multicoloured.

MS5485 $2.75×4 Type **679**×3; Pope John Paull II standing, holding staff 10·00 10·00

680 Poster for *Roustabout*, 1964

2010. Elvis Presley in Film *Roustabout*. Multicoloured.

MS5486 125×90 mm. $6 Type **680** 4·75 5·00

MS5487 90×125 mm. $6 As Charlie Rogers in *Roustabout* (on ladder) 4·75 5·00

MS5488 90×125 mm. $6 Elvis Presley singing 4·75 5·00

MS5489 125×90 mm. $6 Elvis Presley wearing red jacket 4·75 5·00

681 St. George's Lagoon

2010. 300th Anniv of St. George's, Grenada. Multicoloured.

5490	25c. Type **681**	45	45
5491	50c. Church Street, St. George's (vert)	70	70
5492	$1 Market Day, St. George's	1·25	1·25

682 Memorial to Walter Clement Noel (first recorded case)

2010. Sickle Cell Association of Grenada

MS5493 74×120 mm. **682** 25c., 50c., $1, $2 multicoloured 3·50 3·50

MS5494 75×80 mm. **682** $6 multicoloured 4·75 5·00

683 Three Wise Men

2010. Christmas. Multicoloured.

5495	25c. Type **683**	40	25
5496	50c. *Adoration of the Shepherds* (detail) (Guido Reni)	70	45
5497	$1 *Anbetung der Hirten* (detail) (Ribera)	1·25	90
5498	$2 The Star of Bethlehem	1·75	2·25

MS5499 70×100 mm. $6 *Geburt Christi* (Birth of Christ) (Max Bentele) (50×38 mm) 4·75 5·00

684 Rock Beauty (*Holacanthus tricolor*)

2011. Fish. Multicoloured.

5500	25c. Type **684**	40	25
5501	$1.25 Graysby (*Cephalopholis oruentatus*)	1·40	1·50
5502	$1.50 Beaugregory damselfish (*Stegastes leucostictus*)	1·50	1·60
5503	$2 French angelfish (juvenile) (*Pomacanthus paru*)	1·40	1·40

MS5504 100×70 mm. $100 Longsnout butterflyfish (*Chaetodon aculeatus*) (41×30 mm) 80·00 80·00

Nos. 5505/6 are left for possible additions to these definitive stamps.

685 Aerial View, Forbidden City

2011. World Expo 2010 Exhibition, Beijing, China. The Forbidden City, Beijing. Multicoloured.

MS5507 120×141 mm. $2×4 Type **685**; Ancient sundial; Temple roof; Canal 6·00 6·50

MS5508 71×101 mm. $5 Golden Lion (38×51 mm) 4·25 4·50

686 Rabbit

2011. Chinese New Year. Year of the Rabbit. Sheet 131×82 mm. Multicoloured.

MS5509 $2.50 Type **686**×2 4·25 4·50

687 Prince William and Miss Catherine Middleton

2011. Royal Engagement. Multicoloured.

MS5510 $2.50 Type **687**×4 9·00 9·00

MS5511 $2.50 Prince William×2; $2.50 Miss Catherine Middleton×2 9·00 9·00

688 Rat

2011. Chinese Lunar Calendar. Birth Cycles of the Lunar Calendar. Multicoloured.
MS5512 $1×12 Type **688**; Ox; Tiger; Snake; Dragon; Rabbit; Horse; Ram; Monkey; Pig; Dog; Rooster   11·00   12·00

689 Elvis Presley

2011. Elvis Presley Commemoration. Multicoloured.
MS5513 $2.75×4 Type **689**; Elvis Presley wearing black leather jacket; Sitting at dressing room table; Wearing check jacket, head straight   8·50   8·50

MS5514 $2.75×4 Elvis Presley wearing white catsuit; Head and shoulders, wearing black, holding microphone; With guitar, singing; Playing guitar, wearing black   8·50   8·50

690 Princess Diana

2011. 50th Birth Anniv of Princess Diana. Multicoloured.
MS5515 $2.75×4 Type **690**; Princess Diana wearing white headscarf; Wearing red and black check jacket; Wearing dark blue   8·50   8·50

MS5516 $2.75×4 Princess Diana wearing black; Wearing pink and white check jacket and hat; Wearing grey and white striped jacket and white tie-neck blouse; Wearing brown hat and white tie-neck blouse   8·50   8·50

691 Yuri Gagarin
(head of statue)

2011. 50th Anniv of the First Man in Space. Multicoloured.
MS5517 150×100 mm. $2.75×4 Type **691**; Medal showing cosmonaut Gagarin made with spaceship aluminium; Vostok rocket; Gordon Cooper (astronaut) and Mercury Project emblem   8·50   8·50

MS5518 150×100 mm. $2.75×4 Cosmic Conquerors monument, Moscow; Walter Schirra (astronaut) and spacecraft; Yuri Gagarin; Vostok spaceship   8·50   8·50

MS5519 101×70 mm. $6 Vostok spaceship orbiting Earth (horiz)   4·75   4·75
MS5520 101×70 mm. $6 Yuri Gagarin   4·75   4·75

692 Queen Elizabeth II and Pope Benedict XVI

2011. Pope Benedict XVI meets Queen Elizabeth II, Holyroodhouse, Edinburgh, 16 September 2010. Multicoloured.
MS5521 175×130 mm. $3×4 Type **692**; Pope Benedict XVI and Queen Elizabeth II exchanging gifts; Pope Benedict XVI and Queen Elizabeth II meeting schoolchildren; Pope Benedict XVI (pointing) and Queen Elizabeth II   12·00   12·00

MS5522 145×105 mm. $3.50 Queen Elizabeth II (vert); $3.50 Pope Benedict XVI (vert)   8·50   8·50

693 Galileo Galilei
(1564-1642)

2011. Renowned Physicists and the Large Hadron Collider. Multicoloured.
MS5523 140×101 mm. $2.75×4 Type **693**; Sir Isaac Newton (1643-1727); The Large Hadron Collider (1983-); Albert Einstein (1879-1955)   11·00   11·00

MS5524 170×61 mm. $6 The Large Hadron Collider (51×38 mm)   5·50   6·00

694 Qingdao Cross-Sea Bridge

2011. Bridges and Tunnels of the World. Multicoloured.
MS5525 $6 Type **694**   4·75   5·00

MS5526 $6 Qingdao Jiaozhouwan Undersea Tunnel   4·75   5·00

695 Scarlet Macaw
(Ara macao)

2011. Parrots of the Caribbean. Multicoloured.
MS5527 230×85 mm. $2×6 Type **695**; Hyacinth macaw (Anodorhynchus hyacinthinus); Slender-billed parakeet (Enicognathus leptorhynchus); Blue-and-yellow macaw (Ara ararauna); Olive-throated parakeet (Aratinga nana); Burrowing parrot (Cyanoliseus patagonus)   7·00   7·00

MS5528 110×61 mm. $6 Red-and-green macaw (Ara chloropterus)   7·00   7·00

696 Mother Teresa

2011. Mother Teresa Commemoration. Multicoloured.
MS5529 $2.50 Type **696**×2; $2.50 Mother Teresa and Pope John Paul II; $2.50 Mother Teresa and Princess Diana   10·00   10·00

MS5530 $2.50 Mother Teresa and Prince Charles; $2.50 Mother Teresa praying ×2; $2.50 Mother Teresa and Ted Kennedy   10·00   10·00

697 Pres. Abraham Lincoln

2011. Abraham Lincoln (US President 1861-5) Commemoration.
MS5531 140×100 mm. $2.75×4 Type **697**; As Type **697** (deep blue background); As Type **697** (brownish grey background); As Type **697** (reddish-brown background)   8·50   9·00

MS5532 101×140 mm. $2.75×4 Abraham Lincoln (facing towards left): Deep grey background; Lake-brown background; Olive-brown background; Deep lilac background (all horiz)   8·50   9·00

698 William II
(1087-1100)

2011. Kings and Queens of England. Multicoloured.

5533	$2 Type **698**	1·75	1·75
5534	$2 Richard I (1189-99)	1·75	1·75
5535	$2 Edward III (1327-77)	1·75	1·75
5536	$2 Edward IV (1471-83)	1·75	1·75
5537	$2 Henry VIII (1491-1547)	1·75	1·75
5538	$2 Charles I (1625-49)	1·75	1·75
5539	$2 George I (1714-27)	1·75	1·75
5540	$2 George V (1910-36)	1·75	1·75

699 Chocolate Tray-bake

2011. Grenadian Export. Chocolate. Multicoloured.
MS5541 $2.25×9 As Type **699** but showing different patterns in chocolate topping and top left and bottom left stamps showing edge of baking tray   15·00   15·00

MS5542 $2.25×9 showing individual ovoid-shaped chocolate, stamps at left of sheet have darker grey background shading to a lighter pale grey background in stamps at right   15·00   15·00
Stamps from Nos. MS5541/2 are impregnated with a cocoa scent.

700 Tribute in Light

2011. Tenth Anniv of Attack on World Trade Center, New York. Multicoloured.
MS5543 161×110 mm. $2.75×4 Type **700**; Pentagon Memorial, Washington DC; September 11 Memorial, New York; September 11 Memorial, New Jersey   8·50   9·00

MS5544 110×75 mm. $6 New York skyline and US flag (vert)   4·50   4·75

701 Dragon

2011. Chinese New Year. Year of the Dragon. Sheet 70×70 mm. Multicoloured.
MS5545 **701** $8 multicoloured   6·50   7·00

702 Rat

2011. Lunar New Year. Lunar Calendar. Multicoloured.
MS5546 65c.×12 Type **702**; Ox; Tiger; Rabbit; Dragon; Snake; Horse; Sheep; Monkey; Rooster; Dog; Boar   6·00   6·50

703 Pope Benedict XVI

2011. Pope Benedict XVI visits Germany. Multicoloured.
MS5547 $2.75×4 Type **703**; Red City Hall, Berlin; Madonna in the Rose Bower (Stefan Lochner), 1448; Pope Benedict XVI and St. Mary's Cathedral, Erfurt   11·00   11·00

704 Mao Tse-Tung

2011. China 2011 27th Asian International Stamp Exhibition, Wuxi, China. Mao Tse-Tung. Multicoloured.
MS5549 190×90 mm. $3 Type **704**×3   7·00   7·50

MS5550 101×70 mm. $6 Mao Tse-Tung (different)   4·25   4·50

705 Calliope Hummingbird
(Stellula calliope)

2011. Hummingbirds of the Caribbean. Multicoloured.
MS5551 90×191 mm. $2×6 Type **705**; Anna's hummingbird (Calypte anna); Black-chinned hummingbird (Archilochus alexandri); Ruby-throated hummingbird (Archilochus colubris); Costa's hummingbird (Calypte costae); Broad-billed hummingbird (Cynanthus latirostris)   11·00   11·00

MS5552 91×98 mm. $6 Rufous hummingbird (Selasphorus rufus) (vert)   6·00   6·00

706 Pres. John F. Kennedy

2011. 50th Anniv of Inauguration of President John F. Kennedy. Multicoloured.
MS5553 $3×3 Type **706**; Campaigners with 'Kennedy for President' placards; Pres. Kennedy (half-length portrait)   7·00   7·50

MS5554 $3×3 Pres. Kennedy seated; Standing behind microphone; At desk   7·00   7·50

707 Pres. Barack Obama

2011. 50th Birthday of President Barack Obama. Multicoloured.
MS5555 120×120 mm. $3.50×3 Type **707**; Pres. Obama (deep violet background); Pres. Obama (table and woodcarving in background)   7·50   8·00

MS5556 80×81 mm. $6 Pres. Barack Obama (51×38 mm)   4·50   4·75

708 Queen Elizabeth II and Prince Philip, c. 1955

2012. Diamond Jubilee. Multicoloured.
MS5557 180×120 mm. $3.50×4 Type **708**; Princess Elizabeth on wedding day, 1947; Princess Elizabeth with baby Prince Charles, 1948; Queen Elizabeth II with young Prince Charles, c. 1953   13·00   13·00

MS5558 69×100 mm. $9 Queen Elizabeth II with Prince Charles and Princess Anne, c. 1953 (vert)   9·00   9·00

709 Family waiting for Survivors

2012. Centenary of the Sinking of the *Titanic*. Multicoloured.

MS5559 170×150 mm. $3.50×4 Type **709**; Survivors arriving at the docks; Captain Edward J. Smith; RMS *Titanic* sinking ... 13·00 13·00

MS5560 100×100 mm. $9 RMS *Titanic* ... 9·00 9·00

710 Mother Teresa

2012. 15th Death Anniv of Mother Teresa. Multicoloured.

MS5561 150×101 mm. $4×3 Type **710**; Mother Teresa (facing left); Mother Teresa (facing right) ... 11·00 11·00

MS5562 100×70 mm. $4 Mother Teresa in vehicle, talking to woman ... 4·00 4·00

711 Poster for *Live a Little Love a Little*

2012. Elvis Presley in *Live a Little Love a Little*. Multicoloured.

MS5563 125×90 mm. $9 Type **711** ... 7·00 7·00

MS5564 125×90 mm. $9 Elvis Presley holding fan's hand ... 7·00 7·00

MS5565 90×126 mm. $9 As Greg Nolan with dog in *Live a Little Love a Little* (horiz) ... 7·00 7·00

MS5566 91×125 mm. $9 Elvis Presley as Greg Nolan with camera in *Live a Little Love a Little* ... 7·00 7·00

712 Labrador Retriever

2012. Dogs of the World. Multicoloured.

MS5567 150×100 mm. $3.50×3 Type **712**; Bernese mountain dog; Bordeaux mastiff ... 9·00 9·00

MS5568 150×100 mm. $3.50×4 Great Dane; Labrador retriever (black); Chihuahua; Miniature pinscher (all 25×25 mm) ... 12·00 12·00

MS5569 70×100 mm. $9 Shih Tzu (40×40 mm) ... 8·50 8·50

MS5570 70×100 mm. $9 American cocker spaniel (40×40 mm) ... 8·50 8·50

No. MS5571, Type **713** are left for Olympic Games, London issued 27 July 2012, not yet received.

714 Horse

2012. Chinese Zodiac Animals. Multicoloured.

5572 55c. Type **714** ... 70 70
5573 55c. Ram ... 50 50

715 Pope Benedict XVI

2012. Pope Benedict XVI visits Cuba, March 26-28 2012. Multicoloured.

MS5574 151×100 mm. $3.50×4 Type **715**; Pope Benedict XVI meets Fidel Castro; Pope Benedict XVI meets Raul Castro; Pope Benedict XVI gives mass in Santiago ... 10·00 10·00

MS5575 100×70 mm. $9 Pope Benedict XVI gives mass in Havana ... 6·50 6·50

716 Annunciation

2013. Christmas. Paintings by Fra Angelico. Multicoloured.

5576 $1 Type **716** ... 80 80
5577 $1 Archangel Gabriel Annunciate ... 80 80
5578 $2 Virgin Mary Annunciate ... 1·60 1·60
5579 $2 *The Virgin of the Annunciation* ... 1·60 1·60
5580 $5 Virgin and Child ... 4·00 4·50
5581 $5 Adoration of the Magi ... 4·00 4·50

717 Amelia Earhart at First Flying Lesson with Neta Snook, 1921

2013. 75th Anniv (2012) of Disappearance of Amelia Earhart (aviator). Multicoloured.

MS5582 163×186 mm. $2.25×6 Type **717**; Flies as passenger across the Atlantic, 1928; Amelia Earhart sets women's flight speed record of 181 mph, 1930; Amelia Earhart awarded gold medal from Pres. Hoover for solo Atlantic flight, 1932; Amelia Earhart, first woman to fly solo across the Pacific Ocean, 1935; Amelia Earhart and navigator Fred Noonan disappear over the Pacific Ocean, 1937 ... 9·50 9·50

MS5583 100×70 mm. $9 Amelia Earhart and plane ('Flying may not be all plain sailing, but the fun of it is worth the price.') ... 6·50 6·50

718 Adam (*The Creation of Adam*)

2013. 500th Anniv of the Completion of the Sistine Chapel Ceiling by Michelangelo. Multicoloured.

MS5584 129×110 mm. $3.25×4 Type **718**; God (*The Creation of Adam*); *Deluge; The Downfall of Adam and Eve and their Expulsion from the Garden of Eden* ... 9·25 9·25

MS5585 70×110 mm. $8 *The Sacrifice of Noah* (vert) ... 5·75 5·75

719 Princess Diana

2013. 15th Death Anniv of Princess Diana. Multicoloured.

MS5586 $3.50×4 Type **719**; Princess Diana wearing hat with veil; Wearing anorak, looking upwards; Wearing striped dress, pearl necklace and white hat ... 10·00 10·00

MS5587 $3.50×4 Princess Diana wearing bright blue coat and hat; Wearing white hat with red rim and band; Wearing black hooded anorak; Wearing red jacket with brass buttons ... 10·00 10·00

720 Spotted Brazilian Top Shell (*Calliostoma adspersum*)

2013. Seashells of the Caribbean. Multicoloured.

MS5588 150×100 mm. $3.50×4 Type **720**; Accuminate Phos (*Nassaria acuminata*); Florida Fighting Conch (*Strombus alatus*); Jasper Cone (*Conus jaspideus*) ... 7·50 7·50

MS5589 150×100 mm. $3.50×3 Short Abbreviate Coral Shell (*Coralliophila abbreviata*); Winged Surfclam (*Mactrellona alata*); Brown-line Niso (*Niso aeglees*) (60×40 mm) ... 7·50 7·50

MS5590 100×70 mm. $4.50 Pointed Nutclam (*Nuculana acuta*); $4.50 White Pitar (*Pitar albidus*) (both 30×50 mm) ... 6·50 6·50

MS5591 100×70 mm. $9 Boring Turret Snail (*Turritella acropora*) (80×30 mm) ... 6·50 6·50

721 *Heliconius mimicry*

2013. Butterflies of the Caribbean. Multicoloured.

MS5592 150×100 mm. $3.50×4 Type **721**; *Junonia evarete; Heliconius erato petiveranus; Agraulis vanillae* ... 10·00 10·00

MS5593 70×101 mm. $9 *Anartia jatrophae* (38×50 mm) ... 6·50 6·50

722 Elvis Presley

2013. Elvis Presley Classic Hits. Multicoloured.

MS5594 $9 Type **722** (*Love Me*, 1956) ... 6·50 6·50

MS5595 $9 Elvis Presley playing guitar (purple frame) (*Long Legged Girl*, 1967) ... 6·50 6·50

MS5596 $9 Elvis Presley (black frame) (*Indescribably Blue*, 1967) ... 6·50 6·50

MS5597 $9 Elvis Presley holding microphone, singing (red frame) (*Hard Headed Woman*, 1958) ... 6·50 6·50

MS5598 $9 Elvis Presley (red frame) (*I Love You*, 1956) ... 6·50 6·50

OFFICIAL STAMPS

1982. Optd **P.R.G.** (a) Nos. 1085/97 and 1099.

O1	5c. West Indiaman barque, c. 1840	30	40
O2	6c. R.M.S.P. "Orinoco", c. 1851	30	40
O3	10c. Working schooner	30	30
O4	12c. Trimaran at Grand Anse anchorage	30	30
O5	15c. Spice Island cruising yacht "Petite Amie"	30	30
O6	20c. Fishing pirogue	35	30
O7	25c. Harbour police launch	40	30
O8	30c. Grand Anse speedboat	40	30
O9	40c. M.V. "Seimstrand"	50	30
O10	50c. Three-masted schooner "Ariadne"	60	40
O11	90c. M.V. "Geestide"	90	1·00
O12	$1 M.V "Cunard Countess"	90	1·00
O13	$3 Rum-runner	2·25	4·25
O14	$10 Coast-guard patrol boat	6·00	12·00

(b) Nos. 1130/2 and 1134/5.

O15	30c. Prince Charles and Lady Diana Spencer	1·50	2·25
O16	40c. Holyrood House	2·25	2·75
O17	50c. Prince Charles and Lady Diana Spencer	1·25	2·00
O18	$2 Holyrood House	2·25	3·50
O19	$4 Type **268**	5·00	8·00

POSTAGE DUE STAMPS

D1

1892

D8	**D1**	1d. black	4·75	7·50
D9	**D1**	2d. black	12·00	1·75
D10	**D1**	3d. black	17·00	6·00

1892. Inscr SURCHARGE POSTAGE and value.

D4	**13**	1d. on 6d. mauve	£130	1·25
D5	**13**	1d. on 6d. brown	£1800	3·25
D6	**13**	2d. on 6d. mauve	£200	2·50
D7	**13**	2d. on 8d. brown	£3000	13·00

1921. As Type **D1** but inscr "POSTAGE DUE" instead of "SURCHARGE POSTAGE".

D11	**D1**	1d. black	3·00	1·00
D12	**D1**	1½d. black	12·00	28·00
D13	**D1**	2d. black	3·25	1·75
D14	**D1**	3d. black	2·25	4·50

1952. As last, but currency changed.

D15	3c. black	30	12·00
D16	4c. black	30	20·00
D17	6c. black	45	12·00
D18	8c. black	75	17·00

Pt. 1

GRENADINES OF GRENADA (CARRIACOU AND PETITE MARTINIQUE)

The southern part of the group, attached to Grenada. Main islands Petit Martinique and Carriacou. From 1999 stamps were inscribed "Grenada Carriacou and Petite Martinique".

100 cents = 1 dollar.

1973. Royal Wedding. Nos. 582/3 of Grenada optd **GRENADINES**.

1	**196**	25c. multicoloured	15	10
2	**196**	$2 multicoloured	45	50

1974. Stamps of Grenada optd **GRENADINES**.

4	1c. multicoloured (No. 306)	10	10
5	2c. multicoloured (No. 307)	10	10
6	3c. multicoloured (No. 308)	10	10
7	5c. multicoloured (No. 309)	15	10
8	8c. multicoloured (No. 311)	15	10
9	10c. multicoloured (No. 312)	15	10
10	12c. multicoloured (No. 313)	20	10
11	25c. multicoloured (No. 315)	15	10
12	$1 multicoloured (No. 318)	2·50	60
13	$2 multicoloured (No. 319)	3·00	1·50
14	$3 multicoloured (No. 320)	3·00	1·75
15	$5 multicoloured (No. 321)	3·75	2·25

1974. World Cup Football Championship. As Nos. 619/27 of Grenada, but inscr "GRENADA GRENADINES".

16	½c. multicoloured	10	10
17	1c. multicoloured	10	10
18	2c. multicoloured	10	10
19	10c. multicoloured	20	10
20	25c. multicoloured	25	10
21	50c. multicoloured	30	15
22	75c. multicoloured	30	20
23	$1 multicoloured	35	25
MS24	114×76 mm. $2 multicoloured	75	80

1974. Cent of U.P.U. As Nos. 628 etc of Grenada, but inscr "GRENADA GRENADINES".

25	8c. multicoloured	10	10
26	25c. multicoloured	15	10
27	35c. multicoloured	15	10
28	$1 multicoloured	70	40
MS29	172×109 mm. $1 as 15c. and $2 as $1	1·00	1·00

1974. Birth Cent of Sir Winston Churchill. As Nos. 637/9 of Grenada, but inscr "GRENADA GRENADINES".

30	35c. multicoloured	15	10
31	$2 multicoloured	40	45
MS32	129×96 mm. 75c. as 35c. and $1 as $2	35	80

1974. Christmas. As Nos. 640/8 of Grenada, but inscr "GRENADA GRENADINES" and background colours changed.

33	**204**	½c. multicoloured	10	10
34	-	1c. multicoloured	10	10
35	-	2c. multicoloured	10	10
36	-	3c. multicoloured	10	10
37	-	10c. multicoloured	10	10
38	-	25c. multicoloured	10	10
39	-	50c. multicoloured	15	15
40	-	$1 multicoloured	30	25
MS41	117×96 mm. $2 as 1c.		45	60

1975. Big Game Fishing. As Nos. 669 etc of Grenada, but inscr "GRENADA GRENADINES" and background colours changed.

42	½c. multicoloured	10	10
43	1c. multicoloured	10	10
44	2c. multicoloured	10	10
45	10c. multicoloured	15	10
46	25c. multicoloured	20	10
47	50c. multicoloured	20	15
48	70c. multicoloured	25	20
49	$1 multicoloured	35	35
MS50	107×80 mm. $2 multicoloured	60	90

1975. Flowers. As Nos. 678 etc of Grenada, but inscr "GRENADINES".

51	½c. multicoloured	10	10
52	1c. multicoloured	10	10
53	2c. multicoloured	10	10
54	3c. multicoloured	10	10
55	10c. multicoloured	10	10
56	25c. multicoloured	10	10
57	50c. multicoloured	20	15
58	$1 multicoloured	30	20
MS59	102×82 mm. $2 multicoloured	60	70

CANCELLED REMAINDERS*. Some of the following issues have been remaindered, cancelled-to-order, at a fraction of their face value. For all practical purposes these are indistinguishable from genuine postally used copies. Our used quotations, which are indicated by an asterisk, are the same for cancelled-to-order or postally used copies.

---

3 *Christ Crowned with Thorns* (Titian)

1975. Easter. Paintings showing Crucifixion and Deposition by artists listed. Multicoloured.

60	½c. Type **3**	10	10
61	1c. Giotto	10	10
62	2c. Tintoretto	10	10
63	3c. Cranach	10	10
64	35c. Caravaggio	15	10
65	75c. Tiepolo	20	10
66	$2 Velasquez	40	15
MS67	105×90 mm. $1 Titian	60	30

4 *Dawn* (detail from Medici Tomb)

1975. 500th Anniv of Michelangelo. Multicoloured.

68	½c. Type **4**	10	10
69	1c. *Delphic Sibyl*	10	10
70	2c. *Giuliano de Medici*	10	10
71	40c. *The Creation* (detail)	15	10
72	50c. *Lorenzo de Medici*	15	10
73	75c. *Persian Sibyl*	20	10
74	$2 *Head of Christ*	30	15
MS75	118×96 mm. $1 *The Prophet Jeremiah*	75	50

1975. Butterflies. As T **213** of Grenada, but inscr "GRENADINES". Multicoloured.

76	½c. *Morpho peleides*	10	10
77	1c. *Danaus eresimus* ("Danaus gilippus")	10	10
78	2c. *Dismorphia amphione*	10	10
79	35c. *Hamadryas feronia*	35	10
80	45c. *Philaethria dido*	45	10
81	75c. *Phoebis argante*	70	15
82	$2 *Prepona laertes*	1·40	30
MS83	104×77 mm. $1 *Siproeta stelenes*	3·00	3·25

5 Progress "Standard" Badge

1975. 14th World Scout Jamboree, Norway. Multicoloured.

84	½c. Type **5**	10	10
85	1c. Boatman's badge	10	10
86	2c. Coxswain's badge	10	10
87	35c. Interpreter's badge	15	10
88	45c. Ambulance badge	20	10
89	75c. Chief Scout's award	25	10
90	$2 Queen's Scout award	35	15
MS91	106×80 mm. $1 Venture award	55	30

6 The Surrender of Lord Cornwallis

1975. Bicentenary of American Revolution (1976) (1st issue). Multicoloured.

92	½c. Type **6**	10	10
93	1c. Minute-men	10	10
94	2c. Paul Revere's ride	10	10
95	3c. Battle of Bunker Hill	10	10
96	5c. Fifer and drummers	10	10
97	45c. Backwoodsman	15	10
98	75c. Boston Tea Party	20	10
99	$2 Naval engagement	35	10
100	$2 George Washington	35	35
101	$2 White House and flags	35	35
MS102	Two sheets 113×128 mm containing No. 100, and 128×113 mm containing No. 101. Imperf	1·10	1·40

Nos. 100/1 are larger, 35×60 mm.
See also Nos. 176/**MS**183.

---

7 Fencing

1975. Pan-American Games, Mexico City. Multicoloured.

103	½c. Type **7**	10	10
104	1c. Hurdling	10	10
105	2c. Pole-vaulting	10	10
106	35c. Weightlifting	15	10
107	45c. Throwing the javelin	15	10
108	75c. Throwing the discus	15	10
109	$2 Diving	35	15
MS110	78×104 mm. $1 Sprinter	40	20

1975. Nos. 649/68 of Grenada additionally inscr "GRENADINES".

111	½c. Yachts, Point Saline	10	30
112	1c. Yacht Club race, St. George's	10	15
113	2c. Carenage taxi	10	15
114	3c. Large working boats	10	15
115	5c. Deep-water dock, St. George's	10	15
116	6c. Cocoa beans in drying trays	10	15
117	8c. Nutmegs	10	15
118	10c. Rum distillery, River Antoine Estate, c. 1785	10	15
119	12c. Cocoa tree	10	15
120	15c. Fishermen at Fontenoy	10	15
121	20c. Parliament Building	10	40
122	25c. Fort George cannons	10	15
123	35c. Pearls Airport	50	15
124	50c. General Post Office	20	75
125	75c. Carib's Leap, Sauteurs Bay	40	60
126	$1 Carenage, St. George's	60	85
127	$2 St. George's Harbour by night	90	2·00
128	$3 Grand Anse beach	1·10	2·50
129	$5 Canoe Bay and Black Bay	1·50	5·50
130	$10 Sugar-loaf Island	2·25	5·50

8 *Virgin and Child* (Durer)

1975. Christmas. *Virgin and Child* paintings by Artists named.

131	½c. Type **8**	10	10
132	1c. Durer	10	10
133	2c. Correggio	10	10
134	40c. Botticelli	15	10
135	50c. Niccolo da Cremona	15	10
136	75c. Correggio	15	10
137	$2 Correggio	30	15
MS138	114×120 mm. $1 Bellini	60	50

9 Bleeding Tooth

1976. Shells. Multicoloured.

139	½c. Type **9**	10	10
140	1c. Toothed donax	10	10
141	2c. Hawk-wing conch	10	10
142	3c. Atlantic distorsio	10	10
143	25c. Scotch bonnet	40	10
144	50c. King helmet	50	10
145	75c. Queen or pink conch	75	15
MS146	79×105 mm. $2 Atlantic trumpet triton	1·00	70

10 Cocoa Thrush

1976. Flora and Fauna. Multicoloured.

147	½c. "Lignum vitae"	10	10
148	1c. Type **10**	10	10
149	2c. "Eurypelma sp." (spider)	10	10
150	35c. Lesser Antillean Tanager ("Hooded Tanager")	1·25	15
151	50c. "Nyctaginaceae"	1·00	15
152	75c. Grenada dove	2·50	25
153	$1 Marine toad	2·50	25

MS154	108×84 mm. $2 Blue-hooded euphonia	4·00	1·00

11 Hooked Sailfish

1976. Tourism. Multicoloured.

155	½c. Type **11**	10	10
156	1c. Careened schooner, Carriacou	10	10
157	2c. Carriacou Annual Regatta	10	10
158	18c. Boat building on Carriacou	20	10
159	22c. Workboat race, Carriacou Regatta	20	10
160	75c. Cruising off Petit Martinique	30	20
161	$1 Water skiing	40	20
MS162	105×87 mm. $2 Yacht racing at Carriacou	70	75

12 Making a Camp Fire

1976. 50th Anniv of Girl Guides in Grenada. Multicoloured.

163	½c. Type **12**	10	10
164	1c. First aid	10	10
165	2c. Nature study	10	10
166	50c. Cookery	50	15
167	$1 Sketching	75	25
MS168	85×110 mm. $2 Guide playing guitar	1·00	75

13 *Christ Mocked* (Bosch)

1976. Easter. Multicoloured.

169	½c. Type **13**	10	10
170	1c. *Christ Crucified* (Antonello da Messina)	10	10
171	2c. *Adoration of the Trinity* (Durer)	10	10
172	3c. *Lamentation of Christ* (Durer)	10	10
173	35c. *The Entombment* (Van der Weyden)	15	10
174	$3 *The Entombment* (Raphael)	60	30
MS175	57×72 mm. $2 *Blood of the Redeemer* (G. Bellini)	65	70

14 *South Carolina* (frigate)

1976. Bicentenary of American Revolution (2nd issue). Multicoloured.

176	½c. Type **14**	10	10
177	1c. *Lee* (schooner)	10	10
178	2c. *H.M.S. Roebuck* (frigate)	10	10
179	35c. *Andrew Doria* (brig)	40	10
180	50c. *Providence* (sloop)	50	15
181	$1 *Alfred* (frigate)	75	20
182	$2 *Confederacy* (frigate)	1·25	30
MS183	72×85 mm. $3 *Revenge* (cutter)	1·00	1·00

15 Piper Apache

1976. Aircraft. Multicoloured.

184	½c. Type **15**	10	10
185	1c. Beech 50 Twin Bonanza	10	10
186	2c. de Havilland Twin Otter	10	10
187	40c. Britten Norman Islander	30	10
188	50c. de Havilland Heron 2	40	10
189	$2 Hawker Siddeley H.S.748	1·25	25
MS190	71×85 mm. $3 B.A.C. One-Eleven 500	1·00	1·00

16 Cycling

1976. Olympic Games, Montreal. Multicoloured.
191	½c. Type **16**	10	10
192	1c. Pommel horse	10	10
193	2c. Hurdling	10	10
194	35c. Shot putting	10	10
195	45c. Diving	15	10
196	75c. Sprinting	15	10
197	$2 Rowing	35	25
MS198	101×76 mm. $3 Sailing	80	75

17 Virgin and Child (Cima)

1976. Christmas. Multicoloured.
199	½c. Type **17**	10	10
200	1c. The Nativity (Romanino)	10	10
201	2c. The Nativity (Romanino) (different)	10	10
202	35c. Adoration of the Kings (Bruegel)	15	10
203	50c. Madonna and Child (Girolamo)	20	10
204	75c. Adoration of the Magi (Giorgione) (horiz)	20	15
205	$2 Adoration of the Kings (School of Fra Angelico) (horiz)	40	25
MS206	120×100 mm. $3 The Holy Family (Garofalo)	60	2·25

18 Alexander Graham Bell and First Telephone

1977. Centenary of First Telephone Transmission. Designs showing Alexander Graham Bell and telephone. Multicoloured.
207	½c. Type **18**	10	10
208	1c. 1895 telephone	10	10
209	2c. 1900 telephone	10	10
210	35c. 1915 telephone	15	10
211	75c. 1920 telephone	20	10
212	$1 1929 telephone	25	15
213	$2 1963 telephone	35	25
MS214	107×78 mm. $3 Telephone, 1976	1·10	75

19 Coronation Coach

1977. Silver Jubilee. Multicoloured. (a) Perf.
215	35c. Type **19**	10	10
216	$2 Queen entering Abbey	20	10
217	$4 Queen crowned	35	25
MS218	100×70 mm. $5 The Mall on Coronation Night	60	1·25

(b) Imperf×roul. Self-adhesive.
219	35c. Royal visit	15	20
220	50c. Crown of St. Edward	30	80
221	$2 The Queen and Prince Charles	50	1·60
222	$5 Royal Standard	60	1·75

Nos. 219/22 come from booklets.

21 Disrobing of Christ (Fra Angelico)

1977. Easter. Paintings by artists named. Multicoloured.
223	½c. Type **21**	10	10
224	1c. Fra Angelico	10	10
225	2c. El Greco	10	10
226	18c. El Greco	10	10
227	35c. Fra Angelico	15	10
228	50c. Giottino	15	10
229	$2 Antonello da Messina	35	25
MS230	121×94 mm. $3 Fra Angelico	65	65

22 The Virgin adoring the Child (Correggio)

1977. Christmas. Multicoloured.
231	½c. Type **22**	10	10
232	1c. Virgin and Child (Giorgione)	10	10
233	2c. Virgin and Child (Morales)	10	10
234	18c. Madonna della Tenda (Raphael)	10	10
235	35c. Rest on the Flight into Egypt (Van Dyck)	15	10
236	50c. Madonna and Child (Lippi)	15	10
237	$2 Virgin and Child (Lippi) (different)	35	25
MS238	114×99 mm. $3 Virgin and Child with Angels and Saints (Ghirlandaio)	65	65

1977. Royal Visit. Nos. 215/17 optd **ROYAL VISIT W.I. 1977.**
239	35c. Type **19**	10	10
240	$2 Queen entering Abbey	25	20
241	$4 Queen crowned	40	30
MS242	100×70 mm. $5 The Mall on Coronation Night	70	90

24 Life-saving

1977. Caribbean Scout Jamboree, Jamaica. Multicoloured.
243	½c. Type **24**	10	10
244	1c. Overnight hike	10	10
245	2c. Cubs tying knots	10	10
246	22c. Erecting a tent	15	10
247	35c. Gang show limbo dance	25	10
248	75c. Campfire cooking	40	15
249	$3 Sea Scouts in "Mirror" dinghies	80	30
MS250	109×85 mm. $2 Pioneering project—Spring bridge	1·10	90

25 Blast-off

1977. Space Shuttle. Multicoloured.
251	½c. Type **25**	10	10
252	1c. Booster jettison	10	10
253	2c. External tank jettison	10	10
254	22c. Working in orbit	15	10
255	50c. Shuttle re-entry	25	10
256	$3 Shuttle landing	85	30
MS257	85×103 mm. $2 Shuttle being towed	60	70

26 Alfred Nobel and Physiology/Medicine Medal

1978. Nobel Prize Awards. Multicoloured.
258	½c. Type **26**	10	10
259	1c. Physics and Chemistry medal	10	10
260	2c. Peace medal (reverse)	10	10
261	22c. Nobel Institute, Oslo	25	10
262	75c. Peace Prize committee	50	15
263	$3 Literature medal	1·50	30
MS264	127×103 mm. $2 Peace medal and Nobel's will	50	60

27 German Zeppelin Stamp, 1930

1978. 75th Anniv of First Zeppelin Flight and 50th Anniv of Lindbergh's Transatlantic Flight. Multicoloured.
265	5c. Type **27**	20	10
266	15c. French Concorde stamp, 1970	60	10
267	25c. Liechtenstein Zeppelin stamp, 1931	20	10
268	35c. Panama Lindbergh stamp, 1928	20	10
269	50c. Russia Airship stamp, 1931	25	10
270	$3 Spanish Lindbergh stamp, 1930	75	30
MS271	140×79 mm. 75c. U.S.A. Lindbergh stamp, 1927; $2 German LZ-129 Hindenburg stamp, 1936	1·10	90

28 Coronation Ring

1978. 25th Anniv of Coronation. Multicoloured. (a) Horiz designs. Perf.
272	50c. Type **28**	10	10
273	$2 The Orb	25	30
274	$2.50 Imperial State Crown	30	35
MS275	97×67 mm. $5 Queen Elizabeth II	60	60

(b) Vert designs. Roul×imperf. Self-adhesive.
276	18c. Drummer, Royal Regiment of Fusiliers	15	35
277	50c. Drummer, Royal Anglian Regiment	15	45
278	$5 Drum Major, Queen's Regiment	1·00	3·00

30 Le Chapeau de Paille

1978. 400th Birth Anniv of Rubens. Multicoloured.
279	5c. Type **30**	10	10
280	15c. Archilles slaying Hector	15	10
281	18c. Helene Fourment and her Children	15	10
282	22c. Rubens and Isabella Brandt	15	10
283	35c. The Ildefonso Altarpiece	20	10
284	$3 Heads of Negroes (detail)	75	1·00
MS285	85×127 mm. $2 Self-portrait	70	1·00

31 Wright Flyer I

1978. 75th Anniv of Powered Flight.
286	**31**	5c. black, blue and brown	10	10
287	-	15c. black, brown and red	10	10
288	-	18c. black, brown and red	10	10
289	-	25c. black, yellow and green	10	10
290	-	35c. black, pink and purple	15	10
291	-	75c. black, lilac and yellow	25	25
292	-	$3 black, violet and mauve	75	75
MS293		126×83 mm. $2 black, blue and green	75	1·00

DESIGNS—HORIZ: 25c. Wright Flyer III, 1905; 35c. Wright glider No. 1; 75c. Wright Flyer I (different); $3 Various Wright aircraft; $3 Wright Type A. VERT: 15c. Orville Wright; 18c. Wilbur Wright.

32 Audubon's Shearwater

1978. Birds. Multicoloured.
294	5c. Type **32**	50	15
295	10c. Semi-palmated plover ("Northern Ring-necked Plover")	70	15
296	18c. Purple-throated carib ("Garnet-throated Hummingbird") (horiz)	80	15
297	22c. Red-billed whistling duck ("Black-bellied Tree Duck") (horiz)	80	20
298	40c. Caribbean martin (horiz)	1·25	35
299	$1 White-tailed tropic bird ("Yellow-tailed Tropicbird")	1·75	50
300	$2 Long-billed curlew	2·25	75
MS301	78×78 mm. $5 Snowy egret	5·00	2·75

33 Players with Ball

1978. World Cup Football Championship, Argentina. Multicoloured.
302	15c. Type **33**	10	10
303	35c. Running with ball	20	10
304	50c. Player with ball	25	20
305	$3 Heading	80	80
MS306	114×85 mm. $2 Player with ball (different)	80	1·25

34 Captain Cook and Kalaniopu (King of Hawaii), 1778

1978. 250th Birth Anniv of Captain James Cook. Multicoloured.
307	18c. Type **34**	45	10
308	22c. Cook and native of Hawaii	60	15
309	50c. Cook and death scene, 1779	1·00	30
310	$3 Cook and offering ceremony	2·25	1·75
MS311	117×113 mm. $4 H.M.S. "Resolution" (vert)	1·50	1·00

35 Virgin at Prayer

1978. Christmas. Paintings by Durer. Multicoloured.
312	40c. Type **35**	15	10
313	60c. The Dresden Altarpiece	20	10
314	90c. Madonna and Child with St. Anne	25	15
315	$2 Madonna and Child with Pear	50	50
MS316	114×84 mm. $4 Salvator Mundi	1·00	1·40

36 Strelitzia reginae

1979. Flowers. Multicoloured.
317	22c. Type **36**	15	10
318	40c. Euphorbia pulcherrima	25	15
319	$1 Heliconia humilis	45	30
320	$3 Thunbergia alata	80	80

MS321 114×90 mm. $2 *Bougainvillaea glabra*   75   1·00

37 Children with Pig

1979. International Year of the Child. Multicoloured.

322	18c. Type **37**	10	10
323	50c. Children with donkey	20	25
324	$1 Children with goats	25	30
325	$3 Children fishing	65	80
MS326	104×86 mm. $4 Child with coconuts	1·00	1·90

38 20,000 Leagues under the Sea

1979. 150th Birth Anniv of Jules Verne (author). Multicoloured.

327	18c. Type **38**	50	10
328	38c. *From the Earth to the Moon*	55	20
329	75c. *From the Earth to the Moon* (different)	65	35
330	$3 *Five Weeks in a Balloon*	1·25	1·00
MS331	111×86 mm. $4 *Around the World in 80 Days*	1·00	1·60

39 Sir Rowland Hill and Mail Van

1979. Death Centenary of Sir Rowland Hill. Multicoloured.

332	15c. Type **39**	10	10
333	$1 "Britanis" (cargo liner)	20	20
334	$2 Diesel mail train	30	30
335	$3 Concorde	90	70
MS336	85×67 mm. $4 Sir Rowland Hill	75	1·00

40 *Virgin and Child Enthroned* (11th-century Byzantine)

1979. Christmas. Sculptures. Multicoloured.

337	6c. Type **40**	10	10
338	25c. "Presentation in the Temple" (Andre Beauneveu)	10	10
339	30c. *Flight to Egypt* (Utrecht, c. 1510)	10	10
340	40c. *Madonna and Child* (Jacopo della Quercia)	10	10
341	90c. *Madonna della Mela* (Luca della Robbia)	15	15
342	$1 *Madonna and Child* (Antonio Rossellino)	20	20
343	$2 *Madonna and Child* (Antwerp, 1700)	35	35
MS344	125×95 mm. $4 *Virgin*, Krumau	65	1·10

41 Great Hammerhead

1979. Marine Wildlife. Multicoloured.

345	40c. Type **41**	40	30
346	45c. Spot-finned butterflyfish	45	30
347	50c. Permit (fish)	45	40
348	60c. Threaded turban (shell)	65	55
349	70c. Milk conch	75	75
350	75c. Great blue heron	1·25	90
351	90c. Colourful Atlantic moon (shell)	95	1·00
352	$1 Red-footed booby	1·75	1·75
MS353	99×86 mm. $2.50 Collared plover	2·00	1·10

42 Doctor Goofy

1979. International Year of the Child. Walt Disney cartoon characters. Multicoloured.

354	½c. Type **42**	10	10
355	1c. Admiral Mickey Mouse	10	10
356	2c. Fireman Goofy	10	10
357	3c. Nurse Minnie Mouse	10	10
358	4c. Drum Major Mickey Mouse	10	10
359	5c. Policeman Donald Duck	10	10
360	10c. Pilot Donald Duck	10	10
361	$2 Postman Goofy (horiz)	2·25	2·25
362	$2.50 Train driver Donald Duck (horiz)	2·25	2·25
MS363	128×102 mm. $3 Mickey Mouse as fireman	1·75	2·00

1980. First Anniv of Revolution. Nos. 116 and 119/30 optd **PEOPLE'S REVOLUTION 13 MARCH 1979.**

364	6c. Cocoa beans in drying trays	10	10
365	12c. Cocoa tree	10	10
366	15c. Fishermen at Fontenoy	10	10
367	20c. Parliament Building, St. George's	10	10
368	25c. Fort George cannons	15	10
369	35c. Pearls Airport	20	10
370	50c. General Post Office	35	15
371	75c. Carib's Leap, Sauteurs Bay	40	20
372	$1 Carenage, St. George's	55	30
373	$2 St. George's Harbour by night	85	70
374	$3 Grand Anse Beach	1·60	1·60
375	$5 Canoe Bay and Black Bay	2·25	2·50
376	$10 Sugar-loaf Island	3·75	4·25

43 Classroom

1980. 75th Anniv of Rotary International. Multicoloured.

377	6c. Type **43**	10	10
378	30c. Different races encircling Rotary emblem	20	10
379	60c. Rotary executive presenting doctor with cheque	35	20
380	$3 Nurses with young patients	1·25	75
MS381	85×72 mm. $4 Paul P. Harris (founder)	1·00	1·60

44 Yellow-bellied Seedeater

1980. Wild Birds. Multicoloured.

382	25c. Type **44**	50	15
383	40c. Blue-hooded euphonia	55	20
384	90c. Yellow warbler	1·25	65
385	$2 Tropical mockingbird	1·75	1·25
MS386	83×110 mm. $3 Barn Owl	4·00	1·50

45 Running

1980. Olympic Games, Moscow. Multicoloured.

387	30c. Type **45**	20	15
388	40c. Football	15	20
389	90c. Boxing	35	35
390	$2 Wrestling	70	75
MS391	104×75 mm. $4 Athletes in silhouette	75	1·10

1980. "London 1980" International Stamp Exhibition. Nos. 332/5 optd **LONDON 1980.**

392	15c. Mail van	25	15
393	$1 "Britanis" (cargo liner)	85	35
394	$2 Diesel mail train	1·75	1·00
395	$3 Concorde	2·75	2·00

47 Long-jawed Squirrelfish

1980. Fish. Multicoloured.

396A	½c. Type **47**	10	10
397A	1c. Blue chromis	10	10
398A	2c. Four-eyed butterflyfish	10	10
399A	4c. Sergeant major	10	10
400A	5c. Yellow-tailed snapper	10	10
401A	6c. Mutton snapper	10	10
402A	10c. Cocoa damselfish	10	10
403A	12c. Royal gramma	10	10
404A	15c. Cherub angelfish	15	10
405A	20c. Black-barred soldierfish	15	10
406A	25c. Mottled grouper	15	15
407A	30c. Caribbean long-nosed butterflyfish	15	20
408A	40c. Puddingwife	20	25
409A	50c. Midnight parrotfish	25	35
410A	90c. Red-spotted hawkfish	40	55
411A	$1 Hogfish	45	60
412A	$3 Beau Gregory	1·25	1·50
413A	$5 Rock beauty	1·50	1·75
414A	$10 Barred hamlet	2·25	2·75

1980. Christmas. Scenes from Walt Disney's "Bambi". As T **42**. Multicoloured.

415	½c. Bambi with mother	10	10
416	1c. Bambi with quails	10	10
417	2c. Bambi meets Thumper the rabbit	10	10
418	3c. Bambi meets Flower the skunk	10	10
419	4c. Bambi and Faline	10	10
420	5c. Bambi with his father	10	10
421	10c. Bambi on ice	10	10
422	$2.50 Faline with foals	1·75	1·25
423	$3 Bambi and Faline	1·75	1·25
MS424	127×102 mm. $4 Bambi as Prince of the Forest (vert)	2·00	2·00

48 *The Unicorn in Captivity* (15th century unknown artist)

1981. Art Masterpieces. Multicoloured.

425	6c. Type **48**	10	10
426	10c. *The Fighting `Temeraire'* (Turner) (horiz)	10	10
427	25c. *Sunday Afternoon on the Ile de la Grande Jatte* (Seurat) (horiz)	15	15
428	90c. *Max Schmitt in a Single Scull* (Eakins) (horiz)	45	45
429	$2 *The Burial of the Count of Orgaz* (El Greco)	85	85
430	$3 *Portrait of George Washington* (Stuart)	1·10	1·10
MS431	66×101 mm. $5 *Kaiser Karl le Grosse* (detail Dürer)	1·75	2·00

1981. 50th Anniv of Walt Disney's Pluto (cartoon character). As T **42**.

432	$2 Mickey Mouse serving birthday cake to Pluto	1·00	80
MS433	127×101 mm. $4 Pluto in scene from film "Pluto's Dream House"	1·50	1·50

1981. Easter. Walt Disney cartoon characters. As T **42**. Multicoloured.

434	35c. Chip	20	20
435	40c. Dewey	20	20
436	$2 Huey	60	60
437	$2.50 Mickey Mouse	75	75
MS438	126×102 mm. $4 Jimmy Cricket	1·50	1·50

49 Bust of a Woman

1981. Birth Centenary of Picasso. Multicoloured.

439	6c. Type **49**	10	10

440	40c. Woman (study for *Les Demoiselles d'Avignon*)	20	15
441	90c. Nude with raised Arms (*The Dancer of Avignon*)	30	20
442	$4 *The Dryad*	75	75
MS443	103×128 mm. $5 *Les Demoiselles d'Avignon*. Imperf	1·40	1·25

50 Balmoral Castle

1981. Royal Wedding (1st issue). Multicoloured.

444	40c. As 30c.	15	15
445	$2 Type **50**	50	50
446	$4 Prince Charles as parachutist	90	90
MS447	97×84 mm. $5 Royal Coach	70	70
448	30c. Prince Charles and Lady Diana Spencer	35	20
449	40c. Type **50**	45	35

51 Lady Diana Spencer

1981. Royal Wedding (2nd issue). Multicoloured. Self-adhesive.

450	$1 Type **51**	20	35
451	$2 Prince Charles	25	50
452	$5 Prince Charles and Lady Diana Spencer (horiz)	1·25	2·00

52 Amy Johnson (1st solo flight, Britain to Australia by Woman, May 1930)

1981. "Decade for Women". Famous Female Aviators. Multicoloured.

453	30c. Type **52**	45	15
454	70c. Mme. La Baronne de Laroche (1st qualified woman pilot, March 1910)	70	30
455	$1.10 Ruth Nichols (solo Atlantic flight attempt, June 1931)	80	40
456	$3 Amelia Earhart (1st North Atlantic solo flight by woman, May 1932)	1·75	1·10
MS457	90×85 mm. $5 Valentina Nikolayeva-Tereshkova (1st woman in space, June 1963)	1·25	1·40

1981. Christmas. Designs as T **42** showing scenes from Walt Disney's cartoon film "Lady and the Tramp".

458	½c. multicoloured	10	10
459	1c. multicoloured	10	10
460	2c. multicoloured	10	10
461	3c. multicoloured	10	10
462	4c. multicoloured	10	10
463	5c. multicoloured	10	10
464	10c. multicoloured	10	10
465	$2.50 multicoloured	3·25	1·50
466	$3 multicoloured	3·25	1·50
MS467	128×103 mm. $5 multicoloured	5·00	3·00

53 Boeing 747 SCA Carrier

1981. Space Shuttle Project. Multicoloured.

468	10c. Type **53**	30	10
469	40c. Re-entry	65	15
470	$1.10 External tank separation	1·25	45
471	$3 Touchdown	1·75	1·00
MS472	117×98 mm. $5 Launch	2·50	1·60

54 Footballer

1981. World Cup Football Championship, Spain (1982).
473	**54**	20c. multicoloured	15	10
474	-	40c. multicoloured	20	15
475	-	$1 multicoloured	35	30
476	-	$2 multicoloured	65	55
MS477		106×128 mm. $4 multicoloured	1·40	1·60

DESIGNS: 40c. to $4 various designs showing footballers.

55 Mail Van and Stagecoach

1982. Cent of U.P.U. Membership. Multicoloured.
478	30c. Type **55**	30	15
479	40c. U.P.U. emblem	30	15
480	$2.50 "Queen Elizabeth 2" (liner) and sailing ship	1·50	70
481	$4 Concorde and De Havilland D.H.9 biplane	2·25	1·25
MS482	117×78 mm. $5 British Advanced Passenger Train and steam mail trains	3·00	2·25

56 National Sports Meeting

1982. 75th Anniv of Boy Scout Movement and 125th Birth Anniv of Lord Baden-Powell. Multicoloured.
483	6c. Type **56**	15	10
484	90c. Sea scouts sailing	50	30
485	$1.10 Handicraft	65	60
486	$3 Animal tending	1·40	1·40
MS487	100×71 mm. $5 Music around campfire	1·40	1·75

57 *Anartia jatrophae*

1982. Butterflies. Multicoloured.
488	30c. Type **57**	75	30
489	40c. *Chioides vintra*	80	35
490	$1.10 *Cynthia cardui*	1·75	75
491	$3 *Historis odius*	2·75	1·60
MS492	103×77 mm. $5 *Dione juno*	3·25	2·50

58 Prince and Princess of Wales

1982. 21st Birthday of Princess of Wales. Multicoloured.
493	50c. Blenheim Palace	1·25	1·75
494	60c. As 50c.	75	75
495	$1 Type **58**	1·75	2·25
496	$2 Type **58**	1·75	2·00
497	$3 Princess of Wales	2·50	2·75
498	$4 As $3	2·50	2·75
MS499	103×75 mm. $5 Princess Diana (different)	5·50	2·50

59 "New Deal"—Soil Conservation

1982. Birth Centenary of Franklin D. Roosevelt. Multicoloured.
500	30c. Type **59**	25	10
501	40c. Roosevelt and George Washington Carver (scientist)	25	10
502	70c. Civilian conservation corps (reafforestation)	30	20

503	$3 Roosevelt with Pres. Barclay of Liberia, Casablanca Conference, 1943	70	80
MS504	100×72 mm. $5 Roosevelt delivering address at Howard University	1·75	1·75

1982. Birth of Prince William of Wales. Nos. 493/8 optd **ROYAL BABY 21.6.82.**
505	50c. Blenheim Palace	50	75
506	60c. As 50c.	55	60
507	$1 Type **58**	70	1·00
508	$2 Type **58**	1·00	1·25
509	$3 Princess of Wales	1·25	1·75
510	$4 As $3	1·50	1·75
MS511	103×75 mm. $5 Princess Diana (different)	2·10	2·25

60 *Presentation of Christ in the Temple*

1982. Easter. Easter Paintings by Rembrandt. Multicoloured.
512	30c. Type **60**	25	15
513	60c. *Descent from the Cross*	30	10
514	$2 *Raising of the Cross*	45	60
515	$4 *Resurrection of Christ*	80	1·25
MS516	101×126 mm. $5 *The Risen Christ*	2·40	2·00

61 *Santa Fe*, U.S.A.

1982. Famous Trains of the World. Multicoloured.
517	10c. Type **61**	50	15
518	40c. *Mistral*, France	70	20
519	70c. *Rheingold*, Germany	80	45
520	$1 "ET 403", France	1·00	50
521	$1.10 Steam locomotive *Mallard*, Great Britain	1·25	60
522	$2 Tokaido Shinkansen "Hikari", Japan	1·40	90
MS523	121×95 mm. $5 *Settebello*, Italy	1·50	2·00

62 Footballers

1982. World Cup Football Championship Winners.
524	**62**	60c. multicoloured	75	35
525	**62**	$4 multicoloured	2·00	1·25
MS526		92×134 mm. $5 multicoloured	1·50	1·50

1982. Christmas. Scenes from Walt Disney's cartoon film "The Rescuers". As T **42**, but horiz.
527	½c. multicoloured	10	10
528	1c. multicoloured	10	10
529	2c. multicoloured	10	10
530	3c. multicoloured	10	10
531	4c. multicoloured	10	10
532	5c. multicoloured	10	10
533	10c. multicoloured	10	10
534	$2.50 multicoloured	3·25	1·75
535	$3 multicoloured	3·25	1·75
MS536	120×96 mm. $5 multicoloured	5·00	2·75

63 Short-finned Pilot Whale

1982. Save the Whale. Multicoloured.
537	10c. Type **63**	85	55
538	60c. Dall's porpoise	2·00	1·75
539	$1.10 Humpback whale	3·50	2·75
540	$3 Bowhead whale	6·00	7·00
MS541	113×84 mm. $5 Spotted dolphin	4·50	4·00

64 *David and Goliath*

1983. 500th Anniv of Raphael. Multicoloured.
542	25c. Type **64**	15	15
543	30c. "David sees Bathsheba"	15	15
544	90c. "Triumph of David"	30	35
545	$4 "Anointing of Solomon"	70	90
MS546	126×101 mm. $5 "Anointing of David"	80	1·10

65 Voice and Visual Communication

1983. World Communications Year. Multicoloured.
547	30c. Type **65**	10	10
548	60c. Ambulance	25	20
549	$1.10 Westland Whirlwind helicopters	45	45
550	$3 Satellite	1·00	1·00
MS551	127×85 mm. $5 Diver and bottle-nosed dolphin	2·50	2·00

66 Chrysler "Imperial Roadster", 1931

1983. 75th Anniv of Model "T" Ford Car. Multicoloured.
552	10c. Type **66**	15	15
553	30c. Doble steam car, 1925	25	25
554	40c. Ford "Mustang", 1965	25	30
555	60c. Packard tourer, 1930	35	40
556	70c. Mercer "Raceabout", 1913	35	40
557	90c. Corvette "Stingray", 1963	35	40
558	$1.10 Auburn "851 Supercharger Speedster", 1935	40	45
559	$2.50 Pierce-Arrow "Silver Arrow", 1933	65	95
560	$3 Duesenberg dual cowl phaeton, 1929	75	1·25
561	$4 Mercedes-Benz "SSK", 1928	75	1·50
MS562	119×90 mm. $5 McFarlan "Knickerbocker" cabriolet, 1923	1·50	2·50

67 Short Solent 2 Flying Boat

1983. Bicentenary of Manned Flight. Multicoloured.
563	40c. Type **67**	85	20
564	70c. Curtiss R3C-2 seaplane	1·00	35
565	90c. Hawker Nimrod biplane	1·25	40
566	$4 Montgolfier balloon	3·25	2·75
MS567	112×85 mm. $5 LZ-11 "Viktoria Luise" (airship)	1·75	2·00

68 Goofy

1983. Christmas Disney cartoon characters in scenes from "Jingle Bells" (Christmas carol). Multicoloured.
568	½c. Type **68**	10	10
569	1c. Clarabelle Cow	10	10
570	2c. Donald Duck	10	10
571	3c. Pluto	10	10
572	4c. Morty and Ferdie	10	10
573	5c. Huey, Dewey and Louie	10	10
574	10c. Daisy and Chip n'Dale	10	10
575	$2.50 Big Bad Wolf	4·75	5·00
576	$5 Mickey Mouse	5·00	5·50
MS577	102×124 mm. $5 Donald Duck in sleigh	8·00	8·50

69 Weightlifting

1984. Olympic Games, Los Angeles. Multicoloured.
578	30c. Type **69**	20	15
579	60c. Gymnastics	45	35
580	70c. Archery	50	40
581	$4 Sailing	1·90	1·90
MS582	70×102 mm. $5 Basketball	2·25	2·25

70 Frangipani

1984. Flowers. Multicoloured.
583	15c. Type **70**	15	10
584	40c. Dwarf poinciana	30	25
585	70c. Walking iris	55	45
586	$4 Lady's slipper	1·75	2·50
MS587	66×57 mm. $5 Brazilian glory vine	1·50	2·50

71 Goofy

1984. Easter. Multicoloured.
588	½c. Type **71**	10	10
589	1c. Chip and Dale	10	10
590	2c. Daisy Duck and Huey	10	10
591	3c. Daisy Duck	10	10
592	4c. Donald Duck	10	10
593	5c. Merlin and Madam Mim	10	10
594	10c. Flower	10	10
595	$2 Minnie and Mickey Mouse	1·25	2·00
596	$4 Minnie Mouse	1·75	2·75
MS597	126×100 mm. $5 Minnie Mouse (different)	3·00	3·75

72 Bobolink

1984. Songbirds. Multicoloured.
598	40c. Type **72**	1·75	1·50
599	50c. Eastern kingbird	2·00	1·60
600	60c. Barn swallow	2·25	2·00
601	70c. Yellow warbler	2·25	2·00
602	$1 Rose-breasted grosbeak	2·50	2·50
603	$1.10 Common yellowthroat ("Yellowthroat")	2·75	2·75
604	$2 Catbird	3·50	4·50
MS605	71×65 mm. $5 Fork-tailed flycatcher	6·50	5·00

1984. Universal Postal Union Congress, Hamburg. Nos. 585/6 optd **19th U.P.U. CONGRESS HAMBURG.**
606	70c. Walking iris	1·00	1·00
607	$4 Lady's slipper	4·50	5·00
MS608	66×57 mm. $5 Brazilian glory vine	2·25	3·00

74 *Geeststar* (freighter)

1984. Ships. Multicoloured.
609	30c. Type **74**	75	75
610	60c. *Daphne* (liner)	1·00	1·25
611	$1.10 *Southwind* (schooner)	1·25	2·00

612	$4 *Oceanic* (liner)	2·00	5·50
MS613	108×80 mm. $5 Pirate ship	3·00	4·00

1984. 450th Death Anniv of Correggio (painter). As T **296** of Grenada. Multicoloured.

614	10c. "The Hunt—Blowing the Horn"	10	10
615	30c. "St. John the Evangelist" (horiz)	15	15
616	90c. "The Hunt—The Deer's Head"	50	50
617	$4 "The Virgin crowned by Christ" (horiz)	2·00	2·00
MS618	73×63 mm. $5 "Martyrdom of the Four Saints"	2·40	3·00

1984. 150th Birth Anniv of Edgar Degas (painter). As T **297** of Grenada. Multicoloured.

619	25c. "The Song of the Dog"	40	15
620	70c. "Cafe-concert"	70	50
621	$1.10 "The Orchestra of the Opera"	1·50	1·25
622	$3 "The Dance Lesson"	2·75	2·75
MS623	53×73 mm. $5 "Madame Camus at the Piano"	2·40	3·00

1984. "Ausipex" International Stamp Exhibition, Melbourne. As T **298** of Grenada. Multicoloured.

624	$1.10 Queen Victoria Gardens, Melbourne	50	50
625	$4 Ayers Rock	2·00	2·00
MS626	107×76 mm. $5 River Yarra, Melbourne	2·00	3·00

75 Col. Steven's Model (1825)

1984. Railway Locomotives. Multicoloured.

627	20c. Type **75**	55	25
628	50c. *Royal George* (1827)	70	50
629	60c. *Stourbridge Lion* (1829)	75	65
630	70c. *Liverpool* (1830)	80	85
631	90c. *South Carolina* (1832)	90	1·25
632	$1.10 *Monster* (1836)	90	1·50
633	$2 *Lafayette* (1837)	1·10	2·25
634	$4 *Lion* (1838)	1·40	3·75
MS635	Two sheets, each 100×70 mm. (a) $5 Sequin's locomotive (1829). (b) $5 *Adler* (1835). Set of 2 sheets	6·00	8·00

1984. Opening of Point Saline International Airport. Nos. 547, 549 and MS551 optd **OPENING OF POINT SALINE INT'L AIRPORT**.

636	30c. Type **65**	30	25
637	$1.10 Westland Whirlwind helicopters	95	75
MS638	127×85 mm. Diver and bottle-nosed dolphin	4·25	3·50

1984. Christmas. Walt Disney cartoon characters. As T **301** of Grenada. Multicoloured.

639	45c. Donald Duck and nephews knitting Christmas stockings	70	40
640	60c. Donald Duck and nephews sitting on sofa	80	65
641	90c. Donald Duck getting out of bed	1·25	1·00
642	$2 Donald Duck putting presents in wardrobe	2·00	2·50
643	$4 Nephews singing carols outside Donald Duck's window	3·25	4·25
MS644	126×102 mm. $5 Donald Duck filming nephews	4·25	4·00

1985. Birth Bicentenary of John J. Audubon (ornithologist). As T **418** of Ghana. Multicoloured.

645	50c. Blue-winged teal	2·00	60
646	90c. White ibis	2·50	1·25
647	$1.10 Swallow-tailed kite	3·50	2·00
648	$3 Moorhen	4·50	4·75
MS649	82×111 mm. $5 Mangrove cuckoo (vert)	3·25	3·75

See also Nos. 736/40.

76 Kawasaki "750" (1972)

1985. Centenary of the Motor Cycle. Multicoloured.

650	30c. Type **76**	65	45
651	60c. Honda "Goldwing GL1000" (1974) (horiz)	90	1·00
652	70c. Kawasaki "Z650" (1976) (horiz)	1·00	1·10
653	$4 Honda "CBX" (1977)	4·00	6·50
MS654	113×76 mm. $5 BMW "R100RS" (1978)	3·50	4·25

77 Nursing Cadets folding Bandages (Health)

1985. International Youth Year. Multicoloured.

655	50c. Type **77**	70	45
656	70c. Scuba diver and turtle (Environment)	1·00	80
657	$1.10 Yachting (Leisure)	1·60	1·50
658	$3 Boys playing chess (Education)	6·50	7·00
MS659	98×70 mm. $5 Hands touching globe	2·75	3·00

1985. 40th Anniv of International Civil Aviation Organization. As T **305** of Grenada. Multicoloured.

660	5c. Lockheed Lodestar	40	20
661	70c. Hawker Siddeley H.S.748	1·75	55
662	$1.10 Boeing 727-200	2·25	90
663	$4 Boeing 707	3·50	2·50
MS664	87×68 mm. $4 Pilatus Britten Norman Islander	3·50	3·00

78 Lady Baden-Powell (founder) and Grenadian Guide Leaders

1985. 75th Anniv of Girl Guide Movement. Multicoloured.

665	30c. Type **78**	50	20
666	50c. Guide leader and guides on botany field trip	1·00	30
667	70c. Guide leader and guides camping (vert)	1·10	45
668	$4 Guides sailing (vert)	4·00	2·25
MS669	100×73 mm. $5 Lord and Lady Baden-Powell (vert)	3·75	4·25

79 *Chiomara asychis*

1985. Butterflies. Multicoloured.

670	½c. Type **79**	10	20
671	1c. "Anartia amathea"	10	20
672	2c. "Pseudolycaena marsyas"	10	20
673	4c. "Urbanus proteus"	10	20
674	5c. "Polygonus manueli"	15	20
675a	6c. "Battus polydamas"	20	15
676	10c. "Eurema daira"	30	15
677	12c. "Phoebis agarithe"	45	20
678	15c. "Aphrissa statira"	45	20
679	20c. "Strymon simaethis"	60	20
680	25c. "Mestra cana"	60	25
681	30c. "Agraulis vanillae"	60	30
682	40c. "Junonia evarete"	75	45
683	60c. "Dryas julia"	1·00	65
684	70c. "Philaethria dido"	1·10	75
685	$1.10 "Hamadryas feronia"	1·75	1·25
686	$2.50 "Strymon rufofusca"	3·25	3·00
687	$5 "Appias drusilla"	5·00	4·75
688	$10 "Polites dictynna"	8·00	9·00
688b	$20 "Euptychia cephus"	12·00	16·00

80 The Queen Mother before Prince William's Christening

1985. Life and Times of Queen Elizabeth the Queen Mother. Multicoloured.

689	$1 Type **80**	45	60
690	$1.50 In winner's enclosure at Ascot (horiz)	60	75
691	$2.50 With Prince Charles at Garter ceremony, Windsor Castle	85	1·10
MS692	56×85 mm. $5 At opening of Royal York Hospice, London	1·75	3·00

Stamps as Nos. 689/91 but with face values of 70c., $1.10 and $3 exist from additional sheetlets with changed background colours.

81 Scuba Diving

1985. Water Sports. Multicoloured.

693	15c. Type **81**	30	10
694	70c. Boys playing in waterfall	60	45
695	90c. Water skiing	70	55
696	$4 Swimming	1·50	2·25
MS697	103×78 mm. $5 Scuba diver	2·75	3·25

82 Queen or Pink Conch

1985. Marine Life. Multicoloured.

698	60c. Type **82**	75	40
699	90c. Porcupinefish and fire coral	90	60
700	$1.10 Ghost crab	1·25	1·00
701	$4 West Indies spiny lobster	2·75	4·00
MS702	299×70 mm. $5 Long-spined urchin	5·00	4·00

1985. 300th Birth Anniv of Johann Sebastian Bach (composer). As T **309a** of Grenada. Multicoloured.

703	15c. Natural trumpet	50	10
704	60c. Bass viol	85	40
705	$1.10 Flute	1·50	70
706	$3 Double flageolet	2·25	1·75
MS707	110×75 mm. $5 Johann Sebastian Bach	3·25	3·50

1985. Royal Visit. As T **310a** of Grenada. Multicoloured.

708	10c. Arms of Great Britain and Grenada	20	20
709	$1 Queen Elizabeth II (vert)	1·00	1·75
710	$4 Royal Yacht *Britannia*	3·00	4·75
MS711	111×83 mm. $5 Map of Grenada Grenadines	3·00	3·75

1985. 40th Anniv of United Nations Organization. Designs as T **311a** of Grenada showing United Nations (New York) stamps. Multicoloured.

712	$1 Neil Armstrong (first man on Moon) and 1982 Peaceful Uses of Outer Space 20c.	1·10	1·10
713	$2 Gandhi and 1971 Racial Equality Year 13c.	4·75	5·00
714	$2.50 Maimonides (physician) and 1956 World Health Organization 3c.	6·00	6·50
MS715	110×85 mm. $5 U.N. Under-Secretary	2·50	3·00

1985. 150th Birth Anniv of Mark Twain (author). As T **145a** of Gambia showing Walt Disney cartoon characters illustrating scenes from *Letters from Hawaii*. Multicoloured.

716	25c. Minnie Mouse dancing the hula	60	30
717	50c. Donald Duck surfing	90	65
718	$1.50 Donald Duck roasting marshmallow in volcano	2·25	2·25
719	$3 Mickey Mouse and Chip n'Dale canoeing	3·75	4·00
MS720	127×120 mm. $5 Mickey Mouse with cat	4·75	3·75

1985. Birth Bicentenaries of Grimm Brothers (folklorists). As T **145b** of Gambia, but vert, showing Walt Disney cartoon characters in scenes from *The Elves and the Shoemaker*. Multicoloured.

721	30c. Mickey Mouse as the unsuccessful Shoemaker	70	40
722	60c. Two elves making shoes	1·10	85
723	70c. The Shoemaker discovering the new shoes	1·40	1·00
724	$4 The Shoemaker's wife (Minnie Mouse) making clothes for the elves	4·25	5·00
MS725	126×101 mm. $5 The Shoemaker and his wife waving	5·50	5·00

83 *Madonna and Child* (Titian)

1985. Christmas. Religious Paintings. Multicoloured.

726	50c. Type **83**	45	35

727	70c. "Madonna and Child with St. Mary and John the Baptist" (Bugiardini)	55	50
728	$1.10 "Adoration of the Magi" (Di Fredi)	80	1·40
729	$3 "Madonna and Child with Young St. John the Baptist" (Bartolomeo)	1·25	3·75
MS730	112×81 mm. $5 "The Annunciation" (Botticelli)	2·75	6·00

1986. Centenary of Statue of Liberty (1st issue). As T **312a** of Grenada. Multicoloured.

731	5c. Croton Reservoir, New York (1875)	10	10
732	10c. New York Public Library (1986)	10	10
733	70c. Old Boathouse, Central Park (1894)	25	40
734	$4 Boating in Central Park (1986)	1·40	2·25
MS735	103×76 mm. $5 Statue of Liberty (vert)	3·75	4·25

See also Nos. 892/903.

1986. Birth Bicentenary of John J. Audubon (ornithologist) (2nd issue). As T **312b** of Grenada. Multicoloured.

736	50c. Louisiana heron	1·50	1·00
737	70c. Black-crowned night heron	2·00	1·50
738	90c. American bittern	2·25	2·00
739	$1 Glossy ibis	3·75	6·50
MS740	103×74 mm. $5 King eider	6·50	8·50

1986. Visit of President Reagan of U.S.A. Nos. 684 and 687, optd **VISIT OF PRES. REAGAN 20 FEBRUARY 1986**.

741	70c. *Philaethria dido*	1·50	1·25
742	$5 *Appias drusilla*	6·50	8·00

85 Two Footballers

1986. World Cup Football Championship, Mexico. Designs showing footballers.

743	**85**	10c. multicoloured	60	40
744	—	70c. multicoloured	1·75	1·25
745	—	$1 multicoloured	2·00	1·75
746	—	$4 multicoloured	5·00	6·50
MS747		86×104 mm. $5 multicoloured	5·50	5·50

1986. Appearance of Halley's Comet (1st issue). As T **151a** of Gambia. Multicoloured.

748	5c. Nicholas Copernicus (astronomer) and Earl of Rosse's six foot reflector telescope	40	40
749	20c. "Sputnik I" (first satellite) orbiting Earth, 1957	60	40
750	40c. Tycho Brahe's notes and sketch of 1577 Comet	80	60
751	$4 Edmond Halley and 1682 Comet	3·75	4·50
MS752	101×70 mm. $5 Halley's Comet	3·00	3·50

See also Nos. 790/4.
The captions of Nos. 750/1 are transposed.

1986. 60th Birthday of Queen Elizabeth II. As T **151b** of Gambia.

753	2c. black and yellow	10	15
754	$1.50 multicoloured	80	1·00
755	$4 multicoloured	2·00	2·75
MS756	120×85 mm. $5 black and brown	2·00	3·50

DESIGNS: 2c. Princesses Elizabeth and Margaret, Windsor Park, 1933; $1.50, Queen Elizabeth; $4 In Sydney, Australia, 1970; $5 The Royal Family, Coronation Day, 1937.

1986. "Ameripex '86" International Stamp Exhibition, Chicago. As T **315a** of Grenada. Multicoloured.

757	30c. Donald Duck riding mule in Grand Canyon	60	45
758	60c. Daisy Duck, Timothy Mouse and Dumbo on Golden Gate Bridge, San Francisco	85	1·00
759	$1 Mickey Mouse and Goofy in fire engine and Chicago Watertower	1·50	1·75
760	$3 Mickey Mouse as airmail pilot and White House	3·00	4·00
MS761	126×101 mm. $5 Donald Duck and Mickey Mouse watching Halley's Comet over Statue of Liberty	3·75	7·50

1986. Royal Wedding. As T **153b** of Gambia. Multicoloured.

762	60c. Prince Andrew and Miss Sarah Ferguson	55	45
763	70c. Prince Andrew in car	65	55
764	$4 Prince Andrew with Westland Lynx naval helicopter	4·00	3·50
MS765	88×88 mm. $5 Prince Andrew and Miss Sarah Ferguson (different)	4·00	5·50

86 *Hygrocybe firma*

1986. Mushrooms of the Lesser Antilles. Multicoloured.

766	15c. Type **86**	80	40
767	50c. *Xerocomus coccolobae*	1·75	1·25
768	$2 *Volvariella cubensis*	3·50	4·00
769	$3 *Lactarius putidus*	4·50	5·00
MS770	76×80 mm. $5 *Leptonia caeruleopitata*	9·00	12·00

87 Giant Atlantic or Dolobrate Pyram

1986. Sea Shells. Multicoloured.

771	15c. Type **87**	90	50
772	50c. Beau's murex	2·00	1·25
773	$1.10 West Indian fighting conch	2·25	2·75
774	$4 Alphabet conch	3·75	7·00
MS775	109×75 mm. $5 Brown-lined paper bubble	6·50	8·50

1986. World Cup Football Championship Winners, Mexico. Nos. 743/6 optd **WINNERS Argentina 3 W. Germany 2**.

776	**85**	10c. multicoloured	65	40
777	-	70c. multicoloured	1·40	1·10
778	-	$1 multicoloured	1·75	1·40
779	-	$4 multicoloured	4·00	5·50
MS780		86×104 mm. $5 multicoloured	8·00	10·00

88 Common Opossum

1986. Wildlife. Multicoloured.

781	10c. Type **88**	20	20
782	30c. Giant toad	40	40
783	60c. Land tortoise	80	80
784	85c. Murine opossum (vert)	85	85
785	90c. Burmese mongoose (vert)	90	1·00
786	$1.10 Nine-banded armadillo	1·00	1·25
787	$2 Agouti	1·75	2·25
788	$3 Humpback whale	4·00	4·25
MS789	Two sheets, each 103×72 mm. (a) $5 Mona monkey (vert). (b) $5 Iguana. Set of 2 sheets	11·00	14·00

1986. Appearance of Halley's Comet (2nd issue). Nos. 748/51 optd with **T 447a** of Ghana.

790	5c. Nicholas Copernicus (astronomer) and Earl of Rosse's six foot reflector telescope	60	60
791	20c. "Sputnik I" orbiting Earth, 1957	80	50
792	40c. Tycho Brahe's notes and sketch of 1577 Comet	1·00	60
793	$4 Edmond Halley and 1682 Comet	5·00	6·00
MS794	102×70 mm. $5 Halley's Comet	4·00	5·50

1986. Christmas. As **T 318a** of Grenada showing Walt Disney cartoon characters. Multicoloured.

795	25c. Chip n'Dale with hummingbird	50	15
796	30c. Robin delivering card to Mickey Mouse (vert)	50	20
797	50c. Piglet, Pooh and Jose Carioca on beach	65	30
798	60c. Grandma Duck feeding birds (vert)	75	40
799	70c. Cinderella and birds with mistletoe (vert)	80	50
800	$1.50 Huey, Dewey and Louie windsurfing	1·50	2·25
801	$3 Mickey Mouse and Morty on beach with turtle	1·75	3·00
802	$4 Kittens playing on piano (vert)	2·25	4·00
MS803	Two sheets, each 127×102 mm. (a) $5 Mickey Mouse and Willie the Whale. (b) $5 Bambi, Thumper and Blossom in snow (vert). Set of 2 sheets	8·00	11·50

89 Cycling

1986. Olympic Games, Seoul, South Korea (1988). Multicoloured.

804	10c.+5c. Type **89**	75	40
805	50c.+20c. Sailing	75	90
806	70c.+30c. Gymnastics	75	1·10
807	$2+$1 Horse trials	2·00	3·00
MS808	80×100 mm. $3+$1 Marathon	2·50	4·50

90 Aston-Martin "Volante" (1984)

1986. Centenary of Motoring. Multicoloured.

809	10c. Type **90**	25	25
810	30c. Jaguar "MK V" (1948)	45	45
811	60c. Nash "Ambassador" (1956)	60	65
812	70c. Toyota "Supra" (1984)	60	70
813	90c. Ferrari "Testarosa" (1985)	70	90
814	$1 BMW "501B" (1955)	70	95
815	$2 Mercedes-Benz "280 SL" (1968)	1·00	2·00
816	$3 Austro-Daimler "ADR8" (1932)	1·25	2·50
MS817	Two sheets, each 116×85 mm. (a) $5 Morgan "+8" (1977). (b) $5 Checker taxi. Set of 2 sheets	5·50	11·00

1986. Birth Centenary of Marc Chagall (artist). As **T 321a** of Grenada, showing various paintings.

818-857	$1.10×40 multicoloured		
MS858	Two sheets, each 110×95 mm. $5×10 multicoloured (each 104×89 mm). Imperf. Set of 10 sheets	28·00	28·00

1987. America's Cup Yachting Championship. As **T 321b** of Grenada. Multicoloured.

859	25c. *Defender*, 1895	60	40
860	45c. *Galatea*, 1886	80	60
861	70c. *Azzurra*, 1981	1·00	1·00
862	$4 *Australia II*, 1983	2·00	3·50
MS863	113×83 mm. $5 *Columbia* defeating *Shamrock*, 1899 (horiz)	5·00	7·00

1987. 500th Anniv (1992) of Discovery of America by Christopher Columbus (1st issue). As **T 322** of Grenada. Multicoloured.

864	15c. Christopher Columbus	35	25
865	30c. Queen Isabella of Castile	40	30
866	50c. *Santa Maria*	60	50
867	60c. Claiming the New World for Spain	60	60
868	90c. Early Spanish map of Lesser Antilles	80	75
869	$1 King Ferdinand of Aragon	80	80
870	$2 Fort La Navidad (drawing by Columbus)	1·50	2·00
871	$3 Galley and Caribs, Hispaniola (drawing by Columbus)	2·00	2·50
MS872	Two sheets, 104×72 mm. (a) $5 Caribs pearl fishing. (b) $5 *Santa Maria* at anchor. Set of 2 sheets	8·00	11·00

See also Nos. 1191/5, 1224/32, 1366/74, 1494/1500 and 1519/20.

1987. Milestones of Transportation. As **T 322a** of Grenada. Multicoloured.

873	10c. Saunders Roe "SRNI" (first hovercraft), 1959	65	30
874	15c. Bugatti "Royale" (largest car), 1931	70	35
875	30c. Aleksei Leonov and "Voskhod II" (first spacewalk), 1965	90	55
876	50c. C.S.S "Hunley" (first submarine to sink enemy ship), 1864	1·25	75
877	60c. Rolls Royce "Flying Bedstead" (first VTOL aircraft), 1954	1·50	85
878	70c. "Jenny Lind" (first mass produced locomotive class), 1847	1·60	1·25
879	90c. Duryea "Buggvaut" (first U.S petrol-driven car), 1893	1·75	1·25
880	$1.50 Steam locomotive, Metropolitan Railway, London (first underground line), 1863	2·50	2·75
881	$2 S.S. "Great Britain" (first transatlantic crossing by screw-steamship), 1843	3·00	3·25
882	$3 "Budweiser Rocket" (fastest car), 1979	3·25	3·75

1987. "Capex '87" International Stamp Exhibition, Toronto. Game Fish. As **T 323** of Grenada but horiz. Multicoloured.

883	6c. Yellow chub	15	15
884	30c. King mackerel	40	30
885	50c. Short-finned mako	55	55
886	60c. Dolphin (fish)	60	60
887	90c. Skipjack tuna ("Bonito")	75	75
888	$1.10 Cobia	1·00	1·25
889	$3 Tarpon	2·25	2·75
890	$5 Swordfish	2·50	3·25
MS891	Two sheets, each 100×70 mm. (a) $5 Spotted jewfish. (b) $5 Amberjack. Set of 2 sheets	8·00	11·00

1987. Centenary of Statue of Liberty (1986) (2nd issue). As **T 323a** of Grenada. Multicoloured.

892	10c. Cleaning face of statue	20	20
893	15c. Commemorative lapel badges	30	30
894	25c. Band playing and statue	40	40
895	30c. Band on parade and statue	45	45
896	45c. Face of statue	50	50
897	50c. Cleaning head of statue (horiz)	55	55
898	60c. Models of statue (horiz)	65	65
899	70c. Small boat flotilla (horiz)	75	85
900	$1 Unveiling ceremony	85	90
901	$1.10 Statue and Manhattan skyline	90	1·00
902	$2 Parade of warships	1·75	2·00
903	$3 Making commemorative flags	1·90	2·25

1987. Great Scientific Discoveries. As **T 325** of Grenada. Multicoloured.

904	60c. Newton medal	1·00	80
905	$1 Louis Daguerre (inventor of daguerreotype)	1·25	1·00
906	$2 Antoine Lavoisier and apparatus	2·25	3·00
907	$3 Rudolf Diesel and first oil engine	7·00	5·50
MS908	105×75 mm. $5 Halley's Comet	6·00	7·50

No. 907 is inscribed "JAMES WATT" in error.

1987. Bicentenary of U.S. Constitution. As **T 327a** of Grenada. Multicoloured.

909	10c. Washington addressing delegates, Constitutional Convention	25	20
910	50c. Flag and State Seal, Georgia	85	75
911	60c. Capitol, Washington (vert)	85	80
912	$4 Thomas Jefferson (statesman) (vert)	3·25	6·00
MS913	105×75 mm. $5 Alexander Hamilton (New York delegate) (vert)	2·25	4·00

1987. "Hafnia '87" International Stamp Exhibition, Copenhagen. Designs as **T 328** of Grenada, but horiz, illustrating Hans Christian Andersen's fairy tales. Multicoloured.

914	25c. Donald and Daisy Duck in "The Swineherd"	50	30
915	30c. Mickey Mouse, Donald and Daisy Duck in "What the Good Man Does is Always Right"	55	35
916	50c. Mickey and Minnie Mouse in "Little Tuk"	75	75
917	60c. Minnie Mouse and Ferdie in "The World's Fairest Rose"	75	75
918	70c. Mickey Mouse in "The Garden of Paradise"	80	80
919	$1.50 Goofy and Mickey Mouse in "The Naughty Boy"	2·00	2·25
920	$3 Goofy in "What the Moon Saw"	2·75	3·00
921	$4 Alice as "Thumbelina"	3·25	3·50
MS922	Two sheets, each 127×101 mm. (a) $5 Daisy Duck in "Hans Clodhopper". (b) $5 Aunt Matilda and Mickey Mouse in "Elder-Tree Mother". Set of 2 sheets	11·00	12·00

91 *The Virgin and Child with Saints Martin and Agnes*

1987. Christmas. Religious Paintings by El Greco. Multicoloured.

923	10c. Type **91**	40	15
924	50c. "St. Agnes" (detail from "The Virgin and Child with Saints Martin and Agnes")	1·25	75
925	60c. "The Annunciation"	1·25	75
926	$4 "The Holy Family with St. Anne"	4·75	7·25
MS927	75×101 mm. $5 "The Adoration of the Shepherds"	7·50	8·50

1988. Royal Ruby Wedding. As **T 330a** of Grenada. Multicoloured.

928	20c. brown, black and green	50	15
929	30c. brown and black	50	20
930	$2 multicoloured	2·25	2·25
931	$3 multicoloured	2·50	3·25
MS932	76×100 mm. $5 multicoloured	4·50	5·00

DESIGNS: 20c. Queen Elizabeth II with Princess Anne, c. 1957; 30c. Wedding photograph, 1947; $2 Queen with Prince Charles and Princess Anne, c. 1955; $3 Queen Elizabeth (from photo by Tim Graham) 1980; $5 Princess Elizabeth in wedding dress, 1947.

1988. Olympic Games, Seoul. As **T 331** of Grenada showing Walt Disney cartoon characters as Olympic competitors. Multicoloured.

933	1c. Minnie Mouse as rhythmic gymnast (horiz)	10	10
934	2c. Pete and Goofy as pankration wrestlers (horiz)	10	10
935	3c. Huey and Dewey as synchronized swimmers (horiz)	10	10
936	4c. Huey, Dewey and Louie in hoplite race (horiz)	10	10
937	5c. Clarabelle and Daisy Duck playing baseball (horiz)	10	10
938	10c. Goofy and Donald Duck in horse race (horiz)	10	10
939	$6 Donald Duck and Uncle Scrooge McDuck windsurfing (horiz)	4·50	5·50
940	$7 Mickey Mouse in chariot race (horiz)	4·75	5·50
MS941	Two sheets, each 127×101 mm. (a) $5 Mickey Mouse throwing discus in pentathlon. (b) $5 Donald Duck playing tennis. Set of 2 sheets	7·50	9·00

92 Scout signalling with Semaphore Flags

1988. World Scout Jamboree, Australia. Multicoloured.

942	50c. Type **92**	50	35
943	70c. Canoeing	60	50
944	$1 Cooking over campfire (horiz)	70	65
945	$3 Scouts around campfire (horiz)	2·00	3·00
MS946	110×77 mm. $5 Erecting tent	4·00	4·50

1988. Birds. As **T 334** of Grenada. Multicoloured.

947	20c. Yellow-crowned night heron	30	25
948	25c. Brown pelican	30	25
949	45c. Audubon's shearwater	40	35
950	60c. Red-footed booby	50	45
951	70c. Bridled tern	55	55
952	90c. Red-billed tropic bird	70	70
953	$3 Blue-winged teal	1·75	2·25
954	$4 Sora crake ("Sora")	2·00	2·75
MS955	Two sheets, each 105×75 mm. (a) $5 Purple-throated carib. (b) $5 Little blue heron. Set of 2 sheets	6·00	6·50

1988. 500th Birth Anniv of Titian (artist). As **T 166a** of Gambia. Multicoloured.

956	15c. *Man with Blue Eyes*	15	15
957	30c. *The Three Ages of Man* (detail)	20	20
958	60c. *Don Diego Mendoza*	35	35
959	75c. *Emperor Charles V seated*	50	50
960	$1 *A Young Man in a Fur*	60	60
961	$2 *Tobias and the Angel*	1·10	1·40
962	$3 *Pietro Bembo*	1·60	1·90
963	$4 *Pier Luigi Farnese*	1·75	2·25
MS964	110×95 mm. (a) $5 *Sacred and Profane Love* (detail). (b) $5 *Venus and Adonis* (detail). Set of 2 sheets	7·00	8·00

1988. Airships. As **T 336** of Grenada. Multicoloured.

965	10c. "Hindenburg" over Sugarloaf Mountain, Rio de Janeiro, 1937 (horiz)	70	20
966	20c. *Hindenburg* over New York, 1937 (horiz)	85	30
967	30c. U.S. Navy "K" Class airships on Atlantic escort duty, 1944 (horiz)	95	35
968	40c. *Hindenburg* approaching Lakehurst, 1937	1·00	45
969	60c. *Graf Zeppelin* and *Hindenburg* over Germany, 1936	1·25	60
970	70c. *Hindenburg* and *Los Angeles* moored at Lakehurst, 1936 (horiz)	1·25	70
971	$1 *Graf Zeppelin II* over Dover, 1939	1·25	85
972	$2 *Ersatz Deutschland* on scheduled passenger flight, 1912 (horiz)	1·60	1·60

973	$3 *Graf Zeppelin* over Dome of the Rock, Jerusalem, 1931 (horiz)	2·50	2·25
974	$4 *Hindenburg* over Olympic stadium, Berlin, 1936 (horiz)	2·50	2·25
MS975	Two sheets (a) 76×95 mm. $5 LZ-127 *Graf Zeppelin*, 1933. (b) 95×76 mm. $5 LZ-127 *Graf Zeppelin*, 1931 (horiz). Set of 2 sheets	8·00	10·00

93 Bambi and his mother

1988. Disney Animal Cartoon Films.
976- 30c.×54 multicoloured.
1029

MS1030	Six sheets, each 127×102 mm. $5×6 multicoloured. Set of 6 sheets	28·00	30·00

DESIGNS: Scenes from *Bambi*, *Dumbo* $5 (vert), *Lady and the Tramp* $5 (vert), *The Aristocats*, *The Fox and the Hound* and *101 Dalmatians*.

1988. "Sydpex '88" National Stamp Exhibition, Sydney and 60th Birthday of Mickey Mouse. As T **337** of Grenada. Multicoloured.

1031	1c. Mickey Mouse conducting at Sydney Opera House	10	10
1032	2c. Mickey Mouse and Donald Duck at Ayers Rock	10	10
1033	3c. Goofy and Mickey Mouse on sheep station	10	10
1034	4c. Goofy and Mickey Mouse at Lone Pine Koala Sanctuary	10	10
1035	5c. Mickey Mouse, Donald Duck and Goofy playing Australian football	10	10
1036	10c. Mickey Mouse and Goofy camel racing	10	10
1037	$5 Donald Duck and his nephews bowling	4·50	5·00
1038	$6 Mickey Mouse with America's Cup trophy and *Australia II* (yacht)	5·50	6·00
MS1039	Two sheets, each 127×102 mm. (a) $5 Goofy diving on Great Barrier Reef. (b) $5 Donald Duck, Mickey and Minnie Mouse at beach barbecue. Set of 2 sheets	7·50	9·50

1988. Flowering Trees and Shrubs. As T **339** of Grenada. Multicoloured.

1040	10c. Potato tree (vert)	15	15
1041	20c. Wild cotton	15	15
1042	30c. Shower of gold (vert)	20	20
1043	60c. Napoleon's button (vert)	35	30
1044	90c. Geiger tree	60	70
1045	$1 Fern tree	70	80
1046	$2 French cashew	1·25	2·00
1047	$4 Amhrestia (vert)	2·00	3·00
MS1048	Two sheets, each 117×88 mm. (a) $5 African tulip tree (vert). (b) $5 Swamp immortelle. Set of 2 sheets	4·25	5·50

1988. Cars. As T **335** of Grenada. Multicoloured.

1049	$2 Doble "Series E", 1925	1·40	1·25
1050	$2 Alvis "12/50", 1926	1·40	1·25
1051	$2 Sunbeam 3-litre, 1927	1·40	1·25
1052	$2 Franklin "Airman", 1928	1·40	1·25
1053	$2 Delage "D8S", 1929	1·40	1·25
1054	$2 Mors, 1897	1·40	1·25
1055	$2 Peerless "Green Dragon", 1904	1·40	1·25
1056	$2 Pope-Hartford, 1909	1·40	1·25
1057	$2 Daniels "Submarine Speedstar", 1920	1·40	1·25
1058	$2 McFarlan 9.3 litre, 1922	1·40	1·25
1059	$2 Frazer Nash "Lemans" replica, 1949	1·40	1·25
1060	$2 Pegaso "Z102", 1953	1·40	1·25
1061	$2 Siata "Spyder V-8", 1953	1·40	1·25
1062	$2 Kurtis-Offenhauser, 1953	1·40	1·25
1063	$2 Kaiser-Darrin, 1954	1·40	1·25
1064	$2 Tracta, 1930	1·40	1·25
1065	$2 Maybach "Zeppelin", 1932	1·40	1·25
1066	$2 Railton "Light Sports", 1934	1·40	1·25
1067	$2 Hotchkiss, 1936	1·40	1·25
1068	$2 Mercedes-Benz "W163", 1939	1·40	1·25
1069	$2 Aston-Martin "Vantage V8", 1982	1·40	1·25
1070	$2 Porsche "956", 1982	1·40	1·25
1071	$2 Lotus "Esprit Turbo", 1983	1·40	1·25
1072	$2 McLaren "MP4/2", 1984	1·40	1·25
1073	$2 Mercedes-Benz "190E 2.3-16", 1985	1·40	1·25
1074	$2 Ferrari "250 GT Lusso", 1963	1·40	1·25
1075	$2 Porsche "904", 1964	1·40	1·25
1076	$2 Volvo "P1800", 1967	1·40	1·25
1077	$2 McLaren-Chevrolet "M8D", 1970	1·40	1·25
1078	$2 Jaguar "XJ6", 1981	1·40	1·25

1988. "Mickey's Christmas Parade". As T **340a** of Grenada showing Walt Disney cartoon characters. Multicoloured.

1079	$1 Dumbo	65	65
1080	$1 Goofy as Father Christmas	65	65
1081	$1 Minnie Mouse waving from window	65	65
1082	$1 Clarabelle, Mordie and Ferdie watching parade	65	65
1083	$1 Donald Duck's nephews	65	65
1084	$1 Donald Duck as drummer	65	65
1085	$1 Toy soldiers	65	65
1086	$1 Mickey Mouse on wooden horse	65	65
MS1087	Two sheets, each 127×102 mm. (a) $7 Peter Pan and Captain Hook on float (horiz). (b) $7 Mickey Mouse as Father Christmas and Donald Duck in carnival train (horiz). Set of 2 sheets	10·00	11·00

94 Middleweight Boxing (Gold, Henry Maske, East Germany)

1989. Olympic Medal Winners, Seoul (1988). Multicoloured.

1088	15c. Type **94**	40	20
1089	50c. Freestyle wrestling (130 kg) (Bronze, Andreas Schroeder, East Germany)	60	40
1090	60c. Women's team gymnastics (Bronze, East Germany)	70	50
1091	75c. Platform diving (Gold, Greg Louganis, U.S.A.)	60	80
1092	$1 Freestyle wrestling (52 kg) (Gold, Mitsuru Sato, Japan)	90	80
1093	$2 Men's freestyle 4×200 m relay swimming (Bronze, West Germany)	1·40	1·40
1094	$3 Men's 5000 m (Silver, Dieter Baumann, West Germany)	1·60	2·00
1095	$4 Women's heptathlon (Gold, Jackie Joyner-Kersee, U.S.A.)	2·00	2·50
MS1096	Two sheets, each 70×100 mm. (a) $6 Weightlifting (67.5 kg) (Gold, Joachim Kunz, East Germany). (b) $6 Team Three-Day Event (Gold, West Germany). Set of 2 sheets	6·50	8·50

1989. Japanese Art. Paintings by Hiroshige. As T **177a** of Gambia. Multicoloured.

1097	15c. *Crossing the Oi at Shimada by Ferry*	25	25
1098	20c. *Daimyo and Entourage at Arai*	30	30
1099	45c. *Cargo Portage through Goyu*	50	50
1100	75c. *Snowfall at Fujigawa*	75	75
1101	$1 *Horses for the Emperor at Chirifu*	85	85
1102	$2 *Rainfall at Tsuchiyama*	1·60	1·60
1103	$3 *An Inn at Ishibe*	2·25	2·25
1104	$4 *On the Shore of Lake Biwa at Otsu*	2·75	2·75
MS1105	Two sheets, each 102×78 mm. (a) $5 *Fishing Village of Yokkaichi on the Mie*. (b) $5 *Pilgrimage to Atsuta Shrine at Miya*. Set of 2 sheets	4·75	7·00

1989. World Cup Football Championship, Italy (1990) (1st issue). As T **345a** of Grenada. Multicoloured.

1106	15c. World Cup trophy	50	20
1107	20c. Flags of Argentina (winners 1986) and International Federation of Football Associations (FIFA) (horiz)	1·25	20
1108	45c. Franz Beckenbauer (West Germany) with World Cup, 1974	1·00	35
1109	75c. Flags of Italy (winners 1982) and FIFA (horiz)	1·75	55
1110	$1 Pele (Brazil) with Jules Rimet trophy	1·75	85
1111	$2 Flags of West Germany (winners 1974) and FIFA (horiz)	2·25	2·00
1112	$3 Flags of Brazil (winners 1970) and FIFA (horiz)	2·25	2·75
1113	$4 Jules Rimet trophy and Brazil players	2·25	2·75
MS1114	(a) 100×81 mm. $6 Goalkeeper (horiz). (b) 66×95 mm. $6 Péle with Jules Rimet trophy. Set of 2 sheets	8·50	9·00

See also Nos. 1285/9.

1989. North American Railway Locomotives. As T **342** of Grenada. Multicoloured.

1115	$2 Morris & Essex Railroad *Dover*, 1841, U.S.A.	1·50	1·50
1116	$2 Baltimore & Ohio Railroad No. 57 *Memnon*, 1848, U.S.A.	1·50	1·50
1117	$2 Camden & Amboy Railroad *John Stevens*, 1849, U.S.A.	1·50	1·50
1118	$2 Lawrence Machine Shop *Lawrence*, 1853, U.S.A.	1·50	1·50
1119	$2 South Carolina Railroad *James S. Corry*, 1859, U.S.A.	1·50	1·50
1120	$2 Mine Hill & Schuylkill Haven Railroad flexible beam No. 3, 1860, U.S.A.	1·50	1·50
1121	$2 Delaware, Lackawanna & Western Railroad *Montrose*, 1861, U.S.A.	1·50	1·50
1122	$2 Central Pacific Railroad No. 68 *Pequop*, 1868, U.S.A.	1·50	1·50
1123	$2 Boston & Providence Railroad *Daniel Nason*, 1863, U.S.A.	1·50	1·50
1124	$2 Morris & Essex Railroad *Joe Scranton*, 1870, U.S.A.	1·50	1·50
1125	$2 Central Railroad of New Jersey No. 124, 1871, U.S.A.	1·50	1·50
1126	$2 Baldwin tramway steam locomotive, 1876, U.S.A.	1·50	1·50
1127	$2 Lackawanna & Bloomsburg Railroad *Luzerne*, 1878, U.S.A.	1·50	1·50
1128	$2 Central Mexican Railroad No. 150, 1892	1·50	1·50
1129	$2 Denver South Park & Pacific Railroad No. 15, Breckenridge, 1879, U.S.A.	1·50	1·50
1130	$2 Miles Planting & Manufacturing Company plantation locomotive *Daisy*, 1894, U.S.A.	1·50	1·50
1131	$2 Central of Georgia Railroad Baldwin 854 No. 1136, 1895, U.S.A.	1·50	1·50
1132	$2 Savannah, Florida & Western Railroad No. 111, 1900, U.S.A.	1·50	1·50
1133	$2 Douglas, Gilmore & Company contractors locomotive No. 3, 1902, U.S.A.	1·50	1·50
1134	$2 Lehigh Valley Coal Company compressed air locomotive No. 900, 1903, U.S.A.	1·50	1·50
1135	$2 Louisiana & Texas Railroad McKeen motor locomotive, 1908, U.S.A.	1·50	1·50
1136	$2 Clear Lake Lumber Company Type B Climax locomotive No. 6, 1910, U.S.A.	1·50	1·50
1137	$2 Blue Jay Lumber Company Heisler locomotive No. 10, 1912, U.S.A.	1·50	1·50
1138	$2 Stewartstown Railroad petrol locomotive No. 6, 1920s, U.S.A.	1·50	1·50
1139	$2 Bangor & Aroostock Railroad Class G No. 186, 1921, U.S.A.	1·50	1·50
1140	$2 Hammond Lumber Company Mallet locomotive, No. 6, 1923, U.S.A.	1·50	1·50
1141	$2 Central Railway of New Jersey diesel locomotive No. 1000, 1925, U.S.A.	1·50	1·50
1142	$2 Atchison Topeka & Santa Fe Railroad *Super Chief* diesel express, 1935, U.S.A.	1·50	1·50
1143	$2 Norfolk & Western Railroad Class Y-6, 1948, U.S.A.	1·50	1·50
1144	$2 Boston & Maine Railroad Budd diesel railcar, 1949, U.S.A.	1·50	1·50

94a Mickey Mouse and Donald Duck at Ecole Militaire Inflating Balloon

1989. "Philexfrance '89" International Stamp Exn, Paris. Designs showing Walt Disney cartoon characters in Paris. Multicoloured.

1145	1c. Type **94a**	10	10
1146	2c. Mickey and Minnie Mouse on river boat passing Conciergerie	10	10
1147	3c. Mickey Mouse at Hotel de Ville (vert)	10	10
1148	4c. Mickey Mouse at Genie of the Bastille monument (vert)	10	10
1149	5c. Mickey and Minnie Mouse arriving at Opera House	10	10
1150	10c. Mickey and Minnie Mouse on tandem in Luxembourg Gardens	10	10
1151	$5 Mickey Mouse in aeroplane over L'Arch de La Defense (vert)	5·50	6·50
1152	$6 Mickey Mouse at Place Vendome (vert)	5·50	6·50
MS1153	Two sheets, each 127×102 mm. (a) $6 Mickey and Minnie Mouse on scooter in Place de la Concorde. (b) $6 Donald Duck, Mickey and Minnie Mouse in balloon over Versailles. Set of 2 sheets	11·00	13·00

95 Launch of "Apollo 11"

1989. 20th Anniv of First Manned Landing on Moon. Multicoloured.

1154	25c. Type **95**	30	30
1155	50c. Splashdown (horiz)	50	50
1156	60c. Modules in space	60	60
1157	75c. Aldrin setting up experiment (horiz)	70	70
1158	$1 "Apollo 11" leaving Earth orbit (horiz)	80	80
1159	$2 Moving "Apollo 11" to launch site	1·60	1·90
1160	$3 Lunar module "Eagle" leaving Moon (horiz)	2·00	2·50
1161	$4 "Eagle" landing on Moon	2·25	2·75
MS1162	(a) 71×100 mm. $5 Armstrong stepping onto Moon. (b) 101×72 mm. $5 Armstrong's footprint on Moon. Set of 2 sheets	6·50	8·00

1989. Fungi. As T **348** of Grenada. Multicoloured.

1163	6c. *Agaricus purpurellus* (incorrectly inscr "Collybia aurea")	35	25
1164	10c. *Podaxis pistillaris*	35	25
1165	20c. *Hygrocybe firma*	55	45
1166	30c. *Agaricus rufoaurantiacus*	65	55
1167	75c. *Leptonia howellii*	1·40	1·40
1168	$2 *Marasmiellus purpureus*	2·50	2·75
1169	$3 *Marasmius trinitatis*	3·00	3·25
1170	$4 *Collybia aurea* (incorrectly inscr "Hygrocybe martinicensis")	3·25	3·50
MS1171	Two sheets, each 56×71 mm. (a) $6 *Lentinus crinitus* (incorrectly inscr "Agaricus purpurellus"). (b) $6 *Hygrocybe martinicensis* (incorrectly inscr "Lentinus crinitus"). Set of 2 sheets	12·00	13·00

1989. Butterflies. As T **350** of Grenada. Multicoloured.

1172	25c. *Battus polydamas* (inscr "Papilio androgeus")	40	40
1173	35c. *Phoebis sennae*	45	45
1174	45c. *Hamadryas feronia*	55	55
1175	50c. *Cynthia cardui*	55	55
1176	75c. *Ascia monuste*	80	80
1177	90c. *Eurema lisa*	90	90
1178	$2 *Aphrissa statira*	2·00	2·00
1179	$3 *Hypolimnas misippus*	2·50	2·50
MS1180	Two sheets, each 87×115 mm. (a) $6 *Anartia amathea*. (b) $6 *Pseudolycaena marsyas*. Set of 2 sheets	9·00	11·00

96 Ethel Barrymore

1989. 425th Birth Anniv of Shakespeare. Shakespearean Actors. Multicoloured.

1181	15c. Type **96**	35	25
1182	$1.10 Richard Burton	1·50	1·25
1183	$2 John Barrymore	2·25	2·25
1184	$3 Paul Robeson	2·50	2·75
MS1185	103×77 mm. $6 Bando Tamasaburo and Nakamura Kanzaburo	4·50	5·50

97 Buddy Holly

1989. Musicians. Multicoloured.

1186	10c. Type **97**	35	25
1187	25c. Jimmy Hendrix	55	40
1188	75c. Mighty Sparrow	70	70
1189	$4 Katsutoji Kineya	3·00	4·00
MS1190	103×77 mm. $6 Kurt Weill	4·25	4·75

97a Arawaks canoeing

1989. 500th Anniv (1992) of Discovery of America by Columbus (2nd issue). Pre-Columbian Arawak Society. As T **247** of Antigua. Multicoloured.

1191	15c. Type **97a**	25	25
1192	75c. Family and campfire	75	75
1193	90c. Using stone tools	95	95
1194	$3 Eating and drinking	2·50	3·00
MS1195	84×87 mm. $6 Making fire	3·50	4·25

1989. "World Stamp Expo '89" International Stamp Exhibition, Washington. Designs showing Walt Disney cartoon characters illustrating proverbs from *Poor Richard's Almanack*. As T **352** of Grenada. Multicoloured.

1196	1c. Uncle Scrooge McDuck with gold coins in sinking boat	10	10
1197	2c. Robin Hood shooting apple off Friar Tuck	10	10
1198	3c. Winnie the Pooh with honey	10	10
1199	4c. Goofy, Minnie Mouse and Donald Duck exercising	10	10
1200	5c. Pinnochio holding Jimminy Cricket	10	10
1201	6c. Huey and Dewey putting up wallpaper	10	10
1202	8c. Mickey Mouse asleep in storm	15	10
1203	10c. Mickey Mouse as Benjamin Franklin selling "Pennsylvania Gazette"	15	10
1204	$5 Mickey Mouse with chicken, recipe book and egg	4·00	5·00
1205	$6 Mickey Mouse missing carriage	4·50	5·00
MS1206	Two sheets, each 127×102 mm. (a) $6 Mickey Mouse bowing. (b) $6 Mickey Mouse delivering basket of food (vert). Set of 2 sheets	10·50	11·00

1990. Christmas. Paintings by Rubens. As T **352a** of Grenada. Multicoloured.

1207	10c. *The Annunciation*	35	15
1208	15c. *The Flight of the Holy Family into Egypt*	40	15
1209	25c. *The Presentation in the Temple*	55	15
1210	45c. *The Holy Family under the Apple Tree*	70	25
1211	$2 *Madonna and Child with Saints*	2·00	2·50
1212	$4 *The Virgin and Child enthroned with Saints*	3·00	4·00
1213	$5 *The Holy Family*	3·00	4·00
MS1214	Two sheets, each 70×95 mm. (a) $5 *The Adoration of the Magi* (sketch). (b) $5 *The Adoration of the Magi*. Set of 2 sheets	12·00	14·00

1990. "EXPO '90" International Garden and Greenery Exhibition, Osaka. Caribbean Orchids. As T **354** of Grenada. Multicoloured.

1215	15c. Brassacattleya Thalie	30	30
1216	20c. Odontocidium Tigersun	35	35
1217	50c. Odontioda Hambuhren	55	55
1218	75c. Paphiopedium Delrosi	75	75
1219	$1 Vuylstekeara Yokara	95	95
1220	$2 Paphiopedium Geelong	1·75	2·00
1221	$3 Wilsonara Tigerwood	2·00	2·25
1222	$4 Cymbidium Ormoulu	2·50	2·75
MS1223	Two sheets, each 98×68 mm. (a) $6 Odontonia Sappho. (b) $6 Cymbidium Vieux Rose. Set of 2 sheets	11·00	11·50

1990. 500th Anniv (1992) of Discovery of America by Columbus (3rd issue). New World Natural History—Insects. As T **354a** of Grenada. Multicoloured.

1224	35c. *Dynastes hercules* (beetle)	35	35
1225	40c. *Chalcolepidius porcatus* (beetle)	35	35
1226	50c. *Acrocinus longimanus* (beetle)	40	40
1227	60c. *Battus polydamas* (butterfly)	1·00	75
1228	$1 *Orthemis ferruginea* (skimmer)	1·25	95
1229	$2 *Psiloptera variolosa* (beetle)	1·75	1·75
1230	$3 *Hypolimnas misippus* (butterfly)	3·00	3·00
1231	$4 Scarab beetle	3·00	3·00
MS1232	Two sheets, each 102×70 mm. (a) $6 *Calpodes ethlius* (butterfly). (b) *Danaus plexippus* (butterfly). Set of 2 sheets	8·50	9·50

1990. Wildlife. As T **254** of Antigua. Multicoloured.

1233	5c. West Indies giant rice rat	20	20
1234	25c. Agouti	35	35
1235	30c. Humpback whale	70	65
1236	40c. Pilot whale	70	65
1237	$1 Spotted dolphin	95	95
1238	$2 Egyptian mongoose	1·75	2·00
1239	$3 Brazilian tree porcupine	2·25	2·75
1240	$4 American manatee	2·50	3·00
MS1241	Two sheets, each 107×80 mm. (a) $6 Caribbean monk seal. (b) $6 Egyptian mongoose (different). Set of 2 sheets	8·00	9·00

1990. 50th Anniv of Second World War. As T **354b** of Grenada. Multicoloured.

1242	6c. British tanks in France, 1939	30	30
1243	10c. Operation *Crusader*, North Africa, 1941	30	30
1244	20c. Retreat of the Afrika Corps, 1942	40	40
1245	45c. American landing on Aleutian Islands, 1943	50	50
1246	50c. U.S marines landing on Tarawa, 1943	55	55
1247	60c. U.S army entering Rome, 1944	60	60
1248	75c. U.S tanks crossing River Seine, 1944	70	70
1249	$1 Battle of the Bulge, 1944	95	95
1250	$5 American infantry in Italy, 1945	3·00	3·50
1251	$6 B-29 Enola Gay dropping atomic bomb on Hiroshima, 1945	3·50	3·50
MS1252	112×84 mm. $6 St. Paul's Cathedral in London Blitz, 1940	4·00	5·00

1990. "Stamp World London '90" International Stamp Exhibition. As T **193** of Gambia showing Walt Disney cartoon characters at Shakespeare sites. Multicoloured.

1253	15c. Daisy Duck at Ann Hathaway's Cottage (horiz)	50	20
1254	30c. Minnie and Bill Mouse at Shakespeare's birthplace, Stratford	65	35
1255	50c. Minnie Mouse in front of Mary Arden's house, Wilmcote	85	70
1256	60c. Mickey Mouse leaning on hedge in New Place gardens, Stratford (horiz)	1·00	90
1257	$1 Mickey Mouse walking in New Place gardens, Stratford (horiz)	1·40	1·25
1258	$2 Mickey Mouse carrying books in Scholars Lane, Stratford	2·50	2·50
1259	$4 Mickey Mouse and Royal Shakespeare Theatre, Stratford	3·50	4·00
1260	$5 Ludwig von Drake teaching Mickey Mouse at the Stratford Grammar School (horiz)	3·50	4·00
MS1261	Two sheets, each 126×101 mm. (a) $6 Mickey Mouse as Shakespeare. (b) $6 Mickey and Minnie Mouse in rowing boat on River Avon, Stratford (horiz). Set of 2 sheets	11·00	12·00

1990. 90th Birthday of Queen Elizabeth the Queen Mother. As T **194** of Gambia, showing photographs 1970–79.

1262	$2 Queen Mother wearing pink hat and coat	1·10	1·40
1263	$2 Prince Charles and Queen Mother at Garter ceremony	1·10	1·40
1264	$2 Queen Mother in blue floral outfit	1·10	1·40
MS1265	90×75 mm. $6 Queen Mother in Garter robes	4·25	5·00

1990. Stamp World London 90 International Stamp Exhibition (2nd issue). Sheet 97×75 mm containing horiz designs as T **356** of Grenada.

MS1266	$6 green	5·50	6·50

DESIGN: $6 Map of South America and Logo.

1990. Birds. As T **358** of Grenada, but vert. Multicoloured.

1267	25c. Yellow-bellied seedeater	30	30
1268	45c. Carib grackle	50	50
1269	50c. Black-whiskered vireo	55	55
1270	75c. Bananaquit	70	70
1271	$1 White-collared swift	95	95
1272	$2 Yellow-bellied elaenia	1·50	1·50
1273	$3 Blue-hooded euphonia	2·00	2·00
1274	$5 Eared dove	3·25	3·25
MS1275	Two sheets, each 101×72 mm. (a) $6 Mangrove cuckoo. (b) $6 Scaly-breasted thrasher. Set of 2 sheets	8·50	10·00

1990. Crustaceans. As T **359** of Grenada. Multicoloured.

1276	10c. Slipper lobster	20	20
1277	25c. Green reef crab	30	30
1278	65c. Caribbean lobsterette	60	60
1279	75c. Blind deep sea lobster	70	70
1280	$1 Flattened crab	95	95
1281	$2 Ridged slipper lobster	1·75	2·00
1282	$3 Land crab	2·25	2·75
1283	$4 Mountain crab	2·50	2·75
MS1284	Two sheets, each 108×76 mm. (a) $6 Caribbean king crab. (b) $6 Purse crab. Set of 2 sheets	8·00	10·00

98 Lineker, England

1990. World Cup Football Championship, Italy (2nd issue). Multicoloured.

1285	15c. Type **98**	25	25
1286	45c. Burruchaga, Argentina	45	45
1287	$2 Hysen, Sweden	1·75	2·25
1288	$4 Sang Ho, South Korea	2·75	3·75
MS1289	Two sheets, each 76×90 mm. (a) $6 Ramos, U.S.A. (b) $6 Stojkovic, Yugoslavia. Set of 2 sheets	8·50	9·50

1990. Olympic Games, Barcelona (1992). As T **195a** of Gambia. Multicoloured.

1290	10c. Boxing	10	10
1291	25c. Olympic flame	20	20
1292	50c. Football	40	40
1293	75c. Discus throwing	60	60
1294	$1 Pole vaulting	85	85
1295	$2 Show jumping	1·75	2·00
1296	$4 Women's basketball	3·50	3·75
1297	$5 Men's gymnastics	3·00	3·75
MS1298	Two sheets. (a) 101×70 mm. $6 Sailboards. (b) 70×101 mm. $6 Decathlon. Set of 2 sheets	8·50	9·50

1991. 350th Death Anniv of Rubens. As T **195c** of Gambia. Multicoloured.

1299	5c. *Adam and Eve* (Eve detail) (vert)	30	20
1300	15c. *Esther before Ahasuerus* (detail)	50	20
1301	25c. *Adam and Eve* (Adam detail) (vert)	60	25
1302	50c. *Expulsion from Eden*	90	60
1303	$1 *Cain slaying Abel* (detail) (vert)	1·60	1·10
1304	$2 *Lot's Flight*	2·25	2·25
1305	$4 *Samson and Delilah* (detail)	3·50	4·00
1306	$5 *Abraham and Melchizedek*	3·75	4·00
MS1307	Two sheets, each 101×71 mm. (a) $6 *The Meeting of David and Abigail* (detail). (b) $6 *Daniel in the Lions' Den* (detail). Set of 2 sheets	10·00	12·00

1991. Coral Reef Fish. As T **357** of Grenada. Multicoloured.

1308	15c. Barred hamlet	50	25
1309	35c. Long-spined squirrelfish	80	50
1310	45c. Red-spotted hawkfish	85	60
1311	75c. Bigeye	1·25	1·00
1312	$1 Balloonfish ("Spiny puffer")	1·50	1·25
1313	$2 Small-mouth grunt	2·25	2·50
1314	$3 Harlequin bass	2·75	3·25
1315	$5 Creole fish	3·00	3·50
MS1316	Two sheets, each 103×72 mm. (a) $6 Copper sweeper. (b) $6 Royal gramma ("Fairy Basslet"). Set of 2 sheets	8·50	10·00

99 Angel with Star and Lantern

1991. Christmas (1990). Hummel Figurines. Multicoloured.

1317	10c. Type **99**	40	10
1318	15c. Christ Child and Angel playing mandolin	50	15
1319	25c. Shepherd	60	25
1320	50c. Angel with trumpet and lantern	1·10	50
1321	$1 Nativity scene	1·75	95
1322	$2 Christ Child and Angel holding candle	2·75	2·50
1323	$4 Angel with baskets	3·75	4·25
1324	$5 Angels singing	4·00	4·25
MS1325	Two sheets, each 99×122 mm. (a) 5c. As No. 1318; 40c. As No. 1320; 60c. As No. 1321; $3 As No. 1324. (b) 20c. As No. 1319; 75c. As No. 1322; $6 As No. 1323. Set of 2 sheets	10·00	11·00

100 *Brassia maculata*

1991. Orchids. Multicoloured.

1326	5c. Type **100**	30	30
1327	10c. *Oncidium lanceanum*	30	30
1328	15c. *Broughtonia sanguinea*	35	20
1329	25c. *Diacrium bicornutum*	40	20
1330	35c. *Cattleya skinneri*	40	20
1331	45c. *Epidendrum fragrans*	50	25
1332	50c. *Oncidium papilio*	55	30
1333	75c. *Neocogniauxia monophylla*	70	50
1334	$1 *Epidendrum polybulbon*	80	70
1335	$2 *Spiranthes speciosa*	1·40	1·40
1336	$4 *Epidendrum ciliare*	2·25	2·75
1337	$5 *Phais tankervilliae*	2·50	3·00
1338	$10 *Brassia caudata*	4·50	5·50
1339	$20 *Brassavola cordata*	9·25	11·00

1991. Butterflies. As T **363** of Grenada. Multicoloured.

1340	5c. Crimson-patched longwing	40	30
1341	10c. *Morpho helena*	40	30
1342	15c. *Morpho sulkowskyi*	55	35
1343	20c. *Dynastor napoleon*	60	40
1344	25c. *Pieridae callinira*	60	45
1345	30c. *Anartia amathea*	65	50
1346	35c. *Heliconiidae dido*	65	50
1347	45c. *Papilionidae columbus*	75	65
1348	50c. *Nymphalidae praeneste*	85	70
1349	60c. *Panacea prola*	1·00	80
1350	75c. *Dryas julia*	1·00	90
1351	$1 *Papilionidae orthosilaus*	1·25	1·10
1352	$2 *Pyrrhopyge cometes*	1·75	2·00
1353	$3 *Papilionidae paeon*	2·00	2·50
1354	$4 *Morpho cypris*	2·50	3·00
1355	$5 *Choringa*	3·00	3·25
MS1356	Four sheets, each 118×80 mm. (a) $6 *Danaus plexippus*. (b) $6 *Caligo idomenides*. (c) $6 *Nymphalidae amydon*. (d) $6 *Papilio childrenae*. Set of 4 sheets	15·00	15·00

101 Donald and Daisy Duck with Solar-powered Car

1991. Ecology Conservation. Walt Disney cartoon characters. Multicoloured.

1357	10c. Type **101**	60	20
1358	15c. Goofy saving water	70	20
1359	25c. Donald and Daisy on nature hike	90	35
1360	45c. Donald Duck returning chick to nest	1·25	55
1361	$1 Donald Duck and balloons	2·00	1·25
1362	$2 Minnie Mouse and Daisy Duck on hot day	3·00	2·25
1363	$4 Mickey's nephews cleaning beach	3·75	4·25
1364	$5 Donald Duck on pedal generator	3·75	4·25
MS1365	Three sheets, each 127×102 mm. (a) $6 Hiawatha and felled forest. (b) $6 Donald Duck recycling (vert). (c) $6 Mickey Mouse with Arbor Day notice. Set of 3 sheets	14·00	15·00

1991. 500th Anniv (1992) of Discovery of America by Columbus (4th issue). History of Exploration. As T **363a** of Grenada. Multicoloured.

1366	15c. Magellan's *Vitoria* rounding Cape Horn, 1519–21	1·00	50
1367	20c. Drake's *Golden Hind*, 1577–80	1·40	50
1368	50c. Cook's H.M.S *Resolution*, 1768–71	2·00	90
1369	60c. Douglas World Cruiser seaplane, 1924	2·00	80
1370	$1 "Sputnik I" satellite, 1957	2·00	1·00
1371	$2 Gagarin's space flight, 1961	2·25	2·25
1372	$3 Glenn's space flight, 1962	2·50	3·50
1373	$5 Space shuttle, 1981	3·00	3·50
MS1374	Two sheets. (a) 105×78 mm. $6 Bow of *Pinta* (vert). (b) 78×105 mm. $6 Fleet of Columbus. Set of 2 sheets	8·00	10·00

1991. "Phila Nippon '91" International Stamp Exhibition, Tokyo. As T **198c** of Gambia but horiz showing Walt Disney cartoon characters in Japanese scenes. Multicoloured.

1375	15c. Minnie Mouse with silkworms	65	20
1376	30c. Mickey, Minnie, Morty and Ferdie at Torii Gate	85	35
1377	50c. Donald Duck and Mickey Mouse trying origami	1·25	60
1378	60c. Mickey and Minnie diving for pearls	1·40	70
1379	$1 Minnie Mouse in kimono	2·00	1·10
1380	$2 Mickey making masks	2·75	2·50
1381	$4 Donald and Mickey making paper	3·50	3·75
1382	$5 Minnie and Pluto making pottery	3·75	4·00

MS1383 Four sheets, each 122×102 mm. (a) $6 Mickey flower-arranging. (b) $6 Mickey carving a netsuke. (c) $6 Mickey at tea ceremony. (d) $6 Mickey making printing plate. Set of 4 sheets — 16·00 / 16·00

1991. Fungi. As T **364** of Grenada. Multicoloured.

1384	5c. *Pyrrhoglossum pyrrhum*	35	25
1385	45c. *Agaricus purpurellus*	85	50
1386	50c. *Amanita craseoderma*	85	55
1387	90c. *Hygrocybe acutoconica*	1·50	1·25
1388	$1 *Limacella guttata*	1·50	1·25
1389	$2 "*Lactarius hygrophoroides*"	2·00	2·00
1390	$4 *Boletellus cubensis*	3·25	3·50
1391	$5 *Psilocybe caerulescens*	3·25	3·50

MS1392 Two sheets, each 100×70 mm. (a) $6 *Marasmius haematocephalus*. (b) $6 *Lepiota spiculata*. Set of 2 sheets — 12·00 / 13·00

1991. 65th Birthday of Queen Elizabeth II. As T **198a** of Gambia. Multicoloured.

1393	20c. Queen, Prince Philip, Prince Charles and Prince William at Trooping the Colour, 1990	30	20
1394	25c. Queen and Prince Charles at polo match, 1985	30	20
1395	$2 Queen and Prince Philip at Maundy service, 1989	2·00	2·50
1396	$4 Queen with Queen Mother on her 87th birthday, 1987	3·25	3·75

MS1397 68×90 mm. $5 The Queen at Caen Hill, 1990, and Prince Philip at R.A.F. Benson, 1989 — 3·75 / 4·50

1991. Tenth Wedding Anniv of Prince and Princess of Wales. As T **198b** of Gambia. Multicoloured.

1398	5c. Prince and Princess of Wales kissing, 1987	65	25
1399	60c. Portraits of Prince, Princess and sons	1·50	70
1400	$1 Prince Harry in 1988 and Prince William in 1987	1·50	1·10
1401	$5 Princess Diana in 1990 and Prince Charles in 1988	5·50	4·75

MS1402 68×90 mm. $5 Princess with Prince Harry in Majorca, and Prince and Princess with Prince Harry at polo match — 5·50 / 5·00

1991. Death Centenary (1990) of Vincent van Gogh (artist). As T **200b** of Gambia. Multicoloured.

1403	5c. *Two Thistles*	50	30
1404	10c. *Baby Marcelle Roulin*	55	30
1405	15c. *Still Life: Basket with Six Oranges* (horiz)	75	20
1406	25c. *Orchard in Blossom*	90	20
1407	45c. *Armand Roulin*	1·25	35
1408	50c. *Wood Gatherers in Snow* (detail) (horiz)	1·25	50
1409	60c. *Almond Tree in Blossom*	1·50	50
1410	$1 *An Old Man*	2·00	1·25
1411	$2 *The Seine Bridge at Asnieres* (horiz)	2·75	2·50
1412	$3 *Vase with Lilacs, Daises and Anemones*	3·00	3·00
1413	$4 *Self Portrait*	3·25	3·50
1414	$5 *Patience Escalier*	3·25	3·50

MS1415 Three sheets. (a) 127×102 mm. $6 *Quay with Men unloading Sand Barges* (horiz). (b) 127×102 mm. $6 *Sunset: Wheat Fields near Arles* (horiz). (c) 102×127 mm. $6 *Les Alyscamps*. Imperf. Set of 3 sheets — 12·00 / 13·00

102 Sargassum Triggerfish

1991. Reef Fish. Multicoloured.

1416	50c. Type **102**	90	90
1417	50c. Tobaccofish	90	90
1418	50c. Caribbean long-nosed butterflyfish	90	90
1419	50c. Cherub angelfish	90	90
1420	50c. Black jack	90	90
1421	50c. Masked goby and black jack	90	90
1422	50c. Spot-finned hogfish	90	90

1423	50c. Royal gramma ("Fairy basslet")	90	90
1424	50c. Orange-backed bass	90	90
1425	50c. Candy basslet	90	90
1426	50c. Black-capped basslet	90	90
1427	50c. Long-jawed squirrelfish	90	90
1428	50c. Jackknife-fish	90	90
1429	50c. Bigeye	90	90
1430	50c. Short bigeye	90	90

MS1431 106×66 mm. $6 Caribbean flashlight fish — 9·00 / 11·00
Nos. 1416/30 were printed together, *se-tenant*, forming a composite design.

1991. Christmas. Religious Paintings by Martin Schongauer. As T **200c** of Gambia.

1432	10c. black and brown	60	15
1433	35c. multicoloured	1·00	30
1434	50c. multicoloured	1·40	50
1435	75c. multicoloured	1·75	80
1436	$1 multicoloured	2·00	1·25
1437	$2 multicoloured	3·25	3·00
1438	$4 black and brown	4·00	4·25
1439	$5 black, grey and red	4·00	4·50

MS1440 Two sheets, each 102×127 mm. (a) $6 multicoloured. (b) $6 multicoloured. Set of 2 sheets — 9·50 / 11·00
DESIGNS: 10c. *Angel of the Annunciation*; 35c. *Madonna of the Rose Hedge* (detail); 50c. *Madonna of the Rose Hedge* (different detail); 75c. *Nativity* (detail); $1 *Adoration of the Shepherds* (detail); $2 *The Nativity*; $4 *Nativity* (different); $5 *Symbol of St. Matthew*; $6 (No. MS1440a) *Adoration of the Shepherds* (different detail); $6 (No. MS1440b) "*Nativity*".

1992. Great Railways of the World. As T **367** of Grenada. Multicoloured.

1441	75c. Medoc locomotive No. J-S 58, 1857 (Switzerland)	1·10	1·10
1442	75c. Stirling single locomotive No. 1, 1870 (Great Britain)	1·10	1·10
1443	75c. Paris–Lyon–Mediterranee locomotive No. 90, 1877 (France)	1·10	1·10
1444	75c. Standard type, 1880 (U.S.A.)	1·10	1·10
1445	75c. Class 650 *Vittorio Emanuel II*, 1884 (Italy)	1·10	1·10
1446	75c. Johnson single, 1887 (Great Britain)	1·10	1·10
1447	75c. Locomotive No. 999, 1893 (U.S.A.)	1·10	1·10
1448	75c. Class Q1, 1896 (Great Britain)	1·10	1·10
1449	75c. *Claud Hamilton*, 1900 (Great Britain)	1·10	1·10
1450	$1 Class P8, 1906 (Germany)	1·10	1·10
1451	$1 Class P, 1910 (Denmark)	1·10	1·10
1452	$1 Southern Railway Ps4, 1926 (U.S.A.)	1·10	1·10
1453	$1 *Kestrel*, 1932 (Ireland)	1·10	1·10
1454	$1 Southern Pacific Class GS2, 1937 (U.S.A.)	1·10	1·10
1455	$1 Class 12, 1938 (Belgium)	1·10	1·10
1456	$1 Norfolk and Western Railroad Class J No. 600, 1941 (U.S.A.)	1·10	1·10
1457	$1 Alco PA series diesel, 1946 (U.S.A.)	1·10	1·10
1458	$1 Class 4E electric, 1954 (South Africa)	1·10	1·10
1459	$2 Trans Europe Express train, 1957	1·50	1·50
1460	$2 New Haven Railroad Type FL9 diesel, 1960 (U.S.A.)	1·50	1·50
1461	$2 *Hikari* train, 1964 (Japan)	1·50	1·50
1462	$2 Class 103.1 electric, 1970 (Germany)	1·50	1·50
1463	$2 RTG diesel, 1972 (France)	1·50	1·50
1464	$2 ETR 401 Pendolino train, 1976 (Italy)	1·50	1·50
1465	$2 Advanced Passenger Train Class 370, 1981 (Great Britain)	1·50	1·50
1466	$2 Via Rail LRC diesel, 1982 (Canada)	1·50	1·50
1467	$2 MAV BZMOT 601, 1983 (Hungary)	1·50	1·50

MS1468 Two sheets, each 120×80 mm. (a) $6 Werner von Siemens's electric locomotive, 1879 (Germany). (b) ETR 401 Pendolino train, 1976 (Italy). Set of 2 sheets — 11·00 / 11·00

1992. 40th Anniv of Queen Elizabeth II's Accession. As T **202a** of Gambia. Multicoloured.

1469	60c. Swimming jetty on beach	1·10	40
1470	75c. View of Grenadines	1·25	45
1471	$2 Surf on beach	2·50	1·75
1472	$5 Secluded bay	3·75	3·25

MS1473 Two sheets, each 74×92 mm. (a) $6 Plantation house. (b) $6 St. George's. Set of 2 sheets — 9·00 / 9·50

1992. Olympic Games, Barcelona. As T **372** of Grenada. Multicoloured.

1474	10c. Women's backstroke swimming	60	30
1475	15c. Women's handball	65	30
1476	25c. Men's 4×100 m relay	75	30
1477	35c. Men's hammer throw	80	35

1478	50c. Men's 110 m hurdles	90	60
1479	75c. Men's pole vault	1·25	80
1480	$1 Men's volleyball	1·40	1·00
1481	$2 Men's weightlifting	2·50	2·75
1482	$5 Men's gymnastics	3·25	4·00
1483	$5 Football	3·75	4·25

MS1484 Two sheets, each 100×70 mm. (a) $15 Finn class single-handed dinghy sailing. (b) $15 Baseball. Set of 2 sheets — 16·00 / 17·00

1992. Granada '92 Int Stamp Exn, Spain. Spanish Paintings. As T **481a** of Ghana. Multicoloured.

1485	10c. *The Surrender of Seville* (Zurbaran)	30	20
1486	35c. *The Liberation of St. Peter by an Angel* (Antonio de Pereda)	50	35
1487	50c. *Joseph explains the Dreams of the Pharaoh* (Antonio del Castillo Saavedra) (horiz)	75	60
1488	75c. *The Flower Vase* (Juan de Arellano)	1·00	70
1489	$1 *The Duke of Pastrana* (Juan Carreno de Miranda)	1·25	90
1490	$2 *The Annunciation* (detail) (Francisco Rizi)	2·00	2·00
1491	$4 *The Annunciation* (different detail) (Rizi)	3·00	3·50
1492	$5 *Old Women Seated* (attr Antonio Puga)	3·00	3·50

MS1493 Two sheets. (a) 95×120 mm. $6 *The Triumph of Saint Hermenegildo* (Francisco de Herrera the younger) (86×111 mm). (b) 120×95 mm. $6 *Relief of Genoa* (De Pereda) (110×84 mm). Imperf. Set of 2 sheets — 7·00 / 8·00

103 Don Isaac Abarbanel, Minister of Finance

1992. 500th Anniv of Discovery of America by Columbus (5th issue). World Columbian Stamp Expo '92, Chicago. Multicoloured.

1494	10c. Type **103**	15	15
1495	25c. Columbus on voyage	25	25
1496	35c. Look-out sighting land	30	30
1497	50c. King Ferdinand and Queen Isabella of Spain	50	50
1498	60c. Columbus showing map to Queen Isabella	55	55
1499	$5 *Santa Maria* and bird	4·00	5·50

MS1500 Two sheets, each 100×71 mm. (a) $6 Christopher Columbus. (b) $6 Columbus with hand to face. Set of 2 sheets — 7·00 / 8·00

1992. "Genova '92" International Thematic Stamp Exhibition. Hummingbirds. As T **370a** of Grenada. Multicoloured.

1501	5c. Male blue-headed hummingbird	25	30
1502	10c. Female rufous-breasted hermit	25	25
1503	20c. Female blue-headed hummingbird	30	25
1504	45c. Male green-throated carib	45	30
1505	90c. Male Antillean crested hummingbird	60	70
1506	$2 Male purple-throated carib	1·40	1·60
1507	$4 Female purple-throated carib	2·40	2·75
1508	$5 Female Antillean crested hummingbird	2·50	2·75

MS1509 Two sheets, each 104×75 mm. (a) $6 Male Rufous-breasted Hermit. (b) $6 Female Green-throated Carib. Set of 2 sheets — 9·50 / 11·00

1992. 50th Anniv of United Service Organization (forces' entertainment programme). As T **371** of Grenada. Multicoloured.

1510	10c. James Cagney	60	25
1511	15c. Anne Sheridan	60	25
1512	35c. Jerry Colonna	60	25
1513	50c. Spike Jones	70	40
1514	75c. Edgar Bergen	90	55
1515	$1 The Andrews Sisters	1·40	80
1516	$2 Dinah Shore	2·00	2·00
1517	$5 Bing Crosby	4·50	4·50

MS1518 Two sheets, each 107×80 mm. (a) $6 Fred Astaire. (b) $6 Marlene Dietrich. Set of 2 sheets — 7·00 / 7·50
No. 1515 is incorrectly inscribed "THE ANDREW SISTERS".

1992. 500th Anniv of Discovery of America by Columbus (6th issue). Organization of East Caribbean States. As Nos. 2423/4 of Grenada.

1519	$1 Columbus meeting Amerindians	65	65
1520	$2 Ships approaching island	1·25	1·50

1992. Toy Trains from American Manufacturers. As T **372b** of Grenada. Multicoloured.

1521	15c. No. 2220 switcher locomotive, Voltamp (1910)	25	15

1522	25c. Clockwork locomotive of Bridge Port Line, American Miniature Railroad (1907)	35	20
1523	50c. First electric toy locomotive, Ives (1910)	60	40
1524	75c. "J.C. Penney Special" locomotive, American Flyer (1920s)	80	60
1525	$1 Clockwork cast-metal locomotive, Hafner (1916)	95	80
1526	$2 Pull toy copper-plated locomotive, probably Hubley (1900)	1·75	2·00
1527	$4 "Mayflower" locomotive, American Flyer (1928)	3·00	3·50
1528	$5 "Olympian" locomotive, Ives (1929)	3·00	3·50

MS1529 Two sheets. (a) 128×93 mm. $6 Clockwork locomotive, Ives (1910) (50×38½ mm). (b) 142×95 mm. $6 "Statesman" locomotive, American Flyer (50×38½ mm). P 13. Set of 2 sheets — 7·50 / 8·50

1992. Postage Stamp Mega Event, New York. Sheet 100×70 mm containing multicoloured design as T **207a** of Gambia.
MS1530 $6 Brooklyn Bridge — 3·50 / 4·25

1992. Christmas. Religious Paintings. "The Annunciation" by various artists. As T **207b** of Gambia. Multicoloured.

1531	5c. Robert Campin	15	10
1532	15c. Melchior Broederlam	25	10
1533	25c. Fra Filippo Lippi (two-panel diptych)	30	15
1534	35c. Simone Martini	40	20
1535	50c. Lippi (detail from left panel)	55	45
1536	75c. Lippi (detail from right panel)	70	60
1537	90c. Albert Bouts	80	80
1538	$1 D. di Michelino	90	90
1539	$2 Rogier van der Weyden	1·75	2·00
1540	$3 Sandro Botticelli (detail of angel)	2·25	2·75
1541	$4 Botticelli (detail of Virgin Mary)	2·75	3·50
1542	$5 Bernardo Daddi (horiz)	2·75	3·50

MS1543 Three sheets, each 72×97 mm. (a) $6 Van der Weyden (different). (b) $6 Botticelli (as $3). (c) $6 Hubert van Eyck. Set of 3 sheets — 10·50 / 12·00

1992. Gold Record Award Winners. As T **374** of Grenada. Multicoloured.

1544	90c. Leonard Bernstein	1·50	1·25
1545	90c. Ray Charles	1·50	1·25
1546	90c. Bob Dylan	1·50	1·25
1547	90c. Barbra Streisand	1·50	1·25
1548	90c. Frank Sinatra	1·50	1·25
1549	90c. Harry Belafonte	1·50	1·25
1550	90c. Aretha Franklin	1·50	1·25
1551	90c. Garth Brooks	1·50	1·25

MS1552 Two sheets, each 100×70 mm. (a) $3 Charlie Parker; $3 Miles Davis. (b) $3 Johnny Cash; $3 Willie Nelson. Set of 2 sheets — 7·00 / 8·00
Nos. 1544/51 were printed together, *se-tenant*, with a composite background design.

1992. 60th Anniv of Goofy (Disney cartoon character). Scenes from various cartoon films. As T **207c** of Gambia. Multicoloured.

1553	5c. "Father's Day Off", 1953	30	20
1554	10c. "Cold War", 1951	35	20
1555	15c. "Home Made Home", 1951	40	20
1556	25c. "Get Rich Quick", 1951	50	25
1557	50c. "Man's Best Friend", 1952	70	40
1558	75c. "Aquamania", 1961	1·00	55
1559	90c. "Tomorrow We Diet", 1951	1·10	65
1560	$1 "Teachers Are People", 1952	1·25	75
1561	$2 "The Goofy Success Story", 1955	2·00	1·75
1562	$3 "Double Dribble", 1946	2·50	3·00
1563	$4 "Hello Aloha", 1952	2·75	3·25
1564	$5 "Father's Lion", 1952	3·00	3·50

MS1565 Three sheets, each 128×102 mm. (a) $6 "Motor Mania", 1956. (b) $6 "Hold that Pose", 1950 (vert). (c) $6 "Father's Weekend", 1953 (vert). Set of 3 sheets — 12·00 / 13·00

1992. Anniversaries and Events. As T **375** of Grenada. Multicoloured, except No. 1571.

1566	25c. Zeppelin *Viktoria Luise* over Kiel Harbour (horiz)	75	30
1567	50c. Space shuttle "Columbia" landing (horiz)	85	35
1568	75c. German Federal Republic flag and arms (horiz)	85	50
1569	$1.50 Giant anteater (horiz)	1·00	1·00
1570	$2 Scarlet macaw	2·50	2·00
1571	$2 W.H.O. emblem (black and blue) (horiz)	1·50	1·50
1572	$3 Wolfgang Amadeus Mozart	4·00	3·00
1573	$4 The Berlin Airlift (horiz)	3·25	3·50
1574	$4 Repairing "Intelsat VI" satellite in space (horiz)	3·25	3·50
1575	$5 Zeppelin "Hindenburg" on fire (horiz)	3·25	3·50

1576	$5 Admiral Richard Byrd's Ford Trimotor aircraft (horiz)	3·25	3·50

MS1577 Five sheets. (a) 110×80 mm. $6 Zeppelin LZ-4, 1913 (51½×39½ mm). (b) 110×80 mm. $6 First flight of space shuttle "Endeavour" (51½×39½ mm). (c) 110×80 mm. $6 Map of West Germany (39½×51½ mm). (d) 110×80 mm. $6 Jaguar (51½×39½ mm). (e) 98×67 mm. $6 Figaro costume from "The Marriage of Figaro". Set of 5 sheets ... 18·00 20·00

ANNIVERSARIES AND EVENTS: Nos. 1566, 1575, **MS**1577a, 75th death anniv of Count Ferdinand von Zeppelin; 1567, 1574, **MS**1577b, International Space Year; 1568, 1573, **MS**1577c, 25th death anniv of Konrad Adenauer (German statesman); 1569/70, **MS**1577d, Earth Summit '92, Rio; 1571, United Nations World Health Organization Projects; 1572, **MS**1577e, Death bicentenary of Mozart; 1576, 75th anniv of International Association of Lions Clubs.

104 *Atalanta* and *Mischief* (yachts), 1881

1992. History of The Americas Cup Challenge Trophy. Multicoloured.

1578	15c. Type **104**	60	20
1579	25c. "Valkyrie III" and "Defender", 1895	75	30
1580	35c. *Shamrock IV* and *Resolute*, 1920	90	45
1581	75c. *Endeavour II* and *Ranger*, 1937	1·40	70
1582	$1 *Sceptre* and *Columbia*, 1958	1·60	85
1583	$2 *Australia II* and *Liberty*, 1983	2·25	2·25
1584	$4 *Stars & Stripes* and *Kookaburra III*, 1987	3·25	4·00
1585	$5 *New Zealand* and *Stars & Stripes*, 1988	3·25	4·00

MS1586 Two sheets, each 114×85 mm. (a) $6 *America* (schooner), 1851 (57×43 mm). (b) $6 Americas Cup emblems (57×43 mm). Set of 2 sheets ... 10·00 11·00

1993. Dogs of the World. As T **377** of Grenada, but vert. Multicoloured.

1587	35c. Irish setter and Glendalough, Ireland	50	25
1588	50c. Boston terrier and Boston State House, U.S.A.	70	50
1589	75c. Beagle and Temple to Athena, Greece	1·00	60
1590	$1 Weimaraner and Nesselwang, Germany	1·25	85
1591	$3 Norwegian elkhound and Urnes Stave Church, Norway	2·50	3·00
1592	$4 Mastiff and Sphinx, Egypt	2·75	3·00
1593	$5 Akita and Torii Temple, Kyoto, Japan	2·75	3·00
1594	$5 Saluki and Rub'al Khali, Saudi Arabia	2·75	3·00

MS1595 Two sheets, each 99×71 mm. (a) $6 Bull dog, Great Britain. (b) $6 Shar Pei, China. Set of 2 sheets ... 7·50 8·50

1993. Bicentenary of the Louvre, Paris. As T **209b** of Gambia. Multicoloured (except No. 1599).

1596	$1 *Madonna and Child with the young John the Baptist* (Botticelli)	1·00	1·00
1597	$1 *The Buffet* (Chardin)	1·00	1·00
1598	$1 *Return from Market* (Chardin)	1·00	1·00
1599	$1 *Erasmus* (Dürer) (black and grey)	1·00	1·00
1600	$1 *Self-portrait with Eryngium* (Dürer)	1·00	1·00
1601	$1 *Jeanne of Aragon* (Raphael)	1·00	1·00
1602	$1 *La Belle Jardiniere* (detail) (Raphael)	1·00	1·00
1603	$1 *La Belle Jardiniere* (different detail) (Raphael)	1·00	1·00

MS1604 70×100 mm. $6 *King Charles I Hunting* (Van Dyck) (52×85 mm) ... 3·75 4·50

105 *Battus polydamus*

1993. Butterflies. Multicoloured.

1605	15c. Type **105**	40	20
1606	35c. *Astraptes talus*	55	20
1607	45c. *Pseudolycaena marsyas*	55	25
1608	75c. *Siproeta stelenes*	70	50
1609	$1 *Phoebis sennae*	80	60

1610	$2 *Dione juno*	1·40	1·40
1611	$4 *Chlorostrymon simaethis*	2·25	2·75
1612	$5 *Urbanus proteus*	2·50	2·75

MS1613 Two sheets, each 100×70 mm. (a) $6 *Historis odius* ("Orion"). (b) $6 *Heliconius charithonia* ("Zebra"). Set of 2 sheets ... 7·00 8·00

1993. Flowers. As T **380** of Grenada. Multicoloured.

1614	35c. Hibiscus	50	20
1615	35c. Columbine	50	20
1616	45c. Red ginger	50	25
1617	75c. Bougainvillea	70	50
1618	$1 Crown imperial	80	60
1619	$2 Fairy orchid	1·40	1·40
1620	$4 Heliconia	2·25	2·75
1621	$5 Tulip	2·50	2·75

1993. 40th Anniv of Coronation. As T **215a** of Gambia.

1623	35c. multicoloured	30	55
1624	50c. multicoloured	40	60
1625	$2 green and black	1·10	1·40
1626	$4 multicoloured	1·90	2·00

MS1627 70×100 mm. $6 multicoloured ... 6·00 6·50

DESIGNS—(38×27 mm): 35c. Queen Elizabeth II at Coronation (photograph by Cecil Beaton); 50c. Ampulla and spoon; $2 Queen Elizabeth II leaving for Coronation; $4 Prince Harry's christening. (28½×42½ mm)—$6 "Queen Elizabeth II, 1954" (detail) (Pietro Annigoni).

1993. Anniversaries and Events. As T **381** of Grenada. Multicoloured.

1628	15c. *Painter and Model* (Picasso) (horiz)	55	30
1629	35c. Keith Tkachuk and Dmitri Mironov (ice hockey, 1992) (horiz)	1·00	40
1630	50c. Early telescope	85	50
1631	75c. *Gra w Gudziki* (Ludomir Slerdinski) (horiz)	90	90
1632	75c. Willy Brandt and Lyndon Johnson, 1961 (horiz)	90	90
1633	$1 *Artist and his Model* (Picasso) (horiz)	1·00	1·00
1634	$2 *Pocalunek Mongolskiego Ksiecia* (S. Wirkiewicz) (horiz)	1·40	1·40
1635	$4 *The Drawing Lesson* (Picasso) (horiz)	2·25	2·75
1636	$4 Radio telescope	2·25	2·75
1637	$5 Alberto Tomba (Giant Slalom, 1984) (horiz)	2·25	2·75
1638	$5 Willy Brandt and Eleanor Hulles, 1957 (horiz)	2·25	2·75

MS1639 Five sheets. (a) 105×75 mm. $5 Copernicus. (b) 105×75 mm. $6 Picasso (horiz). (c) 75×105 mm. $6 Emil Zogragski (70 metre ski jump, 1984). (d) 75×105 mm. $6 "Allegory" (detail) (Jan Wydra). (e) 105×75 mm. $6 Willy and Rut Brandt (grey and black) (horiz) Set of 5 sheets ... 17·00 19·00

ANNIVERSARIES AND EVENTS: Nos. 1628, 1633, 1635, **MS**1639b, 20th death anniv of Picasso (artist); 1629, 1637, **MS**1639c, Winter Olympic Games '94, Lillehammer; 1630, 1636, **MS**1639a, 450th death anniv of Copernicus (astronomer); 1631, 1634, **MS**1639d, Polska '93 International Stamp Exhibition, Poznan; 1632, 1638, **MS**1639e, 80th birth anniv of Willy Brandt (German politician).

1993. Songbirds. As T **382** of Grenada. Multicoloured.

1640	15c. Painted bunting	80	80
1641	15c. White-throated sparrow	80	80
1642	25c. Common grackle	90	90
1643	25c. Royal flycatcher	90	90
1644	35c. Swallow tanager	95	95
1645	35c. Vermilion flycatcher	95	95
1646	45c. Black-headed bunting	1·00	1·00
1647	50c. Rose-breasted grosbeak	1·00	1·00
1648	75c. Corn bunting	1·25	1·25
1649	75c. Rose-breasted thrush tanager	1·25	1·25
1650	$1 Buff-throated saltator	1·40	1·40
1651	$4 Plush-capped finch	2·75	2·75

MS1652 Two sheets, each 115×86 mm. (a) $6 Pine grosbeak. (b) $6 Bohemian waxwing. Set of 2 sheets ... 12·00 12·00

Nos. 1640/51 were printed together, *se-tenant*, with the backgrounds forming a composite design.
Nos. 1645/6 show the scientific inscriptions transposed between the designs.

1993. Shells. As T **383** of Grenada. Multicoloured.

1653	15c. Hawk-wing conch	35	35
1654	15c. Music volute	35	35
1655	25c. Globe vase and deltoid rock shell	40	40
1656	35c. Spiny Caribbean vase	40	40
1657	35c. American common sundial and common purple janthina	40	40
1658	45c. Toothed donax and gaudy asaphis	40	40
1659	45c. Mouse cone	40	40
1660	50c. Gold-mouthed triton	50	50
1661	75c. Tulip mussel and trigonal tivela	60	60
1662	75c. Common dove shell and chestnut latirus	60	60
1663	$1 Wide-mouthed purpura	70	70
1664	$4 American thorny oyster and Atlantic wing oyster	2·25	2·25

MS1665 Two sheets, each 70×106 mm. (a) $6 Atlantic turkey wing. (b) $6 Zebra or zigzag periwinkle. Set of 2 sheets ... 10·00 10·00

Nos. 1653/64 were printed together, *se-tenant*, with the backgrounds forming a composite design.

1993. Asian International Stamp Exhibitions. As T **219a** of Gambia. Multicoloured. (a) "Indopex '93", Surabaya, Indonesia.

1666	35c. National Museum, Central Jakarta (horiz)	40	20
1667	45c. Sacred wheel and deer (horiz)	45	25
1668	$1 Ramayana relief, Panataran Temple (horiz)	70	60
1669	$1.50 Bullock Carts (Batara Lubis) (horiz)	1·25	1·25
1670	$1.50 *Surat Irsa II* (A. D. Pirous) (horiz)	1·25	1·25
1671	$1.50 *Self-portrait with Goat* (Kartika) (horiz)	1·25	1·25
1672	$1.50 *The Cow-est Cow* (Ivan Sagito) (horiz)	1·25	1·25
1673	$1.50 *Rain Storm* (Sudjana Kerton) (horiz)	1·25	1·25
1674	$1.50 *Story of Pucuk Flower* (Effendi) (horiz)	1·25	1·25
1675	$5 Candi Tikus, Trawulan, East Java (horiz)	2·50	3·00

MS1676 134×105 mm. $6 Banteng cattle (horiz) ... 3·50 4·00

	(b) "Taipei '93", Taiwan.		
1677	35c. Macau Palace Casino, Hong Kong (horiz)	40	20
1678	45c. Stone lion, Ming Tomb, Nanjing (horiz)	45	25
1679	$1 Stone camels, Ming Tomb, Nanjing (horiz)	70	60
1680	$1.50 Nesting quail incense burner (horiz)	1·25	1·25
1681	$1.50 Standing quail incense burner (horiz)	1·25	1·25
1682	$1.50 Seated qilin incense burner (horiz)	1·25	1·25
1683	$1.50 Pottery horse, Han period (horiz)	1·25	1·25
1684	$1.50 Seated caparisoned elephant (horiz)	1·25	1·25
1685	$1.50 Cow in imitation of Delft faience (horiz)	1·25	1·25
1686	$5 Stone lion and elephant, Ming Tomb, Nanjing (horiz)	2·50	3·00

MS1687 134×105 mm. $6 Sumatran tiger, Mt. Leuser National Park ... 3·50 4·00

	(c) "Bangkok 1993", Thailand.		
1688	35c. Three Naga snakes, Chiang Mai's Temple (horiz)	40	20
1689	45c. Sri Mariamman Temple, Singapore (horiz)	45	25
1690	$1 Topiary, Hua Hin Resort (horiz)	70	60
1691	$1.50 *Buddha's Victory over Mara* (horiz)	1·25	1·25
1692	$1.50 *Mythological Elephant* (horiz)	1·25	1·25
1693	$1.50 *Battle with Mara* (Thon Buri) (horiz)	1·25	1·25
1694	$1.50 *Untitled* (Panya Wijinthanasarn) (horiz)	1·25	1·25
1695	$1.50 *Temple Mural* (horiz)	1·25	1·25
1696	$1.50 *Elephants in Pahcekha Buddha's Heaven* (horiz)	1·25	1·25
1697	$5 Pak Tai Temple, Cheung Chau Island (horiz)	2·50	3·00

MS1698 134×105 mm. $6 Monkey from Chiang Kong ... 3·50 4·00

1993. World Cup Football Championship, U.S.A. (1994) (1st issue). As T **221a** of Gambia. Multicoloured.

1699	15c. McCall (Scotland) and Verri (Brazil) (horiz)	70	20
1700	25c. Verri (Brazil) and Maradona (Argentina) (horiz)	75	20
1701	35c. Schillaci (Italy) and Saldana (Uruguay) (horiz)	80	25
1702	45c. Gullit (Holland) and Wright (England) (horiz)	90	35
1703	$1 Verri (Brazil) and Maradona (Argentina) (different) (horiz)	1·25	80
1704	$2 Zubizarreta and Fernandez (Spain) with Albert (Belgium) (horiz)	1·75	1·75
1705	$4 Hagi (Rumania) and McGrath (Ireland) (horiz)	2·50	3·25
1706	$5 Gorriz (Spain) and Scifo (Spain) (horiz)	2·50	3·25

MS1707 Two sheets, each 104×75 mm. (a) $6 Foxboro Stadium, Massachusetts (horiz). (b) $6 Rudi Voeller (Germany). Set of 2 sheets ... 8·00 9·00

See also Nos. 1810/16.

1993. 65th Anniv of Mickey Mouse. Scenes from Walt Disney cartoon films. As T **385** of Grenada.

1708	15c. "Mickey's Rival", 1936	65	25
1709	35c. "The Worm Turns", 1937	80	25
1710	50c. "The Pointer", 1939	95	55
1711	75c. "Society Dog Show", 1939	1·50	90
1712	$1 "A Gentleman's Gentleman", 1941	1·60	1·00
1713	$2 "The Little Whirlwind", 1941	2·25	2·50
1714	$4 "Mickey Down Under", 1948	3·00	3·50
1715	$5 "R'coon Dawg", 1951	3·00	3·50

MS1716 Two sheets, each 127×102 mm. (a) $6 "Lonesome Ghosts", 1937. (b) $6 "Mickey's Garden", 1935 (vert). Set of 2 sheets ... 8·00 8·50

1993. Christmas. Religious Paintings. As T **211b** of Gambia. Black, yellow and red (Nos. 1717, 1721/3 and **MS**1725a) or multicoloured (others).

1717	10c. *Adoration of the Shepherds* (detail) (Dürer)	30	20
1718	25c. *Adoration of the Magi* (detail) (Raphael)	40	20
1719	35c. *Presentation at the Temple* (detail) (Raphael)	45	20
1720	50c. *Adoration of the Magi* (different detail) (Raphael)	55	35
1721	75c. *Adoration of the Shepherds* (different detail) (Dürer)	90	60
1722	$1 *Adoration of the Shepherds* (different detail) (Dürer)	1·00	85
1723	$4 *Adoration of the Shepherds* (different detail) (Dürer)	2·50	3·25
1724	$5 *Presentation at the Temple* (detail) (Raphael)	2·50	3·25

MS1725 Two sheets. (a) 102×128 mm. $6 *Adoration of the Shepherds* (different detail) (Dürer) (horiz). (b) 128×102 mm. $6 *Annunciation* (detail) (Raphael). Set of 2 sheets ... 7·00 8·00

1993. Aviation Anniversaries. As T **386** of Grenada. Multicoloured.

1726	15c. Avro Lancaster	30	25
1727	35c. Blanchard's balloon crossing the River Delaware	15	25
1728	50c. Airship *Graf Zeppelin* over Rio de Janeiro	50	35
1729	75c. Hugo Eckener	65	50
1730	$3 Pres. Washington handing passport to Blanchard	1·40	1·75
1731	$5 Short Sunderland flying boat	2·50	3·00
1732	$5 Eckener in *Graf Zeppelin*	2·50	3·00

MS1733 Three sheets. (a) 76×107 mm. $6 Supermarine Spitfire. (b) 107×76 mm. $6 Blanchard's balloon (vert). (c) 107×76 mm. $6 Eckener with Pres. Hoover. Set of 3 sheets ... 11·50 12·50

ANNIVERSARIES: Nos. 1726, 1731, **MS**1733a, 75th anniv of Royal Air Force; 1727, **MS**1733b, Bicentenary of first airmail flight; 1728/9, 1732, **MS**1733c, 125th birth anniv of Hugo Eckener (airship commander).

1993. Centenaries of Henry Ford's First Petrol Engine (Nos. 1735/6) and Karl Benz's First Four-wheeled Car (others). As T **387** of Grenada. Multicoloured.

1734	25c. Mercedes Benz "300 SLR", 1955	85	25
1735	45c. Ford "Thunderbird", 1957	1·00	25
1736	$4 Ford "150-A" station wagon, 1929	3·50	3·75
1737	$5 Mercedes Benz "540 K"	3·50	3·75

MS1738 Two sheets, 76×107 mm. (a) $6 Mercedes Benz "SSK", 1929. (b) $6 Ford "Model T", 1924. Set of 2 sheets ... 8·00 9·00

1993. Famous Paintings by Rembrandt and Matisse. As T **221c** of Gambia. Multicoloured.

1739	15c. *Hendrickje Stoffels as Flora* (Rembrandt)	40	25
1740	35c. *Lady and Gentleman in Black* (Rembrandt)	50	25
1741	50c. *Aristotle with the Bust of Homer* (Rembrandt)	60	40
1742	75c. *Interior: Flowers and Parakeets* (Matisse)	85	60
1743	$1 *Goldfish* (Matisse)	1·00	95
1744	$2 *The Girl with Green Eyes* (Matisse)	1·75	2·25
1745	$3 *Still Life with a Plaster Figure* (Matisse)	2·00	2·75
1746	$5 *Christ and the Woman of Samaria* (Rembrandt)	2·50	3·25

MS1747 Two sheets. (a) 100×125 mm. $6 *Anna accused of stealing the Kid* (detail) (Rembrandt). (b) 125×100 mm. $6 *Tea in the Garden* (detail) (Matisse) (horiz). Set of 2 sheets ... 8·00 9·00

1994. "Hong Kong '94" International Stamp Exhibition (1st issue). As T **222a** of Gambia. Multicoloured.

1748	40c. Hong Kong 1984 $5 aviation stamp and airliner at Kai Tak Airport	80	85
1749	40c. Grenada Grenadines 1988 20c. airships stamp and junk in Kowloon Bay	80	85

Nos. 1748/9 were printed together, *se-tenant*, forming a composite design.
See also Nos. 1750/5.

1994. "Hong Kong '94" International Stamp Exhibition (2nd issue). Jade Sculptures. As T **222b** of Gambia, but horiz. Multicoloured.

1750	45c. White jade brush washer	65	65
1751	45c. Archaic jade brush washer	65	65
1752	45c. Dark green jade brush washer	65	65
1753	45c. Green jade almsbowl	65	65
1754	45c. Archaic jade dog	65	65
1755	45c. Yellow jade brush washer	65	65

1994. Fungi. As T **390** of Grenada, but with white backgrounds. Multicoloured.

1756	35c. *Hygrocybe hypohaemacta*	45	30
1757	45c. *Cantharellus cinnabarinus*	55	35
1758	50c. *Marasmius haemato-cephalus*	60	40
1759	75c. *Mycena pura*	80	60
1760	$1 *Gymnopilus russipes*	90	80
1761	$2 *Calocybe cyanocephala*	1·40	1·50
1762	$4 *Pluteus chrysophlebius*	2·50	3·00
1763	$5 *Chlorophyllum molybdites*	2·50	3·00
MS1764	Two sheets, each 100×70 mm. (a) $6 *Xeromphalina tenuipes*. (b) *Collybia fibrosipes*. Set of 2 sheets	7·50	8·00

No. 1757 is inscribed "Cantherellus cinnabarinus" and No. 1762 "Pleuteus chrysophlebius", both in error.

1994. Prehistoric Animals. As T **391** of Grenada. Multicoloured.

1765	15c. Spinosaurus	30	25
1766	35c. Apatosaurus (Brontosaurus)	45	30
1767	45c. Tyrannosaurus rex	50	35
1768	55c. Triceratops	50	40
1769	$1 Pachycephalosaurus	85	75
1770	$2 Pteranodon	1·40	1·75
1771	$4 Parasaurolophus	2·50	3·00
1772	$5 Brachiosaurus	2·50	3·00
MS1773	Two sheets, each 100×70 mm. (a) $6 Head of Brachiosaurus (vert). (b) $6 Spinosaurus and Tyrannosaurus rex fighting (vert). Set of 2 sheets	7·50	8·00

1994. 25th Anniv of First Manned Moon Landing. Space Shuttle "Challenger". As T **227a** of Gambia. Multicoloured.

1774	$1.10 "Challenger" crew in training	1·00	1·25
1775	$1.10 Christa McAuliffe (astronaut)	1·00	1·25
1776	$1.10 "Challenger" on launch pad	1·00	1·25
1777	$1.10 Gregory Jarvis (astronaut)	1·00	1·25
1778	$1.10 Ellison Onizuka (astronaut)	1·00	1·25
1779	$1.10 Ronald McNair (astronaut)	1·00	1·25
MS1780	107×76 mm. $6 Judith Resnick (astronaut) (vert)	4·00	4·50

1994. Centenary of International Olympic Committee. Gold Medal Winners. As T **227b** of Gambia. Multicoloured.

1781	50c. Silke Renk (Germany) (javelin), 1992	35	35
1782	$1.50 Mark Spitz (U.S.A.) (swimming), 1972	90	1·40
MS1783	106×77 mm. $6 Japanese team (Nordic skiing), 1994	3·25	3·75

1994. International Year of the Family. As T **391a** of Grenada. Multicoloured.

1784	$1 Grenadines family	60	60

1994. 50th Anniv of D-Day. As T **227c** of Gambia. Multicoloured.

1785	40c. Churchill bridge-laying tank	35	30
1786	$2 Sherman "Firefly" tank leaving landing craft	1·00	1·25
1787	$3 Churchill "Crocodile" flame-thrower	1·60	1·50
MS1788	107×76 mm. $6 Sherman "Crab" flail tank	3·25	3·75

1994. "Philakorea '94" International Stamp Exhibition, Seoul (1st issue). As T **227d** of Gambia. Multicoloured.

1789	40c. Onung Tomb (horiz)	30	30
1790	$1 Stone pagoda, Mt. Namsam (horiz)	55	65
1791	$1 *Admiring Spring in the Country* (left detail) (Sin Yunbok)	55	65
1792	$1 *Admiring Spring in the Country* (right detail)	55	65
1793	$1 *"Woman on Dano Day"* (left detail) (Sin Yunbok)	55	65
1794	$1 *Woman on Dano Day* (right detail)	55	65
1795	$1 *Enjoying Lotuses while Listening to Music* (left detail) (Sin Yunbok)	55	65
1796	$1 *Enjoying Lotuses while Listening to Music* (right detail)	55	65
1797	$1 *Women by a Crystal Stream* (left detail) (Sin Yunbok)	55	65
1798	$1 *Women by a Crystal Stream* (right detail)	55	65
1799	$4 Pusan (horiz)	2·25	2·75
MS1800	70×102 mm. $6 *Blacksmith Shop* (detail) (Kim Duksin)	3·25	3·75

The two details of each painting on Nos. 1791/8 were printed together, se-tenant, each pair forming a composite design.
See also Nos. 1817/31.

1994. Orchids. As T **392** of Grenada. Multicoloured.

1801	15c. *Cattleya aurantiaca*	35	25
1802	25c. *Blettia patula*	40	25
1803	45c. *Sobralia macrantha*	50	30
1804	75c. *Encyclia belizensis*	70	55
1805	$1 *Sophrolaeliocattleya*	85	75
1806	$2 *Encyclia fragrans*	1·40	1·75
1807	$4 *Schombocattleya*	2·50	3·00

1808	$5 *Brassolaeliocattleya*	2·50	3·00
MS1809	Two sheets, each 100×70 mm. (a) $6 *Ornithidium coccineum* (horiz). (b) $6 *Brassavola nodosa* (horiz). Set of 2 sheets	8·50	9·00

1994. World Cup Football Championship, U.S.A. (2nd issue). As T **393** of Grenada. Multicoloured.

1810	75c. Steve Mark (Grenada)	70	70
1811	75c. Jurgen Kohler (Germany)	70	70
1812	75c. Almir (Brazil)	70	70
1813	75c. Michael Windischmann (U.S.A.)	70	70
1814	75c. Guiseppe Giannini (Italy)	70	70
1815	75c. Rashidi Yekini (Nigeria)	70	70
MS1816	Two sheets, each 90×70 mm. (a) $6 Kemari (ancient Japanese game). (b) Hand holding trophy. Set of 2 sheets	7·50	8·50

106 Mickey Mouse and Unjin Miruk Window from Kwanch Ok Temple

1994. "Philakorea '94" International Stamp Exhibition, Seoul (2nd issue). Walt Disney cartoon characters. Multicoloured.

1817	3c. Type **106**	30	40
1818	4c. Goofy imitating statue of Admiral Yi, Chonju	30	40
1819	5c. Cousin Gus and Donald Duck eating dinner	30	40
1820	10c. Mickey playing flute	45	35
1821	15c. Goofy with Tolharubang (statue)	60	20
1822	15c. Type **106**	60	20
1823	20c. Mickey and Minnie at Hyang-Wonjong	60	20
1824	35c. As 4c.	75	25
1825	50c. As 5c.	90	35
1826	75c. As 10c.	1·10	60
1827	$1 As 15c.	1·40	90
1828	$2 As 20c.	2·25	2·50
1829	$4 Mickey as Somori-Kut shaman	3·00	3·50
1830	$5 Minnie holding ceremonial fan	3·00	3·50
MS1831	Two sheets, each 130×103 mm. (a) $6 Minnie beating Buk drum (vert). (b) $6 Mickey in swimming pool at Pugok Hawaii (vert). Set of 2 sheets	8·00	9·00

1994. First Recipients of Order of the Caribbean Community. As Nos. 2750/2 of Grenada. Multicoloured.

1832	25c. Sir Shridath Ramphal	10	10
1833	50c. William Demas	25	30
1834	$2 Derek Walcott	2·75	2·50

1994. Fish. As T **394** of Grenada. Multicoloured.

1835	75c. Porkfish	85	80
1836	75c. Blue chromis	85	80
1837	75c. Caribbean reef shark (facing left)	85	80
1838	75c. Long-spined squirrelfish	85	80
1839	75c. Four-eyed butterflyfish	85	80
1840	75c. Blue head	85	80
1841	75c. Royal gramma	85	80
1842	75c. Sharp-nosed puffer	85	80
1843	75c. Reid's seahorse	85	80
1844	75c. Black-barred soldierfish	85	80
1845	75c. Red-lipped blenny	85	80
1846	75c. Painted wrasse	85	80
1847	75c. Yellow-tailed snapper	85	80
1848	75c. Caribbean reef shark (facing right)	85	80
1849	75c. Great barracuda	85	80
1850	75c. Red-tailed parrotfish	85	80
1851	75c. Blue tang	85	80
1852	75c. Queen angelfish	85	80
1853	75c. Red hind	85	80
1854	75c. Rock beauty	85	80
1855	75c. Queen parrotfish	85	80
1856	75c. Spanish hogfish	85	80
1857	75c. Spotted moray	85	80
1858	75c. Queen triggerfish	85	80
MS1859	Two sheets, each 102×72 mm. (a) $6 Head of queen angelfish. (b) $6 Head of painted wrasse. Set of 2 sheets	8·00	9·00

Nos. 1835/46 and 1847/58 respectively were printed together, se-tenant, forming composite designs.

1994. Christmas. Religious Paintings by Bartolome Murillo. As T **231a** of Gambia. Multicoloured.

1860	15c. *The Annunciation*	30	20
1861	35c. *The Adoration of the Shepherds*	40	20
1862	50c. *Virgin and Child with St. Rose*	50	30

1863	50c. *Flight into Egypt*	50	30
1864	75c. *Virgin and Child*	70	45
1865	$1 *Virgin of the Rosary*	85	70
1866	$4 *The Holy Family*	2·50	3·25
MS1867	Two sheets. (a) 85×95 mm. $6 *Adoration of the Shepherds* (different) (detail). (b) 95×125 mm. $6 *The Holy Family with a Little Bird* (detail). Set of 2 sheets	7·50	8·00

1995. Birds. As T **397** of Grenada. Multicoloured.

1868	25c. Scaly-breasted ground dove ("Ground Dove") (vert)	1·25	40
1869	50c. White-winged dove (vert)	1·75	60
1870	$2 Inca dove (vert)	3·00	2·50
1871	$4 Mourning dove (vert)	4·00	5·50

1995. Centenary of First English Cricket Tour to the West Indies. As T **397a** of Grenada. Multicoloured.

1872	50c. Mike Atherton (England) and Wisden Trophy (vert)	1·10	65
1873	75c. Curtly Ambrose (West Indies) (vert)	1·40	1·10
1874	$1 Brian Lara (West Indies) (vert)	1·50	1·50
MS1875	75×95 mm. $3 West Indian team, 1994	3·00	3·00

107 Aspects of London, National Flag and Map

1995. Capitals of the World. Aspects of various cities, national flags and maps. Multicoloured.

1876	$1 Type **107**	65	70
1877	$1 Cairo	65	70
1878	$1 Vienna	65	70
1879	$1 Paris	65	70
1880	$1 Rome	65	70
1881	$1 Budapest	65	70
1882	$1 Moscow	65	70
1883	$1 Peking ("Beijing")	65	70
1884	$1 Tokyo	65	70
1885	$1 Washington	65	70

108 Pig

1995. Chinese New Year ("Year of the Pig"). Multicoloured designs showing "GRENADA GRENADINES" in colours indicated.

1886	75c. Type **108** (violet)	50	60
1887	75c. Pig (carmine)	50	60
1888	75c. Pig (brown)	50	60
1889	75c. Pig (vermilion)	50	60
MS1890	Two sheets. (a) 106×77 mm. $2 Two pigs (horiz). (b) 67×83 mm. Nos. 1886/9. Set of 2 sheets	3·25	3·50

109 Bull Shark and Diver

1995. Marine Life of the Caribbean. Multicoloured.

1891	$1 Type **109**	75	75
1892	$1 Great white shark	75	75
1893	$1 Octopus and shoal of fish	75	75
1894	$1 Great barracuda	75	75
1895	$1 Green moray	75	75
1896	$1 Spotted eagle ray	75	75
1897	$1 Sea snake	75	75
1898	$1 Stingray	75	75
1899	$1 Grouper	75	75
1900	$1 Dolphins	75	75
1901	$1 Lionfish	75	75
1902	$1 Sea turtle and rock beauty (fish)	75	75
1903	$1 Blue-cheeked butterflyfish and nurse shark	75	75
1904	$1 Queen angelfish	75	75
1905	$1 Grouper and coney	75	75
1906	$1 Rainbow eel and spotted moray	75	75
1907	$1 Sun flower-star and coral crab	75	75
1908	$1 Octopus on sea bed	75	75

MS1909	Two sheets each 107×77 mm. (a) $5 French angelfish. (b) $6 Smooth hammerhead. Set of 2 sheets	6·50	7·00

110 Suffolk Punch

1995. Domestic Animals. Multicoloured.

1910	15c. Type **110**	60	40
1911	25c. Shetland pony	60	40
1912	75c. Blue persian (cat)	60	65
1913	75c. Sorrel abyssinian (cat)	60	65
1914	75c. White angora (cat)	60	65
1915	75c. Brown Burmese (cat)	60	65
1916	75c. Red tabby exotic shorthair (cat)	60	65
1917	75c. Seal-point birman (cat)	60	65
1918	75c. Korat (cat)	60	65
1919	75c. Norwegian forest cat	60	65
1920	75c. Lilac-point Balinese (cat)	60	65
1921	75c. British shorthair (cat)	60	65
1922	75c. Red self longhair (cat)	60	65
1923	75c. Calico Manx (cat)	60	65
1924	75c. Shetland sheepdog	60	65
1925	75c. Bull terrier	60	65
1926	75c. Afghan hound	60	65
1927	75c. Scottish terrier	60	65
1928	75c. Labrador retriever	60	65
1929	75c. English springer spaniel	60	65
1930	75c. Samoyed (dog)	60	65
1931	75c. Irish setter	60	65
1932	75c. Border collie	60	65
1933	75c. Pekingese	60	65
1934	75c. Dachshund	60	65
1935	75c. Weimaraner (dog)	60	65
1936	$1 Arab	85	85
1937	$3 Shire horse	1·75	2·00
MS1938	Two sheets, each 105×75 mm. (a) $6 Seal-point colourpoint (cat). (b) $6 English setter. Set of 2 sheets	7·00	7·50

1995. Centenary (1992) of Sierra Club (environmental protection society). Endangered Species. As T **224a** of Gambia. Multicoloured.

1939	$1 Spotted owl ("Northern Spotted Owl")	90	80
1940	$1 Brown pelican on perch	90	80
1941	$1 Head of brown pelican	90	80
1942	$1 Head of jaguarundi	90	80
1943	$1 Jaguarundi looking over shoulder	90	80
1944	$1 Maned wolf in undergrowth	90	80
1945	$1 American wood stork ("Wood Stork") standing on two legs	90	80
1946	$1 American wood stork standing on one leg	90	80
1947	$1 Close-up of maned wolf	90	80
1948	$1 Brown pelican (horiz)	90	80
1949	$1 Close-up of spotted owl ("Northern Spotted Owl") (horiz)	90	80
1950	$1 Spotted owl ("Northern Spotted Owl") chick (horiz)	90	80
1951	$1 Jaguarundi (horiz)	90	80
1952	$1 Central American spider monkey sitting with young (horiz)	90	80
1953	$1 Central American spider monkey carrying young (horiz)	90	80
1954	$1 Central American spider monkey swinging from branch (horiz)	90	80
1955	$1 American wood stork ("Wood Stork") (horiz)	90	80
1956	$1 Pair of maned wolfs (horiz)	90	80

1995. 18th World Scout Jamboree, Netherlands. As T **403** of Grenada. Multicoloured.

1957	75c. Grenadian scout on beach	60	70
1958	$1 Scout with staff on hill	80	90
1959	$2 Scout saluting and national flag	1·10	1·50
MS1960	107×77 mm. $6 Scout snorkelling	3·50	4·00

1995. 50th Anniv of End of Second World War in Europe. Bombers. As T **237a** of Gambia. Multicoloured.

1961	$2 Avro Type **683** Lancaster	1·50	1·50
1962	$2 Junkers Ju 88	1·50	1·50
1963	$2 North American B-25 Mitchell	1·50	1·50
1964	$2 Boeing B-17 Flying Fortress	1·50	1·50
1965	$2 Petlyakov Pe-2	1·50	1·50
1966	$2 Martin B-26 Marauder	1·50	1·50
1967	$2 Heinkel He 111H	1·50	1·50
1968	$2 Consolidated B-24 Liberator	1·50	1·50
MS1969	105×75 mm. $6 Pres. Truman and newspaper headline (57×43 mm)	3·00	3·50

1995. 50th Anniv of United Nations. As T **404** of Grenada. Multicoloured.

1970	75c. U.N. Headquarters, New York, and flag	60	90
1971	$1 Trygve Lie (first Secretary-General)	80	1·10
1972	$2 U.N. soldier	1·10	1·40
MS1973	101×76 mm. $6 Peace dove over emblem	2·50	3·00

Nos. 1970/2 were printed together, se-tenant, forming a composite design.

1995. 50th Anniv of F.A.O. As T **405** of Grenada. Multicoloured.

1974	75c. Man hoeing	60	90
1975	$1 Woman hoeing	80	1·10
1976	$2 Man and woman hoeing	1·10	1·40
MS1977	106×76 mm. $6 Child eating with chopsticks	2·50	3·00

Nos. 1974/6 were printed together, se-tenant, forming a composite design.

1995. 90th Anniv of Rotary International. As T **406** of Grenada. Multicoloured.

| 1978 | $5 Paul Harris (founder) and logo (horiz) | 2·50 | 3·00 |
| MS1979 | 106×76 mm. $6 Rotary Club and International logos (horiz) | 2·75 | 3·25 |

1995. 95th Birthday of Queen Elizabeth the Queen Mother. As T **239a** of Gambia.

1980	$1.50 brown, light brown and black	1·40	1·40
1981	$1.50 multicoloured	1·40	1·40
1982	$1.50 multicoloured	1·40	1·40
1983	$1.50 multicoloured	1·40	1·40
MS1984	102×127 mm. $6 multicoloured	6·00	5·50

DESIGNS: No. 1980, Queen Elizabeth the Queen Mother (pastel drawing); 1981, At Remembrance Day service; 1982, At desk (oil painting); 1983, Wearing green hat; **MS**1984, Unveiling memorial to Blitz victims.

1995. 50th Anniv of End of Second World War in the Pacific. As T **239b** of Grenada. Multicoloured.

1985	$2 Mitsubishi G4M1 *Betty* (bomber)	1·40	1·50
1986	$2 Japanese submarine "I 14" with seaplane on catapault	1·40	1·50
1987	$2 Mitsubishi GM31 *Nell* (bomber)	1·40	1·50
1988	$2 *Akizuki* (Japanese destroyer)	1·40	1·50
1989	$2 *Kirishima* (Japanese battleship)	1·40	1·50
1990	$2 *Asigari* (Japanese cruiser)	1·40	1·50
MS1991	108×76 mm. $6 Japanese Aichi D3A1 "Val" dive bomber	3·50	3·75

1995. Olympic Games, Atlanta (1996). As T **407** of Grenada. Multicoloured.

1992	15c. Rosemary Ackerman (East Germany) (high jump) (horiz)	50	60
1993	15c. Li Ning (China) (gymnastics) (horiz)	50	60
1994	15c. Denise Parker (U.S.A.) (archery) (horiz)	50	60
1995	$3 Terry Carlisle (U.S.A.) (skeet shooting) (horiz)	2·00	2·50
1996	$3 Kathleen Nord (East Germany) (swimming) (horiz)	2·00	2·50
1997	$3 Brigit Schmidt (East Germany) (canoeing) (horiz)	2·00	2·50
MS1998	Two sheets, each 102×72 mm. (a) $6 Dan Gable and Kikuo Wada (Japan) (wrestling). (b) $6 George Foreman (U.S.A.) (boxing). Set of 2 sheets	7·00	8·00

111 Brown Pelican

1995. Birds of the Caribbean. Multicoloured.

1999	10c. Type **111**	40	40
2000	15c. Black-necked stilt ("Common Stilt")	50	40
2001	25c. Cuban trogon ("Cuban Trogan")	55	30
2002	35c. Greater flamingo ("Flamingo")	60	30
2003	75c. Imperial amazon ("Parrot")	80	45
2004	$1 Pintail ("Pintail Duck")	90	1·00
2005	$1 Great blue heron	1·90	1·90
2006	$1 Jamaican tody	90	1·00
2007	$1 Laughing gull	90	1·00
2008	$1 Purple-throated carib	90	1·00
2009	$1 Red-legged thrush	90	1·00
2010	$1 Ruddy duck	90	1·00
2011	$1 Common shoveler ("Shoveler Duck")	90	1·00
2012	$1 Great red-bellied woodpecker ("West Indian Red-bellied Woodpecker")	90	1·00
2013	$2 Ringed kingfisher	1·40	1·75
2014	$3 Strip-headed tanager	1·75	2·25
MS2015	Two sheets, each 104×73 mm. (a) $5 Village weaver. (b) $5 Blue-hooded euphonia. Set of 2 sheets	7·00	7·50

No. 2001 is inscr "Cuban Trogan", No. 2008 "Purple-throated Carb" and No. 2013 "Ringed King Fisher", all in error.

No. MS2015, carry the "Singapore '95" exhibition logo.

1995. Mickey's Pirate Adventure. Walt Disney cartoon characters. As T **415** of Grenada. Multicoloured.

2016	10c. Goofy and Donald Duck with treasure chests (horiz)	35	25
2017	35c. Mickey and Minnie Mouse at ship's wheel (horiz)	55	25
2018	75c. Mickey, Donald and Goofy opening chest (horiz)	90	55
2019	$1 Big Pete and rats confronting Mickey (horiz)	1·00	75
2020	$2 Mickey, Goofy and Donald in boat (horiz)	1·75	2·00
2021	$5 Goofy fighting rat pirate with mop (horiz)	3·25	4·25
MS2022	Two sheets, each 108×130 mm. (a) $6 Goofy and cannon-balls. (b) $6 Monkey pinching Mickey's nose. Set of 2 sheets	8·00	8·50

1995. Centenary of Nobel Trust Fund. As T **416** of Gambia. Multicoloured.

2023- 75c.×2, $1×27
2051

| MS2052 | Three sheets, each 105×76 mm. (a) $6 Sir Winston Churchill (1953 Literature). (b) $6 Willy Brandt (1971 Peace). (c) $6 Albert Schweitzer (1952 Peace). Set of 3 sheets | 15·00 | 14·00 |

DESIGNS: 75c. W. Arthur Lewis (1979 Economics); Derek Walcott (1992 Literature); $1 Jules Border (1919 Medicine); Rene Cassin (1968 Peace); Verner von Heidenstam (1916 Literature); Jose Echegaray (1904 Literature); Otto Wallach (1910 Chemistry); Corneille Heymans (1938 Medicine); Ivar Giaever (1973 Physics); Sir William Cremer (1903 Peace); John Strutt (1904 Physics); James Franck (1925 Physics); Tobias Asser (1911 Peace); Carl Spitteler (1919 Literature); Christiaan Eijkman (1929 Medicine); Ragnar Granit (1967 Medicine); Frederic Passy (1901 Peace); Louis Neel (1970 Physics); Sir William Ramsay (1904 Chemistry); Philip Noel-Baker (1959 Peace); Heike Onnes (1913 Physics); Fridtjof Nansen (1922 Peace); Sir Ronald Ross (1902 Medicine); Paul Muller (1948 Medicine); Allvar Gullstrand (1911 Medicine); Gerhart Hauptmann (1912 Literature); Hans Spemann (1935 Medicine); Cecil Powell (1950 Physics); Walther Bothe (1954 Physics).

Nos. 2025/33, 2034/42 and 2043/51 respectively were printed together, se-tenant, forming composite designs. No. 2027 (Von Heidenstam) is inscribed "1906" and No. 2044 "Fridtjof Nanser", both in error.

112 Nita Naldi and Rudolph Valentino

1995. Centenary of Cinema. Multicoloured.

2053	$1 Type **112**	75	75
2054	$1 Ramon Novaro and Alice Terry	75	75
2055	$1 Frederic March and Joan Crawford	75	75
2056	$1 Clark Gable and Vivien Leigh	75	75
2057	$1 Barbara Stanwyck and Burt Lancaster	75	75
2058	$1 Warren Beatty and Natalie Wood	75	75
2059	$1 Spencer Tracy and Katharine Hepburn	75	75
2060	$1 Humphrey Bogart and Lauren Bacall	75	75
2061	$1 Omar Sharif and Julie Christie	75	75
2062	$1 Marion Davies	75	75
2063	$1 Marlene Dietrich	75	75
2064	$1 Lillian Gish	75	75
2065	$1 Bette Davis	75	75
2066	$1 Elizabeth Taylor	75	75
2067	$1 Veronica Lake	75	75
2068	$1 Ava Gardner	75	75
2069	$1 Grace Kelly	75	75
2070	$1 Kim Novak	75	75
MS2071	Two sheets. (a) 72×102 mm. $6 Sophia Loren. (b) 102×72 mm. $6 Greta Garbo and John Gilbert (horiz). Set of 2 sheets	7·00	8·00

Nos. 2053/61 and 2062/70 respectively were printed together, se-tenant, forming composite designs.

1995. Racing Cars. As T **423** of Grenada. Multicoloured.

2072	10c. Williams-Renault Formula 1, 1990s	30	20
2073	25c. Porsche "956", Le Mans, 1980s	45	20
2074	35c. Lotus "John Player Special", 1970s	50	20
2075	$1 Ford "GT-40", 1960s	75	45
2076	$2 Mercedes-Benz "W196", 1950s	1·50	2·00
2077	$3 Mercedes "SSK", 1920s	2·00	2·50
MS2078	103×73 mm. $6 Jackie Stewart in Tyrell-Ford, 1971 (vert)	3·75	4·00

113 Man on Donkey

1995. Local Transport. Multicoloured.

| 2079 | 35c. Type **113** | 50 | 25 |
| 2080 | 75c. Local bus | 1·00 | 85 |

1995. Evolution of Sailing Ships. As T **427** of Grenada. Multicoloured.

2081	$1 *Preussen* (full-rigged ship)	90	1·00
2082	$1 Japanese junk	90	1·00
2083	$1 Caribbean pirate ship	90	1·00
2084	$1 *Mayflower* (Pilgrim Fathers)	90	1·00
2085	$1 Chinese junk	90	1·00
2086	$1 *Santa Maria* (Columbus)	90	1·00
MS2087	103×73 mm. $5 Spanish galleon (56×41 mm)	3·25	3·50

1995. Christmas. Religious Paintings. As T **245a** of Gambia. Multicoloured.

2088	10c. *Immaculate Conception* (Piero di Cosimo)	30	20
2089	15c. *St. Michael dedicating Arms to the Madonna* (Le Nain)	35	20
2090	35c. *Annunciation* (Lorenzo di Credi)	55	20
2091	50c. *The Holy Family* (Jacob Jordaens)	70	30
2092	$3 *Madonna and Child* (Lippi)	2·25	3·00
2093	$5 *Madonna and Child with Ten Saints* (Fiorentino)	3·25	4·00
MS2094	102×127 mm. (a) $6 *Adoration of the Shepherds* (detail) (Van Oost). (b) $6 *Holy Family* (detail) (Del Start). Set of 2 sheets	7·50	8·00

114 Symbolic Rat and Candle

1996. Chinese New Year ("Year of the Rat"). Multicoloured, background colours given.

2095	**114**	75c. blue	55	60
2096	**114**	75c. lilac	55	60
2097	**114**	75c. brown	55	60
2098	**114**	75c. green	55	60
MS2099	69×84 mm. Nos. 2095/8	2·00	2·20
MS2100	76×106 mm. $2 Two rats (horiz)	1·40	1·50

The four designs show different Chinese characters.

1996. Works of Art by Durer and Rubens. As T **421** of Grenada. Multicoloured.

2101	15c. *The Centaur Family* (Durer)	30	20
2102	35c. *Oriental Ruler Seated* (Durer)	40	20
2103	50c. *The Entombment* (Durer)	55	30
2104	75c. *Man in Armour* (Rubens)	70	50
2105	$1 *Peace embracing Plenty* (Rubens)	85	75
2106	$2 *Departure of Lot* (Rubens)	1·50	1·75
2107	$3 *The Four Evangelists* (Rubens)	1·75	2·25
2108	$5 *Knight, Death and Devil* (Durer)	3·00	3·75
MS2109	Two sheets, each 101×127 mm. (a) $5 *The Fathers of the Church* (detail) (Rubens). (b) $6 *St. Jerome* (detail) (Durer). Set of 2 sheets	6·50	7·50

115 Mickey and Minnie at New Year's Day "Hopping John" Tradition

1996. Traditional Holidays. Walt Disney cartoon characters. Multicoloured.

2110	25c. Type **115**	50	15
2111	50c. Disney characters dancing around maypole	70	30
2112	75c. Mickey, Minnie and Pluto watching Independence Day fireworks	95	40
2113	90c. Gyro Gearloose and Donald's nephews in Halloween costumes	1·00	90
2114	$3 Donald Duck as Puritan and nephews as Indians on Thanksgiving Day	2·75	3·25
2115	$4 Huey and Dewey with Hanukkah dreidle	2·75	3·50

| MS2116 | Two sheets, each 124×98 mm. (a) $6 Mickey, Minnie and Donald taking part in Caribbean carnival. (b) $6 Traditional pot of gold in St. Patrick's Day parade (vert). Set of 2 sheets | 9·50 | 10·00 |

116 Gateway in Imperial Palace, Peking

1996. "CHINA '96" 9th Asian International Stamp Exhibition, Peking. Multicoloured.

2117	$1 Type **116**	65	70
2118	$1 Eastern end of Great Wall at Shanhaiguan	65	70
2119	$1 Great Wall fortress, Shanhaiguan	65	70
2120	$1 Gate of Heavenly Peace, Peking	65	70
2121	$1 Sun Yat-sen's Mausoleum, Nanjing	65	70
2122	$1 Summer Palace, Peking	65	70
2123	$1 Temple of Heaven, Peking	65	70
2124	$1 Hall of Supreme Harmony, Forbidden City, Peking	65	70
MS2125	Three sheets. (a) 150×100 mm. $2 Traditional Chinese painting (39×50 mm). (b) 90×68 mm. $6 Great Wall of China from the air (39×50 mm). (c) 90×68 mm. $6 Marble Boat, Summer Palace, Peking (50×39 mm). Set of 3 sheets	7·00	7·50

1996. 70th Birthday of Queen Elizabeth II. As T **255a** of Gambia. Multicoloured.

2126	35c. As Type **255a** of Gambia	40	25
2127	$2 Queen wearing tiara and green dress	1·25	1·40
2128	$4 Windsor Castle	2·50	2·75
MS2129	103×125 mm. $6 Queen Elizabeth at Windsor	3·75	4·00

1996. Flowers. As T **430** of Grenada. Multicoloured.

2130	35c. "Camellia "Apple Blossom"	40	25
2131	75c. Odontoglossum	60	60
2132	75c. Cattleya	60	60
2133	75c. Paphiopedilum "Venus's Slipper"	60	60
2134	75c. Laeliocattleya "Marysville"	60	60
2135	75c. Fuchsia "Citation"	60	60
2136	75c. Fuchsia "Amy Lye"	60	60
2137	75c. Clysonimus (butterfly) and temple	60	60
2138	75c. Foxglove (*Digitalis purpurea*)	60	60
2139	75c. Martagon lily (*Lilium martagon*)	60	60
2140	75c. "Tulipa" "Couleur Cardinal"	60	60
2141	75c. Snowdrop (*Galanthus nivalis*)	60	60
2142	75c. "Rosa" "Superstar"	60	60
2143	75c. Crocus "Dutch Yellow Mammoth"	60	60
2144	75c. Japanese lily (*Lilium speciosum*)	60	60
2145	75c. "Lilium" "Joan Evans"	60	60
2146	75c. "Rosa" "Rosemary Harkness"	60	60
2147	90c. Camellia japonica "Extravaganza"	60	60
2148	$1 Chrysanthemum "Primrose Dorothy Else"	60	60
2149	$2 Dahlia "Brandaris"	1·25	1·40
MS2150	Two sheets, each 68×98 mm. (a) $5 Narcissus "Rembrandt". (b) $6 Gladiolus "Flowersong". Set of 2 sheets	6·50	7·50

Nos. 2135/46 were printed together, se-tenant, with the backgrounds forming a composite design.
No. 2135 is inscribed "Fuschcia", No. 2133 "Mammouth" and **MS**2150b "Gladiollus", all in error.

1996. 50th Anniv of UNICEF. As T **258a** of Gambia. Multicoloured.

2151	75c. Child's face (horiz)	55	45
2152	$2 Child with spoon (horiz)	1·10	1·40
2153	$3 Girl sewing (horiz)	1·60	1·90
MS2154	105×75 mm. $6 Mother carrying child	3·00	3·50

1996. 3000th Anniv of Jerusalem. Multicoloured designs as T **424** of Grenada, but horiz.

| MS2155 | 137×47 mm. $1 Pool of Bethesda and *Papaver rhoeas*; $2 Damascus Gate and *Chrysanthemum coronarium*; $3 Church of All Nations and *Myrtus communis*. | 4·00 | 3·75 |
| MS2156 | 82×62 mm. $6 Church of the Holy Sepulchre | 4·00 | 3·75 |

1996. Centenary of Radio. Entertainers. As T **259a** of Gambia. Multicoloured.

| 2157 | 35c. Ed Wynn | 35 | 25 |
| 2158 | 75c. Red Skelton | 55 | 45 |

2159	$1 Joe Penner	65	55
2160	$3 Jerry Colonna	1·75	2·00
MS2161	70×99 mm. $6 Bob Elliot and Ray Goulding (horiz)	3·25	3·75

1996. Olympic Games, Atlanta. Previous Medal Winners. As T **425** of Grenada. Multicoloured.

2162	35c. Los Angeles Memorial Coliseum	35	25
2163	75c. Connie Carpenter-Phinney (U.S.A.) (Cycling)	75	55
2164	$1 Josef Neckermann (Germany) (vert)	70	70
2165	$1 Harry Boldt (Germany) (vert)	70	70
2166	$1 Elena Petouchkova (Russia) (vert)	70	70
2167	$1 Alwin Schockemoehle (Germany) (vert)	70	70
2168	$1 Hans Winkler (Germany) (vert)	70	70
2169	$1 Joe Fargis (U.S.A.) (vert)	70	70
2170	$1 David Broome (Great Britain) (vert)	70	70
2171	$1 Reiner Klimke (Germany) (vert)	70	70
2172	$1 Richard Meade (Great Britain) (vert)	70	70
2173	$1 Julianne McNamara (U.S.A.) (vert)	70	70
2174	$1 Takuti Hayata (Japan) (vert)	70	70
2175	$1 Nikolai Adriana (Russia) (vert)	70	70
2176	$1 Mitch Gaylord (U.S.A.) (vert)	70	70
2177	$1 Ludmilla Tourischeva (Russia) (vert)	70	70
2178	$1 Karin Janz (Germany) (vert)	70	70
2179	$1 Peter Kormann (U.S.A.) (vert)	70	70
2180	$1 Sawoo Kato (Japan) (vert)	70	70
2181	$1 Nadia Comaneci (Rumania) (vert)	70	70
2182	$2 Mohamed Bouchighe (Algeria) (Boxing) (vert)	1·25	1·40
2183	$3 Jackie Joyner Kersee (U.S.A.) (Javelin)	1·75	1·90
MS2184	Two sheets, each 103×74 mm. (a) $5 Child waving flag (vert). (b) $6 William Steinkraus (U.S.A.) (Show jumping). Set of 2 sheets	6·50	7·00

Nos. 2164/72 (equestrians) and 2173/81 (gymnasts) respectively were printed together, *se-tenant*, with the backgrounds forming composite designs.

1996. Classic Cars. As T **426** of Grenada. Multicoloured.

2185	35c. Chevrolet Belair convertible	40	25
2186	50c. V.I.P. car	55	30
2187	75c. Rolls-Royce Torpedo	65	45
2188	$1 Nissan "Cepric" type	70	70
2189	$1 Delaunay-Belleville HB6	70	70
2190	$1 Bugatti Type-15	70	70
2191	$1 Mazda Type 800	70	70
2192	$1 Mercedes 24/100/140 Sport	70	70
2193	$1 MG K3 Rover	70	70
2194	$1 Plymouth Fury	70	70
2195	$2 Mercedes-Benz 500K	1·25	1·40
2196	$3 Bugatti Type-13	1·75	1·90
MS2197	Two sheets, each 106×76 mm. (a) $5 Bugatti "Roadster" Type-55. (b) $6 Lincoln Type-L. Set of 2 sheets	6·50	7·00

1996. Ships. As T **427** of Grenada. Multicoloured.

2198	35c. Grenada schooner	60	25
2199	75c. Grenada schooner (different)	85	45
2200	$1 Athenian triremes, 1000 B.C.	95	95
2201	$1 Egyptian Nile galley, 30 B.C.	95	95
2202	$1 Bangladesh dinghi, 310 B.C.	95	95
2203	$1 Warship of Queen Hatshepsut, 476 B.C.	95	95
2204	$1 Chinese Junk, 200 B.C.	95	95
2205	$1 Polynesian ocean-going canoe, 600 B.C	95	95
2206	$1 "Europa" (liner), 1957	95	95
2207	$1 "Lusitania" (liner), 1906	95	95
2208	$1 "Queen Mary" (liner), 1936	95	95
2209	$1 "Bianca C" (liner)	95	95
2210	$1 "France" (liner), 1952	95	95
2211	$1 "Orion" (liner), 1915	95	95
MS2212	Two sheets, each 104×74 mm. (a) $5 "Queen Elizabeth 2" (liner), 1969 (56×42 mm). (b) $6 Viking longship, 610 (42×56 mm). Set of 2 sheets	6·50	7·00

117 Felix Mendelssohn

1996. Composers. Multicoloured.

2213	$1 Type **117**	90	70

2214	$1 Franz Schubert	90	70
2215	$1 Franz Joseph Haydn	90	70
2216	$1 Robert Schumann	90	70
2217	$1 Ludwig van Beethoven	90	70
2218	$1 Gioacchino Rossini	90	70
2219	$1 George Frederick Handel	90	70
2220	$1 Pyotr Tchaikovsky	90	70
2221	$1 Frederic Chopin	90	70
2222	$1 Bela Bartok	90	70
2223	$1 Giacomo Puccini	90	70
2224	$1 George Gershwin	90	70
2225	$1 Leonard Bernstein	90	70
2226	$1 Kurt Weill	90	70
2227	$1 John Cage	90	70
2228	$1 Aaron Copland	90	70
2229	$1 Sergei Prokofiev	90	70
2230	$1 Igor Stravinsky	90	70
MS2231	Two sheets, each 74×104 mm. (a) $5 Richard Strauss. (b) $6 Wolfgang Amadeus Mozart. Set of 2 sheets	8·50	7·50

Nos. 2213/21 and 2222/30 respectively were printed together, *se-tenant*, with the backgrounds forming composite designs.

1996. Railway Steam Locomotives. As T **429** of Grenada. Multicoloured.

2232	$1.50 Class 38 No. 382, Germany	1·10	1·10
2233	$1.50 *Duchess of Hamilton*, Great Britain	1·10	1·10
2234	$1.50 Class W.P., India	1·10	1·10
2235	$1.50 Class 141R *Americaine*, France	1·10	1·10
2236	$1.50 Class A4 *Mallard*, Great Britain	1·10	1·10
2237	$1.50 Class 18 No. 201, Germany	1·10	1·10
2238	$1.50 Class A2 *Blue Peter*, Great Britain	1·10	1·10
2239	$1.50 Class P36, Russia	1·10	1·10
2240	$1.50 Class QJ, China	1·10	1·10
2241	$1.50 Class 12, Belgium	1·10	1·10
2242	$1.50 Class *Challenger*, U.S.A.	1·10	1·10
2243	$1.50 Class 25, South Africa	1·10	1·10
MS2244	Two sheets, each 100×70 mm. (a) $5 Class *King*, Great Britain. (b) $6 Class *Royal Scot*, Great Britain. Set of 2 sheets	7·00	7·50

1996. Christmas. Religious Paintings. As T **245a** of Gambia. Showing different details from *Suffer Little Children to Come Unto Me* by Van Dyck.

2245	15c. multicoloured	40	20
2246	25c. multicoloured	40	20
2247	$1 multicoloured	1·00	65
2248	$1.50 multicoloured	1·25	1·25
2249	$2 multicoloured	1·60	1·60
2250	$4 multicoloured	2·50	3·25
MS2251	Two sheets, each 106×76 mm. (a) $6 *Suffer Little Children to Come Unto Me* (detail) (Van Dyck) (horiz). (b) $6 *Adoration of the Magi* (Rembrandt) (horiz). Set of 2 sheets	7·50	8·50

118 Man Ho Temple, 1841

1997. "HONG KONG '97" International Stamp Exhibition. Hong Kong Past and Present. T **118** and similar horiz designs. Multicoloured.

MS2252	Five sheets, each 120×96 mm. (a) $3 Type **118**; $3 Man Ho Temple, 1983. (b) $3 St. John's Cathedral, Victoria 1886; $3 St. John's Cathedral, Victoria 1983. (c) $3 Victoria Harbour, 1858; $3 Victoria Harbour, 1983. (d) $3 Waterfront skyscraper; $3 Aerial view of central Victoria. (e) $3 Signing of Treaty of Nanking, 1852. $3 Margaret Thatcher signing The Joint Declaration, 1984. Set of 5 sheets	22·00	20·00

1997. 50th Anniv of UNESCO. As T **273a** of Gambia. Multicoloured.

2253	15c. Temple, Kyoto, Japan	40	20
2254	25c. Roman ruins, Trier, Germany	40	20
2255	$1 Gateway, Mount Taishan, China	80	80
2256	$1 Temple guardian, Kyoto, Japan (vert)	80	80
2257	$1 Temple deity, Kyoto, Japan (vert)	80	80
2258	$1 Temple lamp, Kyoto, Japan (vert)	80	80
2259	$1 Ayutthaya, Thailand (vert)	80	80
2260	$1 Statue, Borobudur Temple, Indonesia (vert)	80	80
2261	$1 Monuments at Pattadakal, India (vert)	80	80
2262	$1 Sleeping buddha, Polonnaruwa, Sri Lanka (vert)	80	80
2263	$1 Sagarmatha National Park, Nepal (vert)	80	80

2264	$1 Congonhas Sanctuary, Brazil (vert)	1·10	1·10
2265	$1 Cartagena, Colombia (vert)	1·10	1·10
2266	$1 Pueblo, Guatemala (vert)	1·10	1·10
2267	$1 Maya statue, Honduras (vert)	1·10	1·10
2268	$1 Popocatepetl Monastery, Mexico (vert)	1·10	1·10
2269	$1 Galapagos Islands, Ecuador (vert)	1·10	1·10
2270	$1 Waterfall, Costa Rica (vert)	1·10	1·10
2271	$1 Glaciares National Park, Argentina (vert)	1·10	1·10
2272	$1.50 Notre Dame Cathedral, Paris, France	1·10	1·10
2273	$1.50 Timbered house, Maulbronn, Germany	1·10	1·10
2274	$1.50 Gateway, Himeji-jo, Japan	1·10	1·10
2275	$1.50 Lion statues, Delphi, Greece	1·10	1·10
2276	$1.50 Palace of Fontainebleau, France	1·10	1·10
2277	$1.50 Scandola Nature Reserve, France	1·10	1·10
2278	$2 Citadel, Dubrovnik, Croatia	1·50	1·60
2279	$4 Angra do Heroismo, Portugal	2·50	3·00
MS2280	Three sheets, each 127×102 mm. (a) $6 Mont St. Michel, France. (b) $6 Ruins of Teotihuacan, Mexico. (c) $6 Temple, Chengde, China. Set of 3 sheets	10·00	11·00

119 Springer Spaniel

1997. Cats and Dogs. Multicoloured.

2281	35c. Type **119**	50	25
2282	45c. Abyssinian blue	50	30
2283	50c. Burmese cream (vert)	50	30
2284	75c. Doberman pinscher	75	50
2285	90c. Persian tortoiseshell and white	75	50
2286	$1 Italian spinone (vert)	85	55
2287	$1.50 Siamese chocolate point	1·10	1·10
2288	$1.50 Oriental shorthair white	1·10	1·10
2289	$1.50 Burmese sable	1·10	1·10
2290	$1.50 Abyssinian tabby	1·10	1·10
2291	$1.50 Persian shaded silver	1·10	1·10
2292	$1.50 Tonkinese natural mink	1·10	1·10
2293	$1.50 Leonberger	1·10	1·10
2294	$1.50 Newfoundland	1·10	1·10
2295	$1.50 Boxer	1·10	1·10
2296	$1.50 St. Bernard	1·10	1·10
2297	$1.50 Silky terrier	1·10	1·10
2298	$1.50 Miniature schnauzer	1·10	1·10
2299	$2 Cocker spaniel (vert)	1·50	1·60
2300	$3 Oriental shorthair agouti (vert)	2·00	2·25
MS2301	Two sheets. (a) 75×105 mm. $6 Sphynx (vert). (b) 105×75 mm. $6 Golden retriever puppy. Set of 2 sheets	7·50	8·00

Nos. 2287/92 (cats) and Nos. 2293/8 (dogs) respectively were printed together, *se-tenant*, with the backgrounds forming composite designs.

1997. Dinosaurs. As T **438** of Grenada. Multicoloured.

2302	45c. Stegosaurus	60	30
2303	90c. Diplodocus	80	50
2304	$1 Pteranodon (vert)	80	55
2305	$1.50 Rhamphorhynchus and head of Brachiosaurus	1·10	1·10
2306	$1.50 Archaeopteryx	1·10	1·10
2307	$1.50 Anurognathus and body of Brachiosaurus	1·10	1·10
2308	$1.50 Head of Albertosaurus	1·10	1·10
2309	$1.50 Herrerasaurus and legs of Brachiosaurus	1·10	1·10
2310	$1.50 Platyhystrix and body of Albertosaurus	1·10	1·10
2311	$1.50 Deinonychus and Ankylasaurus (vert)	1·50	1·60
MS2312	Two sheets, each 103×74 mm. (a) $6 Allosaurus (vert). (b) $6 Hydacrosaurus. Set of 2 sheets	8·00	8·50

Nos. 2305/10 were printed together, *se-tenant*, with the backgrounds forming a composite design.

1997. 300th Anniv of *Mother Goose* Nursery Rhymes. Sheet 72×102 mm containing vert design as T **276a** of Gambia. Multicoloured.

MS2313	$6 Girl and sheep ("Baa, Baa, Black Sheep")	3·50	4·00

1997. 50th Death Anniv of Paul Harris (founder of Rotary International). As T **276b** of Gambia. Multicoloured.

2314	$3 Paul Harris and village women with water pump, Burkina Faso	1·50	1·60
MS2315	78×108 mm. $6 Early Rotary parade float	3·00	3·50

1997. Golden Wedding of Queen Elizabeth and Prince Philip. As T **276c** of Gambia. Multicoloured (except Nos. 2318/19).

2316	$1 Engagement photograph, 1947	1·00	90
2317	$1 Royal coat of arms	1·00	90
2318	$1 Queen Elizabeth and Duke of Edinburgh, 1953 (brown)	1·00	90
2319	$1 Formal portrait of Queen Elizabeth and Prince Philip in uniform (brown)	1·00	90
2320	$1 Sandringham House	1·00	90
2321	$1 Queen Elizabeth and Prince Philip in carriage	1·00	90
MS2322	100×70 mm. $6 Wedding photograph, 1947	5·50	5·00

1997. "Pacific '97" International Stamp Exhibition, San Francisco. Death Centenary of Heinrich von Stephan (founder of the U.P.U.). As T **276d** of Gambia.

2323	$1.50 green	1·10	1·10
2324	$1.50 brown	1·10	1·10
2325	$1.50 violet	1·10	1·10
MS2326	82×118 mm. $6 blue and black	3·25	3·75

DESIGNS: No. 2323, Pony Express, 1860; 2324, Von Stephan and Mercury; 2325, American steam locomotive; **MS**2326 Von Stephan and camel courier, Baghdad.

1997. Birth Bicentenary of Hiroshige (Japanese painter). *100 Famous Views of Edo*. As T **541a** of Ghana but horiz. Multicoloured.

2327	$1.50 Koume Embankment	1·00	1·00
2328	$1.50 Azuma Shrine and the Entwined Camphor	1·00	1·00
2329	$1.50 Yanagishima	1·00	1·00
2330	$1.50 Inside Akiba Shrine, Ukeji	1·00	1·00
2331	$1.50 Distant View of Kinryuzan Temple and Azuma Bridge	1·00	1·00
2332	$1.50 Night View of Matsuchiyama and the San'ya Canal	1·00	1·00
MS2333	Two sheets, each 102×127 mm. (a) $6 Five Pines, Onagi Canal. (b) $6 Spiral Hall, Five Hundred Rakan Temple. Set of 2 sheets	7·00	7·50

1997. 175th Anniv of Brothers Grimm's Third Collection of Fairy Tales. *The Fox and the Geese*. As T **277a** of Gambia. Multicoloured.

2334	$2 Fox and geese	1·60	1·60
2335	$2 Fox with knife and fork and geese	1·60	1·60
2336	$2 Fox asleep and singing geese	1·60	1·60
MS2337	124×96 mm. $6 Fox (horiz)	3·75	4·00

1997. Winter Olympic Games, Nagano, Japan. As T **440** of Grenada. Multicoloured.

2338	90c. Slalom	65	50
2339	$1 Downhill skiing	70	70
2340	$1 Freestyle ski-jumping (blue and green ski suit)	70	70
2341	$1 Curling	70	70
2342	$1 Ski-jumping (pink ski suit)	70	70
2343	$1 Four-man bobsleigh	70	70
2344	$1 Nordic combined	70	70
2345	$1 Speed skating	70	70
2346	$1 Ice hockey	70	70
2347	$1 Cross-country skiing	70	70
2348	$2 One-man luge	1·25	1·40
2349	$2 Men's figure-skating	1·75	1·90
2350	$2 Speed skating (different)	2·75	3·25
MS2351	Two sheets, each 97×67 mm. (a) $6 Figure skating. (b) $6 One-man luge (vert). Set of 2 sheets	6·00	6·50

120 Hong Kong

1997. Return of Hong Kong to China. Multicoloured.

2352	**120**	$1 multicoloured	70	60
2353	-	$1.25 multicoloured	80	85
2354	-	$1.50 mult (63×32 mm)	95	1·00
2355	-	$2 mult (63×32 mm)	1·25	1·40

DESIGNS: $1.25 to $2 Modern Hong Kong shown through inscriptions.

1997. Marine Life. As T **439** of Grenada. Multicoloured.

2356	10c. Wimplefish	10	10
2357	15c. Clown triggerfish	10	10
2358	25c. Ringed emperor angelfish	15	20
2359	35c. Hooded butterflyfish	20	25
2360	45c. Semicircle angelfish	25	30
2361	75c. Scribbled angelfish	40	45
2362	90c. Threadfin butterflyfish	45	50
2363	$1 Clown surgeonfish	60	65
2364	$2 Bottle-nosed dolphin	1·00	1·10
2365	$5 Triggerfish	2·50	2·75
2366	$10 Lionfish	5·00	5·50
2367	$20 Jackknifefish	10·00	10·50

121 Winnie the Pooh as Monday's Child

1997. *Monday's Child* (poem). Disney cartoon characters from Winnie the Pooh illustrating various verses. Multicoloured.

2368	$1 Type **121**	1·25	1·25
2369	$1 Kanga as Tuesday's child	1·25	1·25
2370	$1 Eeyore as Wednesday's child	1·25	1·25
2371	$1 Tigger as Thursday's child	1·25	1·25
2372	$1 Piglet as Friday's child	1·25	1·25
2373	$1 Rabbit as Saturday's child	1·25	1·25
MS2374	128×107 mm. $6 Christopher Robin as Sunday's child	5·50	5·50

122 Snow White kissing Grumpy

1997. Disney Sweethearts. Disney cartoon characters kissing. Multicoloured.

2375	$1 Type **122**	1·10	1·10
2376	$1 Figaro the Cat and Cleo the Fish	1·10	1·10
2377	$1 Peter Pan and Wendy	1·10	1·10
2378	$1 Cinderella and the Prince	1·10	1·10
2379	$1 Ariel and Eric	1·10	1·10
2380	$1 Beauty and the Prince	1·10	1·10
2381	$1 Aladdin and Jasmine	1·10	1·10
2382	$1 Pocahontas and Captain John Smith	1·10	1·10
2383	$1 Phoebus and Esmeralda	1·10	1·10
MS2384	127×102 mm. $6 Georges Hautecourt kissing cats tail (vert)	6·00	6·00

1997. World Cup Football Championship, France (1998). As T **283a** of Gambia.

2385	10c. blue	25	25
2386	20c. multicoloured	30	30
2387	45c. brown	40	30
2388	$1 black	70	70
2389	$1 brown	70	70
2390	$1 black	70	70
2391	$1 brown	70	70
2392	$1 multicoloured	70	70
2393	$1 multicoloured	70	70
2394	$1 black	70	70
2395	$1 brown	70	70
2396	$1 multicoloured	70	70
2397	$1 black	70	70
2398	$1 black	70	70
2399	$1 black	70	70
2400	$1 black	70	70
2401	$1 black	70	70
2402	$1 black	70	70
2403	$1 black	70	70
2404	$1 black	70	70
2405	$1.50 multicoloured	95	1·00
2406	$5 black	2·75	3·00
MS2407	Two sheets. (a) 127×102 mm. $6 black. (b) 102×127 mm. $6 black. Set of 2 sheets	8·50	9·00

DESIGNS—HORIZ: No. 2385, Italian team, 1934; 2386, Angolan team; 2387, Brazilian team, 1958; 2388, Uruguay team, 1950; 2389, Winning England team, 1966; 2390, West German team, 1954; 2391, Uruguayan officials with Jules Rimet trophy, 1930; 2392, West German players celebrating, 1990; 2393, Maradona (Argentine player), 1986; 2394, Brazilian players, 1994; 2395, Argentine players, 1978; 2396, West German player holding World Cup, 1974; 2405, West German team, 1974; 2406, Italian team, 1938; **MS**2407b, Paulao, Angola. VERT: No. 2397, Ademir, Brazil; 2398, Kocsis, Hungary; 2399, Leonidas, Brazil; 2400, Nejedly, Czechoslavakia; 2401, Schiavio, Italy; 2402, Stabile, Uruguay; 2403, Pele, Brazil; 2404, Fritzwalter, West Germany; **MS**2407a, Shearer, England.

1997. Butterflies. As T **444** of Grenada. Multicoloured.

2408	75c. *Polyura dehaani*	65	45
2409	90c. *Polyura dolon*	70	50
2410	$1 *Charaxes candiope*	70	55
2411	$1.50 *Pantaporia punctata*	95	95
2412	$1.50 *Euthalia confucius*	95	95
2413	$1.50 *Euthalia kardama*	95	95
2414	$1.50 *Limenitis albomaculata*	95	95
2415	$1.50 *Hestina assimilis*	95	95
2416	$1.50 *Kallima inachus*	95	95
2417	$1.50 *Euthalia teutoides*	95	95
2418	$1.50 *Euphaedra francina*	95	95
2419	$1.50 *Euphaedra eleus*	95	95
2420	$1.50 *Euphaedra harpalyce*	95	95
2421	$1.50 *Euphaedra cyparissa*	95	95
2422	$1.50 *Euphaedra gausape*	95	95
2423	$1.50 *Euphaedra imperialis*	95	95
2424	$2 *Charaxes etesippe*	1·25	1·40
2425	$3 *Charaxes castor*	1·75	1·90
MS2426	Two sheets, each 106×76 mm. (a) $5 *Charaxes nobilis* (vert). (b) $6 *Charaxes numenes* (vert). Set of 2 sheets	6·50	7·00

Nos. 2412/17 and 2418/23 respectively were printed together, *se-tenant*, with the backgrounds forming composite designs.

123 James Dean

1997. James Dean (actor) Commemoration. Different portaits. Multicoloured.

2427	$1 Type **123**	70	70
2428	$1 Wearing purple jumper	70	70
2429	$1 Wearing stetson and smoking	70	70
2430	$1 Wearing dinner jacket and tie	70	70
2431	$1 Full-face portrait	70	70
2432	$1 Grimacing	70	70
2433	$1 Wearing stetson	70	70
2434	$1 Leaning on arms	70	70
2435	$1 Smoking	70	70

124 *Symphyglossum sanguineum*

1997. Orchids of the World. Multicoloured.

2436	35c. Type **124**	40	25
2437	45c. *Doritaenopsis* "Mythic Beauty"	50	30
2438	75c. *Odontoglossum cervantesii*	65	45
2439	90c. *Cattleya* "Pumpernickel"	70	50
2440	$1 *Vanda* "Patricia Low"	70	55
2441-2449	$1×9 *Lycaste* "Aquila"; *Brassolaeliocattleya* "Dorothy Bertsch"; *Phalaenopsis* "Zuma Urchin"; *Promenaea xanthina*; *Amesiella philippinensis*; *Brassocattleya* "Angel Lace"; *Brassoepidendrum* "Peggy Ann"; *Miltonia seine*; *Sophralaeliocattleya* "Precious Stones"	5·50	
2450-2458	$1×9 *Cymbidium* "Showgirl"; *Disa blackii*; *Phalaenopsis aphrodite*; *Iwanagaara* "Apple Blossom"; *Masdevallia* "Copper Angel"; *Paphiopedilum micranthum*; *Paphiopedilum* "Clare de Lune"; *Laeliocattleya forbesii*; *Dendrobium* "Dawn Maree"	5·50	
2459	$1.50 *Odontonia* "Debutante"	1·00	1·00
2460-2465	$1.50×6 *Miltoniopsis* "Jean Sabourin"; *Cymbidium* "Red Beauty"; *Brassocattleya* "Green Dragon"; *Phalaenopsis* hybrid; *Laeliocattleya* "Mary Ellen Carter"; *Disa* hybrid	5·50	
2466-2471	$1.50×6 *Lycaste macrobulbon*; *Cochleanthes discolor*; *Cymbidium* "Nang Carpenter"; *Paphiopedilum* "Claire de Lune"; *Masdevallia caudata*; *Cymbidium* "Showgirl")	5·50	
2472	$2 *Laeliocattleya* "Mini Purple"	1·25	1·40
2473	$3 *Phragmipedium dominiarum*	1·75	1·90
MS2474	Two sheets, each 76×106 mm. (a) $5 *Phalenopsis* "Medford Star". (b) $6 *Brassolaelio-cattleya* "Dorothy Bertsch". Set of 2 sheets	7·00	7·50

Nos. 2460/5 and 2466/71 respectively were printed together, *se-tenant*, with the backgrounds forming composite designs.

125 *Clitocybe metachroa*

1997. Fungi. Multicoloured.

2475	75c. Type **125**	65	45
2476	90c. *Clavulinopsis helvola*	70	50
2477	$1 *Lycoperdon pyriforme*	70	55
2478	$1.50 *Auricularia auricula-judae*	95	95
2479	$1.50 *Entoloma incanum*	95	95
2480	$1.50 *Coprinus atramentarius*	95	95
2481	$1.50 *Mycena polygramma*	95	95
2482	$1.50 *Lepista nuda*	95	95
2483	$1.50 *Pleurotis cornucopiae*	95	95
2484	$1.50 *Laccaria amethystina*	95	95
2485	$2 *Clathrus archeri*	1·25	1·40
2486	$3 *Lactarius trivialis*	1·75	1·90
MS2487	Two sheets, each 106×76 mm. (a) $6 *Morchella esculenta*. (b) $6 *Amanita muscaria*. Set of 2 sheets	7·50	8·00

126 Ludwig van Beethoven

1997. Classical Composers. Multicoloured.

2488	$1 Type **126**	85	80
2489	$1 Pyotr Tchaikovsky	85	80
2490	$1 Johann Christian Bach	85	80
2491	$1 Frederic Chopin	85	80
2492	$1 Igor Stravinsky	85	80
2493	$1 Franz Joseph Haydn	85	80
2494	$1 Gustav Mahler	85	80
2495	$1 Gioacchino Antonio Rossini	85	80
MS2496	Two sheets, each 106×76 mm. (a) $6 Wolfgang Amadeus Mozart. (b) $6 Franz Schubert. Set of 2 sheets	9·50	9·50

127 Diana, Princess of Wales and Buckingham Palace

1997. Diana, Princess of Wales Commemoration. Multicoloured.

2497	$1.50 Type **127**	1·10	1·10
2498	$1.50 Princess Diana and lake at Althorp	1·10	1·10
2499	$1.50 Princess Diana and Westminster Abbey	1·10	1·10
2500	$1.50 Princess Diana and gates to Althorp	1·10	1·10
2501	$1.50 Princess Diana in pink hat and gates to Kensington Palace	1·10	1·10
2502	$1.50 Princess Diana and Althorp House	1·10	1·10
MS2503	115×80 mm. $6 Holding bouquet (60×40 mm)	3·75	4·00

1997. Christmas. Religious Paintings. As T **448** of Grenada. Multicoloured.

2504	20c. Choir of Angels (Simon Marmion)	30	15
2505	75c. *The Annunciation* (Giotto)	65	45
2506	90c. *Festival of the Rose Garlands* (Albrecht Durer)	70	50
2507	$1.50 *Madonna with Two Angels* (Hans Memling)	95	1·00
2508	$2 *The Ognissanti Madonna* (Giotto)	1·25	1·40
2509	$3 *Angel with Candlestick* (Michelangelo)	1·75	1·90
MS2510	Two sheets, each 114×104 mm. (a) $6*The Rising of the Sun* (detail) (horiz) (Francois Boucher). (b) $6 *Cupid* (detail) (horiz) (Jean-Baptiste Huet). Set of 2 sheets	7·50	7·50

No. 2506 is inscribed "DUER" in error.

1998. Fish. As T **449** of Grenada. Multicoloured.

2511	$1 Queen angelfish	75	75
2512	$1 Clown triggerfish	75	75
2513	$1 Four-spot butterflyfish	75	75
2514	$1 Yellow-tailed damselfish	75	75
2515	$1 Yellow-headed wrasse	75	75
2516	$1 Royal gramma	75	75
2517	$1 Candy basslet	75	75
2518	$1 Smooth trunkfish	75	75
2519	$1 Coral hind	75	75
MS2520	Two sheets. (a) 102×72 mm. $6 Black-finned reef shark. (b) 72×102 mm. $6 Yellow-headed jawfish (vert). Set of 2 sheets	8·50	8·50

Nos. 2511/19 were printed together, *se-tenant*, with the backgrounds forming a composite design.

128 Tiger (hologram)

1998. Chinese New Year ("Year of the Tiger").

2521	**128** $1.50 black on silver foil	1·25	1·25
MS2522	64×76 mm. **128** $3 black on silver foil (52×65 mm)	2·00	2·00

129 *Alabama* (Confederate warship)

1998. Famous Ships. Multicoloured. (a) Ships of the 1860s.

2523	75c. Type **129**	75	75
2524	75c. *Persia* (paddle-steamer)	75	75
2525	75c. *Ariel* (clipper)	75	75
2526	75c. *Florida* (Confederate warship)	75	75
2527	75c. *Great Eastern* (paddle-steamer)	75	75
2528	75c. *Jacob Bell* on fire	75	75
2529	75c. *Star of India* (clipper)	75	75
2530	75c. *Robert E. Lee* (Mississippi paddle-steamer)	75	75
2531	75c. *U.S.S. Passaic* (monitor)	75	75
2532	75c. *Madagascar* (clipper)	75	75
2533	75c. *H.M.S. Devastation* (battleship)	75	75
2534	75c. *General Grant* (clipper)	75	75

(b) Ships of the American Civil War.

2535	$1 Clark Gable as Rhett Butler in *Gone with the Wind* (vert)	75	75
2536	$1 Crew abandoning blockade runner wrecked on Sullivan's Island (vert)	75	75
2537	$1 Margaret Mitchell (author of *Gone with the Wind*) (vert)	75	75
2538	$1 George Alfred Trenholm (ship owner) (vert)	75	75
2539	$1 Dock Street Theatre, Charleston (vert)	75	75
2540	$1 *Howlett* (paddle-steamer) sinking (vert)	75	75
2541	$1 *U.S.S. Tecumseh* on fire (vert)	75	75
2542	$1 City Jail, Charleston (vert)	75	75
MS2543	Two sheets, each 106×76 mm. (a) $6 *Nashville* sinking Union clipper *Harvey Birch* (57×42 mm). (b) $6 *Hatteras* (paddle-steamer) on fire (42×57 mm). Set of 2 sheets	8·00	8·50

130 Concept Strike Fighter

1998. Aircraft Designs of the Future. Multicoloured.

2544	70c. Type **130**	50	40
2545	90c. Concept space shuttle	45	60
2546	$1 Velocity 173 RG Elite	75	75
2547	$1 Davis DA-9	75	75
2548	$1 Concorde	75	75
2549	$1 Voyager	75	75
2550	$1 Factimobile	75	75
2551	$1 RAF 2000	75	75
2552	$1 Boomerang	75	75
2553	$1 N1M Flying Wing	75	75
2554	$2 Concept air and space jet	1·40	1·40
2555	$3 V Jet II	1·75	1·75
MS2556	Two sheets, each 100×70 mm. (a) $6 Concept aeropod. (b) $6 Delmar. Set of 2 sheets	8·00	8·50

131 "Lycaste deppei"

1998. Orchids of the World. Multicoloured.

2557	$1 Type **131**	70	70
2558	$1 *Dendrobium victoriae*	70	70
2559	$1 *Dendrobium nobile*	70	70
2560	$1 *Cymbidium dayanum*	70	70
2561	$1 *Cymbidium* "Starbright"	70	70

2562	$1 Cymbidium giganteum	70	70
2563	$1 Chysis aurea	70	70
2564	$1 Broughtonia sanguinea	70	70
2565	$1 Cattleya guttata	70	70
2566	$1 Calanthe vestita	70	70
2567	$1 Cattleya bicolor	70	70
2568	$1 Laelia anceps	70	70
2569	$1 Epidendrum prismatocarpum	70	70
2570	$1 Coelogyne ochracea	70	70
2571	$1 Doritaenopsis eclantant	70	70
2572	$1 Laelia gouldiana	70	70
2573	$1 Encyclia vitellina	70	70
2574	$1 Maxillaria praestans	70	70
2575	$1 Laelia tenebrosa	70	70
2576	$1.50 Phragmipedium besseae	1·10	1·10
2577	$2 Pschopsis papilio	1·40	1·40
2578	$3 Masdevallia coccinea	1·75	1·75

MS2579 Two sheets, each 29×43 mm.
(a) $6 Masdevallia ignea. (b) $6 Encyclia brassavolae. Set of 2 sheets — 8·00 — 8·50

1998. Seabirds. As T **452** of Grenada. Multicoloured.

2580	75c. Bonaparte's gull (horiz)	60	40
2581	90c. Western sandpiper (horiz)	70	50
2582	$1.50 Common tern (horiz)	1·00	1·00
2583	$1.50 Brown pelican (horiz)	1·00	1·00
2584	$1.50 Black-legged kittiwake and white tern (horiz)	1·00	1·00
2585	$1.50 Herring gull (horiz)	1·00	1·00
2586	$1.50 Lesser noddy (horiz)	1·00	1·00
2587	$1.50 Black-legged kittiwake (horiz)	1·00	1·00
2588	$1.50 Whimbrel (horiz)	1·00	1·00
2589	$1.50 Golden white-tailed tropic bird (horiz)	1·00	1·00
2590	$1.50 Arctic tern (horiz)	1·00	1·00
2591	$1.50 Ruddy turnstone (horiz)	1·00	1·00
2592	$1.50 Blue-eyed cormorant ("Imperial Shag") (horiz)	1·00	1·00
2593	$1.50 Magellan gull (horiz)	1·00	1·00
2594	$2 Great black-backed gull (horiz)	1·40	1·40
2595	$3 Dotterell (horiz)	1·75	1·75

MS2596 Two sheets, each 100×70 mm.
(a) $5 Broad-billed prion (horiz). (b)
$5 Yellow-nosed albatross. Set of
2 sheets — 7·50 — 8·00

1998. International Year of the Ocean. As T **454** of Grenada. Multicoloured.

2597	75c. Great black-backed gull	50	50
2598	75c. Common dolphin	50	50
2599	75c. Seal	50	50
2600	75c. Amazonian catfish	50	50
2601	75c. Shark	50	50
2602	75c. Goldfish	50	50
2603	75c. Cyathopharynx	50	50
2604	75c. Killer whale	50	50
2605	75c. Telmatochromis	50	50
2606	75c. Crab	50	50
2607	75c. Octopus	50	50
2608	75c. Turtle	50	50
2609	90c. Two dolphins	55	55
2610	90c. Seal	55	55
2611	90c. Turtle on rock	55	55
2612	90c. Leopard shark	55	55
2613	90c. Flame angelfish	55	55
2614	90c. Syndontis	55	55
2615	90c. Lamprologus	55	55
2616	90c. "Krptopterus bicirrhus"	55	55
2617	90c. "Pterophyllum scalare"	55	55
2618	90c. Swimming pancake	55	55
2619	90c. Cowfish	55	55
2620	90c. Seahorse	55	55

MS2621 Two sheets, each 98×68
mm. (a) $6 "Tetraodon mbu". (b) $6
Goldfish. Set of 2 sheets — 8·00 — 8·50

Nos. 2597/2608 and 2609/20 respectively were printed together, se-tenant, with the backgrounds forming composite designs.

1998. 50th Anniv of Organization of American States. As T **454a** of Grenada.

2622	$1 violet, orange and black	75	75

1998. 25th Death Anniv of Pablo Picasso (painter). As T **291a** of Gambia. Multicoloured.

2623	45c. Bust of a Woman (vert)	50	30
2624	$2 Three Musicians	1·25	1·25
2625	$3 Studio at La Californie	1·75	1·75

MS2626 102×127 mm. $5 Woman with
a Blue Hat — 3·00 — 3·25

1998. Birth Centenary of Enzo Ferrari (car manufacturer). As T **454b** of Grenada. Multicoloured.

2627	$2 275 GTB	1·50	1·50
2628	$2 340 MM	1·50	1·50
2629	$2 250 GT SWB Berlinetta "Hot Rod"	1·50	1·50

MS2630 104×72 mm. $5 First Ferrari
cabriolet (91×34 mm) — 3·50 — 3·75

1998. 19th World Scout Jamboree, Chile. As T **455** of Grenada. Multicoloured.

2631	90c. Scout greeting	60	40
2632	$1.50 Lord Baden-Powell	90	90

2633	$5 Scout salute	2·50	3·00

MS2634 76×106 mm. $6 Lord Baden-
Powell (vert) — 3·50 — 4·00

1998. 50th Death Anniv of Mahatma Gandhi. As T **455a** of Grenada.

2635	$1 grey, brown and black	1·00	80

MS2636 100×70 mm. $6 grey, brown
and black — 4·00 — 4·00

1998. 80th Anniv of Royal Air Force. As T **292a** of Gambia. Multicoloured.

2637	$2 Tornado GR1	1·60	1·60
2638	$2 BAe Hawk T1A	1·60	1·60
2639	$2 Sepecat Jaguar GR1	1·60	1·60
2640	$2 Harrier GR7	1·60	1·60
2641	$2 Chinook helicopter carrying three loads	1·60	1·60
2642	$2 Silhouette of BAe Harrier GR5	1·60	1·60
2643	$2 Panavia Tornado F3 ADV at sunset	1·60	1·60
2644	$2 Chinook HC2 carrying 105 mm light gun	1·60	1·60

MS2645 Four sheets, each 93×70 mm.
(a) $6 Bristol F2B fighter and head
of golden eagle (bird). (b) $6 Bristol
F2B fighter and montagu's harrier in
flight. (c) $6 Hawker Hunter and EF-
2000 Eurofighter. (d) $6 Tornado and
EF-2000 Eurofighter. Set of 4 sheets — 15·00 — 16·00

1998. Birth Bicentenary of Eugene Delacroix (painter). As T **294** of Gambia. Multicoloured.

2646	$1 The Natchez	80	80
2647	$1 Christ and His Disciples Cross-ing the Sea of Galilee	80	80
2648	$1 Sunset	80	80
2649	$1 Moroccans outside the Walls of Tangier	80	80
2650	$1 The Fireplace	80	80
2651	$1 Forest View with an Oak Tree	80	80
2652	$1 View of the Harbour at Dieppe	80	80
2653	$1 Arab Tax Collectors	80	80

MS2654 85×105 mm. $5 Young Orphan — 3·00 — 3·25

1998. First Death Anniv of Diana, Princess of Wales. As T **293a** of Gambia.

2655	$1.50 multicoloured	60	65

132 Father Christmas and Hare

1998. Disney's Christmas Trains. Walt Disney cartoon characters in train carriages. Multicoloured.

2656	$1 Type **132**	85	85
2657	$1 Giraffe, elephant and tiger	85	85
2658	$1 Three Pigs and Wolf	85	85
2659	$1 Pied Piper, Jiminy Cricket, penguins and children	85	85
2660	$1 Swans, Little Hiawatha and tortoise	85	85
2661	$1 Mickey Mouse as train driver	85	85
2662	$1 Pluto, Chip and Dale	85	85
2663	$1 Donald and Daisy Duck	85	85
2664	$1 Goofy, Huey, Dewey and Louie	85	85
2665	$1 Minnie Mouse and presents	85	85
2666	$1 Piglet as train driver	85	85
2667	$1 Winnie the Pooh and honey	85	85
2668	$1 Rabbit and Owl	85	85
2669	$1 Kanga, Roo and Christopher Robin	85	85
2670	$1 Eeyore and Tigger	85	85

MS2671 Three sheets, each 133×109
mm. (a) $6 Father Christmas and
toy train. (b) $6 Mickey Mouse as
train driver. (c) $6 Rabbit, Winnie
the Pooh, Piglet and Eeyore. Set of
3 sheets — 12·00 — 13·00

1999. Chinese New Year ("Year of the Rabbit"). Sheet 150×76 mm, containing triangular designs as T **435** of Grenada each showing rabbits. Multicoloured. Self-adhesive on gold foil.

MS2672 $1.50, "GRENADA GREN-
ADINES" in green; $1.50 "GRENADA
GRENADINES" in orange; $1.50
"GRENADA GRENADINES" in red — 2·25 — 2·50

133 Troodon

2673	$1 Type **133**	75	75
2674	$1 Camptosaurus	75	75
2675	$1 Parasaurolophus	75	75
2676	$1 Dryosaurus	75	75
2677	$1 Gallimimus	75	75
2678	$1 Camarasaurus	75	75
2679	$1.50 Duckbill (horiz)	1·00	1·00
2680	$1.50 Lambeosaurus (horiz)	1·00	1·00
2681	$1.50 Iguanodon (horiz)	1·00	1·00
2682	$1.50 Euoplocephalus (horiz)	1·00	1·00
2683	$1.50 Triceratops (horiz)	1·00	1·00
2684	$1.50 Brachiosaurus (horiz)	1·00	1·00
2685	$1.50 Ponoptosaurus (horiz)	1·00	1·00
2686	$1.50 Stegosaurus (horiz)	1·00	1·00

1999. "Australia '99" World Stamp Exhibition, Melbourne. Prehistoric Animals. Multicoloured.

MS2687 Three sheets. (a) 106×76
mm. $6 Edmontosaurus (horiz). (b)
76×106 mm. $6 "Tyrannosaurus Rex".
(c) 76×106 mm. $6 Halticosaurus. Set
of 3 sheets — 11·00 — 12·00

134 Great Indian Peninsula Passenger and Mail Locomotive

1999. Steam Trains of the World. Multicoloured.

2688	15c. Type **134**	50	25
2689	75c. Midland Great Western passenger locomotive (Ireland)	60	45
2690	90c. Canada Pacific express locomotive	70	55
2691	$1.50 East Indian Railway express locomotive	1·00	1·00
2692	$2 Victorian Railways suburban tank locomotive (Australia)	1·25	1·25
2693	$2 Eastern Railways compound locomotive (France)	1·25	1·25
2694	$2 Govt Railways Class WF tank locomotive (New Zealand)	1·25	1·25
2695	$2 Burma Railways oil-burning tank locomotive, 1899	1·25	1·25
2696	$2 Federated Malay States Railway Class G steam locomotive, 1899	1·25	1·25
2697	$2 Belfast and Northern Coun-ties Railway narrow-gauge tank locomotive	1·25	1·25
2698	$2 Shunting tank locomotive (Russia)	1·25	1·25
2699	$2 G.N.R. Ivatt large-boilered "Atlantic" type	1·25	1·25
2700	$2 Palatine Railway "Atlantic" type express locomotive (Germany)	1·25	1·25
2701	$2 Belgian State Railways "Dunalastair" type locomo-tive	1·25	1·25
2702	$2 Swedish State Railways Class Cc locomotive	1·25	1·25
2703	$2 Antofagasta and Bolivian Railway tank locomotive (Chile)	1·25	1·25
2704	$2 Bolivian State Fairlie type locomotive	1·25	1·25
2705	$2 Belgian State Railways express locomotive	1·25	1·25
2706	$2 London and South Western Railway Drummond's mixed traffic locomotive	1·25	1·25
2707	$2 Belfast and Northern Coun-ties Railways Compound locomotive	1·25	1·25
2708	$2 Dutch State Railway express passenger locomotive	1·25	1·25
2709	$2 Gothard Railway heavy freight locomotive (Swit-zerland)	1·25	1·25
2710	$2 Waterford, Limerick and Western railway goods locomotive (Ireland)	1·25	1·25
2711	$2 Atchison, Topeka and Santa Fe railway tandem compound express locomo-tive (U.S.A.)	1·25	1·25
2712	$2 Midland Railway Class "Prin-cess of Wales" locomotive (Great Britain)	1·25	1·25
2713	$3 Glasgow and South Western Railway Stirling type locomotive	1·60	1·75

MS2714 Two sheets, each 100×70 mm.
(a) $6 Paris, Lyons and Mediter-
ranean compound locomotive
(France). (b) $6 Italian Southern
Railway compound locomotive. Set
of 2 sheets — 7·50 — 7·50

No. 2701 is inscribed "Dunalastair" in error.

135 Porkfish

1999. Fauna and Flora. Multicoloured.

2715	75c. Type **135**	60	40
2716	90c. Leatherback turtle	70	55
2717	$1 Red-billed tropic bird ("White-tailed Tropicbird") (vert)	70	70
2718	$1 Laughing gull (vert)	70	70
2719	$1 Palm tree (vert)	70	70
2720	$1 Humpback whale (vert)	70	70
2721	$1 Painted bunting (vert)	70	70
2722	$1 Common grackle (vert)	70	70
2723	$1 Green anole (lizard) (vert)	70	70
2724	$1 Morpho peleides (butterfly) (vert)	70	70
2725	$1 Prepona meander (butterfly) (vert)	70	70
2726	$1 Common dolphin (vert)	70	70
2727	$1 Catonephele numilia (but-terfly) (vert)	70	70
2728	$1 Sooty tern (vert)	70	70
2729	$1 Vermilion flycatcher (vert)	70	70
2730	$1 Blue grosbeak (vert)	70	70
2731	$1 Great egret (vert)	70	70
2732	$1 Actinate pellenea (butterfly) (vert)	70	70
2733	$1 Anteos clorinde (butterfly)	70	70
2734	$1 Common iguana (vert)	70	70
2735	$1.50 Ruby-throated hum-mingbird	70	70
2736	$2 Theope eudocia (butterfly)	1·40	1·40

MS2737 Two sheets, each 85×110 mm.
(a) $6 Bananaquit. (b) $6 Beaugre-
gory (fish). Set of 2 sheets — 7·50 — 8·00

Nos. 2717/25 and 2726/34 respectively were printed together, se-tenant, with the backgrounds forming composite designs.

No. 2727 is inscribed "numili" in error.

136 John H. Glenn (astronaut), 1998

1999. John Glenn's (first American to orbit Earth) Return to Space. Multicoloured, except Nos. 2716, 2718 and 2720/1.

2738	$1 Type **136**	70	70
2739	$1 Glenn and Pres. John F. Kennedy (brown and red)	70	70
2740	$1 Inside "Discovery", 1998	70	70
2741	$1 Climbing from "Friendship 7" capsule, 1962 (brown and red)	70	70
2742	$1 Medical checkup	70	70
2743	$1 Climbing into space capsule, 1962 (brown and red)	70	70
2744	$1 As Democratic Senator for Ohio, 1974 (vert) (brown and red)	70	70
2745	$1 In space suit, 1962 (vert)	70	70
2746	$1 Smiling during suit up test, 1998 (vert)	70	70
2747	$1 Preparing for "Discovery" flight (vert)	70	70
2748	$1 At press conference (with microphone) (vert)	70	70
2749	$1 Smiling at camera (wearing glasses) (vert)	70	70
2750	$1 Participating in medical research (vert)	70	70
2751	$1 Posing in space suit, 1998	70	70

No. 2744 was inscribed "Junior Senator form Ohio (1974)" in error.

1999. "iBRA '99" International Stamp Exhibition, Nuremberg. As T **298a** of Gambia. Multicoloured.

2752	35c. Luckenbach (full-rigged ship) and Thurn and Taxis Northern District 1852 ¼sgr. stamp	45	40
2753	45c. Leipzig–Dresden Railway carriage and Schleswig-Holstein 1850 1s.	45	40
2754	$1.50 Leipzig–Dresden Railway carriage and Oldenburg 1852½sgr.	1·50	1·25
2755	$3 Luckenbach (full-rigged ship) and North German Confed-eration 1868 ¼g.	2·25	2·25

MS2756 154×86 mm. $6 Thurn and
Taxis Northern District 1865 ¼sgr.
rouletted pair used on cover — 3·50 — 3·75

1999. 150th Death Anniv of Katsushika Hokusai (Japanese artist). As T **298b** of Gambia. Multicoloured.

2757	$1.50 Fuchu	90	90

2758	$1.50 *Doll Fair at Fikkendana*	90	90
2759	$1.50 *Sumo Wrestlers* (in arm hold)	90	90
2760	$1.50 *Sumo Wrestlers* (in head lock)	90	90
2761	$1.50 *Sojo Henjo*	90	90
2762	$1.50 *Twin Gardens Gateway of Asakusa Kannon Temple*	90	90
2763	$1.50 *A Breeze on a Fine Day*	90	90
2764	$1.50 *Ejiri*	90	90
2765	$1.50 *Horse Drawings* (galloping)	90	90
2766	$1.50 *Horse Drawings* (stationary)	90	90
2767	$1.50 *View along Bank of Sumida River*	90	90
2768	$1.50 *Thunderstorm Below the Mountain*	90	90
MS2769	Two sheets, each 102×72 mm. (a) $6 *Stretching Cloth* (vert). (b) $6 *Kobo Daishi exorcising Demon that causes Sickness* (vert). Set of 2 sheets	7·00	8·00

No. 2762 is inscribed "TWIN GARDAINS GATEWAY" in error.

1999. Tenth Anniv of United Nations Rights of the Child Convention. As T **298c** of Gambia. Multicoloured.

2770	$3 African boy	1·60	1·75
2771	$3 Liv Ullman (UNICEF's first female ambassador)	1·60	1·75
2772	$3 African woman in head scarf	1·60	1·75
MS2773	110×84 mm. $6 Maurice Pate (Founding Director of UNICEF)	2·75	3·25

Nos. 2770/2 were printed together, *se-tenant*, forming a composite design.

1999. "PhilexFrance '99" International Stamp Exhibition, Paris. Railway Locomotives. Two sheets containing horiz designs as T **299d** of Gambia. Multicoloured.

MS2774	(a) 106×81 mm. $6 Paris, Orleans and Mediterranean Railway Cha Pelon type steam locomotive. (b) 106×76 mm. $6 French National Railways Class 7000 high speed electric locomotive. Set of 2 sheets	7·50	8·00

1999. 250th Birth Anniv of Johann von Goethe (German writer). As T **298d** of Gambia.

2775	$3 multicoloured	1·60	1·75
2776	$3 blue and black	1·60	1·75
2777	$3 blue, violet and black	1·60	1·75
MS2778	71×106 mm. $6 brown, chestnut and black	2·75	3·25

DESIGNS—HORIZ: No. 2775, Peasants dancing under linden-tree; 2776, Goethe and Schiller; 2777, Faust dreams of soaring above the mortal. VERT: **MS**2778, Johann von Goethe.

1999. Royal Wedding. As T **298** of Gambia. Multicoloured.

2779	$3 Sophie Rhys-Jones	1·75	1·90
2780	$3 Sophie and Prince Edward	1·75	1·90
2781	$3 Prince Edward	1·75	1·90
MS2782	78×108 mm. $6 Sophie and Prince Edward on wedding day	4·75	5·00

1999. "Queen Elizabeth the Queen Mother's Century". As T **304a** of Gambia.

2783	$2 black and gold	1·40	1·40
2784	$2 multicoloured	1·40	1·40
2785	$2 black and gold	1·40	1·40
2786	$2 multicoloured	1·40	1·40
MS2787	153×157 mm. $6 multicoloured	3·50	3·50

DESIGNS: No. 2783, Lady Elizabeth Bowes-Lyon as a child; 2784, Queen Mother in Rhodesia, 1957; 2785, Queen Mother with Princesses Elizabeth and Anne, 1950; 2786, Queen Mother, 1988. (37×50 mm)—**MS**2787, Queen Mother reviewing Black Watch, Berlin.

138 George Raft

1999. Early Cinema Actors.

2788	**138**	$1 multicoloured	70	70
2789	-	$1 grey and black	70	70
2790	-	$1 grey and black	70	70
2791	-	$1 multicoloured	70	70
2792	-	$1 multicoloured	70	70
2793	-	$1 black and grey	70	70
2794	-	$1 black, blue and grey	70	70
2795	-	$1 multicoloured	70	70
2796	-	$2 multicoloured	1·10	1·10
2797	-	$2 black and grey	1·10	1·10
2798	-	$2 multicoloured	1·10	1·10
2799	-	$2 black and grey	1·10	1·10
MS2800		$6 multicoloured	3·50	3·50

DESIGNS: No. 2791, Fatty Arbuckle; 2792, Buster Keaton; 2795, Harold Lloyd; 2796, James Cagney; 2798, Edward G. Robinson; **MS**2800, Charlie Chaplin. (53×39 mm): No. 2789, George Raft in *Scarface*; 2790, Fatty Arbuckle with nurse; 2793, Buster Keaton on locomotive cow-catcher; 2794, Harold Lloyd hanging on clockface; 2797, James Cagney in *The Public Enemy*; 2799, Edward G. Robinson in *Little Caesar*.

139 "Sputnik I", 1957

1999. Space Exploration. Multicoloured.

2801	$1.50 Type **139**	1·00	1·00
2802	$1.50 "Explorer I", 1958	1·00	1·00
2803	$1.50 "Telstar I" satellite, 1962	1·00	1·00
2804	$1.50 "Maristat I", 1976	1·00	1·00
2805	$1.50 Long Duration Exposure facility, 1984	1·00	1·00
2806	$1.50 Hubble Space Telescope, 1990	1·00	1·00
2807	$1.50 X-15 rocket plane, 1960 (vert)	1·00	1·00
2808	$1.50 "Freedom 7" rocket, 1961 (vert)	1·00	1·00
2809	$1.50 "Friendship 7", 1962 (vert)	1·00	1·00
2810	$1.50 "Gemini 4" rocket and Edward H. White, 1965 (vert)	1·00	1·00
2811	$1.50 Saturn V rocket and Edwin E. Aldrin stepping onto Moon, 1969 (vert)	1·00	1·00
2812	$1.50 Lunar Rover, "Apollo 15" mission, 1971 (vert)	1·00	1·00
MS2813	Two sheets, each 110×85 mm. (a) $6 "Mars Pathfinder", 1997 (55×42 mm); (b) $6 Space shuttle "Columbia", 1981 (55×42 mm). Set of 2 sheets	11·00	11·00

Nos. 2801/6 and 2807/12 were each printed together, *se-tenant*, with the backgrounds forming composite designs.

140 Kirk Douglas

1999. Kirk Douglas (American actor). Multicoloured.

2814	$1.50 Type **140**	90	90
2815	$1.50 As a boxer in *Champion*	90	90
2816	$1.50 As Van Gogh in *Lust for Life*	90	90
2817	$1.50 With white hair and wearing black shirt	90	90
2818	$1.50 In French uniform for *Paths of Glory*	90	90
2819	$1.50 As a cowboy in *The Bad and the Beautiful*	90	90
MS2820	93×106 mm. $6 As Spartacus	3·00	3·25

141 Elvis Presley

1999. Elvis Presley Commemoration. Each grey, silver and black.

2821	$1.50 Type **141**	1·00	1·00
2822	$1.50 Resting chin on hand	1·00	1·00
2823	$1.50 Wearing roll-neck sweater	1·00	1·00
2824	$1.50 Leaning against brick wall	1·00	1·00
2825	$1.50 Singing into microphone	1·00	1·00
2826	$1.50 Singing with eyes closed	1·00	1·00

141a Howard Thurston (magician)

1999. Famous Magicians. Multicoloured.

2826a	$1.50 Type **141a**	90	90
2826b	$1.50 Harry Houdini	90	90
2826c	$1.50 Harry Kellar	90	90

142 Poinsettia and Candle

1999. Christmas. Foliage and Candles. Multicoloured.

2827	15c. Type **142**	15	10
2828	35c. Holly	25	25
2829	75c. Fir tree	60	35
2830	$1.50 Ivy	90	85
2831	$3 Geranium	1·60	2·00
MS2832	83×108 mm. $6 *The Adoration of the Magi* (horiz)	3·25	3·50

No. 2829 is inscribed "FUR TREE" in error.

2000. New Millennium. People and Events of Fourteenth Century (1300–30). As T **471a** of Grenada. Multicoloured.

2833	50c. Robert the Bruce, King of Scotland, 1306	40	40
2834	50c. Fresco by Giotto, 1306	40	40
2835	50c. Mansa Musa, ruler of Mali, 1307	40	40
2836	50c. Dante and *The Divine Comedy*, 1321	40	40
2837	50c. Noh Theatre masks, Japan, 1325	40	40
2838	50c. Staircase, Tenochtitlan (Aztec capital, founded 1325)	40	40
2839	50c. Ibn Batuta on camel (start of journey, 1325)	40	40
2840	50c. Great Munich Fire, 1327	40	40
2841	50c. Grand Duke Ivan I (transfer of capital to Moscow, 1328)	40	40
2842	50c. Archers and castle (beginning of Hundred Years War, 1337)	40	40
2843	50c. Cannon at siege of Calais, 1346 (first recorded use of cannon)	40	40
2844	50c. "Death" (Black Death in Europe, 1348)	40	40
2845	50c. Boccaccio composing *The Decameron*, 1348	40	40
2846	50c. Early Italian spectacles, 1350	40	40
2847	50c. Knight (introduction of plate armour, 1350)	40	40
2848	50c. Junks (completion of Grand Canal of China, 1326) (59×39 mm)	40	40
2849	50c. Maori canoe (Maori migration to New Zealand, 1350)	40	40

143 Dragon

2000. Chinese New Year ("Year of the Dragon"). Sheet 79×60 mm.

MS2850	**143** $4 multicoloured	2·25	2·40

144 Barn Swallow

2000. Birds. Multicoloured.

2851	75c. Type **144**	60	45
2852	90c. Caribbean coot	70	70
2853	$1 Turquoise parrot	70	70
2854	$1 Scarlet-chested parrot	70	70
2855	$1 Red-capped parrot	70	70
2856	$1 Eastern rosella	70	70
2857	$1 Budgerigar	70	70
2858	$1 Superb parrot ("Orange-Flanked Parakeet")	70	70
2859	$1 Mallee ringneck parrot	70	70
2860	$1 Red-rumped parrot	70	70
2861	$1 Yellow-fronted parakeet	70	70
2862	$1 Rainbow lory ("Red-collared Lorikeet")	70	70
2863	$1 Lesser sulphur-crested cockatoo ("Citron-crested Cockatoo")	70	70
2864	$1 Papuan lory ("Stella's Lorikeet")	70	70
2865	$1 Major Mitchell's cockatoo ("Leadbeater's Cockatoo")	70	70
2866	$1 Golden conure	70	70
2867	$1 Red-spotted lorikeet	70	70

2868	$1 Red-shouldered macaw ("Nobel macaw")	70	70
2869	$1 Goffin's cockatoo	70	70
2870	$1 Sun conure	70	70
2871	$1.50 Puerto Rican emerald	1·00	1·00
2872	$1.50 Green mango	1·00	1·00
2873	$1.50 Red-legged thrush	1·00	1·00
2874	$1.50 Green-cheeked amazon ("Red-crowned Parrot")	1·00	1·00
2875	$1.50 Hispaniolan amazon ("Hispaniolan Parrot")	1·00	1·00
2876	$1.50 Yellow-headed parrot ("Yellow-crowned Parrot")	1·00	1·00
2877	$1.50 Yellow-shouldered blackbird	1·00	1·00
2878	$1.50 Troupial	1·00	1·00
2879	$1.50 Green-throated carib	1·00	1·00
2880	$1.50 Nanday conure ("Black-hooded Parakeet")	1·00	1·00
2881	$1.50 Scarlet tanager	1·00	1·00
2882	$1.50 Golden bishop ("Yellow-crowned Bishop")	1·00	1·00
2883	$2 Moorhen ("Common Moorhen")	1·40	1·50
2884	$3 Orange-winged amazon ("Orange-winged Parrot")	1·75	1·90
MS2885	Four sheets. (a) 74×98 mm. $6 Crimson rosella ("Pennant's Parakeet"). (b) 74×98 mm. $6 Scarlet macaw (vert). (c) 75×107 mm. $6 Puerto Rican lizard cuckoo. (d) 75×107 mm. $6 Pin-tailed whydah (vert). Set of 4 sheets	14·00	15·00

Nos. 2853/61, 2862/70, 2871/6 and 2877/82 were each printed together, *se-tenant*, with the backgrounds forming composite designs.

No. 2859 is inscribed "Rigneck", No. 2863 "Cocatoo", No. 2865 "Cockatto" and No. 2869 "GoffinsCocatto", all in error.

145 *Cantharellus cinnabarinus*

2000. Fungi. Multicoloured.

2886	$2 Type **145**	1·25	1·25
2887	$2 *Hygrocybe conica*	1·25	1·25
2888	$2 *Cortinarius violaceus*	1·25	1·25
2889	$2 *Leccinum versipelle*	1·25	1·25
2890	$2 *Russula xerampelina*	1·25	1·25
2891	$2 *Entoloma nitidum*	1·25	1·25
2892	$2 *Lentinus tigrinus*	1·25	1·25
2893	$2 *Mycena flavoalba*	1·25	1·25
2894	$2 *Boletus legaliae* (horiz)	1·25	1·25
2895	$2 *Russula emetica* (horiz)	1·25	1·25
2896	$2 *Cortinarius alboviolaceus* (horiz)	1·25	1·25
2897	$2 *Volvariella bombycina* (horiz)	1·25	1·25
MS2898	Two sheets, each 103×81 mm. (a) $6 *Gomphus floccosus* (horiz). (b) $6 *Collybia dryophila* (horiz). Set of 2 sheets	14·00	15·00

No. 2886 is inscribed "Canharellus", No. 2889 "Lecinum", and No. **MS**2898 (a) "Comphus", all in error.

146 Ferdinand Magellan (Spanish navigator)

2000. New Millennium. Sea Exploration. Multicoloured.

2899	50c. Type **146**	40	40
2900	50c. Ship in storm	40	40
2901	50c. Queen Elizabeth I's hand on globe	40	40
2902	50c. Two wandering albatrosses ("Albatrosses")	40	40
2903	50c. Emperor penguins	40	40
2904	50c. Tahitian woman	40	40
2905	50c. Breadfruit	40	40
2906	50c. Moai (carved statue) on Easter Island	40	40
2907	50c. Maori carving	40	40
2908	50c. Lobster	40	40
2909	50c. Orchid	40	40
2910	50c. Walrus	40	40
2911	50c. Kangaroo	40	40
2912	50c. H.M.S. *Beagle* (Charles Darwin) careened	40	40
2913	50c. Magnificent frigate bird ("Frigatebird")	40	40
2914	50c. Ship and boats in the Strait of Magellan (59×39 mm)	40	40

2915	50c. Captain James Cook (English navigator)	40	40

146a Salvador Allende elected President of Chile, 1970

2000. New Millennium. People and Events of Twentieth Century (1970–79). Multicoloured.

2916	20c. Type **146a**	35	35
2917	20c. Cartoon characters around globe (introduction of Earth Day holiday, 1970)	35	35
2918	20c. Computerized Axial Tomography (CAT) scanner, 1971	35	35
2919	20c. Pres. Richard Nixon in China (re-opening of U.S. relations with People's Republic, 1972)	35	35
2920	20c. Terrorist and flag (murder of Israeli athletes at Munich Olympics 1972)	35	35
2921	20c. Petrol ration sign (OPEC oil price rises, 1973)	35	35
2922	20c. Sydney Opera House, 1973	35	35
2923	20c. Pres. Richard Nixon leaving helicopter (resignation 1974)	35	35
2924	20c. Stylized black hole (new theory, 1974)	35	35
2925	20c. U.S. Bicentennial celebrations, 1976	35	35
2926	20c. Louise Brown, first test tube baby, born 1978)	35	35
2927	20c. Pope John Paul II visiting Poland, 1978	35	35
2928	20c. Ayatollah Khomeini (Iran's Islamic Revolution, 1978)	35	35
2929	20c. Concorde (first flight, 1979)	35	35
2930	20c. Charles de Gaulle (died 1970) and Eiffel Tower	35	35
2931	20c. Pres. Sadat, Prime Minister Begin and Pres. Carter (Camp David Talks 1978/9) (59×39 mm)	35	35
2932	20c. Mother Teresa (Nobel Peace Prize, 1979)	35	35

No. 2932 is inscribed "Noble Peace Prize" in error.

147 Elongate Mbuna ("Slender Mbuna")

2000. Tropical Fish. Multicoloured.

2933	35c. Type **147**	30	25
2934	45c. Pygoplites diacanthus	30	60
2935	75c. Pomacanthus semicirclatus	60	60
2936	75c. Siamese fighting fish	60	60
2937	90c. Zanclus canescens	70	70
2938	$1 Xiphophorus maculatus	70	70
2939	$1 Dwarf pencilfish	70	70
2940	$1 Bumblebee goby	70	70
2941	$1 Black-headed blenny	70	70
2942	$1 Velvet boarfish	70	70
2943	$1 Red-tailed surgeonfish ("Achilles Tang")	70	70
2944	$1 Swordtail	70	70
2945	$1 Moorish idol	70	70
2946	$1 Banded pipefish	70	70
2947	$1 Striped catfish	70	70
2948	$1 Emperor angelfish	70	70
2949	$1 Magenta dottyback ("Strawberryfish")	70	70
2950	$1 Jackknife-fish	70	70
2951	$1 Flame angelfish	70	70
2952	$1 Yellow-tailed ("Clarke's") anemonefish	70	70
2953	$1 Flash-back dottyback	70	70
2954	$1 Coral trout	70	70
2955	$1 Foxface	70	70
2956	$1.65 Bodianus rufus	1·10	1·10
2957	$1.65 Coris aygula	1·10	1·10
2958	$1.65 Centropyge bicolor	1·10	1·10
2959	$1.65 Balistoides conspicillum	1·10	1·10
2960	$1.65 Poecilia reticulata	1·10	1·10
2961	$1.65 Heniochus acuminatus	1·10	1·10
2962	$1.65 Plectorhinchus chaetodonoides	1·10	1·10
2963	$1.65 Bodianus pulchellus	1·10	1·10
2964	$1.65 Acanthurus leucosternon	1·10	1·10
2965	$1.65 Chromileptis altivelis	1·10	1·10
2966	$1.65 Pterophyllum scalare	1·10	1·10
2967	$1.65 Premnas biaculeatus	1·10	1·10

2968	$2 Pennant coralfish ("Wimplefish")	1·40	1·60
2969	$2 Gramma loreto	1·40	1·60
2970	$3 Zebrasoma xanthurum	1·60	1·75

MS2971 Four sheets. (a) 97×68 mm. $6 Harlequin Tuskfish. (b) 97×68 mm. $6 Purple Queen. (c) 93×65 mm. $6 Equetus punctatus. (d) 93×65 mm. $6 Pomacanthus imperator (vert). Set of 4 sheets ... 14·00 15·00

Nos. 2940/7, 2948/55, 2956/61 and 2962/7 were each printed together, se-tenant, with the backgrounds forming composite designs.

No. 2942 is inscribed "CCAPROS APER", No. 2949 "PSEUDOCHROMIS ORPHYREUS", No. 2954 "CEPHALOPHELIS MINIATUS", No. 2962 "PLECTORHYNCHUS CHAETODONOIDS" and No. 2963 "BODIANUS PUCHELLUS", all in error.

2000. 400th Birth Anniv of Sir Anthony Van Dyck (Flemish painter). As T **312a** of Gambia. Multicoloured.

2972	$1.50 Portrait of an Elderly Woman	90	90
2973	$1.50 Head of a Young Woman	90	90
2974	$1.50 Portrait of a Man	90	90
2975	$1.50 Jan van den Wouwer	90	90
2976	$1.50 Portrait of a Young Man	90	90
2977	$1.50 Everhard Jabach	90	90
2978	$1.50 Man in Armour	90	90
2979	$1.50 Portrait of a Young General	90	90
2980	$1.50 Emanuele Filiberto, Prince of Savoy	90	90
2981	$1.50 Donna Polixena Spinola Guzman de Leganes	90	90
2982	$1.50 Luigia Cattaneo Gentile	90	90
2983	$1.50 Giovanni Battista Cattaneo	90	90
2984	$1.50 Marchesa Paolina Adorno Brignole-Sale (1623–25)	90	90
2985	$1.50 Marchesa Geronima Spinola	90	90
2986	$1.50 Marchesa Paolina Adorna Brignole-Sale (1627)	90	90
2987	$1.50 Marcello Durazzo	90	90
2988	$1.50 Marchesa Grimaldi Cattaneo with a Black Page	90	90
2989	$1.50 Young Man of the House of Spinola	90	90
2990	$1.50 Cardinal Bentivoglio	90	90
2991	$1.50 Cardinal Infante Ferdinand	90	90
2992	$1.50 Cesare Alessandro Scaglia, Abbe of Staffarda and Mandanici	90	90
2993	$1.50 A Roman Clergyman	90	90
2994	$1.50 Jean-Charles della Faille	90	90
2995	$1.50 Cardinal Domenico Rivarola	90	90

MS2996 Six sheets. (a) 100×123 mm. $5 Hendrick van der Bergh. (b) 100×123 mm. $5 Jaques le Roy. (c) 100×123 mm. $6 Justus van Meerstraeten. (d) 100×123 mm. $6 Frederik Hendrik, Prince of Orange. (e) 100×123 mm. $6 Maria Louisa de Tassis (horiz). (f) 123×100 mm. $6 Abbot Scaglia adoring the Virgin and Child (horiz). Set of 6 sheets ... 19·00 21·00

Nos. 2972/3 are inscribed "Women", No. 2983 "Cattanaeo" and No. 2992 "Stafford", all in error.

2000. 18th Birthday of Prince William. As T **312b** of Gambia. Multicoloured.

2997	$1.50 Prince William with birthday gift	1·25	1·25
2998	$1.50 In Eton uniform	1·25	1·25
2999	$1.50 Wearing checked shirt	1·25	1·25
3000	$1.50 Wearing grey suit	1·25	1·25

MS3001 100×80 mm. $6 Wearing blue jumper (37×50 mm) ... 4·50 4·50

2000. "EXPO 2000" World Stamp Exhibition, Anaheim, U.S.A. Spacecraft. As T **582a** of Ghana. Multicoloured.

3002	$1.50 "Foton" and comet	1·00	1·00
3003	$1.50 "Sub-Satellite" and rock particle	1·00	1·00
3004	$1.50 Satellite near Eros	1·00	1·00
3005	$1.50 "Explorer 16"	1·00	1·00
3006	$1.50 Space Shuttle Challenger	1·00	1·00
3007	$1.50 Giotto facing right and Halley's Comet	1·00	1·00
3008	$1.50 Circular satellite with aerial (inscr "Foton")	1·00	1·00
3009	$1.50 Giotto facing left (inscr "Sub-Satellite")	1·00	1·00
3010	$1.50 Satellite with solar panels extended (inscr "Near Eros")	1·00	1·00
3011	$1.50 Satellite over planet surface (inscr "Explorer XVI")	1·00	1·00
3012	$1.50 Satellite with folded solar panels (inscr "Astro Challenger")	1·00	1·00
3013	$1.50 Circular satellite with cones on base (inscr "Giotto Halley's Comet")	1·00	1·00

MS3014 Two sheets. (a) 76×106 mm. $6 "Pegasus" over Saturn. (b) 106×76 mm. $6 "Lunar Prospector". Set of 2 sheets ... 7·50 8·00

Nos. 3002/7 and 3008/13 were each printed together, se-tenant, with the backgrounds forming composite designs.

Inscriptions on Nos. 3008/13 repeat those of Nos. 3002/7 in error.

2000. 25th Anniv of "Apollo–Soyuz" Joint Project. As T **582b** of Ghana. Multicoloured.

3015	$3 Thomas P. Stafford (Commander of "Apollo 18")	1·75	1·90
3016	$3 Joint Mission Badge	1·75	1·90
3017	$3 Donald D. Slayton ("Apollo 18")	1·75	1·90

MS3018 70×88 mm. $6 Alexei Leonov (Commander of "Soyuz 19") ... 3·00 3·25

2000. 50th Anniv of Berlin Film Festival. As T **582c** of Ghana. Multicoloured.

3019	$1 James Stewart in Mr. Hobbs takes a Vacation, 1962	1·00	1·00
3020	$1.50 Sachiko Hidari in Kanojo To Kare, 1964	1·00	1·00
3021	$1.50 Juliette Mayniel in Kirmes, 1960	1·00	1·00
3022	$1.50 Le Bonheur, 1965	1·00	1·00
3023	$1.50 La Notte, 1961	1·00	1·00
3024	$1.50 Lee Marvin in Cat Ballou, 1965	1·00	1·00

MS3025 97×103 mm. $6 The Thin Red Line, 1999 ... 3·50 3·75

2000. 175th Anniv of Stockton and Darlington Line (first public railway). As T **582d** of Ghana. Multicoloured.

3026	$3 As Type **582d** of Ghana	2·25	2·25
3027	$3 George Stephenson's Rocket	2·25	2·25

2000. 250th Death Anniv of Johann Sebastian Bach (German composer). Sheet, 75×88 mm, containing vert design as T **312c** of Gambia. Multicoloured.

MS3028 $6 Statue of Johann Sebastian Bach ... 4·50 4·75

2000. Election of Albert Einstein (mathematical physicist) as Time Magazine "Man of the Century". Sheet, 117×90 mm, containing vert design as T **312d** of Gambia. Multicoloured.

MS3029 $6 Albert Einstein ... 3·50 3·75

2000. Centenary of First Zeppelin Flight. As T **582e** of Ghana, each incorporating a portrait of Count Ferdinand von Zeppelin. Multicoloured.

3030	$3 LZ-3, 1906	2·00	2·00
3031	$3 LZ-56, 1915	2·00	2·00
3032	$3 LZ-88, 1917	2·20	2·00

MS3033 118×75 mm. $6 LZ-1, 1900 (50×37 mm) ... 4·25 4·50

2000. Olympic Games, Sydney. As T **582f** of Ghana. Multicoloured.

3034	$2 Frantz Reichel (rugby), Paris (1900)	1·60	1·60
3035	$2 Modern discus-thrower	1·60	1·60
3036	$2 Seoul Sports Complex (1988) and South Korean flag	1·60	1·60
3037	$2 Ancient Greek wrestlers	1·60	1·60

148 Euplagia quadripunctaria

2000. Butterflies and Moths. Multicoloured.

3038	$1.50 Type **148**	1·00	1·00
3039	$1.50 Oenosandra boisduvalii	1·00	1·00
3040	$1.50 Thinopteryx erocopterata	1·00	1·00
3041	$1.50 Euschemon rafflesia	1·00	1·00
3042	$1.50 Milionia isodoxa	1·00	1·00
3043	$1.50 Oysphania euprina	1·00	1·00
3044	$1.50 Thaloina clara	1·00	1·00
3045	$1.50 Zerynthnia rumina	1·00	1·00
3046	$1.50 Attacus atlas	1·00	1·00
3047	$1.50 Lasiocampa quercus	1·00	1·00
3048	$1.50 Pararge schakra	1·00	1·00
3049	$1.50 Arhopala amantes	1·00	1·00
3050	$1.50 Heliconius charithonia	1·00	1·00
3051	$1.50 Dismorphia amphione	1·00	1·00
3052	$1.50 Theela coronata	1·00	1·00
3053	$1.50 Cithaerias esmeralda	1·00	1·00
3054	$1.50 Zerene eurydice	1·00	1·00
3055	$1.50 Theela eudoela	1·00	1·00
3056	$1.50 Catonephele numilia	1·00	1·00
3057	$1.50 Diaethria clymena	1·00	1·00
3058	$1.50 Mesene phareus	1·00	1·00
3059	$1.50 Estigmene aerea	1·00	1·00
3060	$1.50 Marpesia petreus	1·00	1·00
3061	$1.50 Cepheuptychia cephus	1·00	1·00

MS3062 Six sheets. (a) 70×95 mm. $6 Tajuria cippus. (b) 78×97 mm. $6 Ecpantheria serifonia. (c) 75×105 mm. $6 Ornithoptera alexandrae. (d) 127×100 mm. $6 Hyalophora cecropia. (e) 100×73 mm. $2 Cyrestis thyodamos; $2 Papilionidae; $2 Apatura iris; $2 Crypsiphona ocyltaria. (f) 100×73 mm. $2 Hemaris thysbe; $2 Helicopis cupido; $2 Aretia eaja; $2 Erateina staudingeri. Set of 6 sheets ... 23·00 25·00

Nos. 3038/43, 3044/9, 3050/5 and 3056/61 were each printed together, se-tenant, with the backgrounds forming composite designs.

No. 3038 is inscribed "quadripunctama", No. 3041 "Eusehemon zafflesia", No. 3045 "Zerynthia", No. 3048 "Parage", No. 3050 "charitonius", No. 3056 "numili", **MS**3062 (d) "Hyalophor", all in error.

150 Golsdorf Compound Tank Locomotive, Vienna Metropolitan Railway

2000. Railways of the World. Multicoloured.

3066	90c. Type **150**	75	50
3067	$1 Vauxhall, Dublin and Kingstown Railway	75	55
3068	$1.50 Electric railcar, South Jersey Transit	90	90
3069	$1.50 Metroliner, Amtrak	90	90
3070	$1.50 Maglev train, H.S.S.T.	90	90
3071	$1.50 Model E60C electric locomotive, Amtrak	90	90
3072	$1.50 Parsifal diesel express, T.E.E.	90	90
3073	$1.50 Class G.G.I. electric locomotive, Pennsylvania	90	90
3074	$1.50 Electric locomotive, Norwegian State Railways	90	90
3075	$1.50 Diesel-electric locomotive, Jamaica Railway	90	90
3076	$1.50 Diesel-electric locomotive, China	90	90
3077	$1.50 Electric locomotive, Portuguese Railways	90	90
3078	$1.50 "Re-6/6" electric locomotive, Swiss Federal Railways	90	90
3079	$1.50 Dual-purpose electric locomotive, Turkish State Railways	90	90
3080	$1.50 Passenger steam locomotive, Perak Govt Railway	90	90
3081	$1.50 Tank locomotive, Rhondda & Swansea Railway	90	90
3082	$1.50 Aspinal tank locomotive, Lancashire & Yorkshire Railway	90	90
3083	$1.50 Tank locomotive, Northwestern Railway, India	90	90
3084	$1.50 Imperial Mail locomotive, Shanghai–Nanking Railway	90	90
3085	$1.50 Passenger steam locomotive, Danish State Railway	90	90
3086	$1.50 Braithwait steam locomotive, Eastern Counties Railway	90	90
3087	$1.50 Philadelphia, Austria	90	90
3088	$1.50 Stephenson locomotive of 1836	90	90
3089	$1.50 Aigle locomotive, Western Railway, France	90	90
3090	$1.50 Borsig Standard steam locomotive, Germany	90	90
3091	$1.50 Ajax, Great Western Railway	90	90
3092	$2 Metro-Cammell dieselelectric locomotive, Nigerian Railways	1·25	1·25
3093	$3 T.G.V. 001 high-speed turbo train, French National Railways	1·60	1·75

MS3094 Four sheets, each 81×57 mm. (a) $6 The Experiment, U.S.A. (b) $6 Freight steam locomotive, South African Railway. (c) $6 Diesel-electric locomotive, South African Railway. (d) $6 "Prospector" diesel railcar, Western Australia. Set of 4 sheets ... 14·00 15·00

151 Irish Setter

2000. Cats and Dogs. Multicoloured.

3095	45c. Type **151**	45	30
3096	75c. Blue point snowshoe	60	45
3097	90c. Dalmatian	70	55
3098	$1.50 California spangled cat	90	90
3099	$1.50 Russian blue	90	90
3100	$1.50 Seal point Siamese	90	90
3101	$1.50 Black Devon rex	90	90
3102	$1.50 Silver tabby British shorthair	90	90
3103	$1.50 Tricolour Japanese bobtail	90	90
3104	$1.50 Great Dane	90	90
3105	$1.50 Newfoundland	90	90
3106	$1.50 Rottweiler	90	90
3107	$1.50 Bulldog	90	90
3108	$1.50 Japanese spitz	90	90
3109	$1.50 Bull terrier	90	90
3110	$1.50 British white shorthair	90	90
3111	$1.50 Blue-cream American shorthair	90	90
3112	$1.50 Bombay	90	90
3113	$1.50 Red Burmese	90	90
3114	$1.50 Sorrel Abyssinian	90	90

3115	$1.50 Ocicat	90	90
3116	$1.50 Alaskan malamute	90	90
3117	$1.50 Golden retriever	90	90
3118	$1.50 Afghan hound	90	90
3119	$1.50 Long-haired dachshund	90	90
3120	$1.50 Irish terrier	90	90
3121	$1.50 Miniature poodle	90	90
3122	$2 German shepherd	1·25	1·25
3123	$3 Black and white maine coon	1·60	1·75
3124	$4 Brown tabby British shorthair	1·90	2·00

MS3125 Four sheets. (a) 106×76 mm.
$5 Silver Classic Tabby Persian
(horiz). (b) 76×106 mm. $5 Red-
white Bicolor British Shorthair. (c)
106×76 mm. $6 Basset Hound
(horiz). (d) 76×106 mm. $6 Labrador
Retriever. Set of 4 sheets ..... 13·00 14·00

Nos. 3098/103 (cats), 3104/9 (dogs), 3110/15 (cats) and
3116/21 (dogs) were each printed together, *se-tenant*,
with the backgrounds forming composite designs.
No. 3108 is inscribed "Sptz" and No. 3121 "Minature",
both in error.

2000. "Euro 2000" Football Championship. As T **479** of
Grenada. Multicoloured.

3126	$1.50 Tofting (Danish player)	90	90
3127	$1.50 Danish team	90	90
3128	$1.50 Michael Laudrup (Danish player)	90	90
3129	$1.50 Jorgensen (Danish player)	90	90
3130	$1.50 Philips Stadium, Eindhoven	90	90
3131	$1.50 Moller (Danish player)	90	90
3132	$1.50 Thuram (French player)	90	90
3133	$1.50 French team	90	90
3134	$1.50 Barthez (French player)	90	90
3135	$1.50 Zidane (French player)	90	90
3136	$1.50 Jan Breydel Stadium, Bruges	90	90
3137	$1.50 Michel Platini (French player)	90	90
3138	$1.50 Giovanni van Bronckhorst (Dutch player)	90	90
3139	$1.50 Dutch team	90	90
3140	$1.50 Patrick Kluivert (Dutch player)	90	90
3141	$1.50 Johan Cruyff (Dutch player)	90	90
3142	$1.50 Amsterdam Arena Stadium	90	90
3143	$1.50 Zenden (Dutch player)	90	90

MS3144 Three sheets, each 145×96
mm. (a) $6 Bo Johansson (Danish
trainer) (vert). (b) $6 Roger Lemerre
(French trainer) (vert). (c) $6 Frank
Rijkaard (Dutch trainer) (vert). Set
of 3 sheets ..... 10·00 10·50

152 St. Lucia Amazon

2000. "The Stamp Show 2000" International Stamp
Exhibition, London. South American Fauna.
Multicoloured.

3145	75c. Type **152**	60	45
3146	90c. Three-toed sloth	60	45
3147	$1 Hispaniolan solenodon	70	55
3148	$1.50 Red vakari	1·00	1·00
3149	$1.50 St. Andrews virea ("San Andreas Vireo")	1·00	1·00
3150	$1.50 Golden lion tamarin	1·00	1·00
3151	$1.50 American crocodile	1·00	1·00
3152	$1.50 Spectacled caimen	1·00	1·00
3153	$1.50 Rhinoceros iguana	1·00	1·00
3154	$1.50 Jaguarundis	1·00	1·00
3155	$1.50 Andean condor	1·00	1·00
3156	$1.50 Lesser rhea ("Darwin's Rhea")	1·00	1·00
3157	$1.50 Central American tapir	1·00	1·00
3158	$1.50 Jaguar	1·00	1·00
3159	$1.50 Jamaican hutia	1·00	1·00
3160	$2 Thick-billed parrot	1·40	1·50

MS3161 Two sheets, each 106×71 mm.
(a) $6 Kemp Ridley Sea Turtle. (b) $6
Pronghorn. Set of 2 sheets ..... 7·50 8·00

Nos. 3148/53 and 3154/9 were each printed together,
se-tenant, with the backgrounds forming composite designs.

2000. Monarchs of the Millennium. As T **314a** of Gambia.
Multicoloured (except Nos. 3162 and 3166).

3162	$1.50 King Louis XVI of France (lilac, green and brown)	1·00	1·00
3163	$1.50 King Louis XVIII of France	1·00	1·00
3164	$1.50 Kublai Khan's Empress, China	1·00	1·00
3165	$1.50 Queen Mary I of England	1·00	1·00
3166	$1.50 Mohammed Ali, Shah of Iran (black, green and brown)	1·00	1·00
3167	$1.50 Emperor Qianlong of China	1·00	1·00

MS3168 116×136 mm. $6 Grand Duke
Vladimir I of Kiev ..... 3·25 3·50

2000. Popes of the Millennium. As T **314b** of Gambia.
Multicoloured (except No. **MS**3173).

3169	$1.50 Adrian VI	1·40	1·40
3170	$1.50 Paul II	1·40	1·40
3171	$1.50 Callistus III	1·40	1·40
3172	$1.50 Eugene IV	1·40	1·40

MS3173 116×136 mm. $6 Gregory XI
(grey, black and green) ..... 3·50 3·50

153 "Wind"

2000. *The Storm Riders* (Chinese comic series by Ma Wing
Sing). Multicoloured.

3174	$4 Type **153**	1·90	2·00
3175	$4 "Cloud" with sword	1·90	2·00
3176	$4 "Cloud" with dragon	1·90	2·00
3177	$4 "Wind" with waves	1·90	2·00

154 David
Copperfield
(portrait at left
with levitating legs
at right)

2000. David Copperfield (conjurer). Multicoloured.

3178	$1.50 Type **154**	90	90
3179	$1.50 Portrait at right with levitating body at left	90	90
3180	$1.50 Portrait at right with levitating legs at left	90	90
3181	$1.50 Portrait at left with levitating body at right	90	90

2000. "Espana 2000" International Stamp Exhibition,
Madrid. Paintings from the Prado. As T **326a** of
Gambia. Multicoloured.

3182	$1.50 *St. John the Baptist and the Franciscan Maestro, Henricus Werl* (Robert Campin)	90	90
3183	$1.50 *Justice and Peace* (Corrado Giaquinto)	90	90
3184	$1.50 *St. Barbara* (Robert Campin)	90	90
3185	$1.50 *John Fane, 10th Earl of Westmoreland* (Thomas Lawrence)	90	90
3186	$1.50 *The Marchioness of Manzanedo* (Jean-Louis-Ernest Meissonier)	90	90
3187	$1.50 *Mr. Storer* (Martin Archer Shee)	90	90
3188	$1.50 *Isabella Carla Eugenia* (Alonso Sanchez Coello)	90	90
3189	$1.50 *Nobleman with his Hand on his Chest* (El Greco)	90	90
3190	$1.50 *King Philip III* (Juan Pantoja de la Cruz)	90	90
3191	$1.50 Madonna and Child from *The Holy Family with Sts. Ildefonsus and John the Evangelist, and the Master Alonso de Villegas* (Blas del Prado)	90	90
3192	$1.50 *The Last Supper* (Bartolme Carducci)	90.	90
3193	$1.50 St. John from *The Holy Family with Sts. Ildefonsus and John the Evangelist, and the Master Alonso de Villegas*	90	90
3194	$1.50 *St. Dominic of Silos* (Bartolome Bermejo)	90	90
3195	$1.50 *Head of a Prophet* (Jaume Huguet)	90	90
3196	$1.50 *Christ giving His Blessing* (Fernando Gallego)	90	90
3197	$1.50 *The Mystic Marriage of St. Catherine* (Alonso Sanchez Coello)	90	90
3198	$1.50 *St. Catherine of Alexandria* (Fernando Yanez de la Almedina)	90	90
3199	$1.50 *Virgin and Child* (Luis de Morales)	90	90

MS3200 Three sheets, each 110×90
mm. (a) $6 As No. 3192 (horiz). (b)
$6 *The Coronation of the Virgin* (El
Greco) (horiz). (c) $6 As No. 3191.
Set of 3 sheets ..... 9·50 10·00

155 Barbara Taylor
Bradford

2000. Great Writers of the 20th Century: Barbara Taylor
Bradford. Sheet 126×87 mm.

MS3201 **155** $6 multicoloured ..... 3·00 3·50

2000. 60th Anniv of Battle of Britain. As T **327** of
Gambia. Multicolourred.

3202	$1 R.A.F. Pilots running to their planes	1·00	90
3203	$1 Barrage balloons	1·00	90
3204	$1 Supermarine Spitfire B aircraft (fighter)	1·00	90
3205	$1 Princess Elizabeth broadcasting, 1940	1·00	90
3206	$1 Fire Watcher and auxilary fireman	1·00	90
3207	$1 Painting white bands round posts	1·00	90
3208	$1 Bombed building	1·00	90
3209	$1 Air Raid Wardens and auxilary policewoman	1·00	90
3210	$1 Women fire-fighters	1·00	90
3211	$1 Family leaving bombed home	1·00	90
3212	$1 Searchlight	1·00	90
3213	$1 Winston Churchill inspecting bomb damage in Coventry	1·00	90
3214	$1 Rescue team evacuating casualty	1·00	90
3215	$1 Re-united family	1·00	90
3216	$1 After air raid on Buckingham Gate	1·00	90
3217	$1 Aftermath of air raid on Coventry	1·00	90

MS3218 Two sheets, each 106×76 mm.
(a) $6 Hawker Hurricane (fighter).
(b) $6 British family outside air raid
shelter (vert). Set of 2 sheets ..... 9·00 9·00

No. 3215 is inscribed "RESCUSE" in error.

156 Queen
Elizabeth, the
Queen Mother

2000. 100th Birthday of Queen Elizabeth, the Queen
Mother.

3219	**156** $1.50 multicoloured	1·50	1·50

2000. Faces of the Millennium: Queen Elizabeth the
Queen Mother. As T **307a** of Gambia showing
collage of miniature flower photographs.
Multicoloured.

3220	$1 Top of head (face value at left)	1·00	1·00
3221	$1 Top of head (face value at right)	1·00	1·00
3222	$1 Eye and temple (face value at left)	1·00	1·00
3223	$1 Temple (face value at right)	1·00	1·00
3224	$1 Cheek (face value at left)	1·00	1·00
3225	$1 Cheek (face value at right)	1·00	1·00
3226	$1 Chin (face value at left)	1·00	1·00
3227	$1 Neck (face value at right)	1·00	1·00

Nos. 3220/7 were printed together, *se-tenant*, in sheetlets of 8 with the stamps arranged in two vertical columns separated by a gutter also containing miniature
photographs. When viewed as a whole the sheetlet forms
a portrait of the Queen Mother.

2000. Faces of the Millennium: Pope John Paul II. As
T **307a** of Gambia showing collage of miniature
religious photographs. Multicoloured.

3228	$1 Top of head (face value at left)	1·00	1·00
3229	$1 Top of head (face value at right)	1·00	1·00
3230	$1 Ear (face value at left)	1·00	1·00
3231	$1 Temple and eye (face value at right)	1·00	1·00
3232	$1 Neck and collar (face value at left)	1·00	1·00
3233	$1 Cheek and fingertips (face value at right)	1·00	1·00
3234	$1 Shoulder (face value at left)	1·00	1·00
3235	$1 Hands (face value at right)	1·00	1·00

Nos. 3228/35 were printed together, *se-tenant*, in
sheetlets of 8 with the stamps arranged in two vertical
columns separated by a gutter also containing miniature
photographs. When viewed as a whole the sheetlet forms
a portrait of Pope John Paul II.

157 Rat Snake

2001. Chinese New Year. "Year of the Snake".
Multicoloured.

3236	90c. Type **157**	60	70
3237	90c. Mangrove snake	60	70
3238	90c. Boomslang	60	70
3239	90c. Emerald tree boa	60	70
3240	90c. African egg-eating snake	60	70
3241	90c. Chinese green tree viper	60	70

MS3242 74×88 mm. $4 King Cobra ..... 2·25 2·50

2001. Bicentenary of Rijksmuseum, Amsterdam. Dutch
Paintings. As T **330a** of Gambia. Multicoloured.

3243	$1.50 Harpist from *A Music Party* (Rembrandt)	85	90
3244	$1.50 Woman singing from *A Music Party*	85	90
3245	$1.50 Boy and girl from *Rutger Jan Schimmelpenninck with his Wife and Children* (Pierre-Paul Prud'hon)	85	90
3246	$1.50 Girl from *Rutger Jan Schimmelpenninck with his Wife and Children*	85	90
3247	$1.50 *The Syndics* (Thomas de Keyser)	85	90
3248	$1.50 *Marriage Portrait of Isaac Massa and Beatrix van der Laen* (Frans Hals)	85	90
3249	$1.50 Bride from *Marriage Portrait of Isaac Massa and Beatrix van der Laen*	85	90
3250	$1.50 *Winter Landscape with Ice Skaters* (Hendrick Avercamp)	85	90
3251	$1.50 Woman and clerk from *The Spendthrift* (Cornelis Troost)	85	90
3252	$1.50 Beggars from *The Spendthrift*	85	90
3253	$1.50 Two men and a Woman from *The Art Gallery of Jan Gildemeester Jansz* (Adriaan de Lelie)	85	90
3254	$1.50 Man examining painting from *The Art Gallery of Jan Gildemeester Jansz*	85	90
3255	$1.50 Couple with musicians from *Garden Party* (Dirck Hals)	85	90
3256	$1.50 *Still Life with Gilt Goblet* (Willem Claesz Heda)	85	90
3257	$1.50 Two men arguing from *Orestes and Pylades disputing at the Altar* (Pieter Lastman)	85	90
3258	$1.50 Women at altar from *Orestes and Pylades disputing at the Altar*	85	90
3259	$1.50 *Self-portrait in a Yellow Robe* (Jan Lievens)	85	90
3260	$1.50 Couples with monkey from *Garden Party*	85	90
3261	$1.50 Goatherd and goats from *Dune Landscape* (Jan van Goyen)	85	90
3262	$1.50 *The Raampoortje* (Wouter Johannes van Troostwijk)	85	90
3263	$1.50 Houses from *The Ferryboat* (Esaias van de Velde)	85	90
3264	$1.50 *The Departure of a Dignitary from Middleburg* (Adriaen van de Venne)	85	90
3265	$1.50 Cart on ferry from *The Ferryboat*	85	90
3266	$1.50 Group of peasants by fence from *Dune Landscape*	85	90

MS3267 Four sheets. (a) 118×87 mm.
$6 *Anna accused by Tobit of Stealing
a Kid* (Rembrandt). (b) 118×87 mm.
$6 *Cleopatra's Banquet* (Gerard
Lairesse) (horiz). (c) 118×87 mm. $6
View of Tivoli (Isaac de Moucheron)
(horiz). (d) 87×118 mm. $6 *A Music
Party* (Rembrandt). Set of 4 sheets ..... 14·00 15·00

No. 3248 is inscribed "Marraige" and "dr" in error.

158 Greater
Flamingo

2001. Tropical Fauna. Multicoloured.

3268	75c. Type **158**	75	50
3269	90c. Cuban crocodile (horiz)	75	50
3270	$1 Jaguarundi	75	55
3271	$1.50 Red-breasted toucan	1·25	1·25
3272	$1.50 Mexican black howler monkey	1·25	1·25
3273	$1.50 Fieck's pygmy boa	1·25	1·25
3274	$1.50 Red-eyed tree frog	1·25	1·25
3275	$1.50 Caimen	1·25	1·25
3276	$1.50 Jaguar	1·25	1·25
3277	$1.50 Cuban pygmy owl	1·25	1·25
3278	$1.50 Woody spider monkey	1·25	1·25
3279	$1.50 Bee hummingbirds	1·25	1·25
3280	$1.50 Dragonfly, leaf frog and poison dart frog	1·25	1·25
3281	$1.50 Red brocket deer	1·25	1·25
3282	$1.50 Cuban stream anole	1·25	1·25
3283	$2 Wedge-capped capuchin monkey (horiz)	1·50	1·50

MS3284 Two sheets. (a) 72×104 mm. $6 Ocelot. (b) 72×98 mm. $6 Western knight anole. Set of 2 sheets ..... 7·50   8·00

Nos. 3271/6 and 3277/82 were each printed together, *se-tenant*, with the backgrounds forming composite designs.

No. 3271 is inscribed "Red-Breated" in error.

2001. Characters from "Pokemon" (children's cartoon series). As T **332a** of Gambia. Multicoloured.

3285	$1.50 "Bellsprout No. 69"	85	90
3286	$1.50 "Vulpix No. 37"	85	90
3287	$1.50 "Dewgong No. 87"	85	90
3288	$1.50 "Oddish No. 43"	85	90
3289	$1.50 "Dratini No. 147"	85	90
3290	$1.50 "Jigglypuff No. 39"	85	90

MS3291 74×114 mm. $6 "Pikachu No. 25" ..... 3·00   3·25

159 *Scarus vetula*

2001. Endangered Species. Fish. Multicoloured.

3292	75c. Type **159**	75	75
3293	75c. *Scarus taeniopterus*	75	75
3294	75c. *Sparisoma viride*	75	75
3295	75c. *Sparisoma rubripinne*	75	75

160 Falkland Islands Flightless Streamer Duck ("Falklands Streamer Duck")

2001. Caribbean Ducks and Waterfowl. Multicoloured.

3296	$1.50 Type **160**	1·25	1·25
3297	$1.50 Black-crowned night heron	1·25	1·25
3298	$1.50 Muscovy duck	1·25	1·25
3299	$1.50 Ruddy duck	1·25	1·25
3300	$1.50 Northern screamer ("Black necked Screamer")	1·25	1·25
3301	$1.50 White-faced whistling duck	1·25	1·25

MS3302 60×93 mm. $6 Great egret (vert) ..... 4·00   4·25

Nos. 3296/301 were printed together, *se-tenant*, with the backgrounds forming a composite design.

161 Virgie Cary (Shirley Temple) sitting on Chair

2001. Shirley Temple in *The Littlest Rebel*. Showing scenes from the film. Multicoloured.

3303	$2 Type **161**	1·10	1·25
3304	$2 Virgie with her mother (Karen Morley)	1·10	1·25
3305	$2 Virgie with her father, Captain Cary (John Boles)	1·10	1·25
3306	$2 Virgie comforting her mother	1·10	1·25
3307	$2 Virgie with Uncle Billy (Bill Robinson) and Col. Morrison (Jack Holt)	1·10	1·25
3308	$2 Virgie hugging her father	1·10	1·25
3309	$2 Virgie being admonished by Col. Morrison (horiz)	1·10	1·25
3310	$2 Virgie disguised as a negro slave (horiz)	1·10	1·25

3311	$2 Virgie escaping with her father in buggy (horiz)	1·10	1·25
3312	$2 Virgie with Abraham Lincoln (Frank McGlynn Sr.) (horiz)	1·10	1·25

MS3313 105×75 mm. $6 Virgie tap dancing with Uncle Billy ..... 3·00   3·50

2001. Betty Boop (cartoon character). As T **486** of Grenada showing Betty in various geographical locations. Multicoloured.

3314	$1 Flamenco dancing, Spain	65	70
3315	$1 In national dress, Turkey	65	70
3316	$1 Wearing lei, Hawaii	65	70
3317	$1 As belly-dancer, Egypt	65	70
3318	$1 With flower in hair, South Pacific	65	70
3319	$1 Riding horse, Argentina	65	70
3320	$1 Drinking champagne, France	65	70
3321	$1 Sitting in sports car, Hollywood	65	70
3322	$1 As Statue of Liberty, New York	65	70

MS3323 Two sheets, each 90×110 mm. (a) $6 On a gondola, Venice. (b) $6 By river, India. Set of 2 sheets ..... 7·50   8·00

162 Clark Gable smoking Cigar

2001. Birth Centenary of Clark Gable (American film star). Multicoloured.

3324	$1.50 Type **162**	85	90
3325	$1.50 In *Gone With the Wind*	85	90
3326	$1.50 Sitting in director's chair	85	90
3327	$1.50 Signing autograph	85	90
3328	$1.50 Wearing checked tie	85	90
3329	$1.50 In pin-stripe suit with legs crossed	85	90
3330	$1.50 Seated in car	85	90
3331	$1.50 In grey suit	85	90
3332	$1.50 In casual dress	85	90
3333	$1.50 Arm resting on knee	85	90
3334	$1.50 On telephone	85	90
3335	$1.50 In evening dress	85	90

MS3336 Two sheets. (a) 114×88 mm. $6 Wearing U.S. Air Force uniform. (b) 98×110 mm. $6 As Rhett Butler in *Gone With the Wind*. Set of 2 sheets ..... 8·50   9·00

2001. "Philanippon '01" International Stamp Exhibition, Tokyo. Japanese Paintings. As T **493** of Grenada. Multicoloured.

3337	75c. *Daily Life in Edo* (Miyagawa Choshun)	50	45
3338	90c. *Twelve Famous Places in Japan* (Kani Isen'in Naganobu)	60	50
3339	$1 *Along the Sumida River* (Kano Kyuei)	70	75
3340	$1.25 *Cranes* (Kano Eisen'in Michinobu)	80	70
3341	$2 *Courtesan of Yoshiwara* (Katsukawa Shun'ei)	1·25	1·40
3342	$2 *Kiritsubo Chapter* (86×28 mm)	1·25	1·40
3343	$2 *Akahsi Chapter* (86×28 mm)	1·25	1·40
3344	$2 *Hatsune Chapter* (86×28 mm)	1·25	1·40
3345	$2 *E-Awase Chapter* (86×28 mm)	1·25	1·40
3346	$2 Buddha on golden elephant (vert)	1·25	1·40
3347	$2 Buddha on white elephant (vert)	1·25	1·40
3348	$2 Buddha on elephant and temple (vert)	1·25	1·40
3349	$2 Buddha on elephant with crowd (vert)	1·25	1·40
3350	$3 *Bear killing* (unsigned)	1·60	1·75

MS3351 Two sheets. (a) 86×74 mm. $6 *Sage pointing to the Moon* (Katagiri Ranseki). (b) 97×77 mm. $6 Frontispiece from *Devadatta* (Itsukushima-Jinja) (vert). Set of 2 sheets ..... 7·50   8·00

Nos. 3342/5 depicts "Tale of Genji" (Kano Ryusetsu Hidenobu), and 3346/9 illustrates "The Lotus Sutra".

2001. Death Centenary of Queen Victoria. As T **590a** of Ghana. Multicoloured.

3352	$3 Queen Victoria at her Coronation	1·75	1·90
3353	$3 Princess Victoria as a young girl, standing	1·75	1·90
3354	$3 In old age	1·75	1·90

MS3355 107×77 mm. $6 Queen Victoria within royal arms ..... 3·25   3·50

2001. 25th Death Anniv of Mao Tse-tung (Chinese leader). As T **590b** of Ghana. Multicoloured.

3356	$1.50 Young Mao Tse-tung on steps (horiz)	85	90

3357	$1.50 Mao talking with country people on the Long March (horiz)	85	90
3358	$1.50 Visiting a rural market place (horiz)	85	90
3359	$1.50 Explaining doctrines to soldiers (horiz)	85	90

MS3360 93×134 mm. $3 Mao Tse-tung in 1939 proclaiming the People's Republic of China ..... 1·60   1·90

2001. 75th Death Anniv of Claude-Oscar Monet (French painter). As T **590c** of Ghana. Multicoloured.

3361	$1 *The Magpie*	80	80
3362	$1 *La Pointe de la Heve at Low Tide*	80	80
3363	$1 *Regatta at Argenteuil*	80	80
3364	$1 *La Grenouillere (the Frog Pond)*	80	80

MS3365 138×110 mm. $6 *J. F. Jacquemart with Parasol* (vert) ..... 3·50   3·75

2001. 75th Birthday of Queen Elizabeth II. As T **590d** of Ghana. Multicoloured.

3366	$1.25 Princess Elizabeth wearing pearl necklace	1·00	1·00
3367	$1.25 Queen in blue coat with brooch	1·00	1·00
3368	$1.25 Wearing tiara	1·00	1·00
3369	$1.25 Queen Elizabeth in pink	1·00	1·00
3370	$1.25 Queen in Order of the Bath robes	1·00	1·00
3371	$1.25 Wearing blue hat and coat	1·00	1·00
3372	$2 Young Queen in red hat with feathers	1·60	1·60
3373	$2 Queen Elizabeth in evening dress with orders	1·60	1·60
3374	$2 Young Queen wearing tiara	1·60	1·60

MS3375 119×147 mm. $5 Queen Elizabeth at Coronation (38×51 mm) ..... 3·50   3·75

2001. Death Centenary of Giuseppe Verdi (Italian composer). As T **590e** of Ghana. Showing various portraits of the composer.

3376	25c. multicoloured	75	75
3377	75c. multicoloured	1·25	1·25
3378	$2 multicoloured	1·75	1·75
3379	$3 multicoloured	2·00	2·00

MS3380 78×112 mm. $6 multicoloured ..... 5·00   5·00

Nos. 3376/9 were printed together, *se-tenant*, with backgrounds forming a composite design.

2001. Death Centenary of Henri de Toulouse-Lautrec (French painter). As T **590f** of Ghana. Multicoloured.

3381	$1 *Helene V* (horiz)	80	80
3382	$1 *Clownesse* (horiz)	80	80
3383	$1 *Madame Berthe Bady* (horiz)	80	80
3384	$1 *Woman with the Black Boa* (horiz)	80	80

MS3385 55×85 mm. $6 *Loie Fuller at the Folies Bergere* ..... 3·50   3·75

2001. Birth Centenary of Marlene Dietrich (German actress). As T **495** of Grenada. Multicoloured.

3386	$2 Singing on stage	1·25	1·25
3387	$2 With feather boa	1·25	1·25
3388	$2 In floral dress	1·25	1·25
3389	$2 Wearing hat, coat and gloves	1·25	1·25

163 *Creole* (racing schooner), 1927

2001. Ships. Multicoloured.

3390	90c. Type **163**	80	45
3391	$1 *Britannia* (steamer), 1887	80	55
3392	$1.25 *Santa Maria* and Christopher Columbus, 1492	1·00	1·00
3393	$1.25 *Sao Gabriel* and Vasco da Gama, 1498	1·00	1·00
3394	$1.25 *Vitoria* and Ferdinand Magellan, 1519	1·00	1·00
3395	$1.25 *Golden Hind* and Sir Francis Drake, 1577	1·00	1·00
3396	$1.25 H.M.S. *Endeavour* and Captain James Cook, 1768	1·00	1·00
3397	$1.25 H.M.S. *Erebus* and John Franklin	1·00	1·00
3398	$1.25 *William Fawcett* (paddle steamer), 1829	1·00	1·00
3399	$1.25 *Sirius* (paddle steamer), 1838	1·00	1·00
3400	$1.25 *Great Britain* (steam/sail vessel), 1843	1·00	1·00
3401	$1.25 *Oriental* (American clipper), 1849	1·00	1·00
3402	$1.25 *Lightning* (clipper), 1854	1·00	1·00
3403	$1.25 *Great Eastern* (paddle steamer), 1858	1·00	1·00
3404	$1.25 *Mayflower* (Pilgrim Fathers), 1620 (vert)	1·00	1·00
3405	$1.25 *Sv. Petr* (Bering), 1728 (vert)	1·00	1·00

3406	$1.25 H.M.S. *Beagle* (Darwin), 1825 (vert)	1·00	1·00
3407	$1.25 H.M.S. *Challenger* (survey ship), (vert)	1·00	1·00
3408	$1.25 *Vega* (Nordenskjold), 1872 (vert)	1·00	1·00
3409	$1.25 *Fram* (Amundsen and Nansen), 1892 (vert)	1·00	1·00
3410	$2 *Ariel* (clipper), 1865	1·75	1·75
3411	$3 *Sindia* (barque), 1887	2·00	2·00

MS3412 Two sheets, each 60×45 mm. (a) $6 *Cutty Sark* (clipper), 1869. (b) $6 *Challenger* (American clipper), 1851. Set of 2 sheets ..... 10·00   10·00

No. 3405 is inscribed "GABRIEL" in error. The same stamp shows two different incorrect spellings of Bering. No. 3407 is inscribed "1852" in error.

164 *Vanda Singapore* (orchid)

2001. Orchids. Multicoloured.

3413	25c. Type **164**	45	20
3414	50c. *Vanda Joan Warne*	65	30
3415	75c. *Vanda lamellata*	80	45
3416	$1.50 *Papilionanthe teres*	1·25	1·25
3417	$1.50 *Vanda flabellata*	1·25	1·25
3418	$1.50 *Vanda tessellata* (name bottom left)	1·25	1·25
3419	$1.50 *Vanda pumila*	1·25	1·25
3420	$1.50 *Rhynchostylis gigantea*	1·25	1·25
3421	$1.50 *Vandopsis gigantea*	1·25	1·25
3422	$1.50 *Vanda tessellata* (name centre left)	1·25	1·25
3423	$1.50 *Vanda helvola*	1·25	1·25
3424	$1.50 *Vanda brunnea*	1·25	1·25
3425	$1.50 *Vanda stageana*	1·25	1·25
3426	$1.50 *Vanda limbata*	1·25	1·25
3427	$1.50 *Vandopsis tricolor*	1·25	1·25
3428	$2 *Vanda merrillii*	1·75	1·75

MS3429 Two sheets, each 68×97 mm. (a) $6 *Vanda insignis*. (b) $6 *Vandopsis lissochiloides*. Set of 2 sheets ..... 9·00   9·50

No. 3425 is inscribed "STANGEANA" in error.

165 Richard Petty (stock car driver)

2001. Richard Petty (stock car driver). Two sheets each containing vert designs as T **165**. Multicoloured.

MS3430 (a) 92×130 mm. $6 Type **165**. (b) 92×135 mm. $6 Richard Petty being interviewed. Set of 2 sheets ..... 7·50   8·00

166 Dale Earnhardt in Yellow Overalls, 1980

2001. Dale Earnhardt (stock car driver) Commemoration. Multicoloured.

3431	$2 Type **166**	1·10	1·25
3432	$2 With Winston Cup, 1986	1·10	1·25
3433	$2 With Winston Cup, 1987	1·10	1·25
3434	$2 With Winston Cup, 1990	1·10	1·25
3435	$2 With Winston Cup, 1991	1·10	1·25
3436	$2 With Winston Cup, 1993	1·10	1·25
3437	$2 With Winston Cup, 1994	1·10	1·25
3438	$4 Dale Earnhardt's Chevrolet cars (76×52 mm)	1·10	1·25

167 Ferrari F1 86, 1986

2001. Ferrari Formula 1 Racing Cars. Multicoloured.

3439	$1.50 Type **167**		1·00	1·00
3440	$1.50 Ferrari F1 89, 1989		1·00	1·00
3441	$1.50 Ferrari F92A, 1992		1·00	1·00
3442	$1.50 Ferrari F1 93, 1993		1·00	1·00
3443	$1.50 Ferrari 412T1, 1994		1·00	1·00
3444	$1.50 Ferrari F310, 1996		1·00	1·00

168 World Cup Publicity Poster, Brazil, 1950

2001. World Cup Football Championship, Japan and Korea (2002). Designs showing publicity posters and badges from previous World Cups. Multicoloured.

3445	$1.50 Type **168**	1·00	1·00
3446	$1.50 Switzerland, 1954	1·00	1·00
3447	$1.50 Sweden, 1958	1·00	1·00
3448	$1.50 Chile, 1962	1·00	1·00
3449	$1.50 England, 1966	1·00	1·00
3450	$1.50 Mexico, 1970	1·00	1·00
3451	$1.50 Argentina, 1978	1·00	1·00
3452	$1.50 Spain, 1982	1·00	1·00
3453	$1.50 Mexico, 1986	1·00	1·00
3454	$1.50 Italy, 1990	1·00	1·00
3455	$1.50 U.S.A., 1994	1·00	1·00
3456	$1.50 France, 1998	1·00	1·00

MS3457 Two sheets, 88×75 mm. (a) $6 Uruguay, 1930. (b) $6 Detail of World Cup trophy, Japan-Korea, 2002. Set of 2 sheets   8·50   9·00

169 *Coronation of the Virgin (Filipo Lippi)*

2001. Christmas. Italian Renaissance Religious Paintings. Multicoloured.

3458	25c. Type **169**	30	15
3459	75c. *Virgin and Child (Andrea Mantegna)*	70	35
3460	$1.50 *Madonna and Child (Tommaso Masaccio)*	1·25	1·25
3461	$3 *Madonna and Child (Raffaelo Sanzio)*	2·00	2·50

MS3462 96×136 mm. $6 *Virgin and Child enthroned with Angels (Mantegna)*   3·75   4·00

170 *Battle of Solebay, 1672*

2001. Royal Navy Commemoration. Marine Paintings. Multicoloured.

3463	75c. *H.M.S. Renown (battle cruiser), Portsmouth Harbour, 1922* (vert)	70	45
3464	90c. *Battle of the Saintes, 1782* (vert)	85	50
3465	$1.50 Type **170**	1·25	1·25
3466	$1.50 *Royal Prince, 1679*	1·25	1·25
3467	$1.50 *Battle of Texel, 1673*	1·25	1·25
3468	$1.50 *Battle of Scheveningen, 1653*	1·25	1·25
3469	$1.50 *Battle against Barbary Pirates, 1600s*	1·25	1·25
3470	$1.50 *Capture of Royal Charles, 1667*	1·25	1·25
3471	$1.50 *The Glorious First of June, 1794*	1·25	1·25
3472	$1.50 *The Moonlight Battle, 1780*	1·25	1·25
3473	$1.50 *Great Ships of the Jacobean Navy, 1623*	1·25	1·25
3474	$1.50 *Battle of the Gulf of Genoa, 1795*	1·25	1·25
3475	$1.50 *Battle of the Nile, 1798*	1·25	1·25
3476	$1.50 *Battle of St. Lucia, 1778*	1·25	1·25
3477	$2 *Battle of Trafalgar, 1805* (vert)	1·50	1·60
3478	$3 *Henry VIII embarking at Dover, 1520* (vert)	2·00	2·25

MS3479 Two sheets, each 135×67 mm. (a) $6 *H.M.S. Repulse* (battle cruiser), 1924". (b) $6 *Battle of Navarino, 1827.* Set of 2 sheets   9·50   10·00

The date on No. 3466 is incorrect. The *Royal Prince* was sunk by the Dutch in 1666.

---

171 Lady Elizabeth Bowes-Lyon as a Young Child

2001. 101st Birthday of Queen Elizabeth, the Queen Mother.

3480	**171** $2 black and yellow	1·60	1·60
3481	- $2 multicoloured	1·60	1·60
3482	- $2 black and yellow	1·60	1·60
3483	- $2 multicoloured	1·60	1·60

MS3484 151×155 mm. $6 multicoloured   4·00   4·00

DESIGNS: No. 3481, Queen Mother in Rhodesia, 1957; 3482, Queen Elizabeth with Princess Elizabeth and Princess Anne, 1950; 3483, Queen Mother in blue hat, 1988. (37×50 mm); No. MS3484, Queen Mother inspecting Black Watch.

172 John F. Kennedy on P.T. 109

2001. John F. Kennedy (American President) Commemoration. Multicoloured.

3485	$1.50 Type **172**	90	90
3486	$1.50 John Kennedy in chair	90	90
3487	$1.50 Facing left	90	90
3488	$1.50 Facing forward, smiling	90	90
3489	$1.50 Wearing spotted tie	90	90
3490	$1.50 Wearing striped tie	90	90

MS3491 120×82 mm. $6 John Kennedy with Nikita Khrushchev (First Secretary of U.S.S.R.) (horiz)   3·25   3·50

173 Jacqueline Kennedy Onassis

2001. Jacqueline Kennedy Onassis (widow of American president) Commemoration. Multicoloured.

3492	$1.50 Type **173**	90	90
3493	$1.50 Wearing red coat	90	90
3494	$1.50 In green dress	90	90
3495	$1.50 Wearing evening cloak	90	90
3496	$1.50 In matching pink hat and coat	90	90
3497	$1.50 Jacqueline Kennedy Onassis and hot air balloon	90	90

MS3498 Two sheets. (a) 68×83 mm. $6 Portrait with face value at top right. (b) 83×68 mm. $6 Portrait with face value at top left   7·50   8·00

174 General George Patton and Tank

2001. American Military Leaders. Multicoloured.

3499	75c. Type **174**	55	55
3500	75c. General Joseph Stilwell with President and Mrs. Chiang Kai-shek	55	55
3501	75c. Admiral Thomas Kinkaid and marine landing	55	55
3502	75c. General Jonathan Wainwright and Filipino troops	55	55
3503	75c. Lt.-General James Doolittle and aircraft carrier	55	55
3504	75c. General Matthew Ridgway and cheering crowd	55	55
3505	75c. General Maxwell Taylor and B-17s	55	55
3506	75c. Admiral Richmond Turner and island landing	55	55
3507	75c. General Curtis LeMay and heavy bombers	55	55

3508	75c. General Hoyt Vandenberg and fighter aircraft	55	55
3509	75c. General Carl Spaatz and explosion of atomic bomb	55	55
3510	75c. Admiral Raymond Spruance and burning Japanese battleship	55	55
3511	75c. General Omar Bradley and D-Day landings	55	55
3512	75c. General George Marshall and Marine Corps memorial	55	55
3513	75c. General Douglas MacArthur and return to the Philippines	55	55
3514	75c. Admiral William Halsey and carrier landing	55	55
3515	75c. General Dwight Eisenhower and reviewing troops	55	55
3516	75c. Admiral Chester Nimitz and beach landing	55	55
3517	75c. General William Leahy and aircraft carriers	55	55
3518	75c. General Henry Arnold and heavy bomber	55	55
3519	75c. Admiral Ernest King and battleships	55	55
3520	75c. General George Washington and seated with his wife	55	55
3521	75c. General John Pershing and parade	55	55

MS3522 Two sheets, each 150×139 mm. (a) $6 General Dwight Eisenhower (38×49 mm). (b) $6 General Douglas MacArthur (38×49 mm)   7·50   8·00

175 Princess Diana in Evening Dress

2001. 40th Birth Anniv of Diana, Princess of Wales. Multicoloured.

3523	$1.50 Type **175**	1·25	1·25
3524	$1.50 Wearing ski suit	1·25	1·25
3525	$1.50 In pale blue hat	1·25	1·25

176 Nudaurelia cytheria (moth)

2001. Moths. Multicoloured.

3526	75c. Type **176**	65	45
3527	90c. Janomima westwoodi	80	50
3528	$1.50 Actias selene	1·25	1·25
3529	$1.50 Amphicallia bellatrix	1·25	1·25
3530	$1.50 Citheronia regalis	1·25	1·25
3531	$1.50 Arctica caja	1·25	1·25
3532	$1.50 Leto venus	1·25	1·25
3533	$1.50 Alcides zodiaca	1·25	1·25
3534	$1.50 Graellsia isabellae	1·25	1·25
3535	$1.50 Dysphania cuprina	1·25	1·25
3536	$1.50 Automeris io	1·25	1·25
3537	$1.50 Agarista agricola	1·25	1·25
3538	$1.50 Callioratis millari	1·25	1·25
3539	$1.50 Othreis fullonia	1·25	1·25
3540	$1.50 Lasiocampa quercus	1·50	1·60
3541	$3 Chrysiridia riphearia	2·00	2·25

MS3542 Two sheets, each 77×106 mm. (a) $6 *Divana diva* (vert). (b) $6 *Argema mimosae* (vert)   8·50   9·00

No. 3539 is inscribed "Otthreis" in error.

177 Queen Elizabeth in Spotted Dress

2002. Golden Jubilee. Multicoloured.

3543	$2 Type **177**	1·60	1·60
3544	$2 Queen Elizabeth wearing pink hat	1·60	1·60
3545	$2 Queen Elizabeth in evening dress	1·60	1·60
3546	$2 Queen Elizabeth wearing sunglasses	1·60	1·60

MS3547 76×109 mm. $6 Princess Elizabeth with family   4·00   4·25

---

178 Horse on Background of Chinese Characters

2002. Chinese New Year ("Year of the Horse"). Showing different horses.

3548	**178** 75c. multicoloured	65	40
3549	- $1.25 multicoloured	90	95
3550	- $2 multicoloured	1·40	1·60

MS3551 **178** 70×102 mm. $6 black, light orange and orange   3·25   3·75

179 US Flag on Twin Towers

2002. "United We Stand". Support for Victims of 11 September 2001 Attacks.

3552	**179** 80c. multicoloured	60	60

180 Amerigo Vespucci

2002. 550th Birth Anniv of Amerigo Vespucci (explorer).

3553	**180** $1 multicoloured	80	60
3554	- $2 multicoloured	1·40	1·50
3555	- $3 multicoloured	1·90	2·00

MS3556 75×58 mm. $6 multicoloured   3·75   4·00
DESIGNS: $2 to $6 Various portraits.

181 F1 86, 1986

2002. Ferrari Racing Cars. Sheet 147×165 mm containing T **181** and similar horiz designs. Multicoloured.
MS3557 $1.50 Type **181**; $1.50 F1 89, 1989; $1.50 F 92 A, 1992; $1.50 F1 93, 1993; $1.50 412 T1, 1994; $1.50 F310, 1996   4·50   4·75

2002. International Year of Mountains. Two sheets containing horiz designs as T **512** of Grenada. Multicoloured.
MS3558 143×93 mm. $2 Kilimanjaro, Tanzania; $2 Mount Kenya; $2 Mount Kea, Hawaii; $2 Mount Fuji, Japan   4·75   5·50
MS3559 115×65 mm. $6 Ko'olau Mountains, Hawaii   3·25   3·50

182 Waterfall

2002. International Year of Ecotourism. Two sheets containing T **182** and similar horiz designs. Multicoloured.
MS3560 137×105 mm. $1.50 Type **182**; $1.50 Ringed kingfisher; $1.50 Butterfly; $1.50 Rock beauty (fish); $1.50 Cactus; $1.50 Orchid   3·50   3·50
MS3561 80×98 mm. $6 Blue-hooded euphonias   4·75   4·75

183 Olympic Rings
and Skier
(airborne)

2002. Winter Olympic Games, Salt Lake City. Multicoloured.

3562	$3 Type **183**	1·75	1·90
3563	$3 Olympic rings and skier (different)	1·75	1·90
MS3564	82×113 mm. Nos. 3562/3	3·50	3·75

2002. World Scout Jamboree, Thailand. Two sheets each containing multicoloured designs as T **515** of Grenada.

MS3565	107×90 mm. $2 Scout badge and campfire; $2 Scout hiking; $2 Boy scout feeding calf; $2 Girl saluting	4·50	4·75
MS3566	98×70 mm. $2 Scout at seashore (vert)	1·25	1·40

2002. Chiune Sugihara (Japanese Consul-general in Lithuania who rescued Jews, 1939–40) Commemoration. Two sheets each 60×90 mm containing vert designs as T **511** of Grenada.

MS3567	(a) $6 Sugihara and map showing route from Lithuania to Japan. (b) $6 Sugihara and wife Set of 2 sheets	7·50	8·00

184 *Bombus auricomus* (bumble bee)

2002. Flora and Fauna. Miniature sheets containing T **184** and similar multicoloured designs.

MS3568	135×170 mm. $1 Type **184**; $1 *Anax junius* (dragonfly); $1 *Dynastes tityus* (Hercules beetle); $1 *Coccinella novemrotata* (ladybug); $1 *Callicore maimuna* (figure-of-eight butterfly); $1 *Tenodera aridifolia sinensis* (praying mantis)	3·25	3·50
MS3569	135×170 mm. $1 Sperm whale; $1 Bottlenose whale; $1 Sei Whale; $1 Killer whale; $1 Humpback whale ("Humback Whale"); $1 Pygmy sperm whale	3·25	3·50
MS3570	135×170 mm. $2 *Anartia jatrophae*; $2 *Phoebis philea*; $2 *Cepheuptychia cephus*; $2 *Prepona meander*; $2 *Mesene phareus*; $2 *Morpho peleides*	6·50	7·00
MS3571	135×170 mm. $2 *Coprinus comatus*; $2 *Leucocoprinus rachodes*; $2 *Collybia iocephala*; $2 *Lepiota acutesquamosa*; $2 *Morchella crassipes*; $2 *Mycena galericulata*	6·50	7·00
MS3572	Four sheets, each 100×70 mm. (a) $6 *Anax junius* (dragonfly) (horiz). (b) $6 Blue whale (horiz). (c) $6 *Cepheuptychia cephus* (butterfly) (horiz). (d) $6 *Amanita phalloides* (mushroom) Set of 4 sheets	13·00	14·00

No. **MS**3568 shows insects, **MS**3569 shows whales, **MS**3570 shows butterflies and **MS**3571 fungi.

2002. 25th Death Anniv of Elvis Presley. As T **518a** of Grenada. Multicoloured (No. 3573) or black and brown (No. **MS**3574).

3573	$1 Elvis Presley with guitar	1·00	1·00
MS3574	150×215 mm. $1×9 containing nine different portraits of Elvis Presley	7·50	7·50

2002. "Amphilex '02" International Stamp Exhibition, Amsterdam. As T **518b** of Grenada. (a) Dutch Nobel Prize Winners. Sheet 150×100 mm.

MS3575	$1.50 Paul J. Crutzen (Chemistry, 1995) (black and green); $1.50 Nobel medal (black and brown); $1.50 Martinus Veltman (Physics, 1999) (black and mauve); $1.50 Hendrik Lorentz (Physics, 1902) (black and blue); $1.50 Christiaan Eijkman (Medicine, 1929) (black and green); $1.50 Gerard 't Hooft (Physics, 1999) (black and brown)	5·50	5·50

(b) Dutch Lighthouses. Sheet 128×148 mm. Multicoloured.

MS3576	$1.50 Ameland; $1.50 Vlieland; $1.50 Julianadorp; $1.50 Noordwijk; $1.50 Hoek van Holland; $1.50 Goeree	6·50	6·50

(c) Dutch Women's Traditional Costumes. Sheet 120×140 mm containing multicoloured designs, each 36×50 mm.

MS3577	$3 Marken, Noord-Holland; $3 Staphorst, Overijsel; $3 Walchheren, Zeeland	5·50	5·50

185 Teddy Bear holding "HAPPY BIRTHDAY" in Heart

2002. Centenary of the Teddy Bear (1st issue). T **185** and similar vert designs. Multicoloured.

MS3578	140×142 mm. 50c. Type **185**; $1 With waistcoat, briefcase and bowler hat; $2 Wearing raincoat, sunglasses and hat; $5 Wearing boxer shorts with heart pattern	5·00	5·00
MS3579	85×115 mm. 15c. Teddy Bear wearing Guardsmans plumed helmet; $2 Panda teddy bear wearing black hat; $3 Wearing beret and ruff; $4 White teddy bear wearing grey top hat	5·50	5·50

No. **MS**3578 is heart-shaped. See also Nos. 3611/12.

2002. World Cup Football Championship, Japan and Korea. Miniature sheets containing vert designs as T **524** of Grenada. Multicoloured.

MS3580	165×82 mm. $1.50 Oliver Neuville (Germany) and Eddie Pope (USA); $1.50 Claudio Reyna (USA) and Miroslav Klose (Germany); $1.50 Christian Ziege (Germany) and Frankie Hejduk (USA); $1.50 Nadal (Spain) and Jung Hwan Ahn (South Korea); $1.50 Luis Enrique (Spain) and Chong Gug Song (South Korea); $1.50 Park Ji Sung (South Korea) and Mendieta Gaizka (Spain)	5·50	5·50
MS3581	165×82 mm. $1.50 Danny Mills (England) and Ronaldo (Brazil); $1.50 Roque Junior (Brazil) and Emil Heskey (England); $1.50 Sol Campbell (England) and Rivaldo (Brazil); $1.50 Lamine Diatta (Senegal) and Hakan Sukur (Turkey); $1.50 Umit Davala (Turkey) and Khalilou Fadiga (Senegal); $1.50 El Hadji Diouf (Senegal) and Tugay Kerimoglu (Turkey)	5·50	5·50
MS3582	Four sheets, each 82×82 mm. (a) $3 Oliver Kahn (Germany); $3 Brad Friedel (Germany). (b) $3 Chun Soo Lee (South Korea); $3 Juan Carlos Valeron (Spain). (c) $3 David Beckham (England) and Roberto Carlos (Brazil); $3 Ronaldinho (Brazil) and Nicky Butt (England). (d) $3 Alpay Ozalan (Turkey); $3 Khalilou Fadiga (Senegal) Set of 4 sheets	13·00	13·00

2002. Christmas. Religious Paintings. As T **523a** of Grenada. Multicoloured.

3583	15c. *The Redeemer and the Four Apostles* (Carpaccio)	25	10
3584	25c. *The Miracle of the Relic of the Cross* (Carpaccio) (vert)	30	15
3585	50c. *The Presentation in the Temple* (Carpaccio)	40	25
3586	$2 *The Visitation* (Carpaccio)	1·60	1·75
3587	$3 *The Birth of the Virgin* (Carpaccio)	1·90	2·25
MS3588	62×90 mm. $6 *Madonna and Child and Two Angels* (detail) (Cimabue) (vert)	3·25	3·50

186 *Year of Ram* (Ren Yi)

2003. Chinese New Year ("Year of the Ram").

MS3589	**186** 179×108 mm. $1.25×4 multicoloured	3·00	3·25

2003. Columbia Space Shuttle Commemoration. Sheet 183×146 mm, containing vert designs as T **533** of Grenada showing crew members. Multicoloured.

MS3590	$1 David Brown; $1 Commander Rick Husband; $1 Laurel Clark; $1 Kalpana Chawla; $1 Michael Anderson; $1 William McCool; $1 Ilan Ramon	4·50	4·75

2003. Japanese Art. Paintings by Toyohara Kunichika showing Famous Actors. As T **535** of Grenada. Multicoloured.

3591	50c. *Ichikawa Danjuro IX as the Beggar Akushichibyoe Kagekiyo* (vert)	35	25
3592	75c. *Ichikawa Danjuro IX as the Female Demon Ewanari*	55	40
3593	$1.25 *Sawamura Tossho II as Sutewakamaru*	80	80
3594	$3 *Bando Hikosaburo V as Nikki Damjo*	1·60	1·75
MS3595	175×137 mm. $2 *Nakamura Shikan IV as Keyamura Rokusuke*; $2 *Bando Hikosaburo V as Ichimisai no Musume Osono*; $2 *Ichikawa Sadanji I as Wada no Shimobe Busuke*; $2 *Ichikawa Sadanji I as Kiyomizu no Yoshitaka*	4·50	4·75
MS3596	122×82 mm. $6 *Onoe Kikugoro V as Torii Tsuneemon returning to Mikawa* (horiz)	3·25	3·50

2003. 450th Death Anniv of Lucas Cranach the Elder (artist). As T **536** of Grenada. Multicoloured.

3597	25c. *The St. Mary Altarpiece* (detail) (vert)	25	15
3598	$1 *The St. Mary Altarpiece* (different detail) (vert)	70	55
3599	$1.25 "*Altar Piece of the Princes*" (detail) (vert)	80	80
3600	$3 *Frederick the Wise with St. Bartholomew* (detail of altarpiece) (vert)	1·60	1·75
MS3601	150×160 mm. $2 *Judith at the Table of Holofernes* (detail); $2 *St. Catherine Altarpiece* (detail); $2 *Judith killing Holofernes* (detail); $2 *The Martyrdom of St. Catherine* (detail)	4·50	4·75
MS3602	102×123 mm. $6 *Cardinal Albrecht of Brandenbourg as St. Jerome in the Wilderness* (vert)	3·25	3·50

2003. 85th Death Anniv of Gustav Klimt (artist). As T **537** of Grenada. Multicoloured.

3603	15c. *Le Chapeau de Plumes Noires*	20	15
3604	25c. *Le Schloss Kammer am Attersee*	25	15
3605	50c. *Malcesine sur le Lac de Garde*	35	25
3606	75c. *Ferme en Haute-Autriche*	55	40
3607	$1.25 *Portrait d'une Dame*	80	75
3608	$4 *La Frise Beethoven* (detail)	1·90	2·00
MS3609	126×178 mm. $2 *Portrait de la Baronne Elisabeth Bachofen-Echt*; $2 *Portrait d'une Dame*; $2 *Portrait d'Emilie Floge*; $2 *Portrait d'Adele Bloch-Bauer*	4·50	4·75
MS3610	103×81 mm. $6 "*Le Baiser*" (detail). Imperf	3·25	3·50

2003. Centenary of the Teddy Bear (2nd issue). Embroidered Fabric Teddy Bears. As T **538** of Grenada. Self-adhesive. Imperf.

3611	$15 ochre, silver and red	8·00	8·50
MS3612	126×157 mm. No. 3611×4	28·00	29·00

2003. Centenary of Tour de France Cycle Race. As T **540** of Grenada showing past winners. Multicoloured.

MS3613	160×100 mm. $2 Ferdinand Kubler (1950); $2 Hugo Koblet (1951); $2 Fausto Coppi (1952); $2 Louison Bobet (1953)	5·50	5·50
MS3614	160×100 mm. $2 Louison Bobet (1954); $2 Louison Bobet (1955); $2 Roger Walkowiak (1956); $2 Jacques Anquetil (1957)	5·50	5·50
MS3615	160×100 mm. $2 Gastone Nencini (1960); $2 Jacques Anquetil (1961); $2 Jacques Anquetil (1962); $2 Jacques Anquetil (1963)	5·50	5·50
MS3616	Three sheets, each 100×70 mm. (a) $6 Louison Bobet (1953–1955). (b) $6 Jacques Anquetil (1957). (c) $6 Eddy Merckx (1969) Set of 3 sheets	10·00	10·00

187 John Kennedy, Choate Graduate, 1935

2003. 40th Death Anniv of President John F. Kennedy.

MS3617	144×131 mm. $2 Type **187** (agate, black and); $2 John Kennedy, 1946 (multicoloured); $2 With Jacqueline Kennedy on tennis court (multicoloured); $2 With young John F. Kennedy Jnr (multicoloured)	4·50	4·75
MS3618	144×131 mm. $2 With Jacqueline Kennedy (black, brown and grey); $2 Announcing Cuban blockade, 1962 (agate and mauve); $2 Sitting in chair, White House, 1962 (brown and black); $2 Kalpana Kennedy with children at funeral, 1963 (black, mauve and purple)	4·50	4·75

188 Charles Lindbergh

2003. 75th Anniv of First Solo Trans-atlantic Flight. Multicoloured (No. **MS**3620).

MS3619	129×144 mm. $2 Type **188** (blue, grey and red); $2 Lindbergh and Ryan NYP Special *Spirit of St. Louis* (purple, blue and red); $2 Lindbergh and *Spirit of St. Louis* (black and red); $2 Lindbergh (purple, blue and red)	5·00	5·00
MS3620	129×144 mm. $2 Lindbergh (looking forward); $2 Lindbergh (looking left); $2 Lindbergh on arrival in Paris, 1927; $2 Lindbergh and *Spirit of St. Louis*	5·00	5·00

189 La Sagesse

2003. International Year of Freshwater. Multicoloured.

MS3621	150×88 mm. $2 Type **189**; $2 Annadale Falls; $2 Grand Etang	3·25	3·50
MS3622	100×70 mm. $6 St. George	3·25	3·50

2003. Centenary of Circus Clowns. As T **544** of Grenada. Multicoloured.

MS3623	119×194 mm. $2 Anton Pilossian; $2 Victor Vashnikov; $2 Dan Rice; $2 Tom Comet	3·25	3·25
MS3624	146×218 mm. $2 Boxer dog; $2 Macaw; $2 Monigue; $2 Vassily Trofimov	3·25	3·25

No. **MS**3623 shows clowns and is cut in the shape of a clown. No. **MS**3624 shows others circus performers and circus animals and is cut in the shape of an elephant.

190 Wright Flyer

2003. Centenary of Powered Flight. Multicoloured.

MS3625	176×97 mm. $2 Type **190**; $2 NC-4; $2 Douglas World Cruiser; $2 Fokker Eindecker	3·25	3·25
MS3626	176×97 mm. $2 Hansa Brandenburg D.1; $2 B.E.2e; $2 Handley Page 0/400; $2 Avro 504	3·25	3·25
MS3627	176×97 mm. $2 Hawker Hart; $2 Martin B-10; $2 Armstrong Whitworth Siskin IIIA; $2 Loening OL-8	3·25	3·25
MS3628	(a) 67×97 mm. $6 Wright Glider No. III. (b) 106×76 mm. $6 Wright *Flyer II*. (c) 106×76 mm. $6 Gloster Gamecock	7·00	7·00

191 Princess Elizabeth as Young Woman

2003. 50th Anniv of Coronation. Multicoloured.

MS3629	160×86 mm. $3 Type **191**; $3 Queen wearing azure blue; $3 Riding side saddle at Trooping the Colour	3·50	3·50
MS3630	76×106 mm. $6 Queen wearing tiara	3·00	3·00

2003. 21st Birthday of Prince William. As T **547** of Grenada. Multicoloured.

MS3631	160×86 mm. $3 Prince William (half-length photo); $3 Prince William (in close-up); $3 Prince William (looking left)	4·00	4·00
MS3632	106×76 mm. $6 Wearing hat and ski goggles	3·00	3·00

192 Rose-breasted Grosbeak

2003. Birds, Tropical Fish and Flowers of the World. Multicoloured.

3633	25c. Type **192**	30	20
3634	25c. Three-spotted dascyllus ("Domino Damselfish")	30	20
3635	50c. Northern oriole ("Bullock's Oriole")	45	35
3636	50c. Catbird ("Gray Catbird")	45	35
3637	75c. Porcupinefish	60	60
3638	75c. Wild rhododendron (vert)	60	60
3639	$1 Blue grosbeak	90	90
3640	$1 Peony (vert)	90	90
3641	$1.25 Black-tailed damselfish	1·00	1·00
3642	$1.25 Camellia (vert)	1·00	1·00
3643	$2 Reticulate damselfish ("Clown Fish")	1·60	1·60
3644	$2 Laurel (vert)	1·60	1·60
MS3645	110×138 mm. $2 Lazuli bunting; $2 Indigo bunting; $2 Broad-tailed Hummingbird; $2 Scarlet tanager (all vert)	5·00	5·00
MS3646	129×109 mm. $2 Halfmoon triggerfish; $2 Blackeye thicklip ("Half and Half Wrasser"); $2 Pennant coralfish ("Long-fin Banner Fish"); $2 Hump-headed bannerfish ("Butterfly Fish")	4·50	4·50
MS3647	110×130 mm. $2 Apple blossom; $2 Mock orange; $2 Wild rose; $2 Hibiscus (all vert)	4·50	4·50
MS3648	98×68 mm. (a) $6 Barn swallow. (b) $6 Blue-girdled angelfish. (c) $6 Violets (vert)	10·00	10·00

No. **MS3647** is inscribed "ASDA Postage Stamp Mega-Event" on the sheet margin.

193 Madonna and Child (detail), Carnesecchii Tabernacle (Domenico Veneziano)

2003. Christmas. Multicoloured.

3649	35c. Type **193**	25	20
3650	75c. Madonna and Child (detail), Magnoli Altarpiece (Domenico Veneziano)	60	45
3651	90c. Crevole Madonna (detail) (Duccio di Buoninsegna)	70	55
3652	$3 Madonna and Child (detail) (Domenico Veneziano)	1·90	2·25
MS3653	71×96 mm. $6 Madonna and the Child by the Fireplace (detail) (Robert Campin)	3·50	3·75

2003. 300th Anniv of St. Petersburg. "Treasures of the Hermitage". As T **551** of Grenada. Multicoloured.

3654	75c. Abraham and Isaac (Rembrandt)	55	40
3655	$1 David and Jonathan (Rembrandt)	75	60
3656	$1.25 Saint Onuphrus (Juisepe de Ribera)	85	80
3657	$2 Pope Paul III (Titian)	1·75	1·75
MS3658	115×145 mm. $2 Rest on the Flight into Egypt (Murillo); $2 Esther before Ahasuerus (Nicolas Poussin); $2 Abraham's Servant and Rebecca (Jacob Hogers); $2 The Prophet Elisha and Naaman (Lambert Jacobsz) (all horiz)	4·50	4·75
MS3659	(a) 66×78 mm. $6 The Building of Noah's Ark (Guido Reni). Imperf. (b) 78×66 mm. $6 Hagar flees Abram's House (Rubens). Imperf	6·00	6·50

2003. 25th Death Anniv of Norman Rockwell (artist). As T **552** of Grenada. Multicoloured.

MS3660	150×181 mm. $2 The Trumpeter; $2 Waiting for the Vet; $2 The Diving Board; $2 The Discovery	3·50	3·75
MS3661	$6 Day in a Boy's Life (detail) (horiz)	3·50	3·75

2003. 30th Death Anniv of Pablo Picasso (artist). As T **553** of Grenada. Multicoloured.

MS3662	128×168 mm. $2 Jacqueline Sitting; $2 Jacqueline with Flowers; $2 Seated Nude; $2 Woman in Armchair	3·75	4·00
MS3663	74×98 mm. $6 Head of a Woman. Imperf	3·25	3·50

2004. Chinese New Year ("Year of the Monkey"). As T **554** of Grenada. Multicoloured.

MS3664	118×144 mm. $1.50 Cotton-top tamarin; $1.50 Chimpanzee; $1.50 Baboon; $1.50 Bald uakari	3·25	3·50

194 The Mind Landscape of Xie Youyu (Zhao Mengfu)

2004. Hong Kong 2004 International Stamp Exhibition. Paintings by Zhao Mengfu (1254—1322). Multicoloured.

MS3665	120×119 mm. $2 Type **194**; $2 Mountains and trees; $2 Twin Pines; $2 Mountain range and plains	4·00	4·25
MS3666	87×81 mm. $6 Autumn	3·25	3·50

2004. Arthur the Aardvark and Friends. As T **557** of Grenada. Multicoloured.

MS3667	150×183 mm. $1.50 Brain as molecule; $1.50 Binky as pirate; $1.50 Francine as vampire; $1.50 Prunella as fairy; $1.50 Arthur as skeleton; $1.50 Muffy as witch	4·00	4·25
MS3668	150×184 mm. $2 Francine as clown; $2 Buster as Frankenstein's monster; $2 Muffy and spider; $2 Sue Ellen as cat	3·75	4·00
MS3669	150×183 mm. $2 Francine and butterfly; $2 Binky and world map; $2 Brain and maths equation; $2 Arthur and model of planet	3·75	4·00

2004. Marilyn Monroe Commemoration. As T **560** of Grenada.

3670	50c. multicoloured	50	50
MS3671	multicoloured 127×112 mm. $2 black, grey and red; $2 black, grey and red; $2 black, grey and red; $2 black, grey and red	4·25	4·50

DESIGNS: 50c. Wearing halter-neck dress and drop earrings; $2 Wearing white top and short hair; $2 Wearing beret; $2 Wearing white backless dress; $2 With long dark hair and black dress.

195 Deng Xiaoping

2004. Deng Xiaoping (Chinese politician) Commemoration. Sheet 98×68 mm.

MS3672	**195** $6 black, grey and red	3·25	3·50

2004. 25th Anniv of the Pontificate of Pope John Paul II. Sheet 163×153 mm containing horiz designs as T **564** of Grenada. Multicoloured.

MS3673	$2 Pope with Lech Walesa; $2 Pope with Chief Rabbi of Israel, Yisrael Meir Lau; $2 Pope with children; $2 Pope using laptop; $2 Pope wearing mitre and gesturing	6·50	6·50

2004. Olympic Games, Athens, Greece. As T **559** of Grenada. Multicoloured.

3674	25c. Long jump	25	15
3675	50c. Avery Brundage	40	25
3676	$1 Commemorative medal	65	65
3677	$4 Greek vase showing "The Paidotribe" ("Paidotribai")	2·25	2·50

2004. 60th Anniv of D-Day Landings. As T **404** of Dominica. Multicoloured.

3678	25c. Admiral Sir Bertram Ramsay	40	25
3679	50c. Lt Gen. Miles Dempsey	70	50
3680	75c. Bob Shrimpton "Ping", Higher Submarine Detector, HMS Belfast	90	65
3681	$4 Denis Edwards, 6th Airborne Division	2·50	2·75
MS3682	177×107 mm. $2 US troops landing and map of Omaha Beach; $2 Troops moving inland from Omaha Beach; $2 Soldier with rifle and map of Sword Beach; $2 Meeting of German generals and Allied troops leaving landing craft	6·00	6·50
MS3683	177×107 mm. $2 Winston Churchill; $2 Churchill (wearing hat); $2 British link up with Airborne Troops; $2 British troops and map showing Horsa Bridge on Orne River	7·50	7·00
MS3684	100×70 mm. (a) $6 Gunner in British bomber; (b) $6 Assault landing craft coming ashore	7·50	8·00

2004. Bicentenary of Steam Locomotives. Multicoloured. As T **566** of Grenada but horiz.

3685-3693	$1×9 Britannia class; Indian Railways XD class; China Railways KD6 class (USATC S160); SE+CR 01 class; Battle of Britain light Pacific; SR King Arthur class; SR Marsh 13 class; SR N class; SR School class	7·00	7·50
3694-3702	$1×9 LNER V2 class; Sudan Railways locomotive; China Railways DF4 Co Co; LMS 2F with Black 5; LMS Lickey Banker; LMS Princess Royal Pacific; LMS Reboilered Claughton class; LMS Stanier 8F; Midland Railway compound	7·00	7·50
3703-3711	$1×9 SR Merchant Navy Pacific; Gazira Cotton Railway, Sudan; Spanish Railways; LNER 04-1 class; LNER A1 Pacific;LNER A3 class; LNER A4 class Pacific; LNER B1 class; LNER Ivatt Large Atlantic A4 Pacific	7·00	7·50
MS3712	Three sheets, each 97×66 mm. (a) $6 London to Holyhead train. (b) $6 Dublin to Tralee train crossing viaduct. (c) $6 Modern Aberdeen to Penzance train crossing bridge	11·00	12·00

2004. Queen Juliana of the Netherlands Commemoration. As T **568** of Grenada. Multicoloured.

3713	$2 Wedding portrait of Princess Juliana, 1937	1·40	1·40

196 Start of Donkey Race

2004. 40th Carriacou Regatta Festival. Multicoloured.

3714	75c. Type **196**	60	60
3715	90c. Start of model boat race	70	75
3716	$1 Dinghy race (vert)	70	75

2004. Centenary of FIFA (Federation Internationale de Football Association). As T **413** of Dominica. Multicoloured.

MS3717	192×96 mm. $2 David Beckham (England); $2 Marcel Desailly (France); $2 Guido Buchwald (Germany) $2 Alfonso (Spain)	4·50	4·75
MS3718	$6 Bobby Charlton (England)	3·75	4·00

197 Elvis Presley

2004. 50th Anniv of Elvis Presley's First Record. Two sheets, each 187×136 mm, containing T **197** and similar vert designs. Multicoloured.

MS3719	150×100 mm. $2 Type **197**; $2 Wearing spotted shirt, singing with guitar; $2 Wearing shirt, guitar slung over one shoulder; $2 Wearing grey jacket	3·75	4·00
MS3720	$2 Wearing mauve shirt; $2 Wearing spotted shirt, strumming guitar; $2 Wearing jacket and tie, guitar slung over one shoulder; $2 Wearing blue patterned shirt	4·50	4·75

198 Titanic

2004. Ocean Liners. Multicoloured.

3721	25c. Type **198**	30	20
3722	75c. Michaelangelo	70	55
3723	$1 America	85	70
3724	$1.25 Vaterland	1·00	1·00
3725	$2 Deutschland	1·50	1·60
3726	$3 Mauritania	2·00	2·25
MS3727	75×70 mm. $6 Ile de France	3·75	4·00

2004. Ronald Reagan (US President 1981–9) Commemoration. As T **573** of Grenada. Multicoloured.

MS3728	179×107 mm. $2 With Press Secretary James Brady; $2 With German Chancellor Helmut Kohl; $2 Pres. Reagan at desk and with family; $2 With Princess Diana, 1983	4·50	4·75

2004. Centenary of Baseball World Series. As T **574** of Grenada showing George Herman "Babe" Ruth. Multicoloured.

3729	50c. George Herman "Babe" Ruth (white background)	35	35
3730	50c. As No. 2929 (blue background)	35	35
MS3731	1 120×114 mm. $2 Holding bat; $2 Full-face portrait; $2 Facing right; $2 Holding baseball	4·00	4·50

2004. Christmas. 25th Death Anniv of Norman Rockwell (artist). As T **575** of Grenada. Multicoloured.

3732	35c. Follow Me in Merry Measure (1928)	30	25
3733	75c. The Merrie Old Coach Driver (1929)	55	45
3734	90c. Joy to the World (1930)	70	60
3735	$3 Santa Reading His Mail (1935)	1·90	2·25
MS3736	62×80 mm. $6 Wartime Santa (1942). Imperf	3·25	3·50

199 Double Chickens and Peony

2005. Chinese New Year ("Year of the Rooster"). Paintings by Ren Yi. Multicoloured.

MS3737	135×115 mm. 75c.×4 Type **199**	1·75	2·00
MS3738	100×70 mm. $3 A Rooster (59×39 mm)	1·75	2·00

200 Scarlet-bodied Wasp Moth

2005. Moths. Multicoloured.

3739	75c. Type **200**	60	60
3740	90c. Bella moth	70	70
3741	$1 Sphinx moth	70	70
3742	$3 Faithful beauty moth	1·90	2·25
MS3743	93×73 mm. $6 Spotted oleander moth (inscr "Spotted Oleander Caterpillar" in error)	3·50	3·75

201 Heliamphora tatei

2005. Carnivorous Plants of the Caribbean. Multicoloured.

MS3744	150×100 mm. $2 Type **201**; $2 Sarracenia flava and Genlisea pygmaea; $2 Nepenthes bicalcarata; $2 Utricularia intermedia	4·50	4·75
MS3745	93×73 mm. $6 Dionaea muscipula	3·50	3·75

202 Poison Dart Frog

2005. Reptiles of the Caribbean. Multicoloured.

MS3746	150×100 mm. $2 Type **202**; $2 Western Antillean anoles; $2 Black iguana; $2 American crocodile	4·50	4·75
MS3747	93×73 mm. $6 Anolis lizard	3·50	3·75

203 Rice Plants

2005. International Year of Rice (2004). Multicoloured.
MS3748 202×140 mm. $1.50 Type **203**;
$1.50 Rice plants and perched bird;
$1.50 Rice plants and bird (flying
downwards); $1.50 Clump of rice;
$1.50 Rice plants with bird (flying
upwards); $1.50 Two clumps of rice ... 5·00   6·00
MS3749 100×70 mm. $6 Rice farming
in Bali, Indonesia, 1930s (artist anon)
(horiz) ... 3·25   3·50

The stamps in **MS**3748 form a composite design showing a screen painting by Maruyama Oshen of rice plants heavy with grain in autumn.

204 Swiftsure

2005. US National Basketball Association Players. As T **572** of Grenada. Multicoloured.
3750   75c. Tracy McGrady, Houston
       Rockets ... 50   55
3751   75c. Shaquille O'Neal, Miami
       Heat ... 50   55
3752   75c. Steve Nash, Phoenix Suns ... 50   55
3753   75c. Chris Webber, Sacramento
       Kings ... 50   55
3754   75c. Allan Houston, New York
       Knicks ... 50   55
3755   75c. Steve Francis, Orlando
       Magic ... 50   55

2005. Bicentenary of the Battle of Trafalgar.
Multicoloured.
3756   75c. Type **204** ... 85   60
3757 $1 British fleet sailing into Cape
       Trafalgar towards French and
       Spanish fleet (horiz) ... 1·00   85
3758 $2 Captain Alexander Ball ... 1·75   1·75
3759 $3 Vice Admiral Francois Paul
       Brueys d'Aigalliers ... 2·50   2·50
MS3760 96×66 mm. $6 Admiral Aristide Aubert du Petit-Thouars ... 3·75   4·00

2005. 70th Birth Anniv of Elvis Presley. As T **583** of Grenada. Multicoloured.
3761- $1.50×6 With guitar, 1955;
3766   Performing on Milton Berle
       Show, 1956; $1.50 Seated in
       studio, 1958; $1.50 Portrait
       photograph, 1962; Performing for the "68 Special", 1968;
       On tour, 1972 ... 5·50   6·00
3767- $1.50×6 In GI Blues, 1958; Blue
3772   Hawaii, 1961; It Happened at
       the World's Fair, 1963; Harum
       Scarum, 1965; Sitting on car,
       Spinout, 1966; Change of
       Habit, 1969 ... 5·50   6·00

2005. Ozu Yasujiro (film director) Commemoration. As T **584** of Grenada. Multicoloured.
MS3773 145×175 mm. $2 A Mother
Should be Loved, 1934; $2 An Inn in
Tokyo, 1935; $2 Dragnet Gir, 1933; $2
There was a Father, 1942 ... 4·50   5·00

2005. Prehistoric Animals. As T **580** of Grenada.
Multicoloured.
MS3774 Three sheets, each 133×100
mm. (a) Animals: $2 Psittacosaurus;
$2 Deinonychus; $2 Suchomimus;
$2 Smilodon. (b) Fish: $2 Eurypholis;
$2 Ichthyosaurus; $2 Plesiosaur;
$2 Varnerxiphactinus. (c) Birds: $2
Pterosaurus; $2 Archaeopteryx;
Pterosaurian; $2 Microraptor ... 12·00   14·00
MS3775 Three sheets, each 98×69 mm.
(a) Tenotosaurus. (b) $6 Uintatherium. (c) $6 Mammoth (vert) ... 11·00   13·00

2005. 60th Anniv of the End of World War II. "The Route to Victory". As T **587** of Grenada. Multicoloured.
3776 $2 Field Marshal Montgomery
       directing troops forward ... 1·40   1·40
3777 $2 Field Marshal Rommel ... 1·40   1·40

3778 $2 Troops moving forward
       into battle ... 1·40   1·40
3779 $2 German prisoners after Battle of El Alamein ... 1·40   1·40
3780 $2 Russian troops at the gates
       of Berlin ... 1·40   1·40
3781 $2 Two surrendering German
       soldiers ... 1·40   1·40
3782 $2 Berlin in ruins ... 1·40   1·40
3783 $2 Soldier carrying child ... 1·40   1·40
MS3784 Two sheets, each 107×97
mm. (a) $6 Troops attacking, North
African desert. (b) $6 "Give me five
years and you will not recognise
Germany again" (Hitler quotation)
and ruins of Berlin ... 7·00   7·50

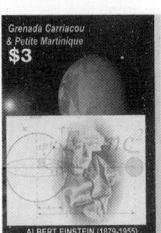

205 "E=mc²" and Sunlight
on Planet Mars

2005. 50th Death Anniv of Albert Einstein (physicist).
Multicoloured.
MS3785 175×80 mm. $3 Type **205**; $3
Albert Einstein; $3 David Ben-Gurion
(first Prime Minister of Israel) ... 6·50   6·50

The two right-hand designs in **MS**2785 form a composite design showing Einstein with David Ben-Gurion.

2005. 60th Anniv of Victory in Japan Day. As T **589** of Grenada. Multicoloured.
3786 $2 P-38 J Lightning ... 1·40   1·40
3787 $2 P-51D Mustang ... 1·40   1·40
3788 $2 F4 fighter plane ... 1·40   1·40
3789 $2 Douglas C-47 Skytrain ... 1·40   1·40
3790 $2 Officer reading VJ Day message to troops ... 1·40   1·40
3791 $2 Chaplain's prayer ... 1·40   1·40
3792 $2 "PEACE" placard ... 1·40   1·40
3793 $2 USS Missouri, Tokyo Bay, 2
       September 1945 ... 1·40   1·40

206 Moses Maimonides

2005. 800th Death Anniv of Moses Maimonides (Rabbi Moses Ben Maimon) (Jewish scholar)).
3794   **206** $2 multicoloured ... 1·50   1·50

207 Pope John Paul II

2005. Pope John Paul II Commemoration.
3795   **207** $3 multicoloured ... 2·00   2·00

2005. Christmas. As T **602** of Grenada. Multicoloured.
3796   35c. Madonna and Child (detail)
       (Andrea del Sarto) ... 25   20
3797   75c. Madonna Pesaro (detail)
       (Tiziano Vecellio) ... 60   45
3798   90c. Madonna and Child (detail)
       (Tiziano Vecellio) ... 70   60
3799 $3 Madonna and Child (detail)
       (Rubens) ... 1·75   2·00
MS3800 100×70 mm. $6 Madonna and
Child (Dominico Veneziano) ... 3·50   4·00

208 Pope John Paul II

2005. Chinese New Year ("Year of the Dog"). Painting of Dog by Chang Dai-Chien.
3801   **208** $1 multicoloured ... 1·00   1·00

209 Pope
Benedict XVI

2006. Election of Pope Benedict XVI.
3802   **209** $2 multicoloured ... 1·40   1·40

2006. 80th Birthday of Queen Elizabeth II. As T **432** of Dominica. Multicoloured.
3803 $3 Wearing white hat and
       jacket, 1960s ... 1·90   1·90
3804 $3 Wearing tiara ... 1·90   1·90
3805 $3 With baby Princess Anne ... 1·90   1·90
3806 $3 Wearing pearls and dark
       blue dress ... 1·90   1·90
MS3807 120×120 mm. $6 Wearing
uniform ... 3·50   3·75

2006. 80th Birth Anniv of Marilyn Monroe (actress). As T **452** of Gambia. Multicoloured.
3808 $3 Marilyn Monroe ... 1·75   1·90

2006. 400th Birth Anniv of Rembrandt Harmenszoon van Rijn (artist). As T **458** of Gambia showing paintings. Multicoloured.
3809   75c. The Strolling Musicians
       (detail) ... 50   35
3810   90c. The Great Jewish Bride
       (detail) ... 60   45
3811 $1 Old Haaringh (detail) ... 65   50
3812 $3 Lady and Gentleman in Black
       (detail of man) ... 1·75   1·90
3813 $3 Lady and Gentleman in Black
       (detail of woman) ... 1·75   1·90
3814 $3 The Shipbuilder and his Wife
       (detail of shipbuilder) ... 1·75   1·90
3815 $3 The Shipbuilder and his Wife
       (detail of wife) ... 1·75   1·90
3816 $4 Beggars receiving Alms at the
       Door of a House (detail) ... 1·90   2·00
3817 $6 Young Woman in a Pearl-
       trimmed Beret (detail) (69×99
       mm) ... 3·25   3·50
3818 $6 Portrait of a Boy (detail)
       (69×99 mm) ... 3·25   3·50

2006. 250th Birth Anniv of Wolfgang Amadeus Mozart (composer). Sheet 100×70 mm containing vert design as T **435** of Dominica. Multicoloured.
MS3819 $6 Don Giovanni (opera) ... 4·00   4·00

210 Space Shuttle Columbia
at Pad 39-A

2006. Space Anniversaries. Multicoloured. (a) 25th Anniv of First Flight of Space Shuttle Columbia.
3820 $2 Type **210** ... 1·40   1·40
3821 $2 Astronauts John Young and
       Robert Crippen ... 1·40   1·40
3822 $2 Columbia first flight take-off ... 1·40   1·40
3823 $2 Columbia in space ... 1·40   1·40
3824 $2 Columbia crew in cabin ... 1·40   1·40
3825 $2 Columbia landing ... 1·40   1·40

2005. (b) Launch of Space Shuttle Discovery.
3826 $3 Mission STS-114
       on pad ... 1·90   1·90
3827   **3826** $3 Mission STS-114 crew ... 1·90   1·90
3828   **3826** $3 Building of first ISS
       elements ... 1·90   1·90
3829   **3826** $3 STS-114 in space walk ... 1·90   1·90

(c) 30th Anniv (2005) of "Apollo"—"Soyuz" Test Project.
3830 $3 Liftoff of "Soyuz 19" from
       Baikonur Cosmodrome,
       Kazakhstan ... 1·90   1·90
3831 $3 ASTP crew ... 1·90   1·90
3832 $3 Soviet and American crew in
       the cabin ... 1·90   1·90
3833 $3 Spacecraft "Soyuz" 19 ... 1·90   1·90
MS3834 Three sheets, each 100×70
mm. (a) $6 "Luna 9" flight apparatus
(first lunar soft landing, 1966). (b) $6
"Venus Express" (first European mission to Venus). (c) $6 Mars Reconnaissance "Orbiter" Set of 3 sheets ... 11·00   13·00

The stamp within No. **MS**3834(c) is incorrectly inscribed "Reconaissance".

2006. 550th Death Anniv of Christopher Columbus. As T **614** of Grenada. Multicoloured.
3835   75c. Pinta (vert) ... 50   35
3836 $1.50 Columbus's fleet setting sail ... 90   70
3837 $2 Santa Maria and map showing voyage ... 1·40   1·50
3838 $3 Columbus discovers San
       Salvador, 1492 ... 1·75   2·00

MS3839 100×70 mm. $6 Christopher
Columbus ... 3·50   3·75

2006. Christmas. Vert designs as T **616** of Grenada showing details from painting Saint Willibrod in Adoration before Mary Mother of God by Rubens. Multicoloured.
3840   25c. Joseph ... 25   20
3841   50c. Cherubs ... 35   30
3842   75c. Madonna and Christ Child ... 50   35
3843 $1 Saint Willibrod ... 65   50
3844 $2 As No. 3840 ... 1·40   1·40
3845 $2 As No. 3841 ... 1·40   1·40
3846 $2 As No. 3842 ... 1·40   1·40
3847 $2 As No. 3843 ... 1·40   1·40

211 LZ-127
Zeppelin

2007. 50th Death Anniv (2006) of Ludwig Durr (Zeppelin designer). Multicoloured.
3848 $3 Type **211** ... 2·25   2·25
3849 $3 Hindenburg's dining room ... 2·25   2·25
3850 $3 Marine Airship L53 ... 2·25   2·25

212 John Kennedy
running for Congress

2007. 90th Birth Anniv of John F. Kennedy (US President 1960–3). Multicoloured.
3851 $2 Type **212** ... 1·50   1·50
3852 $2 Campaign for Congress ... 1·50   1·50
3853 $2 Campaigning in New
       Hampshire ... 1·50   1·50
3854 $2 John Kennedy as President ... 1·50   1·50
3855 $2.50 Naru Island ... 2·00   2·00
3856 $2.50 Lieut. John Kennedy on
       Solomon Islands (in forest,
       wearing cap) ... 2·00   2·00
3857 $2.50 Lieut. Kennedy on
       Solomon Islands (standing
       on boardwalk) ... 2·00   2·00
3858 $2.50 SOS coconut carved by
       John Kennedy ... 2·00   2·00

Nos. 3851/4 ('Elected to the House of Representatives 1946–52') and 3855/8 ('John F. Kennedy Joins the Navy 1941–44').

213 '100' containing Emblem

2007. Centenary of Scouting. Multicoloured.
3859 $2 Type **213** ... 1·50   1·50
MS3860 111×80 mm. $6 As Type **213** ... 4·25   4·25

The stamp within **MS**3860 differs from Type **213** in having different colours and no frame around '100' emblem.

214 Elvis Presley

2007. 30th Death Anniv of Elvis Presley. Multicoloured.
3861 $3 Type **214** ... 2·25   2·25
3862 $3 Elvis Presley playing guitar
       (guitarist in background) ... 2·25   2·25
3863 $3 Seated, with hands resting
       on guitar ... 2·25   2·25
3864 $3 Singing into microphone,
       hands raised ... 2·25   2·25

215 *Wild Boar* (Liu Jiyou)

2007. Chinese New Year ('Year of the Boar'). Multicoloured.
MS3865 85×112 mm. $1×2 Type **215**; $2×2 Type **215** ... 4·25 4·25

216 *Pied-billed Grebe*

2007. Birds of the Caribbean. Multicoloured.

3866	75c. Type **216**	55	40
3867	$1 Black-crowned night-heron	80	65
3868	$1 Turkey vulture	80	65
3869	$2 Hooded warbler (horiz)	1·50	1·50
3870	$2 Northern flicker (horiz)	1·50	1·50
3871	$2 Mockingbird (horiz)	1·50	1·50
3872	$2 Blue tit (horiz)	1·50	1·50
3873	$2 Caspian tern (horiz)	1·50	1·10
3874	$2 Scarlet tanager (horiz)	1·50	1·50
3875	$2 Common nighthawk (horiz)	1·50	1·50
3876	$2 Osprey (horiz)	1·50	1·50
3877	$4 Green honeycreeper	4·00	4·00

MS3878 Three sheets, each 71×100 mm. (a) $5 White-winged parakeet. (b) $5 Blackpoll warbler (horiz). (c) $5 Yellow-green vireo (horiz) ... 11·00 11·00

217 *Goodyera tesselata*

2007. Orchids of the World. Multicoloured.

3879	75c. Type **217**	55	40
3880	$1 Oncidium floridanum	1·10	95
3881	$2 Hexalectris spicata	1·50	1·50
3882	$2 Platanthera grandiflora	1·50	1·50
3883	$2 Platanthera peramoena	1·50	1·50
3884	$2 Cyrtopodium punctatum	1·50	1·50
3885	$2 Spiranthes odorata	1·50	1·50
3886	$2 Platanthera blephariglottis	1·50	1·50
3887	$2 Epipactis helleborine	1·50	50
3888	$2 Cypripedium alaskanum	1·50	1·50
3889	$2 Zeuxine strateumatica	1·50	1·50
3890	$3 Pogonia ophioglossoides	2·25	2·25

MS3891 Three sheets, each 70×100 mm. (a) $6 Macradenia lutescens (horiz). (b) $6 Bletilla striata (horiz). (c) $6 Platanthera chapmanii ... 13·00 13·00

218 *Morchella semilibera*

2007. Fungi of the World. Multicoloured.

3892	75c. Type **218**	55	40
3893	$1 Ganoderma resinaceum	80	65
3894	$1 Helvella crispa	80	65
3895	$2 Aleuria aurantia	1·50	1·50
3896	$2 Boletus sp.	1·50	1·50
3897	$2 Boletellus russellii	1·50	1·50
3898	$2 Otidea onotica	1·50	1·50
3899	$2 Russula sardonia	1·50	1·50
3900	$2 Amanita cruzii	1·50	1·50
3901	$2 Macrocybe titans	1·50	1·50
3902	$2 Amanita microspora	1·50	1·50
3903	$4 Ganoderma sp.	4·00	4·00

MS3904 Three sheets, each 103×73 mm. (a) $5 Cantharellus cibarius. (b) $5 Amanitapolypyramis. (c) $5 Boletellus ananas ... 11·00 11·00

219 *Wicked Stepmother Queen holding Magic Mirror*

2007. Betty Boop in Snow White (cartoon film, 1933). Multicoloured.
MS3905 Two sheets, each 195×175 mm. (a) $1×3 Type **219**; Wicked Stepmother Queen shouting; Bimbo and Koko in knight costumes falling down hole; $2×3 Betty Boop at palace door; Magic mirror pointing at Betty Boop; Betty Boop rolled into snowball (b) $2×4 Queen finding hole; Koko, Bimbo and Queen turned into Hag; Koko as ghost; Betty Boop asleep and Koko and Bimbo turned into ice figures ... 13·00 13·00

MS3906 106×76 mm. $6 Betty Boop fleeing (vert) ... 4·25 4·25

220 *Royal Penguins*

2007. International Polar Year. Penguins. Multicoloured.
MS3907 150×115 mm. $2×6 Type **220** (country inscr at right); Penguins preening, with heads bent (country inscr at top); Head of penguin (foreground) and penguin (country inscr at right); Penguin in foreground) and penguin showing feet (country inscr at bottom); Penguins preening, with heads bent (country inscr at bottom); Penguin (in foreground) and back of penguin (country inscr at left) ... 9·00 9·00

MS3908 100×70 mm. $6 African penguin swimming ... 4·25 4·25

The stamps and margins of No. **MS**3907 forms a composite design showing a colony of royal penguins.

221 *Queen Elizabeth II and Prince Philip*

2007. Diamond Wedding of Queen Elizabeth II and Prince Philip. Multicoloured.

3909	$1.50 Type **221**	1·10	95
3910	$1.50 Queen Elizabeth II	1·10	95

222 *Pope Benedict XVI*

2007. 80th Birthday of Pope Benedict XVI.
3911 **222** $1 multicoloured ... 80 65

223 *Helicopter D-HBKS*

2007. Centenary of the Helicopter. Multicoloured.

3912	$1.50 Type **223**	1·10	95
3913	$1.50 UH-1 Iroquois troop carrier	1·10	95
3914	$1.50 S-65/RH-53D 'Hostage rescue helicopter'	1·10	95
3915	$1.50 UH-1B/C Iroquois helicopter	1·10	95
3916	$1.50 Autogyro	1·10	95
3917	$1.50 BO 105 rescue helicopter	1·10	95

MS3918 100×70 mm. $6 AH-64 Apache armoured gunship ... 4·25 4·25

224 *The Virgin and Child with Saints Jerome and Bartholomew*

2007. Christmas. Multicoloured.

3919	25c. Type **224**	20	25
3920	50c. The Virgin and Child between Saints Thomas and Jerome (Guido Reni)	40	35
3921	75c. The Virgin and Child (Giovanni Batista Salvi)	60	45
3922	$1 The Madonna of Decemviri (Pietro Perugino)	80	65

225 *Rat*

2007. Chinese New Year ('Year of the Rat'). Multicoloured.
3923 **225** $1 multicoloured ... 80 65

226 *Princess Diana*

2007. Tenth Death Anniv of Princess Diana. Multicoloured.

3924	$1.50 Type **226**	1·10	95
3925	$1.50 Wearing dark coat and plumed hat	1·10	95
3926	$1.50 Wearing emerald green	1·10	95
3927	$1.50 As Type **226** in close-up	1·10	95
3928	$1.50 As No. 3925 in close-up	1·10	95
3929	$1.50 As No. 3926 in close-up	1·10	95

MS3930 70×100 mm. $6 Princess Diana and Prince Charles with baby Prince William at his Christening (horiz) ... 4·25 4·25

2008. Elvis Presley Commemoration. As T **636** of Grenada. Multicoloured.

3931	$1.50 Silhouette (back view)	1·10	95
3932	$1.50 Wearing green shirt	1·10	95
3933	$1.50 Silhouette (side view)	1·10	95
3934	$1.50 Playing guitar (seen from back, looking over shoulder)	1·10	95
3935	$1.50 Silhouette (front view)	1·10	95
3936	$1.50 Wearing orange jacket	1·10	95

227 *Aerial View of City of David and Walls of Old City, Jerusalem* (Illustration reduced. Actual size 150×125 mm) (image scaled to 32% of original size)

2008. Israel 2008 World Stamp Championship, Tel-Aviv. Sheet 150×125 mm. Imperf.
MS3937 **227** $6 multicoloured ... 4·25 4·25

228 *Elvis Presley*

2008. Elvis Presley Commemoration. Multicoloured.

3954	$1.50 Type **228**	1·10	95
3955	$1.50 Wearing blue shirt and jeans, striped background	1·10	95
3956	$1.50 Wearing white (seen full length)	1·10	95
3957	$1.50 Wearing blue shirt and jeans (green and black background)	1·10	95
3958	$1.50 Wearing white (seen three quarter length)	1·10	95
3959	$1.50 Wearing red shirt (green, blue and black background)	1·10	95

229 *Bauble in Surf on Beach*

2008. Christmas. Multicoloured.

3960	25c. Type **229**	20	25
3961	50c. 'MERRY CHRISTMAS' and shapes of wrapped parcels in lights	40	35
3962	75c. 'Merry Christmas' written in beach sand and palm fronds	60	45
3963	$1 Christmas lights including outlines of seashells and star (vert)	1·00	85

230 *Mariner 9 and the Valles Marineris on Mars*

2008. 50 Years of Space Exploration and Satellites. Multicoloured.

3964	$2 Type **230**	1·50	1·50
3965	$2 Mariner 9 and technicians	1·50	1·50
3966	$2 Mariner 9 and the Olympus Mons on Mars	1·50	1·50
3967	$2 Valles Marineris on Mars	1·50	1·50
3968	$2 Atlas-Centaur rocket launches Mariner 9	1·50	1·50
3969	$2 Mariner 9 and Mars moon Phobos	1·50	1·50
3970	$2 Venus and Mercury (horiz)	1·50	1·50
3971	$2 Jupiter	1·50	1·50
3972	$2 Earth and Mars	1·50	1·50
3973	$2 Saturn	1·50	1·50
3974	$2 Neptune	1·50	1·50
3975	$2 Uranus	1·50	1·50
3976	$2.50 Mariner 10 and Venus	2·00	2·00
3977	$2.50 Atlas-Centaur rocket and Mariner 10	2·00	2·00
3978	$2.50 Mariner 10 and technicians	2·00	2·00
3979	$2.50 Mariner 10 and Mercury	2·00	2·00
3980	$2.50 Pillars of Creation in the Eagle Nebula	2·00	2·00
3981	$2.50 Orion Nebula	2·00	2·00
3982	$2.50 Crab Nebula	2·00	2·00
3983	$2.50 Horsehead Nebula	2·00	2·00

231 *True Tulip Shell (Fasciolaria tulipa)*

2009. Seashells of the World. Multicoloured.

3984	25c. Type **231**	20	25
3985	50c. Twisted plait olive (Olivancillaria contortuplicata)	40	35
3986	75c. The Junonia (Scaphella junonia)	60	45
3987	$1 Royal comb venus (Pitar dione)	85	60

MS3988 141×101 mm. $2×6 Lion's paw (Lyropecten nodosus); Banded tulip (Fasciolaria lilium); Flame auger (Terebra taurinus); Miniature melo (Micromelo undata); West Indian worm shell (Vermicularia spirata); Mouse cowrie (Cypraea mus) (wrongly spelt 'cowry') (all vert) ... 9·00 9·00

The stamps and margins of No. **MS**3988 form a composite design showing a beach.

232 Blue Chromis (*Chromis cyaneus*)

2009. Tropical Fish. Multicoloured.

3989	$1 Type **232**	80	65
3990	$2 Clown wrasse (*Coris gaimard*)	1·50	1·50
3991	$4 Orange spotted filefish (*Oxymonacanthus longirostris*)	3·00	3·00
3992	$5 Palometa (*Trachinotus goodei*)	3·75	3·75

MS3993 140×100 mm. $2×6
Tiger grouper (*Mycteroperca tigris*);
Bluehead wrasse (*Thalassoma bifasciatum*); Squirrel fish (*Sargocentron speniferun*); Queen parrotfish (*Scarus vetula*); Yellowtail snapper (*Ocyurus chrysurus*); Barred hamlet (*Hypoplectrus puella*) .... 9·00 9·00

The stamps and margins of No. **MS3993** form a composite background design.

233 Pres. Barack Obama

2009. Inauguration of President Barack Obama. Multicoloured.
MS3994 130×100 mm. $2.75×4 Type
233; Facing camera; Speaking, hand
raised; Facing left .... 7·00 7·00
MS3995 100×70 mm. $10 Barack
Obama and Capitol, Washington
(37×50 mm) .... 9·50 9·50

The stamps and margins of Nos. **MS3994/5** form a composite design showing the US flag.

234 Ox Symbols on Prayer Wheels

2009. Chinese New Year. Year of the Ox. Sheet 190×78 mm. Multicoloured.
MS3996 $2.50 Type **234**×4 multi-
coloured .... 8·00 8·00

235 Archery

2009. China 2009 World Stamp Exhibition, Luoyang (1st issue). Sports of the Summer Games. Sheet 138×95 mm containing T **235** and similar vert designs. Multicoloured.
MS3997 Type **235**; Cycling; Wrestling;
Boxing .... 4·00 4·00

236 Qianglong Emperor

2009. China 2009 World Stamp Exhibition (2nd issue). Qianglong Emperor (1736–96). Sheet 150×120 mm containing T **236** and similar vert designs. Multicoloured.
MS3998 Type **236**; Emperor and his
court sitting by table; Sitting at writing desk; Qianglong Emperor (three
quarter length portrait) .... 4·00 4·00

237 Elvis Presley

2009. Elvis Presley Commemoration. Sheet 153×124 mm containing T **237** and similar horiz designs. Multicoloured.
MS3999 Type **237**; In close up (blue inscriptions); Half length, holding microphone (magenta inscriptions); In close-up, singing (turquoise inscriptions) .... 8·00 8·00

238 Caribbean Spiny Lobsters

2009. Endangered Species. Caribbean Spiny Lobster (*Panulirus argus*). Multicoloured.

4000	$3 Type **238**	2·00	2·00
4001	$3 Three lobsters	2·00	2·00
4002	$3 Spiny lobster (side view)	2·00	2·00
4003	$3 Spiny lobster (front view)	2·00	2·00

MS4004 112×165 mm. Nos. 4000/3,
each ×2 .... 16·00 16·00
MS4005 112×94 mm. Nos. 4000/3 .... 7·25 7·25

239 *Psilocybe mexicana*

2009. Fungi of the Caribbean. Multicoloured.

4006	25c. Type **239**	20	25
4007	$1 Crinipellis piceae	1·00	1·00
4008	$2 Psilocybe subcubensis	1·50	1·50
4009	$5 Psilocybe cubensis	3·75	3·75

MS4010 190×90 mm. $2.50×4 *Panaeolus fimicola*; *Psilocybe yungensis*;
Panaeolus subbalteatus; *Russula cremeolilacina* .... 8·00 8·00
MS4011 124×95 mm. $3 *Psilocybe guilartensis*; $3 *Psilocybe aztecorum*
(both 29×40 mm) .... 4·50 4·50

240 Abraham Lincoln as Young Man

2009. Birth Bicentenary of Abraham Lincoln (US President 1861–5). Sheet 175×136 mm containing T **240** and similar vert designs showing portraits. Multicoloured.
MS4012 Type **240**; Older, no beard;
With beard; With beard, head and
shoulders portrait .... 8·00 8·00

241 Pope Benedict XVI

2009. Visit of Pope Benedict XVI to Israel. Sheet 100×150 mm containing T **241** and similar horiz designs. Multicoloured. Litho.
MS4013 Type **241**; Pope Benedict XVI and Israel's President Shimon Peres at the President's residence; Pope visiting the Temple Mount, Jerusalem; Pope visiting Heichal Shlomo, Jerusalem .... 8·00 8·00

242 Don

2009. 25th Anniv of Teenage Mutant Ninja Turtles. Sheet 132×132 mm. containing T **242** and similar vert designs. Multicoloured.
MS4014 Type **242**; Leo; Rafe; Mike .... 8·00 8·00

243 Voyager 1, Saturn and Titan

2009. 40th Anniv of First Manned Moon Landing and International Year of Astronomy. T **243** and similar vert designs. Multicoloured.
MS4015 150×100 mm. $2×6 Type **243**×2; Apollo 11 Lunar Module×2; Voyager 1, Jupiter and its moons Europa, Io, Callisto and Ganymede×2 .... 9·00 9·00
MS4016 100×70 mm. $6 Apollo 11
Lunar Module .... 4·50 4·50

244 John Kennedy Jnr with Pres. Kennedy

2009. Tenth Death Anniv of John Kennedy Jnr. Sheet 130×100 mm containing T **244** and similar vert designs. Multicoloured.
MS4017 Type **244**; John Kennedy Jnr and his mother Jackie Onassis; John Kennedy Jnr; Pres. and Mrs. Kennedy with young John and Caroline .... 8·00 8·00

245 Elvis Presley

2010. 75th Birth Anniv of Elvis Presley. Sheet 190×127 mm containing T **245** and similar vert designs. Multicoloured.
MS4018 Type **245**; On stage, facing left, audience in background; In close-up, singing, facing left; Half kneeling, holding microphone .... 9·50 9·50

246 Elvis Presley as Tulsa McClean

2010. Elvis Presley in GI Blues. Multicoloured.
MS4019 90×125 mm. $6 Type **246** .... 4·25 4·25
MS4020 125×90 mm. $6 Poster for
GI Blues .... 4·25 4·25
MS4021 125×90 mm. $6 Elvis Presley as Tulsa McClean (yellow
background) .... 4·25 4·25
MS4022 90×125 mm. $6 As Tulsa Mc-
Clean (seated on ground) .... 4·25 4·25

247 *Dendrophylax lindenii*

2010. Orchids of the Caribbean. Multicoloured.

4023	$1.20 Type **247**	95	95
4024	$1.80 Scaphyglottis imbricata	1·25	1·25
4025	$3 Encyclia ceratistes	2·25	2·25
4026	$5 Scaphyglottis stellata	4·25	4·25

MS4027 140×100 mm. $2.50×4 *Oncidium excavatum*; *Brassavola nodosa*; *Cattleya gaskelliana*; *Phalaenopsis cultivars* .... 8·00 8·00

MS4028 100×70 mm. $3×2 *Lepanthopsis floripecten*; Equitant *Oncidium* .... 4·25 4·25

248 Pres. Barack Obama

2010. Pres. Barack Obama's Nobel Peace Prize (2009). Sheet 126×178 mm containing T **248** and similar vert designs. Multicoloured.
MS4029 Type **248**; Smiling, facing towards left; Facing camera; Speaking .... 8·00 8·00

249 Pope John Paul II

2010. Fifth Death Anniv of Pope John Paul II. Multicoloured.
MS4030 $2.75×4 Type **249**; Wearing mitre (ceiling pattern at top left corner; Wearing mitre (ceiling pattern at left of stamp); As Type **249** .... 7·00 7·00
MS4031 $2.75×4 Wearing mitre, facing forwards; Wearing mitre, seen in profile; Wearing white skullcap and dark robes; Wearing white skullcap and embroidered robes .... 7·00 7·00

No. **MS4030** has a composite background design showing a ceiling.
No. **MS4031** shows black and white signed photographs.

2010. Centenary of Girlguiding. As T **671** of Grenada. Multicoloured.
MS4032 151×100 mm. $2.75×4 Three guides and leader; Five guides looking out from tent; Three guides in meadow; Four guides .... 7·00 7·00
MS4033 70×100 mm. $6 Five guides
(vert) .... 3·75 3·75

2010. World Cup Football Championship, South Africa. Vert designs as T **672** of Grenada. Multicoloured.
MS4034 130×155 mm. $1.50×6 First Round Group E: Netherlands v. Denmark; Japan v. Cameroon; Netherlands v. Japan; Denmark v. Cameroon; Japan v. Denmark; Cameroon v. Netherlands .... 6·00 6·00
MS4035 130×155 mm. $1.50×6 First Round Group F: Italy v. Paraguay; New Zealand v. Slovakia; Slovakia v. Paraguay; New Zealand v. Italy; Slovakia v. Italy; Paraguay v. New Zealand .... 6·00 6·00
MS4036 130×155 mm. $1.50×6 First Round Group G: Côte d'Ivoire v. Portugal; Brazil v. Korea DPR; Brazil v. Côte d'Ivoire; Portugal v. Korea DPR (inscr 'Portugall'); Korea DPR v. Côte d'Ivoire; Portugal v. Brazil .... 6·00 6·00
MS4037 130×155 mm. $1.50×6 First Round Group H: Honduras v. Chile; Spain v. Switzerland; Chile v. Switzerland; Honduras v. Spain; Spain v. Chile; Switzerland v. Honduras .... 6·00 6·00
MS4038 86×90 mm. $3.50×2 Loftus Versfeld Stadium, Pretoria; Free State Stadium, Bloemfontein .... 5·25 5·25
MS4039 86×90 mm. $3.50×2 Peter Mokaba Stadium, Polokwane; Royal Bafokeng Stadium, Rustenburg .... 5·25 5·25
MS4040 86×90 mm. $3.50×2 Ellis Park Stadium, Johannesburg; Mbombela Stadium, Nelspruitt .... 5·25 5·25

250 Gervais' Beaked Whale (*Mesoplodon europaeus*)

2010. Whales of the Caribbean. Multicoloured.
MS4041 $2×6 Type **250**; Cuvier's beaked whale (*Ziphius cavirostris*); Pygmy sperm whale (*Kogia breviceps*); Melon-headed whale (*Peponocephala electra*); Bryde's whale (*Balaenoptera edeni*); Sperm whale (*Physeter macrocephalus*) .... 7·00 7·00
MS4042 100×70 mm. $6 Humpback whale (*Megaptera novaeangliae*) .... 3·75 3·75

251 Reputed
Self-Portrait, c. 1512

2010. Leonardo da Vinci Commemoration. Multicoloured.

4043	$2 Type **251**	1·25	1·25
4044	$2 Statue of da Vinci outside Uffizi Gallery, Florence, Italy	1·25	1·25
4045	$2 *Vitruvian Man*, c. 1492	1·25	1·25
4046	$2 *La Scapigliata*, c. 1508	1·25	1·25
4047	$2 *Mona Lisa* (detail), c. 1503	1·25	1·25
4048	$2 Study of horses, c. 1490	1·25	1·25
MS4049	$6 *The Last Supper*, c. 1495 (horiz)	3·75	3·75

252 Elvis Presley

2010. 75th Birth Anniv of Elvis Presley (2nd issue). Multicoloured.

MS4050 142×127 mm. $2.75×4 Type **252**; Wearing jacket and tie; Wearing white shirt, facing right; Wearing black jacket, facing left — 7·25 7·25

MS4051 194×160 mm. $2.75×4 Wearing black shirt, holding guitar; Wearing white, facing left; Wearing black leather jacket; Playing guitar (all with black background) — 7·25 7·25

253 Prince William and Miss Catherine Middleton

2011. Royal Engagement. Multicoloured.

MS4052 160×111 mm. $2.50×4 Type **253**×4 — 6·00 6·00

MS4053 160×111 mm. $2.50×4 Miss Catherine Middleton wearing fur hat; Prince William in army uniform; Miss Catherine Middleton; Prince William — 6·00 6·00

MS4054 140×100 mm. $3 Miss Catherine Middleton wearing black hat (horiz) ; $3 Prince William (horiz) — 4·00 4·00

MS4055 140×100 mm. $3 Miss Catherine Middleton wearing beret and scarf ; $3 Prince William — 4·00 4·00

254 Mother Teresa

2011. Indipex 2011 World Philatelic Exhibition, Delhi. Birth Centenary of Mother Teresa. Multicoloured.

MS4056 $2.75×4 Type **254**; Nobel Prize medal (Nobel Peace Prize, 1979); Mother Teresa with baby and portrait photograph; Bharat Ratna Award (1980) — 7·25 7·25

255 Pres. Barack Obama

2011. Indipex 2011 World Philatelic Exhibition, Delhi (2nd issue). President Obama visits India, 6-8 November 2010. Multicoloured.

MS4057 $2.75×4 Type **255**; Barack Obama walking with Indian Prime Minister Manmohan Singh; Barack Obama and Manmohan Singh shaking hands; Barack Obama giving speech — 7·25 7·25

256 Abraham Lincoln

2011. Abraham Lincoln (US President 1861-5) Commemoration. Multicoloured.

MS4058 $2×6 Type **256**; Abraham Lincoln with son; At desk; As young man, no beard, facing right; As younger man, no beard; In close-up — 7·50 7·50

MS4059 $2×6 Head of bronze statue of Abraham Lincoln; Painting of Abraham Lincoln seated in chair; Photograph; Lincoln Memorial statue, Washington DC; Painting of Abraham Lincoln; Head of Abraham Lincoln at Mount Rushmore — 7·50 7·50

257 Pres. John F. Kennedy in the Oval Office, White House

2011. 50th Anniv of the Election of President John F. Kennedy. Multicoloured.

MS4060 140×100 mm. $2.75 Type **257**×4 — 7·25 7·25

MS4061 130×120 mm. $2.75×4 Pres. and Mrs. Kennedy with Caroline and baby John; Pres. and Mrs. Kennedy in evening dress; Pres. and Mrs. Kennedy; Pres and Mrs. Kennedy with Caroline and John aged about 18 months — 7·25 7·25

MS4062 100×70 mm. $6 Pres. John F. Kennedy (colour photo) — 3·75 3·75

MS4063 100×70 mm. $6 Pres. John F. Kennedy (black/white photo) — 3·75 3·75

258 Border Collie

2011. Dogs of the World. Multicoloured.

MS4064 $2.50×4 Type **258**; Briard; Great Dane; Afghan hound — 6·00 6·00

MS4065 $2.50×4 King Charles spaniel; Labrador retriever; German shepherd dog; Weimaraner — 6·00 6·00

259 Princess Diana

2011. 50th Birth Anniv of Princess Diana. Multicoloured.

MS4066 141×100 mm. $2.75×4 Type **259**; Princess Diana with Princes William and Harry; Lady Diana Spencer aged 9; Prince Charles and Princess Diana on honeymoon at Balmoral, 1981 — 7·25 7·25

MS4067 100×70 mm. $6 Princess Diana wearing red hat and jacket and black skirt — 3·75 3·75

260 Pope Benedict XVI with Archbishop of Santiago Julian Barrio

2011. Pope Benedict XVI visits Santiago de Compostela and Barcelona, Spain, 6-7 November 2010. Multicoloured.

MS4068 175×124 mm. $3×4 Type **260**; Pope Benedict XVI holding staff topped with cross; Pope Benedict XVI with Felipe and Letizia, Prince and Princess of Asturias; Pope Benedict XVI giving blessing — 8·00 8·00

MS4069 140×135 mm. $3×4 Pope Benedict XVI; Pope Benedict XVI (side view) dedicating altar of Sagrada Familia Cathedral, Barcelona; Pope Benedict XVI with King Juan Carlos I and Queen Sofia of Spain; Pope Benedict XVI giving speech — 8·00 8·00

261 Pope John Paul II

2011. Beatification of Pope John Paul II. Multicoloured.

MS4070 161×80 mm. $3.30×3 Type **261**; Pope John Paul II kneeling in prayer; Pope John Paul II with hand raised in blessing — 6·50 6·50

MS4071 51×100 mm. $6 Pope John Paul II — 3·75 3·75

262 Duke and Duchess of Cambridge riding in Carriage

2011. Royal Wedding. Multicoloured.

MS4072 150×100 mm. $2.75×4 Type **262**; Duchess of Cambridge (facing left); Prince William (wearing cap); Duke and Duchess of Cambridge leaving Westminster Abbey — 7·25 7·25

MS4073 150×100 mm. $2.75×4 Prince William; Duchess of Cambridge; Household Cavalry in parade; Duke and Duchess of Cambridge waving from Buckingham Palace balcony — 7·25 7·25

MS4074 100×90 mm. $3 Duchess of Cambridge (vert); $3 Prince William (vert) — 2·00 2·00

263 Village Weaver (*Ploceus cucullatus*)

2011. Birds of the World. Multicoloured.

MS4075 150×101 mm. $2.50×4 Type **263**; Belted kingfisher (*Megaceryle alcyon*); Scarlet tanager (*Piranga olivacea*); Semipalmated plover (*Charadrius semipalmatus*) — 6·00 6·00

MS4076 150×101 mm. $2.50×4 Troupial (*Icterus icterus*); Green-throated carib (*Eulampus holosericeus*); Osprey (*Pandion haliaetus*); Green heron (*Butorides virescens*) — 6·00 6·00

MS4077 101×70 mm. $6 Rose-breasted grosbeak (*Pheucticus ludovicianus*) — 3·75 3·75

MS4078 101×70 mm. $6 Merlin (*Falco columbarius*) — 3·75 3·75

264 Dragon

2011. Chinese New Year. Year of the Dragon. Sheet 71×70 mm

MS4079 **264** $8 multicoloured — 5·00 5·00

265 Annunciation (Niccolo di Pietro Gerini)

2011. Christmas. Multicoloured.

4080	25c. Type **265**	20	20
4081	50c. *The Annunciation* (Melchior Broederlam)	30	30
4082	$1 *Coronation of the Virgin* (Giovanni da Milano)	60	60
4083	$2 *Madonna* (André Beauneveu)	1·25	1·25

266 Rat

2011. Lunar New Year. Multicoloured.

MS4084 65c.×12 Type **266**; Ox; Tiger; Rabbit; Dragon; Snake; Horse; Sheep; Monkey; Rooster; Dog; Boar — 4·50 4·50

267 Pipa

2011. China 2011 27th Asian International Stamp Exhibition, Wuxi, China. Traditional Musical Instruments. Multicoloured.

MS4085 160×90 mm. $2×5 Type **267**; Guqin; Dizi; Yangqin; Dagu — 3·25 3·25

MS4086 100×100 mm. $6 Erhu (30×80 mm) — 3·75 3·75

268 *Coltriciella navispora*

2011. Mushrooms of the Caribbean. Multicoloured.

MS4087 181×111 mm. $2×6 Type **268**; *Tylopilus rufonigricans*; *Chroogomphus rutilus*; *Entoloma rugosostriatum*; *Xerocomus amazonicus*; *Coltricia oblectabilis* — 7·50 7·50

MS4088 140×81 mm. $2.50×4 *Tylopilus exiguus*; *Mycena acicula*; *Panaeolus papilionaceus*; *Chroogomphus ochraceus* — 6·00 6·00

MS4089 99×70 mm. $6 *Amanita calochroa* — 3·75 3·75

MS4090 100×70 mm. $6 *Psilocybe cubensis* — 3·75 3·75

269 Giant Ditch Frog (*Leptodactylus fallax*)

2012. Reptiles and Frogs of the Caribbean. Multicoloured.

MS4091 150×100 mm. $3.50×4 Type **269**; Coqui Antillano (*Eleutherodactylus johnstonei*); Gounouj (*Eleutherodactylus amplinympha*); Tink frog (*Eleutherodactylus martinicensis*) — 9·00 9·00

MS4092 150×100 mm. $3.50×4 Puerto Rican crested anole (*Anolis cristatellus cristatellus*); Tropical house gecko (*Hemidactylus mabouia*); Dominican ground lizard (*Ameiva fuscata*); Eyed anole (*Anolis oculatus*) — 9·00 9·00

MS4093 100×70 mm. $9 Red-footed tortoise (*Chelonoidis carbonaria*) — 6·00 6·00

MS4094 100×70 mm. $9 Lesser Antillean iguana (*Iguana delicatissima*) — 6·00 6·00

270 Great Hammerhead (*Sphyrna mokarran*)

2012. Sharks. Multicoloured.
MS4095 $3×5 Type **270**; Reef Shark (*Carcharhinus perezii*); Longfin mako shark (*Isurus paucus*); Lemon shark (*Negaprion brevirostris*); Great white shark (*Carcharodon carcharias*) ... 11·00 11·00

271 Pres. John F. Kennedy

2012. 50th Anniv of Pres. John F. Kennedy's Speech announcing Goal of Reaching the Moon. Multicoloured.
MS4096 140×190 mm. $3.50×4 Type **271**; Pres. Kennedy with John Glenn inspecting the space capsule Friendship 7, Cape Canaveral, 16 November 1963; Apollo NASA emblem; Buzz Aldrin on Moon, 1969 ... 10·00 10·00
MS4097 70×100 mm. $9 John Kennedy and NASA officials standing under Saturn I booster on its launch pad, Cape Canaveral, 16 November 1963 (30×50 mm) ... 8·00 8·00

272 Pope Benedict XVI

2012. 85th Birthday of Pope Benedict XVI. Multicoloured.
MS4098 150×150 mm. $3×4 Type **272**; Pope Benedict XVI with hands clasped; Pope Benedict XVI (side view); Wearing mitre and holding staff ... 8·50 8·50
MS4099 160×70 mm. $3.50×4 Pope Benedict XVI with right arm raised; Facing right; Behind microphone, speaking; In close-up (all 35×35 mm) ... 10·00 10·00
MS4100 100×101 mm. $9 Pope Benedict XVI ... 6·50 6·50

273 John F. Kennedy

2013. 50th Death Anniv of John Fitzgerald Kennedy (1917-63, US President 1961-3). Multicoloured.
MS4101 146×199 mm. $2.50×6 Type **273**; John Kennedy with family members; Sitting at desk, reaching out; Behind microphone, speaking; Seated in chair; At lectern, speaking ... 10·00 10·00
MS4102 70×100 mm. $9 John Kennedy, looking down (vert) ... 6·50 6·50

274 Dusky Dolphin (*Lagenorhynchus obscurus*)

2013. Dolphins. Multicoloured.
MS4103 150×110 mm. $2.75×6 Type **274**; Indo-Pacific Humpback Dolphin (*Sousa chinensis chinensis*); Commerson's Dolphin (*Cephalorhynchus commersoni*); Hector's Dolphin (*Cephalorhynchus hectori*); Atlantic Spotted Dolphin (*Stenella frontalis*); Striped Dolphin (*Stenella coeruleoalba*) ... 11·50 11·50
MS4104 100×70 mm. $9 Spinner Dolphin (*Stenella longirostris*) ... 6·50 6·50

275 'The Investigation on the RMS *Titanic* Begins'

2013. Centenary of the Sinking of the *Titanic*. Multicoloured.
MS4105 120×150 mm. $3.50×4 Type **275**; RMS *Titanic*; RMS *Titanic* hitting iceberg; RMS *Titanic* at night with lights in portholes ... 10·00 10·00
MS4106 100×100 mm. $9 Newspaper vendor and headline 'How the *Titanic* Went Down' (30×50 mm) ... 6·50 6·50

276 Princess Diana

2013. 15th Death Anniv of Princess Diana. Multicoloured.
MS4107 100×165 mm. $3.50×4 Type **276**; Princess Diana wearing tiara and patterned dress; Wearing black and white check dress; Wearing pale mauve jacket ... 10·00 10·00
MS4108 75×100 mm. $9 Princess Diana looking to left and upwards ... 6·50 6·50

277 Pygmy Right Whale (*Caperea marginata*)

2013. Whales. Multicoloured.
MS4109 100×150 mm. $3.50×4 Type **277**; Gray Whale (*Eschrichtius robustus*); Pygmy Killer Whale (*Feresa attenuata*); Bowhead Whale (*Balaena mysticetus*) ... 10·00 10·00
MS4110 70×100 mm. $9 Humpback Whale (*Megaptera novaeangliae*) ... 6·50 6·50

278 Elvis Presley (*Crying in the Chapel*, 1960)

2013. Elvis Presley Classic Hits. Multicoloured.
MS4111 $9 Type **278** ... 6·50 6·50
MS4112 $9 Elvis Presley (purple frame) (*Please Don't Drag That String Around*, 1964) ... 6·50 6·50
MS4113 $9 Elvis Presley wearing stetson, standing by corral (black frame) (*Follow That Dream*, 1962) ... 6·50 6·50
MS4114 $9 Elvis Presley facing microphone singing (red frame) (*You Don't Know Me*, 1968) ... 6·50 6·50
MS4115 $9 Elvis Presley seated (red frame) (*Love Letters*, 1966) ... 6·50 6·50

279 Coronation Portrait

2013. Diamond Jubilee. Multicoloured.
MS4116 150×100 mm. $3.25×4 Type **279**; Queen Elizabeth II wearing tiara and fur-trimmed robe, c. 1965; Queen Elizabeth II wearing diadem, c. 1952; Queen Elizabeth II wearing blue dress, c. 1970 ... 9·25 9·25
MS4117 71×100 mm. $9 Queen Elizabeth II wearing diadem, c. 1952 ... 6·50 6·50

OFFICIAL STAMPS

1982. Optd **P.R.G.** (a) Nos. 400/12 and 414.

O1	5c.	Yellow-tailed snapper	10	20
O2	6c.	Mutton snapper	10	20
O3	10c.	Cocoa damselfish	10	20
O4	12c.	Royal gramma	10	20
O5	15c.	Cherub angelfish	10	20
O6	20c.	Black-barred soldierfish	10	20
O7	25c.	Mottled grouper	10	20
O8	30c.	Long-snouted butterflyfish	15	20
O9	40c.	Puddingwife	15	25
O10	50c.	Midnight parrotfish	20	30
O11	90c.	Redspotted hawkfish	40	55
O12	$1	Hogfish	40	60
O13	$3	Beau Gregory	1·25	2·50
O14	$10	Barred hamlet	4·25	6·50

(b) Nos. 444/6 and 448/9.

O15	30c.	Prince Charles and Lady Diana Spencer	2·00	2·00
O16	40c.	Prince Charles and Lady Diana Spencer	1·60	1·60
O17	40c.	Type **50**	2·00	2·75
O18	$2	Type **50**	2·50	3·50
O19	$4	Prince Charles as parachutist	6·50	8·50

(c) Nos. 473/6.

O20	**54**	20c. multicoloured	10	20
O21	-	40c. multicoloured	15	25
O22	-	$1 multicoloured	35	70
O23	-	$2 multicoloured	70	1·60

Pt. 1

GRENADINES OF ST VINCENT

Part of a group of Islands south of St. Vincent that include Bequia, Mustique, Canouan and Union.

100 cents = 1 dollar.

1973. Royal Wedding. As T 101a of Gibraltar. Multicoloured. Background colours given.

1		25c. green	10	10
2		$1 brown	15	15

1974. Nos. 286/300 of St. Vincent optd GRENADINES OF.

3		1c. Green-backed heron ("Green Heron")	10	10
4		2c. Lesser Antillean bullfinches ("Bullfinch")	15	15
25		3c. St. Vincent amazon ("St. Vincent Parrot")	25	30
6		4c. Rufous-throated solitaire ("Soufriere Bird") (vert)	10	10
7		5c. Red-necked pigeon ("Ramier") (vert)	10	10
8		6c. Bananaquits	10	10
9		8c. Purple-throated carib ("Humming Bird")	10	10
10		10c. Mangrove cuckoo (vert)	10	10
11		12c. Common black hawk ("Black Hawk") (vert)	20	15
12		20c. Bare-eyed thrush	20	20
13		25c. Lesser Antillean tanager ("Prince")	20	20
14		50c. Blue hooded euphonia	30	40
15		$1 Barn owl (vert)	60	75
16		$2.50 Yellow-bellied elaenia ("Crested Elaenia") (vert)	60	1·00
17		$5 Ruddy quail dove	80	1·75

2 Map of Bequia

1974. Maps (1st series).

18	**2**	5c. black, green & deep green	10	10
19	-	15c. multicoloured	10	10
20	-	20c. multicoloured	10	10
21	-	30c. black, pink and red	10	10
22	-	40c. black, violet and purple	10	10
23	-	$1 black, ultramarine and blue	20	20

MAPS: 15c. Prune Island; 20c. Mayreau Island and Tobago Cays; 30c. Mustique Island; 40c. Union Island; $1 Canouan Island.
See also Nos. 85/8.

3a U.P.U. Emblem

1974. Centenary of U.P.U. Multicoloured.

26		2c. Type **3a**	10	10
27		15c. Globe within posthorn	10	10
28		40c. Map of St. Vincent and hand-cancelling	10	10
29		$1 Map of the World	25	15

4 Boat-building

1974. Bequia Island (1st series). Multicoloured.

31		30c. Careening at Port Elizabeth	10	15
32		35c. Admiralty Bay	10	15
33		$1 Fishing-boat race	15	25
34		5c. Type **4**	10	15

See also Nos. 185/88.

5 Music Volute

1974. Shells and Molluscs. Multicoloured.

35A		1c. American thorny oyster	10	10
36A		2c. Zigzag scallop	10	10
37A		3c. Reticulated cowrie-helmet	10	10
38A		4c. Type **5**	10	10
39A		5c. Amber pen shell	10	10
40A		6c. Angular triton	10	10
41A		8c. Flame helmet	10	10
42A		10c. Caribbean olive	10	10
43A		12c. American or common sundial	10	10
44A		15c. Glory of the Atlantic cone	25	20
45B		20c. Flame auger	30	20
46A		25c. King venus	50	20
47A		35c. Long-spined star shell	35	25
48A		45c. Speckled tellin	35	30
49A		50c. Rooster-tail conch	40	25
50B		$1 Green star shell	60	60
51A		$2.50 Antillean or incomparable cone	60	75
52A		$5 Rough file clam	75	80
52cA		$10 Measled cowrie	3·50	1·00

Nos. 38/42, 45, 47 and 49/50 come with and without an imprint below the design.

1974. Birth Centenary of Sir Winston Churchill. As Nos. 403/6 of St. Vincent, but inscr "GRENADINES OF ST. VINCENT" and values (Nos. 53/5) and colours changed.

53	**75**	5c. multicoloured	10	15
54	-	40c. multicoloured	10	15
55	-	50c. multicoloured	10	15
56	-	$1 multicoloured	20	50

6 Cotton House, Mustique

1975. Mustique Island. Multicoloured.

57		5c. Type **6**	10	10
58		35c. "Blue Waters", Endeavour Bay	10	10
59		45c. Endeavour Bay	10	10
60		$1 "Les Jolies Eaux", Gelliceaux Bay	25	20

7 *Danaus plexippus*

1975. Butterflies. Multicoloured.

61		3c. Type **7**	20	10
62		5c. *Agraulis vanillae*	20	10
63		35c. *Battus polydamas*	35	10
64		45c. *Evenus dindymus* and *Junonia evarete*	35	10
65		$1 *Anartia jatrophae*	60	45

8 Resort Pavilion

1975. Petit St. Vincent. Multicoloured.

66		5c. Type **8**	10	10
67		35c. The Harbour	10	20

68	45c. The Jetty	15	20
69	$1 Sailing in coral lagoon	50	1·10

9 Ecumenical Church, Mustique

1975. Christmas. Multicoloured.

70	5c. Type **9**	10	10
71	25c. Catholic Church, Union Island	10	10
72	50c. Catholic Church, Bequia	10	10
73	$1 Anglican Church, Bequia	25	15

10 Sunset Scene

1976. Union Island (1st series). Multicoloured.

74	5c. Type **10**	10	25
75	35c. Customs and Post Office, Clifton	10	20
76	45c. Anglican Church, Ashton	10	20
77	$1 Mail schooner, Clifton Harbour	25	1·00

See also Nos. 242/5.

11 Staghorn Coral

1976. Corals. Multicoloured.

78	5c. Type **11**	10	10
79	35c. Elkhorn coral	20	10
80	45c. Pillar coral	20	10
81	$1 Brain coral	40	20

12 25c. Bicentennial Coin

1976. Bicentenary of American Revolution.

82	**12** 25c. silver, black and blue	10	10
83	- 50c. silver, black and red	20	10
84	- $1 silver, black and mauve	25	20

DESIGNS: 50c. Half-dollar coin; $1 One dollar coin.

1976. Maps (2nd series). As T **2**.

85	5c. black, deep green and green	15	15
86	10c. black, green and blue	15	10
87	35c. black, brown and red	30	20
88	45c. black, red and orange	30	25

Nos. 85/8 exist in 7 different designs to each value as follows: A, Bequia, B, Canouan, C, Mayreau, D, Mustique, E, Petit St. Vincent, F, Prune, G, Union. To indicate any particular design use the appropriate catalogue No. together with the suffix for the island concerned.

13 Station Hill School and Post Office

1977. Mayreau Island. Multicoloured.

89	5c. Type **13**	10	10
90	35c. Church at Old Wall	10	10
91	45c. La Sourciere Anchorage	20	10
92	$1 Saline Bay	35	15

14 Coronation Crown Coin

1977. Silver Jubilee. Multicoloured.

93	25c. Type **14**	15	15
94	50c. Silver Wedding crown	20	10
95	$1 Silver Jubilee crown	20	15

15 Fiddler Crab

1977. Crustaceans. Multicoloured.

96	5c. Type **15**	15	15
97	35c. Ghost crab	25	15
98	50c. Blue crab	30	20
99	$1.25 Spiny lobster	60	90

16 Snorkel Diving

1977. Prune Island. Multicoloured.

100	5c. Type **16**	15	10
101	35c. Palm Island Resort	20	15
102	45c. Casuarina Beach	20	15
103	$1 Palm Island Beach Club	60	1·10

17 Mustique Island

1977. Royal Visit. Surch as in T **17**.

104	**17**	40c. turquoise and green	20	10
105	**17**	$2 ochre and brown	45	25

18 The Clinic, Charlestown

1977. Canouan Island (1st series). Multicoloured.

106	5c. Type **18**	10	15
107	35c. Town jetty, Charlestown	30	15
108	45c. Mail schooner arriving at Charlestown	35	15
109	$1 Grand Bay	40	1·00

See also Nos. 307/10.

19 Tropical Mockingbird

1978. Birds and their Eggs. Multicoloured.

110	1c. Type **19**	10	60
111	2c. Mangrove cuckoo	15	60
112	3c. Osprey	20	60
113	4c. Smooth-billed ani	20	60
114	5c. House wren	20	40
115	6c. Bananaquit	20	40
116	8c. Carib grackle	20	45
117	10c. Yellow-bellied elaenia	20	45
118	12c. Collared plover	30	1·25
119	15c. Cattle egret	30	45
120	20c. Red-footed booby	30	45
121	25c. Red-billed tropic bird	30	45
122	40c. Royal tern	45	1·00
123	50c. Grenada flycatcher ("Rusty-tailed Flycatcher")	45	1·00
124	80c. American purple gallinule ("Purple Gallinule")	70	1·00
125	$1 Broad-winged hawk	75	1·00
126	$2 Scaly-breasted ground dove ("Common Ground Dove")	75	1·60
127	$3 Laughing gull	1·00	1·75
128	$5 Common noddy ("Brown Noddy")	1·00	1·75
129	$10 Grey kingbird	1·25	2·25

19a Worcester Cathedral

1978. 25th Anniv of Coronation. British Cathedrals. Multicoloured.

130	5c. Type **19a**	10	10
131	40c. Coventry Cathedral	10	10
132	$1 Winchester Cathedral	15	20
133	$3 Chester Cathedral	25	45
MS134	130×102 mm. Nos. 130/3	45	80

20 Green Turtle

1978. Turtles. Multicoloured.

135	5c. Type **20**	10	10
136	40c. Hawksbill turtle	15	10
137	50c. Leatherback turtle	15	10
138	$1.25 Loggerhead turtle	40	40

21 Three Kings following Star

1978. Christmas. Scenes and Verses from the Carol *We Three Kings*. Multicoloured.

139	5c. Type **21**	10	10
140	10c. King presenting gold	10	10
141	25c. King presenting frankincense	10	10
142	50c. King presenting myrrh	10	10
143	$2 Kings paying homage to infant Jesus	30	20
MS144	154×175 mm. Nos. 139/43	70	1·25

22 Sailing Yachts

1979. National Regatta.

145	**22**	5c. multicoloured	10	10
146	-	40c. multicoloured	20	10
147	-	50c. multicoloured	25	10
148	-	$2 multicoloured	75	60

DESIGNS: 40c. to $2, Various sailing yachts.

22a Green Iguana

1979. Wildlife. Multicoloured.

149	20c. Type **22a**	10	25
150	40c. Common opossum ("Manicou")	15	25
151	$2 Red-legged tortoise	60	1·10

22b Sir Rowland Hill

1979. Death Centenary of Sir Rowland Hill. Multicoloured.

152	80c. Type **22b**	15	15
153	$1 Great Britain 1d. and 4d. stamps of 1858 with "A10" (Kingstown, St. Vincent) postmark	15	25
154	$2 St. Vincent ½d. and 1d. stamps of 1894 with Bequia postmark	25	40
MS155	165×115 mm. Nos. 124/6 and 152/4	1·40	2·50

22c Young Child

1979. International Year of the Child. Designs showing portraits of young children.

156	**22c** 6c. black, silver and blue	10	10
157	- 40c. black, silver & salmon	10	10
158	- $1 black, silver and buff	15	15
159	- $3 black, silver and lilac	45	30

22d National Flag and "Ixora salicifolia" (flower)

1979. Independence. Multicoloured.

160	5c. Type **22d**	10	10
161	40c. House of Assembly and *Ixora odorata* (flower)	10	10
162	$1 Prime Minister R. Milton Cato and *Ixora javanica* (flower)	20	20

23 False Killer Whale

1980. Whales and Dolphins. Multicoloured.

163	10c. Type **23**	45	30
164	50c. Spinner dolphin	45	35
165	90c. Bottle-nosed dolphin	50	80
166	$2 Short-finned pilot whale ("Blackfish")	1·25	2·25

23a Queen Elizabeth II

1980. "London 1980" International Stamp Exhibition. Multicoloured.

167	40c. Type **23a**	10	15
168	50c. St. Vincent 2c. stamp of 1965	15	15
169	$3 First Grenadines stamps	40	1·25
MS170	165×115 mm. Nos. 122/3, 127 and 167/9	2·00	2·50

23b Running

1980. Sport. Multicoloured.

171	25c. Type **23b**	10	10
172	50c. Sailing	10	10
173	$1 Long-jumping	20	20
174	$2 Swimming	30	30

1980. Hurricane Relief. Nos. 171/4 optd **HURRICANE RELIEF 50c.**

175	**22** 25c.+50c. multicoloured	10	30
176	- 50c.+50c. multicoloured	15	40
177	- $1+50c. multicoloured	20	50
178	- $2+50c. multicoloured	30	70

24 Scene and Verse from the Carol *De Borning Day*

1980. Christmas. Multicoloured.

179	5c. Type **24**	10	10
180	50c. "Mary and de Baby lonely"	10	10
181	60c. "Mary and de Baby weary"	10	10
182	$1 "Mary and de Baby rest easy"	15	15
183	$2 "Star above shine in de sky"	25	25
MS184	159×178 mm. Nos. 179/83	50	1·40

25 Post Office, Port Elizabeth

1981. Bequia Island (2nd series). Multicoloured.

185	50c. Type **25**	15	20
186	60c. Moonhole	15	20
187	$1.50 Fishing boats, Admiralty Bay	30	55
188	$2 "The Friendship Rose" (yacht) at jetty	50	70

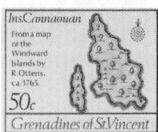

26 Ins. Cannaouan (from map of Windward Islands by R. Ottens, c. 1765)

1981. Details from Early Maps. Multicoloured.

189	50c. Type **26**	30	30
190	50c. Cannouan Is. (from chart by J. Parsons, 1861)	30	30
191	60c. Ins. Moustiques (from map of Windward Islands by R. Ottens, c. 1765)	30	35
192	60c. Mustique Is. (from chart by J. Parsons, 1861)	30	35
193	$2 Ins. Bequia (from map of Windward Islands by R. Ottens, c.1765)	50	75
194	$2 Bequia Is. (from map surveyed in 1763 by T. Jefferys)	50	75

26a Mary

1981. Royal Wedding. Royal Yachts. Multicoloured.

195	50c. Type **26a**	10	15
196	50c. Prince Charles and Lady Diana Spencer	35	40
197	$3 Alexandra	20	30
198	$3 As No. 196	60	90
199	$3.50 Britannia	25	35
200	$3.50 As No. 196	65	90
MS201	120×109 mm. $5 As No. 196	75	75

27 Bar Jack

1981. Game Fish. Multicoloured.

204	10c. Type **27**	15	10
205	50c. Tarpon	30	10
206	60c. Cobia	35	10
207	$2 Blue marlin	1·00	70

28 H.M.S. Experiment (frigate)

1982. Ships. Multicoloured.

208	1c. Type **28**	10	20
209	3c. Lady Nelson (cargo liner)	15	20
210	5c. Daisy (brig)	20	20
211	6c. Carib canoe	10	20
212	10c. Hairoun Star (freighter)	20	10
213	15c. Jupiter (liner)	40	10
214	20c. Christina (steam yacht)	40	10
215	25c. Orinoco (mail paddle-steamer)	40	15
216	30c. H.M.S. Lively (frigate)	40	15
217	50c. Alabama (Confederate warship)	50	30
218	60c. Denmark (freighter)	60	30
219	75c. Santa Maria	1·00	50
220	$1 Baffin (research vessel)	80	55

221	$2 Queen Elizabeth 2 (liner)	1·00	1·00
222	$3 R.Y. Britannia	1·00	1·50
223	$5 Geeststar (freighter)	1·00	1·75
224	$10 Grenadines Star (ferry)	1·25	4·00

29 Prickly Pear Fruit

1982. Prickly Pear Cactus. Multicoloured.

225	10c. Type **29**	15	15
226	50c. Prickly pear flower buds	35	35
227	$1 Flower of prickly pear cactus	60	60
228	$2 Prickly pear cactus	1·25	1·75

30 Anne Neville, Princess of Wales, 1470

1982. 21st Birthday of Princess of Wales. Multicoloured.

229	50c. Type **30**	10	15
230	60c. Coat of arms of Anne Neville	10	15
231	$6 Diana, Princess of Wales	60	80

31 Old and New Uniforms

1982. 75th Anniv of Boy Scout Movement. Multicoloured.

232	$1.50 Type **31**	50	75
233	$2.50 Lord Baden-Powell	60	1·00

1982. Birth of Prince William of Wales. Nos. 224/6 optd **ROYAL BABY** and Island name.

234	50c. Type **30**	10	15
235	60c. Coat of arms of Anne Neville	10	15
236	$6 Diana, Princess of Wales	60	80

Nos. 229/32 exist optd with 5 different island names as follows: A, Bequia, B, Canouan, C, Mayreau, D, Mustique, E, Union Island. To indicate any particular overprint use the appropriate catalogue No. together with the suffix for the island concerned.

33 Silhouette Figures of Mary and Joseph

1982. Christmas. Silhouette of figures. Multicoloured.

237	10c. Type **33**	10	10
238	$1.50 Animals in stable	45	45
239	$2.50 Mary and Joseph with baby Jesus	60	60
MS240	168×99 mm. Nos. 237/9	1·00	2·00

1983. No. 123 surch **45c.**

241	45c. on 50c. Grenada flycatcher	55	30

35 Power Station, Clifton

1983. Union Island (2nd issue). Multicoloured.

242	50c. Type **35**	25	15
243	60c. Sunrise, Clifton harbour	25	15
244	$1.50 Junior Secondary School, Ashton	60	40
245	$2 Frigate Rock and Conch Shell Beach	85	55

36 British Man-of-war

1983. Bicentenary of Treaty of Versailles. Multicoloured.

246	45c. Type **36**	35	15
247	60c. American man-of-war	35	15
248	$1.50 Soldiers carrying U.S flags	75	45
249	$2 British troops in battle	80	55

37 Montgolfier Balloon, 1783

1983. Bicentenary of Manned Flight. Multicoloured.

250	45c. Type **37**	15	15
251	60c. Ayres Turbo Thrush Commander (horiz)	15	15
252	$1.50 Lebaudy-Juillot airship No. 1 La Jaune (horiz)	40	45
253	$2 Space shuttle "Columbia" (horiz)	40	55
MS254	110×145 mm. Nos. 250/3	1·00	1·50

38 Coat of Arms of Henry VIII

1983. Leaders of the World. British Monarchs. Multicoloured.

255	60c. Type **38**	10	25
256	60c. Henry VIII	10	25
257	60c. Coat of Arms of James I	10	25
258	60c. James I	10	25
259	75c. Henry VIII at Hampton Court	10	25
260	75c. Hampton Court	10	25
261	75c. James I at Edinburgh Castle	10	25
262	75c. Edinburgh Castle	10	25
263	$2.50 The Mary Rose	25	35
264	$2.50 Henry VIII and Portsmouth harbour	25	35
265	$2.50 Gunpowder Plot	25	35
266	$2.50 James I and Gunpowder Plot	25	35

39 Quarter Dollar and Half Dollar, 1797

1983. Old Coinage. Multicoloured.

267	20c. Type **39**	10	10
268	45c. Nine Bitts, 1811–14	15	15
269	75c. Twelve Bitts and Six Bitts, 1811–14	25	25
270	$3 Sixty-six Shillings, 1798	80	80

40 Class D13

1984. Leaders of the World. Railway Locomotives (1st series). The first design in each pair shows technical drawings and the second the locomotive at work.

271	5c. multicoloured	10	10
272	5c. multicoloured	10	10
273	10c. multicoloured	10	10
274	10c. multicoloured	10	10
275	15c. multicoloured	10	15

276	15c. multicoloured	10	15
277	35c. multicoloured	10	20
278	35c. multicoloured	10	20
279	45c. multicoloured	10	20
280	45c. multicoloured	10	20
281	60c. multicoloured	15	20
282	60c. multicoloured	15	20
283	$1 multicoloured	15	25
284	$1 multicoloured	15	25
285	$2.50 multicoloured	25	35
286	$2.50 multicoloured	25	35

DESIGNS: Nos. 271/2, Class D13, U.S.A., 1892 (Type **40**); 273/4, High Speed Train 125, Great Britain (1980); 275/6, Class T9, Great Britain (1899); 277/8, Claud Hamilton, Great Britain (1900); 279/80, Class J, U.S.A. (1941); 281/2, Class D16, U.S.A. (1895); 283/4, Lode Star, Great Britain (1907); 285/6, Blue Peter, Great Britain (1948).
See also Nos. 321/26, 351/8, 390/7, 412/9, 443/58, 504/19 and 520/35.

41 Spotted Eagle Ray

1984. Reef Fish. Multicoloured.

287	45c. Type **41**	25	20
288	60c. Queen triggerfish	25	35
289	$1.50 White spotted filefish	40	1·25
290	$2 Schoolmaster	40	1·50

42 R. A. Woolmer

1984. Leaders of the World. Cricketers (1st series). The first design in each pair shows a portrait and the second the cricketer in action.

291	1c. multicoloured	10	10
292	1c. multicoloured	10	10
293	3c. multicoloured	10	10
294	3c. multicoloured	10	10
295	5c. multicoloured	10	10
296	5c. multicoloured	10	10
297	30c. multicoloured	30	30
298	30c. multicoloured	30	30
299	60c. multicoloured	40	40
300	60c. multicoloured	40	40
301	$1 multicoloured	40	40
302	$1 multicoloured	40	40
303	$2 multicoloured	45	70
304	$2 multicoloured	45	70
305	$3 multicoloured	55	80
306	$3 multicoloured	55	80

DESIGNS: Nos. 291/2, R. A. Woolmer (Type **42**); K. S. Ranjitsinhji; 295/6, W. R. Hammond; 297/8, D. L. Underwood; 299/300, W. G. Grace; 301/2, E. A. E. Baptiste; 303/4, A. P. E. Knott; 305/6, L. E. G. Ames.
See also Nos. 331/8 and 364/9.

43 Junior Secondary School

1984. Canouan Island (2nd series). Multicoloured.

307	35c. Type **43**	20	20
308	45c. Police Station	50	25
309	$1 Post Office	50	55
310	$3 Anglican Church	1·00	1·75

1984. Leaders of the World. Railway Locomotives (2nd issue). As T **40**. The first design in each pair shows technical drawings and the second the locomotive at work.

311	1c. multicoloured	10	10
312	1c. multicoloured	10	10
313	5c. multicoloured	10	10
314	5c. multicoloured	10	10
315	20c. multicoloured	15	15
316	20c. multicoloured	15	15
317	35c. multicoloured	15	15
318	35c. multicoloured	15	15
319	60c. multicoloured	25	25
320	60c. multicoloured	25	25
321	$1 multicoloured	25	30
322	$1 multicoloured	25	30
323	$1.50 multicoloured	30	40
324	$1.50 multicoloured	30	40
325	$3 multicoloured	35	55
326	$3 multicoloured	35	55

DESIGNS: Nos. 311/12, Class C62, Japan (1948); 313/14, Class V, Great Britain (1903); 315/16, Richard Trevithick's *Catch-Me-Who-Can*, Great Britain (1808); 317/18, Class E10, Japan (1948); 319/20, *J. B. Earle*, Great Britain (1904); 321/2, No. 762 *Lyn*, Great Britain (1898); 323/4, *Talyllyn*, Great Britain (1865); 325/6, *Cardean*, Great Britain (1906).

44 Lady of the Night

1984. Night-blooming Flowers. Multicoloured.

327	35c. Type **44**	30	30
328	45c. Four o'clock	35	35
329	75c. Mother-in-law's tongue	45	60
330	$3 Queen of the night	1·10	2·75

1984. Leaders of the World. Cricketers (2nd series). As T **42**. The first in each pair listed shows a head portrait and the second the cricketer in action.

331	5c. multicoloured	10	10
332	5c. multicoloured	10	10
333	30c. multicoloured	25	20
334	30c. multicoloured	25	20
335	$1 multicoloured	35	40
336	$1 multicoloured	35	40
337	$2.50 multicoloured	45	80
338	$2.50 multicoloured	45	80

DESIGNS: Nos. 331/2, S. F. Barnes; 333/4, R. Peel; 335/6, H. Larwood; 337/8, Sir John Hobbs.

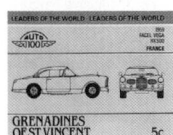

45 Facel "Vega HK500"

1984. Leaders of the World. Automobiles (1st series). The first design in each pair shows technical drawings and the second paintings.

339	5c. black, blue and green	10	10
340	5c. multicoloured	10	10
341	25c. black, lilac and pink	10	10
342	25c. multicoloured	10	10
343	50c. black, blue and orange	15	15
344	50c. multicoloured	15	15
345	$3 black, stone and brown	30	45
346	$3 multicoloured	30	45

DESIGNS: Nos. 339/40, Facel "Vega HK500" (Type **45**); 341/2, BMW "328"; 343/4, Frazer-Nash "TT Replica 1.5L"; 345/6, Buick "Roadmaster Riviera".
See also Nos. 378/85 and 431/42.

46 Three Wise Men and Star

1984. Christmas. Multicoloured.

347	20c. Type **46**	10	10
348	45c. Journeying to Bethlehem	15	25
349	$3 Presenting gifts	70	1·40
MS350	177×107 mm. Nos. 347/9	1·00	2·00

1985. Leaders of the World. Railway Locomotives (3rd series). As T **40**. The first in each pair shows technical drawings and the second the locomotive at work.

351	1c. multicoloured	10	10
352	1c. multicoloured	10	10
353	15c. multicoloured	10	10
354	15c. multicoloured	10	10
355	75c. multicoloured	20	25
356	75c. multicoloured	20	25
357	$3 multicoloured	50	70
358	$3 multicoloured	50	70
MS359	142×122 mm. Nos. 355/8	1·75	6·50

DESIGNS: Nos. 351/2, P.L.M. *Grosse C*, France (1898); 353/4, Class C12, Japan (1932); 355/6, Class D50, Japan (1923); 357/8, *Fire Fly*, Great Britain (1840).

47 Caribbean King Crab

1985. Shell Fish. Multicoloured.

360	25c. Type **47**	20	15
361	60c. Queen or pink conch	30	35
362	$1 White sea urchin	35	60
363	$3 West Indian top shell or wilk	75	2·00

1985. Leaders of the World. Cricketers (3rd series). As T **42** (55, 60c.) the first in each pair showing a head portrait and the second the cricketer in action, or horiz designs showing teams ($2).

364	55c. multicoloured	25	35
365	55c. multicoloured	25	35
366	60c. multicoloured	25	40
367	60c. multicoloured	25	40
368	$2 multicoloured	40	85
369	$2 multicoloured	40	85

DESIGNS—VERT (As T **42**): Nos. 364/5 M. D. Moxon; 366/7, L. Potter. HORIZ (59×42 mm): No. 368, Kent team; 369, Yorkshire team.

48 *Cypripedium calceolus*

1985. Leaders of the World. Flowers. Multicoloured.

370	5c. Type **48**	10	10
371	5c. *Gentiana asclepiadea*	10	10
372	55c. *Clianthus formosus*	15	20
373	55c. *Clemisia coriacea*	15	20
374	60c. *Erythronium americanum*	15	20
375	60c. *Laelia anceps*	15	20
376	$2 *Leucadendron discolor*	35	50
377	$2 *Meconopsis horridula*	35	50

1985. Leaders of the World. Automobiles (2nd series). As T **45**. The first in each pair shows technical drawings and the second paintings.

378	5c. black, yellow and blue	10	10
379	5c. multicoloured	10	10
380	60c. black, yellow and orange	15	15
381	60c. multicoloured	15	15
382	$1 black, green and blue	15	20
383	$1 multicoloured	15	20
384	$1.50 black, blue and green	15	25
385	$1.50 multicoloured	15	25

DESIGNS: Nos. 378/9, Winton (1903); 380/1, Invicta 4½ litre (1932); 382/3, Daimler "SP250 Dart" (1959); 384/5, Brabham "Repco BT19" (1966).

49 Windsurfing

1985. Tourism. Watersports. Multicoloured.

386	35c. Type **49**	15	15
387	45c. Water-skiing	15	15
388	75c. Scuba-diving	15	25
389	$3 Deep-sea game fishing	30	1·40

1985. Leaders of the World. Railway Locomotives (4th series). As T **40**. The first in each pair shows technical drawings and the second the locomotive at work.

390	10c. multicoloured	10	10
391	10c. multicoloured	10	10
392	40c. multicoloured	20	20
393	40c. multicoloured	20	20
394	50c. multicoloured	20	20
395	50c. multicoloured	20	20
396	$2.50 multicoloured	70	80
397	$2.50 multicoloured	70	80

DESIGNS: Nos. 390/1, Class 581 electric train, Japan (1968); 392/3, 231-132BT, Algeria (1936); 394/5, *Slieve Gullion*, Ireland (1913); 396/7, Class *Beattie* well tank, Great Britain (1874).

50 Passion Fruits and Blossom

1985. Fruits and Blossoms. Multicoloured.

398	30c. Type **50**	15	20
399	75c. Guava	25	40
400	$1 Sapodilla	35	55
401	$2 Mango	50	1·10
MS402	145×120 mm. Nos. 398/401	2·00	2·25

51 Queen Elizabeth, the Queen Mother

1985. Leaders of the World. Life and Times of Queen Elizabeth, the Queen Mother. Various vertical portraits.

403	**51**	40c. multicoloured	10	20
404	-	40c. multicoloured	10	20
405	-	75c. multicoloured	15	20
406	-	75c. multicoloured	15	20
407	-	$1.10 multicoloured	15	20
408	-	$1.10 multicoloured	15	20
409	-	$1.75 multicoloured	15	30
410	-	$1.75 multicoloured	15	30
MS411	85×114 mm. $2 multicoloured; $2 multicoloured		50	1·50

Each value, issued in pairs, shows a floral pattern across the bottom of the portraits which stops short of the left-hand edge on the first stamp and of the right-hand edge on the second.

1985. Leaders of the World. Railway Locomotives (5th series). As T **40**. The first design in each pair shows technical drawings and the second the locomotive at work.

412	35c. multicoloured	15	20
413	35c. multicoloured	15	20
414	70c. multicoloured	20	30
415	70c. multicoloured	20	30
416	$1.20 multicoloured	30	40
417	$1.20 multicoloured	30	40
418	$2 multicoloured	40	65
419	$2 multicoloured	40	65

DESIGNS: Nos. 412/13, *Coronation*, Great Britain (1937); 414/15, Class E18, Germany (1935); 416/17, Hayes type, U.S.A. (1854); 418/19, Class 2120, Japan (1890).

1985. Royal Visit. Nos. 199/200, 222, 287, 398 and 407/8 optd **CARIBBEAN ROYAL VISIT 1985** or surch also.

420	**50**	30c. multicoloured	80	1·50
421	**41**	45c. multicoloured	1·00	1·75
422	-	$1.10 multicoloured (No. 407)	1·75	4·00
423	-	$1.10 multicoloured (No. 408)	1·75	4·00
424	-	$1.50 on $3.50 mult (No. 199)	2·00	2·25
425	-	$1.50 on $3.50 mult (No. 200)	20·00	26·00
426	-	$3 multicoloured (No. 222)	2·75	3·75

52 Donkey Man

1985. Traditional Dances. Multicoloured.

427	50c. Type **52**	10	30
428	75c. Cake dance (vert)	15	40
429	$1 Bois-Bois man (vert)	15	55
430	$2 Maypole dance	25	1·10

1986. Leaders of the World. Automobiles (3rd series). As T **45**. The first in each pair shows technical drawings and the second paintings.

431	15c. black, lilac and mauve	10	10
432	15c. multicoloured	10	10
433	45c. black, yellow and brown	10	10
434	45c. multicoloured	10	10
435	60c. black, green and blue	10	25
436	60c. multicoloured	10	25
437	$1 black, brown and green	15	25
438	$1 multicoloured	15	25
439	$1.75 black, yellow and orange	15	35
440	$1.75 multicoloured	15	35
441	$3 multicoloured	25	45
442	$3 multicoloured	25	45

DESIGNS: Nos. 431/2, Mercedes-Benz 4.5 litre (1914); 433/4, Rolls Royce "Silver Wraith" (1954); 435/6, Lamborghini "Countach" (1974); 437/8, Marmon "V-16" (1932); 439/40, Lotus-Ford "49 B" (1968); 441/2, Delage 1.5 litre (1927).

1986. Leaders of the World. Railway Locomotives (6th series). As T **40**. The first in each pair shows technical drawings and the second the locomotive at work.

443	15c. multicoloured	15	10
444	15c. multicoloured	15	10
445	45c. multicoloured	20	20
446	45c. multicoloured	20	20
447	60c. multicoloured	20	30
448	60c. multicoloured	20	30
449	75c. multicoloured	20	35
450	75c. multicoloured	20	35
451	$1 multicoloured	25	40

452	$1 multicoloured	25	40
453	$1.50 multicoloured	25	50
454	$1.50 multicoloured	25	50
455	$2 multicoloured	30	65
456	$2 multicoloured	30	65
457	$3 multicoloured	30	80
458	$3 multicoloured	30	80

DESIGNS: Nos. 443/4, Class T15, Germany (1897); 445/6, Class 13, Great Britain (1900); 447/8, *Halesworth*, Great Britain (1879); 449/50, Class *Problem*, Great Britain (1859); 451/2, Class *Western* diesel, Great Britain (1961); 453/4, Drummond's *Bug*, Great Britain (1899); 455/6, Class *Clan*, Great Britain (1951); 457/8, Class 1800, Japan (1884).

52a Queen Elizabeth II

1986. 60th Birthday of Queen Elizabeth II. Multicoloured.

459	5c. Type **52a**	15	15
460	$1 At Princess Anne's christening, 1950	30	40
461	$4 Princess Elizabeth	60	1·25
462	$6 In Canberra, 1982 (vert)	75	1·50
MS463	85×115 mm. $8 Queen Elizabeth II (different)	1·50	4·50

53 Handmade Dolls

1986. Handicrafts. Multicoloured.

464	10c. Type **53**	10	10
465	60c. Basketwork	20	35
466	$1 Scrimshaw work	30	50
467	$3 Model sailing dinghy	80	2·25

54 Uruguayan Team

1986. World Cup Football Championship, Mexico. Multicoloured.

468	1c. Type **54**	10	10
469	10c. Polish team	10	10
470	45c. Bulgarian player (28×42 mm)	20	30
471	75c. Iraqi player (28×42 mm)	30	40
472	$1.50 South Korean player (28×42 mm)	50	90
473	$2 Northern Irish player (28×42 mm)	60	1·10
474	$4 Portuguese team	75	1·50
475	$5 Canadian team	75	1·50
MS476	Two sheets, 85×114 mm. (a) $1 As No. 474. (b) $3 Type **54**. Set of 2 sheets	1·50	2·75

55 *Marasmius pallescens*

1986. Fungi. Multicoloured.

477	45c. Type **55**	2·25	75
478	60c. *Leucocoprinus fragilissimus*	2·50	1·10
479	75c. *Hygrocybe occidentalis*	2·75	1·60
480	$3 *Xerocomus hypoxanthus*	8·00	7·00

GRENADINES OF ST. VINCENT

60c ROYAL WEDDING 1986

55a Miss Sarah Ferguson and Princess Diana applauding

1986. Royal Wedding (1st issue). Multicoloured.

481	60c. Type **55a**	20	30
482	60c. Prince Andrew at shooting match	20	30
483	$2 Prince Andrew and Miss Sarah Ferguson (horiz)	60	90
484	$2 Prince Charles with Prince Andrew, Princess Anne and Princess Margaret on balcony (horiz)	60	90
MS485	115×85 mm. $8 Duke and Duchess of York in carriage after wedding (horiz)	2·75	4·50

1986. Royal Wedding (2nd issue). Nos. 481/4 optd **Congratulations to T.R.H. The Duke & Duchess of York.**

486	60c. Miss Sarah Ferguson and Princess Diana applauding	30	65
487	60c. Prince Andrew at shooting match	30	65
488	$2 Prince Andrew and Miss Sarah Ferguson (horiz)	1·00	1·25
489	$2 Prince Charles, Prince Andrew, Princess Anne and Princess Margaret on balcony (horiz)	1·00	1·25

56 Brachymesia furcata

1986. Dragonflies. Multicoloured.

490	45c. Type **56**	25	20
491	60c. *Lepthemis vesiculosa*	30	40
492	75c. *Perithemis domitta*	30	45
493	$2.50 *Tramea abdominalis* (vert)	45	1·40

1986. Centenary of Statue of Liberty. Vert views of Statue as T **323a** of Grenada in seperate miniature sheets. Multicoloured.

MS494	Nine sheets, each 85×115 mm. $1.50; $1.75; $2; $2.50; $3; $3.50; $5; $6; $8. Set of 9 sheets	2·50	10·00

57 American Kestrel ("Sparrow Hawk")

1986. Birds of Prey. Multicoloured.

495	10c. Type **57**	75	45
496	45c. Common black hawk ("Black Hawk")	1·90	50
497	60c. Peregrine falcon ("Duck Hawk")	2·25	1·25
498	$4 Osprey ("Fish Hawk")	5·00	6·50

58 Santa playing Steel Band Drums

1986. Christmas. Multicoloured.

499	45c. Type **58**	30	30
500	60c. Santa windsurfing	35	35
501	$1.25 Santa skiing	60	85
502	$2 Santa limbo dancing	1·10	1·60
MS503	166×128 mm. Nos. 499/502	7·00	8·00

1987. Railway Locomotives (7th series). As T **40**. The first in each pair shows technical drawings and the second the locomotive at work.

504	10c. multicoloured	15	10
505	10c. multicoloured	15	10
506	40c. multicoloured	25	25
507	40c. multicoloured	25	25
508	50c. multicoloured	30	30
509	50c. multicoloured	30	30
510	60c. multicoloured	30	30
511	60c. multicoloured	30	30
512	75c. multicoloured	30	40
513	75c. multicoloured	30	40
514	$1 multicoloured	30	50
515	$1 multicoloured	30	50
516	$1.25 multicoloured	30	60
517	$1.25 multicoloured	30	60
518	$1.50 multicoloured	40	75
519	$1.50 multicoloured	40	75

DESIGNS: Nos. 504/5, Class 1001, No. 1275, Great Britain (1874); 506/7, Class 4P Garratt, Great Britain (1927); 508/9, *Papyrus*, Great Britain (1929); 510/11, Class VI, Great Britain (1930); 512/13, Class 40 diesel, No. D200, Great Britain (1958); 514/15, Class 42 *Warship* diesel, Great Britain (1958); 516/17, Class P-69, U.S.A. (1902); 518/19, Class 60-3 Shay, No. 15, U.S.A. (1913).

1987. Railway Locomotives (8th series). As T **40**. The first in each pair shows technical drawings and the second the locomotive at work.

520	10c. multicoloured	15	15
521	10c. multicoloured	15	15
522	40c. multicoloured	25	30
523	40c. multicoloured	25	30
524	50c. multicoloured	30	35
525	50c. multicoloured	30	35
526	60c. multicoloured	30	40
527	60c. multicoloured	30	40
528	75c. multicoloured	30	45
529	75c. multicoloured	30	45
530	$1 multicoloured	30	45
531	$1 multicoloured	30	45
532	$1.50 multicoloured	40	55
533	$1.50 multicoloured	40	55
534	$2 multicoloured	45	70
535	$2 multicoloured	45	70

DESIGNS: Nos. 520/1, Class 142, East Germany (1977); 522/3, Class 120, West Germany (1979); 524/5, Class X, Australia (1954); 526/7, Class 59, Great Britain (1986); 528/9, New York Elevated Railroad *Spuyten Duyvel*, U.S.A. (1875); 530/1, Camden & Amboy Railroad *Stevens* and rebuilt *John Bull*, U.S.A. (1832); 532/3, Class Hl-d, No. 2850, Canada (1938); 534/5, *Pioneer Zephyr* 3-car diesel set, U.S.A. (1934).

59 Queen Elizabeth with Prince Andrew

1987. Royal Ruby Wedding and 150th Anniv of Queen Victoria's Accession.

536	**59** 15c. multicoloured	20	15
537	- 45c. brown, black and yellow	25	20
538	- $1.50 multicoloured	30	55
539	- $3 multicoloured	45	1·00
540	- $4 multicoloured	50	1·25
MS541	85×115 mm. $6 multicoloured	2·00	3·25

DESIGNS: 45c. Queen Victoria and Prince Albert, c. 1855; $1.50, Queen and Prince Philip after Trooping the Colour, 1977; $3 Queen and Duke of Edinburgh, 1953; $4 Queen in her study, c. 1980; Princess Elizabeth, 1947.

60 Banded Coral Shrimp

1987. Marine Life. Multicoloured.

542	45c. Type **60**	55	35
543	50c. Arrow crab and flamingo tongue	60	50
544	65c. Cardinal fish	70	90
545	$5 Moray eel	2·00	4·00
MS546	85×115 mm. $5 Porcupinefish ("Puffer Fish")	2·50	5·00

61 Australia IV

1988. Ocean Racing Yachts. Multicoloured.

547	50c. Type **61**	30	35
548	65c. *Crusader II*	35	50
549	75c. *New Zealand II*	40	60
550	$2 *Italia*	60	1·25
551	$4 *White Crusader*	70	2·00
552	$5 *Stars and Stripes*	70	2·25
MS553	100×140 mm. $1 *Champosa V*	1·25	2·00

62 Seine-fishing Boats racing

1988. Bequia Regatta. Multicoloured.

554	5c. Type **62**	10	15
555	50c. *Friendship Rose* (cruising yacht)	15	30
556	75c. Fishing boats racing	20	45
557	$3.50 Yachts racing	75	2·25
MS558	115×85 mm. $8 Port Elizabeth, Bequia (60×40 mm)	3·25	6·00

63 Britten Norman Islander making Night Approach

1988. Mustique Airways. Multicoloured.

559	15c. Type **63**	10	15
560	65c. Beech Baron aircraft in flight	15	35
561	75c. Britten Norman Islander over forest	15	35
562	$5 Beech Baron on airstrip	1·00	2·25
MS563	115×85 mm. $10 Baleine Falls (36×56 mm)	2·50	5·50

64 *Sv. Pyotr* in Arctic (Bering)

1988. Explorers. Multicoloured.

564	15c. Type **64**	35	20
565	75c. Bering's ships in pack ice	40	30
566	$1 Livingstone's steam launch *Ma-Robert* on Zambesi	40	40
567	$2 Meeting of Livingstone and H. M. Stanley at Ujiji	50	75
568	$3 Speke and Burton at Tabori	50	1·00
569	$3.50 Speke and Burton in canoe on Lake Victoria	50	1·25
570	$4 Sighting the New World, 1492	60	1·40
571	$4.50 Columbus trading with Indians	60	1·50
MS572	Two sheets, each 115×85 mm. (a) $5 Sextant and coastal scene. (b) $5 *Santa Maria* at anchor. Set of 2 sheets	2·50	5·50

65 Asif Iqbal Razvi

1988. Cricketers of 1988 International Season. Multicoloured.

573	20c. Type **65**	40	30
574	45c. R. J. Hadlee	60	50
575	75c. M. D. Crowe	80	80
576	$1.25 C. H. Lloyd	90	1·25
577	$1.50 A. R. Boarder	1·00	1·50
578	$2 M. D. Marshall	1·25	2·00
579	$2.50 G. A. Hick	1·25	2·25
580	$3.50 C. G. Greenidge (horiz)	1·25	2·75
MS581	115×85 mm. $3 As $2	3·75	7·00

66 Pam Shriver

1988. International Tennis Players. Multicoloured.

582	15c. Type **66**	20	20
583	50c. Kevin Curran (vert)	20	30
584	75c. Wendy Turnbull (vert)	25	35
585	$1 Evonne Cawley (vert)	35	50
586	$1.50 Ilie Nastase (vert)	40	65
587	$2 Billie Jean King (vert)	45	75
588	$3 Bjorn Borg (vert)	55	1·25
589	$3.50 Virginia Wade with Wimbledon trophy (vert)	60	1·50
MS590	115×85 mm. $2.25, Stefan Edberg with Wimbledon cup; $2.25, Steffi Graf with Wimbledon trophy	1·50	3·50

No. 584 is inscribed "WENDY TURNBALL" in error.

67 Mickey and Minnie Mouse visiting Fatehpur Sikri

1989. "India-89" International Stamp Exhibition. Designs showing Walt Disney cartoon characters in India. Multicoloured.

591	1c. Type **67**	10	10
592	2c. Mickey and Minnie Mouse aboard "Palace on Wheels" train	10	10
593	3c. Mickey and Minnie Mouse passing Old Fort, Delhi	10	10
594	5c. Mickey and Minnie Mouse on camel, Pinjore Gardens, Haryana	10	10
595	10c. Mickey and Minnie Mouse at Taj Mahal, Agra	15	10
596	25c. Mickey and Minnie Mouse in Chandni Chowk, Old Delhi	20	10
597	$4 Goofy on elephant with Mickey and Minnie Mouse at Agra Fort, Jaipur	3·25	3·50
598	$5 Goofy, Mickey and Minnie Mouse at Gandhi Memorial Cape Comorin	3·00	3·50
MS599	Two sheets, each 127×102 mm. (a) $6 Mickey and Minnie Mouse in vegetable cart, Jaipur. (b) $6 Mickey and Minnie Mouse leaving carriage, Qutab Minar, New Delhi (vert). Set of 2 sheets	8·50	10·00

1989. Japanese Art. As T **177a** of Gambia but horiz. Multicoloured.

600	5c. *The View at Yotsuya* (Hokusai)	20	20
601	30c. *Landscape at Ochanomizu* (Hokuju)	50	50
602	45c. *Itabashi* (Eisen)	60	60
603	65c. *Early Summer Rain* (Kunisada)	75	75
604	75c. *High Noon at Kasumigaseki* (Kuniyoshi)	80	80
605	$1 *The Yoshiwara Embankment by Moonlight* (Kuniyoshi)	1·00	1·00
606	$4 *The Bridge of Boats at Sano* (Hokusai)	2·75	3·00
607	$5 *Lingering Snow on Mount Hira* (Kunitora)	2·75	3·00
MS608	Two sheets, each 103×76 mm. (a) $6 *Colossus of Rhodes* (Kunitora). (b) $6 *Shinobazu Pond* (Kokan). Set of 2 sheets	7·00	8·00

68 Player with Ball and Mt. Vesuvius

1989. World Cup Football Championship, Italy (1st issue). Designs showing players and Italian landmarks. Multicoloured.

609	$1.50 Type **68**	1·40	1·40
610	$1.50 Fallen player, opponent kicking ball and Coliseum	1·40	1·40
611	$1.50 Player blocking ball and Venice	1·40	1·40

612	$1.50 Player tackling and Forum, Rome	1·40	1·40
613	$1.50 Two players competing for ball and Leaning Tower, Pisa	1·40	1·40
614	$1.50 Goalkeeper and Florence	1·40	1·40
615	$1.50 Two players competing for ball and St. Peter's, Vatican	1·40	1·40
616	$1.50 Player kicking ball and Pantheon	1·40	1·40

Nos 609/16 were printed together, *se-tenant*, forming a composite foreground design.
See also Nos. 680/3.

1989. 500th Anniv (1992) of Discovery of America by Columbus (1st issue). Pre-Columbian Arawak Society. As T **97a** of Grenadines of Grenada. Multicoloured.

617	25c. Arawak smoking tobacco	45	30
618	75c. Arawak rolling cigar	75	65
619	$1 Applying body paint	90	80
620	$1.50 Making fire	1·25	1·50
621	$1.50 Cassava production	1·25	1·50
622	$1.50 Woman baking bread	1·25	1·50
623	$1.50 Using stone implement	1·25	1·50
624	$4 Arawak priest	2·50	3·00

MS625 Two sheets, each 70×84 mm. (a) $6 Arawak chief. (b) $6 Men returning from fishing expedition. Set of 2 sheets 11·00 12·00

Nos. 620/3 were printed together, *se-tenant*, forming a composite design.
See also Nos. 818/23 and 864/5.

70 Command Module "Columbia"

1989. 20th Anniv of First Manned Landing on Moon. Multicoloured.

626	5c. Type **70**	40	40
627	40c. Astronaut Neil Armstrong saluting U.S. flag	1·25	85
628	55c. "Columbia" above lunar surface	1·50	1·00
629	65c. Lunar module "Eagle" leaving moon	1·50	1·25
630	70c. "Eagle" on Moon	1·50	1·25
631	$1 "Columbia" re-entering Earth's atmosphere	1·60	1·60
632	$3 "Apollo 11" emblem	3·00	3·25
633	$5 Armstrong and Aldrin on Moon	3·25	3·75

MS634 Two sheets, each 110×82 mm. (a) $6 Launch of "Apollo 11" (vert). (b) $6 "Apollo 11" splashdown. Set of 2 sheets 11·00 12·00

71 *Marpesia petreus*

1989. Butterflies. Multicoloured.

635	5c. Type **71**	50	50
636	30c. *Papilio androgeus*	1·25	60
637	45c. *Strymon maesites*	1·50	65
638	65c. *Junonia coenia*	1·75	1·40
639	75c. *Eurema gratiosa*	2·00	1·50
640	$1 *Hypolimnas misippus*	2·00	1·75
641	$4 *Urbanus proteus*	4·25	4·50
642	$5 *Junonia evarete*	4·25	4·50

MS643 Two sheets. (a) 76×104 mm. $6 *Phoebis agarithe*. (b) 104×76 mm. $6 *Dryas julia*. Set of 2 sheets 15·00 13·00

72 *Solanum urens*

1989. Flowers from St. Vincent Botanical Gardens. Multicoloured.

644	80c. Type **72**	1·50	1·50
645	$1.25 *Passiflora andersonii*	2·00	2·00
646	$1.65 *Miconia andersonii*	2·25	2·25
647	$1.85 *Pitcairnia sulphurea*	2·50	2·50

1989. Christmas. As T **183** of Gambia. Multicoloured.

648	5c. Goofy and Mickey Mouse in Rolls Royce "Silver Ghost", 1907	20	15
649	10c. Daisy Duck driving first Stanley Steamer, 1897	20	15

650	15c. Horace Horsecollar and Clarabelle Cow in Darracq "Genevieve", 1904	25	20
651	45c. Donald Duck driving De-troit electric coupe, 1914	50	40
652	55c. Mickey and Minnie Mouse in first Ford, 1896	55	40
653	$2 Mickey Mouse driving Reo "Runabout", 1904	2·00	2·00
654	$3 Goofy driving Winton mail truck, 1899	2·75	2·75
655	$5 Mickey and Minnie Mouse in Duryea car, 1893	3·50	4·00

MS656 Two sheets, each 127×102 mm. (a) $6 Mickey and Minnie Mouse in Pope-Hartford, 1912. (b) $6 Mickey and Minnie Mouse in Buick "Model 10", 1908. Set of 2 sheets 10·00 12·00

1990. 50th Anniv of Second World War. As T **354c** of Grenada. Multicoloured.

657	10c. Destroyer in action, First Battle of Narvik, 1940	45	25
658	15c. Allied tank at Anzio, 1944	55	35
659	20c. U.S. carrier under attack, Battle of Midway, 1942	60	40
660	45c. North American B-25 Mitchell bombers over Gustav Line, 1944	90	70
661	55c. Map showing Allied zones of Berlin, 1945	95	75
662	65c. German U-boat pursuing convoy, Battle of the Atlantic, 1943	1·00	80
663	90c. Allied tank, North Africa, 1943	1·50	1·40
664	$3 U.S. forces landing on Guam, 1944	3·00	2·75
665	$5 Crossing the Rhine, 1945	4·00	3·75
666	$6 Japanese battleships under attack, Lete Gulf, 1944	4·25	4·25

MS667 100×70 mm. $6 Avro Type **683** Lancaster Mk III on "Dambusters" raid, 1943 6·00 6·00

1990. "Stamp World London 90" International Stamp Exhibition (1st issue). Mickey's Shakespeare Company. As T **193** of Gambia showing Walt Disney cartoon characters. Multicoloured.

668	20c. Goofy as Mark Anthony ("Julius Caesar")	40	20
669	30c. Clarabelle Cow as the Nurse ("Romeo and Juliet")	45	40
670	45c. Pete as Falstaff ("Henry IV")	60	40
671	50c. Minnie Mouse as Portia ("The Merchant of Venice")	65	40
672	$1 Donald Duck as Hamlet ("Hamlet")	1·25	85
673	$2 Daisy Duck as Ophelia ("Hamlet")	2·00	2·00
674	$4 Donald and Daisy Duck as Benedick and Beatrice ("Much Ado About Nothing")	3·50	3·50
675	$5 Minnie Mouse and Donald Duck as Katherine and Petruchio ("The Taming of the Shrew")	3·50	3·50

MS676 Two sheets, each 127×101 mm. (a) $6 Clarabelle as Titania ("A Mid-summer Night's Dream") (vert). (b) $6 Mickey Mouse as Romeo ("Romeo and Juliet") (vert). Set of 2 sheets 11·00 12·00

74 Exhibition Emblem

1990. "Stamp World London 90" International Stamp Exhibition (2nd issue). 150th Anniv of the Penny Black.

677	**74** $1 black, pink and mauve	1·50	1·25
678	- $5 black, lilac and blue	3·75	4·25

MS679 130×100 mm. $6 black and pale blue 5·00 6·00
DESIGNS: $5 Negative image of Penny Black; $6 Penny Black.

74a McCleish, Scotland

1990. World Cup Football Championship, Italy (2nd issue). Multicoloured.

680	25c. Type **74a**	80	40
681	50c. Rasul, Egypt	1·10	80
682	$2 Lindenberger, Austria	2·75	2·75
683	$4 Murray, U.S.A.	3·75	4·25

MS684 Two sheets, each 102×77 mm. (a) $6 Robson, England. (b) $6 Gullit, Netherlands. Set of 2 sheets 16·00 12·00

74b *Paphiopedilum*

1990. "EXPO 90" International Garden and Greenery Exposition, Osaka. Orchids. Multicoloured.

685	5c. Type **74b**	80	50
686	25c. *Dendrobium phalaenopsis* and *Cymbidium* hybrid	1·75	90
687	30c. *Miltonia candida* hybrid	1·75	90
688	50c. *Epidendrum ibaguense* and *Cymbidium* Elliot Rogers	2·25	1·25
689	$1 *Rossioglossum grande*	2·75	1·75
690	$2 *Phalaenopsis* Elisa Chang Lou and *Masdevallia coccinea*	3·25	2·50
691	$4 *Cypripedium acaule* and *Cypripedium calceolus*	3·75	4·00
692	$5 *Orchis spectabilis*	3·75	4·00

MS693 Two sheets, each 108×78 mm. (a) $6 *Dendrobium anosmum*. (b) $6 *Epidendrum ibaguense* and *Phalaenopsis*. Set of 2 sheets 13·00 13·00

75 Scaly-breasted Ground Dove ("Common Ground Dove")

1990. Birds of the Caribbean. Multicoloured.

694	5c. Type **75**	20	20
695	25c. Purple martin	40	40
696	45c. Painted bunting	70	70
697	55c. Blue-hooded euphonia	80	80
698	75c. Blue-grey tanager	1·00	1·00
699	$1 Red-eyed vireo	1·25	1·25
700	$2 Palm chat	2·00	2·00
701	$3 Northern jacana ("North American Jacana")	2·50	2·50
702	$4 Green-throated carib	2·75	2·75
703	$5 St. Vincent amazon ("St. Vincent Parrot")	3·00	3·00

MS704 Two sheets, each 117×87 mm. (a) $3 Magnificent frigate bird; $3 Bananaquit. (b) $6 Red-legged honeycreeper. Set of 2 sheets 9·50 10·00

1991. 90th Birthday of Queen Elizabeth the Queen Mother. As T **194** of Gambia.

705	$2 multicoloured	1·90	1·25
706	$2 multicoloured	1·90	1·25
707	$2 multicoloured	1·90	1·25
708	$2 multicoloured	1·90	1·25
709	$2 multicoloured	1·90	1·25
710	$2 multicoloured	1·90	1·25
711	$2 multicoloured	1·90	1·25
712	$2 multicoloured	1·90	1·25
713	$2 multicoloured	1·90	1·25
714	$2 multicoloured	1·90	1·25
715	$2 multicoloured	1·90	1·25
716	$2 multicoloured	1·90	1·25
717	$2 multicoloured	1·90	1·25
718	$2 multicoloured	1·90	1·25
719	$2 multicoloured	1·90	1·25
720	$2 multicoloured	1·90	1·25
721	$2 multicoloured	1·90	1·25
722	$2 multicoloured	1·90	1·25
723	$2 multicoloured	1·90	1·25
724	$2 multicoloured	1·90	1·25
725	$2 multicoloured	1·90	1·25
726	$2 multicoloured	1·90	1·25
727	$2 multicoloured	1·90	1·25
728	$2 multicoloured	1·90	1·25
729	$2 multicoloured	1·90	1·25
730	$2 multicoloured	1·90	1·25
731	$2 multicoloured	1·90	1·25

MS732 Nine sheets containing details of designs indicated. (a) 120×115 mm. $5 As No. 705. (b) 115×120 mm. $5 As No. 710. (c) 115×120 mm. $5 As No. 712. (d) 115×120 mm. $5 As No. 715. (e) 120×115 mm. $5 As No. 719. (f) 120×115 mm. $5 As No. 720. (g) 120×115 mm. $5 As No. 724. (h) 120×115 mm. $5 As No. 726. (i) 120×115 mm. $5 As No. 730. Set of 9 sheets 30·00 27·00

DESIGNS: No. 705, Lady Elizabeth Bowes-Lyon with sister; 706, Young Lady Elizabeth in long dress; 707, Young Lady Elizabeth wearing a hat; 708, Lady Elizabeth leaning on wall; 709, Lady Elizabeth on pony; 710, Studio portrait; 711, Lady Elizabeth in evening dress; 712, Duchess of York in fur-lined cloak; 713, Duchess of York holding rose; 714, Coronation, 1937; 715, King and Queen with Princess Elizabeth at Royal Lodge, Windsor; 716, Queen Elizabeth in blue hat; 717, King George VI and Queen Elizabeth; 718, Queen Elizabeth with Princess Elizabeth; 719, Queen Elizabeth watching sporting fixture; 720, Queen Elizabeth in white evening dress; 721, Princess Anne's christening, 1950; 722, Queen Mother and policewoman; 723, Queen Mother at ceremonial function; 724, Queen Mother at ceremonial function; 725, Queen Mother in pink coat; 726, Queen Mother in academic robes; 727, Queen Mother in carriage with yellow bouquet; 728, Queen Mother in blue coat and hat; 729, Queen Mother with bouquet; 730, Queen Mother outside Clarence House on her birthday; 731, Queen Mother in turquoise coat and hat.

1991. Death Centenary (1990) of Vincent van Gogh (artist). As T **200b** of Gambia. Multicoloured.

733	5c. *View of Arles with Irises*	40	30
734	10c. *Saintes-Maries* (vert)	40	30
735	15c. *Old Woman of Arles* (vert)	50	30
736	20c. *Orchard in Blossom, bordered by Cypresses*	55	30
737	25c. *Three White Cottages in Saintes-Maries*	55	30
738	35c. *Boats at Saintes-Maries*	70	40
739	40c. *Interior of a Restaurant in Arles*	75	45
740	45c. *Peasant Women* (vert)	80	50
741	55c. *Self-portrait* (vert)	90	60
742	60c. *Pork Butcher's Shop from a Window* (vert)	1·00	70
743	75c. *The Night Cafe in Arles*	1·10	80
744	$1 *2nd Lieut. Millet of the Zouaves*	1·40	95
745	$2 *The Cafe Terrace, Place du Forum, Arles at Night* (vert)	2·25	2·25
746	$3 *The Zouave* (vert)	2·75	3·00
747	$4 *The Two Lovers* (detail) (vert)	3·50	3·75
748	$5 *Still Life*	3·75	4·00

MS749 Four sheets, each 112×76 mm. (a) $5 *Street in Saintes-Maries* (horiz). (b) $5 *Lane near Arles* (horiz). (c) $6 *Harvest at La Crau, with Montmajour in the Background* (horiz). (d) $6 *The Sower*. Imperf. Set of 4 sheets 21·00 19·00

1991. 65th Birthday of Queen Elizabeth II. As T **198a** of Gambia. Multicoloured.

750	15c. Inspecting the Yeomen of the Guard	30	20
751	40c. Queen Elizabeth II with the Queen Mother at the Derby, 1988	55	30
752	$2 The Queen and Prince Philip leaving Euston, 1986	2·00	2·00
753	$4 The Queen at the Common-wealth Institute, 1987	2·75	3·00

MS754 68×90 mm. $5 Queen Elizabeth and Prince Philip with Prince Andrew in naval uniform 4·75 4·75

1991. Tenth Wedding Anniv of Prince and Princess of Wales. As T **198b** of Gambia. Multicoloured.

755	10c. Prince and Princess at polo match, 1987	1·00	30
756	50c. Separate family portraits	1·75	55
757	$1 Prince William and Prince Henry at Kensington Palace, 1991	1·75	1·00
758	$5 Portraits of Prince Charles and Princess Diana	4·75	4·00

MS759 68×90 mm. $5 Separate portraits of Prince and Princess and sons 8·00 5·00

76 Class 150 Steam Locomotive and Map

1991. "Phila Nippon '91" International Stamp Exhibition, Toyko. Japanese Railway Locomotives. Each in black, red and green.

760	10c. Type **76**	80	50
761	25c. Class 7100 locomotive, *Benkei*, 1880	1·10	80
762	35c. Class 8620 steam locomo-tive, 1914	1·40	90
763	50c. Class C53 steamlined steam locomotive, 1928	1·90	1·25
764	$1 Class DD51 diesel-hydraulic locomotive, 1962	2·50	1·90
765	$2 Class KTR001 electric railcar Tango Explorer (inscr "RF 22327")	3·00	3·00
766	$4 Class EF55 electric locomo-tive, 1936	3·50	4·25
767	$5 Class EF58 electric locomo-tive, 1946	3·50	4·25

MS768 Four sheets, each 114×73 mm showing frontal views. (a) $6 Class 9600 steam locomotive (1913) (vert). (b) $6 Class C57 steam locomotive (1937) (vert). (c) $6 Class C62 steam locomotive (1948) (vert). (d) $6 Class 4100 tank locomotive (1912) (vert).
Set of 4 sheets ... 19·00 19·00

77 President Gorbachev and Brandenburg Gate

1991. Anniversaries and Events. Multicoloured.

769	45c. Type **77**	40	40
770	60c. General de Gaulle in Djibouti, 1959	1·25	55
771	65c. "DIE MAUER MUSS WEG!" slogan	65	65
772	80c. East German border guard escaping to West	80	80
773	$1 "Abduction from the Seraglio"	4·75	1·75
774	$1.50 Lilienthal and glider	2·00	1·75
775	$1.75 Trans-Siberian identity plate	4·00	2·75
776	$1.75 Trans-Siberian steam locomotive (vert)	4·00	2·75
777	$2 Czechoslovakia 1918 20h. stamp and scout delivering mail	3·00	3·00
778	$2 Zurich couple maypole dancing	3·00	3·00
779	$2 Man and woman in Vaud traditional costumes	3·00	3·00
780	$2 Georg Laves (architect) and Hoftheater	3·00	3·00
781	$3 Dresden, 1749	8·00	5·00
782	$4 Scouts and cog train on Snowdon (vert)	4·50	5·00

MS783 Eleven sheets. (a) 100×71 mm. $5 Arms of Berlin. (b) 100×71 mm. $5 Berlin police badge. (c) 77×112 mm. $5 De Gaulle in civilian dress. (d) 69×101 mm. $5 General Charles de Gaulle (vert). (e) 75×101 mm. $5 Portrait of Mozart (vert). (f) 75×101 mm. $5 Bust of Mozart (vert). (g) 115×85 mm. $5 Trans-Siberian Class P36 No. 0250 steam locomotive leaving Moscow at night (43×56 mm). (h) 118×89 mm. $5 Jamboree emblem (buff background) (vert). (i) 118×89 mm. $5 Jamboree emblem (bluish violet background) (vert). (j) 101×72 mm. $5 Arms of Appenzell and Thurgau. (k) 101×72 mm. $5 Old Hanover Set of 11 sheets ... 45·00 38·00

Anniversaries and Events:—Nos. 769, 771/2, MS783a/b, Bicentenary of Brandenburg Gate; 770, MS783c/d, Birth centenary of Charles de Gaulle (French statesman); 773, 781, MS783e/f, Death bicentenary of Mozart; 774, Centenary of Otto Lilienthal's gliding experiments; 775/6, MS783g, Centenary of Trans-Siberian Railway; 777, 782, MS783h/i. 50th death anniv of Lord Baden-Powell and World Scout Jamboree, Korea; 778/9, MS783j, 700th anniv of Swiss Confederation; 780, MS783k, 750th anniv of Hanover.

78 Japanese Aircraft and Submarines leaving Truk

1991. 50th Anniv of Japanese Attack on Pearl Harbor. Multicoloured.

784	$1 Type **78**	2·50	1·60
785	$1 Akagi (Japanese aircraft carrier)	2·50	1·60
786	$1 Nakajima B5N2 "Kate" bombers	2·50	1·60
787	$1 Nakajima B5N2 "Kate" bombers attacking Battleship Row	2·50	1·60
788	$1 Burning aircraft, Ford Island airfield	2·50	1·60
789	$1 Doris Miller winning Navy Cross	2·50	1·60
790	$1 U.S.S. West Virginia and Tennessee (battleships) ablaze	2·50	1·60
791	$1 U.S.S. Arizona (battleship) sinking	2·50	1·60
792	$1 U.S.S. New Orleans (cruiser)	2·50	1·60
793	$1 President Roosevelt declaring war	2·50	1·60

78a Pluto pulling Mickey Mouse in Sledge, 1974

1991. Christmas. Walt Disney Company Christmas Cards. Multicoloured.

794	10c. Type **78a**	60	30
795	55c. Mickey, Pluto and Donald Duck watching toy band, 1961	1·25	70
796	65c. "The Same Old Wish", 1942	1·40	85
797	75c. Mickey, Peter Pan, Donald and Nephews with Merlin the magician, 1963	1·50	95
798	$1.50 Mickey and Donald with leprechauns, 1958	2·50	2·50
799	$2 Mickey and friends with book "Old Yeller", 1957	2·75	2·75
800	$4 Mickey controlling Pinocchio, 1953	4·00	4·25
801	$5 Cinderella and Prince dancing, 1987	4·00	4·25

MS802 Two sheets, each 128×102 mm. (a) $6 Santa Claus and American bomber, 1942. (b) $6 Snow White, 1957. Set of 2 sheets ... 14·00 14·00

1992. 40th Anniv of Queen Elizabeth II's Accession. As T 202a of Gambia. Multicoloured.

803	15c. View across bay	75	20
804	45c. Schooner at anchor, Mayreau	1·25	25
805	$2 Hotel on hillside	1·75	1·75
806	$4 Tourist craft at anchor	3·75	3·75

MS807 Two sheets, each 74×97 mm. (a) $6 Beach and palms. (b) $6 Aerial view of hotel by beach. Set of 2 sheets ... 9·50 10·00

78b Big Pete as Hernando Cortes in Mexico

1992. International Stamp Exhibitions. Walt Disney cartoon characters. Multicoloured. (a) "Grenada '92", Spain. Spanish Explorers.

808	15c. Type **78b**	30	15
809	40c. Mickey Mouse as Hernando de Soto at Mississippi River	50	30
810	$2 Goofy as Vasco Nunez de Balboa sights Pacific	1·75	1·75
811	$4 Donald Duck as Francisco Coronado on Rio Grande	2·75	3·00

MS812 127×102 mm. $6 Mickey as Ponce de Leon ... 4·25 4·75

(b) "World Columbian Stamp Expo '92", Chicago. Local Personalities.

813	10c. Mickey Mouse and Pluto outside Walt Disney's birthplace	35	20
814	50c. Donald Duck and nephews in George Pullman's railway sleeping car	1·50	55
815	$1 Daisy Duck as Jane Addams (social reformer) and Hull House	1·60	85
816	$5 Mickey as Carl Sandburg (novelist, poet and historian)	3·75	4·00

MS817 127×102 mm. $6 Daisy as Mrs O'Leary with her cow (source of Chicago Fire of 1871) ... 4·25 4·75

79 King Ferdinand and Queen Isabella of Spain

1992. 500th Anniv of Discovery of America by Columbus (2nd issue). Multicoloured.

818	10c. Type **79**	25	25
819	45c. Santa Maria and Nina in Acul Bay, Haiti	50	50
820	55c. Santa Maria (vert)	55	55
821	$2 Ships of Columbus (vert)	1·40	1·40
822	$4 Wreck of Santa Maria	2·50	2·50
823	$5 Pinta and Nina	2·75	2·75

MS824 Two sheets, each 114×85 mm. (a) $6 Columbus landing on San Salvador. (b) $6 Santa Maria in storm. Set of 2 sheets ... 7·00 8·00

79a Paulogramma sp.

1992. "Genova '92" International Thematic Stamp Exhibition (1st issue). Butterflies. Multicoloured.

825	15c. Type **79a**	75	65
826	20c. Heliconius cydno	80	70

827	30c. Eutresis hypereia	85	75
828	45c. Eurytides columbus (vert)	1·40	1·25
829	55c. Papilio ascolius	1·40	1·00
830	75c. Anaea pasibula	1·40	1·25
831	80c. Heliconius doris	1·40	1·25
832	$1 Perisama pitheas	1·40	1·25
833	$2 Batesia hypochlora	2·00	2·00
834	$3 Heliconius erato	2·50	2·50
835	$4 Elzunia cassandrina	2·75	2·75
836	$5 Sais ivcidice	2·75	2·75

MS837 Three sheets, each 109×79 mm. (a) $6 Oleria tigilla (horiz). (b) $6 Dismorphia orise (horiz). (c) $6 Podotricha telesiphe (horiz). Set of 3 sheets ... 11·00 12·00

See also Nos. 851/62.

79b Entoloma bakeri

1992. Fungi. Multicoloured.

838	10c. Type **79b**	60	50
839	15c. Hydropus paraensis	65	55
840	20c. Leucopaxillus gracillimus	70	60
841	45c. Hygrotrama dennisianum	90	80
842	50c. Leucoagaricus hortensis	90	80
843	65c. Pyrrhoglossum pyrrhum	1·25	1·00
844	75c. Amanita craeoderma	1·25	1·00
845	$1 Lentinus bertieri	1·50	1·25
846	$2 Dennisiomyces griseus	2·00	2·00
847	$3 Xerulina asprata	2·50	2·50
848	$4 Hygrocybe acutoconica	3·00	3·00
849	$5 Lepiota spiculata	3·00	3·00

MS850 Three sheets, each 101×68 mm. (a) $6 Pluteus crysophlebius. (b) $6 Amanita lilloi. (c) $6 Lepiota volvatua. Set of 3 sheets ... 12·00 13·00

1992. "Genova '92" International Thematic Stamp Exhibition (2nd issue). Hummingbirds. As T 370a of Grenada. Multicoloured.

851	5c. Antillean crested hummingbird (female) (horiz)	40	30
852	10c. Blue-tailed emerald (female)	40	30
853	35c. Antillean mango (male) (horiz)	55	45
854	45c. Antillean mango (female) (horiz)	55	45
855	55c. Green-throated carib (horiz)	65	55
856	65c. Green violetear (male)	80	70
857	75c. Blue-tailed emerald (male) (horiz)	90	80
858	$1 Purple-throated carib	1·25	1·00
859	$2 Copper-rumped hummingbird (horiz)	2·25	2·00
860	$3 Rufous-breasted hermit	3·25	2·75
861	$4 Antillean crested hummingbird (male)	4·00	3·50
862	$5 Green-breasted mango (male)	4·25	3·75

MS863 Three sheets, each 105×74 mm. (a) $6 Blue-tailed emerald. (b) $6 Antillean mango. (c) $6 Antillean crested hummingbird. Set of 3 sheets ... 13·00 14·00

1992. 500th Anniv of Discovery of America by Columbus (3rd issue). Organization of East Caribbean States. As T 372a of Grenada. Multicoloured.

864	$1 Columbus meeting Amerindians	75	75
865	$2 Ships approaching island	2·75	2·50

1992. Olympic Games, Albertville and Barcelona. As T 372 of Grenada. Multicoloured.

866	10c. Men's volleyball	70	40
867	15c. Men's gymnastics (horiz)	85	50
868	25c. Men's cross-country skiing	1·00	60
869	30c. Men's 110 m hurdles (horiz)	1·00	60
870	45c. Men's 120 m ski-jumping (horiz)	1·10	70
871	55c. Women's 4×100 m relay (horiz)	1·25	1·00
872	75c. Men's triple jump	1·60	1·00
873	80c. Men's mogul skiing	1·60	1·00
874	$1 Men's 110 m butterfly swimming (horiz)	1·60	1·25
875	$2 "Tornado" Class yachting (horiz)	2·25	1·75
876	$3 Men's decathlon (horiz)	2·50	2·75
877	$5 Show jumping (horiz)	3·75	3·75

MS878 Three sheets, each 101×70 mm. (a) $6 Ice hockey (horiz). (b) $6 Men's single luge (horiz). (c) $6 Football. Set of 3 sheets ... 14·00 14·00

1992. Christmas. Religious Paintings. As T 207b of Gambia. Multicoloured.

879	10c. Our Lady with St. Roch and St. Anthony of Padua (Giorgione)	60	30
880	40c. Anthony of Padua (Master of the Embroidered Leaf)	80	55
881	45c. Madonna and Child (detail) (Orazio Gentileschi)	90	60
882	50c. Madonna and Child with St. Anne (detail) (Da Vinci)	95	65
883	55c. The Holy Family (Crespi)	1·00	70
884	65c. Madonna and Child (Del Sarto)	1·10	80
885	75c. Madonna and Child with Sts. Lawrence and Julian (Gentile da Fabriano)	1·25	90
886	$1 Virgin and Child (detail) (School of Parma)	1·50	1·10
887	$2 Madonna with the Iris (detail) (style of Durer)	2·50	2·25
888	$3 Virgin and Child with St. Jerome and St. Dominic (Lippi)	3·00	3·00
889	$4 Rapolano Madonna (Ambrogio Lorenzetti)	3·50	3·75
890	$5 The Virgin and Child with Angels in a Garden with a Rose Hedge (Stefano da Verona)	3·50	3·75

MS891 Three sheets, each 73×98 mm. (a) $6 Madonna and Child with Grapes (detail) (Cranach the Elder). (b) $6 Virgin and Child with St. John the Baptist (detail) (Botticelli). (c) $6 Madonna and Child with St. Anne (different detail) (Da Vinci). Set of 3 sheets ... 15·00 15·00

80 Nina in Baracoa Harbour

1992. Anniversaries and Events. Multicoloured.

892	10c. Type **80**	2·00	75
893	75c. Airship LZ-3	2·50	1·75
894	75c. Blind man with guide dog	3·50	1·75
895	75c. Training guide dog	3·50	1·75
896	$1 Ships of Columbus	3·50	1·75
897	$1 Adenauer, state arms and German flag	3·00	1·75
898	$1 America III and Il Moro (yachts) with trophy	1·50	1·50
899	$1 Hands breaking bread and emblem (vert)	1·50	1·50
900	$2 "Voyager 2" and planet	3·25	2·50
901	$3 Adenauer and children watching Berlin Airlift	2·75	3·50
902	$4 Airship LZ-37 in flames	3·25	4·00
903	$4 Adenauer and ruins in Cologne	3·00	4·00
904	$5 Mozart with his wife Constanze (vert)	8·00	5·00
905	$5 Adenauer and modern office blocks	3·00	5·00

MS906 Seven sheets. (a) 100×70 mm. $6 Columbus sighting land. (b) 100×70 mm. $6 Count von Zeppelin facing left. (c) 110×70 mm. $6 Count von Zeppelin facing right. (d) 100×70 mm. $6 Konrad Adenauer (vert). (e) 100×70 mm. $6 Konrad Adenauer. (f) 100×70 mm. $6 "Mars Observer" spacecraft. (g) 100×70 mm. $6 Costume for Don Giovanni by Cassandre. Set of 7 sheets ... 35·00 38·00

ANNIVERSARIES AND EVENTS: Nos. 892, 896, MS906a, 500th anniv of discovery of America by Columbus; Nos. 893, 902, MS906b/c, 75th death anniv of Count Ferdinand von Zeppelin (airship pioneer); Nos. 894/5, 75th anniv of International Association of Lions Clubs; Nos. 897, 901, 903, 905, MS906d/e, 25th death anniv of Konrad Adenauer (German statesman); No. 898, Americas Cup yachting championship; No. 899, International Conference on Nutrition, Rome; No. 900, MS906f, International Space Year; No. 904, MS906g, Death bicentenary of Mozart.

81 Olivia and Flaversham

1992. Walt Disney Cartoon Films.

907-	60c.×44 multicoloured.		
950		23·00	24·00

MS951 Ten sheets, each 127×103 mm. $6×10 multicoloured. Set of 10 sheets ... 35·00 38·00

Nos. 907/50 were printed as five se-tenant sheetlets, each of nine different designs except that for "Darkwing Duck" which contains eight vertical designs (Nos. 943/50). The other four sheetlets depict scenes from "The Great Mouse Detective", "Oliver and Company", "The Legend of Sleepy Hollow" and "Ducktales the Movie".

No. MS951 contains two sheets for each film. On one sheet in the pairs for "The Legend of Sleepy Hollow", "Ducktales the Movie" and "Darkwing Duck" the stamp design is vertical.

1992. 15th Death Anniv of Elvis Presley (singer). As T **260** of Dominica. Multicoloured.

952	$1 Elvis Presley	2·75	2·25
953	$1 Elvis with guitar	2·75	2·25
954	$1 Elvis with microphone	2·75	2·25

82 Prince Mickey searching for Bride

1992. "Tales of Uncle Scrooge" (fairy stories). Walt Disney cartoon characters.

955-	60c.×54 multicoloured.		
1008		25·00	26·00

MS1009 Twelve sheets, each 128×102 mm or 102×128 mm. $6×12 multicoloured. Set of 12 sheets   45·00   48·00

Nos. 955/1008 (issued as six sheetlets each of nine different designs) depict scenes from "The Princess and the Pea", "Little Red Riding Hood", "Goldilocks and the Three Bears", "The Pied Piper of Hamelin", "Hop O'-My-Thumb" and "Puss in Boots".

No. **MS**1009 contains two sheets for each story, all being horizontal with the exception of the second sheet for "Puss in Boots". Of the stamp designs in these miniature sheets the two for "Little Red Riding Hood" and one of each for "Goldilocks and the Three Bears", "The Pied Piper of Hamelin" and "Puss in Boots" are vertical.

83 Oleander

1994. Medicinal Plants. Multicoloured.

1010	5c. Type **83**	60	50
1011	10c. Beach morning glory	65	30
1012	30c. Calabash	90	30
1013	45c. Portia tree	1·00	30
1014	55c. Cashew	1·10	40
1015	75c. Prickly pear	1·60	70
1016	$1 Shell ginger	1·75	80
1017	$1.50 Avocado pear	2·50	2·25
1018	$2 Mango	2·75	2·75
1019	$3 Blood flower	3·25	3·75
1020	$4 Sugar apple	3·50	4·50
1021	$5 Barbados lily	3·50	4·50

OFFICIAL STAMPS

1982. Nos. 195/200 optd **OFFICIAL**.

O1	50c. *Mary*	10	15
O2	50c. Prince Charles and Lady Diana Spencer	30	35
O3	$3 *Alexandra*	20	20
O4	$3 Prince Charles and Lady Diana Spencer	65	70
O5	$3.50 *Britannia*	20	20
O6	$3.50 Prince Charles and Lady Diana Spencer	65	70

APPENDIX

The following issues for individual islands in the Grenadines have either been issued in excess of postal needs, or have not been made available to the public in reasonable quantities at face value. Miniature sheets, imperforate sheets etc. are excluded from this listing.

BEQUIA

1984

Leaders of the World. Railway Locomotives (1st series). Two designs for each value, the first showing technical drawings and the second the locomotive at work. 1, 5, 10, 25, 35, 45c., $1.50, $2, each×2.
Grenadines of St. Vincent 1982 Ships definitives (Nos. 208/24) optd **BEQUIA**. 1, 3, 5, 6, 10, 15, 20, 25, 30, 50, 60, 75c., $1, $2, $3, $5, $10.
Leaders of the World. Automobiles (1st series). Two designs for each value, the first showing technical drawings and the second the car in action. 5, 40c., $1, $1.50, each×2.
Leaders of the World. Olympic Games, Los Angeles. 1, 10, 60c., $3, each×2.
Leaders of the World. Railway Locomotives (2nd series). Two designs for each value, the first showing technical drawings and the second the locomotive at work. 1, 5, 10, 35, 75c., $1, $2.50, $3, each×2.
Leaders of the World. Automobiles (2nd series). Two designs for each value, the first showing technical drawings and the second the car in action. 5, 10, 20, 25, 75c., $1, $2.50, $3, each×2.

1985

Leaders of the World. Railway Locomotives (3rd series). Two designs for each value, the first showing technical drawings and the second the locomotive at work. 25, 55, 60c., $2, each×2.
Leaders of the World. Dogs. 25, 35, 55c., $2, each×2.
Leaders of the World. Warships of the Second World War. Two designs for each value, the first showing techni-

cal drawings and the second the ship at sea. 15, 50c., $1, $1.50, each×2.
Leaders of the World. Flowers. 10, 20, 70c., $2.50, each×2.
Leaders of the World. Automobiles (3rd series). Two designs for each value, the first showing technical drawings and the second the car in action. 5, 25, 50c., $1, $1.25, $2, each×2.
Leaders of the World. Railway Locomotives (4th series). Two designs for each value, the first showing technical drawings and the second the locomotive at work. 25, 55, 60, 75c., $1, $2.50, each×2.
Leaders of the World. Life and Times of Queen Elizabeth the Queen Mother. Two designs for each value showing different portraits. 20, 65c., $1.35, $1.80, each×2.
Leaders of the World. Automobiles (4th series). Two designs for each value, the first showing technical drawings and the second the car in action. 20, 45c., $1.50, $2, each×2.

1986

Leaders of the World. Automobiles (5th series). Two designs for each value, the first showing technical drawings and the second the car in action. 25, 50, 65, 75c., $1, $3, each×2.
60th Birthday of Queen Elizabeth II. 5, 75c., $2, $8.
World Cup Football Championship, Mexico. 1, 2, 5, 10, 45, 60, 75c., $1.50, $1.50, $2, $3.50, $6.
Royal Wedding (1st issue). 60c., $2, each×2.
Railway Engineers and Locomotives. $1, $2.50, $3, $4.
Royal Wedding (2nd issue). Previous issue optd "**Congratulations T.R.H. The Duke & Duchess of York**". 60c., $2, each×2.
Automobiles (6th series). Two designs for each value, the first showing technical drawings and the second the car in action. 20, 60, 75, 90c., $1, $3, each×2.

1987

Automobiles (7th series). Two designs for each value, the first showing technical drawings and the second the car in action. 5, 20, 35, 60, 75, 80c., $1.25, $1.75, each×2.
Royal Ruby Wedding. 15, 75c., $1, $2.50, $5.
Railway Locomotives (5th series). Two designs for each value, the first showing technical drawings and the second the locomotive at work. 15, 25, 40, 50, 60, 75c., $1, $2, each×2.

1988

Explorers. 15, 50c., $1.75, $2, $2.50, $3.50, $4.
International Lawn Tennis Players. 15, 45, 80c., $1.25, $1.75, $2, $2.50, $3.

1989

"Philexfrance '89" International Stamp Exhibition, Paris. Walt Disney Cartoon Characters. 1, 2, 3, 4, 5, 10c., $5, $6.

1991

Centenary of Otto Lilienthal's Gliding Experiments. $5.
50th Anniv of Japanese Attack on Pearl Harbor. 50c., $1.
Death Anniv of Mozart. 10, 75c., $4.
50th Death Anniv of Lord Baden-Powell and World Jamboree, Korea. 50c., $1, $2, $3.

1997

Diana, Princess of Wales Commemoration. $1.

2000

Faces of the Millennium: Queen Elizabeth the Queen Mother. Collage of miniature flower photographs. $1×8.

2001

Endangered Species. Turtles. $1.40×4.

2002

Ferrari Racing Cars. $1.10×8.
Chinese New Year ("Year of the Horse"). $1.40×4.
Golden Jubilee. 80c.×4.
25th Death Anniv of Elvis Presley (1st issue). $1 (in sheetlet of 9).
Shirley Temple in Captain January. $1.40×6, $2×4.
Queen Elizabeth the Queen Mother Commemoration. $2×2.
"United We Stand". Support for Victims of 11 September 2001 Terrorist Attacks. $2 (in sheetlet of 4).

2003

Centenary of the Teddy Bear. $2×8.
Chinese New Year ("Year of the Ram"). $1×6.
5th Death Anniv of Diana, Princess of Wales. $2×8.
50th Anniv of General Motors Chevrolet Corvette. $2×4.
40th Death Anniv of President John F. Kennedy. $2×4.
25th Death Anniv of Elvis Presley (2nd issue). 90c.×2 (in sheetlet of 9).
Birds of the Caribbean. 90c., $1, $1.40, $2.

2004

Chinese New Year ("Year of the Monkey"). $1.40×4
Centenary of World Series Baseball. Babe Ruth. 70c.×12
Marilyn Monroe. 70c.×12
Ancient Greece. 30c., 70c., £1, $1.40, $2, $3
Ronald Reagan. $1.40×6
Christmas. 55c., 90c., $1, $4
30th Death Anniv of Pablo Picasso. $2×4
Bicentenary of Steam Locomotives. $2×16
Bicentenary of Steam Locomotives. $1×27

2005

Prehistoric Animals. $2×12
Pope John Paul II Commemoration. 70c, $4
Marine Life. $2×4
Moths. 90c, $1, $1.40, $2
Flowers. $2×4
Liberation of Paris. $2×4
Sinking of the Bismarck. $2×4
60th Anniv of the End of World War II. "The Route to Victory". $2×8
70th Birth Anniv of Elvis Presley. $2×5

2006

80th Birthday of Queen Elizabeth II. $2×4
80th Birth Anniv of Marilyn Monroe. $2×4
50th Death Anniv of Ludwig Durr (Zeppelin engineer). $3×3
50th Anniv of "Loving You" (Elvis Presley). $2.50×4
500th Death Anniv of Christopher Columbus. 20c., 90c., $1.10, $2
Luna 9 $2×6
Mars Reconnaissance Orbiter $3×4

2007

Centenary of World Scouting $3
Diamond Wedding of Queen Elizabeth II and Duke of Edinburgh $1.40×6
Tenth Death Anniv of Diana, Princess of Wales. $1.40×6
Final Flight of Concorde, 2003. $1.40×4
Centenary of the First New York City Taxis. $1.40×6
50th Anniv of Elvis Presley's Purchase of Gracelands. $2×4
90th Birth Anniv of John F. Kennedy (US President 1960–3). $2×8
Halley's Comet, 1986. $2×4
80th Birthday of Pope Benedict XVI. $1
Holocaust Remembrance. $1.40×8

2008

32nd Americas Cup Yachting Championship, Valencia, Spain. $1.20, $1.80, $3, $5
50th Death Anniv (2007) or Qi Baishi. $2×4
Elvis Presley. $1.50×6
150th Anniv of the Apparition of the Virgin Mary to St. Bernadette and Visit of Pope Benedict XVI to Lourdes, France. $2
NBA Basketball. Allen Iverson (Denver Nuggets). $2×3
NBA Basketball. Luis Scola (Houston Rockets). $2×3

2009

Inauguration of President Barack Obama. $2.75×4
Dogs of the World. 75c., 90c., $2, $2.50×4, $3
The Three Stooges. $2×6
Visit of Pope Benedict XVI to Israel. $2.50×4
Elvis Presley Commemoration. Madison Square Gardens, 1972. $2.50×4
40th Anniv of First Manned Moon Manding. $2.50×4

2010

Fifth Death Anniv of Pope John Paul II $2.75×8
Endangered Species. Crabs and Shrimps $2×4
Michael Jackson (singer) Commemoration $2.50×8
Centenary of Girl Guiding $2.50×4
Butterflies of the Caribbean $2.50×4
Pope Benedict XVI at Lourdes, 2008 $2.75

2011

Abraham Lincoln (US President 1861-5) Commemoration $2.75×2
Centenary of First Humans to Reach South Pole $2.75×4
Death Centenary of Henri Dunant (founder of the Red Cross) $2.50×4
Royal Engagement (Prince William and Miss Catherine Middleton) $2.75×6
Personalised stamp $3
150th Anniv of the American Civil War $2.50×20
Orchids of the Caribbean $2×12
Royal Wedding (Prince William and Miss Catherine Middleton) $2.75×8
Insects of the Caribbean $2×5
Butterflies and Moths of the Caribbean $2.75×4
Birds of the World (and their eggs) $2.75×4; $3×3
Butterflies $2.75×4
Tenth Anniv of Attack on World Trade Center, New York $3.50×4
Pres. Barack Obama visits New York City $3.50×4
Pope Benedict XVI $2.75×8

2012

15th Death Anniv of Princess Diana $3×3
Prize Winning Pedigree Dogs $3.50×4
85th Birthday of Pope Benedict XVI $2.75×4
Sea Turtles of the Caribbean $2.50×5
Butterflies of the Caribbean $3.50×4
Dinosaurs $2.75×6
Centenary of Sinking of the Titanic $3.50×4

2013

Diamond Jubilee $3.25×4

CANOUAN

1997

Diana, Princess of Wales Commemoration. $1.

2000

100th Birthday of Queen Elizabeth the Queen Mother. $1.40 (in sheetlet of 6).

2003

40th Death Anniv of President John F. Kennedy. $2×4.
"United We Stand". Support for Victims of 11 September 2001 Terrorist Attacks. $2 (in sheetlet of 4).
25th Death Anniv of Elvis Presley. 90c. (in sheetlet of 9).
Butterflies of the Caribbean. 90c., $1, $1.40, $2.

2007

Centenary of World Scouting. 75c.×20
Centenary of First New York City Taxis. $1.40×6
90th Birth Anniv of John F. Kennedy (US President 1960–3). $2×8
Holocaust Remembrance $1.40×8.
30th Death Anniv of Elvis Presley $1.50×6.
10th Death Anniv of Princess Diana. $2×4.
80th Birthday of Pope Benedict XVI. Photomosaic. $2.25×4.

2008

32nd Americas Cup Yachting Championship, Valencia, Spain. $1.20, $1.80, $3, $5
40th Anniv of Elvis Presley's *68 Special*. $1.40×6

2009

Inauguration of President Barack Obama. $2.75×4

2010

Lech Kaczynski (former President of Poland) Commemoration $2.75
50th Election Anniv of Pres. John F. Kennedy $2.75×8
Pope Benedict XVI Vigil of Prayer in London's Hyde Park $3×3
Pope Benedict XVI meets with Queen Elizabeth II, Edinburgh $3×3

2011

Pres. Abraham Lincoln (US President 1861-5) Commemoration $2.75×8
Elvis Presley Commemoration $2×2; $2.75
5th Death Anniv of Pope John Paul II $2.75×4
Dogs from around the World $2×6
Royal Engagment (Prince William and Miss Catherine Middleton) $2.75×4
Personalised Stamp $3
50th Anniv of NASA $2.50×8
150th Anniv of the American Civil War $2.50×20
Elvis Presley Commemoration $3×7
Birds of the Caribbean $2.50×4
Royal Wedding (Prince William and Miss Catherine Middleton) $3×6
Pres. Obama visits South America $3×6
Pres. Abraham Lincoln Commemoration and 150th Anniv of the American Civil War $2.75×4
Pope Benedict XVI visits Germany $2.75×4
Butterflies of the Caribbean $3.50×8
Orchids $2.75×8
Insects of the Caribbean $2.75×8
50th Birth Anniv of Princess Diana $2.75×4

2012

Stingrays $3.50×4
Marine Mammals $3.50×4
Centenary of the Sinking of the Titanic $3.25×4
Diamond Jubilee $3.75×3

MAYREAU

2006

90th Birth Anniv of John F. Kennedy. $2×8

2007

Diamond Wedding of Queen Elizabeth II and Duke of Edinburgh. $1.40×6
Tenth Death Anniv of Diana, Princess of Wales. $1.40×6
80th Birthday of Pope Benedict XVI. $1.50

2008

32nd Americas Cup Yachting Championship, Valencia, Spain. $1.20, $1.80, $3, $5
Elvis Presley. $1.40×6
35th Anniv of Elvis Presely's *Aloha from Hawaii* Concert. $2×4
NBA Basketball. Lamar Odom (Los Angeles Lakers). $2×3

2009

Inauguration of President Barack Obama. $1.20, $1.80, $3, $5
5 Years of the Pontificate of Pope Benedict XVI. $2.75×4
Endangered Species. Spotted Eagle Ray (*Aetobatus narinari*). $3×4

2010

Fifth Anniv of Pontificate of Pope Benedict XVI $2.75×4
50th Anniv of NASA $2×6; $2.50×4
Michael Jackson (singer) Commemoraton $2×6
Birth Bicentenary of Frederic Chopin (composer) $2.50×4
Dogs from around the World $2.50×4

2011

Abraham Lincoln (US President 1861-5) Commemoration $2.75×8
Elvis Presley Commemoration $2.50×4
Royal Engagement (Prince William and Miss Catherine Middleton) $2.50×4
Personalised Stamp $3
90th Anniv of Albert Einstein's Nobel Prize $2.50×4
Royal Wedding (Prince William and Miss Catherine Middleton) $2.75×5
'Birds of Paradise' $2.75×8
Elvis Presley Commemoration 'The King of Rock n' Roll' $2×5
Orchids $3×6
Butterflies $2.75×8
50th Anniv of Inauguration of Pres. John F. Kennedy $2.50×4
Pope Benedict XVI $2.75×4
10th Anniv of Attack on World Trade Center, New York $2.75×4
50th Birth Anniv of Princess Diana $2.75×4

2012

Centenary of the Sinking of the *Titanic* $3.50×4
Vintage Locomotives $3.25×4

2013

John Glenn's Orbit aboard Friendship 7 $3.50×4
UNESCO World Heritage Sites $3.25×4

MUSTIQUE

1997

Diana, Princess of Wales Commemoration. $1.

2000

Faces of the Millennium: Queen Elizabeth the Queen Mother. Collage of miniature flower photographs. $1×8.

2003

21st Birthday of Prince William of Wales. $3×3.
50th Anniv of Coronation. $3×3.
Centenary of Circus Clowns. $2×4.
50th Anniv of General Motors Chevrolet Corvette. $2×4.
Centenary of General Motors Cadillac. $2×4.
40th Death Anniv of President John F. Kennedy. $2×4.
"United We Stand". Support for Victims of 11 September 2001 Terrorist Attacks. $2 (in sheetlet of 4).
25th Death Anniv of Elvis Presley. 90c. (in sheetlet of 9).
Birds of the Caribbean. $1, $1.10, $1.40, $2

2005

Pope John Paul II Commemoration. $2

2007

Centenary of World Scouting. $1.50×6
Holocaust Remembrance. $1.40×8.

2008

32nd Americas Cup Yachting Championship, Valencia, Spain. $1.20, $1.80, $3, $5
40th Anniv of Elvis Presley's 68 Special. $1.40×6

Tenth Death Anniv of Diana, Princess of Wales. $1.40×6
NBA Basketball. Damon Stoudamire (San Antonio Spurs). $2×3
NBA Basketball. Lamar Odom (Los Angeles Lakers). $2×3

2009

President John F. Kennedy Visits Ireland, June 196'. $2×6
Inauguration of Pres. Barack Obama. $1.20, $1.80, $3, $5
Elvis Presley Commemoration. $2.50×4

2010

Dogs of the World $2×6
Abraham Lincoln (US President 1861-5) Commemoration $2.75×8
NASCAR Greg Biffle $2.75×4
Mushrooms of the Caribbean 25c., $1.25, $1.50, $2×7
50th Anniv of Election of Pres. John F. Kennedy $2.75×4

2011

Michael Jackson Commemoration $$2.75
5th Anniv of Pontificate of Pope Benedict XVI $2.75×2
Royal Engagement (Prince William and Miss Catherine Middleton) $2.50×4
150th Anniv of the American Civil War $2.75×8
Centenary of Discovery of Macchu Picchu $2.50×4
75th Birth Anniv of Elvis Presley $2×6; $2.75×8
5th Death Anniv of Pope John Paul II $2.75×4
Royal Wedding (Prince William and Miss Catherine Middleton) $2.75×5
Birds of the Caribbean $2×6; $2.50×4
Abraham Lincoln (US President 1861-5) Commemoration $2.75×4
Butterflies $2.75×8
Insects of the Caribbean $3.50×8
Orchids $3.50×8
50th Birth Anniv of Princess Diana $2.75×4
President Obama visits Ireland $2.75×4

2012

Centenary of the Sinking of the *Titanic* $3.50×4
50th Anniv of John Glenn's Friendship 7 Space Flight $3.50×4
International Maritime Signal Flags $2.50×6

2013

50th Death Anniv of Pres. John F. Kennedy $3.25×4
40th Anniv of CARICOM $3.25×8
Margaret Thatcher Commemoration $3.25×4

PALM ISLAND

2003

Centenary of the Circus Clown. $2×4.
"United We Stand". Support for Victims of 11 September 2001 Terrorist Attacks. $2 (in sheetlet of 4).
25th Death Anniv of Elvis Presley. 90c. (in sheetlet of 9).
Marine Life of the Caribbean. 50c., 60c., 70c., 90c.

2004

Butterflies. $2×4

TOBAGO CAYS

2003

21st Birthday of Prince William of Wales. $3×3.
50th Anniv of Coronation. $3×3.
50th Anniv of General Motors Chevrolet Corvette. $2×4.
Centenary of General Motors Cadillac. $2×4.
40th Death Anniv of President John F. Kennedy. $2×4.
"United We Stand". Support for Victims of 11 September 2001 Terrorist Attacks. $2 (in sheetlet of 4).

UNION ISLAND

1984

Leaders of the World. British Monarchs. Two designs for each value forming a composite picture. 1, 5, 10, 20, 60c., $3, each×2.
Leaders of the World. Railway Locomotives (1st series). Two designs for each value, the first showing technical drawings and the second the locomotive at work. 5, 60c., $1, $2.
Grenadines of St. Vincent 1982 Ships definitives (Nos. 208/24) optd **UNION ISLAND**. 1, 3, 5, 6, 10, 15, 20, 25, 30, 50, 60, 75c., $1, $2, $3, $5, $10.
Leaders of the World. Cricketers. Two designs for each value, the first showing a portrait and the second the cricketer in action. 1, 10, 15, 55, 60, 75c., $1.50, $3, each×2.
Leaders of the World. Railway Locomotives (2nd series). Two designs for each value, the first showing technical drawings and the second the locomotive at work. 5, 10, 20, 25, 75c., $1, $2.50, $3, each×2.

1985

Leaders of the World. Automobiles (1st series). Two designs for each value, the first showing technical drawings and the second the car in action. 1, 50, 75c., $2.50, each×2.
Leaders of the World. Birth Bicentenary of John J. Audubon (ornithologist). Birds. 15, 50c., $1, $1.50, each×2.
Leaders of the World. Railway Locomotives (3rd series). Two designs for each value, the first showing technical drawings and the second the locomotive at work. 5, 50, 60c., $2, each×2.
Leaders of the World. Butterflies. 15, 25, 75c., $2, each×2.
Leaders of the World. Automobiles (2nd series). Two designs for each value, the first showing technical drawings and the second the car in action. 5, 60c., $1, $1.50, each×2.
Leaders of the World. Automobiles (3rd series). Two designs for each value, the first showing technical drawings and the second the car in action. 10, 55, 60, 75, 90c., $1, $1.50, $2, each×2.
Leaders of the World. Life and Times of Queen Elizabeth the Queen Mother. Two designs for each value showing different portraits. 55, 70c., $1.05, $1.70, each×2.

1986

Leaders of the World. Railway Locomotives (4th series). Two designs for each value, the first showing technical drawings and the second the locomotive at work. 15, 30, 45, 60, 75c., $1.50, $2.50, $3, each×2.
60th Birthday of Queen Elizabeth II. 10, 60c., $2, $8.
World Cup Football Championship, Mexico. 1, 10, 30, 75c., $1, $2.50, $3, $6.
Royal Wedding (1st issue). 60c., $2, each×2.
Automobiles (4th series). Two designs for each value, the first showing technical drawings and the second the car in action. 10, 60, 75c., $1, $1.50, $3, each×2.
Royal Wedding (2nd issue). Previous issue optd as Bequia. 60c., $2, each×2.
Railway Locomotives (5th series). Two designs for each value, the first showing technical drawings and the second the locomotive at work. 15, 45, 60, 75c., $1, $1.50, $2, $3, each×2.

1987

Railway Locomotives (6th series). Two designs for each value, the first showing technical drawings and the second the locomotive at work. 15, 25, 40, 50, 60, 75c., $1, $2, each×2.
Royal Ruby Wedding. 15, 45c., $1.50, $3, $4.
Railway Locomotives (7th series). Two designs for each value, the first showing technical drawings and the second the locomotive at work. 15, 20, 30, 45, 50, 75c., $1, $1.50, each×2.

1989

"Philexfrance 89" International Stamp Exhibition, Paris. Walt Disney Cartoon Characters. 1, 2, 3, 4, 5, 10c., $5, $6.

1997

Diana, Princess of Wales Commemoration. $1.

2000

Faces of the Millennium: Queen Elizabeth the Queen Mother. Collage of miniature flower photographs. $1×8.

2002

Chinese New Year ("Year of the Horse"). $1.40×4.
Endangered Species. Shortfin Mako Shark. $1×4.
"United We Stand". Support for Victims of 11 September 2001 Terrorist Attacks. $2 (in sheetlet of 4).
Queen Elizabeth the Queen Mother Commemoration. $2×3.
Ferrari Cars. $1.10×8.
WWF. Shorefin Mako Shark. $1×16

2003

Centenary of the Teddy Bear. $2×8.
Chinese New Year ("Year of the Ram"). $1×6.
25th Death Anniv of Diana, Princess of Wales. $1.40×6, $2×4.
40th Death Anniv of President John F. Kennedy. $2×4.
25th Death Anniv of Elvis Presley. 90c.×9.
Fish. 90c., $1, $1.40, $2

2004

Chinese New Year ("Year of the Monkey"). "Monkey and Cat" painting by Yi Yuan-Chi. $1.40 (in sheetlet of 4).
Ronald Reagan. $1.40×6
Marilyn Monroe. 75c.×20
Babe Ruth. 75c.×10

2005

25th Anniv of the Pontificate of Pope John Paul II. $2×4
Commemoration of Pope John Paul II. $3×6
Bicentenary of Steam Trains. $1×18
National Basketball Association. 90c.×6
Pope John Paul II Commemoration. 70c.
70th Birth Anniv of Elvis Presley. $2×2

2006

80th Birthday of Queen Elizabeth II. $2×3
500th Death Anniv of Christopher Columbus. 10c., 90c., $2, $3
Venus Express. $2×4
First Flight of Space Shuttle Columbia, 1981. $3×6
400th Birth Anniv of Rembrandt. 50c., 75c., $1, $2×9

2007

90th Birth Anniv of John F. Kennedy. $2×8
Centenary of World Scouting. $4
Diamond Wedding of Queen Elizabeth II and Duke of Edinburgh. $1.40×6
Tenth Death Anniv of Diana, Princess of Wales. $1.40×6; $2×4
80th Birthday of Pope Benedict XVI $1.50
Centenary of the First Helicopter Flight. 10, 25, 90c., $2×4, $5
Elvis Presley through the Decades. $3×4

2009

Inauguration of President Barack Obama. $2.25×3, $2.50×3
Tenth Death Anniv of Diana, Princess of Wales. $2×4
50 Years of Space Exploration and Satellites. $2×8, $2.50×8
40th Anniv of First Manned Moon Landing $2×6; $2.50×4

2010

75th Birth Anniv of Elvis Presley $2.75×8; $3.50×3
NASCAR David Ragan $2.75×4
5th Anniv of Pontificate of Pope Benedict XVI $2.75×4
50th Anniv of Election of President John F. Kennedy $2.75×4
Michael Jackson Commemoration $2.75×8

2011

Abraham Lincoln (US President 1861-5) Commemoration $2.75×8
Royal Engagement (Prince William and Miss Catherine Middleton) $2.75×4
World Cup Football Championship, South Africa (2010) $2.30×28
Beatification of Pope John Paul II $2.75×4
Royal Wedding (Prince William and Miss Catherine Middleton) $2.75×4
World Youth Day. Pope Benedict XVI visits Spain $2.75×4
Abraham Lincoln Commemoration. Gettysburg November 19, 1863 $2.50×4
50th Birth Anniv of Princess Diana $2.75×4
35th Death Anniv of Elvis Presley $1.50×8; $2×5
Spiders $3.50×4
Moths $3.50×4
President Barack Obama $2.75×7
Orchids $2.75×8
Butterflies of the Caribbean $3.50×8

2012

Diamond Jubilee $3.25×4

2013

Cat Breeds $3.25×4
Hummingbirds $3.25×8
Marine Life of the Caribbean $3.25×4

YOUNG ISLAND

2007

90th Birth Anniv of John F. Kennedy. $2×8

2011

Personalised Stamp $3

				Pt. 1

GRIQUALAND WEST

A British colony, later annexed to the Cape of Good Hope and now part of South Africa, whose stamps it uses.

12 pence = 1 shilling; 20 shillings = 1 pound.

1874. Stamp of Cape of Good Hope ("Hope" seated) with pen-and-ink surch.

1	4	1d. on 4d. blue	£1800	£2500

1877. Stamps of Cape of Good Hope ("Hope" seated) optd **G. W.**

2	6	1d. red	£750	£110
3	6	4d. blue	£400	80·00

1877. Stamps of Cape of Good Hope ("Hope" seated) optd **G.W.**

14	6	½d. grey	27·00	27·00
16	6	1d. red	28·00	19·00
6a	4	4d. blue	£450	70·00
26	6	4d. blue	65·00	8·50
27	4	6d. violet	£275	14·00
28	4	1s. green	£250	9·00
29	6	5s. orange	£800	26·00

				Pt. 6

GUADELOUPE

An overseas department of France, formerly a Fr. colony in the W. Indies, consisting of a group of islands between Antigua and Dominica. Now uses the stamps of France.

100 centimes = 1 franc.

1894. French Colonies, "Peace and Commerce" type, surch **G. P. E.** and new value in frame.

6	H	20 on 30c. brown	50·00	60·00
7	H	25 on 35c. black on orange	48·00	55·00

1889. French Colonies, "Commerce" type, surch **GUADELOUPE** and value in figures and words in plain frame.

8	J	3c. on 20c. red on green	1·00	4·00
9	J	15c. on 20c. red on green	9·25	6·50
10	J	25c. on 20c. red on green	9·25	6·50

1889. French Colonies, "Commerce" type, surch **GUADELOUPE** and value in figures and words in ornamental frame.

11	J	5c. on 10c. black on blue	4·25	4·50
12	J	10c. on 40c. red on yellow	13·00	21·00
13	J	15c. on 20c. red on green	14·00	11·00
14	J	25c. on 30c. brown on drab	20·00	23·00

1890. French Colonies, "Commerce" type, surch **5 C. GPE**.

15		5c. on 10c. black on lilac	6·50	5·50
16		5c. on 1f. olive on green	5·50	4·50

1891. French Colonies, "Ceres" and "Commerce" types, optd **GUADELOUPE**.

21	J	1c. black on blue	45	35
22	J	2c. brown on buff	1·40	90
23	J	4c. black on grey	6·00	7·75
24	J	5c. green on light green	4·50	3·75
25	J	10c. black on lilac	25·00	12·00
26	J	15c. blue on light blue	23·00	2·30
27	J	20c. red on green	55·00	50·00
28	J	25c. black on pink	46·00	3·75
19	F	30c. red	£275	£300
29	J	30c. brown on drab	50·00	55·00
30	J	35c. black on orange	£100	85·00
31	J	40c. red on yellow	75·00	65·00
32	J	75c. red on pink	£140	£140
20	F	80c. red	£850	£900
33	J	1f. green	£120	£110

1892. "Tablet" key-type inscr "GUADELOUPE ET DEPENDANCES" in red (1, 5, 15, 25, 50 (No. 52), 75c., 1f.) or blue (others).

34	D	1c. black on blue	85	1·00
35	D	2c. brown on buff	2·50	1·60
37	D	4c. brown on grey	2·00	3·75
38	D	5c. green on light green	3·75	1·20
39	D	10c. black on lilac	16·00	5·50
49	D	10c. red	6·00	1·40
40	D	15c. blue	25·00	45
50	D	15c. grey	10·50	45
41	D	20c. red on green	3·75	12·00
42	D	25c. black on pink	3·75	75
51	D	25c. blue	95·00	£110
43	D	30c. brown on drab	34·00	46·00
44	D	40c. red on yellow	32·00	23·00
45	D	50c. red on pink	28·00	22·00
52	D	50c. brown on blue	16·00	60·00
46	D	75c. brown on yellow	32·00	60·00
47	D	1f. green	28·00	60·00

1903. "Tablet" key-type surch **G & D** (5, 15c., 1f.) or **G et D** (10, 40c.) and new value.

53b		5 on 30c. brown on buff	4·00	9·25
54		10 on 40c. red on yellow	6·50	24·00
55		15 on 50c. red	14·00	19·00
56		40 on 1f. green	9·25	22·00
57		1f. on 75c. brown on yellow	65·00	75·00

49 Mt. Houllemont, Basse-Terre   **50** La Soufriere

51 Pointe-à-Pitre, Grande Terre

1904. Nos. 56/7 further optd **1903** in frame.

59c		40 on 1f. green	60·00	70·00
60c		1f. on 75c. brown on yellow	95·00	95·00

1905. Veiws.

61	49	1c. black on blue	45	20
62	49	2c. brown on yellow	30	10
63	49	4c. brown on grey	50	65
64	49	5c. green	2·75	45
83	49	5c. blue	40	45
65	49	10c. red	4·00	45
84	49	10c. green	2·50	2·30
85	49	10c. red on blue	75	70
66	49	15c. lilac	1·20	35
67	50	20c. red on green	55	35
86	50	20c. green	65	2·50
68	50	25c. blue	2·00	35
87	50	25c. green	1·10	20
69	50	30c. black	4·50	3·25
88	50	30c. red	1·10	2·50
89	50	30c. olive on lilac	2·00	90
70	50	35c. black on yellow	1·80	90
71	50	40c. red on yellow	2·00	1·50
72	50	45c. brown on lilac	3·00	2·75
90	50	45c. red	1·10	2·75
73	50	50c. green on yellow	7·75	4·00
91	50	50c. blue	65	1·40
92	50	50c. mauve	80	55
93	50	65c. blue	3·00	6·50
74	50	75c. red on blue	1·70	2·50
75	51	1f. black on green	1·80	2·50
94	51	1f. blue	1·60	2·20
76	51	2f. red on orange	1·70	4·75
77	51	5f. blue on orange	9·25	25·00

1912. Nos. 37 and 43/4 surch in figures.

78A	D	05 on 4c. brown on grey	1·20	3·25

79A	**D**	05 on 30c. brown on drab	1·70	4·25
80A	**D**	10 on 40c. red on yellow	2·10	4·25

1915. Surch **5c** and red cross.

81	**49**	10c.+5c. red	3·75	4·50
82	**49**	15c.+5c. lilac	1·80	11·50

1924. Surch in figures and bars.

95	**51**	25c. on 5f. blue on orange	45	7·75
96	**51**	65 on 1f. green	1·40	4·00
97	**51**	85 on 1f. green	2·00	8·25
98	**50**	90c. on 75c. blue	1·50	3·50
99	**51**	1f.05 on 2f. red	45	6·00
100	**51**	1f.25 on 1f. blue	65	3·25
101	**51**	1f.50 on 1f. blue	1·50	1·80
102	**51**	3f. on 5f. brown	45	8·25
103	**51**	10f. on 5f. red on yellow	6·00	30·00
104	**51**	20f. on 5f. mauve on red	12·00	32·00

53 Sugar Refinery

54 Saints Harbour

55 Pointe-a-Pitre Harbour

1928

105	**53**	1c. mauve and yellow	35	3·75
106	**53**	2c. red and black	20	90
107	**53**	3c. mauve and yellow	30	5·75
108	**53**	4c. brown and green	20	2·50
109	**53**	5c. green and red	25	1·00
110	**53**	10c. blue and brown	10	10
111	**53**	15c. black and red	20	35
112	**53**	20c. brown and mauve	30	75
113	**54**	25c. olive and blue	60	30
114	**54**	30c. green and deep green	10	10
115	**54**	35c. green	1·00	3·75
116	**54**	40c. mauve and yellow	40	20
117	**54**	45c. grey and purple	70	3·00
118	**54**	45c. deep green and green	1·20	8·50
119	**54**	50c. red and green	35	20
120	**54**	55c. red and blue	1·70	6·00
121	**54**	60c. red and green	50	6·25
122	**54**	65c. red and black	70	70
123	**54**	70c. red and black	45	5·50
124	**54**	75c. green and red	80	1·10
125	**54**	80c. brown and red	90	2·00
126	**54**	90c. red	2·00	2·75
127	**54**	90c. blue and red	90	7·75
128	**55**	1f. blue and red	4·50	1·40
129	**55**	1f. orange and red	3·75	6·50
130	**55**	1f. brown and blue	55	4·25
131	**55**	1f.05 red and blue	3·00	8·50
132	**55**	1f.10 green and orange	5·00	11·00
133	**55**	1f.25 brown and blue	2·00	5·00
134	**55**	1f.25 orange and red	2·50	8·25
135	**55**	1f.40 mauve and blue	2·00	8·00
136	**55**	1f.50 light blue and blue	35	20
137	**55**	1f.60 orange and mauve	2·50	8·00
138	**55**	1f.75 brown and mauve	5·75	1·80
139	**55**	1f.75 blue	14·00	18·00
140	**55**	2f. brown and green	80	65
141	**55**	2f.25 blue	85	7·75
142	**55**	2f.50 green and orange	1·20	8·25
143	**55**	3f. black and brown	55	2·00
144	**55**	5f. red and blue	90	75
145	**55**	10f. brown and mauve	1·10	2·75
146	**55**	20f. red and green	65	7·50

1931. "Colonial Exhibition" key-types inscr "GUADELOUPE".

147	**E**	40c. black and green	5·25	6·25
148	**F**	50c. black and mauve	2·50	4·00
149	**G**	90c. black and red	8·50	19·00
150	**H**	1f.50 black and blue	7·00	12·50

57 Richelieu founding W. India Co., 1635
58 Victor Hughes and Corsairs, 1793

1935. West Indies Tercentenary.

151	**57**	40c. brown	17·00	23·00
152	**57**	50c. red	14·00	12·00

153	**57**	1f.50 blue	14·00	16·00
154	**58**	1f.75 mauve	14·00	12·00
155	**58**	5f. brown	14·00	12·00
156	**58**	10f. green	17·00	12·00

58a Sailing Ships

1937. International Exhibition, Paris.

157	-	20c. violet	1·90	8·25
158	**58a**	30c. green	90	4·00
159	-	40c. red	1·00	8·00
160	-	50c. brown	1·20	3·25
161	-	90c. red	1·10	5·25
162	-	1f.50 blue	1·40	3·50

MS162a 120×100 mm. 3f. blue (as T **58a**). Imperf | 17·00 | 42·00

DESIGNS—VERT: 20c. Allegory of Commerce; 50c. Allegory of Agriculture. HORIZ: 40c. Berber Negress and Annamite; 90c. France with torch of Civilization; 1f.50, Diane de Poitiers.

58b Pierre and Marie Curie

1938. International Anti-cancer Fund.

163	**58b**	1f.75+50c. blue	5·50	34·00

58c

1939. New York World's Fair.

164	**58c**	1f.25 red	2·30	4·00
165	**58c**	2f.25 blue	2·30	3·00

58d Storming the Bastille

1939. 150th Anniv of French Revolution.

166	**58d**	45c.+25c. green and black	8·25	20·00
167	**58d**	70c.+30c. brown & black	8·25	20·00
168	**58d**	90c.+35c. orange & black	9·25	20·00
169	**58d**	1f.25+1f. red and black	9·25	20·00
170	**58d**	2f.25+2f. blue and black	9·75	20·00

1944. Surch **Un franc** (No. 177) or in figures (others). (a) On Nos. 164/5.

178		40c. on 1f.25 red	3·25	7·00
179		40c. on 2f.25 blue	4·25	8·25

(b) On Issue of 1928.

172	**54**	40c. on 35c. green	1·10	6·00
173	**54**	50c. on 25c. olive and blue	65	75
174	**54**	50c. on 65c. red and black	1·10	3·25
177	**54**	1f. on 65c. red and black	75	6·00
175	**54**	1f. on 90c. red	2·50	9·25
176	**54**	1f. on 90c. blue and red	1·40	5·00

(c) On No. 99.

171	**51**	4f. on 1f.05 on 2f. red	5·00	9·25

58e

1944. Mutual Aid and Red Cross Funds.

180	**58e**	5f.+20f. blue	45	8·50

58f Felix Eboue

1945

181	**58f**	2f. black	20	45
182	**58f**	25f. green	65	7·75

63

1945

183	**63**	10c. blue and orange	65	5·00
184	**63**	30c. green and orange	65	3·50
185	**63**	40c. blue and red	75	5·25
186	**63**	50c. orange and green	35	1·00
187	**63**	60c. grey and blue	45	6·25
188	**63**	70c. grey and green	1·00	7·00
189	**63**	80c. green and yellow	75	6·75
190	**63**	1f. purple and green	55	1·30
191	**63**	1f.20 mauve and green	1·00	4·25
192	**63**	1f.50 brown and red	80	1·40
193	**63**	2f. red and blue	90	1·20
194	**63**	2f.40 red and green	1·60	6·25
195	**63**	3f. brown and blue	1·10	50
196	**63**	4f. blue and orange	1·10	1·70
197	**63**	4f.50 orange and green	75	1·70
198	**63**	5f. violet and green	90	2·00
199	**63**	10f. green and mauve	65	45
200	**63**	15f. grey and orange	90	1·00
201	**63**	20f. grey and orange	1·10	75

63a Fairey FC-1

1945. Air.

202	**63a**	50f. green	1·30	4·00
203	**63a**	100f. red	1·50	2·50

63b "Victory"

1946. Air. Victory.

204	**63b**	8f. brown	65	3·00

63c Chad

1946. Air. From Chad to the Rhine.

205	**63c**	5f. olive	1·00	5·50
206	-	10f. blue	1·00	6·00
207	-	15f. purple	1·00	3·25
208	-	20f. red	1·70	7·75
209	-	25f. black	1·00	3·25
210	-	50f. brown	1·20	2·75

DESIGNS: 10f. Koufra; 15f. Mareth; 20f. Normandy; 25f. Paris; 50f. Strasbourg.

64 Woman and Port Basse-Terre
65 Cutting Sugar Cane

66 Guadeloupe Woman
67 Sud Ouest Bretagne over Guadeloupe Woman and Fishing Boats

1947

211	**64**	10c. lake (postage)	10	3·50
212	**64**	30c. brown	10	6·25
213	**64**	50c. green	35	5·75
214	**65**	60c. brown	45	6·50
215	**65**	1f. red	30	5·75
216	**65**	1f.50 blue	90	6·25
217	-	2f. green	1·30	6·75
218	-	2f.50 red	1·70	7·75
219	-	3f. blue	1·70	6·00
220	-	4f. violet	2·20	6·75
221	-	5f. green	2·00	8·25

222	-	6f. red	2·50	2·00
223	-	10f. blue	2·75	5·75
224	-	15f. purple	2·75	4·75
225	-	20f. red	3·25	4·25
226	**66**	25f. green	4·25	8·25
227	**66**	40f. orange	4·00	11·00
228	-	50f. purple (air)	8·25	20·00
229	-	100f. blue	9·25	22·00
230	**67**	200f. red	15·00	30·00

DESIGNS—As Type **66**: 2f. to 3f. Women carrying pineapples; 4f. to 6f. Woman in kerchief facing left; 10f. to 20f. Picking coffee. As Type **67**: 50f. Latecoere 631 flying boat over village; 100f. Short Hythe flying boat landing in bay.

POSTAGE DUE STAMPS

D1

1876

D1	**D1**	15c. black on blue	60·00	50·00
D2	**D1**	25c. black on white	£850	£650
D3	**D1**	30c. black on blue	£110	80·00
D4	**D1**	40c. black on blue	†	£37000
D5	**D1**	40c. black on white	£1100	£850

D3

1884. Imperf.

D8	**D3**	5c. black on white	10·00	18·00
D9	**D3**	10c. black on blue	75·00	65·00
D10	**D3**	15c. black on lilac	£120	75·00
D11	**D3**	20c. black on red	£130	£130
D12	**D3**	30c. black on yellow	£130	£130
D13	**D3**	35c. black on grey	60·00	50·00
D14	**D3**	50c. black on green	22·00	18·00

1903. Postage Due stamps of French Colonies surch **G & D 30** in frame.

D59	**U**	30 on 60c. brown on buff	£275	£300
D61	**U**	30 on 1f. red on yellow	£275	£325

D48 Gustavia Bay, Island of St. Bartholomew

1905

D63	**D48**	5c. blue	20	35
D64	**D48**	10c. brown	35	35
D65	**D48**	15c. green	40	6·75
D66	**D48**	20c. brown on yellow	45	1·20
D67	**D48**	30c. red	55	4·75
D68	**D48**	50c. black	85	7·00
D69	**D48**	60c. orange	75	7·75
D70	**D48**	1f. lilac	1·80	8·50

1926. Surch in figures and words and a percevoir.

D105		2f. on 1f. grey	75	7·50
D106		3f. on 1f. blue	1·80	10·50

D56 Allee Dumanoir, Capesterre

1928

D147	**D56**	2c. mauve and brown	10	3·25
D148	**D56**	4c. brown and blue	10	3·00
D149	**D56**	5c. brown and green	10	2·00
D150	**D56**	10c. yellow and mauve	20	2·00
D151	**D56**	15c. olive and red	20	3·25
D152	**D56**	20c. olive and orange	30	3·00
D153	**D56**	25c. green and red	55	4·00
D154	**D56**	30c. yellow and blue	45	3·00
D155	**D56**	50c. red and brown	50	6·25
D156	**D56**	60c. black and blue	60	6·75
D157	**D56**	1f. red and green	90	4·00
D158	**D56**	2f. red and brown	65	7·75
D159	**D56**	3f. blue and mauve	1·30	7·50

D68 Palms
and Houses

1947

D231	D68	10c. black	10	5·00
D232	D68	30c. green	10	4·75
D233	D68	50c. blue	35	4·75
D234	D68	1f. green	50	7·25
D235	D68	2f. blue	55	6·75
D236	D68	3f. brown	1·10	8·25
D237	D68	4f. purple	1·00	8·75
D238	D68	5f. violet	1·00	9·50
D239	D68	10f. red	1·30	10·00
D240	D68	20f. purple	2·00	11·00

Pt. 22

GUAM

An island in the Pacific Ocean belonging to the United States. Now uses U.S. stamps.

100 cents = 1 dollar.

1899. Stamps of United States optd **GUAM**.

1	1c. green (No. 283)	23·00	28·00
2	2c. red (No. 270)	19·00	28·00
4	3c. violet (No. 271)	£140	£190
5	4c. brown (No. 285)	£150	£190
6	5c. blue (No. 286)	34·00	50·00
7	6c. purple (No. 287a)	£140	£225
8	8c. brown (No. 275)	£140	£225
9	10c. brown (No. 289)	50·00	65·00
11	15c. green (No. 290)	£170	£190
12	50c. orange (No. 278)	£400	£450
13	$1 black (No. 279)	£400	£450

SPECIAL DELIVERY STAMP

1899. Special Delivery stamp of United States optd **GUAM**.

E15	E46	10c. blue (No. E283)	£170	£225

Pt. 15

GUANACASTE

A province of Costa Rica whose stamps it now uses.

100 centavos = 1 peso.

Stamps of Costa Rica optd.

1885. Stamps of 1883 optd **Guanacaste** or **GUANACASTE**.

G1	8	1c. green	2·00	2·00
G36	8	2c. red	1·60	2·00
G3	8	5c. violet	8·00	3·00
G4	8	10c. orange	8·00	8·00
G5	8	40c. blue	15·00	15·00

1887. Stamps of 1887 optd **Guanacaste**.

G37	14	5c. violet	11·00	2·20
G39	14	10c. orange	2·30	2·50

1887. Fiscal stamps optd **Guanacaste** or **GUANACASTE**.

G44	1c. red	£150	£150
G41	2c. blue	25·00	25·00

1889. Stamps of 1889 optd **GUANACASTE**.

G62	17	1c. brown	75	75
G63	17	2c. blue	75	75
G64	17	5c. orange	75	75
G65	17	10c. lake	75	75
G56	17	20c. green	70	75
G57	17	50c. red	1·30	1·10
G59	17	1p. blue	2·75	2·75
G60	17	2p. violet	4·50	4·50
G61	17	5p. olive	27·00	25·00

Pt. 15

GUATEMALA

A republic of Central America; independent since 1847.

1871. 100 centavos = 8 reales = 1 peso.
1927. 100 centavos de quetzal = 1 quetzal.

1 Arms

1871

1	1	1c. bistre	2·00	35·00
2	1	5c. brown	6·00	15·00
3	1	10c. blue	7·75	17·00
4	1	20c. red	6·00	16·00

2

1873

5	2	4r. mauve	£475	£120
6	2	1p. yellow	£250	£150

3 Liberty

1875. Various frames.

7	3	¼r. black	30·00	15·00
8	3	½r. green	30·00	9·50
9	3	1r. blue	30·00	9·50
10	3	2r. red	30·00	9·50

4 Native Indian

1878

11	4	½r. green	2·00	4·75
12	4	2r. red	3·00	9·00
13	4	4r. mauve	3·00	10·00
14	4	1p. yellow	3·50	25·00

5 Resplendent
Quetzal

1879

15	5	¼r. green and brown	11·00	14·00
16	5	1r. green and black	16·00	20·00

For similar stamps, but inscr differently, see Nos. 21/25.

1881. Surch.

17		1c. on ¼r. green and brown	18·00	23·00
18	4	5c. on ½r. green	13·00	20·00
19	5	10c. on 1r. green and black	27·00	35·00
20	4	20c. on 2r. red	70·00	£100

1881. As T **5** inscr "UNION POSTAL UNIVERSAL—GUATEMALA". Centres in green.

21	5	1c. black	4·25	3·00
22	5	2c. brown	4·25	3·00
23	5	5c. red	9·00	3·75
24	5	10c. lilac	4·25	3·00
25	5	20c. yellow	4·25	3·50

7 President J.
Rufino Barrios

Correos Nacionales
150 c. ✸ 150 c.
Guatemala.
150 c. ✸ 150 c.
150 Ctavos.

(8)

1886. Railway stamp variously surch as T **8**.

26	7	25c. on 1p. red	1·10	1·10
27	7	50c. on 1p. red	1·10	1·10
28	7	75c. on 1p. red	1·10	1·10
29	7	100c. on 1p. red	2·10	3·50
30	7	150c. on 1p. red	2·10	3·50

9 Arms of
Guatemala

1886

43a	9	1c. blue	1·70	50
44	9	2c. brown	3·50	50
46	9	5c. violet	4·00	50
47	9	6c. mauve	4·00	50
48	9	10c. red	4·00	50
49	9	20c. green	7·50	1·50
50	9	25c. orange	12·00	2·00

37	9	50c. olive	16·00	4·75
38	9	75c. red	16·00	4·50
39	9	100c. brown	16·00	9·00
40	9	150c. blue	22·00	13·00
41	9	200c. yellow	24·00	13·00

See also Nos. 101/9.

1886. Surch **PROVISIONAL. 1886. 1 UN CENTAVO**.

42h		2c. brown	3·50	2·00

1894. Surch **1894**, bar and value.

55		1c. on 2c. brown	1·50	1·00
51		2c. on 100c. brown	6·50	5·50
57		6c. on 150c. blue	12·00	6·50
53		10c. on 75c. red	8·50	7·00
54		10c. on 200c. yellow	9·75	5·50

1895. Surch **1895 1 CENTAVO** and bar.

59		1c. on 5c. violet	60	50

16 Steamship, arms, portrait of Pres. J. M. Reyna Barrios and locomotive in centre. Arms of El Salvador, Honduras, Nicaragua and Costa Rica in corners

1897. Central American Exhibition.

62	16	1c. black on grey	85	80
63	16	2c. black on green	85	80
64	16	6c. black on orange	85	80
65	16	10c. black on blue	85	80
66	16	12c. black on red	85	80
67	16	18c. black on white	14·50	14·00
68	16	20c. black on red	1·60	1·50
69	16	25c. black on brown	1·60	1·50
70	16	50c. black on brown	1·60	1·50
71	16	75c. black on blue	80·00	75·00
72	16	100c. black on green	1·60	1·50
73	16	150c. black on pink	£160	£200
74	16	200c. black on mauve	1·60	1·50
75	16	500c. black on green	1·60	1·50

1897. Surch **UN CENTAVO 1898**.

76		1c. on 12c. black on red	1·20	1·20

1898. Surch **1898**, bar and value.

77	9	1c. on 5c. violet	1·40	1·40
78	9	1c. on 25c. orange	3·50	3·50
79	9	1c. on 50c. olive	3·00	3·00
80	9	1c. on 75c. red	3·00	3·00
81	9	6c. on 5c. violet	5·50	2·30
82	9	6c. on 10c. red	12·00	12·00
83	9	6c. on 20c. green	6·00	5·00
84	9	6c. on 100c. brown	6·00	5·00
85	9	6c. on 150c. blue	6·00	5·00
86	9	6c. on 200c. yellow	6·00	5·00
87	9	10c. on 20c. yellow	6·00	5·00

20

1898. Fiscal stamps as T **20** optd **CORREOS NACIONALES** or surch **2 CENTAVOS** also.

88	20	1c. blue	2·20	2·10
89	20	2c. on 1c. blue	3·50	3·50

22

1898. Fiscal stamps dated "1898" as T **22** surch **CORREOS NACIONALES** and value.

90	22	1c. on 10c. blue	1·20	1·20
91	22	2c. on 1c. red	5·50	3·00
92	22	2c. on 5c. violet	1·90	1·50
93	22	2c. on 10c. blue	10·50	10·50
94	22	2c. on 25c. red	11·50	11·50
95	22	2c. on 50c. blue	14·50	14·00
96	22	6c. on 1p. violet	6·00	6·50
97	22	6c. on 5p. blue	13·50	11·50
98	22	6c. on 10p. blue	13·50	11·50

1899. Surch **Un 1 Centavo 1899**.

99	9	1c. on 5c. violet	60	35

1900. Surch **1900 1 CENTAVO**.

100		1c. on 10c. red	85	80

1900

101		1c. green	95	35
102		2c. red	95	35
103		5c. blue	3·50	1·80
104		6c. green	1·20	50
105		10c. brown	12·00	1·50
106		20c. mauve	11·00	10·50
107		20c. green	14·50	14·00
108		25c. yellow	11·00	10·50
109		25c. green	14·50	14·00

1901. Surch **1901** and value.

110		1c. on 20c. green	85	80
111		1c. on 25c. orange	95	95
112		2c. on 20c. green	2·40	2·30

1902. Fiscal stamp surch **CORREOS NACIONALES 1902** and value in figures and words.

113	20	1c. on 1c. blue	1·80	1·80
114	20	2c. on 1c. blue	1·80	1·80

1902. Fiscal stamp, dated "1898", surch **CORREOS 1902 Seis 6 Cts**.

115	22	6c. on 25c. green	3·50	3·50

30 Arms   **31** J. Rufino Barrios Statue

35 Statesmen discussing Independence (after painting by E. Bravo)   **47** President Manuel Estrada Cabrera

1902. Inscr "U.P.U. 1902".

116	30	1c. purple and green	50	45
117	31	2c. black and red	50	45
118a	-	5c. black and blue	50	45
119	-	6c. green and yellow	50	45
120	-	10c. blue and orange	60	60
121	35	12½c. black and blue	60	60
122	-	20c. black and red	95	60
141	-	25c. black and blue	85	35
123a	-	50c. blue and brown	70	60
124	-	75c. black and lilac	85	60
125	-	1p. black and brown	1·30	60
126	-	2p. black and orange	1·60	1·30
142	47	5p. black and red	95	95

DESIGNS—HORIZ: 5c. La Reforma Palace; 6c. Temple of Minerva; 10c. Lake Amatitlan; 20c. Cathedral; 25c. G.P.O.; 50c. Columbus Theatre; 75c. Artillery Barracks; 1p. Columbus Monument; 2p. Indian Institute.

1903. Surch **1903 25 CENTAVOS**.

127	9	25c. on 1c. green	1·90	80
128	9	25c. on 2c. red	2·40	40
129	9	25c. on 6c. green	3·75	2·50
130	9	25c. on 10c. brown	12·00	10·50
131	9	25c. on 75c. red	14·50	14·00
132	9	25c. on 150c. blue	14·50	14·00
133	9	25c. on 200c. yellow	16·00	15·00

1908. Surch **1908** and value in figures and words.

134	-	1c. on 10c. blue and orange (No. 120)	50	35
135	35	2c. on 12½c. black and blue	50	50
136	-	6c. on 20c. black and red (No. 122)	70	35

1909. Surch **1909** and value in figures and words.

137	-	2c. on 75c. blk & lil (No. 124)	85	80
138	-	6c. on 50c. bl & brn (No. 123)	50	45
139	-	12½c. on 2p. black and orange (No. 126)	50	45

45 M. Garcia
Granados

1910. Granados Centenary.

140	45	6c. black and bistre	85	60

1911. Surch **1911 Un Centavo**.

143		1c. on 6c. black and bistre	36·00	14·00

1911. Surch **Correos de Guatemala 1911** and value.

144		2c. on 5c. (No. 118a)	2·40	1·20
145		6c. on 10c. (No. 120)	1·90	1·90

1912. Surch **1912** and value.
146	1c. on 20c. (No. 122)	50	45
147	2c. on 50c. (No. 123a)	50	50
148	5c. on 75c. (No. 124)	1·20	1·20

1913. Surch **1913** and value.
149	1c. on 50c. (No. 123a)	35	35
150	6c. on 1p. (No. 125)	50	45
151	12½c. on 2p. (No. 126)	50	45

1916. Surch with value only.
156	**30**	2c. on 1c. purple and green	35	35
152	**30**	6c. on 1c. purple and green	35	35
153	**30**	12½c. on 1c. purple & green	35	35
154	**31**	25c. on 2c. black and red	35	35

59 Pres. Manuel Estrada Cabrera

1917. Re-election of President Cabrera.
| 155 | **59** | 25c. brown and blue | 35 | 35 |

60

1918
| 157 | **60** | 1p.50 blue | 1·00 | 35 |

61 Arms   **64** Technical School

1919. Buildings and Obligatory Tax G.P.O. Rebuilding Fund (No. 158).
158	**61**	12½c. red (obligatory tax)	50	25
159	-	30c. black and red (postage)	3·25	1·20
160	-	60c. black and olive	1·20	70
161	**64**	90c. black and brown	1·20	1·20
162	-	3p. black and green	2·75	40
169	-	1p.50 orange and blue	1·30	35
170	-	5p. green and sepia	4·00	1·90
171	-	15p. red and black	34·00	19·00

DESIGNS—Dated 1918: 30c. Radio station; 60c. Maternity hospital; 3p. Arms. Dated 1921: 1p.50, Monolith at Quirigua; 5p. Garcia Granados Monument; 15p. La Penitenciaria railway bridge, Guatemala City.

1920. Nos. 159/60 surch **1920 2 centavos**.
| 163 | - | 2c. on 30c. black and red | 35 | 35 |
| 164 | - | 2c. on 60c. black and olive | 35 | 35 |

1920. No. 126 surch **25 Centavos** and bars.
| 165 | - | 25c. on 2p. black and orange | 50 | 35 |

68

1920. Telegraph stamp as T **68** optd **CORREOS**.
| 166 | **68** | 25c. green | 35 | 25 |

1921. Surch **1921** and value in words.
| 167 | - | 12½c. on 20c. black and red (No. 122) | 35 | 35 |
| 168 | - | 50c. on 75c. black and lilac (No. 124) | 60 | 35 |

1921. Optd **1921** CORREOS.
| 173 | **63** | 25c. green | 35 | 35 |

1921. Surch **1921** CORREOS DOCE Y MEDIO.
| 172 | **68** | 12½c. on 25c. green | 35 | 35 |

1922. Surch **1922** and value in words.
174	-	12½c. on 20c. (No. 122)	35	35
175	-	12½c. on 60c. (No. 160)	70	70
176	**64**	12½c. on 90c. (No. 161)	85	80
179	-	12½c. on 3p. (No. 162)	35	35
180	-	12½c. on 5p. (No. 170)	70	70
181	-	12½c. on 15p. (No. 171)	70	70
184	-	25c. on 15p. (No. 171)	2·00	2·00
185	-	25c. on 30c. (No. 159)	1·40	1·40
186	-	25c. on 60c. (No. 160)	1·40	1·40
187	-	25c. on 75c. (No. 124)	45	45
188	**64**	25c. on 90c. (No. 161)	1·40	1·40
189	-	25c. on 1p. (No. 125)	35	35
190	-	25c. on 1p.50 (No. 169)	35	35
191	-	25c. on 2p. (No. 126)	55	55
192	-	25c. on 3p. (No. 162)	45	45
193	-	25c. on 5p. (No. 170)	1·10	1·10

80 Independence Centenary Palace   **81** National Palace, Antigua

1922
| 195 | **80** | 12½c. green | 50 | 25 |
| 196 | **81** | 25c. brown | 50 | 25 |

82 Columbus Theatre   **83** Resplendent Quetzal   **84** Garcia Granados Monument

1923
197	**82**	50c. red	70	35
198	**83**	1p. green	3·50	35
199	**84**	5p. orange	1·80	70

1924. Surch **1924** and value.
| 200 | - | 1p. on 1p.50 (No. 169) | 50 | 35 |
| 201 | **84** | 1p.25 on 5p. orange | 70 | 70 |

87 Pres. J. R. Barrios   **88** Dr. L. Montufar

1924
202	-	6c. olive (as No. 119)	25	25
203	**81**	25c. brown	25	25
204	-	50c. red (as No. 123a)	25	25
205	-	1p. brown (as No. 125)	25	25
206	**87**	1p.25 blue	60	25
207	-	2p. orange (as No. 126)	50	35
208	**88**	2p.50 purple	1·40	40
209	-	3p. green (as No. 162)	3·50	70
210	-	15p. black (as No. 171)	7·25	4·25

These all have imprint "PERKINS BACON & CO. LD. LONDRES" at foot.

1925. No. 201 further surch with two bars.
| 211 | **84** | 1p. on 5p. orange | 70 | 70 |

89 Aurora Park   **90** General Post Office

91 National Observatory

1926. Dated "1926".
212	-	6c. bistre (as No. 119)	20	20
213	**89**	12½c. green	20	20
214	**81**	25c. brown	20	20
215	**90**	50c. red	25	25
216	-	1p. brown (as No. 125)	25	25
217	**87**	1p.50 blue	25	25
218	**91**	2p. orange	1·80	1·40
219	**88**	2p.50 purple	2·20	1·80
220	-	3p. green (as No. 162)	60	35
221	-	5p. lilac (as No. 170)	1·40	60
222	-	15p. black (as No. 171)	9·00	4·00

These all have imprint "WATERLOW & SONS LIMITED, LONDRES" at foot.

92 Proposed new G.P.O.

1927. Obligatory Tax. G.P.O. Rebuilding Fund.
| 223 | **92** | 1c. olive | 50 | 35 |

1928. Surch **1928** and value.
224	**91**	½c. de q. on 2p. orange	85	70
225	-	½c. de q. on 5p. lilac (No. 221)	50	35
226	**88**	1c. de q. on 2p.50 purple (No. 219)	50	35

95 Pres. J. R. Barrios   **96** Dr. L. Montufar   **97** Garcia Granados

98 General Orellana   **99** City Arms, Guatemala

1929
227	**91**	½c. green	90	25
228	**81**	1c. sepia	35	25
229	**95**	2c. blue	35	25
230	**96**	3c. lilac	25	25
231	**97**	4c. yellow	35	25
232	**98**	5c. red	70	25
233	-	10c. brown (as No. 119)	60	25
234	-	15c. blue (as No. 125)	85	25
235	**31**	25c. brown	1·40	35
236	**89**	30c. green	1·30	60
237	-	50c. red (as No. 120)	3·00	1·20
238	**99**	1q. black	4·50	70

These all have imprint "T. DE LA RUE & CO. LD. LONDRES" at foot.

1929. Air. Nos. 210 and 222 surch **SERVICIO POSTAL AEREO ANO DE 1928** and new value.
239		3c. on 15p. black (222)	1·70	2·00
240		5c. on 15p. black (222)	85	70
240a		5c. on 15p. black (210)	5·00	3·25
241		15c. on 15p. black (222)	2·40	70
242		20c. on 15p. black (222)	3·50	3·25

1929. Air. Surch **SERVICIO POSTAL AEREO ANO DE 1929 Q0.03.**
| 243 | **88** | 3c. on 2p.50 purple (No. 208) | 1·40 | 1·40 |

1929. Opening of Guatemala–El Salvador Railway. No. 220 surch **FERROCARRIL ORIENTAL 1929** and new value.
| 244 | | 3c. on 3p. green | 1·80 | 2·30 |
| 245 | | 5c. on 3p. green | 1·80 | 2·30 |

1930. Opening of Los Altos Railway. No. 222 surch **FERROCARRIL DE LOS ALTOS Inaugurado en 1929** and value in words.
246		1c. on 15p. black	1·90	2·10
247		2c. on 15p. black	1·90	2·10
248		3c. on 15p. black	1·90	2·10
249		5c. on 15p. black	1·90	2·10
250		15c. on 15p. black	1·90	2·10

104 Bridge and Permanent Way

1930. Opening of Los Altos Railway.
251	-	2c. black and purple	2·10	2·10
252	**104**	3c. black and red	4·00	4·00
253	-	5c. blue and orange	4·00	4·00

DESIGNS: 2c. Quetzaltenango Dam; 5c. Quetzaltenango railway station.

105 Fokker Super Trimotor over Mt. Agua

1930. Air.
| 254 | **105** | 6c. red | 95 | 60 |

1930. Air. Surch **SERVICIO AEREO INTERIOR 1930** and value in words.
255		1c. on 3p. green (No. 220)	60	60
256		2c. on 3p. green	1·80	2·30
257		3c. on 3p. green	1·80	2·30
258		4c. on 3p. green	1·80	2·30
259		10c. on 15p. black (No. 222)	7·75	7·50

1931. Air. Optd **EXTERIOR - 1931**.
| 260 | | 6c. red | 2·10 | 2·00 |

1931. Air. Optd **AEREO EXTERIOR 1931**.
| 261 | **97** | 4c. yellow | 60 | 45 |

1931. Air. Optd **AEREO INTERNACIONAL 1931**.
| 262 | - | 15c. blue (No. 234) | 2·20 | 25 |
| 263 | **89** | 30c. green (No. 236) | 3·50 | 1·20 |

1931. Air. Optd **Primer Vuelo Posta BARRIOS-MIAMI 1931.**
264	**95**	2c. blue	3·50	4·25
265	**96**	3c. lilac	3·50	4·25
266	-	15c. blue (No. 234)	3·50	4·25

1932. Air. Surch **SERVICIO AEREO INTERIOR 1932** and value.
267	**87**	2c. on 1p.50 blue (217)	1·20	80
268	-	3c. on 3p. green (220)	1·20	35
270	-	10c. on 15p. black (222)	12·00	9·50
271	-	15c. on 15p. black (222)	14·50	13·00

114 Monolith of Quirigua

1932
| 272 | **114** | 3c. red | 3·00 | 60 |

See also Nos. 416a/b.

1933. Air. Optd **AEREO INTERIOR 1933**.
| 273 | **97** | 4c. yellow | 35 | 35 |

116 Flag of the Race, Columbus and Tecum Uman

1933. 441st Anniv of Departure of Columbus from Palos.
274	**116**	½c. green	1·10	75
275	**116**	1c. brown	1·80	1·50
276	**116**	2c. blue	1·80	1·50
277	**116**	3c. mauve	1·40	1·20
278	**116**	5c. red	1·80	1·50

1934. Air. (a) Optd **AERO EXTERIOR 1934**.
| 280 | **98** | 5c. red | 2·40 | 35 |
| 281 | - | 15c. blue (No. 234) | 2·40 | 35 |

(b) Optd AERO INTERIOR 1934.
| 279 | **95** | 2c. blue | 85 | 25 |

117 Barrios' Birthplace   **118** Barrios and Agamemnon (freighter)

1935. Birth Centenary of J. R. Barrios.
282	**117**	½c. pink & green (postage)	75	70
283	-	1c. blue and orange	75	70
284	-	2c. black and orange	75	70
285	-	3c. blue and red	75	70
286	-	4c. red and blue	6·75	6·75
287	-	5c. brown and green	5·00	5·00
288	-	10c. red and green	7·25	7·00
289	-	15c. brown and green	7·25	7·00
290	-	25c. black and red	7·25	7·00
291	**118**	10c. blue and brown (air)	2·50	2·50
292	-	15c. brown and grey	2·50	2·50
293	-	30c. violet and red	2·50	1·80

DESIGNS—POSTAGE—HORIZ: 1c. San Lorenzo; 2c. Barrios and Official Decree; 3c. Arms and locomotive; 5c. Telegraph office and Barrios; 10c. Polytechnic School; 15c. Police H.Q.; 25c. Pres. Ubico, arms and Barrios. VERT: 4c. G.P.O. AIR—HORIZ: Barrios and (15c.) tomb, (30c.) statue.

120 Lake Atitlan   **121** Resplendent Quetzal

122 Arms and Map of Guatemala

1935
| 293a | | ½c. blue and green | 35 | 35 |
| 294 | **120** | 1c. red and brown | 35 | 35 |

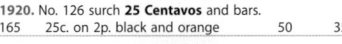

295	**121**	3c. green and orange	1·10	35
296	**121**	3c. green and red	1·10	35
297	-	4c. red and blue	50	35
297a	**122**	5c. brown and blue	1·20	35

DESIGNS—As Type **120**: ½c. Govt. Printing Works; 4c. National Assembly.

123 Lake Amatitlan

1935. Air. (a) Inscr "INTERIOR" (37×17 mm).

298	**123**	2c. brown	35	35
299	-	3c. blue	35	35
300	-	4c. black	35	35
300a	-	4c. blue	35	35
301	-	6c. green	35	35
301a	-	6c. violet	6·00	35
302	-	10c. red	70	35
303	-	15c. orange	95	60
303a	-	15c. green	95	95
304	-	30c. olive	9·00	9·50
304a	-	30c. brown	1·10	70
305	-	50c. purple	27·00	21·00
305a	-	50c. blue	6·00	4·25
306	-	1q. orange	27·00	29·00
306a	-	1q. red	6·75	4·25

DESIGNS: 3c. Puerto Barrios; 4c. San Felipe; 6c., 1q. Different view of Lake Amatitlan; 10c. Livingston; 15c. San Jose; 30c. Atitlan; 50c. La Aurora Airport.

(b) Inscr "EXTERIOR" (34×15 mm) (except Nos. 319/20 which are 46×20 mm).

307	1c. brown	35	35
308	2c. red	35	35
309	3c. mauve	70	35
309a	4c. yellow	2·75	2·10
309b	4c. red	1·40	1·10
310	5c. blue	35	35
310a	5c. orange	35	35
311	10c. brown	70	60
311a	10c. green	70	45
312	15c. red	35	35
312a	15c. orange	35	35
313	20c. blue	4·25	4·25
313a	20c. red	70	35
314	25c. black	5·00	5·00
314a	25c. green	70	35
315	30c. green	2·30	2·20
315a	30c. blue	1·60	35
316	50c. red	11·00	11·50
316a	50c. violet	10·50	11·00
317	1q. blue	38·00	38·00
318	1q. green	11·00	10·50
319	2q.50 olive and red	7·25	5·50
320	5q. blue and orange	11·00	7·00

DESIGNS: 1c. Guatemala City; 2c., 15c. (No. 312) Views of Central Park; 3c. Cerrito del Carmen; 4c. Estuary of R. Dulce; 5c. Plaza J. R. Barrios; 10c. National Liberators' Monument; 15c. (No. 312a) R. Dulce; 20c. Quezaltenango; 25c. Antigua; 30c. Puerto Barrios; 50c. San Jose; 1q. Aurora Airport; 2q.50, Islet; 5q. Rocks on Atlantic Coast.

1936. Obligatory Tax. 65th Anniv of Liberal Revolution. Optd **1871 30 DE JUNIO 1936**.

321	**92**	1c. green	85	80

1936. Obligatory Tax. 115th Anniv of Independence. Optd **1821 15 de SEPTIEMBRE 1936**.

322	1c. green	70	60

1936. Obligatory Tax. National Fair. Optd **FERIA NACIONAL 1936**.

323	1c. olive	85	70

1937. Philatelic Exhibition Fund. Optd **EXPOSICION FILATELICA 1937** or surch **+1** also.

324		1c. olive	85	80
325	**120**	1c.+1c. red and brown	1·20	1·50
326	**121**	3c.+1c. green and orange	1·20	1·50
327	**121**	3c.+1c. green and red	1·20	1·50
328	**122**	5c.+1c. brown and blue	1·20	1·50
329	-	4c.+1c. (No. 300a)	1·30	1·60
330	-	6c.+1c. (No. 301a)	1·30	1·60
331	-	10c.+1c. (No. 311a)	1·30	1·60
332	-	15c.+1c. (No. 312a)	1·30	1·60

128 Resplendent Quetzal

129 General Ubico on horseback

1937. Second Term of Pres. Ubico. (a) Postage.

333	**128**	½c. red and blue	95	70
334	-	1c. brown and grey	70	45

335	-	2c. red and violet	85	45
336	-	3c. blue and purple	70	35
337	-	4c. olive and yellow	3·00	3·00
338	-	5c. purple and red	3·00	2·50
339	-	10c. black and purple	4·25	5·00
340	-	15c. red and blue	3·50	5·00
341	-	25c. violet and orange	4·50	5·25
342	-	50c. orange and green	6·75	8·25
343	**129**	1q. purple and brown	35·00	35·00
344	-	1q.50 brown and olive	35·00	35·00

DESIGNS: As Type **128**—VERT: 1c. Tower of the Reformer; 5c. National Congress entrance; 10c. Customs House. HORIZ: 2c. Union Park, Quezaltenango; 3c. G.P.O; 4c. Government Building, Retalhuleu; 15c. Aurora Airport; 25c. National Fair; 50c. Presidential Guards' Barracks. As Type **129**: 1q.50, Gen. Ubico.

130 Quezaltenango

(b) Air. As T **130**, inscr "INTERIOR" and optd with aeroplane.

345	**130**	2c. black and red	35	35
346	-	3c. black and blue	1·40	1·80
347	-	4c. black and yellow	35	35
348	-	6c. black and green	60	35
349	-	10c. black and purple	3·00	3·25
350	-	15c. black and orange	2·20	1·40
351	-	30c. black and olive	5·50	4·25
352	-	50c. black and blue	7·25	6·50
353	-	75c. black and violet	14·50	15·00
354	-	1q. black and red	16·00	16·00

DESIGNS: 3c. Lake Atitlan; 4c. Progressive colony on Lake Amatitlan; 6c. Carmen Hill; 10c. Relief map; 15c. National University; 30c. Plaza Espana; 50c. Aurora Police Station; 75c. Aurora Amphitheatre; 1q. Aurora Airport.

(c) Air. As T **130** inscr "EXTERIOR" and optd with aeroplane.

355		1c. blue and orange	35	35
356		2c. violet and red	35	35
357		3c. brown and purple	70	70
358		5c. red and green	6·00	4·25
359		10c. green and red	1·80	1·40
360		15c. olive and pink	70	35
361		20c. black and blue	4·25	2·50
362		25c. red and grey	3·50	3·50
363		30c. violet and green	1·80	1·80
364		50c. blue and purple	14·00	14·00
365		1q. purple and olive	14·50	14·50
366		1q.50 brown and red	18·00	18·00

DESIGNS: 1c. Seventh Avenue; 2c. Liberators' Monument; 3c. National Printing Offices; 5c. National Museum; 10c. Central Park; 15c. Escuintla Park; 20c. Mobile Police; 25c. Slaughter-house, Escuintla; 30c. Campo de Marte Stadium; 50c. Plaza Barrios; 1q. Polytechnic; 1q.50, Aurora Airport.

132a George Washington

1938. 150th Anniv of U.S. Constitution. Optd **1787-1789 CL ANIVERSARIO DE LA CONSTITUCION EE. UU. 1937-1939**.

367	**92**	1c. olive (postage)	30	25

MS367b 105×114 mm comprising 4c. brown and red (i); 4c. blue and red (ii); 15c. brown and blue (i); 15c. olive and blue (ii) (air)   8·75   8·50

DESIGNS: 4c. (i) President Roosevelt; 4c. (ii) Map of the Americas; 15c. (i), T **132a**; 15c. (ii) Pan-American Building, Washington.

1938. Obligatory Tax. No. 223 optd **1938**.

368a		1c. olive	50	35

134

1938. First Central American Philatelic Exhibition. (a) Air. As T **134** inscr "PRIMERA EXPOSICION FILATELICA CENTRO AMERICANA".

369	**134**	1c. brown and orange	35	35
370	-	2c. brown and red	35	35
371	-	3c. brown, buff and green	60	60
372	-	4c. brown and purple	85	80
373	-	5c. brown and grey	70	80
374	-	10c. brown and blue	1·40	2·00

DESIGNS: 2c. to 10c. Various portraits as Type **134**.

(b) Postage. No. 223 optd **Primera Exposicion Filatelica Centroamericana 1938**.

375	**92**	1c. olive	60	45

136 Flag of Guatemala

(c) T **136** and similar horiz designs. Flags in national colours, frame colours given.

MS375a 145×96 mm comprising 1c. orange (T **136**); 2c. carmine (El Salvador); 3c. green (Honduras); 4c. purple (Nicaragua); 5c. green (Costa Rica); 10c. bistre (Panama)   3·50   3·50

137 La Merced Church

1939. Optd with flying quetzal. (a) Inland Air Mail. As T **137** inscr "CORREO AEREO INTERIOR".

376	**137**	1c. brown and olive	35	35
377	-	2c. green and red	35	35
378	-	3c. olive and blue	35	35
379	-	4c. green and pink	35	35
380	-	5c. blue and purple	50	35
381	-	6c. grey and orange	60	35
382	-	10c. grey and brown	70	35
383	-	15c. black and purple	1·30	35
384	-	30c. red and blue	1·90	35
385	-	50c. violet and orange	2·75	60
386	-	1q. blue and green	3·75	1·90

DESIGNS: 2c. Christ's Church Ruins, Antigua; 3c. Aurora Airport; 4c. Campo de Marte Stadium; 5c. Cavalry Barracks; 6c. Palace of Justice; 10c. Customs House, San Jose; 15c. Post Office, Retalhuleu; 30c. Municipal Theatre, Quezaltenango; 50c. Customs House, Retalhuleu; 1q. Departmental Palace, Retalhuleu.

(b) Foreign Air Mail. As T **137** inscr "AEREO EXTERIOR" (10c. and 25c.) or "AEREO INTERNACIONAL".

387		1c. brown and sepia	35	35
388		2c. black and green	50	35
389		3c. green and blue	35	35
390		4c. green and brown	35	35
391		5c. red and green	60	35
392		10c. slate and red	3·25	35
393		15c. red and blue	2·75	35
394		20c. yellow and green	95	35
395		25c. olive and purple	95	35
396		30c. grey and red	1·40	35
397		50c. orange and red	2·30	35
398		1q. green and orange	4·50	45

DESIGNS: 1c. Mayan Altar, Aurora Park; 2c. Ministry of Health; 3c. Lake Amatitlan; 4c. Lake Atitlan; 5c. Bridge over Tamazulapa; 10c. National Liberators' Monument; 15c. Palace of the Captains General; 20c. Carmen Hill; 25c. Barrios Square; 30c. Mayan Altar, Archaeological Museum; 50c. Carlos III Fountain; 1q. Antigua.

1939. Obligatory Tax. No. 223 optd **1939**.

399	**92**	1c. olive	60	35

140 National Flower (White Nun)

142 Arms and Map of Guatemala

1939

400	-	½c. brown and green	1·00	35
401	**140**	2c. black and blue	5·50	45
402	-	3c. green and brown	4·75	80
403	-	3c. green and red	4·75	80
404	**142**	5c. red and blue	6·75	2·50

DESIGNS: ½c. Mayan calendar; 3c. Resplendent quetzal.

1939. No. 229 surch **UN CENTAVO**.

405	**95**	1c. on 2c. blue	35	35

1940. Obligatory Tax. No. 223 optd **1940**.

406	**92**	1c. olive	60	35

1940. 50th Anniv of Pan-American Union. (a) Optd **Conmemorativo Union Panamericana 1890-1940**.

407	1c. olive	60	35

(b) Air. Optd **UNION PANAMERICANA 1890-1940 CORREO AEREO**.

408	15c. blue (No. 234)	85	35

1940. Surch with new values.

409	**31**	1c. on 25c. brown	35	35
410	-	5c. on 50c. red (No. 237)	35	35

1941. Obligatory Tax. Optd **1941**.

411	**92**	1c. olive	85	35

1941. Obligatory Tax. Surch **CONSTRUCCION** (twice) and **UN CENTAVO**.

412	**95**	1c. on 2c. blue	50	35

1941. Air. Second Pan-American Health Day. Optd **DICIEMBRE 2 1941 SEGUNDO DIA PAN-AMERICANO DE LA SALUD**.

414		2c. black and green (No. 388)	60	35

1941. Surch ½ **MEDIO CENTAVO** ½.

415	**31**	½c. on 25c. brown	50	45

1942. Obligatory Tax. Surch **CONSTRUCCION 1942 UN CENTAVO**.

416	**95**	1c. on 2c. blue	85	35

1942. As T **114**, but tablet dated "1942".

416a	3c. green	1·40	35
416b	3c. blue	1·40	35

153 Archway between wings of new G.P.O.

1942. Obligatory Tax.

417a	**153**	1c. brown	60	35

154 Guastatoya Vase

1942

418	**154**	½c. brown	50	25
419	-	1c. red	50	25

DESIGN—HORIZ: 1c. Old people's home.

156 Ruins of Zakuleu

157 National Printing Works

158 National Police H.Q.

159 San Carlos Borromeo University, Antigua

1943

420	**156**	½c. brown (postage)	35	25
421	**157**	2c. red	35	25
422	**158**	10c. mauve (air)	70	25
423	**159**	15c. brown	85	25

160 Don Pedro de Alvarado

1943. Air. 400th Anniv of Founding of Antigua.

424	**160**	15c. blue	24·00	16·00

161 Archway between wings of new G.P.O.

1943. Obligatory Tax.

425	**161**	1c. orange	60	35

162 Rafael Maria Landivar

1943. 150th Death Anniv of R. M. Landivar (poet).

426	**162**	5c. blue	50	35

163 National Palace

1944. Inauguration of National Palace.

427	**163**	3c. green (postage)	50	25
444	**163**	5c. red (air)	85	35
445	**163**	10c. lilac	35	35
446	**163**	15c. blue	85	35

1945. Optd **25 de junio de 1944 PALACIO NACIONAL** and bar.

428		3c. blue	70	35

1945. Air. Optd **PALACIO NACIONAL** and bar.

429		5c. red	60	35

165 Archway between wings of new G.P.O.

1945. Obligatory Tax.

430	**165**	1c. orange	60	35
479	**165**	1c. blue	60	35

166 Allegory of the Revolution

1945. Revolution of 20 October 1944.

431	**166**	3c. blue (postage)	50	35
432	**166**	5c. red (air)	95	35
433	**166**	6c. green	95	35
434	**166**	10c. violet	95	35
435	**166**	15c. blue	95	35

1945. Air. Book Fair. No. 389 surch **1945 FERIA DEL LIBRO 2½ CENTAVOS.**

436		2½c. on 3c. green and blue	3·00	2·30

168 Jose Milla y Vidaurre (author) **169** Archbishop Pavo Enriquez de Rivera

1945

437	**168**	1c. green (postage)	50	25
438	**169**	2c. violet	50	35
439	**169**	5c. red (air)	60	35
678	**169**	5c. olive	50	25
679	**169**	5c. blue	50	25
680	**169**	5c. green	50	25
681	**169**	5c. orange	50	25
682	**169**	5c. violet	50	25
683	**169**	5c. grey	50	25
440	**168**	7½c. purple	2·40	1·80
441	**168**	7½c. blue	1·20	60

For stamps as Type **169** but dated "1660 1951" see Nos. 523/27.

170 Torch

1945. First Anniv of Revolution of 20 October 1944.

442	**170**	3c. blue (postage)	35	25
443	**170**	5c. mauve (air)	95	35

MS443a 90×71 mm. No. 443 (×2). Imperf   3·00   1·90

See also Nos. 458/61.

171 Jose Batres y Montufar (military leader and writer)

1945

447	**171**	½c. brown (postage)	35	25
448	**171**	3c. blue	35	25
449	**171**	3c. green	35	35
450	-	10c. green (air)	70	35

DESIGN—HORIZ: 10c. Montufar.

174 Rowland Hill

1946. Centenary of First Postage Stamps.

451		1c. olive & violet (postage)	50	35
452	**174**	5c. brown and grey (air)	50	35
453	-	15c. blue, green and red	85	45

DESIGNS: 1c. U.P.U. Monument, Berne; 15c. Hemispheres and quetzal.

175 Signing the Declaration of Independence

1946. Air. 125th Anniv of Independence.

454	**175**	5c. red	25	25
455	**175**	6c. brown	35	25
456	**175**	10c. violet	50	35
457	**175**	20c. blue	60	35

1947. Air. Second Anniv of Revolution of 20 October 1944. As T **170** but inscr "1944 1946" instead of "1944 1945" and "II" for "I".

458		1c. green	60	35
459		2c. red	60	35
460		3c. violet	60	35
461		5c. blue	60	35

176 Franklin D. Roosevelt

1947. Air.

462	**176**	5c. red	35	35
463	**176**	6c. blue	35	35
464	**176**	10c. blue	50	35
465	**176**	30c. black	2·20	1·40
466	**176**	50c. violet	3·50	3·50
467	**176**	1q. green	6·00	5·75

177 "Labour"

1948. Labour Day and First Anniv of Adoption of Labour Code.

468	**177**	1c. green	60	35
469	**177**	2c. purple	60	35
470	**177**	3c. blue	60	35
471	**177**	5c. red	60	35

1948. Optd **1948.**

472	**142**	5c. red and blue	60	45

1948. Air. Optd **1948 AEREO.**

473		5c. red and blue	60	45

180 Football Match

1948. Air. Fourth Central American and Caribbean Football Championship Games.

474	**180**	3c. black and red	1·20	45
475	**180**	5c. black and green	1·40	70
476	**180**	10c. black and mauve	1·60	1·40
477	**180**	30c. black and blue	3·25	5·25
478	**180**	50c. black and yellow	7·25	7·00

181 Fray Bartolome de Las Casas and Indian

1949. Fray Bartolome de Las Casas ("Apostle of the Indians").

480	**181**	½c. red	35	25
661	**181**	½c. blue	35	25
481	**181**	1c. brown	35	25
662	**181**	1c. violet	35	25
663	**181**	2c. green	60	25
664	**181**	3c. red	50	25
484	**181**	4c. blue	35	25
665a	**181**	4c. brown	35	25

182 Seal of University of Guatemala

1949. Air. Latin-American Universities' Congress.

485	**182**	3c. blue and red	85	70
486	**182**	10c. blue and green	1·70	1·20
487	**182**	50c. blue and yellow	5·00	5·25

183 Gathering Coffee

1950. Tourist Propaganda. (a) Postage.

488	**183**	½c. olive, blue and pink	35	25
489	-	½c. blue and brown	85	35
490	-	1c. olive, brown and yellow	35	25
491	-	1c. green and orange	85	35
492	-	2c. blue, green and red	35	25
493	-	2c. brown and red	85	35
494	-	3c. brown, blue and violet	35	25
495	-	6c. violet, orange & green	50	25

DESIGNS—As Type **183**: ½c. (No. 489), 3c. Cutting sugar canes; 1c. (No. 490), 2c. (No. 493), Agricultural colony; 1c. (No. 491), 2c. (No. 492), Banana trees; 6c. International Bridge.

184 Tecum Uman Monument

(b) Air. Multicoloured centres.

496		3c. red	60	35
497	**184**	5c. lake	60	35
498	-	8c. black	70	35
499	-	13c. brown	1·10	35
500	-	35c. violet	3·50	4·50

DESIGNS—As Type **184**—HORIZ: 3c. Lake Atitlan; 8c. San Cristobal Church; 35c. Momostenango Cliffs. VERT: 13c. Weaver.

185 Footballers

1950. Air. Sixth Central American and Caribbean Games. Inscr "VI JUEGOS DEPORTIVOS 1950".

501	**185**	1c. black and violet	95	35
502	-	3c. black and red	1·10	35
503	-	4c. black and brown	1·40	45
504	-	8c. black and purple	1·70	60
505	-	35c. black and blue	3·75	5·00
506	-	65c. green	7·75	8·25

DESIGNS—HORIZ: 4c. Pole vaulting; 35c. Diving; 65c. Stadium. VERT: 3c. Runners; 8c. Tennis.

186 Ministry of Health Badge

1950. Social Assistance and Public Health Fund.

507	**186**	1c. blue and red (postage)	35	35
508	-	3c. red and green (Nurse)	50	35
509	-	5c. brown and blue (Map)	70	35

MS510 130×80 mm. Nos. 507/9. Imperf or perf   4·25   4·00

187 Nursing School

511		5c. red, green & violet (air)	35	35
512	**187**	10c. green and brown	95	60
513	-	50c. purple, green and red	3·25	4·00
514	-	1q. olive, green and yellow	4·50	4·50

MS515 150×100 mm. Nos. 511/14. Imperf or perf   12·00   11·50

DESIGNS—As Type **187**: 5c. Nurse; 50c., 1q. Zacapa and Roosevelt Hospitals.

1951. No. E479 without surcharge for use as ordinary postage.

517	**E181**	4c. black and green	70	35

1951. 75th Anniv (in 1949) of UPU. Sheet containing stamps similar to Type **5**. Imperf.
MS518 111×69 mm. 1c. carmine (As T **195**); 10c. blue (as T **5**)   3·75   3·75

188 School

1951. Aerial views of schools as T **188**.

519	**188**	½c. brown and violet	60	45
520	-	1c. green and lake	60	45
521	**188**	2c. brown and blue	60	60
522	-	4c. purple and black	60	60

1952. As No. 438 but dated "1660 1951" below portrait.

523	**169**	½c. violet	35	35
524	**169**	1c. red	35	35
525	**169**	2c. green	35	35
526	**169**	4c. orange	70	35
527	**169**	4c. blue	50	25

189 Ceremonial Axehead

1953. Air.

528	**189**	3c. drab and blue	35	35
529	**189**	5c. brown and slate	50	35
530	**189**	10c. slate and violet	70	35

190 Flag and Constitution

1953. Air. Presidential Succession, 1951.

531	**190**	1c. multicoloured	35	25
532	**190**	2c. multicoloured	35	35
533	**190**	4c. multicoloured	50	25

191 R. Alvarez Ovalle
(music), J. J. Palma (words)

1953. National Anthem.

534	**191**	½c. grey and violet	50	35
535	**191**	1c. brown and grey	50	35
536	**191**	2c. olive and brown	50	35
537	**191**	3c. olive and blue	50	35

192 "Work and Play"   **193** Horse Racing

1953. Air. National Fair. Inscr "FERIA NACIONAL".

538	-	1c. red and blue	35	35
539	-	4c. green and orange	1·90	45
540	**192**	5c. brown and green	1·20	60
541	**193**	15c. lilac and brown	1·80	1·50
542	-	20c. blue and red	1·60	1·40
543	-	30c. blue and sepia	1·80	2·00
544	-	50c. black and violet	2·10	2·00
545	-	65c. green and blue	3·75	4·00
546	-	1q. green and red	31·00	19·00

DESIGNS—VERT: 1c. National dance; 4c. National flower (white nun); 30c. Picture and corn cob; 1q. Resplendent quetzal. HORIZ: 20c. Ruins of Zakuleu; 50c. Champion bull; 65c. Cycle-racing.

194 Indian Warrior

1954. Air. National Revolutionary Army Commemoration.

547	**194**	1c. red	50	35
548	**194**	2c. blue	50	35
549	**194**	4c. green	50	35
550	**194**	5c. turquoise	85	35
551	**194**	6c. orange	85	35
552	**194**	10c. violet	1·70	45
553	**194**	20c. sepia	5·00	5·00

1954. As T **5** but inscr "UNION POSTAL UNIVERSAL GUATEMALA" around oval.

554	1c. blue	1·60	35
1222	1c. green	35	30
555	2c. violet	85	35
556	2c. brown	85	35
1222a	2c. blue	35	30
557	3c. red	1·10	35
558	3c. blue	1·10	35
1225	3c. brown	25	20
1226	3c. green	25	20
1227	3c. orange	25	20
559	4c. orange	1·80	35
560	4c. violet	1·60	35
1228	4c. brown	35	30
561	5c. brown	2·40	35
562	5c. red	2·40	35
563	5c. green	1·80	35
564	5c. grey	3·25	35
1228a	5c. mauve	35	30
565	6c. green	2·40	80
1229	6c. blue	45	30

196 Flags of
Guatemala and
ODECA

1954. Air. Third Anniv of Organization of Central American States.

566	**196**	1c. multicoloured	70	60
567	**196**	2c. multicoloured	70	60
568	**196**	4c. multicoloured	70	60

197
Goalkeeper

1955. Golden Jubilee of Football in Guatemala. Inscr "1902–1952".

569	-	4c. violet (Camposeco)	1·60	35
570	-	4c. red (Camposeco)	1·60	35
571	-	4c. green (Camposeco)	1·60	35
572	-	10c. green (Matheu)	4·75	1·20
573	**197**	15c. blue	4·75	3·00

198 Red Cross and
Globe

1956. Red Cross. Inscr "CONMEMORATIVAS CRUZ ROJA".

574	**198**	1c. red & brown (postage)	50	35
575	-	3c. red and green	50	35
576	-	4c. red and black	50	35
577	-	5c.+15c. red and blue	1·60	2·10
578	-	15c. red and lilac	3·50	4·00
579	**198**	25c.+50c. red and blue	3·50	4·00
580	-	35c.+1q. grn & red (air)	8·50	8·75
581	-	50c.+1q. red and blue	8·50	8·75
582	-	1q.+1q. red and green	8·50	8·75

DESIGNS: 3c., 15c. Telephone and red cross; 4c., 5c. Nurse, patient and red cross; 35c. Red Cross ambulance; 50c. Nurse and hospital; 1q. Red Cross nurse.

199 Road Map of   **200** Maya Warrior
Guatemala

1956. Revolution of 1954–55. Inscr "LIBERACION 1954-55".

583	-	½c. violet (postage)	35	35
584	**199**	1c. green	35	35
585	-	3c. sepia	35	35
586	**200**	2c. multicoloured (air)	35	35
587	-	4c. black and red	35	35
588	-	5c. brown and blue	35	35
589	-	6c. blue and sepia	50	35
590	-	20c. brown, blue and violet	2·50	2·20
591	-	30c. olive and blue	3·00	2·75
592	-	65c. green and brown	4·50	3·75
593	-	1q. multicoloured	5·75	5·50
594	-	5q. brown, blue and green	23·00	22·00

DESIGNS: ½c. Liberation dagger symbol; 3c. Oil production; 4c. Family; 5c. Sword smashing Communist emblems; 6c. Hands holding map and cogwheel; 20c. Martyrs' Monument; 30c. Champerico Port; 65c. Telecommunications symbols; 1q. Flags of ODECA countries; 5q. Pres. Armas.

201 Rotary Emblem
and Road Map

1956. Air. 50th Anniv of Rotary International.

595	**201**	4c. bistre and blue	35	35
596	**201**	6c. bistre and green	35	25
597	**201**	35c. bistre and violet	3·00	2·20

1957. Air. Red Cross Fund. Nos. 577/9 optd **AEREO-1957** and ornaments.

598	-	5c.+15c. red and blue	11·50	11·50
599	-	15c.+50c. red and lilac	11·50	11·50
600	**198**	25c.+50c. red and blue	11·50	11·50

203 Esquipulas
Cathedral and
"Black Christ"

1957. Esquipulas Highway Fund. Inscr "PRO-CARRETERA ESQUIPULAS JUNIO 1957".

601	**203**	1½c.+½c. violet and brown (postage)	85	35
602	-	10c.+1q. brown and green (air)	11·00	11·00
603	-	15c.+1q. green and sepia	11·00	11·00
604	-	20c.+1q. slate and brown	11·00	11·00
605	-	25c.+1q. red and lilac	11·00	11·00

DESIGNS—HORIZ: 10c. Esquipulas Cathedral. VERT: 15c. Cathedral and "Black Christ"; 20c. Map of Guatemala and "Black Christ"; 25c. Bishop of Esquipulas.

204 Red Cross, Map and
Resplendent Quetzal

1958. Air. Red Cross.

606	**204**	1c. multicoloured	70	35
607	-	2c. red, brown and blue	50	25
608	-	3c. brown, red and blue	50	25
609	-	4c. red, green and brown	50	25

DESIGNS—VERT: 2c. J. R. Angulo, Mother and Child. HORIZ: 3c. P. de Bethancourt and Invalid; 4c. R. Ayau and Red Cross.

1959. Birth Centenary of R. A. Ovalle (composer of National Anthem). Optd **1858 1958 CENTENARIO.**

610	**191**	½c. grey and violet	60	60

1959. Air. Pres. Castillo Armas Commem. As No. 594 but inscr "LIBERACION 3 DE JULIO DE 1954", etc. Centre in blue and yellow. Frame colours given.

615	-	1c. black	50	35
616	-	2c. red	50	35
617	-	4c. brown	50	35
618	-	6c. green	50	35
619	-	10c. violet	60	45
620	-	20c. green	1·60	1·20
621	-	35c. grey	2·75	2·10

1959. Air. United Nations. Optd **HOMENAJE A LAS NACIONES UNIDAS.**

622	**168**	7½c. blue	1·80	1·90

207 Caravel of 1532
and freighter
Quetzaltenango

1959. Air. Central American Merchant Marine Commemoration.

623	**207**	6c. blue and red	1·60	45

1959. Air. Guatemala's Claim to Belize (British Honduras). As No. 509 optd **BELICE ES NUESTRO** and **AEREO.**

624		5c. brown and blue	85	35

1959. Air. Centenary of First Export of Coffee. No. 589 optd **1859 CENTENARIO PRIMERA EXPORTACION DE CAFE 1959.**

625		6c. blue and sepia	95	35

210 Pres. and Senora
Morales

1959. Air. Visit of President of Honduras.

626	**210**	6c. brown	60	45

211 Red Cross Shield

1960. Red Cross Commemoration. Cross in red.

627	**211**	1c.+1c. blue and brown (postage)	35	60
628	-	3c.+3c. blue and lilac	35	60
629	**211**	4c.+4c. blue and black	35	60
630	-	5c.+5c. blue, pink and red (air)	3·75	4·00
631	-	6c.+6c. green and red	3·75	4·00
632	-	10c.+10c. pink, blue and deep blue	3·75	4·00
633	-	15c.+15c. red, blue and brown	3·75	4·00

634	-	20c.+20c. green, pink and purple	3·75	4·00
635	-	25c.+25c. pink, blue and grey	3·75	4·00
636	-	30c.+30c. multicoloured	3·75	4·00

DESIGNS—3c., 5c. Wounded soldier at Solferino; 6c., 20c. Houses and debris afloat on flood waters; 10c., 25c. Earth, Moon and planets; 15c., 30c. Red Cross H.Q., Guatemala City.

1960. Air. World Refugee Year. Nos. 606/9 optd **ANO MUNDIAL DE REFUGIADOS** or surch also.

637	1c. multicoloured	3·25	2·50
638	2c. red, brown and blue	1·40	1·40
639	3c. brown, red and blue	1·40	1·40
640	4c. red, green and brown	1·40	1·40
641	6c. on 1c. multicoloured	7·75	3·75
642	7c. on 2c. red, brown and blue	3·50	3·00
643	10c. on 3c. brown, red & blue	5·50	5·75
644	20c. on 4c. red, green & brown	6·75	6·50

1960. Air. Founding of City of Melchor de Mencos. No. 589 optd **Fundacion de la cuidad Melchor de Mencos 30-IV-1960.**

645	6c. blue and sepia	1·90	2·10

213 Abraham Lincoln

1960. Air. 150th Birth Anniv of Abraham Lincoln.

646	**213**	5c. slate	35	35
647	**213**	30c. violet	1·70	2·10
648	**213**	50c. slate	8·50	10·00

214 UNESCO
Headquarters, Paris

1960. Air. Inauguration of UNESCO. Headquarters, Paris (1958).

649	**214**	5c. violet and mauve	35	35
650	**214**	6c. sepia and blue	35	35
651	**214**	8c. red and green	60	35
652	**214**	20c. blue and brown	2·20	2·10

1961. Air. Red Cross. Nos. 606/9 optd **MAYO DE 1960.**

653	1c. multicoloured	60	45
654	2c. red, brown and blue	25	45
655	3c. brown, red and blue	60	45
656	4c. red, green and brown	60	45

216 Romulus,
Remus and Wolf

1961. Plaza Italia Inauguration.

657	**216**	3c. blue	95	35

217 Independence
Ceremony

1962. Air. 140th Anniv of Independence.

658	**217**	4c. sepia	35	25
659	**217**	5c. blue	50	25
660	**217**	15c. violet	1·90	95

1962. Air. Malaria Eradication. Optd **1962 EL MUNDO UNIDO CONTRA LA MALARIA.**

666	**214**	6c. sepia and blue	1·30	2·10

219 Dr. Jose Luna

1962. Air. Guatemalan Doctors.

667	219	1c. violet and olive	1·20	35
668	-	4c. green and yellow	1·20	35
669	-	5c. brown and blue	1·20	35
670	-	6c. black and salmon	1·20	35
671	-	10c. brown and green	1·80	35
672	-	20c. blue and mauve	2·10	1·20

DOCTORS: 4c. R. Robles; 5c. N. Esparragoza; 6c. J. Ortega; 10c. D. Gonzalez; 20c. J. Flores.

1962. Air. Pres. Ydigoras's Tour of Central America. No. 589 optd **PRESIDENTE YDIGORAS FUENTES RECORRE POR TIERRA CENTRO AMERICA 14 A 20 DIC. 1962.**

673		6c. blue and sepia	1·70	1·20

1963. Air. New ODECA Charter Commemoration. Optd **CONMEMORACION FIRMA NUEVA CARTA ODECA.—1962.**

674	214	6c. sepia and blue	60	35
675	214	8c. red and green	70	35

222 Girl with Basket of Fruit on head

1963. Air. National Fair, 1960.

676	222	1c. multicoloured	35	25

1963. Air. Presidential Meeting. No. 589 with 11-line opt starting **REUNION PRESIDENTES: KENNEDY.**

677		6c. blue and sepia	8·50	4·25

224 Arms

1963

684	224	10c. red	60	35
685	224	10c. black	60	35
686	224	10c. brown	60	35
687	224	20c. violet	95	45
688	224	20c. blue	95	45

225 Harvester (after "The Reaper", Mathieson)

1963. Air. Freedom from Hunger.

689	225	5c. turquoise	50	35
690	225	10c. blue	95	45

226 Ceiba (national tree)

1963. Air.

691	226	4c. green and sepia	60	35

227 Pedro Bethancourt tending sick man

1964. Campaign for Canonization of Pedro Bethancourt.

692	227	2½c. brown (postage)	35	25
693	227	2½c. blue (air)	25	25
694	227	3c. orange	25	25
695	227	4c. violet	35	25
696	227	5c. green	50	25

228 Patzun Palace

1964. Air. Guatemalan Palaces.

697	228	1c. brown and red	60	35
698	-	3c. green and mauve	60	35
699	-	4c. lake and blue	60	35
700	-	5c. blue and brown	70	35
701	-	6c. blue and green	70	35

PALACES: 3c. Coban; 4c. Retalhuleu; 5c. San Marcos; 6c. Los Capitanes Generales.

229 Municipal Building

1964. Air. New Buildings. (a) As T **229.**

702	229	3c. brown and blue	50	35
703	-	4c. blue and brown	60	45

DESIGN: 4c. Social Security Building.

(b) Designs as Nos. 702/3 but different style frame and inscr, and new designs.

704		3c. green (As No. 703)	85	35
705		4c. slate	85	35
706	229	7c. blue	95	35
707	-	7c. bistre	85	35

DESIGNS: 4c. University Rectory; 7c. (No. 707), Engineering Faculty.

1964. Air. Olympic Games, Tokyo. Optd with Olympic rings and **OLIMPIADAS TOKIO-1964.**

708	204	1c.	1·40	1·60
709	-	2c. (No. 607)	1·40	1·60
710	-	3c. (No. 608)	1·40	1·60
711	-	4c. (No. 609)	1·40	1·60

1964. Air. New York World's Fair. Optd **FERIA MUNDIAL DE NEW YORK.**

712	204	1c.	1·20	1·30
713	-	2c. (No. 607)	1·20	1·30
714	-	3c. (No. 608)	1·20	1·30
715	-	4c. (No. 609)	1·20	1·30

1964. Air. Surch **HABILITADA** 1964 and value.

716	204	7c. on 1c.	50	35
717	-	9c. on 2c. (No. 607)	60	60
718	-	13c. on 3c. (No. 608)	85	70
719	-	21c. on 4c. (No. 609)	1·60	1·30

1964. Air. Eighth Cycle Race. Optd **VIII VUELTA CICLISTICA.**

720	204	1c.	1·80	1·60
721	-	2c. (No. 607)	1·80	1·60
722	-	3c. (No. 608)	1·80	1·60
723	-	4c. (No. 609)	3·25	2·50

234 Pres. Kennedy

1964. Air. Pres. Kennedy Commemoration.

724	234	1c. violet	1·40	85
725	234	2c. green	1·40	85
726	234	3c. brown	1·40	85
727	234	7c. blue	1·40	85
728	234	50c. green	10·50	9·00

1964. Air. 15th UPU Congress, Vienna. Sheet containing two stamps similar to T **224.**
MS729 86×60 mm. 10c. blue; 20c.

		carmine	11·50	12·00

235 Centenary Emblem

1964. Air. Red Cross Centenary. Emblem in silver and red.

730	235	7c. blue	85	45
731	235	9c. orange	85	55
732	235	13c. violet	1·30	95
733	235	21c. green	1·30	1·60

734	235	35c. brown	2·20	2·30
735	235	1q. bistre	6·25	3·75

1964. 15th Anniv (1963) of International Society of Guatemala Collectors. No. 559 optd **HOMENAJE A LA "I.S.G.C." 1948–1963.**

736		4c. orange	70	35

237 Bishop F. Marroquin

1985. Air. 400th Death Anniv of Bishop Marroquin.

737	237	4c. brown and purple	35	25
738	237	7c. sepia and grey	60	25
739	237	9c. black and blue	70	35

1965. Air. Optd **AYUDENOS MAYO 1965.** Emblem in silver and red.

740	235	7c. blue	60	50
741	235	9c. orange	70	60
742	235	13c. violet	75	65
743	235	21c. green	1·10	95
744	235	35c. brown	1·30	1·50

239 Scout Badge

1966. Air. Fifth Regional Scout Training Conference, Guatemala City. Multicoloured.

745		5c. Type **239**	70	65
746		9c. Scouts by campfire	90	85
747		10c. Scout carrying torch and flag	1·10	1·00
748		15c. Scout saluting	1·40	1·30
749		20c. Lord Baden-Powell	2·00	1·90

240 Flags

1966. Air. "Centro America". 145th Anniv of Central American Independence.

750	240	6c. multicoloured	50	20

241 Nefertari's Temple, Abu Simbel

1966. Air. Nubian Monuments Preservation.

751	241	21c. violet and bistre	1·10	55

242 Arms

1966. Air.

752	242	5c. orange	40	20
753	242	5c. green	40	20
754	242	5c. grey	40	25
755	242	5c. violet	40	25
756	242	5c. blue	40	25
757	242	5c. deep blue	40	20
758	242	5c. green	40	20
759	242	5c. green	40	20
760	242	5c. lake	70	25
761	242	5c. green on yellow	75	25

243 Mgr. M. Rossell y Arellano

1966. Air. Monseigneur Rossell Commem.

765	243	1c. violet	30	20
766	243	2c. green	40	20
767	243	3c. sepia	40	20
768	243	7c. blue	60	50
769	243	50c. slate	2·50	2·40

244 Mario M. Montenegro (revolutionary)

1966. Air. Montenegro Commemoration.

770	244	2c. red	30	15
771	244	3c. orange	40	20
772	244	4c. red	50	20
773	244	5c. grey	70	20
774	244	5c. blue	70	20
775	244	5c. green	70	20
776	244	5c. black	70	20

245 Morning Glory

1967. Air. Flowers. Multicoloured.

777	245	4c. Type **245**	60	30
778		8c. "Bird of Paradise" (horiz)	60	30
779		10c. "White Nun" orchid (national flower) (horiz)	85	45
780		20c. "Nymphs of Amatitlan"	1·90	1·30

246 Institute Emblem

1967. Air. Eighth General Assembly of Pan-American Geographical and Historical Institute (1965).

781	246	4c. purple, black & brown	35	20
782	246	5c. blue, black and bistre	70	20
783	246	7c. blue, black and yellow	1·10	30

247 Map of Guatemala and British Honduras

1967. Guatemala's Claim to British Honduras.

784	247	4c. blue, red and green	50	30
785	247	5c. blue, red and yellow	50	30
786	247	6c. blue, grey and orange	50	30

1967. Air. Guatemalan Victory in "Norceca" Football Games. No. 704 optd **GUATEMALA CAMPEON III Norceca Foot-Ball** and football motif.

787		3c. green	2·00	1·40

1967. Air. American Heads of State Meeting, Punta del Este. No. 705 optd **REUNION JEFES DE ESTADO AMERICANO, PUNTA DEL ESTE** etc.

788		4c. slate	1·40	1·40

250 "Peace and Progress"

1967. Air. International Co-operation.
789	250	7c. multicoloured	70	30
790	250	21c. multicoloured	1·10	65

251 Yurrita Church

1967. Air. Religion in Guatemala.
791	251	1c. brown, green and blue	50	30
792	-	2c. brown, pur & salmon	60	30
793	-	3c. indigo, red and blue	60	30
794	-	4c. green, purple & salmon	60	30
795	-	5c. brown, purple & green	60	30
796	-	7c. black, blue and mauve	70	30
797	-	10c. blue, violet and yellow	1·20	35

DESIGNS—HORIZ: 2c. Santo Domingo Church; 3c. San Francisco Church; 7c. Mercy Church, Antigua; 10c. Metropolitan Cathedral. VERT: 4c. Antonio Jose de Irisarri; 5c. Church of the Recollection.

252 Lincoln

1967. Air. Death Centenary (1965) of Abraham Lincoln.
798	252	7c. red and blue	60	30
799	252	9c. black and green	70	30
800	252	11c. black and brown	65	35
801	252	15c. red and blue	80	50
802	252	30c. green and purple	1·80	1·90

1967. Air. Eighth Central American Scout Camporee. Nos. 745/9 optd **VIII Camporee Scout Centroamericano Diciembre 1-8/1967.**
803		5c. Type **239**	50	50
804		9c. Scouts by campfire	80	75
805		10c. Scout carrying torch and flag	1·10	1·00
806		15c. Scout saluting	1·10	1·00
807		20c. Lord Baden-Powell	1·30	1·20

1967. Air. Award of Nobel Prize for Literature to Miguel Angel Asturias (1st issue). Nos. 694/5 optd **"Premio Nobel de Literatura - 10 diciembre 1967 - Miguel Angel Asturias".**
808	227	3c. orange	70	65
809	-	4c. violet	70	65

See also No. 838.

255 UNESCO Emblem and Children

1967. Air. 20th Anniv (1966) of UNESCO.
810	255	4c. green	30	15
811	255	5c. blue	40	20
812	255	7c. grey	50	30
813	255	21c. purple	1·20	1·10

256 Institute Emblem

1967. Air. 25th Anniv of Inter-American Institute of Agricultural Sciences.
814	256	9c. black and green	1·00	95
815	256	25c. red and brown	1·90	1·90
816	256	1q. ultramarine and blue	5·00	4·75

1968. Air. Third Meeting of Central American Presidents. Optd **III REUNION DE PRESIDENTES Nov. 15-18, 1967.**
817	204	1c. (No. 606)	1·20	80
819	-	2c. (No. 607)	1·00	1·00
821	-	3c. (No. 608)	1·00	1·00
823	235	7c. (No. 730)	1·00	1·00
824	235	9c. (No. 731)	1·40	1·40
825	235	13c. (No. 732)	2·00	1·40
826	235	21c. (No. 733)	2·75	1·40
827	235	35c. (No. 734)	2·30	2·40

258 "Madonna of the Choir"

1968. Air. 400th Anniv of "Madonna of the Choir".
828a	258	4c. blue	60	30
829	258	7c. slate	60	30
830	258	9c. green	70	30
830a	258	9c. lilac	75	25
831	258	10c. red	1·00	30
832	258	10c. grey	65	30
832a	258	10c. blue	50	15
833	258	1q. purple	5·00	4·25
834	258	1q. yellow	5·00	4·25

1968. Air. 11th Cycle Race. Nos. 784/6 optd **AEREO XI VUELTA CICLISTICA 1967.**
835	247	4c. blue, red and green	1·10	1·00
836	247	5c. blue, red and yellow	1·10	1·00
837	247	6c. blue, grey and orange	85	85

260 Miguel Angel Asturias

1968. Air. Award of Nobel Prize for Literature to Miguel Angel Asturias.
838	260	20c. blue	1·40	50

1968. Air. Campaign for Conservation of the Forests. No. 789 optd **AYUDA A CONSERVAR LOS BOSQUES.–1968.**
839	250	7c. multicoloured	50	30

1968. Air. Human Rights Year. No. 626 optd **1968.–ANO INTERNACIONAL DERECHOS HUMANOS.–ONU.**
840	210	6c. brown	70	35

1968. Air. Nahakin Scientific Expedition. No. 589 optd **Expedicion Cientifica** etc.
841		6c. blue and sepia	40	35

264 "Visit Guatemala"

1968. Air. Tourism.
842	264	10c. red and green	70	30
843	264	20c. red and black	1·10	75
844	264	50c. blue and red	1·90	1·80

265 Mayan Ball Game Ring and Resplendent Quetzal

1968. Olympic Games, Mexico. Quetzal in green and red.
845	265	1c. black	50	20
850	265	1c. slate	40	30
846	265	5c. yellow	70	30
851	265	5c. pink	70	30
852	265	5c. brown	70	30
853	265	5c. blue	70	70
847	265	8c. orange	80	30
848	265	15c. blue	1·40	30
849	265	30c. violet	2·50	1·30

1968. Air. 20th Anniv of Federation of Central American Universities. No. 705 optd **CONFEDERACION DE UNIVERSIDADES CENTROAMERICANAS 1948 1968.**
854		4c. slate	40	35

267 Presidents Gustavo Diaz Ordaz and Julio Cesar Mendez Montenegro

1968. Air. Exchange Visits of Mexican and Guatemalan Presidents.
855	267	5c. multicoloured	30	30
856	267	10c. blue and ochre	50	30
857	267	25c. blue and ochre	1·20	1·00

268 I.T.U. Emblem and Symbols

1968. Air. Centenary (1965) of I.T.U.
858	268	7c. blue	30	20
859	268	15c. black and green	60	20
859a	268	15c. brown and orange	70	30
860	268	21c. purple	85	55
861	268	35c. red and green	1·20	55
862	268	75c. green and red	3·00	2·75
863	268	3q. brown and red	11·50	9·50

269 Young Girl and Poinsettia

1969. Help for Abandoned Children.
864	269	2½c. ochre, red and green	40	20
865	269	2½c. orange, red and green	60	65
866	269	5c. black, red and green	60	20
867	269	21c. violet, red and green	1·30	1·00

1969. Air. Nos. 845/9 optd **AEREO** and motifs. Quetzal in green and red.
868	265	1c. black	1·00	50
869	265	5c. yellow	1·30	65
870	265	8c. orange	1·20	1·00
871	265	15c. blue	1·40	1·20
872	265	30c. violet	2·00	1·60

271 Dante

1969. Air. 700th Birth Anniv (1965) of Dante.
873	271	7c. blue and plum	50	30
874	271	10c. blue	60	30
875	271	20c. green	85	30
876	271	21c. slate and brown	1·40	95
877	271	35c. violet and green	3·50	2·10

272 Map of Central and South America

1969. Air. 20th Anniv of Latin-American Universities Union.
878	272	2c. mauve and black	30	20
879	-	9c. black and grey	70	30

MS880 118×75 mm. As Nos. 878/9, but colours changed; 2c. blue and black; 9c. black and red. Imperf   1·60   1·40

DESIGN: 26×27 mm 9c. University seal.

273 "Apollo 11" and Moon Landing

1969. Air. First Man on the Moon.
881	273	50c. black and purple	3·50	3·25
882	273	1q. black and blue	5·75	5·75

MS883 111×81 mm. **273** 1q. blue and green. Imperf   8·25   8·00

1970. 50th Anniv of Int Labour Organization. Nos. 847/8 optd **Cincuentenario O.I.T.** and ornaments.
884	265	8c. orange, green and red	60	20
886	265	15c. blue, green and red	85	30

275 Lake Atitlan

1970. Air. Conservation of Atitlan Grebes. Multicoloured.
888	275	4c. Type **275**	1·20	30
889		9c. Family of Atitlan Grebes	1·70	35
890		20c. Young grebe in nest (vert)	3·00	1·00

276 Dr. V. M. Calderon

1970. Air. First Death Anniv of Dr. Victor M. Calderon (medical scientist).
892	276	1c. black and blue	20	20
893	276	2c. black and green	30	20
894	276	9c. black and yellow	70	20

277 Hand holding Bible

1970. Air. 400th Anniv of Spanish Bible.
895	277	5c. multicoloured	40	30

1971. Air. Surch **VALE Q0.50.**
896	268	50c. on 3q. brown and red	2·50	2·40

279 Arms and Newspaper

1971. Air. Stamp Centenary (1st issue) and Centenary of Newspaper "Gaceta de Guatemala".
897	279	2c. blue and red	15	15
899b	279	5c. brown and red	30	30
899	279	25c. blue and red	80	50
899c	279	50c. mauve and brown	1·70	65

See also Nos. 988/9d.

280 Maya Indians and C.A.R.E. Package

1971. 25th Anniv of C.A.R.E. (Co-operative for American Relief Everywhere). Multicoloured.
900		1c. Type **280** (black inscr) (postage)	30	30
901		1c. Type **280** (brown inscr)	30	30

902		1c. Type **280** (violet inscr)	30	30
903		2c. Maya porter and C.A.R.E. parcel (air)	35	25
904		5c. Two Maya warriors and parcel	50	40
905		10c. C.A.R.E. parcel within Maya border	65	45
MS906		141×96 mm. Nos. 900 and 904. Imperf	3·00	3·00
MS907		141×96 mm. Nos. 903 and 905. Imperf	1·40	1·40

SIZES: 2c. (36×30 mm); 50c. (46×27 mm); 10c. (28×31 mm).

281 Decree of 1870

1971. Air. Stamp Centenary. Sheet 140×110 mm containing T **281** and four designs similar to T **1**.
MS908 1c. yellow; 4c, black (T **281**); 5c. brown; 10c. blue; 20c. red   2·50   2·40

282 J. Rufino Barrios, M. Garcia Granados and Emblems

1971. Air. Centenary of Liberal Reforms.

909	**282**	2c. multicoloured	1·00	20
910	**282**	10c. multicoloured	1·90	35
911	**282**	50c. multicoloured	8·25	4·00
912	**282**	1q. multicoloured	14·50	8·00

283 J. A. Chavarry Arrue (stamp engraver) and Leon Bilak (philatelist)

1971. Air. "Homage to Philately".

913	**283**	1c. black and green	30	20
914	**283**	2c. black and brown	40	30
915	**283**	5c. black and orange	60	35

1971. Air. "INTERFER 71" Int Fair, Guatemala. Optd **FERIA INTERNACIONAL "INTERFER–71" 30 Oct. al 21 Nov.**

916	**207**	6c. blue and red	40	20

285 Flag and Map

1971. Air. 150th Anniv of Central American Independence.

917	**285**	1c. blue, black and lilac	25	20
918	**285**	3c. blue, brown and pink	25	20
919	**285**	5c. blue, brown & orange	30	25
920	**285**	9c. blue, black and green	35	25

286 Maya Statue and UNICEF Emblem

1971. Air. 25th Anniv of UNICEF.

921	**286**	1c. green	30	20
921a	**286**	2c. purple	30	25
922	**286**	50c. purple	2·30	2·30
923	**286**	1q. blue	3·75	3·75

287 Boeing "Peashooter" and North American P-51 Mustang

1972. Air. 50th Anniv of Guatemala Air Force.

924	**287**	5c. blue and brown	70	25
925	-	10c. blue	1·30	30

DESIGN—56×32 mm: 10c. Bleriot XI airplane.

1972. Olympic Games, Munich. Sheet No. **MS**518 cut down to size 61×47 mm and optd **JUEGOS OLIMPICOS MUNICH 1972.**
MS926 1c. carmine (As T **5**); 10c. blue (as T **244**)   1·90   1·90

289 Ruins of Capuchin Monastery

1972. Air. Tourism. Ruins of Antigua.

927	**289**	1c. blue and light blue	30	10
928	A	1c. blue and light blue	30	10
929	B	1c. blue and light blue	30	10
930	C	1c. blue and light blue	30	10
931	D	1c. blue and light blue	30	10
932	E	1c. blue and light blue	30	10
933	**289**	2c. black and brown	30	25
934	A	2c. black and brown	30	25
935	B	2c. black and brown	30	25
936	C	2c. black and brown	30	25
937	D	2c. black and brown	30	25
938	E	2c. black and brown	30	25
939	**289**	2½c. black, mauve & silver	60	25
940	A	2½c. black, mauve & silver	60	25
941	B	2½c. black, mauve & silver	60	25
942	C	2½c. black, mauve & silver	60	25
943	D	2½c. black, mauve & silver	60	25
944	E	2½c. black, mauve & silver	60	25
945	**289**	5c. black, blue and orange	95	35
946	A	5c. black, blue and orange	95	35
947	B	5c. black, blue and orange	95	35
948	C	5c. black, blue and orange	95	35
949	D	5c. black, blue and orange	95	35
950	E	5c. black, blue and orange	95	35
951	**289**	20c. black and yellow	85	55
952	A	20c. black and yellow	85	55
953	B	20c. black and yellow	85	55
954	C	20c. black and yellow	85	55
955	D	20c. black and yellow	85	55
956	E	20c. black and yellow	85	55
957	**289**	1q. lt blue, red and blue	5·75	3·00
958	A	1q. lt blue, red and blue	5·75	3·00
959	B	1q. lt blue, red and blue	5·75	3·00
960	C	1q. lt blue, red and blue	5·75	3·00
961	D	1q. lt blue, red and blue	5·75	3·00
962	E	1q. lt blue, red and blue	5·75	3·00

DESIGNS: A, "La Recoleccion" archways; B, Cathedral ruins; C, Santa Clara courtyard; D, San Francisco gateway; E, Fountain, Central Park.
See also Nos. 1230/41.

290 Pres. Carlos Arana Osorio

1973. National Census.

963	**290**	2c. black and blue	20	10
964	-	3c. brown, pink & orange	30	10
965	**290**	5c. purple, mauve & black	40	10
966	-	8c. green, black & emerald	70	20

DESIGNS—VERT: 3c. Pres. Osorio seated; 8c. Pres. Osorio standing.

291 Francisco Ximenez

1973. International Book Year (1972).

967	**291**	2c. black and green	30	20
968	**291**	3c. brown and orange	30	20
969a	**291**	3c. black and yellow	30	20
969	**291**	6c. black and blue	35	25

292 Simon Bolivar and Map

1973. Air. Simon Bolivar, "The Liberator".

970	**292**	3c. black and red	30	20
971	**292**	3c. blue and orange	30	20
972	**292**	5c. black and yellow	35	30
973	**292**	5c. black and green	35	30

293 Eleanor Roosevelt

1973. Air. 90th Birth Anniv (1974) of Eleanor Roosevelt (sociologist).

974	**293**	7c. blue	30	20

294 Star Emblem

1973. Air. Centenary of Polytechnic School.

975	**294**	5c. yellow, brown & blue	40	30

See also Nos. 1000/1.

1973. Air. Nos. 927/32 optd **"II Feria Internacional" INTERFER/73 31 Octubre-Noviembre 18 1973 GUATEMALA.**

976	**289**	1c. blue and light blue	50	35
977	A	1c. blue and light blue	50	35
978	B	1c. blue and light blue	50	35
979	C	1c. blue and light blue	50	35
980	D	1c. blue and light blue	50	35
981	E	1c. blue and light blue	50	35

296 1c. Stamp of 1871

1973. Air. Stamp Centenary (1971). (2nd issue).

988	**296**	1c. brown	30	20
988a	**296**	6c. orange	30	30
988b	**296**	6c. green	30	30
988c	**296**	6c. blue	30	30
988d	**296**	6c. grey	30	30
989	**296**	1q. red	3·75	3·00

297 School Building

1973. Air. Centenary of Instituto Varones, Chiquimula.

990	**297**	3c. multicoloured	30	25
991	**297**	5c. red and black	30	25

1974. No. 863 surch **Desvaloradas a Q0.50** and leaves.

992	**268**	50c. on 3q. brown and red	2·50	2·40

1974. Air. Centenary of Universal Postal Union. Nos. 927/32 optd **UPU HOMENAJE CENTENARIO 1874 1974** and U.P.U. emblem.

993	**289**	1c. blue and light blue	50	35
994	A	1c. blue and light blue	50	35
995	B	1c. blue and light blue	50	35
996	C	1c. blue and light blue	50	35
997	D	1c. blue and light blue	50	35
998	E	1c. blue and light blue	50	35
MS999		141×96 mm	11·50	11·00

300 Barrios and Granados

1974. Air. Centenary (1973) of Polytechnic School (2nd issue).

1000	**300**	6c. red, grey and blue	30	30
1001	**300**	25c. multicoloured	60	35

DESIGN—VERT: 25c. School building.

1974. Air. Protection of the Resplendent Quetzal (Guatemala's national bird). No. 800 surch with bars, **VALE 10c. Proteccion del Ave Nacional el Quetzal** and bird.

1002	**252**	10c. on 11c. black & brn	85	50

302 Costume of San Martin Sacatepequez

1974. Air. Guatemalan Costumes. Multicoloured.

1003		2c. Solola costume	30	30
1004		2½c. Type **302**	30	25
1005		9c. Coban costume	40	30
1006		20c. Chichicastenango costume	70	30

303 Mayan Girl and Resplendent Quetzals

1975. Air. International Women's Year.

1007	**303**	8c. multicoloured	85	30
1008	**303**	20c. multicoloured	1·60	50

304 Rotary Emblem

1975. Air. 50th Anniv of Guatemala City Rotary Club.

1009	**304**	10c. multicoloured	30	10
1010	**304**	15c. multicoloured	55	20

305 I.W.Y. Emblem and Orchid

1975. Air. International Women's Year (2nd series).

1011	**305**	1c. multicoloured	35	30
1012	**305**	8c. multicoloured	50	30
1013	**305**	26c. multicoloured	1·10	40

306 Ruined Village

1976. Air. Earthquake of 4 February 1976. Multicoloured.

1014	1c. Type **306**	20	20
1015	3c. Food queue	20	20
1016	5c. Jaguar Temple, Tikal	20	20
1017	10c. Broken bridge	35	20
1018	15c. Open-air casualty station	55	20
1019	20c. Harvesting sugarcane	55	25
1020	25c. Ruined house	95	30
1021	30c. Reconstruction, Tecpan	1·10	35
1022	50c. Ruined church, Cerrodel Carmen	1·50	50
1023	75c. Clearing debris	2·40	90
1024	1q. Military aid	3·75	1·20
1025	2q. Lake Atitlan	7·00	2·75

MS1026 Three sheets each 112×83 mm. 50c. Map and bell; 1q. Encampment and helicopter; 2q. No. 1025
Set of three sheets 21·00 19·00

Text in panels expresses gratitude for foreign aid.

307 Eagle and Resplendent Quetzal Emblems

1976. Air. Bicentenary of American Revolution. Multicoloured.

1029	1c. Type **307**	30	20
1030	2c. Boston Tea Party	20	20
1031	3c. Thomas Jefferson (after G. Stuart) (vert)	20	20
1032	4c. Eagle and resplendent quetzal emblems (vert)	30	20
1033	5c. *Death of Gen. Warren at Bunker Hill* (detail, Trumbull)	20	20
1034	10c. *Washington reviewing his Ragged Army* (detail, Trego)	30	20
1035	15c. *Washington rallying the Troops at Monmouth* (detail, Leutze)	30	20
1036	20c. Eagle and resplendent quetzal emblems (diff)	55	25
1037	25c. *Meeting of Generals at Yorktown after the Surrender* (detail, Peale)	70	25
1038	30c. *Washington crossing the Delaware* (detail, Leutze)	95	25
1039	35c. Eagle and resplendent quetzal emblems (diff)	1·00	50
1040	40c. *Declaration of Independence* (detail, Trumbull)	1·00	55
1041	45c. *Patrick Henry before Virginia House of Burgesses* (detail, Rothermel) (vert)	1·20	65
1042	50c. *Congress voting Independence* (detail, Savage)	1·60	50
1043	1q. George Washington (after G. Stuart) (vert)	2·75	2·20
1044	2q. Abraham Lincoln (after D. D. Eisenhower) (vert)	4·75	4·25
1045	3q. Benjamin Franklin (after C. W. Peale) (vert)	6·75	5·75
1046	5q. John F. Kennedy (35×55 mm)	11·50	3·75

MS1047 Four sheets (a) 141×103 mm. No. 1043; (b) 147×108 mm. No. 1044; (c) 140×101 mm. No. 1045; (d) 143×105 mm. No. 1046. Imperf Set of four sheets 39·00 34·00

308 Quetzal Coin

1976. Air. 50th Anniv of Quetzal Currency.

1051	**308**	8c. black, orange and blue	30	20
1052	**308**	20c. black, mauve & blue	85	25

309 The Engineers (sculpture)

1976. Air. Centenary of Engineering School, Guatemala City.

1053	**309**	9c. blue	35	20
1054	**309**	10c. green	35	20

310 Sculpture of Christ (Pedro de Mendoza)

1977. Holy Week. Multicoloured.

1055	6c. Type **310** (postage)	50	25
1056	8c. Sculpture of Christ (Lanuza Brothers)	50	25
1057	3c. Statue of Christ (air)	50	25
1058	5c. Statue of Christ (vert)	50	25
1059	7c. Statue of Christ (vert)	50	25
1060	9c. Statue of Christ (vert)	55	25
1061	20c. Statue of Christ and Virgin (vert)	1·10	60
1062	26c. Statue of Christ	1·50	75

MS1063 100×70 mm. 30c. Christ bearing the Cross (horiz) 2·40 2·20

311 Deed to Site of Guatemala City

1977. Air. Bicentenary of Nueva Guatemala de la Asuncion (Guatemala City). Multicoloured.

1064	6c. Type **311**	50	25
1065	7c. City Hall and Bank of Guatemala (horiz)	50	25
1066	8c. Site of first legislative assembly (horiz)	50	25
1067	9c. Archbishop's arms (horiz)	65	25
1068	22c. Arms of Guatemala City	1·00	25

MS1069 Two sheets each 110×80 mm. (a) No. 1067; (b) No. 1068. Imperf Set of two sheets 2·40 2·10

312 Arms of Quetzaltenango

1977. Air. 150th Anniv of Founding of Quetzaltenango.

1071	**312**	7c. black and silver	30	15
1072	-	30c. orange and blue	1·00	35

DESIGN: 30c. City Hall and torch.

313 "Interfer 77" Emblem

1977. Fourth International Fair, Guatemala City.

1073	**313**	7c. multicoloured	30	25

314 Mayan Bas-relief

1977. Air. 14th Congress of Latin Notaries.

1074	**314**	10c. black and red	35	20

315 "The Holy Family"

1977. Air. Christmas. Multicoloured.

1075	1c. Type **315**	30	25
1076	2c. Boy and girl with animals, and Jesus in crib	30	25
1077	4c. Boy and girl with Mary and Jesus	30	25

316 Man from Almolongo

1978. Air. Guatemalan Costumes. Multicoloured.

1078	1c. Type **316**	15	15
1079	2c. Woman from Nebaj	15	15
1080	5c. Couple from San Juan Cotzal	20	15
1081	6c. Couple from Todos Santos	35	15
1082	20c. Couple from Regidores	1·30	25
1083	30c. Woman from San Cristobal	1·30	35

MS1084 70×90 mm. No. 1082 1·50 1·30

317 Virgin of Sorrows, Antigua

1978. Air. Holy Week. Multicoloured.

1085	2c. Type **317**	50	25
1086	4c. Virgin of Mercy, Antigua	50	25
1087	5c. Virgin of Anguish, Yurrita	50	25
1088	6c. Virgin of the Rosary, Santo Domingo	50	25
1089	8c. Virgin of Sorrows, Santo Domingo	50	25
1090	9c. Virgin of the Rosary, Quetzaltenango	50	25
1091	10c. Virgin of the Immaculate Conception, Church of St. Francis	50	25
1092	20c. Virgin of the Immaculate Conception, Cathedral Church	1·20	25

MS1093 71×101 mm. 30c. Pieta, Cavalry Church, Antigua. Imperf 3·50 3·00

318 Footballer

1978. Air. World Cup Football Championship, Argentina.

1094	**318**	10c. multicoloured	35	15

319 Gymnastics

1978. Air. 13th Central American and Caribbean Games, Medellin, Colombia.

1095	**319**	6c. mauve, blue and black	30	25
1096	-	6c. brt blue, blue & black	30	25
1097	-	6c. blue, brt blue & black	30	25
1098	-	6c. blue, mauve and black	30	25
1099	-	8c. mauve, blue and black	30	25

DESIGNS: No. 1096, Volleyball; 1097, Target Shooting; 1098, Weightlifting; 1099, Running.

320 *Cattleya pachecoi*

1978. Air. Orchids. Multicoloured.

1100	1c. Type **320**	30	25
1101	1c. *Sobralia xantholeuca*	35	25
1102	1c. *Cypripedium irapeanum*	35	25
1103	1c. *Oncidium splendidum*	35	25
1104	3c. *Cattleya bowringiana*	40	25
1105	3c. *Encyclia cordigera*	40	25

1106	3c. *Epidendrum imatophyllum*	40	25
1107	3c. *Barkeria skinneri*	40	25
1108	8c. *Spiranthes speciosa*	75	60
1109	20c. *Lycaste skinneri*	2·75	2·40

321 University Seal

1978. Air. 300th Anniv of San Carlos University of Guatemala. Multicoloured.

1110	6c. Type **321**	20	15
1111	7c. Students from different faculties (26×46 mm)	30	15
1112	12c. 17th-century student	35	20
1113	14c. Student and molecular model	55	20

322 Brown and White Children

1978. Air. Guatemalan Children's Year (1977). Multicoloured.

1114	6c. Type **322**	20	15
1115	7c. Child skipping	30	15
1116	12c. "Helping Hand"	35	20
1117	14c. Hands protecting Indian girl	55	20

323 Planting Seedling

1979. Air. Forestry. Multicoloured.

1118	6c. Type **323**	35	25
1119	8c. Burnt forest	35	25
1120	9c. Woodland scene	35	25
1121	10c. Sawmill	35	25
1122	26c. Forest conservation	65	25

MS1123 140×100 mm. Nos. 1118/22 with label showing FAO emblem 2·30 2·10

324 Ocellated Turkey

1979. Air. Wildlife Conservation. Multicoloured.

1124	1c. Type **324**	75	25
1125	3c. White-tailed deer (horiz)	50	25
1126	5c. King vulture	2·40	25
1127	7c. Great horned owl	5·25	1·00
1128	9c. Ocelot	1·10	25

MS1129 98×69 mm. 30c. Resplendent quetzal (35×45 mm) 12·00 11·00

325 Clay Jar

1979. Air. Archaeological Treasures from Tikal. Multicoloured.

1130	2c. Type **325**	50	25
1131	3c. Ceramic head of Mayan woman	65	40
1132	4c. Earring	95	60
1133	5c. Vase	1·10	65
1134	6c. Ceramic figure	1·50	85
1135	7c. Carved bone	1·60	1·00
1136	8c. Striped vase	1·90	1·10
1137	10c. Tripod vase with lid	2·40	1·40

326 Presidential
Guard Headquarters

1979. 30th Anniv of Presidential Guard. Multicoloured.

1138	10c. Type **326** (postage)		30	25
1139	8c. Presidential Guard insignia (air)		30	25

327 National Coat
of Arms

1979. Air. Municipal Arms. Multicoloured.

1140	8c. Type **327**	55	25
1141	8c. Alta Verapaz	55	25
1142	8c. Baja Verapaz	55	25
1143	8c. Chimal Tenango	55	25
1144	8c. Chiquimula	55	25
1145	8c. Escuintla	55	25
1146	8c. Flores (Peten)	55	25
1147	8c. Guatemala	55	25
1148	8c. Huehuetenango	55	25
1149	8c. Izabal	55	25
1150	8c. Jalapa	55	25
1151	8c. Jutiapa	55	25
1152	8c. Mazatenango	55	25
1153	8c. El Progreso	55	25
1154	8c. Quezaltenango	55	25
1155	8c. Quiche	55	25
1156	8c. Retalhuleu	55	25
1157	8c. Sacatepequez	55	25
1158	8c. San Marcos	55	25
1159	8c. Santa Rosa	55	25
1160	8c. Solola	55	25
1161	8c. Totonicapan	55	25
1162	8c. Zacapa	55	25
MS1163	100×72 mm. 50c. First and present national arms. Imperf	4·25	3·75

328 Rotary Emblem and
Girl with Flowers

1980. 75th Anniv of Rotary International. Multicoloured.

1164	4c. Type **328**	95	25
1165	6c. Diamond, emblem and resplendent quetzal	95	25
1166	10c. Paul P. Harris (founder), emblem and resplendent quetzal	1·10	65

329 The Creation
of the World

1981. Air. "Popol Vuh". Designs showing medallic illustrations of Guatemalan history and legends from the Sacred Book of the Ancient Quiches of Guatemala. (a) The Creation.

1167	**329** 1c. black and mauve	10	10
1168	- 2c. black and green	10	10
1169	- 4c. black and blue	35	20
1170	- 8c. black and yellow	70	40
1171	- 10c. black and pink	80	50
1172	- 22c. black and brown	1·90	1·10

(b) The Adventures of Hun Ahpu and Xbalanque.

1173	1c. black and mauve	10	10
1174	4c. black and violet	35	20
1175	6c. black and brown	45	30
1176	8c. black and green	70	40
1177	10c. black and yellow	80	50
1178	26c. black and green	2·10	1·20

(c) The Founding of the Quiche Race.

1179	2c. black and mauve	10	10
1180	4c. black and blue	35	20
1181	6c. black and pink	45	30
1182	8c. black and yellow	70	40
1183	10c. black and green	80	50
1184	30c. black and green	2·50	1·60

(d) The Territorial Expansion of the Quiches.

1185	3c. black and blue	25	10
1186	4c. black and violet	35	20
1187	6c. black and pink	45	30
1188	8c. black and grey	70	40
1189	10c. black and green	80	50
1190	50c. black and mauve	4·25	2·50

DESIGNS—No. 1168, Populating the earth; 1169, Birth of the stick-men; 1170, Destruction of the stick-men; 1171, Creation of the men of corn; 1172, "Thanks to the creator"; 1173, Origin of the twin semi-gods; 1174, Punishment of the Princess Xquic; 1175, Odyssey of Hun Ahpu and Xbalanque; 1176, The test in Xibalba; 1177, Multiplication of the prodigies; 1178, The deification of Hun Ahpu and Xbalanque; 1179, Balam Quitze, father of Caviquib; 1180, Caha Paluma, wife of Balam Quitze; 1181, Balam Acab, father of Nihaibab; 1182, Chomiia, wife of Balam Acab; 1183, Mahucutah, father of Ahau Quiche; 1184, Tzununiha, wife of Mahucutah; 1185, Cotuha, Quiche monarch; 1186, The invincible Cotuha and Iztayul; 1187, Cucumatz, the prodigious king; 1188, Warrior with captive; 1189, "None can conquer or kill the king"; 1190, "This was the greatness of the Quiches".

330 Early and
Modern Telephones
(cent)

1981. Air. Anniversaries.

1191	-	3c. red and black	35	30
1192	-	5c. blue and black	45	30
1193	**330**	6c. multicoloured	60	30
1194	-	7c. multicoloured	70	40
1195	-	12c. multicoloured	1·20	60
1196	-	25c. multicoloured	2·30	1·30

DESIGNS—26×46 mm: 3c. Thomas Edison (centenary of gramophone). 29×39 mm: 7c. Charles Lindbergh (50th anniv of solo Atlantic flight); 12c. Jose Cecilio del Valle (patriot, birth bicentenary); 25c. Jesues Castillo (composer, birth centenary). 46×26 mm: 5c. Spool of film (50th anniv of sound film).

331 Roderico Toledo and
German Chupina (first and
present Police Chiefs)

1981. Air. Centenary of National Police. Multicoloured.

1197	2c. Type **331**	60	30
1198	4c. Police Headquarters	60	30

332 Mayan Sun Calendar

1981. Air. Seventh Latin American Aviculture Congress.

1199	**332**	1c. green, yellow & black	35	30

333 Bernardo
O'Higgins (Chile)

1982. Air. Liberators of the Americas.

1200	**333**	2c. multicoloured	35	30
1201	-	3c. multicoloured	35	30
1202	-	4c. multicoloured	35	30
1203	-	10c. grey and black	35	30

DESIGNS—(31×45 mm): 4c. Jose de San Martin (Argentine); 10c. Miguel Garcia Granados (Guatemala). (26×35 mm): 3c. Jose Artigas (Uruguay).

334 General Barrios and
Bank

1982. Air. Centenary of Banco de Occidente.

1204	**334**	1c. multicoloured	35	30
1205	-	2c. black, red and blue	35	30
1206	-	3c. multicoloured	35	30
1207	-	4c. multicoloured	35	30

DESIGNS—HORIZ: 2c. Bank building. VERT: 3c. Centenary emblem; 4c. Centenary medals.

335 Old and New Bank
Buildings, Guatemala City

1982. Air. 50th Anniv of National Mortgage Bank.

1208	**335**	1c. multicoloured	35	30
1209	-	2c. black, yellow & green	35	30
1210	-	5c. multicoloured	35	30
1211	-	10c. black, yellow & grn	35	30

DESIGNS—HORIZ: 2c. Bank emblem; 10c. Bank and Anniversary emblems. VERT: 5c. Bronze anniversary medallion.

336 Brother Pedro

1983. Air. Blessed Brother Pedro. Multicoloured.

1212	1c. Type **336**	25	20
1213	20c. Apparition of Virgin Mary	95	50

337 I.T.U. and
W.H.O. Emblems
with Ribbons
forming Caduceus

1983. Air. World Communications and Health Day.

1214	**337**	10c. yellow, red and black	45	30

338 Hands holding
Bible

1983. Air. Centenary (1982) of Evangelical Church in Guatemala. Multicoloured.

1215	3c. Type **338**	60	30
1216	5c. Central Evangelical Church	60	30

339 Train crossing Las Vacas
Bridge

1983. Air. Centenary (1980) of Guatemalan Railways. Multicoloured.

1217	10c. Type **339**	1·10	85
1218	25c. General Barrios and trains at station	3·00	1·80
1219	30c. Train crossing Lake Amatitlan Dam	3·50	2·20

340 F.A.O. Emblem and
Starving Children

1983. Air. World Food Day (1981). Multicoloured.

1220	8c. Maize and Globe	35	10
1221	1q. Type **340**	3·25	1·80

1984. Air. As Nos. 927/32 and 945/50 but colours changed. Values inscribed in black.

1230	**289**	1c. black and green	25	20
1231	A	1c. black and green	25	20
1232	B	1c. black and green	25	20
1233	C	1c. black and green	25	20
1234	D	1c. black and green	25	20
1235	E	1c. black and green	25	20
1236	**289**	5c. black and orange	35	20
1237	A	5c. black and orange	35	20
1238	B	5c. black and orange	35	20
1239	C	5c. black and orange	35	20
1240	D	5c. black and orange	35	20
1241	E	5c. black and orange	35	20

341 Pope John Paul II

1984. Air. Papal Visit. Multicoloured.

1242	4c. Type **341**	35	30
1243	8c. Woman kneeling before Pope	35	30

342 Rafael Landivar

1984. Air. 250th Birth Anniv of Rafael Landivar (poet). Multicoloured.

1244	2c. Type **342**	35	30
1245	4c. Landivar's tomb, Antigua Guatemala (horiz)	35	30

343 Casariego y
Acevedo

1984. Air. First Death Anniv of Cardinal Mario Casariego y Acevedo, Archbishop of Guatemala.

1246	**343** 10c. multicoloured	60	30

344 Bank's Emblem

1984. Air. 20th Anniv of Central American Bank for Economic Integration.

1247	**344** 30c. multicoloured	1·60	85

345 Planting Coffee, 1870

1984. Air. Coffee.

1248	**345**	1c. black and brown	25	20
1249	-	2c. black and flesh	25	20
1250	-	3c. black and stone	25	20
1251	-	4c. black and buff	25	20
1252	-	5c. multicoloured	45	30
1253	-	10c. multicoloured	95	50

1254	-	12c. multicoloured	1·20	60
1255	-	25c. multicoloured	2·30	1·30
1256	-	25c. black and brown	£130	10
1257	-	30c. multicoloured	£160	10

DESIGNS: As T **345**: 2c. Harvesting coffee, 1870; 3c. Drying coffee beans, 1870; 4c. Exporting coffee, 1870; 5c. Grafting seedlings; 10c. Instant coffee; 12c. Harvesting and processing coffee; 25c. (1255) Exporting coffee (different). (81×108 mm); 25c. (1256) Women picking coffee. (100×81 mm); 30c. Globe and coffee beans.

346 "Beaver" Cub and Tikal Pyramid

1985. Air. 75th Anniv of Boy Scout Movement. Multicoloured.

1258	5c. Type **346**	35	20
1259	6c. "Wolf" cub and Captains Palace, Old Guatemala	50	25
1260	8c. Scout, xylophone player and countryside	55	35
1261	10c. Rover scout and dancers	70	40
1262	20c. Lord Baden-Powell (founder) and Carlos Cipriani (founder of Guatemalan scouts)	1·50	90

347 Family

1985. Air. Inter-American Family Year.

1263	**347**	10c. multicoloured	55	35

348 Emblem

1985. Air. 25th Anniv of Central American Air Navigation Services Association.

1264	**348**	10c. multicoloured	50	25

349 Morse Key, Samuel Morse, J. Rufino Barrios and Telegraph Aerial

1985. Air. National Telegraph Service.

1265	**349**	4c. black and brown	30	25

350 Olympic Rings and Maya Pelota Player

1986. Air. 90th Anniv of First Modern Olympic Games and Foundation of International Olympic Committee. Multicoloured.

1266	8c. Type **350**	35	25
1267	10c. Rings and Baron Pierre de Coubertin	50	25

351 Rescue Team with Person in Cradle

352 Temple of Minerva, Quetzaltenango

1986. Air. Centenary (1984) of Independence Fair, Quetzaltenango. Multicoloured.

1269	8c. Type **352**	30	20
1270	10c. City arms in courtyard of Quetzaltenango Municipal Palace	35	25

353 Fire behind Fireman carrying Child

1986. Air. Volunteer Firemen (2nd series). Multicoloured.

1271	8c. Type **353**	75	25
1272	10c. Searching rubble after explosion (33×24 mm)	75	30

354 Arms

1986. Air. 25th Anniv (1976) of Association of Telegraphists and Radio-Telegraph Operators.

1273	**354**	6c. multicoloured	30	20

355 Architect with Plans looking at Building

1987. Air. 25th Anniv of San Carlos University Architecture Faculty.

1274	**355**	10c. multicoloured	35	20

356 Emblem and Boeing 727

1987. Air. 40th Anniv of I.C.A.O. Multicoloured.

1275	8c. Type **356**	30	20
1276	10c. Boeing 727 airplane on runway (vert)	35	20

357 Aerial View of Site

1987. Air. Chixoy Hydro-electric Plant.

1277	**357**	2c. multicoloured	30	25

358 Dr. Cayetano Francos y Monroy, Archbishop of Guatemala (founder)

1986. Air. Volunteer Firemen (1st series).

1268	**351**	6c. multicoloured	75	25

See also Nos. 1271/2.

359 Column beside Man studying Book

1987. Air. Regional Book Promotion Centre for Latin America and Caribbean.

1280	**359**	12c. multicoloured	50	25

360 Girls in Traditional Costumes

1987. Coban Folklore Festival. Multicoloured.

1281	50c. Girl weaving	3·25	1·00
1282	1q. Type **360**	6·75	2·10

361 Cesar Branas

1987. Air. Writers (1st series).

1283	**361**	6c. orange and black	30	20
1284	-	8c. red and black	30	20
1285	-	9c. purple and black	30	20

DESIGNS: 8c. Rafael Arevalo Martinez; 9c. Jose Milla y Vidaurre.
See also Nos. 1297/8 and 1307/11.

362 Footballer

1987. Air. Pan-American Games National Football Selection.

1286	**362**	10c. blue and black	35	20

363 Miguel Angel Asturias Cultural Centre

1987

1287	**363**	1c. blue	30	20
1287a	**363**	2c. brown	30	20
1288	**363**	3c. blue	30	20
1289	**363**	4c. mauve	30	20
1290	**363**	5c. orange	30	20
1291	**363**	6c. green	30	20
1292	**363**	7c. red	30	20
1293	**363**	8c. mauve	30	20
1294	**363**	9c. black	30	20
1295	**363**	10c. green	35	25

1988. Air. Writers (2nd series). As T **361**.

1297	4c. red and black	30	20
1298	5c. brown and black	30	20

DESIGNS: 4c. Enrique A. Hidalgo; 5c. Enrique Gomez Carrillo.

364 Stylized Dove

1987. Air. Bicentenary (1981) of St. Joseph Children's College. Multicoloured.

1278	8c. Type **358**	30	20
1279	10c. College emblem	35	25

365 Festival Performers

1988. Air. "Esquipulas II—A Firm Step towards Peace".

1299	**364**	10c. green	50	25
1300	-	40c. red	1·90	1·10
1301	-	60c. blue	2·75	1·60

DESIGNS—HORIZ: 40c. Three stylized doves. VERT: 60c. Stylized dove.

1988. National Folklore Festival, Coban. Sheet 81×100 mm. Imperf.

MS1302	**365**	2q. multicoloured	12·00	11·00

366 St. John and Boys

1989. Death Centenary of St. John Bosco (founder of Salesian Brothers).

1303	**366**	40c. black and gold	1·10	60

367 Birds

1989. Air. Bicentenary of French Revolution.

1304	**367**	1q. red, blue and black	6·00	2·10

368 Madrid Codex (detail)

1990. Air. America. Pre-Columbian Culture. Multicoloured.

1305	10c. Type **368**	2·10	1·20
1306	20c. Tikal Pyramid	4·25	2·50

1990. Air. Writers (3rd series). As T **361**.

1307	1c. mauve and black	30	20
1308	2c. orange and black	30	20
1309	3c. blue and black	30	20
1310	7c. black and green	30	20
1311	10c. black and yellow	30	20

DESIGNS: 1c. Flavio Herrera; 2c. Rosendo Santa Cruz; 3c. Werner Ovalle Lopez; 7c. Clemente Marroquin Rojas; 10c. Miguel Angel Asturias.

369 Games Emblem

1990. Sixth Central American and Caribbean University Games. Multicoloured.

1312	15c. Type **369**	35	25
1313	20c. Mascot holding flame (vert)	55	25
1314	25c. Mascot playing volleyball	75	25
1315	30c. Mascot playing football	85	25
1316	45c. Mascot performing judo movement	1·30	35
1317	1q. Mascot playing baseball	3·00	80
1318	2q. Mascot playing basketball	5·50	1·60
1319	3q. Mascot hurdling	9·00	2·75

370 Family, Cereal and Emblem

1990. Air. 40th Anniv of Central America and Panama Nutrition Institute.

1320	**370**	20c. multicoloured	65	25

371 Palais de l'Athenee, Geneva (venue of founding meeting)

1990. Air. 125th Anniv (1988) of International Red Cross.
| 1321 | **371** | 50c. multicoloured | 1·50 | 40 |

372 Arms

1991. Air. Centenary of National Defence Staff.
| 1322 | **372** | 20c. multicoloured | 55 | 20 |

373 Atitlan Lake

1991. America. Natural World. Multicoloured.
| 1323 | | 10c. Pacaya Volcano in eruption | 30 | 25 |
| 1324 | | 60c. Type **373** | 2·10 | 40 |

374 Martin and Vicente Pinzon

1992. Air. America. 500th Anniv of Discovery of America by Columbus. Each black and green.
| 1325 | | 40c. Type **374** | 1·10 | 50 |
| 1326 | | 60c. Christopher Columbus and "Santa Maria" (vert) | 1·70 | 75 |

375 Crops

1992. Air. 50th Anniv of International Institute for Agricultural Co-operation.
| 1327 | **375** | 10c. multicoloured | 65 | 25 |

376 Emblem

1992. International Anti-AIDS Campaign.
| 1328 | **376** | 1q. multicoloured | 3·00 | 85 |

377 *Encyclia cochleata*

1994. Air. Orchids (1st series). Multicoloured.
1329		50c. Type **377**	1·40	85
1330		1q. *Encyclia vitellina*	2·75	85
1331		2q. *Odontoglossum uroskinneri*	5·25	1·60
See also Nos. 1355/6.

378 Family around Tree

1994. 50th Anniv of 20 October Revolution. Multicoloured.
1332		40c. Type **378**	35	25
1333		60c. Dove on hand (horiz)	55	35
1334		1q. Man holding book and rifle	95	60
1335		2q. Representations of social developments since 1944	1·90	1·20
1336		3q. Three youths supporting torch ("Revolution, Liberty, Justice and Peace")	3·00	1·60

379 City Buildings

1995. Air. Tourism. Multicoloured.
1337		20c. White water rafting	50	25
1338		40c. Windsurfing	50	25
1339		60c. Pleasure boat on Lake Atitlan	65	35
1340		80c. Tourist launch *Crucero*	75	40
1341		1q. Erupting volcano	75	35
1342		2q. Type **379**	1·50	65
1343		3q. Parrots on perch (vert)	2·10	90
1344		4q. Mayan ruins (vert)	3·00	1·30
1345		5q. Ceremony (vert)	3·75	1·80

380 Greeting Crowd

1996. Air. Papal Visit. Pope John Paul II. Multicoloured.
1350		10c. Type **380**	20	15
1351		1q. Holding child	55	50
1352		1q.75 Holding crucifix and wearing mitre	1·00	90
1353		1q.90 Wearing cross and red cloak	1·10	1·00
1354		2q.90 Wearing red hat	1·80	1·60

1996. Air. Orchids (2nd series). As T **377**. Multicoloured.
| 1355 | | 20c. *Phragmipedium caudatum* | 75 | 65 |
| 1356 | | 1q.50 *Odontoglossum laeve* | 5·75 | 5·00 |

381 Carlos Merida

1996. Air. Personalities.
1357	**381**	40c. lt blue, blue & black	30	25
1358	-	50c. brown, blue & black	30	25
1359	-	60c. brown, blue & black	35	35
DESIGNS: 50c. Jose Eulalio Samayoa; 60c. Manuel Montufar y Coronado.

382 University Hall

1997. Buildings. Multicoloured.
| 1360 | | 50c. Type **382** | 35 | 35 |
| 1361 | | 1q. Brewery | 75 | 70 |

383 Breastfeeding

1997. Air. Breastfeeding Campaign.
| 1362 | **383** | 1q. multicoloured | 75 | 65 |

384 Parent and Child (Marion Contreras Castanaza)

1997. 50th Anniv (1996) of UNICEF "Children and Peace". Multicoloured.
| 1363 | | 10c. Type **384** | 30 | 20 |
| 1364 | | 20c. Child riding birds (Marvin Sac Coyoy) (horiz) | 30 | 20 |

385 Child writing (Education)

1997. Air. Public Finance Projects. Multicoloured.
1365		20c. Type **385**	20	20
1366		60c. Child receiving medication (health)	35	25
1367		80c. Road (infrastructure)	55	40
1368		1q. Family (security)	75	50

386 Jorge Rybar (pioneer) and Machinery

1998. Air. 50th Anniv of Guatemala Plastics Industry.
| 1369 | **386** | 10c. multicoloured | 30 | 25 |

387 1875 Postcard and Emblem

1999. Air. 50th Anniv (1998) of El Quetzal (International Society of Guatemala Stamp Collectors).
| 1370 | **387** | 1q. multicoloured | 75 | 65 |

388 Francisco Marroquin (first bishop of Guatemala)

2001. Birth Anniversaries (1999). Multicoloured.
1371		3q. Type **388** (500th anniv)	3·00	2·75
1372		4q. Jacinto Rodriguez Diaz (aviation pioneer) (centenary)	4·00	3·50
1373		8q.75, Miguel Angel Asturias (Nobel Prize winner for Literature) (centenary)	8·75	7·75
1374		10q. Cesar Branas (writer and historian) (centenary)	10·00	8·75

389 Church Architecture, Antigua and Hermano Pedro

2002. Air. Third Visit of Pope John Paul II (50c., 2, 5, 8q.75). 12th Anniv Canonisation of Hermano Pedro (monk and humanitarian) (20, 25c., 1q.). Multicoloured.
1375		20c. Type **389**	25	20
1376		25c. Hermano Pedro holding bell rope	25	20
1377		50c. Hermano Pedro and Pope John Paul II (horiz)	45	40
1378		1q. Nativity, his alms bell and Hermano Pedro (head)	95	85
1379		2q. Pope John Paul II and Archbishop Rudolfo Toruno (horiz)	2·00	1·80
1380		5q. Fountain, part of door lintel and Pope John Paul II (horiz)	5·00	4·50
1381		8q. 75 Pope John Paul II, clock tower and Government Palace (horiz)	8·75	7·75
MS1382	153×128 mm. As Nos. 1375/81		18·00	16·00

390 Guatemalan Flag, Globe, Envelopes, Quetzal Bird and Flags

2002. Air. 125th Anniv of Universal Postal Union (1999). Multicoloured.
1383		20c. Type **390**	25	20
1384		2q. UPU emblem	1·50	1·30
1385		3q. Globe with map of Americas encircled by bird	2·20	2·00
1386		5q. Globe with hands holding envelopes and flags	3·75	3·25

391 Mt. Everest

2002. Air. First Anniv of Jaime Vinals' Ascent of Everest.
| 1387 | **391** | 3q. multicoloured | 2·10 | 1·40 |

392 Children

2002. Air. Centenary of Pan-American Health Organization.
| 1388 | **392** | 4q. multicoloured | 2·50 | 1·90 |

393 Dance of the Conquest Mask, Totonicapan

2003. Masks. Multicoloured.
1389		20c. Type **393**	25	20
1390		2q. Dance of Moors and Christians, Sacatepequez	1·40	1·20
1391		3q. Deer dance, Alta Verapaz	2·10	1·90
1392		4q. Jaguar mask, Deer dance, Totonicapan	2·75	2·50
MS1393	100×71 mm. 5q. Paabanc		3·50	3·00

394 Field Worker and Josemaria Escriva de Balaguer

2003. Birth Centenary of Josemaria Escriva de Balaguer (2002) (founder of Opus Dei (religious organization)). Multicoloured.
1394		20c. Type **394**	25	20
1395		50c. Josemaria Escriva and fisherman	45	40
1396		3q. Facing left	2·30	2·10

1397	10q. Church and Josemaria Escriva	7·50	6·75

395 Man carrying Bananas

2003. 50th Anniv of Regional Organization for Farming Health (OIRSA). Multicoloured.

1398	20c. Type 395	20	20
1399	1q. Hands holding corn	85	75
1400	2q. Cow's face	1·80	1·60
1401	4q. Field of crop	3·25	2·75
1402	5q. Meats	4·50	4·00
1403	10q. Eye and maize	9·00	7·75
MS1404	101×62 mm. 3q. Fruit	1·20	1·00

396 Pier, Punta de Manabique, Izabel Department

2004. Tourism. Izabel Department (1405/7). Multicoloured.

1405	20c. Type 396	20	20
1406	50c. Las Siete Altares, Izabel Department	40	35
1407	1q. Las Escobas waterfalls, Izabel Department	85	75
1408	1q.50 Barrios y Pichilingo harbour (America. Cultural Heritage)	1·40	1·20
1409	2q. Mayan acropolis, Quirigua	1·80	1·60
1410	3q. Livingston beach, Rio Dulce	2·75	2·40
1411	4q. San Felipe castle	3·50	3·25
1412	5q. Sunset, El Estor	4·50	4·00
1413	8q.75 Agua Caliente waterfalls	7·75	7·00
1414	10q. Rio Polochi river	9·00	7·75
MS1415	102×63 mm. 4q. Carving, Mayan acropolis, Quirigua (America. Cultural Heritage)	1·50	1·30

397 Archbishop Quezada Toruno

2004. Archbishop Rudolfo Quezada Toruno's Elevation to Cardinal. Multicoloured.

1416	20c. Type 397	20	20
1417	25c. Wearing vestments and carrying a crosier	20	20
1418	50c. Receiving scroll from Pope John Paul II wearing Cardinal's cappa magna and biretta	40	35
1419	1q. Pope John Paul II receiving Archbishop Quezada Turono wearing skull cap	85	75
1420	2q. Wearing Cardinal's cape and skull cap	1·80	1·60
1421	3q. Wearing Cardinal's cape and skull cap, head and shoulders	2·75	2·40
1422	4q. Speaking at microphone as Archbishop	3·50	3·25
1423	5q. Kissing Pope John Paul II's hand as Cardinal	4·50	4·00
1424	8q.75 With other Archbishops	7·75	7·00
MS1426	102×63 mm. 3q. As No. 1421. Imperf	2·75	2·40

398 *Sarcoramphus papa* (inscr "Sarcoranphus")

2005. Flora and Fauna. America 2003 Endangered Species. Multicoloured.

1427	50c. Type 398	40	35
1428	3q. *Heliconia collinsiana* (vert)	2·75	2·40
1429	5q. *Felis concolor*	4·50	4·00
1430	12q. *Heliconius petiveranus*	8·75	7·70

MS1431	100×64 mm. 12q. *Tapirus vairdii*	10·50	9·25

399 Flags, Water-pipe and Girl

2005. 70th Anniv of Guatemala—Japan Diplomatic Relations. Multicoloured.

1432	1q. Type 399	85	75
1433	8q. Flags, hospital and girl	85	75
MS1434	114×51 mm. 14q. Mount Fuji	10·50	9·25

400 Incense Burner

2005. Pottery. Multicoloured.

1435	1q. Type 400	85	75
1436	2q. Jars with owl faces	1·40	1·20
1437	6q.50 Plate and bowl	4·25	2·10
1438	8q. Lantern	5·50	5·00
MS1439	64×51 mm. 12q. Jars	10·50	9·25

401 Clasped Hands

2005. Centenary of Rotary International. Multicoloured.

1440	2q. Type 401	1·40	1·20
1441	6q.50 Child's face and water droplets	4·25	2·10
MS1442	51×64 mm. 8q. Emblem	5·50	5·00

402 Hand reaching

2006. America. Struggle against Poverty. Multicoloured.

1443	50c. Type 402	40	35
1444	50c. Child's face	40	35
1445	5q. Clasped hands	4·50	4·00
1446	5q. Child's face (different)	4·50	4·00

Nos. 1443/4 and 1445/6, respectively, were issued together, *se-tenant*, forming a composite design.

403 Jose Pardo

2006. Birth Centenary (2005) of Jose Joaquin Pardo Gallardo (historian).

1447	403	3q. multicoloured	2·10	1·90

404 Santa Cruz Hermitage

2006. Churches. Multicoloured.

1448	50c. Type 404	45	40
1449	1q. San Jacinto Church	85	75
1450	2q. San Andreas Xecul Church (vert)	1·40	1·20
1451	3q. El Calvario Church (vert)	2·10	1·90
1452	4q. San Cristobel (vert)	2·75	2·50
1453	5q. La Antigua Cathedral	4·50	4·00
1454	8q. San Pedro Church and Hospital	5·50	5·00
1455	10q. San Pedro Las Huertas Church	7·50	6·75
MS1456	57×70 mm. 14q. Metropolitan Cathedral, Guatemala City	10·50	9·25

405 Nativity (clay)

2006. Christmas. Multicoloured.

1457	20c. Type 405	25	20
1458	6q.50 Nativity (decorated pottery)	5·00	4·75

406 Coffee Grower (Acatenango)

2006. Coffee. Multicoloured.

1459	50c. Type 406	45	40
1460	1q. Antigua	85	75
1461	2q. Atitlan	1·40	1·20
1462	6q.50 Coban	5·00	4·75
1463	8q. Fraijanes	5·50	5·00
1464	10q. Huehue	7·50	6·75
MS1465	102×64 mm. 5q. Oriente; 20q. San Marcos	21·00	19·00

407 Baile de la Conquista

2006. Centenary of Guatemala—Brazil Diplomatic Relations. Multicoloured.

1466	4q. Type 407	2·75	2·50
1467	4q. Maracatua	2·75	2·50

408 Oil Derricks and Petrol Pump

2006. America. Energy Conservation. Multicoloured.

1468	3q. Type 408	2·10	1·90
1469	10q. Switch and solar panels	7·50	6·75

2007. Nos. 1293, 1338/40, 1357, 1359 and 1366 surch.

1470	50c. on 40c. light blue, blue and black (No. 1357) (air)	45	40
1471	50c. on 40c. multicoloured (No. 1338)	45	40
1472	1q. on 60c. multicoloured (No. 1339)	85	75
1473	2q. on 80c. multicoloured (No. 1367)	1·40	1·20
1474	3q. on 60c. grey-brown, blue and black (No. 1359)	2·10	1·90
1475	8q. on 80c. multicoloured (No. 1340)	5·50	5·00
1476	10q. on 60c. multicoloured (No. 1366)	7·50	6·75
1477	5q. on 9c. black (No. 1293) (postage)	4·50	4·00

410 Hand holding Globe

2007. 2006—Year of Honesty and Transparency. Multicoloured.

1478	20c. Type 408	25	20
1479	6q.50 Magnifying glass and finger print (44×25 mm)	5·00	4·75

411 1c. Stamp of 1881 (as No. 21)

2007. 75th Anniv of Guatemala Philatelic Association. Multicoloured.

1480	1q. Type 411	85	75
1481	3q. 2c. Stamp of 1881 (as No. 22)	2·10	1·90
1482	6q.50 5c. Stamp of 1881 (as No. 23)	5·00	4·75
1483	8q. 10c. Stamp of 1881 (as No. 24)	5·50	5·00

MS1484	108×64 mm. 25q. 20c. Stamp of 1881 (as No. 25)	21·00	19·00

412 Early Buildings, Guatemala

2007. Centenary of Uruguay–Guatemala Diplomatic Relations. Multicoloured.

1485	4q. Type 412	2·75	2·50
1486	4q. Colonia del Sacramento	2·75	2·50

Stamps of a similar design were issued by Uruguay.

413 Stylized Children

2007. America. Education for All. Designs showing stylized children. Multicoloured.

1487	4q. Type 413	2·75	2·50
1488	4q. Drawing	2·75	2·50
1489	4q. In house	2·75	2·50
1490	4q. Reading and drawing	2·75	2·50

Nos. 1487/90 were issued together, *se-tenant*, forming a composite design.

414 Holy Family

2007. Christmas. Multicoloured.

1491	20c. Type 414	25	20
1492	6q.50 Three Kings (40×35 mm)	5·00	4·75

415 Emblem

2007. Centenary of World Scouting.

1493	415	20c. multicoloured	25	20

416 Institute Building

2008. Municipal Development Institute.

1494	416	3q. multicoloured	2·10	1·90

417 Gerardi Conedera

2008. Tenth Death Anniv of Juan Jose Gerardi Conedera (bishop and human rights activist).

1495	417	8q. multicoloured	5·50	5·00

418 San Rafael de Matamoros

2008. Forts. Multicoloured.

1496	1q. Type 418	85	75
1497	1q. San Josede Buena Vista	85	75

Nos. 1496/7 were issued together, *se-tenant*, forming a composite design.

419 Mayan Ball Player

Guatemala

2008. Olympic Games, Beijing.
1498	419	6q.50 multicoloured	5·00	4·75

420 *Trogon violaceus braccatus* (violaceous trogon)

2008. Birds. Multicoloured.
1499		50c. Type 420	40	45
1500		1q. *Amazilia beryllina viola* (berylline hummingbird)	85	75
1501		2q. *Turdus rufitorques* (rufous-collared thrush)	1·40	1·20
1502		4q. *Glaucidium brasilianum ridgwayi* (ferruginous pygmy owl)	2·75	2·50
MS1503		108×63 mm. 20q. *Brotogeris jugularis* (inscr 'jularis') (orange-chinned parakeet)	15·00	13·50

421 Embroidered Christmas Rose

2008. Christmas. Multicoloured.
1504		20c. Type 421	25	20
1505		8q. Embroidered Christmas tree	5·50	5·00

422 Virgen Inmaculaada Concepcion (Mary of Immaculate Conception), St. Francis Temple

2008. 500th Anniv of Franciscan Order.
1506	422	3q. multicoloured	2·10	1·90

423 Building Facade

2009. 250th Anniv of Basilica del Senor de Esqipulas.
1507	423	50c. multicoloured	40	45

424 Boats

2009. 50th Anniv of National Marine Defence.
1508	424	1q. multicoloured	85	75

425 Masquerade Ball, Comalapa

2009. America (2008). Festivals. Multicoloured.
1509		50c. Type 425	40	45
1510		2q. Feast of All Saints, Santiago Sacatepequez	1·40	1·20
1511		3q. Marimba dance festival	2·10	1·90
1512		5q. Son dance festival	3·25	2·75
MS1513		82×89 mm. 8q. The brethren and captains festival	5·50	5·50

426 Man, San Juan Atitan

2009. Traditional Costumes. Multicoloured.
1514		50c. Type 426	40	45
1515		1q. Woman, San Juan Sacatepequez	85	75
1516		2q. Woman, Tamahu	1·40	1·20
1517		3q. Woman, San Rafael Petzal	2·10	1·90
1518		4q. Man, Totonicapan	2·75	2·50
1519		5q. Woman, Palzicia	3·25	2·75
1520		8q. Woman, San Pedro San Marcos	5·50	5·00
MS1521		51×64 mm. 10q. Couple, San Juan Cotzal	11·00	11·00

427 Gourd Marimba, 1492 to 1680

2009. Marimba–National Instrument. Multicoloured.
1522		3q. Type 427	2·10	1·90
1523		4q. Marimba on stand, 18th-century	2·75	2·50
1524		5q. Double Marimba, 1892	3·25	2·75
1525		8q. Large concert marimba, 1970	5·50	5·00
1526		10q. Hands playing marimba	11·00	10·50

428 Hands reading and Louis Braille

2009. Birth Bicentenary of Louis Braille (inventor of Braille writing for the blind)
1527	428	1q. multicoloured	85	75

429 Bauble

2009. Christmas. Multicoloured.
1528		20c. Type 429	30	20
1529		50c. Reindeer	40	30
1530		1q. Angel	85	75
1531		6q.50 Star	5·00	4·75

430 Sword, Arms and Monument

2010. 160th (2011) Anniv of Battle of the Arada. Multicoloured..
1532		5q. Type 430	4·00	3·50
1533		5q. Monument and José Rafael Carrera Turcios (first president)	4·00	3·50
MS1534		108×63 mm. 10q. As No. 1533 but design enlarged (vert)	7·50	7·50

EXPRESS LETTER STAMPS

1940. No. 231 optd **EXPRESO**.
E411	97	4c. yellow	2·30	45

E181 Motorcyclist

1948. Surch.
E479	E181	10c. on 4c. blk & grn	5·00	1·30

OFFICIAL STAMPS

O41

1902
O127	O41	1c. green	8·50	5·50
O128	O41	2c. red	8·50	5·50
O129	O41	5c. blue	8·50	4·25
O130	O41	10c. purple	11·50	4·25
O131	O41	25c. orange	11·50	4·25

O100

1929
O239	O100	1c. blue	50	45
O240	O100	2c. sepia	50	45
O241	O100	3c. green	50	45
O242	O100	4c. purple	60	45
O243	O100	5c. lake	60	60
O244	O100	10c. brown	95	95
O245	O100	25c. blue	2·20	1·60

134

1939. Air. Nos. 369/74 optd **OFICIAL OFICIAL**.
O400	134	1c. brown and orange	1·70	1·60
O401	-	2c. brown and red	1·70	1·60
O402	-	3c. brown, buff & green	1·70	1·60
O403	-	4c. brown and purple	1·70	1·60
O404	-	5c. brown and grey	1·70	1·60
O405	-	10c. brown and blue	1·70	1·60

1939. Air. No. MS375a optd **OFFICIAL OFFICIAL** on each stamp in sheet.
MSO405		As No. MS375a	2·50	2·10

Pt. 1

GUERNSEY

An island in the English Channel off N.W. coast of France. Occupied by German Forces from June 1940 to May 1945. "Regional" issues were introduced from 1958 (see after GREAT BRITAIN). The island's postal service was organised as a separate postal administration in 1969.

(a) War Occupation Issues

1

1941
1f	1	½d. green	4·00	3·00
2b	1	1d. red	3·50	2·00
3a	1	2½d. blue	10·00	8·00

(b) Independent Postal Administration

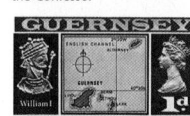

4 Castle Cornet and Edward the Confessor

5 View of Sark

1969
13	4	½d. mauve and black	10	10
14	-	1d. blue and black*	10	10
14b	-	1d. blue and black*	30	30
15	-	1½d. brown and black	10	10
16	-	2d. multicoloured	10	10
17	-	3d. multicoloured	15	15
18	-	4d. multicoloured	20	25
19	-	5d. multicoloured	20	20
20	-	6d. multicoloured	20	40
21	-	9d. multicoloured	30	40
22	-	1s. multicoloured	30	35
23	-	1s.6d. green and black*	25	30
23b	-	1s.6d. green and black*	2·00	1·70
24	-	1s.9d. multicoloured	1·00	1·00
25	-	2s.6d. violet and black	4·00	3·50
26	5	5s. multicoloured	2·50	2·75
27	-	10s. multicoloured	16·00	18·00
28a	-	£1 multicoloured	2·20	2·20

DESIGNS—As Type **4**: 1d. Map and William I; 1½d. Martello tower and Henry II; 2d. Arms of Sark and King John; 3d. Arms of Alderney and Edward III; 4d. Guernsey lily and Henry V; 5d. Arms of Guernsey and Elizabeth I; 6d. Arms of Alderney and Charles II; 9d. Arms of Sark and George III; 1s. Arms of Guernsey and Queen Victoria; 1s.6d., As 1d.; 1s.9d. Guernsey lily and Elizabeth I; 2s.6d. Martello tower and King John. As Type **5**: 10s. View of Alderney; 20s. View of Guernsey.

*On Nos. 14 and 23 the degree of latitude is inscr (incorrectly) as 40° 30'N. On Nos. 14b and 23b it has been corrected to 49° 30'.

19 Isaac Brock as Colonel

1969. Birth Bicent of Sir Isaac Brock. Multicoloured.
29		4d. Type 19	20	20
30		5d. Sir Isaac Brock as Major-General	20	20
31		1s.9d. Isaac Brock as Ensign	90	75
32		2s.6d. Arms and flags (horiz)	90	75

23 H.M.S. *L103* (landing craft) entering St. Peter's Harbour and Hawker Hurricans Mk II

1970. 25th Anniv of Liberation.
33	23	4d. blue	20	20
34	-	5d. brown, lake and grey	40	20
35	-	1s.6d. brown and buff	1·20	1·20

DESIGNS—HORIZ: 5d. H.M.S. *Bulldog* and H.M.S. *Beagle* (destroyers) entering St. Peter Port. VERT: 1s.6d. Brigadier Snow reading Proclamation.

26 Guernsey "Toms"

1970. Agriculture and Horticulture. Multicoloured.
36		4d. Type 26	55	20
37		5d. Guernsey cow	70	20
38		9d. Guernsey bull	2·50	1·30
39		1s.6d. Freesias	2·75	2·40

32 St. Peter's Church, Sark

1970. Christmas. Churches (1st series). Multicoloured.
40		4d. St. Anne's Church, Alderney (horiz)	20	10
41		5d. St. Peter's Church (horiz)	20	10
42		9d. Type 32	1·20	1·00
43		1s.6d. St. Tugual Chapel, Herm	1·50	1·20

See also Nos. 63/6.

34 Martello Tower and King John

1971. Decimal Currency. Nos. 13, etc, but with new colours and decimal values as T **34**.
44		½p. mauve and black (as No. 13)	10	15
45		1p. blue and black (as No. 14b)	10	15
46		1½p. brown & black (as No. 15)	15	15
47		2p. multicoloured (as No. 18)	15	15

48	2½p. multicoloured (as No. 19)		15	10
49	3p. multicoloured (as No. 17)		20	20
50	3½p. multicoloured (as No. 24)		20	20
51	4p. multicoloured (as No. 16)		20	20
52	5p. green and black (as No. 14b)		20	20
53	6p. multicoloured (as No. 20)		20	20
54	7½p. multicoloured (as No. 22)		30	35
55	9p. multicoloured (as No. 21)		75	75
56a	10p. violet & black (as No. 25)		1·50	1·50
57	20p. multicoloured (as No. 26)		70	70
58	50p. multicoloured (as No. 27)		1·50	1·50

35 Hong Kong 2c. of 1862

1971. Thomas De La Rue Commemoration.

59	**35**	2p. purple	35	15
60	-	2½p. red	35	15
61	-	4p. green	1·10	1·10
62	-	7½p. blue	1·40	1·40

DESIGNS (Each showing portraits of Queen Elizabeth and Thomas De La Rue): 2½p. Great Britain 4d. of 1855–7; 4p. Italy 5c. of 1862; 7½p. Confederate States 5c. of 1862.

1971. Christmas. Churches (2nd series). As T 32. Multicoloured.

63	2p. Ebenezer Church, St. Peter Port (horiz)		20	10
64	2½p. Church of St. Pierre du Bois (horiz)		20	10
65	5p. St. Joseph's Church, St. Peter Port		1·10	1·10
66	7½p. Church of St. Philippe de Torteval		1·40	1·40

43 Earl of Chesterfield (1794)

1972. Mail Packet Boats (1st series). Multicoloured.

67	2p. Type **43**		15	10
68	2½p. Dasher (1827)		15	10
69	7½p. Ibex (1891)		40	35
70	9p. Alberta (1900)		60	50

See also Nos. 80/3.

1972. World Conference of Guernsey Breeders, Guernsey. As No. 38 but size 48×29 mm, and additional inscription with face value changed.

71	5p. multicoloured		45	40

48 Bermuda Buttercup

1972. Wild Flowers. Multicoloured.

72	2p. Type **48**		10	10
73	2½p. Heath spotted orchid (vert)		10	10
74	7½p. Kaffir fig		50	50
75	9p. Scarlet pimpernel (vert)		60	60

52 Angels adoring Christ

1972. Royal Silver Wedding and Christmas. Stained-glass Windows from Guernsey Churches. Multicoloured.

76	2p. Type **52**		20	20
77	2½p. The Epiphany		20	20
78	7½p. The Virgin Mary		30	30
79	9p. Christ		45	45

See also Nos. 89/92.

1973. Mail Packet Boats (2nd series). As T 43. Multicoloured.

80	2½p. St. Julien (1925)		10	10
81	3p. Isle of Guernsey (1930)		20	20
82	7½p. St. Patrick (1947)		40	40
83	9p. Sarnia (1961)		45	45

60 Supermarine Sea Eagle Amphibian G-EBGS

1973. 50th Anniv of Air Service. Multicoloured.

84	2½p. Type **60**		10	10
85	3p. Westland Wessex trimotor G-ADEW		10	10
86	5p. de Havilland DH.89 Dragon Rapide G-AGSH *James Hardie*		25	25
87	7½p. Douglas DC-3		35	30
88	9p. Vickers Viscount 800 *Anne Marie*		45	40

65 "The Good Shepherd"

1973. Christmas. Stained-glass Windows from Guernsey Churches. Multicoloured.

89	2½p. Type **65**		20	20
90	3p. Christ at the well of Samaria		20	20
91	7½p. St. Dominic		40	50
92	20p. Mary and the Child Jesus		50	50

69 Princess Anne and Capt. Mark Phillips

1973. Royal Wedding.

93	**69**	25p. multicoloured	75	55

70 John Lockett, 1875

1974. 150th Anniv of Royal National Lifeboat Institution. Multicoloured.

94	2½p. Type **70**		15	15
95	3p. Arthur Lionel, 1912		15	15
96	8p. Euphrosyne Kendal, 1954		30	30
97	10p. Arun, 1972		40	40

74 Private, East Regt, 1815

89 Driver, Field Battery, Royal Guernsey Artillery, 1848

1974. Guernsey Militia. Multicoloured. (a) As T 74.

98	½p. Type **74**		10	10
99	1p. Officer, 2nd North Regt, 1825		10	10
100	1½p. Gunner, Guernsey Artillery, 1787		10	10
101	2p. Gunner, Guernsey Artillery, 1815		10	10
102	2½p. Corporal, Royal Guernsey Artillery, 1868		10	10
103	3p. Field Officer, Royal Guernsey Artillery, 1895		10	10
104	3½p. Sergeant, 3rd Regt, 1867		10	10
105	4p. Officer, East Regt, 1822		10	10
105a	5p. Field Officer, Royal Guernsey Artillery, (1895)		15	15
106	5½p. Colour-Sergeant of Grenadiers, East Regt, 1833		15	15
107	6p. Officer, North Regt, 1832		15	15
107a	6p. Officer, East Regt, 1822		30	30
108	8p. Field Officer, Rifle Company, 1868		25	25
109	9p. Private, 4th West Regt, 1785		25	25
110	10p. Field Officer, 4th West Regt, 1824		30	30

(b) As T 46.

111	20p. Type **89**		60	60
112	50p. Officer, Field Battery, Royal Guernsey Artillery, 1868		1·75	1·60
113	£1 Cavalry Trooper, Light Dragoons, 1814 (horiz)		2·50	2·00

92 Badge of Guernsey and U.P.U. Emblem

1974. Centenary of U.P.U. Multicoloured.

114	2½p. Type **92**		15	15
115	3p. Map of Guernsey		15	15
116	8p. U.P.U. Building, Berne, and Guernsey flag		25	25
117	10p. "Salle des Etats"		30	30

96 Cradle Rock

1974. Renoir Paintings. Multicoloured.

118	3p. Type **96**		20	20
119	5½p. Le Baie de Moulin Huet		20	20
120	8p. Au Bord de la Mer (vert)		40	40
121	10p. Self-portrait (vert)		40	40

100 Guernsey Spleenwort

1975. Guernsey Ferns. Multicoloured.

122	3½p. Type **100**		20	20
123	4p. Sand quilwort		20	20
124	8p. Guernsey quilwort		40	40
125	10p. Least adder's tongue		40	40

104 Victor Hugo House

1975. Victor Hugo's Exile in Guernsey. Multicoloured.

126	3½p. Type **104**		20	20
127	4p. Candie Gardens (vert)		20	20
128	8p. United Europe Oak, Hauteville (vert)		40	40
129	10p. Tapestry Room, Hauteville		40	40
MS130	114×143 mm. Nos. 126/9		1·00	1·00

108 Globe and Seal of Bailiwick

1975. Christmas. Multicoloured.

131	4p. Type **108**		20	20
132	6p. Guernsey flag			
133	10p. Guernsey flag and Alderney shield (horiz)		40	40
134	12p. Guernsey flag and Sark shield (horiz)		40	40

112 Les Hanois

1976. Bailiwick Lighthouses. Multicoloured.

135	4p. Type **112**		20	20
136	6p. Les Casquets		20	20
137	11p. Quesnard		40	40
138	13p. Point Robert		40	40

116 Milk Can

1976. Europa.

139	**116**	10p. brown and green	35	35
140	-	25p. grey and blue	70	70

DESIGN: 25p. Christening cup.

118 Pine Forest, Guernsey

1976. Bailiwick Views. Multicoloured.

141	5p. Type **118**		20	20
142	7p. Herm and Jethou		20	20
143	11p. Grand Greve Bay, Sark (vert)		40	40
144	13p. Trois Vaux Bay, Alderney (vert)		40	40

122 Royal Court House, Guernsey

1976. Christmas. Buildings. Multicoloured.

145	5p. Type **55**		20	20
146	7p. Elizabeth College, Guernsey		20	20
147	11p. La Seigneurie, Sark		40	40
148	13p. Island Hall, Alderney		40	40

126 Queen Elizabeth II

1977. Silver Jubilee. Multicoloured.

149	7p. Type **126**		30	30
150	35p. Queen Elizabeth (half-length portrait)		1·00	1·00

128 Woodland, Talbot's Valley

1977. Europa. Multicoloured.

151	7p. Type **128**		40	40
152	25p. Pastureland, Talbot's Valley		70	70

130 Statue-menhir, Castel

1977. Prehistoric Monuments. Multicoloured.

153	5p. Type **130**		20	20
154	7p. Megalithic tomb, St. Saviour (horiz)		20	20
155	11p. Cist, Tourgis (horiz)		40	40
156	13p. Statue-menhir, St. Martin		40	40

134 Mobile First Aid Unit

1977. Christmas and St. John Ambulance Centenary. Multicoloured.

157	5p. Type **134**		20	20
158	7p. Mobile radar unit		20	20

159		11p. Marine ambulance "Flying Christine II" (vert)	40	40
160		13p. Cliff rescue (vert)	40	40

138 View from Clifton, c. 1830

1978. Old Guernsey Prints (1st series).

161	**138**	5p. black and green	20	20
162	-	7p. black and stone	20	20
163	-	11p. black and pink	40	40
164	-	13p. black and blue	40	40

DESIGNS: 7p. Market Square, St. Peter Port, c. 1838; 11p. Petit-Bo Bay, c. 1839; 13p. The Quay, St. Peter Port, c. 1830.

See also Nos. 249/52.

142 "Prosperity" Memorial

1978. Europa. Multicoloured.

165		5p. Type **142**	20	20
166		7p. Victoria Monument (vert)	35	35

144 Queen Elizabeth II

1978. 25th Anniversary of Coronation.

167	**144**	20p. black, grey and blue	55	55

1978. Royal Visit. As T **62**, but inscr "VISIT OF H.M THE QUEEN AND H.R.H THE DUKE OF EDINBURGH JUNE 28–29, 1978 TO THE BAILIWICK OF GUERNSEY".

168		7p. black, grey and green	30	30

146 Northern Gannet

1978. Birds. Multicoloured.

169		5p. Type **146**	10	10
170		7p. Firecrest	20	15
171		11p. Dartford warbler	30	20
172		13p. Spotted redshank	40	30

150 Solanum

1978. Christmas. Multicoloured.

173		5p. Type **150**	20	20
174		7p. Christmas rose	20	20
175		11p. Holly (vert)	40	40
176		13p. Mistletoe (vert)	40	40

154 One Double Coin, 1830

1979. Coins.

177	**154**	½p. multicoloured	10	10
178	-	1p. multicoloured	10	10
179	-	2p. multicoloured	10	10
180	-	4p. multicoloured	10	10
181	-	5p. black, silver and brown	10	10
182	-	6p. black, silver and red	15	10
183	-	7p. black, silver and green	20	15
184	-	8p. black, silver and brown	25	15

185	-	9p. multicoloured	25	15
186	-	10p. multicoloured (green background)	30	25
187	-	10p. multicoloured (orange background)	30	15
188	-	11p. multicoloured	30	15
189	-	11½p. multicoloured	30	15
190	-	12p. multicoloured	30	15
191	-	13p. multicoloured	30	20
192	-	14p. black, silver and blue	35	20
193	-	15p. black, silver and brown	35	25
194	-	20p. black, silver and brown	60	50
195	-	50p. black, silver and red	1·50	1·00
196	-	£1 black, silver and green	2·25	1·50
197	-	£2 black, silver and blue	4·50	3·00
198	-	£5 multicoloured	9·00	9·00

DESIGNS—VERT (As Type **65**): 1p. Two doubles, 1899; 2p. Four doubles, 1902; 4p. Eight doubles, 1959; 5p. Three pence, 1956; 6p. Five new pence, 1968; 7p. Fifty new pence, 1969; 8p. Ten new pence, 1970; 9p. Half new penny, 1971; 10p. (both) One new penny, 1971; 11p. Two new pence, 1971; 11½p. Half penny, 1979; 12p. One penny, 1977; 13p. Two pence, 1977; 14p. Five pence, 1977; 15p. Ten pence, 1977; 20p. Twenty-five pence, 1972. (26×45 mm): 50p. William I commemorative 10s., 1966; £5 Seal of the Bailiwick, 1977. HORIZ (45×26 mm): £1 Silver Jubilee crown, 1977; £2 Royal Silver Wedding crown, 1972.

175 Pillar-box and Postmark, 1853, and Mail Van and Postmark, 1979

1979. Europa. Communications. Multicoloured.

201		6p. Type **175**	20	20
202		8p. Telephone, 1897 and telex machine, 1979	35	35

177 Steam Tram, 1879

1979. History of Public Transport. Multicoloured.

203		6p. Type **177**	30	30
204		8p. Electric tram, 1896	15	15
205		11p. Motor bus, 1911	40	40
206		13p. Motor bus, 1979	40	40

181 Bureau and Postal Headquarters

1979. Tenth Anniv of Guernsey Postal Administration. Multicoloured.

207		6p. Type **181**	20	20
208		8p. "Mails and telegrams"	25	25
209		13p. "Parcels"	40	40
210		15p. "Philately"	45	45
MS211	120×80 mm. Nos. 207/10		1·10	1·10

185 Major-General Le Marchant

1980. Europa. Personalities. Multicoloured.

212		10p. Type **185**	20	20
213		13½p. Admiral Lord de Saumarez	40	40

187 Policewoman with Lost Child

1980. 60th Anniv of Guernsey Police Force. Multicoloured.

214		7p. Type **187**	30	30
215		15p. Motorcycle escort	40	40
216		17½p. Dog-handler	45	45

190 Golden Guernsey Goat

1980. Golden Guernsey Goats. Multicoloured.

217		7p. Type **190**	20	20
218		10p. Head of goat	20	20
219		13p. Goat	40	40
220		17½p. Goat and kids	45	45

194 Sark Cottage

1980. Christmas. Peter Le Lievre Paintings. Multicoloured.

221		7p. Type **194**	20	20
222		10p. Moulin Huet	25	35
223		13½p. Boats at Sea	35	25
224		15p. Cow Lane (vert)	35	35
225		17½p. Peter Le Lievre (vert)	40	40

199 Polyommatus icarus

1981. Butterflies. Multicoloured.

226		8p. Type **199**	20	20
227		12p. Vanessa atalanta	30	30
228		22p. Aglais urticae	50	50
229		25p. Lasiommata megera	60	60

203 Sailors paying respect to "Le Petit Bonhomme Andriou" (rock resembling head of a man)

1981. Europa. Folklore.

230	**203**	12p. gold, brown & lt brn	50	50
231	-	18p. gold, blue and light blue	60	60

DESIGN: 18p. Fairies and Guernsey lily.

205 Prince Charles

1981. Royal Wedding. Multicoloured.

232		8p. Type **205**	20	20
233		8p. Prince Charles and Lady Diana Spencer	20	20
234		8p. Lady Diana	20	20
235		12p. Type **205**	30	30
236		12p. As No. 233	30	30
237		12p. As No. 234	30	30
238		25p. Royal Family (49×32 mm)	65	65
MS239	104×127 mm. Nos. 232/8		2·50	2·50

209 Sark Launch

1981. Inter-island Transport. Multicoloured.

240		8p. Type **209**	20	20
241		12p. Britten-Norman BN-2A MKIII "short nose" Trislander aircraft	30	30
242		18p. Hydrofoil	40	40

243		22p. Herm catamaran	60	65
244		25p. Sea Trent (coaster)	75	75

214 Rifle Shooting

1981. Int Year for Disabled Persons. Multicoloured.

245		8p. Type **214**	25	25
246		12p. Riding	30	30
247		22p. Swimming	60	60
248		25p. Circuit construction	75	75

1982. Old Guernsey Prints (2nd series). Prints from Sketches by T. Compton. As T **138**.

249		8p. black and blue	30	30
250		12p. black and green	30	30
251		22p. black and brown	60	60
252		25p. black and lilac	70	70

DESIGNS: 8p Jethou; 12p. Fermain Bay; 22p. The Terres; 25p. St. Peter Port.

222 Sir Edgar MacCulloch (founder-president) and Guille-Alles Library, St. Peter Port

1982. Cent of La Societe Guernesiaise. Multicoloured.

253		8p. Type **222**	20	20
254		13p. French invasion fleet crossing English Channel, 1066 ("history")	35	35
255		20p. H.M.S "Crescent", 1793 ("history")	50	50
256		24p. Dragonfly ("entomology")	60	60
257		26p. Common snipe caught for ringing ("ornithology")	70	70
258		29p. Samian bowl, 160–200 A.D. ("archaeology")	80	80

The 13p. and 20p. designs also include the Europa C.E.P.T. emblem.

228 "Sea Scouts"

1982. 75th Anniv of Boy Scout Movement. Multicoloured.

259		8p. Type **228**	25	25
260		13p. "Scouts"	30	30
261		26p. "Cub Scouts"	75	75
262		29p. "Air Scouts"	90	90

232 Midnight Mass

1982. Christmas. Multicoloured.

263		8p. Type **232**	20	20
264		13p. Exchanging gifts	40	40
265		24p. Christmas meal	65	65
266		26p. Exchanging cards	65	65
267		29p. Queen's Christmas message	80	80

237 Flute Player and Boats

1982. Centenary of Boys' Brigade. Multicoloured.

268		8p. Type **237**	30	30
269		13p. Cymbal player and tug o' war	40	40
270		24p. Trumpet player and bible class	65	65
271		26p. Drummer and cadets marching	70	70
272		29p. Boys' Brigade band	80	80

242 Building Albert
Pier Extension, 1850s

1983. Europa. Development of St. Peter Port Harbour. Multicoloured.

273	13p. Type **242**	40	30
274	13p. St. Peter Port harbour, 1983	40	30
275	20p. St. Peter Port, 1680	50	50
276	20p. Artist's impression of future development scheme	50	50

246 View at Guernsey
(Renoir)

1983. Cent of Renoir's Visit to Guernsey. Multicoloured.

277	9p. Type **246**	20	15
278	13p. Children on the Seashore (25×39 mm)	30	30
279	26p. "Marine, Guernsey"	70	70
280	28p. La Bale du Moulin Huet a travers les Arbres	85	80
281	31p. Brouillard a Guernesey	90	90

251 Launching Star of the
West, 1869, and Capt. J.
Lenfestey

1983. Guernsey Shipping (1st series). Multicoloured.

282	9p. Type **251**	20	20
283	13p. Leaving St. Peter Port	30	30
284	26p. Off Rio Grande Bar	70	70
285	28p. Off St. Lucia	85	85
286	31p. Map of 1879–80 voyage	95	95

See also Nos. 415/19.

256 Dame of Sark as Young
Woman

1984. Birth Centenary of Sibyl Hathaway, Dame of Sark. Multicoloured.

287	9p. Type **256**	20	20
288	13p. German occupation, 1940–45	30	15
289	26p. Royal visit, 1957	70	65
290	28p. Chief Pleas	75	70
291	31p. The "Dame of Sark" rose	80	75

261 C.E.P.T. 25th Anniversary Logo

1984. Europa.

292	**261**	13p. light blue, blue & black	40	40
293	**261**	20½p. green, dp green & blk	75	75

262 The Royal Court and
St. George's Flag

1984. Links with the Commonwealth. Multicoloured.

294	9p. Type **262**	20	15
295	31p. Castle Cornet and Union flag	85	85

266 St. Apolline
Chapel

1984. Views. Multicoloured.

296	1p. Little Chapel	10	10
297	2p. Fort Grey (horiz)	10	10
298	3p. Type **266**	10	10
299	4p. Petit Port (horiz)	10	10
300	5p. Little Russel (horiz)	15	10
301	6p. The Harbour, Herm (horiz)	15	15
302	7p. Saints (horiz)	15	15
303	8p. St. Saviour	20	15
304	9p. New Jetty (inscr "Cambridge Berth") (horiz)	20	10
305	10p. Belvoir, Herm (horiz)	30	15
306	11p. La Seigneurie, Sark (horiz)	25	15
306b	12p. Petit Bot	35	15
307	13p. St. Saviours reservoir (horiz)	30	25
308	14p. St. Peter Port	30	20
309	15p. Havelet	35	35
309c	16p. Hostel of St. John (horiz)	40	35
309d	18p. Le Variouf	35	35
310	20p. La Coupee, Sark (horiz)	50	50
310b	21p. King's Mills (horiz)	55	55
310c	26p. Town Church	1·00	1·00
311	30p. Grandes Rocques (horiz)	1·00	1·00
312	40p. Torteval Church	1·00	1·00
313	50p. Bordeaux (horiz)	1·25	1·25
314	£1 Albecq (horiz)	2·10	2·10
315	£2 L' Ancresse (horiz)	4·00	4·00

See also Nos. 398/9a.

289 "A Partridge
in a Pear Tree"

1984. Christmas. "The Twelve Days of Christmas". Multicoloured.

316	5p. Type **289**	15	15
317	5p. "Two turtle doves"	15	15
318	5p. "Three French hens"	15	15
319	5p. "Four colly birds"	15	15
320	5p. "Five gold rings"	15	15
321	5p. "Six geese a-laying"	15	15
322	5p. "Seven swans a-swimming"	15	15
323	5p. "Eight maids a-milking"	15	15
324	5p. "Nine drummers drumming"	15	15
325	5p. "Ten pipers piping"	15	15
326	5p. "Eleven ladies dancing"	15	15
327	5p. "Twelve lords a-leaping"	15	15

301 Sir John
Doyle and Coat
of Arms

1984. 150th Death Anniv of Lt.-General Sir John Doyle. Multicoloured.

328	13p. Type **301**	30	30
329	29p. Battle of Germantown, 1777 (horiz)	75	75
330	31p. Reclamation of Braye du Valle, 1806 (horiz)	75	75
331	34p. Mail for Alderney, 1812 (horiz)	90	90

305 Cuckoo Wrasse

1985. Fish. Multicoloured.

332	9p. Type **305**	30	30
333	13p. Red gurnard	40	40
334	29p. Red mullet	90	90
335	31p. Mackerel	1·00	1·00
336	34p. Oceanic sunfish	1·00	1·00

310 Dove

1985. 40th Anniv of Peace in Europe.

337	**310**	22p. multicoloured	75	75

311 I.Y.Y. Emblem
and Young People of
Different Races

1985. International Youth Year. Multicoloured.

338	9p. Type **311**	25	25
339	31p. Girl Guides cooking over campfire	80	80

313 Stave of Music
enclosing Flags

1985. Europa. European Music Year. Multicoloured.

340	14p. Type **313**	35	35
341	22p. Stave of music and musical instruments	60	55

315 Guide Leader,
Girl Guide and
Brownie

1985. 75th Anniv of Girl Guide Movement.

342	**315**	34p. multicoloured	1·00	1·10

316 Santa Claus

1985. Christmas. Gift-bearers. Multicoloured.

343	5p. Type **316**	25	25
344	5p. Lussibruden (Sweden)	25	25
345	5p. King Balthazar	25	25
346	5p. Saint Nicholas (Netherlands)	25	25
347	5p. La Befana (Italy)	25	25
348	5p. Julenisse (Denmark)	25	25
349	5p. Christkind (Germany)	25	25
350	5p. King Wenceslas (Czechoslovakia)	25	25
351	5p. Shepherd of Les Baux (France)	25	25
352	5p. King Caspar	25	25
353	5p. Baboushka (Russia)	25	25
354	5p. King Melchior	25	25

328 "Vraicing"

1985. Paintings by Paul Jacob Naftel. Multicoloured.

355	9p. Type **328**	20	20
356	14p. Castle Cornet	35	35
357	22p. Rocquaine Bay	65	65
358	31p. Little Russel	1·10	1·10
359	34p. Seaweedgatherers	1·40	1·40

333 Squadron off
Nargue Island, 1809

1986. 150th Death Anniv of Admiral Lord De Saumarez. Multicoloured.

360	9p. Type **333**	35	25
361	14p. Battle of the Nile, 1798	45	30
362	29p. Battle of St. Vincent, 1797	80	70
363	31p. H.M.S Crescent off Cherbourg, 1793	1·25	95
364	34p. Battle of the Saints, 1782	1·25	1·00

338 Profile of
Queen Elizabeth II
(after R. Maklouf)

1986. 60th Birthday of Queen Elizabeth II.

365	**338**	60p. multicoloured	1·50	1·80

339 Northern
Gannet and Nylon
Net ("Operation
Gannet")

1986. Europa. Nature and Environmental Protection. Multicoloured.

366	10p. Type **339**	35	35
367	14p. Whitsun orchid	45	45
368	22p. Guernsey elm	80	80

342 Prince Andrew
and Miss Sarah
Ferguson

1986. Royal Wedding. Multicoloured.

369	14p. Type **342**	40	40
370	34p. Prince Andrew and Miss Sarah Ferguson (different) (47×30 mm)	1·00	1·00

344 Bowls

1986. Sport in Guernsey. Multicoloured.

371	10p. Type **344**	25	20
372	14p. Cricket	35	20
373	22p. Squash	50	45
374	29p. Hockey	90	80
375	31p. Swimming (horiz)	90	80
376	34p. Shooting (horiz)	1·00	90

350 Guernsey Museum
and Art Gallery, Candie
Gardens

1986. Cent of Guernsey Museums. Multicoloured.

377	14p. Type **350**	30	30
378	29p. Fort Grey Maritime Museum	85	85
379	31p. Castle Cornet	85	85
380	34p. National Trust of Guernsey Folk Museum	1·00	1·00

354 While Shepherds Watched their Flocks by Night

1986. Christmas. Carols. Multicoloured.

381	6p. Type **354**	30	30
382	6p. In The Bleak Midwinter	30	30
383	6p. O Little Town of Bethlehem	30	30
384	6p. The Holly and the Ivy	30	30
385	6p. "O Little Christmas Tree	30	30
386	6p. Away in a Manger	30	30
387	6p. Good King Wenceslas	30	30
388	6p. We Three Kings of Orient Are	30	30
389	6p. Hark the Herald Angels Sing	30	30
390	6p. I Saw Three Ships	30	30
391	6p. Little Donkey	30	30
392	6p. Jingle Bells	30	30

366 Duke of Richmond and Portion of Map

1987. Bicentenary of Duke of Richmond's Survey of Guernsey. Sheet 134×103 mm containing T **106** and similar horiz designs showing sections of map. Multicoloured.

MS393 14p. Type **366** North-east; 31p. South-west; 34p. South-east   3·50   3·75

The stamps within No. **MS**393 show a composite design of the Duke of Richmond's map of Guernsey.

367 Post Office Headquarters

1987. Europa. Modern Architecture. Multicoloured.

394	15p. Type **371**	35	30
395	15p. Architect's elevation of Post Office Headquarters	35	30
396	22p. Guernsey Grammar School	50	50
397	22p. Architect's elevation of Grammar School	50	50

1987. Designs as Nos. 306, 306b, 309 and 309c but smaller.

398	11p. La Seigneurie, Sark (22×18 mm)	50	50
398a	12p. Petit Bot (18×22 mm)	40	40
399	15p. Havelet (18×22 mm)	60	60
399a	16p. Hostel of St. John (22×18 mm)	50	50

371 Sir Edmund Andros and La Plaiderie, Guernsey

1987. 350th Birth Anniv of Sir Edmund Andros (colonial administrator). Multicoloured.

400	15p. Type **371**	35	35
401	29p. Governor's Palace, Virginia	1·00	1·00
402	31p. Governor Andros in Boston	1·00	1·00
403	34p. Map of New Amsterdam (New York), 1661	1·40	1·40

375 The Jester's Warning to Young William

1987. 900th Death Anniv of William the Conqueror. Multicoloured.

404	11p. Type **375**	30	30
405	15p. Hastings battlefield	40	35
406	15p. Norman soldier with pennant	40	35
407	22p. William the Conqueror	60	60
408	22p. Queen Matilda and Abbaye aux Dames, Caen	60	60
409	34p. William's coronation regalia and Halley's Comet	90	1·10

381 John Wesley preaching on the Quay, Alderney

1987. Bicentenary of John Wesley's Visit to Guernsey. Multicoloured.

410	7p. Type **381**	20	20
411	15p. Wesley preaching at Mon Plaisir, St. Peter Port	40	40
412	29p. Preaching at Assembly Rooms	80	80
413	31p. Wesley and La Ville Baudu (early Methodist meeting place)	85	85
414	34p. Wesley and first Methodist Chapel, St. Peter Port	1·00	1·00

386 Golden Spur off St. Sampson Harbour

1988. Guernsey Shipping (2nd series). Golden Spur. Multicoloured.

415	11p. Type **386**	50	50
416	15p. Golden Spur entering Hong Kong harbour	50	50
417	29p. Anchored off Macao	1·00	1·00
418	31p. In China Tea Race	1·00	1·00
419	34p. Golden Spur and map showing voyage of 1872–74	1·25	1·25

391 Rowing Boat and Bedford "Rascal" Mail Van

1988. Europa. Transport and Communications. Multicoloured.

420	16p. Type **391**	40	35
421	16p. Rowing boat and Vickers Viscount 800 mail plane	40	35
422	22p. Postman on bicycle and horse-drawn carriages, Sark	70	70
423	22p. Postmen on bicycles and carriage	70	70

Nos. 420/1 and 422/3 were each printed together, *setenant*, the two stamps of each value forming a composite design.

395 Frederick Corbin Lukis and Lukis House, St. Peter Port

1988. Birth Bicentenary of Frederick Corbin Lukis (archaeologist). Multicoloured.

424	12p. Type **395**	30	25
425	16p. Natural history books and reconstructed pot	35	25
426	29p. Lukis directing excavation of Le Creux es Faies and prehistoric beaker	80	85
427	31p. Lukis House Observatory and garden	90	85
428	34p. Prehistoric artifacts	90	90

400 Cougar, Rocky and Annabella (powerboats) and Westland Wessex HU Mk5 Rescue Helicopter off Jethou

1988. World Offshore Powerboat Championships. Multicoloured.

429	16p. Type **400**	35	35
430	30p. *Paul Pilot* (powerboat) in Gouliot Passage	1·10	1·10
431	32p. Start of race at St. Peter Port (vert)	1·20	1·20
432	35p. Admiralty chart showing course (vert)	1·25	1·25

404 Joshua Gosselin and Herbarium

1988. Bicentenary of Joshua Gosselin's "Flora Sarniensis". Multicoloured.

433	12p. Type **404**	25	25
434	16p. Hares-tail grass	35	35
435	16p. Dried hares-tail grass	35	35
436	23p. Variegated catchfly	60	60
437	23p. Dried variegated catchfly	60	60
438	35p. Rock sea lavender	1·20	1·20

410 Coutances Cathedral, France

1988. Christmas. Ecclesiastical Links. Multicoloured.

439	8p. Type **410**	30	30
440	8p. Interior of Notre Dame du Rosaire Church, Guernsey	30	30
441	8p. Stained glass, St. Sampson's Church, Guernsey	30	30
442	8p. Dol-de-Bretagne Cathedral, France	30	30
443	8p. Bishop's throne, Town Church, Guernsey	30	30
444	8p. Winchester Cathedral	30	30
445	8p. St. John's Cathedral, Portsmouth	30	30
446	8p. High altar, St. Joseph's Church, Guernsey	30	30
447	8p. Mont Saint-Michel, France	30	30
448	8p. Chancel, Vale Church, Guernsey	30	30
449	8p. Lychgate, Forest Church, Guernsey	30	30
450	8p. Marmoutier Abbey, France	30	30

422 Le Cat (Tip Cat)

1989. Europa. Children's Toys and Games. Multicoloured.

451	12p. Type **422**	30	20
452	16p. Girl with Cobo Alice doll	40	40
453	23p. Le Colimachaon (hopscotch)	75	85

425 Outline Map of Guernsey

1989. Coil Stamp. No value expressed.

454	**425** (–) blue	90	90
455	**425** (–) green	90	90

No. 454 is inscribed "MINIMUM BAILIWICK POSTAGE PAID" and No. 455 "MINIMUM FIRST CLASS POSTAGE TO UK PAID". They were initally sold at 14p. and 18p. but this was changed in line with postage rate rises.

426 Guernsey Airways de Havilland DH.86 Dragon Express and Mail Van

1989. 50th Anniv of Guernsey Airport (Nos. 456, 458 and 460) and 201 Squadron's Affiliation with Guernsey (Nos. 457, 459 and 461). Multicoloured.

456	12p. Type **426**	35	30
457	12p. Supermarine Southampton II flying boat at mooring	35	30
458	18p. B.E.A. de Havilland DH.89 Dragon Rapide G-AGSH	50	75
459	18p. Short S.25 Sunderland Mk V flying boat taking off	50	75
460	35p. Air U.K. British Aerospace BAe 146	1·00	1·00
461	35p. Avro Shackleton M.R.3	1·00	1·30

432 Queen Elizabeth II (June Mendoza)

1989. Royal Visit.

462	**432** 30p. multicoloured	75	80

433 Ibex at G.W.R. Terminal, St. Peter Port

1989. Centenary of Great Western Railway Steamer Service to Channel Islands. Multicoloured.

463	12p. Type **433**	30	30
464	18p. Great Western (paddle-steamer) in Little Russel	40	40
465	29p. St. Julien passing Casquets Light	80	80
466	34p. Roebuck off Portland	1·00	95
467	37p. Antelope and boat train on Weymouth Quay	1·20	1·10
MS468	115×117 mm. Nos. 463/7	4·00	4·25

438 Two-toed Sloth

1989. Tenth Anniv of Guernsey Zoological Trust. Animals of the Rainforest. Multicoloured.

469	18p. Type **438**	90	90
470	29p. Capuchin monkey	90	90
471	32p. White-lipped tamarin	90	90
472	34p. Common squirrel-monkey	90	90
473	37p. Common gibbon	90	90

443 Star

1989. Christmas. Christmas Tree Decorations. Multicoloured.

474	10p. Type **443**	35	35
475	10p. Fairy	35	35
476	10p. Candles	35	35
477	10p. Bird	35	35
478	10p. Present	35	35
479	10p. Carol-singer	35	35
480	10p. Christmas cracker	35	35
481	10p. Bauble	35	35
482	10p. Christmas stocking	35	35
483	10p. Bell	35	35
484	10p. Fawn	35	35
485	10p. Church	35	35

455 Sark Post Office, c. 1890

1990. Europa. Post Office Buildings.

486	**455** 20p. deep brown, sepia and light brown	45	45
487	– 20p. multicoloured	45	45

488	-	24p. deep brown, sepia and light brown	60	65
489	-	24p. multicoloured	60	65

DESIGNS: No. 487, Sark Post Office, 1990; 488, Arcade Post Office counter, St. Peter Port, c. 1840; 489, Arcade Post Office counter, St. Peter Port, 1990.

459 Penny Black and Mail Steamer off St. Peter Port, 1840

1990. 150th Anniv of the Penny Black. Multicoloured.

490	14p. Type **459**		45	45
491	20p. Penny Red, 1841 and pillar box of 1853		60	60
492	32p. Bisected 2d., 1940 and German Army band		90	90
493	34p. Regional 3d., 1958 and Guernsey emblems		1·00	1·00
494	37p. Independent postal administration 1½d., 1969 and queue outside Main Post Office		1·10	1·10
MS495	151×116 mm. Nos. 490/4		3·75	3·75

No. **MS**495 also commemorates "Stamp World London '90" International Stamp Exhibition.

464 Lt. Philip Saumarez writing Log Book

1990. 250th Anniv of Anson's Circumnavigation. Multicoloured.

496	14p. Type **464**		35	35
497	20p. Anson's squadron leaving Portsmouth, 1740		50	50
498	29p. Ships at St. Catherine's Island, Brazil		80	80
499	34p. H.M.S. *Tryal* (sloop) dismasted, Cape Horn, 1741		1·00	1·00
500	37p. Crew of H.M.S. *Centurion* on Juan Fernandez		1·10	1·10

469 Grey Seal and Pup

1990. Marine Life. Multicoloured.

501	20p. Type **469**		50	50
502	26p. Bottle-nosed dolphin		1·10	1·10
503	31p. Basking shark		1·25	1·25
504	37p. Common porpoise		1·40	1·40

473 Blue Tit and Great Tit

1990. Christmas. Winter Birds. Multicoloured.

505	10p. Type **473**		35	40
506	10p. Snow bunting		35	40
507	10p. Common kestrel ("Kestrel")		35	40
508	10p. Common starling ("Starling")		35	40
509	10p. Western greenfinch ("Greenfinch")		35	40
510	10p. European robin ("Robin")		35	40
511	10p. Winter wren		35	40
512	10p. Barn owl		35	40
513	10p. Mistle thrush		35	40
514	10p. Grey heron ("Heron")		35	40
515	10p. Chaffinch		35	40
516	10p. River kingfisher ("Kingfisher")		35	40

485 Air Raid and 1941 ½d. Stamp

1991. 50th Anniv of First Guernsey Stamps. Multicoloured.

517	37p. Type **485**		1·10	1·10
518	53p. 1941 1d. stamp		1·50	1·50
519	57p. 1944 2½d. stamp		1·50	1·50

488 Visit of Queen Victoria to Guernsey, and Discovery of Neptune, 1846

1991. Europa. Europe in Space. Multicoloured.

520	21p. Type **488**		55	55
521	21p. Visit of Queen Elizabeth II and Prince Philip to Sark, and "Sputnik" (first artificial satellite), 1957		55	55
522	26p. Maiden voyage of "Sarnia" (ferry) and "Vostok I" (first manned space flight), 1961		75	75
523	26p. Cancelling Guernsey stamps, and first manned landing on Moon, 1969		75	75

492 Children in Guernsey Sailing Trust "GP14" Dinghy

1991. Centenary of Guernsey Yacht Club. Multicoloured.

524	15p. Type **492**		45	25
525	21p. Guernsey Regatta		70	40
526	26p. Lombard Channel Islands' Challenge race		80	80
527	31p. Rolex Swan Regatta		90	1·10
528	37p. Old Gaffers' Association gaff-rigged yacht		1·00	1·40
MS529	163×75 mm. As Nos. 524/8, but "GUERNSEY" and face values in yellow		4·00	4·25

497 Pair of Oystercatchers

1991. Nature Conservation. L'Eree Shingle Bank Reserve. Multicoloured.

530	15p. Type **497**		35	20
531	15p. Three ruddy turnstones		35	20
532	15p. Dunlins and ruddy turnstones		35	20
533	15p. Curlew and ruddy turnstones		35	20
534	15p. Ringed plover with chicks		35	20
535	21p. Gull, sea campion and sea radish		35	20
536	21p. Yellow horned poppy		35	20
537	21p. Pair of common stonechats, hare's foot clover and fennel		35	20
538	21p. Hares's foot clover, fennel and slender oat		35	20
539	21p. Sea kale on shore		35	20

Nos. 530/4 and 535/9 were each printed together, *se-tenant*, with the backgrounds forming composite designs.

507 *Rudolph the Red-nosed Reindeer* (Melanie Sharpe)

1991. Christmas. Children's Paintings. Multicoloured.

540	12p. Type **507**		30	15
541	12p. *Christmas Pudding* (James Quinn)		30	15
542	12p. *Snowman* (Lisa Guille)		30	15
543	12p. *Snowman in Top Hat* (Jessica Ede-Golightly)		30	15
544	12p. *Robins and Christmas Tree* (Sharon Le Page)		30	15
545	12p. *Shepherds and Angels* (Anna Coquelin)		30	15
546	12p. *Nativity* (Claudine Lihou)		30	15
547	12p. *Three Wise Men* (Jonathan Le Noury)		30	15
548	12p. *Star of Bethlehem and Angels* (Marcia Mahy)		30	15
549	12p. *Christmas Tree* (Laurel Garfield)		30	15
550	12p. *Santa Claus* (Rebecca Driscoll)		30	15

551	12p. *Snowman and Star* (Ian Lowe)		30	15

519 Queen Elizabeth II in 1952

1992. 40th Anniv of Accession. Multicoloured.

552	23p. Type **519**		50	50
553	28p. Queen Elizabeth in 1977		65	65
554	33p. Queen Elizabeth in 1986		90	90
555	39p. Queen Elizabeth in 1991		1·10	1·10

523 Christopher Columbus

1992. 500th Anniv of Discovery of America by Columbus. Multicoloured.

556	23p. Type **523**		65	60
557	23p. Examples of Columbus's signature		65	60
558	28p. "Santa Maria"		1·20	1·20
559	28p. Map of first voyage		1·20	1·20
MS560	157×77 mm. Nos. 556/9		4·50	5·00

527 Guernsey Calves

1992. 150th Anniv of Royal Guernsey Agricultural and Horticultural Society. Sheet, 93×71 mm.

MS561	527 75p. multicoloured		2·50	2·50

528 Stock

1992. Horticultural Exports. Multicoloured.

562	1p. *Stephanotis floribunda*		10	10
563	2p. Potted hydrangea		10	10
564	3p. Type **528**		10	10
565	4p. Anemones		15	15
566	5p. Gladiolus		15	15
567	6p. *Asparagus plumosus* and *Gypsophila paniculata*		15	15
568	7p. Guernsey lily		20	20
569	8p. Enchantment lily		20	20
570	9p. Clematis "Freckles"		20	25
571	10p. Alstroemeria		25	25
572	16p. Standard carnation (horiz)		50	35
572b	18p. Standard rose		55	45
573	20p. Spray rose		60	50
574	23p. Mixed freesia (horiz)		60	55
575	24p. Standard rose (horiz)		70	60
576	25p. Iris "Ideal" (horiz)		70	60
576b	26p. Freesia "Pink Glow"		70	60
577	28p. Lisianthus (horiz)		80	65
578	30p. Spray chrysanthemum (horiz)		80	70
579	40p. Spray carnation		1·00	1·00
580	50p. Single freesia (horiz)		1·20	1·00
581	£1 Floral arrangement (35×26½ mm)		2·50	2·00
582	£2 Chelsea Flower Show exhibit (35×26½ mm)		5·00	4·00
582a	£3 *Floral Fantasia* (exhibit) (35×28 mm)		7·00	6·00

552 Building the Ship

1992. "Operation Asterix" (excavation of Roman ship). Multicoloured.

583	16p. Type **552**		45	35
584	23p. Loading the cargo		60	50
585	28p. Ship at sea		80	90
586	33p. Ship under attack		95	95
587	39p. Crew swimming ashore		1·10	1·10

557 Tram No. 10 decorated for Battle of Flowers

1992. Guernsey Trams. Multicoloured.

588	16p. Type **557**		45	30
589	23p. Tram No 10 passing Hougue a la Perre		60	35
590	28p. Tram No. 1 at St. Sampsons		75	80
591	33p. First steam tram at St. Peter Port, 1879		90	1·00
592	39p. Last electric tram, 1934		1·10	1·10

562 Man in Party Hat

1992. Christmas. Seasonal Fayre. Multicoloured.

593	13p. Type **562**		45	45
594	13p. Girl and Christmas tree		45	45
595	13p. Woman and balloons		45	45
596	13p. Mince pies and champagne		45	45
597	13p. Roast turkey		45	45
598	13p. Christmas pudding		45	45
599	13p. Christmas cake		45	45
600	13p. Fancy cakes		45	45
601	13p. Cheese		45	45
602	13p. Nuts		45	45
603	13p. Ham		45	45
604	13p. Chocolate log		45	45

Nos. 593/604 were printed together, se-tenant, forming a composite design.

574 Rupert Bear, Bingo and Dog

1993. Rupert Bear and Friends (cartoon characters created by Mary and Herbert Tourtel).

605	**574** 24p. multicoloured		75	75
MS606	116×97 mm. 16p. Airplane and castle; 16p. Professor's servant and Autumn Elf; 16p. Algy Pug; 16p. Baby Badger on sledge; 24p. Bill Badger, Willie Mouse, Reggie Rabbit and Podgy playing in snow; 24p. Type **574**; 24p. The Balloonist avoiding Gregory on toboggan; 24p. Tiger Lily and Edward Trunk		5·75	5·50

The 24p. values in No. MS606 are as Type **574**; the 16p. designs are smaller, each 25½×26 mm.

575 *Tapestry* by Kelly Fletcher

1993. Europa. Contemporary Art. Multicoloured.

607	24p. Type **575**		70	70
608	24p. *Le Marchi a Paissaon* (etching and aquatint, Sally Reed) (48×33½ mm)		70	70
609	28p. *Red Abstract* (painting, Molly Harris)		80	80
610	28p. *Dress Shop, King's Road* (painting, Damon Bell) (48×33½ mm)		80	80

579 Arrest of Guernsey Parliamentarians, Fermain Bay

1993. 350th Anniv of Siege of Castle Cornet. Multicoloured.

611	16p. Type **579**	35	35
612	24p. Parliamentary ships attacking Castle Cornet	60	60
613	28p. Parliamentary captives escaping	75	75
614	33p. Castle cannon firing at St. Peter Port	85	85
615	39p. Surrender of Castle Cornet, 19 December 1651	90	90
MS616	203×75 mm. Nos. 611/15	3·25	4·00

584 Playing Cards

1993. Birth Bicentenary of Thomas de la Rue (printer).

617	**584**	16p. multicoloured	40	45
618	-	24p. multicoloured	65	65
619	-	28p. multicoloured	80	80
620	-	33p. red	95	95
621	-	39p. green	1·10	1·10

DESIGNS: 24p. Fountain pens; 28p. Envelope-folding machine; 33p. Great Britain 1855 4d. stamp; 39p. Thomas de la Rue and Mauritius £1 banknote.

589 "The Twelve Pearls"

1993. Christmas. Stained Glass Windows by Mary-Eily de Putron from the Chapel of Christ the Healer. Multicoloured.

622	13p. Type **589**	30	15
623	13p. "Healing rays"	30	15
624	13p. "Hand of God over the Holy City"	30	15
625	13p. "Wing and Seabirds" (facing left)	30	15
626	13p. "Christ the Healer"	30	15
627	13p. "Wing and Seabirds" (facing right)	30	15
628	13p. "The Young Jesus in the Temple"	30	15
629	13p. "The Raising of Jairus' Daughter"	30	15
630	13p. "Suffer little Children to come unto Me"	30	15
631	13p. "Pilgrim's Progress"	30	15
632	13p. "The Light of the World"	30	15
633	13p. "Raphael, Archangel of Healing, with Tobias"	30	15

601 Les Fouaillages (ancient burial ground)

1994. Europa. Archaeological Discoveries. Multicoloured.

634	24p. Type **601**	55	55
635	24p. Mounted Celtic warrior	55	55
636	30p. Jars, arrow heads and stone axe from Les Fouaillages	80	75
637	30p. Sword, spear head and torque from King's Road burial	80	75

605 Supermarine Spitfires Mk V over Normandy Beaches (image scaled to 52% of original size)

1994. 50th Anniv of D-Day. Sheet 93×71 mm.

MS638	**605** £2 multicoloured	5·00	5·50

Guernsey 16

606 Peugeot "Type 3", 1894

1994. Cent of First Car in Guernsey. Multicoloured.

639	16p. Type **606**	40	40
640	24p. Mercedes "Simplex", 1903	60	45
641	35p. Humber tourer, 1906	90	1·00
642	41p. Bentley sports tourer, 1936	1·00	1·00
643	60p. MG TC Midget, 1948	1·50	1·40

1994. "Philakorea '94" International Stamp Exhibition, Seoul. Sheet 110×90 mm. containing No. 581.

MS644	£1 multicoloured	3·25	3·00

611 Trident (Herm ferry)

1994. 25th Anniv of Guernsey Postal Administration. Multicoloured.

645	16p. Type **611**	35	30
646	24p. Handley Page HPR.7 Herald of Channel Express	55	50
647	35p. Britten Norman BN-2A MkIII Trislander of Aurigny Air Services	85	75
648	41p. Bon Marin de Serk (Sark ferry)	1·00	85
649	60p. Map of Bailiwick	1·40	1·20
MS650	150×100 mm. Nos. 645/9	6·75	7·00

616 Dolls' House

1994. Christmas. Bygone Toys. Multicoloured.

651	13p. Type **616**	40	15
652	13p. Doll	40	15
653	13p. Teddy in bassinette	40	15
654	13p. Sweets in pillar box and playing cards	40	15
655	13p. Spinning top	40	15
656	13p. Building blocks	40	15
657	24p. Rocking horse	75	30
658	24p. Teddy bear	75	30
659	24p. Tricycle	75	30
660	24p. Wooden duck	75	30
661	24p. Hornby toy locomotive	75	30
662	24p. Ludo game	75	30

Nos. 651/6 and 657/62 respectively were printed together, se-tenant, forming composite designs.

628 Seafood "Face"

1995. Greetings Stamps. "The Welcoming Face of Guernsey". Multicoloured.

663	24p. Type **628**	60	55
664	24p. Buckets and spade "face"	60	55
665	24p. Flowers "face"	60	55
666	24p. Fruit and vegetables "face"	60	55
667	24p. Sea shells and seaweed "face"	60	55
668	24p. Anchor and life belts "face"	60	55
669	24p. Glasses, cork and cutlery "face"	60	55
670	24p. Butterflies and caterpillars "face"	60	55
MS671	137×109 mm. Nos. 663/70	4·25	4·25

636 Winston Churchill and Wireless

1995. 50th Anniv of Liberation. Multicoloured.

672	16p. Type **636**	45	30
673	24p. Union Jack and Royal Navy ships off St. Peter Port	60	50
674	35p. Royal Arms and military band	90	90
675	41p. "Vega" (Red Cross supply ship)	90	90
676	60p. Rejoicing crowd	1·50	1·20
MS677	189×75 mm. Nos. 672/6	4·50	4·75

641 Silhouette of Doves on Ground

1995. Europa. Peace and Freedom. Multicoloured.

678	25p. Type **641**	90	90
679	30p. Silhouette of doves in flight	1·10	1·10

The designs of Nos. 678/9 each provide a stereogram or hidden three-dimensional image of a single dove.

643 Prince Charles, Castle Cornet and Bailiwick Arms

1995. Royal Visit.

680	**643**	£1.50 multicoloured	4·50	4·50

1995. "Singapore '95" International Stamp Exhibition. Sheet 110×90 mm. containing No. 581.

MS681	£1 multicoloured	3·75	3·75

644 Part of United Nations Emblem (face value at top left)

1995. 50th Anniv of United Nations. Designs showing different segments of the United Nations Emblem. Each blue and gold.

682	50p. Type **644**	1·10	1·10
683	50p. Face value at top right	1·10	1·10
684	50p. Face value at bottom left	1·10	1·10
685	50p. Face value at bottom right	1·10	1·10

648 "Christmas Trees for Sale in Bern" (Cornelia Huisboum-Weibel)

1995. Christmas. 50th Anniv of UNICEF Multicoloured.

686	13p. Type **648** (face value at left)	40	15
687	13p. "Christmas Trees for Sale in Bern" (face value at right)	40	15
688	13p.+1p. "Evening Snowfall" (Katerina Mertikas) (face value at left)	40	20
689	13p.+1p. "Evening Snowfall" (face value at right)	40	20
690	24p. "It came upon a Midnight Clear" (Georgia Guback) (face value at left)	70	30
691	24p. "It came upon a Midnight Clear" (Georgia Guback) (face value at right)	70	30
692	24p.+2p. "Children of the World" (face value at left)	70	30
693	24p.+2p. "Children of the World" (face value at right)	70	30

Nos. 686/7, 688/9, 690/1 and 692/3 were printed together, se-tenant, each pair forming a composite design.

656 Princess Anne (President, Save the Children Fund) and Children

1996. Europa. Famous Women. Multicoloured.

694	25p. Type **656**	55	50
695	30p. Queen Elizabeth II and people of the Commonwealth	70	75

658 England v. U.S.S.R., 1968 (value at right)

1996. European Football Championship, England. Multicoloured.

696	16p. Type **658**	55	20
697	16p. England v. U.S.S.R., 1968 (value at left)	55	20
698	24p. Italy v. Belgium, 1972 (value at right)	75	25
699	24p. Italy v. Belgium, 1972 (value at left)	75	25
700	35p. Ireland v. Netherlands, 1988 (value at right)	80	40
701	35p. Ireland v. Netherlands, 1988 (value at left)	80	40
702	41p. Denmark v. Germany, 1992 final (value at right)	95	45
703	41p. Denmark v. Germany, 1992 final (value at left)	95	45

666 Maj-Gen. Brock meeting Tecumseh (Indian chief) (image scaled to 44% of original size)

1996. "CAPEX '96" International Stamp Exhibition, Toronto. Sheet 110×90 mm. containing T **666** and similar horiz design.

MS704	24p. Type **666**; £1 Major-General Sir Isaac Brock on horseback, 1812	3·00	2·75

667 Ancient Greek Runner

1996. Centenary of Modern Olympic Games. Ancient Greek Athletes. Each black, yellow and orange.

705	16p. Type **677**	50	40
706	24p. Throwing the javelin	95	90
707	41p. Throwing the discus	1·10	1·20
708	55p. Wrestling (53×31 mm)	1·40	1·50
709	60p. Jumping	1·60	1·70
MS710	192×75 mm. Nos. 705/9	4·50	4·75

No. 708 also includes the "OLYMPHILEX '96" International Stamp Exhibition, Atlanta, logo.

672 Humphrey Bogart as Philip Marlowe

1996. Centenary of Cinema. Screen Detectives. Multicoloured.

711	16p. Type **672**	40	40
712	24p. Peter Sellers as Inspector Clouseau	60	60
713	35p. Basil Rathbone as Sherlock Holmes	85	85
714	41p. Margaret Rutherford as Miss Marple	90	90
715	60p. Warner Oland as Charlie Chan	1·40	1·40

677 The Annunciation

1996. Christmas. Multicoloured.

716	13p. Type **677**	40	40
717	13p. Journey to Bethlehem	40	40
718	13p. Arrival at the inn	40	40
719	13p. Angel and shepherds	40	40

720	13p. Mary, Joseph and Jesus in stable	40	40
721	13p. Shepherds worshipping Jesus	40	40
722	13p. Three Kings following star	40	40
723	13p. Three Kings with gifts	40	40
724	13p. The Presentation in the Temple	40	40
725	13p. Mary and Jesus	40	40
726	13p. Joseph warned by angel	40	40
727	13p. The Flight into Egypt	40	40
728	24p. Mary cradling Jesus (horiz)	40	40
729	25p. The Nativity (horiz)	40	40

691 Holly Blue

1997. Endangered Species. Butterflies and Moths. Multicoloured.

730	18p. Type **691**	55	50
731	25p. Hummingbird hawk- moth	65	60
732	26p. Emperor moth	85	85
733	37p. Brimstone	1·10	1·10
MS734	92×68 mm. £1 Painted Lady	3·00	2·50

No. **MS734** includes the "HONG KONG '97" International Stamp Exhibition logo on the sheet margin.

696 Gilliatt fighting Octopus

1997. Europa. Tales and Legends. Scenes from *Les Travailleurs de la Mer* by Victor Hugo. Multicoloured.

735	26p. Type **696**	70	70
736	31p. Gilliatt grieving on rock	1·00	1·10

698 Shell Beach, Herm

1997. Guernsey Scenes (1st series). Multicoloured. Self-adhesive.

737	18p. Type **698**	60	30
738	25p. La Seigneurie, Sark (vert)	70	60
739	26p. Castle Cornet, Guernsey	80	75

701 19th-century Shipyard, St. Peter Port (image scaled to 44% of original size)

1997. "Pacific '97" World Philatelic Exhibition, San Francisco. Sheet 110×90 mm. containing T **701** and similar horiz design.

MS740	30p. green and gold; £1 multicoloured (*Costa Rica Packet* (barque))	4·00	4·00

See also Nos. 770/3.

702 Transistor Radio, Microphone and Radio Logos

1997. Methods of Communication. Multicoloured.

741	18p. Type **702**	60	60
742	25p. Television, video camera and satellite dish	75	75
743	26p. Fax machine, telephones and mobile phone	75	75
744	37p. Printing press, newspaper and type	1·00	1·00
745	43p. Stamp, coding machine and postbox	1·40	1·50
746	63p. CD, computer and disk	1·60	1·75

708 Teddy Bear making Cake

1997. Christmas. Teddy Bears. Multicoloured.

747	15p. Type **708**	45	45
748	25p. Teddy bears decorating Christmas tree	70	70
749	26p. Two teddy bears in armchair	70	70
750	37p. Teddy bear as Father Christmas	1·00	1·00
751	43p. Teddy bears unwrapping presents	1·10	1·10
752	63p. Teddy bears eating Christmas dinner	1·60	1·60
MS753	123×107 mm. Nos. 747/52	6·00	6·00

714 Visiting Guernsey, 1957

1997. Golden Wedding of Queen Elizabeth and Prince Philip. Multicoloured.

754	18p. Type **714**	50	50
755	25p. Coronation Day, 1953	75	75
756	26p. Royal Family, 1957	75	75
757	37p. On royal yacht, 1972	1·10	1·10
758	43p. Queen Elizabeth and Prince Philip at Trooping the Colour, 1972	1·25	1·25
759	63p. Queen Elizabeth and Prince Philip, 1997	1·75	1·75

No. 755 is inscribed "1947" in error.

720 Tapestry of 11th-century Guernsey (St. Martin)

1998. The Millennium Tapestries Project. Each showing a different century contributed by individual parishes. Multicoloured.

760	25p. Type **720**	70	70
761	25p. 12th-century (St. Saviour)	70	70
762	25p. 13th-century (Vale)	70	70
763	25p. 14th-century (St. Sampson)	70	70
764	25p. 15th-century (Torteval)	70	70
765	25p. 16th-century (Castel)	70	70
766	25p. 17th-century (St. Andrew)	70	70
767	25p. 18th-century (Forest)	70	70
768	25p. 19th-century (St. Pierre du Bois)	70	70
769	25p. 20th-century (St. Peter Port)	70	70

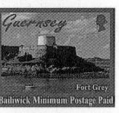

730 Fort Grey

1998. Guernsey Scenes (2nd series). Multicoloured. Self-adhesive.

770	(20p.) Type **730**	1·20	1·20
771	(20p.) Grand Havre	1·20	1·20
772	(25p.) Little Chapel	1·50	1·50
773	(25p.) Guernsey cow	1·50	1·50

Nos. 770/1 are inscribed "Bailiwick Minimum Postage Paid" and were initally sold at 20p. Nos. 772/3 are inscribed "UK Minimum Postage Paid" and were initially sold at 25p.

734 Fairey IIIC, Balloon, Sopwith Camel and Avro 504

1998. 80th Anniv of the Royal Air Force. Multicoloured.

774	20p. Type **734**	50	50
775	25p. Fairey Swordfish, de Havilland DH.82 Tiger Moth, Supermarine Walrus and Gloster Gladiator	60	60
776	30p. Hawker Hurricane, Supermarine Spitfire, Vickers Type **271** Wellington, Short S.25 Sunderland (flying boat), Westland Lysander and Bristol Type **142** Blenheim	70	70
777	37p. de Havilland DH.98 Mosquito, Avro Type **683** Lancaster, british Taylorcraft-tAuster III, Gloster Meteor and Airspeed Horsa glider	90	85
778	43p. English Electric Canberra, Hawker Sea Fury, Bristol Sycamore, Hawker Hunter, Handley Page HP.80 Victor and English Electric BAe Lightning	1·00	1·20
779	63p. Pavania Tornado GRI, BAe Hawk, BAe Sea Harrier, Westland Lynx (helicopter) and Hawker Siddeley (BAe) Nimrod	1·40	1·50

740 Jules Rimet (first President of F.I.F.A) (image scaled to 44% of original size)

1998. 150th Anniv of the Cambridge Rules for Football. Sheet 110×90 mm containing T **173** and similar horiz design.

MS780	30p. Type **740**; £1.75, Bobby Moore and Queen Elizabeth II, 1966	5·50	5·50

741 Girls in Traditional Costume watching Sheep Display, West Show

1998. Europa. Festivals. Multicoloured.

781	20p. Type **741**	70	70
782	25p. Marching band and "Battle of Flowers" exhibit, North Show	80	80
783	30p. Prince Charles, monument and tank, Liberation Day	90	90
784	37p. Goat, dahlias and show-jumping, South Show	1·00	1·00

The 25p. and 30p. incorporate the "EUROPA" emblem.

745 Outward Motorboat　　**763** Royal Yacht *Britannia*

1998. Maritime Heritage. Multicoloured.

785	1p. Type **745**	10	10
786	2p. St. John Ambulance inshore rescue dinghy	10	10
787	3p. Pilot boat, St. Peter Port	10	10
788	4p. *Flying Christine III* (St. John Ambulance launch)	10	10
789	5p. Crab fishing boat	10	10
790	6p. Herm Island ferry	10	10
791	7p. *Sarnia* (St. Peter Port Harbour Authority launch)	15	20
792	8p. *Leopardess* (States' fisheries protection launch)	15	20
793	9p. Trawler	20	25
794	10p. Powerboat (27×27 mm)	20	25
795	20p. Dart 18 racing catamaran (27×27 mm)	40	45
796	30p. 30ft Bermuda-rigged sloop (27×27 mm)	60	65
797	40p. Motor cruiser (27×27 mm)	80	85
798	50p. Ocean-going sailing yacht (27×27 mm)	1·00	1·10
799	75p. Motor yacht *Beaucette Marina* (27×27 mm)	1·50	1·30
800	£1 *Queen Elizabeth 2* (liner) (35×26 mm)	2·00	1·80
801	£3 *Oriana* (liner) (35×26 mm)	6·00	5·50
802	£4 *Queen Mary 2* (liner)	9·00	9·00
803	£5 Type **763**	13·00	10·00

769 Modern Tree, Teletubby and Playstation

1998. 150th Anniv of the Introduction of the Christmas Tree. Multicoloured.

810	17p. Type **769**	1·00	1·00
811	25p. 1960s tinsel tree, toy bus and doll	1·00	1·00
812	30p. 1930s gold foil tree, panda and toy tank	1·00	1·00
813	37p. 1920s tree, model of "Bluebird" and doll	1·25	1·25
814	43p. 1900s tree, teddy bear and toy train	1·25	1·25
815	63p. 1850s tree, wooden doll and spinning top	1·75	1·75
MS816	160×94 mm. Nos. 810/15	7·00	7·00

775 Elizabeth Bowes Lyon, 1907

1999. Life and Times of Queen Elizabeth the Queen Mother. Multicoloured.

817	25p. Type **775**	70	30
818	25p. On wedding day, 1923	70	30
819	25p. Holding Princess Elizabeth, 1926	70	30
820	25p. At Coronation, 1937	70	30
821	25p. Visiting bombed areas of London, 1940 (wearing green hat)	70	30
822	25p. Fishing near Auckland, New Zealand, 1966	70	30
823	25p. At Guernsey function, 1963 (wearing tiara)	70	30
824	25p. Receiving flowers on her birthday, 1992	70	30
825	25p. Presenting trophy, Sandown Park races, 1989	70	30
826	25p. Opening Royal Norfolk Regimental Museum, Norwich, 1990 (wearing blue hat)	70	30

785 Spirit of Guernsey, 1995

1999. 175th Anniv of Royal National Lifeboat Institution. Multicoloured.

827	20p. Type **785**	50	50
828	25p. Sir William Arnold, 1973	60	60
829	30p. Euphrosyne Kendal, 1954	70	70
830	38p. Queen Victoria, 1929	90	90
831	44p. Arthur Lionel, 1912	1·10	1·10
832	64p. Vincent Kirk Ella, 1888	1·50	1·50

791 Burnet Rose and Local Carriage Label

1999. Europa. Parks and Gardens. Herm Island. Designs each showing a different local carriage label. Multicoloured.

833	20p. Type **791**	50	50
834	25p. Atlantic puffin	85	85
835	30p. Small heath butterfly	90	90
836	38p. Shells on Shell Beach	1·30	1·30

795 Prince Edward and Miss Sophie Rhys-Jones

1999. Royal Wedding. Sheet 93×70 mm.

MS837	795	£1 Multicoloured	3·25	3·00

796 Major-General Le Marchant (founder) and Cadet at Sword Drill

1999. Bicentenary of The Royal Military Academy, Sandhurst. Multicoloured.

838	20p. Type **796**	60	60
839	25p. The Duke of York (official sponsor) and Cadet on Horseback	65	55
840	30p. Field-Marshal Earl Haig and cadets on parade	90	90
841	38p. Field-Marshal Viscount Montgomery and bridging exercise	1·25	1·25
842	44p. David Niven (actor) and rifle practice	1·50	1·50
843	64p. Sir Winston Churchill and tank	1·90	1·90

802 The Nativity

1999. Christmas. Wood Carvings by Denis Brehaut from Notre Dame Church. Multicoloured.

844	17p. Type **802**	45	40
845	25p. Virgin Mary and Child	60	55
846	30p. Holy Family	75	70
847	38p. Cattle around manger	90	85
848	44p. Adoration of the Shepherds	1·10	1·20
849	64p. Adoration of the Magi	1·50	1·70
MS850	159×86 mm. Nos. 844/9	5·50	5·50

808 Space Bus (Fallon Ephgrave)

2000. New Millennium. "Stampin' the Future" (children's stamp design competition). Multicoloured.

851	20p. Type **808**	60	45
852	25p. Children holding hands (Abigail Downing)	60	55
853	30p. No Captivity (Laura Martin)	70	65
854	38p. Post Office of the Future (Sarah Haddow)	90	80
855	44p. Solar-powered car (Sophie Medland)	1·20	1·50
856	64p. Woman flying (Danielle McIver)	1·50	1·75

814 Bristol Type 142 Blenheim

2000. 60th Anniv of Battle of Britain. R.A.F. Aircraft. Multicoloured.

857	21p. Type **814**	60	50
858	26p. Hawker Hurricane	70	55
859	36p. Boulton Paul P.28 Defiant II	1·10	85
860	40p. Gloster Gladiator	1·25	95
861	45p. Bristol Type 156 Beaufighter IF	1·40	1·20
862	65p. Supermarine Spitfire IIC	1·75	1·50

820 Guernsey Flag on Kite and "2000"

2000. Europa. Multicoloured.

863	21p. Type **820**	50	45
864	26p. Stylized sails bearing national flowers	60	55
865	36p. "Building Europe"	1·00	1·00
866	65p. Rainbow and three doves	1·60	1·75

824 Iris stylosa

2000. A Botanist's Sketchbook. Restoration of Candie Gardens, St. Peter Port. Multicoloured.

867	26p. Type **824**	70	70
868	26p. Watsonia	70	70
869	26p. Richardia maculata	70	70
870	26p. Narcissus bulbocodium	70	70
871	26p. Triteleia laxa	70	70
872	26p. Tigridia pavonia	70	70
873	26p. Agapanthus umbellatus	70	70
874	26p. Sparaxis	70	70
875	26p. Pancratium maritimum	70	70
876	26p. Nerine sarniensis	70	70

834 Town Church, St. Peter Port

2000. Christmas. Guernsey Churches. Multicoloured.

877	18p. Type **834**	40	40
878	26p. Children leaving St. Sampson's Church	60	55
879	36p. Flying kite by Vale Church	90	85
880	40p. Carol singing outside St. Pierre du Bois Church	95	1·00
881	45p. Building snowman near St. Martin's Church	1·10	1·40
882	65p. Street scene including St. John's Church, St. Peter Port	1·50	1·75
MS883	160×86 mm. Nos. 877/82	6·00	6·00

840 Queen Victoria and Diamond Jubilee Statue

2001. Death Centenary of Queen Victoria. Each incorporating a different portrait of Queen Victoria. Multicoloured.

884	21p. Type **840**	50	50
885	26p. Letter of thanks to Guernsey, 1846	60	55
886	36p. Statues of Queen Victoria and Prince Albert	90	85
887	40p. Stone commemorating 1846 visit	95	95
888	45p. Statue of Prince Albert	1·10	1·10
889	65p. Victoria Tower, 1848	1·50	1·50
MS890	165×80 mm. Nos. 884/9	6·00	7·00

No. **MS**890 includes the logo of the "Hong Kong 2001" Stamp Exhibition on the sheet margin.

846 River kingfisher ("Kingfisher")

2001. Europa. Water Birds. Multicoloured.

891	21p. Type **846**	1·25	1·25
892	26p. Garganey	1·25	1·25
893	36p. Little egret	1·50	1·50
894	65p. Little ringed plover	2·00	2·00

850 Cavalier King Charles Spaniel

2001. Centenary of Guernsey Dog Club. Multicoloured.

895	22p. Type **850**	55	50
896	27p. Miniature schnauzer	65	60
897	36p. German shepherd dog	90	85
898	40p. Cocker spaniel	95	95
899	45p. West highland white terrier	1·10	1·10
900	65p. Dachshund	1·50	1·50

856 La Corbiere Sunset

2001. Island Scenes. Multicoloured. Self-adhesive.

901	(22p.) Type **856**	45	50
902	(22p.) Rue des Hougues	45	50
903	(22p.) St. Saviour's Reservoir	45	50
904	(22p.) Shell Beach, Herm	45	50
905	(22p.) Telegraph Bay, Alderney	45	50
906	(27p.) Alderney Railway	55	60
907	(27p.) Vazon Bay	55	60
908	(27p.) La Coupee, Sark	55	60
909	(27p.) Les Hanois Lighthouse	55	60
910	(27p.) Albecq Beach	55	60

Nos. 901/5 were intended for postage within the Bailiwick and are inscribed "GY". They were each initially sold at 22p. Nos. 906/10 were intended for postage to Great Britain and are inscribed "UK". They were each initially sold at 27p.

866 Droplet of Water on Leaf ("Vision")

2001. Incorporation of Guernsey Post Ltd. Multicoloured.
(a) Square designs as T **193**.

921	22p. Type **866**	45	50
922	27p. Hummingbird ("Understanding")	55	60
923	36p. Butterfly's wing ("Individuality")	70	75
924	40p. Sea shell ("Strength")	80	85
925	45p. Honeycomb ("Community")	90	95
926	65p. Dandelion ("Maturity")	1·20	1·40

(b) Design as No. 28a (1969 £1), but redrawn.

927	£1 View of Guernsey from the sea	5·00	5·50

No. 927 differs from the original 1969 stamp by showing the Queen's portrait without a tiara and by showing "GUERNSEY BAILIWICK" in white instead of grey.

872 "Tree of Joy", St. Peter Port

2001. Christmas. Festive Lights. Multicoloured.

928	19p. Type **872**	40	45
929	27p. Cross, Les Cotils Christian Centre	55	60
930	36p. Les Ruettes Cottage, St. Saviour's	75	80
931	40p. Farmhouse, Le Preel, Castel	1·00	1·10
932	45p. Sark Post Office	1·10	1·20
933	65p. High Street, St. Peter Port	1·50	1·60
MS934	150×100 mm. Nos. 928/33	6·00	6·50

878 Victor Hugo and St. Peter Port

2002. Birth Bicentenary of Victor Hugo (French author). Les Miserables (novel). Multicoloured.

935	22p. Type **878**	45	50
936	27p. Cosette	55	60
937	36p. Valjean	75	80
938	40p. Inspector Javert	90	95
939	45p. Cosette and Marius	1·10	1·10
940	65p. Novel and score for Les Miserables (musical by Alain Boublil and Claude-Michel Schonberg)	1·50	1·60
MS941	150×100 mm. Nos. 935/40	5·50	6·00

The 27p. value reproduces the main image from promotional material for Cameron Mackintosh's musical production.

884 Juggling

2002. Europa. The Circus. Multicoloured.

942	22p. Type **884**	45	50
943	27p. Clowns	55	60
944	36p. Trapeze artists	70	75
945	40p. Knife thrower	80	90
946	45p. Acrobat	90	95
947	65p. High-wire cyclist	1·20	1·40

890 Queen Elizabeth and Crowd

2002. Golden Jubilee. Multicoloured.

948	22p. Type **890**	45	50
949	27p. Queen Elizabeth at St. Peter Port	55	60
950	36p. Queen Elizabeth and Prince Philip at St. Anne's School, Alderney	70	75
951	40p. Queen Elizabeth and La Seigneurie, Sark	80	85
952	45p. At Millennium Stone, L'Ancresse	90	95
953	65p. In evening dress and floodlit Castle Cornet	1·20	1·40

896 Original Pillar Box, Union Street

2002. 150th Anniv of First Pillar Box. Sheet, 55×90 mm.

MS954	896	£1.75 multicoloured	6·50	6·75

897 Family and Ferry, La Maseline

2002. Holidays on Sark. Multicoloured.

955	27p. Type **897**	45	30
956	27p. Passenger tractors	45	30
957	27p. Campsite	45	30
958	27p. Cyclists at La Coupee	45	30
959	27p. Swimming in Venus Pool	45	30
960	27p. La Seigneurie gardens	45	30
961	27p. Posting cards	45	30
962	27p. Carriage ride	45	30
963	27p. Tea at a café	45	30
964	27p. On the beach at Creux Harbour	45	30

907 Elizabeth College and Cadet Corps Parade, 1934

2002. 60th Anniv of Herbert Le Patourel's Victoria Cross. Multicoloured.

965	22p. Type **907**	45	30
966	27p. Captain Le Patourel in action, Tunisia 1942, and V.C	55	60
967	36p. Captain Le Patourel and nurse, 1943	70	75

968	40p. Award ceremony, Cairo, 1943	80	85
969	45p. Major Le Patourel welcomed home to Guernsey, 1948	90	95
970	65p. Hebert Le Patourel carrying the King's Colour, 1968	1·20	1·40

913 Queen Elizabeth the Queen Mother and Bouquet (½-size illustration) (image scaled to 35% of original size)

2002. Queen Elizabeth the Queen Mother Commemoration. Sheet 140×98 mm.

MS971	**913** £2 multicoloured	5·00	5·00

914 Mary and Jesus

2002. Christmas. Multicoloured.

972	22p. Type **914**	50	50
973	27p. Mary, Joseph and Jesus in the stable	70	70
974	36p. Angel appearing to shepherds	1·10	1·10
975	40p. Shepherds with Mary and Jesus	1·25	1·25
976	45p. Three Wise Men	1·50	1·50
977	65p. Stable with star overhead	1·75	1·75
MS978	131×101 mm. Nos. 972/7	5·00	5·00

920 Avro Type 683 Lancaster Bomber and Crew

2003. Memories of the Second World War. 60th Anniv of Operation Tunnel (£1.50) and Dambusters Raid (others) (1st issue). Multicoloured.

979	22p. Type **920**	75	50
980	27p. Flight of Lancaster bombers crossing English coast	75	60
981	36p. Lancaster bombers in enemy searchlights	1·00	75
982	40p. Dropping bouncing bombs	1·00	85
983	£1.50 H.M.S. *Charybdis* (cruiser) and H.M.S. *Limbourne* (destroyer) (40×30 mm)	3·50	3·25

See also Nos. 1027/31 and 1060/4.

925 Hurdling

2003. Island Games, Guernsey. Multicoloured.

984	22p. Type **925**	45	50
985	27p. Cycling	55	60
986	36p. Gymnastics	75	80
987	40p. Sailing	80	85
988	45p. Golf	90	95
989	65p. Running	1·20	1·40
MS990	140×75 mm. Nos. 984/9	5·00	5·00

931 St. Peter Port Harbour ("Naturally Guernsey", 2003)

2003. Europa. Poster Art. Multicoloured.

991	22p. Type **931**	45	50

992	27p. Motor-cruiser off Guernsey ("The islands of Guernsey", 1995)	55	60
993	36p. "Children on the Seashore" (Renoir) ("Holiday Guernsey", 1988)	75	80
994	40p. St. Peter Port Harbour ("Bailiwick of Guernsey", 1978)	80	85
995	45p. St. Peter Port and cliffs ("Guernsey - The Charming Channel Island", 1968)	90	95
996	65p. Secluded bay ("Guernsey", 1956)	1·20	1·40

937 H.M.S. *Guernsey* (image scaled to 41% of original size)

2003. Decommissioning of H.M.S. *Guernsey* (fishery protection patrol vessel). Sheet 117×84 mm.

MS997	**206** £1.50 multicoloured	4·50	4·00

938 Princess Diana and Baby Prince William

2003. 21st Birthday of Prince William of Wales. Multicoloured.

998	27p. Type **938**	55	30
999	27p. Prince William, aged 3, with Prince Charles and Prince Harry at Kensington Palace	55	30
1000	27p. Aged 4, in Parachute Regiment uniform	55	30
1001	27p. Aged 7, with Prince Harry on his first day at Wetherby School	55	30
1002	27p. Aged 8, with Prince Charles at Guards Polo	55	30
1003	27p. Aged 9, on ski slopes with Princess Diana	55	30
1004	27p. On first day at Eton, 1995	55	30
1005	27p. With Prince Charles and Prince Harry at Balmoral, 1997	55	30
1006	27p. Wearing hard hat during Community project in Chile, 2000	55	30
1007	27p. Playing polo, 2002	55	30

948 Letters of Alphabet

2003

1008	**948**	£5 orange, blue and silver	10·00	10·50

The alphabet letters are printed in thermochromic ink which fades from pale orange to white when exposed to heat.

949 Sleeping Boy and Christmas Tree

2003. Christmas. Scenes from Poem *Twas the Night before Christmas* by Clement Clarke Moore. Multicoloured.

1009	10p. Type **949**	20	25
1010	27p. Boy opening shutter to see Santa's sleigh	55	60
1011	36p. Santa on roof with reindeer	70	75
1012	40p. Santa with presents	80	85
1013	45p. Santa leaving presents under Christmas tree	1·20	1·30
1014	65p. Santa in sleigh	1·50	1·70
MS1015	130×104 mm. Nos. 1009/14	4·75	4·75

955 Golden Snub-nosed Monkey

2004. Endangered Species (1st series). Golden Snub-nosed Monkey (*Pygothrix roxellana*). Sheet 120×85 mm.

MS1016	**955** £2 multicoloured	6·50	6·50

See also Nos. **MS1085**, **MS1096**, **MS1173** and **MS1266**.

956 Clematis "Rosemoor"

2004. Raymond Evison's Guernsey Clematis. Multicoloured. Self-adhesive.

1017	(22p.) Type **956**	75	75
1018	(22p.) "Arctic Queen"	75	75
1019	(22p.) "Harlow Carr"	75	75
1020	(22p.) "Guernsey Cream"	75	75
1021	(22p.) "Josephine"	75	75
1022	(27p.) "Blue Moon"	85	85
1023	(27p.) "Wisley"	85	85
1024	(27p.) "Liberation"	85	85
1025	(27p.) "Royal Velvet"	85	85
1026	(27p.) "Hyde Hall"	85	85

Nos. 1017/21 were intended for postage within the Bailiwick and are inscribed "GY". They were each initially sold at 22p. Nos. 1022/6 were intended for postage to Great Britain and are inscribed "UK". They were each initially sold at 27p.

2004. Memories of the Second World War (2nd issue). 60th Anniv of D-Day Landings. As T **920**. Multicoloured.

1027	26p. Supermarine Spitfire	85	85
1028	32p. Landing craft and ship	1·00	1·00
1029	36p. Troops going ashore at Gold Beach	1·20	1·20
1030	40p. Troops in water	1·30	1·30
1031	£1.50 *Vega* (Red Cross supply ship) (40×29 mm)	5·00	5·00

971 Sandcastle, Rider, Bucket and Spade, Deckchair and Canoeist

2004. Europa. Holidays. Multicoloured.

1032	26p. Type **971**	85	85
1033	32p. Pathway sign, walking trails, bench and Guernsey landscapes	1·10	1·10
1034	36p. Lighthouse and yachts in marina, St. Peter Port	1·20	1·20
1035	40p. Glasses of red wine and meals on table	1·30	1·30
1036	45p. Statue-menhir at Castel and Loop Holed Tower, Le Gran'mere statue-menhir, Little Chapel and Victor Hugo statue	1·50	1·50
1037	65p. Guernsey Lily, wildflowers and robin	2·10	2·10

977 Three Crowns (Loyalty)

2004. 800th Anniv of Allegiance to England. Multicoloured.

1038	26p. Type **977**	85	85
1039	32p. Three ships (Trade)	1·10	1·10
1040	36p. Knotted rope (Unity)	1·20	1·20
1041	40p. Three castle turrets (Protection)	1·30	1·30
1042	45p. Three scrolls (Justice)	1·50	1·50
1043	65p. Three leaping fish (Industry)	2·10	2·10
MS1044	140×80 mm. Nos. 1038/43	8·00	8·00

983 Discus Thrower

2004. Olympic Games, Athens, Greece. Multicoloured.

1045	32p. Type **983**	1·00	1·00
1046	36p. Javelin thrower	1·20	1·20
1047	45p. Runners	1·50	1·50
1048	65p. Wrestlers	2·10	2·10
MS1049	152×98 mm. £1 Olympic sports (40×29 mm)	4·75	4·75

988 Little Donkey

2004. Christmas. Multicoloured.

1050	20p. Type **988**	65	25
1051	20p. *While Shepherds Watched*	65	25
1052	20p. *Away in a Manger*	65	25
1053	20p. *Unto Us a Child is Born*	65	25
1054	20p. *We Three Kings*	65	25
1055	32p. Angels wings (33×26 mm)	1·10	1·10
1056	36p. Bauble (33×26 mm)	1·20	1·20
1057	40p. Holly (33×26 mm)	1·30	1·30
1058	45p. Detail of snowman (33×26 mm)	1·50	1·50
1059	65p. Star on top of tree (33×26 mm)	2·20	2·20

Nos. 1050/4 were printed together, se-tenant, with the backgrounds forming a composite design.

2005. Memories of the Second World War (3rd issue). 60th Anniv of Liberation. As T **920**. Multicoloured.

1060	26p. British soldiers in Landrover and welcoming crowd	50	55
1061	32p. Guernsey woman waving and Liberty sign and flags on building	65	70
1062	36p. Parents and children reunited	70	75
1063	40p. Return of local men from Hampshire Regiment	80	85
1064	£1.50 Winston Churchill (40×29 mm)	3·00	3·25

1003 Iris "Dorothea" and "Royal"

2005. Birth Centenary of William J. Caparne (artist and iris breeder). Watercolour paintings of flowers. Multicoloured.

1065	26p. Type **1003**	50	55
1066	32p. Nerine Fothergilli "Major"	65	70
1067	36p. Iris "Garnet"	70	95
1068	40p. Narcissus "Sir Watkin"	85	1·00
1069	45p. Narcissus "Rip van Winkle"	1·00	1·10
1070	65p. Narcissus "Sulphur Phoenix"	1·50	1·50
MS1071	140×85 mm. Nos. 1065/70	5·00	5·50

1009 Spider Crab

2005. Europa. Gastronomy. Seafood and coastal scenes. Multicoloured.

1072	26p. Type **1007**	50	55
1073	32p. Seared red mullet and crab cake	65	70
1074	36p. Lobster salad	70	75
1075	40p. Brill on spinach with local moules	80	85
1076	45p. Prawn salad	90	95
1077	65p. Salmon wrapped in spinach with local moules	1·30	1·40

1015 King George VI

2005. 60th Anniv of Liberation of Guernsey. Multicoloured.

| 1078 | £1 Type **1015** | 2·75 | 2·75 |
| 1079 | £1 Queen Elizabeth II | 2·75 | 2·75 |

1017 Fishing Boat

2005. "Sea Guernsey 2005". Multicoloured.

1080	26p. Type **1017**	50	55
1081	32p. Yacht off Herm Harbour	65	70
1082	36p. Windsurfer	70	75
1083	40p. Sea angler on rocks at Albecq	80	85
1084	65p. Horse and rider on beach, Vazon Bay	1·50	1·40

1022 Basking Shark (image scaled to 40% of original size)

2005. Endangered Species (2nd issue). Basking Shark (*Centorhinus maximas*). Sheet 185×65 mm.

| MS1085 **1022** £2 multicoloured | 5·00 | 5·00 |

1023 Christ holding Guernsey Flag, St. Pierre du Bois

2005. Christmas. Stained-glass Windows from Guernsey and Alderney Parish Churches. Multicoloured.

1086	20p. Type **1023**	40	45
1087	20p. Madonna and Child, St. Saviour	40	45
1088	20p. John baptising Christ, St. Martin	40	45
1089	20p. Christ, the Light of the World, Torteval	40	45
1090	20p. Madonna and Child, St. Sampson	40	45
1091	32p. Madonna and Child, Vale	65	70
1092	36p. Three Kings, Castel	70	75
1093	40p. St. Nicholas, Alderney	80	85
1094	45p. Madonna and Child, St. Andrew	90	95
1095	65p. St. Marguerite, Forest	1·30	1·40

1033 Atlantic Leatherback Turtle

2006. Endangered Species (3rd series). Florida Everglades. Sheet 110×90 mm containing T **1033** and similar horiz design. Multicoloured.

| MS1096 £1 Type **1033**; £1·50 American wood ibis | 6·50 | 6·00 |

1034 Iraq Conflict, 2004

2006. 150th Anniv of the Victoria Cross. Multicoloured.

1097	29p. Type **1034**	60	65
1098	34p. Falklands war, 1982	70	75
1099	38p. Battle of El Alamein, 1942	75	80
1100	42p. Gallipoli campaign, 1915	85	90
1101	47p. Battle of Rorke's Drift, 1879	95	1·00
1102	68p. Charge of the Light Brigade, 1854	1·40	1·50

1040 Pilbeam MP58, British Speed Hill Climb Championship, 1995

2006. Andy Priaulx's Motor Racing Victories. Multicoloured.

1103	29p. Type **1040**	70	70
1104	34p. Renault Spider Cup, 1999	1·00	1·00
1105	42p. British Formula 3, 2001	1·00	1·00
1106	45p. FIA European Touring Car Championship, 2004	1·15	1·15
1107	47p. Nurburgring, Germany, 2005	1·60	1·60
1108	68p. FIA World Touring Car Championship, 2005	1·90	1·90
MS1109 160×100 mm. Nos. 1103/8	6·00	6·00

1046 Brunel and Mailbags at Paddington Station

2006. Birth Bicentenary of Isambard Kingdom Brunel (engineer). Multicoloured.

1110	29p. Type **1046**	60	65
1111	34p. Duke class locomotive No. 3258 *King Arthur* at Paddington Station	70	75
1112	42p. *King Arthur* on Wharncliffe Viaduct	85	90
1113	45p. Loading mail from train onto *Ibex* at Weymouth harbour	90	95
1114	47p. Weymouth & Channel Island steam packet *Ibex*	1·20	1·20
1115	68p. Unloading mail from *Ibex* at St. Peter Port harbour	1·70	1·70

1052 Student working as Waiter in Paris

2006. Europa. Integration. Showing student's gap year travels. Multicoloured.

1116	29p. Type **1052**	70	70
1117	34p. Sphinx, Egypt	1·00	1·00
1118	42p. Great Wall of China	1·00	1·00
1119	45p. Student and aborigines at Ayers Rock, Australia	1·15	1·15
1120	47p. Head of Statue of Liberty, New York	1·60	1·60
1121	68p. Students at Taj Mahal, India	1·90	1·90

1058 Queen Elizabeth II

2006. 80th Birthday of Queen Elizabeth II.

| 1122 | **1058** £10 multicoloured | 22·00 | 22·00 |

1059 Grey Seal

2006. Designation of L'Eree Wetland as Ramsar Site. Multicoloured.

1123	29p. Type **1059**	60	65
1124	34p. Ormer	70	75
1125	42p. Common blenny	85	90
1126	45p. Le Creux es Faies (Neolithic grave)	1·00	95
1127	47p. Yellow horned poppy	1·20	1·00
1128	68p. Oystercatcher	1·50	1·50
MS1129 140×95 mm. Nos. 1123/8	6·50	5·75

1065 A Partridge in a Pear Tree

2006. Christmas. "The Twelve Days of Christmas" (carol). Multicoloured.

1130	22p. Type **1065**	45	50
1131	22p. Two turtle doves	45	50
1132	22p. Three French hens	45	50
1133	22p. Four calling birds	45	50
1134	22p. Five gold rings	45	50
1135	22p. Six geese a-laying	45	50
1136	29p. Seven swans a-swimming	60	65
1137	34p. Eight maids a-milking	70	75
1138	42p. Nine ladies dancing	85	90
1139	45p. Ten lords a-leaping	90	95
1140	47p. Eleven pipers piping	95	1·00
1141	68p. Twelve drummers drumming	1·40	1·50

1077 Departure of Troops on *Queen Elizabeth 2*, Southampton

2007. 25th Anniv of the Battle for the Falklands. Multicoloured.

1142	32p. Type **1077**	75	75
1143	37p. Troops landing at San Carlos Bay	90	90
1144	45p. BAe Sea Harriers flying over SS *Canberra*	1·10	1·10
1145	48p. Lt. Col. H. Jones firing machine gun	1·10	1·10
1146	50p. Westland Sea King helicopter and *Invincible*	1·20	1·50
1147	71p. Troops marching with Union Jack towards Port Stanley	1·70	2·00
MS1148 150×100 mm. Nos. 1142/7	6·75	7·00

1083 Rocks at Albecq

2007. 125th Anniv of La Societe Guernesiaise. Multicoloured. Self-adhesive.

1149	(32p.) Type **1083**	80	80
1150	(32p.) Ivy bee	80	80
1151	(32p.) Vale Church	80	80
1152	(32p.) Common frog	80	80
1153	(32p.) Parasol mushroom	80	80
1154	(37p.) Southern marsh orchid	80	80
1155	(37p.) Shore crab	80	80
1156	(37p.) Alderney blonde hedgehog	80	80
1157	(37p.) Barn owl	80	80
1158	(37p.) Le Trepied dolmen	80	80

Nos. 1149/53 were intended for postage within the Bailiwick, are inscribed "GY" and sold for 32p. each.

Nos. 1154/8 were intended for postage to Great Britain, are inscribed "UK" and sold for 37p. each.

1093 Scouts Camping, 1907

2007. Europa. Centenary of Scouting. Multicoloured.

1159	32p. Type **1093**	75	75
1160	37p. Scout sailing, 1924	90	90
1161	45p. Two scouts fishing from rocks, 1947	1·10	1·10
1162	48p. Scouts making and flying model aircraft, 1968	1·10	1·10
1163	50p. Scouts on caving expedition, 1990	1·50	1·20
1164	71p. Scouts rollerblading, Cambridge Park, St. Peter Port, 2007	2·00	1·70

1099 Mike Hawthorn, 1958

2007. British Formula One World Champions. Multicoloured.

1165	32p. Type **1099**	75	75
1166	32p. Jackie Stewart, 1971	75	75
1167	37p. Graham Hill, 1962	85	85
1168	37p. James Hunt, 1976	85	85
1169	45p. Jim Clark, 1963	1·20	1·10
1170	48p. Nigel Mansell, 1992	1·50	1·10
1171	50p. John Surtees, 1964	1·70	1·20
1172	71p. Damon Hill, 1996	2·50	1·70

1107 Mountain Gorilla (image scaled to 53% of original size)

2007. Endangered Species (4th series). Mountain Gorilla (*Gorilla beringeiberingei*). Sheet 118×84 mm.

| MS1173 **1107** £2·50 multicoloured | 7·00 | 7·00 |

1108 Engagement, c. 1947

2007. Diamond Wedding of Queen Elizabeth II and Duke of Edinburgh. Multicoloured.

1174	32p. Type **1108**	75	75
1175	37p. With baby Princess Anne	90	90
1176	45p. Off-duty, wearing casual clothes	1·10	1·10
1177	48p. On tour	1·10	1·10
1178	50p. With Princes William and Harry	1·20	1·50
1179	71p. In recent years	1·70	1·90

1114 St. Peter Port Harbour

2007. Sea Guernsey. Multicoloured.

1180	32p. Type **1114**	75	75
1181	37p. Fort Grey, Rocquaine Bay	90	90
1182	45p. Point Robert Lighthouse, Sark	1·10	1·10
1183	48p. Islands at dusk (Brecqhou seen from Sark)	1·10	1·10
1184	50p. Vazon Bay	1·50	1·50
1184a	55p. Point Robert Lighthouse, Sark	1·50	1·50
1185	71p. Fontenelle Bay	2·00	1·90

The 45p. value includes the 'sepac' emblem.

No. 1184a is as No. 1182, the 45p. value, but with new value 55p., the current worldwide postcard rate. It has an imprint date '2010' and the sepac emblem omitted

1120 Crystal Angel

2007. Christmas. 'Deck the Halls'. Showing decorations. Multicoloured.

1186	27p. Type **1120**	60	60
1187	27p. Crystal decoration	60	60
1188	27p. Pine cone	60	60
1189	27p. White bauble with leaf design	60	60
1190	27p. Snowflake	60	60
1191	27p. Decoration with star	60	60
1192	32p. Gold bauble	75	75
1193	37p. Candles	90	90
1194	45p. Gold bell	1·10	1·10
1195	48p. Wrapped present with ribbons	1·10	1·10
1196	50p. Spiky star	1·20	1·20
1197	71p. Tree fairy	1·70	1·70

1132 World Touring Car Championship, 2005

2008. Andy Priaulx Triple World Touring Car Champion 2005–2007. Sheet 140×95 mm containing T **1132** and similar horiz designs. Multicoloured.

MS1198	£1 Type **1132**; £1 World Touring Car Championship, 2006; World Touring Car Championship, 2007 (60×48 mm)	7·00	7·50

1133 Beadlet Anemones

2008. Designation of Gouliot Headland and Caves, Sark as RAMSAR Site. Multicoloured.

1199	34p. Type **1133**	80	80
1200	40p. Sand crocus	95	95
1201	48p. Fulmar	1·10	1·10
1202	51p. Sheep's-bit (flower)	1·20	1·20
1203	53p. Thick-lipped grey mullet	1·30	1·30
1204	74p. Light bulb sea-squirt	1·70	1·70
MS1205	140×95 mm. Nos. 1199/204	7·00	7·00

1139 Red Campion

2008. Wild Flowers (1st series). Multicoloured.

1211	10p. Type **1139**	25	25
1212	20p. Great bindweed	45	45
1213	30p. Spear thistle	70	70
1214	40p. Greater bird's-foot trefoil	95	95
1215	50p. Sheep's-bit	1·20	1·20
1216	£1 Marguerite (vert)	2·30	2·30
1217	£2 Sea campion (vert)	4·75	4·75

See also Nos. 1273/83.

1153 'A la perchoine' ('Till the next time')

2008. Europa. The Letter. Designs showing quotations in Guernsiais (Guernsey French) and their English translations. Multicoloured.

1220	34p. Type **1153**	80	80
1221	40p. Banjour	95	95
1222	48p. Oh! Te v	1·10	1·10
1223	51p. Mais oy-ous!	1·20	1·20
1224	53p. Cor chapin!	1·30	1·30
1225	74p. L	1·70	1·70

1159 Mr. Happy

2008. Mr. Men and Little Miss Series of Children's Books by Roger Hargreaves. Multicoloured.

1226	34p. Type **1159**	80	80
1227	40p. Mr. Bump	95	95
1228	48p. Little Miss Naughty	1·10	1·10
1229	51p. Mr. Greedy	1·20	1·20
1230	53p. Mr. Strong	1·30	1·30
1231	74p. Mr. Tickle	1·70	1·70

1165 Pleimont Point

2008. Abstract Guernsey.

1232	(34p.) Type **1165**	80	80
1233	(34p.) Saint's Harbour	80	80
1234	(34p.) Rocks at Albecq	80	80
1235	(34p.) Groynes at Vazon Bay	80	80
1236	(34p.) La Bette Bay	80	80
1237	(40p.) Bordeaux Harbour	95	95
1238	(40p.) St. Saviour's Reservoir	95	95
1239	(40p.) Vazon Bay	95	95
1240	(40p.) St. Peter Port Lighthouse	95	95
1241	(40p.) Petit Port	95	95

Nos. 1232/6 were intended for postage within the Bailiwick and are inscribed 'GY'. They were each initially sold at 34p. Nos. 1237/41 were intended for postage to Great Britain and are inscribed 'UK'. They were each initially sold at 40p.

1175 Ford Model T Touring Car, 1913

2008. Centenary of the Ford Model T. Multicoloured.

1242	34p. Type **1175**	80	80
1243	40p. Delivery van, 1912	95	95
1244	48p. Pick-up, 1925	1·10	1·10
1245	51p. Couplet, 1917	1·20	1·20
1246	53p. First World War army ambulance	1·30	1·30
1247	74p. Roadster, 1912	1·70	1·70

1181 Early Drawing of St. Paul's Cathedral

2008. Guernsey Granite at St. Paul's Cathedral, London. Multicoloured.

1248	34p. Type **1181**	80	80
1249	40p. Cathedral and River Thames, 1860s	95	95
1250	48p. Cathedral during World War II Blitz	1·10	1·10
1251	51p. Cathedral illuminated at night	1·20	1·20
1252	53p. Close-up of St. Paul's Cathedral	1·30	1·30
1253	74p. Cathedral seen from Millennium Bridge	1·70	1·70

Nos. 1248/53 have powdered Guernsey granite applied to the value tablets.

1187 Spruce

2008. Christmas. Festive Foliage. Multicoloured.

1254	29p. Type **1187**	70	70
1255	29p. Christmas cactus	70	70
1256	29p. Ivy	70	70
1257	29p. Cyclamen	70	70
1258	29p. Mistletoe	70	70
1259	29p. Butchers Broom	70	70
1260	34p. Holly	80	80
1261	40p. Poinsettia	95	95
1262	48p. Bracken	1·10	1·10
1263	51p. Hawthorn	1·20	1·20
1264	53p. Clematis 'Peppermint'	1·20	1·20
1265	74p. Pyracantha	1·70	1·70

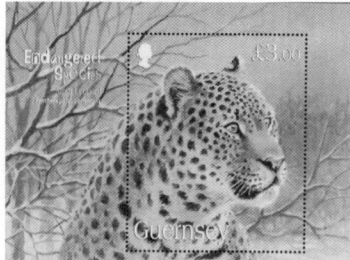

1199 Amur Leopard (image scaled to 41% of original size)

2009. Endangered Species (5th series). Amur Leopard (Panthera pardus orientalis). Sheet 116×84 mm.

MS1266	**1199** £3 multicoloured	8·50	8·50

1200 Land Iguana

2009. 'Darwin's Discoveries'. Multicolored.

1267	36p. Type **1200**	85	85
1268	43p. Wallaby	1·00	1·00

1269	51p. Giant tortoise	1·25	1·25
1270	54p. Marine iguana	1·25	1·25
1271	56p. Guanaco	1·25	1·25
1272	77p. Komodo dragon	1·75	1·75
MS1273	144×80 mm. Nos. 1267/72	7·50	7·50

Nos. 1267/72 commemorate the birth bicentenary of Charles Darwin.

1206 Stinking Onion

2009. Wild Flowers (2nd series). Multicoloured.

1274	1p. Type **1206**	10	10
1275	2p. Common mallow	10	10
1276	3p. Primrose	10	10
1277	4p. Loose-flowered orchid	10	10
1278	5p. Common centaury	10	10
1279	6p. Yellow horned poppy	15	15
1280	7p. Sea kale	20	20
1281	8p. Bluebell	25	25
1282	9p. Sea bindweed	25	25
1283	£3 Common poppy	8·50	8·50

1216 Quasar (digital enhancement)

2009. Europa. Astronomy. 400th Anniv of the Telescope. Multicoloured.

1284	36p. Type **1216**	85	85
1285	43p. Asteroid	1·00	1·00
1286	51p. Satellite View of Sunrays falling on the Earth's Surface	1·25	1·25
1287	54p. Jupiter, Sun in Background (digital composite)	1·25	1·25
1288	56p. The Moon touches the Sun before a Total Eclipse	1·40	1·40
1289	77p. Solar Eruption from the Sun (satellite image)	1·75	1·75

1222 Henry VIII as Young Man

2009. 500th Anniv of the Coronation of King Henry VIII. Multicoloured.

1290	36p. Type **1222**	85	85
1291	43p. Coronation of Henry VIII and Katherine of Aragon, 1509	1·00	1·00
1292	51p. Meeting of Henry VIII and Francis I, Field of the Cloth of Gold, 1520	1·25	1·25
1293	54p. Thomas Wolsey presenting Hampton Court Palace to Henry VIII	1·25	1·25
1294	56p. Henry VIII dancing with Anne Boleyn	1·40	1·40
1295	77p. Henry VIII watching his Navy as Mary Rose sinks, 1545	1·75	1·75

1228 'The Psychedelic 60's'

2009. 40th Anniv of Postal Independence. Multicoloured.

1296	36p. Type **1228**	85	85
1297	43p. 'God Save the 70s'	1·00	1·00
1298	51p. 'The POPular 80s'	1·25	1·25
1299	54p. 'The Urban 90s'	1·25	1·25
1300	56p. 'The Seductive 00s'	1·40	1·40
1301	77p. 'Looking to the Future'	1·75	1·75

1234 Jerbourg Point

2009. Sea Guernsey (2nd series). Multicoloured.

1302	36p. Type **1234**	85	85
1303	43p. Vazon Bay	1·00	1·00
1304	51p. Saints Bay Moorings	1·25	1·25
1305	54p. Le Jaonnet Bay	1·25	1·25
1306	56p. Rocquaine Bay	1·40	1·40
1307	77p. Bordeaux Harbour	1·75	1·75

The 51p. value includes the 'sepac' emblem.

1240 Castel Church

2009. Christmas. Churches. Multicoloured.

1308	31p. Type **1240**	75	75
1309	31p. Torteval Church	75	75
1310	31p. St. Martin's Church	75	75
1311	31p. St. John's Church	75	75
1312	31p. St. Sampson's Church	75	75
1313	31p. St. Peter Port Church	75	75
1314	36p. St. Mathew's Church	85	85
1315	43p. St. Saviour's Church	1·00	1·00
1316	51p. Forest Church	1·25	1·25
1317	54p. St. Andrew's Church	1·25	1·25
1318	56p. Vale Churchmulticoloured	1·40	1·40
1319	77p. St. Peter's Church	1·75	1·75

1252 Asian Elephant (image scaled to 41% of original size)

2010. Endangered Species (6th series). Asian Elephant (Elephas maximus). Sheet 118×84 mm.

MS1320	**1252** £3.07 multicoloured	7·25	7·25

1253 Port a la Jument, Sark

2010. Abstract Guernsey (2nd series). Multicoloured. (a) Ordinary gum.

1321	(48p.) Type **1253**	1·10	1·10
1322	(48p.) The Dog and Lion Rocks-multicoloured	1·10	1·10
1323	(50p.) Fort Grey	1·25	1·25
1324	(58p.) Sunset on West Coast of Guernsey	1·40	1·40
1325	(58p) Slipway at Havelet Bay at Sunrise	1·40	1·40
1326	(80p.) Castle Cornet	1·90	1·90

(b) Self-adhesive.

1327	(48p.) As Type No. **1253**	1·10	1·10
1328	(48p.) As No. 1322	1·10	1·10
1329	(50p.) As No. 1323	1·25	1·25
1330	(58p.) As No. 1324	1·40	1·40
1331	(58p.) As No. 1325	1·40	1·40
1332	(80p.) As No. 1326	1·90	1·90

Nos. 1321/2 and 1327/8 were intended for postage within the Bailiwick and are inscribed 'GY LARGE'. They were each initially sold at 48p.

Nos. 1324/5 and 1330/1 were intended for postage to Great Britain and are inscribed 'UK LARGE'. They were each initially sold at 58p.

Nos. 1323 and 1329 for postage to Europe are inscribed 'EUR' and were initially sold at 50p. each.

Nos. 1326 and 1332 for postage to rest of world are inscribed 'ROW' and were initially sold at 80p. each.

1259 Penny the Postie and Pirate Captain Titch in Boat made from Wooden Chest

2010. Europa. Children's Books. The Adventures of Penny the Postie by Keith Robinson. Multicoloured.

1333	45p. Type **1259**	1·00	1·00
1334	50p. Captain Titch spies enemy Captain Bullybones	1·25	1·25
1335	£2 Captain Titch reclaiming his Stolen Ship	4·50	4·50
MS1336 149×96 mm. Nos. 1333/5		6·75	6·75

1262 Guide kayaking ('Outdoor Activities')

2010. Centenary of Girl Guiding. Embroidered Badges. Multicoloured.

1337	36p. Type **1262**	80	80
1338	45p. Spitfire crossing Search-lights ('Help during WW1&2')	1·00	1·00
1339	48p. Crystal Palace Maze (renovated to celebrate Centenary)	1·10	1·10
1340	50p. Agnes Baden-Powell (founder) wearing First Guide Uniform	1·25	1·25
1341	58p. Mount Everest (Guide trek to base camp, 2009)	1·40	1·40
1342	80p. Queen's Guide Award	1·75	1·75

1268 26 Cornet Street, St. Peter Port

2010. 50th Anniv of the National Trust for Guernsey. Multicoloured.

1343	36p. Type **1268**	80	80
1344	45p. Field of Daffodils at Jerbourg	1·00	1·00
1345	48p. Martello Tower at Fermain Bay, St. Peter Port	1·10	1·10
1346	50p. Ivy Gates, La Rohais, St. Peter Port	1·25	1·25
1347	58p. Pleinmont Headland	1·40	1·40
1348	80p. La Moulin de Quanteraine	1·75	1·75

1274 Loading Gas Masks onto Truck, 1939

2010. 70th Anniv of the Guernsey Evacuation. Multicoloured.

1349	36p. Type **1274**	80	80
1350	45p. Guernsey Children waiting to Leave, 1940	1·00	1·00
1351	48p. German Soldiers leaving Guernsey, 1945	1·10	1·10
1352	50p. Evacuees returning to Guernsey, 1945	1·25	1·25
1353	58p. Queen Elizabeth with Guernsey Children, June 1945	1·40	1·40
1354	80p. Liberation Day, 1946	1·75	1·75

1280 Tennis

2010. 29th Commonwealth Games, Delhi, India. Multicoloured.

1355	36p. Type **1280**	80	80
1356	45p. Bowls	1·00	1·00
1357	48p. Shooting	1·10	1·10
1358	50p. Swimming	1·25	1·25
1359	58p. Athletics	1·40	1·40
1360	80p. Cycling	1·75	1·75

Nos. 1355/60 commemorate the 40th anniv of Guernsey's participation in the Commonwealth Games.

1286 'The Holly and the Ivy'

2010. Christmas Carols. Multicoloured.

1361	31p. Type **1286**	75	75
1362	36p. Little Donkey	80	80
1363	45p. Silent Night	1·00	1·00
1364	48p. I Saw Three Ships	1·10	1·10
1365	50p. Joy to the World	1·25	1·25
1366	58p. Ding Dong Merrily on High	1·40	1·40
1367	80p. We Three Kings	1·75	1·75

1293 Blue Whale (image scaled to 41% of original size)

2011. Endangered Species (7th series). Blue Whale (Balaenoptera musculus). Sheet 118×83 mm

MS1368 **1293** £3 multicoloured		7·00	7·00

1294 Air Raid Precautions Messenger Boy and Boy Evacuee ('Hope')

2011. 90th Anniv of the Royal British Legion. Multicoloured.

1369	36p. Type **1294**	80	80
1370	45p. Royal Navy Veteran Christopher Walsh ('Reflection')	1·00	1·00
1371	52p. World War II Soldiers ('Comradeship')	1·10	1·10
1372	58p. Soldier of 12th Battalion, Hampshire Regiment, training in a Smoke Screen ('Selflessness')	1·25	1·25
1373	65p. Nurse Joyce Collier and Navy Commando ('Service')	1·25	1·25
1374	70p. Soldier receiving Medal ('Dedication')	1·60	1·60
MS1375 140×100 mm. Nos. 1369/74		7·00	7·00

1300 Acorns and Oak Leaves

2011. Europa. Forests. Multicoloured.

1376	45p. Type **1300**	1·10	1·10
1377	52p. Hazelnuts and Hazel leaves	1·50	1·50
1378	£2 Conker and Horse Chestnut leaves	4·75	4·75
MS1379 133×85 mm. Nos. 1375/7		7·25	7·25

1303 Engagement of Prince William to Miss Catherine Middleton, 16 November 2010 (image scaled to 44% of original size)

2011. Royal Wedding. Two sheets, each 110×55 mm

MS1380 **1303** £2 multicoloured		4·75	4·75
MS1381 **1304** £2 multicoloured		4·75	4·75

1305 How to Roast your Pig

2011. The Guernsey Literary and Potato Peel Pie Society (book by Mary Ann Shaffer and Annie Barrows). Multicoloured.

1382	36p. Type **1305**	85	85
1383	47p. Literary Society Bookshelf	1·10	1·10
1384	48p. Arrival of Juliet Ashton at St. Peter Port wearing Red Cloak	1·25	1·25
1385	52p. View through Elizabeth McKenna's Cottage Window	1·25	1·25
1386	61p. Juliet Ashton and Dawsey Adams looking over Moonlit Sea	1·50	1·50
1387	65p. Isola Pribby's Parrot Zenobia	1·60	1·60

1311 Victoria Marina, St. Peter Port

2011. Sea Guernsey (3rd series). Multicoloured.

1388	36p. Type **1311**	90	90
1389	45p. L'Ancresse Bay	1·10	1·10
1390	52p. Bordeaux Harbour Slipway	1·25	1·25
1391	58p. South Coast Sunset	1·40	1·40
1392	65p. Salerie Harbour	1·60	1·60
1393	70p. Petit Port	1·75	1·75

1317 Forest Church (John Shakerley)

2011. Christmas. 'Winter Wonderland'. Winning Entries from Photography Competition. Multicoloured.

1394	31p. Type **1317**	80	80
1395	36p. L'Ancresse Common (Nigel Byrom)	90	90
1396	47p. Guernsey Cows (Sarah Plumley)	1·10	1·10
1397	48p. St. Peter Port (Karen Millard)	1·10	1·10
1398	52p. La Coupée, Sark (Sue Daly)	1·25	1·25
1399	61p. St. Peter's Church (Jason Bishop)	1·50	1·50
1400	65p. Cobo (Eric Ferbrache)	1·60	1·60

1324 Lewis Hamilton

2011. British Formula 1 World Champions (2nd series). Lewis Hamilton (2008) and Jenson Button (2009). Multicoloured.

1401	36p. Type **1324**	90	90
1402	47p. Jenson Button	1·10	1·10
1403	61p. Lewis Hamilton	1·50	1·50
1404	65p. Jenson Button	1·60	1·60
MS1405 140x95 mm. Nos. 1401/4		4·75	4·75

1328 Bengal Tiger (image scaled to 41% of original size)

2012. Endangered Species (8th series). Bengal Tiger (Panthera tigris tigris). Sheet 118×84 mm

MS1406 **1328** £3 multicoloured		7·25	7·25

1329 Coronation of Queen Elizabeth II, 1953, and Birth of Prince Andrew, 1960

2012. Diamond Jubilee. Multicoloured.

1407	36p. Type **1329**	90	90
1408	47p. Queen Elizabeth II presenting World Cup Trophy to England Captain Bobby Moore, 1966, and Launch of Liner QE2, 1967	1·10	1·10
1409	48p. Queen Elizabeth II opened Sydney Opera House, 1973, and attended Olympic Games, Montreal, 1976	1·10	1·10
1410	52p. Queen Elizabeth II Trooping the Colour, 1983, and Prince William and Prince Harry, Wetherby School, 1989	1·25	1·25
1411	61p. Queen Elizabeth II with Nelson Mandela, 1996, and 100th Birthday of Queen Elizabeth the Queen Mother, 2000	1·50	1·50
1412	65p. Queen Elizabeth II in Guernsey, Liberation Day, 2009, and with Pres. Barack Obama, 2011	1·60	1·60
MS1413 141×101 mm. Nos. 1407/12		7·50	7·50

1335 Vazon Bay, Guernsey

2012. Europa. Visit Guernsey. Multicoloured.

1414	(39p.) Type **1335**	95	95
1415	(52p.) Shell Beach, Herm	1·25	1·25
1416	(53p.) Grande Greve, Sark	1·25	1·25
1417	(59p.) Bluestone Bay, Alderney	1·40	1·40
1418	(69p.) Sailing off the Coast of Herm	1·75	1·75
1419	(74p.) La Coupée, Sark	1·75	1·75
MS1420 140×100 mm. Nos. 1414/19		8·00	8·00

No. 1414 was inscr 'GY LETTER', No. 1415 'GY LARGE', No. 1416 'UK LETTER', No. 1417 'INT LETTER 20G', No. 1418 'UK LARGE' and No. 1419 'INT LETTER 40G', and they were originally sold for 39p., 52p., 53p., 59p., 69p. and 74p. respectively.

Nos. 1416/17 have the 'EUROPA' emblem.

1341 Prince William as Volunteer with Raleigh International, Chile, 2000

2012. 30th Birthday of Prince William. Multicoloured.

1421	36p. Type **1341**	90	90
1422	47p. Graduation from St. Andrews University, 2005	1·10	1·10
1423	48p. President of Football Association, 2006	1·25	1·25
1424	52p. Patron of Mountain Rescue, 2007	1·25	1·25
1425	61p. Enduro Africa Charity Motorcyle Ride, 2008	1·50	1·50
1426	65p. RAF Rescue Pilot, 2010	1·60	1·60

1347 Major-General Sir Isaac Brock (leader of British Forces in Canada)

2012. Bicentenary of War of 1812 between United States and Britain. Multicoloured.

1427	£1 Type **1347**	2·40	2·40
1428	£1 Shawnee War Chief Tecumseh (leader of Ohio Native Nations Confederation)	2·40	2·40

1349 Raising Sails

2012. 150th Anniv of the Royal Channel Islands Yacht Club. J-Cup Regatta (2011). Multicoloured.

1429	39p. Type **1349**	95	95
1430	52p. Crew sailing Yacht	1·25	1·25
1431	53p. Two Yachts	1·25	1·25
1432	59p. Three Yachts	1·40	1·40
1433	69p. Crew on Board Yacht	1·75	1·75
1434	74p. Yacht	1·75	1·75

1355 Cart decorated with Flowers

1361 New Narcissus Variety 'Floral Guernsey' (image scaled to 51% of original size)

2012. 20th Anniv of Floral Guernsey. Multicoloured.

1435	39p. Type **1335**	95	95
1436	52p. La Seigneurie Gardens, Sark	1·25	1·25
1437	53p. Flower Display	1·25	1·25
1438	59p. Seaside Garden	1·40	1·40
1439	69p. Seaside Flower Stall	1·75	1·75
1440	74p. Flower Display	1·75	1·75
MS1441	92×98 mm. **1361** £3 multicoloured	7·00	7·00

No. **MS**1441 was cut in the shape of a narcissus flower.

1362 The Ascension

2012. Christmas. The Christmas Story. Multicoloured.

1442	34p. Type **1352**	85	85
1443	39p. Innkeeper shows Mary and Joseph to the Stable	95	95
1444	52p. Jesus is Born in a Stable	1·25	1·25
1445	53p. Angels come down amongst the Shepherds	1·25	1·25
1446	59p. The Three Kings	1·40	1·40
1447	69p. Mary and Baby Jesus	1·75	1·75
1448	74p. Flight to Egypt	1·75	1·75

1369 Giant Panda (image scaled to 41% of original size)

2013. Endangered Species (9th series). Giant Panda (*Ailuropoda melanoleuca*) . Sheet 118×84 mm.
MS1449 **1369** £3 multicoloured	7·00	7·00

1369a Sark's Gold Postbox (image scaled to 34% of original size)

2013. Sark's Gold Postbox. Sheet 140×100 mm.
MS1449a **1369a** £1 multicoloured	2·40	2·40

Sark's postbox was painted gold to commemorate Sark-born Carl Hester's team gold medal in dressage at the Olympic Games, London, 2012.

1370 Tompot Blenny

1376 Black-face Blenny (image scaled to 34% of original size)

2013. Marine Life. Multicoloured.

1450	39p. Type **1370**	95	95
1451	52p. Leopard-spotted Goby	1·25	1·25
1452	53p. Red Gurnard	1·25	1·25
1453	59p. Female Cuckoo Wrasse	1·40	1·40
1454	69p. Male Cuckoo Wrasse	1·75	1·75
1455	74p. John Dory	1·75	1·75
MS1456	140×100 mm. **1376** £5 multicoloured	8·00	8·00

1377 Guernsey Post Daihatsu Hijet Van

2013. Europa. The Postman's Van. Multicoloured.

1457	(40p.) Type **1377**	95	95
1458	(53p.) La Poste Citroen 2CV Van	1·25	1·25
1459	(55p.) Royal Mail Morris 6cwt O-Type Van in Lake District	1·25	1·25
1460	(63p.) Deutsche Bundespost VW Beetle Van	1·40	1·40
1461	(71p.) Posten AB Kalmar Tjorven (DAF)	1·75	1·75
1462	(79p.) U.S. Mail Studebaker Zip Van	1·75	1·75
MS1463	140×100 mm. Nos. 1457/62	8·00	8·00

No. 1457 was inscr 'GY LETTER', No. 1458 'GY LARGE LETTER', No. 1459 'UK LETTER', No. 1460 'INT LETTER 20G', No. 1761 'UK LARGE LETTER' and No. 1762 'INT LETTER 40G' and they were originally sold for 40p., 53p., 55p., 63p., 71p. and 79p. respectively.

1383 Sign of the Mermaid Tavern

2013. Herm Island. Multicoloured.

1464	40p. Type **1383**	95	95
1465	53p. Shell Beach	1·25	1·25
1466	55p. Belvoir Bay	1·25	1·25
1467	63p. Herm Harbour Moorings	1·40	1·40
1468	71p. Fisherman's Beach	1·75	1·75
1469	79p. Gift Shop	1·75	1·75

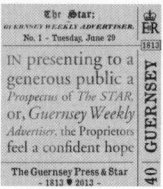

1389 'In presenting to a generous public a Prospectus of The Star, or Guernsey Weekly Advertiser', 29 June 1813

2013. Bicentenary of the *Guernsey Press* and *Star*. Multicoloured.

1470	40p. Type **1389**	95	95
1471	53p. 'The Queen's Diamond Jubilee A Glorious and Wonderful Pageant, *The Star*, 24 June 1897	1·25	1·25
1472	55p. 'Orders of the Commandant' (Evening Press, 1 July 1940) and 1941 1/2d. Stamp printed by *The Guernsey Press*	1·25	1·25
1473	63p. 'Serving the islands for 200 years', *Guernsey Press*, 29 June 2013	1·40	1·40
1474	71p. 'Live Live her Gracious Majesty Queen Elizabeth II', *Evening Press*, 2 June 1953	1·75	1·75
1475	79p. 'Peace and Liberation', *Evening Press*, 9 May 1945	1·75	1·75

1395 Tractor and Hay-kicker

2013. Centenary of the West Show. Multicoloured.

1476	40p. Type **1395**	95	95
1477	53p. Prizewinning Produce	1·25	1·25
1478	55p. Shire Horses pulling Brewery Dray	1·25	1·25
1479	63p. Guernsey Cows	1·40	1·40
1480	71p. Steam Tractor Engine	1·75	1·75
1481	79p. Haymaking in Traditional Dress	1·75	1·75

1401 Duke and Duchess of Cambridge and Prince George (image scaled to 44% of original size)

2013. Birth of Prince George of Cambridge. Sheet 110×55 mm
MS1482 **1401** £3 multicoloured	7·00	7·00

1402 Clematis 'Samaritan Jo'

2013. 'Raymond Evison 25 Years of Gold'. Clematis. Multicoloured.

1483	40p. Type **1402**	95	95
1484	53p. Clematis 'Anna Louise'	1·25	1·25
1485	55p. Clematis 'Chelsea'	1·25	1·25
1486	63p. Clematis 'Edda'	1·40	1·40
1487	71p. Clematis 'The Countess of Wessex'	1·75	1·75
1488	79p. Clematis 'Giselle'	1·75	1·75

Nos. 1483/8 commemorate clematis producer Raymond Evison's 25th gold medal at Chelsea Flower Show.

1408 Santa's Sleigh passing Window

2013. Christmas. When Santa got Stuck up the Chimney. Multicoloured.

1489	35p. Type **1408**	85	85
1490	40p. Santa on Roof	95	95
1491	53p. Santa stuck in Chimney	1·25	1·25
1492	55p. Children pulling Santa out of Chimney	1·25	1·25
1493	63p. Santa sneezing	1·40	1·40
1494	71p. Santa leaving Presents	1·75	1·75
1495	79p. Santa leaving in his Sleigh	1·75	1·75

1415 Horse

2014. Chinese New Year. Year of the Horse. Multicoloured.

1496	40p. Type **1415**	95	95
1497	53p. Cantering Horse	1·25	1·25
1498	55p. Horse kicking	1·25	1·25
1499	63p. Horse	1·40	1·40
1500	71p. Horse rearing	1·75	1·75
1501	79p. Eight Horses	1·75	1·75
MS1502	Nos. 1496/501	8·00	8·00

1421 Sumatran Orangutan (image scaled to 41% of original size)

2014. Endangered Species (10th series). Sumatran Orangutan (*Pongo abelii*)
MS1503 **1421** £3 multicoloured	7·00	7·00

1422 Keys and Wheel

2014. Europa. National Musical Instruments. The Chifournie (hurdy gurdy). Multicoloured.

1504	40p. Type **1422**	95	95
1505	53p. Crank, Tirants and Wheel	1·25	1·25
1506	55p. Wheel and Strings	1·25	1·25
1507	63p. Bridge, Wheel, Strings and Keys	1·40	1·40
1508	71p. Crank, Tirants, Wheel, Tangents and Keys	1·75	1·75
1509	79p. Chifournie	1·75	1·75
MS1510	140×100 mm. Nos. 1504/9	8·00	8·00

1428 St. Peter Port Marina

2014. 50th Anniv of Britain in Bloom. Multicoloured.

1511	(41p.) Type **1428**	95	95
1512	(54p.) White House View, Herm	1·25	1·25
1513	(55p.) Mermaid Beach, Herm	1·25	1·25
1514	(66p.) St. Pierre du Bois	1·50	1·50
1515	(74p.) St. Martin's Church	1·75	1·75
1516	(83p.) Albion Tavern, St. Peter Port	1·75	1·75

Nos. 1511/16 were inscr 'GY LETTER', 'GY LARGE LETTER', 'UK LETTER', 'INT LETTER 20g', 'UK LARGE LETTER' and 'INT LETTER 40g' and were originally sold for 41p., 54p., 55p., 66p., 74p. or 83p.

No. 1514 was inscr 'sepac'.

1434 Map of Guernsey Cartoon Character

2014. Postcrossing (connecting people worldwide through postcards).
1517	(66p.) multicoloured	1·50	1·50

No. 1517 was inscr 'INT LETTER 20g' and originally sold for 66p.

POSTAGE DUE STAMPS

D1 Castle
Cornet

1969. Face values in black.

D1	**D1**	1d. plum	2·00	1·50
D2	**D1**	2d. green	2·00	1·50
D3	**D1**	3d. red	3·00	4·00
D4	**D1**	4d. blue	4·00	5·00
D5	**D1**	5d. ochre	6·00	5·00
D6	**D1**	6d. turquoise	6·00	5·00
D7	**D1**	1s. brown	10·00	9·00

1971. Decimal Currency. Face values in black.

D8	**D1**	½p. plum	10	15
D9	**D1**	1p. green	10	15
D10	**D1**	2p. red	10	15
D11	**D1**	3p. blue	10	15
D12	**D1**	4p. ochre	10	15
D13	**D1**	5p. blue	15	15
D14	**D1**	6p. violet	15	15
D15	**D1**	8p. orange	25	50
D16	**D1**	10p. brown	25	25
D17	**D1**	15p. grey	35	60

D3 St. Peter Port

1977. Face values in black.

D18	**D3**	½p. brown	10	10
D19	**D2**	1p. purple	10	10
D20	**D2**	2p. orange	10	10
D21	**D2**	3p. red	10	15
D22	**D2**	4p. blue	15	15
D23	**D2**	5p. green	15	15
D24	**D2**	6p. brown	15	15
D25	**D2**	8p. brown	15	15
D26	**D2**	10p. blue	15	15
D27	**D2**	14p. green	30	30
D28	**D2**	15p. violet	30	30
D29	**D2**	16p. red	40	30

D4 Milking Cow

1982. Guernsey Scenes, c. 1890.

D30	**D4**	1p. blue and green	15	10
D31	–	2p. brown, lt brown & blue	15	10
D32	–	3p. green and lilac	15	10
D33	–	4p. green and orange	15	15
D34	–	5p. blue and green	15	15
D35	–	16p. blue and light blue	35	40
D36	–	18p. blue and green	40	45
D37	–	20p. green and blue	45	50
D38	–	25p. blue and pink	55	60
D39	–	30p. green and yellow	65	70
D40	–	50p. brown and blue	1·25	1·20
D41	–	£1 lt brown and brown	2·25	2·40

DESIGNS: 2p. Vale Mill; 3p. Sark cottage; 4p. Quay-side, St. Peter Port; 5p. Well, Water Lane, Moulin Huet; 16p. Seaweed gathering; 18p. Upper Walk, White Rock; 20p. Cobo Bay; 25p. Saint's Bay; 30p. La Coupee, Sark; 50p. Old Harbour, St. Peter Port; £1 Greenhouses, Doyle Road, St. Peter Port.

ALDERNEY

The following issues are provided by the Guernsey Post Office for use on Alderney. They are also valid for postal purposes throughout the rest of the Bailiwick of Guernsey.

A1 Island Map

1983. Island Scenes. Multicoloured.

A1	1p. Type **A1**		10	10
A2	4p. Hanging Rock		10	10
A3	9p. States' Building, St. Anne		20	15
A4	10p. St. Anne's Church		25	15
A5	11p. Yachts in Braye Bay		25	20
A6	12p. Victoria St., St. Anne		25	20
A7	13p. Map of Channel		25	20
A8	14p. Fort Clonque		30	25
A9	15p. Corblets Bay and Fort		35	30
A10	16p. Old Tower, St. Anne		35	30
A11	17p. Golf course and Essex Castle		40	35
A12	18p. Old Harbour		40	35
A12a	20p. Quesnard Lighthouse		1·00	1·00
A12b	21p. Braye Harbour		1·00	1·00
A12c	23p. The Island Hall		95	1·00
A12d	24p. "J.T. Daly" (steam locomotive)		1·70	1·70
A12e	28p. "Louis Marchesi of the Round Table" (lifeboat)		2·20	2·20

Nos. A12a/e are larger, 38×27 mm.

A13 Oystercatcher

1984. Birds. Multicoloured.

A13	9p. Type **A13**	1·10	90
A14	13p. Ruddy turnstone ("Turnstone")	1·10	90
A15	26p. Ringed plover	2·50	2·75
A16	28p. Dunlin	2·50	2·75
A17	31p. Curlew	2·50	2·25

A18 Westland Wessex HU.4 Mk5 Helicopter XV732 of The Queen's Flight

1985. 50th Anniv of Alderney Airport. Multicoloured.

A18	9p. Type **A18**	1·40	1·00
A19	13p. Britten Norman BN-2AMkIII "long nose" Trislander	1·70	1·50
A20	29p. de Havilland Heron 1B G-AOXL	3·00	2·75
A21	31p. de Havilland Dragon Rapide DH.89A *Sir Henry Lawrence*	3·50	3·50
A22	34p. Saro A21 G-AHLL Windhover amphibian flying boat G-ABJP "City of Portsmouth"	3·50	3·50

A23 Royal Engineers, 1890

1985. Regiments of the Alderney Garrison. Multicoloured.

A23	9p. Type **A23**	40	30
A24	14p. Duke of Albany's Own Highlanders, 1856	95	80
A25	29p. Royal Artillery, 1855	95	80
A26	31p. South Hampshire Regiment, 1810	1·50	1·30
A27	34p. Royal Irish Regiment, 1782	1·75	1·60

A28 Fort Grosnez

1986. Alderney Forts. Multicoloured.

A28	10p. Type **A28**	80	20
A29	14p. Fort Tourgis	90	80
A30	31p. Fort Clonque	2·50	3·00
A31	34p. Fort Albert	2·50	3·00

A32 *Liverpool* (full-rigged ship), 1902

1987. Alderney Shipwrecks. Multicoloured.

A32	11p. Type **A32**	1·40	1·20
A33	15p. *Petit Raymond* (schooner), 1906	1·50	1·20
A34	29p. *Maina* (yacht), 1910	2·75	3·00
A35	31p. *Burton* (steamer), 1911	3·00	3·25
A36	34p. *Point Law* (oil tanker), 1975	3·50	3·75

A37 Moll's Map of 1724

1989. 250th Anniv of Bastide's Survey of Alderney.

A37	**A37** 12p. multicoloured	30	25
A38	– 18p. black, blue & brown	45	30
A39	– 27p. black, blue and green	95	1·10
A40	– 32p. black, blue and red	1·10	1·10
A41	– 35p. multicoloured	1·50	1·40

DESIGNS: 18p. Bastide's survey of 1739; 27p. Goodwin's map of 1831; 32p. General Staff map of 1943; 35p. Ordnance Survey map, 1988.

A42 H.M.S. *Alderney* (bomb ketch), 1738

1990. Royal Navy Ships named after Alderney.

A42	**A42** 14p. black and bistre	35	20
A43	– 20p. black and brown	50	35
A44	– 29p. black and brown	1·00	1·10
A45	– 34p. black and blue	1·20	1·50
A46	– 37p. black and blue	1·40	1·50

DESIGNS: 20p. H.M.S. *Alderney* "(sixth-rate), 1742; 29p. H.M.S. *Alderney* (sloop), 1755; 34p. H.M.S. *Alderney* (submarine), 1945; 37p. H.M.S. *Alderney* (patrol vessel), 1979.

A47 Wreck of H.M.S. *Victory*, 1744

1991. Automation of The Casquets Lighthouse. Multicoloured.

A47	21p. Type **A47**	80	50
A48	26p. Lighthouse keeper's daughter rowing back to the Casquets	1·90	1·70
A49	31p. MBB-Bolkow Bo105D helicopter G-BATC leaving pad on St. Thomas Tower	2·00	2·20
A50	37p. Northern wheater and yellow wagtail over lighthouse	2·75	3·25
A51	50p. Trinity House vessel *Patricia* and arms	3·75	3·50

A52 Two French Warships on Fire

1992. 300th Anniv of the Battle of La Hogue. Multicoloured.

A52	23p. Type **A52**	1·10	1·00
A53	28p. Crews leaving burning ships	2·40	2·50
A54	33p. French warship sinking	2·75	3·00
A55	50p. *The Battle of La Hogue* (47×32 mm)	3·00	3·50

Nos. A52/4 show details of the painting on the 50p. value.

A56 Spiny Lobster

1993. Endangered Species. Marine Life. Multicoloured.

A56	24p. Type **A56**	60	30
A57	28p. Plumose anemone	60	35
A58	33p. Starfish	70	40
A59	39p. Sea urchin	90	60

Nos. A56/9 were printed together, *se-tenant*, the backgrounds forming a composite design.

A60 Blue-tailed Damselfly, Dark Hair Water Crowfoot and Branched Bur-reed

1994. Flora and Fauna. Multicoloured.

A60	1p. Type **A60**	10	10
A61	2p. White-toothed shrew and flax-leaved St. John's wort	10	10
A62	3p. Fulmar and kaffir fig	10	10
A63	4p. Clouded yellow (butterfly) and red clover	10	10
A64	5p. Bumble bee, prostrate broom and giant broomrape	10	10
A65	6p. Dartford warbler and lesser dodder	15	20
A66	7p. Peacock (butterfly) and stemless thistle	15	20
A67	8p. Mole and bluebell	15	20
A68	9p. Great green grasshopper and common gorse	20	25
A69	10p. Six-spot burnet (moth) and viper's bugloss	20	25
A70	16p. Common blue (butterfly) and pyramidal orchid	55	40
A70b	18p. Small tortoiseshell (butterfly) and buddleia	35	40
A71	20p. Common rabbit and creeping buttercup	40	45
A72	24p. Greater black-backed gull and sand crocus	50	55
A72b	25p. Rock pipit and sea stock	50	55
A72c	26p. Sand digger wasp and sea bindweed (horiz)	50	55
A73	30p. Atlantic puffin and English stonecrop	60	65
A74	40p. Emperor (moth) and bramble	80	85
A75	50p. Pale-spined hedgehog and pink oxalis	1·50	1·20
A76	£1 Common tern and Bermuda grass (horiz)	2·50	2·20
A77	£2 Northern gannet and "Fucus vesiculosus" (seaweed) (horiz)	5·00	4·50

A78 Royal Aircraft Factory SE5A

1995. Birth Cent of Tommy Rose (aviator). Multicoloured.

A78	35p. Type **A78**	95	95
A79	35p. Miles M.19 Master II and other Miles aircraft	95	95
A80	35p. Miles M.57 Aerovan and Miles Monitor M.33	95	95
A81	41p. Miles M.38 Falcon Six winning King's Cup air race, 1935	1·10	1·10
A82	41p. Miles M.2 Hawk Speed Six winning Manx Air Derby, 1947	1·10	1·10
A83	41p. Miles M.3B Falcon Six breaking U.K.–Cape record, 1936	1·10	1·10

A84 Returning Islanders (image scaled to 52% of original size)

1995. 50th Anniv of Return of Islanders to Alderney. Sheet 93×70 mm.

MSA84	**A84** £1.65, multicoloured	5·00	5·00

A85 Signallers training on Alderney

1996. 25th Anniv of Adoption of 30th Signal Regiment by Alderney. Multicoloured.

A85	24p. Type **A85**	45	35
A86	41p. Communications station, Falkland Islands	75	55
A87	60p. Dish aerial and Land Rover, Gulf War	1·10	80
A88	75p. Service with United Nations	1·10	1·10

Nos. A85/8 were printed together, *se-tenant*, forming a composite design.

A89 Cat with Butterfly

1996. Cats. Multicoloured.

A89	16p. Type **A89**	45	35
A90	24p. Blue and white on table	65	40
A91	25p. Tabby kitten grooming blue and white persian kitten	65	65
A92	35p. Red persian under table	1·20	1·20
A93	41p. White cat with tortoise-shell and white in toy cart	1·50	1·70
A94	60p. Siamese playing with wool	2·00	2·00
MSA95	144×97 mm. Nos. A89/94	6·50	6·50

A95 Harold Larwood

1997. 150th Anniv of Cricket on Alderney. Multicoloured.

A96	18p. Type **A95**	50	30
A97	25p. John Arlott	65	35
A98	37p. Pelham J. Warner	1·00	1·20
A99	43p. W. G. Grace	1·20	1·50
A100	63p. John Wisden	1·60	1·70
MSA101	190×75 mm. Nos. A96/100 and label	9·00	9·00

A100 Railway under Construction

1997. Garrison Island (1st series). 150th Anniv of Harbour. Multicoloured.

A102	18p. Type **A100**	45	20
A103	18p. "Ariadne" (paddle steamer) at anchor	45	20
A104	25p. Quarrying stone	65	30
A105	25p. Quarry railway	65	30
A106	26p. Queen Victoria and Prince Albert on Alderney	70	30
A107	26p. Royal Yacht "Victoria and Albert" and guard of honour	70	30
A108	31p. Railway workers greet Queen Victoria	80	35
A109	31p. Royal party in railway wagons	80	35

See also Nos. A116/23, A132/9, A154/61 and A176/83.

A108 Modern Superlite Helmet and Wreck of *Point Law* (oil tanker)

1998. 21st Anniv of Alderney Diving Club. Multicoloured.

A110	20p. Type **A108**	60	40
A111	30p. Cousteau-Gagnan demand valve and wreck of *Stella* (steamer)	85	85
A112	37p. Heinke closed helmet and *Liverpool* (full-rigged ship)	1·20	1·20
A113	43p. Siebe closed helmet	1·70	1·70
A114	63p. Deane open helmet	2·20	2·30
MSA115	190×75 mm. Nos. A110/14 and label	8·00	8·00

1998. Garrison Island (2nd series). As Type **A100**. Multicoloured.

A116	20p. Alderney Post Office	50	25
A117	20p. Traders in Victoria Street	50	25
A118	25p. Court House	60	30
A119	25p. Police Station and fire engine	60	30
A120	30p. St. Anne's Church	70	35
A121	30p. Wedding party at Albert Gate	70	35
A122	37p. *Courier* (ferry) at Braye Bay	85	40
A123	37p. Fishermen at quay	85	40

A121 Stained Glass Window commemorating Mary Rogers (Chief Stewardess) (image scaled to 44% of original size)

1999. Centenary of the Wreck of *Stella* (mail steamer). Sheet 110×90 mm containing Type **A121** and similar horiz design.

MSA124	25p. Type **A121**; £1.75, *Stella* leaving Southampton	6·00	6·00

A122 Solar Eclipse at 10.15 am

1999. Total Eclipse of the Sun (11 August). Designs showing stages of the eclipse. Multicoloured.

A125	20p. Type **A122**	50	50
A126	25p. At 10.51 am	60	60
A127	30p. At 11.14 am	70	70
A128	38p. At 11.16 am	1·00	1·00
A129	44p. At 11.17 am	1·50	1·50
A130	64p. At 11.36 am	1·70	1·90
MSA131	191×80 mm. Nos. A125/30 and label	6·50	6·50

No. MSA131 also includes the "PHILEX FRANCE '99", Paris, and the "iBRA '99", Nuremberg, emblems on the sheet margin.

1999. Garrison Island (3rd series). Forts. As Type **A100**. Multicoloured.

A132	20p. Field gun and crew, Fort Grosnez, c. 1855	45	25
A133	20p. Parade of 9th Bn, Royal Garrison Artillery	45	25
A134	25p. The Arsenal, Fort Albert, c. 1862	55	30
A135	25p. Royal Engineers loading wagons	55	30
A136	30p. 2nd Bn, Royal Scots on parade	65	35
A137	30p. Garrison at work, Fort Tourgis, c. 1865	65	35
A138	38p. Gun emplacement, Fort Houmet Herbe, c. 1870	80	40
A139	38p. Royal Alderney Artillery Militia loading cannon	80	40

Nos. A132/3, A134/5, A136/7 and A138/9 respectively were printed together, *se-tenant*, forming composite designs.

A136 Peregrine Falcon attacking Ruddy Turnstone

2000. Endangered Species. Peregrine Falcon. Multicoloured.

A140	21p. Type **A136**	55	45
A141	26p. Two falcons and prey	60	55
A142	34p. Falcon guarding eggs	1·00	95
A143	38p. Falcon feeding young	1·10	1·00
A144	44p. Falcon and prey	1·60	1·50
A145	64p. Two young falcons	2·25	2·00

A142 Wombles around Map of Alderney

2000. "A Wombling Holiday" (characters from children's television programme). Multicoloured.

A146	21p. Type **A142**	45	45
A147	26p. Alderney and Shansi on beach	55	55
A148	36p. Wellington by lighthouse	95	95
A149	40p. Madame Cholet and Bungo having picnic	1·10	1·10
A150	45p. Tomsk playing golf	1·50	1·50
A151	65p. Orinoco at airport	2·00	2·00
MSA152	160×86 mm. Nos. A146/51	6·50	6·50

A148 Queen Elizabeth the Queen Mother on Alderney, 1984 (image scaled to 52% of original size)

2000. Queen Elizabeth the Queen Mother's 100th Birthday. Sheet 93×70 mm.

MSA153	**A148** £1.50 multicoloured	4·00	4·50

2000. Garrison Island (4th series). Events. As Type **A100**. Multicoloured.

A154	21p. Regimental boxing tournament	45	25
A155	21p. Sports Day, Alderney Gala Week, 1924	45	25
A156	26p. Regimental orchestra playing at Ball	55	30
A157	26p. Garrison Ball in Fort Albert Mess, 1873	55	30
A158	36p. Royal Engineers' colour party, 1859	75	40
A159	36p. Royal Artillery on parade, Queen's 40th Birthday, 1859	75	40
A160	40p. Royal Artillery guard of honour	90	45
A161	40p. Arrival of Maj.-Gen. Marcus Slade, 1863	90	45

Nos. A154/5, A156/7, A158/9 and A160/1 were each printed together, *se-tenant*, forming a composite design.

A157 Queen Elizabeth II

2001. 75th Birthday of Queen Elizabeth II. Sheet 70×70 mm.

MSA162	**A157** £1.75 multicoloured	4·50	4·50

A158 Nurse with Clipboard and Patient in X-Ray

2001. Community Services (1st series). Healthcare. Multicoloured.

A163	22p. Type **A158**	45	50
A164	27p. Nurse with tray and Mignot Memorial Hospital	55	60
A165	36p. Doctor and Princess Anne visiting hospital, 1972	70	75
A166	40p. Nurse from 1960s and maternity unit	80	85
A167	45p. Nurse from 1957 and Queen Elizabeth II laying hospital foundation stone	90	95

A168	65p. Nurse of 1926 with baby and opening of original hospital	1·20	1·40

See also Nos. A197/202, A217/22 and A242/7.

A164 "Feathery" Golf Ball, 1901

2001. 30th Anniv of Alderney Golf Club. Multicoloured.

A169	22p. Type **A164**	45	50
A170	27p. Golfing fashions of the 1920s	55	60
A171	36p. Alderney Golf Course in 1970s	80	75
A172	40p. Modern putter	1·10	1·10
A173	45p. Modern golf gloves and shoes	1·50	1·50
A174	65p. Modern "lofted wood"	1·70	1·70
MSA175	190×75 mm. Nos. A169/74	6·50	6·50

No. MSA175 includes the "Philanippon '01" logo on the sheet margin.

A170 Construction of New Breakwater, 1853

2001. Garrison Island (5th series). The Royal Navy. Multicoloured.

A176	22p. Type **A170**	45	25
A177	22p. Official party inspecting harbour, 1853	45	25
A178	27p. H.M.S. *Emerald*, (steam frigate), 1860	55	30
A179	27p. Disembarking troops from H.M.S. *Emerald*, 1860	55	30
A180	36p. Moored torpedo boats, 1890	70	40
A181	36p. Quick-firing gun on railway wagon, 1890	70	40
A182	40p. H.M.S. *Majestic* (battleship) at anchor, 1901	80	45
A183	40p. Torpedo boats outside harbour, 1901	80	45

Nos. A176/7, A178/9, A180/1 and A182/3 were each printed together, *se-tenant*, each pair forming a composite design.

A178 Queen Elizabeth and Prince Philip arriving at London Airport, Feb 1952 (image scaled to 30% of original size)

2002. Golden Jubilee. Sheet 159×98 mm.

MSA184	**A178** £2 purple and gold	4·00	4·25

A179 Northern Hobby

2002. Migrating Birds (1st series). Raptors. Multicoloured.

A185	22p. Type **A179**	60	50
A186	27p. Black kite	70	60
A187	36p. Merlin	1·00	85
A188	40p. Honey buzzard	1·20	1·00
A189	45p. Osprey	1·50	1·50
A190	65p. Marsh harrier	1·70	1·70
MSA191	170×80 mm. Nos. A185/90	6·50	6·50

See also Nos. A210/MSA216, A235/MSA41 and A259/MS265.

A185 Coal Fire Beacon, 1725

2002. 50th Anniv of Electrification of Les Casquets Lighthouse. Multicoloured.

A192	22p. Type **A185**	50	50
A193	27p. Oil lantern, 1779	60	60
A194	36p. Argand lamp, 1790	75	75
A195	45p. Revolving light, 1818	1·10	1·10
A196	65p. Electric light, 1952	1·50	1·50

No. A196 is inscribed "Elictrification" in error.

2002. Community Services (2nd series). Emergency Medical Aid. As Type **A158**. Multicoloured.

A197	22p. Ambulance technician, and ambulance station	45	50
A198	27p. Ambulance technician using radio, and ambulance	55	60
A199	36p. Doctor, and loading patient onto aircraft	95	95
A200	40p. Pilot, and Brilten-Norman BN-2A MkIII Trislander over Alderney	1·10	1·10
A201	45p. Emergency operator, and patient on stretcher	1·70	1·70
A202	65p. Lifeboatman, and *Roy Barker One* (lifeboat)	2·00	2·00

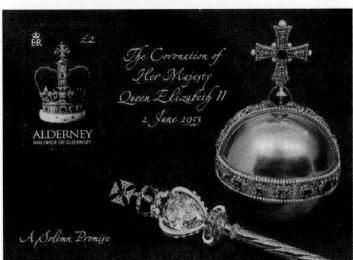

A196 St. Edward's Crown (image scaled to 38% of original size)

2003. 50th Anniv of Coronation. Sheet 128×90 mm.

MSA203	**A196** £2 multicoloured	4·50	4·50

A197 Wright Brothers' *Flyer I*, 1903

2003. Centenary of Powered Flight. Multicoloured.

A204	22p. Type **A197**	60	50
A205	27p. Alcock and Brown's Vickers FB-27 Vimy, 1919	75	75
A206	36p. Douglas DC-3, 1936	1·00	85
A207	40p. de Havilland DH106 Comet 4, 1946	1·20	1·00
A208	45p. British Aerospace/Aerospatiale Concorde, 1969	1·50	1·20
A209	65p. Airbus Industrie Airbus A380	1·50	1·50

2003. Migrating Birds (2nd series). Seabirds. Type **A179**. Multicoloured.

A210	22p. Arctic tern	60	50
A211	27p. Great skua	75	60
A212	36p. Sandwich tern	1·00	75
A213	40p. Sooty shearwater	1·20	1·00
A214	45p. Arctic skua	1·50	1·50
A215	65p. Manx shearwater	2·00	2·00
MSA216	80×170 mm. Nos. A210/15	6·50	6·00

2003. Community Services (3rd series). Alderney Police. As Type **A158**. Multicoloured.

A217	22p. Policeman with clipboard and constables on beat	50	50
A218	27p. Policeman and Land Rover	60	60
A219	36p. Forensic team	80	80
A220	40p. Police constable and policeman with child cyclist	1·00	1·00
A221	45p. Policeman directing traffic and police at scene of accident	1·50	1·50
A222	65p. Policewoman and policeman with customs officer	2·00	2·00

A215 *Hypholoma fasciculare*

2004. Fungi. Multicoloured.

A223	22p. Type **A215**	70	70
A224	27p. *Aleuria aurantia*	85	85
A225	36p. *Coprinus micaceus*	1·20	1·20
A226	40p. *Langermannia gigantean*	1·30	1·30
A227	45p. *Macrolepiota procera*	1·40	1·40
A228	65p. *Xylaria hypoxylon*	2·10	2·10

A221 Boys playing Football, Tourgis Close

2004. Centenary of FIFA (Federation Internationale de Football Association). Multicoloured.

A229	26p. Type **A221**	85	85
A230	32p. Three children playing football, Braye Beach	1·10	1·10
A231	36p. Two boys playing football in playground	1·20	1·20
A232	40p. Teenagers playing football, Arch Bay	1·30	1·30
A233	45p. Football match	1·50	1·50
A234	65p. Father and two children playing football, Arch Bay	2·10	2·10

2004. Migrating Birds (3rd series). Passerines. As Type **A179**. Multicoloured.

A235	26p. Northern wheatear	85	85
A236	32p. Common redstart	1·10	1·10
A237	36p. Yellow wagtail	1·20	1·20
A238	40p. Hoopoe	1·30	1·30
A239	45p. Ring ousel ("Ouzel")	1·50	1·50
A240	65p. Sand martin	2·10	2·10
MSA241	170×80 mm. Nos. A235/40	8·00	8·00

2004. Community Services (4th series). Fire Service. As Type **A158**. Multicoloured.

A242	26p. Fire engine	85	85
A243	32p. Fireman up ladder and fire engine at Fort Tourgis	1·10	1·10
A244	36p. Airport service fire truck	1·20	1·20
A245	40p. Alderney Fire Station	1·30	1·30
A246	45p. Airport training ground	1·50	1·50
A247	65p. Road accident training exercise	2·10	2·10

A239 Mermaid at her Undersea Home

2005. Birth Bicentenary of Hans Christian Andersen. Scenes from *The Little Mermaid*. Multicoloured.

A248	26p. Type **A239**	50	55
A249	32p. Mermaid rescuing drowning Prince	65	70
A250	36p. Mermaid with Sea Witch bargaining her voice for a human life	1·00	1·00
A251	40p. Mermaids waving to Prince and his lover on seashore	2·00	2·00
A252	65p. Mermaid carried away by angels	3·00	3·00

A244 Admiral Horatio Nelson

2005. Bicentenary of Battle of Trafalgar. Multicoloured.

A253	26p. Type **A244**	50	55
A254	32p. HMS *Victory*	65	70
A255	36p. Marine firing musket	70	75
A256	40p. Wounded Nelson with Captain Hardy	80	85
A257	45p. HMS *Victory* in battle with *Redoutable*	1·50	1·70
A258	65p. Admiral James Lord de Saumarez	2·00	2·50

2005. Migrating Birds (4th series). Waders. As Type **A179**. Multicoloured.

A259	26p. Little stint	50	55
A260	32p. Common greenshank	65	70
A261	36p. Golden plover	70	75
A262	40p. Bar-tailed godwit	1·00	85
A263	45p. Green sandpiper	2·00	2·00
A264	65p. Sanderling	3·00	3·00
MSA265	170×80 mm. Nos. A259/64	8·00	8·00

A256 Alderney Arms and Sunset (image scaled to 46% of original size)

2005. 60th Anniv of Return of War Evacuees. Sheet 140×80 mm.

MSA266	**A256** £2 multicoloured	6·00	7·50

A257 Young King Arthur

2006. "The Once and Future King". Multicoloured.

A267	29p. Type **A257**	60	65
A268	34p. Merlyn	70	75
A269	38p. Morgause	1·00	1·00
A270	42p. Queen Guenever	1·50	1·50
A271	47p. Lancelot	1·90	1·90
A272	68p. Mordred	2·20	2·20
MSA273	120×90 mm. Nos. A267/72	8·50	8·50

Nos. A267/**MS**A273 commemorate the birth centenary of Terence Hanbury White, author of "The Once and Future King".

A263 Princess Elizabeth

2006. 80th Birthday of Queen Elizabeth II. Multicoloured.

A274	29p. Type **A263**	30	30
A275	29p. Princess Elizabeth (facing right)	30	30
A276	34p. Queen Elizabeth II, c. 1955	50	50
A277	34p. Wearing brown coat and hat	50	50
A278	42p. Wearing tiara	85	90
A279	42p. Wearing red jacket and red and white hat	85	90
A280	45p. Wearing pale pink hat	90	95
A281	45p. Wearing mauve dress and hat	90	95

A271 Fulmar

2006. Resident Birds (1st series). Seabirds. Multicoloured.

A282	29p. Type **A271**	65	65
A283	34p. Gannet	75	75
A284	42p. Lesser black-backed gull	1·00	1·00
A285	45p. Storm petrel	1·50	1·50
A286	47p. Kittiwake	2·00	2·00
A287	68p. Puffin	3·00	3·00

See also Nos. A316/21, A336/41, A363/368.

A277 *Cerianthus lloydii* (burrowing anemone)

2006. Corals and Anemones. Multicoloured.

A288	1p. Type **A277**	10	10
A289	2p. *Parazoanthus axinellae* (colonial anemone)	10	10
A290	3p. *Corynactis viridis* (jewel anemone colony)	10	10
A291	4p. *Sagartia elegans* (anemone)	10	15
A292	5p. *Alcyonium glomeratum* (red fingers)	10	15
A293	6p. *Metridium senile* (plumose anemone)	10	15
A294	7p. *Eunicella verrucosa* (fan coral)	15	20
A295	8p. *Corynactis viridis* (close-up of jewel anemone)	15	20

A296	9p. *Actinothoe sphyrodeta* (anemone)	20	25
A297	10p. *Anemonia viridis* (snake-locks anemone)	20	25
A298	20p. *Caryophyllia smithii* (Devonshire cup coral)	45	45
A301	40p. *Actinothoe sphyrodeta* (fried egg anemone)	95	95
A304	50p. *Calliactis parasitica* (parasitic anemone)	1·20	1·20
A306	£1 *Actinia equina* (beadlet anemone) (23×29 mm)	2·00	2·10
A307	£2 *Leptopsammia pruvoti* (sunset cup coral) (23×29 mm)	4·00	4·25
A308	£4 *Actinia fragacea* (strawberry anemone)	9·50	9·50

A298 Cushion Starfish

2007. Designation of Alderney West Coast and the Burhou Islands as Ramsar Site. Multicoloured.

A309	32p. Type **A298**	75	75
A310	37p. Gannet colony at Les Etacs	90	90
A311	45p. Spiny squat lobster	1·10	1·10
A312	48p. Grey seal	1·10	1·10
A313	50p. Golden samphire near Fort Clonque	1·20	1·20
A314	71p. Little egret and oyster-catchers	1·70	1·70
MSA315	140×95 mm. Nos. A309/14	6·75	6·75

2007. Resident Birds (2nd series). Passerines. As Type **A271**. Multicoloured.

A316	32p. Blackbird	75	75
A317	37p. Dartford warbler	90	90
A318	45p. Blue tit	1·10	1·10
A319	48p. Wren	1·25	1·25
A320	50p. House sparrow	1·25	1·25
A321	71p. Jackdaw	1·75	1·75

A310 *How the Camel got his Hump*

2007. Rudyard Kipling's *Just So Stories*. Multicoloured.

A322	32p. Type **A310**	75	75
A323	37p. How the Whale got his Throat	90	90
A324	45p. The Elephant	1·10	1·10
A325	48p. How the Leopard got his Spots	1·25	1·25
A326	50p. The Cat that walked by Himself	1·25	1·25
A327	71p. How the Rhinoceros got his Skin	1·75	1·75
MSA328	140×95 mm. Nos. A322/7	7·00	7·00

A316 *Vanessa cardui* (painted lady)

2008. Butterflies. Multicoloured.

A329	34p. Type **A316**	80	80
A330	40p. *Hipparchia semele* (grayling)	95	95
A331	48p. *Callophrys rubi* (green hairstreak)	1·10	1·10
A332	51p. *Pararge aegeria* (speckled wood)	1·20	1·20
A333	53p. *Polyommatus icarus* (common blue)	1·30	1·30
A334	74p. *Melitaea cinxia* (Glanville fritillary)	1·70	1·70
MSA335	140×100 mm. Nos. A329/34	7·00	7·00

2008. Resident Birds (3rd series). Raptors. As Type **A271**. Multicoloured.

A336	34p. Common buzzard	80	80
A337	40p. Peregrine falcon	95	95
A338	48p. Kestrel	1·10	1·10
A339	51p. Barn owl	1·20	1·20
A340	53p. Long-eared owl	1·30	1·30
A341	74p. Sparrowhawk	1·70	1·70

A328 Old Harbour

2008. 25th Anniv of Alderney Stamps. Multicoloured.

A342	34p. Type **A328**	80	80
A343	40p. The Breakwater	95	95
A344	48p. Fort Clonque Causeway	1·10	1·10
A345	51p. Golf Course	1·20	1·20
A346	53p. Hanging Rock	1·30	1·30
A346a	55p. Hanging Rock	1·50	1·50
A347	74p. Fort Clonque	1·70	1·70

A334 Lion Rampant from Alderney Flag

2008

A348	**A334** £5 multicoloured	12·00	12·00

A335 Britten-Norman Islander

2008. 40th Anniv of Aurigny Air Services. Multicoloured.

A349	34p. Type **A335**	80	80
A350	40p. Britten-Norman Trislander	95	95
A351	48p. DHC-6 Twin Otter	1·10	1·10
A352	51p. Short 360	1·20	1·20
A353	53p. Saab 340	1·30	1·30
A354	74p. ATR 72	1·70	1·70
MSA355	140×95 mm. Nos. A349/54	7·00	7·00

A341 Tawny Mining Bee (*Andrena fulva*)

2009. Alderney Bees. Multicoloured.

A356	36p. Type **A341**	90	90
A357	43p. Early bumble bee (*Bombus pratorum*)	1·00	1·00
A358	51p. Bug mining bee (*Colletes daviesanus*)	1·25	1·25
A359	54p. Cuckoo bee (*Nomada goodeniana*)	1·25	1·25
A360	56p. Solitary bee (*Halictus scabiosae*)	1·40	1·40
A361	77p. Honey bee (*Apis mellifera*)	1·75	1·75
MSA362	140×100 mm. Nos. A356/61	8·00	8·00

A347 Turnstone

2009. Resident Birds (4th series). Waders. Multicoloured.

A363	36p. Type **A347**	85	75
A364	43p. Curlew	1·10	1·10
A365	51p. Oystercatcher	1·25	1·25
A366	54p. Snipe	1·25	1·25
A367	56p. Dunlind	1·40	1·40
A368	77p. Ringed Plover	1·60	1·60

A353 Felixstowe F2A Flying Boat with 'Dazzle' Paint over Castle Cornet, 1918

2009. Centenary of Naval Aviation. Multicoloured.

A369	36p. Type **A354**	85	85
A370	43p. Fairey Swordfish NE874 attacking U-boat	1·00	1·00
A371	51p. Blackburn Skuas dive bombing *Scharnhorst*	1·25	1·25
A372	54p. Hawker Sea Fury FB11 (VR930) over Alderney	1·25	1·25
A373	56p. Hawker Seahawk and Sea Furym	1·40	1·40
A374	77p. Agusta Westland HM101 Merlin Helicopter landing on HMS *Daring*	1·75	1·75

A359 Alice West reporting Theft of Bull to Sherlock Holmes

2009. 150th Birth Anniv of Sir Arthur Conan Doyle. Scenes from new story *Sherlock Holmes and the Curious Case of the Alderney Bull*. Multicoloured.

A375	36p. Type **A359**	85	85
A376	43p. Holmes studying Coded Message and Arrest of Herdsman	1·00	1·00
A377	51p. Holmes studying Message on Harbour Wall	1·25	1·25
A378	54p. Sherlock Holmes and Farmer West	1·25	1·25
A379	56p. Holmes and Watson observing Half-Built Lighthouse	1·40	1·40
A380	77p. Arrest of Thief	1·75	1·75

A365 Common Darter (*Sympetrum striolatum*)

2010. Dragonflies. Multicoloured.

A381	36p. Type **A365**	85	85
A382	45p. Emperor dragonfly (*Anax imperator*)	1·10	1·10
A383	56p. Blue-tailed damselfly (*Ischnura elegans*)	1·40	1·40
A384	66p. Brown hawker (*Aeshna grandis*)	1·50	1·50
A385	75p. Black-tailed skimmer (*Orthetrum cancellatum*)	1·75	1·75
A386	83p. Red veined darter (*Sympetrum fonscolumbii*)	2·00	2·00
MSA387	140×100 mm. Nos. A381/6	8·50	8·50

A371 Pilot Keith Gilman

A377 Sir Douglas Bader (birth centenary) (image scaled to 44% of original size)

2010. 70th Anniv of the Battle of Britain. Multicoloured.

A388	36p. Type **A372**	80	80
A389	45p. Hurricanes	1·00	1·00
A390	48p. Pilots scramble	1·10	1·10
A391	50p. Spitfire sortie	1·25	1·25
A392	58p. Air Raid Warden	1·40	1·40
A393	80p. Evacuees	1·75	1·75
MSA394	110×70 mm. A **377** £2 multicoloured	4·50	4·50

A378 Lamp and "Live your life while you have it. Life is a splendid gift"

2010. Death Centenary of Florence Nightingale. Multicoloured.

A395	36p. Type **A378**	80	80
A396	45p. Outstretched Hand and "How very little can be done under a spirit of fear"	1·00	1·00
A397	48p. Hands, Water Bowl and "The very first requirement in a hospital is that it should do the sick no harm"	1·10	1·10
A398	50p. Hands unrolling Bandage and "One's feelings waste themselves in words"	1·25	1·25
A399	58p. Hand writing and "I attribute my success to this – I never gave or took any excuse"	1·40	1·40

A400	80p. Clasped hands and "The greatest things grow by God's Law out of the smallest"	1·75	1·75

A384 Children flying above London

2010. 150th Birth Anniv of J. M. Barrie (author of *Peter Pan and Wendy*). Multicoloured.

A401	36p. Type **A384**	80	80
A402	45p. Captain Hook falling into Crocodile's Jaws	1·00	1·00
A403	48p. Peter visits Captain Hook's Ship	1·10	1·10
A404	50p. Peter waving a Rainbow	1·25	1·25
A405	58p. Children at Top of Neverpeak	1·40	1·40
A406	80p. Bonfire	1·75	1·75
MSA407	110×70 mm. A**390** £3 multicoloured	7·00	7·00

A391 'Oh Christmas Tree'

2010. Christmas Carols. Multicoloured.

A408	31p. Type **A391**	90	90
A409	36p. 'Away in a Manger'	80	80
A410	45p. 'While Shepherds Watched their Flocks by Night'	1·00	1·00
A411	48p. 'Hark the Herald Angels Sing'	1·10	1·10
A412	50p. 'O Holy Night'	1·25	1·25
A413	58p. 'O Little Town of Bethlehem'	1·40	1·40
A414	80p. 'Good King Wenceslas'	1·75	1·75

A398 Elephant Hawk-moth (*Deilephila elpenor*)

2011. Alderney Hawk-moths. Multicoloured.

A415	36p. Type **A398**	80	80
A416	45p. Hummingbird Hawk-moth (*Macroglossum stellatarum*)	1·00	1·00
A417	52p. Convolvulus Hawk-moth (*Agrius convolvuli*)	1·25	1·25
A418	58p. Poplar Hawk-moth (*Laothoe populi*)	1·40	1·40
A419	65p. Striped Hawk-moth (*Hyles livornica*)	1·50	1·50
A420	70p. Privet Hawk-moth (*Sphinx ligustri*)	1·70	1·70
MSA421	140×100 mm. Nos. A415/20	7·50	7·50

A404 Mediterranean Gull (*Icthyaetus melanocephalus*)

2011. Birds of the Bailiwick. Multicoloured.

A422	36p. Type **A404**	85	85
A423	45p. Shelduck (*Tadorna tadorna*)	1·10	1·10
A424	45p. Firecrest (*Regulus ignicapilla*)	1·10	1·10
A425	52p. Balearic Shearwater (*Puffinus mauretanicus*)	1·25	1·25
A426	58p. Woodcock (*Scolopax rusticola*)	1·40	1·40
A427	65p. Little Grebe (*Tachybaptus ruficollis*)	1·60	1·60
MSA428	140×100 mm. Nos. A422/7	7·25	7·25

A410 Queen Elizabeth II and Lt. Philip Mountbatten, July 1949

2011. 85th Birthday of Queen Elizabeth II and 90th Birthday of Prince Philip. Each sepia and silver.

A429	36p. Type **A410**	85	85
A430	45p. Queen Elizabeth II and Prince Philip at Windsor Castle, 6 June 1959	1·10	1·10
A431	48p. Queen Elizabeth II and Prince Philip at Balmoral, 1 June 1972	1·10	1·10
A432	52p. Queen Elizabeth II and Prince Philip at Silver Jubilee Thanksgiving, St. Paul's Cathedral, 7 June 1977	1·25	1·25
A433	58p. Queen Elizabeth II and Prince Philip arriving at St. Paul's Cathedral, 15 June 2006	1·40	1·40
A434	65p. Queen Elizabeth II and Prince Philip at Sikh Temple, Hounslow, London, 15 October 2004	1·60	1·60

A416 Female VAD (Voluntary Aid Detachment) Uniform, c. 1915

2011. Centenary of British Red Cross Uniforms. Multicoloured.

A435	36p. Type **A416**	85	85
A436	47p. Male VAD Uniform, 1915	1·10	1·10
A437	48p. Nurse's Uniform, 1966-78	1·25	1·25
A438	52p. Uniform, 1981-2001	1·25	1·25
A439	61p. Uniform, 2001	1·50	1·50
A440	65p. British Red Cross Work Wear, 2011	1·60	1·60

A422 Victoria Street

2011. Christmas. 'Winter Wonderland'. Multicoloured.

A441	31p. Type **A422**	80	80
A442	36p. St. Anne's Church	90	90
A443	47p. Les Estacs Gannet Colonies	1·10	1·10
A444	48p. Mannez Lighthouse and Santa's Sleigh	1·10	1·10
A445	52p. The Alderney Train	1·25	1·25
A446	61p. Snowman and Children playing at The Breakwater	1·50	1·50
A447	65p. The Harbour	1·60	1·60

A429 *Titanic* leaving Southampton

2012. Centenary of the Sinking of the *Titanic*. Multicoloured.

A448	36p. Type **A429**	1·10	1·10
A449	47p. *Titanic* sailing past Alderney	1·10	1·10
A450	48p. The Grand Staircase	1·10	1·10
A451	52p. Orchestra playing Final Tune	1·25	1·25
A452	61p. Captain Edward J. Smith	1·50	1·50
A453	65p. Lifeboats leaving Titanic	1·50	1·60

A435 Magistrate spares the Terrified Oliver Twist from Apprenticeship as Chimneysweep

2012. Birth Bicentenary of Charles Dickens (writer). Original Illustrations from *Oliver Twist* by George Cruikshank. Each olive-sepia and black.

A454	36p. Type **A435**	90	90
A455	47p. Noah Claypole	1·10	1·10
A456	48p. The Artful Dodger and Charley Bates make Oliver polish their Boots	1·10	1·10
A457	52p. Fagin and Monks appear before Oliver at Maylie's Residence	1·25	1·25
A458	61p. Nancy meeting Rose and Mr. Brownlow on London Bridge	1·50	1·50
A459	65p. Oliver and Rose Maylie see his Mother's Memorial in Village Church	1·60	1·60

A441 Garden Tiger Moth (*Arctia caja*)

2012. Alderney Invertebrates: Tiger Moths and Ermines. Multicoloured.

A460	39p. Type **A441**	95	95
A461	52p. Cream Spot Tiger Moth (*Arctia villica*)	1·25	1·25
A462	53p. Buff Ermine (*Spilosoma lutea*)	1·25	1·25
A463	59p. Ruby Tiger Moth (*Phragmatobia fuliginosa*)	1·40	1·40
A464	69p. Jersey Tiger Moth (*Euplagia quadripunctaria*)	1·75	1·75
A465	74p. Cinnabar (*Tyria jacobaeae*)	1·75	1·75
MSA466	140×100 mm. Nos. A460/5	8·00	8·00

A447 Douglas Quay, Braye Harbour, c. 1800

2012. The History of Alderney Harbour. Multicoloured.

A467	39p. Type **A447**	95	95
A468	52p. Breakwater, completed 1856	1·25	1·25
A469	53p. SS *Courier*, c. 1926	1·25	1·25
A470	59p. Little Crabby Harbour, c. 1985	1·40	1·40
A471	69p. RNLI Lifeboat Roy Barker I, c. 1995	1·75	1·75
A472	74p. Commercial Quay, built 2011	1·75	1·75
MSA473	140×100 mm. Nos. A467/72	8·00	8·00

A453 Angel visits Mary 'Annunciation'

2012. Christmas. The Christmas Story. Multicoloured.

A474	34p. Type **A453**	85	85
A475	39p. No Room at the Inn	95	95
A476	52p. The Birth of Jesus	1·25	1·25
A477	53p. Whilst Shepherds watch their Flocks	1·25	1·25
A478	59p. The Three Kings	1·40	1·40
A479	69p. The Children of Bethlehem visit the Baby Jesus	1·75	1·75
A480	74p. The Flight to Egypt	1·75	1·75

A460 Rose Chafer (*Cetonia aurata*)

2013. Alderney Beetles. Multicoloured.

A481	39p. Type **A460**	95	95
A482	52p. Burying Beetle (*Nicrophorus genus*)	1·25	1·25
A483	53p. Green Tiger Beetle (*Cicindela campestris*)	1·25	1·25
A484	59p. May Bug or Cockchafer (*Melolontha melolontha*)	1·40	1·40
A485	69p. *Netocia morio*	1·75	1·75
A486	74p. Oil Beetle (*Meloegenus*)	1·75	1·75
MSA487	140×100 mm. Nos. A481/6	8·00	8·00

A466 Queen Elizabeth II wearing Imperial State Crown

2013. 60th Anniv of the Coronation. Multicoloured.

A488	40p. Type **A466**	95	95
A489	53p. Coronets and Tiaras from The Goldsmiths and Silversmiths Company, 1953	1·25	1·25
A490	55p. Queen Elizabeth II wearing George IV State Diadem arriving at Westminster Abbey	1·25	1·25
A491	63p. Queen Elizabeth II and Archbishops in Procession down Aisle	1·40	1·40
A492	71p. Queen Elizabeth II (seated in Coronation Chair) and Archbishops	1·75	1·75
A493	79p. Coronation Portrait	1·75	1·75

A472 Rabbit and Beatrix Potter walking Home to Near Sawrey

2013. The Life of Beatrix Potter. Multicoloured.

A494	40p. Type **A472**	95	95
A495	53p. Beatrix Potter feeding Duck	1·25	1·25
A496	55p. Mouse in Onion Patch	1·25	1·25
A497	63p. Dog carrying Branch	1·40	1·40
A498	71p. Beatrix Potter sketching Cat	1·75	1·75
A499	79p. Beatrix Potter in Farmyard	1·75	1·75
MSA500	140×100 mm. Nos. A494/9	8·00	8·00

A478 Santa and Rudolph

2013. Christmas. Rudolph the Red-nosed Reindeer. Multicoloured.

A501	35p. Type **A478**	85	85
A502	40p. Elf comforting Rudolph	95	95
A503	53p. Rudolph with Snowmen	1·25	1·25
A504	55p. Rudolph mocked by Other Reindeer	1·25	1·25
A505	63p. Santa looking into the Fog	1·40	1·40
A506	71p. Rudolph's Glowing Nose	1·75	1·75
A507	79p. Rudolph leading Sleigh	1·75	1·75

A485 7-spot Ladybird (*Coccinella 7-punctata*)

2014. Alderney Ladybirds. Multicoloured.

A508	40p. Type **A485**	95	95
A509	53p. 7-spot Ladybird (*Coccinella 7-punctata*) Newly Hatched	1·25	1·25
A510	55p. 2-spot Ladybird (*Adalia 2-punctata*)	1·25	1·25
A511	63p. Orange Ladybird (*Halyzia 16-guttata*)	1·40	1·40
A512	71p. Harlequin Ladybirds (*Harmonia axyridis*)	1·75	1·75
A513	79p. Harlequin Ladybirds (*Harmonia axyridis*)	1·75	1·75
MSA514	Nos. A508/13	8·00	8·00

A491 William the Conqueror dining with Family after Victory at the Battle of Hastings

A492 William the Conqueror and Knights

A493 The English Nobles and Archbishops surrender

A494 Sword of State and Sceptre presented to William the Conqueror

A495 William the Conqueror crowned by Archbishop Ealdred of York with Geoffrey of Coutances as Translator, Westminster Abbey, 1066

A496 William I acclaimed as King of England and Construction of the White Tower, London

A497 Complete Panel of Tapestry (image scaled to 25% of original size)

2014. Bayeux Tapestry Final Panel (Alderney community project). Multicoloured.

A515	40p. Type **A491**	95	95
A516	53p. William the Conqueror and Knights	1·25	1·25
A517	55p. The English Nobles and Archbishops surrender	1·25	1·25
A518	63p. Sword of State and Sceptre presented to William the Conqueror	1·40	1·40
A519	71p. William the Conqueror crowned by Archbishop Ealdred of York with Geoffrey of Coutances as Translator, Westminster Abbey, 1066	1·75	1·75
A520	79p. William I acclaimed as King of England and Construction of the White Tower, London	1·75	1·75
MSA521	198×49 mm. **A497** £3 multicoloured	7·00	7·00

No. **MSA521** was printed onto cotton and was accompanied by a certificate of authenticity.

Pt. 13

GUINEA

The former French Colony on the W. coast of Africa which became fully independent in 1958.

1959. 100 centimes = 1 franc.
1973. 100 caury = 1 syli.
1986. 100 centimes = 1 franc.

1959. Stamps of Fr. West Africa optd **REPUBLIQUE DE GUINEE** or surch also.

188	-	10f. mult (No. 118)	3·25	3·75
189	20	45f. on 20f. pur, grn & ol	3·75	3·75

10 Pres. Sekou Toure

1959. Proclamation of Independence.

190	10	5f. red	35	10
191	10	10f. blue	55	30
192	10	20f. orange	90	60
193	10	65f. green	2·75	1·60
194	10	100f. violet	4·00	2·50

12 Tamara Lighthouse and Fishing Boats   **13** Flying Doves

1959

201	12	1f. red (postage)	20	10
202	12	2f. green	20	10
203	12	3f. brown	20	10
204	-	5f. blue	40	10
205	-	10f. purple	40	20
206	-	15f. brown	1·20	40
207	-	20f. purple	1·20	35
208	-	25f. brown	2·20	60
209	13	40f. blue (air)	45	35
210	13	50f. green	65	55
211	13	100f. lake	1·30	90
212	13	200f. red	2·75	1·60
213	13	500f. red	7·75	4·50

DESIGNS—VERT: 5f. Palms and dhow; 20f. Pres. Sekou Toure. HORIZ: 10f. Pirogue being launched; 15f. African Elephant (front view); 25f. African Elephant (side view).

14 Mangoes

1959. Fruits in natural colours. Frame colours given.

214	-	10f. red (Bananas)	25	25
215	-	15f. green (Grapefruit)	40	25
216	-	20f. brown (Lemons)	60	30
217	14	25f. blue	80	45
218	-	50f. violet (Pineapple)	1·50	60

15 Lockheed Super Constellation Airliner

1959. Air.

219	15	100f. blue, brown & mauve	2·40	1·30
220	15	500f. mauve, brown & grn	5·75	1·90
221	-	500f. multicoloured	8·25	4·00

DESIGN: 500f. Lockheed Super Constellation airliner on ground.

16 "Raising the Flag"

1959. First Anniv of Independence.

222	16	50f. multicoloured	1·20	60
223	16	100f. multicoloured	2·00	1·00

18 Africans acclaiming U.N. Headquarters Building

1959. U.N.O.

230	18	1f. blue & orange (postage)	15	10
231	18	2f. purple and green	15	10
232	18	3f. brown and red	30	15
233	18	5f. brown and turquoise	30	20
234	18	50f. green, blue & brn (air)	90	70
235	18	100f. green, red and blue	1·60	1·20

Nos. 234/5 are larger (45×26 mm).

19 Eye-testing

1960. National Health. Inscr "POUR NOTRE SANTE NATIONALE".

236	19	20f.+10f. red and blue	95	90
237	-	30f.+20f. violet & orange	1·00	95
238	-	40f.+20f. blue and red	1·60	1·30
239	-	50f.+50f. brown and green	2·50	2·10
240	-	100f.+100f. green & pur	4·00	3·25

DESIGNS—HORIZ: 30f. Laboratory assistant; 40f. Spraying trees. VERT: (28½×40 mm): 50f. Research with microscope; 100f. Operating theatre.

20 "Uprooted Tree"

1960. World Refugee Year.

241	20	25f. multicoloured	70	40
242	20	50f. multicoloured	1·10	75

21 U.P.U. Monument, Berne

1960. First Anniv of Admission to U.P.U. Background differs for each value.

243	21	10f. black and brown	25	10
244	21	15f. lilac and mauve	45	25
245	21	20f. indigo and blue	55	25
246	-	25f. myrtle and green	75	30
247	-	50f. sepia and orange	1·10	55

DESIGN: 25f., 50f. As Type **10** but vert.

1960. Olympic Games. Optd **Jeux Olympiques Rome 1960** and Olympic rings.

248	16	50f. multicoloured (postage)	8·00	7·75
249	16	100f. multicoloured	12·00	11·50
250	15	100f. blue, grn & mve(air)	10·50	7·75
251	15	200f. mauve, brown & grn	18·00	11·00
252	-	500f. multi (No. 221)	47·00	37·00

23 Flag and Map

1960. Second Anniv of Independence.

253	23	25f. multicoloured	50	45
254	23	30f. multicoloured	70	65

1960. 15th Anniv of U.N.O. Optd **XVEME ANNIVERSAIRE DES NATIONS UNIES.** (a) Nos. 214/18. Fruits in natural colours.

255	-	10f. red	30	25
256	-	15f. green	45	25
257	-	20f. brown	55	40
258	14	25f. blue	55	40
259	-	50f. violet	1·10	80

(b) Nos. 230/35.

260	18	1f. blue & orange (postage)	10	10
261	18	2f. purple and green	10	10
262	18	3f. brown and red	10	10
263	18	5f. brown and turquoise	10	10
264	18	50f. green, blue & brn (air)	95	70
265	18	100f. green, red and blue	1·60	1·10

1961. Surch **1961** and value.

266	20	25f.+10f. multicoloured	7·25	7·25
267	20	50f.+20f. multicoloured	7·25	7·25

27 Bohar Reedbuck

1961. Centres in brown, green and blue. Inscriptions and value tablets in colours given.

268	27	5f. turquoise	15	10
269	27	10f. green	15	10
270	27	25f. violet	45	30
271	27	40f. orange	80	40
272	27	50f. red	1·60	60
273	27	75f. blue	2·50	1·00

28 Guinea Flag and Exhibition Hall, Conakry

1961. First Three-Year Plan. Flag in red, yellow and green.

274	28	5f. blue and red	15	10
275	28	10f. brown and red	20	20
276	28	25f. green and red	45	40

29 Helmeted Guineafowl

1961. Guineafowl in purple and blue.

277	29	5f. mauve and blue	15	15
278	29	10f. red and blue	45	15
279	29	25f. red and blue	55	25
280	29	40f. brown and blue	95	40
281	29	50f. bistre and blue	1·30	55
282	29	75f. olive and blue	2·40	95

1961. Protection of Animals. Surch **POUR LA PROTECTION DE NOS ANIMAUX +5 FRS.**

283	27	5f.+5f. turquoise	70	15
284	27	10f.+5f. green	70	25
285	27	25f.+5f. violet	1·90	35
286	27	40f.+5f. orange	2·40	65
287	27	50f.+5f. red	3·50	80
288	27	75f.+5f. blue	5·50	1·30

31 Patrice Lumumba

1962. First Death Anniv of Lumumba (Congo leader).

289	31	10f. multicoloured	40	25
290	31	25f. multicoloured	60	45
291	31	50f. multicoloured	85	50

1962. Malaria Eradication (1st issue). Nos. 236/40 optd with Malaria Eradication emblem and **ERADICATION DE LA MALARIA.**

292	19	20f.+10f. red and blue	55	55
293	-	30f.+20f. violet and orange	65	65
294	-	40f.+20f. blue and red	1·20	1·10
295	-	50f.+50f. brown & green	1·70	1·60
296	-	100f.+100f. green & pur	3·75	3·50

33 King Mohammed V and Map

1962. First Anniv of Casablanca Conference.

297	33	25f. multicoloured	95	40
298	33	75f. multicoloured	2·75	75

34 Mosquito and Emblem

1962. Air. Malaria Eradication (2nd issue).

299	34	25f. black and orange	75	30
300	34	50f. black and red	95	50
301	34	100f. black and green	1·80	80
MS302		103×77 mm. 100f. sepia and green	11·50	11·00

34a Posthorn on North Africa

1962. African Postal Union Commemoration.

303	34a	25f. green, brown & orge	75	20
304	34a	100f. orange and brown	2·30	70

1962. Guinea-fowl stamps surch **POUR LA PROTECTION DE NOS OISEAUX +5 FRS.**

305	29	5f.+5f.	45	25
306	29	10f.+5f.	45	30
307	29	25f.+5f.	95	45
308	29	40f.+5f.	1·30	70
309	29	50f.+5f.	2·20	90
310	29	75f.+5f.	4·25	1·70

36 Bote-player

1962. Native Musicians.

311	36	30c. red, grn & bl (postage)	15	10
312	A	50c. green, brown & salmon	15	10
313	B	1f. purple and green	15	10
314	C	1f.50 turquoise, red & yell	15	10
315	D	2f. green, red and mauve	15	10
316	C	3f. violet, green & turquoise	30	10
317	B	10f. blue, brown and orange	40	25
318	D	20f. red, sepia and olive	45	60
319	36	25f. violet, sepia and olive	60	45
320	A	40f. mauve, green and blue	30	30
321	36	50f. blue, red and rose	45	50
322	A	75f. blue, brown and ochre	3·50	1·00
323	D	100f. blue, red & pink (air)	1·70	70
324	D	200f. red and blue	3·00	1·20
325	E	500f. blue, violet and green	8·25	3·25

DESIGNS—(Musicians playing). HORIZ: A, Bolon; C, Koni; D, Kora; E, Balafon. VERT: B, Flute.

37 Hippopotamus

1962. Wild Game.

326	37	10f. sepia, green and orange	35	10
327	-	25f. brown, sepia and green	55	25
328	-	30f. sepia, yellow and olive	90	45
329	37	50f. sepia, green and blue	1·20	65
330	-	75f. brown, purple and lilac	1·80	85
331	-	100f. sepia, yellow & turq	2·50	1·00

DESIGNS: 25f., 75f. Lion; 30f., 100f. Leopard.

38 Boy at Blackboard

1962. Campaign Against Illiteracy.

332	38	5f. sepia, yellow and red	10	10
333	-	10f. sepia, orange and purple	10	10
334	38	15f. sepia, green and red	35	20
335	-	20f. sepia, turquoise & pur	45	30

DESIGN: 10f., 20f. Teacher at blackboard.

39 Alfa Yaya

1962. African Heroes and Martyrs.

336	39	25f. sepia, turquoise & gold	40	10
337	-	30f. sepia, ochre and gold	55	25
338	-	50f. sepia, purple and gold	85	25
339	-	75f. sepia, green and gold	1·50	55
340	-	100f. sepia, red and gold	2·10	80

PORTRAITS: 30f. King Behanzin; 50f. King Ba Bemba of Sikasso; 75f. Almamy Samory; 100f. Chief Tierno Aliou of the Goumba.

1962. Algerian Refugees Fund. Surch **Aide aux Refugies Algeriens** and premium.

341	33	25f.+15f. multicoloured	95	95
342	33	75f.+25f. multicoloured	1·80	1·80

1962. Air. "The Conquest of Space". Optd with capsule and **La Conquete De L'Espace.**

343	13	40f. blue	75	30
344	13	50f. green	1·00	40
345	13	100f. lake	1·60	75
348	13	200f. red	3·25	1·40

43 Crowned Crane

1962. Birds. Multicoloured.

349	43	Type **43** (postage)	10	10
350		50c. Grey parrot (horiz)	10	10
351		1f. Abyssinian ground hornbill (horiz)	30	10
352		1f.50 White spoonbill (horiz)	30	10
353		2f. Bateleur (horiz)	30	10
354		3f. Type **43**	30	10
355		10f. As 50c. (horiz)	60	30
356		20f. As 1f. (horiz)	95	30
357		25f. As 1f.50 (horiz)	1·20	25
358		40f. As 2f. (horiz)	1·50	45
359		50f. Type **43**	2·20	65
360		75f. As 50c. (horiz)	3·00	80
361		100f. As 1f. (horiz) (air)	2·75	80
362		200f. As 1f.50 (horiz)	5·00	1·50
363		500f. As 2f. (horiz)	10·50	3·50

44 Handball

1963. Sports.

364	44	30c. purple, red and green (postage)	10	10
365	A	50c. violet, lilac and blue	10	10
366	B	1f. sepia, orange and green	10	10
367	C	1f.50 blue, orange & purple	10	10
368	D	2f. blue, turquoise & purple	10	10
369	44	3f. purple, olive and blue	10	10
370	A	4f. violet, mauve and blue	10	10
371	B	5f. sepia, green and purple	20	10
372	C	10f. blue and bright purple	30	10
373	D	20f. blue, orange and red	45	25
374	44	25f. purple, green and black	55	25
375	A	30f. violet, black and blue	55	40
376	B	100f. sepia, lake & grn (air)	1·90	70
377	C	200f. blue, brown & purple	4·00	1·40
378	D	500f. blue, brown & purple	8·75	3·50

DESIGNS: A, Boxing; B, Running; C, Cycling; D, Canoeing.

45 Campaign Emblem

1963. Freedom from Hunger.

379	45	5f. yellow and red	10	10
380	45	10f. yellow and green	15	10
381	45	15f. yellow and brown	30	15
382	45	25f. yellow and olive	45	25

46 *Amauris niavius*

1963. Butterflies. Multicoloured.

383	10c. Type **46** (postage)	10	10
384	30c. *Papilio demodocus*	10	10
385	40c. As 30c.	10	10
386	50c. *Graphum policenes*	10	10
387	1f. *Papilio nireus*	30	10
388	1f.50 Type **46**	30	10
389	2f. *Papilio menestheus*	30	10
390	3f. As 30c.	30	10
391	10f. As 50c.	50	10
392	20f. As 1f.	90	10
393	25f. Type **46**	1·50	25
394	40f. As 2f.	2·00	45
395	50f. As 30c.	2·50	60
396	75f. As 1f.	4·50	95
397	100f. Type **46** (air)	2·50	50
398	200f. As 50c.	4·50	1·10
399	500f. As 2f.	10·00	3·75

47 "African Unity"

1963. Conf of African Heads of State, Addis Ababa.

400	**47**	5f. sepia, blk & turq on grn	10	10
401	**47**	10f. sepia, black and yellow on yellow	15	10
402	**47**	15f. sepia, black & ol on ol	30	10
403	**47**	25f. sepia, black and brown on cinnamon	45	25

48 Capsule encircling Globe

1963. Centenary of Red Cross.

404	**48**	5f. red and green (postage)	10	10
405	**48**	10f. red and blue	35	10
406	**48**	15f. red and yellow	50	25
407	**48**	25f. red and black (air)	85	40
MS408		102×76 mm. 100f. carmine and green	4·25	4·25

1963. Air. First Pan-American Conakry–New York Direct Air Service. Optd **PREMIER SERVICE DIRECT CONAKRY–NEW YORK PAN AMERICAN 30 JUILLET 1963.**

409	**15**	10f. blue, green and mauve	2·75	1·10
410	**15**	200f. mauve, brown & green	4·75	2·20

1963. Olympic Games Preparatory Commission, Conakry. Nos. 364/6 surch **COMMISSION PREPARATOIRE AUX JEUX OLYMPIQUES A CONAKRY**, rings and new value.

411		40f. on 30c. purple, red and green	1·50	1·10
412		50f. on 50c. violet, lilac and blue	2·20	1·70
413		75f. on 1f. sepia, orange & grn	3·75	2·75

51 Jewel Cichlid

1964. Guinea Fish. Multicoloured.

414	30c. Type **51** (postage)	10	10
415	40c. Golden pheasant panchax	10	10
416	50c. Blue gularis	10	10
417	1f. Banded jewelfish and jewel cichlid	10	10
418	1f.50 Yellow gularis	30	10
419	2f. Six-banded lyretail	30	25

420	5f. Type **51**	50	25
421	30f. As 40c.	85	40
422	40f. As 50c.	1·50	70
423	75f. As 1f.	3·25	95
424	100f. As 1f.50 (air)	2·10	80
425	300f. As 2f.	6·75	2·20

52 President Kennedy

1964. Pres. Kennedy Memorial Issue. Flag in red and blue.

426	**52**	5f. violet & black (postage)	10	10
427	**52**	25f. violet and green	45	25
428	**52**	50f. violet and brown	85	40
429	**52**	100f. black and violet (air)	1·90	1·20

53 Pipeline under Construction

1964. Inaug of Piped Water Supply, Conakry.

430	**53**	5f. red	10	10
431	-	10f. violet	15	10
432	-	20f. brown	35	15
433	-	30f. blue	55	25
434	-	50f. green	1·00	50

DESIGNS—HORIZ: 10f. Reservoir; 20f. Joining pipes; 30f. Transporting pipes; 50f. Laying pipes.

54 Ice hockey

1964. Winter Olympic Games, Innsbruck. Rings, frame and tablet in gold.

435	**54**	10f. olive & green (postage)	30	10
436	-	25f. slate and violet	70	25
437	-	50f. black and blue	1·30	60
438	-	100f. black & brn (air)	2·20	95

DESIGNS: 25f. Ski-jumping; 50f. Skiing; 100f. Figure-skating.

1964. Air. Olympic Games, Tokyo (1st issue). Nos. 376/8 optd **JEUX OLYMPIQUES TOKYO 1964** and Olympic rings.

439		100f. sepia, lake and green	1·90	1·30
440		200f. blue, brown and purple	3·50	2·40
441		500f. blue, brown and purple	8·25	5·25

56 Eleanor Roosevelt with Children

1964. 15th Anniv of Declaration of Human Rights.

442	**56**	5f. green (postage)	10	10
443	**56**	10f. orange	10	10
444	**56**	15f. blue	30	10
445	**56**	25f. red	45	25
446	**56**	50f. violet (air)	1·10	50

57 Striped Hyena

1964. Animals.

447	**57**	5f. sepia and yellow	30	10
448	**57**	30f. sepia and blue	55	25
449	-	40f. black and mauve	80	25
450	-	75f. sepia and green	1·60	60
451	-	100f. sepia and ochre	2·20	80
452	-	300f. deep violet and orange	5·75	2·50

ANIMALS: 40f., 300f. African buffalo; 75f., 100f. African elephant.

58 Guinea Pavilion

1964. New York World's Fair.

453	**58**	30f. green and lilac	45	15
454	**58**	40f. green and purple	55	25
455	**58**	50f. green and brown	75	30
456	**58**	75f. blue and red	1·10	50
MS457		Two sheets each 100×76 mm. 59 (a) 100f. orange and blue; (b) 200f. green and carmine Set of 2 sheets	5·75	5·75

See also Nos. 484/**MS**488.

60 Nefertari, Isis and Hathor

1964. Nubian Monuments Preservation. Multicoloured.

458	10f. Type **60** (postage)	30	10
459	25f. Pharaoh in battle	35	10
460	50f. The Nile—partly submerged sphinxes	65	35
461	100f. Rameses II, entrance hall of Great Temple, Abu Simbel	1·50	60
462	200f. Lower part of Colossi, Abu Simbel	2·75	1·10
463	300f. Nefertari (air)	4·75	1·90

61 Athlete with Torch

1965. Olympic Games, Tokyo (2nd issue). Multicoloured.

464	5f. Weightlifter and children (postage)	25	15
465	10f. Type **61**	45	10
466	25f. Pole vaulting	45	25
467	40f. Running	60	40
468	50f. Judo	85	45
469	75f. Japanese hostess	1·50	75
470	100f. Air hostess and Convair Coronado airliner (horiz) (air)	1·90	75
MS471	Two sheets. (a) 85×120 mm. 200f. Sun setting over Mt. Fuji; (b) 120×85 mm. 300f. Snow-clad Mt. Fuji set of 2 sheets	13·00	13·00

62 Doudou (Boke) Mask

1965. Native Masks and Dancers. Multicoloured.

472	20c. Type **62** (postage)	10	10
473	40c. Niamou (Nzerekore) mask	10	10
474	60c. "Yoki" (Boke) statuette	10	10
475	80c. Guekedou dancer	10	10
476	1f. Niamou (Nzerekore) mask	15	10
477	2f. Macenta dancer	15	10
478	15f. Niamou (Nzerekore) mask	30	25
479	20f. Tom-tom beater (forest region)	50	25
480	60f. Macenta "Bird-man" dancer	1·50	45
481	80f. Bassari (Koundara) dancer	1·70	75
482	100f. Karana sword dancer	2·20	90
483	300f. Niamou (Nzerekore) mask (air)	6·50	2·20

1965. New York World's Fair. As Nos. 453/6 but additionally inscr "1965".

484	30f. orange and green	40	15
485	40f. green and red	55	25
486	50f. violet and blue	75	40
487	75f. violet and brown	1·00	55

MS488	Two sheets each 100×70 mm. 59 (a) 100f. green and sepia; (b) 200f. magenta and green Set of 2 sheets	6·50	6·50

63 Metal-work

1965. Native Handicrafts. Multicoloured.

489	15f. Type **63** (postage)	30	10
490	20f. Pottery	30	25
491	60f. Dyeing	85	40
492	80f. Basket-making	1·00	50
493	100f. Ebony-work (air)	1·80	80
494	300f. Ivory-work	5·00	1·80

64 I.T.U. Emblem and Symbols

1965. I.T.U. Centenary.

495	**64**	25f. multicoloured (postage)	45	25
496	**64**	50f. multicoloured	75	40
497	**64**	100f. multicoloured (air)	1·90	70
498	**64**	200f. multicoloured	3·00	1·30

65 Major Grissom | **66** Grissom and Young in "Gemini 2" Spaceship

1965. American and Russian Achievements in Space. Two sheets each 145×215 mm containing fifteen stamps as T **65/6**. Multicoloured.

MS499	America in Space. 5f. Type **65**; 10f. Lt. Com. John W. Young; 15f. Moon from 258 miles; 25f. Moon from 115 miles; 30f. Moon from 58 miles; 100f. Type **66**	11·00	11·00
MS500	Russia in Space. 5f. Col. Pavel Belyayev; 10f. Lt. Col. Alexei Leonov; 15f. Vostoks 3 and 4 in space; 25f. Sputnik over earth; 30f. Vostoks 5 and 6 over earth; 100f. Leonov floating in space	11·00	11·00

67 U.N. Headquarters and I.C.Y. Emblem

1965. I.C.Y.

501	**67**	25f. red and green (postage)	30	15
502	**67**	45f. red and violet	45	25
503	**67**	75f. red and brown	95	50
504	**67**	100f. orange and blue (air)	1·50	70

68 Polytechnic Institute, Conakry

1965. Seventh Anniv of Independence. Multicoloured.

505	25f. Type **68** (postage)	30	10
506	30f. Camayenne Hotel	45	30
507	40f. Gbessia Airport	75	45
508	75f. "28 Septembre" Stadium	1·00	65
509	200f. Polytechnic Institute, North facade	2·20	1·30
510	500f. Ditto, West facade	6·50	3·25

Nos. 509/10 are larger, 53×23 mm.

69 Moon, Globe and Satellite

1965. "To the Moon". Multicoloured.

511		5f. Type **69** (postage)	15	10
512		10f. Trajectory of "Ranger 7"	50	10
513		25f. "Relay" satellite	60	30
514		45f. "Vostok 1, 2" and Globe	95	35
515		100f. "Ranger 7" approaching Moon (vert) (25×36 mm) (air)	1·30	45
516		200f. Launching of "Ranger 7" (vert) (25×36 mm)	2·75	90

Nos. 512/14 are larger, 36×25½ mm.

1965. Gemini 5 and Pictures of Mars Commemoration. Sheet **MS**499 variously optd. The 5, 10 and 100f. are optd in English or French and the 15, 25 and 30f. are optd in French, English and French respectively.

MS517	145×215 mm	10·00	10·00

MS518 155×215 mm. Sheet MS499 optd as last but the 15, 25 and 30f. are optd in English, French and English respectively .... 10·00 | 10·00

70 Sabre Dance, Karana

1966. Guinean Dances. Multicoloured.

519		10c. Type **70** (postage)	10	10
520		30c. Young girls' dance, Lower Guinea	10	10
521		50c. Tiekere musicians, "Eyora" (bamboo) dance, Bandjin- guene (horiz) (36×29 mm)	10	10
522		5f. Doundouba dance, Kouroussa	30	10
523		40f. Bird-man's dance, Macenta	1·50	50
524		100f. Kouyate Kandia, national singer (horiz) (36×29 mm) (air)	1·80	75

See also Nos. 561/6.

1966. Stamp Cent Exn, Cairo. Nos. 460 and 463 optd **CENTENAIRE DU TIMBRE CAIRE 1966**.

525		50f. multicoloured (postage)	95	80
526		300f. multicoloured (air)	3·75	1·80

1966. Pan Arab Games, Cairo (1965). Nos. 464/5, 467/9 optd **JEUX PANARABES CAIRE 1965** and pyramid motif.

527	-	5f. multicoloured (postage)	45	25
528	61	10f. multicoloured	45	25
529	-	40f. multicoloured	90	45
530	-	50f. multicoloured	1·00	70
531	-	75f. multicoloured	1·80	1·10
532	-	100f. multicoloured (air)	1·80	75

MS533 Two sheets as No. **MS**471 optd 200f. and 300f. Price for 2 sheets .... 15·00 | 15·00

73 Vonkou Rocks, Telimele

1966. Landscapes (1st series). Multicoloured.

534		20f. Type **73** (postage)	15	10
535		25f. Artificial lake, Coyah	30	10
536		40f. Waterfalls, Kate	35	15
537		50f. Bridge, Forecariah	55	25
538		75f. Liana bridge	95	45
539		100f. Lighthouse and bay, Boulbinet (air)	85	1·20

See also Nos. 603/608.

74 UNESCO Emblem

1966. 20th Anniv of UNESCO (a) Postage.

540	**74**	25f. multicoloured	70	25

(b) Air. Nos. 509/10 optd **vingt ans 1946 1966** and UNESCO Emblem.

541		200f. multicoloured	2·40	1·50
542		500f. multicoloured	5·75	3·00

76

1966. Guinean Flora and Female Headdresses. Similar designs.

543	**76**	10c. multicoloured (postage)	10	10
544	-	20c. multicoloured	10	10
545	-	30c. multicoloured	10	10
546	-	40c. multicoloured	10	10
547	-	3f. multicoloured	10	10
548	-	4f. multicoloured	10	10
549	-	10f. multicoloured	30	10
550	-	25f. multicoloured	75	15
551	-	30f. multicoloured	95	30
552	-	50f. multicoloured	1·40	35
553	**76**	80f. multicoloured	1·80	60
554	-	200f. multicoloured (air)	4·00	1·30
555	-	300f. multicoloured	5·75	2·20

Nos. 551/555 are 29×42 mm.

1966. Landing of "Luna 9" on Moon. Sheet No. **MS**500 **LUNA 9 FEBRUARY 3 1966**. (a) Inscr English on each stamp.

MS556 145×215 mm. As No MS500 .... 9·00 | 9·00

(b) Inscr French on each stamp.

MS557 145×215 mm. As No MS500 .... 9·00 | 9·00

78 Decade and UNESCO Symbols

1966. Int Hydrological Decade.

558	**78**	5f. red and blue	10	10
559	**78**	25f. red and green	35	10
560	**78**	100f. red and purple	1·20	70

1966. Guinean National Ballet. Designs show various dances as T **70**.

561		60c. multicoloured	10	10
562		1f. multicoloured	10	10
563		1f.50 multicoloured	30	10
564		25f. multicoloured	50	25
565		50f. multicoloured	1·00	50
566		75f. multicoloured	1·70	75

SIZES—VERT: (26×36 mm): 60c., 1f., 1f.50, 50f. HORIZ: (36×29 mm): 25f., 75f.

79 "Village"

1966. 20th Anniv of UNICEF Multicoloured designs showing children's drawings.

567		2f. "Elephant"	10	10
568		3f. "Doll"	10	10
569		10f. "Girl"	10	10
570		20f. Type **79**	30	10
571		25f. "Footballer"	55	25
572		40f. "Still Life"	70	25
573		50f. "Bird in Tree"	85	25

80 Dispensing Medicine

1967. Inauguration of W.H.O. Headquarters, Geneva. Multicoloured.

574	**80**	30f. Type **80**	30	10
575		50f. Doctor examining child	45	25
576		75f. Nurse weighing baby	65	40
577		80f. W.H.O. Building and flag	95	55

81 Niamou Mask

1967. Guinean Masks. Multicoloured.

578		10c. Banda-di (Kanfarade Boke region)	10	10
579		30c. Niamou (N'zerekore region) (different)	10	10
580		50c. Type **81**	10	10
581		60c. Yinadjinkele (Kankan region)	10	10
582		1f. As 10c.	10	10
583		1f.50 As 30c.	10	10
584		5f. Type **81**	25	10
585		25f. As 60c.	30	10
586		30f. As 10c.	45	30
587		50f. As 30c.	85	25
588		75f. As Type **81**	1·40	50
589		100f. As 60c.	2·10	85

82 Research Institute

1967. Pastoria Research Institute. Multicoloured.

590		20c. Type **82** (postage)	10	10
591		30c. *Python regius* (snake)	10	10
592		50c. Extracting snake's venom	10	10
593		1f. *Python sebae*	10	10
594		2f. Attendants handling viper	10	10
595		5f. Gabon viper	15	10
596		20f. *Dendroaspis viridis*	45	10
597		30f. As 5f.	95	20
598		50f. As 1f.	1·80	25
599		75f. As 50c.	2·50	60
600		200f. As 20c. (air)	2·75	1·10
601		300f. As 2f.	5·75	1·80

MS602 105×125 mm. Nos. 596, 599/600 .... 7·00 | 6·25

Nos. 596/601 are 56×26 mm.

1967. Landscapes (2nd series). As T **73**. Multicoloured.

603		5f. Loos Islands (postage)	10	10
604		30f. Tinkisso waterfalls	30	10
605		70f. The "Elephant's Trunk", Kakoulima	65	20
606		80f. Seashore, Ratoma	95	35
607		100f. House of explorer Olivier de Sanderval (air)	1·30	55
608		200f. Aerial view of Conakry	2·00	95

83 People's Palace, Conakry

1967. 20th Anniv of Guinean Democratic Party and Inaug of People's Palace. Multicoloured.

609		5f. Type **83** (postage)	10	10
610		30f. African elephant's head	60	30
611		55f. Type **83**	60	35
612		200f. As 30f. (air)	1·90	1·00

1967. 50th Anniv of Lions Int Landscape series optd **AMITE DES PEUPLES GRACE AU TOURISME 1917 – 1967** and Lions Emblem.

613		5f. (No. 603) (postage)	35	10
614		30f. (No. 604)	45	35
615		40f. (No. 536)	60	30
616		50f. (No. 537)	95	50
617		70f. (No. 605)	1·30	55
618		75f. (No. 538)	2·10	60
619		80f. (No. 606)	2·50	80
620		100f. (No. 539) (air)	2·00	80
621		100f. (No. 607)	2·00	80
622		200f. (No. 608)	4·00	1·60

85 Section of Mural

86 W.H.O. Building, Brazzaville

1967. Air. "World of Tomorrow". Jose Vanetti's Mural, Conference Building, U.N. Headquarters.

623	-	30f. multicoloured	30	15
624	-	50f. multicoloured	55	25
625	85	100f. multicoloured	1·30	55
626	-	200f. multicoloured	2·75	90

MS627 126×85 mm. 50f.×2 100f. Inscr in English or French .... 5·75 | 5·75

DESIGNS: Various sections of mural. The 30, 50, 100f. are horiz designs. MS627 contains two different 50f. vert designs and 100f. similar to T **85**.

1967. Inaug of W.H.O. Building, Brazzaville.

628	86	30f. olive, ochre and blue	45	10
629	86	75f. red, ochre and blue	90	45

87 Human Rights Emblem

1968. Human Rights Year.

630	87	30f. red, green and ochre	50	15
631	87	40f. red, blue and violet	70	25

88 Coyah, Oubreka Region

1968. Regional Costumes and Habitations. Multicoloured.

632		20c. Type **88** (postage)	10	10
633		30c. Kankan Region	10	10
634		40c. Kankan, Upper Guinea	10	10
635		50c. Forest region	10	10
636		60c. Foulamory, Gaoual Region	10	10
637		5f. Cognagui, Koundara Region	10	10
638		15f. As 50c.	25	10
639		20f. As 20c.	40	10
640		30f. As 30c.	55	25
641		40f. Fouta-Djallon, Middle Guinea	95	35
642		100f. Labe, Middle Guinea	2·10	55
643		300f. Bassari, Koundara Region (air)	4·50	1·60

The 60c. to 300f. are larger (60×39 mm).

89 The Village Story-teller

1968. Paintings of African Legends (1st series). Multicoloured.

644		25f. Type **89** (postage)	20	10
645		30f. *The Moon and the Stars*	20	10
646		75f. *Leuk the Hare sells his Sister* (vert)	85	45
647		80f. *The Hunter and the Female Antelope*	95	55
648		100f. *Old Faya's Inheritance* (vert) (air)	1·40	75
649		200f. *Soumangourou Kante killed by Djegue*	2·75	90

MS650 106×141 mm. Nos. 646/9. Imperf .... 11·50 | 11·50

1968. Paintings of African Legends (2nd series). As T **89**. Multicoloured.

651		15f. *Little Demons of Mount Nimba* (postage)	10	10
652		30f. *Lan, the Baby Buffalo* (vert)	30	25
653		40f. *The Nianablas and the Crocodiles*	45	25
654		50f. *Leuk the Hare and the Drum* (vert)	65	25
655		70f. *Malissadio—the Young Girl and the Hippopotamus* (air)	95	25
656		300f. *Little Goune, Son of the Lion* (vert)	4·75	1·60

MS657 106×141 mm. Nos. 653/6. Imperf .... 7·00 | 7·00

90 Olive Baboon

1968. African Fauna. Multicoloured.
658	5f. Type **90** (postage)	30	10
659	10f. Leopards	30	10
660	15f. Hippopotami	45	15
661	20f. Crocodile	75	25
662	30f. Warthog	95	25
663	50f. Kob	1·30	45
664	75f. African buffalo	2·00	60
665	100f. Lions (air)	2·30	50
666	200f. African elephant	4·75	1·30
MS667	Three sheets each 120×100 mm. Nos. 658/60; 661/3 and 664/6 each with *se-tenant* stamp-size label	17·00	12·00

Nos. 665/6 are 50×35 mm.

91 Robert F. Kennedy

1968. "Martyrs of Liberty". Multicoloured.
668	30f. Type **91** (postage)	45	10
669	75f. Martin Luther King	1·00	40
670	100f. John F. Kennedy	1·60	70
671	50f. Type **91** (air)	90	35
672	100f. Martin Luther King	1·90	70
673	200f. John F. Kennedy	4·00	1·60

92 Running

1969. Olympic Games, Mexico (1968). Multicoloured.
674	5f. Type **92** (postage)	10	10
675	10f. Boxing	30	10
676	15f. Throwing the javelin	30	10
677	25f. Football	45	10
678	30f. Steeplechase	55	10
679	50f. Throwing the hammer	70	25
680	75f. Cycling	1·10	40
681	100f. Gymnastics (air)	1·20	45
682	200f. Exercising on rings	2·40	90
683	300f. Pole-vaulting	4·50	1·20

The 25, 100, 200 and 300f. are larger, 57×30 mm. Each design also shows one of three different sculptured figures.

1969. Moon Flight of "Apollo 8". Nos. 514/16 optd APOLLO 8 DEC. 1968 and earth and moon motifs or surch also.
684	30f. on 45f. mult (postage)	1·30	1·20
685	45f. multicoloured	1·30	1·20
686	25f. on 200f. mult (air)	55	45
687	100f. multicoloured	1·70	90
688	200f. multicoloured	3·50	1·40

95 "Tarzan"

1969. "Tarzan" (famous Guinea Chimpanzee). Multicoloured.
689	25f. Type **95**	40	15
690	30f. "Tarzan" in front of Pastoria Institute	50	25
691	75f. "Tarzan" and family	1·00	45
692	100f. "Tarzan" squatting on branch	1·90	65

96 Pioneers lighting Fire

1969. Guinean Pioneer Youth Organization. Multicoloured.
693	5f. Type **96**	10	10
694	25f. Pioneer and village	30	10
695	30f. Pioneers squad	45	10
696	40f. Playing basketball	50	25
697	45f. Two pioneers	70	25
698	50f. Pioneers emblem	90	40
MS699	120×135 mm. Nos. 693/8	3·75	3·00

97 "Apollo" Launch

1969. First Man on the Moon. Multicoloured.
700	25f. Type **97**	30	10
701	30f. View of Earth	30	10
702	50f. Modules descent to the Moon	45	10
703	60f. Astronauts on Moon	55	25
704	75f. Landing module on Moon	75	30
705	100f. Take-off from Moon	1·30	65
706	200f. "Splashdown"	2·75	1·20

No. 705 is 35×71 mm.
The above stamps were issued with English and French inscriptions.

98 Pylon and Heavy Industry

1969. 50th Anniv of I.L.O. Multicoloured.
707	25f. Type **98**	30	10
708	30f. Broadcasting studio	30	10
709	75f. Harvesting	75	25
710	200f. Making pottery	2·30	85

99 Child suffering from Smallpox

1970. Campaign Against Measles and Smallpox. Multicoloured.
711	25f. Type **99**	30	10
712	30f. Mother and child with measles	30	10
713	40f. Inoculating girl	40	25
714	50f. Inoculating boy	60	25
715	60f. Inoculating family	95	35
716	200f. Dr. Edward Jenner	2·75	1·20

100 O.E.R.S. Countries on Map of Africa

1970. Meeting of Senegal River Riparian States Organization (Organisation des Etats Riverains du Fleuve Senegal).
717	**100** 30f. multicoloured	25	25
718	**100** 200f. multicoloured	2·00	1·20

NOTE: The Riparian States are Guinea, Mali, Mauritania and Senegal.

101 Dish Aerial and Open book

1970. World Telecommunications Day.
719	**101** 5f. black and blue	30	10
720	**101** 10f. black and red	30	25
721	**101** 50f. black and yellow	55	25
722	**101** 200f. black and lilac	2·30	1·20

102 Lenin

1970. Birth Centenary of Lenin. Multicoloured.
723	5f. Type **102**	10	10
724	20f. *Lenin in the Smolny* (Serov)	35	10
725	30f. *Lenin addressing Workers* (Serov)	45	25
726	40f. *Lenin speaking to Servicemen* (Vasiliev)	55	30
727	100f. *Lenin with Crowd* (Vasilev)	1·70	65
728	200f. Type **102**	3·25	1·50

103 Congo Tetra

1971. Fish. Multicoloured.
729	5f. Type **103**	10	10
730	10f. Red-spotted gularis	30	10
731	15f. Red-chinned panchax	35	10
732	20f. Six-barred distichodus	40	10
733	25f. Jewel cichlid	50	20
734	30f. Rainbow krib	65	30
735	40f. Two-striped lyretail	90	35
736	45f. Banded jewelfish	1·10	40
737	50f. Red-tailed notho	1·40	50
738	75f. Freshwater butterflyfish	2·20	85
739	100f. Golden trevally	3·00	1·00
740	200f. African mouth-brooder	6·50	2·10

104 Violet-crested Turaco

1971. Wild Birds. Multicoloured.
741	5f. Type **104** (postage)	15	15
742	20f. Golden oriole	45	15
743	30f. Blue headed coucal	75	20
744	40f. Great grey shrike	1·00	40
745	75f. Vulturine guineafowl	2·50	90
746	100f. Southern ground hornbill	3·25	1·20
747	50f. Type **104** (air)	1·50	55
748	100f. As 20f.	3·00	1·10
749	200f. As 75f.	6·50	1·60

105 UNICEF Emblem on Map of Africa

1971. 25th Anniv of UNICEF.
750	**105** 25f. multicoloured	10	10
751	**105** 30f. multicoloured	30	10
752	**105** 50f. multicoloured	55	25
753	**105** 60f. multicoloured	75	25
754	**105** 100f. multicoloured	1·20	60

106 John and Robert Kennedy and Martin Luther King

1972. Air. Martyrs for Peace. Embossed on silver or gold foil.
755	**106** 300f. silver		
756	**106** 1500f. gold, cream and green		

107 Jules Verne and Moon Rocket

1972. Air. Moon Exploration. Embossed on silver or gold foil.
757	**107** 300f. silver
758	**107** 1200f. gold

108 Pres. Richard Nixon

1972. Air. Pres. Nixon's Visit to Peking. Embossed on gold or silver foil.
759	**108** 90f. silver
760	- 90f. silver
761	- 90f. silver
762	- 90f. silver
763	**108** 290f. gold
764	- 290f. gold
765	- 290f. gold
766	- 290f. gold
767	- 1200f. gold and red

DESIGNS—VERT: Nos. 760, 764, Chinese table-tennis player; 761, 765, American table-tennis player; 762, 766, Mao Tse-tung. HORIZ: (45×35 mm): No. 767, Pres. Nixon and Mao Tse-tung.

109 "Flying Flatfish"

1972. Imaginary Space Creatures. Multicoloured.
768	5f. Type **109**	10	10
769	20f. "Radioactive crab"	30	10
770	30f. "Space octopus"	45	10
771	40f. "Rocket-powered serpent"	60	20
772	100f. "Winged eel"	1·30	60
773	200f. "Flying dragon"	2·75	1·10

110 African Child

1972. Racial Equality Year. Multicoloured.
774	15f. Type **110** (postage)	10	10
775	20f. Asiatic child	30	10
776	30f. Indian youth	30	10
777	50f. European girl	75	25
778	100f. Heads of four races	1·20	50
779	100f. As No. 778 (air)	1·50	65

111 "Syncom" and African Map

1972. World Telecommunications Day. Multicoloured.

780	15f. Type **111** (postage)	10	10
781	30f. "Relay"	45	10
782	75f. "Early Bird"	95	25
783	80f. "Telstar"	1·00	40
784	100f. As 30f. (air)	1·50	50
785	200f. As 75f.	3·00	1·00

112 APU Emblem and Dove
with Letter

1972. Tenth Anniv of African Postal Union.

786	**112**	15f. mult (postage)	10	10
787	**112**	30f. multicoloured	30	25
788	**112**	75f. multicoloured	80	30
789	**112**	80f. multicoloured	95	50
790	-	100f. multicoloured (air)	1·20	50
791	-	200f. multicoloured	2·20	95

DESIGNS: 100f. to 200f. APU emblem and airmail envelope.

113 Child
reading Book

1972. International Book Year. Multicoloured.

792	5f. Type **113**	10	10
793	15f. Book with sails	10	10
794	40f. Girl with book and plant	45	10
795	50f. "Key of Knowledge" and open book	75	25
796	75f. "Man" reading book and globe	95	55
797	200f. Open book and laurel sprigs	2·30	95

114 Throwing the
Javelin

1972. Olympic Games, Munich. Multicoloured.

798	5f. Type **114** (postage)	10	10
799	10f. Pole-vaulting	10	10
800	25f. Hurdling	45	10
801	30f. Throwing the hammer	55	10
802	40f. Boxing	75	25
803	50f. Gymnastics (horse)	95	45
804	75f. Running	1·50	55
805	100f. Gymnastics (rings) (air)	2·20	65
806	200f. Cycling	3·75	1·40
MS807	111×75 mm. 300f. Football	6·75	5·75

1972. U.N. Environmental Conservation Conf, Stockholm. Nos. 750/4 optd **UNE SEULE TERRE** and emblem.

808	**105**	25f. multicoloured	45	10
809	**105**	30f. multicoloured	60	30
810	**105**	50f. multicoloured	1·10	40
811	**105**	60f. multicoloured	1·60	50
812	**105**	100f. multicoloured	2·10	95

116 Dimitrov
addressing "Reichstag
Fire" Court

1972. 90th Birth Anniv of George Dimitrov (Bulgarian statesman).

813	**116**	5f. blue, gold and green	10	10
814	-	25f. blue, gold and green	30	10
815	-	40f. blue, gold and green	55	25
816	-	100f. blue, gold and green	1·30	45

DESIGNS: 25f. In Moabit Prison, Berlin, 1933; 40f. Writing memoirs; 100f. G. Dimitrov.

117 Emperor Haile
Selassie

1972. Emperor Haile Selassie of Ethiopia's 80th Birthday. Multicoloured.

817	40f. Type **117**	60	35
818	200f. Emperor Haile Selassie in military uniform	3·00	1·40

118 "Syntomeida
epilais"

1973. Guinean Insects. Multicoloured.

819	5f. Type **118**	25	10
820	15f. *Hippodamia californica*	40	10
821	30f. *Tettigonia viridissima*	1·20	30
822	40f. *Apis mellifica*	1·50	45
823	50f. *Photinus pyralis*	2·00	45
824	200f. *Ancyluris formosissima*	6·25	1·70

119 Dr. Kwame
Nkrumah

1973. Tenth Anniv of Organization of African Unity.

825	**119**	1s.50 black, gold & green	30	10
826	-	2s.50 black, gold & green	45	25
827	-	5s. black, gold and green	75	25
828	-	10s. violet and gold	1·50	50

DESIGNS: Nos. 826/8, different portraits of Dr. Kwame Nkrumah similar to Type **119**.

120 Institute of Applied
Biology, Kindia

1973. 25th Anniv of W.H.O. Multicoloured.

829	1s. Type **120**	10	10
830	2s.50 Preparing vaccine from an egg	40	25
831	3s. Filling ampoules with vaccine	45	25
832	4s. Sterilization of vaccine	55	25
833	5s. Packing vaccines	95	40
834	10s. Preparation of vaccine base	1·50	55
835	20s. Inoculating patient	3·50	1·10

Nos. 833/35 are 48×31 mm.

121 Volcanic Landscape

1973. 500th Birth Anniv of Copernicus. Multicoloured.

836	50c. Type **121**	10	10
837	2s. Sun over desert	30	10
838	4s. Earth and Moon	45	10
839	5s. Lunar landscape	95	25
840	10s. Jupiter	1·60	55
841	20s. Saturn	3·00	85
MS842	133×133 mm. 20s.×4 Copernicus (44×44 mm)	20·00	16·00

122 Loading Bauxite at
Quayside

1974. Air. Bauxite Industry, Bok. Multicoloured.

843	4s. Type **122**	60	10
844	6s. Bauxite train	1·60	50
845	10s. Bauxite mining	2·50	50

123 *Clappertonia
ficifolia*

1974. Flowers of Guinea. Multicoloured.

846	50c. Type **123** (postage)	10	10
847	1s. *Rothmannia longiflora*	·10	10
848	2s. *Oncoba spinosa*	30	10
849	3s. *Venidium fastuosum*	45	10
850	4s. *Bombax costatum*	55	25
851	5s. *Clerodendrum splendens*	1·20	25
852	7s.50 *Combretuni grandiflorum*	1·50	40
853	10s. *Mussaendra erythrophylla*	1·80	55
854	12s. *Argemone mexicana*	2·30	80
855	20s. *Thunbergia alata* (air)	4·00	1·30
856	25s. *Diascia barberae*	4·50	1·60
857	50s. *Kigelia africana*	10·00	2·20

SIZES—VERT: Nos. 847/9, As Type **123**; 850/3, 36×47 mm.
DIAMOND: Nos. 854/7, 61×61 mm.
No. 855 is wrongly inscr "Thunbegia alata".

124 Drummers and Pigeon

1974. Centenary of U.P.U. Multicoloured.

858	5s. Type **124**	40	25
859	6s. Runner and pigeon	95	35
860	7s.50 Monorail train, lorry and pigeon	1·20	50
861	10s. Boeing 707, "United States" (liner) and pigeon	1·50	70
MS862	Two sheets (a) 71×60 mm. 10s. Balloon, canoe and pigeon; (b) 113×95 mm. 20s.×4 Space satellites	17·00	17·00

125 Pioneers
testing Rope-bridge

1974. National Pioneers (Scouting) Movement. Multicoloured.

863	50c. Type **125**	10	10
864	2s. "On safari"	30	10
865	4s. Using field-telephone	45	20
866	5s. Cooking on camp-fire	75	30
867	7s.50 Saluting	1·00	35
868	10s. Playing basketball	1·80	75
MS869	78×60 mm. Nos. 867/8	3·75	4·00

126 Limes

1974. Fruits. Sheet 128×113 mm containing T **126** and similar vert designs. Multicoloured.

MS870	(a) 4s. Type **126**; (b) 4s. Oranges; (c) 5s. Bananas; (d) 5s. Mangoes; (e) 12s. Pineapple	6·50	6·50

127 Chimpanzee

1975. Wild Animals. Multicoloured.

871	1s. Type **127**	30	10
872	2s. Impala	45	25
873	3s. Warthog	55	25
874	4s. Waterbuck	65	30
875	5s. Leopard	95	40
876	6s. Greater kudu	1·10	45
877	6s.50 Common zebra	1·20	55
878	7s.50 African buffalo	1·70	70
879	8s. Hippopotamus	2·40	90
880	10s. Lion	2·75	1·10
881	12s. Black rhinoceros	3·25	1·10
882	25s. African elephant	4·50	1·60
MS883	Three sheets each 96×96 mm. (a) Nos. 871/4; (b) 875/8; (c) Nos. 879/82 (air). Perf or imperf	37·00	18·00

128 Lion and Lioness
beside Pipeline

1975. Tenth Anniv of African Development Bank.

884	5s. Type **128**	95	25
885	7s. African elephants beside pipeline	1·20	25
886	10s. Lions beside pipeline (horiz)	1·70	45
887	20s. African elephant and calf beside pipeline (horiz)	3·50	85

129 Women playing
Saxophones

1976. Int Women's Year (1975). Multicoloured.

888	5s. Type **129**	55	25
889	7s. Women playing guitars	95	30
890	9s. Woman railway shunter	1·50	40
891	15s. Woman doctor	2·20	75
892	20s. Genetics emblems	2·75	1·10
MS893	Two sheets. (a) 70×82 mm. No. 891; (b) 90×125 mm. No. 892×4	16·00	10·50

130 Gymnastics

1976. Olympic Games, Montreal. Multicoloured.

894	3s. Type **130**	45	10
895	4s. Long jump	55	25
896	5s. Throwing the hammer	55	25
897	6s. Throwing the discus	75	25
898	6s.50 Hurdling	80	25
899	7s. Throwing the javelin	95	40
900	8s. Running	1·00	40
901	8s.50 Cycling	1·50	40
902	10s. High-jumping	1·60	55
903	1s. Putting the shot	2·40	85
904	20s. Pole vaulting	3·25	1·10
905	25s. Football	4·00	1·30
MS906	Two sheets. (a) 82×62 mm. 25s. Swimming; (b) 82×112 mm. No. 905×4	22·00	16·00

131 Bell and Early Telephone

1976. Telephone Centenary. Multicoloured.
907	5s. Type **131**	75	15
908	7s. Bell and wall telephone	1·00	25
909	12s. Bell and satellite "Syncom"	1·70	55
910	15s. Bell and satellite "Telstar"	2·50	80

MS911 Two sheets. (a) 70×58 mm. 15s. Bell and telephonist; (b) 110×93 mm. Nos. 907/10 ... 10·00 5·25

132 Collybia fusipes

1977. Mushrooms. Multicoloured.
912	5s. Type **132** (postage)	1·70	35
913	7s. Lycoperdon perlatum	2·50	40
914	9s. Boletus edulis	3·25	65
915	9s.50 Lactarius deliciosus	3·50	80
916	11s.50 Agaricus campestris	5·00	1·40
917	10s. Morchella esculenta (air)	3·50	90
918	12s. Lepiota procera	4·75	1·20
919	15s. Cantharellus cibarius	6·75	1·70

MS920 115×86 mm. Nos. 912 and 914 ... 7·25 3·75

133 Duplex Murex

1977. Sea Shells. Multicoloured.
921	1s. Type **133**	20	10
922	2s. Wavy-leaved turrid	45	20
923	4s. Queen marginella	1·00	40
924	5s. Tympanotonos radula	1·30	45
925	7s. Striped marginella	1·80	50
926	8s. Doris harp	2·10	60
927	10s. Obtuse demoulia	2·75	80
928	20s. Pitted frog shell	5·00	90
929	25s. Adanson's marginella	6·25	1·50

Nos. 927/9 are 50×34 mm.

134 President Sekou Toure

1977. 30th Anniv of Guinean Democratic Party (PDG). Multicoloured.
930	5s. Type **134**	75	25
931	10s. Labourers and oxen	1·20	55
932	20s. Soldier driving tractor	3·00	90
933	25s. Pres. Toure addressing U.N. General Assembly	3·50	1·60
934	30s. Pres. Toure (vert)	4·50	1·80
935	40s. As 30s.	5·50	2·20

MS936 Two sheets. (a) 121×97 mm. Nos. 930/933; (b) 96×76 mm. Nos. 934/935 ... 23·00 21·00

135 Varanus niloticus

1977. Reptiles. Multicoloured.
937	3s. Type **135** (postage)	45	15
938	4s. Hyperolius quinquevittatus	55	20
939	5s. Uromastix	70	25
940	6s. Scincus scincus	1·10	45
941	6s.50 Agama agama	1·40	50
942	7s. Naja melanoleuca	1·90	60
943	8s.50 Python regius	2·30	80
944	20s. Bufo mauritanicus	5·75	1·10
945	10s. Chamaeleo diepis (air)	3·25	60
946	15s. Crocodylus niloticus	4·75	80
947	25s. Testudo elegans	6·75	1·30

136 Eland (male)

1977. Endangered Animals. Multicoloured.
948	1s. Type **136** (postage)	30	10
949	1s. Eland (female)	30	10
950	1s. Eland (young)	30	10
951	2s. Chimpanzee (young)	45	10
952	2s. Chimpanzee	45	10
953	2s. Chimpanzee sitting	45	10
954	2s.50 African elephant	70	25
955	2s.50 African elephant	70	25
956	2s.50 African elephant	70	25
957	3s. Lion	95	25
958	3s. Lioness	95	25
959	3s. Lion Cub	95	25
960	4s. Indian palm squirrel	1·30	25
961	4s. Indian palm squirrel	1·30	25
962	4s. Indian palm squirrel	1·30	25
963	5s. Hippopotamus	1·80	30
964	5s. Hippopotamus	1·80	30
965	5s. Hippopotamus	1·90	30
966	5s. Type **136** (air)	1·30	30
967	5s. As No. 949	1·30	30
968	5s. As No. 950	1·30	30
969	8s. As No. 954	1·90	35
970	8s. As No. 955	1·90	35
971	8s. As No. 956	2·00	35
972	9s. As No. 963	2·20	50
973	9s. As No. 964	2·20	50
974	9s. As No. 965	2·20	50
975	10s. As No. 951	2·50	55
976	10s. As No. 952	2·50	55
977	10s. As No. 953	2·50	55
978	12s. As No. 960	2·75	70
979	12s. As No. 961	2·75	70
980	12s. As No. 962	2·75	70
981	13s. As No. 957	3·25	90
982	13s. As No. 958	3·25	95
983	13s. As No. 959	3·25	95

Issued se-tenant in strips of three within the sheet, each strip showing different views of the same animal.

137 Lenin taking Parade in Red Square, Moscow

1976. 60th Anniv of Russian Revolution. Multicoloured.
984	2s.50 Lenin's first speech in Moscow (postage)	45	10
985	5s. Lenin addressing revolutionary crowd	95	25
986	7s.50 Lenin with militiamen	1·50	30
987	8s. Type **137**	1·80	35
988	10s. Russian ballet (air)	3·00	60
989	30s. Pushkin Monument	6·75	1·30

138 Pres. Giscard d'Estaing at Microphones

1979. Visit of President Giscard d'Estaing of France.
990	**138**	3s. brown and light brown (postage)	50	15
991	–	5s. brown, green and deep green	1·00	20
992	–	6s.50 brown, mauve and deep mauve	1·50	25
993	–	7s. brown, light blue and blue	1·80	30
994	–	8s.50 brown, rose & red	2·50	55
995	–	10s. brown, light violet and violet	3·00	90
996	–	20s. brown, green and deep green	5·75	1·20
997	–	25s. multicoloured (air)	7·25	1·70

DESIGNS—HORIZ: 5s. President Giscard d'Estaing and Sekou Toure in conference; 6s.50, Presidents signing agreement; 7s. Presidents at official meeting; 8s.50, Presidents with their wives; 10s. Presidents in conference; 20s. Toasting the agreement. VERT: 25s. President Giscard d'Estaing.

139 20,000 Leagues Under the Sea

1979. 150th Birth Anniv (1978) of Jules Verne. Multicoloured.
998	1s. Type **139** (postage)	10	10
999	3s. The Children of Captain Grant	45	10
1000	5s. The Mysterious Island	95	30
1001	7s. A Captain of Fifteen Years	1·50	55
1002	10s. The Amazing Adventure of Barsac	2·00	80
1003	20s. Five Weeks in a Balloon (air)	3·00	55
1004	25s. Robur the Conqueror	4·50	80

140 William Henson's Aerial Steam Carriage, 1842

1979. Aviation History. Multicoloured.
1005	3s. Type **140**	45	10
1006	5s. Wright Type A (inscr "Flyer I"), 1903	75	25
1007	6s.50 Caudron C-46O, 1934	95	25
1008	7s. Charles Lindbergh's Spirit of St. Louis, 1927	1·30	25
1009	8s.50 Bristol Beaufighter, 1940	1·70	40
1010	10s. Bleriot XI, 1909	2·10	40
1011	20s. Boeing 727-100, 1963	3·75	80
1012	20s. Concorde	3·75	80

141 Hafla Football Team

1979. Hafla Football Club's Victories. Multicoloured.
1013	1s. Type **141**	10	10
1014	2s. Team members with cup (vert)	30	10
1015	5s. President Toure presenting medals	75	10
1016	7s. President Toure presenting cup (vert)	1·20	40
1017	8s. Ahmed Sekou Toure Cup (vert)	1·60	40
1018	10s. Team captains shaking hands (vert)	1·70	65
1019	20s. The winning goal	3·50	1·20

142 Children dancing round Tree

1980. International Year of the Child. Multicoloured.
1020	2s. Type **142**	30	10
1021	4s. "Heureuse Enfance"	55	10
1022	5s. Steam train (horiz)	95	30
1023	7s. Village (horiz)	1·10	25
1024	10s. Boy climbing tree (horiz)	1·70	40
1025	25s. Children of different races (horiz)	4·25	1·00

143 Buckler Dory

1980. Fish. Multicoloured.
1026	1s. Robust butterflyfish (horiz)	10	10
1027	2s. Blue-pointed porgy (horiz)	30	10
1028	3s. Type **143**	55	10
1029	4s. African hind (horiz)	75	25
1030	5s. Spotted seahorse	95	30
1031	6s. Marine hatchetfish (horiz)	1·20	25
1032	7s. Half-banded snake-eel (horiz)	1·50	25
1033	8s. Flying gurnard	1·70	25
1034	9s. West African squirrel-fish (horiz)	2·00	25
1035	10s. Guinean fingerfish	2·50	25
1036	12s. African sergeant major (horiz)	3·50	60
1037	15s. West African trigger-fish (horiz)	5·00	85

144 Rocket on Launch Pad

1980. Tenth Anniv of 1st Moon Landing. Multicoloured.
1038	1s. Type **144**	10	10
1039	2s. Earth from the Moon	30	10
1040	4s. Armstrong descending from lunar module	45	10
1041	5s. Armstrong on the Moon	75	25
1042	7s. Astronaut collecting samples	95	25
1043	8s. Parachute descent	1·50	40
1044	12s. Winching capsule aboard recovery vessel	2·40	60
1045	20s. Astronauts	4·50	85

145 Dome of the Rock

1981. Palestinian Solidarity.
1046	**145**	8s. multicoloured	1·40	55
1047	**145**	11s. multicoloured	2·50	95

146 Map of Member States and Agricultural Produce

1982. Fifth Anniv of Economic Community of West African States. Multicoloured.
1048	6s. Type **146**	1·20	40
1049	7s. Transport	1·50	55
1050	9s. Heavy industry	2·00	75

147 Ataturk as Soldier

1982. Birth Centenary of Kemal Ataturk (Turkish statesman). Multicoloured.
1051	7s. Type **147** (postage)	1·20	40
1052	10s. Ataturk as statesman	1·70	55
1053	25s. Equestrian statue (horiz)	5·00	1·20
1054	25s. As No. 1053 (air)	5·50	1·00

148 Football

1982. Olympic Games, Moscow. Multicoloured.

1055	1s. Type **148** (postage)	10	10
1056	2s. Basketball	30	10
1057	3s. Diving	45	10
1058	4s. Gymnastics	55	10
1059	5s. Boxing	95	25
1060	6s. High jumping	1·20	25
1061	7s. Running	1·30	40
1062	8s. Long jumping	2·00	60
1063	9s. Fencing (air)	1·70	25
1064	10s. Football (vert)	1·80	45
1065	11s. Basketball (vert)	2·00	60
1066	20s. Diving (vert)	4·25	75
1067	25s. Boxing (vert)	5·00	90

149 Balaidos Stadium, Vigo

1982. World Cup Football Championship, Spain. Football Stadia. Multicoloured.

1068	6s. Type **149** (postage)	95	10
1069	8s. El Molinon, Gijon	1·50	25
1070	9s. San Mames, Bilbao	2·00	50
1071	10s. Sanchez Pizjuan, Seville	2·20	65
1072	10s. Luis Casanova, Valencia (air)	2·75	80
1073	20s. Nou Camp, Barcelona	4·50	1·10
1074	25s. Santiago Bernabeu, Madrid	6·50	1·50

150 Wrestling

1983. Olympic Games, Los Angeles. Multicoloured.

1075	5s. Type **150** (postage)	1·10	30
1076	7s. Weightlifting	1·40	50
1077	10s. Gymnastics	2·10	75
1078	15s. Discus	3·00	1·10
1079	20s. Kayak (air)	4·00	1·10
1080	25s. Equestrian	5·25	1·40
MS1081	89×89 mm. 30s. Running	4·50	1·60

See also Nos. 843/9.

151 Marquis d'Arlandes, Pilatre de Rozier and Montgolfier Balloon, 1783

1983. Bicentenary of Manned Flight. Multicoloured.

1082	5s. Type **151** (postage)	75	25
1083	7s. Jean-Francois Pilatre de Rozier and Montgolfier balloon *Marie Antoinette*, 1784	1·00	40
1084	10s. Henri Dupuy de Lome and airship, 1872 (horiz)	1·50	55
1085	15s. Major A. Parseval and *Airship No. 1*, 1906 (horiz)	2·30	90
1086	20s. Count Zeppelin and airship *Bodensee*, 1919 (horiz) (air)	2·75	90
1087	25s. Balloon *Double Eagle II* and crew, 1978	3·50	1·30
MS1088	81×81 mm. 30s. Nadar and *Le Geant*, 1863, and Santos Dumont and his dirigible, 1919 (horiz 50×41 mm)	4·50	1·60

152 Lungs and Monkey

1983. Centenary of Discovery of Tubercle Bacillus. Multicoloured.

1089	6s. Type **152**	1·40	35
1090	10s. Cow	2·30	50
1091	11s. Robert Koch and microscope	2·40	65
1092	12s. Koch using microscope	2·50	80
1093	15s. Laboratory	3·50	1·00
1094	20s. Scientist with test tube and monkey	4·75	1·30
1095	25s. Doctor examining young boy	6·00	1·60

153 Disabled and Emblem

1983. International Year of Disabled Persons.

1096	**153**	10s. multicoloured	2·75	1·30
1097	**153**	20s. multicoloured	5·75	2·00

154 Mosque, Conakry

1983. 25th Anniv of Independence.

1098	**154**	1s. multicoloured (postage)	15	10
1099	**154**	2s. multicoloured	45	25
1100	**154**	5s. multicoloured	1·10	45
1101	**154**	10s. multicoloured	2·00	65
MS1102	86×109 mm **154** 25s. multicoloured (air)		4·00	1·70

155 Citizens with Scrolls

1983. Tenth Anniv of Mano River Union. Multicoloured.

1103	2s. Type **155** (postage)	35	10
1104	7s. Union emblem	95	40
1105	8s. Map and presidents of Guinea, Sierra Leone and Liberia	1·00	50
1106	10s. Signing the Declaration of Union	1·50	60
MS1107	83×72 mm. 20s. As No. 1106 (air)	3·00	1·70

156 Biathlon

1983. Winter Olympic Games, Sarajevo. Multicoloured.

1108	5s. Type **156** (postage)	75	25
1109	7s. Luge	95	40
1110	10s. Slalom	1·50	55
1111	15s. Speed skating	2·20	80
1112	20s. Ski jump (air)	2·50	75
1113	25s. Ice dancing	3·25	1·20
MS1114	90×90 mm. 30s. Ice Hockey	4·50	1·60

157 Raphael and *Virgin with the Blue Diadem*

1984. Anniversaries (1983). Multicoloured.

1115	5s. Type **157**	75	25
1116	7s. Rubens and *Holy Family*	95	40
1117	10s. Rembrandt and *Portrait of Saskia*	1·80	55
1118	15s. Goethe and scene from *The Young Werther*	2·00	80
1119	20s. Lord Baden-Powell and scout camp	2·75	75

1120	25s. P. P. Harris and speaker at Rotary meeting	3·00	1·20
MS1121	69×90 mm. 30s. John Kennedy and first moon landing	5·00	1·50

158 Abraham Lincoln

1984. Personalities. Multicoloured.

1122	5s. Type **158** (postage)	55	15
1123	7s. Jean-Henri Dunant (founder of Red Cross)	95	35
1124	10s. Gottlieb Daimler (automobile designer)	1·50	45
1125	15s. Louis Bleriot (pilot)	2·30	65
1126	20s. Paul P. Harris (founder of Rotary Club) (air)	2·75	80
1127	25s. Auguste Piccard (ocean explorer)	3·25	1·20
MS1128	100×70 mm. 30s. Anatoli Karpov (world chess champion)	5·25	1·60

159 *The Mystic Marriage of Sts. Catherine and Sebastian* (detail, Correggio)

1984. Paintings. Multicoloured.

1129	5s. Type **159** (postage)	60	15
1130	7s. *The Holy Family* (A. Durer)	1·00	35
1131	10s. *The Veiled Lady* (Raphael)	1·70	45
1132	15s. *Portrait of a Young Man* (A. Durer)	2·50	65
1133	20s. *Portrait of Soutine* (A. Modigliani) (air)	3·00	1·00
1134	25s. *The Esterhazy Madonna* (Raphael)	3·75	1·30
MS1135	77×100 mm. 30s. *Madonna dell Impannata* (Raphael)	5·50	1·60

160 Congo River Steamer and Canoe

1984. Transport. Multicoloured.

1136	5s. Type **160** (postage)	95	30
1137	7s. Airship *Graf Zeppelin*	1·10	40
1138	10s. Daimler car, 1886	2·30	60
1139	15s. Beyer-Garratt steam locomotive	2·50	85
1140	20s. Latecoere seaplane *Comte de la Vaulx* (air)	2·75	90
1141	25s. Savoia Marchetti S-73 airplane	3·25	1·30
MS1142	101×95 mm. 30s. "B" locomotive (46×37 mm)	5·50	1·80

161 W. Hoppe and D. Schauerhammer (bobsleigh)

1984. Winter Olympic Gold Medal Winners. Multicoloured.

1143	5s. Type **161** (postage)	55	25
1144	7s. T. L. Wassberg (cross-country skiing)	85	25
1145	10s. G. Boucher (speed skating)	1·40	55
1146	15s. K. Witt (ladies figure skating)	2·00	75
1147	20s. W. D. Johnson (downhill skiing) (air)	2·75	1·00
1148	25s. U.S.S.R. (ice hockey)	3·25	1·20
MS1149	97×82 mm. 30s. J. Weissflog (ski jumping)	5·00	1·60

162 T. Ruiz and C. Costie (Synchronized Swimming Duet)

1985. Olympic Games Gold Medal Winners. Multicoloured.

1150	5s. Type **162** (postage)	55	25
1151	7s. R. Klimke, H. Krug and U. Sauer, West Germany (team dressage)	85	25
1152	10s. McKee and Buchan, U.S.A. (sailing, "Flying Dutchman" class)	1·40	55
1153	15s. Mark Todd (equestrian three-day event)	2·00	75
1154	20s. Daley Thompson (decathlon) (air)	2·75	1·00
1155	25s. M. Smith, C. Homfeld, L. Burr and J. Fargis, U.S.A. (equestrian team jumping)	3·25	1·20
MS1156	78×78 mm. 30s. Carl Lewis (100, 200 metres, 4×100 metres relay and long jump)	5·75	1·60

163 *Rhodophyllus callidermus*

1985. Fungi. Multicoloured.

1157	5s. Type **163** (postage)	1·00	35
1158	7s. *Agaricus niger*	1·60	50
1159	10s. *Thermitomyces globulus*	2·20	80
1160	15s. *Amanita robusta*	3·00	1·10
1161	20s. *Lepiota subradicans* (air)	3·75	1·40
1162	25s. *Cantharellus rhodophylus*	4·75	1·90
MS1163	69×93 mm. 30s. *Phlebopus silvaticus*	5·25	1·90

164 Hermann Oberth and 2-Stage Conical Motor Rocket

1985. Space Achievements. Multicoloured.

1164	7s. Type **164** (postage)	75	25
1165	10s. "Lunik 1"	1·50	50
1166	15s. "Lunik 2" on Moon, 1959	2·00	65
1167	20s. "Lunik 3" photographing hidden face of Moon	2·75	85
1168	30s. Armstrong, Aldrin and Collins (first manned landing on Moon) (air)	4·25	1·10
1169	35s. Sally Ride (first American woman in space)	5·00	1·40
MS1170	76×94 mm. 50s. Recovering "Palapa V2" satellite	6·75	2·20

165 Maimonides in Jewish Quarter (850th birth anniv)

1985. Anniversaries and Events. Multicoloured.

1171	7s. Type **165** (postage)	85	25
1172	10s. Christopher Columbus departing from Palos, 1492	1·50	45
1173	15s. Frederic Bartholdi and Statue of Liberty (centenary)	2·00	60
1174	20s. Queen Mother with Duke of York and Princess Elizabeth (85th birthday)	2·75	85
1175	30s. Ulf Merbold and space shuttle "Columbia" (air)	4·00	1·00
1176	35s. Prince Charles and Lady Diana Spencer (Royal Wedding)	4·50	1·20
MS1177	95×80 mm. 50s. Prince and Princess of Wales with their children	5·75	2·30

166 Black-billed Cuckoo

1995. Birth Bicentenary of John J. Audubon (ornithologist). Multicoloured.
1178	7s. Type **166** (postage)	1·00	35
1179	10s. Carolina parakeet	1·60	50
1180	15s. American darter (vert)	2·10	75
1181	20s. Red-shouldered hawk	3·00	1·00
1182	30s. Eastern screech owl (air)	4·00	1·20
1183	35s. Brown thrasher (vert)	5·00	1·60
MS1184	64×83 mm. 50s. Mourning dove (wrongly inscr "Zenaidura")	7·50	2·30

167 Blue-point Siamese

1985. Cats and Dogs. Multicoloured.
1185	7s. Type **167** (postage)	95	30
1186	10s. Cocker spaniel	1·50	50
1187	15s. Poodles	2·30	70
1188	20s. Persian blue cat	3·00	85
1189	25s. European tortoiseshell cat	4·00	1·00
1190	30s. German shepherd dog (air)	4·25	1·20
1191	35s. Abyssinian cats	4·75	1·50
1192	50s. Boxer dog	5·50	1·80
MS1193	100×60 mm. 50s. Pyrenean mountain dog and Chartreux cat (49×28 mm)	7·25	2·20

168 Bebeto and Footballers

1985. World Cup Football Championship, Mexico (1986) (1st issue). Multicoloured.
1194	7s. Type **168** (postage)	85	30
1195	10s. Rinat Dassaev	1·50	50
1196	15s. Phil Neal	2·10	75
1197	20s. Jean Tigana	3·00	95
1198	30s. Fernando Chalana (air)	3·75	1·30
1199	35s. Michel Platini	4·75	1·60
MS1200	90×90 mm. 50s. Karl Heinz Rummenigge (49×29 mm)	6·75	2·10

See also Nos. 1268/**MS**1272.

1985. Air. Nos. 1126 and 1119/20 optd.
1201	20s. **80e ANNIVERSAIRE 1905 1985** (1126)	2·50	1·10
1202	20s. **Rassemblement Jambville-1985** (1119)	2·50	1·10
1203	25s. **80e ANNIVERSAIRE 1905 1985** (1120)	3·50	1·50

1985. Nos. 1157/62 surch.
1205	1s. on 5s. Type **163** (postage)	35	10
1206	2s. on 7s. Agaricus niger	75	25
1207	8s. on 10s. Thermitomyces globulus	2·10	50
1208	30s. on 15s. Amanita robusta	6·00	1·20
1209	35s. on 20s. Lepiota subradicans (air)	7·00	1·80
1210	40s. on 25s. Cantharellus rhodophyllus	8·25	2·50
MS1211	69×93 mm. 50s. on 30s. Phlebopus silvaticus	8·75	2·75

171 Class 8 F Locomotive

1985. Trains (1st series). Multicoloured.
1212	7s. Type **171** (postage)	1·10	40
1213	15s. Class III electric locomotive, Germany	2·30	80
1214	25s. Pacific steam locomotive No. 270	3·50	1·20
1215	35s. German electric commuter train Series 420 (air)	5·00	1·80
MS1216	99×88 mm. 50s. "ICE", German high speed train	7·25	2·50

Nos. 1213 and 1215/**MS**1216 commemorate 150th anniv of German railways. See also Nos. 1252/5.

172 Columbus and Pinta

1985. 480th Death Anniv of Christopher Columbus (explorer) (1st issue). Multicoloured.
1217	10s. Type **172** (postage)	1·50	50
1218	20s. Santa Maria	3·00	1·00
1219	30s. Nina (air)	4·00	1·30
1220	40s. Santa Maria and crow's nest	5·75	1·80
MS1221	99×88 mm. 50s. Columbus and Nina	7·25	2·40

See also Nos. 1257**MS**1261.

173 Chopin, aged Eight, playing Piano

1986. International Youth Year. Multicoloured.
1222	10s. Type **173** (postage)	1·50	45
1223	20s. Sandro Botticelli and Birth of Venus	3·00	95
1224	35s. Gioachino Antonio Rossini, aged 15, conducting orchestra	4·50	1·50
1225	25s. Pablo Picasso and Paul as Harlequin (air)	3·75	1·30
MS1226	100×75 mm. 50s. Michelangelo and Doni Tondo (horiz)	7·25	2·40

174 Bayeux Tapestry

1986. Appearance of Halley's Comet. Multicoloured.
1227	5f. Type **174** (postage)	10	10
1228	30f. Comet as seen by the Arabs	30	10
1229	40f. Comet as seen by Montezuma I	45	25
1230	50f. Edmond Halley and trajectory diagram	55	25
1231	300f. Halley and Sir Isaac Newton (air)	2·75	85
1232	500f. Comet, Earth, sun, "Giotto", Soviet and N.A.S.A. space probes	4·50	1·50
MS1233	95×65 mm. 600f. Medal (wrongly inscr Sir Edmund), comet and "Giotto" space probe	6·25	2·10

175 "Challenger" Space Shuttle Memorial Roll

1986. Air. "Challenger" Astronauts Commem. Multicoloured.
1234	100f. Type **175**	1·00	50
1235	170f. Shuttle diagram and Christa McAuliffe holding model	1·70	75
MS1236	65×95 mm. 600f. Shuttle lifting off	6·25	2·10

1986. Various stamps surch. (a) Nos. 1212/15 (Trains).
1237	2f. on 7s. multicoloured	25	10
1238	25f. on 15s. multicoloured	45	20
1239	50f. on 25s. multicoloured	80	30
1240	90f. on 35s. multicoloured	1·40	55
MS1241	99×88 mm. 500f. on 50s. multicoloured	5·25	2·40

(b) Nos. 1217/20 (Columbus).
1242	5f. on 10s. multicoloured	20	20
1243	35f. on 20s. multicoloured	65	45
1244	70f. on 30s. multicoloured	95	30
1245	200f. on 40s. multicoloured	2·40	85
MS1246	99×88 mm. 500f. on 50s. multicoloured	6·00	2·40

(c) Nos. 1222/5 (International Youth Year).
1247	5f. on 10s. mult (postage)	30	10
1248	35f. on 20s. multicoloured	50	25
1249	90f. on 35s. multicoloured	1·30	45
1250	50f. on 25s. mult (air)	60	25
MS1251	100×75 mm. 500f. on 50s. multicoloured	6·00	2·75

177 Dietrich Autorail Diesel Railcar

1986. Trains (2nd series). Multicoloured.
1252	20f. Type **177** (postage)	30	10
1253	100f. Class T.13 steam locomotive No. 7906, Prussia	1·00	25
1254	300f. German steam locomotive No. 01220	2·75	90
1255	400f. Autorail ABH-3 type 5020 diesel train (air)	4·00	1·30
MS1256	87×67 mm. 600f. Renault Autorail ABH 3 and Adler	6·25	1·80

Nos. 1253/4 and **MS**1256 were inscr for the 150th Anniv of German railways.

178 Building Fort Navidad and Map of First Voyage, 1492–93

1986. 480th Death Anniv of Christopher Columbus (explorer) (2nd issue). Multicoloured.
1257	40f. Type **178** (postage)	45	15
1258	70f. Disembarking at Hispaniola and map of second voyage, 1493–96	75	35
1259	200f. Columbus on deck with natives and map of third voyage, 1498–1500	2·00	65
1260	500f. Columbus and crew with natives and map of fourth voyage, 1502–04 (air)	5·50	1·60
MS1261	87×67 mm. 600f. Columbus before King Ferdinand of Spain	6·25	1·80

179 Prince and Princess of Wales and Prince William

1986. Celebrities. Multicoloured.
1262	30f. Type **179** (postage)	35	10
1263	40f. Alain Prost (1985 Formula I world champion)	75	10
1264	100f. Duke and Duchess of York	1·10	40
1265	300f. Elvis Presley (entertainer)	3·50	1·00
1266	500f. Michael Jackson (entertainer) (air)	5·75	1·80
MS1267	109×79 mm. 600f. Marcel Dassault (aircraft engineer) and airplane (47×35 mm)	7·50	2·75

180 Pfaff, Trophy and Satellite

1986. World Cup Football Championship, Mexico (2nd issue). Multicoloured.
1268	100f. Type **180** (postage)	95	25
1269	300f. Michel Platini	2·75	80
1270	400f. Matthaus	3·50	1·20
1271	500f. Diego Maradona (air)	4·50	1·30
MS1272	103×88 mm. 600f. Maradona holding trophy (50×41 mm)	6·25	1·80

181 Judo

1987. Olympic Games, Seoul (1988). Multicoloured.
1273	20f. Type **181** (postage)	30	10
1274	30f. High jumping	30	10
1275	40f. Handball	45	25
1276	100f. Gymnastics	95	30

1277	300f. Javelin throwing (air)	2·75	80
1278	500f. Showjumping	4·75	1·40
MS1279	71×99 mm. 600f. Satellite, stadium and Pierre de Coubertin (founder of modern Olympic Games)	6·25	1·80

182 Rifle shooting

1987. Winter Olympic Games, Calgary (1988) (1st issue). Multicoloured.
1280	50f. on 40f. Type **182** (postage)	45	10
1281	100f. Cross-country skiing	95	25
1282	400f. Ski jumping (air)	4·00	95
1283	500f. Two-man bobsleigh	4·50	1·20
MS1284	116×81 mm. 600f. Women's figure skating and satellite	6·25	1·80

183 Skiing

1987. Winter Olympic Games, Calgary (1988) (2nd issue). Multicoloured.
1285	25f. Type **183** (postage)	30	10
1286	50f. Ice hockey	45	25
1287	100f. Men's figure skating	95	30
1288	150f. Slalom	1·40	40
1289	300f. Speed skating (air)	2·50	75
1290	500f. Four-man bobsleigh	4·50	1·40
MS1291	79×68 mm. 600f. Ski-jumping	6·25	1·80

184 S. K. Doe, Gen. Lansana Conte, Gen. J. Momoh and National Flags

1987. Tenth Anniv of River Mano Reconciliation.
1292	**184** 40f. multicoloured	40	15
1293	**184** 50f. multicoloured	50	20
1294	**184** 75f. multicoloured	75	30
1295	**184** 100f. multicoloured	1·00	40
1296	**184** 150f. multicoloured	1·50	55

185 Dimetrodon

1987. Prehistoric Animals. Multicoloured.
1297	50f. Type **185** (postage)	80	20
1298	100f. Iguanodon	1·70	50
1299	200f. Tylosaurus	3·25	85
1300	300f. Cave bear	4·50	1·30
1301	400f. Sabre-tooth tiger (air)	5·00	1·00
1302	500f. Stegosaurus	6·00	1·20
MS1303	124×78 mm. 600f. Triceratops	7·25	2·10

186 Statue and Portrait of Marquis de Lafayette (revolutionary)

1987. Celebrities. Multicoloured.
1304	50f. Type **186** (230th birth anniv) (postage)	45	10
1305	100f. Ettore Bugatti (motor manufacturer) (40th death anniv) and "White Elephant"	95	50

1306 200f. Gary Kasparov (world chess champion) and game diagram of Kasparov v. Karpov, 1986 — 2·00 60
1307 300f. Flag and George Washington (first U.S. President) (bicentenary of American constitution) — 2·75 90
1308 400f. Boris Becker (tennis player) (air) — 3·50 95
1309 500f. Winston Churchill (statesman) — 4·50 1·20

187 Towers, Chicago, Capitol, Washington and Statue of Liberty, New York (image scaled to 55% of original size)

1987. Air. International Cardiology congress, Chicago, Washington. and New York. Sheet 136×92 mm.
MS1310 187 1500f. multicoloured — 14·00 3·75

188 Tennis Player and Emblem

1987. Olympic Games, Seoul (1988). Tennis.
1311 188 50f. mult (postage) — 45 10
1312 - 100f. multicoloured — 95 30
1313 - 150f. multicoloured — 1·40 45
1314 - 200f. multicoloured — 1·80 55
1315 - 300f. multicoloured (air) — 2·75 85
1316 - 500f. multicoloured — 4·75 1·30
MS1317 95×70 mm. 600f. multicoloured (35×41 mm) — 6·25 1·80
DESIGNS: 100f. to 600f. Various tennis players.

189 Discus thrower and Courtyard of Hospital of the Holy Cross and St. Paul

1987. Olympic Games, Barcelona (1992). Multicoloured.
1318 50f. Type 189 (postage) — 45 10
1319 100f. Statue of Pablo Casals (cellist) and pole vaulter — 95 30
1320 150f. Long jumper and Labyrinth of Horta — 1·40 45
1321 170f. Lizard in Guell Park and javelin thrower — 1·80 55
1322 400f. Gymnast and Church of Mercy (air) — 3·75 1·00
1323 500f. Tennis player and Picasso Museum — 4·75 1·50
MS1324 105×82 mm. 600f. Runner and Miro tapestry (41×50 mm) — 6·25 1·80

190 African Wild Dogs

1987. Endangered Wildlife. Multicoloured.
1325 50f. Type 190 (postage) — 1·20 30
1326 70f. African wild dog — 1·40 45
1327 100f. African wild dogs stalking prey — 1·80 60
1328 170f. African wild dog chasing prey — 2·40 90
1329 400f. South African crowned cranes (air) — 4·50 1·10
1330 500f. Giant eland — 5·50 1·40
MS1331 83×72 mm. 600f. Savanna monkeys (41×35 mm) — 7·25 2·10

191 "Galaxy"–"Grasp"

1988. Space Exploration. Multicoloured.
1332 50f. Type 191 (postage) — 45 10
1333 150f. "Energia"–"Mir" link-up — 1·50 25
1334 200f. NASA space station — 2·00 40
1335 300f. "Ariane-5" rocket depositing satellite payload — 3·00 75
1336 400f. Mars "Rover" space vehicle (air) — 3·75 95
1337 450f. Venus "Vega" space probe — 4·25 1·20
MS1338 108×81 mm. 500f. Mars "Phobos" space probe (41×35 mm) — 5·00 1·80

192 Red-headed Bluebill

1988. Scouts, Birds and Butterflies. Designs showing scouts studying featured animals. Multicoloured.
1339 50f. Type 192 (postage) — 50 10
1340 100f. *Medon nymphalidae* (butterfly) — 1·00 35
1341 150f. Red bishop — 1·50 50
1342 300f. Beautiful sunbird — 3·00 80
1343 400f. *Sophia nymphalidae* (butterfly) (air) — 4·25 1·10
1344 450f. *Rumia nymphalidae* (butterfly) — 4·75 1·40
MS1345 116×88 mm. 750f. *Opus nymphalidae* (butterfly) and rose-ringed parakeet — 7·25 2·30

193 Queen Elizabeth II and Prince Philip

1988. Celebrities. Multicoloured.
1346 200f. Type 193 (40th wedding anniv (1987)) (postage) — 1·80 45
1347 250f. Fritz von Opel (car designer) and "Rak 2 Opel", 1928 — 2·30 55
1348 300f. Wolfgang Amadeus Mozart (composer) — 3·75 80
1349 400f. Steffi Graf (tennis player) — 3·75 90
1350 450f. Edwin "Buzz" Aldrin (astronaut) (air) — 4·00 1·00
1351 500f. Paul Harris (founder of Rotary International) — 4·75 1·20
MS1352 101×77 mm. 750f. Thomas Jefferson (US President) (41×35 mm) — 6·75 2·00

194 Vreni Schneider (Women's Slalom and Giant Slalom)

1988. Calgary Winter Olympic Games Gold Medal Winners. Multicoloured.
1353 50f. Type 194 (postage) — 45 10
1354 150f. Matti Nykaenen (Ski jumping) — 1·40 45
1355 250f. Marina Kiehl (Women's downhill) — 2·30 60
1356 400f. Frank Piccard (Men's super giant slalom) — 3·50 90
1357 100f. Frank-Peter Roetsch (Biathlon) (air) — 95 40
1358 450f. Katarina Witt (Women's figure skating) — 4·00 1·20
MS1359 90×66 mm. 750f. Pirmin Zurbriggen (Men's downhill) — 7·25 2·00

195 Scientist using Microscope

1988. World Health Day. Multicoloured.
1360 50f. Type 195 — 45 10
1361 150f. Nurse vaccinating boy — 1·50 40
1362 500f. Dental check — 4·50 1·30

196 Baron Pierre de Coubertin (founder of modern Olympics)

1988. International Olympic Committee.
1363 196 50f. multicoloured — 45 10
1364 196 100f. multicoloured — 95 25
1365 196 150f. multicoloured — 1·50 45
1366 196 500f. multicoloured — 4·50 1·40

197 Hands exchanging Letter

1988. 25th Anniv of Pan-African Postal Union.
1367 197 50f. multicoloured — 45 10
1368 197 75f. multicoloured — 75 25
1369 197 100f. multicoloured — 95 30
1370 197 150f. multicoloured — 1·40 45

198 Earth Communications Station

1988. Inauguration of MT 20 International Transmission Centre.
1371 198 50f. multicoloured — 45 10
1372 198 100f. multicoloured — 95 30
1373 198 150f. multicoloured — 1·30 50

199 "Helix Nebular"

1989. Appearance of Halley's Comet. Nebulae. Multicoloured.
1374 100f.+25f. Type 199 (postage) — 1·00 25
1375 150f.+25f. Orion — 1·50 40
1376 200f.+25f. "The Eagle" — 2·00 60
1377 250f.+25f. "Triffid" — 2·30 80
1378 300f.+25f. Eta-Carinae (air) — 2·75 80
1379 500f.+25f. NGC 2264 — 5·25 1·20
MS1380 124×99 mm. 750f.+50f. "Horse's Head" and Edmond Halley (astronomer) — 7·50 2·00

200 Diving

1989. Olympic Games, Barcelona (1992) (1st issue). Multicoloured.
1381 50f. Type 200 (postage) — 55 10
1382 100f. Running (vert) — 1·10 25
1383 150f. Shooting — 1·70 40
1384 250f. Tennis (vert) — 2·75 60
1385 400f. Football (air) — 4·50 1·10
1386 500f. Equestrian (dressage) (vert) — 5·50 1·30
MS1387 84×99 mm. 750f. Yachting (vert) — 7·25 2·00

201 Oath of the Tennis Court and Jean Sylvain Bailly (President of National Assembly)

1989. "Philexfrance 89" Stamp Exhibition and Bicentenary of French Revolution. Multicoloured.
1388 250f. Type 201 (postage) — 2·40 65
1389 300f. King addressing the Three Estates and Comte de Mirabeau — 3·00 1·00
1390 400f. 18th July 1790 celebrations and Marquis de La Fayette — 4·00 1·30
1391 450f. The King's arrest at Varennes and Jerome Petion (first President of the Convention) (air) — 4·75 1·40
MS1392 140×103 mm. 750f. Storming of the Bastille and Camille Desmoulins — 7·50 2·30

202 Girl carrying Plants

1989. Tenth Anniv (1987) of International Fund for Agricultural Development. Campaign for Self-sufficiency. Multicoloured.
1393 25f. Type 202 — 30 10
1394 50f. Men irrigating crops — 45 10
1395 75f. Family with cattle — 75 25
1396 100f. Fishermen — 95 25
1397 150f. Harvesting crops — 1·50 40
1398 300f. Pumping water — 3·00 80

203 Buildings, Vehicles and Envelopes on Map

1989. 15th Anniv of Mano River Union. Multicoloured.
1399 150f. Type 203 — 1·80 55
1400 300f. Map and Presidents of member countries — 2·75 80

204 Emblem, Banknotes and Produce

1989. 25th Anniv of African Development Bank.
1401 204 300f. multicoloured — 3·00 1·40

205 Skiing and Super-Tignes

1990. Winter Olympic Games, Albertville (1992). Multicoloured.
1402 150f. Type 205 (postage) — 95 30
1403 250f. Cross-country skiing and Le Lavachet — 2·30 60
1404 400f. Bobsleighing and Val-Claret — 3·75 85
1405 500f. Speed skating and Meribel (air) — 4·75 1·40
MS1406 97×71 mm. 750f. Skiing and Albertville — 7·00 1·80

206 Presidents Bush and Gorbachev (1989 Summit, Malta)

1990. . Multicoloured..

1407	200f. Type **206** (postage)	1·80	45
1408	250f. De Gaulle's appeal to resist, June 1940	3·00	.80
1409	300f. Pope Jean-Paul II, President Gorbachev and dove (1989 meeting)	3·00	75
1410	400f. Concorde and TGV Atlantique express train, France	4·25	85
1411	450f. Robin Yount (cent of Baseball) (air)	4·50	1·00
1412	500f. "Galileo" space probe	5·00	1·40
MS1413	83×100 mm. 750f. Crew of "Apollo 11", 1969 (vert)	7·50	2·00

207 St. Dominic's, Naples

1990. World Cup Football Championship, Italy. Multicoloured.

1414	200f. Type **207** (postage)	1·80	40
1415	250f. Piazza San Carlo, Turin	2·20	60
1416	300f. San Cataldo church, Udine (air)	2·75	75
1417	450f. St. Francis's Church, Udine (air)	4·50	1·20
MS1418	87×72 mm. 750f. Trophy and statue of Dante, Florence	6·50	1·40

1991. "Telecom 91" International Telecommunications Exhibition. Multicoloured.

1419	150f. Type **208**	1·50	75
1420	300f. Emblem (horiz)	2·75	1·40

209 Health Centre

1991. Medecins sans Frontieres.

1421	**209** 300f. multicoloured	3·00	1·40

210 *Madonna della Tenda*

1991. Christmas (1990). Paintings by Raphael. Multicoloured.

1422	50f. Type **210** (postage)	45	10
1423	100f. *Small Cowper Madonna*	95	25
1424	150f. *Tempi Madonna*	1·50	40
1425	250f. *Niccolini Madonna*	2·50	55
1426	300f. *Orleans Madonna* (air)	2·75	75
1427	500f. *Solly Madonna*	4·50	1·20
MS1428	81×105 mm. 750f. *Madonna of the Fisherman*	7·25	1·70

211 Rudi Voller

1991. West Germany, 1990 World Cup Football Champion. West German Players and Goals Scored. Multicoloured.

1429	200f. Type **211** (postage)	2·00	45
1430	250f. Uwe Bein	2·30	60
1431	300f. Pierre Littbarski	2·75	80
1432	400f. Jurgen Klinsmann	4·00	90
1433	450f. Lothar Matthaus (air)	3·25	75
1434	500f. Andreas Brehme	4·50	1·20
MS1435	116×89 mm. 750f. Andreas Brehme	7·00	1·60

212 Fairey Swordfish sinking *Bismarck* (German battleship) and Admirals Raeder and Tovey

1991. Battles of Second World War. Multicoloured.

1436	100f. Type **212** (postage)	1·20	25
1437	150f. Aichi D3A "Val" bombers sinking U.S.S. *Yorktown* (aircraft carrier) and Admirals Yamamoto and Nimitz (Battle of Midway)	1·50	45
1438	200f. American torpedo boat and Admirals Kondo and Halsey (Guadalcanal)	1·80	55
1439	250f. "Crusader III" tanks, Hawker Hurricane Mk II aircraft, Rommel and Montgomery (El Alamein)	2·50	80
1440	300f. "Tiger II" tanks and Generals Guderian and Patton (Ardennes) (air)	3·00	75
1441	450f. Grumman TBF Avenger aircraft sinking *Yamato* (Japanese battleship) and Admiral Kogo and General MacArthur	4·50	1·20
MS1442	120×86 mm. 750f. Boeing "B 17 G Flying Fortress" and Eisenhower	7·00	1·40

1991. Various stamps surch.

1443	100f. on 170f. mult (No. 1321) (postage)	95	45
1444	100f. on 170f. mult (No. 1328)	95	45
1445	100f. on 250f. mult (No. 1388)	95	45
1446	100f. on 400f. mult (No. 1270)	95	45
1447	100f. on 400f. mult (No. 1349)	95	45
1448	100f. on 400f. mult (No. 1356)	95	45
1449	100f. on 400f. mult (No. 1404)	95	45
1450	100f. on 400f. mult (No. 1410)	95	45
1451	100f. on 500f. mult (No. 1362)	95	45
1452	100f. on 500f. mult (No. 1366)	95	45
1453	100f. on 400f. mult (No. 1301) (air)	1·00	45
1454	100f. on 400f. mult (No. 1308)	1·00	45
1455	100f. on 400f. mult (No. 1322)	1·00	45
1456	100f. on 400f. mult (No. 1329)	1·00	45
1457	100f. on 400f. mult (No. 1343)	1·00	45
1458	100f. on 400f. mult (No. 1385)	1·00	45
1459	300f. on 450f. mult (No. 1350)	2·75	90
1460	300f. on 450f. mult (No. 1411)	2·75	90

214 Nat King Cole Trio

1991. Music and Films. Multicoloured.

1461	100f. Type **214** (postage)	1·20	25
1462	150f. Yul Brynner and scene from *The Magnificent Seven*	1·40	40
1463	250f. Judy Garland and scene from *The Wizard of Oz*	2·50	55
1464	300f. Steve McQueen and scene from *Papillon*	2·75	80
1465	500f. Gary Cooper and scene from *Sergeant York*	4·50	80
1466	600f. Bing Crosby and scene from *High Society*	5·50	1·30
MS1467	84×106 mm. 750f. John Wayne and scene from *Conquest of the West*	7·50	1·70

215 Dancer

1991. African Tourism Year. Multicoloured.

1468	100f. Type **215**	1·10	60
1469	150f. Baskets (horiz)	1·70	90
1470	250f. Drum (horiz)	3·00	1·60
1471	300f. Flautist	3·25	2·10

216 Doves, Map and Pope John Paul II

1991. Papal Visit. Litho.

1472	**216** 150f. multicoloured	2·75	1·50

217 "ERS-1" Observation Satellite and Earth

1991. Anniversaries and Events. Multicoloured.

1473	100f. Type **217** (postage)	95	30
1474	150f. *Sunflowers* (Vincent van Gogh, 1888)	1·40	25
1475	200f. Napoleon I (170th death anniv)	2·00	40
1476	250f. Henri Dunant (founder of Red Cross) and Red Cross volunteers	2·30	45
1477	300f. Bicentenary of Brandenburg Gate and second anniversary of fall of Berlin Wall	2·75	60
1478	400f. Pope John Paul II's tour of Africa, 1989	3·75	70
1479	450f. Garry Kasparov and Anatoli Karpov (World Chess Championship, 1990) (air)	4·25	4·50
1480	500f. Boy feeding dove and Rotary International and Lions International emblems	5·25	1·30

218 Care-a-Lot and Care Bears around Globe

1991. Ecology. Care Bear cartoon characters. Multicoloured.

1481	50f. Type **218** (postage)	50	25
1482	100f. Care Bears around sink ("Save Water!")	1·00	45
1483	200f. Care Bears in tree ("Recycle!")	1·90	80
1484	300f. Traffic jam and Care Bear ("Control Noise")	3·00	1·40
1485	400f. Elephant and Care Bear ("Protect Our Wild Life") (horiz)	4·00	2·10
MS1486	Two sheets. (a) 64×95 mm. 500f. Care Bears' emblem and waterfall (39×27 mm) (postage); (b) 95×65 mm. 600f. Scout, tent and Baden-Powell (17th World Scout Jamboree, Korea) (39×26 mm)	4·50	3·00

219 Player, Trophy and Little Five Points

1992. World Cup Football Championship, U.S.A. (1994) (1st issue). Multicoloured.

1487	100f. Type **219** (postage)	95	50
1488	300f. Germany player and Fulton Stadium, Atlanta	3·00	60
1489	400f. Player and Inman Park	3·75	90
1490	500f. Player and Museum of Fine Art (air)	4·50	1·30
MS1491	110×80 mm. 1000f. USA player, "Intelstat VI" satellite and Capitol	6·50	2·10

See also Nos. 1565/MS1569.

220 Emblem

1992. 75th Anniv of Lions International.

1492	**220** 150f. multicoloured	1·40	75
1493	**220** 400f. multicoloured	3·75	2·10

221 Emblem

1992. International Nutrition Conference, Rome.

1494	**221** 150f. mult (postage)	2·10	45
1495	**221** 400f. multicoloured	3·00	45
1496	**221** 500f. multicoloured (air)	3·75	60

222 Scene from *The Devil and Catherine* and Antonin Dvorak (composer)

1992. Anniversaries and Events. Multicoloured.

1497	200f. Type **222** (150th birth (1991)) (postage)	2·10	45
1498	300f. Antonio Vivaldi (composer) (250th death (1991)) and as choirmaster to the Hospital of the Pieta, Venice	3·00	45
1499	350f. Meeting of airship *Graf Zeppelin* and Santos-Dumont's flying boat and Count Ferdinand von Zeppelin (airship pioneer)	3·75	60
1500	400f. Projected locomotive emerging from Channel Tunnel (construction)	4·00	80
1501	450f. Konrad Adenauer (German statesman) and Brandenburg Gate, Berlin (bicentenary of Gate) (air)	4·75	90
1502	500f. Emperor Hirohito of Japan (third death anniv)	5·25	1·40
MS1503	77×115 mm. 750f. Cross-channel locomotive (59×41 mm)	7·50	1·80

223 Charlie Chaplin (actor) and Scene from *Modern Times*

1992. Anniversaries and Events. Multicoloured.

1504	50f. Type **223** (15th death anniv) (postage)	50	30
1505	100f. Pavilion and Christopher Columbus ("Expo '92" World's Fair, Seville)	1·00	30
1506	150f. St. Peter's Square, Rome	1·50	45
1507	200f. Marlene Dietrich (actress, death) in scene from *Shanghai Express*	2·10	60
1508	250f. Michael Schumacher and Formula 1 racing car	2·40	60
1509	300f. Rocket launch and John Glenn (30th anniv of Glenn's three-orbit flight in "Mercury" space capsule)	2·75	75
1510	400f. ill Koch (skipper) and *America 3* (yacht) (winner of Americas Cup) (air)	3·75	1·00
1511	450f. Victory of Washington Redskins in 26th American Superbowl baseball championships	4·50	1·00
1512	500f. Recovery of "Intelsat VI" satellite by "Endeavour" space shuttle	5·00	1·20
MS1513	750f. Brandenburg Gate and Willy Brandt (politician and Mayor of Berlin, 1957–66, death (49×35 mm))	6·75	1·70

1993. 50th Death Anniv (1991) of Robert Baden-Powell (founder of Scouting Movement). Nos. 1339/MS1345 optd **50eme ANNIVERSAIRE DE LA MORT DE BADEN POWEL.**

1515	**192**	50f. mult (postage)	95	25
1516	-	100f. multicoloured	95	25
1517	-	150f. multicoloured	1·40	55
1518	-	300f. multicoloured	75	25
1519	-	400f. multicoloured (air)	3·75	25
1520	-	450f. multicoloured	4·25	25
MS1521		116×87 mm. 750f. multi-coloured	1·40	1·40

1993. Bicentenary of Year One of First Republic of France. Nos. 1388/MS1392 optd **BICENTENAIRE DE L'AN I DE LA REPUBLIQUE FRANCAISE.**

1522	**201**	50f. mult (postage)	2·75	25
1523	-	300f. multicoloured	3·75	25
1524	-	400f. multicoloured	4·75	45
1525	-	450f. multicoloured (air)	5·75	45
MS1526		140×102 mm. 750f. multicoloured	8·50	8·50

1993. Winter Olympic Games, Albertville, Gold Medal Winners. Nos. 1402/MS1406 variously optd.

1527	150f. **SLALOM GEANT Alberto Tomba, Italie** (postage)	1·90	30
1528	250f. **SKI NORDIQUE Vegard Ulvang, Norvege**	2·75	40
1529	400f. **BOB A DEUX G. Weder/D. Acklin, Suisse**	3·75	40
1530	500f. **PATINAGE DE VITESSE Olaf Zinke 1000m., Allemagne** (air)	4·75	40
MS1531	97×71 mm. 750f. As No. 1527	2·75	2·75

1993. World Cup Football Championship, Italy, Results. Nos. 1414/MS1418 optd 1. **ALLEMAGNE** 2. **ARGENTINE** 3. **ITALIE.**

1532	**207**	200f. mult (postage)	1·90	45
1533	-	250f. multicoloured	2·75	60
1534	-	300f. multicoloured	3·25	60
1535	-	450f. multicoloured (air)	4·25	60
MS1536		87×72 mm. 750f. multicoloured	4·75	4·75

1993. Air. Bobby Fischer–Boris Spassky Chess Match (1537) and 75th Anniv of Lions International (1538). Nos. 1479/80 optd.

1537	450f. **RENCONTRE FISCHER - SPASSKY 3 SEPT au 5 NOV 1992 AU MONTENEGRO**	3·75	55
1538	500f. **75eme ANNIVERSAIRE LIONS**	4·75	65

230 West Germany Footballer and Little White House

1993. Olympic Games, Atlanta (1996) (1st issue). Multicoloured.

1539	150f. Type **230** (postage)	1·60	45
1540	250f. Cyclist and Georgia World Congress Center	2·50	75
1541	400f. Basketball player and underground station	4·00	90
1542	500f. Baseball player and steam railroad, New Georgia Railroad (air)	4·75	1·10
MS1543	123×90 mm. 1000f. Table tennis player and Atlanta at night	9·00	9·00

See also Nos. 1623/MS1628.

231 Ice Hockey and "Whale Hunt" (sculpture)

1993. Winter Olympic Games, Lillehammer, Norway (1994). Multicoloured.

1544	150f. Type **231** (postage)	1·40	40
1545	250f. Two-man bobsleigh and Edvard Grieg's house	2·30	75
1546	400f. Biathlon and Fredrikstad Park (air)	3·50	90
1547	450f. Ski jumping and Eidsvoll Manor	4·25	1·20
MS1548	100×72 mm. 1000f. Skiing and Lillehammer	8·75	8·75

232 "Luna 3" and Dark Side of Moon

1993. 25th Anniv (1994) of First Manned Moon Landing. Multicoloured.

1549	150f. Type **232**	1·40	30
1550	150f. "Ranger 7"	1·40	30
1551	150f. "Luna 9"	1·40	30
1552	150f. "Surveyor 1" (first lunar probe)	1·40	30
1553	150f. Lunar "Orbiter 1" and moon	1·40	30
1554	150f. Launch of "Saturn 5" (rocket) carrying "Apollo 11"	1·40	30
1555	150f. "Apollo 11" command module in lunar orbit	1·40	30
1556	150f. Astronaut climbing from "Apollo 11"	1·40	30
1557	150f. "Apollo 12" astronaut recovering "Surveyor 1" camera	1·40	30
1558	150f. Explosion of "Apollo 13"	1·40	30
1559	150f. "Luna 16" probe (first collection of lunar samples by automatic probe)	1·40	30
1560	150f. Lunokhod of "Luna 17" (first lunar vehicle)	1·40	30
1561	150f. Alan Shepard playing golf on moon	1·40	30
1562	150f. First lunar jeep from "Apollo 15" mission	1·40	30
1563	150f. First lunar telescope from "Apollo 16" mission	1·40	30
1564	150f. Astronaut from "Apollo 17" (last "Apollo" mission)	1·40	30

233 San Francisco

1993. World Cup Football Championship, U.S.A. (1994) (2nd issue). Multicoloured.

1565	100f. Type **233** (postage)	1·40	30
1566	300f. Washington D.C.	2·75	55
1567	400f. Renaissance Center, Detroit	3·75	80
1568	500f. Dallas (air)	4·50	1·10
MS1569	106×84 mm. 1000f. New York	9·00	9·00

234 Euparkeria

1993. Prehistoric Animals. Multicoloured.

1570	50f. Type **234**	45	25
1571	50f. Plateosaurus	45	25
1572	50f. Anchisaurus	45	25
1573	50f. Ornithosuchus	45	25
1574	100f. Megalosaurus	95	30
1575	100f. Scelidosaurus	95	30
1576	100f. Camptosaurus	95	30
1577	100f. Ceratosaurus	95	30
1578	250f. Ouranosaurus	2·30	25
1579	250f. Dicraeosaurus	2·30	25
1580	250f. Tarbosaurus	2·30	25
1581	250f. Gorgosaurus	2·30	25
1582	250f. Polacanthus	2·30	25
1583	250f. Deinonychus	2·30	25
1584	250f. Corythosaurus	2·30	25
1585	250f. Spinosaurus	2·30	25
MS1586	170×120 mm. 1000f. "Tyrannosaurus rex" (50×60 mm)	10·00	10·00

235 Prince Johann I of Liechtenstein

1994. Multicoloured. (a) Battle of Austerlitz, 1805.

1587	150f. Type **235**	1·50	75
1588	150f. Marshal Joachim Murat	1·50	75
1589	600f. Napoleon (59×47 mm)	5·50	1·20

Nos. 1587/9 were issued together, se-tenant, forming a composite design of a battle scene.

(b) Battle of the Moskva, 1912.

1590	150f. Marshal Michel Ney	1·60	80
1591	150f. Prince Pyotr Ivanovich Bagration	1·60	80
1592	600f. Napoleon on horseback (59×47 mm)	6·00	1·30

Nos. 1590/2 were issued together, se-tenant, forming a composite design of a battle scene.

(c) Normandy Landings, 1944.

1593	150f. Field-Marshal Erwin Rommel (wrongly inscr "Romel")	1·50	75
1594	150f. Gen. George Patton	1·50	75
1595	600f. Gen. Dwight David Eisenhower (59×47 mm)	5·50	1·20

Nos. 1593/5 were issued together, se-tenant, forming a composite design of a battle scene.

(d) Battle of the Ardennes, 1944.

1596	150f. Lt.-Gen. William H. Simpson	1·50	75
1597	150f. Gen. Heinz Guderian	1·50	75
1598	600f. Tank battle scene (59×47 mm)	5·50	1·20

Nos. 1596/8 were issued together, se-tenant, forming a composite design of a battle scene.

236 Johann Kepler and "Pluto" Space Probe

1994. Astronomers. Multicoloured.

1599	300f. Type **236**	2·75	75
1600	300f. Sir Isaac Newton and "Voyager" space probe	2·75	75
1601	600f. Nicolas Copernicus and "Galileo" space probe (59×47 mm)	4·25	1·20

Nos. 1599/1601 were issued together, se-tenant, forming a composite design.

1994. Winter Olympic Games, Lillehammer. Gold Medal Winners. Nos. 1544/MS1545 variously optd.

1602	150f. **MEDAILLE D'OR SUEDE** (postage)	1·50	75
1603	250f. **G. WEDER D. ACKLIN SUISSE**	2·50	90
1604	400f. **F.B. LUNDBERG NORVEGE** (air)	3·50	1·40
1605	450f. **J. WEISSFLOG ALLEMAGNE**	4·00	1·40
MS1606	100×72 mm. 1000f. T. Moe USA	8·75	8·75

1994. World Cup Football Championship, U.S.A., Winners. Nos. 1565/MS1569 optd 1. **BRESIL** 2. **ITALIE** 3. **SUEDE.**

1607	**233**	100f. mult (postage)	1·30	45
1608	-	300f. multicoloured	2·75	70
1609	-	400f. multicoloured	3·50	90
1610	-	500f. multicoloured (air)	4·50	1·10
MS1611		106×84 mm. 1000f. multicoloured	8·75	8·50

239 Banea Dam

1995. Garafiri Water Management. Multicoloured.

1612	100f. Type **239**	80	40
1613	150f. Donkea	1·20	60
1614	200f. Tinkisso overflow (vert)	1·50	80
1615	250f. Waterfalls	2·00	1·10
1616	500f. Water works, Kinkon	4·00	2·20

240 Red and White Persian

1995. Cats. Multicoloured.

1617	150f. Type **240** (inscr "Tortoise-shell")	75	35
1618	250f. Tabby and white	1·30	65
1619	500f. Black smoke persian ("Smoke long-haired")	2·50	90
1620	500f. Red tabby	2·50	90
1621	500f. Tortoiseshell and white persian ("longhair")	2·50	90
MS1622	48×78 mm. 1000f. Chinchilla (38×30 mm)	5·75	3·75

241 Throwing the Javelin

1995. Olympic Games, Atlanta (1996) (2nd issue). Multicoloured.

1623	150f. Type **241**	40	25
1624	250f. Boxing	75	45
1625	500f. Football	1·30	85
1626	500f. Basketball	1·30	85
1627	500f. Weightlifting	1·30	85
MS1628	48×82 mm. 1000f. Archery (31×39 mm)	4·25	2·75

242 Eurasian Goldfinch

1995. Birds. Multicoloured.

1629	150f. Type **242**	65	35
1630	250f. Nightingale (Luscinia megarhynchos)	1·20	65
1631	500f. Island canary (Serinus canaria)	2·20	90
1632	500f. Chaffinch (Fringilla coelebs)	2·20	90
1633	500f. Western greenfinch (Carduelis chloris)	2·20	90
MS1634	60×75 mm. 1000f. European robin (31×37 mm)	5·75	3·75

243 Mona Monkey

1995. Mammals. Multicoloured.

1635	150f. Type **243**	40	25
1636	250f. Savanna monkey	75	45
1637	500f. Demidoff's galago (Galagoides demidovi)	1·30	85
1638	500f. Hare (Lepus crawshayi) (horiz)	1·30	85
1639	500f. Giant ground pangolin (Manis gigantea) (horiz)	1·30	85
MS1640	49×74 mm. 1000f. African clawless otter (31×39 mm)	5·75	3·75

244 Pup-150 (Great Britain)

1995. Aircraft. Multicoloured.

1641	100f. Type **244**	60	25
1642	150f. Gardan GY-80 "Horizon" (France)	80	60
1643	250f. Piper J-3 Cub (U.S.A.)	1·40	85
1644	500f. Piper PA-28 Cherokee Arrow (U.S.A.)	2·75	1·70

1645	500f. Pilatus PC-6 Porter (Switzerland)	2·75	1·70
1646	500f. Valmet L-90TP Redigo (Finland)	2·75	1·70
MS1647	79×49 mm. 1000f. Stol DO-27 (Germany) (39×30 mm)	5·00	3·75

245 Yoked Oxen

1995. 50th Anniv of F.A.O. Multicoloured.
| 1648 | 200f. Type **245** | 95 | 45 |
| 1649 | 750f. Nutrition lesson | 4·00 | 1·40 |

246 Jacobean Lily

1995. Flowers. Multicoloured.
1650	100f. Type **246**	45	10
1651	150f. Rudbeckia purpurea	75	25
1652	250f. Himalayan blue poppy	1·20	45
1653	500f. Iris "Starshine"	2·30	90
1654	500f. Rose "Gail Borden"	2·90	90
1655	500f. Sweet pea (Lathyrus odoratus)	2·30	90
MS1656	55×70 mm. 100f. Orchid (28×36 mm)	5·00	2·30

247 Players

1995. World Cup Football Championship, France (1998) (1st issue). Multicoloured.
1657	150f. Type **247**	40	25
1658	250f. Player challenging player No. 2	75	45
1659	500f. Players in blue and white shirt and red shirt in tackle	1·30	75
1660	500f. Players Nos. 3 and 10 running after ball	1·30	75
1661	500f. Player No. 2 high-kicking ball	1·30	75
MS1662	90×51 mm. 1000f. Two players opposing player No. 19 (31×39 mm)	5·75	3·00
See also Nos. 1719/**MS**1725.

248 Arab Horse

1995. Arab Horses. Multicoloured.
1663	100f. Type **248**	40	20
1664	150f. Dark brown horse with white star	65	40
1665	250f. Chestnut	1·00	75
1666	500f. Grey	1·70	75
1667	500f. Bay	1·70	75
1668	500f. Bay with harness and rein (horiz)	1·70	1·10
MS1669	69×91 mm. 1000g. Grey (different) (31×39 mm)	5·75	3·00

249 Leccinum nigrescens

1995. Fungi. Multicoloured.
| 1670 | 150f. Type **249** | 40 | 20 |
| 1671 | 250f. Boletus rhodoxanthus | 75 | 35 |

1672	500f. Cantharellus lutescens	1·30	60
1673	500f. Brown roll-rim (Paxillus involutus)	1·30	60
1674	500f. Xerocomus rubellus	1·30	60
MS1675	66×83 mm. 1000f. Gymnoplius junonius (31×38 mm)	3·50	2·00

250 Enterprise, 1832

1995. Veteran Omnibuses. Multicoloured.
1676	250f. Type **250**	1·00	60
1677	300f. Daimler, 1898	1·70	1·00
1678	400f. V.H. Bussing, 1904	2·40	1·30
1679	450f. M.A.N. autobus, 1906	2·80	1·50
1680	500f. M.A.N. autocar, 1934	3·00	1·60

251 Locomotive Tom Thumb, 1829, U.S.A.

1996. Rail Transport. Multicoloured.
1681	200f. Type **251**	95	20
1682	250f. Locomotive Genf, 1858, Switzerland (68×27 mm)	1·20	25
1683	300f. Canterbury Frozen Meat Company Dubs locomotive, 1873, New Zealand	1·80	30
1684	400f. Bagnall fireless steam accumulator locomotive No. 2, Great Britain	2·00	35
1685	450f. Werner von Siemens's first electric locomotive, 1879, and passenger carriage (68×27 mm)	2·30	40
1686	500f. North London Tramways Company tram, 1885–89, Great Britain	3·00	2·50
MS1687	80×90 mm. 1000f. Steam locomotive General, 1862 (39×31 mm)	6·00	4·00

252 Rock Formation

1996. Multicoloured.
1688	200f. Type **252**	95	45
1689	750f. Child	4·00	1·40
1690	1000f. Women carrying faggots	5·00	1·90

253 Red Siskin

1996. Birds. Multicoloured.
1691	200f. Type **253**	95	30
1692	250f. Red-cheeked cordon-bleu	1·20	45
1693	300f. Chestnut-breasted minnikin	1·50	70
1694	400f. Paradise sparrow	1·70	70
1695	450f. Gouldian finch	2·00	80
1696	500f. Red bishop	2·50	90
MS1697	100×70 mm. 1000f. Spotted-sided finch (31×39 mm)	5·00	2·30

254 Bull Terrier

1996. Dogs. Multicoloured.
1698	200f. Type **254**	95	30
1699	250f. Elkhound	1·20	45
1700	300f. Akita	1·50	70

1701	400f. Collie	1·70	70
1702	450f. Rottweiler	2·00	80
1703	500f. Boxer	2·50	90
MS1704	69×89 mm. 1000f. German short-haired setter (31×39 mm)	5·00	2·30

255 Tortoiseshell and White Shorthair

1996. Cats. Multicoloured.
1705	200f. Type **255**	95	30
1706	250f. Bicolour shorthair	1·20	45
1707	300f. Tortoiseshell and white Japanese bobtail	1·50	70
1708	400f. Chocolate point Himalayan	1·80	80
1709	450f. Red longhair	2·10	90
1710	500f. Blue Persian	2·50	1·00
MS1711	109×88 mm. 1000f. Tortoiseshell and white longhair (31×39 mm)	5·50	3·00

256 Chestnut

1996. Fungi. Multicoloured.
1712	200f. Type **256**	80	35
1713	250f. Granular	1·10	45
1714	300f. Destroying angel	1·40	60
1715	400f. Milky blue	1·80	70
1716	450f. Violet cortinarius	1·90	80
1717	500f. Rough-stemmed	2·20	90
MS1718	90×70 mm. 1000f. Hygrophoris (31×39 mm)	4·50	2·30

257 Players

1997. World Cup Football Championship, France (1998) (2nd issue). Multicoloured.
1719	200f. Type **257**	80	30
1720	250f. Player No. 5	1·10	45
1721	300f. Three players	1·40	60
1722	400f. Player dribbling ball past opposition (horiz)	1·00	70
1723	450f. Player No. 12 with opposing player on ground (horiz)	1·99	80
1724	500f. Ball passing lunging goalkeeper (horiz)	2·20	90
MS1725	92×70 mm. 1000f. Goalkeeper looking at ball in net (31×39 mm)	4·50	2·30

258 Paphiopedilum millmoore

1997. Orchids. Multicoloured.
1726	200f. Type **258**	80	30
1727	250f. Paphiopedilum ernest read	1·10	45
1728	300f. Paphiopedilum harrisianum	1·40	60
1729	400f. Paphiopedilum gaudianum	1·80	70
1730	450f. Paphiopedilum papa rohl	1·90	80
1731	500f. Paphiopedilum sea cliff	2·20	90
MS1732	69×89 mm. 1000f. Paphiopedilum gowerianum (31×39 mm)	6·25	3·25

259 Giraffe

1997. Mammals. Multicoloured.
1733	200f. Type **259**	95	30
1734	250f. White rhinoceros (vert)	1·20	45
1735	300f. Warthog	1·50	70
1736	400f. Cheetah	1·70	70
1737	450f. African elephant (vert)	2·00	80
1738	500f. Pygmy hippopotamus	2·50	90
MS1739	90×70 mm. 1000f. Okapi (38×30 mm)	5·00	2·30

260 H.M.S. Captain (turret ship, Great Britain, 1870)

1997. 19th-Century Warships. Multicoloured.
1740	200f. Type **260**	95	30
1741	250f. Kaiser Wilhelm (ironclad, Germany, 1869)	1·20	45
1742	300f. H.M.S. Temeraire (turret ship, Great Britain, 1871)	1·50	70
1743	400f. Mouillage (turret ship, Italy, 1866)	1·70	70
1744	450f. H.M.S. Inflexible (battleship, Great Britain, 1881)	2·00	80
1745	500f. Magenta (ironclad, France, 1862)	2·50	90
MS1746	107×90 mm. 1000f. Redoutable (iron-clad warships, France, 1878) (31×39 mm)	5·00	2·30

261 Siganus trispilos

1997. Fish. Multicoloured.
1747	200f. Type **261**	95	30
1748	250f. Dusky parrotfish	1·20	45
1749	300f. Harlequin tuskfish	1·50	70
1750	400f. Masked unicornfish	1·70	70
1751	450f. "Hypoplectrus gemma"	2·00	80
1752	500f. Red-tailed surgeon-fish	2·50	90
MS1753	90×70 mm. 1000f. Yellow tang (39×31 mm)	5·00	2·30

262 Officer, Von Witerfeldt's Regiment

1997. Prussian Infantry Uniforms. Multicoloured.
1754	200f. Type **262**	95	40
1755	250f. Non-commissioned officer, Von Kanitz's Regiment	1·20	55
1756	300f. Private, Prince Franz von Anhalt-Dessau's Regiment	1·50	70
1757	400f. Private, Von Kalnein's Regiment	2·00	85
1758	450f. Grenadier, Duke Ferdinand of Brunswick's Regiment	2·30	1·00
1759	500f. Grenadier musician, Rekow's Guards Battalion	3·00	1·10
MS1760	91×111 mm. 1000f. Pioneer (31×39 mm)	5·75	2·75

263 Baldwin Steam Locomotive

1997. Steam Locomotives. Multicoloured.
1761	200f. Type **263**	95	40
1762	250f. Steam locomotive No. 1	1·20	55
1763	300f. Vulcan steam locomotive	1·50	70
1764	400f. Commonwealth Edison Company Baldwin steam locomotive No. 2	2·20	85
1765	450f. TCID Railroad steam locomotive No. 108	2·75	1·00
1766	500f. Pittsburgh-Hanover Coal Company steam locomotive No. 3	3·25	1·10
MS1767	110×91 mm. 1000f. Baldwin steam locomotive (39×31 mm)	6·75	3·25

264 14th-century Thai Knight, Rook and King

1997. Chess Pieces. Multicoloured.

1768	200f. Type **264**	75	45
1769	250f. Chinese pawn, king and knight, 1930	1·10	55
1770	300f. Portuguese ivory "seahorse" pawn, queen and king, 1920	1·40	65
1771	400f. German pewter "military" knight, king and pawn	2·30	90
1772	450f. Russian amber queen, king, bishop and knight from reign of Catherine II	2·50	1·00
1773	500f. Max Ernst's designs for queen, king, bishop and knight	3·00	1·20
MS1774	106×90 mm. 1000f. 18th-century French knight (27×36 mm)	5·75	3·75

265 Siberian Husky

1997. Dogs. Multicoloured.

1775	200f. Type **265**	75	45
1776	250f. Teckel	1·10	55
1777	300f. Boston terrier	1·40	65
1778	400f. Basset hound	2·30	90
1779	450f. Dalmatian	2·50	1·00
1780	500f. Rottweiler	3·00	1·20
MS1781	110×80 mm. 1000f. Golden retriever	5·75	3·75

POSTAGE DUE STAMPS

D11

1959

D195	**D11**	1f. green	25	20
D196	**D11**	2f. red	25	20
D197	**D11**	3f. brown	25	20
D198	**D11**	5f. blue	1·23	75
D199	**D11**	10f. orange	20	1·80
D200	**D11**	20f. mauve	5·50	2·50

D17

1959

D224	**D17**	1f. red	25	20
D225	**D17**	2f. orange	25	20
D226	**D17**	3f. lake	50	35
D227	**D17**	5f. green	85	45
D228	**D17**	10f. sepia	1·70	1·10
D229	**D17**	20f. blue	3·25	2·20

APPENDIX

The following stamps have either been issued in excess of postal needs or have not been available to the public in reasonable quantities at face value. Such stamps may be given full listing if there is evidence of regular postal use.

1982

World Cup Winners. Nos. 1068/74 optd.

1983

Olympic Games, Los Angeles. 100s.
Bicentenary of Manned Flight. 100s.
Winter Olympic Games, Sarajevo. 100s.

1984

Winter Olympic Gold Medal Winners. 100s.

1985

Space Achievements. 200s.
Anniversaries and Events. 85th Birthday of Queen Elizabeth the Queen Mother. 100s.

1986

Appearance of Halley's Comet. 1500f.

1987

Winter Olympic Games, Seoul. 1500f.

1989

Embossed on gold foil.Scout and Butterfly. Air 1500f.
Bicentenary of French Revolution. Air 1500f.

1990

Embossed on gold foil. World Cup Football Championship, Italy. Air 1500f.
Winter Olympic Games, Albertville (1992). Air 1500f.
De Gaulle and Free French Forces. Air 1500f.

1992

Embossed on gold foil. Olympic Games, Barcelona. Air 1500f.
World Cup Football Championship, U.S.A. (1994) (1st issue). Air 1500f. (vert design).
Elvis Presley. Air 1500f.
Pope John Paul II's African Tour. Air 1500f.

1993

Embossed on gold foil. Bicentenary of Year One of First Republic of France. Air. Optd on 1989 French Revolution issue. 1500f.
Olympic Games, Atlanta. Air 1500f.
Winter Olympic Games, Lillehammer, Norway. Air 1500f.
World Cup Football Championship, U.S.A. (1994) (2nd issue). Air 1500f. (square design).

1995

Embossed on gold foil. Normandy Landing, 1944. Air. Optd on 1990 De Gaulle Appendix. 1500f.

1997

Dinosaurs. 200fr.; 250fr.; 300f.; 300fr.; 400fr.; 450fr.; 500fr
UNICEF. 200fr.; 300fr.; 750fr.; 1500fr.

1998

Butterflies. 200fr.; 250fr.; 300f.; 300fr.; 400fr.; 450fr.; 500fr.
Cats. 200fr.; 250fr.; 300fr.; 300fr.; 400fr.; 450fr.; 500f.
Diana, Princess of Wales. 200fr.; 300fr.; 750fr.
World Cup Football Championship. 200fr.; 250fr.; 300fr.; 300fr.; 400fr.; 450fr.; 500fr.
German Military Uniforms. 200fr.; 250fr.; 300fr.; 400fr.; 450fr.; 500fr.
Railways. 200fr.; 250fr.; 300fr.; 400fr.; 450fr.; 500fr.
Marine Life. 200fr.×12
Cars. 200fr.; 250fr.; 300fr.; 400fr.; 450fr.; 500fr.
Endangered Species. 200fr.; 250fr.; 300fr.; 400fr.; 450fr.; 750fr, 200fr.×12, 450fr.×6, 750fr.×6
Locomotives of the World. 200fr.×8;300fr.; 300fr.×8; 450fr.×8; 750fr.×8
Aircraft. 200fr.×8;300fr.; 300fr.×8; 450fr.×6; 750fr.×6
Dinosaurs.750fr.×9
Minerals. 750fr.×3
Ships. 450fr.×4; 450fr.×4; 750fr.×4; 750fr.×4; 1500fr.×4
Art. 750fr.×8
Amphibians. 200f.; 300f.; 750f.
Scouting. 200f.; 250f.; 300f.; 400f.; 450f.; 500f.

1999

Horses. 150fr.×6; 450fr.×6; 750fr.×6
Dogs of the World. 750fr.×6
Sculpture. 200fr.; 250fr.; 300fr.; 400fr.; 450fr.; 500fr
Dinosaurs.300fr.×3; 350fr. ×9; 450fr. ×9; 450fr.×8
Return of Macao to China. 650fr.×4; 650fr.×4
Paintings by Zhang Daqain. 330fr.×10
Trains. 100fr.; 200fr.×2; 250fr.×2; 450fr.×4; 300fr.×6; 300fr.×9; 450fr.×9;
Fungi and Insects. 100fr.×3; 150fr.; 300fr.×5; 450fr.×6; 300fr.×9; 450fr.×9;
Birds. 300fr.×2; 300fr.×4; 450fr.×2; 450fr.×6; 500fr.×6; 500fr.×6; 600fr.×2; 750fr.×6
Butterflies. 300fr.×6; 450fr.×6; 750fr.×6
Royal Wedding. 750fr.×6
Paintings by Hokusai. 750fr.×6; 750fr.×6; 3000fr.fr.×6
Goethe Commemoration. 1000fr.×3
Space. 300fr.×2; 450fr.×12; 500fr.×6; 500fr.; 750fr.×6; 750fr.×6
Queen Mother. 3000fr.×4
Cats. 300fr.; 400fr.; 450fr.×6;
Romance of the Three Kingdoms. 460fr.×5; 460fr.×5
Cats. 750f.×3;
Marine Life. 500f.×3
Philex 1999. 200f.; 250f.; 300f.; 400f.; 450f.; 500f.
Trains. 200f.; 280f.; 300f.; 400f.; 450f.; 500f.
Horses. 150f.; 200f.; 300f.; 450f.×2; 750f.
Dinosaurs. 300f.; 450f.×2
Cats. 300f.; 450f.

2000

Millennium. 200fr.×17; 250fr.×5; 300fr.×5
Year of the Dragon. 400fr.×4
Titanic. 750fr.×8
Olympic Games, Sydney. 150fr.×5; 150fr.×5; 210fr.×5; 210fr.×5; 300fr.×5; 300fr.×5; 600fr.×5; 600fr.×5; 750fr.×5; 750fr.×5;
Locomotives. 200fr.×9; 250fr.×5; 300fr.×9; 350fr.×9; 400fr.×9; 900fr.×9
Centenary of First Zeppelin. 300fr.×6; 450fr.×6; 1000fr.×6; 1000fr.×6
Marine Life. 400fr.×2; 450fr.; 750fr.×6; 750fr.×6; 400fr.×2; 450fr.×2; 200fr.×6; 1000fr.×6; 1000fr.×6; 1000fr.×6
Primates. 250f.×4
Aircraft. 750f.×6
Marine Life. 400f.×4; 450f.×4

2001

Flora and Fauna. 300fr.×6; 300fr.×6; 300fr.×6; 750fr.×6; 750fr.×6; 750fr.×6; 750fr.×6; 750fr.×6;
Railways. 200fr.; 300fr.; 950fr.×6; 950fr.×6; 950fr.×6; 4000fr.×6; 4000fr.×6
Personalities. 350fr.×6; 450fr.×6; 600fr.×6; 750fr.×6

1986

Birds. 200fr.; 250fr.; 300fr.; 400fr.; 450fr.; 200fr.; 250fr.; 950fr.×6; 750fr.×6; 750fr.×6; 750fr.×6
Butterflies. 700fr.; 750fr.; 800fr.; 850fr.; 950fr.; 1000fr.; 900fr.×2; 900fr.×6; 900fr.×6; 950fr.×6; 950fr.×6;
Birds. 900fr.×2; 1000fr.×2; 1000fr.×6; 1000fr.×6; 1000fr.×6
Railways. 200fr.×6; 300fr.×6; 750fr.×6; 750fr.×8
Fauna. 200f.×4; 300f.×4; 750f.×4; 750f.×6; 1250f.×4; 1500f.×4; 1750f.×4
Victims of Trade Centre Terrorist Attack. 3500f.×2
Locomotives. 200f.; 300f.; 750f.
Birds. 200f.; 300f.; 500f.; 550f.; 600f.; 650f.

2002

Ships. 750f.×6; 750f.×6
Aircraft. 750fr.×6; 750fr.×6; 750fr.×6; 750fr.×4; 750fr.×6; 750fr.×6; 750fr.×6; 750fr.×6; 750fr.×6; 750fr.×6
Centenary of First Zeppelin. 750fr.×4
Cars. 750fr.×6; 750fr.×6; 750fr.×6;1000fr.×6; 1000fr.×6; 1000fr.×6
Presidents John F Kennedy and Ronald Reagan. 750fr.×3; 750fr.×3
Diana, Princess of Wales. 750fr.×3
Prince William. 750fr.×6; 750fr.×6
Queen Elizabeth II. 1400fr.×4
Elvis Presley. 750fr.×6; 750fr.×6; 750fr.×6; 750fr.×6
Nobel Prize Winners. 750fr.×6; 750fr.×6; 750fr.×6; 750fr.×6
Jaqueline Kennedy Onassis. 1000fr.; 2000fr.; 4000fr.; 1000fr.×6
Personalities. 750fr.×12
Cinema. 750fr.×6; 750fr.×6
Scouts. 200fr.; 300fr.; 5000fr.; 200fr.; 300fr.; 5000fr.; 200fr.; 300fr.; 5000fr.; 200fr.; 750fr.; 5000fr.; 200fr.; 750fr.; 5000fr.; 200fr.; 750fr.; 5000fr.; 200fr.; 750fr.; 5000fr.; 200fr.; 750fr.; 5000fr.; 200fr.; 750fr.; 5000fr.

2003

Space Exploration. 1500fr.×8; 1500fr.×8; 3000fr.×8; 3000fr.×8
Olympic Games, Athens. 750fr.×2; 1500fr.×5; 3000fr.×9
Pope John Paul II. 100fr.; 150fr.; 200fr.; 450fr.; 500fr.; 550fr.; 600fr.; 650fr.; 1000fr.; 1500fr.; 2000fr.; 2500fr.; 7500fr.
Space Exploration. 3000f.×4; 3000f.×4

2006

World Cup Football Championship. 3000f.×4

2007

International Polar Year. 2000f.; 7500f.; 20000f.
Year of the Dolphin. 2000f.; 7500f.; 20000f.
International Heliophysical Year. 2000f.; 7500f.; 20000f.
Year of the Pig. 2000f.; 7500f.; 20000f.
Space Tourism. 3000f.; 10000f.; 15000f.
50th Anniv of Treaty of Rome. 3000f.; 10000f.; 15000f.
Space Exploration. 3000f.; 10000f.; 15000f.
Scouting. 3000f.; 10000f.; 15000f.
Red Cross. 2000f.; 7500f.; 20000f.
Chess. 2000f.; 7500f.; 20000f.
Trains. 2000f.; 7500f.; 20000f.
M. L. Rostropovich. 3000f.; 10000f.; 15000f.
Concorde and Sir Arthur Marshall. 3000f.; 10000f.; 15000f.
Presidential Elections. 3000f.; 10000f.; 15000f.
Water Quality Improvement. 3000f.; 10000f.; 15000f.
Writers and Artists. 3000f.; 10000f.; 15000f.
Moscow Kremlin. 2000f.; 7500f.; 20000f.
Lions. 2000f.; 7500f.; 20000f.
Poverty. 3000f.; 10000f.; 15000f.
Bugatti. 5000f.×6
Historic Cars. 5000f.×6
Chuck Yeager. 5000f.×6
Vietnam War. 5000f.×6
Wernher von Braun. 5000f.×6
Robert Oppenheimer. 5000f.×6
Charles Lindbergh. 5000f.×6
Hindenburg Disaster. 5000f.×6
Buffalo Bill. 5000f.×6
Henry Ford. 5000f.×6
Georges. Guynemer. 5000f.×6
Howard Hughes. 5000f.×6
Red Cross. 5000f.×6
Mars Pathfinder. 5000f.×6
Launch of Saturn Probe. 5000f.×6
Hale Bop Comet. 5000f.×6
Launch of Voyagers 1 and 2. 5000f.×6
Shinkansen High Speed Train. 5000f.×6
Jaques Cousteau. 5000f.×6
Climate Change. 5000f.×6

2008

Dogs and Cats of Celebrities. 5000f.×6
Owls. 5000f.×6
Fungi. 5000f.×6
Orchids. 5000f.×6
Butterflies. 5000f.×6
Sharks. 5000f.×6
Parrots. 5000f.×6
Pandas. 5000f.×6
Turtles. 5000f.×6
Big Cats. 5000f.×6
Whales. 5000f.×6
Polar Animals. 5000f.×6
Bats. 5000f.×6
Marine Fauna. 5000f.×6
Shells and Lighthouses. 5000f.×6
Dinosaurs. 5000f.×6
Endangered Species. 5000f.×6
Elephants and Mammoths. 5000f.×6
Fauna and Fruit. 5000f.×6
Tennis Players. 5000f.×6
Internet. 5000f.×6
400th Anniv of Quebec. 5000f.×6
Arthur C. Clarke. 5000f.×6
Ivan Rebroff. 5000f.×6
Henri Salvador. 5000f.×6
Cyd Charisse. 5000f.×6
Roy Schneider. 5000f.×6
Jaques Brel. 5000f.×6
Stan Swinston. 5000f.×6
Charlton Heston. 5000f.×6
Sydney Pollack. 5000f.×6
Launch of Phoenix Spacecraft. 5000f.×6
Madonna. 5000f.×6
Expo 2010, Shanghai. 5000f.×6
Total Solar Eclipse. 5000f.×6
World Youth Day. 5000f.×6

Simone de Beauvoir. 5000f.×6
First flight of Sukhoi Superjet. 5000f.×6
International Year of the Potato. 5000f.×6
Daytona 500. 5000f.×6
Tenth Anniv of FIM. 5000f.×6
Barcelona World Yacht Race. 5000f.×6
John Shedd Reed Trains. 5000f.×6
Space Shuttle Atlantis. 5000f.×6
Petrol Crisis. 5000f.×6
Transport in Popular Culture. 5000f.×6
Year of Astronomy. 5000f.×6
Disappearence of Steve Fosset. 5000f.×6
Opening of Osaka Higashi Line. 5000f.×6
Mars Overflight. 5000f.×6
New Horizon Space Probe. 5000f.×6
Sebastien Loeb. 5000f.×6
Africarail 2008. 5000f.×6
Edward Lorenz. 5000f.×6
Frank Piasecki. 5000f.×6
John wheeler. 5000f.×6
44th President of USA. 5000f.×6
Cinema. 5000f.×30
Pulitzer Prize. 5000f.×6
Grammy Awards. 5000f.×6
Emmy Awards. 5000f.×6
Year of Astronomy. 5000f.×6
Golden Globe Awards. 5000f.×6
Nobel Peace Prize. 5000f.×6
Football. 5000f.×6
Nobel Prize for Literature. 5000f.×6
International Peace Prize. 5000f.×6
Nobel Prize for Physics. 5000f.×6
Mandrake d'Or for Magicians. 5000f.×6
Fields Medal. 5000f.×6
Nobel Prize for Medicine. 5000f.×6
Turing Prize. 5000f.×6
Sakharov Prize. 5000f.×6
Chinese Rock Stars. 5000f.×6
Chinese Birds. 5000f.×6
Chinese Butterflies. 5000f.×6
Chinese Dogs. 5000f.×6
Chinese Sports. 5000f.×6
Chinese Nobel Prize Winners. 5000f.×6
Chinese Table Tennis Players. 5000f.×6
Chinese Chess Players. 5000f.×6
Chinese Flora. 5000f.×6
Chinese Porcelain. 5000f.×6
Chinese Trains. 5000f.×6
Cats of Asia. 5000f.×6
Chinese Art. 5000f.×6
Chinese Athletes. 5000f.×6
Chinese Emperors. 5000f.×6
Chinese Projects. 5000f.×6
Ancient Chinese Ships. 5000f.×6
China in Africa. 5000f.×6
China 2009 International Stamp Exhibition. 5000f.×6

2009

40th Anniv of First Supersonic Flight. 5000f.×18
Slovakia acceded to Euro Zone. 5000f.×6
Year of Astronomy. 5000f.×6
Barack Obama. 5000f.×6
Year of the Ox. 5000f.×6
Iranian Anniversaries. 5000f.×6
Sustainable Development Summit. 5000f.×6
Birth Bicentenary of Charles Darwin. 5000f.×6
150th Anniv of Publication Origin of Species. 5000f.×6
81st Oscars Ceremony. 5000f.×6
34th Cesar Awards Ceremony. 5000f.×6
Centenary of Louis Bleriot's Flight. 5000f.×6
Abraham Lincoln. 5000f.×6
Death Bicentenary of Jean Bardin. 5000f.×6

Pt. 13

GUINEA-BISSAU

Following an armed rebellion against Colonial rule, the independence of former Portuguese Guinea was recognised on 10 September 1974.

1974. 100 centavos = 1 escudo.
1976. 100 centavos = 1 peso.

77 Amilcar Cabral, Map and Flag

1974. First Anniv of Proclamation of Republic. Country name inscr in white.

426	**77**	1p. multicoloured	50	40
427	**77**	2.5p. multicoloured	75	65
428	**77**	5p. multicoloured	15·00	8·50
429	**77**	10p. multicoloured	2·50	2·00

1975. No. 425 of Portuguese Guinea optd **REP. DA BISSAU**.

430	2e. multicoloured	60	60

79 Amilcar Cabral, Map and Flag

1975. Second Anniv of Proclamation of Republic (1st issue). Country name inscr in black.

431	**79**	1p. multicoloured	45	30
432	**79**	2.5p. multicoloured	60	45
433	**79**	5p. multicoloured	2·50	1·40

434	79	10p. multicoloured	2·50	2·25

See also Nos. 439/440.

80 Amilcar Cabral, Arms and Flag

1975. 51st Birth Anniv of Amilcar Cabral (founder of P.A.I.G.C.).

435	80	1e. multicoloured	20	10
436	80	10e. multicoloured	80	40

81 Family, Arms and Flag

1975. 19th Anniv of P.A.I.G.C. (Partido Africano da Independencia da Guine e do Cabo Verde).

437	81	2e. multicoloured	50	20
438	81	10e. multicoloured	2·00	75

82 Pres. Luis Cabral, Arms and Flag

1975. Second Anniv of Proclamation of Republic (2nd issue).

439	82	3e. multicoloured	40	20
440	82	5e. multicoloured	85	30

83 General Henry Knox (after Stuart) and Cannons of Ticonderoga (after Lovell)

1976. Bicentenary of American Independence (1st issue). Multicoloured.

441	83	5e. Type **83** (postage)	25	15
442		10e. General Putnam and Battle of Bunker Hill	55	30
443		15e. Washington and Crossing of the Delaware	80	35
444		20e. General Kosciuszko and Battle of Saratoga	1·25	50
445		30e. General von Steuben and Valley Forge (air)	1·75	90
446		40e. Lafayette and Monmouth Court House	2·00	1·00
MS447		122×83 mm. 50p. *The Declaration of Independence* (Trumbell)	2·10	2·10

See also Nos. 503/6.

84 Masked Dancer

1976. Dancers. Multicoloured.

448	84	2p. Type **84** (postage)	30	10
449		3p. Dancer and drummer	35	15
450		5p. Dancers on stilts	60	20
451		10p. Dancers with spears and bows (air)	65	40
452		15p. Masked dancer	1·00	50
453		20p. "Devil" dancer	1·50	65
MS454		78×104 mm. 50p. As No. 453	3·50	3·50

1976. Cent of Universal Postal Union (1st issue). Nos. 1448/MS1454 optd **CENTENARIO DA U.P.U. 1874. MEMBRO DA U.P.U. 1974** and emblem.

455	84	2p. multicoloured (post)	10	10
456	-	3p. multicoloured	20	10
457	-	5p. multicoloured	25	15
458	-	10p. multicoloured (air)	50	25
459	-	15p. multicoloured	65	40
460	-	20p. multicoloured	90	50
MS461		78×104 mm. 50p. multicoloured	2·00	2·00

See also Nos. 518/MS524.

1976. Nos. 435/40 surch in new currency.

462		1p. on 1e. multicoloured	10	10
463		2p. on 2e. multicoloured	10	10
464		3p. on 3e. multicoloured	15	10
465		5p. on 5e. multicoloured	25	15
466		10p. on 10e. multicoloured	50	30
467		10p. on 10e. multicoloured	50	30

87 Amilcar Cabral and Funeral

1976. Third Anniv of Amilcar Cabral's Assassination.

468	87	3p. multicoloured	15	10
469	87	5p. multicoloured	20	15
470	87	6p. multicoloured	25	20
471	87	10p. multicoloured	40	25

88 Party Emblem

1976. 20th Anniv of P.A.I.G.C.

472	88	3p. multicoloured	15	15
473	88	15p. multicoloured	65	50
474	88	50p. multicoloured	1·60	1·25

89 Launch of "Soyuz" Spacecraft

1976. Air. "Apollo–Soyuz" Space Link. Multicoloured.

475	89	5p. Type **89**	25	15
476		10p. Launch of "Apollo" spacecraft	45	30
477		15p. Leonov, Stafford and meeting in Space	80	45
478		20p. Eclipse of the Sun	1·25	55
479		30p. Infra-red photograph of Earth	1·75	85
480		40p. Return of Spacecraft to Earth	2·25	95
MS481		117×80 mm. 50p. Spacecraft docking (59×39 mm)	2·00	2·00

90 Bell Telephone of 1876 and Laying First Atlantic Cable

1976. Telephone Centenary. Multicoloured.

482	90	2p. Type **90** (postage)	15	10
483		3p. French telephone of 1890 and first telephone box, 1893	20	10
484		5p. German automatic telephone of 1908 and automatic telephone, 1898	25	10
485		10p. English telephone of 1910 and trans-horizon link, 1963 (air)	55	25
486		15p. French telephone of 1924 and communications satellite	85	45
487		20p. Modern telephone and "Molnya" satellite	1·25	50
MS488		126×83 mm. 50p. Visionphone and people of different races (68×42 mm)	2·00	2·00

91 Women's Figure Skating

1976. Winter Olympic Games, Innsbruck. Multicoloured.

489		1p. Type **91** (postage)	15	10
490		3p. Ice-hockey	30	10
491		5p. Bobsleighing	30	15
492		10p. Pairs figure-skating (air)	55	30
493		20p. Cross-country skiing	1·25	45
494		30p. Speed skating	1·75	85
MS495		116×78 mm. 50p. Slalom skiing	2·25	2·25

92 Footballers and Montreal Skyline

1976. Olympic Games, Montreal. Multicoloured.

496		1p. Type **92**	10	10
497		3p. Pole vaulting	15	10
498		5p. Hurdling	25	15
499		10p. Discus throwing	45	25
500		20p. Running	90	50
501		30p. Wrestling	1·40	75
MS502		120×90 mm. 50p. Cycling (47×38 mm)	2·25	2·25

93 "Viking" orbiting Mars

1976. Bicentenary of American Revolution (2nd issue). Multicoloured. (a) Postage. Horiz designs as T **83**.

503		3p.50 Crispus Attuck and Boston Massacre	30	10
504		5p. Martin Luther King and Capitol	40	20

(b) Air. Success of "Viking" Mission. Vert.

505		25p. Type **93**	1·25	65
506		35p. Lander scooping samples from surface of Mars	1·75	90

94 Amilcar Cabral

1977. Fourth Death Anniv of Amilcar Cabral. Multicoloured.

507		50c. Type **94** (postage)	15	10
508		3p.50 Luis Cabral addressing U.N. Assembly	35	10
509		15p. Type **94** (air)	55	30
510		30p. As No. 508	1·25	50

95 Henri Dunant (Peace, 1901)

1977. 75th Anniv of First Nobel Prizes. Multicoloured.

511		3p.50 Type **95** (postage)	30	10
512		5p. Albert Einstein (Physics, 1921)	35	20
513		6p. Irene and Jean-Frederic Joliot-Curie (Chemistry, 1935)	75	20
514		30p. Alexander Fleming (Medicine, 1945)	1·75	90
515		35p. Ernest Hemingway (Literature, 1954) (air)	2·00	90
516		40p. J. Tinbergen (Economic Sciences, 1969)	2·25	1·00
MS517		101×80 mm. 50p. Nobel Prize medal (56×38 mm)	2·25	2·25

96 Postal Runner and "Telstar" Satellite

1977. Centenary (1974) of Universal Postal Union (2nd issue). Multicoloured.

518		3p.50 Type **96** (postage)	25	15
519		5p. A.E.G. J-II biplane, and satellites circling globe	35	15
520		6p. Mail van and satellite control room	55	15
521		30p. Stage-coach and astronaut cancelling letters on Moon	1·75	50
522		35p. French locomotive (1844) and "Intelsat 4" satellite (air)	6·50	2·75
523		40p. Aircraft and "Apollo"–"Soyuz" link	2·50	90
MS524		115×87 mm. 50p. Chappe's optical telegraph and dish aerial	2·25	2·25

97 Coronation Coach

1977. Silver Jubliee of Queen Elizabeth II. Multicoloured.

525		3p.50 Type **97** (postage)	20	10
526		5p. Coronation ceremony	25	15
527		10p. Yeoman of the Guard and Crown Jewels	45	25
528		20p. Trumpeter sounding fanfare	90	45
529		25p. Royal Horse Guard (air)	1·25	50
530		30p. Royal Family on balcony	1·50	70
MS531		85×102 mm. 50p. Queen Elizabeth, Westminster Abbey and Coronation Chair (39×35 mm)	2·25	2·25

98 Congress Emblem

1977. Third P.A.I.G.C. Congress, Bissau.

532	98	3p.50 multicoloured	25	15

99 *Massacre of the Innocents* (detail)

1977. 400th Birth Anniv of Peter Paul Rubens (artist). Multicoloured.

533		3p.50 Type **99** (postage)	20	10
534		5p. *Rape of the Daughters of Leukippos*	25	15
535		6p. *Lamentation of Christ* (horiz)	35	15
536		30p. *Francisco IV Gonzaga, Prince of Mantua*	1·60	50
537		35p. *The Four Continents* (detail) (horiz) (air)	1·75	50
538		40p. *Marquise Brigida Spinola Doria*	2·25	60
MS539		89×78 mm. 50p. *Wounding of Christ with a Spear*	2·25	2·25

100 Santos-Dumont's Airship *Ballon No. 6*

1978. Airships. Multicoloured.

540		3p.50 Type **100** (postage)	25	15
541		5p. Beardmore airship R-34 crossing Atlantic	35	15

542	10p. *Norge* over North Pole	55	20
543	20p. *Graf Zeppelin* over Abu Simbel	1·40	50
544	25p. *Hindenburg* over New York (air)	1·75	70
545	30p. *Graf Zeppelin*, Concorde airliner and space shuttle	2·25	75
MS546	110×78 mm. 50p. Count Ferdinand von Zeppelin (56×38 mm)	2·75	2·75

101 Footballers, Cup and Poster (Uruguay, 1930)

1978. World Cup Football Championship, Argentina. Multicoloured.

547	3p.50 Type **101** (postage)	20	10
548	5p. "Coupe du Monde, 1938"	25	15
549	10p. Brazil, 1950	55	25
550	20p. Chile, 1962	1·10	45
551	25p. Mexico, 1970 (air)	1·40	50
552	30p. "FIFA World Cup 1974" (Germany)	1·60	65
MS553	102×77 mm. 50p. Argentina 78 emblem	2·25	2·25

DESIGNS: Showing match scenes and posters from previous championships.

102 Black Antelope

1978. Endangered Animals. Multicoloured.

554	3p.50 Type **102** (postage)	30	10
555	5p. Fennec	75	30
556	6p. Secretary bird	1·00	50
557	30p. Hippopotamuses	2·00	65
558	35p. Cheetahs (air)	2·25	65
559	40p. Gorillas	2·50	75
MS560	94×75 mm. 50p. *Cercopithecus erythotis*	2·25	2·25

103 Microwave-antenna

1978. Telecommunications Day.

561	**103**	3p.50 multicoloured	20	15
562	**103**	10p. multicoloured	55	30

104 Child

1978. Children's Day.

563	**104**	50c. blue and green	10	10
564	-	3p. bright red and red	15	10
565	-	5p. light brown and brown	25	15
566	-	30p. brown and red	1·40	1·00

DESIGNS: 3p. Amilcar Cabral and child; 5p. Children; 30p. Two children playing.

105 Reading the Proclamation

1978. 25th Anniv of Coronation of Queen Elizabeth II. Multicoloured.

567	3p. Type **105** (postage)	20	10
568	5p. Queen and Prince Philip in Coronation Coach	25	15
569	10p. Queen and Prince Philip	45	25
570	20p. Mounted drummer	90	45

571	25p. Imperial State Crown and St. Edward's Crown (air)	1·25	50
572	30p. Queen holding orb and sceptre	1·25	65
573	100p. Queen, stained glass window and Imperial State Crown (55×38 mm)	4·50	1·50
MS574	Two sheets (a) 84×105 mm. 50p. Queen on throne with Archbishops (49×40 mm); (b) 87×119 mm. 100p. Coronation Coach (55×38 mm)	7·00	7·00

106 Wright Brothers and Wright Flyer I

1978. History of Aviation. Multicoloured.

575	3p.50 Type **106** (postage)	20	10
576	10p. Alberto Santos-Dumont	45	20
577	15p. Louis Bleriot	75	35
578	20p. Charles Lindbergh (air)	90	40
579	25p. Moon landing	1·25	50
580	30p. Space shuttle	1·50	65
MS581	120×83 mm. 50p. Concorde	3·00	3·00

1978. World Cup Football Championship Results. Nos. 547/52 optd **10 ARGENTINA 20 HOLANDA 30 BRAZIL.**

582	3p.50 multicoloured (postage)	20	10
583	5p. multicoloured	25	15
584	10p. multicoloured	45	25
585	20p. multicoloured	1·10	55
586	25p. multicoloured (air)	1·25	55
587	30p. multicoloured	1·50	70
MS588	102×77 mm. 50p. multicoloured	2·25	2·25

108 *Virgin and Child*, 1497

1978. 450th Death Anniv of Albrecht Durer (artist). Multicoloured.

589	3p.50 Type **108** (postage)	20	10
590	5p. *Virgin and Child*, 1507	25	15
591	6p. *Virgin and Child*, 1512	30	15
592	30p. *Virgin*, 1518	1·40	70
593	35p. *Virgin and Child with St. Anne*, 1519 (air)	1·75	50
594	40p. *Virgin of the Pear*, 1526	2·00	75
MS595	95×85 mm. 50p.*Adoration of the Magi* (49×55 mm)	2·25	1·25

109 Rowland Hill and Wurttemberg 70k. Stamp, 1873

1978. Death Centenary of Rowland Hill.

596	3p.50 Type **109** (postage)	15	10
597	5p. Belgian 10c. stamp, 1849	25	15
598	6p. Monaco 5f. stamp, 1885	30	20
599	30p. Spanish 10r. stamp, 1851	1·40	70
600	35p. Swiss 5r. stamp, 1851 (air)	1·75	50
601	40p. Naples ½t. stamp, 1860	2·00	75
MS602	99×78 mm. 50p. Portuguese Guinea stamp, 1885 (49×41 mm)	2·25	2·25

DESIGNS: 5p. to 40p. show Rowland Hill and stamp.

110 Nurse immunising Child

1979. International Year of the Child (1st issue). Multicoloured.

603	3p.50 Type **110** (postage)	20	10
604	10p. Children drinking	55	25
605	15p. Children with book	1·00	35
606	20p. Space shuttle (air)	1·00	40
607	25p. "Skylab" space station	1·40	50
608	30p. Children playing chess	2·00	75
MS609	117×81 mm. 50p. Children watching space ship orbiting planet	2·25	2·25

See also Nos. 616/**MS619.**

111 Family

1979. National Census.

610	**111**	50c. brown, blue and pink	10	10
611	**111**	2p. brown, blue & lt blue	15	10
612	**111**	4p. brown, blue and yellow	25	15

112 Wave Pattern and Human Figures

1979. World Telecommunications Day. Multicoloured.

613	50c. Type **112**	10	10
614	4p. Wave pattern and human figures (different)	20	15

113 Monument

1979. 20th Anniv of Pindjiuouiti Massacre.

615	**113**	4p.50 multicoloured	30	15

114 Classroom Scene

1980. International Year of the Child (2nd issue). Multicoloured.

616	6p. Type **114** (postage)	30	25
617	10p. Jules Verne and child reading novel (vert)	45	30
618	25p. Locomotive "Northumbrian" (1831), Japanese "Hikari" express train and child with toy steam locomotive (vert)	9·00	1·25
619	35p. Man and child with bows and arrows (vert)	1·60	75
MS620	102×77 mm. 50p. Children with microscope (air)	2·25	2·25

115 Amilcar Cabral, Workers and Children reading Books

1980. Literacy Campaign. Multicoloured.

621	3p.50 Type **115** (postage)	20	10
622	5p. Luis Cabral displaying school textbooks	30	15
623	15p. Type **115** (air)	80	50
624	25p. As No. 622	1·40	75

116 Globe and Cogwheel

1980. Technical Co-operation among Developing Countries.

625	**116**	3p.50 multicoloured	20	10
626	**116**	6p. multicoloured	30	20
627	**116**	10p. multicoloured	45	30

117 Wood Carvings

1980. Handicrafts. Multicoloured.

628	3p. Type **117**	20	10
629	6p. Weaving (horiz)	30	20
630	20p. Bust and statuette (horiz)	1·00	50

118 Ernst Udet

1980. History of Aviation. Air Aces of First World War. Multicoloured.

631	3p.50 Type **118** (postage)	25	15
632	5p. Charles Nungesser	35	25
633	6p. Manfred von Richthofen	55	25
634	30p. Francesco Baracca	1·75	70
635	35p. Willy Coppens de Houthulst (air)	2·10	75
636	40p. Charles Guynemer	2·50	90
MS637	117×80 mm. 50p. Commandant de Rose (37×53 mm)	2·25	2·25

119 Speed Skating

1980. Winter Olympic Games, Lake Placid. Multicoloured.

638	3p. Type **119** (postage)	20	10
639	5p. Downhill	30	20
640	6p. Luge	40	25
641	30p. Cross country skiing	1·75	70
642	35p. Downhill skiing (air)	2·00	75
643	40p. Figure skating	2·40	90
MS644	99×79 mm. 50p. Ice hockey (46×37 mm)	2·25	2·25

120 Putting the Shot

1980. Olympic Games, Moscow. Multicoloured.

645	3p.50 Type **120** (postage)	20	15
646	5p. Gymnastics (ring exercise)	25	20
647	6p. Long jump	35	25
648	30p. Fencing	1·50	70
649	35p. Gymnastics (backward somersault) (air)	1·75	75
650	40p. Running	2·00	90
MS651	84×69 mm. 50p. Olympic emblems and runner (41×50 mm)	2·25	2·25

121 Congress Meeting

1980. 16th Anniv of Cassaca Congress.

652	**121**	3p.50 multicoloured	15	10
653	**121**	6p.50 multicoloured	30	20
654	**121**	10p. multicoloured	40	30

122 Satellites

1981. Space Achievements. Multicoloured.

655	3p.50 Type **122** (postage)	20	10
656	5p. Satellite	25	15
657	6p. Rocket	30	15
658	30p. Space Shuttle "Columbia"	1·75	90
659	35p. "Viking I" (air)	1·75	75
660	40p. U.S.–Soviet space link	2·00	90
MS661 131×80 mm. 50p. "Apollo 11" crew and badge (horiz 59×41 mm)		2·25	2·25

123 Platini (France) and Football Scene

1981. World Cup Football Championship, Spain. Multicoloured.

662	3p.50 Type **123** (postage)	30	10
663	5p. Bettega (Italy)	35	15
664	6p. Rensenbrink (Netherlands)	40	15
665	30p. Rivelino (Brazil)	1·90	80
666	35p. Rummenigge (West Germany) (air)	1·90	80
667	40p. Kempes (Argentina)	2·00	90
MS668 116×82 mm. 50p. Juanito (Spain)		2·25	2·25

124 Lady Diana Spencer with Horse

1981. Wedding of Prince of Wales. Multicoloured.

669	3p.50 Type **124** (postage)	20	15
670	5p. Investiture of Prince of Wales	25	15
671	6p. Lady Diana Spencer with Children	30	15
672	30p. St. Paul's Cathedral	1·25	95
673	35p. Althorp House (air)	1·40	1·00
674	40p. Arms of Prince of Wales	1·50	1·25
MS675 85×103 mm. 50p. Lady Diana Spencer and Prince of Wales		2·00	2·00

125 Eric the Red and Viking Ship

1981. Navigators. Multicoloured.

676	3p.50 Type **125** (postage)	25	15
677	5p. Vasco da Gama and *Sao Gabriel*	30	15
678	6p. Magellan and *Vitoria*	35	20
679	30p. Cartier and *Emerillon*	2·00	1·00
680	35p. Drake and *Golden Hind* (air)	2·50	1·25
681	40p. Cook and H.M.S. *Endeavour*	2·75	1·60
MS682 97×94 mm. 50p. Columbus and *Santa Maria*		3·00	3·00

126 Girl with Bare Feet

1981. Birth Centenary of Pablo Picasso. Multicoloured.

683	3p.50 Type **126** (postage)	20	15
684	5p. Acrobat on Ball	25	15
685	6p. *Pierrot*	30	15
686	30p. *Girl in front of a Mirror*	1·50	95
687	35p. *The First Steps* (air)	2·00	1·00
688	40p. *Woman in Turkish Dress*	2·25	1·25
MS689 93×111 mm. 50p. *Portrait of Sylvette* (41×50 mm)		2·50	2·50

127 Retable of St. Zeno (Mantegna)

1981. Christmas. Multicoloured.

690	3p.50 Type **127** (postage)	20	15
691	5p. *Virgin with Child* (Bellini)	25	15
692	6p. *Virgin and Child with Cherubs* (Mantegna)	30	15
693	25p. *Madonna Campori* (Correggio)	1·50	1·00
694	30p. *Virgin and Child* (Memling) (air)	2·00	1·10
695	35p. *Virgin and Child* (Bellini)	2·25	1·25
MS696 68×117 mm. 50p. *Cortone Triptych* (Fra Angelico) (35×59 mm)		3·00	3·00

128 Archery

1982. 75th Anniv of Boy Scout Movement. Multicoloured.

697	3p.50 Type **128** (postage)	15	10
698	5p. First aid	20	15
699	6p. Bugler	25	15
700	30p. Cub scouts	1·60	80
701	35p. Girl scout in canoe (air)	2·25	90
702	40p. Scouts with model aircraft	2·40	1·25
MS703 100×80 mm. 50p. Scouts playing chess (horiz 47×38 mm)		2·60	2·60

129 Keegan

1982. World Cup Football Championship, Spain. Multicoloured.

704	3p.50 Type **129** (postage)	20	10
705	5p. Rossi	20	15
706	6p. Zico	25	15
707	30p. Arconada	1·60	80
708	35p. Kempes (air)	2·25	1·00
709	40p. Kaltz	2·50	1·10
MS710 100×72 mm. 50p. Player, World Cup and stadium		2·75	2·75

130 Lady Diana Spencer

1982. 21st Birthday of Princess of Wales. Multicoloured.

711	3p.50 Type **130** (postage)	15	10
712	5p. Playing croquet	25	15
713	6p. Lady Diana with pony	30	15
714	30p. Fishing	1·75	80
715	35p. Engagement picture (air)	1·90	90
716	40p. Honeymoon picture	2·00	1·10
MS717 100×80 mm. 50p. Princess of Wales with Prince William (vert)		2·25	2·25

1982. Birth of Prince William of Wales. Nos. 711/**MS**717 optd **21 DE JULHO 1982. GUILHERMO ARTHUR FILIPE LUIS PRINCIPE DE GALES.**

718	3p.50 multicoloured (postage)	20	10
719	5p. multicoloured	25	15
720	6p. multicoloured	30	15
721	30p. multicoloured	1·60	95
722	35p. multicoloured (air)	1·90	1·10
723	40p. multicoloured	2·00	1·25
MS724 100×80 mm. 50p. multicoloured		2·25	2·25

132 National Colours

1982. Visit of President Eanes of Portugal. Multicoloured.

725	4p.50 Type **132**	10	10
726	20p. Doves on national colours	20	10

133 Montgolfier Balloon

1983. Bicentenary of Manned Flight. Multicoloured.

727	50c. Type **133**	10	10
728	2p.50 Charles's hydrogen balloon	15	10
729	3p.50 Charles Green's balloon *Royal Vauxhall*	20	10
730	5p. Gaston Tissandier's balloon *Zenith*	30	10
731	10p. Salomon Andree's balloon *Ornen* over Arctic	60	20
732	20p. Stratosphere balloon *Explorer II*	1·25	40
733	30p. Modern hot-air balloons	2·00	60
MS734 75×87 mm. 50p. Gas balloon (47×47 mm)		3·00	3·00

134 Hamadryas Baboon

1983. African Primates. Multicoloured.

735	1p. Type **134**	10	10
736	1p.50 Gorilla	20	10
737	3p.50 Gelada	30	10
738	5p. Mandrill	40	15
739	8p. Chimpanzee	80	20
740	20p. Eastern black-and-white colobus	1·50	50
741	30p. Diana monkey	2·40	85

135 USA Space Rocket

1983. "Tembal 83" International Thematic Stamp Exhibition, Basle. Sheet 91×57 mm.

MS742 **135** 50p. multicoloured	3·25	3·25

136 Satellite

1983. Cosmonautics Day. Multicoloured.

743	1p. Type **136**	10	10
744	1p.50 Satellite (different)	15	10
745	3p.50 Rocket carrying space shuttle	20	10
746	5p. Satellite (different)	30	15
747	8p. Satellite (different)	60	20
748	20p. Satellite (different)	1·25	45
749	30p. "Soyuz" docking with "Salyut"	2·00	70
MS750 95×54 mm. 50p. "Soyuz"–"Salyut" complex (28×36 mm)		3·25	3·25

137 Woodcut from Caxton's *Game and Playe of Chesse*, Arabian Pawn and Rook

1983. Chess. Multicoloured.

751	1p. Type **137**	15	10
752	1p.50 12th-century European king and knight	15	10
753	3p.50 Mid 18th-century German rook, queen and king	25	10
754	5p. Late 12th/early 13th-century Danish bishop and knight	40	10
755	10p. 18th-century French king and queen	80	25
756	20p. 18th-century Venetian king, knight and queen	1·75	55
757	40p. 19th-century faience knight, queen and rook	3·00	1·10
MS758 83×70 mm. 50p. brown and black (15th-century engraving of chess players) (31×36 mm)		3·50	3·50

138 Vision of Ezekiel

1983. 500th Birth Anniv of Raphael (artist). Multicoloured.

759	1p. Type **138**	10	10
760	1p.50 *Tempi Madonna*	10	10
761	3p.50 *Della Tenda Madonna*	20	10
762	5p. *Orleans Madonna*	25	10
763	8p. *La Belle Jardiniere*	45	20
764	15p. *Small Cowper Madonna*	90	35
765	30p. *St. George and the Dragon*	2·00	60
MS766 74×58 mm. 50p. *Solby Madonna* (31×39 mm)		3·25	3·25

139 Swimming

1983. Olympic Games, Los Angeles (1932 and 1984) (1st issue). Multicoloured.

767	1p. Type **139**	10	10
768	1p.50 Hurdling	15	10
769	3p.50 Fencing	20	10
770	5p. Weightlifting	30	10
771	10p. Marathon	60	15
772	20p. Show jumping	1·10	35
773	40p. Cycling	2·40	65

MS774 86×81 mm. 50p. Stadium   2·60   2·60
See also Nos. 843/**MS**850.

140 Portuguese
Caravel

1983. Brasiliana 83 International Stamp Exhibition, Rio de Janeiro. Sheet 90×89 mm.
MS775 **140** 50p. multicoloured   2·60   2·60

141 Rowland Hill and Penny
Black

1983. World Communications Year. Multicoloured.
776		50c. Type **141**	10	10
777		2p.50 Samuel Morse and morse machine	15	10
778		3p.50 Heinrich Rudolf Hertz and electromagnetic wave diagrams	20	10
779		5p. Lord Kelvin and *Agamemnon* (cable ship)	50	10
780		10p. Alexander Graham Bell and telephones	60	15
781		20p. Guglielmo Marconi and wireless apparatus	1·40	40
782		30p. Vladimir Kosma Zworykin and television	1·60	55
MS783	98×64 mm. 50p. Satellites		3·00	3·00

142 JAAC Emblem

1983. First JAAC Congress. Multicoloured.
784		4p. Crowd and emblem	25	15
785		5p. Type **142**	30	15

143 Speed Skating

1983. Winter Olympic Games, Sarajevo (1st issue). Multicoloured.
786		1p. Type **143**	10	10
787		1p.50 Ski jumping	15	10
788		3p. Cross-country skiing	20	10
789		5p. Bobsleigh	25	10
790		10p. Ice hockey	70	25
791		15p. Ice skating	1·10	30
792		20p. Luge	1·25	35
MS793	94×54 mm. 50p.Skiing		3·25	3·25

See also Nos. 816/**MS**823.

144 Hoeing Vegetable Patch

1983. World Food Day.
794	**144**	1p.50 multicoloured	10	10
795	**144**	2p. multicoloured	15	10
796	**144**	4p. multicoloured	30	15
MS797	60×61 mm. 10p. Man hoeing plantation		75	25

145 U.D.E.M.U.
Emblem

1983. Democratic Union of Women. Multicoloured.
798		4p.50 Type **145**	30	15
799		7p.50 Flag and woman	50	20
800		9p. Woman sewing	70	30
801		12p. Women working on plantation	1·00	45

146 *Canna coccinea*

1983. Flowers. Multicoloured.
802		1p. Type **146**	15	10
803		1p.50 *Bougainvillea litoralis*	20	10
804		3p.50 *Euphorbia milii*	25	10
805		5p. *Delonix regia*	30	10
806		8p. *Bauhinia variegata*	50	15
807		10p. *Spathodea campanulata*	70	20
808		30p. *Hibiscus rosa-sinensis*	2·00	60

147 Guinean
Fingerfish

1983. Fish. Multicoloured.
809		1p. Type **147**	20	15
810		1p.50 Clown loach	25	15
811		3p.50 Spotted climbing-perch	35	20
812		5p. Berthold's panchax	50	20
813		8p. Red-barred lyretail	75	30
814		10p. Two-striped lyretail	1·10	40
815		30p. Lyre-tailed panchax	3·50	1·40

148 Ski Jumping

1984. Winter Olympic Games, Sarajevo (2nd issue). Multicoloured.
816		50c. Type **148**	10	10
817		2p.50 Speed skating	15	10
818		3p.50 Ice hockey	30	10
819		5p. Cross-country skiing	35	10
820		6p. Downhill skiing	60	15
821		20p. Ice skating	1·25	40
822		30p. Two-man bobsleigh	2·00	60
MS823	71×92 mm. 50p. Skiing		3·00	3·00

149 Duesenberg, 1928

1984. 150th Birth Anniv of Gottlieb Daimler (automobile designer). Multicoloured.
824		5p. Type **149**	15	10
825		8p. MG "Midget", 1932	25	10
826		3p. Mercedes, 1928	50	20
827		20p. Bentley, 1928	60	30
828		24p. Alfa Romeo, 1929	85	30
829		30p. Datsun, 1932	1·25	35
830		35p. Lincoln, 1932	1·75	40
MS831	78×112 mm. 100p. Gottlieb Daimler and car (49×42 mm)		3·50	3·50

150 Sud Aviation Caravelle

1984. 40th Anniv of I.C.A.O. Multicoloured.
832		8p. Type **150**	25	10
833		22p. Douglas DC-6B	80	30
834		80p. Ilyushin Il-76	2·25	90

151 *Dona Tadea
Arias de Enriquez*
(Goya)

1984. "Espana 84" International Stamp Exhibition, Madrid. Multicoloured.
835		3p. *Virgin and Child* (Morales)	15	10
836		6p. Type **151**	20	10
837		10p. *Saint Cassilda* (Zurbaran)	30	10
838		12p. *Saints Andrew and Francis* (El Greco)	35	15
839		15p. *Infanta Isabel Clara Eugenia* (Coello)	55	15
840		35p. *Queen Maria of Austria* (Velazquez)	1·40	45
841		40p. *The Trinity* (El Greco)	1·75	55
MS842	76×81 mm. 100p. *The Clothed Maja* (Goya) (49×28 mm)		3·25	3·25

152 Football

1984. Olympic Games, Los Angeles (2nd issue). Multicoloured.
843		6p. Type **152**	15	10
844		8p. Show jumping	25	10
845		15p. Sailing	50	15
846		20p. Hockey	70	20
847		22p. Handball	75	20
848		30p. Canoeing	1·10	35
849		40p. Boxing	1·75	60
MS850	79×92 mm. 100p. Windsurfing		3·75	3·75

153 Fabric
Headdress

1984. "Lubrapex 84" Portuguese–Brazilian Stamp Exhibition, Lisbon. Multicoloured.
851		7p.50 Type **153**	25	15
852		7p.50 Headdress	25	15
853		7p.50 Carved bird headdress	25	15
854		7p.50 Wooden mask	25	15
855		7p.50 Carving of horse	25	15
856		7p.50 Statuette	25	15

154 Tiger

1984. Wild Cats. Multicoloured.
857		3p. Type **154**	15	10
858		6p. Lions	25	10
859		10p. Clouded leopard	35	15
860		12p. Cheetahs	45	20
861		15p. Lynx	60	25
862		35p. Leopard	1·40	55
863		40p. Snow leopard	1·75	65

155 Pearl Throne,
Cameroun

1984. World Heritage. Multicoloured.
864		3p. Type **155**	10	10
865		6p. Antelope (carving), West Sudan	20	10
866		10p. Setial, East Africa	30	15
867		12p. Mask, West African coast	40	20
868		15p. Leopard (statuette), Guinea coast	60	25
869		35p. Carved statuette of woman, Zaire	1·25	50
870		40p. Funeral figures, South-east Africa and Madagascar	1·25	55

156 Amilcar Cabral
making Speech

1984. 60th Birth Anniv of Amilcar Cabral. Multicoloured.
871		5p. Type **156**	15	10
872		12p. Amilcar Cabral in combat dress	35	15
873		20p. Amilcar Cabral memorial	60	25
874		50p. Amilcar Cabral mausoleum	1·50	60

157 Mechanic working on
Engine

1984. 11th Anniv of Independence. Multicoloured.
875		3p. Type **157**	10	10
876		6p. Children in school	20	10
877		10p. Laying bricks	30	10
878		12p. Doctor tending child (vert)	35	20
879		15p. Sewing (vert)	40	20
880		35p. Telephonist and switchboard	1·25	50
881		40p. P.A.I.G.C. headquarters	1·25	55

158 Grey Whales

1984. Whales. Multicoloured.
882		5p. Type **158**	25	10
883		8p. Blue whales	30	15
884		15p. Bottle-nosed dolphins	60	25
885		20p. Sperm whale	70	25
886		24p. Killer whale	85	35
887		30p. Bowhead whale	1·50	40
888		35p. Sei whale	1·75	45

159 *Hypolimnas dexithea*

1984. Butterflies and Moths. Multicoloured.
889		3p. Type **159**	15	15
890		6p. *Papilio arcturus*	20	15
891		10p. *Morpho menelaus terrestris*	35	15
892		12p. *Apaturina erminea*	45	20
893		15p. *Prepona praeneste*	70	25
894		35p. *Ornithoptera paradisea*	1·60	55
895		40p. *Morpho hecuba obidona*	1·60	60

160 Carl Lewis (400
m relay)

1984. Olympic Gold Medallists, Los Angeles.
Multicoloured.

896	6p. Type **160**	15	10
897	8p. Koji Gushiken (men's gymnastics)	15	10
898	15p. Dr. Reiner Klimke (individual dressage)	45	20
899	20p. Tracie Ruiz (synchronized swimming)	55	20
900	22p. May Lou Retton (women's gymnastics)	65	25
901	30p. Michael Gross (100 m freestyle and 100 m butterfly)	90	35
902	40p. Edwin Moses (400 m hurdles)	1·25	50
MS903	54×62 mm. 100p. Daley Thompson (decathlon) (30×38 mm)	2·75	2·75

161 White Mountain Central
Railway locomotive, 1926,
U.S.A.

1984. Locomotives. Multicoloured.

904	5p. Type **161**	20	15
905	8p. Talyllyn Mountain Railway locomotive No. 86, 1886, Great Britain	25	15
906	15p. Wuppetal Overhead Railway, 1901, Germany	50	20
907	20p. Peruvian mountain rack railway locomotive	60	25
908	24p. Steam locomotive, Achensee rack railway, Austria	80	30
909	30p. Vitznau–Rigi rack railway locomotive, Switzerland	1·10	40
910	35p. Vitznau–Rigi rack railway locomotive No. 7, Switzerland	1·60	60
MS911	91×66 mm. 100p. As No. 906 (36×27 mm)	3·50	3·50

162 Harley Davidson Motor Cycle

1985. Centenary of Motor Cycle. Multicoloured.

912	5p. Type **162**	20	15
913	8p. Kawasaki	25	15
914	15p. Honda	45	20
915	20p. Yamaha	70	30
916	25p. Suzuki	1·00	35
917	30p. BMW	1·40	45
918	35p. Moto Guzzi	1·50	50
MS919	90×72 mm. 100p. Daimler single track motor cycle, 1885 (27×36 mm)	3·75	3·75

163 Brown Pelican

1985. Air. Birth Bicentenary of John J. Audubon
(ornithologist). Multicoloured.

920	5p. Type **163**	45	20
921	10p. American white pelican	75	30
922	20p. Great blue heron	1·40	45
923	40p. Greater flamingo	3·00	1·00

164 Clitocybe gibba

1985. Fungi. Multicoloured.

924	7p. Type **164**	35	15
925	9p. Morchella elata	50	20
926	12p. Lepista nuda	75	25
927	20p. Lactarius deliciosus	90	30
928	30p. Russula virescens	1·25	35
929	35p. Chroogomphus rutilus	1·75	50

165 Dunant, Piper Twin
Commanche and Volunteers
attending Patient

1985. 75th Death Anniv of Henri Dunant (Red Cross
founder). Multicoloured.

930	20p. Type **165**	40	15
931	25p. Doctor and volunteer putting patient in ambulance	50	15
932	40p. Helicopter team attending wounded soldier	75	35
933	80p. Volunteers in boat rescuing man from water	1·40	55

166 Long-haired
White Cat

1985. Cats. Multicoloured.

934	7p. Type **166**	20	15
935	10p. Siamese cat	25	15
936	12p. Grey cat	30	15
937	15p. Tortoiseshell cat	40	15
938	20p. Ginger cat	55	20
939	40p. Tabby cat	1·00	35
940	45p. Short-haired white cat	1·40	35
MS941	80×70 mm. 100p. Tabby kittens (39×31 mm)	2·75	2·75

167 Vincenzo Bellini,
1820 Harp and
16th-century Descant
Viol

1985. International Music Year. Composers. Multicoloured.

942	4p. Type **167** (150th death anniv of Bellini)	15	15
943	5p. Robert Schumann (175th birth anniv) and pyramid piano, 1829	15	15
944	7p. Frederic Chopin (175th birth anniv) and piano, 1817	15	15
945	12p. Luigi Cherubini (225th birth anniv), 1720 baryton and 18th-century quinton	20	15
946	20p. Giovanni Battista Pergolesi (275th birth anniv) and harpsichord, 1734	45	15
947	30p. Georg Friedrich Handel (300th birth anniv), 1825 valve trumpet and 18th-century timpani	65	20
948	50p. Heinrich Schutz (400th birth anniv), 17th-century bass viol and 1680 oboe	1·00	45
MS949	77×90 mm. 100p. Johann Sebastian Bach (300th birth anniv) and organ from Thomas Church, Leipzig (28×49 mm3	75	3·75

168 Santa Maria

1985. Sailing Ships. Multicoloured.

950	8p. Type **168**	30	15
951	15p. 16th-century Dutch carrack	40	15
952	20p. Mayflower	50	15
953	30p. St. Louis (French galleon)	75	20
954	35p. Royal Sovereign (galleon), 1660	85	20
955	45p. Soleil Royal (17th- century French warship)	1·25	35
956	80p. 18th-century British naval brig	1·90	60

169 U.N. Emblem,
Rainbow and Peace
Doves

1985. 40th Anniv of U.N.O.

957	**169**	10p. multicoloured	25	15
958	—	20p. blue and brown	50	35

DESIGN: 20p. U.N. emblem in "40".

170 Madonna of the
Rose Garden (detail)

1985. "Italia '85" International Stamp Exhibition, Rome.
Paintings by Botticelli. Multicoloured.

959	7p. Type **170**	15	10
960	10p. Venus and Mars (detail)	15	10
961	12p. St. Augustine in his Study (detail)	20	15
962	15p. Spring (detail)	25	15
963	20p. Virgin and Child (detail)	35	15
964	40p. Virgin and Child with St. John (detail)	1·00	30
965	45p. Birth of Venus (detail)	1·10	35
MS966	73×107 mm. 100p. Virgin and Child with Two Angels (detail) (31×39 mm)	2·50	2·50

171 Youths dancing

1985. International Youth Year. Multicoloured.

967	7p. Type **171**	10	10
968	13p. Windsurfing	20	15
969	15p. Roller skating	20	15
970	25p. Hang-gliding	35	15
971	40p. Surfing	55	25
972	50p. Skateboarding	75	40
973	80p. Free-falling from airplane	1·50	60
MS974	75×75 mm. 100p. Judo (39×31 mm)	3·25	3·25

172 Alfa Touring Car

1986. Anniversaries and Events. Multicoloured.

975	15p. Tail of comet	1·25	50
976	15p. Head of comet	1·25	50
977	15p. Type **172**	1·25	50
978	15p. Frankfurt am Main railway station, 1914	2·25	75

979	15p. Top of trophy	2·50	1·00
980	15p. Base of trophy	2·50	1·00
981	15p. Olympic rings	3·00	1·00
982	15p. View of Barcelona	3·00	1·00
983	15p. Part of space station	1·25	50
984	15p. Deflectors	1·25	50
985	15p. Space station and Shuttle	1·25	50
986	15p. Part of space station and Earth	1·25	50
987	15p. Boris Becker's head and arm	1·50	75
988	15p. Becker's body	1·50	75
989	15p. Lendl's head and arms	1·50	75
990	15p. Lendl's body and legs	1·50	75
MS991	103×67 mm. 100p. Comet and "Giotto" space probe	8·00	8·00

ANNIVERSARIES: Nos. 975/6, Appearance of Halley's Comet; 977, Centenary of motor car; 978, 150th anniv of German railways; 979/80, World Cup Football Championship, Mexico; 981, Olympic Games, Seoul (1988); 982, "500th anniv of discovery of America by Columbus" Exhibition and Olympic Games, Barcelona (1992); 983/6, 25 years of manned space flights; 987/8, Wimbledon Men's Singles champion, 1986; 989/90, Ivan Lendl, winner of U.S. Masters Tournament, 1986.

Nos. 975/90 were printed together in se-tenant sheetlets of 16 stamps, stamps for the same event forming a composite design.

173 Santa Maria

1987. 500th Anniv (1992) of Discovery of America by
Columbus. Multicoloured.

992	50p. Type **173**	2·25	80
993	50p. View of Seville	2·25	80
994	50p. Pedro Alvares Cabral disembarking at Bahia	2·00	60
995	50p. View of Seville (different)	2·25	80
MS996	103×67 mm. 150p. 15th-century galleon in Lisbon harbour	5·75	5·75

1987. Nos. 352/5, 359 and 362/3 of Portuguese Guinea
surch **DA BISSAU** and new value.

997	100p. on 20c. Type **51**	35	15
998	200p. on 35c. African rock python	70	25
999	300p. on 70c. Boomslang	1·10	35
1000	400p. on 80c. West African mamba	1·25	40
1001	500p. on 3e.50 Brown house snake	1·50	50
1002	1000p. on 15e. Striped beauty snake	3·00	1·00
1003	2000p. on 20e. African egg-eating snake (horiz)	6·00	3·00

1987. No. 430 surch **2500,00**.

1004	**76**	2500p. on 2e. mult	7·00	3·25

176 Ice Dancing

1988. Winter Olympic Games, Calgary. Multicoloured.

1005	5p. Type **176**	10	10
1006	10p. Luge	10	10
1007	50p. Skiing	30	15
1008	200p. Downhill skiing	75	30
1009	300p. Ski-bobbing	1·25	40
1010	500p. Ski jumping (vert)	2·00	55
1011	800p. Speed skating (vert)	3·00	1·10
MS1012	90×47 mm. 900p. Two-man luge (39×31 mm)	3·25	3·25

177 Yachting

1988. Olympic Games, Seoul. Multicoloured.

1013	5p. Type **177**	10	10
1014	10p. Equestrian events (horiz)	10	10
1015	50p. High jumping (horiz)	15	10
1016	200p. Rifle shooting (horiz)	70	30
1017	300p. Triple jumping	1·10	40
1018	500p. Tennis	2·00	50
1019	800p. Archery	2·75	1·00

MS1020 70×45 mm. 900p. Football (39×31 mm)   3·00   3·00

178 Football

1988. "Essen 88" Stamp Fair and European Football Championship, Germany.

1021	**178**	5p. multicoloured	10	10
1022	-	10p. multicoloured	10	10
1023	-	50p. multicoloured	15	10
1024	-	200p. multicoloured	70	30
1025	-	300p. multicoloured	1·10	40
1026	-	500p. multicoloured	2·00	50
1027	-	800p. multicoloured	2·75	1·10

MS1028 60×75 mm. 900p. multicoloured   3·00   3·00

DESIGNS: 10 to 900p. Various footballing scenes.

179 Lioness

1988. Animals. Multicoloured.

1029	5p. Type **179**	10	10
1030	10p. Ferruginous pygmy owl	10	10
1031	50p. Hoopoe (horiz)	25	10
1032	200p. Common zebra (horiz)	30	10
1033	300p. African elephant	50	20
1034	500p. Vulturine guineafowl	3·00	1·25
1035	800p. Black rhinoceros	1·25	50

180 Machel

1988. Second Death Anniv of Pres. Samora Machel of Mozambique. Multicoloured.

1036	10p. Type **180**	10	10
1037	50p. With arm raised	10	10
1038	200p. With soldier	30	10
1039	300p. Wearing suit	50	20

181 Henry Dunant (founder)

1988. 125th Anniv of Int Red Cross. Multicoloured.

1040	10p. Type **181**	10	10
1041	50p. Dr. T. Maunoir	10	10
1042	200p. Dr. Louis Appia	30	10
1043	800p. Gustave Moynier	1·25	50

182 Basset Hound

1988. Dogs. Multicoloured.

1044	5p. Type **182**	10	10
1045	10p. Grand bleu de Gascogne	10	10
1046	50p. Italian spinone	10	10
1047	200p. Yorkshire terrier	30	10
1048	300p. Munsterlander	50	20
1049	500p. Pointer	80	30
1050	800p. German shorthaired pointer	1·25	50

MS1051 81×50 mm. 900p. German shepherd (40×32 mm)   1·40   1·40

183 Egyptian Ship, 3300 B.C.

1988. Sailing Ships. Multicoloured.

1052	5p. Type **183**	10	10
1053	10p. Ship of Sahu Re, 2500 B.C. (wrongly inscr "2700 B.C.")	10	10
1054	50p. Ship of Hatshepsut, 1500 B.C	10	10
1055	200p. Ship of Rameses III, 1200 B.C	35	10
1056	300p. Greek trireme, 480 B.C	60	25
1057	500p. Etruscan bireme, 600 B.C	1·00	40
1058	800p. 12th-century Venetian galley	1·50	65

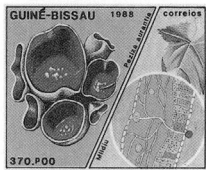

184 Peziza aurantia

1988. Fungi. Multicoloured.

1059	370p. Type **184**	75	30
1060	470p. Morel	1·00	35
1061	600p. Caesar's mushroom	1·25	45
1062	780p. Fly agaric	1·60	55
1063	800p. Deadly amanite	1·60	55
1064	900p. Cultivated mushroom	1·90	70
1065	945p. Pixie stool	2·10	75

185 Francois-Andre Philidor and Rook

1988. "Finlandia 88" International Stamp Exhibition, Helsinki. Chess. Multicoloured.

1066	5p. Type **185**	10	10
1067	10p. Howard Staunton and chessmen	10	10
1068	50p. Adolf Anderssen and queen	10	10
1069	200p. Paul Morphy and pawn	30	10
1070	300p. Wilhelm Steinitz and knight	50	20
1071	500p. Emanuel Lasker and bishop	80	30
1072	800p. Jose Capablanca and king	1·25	50

MS1073 93×62 mm. 900p. Ruy Lopez (37×32 mm)   1·40   1·40

186 Trumpeter, Flag Bearer and Drummer

1988. Abel Djassi Pioneers Organisation. Multicoloured.

1074	10p. Type **186**	10	10
1075	50p. Girls saluting	10	10
1076	200p. Drawing on floor (horiz)	30	10
1077	300p. Playing ball (horiz)	50	20

187 Monument

1988. 400th Anniv of Cacheu. Multicoloured.

1078	10p. Type **187**	10	10
1079	50p. Fort (horiz)	10	10
1080	200p. Early building (horiz)	35	10
1081	300p. Church (horiz)	50	20

188 Woman with Long Hair

1989. Traditional Hairstyles.

1082	**188**	50p. multicoloured	10	10
1083	-	100p. multicoloured	15	10
1084	-	200p. multicoloured	30	10
1085	-	350p. multicoloured	60	25
1086	-	500p. multicoloured	80	30
1087	-	800p. multicoloured	1·25	50
1088	-	1000p. multicoloured	1·60	65

DESIGNS: 50p. to 1000p. Different hairstyles.

189 Bombalon

1989. Traditional Musical Instruments. Multicoloured.

1089	50p. Type **189**	10	10
1090	100p. Flute	15	10
1091	200p. Tambor	35	15
1092	350p. Dondon	65	25
1093	500p. Balafon	90	35
1094	800p. Kora	1·50	60
1095	1000p. Nhanhero	1·75	70

190 Seychelles Blue Pigeon

1989. Birds. Multicoloured.

1096	50p. Type **190**	15	15
1097	100p. Laughing dove	20	15
1098	200p. Namaqua dove	50	30
1099	350p. Purple-breasted ground dove	80	50
1100	500p. African collared dove	1·25	70
1101	800p. Pheasant pigeon	2·10	1·25
1102	1000p. Emerald dove	2·75	1·40

MS1103 71×80 mm. 1500f. Reinwardt's long-tailed pigeon (32×40 mm)   3·75   3·75

191 Pimento

1989. Plants.

1104	**191**	50p. blue	10	10
1105	-	100p. violet	15	10
1106	-	200p. green	35	15
1107	-	350p. red	65	25
1108	-	500p. brown	90	35
1109	-	800p. brown	1·50	60
1110	-	1000p. green	1·75	70

DESIGNS: 100p. Solanum; 200p. "Curcumis peco"; 350p. Tomato; 500p. "Solanum itiopium"; 800p. "Hibiscus esculentus"; 1000p. Baguiche.

192 Madrid Rapid Transit Train No. M-2004, Spain

1989. Trains. Multicoloured.

1111	50p. Type **192**	15	10
1112	100p. Class TEM-2 diesel locomotive, Russia	20	10
1113	200p. Diesel locomotive, Brazil	50	15
1114	350p. Diesel railcar, Spain	95	25
1115	500p. Type 55E electric locomotive, Czechoslovakia	1·40	35
1116	800p. Class Tu-7E diesel shunting locomotive, Russia	2·25	60
1117	1000p. Electric multiple unit, Spain (68×27 mm)	2·60	70

MS1118 89×59 mm. 1500p. Class 593 diesel multiple unit train, Spain (31×39 mm)   3·75   3·75

193 Hurdling

1989. Olympic Games, Barcelona (1992) (1st issue). Multicoloured.

1119	50p. Type **193**	10	10
1120	100p. Boxing	20	10
1121	200p. High jumping	35	15
1122	350p. Sprinters in starting blocks	60	25
1123	500p. Runner leaving starting block	90	35
1124	800p. Gymnastics	1·50	60
1125	1000p. Pole vaulting	1·75	70

MS1126 82×61 mm. 1500p. Football (31×39 mm)   2·60   2·60

See also Nos. 1245/8.

194 "Limelight"

1989. Lilies. Multicoloured.

1127	50p. Type **194**	10	10
1128	100p. "Lilium candidum"	20	10
1129	200p. "Lilium pardalinum"	35	15
1130	350p. "Lilium auratum"	65	25
1131	500p. "Lilium canadense"	90	35
1132	800p. "Enchantment"	1·50	60
1133	1000p. "Black Dragon"	1·75	70

MS1134 43×70 mm. 1500p. "Lilium pyrenaicum" (31×39 mm)   2·60   2·60

195 La Marseillaise (relief by Rude from Arc de Triomphe)

1989. "Philex France 89" International Stamp Exhibition, Paris. Multicoloured.

1135	50p. Type **195**	10	10
1136	100p. Champ de Mars	20	10
1137	200p. Storming of the Bastille	35	15
1138	350p. Fete (27×44 mm)	65	25
1139	500p. Dancing round Tree of Liberty	90	35
1140	800p. Rouget de Lisle singing The Marseillaise	1·50	60
1141	1000p. Storming of the Bastille (different)	1·75	70

MS1142 99×74 mm. 1500p. Motto of the Republic   2·60   2·60

196 Teotihuacan Pot

1989. "Brasiliana 89" International Stamp Exhibition, Rio de Janeiro. Multicoloured.

1143	50p. Type **196**	10	10
1144	100p. Mochica jar	20	10
1145	200p. Jaina statuette	35	15
1146	350p. Nayarit anthrozoomorphic jug	65	25
1147	500p. Inca vase	90	35

1148	800p. Hopewell statuette of mother and child	1·50	60
1149	1000p. Taina mask	1·75	70
MS1150	56×70 mm. 1500p. Ecuador statuette (31×39 mm)	2·75	2·75

197 Players Tackling

1989. World Cup Football Championship, Italy (1990). Multicoloured.

1151	50p. Type **197**	10	10
1152	100p. Players and ball	20	10
1153	200p. Players and ball (different)	35	15
1154	350p. "Scissors" kick	65	25
1155	500p. Goalkeeper	90	35
1156	800p. Foul	1·50	60
1157	1000p. Player scoring goal	1·75	70
MS1158	55×96 mm. 1500p. Legs and ball (37×29 mm)	2·75	2·75

198 Trachodon

1989. Prehistoric Animals. Multicoloured.

1159	50p. Type **198**	10	10
1160	100p. Edaphosaurus (68×22 mm)	20	10
1161	200p. Mesosaurus	35	15
1162	350p. "Elephas primigenius"	65	25
1163	500p. Tyrannosaurus (horiz)	90	35
1164	800p. Stegosaurus (horiz)	1·50	60
1165	1000p. "Cervus megaceros"	1·75	70

No. 1162 is inscribed "Elephius primigienius" in error.

199 Speed Skating

1989. Winter Olympic Games, Albertville (1992). Multicoloured.

1166	50p. Type **199**	10	10
1167	100p. Figure skating	20	10
1168	200p. Ski jumping	35	15
1169	350p. Skiing	65	25
1170	500p. Skiing (different)	90	35
1171	800p. Bobsleighing	1·50	60
1172	1000p. Ice hockey	1·75	70
MS1173	102×61 mm. 1500p. Ice hockey (different) (31×39 mm)	2·75	2·75

200 African Buffalo

1989. Animals.

1174	**200**	50p. brown and red	10	10
1175	-	100p. ultramarine & blue	20	10
1176	-	200p. green & light green	35	15
1177	-	350p. purple and lilac	65	25
1178	-	500p. chestnut and brown	90	35
1179	-	800p. violet & deep violet	1·50	60
1180	-	1000p. deep red and red	1·75	70
1181	-	1500p. red and yellow	2·75	1·10

DESIGNS: 100p. Steppe zebra; 200p. Black rhinoceros; 350p. Okapi; 500p. Rhesus macacque; 800p. Hippopotamus; 1000p. Cheetah; 1500p. Lion.

201 Adoration of Baby Jesus (Fra Filippo Lippi)

1989. Christmas. Multicoloured.

1182	50p. Type **201**	10	10
1183	100p. Adoration of the Kings (Pieter Brueghel)	20	10
1184	200p. Adoration of the Kings (Jan Mostaert)	35	15
1185	350p. Nativity (Albert Durer)	65	25
1186	500p. Adoration of the Kings (Peter Paul Rubens)	90	35
1187	800p. Adoration of the Kings (Roger van der Weyden)	1·50	60
1188	1000p. Adoration of the Kings (Francesco Francia) (horiz)	1·75	70

202 Pope John-Paul II and Map

1990. Papal Visit. Multicoloured.

1189	500p. Type **202**	3·00	1·00
1190	1000p. Pope and couple	3·50	2·00
MS1191	109×137 mm. 1500p. Cathedral (vert)	4·50	2·50

203 Dove flying over Exhibition

1990. Belgica 90 International Stamp Exhibition, Brussels. Sheet 111×122 mm.

MS1192	**203** 3000p. multicoloured	4·00	2·00

204 Cockerel and Hen

1990. "Lubrapex 90" Brazilian–Portuguese Stamp Exhibition, Brasilia. Coop Fowls. Multicoloured.

1193	500p. Type **204**	1·10	50
1194	800p. Common turkey	1·70	1·00
1195	1000p. Duck and ducklings	2·20	1·20
MS1196	112×141 mm. 1500p. Red junglefowl, common turkey, ducks and ducklings	2·50	2·00

205 Radar Rainfall Map

1990. World Meteorology Day. Multicoloured.

1197	1000p. Type **205**	4·50	1·80
1198	3000p. Campbell-Stokes heliograph	13·50	5·00

206 Crying Man and Baby in Womb

1990. 40th Anniv of U.N. Development Programme.

1199	**206** 1000p. multicoloured	4·00	1·50

207 Cotton Plant

1991. Traditional Cotton Weaving. Multicoloured.

1200	400p. Type **207**	1·30	80
1201	500p. Weaver	2·50	1·00
1202	600p. Traditional cloth pattern	3·00	1·20

MS1203	156×228 mm. 150p. Type **207**; 150p. Woman preparing cotton; 150p. Girl spinning cotton; 150p. Picking cotton; 150p. "Earius insulana" (cotton pest) and larvae; 150p. Dyeing cloth; 150p. As No. 1201; 150p. As No. 1202; 150p. Pattern with lozenges and stripes; 150p. Striped pattern	6·50	5·00

208 Mickey Mouse

1991. Carnival Masks. Multicoloured.

1204	200p. Type **208**	50	20
1205	300p. Hippopotamus	70	30
1206	600p. Buffalo	1·40	50
1207	1200p. Buffalo (different)	2·75	1·20

209 Royal Threadfin

1991. Fish. Multicoloured.

1208	300p. Type **209**	30	20
1209	400p. Guinean fingerfish	1·20	55
1210	500p. Goree spadefish	1·70	85
1211	600p. Long-finned pompano	2·20	1·10

210 Fire Engine with Water Cannons

1991. Fire and First Aid Service. Multicoloured.

1212	200p. Type **210**	40	25
1213	500p. Fire engine with ladders	1·50	90
1214	800p. Emergency vehicle with ladders	2·50	1·50
1215	1500p. Ambulance	4·75	2·75

211 Lizard Buzzard

1991. Birds. Multicoloured.

1216	100p. Type **211**	30	15
1217	250p. Crowned crane	1·00	40
1218	350p. Abyssinian ground hornbill	1·30	95
1219	500p. Saddle-bill stork	1·80	1·40
MS1220	111×139 mm. 1500p. Lizard buzzard (different) (40×49)	6·50	4·50

212 "Best Wishes"

1991. Greetings Stamps. Multicoloured.

1221	250p. Type **212**	40	15
1222	400p. Couple embracing ("With love")	60	30
1223	800p. Horn-blower and map of Africa ("Congratulations")	1·50	70
1224	1000p. Doves ("Season's greetings")	2·00	1·00

213 Fula

1992. Traditional Costume. Multicoloured.

1225	400p. Type **213**	40	30

1226	600p. Balanta	50	35
1227	1000p. Fula (different)	80	45
1228	1500p. Manjaco	1·20	55

214 Landolfia owariensis

1992. Fruits. Multicoloured.

1229	500p. Type **214**	25	15
1230	1500p. Dialium guineensis	90	25
1231	2000p. Adansonia digitata	1·30	70
1232	3000p. Parkia biglobosa	2·00	1·10

215 Cigarette and Fruit "Hearts"

1992. World Health Day. "Health in Rhythm with the Heart". Multicoloured.

1233	1500p. Type **215**	1·60	40
1234	4000p. "Heart" running over food	4·25	1·60

216 Cassia alata

1992. "Lubrapex 92" Brazilian–Portuguese Stamp Exhibition, Lisbon. Plants. Multicoloured.

1235	100p. Type **216**	20	10
1236	400p. Perlebia purpurea	40	20
1237	1000p. Caesalpinia pulcherrima	1·20	70
1238	1500p. Adenanthera pavonina	1·80	1·10
MS1239	110×140 mm. 3000p. Caesalpina pulcherrima	3·75	2·50

Nos. 1235/8 were issued together, se-tenant, forming a composite design.

217 Canoe

1992. Canoes. Multicoloured.

1240	750p. Type **217**	35	10
1241	800p. Pirogue	45	15
1242	1000p. Pirogue (different)	1·80	75
1243	1300p. Skiff	2·30	1·00
MS1244	70×96 mm. 1500p. Malachite kingfisher	5·00	3·00

The canoe appears in the margin of No. **MS**1244.

218 Volleyball

1992. Olympic Games, Barcelona (2nd issue). Multicoloured.

1245	600p. Basketball	15	10
1246	1000p. Type **218**	30	10
1247	1500p. Handball	65	25
1248	2000p. Football	1·20	45

219 Afzelia africana

1992. Forest Preservation. Multicoloured.

1249	1000p. Type **219**	30	15
1250	1500p. African mahogany	50	35
1251	2000p. Iroko	1·40	55
1252	3000p. Ambila	2·20	90

220 Sail

1992. 500th Anniv of Discovery of America by Columbus. Sheet 71×96 mm.
MS1253 **220** 5000p. multicoloured   3·00   2·00

221 Colobus

1992. The Red Colobus. Multicoloured.

1254	2000p. Type **221**	1·40	70
1255	2000p. Colobus sitting in tree fork	1·40	70
1256	2000p. Mother and young	1·40	70
1257	2000p. Two colobus on tree branch	1·40	70

222 Puff Adder

1993. Reptiles. Multicoloured.

1258	1500p. Type **222**	30	25
1259	3000p. African dwarf crocodile	1·00	60
1260	4000p. Nile monitor	1·80	1·00
1261	5000p. Rainbow lizard	2·40	1·30
MS1262	130×106 mm. Nos. 1258/61	6·50	5·00

223 "Plan of S. Jose Bissau" (Jose Luis Braun)

1993. Union of Portuguese speaking capital Cities. Sheet 71×97 mm.
MS1263 **223** 6000p. multicoloured   4·00   3·00

224 Waterside Village

1993. Tourism. Multicoloured.

1264	1000p. Type **224**	50	40
1265	2000p. Masked villagers on shore and crops	1·40	80
1266	4000p. Villages on offshore islands	2·75	1·40
1267	5000p. Crops on island	3·75	2·40

Nos. 1264/7 were issued together, *se-tenant*, forming a composite design.

225 Bracelet

1994. Jewellery. Multicoloured.

1268	1500p. Type **225**	60	40
1269	3000p. Tribal mask pendant	1·50	95
1270	4000p. Circles pendant	2·00	1·40
1271	5000p. Filigree pendant	2·50	1·60
MS1272	76×76 mm. 18000p. Detail of tribal mask pendant	11·00	7·50

226 *Erythrina senegalensis*

1994. Medicinal Plants. Multicoloured.

1273	2000p. Type **226**	1·50	50
1274	3000p. *Cassia occidentalis*	2·30	1·40
1275	4000p. *Gardenia ternifolia*	3·00	2·00
1276	6000p. *Cochlospermum tinctorium*	4·50	3·00

227 Player kicking Ball

1994. World Cup Football Championship, U.S.A. Multicoloured.

1277	4000p. Type **227**	1·30	40
1278	5000p. Goalkeeper making save	1·60	55
1279	5500p. Heading the ball	1·80	1·30
1280	6500p. Dribbling the ball	2·20	1·40

228 Common Egg-eater (*Dasypeltis scabra*)

1994. "Philakorea 1994" International and "Singpex '94" Stamp Exhibitions. Snakes. Multicoloured.

1281	5000p. Type **228**	1·70	1·40
1282	5000p. Green snake (*Philothamnus* sp.)	1·70	1·40
1283	5000p. Black-lipped cobra (*Naja melanoleuca*)	1·70	1·40
1284	5000p. African python (*Python sebae*)	1·70	1·40
MS1285	145×105 mm. 15000p. Superb sunbird and tree snake (60×49 mm)	6·00	4·50

229 Collecting Fruits

1995. Palm Oil. Multicoloured.

1286	3000p. Type **229**	40	40
1287	6500p. Crushing fruit	1·50	70
1288	7500p. Palm oil production	2·20	1·20
1289	8000p. Animals and pot of palm oil	2·40	1·40

230 Women fishing

1995. 50th Anniv of United Nations Food and Agriculture Organization. Multicoloured.

1290	3000p. Type **230**	50	40
1291	6500p. Farmer on tractor	1·80	1·20
1292	7500p. Basket of fruit	2·40	1·40
1293	8000p. Women and children queuing	2·50	1·50
MS1294	140×110 mm. Nos. 1292/3	5·00	3·00

231 Hands and Emblem

1995. 50th Anniv of United Nations. Multicoloured.

1295	4000p. Type **231**	60	50
1296	5500p. United Nations emblem	1·60	1·00
1297	7500p. Guinea-Bissau flag and emblem	2·40	1·40
1298	8000p. Hands holding dove and emblem	2·50	1·50
MS1299	95×90 mm. 15000p. Emblem	4·75	3·00

Nos. 1300/10 and Types **232/5** have been left for possible issues of 1998, not seen.

Nos. 1311/20 and Types **235/40** have been left for possible issues of 2000, not seen.

241 *Bolama*

2001. Ships. Multicoloured.

1321	100f. Type **241**	40	25
1322	200f. *Guiné*, 1905–1916	80	60
1323	500f. *Guiné*, 1922–1930	2·00	1·50
1324	750f. *Colonial*	3·00	2·30
1325	1000f. *Guiné*, 1930–1950	4·25	3·00
MS1326	140×112 mm. 5000f. *Rita Maria*	20·00	15·00

242 Bishop Ferrazzetta

2001. Bishop Settimio Arturo Ferrazzetta Commoration. Multicoloured.

1327	250f. Type **242**	1·50	1·20
1328	350f. Wearing black	2·00	1·60
1329	400f. In doorway	2·40	1·80
1330	500f. Facing right	3·00	2·20

243 *Dermochelys coriacea* (leatherback turtle)

2001. Turtles. Multicoloured.

1331	100f. Type **243**	50	40
1332	500f. *Lepidochelys olivacea* (olive Ridley)	1·50	1·00
1333	750f. *Chelonia mydas* (green sea turtle)	2·40	1·80
1334	1000f. *Eretmochelys imbricata* (hawksbill turtle)	3·00	2·40
MS1335	130×90 mm. 5000f. *Caretta caretta* (loggerhead sea turtle)	15·00	12·00

244 Wooden Statue, Nacu

2001. Traditional Art. Multicoloured.

1336	100f. Type **244**	40	35
1337	200f. Incised pots, Balanta	80	60
1338	500f. Pots with handles, Manjaco	2·00	1·50
1339	750f. Woven plate, Fula	4·00	2·10
1340	1000f. Stylized bird, Bijago	4·00	3·00
MS1341	130×90 mm. 1000f. As No. 1340	5·00	4·50

245 *Egretta gularis* (western reef heron)

2001. Waterbirds. Multicoloured.

1342	150f. Type **245**	1·00	80
1343	150f. *Egretta ardesiaca* (black egret)	1·00	80
1344	150f. *Pelicanus onocrotalus* (great white pelican)	1·00	80
1345	150f. *Plectropterus gambensis* (spur-winged goose)	1·00	80
1346	150f. *Egretta garzetta* (little egret)	1·00	8·00
1347	150f. *Anas clypeata* (mallard)	1·00	80
MS1348	150×110 mm. 100f. As Type **245**; 200f. As No. 1343; 250f. As No. 1344; 500f. As No. 1346; 1000f. As No. 1347	14·00	12·00

Nos. 1342/7 were printed, *se-tenant*, forming a composite design.

246 Hippopotamus

2001. Hippopotamus (*Hippopotamus amphibius*). Multicoloured.
1349 **246** 750f. multicoloured   3·50   3·00
MS1350 85×66 mm. 1500f. As Type **246**   7·00   6·00

247 Buffalo at Waterhole

2002. African Buffalo (*Syncerus caffer*). Multicoloured.

1351	115f. Type **247**	85	85
1352	115f. Mother and calf	85	85
1353	115f. Head	85	85
1354	115f. Two buffalo	85	85

248 Flags

2002. United We Stand
1355 **248** 375f. multicoloured   2·30   2·30

249 Seoul (inscr 'Seul') World Cup Stadium, South Korea

2002. World Cup Football Championships, Japan and South Korea

1356	500f. Type **249**	1·30	1·00
1357	750f. Yokohama Stadium, Japan	1·80	1·40
MS1358	120×79 mm. Nos. 1356/7	3·00	3·00

250 Breuget XIV A2 (Lisbon–Guinea, 1925)

2002. History of Aviation. Multicoloured.

1359	150f. Type **250**	1·40	1·00
1360	350f. Dornier Do-J Wal (inscr 'Wal') flying boat (night flight in South Atlantic, 1927)	3·25	2·50
1361	500f. Vickers Valpariso (Lisbon-Guinea–St Tome–Angola–Mozambique, 1928)	4·50	3·50
1362	750f. de Havilland (inscr 'Moth') (Lisbon–Guinea–Angola and back, 1930–31)	7·00	5·25
MS1363	100×70 mm. 1000f. Air cruise over Africa, 1935–36	9·00	8·00

251 *Conus genuanus*

2002. Shells. Multicoloured.

1364	150f. Type **251**	1·40	1·00
1365	350f. *Agaronia hiatula*	1·60	1·40
1366	750f. *Persicula cingulata*	3·50	3·25
1367	1500f. *Tellina madagascariensis* (horiz)	7·00	6·00
MS1368	120×80 mm. No. 1367	7·00	6·00

252 *Sphyraena barracuda* (barracuda)

2002. Fish. Multicoloured.

1369		250f. Type **252**	1·40	1·30
1370		500f. *Luutjanus agennes* (red snapper)	3·00	2·50
1371		750f. *Mugil cephalus* (flathead mullet)	4·25	3·75
MS1372		120×80 mm. 1500f. *Sphyrna* (hammer head shark)	8·50	7·50

APPENDIX

The following stamps have either been issued in excess of postal needs or have not been available to the public in reasonable quantities at face value. Such stamps may be given full listing if there is evidence of regular postal use.

1996

Crustaceans. 5000p.; 7500p.; 10000p.; 15000p.
Olympic Games, Atlanta. 6000p.; 8000p.; 98000p.; 17000p.
Birds. 7000p.; 9000p.; 13000p.; 14000p.
nsects. 5000p.; 10000p.; 12000p.; 13000p.

1997

Animals. 5000p.; 7500p.; 10000p.; 12000p.
Poisonous Animals. 7500p.; 8000p.; 10000p.; 11000p.
20th Anniv of CEDEAO. 25000p.

2001

Olympic Games. 130f.×10; 160f.×10; 170f.×10; 250f.×10; 400f.×10
World Cup. 275f.×18; 300f.×18; 350f.×18
Table Tennis World Championships. 2500f.×2
Orchids. 200f.×9; 350f.×9
Butterflies. 200f.×9; 350f.×9
Goldfish. 250f.×6
Cats. 250f.×6
Minerals. 250f.×6; 300f.×6
Pre-history. 275f.×9
Dogs. 275f.×9; 300f.×9
Fungi. 350f.×6
Tortoises. 500f.×6
Art. 300f.×8; 350f.×8; 400f.×8
Personalities. 350f.×62; 1000f.×31

Pt. 1

GUYANA

Formerly British Guiana. Attained independence on 26 May 1966, and changed its name to Guyana.

100 cents = 1 dollar

CANCELLED REMAINDERS* In 1969 remainders of some issues were put on the market cancelled-to-order in such a way as to be indistinguishable form genuine postally used copies for all practical purposes. Our used quotations which are indicated by an asterisk are the same for cancelled-to-order or postally used copies.

1966. Nos. 331 etc. of British Guiana optd **GUYANA INDEPENDENCE 1966.**

399	**55**	1c. black	10	10
421	-	2c. green	10	10
422	-	3c. green and brown	30	10
400	-	4c. violet	10	10
388	-	5c. red and black	40	10
424	-	6c. green	25	10
401	-	8c. blue	10	10
391	-	12c. black and brown	10	10
435	-	24c. black and orange	8·50	10
393	-	36c. red and black	30	30
405	-	48c. blue and red	30	30
395	-	72c. red and green	1·00	1·50
396	-	$1 multicoloured	7·50	35
397	-	$2 mauve	1·50	1·75
398	-	$5 blue and black	1·00	6·00

74 Flag and Map

1966. Independence. Multicoloured.

408		5c. Type **74**	30	10
409		15c. Type **74**	40	10
410		25c. Arms of Guyana	40	10
411		$1 Arms of Guyana	1·10	1·25

76 Bank Building

1966. Opening of Bank of Guyana.

412	**76**	5c. multicoloured	10	10
413	**76**	25c. multicoloured	10	10

77 British Guiana One Cent Stamp of 1856

1967. World's Rarest Stamp Commemoration.

414	**77**	5c. multicoloured*	10	10
415	**77**	25c. multicoloured*	10	10

78 Chateau Margot

1967. First Anniv of Independence. Multicoloured.

416		6c. Type **78***	10	10
417		15c. Independence Arch*	10	10
418		25c. Fort Island (horiz)*	10	10
419		$1 National Assembly (horiz)	20	15

83 "Millie" (Blue and Yellow Macaw)

1967. Christmas.

441	**83**	5c. yellow, blue, black grn*	10	10
443	**83**	5c. yellow, blue, black red*	10	10
442	**83**	25c. yellow, blue, blk vio*	15	10
444	**83**	25c. yellow, blue, blk grn*	15	10

84 Wicket-keeping

1968. M.C.C.'s West Indies Tour. Multicoloured.

445		5c. Type **84***	10	10
446		6c. Batting*	10	10
447		25c. Bowling*	30	10

87 Pike Cichlid

1968. Multicoloured.

448		1c. Type **87**	10	10
449		2c. Red paranha ("Pirai")	10	10
450		3c. Peacock cichlid ("Lukunani")	10	10
451		5c. Armoured catfish ("Hassar")	10	10
489		6c. Black acara ("Patua")	10	1·00
490		10c. Spix's guan (vert)	45	60
491		15c. Harpy eagle (vert)	60	10
455		20c. Hoatzin (vert)	1·00	10
493		25c. Guianan cock of the rock (vert)	45	10
494		40c. Great kiskadee (vert)	80	1·00
495		50c. Brazilian agouti ("Accouri")	35	15
459		60c. White-lipped peccary	1·50	10
460		$1 Paca ("Labba")	1·00	10
461		$2 Nine-banded armadillo	2·00	2·00
462		$5 Ocelot	1·00	3·00

---

102 *Christ of St. John of the Cross* (Salvador Dali)

1968. Easter.

463	**102**	5c. multicoloured*	10	10
464	**102**	25c. multicoloured*	20	10

103 "Efficiency Year"

1968. "Savings Bonds and Efficiency". Multicoloured.

465		6c. Type **103**	10	10
466		25c. Type **103***	10	10
467		30c. "Savings Bonds"*	10	10
468		40c. "Savings Bonds"*	10	10

105 Open Book, Star and Crescent

1968. 1400th Anniv of Holy Quran.

469	**105**	6c. black, gold and flesh*	10	10
470	**105**	25c. black, gold and lilac*	10	10
471	**105**	30c. black, gold and green*	10	10
472	**105**	40c. black, gold and blue*	10	10

107 Broadcasting Greetings

1968. Christmas.

473	**107**	6c. brown, black and green	10	10
474	**107**	25c. brown, violet green	10	10
475	-	30c. green and turquoise*	10	10
476	-	40c. red and turquoise*	10	10

DESIGNS: 30c. and 40c. Map showing radio link, Guyana–Trinidad.

109 Festival Ceremony

1969. Hindu Festival of Phagwah. Multicoloured.

477		6c. Type **109**	10	10
478		25c. Ladies spraying scent	10	10
479		30c. Type **109**	10	10
480		40c. As No. 478	10	10

111 "Sacrament of the Last Supper" (Dali)

1969. Easter.

481	**111**	6c. multicoloured	10	10
482	**111**	25c. multicoloured	10	10
483	**111**	30c. multicoloured	10	10
484	**111**	40c. multicoloured	10	10

---

112 Map showing "CARIFTA" Countries

1969. First Anniv of "CARIFTA".

500	**112**	6c. red, blue and turquoise	15	15
501	-	25c. lemon, brown and red	15	15

DESIGN—HORIZ: 25c. "Strength in Unity".

114 Building *Independence* (first aluminium ship)

1969. 50th Anniv of I.L.O.

502	**114**	30c. blue, black and silver	40	25
503	-	40c. multicoloured	60	25

DESIGN—HORIZ: 40c. Bauxite processing plant.

116 Scouts raising Flag

1969. Third Caribbean Scout Jamboree and Diamond Jubilee of Scouting in Guyana. Multicoloured.

504		6c. Type **116**	10	10
505		8c. Camp-fire cooking	10	10
506		25c. Type **116**	10	10
507		30c. As 8c.	10	10
508		50c. Type **116**	15	15

118 Gandhi and Spinning-wheel

1969. Birth Centenary of Mahatma Gandhi.

509	**118**	6c. black, brown and olive	75	65
510	**118**	15c. black, brown and lilac	75	65

119 "Mother Sally" Dance Troupe

1969. Christmas. Unissued stamps optd as in T **119**. Multicoloured.

511		5c. Type **119**	10	10
512		6c. City Hall, Georgetown	10	10
513		25c. Type **119**	10	10
514		60c. As 6c.	20	25

121 Forbes Burnham and Map

1970. Republic Day.

515	**121**	5c. sepia, ochre and blue	10	10
516	-	6c. multicoloured	10	10
517	-	15c. multicoloured	15	10

518	-	25c. multicoloured	20	15

DESIGNS—VERT: 6c. Rural self-help. HORIZ: 15c. University of Guyana; 25c. Guyana House.

125 *The Descent from the Cross*

1970. Easter. Paintings by Rubens. Multicoloured.

519	5c. Type **125**		10	10
520	6c. *Christ on the Cross*		10	10
521	15c. Type **125**		20	10
522	25c. As 6c.		20	15

127 "Peace" and U.N. Emblem

1970. 25th Anniv of United Nations. Multicoloured.

523	5c. Type **127**		10	10
524	6c. U.N. emblem, gold-panning and drilling		10	10
525	15c. Type **127**		10	10
526	25c. As 6c.		15	15

128 *Mother and Child* (Philip Moore)

1970. Christmas.

527	**128**	5c. multicoloured	10	10
528	**128**	6c. multicoloured	10	10
529	**128**	15c. multicoloured	15	15
530	**128**	25c. multicoloured	15	15

129 National Co-operative Bank

1971. Republic Day.

531	**129**	6c. multicoloured	10	10
532	**129**	15c. multicoloured	15	15
533	**129**	25c. multicoloured	15	15

130 Racial Equality Symbol

1971. Racial Equality Year.

534	**130**	5c. multicoloured	10	10
535	**130**	6c. multicoloured	10	10
536	**130**	15c. multicoloured	15	15
537	**130**	25c. multicoloured	15	15

131 Young Volunteer felling Tree (from painting by J. Criswick)

1971. First Anniv of Self-help Road Project.

538	**131**	5c. multicoloured	10	10
539	**131**	20c. multicoloured	20	10
540	**131**	25c. multicoloured	20	10
541	**131**	50c. multicoloured	30	1·75

132 Yellow Allamanda

1971. Flowering Plants. Multicoloured.

542	1c. Pitcher Plant of Mt. Roraima		10	10
543	2c. Type **132**		10	10
544	3c. Hanging heliconia		10	10
545	5c. Annatto tree		10	10
546	6c. Cannon-ball tree		10	10
547	10c. Cattleya		3·25	10
548a	15c. Christmas orchid		65	10
549	20c. *Paphinia cristata*		3·00	20
550	25c. Marabunta		5·50	7·50
550ab	25c. Marabunta		45	10
551	40c. Tiger beard		3·50	10
552	50c. *Guzmania lingulata*		40	85
553	60c. Soldier's cap		30	65
554	$1 *Chelonanthus uliginoides*		30	55
555	$2 *Norantea guianensis*		35	55
556	$5 *Odontadenia grandiflora*		55	55

No. 550 shows the flowers facing upwards and has the value in the centre. No. 550ab has the flowers facing downwards with the value to the right.

133 Child praying at Bedside

1971. Christmas. Multicoloured.

557	5c. Type **133**		10	10
558	20c. Type **133**		10	10
559	25c. Carnival masquerader (vert)		10	10
560	50c. As 25c.		20	60

134 Obverse and Reverse of Guyana $1 Coin

1972. Republic Day.

561	**134**	5c. silver, black and red	10	10
562	-	20c. silver, black and red	15	10
563	**134**	25c. silver, black and blue	15	15
564	-	50c. silver, black and green	25	45

DESIGN: 20c., 50c. Reverse and obverse of Guyana $1 coin.

135 Hands and Irrigation Canal

1972. Youman Nabi (Mohammed's Birthday).

565	**135**	5c. multicoloured	10	10
566	**135**	25c. multicoloured	10	10
567	**135**	30c. multicoloured	10	10
568	**135**	60c. multicoloured	20	20

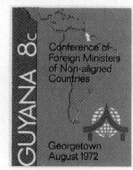

136 Map and Emblem

1972. Conference of Foreign Ministers of Non-aligned Countries.

569	**136**	8c. multicoloured	10	10
570	**136**	25c. multicoloured	10	10
571	**136**	40c. multicoloured	15	15
572	**136**	50c. multicoloured	20	20

137 Hand reaching for Sun

1972. First Caribbean Festival of Arts.

573	**137**	8c. multicoloured	10	10
574	**137**	25c. multicoloured	10	10
575	**137**	40c. multicoloured	15	20
576	**137**	50c. multicoloured	20	25

138 Joseph, Mary and the Infant Jesus

1972. Christmas.

577	**138**	8c. multicoloured	10	10
578	**138**	25c. multicoloured	10	10
579	**138**	40c. multicoloured	15	25
580	**138**	50c. multicoloured	15	25

139 Umana Yana (Meeting-house)

1973. Republic Day. Multicoloured.

581	8c. Type **139**		10	10
582	25c. Bethel Chapel		10	10
583	40c. As 25c.		20	20
584	50c. Type **139**		25	20

140 Pomegranate

1973. Easter. Multicoloured.

585	8c. Type **140**		10	10
586	25c. Cross and map (34×17 mm)		10	10
587	40c. As 25c.		10	10
588	50c. Type **140**		15	15

141 Stylised Blood Cell

1973. 25th Anniv of Guyana Red Cross.

589	**141**	8c. red and black	10	10
590	**141**	25c. red and purple	25	15
591	**141**	40c. red and blue	35	50
592	**141**	50c. red and green	50	1·00

142 Steel-Band Players

1973. Christmas. Multicoloured.

593	8c. Type **142**		10	10
594	25c. Type **142**		20	10
595	40c. "Virgin and Child" stained-glass window (34×47 mm)		40	75
596	50c. As 40c.		40	75

143 Symbol of Progress

1974. Republic Day. Multicoloured.

597	8c. Type **143**		10	10
598	25c. Wai-Wai Indian		10	10
599	40c. Type **143**		15	30
600	50c. As 25c.		15	40

1974. No. 546 surch **8c.**

601	8c. on 6c. multicoloured		10	10

145 Kite with Crucifixion Motif

1974. Easter.

602	**145**	8c. multicoloured	10	10
603	-	25c. black and green	10	10
604	-	40c. black and mauve	10	15
605	**145**	50c. multicoloured	15	25

DESIGN: Nos. 603/4, "Crucifixion" in pre-Columbian style.

146 British Guiana 24c. Stamp of 1874

1974. Centenary of Universal Postal Union.

606	**146**	8c. multicoloured	25	10
607	-	25c. lt green, green black	35	10
608	**146**	40c. multicoloured	35	20
609	-	50c. green, brown black	45	45

DESIGN—VERT (42×25 mm): 25, 50c. U.P.U. emblem and Guyana postman.

147 Guides with Banner

1974. Golden Jubilee of Girl Guides. Multicoloured.

610	8c. Type **147**		20	10
611	25c. Guides in camp		30	15
612	40c. As 25c.		45	40
613	50c. Type **147**		45	45

148 Buck Toyeau

1974. Christmas. Multicoloured.

615	8c. Type **148**		10	10
616	35c. Five-fingers and awaras		10	10
617	50c. Pawpaw and tangerine		15	10
618	$1 Pineapple and sapodilla		30	60
MS619	127×94 mm. Nos. 615/18		70	2·50

1975. No. 544 surch **8c.**

620	8c. on 3c. multicoloured		10	10

149 Golden
Arrow of Courage

1975. Republic Day. Guyana Orders and Decorations.
Multicoloured.

621		10c. Type **149**	10	10
622		35c. Cacique's Crown of Honour	10	15
623		50c. Cacique's Crown of Valour	15	20
624		$1 Order of Excellence	35	60

150 Old Sluice
Gate

1975. Silver Jubilee of International Commission on
Irrigation and Drainage. Multicoloured.

625		10c. Type **150**	10	10
626		35c. Modern sluice gate (horiz)	10	15
627		50c. Type **150**	15	30
628		$1 As 35c.	35	60
MS629		162×121 mm. Nos. 625/8	75	2·75

151 I.W.Y. Emblem and Rock
Drawing

1975. International Women's Year. Designs showing
different rock drawings.

630	**151**	10c. green and yellow	10	10
631	-	35c. violet and blue	15	10
632	-	50c. blue and orange	20	15
633	-	$1 brown and blue	30	45
MS634		178×89 mm. Nos. 630/3	75	3·00

152 Freedom
Monument

1975. Namibia Day. Multicoloured.

635		10c. Type **152**	10	10
636		35c. Unveiling of Monument	15	10
637		50c. Type **152**	25	10
638		$1 As 35c.	35	35

153 G.N.S.
Emblem

1975. First Anniv of National Service.

639	**153**	10c. yellow, green & violet	10	10
640	-	35c. orange, green & violet	10	10
641	-	50c. blue, green and brown	15	15
642	-	$1 mauve, green & lt green	40	40
MS643		196×133 mm. Nos. 639/42	75	2·00

Nos. 640/2 are as Type **153** but have different symbols
within the circle.

154 Court Building, 1875,
and Forester's Badge

1975. Centenary of Guyanese Ancient Order of Foresters.
Multicoloured.

644		10c. Type **154**	10	10
645		35c. Rock drawing of hunter and quarry	25	10
646		50c. Crossed axes and bugle-horn	15	10
647		$1 Bow and arrow	40	40
MS648		129×97 mm. Nos. 644/7	75	2·25

1976. No. 553 surch **35c.**

649		35c. on 60c. Soldier's cap	20	15

156 Shoulder Flash

1976. 50th Anniv of St. John Ambulance in Guyana.

650	**156**	8c. silver, black and mauve	10	10
651	-	15c. silver, black & orange	10	10
652	-	35c. silver, black and green	20	20
653	-	40c. silver, black and blue	25	25

Nos. 651/3 are as Type **156** but show different shoulder flashes.

157 Triumphal
Arch

1976. Tenth Anniv of Independence. Multicoloured.

654		8c. Type **157**	10	10
655		15c. Stylised Victoria Regia lily	10	10
656		35c. "Onward to Socialism"	15	15
657		40c. Worker pointing the way	15	15
MS658		120×100 mm. Nos. 654/7	50	1·50

1976. West Indies Victory in World Cricket Cup. As T
223a of Grenada.

659		15c. Map of the Caribbean	90	1·50
660		15c. Prudential Cup	90	1·50

158 Flame in
Archway

1976. Deepavali Festival. Multicoloured.

661		8c. Type **158**	10	10
662		15c. Flame in hand	10	10
663		35c. Flame in bowl	15	20
664		40c. Goddess Latchmi	15	25
MS665		94×109 mm. Nos. 661/4	50	1·50

159 Festival
Emblem and
"Musical
Instrument"

1977. Second World Black and African Festival of Arts
and Culture, Nigeria.

666	**159**	10c. red, black and gold	10	10
667	**159**	25c. violet, black and gold	15	10
668	**159**	50c. blue, black and gold	20	25
669	**159**	$1 green, black and gold	35	75
MS670		90×157 mm. Nos. 666/9	75	3·00

160 1c. and 5c. Coins

1977. New Coinage.

671	**160**	8c. multicoloured	20	10
672	-	15c. brown, grey and black	25	10
673	-	35c. green, grey and black	45	30
674	-	40c. red, grey and black	50	35
675	-	$1 multicoloured	80	1·25
676	-	$2 multicoloured	1·25	2·75

DESIGNS: 15c.10 and 25c. coins; 35c., 50c. and $1 coins;
40c. $5 and $10 coins; $1 $50 and $100 coins; $2 Reverse
of $1 coin.

161 Hand Pump, c. 1850

1977. National Fire Prevention Week. Multicoloured.

677		8c. Type **161**	1·25	10
678		15c. Steam fire engine, c. 1860	1·60	10
679		35c. Fire engine, c. 1930	1·90	60
680		40c. Fire engine, 1977	1·90	85

162 Cuffy
Monument

1977. Cuffy Monument (commemorating 1763 Slave
Revolt). Multicoloured.

681		8c. Type **162**	10	10
682		15c. Cuffy Monument (different view)	15	10
683		35c. Type **162**	20	20
684		40c. as 15c.	20	30

163 American Manatee

1978. Wildlife Conservation. Multicoloured.

685		8c. Type **163**	65	10
686		15c. Giant sea turtle	85	20
687		35c. Harpy eagle (vert)	4·00	1·50
688		40c. Iguana (vert)	3·50	1·50

164 L.F.S. Burnham (Prime
Minister) and Parliament
Buildings, Georgetown

1978. 25th Anniv of Prime Minister's Entry into
Parliament.

689	**164**	8c. black, violet and grey	10	10
690	-	15c. black, blue and grey	10	10
691	-	35c. black, red and grey	15	20
692	-	40c. black, orange and grey	15	20
MS693		176×118 mm. Nos. 689/92	55	1·00

DESIGNS: 15c. Burnham, graduate and children ("Free Education"); 35c. Burnham and industrial works (Nationalization of Bauxite Industry); 40c. Burnham and village scene
("The Co-operative Village").

165 Dr. George
Giglioli (scientist
and physician)

1978. Nat Science Research Council. Multicoloured.

694		10c. Type **165**	15	10
695		30c. Institute of Applied Science and Technology	20	15
696		50c. Emblem of National Science Research Council	25	25
697		60c. Emblem of Commonwealth Science Council (commemorating the 10th meeting) (horiz)	25	25

166 Prepona
pheridamas

1978. Butterflies. Multicoloured.

698		5c. Type **166**	1·50	10
699		10c. Archonias bellona	1·50	10
700		15c. Eryphanis polyxena	1·50	10
701		20c. Helicopis cupido	1·75	10
702		25c. Nessaea batesii	1·75	10
702a		30c. Nymphidium mantus	1·25	2·50
703		35c. Anaea galanthis	1·75	10
704		40c. Morpho rhetenor (male)	1·75	10
705		50c. Hamadryas amphinome	1·75	20
705a		60c. Papilio androgeus	1·25	1·00
706		$1 Agrias claudina (vert) (25×39 mm)	3·75	20
707		$2 Morpho rhetenor (female) (vert) (25×39 mm)	5·50	35
708		$5 Morpho deidamia (vert) (25×39 mm)	6·50	90
708a		$10 Elbella patrobas (vert) (25×39 mm)	4·50	4·25

168 Amerindian
Stone-chip Grater
in Preparation

1978. National/International Heritage Year. Multicoloured.

709		10c. Type **168**	10	10
710		30c. Cassiri and decorated Amerindian jars	15	10
711		50c. Fort, Kyk-over-al	20	15
712		60c. Fort Island	20	20

169 Dish Aerial by Night

1979. Satellite Earth Station. Multicoloured.

713		10c. Type **169**	10	10
714		30c. Dish aerial by day	20	15
715		50c. Satellite with solar veins	30	15
716		$3 Cylinder satellite	1·00	90

170 Sir Rowland Hill and
British Guiana 1850 12c.
"Cottonreel" Stamp

1979. Death Cent of Sir Rowland Hill. Multicoloured.

717		10c. Type **170**	15	10
718		30c. British Guiana 1856 1c. black on magenta stamp (vert)	20	15
719		50c. British Guiana 1898 1c. Mount Roraima stamp	30	15
720		$3 Printing press used for early British Guiana stamps (vert)	45	80

171 Me and my Sister

1979. International Year of the Child. Children's Paintings. Multicoloured.

721	10c. Type **171**		10	10
722	30c. *Fun with the Fowls* (horiz)		15	15
723	50c. *Two Boys catching Ducks* (horiz)		15	20
724	$3 *Mango Season* (horiz)		45	1·25

172 "An 8 Hour Day"

1979. 60th Anniv of Guyana Labour Union. Multicoloured.

725	10c. Type **172**		10	10
726	30c. "Abolition of Night Baking" (horiz)		10	10
727	50c. "Introduction of the Workmen's Compensation Ordinance"		15	15
728	$3 H. N. Critchlow (founder)		55	90

173 Guyana Flag

1980. Tenth Anniv of Republic.

729	**173**	10c. multicoloured	10	10
730	-	35c. black and orange	30	10
731	-	60c. multicoloured	50	20
732	-	$3 multicoloured	80	90

DESIGNS: 35c. Demerara River Bridge; 60c. Kaieteur Falls; $3 "Makanaima, the Great Ancestral Spirit of the Amerindians".

174 Common Snook

1980. "London 1980" International Stamp Exhibition. Fish. Multicoloured.

733	35c. Type **174**		20	20
734	35c. Trahira ("Haimara")		20	20
735	35c. Electric eel		20	20
736	35c. Golden rivulus		20	20
737	35c. Golden pencilfish		20	20
738	35c. Four-eyed fish		20	20
739	35c. Red piranha ("Pirai")		20	20
740	35c. Smoking hassar		20	20
741	35c. Manta		20	20
742	35c. Festival cichlid ("Flying patwa")		20	20
743	35c. Arapaima		20	20
744	35c. Peacock cichlid ("Lukanani")		20	20

175 Children's Convalescent Home (Community Service)

1980. 75th Anniv of Rotary International. Multicoloured.

745	10c. Type **175**		10	10
746	30c. Georgetown Rotary Club and Rotary International emblems		10	10
747	50c. District 404 emblem (vert)		20	20
748	$3 Rotary anniversary emblem (vert)		80	80

---

176 "C" encircling Globe, Caduceus Emblem and Sea

1980. 25th Anniv of Commonwealth Caribbean Medical Research Council. Multicoloured.

749	10c. Type **176**		10	10
750	60c. Researcher with microscope, Caduceus emblem, stethoscope and beach scene		40	20
751	$3 Caduceus emblem, "C" encircling researcher and island silhouettes		1·10	1·00

177 Virola surinamensis

1980. Christmas. Trees and Foliage. Multicoloured.

752	10c. Type **177**		10	10
753	30c. *Hymenaea courbaril*		20	10
754	50c. *Mora excelsa*		30	15
755	$3 *eltogyne venosa*		80	1·10

GUYANA   30c

178 Brazilian Tree Porcupine

1981. Wildlife. Multicoloured.

756	30c. Type **178**		25	40
757	30c. Red howler		25	40
758	30c. Common squirrel-monkey		25	40
759	30c. Two-toed sloth		25	40
760	30c. Brazilian tapir		25	40
761	30c. Collared peccary		25	40
762a	30c. Six-banded armadillo		25	15
763	30c. Tamandua		25	40
764	30c. Giant anteater		25	40
765	30c. Murine opossum		25	40
766	30c. Brown four-eyed opossum		25	40
767	30c. Brazilian agouti		25	40

1981. Liberation of Southern Africa Conference. No. 635 surch **1981 CONFERENCE $1.05.**

768	$1.05 on 10c. Type **152**		40	30

1981. Royal Wedding (1st issue). Nos. 554 and 556 surch **ROYAL WEDDING 1981** and value.

769c	$3.60 on $5 *Odontadenia grandiflora*		60	65
770	$7.20 on $1 *"helonanthus uliginoides"*		60	60

See also Nos. 841/3 and 930/6.

181 Map of Guyana

1981. Fiscal stamps surch for postal use.

771	**181**	10c. on 3c. black, blue and red	30	10
940	**181**	15c. on 2c. black, blue and grey	50	15
941	**181**	20c. on 2c. black, blue and grey	4·75	30
1029	**181**	25c. on 2c. black, blue and grey	50	10
772	**181**	30c. on 2c. black, blue and grey	45	15
989	**181**	40c. on 2c. black, blue and grey	1·00	15
945	**181**	45c. on 2c. black, blue and grey	1·75	45
773	**181**	50c. on 2c. black, blue and grey	40	15
774	**181**	60c. on 2c. black, blue and grey	45	15
948	**181**	75c. on 2c. black, blue and grey	7·00	25
775	**181**	75c. on 3c. black, blue and red	45	20
949	**181**	80c. on 2c. black, blue and grey	8·50	20
950	**181**	85c. on 2c. black, blue and grey	1·00	25
951	**181**	100c. on 3c. black, blue and red	1·00	35
952	**181**	110c. on 3c. black, blue and red	1·00	30

953	**181**	120c. on 3c. black, blue and red	8·00	35
954	**181**	125c. on 3c. black, blue and red	2·25	35
955	**181**	130c. on 3c. black, blue and red	1·00	35
956	**181**	150c. on 3c. black, blue and red	8·50	40
957	**181**	160c. on 3c. black, blue and red	2·00	40
958	**181**	170c. on 3c. black, blue and red	1·40	45
959	**181**	175c. on 3c. black, blue and red	6·00	45
960	**181**	180c. on 3c. black, blue and red	2·00	60
961	**181**	200c. on 3c. black, blue and red	2·25	45
962	**181**	210c. on 3c. black, blue and red	7·00	50
963	**181**	220c. on 3c. black, blue and red	8·50	50
964	**181**	235c. on 3c. black, blue and red	8·00	50
965	**181**	240c. on 3c. black, blue and red	9·00	50
966	**181**	250c. on 3c. black, blue and red	2·25	50
967	**181**	300c. on 3c. black, blue and red	12·00	55
968	**181**	330c. on 3c. black, blue and red	2·75	65
969	**181**	375c. on 3c. black, blue and red	8·00	75
970	**181**	400c. on 3c. black, blue and red	10·00	75
971	**181**	440c. on 3c. black, blue and red	4·00	75
972	**181**	500c. on 3c. black, blue and red	3·50	1·10
973	**181**	550c. on 3c. black, blue and red	4·00	1·25
974	**181**	625c. on 3c. black, blue and red	2·75	1·75
975	**181**	1500c. on 2c. black, blue and grey	11·00	3·00
976	**181**	2000c. on 2c. black, blue and grey	11·00	3·75

1981. No. 544 surch **7.20.**

775c	720c. on 3c. multicoloured		80·00	15·00

1981. Various stamps optd **1981.**

791	-	15c. mult (No. 491)	17·00	10
810	-	15c. mult (No. 659)	8·00	20
811	-	15c. mult (No. 660)	8·00	35
864	-	15c. mult (No. 548a)	6·00	10
776	**105**	25c. black and lilac	10	10
777	**105**	30c. black, gold and green	15	10
778	-	35c. mult (No. 645)	60	10
792	-	40c. mult (No. 457)	10·00	40
811c	-	40c. mult (No. F5)		£225
812	-	50c. mult (No. 623)	60	20
813	**150**	50c. multicoloured	1·00	20
814	-	50c. blue and orange (No. 632)	24·00	2·25
815	-	50c. mult (No. 646)	2·75	20
816	**159**	50c. blue, black and gold	13·00	2·00
817	-	50c. mult (No. F6)	4·00	20
818	-	60c. mult (No. 731)	60	20
819	-	60c. mult (No. 750)	60	20
820	-	$1 mult (No. 624)	5·00	55
821	**159**	$1 green, black and gold	4·00	30
865	-	$1 mult (No. 554)	40	20
866	-	$2 mult (No. 555)	70	35
823	-	$3 mult (No. 732)	2·00	65
824	-	$5 mult (No. 556)	3·25	1·25

1981. Nos. 545 and 556 surch.

780	75c. on 5c. Annatto tree		50	50
781	210c. on $5 *Odontadenia grandiflora*		80	1·00
781b	220c. on 5c. Annatto tree		£100	8·50

1981. Nos. D8/11 surch **ESSEQUIBO IS OURS.**

782A	D2	10c. on 2c. black	15	10
783A	D2	15c. on 12c. red	15	15
784A	D2	20c. on 1c. green	15	20
786A	D2	55c. on 4c. blue	20	20
788A	D2	65c. on 2c. black	30	15
790A	D2	80c. on 4c. blue	30	20

1981. Nos. 545, 554, 556, 716, 843, F7 and F9 surch.

794	50c. on 5c. Annatto tree (postage)		30	20
795	120c. on $1 *Chelonanthus uliginoides*		75	40
796	140c. on $1 *Chelonanthus uliginoides*		70	40
797	150c. on $2 *Norantea guianensis* (F9)		75	40
798	360c. on $2 *Norantea guianensis* (F9)		3·00	60
799	720c. on 60c. Soldier's Cap (F7)		3·00	1·00

800	220c. on $3 Cylinder satellite		1·75	45
801	250c. on $5 *Odontadenia grandiflora*		1·25	45
802	280c. on $5 *Odontadenia grandiflora*		1·50	50
803	375c. on $5 *Odontadenia grandiflora*		1·75	55
804	$1.10 on $2 *Norantea guianensis* (843) (air)		1·00	1·00

No. 804 has the Royal Wedding opt cancelled by three bars.

1981. No. 448 surch.

805	**87**	15c. on 1c. mult (postage)	70	20
806	**87**	100c. on 1c. mult (air)	70	40
807	**87**	110c. on 1c. multicoloured	70	40

1981. No. 700 optd **ESSEQUIBO IS OURS.**

808	15c. "Eryphanis polyxena"		8·50	25

1981. Various stamps surch.

825	**116**	55c. on 6c. multicoloured	3·00	80
826	**111**	70c. on 6c. multicoloured	1·00	20
827	**111**	100c. on 6c. mult	1·25	20
828	-	100c. on 8c. multicoloured (No. 505)	3·00	20
829	**152**	100c. on $1.05 on 10c. mult (No. 768)	35·00	4·00
830	**116**	110c. on 6c. mult	2·00	30
831	**149**	110c. on 10c. mult	2·50	30
832	**151**	110c. on 10c. green and yellow	6·00	45
834	-	125c. on $2 multicoloured (No. 555)	13·00	80
835	**116**	180c. on 6c. mult	2·25	45
836	**116**	400c. on 6c. mult	3·50	80
837a	**116**	440c. on 6c. mult	1·00	55
838	-	550c. on $10 multicoloured (No. O21)	9·50	1·00
839	-	625c. on 40c. mult (No. F5)	14·00	1·75
840	-	240c. on $3 multicoloured (No. 728)	8·00	75

1981. Royal Wedding (2nd issue). Nos. 544 and 555/6 surch **Royal Wedding 1981** (No. 843 **Air Mail** also) and value.

841	60c. on 3c. Hanging heliconia (postage)		30	35
842	75c. on $5 *Odontadenia grandiflora*		30	35
843	$1.10 on $2 *Norantea guianensis* (air)		30	35

1981. World Cup Football Championship, Spain (1982) (1st issue). No. 781a optd **Espana 82.**

844	220c. on 5c. Annatto tree		2·25	40

See also Nos. 937/9 and 1218.

1981. 150th Birth Anniv of Heinrich von Stephan (founder of U.P.U.) No. 720 surch **1831-1981 Von Stephan 330.**

845	330c. on $3 Printing press used for early British Guiana stamps		1·10	55

1981. No. 489 surch with large figure over smaller figure.

847	12c. on 12c. on 6c. Black acara ("Patua")		20	25
848	15c. on 10c. on 6c. Black acara ("Patua")		15	15
849	15c. on 30c. on 6c. Black acara ("Patua")		15	15
850	15c. on 5c. on 6c. Black acara ("Patua")		15	15
851	15c. on 60c. on 6c. Black acara ("Patua")		15	10

Nos. 847/51 are further surcharges on previously unissued stamps.

214 Coromantyn Free Negro Armed Ranger, c. 1772, and Cuffy Monument

1981. 16th Anniv of Guyana Defence Force. Multicoloured.

853	15c. on 10c. Type **214**		20	10
854	50c. Private, 27th Foot Regiment, c. 1825		30	30
855	$1 on 30c. Private, Col. Fourgeoud's Marines, c. 1775		30	45

856	$1.10 on $3 W.O. and N.C.O., Guyana Defence Force, 1966	35	70

The 15c., $1 and $1.10 values are surcharged on previously unissued stamps.

215 Louis Braille

1981. International Year for Disabled Persons. Famous Disabled People. Multicoloured.

857	15c. on 10c. Type 215	20	10
858	50c. Helen Keller and Rajkumari Singh	30	40
859	$1 on 60c. Beethoven and Sonny Thomas	40	50
860	$1.10 on $3 Renoir	25	55

The 15c., $1 and $1.10 values are surcharged on previously unissued stamps.

1981. No. 489 surch (Nos. 862/3 optd AIR also).

861	12c. on 6c. Black acara ("Patua") (postage)	15	10
862b	50c. on 6c. Black acara ("Patua") (air)	20	15
863	$1 on 6c. Black acara ("Patua")	50	30

1981. Nos. 601, 620, 644, O13, 717, 720, 728, 749, 751 and 755 surch (Nos. 868/9 twice).

867	110c. on 10c. Type 154	3.00	30
868	110c. on 110c. on 8c. on 3c. Hanging heliconia	3.00	40
869	110c. on 110c. on 8c.on 6c. Cannon-ball tree	3.00	40
869b	110c. on 10c. on 25c. Marabunta	2.25	40
870	110c. on 10c. Type 170	2.00	30
871	110c. on 10c. Type 176	8.00	40
872	110c. on $3 Printing press used for early British Guiana stamps	1.75	30
873	110c. on $3 H. N. Critchlow	6.50	45
874	110c. on $3 Caduceus emblem, "C" encircling researcher and island silhouettes	1.50	30
875	110c. on $3 "Peltogyne venosa"	4.00	50

No. 698 surch **Nov 81 50c.**

876	50c. on 5c. Type 166	9.50	20

222 Yellow Allamanda (*Allamanda cathartica*)

1981. Flowers.

877	222	15c. on 2c. lilac, blue and green	15	15
878	-	15c. on 8c. lilac, blue and mauve	15	15

DESIGN: 15c. on 8c. Mazaruni pride (*Sipanea prolensis*). Nos. 877/8 are surcharged on previously unissued stamps.

1981. Air. Human Rights Day. No. 748 surch **Human Rights Day 1981 110 AIR**.

879	110c. on $3 Rotary anniversary emblem	1.00	60

1981. 35th Anniv of UNICEF No. 724 surch **UNICEF 1946 - 1981 125**.

880	125c. on $3 *Mango Season*	1.25	40

1981. "Cancun 81" International Conference. No. 698 surch **Cancun 81 50c.**

880c	50c. on 5c. Type 166	4.50	55

225 Tape Measure and Guyana Metrication Board Van

1982. Metrication. Multicoloured.

881	15c. Type 225		45	45
882	15c. "Metric man"		45	45
883	15c. "Postal service goes metric"		45	45
884	15c. Weighing child on metric scales		45	45
885	15c. Canje Bridge		45	45
886	15c. Tap filling litre bucket		45	45

1982. Various stamps optd **1982**.

887	-	20c. multicoloured (No. 549)	1.00	20
888	105	25c. black, gold and lilac	60	15
889	-	25c. mult (No. 550ab)	1.25	20

See also Nos. 914/17, 919/21, 923/4, 977, 992/8, 1001, 1004, 1006/8, 1015, 1017, 1059, 1117 and OP3/4.

1982. No. 506 optd **POSTAGE** and Nos. 546 and 601 surch.

890	20c. on 6c. Cannon-ball tree	20	10
892	25c. Type 116	1.00	10
893	125c. on 8c. on 6c. Cannon-ball tree	20	20

230 Guyana Soldier and Flag

1982. Savings Campaign.

894	230	$1 multicoloured	30	20

No. 894 is a fiscal stamp optd for postal use. See also Nos. 913 and 990.

1982. 125th Birth Anniv of Lord Baden-Powell and 75th Anniv of Boy Scout Movement. Nos. 543, 545 and 601 surch as given in brackets.

895	15c. on 2c. Type 132 (**BADEN POWELL 1857–1982**)	45	50
896	15c. on 2c. Type 132 (**Scout Movement 1907–1982**)	45	50
897	15c. on 2c. Type 132 (**1907–1982**)	2.25	2.50
898	15c. on 2c. Type 132 (**1857–1982**)	2.25	2.50
899	15c. on 2c. Type 132 (**1982**)	10	10
900	110c. on 5c. Annatto tree (**BADEN POWELL 1857–1982**)	60	20
901	110c. on 5c. Annatto tree (**Scout Movement 1907–1982**)	60	20
902	110c. on 5c. Annatto tree (**1907–1982**)	2.75	3.00
903	110c. on 5c. Annatto tree (**1857–1982**)	2.75	3.00
904	110c. on 5c. Annatto tree (**1982**)	60	20
905	125c. on 8c. on 6c. Cannon-ball tree (**BADEN POWELL 1857–1982**)	60	20
906	125c. on 8c. on 6c. Cannon-ball tree (**Scout Movement 1907–1982**)	60	20
907	125c. on 8c. on 6c. Cannon-ball tree (**1907–1982**)	2.75	3.00
908	125c. on 8c. on 6c. Cannon-ball tree (**1857–1982**)	2.75	3.00
909	125c. on 8c. on 6c. Cannon-ball tree (**1982**)	60	20

1982. 250th Birth Anniv of George Washington. Nos. 718 and 720 surch **Geo Washington 1732 . . . 1982** and value and No. 708 optd **GEORGE WASHINGTON 1732–1982.**

910	100c. on $3 Printing press used for early British Guiana stamps	75	30
911	400c. on 30c. British Guiana 1856 1c. black on purple	1.60	1.25
912	$5 *Morpho deidamia*	13.00	5.50

1982. Savings Campaign. As T 230. Multicoloured.

913	110c. on $5 Guyana male and female soldiers with flag	50	20

No. 913 is a fiscal stamp surch for postal use. See also No. 990.

1982. Easter. Optd **1982** or surch also.

914	111	25c. multicoloured	20	15
915	111	30c. multicoloured	20	15
916	111	45c. on 6c. multicoloured	20	25
917	111	75c. on 40c. multicoloured	35	25

1982. No. 703 surch **20.**

918	20c. on 35c. *Anaea galanthis*	6.00	10

1982. No. F5 optd **1982 180.**

919	180c. on 40c. Tiger beard	3.50	40

1982. Nos. 555/6 optd **1982.**

920	$2 *Norantea guianensis*	80	30
921	$5 *Odontadenia grandiflora*	1.00	70

1982. No. 542 surch **220.**

922	220c. on 1c. Pitcher Plant of Mt. Roraima	1.00	40

1982. Nos. 472 and 684 optd **1982.**

923	105	40c. black, gold and blue	35	15
924	-	40c. multicoloured	50	25

1982. Nos. 469, 751 and 842/3 surch.

925	105	80c. on 6c. black, gold and flesh	30	20
926	105	85c. on 6c. black, gold and flesh	50	20

927	-	160c. on $1.10 on $2 mult (No. 843)	40	30
928	-	210c. on $3 mult (No. 751)	8.00	40
929	-	235c. on 75c. on $5 mult (No. 842)	1.75	60

1982. Royal Wedding (3rd issue). Nos. 841/3 surch.

930	85c. on 60c. on 3c. Hanging heliconia	1.75	60
931	130c. on 60c. on 3c. Hanging heliconia	1.75	60
932	160c. on $1.10 on $2 *Norantea guianensis*	3.50	1.00
933	170c. on $1.10 on $2 *Norantea guianensis*	6.50	4.50
934	210c. on 75c. on $5 *Odontadenia grandiflora*	2.75	40
935	235c. on 75c. on $5 *Odontadenia grandiflora*	3.75	1.40
936	330c. on $1.10 on $2 *Norantea guianensis*	1.75	40

1982. World Cup Football Championship, Spain (2nd issue). Nos. 544, 546 and 554 optd **ESPANA 1982** or surch also.

937	$1 *Chelonanthus uliginosus*	1.00	40
938	110c. on 3c. Hanging heliconia	1.00	25
939	250c. on 6c. Cannon-ball tree	1.40	60

See also No. 1218.

1982. No. 548a optd **1982.**

977	15c. Christmas orchid	9.00	10

1982. No. O26 optd **POSTAGE.**

978	110c. on 6c. Type 116	2.75	35

1982. Air. 21st Birthday of Princess of Wales. Nos. 542, 545 and 555 surch **AIR Princess of Wales 1961– 1982.**

979	110c. on 5c. Annatto tree	1.75	30
980	220c. on 1c. Pitcher Plant of Mt. Roraima	2.00	80
981	330c. on $2 *Norantea guianensis*	2.00	1.25

1982. Birth of Prince William of Wales. Surch **H.R.H Prince William 21st June 1982.** (a) On stamps of British Guiana with additional opt **GUYANA**.

982	50c. on 2c. green (No. 332)	2.00	30
983	$1.10 on 3c. green and brown (No. 333)	2.50	50

(b) On stamps of Guyana previously optd **GUYANA INDEPENDENCE 1966.**

984	50c. on 2c. green (No. 421)	19.00	3.50
985	$1.10 on 3c. green and brown (No. 422)	30.00	3.50
986	$1.25 on 6c. green (No. 424)	60	60
987	$2.20 on 24c. black and orange (No. 435)	1.50	1.50

1982. Savings Campaign. As No. 913 but showing inverted comma before "OURS" in opt.

990	110c. on $5 Guyana male and female soldiers with flag	5.50	75

1982. Italy's Victory in World Cup Football Championship. No. F7 surch **ESPANA 1982 ITALY $2.35.**

991	$2.35 on 180c. on 60c. Soldier's cap	3.75	55

1982. Wildlife Protection. Nos. 687 and 733/8 optd **1982.**

992	35c. Harpy eagle	2.00	40
993	35c. Type 174	2.00	40
994	35c. Trahira ("Haimara")	2.00	40
995	35c. Electric eel	2.00	40
996	35c. Golden rivulus	2.00	40
997	35c. Golden pencilfish	2.00	40
998	35c. Four-eyed fish	2.00	40

1982. Central America and Caribbean Games, Havana. Nos. 542/3 surch **C.A. & CARIB GAMES 1982.**

999	50c. on 2c. Type 132	1.50	25
1000	60c. on 1c. Pitcher plant of Mt. Roraima	1.50	15

1982. No. 730 optd **1982.**

1001	35c. black and orange	50	20

1982. Nos. 841 and 979 further surch.

1002	130c. on 60c. on 3c. Hanging heliconia	40	30
1003	170c. on 110c. on 5c. Annatto tree	70	45

1982. No. 841 surch **1982 440.**

1004	440c. on 60c. on 3c. Hanging heliconia	75	45

1982. Commonwealth Games, Brisbane, Australia. No. 546 surch **Commonwealth GAMES AUSTRALIA 1982 1.25.**

1005	$1.25 on 6c. Cannon-ball tree	1.00	30

1982. Nos. 552, 641 and 719 optd **1982.**

1006	50c. multicoloured (No. 552)	1.50	25
1007	50c. blue, green and brown (No. 641)	1.00	25
1008	50c. multicoloured (No. 719)	60	25

1982. Various Official stamps additionally optd **POSTAGE.**

1009	15c. Christmas Orchid (No. O 23)	15.00	30

1010	50c. *Guzmania lingulata* (No. O14)	90	15
1011	100c. on $3 on $3 Cylinder satellite (No. O19)	1.00	35

1982. International Food Day. No. 617 optd **INT. FOOD DAY 1982.**

1012	50c. Pawpaw and tangerine	7.50	65

1982. International Year of the Elderly. No. 747 optd **INT. YEAR OF THE ELDERLY.**

1013	50c. District 404 emblem	7.00	50

1982. Centenary of Robert Koch's Discovery of Tubercle Bacillus. No. 750 optd **Dr. R. KOCH CENTENARY TBC BACILLUS DISCOVERY.**

1014	60c. Researcher with microscope, Caduceus emblem, stethoscope and beach scene	2.00	30

1982. International Decade for Women. No. 633 optd **1982.**

1015	$1 brown and blue	2.00	60

1982. Birth Centenary of F. D. Roosevelt (American statesman). No. 706 optd **F. D. ROOSEVELT 1882-1982.**

1016	$1 *Agrias claudina*	6.50	50

1982. First Anniv of G.A.C. Inaugural Flight Georgetown to Boa Vista, Brazil. No. 842 optd **1982 GAC Inaug. Flight Georgetown–Boa Vista, Brasil 200.**

1017	200c. on 75c. on $5 *Odontadenia grandiflora*	5.00	1.40

1982. CARICOM Heads of Government Conference, Kingston, Jamaica. Nos. 881/6 surch **50 CARICOM Heads of Gov't Conference July 1982.**

1018	50c. on 15c. Type 225	1.50	50
1019	50c. on 15c. "Metric man"	1.50	50
1020	50c. on 15c. "Postal service goes metric"	1.50	50
1021	50c. on 15c. Weighing child on metric scales	1.50	50
1022	50c. on 15c. Canje Bridge	1.50	50
1023	50c. on 15c. Tap filling litre bucket	1.50	50

1982. Christmas. Nos. 895/9 optd **CHRISTMAS 1982.**

1024	15c. on 2c. Type 132 (surch **BADEN POWELL 1857–1982**)	25	15
1025	15c. on 2c. Type 132 (surch **Scout Movement 1907–1982**)	25	15
1026	15c. on 2c. Type 132 (surch **1907–1982**)	85	75
1027	15c. on 2c. Type 132 (surch **1857–1982**)	85	75
1028	15c. on 2c. Type 132 (surch **1982**)	11.00	12.00

1982. Nos. 543 and 546 surch in figures (no "c" after face value).

1034	15c. on 2c. Type 132	15	10
1035	20c. on 6c. Cannon-ball tree	15	10

See also No. 1086.

1982. No. 489 surch.

1032	50c. on 6c. Black acara ("Patua")	20	15
1033	100c. on 6c. Black acara ("Patua")	40	30

1983. Optd **1983.**

1036	-	15c. mult (No. 655)	3.50	1.50
1037	-	15c. brown, grey and black (No. 672)	3.75	10
1038	-	15c. mult (No. 682)	40	10
1039	214	15c. on 10c. mult	35	10
1040	215	15c. on 10c. mult	1.00	10
1041	-	50c. mult (No. 646)	3.50	25
1042	-	50c. mult (No. 696)	3.50	25
1043	-	50c. mult (No. 719)	1.50	25

See also Nos. 1060/1, 1069/70, 1072/9c, 1096, 1101 and 1110/16.

1983. No. O17 optd **POSTAGE.**

1044	15c. Harpy Eagle	13.00	10

1983. National Heritage. Nos. 710/12 and 778 surch.

1045	90c. on 30c. Cassiri and decorated Amerindian jars	85	50
1046	90c. on 35c. Rock drawing of hunter and quarry	35	20
1047	90c. on 50c. Fort Kyk-over-al	85	50
1048	90c. on 60c. Fort Island	1.25	20

258 Guyana Flag (inscr. "60TH BIRTHDAY ANNIVERSARY")

1983. 60th Birthday of President Burnham and 30 Years in Parliament. Multicoloured.

1049	25c. Type 258		15	20

1050		25c. As T **258** but position of flag reversed and inscr "30th ANNIVERSARY IN PARLIA-MENT"	15	20
1051		$1.30 Youth display (41×25 mm)	40	65
1052		$6 Presidential standard (43½×25 mm)	70	2·75

1983. Surch in words.

1053	**170**	50c. on 10c. mult (No. 717)	2·75	30
1054	-	50c. on 400c. on 30c. mult (No. 911)	3·25	30
1055	**152**	$1 on 10c. mult (No. 635)	7·50	45
1056	**152**	$1 on $1.05 on 10c. mult (No. 768)	6·50	45
1056a	-	$1 on $1.10 on $2 mult (No. 843)	1·00	2·50
1057	-	$1 on 220c. on 5c. mult (No. 844)	7·50	75
1058	-	$1 on 330c. on $2 mult (as No. 981)	3·00	45
1059	-	$1 on $12 on $1.10 on $2 multicoloured (No. P3)	1·75	2·00

See also Nos. 1080/4.

1983. No. 859 optd **1983**.

1060		$1 on 60c. Beethoven and Sonny Thomas	6·00	45

1983. Conference of Foreign Ministers of Non-aligned Countries, New Delhi. No. 569 surch **FIFTY CENTS** and No. 570 optd **1983**.

1061	**136**	25c. multicoloured	75	25
1062	**136**	50c. on 8c. multicoloured	1·00	25

1983. No. 771 further surch **20**.

1064	**181**	20c. on 10c. on 3c. black, blue and red	55	10

1983. Commonwealth Day. Nos. 424 and 435 surch **Commonwealth Day 14 March 1983**, emblem and value.

1065	**60**	25c. on 6c. green	1·00	20
1066	**60**	$1.20 on 6c. green	50	50
1067	**63**	$1.30 on 24c. black and orange	4·00	55
1068	**63**	$2.40 on 24c. black and orange	4·50	1·50

1983. Easter. Nos. 482/3 optd **1983**.

1069	**111**	25c. multicoloured	15	10
1070	**111**	30c. multicoloured	30	15

262

1983. 25th Anniv of International Maritime Organization. British Guiana fiscal stamp optd.

1071	**262**	$4.80 blue and green	2·25	4·25

1983. Optd **1983**.

1072	**152**	50c. mult (No. 637)	1·50	25
1073	**159**	50c. blue, black and yellow (No. 668)	1·50	25
1073a	-	50c. mult (No. 723)	27·00	2·00
1074	-	50c. mult (No. 854)	60	25
1075	-	50c. mult (No. 858)	7·50	25
1076	-	$1 mult (No. 628)	3·00	45
1077	-	$1 mult (No. 638)	3·00	45
1078	-	$1 mult (No. 675)	3·00	45
1079	-	$1 on 30c. mult (No. 855)	1·25	45
1079a	-	$3 mult (No. 720)	27·00	1·50
1079b	-	$3 mult (No. 724)	42·00	3·00
1079c	-	$3 mult (No. 748)	£100	9·50

1983. Surch **FIFTY CENTS**.

1080	**148**	50c. on 8c. mult (No. 615)	1·75	40
1081	**162**	50c. on 8c. mult (No. 681)	6·00	40
1082	**171**	50c. on 10c. mult (No. 721)	3·00	40
1083	-	50c. on 10c. on 25c. mult (No. O13)	8·00	40
1084	-	50c. on 330c. on $3 mult (No. 845)	4·00	40

1983. Surch in figures with c after new face value.

1087	**111**	50c. on 6c. multicoloured (No. 481)	40	30
1098	**105**	15c. on 6c. black, gold and pink (No. 469)	10	10
1099	-	50c. on 6c. multicoloured (No. 489)	30	30
1100	-	20c. on 6c. multicoloured (No. 546)	15	10

1983. No. 489 surch **$1**.

1088		$1 on 6c. Black acara ("Patua")	1·75	30

1983. No. 639 surch **110**.

1089	**153**	110c. on 10c. yellow, green and violet	1·75	50

1983. Nos. 551 and 556 surch.

1090		250c. on 40c. Tiger beard	7·50	55
1091		400c. on $5 Odontadenia grandiflora	5·50	70

1983. World Telecommunications and Health Day. Nos. 842 and 980 further surch.

1092		25c. on 220c. on 1c. Pitcher plant of Mt. Roraima (surch **ITU 1983 25**)	40	40
1093		25c. on 220c. on 1c. Pitcher plant of Mt. Roraima (surch **WHO 1983 25**)	40	40
1094		25c. on 220c. on 1c. Pitcher plant of Mt. Roraima (surch **17 MAY '83 ITU/WHO 25**)	40	40
1095		$4.50 on 75c. on $5 Odontadenia grandiflora (surch **ITU/WHO 17 MAY 1983**)	13·00	1·50
1095a		235c. on 75c. on $5 (No. 929)	1·00	1·00

1983. 30th Anniv of President's Entry into Parliament. Nos. 690 and 692 surch in words, No. 1096 additionally optd **1983**.

1096		$1 on 15c. black, blue and grey	6·00	50
1097		$1 on 40c. black, orange and grey	10·00	50

1983. No. 611 optd **1983**.

1101		25c. Guides in camp	55·00	4·00

1983. 15th World Scout Jamboree, Alberta. Nos. 835/6 and O25 optd **CANADA 1983**, Nos. 1103 and 1105 additionally surch.

1103		$1.30 on 100c. on 8c. multicoloured	1·50	1·00
1104	**116**	100c. on 6c. mult	1·50	1·50
1105	**116**	$3.90 on 400c. on 6c. multicoloured	2·25	3·50

1983. Nos. 659/60 surch.

1106		60c. on 15c. Map of the Caribbean	14·00	55
1107		$1.50 on 15c. Prudential Cup	16·00	2·00

1983. As Nos. 1049/50, but without commemorative inscr above flag.

1108		25c. As Type **258**	25	25
1109		25c. As No. 1050	25	25

1983. Optd **1983**.

1110	**105**	30c. black, gold and green (No. 471)	75	25
1111	-	30c. multicoloured (No. 695)	9·50	50
1112	-	30c. multicoloured (No. 718)	4·50	40
1113	-	30c. multicoloured (No. 722)	8·00	50
1114	-	30c. multicoloured (No. 746)	14·00	50
1115	-	60c. multicoloured (No. 697)	16·00	50
1116	-	60c. multicoloured (No. 731)	5·50	50

1983. No. 553 optd **1982**.

1117		60c. Soldier's cap	4·00	35

1983. Surch.

1118	**157**	120c. on 8c. mult (No. 654)	2·25	40
1119	-	120c. on 10c. red, black and gold (No. 666)	2·25	40
1120	-	120c. on 35c. mult (No. 622)	2·25	40
1121	-	120c. on 35c. orange, green and violet (No. 640)	2·25	40

1983. Nos. 716 and 729 surch.

1122		120c. on 10c. Type **173**	2·00	40
1123		120c. on 375c. on $3 Cylinder satellite	1·75	40

No. 1123 also carries an otherwise unissued surcharge in red reading **INTERNATIONAL SCIENCE YEAR 1982 375**. As issued much of this is obliterated by two heavy bars.

1983. British Guiana No. D1a and Guyana No. D8 surch **120 GUYANA**.

1124	**D 1**	120c. on 1c. green	1·50	45
1125	**D 2**	120c. on 1c. olive	1·50	45

1983. CARICOM Day. No. 823 additionally surch **CARICOM DAY 1983 60**.

1126		60c. on $3 "Makanaima the Great Ancestral Spirit of the Amerindians"	1·00	·35

271 Kurupukari

1983. Riverboats.

1127	**271**	30c. black and red	20	20
1128	-	60c. black and violet	20	35
1129	-	120c. black and yellow	20	60
1130	-	130c. black	25	65
1131	-	150c. black and green	25	80

DESIGNS: 60c. *Makouria*; 120c. *Powis*; 130c. *Pomeroon*; 150c. *Lukanani*.

1983. Unissued Royal Wedding surch similar to No. 843 additionally surch.

1132		$2.30 on $1.10 on $2 Norantea guianensis	60	40
1133		$3.20 on $1.10 on $2 Norantea guianensis	60	40

1983. Bicentenary of Manned Flight and 20th Anniv of Guyana Airways. Nos. 701/2a optd as indicated in brackets.

1134		20c. multicoloured (**BW**)	80	35
1135		20c. multicoloured (**LM**)	80	35
1136		20c. multicoloured (**GY 1963 1983**)	80	35
1137		20c. multicoloured (**JW**)	80	35
1138		20c. multicoloured (**CU**)	80	35
1139		20c. multicoloured (**Mont Golfier 1783-1983**)	80	35
1140		25c. multicoloured (**BGI**)	2·25	1·25
1141		25c. multicoloured (**GEO**)	35	10
1142		25c. multicoloured (**MIA**)	2·25	1·25
1143		25c. multicoloured (**BVB**)	2·25	1·25
1144		25c. multicoloured (**PBM**)	2·25	1·25
1145		25c. multicoloured (**Mont Golfier 1783-1983**)	40	15
1146		25c. multicoloured (**POS**)	2·25	1·25
1147		25c. multicoloured (**JFK**)	2·25	1·25
1148		30c. multicoloured (**AHL**)	80	30
1149		30c. multicoloured (**BCG**)	80	30
1150		30c. multicoloured (**BMJ**)	80	30
1151		30c. multicoloured (**EKE**)	80	30
1152		30c. multicoloured (**GEO**)	80	30
1153		30c. multicoloured (**GFO**)	80	30
1154		30c. multicoloured (**IBM**)	80	30
1155		30c. multicoloured (**Mont Golfier 1783-1983**)	35	15
1156		30c. multicoloured (**KAI**)	80	30
1157		30c. multicoloured (**KAR**)	80	30
1158		30c. multicoloured (**KPG**)	80	30
1159		30c. multicoloured (**KRG**)	80	30
1160		30c. multicoloured (**KTO**)	80	30
1161		30c. multicoloured (**LTM**)	80	30
1162		30c. multicoloured (**MHA**)	80	30
1163		30c. multicoloured (**MWJ**)	80	30
1164		30c. multicoloured (**MYM**)	80	30
1165		30c. multicoloured (**NAI**)	80	30
1166		30c. multicoloured (**ORJ**)	80	30
1167		30c. multicoloured (**USI**)	80	30
1168		30c. multicoloured (**VEG**)	80	30

1983. No. 649 further surch **240**.

1169		240c. on 35c. on 60c. Soldier's cap	2·75	1·25

1983. F.A.O. Fisheries Project. Nos. 448 and 450 surch **FAO 1983** and value.

1170		30c. on 1c. Type **87**	1·00	15
1171		$2.60 on 3c. Peacock cichlid ("Lukunani")	3·50	3·25

277 G.B. 1857 1d. with Georgetown "AO3" Postmark

1983. 125th Anniv of Use of Great Britain Stamps in Guyana. (a) Inscriptions in black.

		(a) Inscriptions in black		
1172	**277**	25c. brown and black	15	10
1173	-	30c. red and black	15	15
1174	-	60c. violet and black	25	30
1175	-	120c. green and black	50	55
		(b) Inscriptions in blue.		
1176	**277**	25c. brown and black	15	15
1177	-	25c. red and black	15	15
1178	-	25c. violet and black	15	15
1179	-	25c. green and black	15	15
1180	**277**	30c. brown and black	15	15
1181	-	30c. red and black	15	15
1182	-	30c. violet and black	15	15
1183	-	30c. green and black	15	15
1184	**277**	45c. brown and black	20	25
1185	-	45c. red and black	20	25
1186	-	45c. violet and black	20	25
1187	-	45c. green and black	20	25
1188	**277**	120c. brown and black	20	55
1189	-	130c. red and black	20	60
1190	-	150c. violet and black	20	70
1191	-	200c. green and black	20	95

DESIGNS: Nos. 1173, 1177, 1181, 1185, 1189, G.B. 1857 4d. red; Nos. 1174, 1178, 1182, 1186, 1190, G.B. 1856 6d. lilac; Nos. 1175, 1179, 1183, 1187, 1191, G.B. 1856 1s. green.

Each design incorporates the "AO3" postmark except Nos. 1189/91 which show mythical post-marks of the Crowned-circle type inscribed "DEMERARA", "BERBICE" or "ESSEQUIBO".

1983. International Communications Year. No. 716 surch **INT. COMMUNICATIONS YEAR 50**.

1192		50c. on 375c. on $3 Cylinder satellite	4·50	30

No. 1192 also carries an otherwise unissued "375" surcharge. As issued much of this surcharge is obliterated by two groups of six horizontal lines.

1983. St. John Ambulance Commemoration. Nos. 650 and 653 surch.

1193	**156**	75c. on 8c. silver, black and mauve	4·50	50
1194	-	$1.20 on 8c. silver, black and blue	6·50	1·00

1983. International Food Day. No. 616 surch **$1.20 Int. Food Day 1983**.

1195		$1.20 on 35c. Five-fingers and awaras	1·00	50

1983. 65th Anniv of I.L.O. and 25th Death Anniv of H. N. Critchlow (founder of Guyana Labour Union). No. 840 further optd **1918-1983 I.L.O.**

1196		240c. on $3 H. N. Critchlow	1·50	1·50

1983. Deepavali Festival. Nos. 661 and 663/4 surch.

1197		25c. on 8c. Type **158**	20	10
1198		$1.50 on 35c. Flame in bowl	1·25	60
1199		$1.50 on 40c. Goddess Latchmi	80	60

1983. No. 732 optd **1982** and No. 798 further optd **1983**.

1200		$3 "Makanaima the Great Ancestral Spirit of the Amerindians"	1·00	70
1201		360c. on $2 Norantea guianensis	1·10	80

1983. Wildlife Protection. Nos. 686 and 688 surch and No. 852 optd **1983**.

1202		30c. Six-banded armadillo	75	15
1203		60c. on 15c. Giant sea turtle	1·25	30
1204		$1.20 on 40c. Iguana	1·75	50

1983. Human Rights Day. No. 1079c optd **Human Rights Day**.

1205		$3 Rotary anniversary emblem	2·00	1·25

1983. Olympic Games, Los Angeles (1984) (1st issue). Nos. 733/44 surch **LOS ANGELES 1984 125**, Nos. 1206/17 further surch **55**.

1206		55c. on 125c. on 35c. Type **174**	25	25
1207		55c. on 125c.on 35c. Trahira ("Haimara")	25	25
1208		55c. on 125c. on 35c. Electric eel	25	25
1209		55c. on 125c.on 35c. Golden rivulus	25	25
1210		55c. on 125c. on 35c. Golden pencilfish	25	25
1211		55c. on 125c. on 35c. Four-eyed fish	25	25
1212		55c. on 125c.on 35c. Red piranha ("Pirai")	25	25
1213		55c. on 125c. on 35c. Smoking hassar	25	25
1214		55c. on 125c. on 35c. Manta	25	25
1215		55c. on 125c. on 35c. Festive cichlid ("Flying patwa")	25	25
1216		55c. on 125c. on 35c. Arapaima	25	25
1217		55c. on 125c. on 35c. Peacock cichlid ("Lukunani")	25	25
1217a		125c. on 35c. Type **174**	8·50	
1217b		125c. on 35c. Trahira ("Hai-mara")	8·50	
1217c		125c. on 35c. Electric eel	8·50	
1217d		125c. on 35c. Golden rivulus	8·50	
1217e		125c. on 35c. Golden pencilfish	8·50	
1217f		125c. on 35c. Four-eyed fish	8·50	
1217g		125c. on 35c. Red piranha ("Pirai")	8·50	
1217h		125c. on 35c. Smoking hassar	8·50	
1217i		125c. on 35c. Manta	8·50	
1217j		125c. on 35c. Festive cichlid ("Flying patwa")	8·50	
1217k		125c. on 35c. Arapaima	8·50	
1217l		125c. on 35c. Peacock cichlid ("Lukunani")	8·50	

See also Nos. 1308/17 and 1420.

1983. No. F7 with unissued ESPANA 1982 surch further optd **1983**.

1218		180c. on 60c. Soldier's cap	3·25	65

1983. Commonwealth Heads of Government Meeting, New Delhi. No. 542 surch **COMMONWEALTH HEADS OF GOV'T MEETING–INDIA 1983 150**.

1219		150c. on 1c. Pitcher plant of Mt. Roraima	4·75	80

1983. Christmas. No. 861 further surch **CHRISTMAS 1983 20c.**

1220		20c. on 12c. on 6c. Black acara ("Patua")	3·00	10

1984. Nos. 838 and F9 optd **POSTAGE**.

1221		$2 Norantea guianensis	3·50	70
1221b		550c. on $10 Elbella patrobas	20·00	8·50

1984. Flowers. Unissued stamps as T 222 surch.

1222		17c. on 2c. lilac, blue and green	4·25	2·25
1223		17c. on 8c. lilac, blue and mauve	4·25	2·25

1984. Republic Day. No. 703 and 705a variously optd or surch.

1224	25c. on 35c. mult (surch **ALL OUR HERITAGE 25**)		50	20
1225	25c. on 35c. mult (surch **1984 25**)		75	30
1226	25c. on 35c. mult (surch **REPUBLIC DAY 25**)		75	30
1227	25c. on 35c. mult (surch **25**)		75	30
1228	25c. on 35c. mult (surch **BERBICE 25**)		4·75	4·75
1229	25c. on 35c. mult (surch **DEMERARA 25**)		4·75	4·75
1230	25c. on 35c. mult (surch **ESSEQUIBO 25**)		4·75	4·75
1232	60c. mult (optd **ALL OUR HERITAGE**)		2·25	75
1233	60c. mult (optd **REPUBLIC DAY**)		2·25	75
1234	60c. mult (optd **1984**)		2·25	75

1984. Guyana Olympic Committee Appeal. Nos. 841/3 surch **OLYMPIC GAMES 84 25c POSTAGE (+2.25 SURTAX)** and rings, the whole surch inverted.

1235	25c. +$2.25 on 60c. on 3c. Hanging heliconia		2·25	6·00
1236	25c. +$2.25 on 75c. on $5 *Odontadenia grandiflora*		2·25	6·00
1237	25c. +$2.25 on £1.10 on $2 *Norantea guianensis*		2·25	6·00

1984. Nature Protection. Various stamps optd **Protecting our Heritage**, some additionally surch.

1238	20c. on 15c. mult (No. 491)		16·00	25
1239	20c. on 15c. mult (No. 791)		16·00	25
1240a	20c. on 15c. mult (No. 1044)		26·00	1·25
1241	25c. mult (No. 550ab)		24·00	25
1242	30c. on 15c. mult (No. 548a)		22·00	30
1243	40c. multicoloured (No. 457)		18·00	30
1244	50c. multicoloured (No. 552)		3·50	30
1245	50c. multicoloured (No. F6)		3·50	30
1246	60c. multicoloured (No. 459)		10·00	30
1247	90c. on 40c. mult (No. 551)		18·00	65
1248	180c. on 40c. mult (No. 919)		18·00	1·00
1250	225c. on 10c. mult (No. 490)		24·00	1·25
1251	260c. on $1 mult (No. 460)		12·00	1·00
1252	320c. on 40c. mult (No. 551)		13·00	2·25
1253	350c. on 40c. mult (No. 551)		22·00	3·00
1254	390c. on 50c. mult (No. 495)		12·00	2·75
1255	450c. on $5 mult (No. 462)		8·00	2·75
1249	$2 multicoloured (No. 461)		55·00	1·75

1984. Easter. Nos. 483 and 916/17 optd **1984** and No. 481 surch **130**.

1256	**111**	30c. multicoloured	20	20
1257	**111**	45c. on 6c. multicoloured	25	25
1258	**111**	75c. on 40c. multicoloured	35	35
1259	**111**	130c. on 6c. multicoloured	65	60

1984. Nos. 937/9 and 991 surch.

1260	75c. on $1 *Chelonanthus uliginosus*		11·00	35
1261	75c. on 110c. on 3c. Hanging heliconia		11·00	35
1262	225c. on 250c. on 6c. Cannon-ball tree		3·00	1·25
1263	230c. on $2.35 on 180c. on 60c. Soldier's cap		3·00	1·00

1984. Nos. 899/901, 904/6 and 909 surch.

1264	20c. on 15c. on 2c. Type **132** (No. 899)		1·50	30
1265	75c. on 110c. on 5c. Annatto tree (No. 904)		10·00	70
1266	90c. on 110c. on 5c. Annatto tree (No. 900)		6·50	85
1267	90c. on 110c. on 5c. Annatto tree (No. 901)		7·50	85
1268	120c. on 125c. on 8c. on 6c. Cannon-ball tree (No. 905)		7·50	1·00
1269	120c. on 125c. on 8c. on 6c. Cannon-ball tree (No. 906)		7·50	1·00
1270	120c. on 125c. on 8c. on 6c. Cannon-ball tree (No. 909)		2·75	1·00

1984. World Telecommunications and Health Day. Nos. 802 and 980 surch.

1271	25c. on 220c. on 1c. Pitcher plant of Mt. Roraima (surch **ITU DAY 1984 25**)		75	75
1272	25c. on 220c. on 1c. Pitcher plant of Mt. Roraima (surch **WHO DAY 1984 25**)		75	75
1273	25c. on 220c. on 1c. Pitcher plant of Mt. Roraima (surch **ITU/WHO DAY 1984 25**)		75	75
1274	$4.50 on 280c. on $5 "*Odontadenia grandiflora*" (surch **ITU/WHO DAY 1984 $4.50**)		2·75	2·75

1984. No. 1005 surch **120**.

1275	120c. on $1.25 on 6c. Cannon-ball tree		7·00	55

1984. World Forestry Conference. No. 755 optd **1984** and Nos. 752/4 and 875 surch.

1276	55c. on 30c. *Hymenaea courbaril*		2·75	45
1277	75c. on 110c. on $3 *Peltogyne venosa*		40	35
1278	160c. on 50c. *Mora excelsa*		75	70
1279	260c. on 10c. Type **177**		1·25	1·25
1280	$3 *Peltogyne venosa*		1·40	1·40

1984. No. 625 surch.

1281	55c. on 110c. on 10c. Type **150**		1·25	30
1282	90c. on 110c. on 10c. Type **150**		1·50	45

Nos. 1281/2 also carry an otherwise unissued 110c. surch.

1984. U.P.U. Congress, Hamburg. Nos. 1188/91 optd **UPU Congress 1984 Hamburg**.

1283	120c. brown and black		50	60
1284	130c. red and black		55	70
1285	150c. violet and black		60	75
1286	200c. green and black		80	90

1984. Nos. 982/3 and 986/7 surch.

1287	45c. on 50c. on 2c. green		60	20
1288	60c. on $1.10 on 3c. olive and brown		3·00	40
1289	120c. on $1.25 on 6c. green		75	65
1290	200c. on $2.20 on 24c. black and orange		8·00	3·25

1984. Nos. 979/80 and 1003 surch and No. 981 optd **1984**.

1291	75c. on 110c. on 5c. Annatto tree		1·75	35
1292	120c. on 170c. on 110c. on 5c. Annatto tree		2·00	55
1293	200c. on 220c. on 1c. Pitcher plant of Mt. Roraima		40·00	2·25
1294	330c. on $2 *Norantea guianensis*		2·50	2·50

1984. CARICOM Day. No. 1200 additionally surch **CARICOM DAY 1984 60**.

1295	60c. on $3 "Makanaima the Great Ancestral Spirit of the Amerindians"		60	30

1984. No. 544 surch **150**.

1296	150c. on 3c. Hanging heliconia		3·50	1·00

1984. CARICOM Heads of Government Conference. No. 544 surch **60 CARICOM HEADS OF GOV'T CONFERENCE JULY 1984**.

1297	60c. on 3c. Hanging heliconia		60	30

301 Children and Thatched School

1984. Cent of Guyana Teachers' Association. Multicoloured.

1298	25c. Type **301**		10	15
1299	25c. Torch and graduates		10	15
1300	25c. Torch and target emblem		10	15
1301	25c. Teachers of 1884 and 1984 in front of school		10	15

1984. 60th Anniv of International Chess Federation. No. 1048 optd or surch also.

1302	25c. on 90c. on 60c. Fort Island (surch **INT. CHESS FED. 1924–1984 25**)		2·50	50
1303	25c. on 90c. on 60c. Fort Island (surch **1984 25**)		3·50	90
1304	75c. on 90c. on 60c. Fort Island (surch **INT. CHESS FED. 1924–1984 75**)		2·50	75
1305	75c. on 90c. on 60c. Fort Island (surch **1984 75**)		3·50	1·25
1306	90c. on 60c. Fort Island (optd **INT. CHESS FED. 1924–1984**)		2·50	80
1307	90c. on 60c. Fort Island (optd **1984**)		3·50	1·50

1984. Olympic Games, Los Angeles (2nd issue). No. 1051 surch.

1308	25c. on $1.30 mult (surch **TRACK AND FIELD 25**)		35	40
1309	25c. on $1.30 mult (surch **BOXING 25**)		40	45
1310	25c. on $1.30 mult (surch **OLYMPIC GAMES 1984 LOS ANGELES 25**)		40	45
1311	25c. on $1.30 mult (surch **CYCLING 25**)		3·25	50
1312	25c. on $1.30 mult (surch **OLYMPIC GAMES 1984 25**)		4·50	1·25
1313	$1.20 on $1.30 mult (surch **TRACK AND FIELD $1.20**)		1·25	1·40
1314	$1.20 on $1.30 mult (surch **BOXING $1.20**)		1·25	1·40
1315	$1.20 on $1.30 mult (surch **OLYMPIC GAMES 1984 LOS ANGELES $1.20**)		1·25	1·40
1316	$1.20 on $1.30 mult (surch **CYCLING $1.20**)		4·75	2·00
1317	$1.20 on $1.30 mult (surch **OLYMPIC GAMES 1984 $1.20**)		4·75	4·50

1984. 60th Anniv of Girl Guide Movement in Guyana. Nos. 900/9 surch **25 GIRL GUIDES 1924-1984**.

1318	25c. on 110c. on 5c. Annatto tree (No. 900)		25	20
1319	25c. on 110c. on 5c. Annatto tree (No. 901)		25	20

1984. Various stamps surch.

1320	25c. on 110c. on 5c. Annatto tree (No. 902)		80	60
1321	25c. on 110c. on 5c. Annatto tree (No. 903)		80	60
1322	25c. on 110c. on 5c. Annatto tree (No. 904)		10·00	11·00
1323	25c. on 125c. on 8c. on 6c. Cannon-ball tree (No. 905)		25	20
1324	25c. on 125c. on 8c. on 6c. Cannon-ball tree (No. 906)		25	20
1325	25c. on 125c. on 8c. on 6c. Cannon-ball tree (No. 907)		80	60
1326	25c. on 125c. on 8c. on 6c. Cannon-ball tree (No. 908)		80	60
1327	25c. on 125c. on 8c. on 6c. Cannon-ball tree (No. 909)		10·00	11·00

1984. Various stamps surch.

1328	20c. on 15c. on 2c. Type **132** (No. 1034)		70	10
1341	25c. on 10c. Cattleya (No. 547)		60·00	2·25
1342	25c. on 15c. Christmas orchid (No. 864)		30·00	50
1343	25c. on 15c. Christmas orchid (No. 548a)		£130	5·50
1346	25c. on 15c. Christmas orchid (No. 977)		18·00	20
1347	25c. on 15c. Christmas orchid (No. 1009)		18·00	20
1348	25c. on 15c. Christmas orchid (No. O23)		18·00	20
1342a	25c. on 35c. on 60c. Soldier's cap (No. 649)		95·00	4·75
1331	60c. on 110c. on 8c. on 3c. Hanging heliconia (As No. 868 but with only one **110**)		38·00	5·00
1332	120c. on 125c. on 8c. on 6c. Cannon-ball tree (No. 893)		7·50	50
1333	120c. on 125c. on $2 *Norantea guianensis* (No. 834)		70·00	7·50
1334	120c. on 125c. on $2 *Norantea guianensis* (No. O20)		6·00	50
1335	120c. on 140c. on $1 *Chelonanthus uliginoides* (No. 796)		5·50	50
1349	130c. on 110c. on $2 *Norantea guianensis* (No. 804)		95·00	6·00
1350	130c. on 110c. on $2 *Norantea guianensis* (No. O22)		1·25	1·25
1336	200c. on 220c. on 1c. Pitcher plant of Mt. Roraima (No. 922)		25·00	1·00
1337	320c. on $1.10 on $2 *Norantea guianensis* (No. 804)		1·50	75
1338	350c. on 375c. on $5 *Odontadenia grandiflora* (No. 803)		5·50	1·00
1339	390c. on $5 *Odontadenia grandiflora* (No. 1091)		6·00	1·25
1340	450c. on $5 *Odontadenia grandiflora* (No. O16)		9·00	3·00
1351a	600c. on $7.20 on $1 *Chelonanthus uliginoides* (No. 770)		50	60

1984. No. 899 optd with fleur-de-lis.

1358a	25c. Marabunta		90·00	4·50

1984. 40th Anniv of I.C.A.O. Nos. 981, 1017 and 1148/68 optd **ICAO** or as indicated.

1361	30c. multicoloured (No. 1148)		1·50	1·00
1362	30c. multicoloured (No. 1149)		1·50	1·00
1363	30c. multicoloured (No. 1150)		1·50	1·00
1364	30c. multicoloured (No. 1151)		1·50	1·00
1365	30c. multicoloured (No. 1152)		1·50	1·00
1366	30c. multicoloured (No. 1153)		1·50	1·00
1367	30c. multicoloured (No. 1154) (optd **IMB/ICAO**)		1·50	1·00
1368	30c. multicoloured (No. 1155) (optd **KCV/ICAO**)		1·50	1·00
1369	30c. multicoloured (No. 1156) (optd **KAI/ICAO**)		1·50	1·00
1370	30c. multicoloured (No. 1157)		1·50	1·00
1371	30c. multicoloured (No. 1158)		1·50	1·00
1372	30c. multicoloured (No. 1155) (optd **1984**)		1·50	1·00
1373	30c. multicoloured (No. 1155) (optd **KPM/ICA**)		1·50	1·00
1374	30c. multicoloured (No. 1159)		1·50	1·00
1375	30c. multicoloured (No. 1160)		1·50	1·00
1376	30c. multicoloured (No. 1161)		1·50	1·00
1377	30c. multicoloured (No. 1155) (optd **PMT/ICAO**)		1·50	1·00
1378	30c. multicoloured (No. 1162)		1·50	1·00
1379	30c. multicoloured (No. 1163)		1·50	1·00
1380	30c. multicoloured (No. 1164)		1·50	1·00
1381	30c. multicoloured (No. 1165)		1·50	1·00
1382	30c. multicoloured (No. 1166)		1·50	1·00
1383	30c. multicoloured (No. 1167)		1·50	1·00
1384	30c. multicoloured (No. 1168)		1·50	1·00
1385	200c. on 330c. on $2 multicoloured (No. 981)		75	85
1386	200c. on 75c. on $5 multicoloured (No. 1017)		3·00	2·00

No. 1385 also carries an otherwise unissued surch **G.A.C. Inaug. Flight Georgetown–Toronto 200**.

1984. Wildlife Protection. Nos. 756/67 optd **1984**.

1387	30c. Type **178**		30	25
1388	30c. Red howler		30	25
1389	30c. Common squirrel-monkey		30	25
1390	30c. Two-toed sloth		30	25
1391	30c. Brazilian tapir		30	25
1392	30c. Collared peccary		30	25
1393	30c. Six-banded armadillo		30	25
1394	30c. Tamandua ("Ant Eater")		30	25
1395	30c. Giant anteater		30	25
1396	30c. Murine opossum		30	25
1397	30c. Brown four-eyed opossum		30	25
1398	30c. Brazilian agouti		30	25

1984. Nos. D10/11 surch **120 GUYANA**.

1399	**D 2**	120c. on 4c. blue	1·50	65
1402	**D 2**	120c. on 12c. red	1·50	65

1984. 175th Birth Anniv of Louis Braille (inventor of alphabet for the blind). No. 1040 surch **$1.50**.

1403	$1.50 on 15c. on 10c. Type **215**		6·50	55

1984. International Food Day. No. 1012 surch **1**.

1404	150c. on 50c. Pawpaw and tangerine		2·50	55

The surcharge places a "1" alongside the original face value and obliterates the "1982" date on the previous overprint.

1984. Birth Centenary of H. N. Critchlow (founder of Guyana Labour Union). No. 873 surch 240 and No. 1196, both optd **1984**.

1405	240c. on 110c. on $3 H. N. Critchlow (No. 873)		1·00	65
1406	240c. on $3 H. N. Critchlow (No. 1196)		7·50	1·25

1984. Nos. 910/12 and 1184/7 surch.

1407	**277**	25c. on 45c. brown and black	15	25
1408	-	25c. on 45c. red and black (No. 1185)	15	25
1409	-	25c. on 45c. violet and black (No. 1186)	15	25
1410	-	25c. on 45c. green and black (No. 1187)	15	25
1411	-	120c. on 100c. on $3 mult (No. 910)	10·00	1·25
1412	-	120c. on 400c. on 30c. mult (No. 911)	1·25	75
1413	-	320c. on $5 multicol (No. 912)	19·00	2·75

1984. Deepavali Festival. Nos. 544/5 surch **MAHA SABHA 1934-1984** and new value.

1414	25c. on 5c. Annatto tree		50	10
1415	$1.50 on 3c. Hanging heliconia		2·75	1·00

1984. A.S.D.A. Philatelic Exhibition, New York. Nos. 1188/91 optd **Philatelic Exhibition New York 1984**.

1416	**277**	120c. brown and black	40	45
1417	-	130c. red and black	45	50
1418	-	150c. violet and black	50	55
1419	-	200c. green and black	70	75

1984. Olympic Games, Los Angeles (3rd issue). Design as No. 1051, but with Olympic rings and inscr "OLYMPIC GAMES 1984 LOS ANGELES".

1420	$1.20 Youth display (41×25 mm)		1·50	70

1984. Nos. 847, 861, 1099 and 1088 surch.

1421	20c. on 12c. on 12c. on 6c. multicoloured (No. 847)		60	10
1422	20c. on 12c. on 6c. mult (No. 861)		95·00	7·00
1423	25c. on 50c. on 6c. mult (No. 1099)		30	10
1424	60c. on $1 on 6c. mult (No. 1088)		45	25

318 Pair of Swallow-tailed Kites on Tree

1984. Christmas. Swallow-tailed Kites. Multicoloured.

1425	60c. Type **318**		3·00	1·75
1426	60c. Swallow-tailed kite on branch		3·00	1·75
1427	60c. Kite in flight with wings raised		3·00	1·75
1428	60c. Kite in flight with wings lowered		3·00	1·75
1429	60c. Kite gliding		3·00	1·75

Nos. 1425/9 were printed together, *se-tenant*, with the backgrounds forming a composite design. Each stamp is inscribed "CHRISTMAS 1982".

319 St. George's Cathedral, Georgetown

1985. Georgetown Buildings. Each black and stone.

1430	25c. Type **319**		10	10
1431	60c. Demerara Mutual Life Assurance Building		15	25
1432	120c. As No. 1431		30	45

1433	120c. Town Hall	30	45
1434	120c. Victoria Law Courts	30	45
1435	200c. As No. 1433	30	75
1436	300c. As No. 1434	30	1·10

Nos. 1432/4 were printed together, *se-tenant*, forming a composite design.

1985. International Youth Year. No. 1420 optd **International Youth Year 1985**.

1437	$1.20 Youth display	3·25	65

Examples of No. 1420 used for this overprint all show the second line of the original inscription as "LOS ANGELLES".

1985. Republic Day. Nos. 1049/50 and 1052 optd or surch **Republic Day 1970-1985**.

1438	25c. Type **238**	50	50
1439	25c. Flag (inscr "30th ANNIVERSARY IN PARLIAMENT")	50	50
1440	120c. on $6 on $6 Presidential standard	1·00	1·00
1441	130c. on $6 on $6 Presidential standard	1·10	1·10

322 Young Ocelot on Branch

1985. Wildlife Protection. Multicoloured.

1442A	25c. Type **322** (green background)	1·75	10
1443A	60c. Young ocelot (different) (brown background)	30	25
1447A	130c. As No. 1446	45	60
1448A	320c. Scarlet macaw (28×46 mm)	3·25	2·00
1449A	330c. Young ocelot reaching for branch (28×46 mm)	90	2·00

1985. Revenue stamp as T **181**, and Nos. 912, 940, 1016 and No. O24 surch.

1450	30c. on 50c. mult (No. O24)	75	10
1451	55c. on 2c. black, blue and grey	75	20
1452	55c. on 15c. on 2c. black, blue and grey (940)	75	20
1453	90c. on $1 mult (No. 1016)	7·50	65
1454	225c. on $5 mult (No. 912)	19·00	2·25
1455	230c. on $5 mult (No. 912)	19·00	2·50
1456	260c. on $5 mult (No. 912)	19·00	3·00

1985. International Youth Year Save the Children Fund Campaign. Nos. 880, 1073a, 1079b and 1082 optd **International Youth Year 1985** or surch also.

1457	50c. "Two Boys catching Ducks" (No. 1073a)	2·25	20
1458	50c. on 10c. Type **171** (No. 1082)	8·00	20
1459	120c. on 125c. on $3 "Mango Season" (No. 880)	2·25	45
1460	$3 "Mango Season" (No. 1079b)	2·25	1·50

1985. 125th Anniv of British Guiana Post Office (1st issue). No. 699 surch 25 and names of post offices and postal agencies open in 1860.

1461	25c. on 10c. mult (**Airy Hall**)	1·50	1·50
1462	25c. on 10c. multicoloured (**Belfield Arab Coast**)	1·50	1·50
1463	25c. on 10c. multicoloured (**Belfield E. C. Dem.**)	1·50	1·50
1464	25c. on 10c. multicoloured (**Belladrum**)	1·50	1·50
1465	25c. on 10c. multicoloured (**Beterver-wagting**)	1·50	1·50
1466	25c. on 10c. mult (**Blairmont Ferry**)	1·50	1·50
1467	25c. on 10c. mult (**Boeraserie**)	1·50	1·50
1468	25c. on 10c. mult (**Brahm**)	1·50	1·50
1469	25c. on 10c. on 10c. mult (**Bushlot**)	1·50	1·50
1470	25c. on 10c. mult (**De Kinderen**)	1·50	1·50
1471	25c. on 10c. multicoloured (**Fort Wellington**)	1·50	1·50
1472	25c. on 10c. mult (**Georgetown**)	1·50	1·50
1473	25c. on 10c. mult (**Hague**)	1·50	1·50
1474	25c. on 10c. mult (**Leguan**)	1·50	1·50
1475	25c. on 10c. mult (**Mahaica**)	1·50	1·50
1476	25c. on 10c. mult (**Mahaicony**)	1·50	1·50
1477	25c. on 10c. multicoloured (**New Amsterdam**)	1·50	1·50
1478	25c. on 10c. mult (**Plaisance**)	1·50	1·50
1479	25c. on 10c. multicoloured (**No. 6 Police Station**)	1·50	1·50
1480	25c. on 10c. mult (**Queenstown**)	1·50	1·50
1481	25c. on 10c. multicoloured (**Vergenoegen**)	1·50	1·50
1482	25c. on 10c. mult (**Vigilance**)	1·50	1·50
1483	25c. on 10c. multicoloured (**Vreed-en-Hoop**)	1·50	1·50
1484	25c. on 10c. mult (**Wakenaam**)	1·50	1·50
1485	25c. on 10c. multicoloured (**Windsor Castle**)	1·50	1·50

See also Nos. 1694/1717, 2140/64 and 2278/2301.

1985. I.T.U./W.H.O. Day. Nos. 1148/68 optd **1985** or with single capital letter.

1486	30c. multicoloured (1148)	1·50	1·50
1487	30c. multicoloured (1149)	1·50	1·50
1488	30c. multicoloured (1150)	1·50	1·50
1489	30c. multicoloured (1151)	1·50	1·50
1490	30c. multicoloured (1152)	1·50	1·50
1491	30c. multicoloured (1153)	1·50	1·50
1492	30c. multicoloured (1154) (**I**)	1·50	1·50
1493	30c. multicoloured (1155) (**T**)	1·50	1·50
1494	30c. multicoloured (1156) (**U**)	1·50	1·50
1495	30c. multicoloured (1157)	1·50	1·50
1496	30c. multicoloured (1158)	1·50	1·50
1497	30c. multicoloured (1155) (**W**)	1·50	1·50
1498	30c. multicoloured (1155) (**H**)	1·50	1·50
1499	30c. multicoloured (1155) (**O**)	1·50	1·50
1500	30c. multicoloured (1159)	1·50	1·50
1501	30c. multicoloured (1160)	1·50	1·50
1502	30c. multicoloured (1161) (**D**)	1·50	1·50
1503	30c. multicoloured (1155) (**A**)	1·50	1·50
1504	30c. multicoloured (1162) (**Y**)	1·50	1·50
1505	30c. multicoloured (1163)	1·50	1·50
1506	30c. multicoloured (1164)	1·50	1·50
1507	30c. multicoloured (1165)	1·50	1·50
1508	30c. multicoloured (1166)	1·50	1·50
1509	30c. multicoloured (1167)	1·50	1·50
1510	30c. multicoloured (1168)	1·50	1·50

1985. No. 861 surch **20**.

1511	20c. on 12c. on 6c. Patua	8·00	25

1985. Tenth Anniv of Caribbean Agricultural Research Development Institute. No. 544 surch **60 CARDI 1975-1985**.

1512	60c. on 3c. Hanging heliconia	6·00	35

1985. No. 839 surch **600**.

1513	600c. on 625c. on 40c. Tiger beard	48·00	4·50

1985. 80th Anniv of Rotary International. Nos. 707 and 879 surch **ROTARY INTERNATIONAL 1905-1985**.

1514	120c. on 110c. on $3 Rotary anniversary emblem	27·00	1·75
1515	300c. on $2 Morpho rhetenor	17·00	5·50

1985. CARICOM Day. No. 1200 surch **CARICOM DAY 1985 60**.

1516	60c. on $3 "Makanaima the Great Ancestral Spirit of the Amerindians"	3·00	40

1985. 135th Anniv of First British Guiana Stamps. No. 870 surch **135th Anniversary Cotton Reel 1850-1985 120**.

1517	120c. on 110c. on 10c. Type **170**	1·75	1·00

Series 1

"REICHENBACHIA" ISSUES. Due to the proliferation of these designs the catalogue uses the book plate numbers as description for each design. The following index gives the species on each plate.

Plate No. 1 (Series 1) *Odontoglossum crispum*
Plate No. 2 (Series 1) *Cattleya percivaliana*
Plate No. 3 (Series 1) *Cypripedium sanderianum*
Plate No. 4 (Series 1) *Odontoglossum rossi*
Plate No. 5 (Series 1) *Cattleya dowiana aurea*
Plate No. 6 (Series 1) *Coelogyne cristata maxima*
Plate No. 7 (Series 1) *Odontoglossum insleayi splendens*
Plate No. 8 (Series 1) *Laelia euspatha*
Plate No. 9 (Series 1) *Dendrobium wardianum*
Plate No. 10 (Series 1) *Laelia autumnalis xanthotropis*
Plate No. 11 (Series 1) *Phalaenopsis grandiflora aurea*
Plate No. 12 (Series 1) *Cattleya lawrenceana*
Plate No. 13 (Series 1) *Masdevallia shuttleworthii* and *M. xanthocorys*
Plate No. 14 (Series 1) *Aeranthus sesquipedalis*
Plate No. 15 (Series 1) *Cattleya mendelii Duke of Marlborough*
Plate No. 16 (Series 1) *Zygopetalum intermedium*
Plate No. 17 (Series 1) *Phaius humblotii*
Plate No. 18 (Series 1) *Chysis bractescens*
Plate No. 19 (Series 1) *Masdevallia backhousiana*
Plate No. 20 (Series 1) *Cattleya citrina*
Plate No. 21 (Series 1) *Oncidium jonesianum* and *Oncidium jonesianum phaeanthum*
Plate No. 22 (Series 1) *Saccolabium giganteum*
Plate No. 23 (Series 1) *Cypripedium io*
Plate No. 24 (Series 1) *Odontoglossum blandum*
Plate No. 25 (Series 1) *Maxillaria sanderiana*
Plate No. 26 (Series 1) *Odontoglossum Edward II*
Plate No. 27 (Series 1) *Vanda teres*
Plate No. 28 (Series 1) *Odontoglossum hallii xanthoglossum*
Plate No. 29 (Series 1) *Odontoglossum crispum hrubyanum*
Plate No. 30 (Series 1) *Oncidium concolor*
Plate No. 31 (Series 1) *Trichopilia suavis alba*
Plate No. 32 (Series 1) *Cattleya superba splendens*
Plate No. 33 (Series 1) *Odontoglossum luteo-purpureum*
Plate No. 34 (Series 1) *Cypripedium niveum*
Plate No. 35 (Series 1) *Stanhopea shuttleworthii*
Plate No. 36 (Series 1) *Laelia anceps percivaliana*
Plate No. 37 (Series 1) *Odontoglossum hebraicum*
Plate No. 38 (Series 1) *Cypripedium oenanthum superbum*
Plate No. 39 (Series 1) *Dendrobium superbiens*
Plate No. 40 (Series 1) *Laelia harpophylla*
Plate No. 41 (Series 1) *Lycaste skinneri* and *alba*
Plate No. 42 (Series 1) *Phalaenopsis stuartiana*
Plate No. 43 (Series 1) *Cattleya trianaei ernesti*
Plate No. 44 (Series 1) *Sobralia xantholeuca*
Plate No. 45 (Series 1) *Odontoglossum crispum kinlesideanum*
Plate No. 46 (Series 1) *Cattleya trianaei schroederiana*
Plate No. 47 (Series 1) *Epidendrum vitellinum*
Plate No. 48 (Series 1) *Laelia anceps stella"* and *barkeriana*
Plate No. 49 (Series 1) *Odontoglossum harryanum"*
Plate No. 50 (Series 1) *Dendrobium leechianum*

Plate No. 51 (Series 1) *Phalaenopsis speciosa*
Plate No. 52 (Series 1) *Laelia elegans schilleriana*
Plate No. 53 (Series 1) *Zygopetalum wendlandi*
Plate No. 54 (Series 1) *Cypripedium elligerum majus*
Plate No. 55 (Series 1) *"Angraecum articulatum*
Plate No. 56 (Series 1) *Laelia anceps sanderiana*
Plate No. 57 (Series 1) *Vanda coerulea*
Plate No. 58 (Series 1) *Dendrobium nobile sanderianum*
Plate No. 59 (Series 1) *Laelia gouldiana*
Plate No. 60 (Series 1) *Odontoglossum grande*
Plate No. 61 (Series 1) *Cypripedium rothschildianum*
Plate No. 62 (Series 1) *Vanda sanderian"*
Plate No. 63 (Series 1) *Dendrobium aureum*
Plate No. 64 (Series 1) *Oncidium macranthum*
Plate No. 65 (Series 1) *Cypripedium tautzianum*
Plate No. 66 (Series 1) *Cymbidium mastersi*
Plate No. 67 (Series 1) *Angraecum caudatum*
Plate No. 68 (Series 1) *Laelia albid"*
Plate No. 69 (Series 1) *Odontoglossum roezlii*
Plate No. 70 (Series 1) *Oncidium ampliatum majus*
Plate No. 71 (Series 1) *Renanthera lowii*
Plate No. 72 (Series 1) *Cattleya warscewiczii*
Plate No. 73 (Series 1) *Oncidium lanceanum*
Plate No. 74 (Series 1) *Vanda hookeriana*
Plate No. 75 (Series 1) *Cattleya labiata gaskelliana*
Plate No. 76 (Series 1) *"Epidendrum prismatocarpum*
Plate No. 77 (Series 1) *Cattleya guttata leopoldi*
Plate No. 78 (Series 1) *Oncidium splendidum*
Plate No. 79 (Series 1) *Odontoglossum hebraicum aspersum*
Plate No. 80 (Series 1) *Cattleya dowiana var chrysotoxa*
Plate No. 81 (Series 1) *Cattleya trianae alba*
Plate No. 82 (Series 1) *Odontoglossum humeanum*
Plate No. 83 (Series 1) *Cypripedium argus*
Plate No. 84 (Series 1) *Odontoglossum luteo-purpureum prionopetalum*
Plate No. 85 (Series 1) *Cattleya rochellensis*
Plate No. 86 (Series 1) *Odontoglossum triumphans*
Plate No. 87 (Series 1) *Phalaenopsis casta*
Plate No. 88 (Series 1) *Oncidium tigrinum*
Plate No. 89 (Series 1) *Cypripedium lemoinierianum*
Plate No. 90 (Series 1) *Catasetum bungerothii*
Plate No. 91 (Series 1) *Cattleya ballantiniana*
Plate No. 92 (Series 1) *Dendrobium brymerianum*
Plate No. 93 (Series 1) *Cattleya eldorado crocata*
Plate No. 94 (Series 1) *Odontoglossum sanderianum*
Plate No. 95 (Series 1) *Cattleya labiata warneri*
Plate No. 96 (Series 1) *Odontoglossum schroderianum*

Series 2

Plate No. 1 (Series 2) *Cypripedium morganiae burfordiense*
Plate No. 2 (Series 2) *Cattleya bowringiana*
Plate No. 3 (Series 2) *Dendrobium formosum*
Plate No. 4 (Series 2) *Phaius tuberculosus*
Plate No. 5 (Series 2) *Odontoglossum crispum mundyanum*
Plate No. 6 (Series 2) *Laelia praestans*
Plate No. 7 (Series 2) *Dendrobium phalaenopsis var staterianum*
Plate No. 8 (Series 2) *Cypripedium boxalli atratum*
Plate No. 9 (Series 2) *Odontoglossum wattianum*
Plate No. 10 (Series 2) *Cypripedium lathamianum inversum*
Plate No. 11 (Series 2) *Paphinia rugosa* and *Zygopetalum xanthinum*
Plate No. 12 (Series 2) *Dendrobium melanodiscus*
Plate No. 13 (Series 2) *Laelia anceps schroderiana*
Plate No. 14 (Series 2) *Phaius hybridus cooksonii*
Plate No. 15 (Series 2) *Disa grandiflora*
Plate No. 16 (Series 2) *Selenipedium hybridum grande*
Plate No. 17 (Series 2) *Cattleya schroederae alba*
Plate No. 18 (Series 2) *Lycaste skinnerii armeniaca*
Plate No. 19 (Series 2) *Odontoglossum excellens*
Plate No. 20 (Series 2) *Laelio-cattleya elegans var blenheimensis*
Plate No. 21 (Series 2) *Odontoglossum coradinei*
Plate No. 22 (Series 2) *Odontoglossum wilckeanum var rothschildianum*
Plate No. 23 (Series 2) *Cypripedium lawrenceanum hyeanum*
Plate No. 24 (Series 2) *Cattleya intermedia punctatissima*
Plate No. 25 (Series 2) *Laelia purpurata*
Plate No. 26 (Series 2) *Masdevallia harryana splendens*
Plate No. 27 (Series 2) *Selenipedium hybridum nitidissimum*
Plate No. 28 (Series 2) *Cattleya mendelii var measuresiana*
Plate No. 29 (Series 20 *Odontoglossum vexillarium* ("miltonia vexillaria")
Plate No. 30 (Series 2) *Saccolabium coeleste*
Plate No. 31 (Series 2) *Cypripedium hybridum youngianum*
Plate No. 32 (Series 2) *Miltonia (hybrida) bleuana*
Plate No. 33 (Series 2) *Laelia grandis*
Plate No. 34 (Series 2) *Cattleya labiata var lueddemanniana*
Plate No. 35 (Series 2) *Odontoglossum coronarium*
Plate No. 36 (Series 2) *Cattleya granulosa var schofieldiana*
Plate No. 37 (Series 2) *Odontoglossum (hybridum) leroyanum*
Plate No. 38 (Series 2) *Cypripedium (hybridum) laucheanum* and *eyermanianum*
Plate No. 39 (Series 2) *Cychnoches chlorochilon*
Plate No. 40 (Series 2) *Cattleya O'Brieniana*
Plate No. 41 (Series 2) *Odontoglossum ramosissimum*
Plate No. 42 (Series 2) *Dendrobium phalaenopsis var"*
Plate No. 43 (Series 2) *Cypripedium (hybridum) polletianum* and *maynardii*
Plate No. 44 (Series 2) *Odontoglossum naevium*
Plate No. 45 (Series 2) *Cypripedium (hybridum) castleanum*
Plate No. 47 (Series 2) *Cattleya amethystoglossa*
Plate No. 48 (Series 2) *Cattleya (hybrida) arnoldiana*
Plate No. 49 (Series 2) *Cattleya labiata*
Plate No. 50 (Series 2) *Dendrobium (hybridum) venus* and "cassiope"
Plate No. 51 (Series 2) *Selenipedium (hybridum) weidlichianum*
Plate No. 52 (Series 2) *Cattleya mossiae var reineckiana"*
Plate No. 53 (Series 2) *Cymbidium lowianum*
Plate No. 54 (Series 2) *Oncidium loxense*
Plate No. 55 (Series 2) *Coelogyne sanderae*
Plate No. 58 (Series 2) *Coelogyne pandurata*
Plate No. 59 (Series 2) *Schomburgkia sanderiana*
Plate No. 60 (Series 2) *Oncidium superbiens*
Plate No. 61 (Series 2) *Dendrobium johnsoniae*
Plate No. 62 (Series 2) *Laelia hybrida behrensiana*
Plate No. 63 (Series 2) Hybrid *Calanthes Victoria Regina*, "Bella" and *Burfordiens"*
Plate No. 64 (Series 2) *Cattleya mendelii* Quorndon House var
Plate No. 65 (Series 2) *Arachnanthe clarkei*
Plate No. 66 (Series 2) *Zygopetalum burtii*
Plate No. 67 (Series 2) *Cattleya (hybrida) parthenia*
Plate No. 68 (Series 2) *Phalaenopsis sanderiana* and *intermedia portei*

Plate No. 69 (Series 2) *Phaius blumei var assamicus*
Plate No. 70 (Series 2) *Angraecum humblotii*
Plate No. 71 (Series 2) *Odontoglossum pescatorei*
Plate No. 72 (Series 2) *Cattleya rex*
Plate No. 73 (Series 2) *Zygopetalum crinitum*
Plate No. 74 (Series 2) *Cattleya lueddemanniana alba*
Plate No. 75 (Series 2) *Cymbidium (hybridum) winnianum*
Plate No. 76 (Series 2) Hybrid *Masdevallias courtauldiana, geleniana* and *measuresian"*
Plate No. 77 (Series 2) *Cypripedium (hybridum) calypso*
Plate No. 78 (Series 2) *Masdevallia chimaera var mooreana*
Plate No. 79 (Series 2) *Miltonia phalaenopsis*
Plate No. 80 (Series 2) *Lissochilus giganteus*
Plate No. 82 (Series 2) *Thunia brymeriana*
Plate No. 83 (Series 2) *Miltonia moreliana*
Plate No. 84 (Series 2) *Oncidium kramerianum*
Plate No. 85 (Series 2) *Cattleya Victoria Regin"*
Plate No. 86 (Series 2) *Zygopetalum klabochorum*
Plate No. 87 (Series 2) *Laelia autumnalis alba*
Plate No. 88 (Series 2) *Spathoglottis kimballiana*
Plate No. 89 (Series 2) *Laelio-cattleya* ("The Hon. Mrs. Astor")
Plate No. 90 (Series 2) *Phaius hybridus amabilis* and *marthiae*
Plate No. 91 (Series 2) *Zygopetalum rostratum*
Plate No. 92 (Series 2) *Coelogyne swaniana*
Plate No. 93 (Series 2) *Laelio-cattleya* (hybrida) *phoebe*
Plate No. 94 (Series 2) *Epidendrum atro-purpureum var randianum*
Plate No. 95 (Series 2) *Dendrobium imperatrix*
Plate No. 96 (Series 2) *Vanda parishii var marriottiana*

331 *Cattleya lawrenceana* (Plate No. 12 (Series 1))

1985. Centenary of Publication of Sanders' *Reichenbachia* (1st issue). Orchids. Multicoloured.

1518	25c. Type **331**	50	30
1519	60c. Plate No. 2 (Series 1)	60	35
1520	60c. Plate No. 7 (Series 1)	60	35
1521	60c. Plate No. 10 (Series 1)	60	35
1522	60c. Plate No. 19 (Series 1)	60	35
1523	60c. Plate No. 31 (Series 1)	60	35
1524	120c. Plate No. 27 (Series 1)	75	55
1525	130c. Plate No. 3 (Series 1)	75	55
1528	130c. Plate No. 18 (Series 1)	5·00	55
1531	130c. Plate No. 29 (Series 1)	3·50	55
1532	130c. Plate No. 30 (Series 1)	3·50	55
1533	200c. Plate No. 4 (Series 1)	3·25	85

See also Nos. 1551/66, 1571/1806, 1597, 1620/1863, 1663/73, 1679/83, 1731/8, 1747/54, 1809/19, 1822, 1868/9, 1872/81, 1884/7, 1907, 1912/15, 1916/24, 1925/9, 2066/73, 2171/8, 2180/2, 2190/3, 2216/18, 2219/20, 2225/7, 2235/42, **MS**2275, 2314/18, 2322/5, 2328, **MS**2332, 2314/18, 2322/5, 2329, 2468/71, 2498/2511 and 2605/8.

332 Arms of Guyana

1985

1535b	**332** 25c. multicoloured	15	20

For Type **332** within frame, see No. 2183.

1985. 85th Birthday of Queen Elizabeth the Queen Mother (1st issue). Nos. 1528 and 1531/2 optd **QUEEN MOTHER 1900-1985**.

1536	130c. Plate No. 18 (Series 1)	80	80
1537	130c. Plate No. 29 (Series 1)	80	80
1538	130c. Plate No. 30 (Series 1)	80	80
MS1539	100×126 mm. 200c.×4 Plate 4 (Series 1)	7·50	5·50

The four stamps in No. **MS**1539 are overprinted **LADY BOWES-LYON 1900-1923, DUCHESS OF YORK 1923-1937, QUEEN ELIZABETH 1937-1952** or **QUEEN MOTHER 1952-1985**.
See also No. **MS**1570.

1985. International Youth Year. Nos. 900/4 surch **25 International Youth Year 1985**.

1540	25c. on 110c. on 5c. multicoloured (900)	25	25
1541	25c. on 110c. on 5c. multicoloured (901)	25	25
1542	25c. on 110c. on 5c. multicoloured (902)	1·00	1·00
1543	25c. on 110c. on 5c. multicoloured (903)	1·00	1·00
1544	25c. on 110c. on 5c. multicoloured (904)	13·00	13·00

1985. 75th Anniv of Girl Guide Movement. No. 612 surch **225 1910-1985**.

1545	225c. on 350c. on 225c. on 40c. Guides in camp	55·00	6·50

No. 1545 also carries two otherwise unissued surcharges at top right.

1985. Birth Bicentenary of John J. Audubon (ornithologist). No. 992 surch **J. J. Audubon 1785-1985 240**.

| 1546 | 240c. on 35c. Harpy eagle | 55·00 | 8·00 |

337 Leaders of the 1763 Rebellion

1985. 150th Anniv (1984) of Abolition of Slavery (1st issue).

1547	**337**	25c. black and grey	25	10
1548	-	60c. black and mauve	20	25
1549	-	130c. black and blue	25	50
1550	-	150c. black and lilac	60	55

DESIGNS: 60c. Damon and Parliament Buildings, Georgetown; 130c. Quamina and Demerara, 1823; 150c. "Den Arendt" (slave ship), 1627.

For these designs in changed colours see Nos. 2552/5.

1985. Centenary of Publication of Sanders' *Reichenbachia* (2nd issue). As T **331** showing orchids. Multicoloured.

1551	25c. Plate No. 52 (Series 1)	2·50	25
1763	55c. Plate No. 9 (Series 1)	55	10
1764	55c. Plate No. 22 (Series 1)	55	10
1765	55c. Plate No. 49 (Series 1)	55	10
1766	55c. Plate No. 64 (Series 1)	55	10
1556	60c. Plate No. 44 (Series 1)	70	35
1557	60c. Plate No. 47 (Series 1)	70	35
1558	120c. Plate No. 36 (Series 1)	2·75	55
1559	130c. Plate No. 16 (Series 1)	2·75	55
1560	130c. Plate No. 38 (Series 1)	2·75	55
1561	150c. Plate No. 32 (Series 1)	2·75	55
1562	150c. Plate No. 34 (Series 1)	2·75	55
1563	150c. Plate No. 35 (Series 1)	2·75	55
1564	150c. Plate No. 41 (Series 1)	2·75	55
1565	150c. Plate No. 48 (Series 1)	2·75	55
1566	150c. Plate No. 62 (Series 1)	2·75	55

1985. Signing of Guyana–Libya Friendship Treaty. No. 621 surch **Guyana/Libya Friendship 1985 150**.

| 1567 | **149** | 150c. on 10c. mult | 9·00 | 2·75 |

1985. Namibia Day. No. 636 surch **150**.

| 1568 | 150c. on 35c. Unveiling of monument | 2·75 | 55 |

1985. World Cup Football Championship, Mexico (1986) (1st issue). No. F2 surch **Mexico 1986 275**.

| 1569 | 275c. on 3c. Hanging heliconia | 25·00 | 6·00 |

See also No. 1727.

1985. 85th Birthday of Queen Elizabeth the Queen Mother (2nd issue). Sheet 120×129 mm containing No. 1529×4 optd as No. MS1539, each stamp surch **200**.

| MS1570 200c. on 130c.×4 Plate No. 20 (Series 1) | 20·00 | 7·50 |

1985. Centenary of Publication of Sanders' *Reichenbachia* (3rd issue). As T **331** showing orchids. Multicoloured.

1571	25c. Plate No. 8 (Series 1)	2·25	20
1572	25c. Plate No. 23 (Series 1)	2·25	20
1573	25c. Plate No. 51 (Series 1)	2·25	20
1574	25c. Plate No. 61 (Series 1)	2·25	20
1575	25c. Plate No. 63 (Series 1)	2·25	20
1576	25c. Plate No. 70 (Series 1)	2·25	20
1577	25c. Plate No. 72 (Series 1)	2·25	20
1578	120c. Plate No. 1 (Series 1) (horiz)	2·25	55
1579	120c. Plate No. 11 (Series 1) (horiz)	2·25	55
1580	120c. Plate No. 28 (Series 1) (horiz)	2·25	55
1767	150c. Plate No. 40 (Series 1) (horiz)	50	20
1768	150c. Plate No. 42 (Series 1) (horiz)	50	20
1769	150c. Plate No. 45 (Series 1) (horiz)	50	20
1584	200c. Plate No. 14 (Series 1) (horiz)	2·50	80
1585	200c. Plate No. 21 (Series 1) (horiz)	2·50	80
1770	200c. Plate No. 43 (Series 1) (horiz)	55	30

1985. 30th Anniv of Commonwealth Caribbean Medical Research Council. Nos. 819, 871, 874, 928 and 1014 optd **1955–1985** or surch also.

1587	-	60c. mult (No. 819)	20	25
1588	-	60c. mult (No. 1014)	20	25
1589	**176**	120c. on 110c. on 10c. multicoloured (No. 871)	40	45
1590		120c. on 110c. on $3 mult (No. 874)	40	45
1592		120c. on 210c. on $3 mult (No. 928)	40	45

1985. 20th Anniv of Guyana Defence Force. No. 856 surch **1965-1985**.

| 1593 | 25c. on $1.10 on $3 W.O. and N.C.O.; Guyana Defence Force, 1966 | 1·00 | 10 |
| 1594 | 225c. on $1.10 on $3 W.O. and N.C.O.; Guyana Defence Force, 1966 | 2·50 | 1·75 |

1985. Fire Prevention. Nos. 678 and 680 optd **1985** and surch.

| 1595 | 25c. on 40c. Fire engine, 1977 | 20·00 | 1·00 |
| 1596 | 320c. on 15c. Steam engine, circa 1860 | 30·00 | 9·50 |

1985. Centenary of Publication of Sanders' *Reichenbachia* (4th issue). As T **331**. Multicoloured.

| 1597 | 60c. Plate No. 55 (Series 1) | 1·75 | 30 |

1985. Columbus Day. Unissued value as T **331** surch **350 CRISTOBAL COLON 1492-1992**. Multicoloured.

| 1598 | 350c. on 120c. Plate No. 65 (Series 1) | 13·00 | 6·00 |

1985. 20th Death Anniv of Sir Winston Churchill. No. 707 optd **SIR WINSTON CHURCHILL 1965-1985**.

| 1599 | $2 *Morpho rhetenor* (female) | 26·00 | 8·00 |

1985. 35th Anniv of International Commission of Irrigation and Drainage. No. 625 with unissued surcharge further surch **1950-1985**.

| 1600 | **150** | 25c. on 110c. on 10c. multicoloured | 75 | 10 |
| 1601 | **150** | 200c. on 110c. on 10c. multicoloured | 1·50 | 1·00 |

1985. 40th Anniv of U.N.O. Nos. 714/16, 800 and O19 optd **United Nations 1945-1985**.

1602	30c. multicoloured (No. 714)	1·75	10
1603	50c. multicoloured (No. 715)	1·75	20
1604	100c. on $3 mult (No. O19)	1·50	40
1605	225c. on 220c. on $3 mult (No. 800)	30·00	4·00
1606	$3 multicoloured (No. 716)	3·50	4·50

1985. Nos. 551/3, O14/15, O18, O21, OP1/2 and F7 optd **POSTAGE**.

1607	30c. on $2 *Norantea guianensis* (No. O18)	50	10
1608	40c. Tiger beard (No. 551)	60·00	1·50
1609	50c. *Guzmania lingulata* (No. 552)	50	20
1610	50c. *Guzmania lingulata* (No. O14)	50	20
1611	60c. Soldier's cap (No. 553)	4·25	25
1612	60c. Soldier's cap (No. O15)	3·50	25
1613	60c. Soldier's cap (No. F7)	1·75	25
1614	$10 *Elbella patrobas* (No. O21)	35·00	9·00
1615	$15 on $1 *Chelonanthus uliginoides* (No. OP1)	8·00	11·00
1616	$20 on $1 *Chelonanthus uliginoides* (No. OP2)	9·00	11·00

1985. Deepavali Festival. Nos. 542/3 surch **Deepavali 1985**.

| 1617 | 25c. on 2c. Type **132** | 2·00 | 25 |
| 1618 | 150c. on 1c. Pitcher plant of Mt. Roraima | 4·50 | 1·75 |

1985. Christmas. Sheet 120×129 mm containing No. 1553×4 optd as No. **MS**1559 surch **Christmas 1985**.

| MS1619 55c.×4 Plate No. 22 (Series 1), each with a different overprint (Type **350**, **Happy New Year**, **Merry Christmas** or **Happy Holidays**) | 8·00 | 4·50 |

1985. Centenary of Publication of Sanders' *Reichenbachia* (5th issue). As T **331** showing orchids. Multicoloured.

1620	25c. Plate No. 59 (Series 1)	1·25	20
1771	30c. Plate No. 53 (Series 1)	30	10
1622	60c. Plate No. 57 (Series 1) (horiz)	1·50	35
1623	60c. Plate No. 73 (Series 1) (horiz)	1·50	35
1624	60c. Plate No. 75 (Series 1) (horiz)	1·50	35
1772	60c. Plate No. 55 (Series 1)	35	15
1773	100c. Plate No. 65 (Series 1)	35	15
1627	120c. Plate No. 37 (Series 1)	2·25	55
1628	120c. Plate No. 46 (Series 1)	2·25	55
1629	120c. Plate No. 56 (Series 1)	2·25	55
1630	120c. Plate No. 58 (Series 1)	2·25	55
1631	120c. Plate No. 67 (Series 1)	2·25	55
1632	130c. Plate No. 66 (Series 1)	2·25	65
1633	150c. Plate No. 26 (Series 1)	2·50	75
1634	200c. Plate No. 33 (Series 1) (horiz)	2·75	85
1774	225c. Plate No. 24 (Series 1)	50	35

The 30, 75, 100 and 225c. values have "GUYANA" in blue.

351 Clive Lloyd (cricketer)

1985. Clive Lloyd's Testimonial Year. Multicoloured.

1636	25c. Type **351**	2·00	95
1637	25c. Clive Lloyd, bat and wicket	55	80
1638	25c. Cricket equipment	55	80
1639	60c. As No. 1638 (25×33 mm)	55	40
1640	$1.30 As No. 1637 (25×33 mm)	55	85
1641	$2.25 Type **351** (25×33 mm)	65	1·50
1642	$3.50 Clive Lloyd with the Prudential Cup (36×56 mm)	65	2·00

1985. Wildlife Protection. Nos. 756/67 optd **1985**.

1643	30c. Type **178**	75	75
1644	30c. Red howler	75	75
1645	30c. Common squirrel-monkey	75	75
1646	30c. Two-toed sloth	75	75
1647	30c. Brazilian tapir	75	75
1648	30c. Collared peccary	75	75
1649	30c. Six-banded armadillo	75	75
1650	30c. Tamandua	75	75
1651	30c. Giant anteater	75	75
1652	30c. Murine opossum	75	75
1653	30c. Brown four-eyed opossum	75	75
1654	30c. Brazilian agouti	75	75

1985. No. 847 surch **20**.

| 1655 | 20c. on 12c. on 12c. on 6c. Black acara ("Patua") | 8·00 | 50 |

1986. Centenary of the Appearance of "Reichenbachia" Volume 1. Nos. 1582 and 1586 optd **REICHENBACHIA 1886-1986**.

| 1657 | 150c. Plate No. 42 (Series 1) | 6·50 | 1·25 |
| 1658 | 200c. Plate No. 43 (Series 1) | 6·50 | 1·40 |

1986. Republic Day. Nos. 1108/9 and 1052 optd **Republic Day 1986** or surch also.

1659	25c. As Type **258**	10	20
1660	25c. As No. 1050	10	20
1661	120c. on $6 Presidential standard	40	50
1662	225c. on $6 Presidential standard	70	1·00

1986. Centenary of Publication of Sanders' *Reichenbachia* (6th issue). As T **331**. Multicoloured.

1663	40c. Plate No. 77 (Series 1)	75	20
1664	45c. Plate No. 54 (Series 1)	75	25
1665	50c. Plate No. 92 (Series 1)	75	25
1666	60c. Plate No. 95 (Series 1)	80	30
1667	75c. Plate No. 5 (Series 1)	85	35
1668	90c. Plate No. 84 (Series 1)	95	40
1669	150c. Plate No. 78 (Series 1)	1·25	60
1670	200c. Plate No. 79 (Series 1)	1·60	80
1671	300c. Plate No. 83 (Series 1)	2·25	1·40
1672	320c. Plate No. 50 (Series 1)	2·25	1·60
1673	360c. Plate No. 85 (Series 1)	2·50	1·75

1986. Easter. No. 481 optd **1986** and surch also.

1674	**111**	25c. on 6c. multicoloured	25	10
1675	**111**	50c. on 6c. multicoloured	40	20
1676	**111**	100c. on 6c. mult	60	40
1677	**111**	200c. on 6c. mult	1·00	70

1986. 60th Anniv of St. John's Ambulance in Guyana. No. 652 surch **1926 1986 150**.

| 1678 | 150c. on 35c. silver, black and green | 3·00 | 75 |

1986. Centenary of Publication of Sanders' *Reichenbachia* (7th issue). As T **331**. Multicoloured.

1679	25c. Plate No. 71 (Series 1) (horiz)	1·50	20
1680	120c. Plate No. 69 (Series 1) (horiz)	2·25	55
1681	150c. Plate No. 87 (Series 1) (horiz)	2·50	65
1682	225c. Plate No. 60 (Series 1) (horiz)	2·50	1·25
1683	350c. Plate No. 94 (Series 1) (horiz)	2·75	2·00

1986. 60th Birthday of Queen Elizabeth II. No. 1526/7 optd **1926 1986 QUEEN ELIZABETH**.

| 1684 | 130c. Plate No. 13 (Series 1) | 7·50 | 2·75 |
| MS1685 100×126 mm. 130c. on 130c., 200c. on 130c., 260c. on 130c., 330c. on 130c., Plate No. 6 (Series 1) | 8·50 | 8·50 |

The original face values on No. **MS**1685 are obliterated by a floral pattern.

1986. Wildlife Protection. Nos. 685, 739/44 and 993/8 surch **Protect the** and value.

1686	60c. on 35c. Type **174**	40	50
1687	60c. on 35c. Trahira ("Haimara")	40	50
1688	60c. on 35c. Electric eel	40	50
1689	60c. on 35c. Golden rivulus	40	50
1690	60c. on 35c. Golden pencilfish	40	50
1691	60c. on 35c. Four-eyed fish	40	50
1691a	60c. on 35c. Red piranha ("Pirai")	12·00	4·50
1691b	60c. on 35c. Smoking hassar	12·00	4·50
1691c	60c. on 35c. Manta	12·00	4·50
1691d	60c. on 35c. Festive cichlid ("Flying patwa")	12·00	4·50
1691e	60c. on 35c. Arapaima	12·00	4·50
1691f	60c. on 35c. Peacock cichlid ("Lukanani")	12·00	4·50
1692	$6 on 8c. Type **163**	3·00	3·50

1986. No. 799 surch **600**.

| 1693 | 600c. on 720c. on 60c. Soldier's cap | 24·00 | 2·75 |

1986. 125th Anniv of British Guiana Post Office (2nd issue). No. 702a surch **25** and names of postal agencies opened between 1860 and 1880.

1694	25c. on 30c. mult (surch **Abary**)	1·50	1·00
1695	25c. on 30c. multicoloured (surch **Anna Regina**)	1·50	1·00
1696	25c. on 30c. multicoloured (surch **Aurora**)	1·50	1·00

1697	25c. on 30c. multicoloured (surch **Bartica Grove**)	1·50	1·00
1698	25c. on 30c. multicoloured (surch **Bel Air**)	1·50	1·00
1699	25c. on 30c. multicoloured (surch **Belle Plaine**)	1·50	1·00
1700	25c. on 30c. multicoloured (surch **Clonbrook**)	1·50	1·00
1701	25c. on 30c. multicoloured (surch **T.P.O. Dem. Railway**)	1·50	1·00
1702	25c. on 30c. multicoloured (surch **Enmore**)	1·50	1·00
1703	25c. on 30c. multicoloured (surch **Fredericksburg**)	1·50	1·00
1704	25c. on 30c. multicoloured (surch **Good Success**)	1·50	1·00
1705	25c. on 30c. mult (surch **1986**)	1·50	1·00
1706	25c. on 30c. multicoloured (surch **Mariabba**)	1·50	1·00
1707	25c. on 30c. multicoloured (surch **Massaruni**)	1·50	1·00
1708	25c. on 30c. mult (surch **Nigg**)	1·50	1·00
1709	25c. on 30c. multicoloured (surch **No. 50**)	1·50	1·00
1710	25c. on 30c. multicoloured (surch **No. 63 Benab**)	1·50	1·00
1711	25c. on 30c. multicoloured (surch **Philadelphia**)	1·50	1·00
1712	25c. on 30c. multicoloured (surch **Sisters**)	1·50	1·00
1713	25c. on 30c. multicoloured (surch **Skeldon**)	1·50	1·00
1714	25c. on 30c. multicoloured (surch **Suddie**)	1·50	1·00
1715	25c. on 30c. multicoloured (surch **Taymouth Manor**)	1·50	1·00
1716	25c. on 30c. mult (surch **Wales**)	1·50	1·00
1717	25c. on 30c. mult (surch **Whim**)	1·50	1·00

1986. 20th Anniv of Independence.

(a) No. 332 of British Guiana surch **GUYANA INDEPENDENCE 1966-1986**, Nos. 424 and 435 of Guyana surch **1986** and No. 656 surch **25**.

1718	25c. on 2c. green (No. 332)	15	10
1719	25c. on 35c. mult (No. 656)	15	10
1720	60c. on 2c. green (No. 332)	25	10
1721	120c. on 6c. green (No. 424)	40	35
1722	130c. on 24c. black and orange (No. 435)	13·00	2·00

(b) Nos. 1188/91 surch **INDEPENDENCE 1966-1986**.

1723	**277**	25c. on 120c. brown, black and blue (No. 1188)	25	40
1724	-	25c. on 130c. red, black and blue (No. 1189)	25	40
1725	-	25c. on 150c. violet and blue (No. 1190)	25	40
1726	-	225c. on 200c. green, black and blue (No. 1191)	65	75

1986. World Cup Football Championship, Mexico (2nd issue). No. 544 surch **MEXICO 1986 225**.

| 1727 | 225c. on 3c. Hanging heliconia | 24·00 | 6·00 |

1986. CARICOM Day. No. 705a optd **CARICOM DAY 1986**.

| 1728 | 60c. "Papilio androgeus" | 12·00 | 75 |

1986. CARICOM Heads of Government Conference, Georgetown. Nos. 544 and 601 surch CARICOM **HEADS OF GOV'T CONFERENCE JULY 1986** and value.

| 1729 | 25c. on 8c. on 6c. Cannonball tree | 2·75 | 30 |
| 1730 | 60c. on 3c. Hanging heliconia | 3·50 | 70 |

1986. Centenary of Publication of Sanders' "Reichenbachia" (8th issue). As T **331**. Multicoloured.

1731	30c. Plate No. 86 (Series 1)	1·50	15
1732	50c. Plate No. 17 (Series 1)	50	20
1733	60c. Plate No. 93 (Series 1)	50	20
1734	100c. Plate No. 68 (Series 1)	2·50	20
1735	130c. Plate No. 91 (Series 1)	2·75	30
1736	250c. Plate No. 74 (Series 1)	75	1·00
1737	260c. Plate No. 39 (Series 1)	75	1·00
1738	375c. Plate No. 90 (Series 1)	4·25	1·50

1986. International Peace Year. Nos. 542 and 546 surch **INT. YEAR OF PEACE** and value.

1739	25c. on 1c. Pitcher plant of Mt. Roraima	80	40
1740	60c. on 6c. Cannon-ball tree	1·75	40
1741	120c. on 6c. Cannon-ball tree	1·75	1·75
1742	130c. on 6c. Cannon-ball tree	1·75	1·75
1743	150c. on 6c. Cannon-ball tree	1·75	1·75

363 Halley's Comet and British Guiana 1907 2c. Stamp

1986. Appearance of Halley's Comet.

1744	**363**	320c. red, black and lilac	40	1·00
1745	-	320c. multicoloured	40	1·00
MS1746		76×50 mm. Nos. 1744/5. Imperf	1·50	2·00

DESIGN: No. 1745, Guyana 1985 320c. scarlet macaw stamp.

1986. Centenary of Publication of Sanders' *Reichenbachia* (9th issue). As T 331. Multicoloured.

1747	40c. Plate No. 96 (Series 1)	2·50	15
1748	45c. Plate No. 81 (Series 1)	30	15
1749	90c. Plate No. 89 (Series 1)	50	20
1750	100c. Plate No. 88 (Series 1)	4·25	20
1751	150c. Plate No. 76 (Series 1)	4·25	35
1752	180c. Plate No. 15 (Series 1)	50	40
1753	320c. Plate No. 82 (Series 1)	60	90
1754	330c. Plate No. 80 (Series 1)	4·00	1·25

1986. No. 489 surch 20.

1755	20c. on 6c. Patua	11·00	40

1986. 50th Anniv of Guyana United Sadr Islamic Association. Nos. 469/70 optd GUSIA 1936-1986, No. 1757 surch also.

1756	**105**	25c. black, gold and lilac	6·00	50
1757	**105**	$1.50 on 6c. black, gold and flesh	11·00	4·50

1986. Regional Pharmacy Conference. No. 545 surch REGIONAL PHARMACY CONFERENCE 1986 130.

1758	130c. on 5c. Annatto tree	11·00	1·75

1986. Centenary of Publication of Sanders' *Reichenbachia* (10th issue). As T 331. Multicoloured.

1809	30c. Plate No. 30 (Series 2)	1·25	15
1810	45c. Plate No. 21 (Series 2) (horiz)	50	15
1811	75c. Plate No. 8 (Series 2)	50	15
1812	80c. Plate No. 42 (Series 2) (horiz)	50	15
1813	90c. Plate No. 4 (Series 2)	55	25
1814	130c. Plate No. 38 (Series 2)	3·00	35
1815	160c. Plate No. 5 (Series 2) (horiz)	3·00	40
1816	200c. Plate No. 9 (Series 2)	75	50
1817	320c. Plate No. 12 (Series 2)	1·75	90
1818	350c. Plate No. 29 (Series 2) (horiz)	2·00	90
1819	360c. Plate No. 34 (Series 2)	5·50	90

1986. 20th Anniv of Independence (2nd issue). As T 332 but additionally inscr "1966–1986" at foot.

1820	25c. multicoloured	20	25

1986. Centenary of Publication of Sanders' *Reichenbachia* (11th issue). Design as No. 1735, but with different face value. Multicoloured.

1822	40c. Plate No. 91 (Series 1)	1·00	15

1986. Nos. 1361/84 surch 120.

1823	120c. on 30c. mult (No. 1361)	2·25	1·75
1824	120c. on 30c. mult (No. 1362)	2·25	1·75
1825	120c. on 30c. mult (No. 1363)	2·25	1·75
1826	120c. on 30c. mult (No. 1364)	2·25	1·75
1827	120c. on 30c. mult (No. 1365)	2·25	1·75
1828	120c. on 30c. mult (No. 1366)	2·25	1·75
1829	120c. on 30c. mult (No. 1367)	2·25	1·75
1830	120c. on 30c. mult (No. 1368)	2·25	1·75
1831	120c. on 30c. mult (No. 1369)	2·25	1·75
1832	120c. on 30c. mult (No. 1370)	2·25	1·75
1833	120c. on 30c. mult (No. 1371)	2·25	1·75
1834	120c. on 30c. mult (No. 1372)	2·25	1·75
1835	120c. on 30c. mult (No. 1373)	2·25	1·75
1836	120c. on 30c. mult (No. 1374)	2·25	1·75
1837	120c. on 30c. mult (No. 1375)	2·25	1·75
1838	120c. on 30c. mult (No. 1376)	2·25	1·75
1839	120c. on 30c. mult (No. 1377)	2·25	1·75
1840	120c. on 30c. mult (No. 1378)	2·25	1·75
1841	120c. on 30c. mult (No. 1379)	2·25	1·75
1842	120c. on 30c. mult (No. 1380)	2·25	1·75
1843	120c. on 30c. mult (No. 1381)	2·25	1·75
1844	120c. on 30c. mult (No. 1382)	2·25	1·75
1845	120c. on 30c. mult (No. 1383)	2·25	1·75
1846	120c. on 30c. mult (No. 1384)	2·25	1·75

1986. 12th World Orchid Conference, Tokyo (1st issue). Unissued design as No. 1731, but with different face value, surch 12th World Orchid Conference TOKYO JAPAN MARCH 1987 650.

1847	650c. on 40c. Plate No. 86 (Series 1)	19·00	6·50

No. 1847 is inscribed "ONTOGLOSSUM TRIUMPHANS" in error.
See also No. 2138.

1986. Columbus Day. Unissued design as No. 1774, but with different face value, surch 1492-1992 CHRISTOPHER COLUMBUS 320.

1864	320c. on 150c. Plate No. 24 (Series 1)	7·00	3·00

1986. International Food Day. Nos. 1170/1 further surch 1986 and value.

1866	50c. on 30c. on 1c. Type 87	6·50	60
1867	225c. on $2.60 on 3c. Peacock cichlid ("Lukunani")	18·00	5·50

1986. Centenary of Publication of Sanders' *Reichenbachia* (12th issue). As T 331, one as No. 1731 with different face value. Multicoloured.

1868	40c. Plate No. 86 (Series 1)	75	15
1869	90c. Plate No. 10 (Series 2)	1·00	30

1986. Air. 40th Annivs of UNICEF and UNESCO No. 706 surch.

1870	120c. on $1 "Agrias claudina" (surch UNICEF 1946-1986 AIR 120)	15·00	12·00
1871	120c. on $1 "Agrias claudina" (surch UNESCO 1946-1986 AIR 120)	15·00	12·00

1986. Centenary of Publication of Sanders' "Reichenbachia" (13th issue). As T 331. Multicoloured.

1872	45c. Plate No. 17 (Series 2)	50	15
1873	50c. Plate No. 33 (Series 2)	50	15
1874	60c. Plate No. 27 (Series 2)	70	15
1875	75c. Plate No. 56 (Series 2)	80	25
1876	85c. Plate No. 45 (Series 2)	16·00	1·25
1877	90c. Plate No. 13 (Series 2)	1·00	30
1878	200c. Plate No. 44 (Series 2)	1·75	55
1879	300c. Plate No. 50 (Series 2)	2·25	1·00
1880	320c. Plate No. 10 (Series 2)	2·25	1·00
1881	390c. Plate No. 6 (Series 2)	2·25	2·00

1986. Deepavali Festival. Nos. 543 and 601 surch Deepavali 1986 and value.

1882	25c. on 2c. Type 132	3·00	50
1883	200c. on 8c. on 6c. Cannon-ball tree	11·00	4·00

1986. Centenary of Publication of Sanders' *Reichenbachia* (14th issue). As T 331, two as Nos. 1732 and 1734 with different face values. Multicoloured.

1884	40c. Plate No. 68 (Series 1)	2·00	25
1885	80c. Plate No. 17 (Series 1)	6·50	90
1886	200c. Plate No. 2 (Series 2)	1·60	1·00
1887	225c. Plate No. 24 (Series 1)	1·60	1·25

1986. Christmas. No. 489 surch CHRISTMAS 1986 20.

1888	20c. on 6c. Black acara ("Patua")	5·00	20
MS1889	215×75 mm. 120c. on 60c.×5 Nos. 1425/9	7·00	7·00

1986. Wildlife Protection. Nos. 756/67 optd 1986.

1894	30c. Type 178	2·50	2·00
1895	30c. Red howler	2·50	2·00
1896	30c. Common squirrel-monkey	2·50	2·00
1897	30c. Two-toed sloth	2·50	2·00
1898	30c. Brazilian tapir	2·50	2·00
1899	30c. Collared peccary	2·50	2·00
1900	30c. Six-banded armadillo	2·50	2·00
1901	30c. Tamandua	2·50	2·00
1902	30c. Giant anteater	2·50	2·00
1903	30c. Murine opossum	2·50	2·00
1904	30c. Brown four-eyed opossum	2·50	2·00
1905	30c. Brazilian agouti	2·50	2·00

1986. No. 1642 surch $15.

1906	$15 on $3.50 Clive Lloyd with Prudential Cup	48·00	22·00

1986. Centenary of Publication of Sanders' *Reichenbachia* (15th issue). Design as No. 1877, but with different face value. Multicoloured.

1907	50c. Plate No. 13 (Series 2)	1·00	25

GUYANA 25c

375 Memorial

1986. President Burnham Commemoration. Multicoloured.

1908	25c. Type 375	10	10
1909	120c. Map of Guyana and flags	30	20
1910	130c. Parliament Buildings and mace	20	20
1911	$6 L. F. Burnham and Georgetown mayoral chain (vert)	60	1·75

1986. Centenary of Publication of Sanders' *Reichenbachia* (16th issue). As Nos. 1765/6, 1874 and 1887 but with different face values. Multicoloured.

1912	50c. Plate No. 49 (Series 1)	75	20
1913	50c. Plate No. 64 (Series 1)	75	20
1914	85c. Plate No. 24 (Series 2)	75	40
1915	90c. Plate No. 27 (Series 1)	11·00	1·50

1986. Centenary of Publication of Sanders' *Reichenbachia* (17th issue). As T 331. Multicoloured.

1916	25c. Plate No. 20 (Series 2)	20	20
1917	30c. Plate No. 7 (Series 2)	45	15
1918	85c. Plate No. 15 (Series 1)	6·50	50
1919	90c. Plate No. 3 (Series 2)	60	20
1920	120c. Plate No. 14 (Series 2)	60	30
1921	130c. Plate No. 32 (Series 2)	60	30
1922	150c. Plate No. 22 (Series 2)	70	45
1923	320c. Plate No. 18 (Series 2)	90	75
1924	330c. Plate No. 28 (Series 2)	90	90

1987. Centenary of Publication of Sanders' *Reichenbachia* (18th issue). As Nos. 1772, 1876, 1886, 1918 and 1923 but with different face values. Multicoloured.

1925	35c. Plate No. 45 (Series 2)	40	15
1926	50c. Plate No. 15 (Series 2)	40	20
1927	50c. Plate No. 55 (Series 1)	40	20
1928	85c. Plate No. 18 (Series 2)	8·00	60
1929	90c. Plate No. 2 (Series 2)	50	30

1987. Tenth Anniv of Guyana Post Office Corporation (1st issue). Unissued designs as Nos. 1771 and 1774, but with different face values, surch or optd G P O C 1977 1987.

1930	$2.25 Plate No. 53 (Series 1)	4·50	75
1931	$10 on 150c. on 150c. Plate No. 24 (Series 1)	11·00	12·00

See also Nos. 2074/80.

1987. Various *Reichenbachia* issues surch.

2380	120c. on 40c. Plate No. 90 (Series 1)	1·00	70
2375	120c. on 40c. Plate No. 91 (No. 1822)	1·00	70
2387	120c. on 50c. Plate No. 9 (Series 1)	60	40
1994	120c. on 50c. Plate No. 49 (Series 1) (No. 1912)	60	40
1995	120c. on 50c. Plate No. 64 (Series 1) (No. 1913)	60	40
2388	120c. on 50c. Plate No. 22 (Series 1)	60	40
2389	120c. on 50c. Plate No. 3 (Series 2)	60	40
2390	120c. on 50c. Plate No. 6 (Series 2)	60	40
2391	120c. on 50c. Plate No. 20 (Series 2)	60	40
2392	120c. on 50c. Plate No. 32 (Series 2)	60	40
2019	120c. on 50c. Plate No. 24 (Series 1)	60	40
2020	120c. on 50c. Plate No. 53 (Series 1)	60	40
2021	120c. on 50c. Plate No. 65 (Series 1)	60	40
1980	120c. on 55c. Plate No. 9 (Series 1) (No. 1763)	50	40
2003	120c. on 55c. Plate No. 49 (Series 1) (No. 1765)	60	40
1981	120c. on 55c. Plate No. 64 (Series 1) (No. 1766)	50	30
2006	120c. on 55c. Plate No. 22 (Series 1) (No. 1764)	60	40
2009	120c. on 55c. Plate No. 15 (Series 1)	60	40
2010	120c. on 55c. Plate No. 81 (Series 1)	60	40
2011	120c. on 55c. Plate No. 82 (Series 1)	60	40
2012	120c. on 55c. Plate No. 89 (Series 1)	60	40
2394	120c. on 60c. Plate No. 2 (Series 1) (No. 1519)	60	30
2027	120c. on 60c. Plate No. 10 (Series 1) (No. 1521)	60	40
2028	120c. on 60c. Plate No. 19 (Series 1) (No. 1522)	60	40
2029	120c. on 60c. Plate No. 31 (Series 1) (No. 1523)	60	40
2030	120c. on 60c. Plate No. 5 (Series 1)	60	40
2403	120c. on 60c. Plate No. 50 (Series 1)	60	40
2404	120c. on 60c. Plate No. 54 (Series 1)	60	40
2405	120c. on 60c. Plate No. 69 (Series 1)	60	40
2034	120c. on 60c. Plate No. 71 (Series 1)	60	40
2406	120c. on 60c. Plate No. 79 (Series 1)	60	40
2036	120c. on 60c. Plate No. 87 (Series 1)	60	40
2407	120c. on 60c. Plate No. 94 (Series 1)	60	40
2038	120c. on 75c. Plate No. 60 (Series 1)	60	40
2039	120c. on 75c. Plate No. 83 (Series 1)	60	40
2040	120c. on 75c. Plate No. 92 (Series 1)	60	40
2041	120c. on 75c. Plate No. 95 (Series 1)	60	40
1933	200c. on 25c. Plate No. 8 (Series 1) (No. 1571)	80	50
1934	200c. on 25c. Plate No. 51 (Series 1) (No. 1573)	80	50
1949	200c. on 25c. Plate No. 52 (Series 1) (No. 1551)	80	50
1951	200c. on 25c. Plate No. 72 (Series 1) (No. 1577)	80	50
1952	200c. on 25c. Plate No. 71 (Series 1) (No. 1679)	80	50
1953	200c. on 30c. Plate No. 86 (Series 1) (No. 1731)	80	50
1954	200c. on 30c. Plate No. 53 (Series 1) (No. 1771)	80	50
1932	200c. on 40c. Plate No. 90 (Series 1)	80	50
1937	200c. on 40c. Plate No. 68 (Series 1) (No. 1884)	80	50
1955	200c. on 40c. Plate No. 77 (Series 1) (No. 1663)	80	50
1956	200c. on 40c. Plate No. 86 (Series 1) (No. 1868)	80	50
1957	200c. on 45c. Plate No. 81 (Series 1) (No. 1748)	80	50
1958	200c. on 45c. Plate No. 77 (Series 1)	80	50
1959	200c. on 45c. Plate No. 78 (Series 1)	80	50
1960	200c. on 45c. Plate No. 85 (Series 1)	80	50
2044	200c. on 45c. Plate No. 84 (Series 1)	60	40
1939	200c. on 50c. Plate No. 92 (Series 1) (No. 1665)	80	50
1940	200c. on 50c. Plate No. 22 (Series 1)	80	50
1961	200c. on 50c. Plate No. 24 (Series 1)	80	50
1962	200c. on 50c. Plate No. 53 (Series 1)	80	50
1963	200c. on 50c. Plate No. 65 (Series 1)	80	50
2046	200c. on 50c. Plate No. 55 (Series 1) (No. 1927)	1·00	50
1941	200c. on 55c. Plate No. 22 (Series 1) (No. 1764)	80	50
1964	200c. on 55c. Plate No. 49 (Series 1) (No. 1765)	80	50
1965	200c. on 55c. Plate No. 17 (Series 1) (No. 1732)	80	50
2050	200c. on 55c. Plate No. 15 (Series 1)	3·50	60
2051	200c. on 55c. Plate No. 81 (Series 1)	3·50	60
2052	200c. on 55c. Plate No. 82 (Series 1)	13·00	1·25
2053	200c. on 55c. Plate No. 89 (Series 1)	3·50	60
1942	200c. on 60c. Plate No. 5 (Series 1)	80	50
1967	200c. on 60c. Plate No. 7 (Series 1) (No. 1520)	80	50
1968	200c. on 60c. Plate No. 10 (Series 1) (No. 1521)	80	50
1969	200c. on 60c. Plate No. 19 (Series 1) (No. 1522)	80	50
1970	200c. on 60c. Plate No. 31 (Series 1) (No. 1523)	80	50
1971	200c. on 60c. Plate No. 44 (Series 1) (No. 1556)	80	50
1972	200c. on 60c. Plate No. 47 (Series 1) (No. 1557)	80	50
1973	200c. on 60c. Plate No. 57 (Series 1) (No. 1622)	80	50
1974	200c. on 60c. Plate No. 73 (Series 1) (No. 1623)	80	50
1975	200c. on 60c. Plate No. 75 (Series 1) (No. 1624)	80	50
1976	200c. on 60c. Plate No. 71 (Series 1)	80	50
1977	200c. on 60c. Plate No. 87 (Series 1)	80	50
1943	200c. on 75c. Plate No. 5 (Series 1) (No. 1667)	80	50
1944	200c. on 75c. Plate No. 60 (Series 1)	80	50
1945	200c. on 75c. Plate No. 92 (Series 1)	80	50
1946	200c. on 85c. Plate No. 18 (Series 2) (No. 1928)	80	50
1947	200c. on 375c. Plate No. 90 (Series 1) (No. 1738)	80	50
1987	225c. on 40c. Plate No. 91 (Series 1) (No. 1822)	70	60
1988	225c. on 40c. Plate No. 90 (Series 1)	70	60
2055	225c. on 40c. Plate No. 86 (Series 1) (No. 1868)	2·50	70
2056	225c. on 40c. Plate No. 68 (Series 1) (No. 1884)	1·00	60
1988a	225c. on 50c. Plate No. 92 (Series 1) (No. 1665)	14·00	3·50
1989	225c. on 50c. Plate No. 22 (Series 1)	70	60
1990	225c. on 50c. Plate No. 55 (Series 1) (No. 1597)	14·00	3·50
1990a	225c. on 60c. Plate No. 95 (Series 1) (No. 1666)	14·00	3·50
1991	225c. on 60c. Plate No. 93 (Series 1) (No. 1733)	70	60
2058	225c. on 65c. Plate No. 76 (Series 1)	1·00	60
2059	225c. on 65c. Plate No. 80 (Series 1)	1·00	60
2060	225c. on 65c. Plate No. 88 (Series 1)	1·00	60
2061	225c. on 65c. Plate No. 96 (Series 1)	1·00	60
1992	225c. on 80c. Plate No. 93 (Series 1)	70	60
1978	225c. on 90c. Plate No. 89 (Series 1) (No. 1749)	80	55
1993	225c. on 150c. Plate No. 42 (Series 1) (No. 1657)	70	60
2062	600c. on 80c. Plate No. 17 (Series 1) (No. 1885)	1·50	1·75
2063	600c. on 80c. Plate No. 39 (Series 1)	1·50	1·75
2064	600c. on 80c. Plate No. 74 (Series 1)	1·50	1·75
2065	600c. on 80c. Plate No. 93 (Series 1)	1·50	1·75

1987. Nos. 1518 and 1572 surch TWO DOLLARS

1935	$2 on 25c. Plate No. 12 (Series 1) (No. 1518)	2·00	60
1936	$2 on 25c. Plate No. 23 (Series 1) (No. 1572)	2·00	90

1987. Various Reichenbachia issues surch 1987

1983	$10 on 25c. Plate No. 53 (Series 1)	3·00	3·50
1984	$12 on 80c. Plate No. 74 (Series 1)	3·25	3·75
1985	$15 on 80c. Plate No. 39 (Series 1)	3·50	4·00
1986	$25 on 25c. Plate No. 53 (Series 1)	6·00	7·00

1987. Centenary of Publication of Sanders' Reichenbachia (19th issue). Multicoloured.

2066	180c. Plate 41 (Series 2)	75	40
2067	240c. Plate 25 (Series 2)	80	50
2068	300c. Plate 85 (Series 2)	8·50	1·50
2069	330c. Plate 82 (Series 2)	9·00	1·75
2070	425c. Plate 87 (Series 2)	9·00	1·75
2071	440c. Plate 88 (Series 2)	9·00	1·75
2072	590c. Plate 52 (Series 2)	1·50	1·75
2073	650c. Plate 65 (Series 2)	1·75	2·00

1987. Tenth Anniv of Guyana Post Office Corporation (2nd issue). Nos. 543, 545, 548a and 601 surch Post Office Corp. 1977-1987.

2074	25c. on 2c. Type 132	25	10
2075	25c. on 5c. Annatto tree	25	10
2076	25c. on 8c. on 6c. Cannon-ball tree	25	10
2077	25c. on 15c. Christmas orchid	5·50	30
2078	60c. on 15c. Christmas orchid	12·00	30
2079	$1.20 on 2c. Type 132	75	75
2080	$1.30 on 15c. Christmas orchid	13·00	3·75

1987. No. 1535b surch 1987 200.

2081	332	200c. on 25c. mult	8·00	2·75

1987. Various Reichenbachia issues optd 1987.

2112	120c. Plate No. 1 (Series 1) (No. 1578)	3·50	75
2113	120c. Plate No. 11 (Series 1) (No. 1579)	2·75	70
2114	120c. Plate No. 28 (Series 1) (No. 1580)	3·25	75
2115	120c. Plate No. 37 (Series 1) (No. 1627)	1·75	70
2116	120c. Plate No. 46 (Series 1) (No. 1628)	9·50	90
2117	120c. Plate No. 56 (Series 1) (No. 1629)	2·75	70
2118	120c. Plate No. 58 (Series 1) (No. 1630)	2·75	70
2132	120c. Plate No. 67 (Series 1) (No. 1631)	60	40
2084	130c. Plate No. 3 (Series 1) (No. 1525)	1·25	40
2093	130c. Plate No. 6 (Series 1) (No. 1759)	1·25	40
2094	130c. Plate No. 20 (Series 1) (No. 1761)	2·00	40
2087	130c. Plate No. 18 (Series 1) (No. 1536)	80	40
2088	130c. Plate No. 29 (Series 1) (No. 1537)	80	40
2089	130c. Plate No. 30 (Series 1) (No. 1538)	80	40
2090	130c. Plate No. 16 (Series 1) (No. 1559)	80	40
2091	130c. Plate No. 66 (Series 1) (No. 1632)	2·00	40
2092	130c. Plate No. 13 (Series 1) (No. 1684)	2·00	40
2109	130c. Plate No. 91 (Series 1) (No. 1735)	60	40
2111	130c. Plate No. 25 (Series 1) (No. 1762)	60	40
2123	150c. Plate No. 40 (Series 1) (No. 1767)	2·50	80
2124	150c. Plate No. 45 (Series 1) (No. 1769)	1·75	70
2125	150c. Plate No. 42 (Series 1) (No. 1657)	7·50	1·00
2137	150c. Plate No. 26 (Series 1) (No. 1633)	60	50
2095	200c. Plate No. 4 (Series 1) (No. 1533)	1·00	50
2096	200c. Plate No. 14 (Series 1) (No. 1584)	1·40	50
2097	200c. Plate No. 21 (Series 1) (No. 1585)	1·00	50
2098	200c. Plate No. 33 (Series 1) (No. 1634)	1·00	50
2099	200c. Plate No. 43 (Series 1) (No. 1658)	2·00	50
2100	200c. Plate No. 79 (Series 1) (No. 1670)	1·00	50
2101	200c. Plate No. 9 (Series 2) (No. 1816)	1·00	50
2102	200c. Plate No. 2 (Series 2) (No. 1886)	3·00	50
2103	250c. Plate No. 74 (Series 1) (No. 1736)	1·00	50
2104	260c. Plate No. 39 (Series 1) (No. 1737)	1·25	60

1987. 12th World Orchid Conference, Tokyo (2nd issue). Nos. 1763 surch 12th World Orchid Conference 650.

2138	650c. on 55c. Plate No. 9 (Series 1)	11·00	6·00

1987. 125th Anniv of British Guiana Post Office (3rd issue). No. 699 surch 25 and names of postal agencies opened by 1885.

2140	25c. on 10c. multicoloured (surch AGRICOLA)	1·75	1·25
2141	25c. on 10c. multicoloured (surch BAGOTVILLE)	1·75	1·25
2142	25c. on 10c. multicoloured (surch BOURDA)	1·75	1·25
2143	25c. on 10c. multicoloured (surch BUXTON)	1·75	1·25
2144	25c. on 10c. multicoloured (surch CABACABURI)	1·75	1·25
2145	25c. on 10c. mult (surch CAR-MICHAEL STREET)	1·75	1·25
2146	25c. on 10c. mult (surch COT-TON TREE)	1·75	1·25
2147	25c. on 10c. multicoloured (surch DUNOON)	1·75	1·25
2148	25c. on 10c. multicoloured (surch FELLOWSHIP)	1·75	1·25
2149	25c. on 10c. multicoloured (surch GROVE)	1·75	1·25
2150	25c. on 10c. multicoloured (surch HACKNEY)	1·75	1·25
2151	25c. on 10c. multicoloured (surch LEONORA)	1·75	1·25
2152	25c. on 10c. mult (surch 1987)	1·75	1·25
2153	25c. on 10c. multicoloured (surch MALLALI)	1·75	1·25
2154	25c. on 10c. multicoloured (surch PROVIDENCE)	1·75	1·25
2155	25c. on 10c. multicoloured (surch RELIANCE)	1·75	1·25
2156	25c. on 10c. multicoloured (surch SPARTA)	1·75	1·25
2157	25c. on 10c. multicoloured (surch STEWARTVILLE)	1·75	1·25
2158	25c. on 10c. multicoloured (surch TARLOGY)	1·75	1·25
2159	25c. on 10c. mult (surch T.P.O. BERBICE RIV.)	1·75	1·25
2160	25c. on 10c. multicoloured (surch T.P.O. DEM. RIV.)	1·75	1·25
2161	25c. on 10c. multicoloured (surch T.P.O. ESSEO. RIV.)	1·75	1·25
2162	25c. on 10c. mult (surch T.P.O. MASSARUNI RIV.)	1·75	1·25
2163	25c. on 10c. multicoloured (surch TUSCHEN (De VRIENDEN)	1·75	1·25
2164	25c. on 10c. multicoloured (surch ZORG)	1·75	1·25

1987. 50th Anniv of First Georgetown to Port-of-Spain Flight by P.A.A. No. 708a optd 28 MARCH 1927 PAA GEO-POS.

2165	$10 "Elbella patrobas"	28·00	13·00

1987. No. 704 surch 25.

2166	25c. on 40c. Morpho rhetenor (male)	16·00	50

1987. Easter. Nos. 481/2 and 484 optd 1987 or surch also.

2167	111	25c. multicoloured	50	10
2168	111	120c. on 6c. mult	75	20
2169	111	320c. on 6c. mult	1·25	90
2170	111	500c. on 40c. mult	1·75	2·25

1987. Centenary of Publication of Sanders' Reichenbachia (20th issue). As T 331. Multicoloured.

2171	240c. Plate No. 47 (Series 2)	80	45
2172	260c. Plate No. 39 (Series 2)	90	55
2173	275c. Plate No. 58 (Series 2) (horiz)	90	55
2174	390c. Plate No. 37 (Series 2) (horiz)	1·10	70
2175	450c. Plate No. 19 (Series 2) (horiz)	1·50	90
2176	460c. Plate No. 54 (Series 2) (horiz)	1·50	90
2177	500c. Plate No. 51 (Series 2)	1·75	1·10
2178	560c. Plate No. 1 (Series 2)	2·00	1·50

1987. No. 706 optd 1987.

2179	167	$1 multicoloured	17·00	1·00

1987. Centenary of Publication of Sanders' Reichenbachia (21st issue). As T 331. Multicoloured.

2180	500c. Plate No. 86 (Series 2)	1·50	1·10
2181	520c. Plate No. 89 (Series 2)	1·50	1·25
2182	$20 Plate No. 83 (Series 2)	4·50	7·00

1987. As T 332 but within frame.

2183	25c. multicoloured	40	40
2184	25c. multicoloured	50	50

No. 2183 has a bird with a short tail (as in Type 332) in the lower part of the arms; No. 2184 has a bird with crest and long tail.

1987. "Capex '87" International Stamp Exhibition, Toronto. Nos. 1744/5 optd CAPEX '87.

2185	363	320c. red, black and lilac	3·00	3·25
2186	-	320c. multicoloured	3·00	3·25

1987. Commonwealth Heads of Government Meeting, Vancouver. Nos. 1066/8 further optd 1987.

2187	$1.20 on 6c. green	1·00	20
2188	$1.30 on 24c. black orange	12·00	1·00
2189	$2.40 on 24c. black orange	15·00	5·00

1987. Centenary of Publication of Sanders' Reichenbachia (22nd issue). As T 331. Multicoloured.

2190	400c. Plate No. 80 (Series 2)	1·25	80
2191	480c. Plate No. 77 (Series 2)	1·50	1·00
2192	520c. Plate No. 94 (Series 2)	1·50	1·50
2193	$25 Plate No. 72 (Series 2)	4·50	8·00

396 Steam Locomotive No. 4 Alexandra

1987. Guyana Railways.

2194	396	$1.20 green	25	30
2195	-	$1.20 green	25	30
2196	-	$1.20 green	25	30
2197	-	$1.20 green	25	30
2198	396	$1.20 purple	25	30
2199	-	$1.20 purple	25	30
2200	-	$1.20 purple	25	30
2201	-	$1.20 purple	25	30
2202	396	$3.20 blue	60	90
2203	-	$3.20 blue	60	90
2204	-	$3.20 blue	60	90
2205	-	$3.20 blue	60	90
2206	-	$3.20 blue	60	90
2207	396	$3.30 black	60	90
2208	396	$3.30 black	60	90
2209	-	$3.30 black	60	90
2210	-	$3.30 black	60	90
2211	-	$3.30 black	60	90
2212	-	$10 multicoloured	60	1·50
2213	-	$12 multicoloured	60	1·50

DESIGNS—As T 396: Nos. 2195, 2199, 2203, 2207, Front view of diesel locomotive; Nos. 2196, 2200, 2204, 2210, Steam locomotive with searchlight; Nos. 2197, 2201, 2205, 2209, Side view of diesel locomotive No. 21. (82×55 mm): No. 2206, Molasses warehouses and early locomotive; No. 2211, Diesel locomotive and passenger train. (88×39 mm): No. 2212, Cattle train and Parika–Rosignol Railway route map; No. 2213, Molasses train and Parika–Rosignol Railway route map.

1987. 50th Anniv of First Flights from Georgetown to Massaruni and Mabaruma. No. 706 optd.

2214	$1 multicoloured (optd FAIREY NICHOLL 8 AUG 1927 GEO-MAZ)	16·00	11·00
2215	$1 multicoloured (optd FAIREY NICHOLL 15 AUG 1927 GEO-MAB)	16·00	11·00

1987. Centenary of Publication of Sanders' Reichenbachia (23rd issue). As T 331. Multicoloured.

2216	200c. Plate No. 43 (Series 2)	7·50	1·75
2217	200c. Plate No. 48 (Series 2)	7·50	1·75
2218	200c. Plate No. 92 (Series 2)	7·50	1·75

1987. Centenary of Publication of Sanders' Reichenbachia (24th issue). No. 2219 surch 600. Multicoloured.

2219	600c. on 900c. Plate No. 74 (Series 2)	6·00	7·00
2220	900c. Plate No. 74 (Series 2)	6·00	7·00

1987. Columbus Day.

2221	225c. on 350c. on 120c. Plate No. 65 (Series 1) (No. 1598 further surch 225)	1·75	80
2222	950c. on 900c. Plate No. 74 (Series 2) (No. 2220 surch 950 CRISTOVAO COLOMBO 1492 – 1992)	3·00	3·50
2223	950c. on 900c. Plate No. 74 (Series 2) (No. 2220 surch 950 CHRISTOPHE COLOMB 1492 – 1992)	3·00	3·50
MS2224	76×50 mm. $20 on 320c.×2 Nos. 1744/5	7·00	9·00

1987. Centenary of Publication of Sanders' Reichenbachia (25th issue). As T 331. Multicoloured.

2225	325c. Plate No. 68 (Series 2) (horiz)	1·50	1·10
2226	420c. Plate No. 95 (Series 2) (horiz)	1·75	1·75
2227	575c. Plate No. 60 (Series 2)	15·00	6·50

1987. Deepavali Festival. Nos. 544/5 surch DEEPAVALI 1987 and new value.

2228	25c. on 3c. Hanging heliconia	3·00	25
2229	$3 on 5c. Annatto tree	9·00	3·75

1987. Christmas. No. 489 surch CHRISTMAS 1987 20, and previously unissued miniature sheet containing Nos. 1425/9 and No. MS1619 surch.

2230	20c. on 6c. Black acara ("Patua")	5·00	20
MS2231	215×75 mm. 120c. on 60c.×5 Nos. 1425/9	8·00	4·00
MS2232	120×129 mm. 225c. on 55c.×4 Plate No. 22 (Series 1), each with a different overprint (Christmas 1985 ,Happy New Year, Merry Christmas or Happy Holidays)	1·60	1·75

1987. Royal Ruby Wedding. Nos. 1684/5 optd 1987 (130c.) or surch 120.

2233	130c. Plate No. 13 (Series 1)	5·50	1·75
MS2234	600c. on 130c. on 130c., 600c. on 200c. on 130c., 600c. on 260c. on 130c., 600c. on 330c. on 130c., Plate No. 6 (Series 1)	9·00	10·00

1987. Centenary of Publication of Sanders' Reichenbachia (26th issue). As T 331. Multicoloured.

2235	255c. Plate No. 61 (Series 2)	5·50	1·25
2236	290c. Plate No. 53 (Series 2)	5·50	1·50
2237	375c. Plate No. 96 (Series 2)	2·00	1·60
2238	680c. Plate No. 64 (Series 2)	15·00	4·50
2239	720c. Plate No. 49 (Series 2)	16·00	7·00
2240	750c. Plate No. 66 (Series 2)	3·00	5·00
2241	800c. Plate No. 79 (Series 2)	3·00	5·50
2242	850c. Plate No. 76 (Series 2)	3·00	5·50

1987. Air. No. 1620 surch AIR 75.

2243	75c. on 25c. Plate No. 59	15·00	1·40

1987. Wildlife Protection. Nos. 756/67 optd 1987, Nos. 1432/4 surch Protect our Heritage '87 320 and Nos. 1631/3, 1752/3 and 1847 optd PROTECT OUR HERITAGE '87.

2244	30c. Type 178	50	40
2245	30c. Red howler	50	40
2246	30c. Common squirrel-monkey	50	40
2247	30c. Two-toed sloth	50	40
2248	30c. Brazilian tapir	50	40
2249	30c. Collared peccary	50	40
2250	30c. Six-banded armadillo	50	40
2251	30c. Tamandua	50	40
2252	30c. Giant anteater	50	40
2253	30c. Murine opossum	50	40
2254	30c. Brown four-eyed opossum	50	40
2255	30c. Brazilian agouti	50	40
2256	120c. Plate No. 67 (Series 1)	1·00	30
2257	130c. Plate No. 66 (Series 1)	1·00	30
2258	150c. Plate No. 26 (Series 1)	1·10	35
2259	180c. Plate No. 15 (Series 1)	1·25	40
2260	320c. Plate No. 82 (Series 1)	1·40	60
2261	320c. on 120c. Demerara Mutual Life Assurance Building	1·40	1·75
2262	320c. on 120c. Town Hall	1·40	1·75
2263	320c. on 120c. Victoria Law Courts	1·40	1·75
2264	650c. on 40c. Plate No. 86 (Series 1)	2·75	3·50

1987. Air. Various "Reichenbachia" issues optd AIR.

2265	60c. Plate No. 55 (Series 1) (No. 1597)	8·50	10·00

1988. World Scout Jamboree, Australia. No. 837a optd AUSTRALIA 1987 JAMBOREE 1988 and Nos. 830, 837a and 1104 surch $10 AUSTRALIA 1987 JAMBOREE 1988.

2266	116	440c. on 6c. mult (No. 837a)	7·50	60
2267	116	$10 on 110c. on 6c. mult (No. 830)	75	90
2268	116	$10 on 180c. on 6c. mult (No. 1104)	75	90
2269a	116	$10 on 440c. on 6c. mult (No. 837)	75	90

1988. Tenth Anniv of International Fund for Agricultural Development. Nos. 448 and 450 surch IFAD For a World Without Hunger.

2270	25c. on 1c. Type 87	3·00	25
2271	$5 on 3c. Lukunani	11·00	8·00

1988. Republic Day. Nos. 545, 548a and 555 surch Republic Day 1988.

2272	25c. on 5c. Annatto tree	20	10
2273	120c. on 15c. Christmas orchid	14·00	1·00
2274	$10 on $2 Noranthea guianensis	2·75	3·75

1988. Centenary of Publication of Sanders' Reichenbachia (27th issue). Four sheets, each 102×127 mm, containing vert designs as T 331. Multicoloured.

MS2275	(a) 320c. Plate No. 46 (Series 2); 330c. Plate No. 55 (Series 2); 350c. Plate No. 57 (Series 2); 500c. Plate No. 81 (Series 2). (b) 320c. Plate No. 55 (Series 2); 330c. Plate No. 46 (Series 2); 500c. Plate No. 81 (Series 2); 500c. Plate No. 57 (Series 2). (c) 320c. Plate No. 57 (Series 2); 330c. Plate No. 81 (Series 2); 350c. Plate No. 55 (Series 2); 500c. Plate No. 46 (Series 2). (d) 320c. Plate No. 81 (Series 2); 330c. Plate No. 57 (Series 2); 350c. Plate No. 55 (Series 2); 500c. Plate No. 46 (Series 2). Set of 4 sheets	18·00	14·00

1988. Centenary of Publication of Sanders' Reichenbachia (28th series). As T 331. Multicoloured.

2276	$10 Plate No. 40 (Series 2)	1·50	2·25
2277	$12 Plate No. 91 (Series 2)	1·50	2·25

1988. 125th Anniv of British Guiana Post Office (4th issue). No. 702a surch 25 and names of postal agencies opened between 1886 and 1900.

2278	25c. on 30c. multicoloured (surch Albouystown)	1·75	1·25
2279	25c. on 30c. multicoloured (surch Anns Grove)	1·75	1·25
2280	25c. on 30c. multicoloured (surch Amacura)	1·75	1·25

2281	25c. on 30c. multicoloured (surch **Arakaka**)	1·75	1·25
2282	25c. on 30c. multicoloured (surch **Baramanni**)	1·75	1·25
2283	25c. on 30c. multicoloured (surch **Cuyuni**)	1·75	1·25
2284	25c. on 30c. multicoloured (surch **Hope Placer**)	1·75	1·25
2285	25c. on 30c. multicoloured (surch **H M P S**)	1·75	1·25
2286	25c. on 30c. mult (surch **Kitty**)	1·75	1·25
2287	25c. on 30c. multicoloured (surch **M'M'Zorg**)	1·75	1·25
2288	25c. on 30c. multicoloured (surch **Maccaseema**)	1·75	1·25
2289	25c. on 30c. mult (surch **1988**)	1·75	1·25
2290	25c. on 30c. multicoloured (surch **Morawhanna**)	1·75	1·25
2291	25c. on 30c. multicoloured (surch **Naamryck**)	1·75	1·25
2292	25c. on 30c. mult (surch **Purini**)	1·75	1·25
2293	25c. on 30c. multicoloured (surch **Potaro Landing**)	1·75	1·25
2294	25c. on 30c. multicoloured (surch **Rockstone**)	1·75	1·25
2295	25c. on 30c. multicoloured (surch **Rosignol**)	1·75	1·25
2296	25c. on 30c. multicoloured (surch **Stanleytown**)	1·75	1·25
2297	25c. on 30c. multicoloured (surch **Santa Rosa**)	1·75	1·25
2298	25c. on 30c. multicoloured (surch **Tumatumari**)	1·75	1·25
2299	25c. on 30c. multicoloured (surch **Weldaad**)	1·75	1·25
2300	25c. on 30c. multicoloured (surch **Wismar**)	1·75	1·25
2301	25c. on 30c. mult (surch **TPO Berbice Railway**)	1·75	1·00

1988. Olympic Games, Seoul (1st issue). Nos. 1206/17 further surch **120 Olympic Games 1988**.

2302	120c. on 55c. on 125c. on 35c. Type **174**	1·60	1·50
2303	120c. on 55c. on 125c. on 35c. Trahira ("Haimara")	1·60	1·50
2304	120c. on 55c. on 125c. on 35c. Electric eel	1·60	1·50
2305	120c. on 55c. on 125c. on 35c. Golden rivulus	1·60	1·50
2306	120c. on 55c. on 125c. on 35c. Golden pencilfish	1·60	1·50
2307	120c. on 55c. on 125c. on 35c. Four-eyed fish	1·60	1·50
2308	120c. on 55c. on 125c. on 35c. Red piranha ("Pirai")	1·60	1·50
2309	120c. on 55c. on 125c. on 35c. Smoking hassar	1·60	1·50
2310	120c. on 55c. on 125c. on 35c. Manta	1·60	1·50
2311	120c. on 55c. on 125c. on 35c. Festive cichlid ("Flying patwa")	1·60	1·50
2312	120c. on 55c. on 125c. on 35c. Arapaima	1·60	1·50
2313	120c. on 55c. on 125c.on 35c. Peacock cichlid ("Lukanani")	1·60	1·50

See also Nos. 2476/95.

1988. Centenary of Publication of Sanders' *Reichenbachia* (29th issue). As T **331**. Multicoloured.

2314	320c. Plate No. 62 (Series 2)	3·75	50
2315	475c. Plate No. 73 (Series 2)	5·50	2·00
2316	525c. Plate No. 36 (Series 2)	6·00	2·25
2317	530c. Plate No. 69 (Series 2)	1·00	2·00
2318	$15 Plate No. 67 (Series 2)	2·50	4·50

1988. CARICOM Day. Nos. 545/6 and 555 surch **Caricom Day 1988** and new value.

2319	25c. on 5c. Annatto tree	25	10
2320	$1.20 on 6c. Cannon-ball tree	1·25	25
2321	$10 on $2 "Norantea guianensis"	4·50	6·00

1988. Centenary of Publication of Sanders' *Reichenbachia* (30th issue). As T **331**. Multicoloured.

2322	700c. Plate No. 62 (Series 2)	1·00	1·75
2323	775c. Plate No. 59 (Series 2)	1·25	2·00
2324	875c. Plate No. 31 (Series 2)	16·00	5·50
2325	950c. Plate No. 78 (Series 2)	1·75	4·50

1988. 40th Anniv of World Health Day. No. 705a optd.

2326	60c. "Papilio androgeus" (optd **WHO 1948-1988**)	22·00	23·00
2327	60c. "Papilio androgeus" (optd **1988**)	35	10

1988. Centenary of Publication of Sanders' *Reichenbachia* (31st issue). As T **331**. Multicoloured.

2328	350c. Plate No. 74 (Series 2)	3·50	1·75

1988. Centenary of Publication of Sanders' *Reichenbachia* (32nd issue). As T **331**, but additionally inscr "1985–1988". Multicoloured.

2329	130c. Plate No. 73 (Series 2)	3·00	35
2330	200c. Plate No. 96 (Series 2)	50	45
2331	260c. Plate No. 16 (Series 2)	6·50	2·50

MS2332 Four sheets, each 102×127 mm. (a) 120c. Plate No. 81 (Series 2); 120c. Plate No. 57 (Series 2); 120c. Plate No. 55 (Series 2); 120c. Plate No. 46 (Series 2). (b) 150c. Plate No. 57 (Series 2); 150c. Plate No. 81 (Series 2); 150c. Plate No. 46 (Series 2); 150c. Plate No. 55 (Series 2). (c) 225c. Plate No. 46 (Series 2); 225c. Plate No. 55 (Series 2); 225c. Plate No. 57 (Series 2); 225c. Plate No. 81 (Series 2). (d) 305c. Plate No. 55 (Series 2); 305c. Plate No. 46 (Series 2); 305c. Plate No. 81 (Series 2); 305c. Plate No. 57 (Series 2). Set of 4 sheets 8·50 6·00

1988. Conservation of Resources

(a) Nos. 1444B/6B optd as T 415 by Gordy Ptg

2333	120c. Young Ocelot (No. 1444) (optd **CONSERVE TREES**)	1·00	80
2334	120c. Young Ocelot (No. 1444) (optd **CONSERVE ELECTRICITY**)	1·00	80
2335	120c. Young Ocelot (No. 1444) (optd **CONSERVE WATER**)	1·00	80
2336	120c. Type **322** (optd **CONSERVE ELECTRICITY**)	1·00	80
2337	120c. Type **322** (optd **CONSERVE WATER**)	1·00	80
2338	120c. Type **322** (optd **CONSERVE TREES**)	1·00	80
2339	120c. Young Ocelot (No. 1446) (optd **CONSERVE WATER**)	1·00	80
2340	120c. Young Ocelot (No. 1446) (optd **CONSERVE TREES**)	1·00	80
2341	120c. Young Ocelot (No. 1446) (optd **CONSERVE ELECTRICITY**)	1·00	80

(b) Nos. 1634, 1670, 1683 and 1774 optd **CONSERVE WATER**.

2342	200c. Plate No. 33 (Series 1)	1·00	1·00
2343	200c. Plate No. 79 (Series 1)	1·00	1·00
2344	225c. Plate No. 24 (Series 1)	1·00	1·00
2345	350c. Plate No. 94 (Series 1)	1·00	1·00

1988. Road Safety Campaign. Nos. 2194/2201 optd.

2346	**396** $1.20 green (optd **BEWARE OF ANIMALS**)	1·50	1·10
2347	– $1.20 green (No. 2195) (optd **BEWARE OF CHILDREN**)	1·50	1·10
2348	– $1.20 green (No. 2196) (optd **DRIVE SAFELY**)	1·50	1·10
2349	– $1.20 green (No. 2197) (optd **DO NOT DRINK AND DRIVE**)	1·50	1·10
2350	**396** $1.20 purple (optd **BEWARE OF ANIMALS**)	1·50	1·10
2351	– $1.20 purple (No. 2199) (optd **BEWARE OF CHILDREN**)	1·50	1·10
2352	– $1.20 purple (No. 2200) (optd **DRIVE SAFELY**)	1·50	1·10
2353	– $1.20 purple (No. 2201) (optd **DO NOT DRINK AND DRIVE**)	1·50	1·10

1988. No. 706 optd **1988** or surch **120**.

2354	$1 *Agrias claudina*	13·00	1·50
2355	120c. on $1 *Agrias claudina*	13·00	1·50

1988. Various *Reichenbachia* issues surch.

2356	120c. on 25c. Plate No. 61 (Series 1) (No. 1574)	1·00	70
2357	120c. on 25c. Plate No. 63 (Series 1) (No. 1575)	1·00	70
2358	120c. on 25c. Plate No. 70 (Series 1) (No. 1576)	1·00	70
2359	120c. on 25c. Plate No. 59 (Series 1) (No. 1620)	1·00	70
2360	120c. on 25c. Plate No. 71 (Series 1) (No. 1679)	1·00	70
2429	120c. on 25c. Plate No. 72 (Series 1) (No. 1577)	1·00	70
2361	120c. on 30c. Plate No. 53 (Series 1) (No. 1771)	1·00	70
2362	120c. on 30c. Plate No. 86 (Series 1) (No. 1731)	1·00	70
2363	120c. on 30c. Plate No. 30 (Series 2) (No. 1809)	1·00	70
2365	120c. on 30c. Plate No. 7 (Series 2)	1·00	70
2366	120c. on 30c. Plate No. 14 (Series 2)	1·00	70
2368	120c. on 30c. Plate No. 22 (Series 2)	1·00	70
2369	120c. on 30c. Plate No. 28 (Series 2)	1·00	70
2371	120c. on 35c. Plate No. 45 (Series 2) (No. 1925)	1·00	70
2372	120c. on 40c. Plate No. 77 (Series 1) (No. 1663)	1·00	70
2374	120c. on 40c. Plate No. 96 (Series 1) (No. 1747)	1·00	70
2377	120c. on 40c. Plate No. 86 (Series 1) (No. 1868)	1·00	70
2378	120c. on 40c. Plate No. 68 (Series 1) (No. 1884)	1·00	70
2381	120c. on 45c. Plate No. 54 (Series 1) (No. 1664)	1·00	70
2382	120c. on 45c. Plate No. 81 (Series 1) (No. 1748)	1·00	70

2383	120c. on 45c. Plate No. 21 (Series 2) (No. 1810)	1·00	70
2384	120c. on 50c. Plate No. 92 (Series 1) (No. 1665)	1·00	70
2385	120c. on 50c. Plate No. 13 (Series 1) (No. 1907)	1·00	70
2386	120c. on 50c. Plate No. 15 (Series 2) (No. 1926)	1·00	70
2393	120c. on 55c. Plate No. 17 (Series 1) (No. 1732)	1·00	70
2395	120c. on 60c. Plate No. 57 (Series 1) (No. 1622)	1·00	70
2397	120c. on 60c. Plate No. 73 (Series 1) (No. 1623)	1·00	70
2398	120c. on 60c. Plate No. 75 (Series 1) (No. 1624)	1·00	70
2400	120c. on 60c. Plate No. 95 (Series 1) (No. 1666)	1·00	70
2401	120c. on 60c. Plate No. 93 (Series 1) (No. 1733)	1·00	70
2402	120c. on 60c. Plate No. 27 (Series 2) (No. 1874)	1·00	70
2408	120c. on 70c. Plate No. 8 (Series 2)	1·00	70
2409	120c. on 70c. Plate No. 9 (Series 2)	1·00	70
2411	120c. on 70c. Plate No. 12 (Series 2)	1·00	70
2413	120c. on 70c. Plate No. 17 (Series 2)	1·00	70
2414	120c. on 80c. Plate No. 39 (Series 1)	1·00	70
2415	120c. on 80c. Plate No. 74 (Series 1)	1·00	70
2416	120c. on 80c. Plate No. 93 (Series 1)	1·00	70
2417	120c. on 85c. Plate No. 45 (Series 2) (No. 1876)	1·00	70
2418	120c. on 85c. Plate No. 24 (Series 2) (No. 1914)	1·00	70
2419	120c. on 85c. Plate No. 15 (Series 2) (No. 1918)	1·00	70
2420	120c. on 85c. Plate No. 18 (Series 2) (No. 1928)	1·00	70
2421	120c. on 90c. Plate No. 84 (Series 1) (No. 1668)	1·00	70
2422	120c. on 90c. Plate No. 89 (Series 1) (No. 1749)	1·00	70
2423	120c. on 90c. Plate No. 10 (Series 2) (No. 1869)	1·00	70
2424	120c. on 90c. Plate No. 13 (Series 2) (No. 1877)	1·00	70
2425	120c. on 90c. Plate No. 27 (Series 2) (No. 1915)	1·00	70
2426	120c. on 90c. Plate No. 2 (Series 2) (No. 1929)	1·00	70
2427	200c. on 80c. Plate No. 42 (Series 1) (No. 1812)	1·00	70
2428	200c. on 90c. Plate No. 4 (Series 1) (No. 1813)	1·00	70
2430	240c. on 140c. Plate No. 30 (Series 2)	1·00	70
2431	240c. on 140c. Plate No. 34 (Series 2)	1·00	70
2432	240c. on 425c. Plate No. 87 (Series 2) (No. 2070)	1·00	70
2433	260c. on 375c. Plate No. 90 (Series 1) (No. 1378)	1·00	70

1988. Conservation of Resources. Various "Reichenbachia" issues optd **CONSERVE OUR RESOURCES**.

2434	100c. Plate No. 65 (Series 1) (No. 1773)	1·25	70
2435	100c. Plate No. 68 (Series 1) (No. 1734)	1·25	70
2436	100c. Plate No. 88 (Series 1) (No. 1750)	1·25	70
2438	120c. Plate No. 27 (Series 1) (No. 1524)	1·25	70
2439	120c. Plate No. 36 (Series 1) (No. 1558)	1·25	70
2440	120c. Plate No. 37 (Series 1) (No. 1627)	1·25	70
2441	120c. Plate No. 56 (Series 1) (No. 1629)	1·25	70
2442	120c. Plate No. 58 (Series 1) (No. 1630)	1·25	70
2443	120c. Plate No. 67 (Series 1) (No. 1631)	1·25	70
2444	120c. Plate No. 69 (Series 1) (No. 1680)	1·25	70
2445	130c. Plate No. 38 (Series 1) (No. 1560)	1·25	70
2446	130c. Plate No. 66 (Series 1) (No. 1632)	1·25	70
2447	130c. Plate No. 91 (Series 1) (No. 1735)	1·25	70
2448	130c. Plate No. 13 (Series 1) (No. 1760)	1·25	70
2449	130c. Plate No. 20 (Series 1) (No. 1761)	1·25	70
2450	150c. Plate No. 26 (Series 1) (No. 1633)	1·25	70
2451	150c. Plate No. 78 (Series 1) (No. 1669)	1·25	70
2452	150c. Plate No. 87 (Series 1) (No. 1681)	1·25	70
2453	150c. Plate No. 76 (Series 1) (No. 1751)	1·25	70
2454	250c. Plate No. 74 (Series 1) (No. 1736)	1·25	70

2455	**396** $3.20 blue	1·50	1·50
2456	– $3.20 blue (No. 2203)	1·50	1·50
2457	– $3.20 blue (No. 2204)	1·50	1·50
2458	– $3.20 blue (No. 2205)	1·50	1·50
2459	– $3.30 black (No. 2207)	1·50	1·50
2460	**396** $3.30 black	1·50	1·50
2461	– $3.30 black (No. 2209)	1·50	1·50
2462	– $3.30 black (No. 2210)	1·50	1·50

1988. Centenary of Publication of Sanders' *Reichenbachia* (33rd issue). As T **331**. Multicoloured.

2468	270c. Plate No. 90 (Series 2)	9·50	70
2469	360c. Plate No. 84 (Series 2)	75	1·00
2470	550c. Plate No. 70 (Series 2) (horiz)	2·00	2·75
2471	670c. Plate No. 71 (Series 2) (horiz)	2·25	3·25

1988. 60th Anniv of Cricket in Guyana. Nos. 1584, 1670, 1681 and 1815 optd **1928 – 1988 CRICKET JUBILEE** or surch also.

2472	200c. Plate No. 14 (Series 1)	25·00	30·00
2473	200c. Plate No. 79 (Series 1)	1·00	65
2474	800c. on 150c. Plate No. 87 (Series 1)	10·00	14·00
2475	800c. on 160c. Plate No. 5 (Series 2)	3·25	3·75

1988. Olympic Games, Seoul. (a) Nos. 1628, 1634, 1671, 1681, 1683, 1814, 1818/19, 1880 and 2069 optd **OLYMPIC GAMES 1988** or surch also.

(a) Nos. 1628, 1634, 1671, 1681, 1683, 1814, 1818/19, 1880 and 2069 optd as T 426 or surch also by Gardy Ptg

2476	120c. Plate No. 46 (Series 1)	50	50
2477	130c. Plate No. 38 (Series 2)	50	50
2478	150c. Plate No. 87 (Series 1)	50	50
2479	200c. Plate No. 33 (Series 1)	50	50
2480	300c. Plate No. 83 (Series 1)	70	70
2481	300c. on 360c. Plate No. 34 (Series 2)	70	70
2482	320c. Plate No. 10 (Series 2)	70	70
2483	330c. Plate No. 82 (Series 2)	70	70
2484	350c. Plate No. 94 (Series 1)	70	70
2485	350c. Plate No. 29 (Series 2)	70	70

(b) Design as No. 1420 but incorrectly inscr "LOS ANGELLES" optd or surch **OLYMPICS 1988** (A) or **KOREA 1988** (B).

2486	$1.20 multicoloured (A)	50	50
2487	$1.20 multicoloured (B)	50	50
2488	130c. on $1.20 mult (A)	50	50
2489	130c. on $1.20 mult (B)	50	50
2490	150c. on $1.20 mult (A)	50	50
2491	150c. on $1.20 mult (B)	50	50
2492	200c. on $1.20 mult (A)	60	60
2493	200c. on $1.20 mult (B)	60	60
2494	350c. on $1.20 mult (A)	70	70
2495	350c. on $1.20 mult (B)	70	70

1988. Columbus Day. Nos. 1672/3 optd or surch **V CENTENARY OF THE LANDING OF CHRISTOPHER COLUMBUS IN THE AMERICAS**.

2496	320c. Plate No. 50 (Series 1)	2·75	60
2497	$15 on 360c. Plate No. 85 (Series 1)	4·75	6·50

1988. Centenary of Publication of Sanders' "Reichenbachia" (34th issue). As T **331**. Multicoloured.

2498	100c. Plate No. 44 (Series 2)	60	55
2499	130c. Plate No. 42 (Series 2) (horiz)	60	55
2500	140c. Plate No. 4 (Series 2)	75	65
2501	160c. Plate No. 50 (Series 2)	75	65
2502	175c. Plate No. 51 (Series 2)	90	75
2503	200c. Plate No. 11 (Series 2)	6·00	1·50
2504	200c. Plate No. 23 (Series 2)	6·00	1·50
2505	200c. Plate No. 26 (Series 2)	6·00	1·50
2506	200c. Plate No. 75 (Series 2)	6·00	1·50
2507	200c. Plate No. 93 (Series 2)	6·00	1·50
2508	250c. Plate No. 79 (Series 2)	1·00	1·00
2509	280c. Plate No. 62 (Series 2)	1·25	1·50
2510	285c. Plate No. 63 (Series 2)	8·50	2·50
2511	380c. Plate No. 35 (Series 2)	9·00	3·00

1988. Christmas (1st issue). Various *Reichenbachia* issues optd or surch.

(a) Optd or surch **SEASON'S GREETINGS**

2512	150c. Plate No. 32 (Series 1) (No. 1561)	80	80
2513	150c. Plate No. 62 (Series 1) (No. 1566)	80	80
2514	225c. Plate No. 60 (Series 1) (No. 1682)	80	80
2515	260c. Plate No. 39 (Series 1) (No. 1737)	80	80
2516	320c. Plate No. 82 (Series 1) (No. 1753)	80	80
2517	330c. Plate No. 80 (Series 1) (No. 1754)	80	80
2518	360c. Plate No. 85 (Series 1) (No. 1673)	80	80
2519	120c. on 100c. Plate No. 6 (Series 1)	80	80

2520	120c. on 100c. Plate No. 13 (Series 1)	80	80
2521	120c. on 100c. Plate No. 20 (Series 1)	80	80
2522	120c. on 100c. Plate No. 25 (Series 1)	80	80
2523	120c. on 100c. Plate No. 40 (Series 1) (horiz)	80	80
2524	120c. on 100c. Plate No. 42 (Series 1) (horiz)	80	80
2525	120c. on 100c. Plate No. 43 (Series 1) (horiz)	80	80
2526	120c. on 100c. Plate No. 45 (Series 1) (horiz)	80	80
2527	225c. Plate No. 24 (Series 1) (No. 1774)	1·50	1·50
2528	225c. on 60c. Plate No. 60 (Series 1) (No. 1682)	1·50	1·50
2530	225c. on 350c. on 120c. Plate No. 65 (Series 1) (No. 2221)	1·50	1·50

MS2531 120×129 mm. 225c. on 55c.×4 Plate No. 22 (Series 1) each with a different overprint (Christmas 1987, Happy New Year, Merry Christmas or Happy Holidays) (No. MS2232) — 4·50 4·50

(b) Optd SEASON'S GREETINGS 1988.

2532	240c. on 180c. Plate No. 15 (Series 1) (No. 1752)	1·00	1·00

1988. Christmas (2nd issue). Nos. 489, 1188/91 and 1449 surch or optd CHRISTMAS 1988.

2533	-	20c. on 6c. mult (No. 489)	35	10
2534	277	120c. brown, black bl	1·00	1·50
2535	-	120c. on 130c. red, black and blue (No. 1189)	1·00	1·50
2536	-	120c. on 150c. violet, black and blue (No. 1190)	1·00	1·50
2537	-	120c. on 200c. green, black and blue (No. 1191)	1·00	1·50
2538	-	500c. on 330c. mult (No. 1449)	2·25	3·00

1988. AIDS Information Campaign. Nos. 707/8a optd or surch with various slogans.

2539	120c. on $5 Morpho deidamia (A)	3·00	3·00
2540	120c. on $5 Morpho deidamia (B)	3·00	3·00
2541	120c. on $5 Morpho deidamia (C)	3·00	3·00
2542	120c. on $5 Morpho deidamia (D)	3·00	3·00
2543	120c. on $5 Morpho deidamia (E)	3·00	3·00
2544	120c. on $10 Elbella patrobas (A)	3·00	3·00
2545	120c. on $10 Elbella patrobas (B)	3·00	3·00
2546	120c. on $10 Elbella patrobas (C)	3·00	3·00
2547	120c. on $10 Elbella patrobas (D)	3·00	3·00
2548	120c. on $10 Elbella patrobas (E)	3·00	3·00
2549	$2 Morpho rhetenor (female) (E)	9·50	2·75
2550	$5 Morpho deidamia (E)	11·00	11·00
2551	$10 Elbella patrobas (E)	13·00	11·00

OVERPRINTS: (A) Be compassionate towards AIDS victims.; (B) Get information on AIDS. it may save your life.; (C) Get the facts. Education helps to prevent AIDS.; (D) Say no to Drugs and limit the spread of AIDS.; (E) Protect yourself from AIDS. Better safe than sorry.

1988. 150th Anniv of Abolition of Slavery (1984) (2nd issue). Designs as Nos. 1547/50, but colours changed.

2552	337	25c. black and brown	20	10
2553	-	60c. black and lilac	25	15
2554	-	130c. black and green	30	70
2555	-	150c. black and blue	35	90

1989. Olympic Medal Winners, Seoul. Nos. 1672, 1923 and 2178 surch SALUTING WINNERS OLYMPIC GAMES 1988.

2556	550c. on 560c. Plate No. 1 (Series 2)	1·50	1·25
2557	900c. on 320c. Plate No. 18 (Series 2)	2·00	2·50
2558	1050c. on 320c. Plate No. 50 (Series 1)	2·50	3·25

1989. Republic Day. Nos. 2194/2201 and 2212 optd REPUBLIC DAY 1989.

2559	396	$1.20 green	70	90
2560	-	$1.20 green (No. 2195)	70	90
2561	-	$1.20 green (No. 2196)	70	90
2562	-	$1.20 green (No. 2197)	70	90
2563	396	$1.20 purple	70	90
2564	-	$1.20 purple (No. 2199)	70	90
2565	-	$1.20 purple (No. 2200)	70	90
2566	-	$1.20 purple (No. 2201)	70	90
2567	-	$10 multicoloured	4·00	5·00

1989. Nos. 2202/5 and 2207/10 surch $5.00.

2568	396	$5 on $3.20 blue	3·25	3·75
2569	-	$5 on $3.20 blue (No. 2203)	3·25	3·75

2570	-	$5 on $3.20 blue (No. 2204)	3·25	3·75
2571	-	$5 on $3.20 blue (No. 2205)	3·25	3·75
2572	-	$5 on $3.30 black (No. 2207)	3·25	3·75
2573	396	$5 on $3.30 black	3·25	3·75
2574	-	$5 on $3.30 black (No. 2209)	3·25	3·75
2575	-	$5 on $3.30 black (No. 2210)	3·25	3·75

1989. Various Reichenbachia issues surch.

2576	120c. on 140c. Plate No. 25 (Series 2)	2·50	2·50
2577	120c. on 140c. Plate No. 52 (Series 2)	2·50	2·50
2578	120c. on 140c. Plate No. 65 (Series 2)	2·50	2·50
2579	120c. on 175c. Plate No. 54 (Series 2)	2·50	2·50
2580	120c. on 140c. Plate No. 38 (Series 2)	2·50	2·50
2581	120c. on 140c. Plate No. 41 (Series 2)	2·50	2·50
2582	170c. on 175c. Plate No. 58 (Series 2)	2·75	2·75
2583	250c. on 280c. Plate No. 66 (Series 2)	3·00	3·00
2584	250c. on 280c. Plate No. 67 (Series 2)	3·00	3·00
2585	300c. on 290c. Plate No. 53 (Series 2) (No. 2236)	3·00	3·00

1989. Nos. 1744/5 and 2185/6 surch TEN DOLLARS $10.00 (Nos. 2586, 2588) or TEN DOLLARS (Nos. 2587, 2589).

2586	363	$10 on 320c. red, black and lilac (No. 1744)	4·50	5·00
2587	-	$10 on 320c. mult (No. 1745)	4·50	5·00
2588	363	$10 on 320c. red, black and lilac (No. 2185)	4·50	5·00
2589	-	$10 on 320c. mult (No. 2186)	4·50	5·00

1989. Nos. O54/7, O59/63 and O65/9 optd POSTAGE or surch also.

2591	125c. on 130c. Plate No. 92 (Series 2)	2·25	2·25
2592	125c. on 140c. Plate No. 36 (Series 2)	2·25	2·25
2593	150c. Plate No. 43 (Series 2)	2·25	2·25
2594	150c. on 175c. Plate No. 31 (Series 2)	2·25	2·25
2595	250c. Plate No. 59 (Series 2)	2·50	2·50
2596	250c. on 225c. Plate No. 26 (Series 2)	2·50	2·50
2597	250c. on 230c. Plate No. 68 (Series 2)	2·50	2·50
2598	250c. on 260c. Plate No. 69 (Series 2)	2·50	2·50
2599	250c. on 275c. Plate No. 90 (Series 2)	2·50	2·50
2600	350c. Plate No. 95 (Series 2)	2·50	2·50
2601	350c. on 330c. Plate No. 23 (Series 2)	2·50	2·50
2602	600c. Plate No. 70 (Series 2)	2·75	3·00
2603	$12 Plate No. 71 (Series 2)	3·25	5·00
2604	$15 Plate No. 84 (Series 2)	3·50	5·50

1989. Centenary of Publication of Sanders' Reichenbachia (35th issue). As T 331. Multicoloured.

2605	200c. on Plate No. 49 (Series 2)	4·00	4·00
2606	200c. Plate No. 53 (Series 2)	4·00	4·00
2607	200c. Plate No. 60 (Series 2)	4·00	4·00
2608	200c. Plate No. 64 (Series 2)	4·00	4·00

1989. No. 1442 surch 250.

2609	322	250c. on 25c. mult	10·00	1·75

1989. 40th Anniv of Guyana Red Cross. No. 1872 surch RED CROSS 1948 1988 and new value.

2610	375c. on 45c. Plate No. 17 (Series 2)	4·50	4·50
2611	425c. on 45c. Plate No. 17 (Series 2)	4·50	4·50

1989. World Health Day. Nos. 1875 and 2239 surch with new value and inscr as indicated.

2612	250c. on 75c. Plate No. 56 (Series 2) surch HEALTH FOR ALL	3·75	3·75
2613	250c. on 75c. Plate No. 56 (Series 2) surch ALL FOR HEALTH	3·75	3·75
2614	675c. on 720c. Plate No. 49 (Series 2) surch ALL FOR HEALTH	4·00	4·50
2615	675c. on 720c. Plate No. 49 (Series 2) surch HEALTH FOR ALL	4·00	4·50

1989. Scouting Anniversaries. Nos. 1873, 1879, 2322, 2509 and unissued value as No. 1873 optd or surch also.

2616	250c. on 50c. Plate No. 33 (Series 2) surch BOY SCOUTS 1909 1989)	1·50	1·50
2617	250c. on 50c. Plate No. 33 (Series 2) surch GIRL GUIDES 1924 1989)	1·50	1·50

2618	250c. on 100c. Plate No. 33 (Series 2) surch BOY SCOUTS 1909 1989)	1·50	1·50
2619	250c. on 100c. Plate No. 33 (Series 2) surch GIRL GUIDES 1924 1989)	1·50	1·50
2620	300c. Note No. 50 (Series 2) (optd BOY SCOUTS 1909 1989)	1·50	1·50
2621	300c. Note No. 50 (Series 2) (optd GIRL GUIDES 1924 1989)	1·50	1·50
2622	$25 on 280c. Plate No. 62 (Series 2) (surch LADY BADEN POWELL 1889 – 1989)	6·00	8·00
2623	$25 on 700c. Plate No. 62 (Series 2) (surch LADY BADEN POWELL 1889 – 1989)	6·00	8·00

The events commemorated are the 80th anniv of Boy Scout Movement in Guyana, 65th anniv of Girl Guide Movement in Guyana and birth centenary of Lady Baden-Powell.

1989. 150 Years of Photography. No. 1881 surch PHOTOGRAPHY 1839 – 1989 and new value.

2624	550c. on 390c. Plate No. 6 (Series 2)	4·25	4·50
2625	650c. on 390c. Plate No. 6 (Series 2)	4·25	4·50

1989. 70th Anniv of International Labour Organization. No. 1875 surch I.L.O. 1919-1989 300.

2627	300c. on 75c. Plate No. 56 (Series 2)	8·50	3·00

1989. Various stamps surch.

2628	80c. on 6c. Plate No. 489	60	20
2629	$1 on 2c. Type 132	60	20
2630	$2.05 on 3c. Hanging heliconia (No. 544)	60	25
2641	$2.55 on 5c. Annatto tree (No. 545)	60	25
2642	$3.25 on 6c. Cannon-ball tree (No. 546)	60	25
2633	$5 on 6c. Type 111	60	30
2634	$6.40 on 10c. "Archonias bel-lona" (No. 699)	9·00	1·00
2648	$6.40 on $3.30 black (No. 2207)	9·00	7·50
2649	$6.40 on $3.30 black (No. 2208)	9·00	7·50
2650	$6.40 on $3.30 black (No. 2209)	9·00	7·50
2651	$6.40 on $3.30 black (No. 2210)	9·00	7·50
2646	640c. on 675 on 720c. Plate No. 49 (Series 2) (No. 2614)	1·75	2·00
2647	640c. on 675c. on 720c. Plate No. 49 (Series 2) (No. 2615)	1·75	2·00
2637a	$7.65 on 35c. Anaea galanthus (No. 703)	9·00	1·50
2638	$7.65 on 40c. Morpho retenor (male) (No. 704)	10·00	1·50
2652	$7.65 on $3.20 blue (No. 2202)	9·00	7·50
2653	$7.65 on $3.20 blue (No. 2203)	9·00	7·50
2654	$7.65 on $3.20 blue (No. 2204)	9·00	7·50
2655	$7.65 on $3.20 blue (No. 2205)	9·00	7·50
2635	$8.90 on 60c. Papilio androgeus (No. 705a)	11·00	1·50
2643	$50 on $2 Morpho rhetenor (female) (No. 707)	22·00	11·00
2644	$100 on $2 Morpho rhetenor (female) (No. 707)	32·00	24·00

1989. CARICOM Day. No. 1878 surch CARICOM DAY 125.

2656	125c. on 200c. Plate No. 44 (Series 2)	5·50	1·00

454 Stalachtis calliope

1989. Butterflies (1st series). Multicoloured.

2657	80c. Type 454	60	10
2658	$2.25 Morpho rhetenor	70	15
2659	$5 Agrias claudia	80	15
2660	$6.40 Marpesia marcella	85	20
2661	$7.65 Papilio zagreus	90	30
2662	$8.90 Chorinea faunus	1·00	30
2663	$25 Euptychia cephus	2·75	2·75
2664	$100 Nessaea regina	7·00	9·00

See also Nos. 2789/2861 and EMS18/19.

455 Kathryn Sullivan (first U.S. woman to walk in space)

1989. 25 Years of Women in Space. Multicoloured.

2665	$6.40 Type 455	70	20
2666	$12.80 Svetlana Savitskaya (first Soviet woman to walk in space)	1·10	45
2667	$15.30 Judy Resnik and Christa McAuliffe and "Challenger" logo	1·10	45
2668	$100 Sally Ride (first U.S. woman astronaut)	8·00	9·00

1989. Centenary of Ahmadiyya (Moslem organization). Nos. 543/5 surch AHMADIYYA CENTENARY 1899-1989.

2669	80c. on 2c. Type 132	5·50	1·00
2670	$6.40 on 3c. Hanging heliconia	17·00	6·50
2671	$8.90 on 5c. Annatto tree	20·00	10·00

457 Head of Harpy Eagle

1990. Endangered Species. Harpy Eagle. Multicoloured.

2672	$2.25 Type 457	75	25
2673	$5 Harpy eagle with monkey prey	1·00	30
2674	$8.90 Eagle on branch (facing right)	1·50	50
2675	$30 Eagle on branch (facing left)	3·25	3·50

458 Channel-billed Toucan

1990. Birds of Guyana. Multicoloured.

2676	$15 Type 458	1·50	70
2677	$25 Blue and yellow macaw	1·75	50
2678	$50 Wattled jacana (horiz)	3·25	2·50
2679	$60 Hoatzin	3·50	2·75

MS2680 Two sheets, each 110×80 mm. (a) $100 Great kiskadee. (b) $100 Amazon kingfisher Set of 2 sheets — 10·00 6·00

1990. 85th Anniv of Rotary International. Optd Rotary International 1905-1990 and emblem

(a) On Nos. 2657/64

2681	80c. Type 454	1·50	30
2682	$2.25 Morpho rhetenor	1·75	50
2683	$5 Agrias claudia	2·25	50
2684	$6.40 Marpesia marcella	2·25	55
2685	$7.65 Papilio zagreus	2·25	55
2686	$8.90 Chorinea faunus	2·50	65
2687	$25 Euptychia cephus	5·00	5·50
2688	$100 Nessaea regina	12·00	14·00

(b) On Nos. 2665/8.

2689	$6.40 Type 455	1·25	40
2690	$12.80 Svetlana Savitskaya (first Soviet woman to walk in space)	1·75	1·00
2691	$15.30 Judy Resnik and Christa McAuliffe with "Challenger" logo	1·75	1·10
2692	$100 Sally Ride (first U.S. woman astronaut)	9·00	11·00

460 Indian Post Runner, 1837

1990. 150th Anniv of the Penny Black and 500th Anniv of Thurn and Taxis Postal Service. Multicoloured.

2693- 2746	$15.30×27, $17.80×9, $20×18	35·00	35·00

MS2747 Three sheets, each 116×86 mm. (a) $150 Post boy. (b) $150 Thurn and Taxis (Northern District) 3gr. of 1852. (c) $150 Thurn and Taxis (Southern District) 6k. of 1852 Set of 3 sheets — 13·00 14·00

Nos. 2693/2746 depict various forms of mail transport.

1990. Ninth Conference of Rotary District 405, Georgetown. Nos. 1759, 1762/3 and 1765/6 surch **ROTARY DISTRICT 405 9th CONFERENCE MAY 1990 GEORGETOWN** and new value.

2748	80c. on 55c. Plate No. 9 (Series 1)	2·50	1·50
2749	80c. on 55c. Plate No. 49 (Series 1)	2·50	1·50
2750	80c. on 55c. Plate No. 64 (Series 1)	2·50	1·50
2751	$6.40 on 130c. Plate No. 6 (Series 1)	9·00	7·50
2752	$6.40 on 130c. Plate No. 25 (Series 1)	9·00	7·50
2753	$7.65 on 130c. Plate No. 25 (Series 1)	9·00	7·50

1990. 90th Birthday of Queen Elizabeth the Queen Mother. Nos. 2657/64 surch **90th Birthday H.M. The Queen Mother.**

2754	80c. Type **454**	2·00	50
2755	$2.25 *Morpho rhetenor*	2·25	60
2756	$5 *Agrias claudia*	2·75	70
2757	$6.40 *Marpesia marcella*	3·00	75
2758	$7.65 *Papilio zagreus*	3·25	80
2759	$8.90 *Chorinea faunus*	3·25	1·00
2760	$25 *Euptychia cephus*	9·00	6·50
2761	$100 *Nessaea regina*	20·00	22·00

See also Nos. **EMS**31/3.

463 Collared Trogon

1990. Birds. Multicoloured.

2762	80c. Marbled wood quail ("Guiana Partridge") (horiz)	30	10
2763	$2.55 Type **463**	40	15
2764	$3.25 Chestnut-tipped toucanet ("Derby Aracari")	40	15
2765	$5 Black-necked aracari	50	20
2766	$5.10 Green aracari	50	30
2767	$5.80 Ivory-billed aracari	50	30
2768	$6.40 Guiana toucanet	50	30
2769	$6.50 Channel-billed toucan ("Sulphur-breasted Toucan")	50	30
2770	$7.55 Red-billed toucan	65	30
2771	$7.65 Toco toucan	65	30
2772	$8.25 Tawny-tufted toucanet ("Natterers Toucanet")	65	30
2773	$8.90 Eared trogon ("Welcome Trogon")	65	30
2774	$9.75 Elegant trogon ("Doubtful Trogon")	65	30
2775	$11.40 Collared trogon ("Banded Aracari")	75	40
2776	$12.65 Golden-headed quetzal ("Golden-headed Train Bearer")	75	40
2777	$12.80 Rufous-breasted hermit	75	40
2778	$13.90 Band tail barbthroat	75	40
2779	$15.30 White-tipped sickle-bill	80	50
2780	$17.80 Black jacobin	90	60
2781	$19.20 Fiery topaz	90	60
2782	$22.95 Tufted coquette	1·00	70
2783	$26.70 Ecuadorian pied-tail	1·00	70
2784	$30 Resplendent quetzal ("Quetzal")	1·00	70
2785	$50 Green-crowned brilliant	1·75	1·25
2786	$100 Emerald-chinned hummingbird	2·75	2·75
2787	$190 Lazuline sabre-wing	4·50	5·00
2788	$225 Beryline hummingbird	4·50	5·50

464 *Melinaea idae*

1990. Butterflies (2nd series). Multicoloured.

2789–	80c., $2.55, $5, $6.40, $7.65,		
2860	$8.90, $10×64, $50 and $100	30·00	35·00

MS2861 Four sheets, each 102×71 mm. (a) $150 "Heliconius aoede". (b) $150 *Phyciodes clio* (horiz). (c) $190 *Thecla hemon*. (d) $190 *Nymphidium caricae* Set of 4 sheets   24·00   27·00

DESIGNS—VERT: $2.55, *Rhetus dysonii*; $5 *Actinote anteas*; $6.40, *Heliconius tales*; $7.65, *Thecla telemus*; $8.90, *Theope eudocia*; $10 (2795). *Heleconius vetustus*; 2796, *Mesosemia eumene*; 2797, *Parides phosphorus*; 2798, *Polystichtis emylius*; 2799, *Xanthocleis aedesia*; 2800, *Doxocopa agathina*; 2801, *Adelpha plesaure*; 2802, *Heliconius wallacei*; 2803, *Notheme eumeus*; 2804, *Melinaea mediatrix*; 2805, *Theritas coronata*; 2806, *Dismorphia orise*; 2807, *Phyciodes ianthe*; 2808, *Morpho aega*; 2809, *Zaretis isidora*; 2810, *Pierella lena*; 2811, *Heliconius silvana*; 2812, *Eunica alcmena*; 2813, *Mechanitis polymnia*; 2814, *Mesosemia ephyne*; 2815, *Thecla erema*; 2816, *Callizona acesta*; 2817, *Stalachtis phaedusa*; 2818, *Battus belus*; 2819, *Nymula phliasus*; 2820, *Parides childrenae*; 2821, *Stalachtis euterpe*; 2822, *Dysmathia portia*; 2823, *Tithorea hermias*; 2824, *Prepona pheridamas*; 2825, *Dismorphia fortunata*; 2826, *Hamadryas amphinome*; $50 *Heliconius vicini*; $100 *Amarynthis meneria*. HORIZ: $10 (2827), *Thecla falerina*; 2828, *Pheles heliconides*; 2829, *Echenias leucocyana*; 2830, *Heliconius xanthocles*; 2831, *Mesopthalma idotea*; 2832, *Parides aeneas*; 2833, *Heliconius numata*; 2834, *Thecla critola*; 2835, *Themone pais*; 2836, *Nymula agle*; 2837, *Adelpha cocala*; 2838, *Anaea eribotes*; 2839, *Prepona demophon*; 2840, *Selenophanes cassiope*; 2841, *Consul hippona*; 2842, *Antirrhaea avernus*; 2843, *Thecla telemus*; 2844, *Thyridia confusa*; 2845, *Heliconius burneyi*; 2846, *Parides lysander*; 2847,*Eunica orphise*; 2848, *Adelpha melona*; 2849, *Morpho menelaus*; 2850, *Nymula phylles*; 2851, *Stalachtis phlegia*; 2852, *Theope barea*; 2853, *Morpho perseus*; 2854, *Lycorea ceres*; 2855, *Archonias bellona*; 2856, *Caeronis chorinaeus*; 2857, *Vila azeca*; 2858, *Nessaea batesii.*

Nos. 2795/2810, 2811/26, 2827/42 and 2843/58 respectively were printed together, *se-tenant*, forming composite designs.

465 *Vanillia inodora*

1990. Flowers. Multicoloured.

2862–	$7.65, $8.90, $10×32,		
2965	$12.80×65, $15.30, $17.80, $20, $25 and $100	28·00	28·00

MS2966 Five sheets. (a) 65×95 mm. $150 *Delonix regia* (horiz). (b) 86×65 mm. $150 *Hexisea bidentata* (horiz). (c) 70×105 mm. $150 *Galeandra devonianal* (horiz). (d) 68×110 mm. $150 *Lecythis ollaria*. (e) 74×104 mm. $190 *Ionopsis utricularioides* Set of 5 sheets   18·00   20·00

DESIGNS—VERT: $8.90, *Epidendrum ibaguense*; $10 (2864), *Dichea muricata*; 2865, *Octomeria erosilabia*; 2866, *Spiranthes orchioides*; 2867, *Brassavola nodosa*; 2868, *Epidendrum rigidum*; 2869, *Brassia caudata*; 2870, *Pleurothallis diffusa*; 2871, *Aspasia variegata*; 2872, *Stenia pallida*; 2873, *Cyrtopodium punctatum*; 2874, *Cattleya deckeri*; 2875, *Cryptarrhena lunata*; 2876, *Cattleya violacea*; 2877, *Caularthron bicornutum*; 2878, *Oncidium carthagenense*; 2879, *Galeandra devoniana*; 2880, *Bifrenaria aurantiaca*; 2881, *Epidendrum ciliare*; 2882, *Dichaea picta*; 2883, *Scaphyglottis violacea*; 2884, *Cattleya percivaliana*; 2885, Map and national flag; 2886, *Epidendrum difforme*; 2887, *Eulophia maculata*; 2888, *Spiranthes tenuis*; 2889, *Peristoria guttata*; 2890, *Pleurothallis pruinosa*; 2891,*Cleistes rosea*; 2892, *Maxillaria variabilis*; 2893, *Brassavola cucullata*; 2894, *Epidendrum moyobambae*; 2895, *Oncidium orthostate*; $12.80, *Maxillaria parkeri*; 2897, *Brassavola martiana*; 2898, *Paphinia cristata*; 2899, *Aganisia pulchella*; 2900, *Oncidium lanceanum*; 2901, *Lockhartia imbricata*; 2902, *Caularthron bilamellatum*; 2903, *Oncidium nanum*; 2904, *Pleurothallis ovalifolia*; 2905, *Galeandra dives*; 2906, *Cycnoches loddigesii*; 2907, *Ada aurantiaca*; 2908, *Catasetum barbatum*; 2909, *Palmorchis pubescens*; 2910, *Epidendrum anceps*; 2911, *Huntleya meleagris*; 2912, *Sobralia sessilis*; $15.30, *Epidendrum nocturnum*; $17.80, *Catasetum discolor*; $20 *Scuticaria hadwenii*; $25 *Epidendrum fragrans*; $100 *Epistephium parviflorum*. HORIZ: $12.80 (2913), *Cochlospermum vitifolium*; 2914, *Eugenia malaccensis*; 2915, *Plumiera rubra*; 2916, *Erythrina glauca*; 2917, *Spathodea campanulata*; 2918, *Jacaranda filicifolia*; 2919, *Samanea saman*; 2920, *Cassia fistula*; 2921, *Abutilon integerrimum*; 2922, *Lagerstroemia speciosa*; 2923, *Tabebuia serratifolia*; 2924, *Guaiacum officinale*; 2925, *Solanum macranthum*; 2926, *Peltophorum roxburghii*; 2927, *Bauhinia variegata*; 2928, *Plumiera alba*; 2929, *Maxillaria camaridii*; 2930, *Vanilla pompona*; 2931, *Stanhopea grandiflora*; 2932, *Oncidium pusillum*; 2933, *Polycycnis vittata*; 2934, *Cattleya lawrenceana*; 2935, *Menadenium labiosum*; 2936, *Rodriguezia secunda*; 2937, *Mormodes buccinator*; 2938, *Otostylis brachystalix*; 2939, *Maxillaria discolor*; 2940, *Liparis elata*; 2941, *Gongora maculata*; 2942, *Koellensteinia graminea*; 2943, *Rudolfiella aurantiaca*; 2944, *Scuticaria steelei*; 2945, *Gloriosa rothschildiana*; 2946, *Pseudocalymma alliaceum*; 2947, *Callichlamys latifolia*; 2948, *Distictis riversii*; 2949, *Maurandya barclaiana*; 2950, *Beaumontia fragrans*; 2951, *Phaseolus caracalla*; 2952, *Mandevilla splendens*; 2953, *Solandra longiflora*; 2954, *Passiflora coccinea*; 2955, *Allamanda cathartica*; 2956, *Bauhinia galpini*; 2957, *Verbena maritima*; 2958, *Mandevilla sauveolens*; 2959, *Phryganocydia corymbosa*; 2960, *Jasminum sambac.*

Nos. 2864/79, 2880/95, 2897/2912, 2913/28, 2929/44 and 2945/60 respectively were printed together, *se-tenant*, forming composite designs.

466 Ivory-billed Woodpecker

1990. Fauna. Multicoloured.

2967–	$12.80×20 (vert designs show-		
2986	ing endangered birds)		
2987–	$12.80×20 (vert designs show-		
3006	ing tropical birds)		
3007–	$12.80×20 (vert designs show-		
3036	ing prehistoric animals)		
3027–	$12.80×20 (horiz designs show-		
3046	ing endangered wildlife)		

DESIGNS—VERT: No. 2968, Cauca guan; 2969, Sun conure; 2970, Resplendent quetzal ("Quetzal"); 2971, Long-wattled umbrellabird; 2972, Banded cotinga; 2973, Blue-throated conure ("Blue-chested Parakeet"); 2974, West Mexican chachalaca ("Rufous-bellied Chachalaca"); 2975, Yellow-faced amazon; 2976, Toucan barbet; 2977, Red siskin; 2978, Guianan cock-of-the-rock ("Cock-of-the-Rock"); 2979, Hyacinth macaw; 2980, Yellow cardinal; 2981, Bare-necked umbrellabird; 2982, Saffron toucanet; 2983, Red-billed curassow; 2984, Spectacled parrotlet; 2985, Lovely cotinga; 2986, Black-bellied gnateater ("Black-breasted Gnateater"); 2987, Swallow-tailed kite; 2988, Hoatzin; 2989, Ruby-topaz hummingbird; 2990, American black vulture; 2991, Rufous-tailed jacamar; 2992, Scarlet macaw; 2993, Rose-breasted thrush tanager; 2994, Toco toucan; 2995, Bearded bellbird; 2996, Blue-crowned motmot; 2997, Green oropendola; 2998, Pompadour cotinga; 2999, Vermilion flycatcher; 3000, Blue and yellow macaw; 3001, White-barred piculet; 3002, Great razor-billed curassow; 3003, Ruddy quail dove; 3004, Paradise tanager; 3005, American darter ("Anhinga"); 3006, Greater flamingo; 3007, Palaelodus; 3008, Archaeotrogon; 3009, Teratornis mirabilis ("Vulture"); 3010, Bradypus tridactylus; 3011, Natalus stramineus bat; 3012, Cebidae; 3013, Cuvieronius; 3014, Phororhacos; 3015, Smilodectes; 3016, Megatherium; 3017, Titanotylopus; 3018, Teleoceras; 3019, Macrauchenia; 3020, Mylodon; 3021, Smilodon; 3022, Glyptodon; 3023, Protohydrocherus; 3024, Archaeohyrax; 3025, Pyrotherium; 3026, Platypittamys. HORIZ: $12.80 (3027), Harpy eagle and hyacinth macaw; 3028, Andean condor; 3029, Amazonian umbrellabird; 3030, Spider monkeys; 3031, Hyacinth macaws; 3032, Red siskin; 3033, Toucan barbet; 3034, Three-toed sloth; 3035, Guanacos; 3036, Spectacled bear; 3037, White-lipped peccary; 3038, Maned wolf; 3039, Jaguar; 3040, Spectacled cayman; 3041, Giant armadillo; 3042, Giant anteater; 3043, South American river otter; 3044, Yapok; 3045, Central American river turtle; 3046, Cauca guan.

Nos. 2967/86, 2987/3006, 3007/26 and 3027/46 respectively were printed together, *se-tenant*, forming composite designs.

No. 2982 is inscribed "Toucanette" and No. 2995 "Bellbird", both in error.

See also **EMS**34/5.

467 National Flag

1991. 25th Anniv of Independence. Sheet 100×70 mm. Litho. Imperf.
MS3047 **467** $225 multicoloured   5·50   6·00

468 Ramon Folist (Cuba) (fencing, 1990)

1991. Winter Olympic Games, Albertville (1st issue), and Olympic Games, Barcelona. Previous Gold Medal Winners. Multicoloured.

3048–	$15.30×9, $17.80×9, $20×18,		
	$25×18 and $30×18	32·00	35·00

MS3120 Three sheets, each 98×70 mm. (a) $150 Johannes Kolehmainen (Finland) (10,000 metres, 1912) (vert). (b) $150 Paavo Nurmi (Finland) (5000 metres, 1924) (vert). (c) $190 Nedo Nadi (Italy) (fencing, 1920) (vert) Set of 3 sheets   11·00   12·00

DESIGNS: $15.30 (3049), Lucien Gaudin (France) (fencing, 1924); 3050, Ole Lilloe-Olsen (Norway) (shooting, 1924); 3051, Morris Fisher (U.S.A.) (rifle shooting, 1924); 3052, Ray Ewry (U.S.A.) (long jump, 1900); 3053, Hubert van Innes (Belgium) (archery, 1900); 3054, Alvin Kraenzlein (U.S.A.) (hurdles, 1900); 3055, Johnny Weissmuller (U.S.A.) (swimming, 1924); 3056, Hans Winkler (West Germany) (show jumping, 1956); $17.80 (3057), Viktor Chukarin (Russia) (gymnastics, 1952); 3058, Agnes Keleti (Hungary) (gymnastics, 1952); 3059, Barbel Wochel (East Germany) (200 metres, 1980); 3060, Eric Heiden (U.S.A.) (speed skating, 1980); 3061, Alvodar Gerevich (Hungary) (fencing, 1932); 3062, Giuseppe Delfino (Italy) (fencing, 1952); 3063, Alexander Tikhonov (Russia) (skiing, 1980); 3064, Pahud de Mortanges (Netherlands) (equestrian, 1932); 3065, Patricia McCormick (U.S.A.) (diving, 1952); $20 (3066), Olga Korbut (Russia) (gymnastics, 1972); 3067, Lyudmila Turischeva (Russia) (gymnastics, 1972); 3068, Lasse Viren (Finland) (10,000 metres, 1972); 3069, George Miez (Switzerland) (gymnastics, 1936); 3070, Roland Matthes (East Germany) (swimming, 1972); 3071, Pal Kovaks (Hungary) (fencing, 1936); 3072, Jesse Owens (U.S.A.) (200 metres, 1936); 3073, Mark Spitz (U.S.A.) (swimming, 1972); 3074, Eduardo Mangiarotti (Italy) (fencing, 1936); 3075, Nelli Kim (Russia) (gymnastics, 1976); 3076, Viktor Krovopuskov (Russia) (fencing, 1976); 3077, Viktor Sidiak (Russia) (fencing, 1976); 3078, Nikolai Andrianov (Russia) (gymnastics, 1976); 3079, Nadia Comaneci (Rumania) (gymnastics, 1976); 3080, Mitsuo Tsukahara (Japan) (gymnastics, 1976); 3081, Yelena Novikova-Belova (Russia) (fencing, 1976); 3082, John Naber (U.S.A.) (swimming, 1976); 3083, Kornella Ender (Rumania) (swimming, 1976); $25 (3084), Lydia Skoblikova (Russia) (speed skating, 1964); 3085, Ivar Ballangrud (Norway) (speed skating, 1936); 3086, Clas Thunberg (Finland) (speed skating, 1928); 3087, Anton Heida (U.S.A.) (gymnastics, 1904); 3088, Akinori Nakayama (Japan) (gymnastics, 1968); 3089, Sixten Jernberg (Sweden) (skiing, 1964); 3090, Yevgeniy Grischin (Russia) (speed skating, 1956); 3091, Paul Radmilovic (East Germany) (waterpolo, 1920); 3092, Charles Daniels (U.S.A.) (swimming, 1904); 3093, Sawao Kato (Japan) (gymnastics, 1968); 3094, Rudolf Karpati (Hungary) (fencing, 1948); 3095, Jeno Fuchs (Hungary) (fencing, 1908); 3096, Emil Zatopek (Czechoslovakia) (10,000 metres, 1948); 3097, Fanny Blankers-Koen (Netherlands) (hurdles, 1948); 3098, Melvin Sheppard (U.S.A.) (4 × 400 metres relay, 1908); 3099, Gert Fredriksson (Sweden) (kayak, 1948); 3100, Paul Elvstrom (Denmark) (sailing, 1948); 3101, Harrison Dillard (U.S.A.) (100 metres, 1948); $30 (3102), Al Oerter (U.S.A.) (discus, 1956); 3103, Polina Atsakhova (Russia) (gymnastics, 1956); 3104, Takashi Ono (Japan) (gymnastics, 1956); 3105, Valentin Muratov (Russia) (gymnastics, 1956); 3106, Henri St. Cyr (Sweden) (equestrian, 1956); 3107, Ian Murray Rose (Australia) (swimming, 1956); 3108, Larisa Latynina (Russia) (gymnastics, 1956); 3109, Carlo Pavesi (Italy) (fencing, 1956); 3110, Dawn Fraser (Australia) (swimming, 1956); 3111, Betty Cuthbert (Australia) (400 metres, 1964); 3112, Vera Caslavska (Czechoslovakia) (gymnastics, 1964); 3113, Galin Kulakova (Russia) (skiing, 1972); 3114, Yukio Endo (Japan) (gymnastics, 1972); 3115, Vladimir Morozov (Russia) (kayak, 1972); 3116, Boris Shaklin (Russia) (gymnastics, 1964); 3117, Don Schollander (U.S.A.) (swimming, 1964); 3118, Gyozo Kulscar (Hungary) (fencing, 1964); 3119, Christian D'Oriloa (France) (fencing, 1956).

Nos. 3048/56, 3057/65, 3066/74, 3075/83, 3084/92, 3093/3101, 3102/10 and 3111/19 respectively were printed together, *se-tenant*, forming composite designs.

Sheetlets containing Nos. 3057/65, 3084/92 and 3111/19 were subsequently re-issued with Nos. 3063, 3086 and 3113 overprinted "ALBERTVILLE '92".

See also Nos. 3186/94 and 3246/54.

1991. 85th Anniv of Rotary International (1990).

(a) Nos. 2789/94 and 2859/60 optd or surch **Paul Percy Harris Founder 1868-1947** and emblem (A) or with Rotary emblem and **1905-1990** (B).

3121	80c. Type **464** (B)	10	10
3122	$2.55 *Rhetus dysonii* (A)	10	10
3123	$5 *Actinote anteas* (A)	10	10
3124	$6.40 *Heliconius tales* (A)	15	15
3125	$7.65 *Thecla telemus* (A)	15	15
3126	$100 on $8.90 on $8.90 *Theope eudocia* (A)	1·75	1·90
3127	$190 on $50 on $50 *Heliconius vicini* (B)	2·75	3·00
3128	$225 on $100 on $100 *Amarynthis meneria* (B)	3·00	3·50

(b) Nos. 2795/2810 optd or surch as Nos. 3121/8 or with emblems and inscriptions of other international organizations.

3129	$10 *Heliconius vetustus* (B)	20	20
3130	$10 *Mesosemia eumene* (optd Boy Scout emblem and **1907–1992**)	20	20
3131	$10 *Parides phosphorus* (optd Lions Club emblem and **1917–1992**)	20	20
3132	$10 *Polystichtis emylius* (A)	20	20
3133	$10 *Xanthocleis aedesia* (optd **125 Years Red Cross** and cross)	20	20
3134	$10 *Doxocopa agathina* (optd with part Rotary emblem)	20	20
3135	$10 *Adelpha plesaure* (optd with part Rotary emblem)	20	20
3136	$10 *Heliconius wallacei* (optd **125 Years Red Cross** and cross)	20	20
3137	$10 *Notheme eumeus* (optd Lions Club emblem and **1917–1992**)	20	20
3138	$10 *Melinaea mediatrix* (optd with part Rotary emblem)	20	20
3139	$10 *Theritas coronata* (optd with part Rotary emblem)	20	20
3140	$10 *Dismorphia orise* (optd Boy Scout emblem and **1907–1992**)	20	20
3141	$50 on $10 on $10 *Phyciodes ianthe* (A)	80	80

3142	$75 on $10 on $10 *Morpho aega* (surch Boy Scout emblem and **1907–1992**)	1·60	1·60
3143	$100 on $10 on $10 *Zaretis isidora* (surch Lions Club emblem and **1917–1992**)	1·75	1·90
3144	$190 on $10 on $10 *Pierella lena* (B)	2·75	3·25

MS3145 Two sheets, each 102×71 mm.
(a) $400 on $150 *Heliconius aoede*.
(b) $500 on $150 *Phyciodes clio* Set
of 2 sheets .... 10·00 10·50

Nos. MS3145a/b only show the new face values on the stamps and have international organization emblems overprinted on the sheet margins.

1991. 65th Birthday of Queen Elizabeth II and 70th Birthday of Prince Philip. As T **198a** of Gambia. Multicoloured.

3146	$12.80 Queen and Prince Philip in evening dress	25	20
3147	$15.30 Queen Elizabeth II	25	20
3148	$100 Queen and Prince Philip	1·25	1·40
3149	$130 Prince Philip	1·50	1·60
3150	$150 Prince Philip in R.A.F. uniform	1·75	1·90
3151	$200 The Queen with Queen Elizabeth the Queen Mother	2·50	2·75

MS3152 68×90 mm. $225 Queen
Elizabeth II .... 3·25 3·50

1991. Tenth Wedding Anniv of Prince and Princess of Wales. As T **198b** of Gambia. Multicoloured.

3153	$8.90 Prince and Princess of Wales	30	20
3154	$50 Separate portraits of Princess and sons	1·00	80
3155	$75 Prince Charles with Prince William	1·25	1·50
3156	$190 Princess Diana with Prince Henry	2·75	3·50

MS3157 68×90 mm. $225 Separate
portraits of Prince Charles, Prince
William and Princess Diana with
Prince Henry .... 3·75 3·75

1991. 75th Anniv of Lions International (1992)

(a) Nos. 2789/94 and 2859/60 optd or surch **Melvin Jones Founder 1880-1961** (A) or with Lions Club emblem and **Lions International 1917–1992** (B)

3158	80c. Type **464** (B)	15	10
3159	$2.55 *Rhetus dysonii* (B)	20	15
3160	$5 *Actinote antea* (A)	30	20
3161	$6.40 *Heliconius tales* (A)	30	25
3162	$7.65 *Thecla telemus* (A)	40	25
3163	$100 on $8.90 on $8.90 *Theope eudocia* (A)	1·50	1·50
3164	$190 on $50 on $50 *Heliconius vicini* (B)	2·50	2·75
3165	$225 on $100 on $100 *Amarynthis meneria* (B)	2·50	2·75

(b) Nos. 2843/58 optd or surch as Nos. 3158/65 or with emblems and inscriptions of other international organizations.

3166	$10 *Thecla telemus* (optd Lions Club emblem and **1917–1992**)	15	15
3167	$10 *Thyridia confusa* (optd Rotary emblem and **1905–1990**)	15	15
3168	$10 *Heliconius burneyi* (optd Boy Scout emblem and **1907–1992**)	15	15
3169	$10 *Parides lysander* (A)	15	15
3170	$10 *Eunica orphise* (optd **125 Years Red Cross** and cross)	15	15
3171	$10 *Adelpha melona* (optd with part Lions Club emblem)	15	15
3172	$10 *Morpho menelaus* (optd with part Lions Club emblem)	15	15
3173	$10 *Nymula phylleus* (optd **125 Years Red Cross** and cross)	15	15
3174	$10 *Stalachtis phlegia* (optd Rotary emblem and **1905–1990**)	15	15
3175	$10 *Theope barea* (optd with part Lions Club emblem)	15	15
3176	$10 *Morpho perseus* (optd with part Lions Club emblem)	15	15
3177	$10 *Lycorea ceres* (optd Boy Scout emblem and **1907–1992**)	15	15
3178	$50 on $10 on $10 *Archonias bellona* (A)	70	70
3179	$75 on $10 on $10 *Caerois chorinaeus* (surch Boy Scout emblem and **1907–1992**)	1·25	1·40
3180	$100 on $10 on $10 *Vila azeca* (surch Rotary emblem and **1905–1990**)	1·50	1·60
3181	$190 on $10 on $10 *Nessaea batesii* (surch Lions Club emblem and **1917–1992**)	2·50	3·00

MS3182 Two sheets, each 102×71 mm.
(a) $400 on $190 *Nymphidium caricae*. (b) $500 on $190 *Thecla hemon*
Set of 2 sheets .... 11·00 12·00

Nos. MS3182a/b only show new face values on the stamps and have international organization emblems overprinted on the sheet margins.

1991. "Phila Nippon '91" International Stamp Exhibition, Tokyo. Sheetlets containing Nos. 2880/95 and 2897/2912, now sold as miniature sheets, and MS2966d with some stamps surch **$50** and inscriptions and exhibition logo on the sheet margins, all in red.

MS3183 135×203 mm. $10×12; $25
on $10; $50 on $10; $75 on $10;
$130 on $10 .... 11·00 12·00

MS3184 135×203 mm. $12.80×12; $25
on $12.80; $50 on $12.80; $75 on
$12.80; $100 on $12.80 .... 11·00 12·00

MS3185 68×110 mm. $250 on $150
"Lecythis ollaria" .... 3·75 4·00

1991. Winter Olympic Games, Albertville (1992) (2nd issue). Nos. 2738/46 optd or surch **ALBERTVILLE 92** or **XVIth Olympic Winter Games in Albertville** (No. 3190).

3186-3194 Set of 9 .... 22·00 23·00

3186- $20 x 6, $70 on $20, $100 on
3194 $20, $190 on $20 ....

1991. John F. Kennedy and Sir Winston Churchill Commemorations. Nos. **MS2966c** and **MS2966e** surch **$600** in black or red.

MS3195 70×105 mm. $600 on $150
Galeandra devoniana (horiz)

MS3196 74×104 mm. $600 on $190
Ionopsis utricularioides

No. MS3195 is additionally overprinted with "IN MEMORIAM John F. Kennedy 1917–1963", "First Man on Moon July 20, 1969" and "Apollo 11" emblem, and No. MS3196 "IN MEMORIAM Sir Winston S. Churchill 1874–1965" and "50th Anniversary World War II" on sheet margins.

474 *Akagi* (Japanese aircraft carrier)

1991. 50th Anniv of Japanese Attack on Pearl Harbor. Each blue, red and black.

3197	$50 Type **474**	1·00	85
3198	$50 Beached Japanese midget submarine	1·00	85
3199	$50 Mitsubishi A6M Zero-Sen fighter	1·00	85
3200	$50 U.S.S. *Arizona* (battleship) under attack	1·00	85
3201	$50 Aichi D3A1 "Val" dive bomber	1·00	85
3202	$50 U.S.S. *California* (battleship) sinking	1·00	85
3203	$50 Curtiss P-40 fighters taking off	1·00	85
3204	$50 U.S.S. *Cassin* and U.S.S. *Downes* damaged in dry dock	1·00	85
3205	$50 Boeing B-17 Flying Fortress crash landing at Bellows Field	1·00	85
3206	$50 U.S.S. *Nevada* (battleship) on fire	1·00	85

475 Brandenburg Gate and Location Plan

1991. Anniversaries and Events. Multicoloured.

3207	$10 Type **475**	20	20
3208	$25 President Bush, President Lech Walesa of Poland and Brandenburg Gate	50	50
3209	$25 Scout handshake	50	50
3210	$30 Scouts hiking at Philmont Scout Ranch	60	60
3211	$40 Jamboree and Scout Movement emblems	70	70
3212	$60 General de Gaulle at Venice, 1944	90	90
3213	$75 De Gaulle with Khrushchev, 1960	1·25	1·25
3214	$75 Mozart and Castle of Laxenburg	2·00	1·50
3215	$75 Caroline Herschel (astronomer) and Old Town Hall, Hanover	1·25	1·25
3216	$75 Map of Switzerland and woman in Valais costume	1·75	1·25
3217	$80 De Gaulle at Algiers, 1958	1·40	1·40
3218	$80 Mozart and death of Leopold II	2·00	1·50
3219	$80 Otto Lilienthal and "Flugzeug Nr. 3"	1·60	1·40
3220	$100 Chancellor Kohl, Foreign Minister Genscher and Brandenburg Gate	1·50	1·50
3221	$100 Lord Baden-Powell (vert)	1·75	1·75
3222	$100 De Gaulle with Pope Paul VI, 1967	2·50	1·75
3223	$100 Mozart and birthplace, Salzburg	2·50	1·75
3224	$100 Class P36 steam locomotive	2·50	1·75

MS3225 Six sheets. (a) 67×99 mm. $150 General De Gaulle (vert). (b) 75×104 mm. $190 General De Gaulle (different) (vert). (c) 101×71 mm. $190 Ceremonial helmet and statues from Brandenburg Gate. (d) 114×83 mm. $190 Rocket-flown commemorative cover, 1960. (e) 73×104 mm. $190 Mozart cameo (vert). (f) 103×74 mm. $190 Arms of Berne and Solothurn Set of 6 sheets .... 17·00 19·00

ANNIVERSARIES and EVENTS—Nos. 3207/8, 3220, MS3225c, Bicentenary of Brandenburg Gate, Berlin; 3209/11, 3221, MS3225d, 17th World Scout Jamboree, Korea; 3212/13, 3217, 3222, MS3225a/b, Birth centenary (1990) of Charles de Gaulle (French statesman); 3214, 3218, 3223, MS3225e, Death bicentenary of Mozart; 3215, 750th anniv of Hanover; 3216, MS3225f, 700th anniv of Swiss Confederation; 3219, Centenary of Otto Lilienthal's first gliding experiments; 3224, Centenary of Trans-Siberian Railway.

No. 3222 is inscribed "Pope John VI" in error.

476 Disney Characters Carol Singing, 1989

1991. Christmas. Walt Disney Christmas Cards. Multicoloured.

3226	80c. Type **476**	10	10
3227	$2.55 Disney characters and carol singers in tram, 1962	15	15
3228	$5 Donald Duck and Pluto with parcel, 1971	20	20
3229	$6.40 "SEASON'S GREETINGS" and Mickey Mouse with candle, 1948	30	20
3230	$7.65 Mickey Mouse as Father Christmas, 1947	30	20
3231	$8.90 Shadow of Pinocchio with candle, 1939	30	20
3232	$50 Three Little Pigs dancing on wolf rug, 1933	1·25	1·25
3233	$50 Conductor and Donald Duck, 1940 (vert)	1·25	1·25
3234	$50 Elephant and ostrich carol singing, 1940 (vert)	1·25	1·25
3235	$50 Hippo, centaurs, Pinocchio and Goofy, 1940 (vert)	1·25	1·25
3236	$50 Snow White, Dopey, Mickey and Minnie, 1940 (vert)	1·25	1·25
3237	$50 Dino, Pluto and Walt Disney, 1940 (vert)	1·25	1·25
3238	$50 Mickey Mouse in sleigh, 1974 (vert)	1·25	1·25
3239	$50 Three Little Pigs, Winnie the Pooh, Bambi and Thumper, 1974 (vert)	1·25	1·25
3240	$50 Baloo, King Louis, Lady and the Tramp, 1974 (vert)	1·25	1·25
3241	$50 Alice, Robin Hood, the Cheshire Cat and Goofy, 1974 (vert)	1·25	1·25
3242	$50 Dumbo, Pinocchio, Peter Pan, Tinkerbelle, Seven Dwarfs and Donald Duck, 1974 (vert)	1·25	1·25
3243	$50 Pluto pulling sleigh, 1974 (vert)	1·25	1·25
3244	$200 Mickey and mice carol singing, 1949	4·00	5·00

MS3245 Eight sheets. (a) 127×101 mm. $260 Mickey, Minnie, Clarabelle and Pluto in mail coach, 1932 (vert). (b) 127×101 mm. $260 Mickey's House, 1935 (vert). (c) 101×127 mm. $260 Jose Carioca, Rooster and Donald Duck on flying carpet, 1944 (vert). (d) 101×127 mm. $260 Casey at the Bat and dancers, 1945. (e) 127×101 mm. $260 Mickey, Donald and Goofy on musical score, 1946. (f) 127×101 mm. $260 Picture of Winnie the Pooh, 1969. (g) 127×101 mm. $260 Father Christmas in chimney, 1969 (vert). (h) 101×127 mm. $260 Letters of film titles forming Mickey Mouse, 1978 (vert) Set of 8 sheets .... 30·00 30·00

477 Gus Gander playing Ice Hockey

1991. Winter Olympic Games, Albertville (1992) (3rd issue). Walt Disney Cartoon Characters. Multicoloured.

3246	$6.40 Type **477**	35	15
3247	$7.65 Mickey and Minnie Mouse in bobsleigh	40	15
3248	$8.90 Donald's Nephews on luge and skis	45	15
3249	$12.80 Goofy freestyle skiing	60	20

3250	$50 Goofy ski jumping	1·75	1·25
3251	$100 Donald and Daisy Duck speed skating	2·50	2·00
3252	$130 Pluto cross-country skiing	2·75	2·75
3253	$190 Mickey and Minnie Mouse ice dancing	3·50	4·50

MS3254 Two sheets, each 125×100 mm. (a) $225 Donald's nephew curling. (b) $225 Donald Duck slalom skiing Set of 2 sheets .... 8·00 8·50

478 Columbus landing on Trinidad

1992. 500th Anniv of Discovery of America by Columbus. Multicoloured.

3255	$6.40 Type **478**	55	40
3256	$7.65 Columbus the map-maker	65	45
3257	$8.90 Fleet blown off course	65	45
3258	$12.80 Map of third voyage and Columbus in chains	65	55
3259	$15.30 Sighting land	65	55
3260	$50 *Nina* and *Pinta*	1·75	1·00
3261	$75 *Santa Maria*	2·00	1·25
3262	$100 Columbus trading with Amerindians	2·25	1·75
3263	$125 Crew and sea monster	2·75	2·75
3264	$130 Columbus landing on San Salvador and map of first voyage	2·75	2·75
3265	$140 Priest and Amerindians	2·75	2·75
3266	$150 Columbus before King Ferdinand and Queen Isabella of Spain	2·75	2·75

MS3267 Three sheets, each 126×91 mm. (a) $280 *Nina* (vert). (b) $280 Columbus (vert). (c) $280 Early map of Caribbean Set of 3 sheets .... 14·00 16·00

479 Tom Mix in *The Great K&A; A Train Robbery*, 1926

1992. Classic Movie Posters. Multicoloured.

3268	$8.90 Type **479**	50	40
3269	$12.80 Richard Dix and Irene Dunne in *Cimarron*, 1931	60	50
3270	$15.30 Fatty Arbuckle in *Buzzin' Around*, 1934	60	50
3271	$25 Tom Tyler in *The Adventures of Captain Marvel*, 1941	80	70
3272	$30 Boris Karloff in *The Mummy*, 1932	1·25	85
3273	$50 Rudolph Valentino in *A Sainted Devil*, 1924	1·40	1·10
3274	$75 Seven posters for *A Tale of Two Cities*, 1935	1·75	1·40
3275	$100 Chester Conklin in *A Tugboat Romeo*, 1916	2·50	1·90
3276	$130 Douglas Fairbanks in *The Thief of Bagdad*, 1924	2·75	2·25
3277	$150 Laurel and Hardy in *Bacon Grabbers*, 1929	3·25	3·00
3278	$190 Marx Brothers in *A Night at the Opera*, 1935	4·00	4·25
3279	$200 Orson Welles in *Citizen Kane*, 1941	4·00	4·25

MS3280 Four sheets. (a) 70×99 mm. $225 Babe Ruth in *Babe Comes Home*, 1927. (b) 70×99 mm. $225 Mae West in *She Done Him Wrong*, 1933. (c) 70×99 mm. $225 Charlie Chaplin in *The Circus*, 1928. (d) 99×70 mm. $225 Poster for never-made film *Zeppelin*, 1933. Imperf Set of 4 sheets .... 15·00 17·00

1992. Easter. Paintings by Dürer. As T **204a** of Gambia. Multicoloured.

3281	$6.40 *The Martyrdom of Ten Thousand* (detail)	25	10
3282	$7.65 *Adoration of the Trinity* (detail of Virgin Mary)	25	10
3283	$12.80 *The Martyrdom of Ten Thousand* (execution detail)	40	20
3284	$15.30 *Adoration of the Trinity* (different detail)	45	25
3285	$50 *The Martyrdom of Ten Thousand* (detail of bishop)	1·00	75
3286	$100 *Adoration of the Trinity* (different detail)	1·50	1·50
3287	$130 *The Martyrdom of Ten Thousand* (different detail)	1·75	2·00
3288	$190 *Adoration of the Trinity* (different detail)	3·25	4·00

MS3289 Two sheets, each 71×101
mm. (a) $225 *The Martyrdom of Ten
Thousand.* (b) $225 *Adoration of the
Trinity* (detail of Christ on cross) Set
of 2 sheets ... 8·00 8·50

1992. Baha'i Holy Year. Surch **BAHA'I HOLY YEAR 1992**
and value.
3290 $6.40 on 60c. Plate No. 10
(Series 1) (No. 1521)
3291 $7.65 on 60c. Plate No. 31
(Series 1) (No. 1523)
3292 $8.90 on 60c. Plate No. 19
(Series 1) (No. 1522)
3293 $50 on 60c. Plate No. 2 (Series
1) (No. 1519)

481 Queen Elizabeth II and
Duke of Edinburgh

1992. 40th Anniv of Queen Elizabeth II's Accession.
Multicoloured.
3294 $8.90 Type **481** ... 75 25
3295 $12.80 Queen at Trooping the
Colour ... 85 30
3296 $100 Queen at Coronation ... 4·00 2·50
3297 $130 Queen in Garter robes ... 4·50 3·25
MS3298 Two sheets, each 119×79 mm.
(a) $225 Queen in Coronation robes.
(b) $225 Queen in blue dress Set
of 2 sheets ... 9·00 9·50

482 Holy Cross Church,
Annai Rupununi

1992. 150th Anniv of Diocese of Guyana. Multicoloured.
3299 $6.40 Type **482** ... 15 10
3300 $50 St. Peter's Church ... 80 65
3301 $100 Interior of St. George's
Cathedral (vert) ... 1·50 1·60
3302 $190 Map of Guyana (vert) ... 2·75 3·75
MS3303 104×70 mm. $225 Religious
symbols ... 3·75 4·50

483 Burmese

1992. Cats. Multicoloured.
3304 $5 Type **483** ... 40 10
3305 $6.40 Turkish van ... 40 10
3306 $12.80 American shorthair ... 60 20
3307 $15.30 Sphynx ... 60 20
3308 $50 Egyptian mau ... 1·25 1·00
3309 $50 Russian blue ... 1·25 1·00
3310 $50 Havana brown ... 1·25 1·00
3311 $50 Himalayan ... 1·25 1·00
3312 $50 Manx ... 1·25 1·00
3313 $50 Cornish rex ... 1·25 1·00
3314 $50 Black Persian ... 1·25 1·00
3315 $50 Scottish fold ... 1·25 1·00
3316 $50 Siamese ... 1·25 1·00
3317 $100 Japanese bobtail ... 1·75 1·25
3318 $130 Abyssinian ... 2·00 1·75
3319 $250 Oriental shorthair ... 3·00 3·25
MS3320 Four sheets, each 99×69 mm.
(a) $250 Chartreuse (vert). (b) $250
Turkish angora (vert). (c) $250 Maine
coon (vert). (d) $250 Chinchilla (vert)
Set of 4 sheets ... 19·00 16·00

484 Red Howler

1992. Animals of Guyana. Multicoloured.
3321 $8.90 Type **484** ... 20 10
3322 $12.80 Ring-tailed coati ... 25 20
3323 $15.30 Jaguar ... 30 20
3324 $25 Two-toed sloth ... 50 30
3325 $50 Giant armadillo ... 1·00 80
3326 $75 Giant anteater ... 1·50 1·75
3327 $100 Capybara ... 1·75 1·90
3328 $130 Ocelot ... 2·00 2·25
MS3329 Two sheets, each 70×100 mm.
(a) $225 Woolly opossum (vert). (b)
$225 Night monkey (vert) Set of
2 sheets ... 8·00 9·00
No. MS3329a is inscribed "WOLLY OPOSSUM" in error.

485 Oligocene Mammoth

1992. Elephants. Multicoloured.
3330 $50 Type **485** ... 1·50 1·50
3331 $50 Mid-Miocene stegodon ... 1·50 1·50
3332 $50 Pliocene mammoth ... 1·50 1·50
3333 $50 Carthaginian elephant
crossing Alps, 219 B.C. ... 1·50 1·50
3334 $50 Ceremonial elephant of
Maharaja of Mysore, India ... 1·50 1·50
3335 $50 Elephant pulling teak
trunks, Burma ... 1·50 1·50
3336 $50 Tiger-hunting by elephant,
India ... 1·50 1·50
3337 $50 Elephant towing raft on
River Kwai, Thailand ... 1·50 1·50
MS3338 110×80 mm. $225 African
elephant ... 6·00 6·00

486 Palomino

1992. Horses. Multicoloured.
3339 $190 Type **486** ... 3·00 3·00
3340 $190 Appaloosa ... 3·00 3·00
3341 $190 Clydesdale ... 3·00 3·00
3342 $190 Arab ... 3·00 3·00
3343 $190 Morgan ... 3·00 3·00
3344 $190 Friesian ... 3·00 3·00
3345 $190 Pinto ... 3·00 3·00
3346 $190 Thoroughbred ... 3·00 3·00
MS3347 109×80 mm. $190 Lipizzaner
(47×29 mm) ... 4·50 4·50
No. 3340 is inscribed "APALOOSA" in error.

1992. International Conference on Nutrition, Rome. Surch
INT. CONFERENCE ON NUTRITION 1992 and value.
3348 $6.40 on 150c. Plate No. 45
(Series 1) (No. 1769)
3349 $7.65 on 150c. Plate No. 42
(Series 1) (No. 1768)
3350 $8.90 on 150c. Plate No. 40
(Series 1) (No. 1767)
3351 $10 on 200c. Plate No. 43
(Series 1) (No. 1658)
3352 $50 on 200c. Plate No. 43
(Series 1) (No. 1658)

488 Marklin Swiss *Crocodile*
Locomotive, 1933

1992. "Genova '92" International Thematic Stamp
Exhibition. Toy Trains from German Manufacturers.
Multicoloured.
3353- $45×9 Made by Marklin: Type
3361 **488**; French tramcar, 1902;
British *Flatiron* tank engine,
1913; German switching
engine, 1970; Third class
carriage, 1909; American
style locomotive, 1904;
Zurich tramcar, 1928; Central
London Railway locomotive
in Paris-Orleans livery, 1904;
British GWR *Great Bear*
locomotive, 1909 ... 6·25 6·50
3362- $45×9 Made by Marklin: LMS
3370 *Precursor* tank engine, 1923;
American *Congressional
Limited* passenger carriage,
1908; Swiss Type "Ae 3/6"
locomotive, 1934; German
Class 80, 1975; British
Southern Railways third
class carriage, 1926; LNWR
Bowen-Cooke tank engine,
1913; London Underground
Two Penny Tube, 1901; French
Paris-Orsay steeplecab, 1920;
Passenger locomotive, 1895 ... 6·25 6·50
3371- $45×9 Made by Marklin:
3379 American style locomotive,
1907; German passenger
carriage, 1908; British Great
Eastern Railway locomotive,
1908; London Underground
steeplecab, 1904; Santa Fe
Railroad diesel locomotive,
1962; British GNR locomotive,
1903; Caledonian Railway
Cardean, 1906; British LNWR
passenger carriage, 1903;
Swiss St. Gotthard Railway
locomotive, 1920 ... 6·25 6·50

3380- $45×9 Made by Marklin: British
3388 LB SCR tank engine No.
22, 1920; Central London
Railway steeplecab locomotive, 1904; German *Borsig*
streamlined, 1935; French
Paris-Lyon-Mediterranee
first class carriage, 1929;
American style locomotive
No. 1021, 1904; French Paris-
Orsay long-nose steeplecab,
1920; British LNER *Cock o' the
North*, 1936; Prussian State
Railways Class P8, 1975; Ger-
man diesel railcar set, 1937 ... 6·25 6·50
3389- $45×9 Marklin North British
3397 Railway *Atlantic*, 1913; Bing
British LNWR *Precursor*, 1916;
Marklin British GWR *King
George V*, 1937; Marklin *Kaiser Train* passenger carriage,
1901; Bing side tank locomo-
tive No. 88, 1904; Marklin
steeplecab, 1912; Marklin
Adler, 1935; Bing British GWR
County of Northampton,
1909; Bing British Midland
Railway *Black Prince*, 1908 ... 6·25 6·50
3398- $45×9 Made by Bing: Midland
3406 Railway "Deeley Type" No.
483, 1909; British Midland
Railway No. 2631, 1903;
German Pacific, 1927; British
GWR third class coach, 1926;
British LSWR "M7" No. 109,
1909; Side tank engine *Pilot*,
1901; British LNWR Webb
Cauliflower, 1912; Side tank
locomotive No. 112, 1910;
British GNR *Stirling Single*,
1904 ... 6·25 6·50
3407- $45×9 Carette tin *Penny Bazaar*
3415 train, 1904; Winteringham
locomotive, 1917; Carette
British Northeastern Railway
Smith Compound, 1905;
Carette S.E. C.R. steam railcar,
1908; Carette British Great
Northern Railway Stirling
Single No. 776, 1903; Carette
British Midland Railways
locomotive No. 1132M, 1911;
Carette London Metropolitan
Railway Co. *Westinghouse*
locomotive No. 5, 1908;
Carette Clestory carriage,
1907; Carette steam railcar
No. 1, 1906 ... 6·25 6·50
3416- $45×9 Made by Bing: Engine
3424 and tender, 1895; British
Midland Railway *Singl*" No.
650, 1913; No. 524/510
reversible locomotive, 1916;
Kaiser Train passenger
carriage, 1902; British rural
station, 1915; British LSWR
M7 tank locomotive, 1909;
Windcutter, 1912; British
Great Central Railway *Sir
Sam Fay*, 1914; Scottish Caledonian Railway *Dunalastair*
locomotive, 1910 ... 6·25 6·50
MS3425 Eight sheets, each 116×83
mm. (a) $350 Bing contractor's loco-
motive No. 18, 1904 (51×39 mm). (b)
$350 Marklin rack railway steeplecab
locomotive, 1908 (51×39 mm). (c)
$350 Bing British GWR *County of
Northampton* locomotive, 1909
(51×39 mm).(d) $350 Marklin French
Paris-Lyon–Mediterranean Pacific
locomotive, 1912 (51×39 mm). (e)
$350 Bing Pabst Blue Ribbon beer
refrigerator wagon, 1925 (51×39
mm). (f) $350 Marklin French *Moun-
tain Etat* locomotive, 1933 (51×39
mm). (g) $350 Marklin German
National Railroad Class 0-1 Pacific
locomotive, 1937 (51×39 mm). (h)
$350 Marklin American *Commodore
Vanderbilt* locomotive, 1937 (51×39
mm) Set of 8 sheets ... 32·00 32·00

1992. Postage Stamp Mega Event, New York. Sheet
100×70 mm, containing multicoloured design as T
207a of Gambia, but vert.
MS3426 $325 Statue of Liberty ... 7·00 8·00

489 Aquarius

1992. Signs of the Zodiac. Multicoloured.
3427 $30 Type **489** ... 85 85
3428 $30 Pisces ... 85 85
3429 $30 Aries ... 85 85
3430 $30 Taurus ... 85 85
3431 $30 Gemini ... 85 85
3432 $30 Cancer ... 85 85
3433 $30 Leo ... 85 85
3434 $30 Virgo ... 85 85
3435 $30 Libra ... 85 85
3436 $30 Scorpio ... 85 85
3437 $30 Sagittarius ... 85 85
3438 $30 Capricorn ... 85 85

490 City Walls and
Two Birds

1992. Bible Stories (1st series). David and Goliath.
Multicoloured.
3439 $25 Type **490** ... 50 50
3440 $25 City walls and one bird
at right ... 50 50
3441 $25 Sun over city gateway ... 50 50
3442 $25 City walls and one bird
at left ... 50 50
3443 $25 City walls and no birds ... 50 50
3444 $25 Philistine army and edge
of shield ... 50 50
3445 $25 Goliath's head and torso ... 50 50
3446 $25 Goliath's arm and spear ... 50 50
3447 $25 Philistine army and
spearhead ... 50 50
3448 $25 Philistine infantry ... 50 50
3449 $25 Philistine cavalry and
infantry ... 50 50
3450 $25 Goliath's shield ... 50 50
3451 $25 Goliath's waist and thigh ... 50 50
3452 $25 David with sling ... 50 50
3453 $25 Israelite soldier with spear ... 50 50
3454 $25 Two Israelite soldiers with
spears and shields ... 50 50
3455 $25 Goliath's right leg ... 50 50
3456 $25 Goliath's left leg (face value
at foot) ... 50 50
3457 $25 David's legs and Israelite
standard ... 50 50
3458 $25 Three Israelite soldiers ... 50 50
3459 $25 Israelite soldier and parts
of two shields ... 50 50
3460 $25 Israelite soldier with sword ... 50 50
3461 $25 Back of Israelite soldier ... 50 50
3462 $25 Israelite soldier leaning
on rock ... 50 50
3463 $25 Israelite soldier looking left ... 50 50
Nos. 3439/63 were printed together, *se-tenant*, forming
a composite design.
See also Nos. 4020/4116.

491 Count Von Zeppelin and
Airship over Lake Constance,
1909

1992. Anniversaries and Events. Multicoloured.
3464 $12.80 Type **491** ... 50 35
3465 $50 "Voyager I" and Jupiter ... 1·50 1·00
3466 $50 Adenauer with Pres.
Kennedy, 1961 ... 1·00 1·00
3467 $100 Aeromedical airlift ... 2·00 2·00
3468 $100 Boutu ("Amazon Dolphin") ... 2·00 2·00
3469 $130 Baby gorilla ... 2·50 2·50
3470 $130 Mobile eye screening unit
and doctor with child ... 2·50 2·50
3471 $130 *Stars and Stripes* (winning
yacht, 1987) ... 2·50 2·50
3472 $130 Lift-off of "Voyager I", 1977 ... 2·50 2·50
3473 $190 Adenauer with President
De Gaulle of France, 1962 ... 3·25 3·25
3474 $225 Von Zeppelin and airship
preparing for take-off, 1905 ... 3·50 3·50
MS3475 Four sheets. (a) 76×105 mm.
$225 Ferdinand von Zeppelin (vert).
(b) 116×80 mm. $225 Earth from
Space (vert). (c) 84×111 mm. $225
Konrad Adenauer (vert). (d) 87×111
mm. $225 "Hyperohus marmoratus
(tree frog)" (vert) Set of 4 sheets ... 15·00 16·00
ANNIVERSARIES and EVENTS: Nos. 3464, MS3475a,
75th death anniv of Count Ferdinand von Zeppelin; 3465,
3472, MS3475b, International Space Year; 3466, 3473,
MS3475c, 75th death anniv of Konrad Adenauer (German
statesman); 3467, United Nations World Health Organization projects; 3468/9, MS3475d, Earth Summit '92, Rio;
3470, 75th anniv of International Association of Lions
Clubs; 3471, Americas Cup Yachting Championship.

492 Hyacinth Macaw

1993. South American Parrots. Multicoloured.
3476 80c. Type **492** ... 30 15
3477 $6.40 Scarlet macaw (preening) ... 50 25
3478 $7.65 Buffon's macaw ("Green
Macaw") (vert) ... 50 25
3479 $15.30 Orange-chinned para-
keet ("Tovi Parakeet") ... 70 50
3480 $50 Blue and yellow macaw ... 1·00 80

3481	$100 Military macaw (vert)	1·50	1·25
3482	$130 Green-winged macaw ("Red and Green Macaw") (vert)	1·75	1·75
3483	$190 Chestnut-fronted macaw ("Severa Macaw")	2·50	3·00

MS3484 Two sheets, each 108×74 mm.
(a) $225 Scarlet macaw. (b) $225
Monk parakeet (vert) Set of 2 sheets 7·00 7·50

493 Crimson Topaz

1993. Birds of Guyana. Multicoloured.

3485	$50 Type **493**	75	75
3486	$50 Bearded bellbird	75	75
3487	$50 Amazonian umbrellabird	75	75
3488	$50 Paradise jacamar	75	75
3489	$50 Paradise tanager	75	75
3490	$50 White-tailed trogon	75	75
3491	$50 Scarlet macaw	75	75
3492	$50 Hawk-headed parrot ("Red-fan Parrot")	75	75
3493	$50 Red-billed toucan	75	75
3494	$50 White-faced antcatcher ("White-plumed Antbird")	75	75
3495	$50 Crimson-hooded manakin	75	75
3496	$50 Guianan cock of the rock	75	75

MS3497 70×100 mm. $325 Tufted
coquette (horiz) 5·00 5·50

Nos. 3485/96 were printed together, *se-tenant*, with the backgrounds forming a composite design.

494 Manatee surfacing

1993. Endangered Species. American Manatee ("Caribbean Manatee"). Multicoloured.

3498	$6.40 Type **494**	60	30
3499	$7.60 Cow and calf feeding	60	30
3500	$8.90 Manatee underwater	60	30
3501	$50 Two manatees	2·25	2·25

495 Tamandua

1993. Animals of Guyana. Multicoloured.

3502	$50 Type **495**	75	75
3503	$50 Pale-throated sloth ("Three-toed Sloth")	75	75
3504	$50 Red howler	75	75
3505	$50 Four-eyed opossum	75	75
3506	$50 Black spider monkey	75	75
3507	$50 Giant otter	75	75
3508	$50 Red brocket	75	75
3509	$50 Brazilian tree porcupine	75	75
3510	$50 Tayra	75	75
3511	$50 Brazilian tapir	75	75
3512	$50 Ocelot	75	75
3513	$50 Giant armadillo	75	75

MS3514 100×70 mm. $325 Paca 4·50 5·00

Nos. 3502/13 were printed together, *se-tenant*, the backgrounds forming a composite design.
No. 3505 is inscribed "Four-eyed Opossium" in error.

496 Pteranodon

1993. Prehistoric Animals. Multicoloured.
3515– $30×12 (Type **496**; Ceara-
3526 dactylus; Eudimorphodon;
Pterodactylus; Stauirko-
saurus; Euoplocephalus;
Tuojiangosaurus; Oviraptor;
Protoceratops; Panaoplo-
saurus; Psittacosaurus;
Corythosaurus) 6·25 7·00

3527–	$30×12 (Sordes; Quetzal-		
3538	coatlus; Archaeopteryx in flight; Rhamphorynchus; Spinosaurus; Anchisaurus; Stegosaurus; Leaellynosaurus; Minmi; Heterdontosaurus; Esothosaurus; Deninonychus)	6·25	7·00
3539–	$30×12 (Archaeopteryx on		
3550	branch; Pteranodon (different); Quetzalcoatlus (three); Protoavis; Dicraeosaurus; Moschops; Lystrosaurus; Dimetrondon; Staurikosaurus; Cacops; Diarthrognathus; Estemmenosuchus)	6·25	7·00

Nos. 3515/26, 3527/38 and 3539/50 respectively were printed together, *se-tenant*, with the backgrounds forming composite designs.

1993. 40th Anniv of Coronation. As T **215a** of Gambia. Multicoloured.

3551	$25 Queen Elizabeth II in Coronation robes (photograph by Cecil Beaton)	85	85
3552	$50 Royal gems	1·25	1·25
3553	$75 Queen Elizabeth and Prince Philip	1·40	1·40
3554	$130 Queen opening Parliament	1·75	2·00

MS3555 69×100 mm. $325 *Queen in
Coronation Robes* (Sir James Gunn)
(28½×42½ mm) 5·00 5·50

497 Gabriel Marquez (author)

1993. Famous People of the Twentieth Century. Multicoloured

(a) Arts and Literature.

3556	$50 Type **497**	75	75
3557	$50 Pablo Picasso (artist)	75	75
3558	$50 Cecil De Mille (film director)	75	75
3559	$50 Martha Graham (dancer)	75	75
3560	$50 Peace dove (inscr "20th Century Arts and Literature")	75	75
3561	$50 Charlie Chaplin (actor)	75	75
3562	$50 Paul Robeson (actor)	75	75
3563	$50 Rudolph Dunbar (musician)	75	75
3564	$50 Louis Armstrong (musician)	75	75

MS3565 100×70 mm. $250 Elvis Presley
(singer) (vert) 3·50 3·50

(b) Science and Medicine.

3566	$50 Louis Leakey (archaeologist and anthropologist)	1·00	75
3567	$50 Jonas Salk (discoverer of polio vaccine)	1·00	75
3568	$50 Hideyo Noguchi (bacteriologist)	1·00	75
3569	$50 Karl Landsteiner (pathologist)	1·00	75
3570	$50 As No. 3550, but inscr "20th Century Science and Medicine"	1·00	75
3571	$50 Sigmund Freud (founder of psychoanalysis)	1·00	75
3572	$50 Louis Pasteur (chemist)	1·00	75
3573	$50 Madame Curie (physicist)	1·00	75
3574	$50 Jean Baptiste Perrin (physicist)	1·00	75

MS3575 100×70 mm. $250 Einstein's
Theory of Relativity equation (vert) 3·50 3·50

(c) Sports Personalities.

3576	$50 O. J. Simpson (American football)	1·10	75
3577	$50 Rohan Kanhai (cricket)	1·10	75
3578	$50 Gabriela Sabatini (tennis)	1·10	75
3579	$50 Severiano Ballesteros (golf)	1·10	75
3580	$50 As No. 3550, but inscr "20th Century Sports"	1·10	75
3581	$50 Franz Beckenbauer (football)	1·10	75
3582	$50 Pele (football)	1·10	75
3583	$50 Wilt Chamberlain (basketball)	1·10	75
3584	$50 Nadia Comaneci (gymnastics)	1·10	75

MS3585 100×70 mm. $250 Jackie
Robinson (baseball) (vert) 3·50 3·50

(d) Peace and Humanity.

3586	$100 Mahatma Gandhi (India)	1·40	1·10
3587	$100 Dalai Lama (Tibet)	1·40	1·10
3588	$100 Michael Manley (Jamaica)	1·40	1·10
3589	$100 Perez de Cuellar (U.N. Secretary-General)	1·40	1·10
3590	$100 Peace dove and globe	1·40	1·10
3591	$100 Mother Teresa (India)	1·40	1·10
3592	$100 Martin Luther King (U.S.A.)	1·40	1·10
3593	$100 Pres. Nelson Mandela (South Africa)	1·40	1·10
3594	$100 Raoul Wallenberg (Sweden)	1·40	1·10

MS3595 100×70 mm. $250 Nobel
Peace Prize scroll (vert) 3·50 3·50

(e) Politics.

3596	$100 Nehru (India)	1·40	1·10
3597	$100 Dr. Eric Williams (Trinidad and Tobago)	1·40	1·10
3598	$100 Pres. John F. Kennedy (U.S.A.)	1·40	1·10
3599	$100 Pres. Hugh Desmond Hoyte (Guyana)	1·40	1·10
3600	$100 Peace dove and map of the Americas	1·40	1·10
3601	$100 Friedrich Ebert (Germany)	1·40	1·10
3602	$100 Pres F. D. Roosevelt (U.S.A.)	1·40	1·10
3603	$100 Mikhail Gorbachev (Russia)	1·40	1·10
3604	$100 Sir Winston Churchill (Great Britain)	1·40	1·10

MS3605 100×70 mm. $250 Flags
of United Nations and member
countries (vert) 3·50 3·50

(f) Transportation and Technology.

3606	$100 Douglas DC-3 cargo plane	1·40	1·25
3607	$100 Space Shuttle	1·40	1·25
3608	$100 Concorde	1·40	1·25
3609	$100 Count Ferdinand von Zeppelin and "Graf Zeppelin"	1·40	1·25
3610	$100 Peace dove and rocket trails	1·40	1·25
3611	$100 Marconi and aerial tower	1·40	1·25
3612	$100 Adrian Thompson (mountaineer) and Mt. Roraima	1·40	1·25
3613	$100 "Hikari" express train, Japan	1·40	1·25
3614	$100 Johann von Neumann and computer	1·40	1·25

MS3615 100×70 mm. $250 Lunar
module "Eagle" on Moon 4·00 4·00

Nos. 3556/64, 3566/74, 3576/84, 3586/94, 3596/3604 and 3606/14 respectively were printed together, *se-tenant*, with composite background designs on Nos. 3586/94, 3596/3604 and 3606/14.
No. 3562 is inscribed "Paul Roebeson" in error.

1881– Picasso *–1973*

498 *Bather, Paris* (Picasso)

1993. Anniversaries and Events. Multicoloured (except No. **MS**3628c).

3616	$15.30 Type **498**	15	20
3617	$25 Willy Brandt with Prime Minister of Israel Golda Meir, 1969 (horiz)	40	40
3618	$50 *Pantaloons* (left half) (Tadeusz Brzozowski)	50	55
3619	$50 Georg Hackl (men's single luge, 1992)	70	70
3620	$50 Astrolabe	70	70
3621	$75 Miedzyrecz Castle	75	80
3622	$100 *Two Nudes* (Picasso)	1·00	1·10
3623	$130 *Pantaloons* (right half) (Tadeusz Brzozowski)	1·25	1·40
3624	$130 Karen Magnussen (women's figure skating, 1972)	1·50	1·50
3625	$190 *Nude seated on a Rock* (Picasso)	1·90	2·25
3626	$190 Willy Brandt at Georgsmarienhutten Steel Mill, 1969 (horiz)	2·25	2·50
3627	$190 Dish aerial	2·25	2·50

MS3628 Five sheets. (a) 104×75 mm.
$300 Copernicus. (b) 75×104 mm.
$325 *The Rescue* (detail) (Picasso).
(c) 104×75 mm. $325 Willy Brandt
giving interview, 1969 (brown and
black). (d) 99×70 mm. $325 *Children
in the Garden* (Wladyslaw Podkowinski) (horiz). (e) 75×104 mm. $325
German four-man bobsleigh team,
1992 Set of 5 sheets 20·00 22·00

ANNIVERSARIES and EVENTS: Nos. 3616, 3622, 3625, **MS**3628b, 20th death anniv of Picasso (artist); 3617, 3626, **MS**3628c, 80th birth anniv (1992) of Willy Brandt (German politician); 3618, 3621, 3623, **MS**3628d, "Polska '93" International Stamp Exhibition, Poznan; 3619, 3624, **MS**3628e, Winter Olympic Games '94, Lillehammer; 3620, 3627, **MS**3628a, 450th death anniv of Copernicus (astronomer).

Nos. 3618 and 3623 were printed together, *se-tenant*, forming a composite design showing the complete painting.

499 Audie Murphy (most decorated U.S. serviceman)

1993. 50th Anniv of Second World War (1st issue). Multicoloured.

3629	$6.40 Type **499**	80	20
3630	$7.65 Allied troops in Normandy (8 June 1944)	80	25
3631	$8.90 American howitzer crew, Battle of Montecassino (18 May 1944)	85	30
3632	$12.80 American aircraft attacking *Yamato* (Japanese battleship), Battle of East China Sea (7 April 1945)	90	50
3633	$15.30 St. Basil's Cathedral, Moscow (Foreign Ministers' Conference, 19 October 1943)	90	50
3634	$50 American troops crossing Rhine at Remagen (7 March 1945)	1·75	75
3635	$100 Boeing B-29 Superfortresses raiding Japan from China (15 June 1944)	2·50	1·75
3636	$130 General Patton and map of Sicily (17 August 1943)	2·75	2·25
3637	$190 Destruction of *Tirpitz* (German battleship) (12 November 1944)	3·75	3·25
3638	$200 American forces in Brittany (1 August 1944)	3·75	3·25
3639	$225 American half-track (ceasefire in Italy, 2 May 1945)	4·00	3·75

MS3640 100×69 mm. $325 Meeting of
American and Russian troops on the
Elbe (25 April 1945) 5·00 6·00

No. 3631 is inscribed "Monte Casino" in error. See also Nos. 3641/60 and 3942/61.

500 R.A.A.F. Bristol Type 156 Beaufighter, Battle of the Bismarck Sea (2-4 March 1943)

1993. 50th Anniv of Second World War (2nd issue). Multicoloured.

3641	$50 Type **500**	80	80
3642	$50 Lockheed P-38 Lightning attacking Admiral Yamamoto's plane, Bougainville (7 April 1943)	80	80
3643	$50 Consolidated B-24 Liberator bombers, Tarawa (17-19 September 1943)	80	80
3644	$50 North American B-25 Mitchell bomber, Rabaul (12 October 1943)	80	80
3645	$50 U.S. Navy aircraft attacking Makin (19 November 1943)	80	80
3646	$50 U.S.A.A.F. bombers on first daylight raid over Germany (27 January 1943)	80	80
3647	$50 R.A.F. de Havilland D.H.98 Mosquito bombers on first daylight raid over Berlin (30 January 1943)	80	80
3648	$50 Allied aircraft over Hamburg (24-30 July 1943)	80	80
3649	$50 Consolidated B-24 Liberators bombing Ploesti oil refineries, Rumania (1 August 1943)	80	80
3650	$50 German nightfighter attacking Allied bombers over Berlin (18 November 1943)	80	80
3651	$50 Japanese aircraft carriers during Operation 1 (7 April 1943)	80	80
3652	$50 Lt. John F. Kennedy's motor torpedo boat U.S.S. *PT109* in Blackett Strait (1 August 1943)	80	80
3653	$50 U.S.S. *Enterprise* (aircraft carrier)	80	80
3654	$50 American battleships bombarding Rabaul (12 October 1943)	80	80
3655	$50 American landing craft at Cape Gloucester (26 December 1943)	80	80
3656	$50 Commissioning of U.S.S. *Bogue* (first anti-submarine escort carrier) (February 1943)	80	80
3657	$50 Grumman FM-2 Wildcat fighters from U.S.S. *Bogue* sinking "U-118"	80	80
3658	$50 U-boat launching torpedo during peak of Battle of the Atlantic (March 1943)	80	80
3659	$50 Surrender of Italian fleet at Malta (10 September 1943)	80	80
3660	$50 H.M.S. *Duke of York* (battleship) sinking *Scharnhorst* (26 December 1943)	80	80

501 Stuart Pearce (England)

1993. World Cup Football Championship, U.S.A. (1994) (1st issue). Multicoloured.

3661	$5 Type **501**	15	10
3662	$6.40 Ronald Koeman (Netherlands)	15	10
3663	$7.65 Gianluca Vialli (Italy)	20	10
3664	$12.80 McStay (Scotland) and Alemao (Brazil)	30	20
3665	$15.30 Ceulemans (Belgium) and Butcher (England)	30	20
3666	$50 Dragan Stojkovic (Yugoslavia)	75	65
3667	$100 Ruud Gullit (Netherlands)	1·25	1·25
3668	$130 Miloslav Kadlec (Czechoslovakia)	1·40	1·50
3669	$150 Ramos (Uruguay) and Berthold (Germany)	1·75	2·00
3670	$190 Baggio (Italy) and Wright (England)	2·25	2·50
3671	$200 Yarentchuck (Russia) and Renquin (Belgium)	2·40	2·75
3672	$225 Timofte (Rumania) and Aleinikov (Russia)	2·50	3·00

MS3673 Two sheets. (a) 101×73 mm. $325 Salvatore Schillaci (Italy) and Jose Pintos (Uruguay) (horiz). (b) 73×101 mm. $325 Rene Higuita (Colombia) Set of 2 sheets — 9·00 9·50

See also Nos. 4142/58.

502 Sir Shridath Ramphal

1993. First Recipients of Order of the Caribbean Community. Multicoloured.

3674	$7.65 Type **502**	60	50
3675	$7.65 William Demas	60	50
3676	$7.65 Derek Walcott	1·00	65

1993. Christmas. Paintings by Rubens and Durer. As T **211b** of Gambia. Each black, yellow and red (Nos. 3678, 3680/1, 3684) or multicoloured (others).

3677	$6.40 *The Holy Family under the Apple Tree* (detail) (Rubens)	15	10
3678	$7.65 *The Virgin in Glory* (detail) (Durer)	15	10
3679	$12.80 *The Holy Family under the Apple Tree* (different detail) (Rubens)	20	15
3680	$15.30 *The Virgin in Glory* (different detail) (Durer)	20	20
3681	$50 *The Virgin in Glory* (different detail) (Durer)	70	55
3682	$130 *The Holy Family under the Apple Tree* (different detail) (Rubens)	1·50	1·60
3683	$190 *The Holy Family under the Apple Tree* (different detail) (Rubens)	2·25	2·50
3684	$250 *The Virgin in Glory* (different detail) (Durer)	2·75	3·25

MS3685 Two sheets. (a) 126×101 mm. $325 *The Holy Family under the Apple Tree* (Rubens). (b) 101×126 mm. $325 *The Virgin in Glory* (woodcut by Durer from *The Life of the Virgin*) Set of 2 sheets — 7·00 8·50

1993. Bicentenary of the Louvre, Paris. As T **209b** of Gambia. Multicoloured.

3686	$50 *Mona Lisa* (Leonardo da Vinci)	60	60
3687- 3694	$50×8 *Self-portrait with Spectacles* (Chardin); *Infanta Maria Theresa* (Velazquez); *Spring* (Arcimboldo); *The Virgin of Sorrows* (Bouts); *The Student* (Fragonard); *Francois I* (Clouet); *Le Condottiere* (Antonello da Messina); *La Bohemienne* (Hals)	4·50	5·00
3695- 3702	$50×8 *The Village Bride* (left detail) (Greuze); *The Village Bride* (centre detail); *The Village Bride* (right detail); *Self-portrait* (Melendez); *The Knight, the Girl and the Mountain* (Baldung-Grien); *The Young Beggar* (Murillo); *The Pilgrims of Emmaus* (left detail) (Le Nain); *The Pilgrims of Emmaus* (right detail)	4·50	5·00

3703- 3710	$50×8 *Woman with a Flea* (detail) (Crespi); *The Woman with Dropsy* (detail) (Dou); *Portrait of a Couple* (Ittenbach); *Cleopatra* (Moreau); *Riches* (Vouet); *Old Man and Young Boy* (Ghirlandaio); *Louis XIV* (Rigaud); *The Drinker* (Pieter de Hooch)	4·50	5·00
3711- 3718	$50×8 *Woman with a Flea* (Crespi); *Self-portrait at Easel* (Rembrandt); *Algerian Women* (detail) (Delacroix); *Head of a Young Man* (Raphael); *Venus and The Graces* (detail) (Botticelli); *Still Life with Chessboard* (detail) (Lubin Baugin); *Lady Macbeth* (Fussli); *The Smoke-filled Room* (detail) (Chardin)	4·50	5·00
3719- 3726	$50×8 *The Virgin with the Rabbit* (Titian); *The Virgin with the Rabbit* (detail of head) (Titian); *The Beautiful Gardener* (detail) (Raphael); *The Lace-maker* (Vermeer); *Jeanne d'Aragon* (detail) (Raphael); *The Astronomer* (Vermeer); *The Rialto Bridge* (detail) (Canaletto); *Sigismond Malatesta* (Piero della Francesca)	4·50	5·00

MS3727 Six sheets, each 95×70 mm. (a) $325 *Mona Lisa* and details (Leonardo da Vinci) (84×56 mm). (b) $325 *The Coronation of Napoleon I* (David) (84×56 mm). (c) $325 *Farmyard* (Jan Brueghel the Younger) (84×56 mm). (d) $325 *The Marriage Feast at Cana* (Veronese) (84×56 mm). (e) $325 *The Fortune-teller* (Caravaggio) (84×56 mm). (f) $325 *The Rialto Bridge* (Canaletto) (84×56 mm) Set of 6 sheets — 23·00 25·00

503 "Donald's Better Self", 1938

1993. Donald Duck Film Posters. Multicoloured.

3728- 3735	$60×8 Type **503**; "Donald's Golf Game", 1938; "Sea Scouts", 1939; "Donald's Penguin", 1939; "A Good Time for a Dime", 1941; "Truant Officer Donald"; "Orphan's Benefit", 1941; "Chef Donald", 1941	7·00	8·00
3736- 3743	$60×8 "The Village Smithy"; "Donald's Snow Fight"; "Donald's Garden"; "Donald's Gold Mine"; "The Vanishing Private"; "Sky Trooper"; "Bellboy Donald"; "The New Spirit", all 1942	7·00	8·00
3744- 3751	$60×8 "Saludos Amigos", 1943; "The Eyes Have It", 1945; "Donald's Crime", 1945; "Straight Shooters", 1947; "Donald's Dilemma", 1947; "Bootle Beetle", 1947; "Daddy Duck", 1948; "Soup's On", 1948	7·00	8·00
3752- 3759	$80×8 "Donald's Happy Birthday", 1949; "Sea Salts", 1949; "Honey Harvester", 1949; "All in a Nutshell", 1949; "The Greener Yard", 1949; "Slide, Donald, Slide", 1949; "Lion Around", 1950; "Trailer Horn", 1950	7·00	8·00
3760- 3767	$80×8 "Bee at the Beach", 1950; "Out on a Limb", 1950; "Corn Chips", 1951; "Test Pilot Donald", 1951; "Lucky Number", 1951; "Out of Scale", 1951; "Bee on Guard", 1951; "Let's Stick Together", 1952	7·00	8·00
3768- 3775	$80×8 "Trick or Treat", 1952; "Don's Fountain of Youth", 1953; "Rugged Bear", 1953; "Canvas Back Duck", 1953; "Dragon Around", 1954; "Grin and Bear It", 1954; "The Flying Squirrel", 1954; "Up a Tree", 1955	7·00	8·00
3776- 3781	$80×8 Scenes from "Pirate Gold": In the crow's nest; Aracuan Bird carrying treasure chest; Donald with treasure map; Donald at souvenir stall; Aracuan Bird with Donald; Donald on jetty (all horiz)	7·00	8·00

MS3782 Five sheets, each 129×103 mm. (a) $500 Book cover of "The Wise Little Hen", 1934 (horiz). (b) $500 Sketch for "Timber", 1941. (c) $500 Fan-card for "The Three Caballeros", 1945 (horiz). (d) $500 Fan-card for "Melody Time", 1948. Imperf. (e) $500 Donald Duck Set of 5 sheets — 27·00 29·00

504 Aladdin

1993. "Aladdin" (film). Disney Cartoon Characters. Multicoloured.

3783- 3790	$7.65×8 Type **504**; Abu the monkey; Jasmine; Rajah the tiger; Jafar; Iago the parrot; The Sultan; The Genie		
3791- 3799	$50×9 Jafar and magic scarab; Tiger Head entrance, Cave of Wonders; Jafar; Aladdin and Abu at breakfast; Aladdin rescuing Jasmine; Aladdin, Jasmine and Abu; Rajah comforts Jasmine; Jafar disguised as an old man; Aladdin and Abu in treasure chamber (all horiz)		
3800- 3808	$65×9 Aladdin with lamp and magic carpet; The Genie measuring Aladdin; Abu turned into an elephant; Aladdin in disguise at palace; Aladdin and Jasmine on magic carpet; Aladdin in disguise, Jasmine and Sultan; Aladdin fighting Jafar; Aladdin and Jasmine; The Genie with suitcase and golf clubs (all horiz)		

MS3809 Four sheets, each 127×102 mm. (a) $325 Aladdin, The Genie, Abu and magic carpet in Cave of Wonders (horiz). (b) $325 Aladdin in disguise on elephant. (c) $325 Aladdin and Jasmine on magic carpet (horiz). (d) $325 The Genie, The Sultan, Jasmine, Aladdin and Abu (horiz) Set of 4 sheets — 18·00 19·00

505 President Dr. Cheddi Jagan

1993. First Anniv of Election of President Jagan.

3810	**505** $6.40 multicoloured	40	30

MS3811 97×69 mm. $325 "REBIRTH OF DEMOCRACY" emblem — 3·50 4·00

1994. "Hong Kong '94" International Stamp Exhibition (1st issue). As T **222a** of Gambia. Multicoloured.

3812	$50 Hong Kong 1984 Royal Hong Kong Jockey Club $1.30 stamp and Happy Valley Racecourse	80	90
3813	$50 Guyana 1992 Movie Posters $190 stamp and Happy Valley Racecourse	80	90

Nos. 3812/13 were printed together, *se-tenant*, with the centre part of each pair forming a composite design.

1994. "Hong Kong '94" International Stamp Exhibition (2nd issue). Ch'ing Dynasty Snuff Boxes (Nos. 3814/19) or Porcelain (Nos. 3820/5). As T **222b** of Gambia. Multicoloured.

3814	$20 Painted enamel in shape of bamboo	35	40
3815	$20 Painted enamel showing woman	35	40
3816	$20 Amber with lions playing ball	35	40
3817	$20 Agate in shape of two gourds	35	40
3818	$20 Glass overlay with dog design	35	40
3819	$20 Glass with foliage design	35	40
3820	$20 Covered jar with dragon design	35	40
3821	$20 Rotating brush-holder	35	40
3822	$20 Covered jar with horses design	35	40
3823	$20 Amphora vase with bats and peaches	35	40
3824	$20 Tea caddy with Fo dogs	35	40
3825	$20 Vase with camellias and peaches design	35	40

1994. Centenary of the Sign for the Mahdi. Nos. 1622/4 and 1634 surch **CENTENARY Sign For The MAHDI 1894-1994** and new value.

3826	$6 on 60c. Plate No. 73 (Series 1) (horiz)		
3827	$20 on 200c. Plate No. 33 (Series 1) (horiz)		
3828	$30 on 60c. Plate No. 57 (Series 1) (horiz)		

3829	$35 on 60c. Plate No. 75 (Series 1) (horiz)		

The surcharges on Nos. 3826 and 3828 show the third line as "MADHI".

1994. Hummel Figurines. As T **501a** of Ghana. Multicoloured.

3830	$20 Girl holding inscribed heart	25	25
3831	$25 Boy with heart under arm	30	30
3832	$35 Baker	40	40
3833	$50 Girl with pot of flowers	60	55
3834	$60 Girl with trumpet, pot plant and bird	70	65
3835	$130 Four girls	1·50	1·50
3836	$190 Boy and two girls with dog	2·25	2·50
3837	$250 Boy with cake and dog	2·75	3·50

MS3838 Two sheets, each 92×124 mm. (a) $6 As No. 3835; $25 No. 3831; $30 As No. 3830; $190 No. 3836. (b) $20 As No. 3832; $35 As No. 3837; $60 No. 3834; $130 As No. 3833 Set of 2 sheets — 6·00 6·50

1994. 75th Anniv of I.L.O. Nos. 1760 and 1629/30 surch **I L O 75th Anniversary 1919-1994** and new value.

3839	$6 on 130c. on 130c. Plate No. 13 (Series 1)		
3840	$30 on 120c. on 120c. Plate No. 58 (Series 1)		
3841	$35 on 120c. on 120c. Plate No. 56 (Series 1)		

1994. Centenary (1992) of Sierra Club (environmental protection society). Endangered Species. As T **224a** of Gambia. Multicoloured.

3842	$70 Red Kangaroo with young	90	90
3843	$70 Head of American alligator	90	90
3844	$70 Head of bald eagle	90	90
3845	$70 Giant panda eating bamboo	90	90
3846	$70 Head of red kangaroo	90	90
3847	$70 Alaskan brown bear sitting	90	90
3848	$70 Bald eagle	90	90
3849	$70 Head of giant panda	90	90
3850	$70 Red kangaroo (horiz)	90	90
3851	$70 Whooping crane facing left (horiz)	90	90
3852	$70 Male whooping crane in courtship display (horiz)	90	90
3853	$70 Whooping crane looking right (horiz)	90	90
3854	$70 Alaskan brown bear and cub (horiz)	90	90
3855	$70 Alaskan brown bear fishing (horiz)	90	90
3856	$70 Bald eagle on branch (horiz)	90	90
3857	$70 Giant panda (horiz)	90	90
3858	$70 American alligator (logo at left) (horiz)	90	90
3859	$70 American alligator (logo at right) (horiz)	90	90
3860	$70 Italian Alps at sunrise (horiz)	90	90
3861	$70 Italian Alps and meadow (horiz)	90	90
3862	$70 Mono Lake at sunset (horiz)	90	90
3863	$70 Rock pinnacles, Mono Lake (horiz)	90	90
3864	$70 Sea lion	90	90
3865	$70 Head of sea lion	90	90
3866	$70 Sea lions on rocks	90	90
3867	$70 Rock pinnacles, Mono Lake	90	90
3868	$70 Sierra Club Centennial emblem (black, brown and green)	90	90
3869	$70 Lake, Italian Alps	90	90
3870	$70 Summit of Matterhorn	90	90
3871	$70 Matterhorn and village	90	90
3872	$70 Clouds over Matterhorn	90	90

1994. Royal Visit. Nos. 3551/4 optd **ROYAL VISIT FEB 19-22, 1994**.

3873	$25 Queen Elizabeth II in Coronation robes (photograph by Cecil Beaton)	2·00	2·00
3874	$50 Royal gems	2·50	2·50
3875	$75 Queen Elizabeth and Prince Philip	3·00	3·00
3876	$130 Queen opening Parliament	3·25	3·25

MS3877 69×100 mm. $325 "Queen in Coronation Robes" (Sir James Gunn) (28½×42½ mm) — 8·00 8·00

509 Cestrum parqui

1994. Flowers. Multicoloured.

3878	$6.40 Type **509**	15	10
3879	$7.65 Brunfelsia calycina	15	10
3880	$12.80 Datura rosei	20	15
3881	$15.30 Ruellia macrantha	20	20

3882	$50 Portlandia albiflora	50	55
3883	$50 Clusia grandiflora	50	55
3884	$50 Begonia haageana	50	55
3885	$50 Fuchsia simplicicaulis	50	55
3886	$50 Guaiacum officinale	50	55
3887	$50 Pithecoctenium cynan-choides	50	55
3888	$50 Sphaeralcea umbellata	50	55
3889	$50 Erythrina poeppigiana	50	55
3890	$50 Steriphoma paradoxa	50	55
3891	$50 Allemanda violacea	50	55
3892	$50 Centropogon cornutus	50	55
3893	$50 Passiflora quadrangularis	50	55
3894	$50 Victoria amazonica	50	55
3895	$50 Cobaea scandens	50	55
3896	$50 Pyrostegia venusta	50	55
3897	$50 Petrea kohautiana	50	55
3898	$50 Hippobroma longiflora	50	55
3899	$50 Cleome hassleriana	50	55
3900	$50 Verbena peruviana	50	55
3901	$50 Tropaeolum peregrinum	50	55
3902	$50 Plumeria rubra	50	55
3903	$50 Selenicereus grandiflorus	50	55
3904	$50 Mandevilla splendens	50	55
3905	$50 Pereskia aculeata	50	55
3906	$50 Ipomoea learii	50	55
3907	$130 Pachystachys coccinea	1·25	1·40
3908	$190 Beloperone guttata	1·90	2·25
3909	$250 Ferdinandusa speciosa	2·50	3·00

MS3910 Two sheets, each 99×70 mm.
(a) $325 Lophospermum erubescens.
(b) $325 Columnea fendleri Set of
2 sheets .... 7·50 8·50

Nos. 3883/94 and 3895/3906 respectively were printed together, se-tenant, forming composite background designs.

1994. 25th Anniv of First Moon Landing (1st issue). As T 227a of Gambia. Multicoloured.

3911	$60 Walter Dornberger and launch of first A-4 rocket	90	90
3912	$60 Rudolph Nebel and "Surveyor 1"	90	90
3913	$60 Robert H. Goddard and "Apollo 7"	90	90
3914	$60 Kurt Debus and view of Earth from Moon ("Apollo 8")	90	90
3915	$60 James T. Webb and "Apollo 9"	90	90
3916	$60 George E. Mueller and "Apollo 10" lunar module	90	90
3917	$60 Wernher von Braun and launch of "Apollo 11"	90	90
3918	$60 Rocco A. Petrone and "Apollo 11" astronaut on Moon	90	90
3919	$60 Eberhard Rees and "Apollo 12" astronaut on Moon	90	90
3920	$60 Charles A. Berry and damaged "Apollo 13"	90	90
3921	$60 Thomas O. Paine and "Apollo 14" before splashdown	90	90
3922	$60 A. F. Staats and "Apollo 15" on Moon	90	90
3923	$60 Robert R. Gilruth and "Apollo 16" astronaut on Moon	90	90
3924	$60 Ernst Stuhlinger and "Apollo 17" crew on Moon	90	90
3925	$60 Christopher C. Kraft and X-30 National Aero-Space Plane	90	90
3926	$60 Rudolf Opitz and Messerschmitt Me 163B Komet (rocket engine), 1943	90	90
3927	$60 Clyde W. Tombaugh and "face" on Mars	90	90
3928	$60 Hermann Oberth and scene from The Girl in the Moon	90	90

MS3929 125×112 mm. $325 Frank J. Everest Jr and "Apollo 11" anniversary logo .... 4·50 5·00

See also Nos. 4169/87.

1994. Centenary of International Olympic Committee. Medal Winners. As T 227b of Gambia. Multicoloured.

3930	$20 Nancy Kerrigan (1994 figure skating silver)	30	30
3931	$35 Sawao Kato (Japan) (1976 gymnastics gold)	50	50
3932	$130 Florence Griffith Joyner (U.S.A.) (1988 100 and 200 metres gold)	1·75	2·00

MS3933 110×80 mm. $325 Mark Wasmeier (Germany) (1994 super giant slalom and giant slalom gold) .... 4·00 4·50

1994. Centenary of First English Cricket Tour to the West Indies (1995). As T 397a of Grenada. Multicoloured.

3934	$20 Clive Lloyd (Guyana and West Indies) (vert)	65	30
3935	$35 Carl Hooper (Guyana and West Indies) and Wisden Trophy	75	50
3936	$60 Graham Hick (England) and Wisden Trophy	1·40	1·50

MS3937 79×100 mm. $200 English team of 1895 (black and brown) .... 3·25 3·00

1994. 50th Anniv of D-Day. Aircraft. As T 227c of Gambia. Multicoloured.

3938	$6 Supermarine Spitfire Mk XI fighter on photo reconnaissance	40	15
3939	$35 North American B-25 Mitchell bomber	85	50
3940	$190 Republic P-47 Thunderbolt fighters	3·00	3·50

MS3941 109×79 mm. $325 Avro Type 683 Lancaster bomber of 419 Squadron .... 4·75 5·00

1994. 50th Anniv of Second World War (3rd issue). As T 500. Multicoloured.

3942	$60 Paratroops drop, D-Day	1·00	80
3943	$60 Glider assault, D-Day	1·00	80
3944	$60 U.S.S. Arkansas (battleship) bombarding Omaha Beach, D-Day	1·00	80
3945	$60 U.S. fighters attacking train	1·00	80
3946	$60 Allied landing craft approaching beaches	1·00	80
3947	$60 Troops in beach obstacles	1·00	80
3948	$60 Commandos leaving landing craft	1·00	80
3949	$60 U.S. flail tank destroying mines	1·00	80
3950	$60 U.S. tank breaking through sea wall	1·00	80
3951	$60 Tanks and infantry advancing	1·00	80
3952	$60 Landings at Anzio (22 January 1944)	1·00	80
3953	$60 R.A.F. attacking Amiens Prison (18 February 1944)	1·00	80
3954	$60 Soviet Army tank in Sevastopol (9 May 1944)	1·00	80
3955	$60 British bren-gun carriers at the Gustav Line (19 May 1944)	1·00	80
3956	$60 D-Day landings (6 June 1944)	1·00	80
3957	$60 "V-1" over London (13 June 1944)	1·00	80
3958	$60 Allies entering Paris (19 August 1944)	1·00	80
3959	$60 German "V-2" rocket ready for launch (8 September 1944)	1·00	80
3960	$60 Sinking of Tirpitz (German battleship) (12 November 1944)	1·00	80
3961	$60 U.S. tanks at Bastogne (29 December 1944)	1·00	80

1994. "Philakorea '94" International Stamp Exhibition, Seoul (1st issue). As T 227d of Gambia. Multicoloured.

3962	$6 Socialist ideals statue, Pyongyang (vert)	10	10
3963	$25 Statue of Admiral Yi Sun-sin (vert)	30	30
3964	$60 Fruits and mountain peaks	70	75
3965	$60 Manchurian crane, bamboo and peaks	70	75
3966	$60 Rising sun and two cranes on pine	70	75
3967	$60 Five cranes on pine and peak	70	75
3968	$60 Three cranes in flight	70	75
3969	$60 Sea, rocky shore and fungi	70	75
3970	$60 Sea, rocky shore and fruit	70	75
3971	$60 Hind at seashore and fruit	70	75
3972	$60 Stag in pine forest	70	75
3973	$60 Deer and fungi by waterfall	70	75
3974	$60 Tops of pines and mountain peaks	70	75
3975	$60 Manchurian crane in flight	70	75
3976	$60 Three cranes on pine tree	70	75
3977	$60 Crane on pine tree	70	75
3978	$60 Top of fruit tree	70	75
3979	$60 Stag and two hinds on mountainside	70	75
3980	$60 Deer and fungi	70	75
3981	$60 Stag by waterfall and hind drinking	70	75
3982	$60 Pine tree, fruit and fungi	70	75
3983	$60 Fungi on mountainside	70	75
3984	$120 Sokkat'ap Pagoda, Pulguksa	1·40	1·60
3985	$130 Village Guardian (statue), Chejudo Island	1·40	1·60

MS3986 Two sheets. (a) 104×73 mm. $325 Europeans at the Korean Court (early lithograph). (b) 73×104 mm. $325 Pagoda by Ch'urae-am Rock Set of 2 sheets .... 7·00 8·00

Nos. 3964/73 and 3974/83, all 23×49 mm, were printed together, se-tenant, in sheetlets of 10, each sheetlet forming a composite design showing panels from a screen painting of longevity symbols from the late Chosun dynasty.

See also Nos. 4117/41.

510 Miki Maya

1994. 80th Anniv of Takarazuka Revue of Japan. Multicoloured.

3987	$20 Type 510	55	60
3988	$20 Fubuki Takane	55	60
3989	$20 Seika Kuze	55	60
3990	$20 Saki Asaji	55	60
3991	$60 Mira Anju (34×47 mm)	75	80
3992	$60 Yuki Amami (34×47 mm)	75	80
3993	$60 Maki Ichiro (34×47 mm)	75	80
3994	$60 Yu Shion (34×47 mm)	75	80

511 Heliconius melpomene

1994. Butterflies. Multicoloured.

3995	$6 Type 511	30	20
3996	$20 Helicopis cupido	60	45
3997	$25 Agrias claudina	65	50
3998	$30 Parides coelus	70	60
3999	$50 Heliconius hecale	85	75
4000	$50 Anaea marthesia	85	75
4001	$50 Brassolis astyra	85	75
4002	$50 Heliconius melpomene	85	75
4003	$50 Haetera piera	85	75
4004	$50 Morpho diana	85	75
4005	$50 Parides coelus	85	75
4006	$50 Catagramma pitheas	85	75
4007	$50 Nessaea obrinus	85	75
4008	$50 Automeris janus	85	75
4009	$50 Papilio torquatus	85	75
4010	$50 Eunica sophonisba	85	75
4011	$50 Ceratinia nise	85	75
4012	$50 Panacea procilla	85	75
4013	$50 Pyrrhogyra neaerea	85	75
4014	$50 Morpho deidamia	85	75
4015	$50 Dismorphia orise	85	75
4016	$60 Morpho diana	1·25	85
4017	$190 Dismorphia orise	3·00	3·00
4018	$250 Morpho deidamia	3·50	3·50

MS4019 Four sheets. (a) 104×76 mm. $325 Anaea eribotes. (b) 104×76 mm. $325 Eunica sophonisba. (c) 110×80 mm. $325 Hamadryas velutina (39×30 mm). (d) 110×80 mm. $325 Agrias claudina (39×30 mm) Set of 4 sheets .... 16·00 17·00

512 Jacob

1994. Bible Stories (2nd series). Multicoloured

(a) Joseph

4020-	$20×24 arranged as blocks of		
4043	4 depicting Jacob giving Joseph a coat of many colours (Type 512 at top left); Joseph thrown into a pit; Joseph sold as a slave; Joseph accused by Potiphar's wife; Joseph interprets Pharoah's dreams; Joseph reunited with his brothers	8·00	8·00

(b) The Parting of the Red Sea.

4044-	$20×24 Palm trees on shore;		
4067	Pyramids; Palm trees on shore and black cloud; Three palm trees; Blue and white dove; Red and white bird; Egyptian army engulfed by sea; Yellow and white dove; Red and green fishes; Egyptian chariot with wall of water at left; Chariots between walls of water; Dolphins; Two doves; Israelites and water to left; Israelites and water to right; Turquoise and purple fishes; Israelites with tree at left; Iraelites with goats; Moses; Israelites with tree at right; Israelites with woman on horse; Israelites with old man and woman carrying pack; Israelites with woman carrying young child; Israelites with cart	8·00	8·00

(c) Ruth.

4068-	$20×24 arranged as blocks of		
4091	6 depicting Ruth and Naomi; Ruth gleaning in cornfield; Boaz establishing kinsman's rights; Naomi with Ruth, Boaz and Obed	8·00	8·00

(d) Daniel in the Lions' Den.

4092-	$20×25 Palm fronds and		
4116	hibiscus flower; Magnificent frigate bird and palm fronds; Magnificent frigate birds and tops of stone pillars; Magnificent frigate bird, pillars and sail at bottom right; Hibiscus, sails of ship and top of pillar; Yellow arum lilies and palm trees; Heads of adult and immature magnificent frigate birds and palm trees; Palm trees, butterfly and stone pillars; Two butterflies and stone pillars; Stone pillar and sailing ship; Great egret (standing); Purple irises and palm trees; Daniel; Angel; Donkey foal; Orchids; Lioness and two cubs; Daniel's legs and lions; Lion; Three crowns; Goat and kid; Kid; Cub and head of lion; Lioness; Great egret in flight	29·00	30·00

Nos. 4020/43, 4044/67, 4068/91 and 4092/4116 respectively were printed together, se-tenant, forming composite designs.

513 Peregrine Falcon

1994. "Philakorea '94" International Stamp Exhibition, Seoul (2nd issue). Birds of the World. Multicoloured.

4117	$35 Type 513	55	55
4118	$35 Great spotted woodpecker	55	55
4119	$35 White-throated kingfisher	55	55
4120	$35 Andean cock of the rock ("Peruvian Cock of the Rock")	55	55
4121	$35 Yellow-headed amazon	55	55
4122	$35 Victoria crowned pigeon	55	55
4123	$35 Little owl	55	55
4124	$35 Common pheasant ("Ring-necked Pheasant")	55	55
4125	$35 Eurasian goldfinch ("Goldfinch")	55	55
4126	$35 Jay	55	55
4127	$35 Keel-billed toucan ("Sulphur-breasted Toucan")	55	55
4128	$35 Blue and white flycatcher ("Japanese Blue Flycatcher")	55	55
4129	$35 Northern goshawk	55	55
4130	$35 Northern lapwing ("Lapwing")	55	55
4131	$35 Long-wattled umbrellabird ("Ornate Umbrellabird")	55	55
4132	$35 Slaty-headed parakeet	55	55
4133	$35 Regent bowerbird	55	55
4134	$35 Egyptian goose	55	55
4135	$35 White-winged crossbill	55	55
4136	$35 Bohemian waxwing ("Waxwing")	55	55
4137	$35 Ruff	55	55
4138	$35 Hoopoe	55	55
4139	$35 Superb starling	55	55
4140	$35 Great jacamar	55	55

MS4141 Two sheets, each 70×100 mm. (a) $325 American bald eagle. (b) $325 Gould's violetear Set of 2 sheets .... 12·00 11·00

514 Paulo Futre (Portugal)

1994. World Cup Football Championship, U.S.A. (2nd issue). Multicoloured.

4142	$6 Type 514	15	10
4143	$35 Lyndon Hooper (Canada)	50	40
4144	$60 Enzo Francescoli (Uruguay)	65	65
4145	$60 Paolo Maldini (Italy)	65	65
4146	$60 Guyana player	65	65
4147	$60 Bwalya Kalusha (Zambia)	65	65
4148	$60 Diego Maradona (Argentina)	65	65
4149	$60 Andreas Brehme (Germany)	65	65
4150	$60 Eric Wynalda (U.S.A.) (pursuing ball)	65	65
4151	$60 John Doyle (U.S.A.)	65	65
4152	$60 Eric Wynalda (U.S.A.) (kicking ball)	65	65
4153	$60 Thomas Dooley (U.S.A.)	65	65
4154	$60 Ernie Stewart (U.S.A.)	65	65

4155	$60 Marcelo Balboa (U.S.A.)	65	65
4156	$60 Bora Milutinovic (U.S.A. coach)	65	65
4157	$190 Freddy Rincon (Colombia)	1·90	3·00

MS4158 Two sheets. (a) 105×75 mm. $325 "94" symbol and player. (b) 75×105 mm. $325 Oller Watson (U.S.A.) Set of 2 sheets   7·50   8·50

Nos. 4145/50 and 4151/6 respectively were printed together, *se-tenant*, forming composite background designs.

515 Anja Fichtel (individual foil, 1988)

1994. Olympic Games, Atlanta (1996) (1st issue). Previous German Gold Medal Winners. Multicoloured.

4159	$6 Type **515**	15	10
4160	$25 Annegret Richter (100 m, 1976) (vert)	35	30
4161	$30 Heike Henkel (high jump, 1992) (vert)	40	35
4162	$35 Armin Hary (100 m, 1960) (vert)	40	40
4163	$50 Heide Rosendahl (long jump, 1972) (vert)	60	65
4164	$60 Josef Neckermann (dressage, 1968) (vert)	90	75
4165	$130 Heike Drechsler (long jump, 1988) (vert)	1·50	1·75
4166	$190 Ulrike Mayfarth (high jump, 1984) (vert)	2·50	2·75
4167	$250 Michael Gross (200 m freestyle and 100 m butterfly, 1984)	3·00	3·50

MS4168 Three sheets. (a) 105×75 mm. $135 Markus Wasmeier (skiing, 1994) (vert); $190 Katja Seizinger (skiing, 1994) (vert). (b) 105×75 mm. $325 Franziska van Almsick (swimming, 1992) (vert). (c) 75×105 mm. $325 Steffi Graf (tennis, 1988, 1992) (vert) Set of 3 sheets   11·00   11·00

See also Nos. 4492/4508 and 4739/88.

516 Dog Laika and Rocket, 1957

1994. 25th Anniv of First Moon Landing (2nd issue). Multicoloured.

4169	$60 Type **516**	90	80
4170	$60 Yuri Gagarin (first man in space), 1961	90	80
4171	$60 John Glenn (first American to orbit Earth), 1962	90	80
4172	$60 Edward White walking in space, 1965	90	80
4173	$60 Neil Armstrong, walking on Moon and "Apollo 11" logo	90	80
4174	$60 "Luna 16" leaving Moon, 1970	90	80
4175	$60 Lunar Module 1 on Moon, 1970	90	80
4176	$60 Skylab 1, 1973	90	80
4177	$60 Astronauts and Apollo–Soyuz link-up, 1975	90	80
4178	$60 "Mars 3"	90	80
4179	$60 "Mariner 10"	90	80
4180	$60 "Voyager"	90	80
4181	$60 "Pioneer"	90	80
4182	$60 "Giotto"	90	80
4183	$60 "Magellan"	90	80
4184	$60 "Galileo"	90	80
4185	$60 "Ulysses"	90	80
4186	$60 "Cassini"	90	80

MS4187 Two sheets, each 142×104 mm. (a) $325 "Apollo 11" astronauts. (b) $325 "Galileo" Set of 2 sheets   8·50   9·00

Nos. 4178/86 were printed together, *se-tenant*, with the backgrounds forming a composite design of Space.

517 South Caroline Railroad *Best Friend of Charleston*, 1830, U.S.A.

1994. History of Trains. Steam Locomotives. Multicoloured.

4188	$25 Type **517**	60	40

4189	$25 South Eastern Railway No. 285, 1882	60	40
4190	$30 Camden Amboy Railway No. 1 *John Bull*, 1831, U.S.A.	60	45
4191	$30 Stephenson "Patentee" type locomotive, 1837	60	45
4192	$30 *Atlantic*, 1832	60	45
4193	$30 *Stourbridge Lion*, 1829, U.S.A.	60	45
4194	$30 Polonceau locomotive, 1854	60	45
4195	$30 *Thomas Rogers*, 1855, U.S.A.	60	45
4196	$30 *Vulcan*, 1858	60	45
4197	$30 *Namur*, 1846	60	45
4198	$30 John Jarvis's *De Witt Clinton*, 1831, U.S.A.	60	45
4199	$30 Seguin locomotive, 1829	60	45
4200	$30 Stephenson's *Planet*, 1830	60	45
4201	$30 Norris locomotive, 1840	60	45
4202	$30 *Sampson*, 1867, U.S.A.	60	45
4203	$30 *Andrew Jackson*, 1832	60	45
4204	$30 *Herald*, 1831	60	45
4205	$30 *Cumberland*, 1845, U.S.A.	60	45
4206	$30 Pennsylvania Railroad Class K, 1880	60	45
4207	$30 Cooke locomotive No. 11, 1885	60	45
4208	$30 *John B. Turner*, 1867, U.S.A.	60	45
4209	$30 Baldwin locomotive, 1871	60	45
4210	$30 Richard Trevithick's locomotive, 1803	60	45
4211	$30 John Stephens's locomotive, 1825	60	45
4212	$30 John Blenkinsop's locomotive, 1814	60	45
4213	$30 *Pennsylvania*, 1803	60	45
4214	$300 Mount Washington Cog Railway locomotive No. 6, 1886	4·00	3·50
4215	$300 Stroudley locomotive *Brighton*, 1872	4·00	3·50

MS4216 Two sheets, each 100×70 mm. (a) $250 Est Railway locomotive, 1878. (b) $300 *Claud Hamilton*, 1900 Set of 2 sheets   9·00   8·00

No. 4198 is inscribed "West Point Foundry 1832 Locomotive" and No. 4202 "Union Iron Works os San Francisco", both error.

1994. Christmas. Religious Paintings. As T **231**a of Gambia. Multicoloured.

4217	$6 *Joseph with the Christ Child* (Guido Reni)	15	10
4218	$20 *Adoration of the Christ Child* (Girolamo Romanino)	30	25
4219	$25 *Adoration of the Christ Child with St. Barbara and St. Martin* (Raffaello Botticini)	35	30
4220	$30 *Holy Family* (Pompeo Batoni)	40	35
4221	$35 *Flight into Egypt* (Bartolommeo Carducci)	45	40
4222	$60 *Holy Family and the Baptist* (Andrea del Sarto)	80	70
4223	$120 *Sacred Conversation* (Cesare de Sesto)	2·00	2·25
4224	$190 *Madonna and Child with Saints Joseph and John the Baptist* (Pontormo)	2·75	3·50

MS4225 Two sheets. (a) 112×93 mm. $325 *Presentation of Christ in the Temple* (Fra Bartolomeo). (b) 85×95 mm. $325 *Holy Family and St. Elizabeth and St. John the Baptist* (Francisco Primaticcio) Set of 2 sheets   7·50   8·00

518 Riker and Dr. Crusher

1994. *Star Trek Generations* (film). Designs showing *Enterprise* crew in 19th-century naval uniforms (Nos. 4226/34) or in 23rd-century (Nos. 4235/43). Multicoloured.

4226	$100 Type **518**	1·75	1·50
4227	$100 Geordi, Dr. Crusher with Lt. Worf in chains	1·75	1·50
4228	$100 Captain Picard	1·75	1·50
4229	$100 Data and Geordi	1·75	1·50
4230	$100 "U.S.S. Enterprise" (sailing ship)	1·75	1·50
4231	$100 Captain Picard and Riker on quarterdeck	1·75	1·50
4232	$100 Data	1·75	1·50
4233	$100 Lt. Worf	1·75	1·50
4234	$100 Dr. Crusher	1·75	1·50
4235	$100 Captain Picard	1·75	1·50
4236	$100 Riker	1·75	1·50
4237	$100 Captain Kirk	1·75	1·50
4238	$100 Soron with phaser	1·75	1·50

4239	$100 Captains Kirk and Picard on horseback	1·75	1·50
4240	$100 Klingon women	1·75	1·50
4241	$100 Captains Kirk and Picard	1·75	1·50
4242	$100 Troi	1·75	1·50
4243	$100 Captain Picard and Data	1·75	1·50
4244	$100 "BOLDLY GO" film poster	1·75	1·50

MS4245 86×103 mm. $500 U.S.S. "Enterprise" from film poster (horiz)   6·00   6·50

519 Cross and Map of Guyana

1994. Centenary of Sisters of Mercy in Guyana.

4246	**519** $60 multicoloured	1·00	80

1994. First Recipients of Order of the Caribbean Community. As T **393**a of Grenada. Multicoloured.

4247	$60 Sir Shridath Ramphal	65	75
4248	$60 William Demas	65	75
4249	$60 Derek Walcott	1·60	75

520 Garfield Sobers congratulating Brian Lara

1995. Brian Lara's Achievements in Cricket. Multicoloured.

4250	$20 Type **520**	55	25
4251	$30 Brian Lara setting world record for highest Test Match score (vert)	60	35
4252	$375 Lara and Chanderpaul	4·75	4·75

MS4253 70×100 mm. $300 Brian Lara (vert)   3·25   3·50

521 Babe Ruth

1995. Birth Centenary of Babe Ruth (baseball player). Each brown and black.

4254	$65 Type **521**	60	80
4255	$65 Preparing to bat (full-length photo)	60	80
4256	$65 Head and shoulders portrait (cap with limp brim)	60	80
4257	$65 In retirement (bare-headed)	60	80
4258	$65 Running (in plain shirt)	60	80
4259	$65 Head and shoulders portrait (cap with emblem and stiff brim)	60	80
4260	$65 Wearing "NEW YORK" shirt	60	80
4261	$65 Preparing to hit (in "NEW YORK" shirt)	60	80
4262	$65 Wearing "YANKEES" shirt	60	80
4263	$65 At base with bat on shoulder (in striped shirt)	60	80
4264	$65 Watching the ball (in striped shirt)	60	80
4265	$65 In cap and coat at Old Timer's Day, Yankee Stadium, 1948	60	80

MS4266 89×118 mm. $500 Babe Ruth (horiz)   5·00   5·25

522 Mickey Mouse as Family Doctor

1995. Disney Characters at Work. Multicoloured.

4267–4275	$30×9 Type **522**; Goofy and optometrist; Daisy Duck as nurse; Scrooge McDuck as psychiatrist; Daisy Duck as physiotherapist; Horace Horsecollar and dentist; Goofy as radiologist; Goofy as pharmacist; Big Pete as chiropractor	4·00	4·50

4276–4284	$30×9 Mickey Mouse as vet; Donald Duck training seals; Ludwig von Duck as animal psychiatrist; Goofy as ornithologist; Daisy Duck grooming Old English sheepdog; Minnie Mouse as herpetologist; Mickey Mouse as pet shop keeper with Pluto; J. Audubon Woodlore as park ranger; Donald Duck as aquarist	4·00	4·50
4285–4293	$30×9 Mickey Mouse as animator with Pluto; Goofy the tailor with Mickey Mouse; Pete the glassblower with Morty; Minnie Mouse painting Clarabelle; Daisy Duck sculpting Donald; Donald Duck as potter; Chip and Dale the watchmakers; Donald Duck the locksmith; Grandma Duck making quilt	4·00	4·50
4294–4301	$35×8 Mickey Mouse as policeman; Donald Duck as fireman; Uncle Scrooge as ambulance driver; Grandma Duck as crossing patrol; Daisy Duck as museum attendant and Donald as visitor; Goofy as census taker and family of rabbits; Horace Horsecollar and Big Pete as street maintenance workers; Donald Duck as sanitation worker at recycling bin (all vert)	4·00	4·50
4302–4309	$35×8 Mickey Mouse with Pluto driving lorry; Mickey Mouse as carpenter sawing; Goofy riding road drill; Minnie Mouse with electric drill; Donald Duck driving forklift; Minnie Mouse and Goofy as construction contractors; Mickey Mouse with Pluto as carpenter making table; Pluto driving bulldozer (all vert)	4·00	4·50
4310–4317	$35×8 Mickey Mouse as plumber; Mickey Mouse the paperboy; Huey, Dewey and Louie moving furniture; Big Pete as handyman; Donald Duck and nephews house painting; Goofy as washing machine repairman; Minnie Mouse as babysitter; Daisy Duck as carer (all vert)	4·00	4·50

MS4318 Six sheets. (a) 132×107 mm. $200 Goofy as surgeon. (b) 107×129 mm. $200 Goofy the zookeeper. (c) 132×107 mm. $200 Ferdie riding Pluto for photographer (vert). (d) 107×129 mm. $200 Horace Horsecollar campaigning for mayor. (e) 132×107 mm. $200 Minnie Mouse as carpenter and puppies. (f) 107×129 mm. $200 Minnie Mouse as maid Set of 6 sheets   25·00   25·00

No. 4271 is inscribed "PHYSICAL THEREPIST" in error.

1995. Centenary of Salvation Army. Nos. 1519 and 1521/3 surch **SALVATION ARMY 1895 – 1995** and new value.

4319	$6 on 60c. Plate No. 10 (Series 1)		
4320	$20 on 60c. Plate No. 19 (Series 1)		
4321	$30 on 60c. Plate No. 2 (Series 1)		
4322	$35 on 60c. Plate No. 31 (Series 1)		

524 Pig

1995. Chinese New Year ("Year of the Pig"). Symbolic pigs. Multicoloured.

4323	$20 Type **524**	60	55
4324	$30 Pig facing left	65	60
4325	$50 Pig facing front (face value bottom right)	80	80
4326	$100 Pig facing front (face value bottom left)	1·25	1·40

MS4327 67×89 mm. $50×4 As Nos. 4323/6   4·00   3·50

MS4328 104×76 mm. $150 Pig's head   3·00   2·75

525 Northern Goshawk ("Goshawk")

1995. Birds. Multicoloured.

4329	$5 Type **525**	40	40
4330	$6 Northern lapwing ("Lapwing")	40	40

4331	$8 Long-wattled umbrellabird ("Ornate Umbrellbird")	40	40
4332	$15 Slaty-headed parakeet	55	50
4333	$19 Regent bowerbird	60	50
4334	$20 Egyptian goose	60	50
4335	$25 White-winged crossbill	75	60
4336	$30 Bohemian waxwing ("Waxwing")	75	60
4337	$35 Ruff	75	65
4338	$60 Hoopoe	1·25	1·00
4339	$100 Superb starling	1·50	1·75
4340	$500 Great jacamar	4·50	5·50

526 Norwegian Forest Cat

1995. "Singapore '95" International Stamp Exhibition. Multicoloured.

4341-4352	$35×12 Cats (Type **526**; Scottish fold; Red Burmese; British blue-hair; Abyssinian; Siamese; Exotic shorthair; Turkish van cat; Black Persian; Black-tipped burmilla; Singapura; Calico shorthair)	4·00	6·50
4353-4364	$35×12 Dogs (Gordon setter; Long-haired chihuahua; Dalmatian; Afghan hound; Old English bulldog; Miniature schnauzer; Clumber spaniel; Pekingese; St. Bernard; English cocker spaniel; Alaskan malamute; Rottweiler)	6·00	6·50
4365-4376	$35×12 Horses (chestnut thoroughbred colt; liver chestnut quarter horse; black Friesian; chestnut Belgian; Appaloosa; Lippizaner; chestnut hunter; British shire; Palomino; pinto ("Seal Brown Point"); Arab; Afghanistan kabardin)	6·00	6·50
MS4377	Three sheets, each 87×71 mm. (a) $300 Maine coon. (b) $300 Golden retriever. (c) $300 American anglo-arab Set of 3 sheets	9·00	9·50

No. 4355 is inscribed "Dalmation", No. 4367 "Freisian" and No. 4370 "Lipizzanas", all in error.

527 Captain John Smith leaving for New World, 1607

1995. "Pocahontas". Characters and scenes from Disney cartoon film. Multicoloured

(a) Vert designs showing characters

4378-4385	$50×8 Pocahontas and Meeko; John Smith; Chief Powhatan; Kocoum; Ratcliffe; Wiggins; Nakoma; Thomas	11·00	12·00

(b) Horiz designs showing film scenes

4386-4394	$8×9 Type **527**; Ratcliffe; Chief Powhatan greeted by his people; Pocahontas standing on cliff; Pocahontas, Nakoma and Meeko in canoe; Powhatan asking Pocahontas to marry Kocoum; Pocahontas receiving her mother's necklace; Pocahontas seeking guidance from Grandmother Willow; Pocahontas watching arrival of "Susan Constant"	4·50	4·50
4395-4403	$30×9 Ratcliffe claiming land for English Crown; Kekata having vision; Meeting of John Smith and Pocahontas; Namantack watching settlers; Powhatan and wounded Namantack; Pocahontas showing John Smith the colours of the wind; Nakoma finds Pocahontas with John Smith; Pocahontas offering John "Indian gold" (corn); Pocahontas, John Smith and Grandmother Willow	7·50	9·00
4404-4412	$35×9 Kocoum telling Pocahontas about the war council; Nakoma telling Kocoum to find Pocahontas; John Smith and Kocoum wrestling over knife; Powhatan sentencing John to death; Pocahontas and Grandmother Willow; Pocahontas saving John Smith; Ratcliffe under arrest; Powhatan draping his cloak over wounded John Smith; Pocahontas and Pocahontas saying goodbye	9·00	11·00

MS4413	Four sheets. (a) 98×120 mm. $300 Meeko. (b) 132×107 mm. $325 Pocahontas hiding. (c) 132×107 mm. $325 Powhatan and Pocahontas. (d) 132×107 mm. $325 Pocahontas kneeling (vert) Set of 4 sheets	30·00	32·00

1995. 95th Birthday of Queen Elizabeth the Queen Mother. As T **239a** of Gambia.

4414	$100 brown, light brown and black	1·50	1·50
4415	$100 multicoloured	1·50	1·50
4416	$100 multicoloured	1·50	1·50
4417	$100 multicoloured	1·50	1·50
MS4418	101×126 mm. $325 multicoloured	4·25	4·50

DESIGNS: No. 4414, Queen Elizabeth the Queen Mother (pastel drawing); 4415, Wearing purple hat; 4416, Wearing turquoise hat; 4417, At desk (oil painting); MS4418, Wearing blue dress and mink stole.

528 Paul Harris (founder) and Rotary Emblem

1995. 90th Anniv of Rotary International. Multicoloured.

4419	**528** $200 multicoloured	2·00	2·50
MS4420	104×74 mm. $300 Rotary emblems	3·00	3·50

529 Girl carrying Sack on Head

1995. 50th Anniv of F.A.O. Multicoloured.

4421	$35 Type **529**	50	65
4422	$60 Man and woman carrying sacks of food aid	80	95
4423	$200 Woman holding sack	2·00	2·40
MS4424	104×74 mm. $300 Bowl of food and F.A.O. emblem	3·00	3·50

Nos. 4421/3 were printed together, se-tenant, forming a composite design.

530 Scouts around Campfire

1995. 18th World Scout Jamboree, Netherlands. Multicoloured.

4425	$20 Type **530**	35	25
4426	$25 Scout on beach	40	30
4427	$30 Scouts hiking	45	35
4428	$35 Scout snorkelling	50	40
4429	$60 Scout saluting and flag of Guyana	90	65
4430	$200 Scout fishing from boat	2·00	2·50
MS4431	Two sheets, each 100×70 mm. (a) $300 Scout putting up tent. (b) Scout canoeing Set of 2 sheets	6·50	7·00

1995. 50th Anniv of End of World War II in Europe. As T **237a** of Gambia. Multicoloured.

4432	$60 American tank during Battle of the Bulge	1·00	90
4433	$60 Allied tanks crossing Siegfried Line	1·00	90
4434	$60 Liberated concentration camp prisoners	1·00	90
4435	$60 Allied plane dropping food to Dutch	1·00	90
4436	$60 U.S. infantry patrol, North Italy	1·00	90
4437	$60 Daily Mail headline announcing Hitler's death	1·00	90
4438	$60 Soviet tanks entering Berlin	1·00	90
4439	$60 Surrender of U858 in U.S. waters	1·00	90
MS4440	105×74 mm. $300 Soviet troops raising flag on Brandenburg Gate (56×42 mm)	3·00	3·25

No. 4433 is incorrectly inscribed "SIGFRIED LINE".

1995. 50th Anniv of End of Second World War in the Pacific. As T **239b** of Gambia. Multicoloured.

4441	$60 P61 Black Widow	1·00	75
4442	$60 PT boat	1·00	75
4443	$60 Martin B-26 Marauder bomber	1·00	75
4444	$60 U.S.S. San Juan (cruiser)	1·00	75
4445	$60 "Gato" class submarine	1·00	75
4446	$60 Destroyer	1·00	75
MS4447	107×77 mm. $300 Cruiser and aircraft carrier	3·00	3·25

531 Thanksgiving (U.S.A.)

1995. Holidays of the World. Multicoloured.

4448	$60 Type **531**	1·00	90
4449	$60 Christmas (Germany)	1·00	90
4450	$60 Hanukkah (Israel)	1·00	90
4451	$60 Easter (Spain)	1·00	90
4452	$60 Carnivale (Brazil)	1·00	90
4453	$60 Bastille Day (France)	1·00	90
4454	$60 Independence Day (India)	1·00	90
4455	$60 St. Patrick's Day (Ireland)	1·00	90
MS4456	105×76 mm. $300 Chinese New Year (China)	3·00	3·25

532 Map of the Americas and U.N. Soldier

1995. 50th Anniv of United Nations. Multicoloured.

4457	$35 Type **532**	55	50
4458	$60 Map of Africa and Western Asia	85	75
4459	$200 Map of Eastern Asia and Australasia with refugees	2·50	3·00
MS4460	74×104 mm. $300 Secretary-General Boutros Boutros Ghali	3·00	3·50

Nos. 4457/9 were printed together, se-tenant, forming a composite design.

533 Four-eyed Butterflyfish

1995. Marine Life. Multicoloured.

4461	$30 Type **533**	70	75
4462	$30 Lemon shark	70	75
4463	$35 Blue-headed wrasse	70	75
4464	$35 Green turtle	70	75
4465	$60 Three-spotted damselfish	70	75
4466	$60 Sawfish	70	75
4467	$60 Sei whales	70	75
4468	$60 Great barracuda	70	75
4469	$60 Mutton snapper	70	75
4470	$60 Hawksbill turtle	70	75
4471	$60 Spanish hogfish	70	75
4472	$60 Queen angelfish	70	75
4473	$60 Porkfish	70	75
4474	$60 Trumpetfish	70	75
4475	$60 Lesser electric ray	70	75
4476	$60 Tiger shark	70	75
4477	$60 Needlefish	70	75
4478	$60 Horse-eyed jack	70	75
4479	$60 Princess parrotfish	70	75
4480	$60 Yellow-tailed snapper	70	75
4481	$60 Spotted snake eel	70	75
4482	$60 Buffalo trunkfish	70	75
4483	$60 Cherubfish angelfish	70	75
4484	$60 French angelfish	70	75
4485	$80 Cocoa damselfish (vert)	90	1·00
4486	$80 Sergeant major (vert)	90	1·00
4487	$80 Beaugregory (vert)	90	1·00
4488	$80 Yellow-tailed damselfish (vert)	90	1·00
4489	$200 Fin-spot wrasse	2·25	2·40
4490	$200 Stingray	2·25	2·40
MS4491	Two sheets, each 100×70 mm. (a) $300 Great white shark. (b) $300 Leatherback turtle Set of 2 sheets	11·00	11·00

Nos. 4461, 4463, 4465 and 4489; Nos. 4462, 4464, 4466 and 4490; Nos. 4467/75; Nos. 4476/84 and Nos. 4485/8 respectively were printed together, se-tenant, the backgrounds forming composite designs.

534 Pole Vaulting

1995. Olympic Games, Atlanta (1996) (2nd issue). Multicoloured.

4492	$60 Type **534**	90	85
4493	$60 Long jumping	90	85
4494	$60 Woman with relay baton	90	85
4495	$60 Wrestling	90	85
4496	$60 Discus (side view)	90	85
4497	$60 Basketball	90	85
4498	$60 Boxing	90	85
4499	$60 Weightlifting	90	85
4500	$60 Shot put	90	85
4501	$60 Man in relay race	90	85
4502	$60 Female gymnast on beam	90	85
4503	$60 Cycling	90	85
4504	$60 Synchronized swimming	90	85
4505	$60 Hurdling	90	85
4506	$60 Male gymnast on pommel horse	90	85
4507	$60 Discus (front view)	90	85
MS4508	Two sheets. (a) 105×75 mm. $300 Athletes at start of race. (b) 75×105 mm. $300 Long jumping Set of 2 sheets	6·50	7·00

Nos. 4492/9 and 4500/7 respectively were printed together, se-tenant, the backgrounds forming composite designs.

535 Sand Martin

1995. Wildlife. Multicoloured.

4509	$20 Type **535**	1·25	1·00
4510	$35 House martin	1·25	1·00
4511	$60 Northern hobby ("Hobby")	1·25	1·00
4512	$60 Olive colobus	1·00	90
4513	$60 Violet-backed starling	1·00	90
4514	$60 Diana monkey	1·00	90
4515	$60 African palm civet	1·00	90
4516	$60 Giraffe and zebras	1·00	90
4517	$60 African linsang	1·00	90
4518	$60 Royal antelope	1·00	90
4519	$60 Duikers	1·00	90
4520	$60 Palm squirrel	1·00	90
4521	$200 Long-tailed skua	1·75	1·40
MS4522	Two sheets, each 110×80 mm. (a) $300 Brush pig and giant forest hog. (b) $300 Chimpanzee Set of 2 sheets	6·50	7·00

Nos. 4509/11 and 4521; and 4512/20 respectively were printed together, se-tenant, forming composite background designs.

536 Queenstown Jama Masjid

1995. Centenary of Queenstown Jama Masjid (mosque), Georgetown.

4523	**536** $60 multicoloured	75	60

537 Woman Soldier with Sub-machine Gun

1995. 30th Anniv of Guyana Defence Force. Multicoloured.

4524	$6 Type **537**	15	10
4525	$60 Soldier with rifle	85	70

538 Bank Logo and Headquarters

1995. 25th Anniv of Caribbean Development Bank.

4526	**538** $60 multicoloured	70	60

1995. Christmas. Religious Paintings. As T **245a** of Gambia. Multicoloured.

4527	$25 Angel of the Annunciation (Carracci)	50	30

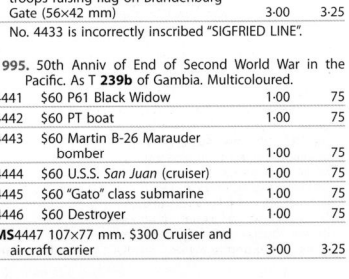

4528	$30 *Virgin of the Annunciation* (Carracci)	55	35
4529	$35 *Assumption of the Madonna* (Carracci)	60	40
4530	$60 *Baptism of Christ* (Carracci)	90	70
4531	$100 *Madonna and Child with Saints* (detail) (Carracci)	1·60	1·75
4532	$300 *Birth of the Virgin* (Carracci)	3·75	5·00

MS4533 Two sheets, each 101×127 mm. (a) $325 *Madonna and Child enthroned with Ten Saints* (Rosso Fiorentino). (b) $325 *Mystic Marriage of St. Catherine* (Carracci) Set of 2 sheets ..... 7·00 8·00

539 John Lennon

1995. 15th Death Anniv of John Lennon (musician).
| 4534 | **539** | $35 multicoloured | 1·00 | 80 |

540 Albrecht Kossel (1910 Medicine)

1995. Centenary of Nobel Trust Fund. Multicoloured.
4535– 4543	$35×9 Type **540**; Arthur H. Compton (1927 Physics); N. M. Butler (1931 Peace); Charles Laveran (1907 Medicine); George R. Minot (1934 Medicine); Henry H. Dale (1936 Medicine); Jacques Monod (1965 Medicine); Alfred Hershey (1969 Medicine); Par Lagerkvist (1951 Literature)	7·00	7·50
4544– 4552	$35×9 Norman F. Ramsey (1989 Physics); Chen Ning Yang (1957 Physics); Earl W. Sutherland Jr. (1971 Medicine); Paul Karrer (1937 Chemistry); Harmut Michel (1988 Chemistry); Richard Kuhn (1938 Chemistry); P. A. M. Dirac (1933 Physics); Victor Grignard (1912 Chemistry); Richard Willstatter (1915 Chemistry)	7·00	7·50
4553– 4561	$35×9 Adolf von Baeyer (1905 Chemistry); Hideki Yukawa (1949 Physics); George W. Beadle (1958 Medicine); Edwin M. McMillan (1951 Chemistry); Samuel C. C. Ting (1976 Physics); Saint-John Perse (1960 Literature); John F. Enders (1954 Medicine); Felix Bloch (1952 Physics); P. B. Medawar (1960 Medicine)	7·00	7·50
4562– 4570	$35×9 Nikolai Basov (1964 Physics); Klas Arnoldson (1908 Peace); Rene Sully-Prudhomme (1901 Literature); Robert W. Wilson (1978 Physics); Hugo Theorell (1955 Medicine); Nelly Sachs (1966 Literature); Hans von Euler-Chelpin (1929 Chemistry); Mairead Corrigan (1976 Peace); Willis E. Lamb Jr. (1955 Physics)	7·00	7·50
4571– 4579	$35×9 Francis Crick (1962 Medicine); Manne Siegbahn (1924 Physics); Eisaku Sato (1974 Peace); Robert Koch (1905 Medicine); Edgar D. Adrian (1932 Medicine); Erwin Neher (1991 Medicine); Henry Taube (1983 Chemistry); Norman Angell (1933 Peace); Robert Robinson (1947 Chemistry)	7·00	7·50
4580– 4588	$35×9 Henri Becquerel (1903 Physics); Igor Tamm (1958 Physics); Georges Kohler (1984 Medicine); Gerhard Domagk (1939 Medicine); Yasunari Kawabata (1968 Literature); Maurice Allais (1988 Economic Sciences); Aristide Briand (1926 Peace); Pavel Cherenkov (1958 Physics); Feodor Lynen (1964 Medicine)	7·00	7·50

MS4589 Six sheets, each 106×76 mm. (a) $300 Lech Walesa (1983 Peace). (b) $300 Heinrich Böll (1972 Literature). (c) $300 Henry A. Kissinger (1973 Peace). (d) $300 Kenichi Fukui (1981 Chemistry). (e) $300 Yasunari Kawabata (1968 Literature). (f) $300 Le Duc Tho (1973 Peace) Set of 6 sheets ..... 23·00 24·00

Nos. 4535/43, 4544/52, 4553/61, 4562/70, 4571/9 and 4580/8 respectively were printed together, *se-tenant*, with the backgrounds forming composite designs.

541 David Copperfield

1995. David Copperfield (magician). Multicoloured.
4590	$60 Type **541**	70	75
4591	$60 David Copperfield in cloak and top hat	70	75
4592	$60 With flaming torch	70	75
4593	$60 David Copperfield in close up	70	75
4594	$60 Head of Statue of Liberty	70	75
4595	$60 David Copperfield climbing rope	70	75
4596	$60 With handcuffs	70	75
4597	$60 With woman dancer	70	75
4598	$60 David Copperfield wearing white shirt	70	75

MS4599 76×106 mm. $300 David Copperfield with rose ..... 3·00 3·50

Nos. 4590/8 were printed together, *se-tenant*, forming a composite background design.

542 Marilyn Monroe

1995. 70th Birth Anniv of Marilyn Monroe (entertainer). Multicoloured.
4600	$60 Type **542**	65	65
4601	$60 Marilyn Monroe with circular earrings	65	65
4602	$60 Marilyn Monroe (red top right corner)	65	65
4603	$60 Marilyn Monroe (signature at bottom right)	65	65
4604	$60 With hair over left eye	65	65
4605	$60 With pink satin at left	65	65
4606	$60 With arm raised	65	65
4607	$60 With pink satin at bottom right	65	65
4608	$60 With square earring	65	65

MS4609 76×105 mm. $300 Marilyn Monroe in pink satin dress (horiz) ..... 3·00 3·25

Nos. 4600/8 were printed together, *se-tenant*, with the background forming a composite design.

543 Rat

1995. Chinese New Year ("Year of the Rat").
4610	**543**	$20 multicoloured	25	20
4611	–	$30 multicoloured (face value bottom left)	35	30
4612	–	$50 multicoloured (face value top right)	65	50
4613	–	$100 multicoloured (face value top left)	1·10	1·25

MS4614 68×92 mm. $50×4 As Nos. 4610/13 ..... 2·40 2·25

MS4615 106×76 mm. $150 multicoloured ..... 2·00 2·25

DESIGNS: $30 to $150 Symbolic rats.

544 City Children

1996. 50th Anniv of UNICEF. Sheet 110×87 mm, containing T **544** and similar horiz designs. Multicoloured.

MS4616 $1100 Type **544**; $1100 Youth worker and children (face value at top right); $1100 City children (face value at bottom right); $1100 Youth worker and children (face value at bottom right) ..... 45·00 45·00

1996. Paintings by Rubens. As T **421** of Grenada. Multicoloured.
4617	$6 *The Garden of Love* (detail)	15	10
4618	$10 *Two Sleeping Children*	20	10
4619	$20 *All Saints Day*	35	20
4620	$25 *Sacrifice of Abraham*	35	25
4621	$30 *The Last Supper*	40	30
4622	$35 *The Birth of Henry of Navarre*	45	30
4623	$40 *Study of standing female saint*	50	35
4624	$50 *The Garden of Love* (different detail)	60	45
4625	$60 *The Garden of Love* (different detail)	70	50
4626	$200 *The Martyrdom of St. Livinus*	2·00	2·25
4627	$200 *St. Francis of Paola*	2·00	2·25
4628	$300 *The Union of Maria de Medici and Henry IV*	3·00	3·75

MS4629 Three sheets. (a) 70×100 mm. $325 *The Three Crosses* (56×84 mm). (b) 100×70 mm. $325 *Decius Mus addressing the Legions* (84×56 mm). (c) 100×70 mm. $325 *Triumph of Henry IV* (84×56 mm) Set of 3 sheets ..... 11·00 12·00

545 Apatosaurus

1996. Prehistoric Animals. Multicoloured.
4630– 4641	$35×12 Type **545**; Archaeopteryx; Dimorphodon; Deinonychus; Coelophysis; Tyrannosaurus; Triceratops; Anatosaurus; Saltasaurus; Allosaurus; Oviraptor; Stegosaurus	5·50	
4642– 4653	$35×12 Ornithomimus; Pteranodon; Rhamphorynchus; Ornitholestes; Brachiosaurus; Parasaurolophus; Ceratosaurus; Camarasaurus; Euoplocephalus; Scutelosaurus; Compsognathus; Stegoceras	5·50	
4654– 4665	$35×12 Eudimorphodon; Criorhynchus; Elasmosaurus; Rhomaleosaurus; Ceresiosaurus; Mesosaurus; Grendelius; Nothosaurus; Mixosaurus; Placodus; Coelacanth; Mosasaurus	5·50	
4666– 4677	$35×12 Tarbosaurus; Hadrosaurus; Polacanthus; Psittacosaurus; Ornitholestes; Yangchuanosaurus; Scelidosaurus; Kentrosaurus; Coelophysis; Lesothosaurus; Plateosaurus; Staurikosaurus (all vert)	5·50	

MS4678 Two sheets, each 101×58 mm. (a) $60 Saurolophus; $60 Muttaburrasaurus; $60 Dicraeosaurus. (b) $60 Heterodontosaurus; $60 Compsognathus; $60 Ornithomimosaure (all vert) Set of 2 sheets ..... 4·50 5·50

MS4679 Five sheets. (a) 106×76 mm. $300 Struthiomimus. (b) 76×106 mm. $300 Tyrannosaurus rex (vert). (c) 76×106 mm. $300 Apatosaurus and Allosaurus. (d) 106×76 mm. $300 Quetzalcoatlus. (e) 106×76 mm. $300 Lagosuchus Set of 5 sheets ..... 19·00 21·00

Nos. 4630/41, 4642/53, 4654/65 and 4666/77 respectively were printed together, *se-tenant*, with the backgrounds forming composite designs.

546 Giant Panda

1996. "CHINA 96" International Stamp Exhibition, Beijing. T **546** and similar vert designs. Multicoloured.

MS4680 130×95 mm. $60 Summer Palace, Beijing (39×51 mm) ..... 1·25 1·40

MS4681 Two sheets, each 146×116 mm. (a) $60 Type **546**; $60 Panda holding bamboo stem; $60 Eating bamboo stalk; $60 On all fours. (b) $60 Panda lying on tree branch (logo at left); $60 Lying on branch (logo at right; $60 Exploring hollow in tree (logo at left); $60 Sitting on trunk (logo at right) Set of 2 sheets ..... 7·00 7·00

The stamps in No. MS4681 form composite designs showing rocks and stream (a) or dead tree (b).

546a Deng Xiaoping writing Inscription

1996. Deng Xiaoping (Chinese leader) Commemoration. Multicoloured.
4681c	$30 Type **546a**	35	40
4681d	$30 Deng Xiaoping addressing meeting (value in red)	35	40
4681e	$30 Signing first day cover for army officer (value in yellow)	35	40
4681f	$30 Waving	35	40
4681g	$30 As No. 4681d (value in yellow)	35	40
4681h	$30 As No. 4681e (value in red)	35	40

MS4681i 73×101 mm. $300 Deng Xiaoping applauding (vert) ..... 3·25 3·50

547 *Morchella esculenta* and *Doryphorella princeps* (leaf beetle)

1996. Fungi of Guyana. Multicoloured.
4682	$20 Type **547**	55	30
4683	$25 Green-spored mushroom	55	30
4684	$30 Common mushroom and leaf beetle	60	40
4685	$35 Pine cone mushroom and *Danaus plexippus* caterpillar	60	40
4686	$60 *Armillaria mellea*	1·25	1·25
4687	$60 *Gomphus floccosus*	1·25	1·25
4688	$60 *Pholiota astragalina*	1·25	1·25
4689	$60 *Helvellaa crispa*	1·25	1·25
4690	$60 *Hygrophorus miniatus*	1·25	1·25
4691	$60 *Omphalotus olearius*	1·25	1·25
4692	$60 *Hygrocybe acutoconica*	1·25	1·25
4693	$60 *Mycena viscosa*	1·25	1·25
4694	$60 Cockle-shell lentinus	80	80
4695	$60 *Volvariella surrecta*	80	80
4696	$60 *Lepiota josserandii*	80	80
4697	$60 *Boletellus betula*	80	80
4698	$60 *Amanita muscaria*	80	80
4699	$60 *Russula claroflava* and *Semiotus angulatus* (click beetle)	80	80
4700	$60 *Dictyophora duplicata* and *Musca domestica* (house fly)	80	80
4701	$60 *Stropharia* and *Editha magnifica* (butterfly hunter)	80	80
4702	$60 *Leotia viscosa*	80	80
4703	$60 *Calostoma cinnabarina*	80	80
4704	$60 Stalkless paxillus	80	80
4705	$60 *Amanita spissa*	80	80

MS4706 Two sheets, each 114×84 mm. (a) $300 *Mycena leaiana* and Yellow grosbeak (bird). (b) $300 *Tubifera ferryginosa*, *Clavulina amethystina* and *Ramaria formosa* (horiz) Set of 2 sheets ..... 8·00 8·50

Nos. 4686 and 4692 are inscribed "Armilluella mellea" and "Hygzocybe acutoconica", both in error.

1996. 70th Birthday of Queen Elizabeth II. As T **255a** of Gambia. Multicoloured.
4707	$100 Queen Elizabeth II	1·40	1·50
4708	$100 Queen wearing green and blue jacket and hat	1·40	1·50
4709	$100 Queen at State Opening of Parliament	1·40	1·50

MS4710 103×125 mm. $325 Queen in Garter robes ..... 4·25 4·50

1996. Commonwealth Pharmacy Week. Unissued values in designs of Nos. 1810 and 1873 surch **COMMONWEALTH PHARMACY WEEK JUNE 16th 22nd 1996.**
| 4711 | $6 on 130c. Plate No. 21 (Series 2) | | |
| 4712 | $60 on 100c. Plate No. 33 (Series 2) | | |

1996. Centenary of Radio. Entertainers. As T **259a** of Gambia. Multicoloured.
4713	$20 Frank Sinatra	50	30
4714	$35 Gene Autry	50	30
4715	$60 Groucho Marx	60	50
4716	$200 Red Skelton	2·00	2·25

MS4717 104×74 mm. $300 Burl Ives ..... 3·50 4·00

549 Hulda Gates

1996. 3000th Anniv of Jerusalem. Multicoloured.

4718	$30 Type **549**	1·00	75
4719	$35 Church of St. Mary Magdalene	1·00	75
4720	$200 Absalom's Tomb, Kidron Valley	3·00	3·00
MS4721	105×76 mm. $300 Children's Holocaust Memorial, Yad Vashem	4·00	4·25

550 Long-billed Starthroat

1996. Birds of the World. Multicoloured.

4722	$60 Type **550**	80	70
4723	$60 Velvet-purple coronet	80	70
4724	$60 Racquet-tailed coquette	80	70
4725	$60 Violet-tailed sylph	80	70
4726	$60 Broad-tailed hummingbird	80	70
4727	$60 Blue-tufted starthroat	80	70
4728	$60 White-necked jacobin	80	70
4729	$60 Ruby-throated hummingbird	80	70
4730	$60 Blue and yellow macaw	80	70
4731	$60 Andean condor	80	70
4732	$60 Guiana crested eagle ("Crested Eagle")	80	70
4733	$60 White-tailed trogon	80	70
4734	$60 Toco toucan	80	70
4735	$60 Great horned owl	80	70
4736	$60 Andean cock-of-the-rock	80	70
4737	$60 Great curassow	80	70

MS4738 Two sheets, each 101×70 mm. (a) $300 Sparkling violetear ("Gould's Sparkling Violet-ear"). (b) $300 Ornate hawk eagle (horiz) Set of 2 sheets ..... 8·50 8·00

Nos. 4722/9 and 4730/7 respectively were printed together, *se-tenant*, the backgrounds forming composite designs.

551 Pancratium (ancient Olympic event)

1996. Olympic Games, Atlanta (3rd issue). Multicoloured.

4739	$20 Type **551**	40	30
4740	$30 Olympic Stadium, Melbourne, 1956	40	30
4741-4749	$50×9 Volleyball; Basketball; Tennis; Table tennis; Baseball; Handball; Hockey; Water polo; Football		5·00
4750/8	$50×9 Cycling; Hurdling; High jumping; Diving; Weightlifting; Canoeing; Wrestling; Gymnastics; Running (all vert)		5·00
4759-4767	$50×9 Florence Griffith-Joyner (track and field) (U.S.A.); Ines Geissler (swimming) (Germany); Nadia Comaneci (gymnastics) (Rumania); Tatiana Gutsu (gymnastics) (Unified team); Ogla Korbut (gymnastics) (Russia); Barbara Krause (swimming) (Germany); Olga Bryzgina (track and field) (Russia); Fanny Blankers-Koen (track and field) (Holland); Irena Szewinska (track and field) (Poland) (all vert)		5·00
4768-4776	$50×9 Gerd Wessig (Germany); Jim Thorpe (U.S.A.); Norman Read (New Zealand); Lasse Viren (Finland); Milt Campbell (U.S.A.); Abebe Bikila (Ethiopia); Jesse Owens (U.S.A.); Viktor Saneev (Russia); Waldemer Cierpinski (Germany) (all track and field) (all vert)		5·00

4777-4785	$50×9 Ditmar Schmidt (handball) (Germany); Pam Shriver (tennis doubles) (U.S.A.); Zina Garrison (tennis doubles) (U.S.A.); Hyun Jung-Hua (table tennis doubles) (Korea); Steffi Graf (tennis) (Germany); Michael Jordan (basketball) (U.S.A.); Karch Kiraly (volleyball) (U.S.A.); "Magic" Johnson (basketball) (U.S.A.); Ingolf Weigert (handball) (Germany) (all vert)		5·00
4786	$60 Leonid Spirin winning 20 kilometre walk, 1956 (vert)	60	60
4787	$200 Lars Hall, Gold medal winner, Modern Pentathlon, 1952 and 1956 (Sweden) (vert)	1·75	2·00

MS4788 Two sheets. (a) 104×74 mm. $300 Carl Lewis, Gold medal winner, track and field, 1984, 1988 and 1992 (U.S.A.). (b) 74×104 mm. $300 U.S.A. defeating Korea at baseball, 1988 Set of 2 sheets ..... 6·50 7·50

Nos. 4741/9, 4750/8, 4759/67, 4768/76 and 4777/85 (the last three showing Gold medal winners) respectively were printed together, *se-tenant*, forming composite background designs.

No. **MS**4788a is inscribed "1985" in error.

552 Mickey's Bait Shop

1996. Mickey Mouse and Friends Outdoors. Multicoloured.

4789	$60 Type **552**	1·00	1·00
4790	$60 Mickey and Pluto as lumberjacks	1·00	1·00
4791	$60 Mickey fishing	1·00	1·00
4792	$80 Donald Duck in BMX bike championships (vert)	1·25	1·25
4793	$80 Goofy as ice hockey superstar (vert)	1·25	1·25
4794	$80 Donald Duck at Malibu Surf City (vert)	1·25	1·25
4795	$100 Mickey as naval captain (vert)	1·40	1·40
4796	$100 Captain Mickey's Seamanship School (vert)	1·40	1·40
4797	$100 Mickey as sailor with ship's wheel and full-rigged sailing ship (vert)	1·40	1·40

MS4798 Five sheets. (a) 124×101 mm. $250 Mickey as Pinkerton detective (vert). (b) 104×126 mm. $250 Mickey as U.S. Marshal (vert). (c) 125×104 mm. $250 Mickey as train conductor and Transcontinental Railroad locomotive. (d) 101×124 mm. $300 Donald Duck as mountaineer. (e) 104×124 mm. $325 Mickey as trapper (vert) Set of 5 sheets ..... 21·00 22·00

553 Two Gun Mickey

1996. Disney Antique Toys. Multicoloured.

4799	$6 Type **553**	50	50
4800	$6 Wood-jointed Mickey figure	50	50
4801	$6 Donald jack-in-the-box	50	50
4802	$6 Rocking Minnie	50	50
4803	$6 Fireman Donald Duck	50	50
4804	$6 Long-billed Donald Duck	50	50
4805	$6 Painted-wood Mickey figure	50	50
4806	$6 Wind-up Jiminy Cricket	50	50

MS4807 Two sheets, each 131×105 mm. (a) $300 Mickey doll. (b) $300 Carousel Set of 2 sheets ..... 10·00 10·00

554 Elvis Presley

1996. 60th Birth Anniv (1995) of Elvis Presley. Multicoloured, background colours given.

4808	**554** $100 red	1·40	1·25

4809	- $100 mauve	1·40	1·25
4810	- $100 brown	1·40	1·25
4811	- $100 blue	1·40	1·25
4812	- $100 purple	1·40	1·25
4813	- $100 blue	1·40	1·25

DESIGNS: Nos. 4809/13, Various portraits.

555 Piece of Meteorite showing Fossil

1996. Mars Meteorite. Sheet 104×76 mm.

MS4814	**555** $50 multicoloured	2·25	1·75

556 Birman

1996. Cats of the World. Multicoloured.

4815	$60 Type **556**	80	70
4816	$60 American curl	80	70
4817	$60 Turkish angora	80	70
4818	$60 European shorthair (Italy)	80	70
4819	$60 Persian (Great Britain)	80	70
4820	$60 Scottish fold	80	70
4821	$60 Sphynx (Canada)	80	70
4822	$60 Malayan (Thailand)	80	70
4823	$60 Cornish rex (Great Britain)	80	70
4824	$60 Norwegian forest (vert)	80	70
4825	$60 Russian shorthair (vert)	80	70
4826	$60 European shorthair (Italy) (vert)	80	70
4827	$60 Birman (vert)	80	70
4828	$60 Ragdoll (U.S.A.) (vert)	80	70
4829	$60 Egyptian mau (vert)	80	70
4830	$60 Persian (Great Britain) (vert)	80	70
4831	$60 Turkish angora (vert)	80	70
4832	$60 Siamese (vert)	80	70

MS4833 Two sheets, each 107×72 mm. (a) $300 Himalayan (U.S.A.). (b) $300 Maine coon (U.S.A.) (vert) Set of 2 sheets ..... 8·00 8·00

Nos. 4815/23 and 4824/32 respectively were printed together, *se-tenant*, with the backgrounds forming composite designs.

557 Hyed Snapper

1996. Marine Life. Multicoloured.

4834	$6 Type **557**	25	15
4835	$6 Angelfish	25	15
4836	$20 Boxfish	35	20
4837	$25 Golden damselfish	35	25
4838	$30 Goblin shark and coelacanth	35	35
4839	$30 "Jason" (American remote-controlled submersible)	35	35
4840	$30 Deep-water invertebrates	35	35
4841	$30 Submarine NR-1	35	35
4842	$30 Giant squid	35	35
4843	$30 Sperm whale	35	35
4844	$30 Volcanic vents and "Alvin" (submersible)	35	35
4845	$30 Air-recycling pressure suits and shipwreck	35	35
4846	$30 "Shinkai" 6500 (submersible)	35	35
4847	$30 Giant tube worms	35	35
4848	$30 Anglerfish	35	35
4849	$30 Six-gill shark	35	35
4850	$30 Autonomous underwater vehicle ABE	35	35
4851	$30 Octopus and viperfish	35	35
4852	$30 Swallower and hatchetfish	35	35
4853	$35 Clown triggerfish	35	30
4854	$60 Red gorgonians	65	65
4855	$60 Soft coral and butterflyfish	65	65
4856	$60 Soft coral and slender snapper	65	65
4857	$60 Common clownfish, anemone and mushroom coral	65	65
4858	$60 Anemone and horse-eyed jack	65	65
4859	$60 Splendid coral trout	65	65
4860	$60 Anemones	65	65
4861	$60 Brain coral	65	65
4862	$60 Cup coral	65	65
4863	$200 Harlequin tuskfish	2·25	2·50

MS4864 Two sheets, each 98×68 mm. (a) $300 Caribbean flower coral. (b) $300 Sea anemone Set of 2 sheets ..... 6·50 7·50

Nos. 4838/52 and 4854/62 respectively were printed together, *se-tenant*, with the backgrounds forming composite designs.

No. 4853 is inscribed "CLOWN TUGGERFISH" in error.

558 Snow White and Reindeer

1996. Christmas. Disney's "Snow White and the Seven Dwarfs". Multicoloured.

4865	$6 Type **558**	30	10
4866	$20 Doc with presents	80	25
4867	$25 Dopey and Sneezy	80	30
4868	$30 Sleepy, Happy and Bashful	80	35
4869	$35 Dopey and Santa Claus	80	40
4870	$60 Dopey with socks at fireplace	1·50	1·00
4871	$100 Dopey and Grumpy	2·50	2·50
4872	$200 Dopey dressed as Santa Claus	3·75	4·50

MS4873 Two sheets, each 122×102 mm. (a) $300 Snow White, Doc and squirrel. (b) $300 Dopey and Christmas tree Set of 2 sheets ..... 12·00 12·00

559 Hotel Tower

1996. 50th Anniv of Hotel Tower, Georgetown.

4874	**559** $30 multicoloured	1·00	40

561 Ox

1997. Chinese New Year (Year of the Ox).

4882	**561** $20 multicoloured	35	25
4883	- $30 multicoloured	50	40
4884	- $35 multicoloured	55	50
4885	- $50 multicoloured	75	80

MS4886 101×72 mm. $150 multicoloured ..... 2·00 2·25

MS4887 68×90 mm. $50 As No. 4882 (value bottom right); $50 As No. 4883 (value bottom left); $50 As No. 4884 (value top right); $50 As No. 4885 (value top left) ..... 2·00 2·25

DESIGNS: Nos. 4883/7 depict symbolic oxen.

562 Mickey with Traditional Box of Sweets

1997. Mickey Mouse and Friends celebrate Chinese New Year. Multicoloured.

4888	$6 Type **562**	40	25
4889	$20 Mickey and Minnie at home with friends	50	35
4890	$25 Mickey and Minnie hanging fortune lantern	50	35
4891	$30 Minnie and Daisy with paper silhouette	55	55
4892	$30 Mickey and friends receiving traditional red money	55	55
4893	$30 Mickey in lion dance	55	55
4894	$30 Mickey preparing Chinese calligraphy wall hangings	55	55
4895	$30 Mickey with symbols of surplus	55	55
4896	$30 Donald Duck playing with fireworks	55	55
4897	$30 Donald, Mickey and Minnie on ox	55	55
4898	$35 Donald Duck and friends at New Year flower market	55	55

4899	$60 Mickey and Minnie as "harmonious man and woman"	90	90
MS4900	Two sheets, each 133×109 mm. (a) $150 Mickey Mouse marching (vert). (b) $200 Mickey and ox Set of 2 sheets	6·50	6·50

563 Burgess Meredith as Ernie Pyle in *The Story of G.I. Joe*

1997. Centenary of Cinema. Second World War Films. Multicoloured.

4901	$50 Type **563**	80	70
4902	$50 M. E. Clifton-James as General Montgomery in *I was Monty's Double*	80	70
4903	$50 Audie Murphy as himself in *To Hell and Back*	80	70
4904	$50 Gary Cooper as Dr. Wassell in *The Story of Dr. Wassell*	80	70
4905	$50 James Mason as Erwin Rommel in *The Desert Fox*	80	70
4906	$50 Manart Kippen as Stalin in *Mission to Moscow*	80	70
4907	$50 Robert Taylor as Col. Paul Tibbets in *Above and Beyond*	80	70
4908	$50 James Cagney as Admiral Bill Halsey in *The Gallant Hours*	80	70
4909	$50 John Garfield as Al Schmid in *Pride of the Marines*	80	70
MS4910	105×75 mm. $300 George C. Scott as Gen. George S. Patton in *Patton* (horiz)	5·50	6·00

564 *Washington in Battle*

1997. Bicentenary of George Washington's Retirement from U.S. Presidency. Multicoloured.

4911	$60 Type **564**	80	60
4912	$60 *Washington taking Presidential Oath*	80	60
4913	$60 *Washington seated in Armchair* (engraving after Chappel)	80	60
4914	$60 *Col. Washington of the Virginia Militia* (Charles W. Peale)	80	60
4915	$60 *George Washington* (Rembrandt Peale)	80	60
4916	$60 *Washington addressing Constitutional Convention* (Junius B. Stearns)	80	60
4917	$60 *Washington on his way to Continental Congress*	80	60
4918	$60 *Washington on a White Charger* (John Faed)	80	60
4919	$60 *Washington surveying* (engraving by G. R. Hall)	80	60
4920	$60 *Washington praying at Valley Forge* (bas-relief)	80	60
4921	$60 *Death of Gen. Mercer at Battle of Princeton* (John Trumbull)	80	60
4922	$60 *Washington taking Command at Cambridge*	80	60
4923	$60 *Washington before Battle of Trenton* (John Trumbull)	80	60
4924	$60 *Washington and his Family at Mount Vernon* (Alonzo Chappel)	80	60
4925	$60 *Washington's Inauguration* (Chappel)	80	60
4926	$60 *Washington* (Adolph Ulrich Wertmuller)	80	60
4927	$60 *Washington accepts Commission as Commander-in-Chief* (Currier & Ives lithograph)	80	60
4928	$60 *Washington* (mezzotint by Sartain)	80	60
4929	$60 *Mount Vernon*	80	60
4930	$60 *Washington with Farm Workers* (print by Junius B. Stearns)	80	60
4931	$60 *Wedding of Nellie Custis* (Ogden)	80	60
4932	$60 *Washington crossing the Delaware* (Leutze)	80	60
4933	$60 *Washington and Gen. Braddock*	80	60

4934	$60 *Washington's Birthplace* (Currier & Ives lithograph)	80	60
4935	$300 *George Washington* (Gilbert Stuart) (66×91 mm)	2·50	3·00
4936	$300 *Washington at Yorktown* (James Peale) (66×91 mm)	2·50	3·00

565 Pres. Kennedy and "Eternal Flame"

1997. 80th Birth Anniv of Pres. John F. Kennedy.

4937	**565** $50 violet	1·00	1·00

No. 4937 is in the same design as the U.S.A. Memorial Issue of 1964.

1997. 50th Anniv of UNESCO. Multicoloured. As T 273a of Gambia.

4938	$20 Hall at Horyu-ji, Japan	20	20
4939	$25 Coastline, Scandola Nature Reserve, France	25	25
4940	$30 Great Wall turret, China	30	30
4941	$35 Bedroom in the Residenz, Wurzburg, Germany	35	30
4942	$60 Monastery of Batalha, Portugal	60	60
4943	$60 Cathedral of Aquisgran, Aachen, Germany (vert)	60	60
4944	$60 Trier Cathedral, Germany (vert)	60	60
4945	$60 Column of Augusta Treveror, Trier (vert)	60	60
4946	$60 The Residenz and garden, Wurzburg (vert)	60	60
4947	$60 Interior of church, Wurzburg (vert)	60	60
4948	$60 The Residenz and lake, Wurzburg (vert)	60	60
4949	$60 Riverside houses, Inselstadt, Bamberg, Germany (vert)	60	60
4950	$60 Cathedral interior, Speyer, Germany (vert)	60	60
4951	$60 Monastery of Thessaloniki, Greece (vert)	60	60
4952	$60 Church tower, Monastery of Mystras, Greece (vert)	4·25	4·25
4953	$60 Interior of Church of Santa Sofia, Thessaloniki (vert)	60	60
4954	$60 Monastery and ruins, Mystras (vert)	60	60
4955	$60 Aerial view of Monastery at Mystras (vert)	60	60
4956	$60 City wall, Thessaloniki (vert)	60	60
4957	$60 Wall painting, Mystras Monastery (vert)	60	60
4958	$60 Paintings in Museum of Byzantine Art, Thessaloniki (vert)	60	60
4959	$60 Monastery of Poblet, Catalonia, Spain (vert)	60	60
4960	$60 Salamanca, Spain (vert)	4·25	4·25
4961	$60 Toledo, Spain (vert)	60	60
4962	$60 Florence Cathedral, Italy (vert)	60	60
4963	$60 Leaning Tower of Pisa, Italy (vert)	60	60
4964	$60 Courtyard and tower, Convent of Cristo in Tomas, Portugal (vert)	60	60
4965	$60 Main door, Convent of Cristo in Tomas (vert)	60	60
4966	$60 Cloisters, Convent of Cristo in Tomas (vert)	60	60
4967	$80 Tower, Horyu-ji, Japan	70	70
4968	$80 Temple with verandah, Kyoto, Japan	70	70
4969	$80 Temple and pillar, Kyoto	70	70
4970	$80 Temples and lake, Horyu-Ji	70	70
4971	$80 Three-storey temple, Horyu-Ji	70	70
4972	$80 University of Virginia, U.S.A.	70	70
4973	$80 Yosemite National Park, U.S.A.	70	70
4974	$80 Yellowstone National Park, U.S.A.	70	70
4975	$80 Olympic National Park, U.S.A.	70	70
4976	$80 Everglades, U.S.A.	70	70
4977	$80 Street, Cuzco, Peru	70	70
4978	$80 Potosi, Bolivia	70	70
4979	$80 Fortress of San Lorenzo, Panama	70	70
4980	$80 Sangay National Park, Ecuador	70	70
4981	$80 Los Glaciares National Park, Argentina	70	70
4982	$200 City walls, Dubrovnik, Croatia	1·75	2·00
MS4983	Four sheets, each 126×101 mm. (a) $300 Golden Buddha, Mount Taishan, China. (b) $300 Monastery garden, Batalha, Portugal. (c) $300 Virgin and Child (statue), Bamberg Cathedral, Germany. (d) $300 Monastery, Mount Athos, Greece Set of 4 sheets	11·00	12·00

566 *Morchella hortensis*

1997. Fungi of the World. Multicoloured.

4984	$6 Type **566**	25	15
4985	$20 *Boletus chrysenteron*	40	20
4986	$25 *Hygrophorus agathosmus*	45	25
4987	$30 *Cortinarius violaceus*	50	30
4988	$35 *Acanthocystis geogenius*	55	30
4989	$60 *Mycena polygramma*	75	50
4990	$80 *Coprinus picaceus*	75	75
4991	$80 *Stropharia umbonatescens*	75	75
4992	$80 *Paxillus involutus*	75	75
4993	$80 *Amanita inaurata*	75	75
4994	$80 *Lepiota rhacodes*	75	75
4995	$80 *Russula amoena*	75	75
4996	$80 *Volvaria volvacea*	75	75
4997	$80 *Psalliota augusta*	75	75
4998	$80 *Tricholoma aurantium*	75	75
4999	$80 *Pholiota spectabilis*	75	75
5000	$80 *Cortinarius armillatus*	75	75
5001	$80 *Agrocybe dura*	75	75
5002	$300 *Hebeloma radicosum*	1·75	2·00
5003	$300 *Coprinus comatus*	2·75	3·00
MS5004	Two sheets, each 76×105 mm. (a) $300 *"Pholiota mutabilis.* (b) $300 *"Amanita muscaria* Set of 2 sheets	7·50	7·00

567 Pineapple Lily

1997. Flowers. Multicoloured.

5005	$6 Type **567**	20	15
5006	$6 Blue columbine	20	15
5007	$20 Petunia	30	20
5008	$25 Lily of the Nile	35	25
5009	$30 Bird of paradise	40	30
5010	$35 African daisy	45	30
5011	$60 Cape lily	60	60
5012	$60 Monarch slipperwort	60	60
5013	$60 Passion flower	60	60
5014	$60 Butterfly iris	60	60
5015	$60 Red-hot poker	60	60
5016	$60 Water lily "Dir G. T. Moore"	60	60
5017	$60 Painted tongue "Superbissima"	60	60
5018	$60 Canariensis orchid	60	60
5019	$60 Annual chrysanthemum	60	60
5020	$80 Tulips	70	70
5021	$80 Liatris	70	70
5022	$80 Roses	70	70
5023	$80 Gerber daisies	70	70
5024	$80 Sunflowers	70	70
5025	$80 Chrysanthemums	70	70
5026	$80 Gazania	70	70
5027	$80 Cape water lily	70	70
5028	$200 Insigne lady's slipper	1·75	2·25
MS5029	105×75 mm. $300 Petunias	3·50	3·75

568 Deng Xiaoping inspecting Rural Sichuan, 1980

1997. Deng Xiaoping (Chinese leader) Commem.

5030	**568** $100 multicoloured	1·00	1·00
MS5031	100×70 mm. $150 Deng Xiaoping on visit to foundry	1·50	1·60

1997. Tenth Anniv of Chernobyl Nuclear Disaster. As T 276a of Gambia. Multicoloured.

5032	$200 As Type **276a** of Gambia	1·75	2·00
5033	$200 As Type **276a** of Gambia, but inscribed "CHABAD'S CHILDREN OF CHERNOBYL" at foot	1·75	2·00

1997. 50th Death Anniv of Paul Harris (founder of Rotary International). As T 276b of Gambia. Mulicoloured.

5034	$200 Paul Harris and volunteers with children ("Health, hunger and humanity")	1·75	2·00

MS5035	77×107 mm. $300 Group of boys ("Mutual respect among all faiths, races and cultures")	2·50	3·00

1997. Golden Wedding of Queen Elizabeth II and Prince Philip. As T 276c of Gambia. Multicoloured (except Nos. 5038/9).

5036	$60 Queen Elizabeth II wearing tiara	90	90
5037	$60 Royal coat of arms	90	90
5038	$60 Wedding photograph, 1947 (black)	90	90
5039	$60 Engagement photograph (black)	90	90
5040	$60 Broadlands, Romsey (honeymoon residence)	90	90
5041	$60 Duke of Edinburgh	90	90
MS5042	99×70 mm. $300 Queen and Duke of Edinburgh	4·00	4·25

1997. "Pacific '97" International Stamp Exhibition, San Francisco. Death Centenary of Heinrich von Stephan (founder of U.P.U.). As T 276d of Gambia.

5043	$100 sepia	1·00	1·25
5044	$100 brown	1·00	1·25
5045	$100 green	1·00	1·25
MS5046	82×118 mm. $300 black and blue	2·75	3·00

DESIGNS: No. 5043, Roman post cart from frieze; 5044, Von Stephan and Mercury; 5045, Cable car, Boston, 1907; MS5046, Von Stephan and ancient Egyptian messenger.

1997. 175th Anniv of Brothers Grimm's Third Collection of Fairy Tales. *Hansel and Gretel.* As T 277a of Gambia. Multicoloured.

5047	$100 Hansel and Gretel lost in forest	1·40	1·40
5048	$100 Gingerbread house	1·40	1·40
5049	$100 Witch	1·40	1·40
MS5050	124×96 mm. $500 Gretel pushing witch into oven (horiz)	6·00	6·50

1997. 300th Anniv of Mother Goose Nursery Rhymes. Multicoloured design as T 276a of Gambia. Sheet 75×101 mm.

MS5051	$300 "Cock-a-doodle-doo" (vert)	3·75	4·00

1997. Birth Bicentenary of Hiroshige (Japanese painter). *One Hundred Famous Views of Edo.* As T 541a of Ghana. Multicoloured.

5052	$80 *Oumayagashi*	1·00	1·00
5053	$80 *Ryogoku Ekoin and Moto-Yanagibashi Bridge*	1·00	1·00
5054	$80 *Pine of Success and Oumayagashi, Asakusa River*	1·00	1·00
5055	$80 *Fireworks at Ryogoku*	1·00	1·00
5056	$80 *Dyers' Quarter, Kanda*	1·00	1·00
5057	$80 *Cotton-goods Lane, Odenma-cho*	1·00	1·00
MS5058	Two sheets, each 102×127 mm. (a) $300 *Suruga-cho.* (b) $300 *Yatsukoji, inside Sujikai Gate* Set of 2 sheets	7·00	8·00

569 Tortoise

1997. "Hong Kong '97" International Stamp Exhibition. Return of Hong Kong to China. Multicoloured.

5059	$80 Type **569**	80	80
5060	$80 Dragon	80	80
5061	$80 Unicorn	80	80
5062	$80 Phoenix	80	80
5063	$80 Barn swallow ("Swallow") and willow (vert)	80	80
5064	$80 River kingfisher ("Kingfisher") and chrysanthemum (vert)	80	80
5065	$80 Common crane ("Crane") and pine (vert)	80	80
5066	$80 Common peafowl ("Peacock") and peony (vert)	80	80
5067	$80 "Bird of Paradise" kite with two tail feathers (vert)	80	80
5068	$80 Large "eyed" kite with blue tail ribbons (vert)	80	80
5069	$80 "Phoenix" kite with "flaming" tail (vert)	80	80
5070	$80 "Insect" kite with red tail ribbons (vert)	80	80
5071	$200 Chinese landscape (face value at top left) (50×75 mm)	2·00	2·25
5072	$200 Chinese landscape (face value at bottom right) (50×75 mm)	2·00	2·25
MS5073	159×110 mm. $500 Junk in Hong Kong harbour (50×75 mm)	4·00	5·00

570 Markus Wasmeier (skier)

1997. Winter Olympic Games, Nagano, Japan (1998). Multicoloured.

5074	$30 Type **570**		35	35
5075	$30 Jens Weissflog (ski-jumper)		35	35
5076	$30 Erhard Keller		35	35
5077	$30 Rosi Mittermaier (skier)		35	35
5078	$30 Gunda Niemann (speed skater)		35	35
5079	$30 Peter Angerer (skier)		35	35
5080	$30 Gorg Thoma (ski-jumper)		35	35
5081	$35 Katja Seizinger (skier)		35	35
5082	$60 Gorg Hackl (luge)		70	70
5083	$60 Gunda Niemann (Germany) (3000 and 5000 m speed skating gold medals, 1992)		70	70
5084	$60 Tony Nash and Robin Dixon (Great Britain) (bobsleigh gold medal, 1964)		70	70
5085	$60 Switzerland (4 man bobsleigh gold medal, 1988)		70	70
5086	$60 Piet Kleine (Holland) (speed skating gold medal, 1976)		70	70
5087	$60 Oksana Baiul (Ukraine) (figure skating gold medal, 1994)		70	70
5088	$60 Cathy Turner (U.S.A.) (500 m speed skating gold medal, 1994)		70	70
5089	$60 Brian Boitano (U.S.A.) (figure skating gold medal, 1988)		70	70
5090	$60 Nancy Kerrigan (U.S.A.) (figure skating silver medal, 1994)		70	70
5091	$200 Katarina Witt (skater)		2·00	2·25

MS5092 Three sheets. (a) 106×81 mm. $300 Jean-Claude Killy (France) (slalom skiing gold medal), 1968. (b) 106×81 mm. $300 Chen Lu (China) (figure skating gold medal, 1992). (c) 76×106 mm. $300 Swiss 4-man bobsleigh team Set of 3 sheets ... 9·50 10·00

No. 5081 is inscribed "KATIA", No. 5087 "BAIUI", No. 5091 "KATHARINA" and No. **MS**5092c "GERMANY", all in error.

571 Chihuahua

1997. Cats and Dogs. Multicoloured.

5093	$20 Type **571**		55	25
5094	$25 Norfolk terrier		55	25
5095	$30 Norwegian forest cat		55	30
5096	$35 Oriental spotted tabby		55	30
5097	$60 Welsh terrier		80	70
5098	$60 Abyssinian (horiz)		80	70
5099	$60 Chocolate colorpoint shorthair (horiz)		80	70
5100	$60 Silver tabby (horiz)		80	70
5101	$60 Persian (horiz)		80	70
5102	$60 Maine coon cat and kitten (horiz)		80	70
5103	$60 Brown-shaded Burmese (horiz)		80	70
5104	$60 Persian kitten (horiz)		80	70
5105	$60 Siamese (horiz)		80	70
5106	$60 British shorthair (horiz)		80	70
5107	$60 Shar-pei		80	70
5108	$60 Chihuahua		80	70
5109	$60 Chow chow		80	70
5110	$60 Sealyham terrier		80	70
5111	$60 Collie		80	70
5112	$60 German shorthair pointer		80	70
5113	$60 Bulldog		80	70
5114	$60 German shepherd dog		80	70
5115	$60 Old English sheepdog		80	70
5116	$200 Asian smoke (cat)		2·00	2·25

MS5117 Two sheets, each 105×76 mm. (a) $300 Manx cat. (b) $300 Tibetan spaniel Set of 2 sheets ... 8·00 8·00

572 Verdin

1997. Birds of the World. Multicoloured.

5118	$25 Type **572**		75	30
5119	$30 Wood thrush (vert)		75	30
5120	$60 Rufous-sided towhee		1·00	50
5121	$80 Groove-billed ani		1·00	90
5122	$80 Green honeycreeper		1·00	90
5123	$80 Emerald toucanet		1·00	90
5124	$80 Wire-tailed manakin		1·00	90
5125	$80 Hoatzin		1·00	90
5126	$80 Rufescent tiger heron ("Tiger Heron")		1·00	90
5127	$80 Magenta-throated woodstar		1·00	90
5128	$80 Anna's hummingbird		1·00	90
5129	$80 Long-tailed hermit		1·00	90
5130	$80 White-tipped sicklebill		1·00	90
5131	$80 Red-footed plumeleteer		1·00	90
5132	$80 Fiery-throated hummingbird		1·00	90
5133	$200 Pygmy nuthatch (vert)		2·25	2·25

MS5134 Two sheets, each 70×100 mm. (a) $300 Pinnated bittern. (b) $300 Keel-billed toucan Set of 2 sheets ... 8·50 8·00

573 Pres. Cheddi Jagan in 1947 and 1997 with National Assembly Building

1997. 50th Anniv of Pres. Cheddi Jagan's Election to Parliament.

5135	**573**	$6 multicoloured	15	15
5136	**573**	$30 multicoloured	50	50

574 Princess Diana

1997. Diana, Princess of Wales Commemoration. Multicoloured.

5137	$80 Type **574**		90	90
5138	$80 Princess Diana in black V-neck dress		90	90
5139	$80 In red dress with diamante pattern on front		90	90
5140	$80 In white evening dress with narrow shoulder straps		90	90
5141	$80 In white evening dress with one shoulder bare		90	90
5142	$80 In lavender dress		90	90

MS5143 Two sheets, each 107×108 mm. (a) $300 In red sleeveless dress (33×51 mm). (b) $300 In white blouse (33×51 mm) Set of 2 sheets ... 7·00 7·50

575 Presidents Clinton (U.S.A.) and Cheddi Jagan (Guyana)

1997. President Clinton's Caribbean Visit. Multicoloured.

5144	$6 Type **575**		15	10
5145	$30 As Type **575**, but different portrait of Pres. Jagan		45	35
5146	$30 Presidents Clinton and Jagan, flags and sunrise over sea (horiz)		45	35
5147	$100 Presidents Clinton and Jagan, flags and sunrise over beach (horiz)		1·50	1·75

576 President Jiang Zemin, Flags, and New York Skyline by Day

1997. Visit of President Jiang Zemin of China to New York. Two sheets, each 125×84 mm, containing T **576** and similar horiz design. Multicoloured.

MS5148 Two sheets. (a) $200 Type **576**. (b) $300 President Jiang Zemin, flags, and New York at night Set of 2 sheets ... 5·50 6·00

1997. Christmas. Paintings. As T **284a** of Gambia. Multicoloured.

5149	$25 Cupid from *The Triumph of Galatea* (Raphael)		30	10
5150	$30 Different Cupid from *The Triumph of Galatea* (Raphael)		30	10
5151	$35 Cupid from *Primavera* (Botticelli)		35	15
5152	$60 *Angel Musicians* (Agostino di Duccio)		70	30
5153	$100 Cupid from illustration No. 1212, *Life Magazine* 28/1/06		1·40	1·50
5154	$200 Angels from *Madonna and Saints* (Rosso Fiorentino)		2·50	3·25

MS5155 Two sheets. (a) 95×105 mm. $300 *The Gardens of Love* (Rubens). (b) 105×95 mm. $300 *Cherubs* (Philippe de Champaigne) Set of 2 sheets ... 8·50 9·00

577 Abraham Lincoln

1997. 75th Anniversaries, 1997–2001. Multicoloured.

5156	$60 Type **577** (Dedication of Lincoln Memorial, Washington, 1922)		85	75
5157	$60 Mask of Tutankhamun (discovery of tomb, 1922)		85	75
5158	$60 Alexander Graham Bell and early telephone, 1922 (75th death anniv)		85	75
5159	$60 John L. Baird and first television, 1923		85	75
5160	$60 President Warren G. Harding, 1923 (75th death anniv)		85	75
5161	$60 Presidency of Calvin Coolidge, 1923		85	75
5162	$60 Skier (first Winter Olympics, Chamonix, France, 1924)		85	75
5163	$60 Sun Yat-sen (Chinese leader), 1925 (75th death anniv)		85	75
5164	$60 Charles Darwin (ban on teaching of evolution, Tennessee, U.S.A., 1925)		85	75
5165	$60 Robert Goddard (first liquid fuel rocket, 1926)		85	75
5166	$60 Richard E. Byrd (first flight over North Pole, 1926)		85	75
5167	$60 Liberty Bell (Sesquicentennial Exposition, Philadelphia, 1926)		85	75

578 Fogarty's Department Store, Georgetown

1997. Buildings in Guyana. Multicoloured.

5168	$6 Type **578**		25	15
5169	$30 St. Rose's High School (150th anniv)		75	50

579 Tiger sitting (face value at bottom right)

1998. Chinese New Year ("Year of the Tiger"). Multicoloured.

5170	$50 Type **579**		50	55
5171	$50 Tiger sitting (face value bottom left)		50	55
5172	$50 Tiger standing (face value top right)		50	55
5173	$50 Tiger standing (face value top left)		50	55

MS5174 102×72 mm. $150 Tiger with Chinese characters in background ... 1·40 1·60

580 Kentrosaurus

1998. Prehistoric Animals. Multicoloured.

5175	$25 Type **580**		40	30
5176	$30 Lesothosaurus		40	30

5177	$35 Stegoceras		40	30
5178	$55 Ceresiosaurus		65	70
5179	$55 Nothosaurus		65	70
5180	$55 Rhomaleosaurus		65	70
5181	$55 Grendelius		65	70
5182	$55 Mixosaurus		65	70
5183	$55 Mesosaurus		65	70
5184	$55 Placodus		65	70
5185	$55 Stethacanthus		65	70
5186	$55 Coelacanth		65	70
5187	$55 Quetzalcoatlus		65	70
5188	$55 Pteranodon		65	70
5189	$55 Peteinosaurus		65	70
5190	$55 Criorhychus		65	70
5191	$55 Pterodaustro		65	60
5192	$55 Eudimorphodon		65	70
5193	$55 Archeopteryx		65	70
5194	$55 Dimorphodon		65	70
5195	$55 Sharovipteryx		65	70
5196	$60 Lagosuchus		65	60
5197	$100 Herrerasaurus		1·00	1·10
5198	$200 Iguanodon		1·90	2·25

MS5199 Two sheets, each 106×76 mm. (a) $300 Yangchuanosaurus (vert). (b) $300 Styracosaurus (vert) Set of 2 sheets ... 6·00 6·50

Nos. 5178/86 and 5187/95 were each printed together, *se-tenant*, with the backgrounds forming composite designs.

581 Bryan Berard

1998. Ice Hockey Players. Multicoloured.

5200	$35 Type **581**		35	35
5201	$35 Ray Bourque		35	35
5202	$35 Martin Brodeur		35	35
5203	$35 Pavel Bure		35	35
5204	$35 Chris Chelios		35	35
5205	$35 Sergei Fedorov		35	35
5206	$35 Peter Forsberg		35	35
5207	$35 Wayne Gretzky		35	35
5208	$35 Dominik Hasek		35	35
5209	$35 Brett Hull		35	35
5210	$35 Jarome Iginla		35	35
5211	$35 Jaromir Jagr		35	35
5212	$35 Paul Kariya		35	35
5213	$35 Saku Koivu		35	35
5214	$35 John LeClair		35	35
5215	$35 Brian Leetch		35	35
5216	$35 Eric Lindros		35	35
5217	$35 Patrick Marleau		35	35
5218	$35 Mark Messier		35	35
5219	$35 Mike Modano		35	35
5220	$35 Chris Osgood		35	35
5221	$35 Zigmund Palffy		35	35
5222	$35 Felix Potvin		35	35
5223	$35 Jeremy Roenick		35	35
5224	$35 Patrick Roy		35	35
5225	$35 Joe Sakic		35	35
5226	$35 Sergei Samsonov		35	35
5227	$35 Teemu Selanne		35	35
5228	$35 Brendan Shanahan		35	35
5229	$35 Ryan Smyth		35	35
5230	$35 Jocelyn Thibault		35	35
5231	$35 Joe Thornton		35	35
5232	$35 Keith Tkachuk		35	35
5233	$35 John Vanbiesbrouck		35	35
5234	$35 Steve Yzerman		35	35
5235	$35 Dainius Zubrus		35	35

582 Argentine Team

1998. World Cup Football Championship, France. Showing competing teams and trophy. Multicoloured.

5236	$30 Type **582**		30	30
5237	$30 Austria		30	30
5238	$30 Belgium		30	30
5239	$30 Brazil		30	30
5240	$30 Bulgaria		30	30
5241	$30 Cameroon		30	30
5242	$30 Chile		30	30
5243	$30 Colombia		30	30
5244	$30 Croatia		30	30
5245	$30 Denmark		30	30
5246	$30 England		30	30

5247	$30 France	30	30
5248	$30 Germany	30	30
5249	$30 Holland	30	30
5250	$30 Iran	30	30
5251	$30 Italy	30	30
5252	$30 Jamaica	30	30
5253	$30 Japan	30	30
5254	$30 Mexico	30	30
5255	$30 Morocco	30	30
5256	$30 Nigeria	30	30
5257	$30 Norway	30	30
5258	$30 Paraguay	30	30
5259	$30 Rumania	30	30
5260	$30 Saudi Arabia	30	30
5261	$30 Scotland	30	30
5262	$30 South Africa	30	30
5263	$30 South Korea	30	30
5264	$30 Spain	30	30
5265	$30 Tunisia	30	30
5266	$30 U.S.A.	30	30
5267	$30 Yugoslavia	30	30

MS5268 Two sheets, each 110×85 mm. (a) $300 Okada, Japan (vert). (b) $300 Nakata, Japan (vert) Set of 2 sheets ... 5·00 5·50

583 Dutch Fluyt

1998. Sailing Ships. Multicoloured.

5269	$80 Type **583**	90	75
5270	$80 *Alastor* (barque)	90	75
5271	$80 *Falcon* (medieval ship)	90	75
5272	$80 *Red Rover* (barque)	90	75
5273	$80 *British Anglesey* (full-rigged ship)	90	75
5274	$80 *Archibald Russell* (barque)	90	75
5275	$80 14th century double-ended Scandinavian ship	90	75
5276	$80 Portuguese caravel	90	75
5277	$80 *Nina* (Columbus)	90	75
5278	$80 *Fannie* (schooner)	90	75
5279	$80 *Vitoria* (Magellan)	90	75
5280	$80 Arab sambook	90	75

MS5281 Two sheets. (a) 76×106 mm. $300 *Half Moon* (Hudson). (b) 106×76 mm. $300 Osberg ship Set of 2 sheets ... 7·50 6·50

No. 5274 is inscribed "ARCHIBALD RUSSEL" in error.

584 J. Bruce Ismay (Managing Director of White Star Line)

1998. 85th Anniv of Sinking of the Titanic (liner). Multicoloured.

5282	$80 Type **584**	1·10	80
5283	$80 Jack Phillips (wireless operator)	1·10	80
5284	$80 Margaret Brown (passenger)	1·10	80
5285	$80 Capt. Edward J. Smith	1·10	80
5286	$80 Frederick Fleet (crew member)	1·10	80
5287	$80 Thomas Andrews (Managing Director of Harland & Wolff)	1·10	80

MS5288 100×70 mm. $300 *Titanic* sinking ... 5·00 3·75

1998. 25th Anniv of Caribbean Community. As T **454a** of Grenada. Multicoloured.

5289	$20 Flags of Grenada and CARICOM	50	20

585 Queen Elizabeth the Queen Mother

1998. 98th Birthday of Queen Elizabeth the Queen Mother.

5290	**585** $90 multicoloured	1·00	90

1998. France's Victory in World Cup Football Championship. Nos. 5239, 5244/5, 5247, 5251, 5258, 5260 and 5262 optd **FRANCE WINNERS**. Multicoloured.

5291	$30 Brazil	30	35

5292	$30 Croatia	30	35
5293	$30 Denmark	30	35
5294	$30 France	30	35
5295	$30 Italy	30	35
5296	$30 Paraguay	30	35
5297	$30 Saudi Arabia	30	35
5298	$30 South Africa	30	35

587 Orville Wright in *Flyer I*, 1903

1998. Aircraft. Multicoloured.

5299	$80 Type **587**	75	75
5300	$80 Bleriot, 1911	75	75
5301	$80 Curtiss Jenny, 1919	75	75
5302	$80 Zeppelin LZ-10 *Schwaben*, 1911	75	75
5303	$80 W-8B, 1923	75	75
5304	$80 DH66, 1926	75	75
5305	$80 A7K Corsair II	75	75
5306	$80 A6E Intruder	75	75
5307	$80 U2 spy plane	75	75
5308	$80 Blackhawk helicopter	75	75
5309	$80 F-16	75	75
5310	$80 Phantom II	75	75

MS5311 Two sheets, each 70×100 mm. (a) $300 A-10 Warthog. (b) $300 HH-65A Dolphin helicopter Set of 2 sheets ... 5·00 5·50

Nos. 5299/304 and 5305/10 were each printed together, *se-tenant*, with the backgrounds forming composite designs.

588 Panda climbing Tree

1998. Giant Pandas. Multicoloured.

5312	$80 Type **588**	75	75
5313	$80 Panda sitting on tree trunk	75	75
5314	$80 Panda climbing bamboo	75	75
5315	$80 Panda chewing bamboo	75	75
5316	$80 Panda snapping bamboo stalk	75	75
5317	$80 Panda eating foliage	75	75

MS5318 100×70 mm. $300 Panda with leaves ... 2·75 3·00

Nos. 5312/17 were printed together, *se-tenant*, with the backgrounds forming a composite design.

589 Mountain Gorilla

1998. Mountain Gorillas. Multicoloured.

5319	$80 Type **589**	75	75
5320	$80 Gorilla climbing tree	75	75
5321	$80 Gorilla eating foliage	75	75
5322	$80 Female gorilla sitting on ground	75	75
5323	$80 Baby gorilla eating twig	75	75
5324	$80 Male gorilla in forest	75	75

MS5325 100×70 mm. $300 Young gorilla eating leaf ... 2·75 3·00

Nos. 5319/24 were printed together, *se-tenant*, with the backgrounds forming a composite design.

590 Christian Lautenschlager in Grand Prix Mercedes, 1914

1998. History of Grand Prix Motor Racing. Multicoloured.

5326	$80 Type **590**	70	70
5327	$80 P. Etancelin in Bugatti Type 35B, 1930	70	70
5328	$80 Louis Chiron in Alfa Romeo P3, 1934	70	70
5329	$80 Richard Seaman in Mercedes-Benz W154, 1938	70	70

5330	$80 Tazio Nuvolari in Auto Union D Type, 1938	70	70
5331	$80 Juan Fangio in Alfa Romeo 158, 1951	70	70
5332	$80 Stirling Moss in Mercedes-Benz W196, 1955	70	70
5333	$80 Phil Hill in Ferrari Dino 246, 1960	70	70
5334	$80 Jack Brabham in Brabham-Repco BT19, 1966	70	70
5335	$80 John Miles in Lotus Ford 72, 1970	70	70
5336	$80 Alain Prost in Renault RE40, 1983	70	70
5337	$80 David Coulthard in McLaren Mercedes MP4/13, 1998	70	70

MS5338 Two sheets, each 100×70 mm. (a) $300 Ferenc Szisz in Grand Prix Renault, 1906 (56×42 mm). (b) $300 Stirling Moss in Maserati 250F, 1956 (56×42 mm) Set of 2 sheets ... 5·00 5·50

591 Comic Book Title (½-size illustration) (image scaled to 51% of original size)

1998. 50th Anniv of Disney's Uncle Scrooge Character. Designs showing text and illustrations from comic book Christmas on Bear Mountain (drawn by C. Barks). Multicoloured.

5339	$35 Type **591**	60	60
5340	$35 Uncle Scrooge sitting in armchair	60	60
5341	$35 Uncle Scrooge looking out window	60	60
5342	$35 James the butler holding telephone	60	60
5343	$35 Uncle Scrooge at foot of staircase	60	60
5344	$35 Donald Duck with open fridge	60	60
5345	$35 Uncle Scrooge entering attic	60	60
5346	$35 Uncle Scrooge in limousine	60	60
5347	$35 Huey, Dewey and Louie at window	60	60
5348	$35 Car in snow	60	60
5349	$35 Ducks in bed	60	60
5350	$35 Donald in chair with nephews	60	60
5351	$35 Donald refusing nephews	60	60
5352	$35 Ducks and rabbit	60	60
5353	$35 Ducks with Christmas tree	60	60
5354	$35 Baby bear climbing down Christmas tree	60	60
5355	$35 Ducks in panic	60	60
5356	$35 Baby bear running	60	60
5357	$35 Ducks searching	60	60
5358	$35 Nephews and tree	60	60
5359	$35 Huey, Dewey and Louie tripping on roller skate	60	60
5360	$35 Frightened nephew	60	60
5361	$35 Baby bear on roller skate	60	60
5362	$35 Donald hiding in light fitting	60	60
5363	$35 Baby bear with chocolate	60	60
5364	$35 Louie climbing Christmas tree	60	60
5365	$35 Baby bear evading Louie	60	60
5366	$35 Nephews searching bedroom	60	60
5367	$35 Donald peering down from light fitting	60	60
5368	$35 Mother bear chasing Donald	60	60
5369	$35 Donald jumping through window	60	60
5370	$35 Bears after eating	60	60
5371	$35 Ducks looking through window	60	60
5372	$35 Donald and sleeping mother bear	60	60
5373	$35 Uncle Scrooge outside cabin	60	60
5374	$35 Uncle Scrooge in bear suit behind sofa	60	60
5375	$35 Uncle Scrooge in bear suit surprised	60	60
5376	$35 Uncle Scrooge with James	60	60
5377	$35 Ducks on Christmas Day	60	60
5378	$35 Donald fainting	60	60

MS5379 220×175 mm. $300 Carl Barks (37×50 mm); $300 Uncle Scrooge pursued by bear (50×37 mm) ... 7·00 7·00

Only issued in stamp booklets in which each pane contains two pairs separated by a horizontal gutter margin showing further parts of the comic strip. Each stamp shows two drawings of which the first in each instance is described for the listing.

1998. 50th Anniv of Organization of American States. As T **454b** of Grenada.

5380	$40 yellow, violet and black	40	30

1998. 25th Death Anniv of Pablo Picasso (painter). As T **291a** of Gambia. Multicoloured.

5381	$25 *Sleeping Peasants*	25	20
5382	$60 *Large Nude in Red Armchair*	55	40
5383	$200 *Female Head* (vert)	1·75	1·90

MS5384 102×126 mm. $300 *Man and Woman* (vert) ... 2·75 3·00

592 James E. West (first Scout executive) and Early Eagle Scouts

1998. 19th World Scout Jamboree, Chile. Multicoloured.

5385	$160 Type **592**	1·40	1·50
5386	$160 Pres. John F. Kennedy greeting Explorers, 1961	1·40	1·50
5387	$160 Walter Schirra (astronaut) receiving Special Merit badge, 1962	1·40	1·50

593 Mahatma Gandhi as Lawyer in South Africa, 1906

1998. 50th Death Anniv of Mahatma Gandhi. Multicoloured.

5388	$100 Type **593**	1·50	1·00
5389	$100 Gandhi on Bengal walk, 1946 (56×42 mm)	1·50	1·00
5390	$100 Gandhi with Jawaharlal Nehru and Sardar Patel, 1948 (56×42 mm)	1·50	1·00
5391	$100 Gandhi during fast, 1947	1·50	1·00

MS5392 70×66 mm. $300 Gandhi and Jawaharlal Nehru (horiz) ... 4·00 3·25

1998. 80th Anniv of Royal Air Force. As T **292a** of Gambia. Multicoloured.

5393	$100 Avro Lancaster B2	1·40	1·00
5394	$100 PBY-5A Catalina amphibian	1·40	1·00
5395	$100 Hawk T1As of Red Arrows	1·40	1·00
5396	$100 Avro Lancaster and De Havilland D.H. 98 Mosquito	1·40	1·00
5397	$100 BAe Hawk T1A	1·40	1·00
5398	$100 C-130 Hercules	1·40	1·00
5399	$100 Panavia Tornado GR1	1·40	1·00
5400	$100 BAe Hawk 200 in desert camouflage	1·40	1·00
5401	$150 BAe Nimrod R1P	1·50	1·25
5402	$150 Panavia Tornado F3 ADV	1·50	1·25
5403	$150 CH-47 Chinook helicopter	1·50	1·25
5404	$150 Panavia Tornado GR1A in front of hangar	1·50	1·25

MS5405 Set of six sheets, each 91×68 mm. (a) $200 Eagle and Bristol F2B fighter. (b) $200 Spitfire and EF2000 Eurofighter. (c) $300 Tiger Moth and EF2000 Eurofighter. (d) $300 Eurofighter. (e) $300 Bristol F2B fighter and two Montagu's harrier (birds). (f) $300 Bristol F2B fighter and Golden eagle Set of 6 sheets ... 15·00 15·00

1998. First Death Anniv of Diana, Princess of Wales. As T **293a** of Gambia.

5406	$60 multicoloured	60	60

1998. Birth Bicentenary of Eugene Delacroix (painter). As T **293** of Gambia. Multicoloured.

5407	$60 *Corner of the Studio* (vert)	70	55
5408	$60 *Count Mornay's Apartment* (vert)	70	55
5409	$60 *Hamlet and the Two Gravediggers* (vert)	70	55
5410	$60 *George Sand* (vert)	70	55
5411	$60 *The Fiancee of Abydos* (vert)	70	55
5412	$60 *The Champs-Elysées* (vert)	70	55
5413	$60 *Lioness* (vert)	70	55
5414	$60 *Alfred Bruyas* (vert)	70	55
5415	$60 *The Sultan of Morocco* (vert)	70	55
5416	$60 *Indian with Kukri* (vert)	70	55
5417	$60 *Man in Turkish Dress* (vert)	70	55
5418	$60 *Studies of Jewish Women* (vert)	70	55
5419	$60 *Arab Horseman giving Signal* (vert)	70	55
5420	$60 *Arab Horsemen charging* (vert)	70	55
5421	$60 *A Seated Moor* (vert)	70	55
5422	$60 *Jewish Woman in Traditional Dress* (vert)	70	55

MS5423 Two sheets, each 100×90 mm. (a) $300 *Death of Sardanpole*. (b) $300 *Jewish Wedding, Morocco* Set of 2 sheets ... 7·50 6·50

594 St. Andrew's Kirk, Georgetown

1999. 180th Anniv of St. Andrew's Kirk, Georgetown. Multicoloured.
5424 $6 Type **594** ... 15 10
5425 $30 Front of church ... 35 25
5426 $60 Front and side of church ... 60 50

595 Rabbit

1999. Chinese New Year ("Year of the Rabbit"). Multicoloured.
5427 $50 Type **595** ... 45 50
5428 $50 Rabbit (face value at bottom left) ... 45 50
5429 $50 Rabbit (face value at top right) ... 45 50
5430 $50 Rabbit (face value at top left) ... 45 50
MS5431 112×70 mm. $150 Rabbit on background of Chinese characters ... 1·25 1·40

596 Pongo driving Steam Locomotive

1999. Disney Trains. Cartoon characters. Multicoloured.
5432 $100 Type **596** ... 1·00 1·00
5433 $100 Puppies watching television ... 1·00 1·00
5434 $100 Perdita, Roger and Anita ... 1·00 1·00
5435 $100 Nanny with puppies ... 1·00 1·00
5436 $100 Horace, Jasper and Cruella De Vil ... 1·00 1·00
5437 $100 Rhino pulling Little John and Friar Tuck ... 1·00 1·00
5438 $100 Maid Marian, Robin Hood and Lady Kluck ... 1·00 1·00
5439 $100 Sir Hiss and Prince John ... 1·00 1·00
5440 $100 Allan-a-Dale on elephant ... 1·00 1·00
5441 $100 Rabbit family and Toby Turtle ... 1·00 1·00
5442 $100 Doc driving train ... 1·00 1·00
5443 $100 Grumpy, Happy, Sleepy and Bashful singing ... 1·00 1·00
5444 $100 Snow White and Prince with diamonds ... 1·00 1·00
5445 $100 Old Witch, animals from forest and Sneezy ... 1·00 1·00
5446 $100 Dopey and racoon on trolley ... 1·00 1·00
5447 $100 Triton driving locomotive ... 1·00 1·00
5448 $100 Flounder with pearls ... 1·00 1·00
5449 $100 Ariel, The Little Mermaid ... 1·00 1·00
5450 $100 Sebastian and friends in band ... 1·00 1·00
5451 $100 Ursula ... 1·00 1·00
MS5452 Five sheets. (a) 127×112 mm. $300 Horace, Jasper and Cruella De Vil (*101 Dalmatians*). (b) 127×112 mm $300 Robin Hood and Little John (*Robin Hood*). (c) 230×180 mm. $200 Doc driving train and $200 Dopey and racoon on trolley (vert) (*Snow White*). (d) 110×27 mm. $300 Ariel kissing statue (*The Little Mermaid*). (e) 127×110 mm. $300 Ariel holding starfish (*The Little Mermaid*) Set of 5 sheets ... 16·00 14·00

Nos. 5432/6 (characters from *101 Dalmatians*), Nos. 5437/41 (*Robin Hood*), Nos. 5442/6 (*Snow White*) and Nos. 5447/51 (*The Little Mermaid*) were each printed together, *se-tenant*, forming composite designs.

597 Huey skateboarding

1999. 70th Birthday of Mickey Mouse. Multicoloured.
5453 $80 Type **597** ... 80 80
5454 $80 Mickey Mouse skateboarding ... 80 80
5455 $80 Dewey skateboarding (purple cap) ... 80 80
5456 $80 Louie skateboarding (red cap) ... 80 80
5457 $80 Goofy skateboarding (lilac boots) ... 80 80
5458 $80 Donald Duck skateboarding (with cap) ... 80 80
5459 $80 Minnie Mouse rollerblading ... 80 80
5460 $80 Goofy rollerblading ... 80 80
5461 $80 Daisy Duck rollerblading (red boots) ... 80 80
5462 $80 Baby Duck rollerblading (yellow wheels) ... 80 80
5463 $80 Donald Duck rollerblading ... 80 80
5464 $80 Mickey Mouse rollerblading (red helmet) ... 80 80
5465 $80 Baby Duck rollerblading (mauve wheels) ... 80 80
5466 $80 Daisy Duck rollerblading (mauve boots) ... 80 80
5467 $80 Mickey Mouse rollerblading (mauve helmet) ... 80 80
5468 $80 Goofy skateboarding (red boots) ... 80 80
5469 $80 Dewey rollerblading ... 80 80
5470 $80 Donald Duck skateboarding (without cap) ... 80 80
MS5471 Three sheets. (a) 112×127 mm. $300 Dewey skateboarding. (b) 127×112 mm. $300 Daisy Duck. (c) 127×112 mm. $300 Goofy (horiz) Set of 3 sheets ... 8·50 8·50

598 *Pelargonium domesticum*

1999. Flowers of the World. Multicoloured.
5472 $60 Type **598** ... 60 60
5473 $60 *Oncidium macranthum* and butterfly ... 60 60
5474 $60 *Bepi orchidglades* ... 60 60
5475 $60 *Helianthus maximiliani* (two flowers) ... 60 60
5476 $60 *Cattleya walkeriana* ... 60 60
5477 $60 *Cattleya frasquita* ... 60 60
5478 $60 *Helianthus maximiliani* (single bloom) ... 60 60
5479 $60 *Paphiopedilum insigne sanderae* and *lilium longifolium* ... 60 60
5480 $60 *Lilium longifolium* ... 60 60
5481 $60 *Dendrobium nobile* ... 60 60
5482 $60 *Phalaenopsis schilleriana* ... 60 60
5483 $60 *Cymbidium alexette* ... 60 60
5484 $60 *Rhododendron nudiflorum* and hummingbird ... 60 60
5485 $60 *Phragmipedium besseae* and *laelia cinnabarina* ... 60 60
5486 $60 *Masdevallia veithiana, laelia cinnabarina* and hummingbird ... 60 60
5487 $60 *Calochortus nuttallii* ... 60 60
5488 $60 *Brassolaelio cattleya* "Puregold" ... 60 60
5489 $60 *Laelia cinnabarina* ... 60 60
5490 $90 *Leptotes bicolor* and *masdevallia ignea* ... 60 60
5491 $90 *Sophrolaelio cattleya* and *anguloa clowesii* ... 60 60
5492 $90 *Laelia pumila* ... 60 60
5493 $90 *Masdevallia ignea* ... 60 60
5494 $90 *Dendrobium phalaenopsis* ... 60 60
5495 $90 *Anguloa clowesii* ... 60 60
MS5496 Two sheets, each 106×75 mm. (a) $300 *Iris pseudacorus*. (b) $300 *Ascocentrum miniatum* (vert) Set of 2 sheets ... 7·50 7·50

Nos. 5472/80, 5481/9 and 5490/5 were each printed together, *se-tenant*, with the backgrounds forming composite designs.
No. **MS**5496b is inscribed "Asocentrum" in error.

599 *Philaethria dido*

1999. Caribbean Butterflies. Multicoloured.
5497 $80 Type **599** ... 80 80
5498 $80 *Papilio troilus* ... 80 80
5499 $80 *Eueides isabella* ... 80 80
5500 $80 *Colobura dirce* ... 80 80
5501 $80 *Agraulis vanillae* ... 80 80
5502 $80 *Callicore maimuna* ... 80 80
5503 $80 *Thecla coronata* ... 80 80
5504 $80 *Battus polydamus* ... 80 80
5505 $80 *Morpho peleides* ... 80 80
5506 $80 *Doxocopa cherubina* ... 80 80
5507 $80 *Metamorpha stelenes* ... 80 80
5508 $80 *Catonephele numili* ... 80 80
MS5509 Two sheets. (a) 76×107 mm. $300 *Papilio cresphontes* (vert). (b) 107×76 mm. $300 *Battus philenor* (vert) Set of 2 sheets ... 5·50 6·00

Nos. 5504 and 5509b are both inscribed "Baltus" in error.

600 Actor from *The Dream*

1999. Akira Kurosawa (Japanese film director) Commemoration. Multicoloured (except No. 5519).
5510 $80 Type **600** ... 70 70
5511 $80 Actor from *Red Beard* ... 70 70
5512 $80 Scene from *Rashomon* ... 70 70
5513 $80 Scene from *Seven Samurai* ... 70 70
5514 $80 Actor from *Kagemusha* ... 70 70
5515 $80 Scene from *Yojimbo* ... 70 70
5516 $130 Akira Kurosawa wearing blue cap (horiz) ... 1·10 1·10
5517 $130 Resting head on right hand (horiz) ... 1·10 1·10
5518 $130 Wearing black jumper (horiz) ... 1·10 1·10
5519 $130 Looking through camera (horiz) (brown and black) ... 1·10 1·10
MS5520 98×68 mm. $300 Actor from *Dreams* ... 2·75 3·00

601 *Boletus aereus*

1999. Fungi. Multicoloured.
5521 $25 *Coprinus atramentarius* (28×33 mm) ... 30 20
5522 $35 *Hebeloma crustuliniforme* (28×33 mm) ... 40 25
5523 $60 Type **601** ... 60 60
5524 $60 *Coprinus comatus* ... 60 60
5525 $60 *Inocybe godeyi* ... 60 60
5526 $60 *Morchella crassipes* ... 60 60
5527 $60 *Lepiota acutesquamosa* ... 60 60
5528 $60 *Amanita phalloides* ... 60 60
5529 $60 *Boletus spadiceus* ... 60 60
5530 $60 *Cortinarius collinitus* ... 60 60
5531 $60 *Lepiota procera* ... 60 60
5532 $60 *Russula ochroleuca* ... 60 60
5533 $60 *Hygrophorus hypotheius* ... 60 60
5534 $60 *Amanita rubescens* ... 60 60
5535 $60 *Boletus satanas* ... 60 60
5536 $60 *Amanita echinocephala* ... 60 60
5537 $60 *Amanita muscaria* ... 60 60
5538 $60 *Boletus badius* ... 60 60
5539 $60 *Hebeloma radicosum* ... 60 60
5540 $60 *Mycena polygramma* ... 60 60
5541 $100 *Russula nigricans* (28×33 mm) ... 90 90
5542 $200 *Tricholoma aurantium* (28×33 mm) ... 1·60 1·75
MS5543 Two sheets. (a) 70×98 mm. $300 *Pluteus cervinus*. (b) 98×70 mm. $300 *Lepiota acutesquamosa* Set of 2 sheets ... 5·50 6·00

No. **MS**5543b is inscribed "Acutesquamoso" in error.

602 Shinkansen 100 Series Bullet Train, Japan (1984)

1999. "Australia '99" International Stamp Exhibition, Melbourne. Trains. Multicoloured (except Nos. 5550/5, each brown, yellow and black, and **MS**5568b/d).
5544 $80 Type **602** ... 1·00 75
5545 $80 Ukrainian ZMGR diesel locomotive, Russia (1983) ... 1·00 75
5546 $80 Rhatische Bahn electric locomotive No. 706, Germany ... 1·00 75
5547 $80 Eurostar T.G.V. train, France (1986) ... 1·00 75
5548 $80 Atlantique T.G.V. train, France (1989) ... 1·00 75
5549 $80 Class 86-6 diesel locomotive No. 86604, Great Britain ... 1·00 75
5550 $80 Joseph Clark steam locomotive, U.S.A. (1868) ... 1·00 75
5551 $80 Diamond Stack Bethel steam locomotive, U.S.A. (1863) ... 1·00 75
5552 $80 New York Central steam locomotive No. 999, U.S.A. (1890) ... 1·00 75
5553 $80 Boston and Maine steam locomotive *Ballardville*, U.S.A. (1876) ... 1·00 75
5554 $80 Portland Rochester Railroad steam locomotive, U.S.A. (1863) ... 1·00 75
5555 $80 Baltimore and Ohio Railroad steam locomotive, U.S.A. (1881) ... 1·00 75
5556 $80 Burlington Northern GP 39-2 diesel locomotive, U.S.A. (1974) ... 1·00 75
5557 $80 CSX GP40-2 diesel locomotive, U.S.A. (1967) ... 1·00 75
5558 $80 Erie Lackawana Railroad GP 9 diesel locomotive, U.S.A. (1956) ... 1·00 75
5559 $80 Amtrak P 42 Genesis No. 82 train, U.S.A. (1993) ... 1·00 75
5560 $80 Erie Railroad S-2 diesel locomotive, U.S.A. (1948) ... 1·00 75
5561 $80 Pennsylvania Railroad S-1 diesel locomotive, U.S.A. (1947) ... 1·00 75
5562 $80 Northern and Western steam locomotive No. 610, U.S.A. (1933) ... 1·00 75
5563 $80 Pennsylvania Railroad M1B Mountain steam locomotive, U.S.A. (1930) ... 1·00 75
5564 $80 Reading Railroad FP7A diesel locomotive, U.S.A. (1951) ... 1·00 75
5565 $80 New York Central steam locomotive No. 765, U.S.A. (1940) ... 1·00 75
5566 $80 Union Pacific steam locomotive No. 3985, U.S.A. (1963) ... 1·00 75
5567 $80 GP 15-15-1 diesel locomotive, U.S.A. (1956) ... 1·00 75
MS5568 Four sheets. (a) 70×98 mm. $300 George Nagelmackers (founder of International Sleeping Car Co.) (vert). (b) 70×98 mm. $300 R. F. Trevithick (engineer, Japanese National Railways) (vert) (violet and black). (c) 70×98 mm. $300 Alfred de Glehn (locomotive designer) (vert) (brown and black). (d) 98×70 mm. $300 George Stephen (president of Canadian Pacific) (vert) (brown and black) Set of 4 sheets ... 11·00 11·00

1999. Royal Wedding. As T **298** of Gambia. Multicoloured.
5569 $150 Sophie Rhys-Jones in multicoloured dress ... 1·25 1·25
5570 $150 Prince Edward with Sophie Rhys-Jones inspecting guard of honour ... 1·25 1·25
5571 $150 Sophie Rhys-Jones wearing grey jacket ... 1·25 1·25
5572 $150 Prince Edward wearing striped shirt ... 1·25 1·25
5573 $150 Prince Edward and Sophie Rhys-Jones at the races ... 1·25 1·25
5574 $150 Sophie Rhys-Jones holding blue folder ... 1·25 1·25
5575 $150 Prince Edward wearing blue shirt ... 1·25 1·25
5576 $150 Sophie Rhys-Jones wearing black outfit ... 1·25 1·25
MS5577 Two sheets, each 83×66 mm. (a) $300 Prince Edward and Sophie Rhys-Jones in front of blossom (horiz). (b) $300 Prince Edward and Sophie Rhys-Jones in front of building (horiz) Set of 2 sheets ... 5·00 5·50

1999. John Glenn's Return to Space. As T **136** of Grenadines of Grenada. Multicoloured.
5578 $100 John Glenn (American astronaut) in spacesuit, 1962 ... 90 90
5579 $100 Relaxing after landing, 1962 ... 90 90

5580	$100 As Senator for Ohio, 1974	90	90
5581	$100 In spacesuit and helmet for Space Shuttle flight, 1998	90	90
5582	$100 In spacesuit without helmet, 1998	90	90

No. 5582 is dated "1992" in error.

1999. "iBRA '99" International Stamp Exhibition, Nuremberg. As T **299a** of Gambia. Multicoloured.

5583	$60 Class E10 electric locomotive, Germany, 1952 (vert)	60	50
5584	$200 Early steam locomotive, Der Adler, Germany, 1835	1·75	1·90

No. 5584 is inscribed "CLASS 01 STEAM EXPRESS TRAIN, GERMANY, 1926" in error.

1999. 150th Death Anniv of Katsushika Hokusai (Japanese artist). As T **299b** of Gambia. Multicoloured.

5585	$80 Travellers climbing a Mountain Path	70	75
5586	$80 Washing Clothes in a River	70	75
5587	$80 The Blind (old man smiling)	70	75
5588	$80 The Blind (man with beard)	70	75
5589	$80 Convolvulus and Tree-frog	70	75
5590	$80 Fishermen hauling a Net	70	75
5591	$80 Hibiscus and Sparrow	70	75
5592	$80 Hydrangea and Swallow	70	75
5593	$80 The Blind (man yawning)	70	75
5594	$80 The Blind (old man frowning)	70	75
5595	$80 Irises	70	75
5596	$80 Lilies	70	75

MS5597 Two sheets, each 101×72 mm. (a) $300 Flowering Cherries at Mount Yoshino (vert). (b) $300 View of Stone Causeway (vert) Set of 2 sheets — 5·00 5·50

1999. Tenth Anniv of U.N. Rights of the Child Convention. As T **299c** of Gambia. Multicoloured.

5598	$150 Two girls	1·25	1·40
5599	$150 Two boys	1·25	1·40
5600	$150 One boy	1·25	1·40

MS5601 $300 Prince Talal, UNICEF special envoy, 1980 — 2·75 3·00

Nos. 5598/600 were printed together, se-tenant, with the backgrounds forming a composite design.

1999. "PhilexFrance '99" International Stamp Exhibition, Paris. Railway Locomotives. Two sheets, each 106×82 mm, containing horiz designs as T **299d** of Gambia. Multicoloured.

MS5602 (a) $300 Class 7000 high-speed locomotive, 1949–55. (b) $300 Class 241-P steam locomotive, 1947–49 Set of 2 sheets — 7·50 7·00

1999. 250th Birth Anniv of Johann von Goethe (German writer). As T **299e** of Gambia.

5603	$150 green, black and blue	1·25	1·40
5604	$150 blue, violet and black	1·25	1·40
5605	$150 blue, brown and black	1·25	1·40

MS5606 78×109 mm. $300 brown, chocolate and black — 2·75 3·00

DESIGNS—HORIZ: No. 5603, Lynceus singing from the watchtower; 5604, Von Goethe and Von Schiller; 5605, The Fallen Icarus. VERT: MS5606, Mephistopheles as a salamander.

603 Kurt Masur (German conductor and musician)

1999. Year of the Older Person. Multicoloured (except No. MS5625).

5607	$50 Type **603**	75	75
5608	$50 Rupert Murdoch (newspaper publisher)	75	75
5609	$50 Margaret Thatcher (former British Prime Minister)	75	75
5610	$50 Pope John Paul II	75	75
5611	$50 Mikhail Gorbachev (Russian leader)	75	75
5612	$50 Ted Turner (American politician)	75	75
5613	$50 Sophia Loren (Italian actress)	75	75
5614	$50 Nelson Mandela (South African leader)	75	75
5615	$50 John Glenn (American astronaut)	75	75
5616	$50 Luciano Pavarotti (Italian opera singer)	75	75
5617	$50 Queen Elizabeth, the Queen Mother	75	75
5618	$50 Jimmy Carter (former American President)	75	75
5619	$100 Ronald Reagan (former American president) in football shirt	80	80
5620	$100 Ronald Reagan wearing black shirt	80	80

5621	$100 Ronald Reagan in military uniform	80	80
5622	$100 Ronald Reagan wearing stetson	80	80
5623	$100 Ronald Reagan feeding chimp with bottle	80	80
5624	$100 Ronald Reagan in evening dress	80	80

MS5625 111×111 mm. $300 Ronald Reagan in star (black) — 2·75 3·00

604 Pope John Paul II praying

1999. Pope John Paul II. Multicoloured.

5626	$80 Type **604**	80	80
5627	$80 Pope John Paul II (face value at top right)	80	80
5628	$80 Pope John Paul II smiling (face value at bottom left)	80	80
5629	$80 With crucifix	80	80
5630	$80 Pope John Paul II wearing black cloak	80	80
5631	$80 Pope John Paul II (face value at bottom right)	80	80

1999. 30th Anniv of First Manned Landing on Moon. As T **298c** of Gambia but horiz. Multicoloured.

5632	$80 Konstantin Tsiolkovsky and first Russian artificial satellite, 1959 (vert)	70	75
5633	$80 Launch of "Apollo 11" (vert)	70	75
5634	$80 Astronaut descending onto Moon (vert)	70	75
5635	$80 Collecting samples of lunar rock (vert)	70	75
5636	$80 "Apollo 11" lunar module, Eagle (vert)	70	75
5637	$80 Splashdown of command module Columbia (vert)	70	75
5638	$80 "Apollo 11" after launch	70	75
5639	$80 "Apollo 11" modules after separation from rocket	70	75
5640	$80 Astronaut leaving Eagle for moon walk	70	75
5641	$80 Seismic experiments equipment	70	75
5642	$80 Eagle leaving Moon	70	75
5643	$80 Eagle after splashdown	70	75

MS5644 Two sheets, each 106×83 mm. (a) $300 Astronaut saluting American flag on Moon. (b) $300 Astronaut Michael Collins Set of 2 sheets — 6·00 6·00

605 Breitling Orbiter 3 (balloon)

1999. First Non-stop Round-the-World Balloon Flight by Breitling Orbiter 3. Multicoloured.

5645	$150 Type **605**	1·25	1·40
5646	$150 Flight logo	1·25	1·40
5647	$150 Bertrand Piccard (balloonist)	1·25	1·40
5648	$150 Brian Jones (balloonist)	1·25	1·40

MS5649 100×70 mm. $300 Breitling Orbiter 3 — 2·75 3·00

606 Sidney Sheldon

1999. Great Authors of the 20th Century. Sidney Sheldon.

5650	**606** $80 multicoloured	70	70

607 Scarlet Macaw ("Marron Macaw")

1999. South American Lories and Parrots. Multicoloured.

5651	$60 Type **607**	60	60
5652	$60 Thick-billed parrot	60	60
5653	$60 Golden-crowned conure	60	60
5654	$60 Yellow-collared macaw	60	60
5655	$60 Double yellow-headed amazon	60	60
5656	$60 Mountain parakeet ("Golden-fronted Parakeet")	60	60
5657	$60 Maroon-bellied conure	60	60
5658	$60 Nanday conure	60	60
5659	$60 Hyacinth macaw	60	60
5660	$60 Blue and yellow macaw ("Blue and Gold Macaw")	60	60
5661	$60 Blue-fronted amazon	60	60
5662	$60 Amazon parrot	60	60
5663	$60 Sun conure	60	60
5664	$60 Orange-chinned parakeet ("Tivi Parakeet")	60	60
5665	$60 Golden conure ("Bavaria's Conure")	60	60
5666	$60 Fairy lorikeet	60	60

MS5667 Two sheets, each 110×85 mm. (a) $300 Jendaya conure (horiz). (b) $300 Grey-cheeked parakeet Set of 2 sheets — 8·00 7·00

Nos. 5651/8 and 5659/66 were each printed together, se-tenant, with the backgrounds forming composite designs.

Nos. 5653, 5657 and 5658 are inscribed "CANURE", "BILLED" and "NANDAYA", all in error.

608 Queen Elizabeth the Queen Mother during Second World War

1999. Queen Elizabeth the Queen Mother's 99th Birthday. Multicoloured.

5668	$60 Type **608**	60	60
5669	$60 Wedding of Duke and Duchess of York, 1923	60	60
5670	$60 Lady Elizabeth Bowes-Lyon as a child	60	60
5671	$60 At Coronation, 1937	60	60
5672	$60 Queen Mother, 1971	60	60
5673	$60 Queen Mother wearing red hat, 1991	60	60
5674	$60 Lady Elizabeth Bowes-Lyon, 1914	60	60
5675	$60 Queen Mother, 1988	60	60
5676	$60 At Royal Agricultural Show during 1950s	60	60
5677	$60 Queen Mother, 1960	60	60

MS5678 50×76 mm. $1000 Queen Mother holding bouquet (43×69 mm). Imperf — 9·00 9·50

1999. "Queen Elizabeth the Queen Mother's Century". As T **305a** of Gambia.

5679	$130 multicoloured	1·25	1·25
5680	$130 black and gold	1·25	1·25
5681	$130 black and gold	1·25	1·25
5682	$130 multicoloured	1·25	1·25

MS5683 154×158 mm. $400 multicoloured — 3·75 4·00

DESIGNS: No. 5679, Duchess of York with Princess Elizabeth, 1928; 5680, Lady Elizabeth Bowes-Lyon, 1981; Queen Elizabeth with Princess Elizabeth, 1940; 5682, Queen Elizabeth the Queen Mother in Venice, 1984. (37×50 mm)—MS5683, Queen Mother in Canada, 1988.

609 Mei Lanfang

1999. "China '99" International Stamp Exhibition, Beijing. 40th Death Anniv of Mei Lanfang (Chinese opera singer). Sheet 118×78 mm.

MS5684	**609** $400 multicoloured	3·00	3·25

610 Wang Guangning

1999. Chinese Football League Players. Multicoloured.

5685	$50 Type **610**	45	50
5686	$50 Gao Feng ("H" emblem)	45	50
5687	$50 Jian Hong (goalkeeper) (bull emblem)	45	50
5688	$50 Gao Zhongxun (Yanbian football club)	45	50
5689	$50 Yao Xia (SCQXFC)	45	50
5690	$50 Zhang Yuning ("E" emblem)	45	50
5691	$50 Zhang Weihua (Matsunichi)	45	50
5692	$50 Dragon logo	45	50
5693	$60 Cai Sheng (winged comma logo)	50	55
5694	$60 Li Weifeng ("A" emblem)	50	55
5695	$60 Xie Zhaoyang (Beijing Guoan)	50	55
5696	$60 Li Xiaopeng (LNTS)	50	55
5697	$60 Hao Haidong (Dalian Wanda)	50	55
5698	$60 Zhang Xiaorui (TEDA)	50	55
5699	$60 Qi Hong (Shenhu)	50	55
5700	$60 Dragon logo	50	55

1999. John F. Kennedy Jr. Commemoration. As T **307** of Gambia. Multicoloured.

5701	$80 John Junior as a child with mother	70	75
5702	$80 John Junior under father's desk	70	75
5703	$80 John and Jacqueline Kennedy as a young couple	70	75
5704	$80 Jacqueline Kennedy	70	75
5705	$80 John Junior with sister, Caroline	70	75
5706	$80 President John Kennedy	70	75
5707	$160 John Junior at father's funeral	1·25	1·40
5708	$160 John Junior as an adult with mother, Jacqueline	1·25	1·40
5709	$160 John Junior in front of U.S. flag	1·25	1·40

1999. Birth Centenary of Enzo Ferrari, 1998 (car manufacturer). As T **564a** of Ghana. Multicoloured.

5710	$30 312 T2 racing car	30	25
5711	$35 553 F.1 racing car	35	25
5712	$60 D 50 racing car	50	40
5713	$100 212 Export sports car	1·00	1·00
5714	$100 410 Superamerica saloon	1·00	1·00
5715	$100 125 S sports car	1·00	1·00
5716	$200 246 F.1 racing car	1·50	1·60
5717	$300 126/C2 racing car	2·25	2·50
5718	$400 312/B2 racing car	2·75	3·00

MS5719 104×70 mm. $300 512 S sports cars (93×35 mm) — 2·50 2·75

611 Inter-American Development Bank Logo

1999. 40th Anniv of Inter-American Development Bank.

5720	**611** $30 multicoloured	40	25

1999. New Millennium (1st issue). People and Events of Eleventh Century (1050–1100). As T **310b** of Gambia. Multicoloured.

5721	$35 Indians with pots (Anasazi trading centre, 1050)	55	55
5722	$35 Catalan "Black Virgin" statue (carved, 1050)	55	55
5723	$35 Horse archer (Seljuk conquest of Armenia, 1064)	55	55
5724	$35 Halley's Comet (appearance, 1066)	55	55
5725	$35 Norman cavalry (Battle of Hastings, 1066)	55	55
5726	$35 William I of England (crowned, 1066)	55	55
5727	$35 Samurai warriors (power of Fujiwara clan checked, 1068)	55	55
5728	$35 Henry IV, Holy Roman Emperor (excommunicated, 1076)	55	55
5729	$35 Timbuktu (founded, 1087)	55	55
5730	$35 Students (foundation of Bologna University, 1088)	55	55
5731	$35 Gondola, Venice (introduction, 1094)	55	55

5732	$35 El Cid (Spanish warrior) (capture of Valencia, 1094)	55	55
5733	$35 Mounted knights (First Crusade, 1095)	55	55
5734	$35 Saracen infantry (capture of Jerusalem, 1099)	55	55
5735	$35 Statue of Guanyin (Chinese deity) (carved, 1100)	55	55
5736	$35 Couple and quote from the Rubaiyat of Omar Khayyam (written, 1100) (55×36 mm)	55	55
5737	$35 Decorating jar (introduction of Syrian style storage jars, 1100)	55	55

1999. New Millennium (2nd issue). People and Events of Twentieth Century (1910–1919). As T **471a** of Grenada. Multicoloured.

5738	$35 Poster for Grafton Gallery's Post Impressionist Exhibition, 1910	60	60
5739	$35 Trial scene and oil rig (Standard Oil case, 1911)	60	60
5740	$35 Harriet Quimby (first American woman pilot, 1911)	60	60
5741	$35 U.S. Senate (declaration of war, 1917)	60	60
5742	$35 Sinking of Titanic, 1912	60	60
5743	$35 Emperor Pu Yi (formation of Chinese Republic, 1913)	60	60
5744	$35 Statue over entrance (opening of Grand Central Station, New York, 1913)	60	60
5745	$35 Archduke Francis Ferdinand of Austria and cavalry (assassinated, 1914)	60	60
5746	$35 Map and lock gates (opening of Panama Canal, 1914)	60	60
5747	$35 Lawrence of Arabia (Arab revolt, 1916)	60	60
5748	$35 Burning buildings, Dublin (Easter Rising, 1916)	60	60
5749	$35 Lenin and revolutionaries (Russian Revolution, 1917)	60	60
5750	$35 Tsar Nicholas II and family (murdered, 1917)	60	60
5751	$35 Treaty of Versailles, 1918	60	60
5752	$35 Three patients and poster (influenza epidemic, 1919)	60	60
5753	$35 Leo Tolstoy and Mark Twain (deaths, 1910) (55×36 mm)	60	60
5754	$35 Walter Gropius and Bauhaus (opened 1919)	60	60

Dates on Nos. 5750 and 5751 are transposed. No. 5754 is inscribed "Bahaus" in error.

1999. Faces of the Millennium. Diana, Princess of Wales. As T **307a** of Gambia. Multicoloured.

5755	$80 Top of head (face value at left)	70	75
5756	$80 Top of head (face value at right)	70	75
5757	$80 Ear (face value at left)	70	75
5758	$80 Eye and temple (face value at right)	70	75
5759	$80 Cheek (face value at left)	70	75
5760	$80 Cheek (face value at right)	70	75
5761	$80 Blue background (face value at left)	70	75
5762	$80 Chin (face value at right)	70	75

Nos. 5755/62 were printed together, se-tenant, in sheetlets of 8 with the stamps arranged in two vertical columns separated by a gutter also containing miniature flower photographs. When viewed as a whole the sheetlet forms a portrait of Diana, Princess of Wales.

GUYANA $100
612 Dragon

2000. Chinese New Year ("Year of the Dragon"). Multicoloured.

5763	$100 Type **612** (face value bottom right)	85	90
5764	$100 Dragon (face value bottom left)	85	90
5765	$100 Dragon (face value top right)	85	90
5766	$100 Dragon (face value top left)	85	90
MS5767	102×70 mm. $300 Dragon on background of Chinese characters	2·50	2·75

613 Cugnot's Steam-powered Fardier (1769)

2000. Cars. Multicoloured.

5768	$100 Type **613**	80	80
5769	$100 Marcus's motor carriage (1875)	80	80
5770	$100 Benz Velo (1894)	80	80

5771	$100 Bordino's steam carriage (1854)	80	80
5772	$100 Benz Motorwagen (1886)	80	80
5773	$100 Black Model T Ford (1908)	80	80
5774	$100 Duesenberg Model A phaeton (1926)	80	80
5775	$100 Mercedes-Benz Model K (1927)	80	80
5776	$100 Rolls-Royce Phantom I (1928)	80	80
5777	$100 Auburn 851 Speedster (1935)	80	80
5778	$100 Mercedes-Benz 540K Cabriolet B (1936)	80	80
5779	$100 Volkswagen Beetle (1949)	80	80
5780	$100 Ford Thunderbird (1957)	80	80
5781	$100 Jaguar XK150 (1957)	80	80
5782	$100 Chevrolet Corvette Stingray (1968)	80	80
5783	$100 BMW 2002 Turbo (1973)	80	80
5784	$100 Porsche 911 Turbo (1975)	80	80
5785	$100 Volkswagen Beetle (1999)	80	80
5786	$100 Daimler (1886)	80	80
5787	$100 Opel Luzman (1898)	80	80
5788	$100 Benz Landaulet Coupe (1899)	80	80
5789	$100 Peugeot Vis-a-vis (1892)	80	80
5790	$100 Benz Patent Motor Car (1886)	80	80
5791	$100 Benz Velo (1894)	80	80
5792	$100 Ford (1896)	80	80
5793	$100 De Dion-Bouton Populare (1903)	80	80
5794	$100 Adler (1900)	80	80
5795	$100 Vauxhall (1904)	80	80
5796	$100 Rolls Royce Silver Ghost (1908)	80	80
5797	$100 Model T Ford (1908) (different)	80	80

MS5798	Five sheets. (a) 105×80 mm. $400 Mercedes Benz 60/70 (1904) (50×38 mm). (b) 105×80 mm. $400 Mercedes Benz Type 320 Cabriolet (1939) (50×38 mm). (c) 105×80 mm. $400 Mercedes Benz 300 SL Gullwing (1954) (50×38 mm). (d) 81×63 mm. $400 Runabout (1910) (50×38 mm). (e) 81×63 mm. $400 Turner Miesse (1904) (50×38 mm) Set of 5 sheets	14·00	15·00

No. 5791 is inscribed "VELD" in error.

614 Top of Head

2000. Faces of the Millennium. George Washington. Designs showing a collage of miniature bank note photographs. Multicoloured.

5799	$80 Type **614**	85	85
5800	$80 Top of head (face value at right)	85	85
5801	$80 Ear (face value at left)	85	85
5802	$80 Cheek (face value at right)	85	85
5803	$80 Right shoulder (face value at left)	85	85
5804	$80 Left shoulder (face value at right)	85	85
5805	$80 Right upper arm (face value at left)	85	85
5806	$80 Left upper arm (face value at right)	85	85

Nos. 5799/806 were printed together, se-tenant, in sheetlets of 8 with the stamps arranged in two vertical columns separated by a gutter also containing miniature photographs. When viewed as a whole the sheetlet forms a portrait of George Washington.

GUYANA $30
615 Hogfish (Lachnolaimus maximus)

2000. Tropical Marine Life. Multicoloured.

5807	$30 Type **615**	30	25
5808	$35 Flamingo-tongue cowrie (Cyphoma gibbosum)	35	25
5809	$60 Permit (Trachinotus falcatus)	60	40
5810	$80 Lionfish (Pterois volitans) (vert)	70	75
5811	$80 Bottle-nosed dolphin (Tursiops truncatus) (vert)	70	75
5812	$80 Jellyfish (Diplulmaris antarctica) (vert)	70	75
5813	$80 Grey angelfish (Pomacanthus arcuatus) (vert)	70	75

5814	$80 Spotted eagle ray (Aetobatus narinari) (vert)	70	75
5815	$80 Grey reef shark (Carcharhinus amblyrhynchos) (vert)	70	75
5816	$80 Sea bass (Sacura margaritacea) (vert)	70	75
5817	$80 Giant octopus (Octopus dolfeini) (vert)	70	75
5818	$80 Great barracuda (Sphyraena barracuda)	70	75
5819	$80 Gulper eel (Saccopharynx sp)	70	75
5820	$80 Sea slug (Chromodoris amoena)	70	75
5821	$80 Blue marlin (Makaira nigricans)	70	75
5822	$80 Killer whale (Orcinus orcai)	70	75
5823	$80 Reid's seahorse (Hippocampus reidi)	70	75
5824	$80 Green sea turtle (Chelonia mydas)	70	75
5825	$80 Sailfin blenny (Emblemaria pandionis)	70	75
5826	$80 Indigo hamlet (Hypoplectrus indigo)	70	75
5827	$80 Scallop (Chlamys hastata)	70	75
5828	$80 Flag rockfish (Sebastes rubrivinctus)	70	75
5829	$80 Lookdown (Selene vomer)	70	75
5830	$80 Orange marginella (Marginella carnea)	70	75
5831	$80 Harbour seal (Phocus vitulina)	70	75
5832	$80 Dolphin fish (Coryphaena hippurus)	70	75
5833	$80 Coney (Epinephelus fulvus)	70	75
5834	$100 Spot-finned hogfish (Bodianus pulchellus)	90	90
5835	$200 Porkfish (Anisotremus virginicus)	1·60	1·75
5836	$300 Orange-throated darter (Etheostoma spectabile)	2·25	2·50

MS5837	Three sheets. (a) 85×110 mm. $400 Snakestar (Asteroschema tenue) (vert). (b) 85×110 mm. $400 Penpoint gunnel (Apodichthys flavidus) (vert). (c) 110×85 mm. $400 Spotted cleaner shrimp (Periclimenes pedersoni (57×42 mm) Set of 3 sheets	11·00	11·00

Nos. 5810/17, 5818/25 and 5826/33 were each printed together, se-tenant, with the backgrounds forming composite designs.

2000. 18th Birthday of Prince William. As T **312b** of Gambia. Multicoloured.

5838	$100 Prince William with Prince Harry	1·00	1·00
5839	$100 As a young boy, holding present	1·00	1·00
5840	$100 Prince William wearing suit and white shirt	1·00	1·00
5841	$100 Wearing suit and blue shirt	1·00	1·00
MS5842	100×80 mm. $400 Dressed for skiing (37×50 mm)	3·75	4·00

2000. "EXPO 2000" World Stamp Exhibition, Anaheim, USA. Space Satellites. As T **582a** of Ghana. Multicoloured.

5843	$100 "Apollo 11"	80	85
5844	$100 "Pioneer" and Saturn	80	85
5845	$100 Nasa/Esa "Soho" Satellite	80	85
5846	$100 Nasa "Mars Orbiter" and Mars	80	85
5847	$100 Space Shuttle and International Space Station	80	85
5848	$100 "Giotto" and Halley's Comet	80	85
5849	$100 "Amsat IIIC" (vert)	80	85
5850	$100 "Sret" (vert)	80	85
5851	$100 "Inspector" (vert)	80	85
5852	$100 "Stardust" (vert)	80	85
5853	$100 "Temisat" (vert)	80	85
5854	$100 "Arsene" (vert)	80	85
5855	$100 "Cesar" with Argentine and Spanish flags	80	85
5856	$100 "Sirio 2" with Italian flag	80	85
5857	$100 "Taos S 80" with French flag	80	85
5858	$100 "Viking" with Swedish flag	80	85
5859	$100 "SCD 1" with Brazilian flag	80	85
5860	$100 "Offeq 1" with Israeli flag	80	85
MS5861	Two sheets. (a) 106×76 mm. $400 "Solar Max". (b) 76×106 mm. $400 Clementine French Satellite "Ariane V 124" (vert)	6·00	6·50

No. 5845 is inscribed "Satellit" in error.

2000. 25th Anniv of "Apollo-Soyuz" Joint Project. As T **582a** of Ghana. Multicoloured.

5862	$200 Thomas Stafford and Vance Brand ("Apollo 18" astronauts)	1·60	1·75
5863	$200 "Apollo 18" command module	1·60	1·75
5864	$200 Thomas Stafford and Valeri Kubasov (Russian cosmonaut)	1·60	1·75
MS5865	88×71 mm. $400 Donald Slayton and Thomas Stafford ("Apollo 18" astronauts) (horiz)	2·75	3·00

2000. 50th Anniv of Berlin Film Festival. As T **582c** of Ghana. Multicoloured.

5866	$100 Das Boot ist Voll, 1981	80	85
5867	$100 David, 1979	80	85
5868	$100 Hong Gooliang, 1988	80	85
5869	$100 Die Ehe der Maria Braun, 1979	80	85
5870	$100 The Whisperers, 1967	80	85
5871	$100 Le Vieil Homme et L'Enfant, 1967	80	85
MS5872	97×103 mm. $400 Love Streams, 1984	3·00	3·25

No. 5871 omits "L'ENFANT" from the film title.

2000. 175th Anniv of Stockton and Darlington Line (first public railway). As T **582c** of Ghana. Multicoloured.

5873	$200 Timothy Hackworth	2·25	2·25
5874	$200 Hackworth's "Sans Pareil" engine	2·25	2·25
5875	$200 Bramhope Tunnel, Otley	2·25	2·25

Nos. 5874 and 5875 are inscribed "Sansareil" and "Branhope", both in error.

GUYANA $400
616 Johann Sebastian Bach

2000. 250th Death Anniv of Johann Sebastian Bach (German composer). Sheet 88×76 mm.

MS5876	**616** $400 multicoloured	5·00	5·00

2000. Election of Albert Einstein (mathematical physicist) as Time Magazine "Man of the Century". Sheet 117×91 mm, containing vert design as T **312d** of Gambia. Multicoloured.

MS5877	$400 Albert Einstein	3·75	3·50

2000. Centenary of First Zeppelin Flight. As T **582c** of Ghana. Multicoloured.

5878	$200 Count von Zeppelin and LZ-1 airship, 1900	2·50	2·00
5879	$200 Von Zeppelin and LZ-2, 1906	2·50	2·00
5880	$200 Von Zeppelin and LZ-9, 1911	2·50	2·00
MS5881	84×114 mm. $400 LZ-127 Zeppelin, 1928 (50×38 mm)	5·00	4·50

2000. Olympic Games, Sydney. As T **582f** of Ghana. Multicoloured.

5882	$160 Henry Robert Pearce (single sculls rower), Los Angeles (1932)	1·25	1·40
5883	$160 Volleyball	1·25	1·40
5884	$160 Olympic Park, Canada (1976) and Canadian flag	1·25	1·40
5885	$160 Ancient Greek athletes	1·25	1·40

GUYANA $100
617 Rohan Kanhai

2000. West Indies Cricket Tour and 100th Test Match at Lord's. Multicoloured.

5886	$100 Type **617**	1·75	1·00
5887	$300 Clive Lloyd	3·25	3·00
MS5888	121×104 mm. $400 Lord's Cricket Ground, London (horiz)	6·00	5·50

GUYANA $150
618 Flags of China and Macau

2000. Return of Macau to Chinese Sovereignty. Sheet 144×119 mm, containing T **618** and similar horiz design. Multicoloured.

MS5889	$150 Type **618**; $150 Downtown Macau	3·25	3·25

2000. Betty Boop (cartoon character). As T **308** of Gambia. Multicoloured.

5890	$80 Betty Boop wearing striped shirt	65	70
5891	$80 With shopping bags	65	70
5892	$80 Kneeling on cushion	65	70
5893	$80 As belly dancer	65	70
5894	$80 Putting on shoe	65	70
5895	$80 Wearing cowboy boots	65	70
5896	$80 Betty Boop dancing	65	70
5897	$80 In flowered trousers	65	70

5898	$80 In black dress	65	70

MS5899 Twenty-two sheets. (a) 137×87 mm. $400 In blue dress and fur stole; (b) 137×87 mm. $400 In polka dot dress; (c) 120×95 mm. $400 Standing in shell; (d) 111×127 mm. $400 In red dress by the sea; (e) 121×95 mm. $400 Wearing brown coat and red scarf; (f) 120×95 mm. $400 With tennis racket; (g) 121×101 mm. $400 Winking; (h) 120×96 mm. $400 Wearing black feather boa and brown hat; (i) 95×133 mm. $400 With sad expression (horiz). (j) 91×143 mm. $400 Wearing ruff; (k) 90×140 mm. $400 Wearing orange t-shirt and baseball hat (horiz). (l) 90×140 mm. $400 Wearing red vest top; (m) 140×90 mm. $400 Wearing pink baseball hat; (n) 90×140 mm. $400 Wearing red dress and orange sash; (o) 89×139 mm. $400 Holding present; (p) 89×139 mm. $400 Wearing party hat (horiz). (q) 89×139 mm. $400 Wearing sailor's hat; (r) 89×139 mm. $400 In red bikini; (s) 89×139 mm. $400 With sunglasses on head; (t) 89×139 mm. $400 In mauve vest top and blue dungarees (horiz). (u) 89×139 mm. $400 In mauve vest top; (v) 89×139 mm. $400 With mauve flower in hair Set of 22 sheets ... 48·00 50·00

2000. Scenes from *I Love Lucy* (American T.V. comedy series). As T **309** of Gambia, but vert. Multicoloured.

5900	$60 Lucy reading a thriller	50	55
5901	$60 Lucy and Ricky talking	50	55
5902	$60 Ricky whispering to Lucy	50	55
5903	$60 Lucy looking out of window	50	55
5904	$60 Lucy behind Ethel	50	55
5905	$60 Ricky holding red scarf over Lucy	50	55
5906	$60 Ethel and Lucy with frying pan	50	55
5907	$60 Ricky with frying pan	50	55
5908	$60 Lucy and Ethel sitting on sofa next to coffee table	50	55

MS5909 Ten sheets. (a) 120×95 mm. $400 Lucy in pink dressing gown. (b) 120×95 mm. $400 Lucy with dustbin lid. (c) 100×134 mm. $400 Lucy wearing glasses. (d) 138×100 mm. $400 Lucy wearing blue hat and green coat. (e) 93×137 mm. $400 Lucy dancing the rumba. (f) 137×100 mm. $400 Lucy wearing green hat. (g) 100×134 mm. $400 Lucy with knives. (h) 137×100 mm. $400 Lucy wearing black hat. (i) 93×137 mm. $400 Lucy in checked shirt. (j) 137×100 mm. $400 Lucy wearing leis Set of 10 sheets ... 21·00 23·00

2000. Scenes from *The Three Stooges* (American T.V. comedy series). As T **310** of Gambia. Multicoloured.

5910	$80 Larry, Moe and Curly (The Three Stooges) with man in green jacket	65	70
5911	$80 Larry and Moe with skeleton	65	70
5912	$80 Shemp with hair standing on end	65	70
5913	$80 Larry, Moe and Curly with fingers in mouths	65	70
5914	$80 Larry, Moe and Curly reading a book	65	70
5915	$80 Larry, Moe and Curly holding man in bowler hat	65	70
5916	$80 Shemp pointing a gun at Larry and Moe	65	70
5917	$80 Moe and Shemp holding Larry (being kicked in stomach by man in blue)	65	70
5918	$80 Moe and Shemp looking at man in window	65	70
5919	$80 Moe pointing syphon bottle at Larry, with Shemp behind	65	70
5920	$80 Larry, Moe and Shemp as cave men (Moe with rock on head)	65	70
5921	$80 Moe with cow	65	70
5922	$80 Shemp with bucket on head	65	70
5923	$80 Moe, Shemp and Larry as cavemen (three wise monkeys)	65	70
5924	$80 Moe, Shemp and Larry as cavemen (Shemp holding large rock)	65	70
5925	$80 Larry, Moe and Shemp wearing pith helmets	65	70
5926	$80 Moe, Shemp and Larry in front of painting	65	70
5927	$80 Moe, Larry and Shemp with false beards	65	70

MS5928 Four sheets (a) 92×122 mm. $400 Shemp wearing tam-o'-shanter (vert). (b)122×92 mm. $400 Larry with skeleton. (c) 131×103 mm. $400 Larry with lady in blue dress (vert). (d) 131×103 mm. $400 Moe being pulled by collar Set of 4 sheets ... 9·00 12·00

619 Outline Drawing of Dove on Head

2000. Third Annual Caribbean Media Conference, Georgetown.

5929	**619**	$100 multicoloured	1·00	85

2000. "Euro 2000" Football Championship. As T **316** of Gambia. Multicoloured.

5930	$80 Turkish team	70	75
5931	$80 Slovenian team	70	75
5932	$80 Yugoslavian team	70	75
5933	$80 Swedish team	70	75
5934	$80 Belgian team	70	75
5935	$80 Spanish team	70	75
5936	$80 French team	70	75
5937	$80 English team	70	75
5938	$80 Danish team	70	75
5939	$80 German team	70	75
5940	$80 Italian team	70	75
5941	$80 Dutch team	70	75
5942	$80 Portuguese team	70	75
5943	$80 Romanian team	70	75
5944	$80 Czech team	70	75
5945	$80 Norwegian team	70	75

MS5946 Two sheets, each 102×80 mm. (a) $400 Stefan Kuntz, 1966 (vert). (b) $400 Jurgen Klinsmann holding trophy, 1996 (vert) Set of 2 sheets ... 6·50 7·00

620 Lee Hyo-Ri (Korean singer)

2000. Fine Killing Liberty (FIN.K.L), Korean Girl Group. Multicoloured (except No. 5954).

5947	$80 Type **620**	70	75
5948	$80 Ok Ju-Hyun (head tilted to left)	70	75
5949	$80 Lee Jin (looking sideways)	70	75
5950	$80 Lee Jin (facing forwards)	70	75
5951	$80 FIN.K.L	70	75
5952	$80 Sung Yu-Ri (head tilted to left)	70	75
5953	$80 Lee Hyo-Ri (no hat)	70	75
5954	$80 Sung Yu-Ri (facing forwards) (purple, black and blue)	70	75
5955	$80 Ok Ju-Hyun smiling	70	75

621 Amanita calyptroderma

2000. "The Stamp Show 2000" International Stamp Exhibition, London. Fungi. Multicoloured.

5956	$100 Type **621**	85	90
5957	$100 Polyporus brumalis	85	90
5958	$100 Hygrophorus pudorinus	85	90
5959	$100 Aeryginosa strophoria geophila	85	90
5960	$100 Amanita muscaria	85	90
5961	$100 Armillaria mellea	85	90
5962	$100 Hygrophoracea	85	90
5963	$100 Russula xerampelina	85	90
5964	$100 Hygrophorus coccineus	85	90
5965	$100 Psilocybe stuntzii	85	90
5966	$100 Rhodotus palmatus	85	90
5967	$100 Lactarius indigo	85	90
5968	$100 Gomphus floccosus	85	90
5969	$100 Amanita caesarea	85	90
5970	$100 Leotia viscose	85	90
5971	$100 Entoloma salmoneum	85	90
5972	$100 Cheimonophyllum candidissimus	85	90
5973	$100 Cortinarius multiformis	85	90

MS5974 Three sheets. (a) 99×69 mm. $400 Marasmius rotula. (b) 69×99 mm. $400 Volvariella pusilla (vert). (c) 99×69 mm. $400 Trametes versicolour Set of 3 sheets ... 9·00 9·50

Nos. 5956/61, 5962/7 and 5968/73 were each printed together, se-tenant, with the backgrounds forming composite designs.

Nos. 5956/8, 5961/2, 5964/5, 5967, 5969, 5972, **MS**5974a and **MS**5974c are inscribed "calyptzoderma", "crumalis", "pydorinus", "Armillariella", "Hygrophotaceae", "cocineus", "psilcybe stuntaii", "lactaius", "Aminita", "candidissimis", "zotula" and "Tzametes", all in error.

622 Bougainvillea spectabilis

2000. Flowers. Multicoloured.

5975	$35 Type **622**	35	25
5976	$60 Euphorbia milii	60	40
5977	$100 Cordia sebestena (vert)	80	85
5978	$100 Heliconia wagneriana (vert)	80	85
5979	$100 Dendrobium phalaenopsis (vert)	80	85
5980	$100 Passiflora caerulea (vert)	80	85
5981	$100 Oncidium nubigenum (vert)	80	85
5982	$100 Hibiscus rosa-sinensis (vert)	80	85
5983	$100 Lantana camara	80	85
5984	$100 Jatropha integerrima	80	85
5985	$100 Plumeria alba	80	85
5986	$100 Strelitzia reginae	80	85
5987	$100 Clerodendrum splendens	80	85
5988	$100 Thunbergia grandiflora	80	85
5989	$200 Catharanthus roseus	1·50	1·60
5990	$300 Ipomoea carnea	2·10	2·25

MS5991 Two sheets (a) 83×103 mm. $400 Cattleya granulose (vert). (b) 103×83 mm. $400 Guzmania lingulata Set of 2 sheets ... 6·00 6·50

Nos. 5983/8 were printed together, se-tenant, the backgrounds forming a composite design.

623 Russelia equisetiformis

2000. Flowers of Central America. Multicoloured.

5992	$35 Type **623**	35	25
5993	$60 Sprekelia formosissima	60	40
5994	$100 Bignonia capreolata	80	85
5995	$100 Calceolaria herbeo-hybrida	80	85
5996	$100 Canna generalis	80	85
5997	$100 Bauhinia grandiflora	80	85
5998	$100 Amaranthus caudatus	80	85
5999	$100 Abutilon megapotamicum	80	85
6000	$100 Ipomoea tricolor ("Morning Glory")	80	85
6001	$100 Lantana camara	80	85
6002	$100 Cantua buxifolia	80	85
6003	$100 Fuschia	80	85
6004	$100 Eichhornia crassipes	80	85
6005	$100 Cosmos sulphureus	80	85
6006	$200 Passiflora quadrangularis	1·50	1·60
6007	$300 Mirabilis jalapa	2·10	2·25

MS6008 Two sheets, each 100×70 mm. (a) $400 Oeceoclades maculate. (b) $400 Passiflora van-volxemii ("Tasconia") ... 6·00 6·50

No. 6004 is inscribed "Eichhornia", in error.

2000. Victims of Munich Olympics Massacre (1972) Commemoration. As T **328** of Gambia showing Israeli athletes and officials. Multicoloured.

6009	$40 Yaakov Springer (weightlifting referee)	75	50
6010	$40 Andrei Schpitzer (fencing referee)	75	50
6011	$40 Amitsur Shapira (athletics coach)	75	50
6012	$40 David Berger (weightlifter)	75	50
6013	$40 Ze'ev Friedman (weight-lifter)	75	50
6014	$40 Joseph Gottfreund (wrestling referee)	75	50
6015	$40 Moshe Weinberg (wrestling referee)	75	50
6016	$40 Kahat Shor (shooting coach)	75	50
6017	$40 Mark Slavin (wrestler)	75	50
6018	$40 Eliezer Halffin (wrestler)	75	50
6019	$40 Joseph Romano (weight-lifter)	75	50
6020	$40 Munich Olympics stadium	75	50

MS6021 127×101 mm. $400 Israeli athlete with Olympic torch (vert) ... 4·50 4·00

2000. Queen Elizabeth the Queen Mother's 100th Birthday. As T **318** of Gambia. Multicoloured.

6022	$100 Queen Elizabeth the Queen Mother	1·50	1·50

624 Heads of Two Angels

2000. Christmas and Holy Year. Multicoloured.

6023	$60 Type **624**	50	40
6024	$90 Two angels	80	60
6025	$120 Heads of two angels (different)	1·00	75
6026	$180 As $90	1·40	1·60
6027	$180 Type **624**	1·40	1·60
6028	$180 As $120	1·40	1·60
6029	$180 Two angels with drapery	1·40	1·60
6030	$400 As No. 6029	3·00	3·25

MS6031 121×110 mm. $400 Holy Child (horiz) ... 3·25 3·50

625 Snake

2001. Chinese New Year ("Year of the Snake"). Multicoloured.

6032	$80 Type **625**	70	70
6033	$80 Snake (face value at top right)	70	70
6034	$80 Snake (face value at bottom right)	70	70
6035	$80 Snake (face value at bottom left)	70	70

MS6036 85×65 mm. $250 Snake (vert) ... 2·00 2·50

626 Prime Minister's Residence, Georgetown

2001. Tourist Attractions. Multicoloured.

6037	$90 Type **626**	1·00	1·00
6038	$90 Kaieteur Falls (vert)	1·00	1·00

2001. Faces of the Millennium. Queen Elizabeth the Queen Mother's 100th Birthday. As T **307a** of Gambia showing collage of miniature flower photographs. Multicoloured.

6039	$80 Top left side of head	75	75
6040	$80 Top right side of head	75	75
6041	$80 Eye and temple	75	75
6042	$80 Temple	75	75
6043	$80 Right cheek	75	75
6044	$80 Left cheek	75	75
6045	$80 Chin	75	75
6046	$80 Neck	75	75

Nos. 6039/46 were printed together, se-tenant, in sheetlets of 8 with the stamps arranged in two vertical columns separated by a gutter also containing miniature photographs. When viewed as a whole, the sheetlet forms a portrait of the Queen Mother.

2001. Faces of the Millennium: 80th Birthday of Pope John Paul II. As T **307a** of Gambia showing collage of miniature religious photographs. Multicoloured.

6047	$100 Back of head	1·10	1·10
6048	$100 Front of forehead	1·10	1·10
6049	$100 Ear	1·10	1·10
6050	$100 Eye	1·10	1·10
6051	$100 Neck	1·10	1·10
6052	$100 Cheek	1·10	1·10
6053	$100 Shoulder of robe	1·10	1·10
6054	$100 Hands	1·10	1·10

Nos. 6047/54 were printed together, se-tenant, in sheetlets of 8 with the stamps arranged in two vertical columns separated by a gutter also containing miniature photographs. When viewed as a whole, the sheetlet forms a portrait of the Pope.

627 Chow Yun-Fat

2001. Chow Yun-Fat (Hong Kong actor). Multicoloured.

6055	$60 Type **627**	50	55
6056	$60 Wearing maroon coat	50	55
6057	$60 Wearing dark suit and grey shirt	50	55
6058	$60 In cream jacket, black shirt and white T-shirt	50	55
6059	$60 Wearing dark suit, white shirt and grey tie	50	55
6060	$60 In dark overcoat	50	55

2001. Characters from Pokemon (children's cartoon series). As T **332a** of Gambia. Multicoloured.

6061	$100 "Staryu No. 120"	85	85
6062	$100 "Seaking No. 119"	85	85
6063	$100 "Tentacool No. 72"	85	85
6064	$100 "Magikarp No. 129"	85	85
6065	$100 "Seadra No. 117"	85	85
6066	$100 "Goldeen No. 118"	85	85
MS6067	74×114 mm. $400 "Horsea No. 116" (vert)	1·10	1·10

628 Boxer Dog

2001. "Hong Kong 2001" Stamp Exhibition. Cats and Dogs. Multicoloured.

6068	$35 Type **628**	35	25
6069	$60 Cinnamon ocicat	55	55
6070	$60 Devon Rex	55	55
6071	$60 Egyptian Mau	55	55
6072	$60 Turkish angora	55	55
6073	$60 Sphynx	55	55
6074	$60 Persian	55	55
6075	$60 American wirehair	55	55
6076	$60 Exotic shorthair	55	55
6077	$60 American curl	55	55
6078	$80 Airedale terrier	70	70
6079	$80 Greyhound	70	70
6080	$80 Afghan hound	70	70
6081	$80 Samoyed	70	70
6082	$80 Field spaniel	70	70
6083	$80 Scottish terrier	70	70
6084	$80 Brittany spaniel (brown and white)	70	70
6085	$80 Boston terrier	70	70
6086	$100 Smooth dachshund	90	90
6087	$300 White Manx	2·50	2·75
MS6088	Two sheets, each 100×80 mm. (a) $400 Birman (cat). (b) $400 Dalmatian Set of 2 sheets	6·50	7·00

Nos. 6070/7 (cats) and 6078/85 (dogs) were each printed together, se-tenant, with the backgrounds forming composite designs. No. 6081 is inscribed "Samoyeo" in error. Nos. 6070/85 and **MS**6088 all show the "Hong Kong 2001" logo on the sheet margins.

629 "Tom"

2001. Cats and Dogs of the Cinema. Multicoloured.

6089	$100 Type **629**	90	90
6090	$100 "Puff" (Siamese)	90	90
6091	$100 "Jag" (silver tabby)	90	90
6092	$100 "Fritz" (Burmese, with paw curled)	90	90
6093	$100 "Smokey" (Burmese)	90	90
6094	$100 "Thor" (white cat)	90	90
6095	$100 "Pup" (small black and tan dog)	90	90
6096	$100 "Yogi" (white dog in snow)	90	90
6097	$100 "Hooch" (mastiff)	90	90
6098	$100 "Huxley Blu" (collie)	90	90
6099	$100 "Snowflake" (small white dog)	90	90
6100	$100 "Red" (Irish setter)	90	90
MS6101	Two sheets, each 67×86 mm. (a) $400 "Spike" (kitten). (b) $400 "Baron of Fillmore" (German shepherd dog) Set of 2 sheets	6·50	7·00

630 Chihuahua

2001. Dogs and Cats in the Caribbean. Multicoloured.

6102	$35 Type **630**	35	25
6103	$60 Persian tabby	60	40
6104	$80 Rottweiler	70	70
6105	$80 German shepherd	70	70
6106	$80 Burmese mountain dog	70	70
6107	$80 Shar Pei	70	70
6108	$80 Dachshund	70	70
6109	$80 Jack Russell	70	70
6110	$80 Boston terrier	70	70
6111	$80 Corgi	70	70
6112	$80 American shorthair	70	70
6113	$80 Somali	70	70
6114	$80 Balinese	70	70
6115	$80 Egyptian Mau	70	70
6116	$80 Scottish fold	70	70
6117	$80 Sphynx	70	70
6118	$80 Korat	70	70
6119	$100 Colourpoint shorthair	90	90
6120	$200 Cocker spaniel	1·60	1·75
MS6121	Two sheets, each 76×86 mm. (a) $400 Beagle. (b) $400 Abyssinian (cat) Set of 2 sheets	6·50	7·00

Nos. 6104/11 (dogs) and 6112/18 (cats) were each printed together, se-tenant, with the backgrounds forming composite designs that extend onto the sheetlet margins.

$300

GUYANA

631 George Washington

2001. George Washington (American president) Commemoration.

6122	**631** $300 multicoloured	2·50	2·75

632 Hello Kitty in Alice in Wonderland

2001. Hello Kitty (cartoon character). Twelve sheets, each 100×100 mm, containg vert designs as T **632** of Hello Kitty in European (No. **MS**6120a/f) or Japanese (No. **MS**6120g/l) fairy tales. Multicoloured.

MS6123	(a) $400 Type **632**. (b) $400 Cinderella. (c) $400 Heidi. (d) $400 The Wizard of Oz. (e) $400 Peter Pan. (f) $400 Little Red Riding Hood. (g) $400 Three in a Boat. (h) $400 Bamboo Princess. (i) $400 The Fisherman. (j) $400 Up a Tree. (k) $400 On a Bear. (l) $400 In the Snow Set of 12 sheets	32·00	35·00

633 American Securities and Exchange Commission Office (founded 1934)

2001. People and Events of Early 20th Century. Multicoloured.

6124	$60 Type **633**	85	60
6125	$60 Herbert Hoover (American President, elected 1928)	85	60
6126	$60 Al Jolson in The Jazz Singer (first talking film, 1927)	85	60
6127	$60 J. Edgar Hoover (Director of F.B.I., appointed 1924)	85	60
6128	$60 Alexander Fleming (discovered penicillin, 1928)	85	60
6129	$60 Radio and microphone (Federal Communications Commission set up, 1927)	85	60
6130	$60 Charles Lindbergh (first solo transatlantic flight, 1927)	85	60
6131	$60 Albert Einstein (awarded Nobel physics prize, 1921)	85	60
6132	$60 Paul von Hindenburg (German leader, died 1934, succeeded by Hitler)	85	60
6133	$60 American flag and certificate (American Social Security Act, 1935)	85	60
6134	$60 Amelia Earhart (first solo flight from Hawaii to California)	85	60
6135	$60 Marcus Garvey (founder of Universal Negro Improvement Association, prison sentence commuted and deported, 1927)	85	60

$60
GUYANA

634 Ronald Reagan

2001. 90th Birthday of Ronald Reagan (American President). Multicoloured (except Nos. 6136/8).

6136	$60 Type **634** (lilac and black)	60	60
6137	$60 With chimp in Bedtime for Bonzo (lilac and black)	60	60
6138	$60 Wearing cowboy hat (grey and black)	60	60
6139	$60 In dark suit and black tie	60	60
6140	$60 With Nancy Reagan	60	60
6141	$60 Pointing	60	60
6142	$60 Getting into car and waving	60	60
6143	$60 Signing reduction of nuclear arms treaty with Mikhail Gorbachev, 1987	60	60
6144	$60 Helping demolish Berlin Wall, 1989	60	60
6145	$60 With President Clinton	60	60

GUYANA $25

635 Girl at a Hot Spring Resort (Hashiguchi Goyo)

2001. "Philanippon '01" International Stamp Exhibition, Tokyo. Japanese Paintings. Multicoloured.

6146	$25 Type **635**	20	20
6147	$25 Hanaogi with Maidservant (Eishosai Choki)	20	20
6148	$30 Morokoshi of the Echizenya (Rekisentei Eiri)	25	25
6149	$30 Courtesan receiving a Letter of Invitation (Suzuki Harunobu)	25	25
6150	$35 Mother and Daughter on an Outing (Katsushika Hokusai)	30	30
6151	$35 Two Girls on Way to (or from) the Bathhouse (S. Harunobu)	30	30
6152	$60 Matron in Love (Kitagawa Utamaro)	55	55
6153	$60 "Girl and Frog" (S. Harunobu)	55	55
6154	$80 Insects, reptiles and amphibians at a Pond (38×72 mm)	70	70
6155	$80 Rose Mallow and Fowl (38×72 mm)	70	70
6156	$80 Rooster, Sunflower and Morning Glories (38×72 mm)	70	70
6157	$80 Group of Roosters (38×72 mm)	70	70
6158	$80 Black Rooster and Nandina (38×72 mm)	70	70
6159	$80 Birds and Autumn Maples (38×72 mm)	70	70
6160	$80 Wagtail and Roses (38×72 mm)	70	70

6161	$80 Cockatoos in a Pine (38×72 mm)	70	70
6162	$100 Three Beauties of High Fame (K. Utamaro)	85	85
6163	$100 The Courtesan Midorigi (Chokosai Eisho)	85	85
6164	$100 Bridge (38×72 mm)	85	85
6165	$100 Causeway and summer house (38×72 mm)	85	85
6166	$100 Island in lake with single tree (38×72 mm)	85	85
6167	$100 Rocky islet and waterfalls tumbling into lake (38×72 mm)	85	85
6168	$100 Shugakuin Imperial Villa with Japanese letters (38×72 mm)	85	85
6169	$100 Trees with Japanese letters (38×72 mm)	85	85
6170	$120 Girls After the Bath (K. Utamaro) (38×72 mm)	85	85
6171	$120 Summer Evening on Riverbank at Hama-Cho (Torii Kiyonaga) (38×72 mm)	90	90
6172	$120 A Beauty in the Wind (Kaigetsudo Ando) (38×72 mm)	90	90
6173	$120 Sisters (Shimainozu) (Tsuji Kako) (38×72 mm)	90	90
6174	$120 Kasamori Osen (S. Harunobu) (38×72 mm)	90	90
6175	$160 Ichikawa Ebizo behind Screen (30×38 mm)	1·25	1·25
6176	$160 Ichikawa Ebizo in red jacket (30×38 mm)	1·25	1·25
6177	$160 Ichikawa Ebizo with musicians (30×38 mm)	1·25	1·25
6178	$160 Ichikawa Ebizo being dressed as warrior (30×38 mm)	1·60	1·75
6179	$200 Girl breaking off Branch of Flowering Tree (S. Harunobu)	1·60	1·75
6180	$200 Maiko (Tsuchida Bakusen)	1·60	1·75
MS6181	Five sheets. (a) 120×80 mm. $400 "Wintry Sky (Higashibara Hosen). (b)120×80 mm. $400 Woman holding a Flower (Kajiwara Hisako). (c) 120×80 mm. $400 Palace of Immortals in an Autumn Valley (Okochi Yako). (d) 80×120 mm. $400 Fish and Octopus from the Colourful Realm of living Beings (I. Jakuchu). (e) 80×120 mm. $400 Portrait of Takami Senseki (Watanabe Kazan). All imperf set of 5 sheets	14·00	15·00

Nos. 6154/61 (paintings by Ito Jakuchu), 6164/9 "Procession to the Shugakuin Imperial Villa" by Kakimoto Sesshin), 6170/4 (Japanese Women) and 6175/8 "Ichikawa Ebizo (actor) by Toshusai Sharaku) were each printed together, se-tenant, in sheetlets of 4, 5, 6 or 8 with enlarged inscribed margins.
Nos. 6164/9 and 6175/8 each form a composite design.

Guyana $200

636 Queen Victoria, 1850

2001. Death Centenary of Queen Victoria. Multicoloured.

6182	$200 Type **636**	2·00	2·00
6183	$200 Queen Victoria, 1843	2·00	2·00
6184	$200 Queen Victoria wearing crown, 1859	2·00	2·00
6185	$200 Queen Victoria in feathered hat, 1897	2·00	2·00
6186	$200 Princess Victoria, 1829	2·00	2·00
6187	$200 Queen Victoria with hair in bun, 1837	2·00	2·00
6188	$200 In uniform for troop review, 1840	2·00	2·00
6189	$200 Wearing crown and white veil, 1897	2·00	2·00
MS6190	Two sheets, each 88×120 mm. (a) $400 Queen Victoria. (b) $400 Queen Victoria in old age Set of 2 sheets	12·00	12·00

2001. 75th Death Anniv of Claude-Oscar Monet (artist). As T **339** of Gambia. Multicoloured.

6191	$150 Village Street near Honfleur	1·25	1·40
6192	$150 Road to Chailly	1·25	1·40
6193	$150 Train in the Countryside	1·25	1·40
6194	$150 Quai du Louvre	1·25	1·40
MS6195	136×111 mm. $400 Flowering Garden (vert)	3·50	3·75

2001. 75th Birthday of Queen Elizabeth II. As T **340** of Gambia. Multicoloured.

6196	$150 Queen Elizabeth wearing pink hat	1·75	1·75
6197	$150 Wearing red coat and hat	1·75	1·75
6198	$150 Wearing white turban style hat	1·75	1·75
6199	$150 Wearing tiara	1·75	1·75
MS6200	80×110 mm. $400 Queen Elizabeth wearing yellow dress and pearls (38×50 mm)	4·50	4·75

2001. Death Centenary of Giuseppe Verdi (Italian composer). Vert designs as T **342** of Gambia. Multicoloured.

6201	$160 Verdi (face value at bottom left)	2·25	2·25
6202	$160 Rigoletto and score	2·25	2·25
6203	$160 Ernani and opera score	2·25	2·25
6204	$160 Verdi (face value at bottom right)	2·25	2·25
MS6205	77×117 mm. $400 Verdi	5·00	5·00

Nos. 6201/4 were printed together, *se-tenant*, with the backgrounds forming a composite design.

2001. Death Centenary of Henri de Toulouse-Lautrec (artist). As T **343** of Gambia. Multicoloured.

6206	$160 *Maurice Joyant in the Baie de Somme* (horiz)	1·75	1·75
6207	$160 *Monsieur Boileau* (horiz)	1·75	1·75
6208	$160 *Monsieur, Madame and the Dog* (horiz)	1·75	1·75
MS6209	66×85 mm. $400 *"Monsieur"*	4·50	4·50

637 Top Right of Head

2001. Faces of the Millennium. John F. Kennedy. Showing collage of miniature photographs from Kennedy's years as President. Multicoloured.

6210	$80 Type **637**	65	70
6211	$80 Top left of head	65	70
6212	$80 Top of right cheek	65	70
6213	$80 Top of left cheek	65	70
6214	$80 Bottom of right cheek	65	70
6215	$80 Bottom of left cheek	65	70
6216	$80 Bottom right of chin	65	70
6217	$80 Bottom left of chin	65	70

Nos. 6210/17 were printed together, *se-tenant*, in sheetlets of 8 with the stamps arranged in two vertical columns separated by a gutter also containing miniature photographs. When viewed as a whole, the sheetlet forms a portrait of JFK.

2001. 75th Birthday of Queen Elizabeth II. As T **368** of Dominica.

6218	$80 multicoloured	1·00	1·10

No. 6218 was also issued, in the same format, inscribed "In Celebration of the 50th Anniversary of H.M. Queen Elizabeth II's Accession to the Throne' in the margin.

638 Rainbow Lory ("Rainbow Lorikeet")

2001. Tropical Birds. Multicoloured.

6219	$100 Type **638**	1·40	1·40
6220	$100 King bird of paradise	1·40	1·40
6221	$100 Canary-winged parakeet ("Yellow-Chevroned Parakeet")	1·40	1·40
6222	$100 Masked lovebird	1·40	1·40
6223	$100 Scarlet ibis	1·40	1·40
6224	$100 Toco toucan	1·40	1·40
6225	$100 Hyacinth macaw	1·40	1·40
6226	$100 Wire-tailed manakin	1·40	1·40
6227	$100 Scarlet macaw	1·40	1·40
6228	$100 Sun conure ("Sun Parakeet")	1·40	1·40
6229	$100 Roseate spoonbill	1·40	1·40
6230	$100 Red-billed toucan	1·40	1·40
MS6231	Two sheets, each 85×110 mm. (a) $400 Eclectus parrot (vert). (b) $400 Sulphur-crested cockatoo (vert) Set of 2 sheets	6·50	6·00

Nos. 6219/24 and 6225/30 were each printed together, *se-tenant*, with the backgrounds forming composite designs.

639 Alamosaurus head

2001. "Vegaspex 2001", Nevada. Prehistoric Creatures. Multicoloured.

6232	$20 Allosaurus (vert)	30	15
6233	$30 Spinosaurus (vert)	40	25
6234	$35 Pteranodon (vert)	40	25

6235	$60 Cetiosaurus (vert)	50	40
6236	$60 Type **639**	60	65
6237	$100 Archaeopteryx	60	65
6238	$100 Pachycephalosaurus head and Alamosaurus body	60	65
6239	$100 Parasaurolophus	60	65
6240	$100 Edmontosaurus head	60	65
6241	$100 Triceratops	60	65
6242	$100 Brachiosaurus head, neck and back	60	65
6243	$100 Dimorphodon	60	65
6244	$100 Coelophysis head and Brachiosaurus body	60	65
6245	$100 Velociraptor	60	65
6246	$100 Antrodemus	60	65
6247	$100 Euparkeria	60	65
6248	$100 Brachiosaurus head and neck	60	65
6249	$100 Pteranodon	60	65
6250	$100 Compsognathus and Brachiosaurus neck	60	65
6251	$100 Corythosaurus	60	65
6252	$100 Allosaurus	60	65
6253	$100 Torosaurus	60	65
6254	$100 Ichthyostega	60	65
6255	$100 Eryops	60	65
6256	$100 Ichthyosaur	60	65
6257	$100 Pliosaur	60	65
6258	$100 Dunklosteus	60	65
6259	$100 Eogyrinus	60	65
6260	$200 Archaeopteryx (vert)	1·25	1·25
6261	$300 Parasaurolophus (vert)	2·00	2·00
MS6262	Four sheets. (a) 88×68 mm. $400 Pteranodon. (b) 88×68 mm. $400 Ichthyosaur. (c) 88×68 mm. $400 Torosaurus. (d) 68×88 mm. $400 Brachiosaurus (vert) Set of 4 sheets	14·00	12·00

Nos. 6236/41, 6242/7, 6248/53 and 6254/9 were each printed together, *se-tenant*, with the backgrounds forming composite designs.

640 Elephant

2001. Tropical Rainforest. Multicoloured.

6263	$35 Mandrill (vert)	40	25
6264	$80 Type **640**	60	55
6265	$80 Impala	60	55
6266	$80 Leopard head and shoulders	60	55
6267	$80 Grey parrot and leopard body	60	55
6268	$80 Hippopotamus	60	55
6269	$80 Pygmy chimp	60	55
6270	$80 African green python	60	55
6271	$80 Mountain gorilla	60	55
6272	$80 Three-toed sloth	60	55
6273	$80 Lion tamarind	60	55
6274	$80 Ring-tailed lemur	60	55
6275	$80 Sugar glider	60	55
6276	$80 Toco toucan	60	55
6277	$80 Trogon	60	55
6278	$80 Pygmy marmoset	60	55
6279	$80 Poison arrow frog	60	55
6280	$100 Leaf-cutting ants	70	75
MS6281	Two sheets, each 110×85 mm. (a) $400 Tapir (vert). (b) $400 Sable antelope (vert) Set of 2 sheets	5·50	5·50

Nos. 6264/71 and 6272/9 were each printed together, *se-tenant*, with the backgrounds forming composite designs.

641 Prince Willem-Alexander of Orange and Miss Maxima Zorreguieta

2002. Royal Wedding. Multicoloured.

MS6282 158×240 mm. $120 Type **641**; $120 Prince Willem-Alexander on right and Miss Maxima on left; $120 Prince Willem-Alexander on left and Miss Maxima on right; $120 Hugging from the side; $120 Prince Willem-Alexander; $120 Miss Maxima   4·25   4·25

642 U.S. Flag as Statue of Liberty and Flag of Guyana

2002. "United We Stand". Support for Victims of 11 September 2001 Terrorist Attacks.

MS6283 120×120 mm. **642** $200 ×4 multicoloured   4·75   4·75

643 Queen Elizabeth II

2002. Golden Jubilee (1st issue). Multicoloured.

MS6284 132×100 mm. $150 Type **643**; $150 Queen Elizabeth and Prince Philip; $150 Queen Elizabeth and Prince Philip waving; $150 Queen Elizabeth and horse   6·00   4·50

MS6285 76×109 mm. $400 Queen Elizabeth and Princess Margaret   3·75   3·25

See also Nos. **MS6370/** and **MS6371.**

644 Harold C. Urey (Chemistry, 1934)

2002. Nobel Prize Winners (1st issue). Multicoloured.

MS6286 Two sheets each 183×129 mm. (a) $100 Type **644**; $100 Willard F. Libby (Chemistry, 1960); $100 Frederick Sanger (Chemistry, 1958 and 1980); $100 Teodor Svedberg (Chemistry, 1926); $100 Cyril N. Hinshelwood (Chemistry, 1956); $100 Nicolay Semenov (Chemistry, 1956). (b) $100 Alexander Todd (Chemistry, 1957); $100 John Steinbeck (Literature, 1962); $100 Edward C. Kendall (Physiology and Medicine, 1950); $100 Frederick G. Banting (Physiology and Medicine, 1923); $100 Charles Nicolle (Physiology and Medicine, 1928); $100 Charles Richet (Physiology and Medicine, 1913) Set of 2 sheets   8·50   8·50

MS6287 Three sheets each 106×75 mm. (a) $400 International Red Cross (Peace, 1917). (b) $400 John J. R. MacLeod (Physiology and Medicine, 1923). (c) $400 Derek H. R. Barton (Chemistry, 1969) Set of 3 sheets   8·50   8·50

2002. Nobel Prize Winners (2nd issue). Albert Einstein Photomosaic. Sheet 160×244 mm containing vert designs as T **637** showing miniature scientific images. Multicoloured.

MS6288 $80 Left of forehead; $80 Right of forehead; $80 Left eye; $80 Right eye; $80 Left cheek; $80 Right cheek; $80 Left of jaw; $80 Right of jaw   6·00   4·50

The stamps of No. **MS6288** were printed in two vertical columns of 4, separated by a central gutter. When viewed as a whole, the miniature sheet forms a portrait of Albert Einstein.

645 Chinese Character meaning "Horse" (Qin Dynasty)

2002. Chinese New Year ("Year of the Horse"). Multicoloured.

6289	$100 Type **645**	60	65
6290	$100 Yin Dynasty	60	65
6291	$100 Tang Dynasty	60	65
6292	$100 Shang and Zhou Dynasties	60	65

MS6293 125×116 mm. (a) $150 Decorated person riding purple horse; (b) $150 Decorated Person riding orange horse. (37×50 mm)   1·90   1·90

Nos. 6282/5 show Chinese characters for "Horse" from various dynasties and an explanation of the Chinese characters inscribed on the bottom margin.

646 Obdulio Varela (Uruguay) (Brazil, 1950)

2002. World Cup Football Championship, Japan and South Korea. Tournament posters. Multicoloured.

6294	$100 Type **646**	60	65
6295	$100 Jules Rimet (Switzerland, 1954)	60	65
6296	$100 Pele and team mates (Brazil) (Sweden, 1958)	60	65
6297	$100 Zito (Brazil) (Chile, 1962)	60	65
6298	$100 English players (England, 1966)	60	65
6299	$100 Jairzinho (Brazil) (Mexico, 1970)	60	65
6300	$100 Daniel Passarella (Argentina) (Argentina, 1978)	60	65
6301	$100 Paolo Rossi (Italy) (Spain, 1982)	60	65
6302	$100 Diego Maradona (Argentina) (Mexico, 1986)	60	65
6303	$100 Lothar Matthaus and Rudi Voller (West Germany) (Italy, 1990)	60	65
6304	$100 Brazilian players (U.S.A., 1994)	60	65
6305	$100 Zinedine Zidane (France) (France, 1998)	60	65
MS6306	Two sheets, each 88×75 mm. (a) $400 Detail of Jules Rimet Trophy (Uruguay, 1930). (b) $400 Detail of World Cup Trophy (Japan and South Korea, 2002) Set of 2 sheets	4·75	4·75

647 The Devil's Tower, U.S.A

2002. International Year of Mountains (1st issue). Multicoloured.

MS6307 136×95 mm. $200 Type **647**; $200 Schreckhorn, Switzerland; $200 Mt. Rainer (U.S.A); $200 Mt. Everest, Tibet   4·75   4·75

MS6308 84×56 mm. $400 Mt. McKinley   2·40   2·40

2002. International Year of Mountains (2nd issue). As T **647**.

6309	$80 Mt. Kosciuszko, Australia	75	65
6310	$100 Mt. Elbrus, Russia	1·00	75
6311	$150 Mt. Vinson, Antarctica	1·40	1·75
MS6312	73×90 mm. $400 Mt. Everest, Nepal	3·50	3·50

648 Skiing

2002. Winter Olympic Games, Salt Lake City. Multicoloured.

6313	$200 Type **648**	1·50	1·50
6314	$200 Ice Skating	1·50	1·50
MS6315	82×113 mm. Nos. 6313/14	3·00	3·00

649 Owl

2002. United Nations Year of Eco Tourism. Multicoloured.

MS6316 81×137 mm. $100 Type **649**; $100 Waterfall; $100 Baboon; $100 Butterfly; $100 Flower; $100 Ferret   6·00   6·00

MS6317 86×69 mm. $400 Leopard   3·25   3·25

650 Environmental Science Merit Badge

2002. 20th World Scout Jamboree, Thailand. Multicoloured.
MS6318 161×67 mm. $200 Type **650**; $200 World Citizen Merit badge; $200 Life Saving Merit badge — 5·50 / 5·50
MS6319 98×67 mm. $400 Jamboree mascot saluting — 3·75 / 3·75

651 Kaieteur Falls, Guyana

2002. 30th Anniv of Diplomatic Relations with Republic of China. Multicoloured.
6320 $100 Type **651** — 80 / 80
6321 $100 Great Wall of China — 80 / 80

652 Volunteer Cleaning Globe and Emblem

2002. International Year of Volunteers. Multicoloured.
6322 $35 Type **652** — 35 / 25
6323 $60 Two styles of emblem — 55 / 40
6324 $300 Volunteer "embracing the nation" — 2·50 / 3·00

653 Sperm Whale

2002. Whales. Multicoloured.
MS6325 140×67 mm. $100 Type **653**; $100 Pygmy Sperm whale; $100 Blue whale; $100 Bottlenose whale; $100 Killer whale; $100 True's Beaked whale — 7·00 / 6·50
MS6326 75×62 mm. $400 Beluga whale — 4·75 / 4·50

654 Masdevallia tovarensis

2002. Orchids. Multicoloured.
MS6327 94×103 mm. $100 Type **654**; $100 Encyclia vitellina; $100 Dendrobium nobile; $100 Masdevallia falcate; $100 Calanthe vestita; $100 Brassolaelia cattleya — 7·00 / 6·50
MS6328 74×62 mm. $400 Brassavola nodosa (horiz) — 4·75 / 4·50

2002. Birds. As T **654**. Multicoloured.
MS6329 94×103 mm. $100 Flycatcher; $100 Barbary shrike; $100 Red-faced mousebird; $100 Red-footed booby; $100 White-fronted goose; $100 Great crested grebe — 7·00 / 6·50
MS6330 74×62 mm. $400 Whiskered tern — 4·75 / 4·50

2002. Butterflies. As T **654**. Multicoloured.
MS6331 94×103 mm. $100 Sweet oil butterfly; $100 Swallowtail; $100 Southern white admiral; $100 Pre-pona pheridamas; $100 Plain tiger; $100 Common eggfly — 7·00 / 6·50
MS6332 62×75 mm. $400 Zebra butterfly — 4·75 / 4·50

2002. Moths. As T **654**. Multicoloured.
MS6333 94×103 mm. $100 Burgena varia; $100 Mimas tiliae; $100 Hyles euphorbiae; $100 Eligma laetipicta; $100 Autometris io; $100 Hyloicus pinastri — 6·50 / 6·00
MS6334 75×62 mm. $400 Callimorpha quadripuntaria — 4·50 / 4·25

655 Elvis Presley

2002. 25th Death Anniv of Elvis Presley. Multicoloured.
MS6335 Two sheets each 200×170 mm. (a) $60 Type **655**×9. (b) $60 Elvis in army uniform in front of U.S. flag×9 Set of 2 sheets — 7·00 / 6·00

656 Popeye

2002. Popeye (cartoon character). Multicoloured.
MS6336 187×125 mm. $100 Type **656**; $100 Olive Oyl; $100 Wimpy; $100 Eugene the Jeep; $100 Sweet Pea racing for ball; $100 Sweet Pea holding tennis ball — 4·25 / 4·25
MS6337 118×86 mm. $400 Popeye wearing white tennis shirt — 2·40 / 2·40

657 Ronald Reagan

2003. Ronald Reagan (President of U.S.A 1981–1989). T **657** and Multicoloured.
MS6338 167×136 mm. $100 Ronald Reagan and eagle; $100 Type **657**; $100 In front of Mt. Rushmore; $100 Kissing Nancy Reagan; $100 With hand to forehead and White House; $100 On horseback — 3·50 / 3·50
MS6339 106×76 mm. $400 Ronald Reagan and Mikhail Gorbachev shaking hands (horiz) — 2·40 / 2·40

658 Ram

2003. Chinese New Year ("Year of the Ram").
MS6340 **658** 109×86 mm. $100×4 multicoloured — 3·75 / 3·75

659 John F. Kennedy

2003. John F. Kennedy Commemoration. T **659** and similar multicoloured designs.
MS6341 158×128 mm. $100 Addressing the nation; $100 Type **659**; $100 Space scene in background; $100 With miniature model of White House; $100 In front of rocket; $100 Jackie Kennedy at funeral — 4·50 / 4·50
MS6342 106×76 mm. $400 John F. Kennedy and Jackie Kennedy in open top car (horiz) — 3·25 / 3·25

660 Princess Diana

2003. Diana, Princess of Wales Commemoration. Multicoloured.
MS6343 157×127 mm. $100 Type **660**; $100 Wearing tiara; $100 Wearing high collared top; $100 Wearing wedding veil; $100 Looking straight ahead; $100 Looking left — 4·50 / 4·50
MS6344 104×75 mm. $400 Wearing pink and black hat and pearl choker — 3·25 / 3·25

661 The Actor Nakamura Shikan IV

2003. Famous Actors in Japanese Art. Paintings by Toyohara Kunichika. Multicoloured.
6345 $60 Type **661** — 55 / 40
6346 $80 The Actor Ichikawa Danjuro IX as Sukeroku (1883) — 70 / 55
6347 $100 The Actor Onoe Tatsunosuke — 85 / 70
6348 $300 The Actor Ichikawa Sadanji I as Kyusuke — 2·40 / 2·75
MS6349 182×143 mm. $150 The Actor Kawarazak Sansho as Watonai; $150 The Actor Ichikawa Danjuro IX as Kamakura Gongoro Kagemasa; $150 The Actor Ichikawa Sadanji I as Sadajkuro; $150 The Actor Ichikawa Danjuro IX as Sukeroku (1898) — 4·50 / 4·50
MS6350 127×83 mm. $400 The Actor Ichikawa Danjuro IX as Kato Shukeigashira Kiyomasa (horiz) — 3·25 / 3·25

662 Tension Red

2003. Wassily Kandinsky (artist) Commemoration. Multicoloured.
6351 $25 Type **662** — 25 / 20
6352 $30 Black Accompanimen — 30 / 25
6353 $35 Calm Tension — 30 / 25
6354 $60 Hard and Soft — 50 / 40
6355 $100 Yellow Point (horiz) — 75 / 65
6356 $300 Composition VIII (horiz) — 2·00 / 2·50
MS6357 130×156 mm. $150 Red Oval, 1920; $150 On the White II, 1923; $150 Mutual Agreement, 1942; $150 Inclination, 1931 — 4·50 / 4·50
MS6358 Two sheets each 104×84 mm. (a) $400 White Center, 1921. (b) $400 Black Weft, 1922. Imperf — 6·50 / 6·50

663 Portrait of a Man

2003. 450th Death Anniv of Lucas Cranach the Elder (artist). Multicoloured.
6359 $35 Type **663** — 30 / 25
6360 $60 Portrait of a Woman — 50 / 40
6361 $100 Duchess Catherine of Mecklenburg (detail) — 80 / 65
6362 $200 Portrait of Duke Henry of Saxony (detail) — 1·50 / 1·75

MS6363 160×117 mm. $150 The Virgin, c. 1518 (detail); $150 The Virgin and Child Under the Apple Tree (detail); $150 The Virgin(detail); $150 The Virgin — 4·50 / 4·50
MS6364 93×130 mm. $400 The Virgin and Child Holding a Piece of Bread (detail) — 3·25 / 3·25

664 Outline of Guyana

2003. 30th Anniv of the Caribbean Community ("CARICOM"). Multicoloured.
6365 $20 Type **664** — 20 / 10
6366 $60 Bank of Guyana (horiz) — 50 / 40
6367 $100 Hands holding torch — 80 / 65
6368 $160 AIDS ribbon and stethoscope — 1·40 / 1·75

665 Queen Elizabeth II

2003. Golden Jubilee (2nd issue). Multicoloured.
MS6370 166×108 mm. $200 Type **665**; $200 Wearing purple top; $200 Wearing pink top — 6·50 / 6·50
MS6371 76×106 mm. $400 Wearing Imperial State Crown — 4·50 / 4·50

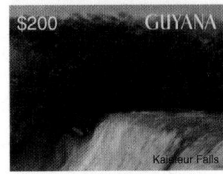

666 Top of Kaieteur Falls

2003. International Year of Freshwater. Multicoloured.
MS6372 143×150 mm. $200 Type **666**; $200 Middle of Kaieteur Falls; $200 Kaieteur Falls and part of Cliffside — 5·50 / 5·50
MS6373 76×106 mm. $400 Amazon River — 4·00 / 4·00

667 Jacques Anquetil (1964)

2003. Centenary of Tour de France Cycle Race. Multicoloured.
MS6374 163×104 mm. $150 Type **667**; $150 Felice Gimondi (1965); $150 Lucien Aimar (1966); $150 Roger Pingeon (1967) — 6·50 / 6·50
MS6375 106×76 mm. $400 Jan Janssen (1968) — 4·50 / 4·50

668 Brown Teddy Bear

2003. Centenary of Teddy Bears. Multicoloured.
MS6376 178×140 mm. $80 Type **668**×9; lilac; green; blue; light green; light blue; stone; mauve; pale green; light mauve — 4·50 / 4·50
MS6377 178×102 mm. $150 Bear dressed in red dress and white apron; $150 Blue bear dressed in yellow bow tie; $150 Bear decorated with fairy lights and star; $150 Bear dressed in blue dress and ribbon — 3·50 / 3·50

669 Prince William
as a Baby

2003. 21st Birthday of Prince William. Multicoloured.
MS6378 166×108 mm. $200 Type **669**;
$200 Wearing round neck sweater;
$200 Wearing christening robe   5·50   5·00

MS6379 76×106 mm. $400 Wearing
blue shirt and tie   3·75   3·50

670 Sixty Special (1948)

2003. Centenary of the Cadillac. Multicoloured.
MS6380 126×176 mm. $150 Type **670**;
$150 Fleetwood Sixty Special (1966);
$150 Eldorado (1967); Eldorado
Convertible (1976)   3·50   3·50

MS6381 90×126 mm. $400 Red vintage
Cadillac   3·25   3·25

671 Corvette Stingray (1964)

2003. 50th Anniv of the Corvette. Multicoloured.
MS6382 146×126 mm. $150 Type
671; $150 Corvette Stingray (1963);
$150 Corvette Stingray (1966);
Corvette (1969)   3·50   3·50

MS6383 126×90 mm. $400 Corvette
(1971)   3·25   3·25

672 AVRO Plane (Sir Alliot
Verdon Roe)

2003. Centenary of Powered Flight. Multicoloured.
6384 $100 Type **672**   1·50   1·00
6385 $160 First British powered flight   2·50   2·50
MS6386 Two sheets. (a) 186×106 mm.
$150 Wright Brothers' plane; $150
SPAD 13; $150 Sopwith F.1; $150
Albatross D.II. (b) 106×186 mm. $150
Nieuport 17; $150 Scout Experimen-
tal 5a; $150 De Havilland 4; $150
Wright Brothers plane (black crosses
on tail) Set of 2 sheets   7·50   7·50

MS6387 Two sheets each 76×106
mm. (a) $400 Fokker D.VIIs. (b) $400
Wright Brothers plane over water   7·50   7·50

673 Grecian
Shoemaker

2003. Butterflies. Multicoloured.
6388 $20 Type **673**   25   15
6389 $55 Clorinde   70   35
6390 $80 Orange-barred sulphur   1·00   55
6391 $100 The atala   1·25   65
6392 $160 White peacock   1·75   1·25
6393 $200 Polydamas swallowtail   2·00   1·40
6394 $300 Giant swallowtail   3·00   2·25
6395 $400 Banded king shoemaker   4·00   3·50
6396 $500 Blue night   4·50   3·75
6397 $1000 Orange theope   8·00   8·00
6398 $2000 Small lace-wing   15·00   17·00
6399 $3000 Common morpho   20·00   22·00

674 Clitocybe clavipes

2003. Mushrooms. Multicoloured.
6400 $20 Type **674**   40   30
6401 $20 Clitocybe gibba   40   30
6402 $30 Calocybe carnea   50   25
6403 $300 Marasmius   3·50   4·00
MS6404 133×92 mm. $150 Amanita
spissa; $150 Boletus aestivalis; $150
Boletus rubellus; $150 Clathrus archeri   6·00   6·00

MS6405 96×66 mm. $400 Volvariella
bombycina   4·25   4·25

675 Toucan

2003. Endangered Species. Toucan. Multicoloured.
6406 $100 Toucan with chick   1·75   1·50
6407 $100 Type **675**   1·75   1·50
6408 $100 Two Toucans on branch   1·75   1·50
6409 $100 One Toucan on branch   1·75   1·50
MS6410 204×169 mm. Designs as Nos.
6406/9, each×2   11·00   9·00

676 Begonia sedeni

2003. Flowers. Multicoloured.
6411 $20 Type **676**   30   15
6412 $30 Dahlia   40   25
6413 $35 Eschecholzia californica   40   30
6414 $300 Lupinus perennis   3·50   4·00
MS6415 116×116 mm. $150 Aga-
panthus africanus; $150 Hyacinth
cultivars; $150 Protea linearis; $150
Hippestrum aulicum   6·00   6·00

MS6416 66×96 mm. $400 Crocus
sativus (horiz)   4·25   4·25

677 Regal Tang

2003. Fish. Multicoloured.
6417 $25 Type **677**   35   20
6418 $60 Pajama tang   70   40
6419 $100 Coral beauty   1·10   80
6420 $200 Emperor angelfish   1·90   2·25
MS6421 145×100 mm. $150 High
hat; $150 Regal angelfish; $150 Fire
clown; $150 Domino damselfish   6·00   6·00
MS6422 66×96 mm. $400 Tomato
clown   4·25   4·25

678 Common Tenrec

2003. Animals. Multicoloured.
6423 $25 Type **678**   30   20
6424 $60 Woolly monkey (vert)   70   40
6425 $100 Gundi   1·10   85
6426 $200 Hooded seal   1·90   2·25
MS6427 135×127 mm. $150 Prevost's
squirrel; $150 Mountain tapir; $150
Sea otter; $150 Indus dolphin   6·00   6·00
MS6428 67×96 mm. $400 Peter's disk-
winged bat (vert)   4·25   4·25

679 Princess
Catharina-Amalia

2003. Birth of Princess Catharina-Amalia of the
Netherlands. Sheet 185×115 mm containing T **679**
and similar vert designs. Multicoloured.
MS6429 $200 Type **679**; $200 Prince
Willem-Alexander and Princess
Catharina-Amalia; $200 Princess
Catharina-Amalia (looking to left)   5·50   5·50
No. **MS**6429 is cut around in the shape of a baby.

680 Handshake

2003. 35th Anniv of Guyana—Brazil Diplomatic Relations.
6430   **680** $20 multicoloured   75   50

681 Dark Brown Monkey

2004. Chinese New Year ("Year of the Monkey"). Sheet
140×117 mm containing T **681** and similar vert
designs. Multicoloured.
MS6431 $100 Type **681**; $100 Black
and white monkey; $100 Light
brown monkey; $100 Red Howler
Monkey   3·75   3·75

682 Concubines of
Emperor Chu

2004. Hong Kong 2004 International Stamp Exhibition.
Paintings by Tang Yin. T **682** and similar
multicoloured designs.
MS6432 140×140 mm. $150 Type
682; $150 Woman standing on
boardwalk; $150 Woman standing
on rocky slope; $150 Mountain
landscape   4·50   4·75
MS6433 108×78 mm. $400 Mountain
Scene (horiz)   3·25   3·50

683 "Doctor and Doll"

2004. 25th Death Anniv of Norman Rockwell (artist).
Multicoloured.
MS6434 142×173 mm. $150 Type
683; $150 Babysitter with Screaming
Infant; $150 Girl with Black Eye; $150
Checkup   4·50   4·50
MS6435 95×103 mm. $400 Girl running
with Wet Canvas (Wet Paint) (detail)
(horiz)   3·25   3·25

684 Mercury giving Bacchus to
Nymphs to Raise (Laurent de la
Hyre)

2004. 300th Anniv of St. Petersburg. "Treasures of the
Hermitage". Multicoloured.
6436 $35 Type **684**   35   25
6437 $60 Satyr and Bacchante (Nico-
las Poussin) (vert)   60   40
6438 $100 Parting of Abelard and
Eloisa (Angelica Kauffmann)   90   75
6439 $200 Pastoral Scene (Francois
Boucher)   1·60   2·00
MS6440 147×126 mm. $150 The
Union of Earth and Water (Rubens);
$150 Hercules between Love and
Wisdom (Pompeo Girolano Batoni);
$150 Innocence choosing Love over
Wealth (Pierre-Paul Prud'hon); $150
Mars and Venus (Joseph-Marie Vien)
(all vert)   5·50   5·50
MS6441 Two sheets. (a) 77×55 mm.
$400 Allegory of Virtuous Life
(Hendrik van Balen). (b) 55×77 mm.
$400 Statue of Ceres (Rubens). Both
imperf. Set of 2 sheets   7·00   7·00

685 Woman in Yellow Hat

2004. 30th Death Anniv (2003) of Pablo Picasso (artist).
Multicoloured.
MS6442 130×167 mm. $150 Type **685**;
$150 Seated Woman; $150 Head of a
Woman; $150 Large Profile   5·50   5·50
MS6443 72×98 mm. $400 Seated
Woman. Imperf   3·50   3·50

686 A Woman Bathing

2004. Paintings by Rembrandt. Multicoloured.
6444 $35 Type **686**   45   25
6445 $60 Flora   75   40
6446 $100 The Poet, Jan Hermansz
Krul   1·10   75
6447 $200 Portrait of a Young Man   1·90   2·25
MS6448 182×183 mm. $150 The
Apostle James; $150 The Apostle
Bartholomew; $150 The Evangelist
Matthew inspired by an Angel; $150
The Apostle Peter Standing   5·50   5·50
MS6449 113×146 mm. $400 Balaam
and the Ass   3·75   3·75

687 Uruguay (1930)

2004. Centenary of FIFA (Federation Internationale de
Football Association). World Cup winning teams.
Multicoloured.
6450 $80 Type **687**   50   55
6451 $80 Italy (1934)   50   55
6452 $80 Italy (1938)   50   55
6453 $80 Uruguay (1950)   50   55
6454 $80 Germany (1954)   50   55
6455 $80 Brazil (1958)   50   55
6456 $80 Brazil (1962)   50   55
6457 $80 England (1966)   50   55
6458 $80 Brazil (1970)   50   55

688 Poster for Olympic
Games, Stockholm, 1912

2004. Olympic Games, Athens. Multicoloured.

6459	$60 Type **688**	45	40
6460	$80 Competitor in high jump, Los Angeles, 1932 (horiz)	65	65
6461	$100 Commemorative medal for Olympic Games, Los Angeles, 1932	90	85
6462	$200 Ancient Greek athletes in 192 metre first foot race (horiz)	1·75	2·00

2004. European Football Championship, Portugal. Commemoration of Match between France and Spain (1984). As T **407** of Dominica. Multicoloured.

MS6463	147×85 mm. $150 Michelle Platini; $150 Luis Arconada; $150 Bruno Bellone; $150 Parc des Princes Stadium, Paris	5·50	6·00
MS6464	96×85 mm. $400 Winning French team, 1984 (50×37 mm)	3·25	3·50

2004. 25th Anniv of Pontificate of Pope John Paul II. Sheet 164×154 mm containing horiz designs as T **408** of Dominica. Multicoloured.

MS6465	$100 Pope John Paul II with Fidel Castro, 1998; $100 With US President Clinton, 1999; $100 Audience with Pope, 2000; $100 Pope in prayer, 2003; $100 In popemobile, 2003	6·00	5·50

689 Deng Xiaoping

2004. Birth Centenary of Deng Xiaoping (Chinese leader). Sheet 95×65 mm.

MS6466	**689** $400 multicoloured	3·50	3·75

2004. Centenary of FIFA (Federation Internationale de Football Association). As T **413** of Dominica. Multicoloured.

MS6467	192×96 mm. $150 Alf Ramsey (England); $150 Pele (Brazil); $150 Lothar Matthaus; $150 Dennis Bergkamp (Holland)	5·50	6·00
MS6468	107×86 mm. $400 Fabien Barthez (France)	3·50	3·75

690 Michael Wittmann, 101st Sturmmorser Kompanie

2004. 60th Anniv of D-Day Landings. Multicoloured.

MS6469	97×137 mm. $150 Type **690**; $150 Lt. Robert Edlin, 2nd Battalion Army Ranger; $150 CSM Stanley Hollis, 6th Green Howards; $150 Kurt Meyer, 12th SS Panzer Division	7·00	6·50
MS6470	156×109 mm. $150 Rear Adm. John Hall; $150 Rear Adm. Carlton Bryant; $150 Gen. Dwight Eisenhower; $150 Gen. H. Arnold	7·00	6·50
MS6471	133×97 mm. $150 Anti-aircraft battery and map of Utah Beach ("Operation Overlord begins"); $150 Troops in landing craft storm Normandy beaches; $150 Troops drop behind enemy lines; $150 Churchill announces landings a success (all horiz)	7·00	6·50
MS6472	137×97 mm. $150 Royal Scots Fusiliers; $150 2nd Company 101st Heavy Tank Battalion; $150 Six-pounder anti-tank gun of the 7th Green Howards; $150 229th Engineer Combat Battalion (all horiz)	7·00	6·50
MS6473	Four sheets. (a) 97×66 mm. $400 Maj. Gen. Maxwell Taylor (horiz). (b) 67×97 mm. $400 T/Sgt. Clifton Barker, 743rd Tank Battalion. (c) 97×66 mm. $400 Tank battle, Cotentin Peninsula, Normandy (horiz). (d) 97×66 mm. $400 Seaforth Highlanders of Canada (horiz)	14·00	13·00

691 *Hercules*, United States

2004. Bicentenary of Steam Locomotives. Multicoloured.

6474-	$150×9 Type **691**; *Stirling* 8ft
6477	Single Class, Great Britain; Class YP, India; Class 01.10, Germany	6·50	6·50

6478-	$150×9 GWR "King" Class, Great
6481	Britain; 4500 Class, France; Class F, Sweden; Class 231C, France	6·50	6·50
6482-	$150×9 Train near Santa Fe
6485	Depot; LD Porta; D9000 Royal Scots Grey; French TGV train	6·50	6·50

MS6486	Four sheets, each 156×84 mm. (a) $150×4 Western Railway, France, 1856; Dutch State Railway, 1880; Southern Railway, England, 1890; Madras and Southern Mahratta Railway, India, 1891. (b) $150×4 Shantung Railway, China, 1919; Great Indian Peninsula Railway, 1898; Cumberland Valley Railroad, USA, 1851; Central Pacific Railroad, USA, 1863. (c) $150×4 Great Northern Railway, Ireland, 1876; London and Northwestern Railway, 1873; Shanghai—Nanking Railway, China, 1910; London, Brighton and South Coast Railway, 1846. (d) $150×4 Baltimore and Ohio Railroad, USA, 1856; Utica and Schenectady Railroad, USA, 1837; Great Southern Railway, Spain, 1913; Victorian Government Railway, Australia, 1906	20·00	20·00
MS6487	Seven sheets. (a) 97×68 mm. $400 TGV Atlantique train. (b) 97×68 mm. $400 *Northumbrian*, Great Britain (vert). (c) 67×97 mm. $400 No. 999, United States. (d) 97×68 mm. $400 Austrian State Railway, 1868 (e) 97×68 mm. $400 Pennsylvania Railroad, 1848 (f) 97×68 mm. $400 Netherlands State Railway, 1886 (g) 97×68 mm. $400 London, Midland and Scottish Railway, 1923	26·00	26·00

No. **MS**6486a/d consist of four stamps in two horizontal pairs, each pair forming a composite background design showing a railway in a landscape.

692 Mexican Funnel-eared Bat

2005. Fauna and Flora of South America. Multicoloured.

6488	$160 Type **692**	1·75	1·75
6489	$160 Greater bulldog bat	1·75	1·75
6490	$160 Vampire bat	1·75	1·75
6491	$160 Geoffroy's tailess bat	1·75	1·75
6492	$160 Blue passion flower (vert)	1·75	1·75
6493	$160 Scarlet passion flower (vert)	1·75	1·75
6494	$160 Passion vine (vert)	1·75	1·75
6495	$160 Bromeliad flower (vert)	1·75	1·75
MS6496	Two sheets, each 110×97 mm. (a) $160×4 Fish: Velvet cichlid; Freshwater stingray; Splash tetra; Red piranha. (b) $160×4 Reptiles: Red-foot tortoise; Emerald tree boa; Green iguana; Cuvier's dwarf caiman	14·00	14·00
MS6497	Two sheets, each 100×70 mm. (a) $400 Short-tailed fruit bat (vert). (b) $400 Epiphytic blueberry (vert). (c) $400 Tambaqui (vert). (d) $400 Eyelash viper	15·00	15·00

693 Dark Brown Rooster

2005. Chinese New Year ("Year of the Rooster"). Multicoloured.

6498	$50 Type **693**	75	75
6499	$50 White rooster	75	75

694 Moeritherium

2005. Prehistoric Animals. Multicoloured.

MS6500	Three sheets, each 177×96 mm. (a) $150×4 Moeritherium; Deinonychus; Ophthalmosaurus; Grendelius. (b) $150×4 Eustreptospondylus; Rhamphorhynchus; Utahraptor; Enteledonts. (c) $150×4 Spinosaurus; Tarbosaurus; Coelophysis; Sinosauropteryx prima	14·00	14·00
MS6501	(a) 100×70 mm. $400 Ophtalmosaurus baby. (b) 100×70 mm. $400 Iguanodon bernissartensis (vert). (c) 70×100 mm. $400 Velociraptors hatching from eggs (vert)	13·00	13·00

The stamps within Nos. **MS**6500a/c form composite background designs.

---

695 Ringbang Emblem, Guyana Landscape and Eddy Grant

2005. Eddy Grant (singer and music producer). Multicoloured.

6502	$20 Type **695**	20	15
6503	$80 Eddy Grant and Ringbang emblem	65	65
6504	$190 Eddy Grant (blue background) (38×49 mm)	1·60	1·75
6505	$190 As No. 6504 (stone background) (38×49 mm)	1·60	1·75
6506	$190 As No. 6504 (lavender background) (38×49 mm)	1·60	1·75
6507	$190 As No. 6504 (lilac background) (38×49 mm)	1·60	1·75
MS6508	100×70 mm. $400 Eddy Grant singing with guitar (38×49 mm)	3·25	3·50

696 Chamberlain on Peace Mission to Nazi Germany, 1938

2005. 60th Anniv of Victory in Europe Day. Multicoloured.

6509	$200 Type **696**	2·50	2·50
6510	$200 RAF Spitfire	2·50	2·50
6511	$200 VE Day poster and cover of *The Illustrated London News*	2·50	2·50
MS6512	100×70 mm. $400 Netherlands 1945 Liberation stamp (vert)	4·50	4·75

697 Japanese Attack on Pearl Harbour, 1945

2005. 60th Anniv of Victory in Japan Day. Multicoloured.

6513	$200 Type **697**	2·50	2·50
6514	$200 Iwo Jima War Memorial, Harlington, Texas	2·50	2·50
6515	$200 "JAPAN SURRENDERS!" newspaper headline	2·50	2·50
MS6516	100×70 mm. $400 US Navy "Seabees" celebrating Japanese surrender	4·50	4·75

2005. Pope John Paul II Commemoration. As T **600** of Grenada. Multicoloured.

6517	$300 Pope John Paul II with US President Ronald Reagan	3·00	3·00

2005. 75th Anniv of First World Cup Football Championship, Uruguay. As T **420** of Dominica showing scenes from World Cup, Switzerland, 1954. Multicoloured.

6518	$150 German Federal Republic team	1·40	1·50
6519	$150 Winning goal in net and Gyula Grosics (Hungarian goalkeeper), Germany v. Hungary final	1·40	1·50
6520	$150 Wankdorf Stadium, Berne	1·40	1·50
6521	$150 Helmut Rahn about to score winning goal for West Germany	1·40	1·50
MS6522	115×90 mm. $400 Victorious German team members	3·25	3·50

698 Friedrich von Schiller

2005. Death Bicentenary of Friedrich von Schiller (poet and dramatist). Multicoloured.

6523	$200 Type **698**	2·25	2·25
6524	$200 Schiller and his house, Gohlis, Saxony	2·25	2·25
6525	$200 Ludwig von Beethoven (composer)	2·25	2·25
6526	$400 Schiller, Beethoven and *Ode to Joy* (written by Schiller, set to music by Beethoven) (60×55 mm)	4·50	4·50

---

699 Jules Verne

2005. Death Centenary of Jules Verne (writer). Multicoloured.

6527	$150 Type **699**	1·75	1·75
6528	$150 Interior of space capsule in *From the Earth to the Moon*	1·75	1·75
6529	$150 Space capsule in *From the Earth to the Moon*	1·75	1·75
6530	$150 Apollo 11 command module, 1969	1·75	1·75
MS6531	100×70 mm. $400 Neil Armstrong and lunar module on Moon, 1969 (horiz)	4·75	4·75

2005. Bicentenary of the Battle of Trafalgar. As T **423** of Dominica. Multicoloured.

6532	$25 Vice-Admiral Collingwood (vert)	60	30
6533	$35 Admiral Nelson wounded, Battle of Santa Cruz, 1797 (vert)	70	40
6534	$60 Nelson's funeral car arriving at St. Paul's Cathedral, 1806 (vert)	1·10	55
6535	$80 Admiral Lord Nelson and Flag Captain Thomas Hardy (vert)	1·40	65
6536	$100 First shots fired in Battle of Trafalgar	1·60	1·00
6537	$300 British ship hoisting signals to begin pincer movement (vert)	4·50	5·50
MS6538	70×100 mm. $400 Admiral Lord Nelson (vert)	5·50	5·50

700 Dental Examination

2005. Centenary of Rotary International. Multicoloured.

MS6539	140×109 mm. $150 Type **700**; $150 Carl-Wilhelm Steinhammar (2005 President-elect); $150 First Couple—District of Guyana	4·75	4·75
MS6540	100×70 mm. $400 Homer Wood (horiz)	4·25	4·25

The stamps within No. **MS**6540 form a composite background design.

701 *The Travelling Companion*

2005. Birth Bicentenary of Hans Christian Andersen (writer). Multicoloured.

6541	$200 Type **701**	1·75	1·90
6542	$200 *The Shadow*	1·75	1·90
6543	$200 *The Drop of Water*	1·75	1·90
MS6544	100×70 mm. $400 *The Emperor's New Suit* (50×38 mm)	3·25	3·50

702 "Luna 9"

2006. Space Anniversaries. Multicoloured.

(a) 40th Anniv of "Luna 9" Moon Landing

6545	$160 Type **702**	2·00	2·00
6546	$160 "Luna 9" capsule	2·00	2·00
6547	$160 Moon's *Oceanus Procellarum*	2·00	2·00
6548	$160 Sergei Korolev	2·00	2·00
6549	$160 Image of Moon's surface	2·00	2·00
6550	$160 Take-off of Molniya 8K78M rocket	2·00	2·00

(b) Muse Itokawa Comet Encounter.

6551	$200 Take-off of MV-5 rocket (vert)	2·25	2·25
6552	$200 Spacecraft *Hayabusa* (vert)	2·25	2·25
6553	$200 Itokawa composite colour image (vert)	2·25	2·25
6554	$200 Projected return to Earth (vert)	2·25	2·25

(c) 25th Anniv of First Flight of Space Shuttle Columbia.
6555 $200 Launch of space shuttle Columbia (vert) 2·25 2·25
6556 $200 Astronaut Robert Crippen (vert) 2·25 2·25
6557 $200 Astronaut John Young (vert) 2·25 2·25
6558 $200 Mission control (vert) 2·25 2·25

(d) Launch of Space Shuttle Discovery.
6559 $200 SS *Discovery* docked at ISS Destiny Laboratory 2·25 2·25
6560 $200 Astronaut Stephen Robinson attached to foot restraint on ISS Canadarm2 2·25 2·25
6561 $200 SS *Discovery* seen from ISS during docking operations 2·25 2·25
6562 $200 SS *Discovery* safe return 2·25 2·25
MS6563 Four sheets each 98×68 mm. (a) $400 Lunar Reconnaissance Orbiter. (b) $400 *Hayabusa* spacecraft over Asteroid Itokawa. (c) $400 Calipso satellite. (d) $400 Venus Express (first European mission to Venus) 15·00 15·00

2006. 80th Birthday of Queen Elizabeth II. As T **432** of Dominica. Multicoloured.
6564 $200 Queen Elizabeth II and Parliament Building, Guyana, 1966 2·50 2·50
6565 $200 Queen Elizabeth wearing black edged fawn jacket and hat, c. 1990 2·50 2·50
MS6566 120×120 mm. $400 Queen Elizabeth, c. 1955 and flags of Guyana and Great Britain 6·00 6·00

703 De Beers Zeppelin NT

2006. Hot Air Balloons and Airships. Multicoloured.
6567 $200 Type **703** 2·25 2·25
6568 $200 Lockhead Martin LTA 2004 2·25 2·25
6569 $200 Stratellite concept airship 2·25 2·25
MS6570 100×70 mm. $400 Skybus airship, Switzerland 4·50 4·50

2006. 400th Birth Anniv of Rembrandt Harmenszoon van Rijn (artist). As T **458** of Gambia. Multicoloured.
6571 $160 Man playing violin 1·90 1·90
6572 $160 Woman wearing shawl 1·90 1·90
6573 $160 Man playing harp 1·90 1·90
6574 $160 Woman with sheet music 1·90 1·90
MS6575 57×84 mm. $400 "Old Man with a Jewelled Cross" (detail). Imperf 4·50 4·50
Nos. 6571/4 all show details from painting "The Music Makers".

704 Nina

2006. 500th Death Anniv of Christopher Columbus. Multicoloured.
6576 $300 Type **704** 4·00 4·00
6577 $300 *Pinta* 4·00 4·00
6578 $300 *Santa Maria* 4·00 4·00

705 British Guiana 1856 1c. Black on Magenta Stamp

2006. 150th Anniv of Printing of the World's Rarest Stamp. Sheet 100×68 mm.
MS6579 **705** $400 multicoloured 4·50 4·50

706 Japanese Kemari Player, 7th-century

2006. World Cup Football Championship, Germany. History of Soccer. Sheet 102×127 mm containing T **706** and similar vert designs. Multicoloured.
MS6580 $80 Type **706**; $100 Kemari game, 7th-century; $160 Chinese Tsu Chu game, 2500BC; $300 1986 50f. Chinese stamp showing tsu chu game, 2500BC 6·00 6·50

707 Betty Boop with Hat and Cane

2006. Betty Boop. Multicoloured.
6581 $100 Type **707** 80 80
6582 $100 Seated on chair, holding mirror 80 80
6583 $100 With bouquet of red roses 80 80
6584 $100 Standing on grating with dress blowing upwards 80 80
6585 $100 With microphone 80 80
6586 $100 Lifting dress to show heart-shaped garter 80 80
MS6587 72×102 mm. $200 Seated, wearing black dress (horiz); $200 In car (horiz) 3·25 3·50

708 Marilyn Monroe

2007. 80th Birth Anniv (2006) of Marilyn Monroe (actress). Multicoloured.
6588 $200 Type **708** 1·60 1·60
6589 $200 Wearing pink dress, standing sideways with head and shoulders turned towards camera 1·60 1·60
6590 $200 Wearing pink dress, standing sideways with head turned towards camera 1·60 1·60
6591 $200 In close-up, speaking 1·60 1·60
MS6592 70×100 mm. $400 In close-up, smiling 2·75 3·00

709 Bletia florida

2007. Orchids. Multicoloured.
6593 $25 Type **709** 50 30
6594 $35 Basiphyllaea corallicola 60 35
6595 $60 Calopogon multiflorus 80 50
6596 $160 Cypripedium acaule 1·75 1·75
6597 $160 Calopogon tuberosus 1·75 1·75
6598 $160 Calopogon pallidus 1·75 1·75
6599 $160 Bletia patula 1·75 1·75
6600 $300 Bletia purpurea 1·75 1·75
MS6601 66×95 mm. $400 Cypripedium reginae 4·50 4·50

710 Summer Tanager

2007. Birds of South America. Multicoloured.
6602 $25 Type **710** 60 30
6603 $35 Gray-cheeked thrush 70 35
6604 $60 Blackpoll warbler 90 50
6605 $160 Golden-tailed warbler (vert) 2·00 2·00
6606 $160 Blue-crowned parakeet (vert) 2·00 2·00
6607 $160 White-winged parakeet (vert) 2·00 2·00
6608 $160 Yellow-green vireo (vert) 2·00 2·00
6609 $300 Thick-billed parrot 3·75 3·75
MS6610 95×66 mm. (a) $400 Bobolink (vert). (b) $400 Pacific golden plover (vert) 11·00 11·00

711 Morpho vitrea

2007. Butterflies of South America. Multicoloured.
6611 $25 Type **711** 60 40
6612 $35 Rothschildia Hesperus 70 50
6613 $60 Anaea nessus 90 60
6614 $300 Dryas iulia 3·50 3·75
MS6615 $160×4 Callithea sapphire; Prepona buckleyana; Lycorea pasinuntia; Danaus eresimus 8·00 8·00
MS6616 Two sheets, each 100×70 mm. (a) $400 Eurytides protesilaus. (b) $400 Cithaerias aurorina 9·50 9·50
The stamps and margins of No. MS6615 form a composite background design showing a butterfly's wing.

712 Chartreux

2007. Cats. Multicoloured.
6617 $25 Type **712** 50 40
6618 $35 Siamese Seal snowshoe point 60 50
6619 $60 Maine coon 80 60
6620 $300 Turkish angora 3·25 3·50
MS6621 70×101 mm. $400 Blue Burmese (vert) 4·50 4·50

713 Papillon

2007. Dogs. Multicoloured.
6622 $160 Type **713** 2·25 2·25
6623 $160 Dogue de Bordeaux 2·25 2·25
6624 $160 Cavalier King Charles spaniel 2·25 2·25
6625 $160 Neapolitan mastiff 2·25 2·25
MS6626 70×100 mm. $400 Basset hound wearing tweed hat 4·75 4·75

714 Mozart in 1770

2007. 250th Birth Anniv (2006) of Wolfgang Amadeus Mozart (composer). Multicoloured.
6627 $190 Type **714** 2·75 2·75
6628 $190 Mozart in 1762 2·75 2·75
6629 $190 Mozart, c. 1789 2·75 2·75
6630 $190 Portrait by Joseph Grassi 2·75 2·75

715 Lord Robert Baden-Powell (founder), Peace Dove and Globe

2007. Centenary of World Scouting and 21st World Scout Jamboree, England. Multicoloured.
6631 $180 Type **715** 2·25 2·25
6632 $180 Scouts rafting 2·25 2·25
6633 $180 Scouts in tug-of-war 2·25 2·25
MS6634 111×80 mm. $400 Peace dove (vert) 4·50 4·50

716 Pig

2007. Chinese New Year ("Year of the Pig"). Multicoloured.
6635 $55 Type **716** 55 55

6636 $80 Pig (facing right) 75 75
6637 $100 As Type **716** 1·10 1·10
6638 $160 As No. 6636 1·50 1·50

717 Oath of Office

2007. 90th Birth Anniv of John F. Kennedy (US President 1960–3). Multicoloured.
MS6639 Two sheets, each 108×130 mm. (a) $80 Type **717**; $100 Inaugural speech; $160 John Kennedy; $190 With Jacqueline Kennedy at Inaugural Ball. (b) $80 The Peace Corps; $100 The Space Program; $160 Civil Rights; $190 John Kennedy, 1941 12·00 12·00

718 Elvis Presley

2007. 30th Death Anniv of Elvis Presley. Multicoloured.
6640 $160 Type **718** 1·75 1·75
6641 $160 Poster in bright scarlet and brown-rose 1·75 1·75
6642 $160 Young Elvis Presley (wearing black shirt) 1·75 1·75
6643 $160 Wearing sunglasses, facing left 1·75 1·75

2007. World Cup Cricket, West Indies. As T **448** of Dominica. Multicoloured.
6644 $100 Outline map and flag of Guyana 1·75 80
6645 $200 Victorious Guyana team, Stanford 20/20 (horiz) 3·25 3·25
MS6646 117×90 mm. $500 World Cup Cricket emblem 6·00 6·00

719 Pope Benedict XVI

2007. 80th Birthday of Pope Benedict XVI.
6647 **719** $80 multicoloured 1·25 1·25

720 Concorde Prototype 002 rolled out, Filton, September 1968

2007. Concorde. Multicoloured.
6648 $100 Type **720** 1·50 1·50
6649 $100 Prototype 002 (seen from above, gangway down), Filton, September 1968 1·50 1·50
6650 $100 Concorde and Red Arrows, 1985 1·50 1·50
6651 $100 Silhouettes of Concorde, Red Arrows and *Queen Elizabeth II* 1·50 1·50
Nos. 6650/1 commemorate Concorde's flight in formation with the Red Arrows and the liner *Queen Elizabeth* in 1985.

721 Hockey

2008. Olympic Games, Beijing. Multicoloured.
6652 $100 Type **721** 1·40 1·40

6653	$100 Basketball	1·40	1·40
6654	$100 Judo	1·40	1·40
6655	$100 Shooting	1·40	1·40

722 Emblem and 'Carifesta X'

2008. Carifesta Caribbean Festival of Arts, Guyana. Multicoloured, background colours given.

6656	**722**	$20 red	35	30
6657	**722**	$55 green and yellow	60	40
6658	**722**	$80 green	75	75
6659	**722**	$160 yellow	1·50	1·75

723 St. Stanislaus College, Georgetown

2008. 150th Anniv (2007) of Jesuits in Guyana. Multicoloured.

6660	$80 Type **723**	75	65
6661	$100 Sacred Heart Church, 1861–2004, Georgetown	95	65
6662	$160 Fr. Cuthbert Cary-Elwes, missionary among the Amerindians, 1909–23	1·50	1·75

724 Sir James Douglas

2008. 150th Anniv of Appointment of Sir James Douglas (born in Guyana) as First Governor of British Colombia, Canada. Sheet 70×100 mm.
MS6663 multicoloured 1·75 1·75

725 White Peony

2009. China 2009 World Stamp Exhibition, Luoyang (1st issue). Peonies.

6664	**725**	$80 multicoloured	50	55

726 Red Peony

2009. China 2009 World Stamp Exhibition, Luoyang (2nd issue). The Art of Wang Hui (1632–1717). Sheet 150×120 mm containing T **726** and similar horiz designs. Multicoloured.
MS6665 Type **726**; River valley and coast; Clouds and forest; Coastal rocks with pines 5·50 5·50

727 Elvis Presley

2009. Elvis Presley Commemoration. Sheet 128×190 mm containing T **727** and similar vert designs. Multicoloured.
MS6666 Type **727**; Wearing orange jacket; Wearing white jacket; In profile; In close-up, singing into microphone; Wearing black shirt 8·50 8·50

728 Pres. Barack Obama

2009. Inauguration of Pres. Barack Obama. Sheet 107×145 mm containing T **728** and similar vert designs showing Pres. Obama. Multicoloured.
MS6667 Type **728**; In profile; Wearing red tie; Wearing pale grey tie 4·50 4·50

729 50th Anniversary Commemorative Magazine

2009. 50th Anniv of Rotary Club of Georgetown, Guyana. Sheet 140×90 mm containing T **729** and similar horiz designs. Multicoloured.
MS6668 $80 Type **729**; $80 'Christmas Cheers for the Elderly'; $160 Poster showing people in wheelchairs ('Physically challenged sports'); $160 Boy receiving award 4·50 4·50

730 500 F2, 1952

2009. Ferrari Racing Cars. Sheet 120×100 mm containing T **730** and similar horiz designs. Multicoloured.
MS6669 $200×4 Type **730**; 500 F2, 1953; 246 F1, 1958; 312 T2, 1976 6·50 6·50

730a Takutu Bridge

2009. Opening of Takutu Bridge linking Guyana to Brazil. Sheet 100×70 mm.
MS6669a multicoloured 3·50 3·50

731 Guyana Scouts Centenary Parade

2009. Centenary of Scouting in Guyana and 14th Caribbean Scout Jamboree, Georgetown. Multicoloured.

6670	$55 Type **731**	35	40
6671	$55 Archery (vert)	35	40
6672	$80 Helping the homeless	50	55
6673	$80 Erecting shelter at Scout jamboree	50	55
6674	$160 '1909 Scouting Guyana 2009' and national flag	1·40	1·50
6675	$160 '2009 14th Caribbean Scout jamboree Celebrating 100 years of Scouting in Guyana'	1·40	1·50

732 Trevor Ariza (Los Angeles Lakers)

2009. NBA Basketball Finals. Multicoloured.

6676	$90 Type **732**	65	70
6677	$90 Shannon Brown	65	70
6678	$90 Jordan Farmar	65	70
6679	$90 Andrew Bynum	65	70
6680	$90 Kobe Bryant	65	70
6681	$90 Derek Fisher	65	70
6682	$90 Pau Gasol	65	70
6683	$90 Lamar Odom	65	70
6684	$90 Luke Walton	65	70
6685	$90 Rafer Alston	65	70
6686	$90 Marcin Gortat	65	70
6687	$90 Rashard Lewis	65	70
6688	$90 Courtney Lee	65	70
6689	$90 Dwight Howard	65	70
6690	$90 Jameer Nelson	65	70
6691	$90 Mickael Pietrus	65	70
6692	$90 J. J. Redick	65	70
6693	$90 Hedo Turkoglu	65	70

Nos. 6676/84 show players from Los Angeles Lakers, the 2009 NBA champions.
Nos. 6685/93 show players from Orlando Magic, the 2009 Eastern Conference champions.

733 Michael Jackson

2009. Michael Jackson Commemoration. Two sheets, each 178×127 mm, containing T **733** and similar multicoloured designs.
MS6694 Type **733**; With arm raised and other hand on belt buckle; Seen from side, right arm outstretched; Both hands at waist level 6·00 6·00
MS6695 Wearing red waistcoat; Wearing black hat, black glittery jacket and white T shirt; Wearing black sequinned jacket and white T shirt; Wearing red T shirt with black diagonal band (all horiz) 6·00 6·00

734 Parliament Building, Georgetown

2009. 60th Anniv of the Commonwealth. Sheet 170×114 mm.. Multicoloured.
MS6696 $60 Type **734**×6 2·50 2·50

735 National Library, Georgetown

2009. Centenary of National Library, Georgetown. Sheet 120×100 mm containing T **735** and similar horiz designs. Multicoloured.
MS6697 Type **735**; Aerial view; Students in library; Students in library (black and white photo) 4·00 4·00

736 J-8II

2009. Centenary of Chinese Aviation and Aeropex 2009 Exhibition, Beijing. T **736** and similar horiz designs showing fighter jets. Multicoloured.
MS6698 145×95 mm. $150×4 Type **736**; Shenyang J-811; Shenyang J-11; Shentang J-10 (pale blue background); (blue sky and white clouds background) 5·00 5·00
MS6699 120×80 mm. $400 Shenyang J-10 (50×37 mm) 3·25 3·25

737 Pope John Paul II and Cardinal Joseph Ratzinger

2009. Pope Benedict XVI and Pope John Paul II. Multicoloured.
MS6700 120×140 mm. $200×4 As Type **737** 3·25 3·25
MS6701 110×100 mm. $400×2 Cardinal Joseph Ratzinger; Pope John Paul II 6·50 6·50

The stamps within MS6700 are all as Type **737** with a yellow border at the foot of the stamp which depicts portions of the sheet background illustration of the portico of St. Peter's Basilica.
A $2000 gold stamp containing a multicoloured illustration of Pope Benedict XVI was issued on the same date

738 Rat

2010. Chinese Lunar Calendar. Multicoloured.
MS6702 $45×12 Type **738**; Ox; Tiger; Rabbit; Dragon; Snake; Horse; Ram; Monkey; Cock; Dog; Pig 3·50 3·50

739 Tiger

2010. Chinese New Year. Year of the Tiger. Multicoloured.
MS6703 $450 Type **739**; $450 As Type **739** but red background and white frame 7·75 7·75

740 Anniversary Emblem

2010. 40th Anniv of Republic. Multicoloured.
MS6704 $80×4 Type **740**; Masqueraders; Mash Float Parade; Children's Costume Parade 3·50 3·50

(741)

2010. Haiti Earthquake Relief

6705	$160 Golden-tailed warbler (vert)	1·40	1·50
6706	$160 Blue-crowned parakeet (vert)	1·40	1·50
6707	$160 White-winged parakeet (vert)	1·40	1·50
6708	$160 Yellow-green vireo (vert)	1·40	1·50

742 Princess Diana

2010. Princess Diana Commemoration. Multicoloured.
MS6709 $225×4 Type **742**; Wearing fawn cap with large tassel at left; Wearing white; Wearing bright blue brimmed hat with feather 6·75 6·75
MS6710 $225×4 Wearing tiara; Wearing white and red patterned jacket and red hat with black band; Wearing black blouse with red cuffs and collar with gold pattern; Wearing Royal Navy cap and blue jacket 6·75 6·75

743 Pres Obama at Great Hall of People, Beijing

2010. Visit of Pres. Barack Obama to China. Multicoloured.
MS6711 $300 Type **743**; $300 Pres. Hu Jintao (China) 7·50 7·50

744 Elvis Presley as Deke Rivers in *Loving You*

2010. Elvis Presley in *Loving You* (film), 1957. Multicoloured.

MS6712 125×90 mm. $500 Type **744**		4·50	4·50
MS6713 90×125 mm. $500 Playing guitar, wearing western shirt		4·50	4·50
MS6714 90×125 mm. $500 Playing guitar, wearing denim jacket		4·50	4·50
MS6715 125×90 mm. $500 Poster for *Loving You*		4·50	4·50

745 Guyana Flag

2010. National Stamp

6716	**745**	$160 multicoloured	1·25	1·25

746 Three Guides

2010. Centenary of Girlguiding. Multicoloured.

MS6717 150×100 mm. $275×4 Type **746**; Two guides in dark blue uniforms; Three guides in light blue uniforms with yellow necktie; Four guides on ropewalk		8·25	8·25
MS6718 70×100 mm. $450 Guide saluting (vert)		3·50	3·50

747 'Don't be a Joker Drugs Kill'

2010. UNICEF Rights of the Child. Winning Entries in Children's Postage Stamp Design Competition. Multicoloured.

MS6719 $100×4 Type **747**; "The Right not to be Mistreated'; 'The Right to Live with a Family'; 'The Right not to Witness Domestic Violence'		3·00	3·00

748 Map showing Bartica ('gateway to the Interior')

2010. Tenth Anniv of Porkknocker Day. Multicoloured.

MS6720 $100×4 Type **748**; Cyrilda de Jesus (porkknocker miner); Dick Manning (porkknocker); Mazaruni gold nuggets and diamonds		3·00	3·00

749 Joan Capdevila

2011. World Cup Football, South Africa. Multicoloured.

MS6721 131×150 mm. $120×6 Netherlands v. Spain: Type **749**; Arjen Robben; Pedro; Gregory van der Wiel; Xabi Alonso; Wesley Sneijder		5·50	5·50
MS6722 131×150 mm. $120×6 Uruguay v. Germany: Dennis Aogo; Diego Forlan; Bastian Schweinsteiger; Martin Caceres; Stefan Kiessling; Maximiliano Pereira		5·50	5·50
MS6723 85×90 mmm. $550 Andres Iniesta (Spain)		4·25	4·25
MS6724 85×90 mm. $550 Thomas Mueller (Germany)		4·25	4·25

750 Deng Xiaoping

2010. Beijing 2010 International Stamp and Coin Expo. Leaders of China. Multicoloured.

MS6725 $150×4 Qin Shi Huang (259-210 BC, first Emperor of China): Painting (pale grey background); Sculpture; Painting (pale yellow background); Inscription 'QIN SHI HUANG THE FIRST EMPEROR OF CHINA'		4·50	4·50
MS6726 $150×4 Deng Xiaoping (1904-97, Paramount Leader of the People's Republic of China): Type **750**; Full face, in close-up; Facing right; Facing left		4·50	4·50
MS6727 $150×4 Jiang Zemin (President of People's Republic of China, 1993-2003): Wearing orange scarf; Photographed facing forward; Looking down to right; Looking left and smiling		4·50	4·50

751 Rabbit running

2011. Chinese New Year. Year of the Rabbit.

MS6728 $200 Type **751**; $200 Rabbit (sitting)		3·00	3·00

752 *The Adoration of the Magi* (Hieronymus Bosch)

2011. Christmas. Multicoloured.

6729	$80 Type **752**		60	60
6730	$100 *The Adoration of the Magi* (Peter Paul Rubens), c. 1634		75	75
6731	$225 *Madonna and Child* (Carlo Crivelli), c. 1490		1·75	1·75
6732	$500 *The Flight into Egypt* (Lucas Cranach the Elder)		3·75	3·75

753 Pope John Paul II

2011. Fifth Death Anniv of Pope John Paul II. Multicoloured.

MS6733 $225×4 Type **753**; Wearing white robe and skull cap; With staff and mitre (white robe); Praying, facing left		6·75	6·75
MS6734 $225×4 Pope John Paul II (wearing red cassock and robe and white skull cap; Wearing white robe and skull cap, facing left; With staff and mitre (wearing red robe); Wearing red robe and white skull cap, looking down		6·75	6·75

754 Pope Benedict XVI

2011. Fifth Anniv of Pontificate of Pope Benedict XVI. Multicoloured.

MS6735 119×138 mm. $225 Type **754**×4		6·75	6·75
MS6736 182×95 mm. $225 Pope Benedict XVI (in close-up)×4		6·75	6·75

755 Abraham Lincoln

2011. Abraham Lincoln (US President 1861-5) Commemoration. Multicoloured.

MS6737 141×101 mm. $225×4 Type **755** and as Type **755** but with pink, greenish grey and lilac tinged backgrounds		6·75	6·75
MS6738 101×131 mm. $225 Young Abraham Lincoln (without beard) ×2; $225 Older Abraham Lincoln (with beard)×2		6·75	6·75

756 UNITEC-1

2011. International Year of Astronomy (2009). Multicoloured.

MS6739 Japanese Space Probes $225×4 Type **756**; IKAROS solar sail; KSAT Negai; Waseda-sat2		6·75	6·75
MS6740 Mars Exploration $255×4 Phobos-Grunt arrival; Phobos-Grunt landing; Mars Reconnaissance Orbiter; Phobos-Grunt liftoff		7·75	7·75

757 Prince William and Miss Catherine Middleton

2011. Royal Engagement. Multicoloured.

MS6741 100×151 mm. $200 Type **757**×4		6·00	6·00
MS6742 Colour photos: $200×4 Prince William and Miss Catherine Middleton in St. James' Palace; Prince William and Miss Catherine Middleton (in profile); Miss Catherine Middleton; Prince William		6·00	6·00
MS6743 Black/white photos: $225 Prince William; $225 Miss Catherine Middleton		3·50	3·50
MS6744 100×70 mm. $450 Prince William and Miss Catherine Middleton in St. James' Palace (different)		3·50	3·50

758 Lieut. Col. John Pegram, Brigadier General William S. Rosecrans and Engagement at Rich Mountain, 1861

2011. 150th Anniv of the American Civil War. Multicoloured.

MS6745 $225×4 Type **758**; Lieut.-Col. Pegram, Brigadier General Rosecrans and Battle of Rich Mountain (in deep blue); Lieut.-Col. Pegram, Brigadier General Rosecrans and Battle of Rich Mountain (in maroon); Lieut.-Col. Pegram, Brigadier General Rosecrans and Confederate Prisoners, Rich Mountain		6·75	6·75
MS6746 $225×4 Brigadier General James Longstreet, General Daniel Tyler and: Blackburn's Ford; Member's of Longstreet's Brigade; Fairfax County Courthouse; Battle of Blackburn's Ford, 1861		6·75	6·75
MS6747 $225×4 Brigadier General Joseph E. Johnston, Brigadier General Irvin McDowell and: First Battle of Bull Run, 1861; Confederate fortifications, Manassas; Union Charge at Bull Run; Henry House in ruins		6·75	6·75

759 Mother Teresa praying

2011. Birth Centenary of Mother Teresa. Multicoloured.

MS6748 $225 Type **759**×4		6·75	6·75

760 Temple of Shiva

2011. Indipex 2011 International Stamp Exhibition, New Delhi. Sites and Scenes of India. Multicoloured.

MS6749 141×130 mm. $225×4 Type **760**; Ramnagar Fort; Kangra Valley; Khajuraho Temple		6·75	6·75
MS6750 141×130 mm. $225×4 Interior of Taj Mahal; Dome of Taj Mahal; Taj Mahal at sunset; Exterior walls of Taj Mahal		6·75	6·75
MS6751 71×101 mm. $450 Statue of Shiva (38×51 mm)		3·00	3·00

761 Bush Dogs drinking

2011. Endangered Species. Bush Dog (*Speothos venaticus*). Multicoloured.

6752	$150 Type **761**		1·10	1·10
6753	$150 Female with three pups		1·10	1·10
6754	$150 Female in den with two pups		1·10	1·10
6755	$150 Head of bush dog		1·10	1·10
MS6756 100×140 mm. Nos. 6752/5, each ×2			8·75	8·75

762 Shivnarine Chanderpaul

2011. Cricket World Cup, India, Sri Lanka and Bangladesh. Multicoloured.

6757	$100 Type **762**		75	75
6758	$150 Sardar Patel Stadium, Ahmedabad (horiz)		1·10	1·10
MS6759 148×100 mm. $300 Trophy (30×40 mm)			2·25	2·25

763 Pres. Kennedy in Stadium

2011. 50th Anniv of Inauguration of President John F. Kennedy. Multicoloured.

MS6760 170×130 mm. $175 Type **763**×2; $175 Pres. Kennedy in front of microphones speaking×2; $175 In close-up×2		7·75	7·75
MS6761 153×133 mm. $225×4 With Jackie Kennedy (wearing white dress); Presidential Campaign badge; Pres. Kennedy speaking; With Jackie Kennedy (wearing red dress)		6·75	6·75

764 Pres. Barack Obama

2011. 50th Birthday of Pres. Barack Obama. Multicoloured.

MS6762 $225 Type **764**×2; Pres. Obama (bright blue background)×2		6·75	6·75
MS6763 $225 Pres. Obama (ochre background)×2; $225 Pres. Obama (lake-brown background)×2		6·75	6·75

765 Prince William

2011. Royal Wedding. Multicoloured.
MS6764 150×100 mm. $250×4 Black
and white photos: Type **765**; Prince
William and Duchess of Cambridge;
Procession; Duchess of Cambridge ... 7·50 7·50

MS6765 150×100 mm. $275×3 Colour
photos: Prince William and Duchess
of Cambridge leaving Westminster
Abbey; Prince William and Duchess
of Cambridge in carriage; Prince William holding her hand (all vert) ... 6·25 6·25

MS6766 100×90 mm. $500 Prince
William and Duchess of Cambridge
kissing on Buckingham Palace
balcony (38×51 mm) ... 3·75 3·75

766 Elvis Presley in
Jailhouse Rock

2011. Elvis Presley Commemoration. Multicoloured.
MS6767 130×100 mm. $225×4 *Jailhouse
Rock* (film): Type **766**; Playing guitar
and singing (half length photo);
Playing guitar and singing (three
quarter length); Dancing and singing,
jailhouse bars in background ... 6·75 6·75

MS6768 130×100 mm. $225×4 Aloha
from Hawaii: Outdoors, wearing
lei; In concert holding microphone
(half length photo, in half profile);
In concert holding microphone
(head and shoulders, in profile); With
hand raised ... 6·75 6·75

MS6769 146×146 mm. $225×4 Albums:
Blue Hawaii; *Elvis Gold Records Vol 4*;
ELVIS PRESLEY; *Moody Blue* ... 6·75 6·75

MS6770 146×146 mm. $225×4 Albums:
Viva Las Vegas; *Elvis Welcome to My
World*; *ELVIS*; *I Got Stung* ... 6·75 6·75

767
*Pseudotulostoma
volvata*

**2011. International Year of Forests. Mushrooms of the
Caribbean. Multicoloured.**
MS6771 170×100 mm. $150×6 Type
767; *Inocybe ayangannae*; *Amanita
perphaea*; *Entoloma olivaceocolora-
tum*; *Panaeolus cyanescens*; *Tylopilus
vinaceipallidus* ... 6·75 6·75

MS6772 100×130 mm. $225×4
Boletellus dicmyophilus; *Inocybe
epidendron*; *Tilopilus pakaraimensis*;
Amanita aurantiobrunnea ... 6·75 6·75

MS6773 70×100 mm. $475 *Amauro-
derma gusmanianum* ... 3·50 3·50

MS6774 70×100 mm. $475 *Craterellus
excelsus* ... 3·50 3·50

768 Princess Diana

2011. 50th Birth Anniv of Princess Diana. Multicoloured.
MS6775 140×100 mm. $275×3 Type
768; Princess Diana wearing white
jacket and headscarf; Prince Charles
and Princess Diana on honeymoon
at Balmoral, 1981 ... 6·25 6·25

MS6776 100×100 mm. $450 Princess
Diana wearing winter coat and hat
(51×38 mm) ... 3·50 3·50

769 Rat

770 King Edward
VIII

2012. Chinese Zodiac Animals. Multicoloured.
MS6777 550×12 Type **769**; Ox; Tiger;
Rabbit; Dragon; Snake; Horse; Sheep;
Monkey; Rooster; Dog; Boar ... 4·50 4·50

**2012. 75th Anniv of Accession of King Edward VIII (1st
issue). Multicoloured.**
MS6778 150×100 mm. $300 Type
770×3 ... 6·75 6·75

MS6779 71×140 mm. $700 King Ed-
ward VIII in uniform (50×30 mm) ... 5·25 5·25
Nos. **MS**6778/9 are wrongly inscr 'KING EDWARD XIII'.

**2012. 75th Anniv of Accession of King Edward VIII (2nd
issue). As Nos. MS6778/9 but with inscriptions on
stamps and sheet margins corrected to 'King Edward
VIII'**
MS6780 150×100 mm. $300×3 As
Type **770**×3 ... 6·75 6·75

MS6781 71×140 mm. $700 King Ed-
ward VIII in uniform (50×30 mm) ... 5·25 5·25

771 Anhinga (*Anhinga
anhinga*)

2012. Birds of South America (1st series). Multicoloured.
MS6782 135×90 mm. $160×4 Type
771; Least Grebe (*Tachybaptus
dominicus*); Scarlet Ibis (*Eudocimus
ruber*); Neotropic Cormorant (*Phalacrocorax brasilianus*) ... 4·75 4·75

MS6783 135×90 mm. $160×4 Northern
Caracara (*Caracara cheriway*); Cocoi
Heron (*Ardea cocoi*); Tricolored
Heron (*Egretta tricolor*); Jabiru (*Jabiru
mycteria*) ... 4·75 4·75

MS6784 100×70 mm. $400 White-tailed
Kite (*Elanus leucurus*) (vert) ... 3·00 3·00

MS6785 100×70 mm. $400 Glossy Ibis
(*Plegadis falcinellus*) ... 3·00 3·00

772 Iphiclus Sister (*Adelpha
iphiclu*)

2012. Butterflies of the World. Multicoloured.
MS6786 100×150 mm. $250×4 Type
772; Gaudy Altinote (*Altinote negra
sobrina*); Gulf Fritillary (*Agraulis vanil-
lae*); Tiger Crescent (*Eresia eunic*) ... 7·50 7·50

MS6787 100×150 mm. $250×4 Orange-
banded Gem (*Crocozona coecias*);
Red-barred Amarynthis (*Amarynthis
meneria*); Thesprotia Sister (*Adelpha
thesprotia*); Orange-barred Sister
(*Adelpha saundersii*) ... 7·50 7·50

MS6788 71×100 mm. $500 White-
barred Sister (*Adelpha epione*)
(38×50 mm) ... 3·75 3·75

MS6789 71×100 mm. $500 Blue Dusky-
wing (*Anastrus neaeris*) (38×50 mm) ... 3·75 3·75

REPTILES
Giant Tortoise, Chelonoidis nigra

773 Giant Tortoise
(*Chelonoidis nigra*)

2012. Reptiles of South America. Multicoloured.
MS6790 150×101 mm. $250×4 Type
773; Caiman Lizard (*Dracaena guian-
ensis*); Marine Iguana (*Amblyrhynchus
cristatus*); Milk Snake (*Lampropeltis
triangulum*) ... 7·50 7·50

MS6791 150×101 mm. $250×4
Rainbow Whiptail (*Cnemidophorus
lemniscatus*); Emerald Tree Boa
(*Corallus caninus*); Green Vine Snake
(*Oxybelis fulgidus*); Green Iguana
(*Iguana iguana*) ... 7·50 7·50

MS6792 100×101 mm. $700 Spectacled
Caiman (*Caiman crocodylus*) (50×30
mm) ... 5·25 5·25

MS6793 100×101 mm. $700 Boa Con-
strictor (*Boa constrictor*) (30×80 mm) ... 5·25 5·25

774 Wenlock

2012. Olympic Games, London. Mascots. Multicoloured.
MS6794 $125 Type **774**×4; $125
Mandeville×4 ... 3·75 3·75

775 Tian'anmen, China

**2012. 40th Anniv of Diplomatic Relations between
Guyana and People's Republic of China.
Multicoloured.**
MS6795 $350 Type **775**; $350 Guyana
International Conference Centre ... 5·25 5·25

776 *Ada aurantiaca*

2012. Orchids of South America. Multicoloured.
MS6796 170×101 mm. $250×4 Type
776; *Cattleya labiata*; *Masdevallia
haryana*; *Masdevallia davisii* ... 7·50 7·50

MS6797 101×70 mm. $700 *Zygopeta-
lum clayi* ... 5·25 5·25

777 *Melampus*
(*Melampus*) *coffeus*

2012. Seashells of the Caribbean. Multicoloured.
MS6798 151×100 mm. $175×6
Type **777**; *Nerita fulgurans*; *Nerita
peloronta*; *Littorina nebulosa*; *Tectar-
ius muricatus*; *Hyalina avena* ... 7·75 7·75

MS6799 151×100 mm. $225×4 *Cassis
flammea*; *Liguus virgineus*; *Trigonos-
toma rugosum*; *Neritina virginea* ... 6·75 6·75

MS6800 100×71 mm. $500 *Cymatium
raderi* ... 3·75 3·75

MS6801 100×71 mm. $500 *Cassis
madagascariensis* ... 3·75 3·75

778 Grey Wolf (*Canis lupus*)

2012. The Evolution of Dogs. Multicoloured.
MS6802 250×180 mm. $225×5 Type
778; Canaan Dog; Maltese; Greyhound; Golden Retriever ... 8·50 8·50

MS6803 161×100 mm. $250×4 Coyote
(*Canis latrans*); Alaskan Huskey; Red
Fox (*Vulpes vulpes*); Yorkshire Terrier ... 7·50 7·50

MS6804 70×100 mm. $700 Dalmation
(vert) ... 5·25 5·25

MS6805 70×100 mm. $700 Bullmastiff
(vert) ... 5·25 5·25

779 Jaguar
(*Panthera onca*)

2012. Wildlife of South America. Multicoloured.
MS6806 110×159 mm. $300×3 Type
779; Toucan (*Ramphastos vitellinus*);
Chinchilla (*Chinchilla lanigera*) ... 6·75 6·75

MS6807 70×120 mm. $350 Llama (fac-
ing right); $350 Llama (facing left) ... 5·25 5·25

780 Killer Whale (*Orcinus orca*)

2012. Whales. Multicoloured.
MS6808 179×110 mm. $300×3 Type
780; Humpback Whale (*Megaptera
novaeangliae*); Blue Whale (*Balaenoptera musculus*) ... 6·75 6·75

MS6809 100×90 mm. $700 Beluga
Whale (*Delphinapterus leucas*) (80×30
mm) ... 5·25 5·25

781 Spinner Dolphin

2012. Dolphins. Multicoloured.
MS6810 130×101 mm. $300×3 Type
781; Atlantic Spotted Dolphin;
Amazon River Dolphin ... 6·75 6·75

MS6811 130×101 mm. $300×3
Clymene Dolphin; Dusky Dolphin;
White Sided Dolphin ... 6·75 6·75

MS6812 100×71 mm. $700 Common
Dolphin ... 5·25 5·25

MS6813 100×71 mm. $700 Bottlenose
Dolphin (vert) ... 5·25 5·25

782 Joel

**2012. 500th Anniv of Completion of the Sistine Chapel
Ceiling by Michelangelo. Multicoloured.**
MS6814 191×80 mm. $225×3 Type
782; Daniel; The Libyan Sibyl ... 5·00 5·00

MS6815 130×70 mm. $350
Michelangelo (vert); $350 Ancestors
of Christ (vert) ... 5·25 5·25

783 Princess Diana

2012. 15th Death Anniv of Princess Diana. Multicoloured.
MS6816 $250×4 Type **783**; Princess
Diana wearing white hat and white
jacket with gold braids; Wearing
tiara and turquoise dress; Wearing
beige hat and jacket ... 7·50 7·50

MS6817 $250×4 Princess Diana
wearing red jacket and lei; Wearing
spotted dress and pearl necklace;
Wearing jacket and tie; Wearing pale
yellow jacket and leis ... 7·50 7·50

784 Elvis Presley

2012. Elvis Presley Classic Hits. Multicoloured.
MS6818 $700 Type **784** (*Big Boss Man*) ... 5·25 5·25

MS6819 $700 Elvis Presley wearing
white, arms outstretched (purple
frame) (*Way Down*) ... 5·25 5·25

MS6820 $700 Wearing dark brown
shirt and white tie (blue-black
frame) (*Stuck on You*) ... 5·25 5·25

MS6821 $700 Elvis Presley reading
(orange-red frame) (*I Gotta Know*) ... 5·25 5·25

MS6822 $700 Wearing white jacket
(orange-red frame) (*It Feels So Right*) ... 5·25 5·25

785 Rabbits

2012. Chinese Zodiac Animals. Multicoloured.
6823	$50 Type **785**		40	40
6824	$50 Tiger		40	40

786 *Bunchosia argentea*

2013. Blossoms and Plants. Multicoloured.
MS6825 100×101 mm. $225×4 Type **786**; *Strelitzia reginae*; *Aechmea chantinii*; *Acanthocereus tetragonus* — 6·75 6·75
MS6826 100×100 mm. $225×4 *Asclepias curassavica*; *Passiflora tarminiana*; *Heliconia bihai*; *Aphelandra squarrosa* — 6·75 6·75
MS6827 100×101 mm. $710 *Iris germanica* (38×51 mm) — 5·25 5·25

787 Great White Shark (*Carcharodon carcharias*)

2013. Sharks. Multicoloured.
MS6828 117×151 mm. $225×6 Type **787**; Mako Shark (*Isurus oxyrinchus*); Great Hammerhead (*Sphyrna mokarranv*); Blue Shark (*Prionace glauca*); Blacktip Reef Shark (*Carcharhinus melanopterus*); Nurse Shark (*Ginglymostoma cirratum*) — 10·00 10·00
MS6829 90×100 mm. $710 Whale Shark (*Rhincodon typus*) (80×30 mm) — 5·25 5·25

788 Marine Life (image scaled to 58% of original size)

2013. World Environment Day. Multicoloured.
MS6830 160×175 mm. $275×3 Type **788**; Outline map of Australia, New Guinea and New Zealand and diver, Hammerhead Shark, ray and other marine life; Whale, turtle and other marine life — 6·25 6·25
MS6831 51×90 mm. $710 White heart emblem (circular, 38 mm) — 5·25 5·25

789 *Madonna and Child, c. 1470-5 (Andrea del Verrocchio)*

2013. History of Art. Renaissance Era Madonnas (MS6832) and Mannerism (others). Multicoloured.
MS6832 140×140 mm. $275×3 Type **789**; *Madonna, c. 1473* (Carlo Crivelli); *Madonna, 1512-16* (Mathis Gothart Grünewald) — 6·25 6·25
MS6833 140×140 mm. $275×3 *Portrait of Ugolino Martelli, 1535* (Agnolo Bronzino); *Sacrifice of Isaac, c. 1586* (Paolo Veronese); *The Ignudi, 1509* (Michelangelo) — 6·25 6·25
MS6834 90×120 mm. $710 *Penitent Magdalene, c. 1598-1602* (Tintoretto) (horiz) — 5·25 5·25

790 Snake

2013. Chinese New Year. Year of the Snake. Multicoloured.
MS6835 170×211 mm. $80 Chinese calligraphic character for snake×4; $80 Type **790**×16 — 12·00 12·00
MS6836 119×101 mm. $225 Green snake (30×40 mm)×4 — 6·75 6·75

791 *Danaus gilippus berenice*

2013. Butterflies. Multicoloured.
MS6837 $150×6 Type **791**; *Lycorea halia cleobaea*; *Hypothyris lycaste*; *Danaus gilippus thersippus*; *Danaus plexippus*; *Libytheana fulvescens* — 6·75 6·75
MS6838 $200×6 *Battus philenor orsua*; *Dismorphia eunoe desine*; *Dismorphia spio*; *Lieinix viridifascia*; *Lyropteryx lyra cleadas*; *Neophasia terlooii* — 9·00 9·00

792 Wallace Hartley (violinist and bandleader)

2013. Centenary (2012) of Sinking of the *Titanic*. Multicoloured.
MS6839 181×101 mm. $200×6 Type **792**; Georges Krins (violinist); John Law Hume (violinist); John Wesley Woodward (cellist); Percy Cornelius Taylor (cellist); Theodore Ronald Brailey (pianist) — 9·00 9·00
MS6840 119×71 mm. $700 RMS *Titanic* (80×30 mm) — 5·25 5·25

793 Black-backed Tanager (*Tangara peruviana*)

2013. Birds of South America (2nd series). Multicoloured.
MS6841 50×170 mm. $225×4 Type **793**; Golden-hooded Tanager (*Tangara larvata*); Turquoise Tanager (*Tangara mexicana*); Burnished-buff Tanager (*Tangara cayana*) — 6·75 6·75
MS6842 70×101 mm. $710 Golden Tanager (*Tangara arthus*) (38×50 mm) — 5·25 5·25

794 Pope Benedict XVI at the Wailing Wall, Jerusalem

2013. Papal Retrospectives. Visits of Pope Benedict XVI to Israel, 2009 and Great Britain, 2010. Multicoloured.
MS6843 101×175 mm. $225×4 Type **794**; Pope Benedict XVI with Pres. Shimon Peres of Israel; Behind microphones; Wearing green cloak, holding staff — 6·75 6·75
MS6844 101×175 mm. $225×4 Pope Benedict XVI with Queen Elizabeth II and Prince Philip; Pope Benedict holding incense, followed by churchmen in prayer; Wearing mitre and holding staff; Holding communion chalice — 6·75 6·75
MS6845 70×125 mm. $710 Pope Benedict XVI facing Wailing Wall, Jerusalem — 5·25 5·25
MS6846 70×125 mm. $710 Pope Benedict XVI in Great Britain, Union flag in background — 5·25 5·25

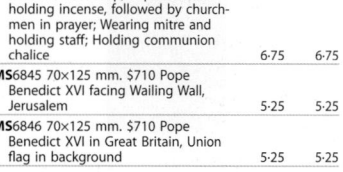

795 Mars Rover

2013. Mars Exploration. Multicoloured.
MS6847 $225×4 Mars Rover; Mars Spirit; Curiosity; Mars Reconnaissance Orbiter — 6·75 6·75
MS6848 $225×4 Mariner 4; Mariner 9; Phoenix; Odyssey — 6·75 6·75

>> Family

796 John Kennedy and Family

2013. 50th Death Anniv of Pres. John F. Kennedy. Multicoloured.
MS6849 149×120 mm. $225×4 Type **796**; Pres. Kennedy with Nikita Krushchev; With Dr. Martin Luther King and others; Inspecting space capsule, Cape Canaveral, 23 February 1963 — 6·75 6·75
MS6850 100×71 mm. $355×2 Presidential campaign poster: Left portion showing John Kennedy; Right portion showing Lyndon Johnson (both 30×40 mm) — 5·25 5·25

797 Muhammad Ali

2013. Muhammad Ali (boxer). Multicoloured.
MS6851 180×120 mm. $225×4 Type **797**; Muhammad Ali wearing white robe, hands at waist level; In close-up; Wearing white robe, right hand raised — 6·75 6·75

798 *Ex-Varyag*

2013. Aircraft Carriers. Multicoloured.
MS6852 150×151 mm. $250×4 Type **798**; *Foch* (R99); USS *Yorktown* (CV-10); *Guiseppe Garibaldi* (551) — 7·50 7·50
MS6853 101×100 mm. $700 *Admiral Flota Sovetskogo Soyuza Kuznetsov* (50×38 mm) — 5·25 5·25

EXPRESS LETTER STAMPS

1986. Various stamps surch **EXPRESS** and new values.
E1	$12 on 350c. on 120c. multicoloured (No. 1598)		7·00	7·00
E2	$15 on 40c. multicoloured (No. 1868)		9·00	9·00
E3	$20 on $6.40 multicoloured		7·00	7·00
E4	$25 on 25c. multicoloured (as No. 1771, but value changed)		13·00	13·00

No. E3 was previously a miniature sheet for Halley's Comet containing two 320c. stamps. As surch the original values on both designs have been cancelled and replaced by a single $20 face value.

1987. No. E3 additionally optd with small Maltese cross above surch.
E5	$20 on $6.40 multicoloured		7·00	7·00

1987. Centenary of Publication of Sanders' *Reichenbachia*. As T **331** additionally inscr "EXPRESS". Multicoloured.
E6	$15 Plate No. 11 (Series 2)		6·00	6·00
E7	$20 Plate No. 93 (Series 2)		3·50	4·00
E8	$25 Plate No. 63 (Series 2)		5·00	6·50
E9	$45 Plate No. 35 (Series 2)		8·00	10·00

1987. Nos. 1744/5 imperf between surch **EXPRESS FORTY DOLLARS** and star.
E10	$40 on $6.40 multicoloured		12·00	12·00

1987. No. E2 additionally optd **1987**.
E11	$15 on 40c. multicoloured		11·00	7·00

1988. Nos. 2206 and 2211 surch **SPECIAL DELIVERY** and new value.
E12	$40 on $3.20 blue		10·00	11·00
E13	$45 on $3.30 black		10·00	11·00

1989. Imperf between pairs of Nos. 1744/5 and 2185/6 surch **EXPRESS FORTY DOLLARS** (without stars).
E14	$40 on $6.40 multicoloured (Nos. 1744/5)		6·00	6·50
E15	$40 on $6.40 multicoloured (Nos. 2185/6)		6·00	6·50

1989. Nos. 2206 and 2211 surch **SPECIAL DELIVERY** and new value.
E16	$190 on $3.30 black		17·00	19·00
E17	$225 on $3.20 blue		18·00	20·00

1989. Butterflies. Two sheets, each 97×67 mm, containing vert designs as T **454** optd EXPRESS. Multicoloured.
EMS18	$130 *Phareas coeleste*		5·00	5·00
EMS19	$190 *Papilio torquatus*		6·00	6·00

1989. Women in Space. Sheet 92×67 mm, containing vert design as T **455** optd EXPRESS. Multicoloured.
EMS20	$190 Valentina Tereshkova (first woman cosmonaut)		4·25	4·50

1989. "World Stamp Expo '89" International Stamp Exhibition, Washington. Nos. EMS18/19 optd with logo.
EMS21	$130 *Phareas coeleste*		4·00	4·00
EMS22	$190 *Papilio torquatus*		4·50	4·50

Nos. EMS21/22 show additional overprints on sheet margins.

1990. 85th Anniv of Rotary International. Nos. EMS18/20 optd **ROTARY INTERNATIONAL 1905–1990** and emblem on sheet margins only.
EMS23	$130 *Phareas coeleste*		4·00	4·00
EMS24	$190 *Papilio torquatus*		6·50	6·50
EMS25	$190 Valentina Tereshkova (first woman cosmonaut)		4·25	6·00

1990. "Stamp World London '90" International Stamp Exhibition. Nos. EMS18/20 optd **Stamp World London '90** and emblem on sheet margins only.
EMS26	$130 *Phareas coeleste* (R.)		3·75	3·75
EMS27	$190 *Papilio torquatus*		5·50	5·50
EMS28	$190 Valentina Tereshkova (first woman cosmonaut)		4·00	5·50

1990. "Belgica '90" International Stamp Exhibition, Brussels. Nos. EMS18 and EMS20 additionally optd **BELGICA PHILATELIC EXPOSITION 1990** and emblem in black on sheet margins only.
EMS29	$130 *Phareas coeleste*		4·00	4·00
EMS30	$190 Valentina Tereshkova (first woman cosmonaut)		4·50	5·00

1990. 90th Birthday of Queen Elizabeth the Queen Mother. Nos. EMS18/20 optd **90TH BIRTHDAY H.M. THE QUEEN MOTHER** on sheet margins only.
EMS31	$130 *Phareas coeleste*		3·50	3·50
EMS32	$190 *Papilio torquatus*		4·00	4·00
EMS33	$190 Valentina Tereshkova (first woman cosmonaut)		4·00	4·00

1990. Fauna. Two sheets, each 110×80 mm, containing vert designs as T **466**, but larger (40×55 mm) inscr EXPRESS. Multicoloured.
EMS34	$130 Harpy Eagle		4·50	4·50
EMS35	$150 Ocelot		4·50	4·50

OFFICIAL STAMPS

1981. Nos. 556, F4a and F6/7 optd **OPS** or surch also.
O13	10c. on 25c. Marabunta		3·50	2·25
O14	50c. *Guzmania lingulata*		1·00	30
O15	60c. Soldier's cap		1·00	20
O16	$5 *Odontadenia grandiflora*		1·75	1·75

1981. Nos. 491, 708a, 716, 804, 834 and F9 optd **OPS** or surch also.
O17	15c. Harpy eagle (postage)		9·50	65
O18	30c. on $2 *Norantea guianensis* (F9)		45	30
O19	100c. on $3 Cylinder satellite		2·00	40
O20	125c. on $2 *Norantea guianensis*		1·00	60
O21	$10 *Elbella patrobas*		12·00	11·00
O22	$1.10 on $2 *Norantea guianensis* (804) (air)		1·00	2·00

1981. Nos. 548a, 719, 828 and 830 optd **OPS** or surch also.
O23	15c. Christmas orchid		9·50	1·50
O24	50c. British Guiana 1898 1c. stamp		1·25	35
O25	100c. on 8c. Camp-fire cooking		1·25	50
O26	110c. on 6c. Type **116**		2·00	1·25

1982. Various stamps optd **OPS**.
O27	-	20c. multicoloured (No. 701)	8·00	80
O28	**136**	40c. multicoloured	1·00	15
O29	-	40c. red, grey and black (No. 674)	1·00	15
O30	-	$2 multicoloured (No. 676)	7·00	75

1982. Nos. 911 and 980 optd or surch **OPS.**

O31	250c. on 400c. on 30c. multicoloured (postage)	80	60
O32	200c. on 1c. multicoloured (air)	1·00	60

1982. No. F9 optd **OPS.**

| O33 | $2 *Norantea guianensis* | 8·00 | 2·00 |

1982. Air. No. 979 optd **OPS.**

| O34 | 110c. on 5c. Annatto tree | 1·25 | 40 |

1984. No. 912 surch **OPS.**

O35	150c. on $5 multicoloured	6·00	2·75
O36	200c. on $5 multicoloured	6·50	3·00
O37	225c. on $5 multicoloured	6·50	3·25
O38	230c. on $5 multicoloured	6·50	3·25
O39	260c. on $5 multicoloured	6·50	3·50
O40	320c. on $5 multicoloured	8·00	4·00
O41	350c. on $5 multicoloured	8·50	4·50
O42	600c. on $5 multicoloured	10·00	6·50

1984. Nos. O32 and O34 surch and No. 981 optd **OPS.**

O43	25c. on 110c. on 5c. Annatto tree	1·50	40
O44	30c. on 110c. on 5c. Annatto tree	1·50	45
O45	45c. on 220c. on 1c. Pitcher plant of Mt. Roraima	1·60	55
O46	55c. on 110c. on 5c. Annatto tree	1·75	60
O47	60c. on 220c. on 1c. Pitcher plant of Mt. Roraima	1·75	60
O48	75c. on 220c. on 1c. Pitcher plant of Mt. Roraima	2·00	70
O49	90c. on 220c. on 1c. Pitcher plant of Mt. Roraima	2·00	80
O50	120c. on 220c. on 1c. Pitcher plant of Mt. Roraima	2·25	1·25
O51	130c. on 220c. on 1c. Pitcher plant of Mt. Roraima	2·25	1·25
O52	330c. on $2 *Norantea guianensis*	4·00	4·00

1987. Centenary of Publication of Sanders' *Reichenbachia*. As T **331** additionally inscr "OFFICIAL". Multicoloured.

O53	120c. Plate No. 48 (Series 2)	2·00	45
O54	130c. Plate No. 92 (Series 2)	2·00	45
O55	140c. Plate No. 36 (Series 2)	75	35
O56	150c. Plate No. 43 (Series 2)	2·00	50
O57	175c. Plate No. 31 (Series 2)	80	40
O58	200c. Plate No. 61 (Series 2)	2·00	60
O59	225c. Plate No. 26 (Series 2)	2·00	60
O60	230c. Plate No. 68 (Series 2) (horiz)	50	50
O61	250c. Plate No. 59 (Series 2)	50	60
O62	260c. Plate No. 69 (Series 2)	50	60
O63	275c. Plate No. 90 (Series 2)	2·00	75
O64	320c. Plate No. 75 (Series 2)	2·00	80
O65	330c. Plate No. 23 (Series 2)	3·50	1·00
O66	350c. Plate No. 95 (Series 2) (horiz)	50	80
O67	600c. Plate No. 70 (Series 2) (horiz)	75	1·60
O68	$12 Plate No. 71 (Series 2) (horiz)	1·40	2·50
O69	$15 Plate No. 84 (Series 2)	1·50	2·75

OFFICIAL PARCEL POST STAMPS

1981. Nos. P1/2 optd **OPS.**

| OP1 | $15 on $1 *Chelonanthus uliginoides* | 10·00 | 2·25 |
| OP2 | $20 on $1 *Chelonanthus uliginoides* | 10·00 | 2·75 |

1983. No. 843 surch **OPS Parcel Post $12.00** and additionally optd **1982**.

| OP3 | $12 on $1.10 on $2 *Norantea guianensis* | 80·00 | 17·00 |

1983. No. OP3 with additional **OPS** opt.

| OP4 | $12 on $1.10 on $2 *Norantea guianensis* | 22·00 | 4·50 |

1983. No. P4 optd **OPS.**

| OP5 | $12 on $1.10 on $2 *Norantea guianensis* | 7·50 | 4·00 |

1981. No. 554 surch **PARCEL POST** and new value.

| P1 | $15 on $1 *Chelonanthus uliginoides* | 10·00 | 3·00 |
| P2 | $20 on $1 *Chelonanthus uliginoides* | 10·00 | 6·00 |

1983. No. 843 surch **PARCEL POST $12.00.**

| P3 | $12 on $1.10 on $2 *Norantea guianensis* | 2·25 | 2·50 |

1983. Unissued Royal Wedding surch, similar to No. 843, further surch **Parcel Post $12.00.**

| P4 | $12 on $1.10 on $2 *Norantea guianensis* | 1·00 | 1·00 |

1985. No. 673 surch **TWENTY FIVE DOLLARS PARCEL POST 25.00.**

| P5 | $25 on 35c. green, grey and black | 28·00 | 19·00 |

POSTAGE DUE STAMPS

D2

1987

D8	D2	1c. green	25	3·75
D9	D2	2c. black	25	3·75
D10	D2	4c. blue	25	3·75
D11	D2	12c. red	35	3·75

POSTAL FISCAL STAMPS

1975. Nos. 543/5 and 550ab/6 optd **REVENUE ONLY.**

F1	2c. Type **132**	50	40
F2	3c. Hanging heliconia	50	50
F3	5c. Annatto tree	75	30
F4	25c. Marabunta	3·25	30
F5	40c. Tiger beard	5·50	30
F6	50c. *Guzmania lingulata*	70	40
F7	60c. Soldier's cap	75	50
F8	$1 *Chelonanthus uliginoides*	75	1·25
F9	$2 *Norantea guianensis*	1·00	2·75
F10	$5 *Odontadenis grandiflora*	1·75	9·00

Although intended for fiscal use Nos. F1/F10 were allowed by the postal authorities as an "act of grace" to do duty as postage stamps until 30 June 1976.

Pt. 1

GWALIOR

A "convention" state of Central India.

12 pies = 1 anna; 16 annas = 1 rupee.

1885. Queen Victoria stamps of India optd **GWALIOR** at foot and native opt at top.

1	23	½a. turquoise	£190	40·00
6	-	1a. purple	£120	40·00
6	-	1a.6p. brown	£130	
3	-	2a. blue	£100	22·00
8	-	4a. green (No. 69)	£150	
9	-	6a. brown (No. 80)	£150	
10	-	8a. mauve	£110	
11	-	1r. grey (No. 101)	£110	

Queen Victoria stamps of India optd **GWALIOR** at foot and native opt at top.

1885. Queen Victoria

17	-	9p. red	40·00	75·00
16c	23	½a. turquoise	1·00	10
18	-	1a. purple	3·00	20
20c	-	1a.6p. brown	2·25	2·25
21c	-	2a. blue	5·00	10
23	-	2a.6p. green	15·00	26·00
25c	-	3a. orange	7·50	15
14	-	4a. green (No. 69)	50·00	26·00
27c	-	4a. green (No. 69)	9·50	1·75
29	-	6a. brown (No. 80)	7·00	14·00
30c	-	8a. mauve	10·00	2·25
33c	-	1r. grey (No. 101)	7·00	6·00
34	37	1r. green and red	13·00	9·00
35	38	2r. red and orange	6·00	3·00
36	38	3r. brown and green	8·50	3·50
37	38	5r. blue and violet	15·00	6·50

1899. Queen Victoria.

38	40	3p. red	50	20
39	40	3p. grey	8·00	60·00
40	23	½a. green	2·50	2·25
41	-	1a. red	1·25	35
42	-	2a. lilac	5·00	7·50
43	-	2½a. blue	4·00	9·50

1903. King Edward VII

46A	41	3p. grey	1·50	20
48A	-	½a. green (No. 122)	20	10
49A	-	1a. red (No. 123)	20	10
50A	-	2a. lilac	3·25	1·25
52B	-	2a.6p. blue	2·50	12·00
53A	-	3a. orange	3·25	35
54A	-	4a. olive	5·50	40
56B	-	6a. bistre	12·00	1·75
57A	-	8a. mauve	9·00	2·25
59B	-	12a. purple on red	6·50	3·25
60A	-	1r. green and red	7·00	1·75
61B	52	2r. red and orange	9·00	11·00
62B	52	3r. brown and green	35·00	70·00
63B	52	5r. blue and violet	21·00	28·00

1907. King Edward VII inscr "INDIA POSTAGE AND REVENUE".

65	-	½a. green (No. 149)	2·50	20
66	-	1a. red (No. 150)	1·50	20

1912. King George V

67	55	3p. grey	10	10
68	58	½a. green	60	10
102	79	½a. green	60	20

88	80	9p. green	4·75	30
69	57	1a. red	30	10
80	57	1a. brown	1·10	10
103	81	1a. brown	20	10
90	82	1a.3p. mauve	75	15
81	58	1½a. brown (No. 165)	4·00	75
82	58	1½a. red	20	20
70	59	2a. purple	2·00	30
91	70	2a. lilac	75	30
104	59	2a. red	4·75	3·50
83	61	2½a. blue	4·25	1·75
84	61	2½a. orange	35	50
71	62	3a. orange	1·00	15
92	62	3a. blue	1·50	40
72	63	4a. olive	75	60
93	71	4a. green	2·00	1·00
73a	64	6a. bistre	2·50	1·50
74	65	8a. mauve	4·50	1·50
75	66	12a. red	2·25	4·00
76	67	1r. brown and green	17·00	1·50
77	67	2r. red and brown	10·00	4·00
78	67	5r. blue and violet	30·00	6·50

1922. No. 192 (King George V) optd **GWALIOR** only.

79	57	9p. on 1a. on 1a. red	10	50

1928. King George V. Optd in larger type (19 mm long).

96	67	1r. brown and green	6·00	6·50
97w	67	2r. red and orange	8·00	4·50
98	67	5r. blue and violet	29·00	32·00
99	67	10r. green and red	95·00	55·00
100	67	15r. blue and olive	£160	90·00
101	67	25r. orange and blue	£375	£225

1938. King George VI

105	91	3p. slate	15·00	10
106	91	½a. brown	15·00	10
107	91	9p. green	70·00	4·75
108	91	1a. red	14·00	15
109	91	3a. green (No. 253)	50·00	6·00
110	91	4a. brown (No. 255)	70·00	4·50
111	91	6a. green (No. 256)	10·00	16·00
112	93	1r. slate and brown	13·00	1·75
113	93	2r. purple and brown	25·00	12·00
114	93	5r. green and blue	32·00	45·00
115	93	10r. purple and red	32·00	48·00
116	93	15r. brown and green	90·00	£225
117	93	25r. slate and purple	80·00	£180

1942. King George VI.

118	100a	3p. slate	45	10
119	100a	½a. mauve	1·00	10
120	100a	9p. green	1·25	10
121	100a	1a. red	1·00	10
122	101	1½a. violet	10·00	1·25
123	101	2a. red	1·50	20
124	101	3a. violet	8·50	2·75
125	102	4a. brown	5·00	20
126	102	6a. green	14·00	27·00
127	102	8a. violet	2·00	2·00
128	102	12a. purple	8·00	24·00

OFFICIAL STAMPS

Stamps of India overprinted with native inscription at top and bottom, unless otherwise stated.

1895. Queen Victoria.

O1	23	½a. turquoise	1·50	10
O3	-	1a. purple	5·00	10
O5	-	2a. blue	4·50	50
O7	-	4a. green (No. 96)	5·50	2·25
O9	-	8a. mauve	8·00	2·75
O10	37	1r. green and red	13·00	3·50

1901. Queen Victoria.

O23	40	3p. red	2·50	25
O24	40	3p. grey	2·50	3·75
O26	23	½a. green	1·50	10
O27	-	1a. red	9·00	10
O28	-	2a. lilac	3·00	2·25

1903. King Edward VII

O29	41	3p. grey	70	10
O41	-	½a. green (No. 122)	7·00	15
O32	-	1a. red (No. 123)	1·10	10
O33a	-	2a. lilac	4·00	30
O44	-	4a. olive	3·75	1·00
O36	-	8a. mauve	16·00	70
O38	-	1r. green and red	5·00	2·50

1907. King Edward VII inscr "POSTAGE & REVENUE".

O48	-	1a. red (No. 150)	12·00	15
O49	-	½a. green (No. 149)	1·75	15

1913. King George V.

O53a	57	1a. red	50	10
O51	55	3p. grey	1·00	20
O62	56	½a. green	10	10
O73	79	½a. green	15	15
O63	80	9p. green	20	15
O64	57	1a. brown	10	10

O74	81	1a. brown	15	15
O65	82	1a.3p. mauve	50	15
O55	59	2a. purple	2·75	1·25
O66	70	2a. lilac	20	15
O75	59	2a. red	20	40
O67	71	4a. green	1·75	30
O77	63	4a. olive	60	75
O68	65	8a. mauve	75	1·40
O58	67	1r. brown and green	45·00	38·00

1922. No. O97 (King George V Official) optd **GWALIOR** only.

O59	57	9p. on 1a. on 1a. red	10	30

1927. King George V. Optd in large type (21 mm long).

O69	67	1r. brown and green	1·25	2·00
O70	67	2r. red and orange	30·00	30·00
O71	67	5r. blue and violet	40·00	£275
O72	67	10r. green and red	£225	£650

1938. King George VI.

O78	91	½a. brown	7·50	30
O79	91	1a. red	3·75	20
O91	93	1r. slate and brown	15·00	27·00
O92	93	2r. purple and brown	18·00	£140
O93	93	5r. green and blue	30·00	£750
O94	93	10r. purple and red	80·00	£1600

1940. King George VI. Optd at bottom only.

O80	O20	3p. slate	50	10
O81	O20	½a. brown	13·00	25
O82	O20	½a. purple	1·50	10
O83	O20	9p. green	1·00	70
O84	O20	1a. red	2·25	10
O85	O20	1a.3p. brown	70·00	1·75
O86	O20	1a.6p. violet	1·00	30
O87	O20	2a. orange	1·00	30
O88	O20	4a. brown	1·25	3·50
O89	O20	8a. violet	7·00	11·00

1942. No. O65 surch **1A 1A** and bar.

O90	82	1a. on 1a.3p. mauve	26·00	3·25

Pt. 15

HAITI

The W. portion of the island of Hispaniola in the West Indies. A republic, independent from 1804.

100 centimes = 1 gourde or piastre.

1 Liberty

1881. Imperf.

1	1	1c. red	8·25	5·00
2	1	2c. purple	10·00	5·00
3	1	3c. bistre	18·00	7·50
4	1	5c. green	31·00	15·00
5	1	7c. blue	20·00	3·75
6	1	20c. brown	75·00	28·00

1882. Perf.

7	1	1c. red	5·25	1·90
9	1	2c. purple	8·50	2·50
12	1	3c. bistre	10·50	3·00
15	1	5c. green	7·00	1·30
17	1	7c. blue	9·50	1·90
20	1	20c. brown	11·00	2·40

2 Pres. Salomon

1887

24	2	1c. lake	35	30
25	2	2c. mauve	90	65
26	2	3c. blue	65	40
27	2	5c. green	4·25	50

1890. Surch **DEUX 2 CENT.**

28	2	2c. on 3c. blue	60	50

4 Tree with Leaves upright

1891. Tree with leaves upright.

29	4	1c. mauve	45	30
30	4	2c. blue	65	30
31	4	3c. lilac	90	40
31a	4	3c. grey	80	50
32	4	5c. orange	3·00	45
33	4	7c. red	6·75	2·50

1892. Surch DEUX 2 CENT.

34		2c. on 3c. lilac	1·20	85
34a		2c. on 3c. grey	1·40	95

5 Tree with Leaves drooping

1893. Tree with leaves drooping.

35a	5	1c. purple	35	15
41	5	1c. blue	50	65
36	5	2c. blue	45	20
42	5	2c. red	60	1·10
37	5	3c. lilac	65	40
43	5	3c. brown	50	1·10
38	5	5c. orange	2·50	45
44	5	5c. green	60	1·10
39	5	7c. red	45	20
45	5	7c. grey	80	1·60
40	5	20c. brown	1·60	1·00
46	5	20c. orange	1·00	2·10

1898. Surch DEUX 2 CENT.

47		2c. on 20c. brown	1·20	80
48		2c. on 20c. orange	80	60

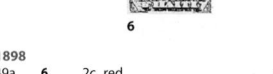

6

1898

49a	6	2c. red	45	20
50a	6	5c. green	45	20

8 Pres. Simon Sam　　**9**

1898

51	8	1c. blue	15	10
67	9	1c. green	15	10
52	8	2c. orange	15	15
68	9	2c. red	15	15
53	8	3c. green	15	15
54	9	4c. red	15	15
55	8	5c. brown	15	15
69	9	5c. blue	15	15
56	8	7c. grey	15	15
57	9	8c. red	15	15
58	9	10c. orange	15	15
59	9	15c. olive	55	40
60	8	20c. black	55	40
61	8	50c. lake	65	45
62	8	1g. mauve	2·00	1·50

1902. Optd MAI Gt Pre 1902 in frame.

70	8	1c. blue	55	40
71	9	1c. green	40	40
72	8	2c. orange	70	65
73	9	2c. red	40	25
74	8	3c. green	40	40
75	9	4c. red	55	50
76	8	5c. brown	1·10	1·00
77	8	5c. blue	40	40
78	8	7c. grey	85	80
79	9	8c. red	85	80
80	9	10c. orange	85	80
81	8	15c. olive	4·00	2·50
82	8	20c. black	4·00	4·00
83	8	50c. lake	9·75	5·50
84	8	1g. mauve	15·00	13·00

12 Arms　　**13** J.-J. Dessalines

1904. Cent of Independence. Optd 1804 POSTE PAYE 1904 in frame. T 12 and portraits as T 13.

89	12	1c. green	45	40
90		2c. black and red	45	40
91		5c. black and blue	45	40
92	13	7c. black and red	45	40
93		10c. black and yellow	45	40

94		20c. black and grey	45	40
95		50c. black and olive	45	40

DESIGNS—2, 5c. Toussaint l'Ouverture; 20, 50c. Petion.

1904. Nos. 89/95 but without opt.

No.	Description		
96	1c. green	30	30
97	2c. black and red	30	30
98	5c. black and blue	30	30
99	7c. black and red	30	30
100	10c. black and yellow	30	30
101	20c. black and grey	30	30
102	50c. black and olive	30	30

15 Pres. Nord Alexis

1904. External Mail. Optd 1804 POSTE PAYE 1904 in frame.

103	15	1c. green	55	50
104	15	2c. red	55	50
105	15	5c. blue	55	50
106	15	10c. brown	55	50
107	15	20c. orange	55	50
108	15	50c. plum	55	50

1904. Nos. 103/108, but without opt.

No.	Description		
109	1c. green	30	30
110	2c. red	30	30
111	5c. blue	30	30
112	10c. brown	30	30
113	20c. orange	30	30
114	50c. plum	30	30

1906. Optd SERVICE EXTERIEUR PROVISOIRE EN PIASTRES FORTES in oval.

117	8	1c. blue	1·10	75
118	9	1c. green	60	60
119	8	2c. orange	2·00	1·90
120	9	2c. red	1·10	1·00
121	8	3c. green	1·10	1·00
122	9	4c. red	4·75	3·75
123	8	5c. brown	6·00	4·50
124	8	5c. blue	85	50
125	8	7c. grey	4·00	3·75
126	9	8c. red	85	80
127	9	10c. orange	1·60	95
128	9	15c. olive	2·00	1·00
129	8	20c. black	4·75	3·75
130	8	50c. lake	4·75	3·00
131	8	1g. mauve	9·50	6·00

19 Pres. Nord Alexis　　**20** Arms

1906

No.	T	Description		
132	19	1c. de g. blue	30	20
133	20	2c. de g. orange	40	20
134	20	2c. de g. yellow	60	25
135	19	3c. de g. grey	35	20
136	20	7c. de g. green	1·10	40

21 Iron Market, Port-au-Prince

1906. Currency changed from "gourdes" to "piastres".

No.	T	Description		
137		1c. de p. green	30	25
138	19	2c. de p. red	40	25
139	21	3c. de p. sepia	55	25
140	21	3c. de p. orange	6·25	3·00
141		4c. de p. red	55	30
167		4c. de p. olive	11·50	8·25
142	19	5c. de p. blue	2·00	25
143		7c. de p. grey	1·60	75
168		7c. de p. red	38·00	28·00
144		8c. de p. red	1·60	70
169		8c. de p. olive	23·00	17·00
145		10c. de p. orange	1·10	25
170		10c. de p. brown	23·00	17·00
146		15c. de p. olive	2·00	80
171		15c. de p. yellow	11·50	5·50
147	19	20c. de p. blue	2·00	80
148	20	50c. de p. red	3·00	2·10
172	20	50c. de p. yellow	11·50	8·25
149		1pi. red	6·50	4·00
173		1pi. red	11·50	10·00

DESIGNS—As Type **21**: 4c. Palace of Sans Souci-Milot; 7c. Independence Palace, Gonaives; 8c. Entrance to Catholic College, Port-au-Prince; 10c. Catholic Monastery and Church, Port-au-Prince; 15c. Government Offices, Port-au-Prince; 1pi. President's Palace, Port-au-Prince.

1906. Surch with value in double-lined frame. Without opt.

154	15	1c. on 5c. blue	35	30
155	15	1c. on 10c. brown	45	20
156	15	1c. on 20c. orange	35	20
157	15	2c. on 10c. brown	35	20
158	15	2c. on 20c. orange	35	35
159	15	2c. on 50c. plum	45	35

24 Pres. A. T. Simon

1910

160	24	1c. de g. black and red	25	20
161	24	2c. de g. black and red	60	45
162	24	5c. de p. black and blue	11·50	65
163	24	20c. de p. black and green	9·50	6·50

25 Pres. C. Leconte

1912. Various frames.

164	25	1c. de g. lake	35	35
165	25	2c. de g. orange	45	35
166	25	5c. de g. blue	80	35

1914. Optd GL O.Z. 7 FEV. 1914 in frame. A. On 1898 issue.

174	9	8c. red	11·50	8·75

B. On 1904 issue, without opt.

175	15	1c. green (No. 109)	29·00	24·00
176	15	2c. red	29·00	24·00
177	15	5c. blue	60	35
178	15	10c. brown	60	35
179	15	20c. orange	95	45
180	15	50c. plum	2·30	1·10

C. On pictorial stamps of 1906.

181	20	1c. de g. yellow	45	35
182	19	3c. de g. grey	45	35

D. On pictorial stamps of 1906.

183	20	1c. de p. green (No. 137)	45	35
184	19	2c. de p. red (No. 138)	60	35
185	21	3c. de p. sepia (No. 139)	95	55
186	21	3c. de p. orange (No. 140)	45	35
187		4c. de p. red (No. 141)	95	45
198		4c. de p. olive (No. 167)	2·50	1·30
188		7c. de p. grey (No. 143)	2·30	2·20
200		7c. de p. red (No. 168)	5·75	5·50
189		8c. de p. red (No. 144)	4·00	3·75
201		8c. de p. olive (No. 169)	7·50	7·25
190		10c. de p. orange (No. 145)	1·20	55
202		10c. de p. brown (No. 170)	3·00	1·90
191		15c. de p. olive (No. 146)	3·25	3·00
203		15c. de p. yellow (No. 171)	2·50	1·30
192	19	20c. de p. blue (No. 147)	3·00	1·10
194	20	50c. de p. red (No. 148)	5·25	5·00
204	20	50c. de p. yellow (No. 172)	8·75	8·25
195		1pi. red (No. 149)	5·25	5·00
205		1pi. red (No. 173)	9·50	8·75

E. On stamp of 1910.

193	24	20c. de p. black and green	3·50	3·25

F. On stamps of 1912.

No.	T	Description		
196	25	1c. de g. lake	45	35
197	25	2c. de g. orange	60	45
199	25	5c. de p. blue	95	35

1914. Stamps of 1904, without the opt, surch GL O.Z 7 FEV 1914 7 CENT in diamond frame.

213	15	7c. on 20c. orange (No. 113)	45	20
214	15	7c. on 50c. plum (No. 114)	40	20

1914. Pictorial stamps of 1906 (Nos. 148/73), surch GL OZ 1 CENT DE PIASTRE 7 FEV. 1914 in frame.

215	20	1c. on 50c. red	45	35
216	20	1c. on 50c. yellow	60	45
217		1c. de p. on 1p. red	60	45
218		1c. de p. on 1p. red	60	45

38

1915

219		2c. de g. black and yellow	80	
220	38	5c. de g. black and green	1·30	
221		7c. de g. black and red	80	

PORTRAIT: 2, 7c. O. Zamor.

1915. As T 24, inscr "EMISSION 1914".

222		1c. de p. black and green	2·50	
223		3c. de p. black and olive	25	
224		5c. de p. black and blue	45	
225		7c. de p. black and orange	1·20	
226		10c. de p. black and brown	35	
227		15c. de p. black and olive	45	
228		20c. de p. black and brown	45	

DESIGNS: 1c., 5c., 10c., 15c. O. Zamor; 3c., 20c. Arms; 7c. T. Auguste.

1915. Surch with figure in frame.

229	1	on 5c. blue (No. 111)	1·40	1·30
230	1	on 7c. grey (No. 143)	45	45
231	1	on 10c. brown (No. 112)	60	55
232	1	on 20c. orange (No. 107)	45	45
233	1	on 20c. orange (No. 113)	80	75
234	1	on 50c. plum (No. 108)	2·10	55
235	1	on 50c. plum (No. 114)	45	45
236	2	on 1pi. red (No. 172)	45	45

1917. Surch GOURDE and value in frame. A. On provisional stamps of 1906.

No.	T	Description		
237	8	1c. on 50c. lake (No. 130)	23·00	17·00
238	8	1c. on 1g. mauve (No. 131)	26·00	20·00

B. On pictorial stamps of 1906.

No.	T	Description		
239		1c. on 4c. de p. red (No. 141)	60	55
240		1c. on 4c. de p. olive (No. 167)	60	55
241		1c. on 7c. de p. red (No. 168)	45	45
242		1c. on 10c. de p. orange (No. 145)	60	55
243		1c. on 15c. de p. yellow (No. 171)	45	45
244	19	1c. on 20c. de p. blue (No. 147)	60	55
246	24	1c. on 20c. de p. black and green (No. 163)	60	55
247	20	1c. on 50c. de p. red (No. 148)	60	55
249		1c. on 50c. de p. yellow (No. 172)	1·50	1·30
250		1c. on 1p. red (No. 173)	1·20	1·20
251	21	2c. on 3c. de p. sepia (No. 139)	60	55
252	21	2c. on 3c. de p. orange (No. 140)	60	55
253		2c. on 8c. de p. red (No. 144)	60	55
255		2c. on 8c. de p. olive (No. 169)	45	45
256		2c. de p. on 10c. brown (No. 170)	45	20
257		2c. on 15c. de p. olive (No. 146)	60	55
258		2c. on 15c. de p. yellow (No. 171)	60	55
259	19	2c. on 20c. de p. blue (No. 147)	60	55
260		5c. on 10c. de p. brown (No. 170)	80	75
261		5c. on 15c. de p. yellow (No. 171)	4·00	3·75

1919. For inland use. Provisionals of 1914. (a) Surch with new value without frame.

262		1c. on 15c. de p. olive (No. 191)	45	45
263	19	1c. on 20c. de p. blue (No. 192)	45	45
264	24	1c. on 20c. de p. black and green (No. 193)	45	45
265		1c. on 1p. red (No. 205)	45	45
267		1c. on 1p. red (No. 205)	45	45

(b) Surch with new value in frame.

268		2c. on 4c. de p. red (No. 187)	45	45
269		2c. on 8c. de p. red (No. 189)	60	55
270		2c. on 8c. de p. olive (No. 201)	45	45
271	24	2c. on 20c. de p. black and green	60	55
272	20	2c. on 50c. de p. red (No. 194)	35	20
274	20	2c. on 50c. de p. yellow (No. 204)	45	35
275		2c. on 1p. red (No. 195)	2·30	2·00
276		2c. on 1p. red (No. 205)	1·80	1·70

277	21	3c. on 3c. de p. sepia (No. 185)	45	45
278	-	3c. on 7c. de p. red (No. 200)	45	35
279	21	5c. on 3c. de p. sepia (No. 185)	45	35
280	21	5c. on 3c. de p. orange (No. 186)	1·70	1·50
281	-	5c. on 4c. de p. red (No. 187)	60	55
282	-	5c. on 4c. de p. olive (No. 198)	35	35
283	-	5c. on 7c. de p. grey (No. 188)	35	35
284	-	5c. on 7c. de p. red (No. 200)	45	45
285	15	5c. on 7c. on 20c. orange (No. 213)	45	45
286	15	5c. on 7c. on 50c. plum (No. 214)	3·25	3·00
287	19	5c. on 10c. de p. orange (No. 190)	45	45
288	-	5c. on 15c. de p. yellow (No. 203)	45	45
289	-	5c. on 10c. de p. orange (No. 190)	45	45

No. 289 has the word "PIASTRE" in the surcharge.

1919. Postage Due stamps surch **POSTES** and new value in frame.

290	D23	5c. de g. on 10c. de p. purple (No. D211)	35	35
291	D23	5c. de g. on 50c. de p. olive (No. D153)	10·00	7·75
292	D23	5c. de g. on 50c. de p. olive (No. D212)	45	45

48 "Agriculture"

1920

294	48	3c. de g. orange	35	35
295	48	5c. de g. green	35	35
296	-	10c. de g. red	45	35
297	-	15c. de g. violet	45	35
298	-	25c. de g. blue	60	45

DESIGN: 10c., 15c., 25c. "Commerce".

| **50** Pres. L. J. Borno | **51** Christophe's Citadel |

54 Coffee

1924

299	50	5c. green	35	20
300	51	10c. red	35	20
301	-	20c. blue	80	35
304	54	35c. green	3·50	55
302	50	50c. black and orange	80	35
303	-	1g. olive	1·50	45

DESIGNS—VERT: 20c. Map of W. Indies. HORIZ: 1g. National Palace.

55 Pres. Borno

1929. Frontier Agreement between Haiti and Dominican Republic.

| 305 | 55 | 10c. red | 45 | 35 |

56 Fokker Super Trimotor over Port-au-Prince

1929. Air.

306	56	25c. green	45	35
307	56	50c. violet	60	35
308	56	75c. red	1·50	1·10
309	56	1g. blue	1·60	1·40

57 Salomon and S. Vincent

1931. 50th Anniv of U.P.U. Membership.

| 310 | 57 | 5c. green | 1·20 | 45 |
| 311 | - | 10c. red (S. Vincent) | 1·20 | 45 |

1933. Air. "Columbia" New York–Haiti Flight. Surch **COLUMBIA VOL-DIRECT N.-Y.–P.AU-P. BOYD-LYON 60 CTS.**

| 311a | | 60c. on 20c. blue (No. 301) | 60·00 | 65·00 |

| **59** Pres. S. Vincent | **60** Prince's Aqueduct |

1933. T 59 and designs as T **60.**

312	59	3c. orange	25	10
313	59	3c. green	25	10
316	60	5c. green	25	10
317	60	5c. olive	45	20
318	-	10c. red	45	20
320	-	10c. brown	45	15
321	-	25c. blue	80	20
322	-	50c. brown	2·30	50
323	-	1g. green	2·30	50
324	-	2g.50 olive	4·00	80

DESIGNS: 10c. Fort National; 25c. Palace of Sans Souci; 50c. Christophe's Chapel, Milot; 1g. King's Gallery, Citadel; 2g.50, Vallieres Battery.

62 Fokker Super Trimotor over Christophe's Citadel

1933. Air.

325	62	50c. orange	4·75	75
326	62	50c. olive	4·75	75
327	62	50c. red	3·00	1·70
328	62	50c. black	1·80	75
329	62	60c. brown	95	45
330	62	1g. blue	1·50	45

63 Alexandre Dumas and his Father and Son

1935. Visit of French Delegation to West Indies.

331	63	10c. brown and red (postage)	80	35
332	63	25c. brown and blue	1·50	45
333	63	60c. brown and violet (air)	4·00	2·20

64 Arms of Haiti, and George Washington

1938. Air. 150th Anniv of U.S. Constitution.

| 334 | 64 | 60c. blue | 60 | 35 |

1939. Surch **25c** between bars.

| 335 | 54 | 25c. on 35c. green | 80 | 35 |

66 Pierre de Coubertin

1939. Port-au-Prince Athletic Stadium Fund.

336	66	10c.+10c. red (postage)	25·00	25·00
337	66	60c.+40c. violet (air)	22·00	22·00
338	66	1g.25+60c. black	22·00	22·00

67

1941. Third Caribbean Conference.

339	67	10c. red (postage)	95	45
340	67	25c. blue	80	35
341	67	60c. olive (air)	3·00	75
342	67	1g.25 violet	3·00	55

68 Our Lady of Perpetual Succour

1942. Our Lady of Perpetual Succour (National Patroness).

343	68	3c. purple (postage)	35	20
344	68	5c. green	45	20
345	68	10c. red	45	20
346	68	15c. orange	60	45
347	68	20c. brown	60	45
348	68	25c. blue	1·20	45
349	68	50c. red	1·60	65
350	68	2g.50 brown	5·25	1·30
351	68	5g. violet	10·50	4·00

The 5g. is larger (32½×47 mm).

352		10c. olive (air)	35	20
353		25c. blue	45	35
354		50c. green	80	35
355		60c. red	1·20	45
356		1g.25 black	2·30	45

MS357 Three sheets each 140×128 mm. (a) Nos. 352, 354; (b) 353, 355; (c) No. 356 ... 14·00 13·00

69 Admiral Killick and Flagship *Crete-a-Pierrot*

1943. 41st Death Anniv of Admiral Killick.

358	69	3c. orange (postage)	35	20
359	69	5c. green	45	35
360	69	10c. red	45	35
361	69	25c. blue	60	35
362	69	50c. olive	1·20	45
363	69	5g. brown	5·25	2·75
364	69	60c. violet (air)	60	35
365	69	1g.25 black	1·80	1·40

1944. Surch (a) **Postage**.

366	59	0.02 on 3c. green	25	20
367	59	0.05 on 3c. green	35	35
368	68	0.10 on 15c. orange	35	20
369	69	0.10 on 25c. blue	35	20
370	-	0.10 on 1g. olive (No. 303)	45	35
371	-	0.20 on 2g.50 olive (No. 324)	45	35

(b) Air.

| 372 | 62 | 0.10 on 60c. brown | 45 | 35 |

71

1944. Obligatory Tax. United Nations Relief Fund.

373	71	5c. blue	1·20	55
374	71	5c. black	1·20	55
375	71	5c. olive	1·20	55
376	71	5c. violet	1·20	55
377	71	5c. brown	1·20	55
378	71	5c. green	1·20	55
379	71	5c. red	1·20	55

72 Nurse and Wounded Soldier

1945. Red Cross stamps. Cross in red.

381	72	3c. black (postage)	10	10
382	72	5c. green	20	10
383	72	10c. orange	25	15
384	72	20c. brown	25	15
385	72	25c. blue	35	20
386	72	35c. orange	45	20
387	72	50c. red	45	20
388	72	1g. olive	80	35
389	72	2½g. violet	2·30	45
390	72	20c. orange (air)	35	20
391	72	25c. blue	35	20
392	72	50c. brown	35	20
393	72	60c. purple	45	20
394	72	1g. yellow	1·20	35
395	72	1g.25c. red	1·00	35
396	72	1g.35c. green	1·00	55
397	72	5g. black	6·50	2·20

73 Franklin D. Roosevelt

1946. Air.

| 398 | 73 | 20c. black | 35 | 20 |
| 399 | 73 | 60c. black | 45 | 20 |

74 Capois-la-Mort

1946

400	74	3c. orange (postage)	20	10
401	74	5c. green	20	10
402	74	10c. red	20	10
403	74	20c. black	20	10
404	74	25c. blue	25	15
405	74	35c. orange	35	20
406	74	50c. brown	45	35
407	74	1g. olive	45	35
408	74	2g.50 grey	1·20	45
409	74	20c. red (air)	20	15
410	74	25c. green	20	15
411	74	50c. orange	25	15
412	74	60c. purple	35	15
413	74	1g. slate	45	15
414	74	1g.25 violet	65	35
415	74	1g.35 black	65	45
416	74	5g. red	2·00	1·10

75 J.-J. Dessalines

1947. 141st Death Anniv of Emperor Jean-Jacques Dessalines, founder of National Independence.

417	75	3c. orange (postage)	10	10
418	75	5c. green	10	10
419	75	5c. violet	60	15
420	75	10c. red	20	10
421	75	25c. blue	35	15
422	75	20c. brown (air)	35	15

1947. Surch.

423	74	10c. on 35c. orge (postage)	35	20
424	74	5c. on 1g.35 black (air)	50	35
425	74	30c. on 50c. orange	45	35
426	74	30c. on 1g.35 black	45	35

77 Sanatorium and Mosquito

1949. Air. Anti-T.B. and Malaria Fund. Cross in red.

427	77	20c.+20c. sepia	9·50	5·50
428	77	30c.+30c. green	9·50	5·50
429	77	45c.+45c. brown	9·50	5·50
430	77	80c.+80c. violet	9·50	5·50
431	77	1g.25+1g.25 red	9·50	5·50
432	77	1g.75+1g.75 blue	9·50	5·50

MS433 Two sheets each 120×80 mm.
(a) No. 431; (b) No. 432 — 60·00 40·00

78 Washington, Dessalines and Bolivar

1949. Obligatory Tax. Bicent of Port-au-Prince.

434	78	5c. red	45	35
435	78	5c. brown	45	35
436	78	5c. orange	45	35
437	78	5c. grey	45	35
438	78	5c. violet	45	35
439	78	5c. blue	45	35
440	78	5c. green	45	35
441	78	5c. black	45	35

79 Arms of Port-au-Prince

80 Columbus and *Santa Maria*

1950. Bicentenary of Port-au-Prince Exhibition. (a) Postage. Multicoloured arms.

442	79	10c. red	35	20

(b) Air.

443	80	30c. blue and grey	80	45
444	-	1g. black (Pres. D. Estime)	80	45

1950. 75th Anniv of U.P.U. Optd U P U 1874 1949 or surch also.

445	78	3 on 5c. grey (postage)	20	15
446	78	5c. green	35	20
447	78	10 on 5c. red	35	20
448	78	20 on 5c. blue	45	45
449	74	30 on 25c. green (air)	35	20
450	74	1g. slate	50	45
451	74	1.50 on 1g.35 black	1·50	1·30

83 Cocoa

1951. National Products.

456	83	5c. green (postage)	35	20
457	-	30c. orange (Bananas) (air)	1·20	35
458	-	80c. pink and green (Coffee)	3·00	55
459	-	5g. grey (Sisal)	10·00	3·25

84 Isabella the Catholic

1951. Air. Fifth Birth Cent of Isabella the Catholic.

460	84	15c. brown	25	20
461	84	30c. blue	35	35

85 Pres. Magloire and Nursery, La Saline

1953. Projects realized by Pres. Magloire. Designs with medallion of president.

462	85	5c. green (postage)	20	10
463	-	10c. red	25	15
464	-	20c. blue (air)	35	20
465	-	30c. brown	35	20
466	-	1.50g. black	75	45
467	-	2.50g. violet	1·40	75

DESIGNS—HORIZ: 10c. Road-making; 20c. Anchorage, Cap-Haitien; 30c. Workers' estate, St. Martin; 1.50g. Old Cathedral restoration; 2.50g. School canteen.

1953. 150th Death Anniv of Toussaint l'Ouverture. No. 405 surch 7 AVRIL 1803 - 1953 50.

469	74	50c. on 35c. orange	45	35

1953. Air. 150th Anniv of National Flag. Surch 18 MAI 1803 - 1953 50.

470		50c. on 60c. purple	35	20
471		50c. on 1g.35 black	35	20

87 J.-J. Dessalines and Pres. Magloire

88 Toussaint l'Ouverture

89 Marie-Jeanne and Lamartiniere on La Crete-a-Pierrot

1954. 150th Anniv of Independence. (a) As T 87/8.

472	87	3c. black and blue (postage)	10	10
473	88	5c. black and green	25	15
474	-	5c. black and green	25	15
475	-	5c. black and green	35	25
476	-	5c. black and green	25	15
477	87	10c. black and red	25	15
478	-	15c. black and lilac	35	20
479	88	50c. black and green (air)	40	25
480	-	50c. black and green	40	25
481	-	50c. black and red	40	25
482	-	50c. black and brown	40	25
483	-	50c. black and blue	40	25
484	-	1g. black and grey	70	45
485	-	1g.50 black and mauve	1·30	95
486	87	7g.50 black and orange	5·00	4·50

PORTRAITS—As Type 88. Nos. 474, 482, Lamartiniere; Nos. 475, 482, Boisrond-Tonnerre; Nos. 476, 483, 485, A. Petion; No. 478, Capois-La-Mort; No. 480, J. J. Dessalines; No. 481, H. Christophe.
For stamps as No. 480 without dates see Nos. 533/4.

(b) As T 89.

487	89	25c. orange (postage)	35	20
488	-	25c. slate	35	20
489	89	50c. red (air)	35	20
490	89	50c. black	35	30
491	-	50c. pink	35	20
492	-	50c. blue	35	20

DESIGN—HORIZ: Nos. 488, 491, 492, Battle of Vertieres; Nos. 489/92 are larger (31½×26 mm).

90 Mme. Magloire

1954. Mme. Magloire.

493	90	10c. orange (postage)	25	15
494	90	10c. blue	25	15
495	90	20c. red (air)	20	15
496	90	50c. brown	35	35
497	90	1g. green	45	35
498	90	1g.50 red	65	45
499	90	2g.50 green	1·00	80
500	90	5g. blue	2·50	2·00

91 Tomb and Arms of King Henri Christophe

92 Christophe, Citadel and Pres. Magloire

1954. Restoration of Christophe's Citadel. (a) T 91. Flag in black and red.

501	91	10c. red (postage)	25	15
502	91	50c. orange (air)	35	20
503	91	1g. blue	70	45
504	91	1g.50 green	1·00	55
505	91	2g.50 grey	1·60	80
506	91	5g. red	3·00	1·70

(b) T 92.

507	92	10c. red (postage)	20	15
508	92	50c. black and orange (air)	35	20
509	92	1g. black and blue	70	45
510	92	1g.50 black and green	1·00	55
511	92	2g.50 black and grey	1·60	80
512	92	5g. black and red	3·00	1·70

93 Columbus's Drawing of Fort de la Nativite

1954. Air.

513	93	50c. red	60	45
514	93	50c. slate	60	45

94 Sikorsky S-55 Helicopter over Ruins

1955. Obligatory Tax. Cyclone "Hazel" Relief Fund (1st issue).

515	94	10c. blue	25	15
516	94	10c. green	25	15
517	94	10c. orange	25	15
518	94	10c. black	25	15
519	94	20c. red	30	15
520	94	20c. green	30	15

95 Sikorsky S-55 Helicopter

1955. Obligatory Tax. Cyclone "Hazel" Relief Fund (2nd issue).

521	95	10c. black and grey (postage)	25	15
522	95	20c. deep blue and blue	30	15
523	95	10c. red and brown (air)	25	15
524	95	20c. red and pink	30	15

96 J.-J. Dessalines

1955. Dessalines Commemoration.

525	96	3c. black and brown (postage)	15	10
526	96	5c. black and lilac	15	10
527	96	10c. black and red	20	10
528	96	10c. black and pink	15	10
529	96	25c. black and blue	25	15
530	96	25c. black and light blue	25	15
531	96	20c. black and green (air)	15	10
532	96	20c. black and orange	15	10

1955. Air. As No. 480 but without dates and colours changed.

533		50c. black and blue	35	20
534		50c. black and grey	35	20

97 Pres. Magloire and Monument

1955. 21st Anniv of Haitian Army.

535	97	10c. blue and black (postage)	35	20
536	97	10c. red and black	35	20
537	97	1g.50 green and black (air)	60	20
538	97	1g.50 blue and black	60	20

98 Mallard

99 Douglas DC-4, Liner and Map

1955

539		10c. blue (postage)	1·30	25
540	98	25c. green and turquoise	1·80	30
541	99	50c. black and grey (air)	65	20
542	-	50c. red and grey	40	20
543	99	75c. green and turquoise	90	45
544	-	1g. olive and blue	75	25
545	-	2g.50 orange	8·25	1·50
546	98	5g. red and buff	12·50	2·50

DESIGNS—VERT: 10c., 2g.50, Greater flamingo. HORIZ: 50c. (No. 542), 1g. Car on coast road.

100 Immanuel Kant

1956. Tenth Anniv of First Int Philosophical Congress.

547	100	10c. blue (postage)	25	15
548	100	50c. brown (air)	35	20
549	100	75c. green	45	35
550	100	1g.50 mauve	1·10	45

MS551 155×50 mm. Nos. 548/9 and 1g.25 indigo in same design 7·00 4·50

101 Zim Basin and Waterfall

1957

552	101	10c. orange and blue (postage)	25	10
553	101	50c. green and turq (air)	35	20
554	101	1g.50 green and blue	55	35
555	101	2g.50 blue and light blue	85	55
556	101	5g. violet and blue	2·00	1·40

102 J.-J. Dessalines and Monument

1958. Birth Bicentenary of J. J. Dessalines.

557	102	5c. green and black (postage)	25	10
558	102	10c. red and black	25	10
559	102	25c. blue and black	35	10
560	102	20c. grey and black (air)	25	10
561	102	50c. orange and black	60	35

103 The "Atomium"

1958. Brussels International Exhibition.

562	103	50c. brown (postage)	35	20
563	-	75c. green	35	20
564	103	1g. violet	65	20
565	-	1g.50 orange	65	35
566	103	2g.50 red (air)	1·00	45
567	-	5g. blue	1·20	75

MS568 108×69 mm. Nos. 566/7. Imperf 3·75 3·50
DESIGN—HORIZ: 75c. 1g.50 and 5g. Exhibition view.

104 Sylvio Cator making Long Jump

1958. Sylvio Cator (athlete) Commemoration.

569	104	5c. green (postage)	15	10
570	104	10c. brown	15	10
571	104	20c. purple and mauve	20	10
572	-	50c. black (air)	25	15
573	-	50c. green	25	15
574	-	1g. brown	45	35

575 - 5g. black and grey 2·00 75

DESIGN—HORIZ: Nos. 572/75, Sylvio Cator making long jump (head-on view).

1958. Red Cross. Nos. 564/66 surch with red cross and **+50 CENTIMES**.

576	103	1g.+50c. violet (postage)	2·30	2·20
577	-	1g.50+50c. orange	2·30	2·20
578	103	2g.50+50c. red (air)	2·30	2·20

106 Head of U.S. Satellite

1958. I.G.Y. Inscr as in T **106**.

579	106	10c. lake and turq (postage)	25	15
580	-	20c. black and orange	1·10	45
581	-	50c. red and green	65	25
582	-	1g. black and blue	75	25
583	106	50c. lake and blue (air)	45	25
584	-	1g.50 brown and red	2·75	65
585	-	2g. red and blue	1·80	35

MS586 82×112 mm. Nos. 583/5. Imperf 7·00 6·50

DESIGNS: 20c., 1g.50, King penguins on iceflow; 50c., 2g. Giant radio telescope; 1g. Ocean-bed exploration.

107 Duvalier

1958. First Anniv of Installation of President Francois Duvalier. Commemorative inscr in blue.

587	107	10c. blk & pink (postage)	25	10
588	107	50c. black and green	35	20
589	107	1g. black and red	45	35
590	107	5g. black and salmon	2·10	1·40
591	-	50c. black and red (air)	85	20
592	-	2g.50 black and orange	1·20	55
593	-	5g. black and mauve	1·60	1·10
594	-	7g.50 black and green	2·40	1·80

MS595 132×78 mm. Nos. 590 and 593/4 8·25 7·75

DESIGN: Nos. 591/94 as Type 107 but horiz.

1958. As T **107** but without commem. inscr. (a) Postage. Vert portrait.

596		5c. black and blue	10	10
597		10c. black and pink	10	10
598		20c. black and yellow	15	15
599		50c. black and green	25	15
600		1g. black and red	45	35
601		1g.50 black and pink	60	45
602		2g.50 black and lavender	80	45
603		5g. black and salmon	1·50	1·00

(b) Air. Horiz portrait.

604		50c. black and red	35	20
605		1g. black and violet	45	20
606		1g.50 black and brown	65	35
607		2g. black and pink	85	35
608		2g.50 black and orange	95	45
609		5g. black and mauve	1·80	1·10
610		7g.50 black and green	2·50	1·40

108 Map of Haiti

1958. United Nations.

611	108	10c. red (postage)	20	10
612	108	25c. green	25	15
613	-	50c. red and blue (air)	35	20
614	108	75c. blue	35	20
615	108	1g. brown	45	35

MS616 109×67 mm. Nos. 613 and 615. Imperf 3·00 3·00

DESIGN: 50c. Flags of Haiti and U.N.

1959. Tenth Anniv of Declaration of Human Rights. Nos. 611/15 optd **10TH ANNIVERSARY OF THE UNIVERSAL DECLARATION OF HUMAN RIGHTS**.

(a) Postage. (i) English.

| 617 | | 10c. red | 25 | 15 |
| 618 | | 25c. green | 35 | 20 |

(ii) French.

| 617 | | 10c. red | 25 | 15 |
| 618 | | 25c. green | 35 | 20 |

(iii) Portuguese.

| 617 | | 10c. red | 25 | 15 |
| 618 | | 25c. green | 35 | 20 |

(iv) Spanish.

| 617 | | 10c. red | 25 | 15 |
| 618 | | 25c. green | 35 | 20 |

(b) Air. (i) English.

619	-	20c. red and blue	50	50
620	108	75c. blue	70	70
621	108	1g. brown	1·30	1·20

(ii) French.

619	-	20c. red and blue	50	50
620	108	75c. blue	70	70
621	108	1g. brown	1·30	1·20

(iii) Portuguese.

619	-	20c. red and blue	50	50
620	108	75c. blue	70	70
621	108	1g. brown	1·30	1·20

(iv) Spanish.

619	-	20c. red and blue	50	50
620	108	75c. blue	70	70
621	108	1g. brown	1·30	1·20

Overprinted alternately in different languages through the sheet of 25.

110 Pope Pius XII with Children

1959. Pope Pius XII Commemoration. Inscr "PIE XII PAPE DE LA PAIX".

622	110	10c. olive and blue (postage)	15	10
623	-	50c. brown and green	35	20
624	-	2g. sepia and lake	80	45
625	110	50c. violet and green (air)	25	15
626	-	1g.50 brown and olive	55	35
627	-	2g.50 blue and purple	85	35

DESIGNS: 50c. (No. 623), 1g.50, Pope at prayer; 2g., 2g.50, Pope giving blessing.

1959. Red Cross. (a) United Nations stamps surch with red cross and **+25 CENTIMES**.

628	108	10c.+25c. (postage)	35	20
629	108	25c.+25c.	35	20
630	-	50c.+25c. (air)	35	30
631	108	75c.+25c.	40	40
632	108	1g.+25c.	60	55

(b) Pope Pius XII stamps surch with red cross and **+50 CENTIMES**.

633	110	10c.+50c. (postage)	65	45
634	-	50c.+50c.	65	50
635	-	2g.+50c.	1·00	80
636	110	50c.+50c. (air)	85	80
637	-	1g.50+50c.	85	80
638	-	2g.50+50c.	1·00	1·00

111 Abraham Lincoln when a young man

1959. 150th Birth Anniv of Abraham Lincoln.

639	111	50c. purple and blue (postage)	35	20
640	-	1g. brown and green (air)	45	35
641	-	2g. myrtle and green	60	45
642	-	2g.50 blue and buff	65	35

MS643 120×105 mm. Nos. 639/42. Imperf 2·40 2·30

PORTRAITS of Lincoln (bearded): 1g. Looking right; 2g., 2g.50, Looking left. The designs include various buildings associated with Lincoln.

1959. World Refugee Year (1st issue). Nos. 639/42 surch **Nations Unies ANNEE DES REFUGIES 1959-1960 + 20 Centimes**.

644	111	50c.+20c. purple and blue (postage)	70	65
645	-	1g.+20c. brown and green (air)	85	70
646	-	2g.+20c. myrtle and green	90	85
647	-	2g.50+20c. blue and buff	95	90

MS648 120×105 mm. As Nos. 644/7 but each stamp surch **50c.** Imperf 23·00 22·00

113 Chicago's First House and Modern Skyline

1959. Third Pan-American Games, Chicago.

649	113	25c. sepia and blue (postage)	35	20
650	-	50c. multicoloured	45	35
651	-	75c. sepia and blue	60	45
652	-	50c. brown & turq (air)	60	20
653	113	1g. turquoise and purple	85	35
654	-	1g.50 multicoloured	1·10	45

DESIGNS—HORIZ: 50c., 1g.50, Discus-thrower and Haitian flag. VERT: 50c. (air), 75c. J. B. Paul Dessables (founder of Chicago) and map.

114

1959. Obligatory Tax. Literacy Fund. (a) Postage. (i) Size 40×23 mm.

655	114	5c. green	20	15
656	114	10c. black	20	15
657	114	10c. red	20	15

(ii) Size 29×17 mm.

658		5c. green	20	15
659		5c. red	20	15
660		10c. blue	20	15

(b) Air. Size 29×17 mm.

661		5c. yellow	20	15
662		5c. blue	20	15
663		10c. orange	20	15

1959. Sports Fund. Nos. 649/54 surch **POUR LE SPORT + 0.75 CENTIMES**.

664		25c.+75c. sepia and blue (postage)	60	55
665		50c.+75c. multicoloured	80	55
666		75c.+75c. sepia and blue	80	55
667		50c.+75c. brown and turq (air)	85	70
668		1g.+75c. turquoise and purple	85	70
669		1g.50+75c. multicoloured	85	70

1960. UNICEF Commem. Nos. 600 and 607/8 surch **Hommage a l'UNICEF +G.0,50**.

670		1g.+50c. black and red (postage)	80	80
671		2g.+50c. black and pink (air)	85	85
672		2g.50+50c. black and orange	1·50	1·50

1960. Winter Olympic Games. Nos. 650 and 652/4 optd with Olympic rings and **VIIIEME JEUX OLYMPIQUES D'HIVER CALIFORNIE USA 1960**.

673		50c. multicoloured (postage)	1·50	1·10
674		50c. brown and turquoise (air)	1·10	1·10
675		1g. turquoise and purple	1·60	1·60
676		1g.50 multicoloured	2·10	2·10

118 "Uprooted Tree"

1960. World Refugee Year (2nd issue).

677	118	10c. green and orange (postage)	15	10
678	118	50c. purple and violet	35	20
679	118	50c. brown and blue (air)	35	20
680	118	1g. red and green	45	35

MS681 134×76 mm. Nos. 677/80. Imperf 5·00 4·75

1960. Surch in figures.

| 682 | 96 | 5c. on 3c. black and brown | 20 | 15 |
| 683 | 96 | 10c. on 3c. black and brown | 30 | 15 |

1960. 28th Anniv of Haitian Red Cross. 1945 Red Cross stamps optd **"28eme ANNIVERSAIRE"** or surch also.

684	72	1g. on 2½g. violet (postage)	80	45
685	72	2½g. violet	1·20	90
686	72	20c. on 1g.35 green (air)	35	45
687	72	50c. on 60c. purple	60	35
688	72	50c. on 1g.35 green	35	35
689	72	50c. on 2½g. violet	35	35
690	72	60c. purple	35	35
691	72	1g. on 1g.35 green	55	45
692	72	1g.35 green	60	45

| 693 | 72 | 2g. on 1g.35 green | 1·20 | 90 |

No. 689 is also optd **Avion**.

121 "Sugar Queen, 1960" and Beach

1960. Election of Miss Claudinette Fouchard ("Miss Haiti") as World "Sugar Queen, 1960".

694	-	10c. violet and brown (postage)	25	15
695	-	20c. black and brown	35	15
696	121	50c. brown and blue	60	20
697	-	1g. brown and green	1·20	35
698	-	50c. brown and mauve (air)	65	20
699	121	2g.50 brown and blue	1·60	45

DESIGNS: Sugar Queen and—10c., 1g. Plantation (different views); 20c., 50c. Harvesting.

1960. Education Campaign. Surch **ALPHABETISATION** and premium.

700	118	10c.+20c. green and orange (postage)	30	15
701	118	10c.+30c. green and orange	35	20
702	118	50c.+20c. purple and violet	35	20
703	118	50c.+30c. purple and violet	50	45
704	118	50c.+20c. black and blue (air)	35	30
705	118	50c.+30c. black and blue	60	50
706	118	1g.+20c. red and green	80	65
707	118	1g.+30c. red and green	80	65

123 Olympic Torch, Victory Parade at Athens, 1896, and Melbourne Stadium

1960. Olympic Games, Rome.

708	123	10c. blk and orge (postage)	10	10
709	-	20c. blue and red	15	10
710	-	50c. green and brown	35	20
711	-	1g. blue and black	45	35
712	-	50c. purple and bistre (air)	35	20
713	-	1g.50 mauve and green	60	20
714	-	2g.50 slate, purple and blk	85	35

MS715 104×57 mm. Nos. 711 and 714. Imperf 3·00 3·00

DESIGNS: 20c. and 1g.50, "The Discus-thrower" and Rome Stadium; 50c. (No. 710), Pierre de Coubertin (founder) and Athletes Parade, Melbourne; 50c. (No. 712), As Type 123 but P. de Coubertin inset; 1g. Athens Stadium, 1896; 2g.50, Victory Parade, Athens, 1896, and Athletes' Parade, Melbourne.

1960. Nos. 710/3 surch **+25 CENTIMES**.

716		50c.+25c. grn and brn (postage)	35	20
717		1g.+25c. blue and black	45	35
718		50c.+25c. purple and bistre (air)	35	20
719		1g.50+25c. mauve and green	55	40

125 Occide Jeanty

1960. Birth Cent of Occide Jeanty (composer).

720	125	10c. purple and orange (postage)	25	10
721	-	20c. purple and blue	35	20
722	125	50c. sepia and green	45	35
723	125	50c. blue and yellow	40	20
724	-	1g.50 slate and mauve	65	20

DESIGN: 20c., 1g.50, Jeanty and Capitol, Port-au-Prince.

126 U.N., New York

1960. 15th Anniv of U.N.O.

731	**126**	1g. black and grn (postage)	45	35
732	**126**	50c. black and red (air)	35	20
733	**126**	1g.50 black and blue	45	35
MS734		106×77 mm. Nos. 731/3. Imperf	2·30	2·20

127 Sud Aviation Caravelle

1960. Air. Aviation Week.

735	**127**	20c. blue and red	15	10
736	-	50c. brown and green	40	20
737	-	50c. blue and green	40	20
738	-	50c. black and green	40	20
739	**127**	1g. green and red	90	20
740	-	1g.50 pink and blue	95	35
MS741		80×125 mm. Nos. 738/40. Imperf	2·30	1·90

DESIGNS: 50c. (3) Boeing 707 airliner and Wright *Flyer I*; 1g.50, Boeing 707 and 60c. "Columbia" stamp of 1933.

1961. UNICEF Child Welfare Fund. Surch **UNICEF +25 centimes**.

748	**126**	1g.+25c. black and green (postage)	45	35
749	**126**	50c.+25c. black and red (air)	35	20
750	**126**	1g.50+25c. black and blue	55	40

129 Alexandre Dumas (father and son)

1961. Alexandre Dumas Commemoration.

751	-	5c. brown and blue (postage)	15	10
752	-	10c. black, purple and red	15	10
753	**129**	50c. blue and red	35	20
754	-	50c. black and blue (air)	45	20
755	-	1g. red and black	60	35
756	-	1g.50 black and green	80	45

DESIGNS—HORIZ: 5c. Dumas' House; 50c. (No. 754), A. Dumas and "The Three Musketeers". VERT: 10c. A. Dumas and horseman in "Twenty Years After"; 1g. A. Dumas (son) and "The Lady of the Camellias" (Marguerite Gauthier); 1g.50, A. Dumas, and "The Count of Monte Cristo".

130 Pirates

1961. Tourist Publicity.

761	-	5c. yellow and blue (postage)	15	10
762	**130**	10c. yellow and mauve	15	10
763	-	15c. orange and green	20	10
764	-	20c. orange and brown	25	15
765	-	50c. yellow and blue	35	20
766	-	20c. yellow and blue (air)	25	10
767	-	50c. orange and violet	45	20
768	-	1g. yellow and green	50	35

DESIGNS: Nos. 761, 768, Map of Tortuga; No. 763, Two pirates on beach; Nos. 764, 766, Pirate ships attacking galleon; Nos. 765, 767, Pirate in rigging.

1961. Re-election of Pres. Duvalier. Optd **Dr. F. Duvalier President 22 Mai 1961**.

769	**102**	5c. green and blk (postage)	10	10
770	**102**	10c. red and black	15	10
771	**102**	25c. blue and black	25	15
772	**74**	2g.50 grey	95	55
773	**102**	20c. grey and black (air)	15	10
774	**102**	50c. mauve and blue	25	20
775	**99**	75c. green and turquoise	35	35

1961. Air. 18th World Scout Conference, Lisbon. Nos. 735 and 739/40 surch **18e CONFERENCE INTERNATIONALE DU SCOUTISME MONDIAL. LISBONNE SEPTEMBRE 1961 +0,25** and Scout emblem.

776	-	20c.+25c. blue and red	30	25
777	-	1g.+25c. green and red	40	30
778	-	1g.50+25c. pink and blue	50	45
MS779		No. MS741 surch. Imperf	22·00	22·00

1961. U.N. and Haitian Malaria Eradication Campaign. Surch **OMS SNEM +20 CENTIMES**.

780	**126**	1g.+20c. black and green (postage)	70	55
781	**126**	50c.+20c. black and red (air)	1·30	1·20
782	**126**	1g.50+20c. black and blue	1·80	1·70

1961. Duvalier-Ville Reconstruction Fund Nos. 598, 600, 602, 604/5 and 608/10 surch with UNICEF emblem, **Duvalier-Ville** and premium.

783	-	20c.+25c. black and yellow (postage)	25	20
784	-	25c.+25c. black and red (air)	35	35
785	-	1g.+50c. black and violet	45	45
786	-	5g.+50c. black and mauve	95	90
787	-	1g.+50c. black and red	45	45
788	-	2g.50+50c. black and blue	80	55
789	-	2g.50+50c. black and orange	55	50
790	-	7g.50+50c. black and green	1·30	1·10

1962. Colonel Glenn's Space Flight. Nos. 761, 768 optd **EXPLORATION SPATIALE JOHN GLENN** and outline of capsule or surch also.

795	-	50c. on 5c. yell and bl (postage)	35	20
796	-	1g.50 on 5c. yellow and blue	1·20	75
797	-	1g. yellow and green (air)	45	35
798	-	2g. on 1g. yellow and green	1·20	90

136 Campaign Emblem

1962. Malaria Eradication.

799	**136**	5c. blue and red (postage)	15	10
800	-	10c. green and brown	15	10
801	**136**	50c. red and blue	35	20
802	-	20c. red and violet (air)	15	10
803	**136**	50c. red and green	35	20
804	-	1g. blue and orange	45	35
MS805		140×70 mm. Nos. 801 and 803/4 in slightly different colours. Imperf	2·30	2·20

DESIGN: 10c., 20c., 1g. As Type **136** but with long side of triangle at top.
See also No. MS826.

1962. World Refugee Year (3rd issue). As T **118** but additionally inscr **"1962"** and colours changed.

806	**118**	10c. orange and blue (postage)	15	15
807	**118**	50c. green and mauve	35	35
808	**118**	50c. brown and blue (air)	30	25
809	**118**	1g. black and buff	35	35
MS810		133×76 mm. Nos. 806/9. Imperf	2·30	2·20

137 Scout Badge

1962. 22nd Anniv of Haitian Boy Scout Movement.

811	**137**	3c. orange and violet (postage)	15	15
812	-	5c. brown, olive and black	15	15
813	-	10c. brown, black and green	15	15
814	**137**	25c. black, lake and olive	20	15
815	-	50c. green, violet and red	35	20
816	-	20c. slate, green and purple (air)	20	15
817	**137**	50c. brown, green and red	45	35
818	-	1g.50 turq, sepia and brown	60	35
MS819		102×60 mm. Nos. 817/18. Imperf	1·40	1·30

DESIGNS—VERT: 5c., 20c., 50c. (post) Scout and camp. HORIZ: 10c., 1g.50, Lord and Lady Baden-Powell.

1962. Surch with premium. (a) Nos. 799/804.

820	**136**	5c.+25c. (postage)	25	20
821	-	10c.+25c.	25	20
822	**136**	50c.+25c.	35	20
823	-	20c.+25c. (air)	25	20
824	**136**	50c.+25c.	35	20
825	-	1g.+25c.	45	35
MS826		140×70 mm. As No. MS810 but sheet additionally inscribed "Contribution d'Haiti a l'OM" below stamps	1·80	1·70

(b) Nos. 806/9.

827	**118**	10c.+20c. (postage)	25	20
828	**118**	50c.+20c.	35	35
829	**118**	50c.+20c. (air)	35	35
830	**118**	1g.+20c.	45	35

1962. Air. Port-au-Prince Airport Construction Fund. Optd **AEROPORT INTERNATIONAL 1962**, with No. 832 additionally optd **Poste Aerienne**.

831	-	20c. No. 816	25	20
832	-	50c. No. 815	35	20
833	**137**	50c. No. 817	35	20
834	-	1g.50 No. 818	50	35

140 Tower, World's Fair

1962. "Century 21" Exn (World's Fair), Seattle.

835	**140**	10c. purple and blue (postage)	10	10
836	**140**	20c. blue and red	15	10
837	**140**	50c. green and yellow	35	20
838	**140**	1g. red and green	45	35
839	**140**	50c. black and lilac (air)	35	15
840	**140**	1g. red and grey	50	35
841	**140**	1g.50 purple and orange	60	35
MS842		133×82 mm. Nos. 840/1. Imperf	3·00	2·75

141 Town plan and 1904 10c. stamp

1963. Duvalier-ville Commemoration.

843	**141**	5c. black, yellow and violet (postage)	10	10
844	**141**	10c. black, yellow and red	15	10
845	**141**	25c. black, yellow and grey	25	20
846	-	50c. brown and orange (air)	25	20
847	-	1g. brown and blue	65	35
848	-	1g.50 brown and green	80	45

DESIGN: Nos. 846/8 Houses and 1881 2c. stamp.

1963. "Peaceful Uses of Outer Space". Nos. 837/38 and 841/2 optd **UTILISATIONS PACIFIQUES DE L'ESPACE** and space capsule.

853	**140**	50c. green and yellow (postage)	60	35
854	**140**	1g. red and green	1·20	45
855	**140**	1g. red and grey (air)	1·20	55
856	**140**	1g.50 purple and orange	1·50	95

1963. Literacy Campaign. Surch **ALPHABETISATION + 0,10**.

857	**141**	25c.+10c. (postage)	20	15
858	-	50c.+10c. (No. 846) (air)	35	20
859	-	1g.50+10c. (No. 848)	45	35

143 Harvesting

1963. Freedom from Hunger.

860	**143**	10c. orange and black (postage)	10	10
861	**143**	20c. turquoise and black	15	15
862	**143**	50c. mauve and black (air)	35	20
863	**143**	1g. green and black	45	35

144 Dag Hammarskjold and U.N. Emblem

1963. Air. Dag Hammarskjold Commemoration. Portrait in blue.

864	**144**	20c. brown and bistre	15	10
865	**144**	50c. red and blue	35	20
866	**144**	1g. blue and mauve	35	20
867	**144**	1g.50 green and grey	60	45
MS868		110×65 mm. Nos. 865 and 868 (but in brown and light brown). Imperf	1·80	1·70

Nos. 864/67 were printed in sheets of 25 (5×5) with a map of Sweden in the background covering most stamps in the second and third vertical rows.

145 Dessalines Statue

1963. Dessalines Commemoration.

869	**145**	5c. red and brown (postage)	15	10
870	**145**	10c. blue, green and ochre	15	10
871	**145**	50c. green and brown (air)	25	15
872	**145**	50c. purple, violet and blue	25	15

146 "Alphabet-isation"

1963. Obligatory Tax. Education Fund.

873	**146**	10c. red (postage)	10	10
874	**146**	10c. blue	10	10
875	**146**	10c. olive	10	10
876	**146**	10c. brown (air)	10	10
877	**146**	10c. violet	10	10
878	**146**	10c. violet	10	10

See also Nos. 974/78, 1157/63 and 1260/1.

1964. Mothers' Festival. Optd **FETE DES MERES 1964** or surch also.

879	**145**	10c. blue, green and ochre (postage)	15	10
880	**145**	50c. green and brown (air)	35	20
881	**145**	50c. purple, violet and blue	35	20
882	**145**	1g.50 on 80c. pink and green (No. 458)	50	35

1964. Winter Olympic Games, Innsbruck. Surch **JEUX OLYMPIQUES D'HIVER INNSBRUCK 1964 0.50+0.10**, Olympic rings and Games emblem.

883	**137**	50c.+10c. on 3c. (postage)	55	35
884	**137**	50c.+10c. on 5c. (No. 812)	55	35
885	-	50c.+10c. on 10c. (No. 813)	55	35
886	**137**	50c.+10c. on 25c.	55	35
887	**101**	50c.+10c. on 2g.50 (air)	80	70

1964. Air. Red Cross Cent (1963). Optd **18631963** and Centenary Emblem, on surch also. Portrait in blue.

888	**144**	20c. brown and bistre	30	15
889	**144**	50c. red and blue	35	20
890	**144**	1g. blue and mauve	50	35
891	**144**	1g.50 green and grey	60	45
892	**144**	2g.50+1g.25 on 1g.50 green and grey	1·20	1·00

150 Weightlifting

1964. Olympic Games, Tokyo (1st issue).

893	**150**	10c. sepia and blue (postage)	15	10
894	**150**	25c. sepia and salmon	20	15
895	-	50c. sepia and mauve	35	20
896	**150**	50c. sepia and purple (air)	35	20
897	-	50c. sepia and green	35	20
898	-	75c. sepia and yellow	45	35
899	-	1g.50 sepia and grey	60	45
MS900		75×89 mm. Nos. 896/9 in new colours. Imperf	2·30	2·20

DESIGN: Nos. 895, 896/9, Hurdling.

151 Our Lady of Perpetual Succour and Airport

1964. International Airport.

901	**151**	10c. black and ochre (postage)	20	10
902	**151**	25c. black and turquoise	25	15
903	**151**	50c. black and green	35	20

904	151	1g. black and red	45	35
905	151	50c. black and orange		
		(air)	35	20
906	151	1g.50 black and mauve	60	35
907	151	2g.50 black and violet	1·20	55

1965. International Airport Opening. Optd **1965.**

908		10c. black and ochre (postage)	15	10
909		25c. black and turquoise	25	20
910		50c. black and green	35	20
911		1g. black and red	45	35
912		50c. black and orange (air)	35	20
913		1g.50 black and mauve	60	35
914		2g.50 black and violet	95	65

1965. Olympic Games. Tokyo (2nd issue). Nos. 893/9 surch **+5 c.**

915	150	10c.+5c. (postage)	15	10
916	-	25c.+5c.	25	20
917	-	50c.+5c.	45	35
918	150	50c.+5c. (air)	35	20
919	-	50c.+5c.	35	20
920	-	75c.+5c.	45	35
921	-	1g.50+5c.	70	55
MS922 No. MS900 surch **25c.**			9·50	8·75

154 Unisphere

1965. New York World's Fair.

923	154	10c. multicoloured (postage)	15	10
924	-	20c. purple and yellow	25	15
925	154	50c. multicoloured	35	20
926	154	50c. blue and yellow (air)	35	20
927	-	1g.50 black and yellow	45	35
928	154	5g. multicoloured	2·10	1·70

DESIGN: 20c., 50c. (No. 926), 1g.50, "Reaching for the Stars" (statue).

1965. Haitian Merchant Marine Commemoration.

929	155	10c. multicoloured (postage)	15	10
930	155	50c. multicoloured	35	20
931	155	50c. multicoloured (air)	35	20
932	155	1g.50 multicoloured	65	45

155 Likala (freighter) in Port

1965. Air 20th Anniv of U.N. Optd **O.N.U. 1945-1965.** Portrait in black.

933	144	20c. brown and bistre	15	10
934	144	50c. red and blue	35	20
935	144	1g. blue and mauve	45	35
936	144	1g.50 green and grey	60	45

157 I.T.U. Emblem and Symbols

1965. Centenary of I.T.U.

937	157	10c. mult (postage)	15	10
938	157	25c. multicoloured	25	10
939	157	50c. multicoloured	35	15
940	157	50c. multicoloured (air)	35	15
941	157	1g. multicoloured	45	35
942	157	1g.50 multicoloured	75	45
943	157	2g. multicoloured	1·10	55
MS944 116×67 mm. Nos. 940 and 943. Imperf			12·00	10·00

1965. 25th Anniv of U.N.E.S.C.O. Nos. 937/41 optd **20e Anniversaire UNESCO.**

945		10c. mult	25	20
946		25c. multicoloured	30	25
947		50c. multicoloured		50	40
948		50c. multicoloured (air)	1·20	45
949		1g. multicoloured	2·30	75
MS950 116×67 mm. No. MS944 optd			23·00	

158 Cathedral Facade

1965. Bicentenary of Cathedral of Our Lady of the Assumption, Port-au-Prince. Multicoloured.

951		5c. Type **158**	15	10
952		10c. High Altar (vert)	15	10
953		25c. "Our Lady of the Assumption" (painting) (vert)	25	15
954		50c. Type **158** (air)	35	20
955		1g. High Altar (vert)	60	45
956		7g.50 As 25c. but larger, 38×51 mm	2·30	2·00

159 Passiflora quadrangularis

1965. Haitian Flowers. Multicoloured.

957		3c. Type **159** (postage)	15	15
958		5c. Sambucus canadensis	15	15
959		10c. Hibiscus esculentus	15	15
960		15c. As 5c.	25	15
961		50c. Type **159**	45	35
962		50c. Type **159** (air)	35	20
963		50c. As 5c.	35	20
964		50c. As 10c.	35	20
965		1g.50 As 5c.	60	45
966		1g.50 As 10c.	60	45
967		5g. Type **159**	1·80	1·40

160 Amulet

1966. "Culture". Multicoloured.

968		5c. Type **160** (postage)	15	15
969		10c. Carved stool and Veve decoration (horiz)	15	15
970		50c. Type **160**	35	20
971		50c. Carved stool and Veve decoration (horiz) (air)	35	20
972		1g.50 Type **160**	60	45
973		2g.50 Modern abstract painting (52×37 mm)	1·30	75

1966. Obligatory Tax. Education Fund. As T **146** but larger (17×25½ mm).

974	146	10c. green (postage)	20	15
975	146	10c. violet	20	15
977	146	10c. orange (air)	20	15
978	146	10c. blue	20	15

1966. State Visit of Emperor Haile Selassie of Ethiopia. Nos. 969 and 971/3 optd **Hommage Haile Selassie 1er 24-25 Avril 1966.**

979	-	10c. multicoloured (postage)	25	20
980	-	50c. multicoloured (air)	35	20
981	160	1g.50 multicoloured	60	45
982	-	2g.50 multicoloured	1·20	90

162 Astronauts and "Gemini" Capsules

1966. Space Rendezvous. Astronauts and capsules in brown.

983	162	5c. indigo and blue (postage)	15	15
984	162	10c. violet and blue	15	15
985	162	25c. green and blue	25	20
986	162	50c. red and blue	35	20
987	-	50c. indigo and blue (air)	35	20
988	-	1g. green and blue	45	35
989	-	1g.50 red and blue	60	45

DESIGN: Nos. 987/9, Astronauts and "Gemini" capsules (different arrangement).

163 Football and Pres. Duvalier

1966. Caribbean Football Championships. Portrait in black. (i) Inscr "CHAMPIONNAT DE FOOTBALL DES CARAIBES".

990	163	5c. green and flesh (postage)	15	15
991	-	10c. green and blue	15	15
992	163	15c. green and apple	25	15
993	163	50c. green and lilac	35	20
994	163	50c. purple and sage (air)	35	20
995	-	1g.50 purple and pink	60	45

(ii) As Nos. 990/5 but additionally inscr **COUPE DR. FRANCOIS DUVALIER 22 JUIN.**

996	163	5c. green and flesh (postage)	15	15
997	-	10c. green and blue	15	10
998	163	15c. green and apple	20	15
999	-	50c. green and lilac	35	20
1000	163	50c. purple and sage (air)	35	35
1001	-	1g.50 purple and pink	60	45

DESIGN: 10c., 50c. (No. 991, 993), 1g.50, Footballer and Pres. Duvalier.

164 Audio-visual Aids

1966. National Education.

1002		5c. purple, green and pink (postage)	15	15
1003		10c. sepia, lake and brown	15	15
1004	164	25c. violet, blue and green	25	20
1005	-	50c. pur, grn and yell (air)	35	20
1006	-	1g. sepia, brown and orge	45	35
1007	164	1g.50 blue, turq and grn	60	45

DESIGNS—VERT: 5c., 50c. Young Haitians walking towards ABC "sun"; 10c., 1g. Scouting—hat, knot and saluting hand.

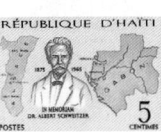

165 Dr. Albert Schweitzer and Maps of Alsace and Gabon

1967. Schweitzer Commemoration. Multicoloured.

1008	165	5c. Type **165** (postage)	15	15
1009		10c. Dr. Schweitzer and organ pipes	15	15
1010		20c. Dr. Schweitzer and Hospital Deschapelles, Haiti	35	20
1011		50c. As 20c. (air)	45	35
1012		1g. As 5c.	45	35
1013		1g.50 Type **165**	60	45
1014		2g. As 10c.	80	65

166 J.-J. Dessalines and Melon

1967. Dessalines Commemoration. With Portrait of Dessalines. Multicoloured.

1015	166	5c. Type **166** (postage)	15	15
1016		10c. Chou (cabbage)	15	15
1017		20c. Mandarine (orange)	25	20
1018		50c. Mirliton (gourd)	35	20
1019		50c. Type **166** (air)	35	20
1020		1g. As 20c.	45	35
1021		1g.50 As 20c.	60	45

1967. World Scout Jamboree, Idaho. Nos. 957/8, 960/1, 963 and 965 surch **12e Jamboree Mondial 1967** or with additional premium only.

1022		10c.+10c. on 5c. (postage)	10	10
1023		15c.+10c.	15	15
1024		50c. on 3c.	25	20
1025		50c.+10c.	25	35
1026		50c.+10c.	25	20
1027		1g.50+50c.	60	45

1967. World Fair, Montreal. Nos. 968/70 and 972 optd **EXPO CANADA 1967** and emblem, also surch with new values (1g. and 2g.).

1028	160	5c. multicoloured (postage)	15	15
1029	-	10c. multicoloured	15	15
1030	160	50c. multicoloured	25	20
1031		1g. on 5c. multicoloured	45	35
1032	160	1g.50 multicoloured (air)	60	45
1033	160	2g. on 1g.50 mult	95	65

169 Head of Duvalier and Guineafowl Emblem

1967. Tenth Anniv of Duvalierists Revolution.

1034	169	5c. gold and red (postage)	15	15
1035	169	10c. gold and blue	15	15
1036	169	25c. gold and brown	25	15
1037	169	50c. gold and purple	35	20
1038	169	1g. gold and green (air)	45	35
1039	169	1g.50 gold and violet	60	45
1040	169	2g. gold and red	95	65

170 "Literacy"

1967. National Education. Multicoloured.

1041		5c. Type **170** (postage)	15	15
1042		10c. "Scouting" (Scout badge) (vert)	15	15
1043		25c. "Visual Aids" (slide projection)	25	15
1044		50c. Type **170** (air)	25	20
1045		1g. As 10c. (vert)	45	35
1046		1g.50 As 25c.	60	45

1968. Olympic Games, Mexico. Nos. 990, 992 and 995 surch **MEXICO 1968** with Olympic rings and value or optd only (1g.50).

1047	163	50c. on 15c. (postage)	35	20
1048	163	1g. on 5c.	45	35
1049	-	1g.50 (air)	60	45
1050	-	2g.50+1g.25 on 1g.50	1·40	1·10

1968. Winter Olympic Games, Grenoble. Nos. 986/9 optd Xeme **JEUX OLYMPIQUES D'HIVER–GRENOBLE 1968** and Games emblem.

1051	162	50c. red and blue (postage)	80	75
1052	-	50c. indigo and blue (air)	60	35
1053	-	1g. green and blue	1·20	55
1054	-	1g.50 red and blue	2·10	1·00

173 Bois Caiman Ceremony

1968. Slaves' Revolt Commemoration.

1055	173	5c. multicoloured (postage)	10	10
1056	173	10c. multicoloured	15	10
1057	173	25c. multicoloured	20	15
1058	173	50c. multicoloured	35	20
1059	173	50c. multicoloured (air)	35	20
1060	173	50c. multicoloured	35	20
1061	173	1g. multicoloured	45	35
1062	173	1g. multicoloured	45	35
1063	173	1g.50 multicoloured	70	55
1064	173	2g. multicoloured	80	65
1065	173	5g. multicoloured	1·80	1·30

Nos. 1060 and 1062/4 are in a larger size—49½×36 mm.

174 "The Unknown Slave"

1968. Inaug of Slavery Freedom Monument.

1066	174	5c. black and blue (postage)	15	15
1067	174	10c. black and brown	15	10
1068	174	20c. black and violet	10	15
1069	174	25c. black and blue	25	20
1070	174	50c. black and green	35	20
1071	174	50c. black and ochre (air)	35	20
1072	174	1g. black and red	45	35
1073	174	1g.50 black and orange	70	45

1968. Air. Nos. 1044/6 surch **CULTURE + 0.10.**

1074	170	50c.+10c. multicoloured	35	20
1075	-	1g.+10c. multicoloured	45	35
1076	-	1g.50+10c. multicoloured	60	45

176 Various Arms
and Palm

1968. Consecration of Haitian Bishopric.

1077	176	5c. multicoloured (postage)	15	15
1078	-	10c. multicoloured	15	10
1079	-	25c. multicoloured	20	15
1080	176	50c. multicoloured (air)	35	20
1081	-	1g. multicoloured	45	35
1082	-	1g.50 multicoloured	60	45
1083	-	2g.50 multicoloured	1·20	90

DESIGNS—HORIZ: (50×30 mm): 10c., 1g., 2g.50, Virgin Mary; 25c., 1g.50, Cathedral, Port-au-Prince.

177 Boeing 727-100 over
Control Tower

1968. Inauguration of Duvalier Airport, Port-au-Prince. Portrait in black.

1084	177	5c. brown and blue (postage)	15	15
1085	177	10c. brown and blue	15	10
1086	177	25c. brown and lilac	25	15
1087	-	50c. purple and violet (air)	35	20
1088	-	1g.50 purple and blue	60	45
1089	-	2g.50 purple and turquoise	80	75

DESIGN: 50c., 1g.50, 2g.50, Boeing 727-100 over airport entrance.

178 President Duvalier,
Emblems and Map

1968. Air. Fourth Anniv of Francois Duvalier's "Life Presidency". Die-stamped in gold.

1090	178	30g. gold, black and red	35·00	33·00

179 Slave breaking
Chains

1968. "Revolt of the Slaves" (1791).

1091	179	5c. mauve, purple and blue (postage)	15	15
1092	179	10c. mauve, pur and orge	15	10
1093	179	25c. mauve, pur and ochre	25	15
1094	179	50c. mauve, pur and lil (air)	35	20
1095	179	1g. mauve, purple and grn	45	35
1096	179	1g.50 mauve, pur and bl	60	45
1097	179	2g. mauve, purple and turq	70	55

180 "Learning the
Alphabet"

1968. "National Education". Multicoloured.

1098		5c. Type **180** (postage)	15	15
1099		10c. Children watching TV screen ("Education by Audio-visual Methods")	15	10
1100		50c. Hands with ball ("Education Through Sport")	35	20
1101		50c. As No. 1099 (air)	35	20
1102		1g. As No. 1100	45	35
1103		1g.50 As No. 1099	60	45

181 Boesman
and Balloon

1968. Air. Boesman's Balloon Flight.

1104	181	70c. brown and green	60	45
1105	181	1g.75 brown and blue	1·20	90

182 Airmail Cachet
of 1925

1968. Air. Galiffet's Balloon Flight of 1784. Each black and purple on mauve.

1106		70c. Airplane and "AVION" ("2 May 1925")	45	55
1107		70c. Type **182**	45	55
1108		70c. "AVION" and airplane ("28 March 1927")	45	55
1109		70c. "HAITI POSTE AVION" and airplane ("12 July 1927")	45	55
1110		70c. Airplane and "AVION" within ring ("13 Sept 1927")	45	55
1111		70c. "LINDBERGH" and airplane ("6th February 1928")	45	55

Nos. 1106/11 were issued together *se-tenant* within a small sheet containing two blocks of six (3×2) with an overall background design representing Galiffet's balloon.

183 Churchill as Elder Brother
of Trinity House

1968. Churchill Commemoration. Multicoloured.

1112		3c. Type **183** (postage)	10	10
1113		5c. Churchill painting	10	10
1114		10c. As Knight of the Garter	15	10
1115		15c. 79th birthday portrait and troops	20	15
1116		20c. Churchill and Farman M.F.7 floatplane	20	15
1117		25c. Karsh portrait and taking leave of the Queen	25	20
1118		50c. Giving "V" sign and Houses of Parliament	35	20
1119		50c. As No. 1116 (air)	35	20
1120		75c. As No. 1115	45	35
1121		1g. As No. 1117	60	45
1122		1g.50 As No. 1118	70	55

MS1123 101×75 mm. 3g. Karsh portrait and Arms (horiz) — 3·50 3·25

1969. Nos. 1070/2 surch.

1124	174	70c. on 50c. (postage)	45	35
1125	174	70c. on 50c. (air)	45	35
1126	174	1g.75 on 1g.	70	45

185 Blue-hooded
Euphonia

1969. Birds. Multicoloured.

1127		5c. Type **185** (postage)	1·60	45
1128		10c. Hispaniolan trogon	1·60	45
1129		20c. Palm chat	1·90	45
1130		25c. Stripe-headed tanager	2·20	55
1131		50c. Type **185**	3·00	55
1132		50c. As 10c. (air)	2·50	75
1133		1g. Black-cowled oriole	3·00	1·30
1134		1g.50 As 25c.	3·75	1·80
1135		2g. Hispaniolan woodpecker	4·25	2·20

186 "Theato, Paris-1900"

1969. Winners of Olympic Marathon showing commemorative inscr and stamp of "host" country. Multicoloured.

1136		5c. "Louis, Athens-1896" (postage)	15	15
1137		10c. Type **186**	25	20
1138		15c. "Hicks, St. Louis-1904"	25	20
1139		20c. "Hayes, London-1908"	45	35
1140		20c. "McArthur, Stockholm-1912"	45	45
1141		25c. "Kolehmainen, Antwerp-1920"	70	65
1142		25c. "Steenroos, Paris-1924"	70	65
1143		25c. "El Ouafi, Amsterdam-1928"	70	65
1144		30c. "Zabala, Los Angeles-1932" (air)	80	75
1145		50c. "Son, Berlin-1936"	1·20	1·10
1146		60c. "Cabrera, London-1948"	1·60	1·50
1147		75c. "Zatopek, Helsinki-1952"	2·30	2·20
1148		75c. "Mimoun, Melbourn-1956"	2·30	2·20
1149		90c. "Bikila, Rome-1960"	2·50	2·40
1150		1g. "Bikila, Tokyo-1964"	3·25	3·00
1151		1g.25 "Wolde, Mexico-1968"	4·50	4·25

MS1152 Two sheets each 128×71 mm. 1g.50 Design as No. 1144; 2g. Design as No. 1151 — 28·00 26·00

Nos. 1136, 1139, 1142 and 1149 are larger, size 66×36 mm.

187 Pylons and
Electric Light Bulb

1969. Construction of Duvalier Hydro-electric Scheme.

1153	187	20c. violet and blue (postage)	15	10
1154	187	20c. blue and violet (air)	25	15
1155	187	25c. green and red	25	15
1156	187	25c. red and green	25	15

189 Practising the
Alphabet

1969. Obligatory Tax. Education Fund. As Nos. 974/8.

1157	146	10c. brown (postage)	25	20
1158	146	10c. blue	25	20
1159	146	10c. purple (air)	25	20
1160	146	10c. red	25	20
1161	146	10c. yellow	25	20
1162	146	10c. green	25	20
1163	146	10c. maroon	25	20

1969. 50th Anniv of League of Red Cross Societies. Various stamps surch **50 eme. Anniversaire de la Ligue des Societes de la Croix Rouge.**

1164		10c.+10c. (No. 1099) (postage)	15	10
1165		50c.+20c. (No. 1100)	45	35
1166		50c.+20c. (No. 1101) (air)	45	35
1167		1g.50+25c. (No. 1103)	80	45

1969. "National Education". Multicoloured.

1168		5c. Type **189** (postage)	15	15
1169		10c. Children at play (vert)	15	10
1170		50c. Audio-visual education (vert)	25	15
1171		50c. As No. 1170 (vert) (air)	25	20
1172		1g. Type **189**	45	35
1173		1g.50 As No. 1169 (vert)	70	45

190 I.L.O. Emblem

1969. 50th Anniv of I.L.O.

1174	190	5c. green and black (postage)	15	15
1175	190	10c. brown and black	15	10
1176	190	20c. blue and black	20	15
1177	190	25c. red and black (air)	25	20
1178	190	70c. orange and black	60	35
1179	190	1g.75 violet and black	1·20	65

191 Papilio zonaria

1969. Haitian Butterflies. Multicoloured.

1180		10c. Type **191** (postage)	1·10	35
1181		20c. Zerene cesonia	2·30	50
1182		25c. Papilio machaonides	3·50	55
1183		50c. Danaus eresimus (air)	4·75	70
1184		1g.50 Anaea marthesia	9·75	1·70
1185		2g. Prepona antimache	14·00	2·75

192 Dr. Martin Luther
King

1970. Dr. Martin Luther King (American Civil Rights leader) Commemoration.

1186	192	10c. brown, red and ochre (postage)	15	10
1187	192	20c. black, red and blue	15	10
1188	192	25c. black, red and pink	20	20
1189	192	50c. black, red and green (air)	40	30
1190	192	1g. black, red and orange	50	40
1191	192	1g.50 black, red and blue	60	50

193 Laeliopsis
dominguensis

1970. Haitian Orchids. Multicoloured.

1192		10c. Type **193** (postage)	15	10
1193		20c. Oncidium haitiense	30	30
1194		25c. Oncidium calochilum	40	30
1195		50c. Tetramicra elegans (air)	40	30
1196		1g.50 Epidendrum truncatum	70	50
1197		2g. Oncidium desertorum	1·00	75

194 U.P.U. Monument
Berne, and Map of Haiti

1970. 16th U.P.U. Congress, Tokyo.

1198	194	10c. brown, black and green (postage)	15	10
1199	-	25c. yellow, black and red	20	20
1200	-	50c. green, black and blue	30	20
1201	-	50c. brn, blk and vio (air)	30	20
1202	-	1g.50 yellow, blk and red	60	40
1203	194	2g. brown, black and green	85	60

MS1204 130×74 mm. Nos. 1201/3. Imperf — 2·10 1·90

DESIGNS—VERT: 25c., 1g.50, Stylized "propeller". HORIZ: 50c. (both), Doves and globe.

195 Map, Dam
and Generator

1970. Construction of Duvalier Central Hydro-electric Power Station. Multicoloured.

1205		20c. Type **195** (postage)	20	10
1206		25c. Map, dam and pylon	20	15

1970. 25th Anniv of United Nations. Nos. 1200/203 optd **XXVe ANNIVERSAIRE O.N.U.** and emblem.

1207	-	50c. green, black and blue (postage)	30	20
1208	-	50c. brown, blk and blue (air)	30	20
1209	-	1g.50 yellow, black and red	60	40
1210	194	2g. brown, black and green	85	60

MS1211 130×73 mm. As Nos. 1208/10. Imperf — 2·10 1·90

197 Power Station and Pylon

1970. Obligatory Tax. Duvalier Hydro-electric Project.

1212	**197**	20c. brown and lilac (postage)	20	10
1213	**197**	20c. grey and brown (air)	20	10
1214	**197**	20c. violet and blue	20	10
1214a	**197**	25c. black and olive		

See also No. 1268.

198 Fort Nativity, 1492

1970. Christmas.

1215	**198**	3c. brn and yell (postage)	15	10
1216	**198**	5c. black and green	25	20
1217	-	1g.50 multicoloured (sepia panel) (air)	60	40
1218	-	1g.50 mult (blue panel) (air)	60	40
1219	-	2g. multicoloured	1·00	60

DESIGN—SQUARE (33×33 mm): Nos. 1217/19, "Haitian Nativity" (Toussaint Auguste).

199 The Oriental (Rembrandt)

1971. Paintings. Multicoloured.

1220	**199**	5c. Type 199 (postage)	15	15
1221		10c. The Ascension (C. Bazile)	15	15
1222		20c. Irises in a vase (Van Gogh)	20	15
1223		50c. The Baptism of Christ (C. Bazile)	30	20
1224		50c. The Nativity (R. Benoit) (air)	30	20
1225		1g. Head of a Negro (Rubens)	50	40
1226		1g.50 As 10c.	65	50

MS1227 Two sheets each 66×86 mm. (a) 3g. Young Mother Sewing (Cassatt); (b) 3g. The Card-players (Cezanne) (25×37 mm). Imperf 2·30 2·30

200 Football

1971. World Cup Football Championship, Mexico (1970).

1228	**200**	5c. black and orange	15	10
1229	**200**	50c. black and brown	40	30
1230	-	50c. black, yellow and pink	40	30
1231	-	1g. black, yellow and lilac	60	40
1232	**200**	1g.50 black and drab	70	50
1233	-	5g. black, yellow and grey	2·10	1·40

MS1234 84×66 mm. 70c. black and violet (T **200**); 1g. multicoloured (Jules Rimet Cup). Imperf 10·50 7·75

DESIGNS: Nos. 1230/31, 1233, Jules Rimet Cup.

1971. Inauguration of Duvalier Central Power Station. Surch INAUGURATION 22-7-71 and premium.

1235	**195**	20c.+50c. multicoloured	40	30
1236	-	25c.+1g.50 multicoloured (No. 1206)	70	40

202 Balloon and Airmail Stamp of 1929

1971. Air. 40th Anniv of Airmail Service (1969).

1237	**202**	20c. black, red and blue	20	15
1238	**202**	50c. black, red and blue	35	20
1239	-	1g. black and orange	80	40
1240	-	1g.50 black and mauve	1·20	50

MS1241 85×71 mm. 50c. purple and emerald 5·75 3·75

DESIGNS: Nos. 1239/40, Concorde and 1929 air stamp; MS1241, 1929 50c. Air stamp.

1971. Obligatory Tax. Education Fund. Nos. 1205/6 surch ALPHABETISATION and value.

1242	**195**	20c.+10c. multicoloured	30	20
1243	-	25c.+10c. multicoloured	30	20

1972. Air. INTERPEX International Stamp Exhibition, New York Nos. 1237/40 optd INTERPEX 72 and emblem.

1244	**202**	20c. black, red and blue	20	10
1245	**202**	50c. black, red and blue	30	30
1246	-	1g. black and orange	50	40
1247	-	1g.50 black and mauve	60	50

205 J.-J. Dessalines and Emblem

1972. Jean-Jacques Dessalines ("founder of Haiti") Commemoration (1st issue).

1248	**205**	5c. black and grn (postage)	15	10
1249	**205**	10c. black and blue	20	20
1250	**205**	25c. black and orange	20	20
1251	**205**	50c. black and green (air)	30	20
1252	**205**	2g.50 black and lilac	1·00	60

See also Nos. 1304/10, 1343/52, 1357/60, 1413/17 and 1451/2.

1972. Air. Fifth "Haipex" Congress. Nos. 1237/40 optd HAIPEX 5eme. CONGRES and emblem.

1253	**202**	20c. black, red and blue	15	10
1254	-	50c. black, red and blue	30	20
1255	-	1g. black and orange	40	30
1256	-	1g.50 black and mauve	60	40

1972. Air. Belgica 72 Stamp Exhibition, Brussels. Nos. 1238/40 optd BELGICA 72 and emblem.

1257		50c. black, red and blue	30	20
1258		1g. black and orange	40	30
1259		1g.50 black and mauve	60	40

1972. Obligatory Tax. As Nos. 974/8.

1260	**146**	5c. red	20	20
1261	**146**	5c. blue	20	20

208 "Sun" and "EXPO" Emblem

1972. EXPO 70 World Fair, Osaka, Japan (1970).

1262	**208**	10c. multicoloured (postage)	15	10
1263	-	25c. multicoloured	20	20
1264	-	50c. multicoloured (air)	30	20
1265	-	1g. multicoloured	50	30
1266	-	1g.50 multicoloured	60	40
1267	-	2g.50 multicoloured	85	50

DESIGNS—HORIZ: Nos. 1264/7, Sun Tower and emblem.

1972. Obligatory Tax. Duvalier Hydro-electric Project. As Nos. 1212/14.

1268	**197**	20c. brown and blue	20	20

209 Basket Vendors

1973. 20th Anniv of Caribbean Travel Assn. Multicoloured.

1269		50c. Type 209	30	20
1270		80c. Postal bus service	40	30
1271		1g.50 Type 209	60	40
1272		2g.50 As 80c.	1·20	70

1973. Air. Education Fund. As Nos. 977/8 but larger size 17×25 mm.

1273	**146**	10c. brown and blue	30	20
1274	**146**	10c. brown and green	30	20
1275	**146**	10c. brown and orange	30	20

210 Headquarters and Map

1973. Air. 70th Anniv of Pan-American Health Organization. Multicoloured.

1276	**210**	50c. multicoloured	30	20
1277	**210**	80c. multicoloured	40	30
1278	**210**	1g.50 multicoloured	50	40
1279	**210**	2g. multicoloured	65	50

211 Miniature Melo

1973. Marine Life. Multicoloured.

1280		5c. Type 211 (postage)	15	15
1281		10c. Nemaster rubiginosa	20	15
1282		25c. Cyerce cristallina	35	20
1283		50c. Desmophyllum riisei	60	20
1284		50c. Platypodia spectabilis (air)	60	30
1285		85c. Goniaster tessellatus	85	30
1286		1g.50 Stephanocyathus diadema	1·10	40
1287		2g. Phyllangia americana	1·40	50

211a Royal Gramma

1973. Fish. Multicoloured.

1288		10c. Type 211a (postage)	30	20
1289		40c. Blue tang	40	30
1290		50c. Black-capped basslet (air)	40	30
1291		85c. Rock beauty	50	40
1292		1g.50 Peppermint basslet	75	50
1293		5g. Creole wrasse	2·50	1·20

212 Haitian Flag

1973. Air.

1294	**212**	80c. black and red	40	30
1295		80c. black and red	40	30
1296	-	1g.85 black and red	85	60
1297	-	1g.85 black and red	85	60

DESIGNS—As Type **212**: No. 1295, Flag and arms (framed). (47×29 mm): No. 1296, Flag and arms; No. 1297, Flag and Pres. Jean-Claude Duvalier.

213 Football Stadium

1973. World Cup Football Championship. Preliminary Games between Caribbean Countries.

1298	**213**	10c. green, black and brown (postage)	15	10
1299	-	20c. mauve, black and brown	20	20
1300	**213**	50c. green, black and red (air)	30	20
1301	**213**	80c. green, black and blue	40	30
1302	-	1g.75 green, black and brn	85	40
1303	-	10g. green, black and brn	3·00	2·10

DESIGNS: 20c., 1g.75, 10g. World Cup stamp of 1971.

214 J.-J. Dessalines

1974. Jean-Jacques Dessalines Commemoration (2nd issue).

1304	**214**	10c. green and blue (postage)	15	10
1305	**214**	20c. black and red	20	20
1306	**214**	25c. violet and brown	20	20
1307	**214**	50c. blue and brown (air)	30	20
1308	**214**	80c. brown and grey	40	30
1309	**214**	1g. purple and green	50	40
1310	**214**	1g.75 green and mauve	85	50

215 Symbol of Solar System

1974. 500th Birth Anniv (1973) of Nicolas Copernicus (astronomer). Multicoloured.

1311		10c. Type 215 (postage)	15	10
1312		25c. Copernicus	20	20
1313		50c. Type 215 (air)	30	20
1314		50c. As 25c.	30	20
1315		80c. Type 215	40	30
1316		1g. As 25c.	50	40
1317		1g.75 Type 215	85	50

MS1318 96×65 mm. 1g.50 Type 215; 2g.50 As 25c. Imperf 2·10 1·90

216 Pres. Jean-Claude Duvalier

1974

1319	**216**	10c. green and gold (postage)	15	10
1320	**216**	20c. purple and gold	20	20
1321	**216**	50c. blue and gold	30	20
1322	**216**	50c. purple and gold (air)	30	20
1323	**216**	80c. red and gold	40	30
1324	**216**	1g. purple and gold	50	40
1325	**216**	1g.50 blue and gold	85	60
1326	**216**	1g.75 violet and gold	1·00	65
1327	**216**	5g. grey and gold	2·50	1·40

1975. Air. Nos. 1296/7 surch.

1328		80c. on 1g.85 black and red	50	40
1329		80c. on 1g.85 black and red	50	40

1975. Air. Centenary of U.P.U. Nos. 1296/7 optd 1874 UPU 1974 100 ANS.

1330		1g.85 black and red	85	60
1331		1g.85 black and red	85	60

219 Haiti 60c. Stamp of 1937

1976. Bicentenary of American Revolution.

1332	**219**	10c. multicoloured (postage)	20	20
1333	-	50c. multicoloured (air)	30	20
1334	-	80c. multicoloured	50	30
1335	-	1g.50 multicoloured	50	30
1336	-	7g.50 multicoloured	2·50	1·70

DESIGN: 50c. to 7g.50, text with names of Haitians at Siege of Savannah.

1976. Surch.

1337	**205**	80c. on 25c. black and pink (postage)	50	30
1338	-	80c. on 10c. multicoloured (No. 1288)	50	30
1339	**214**	80c. on 25c. violet and brn	50	30
1340	**215**	80c. on 10c. multicoloured	50	30
1341	**205**	80c. on 85c. multicoloured (No. 1285) (air)	50	30
1342	-	80c. on 80c. multicoloured (No. 1291)	50	30

1977. Jean-Jacques Dessalines Commemoration (3rd issue).

1343	**205**	20c. black and brown (postage)	15	10
1344	**205**	50c. black and mauve	30	20
1345	**205**	75c. black and yellow (air)	30	30
1346	**205**	1g. black and blue	30	30
1347	**205**	1g.25 black and olive	40	30

1348	205	1g.50 black and grey	40	30
1349	205	1g.75 black and red	50	40
1350	205	2g. black and yellow	60	50
1351	205	5g. black and blue	1·60	95
1352	205	10g. black and brown	3·00	1·90

1977. Air. Lindbergh's Transatlantic Flight Nos. 1313/14 and 1316/17 optd or surch **C. LINDBERGH. N.Y.-PARIS 1927-1977.**

1353		1g. Copernicus	40	30
1354		1g.25 on 50c. Type **215**	50	40
1355		1g.25 on 50c. Copernicus	50	40
1356		1g.25 on 1g.75 Type **215**	50	40

1977. Jean-Jacques Dessalines Commemoration (4th issue).

1357		10c. black and mauve (postage)	15	10
1358		50c. black and brown	30	20
1359		80c. black and green (air)	40	30
1360		1g. black and brown	50	40

1977. Air. Various stamps surch **G. O.80.**

1361	-	80c. on 1g.50 multicoloured (No. 1266)	50	30
1362	-	80c. on 2g.50 multicoloured (No. 1267)	50	30
1363	-	80c. on 1g.85 black and red (No. 1296)	50	30
1364	215	80c. on 1g.75 multicoloured	50	30
1365	216	80c. on 1g.75 violet and gold	50	30
1366	-	80c. on 1g.50 multicoloured (No. 1335)	50	30

1978. Surch **1.00.**

1367	205	1g. on 20c. black and brn	40	30
1368	205	1g. on 1g.75 black and red	40	30
1369	205	1g.25 on 75c. black and yellow	40	30
1370	205	1g.25 on 1g.50 black and green	40	30

Nos. 1368/70 have the inscription "AVION" obliterated by the surcharge.

224 J.-C. Duvalier Telecommunications Stations

1978. Telephone Centenary (1976). Multicoloured.

1372		10c. Type **224** (postage)	15	15
1373		20c. Video telephone	20	20
1374		50c. Alexander Graham Bell (vert)	30	20
1375		1g. Satellite over Earth (air)	40	30
1376		1g.25 Type **224**	50	40
1377		2g. Wall telephone, 1890 (vert)	70	50

225 Flag-raising Ceremony

1978. Olympic Games, Montreal (1976). Multicoloured.

1378		5c. Type **225** (postage)	15	10
1379		25c. Cycling	20	20
1380		50c. High jump	30	20
1381		1g.25 Horse jumping (air)	60	50
1382		2g.50 Basketball	1·20	95
1383		5g. Yachting	2·75	1·20

226 Mother feeding Baby

1979. 50th Anniv of Inter-American Child Institute. Multicoloured.

1384		25c. Type **226** (postage)	20	20
1385		1g.25 Type **226** (air)	50	40
1386		2g. Nurse vaccinating child	70	50

227 Mother feeding Child

1979. 30th Anniv of Co-operative for American Relief Everywhere (CARE). Multicoloured.

1387		25c. Type **227** (postage)	20	20
1388		50c. Type **227**	30	20
1389		1g. Spinning cotton (air)	60	50
1390		1g.25 As No. 1389	85	60
1391		2g. As No. 1389	1·20	75

228 Human Rights Emblem

1979. 30th Anniv of Declaration of Human Rights.

1392	228	25c. multicoloured (postage)	25	20
1393	228	1g. multicoloured (air)	60	50
1394	228	1g.25 multicoloured	85	60
1395	228	2g. multicoloured	1·20	75

229 Anteor Firmin and Book

1979. International Anti-Apartheid Year.

1396	229	50c. pink and brown (postage)	35	20
1397	229	1g. green and brown (air)	70	50
1398	229	1g.25 blue and brown	85	60
1399	229	2g. olive and brown	1·30	75

230 Children playing

1979. International Year of the Child.

1400	230	10c. multicoloured (postage)	15	10
1401	230	25c. multicoloured	20	20
1402	230	50c. multicoloured	30	20
1403	230	1g. multicoloured (air)	60	50
1404	230	1g.25 multicoloured	85	60
1405	230	2g.50 multicoloured	2·30	95
1406	230	5g. multicoloured	3·00	1·40

1980. Air. Wedding of President Duvalier. Nos. 1322 and 1325/6 optd **27 5 80 JOUR FASTE.**

1407	216	50c. purple and gold	30	20
1408	216	1g.50 blue and gold	85	40
1409	216	1g.75 violet and gold	1·00	50

1980. Nos. 1252, 1357 and 1359 surch **TIMBRE POSTE** with value changed.

1410	205	1g. on 2g.50 black and lil	50	40
1411	205	1g.25 on 10c. blk and mve	60	50
1412	205	1g.25 on 80c. blk and grn	60	50

1980. Jean-Jacques Dessalines Commemoration (5th issue).

1413		25c. black and orange (postage)	25	15
1414		1g. black and grey (air)	50	40
1415		1g.25 black and pink	60	50
1416		2g. black and green	1·00	75
1417		5g. black and blue	2·10	1·40

233 Henri Christophe Citadel

1980. World Tourism Conference, Manila. Multicoloured.

1418		5c. Type **233** (postage)	15	10
1419		25c. Sans-Souci Palace	20	20
1420		25c. Vallieres market	30	20
1421		1g. Type **233** (air)	50	40
1422		1g.25 As No. 1419	60	50
1423		1g.50 Carnival dancers	85	50
1424		2g. Women with flowers	1·00	75
1425		2g.50 As No. 1424	1·20	95

234 Players and Flag of Uruguay (1930)

1980. 50th Anniv of First World Cup Football Championship. Multicoloured.

1426		10c. Type **234** (postage)	15	10
1427		20c. Italy (1934)	15	15
1428		25c. Italy (1938)	20	20
1429		50c. Uruguay (air)	30	20
1430		75c. West Germany (1954)	40	30
1431		1g. Brazil (1958)	60	40
1432		1g.25 Brazil (1962)	70	50
1433		1g.50 England (1966)	95	60
1434		1g.75 Brazil (1970)	1·10	75
1435		2g. West Germany (1974)	1·20	85
1436		5g. Argentina (1978)	3·00	1·90

235 *Woman with Birds and Flowers* (Hector Hyppolite)

1981. Paintings. Multicoloured.

1437		5c. Type **235** (postage)	15	10
1438		10c. *Going to Church* (Gregoire Etienne)	15	15
1439		20c. *Street Market* (Petion Savain)	15	15
1440		25c. *Market Sellers* (Michele Manual)	20	15
1441		50c. Type **235** (air)	30	20
1442		1g. As No. 1438	60	50
1443		2g. As No. 1439	1·10	75
1444		5g. As No. 1440	2·10	1·40

1981. Various stamps surch **1.25.**

1445	233	1g.25 on 5c. multicoloured (postage)	60	50
1446	235	1g.25 on 5c. multicoloured	60	50
1447	-	1g.25 on 10c. multicoloured (No. 1438)	60	50
1448	-	1g.25 on 20c. multicoloured (No. 1427)	60	50
1449	-	1g.25 on 1g.50 multicoloured (No. 1423) (air)	60	50
1450	205	2g. on 5g. black and blue (No. 1417)	80	60

The surcharge on No. 1446 is inverted.

1982. Jean-Jacques Dessalines ("founder of Haiti") Commemoration (6th issue).

1451		1g.25 black and brown	60	50
1452		2g. black and violet	1·00	75

237 President Duvalier, Dish Aerial and Freighter at Quayside

1982. Tenth Anniv of Duvalier Reforms ("Jean-Claudisme").

1453	237	25c. green and black	20	20
1454	237	50c. green and black	30	20
1455	237	1g. purple and black	50	40
1456	237	1g.25 blue and black	60	50
1457	237	2g. orange and black	1·00	75
1458	237	5g. orange and black	2·10	1·40

1982. Nos. 1453 and 1455/7 optd **1957- 1982 25 ANS DE REVOLUTION.**

1459		25c. green and black	20	20
1460		1g. purple and black	50	40
1461		1g.25 blue and black	60	50
1462		2g. orange and black	1·00	75

239 Scouts planting Trees

1983. 75th Anniv of Boy Scout Movement. Multicoloured.

1463		5c. Type **239** (postage)	15	10
1464		10c. Lord Baden-Powell (vert)	20	20
1465		25c. Scout teaching villagers to read	20	20
1466		50c. As No. 1464	35	20
1467		75c. As No. 1465 (air)	75	30
1468		1g. Type **239**	90	40
1469		1g.25 As No. 1465	1·30	60
1470		2g. As No. 1464	1·70	75

240 Our Lady of Perpetual Succour

1983. Centenary of Miracle of Our Lady of Perpetual Succour.

1471	240	10c. mult (postage)	15	10
1472	240	20c. multicoloured	20	15
1473	240	25c. multicoloured	20	15
1474	240	50c. multicoloured	30	20
1475	240	75c. multicoloured (air)	40	30
1476	240	1g. multicoloured	50	40
1477	240	1g.25 multicoloured	60	50
1478	240	1g.50 multicoloured	85	60
1479	240	1g.75 multicoloured	95	70
1480	-	2g. multicoloured	1·10	75
1481	-	5g. multicoloured	2·00	1·40

MS1482 Two sheets each containing No. 1481. (a) 90×115 mm; (b) 115×90 mm   4·00   3·50

Nos. 1480/1 differ slightly in design of the frame.

241 Arms of Haiti and U.P.U. Monument, Berne

1983. Centenary (1981) of U.P.U. Membership.

1483	241	5c. brown, red and black (postage)	15	15
1484	-	10c. brown, black and blue	25	20
1485	-	25c. green, black and red	25	20
1486	-	50c. green, red and black	25	20
1487	-	75c. lilac, black and blue (air)	45	30
1488	-	1g. blue, red and black	60	40
1489	-	1g.25 blue, black and red	70	50
1490	-	2g. blue, black and red	1·20	75

DESIGNS: 50c., 1g. Type **241**; 10, 75c. L. F. Salomon and J. C. Duvalier; 25c., 1g.25, 2g. First Haitian stamp and U.P.U. Monument, Berne.

242 Argentine and Belgian Footballers

1983. World Cup Football Championship, Spain.

1491	242	5c. black and bl (postage)	15	10
1492	-	10c. black and brown	20	20
1493	-	20c. black and green	20	20
1494	-	25c. black and green	20	20
1495	-	50c. black and yellow	30	20
1496	-	1g. multicoloured	50	40
1497	-	1g.25 multicoloured	60	50
1498	-	1g.50 multicoloured	85	60
1499	-	2g. multicoloured	1·00	75
1500	-	2g.50 multicoloured	1·20	95

DESIGNS—VERT: 10c. Northern Ireland and Yugoslavia; 20c. England and France; 25c. Spain and Northern Ireland; 50c. Italian player with Cup. HORIZ: 1g. Brazil and Scotland; 1g.25, Northern Ireland and France; 1g.50, Poland and Cameroun; 2g. Italy and West Germany; 2g.50, Argentine and Brazil.

243 1c. Stamp of 1881

1984. Stamp Centenary (1981).

1501	**243**	5c. multicoloured (postage)	15	10
1502	-	10c. multicoloured	25	20
1503	-	25c. multicoloured	25	20
1504	-	50c. multicoloured	30	20
1505	-	75c. yellow, brown and silver (air)	40	30
1506	-	1g. blue, red and gold	50	40
1507	-	1g.25 multicoloured	60	50
1508	-	2g. gold, brown and green	1·00	75

DESIGNS: 10c. 1881 2c. stamp; 25c., 1881 3c. stamp; 50c. 1881 7c. stamp; 1g. Pres. Salomon; 1g.25, 2g. Pres. Duvalier.

244 Modern Communications Equipment

1984. World Communications Year.

1509	**244**	25c. blue and purple	20	20
1510	**244**	50c. blue and olive	30	20
1511	-	1g. orange, brown and grn	50	40
1512	-	1g.25 orange, brown and blue	60	50
1513	-	2g. blue, orange and black	1·00	75
1514	-	2g.50 blue, bistre and blk	1·20	95

DESIGNS—VERT: 1g., 1g.25, Pres. Petion's drum; 2g., 2g.50, W.C.Y. emblem as satellite over globe.

245 Javelin-thrower, Runner and Polevaulter

1984. Olympic Games, Los Angeles.

1515	**245**	5c. black, green and red	15	10
1516	**245**	10c. black, olive and red	20	20
1517	-	25c. black, green and red	20	20
1518	-	50c. black, ochre and red	30	20
1519	-	1g. black, blue and red	50	40
1520	-	1g.25 black, blue and orge	70	50
1521	-	2g. black, violet and red	1·00	75
MS1522	52×72 mm. 2g.50 black, green and orange		1·70	95

DESIGNS—HORIZ: 25c., 50c. Hurdler. VERT: 1g. to 2g.50, Long jumper.

246 Head of "The Unknown Indian", Toussaint Square, Louverture

1984. 500th Anniv of Arrival of Europeans in America (1st issue).

1523	**246**	5c. multicoloured (postage)	30	20
1524	**246**	10c. multicoloured	30	25
1525	**246**	25c. multicoloured	30	25
1526	**246**	50c. multicoloured	45	30
1527	-	1g. multicoloured (air)	60	40
1528	-	1g.25 multicoloured	90	55
1529	-	2g.50 multicoloured	2·50	1·30
MS1530	124×79 mm. Nos. 1526 and 1529		7·75	6·75

DESIGN: 1 to 2g. "The Unknown Indian". See also Nos. 1539/44.

247 Simon Bolivar and Alexandre Petion

1985. Birth Bicentenary of Simon Bolivar. Multicoloured.

1531	5c. Type **247** (postage)		15	15

1532	25c. Bolivar and Alexandre Petion (different)	25	20
1533	50c. Bolivar and flags of members of Grand Colombian Confederation	30	20
1534	1g. Type **247** (air)	50	40
1535	1g.25 As No. 1532	60	50
1536	2g. Type **247**	1·00	75
1537	7g.50 As No. 1532	3·00	1·90
MS1538	90×61 mm. 4g.50 As No. 1533	2·75	1·70

248 Chief Henri

1986. 500th Anniv of Arrival of Europeans in America (2nd issue).

1539	**248**	10c. multicoloured (postage)	45	20
1540	**248**	25c. multicoloured	45	20
1541	**248**	50c. multicoloured	50	20
1542	-	1g. multicoloured (air)	85	40
1543	-	1g.25 multicoloured	1·10	50
1544	-	2g. multicoloured	1·70	75
MS1545	69×89 mm. 3g. mult		7·75	7·00

DESIGN: 1 to 3g. Chief Henri hunting.

1986. Various stamps surch.

1546	**241**	25c. on 5c. brown, red and black (postage)	25	20
1547	**242**	25c. on 5c. black and blue	25	20
1548	**243**	25c. on 5c. multicoloured	25	20
1549	-	25c. on 75c. multicoloured (1430) (air)	25	20
1550	-	25c. on 75c. multicoloured (1467)	25	20
1551	-	25c. on 1g.50 multicoloured (1122)	25	20

250 Planting Saplings

1986. International Youth Year (1985). Multicoloured,

1552	10c. Type **250** (postage)	15	10
1553	25c. I.Y.Y. emblem	20	20
1554	50c. Boy and girl scouts and flag	30	20
1555	1g. Type **250** (air)	50	40
1556	1g.25 As No. 1553	60	50
1557	2g. As No. 1554	1·00	75
MS1558	100×80 mm. 3g. green, red and black	4·75	4·25

251 Dove above Peace Year Emblem on Globe

1987. International Peace Year (1986) and 40th Anniv of United Nations Educational, Scientific and Cultural Organization.

1559	**251**	10c. multicoloured (postage)	20	20
1560	**251**	25c. multicoloured	20	20
1561	**251**	50c. multicoloured	30	20
1562	**251**	1g. multicoloured (air)	50	40
1563	**251**	1g.25 multicoloured	60	50
1564	**251**	2g.50 multicoloured	1·20	95
MS1565	56×66 mm. 2g. multicoloured		1·60	1·50

252 Peralte and Flag

1989. Charlemagne Peralte Commemoration.

1566	**252**	25c. multicoloured	20	20
1567	**252**	50c. multicoloured	30	20
1568	**252**	1g. multicoloured (air)	50	40
1569	**252**	2g. multicoloured	1·00	75

1570	**252**	3g. multicoloured	1·60	1·20
MS1571	102×85 mm. No. 1569		2·10	1·90

253 Slaves and Tree forming Fist

1991. Bicentenary of Uprising of Slaves. Multicoloured.

1572	25c. Type **253** (postage)	25	20
1573	50c. Type **253**	40	25
1574	1g. Gathering of slaves around fire (air)	75	50
1575	2g. As No. 1574	1·50	95
1576	3g. As No. 1574	2·30	1·40
MS1577	132×85 mm. 50c. No. 1573; 2g. No. 1575	6·50	6·00

254 Amerindian watching Europeans landing

1993. America. 500th Anniv (1992) of Discovery of America by Columbus. Multicoloured.

1578	25c. Type **254** (postage)	20	20
1579	50c. Type **254**	30	20
1580	1g. Columbus's fleet at anchor and rowing boats on shore (vert) (air)	50	40
1581	2g. As No. 1580	1·00	75
1582	3g. As No. 1580	1·60	1·20
MS1583	120×82 mm. Nos. 1580/1	7·25	6·75

255 Map of Haiti and Emblem

1995. 25th General Assembly of Organization of American States. Multicoloured.

1584	50c. Type **255**	30	20
1585	75c. Type **255**	40	30
1586	1g. Map of Americas and emblems (vert)	50	40
1587	2g. As No. 1586	1·00	75
1588	3g. As No. 1586	1·60	1·20
1589	5g. As No. 1586	2·30	1·40
MS1590	72×59 mm. 7g.50 Type **255**	4·25	3·25

256 Dove holding Flags in Beak

1995. 50th Anniv of U.N.O. Multicoloured.

1591	50c. Type **256** (postage)	35	20
1592	75c. Type **256**	45	30
1593	1g. Dove with olive branch flying over flags (air)	60	40
1594	2g. As No. 1593	1·30	75
1595	3g. As No. 1593	2·00	1·10
1596	5g. As No. 1593	3·00	1·90
MS1597	103×84 mm. 5g. Dove carrying olive branch	6·00	4·50

1996. Various stamps surch **XXIIIES JEUX OLYMPIQUES LOS ANGELES 1984.**

1598	2g. on 1g.25 black, blue and orange (1520) (postage)	50	40
1599	2g. on 1g.25 multicoloured (1556) (air)	1·00	75
1600	3g. on 1g.25 multicoloured (1535)	2·10	1·50
1601	3g. on 1g.25 multicoloured (1477)	3·00	2·30

259 Players

1996. Olympic Games, Atlanta. Multicoloured. (a) Centenary of Volleyball.

1605	50c. Type **259**	30	20
1606	75c. Umpire and players	40	30

1607	1g. Players holding Olympic Flame	50	40
1608	2g. Players jumping for ball	1·00	75

(b) 1984 Medal Winners.

1609	3g. 400 m hurdles (U.S.A.)	60	40
1610	10g. Decathlon (gold, Great Britain)	2·00	1·40
MS1611	110×80 mm. 15g. Volleyball player	5·75	5·25

Nos. 1605/6 were issued together, se-tenant, forming a composite design of a match scene and Nos. 1607/8 a composite design of a map.

260 "Virgin and Child" (Jacopo Bellini)

1996. Christmas. Multicoloured.

1612	2g. Type **260**	40	30
1613	3g. "Adoration of the Shepherds" (Bernardo Strozzi)	60	50
1614	6g. "Virgin and Child" (Giovanni Bellini)	1·30	95
1615	10g. "Virgin and Child" (Francesco Mazzola)	2·30	1·50
1616	25g. "Adoration of the Magi" (Gentile da Fabriano)	5·75	4·00
MS1617	106×76 mm. 25g. "Nativity" (Jan de Beer)	4·25	3·75

261 Children in Street

1997. 50th Anniv (1996) of UNICEF.

1618	**261**	4g. multicoloured	60	40
1619	**261**	5g. multicoloured	70	60
1620	**261**	6g. multicoloured	85	60
1621	**261**	10g. multicoloured	1·40	1·20
1622	**261**	20g. multicoloured	3·00	2·10
MS1622a	100×70 mm. 25g. Crowd		4·25	3·75

262 Sleeping Beauty

1998. 175th Anniv (1997) of Third Collection of Fairy Tales by Brothers Grimm. Multicoloured.

1623	2g. Type **262**	1·00	95
1624	3g. Snow White	1·60	1·40
1625	4g. Sleeping Beauty and Prince	2·10	1·90
1626	6g. Man in bed (Water of Life)	3·00	3·00
1627	10g. Cinderella	5·75	5·25
1628	20g. Serving patient with the Water of Life	11·50	10·50
MS1629	195×150 mm. As Nos. 1623/8 but each with decorated frame and size 37×50 mm	12·00	11·00

263 Cocoa Beans

1998. Grande Arche Roof Competition, Paris. "Haiti: Women and Creation". Multicoloured.

1630	2g. Type **263**	1·40	1·40
1631	3g. Swords and flags	2·10	1·90
1632	5g. Boy with model churches	3·50	3·50
1633	6g. Woman with artist's palette and brush	4·25	4·00
MS1634	80×110 mm. 15g. La Grande Arche	11·50	10·50

264 Animals, Birds and Coastline

1999. Nature Protection. Sheet 100×85 mm.

MS1635	**264**	20g. multicoloured	3·00	3·00

265 *Hyla vasta*

1999. Endangered Species. Amphibians and Reptiles. Multicoloured.

1636		2g. Type **265**	40	40
1637		2g. *Cyclura ricordii*	40	40
1638		4g. Head of *Hyla vasta*	70	70
1639		4g. Head of *Cyclura ricordiii*	70	70

266 *Priotelus roseigaster*

1999. Birds. Multicoloured.

1640		2g. Type **266**	40	40
1641		4g. *Xenoligea mantana* (inscr "Xenoligeo mantana")	70	70
1642		10g. *Phoenicophilus polio-cephalus*	1·60	1·40
1643		20g. *Phoenicopterus rubber*	3·00	3·00
MS1644		120×90 mm. Nos. 1640/3	6·25	5·75

267 Diamond Sutra (868 AD) (first moveable type) (11th-century)

1999. Chinese Inventions. Multicoloured.

1645		2g. Type **267**	30	30
1646		3g. Paper making (2nd-century BC)	50	50
1647		6g. Cannon (gunpowder 9th-century)	1·00	95
1648		10g. Compass (4th-century BC)	1·70	1·50
MS1649		171×121 mm. Nos. 1645/8	3·00	3·00

268 The Nativity   **269** Flight into Egypt

1999. Christmas.

1650	**268**	1g. multicoloured	10	10
1651	**268**	3g. multicoloured	40	40
1652	**268**	5g. multicoloured	70	70
1653	**269**	10g. multicoloured	1·60	1·40
1654	**269**	15g. multicoloured	2·30	2·10
1655	**269**	20g. multicoloured	3·00	2·75

270 Pirogue

2000. Tourism. Multicoloured.

1656		2g. Type **270**	40	40
1657		3g. Child	50	50
1658		4g. Bassin Zim waterfall (vert)	70	70
1659		5g. Ardadins Island (vert)	95	85
1660		6g. Gingerbread house	1·30	1·20
1661		10g. National Palace	1·70	1·50
1662		20g. Peligre Lake (vert)	2·10	1·90
MS1663		Two sheets. (a) 130×180 mm. Nos. 1656/72. (b) 78×100 mm. 25g. Sail boat (vert)	8·25	7·75

271 Open Book

2001. Air. Bicentenary of the Constitution.

1664	**271**	1g. multicoloured	20	10
1665	**271**	2g. multicoloured	40	40
1666	**271**	5g. multicoloured	95	85
1667	**271**	10g. multicoloured	1·70	1·50
1668	**271**	25g. multicoloured	2·50	2·40
1669	**271**	50g. multicoloured	3·00	3·00
MS1670		141×100 mm. 25g.×2, Toussaint Louverture; As Type **271**	5·25	4·75

272 Toussaint Louverture

2003. Death Bicentenary of Toussaint Louverture.

1671	**272**	1g. multicoloured	20	10
1672	**272**	2g. multicoloured	40	40
1673	**272**	3g. multicoloured	50	50
1674	**272**	5g. multicoloured	95	85
1675	**272**	6g. multicoloured	1·30	1·20
1676	**272**	10g. multicoloured	1·70	1·50
MS1677		160×220 mm. **272** 15g. multicoloured. Imperf	2·10	1·90

281 Child, Aircraft and Relief Parachutes

2010. Earthquake, 12 January 2010. Multicoloured.

1701		25g. Type **281**	2·10	1·80
1702		25g. Red Cross worker holding infant	2·10	1·80
1703		25g. Red Cross workers and rescue dog	2·10	1·80
1704		25g. Delivering aid	2·10	1·80
1705		25g. Red Cross ship	2·10	1·80
1706		25g. Bandaging child	2·10	1·80
1707		25g. Damaged building and woman	2·10	1·80
1708		25g. Government building before and after earthquake	2·10	1·80
MS1709		148×188 mm. 15g. Post Office before earthquake; 15g. Post Office and vehicle before earthquake; 25g. Post Office demolished and two survivors; 25g. Post Office demolished and blue posts; 25g. Post Office rubble and survivor; 50g. Post Office as rubble; 50g. Four survivors and Post Office ruins	9·50	9·50

It is reported that Nos. 1701/8 were printed without governmental authority and will, if necessary, be removed from the listing if and when confirmed by the Postal Authority of Haiti.

OFFICIAL STAMPS

1960. Nos. 736/40 optd OFFICIEL.

O742	-	50c. brown and green	†	55
O743	-	50c. blue and green	†	55
O744	-	50c. black and green	†	55
O745	127	1g. green and red	†	75
O746	-	1g.50 pink and blue	†	1·20
MSO747		No. MS741 optd UNICEF+25 centimes on each stamp	†	3·25

The above were only issued precancelled.

O135 Dessalines' Statue

1962. Air. (a) Size 20½×37½ mm.

O791	**O135**	50c. sepia and blue	45	35
O792	**O135**	1g. red and blue	70	45
O793	**O135**	1g.50 blue and bistre	95	65

(b) Size 30½×40 mm.

O794		5g. green and red	2·50	2·20

PARCEL POST STAMPS

1960. Optd COLIS POSTAUX.

P725	102	5c. green and blk (postage)	10	10
P726	102	10c. red and black	20	15
P727	102	25c. blue and black	30	20
P728	74	2g.50 brown	2·40	2·20
P729	102	50c. orange and black (air)	45	35
P730	101	5g. violet and blue	3·00	2·40

P130 Arms

1961

P757	**P130**	50c. violet and bistre (postage)	45	35
P758	**P130**	1g. blue and red	70	45
P759	**P130**	2g.50 lake and grn (air)	1·80	1·30
P760	**P130**	5g. green and orange	2·30	1·50

POSTAGE DUE STAMPS

D10

1898

D63	**D10**	2c. blue	45	35
D64	**D10**	5c. brown	80	55
D65	**D10**	10c. orange	1·20	80
D66	**D10**	50c. grey	2·00	1·10

1902. Optd MAI Gt Pre 1902 in frame.

D85		2c. blue	1·30	90
D86		5c. brown	1·10	70
D87		10c. orange	1·50	75
D88		50c. grey	8·25	4·00

D23

1906

D150	**D23**	2c. red	90	50
D151	**D23**	5c. blue	2·40	2·30
D152	**D23**	10c. purple	2·40	2·30
D153	**D23**	50c. olive	8·50	5·00

1914. Optd GL O. Z 7 FEV. 1914 in frame.

D206	**D10**	5c. brown	95	55
D207	**D10**	10c. orange	80	75
D208	**D10**	50c. grey	5·25	3·25

1914. Optd GL O. Z 7 FEV. 1914 in frame.

D209	**D 23**	2c. red	70	45
D210	**D 23**	5c. blue	1·10	65
D211	**D 23**	10c. purple	4·00	3·25
D212	**D 23**	50c. olive	7·00	4·50

D83

1951

D452	**D83**	10c. red	20	15
D453	**D83**	20c. brown	25	20
D454	**D83**	40c. green	35	35
D455	**D83**	50c. yellow	45	45

SPECIAL DELIVERY STAMP

S 86 G.P.O.

1953

E468	**S 86**	25c. red	55	40

APPENDIX

The following stamps have either been issued in excess of postal needs or have not been available to the public in reasonable quantities at face value. Such stamps may later be given full listing if there is evidence of regular postal use.

1968

Medal Winners, Winter Olympic Games, Grenoble. Postage 5, 10, 20, 25, 50c., 1g.50; Air 2g.

1969

Moon Landing of "Apollo 11". Optd on 1969 Birds issue. Nos. 1132/5. Air 50c., 1g.50, 2g.

Space Flights of "Apollo 7" and "Apollo 8". Postage 10, 15, 20, 25c.; Air 70c., 1g., 1g.25, 1g.50.

1970

Moon Mission of "Apollo 12". Postage 5, 10, 15, 20, 25, 30, 40, 50c.; Air 25, 30, 40, 50, 75c., 1g., 1g.25, 1g.50.

1971

Safe Return of "Apollo 13". Optd on 1970 "Apollo 12" issue. Postage 5, 10, 15, 20, 25, 30, 40, 50c.; Air 25, 30, 40, 50, 75c., 1g., 1g.25, 1g.50.

1972

Gold Medal Winners Olympic Games, Munich. Air 50, 75c., 1g.50, 2g.50, 5g.

1973

American and Russian Space Exploration. Postage 5, 10, 20, 25, 50c., 2g.50, 5g.; Air 50, 75c., 1g.50, 2g.50, 5g.

Moon Mission of "Apollo 17". Optd on 1973 Space Exploration issue. 50c., 2g.50, 5g.

Pt. 7

HAMBURG

A port in north-west Germany, formerly a Free City. In 1867 it joined the North German Confederation.

16 schillinge = 1 mark.

1

1859. Imperf.

1	1	½s. black	£140	£900
2	1	1s. brown	£140	£140
3	1	2s. red	£140	£150
4	1	3s. blue	£140	£190
6	1	4s. green	£180	£1900
7	1	7s. orange	£140	70·00
10	1	9s. yellow	£275	£3000

3   **4**

1864. Imperf.

11	3	1¼s. lilac	£900	£1400
15	3	1¼s. grey	£120	£120
17	3	1¼s. blue	£900	£1800
18	4	2½s. green	£200	£200

1864. Perf.

19	1	½s. black	11·00	18·00
20	1	1s. brown	18·00	26·00
21	3	1¼s. mauve	£130	18·00
25	1	2s. red	22·00	29·00
27	4	2½s. green	£170	55·00
30	1	3s. blue	60·00	55·00
33	1	4s. green	£300	60·00
34	1	7s. orange	£225	£180
37	1	7s. mauve	16·00	23·00
38	1	9s. yellow	39·00	£3000

5

1866. Roul.

44	5	1¼s. mauve	55·00	55·00
45	5	1½s. pink	18·00	£190

1867. Perf.

46	1	2½s. green	18·00	£120

HANOVER

In north-east Germany. An independent kingdom until 1866, when it was annexed by Prussia.

1850. 12 pfennige = 1 gutegroschen.
  24 gutengroschen = 1 thaler.
1858. 10 (new) pfennige = 1 (new) groschen.
  30 (new) groschen = 1 thaler.

2

1850. On coloured paper. Imperf.

1	2	1ggr. black on blue	£5500	70·00
2	2	1ggr. black on green	£130	13·00
3	2	⅟₃₀th. black on orange	£170	75·00
4	2	⅟₃₀th. black on red	£170	75·00
5	2	⅟₁₅th. black on blue	£275	£120
6	2	⅟₁₀th. black on orange	£325	90·00

1853. Imperf.

18	4	3pf. pink	£190	£225

4

1855. With coloured network. Imperf.

12	4	3pf. pink and black	£450	£400
14	2	1ggr. black and green	£110	18·00
15	2	⅟₃₀th. black and pink	£225	47·00
16	2	⅟₁₅th. black and blue	£170	£110
10	2	⅟₁₀th. black and orange	£325	£225

5 King George V

1859. Imperf.

23	5	1gr. pink	5·50	6·50
25a	5	2gr. blue	22·00	65·00
28	5	3gr. yellow	£225	£140
29	5	3gr. brown	39·00	80·00
31	5	10gr. green	£375	£1300

6

1860. Imperf.

32a	6	½gr. black	£250	£300

1863. Imperf.

34	4	3pf. green	£550	£1400

1864. Roul.

35a	4	3pf. green	45·00	90·00
36a	6	½gr. black	£375	£375
37a	5	1gr. pink	17·00	11·50
38	5	2gr. blue	£170	90·00
39a	5	3gr. brown	£100	£100

HATAY

Hatay was returned to Turkey in June 1939.

1939. 100 santims = 40 paras = 1 kurus.

1939. Stamps of Turkey surch HATAY DEVLETI and value.

32	112	10s. on 20pa. orange	80	40
33	112	25s. on 1k. green	80	40
34	112	50s. on 2k. violet	80	40
35	112	75s. on 2½k. blue	80	40
36	112	1k. on 4k. grey	40	1·20
37	112	1k. on 5k. red	80	40
38	112	1½k. on 3k. brown	1·20	55
39	112	2½k. on 4k. grey	1·60	80
40	112	5k. on 8k. blue	4·75	2·40
41	112	12½k. on 20k. green	7·00	3·50
42	112	20k. on 25k. blue	8·00	4·00

9 Map of Hatay   **10** Flag of Hatay

1939

48	9	10pa. orange and blue	45	15
49	9	30pa. violet and blue	55	25
50	9	1½k. olive and blue	80	40
51	-	2½k. green	85	40
52	-	3k. blue	95	45
53	-	5k. red	1·20	55
54	10	6k. red and blue	1·30	65
55	10	7½k. red and green	1·30	80
56	10	12k. red and violet	2·00	1·20
57	10	12½k. red and blue	2·40	1·20
58	-	17½k. red	4·75	2·40
59	-	25k. olive	6·00	2·75
60	-	50k. blue	13·50	6·25

DESIGNS—HORIZ: 2½, 3, 5k. Lions of Antioch; 17½, 25, 50k. Parliament House, Antioch.

1939. Commemorating Turkish Annexation. Optd T. C. ilhak tarihi 30-6-1939.

65	9	10pa. orange and blue	65	25
66	9	30pa. violet and blue	80	40
67	9	1½k. olive and blue	80	40
68	-	2½k. green (No. 51)	1·20	55
69	-	3k. blue (No. 52)	1·30	65
70	-	5k. red (No. 53)	1·30	65
71	10	6k. red and blue	1·30	65
72	10	7½k. red and green	1·60	80
73	10	12k. red and violet	2·00	95
74	10	12½k. red and blue	2·00	1·00
75	-	17½k. red (No. 58)	4·25	2·40
76	-	25k. olive (No. 59)	8·75	4·25
77	-	50k. blue (No. 60)	17·00	9·50

POSTAGE DUE STAMPS

1939. Postage Due stamps of Turkey optd HATAY DEVLETI or surch also.

D43	D121	1k. on 2k. blue	1·60	80
D44	D121	3k. violet	3·25	1·60
D45	D121	4k. on 5k. green	3·25	1·60
D46	D121	5k. on 12k. red	4·00	2·40
D47	D121	12k. red	47·00	24·00

D11 Castle at Antioch

1939

D61	D11	1k. red	1·60	80
D62	D11	3k. brown	2·00	80
D63	D11	4k. green	2·75	80
D64	D11	5k. grey	4·00	1·20

1939. Nos. D61/4 optd T. C. ilhak tarihi 30-6-1939.

D73	1k. red		2·75	1·20
D74	3k. brown		3·25	1·20
D75	4k. green		4·00	1·60
D76	5k. grey		4·25	1·60

HAWAII

A group of islands in the central Pacific, an independent kingdom till 1893 when a provisional government was set up. Annexed in 1898 by the United States. Now a State of the U.S.A.

100 cents = 1 dollar.

1

1851. Inscr "Hawaiian Postage". Imperf.

1	1	2c. blue	£750000	£340000
2	1	5c. blue	£70000	£40000
3	1	13c. blue	£35000	£30000

On Nos. 1/2 the value is expressed in words.

1852. Inscr "H.L. & US. Postage". Imperf.

4		13c. blue	£45000	£32000

3 Kamehameha III

1853. Imperf.

18	3	5c. blue		28·00
19	3	13c. red		£275

5

1859. Inter-island post.

9	5	1c. blue	£18000	£12000
12	5	1c. black	£1000	£2000
10	5	2c. blue	£7000	£5500
14d	5	2c. black	£1100	£800

6 Kamehameha IV

1862. Imperf.

22	6	2c. red		65·00

7 Princess Victoria Kamamalu

1864. Perf.

27	7	1c. mauve	12·50	10·00
41	-	2c. red	75·00	25·00
42	-	5c. blue	20·00	4·50
30	-	6c. green	34·00	12·50
31	-	18c. red	£110	45·00

DESIGNS: 2c. Kamehameha IV; 5c., 6c. Portraits of Kamehameha V; 18c. H.E. Mataio Kekuanaoa.

12

1865. Inter-island post.

32	12	1c. blue		£400
33	12	2c. blue		£400
34	12	5c. blue on blue	£750	£1300
35	-	5c. blue on blue	£1100	£800

DESIGN: No. 35, As Type **12** but inscr "HAWAIIAN POSTAGE" on left side of frame.

16 Princess Likelike

1875

38	16	1c. blue	8·00	11·50
39	16	1c. green	3·50	2·75
36	-	2c. brown	10·00	4·00
40b	-	2c. red	5·50	1·40
44	-	10c. black	48·00	27·00
45	-	10c. red	45·00	17·00
46	-	10c. brown	41·00	13·50
37	-	12c. black	75·00	39·00
47	-	12c. lilac	£100	£45
48	-	15c. brown	75·00	34·00
49	-	25c. purple	£170	70·00
50	-	50c. red	£225	95·00
51	-	$1 red	£275	£325

DESIGNS: 2c. King Kalakaua; 10c. Same in uniform; 12c. Queen Leleiohoku; 15c. Queen Kapiolani; 25c. Statute of Kamehameha I; 50c. King Lunalilo; $1, Queen Emma Kaleleonalani.

22 Princess (later Queen) Liliuokalani

1890

53	22	2c. violet	5·75	1·70

1893. Stamps of 1864, 1875 and 1889, optd Provisional GOVT. 1893.

54	7	1c. mauve	10·00	14·00
55	16	1c. blue	9·75	14·00
56	16	1c. green	2·00	3·50
57	-	2c. brown	13·50	27·00
58	22	2c. violet	1·70	2·00
67	-	2c. red (No. 41)	90·00	£100
68	-	2c. red (No. 40b)	1·70	3·25
60	-	5c. blue	8·50	3·50
61	-	6c. green	12·50	20·00
62	-	10c. black	12·50	20·00
70	-	10c. red	20·00	34·00
71	-	10c. brown	10·00	17·00
64	-	12c. black	12·50	25·00
65	-	12c. lilac	£190	£275
73	-	15c. brown	27·00	41·00
74	-	18c. red	34·00	48·00
66	-	25c. purple	36·00	55·00
75	-	50c. red	85·00	£130
76	-	$1 red	£150	£225

24 Arms

1894

77	24	1c. orange	2·75	1·70
89	24	1c. green	2·00	1·70
78	-	2c. brown	3·25	90
90	-	2c. blue	1·90	1·40
79	26	5c. red	5·50	2·00
91	26	5c. blue	9·00	4·00
80	-	10c. green	8·50	6·25
81	-	12c. blue	17·00	25·00
82	-	25c. blue	25·00	20·00

DESIGNS—HORIZ: 2c. Honolulu; 12c. "Arawa" (steamer). VERT: 10c. Star and palms; 25c. President S. B. Dole.

26 Statue of King Kamehameha I

OFFICIAL STAMPS

O30 Secretary L. A. Thurston

1896

O83	O30	2c. green	55·00	25·00
O84	O30	5c. brown	55·00	25·00
O85	O30	6c. blue	55·00	25·00
O86	O30	10c. red	55·00	25·00
O87	O30	12c. orange	55·00	25·00
O88	O30	25c. violet	55·00	25·00

HELIGOLAND

An island off the N. coast of Germany, ceded to that country by Great Britain in 1890.

1867. 16 schillings = 1 mark.
1875. 100 pfennig = 1 mark.

Many of the Heligoland stamps found in old collections and the majority of those offered at a small fraction of catalogue prices today, are reprints which have very little value.

1

1867. Perf (½, 1, 2 and 6 sch. also roul).

5	1	¼sch. green and red	35·00	£1600
6b	1	½sch. green and red	£110	£170
7	1	¾sch. red and green	50·00	£1200
8a	1	1sch. red and green	£140	£200
9	1	1½sch. green and red	95·00	£275
3	1	2sch. red and green	18·00	65·00
4	1	6sch. green and red	20·00	£275

2   **3**   **4**

5

1875

10	2	1pf. (¼d.) green and red	18·00	£550
11	2	2pf. (½d.) red and green	19·00	£650
12a	3	3pf. green, red and yellow	£170	£900
13	2	5pf. (¾d.) green and red	22·00	20·00
14a	2	10pf. (1½d.) red and green	17·00	23·00
15b	3	20pf. (2½d.) green, red and yellow	24·00	30·00
16	2	25pf. (3d.) green and red	24·00	29·00
17	2	50pf. (6d.) red and green	26·00	42·00
18	4	1m. (1s.) green, red and black	£170	£200
19	5	5m. (5s.) green, red and black	£225	£950

Pt. 17

HOI-HAO (HOIHOW)

An Indo-Chinese post office in China, closed in 1922.

1901. 100 centimes = 1 franc.
1918. 100 cents = 1 piastre.

HOI HAO
州瓊
(1)

1902. Stamps of Indo-China "Tablet" key-type, optd with T **1**. Chinese characters read "HOI-HAO" and are the same on every value.

1	D	1c. black on blue	4·75	4·00
2	D	2c. brown on yellow	6·25	5·00
3	D	4c. red on grey	4·75	4·25
4	D	5c. green	4·75	6·00
5	D	10c. black on lilac	11·00	11·00
6	D	15c. blue	£2500	£1200
7	D	15c. grey	4·75	4·00
8	D	20c. red on green	48·00	50·00
9	D	25c. black on red	18·00	8·75
10	D	30c. brown	70·00	80·00
11	D	40c. red on yellow	60·00	75·00
12	D	50c. red on rose	65·00	80·00
13	D	75c. brown on orange	£300	£250
14	D	1f. olive	£1100	£800
15	D	5f. mauve on lilac	£850	£700

1903. Stamps of Indo-China, "Tablet" key-type, surch as T **1**. Chinese characters indicate the value and differ for each denomination.

16		1c. black on blue	3·50	3·25
17		2c. brown on yellow	4·50	5·00
18		4c. red on grey	4·75	9·50
19		5c. green	4·75	10·00
20		10c. red	4·25	3·75
21		15c. grey	4·25	8·25
22		20c. red on green	14·00	22·00
23		25c. blue	4·00	5·00
24		25c. black on red	10·00	12·50
25		30c. brown	7·25	12·50
26		40c. red on yellow	85·00	£100
27		50c. red on rose	46·00	90·00
28		50c. brown on blue	£180	£170
29		75c. brown on orange	80·00	90·00
30		1f. olive	£110	£110
31		5f. mauve on lilac	£250	£225

1906. Stamps of Indo-China surch **HOI-HAO** and with value in Chinese.

32	8	1c. olive	4·75	8·00
33	8	2c. red on yellow	4·25	6·25
34	8	4c. mauve on blue	4·25	5·25
35	8	5c. green	9·50	13·00
36	8	10c. red	9·50	13·00
37	8	15c. brown on blue	11·50	13·00
38	8	20c. red on green	10·00	17·00
39	8	25c. blue	13·00	15·00
40	8	30c. brown on cream	19·00	25·00
41	8	35c. black on yellow	23·00	44·00
42	8	40c. black on grey	18·00	55·00
43	8	50c. brown	34·00	60·00
44	D	75c. brown on orange	85·00	85·00
45	8	1f. green	65·00	80·00
46	8	2f. brown on yellow	70·00	85·00
47	D	5f. mauve on lilac	£140	£150
48	8	10f. red on green	£180	£170

1908. Native types of Indo-China surch **HOIHAO** (1 to 50c.) or **HOI-HAO** (others) and with value in Chinese.

49	10	1c. black and olive	1·20	85
50	10	2c. black and brown	1·40	1·50
51	10	4c. black and blue	1·90	2·00
52	10	5c. black and green	2·10	3·00
53	10	10c. black and red	4·00	4·50
54	10	15c. black and violet	9·00	12·50
55	11	20c. black and violet	9·00	15·00
56	11	25c. black and blue	7·75	16·00
57	11	30c. black and brown	8·75	21·00
58	11	35c. black and green	10·50	22·00
59	11	40c. black and brown	7·50	17·00
60	11	50c. black and red	12·50	29·00
61	12	75c. black and orange	19·00	33·00
62	12	1f. black and red	46·00	65·00
63	12	2f. black and green	65·00	80·00
64	12	5f. black and blue	£110	£140
65	12	10f. black and violet	£160	£150

1919. Stamps as last surch in addition with value in figures and words.

66	10	⅖c. on 1c. black and olive	1·80	7·50
67	10	⅘c. on 2c. black and brown	1·20	6·00
68	10	1⅗c. on 4c. black and blue	3·00	8·25
69	10	2c. on 5c. black and green	2·75	3·50
70	10	4c. on 10c. black and red	4·25	9·25
71	10	6c. on 15c. black and violet	2·75	3·00
72	11	8c. on 20c. black and violet	6·50	11·50
73	11	10c. on 25c. black and blue	11·00	18·00
74	11	12c. on 30c. black & brown	3·50	9·25
75	11	14c. on 35c. black and green	4·50	10·00
76	11	16c. on 40c. black & brown	3·50	11·00
77	11	20c. on 50c. black and red	6·50	8·25
78	12	30c. on 75c. black & orange	6·50	12·50
79	-	40c. on 1f. black and red	17·00	32·00
80	-	80c. on 2f. black and green	60·00	65·00
81	-	2p. on 5f. black and blue	90·00	£130
82	-	4p. on 10f. black and violet	£225	£225

Pt. 15

HONDURAS

A republic of C. America, independent since 1838.

1866. 8 reales = 1 peso.
1878. 100 centavos = 1 peso.
1933. 100 centavos = 1 lempira.

1 Seal of Honduras

1866. Imperf.

1	1	2r. black on green	65	
2	1	2r. black on red	65	

5 Pres. F. Morazan

1878. Perf.

31	5	1c. violet	60	60
32	5	2c. brown	60	60
33	5	½r. black	4·50	60
34	5	1r. green	25·00	1·20
35	5	2r. blue	3·75	4·75
36	5	4r. red	5·00	9·25
37	5	1p. orange	6·25	19·00

6

1890

45	6	1c. green	35	35
46	6	2c. red	35	35
47	6	5c. blue	35	35
48	6	10c. orange	50	50
49	6	20c. bistre	50	50
50	6	25c. red	50	50
51	6	30c. violet	60	70
52	6	40c. blue	60	95
53	6	50c. brown	75	95
54	6	75c. green	75	2·40
55	6	1p. lake	85	3·00

8 President Bogran

1891

56	8	1c. blue	35	35
57	8	2c. brown	35	35
58	8	5c. green	35	35
59	8	10c. red	35	35
60	8	20c. lake	35	70
61	8	25c. red	50	70
62	8	30c. grey	50	70
63	8	40c. green	50	70
64	8	50c. sepia	60	95
65	8	75c. violet	60	1·60
66	8	1p. brown	60	1·90
67	-	2p. black and brown	1·90	6·00
68	-	5p. black and violet	1·90	7·25
69	-	10p. black and green	1·90	7·25

DESIGN (LARGER): 2, 5, 10p. Pres. Bogran facing left.

10

1892. 400th Anniv of Discovery of America.

70	10	1c. grey	75	60
71	10	2c. blue	75	60
72	10	5c. green	75	60
73	10	10c. green	75	60
74	10	20c. red	75	60
75	10	25c. brown	85	70
76	10	30c. blue	85	70
77	10	40c. orange	85	1·10
78	10	50c. brown	1·10	1·10
79	10	75c. lake	1·20	1·60
80	10	1p. violet	1·20	1·70

11 Gen. Cabanas

1893

81	11	1c. green	35	1·80
82	11	2c. red	35	1·80
83	11	5c. blue	35	1·80
84	11	10c. brown	35	1·80
85	11	20c. brown	35	1·80
86	11	25c. blue	35	1·80
87	11	30c. orange	60	1·80
88	11	40c. black	60	1·80
89	11	50c. sepia	60	1·80
90	11	75c. violet	75	1·80
91	11	1p. brown	75	2·20

12

1895

92	12	1c. red	35	35
93	12	2c. blue	35	35
94	12	5c. grey	35	60
95	12	10c. lake	50	60
96	12	20c. lilac	50	70
97	12	30c. lilac	50	1·10
98	12	50c. brown	60	1·60
99	12	1p. green	75	1·90

13 President Arias

1896

100	13	1c. red	35	50
101	13	2c. brown	35	50
102	13	5c. purple	35	50
103	13	10c. red	50	50
104	13	20c. green	1·00	60
105	13	30c. blue	85	85
106	13	50c. lake	1·20	1·20
107	13	1p. sepia	1·70	1·80

14 Steam Train

1898

108	14	1c. brown	50	35
109	14	2c. red	50	35
110	14	5c. blue	50	35
111	14	6c. purple	85	60
112	14	10c. blue	90	60
113	14	20c. bistre	1·90	1·70
114	14	50c. orange	4·00	3·75
115	14	1p. green	4·75	5·50

16 General Santos Guardiola

1903

118	16	1c. green	50	25
119	16	2c. red	50	25
120	16	5c. blue	50	35
121	16	6c. lilac	50	35
122	16	10c. brown	50	35
123	16	20c. blue	60	50
124	16	50c. red	1·60	1·30
125	16	1p. orange	1·60	1·30

17 President Medina

1907. Perf or imperf.

127	17	1c. green	25	25
136	17	1c. black	21·00	21·00
128a	17	2c. red	35	35
129	17	5c. blue	35	35
130	17	6c. violet	50	35
131	17	10c. sepia	50	50
132	17	20c. blue	1·10	95
133	17	50c. red	1·40	1·30
134	17	1p. orange	1·90	1·80

1910. Surch in figures.

137	17	1 on 20c. blue	9·25	7·25
138		5 on 20c. blue	9·25	7·25
139		10 on 20c. blue	9·25	7·25

20

1911

140	20	1c. violet	50	25
141	20	2c. green	50	25
142	20	5c. red	50	25
143	20	6c. blue	60	35
144	20	10c. blue	75	50
145	20	20c. yellow	75	60
146	20	50c. brown	2·50	2·20
147	20	1p. olive	3·00	2·40

1911. Optd **XC Aniversario de la Independencia**.

157	23	2c. green	22·00	22·00

23

1912. Election of President Manuel Bonilla.

158	23	1c. red	15·00	14·50

1913. 90th Anniv of Independence. Surch **2 CENTAVOS**.

159	20	2c. on 1c. violet	1·60	95

1913. Surch in figures and words.

161		2c. on 1c. violet	8·75	7·25
162		2c. on 10c. blue	3·50	3·00
163		2c. on 20c. yellow	8·75	8·50
164		5c. on 1c. violet	2·40	1·80
165		5c. on 10c. blue	3·75	2·20
166		6c. on 1c. violet	3·75	3·00

26 Gen. T. Sierra   **27** Gen. M. Bonilla

1913

167	26	1c. brown	25	25
168	26	2c. red	35	25
169	27	5c. blue	50	25
170	27	5c. blue	50	25
171	27	6c. violet	60	35

172	27	6c. mauve	50	35
173	26	10c. blue	1·00	95
174	26	10c. brown	1·60	1·60
175	26	20c. brown	1·20	1·10
176	27	50c. red	2·50	2·40
177	27	1p. green	3·00	3·00

1914. Surch.

178	26	1c. on 2c. red	1·00	95
179	26	1c. on 2c. red	1·60	1·20
180	27	5c. on 6c. violet	2·50	2·40
181	26	5c. on 10c. brown	3·00	2·20
182	26	10c. on 2c. red	2·50	2·40
184	27	10c. on 6c. violet	3·00	3·00
185	27	10c. on 50c. red	8·00	6·00

32 Railway Bridge over River Ulua at Pimienta

1915. Dated "1915".

186	32	1c. brown	25	25
187	32	2c. red	25	25
188	-	5c. blue	35	25
189	-	6c. violet	50	25
190	32	10c. blue	1·00	25
191	32	20c. brown	1·60	1·20
192	-	50c. red	1·90	1·80
193	-	1p. green	3·00	3·00

DESIGN: 5c., 6c., 50c., 1p. Bonilla Theatre.

34 Pres. Francisco Bertrand

1916

194	34	1c. orange	2·50	2·40

1918. No. O206 optd CORRIENTE and bar.

195		5c. blue	2·50	1·80

36 Statue of Francisco Morazan

1919. Dated "1919" at top.

196	36	1c. brown	25	25
197	36	2c. red	35	25
198	36	5c. red	35	25
199	36	6c. mauve	35	25
200	36	10c. blue	35	35
201	36	15c. blue	1·00	25
202	36	15c. violet	75	25
203	36	20c. brown	1·20	35
204	36	50c. brown	5·00	3·00
205	36	1p. green	9·25	24·00

36a

1920. Assumption of Power by Gen. R. L. Gutierrez.

206	36a	2c. red	3·00	3·00
207	36a	2c. gold (51×40 mm)	15·00	14·50
208	36a	2c. silver (51×40 mm)	15·00	14·50
209	36a	2c. red (51×40 mm)	15·00	14·50

1921. As T 36, but dated "1920" at top.

210	36	6c. purple	12·50	6·00

1922. Surch VALE SEIS CTS.

211		6c. on 2c. red	60	60

1923. Surch HABILITADO VALE and value in words and figures.

212		$0.10 on 1c. brown	1·90	1·80
213		$0.50 on 2c. red	2·50	2·40
214		1p. on 5c. red	4·25	4·25

39 Dionisio de Herrera

1923

215	39	1c. olive	35	25
216	39	2c. red	50	25
217	39	6c. purple	50	25
218	39	10c. blue	50	25
219	39	20c. brown	1·00	50
220	39	50c. red	2·20	1·30
221	39	1p. green	5·00	3·50

40 M. Paz Baraona

1925. Inaug of President Baraona. Imperf or perf.

222A	40	1c. blue	2·50	2·40
224B	40	1c. red	11·00	11·00
225B	40	1c. brown	11·00	11·00

1925. Air. Nos. 186/93 optd AERO CORREO or surch also.

227		5c. blue	£110	£110
229		10c. blue	£225	£225
231		20c. brown	£225	£225
235		25c. on 1c. brown	£160	£160
236		25c. on 5c. blue	£275	£275
236c		25c. on 10c. blue	£84000	
237		25c. on 20c. brown	£250	£250
233		50c. red	£550	£350
234		1p. green	£750	£700

1926. Optd Acuerdo Mayo 3 de 1926 HABILITADO.

238	36	6c. mauve	1·60	1·30

1926. Optd HABILITADO 1926.

242	32	2c. red	35	35
243	36	2c. red	35	35

1926. Optd 1926.

239	-	6c. violet (No. 189)	2·75	2·75
240	36	6c. violet	3·00	3·00

1926. Surch Vale 6 Cts. 1926 and bar.

243d		6c. on 10c. blue	60	25

1927. Surch vale 6 cts. 1927 and bar.

244		6c. on 15c. violet	1·00	95
245	32	6c. on 20c. brown	1·00	95
246	36	6c. on 20c. brown	75	70

47 Copan Ruins

1927. Various designs as T 47.

247	-	1c. blue (Road)	35	25
248	47	2c. red	35	25
249	-	5c. purple (Pine tree)	35	25
250	-	5c. blue (Pine tree)	20·00	8·50
251	-	6c. black (Palace)	1·00	70
252	-	6c. blue (Palace)	1·00	60
253	-	10c. blue (P. Leiva)	1·00	25
254	-	15c. blue (Pres. Soto)	1·20	60
255	-	20c. blue (Lempira)	1·60	70
256	-	30c. brown (Map)	2·00	1·20
257	-	50c. green (Pres. Lindo)	3·25	1·90
258	-	1p. red (Columbus)	6·25	3·00

50 President Colindres and Vice-President Chavez

1929. Installation of President Colindres.

259	50	1c. lake	3·75	3·50
260	-	2c. green	3·75	3·50

DESIGN—VERT: 2c. Pres. Colindres.

51a L. Garay (Pilot)

1929. Air. Planned Flight from New York to Honduras.

260a	51a	50c. carmine	2·75	2·40

1929. Air. No. 260a surch.

260b		50c.+5c. carmine	60	35
260c		50c.+10c. carmine	75	50
260d		50c.+15c. carmine	1·00	60
260e		50c.+20c. carmine	1·40	95

The flight did not take place, however, the stamps were sold at the post office and had validity. The face value was for the pilot and the premium for the Department of Public Health for a tuberculosis hospital.

1929. Air. (a) Surch Servicio aereo Vale, value and 1929.

262	39	5c. on 20c. brown	1·90	1·80
263	39	10c. on 50c. red	3·00	2·40
264	39	15c. on 1p. green	5·00	4·75
261	39	25c. on 50c. red	6·25	4·75

(b) Surch Servicio Aereo Internacional 1929 and value.

265		5c. on 10c. blue	75	70
266		20c. on 50c. red	1·50	1·40

1929. Herrera Monument type, dated "1924–1928". Surch Vale 1 cts. XI 1929.

267	-	6c. on 6c. mauve	1·00	95

1929. Nos. 247/58 optd 1929a1930.

268	-	1c. blue	35	25
269	47	2c. red	60	35
270	-	5c. purple	50	35
271	-	5c. blue	1·40	95
272	-	6c. black	3·00	2·75
273	-	6c. blue	50	25
274	-	10c. blue	50	25
275	-	15c. blue	60	35
276	-	20c. blue	60	50
277	-	30c. brown	1·00	70
278	-	50c. green	2·50	1·20
279	-	1p. green	6·25	3·00

1930. Air. No. O264 optd HABILITADO Servicio Aereo Internacional 1930.

281		50c. green and yellow	1·60	1·60

1930. Air. Surch Servicio Aereo Internacional Vale, value and 1930.

282	39	5c. on 10c. blue	75	70
284	39	5c. on 20c. brown	£160	£160
285	39	10c. on 20c. brown	1·00	95
287	-	25c. on 50c. red (No. 192)	1·40	1·30

1930. Air. Surch Vale and value in addition in large letters and figures.

290	39	10c. on 5c. on 20c. brown (No. 284)	1·20	1·20
291	39	10c. on 10c. on 20c. brown (No. 285)	£120	£120
292	-	50c. on 25c. on 1p. green (No. 193)	5·50	5·50

1930. Air. Surch Servicio aereo Vale, value and Marzo–1930.

293	39	5c. on 10c. blue	75	60
294	39	15c. on 20c. brown	1·00	70
295	-	20c. on 50c. red (No. 192)	1·50	1·30

1930. Surch Vale, value and 1930.

297	39	1c. on 10c. blue	60	50
298	39	2c. on 10c. blue	60	50

1930. Nos. O259/60 optd Habilitado para el servicio publico 1930.

299	-	1c. blue	75	70
300	O50	2c. red	1·50	1·40

1930. Air. Surch Servicio aereo Vale 5 centavos oro Mayo.

301	39	5c. on 20c. brown	1·90	1·80

1930. Air. Nos. O264/5 optd. HABILITADO Servicio Aereo MAYO 1930.

302		20c. blue	1·90	1·80
303		50c. green and yellow	1·90	1·80
304		1p. red	2·50	2·40

1930. Optd Habilitado julio.–1930.

305	32	1c. brown	1·20	1·20
306	36	1c. brown	21·00	21·00
309	39	1c. olive	50	35
310	39	2c. red	1·20	1·20
307	36	20c. brown	21·00	21·00
308	36	$0.50 on 2c. red (No. 213)	£120	£120

66 Title Page, First Issue Government Gazette

1930. Newspaper Centenary.

311	66	2c. blue	1·20	1·20
312	66	2c. orange	1·20	1·20
313	66	2c. red	1·20	1·20

67 National Palace, Tegucigalpa

1930. Air.

314	67	5c. yellow	60	35
315	67	10c. red	1·10	70
316	67	15c. green	1·50	95
317	67	20c. violet	1·70	85
318	67	1p. brown	6·25	5·50

68 Pres. Baraona   **69** Amapala

1931

319	68	1c. sepia	70	25
320	-	2c. red	70	25
321	-	5c. violet	85	25
322	-	6c. green	85	25
323	69	10c. brown	1·40	35
324	-	15c. blue	1·60	35
325	-	20c. black	3·25	50
326	-	50c. olive	4·25	1·90
327	-	1p. slate	8·75	3·25

DESIGNS—As Type **68**: 2c. Pres. Bonilla; 15c. Copan Ruins; 20c. Columbus. As Type **69**: 5c. Lake Yojoa; 6c. Tegucigalpa Palace; 50c. Discovery of America; 1p. Loarq Bridge at Loarq.

1931. Nos. 319/27 and 314/18 optd T.S.de.C.

328	68	1c. sepia (postage)	50	35
329	-	2c. red	75	35
330	-	5c. violet	85	50
331	-	6c. green	85	50
332	69	10c. brown	1·20	50
333	-	15c. blue	1·40	70
334	-	20c. black	2·50	70
335	-	50c. olive	7·50	6·00
336	-	1p. slate	9·50	8·50
337	67	5c. yellow (air)	3·75	3·50
338	67	10c. red	5·50	5·50
339	67	15c. green	9·25	9·00
339a	67	20c. violet	9·25	9·00
339b	67	1p. brown	19·00	18·00

1931. Air. Surch Servicio aereo interior Vale 15 cts Octubre 1931.

340	39	15c. on 20c.	5·00	3·50
342	36	15c. on 20c. (No. O218)	7·50	6·00
344a	32	15c. on 20c. (No. O209)	10·00	9·75
344c	39	15c. on 20c. (No. O226)	4·25	4·00
343	-	15c. on 50c. (No. O210)	7·50	6·00
346	36	15c. on 50c. (No. O219)	4·75	3·75
341	-	15c. on 1p. (No. O265)	7·50	6·00

Nos. 342/3 come with or without the original OFICIAL overprint obliterated.

1932. Air. Surch S.–Aereo VI. 15 cts. XI 1931.

347	39	15c. on 20c. brown	5·00	4·25
348	36	15c. on 50c. (No. O219)	5·00	4·25
349	-	15c. on 50c. (No. O264)	4·75	4·00
350	-	15c. on 1p. (No. O265)	4·75	3·00

1932. Air. Nos. O328/36 optd Servicio Aereo Exterior. Habilitado X. 1931.

350c	O70	1c. blue	50	50
350d	O70	2c. purple	1·10	1·10
350e	O70	5c. olive	1·40	1·30
350f	O70	6c. red	1·40	1·30
350g	O70	10c. green	1·60	1·60
350h	O70	15c. brown	2·75	2·40
350i	O70	20c. brown	2·75	2·40
350j	O70	50c. violet	2·00	1·90
350k	O70	1p. orange	2·75	2·40

1932. Nos. O223/25 surch Aereo interior VALE 15 Cts. 1932.

351	39	15c. on 2c. red	1·00	95
352	39	15c. on 6c. purple	1·00	95
353	39	15c. on 10c. blue	1·00	95

78 Pres. Carias and Vice-Pres. Williams

1933. Inauguration of Pres. Carias.

355	78	2c. red	75	60
356	78	6c. green	1·00	70
357	78	10c. blue	1·20	85
358	78	15c. orange	1·50	95

79 Flag of the Race

1933. 441st Anniv of Departure of Columbus from Palos.

359	**79**	2c. blue	90	70
360	**79**	6c. yellow	1·10	85
361	**79**	10c. violet	1·40	1·10
362	**79**	15c. violet	1·90	1·40
363	**79**	50c. red	7·50	6·00
364	**79**	1l. green	12·50	12·00

80 Pres. T. Carias

1935. Inscr as in T **80**.

365	-	1c. green	60	25
366	**80**	2c. red	60	25
367	-	5c. blue	60	35
368	-	6c. brown	60	35

DESIGNS: 1c. Masonic Temple, Tegucigalpa; 5c. National Flag; 6c. Pres. T. E. Palma.

82 Tegucigalpa

1935. Air. Inscr as in T **82**.

369	-	8c. blue	25	25
370	**82**	10c. grey	35	25
371	-	15c. olive	75	25
372	-	20c. green	1·20	60
373	-	40c. brown	1·40	35
374	-	50c. yellow	12·50	4·75
375	-	1l. green	4·50	3·50

DESIGNS: 8c. G.P.O. and Congress Building; 15c. Map of Honduras; 20c. Presidential Palace and Mayol Railway Bridge; 40c. Different view of Tegucigalpa; 50c. Great horned owl; 1l. National Arms.

84 President Carias and Carias Bridge

1937. Re-election of President Carias.

376	**84**	6c. red and olive	1·20	60
377	**84**	21c. green and violet	2·50	1·20
378	**84**	46c. orange and brown	3·00	2·20
379	**84**	55c. blue and black	5·00	3·50

85 Book of the Constitution and Flags of U.S. and Honduras

1937. Air. 150th Anniv of U.S. Constitution.

380	**85**	46c. multicoloured	3·00	1·80

86 Comayagua Cathedral

1937. Air. 400th Anniv of Comayagua.

381	**86**	2c. red	35	25
382	-	8c. blue	75	35
383	-	15c. black	1·10	70
384	-	50c. brown	6·75	3·00

DESIGNS: 8c. Founding of Comayagua; 15c. Portraits of Caceres and Carias; 50c. Lintel of Royal Palace.

90 Arms of Honduras   **91** Copan Ruins

1939. Dated "1939 1942".

385	**90**	1c. yellow (postage)	25	25

386	-	2c. red	25	25
387	-	3c. red	35	25
388	-	5c. orange	50	35
389	-	8c. blue	60	50

DESIGNS: 2c. Central District Palace; 3c. Map of Honduras; 5c. Choluteca Bridge; 8c. National flag.

390	**91**	10c. brown (air)	35	10
391	-	15c. blue	50	10
392	-	21c. slate	85	10
393	-	30c. green	1·10	25
394	-	40c. violet	1·90	25
395	-	46c. brown	1·90	1·10
396	-	55c. green	2·40	1·40
397	-	66c. black	3·75	2·10
398	-	1l. olive	4·25	1·30
399	-	2l. red	6·25	4·25

DESIGNS: 15c. Pres. Carias; 21c. Mayan Temple; 30c. J. C. del Valle; 40c. The Presidency; 46c. Statue of Lempira; 55c. Suyapa Church; 66c. J. T. Reyes; 1l. Choluteca Hospital; 2l. R. Rosa.

92 Flags of Honduras, U.S.A., and Francisco Morazan

1940. Air. 50th Anniv of Pan-American Union. Sheet 130×114 mm containing T **92** and similar multicoloured designs with different inset portraits.

MS399a	14c. Type **92**; 16c. Washington, J.C. del Valle; 40c. Bolivar	5·50	5·50

1940. Air. Dedication of Columbus Memorial Lighthouse. Official stamps optd **Correo Aereo Habilitado para Servicio Publico Pro-Faro-Colon-1940**.

400	**O92**	2c. blue and green	25	25
401	**O92**	5c. blue and orange	35	35
402	**O92**	8c. blue and brown	35	35
403	**O92**	15c. blue and red	75	70
404	**O92**	46c. blue and olive	1·00	95
405	**O92**	50c. blue and violet	1·20	1·20
406	**O92**	1l. blue and brown	5·00	4·75
407	**O92**	2l. blue and red	11·00	11·00

97 Francisco Morazan

1941. Obligatory Tax. Death Centenary of Gen. Morazan.

408	**97**	1c. brown	60	25

98 Red Cross

1941. Obligatory Tax. Red Cross.

409	**98**	1c. blue and red	35	25

1941. Air. Official stamps optd **Habilitada para el Servicio Publico 1941**.

410	**O92**	5c. blue and orange	5·00	35
411	**O92**	8c. blue and brown	7·50	35

1941. Air. Official stamps surch **Rehabilitada para el Servicio Publico 1941 Vale** and value in words.

412	3c. on 2c. blue and green	60	35
413	8c. on 2c. blue and green	75	60
414	8c. on 15c. blue and red	75	25
415	8c. on 46c. blue & olive	1·20	70
416	8c. on 50c. blue & violet	1·50	70
417	8c. on 1l. blue & brown	2·00	1·40
418	8c. on 2l. blue and red	2·50	2·20

1942. Air. Surch **Correo Aereo** and value.

419	8c. on 15c. blue (No. 391)	1·20	35
420	16c. on 46c. brown (No. 395)	1·20	35

102 Morazan's Birthplace   **103** Tomb

1942. Air. Death Centenary of Gen. Morazan.

421	-	2c. orange	25	10
422	-	5c. blue	25	10
423	**102**	8c. purple	25	10
424	**103**	14c. black	50	35
425	-	16c. olive	25	25
426	-	21c. blue	1·60	1·20

427	-	1l. blue	4·25	3·50
428	-	2l. brown	11·00	10·50

DESIGNS—HORIZ: 2c. Commemoration plate; 5c. Battle of La Trinidad; 16c. Morazan's monument (as in Type **36**); 21c. Church where Morazan was baptised; 1l. Arms of C. American Federation. VERT: 2l. Morazan.

105 Coat of Arms   **106** Western Hemisphere

1943. Air.

429	**105**	1c. green	25	25
430	-	2c. blue	25	25
431	-	5c. green	50	25
432	-	6c. green	35	25
433	-	8c. purple	35	25
434	-	10c. brown	50	25
435	-	15c. red	50	25
436	-	16c. red	60	25
437	-	21c. blue	1·00	25
438	-	30c. brown	75	25
439	-	40c. red	75	25
440	-	55c. black	1·50	85
441	-	1l. brown	2·50	2·20
442	**106**	2l. lake	8·00	5·50
443	-	5l. orange	20·00	19·00

DESIGNS—HORIZ: 2c. National flag; 5c. Cattle; 8c. Rosario; 15c. Tobacco plant; 21c. Orchid; 30c. Oranges; 40c. Wheat; 5l. Map of Honduras. VERT: 6c. Banana Tree; 10c. Pine tree; 16c. Sugar cane; 55c. Coconut palms; 1l. Maize.

114 Agricultural College

1944. Air. Inauguration of Pan-American Agricultural College.

444	**114**	21c. green	60	35

1944. Optd **HABILITADO 1944-45**.

445	**90**	1c. yellow	50	50
446	-	2c. red (No. 386)	1·60	95

1945. Air. Surch **Correo Aereo HABILITADO Acd. No 798-1945** and value.

447	1c. on 50c. (No. 384)	10	10
448	**86**	2c. on 2c. red	10	10
449	8c. on 15c. (No. 383)	25	25
450	**91**	10c. on 10c. brown	60	50
451	15c. on 15c. (No. 391)	35	25
452	30c. on 21c. (No. 392)	7·50	4·75
453	40c. on 40c. (No. 394)	3·00	1·70
454	1l. on 46c. (No. 395)	3·00	2·40
455	2l. on 66c. (No. 397)	7·50	4·75

1945. Air. Allied Victory in Europe. MS399a optd **VICTORIA DE LAS NACIONES UNIDAS ALEMANIA SE RINDE INCONDICIONALMENTE 8 DE MAYO DE 1945 ACDO. No. 1231 QUE AUTORIZA LA CONTRAMARCA**.

MS455a 103×114 mm	6·25	4·75

117 Flag, mother and child

1945. Obligatory Tax. Red Cross.

456	**117**	1c. brown and red	35	25
456a	-	1c. red and brown	35	25

DESIGN: No. 456a, Red Cross.

118 Arms of Honduras

1946. Air. Coats of Arms.

457	**118**	1c. red	25	25
458	-	2c. orange	25	25
459	-	5c. violet	35	25
461	-	15c. purple	1·00	25
462	-	21c. blue	1·20	35
463	-	1l. green	4·25	1·90
464	-	2l. grey	7·50	3·50

ARMS: 2c. Von Gracias and Trujillo; 5c. Comayagua and S. J. de Olancho; 15c. Comayagua and S. J. de Puerto Caballos; 21c. Comayagua and Tencoa; 1l. Jerez de la Frontera de Choluteca and San Pedro de Zula; 2l. San Miguel de Heredia de Tegucigalpa.

119 Broken Column and F. D. Roosevelt

1946. Air. Allied Victory over Japan and Death of Pres. Roosevelt. (a) Inscr "F.D.R.".

460	**119**	8c. brown	1·20	60

(b) Inscr "FRANKLIN D. ROOSEVELT".

465	8c. brown	75	35

120 Honduras and Copan Antiquities

1947. Air. First International Conference of Caribbean Archaeologists. Various frames.

466	**120**	16c. brown	35	25
467	**120**	22c. yellow	60	35
468	**120**	40c. orange	1·20	95
469	**120**	1l. blue	1·50	1·20
470	**120**	2l. mauve	6·25	4·75
471	**120**	5l. brown	15·00	11·00

121 Flag and Arms of Honduras   **122** Galvez, Carias and Lozano

123 National Stadium   **124** President Galvez

1949. Air. Inauguration of President Juan Manuel Galvez. Inscr "CONMEMORATIVA DE LA SUCESION PRESIDENCIAL", etc.

472	**121**	1c. blue	10	10
473	**124**	2c. red	10	10
474	-	5c. blue	10	10
475	-	9c. brown	10	10
476	-	15c. brown	10	10
477	**122**	21c. black	25	25
478	**123**	30c. olive	1·20	60
479	-	40c. grey	25	25
480	-	1l. brown	1·90	1·20
481	-	2l. violet	5·00	3·25
482	-	5l. brown	12·50	7·25

DESIGNS—HORIZ: 40c. Toncontin Customs House; 5l. Galvez and Lozano. VERT: 5c., 15c. Lozano (different frames); 9c. Galvez; 1l. Palace of Tegucigalpa; 2l. Carias.

1951. Air. 75th Anniv of U.P.U. Optd **U.P.U. 75 Aniversario 1874-1949**.

483	**120**	16c. green	1·00	60
484	-	22c. yellow	1·20	95
485	-	40c. orange	1·20	1·20
486	-	1l. blue	3·00	1·80
487	-	2l. mauve	6·25	4·75
488	-	5l. brown	37·00	30·00
MS488a 103×114 mm. Imperf	£375	£350

1951. Air. Founding of Central Bank. Nos. 472/81 optd **Conmemorativa Fundacion Banco Central Administracion Galvez–Lozano Julio 1o. de 1950**.

489	1c. blue	10	10
490	2c. red	10	10
491	5c. blue	10	10
492	9c. brown	10	10
493	15c. brown	25	10
494	21c. black	35	25
495	30c. olive	75	60
496	40c. grey	1·20	85
497	1l. brown	3·75	1·90
498	2l. violet	9·50	6·25

127 Discovery of America

128 Isabella the Catholic

1952. Air. 500th Anniv of Birth of Isabella the Catholic.

499	127	1c. slate and orange	10	10
500	-	2c. brown and blue	10	10
501	-	8c. sepia and green	25	25
502	128	16c. black and blue	75	60
503	-	30c. green and violet	1·20	1·20
504	-	1l. black and red	2·50	1·90
505	127	2l. violet and brown	5·25	4·25
506	128	5l. olive and purple	10·50	9·50

DESIGNS—HORIZ: 2c.1l. King Ferdinand and Queen Isabella receive Columbus; 8c. Surrender of Granada; 30c. Queen Isabella pledging her jewels.

1953. Air. Surch **HABILITADO 1953** and value.

507	122	5c. on 21c. black	35	10
508	122	8c. on 21c. black	75	25
509	122	16c. on 21c. black	1·40	50

1953. Air. Nos. O507/509 and O512/14 surch **HABILITADO 1953** and value or optd only.

510	127	10c. on 1c. olive & purple	25	10
511	127	12c. on 1c. olive & purple	25	25
512	-	15c. on 2c. violet & brn	35	25
513	-	20c. on 2c. violet & brn	75	60
514	-	24c. on 2c. violet & brn	75	60
515	-	25c. on 2c. violet & brn	75	60
516	-	30c. on 8c. black and red	75	60
517	-	35c. on 8c. black and red	85	70
518	-	50c. on 8c. black and red	1·20	95
519	-	60c. on 8c. black and red	1·60	1·20
520	-	1l. sepia and green	3·50	2·75
521	127	2l. brown and blue	8·25	6·50
522	128	5l. slate and orange	20·00	17·00

130 U.N. Emblem

1953. Air. United Nations. Inscr as in T **130**.

523	-	1c. blue and black	10	10
524	130	2c. blue and black	10	10
525	-	3c. violet and black	25	10
526	-	5c. green and black	25	10
527	-	15c. brown and black	60	35
528	-	30c. brown and black	1·20	70
529	-	1l. red and black	10·00	70
530	-	2l. orange and black	12·50	95
531	-	5l. green and black	25·00	18·00

DESIGNS: 1c. U.N. and Honduras flags; 3c. U.N. Building, New York; 5c. Arms of U.S.A.; 15c. Pres. J. M. Galvez; 30c. Indian girl (U.N.I.C.E.F.); 1l. Refugee mother and child (U.N.R.R.A.); 2l. Torch and open book (U.N.E.S.C.O.); 5l. Cornucopia (F.A.O.).

1955. Air. 50th Anniv of Rotary International. Nos. O532/38 optd with rotary emblem, **1905 1955**, clasped hands and laurel sprigs or surch also.

532		1c. blue and black	25	25
533		2c. green and black	25	25
534		3c. orange and black	25	25
535		5c. red and black	25	25
536		8c. on 1c. blue and black	25	25
537		10c. on 2c. green and black	25	25
538		12c. on 3c. orange and black	35	25
539		15c. sepia and black	35	35
540		30c. purple and black	1·50	1·20
541		1l. olive and black	27·00	24·00

1956. Air. Tenth Anniv of U.N.O. Nos. O523/5 and 527/31 optd **ONU X ANIVERSARIO 1945-1955**.

542		1c. blue and black	25	25
543		2c. green and black	25	25
544		3c. orange and black	35	25
545		5c. red and black	35	35
546		15c. brown and black	50	35
547		30c. brown and black	75	60
548		1l. red and black	5·50	3·75
549		2l. orange and black	8·00	7·25
550		5l. green and black	21·00	19·00

133 J. Lozano Diaz

134 Southern Highway

1956. Air.

551	-	1c. blue and black	25	25
552	133	2c. blue and black	25	25
553	134	3c. sepia and black	25	25
554	-	4c. purple and black	25	25
555	-	5c. red and black	25	25
556	-	8c. multicoloured	25	25
557	-	10c. green and black	25	25
558	-	12c. green and black	25	25
559	-	15c. black and red	25	25
560	-	20c. blue and black	25	25
561	133	24c. purple and black	35	25
562	-	25c. green and black	35	35
563	-	30c. red and black	50	35
564	-	40c. brown and black	60	35
565	-	50c. turquoise and black	75	50
566	-	60c. orange and black	1·00	70
567	-	1l. purple and black	2·50	1·60
568	-	2l. red and black	5·00	3·50
569	-	5l. lake and black	10·50	7·75

DESIGNS—HORIZ: 1c. Suyapa Basilica; 8c. Landscape and cornucopia; 10c. National Stadium; 12c. United States School; 15c. Projected Central Bank of Honduras; 20c. Legislative Building; 25c. Projected Development Bank; 30c. Toncontin Airport; 40c. J. R. Molina Bridge; 60c. Treasury Building; 1l. Blood Bank. VERT: 4c. Dona de Estrada Palma; 5c. Dona de Morazan; 50c. Peace Memorial; 2l. Electrical Communications Building; 5l. Presidential Palace.

135 Revolutionary Flag

1957. Air. Revolution of October 21, 1956. Frames in black.

570	135	1c. blue and yellow	10	10
571	-	2c. purple, green & orange	10	10
572	135	5c. blue and pink	25	10
573	-	8c. violet, olive and orange	25	10
574	-	10c. brown and violet	25	25
575	135	12c. blue and turquoise	35	25
576	-	15c. brown and green	60	35
577	-	30c. grey and pink	75	60
578	-	1l. brown and blue	3·75	2·10
579	-	2l. grey and green	6·25	3·75

DESIGNS: 2c., 8c. Obelisk and mountains; 10c., 15c., 1l. Indian with bow and arrow; 30c., 2l. Arms of 1821.

NOTE.—In July 1958 after stocks of current issues had been looted, eighteen different facsimile signatures validated the remaining stamps for use.

136 Flags of Honduras and the U.S.A. and Book

1958. Air. Bi-national Centre Commemoration. (Institute of American Culture). Flags in national colours.

580	136	1c. blue	25	10
581	136	2c. red	25	10
582	136	5c. green	25	10
583	136	10c. brown	35	25
584	136	20c. orange	60	35
585	136	30c. red	75	50
586	136	50c. grey	1·00	60
587	136	1l. yellow	2·00	1·70
588	136	2l. olive	3·25	2·75
589	136	5l. blue	7·50	6·00

137 Abraham Lincoln

1959. Air. 150th Birth Anniv of Abraham Lincoln. Flags in blue and red.

590	137	1c. green	25	25
591	-	2c. blue	25	25
592	-	3c. violet	25	25
593	-	5c. red	25	25
594	-	10c. slate	35	25
595	-	12c. sepia	35	25
596	137	15c. orange	50	25
597	-	25c. purple	85	35
598	-	50c. blue	1·10	70
599	-	1l. brown	2·50	1·60
600	-	2l. olive	4·00	2·40
601	-	5l. yellow	8·00	5·50

MS601a 180×140 mm. As Nos. 590, 592, 594, 597, 599 and 601. Imperf — 15·00 12·00

DESIGNS—HORIZ: 2c., 25c. Lincoln's birthplace; 3c., 50c. Gettysburg Address; 5c., 1l. Lincoln at conference to free slaves; 10c., 2l. Assassination of Lincoln; 12c., 5l. Lincoln Memorial, Washington.

138 Henri Dunant

1959. Obligatory Tax. Red Cross.

602	138	1c. red and blue	35	25
647	138	1c. red and green	35	25
648	138	1c. red and brown	35	25

Nos. 647/8 have no frame around portrait and values are at left.

139 Constitution of 21 December 1957

1959. Air. Second Anniv of New Constitution. Inscr "21 DE DICIEMBRE DE 1957".

603	139	1c. red, blue and brown	10	10
604	-	2c. brown	10	10
605	-	3c. blue	10	10
606	-	5c. orange	25	10
607	139	10c. red, blue and green	35	25
608	-	12c. red	50	25
609	-	25c. violet	1·20	70
610	-	50c. grey-blue	2·20	95

DESIGNS—HORIZ: 2, 12c. Inaug of Pres. R. V. Morales. VERT: 3, 25c. Pres. R. V. Morales; 5, 50c. Flaming torch.

140 King Alfonso XIII of Spain and Map

1961. Air. Settlement of Boundary Dispute with Nicaragua.

611	140	1c. blue	10	10
612	-	2c. pink	1·10	70
613	-	5c. green	25	25
614	-	10c. brown	25	25
615	-	20c. red	60	60
616	-	50c. brown	1·40	85
617	-	1l. slate	2·20	1·70

DESIGNS: 2c. 1906 award (document); 5c. Arbitration commission, 1907; 10c. International Court of Justice, The Hague; 20c. 1960 award (document); 50c. Pres. Morales Foreign Minister Puerto and map; 1l. Presidents Davila and Morales.

1964. Air. Freedom from Hunger. Flags in National colours. Optd **FAO Luncha Contra el Hambre**.

621	136	1c. blue	25	25
622	136	2c. red	25	25
623	136	5c. green	35	35
624	136	30c. red	1·90	1·80
625	136	2l. olive	8·00	7·75

1964. Air. Olympic Games, Tokyo. Optd with Olympic Rings and **1964**.

626	-	1c. blue & black (No. 523)	25	25
627	130	2c. blue and black	35	35
628	-	3c. violet & blk (No. 525)	60	60
629	-	5c. brn & blk (No. 527)	1·20	1·20

See also No. O646.

144 Ancient Stadium

1964. Air. "Homage to Sport" and Olympic Games, Tokyo.

630	144	1c. black and green	10	10
631	-	2c. black and mauve	25	10
632	-	5c. black and blue	25	10
633	-	8c. black and grey-green	35	25
634	144	10c. black and bistre	75	60
635	-	12c. black and yellow	1·00	60
636	-	1l. black and buff	3·00	1·80
637	-	2l. black and olive	6·75	6·00
638	144	3l. black and red	8·75	8·50

MS638a 130×110 mm. Nos. 632/3, 635 and 638 — 60·00 60·00

DESIGNS: 2c., 12c. Boundary stones; 5c., 1l. Mayan ball player; 8c., 2l. Olympic Stadium, Tokyo.

1964. Air. Surch.

639	-	4c. on 5c. (No. 593)	25	25
618	137	6c. on 15c.	35	25
619	-	8c. on 25c. (No. 597)	50	25
640	-	10c. on 15c. (No. 476)	25	25
620	-	10c. on 50c. (No. 598)	60	35
641	-	12c. on 16c. (No. 425)	35	25
642	-	12c. on 21c. (No. 426)	35	35
643	120	12c. on 22c.	35	35
644	120	30c. on 1l.	85	50
645	-	40c. on 1l. (No. 480)	1·20	85
646	120	40c. on 2l.	1·20	85

See also Nos. 716/18 and O647/18.

1965. Air. Presidential Investiture of General Lopez. Optd **Toma de Posesion General Oswaldo Lopez A. Junio 6, 1965**. Flags in blue and red.

649	137	1c. green	10	10
650	-	2c. green	10	10
651	-	3c. violet (No. 592)	25	25
652	-	5c. red (No. 593)	25	25
653	137	15c. orange	35	25
654	-	25c. purple (No. 597)	60	50
655	-	50c. red	1·20	1·10
656	-	2l. olive (No. 600)	4·50	3·75
657	-	5l. yellow (No. 601)	10·00	9·00

147 Ambulance and Clinic

1965. Air. Order of Malta Campaign Against Leprosy.

658	147	1c. blue	60	60
659	-	5c. green	60	60
660	-	12c. black	85	85
661	-	1l. brown	3·25	3·25

DESIGNS: 5c. Hospital; 12c. Patients receiving treatment; 1l. Map of Honduras.

148 Father Subirana

1965. Air. Death Cent of Father Manuel de Jesus Subirana. Centres in black and gold; inscr in black.

662	-	1c. violet	10	10
663	-	2c. flesh	10	10
664	148	8c. pink	25	25
665	-	10c. purple	25	25
666	-	12c. brown	35	35
667	-	20c. green	75	60
668	-	1l. sage	3·00	2·75
669	-	2l. blue	5·50	4·50

MS670 99×148 mm. Nos. 664, 666 and 668/9 — 31·00 24·00

DESIGNS: 1c. Abraham, Jicaque Indian; 2c. Allegory of Catechism; 10c. Msgr. Juan de Jesus Zepeda; 12c. Pope Pius IX; 20c. Subirana's Tomb, Yoro; 1l. Hermitage; 2l. Jicaque Indian woman and child.

1965. Air. Churchill Commemoration. Nos. 499/500 and 470 optd **IN MEMORIAM Sir Winston Churchill 1874-1965**.

671	127	1c. black and orange	60	60
672	-	2c. brown and blue	1·20	1·20
673	-	2l. mauve	10·50	10·50

See also No. O674.

1966. Air. Pope Paul's Visit to U.N. Organisation. Nos. 662/68 optd **CONMEMORATIVA Visita S. S. Pablo VI a la ONU. 4-X-1965**.

675	-	1c. violet	10	10
676	-	2c. flesh	10	10
677	148	8c. pink	35	25
678	-	10c. purple	60	35
679	-	12c. brown	60	35
680	-	20c. green	85	70
681	-	1l. sage	5·00	4·25

151 2r. Stamp of
1866

1966. Air. Stamp Centenary. Inscriptions in black (1c., 2c.)
or in gold (others).

682	**151**	1c. black, green and gold	10	10
683	-	2c. blue, black and orange	10	10
684	-	3c. purple and red	25	10
685	-	4c. indigo and blue	25	10
686	-	5c. purple and mauve	4·50	1·30
687	-	6c. violet and lilac	25	25
688	-	7c. slate and turquoise	25	25
689	-	8c. indigo and blue	25	25
690	-	9c. blue and cobalt	25	25
691	-	10c. black and olive	25	25
692	-	12c. yellow, black & green	25	25
693	-	15c. purple and mauve	35	35
694	-	20c. black and orange	35	35
695	-	30c. blue and yellow	75	60
696	-	40c. multicoloured	1·10	95
697	-	1l. green and emerald	2·75	1·70
698	-	2l. black and grey	5·50	4·00
MS699		139×121 mm. Nos. 682/3, 691/2 and 697/8	6·75	6·75

DESIGNS—VERT: 2c. Honduras; 5c. air stamp of 1925; 3c.
T. Estrada Palma, 1st Director of Posts; 8c. Sir Rowland
Hill; 10c. Pres. Arellano; 12c. Postal emblem; 15c. H. von
Stephan; 30c. Honduras flag; 40c. Honduras arms; 1l.
U.P.U. Monument, Berne; 2l. J. M. Medina (statesman).
HORIZ: 4c. Post Office, Tegucigalpa; 5c. Steam locomotive
No. 59; 6c. 19th-century mule transport; 7c. 19th-century
sorting office; 9c. Mail van; 20c. Curtiss C-46 Commando
mail plane.

See also No. E700.

1966. Air. World Cup Football Championship, Final
Match between England and West Germany. Optd
**CAMPEONATO DE FOOTBALL Copa Mundial 1966
Inglaterra-Alemania Wembley, Julio 30.**

701		2c. vio & brn (No. O508)	25	25
702	**128**	16c. black and blue	60	60
703	**127**	2l. violet and brown	13·50	13·50

1967. Air. 20th Anniv of U.N.O. Nos. 662/4 and 666/9
optd **CONMEMORATIVA del XX Aniversario ONU
1966.**

704	-	1c. violet	25	25
705	-	2c. flesh	25	25
706	**148**	8c. pink	35	25
707	-	12c. brown	50	25
708	-	20c. green	60	25
709	-	1l. sage	1·90	60
710	-	2l. blue	5·25	5·00

1967. Birth Bicentenary of Simeon Canas y Villacorta
(slave liberator). Nos. 551, 553, 559, 552 and 568.
Optd **Simeon Canas y Villacorta Libertador de los
esclavos en Centro America 1767-1967.**

711		1c. blue and black	25	25
712		3c. sepia and black	50	35
713		15c. black and red	85	70
714		25c. green and black	1·60	1·20
715		2l. red and black	3·75	3·00

1967. Air. Nos. E570 and 480/1 surch.

716	**E135**	10c. on 20c. grey, black and red	60	25
717	-	10c. on 1l. brown	60	25
718	-	10c. on 2l. violet	60	25

156 J. C. del Valle
(Honduras)

1967. Air. Founding of Central-American Journalists'
Federation.

719	**156**	11c. black, blue and gold	25	25
720	-	12c. black, yellow and blue	25	25
721	-	14c. black, green and silver	25	25
722	-	20c. black, green & mauve	25	25
723	-	30c. black, yellow and lilac	35	25
724	-	40c. gold, blue and violet	1·50	1·20
725	-	50c. green, red and olive	1·60	1·20

DESIGNS: 12c. Ruben Dario (Nicaragua); 14c. J. B. Mon-
tufar (Guatemala); 20c. F. Gavidia (El Salvador); 30c. J.
M. Fernandez (Costa Rica); 40c. Federation emblem; 50c.
Central American map.

157 Olympic Rings and
Flags of Mexico and
Honduras

1968. Air. Olympic Games, Mexico. Multicoloured.

726		1c. Type **157**	25	25
727		2c. Type **157**	35	35
728		5c. Italian flag and boxing	60	60
729		10c. French flag and skiing	75	70
730		12c. West German flag and show-jumping	85	85
731		50c. British flag and athletics	5·25	5·00
732		1l. U.S. flag and running	8·00	7·75
MS733		110×70 mm. **157** 20c. multicol-oured; 40c. multicoloured	12·50	12·00

158 J. F. Kennedy and
Rocket Launch

1968. Air. International Telecommunications Union
Centenary. Multicoloured.

734		1c. Type **158**	25	25
735		2c. Dish aerial and telephone	25	25
736		3c. Dish aerial and television	25	25
737		5c. Dish aerial, globe and I.T.U. emblem as satellite	60	60
738		8c. "Early Bird" satellite	85	85
739		10c. Type **158**	1·00	95
740		20c. Type **158**	1·20	1·20

1969. Air. Robert F. Kennedy Commemoration. Nos. 734
and 739/40 optd **In-Memoriam Robert F. Kennedy
1925-1968.**

741		1c. multicoloured	75	50
742		10c. multicoloured	75	50
743		20c. multicoloured	75	50

1969. Air. Gold Medal Winners, Olympic Games. Nos.
735/8 optd **Medallas de Oro Mexico 1968.**

744		2c. multicoloured	50	35
745		3c. multicoloured	75	65
746		5c. multicoloured	1·20	1·00
747		8c. multicoloured	1·80	1·60

161 Patient and
Nurse

1969. Obligatory Tax. Red Cross.

748	**161**	1c. red and blue	35	25

162 Rocket Launch

1969. Air. First Man on the Moon. Multicoloured.

749		5c. Type **162**	10	10
750		10c. Moon	25	10
751		12c. Lunar landing module leaving space-ship (horiz)	35	10
752		20c. Astronaut on Moon (horiz)	85	35
753		24c. Lunar landing module taking off from Moon	1·10	60
754		30c. Capsule re-entering Earth's atmosphere (horiz)	1·60	85

1970. No. E700 optd with **"HABILITADO"** for use as
ordinary postage stamp.

755		20c. brown, orange and gold	1·20	95

1970. Air. Various stamps surch in figures.

756	**151**	4c.+1c. (No. 682)	35	25
757		4c.+3c. (No. 525)	35	25
758	-	5c.+1c. (No. 662)	50	25
759		5c.+7c. (No. 688)	35	25
760		8c.+2c. (No. 663)	1·00	50
761	-	10c.+2c. (No. 500)	1·20	60
762	**133**	10c.+2c. (No. 552)	1·20	60
763	-	10c.+3c. (No. 553)	1·20	60
764	**134**	10c.+3c. (No. 553)	1·20	60
765	-	10c.+3c. (No. 684)	1·20	60
766	-	10c.+9c. (No. 690)	50	25

767	**156**	10c.+11c. (No. 719)	50	25
768	-	12c.+14c. (No. 721)	60	35
769	**E135**	12c.+20c. (No. E570)	60	35
770	-	12c.+1l. (No. 480)	60	35
771	-	15c.+12c. (No. 783)	1·60	85
772	-	30c.+12c. (No. 783)	2·00	1·20
773	-	40c.+24c. (No. 753)	3·25	2·40
774	-	40c.+50c. (No. 731)	3·25	2·40

1970. Air. Safe Return of "Apollo 13". Nos. 749/54 optd
**Admiracion al Rescate del Apolo XIII, James A.
Lovell, Fred W. Haise Jr., John L. Swigert Jr.**

775	-	10c. multicoloured	10	10
776	-	10c. multicoloured	25	25
777	-	12c. multicoloured	35	25
778	-	20c. multicoloured	60	50
779	-	24c. multicoloured	75	60
780	-	30c. multicoloured	1·20	1·10

165 J. A. Sanhueza
(firefighter)

1970. Air. Campaign Against Forest Fires. Multicoloured.

781		5c. Type **165**	25	25
782		8c. R. Ordonez Rodriguez (firefighter)	35	25
783		12c. Fire Brigade emblems (horiz)	50	25
784		20c. Flag, map and emblems	75	50
785		1l. Emblems, and flags of Hon-duras, U.N. and U.S.A.	4·25	2·40
MS786		120×130 mm. Nos. 781/4 (sold at 1l.45). Imperf	4·25	3·50

166 Hotel Honduras
Maya

1970. Air. Opening of Hotel Honduras Maya, Tegucigalpa.

787	**166**	12c. black and blue	60	35

1972. Air. 50th Anniv of Honduras Masonic Grand Lodge.
Nos. 749 and 751/3. optd **Aniversario Gran Logia
de Honduras 1922-1972** or surch also.

791		5c. multicoloured	1·20	60
792		12c. multicoloured	1·60	1·10
793		1l. on 20c. multicoloured	4·25	3·25
794		2l. on 24c. multicoloured	8·00	6·25

168 Soldiers' Bay, Guanaja

1972. Air. 150th Anniv of Independence (1970).
Multicoloured.

795		4c. Type **168**	25	10
796		5c. Bugler sounding "Last Post" (vert)	25	10
797		6c. Lake Yojoa	25	10
798		7c. *The Banana Carrier* (R. Aguilar) (vert)	25	10
799		8c. Soldiers marching and fly-past	35	10
800		9c. *Brassavola digbyana* (na-tional flower) (vert)	35	10
801		10c. As 9c.	50	25
802		12c. Machine-gunner	50	25
803		15c. Tela beach at sunset	60	25
804		20c. Stretcher-bearers	60	25
805		30c. *San Antonio de Oriente* (A. Velasquez)	85	60
806		40c. Ruins of Copan	1·50	70
807		50c. *Woman from Huacal* (P. Zelaya Sierra)	1·50	70
808		1l. Trujillo Bay	3·50	2·40
809		2l. As 9c.	4·25	3·00
MS810		Four sheets each 122×112 mm. (a) Nos. 795, 799, 802 and 808; (b) Nos. 796/7, 804 and 807; (c) Nos. 798, 803 and 805/6; (d) Nos. 800/1 and 809 Set of four sheets	16·00	16·00

169 Sister Maria
Rosa and Child

1972. Air. "S.O.S." Children's Villages in Honduras. Each
brown, green and gold.

812		10c. Type **169**	35	25
813		15c. "S.O.S. Villages" emblem (horiz)	60	35
814		30c. Father J. T. Reyes (educa-tionalist)	75	50
815		40c. First Central American "S.O.S." village (horiz)	85	60
816		1l. "Future Citizen" (boy)	2·50	1·90

170 Map of Honduras

1973. Air. 25th Anniv of National Cartographic Service
(10c.) and Joint Cartographic Work (12c.).

817	**170**	10c. multicoloured	75	50
818	-	12c. multicoloured	1·00	70

DESIGN: 12c. Similar to Type **170** but with two badges
and inscr "25 Anos de Labor Cartografica Conjunta".

171 Illustration from
Habitante de la Osa

1973. Air. 25th Anniv of U.N.E.S.C.O. and Juan Ramon
Molina (poet) Commem. Multicoloured.

819	**171**	8c. Type **171**	35	10
820		20c. Juan Ramon Molina	1·00	60
821		1l. Illustration from *Tierras Mares y Cielos*	2·50	1·40
822		2l. U.N.E.S.C.O. emblem	4·25	3·25
MS823		140×128 mm. Nos. 819/22	9·25	8·50

1973. Air. Census and World Population Year. Various
stamps optd **Censos de Poblacion y Vivienda,
marzo 1974. 1974 Ano Mundial de Poblacion.**

824	**169**	10c. brown, green and gold	25	25
828	**170**	10c. multicoloured	25	25
829	-	12c. mult (No. 818)	25	25
825	-	15c. brown, green and gold (No. 813)	25	25
826	-	30c. brown, green and gold (No. 814)	60	50
827	-	40c. brown, green and gold (No. 815)	60	50

1974. Air. Various stamps surch.

830		2c. on 1c. blue and black (No. 551)	25	10
831	**137**	2c. on 1c. green	25	10
832	-	3c. on 1c. blue and black (No. 551)	25	10
833	**137**	3c. on 1c. green	25	10
834	-	16c. on 1c. bl & blk (551)	25	10
835	**135**	16c. on 1c. bl, yell & blk	25	10
836	**137**	16c. on 1c. green	25	10
837	-	16c. on 1c. mult (O602)	75	50
838	-	16c. on 1c. violet (662)	25	10
841	**171**	18c. on 8c. mult	35	25
839	**170**	18c. on 10c. mult	35	25
842	**169**	18c. on 10c. mult	35	25
840	-	18c. on 12c. mult (818)	85	25
843	-	50c. on 30c. mult (814)	1·20	35
847	-	1l. on 30c. mult (814)	2·10	1·40
846	-	1l. on 50c. blue (610)	2·50	1·90
844	**137**	1l. on 2l. mauve	2·50	1·90
845	-	1l. on 2l. violet (No. 481)	2·50	1·90

1974. Air. Honduras' Children's Villages. 25th Anniv.
Nos. 786/9 optd **1949-1974 SOS Kinderdorfer
Internacional Honduras-Austria.**

851	**169**	10c. multicoloured	25	10
852	-	15c. multicoloured	50	35
853	-	30c. multicoloured	60	50
854	-	40c. multicoloured	85	70

175 Flags of West
Germany and Austria

1975. Air. Centenary (1974) of U.P.U. Multicoloured.

855	1c. Type **175**		25	25
856	2c. Belgium and Denmark		25	25
857	3c. Spain and France		25	25
858	4c. Hungary and Russia		25	25
859	5c. Great Britain and Italy		25	25
860	10c. Norway and Sweden		25	25
861	12c. Honduras		35	35
862	15c. United States and Switzerland		50	50
863	20c. Greece and Portugal		60	60
864	30c. Rumania and Yugoslavia		1·10	1·10
865	1l. Egypt and France		2·75	2·75
866	2l. Luxembourg and Turkey		5·50	5·50
MS867	150×122 mm. As Nos. 855/66 but different backgrounds		19·00	18·00

176 Jalteva Youth Centre

1976. Air. International Women's Year (1975). Multicoloured.

868	8c. Humuya Youth Centre		25	10
869	16c. Type **176**		35	25
870	18c. Sra Arellano and I.W.Y. emblem		35	25
871	30c. El Carmen Youth Centre, San Pedro Sula		60	35
872	55c. Flag of National Social Welfare Organization (vert)		1·10	85
873	1l. Sports and recreation grounds, La Isla		1·80	1·20
874	2l. Women's Social Centre		4·25	2·50

177 "CARE"
Package

1976. Air. 20th Anniv of "CARE" (Co-operative for American Relief Everywhere) in Honduras.

875	**177**	1c. blue and black	10	10
876	-	5c. mauve and black	10	10
877	**177**	16c. red and black	25	25
878	-	18c. green and black	35	25
879	**177**	30c. blue and black	60	50
880	-	50c. green and black	1·00	70
881	**177**	55c. brown and black	1·00	70
882	-	70c. purple and black	1·20	95
883	**177**	1l. blue and black	1·70	1·20
884	-	2l. orange and black	3·75	2·50

DESIGN—HORIZ: 5c., 18c., 50c., 70c., 2l. "CARE" on globe. Each of the above stamps has a different inscription detailing "CARE's" various fields of activities in Honduras.

178 White-tailed
Deer in Burnt
Forest

1976. Air. Forest Protection. Multicoloured.

885	10c. Type **178**		25	10
886	16c. COHDEFOR emblem		25	25
887	18c. Forest stream (horiz)		35	25
888	30c. Live and burning trees		75	35
889	50c. Type **178**		1·00	70
890	70c. Protection emblem		1·40	95
891	1l. Forest of young trees (horiz)		1·80	1·40
892	2l. As 30c.		4·25	3·00

COHDEFOR = Corporacion Hondurena de Desarollo Forestal.

179 Boston Tea
Party and "Liberty"
Flag

1976. Air. Bicentenary of American Revolution. Multicoloured.

894	1c. Type **179**		10	10
895	2c. Hoisting the "Liberty and Union" flag		10	10
896	3c. Battle of Bunker Hill and Pine Tree flag		10	10
897	4c. Loading stores aboard *Washington* and "An Appeal to Heaven" flag		10	10
898	5c. First naval ensign and navy warship		35	35
899	6c. Presidential Palace, Tegucigalpa, and Honduras flag		25	25
900	18c. Capitol, Washington and U.S. flag		75	70
901	55c. Washington at Valley Forge and Grand Union flag		1·00	95
902	2l. Battle scene and Bennington flag		3·50	3·25
903	3l. Betsy Ross flag		5·75	5·75
MS904	Three sheets each 110×85 mm. (a) Nos. 896 and 899/901; (b) Nos. 894, 897 and 902; (c) Nos. 895, 898 and 903. Imperf		19·00	18·00

180 Queen Sophia
of Spain

1977. Air. Visit of King and Queen of Spain. Multicoloured.

905	16c. Type **180**		25	25
906	18c. King Juan Carlos		25	25
907	30c. Queen Sophia and King Juan Carlos		60	50
908	2l. Arms of Honduras and Spain (horiz)		2·75	2·40

181 Mayan Stelae

1978. Air. Honduras 78. Stamp Exhibition. Multicoloured.

909	15c. Type **181**		25	25
910	18c. Giant head		60	25
911	30c. Kneeling figure		85	70
912	55c. Sun God		1·50	1·20
MS913	160×110 mm. 1l.50 Mayan pelota court. Imperf		4·00	3·75

182 Del Valle's Birthplace

1978. Air. Birth Bicentenary of Jose Cecelio del Valle. Multicoloured.

914	8c. Type **182**		10	10
915	14c. La Merced Church, Choluteca		10	10
916	15c. Baptismal font (vert)		25	10
917	20c. Reading Independence Act		25	10
918	25c. Portrait, documents and map of Central America		35	25
919	40c. Portrait (vert)		60	35
920	1l. Monument, Choluteca (vert)		1·60	1·10
921	3l. Bust (vert)		5·50	4·25

183 Rural Heath Centre

1978. Air. 75th Anniv (1977) of Panamerican Health Organization. Multicoloured.

922	5c. Type **183**		10	10
923	6c. Child at water tap		10	10
924	10c. Los Laureles Dam, Tegucigalpa		25	10
925	20c. Rural aqueduct		35	25
926	40c. Teaching hospital, Tegucigalpa		75	50
927	2l. Parents and child		2·75	2·20
928	3l. Vaccination of child		4·00	3·00
929	5l. Panamerican Health Organization Building, Washington		5·75	5·00

184 Luis Landa and
"Botanica"

1978. Air. Birth Centenary of Professor Luis Landa (botanist). Multicoloured.

930	14c. Type **184**		10	10
931	16c. Map of Honduras		25	10
932	18c. Medals received by Landa		25	10
933	30c. Birthplace, San Ignacio		35	35
934	2l. "Brassavola" (national flower)		4·00	2·50
935	3l. Women's normal school		5·50	5·00

1978. Air. Argentina's Victory in World Cup Football Championship. Nos. 909/12 optd with **Argentina Campeon Holanda sub-Campeon XI Campeonato Mundial de Football** and emblem.

936	**181**	15c. multicoloured	25	10
937	-	18c. multicoloured	35	25
938	-	30c. multicoloured	60	35
939	-	55c. multicoloured	1·20	70
MS940	160×110 mm. 1l.50 multicoloured		41·00	

186 Central University

1978. Air. 400th Anniv of Founding of Tegucigalpa.

941	**186**	6c. brown and black	10	10
942	-	6c. multicoloured	10	10
943	-	8c. brown and black	10	10
944	-	8c. multicoloured	10	10
945	-	10c. brown and black	10	10
946	-	10c. multicoloured	10	10
947	-	16c. brown and black	10	10
948	-	16c. multicoloured	10	10
949	-	20c. brown and black	25	10
950	-	20c. multicoloured	25	10
951	-	40c. brown and black	35	35
952	-	40c. multicoloured	35	35
953	-	50c. brown and black	85	60
954	-	50c. multicoloured	85	60
955	-	5l. brown and black	9·75	8·25
956	-	5l. multicoloured	9·75	8·25
MS957	160×110 mm. 1l.50 multicoloured		4·25	4·25

DESIGNS—HORIZ: No. 942, University City; No. 943, Manuel Bonilla Theatre; No. 944, Present Manuel Bonilla Theatre; No. 947, National Palace; No. 948, Presidential House; No. 949, General San Felipe Hospital; No. 950, Teaching Hospital; No. 951, Parish Church and Convent of San Francisco; No. 952, Metropolitan Cathedral; No. 953, Old view of Tegucigalpa; No. 954, Modern view of Tegucigalpa; **MS**957, Aerial view of Tegucigalpa. VERT: No. 945, Court House; No. 946, North Boulevard highway intersection; No. 955, Arms of San Miguel de Tegucigalpa; No. 956, President Marco Aurelio Soto.

187 Footballers jumping
for Ball

1978. Air. Seventh Youth Football Championship of Central American Football League. Multicoloured.

958	15c. Type **187**		25	10
959	30c. Goalkeeper (horiz)		60	10
960	55c. Tackling		85	35
961	1l. Goalkeeper and players (horiz)		1·80	1·10
962	2l. Players at goalmouth (horiz)		3·00	2·40

188 National Postal Emblem

1979. Air. Centenary of Honduras's U.P.U. Membership (1st issue). Multicoloured.

963	2c. Type **188**		10	10
964	15c. U.P.U. emblem		25	25
965	25c. Roman Rosa (vert)		50	50
966	50c. Marco Aurelio Soto (vert)		1·00	95

See also Nos. 975/6.

189 Rotary Emblem and
"50"

1979. Air. 50th Anniv of Tegucigalpa Rotary Club.

967	**189**	3c. orange, turquoise and bistre	10	10
968	**189**	5c. green, emerald and bistre	10	10
969	**189**	50c. ochre, mauve and bistre	85	60
970	**189**	2l. blue, violet and bistre	2·75	2·40

190 Map of Caratasca
Lagoon

1979. Air. 50th Anniv of Pan-American Institute of History and Geography. Multicoloured.

971	5c. Type **190**		10	10
972	10c. Aerial view of Fort San Fernando de Omoa		10	10
973	24c. Institute anniversary emblem (vert)		35	25
974	5l. Map of Santanilla Islands		6·25	5·50

191 Model of New General Post
Office Building

1980. Air. Centenary (1979) of U.P.U. Membership (2nd issue).

975	**191**	24c. multicoloured	35	25
976	-	3l. brown, yellow & black	4·00	3·50

DESIGN: 3l. 19th century Post Office.

192 *Landscape*
(Roman E.
Cooper)

1980. Air. International Year of the Child (1979). Multicoloured.

977	1c. *Workers in a Field* (J. E. Mejia) (horiz)		25	25
978	5c. Type **192**		25	25
979	15c. *Sitting boy* (D. M. Zavala)		25	25
980	20c. I.Y.C. emblem		35	35
981	30c. *Beach scene* (M. A. Hernandez) (horiz)		60	60
MS982	105×79 mm. 1l. United Nation's Children's Fund (UNICEF) emblem		2·20	2·20

193 Hill and "Maltese
Cross" Cancellations

1980. Air. Death Centenary (1979) of Sir Rowland Hill. Multicoloured.

983	1c. Type **193**		10	10
984	2c. Great Britain "Penny Black"		10	10
985	5c. 1866 Honduras 2r. green		25	25

986	10c. 1866 Honduras 2r. rose	35	35
987	15c. Honduras postal emblem	75	70
988	20c. Flags of Honduras and United Kingdom	85	85
MS989	105×79 mm. 1l. Stamp Centenary stamp, 1966 (46×34 mm)	1·90	1·80

Nos. 987/8 are 46×34 mm.

194 Visitacion Padilla (founder of Honduras section)

1981. Air. 50th Anniv of Inter-American Women's Commission. Multicoloured.

990	2c. Type **194**	25	25
991	10c. Maria Trinidad del Cid (founder of Honduras section)	25	25
992	40c. Intubucana Indian mother and child	60	50
993	1l. Emblem (horiz)	1·40	1·20

195 O'Higgins during the Liberation of Chile (Cosmo San Martin)

1981. Air. Bernardo O'Higgins Commemoration. Multicoloured.

994	16c. Type **195**	25	25
995	20c. Don Ambrosio O'Higgins (father) (vert)	25	25
996	30c. Bernardo O'Higgins (Jose Gil de Castro) (vert)	35	35
997	1l. Bernardo O'Higgins laying-down Office (M. Antonio Caro)	1·50	85

196 National Sports Emblem

1981. Air. World Cup Football Championship Preliminary Round. Multicoloured.

998	20c. Type **196**	75	35
999	50c. Footballer and map of Honduras	1·70	1·30
1000	70c. Flags of Honduras, CONCACAF and FIFA	2·50	1·80
1001	1l. National stadium	3·75	2·10
MS1002	110×80 mm. 1l.50 Type **196**	3·00	2·40

197 Curtiss Condor II Biplane

1983. Air. 50th Anniv of Honduras Air Force. Multicoloured.

1003	3c. Type **197**	10	10
1004	15c. North America Texan	25	10
1005	25c. Chance Vought F4U-5 Corsair	50	35
1006	65c. Douglas C-47 Skytrain	1·00	60
1007	1l. Cessna Dragonfly	1·50	95
1008	2l. Dassault Super Mystere SMB-11	3·00	2·40
MS1009	80×55 mm. 11.55 Air Force Headquarters and Bell "UH-1H" helicopter	3·00	3·00

198 U.P.U. Monument, Berne

1983. Air. Election to U.P.U. Executive Council (1979). Multicoloured.

1010	16c. Type **198**	25	25
1011	18c. 18th U.P.U. Congress emblem	25	25

1012	30c. Honduras's postal emblem	35	35
1013	55c. View of Rio de Janeiro	75	70
1014	2l. "Stamp" showing pigeon on globe (vert)	2·75	2·75
MS1015	80×110 mm. 1l. mult	1·50	1·40

DESIGNS—HORIZ: 18c. 18th UPU Congress emblem; 30c. Honduras's postal emblem; 55c. View of Rio de Janeiro. VERT: 1, 2l. "Stamp showing pigeon on globe.

199 I.Y.D.P. Emblem

1983. Air. International Year of Disabled Persons.

1016	**199** 25c. multicoloured	60	50

200 National Library, Tegucigalpa

1983. Air. Centenary (1980) of National Library and Archives. Multicoloured.

1017	9c. Type **200**	25	15
1018	1l. Books	1·10	45

1983. Air. Papal Visit. Nos. 951/2 optd **CONMEMORATIVA DE LA VISITA DE SS. JUAN PABLO II 8 de marzo de 1983.**

1019	40c. brown and black	3·00	2·40
1020	40c. multicoloured	3·00	2·40

202 Agricultural Produce

1983. Air. World Food Day (1981).

1021	**202** 65c. multicoloured	70	70

203 Hands reaching for Open Book

1983. Air. Literacy Campaign (1980). Multicoloured.

1022	40c. Type **203**	55	45
1023	1l.50 Family with books	2·20	1·70

204 Motorway Bridge over River Comayagua

1983. 20th Anniv of Inter-American Development Bank. Multicoloured.

1024	1l. Type **204**	1·60	85
1025	2l. Luis Borgran Technical Institute	2·75	1·70

205 Arms

1984. Air. Second Anniv of Return of Constitutional Government. Multicoloured.

1026	20c. Type **205**	25	15
1027	20c. President Roberto Suazo Cordova	25	15

206 Hand, Dove and Map on Globe

1984. "Internationalization of Peace".

1028	**206** 78c. black, blue and green	90	70
1029	**206** 85c. black, orange & grn	1·00	35
1030	**206** 95c. black, orange & grn	1·10	45
1031	**206** 1l.50 black, red & green	1·80	60
1032	**206** 2l. black, lt grn & green	2·00	80
1033	**206** 5l. black, purple & green	5·50	1·90

207 Front Page of La Gaceta

1984. Air. 150th Anniv of La Gaceta.

1034	**207** 10c. brown, black and green	25	15
1035	**207** 20c. brown, black and sepia	35	25

1986. Various stamps surch.

1036	**184** 60c. on 14c. multicoloured (postage)	80	45
1037	**177** 5c. on 1c. blue and black (air)	10	10
1038	- 10c. on 8c. multicoloured (No. 868)	10	10
1039	**176** 20c. on 16c. multicoloured	25	15
1040	- 50c. on 14c. multicoloured (No. 915)	50	25
1041	- 85c. on 6c. multicoloured (No. 942)	90	50
1042	**186** 85c. on 6c. brown and blk	90	50
1043	- 95c. on 6c. brown and blk	1·10	50
1044	- 95c. on 6c. multicoloured (No. 942)	1·10	70
1045	**177** 1l. on 1c. blue and black	1·20	85

1986. Air. Exfilhon '86 Stamp Exhibition and World Cup Winners. Nos. 951/2 optd.

1046	40c. "EXFILHON '86/ ARGENTINA CAMPEON/ MEXICO '86" (951)	45	25
1047	40c. "EXFILHON '86/ ALEMANIA FEDERAL Sub Campeon/ MEXICO'86" (952)	45	25
1048	40c. "EXFILHON '86/ "FRANCIA TERCER LUGAR"/ MEXICO'86" (952)	45	25
1049	40c. "EXFILHON '86"/ "BELGICA–CUARTO LUGAR"/ MEXICO'86" (951)	45	25

210 Phulapanzak

1986. Air. Tourism. Multicoloured.

1050	20c. Type **210**	25	15
1051	78c. Aerial view of Bahia Island beach and jetty (horiz)	70	35
1052	85c. Yacht off Bahia Islands (horiz)	90	45
1053	95c. Yojoa lake	1·00	45
1054	1l. Woman painting pottery	1·10	50
MS1055	84×58 mm. 1l.50 San Fernando Castle, Omoa (80×55 mm). Imperf	1·80	1·70

211 Pres. Jose Azcona and Flag

1987. Air. First Anniv of Democratic Government.

1056	**211** 20c. multicoloured	35	15
1057	**211** 85c. multicoloured	1·40	50

212 Edward Warner Award Medal

1987. 25th Anniv (1985) of Central American Air Navigation Services Association. Multicoloured.

1058	2c. Type **212**	20	15
1059	5c. Flags of member countries (horiz)	20	15
1060	60c. Transmission mast, arrows and airplane (horiz)	70	25
1061	75c. Emblem	90	35
1062	1l. Members' flags and emblem	1·30	45
MS1063	100×80 mm. 1l.50 As No. 1062	2·20	2·20

213 Eupatorium cyrillinelsonii

1987. Air. Flowering Plants. Multicoloured.

1064	10c. Type **213**	25	15
1065	20c. Salvia ernestivargasii	35	25
1066	95c. Robinsonella erasmi-sosae	90	50

214 Turquoise-browed Motmot

1987. Air. Birds. Multicoloured.

1067	50c. Type **214**	1·80	35
1068	60c. Keel-billed toucan	2·20	45
1069	85c. Yellow-headed amazon	3·25	60

215 Family and House on Emblem

1987. 30th Anniv of Housing Institute.

1070	**215** 5c. multicoloured	20	15
1071	- 95c. black, brown & blue	90	45

DESIGN: 95c. Emblem.

216 Emblem

1987. Air. 30th Anniv of Honduras National Autonomous University.

1072	**216** 1l. red, black and yellow	1·30	60

217 Emblem

1987. Air. 50th Anniv of Honduras Red Cross.

1073	**217** 20c. red and blue	35	25

218 Emblem of President

1988. Air. 17th Lions International Latin-American and Caribbean Forum, Honduras.

| 1074 | 218 | 95c. blue and yellow | 1·10 | 45 |

219 1913 Headquarters Building, La Ceiba

1988. Air. 75th Anniv of Banco Atlantida.

1075		10c. Type **219**	20	10
1076		85c. Present headquarters building, Tegucigalpa	1·20	60
MS1077	112×81 mm. Nos. 1075/6 (sold at 1l.). No. gum		1·30	1·30

1988. Nos. 941/4 surch.

1078		5c. on 6c. brown and black	20	10
1079		5c. on 6c. multicoloured	20	10
1080		20c. on 8c. brown and black	30	15
1081		20c. on 8c. multicoloured	30	15

221 Postal Messenger

1988. Air. Exfilhon 88 Stamp Exhibition, Honduras.

1082	221	85c. brown	90	50
1083	-	2l. brown and red	2·20	1·40
MS1084	115×83 mm. 3l. orange-brown and ultramarine (Ship carrying mail). Imperf		3·50	3·50

DESIGN: 2l. Handstamp on cover.

222 Athletes

1988. Air. Olympic Games, Seoul.

1085	222	85c. black, yellow & mve	1·00	50
1086	-	1l. yellow, black & orge	1·30	70
MS1087	114×83 mm. 4l. Single sculls designs as Nos. 1085/6. Imperf		4·50	4·25

DESIGN: 1l. Ball games equipment.

223 Three-legged Tub

1988. Air. 500th Anniv (1992) of Discovery of America by Christopher Columbus. Multicoloured.

1088		10c. Type **223**	35	15
1089		25c. Bowl (horiz)	80	25
1090		30c. Dish with legs shaped as animal heads (horiz)	1·10	35
1091		50c. Jug	1·80	50
MS1092	114×83 mm. 1l.Square dish. Imperf		3·50	3·50

1989. Air. Various stamps surch.

1093	-	10c. on 16c. brown and black (No. 947)	20	10
1094	-	10c. on 16c. multicoloured (No. 948)	20	10
1095	-	15c. on 6c. multicoloured (No. 923)	20	15
1096	195	20c. on 16c. multicoloured	45	15
1097	176	50c. on 16c. multicoloured	70	40
1098	-	95c. on 18c. multicoloured (No. 910)	1·30	50
1099	-	1l. on 16c. multicoloured (No. 836)	1·30	1·00

1990. Air. Fourth Central American Games. Nos. 887 and 878 surch **IV Juegos Olimpicos Centroamericanos** and value.

| 1101 | | 75c. on 18c. multicoloured | 1·10 | 85 |
| 1102 | | 85c. on 18c. green and black | 1·20 | 95 |

1990. Air. Nos. 915 and 870 surch **L. 0.20.**

| 1103 | | 20c. on 14c. multicoloured | 25 | 15 |
| 1104 | | 20c. on 18c. multicoloured | 25 | 15 |

1990. Air. 50th Anniv (1989) of I.H.C.I. Nos. 930 and 915 surch **50 Aniversario IHCI 1939–1989** and new value.

| 1105 | 184 | 20c. on 14c. mult | 20 | 10 |
| 1106 | - | 1l. on 14c. multicoloured | 65 | 45 |

228 Monkey swinging through Trees

1990. Air. The Black-handed Spider Monkey. Multicoloured.

1107		10c. Type **228**	1·70	95
1108		10c. Mother and baby	1·70	95
1109		20c. Monkey swinging through trees (different)	3·00	1·50
1110		20c. Mother and baby (different)	3·00	1·50

1990. Air. World Cup Football Championship, Italy. No. 960 surch **ITALIA '90 L.1.00.**

| 1111 | | 1l. on 55c. multicoloured | 65 | 45 |
| MS1112 | 110×80 mm. 1l.50 multicoloured (optd **CAMPEONATO MUNDIAL/DE FUTBOL/ITALIA '90**) and mascot | | 90 | 85 |

230 Institute Building

1990. Air Centenary of Luis Bogran Technical Institute, Tegucigalpa.

1113	230	20c. red, black and green	20	10
1114	-	85c. multicoloured	65	45
MS1115	114×82 mm. **230** 2l. red, black and emerald		1·60	1·60

DESIGN: 85c. Cogwheel, globe and Institute emblem.

231 Emblem

1990. Air. 45th Anniv of F.A.O.

| 1116 | 231 | 95c. multicoloured | 70 | 50 |

232 Santa Maria, Shoreline, Fish and Fruit

1990. America. The Natural World. Multicoloured.

| 1117 | | 20c. Type **232** | 20 | 15 |
| 1118 | | 1l. Maize, fish, fruit and palm (horiz) | 70 | 50 |

233 Congress Emblem

1990. Air. 30th Anniv and 17th Congress of Inter-American Construction Industry Federation.

| 1119 | 233 | 20c. black and green | 20 | 10 |
| 1120 | - | 1l. black and blue | 70 | 50 |

DESIGN—HORIZ: 1l. Jose Cecilio del Valle Palace, Tegucigalpa (Ministry of Foreign Relations).

234 Virgin and Child with Apostles

1990. Air. Christmas. Multicoloured.

1121		20c. Type **234**	20	10
1122		95c. Virgin and Child (vert)	70	45
MS1123	101×82 mm. 3l. Poinsettia. Imperf		2·20	2·20

235 St. John Bosco (founder) (after Mario Caffaro Roke)

1990. Air. 80th Anniv of Salesian Brothers in Honduras. Multicoloured.

| 1124 | | 75c. Type **235** | 55 | 35 |
| 1125 | | 1l. Bosco and National Youth Sanctuary, Tegucigalpa | 80 | 50 |

236 Pres. Callejas

1991. Air. First Anniv of Presidency of Rafael Leonardo Callejas. Multicoloured.

| 1126 | | 30c. Type **236** | 20 | 10 |
| 1127 | | 2l. Pres. Callejas wearing sash | 1·40 | 95 |

237 Strymon melinus

1991. Air. Butterflies. Multicoloured.

1128		85c. Type **237**	90	45
1129		90c. *Diorina* sp.	1·20	50
1130		1l.50 *Hyalophora cecropia*	1·80	80
MS1131	114×82 mm. 5l. "Papilio polixenes". Imperf		3·50	3·25

238 Rhyncholaelia glauca

1991. Air. Orchids. Multicoloured.

1132		30c. Type **238**	20	10
1133		50c. *Oncidium splendidum* (vert)	35	25
1134		95c. *Laelia anceps* (vert)	70	50
1135		1l.50 *Cattleya skinneri*	1·40	1·00

239 International Latin Lawyers Union Emblem and Flags

1991. Air. Sixth Caribbean and North and Central American Lawyers' Day.

| 1136 | 239 | 50c. multicoloured | 45 | 25 |

241 Emblem, Flags and Carving

1991. Air. 25th Anniv of Italian–Latin American Institute.

| 1138 | 241 | 1l. multicoloured | 70 | 45 |

242 Meeting of Old and New Worlds

1991. Air. Espamer '91 Spain–Latin America Stamp Exhibition, Buenos Aires.

| 1139 | 242 | 2l. multicoloured | 2·20 | 85 |
| MS1140 | 102×83 mm. **242** 5l. multicoloured. Imperf | | 3·50 | 3·50 |

243 Valle

1991. Air. Birth Centenary of Rafael Heliodoro Valle.

| 1141 | 243 | 2l. black and red | 1·30 | 95 |

244 Show Jumping

1991. Air. 11th Pan-American Games, Havana. Multicoloured.

1142		30c. Type **244**	20	10
1143		85c. Judo	65	45
1144		95c. Swimming	70	45
MS1145	115×83 mm. 5l. Swimmers diving into pool. Imperf		3·50	3·50

245 St. Manuel de Colohete's Church, Gracias, Lempira

1991. Air. Churches. Multicoloured.

1146		30c. Type **245**	20	10
1147		95c. Church of Mercy, Gracias, Lempira	70	45
1148		1l. Comayagua Cathedral	70	45

246 Stone Carving and Cobs of Corn

1991. Air. America. Pre-Columbian Civilizations. Multicoloured.

1149		25c. Type **246**	20	10
1150		40c. Stone carving, dried corn and map	40	20
1151		1l.50 Stone carving and map of Honduras	1·10	70

247 Means of Control

1991. Air. Fourth International Congress on Pest Control. Multicoloured.

1152		30c. Type **247**	55	15
1153		75c. Hoeing crop (scientific co-operation)	1·30	35
1154		1l. Co-operation of scientists and producers	1·80	50
MS1155	115×83 mm. 5l. Biological control. Imperf		3·50	3·50

248 Poinsettias in Basket

1991. Christmas. Multicoloured.

| 1156 | | 1l. Type **248** | 70 | 45 |
| 1157 | | 2l. Poinsettia in chicken-shaped pot | 1·50 | 95 |

249 *Taking Possession of
the New Continent* (Enrique
Escher)

1992. Air. 75th Anniv of Savings Bank of Honduras.
Multicoloured.

1158	85c. Type **249**	55	35
1159	1l. *First Celebration of Mass in the Americas* (Maury Flores)	70	45
MS1160	114×83 mm. 5l. As T **249** but larger. Imperf	3·50	3·50

250 Presidents Callejas
and Cossiga of Italy

1992. Air. Second Year in Office of President Rafael
Leonardo Callejas. Multicoloured.

| 1161 | 20c. Type **250** | 15 | 10 |
| 1162 | 2l. Callejas with Pope | 1·30 | 85 |

251 *View From Crow's
Nest*

1992. Air. America 1991. 500th Anniv of Discovery of
America. Multicoloured.

1163	90c. Type **251**	70	50
1164	1l. Fleet	80	60
1165	2l. Ship approaching island	1·80	1·30

252 Skiing

1992. Winter Olympic Games, Albertville. Multicoloured.

| 1166 | 50c. Type **252** | 25 | 15 |
| 1167 | 3l. Jenny Palacios de Stillo (cross-country skier) | 2·00 | 1·30 |

253 Athletics

1992. Olympic Games, Barcelona. Multicoloured.

1168	20c. Type **253**	20	10
1169	50c. Tennis	35	15
1170	85c. Football	65	45

254 *Seller* (Manuel
Rodriguez)

1992. Mother's Day. Paintings. Multicoloured.

1171	20c. Type **254**	20	10
1172	50c. *Grandmother and Baby* (Manuel Rodriguez)	25	15
1173	5l. *Sellers* (Maury Flores)	3·25	2·20

255 *Chlosyne janais*

1992. Butterflies. Multicoloured.

1174	25c. Type **255**	25	15
1175	85c. *Agrilus vanillae*	80	45
1176	3l. *Morpho granadensis*	2·75	1·30

| MS1177 | 107×76 mm. 5l. *Dryadula phalusa*. Imper | 4·25 | 4·00 |

256 *Bougainvillea glabra
"Napoleon"*

1992. Air. Flowers. Multicoloured.

1178	20c. Type **256**	25	15
1179	30c. *Canna indica*	25	15
1180	75c. *Epiphyllum* sp.	70	50
1181	95c. *Sobralia macrantha*	1·00	70

257 Dam

1992. Air. General Francisco Morazan Hydroelectric
Project. Multicoloured.

| 1182 | 85c. Type **257** | 55 | 35 |
| 1183 | 4l. Inner view of dam (horiz) | 2·75 | 1·70 |

258 Crops

1992. Air. 50th Anniv of Inter-American Institute for
Agricultural Co-operation.

| 1184 | **258** | 95c. multicoloured (white background) | 65 | 50 |
| 1185 | **258** | 95c. multicoloured (black background) | 65 | 50 |

259 *Huancasco*
(Arturo Lopez
Rodezno)

1992. Air. Children's Day. Multicoloured.

1186	25c. Type **259**	20	10
1187	95c. *Bougainvillea* (Enrique Escher)	65	35
1188	2l. *Melissa* (Cesar Ordonez)	1·30	85

260 Morazan on
Horseback (after
Francisco Cisneros)

1992. Air. Birth Bicentenary of General Francisco
Morazan. Multicoloured.

1189	5c. Type **260**	20	15
1190	10c. Statue of Morazan, Ampala	20	15
1191	50c. Morazan's watch and sword (horiz)	25	15
1192	95c. Josefa Lastiri de Morazan (wife)	65	45
MS1193	77×107 mm. 5l. *The Glory of Morazan* (after Zuniga Figueroa). Imperf	3·25	2·50

261 Globe as Pot filled
with Food

1992. Air. Int Nutrition Conference, Rome.

| 1194 | **261** | 1l.05 multicoloured | 70 | 50 |

262 Cinnamon
Hummingbird

1992. Air. Exfilhon '92 National Stamp Exhibition,
Tegucigalpa. Multicoloured.

1195	1l.50 Type **262**	1·80	1·70
1196	2l.45 Scarlet macaw	2·75	2·50
MS1197	76×108 mm. 5l. Resplendent quetzal (*Pharomachrus mocinno*). Imperf	3·50	3·50

263 Bee-keeping

1992. Air. 50th Anniv of Pan-American School of
Agriculture. Multicoloured.

1198	20c. Type **263**	10	10
1199	85c. Tending goats	55	35
1200	1l. Ploughing with oxen	65	45
1201	2l. Hoeing (vert)	1·30	85

264 Fruit, Locomotive,
Clock and Bridge

1992. Air. Centenary of El Progreso (City).

| 1202 | **264** | 1l.55 multicoloured | 1·20 | 70 |

265 Amerindian
Village

1992. Air. America. 500th Anniv of Discovery of America
by Columbus. Multicoloured.

| 1203 | 35c. Type **265** | 20 | 10 |
| 1204 | 5l. Columbus's landing party meeting Amerindians | 2·50 | 1·80 |

266 Columbus's
Fleet and Landing
Craft

1992. Air. 500th Anniv of Discovery of America by
Columbus. Details of "The First Mass" by Roque
Zelaya. Multicoloured.

1205	95c. Type **266**	55	45
1206	1l. Mass (horiz)	70	50
1207	2l. View of village (horiz)	1·40	1·10

267 Road and Bridge

1992. Air. First Central America–Panama Highway
Maintenance Congress, San Pedro Sula.
Multicoloured.

| 1208 | 20c. Type **267** | 20 | 10 |
| 1209 | 85c. Bulldozer | 55 | 35 |

268 The Greasy
Pole

1992. Air. Christmas. Multicoloured.

| 1210 | 20c. Type **268** | 20 | 10 |
| 1211 | 85c. Crib, San Antonio de Flores (horiz) | 55 | 35 |

269 Globes, Children and
Emblem

1992. Air. 90th Anniv of Pan-American Health
Organization.

| 1212 | **269** | 3l.95 multicoloured | 2·30 | 1·90 |

1992. Air. Nos. 894 and 899/900 surch.

1213	**179**	20c. on 1c. multicoloured	20	15
1214	–	20c. on 6c. multicoloured	25	15
1215	–	85c. on 18c. mult	55	35

271 Pres. Callejas
at Ceremony

1993. Air. Third Year of Rafael L. Callejas's Presidential
Term and International Court of Justice's Decision on
Border with El Salvador. Multicoloured.

| 1216 | 90c. Type **271** | 55 | 35 |
| 1217 | 1l.05 Map (horiz) | 65 | 45 |

272 Mother and
Child

1993. Air. Mother's Day. Multicoloured.

| 1218 | 50c. Type **272** | 25 | 15 |
| 1219 | 95c. Mother and child (different) | 55 | 35 |

273 American Manatee

1993. Air. Endangered Mammals. Multicoloured.

1220	85c. Type **273**	65	45
1221	2l.45 Puma	1·60	1·30
1222	10l. Jaguar (vert)	5·75	3·75

274 Scarlet Macaws

1993. Air. National Symbols. Multicoloured.

| 1223 | 25c. Type **274** | 1·30 | 1·00 |
| 1224 | 95c. White-tailed deer | 1·60 | 1·40 |

1993. Air. Various stamps surch.

1225	–	20c. on 3c. multicoloured (No. 896)	25	15
1226	**189**	20c. on 3c. orange, blue and bistre	25	15
1227	**197**	20c. on 3c. multicoloured	25	15
1228	–	20c. on 8c. multicoloured (No. 868)	25	15
1229	**182**	20c. on 8c. multicoloured	25	15

1230	176	50c. on 16c. multicoloured	25	15
1231	177	50c. on 16c. red and black	25	15
1232	-	50c. on 16c. multicoloured (No. 886)	25	15
1233	180	50c. on 16c. multicoloured	25	15
1234	-	50c. on 16c. multicoloured (No. 931)	45	15
1235	195	50c. on 16c. multicoloured	45	25
1236	-	50c. on 18c. multicoloured (No. 870)	25	15
1237	-	50c. on 18c. multicoloured (No. 910)	25	15
1238	-	50c. on 18c. mauve and black (No. 1011)	25	15
1239	-	85c. on 18c. green and black (No. 878)	45	35
1240	-	85c. on 18c. multicoloured (No. 906)	45	35
1241	-	85c. on 18c. multicoloured (No. 932)	55	35
1242	-	85c. on 18c. multicoloured (No. 937)	45	35
1243	-	85c. on 24c. multicoloured (No. 973)	45	35
1244	191	85c. on 24c. multicoloured	45	35

276 30r. "Bull's Eye" Stamp

1993. Air. 150th Anniv of First Brazilian Stamps. Multicoloured.

1245		20c. Type **276**	20	10
1246		50c. 60r. "Bull's eye" stamp	25	15
1247		95c. 90r. "Bull's eye" stamp	55	45

277 Atlantida

1993. Air. Departments. Multicoloured.

1248		20c. Type **277**	15	10
1249		20c. Colon	15	10
1250		20c. Cortes	15	10
1251		20c. Choluteca	15	10
1252		20c. El Paraiso	15	10
1253		20c. Francisco Morazan	15	10
1254		50c. Comayagua (vert)	35	25
1255		50c. Copan (vert)	35	25
1256		50c. Intibuca (vert)	35	25
1257		50c. Bahia Islands (vert)	35	25
1258		50c. Lempira (vert)	35	25
1259		50c. Ocotepeque (vert)	35	25
1260		1l.50 La Paz	90	80
1261		1l.50 Olancho	90	80
1262		1l.50 Santa Barbara	90	80
1263		1l.50 Valle	90	80
1264		1l.50 Yoro	90	80
1265		1l.50 Gracias a Dios	90	80

278 Muscovy Duck

1993. Air. America. Endangered Birds. Multicoloured.

1266		20c. Ornate hawk eagle (vert)	25	15
1267		80c. Type **278**	1·10	70
1268		2l. Harpy eagle	2·75	1·70

279 Painting by Julia Padilla

1993. Air. 40th Anniv of United Nations Development Programme.

1269	279	95c. multicoloured	55	35

280 Church

1993. Air. Christmas. Paintings by Aida Lara de Pedemonte. Multicoloured.

1270		20c. Type **280**	20	10
1271		85c. Flower vendor	45	35

281 Ramon Rosa

1993. Air. Personalities. Multicoloured.

1272		25c. Type **281**	20	10
1273		65c. Jesus Aguilar Paz	35	25
1274		85c. Augusto Coello	45	35

282 Grey Angelfish

1993. Air. Fish. Multicoloured.

1275		20c. Type **282**	25	15
1276		85c. Queen angelfish	55	45
1277		3l. Banded butterflyfish	1·90	1·50

283 Norma Callejas planting Tree

1994. Air. Fourth Year of Rafael L. Callejas's Presidential Term. Multicoloured.

1278		95c. Type **283**	45	35
1279		1l. Pres. Callejas and Government House (horiz)	45	35

284 Family with Rushes (Aida Lara de Pedemonte)

1994. International Year of the Family.

1280	284	1l. multicoloured	45	35

285 Dove and Maps on Globe

1994. Air. International Peace and Development in Central America Conference, Tegucigalpa.

1281	285	1l. multicoloured	45	35

286 Madonna and Child

1994. Air. Christmas. Paintings by Gelasio Gimenez. Multicoloured.

1282		95c. Type **286**	45	35
1283		1l. Holy Family	55	45

287 "Family Scene" (Delmer Mejia)

1995. Air. 50th Anniv of U.N.O. Multicoloured.

1284		1l. *The Sowing: Ecological Family* (Elisa Dulcey)	55	45
1285		2l. Type **287**	90	80
1286		3l. Anniversary emblem	1·30	1·20

288 Pres. Reina

1995. Air. First Anniv of Presidency of Carlos Roberto Reina. Multicoloured.

1287		80c. Type **288**	45	35
1288		95c. Pres. Reina with arms raised (horiz)	45	35
1289		1l. Pres. Reina at summit conference (horiz)	55	45

289 Postman loading Mail Van

1995. Air. America. Postal Transport. Paintings by Ramiro Rodriguez Zelaya. Multicoloured.

1290		1l.50 Type **289**	70	60
1291		2l. Postman on motor cycle	90	80

290 *Boletellus russelli*

1995. Air. Fungi. Multicoloured.

1292		1l. *Marasmius cohaerens* (horiz)	45	35
1293		1l. Blue leg (*Lepista nuda*) (horiz)	45	35
1294		1l. *Polyporus pargamenus* (horiz)	45	35
1295		1l. *Fomes* sp. (horiz)	45	35
1296		1l. *Paneolus sphinctrinus* (horiz)	45	35
1297		1l. *Hygrophorus aurantiaca* (horiz)	45	35
1298		1l.50 The blusher (*Amanita rubescens*)	65	50
1299		1l.50 *Boletus frostii*	65	50
1300		1l.50 *Fomes annosus*	65	50
1301		1l.50 *Psathyrella* sp.	65	50
1302		1l.50 Type **290**	65	50
1303		1l.50 *Marasmius spegazzinii*	65	50
1304		2l. *Amanita* sp.	90	80
1305		2l. Golden tops (*Psilocybe cubensis*)	90	80
1306		2l. Royal boletus (*Boletus regius*)	90	80
1307		2l. Black trumpet (*Craterellus cornucopioides*)	90	80
1308		2l. *Auricularia delicata*	90	80
1309		2l. *Clavariadelphus pistilaris*	90	80
1310		2l.50 *Scleroderma aurantium* (horiz)	1·10	95
1311		2l.50 *Amanita praegraveolens* (horiz)	1·10	95
1312		2l.50 Chanterelle (*Cantharellus cibarius*) (horiz)	1·10	95
1313		2l.50 *Geastrum triplex* (horiz)	1·10	95
1314		2l.50 *Russula emetica* (horiz)	1·10	95
1315		2l.50 *Boletus pinicola* (horiz)	1·10	95
1316		3l. *Fomes versicolor* (horiz)	1·30	1·20
1317		3l. *Cantharellus purpurascens* (horiz)	1·30	1·20
1318		3l. *Lyophyllum decastes* (horiz)	1·30	1·20
1319		3l. Oyster fungus (*Pleurotus ostreatus*) (horiz)	1·30	1·20
1320		3l. *Boletus ananas* (horiz)	1·30	1·20
1321		3l. Caesar's mushroom (*Amanita caesarea*) (horiz)	1·30	1·20

291 "Food for All"

1995. Air. 50th Anniv of F.A.O.

1322	291	3l. multicoloured	90	50

292 Family and Farm over Globe

1995. Air. 50th Anniv of CARE (Co-operative for Assistance and Remittances Overseas). Multicoloured.

1323		1l.40 Type **292**	65	50
1324		5l.40 Crop farming	2·20	1·90
1325		5l.40 Keel-billed toucan, orchid, planting tree and animals at waterfall	2·20	1·90

293 Archaeological Site (½-size illustration)

1995. Air. El Puente Archaeological Park. Sheet 83×58 mm. Imperf.

MS1326	293	20l. multicoloured	7·25	7·00

294 People around Japanese Character

1995. 20th Anniv of Japanese Overseas Co-operation Voluntary Workers in Honduras. Multicoloured.

1327		1l.40 Type **294** (postage)	65	50
1328		4l.30 Amerindian-style figures on pages of leaflet (horiz) (air)	1·40	1·30
1329		5l.40 Volunteer and people in traditional costumes (horiz)	1·90	1·70

295 Scorpion Mud Turtle

1995. Air. America. Environmental Protection. Multicoloured.

1330		1l.40 Type **295**	55	45
1331		4l.54 *Alpinia purpurata* (flower) (vert)	1·40	1·30
1332		10l. Common caracara (*Caracara*) (vert)	3·25	3·00

296 *Agalychnis* sp.

1995. Air. Reptiles and Amphibians. Multicoloured.

1333		5l.40 Type **296**	2·20	2·20
1334		5l.40 Iguana	2·20	2·20

297 Bell

1995. Air. Christmas. Multicoloured.

1335		1l.40 Type **297**	55	50

1336	5l.40 Crib figures (horiz)	2·20	2·10
1337	6l.90 Deer (carving)	2·75	2·50

298 "SICA" over Map

1996. Air. Third Anniv of Central American Integration System. Multicoloured.

1338	1l.40 Type **298** (signing of Protocol, 1991)	45	45
1339	4l.30 Emblem	1·50	1·50
1340	5l.40 Presidents of Central American countries at 17th Summit	2·00	1·90

299 Allegorical Design

1996. Air. United Nations Decade against Drug Abuse and Drug Trafficking. Multicoloured.

1341	1l.40 Type **299**	45	45
1342	5l.40 Woman's head with butterfly as hat (vert)	1·80	1·70
1343	10l. Guitar and bar of music	2·75	2·50

300 Traditional Headdress

1996. Air. Bicentenary of Arrival of Garifunas Tribe in Honduras. Multicoloured.

1344	1l.40 Type **300**	45	35
1345	5l.40 Tribesmen dancing to music (horiz)	1·80	1·40
1346	10l. Drums (horiz)	2·75	2·20

301 Steam Locomotive "San Jose"

1996. Air. Exfilhon 96 National Stamp Exn, Tegucigalpa. Railway Locomotives. Multicoloured.

1347	5l.40 Type **301**	1·80	1·70
1348	5l.40 Diesel railcar No. 203	1·80	1·70
MS1349	75×52 mm. 20l.+2l. Locomotive *San Jose.* Imperf	7·25	7·00

302 Football

1996. Air. Sixth Central American Games, San Pedro Sula (1997). Multicoloured.

1350	4l.30 Type **302**	1·30	85
1351	4l.54 Volleyball and games emblem	1·40	90
1352	5l.40 Games mascot (vert)	1·80	1·10

303 Honduran and International Badges

1996. Air. 75th Anniv of Honduran Scouts' Association. Multicoloured.

1353	2l.15 Type **303**	55	35
1354	5l.40 Anniversary emblem (vert)	1·80	1·00
1355	6l.90 Scout feeding deer (vert)	2·20	1·30

304 Poinsettia and Candles

1996. Air. Christmas. Multicoloured.

1356	1l.40 Type **304**	55	35
1357	3l. Poinsettia	1·30	75
1358	5l.40 As Type **304** but vert	2·75	1·40

305 Opatoro Man

1997. Air. America (1996). Traditional Costumes. Multicoloured.

1359	4l.55 Type **305**	1·30	75
1360	5l.40 Jocomico woman	1·80	1·00
1361	10l. Intibuca couple	3·25	1·80

306 Children playing in River (Oscar Moncada)

1997. Air. 20th Anniv of Honduran Plan and 60th Anniv of International Plan. Multicoloured.

1362	1l.40 Type **306**	55	30
1363	5l.40 Girl beside river (Nataly Alexandra Reyes) (horiz)	1·80	95
1364	9l.70 Street (Walter Enrique Martinez) (horiz)	3·00	2·40

307 Red-tailed Hawk

1997. Birds. Multicoloured.

1365	1l.40 Type **307** (postage)	55	35
1366	1l.50 Keel-billed toucan	55	35
1367	2l. Red-billed whistling duck	70	50
1368	2l.15 Collared forest falcon	80	60
1369	3l. Common caracara	1·10	85
1370	5l.40 King vulture (air)	2·00	1·70
MS1371	57×84 mm. 20l. As No. 1370 (41×61 mm). Imperf	6·75	6·50

308 Von Stephan

1997. Air. Death Centenary of Dr. Heinrich von Stephan (founder of U.P.U.).

1372	**308** 5l.40 multicoloured	1·40	80

309 Children and Adults in Room (Yorvin Ramon Toro)

1997. Air. World Population Day. Multicoloured.

1373	1l.40 Type **309**	45	25
1374	6l.90 Family group and house (Marvin Lamberth Harry)	1·80	85

310 *Rothschildia forbesi*

1997. Air. Butterflies and Moths. Multicoloured.

1375	1l. Type **310**	25	15
1376	1l.40 *Parides photinus*	35	15
1377	2l.15 Emperor	55	45
1378	3l. Jamaican kite swallowtail	90	70
1379	4l.30 *Parides iphidamas*	1·30	1·00
1380	5l.40 Monarch	1·80	1·30

MS1381	89×64 mm. 20l.+2l. *Hamadryas arinome.* Imperf	4·50	3·50

311 St. Theresa

1997. Air. Death Centenary of St. Theresa of Lisieux. Multicoloured.

1382	1l.40 Type **311**	45	30
1383	5l.40 St. Theresa (different)	1·30	70

312 Observatory

1997. Air. 150th Anniv of National University and 40th Anniv of Free University. Multicoloured.

1384	1l.40 Type **312**	35	25
1385	5l.40 Statue of Fr. Jose Trinidad Reyes (founder)	1·30	70
1386	10l. Woman with book guiding boy	2·30	1·30

313 Diana, Princess of Wales

1997. Air. Diana, Princess of Wales Commemoration. Multicoloured.

1387	1l.40 Type **313**	35	25
1388	5l.40 Visiting minefield (horiz)	1·80	85

MS1389	57×83 mm. 20l. Mother Teresa (founder of Missionaries of Charity) and Princess of Wales. Imperf	5·50	3·50

314 Children around Statue (Nelson Leonel Rodriguez)

1997. Air. 37th Anniv of Alcoholics Anonymous (rehabilitation organization).

1390	**314** 5l.40 multicoloured	1·60	85

315 "Christ of Picacho" (statue)

1997. Air. Christmas. Multicoloured.

1391	1l.40 Type **315**	35	25
1392	5l.50 "Virgin of Suyapa"	1·40	1·00

316 Basketball

1997. Air. Sixth Central American Games, San Pedro Sula. Multicoloured.

1393	1l.40 Type **316**	45	35
1394	1l.40 Baseball (batting)	45	35
1395	1l.40 Football	45	35
1396	1l.40 Squash	45	35
1397	1l.40 Volleyball	45	35
1398	1l.40 Handball	45	35
1399	1l.40 Bowls	45	35
1400	1l.40 Table tennis	45	35
1401	1l.40 Rings on map of Honduras	45	35
1402	1l.40 Baseball (bowling)	45	35
1403	1l.50 Taekwondo (kicking)	55	45
1404	1l.50 Karate (one hand raised)	55	45
1405	1l.50 Judo (bowing)	55	45
1406	1l.50 Wrestling	55	45
1407	1l.50 Weightlifting	55	45
1408	1l.50 Boxing	55	45
1409	1l.50 Body-building	55	45
1410	1l.50 Fencing	55	45
1411	1l.50 Games emblem	55	45
1412	1l.50 Shooting	55	45
1413	2l.15 Cycling (on bicycle)	70	60
1414	2l.15 Road cycle racing (running beside bicycle)	70	60
1415	2l.15 Swimming	70	60
1416	2l.15 Water polo	70	60
1417	2l.15 Hurdling	70	60
1418	2l.15 Gymnastics (ring exercise)	70	60
1419	2l.15 Horse riding	70	60
1420	2l.15 Tennis	70	60
1421	2l.15 Pedrito Pichete (Games mascot)	70	60
1422	2l.15 Chess	70	60

317 *Cichlasoma dovii*

1997. Air. Fish. Multicoloured.

1423	1l.40 Type **317**	35	25
1424	2l. *Cichlasoma spilurum* (facing left)	55	45
1425	3l. *Cichlasoma spilurum* (facing right)	70	60
1426	5l.40 *Astyanay fasciatus*	1·30	1·00

318 Queen Triggerfish

1998. Air. 50th Anniv of Bancahsa. Marine Life of Bahia Coral Reef. Multicoloured.

1427	2l.50 Type **318**	90	70
1428	2l.50 White grunt (*Haemulon plumieri*)	90	70
1429	2l.50 French angelfish (*Pomacanthus paru*)	90	70
1430	2l.50 Wrasse (juvenile) (*Halichoeres garnoti*)	90	70
1431	2l.50 Grey angelfish (complete fish) (*Pomacanthus arcuatus*)	90	70
1432	2l.50 Queen angelfish (*Holacanthus ciliaris*)	90	70
1433	2l.50 Diver and *Pseud opterogorgia* (coral)	90	70
1434	2l.50 Diver's oxygen tank and *Pseud opterogorgia*	90	70
1435	2l.50 Six fingers of pillar coral (*Dendrogyra cylindrus*) (inscr in Latin)	90	70
1436	2l.50 Squirrelfish facing right (*Holocentrus adscensionis*)	90	70
1437	2l.50 Three fingers of pillar coral (*Dendrogyra cylindrus*) (inscr in Latin)	90	70
1438	2l.50 *Stegastes fuscu* (fish)	90	70
1439	2l.50 *Gorgonia mariae* (coral)	90	70
1440	2l.50 Three fingers of pillar coral (inscr in English)	90	70
1441	2l.50 Head of grey angelfish (*Pomacanthus arcuatus*)	90	70
1442	2l.50 Squirrelfish facing left (*Holocentrus adscensionis*)	90	70
1443	2l.50 *Eusmilia fastigiata* (coral)	90	70
1444	2l.50 Midnight parrotfish (*Scarus coelestinus*)	90	70
1445	2l.50 One finger of pillar coral (inscr in English)	90	70
1446	2l.50 Hogfish (*Lachnolaimus maximus*)	90	70

Nos. 1427/46 were issued together, *se-tenant,* forming a composite design.

319 Postman on Motor Cycle

1998. Air. America (1997). Postal Service. Multicoloured.

1447	5l.40 Type **319**	1·30	85
1448	5l.40 Post Office	1·30	85

320 Sculpted Skull from Temple 16

1998. Air. Maya Culture. Multicoloured.

1449	1l. Type **320**	35	25
1450	1l.40 Stone carving	45	35
1451	2l.15 Steles H and F	65	50
1452	5l.40 Carved water vessel	1·30	1·00
MS1453	89×64 mm. 20l. Temple ruins, Copan. Imperf	4·50	2·50

321 Players and Trophy

1998. Air. World Cup Football Championship, France. Multicoloured.

1454	5l.40 Type **321**	1·30	85
1455	10l. Players in tackle and trophy (vert)	2·75	1·70
MS1456	67×95 mm. 10l. Tegucigalpa Stadium, Honduras (63×42 mm); 10l. St. Denis Stadium, France (63×46 mm)	8·00	7·75

322 Green Iguana

1998. Air. Reptiles. Multicoloured.

1457	1l.40 Type **322**	35	25
1458	2l. Eyelash viper	55	45
1459	3l. Green lizards	80	70
1460	5l.40 Coral snake	1·40	1·00
MS1461	89×63 mm. 20l.+2l. Turtle. Imperf	3·50	2·20

323 Robin giving Gift to Girl

1998. Air. Christmas. Multicoloured.

1462	3l. Type **323**	65	45
1463	5l.40 Child Jesus in crib (horiz)	1·20	85
1464	10l. Child leading donkey	2·20	1·70

324 Flores and his Wife greeting Pope

1999. Air. First Anniv of Inauguration of President Carlos Roberto Flores.

1465	5l.40 Type **324**	1·30	85
1466	10l. President and Mary Flores (vert)	2·00	1·30

325 Floods, Central Zone

1999. Air. Hurricane Mitch Victims' Fund. Multicoloured.

1467	5l.40 Type **325**	1·10	1·00
1468	5l.40 Man carrying boy on back through flood and black-tailed trogon	1·10	1·00
1469	5l.40 Prince Felipe of Spain and Mary Flores (President's wife)	1·10	1·00
1470	5l.40 Child crying and orchid	1·10	1·00
1471	5l.40 People clearing timber in Comayaguela and orchid	1·10	1·00
1472	5l.40 People wading through flood in North Zone and spectacled owl	1·10	1·00
1473	5l.40 Destruction of La Hoya quarter, Tegucigalpa, and orchid	1·10	1·00
1474	5l.40 Soldier helping woman and child in North Zone and lance-tailed manakin	1·10	1·00
1475	5l.40 Collapsed houses in rural zone and orchids	1·10	1·00
1476	5l.40 Collapsed bridge and damaged motor cars ("Red Vial") and red-capped manakin	1·10	1·00
1477	5l.40 Damaged houses, motor cars and uprooted trees ("Red Vial") and orchids	1·10	1·00
1478	5l.40 Mexican soldiers with dogs and airplane	1·10	1·00
1479	5l.40 Two children swimming in North Zone and sinaloa martin	1·10	1·00
1480	5l.40 Mary and President Flores with Hillary Clinton (wfe of U.S. President)	1·10	1·00
1481	5l.40 Crowd before collapsed building in South Zone and rufous motmot	1·10	1·00
1482	5l.40 President Flores and George Bush (U.S. President, 1988–92)	1·10	1·00
1483	5l.40 Three men digging out rubble and tufted jay	1·10	1·00
1484	5l.40 Helicopter on beach and orchid	1·10	1·00
1485	5l.40 Car submerged under flood water in North Zone and bare-necked umbrel-labird	1·10	1·00
1486	5l.40 Tipper Gore (U.S. Vice-president's wife) and Mary Flores in flooded building	1·10	1·00
1487	5l.40 Flooded banana planta-tion and orchid	1·10	1·00
1488	5l.40 Tegucigalpa submerged under flood water and red-breasted blackbird and green bird	1·10	1·00
1489	5l.40 Traffic jam behind rocks from landslide ("Red Vial")	1·10	1·00
1490	5l.40 Comayaguela and ridg-way's cotinga	1·10	1·00
1491	5l.40 Destruction of Comay-aguela street and orchid	1·10	1·00
1492	5l.40 People carrying plank in Eastern Zone and scarlet macaw	1·10	1·00
1493	5l.40 Mexican truck being filled with debris and orchid	1·10	1·00
1494	5l.40 Bulldozer clearing street and white-tipped sicklebill	1·10	1·00
1495	5l.40 President Flores and Presi-dent Chirac of France	1·10	1·00
1496	5l.40 Comayaguela commercial zone flooded and tooth-billed hummingbird	1·10	1·00
1497	5l.40 People looking at flood water in Tegucigalpa and lineated woodpecker	1·10	1·00
1498	5l.40 Stranded BMW motor car in Comayaguela street and hoffmann's conure	1·10	1·00

326 Pilar Salinas

1999. Air. America (1998). Famous Women. Multicoloured.

1499	2l.60 Type **326**	55	35
1500	7l.30 Clementina Suarerz (poet)	1·60	85
1501	10l.65 Mary Flores (President's wife)	2·30	1·40

327 Enka Orellana breast-feeding Baby

1999. Air. Mothers' Day. Multicoloured.

1502	20l. Type **327**	4·00	3·00
1503	30l. Paphiopedilum urbanianum (horiz)	5·75	4·00
1504	50l. Miltoniopsis vexillaria (horiz)	9·75	6·00

1999. No. 748 surch.

1505	2l.60 on 1c. blue and red	70	45
1506	7l.85 on 1c. blue and red	2·00	1·40
1507	10l.65 on 1c. blue and red	2·75	1·90
1508	11l.55 on 1c. blue and red	3·00	2·10
1509	12l.45 on 1c. blue and red	3·25	2·30
1510	13l.85 on 1c. blue and red	3·50	2·50

329 Orange-fronted Conure

1999. Air. 30th Anniv of Sogerin Bank. Birds. Multicoloured.

1511	3l. Type **329**	70	45
1512	3l. White-fronted amazon (Amazona albifrons)	70	45
1513	3l. Yellow-naped amazon (Amazona auropalliata)	70	45
1514	3l. Red-lored amazon (Amazona autumnalis)	70	45
1515	3l. Sun-bittern (Eurypga helias)	70	45
1516	3l. Great curassow (Crax rubra)	70	45
1517	3l. Orange-chinned parakeet (Brotogeris jugularis)	70	45
1518	3l. White-capped parrot (Pionus senilis)	70	45
1519	3l. Brown-throated conure (Aratinga rubritorques)	70	45
1520	3l. Great tinamou (Tinamus major)	70	45
1521	5l. King vulture (Sarcorhamphus papa)	1·30	85
1522	5l. White hawk (Leucopternis albicollis)	1·30	85
1523	5l. Harpy eagle (Harpia harpyja)	1·30	85
1524	5l. Spectacled owl (Pulsatrix perspicillata)	1·30	85
1525	5l. Ornate hawk eagle (Spiza-etus ornatus)	1·30	85
1526	5l. Resplendent quetzal (Pha-romachrus mocinno)	1·30	85
1527	5l. Emerald toucanet (Aulaco-rhynchus prasinus)	1·30	85
1528	5l. Honduras emerald (Amazilia luciae)	1·30	85
1529	5l. Scarlet macaw (Ara macao)	1·30	85
1530	5l. Yucatan woodpecker (Centu-ras pygmaeus)	1·30	85
1531	10l. Jabiru (Jabiru mycteria) (wrongly inscr "Jaberu")	2·20	1·50
1532	10l. Hook-billed kite (Chondro-hierax uncinatus)	2·20	1·50
1533	10l. Resplendent quetzal (Pharomachrus mocinno) (different)	2·20	1·50
1534	10l. Keel-billed toucan (Ram-phastos sulfuratus)	2·20	1·50

Nos. 1511/30 were issued together, se-tenant, forming a composite design.

330 Salvador Moncada (scientist) and Pipette

1999. Air. New Millennium. Multicoloured.

1535	2l. Type **330**	45	35
1536	8l.65 Albert Einstein (scientist, formulator of Theory of Relativity, 1905)	1·40	1·00
1537	10l. Wilhelm Rontgen (scientist, discoverer of X-rays, 1895)	1·70	1·40
1538	14l.95 George Stephenson (engineer) (inventor of steam locomotive, 1829) and Rocket (horiz)	2·75	2·00

331 Headquarters

1999. Air. 40th Anniv of Inter-American Development Bank.

1539	**331**	18l.30 multicoloured	3·50	2·20

332 Josemaria Escriva de Balaguer (founder)

1999. Air. 70th Anniv (1998) of Founding of Opus Dei (religious organization).

1540	**332**	2l.60 multicoloured	70	45
1541	**332**	16l.40 multicoloured	3·75	2·20

333 Statue and View of Cedros, Francisco Morazan Province

1999. Air. 175th Anniv of National Congress. Multicoloured.

1542	4l.30 Type **333**	90	45
1543	10l. Rafael Pineda Ponce (Congress President) and building	2·10	1·40

334 St. Peter

2000. Holy Year 2000. Multicoloured.

1544	4l. Open gateway into garden	1·00	70
1545	4l.30 Type **334**	1·10	80
1546	4l.30 As Type **334**, but with country name and face value in yellow	1·10	80
1547	6l.90 Jesus (statue) and Jerusa-lem (horiz)	1·70	1·20
1548	7l.30 Pope John Paul II address-ing crowd (horiz)	1·90	1·30
1549	10l. Pope John Paul II	2·75	1·80
1550	14l. Pope John Paul II and Pres. Carlos Roberto Flores	3·00	2·10
1551	14l. As No. 1550 but with country name at right	3·50	2·40

335 Pres. Flores and Reunion Consultative Group, Stockholm, Sweden

2000. Second Anniv of Inauguration of President Carlos Roberto Flores. Multicoloured.

1552	10l. Type **335**	2·50	1·80
1553	10l.65 Flores and General Mario Hung Pacheco	2·75	1·90

336 Left Half of Marimba

2000. Air. Musical Instruments. Multicoloured.

1554	1l.40 Type **336**	45	35
1555	1l.40 Right half of Marimba	45	35
1556	1l.40 Ayotl	45	35
1557	2l.60 Maracas	80	65
1558	2l.60 Guiro	80	65
1559	2l.60 Chinchin	80	65
1560	2l.60 Raspador	80	65
1561	2l.60 Quijada de Caballo	80	65
1562	3l. Fish-shaped whistle	90	70
1563	3l. Aztec drum	90	70
1564	3l. Whistle ("Pito Zoomorfo de un tono")	90	70
1565	3l. Whistle ("Pito Zoomorfo de dos tonos")	90	70
1566	3l. Tun	90	70
1567	4l. Tecomate	1·10	85
1568	4l. Deerskin drum	1·10	85
1569	4l. Guacalitos	1·10	85

1570	4l. Women standing to left of marimba	1·10	85
1571	4l. Men standing to right of marimba	1·10	85
1572	10l. Maya drum	3·25	2·50
1573	10l. Teponaxtle	3·25	2·50
MS1574a	Inscribed Pro filatelia in black, 221×139 mm. 10l.+1l. Drummer, Garifuna (horiz); 10l.+1l. Tolteca drum (horiz); 10l.+1l. Flutes (horiz); 10l.+1l. Chirimia (horiz); 10l.+1l. Maya drum (different) (horiz); 10l.+1l. Man blowing conch shell (horiz)	15·00	14·50
MS1574b	As MS1574a but inscription Pro filatelia in red	17·00	16·00

337 Man

2000. 50th Anniv of Central Honduras Bank. Paintings by Pablo Zelaya Sierra. Multicoloured.

1575	1l.40 Type **337**	45	35
1576	1l.40 Dog barking	45	35
1577	1l.40 View of town on hillside	45	35
1578	1l.40 Back of woman's head	45	35
1579	1l.40 Woman holding bowl	45	35
1580	2l. Building surrounded by trees	70	60
1581	2l. Old woman wearing black gown	70	60
1582	2l. Two women talking	70	60
1583	2l. Woman wrapped in white sheet	70	60
1584	2l. View of walled town	70	60
1585	2l.60 Birds and animals	90	70
1586	2l.60 Trees	90	70
1587	2l.60 Nun beside harp	90	70
1588	2l.60 Archers	90	70
1589	2l.60 Moon over sea	90	70
1590	2l.60 Sculpture of woman's head	90	70
1591	2l.60 Gardener in grounds of large house	90	70
1592	2l.60 Sculpture of man's head and open fan	90	70
1593	10l. Lemons on white table cloth	3·50	3·00
1594	10l. Pile of books	3·50	3·00

338 1925 25c. on 10c. Airmail Stamp

2000. Air. 75th Anniv of Honduras Airmail Stamps. Multicoloured.

1595	7l.30 Type **338**	1·80	90
1596	10l. Thomas Canfield Pounds (founder of Central American Airline) (vert)	2·50	1·30
1597	10l.65 General Rafael Lopez Gutierrez (President of Honduras, 1920–24) (vert)	2·75	1·40
MS1598	111×89 mm. 50l.+5l. Biplane and Sumner B. Margan (pilot) (80×59 mm)	18·00	17·00

339 Flower and Rifle

2000. Air. America (1999). A New Millennium without Arms. Multicoloured.

1599	10l. Type **339**	2·75	1·80
1600	10l.65 White dove and soldier	3·25	1·90
1601	14l. Steam train and bomb (horiz)	4·00	2·50

340 Ivan Guerrero and Mario Chirinos (football)

2000. Air. Olympic Games, Sydney. Multicoloured.

1602	2l.60 Type **340**	1·30	1·10
1603	10l.65 Ramon Valle (swimming) (vert)	4·50	3·50

1604	12l.45 Gina Coello (running) (vert)	5·00	4·00
MS1605	122×90 mm. 4l.30 Swimming; 4l.30 Danilo Turcios (football); 10l.65 David Suazo (football); 10l.65 Pedro Ventura (running). Perf or imperf	8·50	8·25

L.48.50+

(341)

2000. No. MS913 surch with T **341** in black and red.

MS1606	160×110 mm. 48l.50 on 1l.50, Mayan pelota court	13·00	12·50

342 Children and White-crowned Parrot

2000. Air. International Year of Volunteers. Multicoloured.

1607	2l.60 Type **342**	70	45
1608	10l.65 Boy and flower	2·75	1·70

343 Mary and Jesus

2000. Air. Christmas. Multicoloured.

1609	1l.60 Type **343**	70	45
1610	7l.30 Nativity (vert)	2·20	1·30
1611	14l. Pavement art	2·75	1·40

344 Yellow-naped Amazon (*Amazona auroalliata*)

2001. Air. America. AIDS Awareness Campaign. Monogamy. Multicoloured.

1612	2l.60 Type **344**	45	35
1613	4l.30 Common ground dove (*Columbina passerine*) (horiz)	75	60
1614	10l.65 Scarlet macaw (*Ara macao*)	2·30	2·00
1615	20l. Harpy eagle (*Aguila harpia*)	4·50	3·50

2001. Air. Various stamps surch.

1616	2l. on 16c. brown and black (No. 947)	35	25
1617	2l. on 16c. multicoloured (No. 948)	35	25
1618	2l.60 on 3c. orange, blue and brown (No. 967)	45	35
1619	2l.60 on 3c. multicoloured (No. 1003)	45	35
1620	2l.60 on 8c. multicoloured (No. 914)	45	35
1621	2l.60 on 16c. multicoloured (No. 931)	45	35
1622	3l. on 16c. multicoloured (No. 886)	55	45
1623	4l. on 9c. multicoloured (No. 1017)	55	45
1624	4l.30 on 6c. multicoloured (No. 899)	70	50
1625	7l.30 on 6c. brown and black (No. 941)	1·30	60
1626	7l.30 on 6c. multicoloured (No. 942)	1·30	60
1627	10l. on 6c. orange-red and black (No. 877)	1·80	85
1628	10l.65 on 16c. multicoloured (No. 994)	2·00	1·00

1629	14l. on 16c. multicoloured (No. 905)	3·25	1·40

346 Cardinal Rodriguez as a Child with his Father

2001. Air. Cardinal Oscar Andreas Rodriguez. Multicoloured.

1630	2l.60 Type **346**	90	70
1631	2l.60 Seated, wearing white vestments	90	70
1632	2l.60 Seated, at Seminary, 1964	90	70
1633	2l.60 Consecration as Arch-bishop	90	70
1634	2l.60 At home, 1960	90	70
1635	2l.60 Kneeling before Pope John Paul II and other clergy, Vatican, 2001	90	70
1636	2l.60 Celebrating Mass, 1970	90	70
1637	2l.60 Woman wearing dark glasses, Cardinal Rodriguez and crowd, Vatican	90	70
1638	2l.60 Pope John Paul II and Cardinal Rodriguez wearing sash, 1993	90	70
1639	2l.60 Leaving airplane as Cardinal, 2001	90	70
1640	10l.65 Woman, Cardinal Rodriguez and Pope John Paul II, 1993 (47×40 mm)	3·50	3·00
1641	10l.65 Audience with Pope John Paul II, 2001 (47×40 mm)	3·50	3·00
1642	10l.65 Receiving cardinal ring from Pope John Paul II (47×40 mm)	3·50	3·00
1643	10l.65 Addressing crowd, 2001 (47×40 mm)	3·50	3·00
1644	10l.65 Kneeling before Pope John Paul II, Rome, 1993 (47×40 mm)	3·50	3·00
1645	10l.65 Pope John Paul II and Cardinal Rodriguez, 2000 (47×40 mm)	3·50	3·00
1646	15l. As No. 1645 enlarged to show crowd (164×132 mm)	4·50	3·50

347 Stylized Mother and child

2001. Air. 50th Anniv of United Nations High Commissioner for Refugees. Multicoloured.

1647	2l.60 Type **347**	90	60
1648	10l.65 Refugees (horiz)	3·50	2·30

348 Jug

2001. Air. 50th Anniv of Banco Occidente. Mayan Ceramics. Multicoloured.

1649	2l. Type **348**	70	60
1650	2l. Man-shaped jar	70	60
1651	2l. Seated figure with raised arms	70	60
1652	2l. Three-legged cylindrical vase	70	60
1653	2l. Textured censer with crouching animal on lid	70	60
1654	3l. Seated figure (scribe)	1·10	85
1655	3l. Cylindrical decorated jar	1·10	85
1656	3l. Three conjoined pots	1·10	85
1657	3l. Head	1·10	85
1658	3l. Man-shaped jar, arms forming handles	1·10	85
1659	5l. Decorated pot with handles and legs	1·80	1·40
1660	5l. Curved pot with lip and handles	1·80	1·40
1661	5l. Censer with large animal on lid	1·80	1·40
1662	5l. Seated figure with hands on knees	1·80	1·40
1663	5l. Man-shaped jar showing teeth	1·80	1·40

1664	6l.90 Pot with handles and narrow base	2·30	1·90
1665	6l.90 Seated figure with hands on knees (different)	2·30	1·90
1667	6l.90 Jar in shape of seated figure holding pole	2·30	1·90
1668	6l.90 Tall cylindrical vase	2·30	1·90
1669	6l.90 Textured pot with animal-shaped handles	2·30	1·90

349 Juan Ramon Molina Bridge

2001. Air. Honduras–Japan Diplomatic Relations. Sheet 153×127 mm containing T **349** and similar horiz designs showing views of bridge. Multicoloured.

MS1670	2l.60 Type **349**; 10l.65, Side view; 13l.65 From beneath	11·50	11·00

350 Turquoise-browed Motmot, Lago de Yojoa

2002. Air. America (2001). UNESCO World Heritage Sites. Multicoloured.

1671	10l. Type **350**	3·50	3·00
1672	10l.65 Iguana, Islas del Cisne	3·50	3·00
1673	20l. Chrysina quetzalcoatli, Cataratas de Pulaphanzhak (horiz)	7·25	5·75

351 Centenary Emblem

2002. Air. Centenary of Pan American Health Organization.

1674	**351** 10l. multicoloured	3·50	3·50

352 Statues and Buildings

2002. Air. Inauguration of Miguel Pastor, Mayor of Tegucigalpa. Multicoloured.

1675	1l.40 Type **352**	55	45
1676	1l.40 Chimpanzee dropping banana skin in rubbish bin	55	45
1677	1l.40 Municipal building	55	45
1678	2l.60 Flags and Mayor Pastor (27×35 mm)	90	70
1679	2l.60 Mayor Pastor sitting under tree (27×35 mm)	90	70
1680	2l.60 With elderly woman (27×35 mm)	90	70
1681	2l.60 With children (27×35 mm)	90	70
1682	2l.60 Mayor Pastor crouching (27×35 mm)	90	70
1683	2l.60 With family (27×35 mm)	90	70
1684	10l. Mayor Pastor and committee members	3·50	3·00
1685	10l. Mayor Pastor and guests on roof top	3·50	3·00
1686	10l.65 Type **352** (114×75 mm)	3·75	3·00

353 Natives and Cross

2002. Air. America. Literacy Campaign. Two sheets, each 114×92 mm containing T **353** and similar horiz designs. Multicoloured.

MS1687	(a) 2l.60 Type **353**; 3l. Santa Barbara fortress, Trujillo; 10l. "400 Years of History" (detail) (Mario Castillo); 10l. Arrival of missionaries (500th anniv of arrival of first Catholics on mainland America); (b) 10l.65 River and forest; 12l.45 Natives landing on beach; 13l.65 Spaniards landing craft; 20l. Spanish ship (500th anniv of discovery of Honduras)	10·00	9·75

354 Building and Emblems

2002. Tenth Anniv of Banco del Pais, Tegucigalpa.

1688	**354**	2l. multicoloured	35	30
1689	**354**	2l.60 multicoloured	45	35
1690	**354**	10l. multicoloured	1·60	1·30
1691	**354**	10l.65 multicoloured	1·70	1·40

355 *Vanilla planifolia*

2002. Air. Orchids. Multicoloured.

1692	1l.40 Type **355**	25	20
1693	2l.60 *Lycaste virginalis* (inscr "viriginalis")	45	35
1694	3l. *Coelia bella*	55	45
1695	4l.30 *Chysis laevis*	70	60
1696	8l.65 *Myrmecophilia brysiana*	1·40	1·20
1697	10l. *Rhyncholaelia digbyana* (inscr "Rhyncolaelia")	1·60	1·30
MS1698	96×66 mm. 20l. *Mormodes aromatica*. Imperf	3·50	3·50

356 The Nativity (figurines)

2002. Air. Christmas. Multicoloured.

1699	2l.60 Type **356**	45	35
1700	10l.65 Nativity (painting)	1·70	1·40
1701	14l. Crowd and outdoor Nativity	2·30	1·90

357 Children

2002. Air. 120th Anniv of PANI (social awareness organization). Multicoloured.

1702	2l.60 Type **357**	45	35
1703	10l. Elderly men	1·60	1·30
1704	10l.65 Carving, instruments, building and birds (vert)	1·70	1·40

358 *Chrysina spectabilis*

2003. Air. 90th Anniv of Banco Atlantida. Insects. Multicoloured.

170-1712	2l. 60×4, *Chrysina cusuquensis; Calomacraspis haroldi; Pelidnota strigosa; Odontocheila tawahka*	1·80	1·40
1705-1708	2l.×4, Type **358**; *Chrysina strasseni; Viridimicus omensis; Hoplopyga liturata*	1·40	1·20
1713-1716	3l.×4, *Chrysina cavei; Macropoides crassipes; Pelidnota velutipes; Tragidion cyanovestis*	2·20	1·80
1717-1720	4l.×4, *Chrysina pastori; Platycoelia humeralis; Phanaeus eximius; Acanthoderes cavei*	2·80	2·40
1721-1724	10l. 65×4, *Chrysina quetzalcoatli; Cyclocephala abrelata; Aegithus rufipennis; Callipogon barbatum*	6·75	5·50
MS1725	120×72 mm. 10l.×3, Eggs; Larva; Pupa	4·50	4·25

359 Schoolchildren

2003. Air. World Food Programme. Multicoloured.

1726	2l.60 Type **359**	45	35
1727	6l.90 Girl eating from red bowl	1·20	95
1728	10l.65 Child eating, spoon in right hand	1·70	1·40

360 Pope John Paul II

2003. Air. 25th Anniv of Pontificate of Pope John Paul II. 20th Anniv of visit of Pope John Paul II to Honduras. Sheet 185×82 mm containing T **360** and similar vert designs. Multicoloured.

MS1729	13l.65 Type **360**; 14l.55 Disembarking from aircraft; 15l.45 Wearing mitre; 16l.65 Holding rosary	9·25	9·00

361 Foodstuffs

2003. Air. 50th Anniv of OIRSA (Organization for Farming Health). Multicoloured.

1730	2l.60 Type **361**	55	45
1731	10l. Vegetables as eye	2·00	1·60
1732	10l.65 Emblem	2·10	1·70
1733	14l. Basket of vegetables	2·75	2·10
1734	20l. Sweet corn, squash and fish	3·75	3·00

362 Llama Bridge

2003. Air. Bridges. Sheet 169×182 mm containing T **362** and similar horiz designs. Multicoloured.

MS1735	3l. Type **362**; 3l. Sol Naciente; 4l.30 Rio Hondo; Iztoca; 4l.30 El Chile; 10l. La Democracia; 10l. Guasaule	9·00	8·50

363 Flag and Emblem

2003. Air. Telethon. Multicoloured.

1736	1l.40 Type **363**	25	20
1737	2l.60 Emblem and outstretched hand	55	45
1738	7l.30 As No. 1737 but design enlarged	1·40	1·20
1739	10l. Map and emblem	1·80	1·40

364 Angel

2003. Air. Christmas. Multicoloured.

1740	10l.65 Type **364**	1·80	1·40
1741	14l. The Nativity	2·75	2·10

365 *Arantinga strenua*

2003. Air. America. Endangered Species. Birds. Sheet 94×105 mm containing T **365** and similar vert designs. Multicoloured.

MS1742	10l. Type **365**; 10l.65 *Falco deiroleucus*; 14l. *Spizaetus melanoleucos*; 20l. *Amazona xantholora*	7·25	7·00

Nos. 1743/54 and Type **366** have been left for 'Fauna', issued on 24 May 2004, not yet received.
Nos. 1755/59 and Type **367** have been left for 'Shells', issued on 19 July 2004, not yet received.
No. 1760 and Type **368** have been left for 'Surcharges', issued on 13 August 2004, not yet received.
Nos. 1761/65 and Type **369** have been left for 'Football', issued on 13 September 2004, not yet received.

370 Journey to Bethlehem

2004. Air. Christmas. Multicoloured.

1766	2l.60 Type **370**	55	45
1767	7l.85 Santa enclosed in bauble	1·50	1·30
1768	10l.65 Three kings	2·10	1·70
1769	20l. The Nativity	3·75	3·00

371 Family

2005. Air. Family Unity. Multicoloured.

1770	10l. Type **371**	2·00	1·60
1771	20l. Virgen de Suyapa (Virgin of Suyapa) (vert)	3·75	3·00

372 Paul Harris (founder) and Early Leaders

2005. Air. Centenary of Rotary International. Multicoloured.

1772	2l.60 Type **372**	55	40
1773	5l. Rotary emblem (vert)	1·00	85
1774	8l. Community bank and Rotary emblems	1·70	1·40
1775	10l.65 Polio plus emblem	2·10	1·70
1776	14l. Carved monument	2·75	2·10

373 Pope John Paul II

2005. Air. Pope John Paul II Commemoration. Multicoloured.

1777	10l. Type **373**	2·00	1·60
1778	15l. Facing left	2·75	2·40

No. 1779 is left for stamp not yet received.

374 Macaws

2005. Air. 75th Anniv of Medical Review. Sheet 92×118 mm T **374** and similar vert designs. Multicoloured.

MS1784	25l.×4, Type **374**; Macaw and bananas; Cockerel; Turkeys	19·00	19·00

Nos. 1780/83 have been left for single stamps not yet received.
No. 1785 is vacant.

376 One Hundred Sacks of Rice (play)

2003. Air. 70th Anniv of Honduras–Japan Diplomatic Relations. Multicoloured.

1836	8l. Type **376**	1·70	1·40
1837	15l. Emblem	2·75	2·40
1838	30l. National Congress and Princess Sayako of Japan	5·50	4·75
MS1839	106×99 mm. 25l.×4, Japanese ceramics; Cherry blossom and *Rhyncholaelia digbyana*; Mayan ceramic; Mount Fuji and Pico bonito National Park	19·00	19·00

Nos. 1786/1835 and Type **375** have been left for 'Surcharges', issued on 3 June 2005, not yet received.

377 Jose Trinidad Cabanas

2005. Air. Birth Bicentenary of Jose Trinidad Cabanas (president 1852–1855). Multicoloured.

1840	3l. Type **377**	60	45
1841	8l. University City (horiz)	1·70	1·40
1842	15l. As older man	2·75	2·40

378 Emblem

2005. Air. Water Capital. Multicoloured.

1843	30l. Type **378**	5·50	4·75
MS1844	99×73 mm. 50l. As Type **378**	9·25	9·25

Nos. 1845/49 and Type **379** have been left for 'Mail Transport', issued on 6 December 2005, not yet received.
No. 1850 and Type **380** have been left for 'Fungi', issued 2005, not yet received.
Nos. 1851/54 and Type **381** have been left for 'Surcharges', issued 2005, not yet received.
Nos. 1855/6 and Type **382** have been left for 'Winter Olympic Games, Turin', issued on 24 January 2006, not yet received.

383 Ruins, Copan

2006. Air. Debt Reduction. Multicoloured.

1857	14l. Type **383**	2·75	2·10
1858	15l. Flags of supporting countries	2·75	2·40
1859	30l. Ricardo Maduro (pres. 2002–2006) (vert)	5·50	4·75

No. 1860 is vacant.
Nos. 1861/63 and Type **384** have been left for '70th Anniv of Chamber of Commerce', issued 2006, not yet received.
Nos. 1864/5 and Type **385** have been left for 'Honduras–Brazil Diplomatic Relations', issued 2006, not yet received.
No. 1866 and Type **386** have been left for 'Honduras–Japan Friendship', issued 2006, not yet received.

387 Roberto Micheletti Bain (pres. Congress), Manuel Zelaya (pres. 2006–) and Vilma Cecilia Morales (pres. supreme court)

2007. Air. 25th Anniv of National Constitution. Multicoloured.

1867	5l. Type **387**	1·00	85
1868	10l. First constituent assembly meeting venue	2·00	1·60
1869	15l. Presidential palace (1922–91) (vert)	2·75	2·40
1870	20l. Legislative building	3·75	3·00

Nos. 1871/76 and Type **388** have been left for '50th Anniv of Central Bank', issued on 13 March 2007, not yet received.
No. 1877 and Type **389** have been left for 'Children's Rights', issued on 18 October 2007, not yet received.

390 Launch

2007. 50th Anniv of Space Exploration. Sputnik. Sheet 79×100 mm containing T **390** and similar multicoloured designs.
MS1878 25l. Type **390**; 35l. *Sputnik*; 50l. Orbit (60×40 mm) ... 4·75 ... 3·75

Nos. 1879/80; 1882; 1886; 1888; 1890/1 and 1894/5 have been left for stamps not yet received.

2007. Air. Various stamps surch.

1881	2l. on 8l.65 multicoloured (1696)		40	35
1883	3l. on 1l.40 multicoloured (1692)		60	45
1884	3l. on 1l.40 multicoloured (1736)		60	45
1885	3l. on 2l.60 multicoloured (1737)		60	45
1887	3l. on 7l.30 multicoloured (1738)		60	45
1889	3l. on 18l.30 multicoloured (1539)		60	45
1892	5l. on 2l.60 multicoloured (1693)		1·50	1·30
1893	5l. on 4l.30 multicoloured (1695)		1·50	1·30

392 Struggle against Poverty

2008. Air. Exfilhon 2008 Stamp Exhibition. America–2005, 2006, 2007 and 2008. Sheet 108×92 mm containing T **392** and similar horiz designs. Multicoloured.
MS1896 2l. Type **392**; 3l. Alternative energy; 5l. Education for all; 10l. National festivals ... 4·50 ... 4·50

393 *Medusa de las Islas*

2008. Air. Paintings by Gaye–Darlene Bidart de Satulsky. Sheet 110×155 mm containing T **393** and similar vert designs. Multicoloured.
MS1897 3l. Type **393**; 3l. *Nido de Amor*; 3l. *Guitarrista Isleno*; 5l. *'M' Hombre Cruz*; 5l. *Amor a Martillazors*; 5l. *Sor Maria Rosa*; 5l. *Islena, Luna y Mar*; 5l. *Clementina Suarez*; 5l. *La Naranjera*; ... 7·75 ... 7·75

394 Olympic Torch

2008. Air. Olympic Games, Beijing. Multicoloured.

1898	3l. Type **394**		60	45
1899	5l. Athletics		1·00	85
1900	5l. Judo		1·00	85
1901	25l. Football		4·75	3·75

395 'El Emprendedor'

2008. Air. Centenary of Honduras–Mexico Diplomatic Relations. Sheet 139×113 mm containing T **395** and similar multicoloured designs, inscriptions given.
MS1902 5l. Type **395**; 10l. 'La Estrellas se aceranal Aguia'; 15l. 'Hermano de Antano' (horiz); 20l. 'Lazos y Vientos de Amistad'; 25l. 'Eclipse Maya' (horiz); 50l. 'Ciclico' (horiz) ... 19·00 ... 19·00

No. 1903 is vacant.

396 Juan Ramon Molina

2008. Air. Death Centenary of Juan Ramon Molina (writer). Multicoloured.

1904	10l. Type **396**		2·00	1·60
1905	25l. Bust		4·75	3·75

397 School Building

2009. Air. Supporting Education. Escuela Normal 'Espana', Villa Ahumada, Danli. Multicoloured.

1906	2l. Type **397**		45	35
1907	5l. Emblem		1·50	1·30

398 Hopscotch

2009. Air. Games. Multicoloured.

1908	3l. Type **398**		60	45
1909	10l. Kite flying		2·00	1·60
1910	20l. Spinning top		3·75	3·00
1911	50l. Children playing games		9·00	7·75

EXPRESS LETTER STAMPS

1953. No. O507 surch **ENTREGA INMEDIATA 1953 L 0.20.**
E523 **127** 20c. on 1c. olive & pur ... 3·75 ... 1·80

1956. Air. Optd **ENTREGA INMEDIATA** as in Type E**135**.
E570 **E135** 20c. grey and black ... 1·40 ... 60

1966. Stamp Cent. Design similar to T **144**.
E700 20c. brown, gold & lt brown ... 85 ... 40
DESIGN—HORIZ: 20c. Motor cyclist.

E135 Lockheed Constellation

1972. As T **168**, but inscr "ENTREGA INMEDIATA". Multicoloured.
E811 20c. Chance Vought F4U-5 Corsair fighter aircraft ... 60 ... 60

1975. No. E811 surch.
E848 60c. on 20c. multicoloured ... 1·90 ... 1·20

1976. As T **178**.
E893 60c. Deer in forest ... 1·20 ... 85

OFFICIAL STAMPS
Various stamps overprinted OFICIAL.

1890. Stamps of 1890.

O56	**6**	1c. yellow	35
O57	**6**	2c. yellow	35
O58	**6**	5c. yellow	35
O59	**6**	10c. yellow	35
O60	**6**	20c. yellow	35
O61	**6**	25c. yellow	35
O62	**6**	30c. yellow	35
O63	**6**	40c. yellow	35
O64	**6**	50c. yellow	35
O65	**6**	75c. yellow	35
O66	**6**	1p. yellow	35

1891. Stamps of 1891.

O70	**8**	1c. yellow	35
O71	**8**	2c. yellow	35
O72	**8**	5c. yellow	35
O73	**8**	10c. yellow	35
O74	**8**	20c. yellow	35
O75	**8**	25c. yellow	35
O76	**8**	30c. yellow	35
O77	**8**	40c. yellow	35
O78	**8**	50c. yellow	35
O79	**8**	75c. yellow	35
O80	**8**	1p. yellow	35

1898. Stamps of 1898.

O116	**14**	5c. blue	60
O117	**14**	10c. blue	1·20
O118	**14**	20c. bistre	1·90
O119	**14**	50c. orange	3·75
O120	**14**	1p. green	5·00

1911. Stamps of 1911.

O148	**20**	1c. violet	2·20	85
O149	**20**	2c. green	1·40	95
O150	**20**	5c. red	2·20	1·80
O151	**20**	6c. blue	4·00	3·00
O152	**20**	10c. blue	2·20	1·80
O153	**20**	20c. yellow	7·50	7·25
O154	**20**	50c. brown	12·50	10·50
O155	**20**	1p. olive	19·00	14·50

1914. No. O150 and O148 surch.

O186		1c. on 5c. red	2·75	2·20
O187		2c. on 5c. red	3·00	2·20
O188		10c. on 1c. violet	5·50	4·75
O189		10c. on 5c. red	31·00	30·00
O190		20c. on 1c. violet	4·25	3·50

1914. No. O190 and O146 surch **OFICIAL** and value.

O191		10c. on 20c. on 1c. violet	31·00	30·00
O193		20c. on 50c. brown	7·50	7·25

1915. Stamps of 1913.

O194	**26**	1c. brown	40	40
O195	**26**	2c. red	40	40
O197	**27**	5c. blue	45	45
O198	**27**	6c. violet	1·50	1·40
O199	**26**	10c. brown	1·20	1·20
O200	**26**	20c. brown	3·00	2·75
O202	**27**	50c. red	5·75	5·75

1915. No. 168 surch **OFICIAL $0.01.**
O203 **26** 1c. on 2c. red ... 3·00 ... 3·00

1915. Stamps of 1915.

O204	**32**	1c. brown	35	35
O205	**32**	2c. red	50	50
O206		5c. blue	50	50
O207		6c. violet	60	60
O208	**32**	10c. blue	75	70
O209	**32**	20c. brown	1·00	95
O210		50c. red	2·50	2·40
O211		1p. green	5·00	4·75

1921. Stamps of 1919.

O212	**36**	1c. brown	3·75	3·50
O213	**36**	2c. red	10·00	9·75
O214	**36**	5c. red	10·00	9·75
O215	**36**	6c. mauve	85	85
O216	**36**	10c. blue	1·00	95
O217	**36**	15c. blue	1·20	1·20
O218	**36**	20c. brown	1·60	1·60
O219	**36**	50c. brown	2·20	2·20
O220	**36**	1p. green	4·25	4·25

1925. Stamps of 1923.

O222	**39**	1c. olive	25	25
O223	**39**	2c. red	35	35
O224	**39**	6c. purple	50	50
O225	**39**	10c. blue	75	70
O226	**39**	20c. brown	1·10	1·10
O227	**39**	50c. red	2·00	1·90
O228	**39**	1p. green	3·00	3·00

O50 J. R. Molina

1929

O259		1c. blue	25	10
O260	**O50**	2c. red	25	25
O261		5c. violet	50	50
O262		10c. green	60	50
O263		20c. blue	75	70
O264		50c. green and yellow	1·50	1·40
O265		1p. brown	3·00	3·00

DESIGNS: J. C. Valle; 5c. Coffee tree; 10c. J. T. Reyes; 20c. Tegucigalpa Cathedral; 50c. Lake Yojoa; 1p. Wireless station.

1930. Air. Nos. O224/8 surch **Servicio aereo Vale 5 centavos VI-1930** or optd **Servicio aereo Habilitado VI-1930.**

O319	**39**	5c. on 6c. purple	1·40	1·30
O320	**39**	6c. purple	£120	£120
O321	**39**	10c. blue	1·60	1·60
O322	**39**	20c. brown	1·60	1·60
O323	**39**	50c. red	2·00	1·90
O324	**39**	1p. green	1·60	1·60

O70 Tegucigalpa

1931

O328	**O70**	1c. blue	35	25
O329	**O70**	2c. purple	50	35
O330	**O70**	5c. olive	60	50
O331	**O70**	6c. red	60	50
O332	**O70**	10c. green	75	50
O333	**O70**	15c. brown	1·00	60
O334	**O70**	20c. brown	1·20	85
O335	**O70**	50c. violet	1·50	1·10
O336	**O70**	1p. orange	2·75	2·75

1933. Air. Various stamps surch **Aereo Oficial Vale 1933** and new value.

O354	**66**	20c. on 2c. blue	5·00	4·75
O355	**66**	20c. on 2c. orange	5·00	4·75
O356	**66**	20c. on 2c. red	5·00	4·75
O357	**66**	40c. on 2c. orange	4·50	4·25
O358	**66**	40c. on 2c. red	6·75	6·75
O360	-	40c. on 5c. purple (249)	6·75	6·75
O361	-	40c. on 5c. blue (250)	9·25	9·00
O362	-	40c. on 5c. purple (270)	6·75	6·75
O363	-	40c. on 5c. blue (271)	12·50	12·00
O364	-	40c. on 5c. violet (O261)	2·40	2·40
O372	**39**	60c. on 5c. purple (O224)	1·50	1·40
O365	-	70c. on 5c. blue (188)	8·00	7·75
O374	-	70c. on 5c. blue (O206)	8·00	7·75
O366	**39**	70c. on 10c. blue	7·50	7·25
O375	**32**	70c. on 10c. blue (O208)	12·50	12·00
O377	**36**	70c. on 10c. blue (O216)	5·50	5·50
O378	**39**	70c. on 10c. blue (O225)	7·50	7·25
O380	**36**	70c. on 15c. blue (O217)	£150	£140
O381	**36**	90c. on 10c. blue (O216)	8·00	7·75
O382	**36**	90c. on 15c. blue (O217)	5·75	5·50
O383	**39**	1l. on 2c. red	2·10	2·10
O367	-	1l. on 20c. brown	2·10	2·10
O384	**36**	1l. on 20c. brown (O218)	5·75	5·50
O385	**39**	1l. on 20c. brown (O226)	5·00	4·75
O368	**39**	1l. on 50c. red	16·00	15·00
O386	**36**	1l. on 50c. brown (O219)	3·00	3·00
O387	**39**	1l. on 50c. red (O227)	6·75	6·75
O369	**36**	1.20l. on 1p. green	2·50	2·40
O388	-	1.20l. on 1p. grn (O211)	13·50	10·50
O389	**39**	1.20l. on 1p. grn (O288)	2·50	2·40

1935. Stamps of 1931 optd **HABILITADO 1935-1938** between thick lines.

O390	**O70**	1c. blue	35	35
O391	**O70**	2c. purple	35	35
O392	**O70**	5c. olive	50	50
O393	**O70**	6c. red	60	60
O394	**O70**	10c. green	60	60
O395	**O70**	15c. brown	75	70
O396	**O70**	20c. brown	1·50	1·40
O397	**O70**	50c. violet	5·50	5·50

O92 Coat of Arms and National Flag

1939. Air.

O400	**O92**	2c. blue and green	25	25
O401	**O92**	5c. blue and orange	25	25
O402	**O92**	8c. blue and brown	25	25
O403	**O92**	15c. blue and red	35	25
O404	**O92**	46c. blue and olive	60	35
O405	**O92**	50c. blue and violet	75	35
O406	**O92**	1l. blue and brown	2·50	1·80
O407	**O92**	2l. blue and red	5·00	3·25

1952. Air. 500th Birth Anniv of Isabella the Catholic. As Nos. 499/506 but colours changed, optd **OFICIAL.**

O507	**127**	1c. olive and purple	10	10
O508	-	2c. violet and brown	25	25
O509	-	8c. black and red	35	35
O510	**128**	16c. green and violet	50	50
O511	-	30c. black and blue	75	70
O512	-	1l. sepia and green	2·00	1·90
O513	**127**	2l. brown and blue	4·00	3·75
O514	**128**	5l. slate and orange	10·50	10·00

1953. Air. United Nations. As Nos. 523/31 but colours changed (except 1c.), optd **OFICIAL.**

O532	-	1c. blue and black	25	25
O533	**130**	2c. green and black	25	25
O534	-	3c. orange and black	25	25
O535	-	5c. red and black	25	25
O536	-	15c. sepia and black	35	25
O537	-	30c. purple and black	60	50
O538	-	1l. olive and black	6·25	3·50
O539	-	2l. purple and black	7·50	4·25
O540	-	5l. blue and black	19·00	10·50

1956. Air. As Nos. 551/69 but colours changed, optd **OFICIAL.**

O570	1c. lake and black	25	25
O571	2c. red and black	25	25
O572	3c. purple and black	25	25
O573	4c. orange and black	25	25
O574	5c. turquoise and black	25	25
O575	8c. multicoloured	25	25
O576	10c. brown and black	25	25
O577	12c. red and black	25	25
O578	15c. black and red	25	25
O579	20c. olive and black	25	25
O580	24c. blue and black	35	25
O581	25c. purple and black	35	25
O582	30c. green and black	35	25
O583	40c. orange and black	35	35
O584	50c. red and black	60	50
O585	60c. purple and black	60	60
O586	1l. sepia and black	2·50	1·60
O587	2l. blue and black	5·00	3·50
O588	5f. blue and black	10·50	7·75

1957. Air. Revolution of 21 October 1956. Nos. 570/9 optd **OFICIAL.** Frames in black.

O589	1c. blue and yellow	10	10
O590	2c. purple, green and orange	10	10
O591	5c. blue and pink	10	10
O592	8c. violet, olive and orange	10	10
O593	10c. brown and violet	25	25
O594	12c. blue and turquoise	25	25
O595	15c. brown and green	35	35
O596	30c. grey and pink	85	85
O597	1l. brown and blue	2·75	2·75
O598	2l. grey and green	6·25	6·00

1959. Air. Abraham Lincoln. 150th Birth Anniv No. 590/601 but colours changed and optd **OFICIAL.** Flags in blue and red.

O602	1c. yellow	25	25
O603	2c. olive	25	25
O604	3c. brown	25	25
O605	5c. blue	25	25
O606	10c. purple	25	25
O607	12c. orange	25	25
O608	15c. sepia	25	25
O609	25c. slate	35	25
O610	50c. red	60	35
O611	1l. violet	1·20	95
O612	2l. blue	3·50	1·80
O613	5l. green	7·00	6·25
MSO614	180×140 mm. As Nos. O603, O605, O607/8, O610 and O612. Imperf	4·25	3·50

1964. Air. Pres. Kennedy Memorial Issue. Optd **IN MEMORIAM JOHN F. KENNEDY 22 NOVIEMBRE 1963.**

O626	1c. yellow (No. O602)	10	10
O627	2c. olive (No. O603)	25	25
O628	3c. brown (No. O604)	35	25
O629	5c. blue (No. O605)	60	50
O630	15c. sepia (No. O608)	2·50	2·20
O631	50c. red (No. O610)	12·00	10·50
MSO632	On No. **MS**614	75·00	70·00

1964. Air. Nos. O611/14 surch.

O647	10c. on 50c. red	35	35
O648	12c. on 15c. sepia	50	35
O649	12c. on 25c. slate	50	35
O621	20c. on 25c. slate	75	50

1964. Air. Olympic Games, Tokyo. Optd with Olympic Rings and **1964.**

O632	2l. purple & black (No. O539)	10·00	9·75

1965. Air. Nos. 630/38 optd **OFICIAL.**

O650	144	1c. black and green	10	10
O651	-	2c. black and mauve	10	10
O652	-	5c. black and blue	25	25
O653	-	8c. black and green	25	25
O654	144	10c. black and bistre	50	50
O655	-	12c. black and yellow	60	60
O656	-	1l. black and buff	5·50	5·50
O657	-	2l. black and olive	10·50	10·00
O658	144	3l. black and red	14·00	13·50

1965. Air. Churchill Commem. Optd **IN MEMORIAM Sir Winston Churchill 1874-1965.**

O674	128	16c. green and violet	1·50	1·40

1971. Air. Various official stamps surch in figures.

O789	-	10c. on 2c. (O603)	50	35
O788	134	10c. on 3c. (O572)	50	35
O790	-	10c. on 3c. (O604)	50	35

1974. Air. Nos. O570 and O602 surch.

O849	2c. on 1c. lake and black	25	10
O850	2c. on 1c. yellow	25	10

Pt. 1, Pt. 17

HONG KONG

Former British colony at the mouth of the Canton R., consisting of the island of Hong Kong and peninsula of Kowloon. Under Japanese Occupation from 25 December 1941, until liberated by British forces on 16 September 1945.

Hong Kong became a Special Administrative Region of the People's Republic of China on 1 July 1997.

Hong Kong.
100 cents = 1 Hong Kong dollar.

Japanese Occupation of Hong Kong.
100 sen = 1 yen.

1

1862

8a	1	2c. brown	£130	7·50
34	1	4c. grey	29·00	3·00
10	1	6c. lilac	£450	19·00
11b	1	8c. yellow	£475	15·00
12a	1	12c. blue	32·00	9·00
22	1	16c. yellow	£1900	65·00
4	1	18c. lilac	£650	55·00
14	1	24c. green	£650	12·00
15a	1	30c. red	£900	15·00
16	1	30c. mauve	£275	5·50
17a	1	48c. red	£950	32·00
18	1	96c. olive	£80000	£750
19	1	96c. grey	£1500	65·00

1877. Surch in figures and words, thus **5 cents.**

23	5c. on 8c. yellow	£1100	£110
24	5c. on 18c. lilac	£950	65·00
25	10c. on 12c. blue	£1000	55·00
26	10c. on 16c. yellow	£4250	£150
27	10c. on 24c. green	£1500	£100
20	16c. on 18c. lilac	£2250	£150
21	28c. on 30c. mauve	£1500	50·00

1880

33	2c. red	55·00	2·75
56	2c. green	28·00	85
57	4c. red	21·00	85
35	5c. blue	42·00	85
58	5c. yellow	26·00	85
30	10c. mauve	£850	17·00
37a	10c. green	£180	2·00
38	10c. purple on red	45·00	1·75
59	10c. blue	50·00	2·50
39a	30c. green	£110	27·00
61	30c. brown	60·00	26·00
31	48c. brown	£1500	£110

1885. Surch in figures and words, thus **20 CENTS.**

54	10c. on 30c. green	£600	£1200
40	20c. on 30c. red	£200	6·00
45a	20c. on 30c. green	£110	£150
41	50c. on 48c. brown	£400	45·00
46	50c. on 48c. purple	£300	£325
42	$1 on 96c. olive	£750	85·00
47	$1 on 96c. purple on red	£800	£350
53a	$1 on 96c. black	£2750	£3750

1891. Surch in figures and words, thus **7 cents.**

43	7c. on 10c. green	95·00	10·00
44	14c. on 30c. mauve	£200	80·00

弍	五十	壹員
13 (20c.)	**14** (50c.)	**15** ($1)

1891. T **1** surch with figures and words and with Chinese surch also.

55	-	10c. on 30c. green	75·00	90·00
48a	13	20c. on 30c. green	42·00	9·50
49	14	50c. on 48c. purple	80·00	5·50
50	15	$1 on 96c. purple on red	£450	22·00
52a	15	$1 on 96c. black	£200	27·00

The Chinese surch on No. 55 is larger than Type **13.**

1891. 50th Anniv of Colony. Optd **1841 Hong Kong JUBILEE 1891.**

51	1	2c. red	£475	£130

20

1903

62	20	1c. purple and brown	2·00	50
91	20	1c. brown	8·50	1·00
77	20	2c. green	24·00	2·75

78a	20	4c. purple on red	23·00	2·00
93	20	4c. red	18·00	40
79a	20	5c. green and orange	22·00	7·00
94	20	6c. brown and purple	35·00	8·00
66	20	8c. grey and violet	15·00	1·50
81	20	10c. purple and blue on blue	32·00	1·25
95	20	10c. blue	60·00	40
68	20	12c. green & purple on yell	12·00	5·50
83a	20	20c. grey and brown	60·00	3·50
96	20	20c. purple and green	50·00	45·00
84	20	30c. green and black	65·00	32·00
97	20	30c. purple and yellow	65·00	42·00
85	20	50c. green and purple	£110	16·00
98	20	50c. black on green	50·00	19·00
86	20	$1 purple and olive	£200	42·00
87a	20	$2 grey and red	£300	£130
99	20	$2 red and black	£400	£425
88	20	$3 grey and blue	£350	£325
89	20	$5 purple and green	£550	£475
76	20	$10 grey and orange on blue	£1400	£475

24

1912

117	24	1c. brown	2·25	40
118	24	2c. green	6·00	1·00
118c	24	2c. grey	25·00	10·00
119	24	3c. grey	14·00	2·00
120	24	4c. red	7·50	70
121	24	5c. violet	22·00	30
103	24	6c. orange	7·00	2·75
104	24	8c. grey	35·00	9·50
123	24	8c. orange	7·00	2·00
124	24	10c. blue	10·00	30
106	24	12c. purple on yellow	11·00	12·00
125	24	20c. purple and olive	11·00	30
126	24	25c. purple	9·00	2·25
127	24	30c. purple and orange	13·00	2·00
128	24	50c. black on green	29·00	30
129	24	$1 purple and blue on blue	50·00	50
130	24	$2 red and black	£140	9·00
131	24	$3 green and purple	£200	70·00
132	24	$5 green and red on green	£500	80·00
116	24	$10 purple and black on red	£600	£110

1935. Silver Jubilee. As T **10a** of Gambia.

133		3c. blue and black	4·00	4·50
134		5c. green and blue	8·50	3·50
135		10c. brown and blue	22·00	1·75
136		20c. grey and purple	40·00	11·00

1937. Coronation. As T **10b** of Gambia.

137		4c. green	4·50	7·00
138		15c. red	10·00	3·25
139		25c. blue	13·00	5·50

29 King George VI

1938

140	29	1c. brown	1·75	4·75
141	29	2c. grey	2·00	30
142a	29	4c. orange	4·75	3·25
143	29	5c. green	1·25	20
144	29	8c. brown	1·75	3·25
145b	29	10c. violet	8·00	1·75
146	29	15c. red	2·00	30
147	29	20c. black	1·25	30
148	29	20c. red	12·00	40
149	29	25c. blue	29·00	4·00
150	29	25c. olive	7·00	4·00
151a	29	30c. violet	27·00	11·00
152	29	30c. blue	7·00	20
153c	29	50c. purple	12·00	20
154	29	80c. red	6·00	1·00
155	29	$1 purple and blue	8·00	4·25
156	29	$1 orange and green	25·00	30
157	29	$2 orange and green	80·00	38·00
158a	29	$2 violet and red	55·00	1·00
159	29	$5 purple and red	70·00	50·00
160	29	$5 green and violet	80·00	22·00
161	29	$10 green and violet	£700	£140
162	29	$10 violet and blue	£140	55·00

30 Street Scene

1941. Centenary of British Occupation. Dated "1841 1941".

163	30	2c. orange and brown	8·00	2·50
164	-	4c. purple and red	9·50	5·00
165	-	5c. black and green	3·50	50
166	-	15c. black and red	9·50	3·00
167	-	25c. brown and blue	19·00	9·00
168	-	$1 blue and orange	50·00	13·00

DESIGNS—HORIZ: 4c. *Empress of Japan* (liner) and junk; 5c. University; 15c. Harbour; $1 *Falcon* (clipper) and Short S.23 Empire "C" Class flying boat. VERT: 25c. Hong Kong Bank.

For Japanese issues see "Japanese Occupation of Hong Kong".

36 King George VI and Pheonix

1946. Victory.

169	36	30c. blue and red	3·50	2·25
170	36	$1 brown and red	3·75	75

1948. Silver Wedding. As T **11b/11c** of Gambia.

171	10c. violet	3·75	1·50
172	$10 red	£325	£130

1949. U.P.U. As T **11d/11g** of Gambia.

173	10c. violet	4·50	1·00
174	20c. red	17·00	6·00
175	30c. blue	15·00	6·00
176	80c. mauve	35·00	8·00

1953. Coronation. As T **11h** of Gambia.

177	10c. black and purple	3·50	30

1954. As T **29** but portrait of Queen Elizabeth, facing left.

178		5c. orange	1·75	20
179		10c. lilac	2·50	10
180a		15c. green	4·50	1·75
181		20c. brown	6·00	30
182a		25c. red	4·00	3·75
183		30c. grey	5·00	20
184		40c. blue	6·50	20
185		50c. purple	6·50	20
186		65c. grey	20·00	17·00
187		$1 orange and green	7·50	20
188		$1.30 blue and red	24·00	3·00
189		$2 violet and red	12·00	1·00
190		$5 green and purple	75·00	3·75
191		$10 violet and blue	65·00	13·00

38 University Arms

1961. Golden Jubilee of Hong Kong University.

192	38	$1 multicoloured	3·25	2·00

39 Statue of Queen Victoria

1962. Stamp Centenary.

193	39	10c. black and mauve	45	10
194	39	20c. black and blue	1·50	2·25
195	39	50c. black and bistre	2·75	40

40 Queen Elizabeth II (after Annigoni)

1962

196	40	5c. orange	75	60
223	40	10c. violet	70	70
198	40	15c. green	3·25	3·75
199	40	20c. brown	2·50	2·00
200	40	25c. red	3·00	4·75

201	40	30c. blue	2·50	10
202	40	40c. turquoise	5·00	70
203	40	50c. red	1·75	30
230	40	65c. blue	6·50	10·00
231	40	$1 sepia	18·00	1·75
206	-	$1.30 multicoloured	2·75	20
207	-	$2 multicoloured	5·00	1·00
208	-	$5 multicoloured	14·00	1·75
209	-	$10 multicoloured	25·00	3·00
210	-	$20 multicoloured	80·00	26·00

Nos. 206/10 are as T **40** but larger 26×40½ mm.

1963. Freedom from Hunger. As T **20a** of Gambia.
211		$1.30 green	27·00	7·00

1963. Cent of Red Cross. As T **20b** of Gambia.
212		10c. red and black	1·50	30
213		$1.30 red and blue	9·50	8·00

44 ITU Emblem

1965. Centenary of I.T.U.
214		10c. purple and yellow	1·50	25
215		$1.30 olive and green	8·50	5·50

45 ICY Emblem

1965. International Co-operation Year
216		10c. purple and turquoise	1·50	25
217		$1.30 green and lavender	10·00	5·50

46 Winston Churchill and St Paul's Cathedral in Wartime

1966. Churchill Commemoration
218		10c. blue	2·50	15
219		50c. green	2·75	30
220		$1.30 brown	10·00	3·00
221		$2 violet	20·00	10·00

47 WHO Building

1966. Inauguration of W.H.O. Headquarters, Geneva
237		10c. black, green and blue	1·50	30
238		50c. black, purple and ochre	4·50	1·75

48 'Education'

48a 'Science'

48b 'Culture'

1966. 20th Anniv of U.N.E.S.C.O.
239		10c. multicoloured	2·50	20
240		50c. yellow, violet and olive	5·50	90
241		$2 black, purple and orange	32·00	20·00

49 Rams' Heads on Chinese Lanterns

1967. Chinese New Year ("Year of the Ram").
242	49	10c. red, olive and yellow	2·00	50
243	-	$1.30 green, red and yellow	13·00	9·00

DESIGN: $1.30, Three rams.

50 Cable Route Map

1967. Completion of Malaysia–Hong Kong Link of SEACOM Telephone Cable.
244	50	$1.30 blue and red	6·00	2·25

51 Rhesus Macaques in Tree

1968. Chinese New Year ("Year of the Monkey").
245	51	10c. gold, black and red	2·00	50
246	-	$1.30 gold, black and red	13·00	10·00

DESIGN: $1.30, Family of rhesus macaques.

52 *Iberia* (liner) at Ocean Terminal

1968. Sea Craft.
247	52	10c. multicoloured	1·75	15
248	-	20c. blue, black and brown	2·50	1·75
249	-	40c. orange, black & mauve	8·50	14·00
250	-	50c. red, black and green	5·50	75
251	-	$1 yellow, black and red	9·00	8·00
252	-	$1.30 blue, black and pink	27·00	4·25

DESIGNS: 20c. Pleasure launch; 40c. Car ferry; 50c. Passenger ferry; $1 Sampan; $1.30, Junk.

53 "Bauhinia blakeana"

1968. Multicoloured.
253		65c. Type **53**	8·00	50
254		$1 Arms of Hong Kong	8·00	40

55 "Aladdin's Lamp" and Human Rights Emblem

1968. Human Rights Year.
255	55	10c. orange, black and green	75	75
256	55	50c. yellow, black & purple	1·75	2·25

56 Cockerel

1969. Chinese New Year ("Year of the Cock"). Multicoloured.
257		10c. Type **56**	2·00	1·00
258		$1.30 Cockerel (vert)	26·00	9·00

58 Arms of Chinese University

1969. Establishment of Chinese University of Hong Kong.
259	58	40c. violet, gold and blue	1·75	2·25

59 Earth Station and Satellite

1969. Opening of Communications Satellite Tracking Station.
260	59	$1 multicoloured	4·50	2·50

60 Chow's Head

1970. Chinese New Year ("Year of the Dog"). Multicoloured.
261		10c. Type **60**	2·50	1·00
262		$1.30 Chow standing (horiz)	30·00	10·00

62 "Expo '70" Emblem

1970. World Fair, Osaka. Multicoloured.
263		15c. Type **62**	65	85
264		25c. "Expo '70" emblem and junks (horiz)	1·40	1·50

64 Plaque in Tung Wah Hospital

1970. Centenary of Tung Wah Hospital.
265	64	10c. multicoloured	50	25
266	64	50c. multicoloured	1·00	1·50

65 Symbol

1970. Asian Productivity Year.
267	65	10c. multicoloured	1·00	60

66 Pig

1971. Chinese New Year ("Year of the Pig").
268	66	10c. multicoloured	2·50	90
269	66	$1.30 multicoloured	20·00	11·00

67 "60" and Scout Badge

1971. Diamond Jubilee of Scouting in Hong Kong.
270	67	10c. black, red and yellow	75	10
271	67	50c. black, green and blue	2·50	1·00
272	67	$2 black, mauve and violet	13·00	12·00

68 Festival Emblem

1971. Hong Kong Festival.
273	68	10c. orange and purple	1·00	20
274	-	50c. multicoloured	1·75	1·00

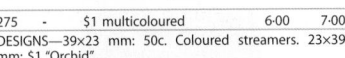

275	-	$1 multicoloured	6·00	7·00

DESIGNS—39×23 mm: 50c. Coloured streamers. 23×39 mm: $1 "Orchid".

69 Stylized Rats

1972. Chinese New Year. ("Year of the Rat").
276	69	10c. red, black and gold	2·50	50
277	69	$1.30 red, black and gold	28·00	11·00

70 Tunnel Entrance

1972. Opening of Cross-Harbour Tunnel.
278	70	$1 multicoloured	4·50	2·25

1972. Royal Silver Wedding. As T **98** of Gibraltar, but with Phoenix and Dragon in background.
279		10c. multicoloured	30	15
280		50c. multicoloured	1·10	1·40

72 Ox

1973. Chinese New Year ("Year of the Ox").
281	72	10c. orange, brown & black	75	50
282	-	$1.30 yellow, orange & black	3·50	6·00

DESIGN—HORIZ: $1.30, Ox.

73 Queen Elizabeth II

1973
311	73	10c. orange	55	30
284	73	15c. green	7·00	9·50
313	73	20c. violet	50	10
286	73	25c. brown	11·00	8·50
315	73	30c. blue	70	70
316	73	40c. blue	1·25	2·50
289	73	50c. red	1·50	60
318	73	60c. lavender	1·75	2·50
290	73	65c. brown	16·00	14·00
320	73	70c. yellow	1·75	75
321	73	80c. red	2·25	3·25
321c	73	90c. brown	4·00	2·50
291	73	$1 green	2·25	80
323	-	$1.30 yellow and violet	2·50	30
324	-	$2 green and brown	3·00	1·75
324c	-	$5 pink and blue	4·75	1·75
324d	-	$10 pink and green	5·00	6·00
324e	-	$20 pink and black	9·00	12·00

Values of $1.30 and above are size 27×32 mm.

1973. Royal Wedding. As T **101a** of Gibraltar. Multicoloured. Background colours given.
297		50c. brown	50	15
298		$2 mauve	1·50	2·00

75 Festival Symbols forming Chinese Character

1973. Hong Kong Festival.
299	75	10c. red and green	40	10
300	-	50c. mauve and orange	1·50	95
301	-	$1 green and mauve	3·50	4·00

DESIGNS—Festival symbols arranged to form a Chinese character: 10c. "Hong"; 50c. "Kong"; $1 "Festival".

76 Tiger

1974. Chinese New Year ("Year of the Tiger").

302	**76**	10c. multicoloured	2·00	50
303	-	$1.30 multicoloured	6·50	12·00

DESIGN—VERT: $1.30, similar to Type **76**.

77 Chinese Mask

1974. Arts Festival.

304	**77**	10c. multicoloured	75	10
305	-	$1 multicoloured	3·25	4·25
306	-	$2 multicoloured	5·50	8·50
MS307	159×94 mm. Nos. 304/6		30·00	35·00

DESIGNS: $1, $2, Chinese masks similar to T **77**.

78 Pigeons with Letters

1974. Centenary of U.P.U.

308	**78**	10c. blue, green and black	40	10
309	-	50c. mauve, orange & black	75	40
310	-	$2 multicoloured	2·25	4·00

DESIGNS: 50c. Globe within letters; $2 Hands holding letters.

79 Stylized Hare

1975. Chinese New Year (Year of the Hare)

327	**79**	10c. silver and red	1·00	60
328	-	$1.30 gold and green	5·00	6·50

80 Queen Elizabeth II, the Duke of Edinburgh and Hong Kong Arms

1975. Royal Visit.

329	**80**	$1.30 multicoloured	2·00	1·50
330	**80**	$2 multicoloured	3·00	3·75

81 Mid-Autumn Festival

1975. Hong Kong Festivals of 1975. Multicoloured.

331	**81**	50c. Type **81**	2·00	50
332		$1 Dragon-boat Festival	6·50	2·50
333		$2 Tin Hau Festival	25·00	9·50
MS334	102×83 mm. Nos. 331/3		60·00	35·00

82 Melodious Laughing Thrush ("The Hwamei")

1975. Birds. Multicoloured.

335	50c. Type **82**	2·50	50
336	$1.30 Chinese bulbul	7·00	3·50
337	$2 Black-capped kingfisher	13·00	11·00

83 Dragon

1976. Chinese New Year ("Year of the Dragon").

338	**83**	20c. mauve, purple and gold	75	10
339	-	$1.30 green, red and gold	4·00	2·50

DESIGN: $1.30, As Type **83** but dragon reversed.

84 "60" and Girl Guides Badge

1976. Diamond Jubilee of Girl Guides. Multicoloured.

354	20c. Type **84**	50	10
355	$1.30 Badge, stylized diamond and "60"	4·00	4·00

85 "Postal Services" in Chinese Characters

1976. Opening of New G.P.O.

356	**85**	20c. green, grey and black	75	10
357	-	$1.30 orange, grey and black	2·25	1·50
358	-	$2 yellow, grey and black	4·25	4·00

DESIGNS: $1.30, Old G.P.O.; $2 New G.P.O.

86 Tree Snake on Branch

1977. Chinese New Year ("Year of the Snake"). Multicoloured.

359	20c. Type **86**	50	15
360	$1.30 Snake facing left	2·00	3·50

87 Presentation of the Orb

1977. Silver Jubilee. Multicoloured.

361	20c. Type **87**	40	10
362	$1.30 The Queen's visit, 1975	1·00	75
363	$2 The Orb (vert)	1·25	1·50

88 Tram Cars

1977. Tourism. Multicoloured.

364	20c. Type **88**	55	10
365	60c. Star ferryboat	1·75	10
366	$1.30 The Peak Railway	2·00	2·00
367	$2 Junk and sampan	2·00	3·50

89 Buttercup Orchid

1977. Orchids. Multicoloured.

368	20c. Type **89**	1·25	20
369	$1.30 Lady's slipper orchid	3·00	1·50
370	$2 Susan orchid	5·00	4·50

90 Horse

1978. Chinese New Year ("Year of the Horse").

371	**90**	20c. mauve, olive and bistre	50	10
372	**90**	$1.30 orange, brn & lt brn	2·75	4·50

91 Queen Elizabeth II

1978. 25th Anniv of Coronation.

373	**91**	20c. mauve and blue	40	10
374	**91**	$1.30 blue and mauve	1·00	1·75

92 Girl and Boy holding Hands

1978. Centenary of Po Leung Kuk (children's charity). Multicoloured.

375	20c. Type **92**	25	15
376	$1.30 Ring of children	1·00	2·00

93 Electronics Industry

1979. Hong Kong Industries.

377	**93**	20c. yellow, olive & orange	30	10
378	-	$1.30 multicoloured	80	1·75
379	-	$2 multicoloured	85	2·25

DESIGNS: $1.30, Toy industry; $2 Garment industry.

94 *Precis orithya*

1979. Butterflies. Multicoloured.

380	20c. Type **94**	45	10
381	$1 *Graphium sarpedon*	85	55
382	$1.30 *Heliophorus epicles*	90	1·00
383	$2 *Danaus genutia*	1·25	3·75

95 Diagrammatic View of Railway Station

1979. Mass Transit Railway. Multicoloured.

384	20c. Type **95**	45	10
385	$1.30 Diagrammatic view of car	1·00	55
386	$2 Plan showing route of railway	1·00	2·00

96 Tsui Shing Lau Pagoda

1980. Rural Architecture.

387	**96**	20c. black, mauve & yellow	35	20
388	-	$1.30 multicoloured	60	80
389	-	$2 multicoloured	80	2·00

DESIGNS—HORIZ: $1.30, Village house, Sai O; $2 Ching Chung Koon Temple.

97 Queen Elizabeth the Queen Mother

1980. 80th Birthday of The Queen Mother.

390	**97**	$1.30 multicoloured	1·00	1·25

98 Botanical Gardens

1980. Parks. Multicoloured.

391	20c. Type **98**	20	15
392	$1 Ocean Park	35	35
393	$1.30 Kowloon Park	40	50
394	$2 Country parks	70	2·25

99 Red-spotted Grouper

1981. Fish. Multicoloured.

395	20c. Type **99**	25	15
396	$1 Golden thread-finned bream	50	45
397	$1.30 Scar-breasted tuskfish	55	60
398	$2 Blue-barred orange parrotfish	70	2·25

100 Wedding Bouquet from Hong Kong

1981. Royal Wedding. Multicoloured.

399	20c. Type **100**	20	10
400	$1.30 Prince Charles in Hong Kong	45	30
401	$5 Prince Charles and Lady Diana Spencer	1·25	2·25

101 Suburban Development

1981. Public Housing.

402	**101**	20c. multicoloured	20	10
403	-	$1 multicoloured	55	40
404	-	$1.30 multicoloured	60	65
405	-	$2 multicoloured	70	1·75
MS406	148×105 mm. Nos. 402/5		3·50	5·50

DESIGNS: $1 to $2, Various suburban developments.

102 Victoria from the Harbour, c.1855

1982. Hong Kong Port, Past and Present. Multicoloured.

407		20c. Type **102**	50	15
408		$1 West Point, Hong Kong, 1847	1·25	80
409		$1.30 Fleet of junks	1·40	85
410		$2 Liner Queen Elizabeth 2 at Hong Kong	2·50	3·00

103 Large Indian Civet

1982. Wild Animals.

411	**103**	20c. black, pink and brown	25	15
412	-	$1 multicoloured	45	45
413	-	$1.30 black, green & orange	50	55
414	-	$5 black, brown and yellow	1·25	3·25

DESIGNS: $1 Chinese pangolin; $1.30, Chinese porcupine; $5 Indian muntjac.

104 Queen Elizabeth II

1982

415	**104**	10c. light red, red & yellow	80	60
416	**104**	20c. blue, violet & lavender	1·00	1·00
417	**104**	30c. lt violet, violet & pink	1·50	30
418	**104**	40c. red and blue	1·50	30
475	**104**	50c. chestnut, brn & grn	1·00	40
476	**104**	60c. purple and grey	1·50	1·10
477	**104**	70c. green, myrtle & yellow	3·50	1·00
478	**104**	80c. bistre, brown & green	3·75	3·50
479	**104**	90c. dp green, grn & turq	4·50	75
480	**104**	$1 dp orange, orange & red	1·75	40
481	**104**	$1.30 blue and mauve	2·50	45
482	**104**	$1.70 dp blue, blue & grn	4·00	1·50
483	**104**	$2 blue and pink	3·75	1·50
484	-	$5 red, purple and yellow	10·00	3·75
485	-	$10 brown and light brown	9·50	5·00
486	-	$20 red and blue	10·00	7·50
487	-	$50 red and grey	32·00	27·00

Nos. 484/7 are as Type **104** but larger, 26×30 mm.

106 Table Tennis

1982. Sport for the Disabled. Multicoloured.

431	**106**	30c. Type **106**	50	10
432		$1 Racing	75	80
433		$1.30 Basketball	2·75	1·50
434		$5 Archery	3·75	6·50

107 Dancing

1983. Performing Arts.

435	**107**	30c. light blue and blue	40	10
436	-	$1.30 red and purple	1·25	1·25
437	-	$5 green and deep green	3·00	5·00

DESIGNS: $1.30, "Theatre"; $5 "Music".

108 Aerial View of Hong Kong

1983. Commonwealth Day. Multicoloured.

438	**108**	30c. Type **108**	70	10
439		$1 Liverpool Bay (container ship)	1·50	1·25
440		$1.30 Hong Kong flag	1·50	1·25
441		$5 Queen Elizabeth II and Hong Kong	3·00	6·50

109 Victoria Harbour

1983. Hong Kong by Night. Multicoloured.

442	**109**	30c. Type **109**	1·25	15
443		$1 Space Museum, Tsim Sha Tsui Cultural Centre	3·00	1·50
444		$1.30 Fireworks display	4·00	2·00
445		$5 "Jumbo", floating restaurant	11·00	10·00

110 Old and new Observatory Buildings

1983. Centenary of Hong Kong Observatory.

446	**110**	40c. orange, brown & black	75	10
447	-	$1 mauve & blk	1·50	1·25
448	-	$1.30 blue, dp blue & black	1·75	1·40
449	-	$5 yellow, green and black	5·00	9·00

DESIGNS: $1 Wind measuring equipment; $1.30, Thermometer; $5 Ancient and modern seismometers.

111 de Havilland D.H.86 Dragon Express Dorado (Hong Kong– Penang Service, 1936)

1984. Aviation in Hong Kong. Multicoloured.

450	**111**	40c. Type **111**	1·00	15
451		$1 Sikorsky S-42B flying boat (San Francisco–Hong Kong Service, 1937)	1·75	1·50
452		$1.30 Cathay-Pacific Boeing 747 jet leaving Kai Tak Airport	2·00	1·50
453		$5 Baldwin brothers' balloon, 1891 (vert)	4·75	11·00

112 Map by Capt. E. Belcher, 1836

1984. Maps of Hong Kong. Multicoloured.

454	**112**	40c. Type **112**	1·00	20
455		$1 Bartholomew map of 1929	1·75	1·25
456		$1.30 Early map of Hong Kong waters	2·00	1·75
457		$5 Chinese-style map of 1819	10·00	12·00

113 Cockerel

1984. Chinese Lanterns. Multicoloured.

458	**113**	40c. Type **113**	1·00	15
459		$1 Dog	2·00	1·40
460		$1.30 Butterfly	3·00	1·75
461		$5 Fish	9·50	12·00

114 Jockey on Horse and Nurse with Baby ("Health Care")

1984. Centenary of Royal Hong Kong Jockey Club. Designs showing aspects of Club's charity work. Multicoloured.

462		40c. Type **114**	1·25	20
463		$1 Disabled man playing handball ("Support for Disabled")	2·00	1·75
464		$1.30 Ballerina ("The Arts")	3·00	2·00
465		$5 Humboldt penguins ("Ocean Park")	9·00	11·00
MS466	178×98 mm. Nos. 462/5		23·00	25·00

115 Hung Sing Temple

1985. Historic Buildings. Multicoloured.

467		40c. Type **115**	60	20
468		$1 St. John's Cathedral	1·00	1·10
469		$1.30 The Old Supreme Court Building	1·10	1·25
470		$5 Wan Chai Post Office	4·50	9·00

116 Prow of Dragon Boat

1985. Tenth International Dragon Boat Festival. Designs showing different parts of dragon boat. Multicoloured.

488		40c. Type **116**	50	15
489		$1 Drummer and rowers	1·75	1·25
490		$1.30 Rowers	3·00	1·60
491		$5 Stern of boat	9·25	11·00
MS492	190×100 mm. Nos. 488/91		18·00	18·00

117 The Queen Mother with Prince Charles and Prince William, 1984

1985. Life and Times of Queen Elizabeth the Queen Mother. Multicoloured.

493		40c. At Glamis Castle, aged 7	60	10
494		$1 Type **117**	1·75	1·25
495		$1.30 The Queen Mother, 1970 (from photo by Cecil Beaton)	2·00	1·40
496		$5 With Prince Henry at his christening (from photo by Lord Snowdon)	3·25	5·50

118 Melastoma

1985. Native Flowers. Multicoloured.

497		40c. Type **118**	1·25	20
498		50c. Chinese lily	1·25	40
499		60c. Grantham's camellia	1·50	1·25
500		$1.70 Narcissus	2·25	1·25
501		$1.70 Bauhinia	2·75	1·50
502		$5 Chinese New Year flower	5·00	12·00

119 Hong Kong Academy for Performing Arts

1985. New Buildings. Multicoloured.

503		50c. Type **119**	65	15
504		$1.30 Exchange Square (vert)	1·00	70
505		$1.70 Hong Kong Bank Headquarters (vert)	1·25	75
506		$5 Hong Kong Coliseum	2·00	7·50

120 Halley's Comet in the Solar System

1986. Appearance of Halley's Comet. Multicoloured.

507		50c. Type **120**	1·25	20
508		$1.30 Edmond Halley and Comet	1·50	1·40
509		$1.70 Comet over Hong Kong	1·75	1·50
510		$5 Comet passing the Earth	6·50	11·00
MS511	135×80 mm. Nos. 507/10		17·00	21·00

120a At Wedding of Miss Celia Bowes-Lyon, 1931

1986. 60th Birthday of Queen Elizabeth II. Multicoloured.

512		50c. Type **120a**	50	10
513		$1 Queen in Garter procession, Windsor Castle, 1977	85	60
514		$1.30 In Hong Kong, 1975	1·10	70
515		$1.70 At Royal Lodge, Windsor, 1980 (from photo by Norman Parkinson)	1·25	75
516		$5 At Crown Agents Head Office, London, 1983	4·00	6·50

121 Mass Transit Train, Boeing 747 Airliner and Map of World

1986. "Expo '86" World Fair, Vancouver. Multicoloured.

517		50c. Type **121**	80	30
518		$1.30 Hong Kong Bank Headquarters and map of world	1·50	1·00
519		$1.70 Container ship and map of world	2·25	1·40
520		$5 Dish aerial and map of world	5·00	8·00

122 Hand-liner Sampan

1986. Fishing Vessels. Designs showing fishing boat and outline of fish. Multicoloured.

521		50c. Type **122**	80	15
522		$1.30 Stern trawler	1·50	1·10
523		$1.70 Long liner junk	1·75	1·40
524		$5 Junk trawler	5·50	9·50

123 The Second Puan Khequa (attr Spoilum)

1986. 19th-century Hong Kong Portraits. Multicoloured.

525		50c. Type **123**	40	15
526		$1.30 Chinese Lady (19th-century copy)	1·25	1·25
527		$1.70 Lamqua (self-portrait)	1·40	1·40
528		$5 Wife of Wo Hing Qua (attr G. Chinnery)	3·25	6·50

124 Rabbit

1987. Chinese New Year ("Year of the Rabbit"). Designs showing stylized rabbits.

529	**124**	50c. Type **124**	75	15
530	-	$1.30 multicoloured	1·40	1·10
531	-	$1.70 multicoloured	1·50	1·10
532	-	$5 multicoloured	6·00	6·50
MS533	133×84 mm. Nos. 529/32		25·00	26·00

Nos. 530/1 have the "0" omitted from their face values.

125 *Village Square, Hong Kong Island, 1838 (Auguste Borget)*

1987. 19th-century Hong Kong Scenes. Multicoloured.

534	50c. Type **125**	80	15
535	$1.30 *Boat Dwellers, Kowloon Bay, 1838 (Auguste Borget)*	2·25	1·25
536	$1.70 *Flagstaff House, 1846 (Murdoch Bruce)*	2·75	1·40
537	$5 *Wellington Street, late 19th-century (C. Andrasi)*	7·50	11·00

126 Queen Elizabeth II and Central Victoria

1987

538B	**126**	10c. multicoloured	75	65
539A	**126**	40c. multicoloured	1·75	2·50
602	**126**	50c. multicoloured	1·25	1·00
603	**126**	60c. multicoloured	1·75	30
604	**126**	70c. multicoloured	2·50	2·00
605	**126**	80c. multicoloured	2·00	1·75
606	**126**	90c. multicoloured	1·75	1·25
607	**126**	$1 multicoloured	2·25	1·00
607a	**126**	$1.20 multicoloured	3·50	3·75
608	**126**	$1.30 multicoloured	3·50	2·00
609	**126**	$1.40 multicoloured	3·50	1·25
547A	**126**	$1.70 multicoloured	3·00	80
610	**126**	$1.80 multicoloured	1·75	60
611	**126**	$2 multicoloured	2·50	50
611a	**126**	$2.30 multicoloured	3·50	3·75
612	-	$5 multicoloured	6·00	1·75
613	-	$10 multicoloured	9·00	6·00
614	-	$20 multicoloured	13·00	11·00
615	-	$50 multicoloured	19·00	22·00

DESIGNS—25×31 mm: Queen Elizabeth II and $5 Kowloon; $10 Victoria Harbour; $20 Legislative Council Building; $50 Government House.

With the exception of Nos. 607a and 611a which are dated, all the above exist with or without a date in the design.

127 Hong Kong Flag

1987

554a	**127**	10c. multicoloured	1·00	1·00
554b	-	50c. brown, red and black	1·25	1·75
554c	-	80c. mauve, green & blk	1·50	3·25
554d	-	90c. blue, brown & black	1·50	2·00
554e	-	$1.30 green, blue & black	2·00	2·75
554f	-	$2.30 brown, violet & blk	2·25	3·75

DESIGN: 50c. to $2.30, Map of Hong Kong.

128 Alice Ho Miu Ling Nethersole Hospital, 1887

1987. Hong Kong Medical Centenaries. Multicoloured.

555	50c. Type **128**	1·25	20
556	$1.30 Matron and nurses, Nethersole Hospital, 1891	2·50	1·40
557	$1.70 Scanning equipment, Faculty of Medicine	3·00	1·40
558	$5 Nurse and patient, Faculty of Medicine	9·00	9·00

129 Casual Dress with Fringed Hem, 220–589

1987. Historical Chinese Costumes. Multicoloured.

559	50c. Type **129**	55	10

560	$1.30 Two-piece dress and wrap, 581–960	1·40	1·25
561	$1.70 Formal dress, Song Dynasty, 960–1279	1·50	1·50
562	$5 Manchu empress costume, 1644–1911	4·00	7·50

130 Dragon

1988. Chinese New Year ("Year of the Dragon"). Designs showing dragons.

563	**130**	50c. multicoloured	60	15
564	-	$1.30 multicoloured	1·25	1·00
565	-	$1.70 multicoloured	1·50	1·10
566	-	$5 multicoloured	2·75	5·50
MS567	134×88 mm. Nos. 563/6		9·00	12·00

131 White-throated Kingfisher ("White-breasted Kingfisher")

1988. Hong Kong Birds. Multicoloured.

568	50c. Type **131**	1·00	30
569	$1.30 Fukien niltava	2·00	1·60
570	$1.70 Black kite	2·50	1·75
571	$5 Lesser pied kingfisher	4·00	7·00

132 Chinese Banyan

1988. Trees of Hong Kong. Multicoloured.

572	50c. Type **132**	35	10
573	$1.30 Hong Kong orchid tree	70	65
574	$1.70 Cotton tree	90	85
575	$5 Schima	2·50	5·50
MS576	135×85 mm. Nos. 572/5	10·00	7·50

133 Lower Terminal, Peak Tramway

1988. Centenary of The Peak Tramway. Multicoloured.

577	50c. Type **133**	35	10
578	$1.30 Tram on incline	70	1·00
579	$1.70 Peak Tower Upper Terminal	90	1·25
580	$5 Tram	2·50	5·00
MS581	160×90 mm. Nos. 577/80	8·50	9·00

134 Hong Kong Catholic Cathedral

1988. Centenary of Hong Kong Catholic Cathedral.

582	**134**	60c. multicoloured	1·25	1·50

135 Deaf Girl

1988. Community Chest Charity.

583	**135**	60c.+10c. +10c. black, red & bl	60	1·25
584	-	$1.40+20c. +20c. black, red and green	75	1·40
585	-	$1.80+30c. +30c. black, red and orange	90	1·75
586	-	$5+$1 +$1 black, red & brn	1·50	5·00

DESIGNS: $1.40, Elderly woman; $1.80, Blind boy using braille typewriter; $5 Mother and baby.

136 Snake

1989. Chinese New Year ("Year of the Snake"). Multicoloured.

587	60c. Type **136**	45	15
588	$1.40 Snake and fish	1·75	70
589	$1.80 Snake on branch	1·90	85
590	$5 Coiled snake	5·00	7·25
MS591	135×85 mm. Nos. 587/90	12·00	7·50

137 Girl and Doll

1989. Cheung Chau Bun Festival. Multicoloured.

592	60c. Type **137**	55	15
593	$1.40 Girl in festival costume	1·25	80
594	$1.80 Paper effigy of god Taai Si Wong	1·40	90
595	$5 Floral gateway	3·50	6·00

138 Twins (wood carving, Cheung Yee)

1989. Modern Art. Multicoloured.

596	60c. Type **138**	50	15
597	$1.40 *Figures* (acrylic on paper, Chan Luis)	1·25	80
598	$1.80 *Lotus* (copper sculpture, Van Lau)	1·40	90
599	$5 *Zen Painting* (ink and colour on paper, Lui Shou-kwan)	3·00	4·75

139 Lunar New Year Festivities

1989. Hong Kong People. Multicoloured.

616	60c. Type **139**	75	10
617	$1.40 Shadow boxing and horse racing	2·00	80
618	$1.80 Foreign-exchange dealer and traditional builder	2·00	90
619	$5 Multi-racial society	4·50	8·00

140 University of Science and Technology

1989. Building for the Future.

620	**140**	60c. black, yellow & brn	45	15
621	-	70c. blk, pale pink & pink	50	40
622	-	$1.30 black, lt green & grn	1·00	1·00
623	-	$1.40 black, lt blue & blue	1·00	70
624	-	$1.80 black, turquoise & bl	1·25	1·00
625	-	$5 brown, orange and red	6·50	8·50

DESIGNS: 70c. Cultural Centre; $1.30, Eastern Harbour motorway interchange; $1.40, New Bank of China Building; $1.80, Convention and Exhibition Centre; $5 Mass Transit electric train.

141 Prince and Princess of Wales and Hong Kong Skyline

1989. Royal Visit. Multicoloured.

626	60c. Type **141**	1·50	30
627	$1.40 Princess of Wales	2·50	1·10
628	$1.80 Prince of Wales	1·75	1·10
629	$5 Prince and Princess of Wales in evening dress	7·50	9·00
MS630	128×75 mm. No. 629	13·00	9·00

143 Horse

1990. Chinese New Year ("Year of the Horse").

631	**143**	60c. multicoloured	55	20
632	-	$1.40 multicoloured	1·75	1·25
633	-	$1.80 multicoloured	1·90	1·25
634	-	$5 multicoloured	6·50	9·50
MS635	135×85 mm. Nos. 631/4		13·00	10·00

DESIGNS: $1.40 to $5, Different horse designs.

144 Chinese Lobster Dish

1990. International Cuisine. Designs showing various dishes. Multicoloured.

636	60c. Type **144**	60	15
637	70c. Indian	60	50
638	$1.30 Chinese vegetables	1·00	1·25
639	$1.40 Thai	1·00	70
640	$1.80 Japanese	1·25	95
641	$5 French	4·25	8·50

145 Air Pollution and Clean Air

1990. U.N. World Environment Day. Multicoloured.

642	60c. Type **145**	40	15
643	$1.40 Noise pollution and music	85	80
644	$1.80 Polluted and clean water	1·00	80
645	$5 Litter on ground and in bin	2·75	4·00

1990. "New Zealand 1990" International Stamp Exhibition, Auckland. Sheet 130×75 mm, containing design as No. 613.

MS646	$10 multicoloured	80·00	85·00

146 Street Lamp and Des Voeux Road, 1890

1990. Centenary of Electricity Supply.

647	**146**	60c. black, bistre & brown	60	15
648	-	$1.40 multicoloured	1·00	80
649	-	$1.80 black, bistre and blue	1·25	80
650	-	$5 multicoloured	2·25	4·50
MS651		155×85 mm. Nos. 648 and 650	4·50	6·00

DESIGNS: $1.40, Street Lamp and *Jumbo* (floating restaurant), 1940; $1.80, Street lamp and pylon, 1960; $5 Street lamp and Hong Kong from harbour, 1980.

147 Christmas Tree and Skyscrapers

1990. Christmas. Multicoloured.

652	50c. Type **147**	25	10
653	60c. Dove with holly	25	15
654	$1.40 Firework display	80	40
655	$1.80 Father Christmas hat on skyscraper	1·00	50
656	$2 Children with Father Christmas	1·40	1·40
657	$5 Candy stick with bow and Hong Kong skyline	3·00	6·00

148 Ram

1991. Chinese New Year ("Year of the Ram").

658	**148**	60c. multicoloured	25	15
659	-	$1.40 multicoloured	65	60
660	-	$1.80 multicoloured	80	75
661	-	$5 multicoloured	2·75	5·50
MS662		135×85 mm. Nos. 658/61	6·50	7·50

DESIGNS: $1.40 to $5, Different ram designs.

149 Letter "A", Clock, Teddy Bear and Building Bricks (Kindergarten)

1991. Education. Multicoloured.

663	80c. Type **149**	50	20
664	$1.80 Globe, laboratory flask and mathematical symbols (Primary and Secondary)	1·25	80
665	$2.30 Machinery (Vocational)	1·40	1·40
666	$5 Mortar board, computer and books (Tertiary)	3·50	6·50

150 Rickshaw

1991. 100 Years of Public Transport. Multicoloured.

667	80c. Type **150**	30	15
668	90c. Double-decker bus	70	75
669	$1.70 Harbour ferry	1·10	1·25
670	$1.80 Double-deck tram	1·40	80
671	$2.30 Mass Transit electric train	2·00	2·25
672	$5 Jetfoil	3·50	6·50

151 Victorian Pillar Box and Cover of 1888

1991. 150th Anniv of Hong Kong Post Office. Multicoloured.

673	80c. Type **151**	50	15
674	$1.70 Edwardian pillar box and cover	1·00	1·00
675	$1.80 King George V pillar box and cover of 1935	1·10	75
676	$2.30 King George VI pillar box and cover of 1938	1·50	2·00
677	$5 Queen Elizabeth II pillar box and cover of 1989	4·00	7·50
MS678	130×75 mm. $10 As No. 677	13·00	16·00

See also Nos. **MS**745 and **MS**899.

152 Bronze Buddha, Lantau Island

1991. Landmarks.

679	**152**	80c. red and black	50	15
680	-	$1.70 green and black	1·00	1·25
681	-	$1.80 violet and black	1·75	80
682	-	$2.30 blue and black	1·25	2·00
683	-	$5 orange and black	3·50	7·25

DESIGNS: $1.70, Peak Pavilion; $1.80, Clocktower of Kowloon–Canton Railway Station; $2.30, Catholic Cathedral; $5 Wong Tai Sin Temple.

1991. "Phila Nippon '91" International Stamp Exhibition, Tokyo. Sheet 130×75 mm, containing design as No. 613.

MS684	$10 multicoloured	32·00	30·00

1991. Olympic Games, Barcelona (1992) (1st issue). Sheet 130×75 mm, containing design as No. 613.

MS685	$10 multicoloured	18·00	18·00

See also Nos. 696/700 and **MS**722.

153 Monkey

1992. Chinese New Year ("Year of the Monkey").

686	**153**	80c. multicoloured	40	15
687	-	$1.80 multicoloured	80	70
688	-	$2.30 multicoloured	1·25	1·75
689	-	$5 multicoloured	2·75	7·00
MS690		135×85 mm. Nos. 686/9	9·50	12·00

DESIGNS: $1.80 to $5, Different monkey designs.

1992. 40th Anniv of Queen Elizabeth II's Accession. As T **179a** of Gibraltar. Multicoloured.

691	80c. Royal barge in Hong Kong harbour	30	15
692	$1.70 Queen watching dancing display	60	70
693	$1.80 Fireworks display	60	35
694	$2.30 Three portraits of Queen Elizabeth	90	1·00
695	$5 Queen Elizabeth II	1·50	3·25

154 Running

1992. Olympic Games, Barcelona (2nd issue). Multicoloured.

696	80c. Type **154**	40	20
697	$1.80 Swimming and javelin	90	1·00
698	$2.30 Cycling	2·00	2·00
699	$5 High jump	2·25	5·50
MS700	130×75 mm. As Nos. 696/9*	9·00	9·50

*The stamps from No. **MS**700 show the inscriptions in different colours, instead of the black on Nos. 696/9. The designs of the $1.80 and $5 values from the miniature sheet have also been rearranged so that "HONG KONG" and the Royal Cypher occur at the right of the inscription.

1992. "World Columbian Stamp Expo '92" Exhibition, Chicago. Sheet 130×75 mm, containing design as No. 613, but colours changed.

MS701	$10 multicoloured	3·00	6·50

155 Queen Elizabeth II

1992

714	-	$5 bright blue-green, black and light green	2·00	2·00
702	**155**	10c. mauve, blk & cerise	30	50
702b	**155**	20c. black, indigo & bl	1·00	1·75
703	**155**	50c. red, black and yellow	30	30
704	**155**	60c. blue, black and light blue	2·00	2·00
705	**155**	70c. mauve, black and lilac	2·00	1·25
706	**155**	80c. mauve, black and pink	30	45
707	**155**	90c. green, blk & grey	30	60
708	**155**	$1 brown, black and yellow	35	20
708b	**155**	$1.10 red, black & orge	3·00	2·25
709	**155**	$1.20 violet, blk & lilac	45	25
757c	**155**	$1.30 blue, black and orange	50	1·00
709c	**155**	$1.40 green, black and yellow	3·00	1·75
709d	**155**	$1.50 brown, black and blue	2·25	3·00
709e	**155**	$1.60 green, black and lilac	2·00	2·50
710	**155**	$1.70 ultram, blk & bl	1·00	1·00
711	**155**	$1.80 mauve, black and grey	1·25	55
711a	**155**	$1.90 green, black and stone	1·00	2·00
764	**155**	$2 blue, black and green	60	80
712b	**155**	$2.10 red, black & green	2·25	2·25
713	**155**	$2.30 brown, black and pink	2·50	75
759	**155**	$2.40 blue, blk & grey	1·10	2·50
713b	**155**	$2.50 green, black and yellow	2·25	2·50
713c	**155**	$2.60 choc, blk & brn	1·50	2·75
713d	**155**	$3.10 brown, black and blue	2·25	1·00
759e	**155**	$5 green, black & lt grn	1·50	3·25
715	-	$10 brown, black and cinnamon	2·00	2·75
716	-	$20 red, black & orange	4·25	4·50
717	-	$50 dp grey, blk & grey	8·50	11·00

Nos. 715/17 are as Type **155**, but larger, 26×30 mm.

156 Stamps and Perforation Gauge

1992. Stamp Collecting. Multicoloured.

718	80c. Type **156**	30	25
719	$1.80 Handstamp of 1841, 1891 Jubilee overprint and tweezers	60	75
720	$2.30 Stamps of 1946 and 1949 under magnifying glass	85	1·25
721	$5 2c. of 1862 and watermark detector	2·00	4·00

1992. Olympic Games, Barcelona (3rd issue). As No. **MS**700, but additionally inscribed "To Commemorate the Opening of the 1992 Summer Olympic Games 25 July 1992", in English and Chinese, at foot of sheet.

MS722	130×75 mm. As Nos. 696/9	3·25	6·00

1992. "Kuala Lumpur '92" International Stamp Exhibition. Sheet 130×75 mm, containing design as No. 715, but colours changed.

MS723	$10 blue, black and light blue	3·25	7·00

157 Principal Male Character

1992. Chinese Opera. Multicoloured.

724	80c. Type **157**	1·25	25
725	$1.80 Martial character	2·00	1·60
726	$2.30 Principal female character	2·25	2·50
727	$5 Comic character	4·50	10·00

158 Hearts

1992. Greetings Stamps. Multicoloured.

728	80c. Type **158**	30	20
729	$1.80 Stars	55	60
730	$2.30 Presents	75	1·00
731	$5 Balloons	1·60	3·50

159 Cockerel

1993. Chinese New Year ("Year of the Cock").

732	**159**	80c. Type **159**	30	20
733	-	$1.80 multicoloured	70	80
734	-	$2.30 multicoloured	95	1·25
735	-	$5 multicoloured	1·75	4·25
MS736		133×84 mm. Nos. 732/5	4·00	6·50

DESIGNS: $1.80 to $5, Different cock designs.

160 Pipa

1993. Chinese String Musical Instruments. Multicoloured.

737	80c. Type **160**	40	20
738	$1.80 Erhu	70	75
739	$2.30 Ruan	85	1·25
740	$5 Gehu	1·50	3·75

161 Central Waterfront, Hong Kong in 1954

1993. 40th Anniv of Coronation. Multicoloured.

741	80c. Type **161**	40	20
742	$1.80 Hong Kong in 1963	70	75
743	$2.30 Hong Kong in 1975	90	1·25
744	$5 Hong Kong in 1992	1·75	4·00

1993. 150th Anniv of Hong Kong Post Office (2nd issue). Sheet 130×75 mm, containing design as No. 715.

MS745	$10 brown, black and cinnamon	3·50	6·00

1993. "Hong Kong '94" International Stamp Exhibition. Sheet 115×78 mm, containing design as No. 715, but colours changed.

MS746	$10 purple, black, yellow and blue	3·50	5·00

162 University of Science and Technology Building and Student

1993. Hong Kong's Contribution to Science and Technology. Multicoloured.

747	80c. Type **162**	25	20
748	$1.80 Science Museum building and energy machine exhibit	40	40
749	$2.30 Governor's Award and circuit board	60	90
750	$5 Dish aerials and world map	1·25	3·50

1993. "Bangkok '93" International Stamp Exhibition. Sheet 131×75 mm, containing design as No. 715, but colours changed.

MS751	$10 emerald, deep green and green	2·75	3·75

163 Red Calico Egg-fish

1993. Goldfish. Multicoloured.

752	$1 Type **163**	50	20

753		$1.90 Red cap oranda	80	50
754		$2.40 Red and white fringetail	1.00	1.25
755		$5 Black and gold dragon-eye	1.75	5.00
MS756		130×75 mm. Nos. 752/5	4.75	8.50

164 Dog

1994. Chinese New Year ("Year of the Dog").

766	**164**	$1 multicoloured	30	20
767	-	$1.90 multicoloured	50	55
768	-	$2.40 multicoloured	70	1.00
769	-	$5 multicoloured	1.75	4.00
MS770		133×84 mm. Nos. 766/9	5.50	8.00

DESIGNS: $1.90 to $5, Different dog designs.

1994. "Hong Kong '94" International Stamp Exhibition. Sheet 130×75 mm, containing design as No. 714.

| MS771 | **155** | $5 green, black and light green | 2.00 | 5.00 |

165 Modern Police Constables on Traffic Duty

1994. 150th Anniv of Royal Hong Kong Police Force. Multicoloured.

772	**165**	$1 Type **165**	30	20
773		$1.20 Marine policeman with binoculars	40	50
774		$1.90 Police uniforms of 1950	55	50
775		$2 Tactical firearms unit officer with sub-machine gun	75	1.00
776		$2.40 Early 20th-century police uniforms	90	1.25
777		$5 Sikh and Chinese constables of 1900	2.75	4.25

166 Dragon Boat Festival

1994. Traditional Chinese Festivals. Multicoloured.

778	**166**	$1 Type **166**	35	20
779		$1.90 Lunar New Year	60	70
780		$2.40 Seven Sisters Festival	85	1.25
781		$5 Mid-Autumn Festival	1.75	4.25

1994. Conference of Commonwealth Postal Administrations, Hong Kong. Sheet 134×83 mm, containing design as No. 715.

| MS782 | | $10 brown, black and cinnamon | 4.00 | 7.00 |

167 Swimming

1994. 15th Commonwealth Games, Victoria, Canada. Multicoloured.

783	**167**	$1 Type **167**	25	20
784		$1.90 Bowls	40	55
785		$2.40 Gymnastics	50	1.00
786		$5 Weightlifting	90	3.25

168 Dr. James Legge and Students

1994. Dr. James Legge (Chinese scholar) Commemoration.

| 787 | **168** | $1 multicoloured | 1.00 | 1.00 |

169 Alcyonium Coral

1994. Corals. Multicoloured.

788		$1 Type **169**	25	20
789		$1.90 Zoanthus	35	60
790		$2.40 Tubastrea	45	1.00
791		$5 Platygyra	80	3.00
MS792		130×75 mm. Nos. 788/91	4.50	7.00

170 Pig

1995. Chinese New Year ("Year of the Pig").

793	**170**	$1 multicoloured	30	30
794	-	$1.90 multicoloured	60	80
795	-	$2.40 multicoloured	60	1.10
796	-	$5 multicoloured	1.25	4.00
MS797		130×84 mm. Nos. 793/6	4.25	6.50

DESIGNS: $1.90 to $5, Different pig designs.

171 Hong Kong Rugby Sevens

1995. International Sporting Events in Hong Kong. Multicoloured.

798		$1 Type **171**	45	20
799		$1.90 The China Sea Yacht Race	60	80
800		$2.40 International Dragon Boat Races	85	1.10
801		$5 Hong Kong International Horse Races	1.75	4.25

172 Tsui Shing Lau Pagoda

1995. Hong Kong Traditional Rural Buildings. Multicoloured.

802		$1 Type **172**	30	25
803		$1.90 Sam Tung Uk village	45	65
804		$2.40 Lo Wai village	60	1.10
805		$5 Man Shek Tong house	1.10	3.50

173 Regimental Badge

1995. Disbandment of the Royal Hong Kong Regiment. Multicoloured.

806		$1.20 Type **173**	70	25
807		$2.10 Regimental guidon (horiz)	80	65
808		$2.60 Colour of Hong Kong Volunteer Defence Corps, 1928 (horiz)	80	1.10
809		$5 Cap badge of Royal Hong Kong Defence Force, 1951	1.10	4.00

1995. "Singapore '95" International Stamp Exhibition. Sheet 130×75 mm, containing design as No. 715, but colours changed.

| MS810 | | $10 mauve, green, yellow and lilac | 4.00 | 6.50 |

1995. 50th Anniv of End of Second World War. Sheet 130×75 mm, containing design as No. 715.

| MS811 | | $10 brown, black and cinnamon | 4.50 | 7.00 |

174 Bruce Lee

1995. Hong Kong Film Stars. Multicoloured.

812		$1.20 Type **174**	2.00	75
813		$2.10 Leung Sing-por	2.25	1.40
814		$2.60 Yam Kim-fai	3.00	2.25
815		$5 Lin Dai	3.50	5.00

175 Rat

1996. Chinese New Year ("Year of the Rat").

816	**175**	$1.20 multicoloured	25	30
817	-	$2.10 multicoloured	50	55
818	-	$2.60 multicoloured	50	65
819	-	$5 multicoloured	1.50	1.75
MS820		133×85 mm. Nos. 816/19	3.50	3.50

DESIGNS: $2.10 to $5, Rats (different).

1996. Visit "HONG KONG '97" Stamp Exhibition (1st issue). Sheet 130×80 mm, containing design as No. 715, but colours changed.

| MS821 | | $10 orange, black and green | 4.00 | 6.50 |

See also Nos. MS827, MS841 and MS872/3.

176 Rhythmic Gymnastics

1996. Olympic Games, Atlanta. Multicoloured with Royal cypher and face values in black and Olympic rings multicoloured.

822		$1.20 Type **176**	20	25
823		$2.10 Diving	35	65
824		$2.60 Athletics	40	75
825		$5 Basketball	1.90	3.25

| MS826 | | 130×75 mm. As Nos. 822/5, but Royal Cypher and Olympic Rings in gold and face values in black (medal in bottom sheet margin) | 2.50 | 4.25 |

See also Nos. 832/5.

1996. Visit "HONG KONG '97" Stamp Exhibition (2nd issue). Sheet 130×80 mm, containing design as No. 715, but colours changed.

| MS827 | | $10 green, deep green and violet | 2.50 | 3.00 |

177 Painted Pottery Basin, c. 4500–3700 B.C.

1996. Archaeological Discoveries. Multicoloured.

828		$1.20 Type **177**	45	25
829		$2.10 Stone "yue" (ceremonial axe), c. 2900–2200 B.C.	50	65
830		$2.60 Stone "ge" (halberd), c. 2200–1500 B.C.	55	1.00
831		$5 Pottery tripod, c. 25–220 A.D.	1.00	2.50

1996. Opening of Centennial Olympic Games, Atlanta. Designs as Nos. 822/5, but with Royal Cypher and Olympic Rings in gold and face values in colours quoted.

832		$1.20 Type **176** (mauve)	35	25
833		$2.10 As No. 823 (blue)	40	60
834		$2.60 As No. 824 (green)	45	90
835		$5 As No. 825 (red)	1.00	2.75

| MS836 | | 130×75 mm. As No. MS826, but with medal in top margin | 2.75 | 4.50 |

The stamps in Nos. MS826 and MS836 are similar. The miniature sheets differ in the marginal inscriptions and illustrations. No. MS826 is inscribed "1996 OLYMPIC GAMES" and has a Gold Medal in the bottom margin. No. MS836 is inscribed "TO COMMEMORATE THE OPENING OF THE CENTENNIAL OLYMPIC GAMES 19 JULY 1996" and has the medal in the top margin.

178 Pat Sin Leng Mountain

1996. Mountains. Multicoloured.

837		$1.30 Type **178**	45	35
838		$2.50 Ma On Shan (40×35 mm)	65	1.00
839		$3.10 Lion Rock (35×40 mm)	85	1.40
840		$5 Lantau Peak (25×46½ mm)	1.10	2.75

1996. Visit "HONG KONG '97" Stamp Exhibition (3rd issue). Sheet 130×80 mm, containing design as No. 715, but colours changed.

| MS841 | | $10 green, black and red | 2.50 | 3.50 |

1996. Hong Kong Team's Achievements at Atlanta Olympic Games. Sheet 130×75 mm, containing No. 715.

| MS842 | | $10 brown, black and cinnamon | 2.75 | 3.25 |

179 Main Building, University of Hong Kong, 1912

1996. Urban Heritage. Multicoloured.

843		$1.30 Type **179**	30	70
844		$2.50 Western Market, 1906	50	85
845		$3.10 Old Pathological Institute, 1905	55	1.00
846		$5 Flagstaff House, 1846	70	2.25

1996. Serving the Community. Sheet 130×75 mm, containing design as No. 619, but smaller, 25×35 mm. Multicoloured.

| MS847 | | $5 Multi-racial society | 1.00 | 1.25 |

180 Part of Hong Kong Skyline

1997

848	**180**	10c. purple and pink	15	30
849	-	20c. brown and red	30	30
850	-	50c. green and orange	20	40
851	-	$1 blue and yellow	30	20
852	-	$1.20 green and yellow	30	50
853	-	$1.30 violet and green	30	25
854	-	$1.40 purple and green	30	50
855	-	$1.60 green and green	30	60
856	-	$2 green and blue	40	50
857	-	$2.10 turquoise and blue	40	60
858	-	$2.50 violet and mauve	50	1.00
859	-	$3.10 purple and mauve	60	70
860	-	$5 mauve and orange	1.25	1.00
861	-	$10 multicoloured (28×32 mm)	2.00	2.50
862	-	$20 multicoloured (28×32 mm)	3.50	5.00
863	-	$50 multicoloured (28×32 mm)	8.00	11.00
MS864		273×53 mm. Nos. 848/60	3.50	4.00
MS865		95×72 mm. Nos. 861/3	13.00	13.50

DESIGNS: 20c. to $50, Different sections of Hong Kong skyline.

See also Nos. MS872/3 and MS892.

1997. Visit "HONG KONG '97" Stamp Exhibition (4th issue). Sheet 130×80 mm, containing No. 861, with marginal illustration in violet.

| MS872 | | $10 multicoloured | 2.00 | 3.50 |

1997. Visit "HONG KONG '97" Stamp Exhibition (5th issue). Sheet 130×80 mm, containing No. 861, with marginal illustration in brown.

| MS873 | | $10 multicoloured | 2.00 | 3.50 |

181 Ox

1997. Chinese New Year ("Year of the Ox").

874	**181**	$1.30 multicoloured	25	25
875	**181**	$2.50 multicoloured	40	55
876	**181**	$3.10 multicoloured	55	90
877	**181**	$5 multicoloured	85	2.00
MS878		133×84 mm. Nos. 874/7	1.75	3.00

182 Yellow-breasted Bunting

1997. Migratory Birds. Multicoloured.

884		$1.30 Type **182**	40	35
885		$2.50 Great knot	50	55
886		$3.10 Falcated teal	65	90
887		$5 Black-faced spoonbill	85	2.00

183 Hong Kong Stadium

1997. Modern Landmarks. Multicoloured.

888	$1.30 Type **183**		30	25
889	$2.50 Peak Tower		60	55
890	$3.10 Hong Kong Convention and Exhibition Centre		85	1·10
891	$5 Lantau bridge		1·40	2·50
MS892	130×76 mm. No. 891		1·00	1·75

1997. Paralympic Games, Atlanta (1996). Sheet 130×75 mm, containing No. 861.
MS898	$10 multicoloured		1·50	2·25

1997. History of the Hong Kong Post Office. Sheet 130×75 mm, containing design as No. 677, but redrawn smaller, 22×38 mm.
MS899	$5 multicoloured		1·00	1·75

184 House of Sam Tung Uk

1997. Establishment of Hong Kong as Special Administrative Region of People's Republic of China. Multicoloured.

900	$1.30 Type **184**		45	40
901	$1.60 Hong Kong Bank and vehicles		55	40
902	$2.50 Buildings and Hong Kong Convention and Exhibition Centre		80	50
903	$2.60 Container Terminal		90	50
904	$3.10 Junks and dolphins		1·10	60
905	$5 Bauhinia flower and clouds		1·70	60
MS906	131×75 mm. No. 905		2·75	2·30

185 Graphs and Hong Kong Bank (Finance and Banking)

1997. World Bank Group and International Monetary Fund Annual Meetings. Multicoloured.

907	$1.30 Type **185**		45	40
908	$2.50 Share prices (Investment) and Stock Exchange		80	60
909	$3.10 Map on printed circuit and dish aerial (Trade and Telecommunications)		1·10	80
910	$5 Satellite image and road junctions (Infrastructure and Transport)		1·70	1·20

186 Clam

1997. Sea Shells. Multicoloured.

911	$1.30 Type **186**		45	40
912	$2.50 Cowrie		80	60
913	$3.10 Cone		1·10	80
914	$5 Murex		1·70	1·20

187 Tiger

1998. Chinese New Year ("Year of the Tiger").

915	**187**	$1.30 multicoloured	55	30
916	**187**	$2.50 multicoloured	80	60
917	**187**	$3.10 multicoloured	1·10	70
918	**187**	$5 multicoloured	1·40	80
MS919	133×84 mm. Nos. 915/18		6·75	6·50

188 *Star*, 1900s

1998. Centenary of *Star* Ferry. Multicoloured.

920	$1.30 Type **188**		45	40
921	$2.50 *Star*, 1910s–20s		80	60
922	$3.10 *Star*, 1920s–1950s		1·10	70
923	$5 *Star*, 1950s onwards		1·60	80

189 Observation Lounge

1998. Inauguration of Hong Kong International Airport, Chek Lap Kok. Multicoloured.

924	$1.30 Type **189**		45	40
925	$1.60 Couple boarding train		55	50
926	$2.50 Train and suspension bridge		80	60
927	$2.60 Concourse and mail vans at Airmail Centre		90	65
928	$3.10 Aircraft in bays		1·10	80
929	$5 Airplane taking off		1·80	1·20
MS930	145×79 mm. No. 929		2·75	2·50

190 De Havilland D.H.86 Dragon Express *Dorado* (Hong Kong—Penang Service, 1936)

1998. Closure of Kaj Tak Airport. Sheet 130×75 mm.
MS931	190 $5 multicoloured		2·75	2·50

Type 190 is a redrawn version of Type **111**.

191 Grasshopper and Cub Scouts and Knot

1998. 85th Anniv of Hong Kong Scout Association. Multicoloured.

932	$1.30 Type **191**		45	40
933	$2.50 Two scouts, knot, watch-tower and tents		80	70
934	$3.10 Two venture scouts, knot, sailing dinghies and helicopter		1·10	80
935	$5 Rover scout and adult leader, knot and buildings		1·70	1·00

192 Graphic Design

1998. Hong Kong Design. Multicoloured.

936	$1.30 Type **192**		45	40
937	$2.50 Product design		80	70
938	$3.10 Interior design		1·00	90
939	$5 Fashion design		1·70	1·00

193 Dragonfly Kite

1998. Kites. Multicoloured.

940	$1.30 Type **193**		45	40
941	$2.50 Dragon kite		80	70
942	$3.10 Butterfly kite		1·00	90
943	$5 Goldfish kite		1·70	1·20
MS944	135×85 mm. Nos. 940/3		4·50	4·00

194 Rabbit ("Kung Hei Fat Choi")

1999. Chinese New Year ("Year of the Rabbit"). Multicoloured.

945	$1.30 Type **194**		45	40
946	$2.50 Rabbit and scroll ("Good Health")		80	70
947	$3.10 Rabbit and tangerine ("Good Luck")		1·10	90
948	$5 Rabbit and sweet tray ("May all your wishes come true")		1·70	1·20

The gold panels of the designs can be scratched off to reveal a greeting in Chinese characters as given in brackets. Prices for Nos. 945/8 are for examples with the gold panels intact.

195 Rabbit

1999. Chinese Lunar Cycle. Sheet 250×48 mm containing similar designs to 1987-98 New Year issues but with inscriptions as in T **195** and some face values altered. Multicoloured.

MS949	$1.30 As Type **175**; $1.30 As Type **181**; $1.30 As Type **187**; $1.30 As Type **195**; $1.30 As Type **170**; $1.30 As Type **130**; $1.30 As No. 768; $1.30 As Type **136**; $1.30 As No. 735; $1.30 As Type **53**; $1.30 As Type **148**; $1.30 As Type **143**		7·75	7·75

196 Calligraphy

1999. International Year of the Elderly. Multicoloured.

950	$1.30 Type **196**		45	40
951	$2.50 Holding bird cage		80	70
952	$3.10 Playing chess		1·10	90
953	$5 Holding walking stick (voluntary services)		1·70	1·20

1999. Hong Kong Team's Achievements at 13th Asian Games, Bangkok (1998). Sheet 135×85 mm.
MS954	Nos. 856/7		4·00	4·00

197 An An

1999. Presentation of Giant Pandas An An and Jia Jia to Hong Kong. Sheet 132×78 mm.
MS955	197 $10 multicoloured		6·25	6·25

198 Bus

1999. Public Transport. Multicoloured.

956	$1.30 Type **198**		45	40
957	$2.40 Minibus		80	60
958	$2.50 Tram		1·00	80
959	$2.60 Taxi		1·30	80
960	$3.10 "Airport Express" train		1·60	1·10

199 Hong Kong Harbour

1999. Hong Kong–Singapore Joint Issue. Multicoloured.

961	$1.20 Type **199**		35	30
962	$1.30 Singapore skyline		45	40
963	$2.50 Giant Buddha, Lantau Island, Hong Kong		80	70
964	$2.60 Merlion statue, Sentosa Island, Singapore		90	75
965	$3.10 Street scene, Hong Kong		1·10	90
966	$5 Bugis Junction, Singapore		1·80	1·20
MS967	133×76 mm. Nos. 961/6		5·25	5·25

1999. "China 1999" International Stamp Exhibition, Peking. Sheet 130×75 mm.
MS968	No. 861		4·00	4·00

200 Flags of Hong Kong and People's Republic, and Hong Kong

1999. 50th Anniv of People's Republic of China. Multicoloured.

969	$1.30 Type **200**		80	40
970	$2.50 "Bauhinia blakeana" and Hong Kong harbour		1·00	70
971	$3.10 Chinese dragon dance		1·30	90
972	$5 Firework display over Hong Kong		2·10	1·40

201 Museum of Tea Ware

1999. Hong Kong Landmarks and Tourist Attractions. Multicoloured

(a) Size 24×29 mm (10c. to $5) or 26×31 mm (others)

973	10c. Type **201**		20	20
974	20c. St. John's Cathedral		20	20
975	50c. Legislative Council building		20	20
976	$1 Tai Fu Tai		35	20
977	$1.20 Wong Tai Sin Temple		45	20
978	$1.30 Victoria Harbour		45	20
979	$1.40 Hong Kong Railway Museum		45	20
980	$1.60 Tsim Sha Tsui clocktower		55	25
980a	$1.80 Hong Kong Stadium		60	30
980b	$1.90 Western Market		65	30
981	$2 Happy Valley racecourse		80	35
982	$2.10 Kowloon–Canton Railway		85	35
982a	$2.40 Repulse Bay		1·00	40
983	$2.50 Chi Lin Nunnery, Kowloon		1·00	40
983b	$3 The Peak Tower		1·30	45
984	$3.10 Giant Buddha, Po Lin Monastery, Lantau Island		1·30	45
985	$5 Pagoda, Aw Boon Haw Gardens		1·70	50
986	$10 Tsing Ma bridge		2·75	1·50
986a	$13 Hong Kong Cultural Centre		5·00	2·50
987	$20 Hong Kong Convention and Exhibition Centre		6·00	3·50
988	$50 Hong Kong International Airport		16·00	7·25
MS989	210×153 mm. Nos. 973/85		7·75	7·75
MS990	118×89 mm. 986/8		28·00	28·00

(b) Size 20×24 mm.

991	10c. As Type **201**		1·00	1·00
992	50c. As No. 975		1·00	1·00
993	$1.30 As No. 978		2·50	1·50
993a	$1.40 As No. 979		1·60	50
994	$1.60 As No. 980		3·00	1·75
994a	$1.80 As No. 980a		1·80	60
994b	$2.40 As No. 982a		2·00	70
994c	$3 As No. 984		4·00	2·50

202 Dolphins

1999. Endangered Species. Indo-Pacific Hump- backed Dolphin ("Chinese White Dolphin").

995	**202**	$1.30 multicoloured	55	40
996	-	$2.50 multicoloured	90	70
997	-	$3.10 multicoloured	1·10	90
998	-	$5 multicoloured	1·90	1·20
MS999	150×80 mm. Nos. 995/8		5·50	5·50

DESIGNS: $2.50 to $5 Various designs showing dolphins as Type **202**.

203 Dragon Boat Race (fire) and City Skyline (metal)

1999. New Millennium (1st issue). The Five Elements. Sheet 130×75 mm containing T **203** and similar horiz designs. Multicoloured.

MS1000	$5 Type **203**; $5 Tsing Ma bridge (wood) and birds flying over Mai Po Marshes (water)	4·50	4·50

204 Victoria Harbour

2000. New Millennium (2nd issue).

1001	**204**	$50 multicoloured	28·00	28·00

No. 1001 is embossed with 22 carat gold.

205 Scales on Globe (Au Chung-yip)

2000. New Millennium (3rd issue). Winning Entries in Children's Millennium Stamp Design Competition. Multicoloured.

1002	**205**	$1.30 Type **205**	45	30
1003		$2.50 Globe, space shuttle, houses and children watering (Cheung Hang)	90	70
1004		$3.10 Planets (Valerie Teh)	1·00	80
1005		$5 Planets, spacecraft and satellite (Tsui Ming-yin)	1·60	1·10

206 Dragon

2000. Chinese New Year ("Year of the Dragon").

1006	**206**	$1.30 multicoloured	45	35
1007	-	$2.50 multicoloured	90	70
1008	-	$3.10 multicoloured	1·00	80
1009	-	$5 multicoloured	1·70	1·20
MS1010	Two sheets, each 135×85 mm. (a) Nos. 1006/9. (b) $5 No. 1009. Imperf Set of 2 sheets		18·00	18·00

DESIGNS: $2.50 to $5 Various dragons.

2000. Establishment of the Certification Authority (1st issue). Sheet 140×90 mm containing design as No. 986.

MS1011	$10 multicoloured	4·50	4·50

2000. Visit "HONG KONG 2001" Stamp Exhibition (1st issue). Sheet 130×74 mm containing design as No. 986, and with marginal illustrations showing bird.

MS1012	$10 multicoloured	5·50	5·50

See also Nos. **MS1017**, **MS1022**, **MS1027**, **MS1028**, **MS1037** and **MS1052**.

207 Hong Kong Heritage Museum, Sha Tin

2000. Museums and Libraries. Multicoloured.

1013	$1.30 Type **207**	65	40
1014	$2.50 Central Library, Causeway Bay	1·20	80

1015	$3.10 Museum of Coastal Defence, Shau Kei Wan	1·30	90
1016	$5 Museum of History, Tsim Sha Tsui East	2·10	1·60

2000. Visit "HONG KONG 2001" Stamp Exhibition (2nd issue). Sheet 130×75 mm containing design as No. 986, and with marginal illustration showing flowers.

MS1017	$10 multicoloured	4·50	4·50

208 Patient and Nurse (Blood Transfusion)

2000. 50th Anniv of Hong Kong Red Cross. Multicoloured.

1018	$1.30 Type **208**	55	40
1019	$2.50 Doctor and child (Special Education and Care for the Disabled)	1·00	70
1020	$3.10 Man distributing blankets (Disaster relief)	1·10	80
1021	$5 Volunteer and young man (Youth and Voluntary services)	1·80	1·20
MS1022	130×75 mm. Nos. 1018/21	4·75	4·75

209 Lantern Fly

2000. Insects. Multicoloured.

1023	$1.30 Type **209**	65	35
1024	$2.50 Yellow-spotted emerald	1·10	65
1025	$3.10 Hong Kong birdwing (butterfly)	1·20	80
1026	$5 Red-cap tortoise beetle	2·00	1·60
MS1027	130×75 mm. Nos. 1023/6	5·25	5·25

210 Lion Rock

2000. Visit "HONG KONG 2001" Stamp Exhibition (3rd issue). Sheet 130×75 mm.

MS1028	**210**	$10 multicoloured	4·50	4·50

211 Cycling and Tennis

2000. Olympic Games, Sydney. Multicoloured.

1029	$1.30 Type **211**	55	45
1030	$2.50 Table tennis and running	1·00	90
1031	$3.10 Wrestling and rowing	1·20	1·00
1032	$5 Diving and wind surfing	1·90	1·30

212 View of Street (Establishment of Chamber, 1900)

2000. Centenary of General Chamber of Commerce. Multicoloured.

1033	$1.30 Type **212**	55	45
1034	$2.50 Old and new headquarters (relocation, 1922)	1·00	90
1035	$3.10 Victims of Pak Tin village fire receiving aid	1·20	1·00
1036	$5 Man using abacus and hand using mouse	1·90	1·60

---

213 Corals

2000. Visit "HONG KONG 2001" Stamp Exhibition (4th issue). 129×75 mm.

MS1037	**213**	$10 multicoloured	4·50	4·50

2000. I.T.U. Telecome, Asia 2000. Sheet 130×75 mm containing design as No. 986.

MS1038	$10 multicoloured	4·50	4·50

214 Hong Kong Convention and Exhibition Centre

2000. New Millennium (4th issue). Sheet 91×151 mm.

MS1039	**214**	$20 multicoloured	7·25	7·25

215 Snake

2001. Chinese New Year ("Year of the Snake").

1040	**215**	$1.30 multicoloured	55	45
1041	-	$2.50 multicoloured	1·00	90
1042	-	$3.10 multicoloured	1·20	1·00
1043	-	$5 multicoloured	1·90	1·60
MS1044	Two sheets, each 135×85 mm. (a) $5 Nos. 1040/3. (b) $5 No. 1043. Imperf		7·75	7·75

DESIGNS: $2.50 to $5 Showing various snakes.

216 Leaves and Pebbles ("Happy Memories")

2001. Greetings Stamps. Multicoloured.

1045	$1.30 Type **216**	45	35
1046	$1.60 Swans ("Happy Valentine's Day")	55	45
1047	$2.50 Chicks ("Happy Birthday")	1·10	80
1048	$2.60 Cherry blossom ("Happy New Year")	1·10	80
1049	$3.10 Bamboo ("A Successful Year")	1·30	1·00
1050	$5 Poinsettia ("Merry Christmas")	1·90	1·70

217 Dragon ("Year of the Dragon")

2001. "HONG KONG 2001" Stamp Exhibition. Sheet 135×90 mm.

MS1051	$50 Type **217**; $50 Snake ("Year of the Snake")	45·00	45·00

218 Schima tree

2001. Visit "HONG KONG 201" Stamp Exhibition (5th issue). Sheet 130×75 mm.

MS1052	**218**	$5 multicoloured	2·40	2·20

---

219 Tai Tam Tuk Reservoir

2001. 150th Anniv of Hong Kong's Public Water Supply. Multicoloured.

1053	$1.30 Type **219**	60	45
1054	$2.50 Plover Cove Reservoir	1·10	90
1055	$3.10 Guangdong to Hong Kong water pipeline	1·30	1·10
1056	$5 Water monitoring equipment and chemical symbols	2·00	1·80

220 Ng Cho-fan and Pak Yin

2001. Hong Kong Film Stars. Multicoloured.

1057	$1.30 Type **220**	60	45
1058	$2.50 Sun Ma Si-tsang and Tang Bik-wan	1·10	90
1059	$3.10 Cheung Wood-yau and Wong Man-lei	1·30	1·10
1060	$5 Mak Bing-wing and Fung Wong-nui	2·00	1·80

2001. Ninth National Games, Guangzhou, People's Republic of China. Preliminary Contest for Sanda (discipline in National Game), Hong Kong. Sheet 130×75 mm containing design as No. 985 and with marginal illustrations showing boxing gloves.

MS1061	$5 multicoloured	2·75	2·75

221 Dragon Boat and Sydney Opera House

2001. Dragon Boat Racing. Multicoloured.

1062	$5 Type **221**	2·20	1·80
1063	$5 Dragon boat racing and Hong Kong Convention and Exhibition Centre	2·20	1·80
MS1064	106×70 mm. Nos. 1062/3	4·75	4·75

222 Emblem

2001. Choice of Beijing as 2008 Olympic Host City.

1065	**222**	$1.30 multicoloured	1·20	80

2001. "PHILA NIPPON 02" International Stamp Exhibition, Tokyo. Sheet 130×75 mm containing design as No. 986.

MS1066	$10 multicoloured	4·75	4·75

223 Pouring Tea (Gongfu tea)

2001. Tea Culture. Multicoloured.

1067	$1.30 Type **223**	60	45
1068	$2.50 Hong Kong style tea	1·10	90
1069	$3.10 Pouring water (Yum Cha and Dim Sum)	1·40	1·10
1070	$5 Pouring hot water in to tea pot	2·20	1·80

224 Centella asiatica

2001. Medicinal Herbs. Multicoloured.

1071	$1.30 Type **224**	60	45
1072	$2.50 *Lobelia chinensis*	1·10	90
1073	$3.10 *Gardenia jasminoides*	1·40	1·10
1074	$5 *Scutellaria indica*	2·20	1·80

225 Child dressed as Bear

2001. Children's Stamps. Self-adhesive gum.

1075	$1.30 Type **225**	60	45
1076	$2.50 Child dressed as duck	1·10	90
1077	$3.10 Child dressed as pot plant	1·40	1·10
1078	$5 Child dressed as bee	2·20	1·80
MS1079	130×92 mm. Nos. 1075/8	5·75	5·75

The stamps had portions of the design left white for users to colour as they wished. Such embellishments did not affect the postal validity of the stamps.

226 Horse

2002. Chinese New Year ("Year of the Horse").

1080	**226**	$1.30 multicoloured	60	45
1081	–	$2.50 multicoloured	1·10	90
1082	–	$3.10 multicoloured	1·40	1·10
1083	–	$5 multicoloured	2·20	1·80
MS1084		Two sheets, each 135×85 mm. (a) Nos. 1080/3. (b) No. 1083. Imperf	8·25	8·25

DESIGNS: Nos. 1081/3, showing horses.

2002. Serving the Community Festival 2002. Sheet 75×130 mm, containing design as No. 985.

MS1085	$5 multicoloured	3·00	3·00

227 Snake

2002. Chinese New Year ("Year of the Snake"). Sheet 135×90 mm.

MS1086	$50 Type **227**; $50 Horse ("Year of the Horse")	55·00	55·00

No. **MS**1086 has the snake and the horse embossed in gold and silver foil.

228 "Lines in Motion" (detail, Chui Tze-hung)

2002. Modern Art. Multicoloured.

1087	$1.30 Type **228**	60	45
1088	$2.50 "Volume and Time" (detail, Hon Chi-fun)	1·10	90
1089	$3.10 "Bright Sun" (sculpture, detail, Aries Lee)	1·30	1·10
1090	$5 "Midsummer" (detail, Irene Chou)	2·00	1·80

229 Face and Periodic Table (Education)

2002. Information Technology. Multicoloured.

1091	$1.40 Type **229**	60	45
1092	$2.40 Face, world map and internet symbols (communications)	95	80
1093	$3 Face, film and musical notes (entertainment)	1·20	1·00
1094	$5 Face, buildings and city (commerce)	2·00	1·80

230 Player and Football

2002. World Cup Football Championship. Japan and South Korea. Multicoloured.

1095	$1.40 Type **230**	85	55
1096	$1.40 Players tackling and crowd	85	55

231 North Atlantic Pink Tree Coral, Pacific Orange Cup Coral and North Pacific Horn Coral

2002. Corals. Multicoloured.

1097	$1.40 Type **231**	60	45
1098	$2.40 North Atlantic giant orange tree coral and black coral	95	80
1099	$3 *Dendronepthea gigantea* and *Dendronepthea*	1·20	1·00
1100	$5 *Tubastrea* and *Echinogorgia* and island	1·90	1·70
MS1101	161×85 mm. Nos. 1097/1100	4·75	4·75

Stamps in similar designs were issued by Canada.

232 Hong Kong Buildings and Train

2002. Fifth Anniv of Beijing—Kowloon Through Train Service. Multicoloured.

1102	$1.40 Type **232**	60	45
1103	$2.40 Wuhan—Changjiang Bridge and train	95	80
1104	$3 Pagodas, Shaolin Monastery, Zhengzhou and train	1·20	1·00
1105	$5 Temple of Heaven, Beijing and front of train	1·90	1·70

Nos. 1102/5 were issued together, forming a composite design of a train.

233 Chinese White Dolphins and Coral

2002. Fifth Anniv of Hong Kong's Status as Special Administrative Region of People's Republic of China. Multicoloured.

1106	$1.40 Type **233**	60	45
1107	$2.40 School children and bauhinia flowers	95	80
1108	$3 Birds in flight over Hong Kong airport	1·20	1·00
1109	$5 Flags of China and Hong Kong, buildings and fireworks	1·90	1·50
MS1110	135×85 mm. Nos. 1106/9	4·75	4·75

2002. "PHILAKOREA 2002" World Stamp Exhibition, Seoul, South Korea. Sheet 131×75 mm, containing design as No. 986.

MS1111	$10 multicoloured	4·75	4·75

2002. "AMPHILEX 2002" World Stamp Exhibition, Amsterdam. Sheet 130×75 mm, containing design as No. 986.

MS1112	$10 multicoloured	4·75	4·75

2002. Hukou Waterfall Shanxi, People's Republic of China. Sheet 140×90 mm, containing design as No. 986.

MS1113	$10 multicoloured	4·75	4·75

234 Ping Chau

2002. Geology of Hong Kong. Multicoloured.

1114	$1.40 Type **234**	60	45
1115	$2.40 Port Island	95	80
1116	$3 Po Pin Chau	1·40	1·10
1117	$5 Lamma Island	3·50	2·20
MS1118	136×81 mm. Nos. 1114/17	6·50	6·50

235 Radar Signal and Luopan (fengshui compass)

2002. Cultural Diversity. Multicoloured.

1119	10c. Type **235**	25	10
1120	20c. Calculator and abacus	25	10
1121	50c. Incense coils and stained-glass window	25	10
1122	$1 Chair and Luohan (bed)	35	20
1123	$1.40 Dim Sum (dumplings) and loaves of bread	50	30
1124	$1.80 Cutlery and chopsticks	60	35
1125	$1.90 Canned drinks and tea caddies	65	40
1126	$2 European and oriental wedding cakes	70	45
1127	$2.40 Erhu (stringed instrument) and violin	85	50
1128	$2.50 Oriental letterbox and internet symbol	90	55
1129	$3 Yachts and Dragon boat	1·10	65
1130	$5 Traditional tiled roof and modern office block	1·80	1·00
1131	$10 Ballet dancers and Chinese opera character	3·50	1·10
1132	$13 Chess pieces and Xiangqi pieces (Chinese chess)	4·75	1·70
1133	$20 Christmas lights and mid-autumn festival lantern	7·25	2·20
1134	$50 Sculptures "Oval with points" (Henry Moore) and "Tai Chi series: Single Whip" (Ju Ming)	18·00	6·25
MS1135	Two sheets (a) 210×150 mm. Nos. 1119/30 (b) 122×101 mm. Nos. 1131/4	36·00	36·00

236 Christmas Tree

2002. Christmas. Multicoloured.

1146	$1.40 Type **236**	50	45
1147	$2.40 Bauble	85	80
1148	$3 Snowman	1·20	90
1149	$5 Bell	1·80	1·30

237 Train and Station (Main Street)

2003. Disneyland Hong Kong. Multicoloured.

1150	$1.40 Type **237**	60	45
1151	$2.40 Castle (Fantasyland)	95	80
1152	$3 Tree house (Adventureland)	1·10	90
1153	$5 Pylons (Tomorrowland)	1·80	1·30
MS1154	135×85 mm. Nos. 1150/3	4·75	4·75

Nos. 1150/**MS**1154 each have an embossed figure of Mickey Mouse in the lower left corner.

238 Argali Ram

2003. Chinese New Year ("Year of the Ram"). Multicoloured.

(a) Two phosphor bands

1155	$1.40 Type **238**	60	45
1156	$2.40 Sheep	95	80
1157	$3 Tahr ram	1·10	90
1158	$5 Gazella ram	1·80	1·30
MS1159	Two sheets, each 135×85 mm. (a) Nos. 1155/8; (b) $5 No. 1158 Set of 2 sheets	8·25	8·25

(b) One phosphor band

1160	$10 As No. 1008 ("Year of the Dragon")	3·50	2·75
1161	$10 As No. 1042 ("Year of the Snake")	3·50	2·75
1162	$10 As No. 1081 ("Year of the Horse")	3·50	2·75
1163	$10 As No. 1158 ("Year of the Ram")	3·50	2·75

(c) Size 38×51 mm. Ordinary paper.

MS1164	135×90 mm. $50 As No. 1162 ("Year of the Horse") (37×50 mm); $50 As No. 1157 (37×50 mm)	43·00	44·00

No. **MS**1164 has the horse and ram embossed with gold and silver foil.

239 Letter Writing

2003. Traditional Trades and Crafts. Multicoloured.

1165	$1.40 Type **239**	60	45
1166	$1.80 Bird cage maker (vert)	70	55
1167	$2.40 Qipao tailoring (women's clothes)	85	65
1168	$2.50 Hairdressing (vert)	95	80
1169	$3 Making dough figures (vert)	1·10	90
1170	$5 Olive seller	1·80	1·30
MS1171	219×123 mm. Nos. 1165/70	6·25	6·25

240 Hong Kong Skyline

2003. Hong Kong 2004 International Stamp Exhibition (1st issue). Sheet 135×85 mm.

MS1172	**240**	$10 multicoloured	4·75	4·75

See also Nos. **MS**1190, **MS**1213 and 1214/1230.

241 The Master-of-Nets Garden, Suzhou

2003. Mainland Landscapes (1st issue). Sheet 140×90 mm.

MS1173	**241**	$10 multicoloured	4·75	4·75

See also Nos. **MS**1243, **MS**1324, **MS**1349, **MS**1447 and **MS**1495.

242 Fukien Tea (semi-cascade)

2003. Miniature Landscapes. Multicoloured.

1174	$1.40 Type **242**	60	45
1175	$2.40 Hedge Sageretia (informal upright)	95	75
1176	$3 Fire-thorn (cascade) (vert)	1·20	95
1177	$5 Chinese Hackberry (root on rock) (vert)	1·80	1·40

243 Ear-spot Angelfish

2003. Aquarium Fish. Multicoloured.

1178	$1.40 Type **243**	50	40
1179	$2.40 Copper-banded but-terflyfish	85	65
1180	$3 Dwarf gourami	1·20	95
1181	$5 Red discus	1·70	1·30

244 Bottles and Man holding Firework ("Celebrations")

2003. Greetings Stamps. With service indicator. Multicoloured.

(a) Postage

1182	($1.40) Type **244** ("Local Mail Postage")	60	45
1183	($1.40) Man and heart-shaped tree ("Care and Love")	60	45

(b) AIR

1184	($3) No. 1182 ("Air Mail Postage")	1·20	95
1185	($3) No. 1183	1·20	95

No. 1182/3 were for use on letters up to 30 grams within Hong Kong and 1184/5 were for use on airmail letters up to 20 grams to addresses outside Hong Kong.

245 Pied Avocet

2003. Water Birds. Multicoloured.

1186	$1.40 Type **245**	50	40
1187	$2.40 Horned grebe	70	55
1188	$3 Great crested grebe	1·10	85
1189	$5 Black-throated diver	1·80	1·40

Stamps of the same design were issued by Sweden.

246 Sha Tin Park

2003. Hong Kong 2004 International Stamp Exhibition (2nd issue). Sheet 135×85 mm.

MS1190 **246** $10 multicoloured	4·75	4·75

247 Astronaut and Satellite

2003. First Chinese Manned Space Flight. Multicoloured.

1191	$1.40 Type **247**	95	75
1192	$1.40 Shenzhou-5 space craft	95	75

248 Drum

2003. Traditional Instruments. Multicoloured.

1193	$1.40 Type **248**	50	40
1194	$2.40 Clappers	85	65
1195	$3 Cymbals	1·20	95
1196	$5 Gongs	1·70	1·30

MS1197 130×75 mm. $13 Bell (35×45 mm)	4·75	4·75

249 Potola Palace, Lhasa

2003. UNESCO World Heritage Sites in China. Multicoloured.

1198	$1.40 Type **249**	50	40
1199	$1.80 Imperial Palace, Beijing (47×39 mm)	70	55
1200	$2.40 First Qin Emperor's Mausoleum, Shaanxi Province (47×39 mm)	85	65
1201	$2.50 Mount Huangshan, Anhui Province (39×47 mm)	90	70
1202	$3 Old Town, Lijang (39×47 mm)	1·10	85
1203	$5 Jiuzhaigou valley, Sichuan Province (77×30 mm)	1·60	1·20

250 Building Development and People on Walkways

2003. Development of Public Housing. Multicoloured.

1204	$1.40 Type **250**	60	45
1205	$2.40 L-shaped development and women through window	95	75
1206	$3 High-rise development and man reading with children	1·20	95
1207	$5 High-rise development and family walking in park	1·80	1·40

251 Monkey

2004. New Year. (Year of the Monkey). Multicoloured.

1208	$1.40 Type **251**	50	40
1209	$2.40 Mother and baby	85	65
1210	$3 Walking	95	75
1211	$5 Holding branch	1·60	1·20

MS1212 Two sheets, each 136×85 mm (a/b). (a) Nos. 1208/11. (b) As No. 1211. Imperf. (c) 135×90 mm $50×2, As No. 1155 (38×52 mm); As No. 1211 (38×52 mm) Set of 2 sheets	3·00	3·00

252 Round Pudding and Greeting

2004. Hong Kong 2004 International Stamp Exhibition (3rd issue). Tourism. Six sheets, each 135×86 mm containing T **252** and similar horiz designs. Multicoloured.

MS1213 (a) $10 Type **252**; (b) $10×2, As No. MS1213a; (c) $10 New Year parade; (d) $10 Jade pendant; (e) $10 Fire dragon	22·00	22·00

2004. Hong Kong 2004 International Stamp Exhibition (4th issue). Hong Kong Landmarks and Tourist Attractions. Multicoloured.

1214	$1.40 As Type **201**	35	30
1215	$1.40 As No. 973	35	30
1216	$1.40 As No. 974	35	30
1217	$1.40 As No. 975	35	30
1218	$1.40 As No. 976	35	30
1219	$1.40 As No. 977	35	30
1220	$1.40 As No. 978	35	30
1221	$1.40 As No. 979	35	30
1222	$1.40 As No. 980a	35	30

1223	$1.40 As No. 980b	35	30
1224	$1.40 As No. 981	35	30
1225	$1.40 As No. 982	35	30
1226	$1.40 As No. 982a	35	30
1227	$1.40 As No. 983	35	30
1228	$1.40 As No. 984	35	30
1229	$1.40 As No. 984b	35	30
1230	$1.40 As No. 985	35	30
1231	$1.40 As No. 986	35	30
1232	$1.40 As No. 986a	35	30
1233	$1.40 As No. 987	35	30
1234	$1.40 As No. 988	35	30

253 Hong Kong Team

2004. Rugby Sevens. Multicoloured.

1235	$1.40 Type **253**	50	40
1236	$2.40 New Zealand team	85	65
1237	$3 Hong Kong Stadium	1·10	85
1238	$5 Westpac Stadium, Wellington	1·60	1·20

Stamps of the same design were issued by New Zealand.

254 Scissors, Paper, Stone (Ka-lai Tsoi)

2004. Winning Entries in Children's Stamp Design Competition. Games. Multicoloured.

1239	$1.40 Type **254**	50	40
1240	$2.40 Chinese chess (Belinda Hoi-yan Chan)	85	65
1241	$3 Bubble blowing (April Nga-pui Yuen)	1·10	85
1242	$5 Hopscotch (Chap-yin Lui)	1·60	1·20

255 The Chen Clan Academy, Guangzhou

2004. Mainland Landscapes (2nd series). Sheet 140×90 mm.

MS1243 **255** $10 multicoloured	3·75	3·75

256 First Tram (1904)

2004. Centenary of Hong Kong Tramway.

1244	$1.40 Type **256**	50	40
1245	$2.40 Open-topped tram	70	55
1246	$3 Canvas-topped tram	1·20	95
1247	$5 Modern tram	1·80	1·40

MS1248 Two sheets, each 136×85 mm. (a) Nos. 1240/3; (b) $5 Millennium new tram Set of 2 sheets	7·25	7·25

257 Soldiers, Sailors and Airmen

2004. Armed Forces. Multicoloured.

1249	$1.40 Type **257**	50	40
1250	$1.80 Serviceman giving blood	60	45
1251	$2.40 Servicemen and children	70	55
1252	$2.50 Soldiers	85	65
1253	$3 Sailors	1·10	85
1254	$5 Airmen	1·60	1·20

258 Preparing to Dive

2004. Olympic Games, Athens. Sports. Multicoloured.

1255	$1.40 Type **258**	50	40
1256	$1.40 Diver twisting forward	50	40
1257	$1.40 Descending with arms extended	50	40
1258	$1.40 Entering water	50	40
1259	$1.40 Volleyball player with bent knees	50	40
1260	$1.40 Jumping to hit ball	50	40
1261	$1.40 Hitting ball	50	40
1262	$1.40 Opponent trying to save	50	40
1263	$1.40 Two cyclists	50	40
1264	$1.40 Cyclist	50	40
1265	$1.40 Cyclists at speed	50	40
1266	$1.40 Victory salute	50	40
1267	$1.40 Badminton player preparing to hit shuttlecock	50	40
1268	$1.40 Player with arm extended	50	40
1269	$1.40 Player leaning backwards	50	40
1270	$1.40 Player leaning to right	50	40
1271	$1.40 Start of relay race	50	40
1272	$1.40 Runners	50	40
1273	$1.40 Baton exchange	50	40
1274	$1.40 Runner with baton raised	50	40

MS1275 130×75 mm. $5×2, Classical Olympic runner; Modern runner	3·50	3·50

259 Flags and Deng Xiaoping

2004. Birth Centenary of Deng Xiaoping (leader of China, 1978–89). Two sheets containing T **259** and similar horiz designs. Multicoloured.

MS1276 (a) 175×130 mm. $1.40 Type **259**; $1.40 Wearing blue suit, each×4 (b) 130×75 mm. $10 As young man	8·50	8·50

260 First Bronze Coin, 1863

2004. Currency. Multicoloured.

1277	$1.40 Type **260**	50	40
1278	$2.40 First silver coin, 1866	70	55
1279	$3 First paper currency, 1935	1·10	85
1280	$5 Gold coin to commemorate Hong Kong Special Administrative Region, 1997	1·60	1·20

MS1281 (a) 130×80 mm. Nos. 1277/80 (b) 130×75 mm. $5 Reverse of $10 dollar coin, 1997	6·00	6·00

261 Building and Bridge

2004. Development of Pearl River Delta Region. Multicoloured.

1282	$1.40 Type **261**	50	40
1283	$2.40 Container and crane	70	55
1284	$3 Views of Hong Kong, Guangdong and Macau	1·10	85
1285	$5 Harbour views and men shaking hands	1·60	1·20

262 Straw Mushrooms

2004. Fungi. Multicoloured.

1286	$1.40 Type **262**	50	40

1287	$2.40 Red-orange mushroom	70	55
1288	$3 Violet marasmius	1·10	85
1289	$5 Lingzhi	1·60	1·20

MS1290 (a) 130×85 mm. Nos. 1286/9.
(b) 130×75 mm. $5 Hexagon fungus   6·75   6·75

263
Clothes Peg
(A)

2005. Greetings Stamps. Alphabet. Sheet 230×162 mm containing T **263** and similar vert designs showing household objects as letters of the alphabet. Multicoloured

(a) Ordinary gum

MS1291 $1.40×30, Type **263**×2; Scissors handle (B); Lamp (C); Plastic lid (D); Rack (E) x 2; Gauge (F); Clamp (G); Bamboo (H); Torch (I) x 2; Cleaning mop (J); Stapler (K); Sock (L); Maths equipment (M); Swiss Army knife (N); Elastic band (O) x 2; Sieve (P); Stainless steel ring (Q); Sunglasses (R); Coat hanger (S); Brush (T); Flip flops (U); Drawing compass (V); Corkscrew (W); Tap (X); Meat skewer (Y); Paint roller (Z)   14·50   14·50

(b) Self-adhesive gum

MS1291a $1.40×30, Type **263**×2; Scissors handle (B); Lamp (C); Plastic lid (D); Rack (E)×2; Gauge (F); Clamp (G); Bamboo (H); Torch (I)×2; Cleaning mop (J); Stapler (K); Sock (L); Maths equipment (M); Swiss Army knife (N); Elastic band (O)×2; Sieve (P); Stainless steel ring (Q); Sunglasses (R); Coat hanger (S); Brush (T); Flip flops (U); Drawing compass (V); Corkscrew (W); Tap (X); Meat skewer (Y); Paint roller (Z)   14·50   14·50

The stamps and margin of **MS**1291 form a composite design.

264 Rooster

2005. New Year. (Year of the Rooster). Multicoloured.

1292	$1.40 Type **264**	50	40
1293	$2.40 With black neck feathers	85	65
1294	$3 With leg raised	95	75
1295	$5 Crowing	1·60	1·20

MS1296 Three sheets. (a) 136×85 mm Nos. 1292/5. (b) 136×85 mm As No. 1295. Imperf. (c) 135×90 mm $50×2, As No. 1209 (38×52 mm); As No. 1292 (38×52 mm)   4·00   4·00

No. **MS**1296c has the ram and monkey embossed with gold and silver foil.

265 "The Ugly Duckling"

2005. Birth Bicentenary of Hans Christian Andersen (writer).

1297	**265**	$1.40 blue	50	40
1298	-	$2.40 green	85	65
1299	-	$3 orange	95	75
1300	-	$5 magenta	1·60	1·20

DESIGNS: $1.40 Type **265**; $2.40 "The Little Mermaid"; $3 "The Little Match Girl"; $5 "The Emperor's New Clothes".

266 Opera House, Sydney

2005. Pacific Explorer 2005 International Stamp Exhibition, Australia. Sheet 130×75 mm.
MS1301 **266** $10 multicoloured   3·75   3·75

267 Variegated Pearl-scale

2005. Goldfish. Multicoloured.

1302	$1.40 Type **267**	50	40
1303	$2.40 Red and white swallowtail	85	65
1304	$3 Pale bronze egg phoenix	45	95	75
1305	$5 Blue wenyu	1·60	1·20

MS1306 Two sheets, each 130×75 mm. (a) Nos. 1302/5. (b) $5 Red and white dragon-eye (45×35 mm)   6·25   6·25

268 Zheng He

2005. 600th Anniv of the Voyages of Zheng He (Ma Sanbao). Multicoloured.

1307	$1.40 Type **268**	50	40
1308	$1.40 Giraffe, jars and ship	50	40
1309	$1.40 Ships and compass	50	40

MS1310 139×80 mm. $10 Nine-masted "Treasure ship" (50×30 mm)   3·50   3·50
Stamps of a similar design were issued by China and Macau.

269 Coloured Shapes

2005. Creative Industries. Multicoloured.

1311	$1.40 multicoloured	50	40
1312	$2.40 green and black	85	65
1313	$3 scarlet, black and bronze	95	75
1314	$5 multicoloured	1·60	1·20

DESIGNS: $1.40 Type **269** (advertising, architecture and design); $2.40 Digital symbols (digital entertainment, publishing and computers); $3 Coloured grids (media); $5 Streamers (arts, antiques, crafts and performing arts).

270 Early Compass

2005. Chinese Inventions. Multicoloured.

1315	$1.40 Type **270**	50	40
1316	$2.40 Printing	85	65
1317	$3 Gunpowder	95	75
1318	$5 Paper making	1·60	1·20

271 Mickey and Minnie (Main Street, USA)

2005. Disneyland Hong Kong. Grand Opening. Multicoloured.

1319	$1.40 Type **271**	50	40
1320	$2.40 Dumbo (Fantasyland)	85	65
1321	$3 Simba and Nala (Adventureland)	95	75
1322	$5 Pluto (Tomorrowland)	1·60	1·20

MS1323 Three sheets, each 135×85 mm. (a) Nos. 1319/22. (b) $5 Mickey. (c) $50 As No. **MS**1323b   28·00   28·00
No. **MS**1323c has Mickey embossed with gold foil.

272 Qiantang Bore

2005. Mainland Scenery (3rd issue). Sheet 141×90 mm.
MS1324 **272** $10 multicoloured   4·00   4·00

273 Boat, Tai O, Hong Kong

2005. Fishing Villages. Multicoloured.

1325	$1.40 Type **273**	50	40
1326	$2.40 Fisherman and boats, Aldeia da Carrasqueira	85	65
1327	$3 Wrapped fish, Tai O	95	75
1328	$5 Moorings and pier, Aldeia da Carrasqueira	1·60	1·20

Nos. 1325 and 1327, and 1326 and 1328, respectively were issued together, *se-tenant*, each pair forming a composite design. Stamps of the same design were issued by Portugal.

274 Wong ka Kui

2005. Pop Singers. Multicoloured.

1329	$1.40 Type **274**	70	55
1330	$1.80 Danny Chan	95	75
1331	$2.40 Roman Tam	1·10	85
1332	$3 Leslie Chung	1·20	95
1333	$5 Anita Mui	1·80	1·40

275 Dog

2006. New Year. (Year of the Dog). Multicoloured.

1334	$1.40 Type **275**	50	40
1335	$2.40 Pekinese	85	65
1336	$3 German shepherd	95	75
1337	$5 Beagle	1·60	1·20

MS1338 Two sheets, each 136×85 mm. (a) Nos. 1334/7. (b) As No. 1337. Imperf   6·25   6·25
MS1339 135×90 mm Size 38×52 mm. $50×2, As No. 1292; As No. 1335   42·00   42·00

No. **MS**1339 has the rooster and dog embossed with gold and silver foil.

276 Lantern enclosing Woman

2006. Chinese Lanterns. Multicoloured.
MS1340 108×131 mm. $1.40×2, Type 276×2; $1.80×2, Lantern enclosing flowers×2; $2.40×2, Lantern enclosing birds×2   5·25   5·25
MS1341 130×75 mm $5 Children holding dragon lantern (38×49 mm)   6·00   6·00

277 Bear wearing Hakka Costume (Yuen-ching Lee)

2006. Dress up Bear. Winning Entries in Children's Design a Stamp Competition. Multicoloured.

1342	$1.40 Type **277**	50	40
1343	$1.80 Wearing wedding costume (Sean Sheung-nam Lam)	70	55
1344	$2.40 Wearing pleated skirt (Chun-hin Chow)	85	65

1345	$2.50 Wearing embroidered apron and shoes (Hong-wan Lau)	90	70
1346	$3 Wearing striped top and hat (Man-lok Chiu)	1·20	95
1347	$5 Wearing leaf skirt (Michelle Hiu-tung Lau)	1·80	1·40

MS1348 115×115 mm. Nos. 1342/7   6·00   6·00

278 Mount Taishan

2006. Mainland Scenery (4th issue). Sheet 140×90 mm.
MS1349 **278** $10 multicoloured   3·25   3·25

279 Rainbow

2006. Washington 2006 Philatelic Exhibition. Sheet 130×75 mm.
MS1350 **279** $10 multicoloured   3·25   3·25

280 "Respect makes a Successful Marriage"

2006. Chinese Idioms. Multicoloured.

1351	$1.40 Type **280**	50	40
1352	$2.40 "Reading is always rewarding"	85	65
1353	$3 "Prepare for success"	95	75
1354	$5 "All in the same boat"	1·60	1·20

MS1355 135×85 mm. Nos. 1351/4   4·00   4·00

281 Central and Western District

2006. Hong Kong Districts. Multicoloured.

1356	$1.40 Type **281**	50	40
1357	$1.40 Eastern	50	40
1358	$1.40 Southern	50	40
1359	$1.40 Wan Chai	50	40
1360	$1.40 Yau Tsim Mong	50	40
1361	$1.40 Wong Tai Sin	50	40
1362	$1.40 Kwun Tong	50	40
1363	$1.40 Sham Shui Po	50	40
1364	$1.40 Kowloon City	50	40
1365	$1.40 Sai Kung	50	40
1366	$1.40 Kwai Tsing	50	40
1367	$1.40 Tai Po	50	40
1368	$1.40 North	50	40
1369	$1.40 Tsuen Wan	50	40
1370	$1.40 Sha Tin	50	40
1371	$1.40 Tuen Mun	50	40
1372	$1.40 Yuen Long	50	40
1373	$1.40 Islands district	50	40

282 Fireworks over Victoria Harbour

2006. Fireworks. Multicoloured.

1374	$5 Type **282**	1·60	1·20
1375	$5 Fireworks over Giant Ferris Wheel, Vienna, Austria	1·60	1·20

MS1376 146×85 mm. $50×2, As Type **282**; As No. 1375   34·00   34·00

MS1376 has crystals applied to the surface of the stamps and was sold in a folder.
Stamps of a similar design were issued by Austria.

283 Love

2006. International Day of Peace. Multicoloured.

1377	$1.40 Type **283**	50	40
1378	$1.80 Peace	60	45
1379	$2.40 Hope	70	55
1380	$3 Caring	95	75
1381	$5 Harmony	1·60	1·20
MS1382	150×85 mm. Nos. 1377/81	4·00	4·00

284 Security Bus

2006. Government Transport. Multicoloured.

1383	$1.40 Type **284**	50	40
1384	$1.80 Mobile X-ray unit	60	45
1385	$2.40 Hydraulic lift fire appliance	70	55
1386	$2.50 Super Puma helicopter	80	60
1387	$3 Traffic Control motorcycle	95	75
1388	$5 Immigration Dept launch	1·60	1·20

285 Sun Yat-Sen

2006. 140th Birth Anniv of Sun Yat-Sen (revolutionary). Multicoloured.

1389	$1.40 Type **285**	50	40
1390	$2.40 Seated wearing suit	85	65
1391	$3 Standing wearing suit	95	75
1392	$5 As older man	1·70	1·30
MS1393	130×75 mm. $5 Seated wearing traditional dress	2·20	2·20

286 Bottles

2006. Greetings Stamps. Multicoloured.

(a) Inscr "Local Mail Postage"

1394	($1.40) Type **286** (postage)	50	40
1395	($1.40) Hearts	50	40

(b) AIR. Inscr "Air Mail Postage"

1396	($3) Glasses (air)	95	75
1397	($3) Flowers	95	75

287
White-bellied
Sea Eagle

2006. Birds. Multicoloured.

(a) Two phosphor bands (1398/403) or one phosphor band (others)

1398	10c. Type **287**	10	10
1399	20c. Collared scops owl	20	15
1400	50c. Scarlet minivet	25	20
1401	$1 Kingfisher	35	30
1402	$1.40 Fork-tailed sunbird	50	40
1403	$1.80 Roseate tern	60	45
1404	$1.90 Black-faced spoonbill	60	45
1405	$2 Little egret	65	50
1406	$2.40 Greater painted snipe	85	65
1407	$2.50 Swallow	90	70
1408	$3 Red-whiskered bulbul	95	75
1409	$5 Long-tailed shrike	1·60	1·20

(b) Size 28×33 mm. One phosphor band

1410	$10 White wagtail	3·00	2·30
1411	$13 Northern shoveler	4·25	3·25
1412	$20 Magpie	6·00	4·75
1413	$50 Dalmatian pelican	14·50	11·50
MS1414	220 ×160 mm. Nos. 1398/409	7·00	7·00
MS1415	150×90 mm. Nos. 1410/13	28·00	28·00

MS1416   130×75 mm. Size 28×33 mm. $10 As No. 1410 (white wagtail) (21.9.10)   3·25   3·25

Numbers have been left for additions to this series.

288 Pig and Piglet

2007. New Year. (Year of the Pig). Multicoloured.

(a) Two phosphor bands ($1.40) or one phosphor band (others)

1425	$1.40 Type **288**	50	40
1426	$2.40 Pot-bellied pig	70	55
1427	$3 Spotted pig	95	75
1428	$5 Piglet	1·40	1·10
MS1429	Two sheets, each 135×85 mm. (a) Nos. 1425/8; (b) $5 No. 1428	6·00	6·00

(b) One phosphor band

1430	$10 As No. 1210 ("Year of the Monkey")	3·00	2·30
1431	$10 As No. 1292 ("Year of the Rooster")	3·00	2·30
1432	$10 As No. 1335 ("Year of the Dog")	3·00	2·30
1433	$10 As No. 1417 ("Year of the Pig")	3·00	2·30

(c) Size 38×51 mm

MS1434   136×90 mm. $50 As No. 1337 ("Year of the Dog"); $50 As No. 1425   38·00   38·00

289 Robert Baden-Powell (founder)

2007. Centenary of World Scouting. Multicoloured.

1435	$1.40 Type **289**	50	40
1436	$2.40 Emblem and compass	70	55
1437	$3 Rucksack and reef knot	95	75
1438	$5 Scouts	1·40	1·10
MS1439	130×75 mm. Nos. 1435/8	3·75	3·75

290 Two Rabbits (Spot the differences)

2007. Children's Stamps. Bunny Fun and Games. Multicoloured.

1440	$1.40 Type **290**	50	40
1441	$1.80 Outline (colour in dotted areas)	60	45
1442	$2.40 Maize (trace your way out)	70	55
1443	$2.50 Rabbit and Easter eggs (hunt for Easter eggs)	80	60
1444	$3 Tree containing rabbits (spot ten rabbits)	95	75
1445	$5 Rabbit in egg (look for a star)	1·40	1·10
MS1446	140×90 mm. Nos. 1440/5	4·75	4·75

291 Shilin, Kunming

2007. Mainland Scenery (5th issue). Sheet 130×90 mm.
MS1447 **291** $10 multicoloured   3·00   3·00

292 Southern Lion Dance

2007. Lion Dance and Martial Arts. Multicoloured.

1448	$1.40 Type **292**	50	40
1449	$2.40 Nanquan	70	55
1450	$3 Northern lion dance	95	75
1451	$5 Beitui	1·40	1·10
MS1452	130×90 mm. Nos. 1448/51	3·75	3·75

Nos. 1448/51 each has a small gold symbol signifying the design in lower left ($1.40 and $5) or right ($2.40 and $3) corners.

293 *Faunis eumeus*

2007. Butterflies. Multicoloured.

1453	$1.40 Type **293**	50	40
1454	$1.80 Prioneris philpnome	60	45
1455	$2.40 Polyura nepenthes	70	55
1456	$3 Tajura maculata	95	75
1457	$5 Acraea issoria	1·40	1·10

294 Children

2007. Tenth Anniv of Re-unification of Hong Kong. Multicoloured.

1458	$1.40 Type **294**	50	40
1459	$1.40 Forever Blooming Bauhinia	60	45
1460	$1.80 Heritage Museum	60	45
1461	$2.40 Tsing Ma bridge	70	55
1462	$2.50 International Wetland Park	80	60
1463	$3 Two IFC building	95	75
1464	$5 Fireworks over city	1·40	1·10
MS1465	130×91 mm. Size 30×60 mm. $10×3, Victoria Harbour waterfront	8·00	8·00
MS1465a	110×150 mm. No. 1459 and Nos. 5189/91 of China	12·00	12·00

The stamps and margins of MS1465 form a composite view of Victoria Harbour waterfront from the sea.

A stamp of a similar design to No. 1459 was issued by China.

295 Symbols of Transport and Guardian God

2007. Bangkok 2007, International Philatelic Exhibition. Sheet 130×75 mm.
MS1466 **295** $10 multicoloured   3·00   3·00

296 Scales and People of Many Nations (Human Rights)

2007. Civil Responsibility. Multicoloured.

1467	$1.40 Type **296**	60	45
1468	$2.40 Buildings with faces (Rule of Law)	70	55
1469	$3 Clasped hands (Social Participation)	95	75
1470	$5 Rainbow and hands enclosing fruit (Corporate Citizenship)	1·40	1·10

297 Tin Hau Temple, Causeway Bay

2007. Official Monuments. Multicoloured.

1471	$1.40 Type **297**	60	50
1472	$1.80 Old Post Office, Wan Chai	70	55
1473	$2.40 Former Central Police Station Compound	75	55
1474	$2.50 Former Yamen building, Kowloon Walled City	80	60
1475	$3 Kun Lung Gate Tower, Lung Yeuk Tau	1·00	75
1476	$5 Tang Lung Chai lighthouse	1·50	1·10
MS1477	145×78 mm. Nos. 1471/6	5·25	5·25

298 Stocking

2007. Christmas. Multicoloured.

1478	$1.40 Type **298**	60	50
1479	$2.40 Gingerbread man	75	55
1480	$3 Inscribed bell	85	65
1481	$5 Snowman	1·40	1·10

299 Qing Dynasty Carved Chair

2007. Woodcraft. Multicoloured.

1482	$5 Type **299**	1·20	95
1483	$5 Wooden bowls	1·20	95
MS1484	106×70 mm. Nos. 1482/3	2·75	2·75

Stamps of a similar design were issued by Finland.

300 Firework

2007. Greetings Stamps. With service indicator. Multicoloured

(a) Inscr "Local Mail Postage"

1485	($1.40) Type **300**	60	50
1486	($1.40) Two birds	60	50

(b) AIR. Inscr "Air Mail Postage"

1487	($3) Parcels and balloons	85	65
1488	($3) Slippers	85	65

No. 1485/6 were for use on letters up to 30 grams within Hong Kong and 1487/8 were for use on airmail letters up to 20 grams to addresses outside Hong Kong.

301 Rat

2008. New Year. (Year of the Rat). Multicoloured.

(a) Two phosphor bands ($1.40) or one phosphor band (others)

1489	$1.40 Type **301**	35	30
1490	$2.40 Rat seated	60	50
1491	$3 Rat facing left	85	65
1492	$5 Rat facing right	1·40	1·10
MS1493	Two sheets, each 135×85 mm. (a) Nos. 1489/92 (b) $5 As No. 1492	5·25	5·25

(b) Size 38×51 mm

MS1494   136×90 mm. $50 As No. 1425 ('Year of the Pig'); $50 As No. 1492   31·00   31·00

302 Huanglong

2008. Mainland Scenery (6th issue). Sheet 140×90 mm.
MS1495 **302** $10 multicoloured   3·00   3·00

303 Hibiscus

2008. Flowers. Multicoloured.

1496	$1.40 Type **303**	35	30
1497	$1.80 Cotton tree blooms	50	40
1498	$2.40 Allamanda	60	50
1499	$2.50 Azalea	70	55
1500	$3 Lotus blossom	85	65
1501	$5 Morning glory	1·40	1·10
MS1502	220×123 mm. Nos. 1496/501	4·50	4·50

304 Bauhinia
(Yu-tong Chua)

2008. Paper Folding. Multicoloured.

1503	$1.40 Type **304**	45	30
1504	$1.80 Bear (Shing-him (Bernard) Yeung) (horiz)	55	40
1505	$2.40 New Year decorations (Wing-tung Lau; Ka-wing Cheung)	70	50
1506	$2.50 Rainbow and lotus blossom (Hiu-yu Chau; Hiu-ling Wong) (horiz)	80	55
1507	$3 Koala bears and monkey holding banana (Wing-tung Lo; Ka-wing Cheung) .	1·00	70
1508	$5 Christmas scene and Santa Claus (Po-chu Yeung and Lesley Chu; Hon-keung and Hazel Li Hin) (horiz)	1·60	1·10
MS1509	218×122 mm. Nos. 1503/8	5·25	5·25

305 Flower Hat
Jellyfish

2008. Jellyfish. Multicoloured.

1510	$1.40 Type **305**	45	30
1511	$1.80 Octopus jellyfish (horiz)	55	40
1512	$2.40 Brown sea nettle	70	50
1513	$2.50 Moon jellyfish (horiz)	80	55
1514	$3 Lion's mane jellyfish	1·00	70
1515	$5 Pacific sea nettle	1·60	1·10
MS1516	135×85 mm. Nos. 1510/15	5·25	5·25

306 Ying Ying and Le Le

2008. Pandas. Multicoloured.

1517	$1.40 Type **306**	45	30
1518	$2.40 Ying Ying	70	50
1519	$3 Le Le	1·00	70
1520	$5 Ying Ying and Le Le in tree	1·60	1·10
MS1521	176×210 mm. Nos. 1517/20, each×2	7·25	7·25

307 Show Jumping

2008. Olympic Games, Beijing. Equestrian Events in Hong Kong. Multicoloured.

1522	$1.40 Type **307**	45	30
1523	$2.40 Dressage	70	50
1524	$3 Eventing	1·00	70
1525	$5 Stylized winning horse and rider	1·60	1·10
MS1526	135×85 mm. Nos. 1522/5	3·75	3·75

308 Cityscape

2008. Praga 2008 International Stamp Exhibition, Prague, Czech Republic. Sheet 130×75 mm. Multicoloured.

MS1527	**308** $10 multicoloured	3·25	3·25

309 Chwibari
(Bongsan Mask
Dance)

2008. Masks. Multicoloured.

1528	$5 Type **309**	1·60	1·10
1529	$5 Big Head Buddha (Chinese Lion Dance)	1·60	1·10
MS1530	106×70 mm. $5×2, Nos. 1528/9	3·25	3·25

Stamps of a similar design were issued by Korea.

310 Justice

2008. The Judiciary. Multicoloured.

1531	$1.40 Type **310**	65	45
1532	$2.40 Court building	1·00	70
1533	$3 Barristers and judges	1·40	1·00
1534	$5 Gavel	2·30	1·60
MS1535	136×85 mm. Nos. 1531/4	5·25	5·25

311 Ox

2009. New Year. (Year of the Ox). Multicoloured.

(a) Two phosphor bands ($1.40) or one phosphor band (others)

1536	$1.40 Type **311**	55	45
1537	$2.40 Friesian cow	85	70
1538	$3 Yak	1·20	1·00
1539	$5 Water buffalo	2·00	1·60
MS1540	135×85 mm. Nos. 1536/8	4·75	5·00
MS1541	135×85 mm. $5 No. 1539. Imperf	2·00	2·00

(b) Size 38×51 mm.

MS1542	136×90 mm. $50 As No. 1489 (Year of the Rat); $50 As No. 1536	37·00	37·00

No. MS1542 has the rat and ox embossed with gold and silver foil.

312 Mount Tianshan

2009. Mainland Scenery (7th issue). Sheet 140×90 mm. Multicoloured.

MS1543	**312** $10 multicoloured	3·75	3·75

313 Peony and *Bauhinia blakeana* (flowers of Hong Kong and Luoyang)

2009. China 2009 International Stamp Exhibition, Luoyang. Sheet 130×75 mm.

MS1544	**313** $5 multicoloured	1·70	1·70

314 Tangram Pieces as
Figure

2009. Hong Kong 2009, 23rd Asian International Stamp Exhibition. Sheet 135×85 mm.

MS1545	**314** $50 multicoloured	18·00	18·00

315 Calligraphy
(Wang Duo)

2009. Hong Kong Museums Collections. Multicoloured.

1546	$1.40 Type **315**	55	45
1547	$1.80 Mountains (Wang Yuanqi)	70	55
1548	$2.40 Calligraphy (Wang Xizhi)	85	70
1549	$2.50 Moon and bird on blossom branch	1·00	80
1550	$3 Fan (Ju Lian) (horiz)	1·20	1·00
1551	$5 Calligrapher and assistants (Gu Huai) (horiz)	2·00	1·60
MS1552	140×90 mm. Nos. 1546/51	6·00	6·00

316 Flowers

2009. Greetings Stamps. With service indicator. Showing felt applique. Multicoloured

(a) Inscr 'Local Mail Postage'

1553	($1.40) Type **316**	60	50
1554	($1.40) Lion costume	60	50

(b) Air. Inscr 'Air Mail Postage'.

1555	($3) Conical hats and musical notes	1·00	80
1556	($3) Butterflies	1·00	80

No. 1553/4 were for use on letters up to 30 grams within Hong Kong and 1555/6 were for use on airmail letters up to 20 grams to addresses outside Hong Kong.

317 Sniffer Dog

2009. Centenary of Customs and Excise Service. Multicoloured.

1557	$1.40 Type **317**	45	35
1558	$2.40 Custom and Excise vehicle	75	60
1559	$3 Coast guard vessel	1·00	80
1560	$5 Service men	1·60	1·30
MS1561	135×85 mm. Nos. 1557/60	3·75	3·75

318 Victoria Harbour and
Tiananmen Square

2009. 60th Anniv of People's Republic of China. T **318** and similar vert (MS1569) or fan shaped (others) designs. Multicoloured.

1562	$1.40 Type **318**	45	35
1563	$1.80 National flag and 'Forever Blooming Bauhinia' (symbol of Hong Kong)	50	40
1564	$2.40 National stadium	75	60
1565	$2.50 CZ-2F rocket	80	65
1566	$3 Temple of Heaven, Beijing	1·10	85
1567	$5 Dragon and Great Wall of China	1·70	1·40
MS1568	140×90 mm. Nos. 1562/7	5·25	5·25
MS1569	140×90 mm. $5×2, Forbidden City; Hong Kong skyline	4·25	4·25

319 Hong Kong Player

2009. Hong Kong–Brazil Diplomatic Relations. Football. Multicoloured.

1570	$1.40 Type **319**	45	35
1571	$2.40 Hong Kong goalkeeper	75	60
1572	$3 Brazilian player	1·00	80
1573	$5 Brazilian player (different)	1·60	1·30
MS1574	135×85 mm. Nos. 1570/3	3·50	3·50

320 Judo, Rugby Sevens and
Kayaking

2009. East Asian Games, Hong Kong. Designs showing athletes, colours of athletes given. Multicoloured.

1575	$1.40 Type **320**	35	30
1576	$1.40 Badminton, athletics, martial arts and rifle shooting (gold)	35	30
1577	$2.40 Cycling, weightlifting and tennis (silver)	55	45
1578	$2.40 Men's volleyball, hockey, women's table tennis and diving (silver)	55	45
1579	$3 Men's table tennis, women's volleyball, dance and snooker (bronze)	1·40	1·10
1580	$3 Wind surfing, football, basketball and taekwando (bronze)	1·40	1·10
MS1581	150×90 mm. Nos. 1575/81	4·25	4·25

321 Tower and
Suspension
Cables

2009. Opening of Stonecutters Bridge. Multicoloured.

1582	$1.40 Type **321**	45	35
1583	$2.40 Aerial view of bridge	75	60
1584	$3 Bridge from river	1·10	90
1585	$5 Aerial view of tower and suspension cables	1·70	1·40
MS1586	150×90 mm. Nos. 1582/5	4·00	4·00

322 Tiger

2010. Chinese New Year (Year of the Tiger). Multicoloured.

(a) Two phosphor bands ($1.40) or one phosphor band (others)

1587	$1.40 Type **322**	45	35
1588	$2.40 Facing left	75	60
1589	$3 Seated	1·10	90
1590	$5 White tiger	1·70	1·40
MS1591	135×85 mm. Nos. 1587/90	4·00	4·00
MS1592	135×85 mm. $5 No. 1590	1·70	1·70

(b) Size 38×51 mm

MS1593	136×90 mm. $50 As No. 1537 (Year of the Ox); $50 As No. 1588	27·00	27·00

No. MS1593 has the ox and tiger embossed with gold and silver foil.

323 Fujian Tolou

2010. Mainland Scenery (8th issue). Sheet 140×90 mm

MS1594	**323** $10 multicoloured	3·75	3·75

324 Skyline with Dragon's
Head

2010. Expo 2010, Shanghai. Multicoloured.

1595	$1.40 Type **324**	45	40
1596	$2.40 Skyline on leaf	75	65
1597	$3 Skyline on bridge	1·20	1·10
1598	$5 Skyline on profiled head	1·90	1·60
MS1599	135×85 mm. Nos. 1595/8	4·25	4·25

325 Symbols of Hong Kong and London

2010. London 2010 Festival of Stamps
MS1600 **325** $10 bright scarlet and
deep ultramarine   3·75   3·75

326 Pottinger Street

2010. Streets of Hong Kong. Multicoloured.
1601	$1.40 Type **326**	55	50
1602	$1.40 Nathen Road	55	50
1603	$2.40 Temple Street	95	80
1604	$2.40 Hollywood Road	95	80
1605	$3 Des Voeux Road West	1·20	1·10
1606	$3 Stanley Market	1·20	1·10
MS1607	140×90 mm. Nos. 1601/6	5·00	5·00

327 Paradise Fish (only
freshwater fish named after
the territory)

2010. Biodiversity. Multicoloured.
1608	$1.40 Type **327**	45	40
1609	$2.40 Romer's tree frog (small-est frog species found in Hong Kong)	75	65
1610	$3 *Sinopora hongkongensis* (plant first discovered in Tai Mo Shan and new to science)	1·20	1·00
1611	$5 *Fukienogomphus choifongae* (dragonfly first discovered in Wu Kau Tang and new to science)	1·70	1·50
MS1612	135×85 mm. Nos. 1608/11	4·00	4·00

328 Steam
Locomotive and
Hong Kong
Railway Museum.

2010. Centenary of Hong Kong Railway. Multicooured.
1613	$1.40 Type **328**	30	25
1614	$1.80 Diesel locomotive and Clock Tower of old Kowloon–Canton Railway terminus, Tsim Sha Tsui	45	40
1615	$2.40 Electric locomotive and old Hung Hom terminus	80	70
1616	$2.50 MTR Passenger train and International Finance Centre, above MTR Hong Kong Station	1·10	90
1617	$3 Kowloon–Guangzhou through train and MTR Hung Hom Station	1·20	1·10
1618	$5 Airport Express train and Hong Kong International Airport	1·70	1·50
MS1619	135×85 mm. Nos. 1613/18	5·00	4·75
MS1620	135×85 mm. $20 As Type **328** (38×51 mm)	5·50	5·50

329 Harbour of Hong Kong
(Hei-chun Man)

2010. Hong Kong in My Eyes. Multicooured.
1621	$1.40 Type **329**	45	40
1622	$2.40 Beautiful Hong Kong (Ying-jun Tan)	75	65
1623	$3 *Hong Kong is Fun* (Tsz-yu Soong)	1·20	1·00
1624	$5 *City Beat* (Yvette Chantal Yao)	1·70	1·50
MS1625	135×85 mm. Nos. 1621/4	4·00	4·00

330 Dwelling with
Scaffolding

2010. Redevelopment. Multicoloured.
1626	$1.40 Type **330**	45	40
1627	$2.40 Work	80	70
1628	$3 Transport	1·20	1·10
1629	$5 Community	1·70	1·50
MS1630	150×85 mm. Nos. 1626/9	4·25	4·25

331 Cape D'Aguilar

2010. Lighthouses. Multicoloured.
1631	$1.40 Type **331**	45	40
1632	$1.80 Old Green Island	55	50
1633	$2.40 New Green Island	80	70
1634	$3 Tang Lung Chau	1·20	1·10
1635	$5 Waglan	1·70	1·50
MS1636	150×85 mm. Nos. 1631/5	4·25	4·25

332 Rabbit

2011. Chinese New Year. (Year of the Rabbit). Multicoloured.

(a) Two phosphor bands ($1.40) or one phosphor band (others)
1637	$1.40 Type **332**	45	40
1638	$1.40 Wild rabbit	80	70
1639	$3 Brown and white rabbit	1·20	1·10
1640	$5 Long-haired dwarf rabbit	1·70	1·50
MS1641	210×150 mm. $1.40×12, As Type **301**; As No. 1537; As Type **322**; As Type **332**; As Type **206**; As Type **288**; As Type **215**; As No. 1335; As Type **264**; As No. 1211; As No. 1157; As Type **226**	5·50	5·50
MS1642	135×85 mm. As Nos. 1637/40	4·25	4·25
MS1643	135×85 mm. As No. 1640	1·70	1·70

(b) One phosphor band. Flocked paper. Litho Cartor.
1644	$10 As No. 1492	3·00	2·75
1645	$10 As Type **311**	3·00	2·75
1646	$10 As Type **322**	3·00	2·75
1647	$10 As No. 1639	3·00	2·75

(c) Size 38×51 mm. Ordinary paper. Litho, embossed and foil stamped Cartor.
MS1648	136×90 mm. $50×2, As No. 1589; As Type **332**	27·00	27·00

No. **MS**1648 has the tiger and rabbit embossed with gold and silver foil.

333 Farman Biplane Replica
(on display at Hong Kong
International Airport Passenger
Terminal)

2011. Centenary of Powered Flight. Multicoloured.
MS1649	$3×2, Type **333**; Lift-off of Far-man biplane (flown by Charles Van den Born), from tidal flats	2·00	2·00

334 Note and Leaf
on Diary Page
(planting trees)

2011. Tenth Anniv of International Year of Volunteers
1650	$1.40 Type **334**	45	40
1651	$2.40 Internet recruitment leaflet to rally support for community charity event	80	70
1652	$3 Email brings good news on school redevelopment	1·20	1·10
1653	$5 Calendar reminder of upcoming home visit with elderly volunteer	1·70	1·50
MS1654	135×90 mm. $5 'VOLUNTEER-ISM' (36×35 mm (heart-shaped))	1·90	1·90

335 Tap and Globe as
Droplet of Water
('Conserve Water')

2011. Green Living. Multicoloured.
1655	$1.40 Type **335**	45	40
1656	$2.40 Clouds, tree and globe as sun ('Clean Air')	80	70
1657	$3 Low energy light bulb and globe as lamp ('Save Energy')	1·20	1·10
1658	$5 Globe, recycle emblem, can, bottle and paper ('Recycle')	1·70	1·50
MS1659	122×78 mm. $5 Plantlet growing from globe ('Treasure the Earth')	1·90	1·90

336 'Founding, 1861'

2011. 150th Anniv of Hong Kong General Chamber of Commerce. Multicoloured.
1660	$1.40 Type **336**	45	40
1661	$2.40 Shipyard ('Issue of Certifi-cates of Origin, 1923')	80	70
1662	$3 'Sponsorship for Good Citizen Award, 1973'	1·20	1·10
1663	$5 'Entry into China Market, 1978'	1·70	1·50
MS1664	135×85 mm. Nos. 1660/3	4·25	4·25

337 'Mutual Help in Hard
Times'

2011. Children Stamps. Chinese Idioms and Their Stories. Multicoloured.
1665	$1.40 Type **337**	45	40
1666	$1.80 'Water drops wear away rocks'	55	50
1667	$2.40 'Prctise makes perfect'	80	70
1668	$3 'Save to give'	1·20	1·10
1669	$5 'As deft as a master butcher'	1·70	1·50
MS1670	150×85 mm. As Nos. 1665/9, but with parts of the design printed without colour	5·00	5·00

338 Dunhuang
Grottoes

2011. Mainland Scenery (10th issue). Dunhuang Grottoes (**MS**1671) or Complete Mainland Scenery Series (**MS**1672). Multicoloured.
MS1671	140×90 mm. $10 Type **338**	3·75	3·25

MS1672	210×149 mm. $2.40×9, Qiang-tang Bore (As Type **272**) (76×30 mm.); Dunhuang Grottoes (As Type **338**); Mount Tianshan (As Type **312**) (45×28 mm.); Fujian Tulou (As Type **323**) (45×28 mm.); Master of Nets' Garden (As Type **241**) (45×40 mm.); Glen Clan Academy (As Type **255**) (45×28 mm.); Shilin (As Type **291**) (45×28 mm.); Mount Taishan (As Type **278**) (45×28 mm.)	7·50	7·50

339 Early and Modern Post Boxes

2011. 170th Anniv of Hong Kong Postal Service. Sheet 130×75 mm
MS1673	**339** $10 multicoloured	3·75	3·75

340 Main Building in 1910 and
the Golden Trowel

2011. Centenary of University of Hong Kong. Multicoloured.
1674	$1.40 Type **340**	45	40
1675	$1.80 Main Building in 1912 and Fête and Bazaar poster	55	50
1676	$2.40 Union Building in 1919, Main Building in the background and statue of Dr. Sun Yat-sen	80	70
1677	$2.50 Roofless Main Building in 1946 and Mace	85	75
1678	$3 Main Building and West Gate, 1940's, and inkstand	1·20	1·10
1679	$5 Main Building and courtyard, today, and Coat of Arms	1·70	1·50
MS1680	130×75 mm. $5 Letters Patent from College of Arms granting Full Coat of Arms (35×45mm)	1·90	1·90

341 Monument to
72 Martyrs of
Huanghuagang

2011. Centenary of Xinhai Revolution (Revolution of 1911). Each black and carmine-vermilion.
1681	$1.40 Type **341**	45	40
1682	$2.40 Wuchang Uprising	80	70
1683	$3 Cai Yuanpei and Zhang Tai-yan, leaders of Guangfuhui (Restoration Society), Huang Xing and Song Jiaoren, (founders of Huaxinghui (Society for the Revival of China)) (forerunners of Xinhai Revolution)	1·20	1·10
1684	$5 Sun Yat-sen assuming office of Provisional President	1·70	1·50
MS1685	130×75 mm. $5×2, Central School (present-day Queen's Col-lege), Hong Kong where Sun Yat-sen was educated (horiz); Sun Yat-sen's election as president of Tongmen-ghui and his proclamation in Min Bao (horiz)	3·75	3·75

342 Lion's Head Rice
Flour Figurine (Hong
Kong)

2011. Handicrafts. Multicoloured.
1686	$5 Type **342**	1·90	1·60
1687	$5 Painted egg (Romania)	1·90	1·60
MS1688	135×85 mm. Nos. 1686/7	3·75	3·75

343 Headdress from Cantonese Opera

2011. Hong Kong Museums' Collections. Multicoloured.
1689	$1.40 Type **343**	45	40
1690	$1.80 Qipao (women's dress)	55	50
1691	$2.40 Silver footed bowl decorated in repoussé (horiz)	80	70
1692	$2.50 Sequined reversible palace costume (horiz)	85	75
1693	$3 Green glazed barrel for herbal tea (horiz)	1·20	1·10
1694	$5 Baby-carrier with head support (horiz)	1·70	1·50
MS1695	145×95 mm. Nos. 1689/94	5·25	5·25

344 Chief Executive's Office, Central Government Offices and Legislative Council Complex

2011. Tamar Development Project. Sheet 140×90 mm
MS1696	**344** $10 multicoloured	3·75	3·75

345 Fire Dragon and Joss Sticks

2012. Chinese New Year (Year of the Dragon). Multicoloured.

(a) Two phosphor bands ($1.40) or one phosphor band (others). Granite paper
1697	$1.40 Type **345**	45	40
1698	$2.40 Golden dragon	80	70
1699	$3 Dragon dance head	1·20	1·10
1700	$5 Long thin dragon	1·70	1·50
MS1701	136×90 mm. $10 Flying dragon	4·75	4·75
MS1702	210×150 mm. $1.40×12, As No. 1007 (dragon); As No.1041 (snake); As T **226** (horse); As No. 1157 (ram); As No. 1211 (monkey); As No. 1294 (cockerel); As T **288** (pig); As No. 1492 (rat); As T **311** (ox); As No. 1588 (tiger); As T **332** (rabbit)	5·25	5·25
MS1703	210×150 mm. $1.40×12, As T **217** (dragon); As T **215** (snake); As No. 1081 (horse); As T **238** (ram); As No. 1209 (monkey); As No. 1295 (cockerel); As No. 1337 (dog); As No. 1426 (pig); As T **301** (rat); As No. 1537 (ox); As No. 1589 (tiger); As No. 1639 (rabbit)	5·25	5·25

(b) Silk-faced paper. Granite paper. Miniature sheet
MS1704	80×80 mm. $50 Flying dragon (design as stamp of **MS**1701 but multicoloured) (45×45 mm)	25·00	25·00

(c) Size 38×51 mm. Ordinary paper. Miniature sheet
MS1705	136×90 mm. $50×2, As Type **332**; Dragon	25·00	25·00

No. **MS**1703 has the rabbit and dragon embossed with gold and silver foil.

346 College Building

2012. 150th Anniv of Queen's College. Multicoloured.
MS1706	130×75 mm. $10 Type **346**	4·25	4·25
MS1707	120×130 mm. $10×4, As Type **346**, glitter applied to shield outline; As Type **346**, varnish applied to central design and bronze face value; As Type **346**, arms and building embossed; As Type **346**, building and face value gold foil die-stamped	20·00	20·00

347 Château Douglas (painting)

2012. Art of France and Hong Kong. Multicoloured.
1708	$1.40 Type **347**	40	40
1709	$2.40 Crab #4 (Yee Cheung)	70	70
1710	$3 The Racetrack (painting) (Edgar Degas)	1·10	1·10
1711	$5 Le Cheval (sculpture) (Raymond Duchamp-Villon)	1·50	1·50
MS1712	140×90 mm. As No. 1708/11	3·50	3·50

348 Tin Hau Festival

2012. Hong Kong Festivals. Multicoloured.
1713	$1.40 Type **348**	40	40
1714	$2.40 Kwun Yum Festival	70	70
1715	$3 Birthday of Buddha	1·10	1·10
1716	$5 Tuen Ng Festival	1·50	1·50
MS1717	135×85 mm. $5 Mid Autumn Festival	2·00	2·00

349 Beagle (Ministry of Agriculture, Fisheries and Conservation)

2012. Working Dogs in Government Service. Multicoloured.
1718	$1.40 Type **349**	40	40
1719	$1.80 German Shepherd (Correctional Services)	50	50
1720	$2.40 Springer Spaniel (Customs and Excise)	70	70
1721	$2.50 Golden Labrador (Fire Services)	85	85
1722	$3 Black Labrador (Food and Environmental Hygiene)	1·10	1·10
1723	$5 Malinois (Hong Kong Police)	1·50	1·50
MS1724	135×85 mm. $5 As Nos. 1718/23, head and shoulders only (detail) (100×40 mm)	2·00	2·00

350 Statue of Justice

2012. 15th Anniv of Establishment of Hong Kong Special Administrative Region. Multicoloured.
MS1725	$5×3, Type **350**; Skyscrapers; Chek Lap Kok Airport	6·00	6·00

351 Stylized Windsurfer and '2'

2012. Olympic Games, London. Multicoloured.
1726	$1.40 Type **351**	40	40
1727	$2.40 Handball player, archer and '0'	70	70
1728	$3 Tennis player, cyclist and '1'	1·10	1·10
1729	$5 Swimmer and '2'	1·50	1·50
MS1730	135×85 mm. As Nos. 1726/9 (composite design)	3·50	3·50

352 Egg Tarts and Milk Tea

2012. Hong Kong Delicacies. Multicoloured.
1731	$1.40 Type **352**	40	40
1732	$2.40 Wonton noodles	70	70
1733	$3 Roast goose	1·10	1·10
1734	$5 Seafood	1·50	1·50
MS1735	135×85 mm. As No. 1731/4	3·50	

353 The Great Wall of China

2012. World Heritage Sites in China (1st Series). The Great Wall. Sheet 140×90 mm
MS1736	**353** $10 multicoloured		

354 Capricorn

2012. Signs of the Western Zodiac. Multicoloured.

(a) Ordinary gum
1737	$1.40 Type **354**	40	40
1738	$1.40 Aquarius	40	40
1739	$1.40 Pisces	40	40
1740	$1.40 Aries	40	40
1741	$1.40 Taurus	40	40
1742	$1.40 Gemini	40	40
1743	$1.40 Cancer	40	40
1744	$1.40 Leo	40	40
1745	$1.40 Virgo	40	40
1746	$1.40 Libra	40	40
1747	$1.40 Scorpio	40	40
1748	$1.40 Sagittarius	40	40
MS1749	210×150 mm. As Nos. 1737/48	5·00	5·00

(b) Booklet stamps. Self-adhesive
1750	$1.40 As Type **354**	40	40
1751	$1.40 As No. 1738	40	40
1752	$1.40 As No. 1739	40	40
1753	$1.40 As No. 1740	40	40
1754	$1.40 As No. 1741	40	40
1755	$1.40 As No. 1742	40	40
1756	$1.40 As No. 1743	40	40
1757	$1.40 As No. 1744	40	40
1758	$1.40 As No. 1745	40	40
1759	$1.40 As No. 1746	40	40
1760	$1.40 As No. 1747	40	40
1761	$1.40 As No. 1748	40	40

355 Cosmoscarta bispecularis

2012. Insects. Multicoloured.
1762	$1.40 Type **355**	40	40
1763	$1.80 Flower Mantis (Creobroter gemmatus) (inscr 'Flower Mantid' Creobroter gemmata)	50	50
1764	$2.40 China-mark Eristena (inscr 'Mangrove china-mark')	70	70
1765	$2.50 White Dragontail (Lamproptera curius)	85	85
1766	$3 Four-spot Midget (Mortonagrion hirosei)	1·10	1·10
1767	$5 Bent-winged Firefly (Pteroptyx maipo)	1·50	1·50
MS1768	145×95 mm. Nos. 1763/7	7·00	7·00

356 1862 2c. Stamp (As Type 1), Quill pen and Ink Well

2012. 150th Anniv of Stamp Issuance in Hong Kong
1769	$1.40 Type **356**	40	40
1770	$1.80 Fountain pen and 1862 8c. stamp	50	50
1771	$2.40 Ballpoint pen and 1862 12c. stamp	70	70
1772	$2.50 1862 18c. stamp and typewriter	85	85
1773	$3 1862 24c. stamp and keyboard	1·10	1·10
1774	$5 Quick responce code and 1862 48c. stamp	1·50	1·50
MS1775	130×75 mm. $10 1862 96c. stamp and barcode (65×24mm)	7·00	7·00

357 Stylised Snake

2013. Chinese New Year (Year of the Snake). Multicoloured.

(a) Two phosphor bands ($1.40) or one phosphor band (others)
1776	$1.40 Type **357**	40	40
1777	$2.40 Snake	70	70
1778	$3 Snake glyphs	1·10	1·10
1779	$5 Jade snake	1·50	1·50
MS1780	135×85 mm. $10 Multicoloured snake breathing fire (45×45 mm)	5·00	5·00

(b) Silk-faced paper. Miniature sheet
MS1781	80×80 mm. $50 Multicoloured snake breathing fire (design as stamp of **MS**1780) (45×45 mm)	20·00	20·00

(c) Size 45×28 mm. Miniature sheet
MS1782	136×90 mm. $50×2, Dragon (As No. 1700); As Type **357**	30·00	30·00

No. **MS**1782 has the snake applied as 22-carat gold-plated lace metal.

359 My Dog

2013. Children's Stamps. My Pet and I. Multicoloured.
MS1793	140×90 mm. $1.40 Type **359**; $1.80 My Cat; $2.40 My Tortoise; $2.50 My Guinea Pig; $3 My Rabbit; $5 My Hamster	10·00	10·00

360 YHA Mei Ho House Youth Hostel

2013. Revitalisation of Historic Buildings in Hong Kong. Multicoloured.
1794	$1.40 Type **360**	40	40
1795	$1.80 Fong Yuen Study Hall, Yuen Yuen Institute	50	50
1796	$2.40 Jao Tsung-I Academy	70	70
1797	$2.50 Hong Kong Baptist University School of Chinese Medicine – Lui Seng Chun	85	85
1798	$3 Tai O Heritage Hotel	1·10	1·10
1799	$5 SCAD Hong Kong	1·50	1·50
MS1800	180×75 mm. Nos. 1794/9 (65×24mm)	7·00	7·00

361 Kai Tak Cruise Terminal (image scaled to 49% of original size)

2013. Kai Tak Cruise Terminal
MS1801	**361** $10 multicoloured	5·50	5·50
MS1802	**361** $20 multicoloured	12·00	12·00

362 Chinese Newly Weds

2013. Chinese and Western Wedding Customs. Multicoloured.

1803	$1.40 Type **362**	40	40
1804	$1.80 Western newly weds	50	50
1805	$2.40 Gift Presentation (traditional Chinese pre-wedding etiquette)	70	70
1806	$2.50 Western couple cutting the cake	85	85
1807	$3 Dragon and phoenix (auspicious Chinese marriage symbols)	1·10	1·10
1808	$5 Western white wedding with bells and archway	1·50	1·50
MS1809	135×90 mm. $10 Chinese and western newly weds (100×40 mm)	7·00	7·00

363 Jade Dragon Snow Mountain and Wanjuan Pavilion, Mu's Mansion

2013. World Heritage Sites in China (2nd Series). Old Town of Lijiang. Sheet 140×90 mm

MS1810 **363**	$10 multicoloured	5·00	5·00

364 Tilling Stevens Bus (1947)

2013. Hong Kong Buses. Multicoloured.

1811	$1.40 Type **364**	40	40
1812	$1.80 Daimler A (1949)	50	50
1813	$2.40 Single-decker Albion Coach (1975)	70	70
1814	$2.50 Leyland Olympian 11m (1988)	85	85
1815	$3 Volvo Olympian 11m (1995)	1·10	1·10
1816	$5 Dennis Trident (1997)	1·50	1·50
MS1817	140×90 mm. $5 Euro V Bus (100×40mm)	7·00	7·00
MS1818	140×90 mm. $20 Euro V Bus (different) (100×40mm)	12·00	12·00

365 *Thanksgiving* (Chan Tung Mui)

2013. Inclusive Arts. Multicoloured.

1819	$1.70 Type **365**	50	50
1820	$2.90 *Always by your Side* (Cheng Kai Man)	1·10	1·10
1821	$3.70 *The Vitality of Hong Kong* (Ko Nam)	1·25	1·25
1822	$5 *How are you?* (Liu Tung Mui)	1·50	1·50
MS1823	135×90 mm. Nos. 1819/22	7·00	7·00

366 Symbols of Green Energy Generation

2013. Innovation and Technology. Multicoloured.

1824	$1.70 Type **366** (Green technology)	50	50
1825	$2.20 Computer code (Information and communication technology)	65	65
1826	$2.90 ECG chart (Chinese medicine)	1·00	1·00
1827	$3.10 Stylized sweetcorn (Biotechnology)	1·20	1·20
1828	$3.70 'NANO' (nano technology and advanced materials)	1·30	1·30
1829	$5 Radio waves (Radio frequency identification)	2·00	2·00
MS1830	190×105 mm. Nos. 1824/9	8·00	8·00

367 Legislative Complex, 2011

2013. Our Legislative Council. Multicoloured.

1831	$1.70 Type **367**	50	50
1832	$2.90 Old Supreme Court building, Central Hong Kong (1985 to November 2011)	1·00	1·00
1833	$3.70 Council chamber in new Complex	1·30	1·30
1834	$5 President's chair in old legislative room	1·50	1·50
MS1835	135×85 mm. Nos. 1831/4	6·00	6·00

POSTAGE DUE STAMPS

D1 Post-office Scales

1923

D1ab	**D1**	1c. brown	30	1·00
D2a	**D1**	2c. green	11·00	5·00
D3a	**D1**	4c. red	30·00	5·00
D7a	**D1**	4c. orange	2·50	10·00
D18	**D1**	5c. red (21×18 mm)	2·00	4·75
D4	**D1**	6c. yellow	32·00	13·00
D8	**D1**	6c. red	5·50	5·50
D9	**D1**	8c. brown	4·50	32·00
D15	**D1**	10c. violet	3·50	7·00
D5	**D1**	10c. blue	27·00	8·50
D16	**D1**	20c. black	6·00	3·00
D22	**D1**	50c. blue	4·50	10·00

1976. As Type D **1** but smaller design 21×17 mm with redrawn value.

D25a	10c. violet	80	2·00
D26a	20c. grey	1·50	2·25
D27a	50c. blue	1·50	2·75
D28a	$1 yellow	1·40	4·00

D2

1987

D31	**D2**	10c. green	10	60
D32	**D2**	20c. brown	10	60
D33	**D2**	50c. violet	10	20
D34	**D2**	$1 orange	15	20
D35	**D2**	$5 blue	80	1·60
D36	**D2**	$10 red	1·60	3·00

D3

2004

D37	**D 3**	10c. ultramarine	10	15
D38	**D 3**	20c. blue	10	15
D39	**D 3**	50c. orange	25	25
D40	**D 3**	$1 pink	60	70
D41	**D 3**	$5 green	1·40	1·60
D42	**D 3**	$10 magenta	3·00	3·25

JAPANESE OCCUPATION OF HONG KONG

(1)   (2)

1945. Stamps of Japan surch as T **1** (No. J1) or T **2**.

J1	**126**	1.50yen on 1s. brown	38·00	26·00
J2	**84**	3yen on 2s. red	12·00	26·00
J3	**84**	5yen on 5s. red (No. 396)	£900	£150

HORTA

A district of the Azores for which separate issues were used from 1892 to 1905.

1865. 1000 reis = 1 milreis.

1892. As T **4** of Funchal, but inscr "HORTA".

4	5r. yellow	3·75	2·75
5	10r. mauve	3·75	3·50
6	15r. brown	3·75	3·50
7	20r. lilac	4·50	4·25
2	25r. green	7·00	1·80
8	50r. blue	11·00	5·00
22	75r. red	12·50	8·00
10	80r. green	16·00	14·50
23	100r. brown on yellow	70·00	60·00
24	150r. red on rose	80·00	65·00
25	200r. blue on blue	80·00	65·00
26	300r. blue on brown	80·00	65·00

1897. "King Carlos" key-type inscr "HORTA". Name and value in red (Nos. 46 and 41) or black (others).

28	S	2½r. grey	80	40
29	S	5r. orange	80	40
30	S	10r. green	80	40
31	S	15r. brown	11·00	8·00
42	S	15r. green	2·10	1·60
32	S	20r. lilac	2·10	1·70
33	S	25r. green	3·75	1·40
43	S	25r. red	2·10	1·00
34	S	50r. blue	4·25	1·80
45	S	65r. blue	1·50	1·10
35	S	75r. red	4·00	1·80
46	S	75r. brown on yellow	17·00	15·00
36	S	80r. mauve	2·20	1·40
47	S	100r. blue on blue	4·00	1·40
47	S	115r. red on pink	2·75	2·10
48	S	130r. brown on yellow	2·75	2·10
38	S	150r. brown on yellow	2·75	1·40
49	S	180r. black on pink	2·75	2·10
39	S	200r. purple on pink	8·00	6·75
40	S	300r. blue on pink	14·00	10·50
41	S	500r. black on blue	19·00	17·00

HUNGARY

A country in central Europe. A Kingdom ruled by the Emperor of Austria until 1918. A Republic was then proclaimed, and later a Soviet style constitution was adopted. In 1919 parts of the country were occupied by France, Serbia and Rumania, including Budapest. Following the withdrawal of the Rumanians a National Republic was instituted, and in 1920 Hungary was declared a Monarchy with Admiral Nicholas Horthy as Regent. In 1946 Hungary became a Republic again.

Hungary.
1858. 100 krajczar = 1 forint.
1900. 100 filler (heller) = 1 korona (krone).
1926. 100 filler = 1 pengo.
1946. 100 filler = 1 forint.

Szeged.
100 filler = 1 korona.

1

1871

8	**1**	2k. yellow	£100	17·00
9	**1**	3k. green	£225	65·00
10	**1**	5k. red	£100	2·30
11	**1**	10k. blue	£500	37·00
12	**1**	15k. brown	£600	50·00
13	**1**	25k. lilac	£325	£130

2

1874

29b	**2**	2k. lilac	1·60	40
30b	**2**	3k. green	1·60	40
31b	**2**	5k. red	8·00	40
32b	**2**	10k. blue	4·75	55
28a	**2**	20k. grey	10·00	85

1888. Numerals in black on the krajczar values, in red on the forint values, as T **N4**.

39a	1k. black	18·00	2·20
40	2k. mauve and light mauve	£180	49·00
41	3k. green and light green	60·00	17·00
42	5k. red and pink	60·00	2·75
43	8k. orange and yellow	11·00	1·60

44a	10k. blue	9·75	1·40
45	12k. brown and green	15·00	1·60
46	15k. red and blue	11·00	1·60
47a	20k. grey	16·00	5·50
48	24k. purple and red	38·00	2·20
62B	30k. olive and brown	9·75	6·50
63	50k. red and orange	14·50	22·00
1	1fo. grey and silver	£225	6·50
38i	3fo. brown and gold	14·00	8·75

7 "Turul" (mythical bird of the Magyars)

8 King Francis Joseph wearing Hungarian Crown

1900. Figures of value in black.

99	**7**	1f. grey	30	10
100	**7**	2f. yellow	20	10
118	**7**	3f. orange	10	10
67	**7**	4f. mauve	85	45
102	**7**	5f. green	20	10
69b	**7**	6f. purple	1·10	55
103	**7**	6f. drab	30	10
120	**7**	6f. green	10	10
121	**7**	10f. red	10	10
105	**7**	12f. lilac	55	10
122	**7**	12f. lilac on yellow	15	10
123	**7**	16f. green	15	15
124	**7**	20f. brown	20	10
125	**7**	25f. blue	20	10
126	**7**	30f. brown	20	10
127	**7**	35f. purple	20	10
111	**7**	50f. red	95	10
128	**7**	50f. red on blue	20	10
112	**7**	60f. green	5·50	20
130	**7**	60f. green on pink	90	10
131	**7**	70f. brown and green	30	10
132	**7**	80f. violet	30	10
133	**8**	1k. red	2·00	10
134	**8**	2k. blue	4·50	10
81	**8**	3k. blue	£160	8·00
135	**8**	5k. red	4·75	2·00

12

1913. Flood Charity stamps. As T **7/8**, but with label as T **12**.

136	**12**	1f.+2f. grey	1·20	1·20
137	**12**	2f.+2f. yellow	60	60
138	**12**	3f.+2f. orange	60	60
139	**12**	5f.+2f. green	60	60
140	**12**	6f.+2f. drab	1·20	1·20
141	**12**	10f.+2f. red	60	25
142	**12**	12f.+2f. lilac on yellow	1·70	1·70
143	**12**	16f.+2f. green	1·20	1·20
144	**12**	20f.+2f. brown	3·00	2·30
145	**12**	25f.+2f. blue	1·20	80
146	**12**	30f.+2f. brown	1·70	1·20
147	**12**	35f.+2f. purple	1·70	80
148	**12**	50f.+2f. lake on blue	6·00	3·00
149	**12**	60f.+2f. green on red	7·25	1·70
150	**8**	1k.+2f. red	29·00	14·00
151	**8**	2k.+2f. blue	65·00	60·00
152	**8**	5k.+2f. red	29·00	23·00

1914. War Charity. Nos. 136/52 (with labels) surch **Hadi segely Ozvegyeknek es arvaknak ket (2) filler**.

153	**12**	1f.+2f. grey	1·20	60
154	**12**	2f.+2f. yellow	1·20	60
155	**12**	3f.+2f. orange	1·20	60
156	**12**	5f.+2f. green	60	25
157	**12**	6f.+2f. drab	1·20	60
158	**12**	10f.+2f. red	60	25
159	**12**	12f.+2f. lilac on yellow	1·40	60
160	**12**	16f.+2f. green	1·40	60
161	**12**	20f.+2f. brown	1·70	80
162	**12**	25f.+2f. blue	1·70	80
163	**12**	30f.+2f. brown	2·30	80
164	**12**	35f.+2f. purple	5·75	1·70
165	**12**	50f.+2f. lake on blue	3·00	1·70
166	**12**	60f.+2f. green on red	8·75	1·70
167	**8**	1k.+2f. red (No. 150)	75·00	47·00
168	**8**	2k.+2f. blue (No. 151)	29·00	41·00
169	**8**	5k.+2f. red (No. 152)	30·00	35·00

1915. War Charity. Stamps of 1900 (without labels) surch as last round the stamp.

170	**7**	1f.+2f. grey	10	10
171	**7**	2f.+2f. yellow	10	10

172	7	3f.+2f. orange	10	10
173	7	5f.+2f. green	10	10
174	7	6f.+2f. drab	10	10
175	7	10f.+2f. red	10	10
176	7	12f.+2f. lilac on yellow	10	10
177	7	16f.+2f. green	60	60
178	7	20f.+2f. brown	60	60
179	7	25f.+2f. blue	25	25
180	7	30f.+2f. brown	25	25
181	7	35f.+2f. purple	35	35
182	7	50f.+2f. lake on blue	60	60
183	7	60f.+2f. green on red	1·20	1·20
185	8	1k.+2f. red (No. 133)	1·90	1·90
186	8	2k.+2f. blue (No. 134)	5·75	5·75
187	8	5k.+2f. red (No. 135)	14·00	14·00

18 Harvesters

1916. As T **18** but with white figures in top corners.

243	18	10f. red	95	35
244	18	15f. purple	95	35

19 Parliament Buildings, Budapest

1916. Inscr "MAGYAR KIR. POSTA".

245		2f. brown	10	10
246		3f. red	10	10
247		4f. slate	10	10
248		5f. green	10	10
249		6f. blue	10	10
250		10f. red	1·20	10
251		15f. violet	10	10
252		20f. brown	10	10
253		25f. blue	10	10
254		35f. brown	10	10
255		40f. olive	10	10
256	19	50f. purple	25	10
257	19	75f. blue	25	10
258	19	80f. green	25	10
259	19	1k. lake	25	10
260	19	2k. brown	25	10
261	19	3k. grey and violet	1·20	25
262	19	5k. brown	1·40	10
263	19	10k. mauve and brown	1·70	1·00

In Type **19** the colours of the centres differ slightly from those of the frames.

For later issues in Types **18** and **19**, see Nos. 372/86 and 404/11.

20 In Trenches   **22** "Turul" at bay

1916. War Charity.

264	20	10f.+2f. red	25	25
265	-	15f.+2f. violet	35	35
266	22	40f.+2f. lake	50	50

DESIGN: 15f. Hand to hand combat.

23 Queen Zita

1916. Coronation.

267	23	10f. mauve	85	85
268	-	15f. red (Emperor Charles IV)	85	85

1917. War Charity Exhibition. Nos. 243/4 surch **Jozsef foherczeg vezerezredes hadi kiallitasa 1 korona** (= "Prince Joseph. Chief Colonel General War Exhibition").

269	18	10f.+1k. red	85	85
270	18	15f.+1k. violet	85	85

1918. Air. Surch **REPULO POSTA** and value.

271	19	1k.50 on 75f. blue	19·00	24·00
272	19	4k.50 on 2k. brown	18·00	22·00

27 Charles IV   **28** Zita

1918

273	27	10f. red	25	25

274	27	15f. violet	25	25
275	27	20f. brown	25	25
276	27	25f. blue	25	25
277	28	40f. olive	25	25
278	28	50f. purple	25	25

1918. Optd **KOZTARSASAG**. (a) War Charity Stamps (Nos. 264/6).

279	20	10+2f. red	25	25
280	-	15+2f. violet	25	25
281	22	40+2f. red	25	25

(b) Harvesters and Parliament.

282	18	2f. brown	15	15
283	18	3f. red	15	15
284	18	4f. grey	15	15
285	18	5f. green	15	15
286	18	6f. blue	15	15
287	18	10f. red	15	15
288	18	20f. brown	15	15
289	18	40f. green	15	15
290	19	1k. red	15	15
291	19	2k. brown	40	55
292	19	3k. grey and violet	70	90
293	19	5k. brown	2·75	3·50
294	19	10k. mauve and brown	3·00	3·50

(c) Charles and Zita.

295	27	10f. pink	10	15
296	27	15f. purple	10	15
297	27	20f. brown	10	15
298	27	25f. blue	15	15
299	28	40f. green	45	55
300	28	50f. purple	25	25

1919. As T **18/19**, but inscr "MAGYAR POSTA".

301	18	2f. brown	10	10
302	18	4f. grey	10	10
303	18	5f. green	10	10
304	18	6f. blue	10	10
305	18	10f. red	20	10
306	18	15f. violet	10	10
307	18	20f. brown	10	10
308	18	20f. green	10	10
309	18	25f. blue	10	10
310	18	40f. green	10	10
311	18	40f. red	10	10
312	18	45f. orange	10	10
313	19	50f. purple	10	10
314	19	60f. blue and brown	10	10
315	19	95f. blue	10	10
316	19	1k. red	10	10
317	19	1k. blue and indigo	10	10
318	19	1k.20 green	10	20
319	19	1k.40 green	10	20
320	19	2k. brown	10	10
321	19	3k. grey and violet	15	20
322	19	5k. brown	10	55
323	19	10k. mauve and brown	85	70

32 Karl Marx

1919

324	32	20f. red and brown	90	90
325	-	45f. green and orange	90	90
326	-	60f. brown and grey	6·75	6·75
327	-	75f. brown and red	6·75	6·75
328	-	80f. brown and olive	6·75	6·75

PORTRAITS: 45f. S. Petofi; 60f. Ignacs Martinovics; 75f. G. Dozsa; 80f. F. Engels.

1919. Nos. 301 etc optd **MAGYAR TANACSKOZTARSASAG**. (second word hyphenated on 2 to 45f.) (= "Hungarian Soviet Republic").

329	18	2f. brown	30	40
330	18	3f. purple	30	40
331	18	4f. grey	30	40
332	18	5f. green	30	40
333	18	6f. blue	30	40
334	18	10f. red	30	40
335	18	15f. violet	30	40
336	18	20f. brown	30	40
337	18	25f. blue	30	40
338	18	40f. green	30	40
339	18	45f. orange	30	40
340	19	50f. purple	30	40
341	19	95f. blue	30	40
342	19	1k. red	30	40
343	19	1k.20 green	1·20	1·20
344	19	1k.40 green	1·20	1·20
345	19	2k. brown	1·80	1·80
346	19	3k. grey and violet	1·80	1·80
347	19	5k. brown	1·80	1·80
348	19	10k. mauve and brown	2·40	2·40

1919. Entry of National Army into Budapest. Nos. 303 etc optd **A nemzeti hadsereg bevonulasa. 1919. XI/16.**

348a	18	5f. green	1·00	1·00
348b	18	10f. red	1·00	1·10
348c	18	15f. violet	1·00	1·10
348d	18	20f. brown	1·00	1·10
348e	18	25f. blue	1·00	1·10

(36)   (37)

1920. Nos. 329/48 optd with T **36** (2 to 45f.) or **37** (others).

349		2f. brown	1·50	1·50
350		3f. purple	30	30
351		4f. grey	1·50	1·50
352		5f. green	20	20
353		6f. blue	35	35
354		10f. red	20	20
355		15f. violet	20	20
356		20f. brown	20	20
357		25f. blue	30	30
358		40f. green	1·90	1·90
359		45f. orange	1·90	1·90
360	19	50f. purple	1·90	1·90
361	19	95f. blue	1·90	1·90
362	19	1k. red	1·90	1·90
363	19	1k.20 green	2·30	2·30
364	19	1k.40 green	2·30	2·30
365	19	2k. brown	13·00	13·00
366	19	3k. grey and violet	13·00	13·00
367	19	5k. brown	45	45
368	19	10k. mauve and brown	13·00	13·00

38 Returning P.O.W.

1920. Returned Prisoners-of-War Fund.

369B	38	40f.+1k. lake	1·90	1·90
370A	-	60f.+2k. brown	3·00	3·00
371A	-	1k.+5k. blue	1·60	1·60

DESIGNS—HORIZ: 60f. Prison Camp. VERT: 1k. Family Reunion.

1920. Re-issue of T **18** inscr "MAGYAR KIR. POSTA".

372	18	5f. brown	15	15
373	18	10f. purple	15	15
374	18	40f. red	15	15
375	18	50f. green	15	15
376	18	50f. blue	15	15
377	18	60f. black	15	15
378	18	1k. green	15	15
379	18	1½k. purple	15	15
380	18	2k. blue	15	15
381	18	2½k. green	20	15
382	18	3k. brown	20	15
383	18	4k. red	15	15
384	18	4½k. violet	30	15
385	18	5k. brown	25	15
386	18	6k. blue	25	15
387	18	10k. brown	25	15
388	18	15k. black	35	15
389	18	20k. red	35	15
390	18	25k. orange	35	15
391	18	40k. green	35	15
392	18	50k. blue	35	15
393	18	100k. purple	40	15
394	18	150k. green	60	15
395	18	200k. green	60	15
396	18	350k. violet	1·80	40
442	18	300k. red	40	15
443	18	400k. blue	40	15
444	18	500k. black	40	25
445	18	600k. bistre	40	25
446	18	800k. yellow	50	40

1920. Air. No. 263 surch **LEGI POSTA** and value.

401	19	3k. on 10k. mauve & brn	3·75	4·50
402	19	8k. on 10k. mauve & brn	3·75	4·50
403	19	12k. on 10k. mauve & brn	3·75	4·50

1920. Re-issue of T **19** inscr "MAGYAR KIR. POSTA".

404		2k.50 blue	25	15
405		3k.50 grey	30	15
406		10k. brown	60	15
407		15k. grey	25	15
408		20k. red	35	20
409		25k. orange	40	15
410		30k. lake	50	15
411		40k. green	50	15

412		50k. blue	65	15
413		100k. brown	65	15
414		400k. green	1·00	40
415		500k. violet	75	20
416		1000k. red	1·80	25
448		2000k. red	1·90	75

42 Madonna and Child

1921

418	42	50k. blue and brown	65	50
419	42	100k. brown and bistre	1·30	75
420	42	200k. ultramarine and blue	1·30	40
421	42	500k. mauve and purple	1·50	40
422	42	1000k. purple and mauve	1·70	40
423	42	2000k. mauve and green	2·75	90
424	42	2500k. brown and bistre	2·40	65
425	42	3000k. mauve and red	3·00	65
426	42	5000k. light green and green	3·25	1·50
427	42	10000k. blue and violet	4·50	1·50

44 Statue of Petofi in National Dress   **45** John, the hero, on flying dragon   **47** Death of Petofi

1923. Birth Centenary of Petofi (poet).

428	44	10k. (+ 10k.) blue	1·30	1·30
429	45	15k. (+ 15k.) blue	2·50	2·50
430	-	25k. (+ 25k.) brown	1·30	1·30
431	47	40k. (+ 40k.) red	3·75	3·75
432	-	50k. (+ 50k.) purple	3·75	3·75

DESIGNS—VERT (As Type **45**): 25k. Petofi; 50k. Petofi addressing the people.

49 Icarus over Budapest

1924. Air.

433	49	100k. pink and brown	4·00	4·00
434	49	500k. light green and green	4·00	4·00
435	49	1000k. brown and bistre	4·00	4·00
436	49	2000k. blue and deep blue	4·00	4·00
436a	49	5000k. mauve and purple	6·25	6·25
436b	49	10000k. purple and red	6·25	6·25

50

1924. Tuberculosis Relief Fund.

437	50	300k. (+ 300k.) blue	7·50	7·50
438	-	500k. (+ 500k.) brown	7·50	7·50
439	-	1000k. (+ 1000k.) green	7·50	7·50

DESIGNS: 500k. Mother and child; 1000k. Bowman.

53 M. Jokai

1925. Birth Centenary of Maurus Jokai (novelist).

449	53	1000k. brown and green	9·50	8·75
450	53	2000k. brown	3·25	1·30
451	53	2500k. brown and blue	9·50	8·75

55

1925. Sports Association Fund.

452	-	100k.(+100k.) brn & grn	6·25	3·75

453	-	200k.(+200k.) grn & brn	6·25	5·00
454	-	300k.(+300k.) blue	15·00	7·00
455	-	400k.(+400k.) green & bl	15·00	8·75
456	-	500k.(+500k.) purple	16·00	9·50
457	-	1000k.(+1000k.) red	19·00	10·00
458	55	2000k.(+2000k.) purple	21·00	10·50
459	-	2500k.(+2500k.) sepia	25·00	11·50

DESIGNS—HORIZ: 100k. Athletes; 500k. Fencing. VERT: 200k. Skiing; 300k. Skating; 400k. Diving; 1000k. Scouts; 2500k. Hurdles.

  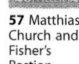

56 Crown of St. Stephen

57 Matthias Church and Fisher's Bastion

58 Royal Palace, Budapest

59

60 Madonna and Child

1926. T 59 is without boat.

460	56	1f. black	1·00	25
461	56	2f. blue	1·00	25
462	56	3f. orange	1·00	25
463	56	4f. mauve	1·00	25
464	56	6f. green	1·00	25
465	56	8f. mauve	2·00	25
466	57	10f. blue	2·00	25
467	57	16f. violet	2·00	25
468	57	20f. red	2·00	25
469	57	25f. brown	2·00	25
470	59	30f. green	6·25	40
471	58	32f. violet	6·25	25
472	58	40f. blue and deep blue	9·50	25
473	59	46f. blue	8·25	40
474	59	50f. black	8·50	40
475	59	70f. red	9·50	40
476	60	1p. green	65·00	1·30
477	60	2p. red	65·00	1·90
478	60	5p. blue	65·00	9·50

See also Nos. 502/6.

61 The fabulous "Turul"

62 Mercury astride a "Turul"

1927. Air.

478a	61	4f. orange	65	65
479	61	12f. green	2·00	90
480	61	16f. brown	2·00	90
481	61	20f. red	2·00	90
482	61	32f. purple	6·25	3·25
483	61	40f. blue	5·00	1·90
484	62	50f. red	5·00	1·90
485	62	72f. olive	6·25	2·10
486	62	80f. violet	7·00	2·50
487	62	1p. green	6·25	2·75
488	62	2p. red	12·50	4·50
489	62	5p. blue	44·00	45·00

66 Royal Palace, Budapest

1928. T 66 has the boat in a different place and a redrawn frame.

502	66	30f. green	6·25	15
503	66	32f. purple	8·75	40
504	66	40f. blue	8·75	25
505	66	46f. green	8·75	25
506	66	50f. brown	8·25	25

67 St. Stephen

1928. 890th Death Anniv of St. Stephen of Hungary.

507	67	8f. green	1·90	65
508	67	16f. red	1·90	65
509	67	32f. blue	7·50	4·50

1929. Colours changed.

510	8f. red	1·30	50
511	16f. violet	1·50	65
512	32f. bistre	6·25	3·25

68 Admiral Horthy

1930. Tenth Anniv of Regency.

513	68	8f. green	1·90	30
514	68	16f. violet	1·90	40
515	68	20f. red	11·50	1·50
516	68	32f. brown	9·50	4·50
517	68	40f. blue	12·50	1·90

69 St. Emeric

1930. 900th Death Anniv of St. Emeric.

518	69	8f.+2f. green	1·90	1·30
519	-	16f.+4f. purple	2·50	1·30
520	-	20f.+4f. red	6·25	3·75
521	-	32f.+8f. blue	8·75	6·25

DESIGNS—VERT: 16f. St. Stephen and Queen Gisela; 20f. St. Ladislas. HORIZ: 32f. Sts. Gellert and Emeric.

1931. Surch.

526	56	2 on 3f. orange	3·25	40
527	56	6 on 8f. mauve	3·25	25
528	57	10 on 16f. violet	3·25	25
525	57	20 on 25f. brown	3·75	1·90

1931. Air. Optd Zeppelin 1931.

529	62	1p. orange	£130	£130
530	62	2p. purple	£130	£130

73 St. Elizabeth

1932. 700th Death Anniv of St. Elizabeth of Hungary.

531	73	10f. blue	1·30	65
532	73	20f. red	1·30	65
533	-	32f. purple	7·50	65
534	-	40f. blue	5·75	1·90

DESIGN—18×28 mm: 32, 40f. St. Elizabeth giving cloak to the poor.

75 Madonna and Child

1932

535	75	1p. green	65·00	2·75
536	75	2p. red	65·00	4·25
537	75	5p. blue	£190	14·00
538	75	10p. brown	£225	90·00

1932. No. 527 further surch 2.

540	56	2 on 6 on 8f. mauve	3·50	95

77

1932. Famous Hungarians.

541	-	1f. grey	90	15
542	-	2f. orange	90	15
543	-	4f. blue	90	15
543a	77	5f. brown	1·30	25
544	-	6f. green	90	15
545	-	10f. green	90	15
546	-	16f. violet	90	25
547	-	20f. red	1·50	25
547a	-	25f. green	2·50	25
548	-	30f. brown	1·50	40
549	-	32f. purple	2·50	40
550	-	40f. blue	4·50	1·50
551	-	50f. green	4·50	1·50
552	-	70f. red	6·25	1·00

DESIGNS: 1f. I. Madach, poet, 1823–64; 2f. J Arany, poet, 1817–82; 4f. I. Semmelweis, physician, 1818–65; 5f. F. Kolcsey, poet, 1790–1838; 6f. L. Eotvos, physicist, 1848–1919; 10f. I. Szechenyi, statesman, 1791–1860; 16f. F. Deak, statesman, 1803–76; 20f. F. Liszt, composer, 1811–86; 25f. M. Vorosmarty, poet, 1800–55; 30f. L. Kossuth, statesman, 1802–94; 32f. I. Tisza, statesman, 1861–1918; 40f. M. Munkacsy, painter, 1844–1900; 50f. S. Korosi Csoma, explorer, 1784–1842; 70f. F. Bolyai, mathematician, 1775–1856.

1932. Surch 10.

553	59	10 on 70f. red	6·25	65

79 "Justice for Hungary" over Danube

80 Gift Plane from Mussolini

1933. Air.

554	79	10f. green	3·25	65
555	79	16f. violet	3·25	65
556	80	20f. red	9·50	1·30
557	80	40f. blue	9·50	1·30
558	-	48f. black	25·00	3·25
559	-	72f. brown	65·00	3·75
560	-	1p. green	65·00	4·50
561	-	2p. red	95·00	25·00
562	-	5p. grey	£190	£225

DESIGNS—VERT: As Type 80: 48, 72f. "Spirit of Flight" on wing of Lockheed Model 8A Sirius; 1, 2, 5p. Mercury and propeller.

83 "The Stag of Hungary"

1933. International Scout Jamboree, Godollo.

563	83	10f. green	1·90	1·30
564	83	16f. red	6·25	3·75
565	83	20f. red	4·50	1·90
566	83	32f. yellow	14·00	9·50
567	83	40f. blue	15·00	6·25

1934. Second Hungarian Philatelic Exhibition, Budapest, and Jubilee of First Hungarian Philatelic Society (L.E.H.E.). Sheet 64×76 mm containing No. 547 in changed colour.

MS568	20f. red	£225	£180

84 Ferenc Rakoczi II

1935. Death Bicentenary of Prince Rakoczi.

569	84	10f. green	1·90	65
570	84	16f. violet	11·50	5·00
571	84	20f. red	3·25	1·90
572	84	32f. red	15·00	9·50
573	84	40f. blue	19·00	11·50

85 Cardinal Peter Pazmany

1935. Tercentenary of Budapest University.

574	85	6f. green	3·25	1·50
575	-	10f. green	65	40
576	85	16f. violet	4·50	2·50
577	85	20f. mauve	65	65
578	-	32f. red	7·50	5·25
579	-	40f. blue	6·25	5·25

DESIGN—HORIZ (35×25 mm): 10f., 32f., 40f. Pazmany signing deed.

87 Fokker F.VIIb/3m

1936. Air.

580	87	10f. green	1·30	65
581	87	20f. red	1·30	65
582	87	36f. brown	1·30	65
583	-	40f. blue	1·30	65
584	-	52f. orange	1·90	65
585	-	60f. violet	24·00	3·25
586	-	80f. green	5·00	65
587	-	1p. green	5·00	90
588	-	2p. lake	6·25	3·25
589	-	5p. blue	25·00	25·00

DESIGNS: 40f. to 80f. Fokker F.VIIb/3m over Parliament Buildings; 1p. to 5p. Fokker F.VIIb/3m (different).

88 Ancient Buda

1936. 250th Anniv of Recapture of Buda from Turks.

590	88	10f. green	1·30	40
591	-	16f. mauve	7·50	5·00
592	-	20f. red	1·30	40
593	-	32f. brown	7·50	5·00
594	88	40f. blue	7·50	5·00

DESIGNS: 16f. Angel of Peace over Buda; 20f. Arms of Buda; 32f. Colour bearer and bugler.

89 "Commerce", "May Fair, 1937" and R. Danube

1937. Budapest International Fair.

595	89	2f. orange	25	10
596	89	6f. green	65	15
597	89	10f. green	90	25
598	89	20f. red	1·90	65
599	89	32f. violet	2·50	90
600	89	40f. blue	2·75	1·30

90 St. Stephen, the Church Builder

1938. 900th Death Anniv of St. Stephen. (1st issue).

601	-	1f. violet	65	25
602	90	2f. sepia	25	25
603	-	4f. blue	1·30	25
604	-	5f. mauve	1·90	25
605	-	6f. green	2·50	25
606	-	10f. red	1·90	25
607	90	16f. violet	3·25	90
608	-	20f. red	1·90	25
609	-	25f. green	2·50	1·30
610	-	30f. bistre	3·75	25
611	-	32f. red on yellow	3·75	3·25
612	-	40f. blue	3·75	25
613	-	50f. purple on green	4·50	25
614	-	70f. green on blue	7·00	90

MS614a 146×106 mm. No. 608 for 34th International Eucharistic Congress and Philatelic Exhibition, Budapest 50·00 44·00

DESIGNS: 1f., 10f. Abbot Astrik receiving Crown from Pope; 4f., 20f. St. Stephen enthroned; 5f., 25f. St. Gellert and St. Stephen; 6f., 30f. St. Stephen offering Crown to Virgin Mary; 32f., 50f. St. Stephen; 40f. Madonna and Child; 70f. Crown of St. Stephen.

See also Nos. 620/MS621a.

92 Admiral Horthy

1938. Admiral Horthy.

615	92	1p. green	4·50	25
616	92	2p. sepia	5·00	25
617	92	5p. blue	6·25	2·75

93 Eucharistic Symbols

1938. 34th International Eucharistic Congress.

618	-	16f.+16f. blue	8·25	8·25
619	**93**	20f.+20f. red	8·25	8·25

MS619a 130×149 mm 6f.+6f. green;
10f.+10f. red; 16f.+16f. blue; 20f.+20f.
red; 32f.+32f. purple; 40f.+40f. blue;
50f.+50f. mauve 75·00 75·00

DESIGNS: 6f. St. Stephen; 10f.St. Emeric; 16f. (619), St Ladislas; 16f. St. Laszio; 20f. Offering crown to Virgin Mary; 32f. St. Elizabeth; 40f. Bishop Maurice and Pecs Cathedral; 50f. St. Margaret.

94 St. Stephen the Victorious

1938. 900th Death Anniv of St. Stephen (2nd issue).

620	**94**	10f.+10f. purple	5·00	5·00
621	-	20f.+20f. red	5·00	5·00

MS621a 153×113 mm. 6f.+6f. green;
10f.+10f. red; 16f.+16f. brown;
20f.+20f. red; 32f.+32f. blue; 40f.+40f.
blue; 50f.+50f. purple 65·00 70·00

DESIGNS: St. Stephen the missionary; 16f. On throne; 20f. Offering crown to Virgin Mary; 32f. Receiving bishops and monks; 40f. Queen Gisela, St. Stephen and St. Emeric; 50f. On bier.

95 Debrecen College

1938. 400th Anniv of Debrecen College.

622	**95**	6f. green	65	15
623	-	10f. brown	65	15
624	-	16f. red	65	40
625	-	20f. red	65	25
626	-	32f. green	1·50	1·10
627	-	40f. blue	1·50	90

DESIGNS—HORIZ: 10, 20f. 18th and 19th-cent views of College. VERT: 16f. 18th-century students as firemen; 32f. Prof. Marothi; 40f. Dr. Hatvani.

1938. Acquisition of Czech Territory. As Nos. 608 and 614 optd HAZATERES 1938.

628		20f. red	3·25	2·50
629		70f. brown on blue	3·25	2·50

100 Statue representing Northern Provinces

1939. "Hungary for Hungarians" Patriotic Fund.

630	**100**	6f.+3f. green	1·50	90
631	-	10f.+5f. green	90	65
632	-	20f.+10f. red	90	65
633	-	30f.+15f. green	1·90	1·30
634	-	40f.+20f. blue	2·50	1·30

DESIGNS: 10f. Fort at Munkacs; 20f. Admiral Horthy leading troops into Komarom; 30f. Cathedral of St. Elizabeth of Hungary, Kassa; 40f. Girls offering flowers to soldiers.

101 Crown of St. Stephen

102 Esztergom Basilica

1939. Crown of St. Stephen.

635	**101**	1f. brown	15	15
636	**101**	2f. green	15	15
690	**101**	3f. brown	15	15
637	**101**	4f. brown	15	15
638	**101**	5f. violet	15	15
639	**101**	6f. green	15	15
693	**101**	8f. green	15	15
640	**101**	10f. brown	15	15
695	**101**	12f. red	15	15
641	**101**	16f. violet	15	15
642	-	20f. red	15	15
697	-	24f. red	15	15
643	-	25f. blue	15	15
699	-	30f. mauve	15	15
645	-	32f. brown	25	15
700	**102**	40f. green	25	25
701	-	50f. green	25	25
702	-	70f. red	25	25
698	-	80f. brown	65	25

DESIGNS—As T **101**: 20, 24f. St. Stephen; 25, 80f. Madonna and Child. As T **102**: 30f. Buda Cathedral; 32f. Debrecen Reformed Church; 50f. Budapest Evangelical Church; 70f. Kassa Cathedral.

For further issues in these designs, see Nos. 751/5.

103 Guides' Salute

1939. Girl Guides' Rally, Godollo. Inscr "I. PAX-TING".

649	**103**	2f. orange	75	50
650	-	6f. green	75	50
651	-	10f. brown	1·30	75
652	-	20f. pink	1·90	1·30

DESIGNS: 6f. Lily symbol and Hungarian arms; 10f. Guide and girl in national costume; 20f. Dove of peace.

104 Memorial Tablets

1939. National Protestant Day and Int Protestant Cultural Fund.

653	**104**	6f.+3f. green	1·50	90
654	-	10f.+5f. purple	1·50	90
655	-	20f.+10f. red	2·30	1·90
656	-	32f.+16f. brown	2·50	2·50
657	-	40f.+20f. blue	3·25	3·00

MS657a 77×112 mm. No. 656 32f.
brown. Perf or imperf 65·00 65·00

DESIGNS—HORIZ: 10f., 20f. G. Karoli and A. Molnar di Szenci (translators of the Bible and the Psalms). VERT: 32f. Prince Gabriel Bethlen; 40f. Zsuzsanna Lorantffy.

106 Boy Scout with Kite

1940. Admiral Horthy Aviation Fund.

658	**106**	6f.+6f. green	90	90
659	-	10f.+10f. brown	1·50	1·50
660	-	20f.+20f. red	2·10	2·10

DESIGNS: 10f. "Spirit of Flight"; 20f. St. Elizabeth carrying Crown and Cross of St. Stephen.

107 Regent and Szeged Cathedral

1940. 20th Anniv of Regency.

661	**107**	6f. green	25	25
662	-	10f. brown and olive	40	40
663	-	20f. red	90	90

DESIGNS: 10f. Admiral Horthy (dated "1920 1940"); 20f. Kassa Cathedral and Angelic bellringer (dated "1939").

108 Stemming the Flood

1940. Flood Relief Fund.

664	**108**	10f.+2f. purple	65	40
665	**108**	20f.+4f. orange	65	40
666	**108**	20f.+50f. brown	1·90	2·00

MS666a 77×112 mm. T **108**. 20f.+1p.
green 8·25 8·25

109 Hunyadi Family Arms

110 Hunyadi Castle

1940. 500th Birth Anniv of King Matthias Hunyadi and Cultural Institutes Fund.

667	**109**	6f.+6f. green	90	90
668	**110**	10f.+5f. brown	90	90
669	-	16f.+8f. olive	1·10	1·10
670	-	20f.+10f. red	1·10	1·10

671	-	32f.+16f. grey	1·50	1·50

MS671a 89×113 mm. 20f.+1p. green
(as No. 670) 8·25 8·25

DESIGNS—VERT: 16f. Bust of King Matthias (dated "1440–1490"); 32f. Corvin Codex (dated "1473"). HORIZ: 20f. Equestrian Statue of King Matthias.

111 Crown of St. Stephen

1940. Recovery from Rumania of North-Eastern Transylvania.

672	**111**	10f. green and yellow	65	25

112 Madonna and Martyr

1940. Transylvanian Relief Fund. Various designs dated "1940".

673	-	10f.+50f. green	1·50	1·50
674	**112**	20f.+50f. red	1·60	1·60
675	-	32f.+50f. brown	2·00	2·00

DESIGNS: 10f. Prince Csaba and soldier; 32f. Mother offering child to Fatherland.

113 Spirit of Music

1940. Artists' Relief Fund. Inscr "MAGYAR MUVESZETERT".

676	**113**	6f.+6f. green	2·10	1·90
677	-	10f.+10f. brown	2·10	1·90
678	-	16f.+16f. violet	2·10	1·90
679	-	20f.+20f. red	2·10	1·90

MS679a 123×84 mm. 6f.+6f. brown;
10f.+10f. red; 16f.+16f. green;
20f.+20f. lilac 9·50 9·50

DESIGNS—VERT: 10f. Sculpture; 16f. Painting. HORIZ: 20f. Poetry (Pegasus).

114 Pilot

1941. Air. Horthy Aviation Fund. Various allegorical designs inscribed "HORTHY MIKLOS NEMZETI REPULO ALAP".

680	**114**	6f.+6f. olive	90	90
681	-	10f.+10f. brown	90	90
682	-	20f.+20f. red	90	90
683	-	32f.+32f. blue	2·50	2·50

DESIGNS: 10f. Youth releasing model glider; 20f. Glider; 32f. Madonna.

1941. Acquisition of Yugoslav Territory. Overprinted DEL-UISSZATER ("The South Comes Home").

684	**101**	10f. brown	65	15
685	-	20f. red (No. 642)	65	15

116 Admiral Horthy

1941

686A	**116**	1p. green and yellow	40	25
687B	**116**	2p. brown and yellow	40	40
688B	**116**	5p. purple and yellow	1·30	50

118 Szechenyi

119 Giant opening Straits of Kazan

1941. 150th Birth Anniv of Count Szechenyi.

703	**118**	10f. olive	25	15
704	-	16f. green	40	25
705	**119**	20f. red	40	25
706	-	32f. orange	90	50
707	-	40f. blue	1·00	50

DESIGNS: 16f. Count Szechenyi and Academy of Science; 32f. Budapest Chain Bridge; 40f. Mercury, Locomotive and "Szent Istvan" (river steamer).

120 Infantry in Action

1941. Soldiers' Gifts Fund. Inscr "HONVEDEINK KARACSONYARA 1941". (a) 1st issue.

708	**120**	8f.+12f. green	75	65
709	-	12f.+18f. brown	75	65
710	-	20f.+30f. blue	90	65
711	-	40f.+60f. brown	90	65

DESIGNS: 12f. Artillery; 20f. Tanks; 40f. Cavalryman and cyclist.

(b) 2nd Issue (for Christmas gifts).

712		20f.+40f. red	3·75	3·75

DESIGN: Soldier in helmet; cross and sword.

121 Pilot and Airplane

1942. Air. Horthy Aviation Fund. Inscr "HORTHY MIKLOS NEMZETI REPULO ALAP".

713	**121**	8f.+8f. green	1·30	1·30
714	-	12f.+12f. blue	1·30	1·30
715	-	20f.+20f. brown	1·30	1·30
716	-	30f.+30f. red	1·30	1·30

DESIGNS—VERT: 30f. Airmen and Turul. HORIZ: 12f. Aircraft and horsemen; 20f. Airplane and archer.

122 Blood Transfusion

1942. Red Cross Fund. Cross in red.

717	**122**	3f.+18f. green	2·10	2·10
718	-	8f.+32f. brown	2·10	2·10
719	-	12f.+50f. purple	2·10	2·10
720	-	20f.+1p. blue	2·10	2·10

DESIGNS: 8f. First aid; 12f. Wireless and carrier-pigeon service; 20f. Bereaved parents and orphans.

123 Vice-regent Stephen Horthy

1942. Air. Mourning for Stephen Horthy and Horthy Aviation Fund.

721	-	20f. black	65	65
722	**123**	30f.+20f. violet	75	75

No. 721 is squarer in shape than No. 722 and is dated "1904–1942".

124 Stephen Horthy's Widow

1942. Red Cross Fund. Cross and Crown in red.

723	**124**	6f.+1p. blue	4·50	4·50
724	-	8f.+32f. brown	4·50	4·50
725	-	20f.+1p. brown	4·50	4·50

DESIGNS—HORIZ: 8f. Nurse and wounded soldier. VERT: 20f. Stephen Horthy's mother.

125 King Ladislas

1942. Cultural Funds.

726	**125**	6f.+6f. brown	90	90
727	-	8f.+8f. green	90	90
728	-	12f.+12f. brown	90	90
729	-	20f.+20f. green	90	90
730	-	24f.+24f. brown	90	90

| 731 | - | 30f.+30f. red | 90 | 90 |

DESIGNS—Statuettes: 8f. Ladislas on horseback; 20f. Bela IV with architect; 30f. Lajos the Great enthroned. King's heads; 12f. Bela IV; 24f. Lajos the Great.

126 Prince Arpad   **127** St. Stephen's Crown

1943. Prince Arpad.

732	**126**	1f. grey	15	15
733	-	2f. orange	15	15
734	-	3f. blue	15	15
735	-	4f. brown	15	15
736	-	5f. red	15	15
737	-	6f. lilac	15	15
738	-	8f. green	15	15
739	-	10f. brown	20	15
740	-	12f. green	20	15
741	-	18f. black	20	15
742	**127**	20f. brown	20	15
743	-	24f. purple	25	15
744	**127**	30f. red	25	15
745	-	30f. red	25	15
746	**127**	50f. blue	25	15
747	**127**	80f. brown	25	15
748	**127**	1p. green	25	15
749	**127**	2p. brown	35	65
750	**127**	5p. purple	50	1·30

DESIGNS: 2f. King Ladislas; 3f. Miklos Toldi; 4f. Janos Hunyadi; 5f. Pal Kinizsi; 6f. Miklos Zrinyi; 8f. Ferenc Rakoczi II; 10f. Andre Hadik; 12f. Artur Gorgey; 18f. and 24f. Madonna; 30f. (No. 745), St. Margaret.

1943. As T **102** (designs and colours changed).

751	-	30f. red	25	15
752	-	40f. grey	25	15
753	**102**	50f. blue	25	15
754	-	70f. green	25	15
755	-	80f. brown	25	15

DESIGNS: 30f. Kassa Cathedral; 40f. Debrecen Reformed Church; 70f. Budapest Evangelical Church; 80f. Buda Cathedral.

128 Mounted Archer

1943. Wounded Soldiers' Relief Fund. Inscr as in T **128**.

756	**128**	1f.+1f. grey	15	15
757	-	3f.+1f. lilac	75	1·30
758	-	4f.+1f. brown	25	20
759	-	8f.+2f. green	25	20
760	-	12f.+2f. brown	25	20
761	-	20f.+2f. brown	25	20
762	-	40f.+4f. grey	30	20
763	-	50f.+6f. brown	40	20
764	-	70f.+8f. blue	50	40

DESIGNS—VERT: 3f., 4f. Magyar soldier with battle-axe and buckler; 8f. Warrior with shield and sword; 20f. Musketeer; 50f. Artilleryman; 70f. Magyar Arms. HORIZ: 12f. Lancer; 40f. Hussar.

129 Model Glider

1943. Air. Horthy Aviation Fund. Inscr "HORTHY MIKLOS NEMZETI REPULO ALAP".

765	**129**	8f.+8f. green	1·30	1·10
766	-	12f.+12f. blue	1·30	1·10
767	-	20f.+20f. brown	1·30	1·10
768	-	30f.+30f. red	1·30	1·10

DESIGNS: 12f. Gliders in flight; 20f. White-tailed sea eagle and aircraft; 30f. Cant Z.1007 bis Alcione bomber and gliders.

130 Shepherds and Angels

1943. Christmas.

769	**130**	4f. green	40	40
770	-	20f. blue	40	40
771	-	30f. red	40	40

DESIGNS: 20f. Nativity; 30f. Adoration of the Wise Men.

131 Nurse and Soldier

1944. Red Cross Fund. Cross and Crown in red.

772	**131**	20f.+20f. brown	90	75
773	-	30f.+30f. brown	90	75
774	-	50f.+50f. purple	90	75
775	-	70f.+70f. blue	90	75

DESIGNS: 30f. Soldier, nurse, mother and child; 50f. Nurse shielding a lamp over the Fallen; 70f. Soldier with crutches, nurse and sapling.

132 Drummer and Flags

1944. 50th Death Anniv of Kossuth (statesman).

776	-	4f. brown	40	25
777	**132**	20f. green	40	25
778	-	30f. red	40	25
779	-	50f. blue	40	25

DESIGNS—VERT: 4f. Kossuth and family group; 50f. Portrait. HORIZ: 30f. Kossuth speaking before an assembly.

133 St. Elizabeth

1944. Famous Women.

780	**133**	20f. bistre	40	40
781	-	24f. purple	40	40
782	-	30f. red	40	40
783	-	50f. blue	40	40
784	-	70f. red	40	40
785	-	80f. brown	40	40

PORTRAITS: 24f. St. Margaret; 30f. Elizabeth Szilagyi; 50f. Dorothy Kanizsai; 70f. Zsuzsanna Lorantffy; 80f. Ilona Zrinyi.

1945. Stamps as Nos. 732/48, surch **FELSZABADULAS** (= Liberation) **1945 apr 4** and value. On yellow or blue surface-tinted paper (same price).

786	-	10f. on 1f. grey	2·50	2·50
787	-	20f. on 3f. blue	2·50	2·50
788	-	30f. on 4f. brown		2·50
789	-	40f. on 6f. blue	2·50	2·50
790	-	50f. on 8f. green	2·50	2·50
791	-	1p. on 10f. brown	2·50	2·50
792	-	150f. on 12f. green	2·50	2·50
793	-	2p. on 18f. black	2·50	2·50
794	-	3p. on 20f. brown	2·50	2·50
795	-	5p. on 24f. purple	2·50	2·50
796	-	6p. on 50f. blue	2·50	2·50
797	-	10p. on 80f. brown	2·50	2·50
798	-	20p. on 1p. green	2·50	2·50

135 Bajcsy-Zsilinszky

1945. Bajcsy-Zsilinszky (patriot).

| 799 | **135** | 1p.+1p. purple | 1·30 | 1·30 |

1945. Provisionals. 1st issue. Surch **1945** and value. (a) On stamps of 1943, Nos. 732/50, surface-tinted paper.

800	-	10f. on 4f. brown on blue	15	15
801	-	10f. on 10f. brown on blue	40	40
802	-	10f. on 12f. green on yellow	15	15
803	-	20f. on 1f. grey on yellow	15	15
804	-	20f. on 18f. black on yellow	15	15
805	-	28f. on 5f. red on blue	15	15
806	-	30f. on 30f. red on blue (No. 745)		15	15
807	-	30f. on 30f. red on blue (No. 744)		15	15
808	-	40f. on 24f. purple on yellow	15	15
809	-	42f. on 20f. brown on yellow	15	15
810	-	50f. on 50f. blue on yellow	15	15
811	-	60f. on 8f. green on yellow	15	15
812	-	1p. on 80f. brown on blue	15	15
813	-	1p. on 1p. green on yellow	15	15
814	-	150f. on 6f. blue on yellow	1·50	1·50
815	-	2p. on 2p. brown on blue	15	15
816	-	3p. on 3f. blue on yellow	40	40
817	-	5p. on 5p. purple on yellow	15	15
818	-	10p. on 2f. orange on blue	12·50	12·50

(b) On Famous Women Series of 1944 (Nos. 780/5), surface-tinted paper.

| 819 | - | 20f. on 20f. bistre on blue | 15 | 15 |

820	-	30f. on 30f. red on blue	15	15
821	-	40f. on 24f. purple on yellow	15	15
822	-	50f. on 50f. blue on yellow	15	15
823	-	80f. on 80f. brown on yellow	15	15
824	-	1p. on 70f. red on blue	25	25

1945. Provisionals. 2nd issue. Surch **1945** and value. (a) On stamps of 1943, Nos. 732/48, surface-tinted paper.

825	-	40f. on 10f. brown on blue	15	15
826	-	1p. on 20f. brown on yellow	15	15
827	-	1.60p. on 12f. green on yellow	15	15
828	-	2p. on 4f. brown on blue	15	15
829	-	4p. on 30f. red on blue (No. 744)		15	15
830	-	5p. on 8f. green on yellow	15	15
831	-	6p. on 50f. blue on yellow	15	15
832	-	7p. on 1p. green on yellow	15	15
833	-	9p. on 1f. grey on yellow	15	15
834	-	10p. on 80f. brown on blue	15	15

(b) On Famous Women Series of 1944. (Nos. 780/3), surface-tinted paper.

835	-	80f. on 24f. purple on yellow	15	15
836	-	3p. on 50f. blue on yellow	15	15
837	-	8p. on 20f. bistre on blue	15	15
838	-	20p. on 30f. red on blue	15	15

1945. National High School Fund. Nos. 776/9, with coloured surfaces, surch **BEKE A NEPFOISKOLAKERT**, new value and premium.

839	**132**	3p.+9p. on 20f. green on yellow	65	1·10
840	-	4p.+12p. on 4f. brown on blue	65	1·10
841	-	8p.+24p. on 50f. blue on yellow	65	1·10
842	-	10p.+30p. on 30f. red on blue	65	1·10

138 Mining

1945. Int Trade Union Conference, Paris.

843	**138**	40f. grey	8·75	10·00
844	-	1p.60 brown	8·75	10·00
845	-	2p. green	8·75	10·00
846	-	3p. purple	8·75	10·00
847	-	5p. red	8·75	10·00
848	-	8p. brown	8·75	10·00
849	-	10p. red	8·75	10·00
850	-	20p. green	8·75	10·00

DESIGNS: Trade Symbols—1p.60, Hammer and anvil (ironworking); 2p. Winged wheel (railway workers); 3p. Trowel and bricks (building); 5p. Plough (agriculture); 8p. Carrier pigeon (communications); 10p. Compasses (engineering); 20p. Winged pen and book (clerks).

139 I. Sallai and S. Furst

1945. National Relief Fund.

851	**139**	2p.+2p. brown	2·50	2·75
852	-	3p.+3p. red	2·50	2·75
853	-	4p.+4p. violet	2·50	2·75
854	-	6p.+6p. green	2·50	2·75
855	-	10p.+10p. red	2·50	2·75
856	-	15p.+15p. olive	2·50	2·75
857	-	20p.+20p. brown	2·50	2·75
858	-	40p.+40p. blue	2·50	2·75

PORTRAITS: 3p. L. Kabok and I. Monus; 4p. F. Rozsa and Z. Schonherz; 6p. A. Koltoi and P. Knurr; 10p. G. Sarkozi and I. Nagy; 15p. V. Tartsay and J. Nagy; 20p. J. Kiss and E. Bajcsy-Zsilinszky; 40p. E. Sagvari and O. Hoffmann.

1945. Provisionals (3rd issue). Nos. 738, 740/1 and 745 (coloured surfaces) surch **1945** and new value.

859	-	40p. on 8f. green on yellow	15	15
860	-	60p. on 18f. black on yellow	15	15
861	-	100p. on 12f. green on yellow	15	15
862	-	300p. on 30f. red on blue	25	25

140 Reconstruction

1945

863	**140**	12p. olive	65	65
864	**140**	20p. green	25	40
865	**140**	24p. brown	65	65
866	**140**	30p. black	25	40
867	**140**	40p. green	25	40
868	**140**	60p. red	25	40
869	**140**	100p. orange	25	40
870	**140**	120p. blue	25	40
871	**140**	140p. red	90	1·00

872	**140**	200p. brown	25	40
873	**140**	240p. blue	25	40
874	**140**	300p. red	25	40
875	**140**	500p. green	25	40
876	**140**	1000p. purple	25	40
877	**140**	3000p. red	25	40

Owing to the collapse of the pengo, the following stamps were overprinted to show the postage rate for which they were valid, and they were sold at the appropriate rate for the day. **Any** or **Nyomtatv** = Sample Post or Printed Matter. **Hlp** or **Helyi lev. lap** = Local Postcard. **Hl** or **Helyi level** = Local Letter. **Tlp** or **Tavolsagi lev.-lap** = Inland Postcard. **Tl** or **Tavolsagi level** = Inland Letter. **Ajl** or **Ajanlas** = Registered Letter. **Cs.** or **Csomag** = Parcel.

1946. Optd as above. (a) First Issue.

878	**126**	"Any. 1" on 1f. grey	15	15
879	-	"Hlp. 1" on 8p. on 20f. bistre on blue (No. 837)		15	15
880	-	"Hl. 1" on 50f. blue (No. 783)		15	15
881	-	"Tlp. 1" on 4f. brown (No. 735)		15	15
882	-	"Tl. 1" on 10f. brown (No. 739)		15	15
883	**133**	"Ajl. 1" on 20f. bistre	15	15
883b	**127**	"Cs. 5-1" on 30f. red (No. 744)		31·00	31·00
884	-	"Cs. 5-1" on 70f. red (No. 784)		15	15
885	-	"Cs. 10-1" on 70f. red (No. 784)		15	15
885a	**127**	"Cs. 10-1" on 80f. brown (No. 747)		50·00	50·00

(b) Second Issue.

886	**126**	"Any. 2" on 1f. grey	25	25
887	-	"Hlp. 2" on 8p. on 20f. bistre on blue (No. 837)		25	25
888	-	"Hl. 2" on 40f. on 10f. brown on blue (No. 825)		25	25
889	-	"Tlp. 2" on 4f. brown (No. 735)		25	25
890	-	"Tl. 2" on 10f. on 4f. brown on blue (No. 800)		25	25
891	-	"Ajl. 2" on 12f. green (No. 740)		25	25
892	-	"Cs. 5-2" on 24f. purple (No. 781)		25	25
893	-	"Cs. 10-2" on 80f. brown (No. 785)		25	25

(c) Third Issue.

894	-	"Nyomtatv. 20gr." on 60f. on 8f. green on yellow (No. 811)		25	25
895	-	"Helyi lev.-lap" on 2f. bistre on blue (as No. 780)		25	25
896	-	"Helyi level" on 10f. brown on blue (as No. 739)		25	25
897	-	"Tavolsagi lev.-lap" on 4f. brown (No. 735)		25	25
898	-	"Tavolsagi level" on 18f. black (No. 741)		25	25
899	-	"Ajanlas" on 24f. purple (No. 781)		25	25
900	-	"Csomag 5 kg" on 2p. on 4f. brown on blue (No. 828)		25	25
901	-	"Csomag 10kg." on 30f. red on blue (as No. 782)		25	25

ez(er) p. = thousand pengos.
m(illio) p. = million pengos.
m.p. (milpengo) = million pengos.
md.p. (milliard. p) = thousand million pengos.
b.p. (billio. p) = million billion pengos.
ez. ap (ezer adopengo) = thousand "tax" pengos.
m. ap. (millio adopengo) = million "tax" pengos.

143

1946. Foundation of Republic.

| 902 | **143** | 3ez. p. brown | 25 | 25 |
| 903 | **143** | 15ez. p. blue | 25 | 25 |

144

1946

904	**144**	4ez. p. brown	25	25
905	**144**	10ez. p. red	25	25
906	**144**	15ez. p. brown	25	25
907	**144**	20ez. p. brown	25	25
908	**144**	30ez. p. purple	25	25
909	**144**	50ez. p. grey	25	25
910	**144**	80ez. p. brown	25	25
911	**144**	100ez. p. red	25	25
912	**144**	160ez. p. green	25	25

913	144	200ez. p. green	25	25
914	144	500ez. p. red	25	25
915	144	640ez. p. olive	25	25
916	144	800ez. p. violet	25	25

145

1946. 75th Anniv of First Hungarian Stamps.

917	145	500+500ez. p. green	3·25	3·50
918	145	1+1m. p. brown	3·25	3·50
919	145	1.5+1.5m. p. red	3·25	3·50
920	145	2+2m. p. blue	3·25	3·50

146

1946

921	146	1m.p. red	40	65
922	146	2m.p. blue	40	65
923	146	3m.p. brown	40	65
924	146	4m.p. grey	40	65
925	146	5m.p. violet	40	65
926	146	10m.p. green	40	65
927	146	20m.p. red	40	65
928	146	50m.p. green	40	65

147
Posthorn
and Arms

1946

929	147	100m.p. red	30	65
930	147	200m.p. red	30	65
931	147	500m.p. red	30	65
932	147	1000m.p. red	30	65
933	147	2000m.p. red	30	65
934	147	3000m.p. red	30	65
935	147	5000m.p. red	30	65
936	147	10,000m.p. red	30	65
937	147	20,000m.p. red	30	65
938	147	30,000m.p. red	30	65
939	147	50,000m.p. red	30	65

148 Posthorn

1946

940	148	100md.p. green and red	40	65
941	148	200md.p. green and red	40	65
942	148	500md.p. green and red	40	65

149 Dove
and Letter

1946

943	149	1b.p. black and red	25	65
944	149	2b.p. black and red	25	65
945	149	5b.p. black and red	25	65
946	149	10b.p. black and red	25	65
947	149	20b.p. black and red	25	65
948	149	50b.p. black and red	25	65
949	149	100b.p. black and red	25	65
950	149	200b.p. black and red	25	65
951	149	500b.p. black and red	25	65
952	149	1000b.p. black and red	25	65
953	149	10,000b.p. black and red	1·10	1·30
954	149	50,000b.p. black and red	1·10	1·30
955	149	100,000b.p. black and red	1·10	1·30
956	149	500,000b.p. black and red	1·10	1·30

150 Locomotive
"Heves", 1846

1946. Centenary of Hungarian Railways.

957	150	10000ap. brown	5·50	5·75
958	-	20000ap. blue	5·50	5·75
959	-	30000ap. green	5·50	5·75
960	-	40000ap. red	5·50	5·75

DESIGNS: 20000ap. Class 424 steam locomotive; 30000ap. Class V44 electric locomotive; 40000ap. *Arpad* diesel railcar, 1935.

151 Posthorn

1946

961	151	5ez. ap. green and black	25	65
962	151	10ez. ap. green and black	25	65
963	151	20ez. ap. green and black	25	65
964	151	50ez. ap. green and black	25	65
965	151	80ez. ap. green and black	25	65
966	151	100ez. ap. green and black	25	65
967	151	200ez. ap. green and black	25	65
968	151	500ez. ap. green and black	25	65
969	151	1m. ap. red and black	65	1·30
970	151	5m. ap. red and black	65	1·30

152 Industry	**153** Agriculture

1946. Currency Reform.

971	152	8fi. brown	25	15
972	152	10fi. brown	25	15
973	152	12fi. brown	25	15
974	152	20fi. brown	25	15
975	152	30fi. brown	25	15
976	152	40fi. brown	25	15
977	152	60fi. brown	25	15
978	153	1fo. green	1·00	15
979	153	1fo. 40 green	1·00	15
980	153	2fo. green	1·90	15
981	153	3fo. green	6·25	15
982	153	5fo. green	1·90	15
983	153	10fo. green	3·75	65

154 Ceres

1946. Agricultural Fair.

984	154	30fi.+60fi. green	7·50	8·75
985	154	60fi.+1fo. 20 red	7·50	8·75
986	154	1fo.+2fo. blue	7·50	8·75

155 Liberty
Bridge

1947. Air. Views.

987	-	10fi. red	25	15
988	-	20fi. grey	25	15
989	155	50fi. brown	65	15
990	-	70fi. green	80	15
991	-	1fo. blue	2·00	15
992	-	1fo. 40 brown	2·00	25
993	-	3fo. green	2·00	25
994	-	5fo. lilac	8·00	2·10

DESIGNS: 10fi. Loyalty Tower, Sopron; 20fi. Esztergom Cathedral; 70fi. Palace Hotel, Lillafured; 1fo. Vajdahunyad Castle, Budapest; 1fo. 40, Visegrad Fortress; 3fo. *Falcone* (racing yacht) on Lake Balaton; 5fo. Parliament Buildings and Kossuth Bridge.

156 Gyorgy
Dozsa

1947. Liberty issue.

995	156	8fi. red	65	15
996	-	10fi. blue	65	15

997	-	12fi. brown	65	15
998	-	20fi. green	95	15
999	-	30fi. brown	95	15
1000	-	40fi. purple	1·20	15
1001	-	60fi. red	1·20	15
1002	-	1fo. blue	1·30	15
1003	-	2fo. violet	2·75	65
1004	-	4fo. green	4·00	95

PORTRAITS: 10fi. A. Budai Nagy; 12fi. T. Esze; 20fi. I. Martinovics; 30fi. J. Batsanyi; 40fi. L. Kossuth; 60fi. M. Tancsics; 1fo. S. Petofi; 2fo. E. Ady; 4fo. A. Jozsef.

157 Doctor
examining X-Ray

1947. Welfare Organizations. Inscr "SIESS! ADJ! SEGITS!" (trans. "Come! Give! Help!").

1005	-	8fi.+50fi. blue	6·00	8·00
1006	157	12fi.+50fi. brown	6·00	8·00
1007	-	20fi.+50fi. green	6·00	8·00
1008	-	60fi.+50fi. red	2·50	1·30

DESIGNS: 8fi. Doctor testing syringe; 20fi. Nurse and child; 60fi. Released prisoner-of-war.

158 Emblem of
Peace

1947. Peace Treaty.

1009	158	60fi. red	80	40

159 Liberty
Statue

1947. 30th Anniv of Soviet Union and Hungarian–Soviet Cultural Society Fund.

1010	-	40fi.+40fi. brn & grn	6·75	6·75
1011	159	60fi.+60fi. grey and red	3·25	3·25
1012	-	1fo.+1fo. black & blue	6·75	6·75

PORTRAITS: 40fi. Lenin; 1fo. Stalin.

161 Savings Bank

1947. Savings Day. Inscr "TAKAREKOS JELENBOLDOG JOVO".

1013	-	40fi. red (beehive)	65	25
1014	161	60fi. red	65	25

162 16th-century Mail
Coach

1947. Stamp Day.

1015	162	30fi. (+ 50fi.) brown	14·50	14·50

165 Arms of
Hungary

1948. Centenary of Insurrection.

1016	-	8fi. red	25	15
1017	-	10fi. blue	25	15
1018	-	12fi. brown	40	15
1019	-	20fi. green	80	15
1020	-	30fi. brown	40	15
1021	-	40fi. purple	40	15
1022	-	60fi. red	1·60	15
1023	165	1fo. blue	1·60	15

1024	165	2fo. brown	3·25	40
1025	165	3fo. olive	4·00	80
1026	165	4fo. red	6·75	1·30

DESIGNS—HORIZ: 8fi., 40fi. Hungarian independence flag; 10fi. Printing press; 12fi. Latticed window; 20fi. Shako, trumpet and sword; 30fi., 60fi. Slogan.

167 Johann Gutenberg

1948. Air. Explorers and Inventors.

1027	167	1fi. red	40	40
1028	-	2fi. mauve	40	40
1029	-	4fi. blue	40	40
1030	-	5fi. brown	55	55
1031	-	6fi. green	55	55
1032	-	8fi. purple	55	55
1033	-	10fi. brown	65	65
1034	-	12fi. green	65	65
1035	-	30fi. red	2·30	2·30
1036	-	40fi. violet	2·75	2·75

PORTRAITS: 2fi. Christopher Columbus; 4fi. Robert Fulton; 5fi. George Stephenson; 6fi. David Schwarz and Count Ferdinand von Zeppelin; 8fi. Thomas Edison; 10fi. Louis Bleriot; 12fi. Roald Amundsen; 30fi. Kalman Kando; 40fi. Alexander Popov.

168 Chain Bridge,
Budapest

1948. Air. Re-opening of Budapest Chain Bridge. Sheets 74×65 mm.

MS1036a		2fo.+18fo. Red	£160	£160
MS1036b	168	3fo.+18fo. blue	£160	£160

DESIGN: 20fo. Shows a more distant view of the bridge.

169 Lorand Eotvos

1948. Birth Centenary of L. Eotvos (physicist).

1037	169	60fi. red	2·00	65

170 William Shakespeare

1948. Air. Writers.

1038	170	1fi. blue	40	40
1039	-	2fi. red	40	40
1040	-	4fi. green	40	40
1041	-	5fi. mauve	55	55
1042	-	6fi. blue	55	55
1043	-	8fi. brown	55	55
1044	-	10fi. red	65	65
1045	-	12fi. violet	65	65
1046	-	30fi. brown	2·30	2·30
1047	-	40fi. brown	2·75	2·75

PORTRAITS: 2fi. Voltaire; 4fi. Goethe; 5fi. Byron; 6fi. Victor Hugo; 8fi. Edgar Allan Poe; 10fi. Petofi; 12fi. Mark Twain; 30fi. Tolstoy; 40fi. Gorki.

171 Globe and
Pigeon

1948. Fifth National Philatelic Exhibition.

1048	171	30fi. blue	8·00	8·00

Sold at 1fo.30 (incl 1fo. entrance fee).

172 Symbolizing
Industry,
Agriculture and
Culture

1948. 17th Trades' Union Congress.

1049	172	30fi. red	1·30	1·30

173 Agricultural Worker

1949. International Women's Day.
| 1050 | **173** | 60fi.+60fi. mauve | 2·75 | 2·75 |

174 Reproduction of T **32**

1949. 30th Anniv of Bolshevist Regime.
| 1051 | **174** | 40fi. brown and red | 65 | 65 |
| 1052 | – | 60fi. olive and red | 65 | 65 |
DESIGN: 60fi. Reproduction of No. 325.

175 Pushkin holding Torch and Scroll

1949. 150th Birth Anniv of A. S. Pushkin (poet).
| 1053 | **175** | 1fo.+1fo. red | 13·50 | 13·50 |
MS1053a 52×62 mm. 1fo.+1fo. Red | 20·00 | 20·00 |
DESIGN—HORIZ: No. **MS**1053a, Puhkin writing.

176 Symbolising Workers of Five Continents

1949. Second World Federation of Trade Unions Congress, Milan. Flag in red.
1054	**176**	30fi. brown	4·75	4·75
1055	**176**	40fi. purple	4·75	4·75
1056	**176**	60fi. red	4·75	4·75
1057	**176**	1fo. blue	4·75	4·75

177 Sandor Petofi

1949. Death Centenary of Petofi (poet).
1058	**177**	40fi. purple	95	55
1059	**177**	60fi. red	65	25
1060	**177**	1fo. blue	80	40
1096	**177**	40fi. brown	95	55
1098	**177**	1fo. green	80	55

178 Heads and Globe

1949. World Youth Festival, Budapest.
1061	**178**	20fi. brown	1·60	1·60
1062	–	30fi. green	2·00	2·00
1063	–	40fi. bistre	2·75	2·75
1064	–	60fi. red	2·75	2·75
1065	–	1fo. blue	3·50	3·50
MS1065a 100×130 mm. Nos. 1061/5, but colours changed | 60·00 | 60·00 |
DESIGNS: 30fi. Three clenched fists; 40fi. Man breaking chains; 60fi. Young people and banner; 1fo. Workers and tractor.

179 Hungarian Coat-of-Arms

1949. Ratification of Constitution. Arms in blue, brown, red and green.
1066A	**179**	20fi. green	2·00	95
1067B	**179**	60fi. red	1·60	65
1068B	**179**	1fo. blue	1·70	65

181 Globes and Posthorn

1949. 75th Anniv of U.P.U.
1069	**181**	60fi. red (postage)	95	95
1070	**181**	1fo. blue	95	95
1071	–	2fo. brown (air)	2·00	2·00
MS1072 128×98 mm. 3fo. (×4) brown and red | £750 | £750 |
DESIGN: 2, 3fo. Lisunov Li-2 airplane replaces posthorn.

182 Chain Bridge

1949. Centenary of Budapest Chain Bridge.
1073	**182**	40fi. green (postage)	95	65
1074	**182**	60fi. brown	95	65
1075	**182**	1fo. blue	95	65
1076	**182**	1fo.60 red (air)	2·00	1·30
1077	**182**	2fo. olive	2·00	1·30
MS1077a 136×100 mm. 50 fo. Lilac | £600 | £600 |
DESIGN—VERT: 50fo. Drawing board, plans, etc.

183 Postman and Forms of Transport

1949. Air. Stamp Day.
| 1078 | **183** | 50fi. grey | 10·00 | 10·00 |

184 Joseph Stalin

1949. Stalin's 70th Birthday.
1079	**184**	60fi. red	1·30	55
1080	**184**	1fo. blue	2·00	80
1081	**184**	2fo. brown	2·75	1·60

185 Miners

1950. Five Year Plan.
1082B	**185**	8fi. grey	1·30	15
1083B	–	10fi. purple	65	15
1084B	–	12fi. red	65	15
1085B	–	20fi. green	65	15
1086B	–	30fi. purple	80	15
1087B	–	40fi. brown	1·60	15
1088B	–	60fi. red	1·60	15
1089B	–	1fo. violet and yellow	2·00	15
1090B	–	1fo.70 green and yellow	3·25	15
1091B	–	2fo. red and orange	4·00	45
1092B	–	3fo. blue and buff	4·25	55
1093B	–	4fo. green and orange	4·75	65
1094B	–	5fo. purple and yellow	8·00	1·90
1095B	–	10fo. brown and yellow	10·00	4·75
DESIGNS: 10fi. Iron foundry; 12fi. Power station; 20fi. Textiles; 30fi. Factory workers' entertainment; 40fi. Mechanical farming; 60fi. Village co-operative office; 1fo. Class 303 steam locomotive on bridge; 1fo.70, Family at health resort; 2fo. Soldier and tank; 3fo. Freighter and Lisunov Li-2 airplane; 4fo. Cattle; 5fo. Draughtsman and factory; 10fo. Sportsman, woman and football match.

186 Philatelic Museum

1950. 20th Anniv of P.O. Philatelic Museum.
| 1099 | **186** | 60fi. brown and black (postage) | 13·50 | 13·50 |
| 1100 | – | 2fo. red and yellow (air) | 16·00 | 16·00 |
DESIGN—HORIZ: 2fo. Globe, coach, Douglas DC-4 airliner and stamps.

188 Family Greeting Soviet Troops

1950. Fifth Anniv of Liberation.
1101	**188**	40fi. black	2·00	1·30
1102	**188**	60fi. lake	1·30	25
1103	**188**	1fo. blue	1·30	65
1104	**188**	2fo. brown	2·00	95

189 Chess Match

1950. First International Candidates Chess Tournament, Budapest. Designs incorporate rook and chessboard.
1105	**189**	60fi. mauve (postage)	3·25	95
1106	–	1fo. blue	6·75	2·00
1107	–	1fo.60 brown (air)	10·00	3·50
DESIGNS: 1fo. Trade Union Building; 1fo.60, Map.

190 Workers and Star

1950. May Day. Inscr as in T **190**.
1108	**190**	40fi. brown	3·50	1·30
1109	–	60fi. red	1·60	25
1110	**190**	1fo. blue	3·00	95
DESIGN: 60fi. Two workers.

191 Workers and Flag

1950. World Federation of Trade Unions Congress, Budapest.
1111	**191**	40fi. green (postage)	3·50	1·30
1112	**191**	60fi. red	1·60	35
1113	–	1fo. brown (air)	3·00	95
DESIGNS: 40fi. Statue, dove and globes; 1fo. Globes, Chain Bridge and Parliament Buildings.

192 Baby and Nursery

1950. Children's Day.
1114	**192**	20fi. brown and grey	2·75	2·30
1115	–	30fi. mauve and brown	1·10	40
1116	–	40fi. green and blue	1·10	40
1117	–	60fi. red and brown	£1600	£1600
1117a	–	60fi. red and brown	1·10	40
1118	–	1fo.70 blue and green	2·30	1·30
DESIGNS: 30fi. Baby boy and holiday scene; 40fi. Schoolgirl and classroom; 60fi. Pioneer boy and camp; 1fo.70, Pioneer boy and girl and model glider class.
No. 1117 is inscr "UTANPOTLASUNK A JOVO HARCAIHOZ" and No. 1117a is inscr "SZABAD HAZABAN BOLDOG IFJUSAG".

193 Workers and Globe

1950. First Congress of Young Workers, Budapest.
| 1119 | **193** | 20fi. green | 1·60 | 80 |

1120	–	30fi. orange	40	25
1121	–	40fi. brown	40	25
1122	–	60fi. mauve	1·10	40
1123	–	1fo.70 green	3·00	95
DESIGNS—HORIZ: 30fi. Foundry worker and cauldron. VERT: 40fi. Man, woman and banner; 60fi. Workers, banner and Liberty Statue; 1fo.70, Three workers and banner.

194 Peonies

1950. Flowers.
1124	**194**	30fi. purple and green	1·90	65
1125	–	40fi. green, yellow & mve	1·90	75
1126	–	60fi. brown, yellow & grn	3·25	1·00
1127	–	1fo. violet, red and green	6·25	4·50
1128	–	1fo.70 violet, grn & lilac	6·00	2·75
DESIGNS: 40fi. Pasque flowers; 60fi. Yellow pheasant's-eye; 1fo. Geranium; 1fo.70, Campanulas.

195 Miner

1950. Second National Inventions Exhibition.
1129	**195**	40fi. brown	2·50	75
1130	–	60fi. red	2·10	65
1131	–	1fo. blue	3·25	1·40
DESIGNS: 60fi. Turner; 1fo. Building factory.

196 Liberty Statue

1950. Air.
1132	**196**	20fi. red	25	15
1133	–	30fi. violet	25	15
1134	–	70fi. purple	65	15
1135	–	1fo. brown	65	15
1136	–	1fo.60 blue	1·30	15
1137	–	2fo. red	1·50	15
1138	–	3fo. black	1·90	15
1139	–	5fo. blue	3·25	90
1140	–	10fo. brown	9·50	1·50
1140a	–	20fo. green	19·00	8·25
DESIGNS—VERT: 30fi. Crane and buildings; 70fi. Diosgyor steelworks; 1fo. "Stalinyec" tractor; 1fo.60, "Szeged" (freighter); 2fo. Combine harvester; 3fo. Class 303 steam locomotive; 5fo. Matyas Rakosi steel-mill; 10, 20fo. Lisunov Li-2 airplane at Budaors airport.
For No. 1139 but on silver paper see No. 1437.

198 Worker signing Peace Petition

1950. Peace Propaganda.
1141	**198**	40fi. brown and blue	16·00	16·00
1142	–	60fi. green and orange	3·75	3·75
1143	–	1fo. brown and green	16·00	16·00
DESIGNS—VERT: 60fi. Girl holding dove. HORIZ: 1fo. Soldier, mother and children.

199 Swimmers

1950.
1144	**199**	10fi. blue and light blue (postage)	15	15
1145	–	20fi. brown and orange	15	15
1146	–	1fo. green and olive	1·30	90
1147	–	1fo.70 red and vermilion	1·90	1·50
1148	–	2fo. violet and brown	3·75	2·10
1149	–	30fi. mauve & violet (air)	65	25
1150	–	40fi. blue and green	1·30	25
1151	–	60fi. orange, brown & grn	1·90	65
1152	–	70fi. brown and grey	2·50	90
1153	–	3fo. chestnut and brown	5·75	2·10

DESIGNS—POSTAGE: 20fi. Vaulting; 1fo. Mountaineering; 1fo.70, Basketball; 2fo. Motor cycling. AIR: 30fi. Volleyball; 40fi. Throwing the javelin; 60fi. Emblem of "Ready for work and action" movement; 70fi. Football; 3fo. Gliding.

200 Jozef Bem and Battle of Piski

1950. Death Centenary of Gen. Bem.

1154	200	40fi. brown	1·50	65
1155	200	60fi. red	1·50	65
1156	200	1fo. blue	3·25	90
MS1156a 98×78 mm. 200 2fo. (+2fo.) purple. Imperf			65·00	65·00

201 Workers and Soldier

1951. Second Hungarian Communist Party Congress.

1157	201	10fi. green	65	25
1158	-	30fi. brown	90	65
1159	-	60fi. red	1·30	90
1160	-	1fo. blue	2·10	1·30

DESIGNS—HORIZ: 30fi. Workers, soldier and banner; 60fi. Portrait and four workers with flags. VERT: 1fo. Procession with banner.

202 Flags

1951. Hungarian–Soviet Amity. Inscr "MAGYAR SZOVJET BARATSAG HONAPJA 1951".

1161	202	60fi. red	65	25
1162	-	1fo. violet	1·30	65

DESIGN: 1fo. Hungarian and Russian workers.

203 Mare and Foal

1951. Livestock Expansion Plan.

1163	203	10fi. brown and ochre (postage)	40	25
1164	-	30fi. brown and red	65	65
1165	-	40fi. brown and green	90	65
1166	-	60fi. brown and orange	1·30	90
1167	203	20fi. brown & green (air)	50	40
1168	-	70fi. ochre and brown	1·30	1·00
1169	-	1fo. brown and blue	5·00	2·10
1170	-	1fo.60 chestnut & brown	8·75	3·25

DESIGNS: 30, 70fi. Sow and litter; 40fi., 1fo. Ewe and lamb; 60fi., 1fo.60, Cow and calf.

204 Worker

1951. May Day. Inscr "1951 MAJUS".

1171	204	40fi. brown	1·40	1·30
1172	-	60fi. red	1·30	25
1173	-	1fo. blue	1·30	90

DESIGNS—VERT: 60fi. People with banners. HORIZ: 1fo. Labour Day rally.

205 Leo Frankel **206** Street-fighting

1951. 80th Anniv of Paris Commune.

1174	205	60fi. brown	1·30	25
1175	206	1fo. blue and red	1·90	65

207 Children's Heads

1951. Int Children's Day. Inscr "NEMZETKOZI GYERMEKNAP 1951".

1176	207	30fi. brown	65	25
1177	-	40fi. green	90	25
1178	-	50fi. brown	90	65
1179	-	60fi. mauve	1·30	65
1180	-	1fo.70 blue	1·90	1·90

DESIGNS: 40fi. Flying model airplane; 50fi. Diesel train on Budapest Pioneer Railway; 60fi. Chemistry experiment; 1fo.70, Blowing bugle.

208 Ganz Wagon Works

1951. Rebuilding Plan (1st series).

1180a		8fi. green	90	15
1180b		10fi. violet	90	15
1180c		12fi. red	90	15
1181	208	20fi. green	90	25
1182	-	30fi. orange	1·10	25
1183	-	40fi. brown	1·10	25
1183a	-	50fi. blue	1·30	25
1184	-	60fi. red	1·50	25
1184a	-	70fi. brown	1·90	25
1184b	-	80fi. purple	1·90	25
1185	-	1fo. blue	2·50	25
1185a	-	1fo.20 red	3·25	25
1185b	-	1fo.70 blue	2·10	25
1185c	-	2fo. green	2·10	25
1186	-	3fo. purple	3·75	25
1186a	-	4fo. olive	4·00	40
1186b	-	5fo. black	6·25	40

BUILDINGS: 8fi. Stalin School; 10fi. Szekesfehervar railway station; 12fi. Ujpest medical dispensary; 30fi. Flats; 40fi. Central Railway Station, Budapest; 50fi. Inota power station; 60fi. Matyas Rakosi Cultural Institute; 70fi. Hajdunanas grain elevator; 80fi. Tiszalok dam; 1fo. Kilian Road School; 1fo.20, Mining Apprentices Institute, Ajkacsingervolgy; 1fo.70, Iron and Steel Apprentices Institute, Csepel; 2fo. Cultural Centre, Hungarian Optical Works; 3fo. Building Workers' Union Headquarters; 4fo. Miners' Union Headquarters; 5fo. Flats.

See also Nos. 1296/1304.

209 Gorky

1951. 15th Death Anniv of Maksim Gorky (Russian writer).

1187	209	60fi. red	40	25
1188	209	1fo. blue	75	40
1189	209	2fo. purple	2·50	1·30

210 Engineers and Tractors

1951. First Anniv of Five Year Plan.

1190	210	20fi. sepia (postage)	25	25
1191	-	30fi. blue	40	30
1192	-	40fi. red	90	40
1193	-	60fi. brown	1·00	40
1194	-	70fi. brown (air)	1·40	65
1195	-	1fo. green	1·50	90
1196	-	2fo. purple	2·10	1·30

DESIGNS: 30fi. Doctor X-raying patient; 40fi. Workman instructing apprentices; 60fi. Girl driving tractor; 70fi. Electrical engineers constructing pylon; 1fo. Young people and recreation home; 2fo. Lisunov Li-2 airplane over Stalin (later Arpad) Bridge.

211 1871 Stamp without portrait and Hungarian Arms

1951. 80th Anniv of First Hungarian Postage Stamp.

1197	211	60fi. green	3·75	3·75
1198	211	1fo.+1fo. red	19·00	19·00
1199	211	2fo.+2fo. blue	21·00	21·00
MS1199a Air. Three sheets each 78×97 mm. Nos. 1197/9 Set of 3 sheets			£275	£275

212 Soldiers Parading

1951. Army Day.

1200	212	1fo. brown (postage)	2·10	40
1201	-	60fi. blue (air)	1·30	40

DESIGN—VERT: 60fi. Tanks and Liberty Statue.

213 Lily of the Valley

1951. Flowers.

1202		30fi. violet, blue and green	65	25
1203	213	40fi. myrtle and green	2·10	1·00
1204	-	60fi. red, pink and green	1·50	65
1205	-	1fo. blue, red and green	2·50	1·30
1206	-	1fo.70 brown, yell & grn	5·75	3·75

FLOWERS: 30fi. Cornflowers; 60fi. Tulips; 1fo. Poppies; 1fo.70, Cowslips.

214 Revolutionaries and Flags

1951. 34th Anniv of Russian Revolution.

1207	214	40fi. green	1·50	90
1208	-	60fi. blue	1·30	65
1209	-	1fo. red	1·50	90

DESIGNS: 60fi. Lenin addressing revolutionaries; 1fo. Lenin and Stalin.

215 Parade before Stalin Statue

1951. Stalin's 72nd Birthday.

1210	215	60fi. red	2·30	1·00
1211	215	1fo. blue	2·30	1·00

216 Bolshoi State Theatre, Moscow

1952. Views of Moscow.

1212	216	60fi. lake and green	75	25
1213	-	1fo. brown and red	1·10	50
1214	-	1fo.60 olive and lake	1·90	1·00

DESIGNS: 1fo. Lenin Mausoleum; 1fo.60, Kremlin.

217 Rakosi and Peasants **218** Rakosi

1952. 60th Birth Anniv of Rakosi.

1215	217	60fi. purple	1·30	65
1216	218	1fo. brown	1·30	65
1217	-	2fo. blue	3·25	1·30

DESIGN: 2fo. Rakosi and foundry workers.

219 L. Kossuth

1952. Heroes of 1848 Revolution.

1218	219	20fi. green	25	25
1219	-	30fi. purple (Petofi)	40	25
1220	-	50fi. black (Bem)	75	40
1221	-	60fi. lake (Tancsics)	90	40
1222	-	1fo. blue (Damjanich)	1·00	65
1223	-	1fo.50 brown (Nagy)	1·30	1·30

220 Pied Avocet

1952. Air. Birds.

1224	220	20fi. black and green	25	15
1225	-	20fi. black and green	25	15
1226	-	40fi. black, yellow & brn	40	25
1227	-	50fi. black and orange	50	25
1228	-	60fi. black and red	75	40
1229	-	70fi. black, orange & red	90	50
1230	-	80fi. black, yellow & grn	1·30	65
1231	-	1fo. black, red and blue	1·50	75
1232	-	1fo.40 multicoloured	1·50	75
1233	-	1fo.60 black, grn & brn	2·10	1·10
1234	-	2fo.50 black and purple	4·50	1·90

DESIGNS: 30fi. White stork; 40fi. Golden oriole; 50fi. Kentish plover; 60fi. Black-winged stilt; 70fi. Lesser grey strike; 80fi. Great bustard; 1fo. Western red-footed falcon; 1fo.40, European bee eater; 1fo.60, Glossy ibis; 2fo.50, Great egret.

1952. Budapest Philatelic Exn. No. 1050 with bars obliterating inscription and premium.

1235	173	60fi. mauve	75·00	75·00

222 Drummer and Flags

1952. May Day. Inscr "1952 MAJUS I".

1236	222	40fi. red and green	2·50	1·00
1237	-	60fi. red and brown	1·90	1·00
1238	-	1fo. red and brown	1·90	1·00

DESIGNS: 60fi. Workers; 1fo. Workman and globe.

223 Running

1952. 15th Olympic Games, Helsinki.

1239	223	30fi. brown (postage)	1·00	25
1240	-	40fi. green	1·00	25
1241	-	60fi. red	1·50	25
1242	-	1fo. blue	2·50	50
1243	-	1fo.70 orange (air)	3·25	1·90
1244	-	2fo. brown	3·75	2·00

DESIGNS: 40fi. Swimming; 60fi. Fencing; 1fo. Gymnastics; 1fo.70, Throwing the hammer; 2fo. Stadium.

224 Leonardo da Vinci

1952. Air. 500th Birth Anniv of Leonardo da Vinci and 150th Birth Anniv of Victor Hugo.

1245	224	1fo.60 blue	1·50	90
1246	-	2fo. purple (Victor Hugo)	2·50	1·50

225 Train and Railwayman

1952. Railway Day. Inscr "1952 VIII 10".

1247	225	60fi. brown	1·50	65
1248	-	1fo. green	2·10	65

DESIGN: 1fo. Railway tracks.

226 Mechanical
Coal-cutter

1952. Miners' Day. Inscr as in T **226**.
| 1249 | **226** | 60fi. brown | 1·50 | 40 |
| 1250 | - | 1fo. green | 2·10 | 65 |

DESIGN: 1fo. Miners operating machinery.

227 L. Kossuth

1952. 150th Birth Anniv of Kossuth (statesman).
1251	**227**	40fi. olive on pink	1·50	40
1252	-	60fi. black on blue	65	40
1253	**227**	1fo. lilac on yellow	1·50	90

DESIGN: 60fi. Statue of Kossuth.

228 Gy Dozsa

1952. Army Day. Inscr as T **228**.
1254		20fi. lilac (J. Hunyadi)	40	15
1255		30fi. green (T **228**)	40	15
1256		40fi. blue (M. Zrinyi)	40	15
1257		60fi. purple (I. Zrinyi)	75	65
1258		1fo. turquoise (B. Vak)	1·30	65
1259		1fo.50 brown (A. Stromfeld)	2·50	90

229 Boy, Girl and Stamp
Exhibition

1952. Air. Stamp Day. Inscr "XXV. BELYEGNAP 1952".
| 1260 | | 1fo.+1fo. blue | 12·50 | 12·50 |
| 1261 | **229** | 2fo.+2fo. red | 12·50 | 12·50 |

DESIGN: 1fo. Children examining stamps.

230 Lenin and
Revolutionary Council

1952. 35th Anniv of Russian Revolution.
1262	**230**	40fi. olive and purple	2·50	65
1263	-	60fi. olive and black	1·30	25
1264	-	1fo. olive and red	2·50	65

DESIGNS: 60fi. Stalin and Cossacks; 1fo. Marx, Engels, Lenin, Stalin and Spassky Tower.

231 Harvester

1952. Third Hungarian Peace Congress. Inscr as in T 231.
| 1265 | **231** | 60fi. red on yellow | 1·30 | 25 |
| 1266 | - | 1fo. brown on green | 1·30 | 65 |

DESIGN—HORIZ: 1fo. Workers' discussion group.

232 Tunnel Construction

1953. Budapest Underground Railway. Inscr "BUDAPESTI FOLDALATTI GYORSVASUT".
| 1267 | **232** | 60fi. green | 1·90 | 65 |
| 1268 | - | 1fo. lake | 1·90 | 90 |

DESIGN—HORIZ: 1fo. Underground map and station.

233 Russian Flag and
Tank

1953. Tenth Anniv of Battle of Stalingrad.
| 1269 | **233** | 40fi. red | 1·90 | 25 |
| 1270 | - | 60fi. brown | 1·90 | 90 |

DESIGN: 60fi. Soldier, map and flags.

234 Eurasian
Red Squirrel

1953. Air. Forest Animals.
1271	**234**	20fi. brown and olive	40	25
1272	-	30fi. sepia and brown	50	40
1273	-	40fi. sepia and green	55	50
1274	-	50fi. sepia and brown	75	65
1275	-	60fi. brown and turquoise	1·00	75
1276	-	70fi. brown and olive	1·10	90
1277	-	80fi. brown and green	1·50	1·30
1278	-	1fo. brown and green	2·00	1·50
1279	-	1fo.50 black and bistre	4·25	2·10
1280	-	2fo. sepia and brown	4·50	2·50

DESIGNS—HORIZ: 30fi. West European hedgehog; 40fi. Brown hare; 60fi. European otter; 70fi. Red fox; 1fo. Roe deer; 1fo.50, Wild boar. VERT: 50fi. Beech marten; 80fi. Fallow deer; 2fo. Red deer.

235 Stalin

1953. Death of Stalin.
| 1281 | **235** | 60fi. black | 65 | 40 |
| **MS**1281a 51×72 mm. 2fo. purple (T **235**) | | | 50·00 | 50·00 |

236 Rest Home,
Galyateto

1953. Workers' Rest Homes.
1282	**236**	30fi. brown (postage)	25	15
1283	-	40fi. blue	35	15
1284	-	50fi. ochre	40	25
1285	-	60fi. green	50	25
1286	-	70fi. red	65	40
1287	-	1fo. turquoise (air)	90	50
1288	-	1fo.50 purple	1·30	65

DESIGNS: 40fi. Terrace, Mecsek; 50fi. Parad Spa; 60fi. Sports field, Kekes; 70fi. Balaton-fured Spa; 1fo. Children paddling at Balaton; 1fo.50, Lillafured Rest Home.

237 Young
People and
Banners

1953. May Day.
| 1289 | **237** | 60fi. brown & red on yell | 1·30 | 40 |

238 Karl Marx

1953. 70th Death Anniv of Karl Marx.
| 1290 | **238** | 1fo. black on pink | 1·30 | 40 |

See also No. 2354.

239 Peasants and Flag

1953. 250th Anniv of Rakoczi Rebellion.
1291	**239**	20fi. orange & grn on grn	1·30	90
1292	-	30fi. orange and purple	1·50	1·30
1293	-	40fi. orange & blue on pk	1·90	1·50
1294	-	60fi. orange & grn on yell	3·25	2·50
1295	-	1fo. red & brown on yell	4·50	3·25

DESIGNS: 30fi. Drummer and insurgents; 40fi. Battle scene; 60fi. Cavalryman attacking soldier; 1fo. Ferenc Rakoczi II.

1953. Rebuilding Plan (2nd series). As T **208**.
1296		8fi. green	40	15
1297		10fi. lilac	65	15
1298		12fi. red	1·30	15
1299a		20fi. green	2·50	25
1300		30fi. orange	1·30	15
1301		40fi. brown	1·90	15
1302		50fi. blue	1·90	15
1303a		60fi. red	5·00	25
1304		70fi. brown	2·50	25

BUILDINGS: 8fi. Day nursery, Ozd; 10fi. Nursing school, Szombathely; 12fi. Workers houses, Komlo; 20fi. Department store, Ujpest; 30fi. Factory, Maly; 40fi. General Hospital, Fovaros; 50fi. Gymnasium, Sztalinvaros; 60fi. Post Office, Csepel; 70fi. Blast-furnace, Diosgyor.

240 Cycling

1953. Opening of People's Stadium. Budapest. Inscr "1953 NEPSTADION".
1313	**240**	20fi. brown and orange (postage)	15	15
1314	-	30fi. brown and green	15	15
1315	-	40fi. brown and blue	25	15
1316	-	50fi. brown and olive	30	15
1317	-	60fi. brown and yellow	40	15
1318	-	80fi. brown & turq (air)	65	25
1319	-	1fo. brown and purple	90	40
1320	-	2fo. brown and green	2·10	1·30
1321	-	3fo. brown and red	3·25	1·30
1322	-	5fo. turquoise and brown	5·00	3·25

DESIGNS: 30fi. Swimming; 40fi. Gymnastics; 50fi. Throwing the discus; 60fi. Wrestling; 80fi. Water polo; 1fo. Boxing; 2fo. Football; 3fo. Running; 5fo. Stadium.

241 Kazar

1953. Provincial Costumes.
1323	**241**	20fi. green	1·90	65
1324	-	30fi. brown	2·50	65
1325	-	40fi. blue	3·25	65
1326	-	60fi. red	4·50	2·50
1327	-	1fo. turquoise	5·00	2·50
1328	-	1fo.70 green	6·25	3·75
1329	-	2fo. red	10·00	5·00
1330	-	2fo.50 purple	12·50	10·00

PROVINCES: 30fi. Ersekcsanad; 40fi. Kalocsa; 60fi. Sioagard; 1fo. Sarkoz; 1fo.70, Boldog; 2fo. Orhalom; 2fo.50, Hosszuheteny.

242 Postwoman
Delivering Letters

1953. Stamp Day.
| 1331 | **242** | 1fo.+1fo. turquoise | 6·25 | 6·25 |
| 1332 | **242** | 2fo.+2fo. lilac | 6·25 | 6·25 |

1953. Air. Hungarian Football Team's Victory at Wembley. No. 1320 optd **LONDON-WEMBLEY 1953. XI 25. 6:3**.
| 1333 | | 2fo. brown and green | 35·00 | 31·00 |

244 Bihari

1953. Air. Hungarian Composers.
1334	**244**	30fi. grey and brown	40	25
1335	-	40fi. orange and brown (Erkel)	50	30
1336	-	60fi. green & brn (Liszt)	65	40
1337	-	70fi. red and brown (Mosonyi)	75	50
1338	-	80fi. blue and brown (Goldmark)	90	65
1339	-	1fo. bistre and brown (Bartok)	1·30	1·00
1340	-	2fo. lilac and brown (Kodaly)	2·10	1·90

245 Lenin

1954. 30th Death Anniv of Lenin.
1341	**245**	40fi. green	1·90	1·30
1342	-	60fi. brown	2·50	65
1343	-	1fo. lake	3·75	65

DESIGNS: 60fi. Lenin addressing meeting; 1fo. Profile portrait of Lenin.

246 Turnip
Beetle

1954. Air. Insects.
1344	**246**	30fi. brown and orange	55	40
1345	-	40fi. brown and green	65	50
1346	-	50fi. black and red	90	70
1347	-	60fi. brown, yell & lilac	1·00	75
1348	-	80fi. claret, purple & grn	1·40	1·10
1349	-	1fo. black and brown	1·60	1·30
1350	-	1fo.20 brown and green	1·90	1·50
1351	-	1fo.50 dp brown & brn	2·50	1·90
1352	-	2fo. brown and chestnut	3·25	2·50
1353	-	3fo. brown and green	4·75	3·25

INSECTS—HORIZ: 40fi. Crawling cockchafer; 50fi. Longhorn beetle; 60fi. Hornet; 1fo.20, European field cricket; 1fo.50, European rhinoceros beetle; 2fo. Stag beetle. VERT: 80fi. Apple beetle; 1fo. Corn beetle; 3fo. Great silver water beetle.

247 Mother and Baby

1954. Child Welfare.
1354		30fi. blue (postage)	40	20
1355	**247**	40fi. bistre	65	25
1356	-	60fi. lilac	90	40
1357	-	1fo. green (air)	1·50	65
1358	-	1fo.50 red	2·10	75
1359	-	2fo. turquoise	3·75	1·90

DESIGNS: 30fi. Woman having blood-test; 60fi. Doctor examining child; 1fo. Children in creche; 1fo.50, Doctor, mother and child; 2fo. Children in nursery school.

248 Worker and Flag

1954. 35th Anniv of Proclamation of Hungarian Soviet Republic.

1360		40fi. blue and red	2·50	2·30
1361	**248**	60fi. brown and red	6·25	3·75
1362	-	1fo. black and red	8·75	5·00

DESIGNS—HORIZ: 40fi. Worker reading book; 1fo. Soldier with rifle.

249 Maypole

1954. May Day. Inscr "1954-MAJUS I".

1363	**249**	40fi. olive	65	15
1364	-	60fi. red	65	25

DESIGN: 60fi. Worker and flag.

250 Agricultural Worker

1954. Third Hungarian Communist Party Congress, Budapest.

1365	**250**	60fi. red on yellow	1·00	50

251 Boy building Model Glider

1954. Air.

1366	**251**	40fi. grey and brown	40	20
1367	-	50fi. brown and grey	45	25
1368	-	60fi. grey and brown	50	30
1369	-	80fi. brown and violet	55	40
1370	-	1fo. grey and brown	65	50
1371	-	1fo.20 brown and green	90	65
1372	-	1fo.50 grey and purple	2·50	
1373	-	2fo. brown and blue	3·25	2·10

DESIGNS—As Type **251**: 60fi. Gliders; 1fo. Parachutists; 1fo.50, Lisunov Li-2 airplane. 43×43 mm; 50fi. Boy flying model airplane; 80fi. Libis KB-6T Matajur aircraft and hangar; 1fo.20, Letov C-4 biplane; 2fo. Mikoyan Gurevich MiG-15 jet fighters.

252 Hungarian National Museum

1954. Fifth Anniv of Constitution.

1374	**252**	40fi. blue	2·10	1·30
1375	-	60fi. brown	1·90	75
1376	-	1fo. brown	2·10	1·00

DESIGNS: 60fi. Hungarian Coat of Arms; 1fo. Dome of Parliament Buildings, Budapest.

253 Paprika

1954. Fruit. Multicoloured.

1377	**253**	40fi. Type **253**	95	35
1378	-	50fi. Tomatoes	95	35
1379	-	60fi. Grapes	95	35
1380	-	80fi. Apricots	1·10	50
1381	-	1fo. Apples	1·40	60
1382	-	1fo.20 Plums	2·10	1·20
1383	-	1fo.50 Cherries	4·25	2·40
1384	-	2fo. Peaches	6·00	3·00

254 M. Jokai

1954. 50th Death Anniv of Jokai (novelist).

1385	**254**	60fi. green	1·30	65
1386	**254**	1fo. purple	2·50	1·90

255 C. J. Apacai

1954. Hungarian Scientists.

1387	**255**	8fi. black on yellow	15	15
1388	-	10fi. lake on pink	15	15
1389	-	12fi. black on blue	15	15
1390	-	20fi. brown on yellow	15	15
1391	-	30fi. blue on pink	25	15
1392	-	40fi. green on yellow	30	15
1393	-	50fi. brown on green	40	20
1394	-	60fi. blue on pink	50	25
1395	-	1fo. olive	80	25
1396	-	1fo.70 red on yellow	1·30	40
1397	-	2fo. turquoise	2·00	50

PORTRAITS: 10fi. S. Korosi Csoma; 12fi. A. Jedlik; 20fi. I. Semmelweis; 30fi. J. Irinyi; 40fi. F. Koranyi; 50fi. A. Vambery; 60fi. K. Than; 1fo. O. Herman; 1fo.70, T. Puskas; 2fo. E. Hogyes.

256 Speed Skaters

1955. Air. Winter Sports.

1398		40fi. brown, blue & black	1·00	40
1399		50fi. red, green and brown	1·00	40
1400		60fi. red, blue and brown	1·30	65
1401		80fi. green, brown & blk	1·60	65
1402		1fo. red, blue and brown	2·50	1·30
1403	**256**	1fo.20 red, green & blk	2·50	1·90
1404		1fo.50 red, green & brn	3·75	2·30
1405		2fo. red, green and brown	4·00	2·50

DESIGNS—VERT: 40fi. Boys on toboggan; 60fi. Ice-yacht; 1fo. Ski jumper; 1fo.50, Skier turning. HORIZ: 50fi. Cross-country skier; 80fi. Ice-hockey players; 2fo. Figure skaters.

257 Blast Furnace

1955. Tenth Anniv of Liberation.

1406		40fi. brown and red	80	40
1407	**257**	60fi. red and green	90	50
1408	-	1fo. green and brown	1·60	1·00
1409	-	2fo. brown and green	2·20	1·50

DESIGNS—VERT: 40fi. Reading room; 2fo. Liberty statue. HORIZ: 1fo. Combine harvester.

258 "1st May"

1955. May Day.

1410	**258**	1fo. red	80	40

259 State Printing Works

1955. Centenary of Hungarian State Printing Office.

1411	**259**	60fi. brown and green	65	40

MS1411a 97×77 mm. Air. T **259** 5fo.				
		red and green	50·00	50·00

260 Young Workers and Flag

1955. Second Congress of Young Workers' Federation.

1412	**260**	1fo. brown	80	40

261 Postilion

1955. Opening of P.O. Museum.

1413	**261**	1fo. purple	80	40

262 Radio Mechanic

1955. Workers.

1414		8fi. brown	15	15
1415	-	10fi. turquoise	15	15
1416	-	12fi. orange	15	15
1417	**262**	20fi. olive	15	15
1418	-	30fi. red	15	15
1419	-	40fi. brown	15	15
1420	-	50fi. blue	15	15
1421	-	60fi. red	20	15
1422	-	70fi. olive	20	15
1423	-	80fi. purple	25	15
1424	-	1fo. blue	25	15
1425	-	1fo.20 bistre	60	15
1426	-	1fo.40 green	65	15
1427	-	1fo.70 lilac	85	15
1428	-	2fo. lake	90	15
1429	-	2fo.60 red	1·30	15
1430	-	3fo. green	1·60	15
1431	-	4fo. blue	5·25	15
1432	-	5fo. brown	3·25	15
1433	-	10fo. violet	5·75	15

DESIGNS: 8fi. Market gardener; 10fi. Fisherman; 12fi. Bricklayer; 30fi. Potter; 40fi. Railway guard; 50fi. Shop assistant; 60fi. Post Office worker; 70fi. Herdsman; 80fi. Mill-girl; 1fo. Boat-builder; 1fo.20, Carpenter; 1fo.40, Tram conductor; 1fo.70, Swineherd; 2fo. Welder; 2fo.60, Tractor-driver; 3fo. Horse and groom; 4fo. Bus driver; 5fo. Telegraph lineman; 10fo. Miner.

263 M. Csokonai Vitez

1955. Hungarian Poets.

1434	**263**	60fi. black	1·30	25
1435	-	1fo. blue	1·30	65
1436	-	2fo. red	1·30	90

PORTRAITS: 1fo. M. Vorosmarty; 2fo. A. Jozsef.

1955. Air. Light Metal Industries Int Congress, Budapest. As No. 1139.

1437		5fo. blue on silver	28·00	28·00

264 Bela Bartok

1955. Tenth Death Anniv of Bartok (composer).

1438	**264**	60fi. brown (postage)	1·30	25
1439	**264**	1fo. green (air)	3·25	2·75
1440	**264**	1fo. brown	5·75	3·75

265 "Hargita" Diesel Multiple Unit

1955. Transport.

1441	**265**	40fi. brown and green	40	15
1442	-	60fi. bistre and green	50	25
1443	-	80fi. brown and green	65	40
1444	-	1fo. green and brown	90	65
1445	-	1fo.20 black and brown	1·30	90
1446	-	1fo.50 brown and black	1·60	1·00
1447	-	2fo. brown and green	2·20	1·30

DESIGNS: 60fi. Motor coach; 80fi. Motor cyclist; 1fo. Lorry; 1fo.20, Class 303 steam locomotive; 1fo.50, Tipper; 2fo. Beke (freighter).

266 Puli Sheepdog

1956. Hungarian Dogs.

1448	**266**	40fi. black, red and yellow	40	15
1449	-	50fi. black, buff and blue	50	20
1450	-	60fi. black, red and green	65	25
1451	-	80fi. black, orge & grey	80	40
1452	-	1fo. black, orange & turq	90	50
1453	-	1fo.20 black, brn & orge	1·30	65
1454	-	1fo.50 black, buff & bl	1·90	90
1455	-	2fo. black, brown & mve	3·25	1·50

DESIGNS—RECTANGULAR (36×26 mm): 50fi. Puli and cattle; 1fo.50, Kuvasz sheepdog and cottage. (27×35 mm): 80fi. Hungarian retriever. (27×38 mm): 1fo. Hungarian retriever carrying mallard. As Type **266**: 60fi. Pumi; 1fo.20, Kuvasz sheepdog; 2fo. Komondor sheepdog.

268 Pioneers' Badge

1956. Tenth Anniv of Pioneers Movement.

1456	**268**	1fo. red	65	25
1457	**268**	1fo. grey	65	25

269 Hunyadi on Horseback

1956. 500th Death Anniv of Janos Hunyadi.

1458	**269**	1fo. brown on yellow	90	90

270 Miner

1956. Miners' Day.

1459	**270**	1fo. blue	80	40

271 Horse-jumping

1956. Olympic Games. Inscr "1956". Centres in brown.

1460		20fi. blue (Canoeing)	20	20
1461	**271**	30fi. olive	25	20
1462	-	40fi. brown (Fencing)	35	20
1463	-	60fi. turquoise (Hurdling)	40	20
1464	-	1fo. red (Football)	50	25
1465	-	1fo.50 violet (Weightlifting)	80	40
1466	-	2fo. green (Gymnastics)	1·30	75
1467	-	3fo. mauve (Basketball)	2·50	1·30

272 Chopin

1956. Hungarian–Polish Philatelic Exn, Budapest.

1468		1fo. blue (Liszt)	3·25	3·25
1469	**272**	1fo. mauve	3·25	3·25

1957. Hungarian Red Cross Fund. Nos. 1417 etc., surch with shield, cross and premium.

1470	262	20fi.+20fi. olive	25	25
1471	-	30fi.+30fi. red	65	40
1472	-	40fi.+40fi. brown	80	65
1473	-	60fi.+60fi. red	90	75
1474	-	1fo.+1fo. blue	1·90	1·60
1475	-	2fo.+2fo. lake	3·25	2·10

274 Dr. L. Zamenhof

1957. Air. 70th Anniv of Esperanto.

1476		60fi. brown	80	40
1477	274	1fo. green	1·00	50

DESIGN—HORIZ: 60fi. Esperanto Star.

275 Letters, Letter-box and Globe

1957. Air. Hungarian Red Cross Fund. Cross in red.

1478	275	60fi.+30fi. brown	50	35
1479	-	1fo.+50fi. lilac	65	40
1480	-	2fo.+1fo. red	1·90	50
1481	-	3fo.+1fo.50 blue	2·50	1·90
1482	-	5fo.+2fo.50 grey	4·50	3·25
1483	-	10fi.+5fo. green	7·75	5·00

DESIGNS: 1fo. Postal coach; 2fo. Top of telegraph pole; 3fo. Radio aerial mast; 5fo. Desk telephone; 10fo. (46×31 mm) Posthorn.

276 Janos Arany

1957. 75th Death Anniv of Janos Arany (poet).

1484	276	2fo. blue	1·00	40

277 Arms

1957. Inauguration of National Emblem.

1485	277	60fi. red	65	25
1486	277	1fo. green	1·30	40

278 Congress Emblem

1957. Fourth W.F.T.U. Congress, Leipzig.

1487	278	1fo. red	65	40

279 Courier

1957. Air. Stamp Day.

1488	279	1fo.(+4fo.) brown and bistre on cream	1·30	1·30
1489	-	1fo.(+4fo.) brown and bistre on cream	1·30	1·30

DESIGN: No. 1489, Tupolev Tu-104A airplane over Budapest.

280 Dove of Peace and Flags

1957. 40th Anniv of Russian Revolution. Flags multicoloured.

1490	280	60fi. black and grey	40	15
1491	-	1fo. black and drab	80	40

DESIGN: 1fo. Lenin.

281 Komarom Tumbler Pigeons

1957. Int Pigeon-fanciers' Exn, Budapest.

1492	281	30fi. brown, yellow and green (postage)	15	15
1493	-	40fi. black and brown	15	15
1494	-	60fi. grey and blue	40	15
1495	-	1fo. brown and grey	80	15
1496	-	2fo. grey and mauve	1·40	75
1497	-	3fo. grn, grey & red (air)	1·60	90

DESIGNS: 40fi. Two short-beaked Budapest pigeons; 60fi. Giant domestic pigeon; 1fo. Three Szeged pigeons; 2fo. Two Hungarian fantail pigeons; 3fo. Two carrier pigeons.

IMPERFORATE STAMPS. Most modern Hungarian stamps issued up to the end of 1991 also exist imperforate.

282 Television Building

1958. Inauguration of Hungarian Television Service.

1498	282	2fo. purple	1·90	75
MS1498a		49×70 mm. **282** 2fo. (+23fo.) green	60·00	60·00

283 Mother and Child

1958. Savings Campaign.

1499	283	20fi. deep green and green	25	15
1500	-	30fi. purple and green	40	15
1501	-	40fi. brown and bistre	80	15
1502	-	60fi. myrtle and red	90	15
1503	-	1fo. brown and green	1·60	15
1504	-	2fo. green and orange	2·20	1·50

DESIGNS: 30fi. Old man feeding pigeons; 40fi. Schoolboys with savings stamps; 60fi. "The Cricket and the Ant."; 1fo. Bees on honeycomb; 2fo. Hands holding banknotes.

284 Hungarian Pavilion

1958. Air. Brussels International Exhibition. Inscr "BRUXELLES 1958".

1505	284	20fi. brown and red	40	15
1506	-	40fi. sepia and blue	40	15
1507	-	60fi. sepia and red	40	15
1508	-	1fo. brown and ochre	65	15
1509	-	1fo.40 multicoloured	90	15
1510	-	2fo. sepia and brown	1·30	15
1511	-	3fo. sepia and green	2·20	90
1512	-	5fo. multicoloured	4·00	1·90
MS1512a		72×98 mm. 10fo. mauve	50·00	50·00

DESIGNS—HORIZ: 40fi. Map of Hungary and exhibits; 60fi. Parliament Buildings, Budapest; 1fo. Chain Bridge, Budapest; 1fo.40, Arms of Belgium and Hungary and Exhibition emblem; 5fo. Exhibition emblem. VERT: 2fo. "Mannekin Pis" statue, Brussels; 3fo. Town Hall, Brussels; 10fo. Girl in national costume as T 241.

285 Arms of Hungary

1958. First Anniv of Amended Constitution. Arms multicoloured.

1513	285	60fi. red	25	15
1514	285	1fo. green	50	25
1515	285	2fo. drab	1·00	50

286 Youth with Book

1958. Fifth Youth Festival, Keszthely.

1516	286	1fo. brown	1·00	1·00

287 Town Hall, Prague and Posthorn

1958. Organization of Socialist Countries' Postal Administrations Conference, Prague.

1517	287	60fi. green (postage)	80	40
1518	-	1fo. lake (air)	80	40

DESIGN: 1fo. Prague Castle, telegraph pole and wires.

288 *Linum dolomiticum*

1958. Flowers.

1519	288	20fi. yellow and purple	25	15
1520	-	30fi. brown and blue	40	15
1521	-	40fi. brown, buff & sepia	75	15
1522	-	60fi. mauve and green	90	15
1523	-	1fo. green and red	1·40	40
1524	-	2fo. yellow and green	2·75	50
1525	-	2fo.50 pink and blue	3·25	1·00
1526	-	3fo. pink, lt green & grn	4·00	1·40

FLOWERS—TRIANGULAR: 30fi. *Kitaibelia vitifolia*; 2fo.50, *Dianthus collinus*; 3fo. *Rosa sancti andreae*. VERT: (20½×31 mm): 40fi. *Doronicum hungaricum*; 60fi. *Colchicum arenarium*; 1fo. *Helleborus purpuracens*; 2fo. *Hemerocallis lilioasphodelus*.

For miniature sheet containing stamps as T **288**, see No. **MS**1533a.

289 Table-tennis Bat and Ball

1958. European Table-tennis and Swimming Championships, and World Wrestling Championships, Budapest.

1527	289	20fi. red on pink	15	15
1528	-	30fi. olive on green	25	15
1529	-	40fi. purple on yellow	40	15
1530	-	60fi. brown on blue	65	25
1531	-	1fo. blue on blue	90	50
1532	-	2fo.50 red on yellow	1·90	1·10
1533	-	3fo. blue on turquoise	3·25	1·60

DESIGNS—VERT: 30fi. Table-tennis player; 40fi. Wrestlers; 1fo. Water-polo player; 2fo.50, High-diver. HORIZ: 60fi. Wrestlers; 3fo. Swimmer.

1958. International Philatelic Federation Congress, Brussels.

MS1533a		111×111 mm. Nos. 1519/20 and 1525/6 in new colours	50·00	50·00

290

1958. Air. (a) Int Correspondence Week.

1534	290	60fi. bistre and purple	65	25
1535	-	1fo. bistre and blue	90	65

(b) National Stamp Exhibition, Budapest.

1536		1fo.(+2fo.) bistre and red	1·40	1·40
1537	290	1fo.(+2fo.) bistre and green	1·40	1·40

DESIGNS: No. 1535, Posthorn, envelope and transport; No. 1536, Stamp and magnifier.

291 Airliner over Millennium Monument Budapest

1958. Air. 40th Anniv of First Hungarian Air Mail Stamp.

1538	291	3fo. purple, red and drab	1·30	65
1539	-	5fo. blue, red and drab	2·50	90

DESIGN: 5fo. Airliner over Sopron Tower.

For similar stamps but without commemorative inscription see Nos. 1542/51.

292 Red Flag

1958. 40th Anniv of Hungarian Communist Party and Founding of the "Red Journal".

1540	292	1fo. red and brown	65	25
1541	-	2fo. red and blue	90	65

DESIGN: 2fo. Hand holding up the newspaper "Voros Ujsag" (Red Journal).

1958. Air. As T **291** but with "LEGIPOSTA" at top in place of commem inscription. On cream paper.

1542		20fi. green and red	15	15
1543		30fi. violet and red	15	15
1544		70fi. purple and red	25	15
1545		1fo. blue and red	40	15
1546		1fo.60 purple and red	65	25
1547		2fo. green and red	75	25
1548		3fo. brn & red	90	40
1549	291	5fo. green and red	1·50	50
1550	-	10fo. blue and red	4·50	1·00
1551	-	20fo. sepia and red	9·50	2·50

DESIGNS: Airliner over: 20fi. Town Hall, Szeged; 30fi. Sarospatak Castle; 70fi. Town Hall, Gyor; 1fo. Opera House, Budapest; 1fo.60, Old City of Veszprem; 2fo. Chain Bridge, Budapest; 3fo. Sopron Tower; 10fo. Danube Embankment, Budapest; 20fo. Budapest Cathedral.

293 Rocket approaching the Moon

1959. I.G.Y. Achievements.

1552		10fi. brown and red	25	15
1553		20fi. black and blue	65	15
1554		30fi. buff and green	90	25
1555		40fi. light blue and blue	1·30	40
1556	293	60fi. green and blue	1·40	65
1557	-	1fo. brown and red	1·60	75
1558	-	5fo. brown & deep brown	3·75	1·30

DESIGNS—(31½×21 mm): 10fi. Eotvos torsion balance (gravimetry); 20fi. Ship using echo-sounder (oceanography); 30fi. "Northern Lights" and polar scene. (35½×26½ mm): 40fi. Russian polar camp and Antarctic route map; 1fo. Observatory and the sun; 5fo. Russian "Sputnik" and American "Vanguard" (artificial satellites).

See also No. 1605.

294 Revolutionary

1959. 40th Anniv of Proclamation of Hungarian Soviet Republic.

1559	294	20fi. red and purple	15	15
1560	294	60fi. red and blue	50	25
1561	294	1fo. red and brown	1·10	50

295 Rose

1959. May Day.

1562	**295**	60fi. red, green and lilac	65	25
1563	**295**	1fo. red, green and brown	90	40

296 Nagy Model of Locomotive "Deru", 1847

1959. Transport Museum

1564	**296**	20fi. mult (postage)	15	15
1565	-	30fi. green, black and buff	25	15
1566	-	40fi. multicoloured	40	15
1567	-	60fi. multicoloured	50	15
1568	-	1fo. multicoloured	75	25
1569	-	2fo. multicoloured	1·30	25
1570	-	2fo.50 multicoloured (blue background)	1·50	35
1571	-	3fo. multicoloured (air)	3·75	2·30

DESIGNS—HORIZ: 30fi. Ganz diesel railcar; 60fi. Csonka motor car; 1fo. Ikarusz rear-engine motor coach; 2fo. First Lake Balaton steamer *Kisfaludy*; 2fo.50, Stagecoach; 3fo. Aladar Zselyi's monoplane. VERT: 40fi. Early railway sema-phore signal.

See also No. 1572.

1959. Int Philatelic Federation Congress, Hamburg. As No. 1570 but colours changed.

1572		2fo.50 multicoloured (yellow background)	3·25	3·25

297 Posthorn

1959. Organization of Socialist Countries' Postal Administration Conference, Berlin.

1573	**297**	1fo. red	1·30	1·30

298 Great Cormorant

1959. Water Birds. Inscr "1959".

1574	**298**	10fi. black and green	25	15
1575	-	20fi. green and blue	40	15
1576	-	30fi. violet, myrtle & orge	65	25
1577	-	40fi. grey and green	75	65
1578	-	60fi. brown and purple	90	70
1579	-	1fo. black and turquoise	1·10	75
1580	-	2fo. black and red	2·10	90
1581	-	3fo. brown and bistre	3·25	1·90

DESIGNS: 20fi. Little egret; 30fi. Purple heron; 40fi. Great egret; 60fi. White spoonbill; 1fo. Grey heron; 2fo. Squacco heron; 3fo. Glossy ibis.

299 10th-century Man-at-Arms

1959. 24th World Fencing Championships, Budapest. Inscr as in T 299.

1582	**299**	10fi. black and blue	15	15
1583	-	20fi. black and lemon	15	15
1584	-	30fi. black and violet	25	15
1585	-	40fi. black and red	25	15
1586	-	60fi. black and purple	40	15
1587	-	1fo. black and turquoise	75	15

1588	-	1fo.40 black and orange	1·30	25
1589	-	3fo. black and green	2·50	90

DESIGNS (Evolution of Hungarian swordsmanship): 20fi. 15th-century man-at-arms; 30fi. 18th-century soldier; 40fi. 19th-century soldier; 60fi. 19th-century cavalryman. Fenc-er: at the assault (1fo.); on guard (1fo.40); saluting (3fo.).

300 Bathers at Lake Balaton

1959. Lake Balaton Summer Courses.

1590	-	30fi. bl on yell (postage)	15	15
1591	-	40fi. red on green	25	15
1592	**300**	60fi. brown on pink	40	15
1593	-	1fo.20 violet on pink	90	25
1594	-	2fo. red on yellow	1·50	50
1595	-	20fi. green (air)	15	15
1596	-	70fi. blue	40	15
1597	-	1fo. red and blue	65	25
1598	-	1fo.70 brown on yellow	1·30	90

DESIGNS—VERT: 20fi. Tihany (view); 30fi. "Kek Madar" (yacht); 70fi. *Tihany* (waterbus); 1fo. Waterlily and view of Heviz; 1fo.20, Anglers; 1fo.70, Saturnus (yacht) and statue of fisherman (Balaton pier); 2fo. Holiday-makers and *Beloi-annis* (lake steamer). HORIZ: 40fi. Vintner with grapes.

301

1959. 150th Death Anniv of Haydn (composer).

1599	**301**	40fi. yellow and purple	65	25
1600	-	60fi. buff and slate	1·30	25
1601	-	1fo. orange and violet	1·90	40

MS1601a 94×76 mm. 3fo. purple; 3fo. green (each 27×35 mm) | 19·00 | 19·00

DESIGNS—HORIZ: 60fi. Fertod Chateau. VERT: 1fo. Hay-den; 3fo (purple) "J h" and music score; 3fo. Green "F SCH" and prose quotation.

No. **MS**1601a also commemorates Schiller's birth bi-centenary.

1959. Birth Bicentenary of Schiller (poet). As T **301** but inscr "F. SCHILLER" etc.

1602	-	40fi. yellow and olive	65	25
1603	-	60fi. pink and blue	1·30	25
1604	-	1fo. yellow and purple	1·90	40

DESIGNS—VERT: 40fi. Stylized initials "F" and "Sch" and Schiller's birthplace; 1fo. Schiller. HORIZ: 60fi. Pegasus.
See also No. **MS**1601a.

1959. Landing of Russian Rocket on the Moon. As T **293** with addition of Russian Flag and "22 h 0234" on Moon in red.

1605	**293**	60fi. green and blue	90	40

302 Shepherd with Letter

1959. Stamp Day and National Stamp Exn.

1606	**302**	2fo. purple	3·25	3·25

303 "Taking Delivery"

1959. International Correspondence Week.

1607	**303**	60fi. multicoloured	90	40

304 Lenin and Szamuely

1959. Russian Stamp Exhibition, Budapest.

1608	**304**	20fi. brown and red	15	15
1609	-	40fi. lake & brown on bl	40	25
1610	-	60fi. buff and blue	65	50
1611	-	1fo. multicoloured	90	75

DESIGNS: 40fi. Pushkin; 60fi. Mayakovsky; 1fo. Arms with hands clasping flag.

305 Swallowtail

1959. Butterflies and Moths. Butterflies in natural colours, background colours given.

1612	**305**	20fi. black and green (postage)	65	25
1613	-	30fi. black and blue	65	25
1614	-	40fi. black and brown	90	40
1615	-	60fi. black and bistre	1·30	65
1616	-	1fo. black and green (air)	1·90	75
1617	-	2fo. black and lilac	4·00	1·50
1618	-	3fo. black and green	6·25	2·50

DESIGNS—HORIZ: 30fi. Hebe tiger moth; 40fi. Adonis blue; 2fo. Death's-head hawk moth. VERT: 60fi. Purple em-peror; 1fo. Scarce copper; 3fo. Red emperor.

306

1959. Seventh Socialist Workers' Party Congress. Flag in red and green.

1619	**306**	60fi. brown	25	15
1620	-	1fo. red	50	25

DESIGN: 1fo. Flag inscr "MSZMP VII. KONGRESSZUSA".

307 "Fairy Tales"

1959. Fairy Tales (1st series). Centres and inscr in black.

1621	**307**	20fi. multicoloured	25	15
1622	-	30fi. pink	40	15
1623	-	40fi. turquoise	65	20
1624	-	60fi. blue	90	25
1625	-	1fo. yellow	1·00	50
1626	-	2fo. green	1·30	65
1627	-	2fo.50 salmon	1·90	70
1628	-	3fo. red	1·90	75

FAIRY TALE SCENES: 30fi. *The Sleeping Beauty*; 40fi. *Mat the Goose*; 60fi. *The Cricket and the Ant*; 1fo. *Mashenka and the Bears*; 2fo. *The Babes in the Wood*; 2fo.50, *The Pied Piper of Hamelin*; 3fo. *Little Red Riding Hood*.
See also Nos. 1702/9 and 2133/41.

308 Sumeg Castle

1960. Hungarian Castles. On white paper.

1629	**308**	8fi. purple	15	15
1630	-	10fi. brown	15	15
1631	-	12fi. blue	15	15
1632	-	20fi. green	15	15
1633	-	30fi. brown	15	15
1634	-	40fi. turquoise	15	15
1635	-	50fi. brown	15	15
1636	-	60fi. red	40	15
1637	-	70fi. green	40	15
1638	-	80fi. purple	25	15
1639	-	1fo. blue	40	15
1640	-	1fo.20 purple	50	15
1641	-	1fo.40 blue	50	15
1642	-	1fo.70 lilac ("SOMLO")	50	15
1642a	-	1fo.70 lilac ("SOMLYO")	90	25
1643	-	2fo. bistre	90	15
1644	-	2fo.60 blue	1·30	15
1645	-	3fo. brown	1·30	25
1646	-	4fo. violet	1·80	15
1647	-	5fo. green	2·10	50
1648	-	10fo. red	4·50	75

CASTLES—As Type **308**: 10fi. Kisvarda; 12fi. Szigliget; 20fi. Tata; 30fi. Diosgyor; 40fi. Simon Tornya; 50fi. Fuzer; 60fi. Sarospatak; 70fi. Nagyvazsony; 80fi. Egervar. 28½×21½ mm: 1fo. Vitany; 1fo.20, Sirok; 1fo.40, Siklos; 1fo.70, Som-lyo; 2fo. Boldogko; 2fo.60, Holloko; 4fo. Eger. 21½×28½ mm: 3fo. Csesznek; 5fo. Koszeg; 10fo. Sarvar.
See also Nos. 1694/700.

309 Halas Lace

1960. Halas Lace (1st series). Designs showing lace as T **309**. Inscriptions and values in orange.

1649	**304**	20fi. sepia	25	10
1650	-	30fi. violet	35	10
1651	-	40fi. turquoise	50	25
1652	-	60fi. brown	70	35
1653	-	1fo. green	1·30	60
1654	-	1fo.50 green	1·40	70
1655	-	2fo. blue	2·75	1·10
1656	-	3fo. red	4·75	1·40

Nos. 1650/1, 1654/5 are larger 38×44 mm.
See also Nos. 1971/8.

310 Cross-country Skiing

1960. Winter Olympic Games.

1657	**310**	30fi. bistre and blue	25	10
1658	-	40fi. bistre and green	25	10
1659	-	60fi. bistre and red	50	10
1660	-	80fi. bistre and violet	60	25
1661	-	1fo. bistre and turquoise	1·20	60
1662	-	1fo.20 bistre and lake	1·20	70
1663	-	2fo.+1fo. mult	3·50	85

DESIGNS: 40fi. Ice hockey; 60fi. Ski jumping; 80fi. Speed skating; 1fo. Skiing; 1fo.20, Figure skating; 2fo. Games emblem.

311 Kato Haman

1960. Celebrities and Anniversaries. Portrait as T **311**.

1664	60fi. purple (T **311**)	35	10
1665	60fi. brown (Clara Zetkin)	35	10
1666	60fi. violet (Garibaldi)	35	10
1667	60fi. green (I. Turr)	35	10
1668	60fi. red (I. Tukory)	35	10
1669	60fi. deep blue and blue (O. Herman)	35	10
1670	60fi. brown (Beethoven)	35	10
1671	60fi. red (F. Mora)	35	10
1672	60fi. black and grey (B. I. Toth)	35	10
1673	60fi. purple and mauve (D. Banki)	35	10
1674	60fi. deep green and green (A. G. Pattantyus)	35	10
1675	60fi. blue and cobalt (I. P. Sem-melweis)	35	10
1676	60fi. brown (Joliot-Curie)	35	10
1677	60fi. red (F. Erkel)	35	10
1678	60fi. blue and light blue (J. Bolyai)	35	10
1679	60fi. red (V. I. Lenin)	35	10

COMMEMORATIVE EVENTS: Nos. 1664/5, Int Women's Day: 1666, Centenary of Sicilian Expedition; 1669, 125th Birth Anniv; 1670, Martonvasar Beethoven Concerts: 1671, Szeged Festival: 1672, Miners' Day: 1677, 150th Birth An-niv; 1678, Birth Centenary; 1679, 90th Birth Anniv.

312 Yellow Pheasant's-eye and Quill

1960. Stamp Exhibition Budapest.

1680	**312**	2fo.(+4fo.) yellow, green and brown	2·20	2·20

313 Soldier

1960. 15th Anniv of Liberation.

1681	**313**	40fi. brown and red	60	35
1682	-	60fi. red, green and brown	1·20	50

DESIGN—HORIZ: 60fi. Student with flag (inscr "1945 FEL-SZABADULASUNK... 1960").

314 Rowing

1960. Summer Olympic Games. Centres and inscr in black (3fo. multicoloured). Circular frames in bistre. Background colours given.

1683	10fi. blue (T **314**)	10	10
1684	20fi. brown (Boxing)	10	10
1685	30fi. lilac (Archery)	10	10
1686	40fi. ochre (Discus)	10	10
1687	50fi. red (Ball game)	10	10
1688	60fi. green (Javelin)	25	10
1689	1fo. purple (Horse-riding)	60	10
1690	1fo.40 blue (Wrestling)	70	10
1691	1fo.70 brown (Swordplay)	1·20	25
1692	2fo.+1fo. red (Romulus, Remus and Wolf)	1·30	35
1693	3fo. grey (Olympic Rings and Arms of Hungary)	3·50	1·40
MS1693a	67×95 mm. 10fo. multi-coloured	30·00	30·00

1960. International Philatelic Federation Congress, Warsaw. Sheet 161×122 mm containing four of No. 1656, each in different colours, side by side with commemorative labels.

MS1693b	3fo. (×4)	18·00	18·00

1960. Hungarian Castles. As Nos. 1629, 1632/3, 1636/7 and 1641/2 but printed on coloured paper.

1694	8fi. purple on blue	10	10
1695	20fi. bronze on green	25	10
1696	30fi. brown on yellow	25	10
1697	60fi. red on pink	35	10
1698	70fi. green on blue	60	10
1699	1fo.40 blue on blue	85	10
1700	1fo.70 lilac on blue ("SOMLO")	1·90	25

315 Girl in Mezokovesd Provincial Costume

1960. Stamp Day.

1701	**315**	2fo.(+4fo.) mult	3·00	3·00

316 The Turnip

1960. Fairy Tales (2nd series). Multicoloured.

1702	20fi. Type **316**	10	10
1703	30fi. Snow White and the Seven Dwarfs	10	10
1704	40fi. The Miller, Son and Donkey	25	10
1705	60fi. Puss in Boots	35	20
1706	80fi. The Fox and the Raven	60	25
1707	1fo. The Maple-wood Pipe	1·20	35
1708	1fo.70 The Stork and the Fox	1·40	60
1709	2fo. Momotaro (Japanese tale)	3·00	70

317 F. Rozsa

1961. Celebrities and Anniversaries. Portraits as T **317**.

1710	1fo. brown (T **317**)	35	10
1711	1fo. turquoise (G. Kilian)	35	10
1712	1fo. red (J. Rippi-Ronai)	35	10
1713	1fo. olive (S. Latinka)	35	10
1714	1fo. green (M. Zalka)	35	10
1715	1fo. lake (J. Katona)	35	10

COMMEMORATIVE EVENTS: No. 1710, Press Day; No. 1711, Gyorgy Kilian Sports Movement; No. 1712, Birth Cent; No. 1713, 75th Birth Anniv; No. 1714, 65th Birth Anniv.

318 Eastern Grey Kangaroo with Young

1961. Budapest Zoo Animals. Inscr "ZOO 1961".

1716	**318**	20fi. black and orange	25	10
1717	-	30fi. sepia and green	35	10
1718	-	40fi. brown and chestnut	50	10
1719	-	60fi. grey and mauve	60	10
1720	-	80fi. yellow and black	70	10
1721	-	1fo. brown and green	1·10	25
1722	-	1fo.40 sepia and turquoise	1·60	25
1723	-	2fo. black and red	1·80	95
1724	-	2fo.60 brown and violet	2·40	1·40
1725	-	3fo. multicoloured	3·75	1·80

DESIGNS—HORIZ: 30fi. American bison; 60fi. Indian elephant and calf; 80fi. Tiger and cubs; 1fo.40, Polar bear; 2fo. Common zebra and foal; 2fo.60, European bison cow with calf. VERT: 40fi. Brown bear; 1fo. Ibex; 3fo. Main entrance, Budapest Zoo.

319 Child chasing Butterfly

1961. Health. Inscr "1961". Cross in red.

1726	**319**	30fi. black, purple & brn	10	10
1727	-	40fi. sepia, blue & turq	25	10
1728	-	60fi. yellow, grey & violet	30	10
1729	-	1fo. multicoloured	35	10
1730	-	1fo.70 yellow, blue & grn	95	25
1731	-	4fo. green and grey	2·10	85

DESIGNS—As Type 319: 40fi. Patient on operating table. LARGER (29½×35 mm): 60fi. Ambulance and stretcher; 1fo. Traffic lights and scooter; 1fo.70, Syringe and jars; 4fo. Emblem of Health Department.

320 Launching of Rocket "Vostok"

1961. World's First Manned Space Flight. Inscr "1961. IV.12".

1732	**320**	1fo. brown and blue	1·80	1·20
1733	-	2fo. brown and blue	5·50	4·75

DESIGN: 2fo. Gagarin and "Vostok" in flight.

321 Roses

1961. May Day.

1734	**321**	1fo. red and green	60	25
1735	-	2fo. red and green	1·20	60

DESIGN: 2fo. As Type 321 but roses and inscr reversed.

322 "Venus" Rocket

1961. Launching of Soviet "Venus" Rocket. Inscr "VENUSZ RAKETA 1961 11.12".

1736	**322**	40fi. black, bistre and blue	70	70
1737	-	60fi. black, bistre and blue	1·20	1·20
1738	-	80fi. black and blue	1·30	1·30
1739	-	2fo. bistre and violet-blue	3·50	3·50

DESIGNS: 60fi. Separation of rocket capsule in flight; 80fi. Capsule and orbit diagram; 2fo. Allegory of flying woman and crescent moon.

323 Conference Emblem, Letter and Transport

1961. Organization of Socialist Countries' Postal Administrations Conference.

1740	**323**	40fi. black and orange	55	10
1741	-	60fi. black and mauve	65	10
1742	-	1fo. black and blue	1·10	75

DESIGNS: 60fi. Television aerial; 1fo. Radar receiving equipment.

324 Hungarian Flag

1961. International Stamp Exhibition, Budapest. (a) 1st issue. Background in silver.

1743	**324**	1fo. red, green and black	65	60
1744	-	1fo.70 multicoloured	1·30	1·10
1745	-	2fo.60 multicoloured	1·90	1·20
1746	-	3fo. multicoloured	2·50	1·90

(b) 2nd issue. Background in gold. Inscriptions at left altered on 1fo. and 3fo.

1747	**324**	1fo. red, green and black	80	75
1748	-	1fo.70 multicoloured	1·30	1·20
1749	-	2fo.60 multicoloured	1·90	1·90
1750	-	3fo. multicoloured	2·30	2·20

DESIGNS: 1fo.70, Late spider orchids; 2fo.60, Small tortoiseshell; 3fo. Eurasian goldfinch.
See also Nos. 1765/8.

325 George Stephenson

1961. Communications Ministers' Conference, Budapest. Inscr "KOZLEKEDESUGYI", etc.

1751	**325**	60fi. olive	25	10
1752	-	1fo. bistre, black and blue	65	10
1753	-	2fo. brown	1·00	35

DESIGNS: 1fo. Communications emblems; 2fo. J. Landler (Minister of Communications).

326 Football and Club Badge

1961. 50th Anniv of VASAS Sports Club. Badge in gold, red and blue.

1754	**326**	40fi. orange, black and gold	15	10
1755	-	60fi. green, black and gold	40	10
1756	-	1fo. bistre, black and gold	50	35
1757	-	2fo.+1fo. blue, blk & gold	1·60	1·10

DESIGNS: 60fi. Wrestling; 1fo. Vaulting; 2fo. Sailing.

327 Three Racehorses

1961. Racehorses.

1758	**327**	30fi. multicoloured	25	10
1759	-	40fi. multicoloured	40	25
1760	-	60fi. multicoloured	65	35
1761	-	1fo. black, green and orange	75	60
1762	-	1fo.70 sepia, black and green	1·50	75
1763	-	2fo. black, blue and brown	1·90	1·40
1764	-	3fo. multicoloured	3·25	1·90

DESIGNS: 40fi. Three hurdlers; 60fi. Trotting race (two horses); 1fo. Trotting race (three horses); 1fo.70, Two racehorses and two foals; 2fo. Hungarian trotter Baka; 3fo. 19th century champion mare, Kincsem.

328 Budapest

1961. Stamp Day and International Stamp Exhibition, Budapest (3rd issue). Designs as T **328**.

1765	**328**	2fo.+1fo. bl, brn & ol	2·30	2·30
1766	-	2fo.+1fo. bl, brn & ol	2·30	2·30
1767	-	2fo.+1fo. bl, brn & ol	2·30	2·30
1768	-	2fo.+1fo. bl, brn & ol	2·30	2·30

Nos. 1765/8 are printed together in sheets of 40 (4×10) with one vertical row of each design. Horizontal strips of four form a composite panorama of Budapest.

329 Music, Keyboard and Silhouette

1961. 150th Birth and 75th Death Anniv of Liszt (composer).

1769	**329**	60fi. black and gold	60	25
1770	-	1fo. black	80	60
1771	-	2fo. green and blue	1·70	1·20
MS1771a	71×98 mm. 10fo. multi-coloured	17·00	17·00

DESIGNS—VERT: 1fo. Statue; 10fo. Head profile over piano keys. HORIZ: 2fo. Music Academy.

330 Lenin

1961. 22nd Soviet Communist Party Congress, Moscow.

1772	**330**	1fo. brown	60	25

331 Monk's Hood

1961. Medicinal Plants. Multicoloured.

1773	20fi. Type **331**	10	10
1774	30fi. Centaury	10	10
1775	40fi. Blue iris	25	10
1776	60fi. Thorn-apple	35	10
1777	1fo. Purple hollyhock	80	15
1778	1fo.70 Hop	1·20	25
1779	2fo. Poppy	1·70	60
1780	3fo. Mullein	2·30	1·00

332 Nightingale

1961. Birds of Woods and Fields. Multicoloured. Inscr "1961".

1781	30fi. Type **332**	10	10
1782	40fi. Great tit	25	10
1783	60fi. Chaffinch (horiz)	35	10
1784	1fo. Jay	60	15
1785	1fo.20 Golden oriole (horiz)	70	25
1786	1fo.50 Blackbird (horiz)	1·20	35
1787	2fo. Yellowhammer	1·40	40
1788	3fo. Northern lapwing (horiz)	2·30	80

333 M. Karolyi

1962. Celebrities and Anniversaries. Inscr "1962".

1789	**333**	1fo. sepia	35	10
1790	-	1fo. brown (F. Berkes)	35	10
1791	-	1fo. blue (J. Pech)	35	10
1792	-	1fo. violet (A. Chazar)	35	10
1793	-	1fo. blue (Dr. F. Hutyra)	35	10
1794	-	1fo. red (G. Egressy)	35	10

ANNIVERSARIES: Nos. 1789/90, 5th Co-operative Movement Congress; 1791, 75th anniv of Hydrographic Institute; 1792, 50th anniv of Sports Club for the Deaf; 1793, 175th anniv of Hungarian Veterinary Service; 1794, 125th anniv of National Theatre.

333a Globe and Gagarin, Titov and Glenn (image scaled to 59% of original size)

1962. World Space Flights of Gagarin, Titov and Glenn. Sheet 109×70 mm.
MS1794a **333a** 10fo. multicoloured   17·00   17·00

334 Railway Signals

1962. 14th Int Railwaymen's Esperanto Congress.
1795 **334** 1fo. green   30   10

335 Green Swordtail

1962. Ornamental Fish. Inscr "1962". Multicoloured.
1796	**335**	20fi. Type **335**	10	10
1797		30fi. Paradise fish	10	10
1798		40fi. Fan-tailed guppy	15	10
1799		60fi. Siamese fighting fish	25	10
1800		1fo. Tiger barb	35	10
1801		1fo. Freshwater angelfish	60	25
1802		1fo.20 Sunfish	70	35
1803		1fo.50 Lyretail panchax	1·00	45
1804		2fo. Neon tetra	1·30	60
1805		3fo. Blue discus	1·70	1·30

336 Flags of Argentina and Bulgaria

1962. World Football Championships, 1962. Inscr "CHILE 1962". Flags in national colours: ball, flagpole, value, etc., in bistre.
1806		30fi. mauve	25	10
1807		40fi. green	35	15
1808		60fi. lilac	60	25
1809		1fo. blue	70	35
1810	**336**	1fo.70 orange	1·40	45
1811		2fo. turquoise	1·60	50
1812		3fo. red	1·70	60
1813		4fo.+1fo. green	3·50	1·20

MS1813a 72×92 mm. 10fo. multicoloured   11·50   11·50

FLAGS: 30fi. Colombia and Uruguay; 40fi. U.S.S.R. and Yugoslavia; 60fi. Switzerland and Chile; 1fo. German Federal Republic and Italy; 2fo. Hungary and Great Britain; 3fo. Brazil and Mexico; 4fo. Spain and Czechoslovakia. The two flags on each stamp represent the football teams playing against each other in the first round. VERT: (28½×39 mm)—10fo. Goal keeper and map.

337 Gutenberg

1962. Centenary of Hungarian Printing Union.
1814	**337**	1fo. blue	35	10
1815		1fo. brown	35	10

PORTRAIT: No. 1815, Miklos Kis (first Hungarian printer).

338 Campaign Emblem

1962. Malaria Eradication.
1816 **338** 2fo.50 bistre and black   1·70   80
MS1816a 111×76 mm. 2fo.50 (×4) green and black   15·00   15·00

339 "Beating Swords into Ploughshares"

1962. World Peace Congress, Moscow.
1817 **339** 1fo. brown   35   10

340 Festival Emblem

1962. World Youth Festival, Helsinki.
1818 **340** 3fo. multicoloured   1·20   45

341 Icarus

1962. Air. Development of Flight.
1819	**341**	30fi. bistre and blue	10	10
1820		40fi. blue and green	25	10
1821		60fi. red and blue	35	10
1822		80fi. silver, blue & turq	45	10
1823		1fo. silver, blue & purple	60	15
1824		1fo.40 orange and blue	70	35
1825		2fo. brown and turquoise	95	45
1826		3fo. blue, silver and violet	1·20	60
1827		4fo. silver, black & green	1·70	70

DESIGNS: 40fi. Modern glider and Lilienthal monoplane glider; 60fi. Zlin Trener 6 and Rakos's monoplane; 80fi. Airship "Graf Zeppelin" and Montgolfier balloon; 1fo. Ilyushin Il-18B and Wright Flyer I; 1fo.40, Nord 3202 sports airplane and Peter Nesterov's Nieuport biplane; 2fo. Mil Mi-6 helicopter and Asboth's helicopter; 3fo. Myasichev Mya-4 airliner and Zhukovsky's wind tunnel; 4fo. Space rocket and Tsiolkovsky's rocket.

342 Hybrid Tea

1962. Rose Culture. Roses in natural colours. Background colours given.
1828		20fi. brown	25	10
1829	**342**	40fi. myrtle	45	10
1830		60fi. violet	60	10
1831		80fi. red	80	15
1832		1fo. myrtle	1·20	45
1833		1fo.20 orange	1·40	60
1834		2fo. turquoise	3·00	80

ROSES: 20fi. Floribunda; 60fi. to 2fo. Various hybrid teas.

343 Globe, "Vostok 3" and "Vostok 4"

1962. Air. First "Team" Manned Space Flight.
1835	**343**	1fo. brown and blue	80	60
1836		2fo. brown and blue	1·70	1·20

DESIGN: 2fo. Cosmonauts Nikolaev and Popovich.

344 Weightlifting

1962. European Weightlifting Championships, Budapest.
1837 **344** 1fo. brown   80   35

345 Austrian 2kr. stamp of 1850

1962. 35th Stamp Day.
1838	**345**	2fo.+1fo. brown & yell	1·70	1·70
1839	-	2fo.+1fo. brown & pk	1·70	1·70
1840	-	2fo.+1fo. brown & bl	1·70	1·70
1841	-	2fo.+1fo. brown & grn	1·70	1·70

MS1841a 91×110 mm. Nos. 1838/41 in block of four   10·50   10·50

DESIGNS: Hungarian stamps of: No. 1839, 1919 (75fi. Dozsa); No. 1840, 1955 (1fo. 50 Skiing); No. 1841, 1959 (3fo. "Vanessa atalanta").

346 Primitive and Modern Oilwells

1962. 25th Anniv of Hungarian Oil Industry.
1842 **346** 1fo. green   35   10

347 Gagarin

1962. Air. Astronautical Congress, Paris.
1843	**347**	40fi. ochre and purple	25	10
1844	-	60fi. ochre and green	60	15
1845	-	1fo. ochre and turquoise	80	25
1846	-	1fo.40 ochre and brown	1·20	35
1847	-	1fo.70 ochre and blue	1·60	60
1848	-	2fo.60 ochre and violet	1·70	80
1849	-	3fo. ochre and brown	3·00	1·40

ASTRONAUTS: 60fi. Titov; 1fo. Glenn; 1fo.40, Scott Carpenter; 1fo.70, Nikolaev; 2fo.60, Popovich; 3fo. Schirra.

348 Cup and Football

1962. "Budapest Vasas" Football Team's Victory in Central European Cup Competition.
1850 **348** 2fo.+1fo. mult   1·20   95

349 Osprey

1962. Air. Birds of Prey. Multicoloured.
1851		30fi. Eagle owl	25	10
1852		40fi. Type **349**	25	25
1853		60fi. Marsh harrier	60	35
1854		80fi. Booted eagle	80	60
1855		1fo. African fish eagle	1·20	80
1856		2fo. Lammergeier	1·70	95
1857		3fo. Golden eagle	2·30	1·20
1858		4fo. Common kestrel	3·00	1·40

350 Racing Motor Cyclist

1962. Motor Cycle and Car Sports. Multicoloured.
1859	**350**	20fi. Type **350**	10	10
1860		30fi. Sidecar racing	15	10
1861		40fi. "Scrambling" (hill climb)	25	10
1862		60fi. Dirt-track racing	35	15
1863		1fo. Wearing "garland"	70	25
1864		1fo.20 Speed trials	80	35
1865		1fo.70 Sidecar trials	1·30	40
1866		2fo. "Go-kart" racing	1·50	45
1867		3fo. Car racing	1·70	1·40

351 Ice Skater

1963. European Figure Skating and Ice Dancing Championships, Budapest.
1868	**351**	20fi. green, brown & lilac	10	10
1869	-	40fi. black, brn & salmon	25	15
1870	-	60fi. multicoloured	60	35
1871	-	1fo. multicoloured	80	45
1872	-	1fo.40 multicoloured	1·20	60
1873	-	2fo. red, brown and green	1·70	80
1874	-	3fo. multicoloured	3·00	1·20

MS1874a 66×94 mm. 10fo. multicoloured   11·50   11·50

DESIGNS—VERT: 40fi., 2fo. Skater leaping; 60fi., 1fo. Pairs dancing; 1fo.40, Skater turning; 10fo. (29×38 mm), Figure skater and flags. HORIZ: 3fo. Pair dancing.

352 J. Batsanyi

1963. Celebrities and Anniversaries.
1875		40fi. lake (Type **352**)	10	10
1876		40fi. green (F. Entz)	10	10
1877		40fi. blue (I. Markovits)	25	10
1878		40fi. olive (L. Weiner)	25	10
1879		60fi. purple (Dr. F. Koranyi)	60	10
1880		60fi. bronze (G. Gardonyi)	25	10
1881		60fi. brown (P. de Coubertin)	60	10
1882		60fi. violet (J. Eotvos)	35	10

ANNIVERSARIES: No. 1875, Revolutionary, birth bicent; No. 1876, Horticulture College founder, Horticulture cent; No. 1877, Inventor, Hungarian Shorthand, cent; No. 1878, Composer, Budapest Music Competitions; No. 1879, Tuberculosis researcher, 50th death anniv; No. 1880, Novelist, birth cent; No. 1881, Olympic Games reviver, birth cent; No. 1882, Author, 150th birth anniv.

353 Bulgarian 21. Rocket Stamp of 1959

1963. Organization of Socialist Countries Postal Administrations Conference, Budapest.
1883	-	20fi. red, yellow and green	10	10
1884	**353**	30fi. red, brown & purple	10	10
1885	-	40fi. purple and blue	10	10
1886	-	50fi. violet and blue	15	10
1887	-	60fi. multicoloured	25	10
1888	-	80fi. turquoise, black & bl	35	10
1889	-	1fo. multicoloured	45	10
1890	-	1fo.20 yellow, violet & bl	50	15
1891	-	1fo.40 blue, red & brown	60	15
1892	-	1fo.70 brn, grn & lt brn	1·00	25
1893	-	2fo. orange, blue & pur	1·20	35
1894	-	2fo.60 violet, red & grn	1·30	1·20

DESIGNS: Various "space" stamps—HORIZ: 20fi. Albania 11.50 (1962); 40fi. Czechoslovakia 80h. (1962); 50fi. China 8f. (1962); 60fi. N. Korea 10ch. (1961); 80fi. Poland 40g. (1959); 1fo. Hungary 60fi. (1961); 1fo.40, East Germany 25pf. (1961); 1fo.70, Rumania 1l.20 (1957); 2fo.60, N. Vietnam 6x. (1961). VERT: 1fo.20, Mongolia 30m. (1959); 2fo. Russia 6k. (1961).

354 Fair Emblem

1963. International Fair, Budapest.
| 1895 | **354** | 1fo. violet | 60 | 10 |

355 Erkel (composer)

1963. Students' Erkel Memorial Festival, Gyula.
| 1896 | **355** | 60fi. brown | 60 | 10 |

356 Roses

1963. Fifth National Rose Show, Budapest.
| 1897 | **356** | 2fo. red, green and brown | 1·20 | 10 |

357 Helicon Monument

1963. Tenth Youth Festival, Keszthely.
| 1898 | **357** | 40fi. blue | 10 | 10 |

358 Chain Bridge and "Snow White" (Danube steamer)

1963. Transport and Communications.
1899	**358**	10fi. blue	10	10
1900	-	20fi. green	10	10
1901	-	30fi. blue	10	10
1902	-	40fi. orange	10	10
1902b	-	40fi. grey	35	35
1903	-	50fi. brown	10	10
1904	-	60fi. red	10	10
1905	-	70fi. olive	10	10
1906	-	80fi. brown	10	10
1906a	-	1fo. brown	25	25
1907	-	1fo. purple	25	10
1908	-	1fo.20 brown	2·00	60
1909	-	1fo.20 violet	10	10
1910	-	1fo.40 green	35	10
1911	-	1fo.70 brown	45	10
1912	-	2fo. turquoise	60	10
1913	-	2fo.50 purple	70	25
1914	-	2fo.60 olive	80	25
1915	-	3fo. blue	60	10
1916	-	4fo. blue	80	10
1917	-	5fo. brown	1·20	10
1918	-	6fo. ochre	1·30	10
1919	-	8fo. mauve	2·00	45

| 1920 | - | 10fo. green | 2·30 | 1·20 |

DESIGNS—As Type **358**: HORIZ: 20fi. Tramcar; 30fi. Open-deck bus; 40fi. (No. 1902), Articulated bus; 40fi. (No. 1902b), Budapest 100 Post Office; 50fi. Railway truck with gas cylinders; 60fi. Trolley bus; 70fi. Railway T.P.O. coach; 80fi. Motor cyclist. VERT: 1fo. (No. 1906a), Hotel Budapest. 28½×21 mm: 1fo. (No. 1907) Articulated trolley bus; 1fo.40, Postal coach; 1fo.70, Diesel-electric multiple unit train; 2fo. T.V. broadcast coach; 2fo.50, Tourist coach; 2fo.60, Signalbox and train; 3fo. Parcels conveyor; 5fo. Railway fork-lift truck; 6fo. Telex operator; 8fo. Telephonist and map; 10fo. Postwoman. 21×28½ mm: 1fo.20, (No. 1908), Mail plane and trolley on tarmac; 1fo.20, (No. 1909), Control tower, Miskolc; 4fo. Pylon, Pecs.
See also Nos. 2767/70.

359 Holidaymaker and *Beloiannis* (lake steamer)

1963. Centenary of Siofok Resort, Lake Balaton.
1921		20fi. black, green and red	60	25
1922	**359**	40fi. multicoloured	60	25
1923	-	60fi. orange, brown & bl	60	35

DESIGNS—TRIANGULAR: 20fi. *Tihany* (water bus); 60fi. Yacht.

359a Spaceship over Globe

1963. Air. Space Flights of "Vostok 5" and "Vostok 6". Sheet 64×94 mm.
| **MS**1923a | **359a** | 10fo. light blue, blue and gold | 14·00 | 14·00 |

360 Mail Coach and Arc de Triomphe, Paris

1963. Centenary of Paris Postal Conference.
| 1924 | **360** | 1fo. red | 60 | 25 |

361 Performance in front of Szeged Cathedral

1963. Summer Drama Festival, Szeged.
| 1925 | **361** | 40fi. blue | 25 | 25 |

362 Child with towel

1963. Red Cross Centenary. Inscr "1863–1963". Multicoloured.
1926		30fi. Type **362**	10	10
1927		40fi. Girl with medicine bottle and tablets	10	10
1928		60fi. Girls of three races	25	10
1929		1fo. Girl and "heart"	35	15
1930		1fo.40 Boys of three races	60	25
1931		2fo. Child being medically examined	70	35
1932		3fo. Hands tending plants	2·00	70

363 Pylon and Map

1963. Village Electrification.
| 1933 | **363** | 1fo. black and grey | 60 | 25 |

364 Karancssag

1963. Provincial Costumes.
1934	**364**	20fi. lake	25	10
1935	-	30fi. green (Kapuvar)	30	15
1936	-	40fi. brown (Debrecen)	35	25
1937	-	60fi. blue (Hortobagy)	60	30
1938	-	1fo. red (Csokoly)	80	35
1939	-	1fo.70 violet (Dunantul)	95	50
1940	-	2fo. turquoise (Bujak)	1·20	60
1941	-	2fo.50 red (Alfold)	1·40	1·00
1942	-	3fo. blue (Mezokovesd)	3·00	1·20

365 Hyacinth

1963. Stamp Day. Flowers. Multicoloured.
1943		2fo.+1fo. Type **365**	1·30	1·30
1944		2fo.+1fo. Narcissus	1·30	1·30
1945		2fo.+1fo. Chrysanthemum	1·30	1·30
1946		2fo.+1fo. Tiger lily	1·30	1·30
MS1946a		76×91 mm. Nos. 1943/6 but smaller (20×27 mm) in block of four	6·50	6·50

366 Skiing (slalom)

1963. Winter Olympic Games, Innsbruck, 1964. "MAGYAR" and emblems red and black; centres brown: background colours given.
1947	**366**	40fi. green	10	10
1948	-	60fi. violet	10	10
1949	-	70fi. blue	15	10
1950	-	80fi. green	25	10
1951	-	1fo. orange	35	15
1952	-	2fo. blue	80	25
1953	-	2fo.60 purple	2·00	80
1954	-	4fo.+1fo. blue	2·30	95

DESIGNS: 60fi. Skiing (biathlon); 70fi. Ski jumping; 80fi. Rifle-shooting on skis; 1fo. Figure skating (pairs); 2fo. Ice hockey; 2fo.60, Speed skating; 4fo. Bobsleighing.

367 Calendar

1963. New Year Issue. Hungarian Postal and Philatelic Museum Fund. Multicoloured.
1955		20fi. Type **367**	10	10
1956		30fi. Young chimney-sweep with glass of wine	10	10
1957		40fi. Four-leafed clover	10	10
1958		60fi. Piglet in top-hat	10	10
1959		1fo. Young pierrot	35	15
1960		2fo. Chinese lanterns and mask	60	25
1961		2fo.50+1fo.20 Holly, mistletoe, clover and horseshoe	95	35
1962		3fo.+1fo.50 Piglets with balloon	2·00	70

SIZES: As Type **367**—HORIZ: 20fi., 1fo., 3fo. VERT: 40fi. LARGER (28×38 mm.): 30fi., 60fi., 2fo., 2fo.50.

368 Moon Rocket

1964. Space Research. Multicoloured.
1963		30fi. Type **368**	25	10
1964		40fi. Venus rocket	35	10
1965		60fi. "Vostok 1" (horiz)	45	15
1966		1fo. U.S. spaceship	60	20
1967		1fo.70 Soviet team space flights	1·00	25
1968		2fo. "Telstar" (horiz)	1·20	35
1969		2fo.60 Mars rocket	1·30	60
1970		3fo. "Space Research" (rockets and tracking equipment) (horiz)	1·70	70

368a Skier racing

1964. Winter Olympic Games, Innsbruck, 1964. Sheet 65×60 mm.
| **MS**1970a | **368a** | 10fo. multicoloured | 8·75 | 8·75 |

369 Swans

1964. Halas Lace (2nd series). Lace patterns die-stamped in white on black; inscriptions black.
1971	**369**	20fi. green	25	10
1972	-	30fi. yellow	60	10
1973	-	40fi. red	80	15
1974	-	60fi. olive	1·20	20
1975	-	1fo. orange	1·40	25
1976	-	1fo.40 blue	1·70	30
1977	-	2fo. turquoise	2·00	60
1978	-	2fo.60 violet	2·50	80

LACE PATTERNS—VERT: (38½×45 mm.): 30fi. Peacocks; 40fi. Pigeons; 60fi. Peacock; 1fo. Deer; 1fo.40, Fisherman; 2fo. Pigeons. As Type **369**: 2fo.60, Butterfly.

370 Armour and Swords

371 Basketball

372 Dozsa and Kossuth

373 Fair and Emblem

374 "Breasting the Tape"

1964. Anniversaries and Events of 1964. Designs as T **370/4**, some showing portraits. (a) As T **370**.
1979		60fi. purple (I. Madach)	25	25
1980		60fi. olive (E. Szabo)	35	25
1981		60fi. olive (A. Fay)	35	25

1982	1fo. red (Skittles)	60	25
1983	2fo. brown (T **370**)	60	25

ANNIV OR EVENT: No. 1979, (author, death cent.); No. 1980, (founder of Municipal Libraries, 60th anniv); No. 1981, (death cent.); No. 1982, (1st European Skittles Championships, Budapest); No. 1983, (50th anniv of Hungarian Fencing Assn.).

(b) As T 371.

1984	60fi. turquoise (Stalactites and stalagmites)	25	25
1985	60fi. blue (Bauxite excavator)	35	25
1986	1fo. green (Forest and waterfall)	60	25
1987	2fo. brown (Galileo)	80	25
1988	2fo. lake (Shakespeare)	80	25
1989	2fo. blue (T **371**)	1·70	60
1990	60fi. red (K. Marx)	35	25

ANNIV OR EVENT—VERT: No. 1984, (Aggteleki Cave); No. 1985, (30th anniv or Hungarian Aluminium Production); No. 1986, (National Forestry Federation Congress); No. 1987, (400th birth anniv); No. 1988 (400th birth anniv); No. 1989, (European Women's Basketball Championships). HORIZ: No. 1990, (cent of "First International").

(c) As T 372.

1991	1fo. blue (T **372**)	60	25
1992	3fo.+1fo.50, black, grey and orange (Sports Museum, Budapest)	1·40	35

ANNIV OR EVENT: No. 1991, (60th Anniv of City of Cegled); No. 1992, (Lawn Tennis Historical Exn, Budapest).

(d) T 373.

1993	1fo. green (Budapest Int Fair)	60	25

(e) As T 374.

1994	60fi. slate ("Alba Regia" statue)	35	25
1995	1fo. brown (M. Ybl)	60	25
1996	2fo. brown (T **374**)	80	25
1997	2fo. dull pur (Michelangelo)	80	25

ANNIV OR EVENT: No. 1994, (Szekesfehervar Days); No. 1995, (architect, 150th birth anniv); No. 1996, (50th anniv of Hungarian–Swedish Athletic Meeting); No. 1997, (400th death anniv).

375 Eleanor Roosevelt

1964. Eleanor Roosevelt Commemoration.

1998	**375**	2fo. ochre, deep brown and brown	80	60

MS1998a 112×76 mm. 4×2 fo. (each 39×20 mm) in different colours, showing portrait 5·25 5·25

376 Fencing

1964. Olympic Games, Tokyo. Multicoloured.

1999	30fi. Type **376**	10	10
2000	40fi. Gymnastics	10	10
2001	60fi. Football	10	10
2002	80fi. Horse-jumping	10	10
2003	1fo. Running	25	10
2004	1fo.40 Weightlifting	35	10
2005	1fo.70 Gymnastics (trapeze)	45	10
2006	2fo. Throwing the hammer, and javelin	70	15
2007	2fo. 50 Boxing	1·50	60
2008	3fo.+1fo. Water-polo	1·70	95

377 Peaches (*Magyar Kajszi*)

1964. National Peaches and Apricots Exhibition, Budapest. Designs of peaches or apricots. Multicoloured.

2009	40fi. "J.H. Hale"	10	10
2010	60fi. Type **377**	10	10
2011	1fo. "Mandula Kajszi"	35	10
2012	1fo.50 "Borsi Rozsa"	60	10
2013	1fo.70 "Alexander"	80	15

2014	2fo. "Champion"	1·20	25
2015	2fo.60 "Elberta"	1·40	60
2016	3fo. "Mayflower"	2·50	80

378 Lilac

1964. Stamp Day. Multicoloured.

2017	2fo.+1fo. Type **378**	1·40	1·40
2018	2fo.+1fo. Mallard	1·40	1·40
2019	2fo.+1fo. Gymnast	1·40	1·40
2020	2fo.+1fo. Rocket and globe	1·40	1·40

MS2020a 85×100 mm. Nos. 2017/20 but smaller (20×27½ mm) in block of four 6·50 6·50

378a Mt. Fuji and Stadium

1964. Air. Summer Olympic Games, Tokyo. Sheet 56×83 mm.
MS2020b **378a** 10fo. multicoloured 10·50 10·50

379 Pedestrian Road Crossing

1964. Road Safety. Multicoloured.

2021	20fi. Type **379**	25	10
2022	60fi. Child with ball running into road	60	10
2023	1fo. Woman and child waiting to cross road	80	60

379a Venus, Rocket and Globe

1964. Three-manned Space Flight. Sheet 87×74 mm.
MS2023a **379a** 10fo. multicoloured 10·50 10·50

380 Arpad Bridge, Budapest

1964. Opening of Reconstructed Elizabeth Bridge, Budapest.

2024	**380**	20fi. grey, green and blue (postage)	10	10
2025	-	30fi. green, blue & brown	10	10
2026	-	60fi. brown, grn & dp brn	35	10
2027	-	1fo. brown, bl & dp brn	70	10
2028	-	1fo.50 grey, blue & brn	1·20	25
2029	-	2fo. grey, green & brown	1·50	60
2030	-	2fo.50 grey, blue & brn	2·30	1·30

(b) Air.

MS2030a 95×49 mm. 10fo. green 10·50 10·50
BUDAPEST BRIDGES: 30fi. Margaret; 60fi. Chain; 1fo. Elizabeth; 1fo.50, Liberty; 2fo. Petofi; 2fo.50, South; 10fo. Elizabeth (different).

381 Common Pheasant

1964. "Hunting". Multicoloured.

2034	20fi. Type **381**	10	10
2035	30fi. Wild boar	10	10
2036	40fi. Grey partridges	15	10
2037	60fi. Brown hare	25	10
2038	80fi. Fallow deer	35	10

2039	1fo. Mouflon	60	10
2040	1fo.70 Red deer	1·20	15
2041	2fo. Great bustard	1·30	25
2042	2fo.50 Roe deer	1·40	60
2043	3fo. Emblem of Hunters' Federation	2·30	1·20

382 Horse-riding and Medals

1965. Olympic Games, Tokyo—Hungarian Winners' Medals. Medals: Gold and brown (G); Silver and black (S); Bronze and brown (B).

2044	20fi. brown and olive (G)	10	10
2045	30fi. brown and violet (S)	10	10
2046	50fi. brown and olive (G)	10	10
2047	60fi. brown and light blue (G)	15	10
2048	70fi. brown, slate & stone (B)	25	10
2049	80fi. brown and green (G)	35	15
2050	1fo. brown, violet & mauve (S)	60	25
2051	1fo.20 brown and blue (S)	80	35
2052	1fo.40 brown and grey (S)	1·20	45
2053	1fo.50 brown and bistre (G)	1·40	60
2054	1fo.70 brown and red (S)	1·70	80
2055	3fo. brown and turquoise (G)	2·30	1·40

DESIGNS: 20fi. Type **382**; 30fi. Gymnastics; 50fi. Rifle-shooting; 60fi. Water-polo; 70fi. Putting the shot; 80fi. Football; 1fo. Weightlifting; 1fo.20, Canoeing; 1fo.40, Throwing the hammer; 1fo.50, Wrestling; 1fo.70, Throwing the javelin; 3fo. Fencing.

383 Mil Mi-4 Helicopter and Polar Station

1965. International Quiet Sun Year.

2056	**383**	20fi. orange, black & blue	10	10
2057	-	30fi. green, black & grey	10	10
2058	-	60fi. yellow, black & mve	10	10
2059	-	80fi. yellow, black & grn	25	10
2060	-	1fo.50 multicoloured	45	10
2061	-	1fo.70 black, mauve & bl	60	15
2062	-	2fo. red, black and blue	70	25
2063	-	2fo.50 yellow, blk & brn	1·20	60
2064	-	3fo. black, blue & yellow	1·70	1·20

MS2065 62×85 mm. 10fo. black, orange and blue 5·75 5·75
DESIGNS: 30fi. Rocket and radar aerials; 60fi. Rocket and diagram; 80fi. Radio telescope; 1fo.50, Compass needle on Globe; 1fo.70, Weather balloon; 2fo. Northern Lights and Adelie Penguins; 2fo.50, Space satellite; 3fo. I.Q.S.Y. emblem and world map; 10fo. Sun flares, snow crystals and rain.

384 Asters

1965. 20th Anniv of Liberation. Multicoloured.

2066	20fi. Type **384**	10	10
2067	30fi. Peonies	10	10
2068	50fi. Carnations	15	10
2069	60fi. Roses	25	10
2070	1fo.40 Lilies	60	10
2071	1fo.70 Godetia	70	15
2072	2fo. Gladiolus	75	25
2073	2fo.50 Parrot tulips	80	60
2074	3fo. Mixed bouquet	2·00	1·20

385 Leonov in Space

1965. Air. "Voskhod 2" Space Flight.

2075	**385**	1fo. grey and violet	60	25
2076	-	2fo. brown and purple	1·70	1·40

DESIGN: 2fo. Belyaev and Leonov.

386 Red Head (after Leonardo da Vinci)

1965. Int Renaissance Conference, Budapest.

2077	**386**	60fi. brown and ochre	45	10

387 Nikolaev, Tereshkova and View of Budapest

1965. Visit of Astronauts Nikolaev and Tereshkova.

2078	**387**	1fo. brown and blue	60	10

388 I.T.U. Emblem and Symbols

1965. Centenary of I.T.U.

2079	**388**	60fi. blue	35	10

389 Reproduction of Austria Type 109

1965. International Philatelic Exhibition, Vienna ("WIPA 1965"). Sheet 102×75 mm containing two of T **389** and two labels showing commemorative covers.
MS2080 **389** 2fo. (×2) blue and grey 1·00 1·00

390 French 13th-cent Tennis

1965. "History of Tennis".

2081	**390**	30fi. lake on buff	10	10
2082	-	40fi.+10fi. blk on lilac	10	10
2083	-	60fi.+10fi. green on bis	25	10
2084	-	70fi.+30fi. pur on turq	35	10
2085	-	80fi.+40fi. blue on lav	60	15
2086	-	1fo.+50fi. green on yell	70	25
2087	-	1fo.50+50fi. brown on green	80	35
2088	-	1fo.70+50fi. blk on bl	1·20	60
2089	-	2fo.+1fo. red on green	1·30	80

DESIGNS: 40fi. Hungarian 16th-cent game; 60fi. French 18th-cent "long court"; 70fi. 16th-cent "tennys courte"; 80fi. 16th-cent court at Fontainebleau; 1fo. 17th-cent game; 1fo.50, W. C. Wingfield and Wimbledon Cup, 1877; 1fo.70, Davis Cup, 1900. 2fo. Bela Kehrling in play.

391 Marx and Lenin

1965. Organization of Socialist Countries' Postal Administrations Congress, Peking.

2090	**391**	60fi. multicoloured	35	10

392 I.C.Y. Emblem and Pulleys

1965. International Co-operation Year.

2091	**392**	2fo. red	60	10

MS2092 75×98 mm T **392** but smaller (21×29 mm) in blokc of four, each in a different colour   5·25   5·25

393 Equestrian Act

1965. "Circus 1965". Multicoloured.

2093	**393**	Type **393**	10	10
2094		30fi. Musical clown	15	10
2095		40fi. Performing elephant	25	10
2096		50fi. Performing seal	35	15
2097		60fi. Lions	60	25
2098		1fo. Wild cat leaping through burning hoops	70	35
2099		1fo.50 Black panthers	1·20	35
2100		2fo.50 Acrobat with hoops	1·40	60
2101		3fo. Performing panther and dogs	2·00	80
2102		4fo. Bear on bicycle	3·00	2·10

394 Rescue Boat

1965. Danube Flood Relief.

2103	**394**	1fo.+50fi. brown & bl	1·70	1·70

MS2104 113×79 mm. 10fo.+5 fo. brown (Another rescue boat as T **394**)   5·75   5·75

395 Dr. I. Semmelweis

1965. Death Centenary of Ignac Semmelweis (physician).

2105	**395**	60fi. brown	35	25

396 Running

1965. University Games, Budapest. Multicoloured (except **MS**2115).

2106	**396**	Type **396**	10	10
2107		30fi. Start of swimming race	10	10
2108		50fi. Diving	10	10
2109		60fi. Gymnastics	20	10
2110		80fi. Tennis	25	10
2111		1fo.70 Fencing	60	15
2112		2fo. Volleyball	70	25
2113		2fo.50 Basketball	1·20	60
2114		4fo. Water-polo	1·70	1·60

MS2115 195×75 mm. Horiz design (38×28 mm) showing stadium. 10fo. chestnut, ochre and grey   8·75   8·75

397 Congress Emblem

1965. Sixth W.F.T.U. Congress, Warsaw.

2116	**397**	60fi. blue	35	10

398 Phyllocactus hybridum

1965. Succulents and Orchids. Multicoloured.

2117		20fi. Type **398**	10	10
2118		30fi. Cattleya warszewiczii	10	10
2119		60fi. Rebutia calliantha	20	10
2120		70fi. Paphiopedilum hybridum	25	10
2121		80fi. Opuntia rhodantha	60	10
2122		1fo. Laelia elegans	70	10
2123		1fo.50 Zygocactus truncatus	80	15
2124		2fo. Strelitzia reginae	1·20	25
2125		2fo.50 Lithops weberi	1·40	60
2126		3fo. Victoria amazonica	3·00	1·20

399 Reproduction of No. 1127

1965. Stamp Day. Designs show reproductions of Hungarian stamps. Multicoloured.

2127		2fo.+1fo. Type **399**	1·50	1·50
2128		2fo.+1fo. No. 1280	1·50	1·50
2129		2fo.+1fo. No. 1873	1·50	1·50
2130		2fo.+1fo. No. 1733	1·50	1·50

MS2131 100×85 mm. Nos. 2127/30 but smaller   7·50   7·50

400 F.I.R. Emblem

1965. Fifth International Federation of Resistance Fighters Congress, Budapest.

2132	**400**	2fo. blue	80	25

401 The Magic Horse

1965. Fairy Tales (3rd series). Scenes from *The Arabian Nights Entertainments*. Multicoloured.

2133		20fi. Type **401**	10	10
2134		30fi. Sultan Schahriah and Scheherazade	10	10
2135		50fi. Sinbad's 5th Voyage (ship)	10	10
2136		60fi. Aladdin and Genie of the Lamp	25	10
2137		80fi. Haroun al Rashid	35	10
2138		1fo. The Magic Carpet	80	25
2139		1fo.70 The Fisherman and the Genie	1·20	45
2140		2fo. Ali Baba	1·40	80
2141		3fo. Sinbad's 2nd Voyage (roc—legendary bird)	2·30	1·20

402 "Mariner 4"

1965. Air. Space Research.

2142	**402**	20fi. black, yellow & blue	25	10
2143	-	30fi. violet, yellow & brn	25	10
2144	-	40fi. brown, mauve & bl	45	10

2145	-	60fi. multicoloured	60	25
2146	-	1fo. multicoloured	1·20	35
2147	-	2fo.50 black, grey & pur	1·70	60
2148	-	3fo. black, green & brn	2·30	80

MS2149 105×85 mm. 10fo. multi-coloured   7·50   7·50

DESIGNS—VERT: 30fi. "San Marco" (Italian satellite); 40fi. "Molnyija 1" (Polish satellite); 60fi. Moon rocket; 1fo. "Sha-pir" rocket; 2fo.50, "Szonda 3" satellite; 3fo. "Syncom 3" satellite. HORIZ: 10fo. Satellites orbiting Globe.

403 Scarlet Tiger Moth

1966. Butterflies and Moths. Multicoloured.

2150		20fi. Type **403**	10	10
2151		60fi. Orange tip	25	10
2152		70fi. Meleager's blue	60	10
2153		80fi. Scarce swallowtail	70	10
2154		1fo. Common burnet	80	10
2155		1fo.50 Southern festoon	95	35
2156		2fo. Camberwell beauty	1·20	45
2157		2fo.50 Nettle-tree butterfly	1·40	45
2158		3fo. Clouded yellow	1·90	1·20

404 Bela Kun

1966. Anniversaries of 1966.

2159		60fi. black and red (T **404**)	35	25
2160		60fi. black and blue (T. Esze)	80	25
2161		1fo. violet (Shastri)	60	25
2162		2fo. brown and ochre (I. Szechenyi)	80	25
2163		2fo. sepia and bistre (M. Zrinyi)	80	25
2164		2fo. sepia and green (S. Koranyi)	80	25

EVENTS: No. 2159, 80th Birth anniv (workers' leader); 2160, (after statue by M. Nemeth) 300th Birth anniv (war hero); 2161, Death commem (Indian Prime Minister); 2162, 175th Birth anniv (statesman); 2163, 400th Death anniv (military commander); 2164, Birth cent (scientist).

405 "Luna 9" in Space

1966. Moon Landing of "Luna 9".

2165	**405**	2fo. black, yellow & violet	60	25
2166	-	3fo. black, yellow & blue	1·70	1·20

DESIGN—HORIZ: 3fo. "Luna 9" on Moon.

406 Crocus

1966. Flower Protection. Multicoloured.

2167		20fi. Type **406**	40	10
2168		30fi. European cyclamen	50	25
2169		60fi. Ligularia	80	35
2170		1fo.40 Orange lily	1·20	45
2171		1fo.50 Fritillary	1·40	80
2172		3fo. "Dracocephalum ruyschiana	2·50	1·20

407 Order of Labour (bronze)

1966. Hungarian Medals and Orders. Multicoloured.

2173		20fi. Type **407**	10	10
2174		30fi. Order of Labour (silver)	10	10
2175		50fi. Banner Order of Republic, 3rd class (21½×28½ mm)	10	10
2176		60fi. Order of Labour (gold)	10	10
2177		70fi. Banner Order of Republic, 2nd class (25×30½ mm)	25	10
2178		1fo. Red Banner Order of Labour	35	15
2179		1fo.20 Banner Order of Republic, 1st class (28½×38 mm)	45	35
2180		2fo. Order of Merit of Republic	95	60
2181		2fo.50 Hero of Socialist Labour	1·40	95

408 Early Transport and Budapest Railway Station, 1846

1966. Re-opening of Transport Museum, Budapest.

2182	**408**	1fo. brown, green & yell	60	25
2183	-	2fo. blue, brown & green	1·20	60

DESIGN: 2fo. Modern transport and South Station, Buda-pest.

409 Barn Swallows

1966. Protection of Birds. Multicoloured.

2184		20fi. Type **409**	25	10
2185		30fi. Long-tailed tits	35	10
2186		60fi. Red crossbill	60	15
2187		1fo.40 Middle-spotted wood-pecker	1·40	35
2188		1fo.50 Hoopoe	1·70	70
2189		3fo. Forest and emblem of Na-tional Forestry Association	2·50	1·40

410 W.H.O. Building

1966. Inauguration of W.H.O. Headquarters, Geneva.

2190	**410**	2fo. black and blue	80	25

411 Football

1966. World Cup Football Championships (1st issue). Sheet 76×108 mm.

MS2191 **411** 10fo. multicoloured   10·00   10·00

See also Nos. 2194/2202.

412 Nuclear Research Institute

1966. Tenth Anniv of United Nuclear Research Institute, Dubna (U.S.S.R.).

2192	**412**	60fi. black and green	80	25

413 Buda Fortress, after Schedel's "Chronicle" (1493)

1966. 20th Anniv of U.N.E.S.C.O. and 72nd Executive Board Session, Budapest.

2193	**413**	2fo. violet and blue	1·20	35

414 Jules Rimet, Football and Cup

1966. World Cup Football Championship (2nd issue). Multicoloured.

2194	**20fi.**	Type **414**	10	10
2195	30fi.	Montevideo, 1930	25	10
2196	60fi.	Rome, 1934	35	10
2197	1fo.	Paris, 1938	45	10
2198	1fo.40	Rio de Janeiro, 1950	60	15
2199	1fo.70	Berne, 1954	1·00	25
2200	2fo.	Stockholm, 1958	1·20	60
2201	2fo.50	Santiago de Chile, 1962	1·70	80
2202	3fo.+1fo.	World Cup emblem on Union Jack, and map of England	2·50	2·00

415 Girl Pioneer and Emblem

1966. 20th Anniv of Hungarian Pioneers Movement.

2203	**415**	60fi. red and violet	80	25

416 Fire Engine

1966. Centenary of Voluntary Fire Brigades.

2204	**416**	2fo. black and orange	1·20	60

417 Red Fox

1966. Hunting Trophies. Multicoloured.

2205	**20fi.**	Type **417**	10	10
2206	60fi.	Wild boar	25	10
2207	70fi.	Wild cat	35	10
2208	80fi.	Roe deer	35	10
2209	1fo.50	Red deer	60	15
2210	2fo.50	Fallow deer	70	25
2211	3fo.	Mouflon	1·70	95

418 Throwing the Discus

1966. Eighth European Athletic Championships, Budapest. Multicoloured.

2212	**20fi.**	Type **418**	10	10
2213	30fi.	High-jumping	25	10
2214	40fi.	Throwing the javelin	35	10
2215	50fi.	Throwing the hammer	45	10
2216	60fi.	Long-jumping	70	15
2217	1fo.	Putting the shot	1·20	35
2218	2fo.	Pole-vaulting	2·00	95
2219	3fo.	Running	3·00	1·20
MS2220	105×75 mm. 10fo. Hurdling		10·50	10·50

419 Archery

1966. Stamp Day. Multicoloured.

2221	2fo.+50fi.	Types **419**	1·50	1·50
2222	2fo.+50fi.	Grapes	1·50	1·50
2223	2fo.+50fi.	Poppies	1·50	1·50
2224	2fo.+50fi.	Space dogs	1·50	1·50
MS2225	98×84 mm. Nos. 2221/4		7·00	7·00

420 Helsinki

1966. Air.

2226	**420**	20fi. red	10	10
2227	-	50fi. brown	10	10
2228	-	1fo. blue	25	10
2229	-	1fo.10 black	30	10
2230	-	1fo.20 orange	35	10
2231	-	1fo.50 green	40	10
2232	-	2fo. blue	50	15
2233	-	2fo.50 red	60	25
2234	-	3fo. green	65	30
2235	-	4fo. brown	3·00	2·10
2236	-	5fo. violet	1·20	35
2237	-	10fo. blue	3·00	60
2238	-	20fo. green	4·75	1·20

DESIGNS—Ilyushin Il-18 over: 50fi. Athens; 1fo. Beirut; 1fo.10, Frankfurt; 1fo.20, Cairo; 1fo.50, Copenhagen; 2fo. London; 2fo.50, Moscow; 3fo. Paris; 4fo. Prague; 5fo. Rome; 10fo. Damascus; 20fo. Budapest.

For 2fo.60 in similar design see No. 2369.

421 Girl in the Woods (after Barabas)

1966. Paintings in Hungarian National Gallery (1st series). Multicoloured.

2239	**60fi.**	Type **421**	60	25
2240	1fo.	Mrs. Istvan Bitto (Barabas)	80	35
2241	1fo.50	Laszlo Hunyadi Farewell (Benczur)	1·40	60
2242	1fo.70	Woman Reading (Benczur) (horiz)	2·00	70
2243	2fo.	The Faggot-carrier (Munkacsy)	2·30	80
2244	2fo.50	The Yawning Apprentice (Munkacsy)	2·50	85
2245	3fo.	Woman in Lilac (Szinyei)	3·50	95
MS2246	97×79 mm. 10fo. Picnic in May (Szinyei)		16·00	16·00

See also Nos. 2282/8, 2318/MS2325, 2357/MS2364, 2411/MS2418, 2449/MS2456 and 2525/MS2532.

422 "Vostok 3" and "Vostok 4" (Nikolaev and Popovich)

1966. Twin Space Flights. Multicoloured.

2247	**20fi.**	Type **422**	10	10
2248	60fi.	Borman and Lovell, Schirra and Stafford	30	10
2249	80fi.	Bykovsky and Tereshkova	35	10
2250	1fo.	Stafford and Cernan	60	10
2251	1fo.50	Belyaev and Leonov (Leonov in space)	80	35
2252	2fo.	McDivitt and White (White in space)	1·20	45
2253	2fo.50	Komarov, Feoktistov and Yegorov	2·00	70
2254	3fo.	Conrad and Gordon	2·50	80

423 Kitaibel and Kitaibelia vitifolia

1967. 150th Death Anniv of Pal Kitaibel (botanist). Carpathian Flowers. Multicoloured.

2255	**20fi.**	Type **423**	10	10
2256	60fi.	Dentaria glandulosa	35	10
2257	1fo.	Edraianthus tenuifolius	45	10
2258	1fo.50	Althaea pallida	80	25
2259	2fo.	Centaurea mollis	1·00	35
2260	2fo.50	Sternbergia colchiciflora	2·00	45
2261	3fo.	Iris hungarica	2·10	1·30

424 Militiaman

1967. Tenth Anniv of Workers' Militia.

2262	**424**	2fo. blue	80	25

425 Faustus Verancsics' Parachute Descent, 1617

1967. Air. "Aerofila 67". Airmail Stamp Exhibition, Budapest. (a) 1st issue.

2263	2fo.+1fo.	sepia and yellow	1·50	1·50
2264	2fo.+1fo.	sepia and blue	1·50	1·50
2265	2fo.+1fo.	sepia and green	1·50	1·50
2266	2fo.+1fo.	sepia and pink	1·50	1·50
MS2267	116×90 mm. Nos. 2263/6		7·00	7·00

(b) 2nd issue.

2268	2fo.+1fo.	blue and green	1·50	1·50
2269	2fo.+1fo.	blue and orange	1·50	1·50
2270	2fo.+1fo.	blue and yellow	1·50	1·50
2271	2fo.+1fo.	blue and pink	1·50	1·50
MS2272	116×90 mm. Nos. 2268/71		7·00	7·00

DESIGNS: No. 2263, Type **425**; No. 2264, David Schwartz's aluminium airship, 1897; No. 2265, Erno Horvath's monoplane, 1911; No. 2266, PKZ-2 helicopter, 1918; No. 2268, Parachutist; No. 2269, Mil Mi-1 helicopter; No. 2270, Tupolev Tu-154 airliner; No. 2271, "Luna 12".

426 I.T.Y. Emblem and Transport

1967. International Tourist Year.

2273	**426**	1fo. black and blue	60	25

427 Milton, after Orial Petrics

1967. "Amphilex" Stamp Exhibition, Amsterdam. Sheet 81×91 mm.

MS2274	**427**	10fo. multicoloured	10·50	10·50

428 Ferenc Deak (paddle-steamer), Schonbuchel Castle and Austrian Flag

1967. 25th Session of Danube Commission. Vessels of Mahart Shipping Company.

2275	**428**	30fi. multicoloured	60	25
2276	-	60fi. multicoloured	80	45

2277	-	1fo. multicoloured	1·70	60
2278	-	1fo. multicoloured	3·50	1·00
2279	-	1fo.70 multicoloured	5·25	1·20
2280	-	2fo. multicoloured	5·75	2·30
2281	-	2fo.50 multicoloured	8·75	3·00

DESIGNS (Vessels, backgrounds and flags): 60fi. River-bus Revfulop Bratislava Castle, Czechoslovakia; 1fo. Diesel passenger boat Hunyadi, Buda Castle, Hungary; 1fo.50, Diesel tug Szekszard, Golubac Castle, Yugoslavia; 1fo.70, Tug Miscolc, Vidin Castle, Bulgaria; 2fo. Motor-freighter Tihany, Galati shipyard. Rumania; 2fo.50, Hydrofoil Siraly I, port of Izmail, U.S.S.R.

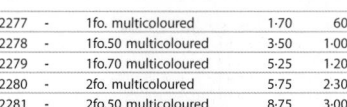

429 Szidonia Deak (A. Gyorgyi)

1967. Paintings in National Gallery, Budapest (2nd series). Multicoloured.

2282	**60fi.**	Liszt (M. Munkacsy)	35	25
2283	1fo.	Self-portrait (S. Lanyi)	60	30
2284	1fo.50	Portrait of a Lady (J. Borsos)	80	35
2285	1fo.70	The Lovers (after P. Szinyei Merse) (horiz)	1·30	40
2286	2fo.	Type **429**	1·40	45
2287	2fo.50	National Guardsman (J. Borsos)	1·60	60
2288	3fo.	Louis XV and Madame Dubarry (G. Benczur)	1·90	70

430 Poodle

1967. Dogs. Multicoloured.

2289	**30fi.**	Type **430**	15	10
2290	60fi.	Collie (23½×35 mm)	25	10
2291	1fo.	Pointer	45	10
2292	1fo.40	Fox terriers (23½×35 mm)	80	15
2293	1fo.70	Pumi	1·20	35
2294	3fo.	Alsatian (23½×35 mm)	1·40	80
2295	4fo.	Puli	2·50	1·40

431 Sterlet

1967. 14th International Anglers' Federation Congress, and World Angling Championships, Dunaujvaros. Multicoloured.

2296	**20fi.**	Type **431**	10	10
2297	60fi.	Zander	25	10
2298	1fo.	Common carp	35	10
2299	1fo.70	Wels	95	15
2300	2fo.	Northern pike	1·20	35
2301	2fo.50	Asp	1·40	70
2302	3fo.+1fo.	Anglers' and C.I.P.S. (Federation) emblem	2·50	1·30

432 Prince Igor (Borodin)

1967. Popular Operas. Designs showing scenes from various operas. Multicoloured.

2303	**20fi.**	Type **432**	25	10
2304	30fi.	Der Freischutz (Weber)	25	10
2305	40fi.	The Magic Flute (Mozart)	60	15
2306	60fi.	Bluebeard's Castle (Bartok)	80	25
2307	80fi.	Carmen (Bizet) (vert)	1·20	35
2308	1fo.	Don Carlos (Verdi) (vert)	1·40	60
2309	1fo.70	Tannhauser (Wagner) (vert)	1·70	1·20
2310	3fo.	Laszlo Hunyadi (Erkel) (vert)	2·30	2·10

433 "Teaching"
(14th-cent class)

1967. 600th Anniv of Higher Education in Hungary.
| 2311 | **433** | 2fo. green and gold | 1·40 | 25 |

434 Faculty Building

1967. 300th Anniv of Political Law and Science Faculty, Lorand Eotvos University, Budapest.
| 2312 | **434** | 2fo. green | 1·40 | 25 |

435 *Lenin as Teacher*

1967. 50th Anniv of October Revolution. Multicoloured.
2313	60fi. Type **435**	25	10
2314	1fo. *Lenin*	25	10
2315	3fo. *Lenin aboard the Aurora*	1·20	60

436 "Venus 4"

1967. Landing of "Venus 4" on planet Venus.
| 2316 | **436** | 5fo. multicoloured | 2·00 | 1·50 |

437 19th-centenary Mail Coach

1967. Centenary of Hungarian Postal Administration. Sheet 85×95 mm.
| MS2317 | **437** | 10fo. multicoloured | 5·75 | 5·75 |

437a *Brother and Sister* (A. Fenyes)

1967. Paintings in National Gallery, Budapest (3rd series). Multicoloured.
2318	60fi. Type **437a**	25	10
2319	1fo. *Boys Wrestling on Beach* (O. Glatz)	60	10
2320	1fo.50 *October* (K. Ferenczy)	75	15
2321	1fo.70 *Women by the River* (I. Szonyi) (horiz)	80	25
2322	2fo. *Godfather's Breakfast* (I. Csok)	85	30
2323	2fo.50 *The Eviction Order* (G. Derkovits)	1·00	60
2324	3fo. *Self-Portrait* (T. Csontvary)	1·20	80
MS2325	78×100 mm. 10fo. *The Apple Pickers* (B. Uitz) (larger 37½×60 mm)	2·25	3·00

"Women by the River" (1fo.70) is in a private collection in Budapest.
See also Nos. 2357/MS2364 and 2411/MS2418.

438 Rifle-shooting on Skis

1967. Winter Olympic Games, Grenoble. Multicoloured.
2326	30fi. Type **438**	10	10
2327	60fi. Figure skating (pairs)	25	10
2328	1fo. Bobsleighing	35	10
2329	1fo.40 Downhill skiing	60	15
2330	1fo.70 Figure skating	80	25
2331	2fo. Speed skating	95	45
2332	3fo. Ski jumping	1·20	80
2333	4fo. Ice stadium, Grenoble	1·70	1·20
MS2334	116×99 mm. 10fo. Ice hockey goal keeper (61×61 mm)	4·75	4·75

439 Kalman Kando, Class V43 Electric Locomotive and Map

1968. Kando Commemoration.
| 2335 | **439** | 2fo. blue | 80 | 25 |

440 Cat

1968. Cats. Multicoloured.
2336	20fi. Type **440**	25	10
2337	60fi. Cream angora	35	25
2338	1fo. Smoky angora	60	30
2339	1fo.20 Domestic kitten	70	35
2340	1fo.50 White angora	1·20	60
2341	2fo. Striped angora	1·40	80
2342	2fo.50 Siamese	2·00	95
2343	5fo. Blue angora	3·50	1·40

441 Zoltan Kodaly (composer)

1968. Kodaly Commemoration.
| 2344 | **441** | 5fo. multicoloured | 2·00 | 1·20 |

442 City Hall, Arms, Grapes and Apricot

1968. 600th Anniv of Kecskemet.
| 2345 | **442** | 2fo. brown | 80 | 25 |

443 White Stork

1968. International Council for Bird Preservation Congress, Budapest. Protected Birds. Multicoloured.
2346	20fi. Type **443**	25	10
2347	50fi. Golden orioles	35	15
2348	60fi. Imperial eagle	45	25
2349	1fo. Western red-footed falcons	60	30
2350	1fo.20 Eurasian scops owl	70	35
2351	1fo.50 Great bustard	80	40
2352	2fo. European bee eaters	2·30	60
2353	2fo.50 Greylag goose	3·00	1·30

444 Karl Marx

1968. 150th Birth Anniv of Karl Marx.
| 2354 | **444** | 1fo. purple | 60 | 25 |

See also No. 1290.

445 Icarus falling in space

1968. In Memoriam. Astronauts White, Gagarin and Komarov. Sheet 95×77 mm.
| MS2355 | **445** | 10fo. multicoloured | 5·75 | 5·75 |

446 Student

1968. 150th Anniv of Mosonmagyarovar Agricultural College.
| 2356 | **446** | 2fo. green | 80 | 25 |

1968. Paintings in National Gallery, Budapest (4th series). As T **437a**. Multicoloured.
2357	40fi. *Girl with a Pitcher* (Goya)	10	10
2358	60fi. *Head of an Apostle* (El Greco)	25	10
2359	1fo. *Boy with Apples* (Nunez) (horiz)	45	25
2360	1fo.50 *The Repentant Magdalen* (El Greco)	95	35
2361	2fo.50 *The Breakfast* (Velasquez) (horiz)	1·40	40
2362	4fo. *St. Elizabeth* (detail from *The Holy Family*; El Greco)	1·60	95
2363	5fo. *The Knife-grinder* (Goya)	1·70	1·20
MS2364	88×95 mm. 10fo. *Portrait of a Girl* (Palma Vecchio)	3·00	3·75

447 Lake Steamer, Flags and Badacsony Hills

1968. Lake Balaton Resorts. Multicoloured.
2365	20fi. Type **447**	25	10
2365a	40fi. As Type **447**	25	10
2366	60fi. Tihany peninsula, tower and feather	25	10
2367	1fo. Yachts and buoy, Balatonalmadi	25	10
2368	2fo. Szigliget bay, vineyard, wine and fish	60	25

448 Ilyushin Il-18 over St. Stephen's Cathedral, Vienna

1968. Air. 50th Anniv of Budapest–Vienna Airmail Service.
| 2369 | **448** | 2fo.60 violet | 1·20 | 35 |

449 Class 424 Steam Locomotive No. 176

1968. Centenary of Hungarian State Railways.
| 2370 | **449** | 2fo. multicoloured | 2·00 | 60 |

450 Grazing Stud

1968. Horse-breeding on the Hortobagy "puszta" (Hungarian steppe). Multicoloured.
2371	30fi. Type **450**	15	10
2372	40fi. Horses in storm	15	10
2373	60fi. Grooms horse-racing	25	10
2374	80fi. Horse-drawn sleigh	45	10
2375	1fo. Four-in-hand	60	30
2376	1fo.40 Seven-in-hand	70	35
2377	2fo. Driving five horses	85	40
2378	2fo.50 Groom preparing evening meal	95	60
2379	4fo. Five-in-hand	1·20	95

451 M. Tompa

1968. Death Centenary of Mihaly Tompa (poet).
| 2380 | **451** | 60fi. violet | 35 | 10 |

452 Festival Emblem, Bulgarian and Hungarian Couples in National Costume

1968. Ninth World Youth Festival, Sofia.
| 2381 | **452** | 60fi. multicoloured | 35 | 10 |

453 Breasting the Tape

454 Swimming

1968. Air. Olympic Games, Mexico. Multicoloured.
| MS2382 | 81×101 mm. **453** 10fo. multicoloured (postage) | 6·50 | 6·50 |

2383	20fi. Type **454** (air)	10	10
2384	60fi. Football	10	10
2385	80fi. Wrestling	10	10
2386	1fo. Canoeing	15	10
2387	1fo.40 Gymnastics	35	10
2388	2fo.+1fo. Horse-jumping	1·20	35
2389	3fo. Fencing	1·40	45
2390	4fo. Throwing the Javelin	1·70	65

455 Baja Plate, 1870

1968. Stamp Day. Hungarian Ceramics. Multicoloured.

2391	**455**	1fo.+50fi. Type **455**	1·20	1·20
2392		1fo.+50fi. West Hungarian jug, 1618	1·20	1·20
2393		1fo.+50fi. Tiszafured flagon, 1847	1·20	1·20
2394		1fo.+50fi. Mezocsat flask, 1848	1·20	1·20

MS2395 74×96 mm. 2fo.+50fi. North Hungarian jug, 1672; 2fo.+50fi. Mezocsat plate, 1843; 2fo.+50fi. Moragy plate, 1860; 2fo.+50fi. Debrecen pitcher, 1793 ... 5·75 5·75

The designs from the miniature sheet are smaller, measuring 25×35 mm.

456 Society Emblem

1968. "Hungarian Society for Popularization of Scientific Knowledge".

2396	**456**	2fo. black and blue	80	25

457 Rocket Hesperus

1968. Garden Flowers. Multicoloured.

2397	**457**	20fi. Type **457**	35	10
2398		60fi. Pansy	45	10
2399		80fi. Zinnias	60	35
2400		1fo. Morning Glory	95	45
2401		1fo.40 Petunia	1·20	60
2402		1fo.50 Purslane	1·40	65
2403		2fo. Michaelmas daisies	1·60	70
2404		2fo.50 Dahlia	1·70	1·20

458 Two Girls waving Flags

1968. Children's Stamp Designs for 50th Anniv of Hungarian Communist Party. Multicoloured.

2405	**458**	40fi. Type **458**	35	10
2406		60fi. Children with flags and banner	80	25
2407		1fo. Pioneer bugler in camp	1·40	60

459 "Workers of the World Unite" (Bertalan Por's 1918 poster)

1968. 50th Anniv of Hungarian Communist Party.

2408	**459**	1fo. black, red and gold	35	25
2409	-	2fo. multicoloured	45	35

DESIGN—HORIZ: 2fo. "Martyrs" (statue by Zoltan Kiss).

460 Human Rights Emblem

1968. Human Rights Year.

2410	**460**	1fo. brown	80	25

1968. Paintings in National Gallery, Budapest (5th series). Italian Masters. As T **437a**. Multicoloured.

2411		40fi. *Esterhazy Madonna* (Raphael)	10	10
2412		60fi. *The Annunciation* (Strozzi)	10	10
2413		1fo. *Portrait of a Young Man* (Raphael)	25	10
2414		1fo.50 *The Three Graces* (Naldini)	60	10
2415		2fo.50 *Portrait of a Man* (Sebastian del Piombo)	1·00	35
2416		4fo. *The Doge Marcantonio Trevisani* (Titian)	1·70	80
2417		5fo. *Venus, Cupid and Jealousy* (Bronzino)	2·50	1·30

MS2418 116×73 mm. 10fo. *Bathsheba bathing* Ricci). Imperf ... 6·50 6·50

461 Endre Ady

1969. 50th Death Anniv of Endre Ady (poet).

2419	**461**	1fo. black, purple & gold	60	25

462 Press Emblem

1969. Centenary of Athenaeum Press.

2420	**462**	2fo. multicoloured	80	25

463 "Apollo 8" entering Moon Orbit

1969. Air. Moon Flight of "Apollo 8". Sheet 111×81 mm.

MS2421 **463** 10fo. multicoloured ... 70 70

464 Throwing the Javelin

1969. Olympic Gold Medal Winners. Multicoloured.

2422	**464**	40fi. Type **464**	15	10
2423		60fi. Canoeing	25	10
2424		1fo. Football	30	10
2425		1fo.20 Throwing the Hammer	35	15
2426		2fo. Fencing	50	25
2427		3fo. Wrestling	60	30
2428		4fo. Kayak-canoeing	1·40	35
2429		5fo. Horse-jumping	1·70	95

MS2430 111×84 mm. 10fo. Ancient Greek Athlete and Olympic Flame ... 7·50 7·50

465 Poster by O. Danko

1969. 50th Anniv of Proclamation of Hungarian Soviet Republic.

2431	**465**	40fi. black, red and gold	10	10
2432	-	60fi. black, red and gold	10	10
2433	-	1fo. black, red and gold	35	15
2434	-	2fo. multicoloured	60	25
2435	-	3fo. multicoloured	1·20	60

MS2436 97×71 mm. 10fo. black, red and grey ... 4·75 4·75

DESIGNS: 60fi. "Lenin" by unknown artist; 1fo. "Young Man Breaking Chains" (R. Steiner); 2fo. "Worker" (I. Foldes and G. Vegh); 3fo. "Soldier" (unknown artist). HORIZ—(52×40 mm): 10fo. "Workers with Banner" (R. Bereny).

466 Space Link-up of "Soyuz 4" and "Soyuz 5"

1969. Air. Space Flights of "Soyuz 4" and "Soyuz 5". Multicoloured.

2437	**466**	2fo. Type **466**	80	80
2438		2fo. Link-up and astronauts "walking" in Space	80	80

467 Jersey Tiger Moth

1969. Butterflies and Moths. Multicoloured.

2439	**467**	40fi. Type **467**	25	10
2440		60fi. Eyed hawk moth	25	10
2441		80fi. Painted lady	25	10
2442		1fo. Foxy charaxes	30	10
2443		1fo.20 Lesser fiery copper	40	10
2444		2fo. Large blue	80	25
2445		3fo. Dark crimson underwing	1·60	60
2446		4fo. Peacock	1·70	1·20

468 I.L.O. Emblem

1969. 50th Anniv of Int Labour Organisation.

2447	**468**	1fo. brown and red	60	25

469 Chain Bridge, Budapest

1969. "Budapest 71" Stamp Exhibition.

2448	**469**	5fo.+2fo. multicoloured	2·30	2·30

470 Black Pigs (Gauguin)

1969. Paintings in National Gallery, Budapest (6th series). French Masters. Multicoloured.

2449	**470**	40fi. Type **470**	15	10
2450		60fi. *The Ladies* (Toulouse-Lautrec) (horiz)	25	10
2451		1fo. *Venus on Clouds* (Vouet)	35	15
2452		2fo. *Lady with Fan* (Manet) (horiz)	80	25
2453		3fo. *Petra Camara* (Chasseriau)	1·70	35
2454		4fo. *The Cowherd* (Troyon) (horiz)	2·30	70
2455		5fo. *The Wrestlers* (Courbet)	2·50	1·20

MS2456 75×97 mm. 10fo. *Pomona* (Fouche) ... 7·00 7·00

471 Vac

1969. Danube Towns. Multicoloured.

2457	**471**	40fi. Type **471**	10	10
2458		1fo. Szentendre	10	10
2459		1fo.20 Visegrad	60	10
2460		3fo. Esztergom	95	25

472 "PAX"

1969. 20th Anniv of Int Peace Movement.

2461	**472**	1fo. gold, dp blue & blue	60	25

473 Astronauts on Moon

1969. Air. First Man on the Moon (1st issue). Sheet 133×89 mm.

MS2462 **473** 10fo. multicoloured ... 10·50 10·50

See also Nos. 2487/94.

474 Zelkova Leaf (fossil)

1969. Centenary of Hungarian Geological Institute. Minerals and Fossils. Multicoloured.

2463	**474**	40fi. Type **474**	15	10
2464		60fi. Greenockite calcite sphalerite crystals	25	10
2465		1fo. Hungarian herring (fossilized fish)	30	10
2466		1fo.20 Quartz crystals	35	15
2467		2fo. "Reineckia crassicostata" (ammonite)	45	25
2468		3fo. Copper ore	95	35
2469		4fo. "Placochelys placodonta" (fossilized turtle)	1·70	95
2470		5fo. Cuprite crystals	3·00	1·20

475 Okorag Stirrupcup, 1880

1969. Stamp Day. Hungarian Folk Art. Wood-carvings. Multicoloured.

2471		1fo.+50fi. Type **475**	1·40	1·40
2472		1fo.+50fi. Felsotizavidek jar, 1898	1·40	1·40
2473		1fo.+50fi. Somogyharsagy pot, 1935	1·40	1·40
2474		1fo.+50fi. Alfold smoking-pipe, 1740	1·40	1·40

MS2475 75×96 mm. 2fo.+50fi. ×4 (a) Csorna panel, 1879; (b) Okany mug, 1914; (c) Sellye casket, 1899; (d) Lengyeltoti box, 1880 ... 5·75 5·75

The designs in **MS**2475 are smaller, each 31×40 mm.

476 *The Scientist at his Table* (Rembrandt)

1969. Int "History of Art" Congress, Budapest.

2476	**476**	1fo. sepia	60	25

477 Horse-jumping

1969. World Pentathlon Championships, Budapest. Multicoloured.

2477	40fi. Type **477**		30	15
2478	60fi. Fencing		60	35
2479	1fo. Pistol-shooting		95	60
2480	2fo. Swimming		1·00	70
2481	3fo. Running		1·20	95
2482	5fo. All five sports		2·30	1·40

478 Postcard and Letterbox

1969. Centenary of First Hungarian Postcard.

2483	**478**	60fi. ochre and red	35	25

479 Mahatma Gandhi

1969. Birth Centenary of Mahatma Gandhi.

2484	**479**	5fo. multicoloured	1·70	1·20

480 Hemispheres

1969. World Trade Unions Federations Congress, Budapest.

2485	**480**	2fo. blue and brown	80	25

481 Janos Nagy (self-portrait)

1969. 50th Death Anniv of Janos Nagy (painter).

2486	**481**	5fo. multicoloured	1·70	1·20

482 "Flight to the Moon" (after Jules Verne)

1969. Air. First Man on the Moon (2nd issue). Multicoloured.

2487	40fi. Type **482**		10	10
2488	60fi. Tsiolkovsky's "space station"		25	10
2489	1fo. "Luna 1"		35	10
2490	1fo.50 "Ranger 7"		70	15
2491	2fo. "Luna 9"		95	25
2492	2fo.50 "Apollo 8"		1·00	35
2493	3fo. "Soyuz 4" and "5"		1·40	70
2494	4fo. "Apollo 10"		1·70	1·00

483 St John the Evangelist (Van Dyck)

1969. Dutch Paintings in Hungarian Museums. Multicoloured.

2495	40fi. Type **483**		10	10
2496	60fi. Peasants (P. de Molyn)		10	10
2497	1fo. Boy lighting Pipe (H. Terbruggen)		45	15
2498	2fo. The Musicians (detail, Jan Steen)		80	25
2499	3fo. Woman reading Letter (P. de Hooch)		1·50	35
2500	4fo. The Fiddler (Dirk Hals)		1·70	70
2501	5fo. J. Asselyn (Frans Hals)		2·30	1·40

MS2502 73×97 mm. 10fo. *Mucius Scaevola before Porsenna* (Rubens and Van Dyck) — 5·75 — 5·75

484 Kiskunfelegyhaza Pigeon

1969. International Pigeon Exhibitionn, Budapest.

2503	**484**	1fo. multicoloured	60	25

485 Daimler (1886)

1970. Air. Old Motor Cars. Multicoloured.

2504	40fi. Type **485**		35	10
2505	60fi. Peugeot (1894)		45	15
2506	1fo. Benz (1901)		60	35
2507	1fo.50 Cudell (1902)		70	45
2508	2fo. Rolls-Royce (1908)		1·00	60
2509	2fo.50 Ford "T" (1908)		1·20	80
2510	3fo. Vermorel (1912)		1·70	95
2511	4fo. Csonka (1912)		2·30	1·20

486 View of Budapest

1970. "Budapest 71" Stamp Exhibition and Centenary of Hungarian Stamps (1st series). Multicoloured. Background colours given.

2512	**486**	2fo.+1fo. brown	1·00	1·00
2513	–	2fo.+1fo. lilac	1·00	1·00
2514	–	2fo.+1fo. blue	1·00	1·00

DESIGNS: Nos. 2513/4 show different views of Budapest, in style as Type **486**.
See also Nos. 2572/**MS**2576 and 2604/**MS**2608.

487 "Soyuz 6, 7, 8"

1970. Air. Space Exploration. Multicoloured.

2515	3fo.(×4) Type **487**		1·20	1·20
2516	3fo.(×4) Astronauts on Moon ("Apollo 12")		1·20	1·20

Nos. 2515/6 were only available each in small sheets of four, and are priced thus.

488 Underground Train at Station

1970. Opening of Budapest Underground Railway.

2517	**488**	1fo. blue, turquoise & blk	60	25

489 Budapest Panorama, 1945 (image scaled to 37% of original size)

490 Cloud Formation, Satellite and Globe

1970. Centenary of Hungarian Meteorological Service.

2519	**490**	1fo. multicoloured	60	25

491 Lenin

1970. Birth Centenary of Lenin. Multicoloured.

2520	1fo. Lenin Statue, Budapest		25	10
2521	2fo. Type **491**		60	35

492 Lehar and Music

1970. Birth Cent of Franz Lehar (composer).

2522	**492**	2fo. multicoloured	80	35

493 Fujiyama and Hungarian Pavilion

1970. Air. Expo 70. Multicoloured.

2523	2fo. Type **493**		1·20	1·20
2524	3fo. Tower of the Sun and Peace Bell		1·70	1·70

494 Samson and Delilah (M. Rocca)

1970. Paintings in National Gallery, Budapest (7th series). Multicoloured.

2525	40fi. Type **494**		10	10
2526	60fi. *Joseph's Dream* (G. B. Langetti)		25	10
2527	1fo. *Clio* (P. Mignard)		35	15
2528	1fo.50 Venus and Satyr (S. Ricci) (horiz.)		45	25
2529	2fo.50 Andromeda (F. Furini)		95	35
2530	4fo. *Venus, Adonis and Cupid* (L. Giordano)		1·50	80
2531	5fo. *Allegory* (woman) (C. Giaquinto)		1·70	1·20

MS2532 100×85 mm. 10fo. *Diane and Callisto* (Janssens) (horiz) — 7·00 — 7·00

The design of **MS**2532 is larger, 64×46 mm.

495 "Apollo 13" over Moon

1970. 25th Anniv of Liberation. Sheet 159×83 mm containing T **489** and similar horiz design. Multicoloured.

MS2518 5fo. ×2 (a) Type **489**; (b) Budapest panorama, 1970 — 5·75 — 5·75

496 Beethoven (from statue at Martonvasar)

1970. Birth Bicentenary of Beethoven.

2534	**496**	1fo. green, lilac & yellow	1·40	35

497 Foundryman

1970. Bicentenary of Diosgyor Foundry, Miskolc.

2535	**497**	1fo. multicoloured	60	25

498 St. Stephen

1970. 1,000th Birth Anniv of St. Stephen (King Stephen I of Hungary).

2536	**498**	3fo. multicoloured	1·40	45

499 Rowing Four

1970. 17th European Women's Rowing Championships, Lake Tata.

2537	**499**	1fo. multicoloured	80	25

500 Illuminated Initial

1970. Stamp Day. Paintings and Illuminated Initials from Codices of King Matthias.

2538	1fo.+50fi. Type **500**		1·40	1·40
2539	1fo.+50fi. "N" and flowers		1·40	1·40
2540	1fo.+50fi. "O" and ornamentation		1·40	1·40
2541	1fo.+50fi. "King Matthias"		1·40	1·40

MS2542 66×86 mm. 2fo.+50fi. ×4 (a) "Bishop Ransanus with King Matthias and Queen Beatrix"; (b) "Q" and "Old Humanist"; (c) "C" and "Appianus of Alexandria"; (d) "A" and "King David on Throne" — 7·50 — 7·50

501 "Soyuz 9" on Transporter

1970. Air. "Soyuz 9" Space Mission. Sheet 108×87 mm containing T **501** and three similar horiz designs. Multicoloured.

MS2543 2fo.50 ×4 (a) Type **501**; (b) Launch; (c) In flight; (d) Cosmonauts — 5·25 — 5·25

1970. Air. Space Flight of "Apollo 13". Sheet 112×90 mm containing T **495** and three other similar horiz designs. Multicoloured.

MS2533 2fo.50 ×4 (a) Type **495**; (b) In flight; (c) Descent; (d) In sea — 5·25 — 5·25

502 "Bread" (sculpture by I. Szabo) and F.A.O. Emblem

1970. Seventh F.A.O. European Regional Conference, Budapest.
2544 **502** 1fo. multicoloured 60 25

503 Boxing

1970. 75th Anniv of Hungarian Olympic Committee. Multicoloured.
2545 40fi. Type **503** 10 10
2546 60fi. Canoeing 10 10
2547 1fo. Fencing 25 15
2548 1fo.50 Water-polo 35 25
2549 2fo. Gymnastics 95 35
2550 2fo.50 Throwing the Hammer 95 45
2551 3fo. Wrestling 1·20 60
2552 5fo. Swimming 1·30 65

504 Family and "Flame of Knowledge"

1970. Fifth Education Congress, Budapest.
2553 **504** 1fo. blue, green & orange 60 25

505 Chalice of Benedek Suky, c. 1400

1970. Goldsmiths' Craft. Treasures from Budapest National Museum and Esztergom Treasury. Multicoloured.
2554 40fi. Type **505** 10 10
2555 60fi. Altar-cruet, c. 1500 10 10
2556 1fo. "Nadasdy" goblet, 16th-century 25 10
2557 1fo.50 Coconut goblet with gold case, c. 1600 45 15
2558 2fo. Silver tankard of M. Toldalaghy, c. 1623 60 35
2559 2fo.50 Communion-cup of G.I. Rakoczi, c. 1670 95 45
2560 3fo. Tankard, c. 1690 1·20 60
2561 4fo. "Bell-flower" cup, c. 1710 1·70 1·20

506 The Virgin and Child ("Giampietrino", G. Pedrini)

1970. Paintings. Religious Art from Christian Museum, Esztergom. Multicoloured.
2562 40fi. Type **506** 10 10
2563 60fi. Love (G. Lazzarini) 10 10
2564 1fo. Legend of St. Catherine of Alexandria ("Master of Bat") 25 15
2565 1fo.50 Adoration of the Shepherds (F. Fontebasso) (horiz.) 70 25
2566 2fo.50 Adoration of the Magi (Master of Aranyosmarot) 1·40 35

2567 4fo. Temptation of St. Anthony the Hermit (J. de Cock) 1·90 70
2568 5fo. St. Sebastian (Palmezzano) 2·00 80
MS2569 72×84 mm. 10fo. The Maid and the Unicorn (unknown Lombard painter) 7·50 7·50

507 Mauthausen Camp Memorial (A. Makrisz)

1970. 25th Anniv of Liberation of Concentration Camps.
2570 **507** 1fo. brown and blue 60 25

508 "Luna 16" in Flight

1971. Air. "Luna 16" Space Mission. Sheet 108×87 mm containing T **508** and three other similar horiz designs. Multicoloured.
MS2571 2fo.50 ×4 (a) Type **508**; (b) Parachute landing; (c) On Moon's surface; (d) Nosecone 5·25 5·25

509 Budapest, 1470

1971. "Budapest 71" Stamp Exhibition and Centenary of Hungarian Stamps (2nd series). "Budapest Through the Ages".
2572 **509** 2fo.+1fo. black & yell 1·00 1·00
2573 - 2fo.+1fo. black & mve 1·00 1·00
2574 - 2fo.+1fo. black & grn 1·00 1·00
2575 - 2fo.+1fo. black & orge 1·00 1·00
MS2576 110×75 mm. 2fo.+1fo. ×4 (a) black and orange; (b) black and pale green; (c) black and violet; (d) black and mauve 4·75 4·75
DESIGNS: Budapest in: No. 2573, 1600; No. 2574, 1638; No. 2575, 1770. Smaller (40×18 mm)—No. MS2575, Budapest in (a) 1777, (b) 1850, (c) 1895, (d) 1970.

510 "Lunokhod 1" on Module

1971. Air. Moon Mission of "Luna 17" and "Lunokhod 2". Sheet 108×87 mm containing T **510** and three other similar horiz designs. Multicoloured.
MS2577 2fo.50 ×4 (a) Type **510**; (b) "Luna 17" leaving Earth; (c) "Luna 17" nearing Moon; (d) "Lunokhod 1" on Moon's surface 5·25 5·25

511 "The Marseillaise" (sculpture by Rude)

1971. Centenary of Paris Commune.
2578 **511** 3fo. brown and green 1·30 60

512 Bela Bartok

1971. 90th Birth Anniv of Bela Bartok (composer).
2579 **512** 1fo. black, grey and red 1·40 25

513 Gyor in 1594

1971. 700th Anniv of Gyor.
2580 **513** 2fo. multicoloured 80 35

514 Astronauts on Moon

1971. Air. "Apollo 14" Moon Mission. Sheet 120×70 mm.
MS2581 **514** 10fo. multicoloured 5·75 5·75

1971. Birth Centenary of Andras L. Achim (peasant leader). Portrait in similar style to T **512**.
2582 1fo. black, grey and green 60 25

516 Hunting European Bison

1971. World Hunting Exhibition, Budapest. Multicoloured.
2583 40fi. Type **516** (postage) 25 10
2584 60fi. Hunting wild boar 35 25
2585 80fi. Deer-stalking 60 30
2586 1fo. Falconry 95 35
2587 1fo.20 Stag-hunting 1·00 45
2588 2fo. Great bustards with young 1·20 60
2589 3fo. Netting fish 1·70 70
2590 4fo. Angling 2·30 80

MS2591 145×100 mm. 10fo. Herd of roe deer (air) 8·75 8·75
The design of the 10fo. is larger, 72×46 mm.

517 Portrait of a Man (Durer)

1971. 500th Birth Anniv of Albrecht Durer (artist). Sheet 80×100 mm.
MS2592 **517** 10fo. multicoloured 4·75 4·75

518 Emblem on Flower

1971. 25th Anniv of Hungarian Young Pioneers.
2593 **518** 1fo. multicoloured 1·20 25

519 F.I.R. Emblem

1971. 20th Anniv of International Federation of Resistance Fighters.
2594 **519** 1fo. multicoloured 1·20 25

520 Walking in the Garden (Toyokuni School)

1971. Japanese Colour Prints from Ferenc Hopp Collection, Budapest. Multicoloured.
2595 40fi. Type **520** 10 10
2596 60fi. Geisha in boat (Yeishi) 15 10
2597 1fo. Woman with scroll-painting (Yeishi) 35 15
2598 1fo.50 Oirans (Kiyonaga) 60 25
2599 2fo. Awabi Fishers (Utamaro) 95 30
2600 2fo.50 Seated Oiran (Harunobu) 1·00 35
2601 3fo. Peasant Girl carrying Faggots (Hokusai) 1·20 1·00
2602 4fo. Women and Girls Walking (Yeishi) 1·70 1·40

521 Locomotive Bets and Route Map (1846)

1971. 125th Anniv of Hungarian Railways.
2603 **521** 1fo. multicoloured 80 25

522 Hungarian Newspaper Stamp of 1871

1971. "Budapest 71" Stamp Exhibition and Centenary of Hungarian Stamps (3rd series). Multicoloured.
2604 2fo.+1fo. Type **522** 1·40 1·40
2605 2fo.+1fo. 45f. "Petofi" stamp of 1919 1·40 1·40
2606 2fo.+1fo. 40k. "Harvesters" stamp of 1920 1·40 1·40
2607 2fo.+1fo. 16f.+16f. "Art" stamp of 1940 1·40 1·40
MS2608 115×99 mm. 2fo.+1fo. ×4 (a) 60f.+60f. "Liberty" stamp of 1947; (b) 2fo. "Costume" stamp of 1953; (c) 2fo. Air stamp of 1958; (d) 1fo. "Space" stamp of 1965 5·75 5·75

523 Griffin with Inking Balls

1971. Centenary of State Printing Office, Budapest.
2609 **523** 1fo. multicoloured 80 80

524 O.I.J. Emblem and Page of "Magyar Sajto"

1971. 25th Anniv of Int Organisation of Journalists.
2610 **524** 1fo. gold and blue 60 25

525 Volkov, Dobrovolsky and Patsaev (image scaled to 53% of original size)

1971. Air. "Soyuz 11" Cosmonauts Memorial Issue. Sheet 133×90 mm.
MS2611 **525** 10fo. multicoloured 5·75 5·75

526 J. Winterl (founder) and *Waldsteinia geoides*

1971. Bicentenary of Botanical Gardens, Budapest. Multicoloured.

2612	40fi. Type **526**	10	10
2613	60fi. *Bromeliaceae*	20	10
2614	80fi. *Titanopsis calcarea*	25	15
2615	1fo. *Vinca herbacea*	35	20
2616	1fo.20 *Gymnocalycium mih- anovichii*	45	25
2617	2fo. *Nymphaea gigantea*	95	35
2618	3fo. *Iris arenaria*	1·20	60
2619	5fo. *Paeonia banatica*	2·30	1·20

527 Horse-racing

1971. Equestrian Sport. Multicoloured.

2620	40fi. Type **527**	15	10
2621	60fi. Trotting	25	10
2622	80fi. Cross-country riding	35	10
2623	1fo. Show-jumping	45	10
2624	1fo.20 Start of race	60	15
2625	2fo. Polo	95	35
2626	3fo. Steeplechasing	1·40	70
2627	5fo. Dressage	2·30	1·30

528 Execution of Koppany

1971. Miniatures from the *Illuminated Chronicle* of King Lajos I of Hungary. Multicoloured.

2628	40fi. Type **528**	20	10
2629	60fi. *The Pursuit of King Peter*	25	10
2630	1fo. *Bazarad's Victory over King Karoly I*	35	15
2631	1fo.50 *The Strife between King Salamon and Prince Geza*	70	25
2632	2fo.50 *The Founding of Obuda Monastery by King Stephen and Queen Gisela*	1·00	35
2633	4fo. *Reconciliation of King Ka- lman and his brother, Almos*	1·60	80
2634	5fo. *King Ladislas I supervising the construction of Nagyvarad Church*	1·70	1·20
MS2635	84×87 mm. 10fo. *The Funeral of Prince Emeric and the Binding of Vazul*	5·25	5·25

The design of the 10fo. is larger, 51×60 mm.

529 Racial Equality Year Emblem

1971. Racial Equality Year.

2636	**529** 1fo. multicoloured	60	25

530 Ice Hockey

1971. Winter Olympic Games, Sapporo, Japan (1972). Multicoloured.

2637	40fi. Type **530**	10	10
2638	60fi. Downhill skiing	25	10
2639	80fi. Figure skating (female)	30	10
2640	1fo. Ski jumping	35	10

2641	1fo.20 Cross-country skiing	60	15
2642	2fo. Figure skating (male)	70	25
2643	3fo. Bobsleighing	95	80
2644	4fo. Rifle-shooting (Biathlon)	1·20	1·30
MS2645	133×89 mm. 10fo. Buddha	7·50	7·50

The design of the 10fo. is larger, 89×51 mm.

531 Astronauts aboard Moon Rover

1972. Air. Moon Flight of "Apollo 15". Sheet 120×76 mm.

MS2646	**531** 10fo. multicoloured	5·75	5·75

532 Class 303, 1950

1972. Railway Steam Locomotives. Multicoloured.

2647	40fi. Type **532**	30	10
2648	60fi. Class P6, 1902, Prussia	35	15
2649	80fi. Class 380, 1894, Italy	60	35
2650	1fo. Class P36, 1950, Russia	55	15
2651	1fo.20 Heisler locomotive, Japan	60	30
2652	2fo. Scottish Caledonian tank locomotive, 1837	1·40	70
2653	4fo. Class 166, 1882, Austria	1·70	1·20
2654	5fo. Locomotive "Continent", 1854	2·30	1·40

533 J. Pannonius (A. Mantegna)

1972. 500th Death Anniv of Janus Pannonius (poet).

2655	**533** 1fo. multicoloured	35	25

534 "Mariner 9"

1972. Exploration of Mars. Multicoloured.

2656	2fo. Type **534**	80	80
2657	2fo. "Mars 2 and 3"	80	80

535 Doorway of Csempeszkopacs Church

1972. Protection of Monuments.

2658	**535** 3fo. green	1·40	60

536 Hungarian Greyhound

1972. Dogs. Multicoloured.

2659	40fi. Type **536**	15	10
2660	60fi. Afghan hound (head)	25	10
2661	80fi. Irish wolfhound	30	15
2662	1fo.20 Borzoi (head)	45	25
2663	2fo. Greyhound	95	35
2664	4fo. Whippet (head)	2·10	60
2665	6fo. Afghan hound	2·30	1·40

537 J. Imre, E. Grosz and L. Blaskovics

1972. First European Oculists' Congress, Budapest. Famous Oculists.

2666	**537** 1fo. brown and red	1·20	25
2667	- 2fo. brown and blue	1·70	95

DESIGN: 2fo. A. Gullstrand, V. P. Filatov and J. Gonin.

538 Footballers and Flag of Hungary

1972. Air. European Football Championships. Footballers and Flags of participating countries. Multicoloured.

2668	40fi. Type **538**	25	15
2669	60fi. Rumania	30	25
2670	80fi. West Germany	35	30
2671	1fo. England	60	45
2672	1fo.20 Yugoslavia	80	50
2673	2fo. Russia	1·40	60
2674	4fo. Italy	2·10	70
2675	5fo. Belgium	2·30	1·20

539 "V. Miskolcz" postmark, 1818–43

1972. Stamp Day.

2676	**539** 2fo.+1fo. black & blue	1·20	1·20
2677	- 2fo.+1fo. black & yell	1·20	1·20
2678	- 2fo.+1fo. black & grn	1·20	1·20
2679	- 2fo.+1fo. mult	1·20	1·20
MS2680	105×90 mm. 2fo.+1fo. ×4 (a) Wax impression of signet ring, 1953; (b) Letter of Rakoczi era, 1705; (c) Courier letter of 1708; (d) V. Tokai postmark, 1752	7·50	7·50

DESIGNS: No. 2677, "Szegedin" postmark, 1827–48; 2678, "Esztergom" postmark, 1848–51; 2679, "Budapest 71" stamp cent, cancellation, 1971.

540 Girl reading Book

1972. International Book Year.

2681	**540** 1fo. multicoloured	70	25

541 Roses

1972. National Rose Exhibition.

2682	**541** 1fo. multicoloured	80	25

542 Globe and Olympic Rings

1972. Air. Olympic Games, Munich (1st issue). Sheet 117×68 mm.

MS2683	**542** 10fo. multicoloured	16·00	16·00

See also Nos. 2687/MS2695.

543 G. Dimitrov

1972. 90th Birth Anniv of Georgi Dimitrov (Bulgarian leader).

2684	**543** 3fo. multicoloured	80	45

544 "St. Martin and the Beggar"

1972. "Belgica '72" Stamp Exhibition, Brussles. Sheet 69×94 mm.

MS2685	**544** 10fo. multicoloured	4·75	4·75

545 Gy. Dozsa

1972. 500th Birth Anniv of Gyorgy Dozsa (revolutionary).

2686	**545** 1fo. multicoloured	60	25

546 Football

1972. Olympic Games, Munich (2nd issue). Multicoloured.

2687	40fi. Type **546** (postage)	10	10
2688	60fi. Water-polo	10	10
2689	80fi. Javelin-throwing	20	10
2690	1fo. Kayak-canoeing	25	10
2691	1fo.20 Boxing	60	10
2692	2fo. Gymnastics	80	15
2693	3fo.+1fo. Wrestling	1·40	45
2694	5fo. Fencing	2·30	1·20

MS2695	115×90 mm. 10fo. Show- jumping (air)	7·00	7·00

The design on the 10fo. is larger, 43×43 mm.

547 Prince Geza indicating Site of Szekesfehervar

1972. Millenary of Szekesfehervar and 750th Anniv of "Aranybulla" (legislative document). Multicoloured.

2696	40fi. Type **547**	10	10
2697	60fi. King Stephen and shield	10	10
2698	80fi. Soldiers and cavalry	20	10
2699	1fo.20 King Stephen drawing up legislation	45	15
2700	2fo. Mason sculpting column	95	25
2701	4fo. Merchant displaying wares to King Stephen	1·70	45
2702	6fo. Views of Szekesfehervar and Palace	2·30	80

MS2703	136×90 mm. 10fo. King Andrew II at presentation of "Arany- bulla" to the court	5·25	5·25

The design on the 10fo. is larger, 95×47 mm.

548 Parliament Building, Budapest

1972. Constitution Day. Multicoloured.
| 2704 | 5fo. Type **548** | 1·40 | 25 |
| 2705 | 6fo. Parliament in session | 1·70 | 60 |

549 Eger and "Bulls Blood"

1972. World Wines Competition, Budapest Multicoloured.
| 2706 | 1fo. Type **549** | 60 | 10 |
| 2707 | 2fo. Tokay and "Tokay Aszu" | 1·70 | 60 |

550 Ear of Wheat and Emblems on Open Book

1972. 175th Anniv of Georgikon Agricultural Academy, Keszthely.
| 2708 | **550** | 1fo. multicoloured | 35 | 25 |

551 "Rothschild" Vase

1972. Herendi Porcelain. Multicoloured.
2709	40fi. Type **551**	20	10
2710	60fi. "Poisson" bonboniere	25	10
2711	80fi. "Victoria" vase	30	10
2712	1fo. "Miramare" dish	35	10
2713	1fo.20 "Godollo" pot	45	15
2714	2fo. "Empire" tea-set	70	25
2715	4fo. "Apponyi" dish	1·40	80
2716	5fo. "Baroque" vase	1·70	80

The 60fi., 1fo.20, and 4fo. are size 34×36 mm.

552 Class M62 Diesel Train and U.I.C. Emblem

1972. 50th Anniv of Int Railway Union.
| 2717 | **552** | 1fo. red | 80 | 25 |

553 Commemorative Emblem

1972. 25th Anniv of National Economy Plan.
| 2718 | **553** | 1fo. yellow, sepia & brn | 60 | 25 |

554 River Steamer and Old Obuda

1972. Centenary of Unification of Buda, Obuda and Pest as Budapest.
2719	**554**	1fo. purple and blue	35	10
2720	-	1fo. blue and purple	35	10
2721	-	2fo. green and brown	60	15
2722	-	2fo. brown and green	60	15
2723	-	3fo. brown and green	70	35
2724	-	3fo. green and brown	70	35

DESIGNS: No. 2720, River hydrofoil and modern Obuda; 2721, Buda, 1872; 2722, Budapest, 1972; 2723, Pest, 1872; 2724, Parliament Buildings, Budapest.

555 Congress Emblem within Ear

1972. Int Audiological Congress, Budapest.
| 2725 | **555** | 1fo. multicoloured | 60 | 25 |

556 "Apollo 16"

1972. Air. Moon Flight of "Apollo 16". Sheet 120×75 mm.
| MS2726 **556** | 10fo. multicoloured | 5·25 | 5·25 |

557 Postbox, Bell Telephone and Satellite "Molnya"

1972. Reopening of Postal and Philatelic Museums, Budapest. Multicoloured.
| 2727 | 4fo.+2fo. Type **557** | 1·70 | 1·70 |
| 2728 | 4fo.+2fo. Globe, posthorn and stamps | 1·70 | 1·70 |

558 Miklos Radnoti (poet)

1972. Radnoti Commemoration.
| 2729 | **558** | 1fo. multicoloured | 35 | 25 |

559 F. Martos

1972. 75th Birth Anniv of Flora Martos (patriot).
| 2730 | **559** | 1fo. multicoloured | 35 | 25 |

560 "The Muses" (J. Rippl-Ronai)

1972. Stained Glass Windows. Multicoloured.
2731	40fi. Type **560**	20	10
2732	60fi. "16th-century Scribe" (F. Sebestenyl)	20	15
2733	1fo. "Exodus to Egypt" (K. Lotz and B. Szekely)	35	20
2734	1fo.50 "Prince Arpad's Messenger" (J. Percz)	60	25

561 "Textiles"

1972. Opening of Textiles Technical Museum, Budapest.
| 2738 | **561** | 1fo. multicoloured | 80 | 25 |

562 Main Square, Szarvas

1972. Views.
2739	**562**	40fi. brown and orange	10	10
2739a	-	40fi. black and green	10	10
2740	-	1fo. blue and light blue	15	10
2741	-	1fo. brown and yellow	15	10
2742	-	3fo. green and blue	60	25
2743	-	4fo. red and orange	60	25
2743a	-	4fo. brown and pink	1·20	35
2744	-	5fo. blue and cobalt	60	10
2745	-	6fo. brown and red	1·70	25
2746	-	7fo. violet and lilac	1·20	35
2747	-	8fo. deep green & green	1·20	10
2748	-	10fo. brown and yellow	1·20	25
2749	-	20fo. multicoloured	4·75	80
2750	-	50fo. multicoloured	9·25	3·00

DESIGNS: 21×18 mm: 40fi. (No. 2739a) Rotunda (public health centre), Vasvar; 1fo. (No. 2740) Salgotarjan; 1fo. (No. 2741) Nyirbator. 28×22 mm: 3fo. Tokay; 4fo. (No. 2743) Esztergom; 4fo. (No. 2743a) Szentendre; 5fo. Szolnok; 6fo. Dunaujvaros; 7fo. Kaposvar; 8fo. Vac; 10fo. Kiskunfelegyhaza; 20fo. Veszprem; 50ra. Pecs.

563 S. Petofi

1972. 150th Birth Anniv of Sandor Petofi (poet and patriot).
2762		1fo. red	25	10
2763	**563**	2fo. lilac	60	15
2764	-	3fo. green	95	45

DESIGNS: 1fo. Petofi making speech in Cafe Pilvax; 3fo. Petofi on horseback during War of Independence, 1848–49.

564 Arms of U.S.S.R.

1972. 50th Anniv of U.S.S.R.
| 2765 | **564** | 1fo. multicoloured | 35 | 25 |

565 Code Map and Crow Symbol

1973. Introduction of Postal Codes.
| 2766 | **565** | 1fo. black and red | 35 | 25 |

1973. As Nos. 1912, 1915/16 and 1918 but smaller.
2767	2fo. blue (22×19 mm)	45	25
2768	3fo. blue (22×19 mm)	60	45
2769	4fo. green (19×22 mm)	95	60
2770	6fo. ochre (22×19 mm)	1·40	1·00

2735	2fo.50 "The Nativity" (L. Sztehlo)	95	30
2736	4fo. "Prince Arpad and Leaders" (K. Kernstock)	1·40	60
2737	5fo. "King Matthias reprimands the Rich Aristocrats" (J. Haranghy)	1·70	95

566 Astronaut on Moon

1973. Air. Moon Flight of "Apollo 17". Sheet 69×110 mm.
| MS2771 **566** | 10fo. multicoloured | 7·00 | 7·00 |

567 I. Madach

1973. 150th Birth Anniv of Imre Madach (writer).
| 2772 | **567** | 1fo. multicoloured | 60 | 25 |

568 Carnival Mask

1973. Busho-Walking Ceremony, Mohacs. Carnival Masks.
2773	**568**	40fi. multicoloured	15	10
2774	-	60fi. multicoloured	25	10
2775	-	80fi. multicoloured	35	10
2776	-	1fo.20 multicoloured	70	15
2777	-	2fo. multicoloured	95	35
2778	-	4fo. multicoloured	1·20	60
2779	-	6fo. multicoloured	2·30	95

569 Copernicus

1973. 500th Birth Anniv of Copernicus.
| 2780 | **569** | 3fo. blue | 1·70 | 80 |

570 "Venus 8"

1973. Air. Space Flight of "Venus 8". Sheet 110×93 mm.
| MS2781 **570** | 10fo. multicoloured | 5·75 | 5·75 |

571 Show-jumping (Pentathlon) and Gold Medal

1973. Hungarian Medal Winners, Olympic Games, Munich. Multicoloured.
2782	40fi. Type **571**	10	10
2783	60fi. Weightlifting (Gold)	25	10
2784	1fo. Canoeing (Silver)	45	10
2785	1fo.20 Swimming (Silver)	60	15
2786	1fo.80 Boxing (Gold)	65	25

2787	4fo. Wrestling (Gold)		1·20	60
2788	6fo. Fencing (Gold)		1·70	95

572 Biological Man

1973. 25th Anniv of W.H.O.

2790	**572**	1fo. brown and green	35	25

573 Winter Wrens

1973. Air. Hungarian Birds. Multicoloured.

2791	40fi. Type **573** (postage)	25	10
2792	60fi. Rock thrush	30	10
2793	80fi. European robins	40	10
2794	1fo. Firecrests	60	25
2795	1fo.20 Linnets	85	35
2796	2fo. Blue tits	95	45
2797	4fo. Bluethroat	1·40	50
2798	5fo. Grey wagtails	1·70	60

MS2789 132×88 mm. 10fo. Girl igniting Olympic Flame (air)	4·50	60

The design of the 10fo. is larger, 83×46 mm.

574 Soldier and Weapons

1973. Military Stamp Collectors' Exhibition, Budapest.

2799	**574**	3fo. multicoloured	80	35

575 "Budapest 61" 1fo. Stamp

1973. "IBRA 73" Stamp Exn, Munich, and "POLSKA `73", Poznan. Reproductions of Hungary Exhibition stamps. Multicoloured.

2800	40fi. Type **575** (postage)	10	10
2801	60fi. "Budapest 61" 1fo.70 stamp	10	10
2802	80fi. "Budapest 61" 2fo.60 stamp	25	10
2803	1fo. "Budapest 61" 3fo. stamp	35	10
2804	1fo.20 "Budapest 71" 2fo. stamp	40	10
2805	2fo. "Budapest 71" 2fo. stamp	60	25
2806	4fo. "Budapest 71" 2fo. stamp	1·20	60
2807	5fo. "Budapest 71" 2fo. stamp	1·30	65

MS2808 130×81 mm. 10fo. Bavaria's first stamp, Town Hall and Olympic complex, Munich (air)	5·25	5·25

The design of the 10fo. is larger, 83×46 mm.

576 Setting Type and Preparing Ink

1973. 500th Anniv of Book-printing in Hungary.

2809	**576**	1fo. black and gold	25	10
2810	-	3fo. black and gold	95	25

DESIGN: 3fo. Printer operating press.

577 Storm over Hortobagy Puszta

1973. Paintings by Csontvary Kosztka. Multicoloured.

2811	40fi. Type **577**	10	10
2812	60fi. Mary's Well, Nazareth	20	10
2813	1fo. Carriage drive by Moonlight (vert)	30	25
2814	1fo.50 Pilgrimage to the Lebanese Cedars (vert)	45	10
2815	2fo.50 The Lone Cedar	60	25
2816	4fo. Waterfall at Jajce	1·30	60
2817	5fo. Ruins of Greek Theatre at Taormina	1·40	95

MS2818 114×75 mm. 10fo. Riding at the Seaside	4·75	4·75

The design of the 10fo. is larger, 91×43 mm.

578 "Europa" Poster

1973. European Security and Co-operation Conference, Helsinki.

2819	**578**	2fo.50 brown and black	3·75	3·75

579 Rosa gallica

1973. Wild Flowers. Multicoloured.

2820	40fi. Type **579**	10	10
2821	60fi. Cyclamen europaeum	10	10
2822	80fi. Pulmonaria mollissima	25	10
2823	1fo.20 Bellis perennis	45	15
2824	2fo. Adonis vernalis	80	25
2825	4fo. Viola cyanea	1·40	60
2826	6fo. Papaver rhoeas	2·10	1·20

580 "Let's be friends...!"

1973. Road Safety.

2827	**580**	40fi. green and red	10	10
2828	-	60fi. violet and orange	15	10
2829	-	1fo. blue and red	35	25

DESIGNS: 60fi. "Not even a glass!" (hand reaching for tumbler); 1fo. "Cyclist – use a lamp" (car running down cyclist).

581 Silver "Eagle" Disc

1973. Jewelled Treasures, National Museum. Multicoloured.

2830	2fo.+50fi. Type **581**	1·40	1·40
2831	2fo.+50fi. Serpent's head ring	1·40	1·40
2832	2fo.+50fi. "Loving couple" buckle	1·40	1·40
2833	2fo.+50fi. Silver "floral" buckle	1·40	1·40

MS2834 75×101 mm. 2fo.+50fi. ×4 (a) Opaline pendant; (b) Jewelled buckle; (c) Floral pin; (d) Rosette pendant	6·50	6·50

The designs in MS2834 are each 25×36 mm.

582 "Skylab" photographing Earth

1973. Air. "Skylab" Space-station. Sheet 114×75 mm.

MS2835 **582** 10fo. multicoloured	6·50	6·50

583 The Three Kings (Master of the High Altar, Szmrecsany)

1973. Esztergom Millennium. "Old Master" Paintings in the Christian Museum. Mulicoloured.

2836	40fi. Type **583**	10	10
2837	60fi. Angels making Music (Master "B.E.")	10	10
2838	1fo. The Adoration of the Magi (anon.)	35	15
2839	1fo.50 The Annunciation (Szmrecsany Master)	50	20
2840	2fo.50 Angels making Music (different Master "B.E.")	60	25
2841	4fo. The Visitation of Mary and Elizabeth (Szmrecsany Master)	1·00	35
2842	5fo. The Legend of St. Catharine of Alexandria (Master Bati)	1·20	95

MS2843 73×101 mm. 10fo. The Birth of Jesus (Szmrecsany Master)	5·25	5·25

584 Csokonai's Statue, Debrecen

1973. Birth Bicentenary of M. Csokonai Vitez (poet).

2844	**584**	2fo. multicoloured	80	25

585 J. Marti

1973. 120th Birth Anniv of Jose Marti (Cuban patriot).

2845	**585**	1fo. brown, red and blue	35	25

586 B. Pesti

1973. 30th Death Anniv of Barnabas Pesti (patriot).

2846	**586**	1fo. lt brown, brown & bl	35	25

588 Kayak-canoeing

1973. World Aquatic Sports Championships, Belgrade and Tampere. Multicoloured.

2855	40fi. Type **588**	10	10

2856	60fi. Water polo	10	10
2857	80fi. Men's solo kayak	30	10
2858	1fo.20 Swimming	35	10
2859	2fo. Men's kayak fours	60	15
2860	4fo. Men's solo canoe	1·20	60
2861	6fo. Men's double canoe	1·50	95

589 Map of Europe

1974. European Security and Co-operation Conference, Geneva. Sheet 143×71 mm containing two stamps as T **589** together with a double-size label depicting Geneva.

MS2862 **589** 50fo.×2 gold, blue and green	11·50	11·50

590 Lenin

1974. 50th Death Anniv of Lenin.

2863	**590**	2fo. brown, blue and gold	95	25

591 J. Boczor, I. Bekes and T. Elek

1974. Hungarian Heroes of the French Resistance.

2864	**591**	3fo. multicoloured	1·20	35

592 "Comecon" Building, Moscow, and Flags

1974. 25th Anniv of Council for Mutual Economic Aid.

2865	**592**	1fo. multicoloured	60	25

593 Savings Bank Emblem, Note and Coins

1974. 25th Anniv of National Savings Bank.

2866	**593**	1fo. multicoloured	35	25

594 "Mariner 4" on course for Mars

1974. Mars Research Projects. Multicoloured.

2867	40fi. Type **594** (postage)	10	10
2868	60fi. "Mars 2" approaching Mars	10	10
2869	80fi. "Mariner 4" space probe	35	10
2870	1fo. Mt. Palomar telescope and Mars photo	60	10
2871	1fo.20 "Mars 3" on planet's surface	80	15
2872	5fo. "Mariner 9" approaching Mars and satellites	1·90	60
2873	6fo. G. Schiaparelli and Martian "canals" map (air)	2·00	1·40

MS2874 96×91 mm. 10fo. "Mars 7" in Space	4·75	4·75

595 Pres. Salvador Allende

1974. Pres. Allende of Chile Commemoration.
| 2875 | 595 | 1fo. multicoloured | 35 | 25 |

596 Mona Lisa (Leonardo da Vinci)

1974. Exhibition of Mona Lisa in Japan.
| 2876 | 596 | 4fo. multicoloured | 17·00 | 17·00 |

597 2k. Stamp of 1874 and Mallow

1974. Centenary of Hungarian "Envelope Design" Stamps. Sheet 103×87 mm containing T **597** and similar horiz design. Multicoloured.
MS2877 2fo.50 ×5 (a) Type **597**; (b) 3k. stamp and aster; (c) 5k. stamp and daisy; (d) 10k. stamp and columbine   4·75   4·75

598 Dove with Letter

1974. Centenary of U.P.U. Multicoloured.
2878	598	40fi. Type 598	10	10
2879		60fi. Mail coach	10	10
2880		80fi. Early mail van and postbox	35	10
2881		1fo.20 Balloon post	45	15
2882		2fo. Diesel mail train	95	25
2883		4fo. Post-bus	1·40	60
2884		6fo. Tupolev Tu-154 mail plane	1·90	1·20
MS2885 132×106 mm. 2fo.50 ×4 (a) As 60fi.; (b) As 80fi. but design reversed; (c) As 6fo.; (d) "Apollo 15"   6·50   6·50

The designs in MS2885 are smaller, 45×30 mm. and are redrawn so that only part of the U.P.U. Monument falls on each stamp.

599 Swiss 2½r. "Basle Dove" Stamp of 1845

1974. "Internaba 1974" Stamp Exhibition, Basle.
| 2886 | 599 | 3fo. multicoloured | 2·30 | 2·30 |

600 13th-century miniature from King Alfonso X's Book of Chess, Dice and Tablings and Pawn

1974. 50th Anniv of International Chess Federation and 21st Chess Olympiad, Nice.
| 2887 | 600 | 40fi. black, green and blue | 30 | 10 |

2888	-	60fi. black, brown & lilac	60	15
2889	-	80fi. black, yellow & grn	95	25
2890	-	1fo.20 black, yellow and lilac	1·20	35
2891	-	2fo. black, stone and blue	1·50	45
2892	-	4fo. black, yellow & pink	1·70	1·00
2893	-	6fo. black, brown & grn	2·00	1·20
DESIGNS: 60fi. 15th-century woodcut from "The Game and Playe of Chesse" by William Caxton and knight; 80fi. 15th-century illustration from Italian chess book and bishop; 1fo.20, "The Chess Players" (17th-century engraving by Jacob van der Heyden) and rook; 2fo. Kempelen's chess playing machine (1769) and king; 4fo. Geza Maroczy (Hungarian master) and queen; 6fo. View of Nice and tournament emblem.

601 Passenger Train, 1874

1974. Centenary of the Budapest Rack Railway. Sheet 132× 96 mm. containing T **601** and similar horiz designs. Multicoloured.
MS2894 2fo.50 Type **601**; 2fo.50 Goods train, 1874; 2fo.50 Passenger train, 1929; 2fo.50 Passenger train, 1973   7·50   7·50

602 Congress Emblem

1974. Fourth International Economists' Congress, Budapest.
| 2895 | 602 | 2fo. black, blue and silver | 1·20 | 25 |

603 Woman Bathing (K Lotz)

1974. Nudes. Paintings. Multicoloured.
2896	603	40fi. Type 603	20	10
2897		60fi. Awakening (K. Brocky)	25	10
2898		1fo. Venus and Cupid (K. Brocky) (horiz)	60	25
2899		1fo.50 After Bathing (K. Lotz)	80	35
2900		2fo.50 Honi soit qui mal y pense (reclining nude) (I. Csok) (horiz)	1·20	60
2901		4fo. After Bathing (B. Szkely)	1·70	75
2902		5fo. Devotion (E. Korb)	1·70	80
MS2903 75×102 mm. 10fo. Lark (P.M. Szinyei) (50×71 mm)   7·50   7·50

604 Mimi (Czobel)

1974. 91st Birth Anniv of Bela Czobel (painter).
| 2904 | 604 | 1fo. multicoloured | 1·70 | 25 |

605 "Intersputnik" Satellite Tracking Radar

1974. 25th Anniv of Technical and Scientific Co-operation between Hungary and Soviet Union.
| 2905 | 605 | 1fo. violet and blue | 45 | 10 |
| 2906 | - | 3fo. mauve and green | 1·30 | 15 |

DESIGN—HORIZ: 3fo. Power installations.

606 Neruda

1974. Pablo Neruda (Chilean poet) Commemoration.
| 2907 | 606 | 1fo. brown, deep brown and blue | 35 | 25 |

607 Swedish 3s. Stamp, 1855, and "Swedish Lion"

1974. "Stockholmia 74" International Stamp Exhibition.
| 2908 | 607 | 3fo. green, blue and gold | 2·00 | 2·00 |

608 Tanks and Infantry

1974. Military Day.
2909	608	1fo. black, red and gold (postage)	35	10
2910	-	2fo. blk, grn & gold (air)	60	25
2911	-	3fo. black, blue and gold	80	45
DESIGNS—VERT: 2fo. Guided missile and radar. HORIZ: 3fo. Parachutist, helicopter and jet fighter.

609 J. A. Segner and Moon

1974. 270th Birth Anniv of Janos Segner (scientist).
| 2912 | 609 | 3fo. multicoloured | 1·30 | 35 |

610 Hansa Brandenburg C-1 Biplane, 1918

1974. Air. "Aerofila 1974" International Airmail Exhibition, Budapest. Multicoloured.
2913	610	2fo.+1fo. Type 610	1·70	1·70
2914		2fo.+1fo. Airship Graf Zeppelin	1·70	1·70
2915		2fo.+1fo. Hot air balloon	1·70	1·70
2916		2fo.+1fo. Mil Mi-1 helicopter	1·70	1·70
MS2917 107×92 mm. 2fo.+1fo. Hungarian 1k.50 stamp, 1918; 2fo. + 1fo. Hungarian 500k. stamp, 1924; 2fo.+1fo. Hungarian 3fo. stamp, 1970; 2fo. + 1fo. Hungarian 3fo. stamp, 1970; 2fo.+1fo. Hungarian 10fo. stamp, 1972   7·00   7·00

611 Purple Tiger Moth

1974. Butterflies and Moths. Multicoloured.
2918	611	40fi. Type 611	25	10
2919		60fi. Marbled white	45	15
2920		80fi. Apollo	60	25

2921		1fo. Spurge hawk moth	70	35
2922		1fo.20 Clifden's nonpareil	95	60
2923		5fo. Purple emperor	2·20	95
2924		6fo. Purple-edged copper	2·30	1·40

612 Istvan Pataki

1974. Hungarian Antifascist Martyrs. Multicoloured.
| 2925 | 612 | 1fo. Type 612 | 35 | 10 |
| 2926 | | 1fo. Robert Kreutz | 35 | 10 |

613 Mother and Child

1974. "Mothers".
| 2927 | 613 | 1fo. black, yellow & blue | 35 | 10 |

614 Puppy

1974. Young Animals. (1st series). Multicoloured.
2928	614	40fi. Type 614	15	10
2929		60fi. Kittens (horiz)	20	15
2930		80fi. Rabbit	25	20
2931		1fo.20 Foal (horiz)	35	25
2932		2fo. Lamb	80	35
2933		4fo. Calf (horiz)	1·40	60
2934		6fo. Piglet	1·70	1·50
See also Nos. 3014/20.

615 Lambarene Hospital

1975. Birth Centenary of Dr. Albert Schweitzer (Nobel Peace Prize Winner). Multicoloured.
2935	615	40fi. Type 615	10	10
2936		60fi. Casualty being treated	20	10
2937		80fi. Casualty being transported by canoe	25	10
2938		1fo.20 Charitable goods arriving by freighter	35	10
2939		2fo. View of Lambarene, doves, globe and Red Cross emblem	80	15
2940		4fo. Schweitzer's Nobel Peace Prize medal and inscription	1·40	35
2941		6fo. Schweitzer and organ-pipes	1·90	80

616 F. Bolyai

1975. Birth Bicentenary of Farkas Bolyai (mathematician).
| 2942 | 616 | 1fo. grey and red | 60 | 25 |

617 Carrier-pigeon

618 Karolyi

1975. Birth Centenary of Count Mihaly Karolyi (politician).
2944	**618**	1fo. brown and blue	60	25

619 Woman's Head

1975. International Woman's Year.
2945	**619**	1fo. black and blue	60	25

620 "Railway Rebuilding"

1975. 30th Anniv of Liberation. Multicoloured.
2946		40fi. Type **620**	10	10
2947		60fi. Hammer and sickle representing agriculture	25	10
2948		2fo. Blacksmith's hammer representing Communist party action	60	15
2949		4fo. Power hammer as "3" representing the "Three Year Heavy Industry Plan"	1·20	25
2950		5fo. Blocks of Flats representing "developed socialist society"	1·40	70

621 1915 "Arrow"

1975. 75th Anniv of Hungarian Automobile Club. Vintage Motor Cars. Multicoloured.
2951		40fi. Type **621**	25	10
2952		60fi. 1911 "Swift"	30	10
2953		80fi. 1908 Ford "T"	35	25
2954		1fo. 1901 Mercedes	60	35
2955		1fo.20 1912 Panhard Levassor	70	60
2956		1fo. 1906 Csonka	2·00	80
2957		6fo. Hungarian Automobile Club and international motoring organizations' emblems	3·75	1·20

622 Creation of Adam (from ceiling of Sistine Chapel) (image scaled to 51% of original size)

1975. 500th Birth Anniv of Michelangelo. Sheet 126×90 mm.
MS2958	**622**	10fo. multicoloured	8·75	8·75

623 Academy Building

1975. 150th Anniv of National Academy of Sciences. Multicoloured.
2959		1fo. Type **623**	60	25
2960		2fo. Dates "1825" and "1975"	1·00	60
2961		3fo. Count Istvan Szechenyi (statesman)	1·20	80

1975. Air. Pigeon-racing Olympics, Budapest.
2943	**617**	3fo. multicoloured	1·70	1·70

624 Olympic Stadium, Moscow

1975. "Socphilex V" International Stamp Exhibition, Moscow.
2962	**624**	5fo. multicoloured	3·00	3·00

625 French 1f. Stamp, 1964

1975. "Arphila 75" International Stamp Exhibition, Paris.
2963	**625**	5fo. multicoloured	2·30	2·30

626 Electric Railway Locomotive and Transformer

1975. 75th Anniv of Hungarian Electro-technical Association.
2964	**626**	1fo. multicoloured	1·20	25

627 "Sputnik 2"

1975. Air. "Apollo–Soyuz" Space Link. Multicoloured.
2965		40fi. Type **627**	10	10
2966		60fi. "Mercury Atlas 5"	10	10
2967		80fi. "Lunokhod 1" (moon vehicle)	25	10
2968		1fo.20 "Apollo 15" (moon vehicle)	35	15
2969		2fo. Launch of "Soyuz" from Baikonur	70	25
2970		4fo. Launch of "Apollo"	1·70	60
2971		6fo. "Apollo–Soyuz" link-up	2·30	1·20
MS2972		129×100 mm. 10fo. "Apollo" and "Soyuz" in linking manoeuvre (65×42 mm)	5·75	5·75

628 Sword, Epee, Rapier, and Globe

1975. World Fencing Championships, Budapest.
2973	**628**	1fo. multicoloured	35	25

629 Whale Pavilion

1975. International Exposition, Okinawa (1st issue). Sheet 116×95 mm.
MS2974	**629**	10fo. multicoloured	4·00	4·00
See also Nos. 2986/92.

630 Map of Europe and Cogwheel (image scaled to 53% of original size)

1975. Air. European Security and Co-operation Conference, Helsinki. Sheet 157×82 mm.
MS2975	**630**	10fo. multicoloured	7·00	7·00

631 A. Zimmermann

1975. Birth Centenary of Dr. Agoston Zimmermann (veterinary surgeon).
2976	**631**	1fo. dp brown, brn & bl	35	25

632 Branches of Tree symbolizing 14 Languages

1975. Int Finno-Ugrian Congress, Budapest.
2977	**632**	1fo. multicoloured	60	25

633 (image scaled to 51% of original size)

1975. Air. Hungarian Stamps since 1945. Sheet 150×95 mm. Multicoloured.
MS2978		Hungarian 1fo. Stamp, 1964, 2fo. Stamp, 1961 and 2fo.50 Stamp, 1973	6·50	6·50

634 Anjou Wall Fountain

1975. Stamp Day. Preservation of Monuments. Monuments in Visegrad Palace. Multicoloured.
2979		2fo.+1fo. Type **634**	2·30	2·30
2980		2fo.+1fo. Anjou well house	2·30	2·30
2981		2fo.+1fo. Hunyadi wall fountain	2·30	2·30
2982		2fo.+1fo. Hercules fountain	2·30	2·30
MS2983		128×100 mm. 2fo.+1fo. Detail of Hunyadi wall fountain (26×37 mm); 2fo.+1fo. Madonna of Visegrad (52×37 mm); 2fo.+1fo. Detail of Hercules fountain (26×37 mm); 2fo.+1fo. View of Visegrad in 1480 (105×37 mm)	7·00	7·00

635 Hungarian Arms and Map

1975. 25th Anniv of Hungarian Council System. Multicoloured.
2984		1fo. Type **635**	35	10
2985		1fo. Voters participating in council election	35	10

636 Ocean Pollution

1975. International Exposition, Okinawa. Environmental Protection (2nd issue). Multicoloured.
2986		40fi. Type **636**	10	10

2987		60fi. Strangled rose (water pollution)	15	10
2988		80fi. Clown anemonefish struggling for uncontaminated water (river pollution)	25	10
2989		1fo. Dead carnation (soil pollution)	35	10
2990		1fo.20 Falling bird (air pollution)	60	15
2991		5fo. Infected lung (smoke pollution)	1·50	45
2992		6fo. Healthy and skeletal hands (life and death)	2·00	1·20

637 Mariska Gardos (writer) (1885–1973)

1975. Birth Anniv of Celebrities. Each black and red.
2993		1fo. Type **637**	35	10
2994		1fo. Imre Tarr (soldier) (1900–1937)	35	10
2995		1fo. Imre Meso (Communist martyr) (1905–1956)	35	10

638 Treble Clef, Organ and Orchestra

1975. Centenary of Ferenc Liszt Music Academy, Budapest.
2996	**638**	1fo. multicoloured	35	25

639 18th-century Icon of Szigetcsep

1975. Hungarian Icons depicting the Virgin and Child. Multicoloured.
2997		40fi. Type **639**	10	10
2998		60fi. 18th-century Icon of Graboc	25	10
2999		1fo. 18th-century Icon of Esztergom	45	10
3000		1fo.50 18th-century Icon of Vatoped	80	15
3001		2fo.50 17th-century Icon of Tottos	1·20	25
3002		5fo. 17th-century Icon of Gyor	1·60	45
3003		5fo. 18th-century Icon of Kazan	1·70	1·50

640 Mother and Child, Flags and Radar Equipment

1975. 20th Anniv of Warsaw Treaty.
3004	**640**	1fo. multicoloured	35	25

641 Ice Hockey

1975. Winter Olympic Games, Innsbruck. Multicoloured.
3005		40fi. Type **641**	25	10
3006		60fi. Slalom skiing	25	10
3007		80fi. Slalom skiing (different)	30	10
3008		1fo.20 Ski jumping	45	10
3009		2fo. Speed skating	70	25
3010		4fo. Cross-country skiing	1·40	60
3011		5fo. Bobsleighing	1·90	80
MS3012		130×80 mm. 10fo. Pairs figure skating (65×42 mm)	5·75	5·75

642 Banknotes of 1925 and 1975

1976. 50th Anniv of State Banknote Printing Office, Budapest.

3013	**642**	1fo. multicoloured	70	25

1976. Young Animals (2nd series). As T **614**. Multicoloured.

3014	40fi. Wild boars (horiz)	10	10
3015	60fi. Eurasian red squirrels	20	10
3016	80fi. Lynx (horiz)	25	10
3017	1fo.20 Wolf cubs	35	10
3018	2fo. Red fox cubs (horiz)	70	15
3019	4fo. Brown bear cubs	1·40	60
3020	6fo. Lion cubs (horiz)	2·10	80

643 Alexander Graham Bell, Telecommunications Satellite and Dish Aerial

1976. Telephone Centenary.

3021	**643**	3fo. multicoloured	1·40	1·40

644 *Horses in Storm* (K. Lotz)

1976. Air. Tourist Publicity. Paintings. Sheet 95×135 mm containing T **644** and similar square design. Multicoloured.

MS3022 5fo. Type **644**; 5fo. *Morning at Tihany* (J. Halapy)	4·75	4·75

645 *Clash between Rakoczi's Kuruts and Hapsburg Soldiers*

1976. 300th Birth Anniv of Prince Ferenc Rakoczi II (soldier). Paintings. Multicoloured.

3023	40fi. Type **645**	10	10
3024	60fi. *Meeting of Rakoczi and Tamas Esze*	25	10
3025	1fo. *The Parliament of Onod* (Mor Than)	60	15
3026	2fo. *Kuruts' Encampment*	1·20	25
3027	3fo. *Ilona Zrinyi* (Rakoczi's mother) (vert)	2·30	35
3028	4fo. *Kuruts Officers* (vert)	3·00	80
3029	5fo. *Prince Rakoczi II* (A. Manyoki) (vert)	4·00	1·40

646 Metric System Act, 1876

1976. Centenary of Introduction of Metric System into Hungary. Multicoloured.

3030	1fo. Type **646**	25	10
3031	2fo. Istvan Krusper (scientist) and vacuum balance	80	35
3032	3fo. Interferometer, space rocket and emblem	1·20	60

647 Knight

1976. Stamp Day. Gothic Statues from Buda Castle.

3033	2fo.50+1fo. Type **647**	1·30	1·30
3034	2fo.50+1fo. Armour bearer	1·30	1·30
3035	2fo.50+1fo. Apostle	1·30	1·30
3036	2fo.50+1fo. Bishop	1·30	1·30
MS3037	107×100 mm. 2fo.50+1fo. Man wearing brimmed hat; 2fo.50+1fo. Woman in wimple; 2fo.50+1fo. Man wearing cloth hat; 2fo.50+1fo. Man in fur cap	4·00	4·00

The designs in **MS** are horiz, 35×28 mm, and show statue heads only.

648 U.S. 6c. Stamp, 1968

1976. "Interphil '76" Int Stamp Exhibition, Philadelphia.

3038	**648**	5fo. multicoloured	2·50	2·50

649 "Children Playing" (E. Gebora) within "30"

1976. 30th Anniv of Hungarian Pioneers Movement.

3039	**649**	1fo. multicoloured	45	25

650 Truck, Tractor and Safety Headgear with Emblem

1976. Industrial Safety.

3040	**650**	1fo. multicoloured	45	25

651 "Intelstar IV" Telecommunications Satellite

1976. Olympic Games, Montreal. Multicoloured.

3041	40fi. Type **651** (postage)	10	10
3042	60fi. Horse-jumping	15	10
3043	1fo. Swimming	25	10
3044	2fo. Canoeing	35	10
3045	3fo. Fencing	80	15
3046	4fo. Javelin-throwing	1·20	35
3047	5fo. Gymnastics	1·40	60
MS3048	135×85 mm. 20fo. black, grey and red (air)	9·25	9·25

DESIGN: 44×57 mm. 20fo. Olympic Stadium, Montreal.

652 Danish 1851 4 R.B.S. Stamp and *Little Mermaid* Statue

1976. "Hafnia '76" International Stamp Exhibition, Copenhagen.

3049	**652**	3fo. multicoloured	2·00	2·00

653 *Flora* (Titian)

1976. 400th Death Anniv of Titian (painter).

3050	**653**	4fo. multicoloured	1·40	35

654 *Discovery of King Lajos II's Body* (B. Szekely)

1976. 450th Anniv of Battle of Mohacs. Sheet 82×81 mm.

MS3051	**654**	20fo. multicoloured	5·75	5·75

655 Pal Gyulai (1826–1909)

1976. Writers' Anniversaries.

3052	**655**	2fo. black and red	70	25
3053	-	2fo. black, yellow & gold	70	25

DESIGN: No. 3053, Daniel Berzsenyi (1776–1836).

656 "Hussar" (Zs. Kisfaludy-Strobl)

1976. 150th Anniv of Herend China Factory.

3054	**656**	4fo. multicoloured	1·40	25

657 Tuscany 1q. Stamp, 1851 and Arms of Milan

1976. "Italia '76" International Stamp Exhibition, Milan.

3055	**657**	5fo. multicoloured	5·25	5·25

658 Russian Dancer, Flags and Building

1976. Second Anniv of House of Soviet Culture and Science, Budapest.

3056	**658**	1fo. multicoloured	35	25

659 Ignac Bogar

1976. Hungarian Labour Movement Celebrities.

3057	**659**	1fo. brown and red	35	10
3058	-	1fo. brown and red	35	10
3059	-	1fo. brown and red	35	10

PORTRAITS: No. 3058, Rudolf Golub; No. 3059, Jozsef Madzsar.

660 Dr. F. Koranyi and Dispensary

1976. 75th Anniv of Koranyi T.B. Dispensary.

3060	**660**	2fo. multicoloured	80	25

661 Launch of "Viking" Mission

1976. Air. Space Probes to Mars and Venus. Multicoloured.

3061	40fi. Type **661**	10	10
3062	60fi. "Viking" in flight	20	10
3063	1fo. "Viking" on Mars	25	10
3064	2fo. Launch of "Venera"	60	15
3065	3fo. "Venera 9" in flight	95	25
3066	4fo. "Venera 10" descending to Venus	1·40	35
3067	5fo. "Venera" on Venus	1·70	1·20
MS3068	97×81 mm. 20fo. "Viking 1" landing on Mars (42×65 mm)	5·25	5·25

662 Locomotive No. 4, 1875

1976. Centenary of Gyor-Sopron Railway. Multicoloured.

3069	40fi. Type **662**	20	10
3070	60fi. Locomotive No. 17, 1885	25	10
3071	1fo. Rail-bus. 1925	35	10
3072	2fo. Steam locomotive, 1920	80	15
3073	3fo. Diesel railcar, 1926	1·30	25
3074	4fo. Diesel railcar, 1934	2·00	60
3075	5fo. Diesel railcar, 1971	2·30	1·20

663 Tree Foliage and Map

1976. "Afforestation of 1,000,000th Hectare".

3076	**663**	1fo. multicoloured	70	25

664 Weightlifting and Wrestling (silver medals)

1976. Olympic Games, Montreal. Hungarian Medal-winners. Multicoloured.

3077	40fi. Type **664**	10	10
3078	60fi. Men's solo kayak and Women's pairs kayak (silver medals)	25	10
3079	1fo. Men's gymnastics (horse) (gold medal)	35	15
3080	4fo. Women's rapier (gold medal)	1·50	60
3081	6fo. Men's javelin (gold medal)	3·00	1·50
MS3082	80×95 mm. 20fo. Water-polo (Gold medal)	5·75	5·75

665 White Spoonbill

1977. Birds of Hortabagy National Park. Multicoloured.

3083	40fi. Type **665**	25	10
3084	60fi. White stork	35	15
3085	1fo. Purple heron	60	25
3086	2fo. Great bustard	70	35
3087	3fo. Common crane	1·20	60
3088	4fo. Pied wagtail	2·00	80
3089	5fo. Garganey	3·00	1·20

666 Imre Abonyi (champion driver) and Carriage, 1976

1977. Historic Horse-drawn Vehicles. Multicoloured.

3090	40fi. Type **666**	20	10
3091	60fi. Omnibus, 1870	25	10
3092	1fo. Hackney-carriage, 1890	30	10
3093	2fo. 19th-century mail coach	60	15
3094	3fo. 18th-century covered wagon	1·20	25
3095	4fo. Coach, 1568	1·50	60
3096	5fo. Saint Elizabeth's carriage, 1430	1·90	1·00

667 Common Peafowl

1977. Peafowl and Pheasants. Multicoloured.

3097	40fi. Type **667**	20	10
3098	60fi. Green peafowl	25	10
3099	1fo. Congo peafowl	30	10
3100	3fo. Great Argus pheasant	95	25
3101	4fo. Himalayan monal pheasant	1·70	35
3102	6fo. Burmese peacock- pheasant	2·30	1·40

668 Front Page of *Nepszava* and Printing Works

1977. Centenary of Newspaper "Nepszava".

3103	**668**	1fo. black, red and gold	35	25

669 *Flower painting* (Mihaly Munkacsy)

1977. Flower Paintings by Hungarian Artists. Multicoloured.

3104	40fi. Type **669**	10	10
3105	60fi. Jakab Bogdany	15	10
3106	1fo. Istvan Csok (horiz)	25	15
3107	2fo. Janos Halapy	60	25
3108	3fo. Jozsef Rippl-Ronai (horiz)	1·20	35
3109	4fo. Janos Tornyai	1·50	60
3110	5fo. Jozsef Koszta	1·90	1·50

670 Isaac Newton and Lens

1977. 250th Death Anniv of Isaac Newton (mathematician).

3111	**670**	3fo. black, brown and red	1·40	1·40

671 Children Running

1977. Youth Sports.

3112	**671**	3fo.+1fo. 50 mult	1·70	1·20

672 "Acrofila 74" 2fo.+1fo. Stamp

1977. Stamp Exhibitions.

3113	**672**	3fo. multicoloured	2·00	2·00

673 Janos Vajda

1977. 150th Birth Anniv of Janos Vajda (poet).

3114	**673**	1fo. stone, black & green	45	25

674 Netherlands 5c. Stamp, 1852

1977. "Amphilex 77" International Stamp Exhibition, Amsterdam.

3115	**674**	3fo. multicoloured	1·90	1·90

675 "Wedding at Nagyrede" Dance

1977. 25th Anniv of State Folk Ensemble.

3116	**675**	3fo. multicoloured	1·70	25

676 *Bathsheba at the Fountain*

1977. 400th Birth Anniv of Peter Paul Rubens. Sheet 70×94 mm.

MS3117	**676**	20fo. multicoloured	14·00	14·00

677 View of Sopron (from medieval engraving), Arms and Fidelity Tower

1977. 700th Anniv of Sopron.

3118	**677**	1fo. multicoloured	3·00	3·00

678 Kincsem (champion racehorse)

1977. 150th Anniv of Horse Racing in Hungary.

3119	**678**	1fo. multicoloured	2·30	2·30

679 East German 10pf. Stamp, 1957

1977. "Sozphilex 77" Stamp Exhibition, East Berlin.

3120	**679**	3fo. multicoloured	2·00	2·00

680 Scythian Iron Bell (6th century B.C.)

1977. Stamp Day and 175th Anniv of Hungarian National Museum. Art Treasures.

3121	**680**	2fo. brown and blue	1·20	1·20
3122	-	2fo. brown and violet	1·20	1·20
3123	-	2fo. brown & deep brown	1·20	1·20
3124	-	2fo. gold and mauve	1·20	1·20
MS3125	73×83 mm. 10fo. multicoloured		7·00	7·00

DESIGNS: No. 3122, Bronze candlestick, 12-13th century; 3123, Copper aquamanile, 13th century; 3124, Cast gold Christ (from crucifix), 11th century. 32×47 mm—10fo. Plate from crown of Constantinus Monomakhosz, 11th century.

681 "Sputnik 1"

1977. Space Research. Multicoloured.

3126	40fi. Type **681** (postage)	10	10
3127	60fi. "Skylab"	15	10
3128	1fo. "Soyuz–Salyut 5" space station	25	10
3129	3fo. "Luna 24"	80	15
3130	4fo. "Mars 3"	2·00	30
3131	6fo. "Viking"	2·30	1·40
MS3132	98×78 mm. 20fo. Viking Lander on Mars (air)		7·50	7·50

682 Map, Dove and "Europa"

1977. Air. European Security Conference, Belgrade. Sheet 125×75 mm.

MS3133	**682**	20fo. multicoloured	7·00	7·00

683 Tupolev Tu-154

1977. Air.

3134	**683**	60fl. black and orange	15	10
3135	-	1fo.20 black and lilac	20	10
3136	-	2fo. black and orange	30	10
3137	-	2fo.40 black & turquoise	35	10
3138	-	4fo. black and blue	60	10
3139	-	5fo. black and mauve	80	15
3140	-	10fo. black and blue	2·00	30
3141	-	20fo. black and green	4·00	80

DESIGNS—As T **683**: 1fo.20, Douglas DC-8-62; 2fo. Ilyushin Il-62M; 2fo.40, Airbus Industrie A300B4; 4fo. Boeing 747; 5fo. Tupolev Tu-144; 10fo. Concorde. 38×28 mm: 20fo. Ilyushin Il-86.

684 Montgolfier Brothers and Balloon

1977. Air. Airships. Multicoloured.

3142	40fi. Type **684**	10	10
3143	60fi. David Schwarz and his aluminium airship	20	10
3144	1fo. Alberto Santos-Dumont and airship *Ballon No. 5* over Paris	30	10
3145	2fo. K. E. Tsiolkovsky and airship *Lebedi* over Kremlin	60	10
3146	3fo. Roald Amundsen and airship *Norge* over North Pole	80	25
3147	4fo. Hugo Eckener and airship *Graf Zeppelin* over Mount Fuji	1·40	30
3148	5fo. Ferdinand Zeppelin and *Graf Zeppelin* over Chicago World Exhibition	2·30	80
MS3149	98×78 mm. 20fo. Airship LZ-127 *Graf Zeppelin* over Budapest (58×36 mm)		7·00	7·00

685 Feet Immersed in Water

1977. World Rheumatism Year.

3150	**685**	1fo. multicoloured	70	25

686 Ervin Szabo

1977. Anniversaries.

3151	-	1fo. black and red	35	25
3152	**686**	1fo. grey, black and red	35	25

DESIGNS: No 3151, Jamos Szanto Kovacs (agrarian socialist movement leader, 125th birth anniv); 3152, Type **686** (director of Municipal Libraries, journalist and labour movement leader, birth centenary).

687 Monument to Hungarian Participants, Omsk

1977. 60th Anniv of Russian Revolution.

3153	**687**	1fo. black and red	35	25

688 Endre Ady

1977. Birth Centenary of Endre Ady (poet).
| 3154 | **688** | 1fo. blue | 60 | 60 |

689 Lesser Panda

1977. Bears. Multicoloured.
3155	40fi.	Type **689**	15	10
3156	60fi.	Giant panda	20	10
3157	1fo.	Asiatic black bear	40	15
3158	4fo.	Polar bear	1·50	25
3159	6fo.	Brown bear	3·50	1·20

690 Austrian Flag
and Passenger
Ship

1977. 30th Anniv of Re-establishment of Danube Commission. Sheet 130×93 mm containing T **690** and similar horiz designs.
| MS3160 | 2fo.×11 multicoloured | 14·00 | 14·00 |

DESIGNS—Flags and ships of : Austria, Bulgaria, Czechoslovakia, France, Netherlands, Yugoslavia, Hungary, West Germany, Rumania, Switzerland, Soviet Union.

691 Border-country
Lancer, 17th-cent

1978. Hussars. Multicoloured.
3161	40fi.	Type **691**	15	10
3162	60fi.	Kuruts horseman, 1710	20	10
3163	1fo.	Baranya hussar, 1762	30	10
3164	2fo.	Palatine Hussars officer, 1809	60	15
3165	4fo.	Alexander Hussar, 1848	1·20	45
3166	6fo.	Trumpeter, 5th Honved Regiment, 1900	2·50	80

692 Moon Station

1978. Air. Science Fiction in Space Research. Multicoloured.
3167	40fi.	Type **692**	10	10
3168	60fi.	Moon settlement	15	10
3169	1fo.	Phobos	30	10
3170	2fo.	Exploring an asteroid	60	10
3171	3fo.	Spacecraft in gravitational field of Mars	80	10
3172	4fo.	One of Saturn's rings	1·40	25
3173	5fo.	"Jupiter 3"	1·70	70

693 School of Arts and Crafts

1978. Bicentenary of School of Art and Crafts.
| 3174 | **693** | 1fo. multicoloured | 35 | 25 |

694 Profile Heads

1978. Youth Stamp Exhibition, Hatvan.
| 3175 | **694** | 3fo.+1fo.50 silver, red and black | 3·50 | 3·50 |

695 "Generations"
(Gyula Derkovits)

1978. "Socphilex 78" Stamp Exhibition, Szombathely.
| 3176 | **695** | 3fo.+1fo.50 mult | 1·70 | 1·70 |

696 Louis Bleriot

1978. Air. Famous Aviators and their Airplanes. Multicoloured.
3177	40fi.	Type **696**	15	10
3178	60fi.	John Alcock and Arthur Whitten Brown	20	10
3179	1fo.	Albert C. Read	25	10
3180	2fo.	Hermann Kohl, Gunther Hunefeld and James Fitzmaurice	70	15
3181	3fo.	Amy Johnson and Jim Mollison	1·00	25
3182	4fo.	Georgy Endresz and Sandor Magyar	1·50	30
3183	5fo.	Wolfgang von Gronau	1·90	1·20
MS3184	96×79 mm. 20fo. Wright Brothers and *Flyer* (74×25 mm)	7·00	7·00

697 Glass Vase and
Glass-blowing Tube

1978. Centenary of Ajka Glass Works.
| 3185 | **697** | 1fo. multicoloured | 35 | 25 |

698 West Germany and
Poland

1978. World Cup Football Championship, Argentina. Multicoloured.
3186	2fo.	Type **698**	80	35
3187	2fo.	Hungary and Argentina	80	35
3188	2fo.	France and Italy	80	35
3189	2fo.	Tunisia and Mexico	80	35
3190	2fo.	Sweden and Brazil	80	35
3191	2fo.	Spain and Austria	80	35
3192	2fo.	Peru and Scotland	80	35
3193	2fo.	Iran and Netherlands	80	35
MS3194	98×76 mm. 20fo. World Cup emblem and goal mouth (37×27 mm)	8·25	8·25

699 Canadian 3d. Stamp, 1851

1978. "Capex 78" International Stamp Exhibition, Toronto.
| 3195 | **699** | 3fo. multicoloured | 1·70 | 1·70 |

| **700** Diesel MK 45 Locomotive | **702** Festival Emblem |

1978. 30th Anniv of Budapest Pioneer Railway.
| 3196 | **700** | 1fo. multicoloured | 35 | 25 |

701 Leif Eriksson

1978. Explorers. Two sheets each 130×100 mm containing horiz designs as T **701**.
| MS3197 | Two sheets (a) 2fo. ×4 yellow and black (T **701**); orange and black (Christopher Columbus); orange and black (Vasco da Gama); pink and black (Ferdinand Magellan). (b) 2fo. ×4 yellow and black (Sir Francis Drake); apple green and black (Henry Hudson); green and black (James Cook); light blue and black (Robert Peary) 2 sheets | 14·00 | 14·00 |

702 Festival
Emblem

1978. 11th World Youth and Students' Festival, Havana. Multicoloured.
| 3198 | 1fo. | Type **702** | 35 | 10 |
| 3199 | 1fo. | Map of Cuba and emblem | 35 | 10 |

703 Human Torso
and Heart

1978. World Hypertension Year.
| 3200 | **703** | 1fo. red, black and blue | 35 | 10 |

704 Jules Verne and illustration
from *A Journey to the Moon*

1978. Air. 150th Birth Anniv of Jules Verne (novelist). Sheet 97×78 mm.
| MS3201 | **704** | 20fo. black and yellow | 7·00 | 7·00 |

705 Dove and Fist
holding Olive
Branch

1978. 20th Anniv of Communist Party Review "Peace and Socialism".
| 3202 | **705** | 1fo. red and black | 35 | 10 |

706 Vladimir Remek cancelling
Letters, "Salyut 6" and "Soyuz 28"

1978. Air. "Praga 1978" International Stamp Exhibition, Prague.
| 3203 | **706** | 3fo. multicoloured | 1·70 | 1·70 |

707 Toshiba Automatic Letter
Sorting Equipment

1978. Automation of Letter Sorting.
| 3204 | **707** | 1fo. multicoloured | 60 | 60 |

708 Putto offering Grapes

1978. Stamp Day. Mosaics. Multicoloured.
3205	2fo.	Type **708**	2·50	2·50
3206	2fo.	Tiger	2·50	2·50
3207	2fo.	Bird	2·50	2·50
3208	2fo.	Dolphin	2·50	2·50
MS3209	88×61 mm. 10fo. Hercules aiming arrow at Centaur Nessus fleeing with Nymph Deianeira (51×32 mm)	11·50	11·50

709 Methods of
Communication

1978. Organization of Socialist Countries' Postal Administrations Conference, Tbilisi.
| 3210 | **709** | 1fo. multicoloured | 60 | 25 |

710 Imre Thokoly

1978. 300th Anniv of Thokoly's Revolt.
| 3211 | **710** | 1fo. black and yellow | 60 | 25 |

711 Hungarian Regalia

1978. Return of Hungarian Regalia. Sheet 76×96 mm.
| MS3212 | **711** | 20fo. multicoloured | 10·50 | 10·50 |

712 "The Red Coach" (novel)

1978. Birth Centenary of Gyula Krudy (novelist).
| 3213 | **712** | 3fo. red and black | 1·00 | 25 |

713 St. Ladislas (bust,
Gyor Cathedral)

1978. 900th Anniv of Accession of St. Ladislas.
| 3214 | **713** | 1fo. multicoloured | 70 | 25 |

714 Buildings and Arms of Koszeg

1978. 650th Anniv of Koszeg.
3215 **714** 1fo. multicoloured ... 70 ... 25

715 Samu Czaban and Gizella Berzeviczy

1978. Birth Centenaries of Samu Czaban and Gizella Berzeviczy (teachers).
3216 **715** 1fo. multicoloured ... 70 ... 60

716 Communist Party Emblem

1978. 60th Anniv of Hungarian Communist Party.
3217 **716** 1fo. red, grey and black ... 25 ... 10

717 "Girl cutting Bread"

1978. Ceramics by Margit Kovacs. Multicoloured.
3218 1fo. Type **717** ... 45 ... 10
3219 2fo. "Girl with Pitcher" ... 60 ... 35
3220 3fo. "Boy Potter" ... 1·20 ... 60

718 Self-portrait in Fur Coat

1978. 450th Death Anniv of Albrecht Durer (artist). Multicoloured.
3221 40fi. *Madonna with Child* ... 10 ... 10
3222 60fi. *Adoration of the Magi* (horiz) ... 10 ... 10
3223 1fo. Type **718** ... 25 ... 10
3224 2fo. *St. George* ... 60 ... 10
3225 3fo. *Nativity* (horiz) ... 1·20 ... 15
3226 4fo. *St. Eustace* ... 1·40 ... 25
3227 5fo. *The Four Apostles* ... 2·00 ... 1·20
MS3228 78×99 mm. 20fo. sepia and stone (*Dancing Peasant Couple*) (36×59 mm) ... 7·00 ... 7·00

719 Human Rights Emblem

1979. 30th Anniv of Declaration of Human Rights.
3229 **719** 1fo. blue and light blue ... 1·70 ... 1·70

720 Child with Dog

1979. International Year of the Child (1st issue). Multicoloured.
3230 1fo. Type **720** ... 1·20 ... 1·20
3231 1fo. Family group ... 1·20 ... 1·20
3232 1fo. Children of different races ... 7·00 ... 7·00
See also Nos. 3287/93.

721 *Soldiers of the Red Army, Forward!* (poster by Bela Uitz)

1979. 60th Anniv of First Hungarian Soviet Republic.
3233 **721** 1fo. black, red and grey ... 25 ... 10

722 "Girl Reading" (Ferenc Kovacs)

1979. Youth Stamp Exhibition, Bekescsaba.
3234 **722** 3fo.+1fo.50 grey, blue and black ... 1·20 ... 1·20

723 Chessmen and Cup

1979. 23rd Chess Olympiad, Buenos Aires (1978).
3235 **723** 3fo. multicoloured ... 2·00 ... 1·70

724 Alexander Nevski Cathedral, Sofia, and First Bulgarian Stamp

1979. "Philaserdica 79" International Stamp Exhibition, Sofia.
3236 **724** 3fo. multicoloured ... 1·50 ... 1·50

725 Stephenson's Rocket, 1829

1979. International Transport Exhibition, Hamburg. Depicting development of the railway. Multicoloured.
3237 40fi. Type **725** ... 25 ... 10
3238 60fi. Siemens's electric locomotive, 1879 ... 40 ... 10
3239 1fo. Locomotive *Pioneer*, 1851 (wrongly dated "1936") ... 65 ... 20
3240 2fo. Hungarian Class MAV I.e pulling *Orient Express*, 1883 ... 75 ... 25
3241 3fo. *Trans-Siberian Express*, 1898 ... 1·30 ... 50
3242 4fo. Japanese *Hikari* express train, 1964 ... 1·90 ... 75
3243 5fo. German *Transrapid 05* Maglev train, 1979 ... 2·10 ... 1·50
MS3244 78×95 mm. 20fo. European railway map (51×36 mm) ... 10·50 ... 10·50

726 Soyuz Gas Pipeline and Compressor Station

1979. 30th Anniv of Council of Mutual Economic Aid. Multicoloured.
3245 1fo. Type **726** ... 25 ... 10
3246 2fo. Pylon and dam, Lenin hydro-electric power station, Dnepropetrovsk ... 65 ... 20
3247 3fo. Council building, Moscow ... 90 ... 25

727 Zsigmond Moricz (after J. Rippl-Ronai)

1979. Birth Centenary of Zsigmond Moricz (writer).
3248 **727** 1fo. multicoloured ... 25 ... 10

728 City Hall, Helsinki (1952 Games)

1979. Olympic Games, Moscow (1980) (1st issue). Multicoloured.
3249 40fi. Type **728** ... 15 ... 10
3250 60fi. Colosseum, Rome (1960) ... 25 ... 10
3251 1fo. Asakusa Temple, Tokyo (1964) ... 65 ... 20
3252 2fo. Cathedral, Mexico City (1968) ... 90 ... 25
3253 3fo. Frauenkirche, Munich (1972) ... 1·30 ... 35
3254 4fo. Modern quarter, Montreal (1976) ... 1·50 ... 60
3255 5fo. Lomonosov University, Moscow, and Misha the bear (mascot) (1980) ... 2·10 ... 1·20
See also Nos. 3323/29.

729 *Child with Horse and Greyhounds* (Janos Vaszary)

1979. Animal Paintings. Multicoloured.
3256 40fi. Type **729** ... 20 ... 10
3257 60fi. *Coach and Five* (Karoly Lotz) ... 25 ... 10
3258 1fo. *Lads on Horseback* (Celesztin Pallya) ... 40 ... 25
3259 2fo. *Farewell* (Karoly Lotz) ... 65 ... 35
3260 3fo. *Horse Market* (Celeztin Pallya) ... 90 ... 60
3261 4fo. *Wandering* (Bela Ivanyi-Grunwald) ... 1·30 ... 85
3262 5fo. *Ready for Hunting* (Karoly Sterio) ... 2·50 ... 1·20

730 Sturgeon, Cousteau's Ship *Calypso* and Black Sea

1979. Sea and River Purity.
3263 **730** 3fo. multicoloured ... 1·30 ... 25

731 Globe and Five Pentathlon Sports

1979. Pentathlon World Championship, Budapest.
3264 **731** 2fo. multicoloured ... 1·30 ... 35

732 Stephen I Denarius (reverse)

1979. Ninth International Numismatic Congress, Berne. Designs showing old Hungarian coins. Multicoloured.
3265 1fo. Type **732** ... 20 ... 25
3266 2fo. Bela III copper coin (obverse) ... 65 ... 60
3267 3fo. Louis the Great groat (reverse) ... 90 ... 85
3268 4fo. Matthias I gold forint (obverse) ... 1·30 ... 1·20
3269 5fo. Wladislaw II gulden (reverse) ... 1·50 ... 1·50

733 Design for Proposed Hungarian Stamp of 1848

1979. Stamp Day. Sheet 70×56 mm.
MS3270 **733** 10fo. multicoloured ... 7·50 ... 7·50

734 Light Passenger Locomotive

1979. Centenary of Gyor–Sopron–Ebenfurt Railway. Sheet 98×79 mm containing T **734** and similar horiz designs. Multicoloured.
MS3271 5fo. Type **734**; 5fo. Class 424 steam locomotive; 5fo. Class 520 locomotive; 5fo. Diesel locomotive Type M41 ... 7·50 ... 7·50

735 Flags and Globe filled with Coins

1979. World Savings Day.
3272 **735** 1fo. multicoloured ... 25 ... 10

736 "Vega-Chess" (Victor Vasarely)

1979. Modern Art.
3273 **736** 1fo. multicoloured ... 50 ... 25

737 European Otter

1979. Protected Animals. Multicoloured.
3274	40fi. Type **737**	25	10
3275	60fi. Wild cat	30	10
3276	1fo. Pine marten	40	10
3277	2fo. Eurasian badger	75	20
3278	4fo. Steppe polecat	1·50	60
3279	6fo. Beech marten	3·75	1·40

738 Ski Jumping

1979. Air. Winter Olympic Games, Lake Placid (1980). Multicoloured.
3280	40fi. Type **738**	30	10
3281	60fi. Figure skating	65	20
3282	1fo. Slalom	70	35
3283	2fo. Ice hockey	1·30	50
3284	4fo. Bobsleigh	1·90	60
3285	6fo. Cross-country skiing	2·50	1·90
MS3286	97×73 mm. 20fo. Ice dancing (square, 49×49 mm)	8·25	8·25

739 Tom Thumb

1979. International Year of the Child (2nd issue). Designs depicting children's stories. Multicoloured.
3287	40fi. Type **739**	25	10
3288	60fi. *The Ugly Duckling* (Andersen)	65	10
3289	1fo. *The Fisher and the Goldfish*	75	20
3290	2fo. *Cinderella*	1·30	25
3291	3fo. *Gulliver's Travels* (Swift)	1·40	35
3292	4fo. *The Little Pig and the Wolves*	1·50	60
3293	5fo. *Gallant John*	2·50	1·00
MS3294	78×98 mm. 20fo. *Fairy Ilona*	8·25	8·25

740 Achillea and Bee-eating Beetles

1980. Pollination. Multicoloured.
3295	40fi. Type **740**	20	10
3296	60fi. Gaillardia and bee	25	10
3297	1fo. Rudbeckia and red admiral	40	10
3298	2fo. Dog rose and rose chafer	75	20
3299	4fo. *Petroselinum hortense* and striped bug	1·50	35
3300	6fo. Achillea and longhorn beetle	2·40	1·20

741 Hanging Gardens of Babylon

1980. Seven Wonders of the Ancient World. Multicoloured.
3301	40fi. Type **741**	15	10
3302	60fi. Temple of Artemis, Ephesus	20	10
3303	1fo. Statue of Zeus, Olympia	25	10

3304	2fo. Mausoleum of Halicarnassus	65	20
3305	3fo. Colossus of Rhodes	1·00	25
3306	4fo. Pharos, Alexandria	1·40	35
3307	5fo. Pyramids of Egypt	3·00	1·00

742 Gabor Bethlen (copperplate)

1980. 400th Birth Anniv of Gabor Bethlen (Prince of Transylvania).
3308	**742** 1fo. multicoloured	25	10

743 Tihany Abbey

1980. 925th Anniv of Foundation of Tihany Abbey.
3309	**743** 1fo. multicoloured	25	10

744 Easter Sepulchre

1980. Easter Sepulchre of Garamszentbenedek. Designs showing details of sepulchre. Multicoloured.
3310	1fo. Type **744**	25	25
3311	2fo. Three Marys	65	60
3312	3fo. Apostle Jacob	1·00	1·00
3313	4fo. Apostle Thaddeus	1·30	1·20
3314	5fo. Apostle Andrew	1·60	1·60

745 Bunch of Wild Flowers

1980. 35th Anniv of Liberation.
3315	**745** 1fo. multicoloured	40	25

746 Watch symbolising Environmental Protection

1980. Youth Stamp Exhibition, Dunaujvaros.
3316	**746** 3fo.+1fo.50 mult	1·30	1·30

747 Attila Jozsef

1980. 75th Birth Anniv of Attila Jozsef (poet).
3317	**747** 1fo. green and red	40	25

748 "Madonna and Child" Stamp of 1921 with Inverted Centre

1980. 50th Anniv of Hungarian Stamp Museum.
3318	**748** 1fo. multicoloured	2·30	2·30

749 Great Britain 2d. Blue and Life Guard

1980. "London 1980" International Stamp Exhibition.
3319	**749** 3fo. multicoloured	1·30	1·30

750 Soviet and Hungarian Cosmonauts

1980. Air. Soviet-Hungarian Space Flight.
3320	**750** 5fo. multicoloured	2·50	60

751 Margit Kaffka

1980. Birth Centenary of Margit Kaffka (writer).
3321	**751** 1fo. yellow, black & vio	40	25

752 Norwegian 1951 Olympic Stamp and Statue "Mother and Child" (Gustav Vigeland)

1980. "Norwex 80" International Stamp Exhibition, Oslo.
3322	**752** 3fo. multicoloured	1·50	1·50

753 Handball

1980. Air. Olympic Games, Moscow (2nd issue). Multicoloured.
3323	40fi. Type **753**	15	10
3324	60fi. Double kayak	20	10
3325	1fo. Running	25	10
3326	2fo. Gymnastics	65	10
3327	3fo. Show-jumping (modern pentathlon)	1·00	20
3328	4fo. Wrestling	1·60	60
3329	5fo. Water polo	1·90	1·50
MS3330	71×87 mm. 20fo. Runners with Olympic flame	8·25	8·25

754 Endre Hogyes (physician) and Congress Emblem

1980. 28th International Congress of Physiological Sciences, Budapest.
3331	**754** 1fo. multicoloured	30	10

755 B. Farkos, V. Kubasov and Space Station

1980. Air. Soviet-Hungarian Space Flight (2nd issue). Sheet 72×93 mm.
MS3332	**755** 20fo. multicoloured	10·50	10·50

756 Zoltan Schonherz

1980. 75th Birth Anniv of Zoltan Schonherz (Workers' Movement member).
3333	**756** 1fo. multicoloured	30	10

757 Decanter

1980. Stamp Day. Glassware. Multicoloured.
3334	1fo. Type **757**	40	25
3335	2fo. Wine glass, Budapest	75	60
3336	3fo. Drinking glass, Zay-Ugrocz	1·30	85
MS3337	68×79 mm. 10fo. Drinking glass, Pecs (25×35 mm)	4·50	4·50

758 Greek Athletes and Olympic Gold Medal

1980. Air. Olympic Champions. Sheet 84×65 mm.
MS3338	**758** 20fo. multicoloured	7·00	7·00

759 Bertalan Por (self-portrait)

1980. Birth Centenary of Bertalan Por (artist).
3339	**759** 1fo. multicoloured	30	20

760 Greylag Goose

1980. Protected Birds. Multicoloured.
3340	40fi. Type **760**	15	10
3341	60fi. Black-crowned night herons	25	10
3342	1fo. Common shovelers	30	20
3343	2fo. White-winged black tern	65	25
3344	4fo. Great crested grebes	1·90	85
3345	6fo. Black-winged stilts	3·25	1·50
MS3346	75×95 mm. 20fo. Great egrets (40×63 mm)	6·25	6·25

761 Peace Dove and Map of Europe

1980. European Security and Co-operation Conference, Madrid. Sheet 99×78 mm.

| MS3347 | **761** | 20fo. multicoloured | 3·75 | 3·75 |

762 Johannes Kepler

1980. 350th Death Anniv of Johannes Kepler (astronomer).

| 3348 | **762** | 1fo. multicoloured | 65 | 25 |

763 Karoly Kisfaludy

1980. 150th Death Anniv of Karoly Kisfaludy (dramatist and poet).

| 3349 | **763** | 1fo. multicoloured | 50 | 20 |

764 U.N. Building, New York

1980. 25th Anniv of United Nations Membership. Multicoloured.

3350	**764**	40fi. Type **764**	15	10
3351		60fi. U.N. building, Geneva	20	10
3352		1fo. International Centre, Vienna	25	10
3353		2fo. U.N. and Hungarian flags	65	20
3354		4fo. U.N. emblem and Hungarian arms	1·30	25
3355		6fo. World map	3·75	2·10

765 Ferenc Erdei

1980. 70th Birth Anniv of Ferenc Erdei (agricultural economist and politician).

| 3356 | **765** | 1fo. multicoloured | 25 | 10 |

766 Bela Szanto

1981. Birth Centenary of Bela Szanto (founder member of Hungarian Communist Party).

| 3357 | **766** | 1fo. multicoloured | 25 | 10 |

767 Lajos Batthyany (after Miklos Barabas)

1981. 175th Birth Anniv of Lajos Batthany (politician).

| 3358 | **767** | 1fo. multicoloured | 25 | 10 |

768 Cheetah

1981. Air. Birth Centenary of Kalman Kittenberger (explorer and zoologist). Multicoloured.

3359		40fi. Type **768**	20	10
3360		60fi. Lion	20	10
3361		1fo. Leopard	30	20
3362		2fo. Black rhinoceros	65	25
3363		3fo. Greater kudu	1·00	30
3364		4fo. African elephant	1·40	35
3365		5fo. Kittenberger and Hungarian National Museum	3·25	1·90

769 *Graf Zeppelin* over Tokyo

1981. Air. "Luraba" International Exhibition of Aero- and Astro-philately, Lucerne. *Graf Zeppelin* Flights. Multicoloured.

3366		1fo. Type **769** (first round-the-world flight, 1929)	25	10
3367		2fo. Franz Josef Land and icebreaker *Malygin* (Polar flight, 1931)	50	20
3368		3fo. Nine-arch Bridge, Hortobagy (Hungary flight, 1931)	75	25
3369		4fo. Hostentor, Lubeck (Baltic flight, 1931)	1·00	30
3370		5fo. Tower Bridge (England flight, 1931)	1·10	35
3371		6fo. Federal Palace, Chicago (World Exhibition flight, 1933)	1·30	50
3372		7fo. Lucerne (1st Swiss flight, 1929)	1·90	1·60

770 Bela Bartok (after Ferenczy Beni)

1981. Birth Centenary of Bela Bartok (composer). Sheet 100×80 mm containing T **770** and similar vert design. Multicoloured.

| MS3373 | | 10fo. Type **770**; 10fo. Illustration for "Cantata Profana" | 8·25 | 8·25 |

771 Flag of House of Arpad (11th century)

1981. Historical Hungarian Flags. Multicoloured.

3374		40fi. Type **771**	20	10
3375		60fi. Hunyadi Family flag (15th century)	40	15
3376		1fo. Flag of Gabor Bethlen (1600)	75	20
3377		2fo. Flag of Ferenc Rakoczi II (1706)	1·10	25
3378		4fo. "Honved" (1848–49)	1·50	35
3379		6fo. Troop Flag (1919)	2·10	1·10

772 Red Deer seen through Binoculars

1981. Centenary of Association of Hungarian Huntsmen.

| 3380 | **772** | 2fo. multicoloured | 65 | 25 |

773 First Hungarian Telephone Exchange

1981. Centenary of First Hungarian Telephone Exchange, Budapest.

| 3381 | **773** | 2fo. multicoloured | 1·30 | 25 |

774 Henri Dunant (founder) and Map of Europe

1981. Third European Conference of Red Cross and Red Crescent Societies, Budapest. Sheet 98×78 mm.

| MS3382 | **774** | 20fo. multicoloured | 6·25 | 6·25 |

775 Red Cross, Transport and Globe

1981. Centenary of Hungarian Red Cross.

| 3383 | **775** | 2fo. orange and red | 65 | 25 |

776 Airship LZ-127 *Graf Zeppelin*

1981. "WIPA 1981" International Stamp Exhibition, Vienna. Sheet 80×60 mm containing T **776** and similar horiz designs depicting "WIPA 1933" souvenir labels.

| MS3384 | | 5fo. green and black (Type **776**); 5fo. purple and black (Rocket); 5fo. brown and black (Dispatch rider); 5fo. blue and black (Sailing ship) | 8·25 | 8·25 |

777 I.Y.D.P. Emblem and Person pushing Wheelchair

1981. International Year of Disabled Persons.

| 3385 | **777** | 2fo.+1fo. green & yell | 1·90 | 1·20 |

778 Young People and Factory

1981. Tenth Young Communist League Congress, Budapest.

| 3386 | **778** | 4fo.+2fo. mult | 2·50 | 2·50 |

779 Stephenson and "Locomotion"

1981. Birth Bicentenary of George Stephenson (railway pioneer).

| 3387 | **779** | 2fo. yellow, grey & brown | 1·30 | 35 |

780 Bela Vago

1981. Birth Centenary of Bela Vago (founder member of Hungarian Communist Party).

| 3388 | **780** | 2fo. green and brown | 90 | 25 |

781 Alexander Fleming

1981. Birth Centenary of Alexander Fleming (discoverer of penicillin).

| 3389 | **781** | 2fo. multicoloured | 90 | 35 |

782 Bridal Chest from Szentgal

1981. Stamp Day. Bridal Chests. Multicoloured.

3390		1fo. Type **782**	65	50
3391		2fo. Chest from Hodmezovasarhely	1·30	1·10
MS3392		76×55 mm. 10fo. Chest from Bacs (43×23 mm)	7·00	7·00

783 Calvinist College

1981. 450th Anniv of Calvinist College, Papa.

| 3393 | **783** | 2fo. multicoloured | 90 | 25 |

784 Hands holding F.A.O. Emblem

1981. World Food Day.

| 3394 | **784** | 2fo. multicoloured | 1·90 | 25 |

785 German Costume

1981. National Costumes of Hungarian Ethnic Minorities. Multicoloured.

3395		1fo. Slovakian costume	1·80	1·80
3396		2fo. Type **785**	1·80	1·80
3397		3fo. Croatian costume	1·80	1·80
3398		4fo. Rumanian costume	1·80	1·80

786 "Franz I" (1830) and *Ferene Deak* on 30fi. Stamp

1981. 125th Anniv of Danube Commission. Paddlesteamers and Danube Commission stamps issued in 1967. Multicoloured.

3399		1fo. Type **786**	40	25
3400		1fo. *Arpad* (1834) and *Revfulop* on 60fi. stamp	45	30
3401		2fo. *Szechenyi* (1853) and *Hunyadi* on 1fo. stamp	65	50
3402		2fo. *Grof Szechenyi Istvan* (1896) and *Szekszard* on 1fo.50 stamp	70	50
3403		4fo. *Zsofia* (1914) and *Miscolc* on 1fo.70 stamp	1·10	85
3404		6fo. *Felszabadulas* (1917) and *Tihany* on 2fo. stamp	2·00	1·50
3405		8fo. *Rakoczi* (1964) and *Siraly I* on 2fo.50 stamp	2·75	1·90

MS3406 96×77 mm. 20fo. Hydrofoil
Solyom and 1fo. stamp (49×39 mm)   7·00   7·00

787 "Mother
Breast-feeding"
(pottery,
Margit Kovacs)

1981. Christmas. Multicoloured.
3407   1fo. Type **787**   65   35
3408   2fo. "Madonna of Csurgo"
(bronze Amerigo Tot)   1·30   50

788 Pen Pals
(Rockwell)

1981. Illustrations by Norman Rockwell and Anna
Lesznai. Multicoloured.
3409   1fo. Type **788**   20   20
3410   2fo. Courting under the Clock at
Midnight (Rockwell)   30   25
3411   2fo. Maiden Voyage (Rockwell)   30   25
3412   4fo. Threading the Needle
(Rockwell)   1·30   1·10
3413   4fo. At the End of the Village
(detail) (Lesznai)   1·30   1·10
3414   5fo. Dance (detail) (Lesznai)   1·90   1·70
3415   6fo. Sunday (detail) (Lesznai)   2·10   2·10

789 La Tolette

1981. Birth Centenary of Pablo Picasso (artist). Sheet
61×86 mm.
MS3416 **789** 20fo. multicoloured   8·25   8·25

790 Militiaman at
Shooting Practice

1982. 25th Anniv of Workers' Militia. Multicoloured.
3417   1fo. Type **790**   25   20
3418   4fo. Three generations of
militiamen   1·30   35

791 Congress
Emblem and
Havana

1982. Tenth World Trade Unions Federation Congress,
Havana.
3419   **791** 2fo. multicoloured   65   25

792 Gyula
Alpari

1982. Birth Centenary of Gyula Alpari (journalist).
3420   **792** 2fo. yellow, purple & brn   65   25

---

793 Dr. Robert
Koch

1982. Centenary of Discovery of Tubercle Bacillus.
3421   **793** 2fo. multicoloured   65   25

794 Tennis
Racket and
Ball

1982. Youth Stamp. European Junior Tennis Cup.
3422   **794** 4fo.+2fo. mult   1·90   1·90

795 Hungary v. Egypt, 1934

1982. World Cup Football Championship, Spain.
Multicoloured.
3423   1fo. Type **795**   40   10
3424   1fo. Italy v. Hungary, 1938   40   10
3425   2fo. West Germany v. Hungary,
1954   75   20
3426   2fo. Hungary v. Mexico, 1958   75   20
3427   4fo. Hungary v. England, 1962 1·50   25
3428   6fo. Hungary v. Brazil, 1966   1·90   35
3429   8fo. Argentina v. Hungary, 1978 2·50   1·50
MS3430 100×68 mm. 10fo. Barcelona
stadium; 10fo. Madrid stadium   7·50   7·50

796 Table Tennis
Player and Map of
Europe

1982. European Table Tennis Championship, Budapest.
3431   **796** 2fo. multicoloured   1·00   25

797 "Pascali"

1982. Roses. Multicoloured.
3432   1fo. Type **797**   40   10
3433   1fo. "Michele Meilland"   40   10
3434   2fo. "Diorama"   75   20
3435   2fo. "Wendy Cussons"   75   20
3436   3fo. "Blue Moon"   1·10   25
3437   3fo. "Invitation"   1·10   25
3438   4fo. "Tropicana"   2·10   1·40
MS3439 70×92 mm. 10fo. Bunch of
roses (35×57 mm)   6·25   6·25

798 Georgi
Dimitrov

1982. Birth Centenary of Georgi Dimitrov (Bulgarian
statesman).
3440   **798** 2fo. grey, green & brown   65   60

799 "Columbia"
Space Shuttle

1982. Space Research. Multicoloured.
3441   1fo. Type **799**   25   10
3442   1fo. Neil Armstrong (first man
on Moon)   25   10
3443   2fo. A. Leonov (first space-
walker)   65   20
3444   2fo. Yuri Gagarin (first man
in space)   65   20
3445   4fo. Laika (first dog in space)   1·30   25
3446   4fo. "Sputnik I" (first artificial
satellite)   1·30   25
3447   6fo. K. E. Tsiolkovsky (Russian
scientist)   2·00   1·00

800 Watermark

1982. Bicentenary of Diosgyor Paper-mill.
3448   **800** 2fo. multicoloured   65   25

801 Rubik Cube

1982. World Rubik Cube Championship, Budapest.
3449   **801** 2fo. multicoloured   65   25

802 World Cup 20fi. Stamp, 1966,
and Paris Arms

1982. "Philexfrance 82" International Stamp Exhibition,
Paris. Sheet 98×72 mm.
MS3450 **802** 20fo.+10fo. mult   6·25   6·25

803 Col. Mihaly
Kovats (after S.
Finta)

1982. 250th Birth Anniv of George Washington. Sheet
90×72 mm containing T **803** and similar vert design.
Multicoloured.
MS3451 5fo. Type **803**; 5fo. Washington
on horseback (after F. Kemmelmeyer)   5·00   5·00

804 Blood
Drop

1982. World Haematology Congress, Budapest.
3452   **804** 2fo. multicoloured   65   25

---

805 Zirc Abbey and
Seal of King Bela III

1982. 800th Anniv of Zirc Abbey.
3453   **805** 2fo. multicoloured   65   25

806 Fishermen's
Bastion, Budapest

1982. Stamp Day. Multicoloured.
3454   4fo.+2fo. Type **806**   1·90   1·90
3455   4fo.+2fo. Cupola of Parliament,
Budapest   1·90   1·90

807 Budapest (image scaled to 59% of original size)

1982. Tenth Anniv of European Security and Co-
operation Conference, Brussels. Sheet 100×84 mm.
MS3456 **807** 20fo.+10fo. mult   5·75   5·75

808 Kner
Emblem

1982. Centenary of Kner Printing Office, Gyoma.
3457   **808** 2fo. yellow, black
and red   65   25

809 Agricultural Symbols on
Map of Hungary

1982. "Agrofila '82" Stamp Exhibition, Godollo.
3458   **809** 5fo. multicoloured   1·90   1·90

810 Horse-drawn Bus and
Underground Train

1982. 150th Anniv of Public Transport in Budapest.
3459   **810** 2fo. multicoloured   65   25

811 Budapest
Polytechnic
University

1982. Bicentenary of University Engineering Education.
3460   **811** 2fo. brown, stone & blue   65   25

812 Gyorgy
Boloni

1982. Birth Centenary of Gyorgy Boloni (journalist).
3461 **812** 2fo. yellow, brown and
deep brown   65   25

813 Lenin

1982. 65th Anniv of Russian Revolution.
3462 **813** 5fo. multicoloured   1·50   25

814 Vuk and Bird

1982. Vuk the Fox Cub (cartoon character). Multicoloured.
3463   1fo. Type **814**   25   10
3464   1fo. Two dogs   25   10
3465   2fo. Vuk and cock   75   20
3466   2fo. Vuk and owl   75   20
3467   4fo. Vuk and geese   1·50   20
3468   6fo. Vuk and frog   2·50 1·00
3469   8fo. Vuk, old fox and butterflies 3·25 1·70

815 St. Stephen
(sculpture, Imre
Varga)

1982. Works of Art in Hungarian Chapel, Vatican.
Multicoloured.
3470   2fo. Type **815**   75   75
3471   2fo. *Pope Silvester II making
donation to St. Stephen*
(37×18 mm)   75   75
3472   2fo. *St. John of Capistrano ringing Angelus to commemorate
Hungarian victory over
Turks"* (37×18 mm)   75   75
3473   2fo. *Pope Paul VI showing Cardinal Lekai site of Hungarian
Chapel* (37×18 mm)   75   75
3474   2fo. *Pope John Paul II consecrat-
ing chapel* (37×18 mm)   75   75
3475   2fo. *Madonna* (sculpture, Imre
Varga)   75   75

Nos. 3471/5 were printed together, *se-tenant*, forming
a composite design of a relief by Amerigo Tot.

816 Dog and
Cat crossing
road

1982. New Year.
3476 **816** 2fo. multicoloured   65   25

817 Zoltan Kodaly

1982. Birth Centenary of Zoltan Kodaly (composer). Sheet
66×95 mm.
MS3477 **817** 20fo. brown and stone   5·75   5·75

818 Goethe (after
Heinrich Kolbe)

1982. 150th Death Anniv of Johann Wolfgang Goethe
(writer). Sheet 93×74 mm.
MS3478 **818** 20fo. multicoloured   6·25   6·25

819 Raven and
Envelope Address
Marks

1983. Tenth Anniv of Postal Codes.
3479 **819** 2fo. black, grey and red 65   25

820 *Ship of Peace* (Endre
Szasz)

1983. Budapest Spring Festival.
3480 **820** 2fo. grey, gold and black 65   25

821 Student at
School Door

1983. Youth Stamp Exhibition, Baja.
3481 **821** 4fo.+2fo. mult   1·90   1·90

822 Gyula
Juhasz

1983. Birth Cent of Gyula Juhasz (writer).
3482 **822** 2fo. dp brown, brn & blk 65   25

823 Menner's Balloon,
1811

1983. Air. Bicent of Manned Flight. Multicoloured.
3483   1fo. Type **823** (1st manned
flight in Hungary)   25   10
3484   1fo. Captive observation balloon at Budapest Exhibition,
1896   25   10
3485   2fo. Pursuit race, 1904   65   10
3486   2fo. Hot-air balloon *Pannonia*,
1977   65   10
3487   4fo. Hot-air balloon *Malev*, 1981 1·30   20
3488   4fo. Hungarian National De-
fence Union balloon, 1982 1·30   20
3489   5fo. Non-rigid airship over Mecsek television tower, 1981 1·50   75
MS3490 88×74 mm. 20fo. Hot-air balloons (39×49 mm)   5·75   5·75

824 Szentgotthard
Monastery and Seal

1983. 800th Anniv of Szentgotthard.
3491 **824** 2fo. multicoloured   65   25

825 Watermill, Tapolca

1983. "Tembal 83" Thematic Stamps Exhibition, Basel.
3492 **825** 5fo. multicoloured   1·90   1·90

826 Parliament Buildings,
Budapest

1983. Fifth Inter-Parliamentary Union Conference,
Budapest. Sheet 95×77 mm.
MS3493 **826** 20fo. multicoloured   5·75   5·75

827 Jeno Hamburger

1983. Birth Centenary of Jeno Hamburger (doctor and
revolutionary).
3494 **827** 2fo. brown, blue and red 65   25

828 *Giovanna
d'Aragona*

1983. 500th Birth Anniv of Raphael (artist). Multicoloured.
3495   1fo. Type **828**   20   10
3496   1fo. *Lady with Unicorn*   20   10
3497   2fo. *Madonna of the Chair*   40   10
3498   2fo. *Madonna of the Grand Duke* 40   10
3499   4fo. *La Muta*   1·10   25
3500   6fo. *Lady with a Veil*   1·60   35
3501   8fo. *La Fornarina*   2·10   75
MS3502 66×89 mm. 20fo. *Esterhazy
Madonna* (24×37 mm)   7·00   7·00

829 Vagi and
Newspapers

1983. Birth Centenary of Istvan Vagi (secretary of
Socialist Workers' Party).
3503 **829** 2fo. multicoloured   65   25

830 Bolivar and
Map of Americas

1983. Birth Bicent of Simon Bolivar.
3504 **830** 2fo. multicoloured   65   25

831 Globe and
Congress
Emblem

1983. 68th Universal Esperanto Congress, Budapest.
3505 **831** 2fo. multicoloured   65   25

832 Martin Luther

1983. 500th Anniv of Martin Luther (religious reformer).
Sheet 80×65 mm.
MS3506 **832** 20fo. multicoloured   7·00   7·00

833 Lesser Spotted
Eagle

1983. Birds of Prey. Multicoloured.
3507   1fo. Type **833**   25   10
3508   1fo. Imperial eagle   25   10
3509   2fo. White-tailed sea eagle   65   10
3510   2fo. Western red-footed falcon 65   10
3511   4fo. Saker falcon   1·30   60
3512   6fo. Rough-legged buzzard   2·30 1·20
3513   8fo. Common buzzard   3·25 2·10

834 Bee
collecting
Pollen

1983. 29th Apimondia (Bee Keeping) Congress, Budapest.
3514 **834** 1fo. multicoloured   25   10

835 Old National Theatre
(after R. Alt)

1983. Stamp Day. Engravings of Budapest Buildings.
3515 **835** 4fo.+2fo. yellow, brown
and black   2·10   2·10
3516   -   4fo.+2fo. yellow, brown
and black   2·10   2·10
MS3517 80×63 mm. 20fo.+10fo. yellow
and brown   7·00   7·00
DESIGNS:—As T **835**: No. 3516, Municipal concert hall,
Pest (after H. Luders). 27×44 mm—**MS**3517, Holy Trinity
Square, Buda (after Rudolf Alt).

836 *Fruit-piece*

1983. Birth Centenary of Bela Czobel (artist).
3518 **836** 2fo. multicoloured   65   25

837 "Molnya"
Satellite and Kekes
TV Tower

1983. World Communications Year. Multicoloured.

3519	1fo. Type **837**		25	10
3520	1fo. Dish aerials and rockets		25	10
3521	2fo. Manual telephone exchange and modern "TMM-81" telephone		65	10
3522	3fo. Computer terminal		90	25
3523	5fo. Automatic letter-storing equipment		1·50	35
3524	8fo. Teletext and newspaper mastheads		2·50	60
MS3525	70×90 mm. 20fo. "Molnya" satellite (29×44 mm)		7·00	7·00

838 Flags
encircling
Globe

1983. 34th International Astronautical Federation Congress, Budapest.

3526	**838**	2fo. multicoloured	65	25

839 Kremlin, Moscow

1983. "Sozphilex '83" Stamp Exhibition, Moscow.

3527	**839**	2fo. multicoloured	90	90

840 Congress Palace, Madrid

1983. European Security and Co-operation Conference, Madrid. Sheet 98×78 mm.

MS3528	**840** 20fo. multicoloured	5·00	5·00

841 Babits (after
Jozsef
Rippl-Ronai)

1983. Birth Cent of Mihaly Babits (writer).

3529	**841**	2fo. multicoloured	65	25

842 Madonna with
Rose

1983. Christmas. Multicoloured.

3530	1fo. Type **842**		25	10
3531	2fo. Altar painting, Csik-menasag		65	20

843 Zanka

1983. Hungarian Resorts. Multicoloured.

3532	1fo. Type **843**	40	10
3533	2fo. Hajduszoboszlo	50	10
3534	5fo. Heviz	1·30	25

844 Ice Dancing

1983. Winter Olympic Games, Sarajevo.

3535	**844**	1fo. multicoloured	25	10
3536	-	1fo. multicoloured	25	10
3537	-	2fo. multicoloured (man lifting girl)	65	10
3538	-	2fo. multicoloured	65	10
3539	-	4fo. multicoloured (man with both arms bent)	1·30	25
3540	-	4fo. multicoloured (man with one arm outstretched)	1·30	25
3541	-	6fo. multicoloured	1·40	50
MS3542	70×70 mm. 20fo. multicoloured (49×39 mm)		6·25	6·25

DESIGNS: Nos. 3536/42, Different ice dancing designs.

845 Virgin with
Six Saints
(Tiepolo)

1984. Paintings Stolen from Museum of Fine Arts, Budapest. Sheet 130×98 mm containing T **845** and similar multicoloured designs.

MS3543 2fo. Type **845**; 2fo. Esterhazy Madonna (Raphael); 2fo. Portrait of Giorgione (imitator of Giorgione); 2fo. Portrait of a Woman (Tintoretto); 2fo. "Pietro Bempo" (Raphael); 2fo. Portrait of a Man (Tintoretto); 8fo. Rest on the Flight into Egypt (Tiepolo) (47×32 mm) ... 7·00 7·00

846 Csoma (statue)
and Sepulchre,
Darjeeling

1984. Birth Bicentenary of Sandor Korosi Csoma (traveller and philologist).

3544	**846**	2fo. multicoloured	65	25

847 "Energy"
and Sun

1984. Save Energy Campaign.

3545	**847**	1fo. red and black	25	10

848 Parent
and Child

1984. Youth Stamp.

3546	**848**	4fo.+2fo. mult	2·10	2·10

849 40fi. Goya
Stamp, 1968

1984. International Stamp Exhibitions. Sheet 125×104 mm containing T **849** and similar vert designs. Multicoloured.

MS3547 4fo. Type **849** ("Espana 84", Madrid); 4fo. 20fi. kangaroo stamp, 1961 ("Ausipex 84", Melbourne); 4fo. 1fo. Schiller stamp, 1959 ("Philatelia '84", Stuttgart) ... 5·00 5·00

850 Hair Ornaments from
Rakamaz

1984. Archaeological Finds.

3548	**850**	1fo. stone and brown	25	10
3549	-	1fo. stone and brown	25	10
3550	-	2fo. stone and brown	50	10
3551	-	2fo. stone and brown	50	10
3552	-	4fo. stone and brown	90	25
3553	-	6fo. stone and brown	1·50	35
3554	-	2fo. stone and brown	50	20

DESIGNS: No. 3549, Purse plates from Szolnok-Strazsahalom and Galgocz; 3550, Hair ornaments from Sarospatak; 3551, St. Stephen's sword (Prague) and Attila's sword (Aachen); 3552, Bowl from Ketpo; 3553, Stick handles from Hajdudorog and Szabadattyan; 3554, Saddle-bow from Izsak and bit and stirrups from Muszka.

851 Cracow
and Emblem

1984. 25th Session of Permanent Committee of Posts and Telecommunications, Cracow, Poland.

3555	**851**	2fo. multicoloured	65	25

852 Epiphile dilecta

1984. Butterflies. Multicoloured.

3556	1fo. Type **852**	30	10
3557	1fo. Agrias sara	30	10
3558	2fo. Blue morpho (Morpho cypris)	65	25
3559	2fo. Ancyluris formosissima	65	25
3560	4fo. African monarch	1·30	35
3561	6fo. Catagramma cynosura	1·90	60
3562	8fo. Paradise birdwing	2·50	75

No. 3557 is inscribed "Agra sara".

853 "Archer"

1984. Birth Centenary of Zsigmond Kisfaludy Strobl (sculptor).

3563	**853**	2fo. brown and yellow	65	25

854 Hevesi

1984. Birth Centenary of Akos Hevesi (activist in working-class movement).

3564	**854**	2fo. multicoloured	65	25

855 Doves
around Map of
Hungary

1984. Peace Festival, Pusztavacs.

3565	**855**	2fo. multicoloured	65	25

856 World
Map and
Airplane

1984. World Aerobatics Championship, Bekescsaba.

3566	**856**	2fo. multicoloured	65	25

857 Four-in-hand

1984. World Team-driving Championships, Szilvasvarad.

3567	**857**	2fo. multicoloured	65	25

858 Conference
Emblem

1984. 14th Organization of Socialist Countries' Postal Administrations Conference, Budapest.

3568	**858**	2fo. multicoloured	65	25

859 Four-handled Vase

1984. Stamp Day. Multicoloured.

3569	1fo. Type **859**	40	10
3570	2fo. Platter with flower decoration	90	25
MS3571	80×63 mm. 10fo. Cover with 1874 3k. stamp (44×27 mm)	4·50	4·50

860 Music crowned by Fame
(fresco, Mor Than)

1984. Reopening of Budapest Opera House. Multicoloured.

3572	1fo. Type **860**	25	10
3573	2fo. Central staircase	65	25
3574	5fo. Auditorium	1·30	50
MS3575	80×65 mm. 20fo. Facade and floor plan (49×39 mm)	6·25	6·25

861 Atrium Hyatt Hotel

1984. Budapest Hotels along the Danube. Multicoloured.

3576	1fo. Type **861**	25	10
3577	2fo. Duna Intercontinental	50	25
3578	4fo. Forum	75	25
3579	4fo. Thermal Hotel, Margaret Island	75	25
3580	5fo. Hilton	1·00	35
3581	8fo. Gellert	1·80	50

MS3582 78×55 mm. 20fo. Hilton (different) (36×25 mm)   6·25   6·25

862 Cep (*Boletus edulis*)

1984. Edible Mushrooms. Multicoloured.

3583	1fo. Type **862**	65	20
3584	1fo. Scotch bonnet (*Marasmius orcades*)	65	20
3585	2fo. Common morel (*Morchella esculenta*)	1·00	20
3586	2fo. Field mushroom (*Agaricus campester*)	1·00	20
3587	3fo. Chanterelle (*Cantharellus cibarius*)	1·50	35
3588	3fo. Parasol mushroom (*Macrolepiota procera*)	1·50	35
3589	4fo. Boot-lace fungus	2·10	60

863 Kato Haman (Labour Movement leader)

1984. Birth Centenaries.

| 3590 | **863** | 2fo. brown, gold and black | 65 | 25 |
| 3591 | - | 2fo. brown, gold and black | 65 | 25 |

DESIGN: No. 3591, Bela Balazs (writer).

864 Virgin and Child (small altar, Trencseny)

1984. Christmas.

| 3592 | **864** | 1fo. multicoloured | 40 | 10 |

865 Torah Crown (Buda)

1984. Reopening of Jewish Museum, Budapest. Multicoloured.

3593	1fo. Type **865**	25	10
3594	1fo. Chalice (Moscow)	25	10
3595	2fo. Torah shield (Vienna)	50	10
3596	2fo. Elias chalice (Warsaw)	50	10
3597	4fo. Esrog holder (Augsburg)	75	25
3598	6fo. Candle holder (Warsaw)	1·30	35
3599	8fo. Urn (Pest)	1·80	60

866 Barn Owl

1984. Owls. Multicoloured.

3600	1fo. Type **866**	50	20
3601	1fo. Little owl	50	20
3602	2fo. Tawny owl	90	20
3603	2fo. Long-eared owl	90	20
3604	4fo. Snowy owl	1·40	45
3605	6fo. Ural owl	1·90	70
3606	8fo. Eagle owl	2·50	85

867 Long Jumping and Emblem

1985. 90th Anniv of Hungarian Olympic Committee. Sheet 86×70 mm.

MS3607 **867** 20fo. multicoloured   7·00   7·00

868 Novi Sad Bridge, Yugoslavia

1985. Danube Bridges. Multicoloured.

3608	1fo. Type **868**	25	10
3609	1fo. Baja, Hungary	25	10
3610	2fo. Arpad bridge, Budapest	50	10
3611	2fo. Bratislava, Czechoslovakia	50	10
3612	4fo. Reichsbrucke bridge, Vienna	1·00	25
3613	6fo. Linz, Austria	1·30	50
3614	8fo. Regensburg, West Germany	1·90	60

MS3615 65×80 mm. 20fo. Elizabeth and Chain Bridges, Budapest (49×39 mm)   6·25   6·25

869 Laszlo Rudas

1985. Birth Centenary of Laszlo Rudas (philosopher and socialist).

| 3616 | **869** | 2fo. brown, gold & black | 65 | 25 |

870 Woman and Flowers

1985. International Women's Day.

| 3617 | **870** | 2fo. multicoloured | 65 | 25 |

871 1925 200k. Skiing Stamp

1985. "Olymphilex `85" International Olympic Stamps Exhibition, Lausanne.

| 3618 | **871** | 4fo. green, gold and blue | 1·30 | 35 |
| 3619 | - | 5fo. blue, brown and gold | 1·40 | 50 |

DESIGN: 5fo. 1925 300k. Skating stamp.

872 Liberty Bridge, Liberation Statue and Fireworks

1985. 40th Anniv of Liberation. Sheet 70×95 mm.

MS3620 **872** 20fo. multicoloured   6·25   6·25

873 Little Red Riding Hood

1985. Birth Centenary of Jacob Grimm (folklorist).

| 3621 | **873** | 4fo.+2fo. mult | 1·90 | 1·90 |

874 Gyorgy Lukacs

1985. Birth Centenary of Gyorgy Lukacs (philosopher).

| 3622 | **874** | 2fo. multicoloured | 65 | 25 |

875 Title Page

1985. 300th Anniv of Totfalusi Bible.

| 3623 | **875** | 2fo. black and gold | 65 | 25 |

876 Peter Pazmany (founder)

1985. 350th Anniv of Lorand Eotvos University.

| 3624 | **876** | 2fo. grey and red | 65 | 60 |

877 Boxing

1985. 26th European Boxing Championships, Budapest.

| 3625 | **877** | 2fo. multicoloured | 65 | 25 |

878 Women Footballers

1985. International Youth Year. Multicoloured.

3626	1fo. Type **878**	25	10
3627	2fo. Windsurfing	50	10
3628	2fo. Women exercising	50	10
3629	4fo. Karate	1·00	25
3630	4fo. Go-karting	1·00	25
3631	5fo. Hang gliding	1·30	35
3632	6fo. Skate-boarding	1·40	50

879 Monorail Train

1985. "Expo '85" World's Fair, Tsukuba. Multicoloured.

| 3633 | 2fo. Type **879** | 65 | 25 |
| 3634 | 4fo. Fuyo Theatre | 1·30 | 35 |

880 Common Flicker

1985. Birth Bicentenary of John J. Audubon (ornithologist). Multicoloured.

3635	2fo. Type **880** (postage)	90	20
3636	2fo. Bohemian waxwing	90	20
3637	2fo. Pileated woodpecker	90	20
3638	4fo. Northern oriole	1·50	35
3639	4fo. Common flicker (air)	1·50	35
3640	6fo. Common cardinal	2·10	60

881 Nonius XXXVI

1985. Bicentenary of Horsebreeding at Mezohegyes. Multicoloured.

3641	1fo. Type **881**	40	10
3642	2fo. Furioso XXIII	75	10
3643	4fo. Gidran I	1·40	35
3644	4fo. Ramses III	1·40	35
3645	6fo. Krozus I	2·10	50

882 Hand pointing to Cracked Earth (Imre Varga)

1985. Fifth Congress of International Association of Physicians against Nuclear War, Budapest.

| 3646 | **882** | 2fo. multicoloured | 65 | 25 |

883 Handel, Kettledrum and Horn

1985. Music Year. Multicoloured.

3647	1fo. Type **883** (300th birth anniv)	30	10
3648	2fo. Bach and Thomas Church organ, Leipzig (300th birth anniv)	55	25
3649	4fo. Luigi Cherubini, harp, bass violin and baryton (225th birth anniv)	90	60
3650	4fo. Chopin and piano (175th birth anniv)	90	60
3651	5fo. Mahler, viola, double horn and kettledrum (125th birth anniv)	1·30	75
3652	6fo. Ferenc Erkel, viola and bass tuba (175th birth anniv)	1·50	1·20

884 Red Square and Emblem

1985. 12th World Youth and Students' Festival, Moscow. Sheet 89×69 mm.

MS3653 **884** 20fo. multicoloured   6·25   6·25

885 Finlandia Palace

1985. Tenth Anniv of Helsinki Agreement. Sheet 92×75 mm.
MS3654 **885** 20fo. multicoloured 6·25 6·25

886 Key with Globe as Head

1985. World Tourism Day.
3655 **886** 2fo. multicoloured 65 25

887 Flags on Computer Keyboards

1985. "COMNET '85" Computer Networks Conference, Budapest.
3656 **887** 4fo. multicoloured 90 25

888 Budapest

1985. European Security and Co-operation Conference, Budapest.
MS3657 **888** 20fo. multicoloured 7·50 7·50

889 Water Holder

1985. Stamp Day. Haban Ceramics. Multicoloured.
3658 **889** 1fo. Type **889** 40 40
3659 2fo. Tankard with cover 90 90
MS3660 80×60 mm. 10fo. Hexagonal medicine holder 6·25 6·25

890 Italian 1960 5l. Stamp

1985. "Italia '85" International Stamp Exhibition, Rome.
3661 **890** 5fo. multicoloured 1·90 1·90

891 Dove and U.N. Emblem

1985. 40th Anniv of United Nations Organization.
3662 **891** 4fo. turquoise, bl & dp bl 90 25

892 Red Lily

1985. Lily Family. Multicoloured.
3663 1fo. Type **892** 25 10
3664 2fo. Turk's-cap lily 50 10
3665 2fo. Dog's tooth violet 50 10
3666 4fo. Tiger lily 1·00 20
3667 4fo. Snake's-head fritillary 1·00 20
3668 5fo. Day lily 1·30 35
3669 6fo. *Bulbocodium vernum* 1·90 50

893 Carol Singers

1985. Christmas.
3670 **893** 2fo. multicoloured 65 25

894 Istvan Ries

1985. Birth Centenary of Istvan Ries (Minister of Justice).
3671 **894** 2fo. multicoloured 65 25

895 Three Houses under One Roof

1985. S.O.S. Childrens' Village.
3672 **895** 4fo.+2fo. multicoloured 2·10 2·20

896 Fantic "Sprinter", 1984

1985. Centenary of Motor Cycle.
3673 **896** 1fo. black, orange & blue 30 10
3674 - 2fo. black, yellow & blue 50 10
3675 - 2fo. black, green and grey 50 10
3676 - 4fo. multicoloured 1·00 15
3677 - 4fo. black, green and grey 1·00 20
3678 - 5fo. multicoloured 1·30 35
3679 - 6fo. multicoloured 1·90 60
DESIGNS: No. 3674, Harley-Davidson "Duo-Glide", 1960; 3675, Suzuki "Katana GSX", 1983; 3676, BMW "R47", 1927; 3677, Rudge-Whitworth, 1935; 3678, NSU, 1910; 3679, Daimler, 1885.

897 "Ice" Satellite and Dinosaurs

1986. Air. Appearance of Halley's Comet. Multicoloured.
3680 2fo. Type **897** 65 10
3681 2fo. "Vega" satellite and detail of Bayeux Tapestry showing comet 65 10
3682 2fo. "Suisei" satellite and German engraving of 1507 65 10
3683 4fo. "Giotto" satellite and "The Magi" (tapestry after Giotto) 1·30 25

3684 4fo. "Astron" satellite and Virgo, Leo, Corvus, Crater and Hydra constellations 1·30 25
3685 6fo. Space shuttle and Edmond Halley (wrongly inscr "Edmund") 1·90 60

898 Bela Kun

1986. Birth Centenary of Bela Kun (Communist Party leader).
3686 **898** 4fo. multicoloured 90 25

899 "Challenger" (space shuttle)

1986. Challenger Astronauts Commemoration. Sheet 92×79 mm.
MS3687 **899** 20fo. multicoloured 8·25 8·25

900 Guide Dog

1986. The Blind.
3688 **900** 4fo. multicoloured 90 25

901 Running for Ball

1986. World Cup Football Championship, Mexico. Multicoloured.
3689 2fo. Type **901** 65 10
3690 2fo. Heading ball 65 10
3691 4fo. Tackling 1·30 25
3692 4fo. Goalkeeper diving for ball 1·30 25
3693 4fo. Goalkeeper catching ball 1·30 25
3694 6fo. Tackling (different) 1·90 60
MS3695 80×60 mm. 20fo. Team celebrating (40×30 mm) 7·00 7·00

902 Cable Railway

1986. Re-opening of Buda Castle Cable Railway.
3696 **902** 2fo. brown, yell & orge 65 25

903 Rose "Yankee Doodle"

1986. "Ameripex '86" International Stamp Exhibition, Chicago. Sheet 80×100 mm containing T **903** and similar vert designs. Multicoloured.
MS3697 5fo. Type **903**; 5fo. Rose "America"; 10fo. Statue of George Washington, Budapest and exhibition emblem (25×70 mm) 5·75 5·75

904 Japanese and Hungarian Dolls

1986. Hungarian Days in Tokyo.
3698 **904** 4fo. multicoloured 90 25

905 Fay

1986. Birth Bicentenary of Andras Fay (writer, politician and founder of First Hungarian Savings Bank Union).
3699 **905** 4fo. brown & pale brown 90 90

906 Flag and "40"

1986. Youth Stamp. 40th Anniv of Young Pioneers Movement.
3700 **906** 4fo.+2fo. multicoloured 1·90 1·90

907 Ferrari Racing Cars, 1961 and 1985

1986. Centenary of Motor Car. Multicoloured.
3701 2fo. Type **907** 65 10
3702 2fo. Alfa Romeo racing cars, 1932 and 1984 65 10
3703 2fo. Volkswagen "Beetle", 1936, and Porsche "959", 1986 65 10
3704 4fo. Renault "14 CV", 1902, and "5 GT Turbo", 1985 1·30 25
3705 4fo. Fiat "3 1/2", 1899, and "Ritmo", 1985 1·30 25
3706 6fo. Daimler, 1886, and Mercedes-Benz "230 SE", 1986 1·90 60

908 *Wasa* (Swedish ship of the line), 1628

1986. "Stockholmia '86" Int Stamp Exhibition.
3707 **908** 2fo. multicoloured 1·40 1·40

909 Moritz Kaposi (cancer specialist)

1986. 14th International Cancer Congress, Budapest.
3708 **909** 4fo. multicoloured 90 25

910 *Recapture of Buda Castle* (Gyula Benczur)

1986. 300th Anniv of Recapture of Buda from Turks.
3709 **910** 4fo. multicoloured 90 25

911 *Tranquillity*

1986. Stamp Day. Multicoloured.

3710	2fo. Type **911**	65	65
3711	2fo. *Confidence*	65	65
MS3712 80×60 mm. 10fo. *Hope* (28×49 mm)		5·75	5·75

912 Fragment of 15th-cent Carpet from Anatolia

1986. Fifth International Oriental Carpets and Tapestry Conference, Vienna and Budapest.

3713	**912**	4fo. multicoloured	90	25

913 Model of New Theatre

1986. National Theatre, Budapest. Sheet 63×85 mm.

MS3714 **913** 20fo.+10fo. brown, stone and light brown		7·00	7·00

914 Piano and Liszt

1986. 175th Birth Anniv of Franz Liszt (pianist and composer).

3715	**914**	4fo. deep green and green	90	25

915 Dove

1986. International Peace Year.

3716	**915**	4fo. multicoloured	1·30	1·30

916 Hofburg Palace, Vienna, and Map

1986. European Security and Co-operation Conference Review Meeting, Vienna. Sheet 65×80 mm.

MS3717 **916** 20fo. multicoloured		6·25	6·25

917 Pogany

1986. Birth Centenary of Jozsef Pogany (writer and journalist).

3718	**917**	4fo. multicoloured	90	25

918 Munnich

1986. Birth Centenary of Ferenc Munnich (former Prime Minister).

3719	**918**	4fo. multicoloured	90	25

919 Heads

1986. 12th General Assembly of World Federation of Democratic Youth, Budapest.

3720	**919**	4fo. multicoloured	90	25

920 Apricots ("Kajszi" C.235)

1986. Fruit. Multicoloured.

3721	2fo. Type **920**	65	10
3722	2fo. Cherries ("Good bearer of Erd")	65	10
3723	4fo. Apples ("Jonathan" M.14)	1·30	25
3724	4fo. Raspberries ("Nagymaros")	1·30	25
3725	4fo. Peaches ("Piroska")	1·30	25
3726	6fo. Grapes ("Zalagyongye")	2·50	35

921 Forgach Castle, Szecseny

1986. Castles. Inscr "MAGYAR POSTA".

3727	**921**	2fo. bistre and yellow	30	10
3728	-	3fo. green and light green	40	10
3729	-	4fo. blue and light blue	50	10
3730	-	5fo. red and pink	65	10
3731	-	6fo. brown and orange	75	10
3732	-	8fo. red and orange	1·00	10
3733	-	10fo. brown and ochre	1·00	25
3734	-	20fo. green and yellow	2·00	60
3735	-	30fo. light green and green	2·75	85
3736	-	40fo. blue and light blue	3·25	1·20
3737	-	50fo. deep red and red	4·50	1·50
3738	-	70fo. deep grey and grey	6·25	2·10
3739	-	100fo. violet and lilac	8·25	3·00

DESIGNS: 3fo. Savoya Castle, Rackeve; 4fo. Batthyany Castle, Kormend; 5fo. Szechenyi Castle, Nagycenk; 6fo. Rudnyanszky Castle, Nagyteteny; 8fo. Szapary Castle, Buk; 10fo. Festetics Castle, Keszthely; 20fo. Brunswick Castle, Martonvasar; 30fo. De La Motte Castle, Noszvaj; 40fo. L'Huillier-Coburg Castle, Edeleny; 50fo. Teleki-Degenfeld Castle, Szirak; 70fo. Magochy Castle, Pacin; 100fo. Esterhazy Castle, Fertod.
See also Nos. 3888 and 4045/9.

922 Wild Cat

1986. Protected Animals. Multicoloured.

3740	2fo. Type **922**	75	15
3741	2fo. European otter	75	15
3742	2fo. Stoat	75	15
3743	4fo. Eurasian red squirrel	1·30	25
3744	4fo. East European hedgehog	1·30	25
3745	6fo. European pond turtle	1·90	50

923 St. Stephen I (coronation cloak, 1030)

1986. Kings (1st series).

3746	**923**	2fo. brown, blue and red	50	10
3747	-	2fo. brown, grey and red	50	10
3748	-	4fo. brown, green and red	1·10	25
3749	-	4fo. brown, grey and red	1·10	25
3750	-	6fo. brown, blue and red	1·60	45

DESIGNS: No. 3747, Geza I (enamel portrait on Hungarian crown, 1070); 3748, St. Ladislas I (Gyor Cathedral, 1400); 3749, Bela III (Kalocsa Cathedral statue, 1200); 3750, Bela IV (Jak church statue, 1230).
See also Nos. 3835/7.

924 Death Cap ("Amanita phalloides")

1986. Fungi. Multicoloured.

3751	2fo. Type **924**	50	20
3752	2fo. Fly agaric (*Amanita muscaria*)	50	20
3753	2fo. Red-staining inocybe (*Inocybe patouillardi*)	50	20
3754	4fo. Olive-wood pleurotus (*Omphalotus olearius*)	1·00	45
3755	4fo. Panther cap (*Amanita pantherina*)	1·00	45
3756	6fo. Beefsteak morel	1·50	75

925 Banded Gourami

1987. Fish. Multicoloured.

3757	2fo. Type **925**	50	10
3758	2fo. Thread-finned rainbowfish (*Iriathorina werneri*)	50	10
3759	2fo. Zebra mbuna (*Pseudotropheus zebra*)	50	10
3760	4fo. Ramirez dwarf cichlid (*Papiliochromis ramirezi*)	1·00	35
3761	4fo. Multicoloured lyretail (*Aphyosemion multicolor*)	1·00	35
3762	6fo. Bleeding-heart tetra (*Hyphessobrycon erythrostigma*)	1·50	50

926 "Sitting Woman"

1987. Birth Centenary of Bela Uitz (painter).

3763	**926**	4fo. multicoloured	75	25

927 Abstract

1987. Birth Centenary of Lajos Kassak (writer and painter).

3764	**927**	4fo. black and red	75	25

928 Flag, Books, Torch and Dove

1987. 30th Anniv of Young Communist League.

3765	**928**	4fo.+2fo. mult	2·00	2·00

929 Hippocrates (medical oath)

1987. Pioneers of Medicine (1st series).

3766	**929**	2fo. brown and blue	50	10
3767	-	4fo. green and black	1·10	25
3768	-	4fo. blue and black	1·10	25
3769	-	4fo. brown and black	1·10	25
3770	-	6fo. brown and black	1·80	45

DESIGNS: No. 3767, Avicenna (*Kanun* book of medical rules); 3768, Ambroise Pare (improved treatment of wounds); 3769, William Harvey (circulation of blood); 3770, Ignac Semmelweis (aseptic treatment of wounds).
See also Nos. 3939/43.

930 Food Jar, Hodmezovasarhely

1987. Neolithic and Copper Age Art. Multicoloured.

3771	**930**	2fo. brown and green	65	10
3772	-	4fo. brown and flesh	1·30	25
3773	-	4fo. brown and pink	1·30	25
3774	-	5fo. brown and green	1·50	45

DESIGNS: No. 3772, Altar, Szeged; 3773, Statue with sickle, Szegvar-Tuzkoves; 3774, Vase with face, Center.

931 King Matthias's Cross

1987. Re-opening of Esztergom Cathedral Treasury. Sheet 64×80 mm.

MS3775 **931** 20fo. multicoloured		5·00	5·00

932 Old and Modern Ambulances

1987. Centenary of Hungarian First Aid Association.

3776	**932**	4fo. multicoloured	75	25

933 Toronto ("Capex '87")

1987. International Stamp Exhibitions. Multicoloured.

3777	5fo. Type **933**	1·90	1·90
3778	5fo. "Olymphilex 87" building, Rome	1·90	1·90
3779	5fo. "Hafnia 87" building, Copenhagen	1·90	1·90

934 Jozsef Marek

1987. Bicentenary of University of Veterinary Sciences, Budapest.

3780	**934**	4fo. silver, blue and black	75	25

935 Teleki, Route Map and Porters

1987. Centenary of Samuel Teleki's African Expedition.
3781 **935** 4fo. multicoloured 75 25

936 Printing Shop (17th-century wood-print, Abraham von Werdt)

1987. 125th Anniv of Hungarian Printing, Paper and Press Workers' Union.
3782 **936** 4fo. brown and stone 75 25

937 James Cook and H.M.S. "Resolution"

1987. Antarctic Exploration. Multicoloured.
3783 2fo. Type **937** 50 20
3784 2fo. Fabian von Bellingshausen and seals 50 20
3785 2fo. Ernest Shackleton and emperor penguins 50 20
3786 4fo. Roald Amundsen and huskies 1·10 35
3787 4fo. Robert F. Scott and *Terra Nova* 1·10 35
3788 6fo. Richard Byrd and Ford Trimotor *Floyd Bennett* 1·50 55
MS3789 86×70 mm. 20fo. Mirnyi Research Station (32×42 mm) 11·50 11·50

938 Old and New Railway Emblems and Institute

1987. Cent of Railway Officers' Training Institute.
3790 **938** 4fo. black and blue 75 25

939 Flowers and Dolphin

1987. Stamp Day. Carvings from Buda Castle.
3791 **939** 2fo. indigo, blue & azure 65 65
3792 - 4fo. olive, green & turq 1·30 1·30
MS3793 68×88 mm. 10fo. agate, grey and lilac 5·00 5·00
DESIGNS: 4fo. King Matthias's arms; 10fo. Capital of Column.

940 Jesse Altar

1987. Gyongyospata Church.
3794 **940** 4fo. multicoloured 2·00 2·00

941 "Orchis purpurea"

1987. Orchids. Multicoloured.
3795 2fo. Type **941** 50 10
3796 2fo. *Cypripedium calceolus* 50 10
3797 4fo. *Ophrys scolopax* 1·00 20
3798 4fo. *Himantoglossum hircinum* 1·00 20
3799 5fo. *Cephalanthera rubra* 1·30 25
3800 6fo. *Epipactis atrorubens* 1·60 35
MS3801 40×60 mm. 20fo. Orchids (24×33 mm) 7·00 7·00

942 Speed Skating

1987. Winter Olympic Games, Calgary. Multicoloured.
3802 2fo. Type **942** 50 10
3803 2fo. Cross-country skiing 50 10
3804 4fo. Biathlon 1·00 20
3805 4fo. Ice hockey 1·00 20
3806 4fo. Four-man bobsleigh 1·00 20
3807 6fo. Ski jumping 1·80 35
MS3808 50×60 mm. 20fo. Slalom (24×41 mm) 6·25 6·25

943 Clasped Hands and Map

1987. U.S.–Soviet Strategic Arms Reduction Talks, Washington. Sheet 78×82 mm.
MS3809 **943** 20fo. multicoloured 6·25 6·25

945 The White Crane (Japanese folk tale)

1987. Fairy Tales. Multicoloured.
3816 2fo. Type **945** 65 20
3817 2fo. *The Fox and the Raven* (Aesop) 65 20
3818 4fo. *The Hare and The Tortoise* (Aesop) 1·30 25
3819 4fo. *The Ugly Duckling* (Hans Christian Andersen) 1·30 25
3820 6fo. *The Brave Little Lead Soldier* (Hans Christian Andersen) 1·90 55

946 Zeppelin and Airship LZ-2

1988. 150th Birth Anniv of Ferdinand von Zeppelin (airship pioneer).
3821 **946** 2fo. black and blue 50 20
3822 - 4fo. deep brown & brown 1·30 30
3823 - 4fo. purple and lilac 1·30 30
3824 - 8fo. olive and green 1·90 55
DESIGNS: No. 3822, LZ-4; 3823, *Schwaben*; 3824, *Graf Zeppelin*.

947 Skater

1988. World Figure Skating Championships, Budapest. Skaters from 19th-century to date. Multicoloured.
3825 2fo. Type **947** 50 10
3826 2fo. Man wearing hat 50 10
3827 4fo. Woman 1·00 20
3828 4fo. Man in hat and coat 1·00 20
3829 5fo. Woman in modern skating dress 1·10 25
3830 6fo. Pair 1·30 35
MS3831 89×72 mm. 20fo. Pair (different) (32×47 mm) 6·25 6·25

948 Woman's Head

1988. Stamp Day. "Socfilex" International Stamp Exhibition, Kecskemet. Sheet 72×54 mm.
MS3832 **948** 20fo.+10fo. mult 7·50 7·50

949 Monus

1988. Birth Centenary of Illes Monus (newspaper editor).
3833 **949** 4fo. blue, red and black 75 25

950 18th-cent Postmaster's Uniform

1988. Stamp Exhibitions.
MS3834 **950** 4fo. black and stone 2·10 2·10

1988. Kings (2nd series). As T **923**.
3835 2fo. brown, green and red 50 10
3836 4fo. brown, blue and red 1·00 25
3837 6fo. brown, violet and red 1·50 35
DESIGNS: 2fo. Karoly I (Charles Robert) (detail of decorated initial from "Illuminated Chronicle", 1358); 4fo. Lajos the Great (relief, St. Simeon's reliquary, Zara, 1380); 6fo. Zsigmond (Sigismund of Luxembourg) (after great seal, 1433).

951 Rowing

1988. Olympic Games, Seoul. Multicoloured.
3838 2fo. Type **951** 50 10
3839 4fo. Hurdling 1·00 35
3840 4fo. Fencing 1·00 35
3841 6fo. Boxing 1·90 60
MS3842 70×80 mm. 20fo. Tennis (31×40 mm) 7·50 7·50

952 Computer Drawing of Head

1988. Sixth Anniv of "Dilemma" (first computer-animated film).
3843 **952** 4fo. multicoloured 75 25

953 Card and Emblem

1988. Eurocheque Congress, Budapest.
3844 **953** 4fo. multicoloured 75 25

954 "Santa Maria", 1492

1988. Ships. Multicoloured.
3845 2fo. Type **954** 65 25
3846 2fo. *Mayflower*, 1620 65 25
3847 2fo. *Sovereign of the Seas*, 1637 65 25
3848 4fo. *Jylland* (steam warship), 1860 1·40 35
3849 6fo. *St. Jupat* (yacht), 1985 2·00 60

955 Damaged Head

1988. Anti-drugs Campaign.
3850 **955** 4fo. multicoloured 75 25

956 Green-winged Teal (Anas crecca)

1988. Wild Ducks. Multicoloured.
3851 2fo. Type **956** 55 25
3852 2fo. Common goldeneye (*Bucephula clangula*) 55 25
3853 4fo. European wigeon (*Anas penelope*) 1·40 35
3854 4fo. Red-crested pochard (*Netta rufina*) 1·40 35
3855 6fo. Gadwell 2·10 60
MS3856 90×73 mm. 20fo. Mallard (*Anas platyrhynchos*) 6·25 6·25

957 Steam Train

1988. Exhibits in Toy Museum, Kecskemet. Multicoloured.
3857 2fo. Type **957** 65 20
3858 2fo. See-saw 65 20
3859 4fo.+2fo. Pecking chicks 1·90 50
3860 5fo. Johnny Hussar 1·30 35

958 Facade

1988. 450th Anniv of Debrecen Calvinist College.
3861 **958** 4fo. multicoloured 75 25

959 Congress Emblem

1988. 58th American Society of Travel Agents Congress, Budapest.
3862 **959** 4fo. multicoloured 75 25

960 Lloyd C.II Biplane

1988. Air. Hungarian Biplanes.

3863	**960**	1fo. green	15	10
3864	-	2fo. purple	25	10
3865	-	4fo. bistre	65	25
3866	-	10fo. blue	1·60	55
3867	-	12fo. red	2·00	60

DESIGNS: 2fo. Hansa Brandenburg C-I; 4fo. UFAG C-I; 10fo. Gerle 13 scout plane; 12fo. WM 13 trainer.

961 Post Official's Collar and Badge

1988. Centenary of Post Office Training School.

3868	**961**	4fo. red, blue and brown	75	25

962 Baross and Postal Savings Bank, Budapest

1988. Stamp Day. 140th Birth Anniv of Gabor Baross (politician). Multicoloured.

3869		2fo. Type **962**	65	60
3870		4fo. Baross with telephone and telegraph equipment	1·30	1·20
MS3871		80×70 mm. 10fo. Baross and East Railway Station, Budapest	5·00	5·00

963 Lengyel

1988. Birth Centenary of Gyula Lengyel (labour movement activist).

3872	**963**	4fo. multicoloured	75	25

964 Christmas Tree

1988. Christmas.

3873	**964**	2fo. multicoloured	65	10

965 Richard Adolf Zsigmondy (chemistry, 1925)

1988. Nobel Prize Winners.

3874	**965**	2fo. deep brown & brown	50	10
3875	-	2fo. deep green and green	50	10
3876	-	2fo. deep brown & brown	50	10
3877	-	4fo. dp mauve & mauve	90	20
3878	-	4fo. green and grey	90	20
3879	-	6fo. brown & light brown	1·40	35

DESIGNS: No. 3875, Robert Barany (medicine, 1914,); 3876, Gyorgy Hevesy (chemistry, 1943); 3877, Albert Szent-Gyorgyi (chemistry, 1937); 3878, Gyorgy Bekesy (medicine, 1961); 3879, Denes Gabor (physics, 1971).

966 Szakasits

1988. Birth Centenary of Arpad Szakasits (President, 1948–50).

3880	**966**	4fo. multicoloured	75	25

967 Stadium and Emblem

1988. Hungarian Medals at Seoul Olympic Games. Sheet 70×90 mm.

MS3881	**967**	20fo. multicoloured	7·00	7·00

968 Silver Teapot from Pest, 1846

1988. Metal Work.

3882	**968**	2fo. blue and brown	75	10
3883	-	2fo. deep brown & brown	75	10
3884	-	4fo. lilac and brown	1·50	35
3885	-	5fo. green and brown	1·90	50

DESIGNS: No. 3883, 18th-century silver pot, Buda; 3884, Silver sugar basin from Pest, 1822; 3885, Pierced cast iron plate from Resicabanya, 1850.

969 Emblem

1989. Foundation of Post and Savings Bank Company.

3886	**969**	5fo. blue, silver and black	75	25

970 Wallisch

1989. Birth Centenary of Kalman Wallisch (workers' movement activist).

3887	**970**	3fo. blue and red	65	10

971 Festetics Castle, Keszthely

1989

3888	**971**	10fo. brown and bistre	1·10	25

972 Athletes

1989. Second International Indoor Athletics Championships, Budapest.

3889	**972**	3fo. multicoloured	65	10

973 Houses of Parliament and Big Ben London

1989. Centenary of Interparliamentary Union. Sheet 78×90 mm containing T **973** and similar vert design. Multicoloured.

MS3890		10fo. Type **973**; 10fo. Parliament Building, Budapest	5·75	5·75

974 Gyetvai

1989. Birth Centenary of Janos Gyetvai (journalist).

3891	**974**	3fo. green and red	65	10

975 "Sky-high Tree" (detail, carpet)

1989. 27th National Youth Stamp Exn, Veszprem.

3892	**975**	5fo.+2fo. mult	1·90	1·90

976 O Bajan

1989. Bicentenary of Babolina Stud Farm. Multicoloured.

3893	**976**	3fo. Type **976**	90	90
3894		3fo. Stud officer	90	90
3895		3fo. Gazal II	90	90

977 Disabled People and "ART '89"

1989. "Art '89" International Festival of Disabled People and their Artist Friends.

3896	**977**	5fo. multicoloured	75	25

978 Arrangement of Narcissi, Crocuses and Violets

1989. Flower Arrangements. Multicoloured.

3897	**978**	2fo. Type **978**	40	10
3898		3fo. Irises, tulips and lilies (horiz)	65	10
3899		3fo. Roses and chrysanthemums	65	10
3900		5fo. Dahlias and lilies (horiz)	1·30	35
3901		10fo. Roses, Chinese lanterns and holly	2·50	60

979 Birds

1989. Bicentenary of French Revolution.

3902	**979**	5fo. black, red and blue	75	25

MS3903	80×70 mm. **979**	20fo. black, red and blue (49×28 mm)	7·50	7·50

980 Model of Veszto Church

1989. Veszto Church Excavation.

3904	**980**	3fo. multicoloured	65	10

981 Photographer with Camera

1989. 150th Anniv of Photography.

3905	**981**	5fo. lt brown, blk & brn	75	25

982 Turistvandi Water-mill

1989. Mills. Multicoloured.

3906		2fo. Type **982**	40	10
3907		3fo. Szarvas horse-driven mill	65	20
3908		5fo. Kiskunhalas windmill	1·00	35
3909		10fo. Shipmill, River Drava	2·30	60

983 Footprint and U.S. Flag

1989. 20th Anniv of First Manned Landing on Moon. Sheet 80×70 mm.

MS3910	**983**	20fo. multicoloured	5·75	5·75

984 Messenger Glider

1989. "Old Timer" Rally, Budakeszi Airport, and 60th Anniv of Gliding in Hungary. Multicoloured.

3911		3fo. Type **984**	65	25
3912		5fo. Pal glider	1·10	50

985 Sand Lizard

1989. Endangered Reptiles. Multicoloured.

3913		2fo. Type **985**	40	10
3914		3fo. Green lizard	65	15
3915		5fo. Grass snake (Natrix natrix)	1·10	25
3916		5fo. Orsinis's viper (Vipera rakosiensis)	1·10	25
3917		10fo. European pond terrapin	2·30	60

986 Competitors

1989. 31st World Modern Pentathlon Championships, Budapest.

3918	**986**	5fo. multicoloured	75	25

1989. Nos. 3851 and 3853 surch.

| 3919 | 3fo. on 2fo. multicoloured | 1·60 | 50 |
| 3920 | 5fo. on 4fo. multicoloured | 1·90 | 85 |

988 Baradla Cave, Aggtelek

1989. Tenth World Speleology Congress, Budapest. Multicoloured.

3921	3fo. Type **988**	50	10
3922	5fo. Szemlohegy cave, Budapest	90	25
3923	10fo. Anna Cave, Lillafured	1·90	35
3924	12fo. Tapolca cave lake, Miskolctapolca	2·30	60

989 Carriage

1989. World Two-in-Hand Carriage Driving Championship, Balatonfenyves.

| 3925 | **989** | 5fo. multicoloured | 1·50 | 25 |

990 Zsuzsa Kossuth (War of Independence nurse)

1989. Stamp Day. 125th Anniv of Red Cross Movement.

3926	**990**	5fo. black, blue and red	90	90
3927	–	10fo. multicoloured	1·90	1·90
MS3928	82×65 mm. 20fo.+10fo. mult		8·25	8·25

DESIGNS: 10fo. Florence Nightingale (nursing pioneer) and decoration. 27×44 mm—20fo. *Battle of Solferini* (Carlo Bossoli).

991 Memorial Statue, Arad

1989. 140th Death Anniv of "Martyrs of Arad". Sheet 110×75 mm.

| MS3929 | **991** | 20fo.+10fo. mult | | 8·25 | 8·25 |

The surcharge was for the erection of a new statue.

992 Stamp and Miniature Sheets

1989. Pro Philatelia. Sheet 72×92 mm.

| MS3930 | **992** | 50fo. multicoloured | 15·00 | 15·00 |

993 Flowers and Broken Barbed Wire

1989. Dismantling of Electrified Fence on Western Border.

| 3931 | **993** | 5fo. multicoloured | 1·00 | 25 |

994 *Conquest of Hungary (Mor Than)*

1989. 1100th Anniv of Arpad as Prince of the Magyars.

| 3932 | **994** | 5fo. multicoloured | 1·50 | 25 |

995 Flight into Egypt

1989. Christmas.

| 3933 | **995** | 3fo. multicoloured | 1·30 | 25 |

996 Nehru

1989. Birth Centenary of Jawaharlal Nehru (Indian statesman).

| 3934 | **996** | 3fo. brown and stone | 1·30 | 25 |

997 *Miska (Dezso Korniss)*

1990. Modern Hungarian Paintings. Multicoloured.

3935	3fo. Type **997**	65	10
3936	5fo. *Sunrise* (Lajos Kassak)	1·30	25
3937	10fo. *Grotesque Burial* (Endre Balint)	2·50	35
3938	12fo. *Remembered Toys* (Tihamer Gyarmathy)	3·00	60

1989. Pioneers of Medicine (2nd series). As T **929**.

3939	3fo. green	75	10
3940	3fo. brown	75	10
3941	4fo. black	1·00	20
3942	6fo. grey	1·50	25
3943	10fo. purple	2·50	60

DESIGNS: No. 3939, Claudius Galenus (anatomist and physiologist); 3940, Paracelsus (pharmacy); 3941, Andreas Vesalius (dissection); 3942, Rudolf Virchow (pathology of cells); 3943, Ivan Petrovich Pavlov (blood circulation, digestion and nervous system).

998 Hands holding Coin

1990. 150th Anniv of Savings Banks in Hungary.

| 3944 | **998** | 5fo. multicoloured | 90 | 25 |

999 Sewing Machine

1990. 125th Anniv of Singer Sewing Machine.

| 3945 | **999** | 5fo. brown and cinnamon | 90 | 25 |

1000 Wall Telephone and Jozsefvaros Telephone Exchange

1990. Posts and Telecommunications. Multicoloured.

| 3946 | 3fo. Type **1000** | 40 | 10 |
| 3947 | 5fo. Pillar box and Head Post Office, Budapest | 75 | 10 |

1001 Northern Bullfinch (*Pyrrhula pyrrhula*)

1990. Birds. Multicoloured.

3960	3fo. Type **1001**	75	25
3961	3fo. River kingfisher (*Alcedo atthis*)	75	25
3962	3fo. Syrian woodpecker (*Dendrocopos syriacus*)	75	25
3963	5fo. Hoopoe (*Upupa epops*)	1·40	35
3964	5fo. European bee eater (*Merops apiaster*)	1·40	35
3965	10fo. European roller	2·50	70

1002 *Protea compacta*

1990. African Flowers. Multicoloured.

3966	3fo. Type **1002**	75	10
3967	3fo. *Leucadendron spissifolium*	75	10
3968	3fo. Leucadendron tinctum pubibracteolatum	75	10
3969	5fo. *Protea barbigera*	1·40	25
3970	5fo. *Protea lepidocarpodendron neriifolia*	1·40	25
3971	10fo. *Protea cynaroides*	2·50	60
MS3972	64×82 mm. 20fo. Mixed bouquet (25×36 mm)	8·25	8·25

1003 Sarospatak Teachers' Training School

1990. 28th National Youth Stamp Exhibition, Sarospatak.

| 3973 | **1003** | 8fo.+4fo. mult | 2·50 | 2·50 |

1004 Janos Hunyadi (regent)

1990. The Hunyadis. Multicoloured.

| 3974 | 5fo. Type **1004** | 90 | 25 |
| 3975 | 5fo. King Matthias I Corvinus | 90 | 25 |

1005 Penny Black

1990. "Stamp World London 90" International Stamp Exhibition. 150th Anniv of the Penny Black. Sheet 88×60 mm.

| MS3976 | **1005** | 20fo. multicoloured | 7·00 | 7·00 |

1006 Gaspar Karoli (statue)

1990. 400th Anniv of Publication of Karoli Bible (first Hungarian translation).

| 3977 | **1006** | 8fo. cream, green & red | 2·00 | 2·00 |

1007 Footballers

1990. World Cup Football Championship, Italy.

3978	**1007**	3fo. multicoloured	65	10
3979	–	5fo. multicoloured (ball on ground)	1·10	20
3980	–	5fo. multicoloured (ball in air)	1·10	20
3981	–	8fo. multicoloured (dribbling)	1·80	25
3982	–	8fo. mult (heading ball into goal)	1·80	25
3983	–	10fo. multicoloured	2·30	35
MS3984	95×70 mm. 20fo. mult		7·00	7·00

DESIGNS: Nos. 3979/84, Various footballing scenes.

1008 Hand writing with Quill Pen

1990. 300th Birth Anniv of Kelemen Mikes (writer).

| 3985 | **1008** | 8fo. black and gold | 1·50 | 25 |

1009 *Weaver* (Noemi Ferenczy)

1990. Birth Centenaries of Noemi and Beni Ferenczy (artists).

| 3986 | **1009** | 3fo. multicoloured | 1·00 | 15 |
| 3987 | – | 5fo. black and brown | 1·60 | 20 |

DESIGN: 5fo. Bronze figure (Beni Ferenczy).

1010 Kazinczy

1990. 159th Death Anniv of Ferenc Kazinczy (writer and language reformer).

| 3988 | **1010** | 8fo. multicoloured | 1·30 | 15 |

1011 Kolcsey (after Anton Einsle)

1990. Birth Bicentenary of Ferenc Kolcsey (composer of national anthem).

| 3989 | **1011** | 8fo. multicoloured | 1·30 | 15 |

1012 "St. Stephen" (carving in Parliament Hall) and Arms

1990. New State Arms.

| 3990 | **1012** | 8fo. multicoloured | 1·30 | 15 |
| MS3991 | 70×90 mm. 20fo. Arms (33×49 mm) | | 7·00 | 7·00 |

1013 Cabernet
Franc Grapes,
Hajos

1990. Wine Grapes and Regions (1st series). Multicoloured.

3992	3fo. Type **1013**	50	10
3993	5fo. Cabernet Sauvignon, Villany	90	15
3994	8fo. Riesling, Badacsony	1·40	20
3995	8fo. Kadarka, Szekszard	1·40	20
3996	8fo. Leanyka, Eger	1·40	20
3997	10fo. Furmint, Tokaj-Hegyalja	1·90	25

See also Nos. 4363/5, 4436/7, 4521/2, 4596/7, 4686/7, 4895/6 and 5034/6.

1014 *Feast*

1990. Stamp Day. Paintings by Ender Szasz. Multicoloured.

3998	8fo. Type **1014**	1·30	1·30
3999	12fo. *Message*	2·10	2·10
MS4000 70×90 mm. 20fo.+10fo. *Yesterday* (39×44 mm)		7·50	7·50

1015 Tarbosaurus

1990. Prehistoric Animals. Multicoloured.

4001	3fo. Type **1015**	50	10
4002	5fo. Brontosaurus	90	15
4003	5fo. Dimorphodon	1·40	20
4004	5fo. Stegosaurus	1·40	20
4005	8fo. Platybelodon	1·40	20
4006	10fo. Mammoth	1·90	60

1016 Dinosaurs
reading

1990. International Literacy Year.

4007	**1016**	10fo. multicoloured	1·90	25

1017 Bird holding Letter

1990. 60th Anniv of Stamp Museum, Budapest.

4008	**1017**	5fo. red and green	90	25

1018 *Great
Courier* (detail,
Albrecht Durer)

1990. Pro Philatelia. 500th Anniv of Regular European Postal Services. Sheet 90×71 mm.
MS4009 **1018** 50fo. black, red and yellow 9·50 9·50

1019 Book-shaped
Travelling Clock, by
M. Fenich and M.
Wolff, 1576

1990. Clocks. Multicoloured.

4010	3fo. Type **1019**	50	10
4011	5fo. Clock by Hans Schmidt, 1643	1·00	15
4012	5fo. Rococo style clock by J. M. Welz, 1790	1·00	15
4013	10fo. Clock by Johann Hillrich, 1814	2·30	75

1020 *Madonna
and Child*
(Sandro
Botticelli)

1990. Christmas.

4014	**1020**	5fo. multicoloured	90	25

1021 Lorand
Eotvos (inventor)
and Torsion
Pendulum

1991. Centenary of Torsion Pendulum.

4015	**1021**	12fo. multicoloured	1·90	25

1022
*Mandevilla
splendens*

1991. Flowers of the Americas. Multicoloured.

4016	5fo. Type **1022**	40	10
4017	7fo. *Lobelia cardinalis*	65	15
4018	7fo. Cup and saucer flower	65	15
4019	12fo. *Steriphoma paradoxa*	1·10	25
4020	15fo. Shrimp plant	1·30	75
MS4021 58×80 mm. 20fo. Mixed bouquet (27×43 mm)		6·25	6·25

1023 Post Office,
Budapest

1991. Hungarian Full Membership of Council of Europe and Entry into C.E.P.T. (European Posts and Telecommunications Conference). Multicoloured.

4022	5fo. Type **1023**	5·00	5·00
4023	7fo. Post Office, Pecs	5·75	5·75

1024 "Ulysses"
Jupiter Probe

1991. Europa. Europe in Space. Multicoloured.

4024	12fo. Type **1024**	3·75	2·50

4025	30fo. "Cassini" and "Huygens" (wrongly inscr "Hughes") Saturn probes	8·75	5·00

1025 *Peter and the Wolf* (tapestry,
Gabriella Hajnal)

1991. Youth Stamp.

4026	**1025**	12fo.+6fo. mult	1·50	1·50

1026 Gorilla

1991. 125th Anniv of Budapest Zoological and Botanic Gardens. Multicoloured.

4027	7fo. Type **1026**	65	50
4028	12fo. Polar bear	1·00	85
4029	12fo. Rhinoceros	1·00	85
4030	12fo. Keel-billed toucan	1·00	85
4031	20fo. Orchid and glasshouse	1·90	1·60

1027 Teleki

1991. 50th Death Anniv of Count Pal Teleki (Prime Minister, 1920–21 and 1939–41).

4032	**1027**	12fo. brn, cinn & blk	1·50	1·50

1028 Map, Emblem
and Fencers

1991. 44th World Fencing Championships, Budapest.

4033	**1028**	12fo. multicoloured	1·50	1·50

1029 Mariapocs

1991. Visit of Pope John Paul II (1st issue). Shrines to Virgin Mary. Multicoloured.

4034	7fo. Type **1029**	65	50
4035	12fo. Mariagyud	1·00	85
4036	12fo. Celldomolk	1·00	85
4037	12fo. Mariaremete	1·00	85
4038	20fo. Esztergom	1·90	1·60

1030 *Appeggi Landscape* and Marko

1991. Birth Bicent of Karoly Marko (painter).

4039	**1030**	12fo. multicoloured	1·50	1·50

1031 Lilienthal and
Monoplane Gliders, 1891

1991. Centenary of First Heavier-than-Air Manned Flight by Otto Lilienthal.

4040	**1031**	7fo. black, ochre & brn	65	50
4041	-	12fo. black, drab & bis	90	75
4042	-	20fo. dp blue, azure & bl	1·50	1·30
4043	-	30fo. black, lilac & vio	2·50	2·10

DESIGNS: 12fo. Wright brothers' Flyer 1, 1903; 20fo. Santos-Dumont's "14 bis", 1906; 30fo. Aladar Zselyi's monoplane, 1910.

1032 Players

1991. Centenary of Basketball.

4044	**1032**	12fo. multicoloured	1·50	1·50

1991. Castles. Inscr "MAGYARORSZAG". As T **921**.

4045	7fo. brown and sepia	65	50
4047	12fo. ultramarine and blue	1·00	85
4049	15fo. brown and green	1·00	85

DESIGNS—32×25 mm; 7fo. Esterhazy Castle, Papa; 12fo. Dory Castle, Mihaly, 35×26 mm; 15fo. Festetics Castle, Keszthely.

1033 Pope John Paul II

1991. Papal Visit (2nd issue). Sheet 60×80 mm.
MS4055 **1033** 50fo. black and blue 8·25 8·25

1034 Map of Europe
and Congress
Emblem

1991. Third International Hungarian Philological Society Congress, Szeged.

4056	**1034**	12fo. multicoloured	1·50	1·30

1035 Szechenyi

1991. Birth Bicentenary of Count Istvan Szechenyi (social reformer).

4057	**1035**	12fo. red	1·50	1·30

1036 Mozart as
Child

1991. Stamp Day. Death Bicentenary of Wolfgang Amadeus Mozart (composer). Multicoloured.

4058	12fo. Type **1036**	1·30	1·00
4059	20fo. Mozart as youth	2·10	1·80
MS4060 80×61 mm. 30fo.+15fo. Mozart as man (24×36 mm)		7·50	7·50

1037 "Telecom 91"

1991. "Telecom 91" International Telecommunications Exhibition, Geneva.

4061	**1037**	12fo. multicoloured	1·50	1·30

1991. 35th Anniv of 1956 Uprising, No. 4047 optd **A FORRADALOM EMLEKERE 1956 1991**.

4062	12fo. ultramarine and blue	1·50	1·30

1039 Sebastian
Cabot

1991. 500th Anniv (1992) of Discovery of America by
Columbus. Multicoloured.

4063	7fo. Type **1039**	65	50
4064	12fo. Amerigo Vespucci	90	75
4065	12fo. Hernan Cortes	90	75
4066	15fo. Ferdinand Magellan	1·30	1·00
4067	20f. Francisco Pizarro	1·90	1·60
MS4068 85×71 mm. 30fo. Columbus (21×33 mm)		4·00	4·00

1040 Arms of
Order

1991. Postal Convention with Sovereign Military Order of
Malta.

4069	**1040** 12fo. multicoloured	1·50	1·30

1041 "Virgin of
Mariapocs"

1991. Christmas. Multicoloured.

4070	7fo. Type **1041**	90	75
4071	12fo. "Virgin of Mariaremete"	1·30	1·00

1042 Flower

1991. Human Rights.

4072	**1042** 12fo. multicoloured	1·50	1·30

1043 Biathlon

1991. Winter Olympic Games, Albertville (1992).
Multicoloured.

4073	7fo. Type **1043**	65	50
4074	12fo. Slalom	90	75
4075	15fo. Four-man bobsleigh	1·30	1·00
4076	20fo. Ski jumping	1·50	1·30
4077	30fo. Ice hockey	2·50	2·10
MS4078 73×54 mm. 30fo. Ice skating (pairs) (26×36 mm)		6·25	6·25

1044 1871 25k.
Stamp

1991. Pro Philatelia. Sheet 90×71 mm.

MS4079 **1044** 50fo. violet		7·50	7·50

1045 Arms

1992. 350th Anniv of Piarist Order in Hungary.

4080	**1045** 10fo. gold, blue and ultramarine	75	65

1046 Holloko

1992. U.N.E.S.C.O. World Heritage Site.

4081	**1046** 15fo. multicoloured	1·90	1·60

1047 Swimming

1992. Olympic Games, Barcelona. Multicoloured.

4082	7fo. Type **1047**	1·30	1·00
4083	9fo. Cycling	1·90	1·60
4084	10fo. Gymnastics	1·90	1·60
4085	15fo. Running	3·25	2·50

1048 *Indian's
Head* Map

1992. "Expo '92" World's Fair, Seville. Fantasy Maps.
Multicoloured.

4086	10fo. Type **1048**	1·30	1·00
4087	10fo. Islands, sea monsters and *Santa Maria* forming face	1·30	1·00
4088	15fo. *Conquistador's head* map	1·90	1·60
4089	15fo. Navigation instruments and map forming face	1·90	1·60

1049 Comenius

1992. 400th Birth Anniv of Jan Komensky (Comenius)
(educationist).

4090	**1049** 15fo. multicoloured	1·50	1·30

1050 Mindszenty

1992. Birth Centenary of Cardinal Jozsef Mindszenty,
Archbishop of Esztergom.

4091	**1050** 15fo. brn, cream & red	1·50	1·30

1051 Statue of
Mayan Man

1992. Europa. 500th Anniv of Discovery of America by
Columbus. Multicoloured.

4092	15fo. Type **1051**	2·50	1·60
4093	40fo. Statue of Mayan woman	6·25	3·75

1052 Self-portrait
(Renata Toth)

1992. Youth Stamps. Children's Drawings. Multicoloured.

4094	9fo.+4fo. Type **1052**	90	75
4095	10fo.+4fo. *The Sun Shines for Me* (Sandor Pusoma) (horiz)	90	75
4096	15fo.+4fo. *I will be a Beauty King* (Endre Knipf)	1·30	1·00

1053 Gymnasts and Emblem

1992. European Gymnastics Championships, Budapest.

4097	**1053** 15fo. multicoloured	1·50	1·30

1054 St. Margaret
(after J. S. Scott)

1992. 750th Birth Anniv of St. Margaret.

4098	**1054** 15fo. turq, lt bl & bl	1·30	1·00

1055 Saker Falcon

1992. Birds of Prey. Multicoloured.

4099	9fo. Type **1055**	65	50
4100	10fo. Booted eagle	75	65
4101	15fo. Short-toed eagle	1·10	95
4102	40fo. Red kite	2·75	2·30

1056 Wallenberg

1992. 80th Birth Anniv of Raoul Wallenberg (Swedish
diplomat).

4103	**1056** 15fo. grey, red and green	1·00	85

1057 Millennium
Monument,
Budapest

1992. Third World Federation of Hungarians Congress,
Budapest.

4104	**1057** 15fo. multicoloured	1·00	85

1058 Theodore von
Karman (space pioneer,
birth centenary (1991))

1992. Anniversaries.

4105	**1058** 15fo. grey, black and deep grey	90	75
4106	– 40fo. grey, black & brn	2·75	2·30

DESIGN: 40fo. Neumann Janos (mathematician, 35th
death anniv).

1059 Current
Hungarian Post Emblem

1992. Stamp Day. "Eurofilex '92" International Postal
History Exhibition, Budapest.

4107	**1059** 10fo.+5fo. multicoloured	1·30	1·00
4108	**1059** 15fo.+5fo. multicoloured	1·90	1·60
MS4109 91×66 mm. 50fo.+20fo. brown, cinnamon and black		5·75	5·75

DESIGNS—VERT Hungarian Royal Post emblem, 1867.
39×29 mm—50fo. *Postal Riders* (etching, Ferenc Helbing).
See also No. 4111.

1060 Church of the
Holy Family,
Barcelona, and
Medals

1992. Hungarian Olympic Games (Barcelona) Medal
Winners. Sheet 61×80 mm.

MS4110 **1060** 50fo.+20fo. mult		6·25	6·25

1992. As No. 4108 but without premium and
commemorative inscription.

4111	15fo. multicoloured	1·40	1·10

1061 Entwined
Cables

1992. "Europa Telecom '92" Telecommunications
Exhibition, Budapest.

4112	**1061** 15fo. multicoloured	1·00	85

1062 Istvan
Bathory (King
Stefan I of Poland)

1992. Princes of Transylvania. Multicoloured.

4113	10fo. Type **1062**	65	50
4114	15fo. Istvan Bocskai	90	75
4115	40fo. Gabor Bethlen	3·25	2·50

1063 Pieces on
Board

1992. Tenth European Chess Team Championship,
Debrecen.

4116	**1063** 15fo. multicoloured	2·00	1·70

1064 *Clianthus
formosus*   **1065** Postal Rider
of Prince Ferenc
Rakoczi II,
1703–11

1992. Australian Flowers. Multicoloured.

4117	9fo. Type **1064**	65	50
4118	10fo. *Leschenaultia biloba*	90	75
4119	15fo. *Anigosanthos manglesii*	1·30	1·00
4120	40fo. *Comesperma ericinum*	3·00	2·50
MS4121 64×83 mm. 50fo. Mixed flowers (31×41 mm)		6·25	6·25

1065 Postal Rider of Prince Ferenc Rakoczi II, 1703–11

1992. Post Office Uniforms. Multicoloured.
4122	10fo. Type **1065**		90	75
4123	15fo. Postmen, 1874		1·30	1·00

1066 "Holy Family" (iron relief, 1850)

1992. Christmas.
4124	**1066**	15fo. black and blue	1·10	95

1067 Arachnis flos-aeris

1993. Asian Flowers. Multicoloured.
4125	10fo. Type **1067**		65	50
4126	10fo. Dendrobium densiflorium		65	50
4127	15fo. Lilium speciosum		1·30	1·00
4128	15fo. Meconopsis aculeata		1·30	1·00
MS4129	64×83 mm. 50fo. Mixed bouquet (31×41 mm)		7·50	7·50

1068 Shield Decoration of Deer

1993. Scythian Remains in Hungary. Multicoloured.
4130	10fo. Type **1068**		90	75
4131	17fo. Gilt-silver embossed deer		1·50	1·30

1069 Single Sculls

1993. Centenary of Rowing Association.
4132	**1069**	17fo. multicoloured	1·50	1·30

1070 Queen Beatrix and King Matthias I Corvinus (detail of Missal)

1993. King Matthias I Corvinus's "Missale Romanum".
4133	**1070**	15fo. multicoloured	1·80	1·50
MS4134	106×156 mm. 40fo. Illustration from missal (59×39 mm)		4·50	4·50

1071 Animals in Wood

1993. Youth Stamps. Tapestries by Erzsebet Szekeres. Multicoloured.
4135	10fo.+5fo. Type **1071**		1·30	1·00
4136	17fo.+8fo. Animals in tree hiding from dragons		2·10	1·80

1072 Competitors and Globe

1993. World Motocross Championships, Cserenfa.
4137	**1072**	17fo. multicoloured	75	65

1073 Diagram of Solar System and Copernicus

1993. "Polska'93" International Stamp Exn.
4138	**1073**	17fo. multicoloured	75	65

1074 Paks Catholic Church

1993. Europa. Contemporary Art. Architecture by Imre Makovecz. Multicoloured.
4139	17fo. Type **1074**		1·30	1·00
4140	45fo. Hungarian pavilion at "Expo '92" World's Fair, Seville		2·75	2·30

1075 Cauliflower Clavaria

1993. Fungi. Multicoloured.
4141	10fo. Type **1075**		50	40
4142	17fo. Death trumpet		75	65
4143	45fo. Caesar's mushroom		2·50	2·10

1076 St. Christopher (Albrecht Durer)

1993. European Year of the Aged.
4144	**1076**	17fo. black, cream and silver	75	65

1077 Class 326 and 424 Steam Locomotives

1993. 125th Anniv of Hungarian Railways.
4145	**1077**	17fo. blue and cobalt	75	65

1078 Rowing Boat approaching Town

1993. 900th Anniv of Mohacs.
4146	**1078**	17fo. brown, cinnamon and red	75	65

1079 Poplar Admiral

1993. Butterflies. Multicoloured.
4147	10fo. Type **1079**		50	40
4148	17fo. Aricia artaxerxes		1·00	85
4149	30fo. Plebejides pylaon		1·60	1·40

1080 Kalman Latabar

1993. Great Humourists. Multicoloured.
4150	17fo. Type **1080**		90	75
4151	30fo. Charlie Chaplin		1·60	1·40

1081 Ribbon Dove over North-western Europe

1993. 20th Anniv of European Security and Co-operation Conference, Helsinki. Sheet 82×62 mm.
MS4152	**1081**	50fo. multicoloured	3·75	3·75

1082 Solar Panel absorbing Sun's Rays

1993. International Solar Energy Society Congress, Budapest.
4153	**1082**	17fo. multicoloured	75	65

1083 Laszlo Nemeth

1993. Writers. Each blue and azure.
4154	17fo. Type **1083**		90	75
4155	17fo. Dezso Szabo		90	75
4156	17fo. Antal Szerb		90	75

1084 Zoltan Nagy and 1953 20fi. Stamp

1993. Stamp Day. Designers. Multicoloured.
4157	10fo.+5fo. Type **1084**		75	65
4158	17fo.+5fo. Sandor Legrady and 1938 50f. stamp		1·30	1·00
MS4159	56×75 mm. 50fo.+20fo. Ferenc Helbing and 1932 10p. stamp (35×26 mm)		4·50	4·50

1085 Arms

1993. 175th Anniv of Faculty of Agronomics, Pannon Agricultural University, Magyarovar.
4160	**1085**	17fo. multicoloured	1·00	85

1086 Szent Istvan, 1892

1993. Hungarian Ships. Multicoloured.
4161	10fo. Type **1086**		50	40
4162	30fo. Szent Istvan (battleship), 1915		1·80	1·50

1087 Prehistoric Man and Skull (Vertesszolos)

1993. Palaeolithic Remains in Hungary. Multicoloured.
4163	17fo. Type **1087**		90	75
4164	30fo. Men round fire and stone tool (Szeleta Cave, Lillafured)		1·60	1·40

1088 Route-map of Central Europe

1993. Roman Roads. Sheet 80×65 mm.
MS4165	**1088**	50fo. multicoloured	4·50	4·50

1089 Madonna and Child (altarpiece by F. A. Hillebrant, Szekesteheervar Cathedral)

1993. Christmas.
4166	**1089**	10fo. multicoloured	65	50

1090 Szechenyi Chain Bridge

1993. "Expo '96" World's Fair, Budapest (1st issue).
4167	**1090**	17fo. dp green & green	75	65
4168	-	30fo. purple and claret	1·40	1·10
4169	-	45fo. dp brown & brown	2·10	1·80

DESIGNS—HORIZ: 30fo. Opera House. VERT: 45fo. Matthias Church.
See also Nos. 4236/8 and 4268/9.

1091 Antall

1993. Joszef Antall (Prime Minister since 1990) Commemoration.
4170	**1091**	19fo. multicoloured	1·00	85
MS4171	70×50 mm. No. 4170		2·30	2·30

1092 Skiing

1994. Winter Olympic Games, Lillehammer, Norway. Multicoloured.
4172	12fo. Type **1092**		75	65
4173	19fo. Ice hockey		1·10	95

1093 Douglas DC-3

1994. 50th Anniv of I.C.A.O.
4174	**1093**	56fo. multicoloured	2·75	2·30

1094 *Golgotha*
(detail, Mihaly
Munkacsy)

1994. Easter.
4175	**1094**	12fo. multicoloured	65	50

1095 Mihaly
Munkacsy
(self-portrait)

1994. Artists' 150th Birth Anniversaries. Multicoloured.
4176		12fo. Gyula Benczur (self-portrait)	65	50
4177		19fo. Type **1095**	90	75

1096 Kossuth

1994. Death Centenary of Lajos Kossuth (Governor of
1849 Republic).
4178	**1096**	19fo. multicoloured	1·00	85

1097 Hen with Chicks

1994. The Great Bustard. Multicoloured.
4179		10fo. Type **1097**	65	50
4180		10fo. Bustards taking off	65	50
4181		10fo. Cock in mating display	65	50
4182		10fo. Hen with chicks (different)	65	50

1098 Bem

1994. Birth Bicentenary of Jozsef Bem (revolutionary).
4183	**1098**	19fo. multicoloured	1·00	85

1099 Discovery
of Franz Josef
Land (120th
anniv)

1994. Europa. Discoveries. Multicoloured.
4184		19fo. Type **1099**	1·30	1·00
4185		50fo. Mark Aurel Stein and Buddha (expeditions in Asia)	2·50	2·10

1100 *The Little
Prince*

1994. Youth Stamp. 50th Anniv of Disappearance of
Antoine de Saint-Exupery (writer and pilot).
4186	**1100**	19fo.+5fo. mult	1·30	1·30

1101 Balint Balassi
(poet, 400th
death)

1994. Writers' Anniversaries.
4187	**1101**	19ft. pink and brown	90	75
4188	-	19ft. stone and grey	90	75

DESIGN: No. 4188, Miklos Josika (novelist, birth bicentenary).

1102 Horsemen

1994. 1100th Anniv (1996) of Magyar Conquest (1st
issue). Multicoloured.
4189		19ft. Type **1102**	90	75
4190		19ft. Arpad and standard bearers (58×39 mm)	90	75
4191		19ft. Mounted archer	90	75

    Nos. 4189/91 were issued together, *se-tenant*, forming a composite design of a detail of the painting *in the round* commissioned to celebrate the millenary of the Conquest.
    See also Nos. 4240/2 and 4275/7.

1103 Athens Stadium, 1896

1994. Centenary of International Olympic Committee.
Multicoloured.
4192		12ft. Olympic medals of 1896 and 1992	40	30
4193		19ft. Type **1103**	75	65
4194		19ft. Ancient Greek athletes, Olympic flag and flame	75	65
4195		35ft. Pierre de Coubertin (founder)	1·40	1·10

1104 Elvis Presley
and Players

1994. World Cup Football Championship, U.S.A. American
Entertainers. Multicoloured.
4196		19ft. Type **1104**	75	65
4197		19ft. Marilyn Monroe and players	75	65
4198		35ft. John Wayne and players	1·30	1·00

1105 Family

1994. International Year of the Family.
4199	**1105**	19fo. multicoloured	75	65

1106 Summer
Snowflake

1994. European Flowers. Multicoloured.
4200		12fo. Type **1106**	50	40
4201		19fo. Common rock-rose	75	65
4202		35fo. *Eryngium alpinum*	1·30	1·00
4203		50fo. Pennycress	1·90	1·60
MS4204	64×83 mm. 100fo. Mixed bouquet (31×40 mm)		5·00	5·00

1107 Heinrich von
Stephan (founder) and
Emblem

1994. 120th Anniv of Universal Postal Union.
4205	**1107**	19fo. grey, brown & blk	75	65
4206	-	35fo. blue, brown & blk	1·30	1·00
MS4207	98×71 mm. 50fo.+25fo. brown, black and blue (Heinrich von Stephan) (vert); 50fo.+25 fo. brown, black and violet (Gervay Mihaly) (vert)		5·75	5·75

DESIGN: 35fo. Gervay Mihaly (first Director General of
Posts) and U.P.U. emblem.

1108 Csik Megye

1994. Traditional Patterns.
4208		1fo. violet and black	15	10
4209		2fo. multicoloured	15	10
4210		3fo. multicoloured	15	10
4210a		5fo. multicoloured	15	10
4211		9fo. multicoloured	20	15
4212	**1108**	11fo. multicoloured	25	20
4213	-	12fo. multicoloured	40	30
4214	-	13fo. multicoloured	40	30
4215	-	14fo. multicoloured	40	30
4216	-	16fo. multicoloured	45	35
4217	-	17fo. black, grey & red	40	30
4218	-	19fo. multicoloured	75	65
4219	-	22fo. multicoloured	75	65
4220	-	24fo. multicoloured	65	50
4220a	-	24fo. multicoloured	65	50
4220b	-	27fo. multicoloured	75	65
4221	-	32fo. multicoloured	1·00	85
4222	-	35fo. multicoloured	1·30	1·00
4223	-	38fo. multicoloured	1·40	1·10
4224	-	40fo. multicoloured	1·50	1·30
4225	-	50fo. multicoloured	2·50	2·10
4225a	-	65fo. black, red and grey	1·30	1·00
4226	-	75fo. multicoloured	1·90	1·60
4226a	-	79fo. multicoloured	1·00	85
4227	-	80fo. multicoloured	2·00	1·70
4228	-	90fo. multicoloured	1·90	1·60
4229	-	100fo. multicoloured	1·50	1·30
4229a	-	200fo. multicoloured	3·75	3·25
4230	-	300fo. multicoloured	6·25	5·25
4231	-	500fo. multicoloured	10·00	8·25

DESIGNS: 1fo. Torocko; 2fo. Buzsak; 3fo. Vas megye (flowers); 5fo. Rabakoz; 9, 24fo. (4220) Felfold; 12, 27fo. Vas megye (birds); 13, 32fo. Debrecen; 14, 80fo. Sarkoz; 16fo. Csiki-Medence; 17, 35, 65fo. Dunantul; 19, 24fo. (4220a) Kalocsa; 22, 90fo. Kalocsa (different); 38, 75fo. Oroshaza; 40fo. Kalotaszeg; 50fo. Szentgal; 79fo. Moldvai csango; 100fo. Szecseny videke; 200fo. Mezokovesd; 500fo. Szolnok megye.

1109 Budapest

1994. Conference of Security and Co-operation in Europe
Summit, Budapest. Sheet 92×70 mm.
MS4232	**1109**	100fo. multicoloured	5·00	5·00

1110 Hebrew
Tombstone

1994. Holocaust Victims' Commemoration.
4233	**1110**	19fo. multicoloured	1·00	85

1111 Nativity

1994. Christmas. Paintings by Pal Molnar. Multicoloured.
4234		12fo. Type **1111**	65	50
4235		35fo. *Flight into Egypt* (31×29 mm)	1·30	1·00

1112 National Museum

1994. "Expo '96" World's Fair, Budapest (2nd issue).
Budapest landmarks.
4236	**1112**	19fo. green	75	65
4237	-	19fo. brown	75	65
4238	-	19fo. violet	75	65

DESIGNS: No. 4237, University of Technical Sciences; 4238,
Vajdahunyad Castle.

1113 *Ferencz
Jozsef I*
(paddle-steamer) and *Baross*
(container ship)

1995. Centenary of Hungarian Shipping Company.
4239	**1113**	22fo. multicoloured	1·00	85

1995. 1100th Anniv (1996) of Magyar Conquest (2nd
issue). As T **1102**. Multicoloured.
4240		22fo. Ox cart	90	75
4241		22fo. Arpad's consort in ox cart (59×39 mm)	90	75
4242		22fo. Men and pack ox	90	75

    Nos. 4240/2 were issued together, *se-tenant*, forming a composite design of a detail of the painting *in the round* commissioned to celebrate the millenary of the Conquest.

1114 Lamb of
God

1995. Easter.
4243	**1114**	14fo. purple and black	75	65

1115 Paddle-steamer

1995. 150th Anniv of Steamer Service on River Tisza
(14fo.) and Birth Bicentenary of Pal Vasarhelyi
(engineer) (60fo.). Multicoloured.
4244		14fo. Type **1115**	50	40
4245		60fo. Vasarhelyi (after Miklos Barabas) and survey ship	2·10	1·80

1116 Weather Map and
Barometer

1995. Anniversaries. Multicoloured.
4246		22fo. Type **1116** (125th anniv of Hungarian Meteorological Service)	1·00	85
4247		22fo. Emblem (50th anniv of F.A.O.) (25×41 mm)	1·00	85
4248		22fo.+10fo. John the Hero (150th anniv of poem by Petofi) (37×45 mm)	1·30	1·00

No. 4248 is the 1995 Youth Stamp.

1117 White Stork
and Frog

1995. European Nature Conservation Year. Multicoloured.
4249		14fo. Type **1117**	1·00	85
4250		14fo. Red squirrel	1·00	85
4251		14fo. Blue tit	1·00	85
4252		14fo. Butterfly and hedgehog	1·00	85

Nos. 4249/52 were issued together, *se-tenant*, forming a composite design.

1118 Allied Flags
forming Dove over
Map of Europe

1995. Europa. Peace and Freedom.
4253	**1118**	22fo. multicoloured	1·90	1·60

1119 Gymnastics and
Ferenc Kemeny
(founder)

1995. Centenary of Hungarian Olympic Committee. Multicoloured.
4254		22fo. Type **1119**	90	75
4255		60fo. Throwing the javelin	2·30	1·90
4256		100fo. Fencing	3·75	3·25

1120 Exhibition Emblem

1995. "Olympiafila '95" International Olympic and Sports Stamps Exhibition, Budapest.
4257	**1120**	22fo.+11fo. mult (rings in yellow)	1·40	1·10
4258	**1120**	22fo.+11fo. mult (rings in purple)	1·40	1·10

1121 Saint
Ladislas (detail of
fresco,
Szekelyderzs
Castle Chapel)

1995. 900th Death Anniv of St. Ladislas, King of Hungary.
4259	**1121**	22fo. multicoloured	90	75

1122 Almasy

1995. Birth Centenary of Laszlo Almasy (explorer).
4260	**1122**	22fo. multicoloured	1·30	1·00

1123 Museum of Applied Arts, Budapest, and Lechner

1995. 150th Birth Anniv of Odon Lechner (architect).
4261	**1123**	22fo. multicoloured	1·30	1·00

1124 K XVIII 1923
(Laszlo
Moholy-Nagy)

1995. Artists' Birth Centenaries. Multicoloured.
4262		22fo. Type **1124**	1·10	95
4263		22fo. *The Fiddler* (Aurel Bernath)	1·10	95

1125 College
Building and Jozsef
Eotvos (founder)

1995. Centenary of Eotvos College.
4264	**1125**	60fo. multicoloured	2·50	2·10

1126 Postal Carriage and
Map of Postal Routes

1995. Stamp Day. Multicoloured.
4265		22fo. Type **1126**	65	50
4266		40fo. Airplane and route map	1·30	1·00
MS4267		80×61 mm. 100fo.+30fo. Children looking at stamp album (29×44 mm)	5·00	5·00

1995. "Expo '96" World's Fair, Budapest (3rd issue). As T **1112** showing Budapest landmarks.
4268		22fo. grey	75	65
4269		22fo. purple	75	65

DESIGNS: No. 4268, West Railway Station; 4269, Music Hall.

1127 Anniversary
Emblem

1995. 50th Anniv of U.N.O.
4270	**1127**	60fo. multicoloured	1·90	1·60

1128 Sparklers

1995. Christmas. Multicoloured.
4271		14fo. Type **1128**	40	30
4272		60fo. Three wise men in stable	1·80	1·50

1129 St Elizabeth
bathing Leper

1995. Saint Elizabeth of Hungary.
4273	**1129**	22fo. multicoloured	90	75

1130 Nobel Medals

1995. Centenary of Nobel Trust Fund.
4274	**1130**	100fo. multicoloured	4·00	3·25

1996. 1100th Anniv of Magyar Conquest (3rd issue). As T **1102**. Multicoloured.
4275		24fo. Rejoicing crowd	75	65
4276		24fo. Shaman presenting sacrificial white horse (59×39 mm)	75	65
4277		24fo. Bards	75	65

Nos. 4275/7 were issued together, *se-tenant*, forming a composite design.

1131 Leather
Purse

1996. Ninth-century Relics from Kares Cemeteries. Multicoloured.
4278		24fo. Type **1131**	75	65
4279		24fo. Gold and silver sabre hilt	75	65

1132 Monastery (after
Xaver Zsoldos)

1996. Millenary of Pannonhalma Monastery (1st issue). Sheet 100×80 mm.
MS4280	**1132**	100fo. violet	3·50	3·50

See also Nos. 4290/1 and 4305/6.

1133 Headquarters

1996. Centenary of Journalists' Association.
4281	**1133**	50fo. multicoloured	1·40	1·10

1134 Emblem

1996. Promotion of Hungarian Production.
4282	**1134**	24fo. black, red & green	75	65

1135 Swimming

1996. Centenary of Modern Olympic Games and Olympic Games, Atlanta. Multicoloured.
4283		24fo. Type **1135**	65	50
4284		50fo. Tennis (Csilla Orosz)	1·30	1·00
4285		75fo. Canoeing	1·90	1·60

1996. 1100th Anniv of Magyar Conquest (4th issue). As T **1102** Sheet 150×190 mm containing previous designs. Multicoloured.
MS4286		19fo. ×3 Nos. 4189/91; 22fo. ×3 Nos. 4240/2; 24fo. ×3 Nos. 4275/7	8·25	8·25

1136 First Carriage

1996. Centenary of Budapest Underground Railway.
4287	**1136**	24fo. multicoloured	75	65

1137 Queen Gizella (wife of St. Stephen)

1996. Europa. Famous Women. Hungarian Queens. Multicoloured.
4288		24fo. Type **1137**	1·00	85

4289		75fo. Queen Elisabeth (wife of Francis Joseph I)	2·75	2·30

1138 Triumphal Arch
(entrance to
Cathedral)

1996. Millenary of Pannonhalma Monastery (2nd issue).
4290	**1138**	17fo. brown	50	35
4291	-	24fo. blue	70	50

DESIGN: 24fo. Monks gathered in cloisters.

1139 Bird and
"DRUG"

1996. International Day against Drug Abuse.
4292	**1139**	24fo. multicoloured	85	65

1140 Denes Mihaly
(television pioneer)

1996. Inventors. Multicoloured.
4293		24fo. Type **1140**	70	50
4294		50fo. Laszlo Biro and ballpoint pen	1·40	1·00
4295		75fo. Zoltan Bay and Moon radar	2·10	1·60

1141 Laszlo Vitez
(puppet)

1996. Youth Stamp. Puppet Festival, Budapest.
4296	**1141**	24fo.+10fo. multicoloured	1·10	85

1142 *Heves*, 1846

1996. 150th Anniv of Hungarian Railways. Steam Locomotives. Multicoloured.
4297		17fo. Class 303	55	40
4298		24fo. Class 325	95	70
4299		24fo. Type **1142**	95	70

On No. 4299 the nameplate is inscribed "PEST".

1143 Pyramid

1996. Second European Mathematics Congress, Budapest.
4300	**1143**	24fo. multicoloured	95	65

1144 Hungarian
Long-horned Wood Beetle
(*Ropalopus ungaricus*)

1996. "NATUREXPO '96" International Nature Conservation Exhibition, Budapest. Multicoloured.

4301	13fo. Type **1144**	50	35
4302	13fo. Lynx ("Lynx lynx")	50	35
4303	13fo. Siberian iris ("Iris sibirica")	50	35
4304	13fo. Great egret ("Egretta alba")	50	35

1996. Millenary of Pannonhalma Monastery (3rd issue). As T **1138**.

| 4305 | 17fo. brown | 65 | 45 |
| 4306 | 24fo. green | 80 | 55 |

DESIGNS: 17fo. Refectory; 24fo. Main library.

1145 Homage to Prince Arpad (from *Vienna Picture Chronicle*)

1996. Stamp Day. "Budapest '96" International Stamp Exhibition, Budapest. Multicoloured.

4307	17fo. Type **1145**	65	45
4308	24fo. Prince Arpad on horseback and soldiers (from *Vienna Picture Chronicle*)	80	55
MS4309	92×72 mm. 150fo.+50fo. 1944 1f. Prince Arpad stamp, first page of Deeds of Hungarians and detail of *Compact sealed with Blood* (mural by Bertalan Szekely, Kecskemet Town Hall)	5·50	5·50

1146 1871 10k. Engraved Stamp

1996. World Convention of Hungarian Stamps and Postal History.

| 4310 | **1146** 24fo. multicoloured | 80 | 55 |

1147 Map and Paddle-steamer *Kisfaludy*

1996. 150th Anniv of Steamer Service on Lake Balaton.

| 4311 | **1147** 17fo. multicoloured | 80 | 55 |

1148 Mastheads and Demonstration

1996. 40th Anniv of 23 October Uprising. Multicoloured.

4312	13fo. Type **1148**	50	35
4313	16fo. Newspaper, burning flag and motor vehicle	50	35
4314	17fo. Men with rifles and newspaper	65	45
4315	24fo. Newspaper and Imre Nagy (Prime Minister, Oct–Nov 1956)	80	55
MS4316	76×75 mm. 40fo. Imre Nagy and government members (44×29 mm)	2·40	2·40

1149 Atlanta and Medals

1996. Hungarian Medal Winners at Olympic Games. Sheet 85×55 mm.

| MS4317 | **1149** 150fo. multicoloured | 5·50 | 5·50 |

1150 *Madonna and Child with Two Angels* (Matteo di Giovanni)

1996. Christmas. Multicoloured.

| 4318 | 17fo. Type **1150** | 65 | 45 |
| 4319 | 24fo. *Adoration of the Wise Men* (Salzburg Master) | 80 | 55 |

1151 List of Years

1996. 50th Anniv of UNICEF.

| 4320 | **1151** 24fo. multicoloured | 80 | 55 |

1152 Bust, Book, Quill and Shield

1996. Birth Bicentenary of Miklos Wesselenyi (writer).

| 4321 | **1152** 24fo. multicoloured | 80 | 55 |

1153 Kalman Mikszath and Characters

1997. Writers' Birth Anniversaries. Multicoloured.

| 4322 | 27fo. Type **1153** (150th anniv) | 80 | 55 |
| 4323 | 27fo. Aron Tamasi (cent) | 80 | 55 |

1154 Baranya

1997. Arms. Multicoloured. (a) As T **1154**.

4324	27fo. Type **1154**	80	55
4325	27fo. Bacs-Kiskun	80	55
4326	27fo. Bekes	80	55
4327	27fo. Borsod-Abauj-Zemplen	80	55
4328	27fo. Fejer	80	55
4329	27fo. Gyor-Moson-Sopron	80	55
4330	27fo. Heves	80	55
4331	27fo. Jasz-Nagykun-Szolnok	80	55
4332	27fo. Komarom-Esztergom	80	55
4333	27fo. Nograd	80	55
4334	27fo. Pest	80	55
4335	27fo. Somogy	80	55
4336	27fo. Tolna	80	55
4337	27fo. Vas	80	55
4338	27fo. Veszprem	80	55
4339	27fo. Zala	80	55

(b) Size 50×32 mm.

4340	27fo. Hajdu-Bihar	80	55
4341	27fo. Budapest	80	55
4342	27fo. Csongrad	80	55
4343	27fo. Szabolcs-Szatmar-Bereg	80	55
MS4344	Four sheets, each 78×125 mm. (a) Nos. 4324/33 and 4340 plus label; (b) Nos. 4328/33; (c) Nos. 4334/9; (d) Nos. 4341/3 Set of 4 sheets	16·00	16·00

1155 Badge, Camp and Sailing

1997. 90th Anniv of Scout Movement.

| 4345 | **1155** 20fo. multicoloured | 80 | 55 |

1156 Book, Knight and Arany

1997. 150th Anniv of Composition of "Miklos Toldi" by Janos Arany (winning entry in poetry competition).

| 4346 | **1156** 27fo.+10fo. multicoloured | 95 | 65 |

1157 St. Adalbert

1997. Death Millenary of St. Adalbert (Bishop of Prague).

| 4347 | **1157** 80fo. lilac | 2·75 | 2·00 |

1158 Emblem and City

1997. World Customs' Union Conference, Budapest.

| 4348 | **1158** 90fo. multicoloured | 2·40 | 1·70 |

1159 Gemsboks

1997. African Animals. Multicoloured.

4349	16fo. Type **1159**	50	35
4350	20fo. Common zebras	65	45
4351	20fo. Black rhinoceroses	65	45
4352	27fo. Lions	80	55
MS4353	91×64 mm. 90fo. African elephants	4·50	4·50

1160 *The Enchanted Hart*

1997. Europa. Tales and Legends. Multicoloured.

| 4354 | 27fo. Type **1160** | 95 | 65 |
| 4355 | 90fo. King St. Stephen overseeing burial of Prince Geza (death millenary) | 3·00 | 2·10 |

1161 Schraetzer (*Gymnocephalus schraetzer*)

1997. Fish. Multicoloured.

4356	20fo. Type **1161**	50	35
4357	20fo. Bullhead *Cottus gobio*	50	35
4358	20fo. Schneider *Alburnoides bipunctatus*	50	35
4359	20fo. Spiny loach (*Cobitis taenia*)	50	35

Nos. 4356/9 were issued together, *se-tenant*, forming a composite design.

1162 St. Jadwiga (after Peter Prokop)

1997. Canonization of Queen Jadwiga of Poland.

| 4360 | **1162** 90fo. multicoloured | 2·40 | 1·70 |

1163 Janos Selye

1997. Int Congress on Stress, Budapest.

| 4361 | **1163** 90fo. multicoloured | 2·40 | 1·70 |

1997. No. 4220 surch **60 f.**

| 4362 | 60fo. on 24fo. multicoloured | 1·40 | 1·00 |

1997. Wine Grapes and Regions (2nd series). As T **1013**. Multicoloured.

4363	27fo. Harslevelu, Gyongyos	65	55
4364	27fo. Nemes Kadarka, Kiskoros	65	55
4365	27fo. Teltfurtu Ezerjo, Mor	65	55

1165 Flower surrounded by Flood Waters

1997. Flood Relief Funds.

| 4366 | **1165** 27fo.+100fo. mult | 3·25 | 2·75 |

1166 Postman and Csonka Tricycle, 1900

1997. Stamp Day. Multicoloured.

4367	27fo.+5fo. Type **1166**	80	65
4368	55fo.+5fo. Registered letter receiving-machine, 1906 (vert)	1·60	1·30
MS4369	82×68 mm. 90fo.+30fo. Csonka post van, 1905	8·00	8·00

1167 Nativity

1997. Christmas. Multicoloured.

| 4370 | 20fo. Type **1167** | 50 | 40 |
| 4371 | 27fo. Adoration of the Wise Men | 80 | 65 |

1168 Weightlifter

1997. 68th World Weightlifting Championships, Thailand.

| 4372 | **1168** 90fo. multicoloured | 2·40 | 2·00 |

1169 Skiing

1998. Winter Olympic Games, Nagano, Japan. Multicoloured.

| 4373 | 30fo. Type **1169** | 65 | 55 |
| 4374 | 100fo. Snowboarding | 2·40 | 1·80 |

1170 Szechenyi with Camera

1998. Birth Centenary of Zsigmond Szechenyi (travel writer).

| 4375 | **1170** 60fo. multicoloured | 1·70 | 1·30 |

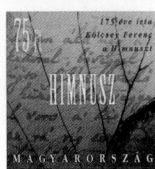

1171 Leaf and Lyrics

1998. 175th Anniv of National Hymn by Ferenc Kolcsey.
4376	**1171**	75fo. multicoloured	2·00	1·60

1172 Balint Postas holding Envelope

1998. Introduction of Balint Postas (post mascot). Multicoloured.
4377	23fo. Type **1172**		65	55
4378	24fo. Balint Postas bowing		75	60
4379	30fo. Balint Postas with arms outstretched		85	65
4380	65fo. Balint Postas flying		1·70	1·30

1173 Hearts and Post Box

1998. St. Valentine's Day.
4381	**1173**	24fo. multicoloured	85	65

1174 Szilard

1998. Birth Centenary of Leo Szilard (scientist).
4382	**1174**	50fo. multicoloured	1·30	1·10

1175 Sandor Petofi (poet)

1998. 150th Anniv of March Revolution, 1848. Multicoloured.
4383	23fo. Type **1175**		65	55
4384	24fo. Mihaly Tancsics (politician and workers' newspaper editor) and inkwell		75	60
4385	30fo. Lajos Kossuth (Governor of 1849 Republic) and coin		85	65
MS4386	78×65 mm. 150fo.+50fo. Leaders of the Revolution (44×29 mm)		6·75	6·75

1176 The Resurrection of Christ (El Greco)

1998. Easter.
4387	–	24fo. red and black	65	55
4388	**1176**	30fo. multicoloured	1·00	80
DESIGN: 27×39 mm—24fo. Dots forming outline of egg.

1177 Vase

1998. Ceramics. Multicoloured.
4389	20fo. Type **1177**		50	40
4390	24fo. Bowl decorated with butterflies (horiz)		60	45
4391	30fo. Spiral vase		65	55
4392	95fo. Bowl with lid (horiz)		2·50	2·00

1178 Postman

1998. Stamp Day. 250th Anniv of Inauguration of Postal Service by Empress Maria Theresa. Multicoloured.
4393	24fo.+10fo. Type **1178**		1·00	80
4394	30fo.+10fo. Mounted courier		1·10	85
MS4395	80×61 mm. 150fo. Horse-drawn post coach		6·00	6·00

1179 American Bison

1998. American Animals. Multicoloured.
4396	23fo. Type **1179**		65	55
4397	24fo. Brown bear		75	60
4398	24fo. Mississippi alligator		75	60
4399	30fo. Ocelot		85	65
MS4400	90×60 mm. 150fo. Marvellous spatule-tail		5·00	5·00

1180 Jendrassik

1998. Birth Centenary of Gyorgy Jendrassik (engineer).
4401	**1180**	100fo. blue	2·75	2·10

1181 Hurdling

1998. European Light Athletics Championships, Budapest. Multicoloured.
4402	24fo. Type **1181**		50	40
4403	65fo. High jumping		1·50	1·20
4404	80fo. Throwing the hammer		2·20	1·70

1182 Canoe

1998. World White-water Canoeing Championships, Szeged.
4405	**1182**	30fo. multicoloured	85	65

1183 Players

1998. World Cup Football Championship, France. Multicoloured.
4406	30fo. Type **1183**		65	55
4407	110fo. Players with ball on ground		2·75	2·10
Nos. 4406/7 were issued together, *se-tenant*, forming a composite design.

1184 Baross (after Miklos Barabos)

1998. 150th Birth Anniv of Gabor Baross (politician).
4408	**1184**	60fo. multicoloured	1·70	1·30

1185 Signalman and Pioneers in Railway Carriage

1998. 50th Anniv of Budapest Pioneer Railway.
4409	**1185**	24fo. multicoloured	85	65

1186 Congress Emblem

1998. World Congress of Computer Technology, Vienna and Budapest.
4410	**1186**	65fo. multicoloured	1·90	1·50

1187 Carved Poles

1998. Europa. National Festivals. Multicoloured.
4411	50fo. Type **1187** (Republic Day)		2·20	1·70
4412	60fo. Carved shield and corn (National Day)		2·75	2·10

1188 Emblem

1998. 60th Anniv of Hungarians Abroad Organization.
4413	**1188**	100fo. multicoloured	3·00	2·30

1189 Hortobagyi National Park

1998. National Parks (1st series). Multicoloured.
4414	24fo. Type **1189**		50	40
4415	70fo. Kiskunsagi National Park		1·90	1·50
See also Nos. 4438/9, 4507/8 and 4559/61.

1190 *Adoration of the Shepherds* (Agnolo Bronzino)

1998. Christmas. Multicoloured.
4416	20fo. Type **1190**		65	55
4417	24fo. *Madonna and Child Enthroned* (Carlo Crivelli) (vert)		75	60
For 24fo. as Type **1190** see No. 4485.

1191 Easter Eggs

1999. Easter. Multicoloured.
4418	27fo. Type **1191**		65	55
4419	32fo. Head of Christ (Ferenc Svindt) (37×52 mm)		85	65

1192 "Self-portrait" (wood carving, Jeno Szervatiusz)

1999. International Year of the Elderly.
4420	**1192**	32fo. multicoloured	85	65

1193 "Novara" (full-rigged ship)

1999. Sailing Ships. Multicoloured.
4421	32fo. Type **1193**		65	55
4422	79fo. *Phoenix* (barge)		1·70	1·30
4423	110fo. *Folyami Vitorlas* (galley)		2·75	2·10

1194 Path of Eclipse

1999. Total Solar Eclipse (11 Aug). Sheet 105×76 mm.
MS4424	**1194**	1999fo. multicoloured	47·00	47·00

1195 Artur Gorgey (commander of Upper Danube)

1999. 150th Anniv of 1848–49 Uprising. Multicoloured.
4425	24fo. Type **1195**		65	55
4426	27fo. Lajos Batthyany (politician)		75	60
4427	32fo. General Jozef Bem		85	65
MS4428	78×65 mm. 100fo. *The Battle of Tapioticske* (detail, Mor Than) (44×27 mm)		3·00	3·00

1196 Scene from "Bobo and the Hare" (animated film)

1999. Youth Stamp.
4429	**1196**	52fo.+25fo. mult	1·70	1·30

1197 Cathedrals within Map and Emblem

1999. 50th Anniv of North Atlantic Treaty Organization.
4430	**1197**	110fo. multicoloured	3·25	2·75

1198 The Five Sports

1999. Fifth World Pentathlon Championship, Budapest. Sheet 86×70 mm.
MS4431	**1198**	100fo. multicoloured	3·00	3·00

1199 Papai

1999. 350th Birth Anniv of Ferenc Pariz Papai (scientist, physician and lexicographer).

4432	**1199**	50fo. green and orange	1·00	80

1200 Science Academy, Budapest

1999. World Science Congress, Budapest.

4433	**1200**	65fo. multicoloured	1·20	90

1201 Anniversary Badge on Scroll

1999. Centenary of Ferencvaros Sports Club.

4434	**1201**	100fo. multicoloured	1·90	1·50

1202 Council Flag

1999. 50th Anniv of Council of Europe.

4435	**1202**	50fo. multicoloured	2·50	2·00

1203 Juhfark, Somlo

1999. Wine Grapes and Regions (3rd series). Multicoloured.

4436	24fo. Type **1203**	50	40
4437	27fo. Kekfrankos, Sopron	60	45

1999. Europa. Parks and Gardens. National Parks (2nd series). As T **1189**. Multicoloured.

4438	27fo. Aggtelek National Park	2·50	2·00
4439	32fo. Bukk National Park	2·75	2·10

1204 Bengali Tiger

1999. Asian Animals. Multicoloured.

4440	27fo. Type **1204**	85	65
4441	32fo. Giant panda	90	75
4442	52fo. Black leopard	1·30	1·10
4443	79fo. Orang-utan	1·70	1·30
MS4444	78×75 mm. 100fo. Mandarin (49×29 mm)	6·00	6·00

1205 Title Page of Decree

1999. Stamp Day. 250th Anniv of Decree by Empress Maria Theresa establishing Regular Mail Coach Service. Multicoloured.

4445	32fo.+15fo. Type **1205**	1·00	80
4446	52fo.+20fo. Passengers boarding coach and woman with letters	1·30	1·10
MS4447	75×60 mm. 150fo. Horses and mail coach (31×41 mm)	4·25	4·25

1206 Common Poppy

1999. Greetings Stamps. Flowers. Multicoloured.

4448	27fo. Type **1206**	50	40
4449	32fo. Trumpet gentian	85	65

1207 Cukor

1999. Birth Centenary of George Cukor (film director).

4450	**1207**	50fo. multicoloured	1·20	90

1208 U.P.U. Emblem

1999. 125th Anniv of Universal Postal Union. "China '99" International Stamp Exhibition, Peking.

4451	**1208**	32fo. multicoloured	85	65

1209 Woodcut by Samuel Mikoviny (from "Notitia Hungarie" by Matyas Bel)

1999. International Book Fair, Frankfurt.

4452	**1209**	40fo. multicoloured	85	65

1210 High-backed Chair, Szepesseg (17th century)

1999. Antique Furniture.

4453	-	1fo. green and yellow	15	15
4454	-	2fo. green and black	15	15
4455	-	3fo. red and black	15	15
4456	-	4fo. brown	15	15
4457	-	5fo. deep blue and blue	15	15
4458	-	6fo. brown and sepia	15	15
4459	-	7fo. brown and pink	15	15
4460	-	8fo. black and grey	10	10
4460a	-	9fo. violet and maroon	10	10
4461	**1210**	10fo. bistre and black	10	10
4464	-	20fo. green and black	25	20
4467	-	26fo. green and black	35	25
4468	-	29fo. green and black	40	35
4469	-	30fo. mauve and black	50	40
4470	-	31fo. dp mauve and mve	60	45
4470a	-	32fo. pink and red	65	55
4470b	-	33fo. pink and red	75	60
4470c	-	35fo. pink and red	85	65
4471	-	40fo. brown & lt brown	90	75
4472	-	50fo. blue and black	1·00	80
4474	-	60fo. olive and green	1·30	1·10
4475	-	65fo. ochre and brown	1·40	1·10
4476	-	70fo. rose and black	1·50	1·20
4478	-	80fo. grey and black	1·70	1·30
4480	-	90fo. lilac and purple	1·90	1·50
4481	-	100fo. brown and black	2·00	1·60
4482	-	134fo. ochre and brown	3·00	2·40
4483	-	200fo. blue and green	4·25	3·25
4484	-	210fo. green and olive	4·75	3·75
4484a	-	230fo. blue-green and bottle green	5·00	4·00
4484b	-	300fo. red and rosine	6·00	4·50
4484c	-	500fo. blue and cobalt	10·00	8·00
4484d	-	1000fo. olive and bistre	20·00	16·00

DESIGNS—VERT: 1fo. Wooden stool, 1910; 2fo. Heves County wooden chair, 1838; 3fo. 19th-century gilded chair; 4fo. Armchair by Geza Marota; 5fo. Chair by Odon Farago; 6fo. Wooden chair by Marton Kovacs; 7fo. Ornate chair, 1853; 8fo. 19th-century chair; 9fo. 18th-century wooden armchair; 20fo. Armchair by Karoly Lingel, 1915; 26, 31fo. Neo-Gothic chair, 1850; 29fo. Magyargee wooden chair, 1879; 30fo. Armchair by Karoly Nagy, 1935; 32, 33fo. Ornate backed chair, 1890; 35fo. 18th-century carver; 40fo. Ornate chair, 1896; 50fo. Prince Pal Esterhazy's armchair (16th-century); 60fo. Chair, 1840; 65fo. Cane-bottomed ornate armchair, 1920; 70fo. Chair with umbrella-shaped back, 1820; 80fo. High backed chair; 90fo. Upholstered armchair by Lajos Kozma. HORIZ: 100fo. Couch by Lajos Kozma, 1920; 134fo. Double-seated chair, 1900; 200fo. Ornate couch, 1810; 210fo., 230fo. Love seat (1900); 300fo. 18th-century settee; 500fo. Rococo settee, 1880; 1000fo. Vassily chair by Marcel Breuer, 1925.

1211 Three Wise Men (Zsuzsa Demeter)

1999. Christmas. Multicoloured.

4485	24fo. Type **1190**	65	55
4486	27fo. Type **1211**	75	60
4487	32fo. "Madonna and Child" (stained glass window, Miksa Roth) (vert)	85	65

1212 Wigner

1999. 97th Birth Anniv of Jeno Wigner (physicist).

4488	**1212**	32fo. blue	85	65

1213 Paddle-steamer passing under Bridge

1999. 150th Anniv of Chain Bridge, Budapest. Sheet 87×57 mm.

MS4489	**1213** 150fo. blue, red and green	3·25	3·25

1214 Coronation Sceptre

2000. New Millenium.

4490	**1214**	28fo. bistre and purple	50	40
4491	**1214**	30fo. bistre and purple	65	55
4492	-	34fo. multicoloured	75	60
4493	-	36fo. multicoloured	85	65
4494	-	40fo. multicoloured	90	75

DESIGN:—34, 36, 40fo. Millennium flag.

1215 Miklos Kis Misztotfalusi (printer, 350th anniv)

2000. Birth Anniversaries.

4495	**1215**	30fo. grn, stone & brn	85	65
4496	-	40fo. blue, stone & brn	1·20	90
4497	-	50fo. red, stone & brn	1·30	1·10
4498	-	80fo. brown and stone	2·00	1·60

DESIGNS—40fo. Anyos Jedlik (physicist, bicentenary); 50fo. Jeno Kvassay (engineer, 150th anniv); 80fo. Jeno Barcsay (artist, centenary).

1216 Fekete and Animal Characters

2000. Youth Stamp. Birth Centenary of Istvan Fekete (writer).

4499	**1216**	60fo.+30fo. mult	2·20	1·70

1217 Hungarian Cultural Foundation and Exhibition Emblem

2000. "Hunphilex 2000" Stamp Exn, Budapest.

4500	**1217**	200fo.+100fo. mult	6·75	5·25

1218 Mihaly Vorosmarty (poet, bicentenary)

2000. Birth Anniversaries.

4501	**1218**	50fo. green and black	1·00	80
4502	-	50fo. brown and black	1·00	80
4503	-	50fo. green and black	1·00	80
4504	-	50fo. brown and black	1·00	80
4505	-	50fo. green and black	1·00	80

DESIGNS: No. 4502, Mari Jaszai (actress, 150th anniv); 4503, Sandor Marai (writer, centenary); 4504, Lujza Blaha (actress, 150th anniv); 4505, Lorinc Szabo (poet and translator, centenary).

1219 Symbolic Easter Eggs

2000. Easter. Multicoloured.

4506	26fo. Type **1219**	50	40
4507	28fo. Decorated egg (29×31 mm)	60	45

2000. National Parks (3rd series). As T **1189**. Multicoloured.

4508	29fo. Ferto-Hansag National Park	65	55
4509	34fo. Duna-Drava National Park	75	60

1220 Airport Building and Lisunov Li-2 Airplane

2000. 50th Anniv of Ferihegy International Airport.

4510	**1220**	136fo. multicoloured	2·50	2·00

1221 Banded Wren

2000. Australian Animals. Multicoloured.

4511	26fo. Type **1221**	60	45
4512	28fo. Opossum	65	55
4513	83fo. Koala	1·70	1·30
4514	90fo. Red kangaroo	1·90	1·50
MS4515	107×70 mm. 110fo. Duck-billed platypus	3·00	3·00

1222 Jigsaw
Puzzle

2000. Europa. Multicoloured.
4516	34fo. Type **1222**		2·75	2·10
4517	54fo. "Building Europe"		3·50	2·75

1223 Boat on Corinthian
Canal, and Istvan Turr
(engineer)

2000. "EXPO 2000" World's Fair, Hanover, Germany.
4518	**1223**	80fo. multicoloured	1·90	1·50

1224 Bisected and
Complete 6k. Austrian
Empire Stamps

2000. "WIPA 2000" International Stamp Exhibition, Vienna. 150th Anniv of Hungarian Stamps.
4519	**1224**	110fo. multicoloured	2·20	1·70

1225 Queen
Gizella I

2000. Stamp Day. Showing decorative figures from Coronation Gown. Multicoloured.
4520	26fo. Type **1225**		50	40
4521	28fo. King Istvan I		60	45

1226 Balatonfured-Csopak

2000. Wine Grapes and Regions (4th series). Multicoloured.
4522	29fo. Type **1226**		50	40
4523	34fo. Aszar-Neszmely		65	55

1227 Evangelical
Church, Budapest

2000. Churches. Multicoloured.
4524	30fo. Type **1227**		65	55
4525	30fo. St. Anthony's Friars' Church, Eger		65	55
4526	30fo. Reformed Church, Takos		65	55
4527	30fo. Abbey Church, Jak		65	55

1228 Globe

2000. Millennium. Sheet 120×70 mm.
MS4528	**1228**	2000fo. multicoloured	37·00	37·00

1229 Boeing
767-200

2000. 90th Anniv of Hungarian Aviation.
4529	**1229**	120fo. multicoloured	3·75	3·00

1230 King Laszlo, 1077–95

2000. New Millennium (1st series). Multicoloured.
4530	50fo. Type **1230**		90	70
4531	50fo. Issue of Golden Bull (charter of rights for freemen) by King Andrew II, 1222		90	70
4532	50fo. St. Elizabeth and the Mongol invasion, 1241		90	70
4533	50fo. Reign of King Sigismund, 1395–1437		90	70
4534	50fo. Janos Hunyadi (regent) and Janos Kapisztran		90	70
4535	50fo. Reign of King Matthias, 1458–90		90	70
4536	50fo. The Crucifixion, Miklos Zrinyi (military commander) and Siege of Szigetvas, 1566		90	70
4537	50fo. Horseman, battle scenes and the recapture of Buda Castle and Gyor		90	70
4538	50fo. People outside Church, Transylvania		90	70
4539	50fo. Peter Pazmany (founder) and University, Budapest, 1635		90	70

Nos. 4530/4 and 4535/9 were issued together, *se-tenant*, forming a composite design.
See also Nos. 4585/**MS**4595.

1231 Detail of
Coronation Gown

2000. "HUNPHILEX 2000" International Stamp Exhibition, Budapest. Multicoloured.
MS4540 93×72 mm. 200fo.+100fo. Type **1231**	7·25	7·25

1232 Dohany
Utca Synagogue,
Budapest

2000. Hungary–Israel Joint Issue.
4541	**1232**	120fo. multicoloured	2·20	1·80

1233 Mary and
Jesus leaving
Bethlehem

2000. Christmas. Multicoloured.
4542	26fo. Type **1233**		45	35
4543	28fo. Church (27×28 mm)		50	40
4544	29fo. Christmas tree (27×28 mm)		50	40
4545	34fo. Nativity scene on watch face (32×36 mm)		60	50

1234 Emblem and Writing Desk

2000. 50th Anniv of Convention on Human Rights.
4546	**1234**	50fo. multicoloured	1·50	1·20

1235 Rifle Shooting

2000. Olympic Games, Sydney. Multicoloured.
4547	30fo. Type **1235**		45	35
4548	40fo. Weightlifting		75	60
4549	80fo. Gymnastics		1·50	1·20
MS4550 85×63 mm. 120fo. Two-man kayak			3·00	3·00

1236 Eger Castle
and Extract from
Poem

2001. Youth Stamp. Centenary of Eclipse of the Crescent Moon (poem by Geza Gardonyi).
4551	**1236**	60fo.+30fo. mult	2·00	1·60

1237 Profiles

2001. European Year of Languages.
4552	**1237**	100fo. multicoloured	2·75	2·20

1238 Man
blowing Trumpet

2001. Greetings Stamps. Multicoloured.
4553	36fo. Type **1238**		55	45
4554	36fo. Couple dancing		55	45
4555	36fo. Baby in cradle		55	45
4556	36fo. Clown		55	45
4557	36fo. Woman and child		55	45

1239 Ice-skater

2001
4558	**1239**	140fo. multicoloured	2·75	2·20

1240 Easter Eggs and
Rabbit

2001. Easter.
4559	**1240**	28fo. multicoloured	95	75

2001. National Parks (4th series). As T 1189. Multicoloured.
4560	28fo. Upper Balaton National Park		60	50
4561	36fo. Koros-Maros National Park		65	55
4562	70fo. Duna-Ipoly National Park		1·30	1·10

1241 Mk 48 Diesel
Locomotive, Lillafured State
Forest Railway

2001. Light Railways. Multicoloured.
4563	31fo. Type **1241**		60	50
4564	36fo. 490 series steam locomotive, Keeskemet Light Railway		65	55
4565	100fo. 394 series steam locomotive, Szechenyi Railway Museum		2·00	1·60

1242 Emblem and
Vegetation

2001. Anniversaries. Multicoloured.
4567	70fo. Type **1242** (50th anniversaries of International Plant Protection Convention and European and Mediterranean Plant Protection Organization)	1·10	85
4568	80fo. Globe, people and emblem (50th anniv of United Nations High Commissioner for Refugees)	1·20	95

1243 Door Inlay, St.
Adalbert Basilica

2001. Millenary of Archdiocese of Esztergom.
4569	**1243**	124fo. multicoloured	2·40	1·90

1244 Ringed Seal (*Phoca
hispida*)

2001. Animals. Multicoloured.
4570	28fo. Type **1244**		55	45
4571	36fo. Wolf (*Canis lupus*)		65	55
4572	70fo. Herman's tortoise (*Testudo hermanni*)		1·20	95
4573	90fo. River kingfisher (*Alcedo atthis*)		1·60	1·30
MS4574 90×66 mm. 200fo. Red deer males (*Cervus elaphus*)			4·00	4·00

1245 Chest containing
Water

2001. Europa. Water Resources. Multicoloured.
4575	36fo. Type **1245**		95	75
4576	90fo. Open globe filled with water		2·40	1·90

1246 1871 1k.
Newspaper
Stamp

2001. Stamp Day. 130th Anniv of Hungarian Stamps. Multicoloured.
4577	36fo. Type **1246**		65	55
4578	90fo. 1871 3k. stamp		1·50	1·20
MS4579 60×75 mm. 200fo.+40fo. *Pigeon Post* (Miklos Barabas) (39×49 mm)			4·75	4·75

1247 Players

2001. European Water Polo Championship, Budapest.
4580	**1247**	150fo. multicoloured	2·75	2·20

1248 Scout's Hats

2001. Fourth European Conference of Former Scouts and Guides, Budapest.
4581 **1248** 150fo. multicoloured ... 2·75 ... 2·20

1249 Drawing (Aladar Korosfoi-Kriesch)

2001. Art Anniversaries.
4582 **1249** 100fo. blue, mauve and lilac ... 2·00 ... 1·60
4583 − 150fo. black and blue (49×21 mm) ... 2·75 ... 2·20
DESIGNS—VERT: 100fo. Type **1249** (centenary of Godollo Artists' Colony). HORIZ: 150fo. Emblems representing different branches of the arts (centenary of FESZEK Club).

1250 Athletics Race

2001. World Youth Athletics Championship, Debrecen.
4584 **1250** 140fo. multicoloured ... 2·50 ... 2·00

1251 Ferenc Rakovic and Ilona Zrinyi

2001. New Millennium (2nd series). Multicoloured.
4585 **1251** 50fo. Type **1251** ... 80 ... 65
4586 50fo. Terezia Maria and royal horse guard ... 80 ... 65
4587 50fo. Istvan Szechenyi and Chain Bridge ... 80 ... 65
4588 50fo. Newspaper headline and man on horseback ... 80 ... 65
4589 50fo. Janos Arany, *The Solitary Cedar* (detail, Tivadar Csontvary Kosztka) and Parliament buildings ... 80 ... 65
4590 50fo. First World War soldiers and map ... 80 ... 65
4591 50fo. Mihaly Babits ... 80 ... 65
4592 50fo. Chain Bridge and Bishop Vilmos Apor ... 80 ... 65
4593 50fo. Tanks and soldiers (Revolution, 1956) and Zoltan Kodaly (composer) ... 80 ... 65
4594 50fo. Young children and Millennium flag ... 80 ... 65
MS4595 105×75 mm. 2001fo. Crown (39×31 mm) ... 33·00 ... 33·00

1252 Pannonhalma-Sokoroalja

2001. Wine Grapes and Regions (5th series). Multicoloured.
4596 **1252** 60fo. Type **1252** ... 1·10 ... 85
4597 70fo. Balatonboglar ... 1·30 ... 1·10

1253 Common Peacock (30 m mosaic)

2001. Guinness Record Attempt by Hungarian Post Office to Create World's Largest Mosaic from Used Postage Stamps.
4598 **1253** 10fo. multicoloured ... 40 ... 30

1254 Bridge

2001. Reconstruction of Maria Valeria Bridge, Estergom–Parkany.
4599 **1254** 36fo. multicoloured ... 80 ... 65

1255 Angel and Decorations

2001. Christmas.
4600 **1255** 36fo. multicoloured ... 80 ... 65

1256 1871 2k. Stamp and Emblem

2001. 150th Anniv of Hungarian Stamp Printing.
4601 **1256** 150fo. multicoloured ... 2·75 ... 2·20

1257 Ice Hockey Player

2002. Winter Olympic Games, Salt Lake City, U.S.A.
4602 **1257** 160fo. multicoloured ... 3·00 ... 2·40

1258 Soldiers fighting (Defence of Eger Castle)

2002. Youth Stamp. 450th Anniv of War with Ottoman Empire. Sheet 120×68 mm containing T **1258** and similar multicoloured designs.
MS4603 50fo. Type **1258**; 50fo. Istvan Losonczy and Turkish soldiers, Timisoara; 100fo. + 50fo. Soldiers and pages (Battle of Dregely Castle) (39×29 mm) ... 4·50 ... 4·50

1259 Ordinary "Penny-farthing" Bicycle

2002. History of the Bicycle. Multicoloured.
4604 **1259** 40fo. Type **1259** ... 80 ... 65
4605 40fo. Tricycle, 1900s ... 80 ... 65
4606 40fo. Karoly Iszer (chairman of Budapest Sport Club) ... 80 ... 65
4607 40fo. Four-man cycle ... 80 ... 65

1260 Easter Eggs

2002. Easter.
4608 **1260** 30fo. multicoloured ... 55 ... 45

1261 Libelle

2002. Aviation. Multicoloured.
4609 **1261** 180fo. Type **1261** ... 3·00 ... 2·50
4610 190fo. Hungarian Lloyd Aircraft and Engine Factory biplane ... 3·25 ... 2·75

1262 Lajos Kossuth

2002. Birth Anniversaries. Multicoloured.
4611 **1262** 33fo. Type **1262** (statesman, bicentenary) ... 55 ... 45
4612 134fo. Janos Bolyai (mathematician, bicentenary) ... 2·40 ... 1·90
4613 150fo. Gyula Illyes (poet and writer, centenary) ... 2·50 ... 2·00

1263 Stage Set for *The Tragedy of Man* (Imre Madach)

2002. Inauguration of New National Theatre, Budapest. Sheet 85×60 mm.
MS4614 **1263** 500fo. multicoloured ... 8·75 ... 8·75

1264 Parliament Building

2002. Centenary of Inauguration of Parliament Building. Sheet 97×67 mm.
MS4615 **1264** 500fo. multicoloured ... 8·75 ... 8·75

1265 "S.O.S."

2002. Environmental Protection.
4616 **1265** 158fo. multicoloured ... 2·75 ... 2·20

1266 Book of Psalms of King David

2002. Bicentenaries of Hungarian National Museum and National Szechenyi Library. Exhibits from the institutions. Multicoloured.
MS4617 150fo. Type **1266**; 150fo. Illumination from the second volume of King Matthias's Book of Rites; 150fo. Civil Guard of Pest Standard, 1848; 150fo. Holy water basin, 1903 ... 10·50 ... 10·50

1267 Deer

2002. Centenary of Halas Lace. Multicoloured.
4618 **1267** 100fo. Type **1267** ... 1·90 ... 1·50
4619 110fo. Swan ... 2·00 ... 1·60
4620 140fo. Couple ... 2·50 ... 2·00

1268 Wild Cat (*Felis sylvestris*)

2002. Fauna. Multicoloured.
4621 **1268** 30fo. Type **1268** ... 55 ... 45
4622 38fo. Crimean bull lizard (*Podarcis taurica*) ... 65 ... 55
4623 110fo. Jay (*Garrulus glandarius*) ... 2·00 ... 1·60
4624 160fo. Alpine longhorn beetle (*Rosalia alpina*) ... 3·00 ... 2·40
MS4625 90×65 mm. 500fo. Sterlet (*Acipenser ruthenus*) ... 8·75 ... 8·75

1269 Elephant

2002. Europa. Circus.
4626 **1269** 62fo. multicoloured ... 2·00 ... 1·60

1270 Players

2002. World Cup Football Championship, Japan and South Korea.
4627 **1270** 160fo. multicoloured ... 3·00 ... 2·40

1271 Dog and Kennel (Etesd meg)

2002. Greetings Stamps. Designs as Nos. 4448/9 but with change of face value.
4628 30fo. Common poppy ... 55 ... 45
4629 38fo. Trumpet gentian ... 65 ... 55

2002. Greetings Stamps. Self-adhesive. Multicoloured.
4630 38fo. Type **1271** ... 65 ... 55
4631 38fo. Washing line (Megszulettem!) ... 65 ... 55
4632 38fo. Present outside house (Sok boldogsagot!) ... 65 ... 55
4633 38fo. Sofa and plant (Ontozdmeg...!) ... 65 ... 55
4634 38fo. Man in room (Ennyire szeretlek!) ... 65 ... 55
Nos. 4630/4 were issued together, *se-tenant*, forming a composite design.

1272 "Stone-pelter" (Karoly Ferenczy)

2002. Art. Multicoloured.
4635 62fo. Type **1272** ... 1·10 ... 85
4636 188fo. *Ballerina* (statue, Ferenc Medgyessy) (vert) ... 3·50 ... 2·75

1273 Buda Castle

2002. UNESCO World Heritage Sites. Multicoloured.
4637 100fo. Type **1273** ... 2·00 ... 1·60
4638 150fo. Holloko, Nograd ... 2·75 ... 2·20
4639 180fo. Aggtelek-Carst Caves (horiz) ... 3·25 ... 2·75

1274 Facade and Statue

2002. Millenary of Kalocsa Archdiocese.
4640 **1274** 150fo. multicoloured ... 2·75 ... 2·20

1275 Insulin Molecule, Hand holding Syringe and Map of Europe

2002. Medical Events in 2002. Multicoloured.

4641	100fo. Type **1275** (38th European Diabetes Association Congress)	1·70	1·40
4642	150fo. Arms, arrows and map of Europe (16th European Society of Elbow and Shoulder Surgeons Congress)	2·75	2·20

1276 "Pound Cake Madonna"

2002. 75th Anniv of Stamp Day. Birth Centenary of Margit Kováacs (ceramicist). Multicoloured.

4643	33fo. Type **1276**	55	45
4644	38fo. Family Photograph Album	65	55
MS4645	86×72 mm. 400fo.+200fo. St. George, The Dragon Slayer (25×36 mm)	10·00	10·00

1277 "Adoration of the Magi"

2002. Christmas. Paintings by Erzsebet Udvardi. Multicoloured.

4646	30fo. Type **1277**	50	40
4647	38fo. Bethelem	65	50

1278 Gymnast

2002. World Gymnastics Championships, Debrecen.

4648	**1278**	160fo. multicoloured	2·50	2·10

1279 Rakoczi Mansion, Tekirdag

2002. Cultural Heritage. Multicoloured.

4649	40fo. Type **1279**	75	60
4650	110fo. Pasha Gazi Kasim Mosque, Pecs	2·00	1·70

Stamps in similar designs were issued by Turkey.

1280 John von Neuman

2003. Birth Anniversaries. Multicoloured.

4651	32fo. Type **1280** (computing pioneer) (centenary)	50	40
4652	40fo. Rezso Soo (botanist) (centenary)	75	60
4653	60fo. Karoly Zipernowsky (electrical engineer) (150th)	1·00	85

1281 Frankenthal Coffee Set

2003. Herend Porcelain. Sheet 138×71 mm containing T 1281 and similar vert designs. Multicoloured.

MS4654	150fo. Type **1281**; 150fo. Blue coffee pot, cup and saucer; 150fo. Tall vase; 150fo. Siang Noir shell bowl and jug	10·00	10·00

1282 Retreating Soldiers

2003. 60th Anniv of Second Royal Hungarian Army's Defeat at the River Don.

4655	**1282**	40fo. multicoloured	75	60

1283 Crucifixion

2003. Easter.

4656	**1283**	32fo. multicoloured	50	40

1284 Title Page

2003. Sport (1st issue). Centenary of Nemzeti Sport (sports magazine).

4657	**1284**	150fo. multicoloured	2·50	2·10

See also Nos. 4670 and 4673.

1285 Church

2003. Greetings Stamps. Multicoloured. Self-adhesive.

4658	40fo. Type **1285**	65	50
4659	40fo. Two flowers	65	50
4660	40fo. Flower	65	50
4661	40fo. Decorated eggs	65	50
4662	40fo. Candles in window and Christmas tree	65	50

1286 BMX Cyclist

2003. Youth Stamps. Extreme Sports. Multicoloured.

4663	100fo. Type **1286**	1·80	1·40
4664	100fo. Snowboarding	1·80	1·40
4665	100fo. Parachuting	1·80	1·40
4666	100fo.+50t. White water canoeing	2·50	2·10

1287 Rogner Hotel, Heviz

2003. Tourism. Spa Hotels. Multicoloured.

4667	110fo. Type **1287**	1·90	1·60
4668	120fo. Helia Hotel, Budapest	2·10	1·80

1288 Gerle 13 Aircraft, 1933

2003. Hungarian Aviation. Multicoloured.

4669	142fo. Type **1288**	2·50	2·10
4670	160fo. L-2 Roma, 1925	2·75	2·30

1289 Columbia

2003. Space Shuttle Columbia Memorial. Sheet 92×72 mm.

MS4671	**1289**	500fo. multicoloured	8·25	8·25

1290 Championship Emblem

2003. Sport (2nd issue). World Division I Ice Hockey Championship, Budapest.

4672	**1290**	110fo. multicoloured	1·90	1·60

1291 Stadium

2003. Sport (3rd issue). Budapest Sports Arena.

4673	**1291**	120fo. multicoloured	2·10	1·80

1292 Hand holding Quill Pen

2003. Signing of Treaty of Accession to the European Union. (1st Issue). Sheet 106×70 mm.

MS4674	**1292**	500fo. multicoloured	9·50	9·50

See also Nos. 4692/3, 4714, 4722 and **MS**4725.

1293 Police Motorcyclist

2003. Police Service.

4675	**1293**	65fo. multicoloured	1·10	95

1294 Statue of Seated Woman (Danubius fountain)

2003. Stamp Day. Multicoloured.

4676	35fo. Type **1294**	65	50
4677	40fo. Statue of seated woman (Danubius fountain) (different)	75	60
MS4678	81×60 mm. 400fo.+100fo. "Calvin Square" (Jozsef Molnar)	8·75	8·75

1295 Kuruc Sabre, Sword and Mace

2003. 300th Anniv of Rakoczi's War of Independence. Sheet 121×61 mm containing T 1295 and similar vert designs. Multicoloured.

MS4679	120fo. Type **1295**; 120fo. Coins; 120fo. Old National flag, pipes and drums; 120fo. Pistols and powder horn	8·25	8·25

1296 Steppe Polecat (Mustela eversmanni)

2003. Fauna. Multicoloured.

4680	30fo. Type **1296**	65	50
4681	38fo. Short-toed lark (Calandrella brachydactyla)	75	60
4682	110fo. European tree frog (Hyla arborea)	1·90	1·60
4683	160fo. European weatherfish (Misgurnus fossilis)	2·00	1·70
MS4684	90×65 mm. 500fo. Ladybird spider (Eresus cinnaberinus) (inscr "cinnabarinus")	8·75	8·75

1297 Only Posters (Istvaán Orosz)

2003. Europa. Poster Art.

4685	**1297**	65fo. red, yellow and black	1·90	1·60

1298 Bukkaljai

2003. Wine Grapes and Regions (6th series). Multicoloured.

4686	60fo. Type **1298**	1·00	85
4687	130fo. Balaton-felvideki	2·10	1·80

1299 King Ladislaus and Unknown Queen (image scaled to 46% of original size)

2003. King Ladislaus' Robe (11th-century). Sheet 108×70 mm.

MS4688	**1299**	300fo. multicoloured	5·00	5·00

1300 Bishop Gerard and Angel (sculpture, Imre Varga)

2003. Art. Multicoloured.

4689	32fo. Type **1300**	65	50
4690	60fo. "Roman Bridge at Mostar" (Tivadar Csontvary Kosztka) (horiz)	1·00	85

1301 Crowds and Anniversary Emblem

2003. 50th Anniv of People's Stadium. 50th Anniv of Hungarian Football Team's Victory over England. Sheet 103×68 mm containing T 1301 and similar horiz design.

MS4691	**1301**	250fo. Type **1301**; 250fo. Goal and players	8·75	8·75

1302 European Union Emblem as Clock Face

2003. Hungary's Accession to European Union (2nd issue). Multicoloured.

4692	**1302**	115fo. Type **1302**	2·50	2·10
4693		130fo. As No. 4692 but with clock hands moved forward	3·25	2·50

1303 Fruit and Vegetables

2003. Nutrition.

4694	**1303**	120fo. multicoloured	1·90	1·60

1304 Feet and Cycle Wheel

2003. European Car-free Day.

4695	**1304**	150fo. multicoloured	2·50	2·10

1305 *Dactylorhiza fuchsia sooana*

2003. Birth Centenary of Rezso Soo (botanist).

4696	**1305**	44fo. multicoloured	75	60

1306 The Illuminated Chronicle

2003. Ancient Books. Multicoloured.

4697	**1306**	44fo. Type **1306**	75	60
4698		44fo. The Book of Zhou Rites	75	60

Stamps of a similar design were issued by Republic of China.

1307 Ferenc Deak

2003. 200th Birth Anniv of Ferenc Deak (politician). Sheet 99×68 mm.

MS4699	**1307**	500fo. multicoloured	8·75	8·75

1308 Reindeer

2003. Christmas. Multicoloured.

4700	**1308**	35fo. Type **1308**	65	50
4701		44fo. Angels, tree and house	75	60

1309 Globe and Computer Screen

2003. World Science Forum, Budapest. Sheet 87×62 mm.

MS4702	**1309**	500fo. multicoloured	8·75	8·75

1310 Jozsef Bajza

2004. Birth Anniversaries. Multicoloured.

4703		40fo. Balint Balassi (writer) (150th)	65	50
4704		44fo. Type **1310** (writer) (200th)	75	60
4705		80fo. Andras Janos Segner (mathematician) (300th)	1·40	1·10

1311 *Muki* Diesel Engine, Kemence Railway Museum

2004. Light Railways. Multicoloured.

4706		120fo. Type **1311**	2·00	1·70
4707		150fo. *Rezet* steam engine, Cemenc State Forest Railway	2·50	2·10

1312 Masks and Bonfire (Busojaras)

2004. Festivals. Sheet 160×45 mm containing T **1312** and similar horiz designs. Multicoloured.

MS4708		60fo.×4 Type **1312**; Flowers (Viragkarneval); Grapes and wine glass (Borfesztival); Trumpet, scroll and drum (Karnevalok)	4·00	4·00

1313 Puli

2004. Youth Stamps. Dogs. Sheet 140×70 mm containing T **1313** and similar vert designs.

MS4709		100fo. Type **1313**; 100fo. Greyhound; 100fo. Mudi; 100fo.+50fo. Vizsla	7·00	7·00

1314 "e"

2004. European Information Technology Ministerial Conference, Budapest.

4710		40fo. Type **1314** (blue and light blue)	65	50
4711		40fo. "e" (purple and yellow)	65	50
4712		40fo. "e" (orange and pink)	65	50
4713		40fo. "e" (green and red)	65	50

1315 Clock-face

2004. Hungary's Accession to European Union (3rd issue).

4714	**1315**	100fo. multicoloured	2·50	2·10

1316 Athletes

2004. Tenth World Indoor Athletics Championship, Budapest.

4715	**1316**	120fo. multicoloured	1·30	1·00

1317 Rabbit and Egg

2004. Easter.

4716	**1317**	48fo. multicoloured	2·00	1·70

1318 Buk Hotel, Bukfurdo

2004. Tourism. Spa Hotels. Multicoloured.

4717		120fo. Type **1318**	2·00	1·70
4718		150fo. Aqua Sol Hotel, Hajduszoboszlo	2·50	2·10

1319 St. Martin's Monastery, Pannonia

2004. UNESCO World Heritage Sites. Multicoloured.

4719		150fo. Type **1319**	2·50	2·10
4720		170fo. Tern, cattle and horses, Hortobagy National Park (horiz)	2·75	2·30

1320 Stone inscribed with Star of David

2004. 60th Anniv of Hungarian Holocaust.

4721	**1320**	160fo. multicoloured	2·50	2·10

1321 Clock-face

2004. Hungary's Accession to European Union (4th issue).

4722	**1321**	190fo. multicoloured	4·50	3·50

1322 Twin-handled Vase

2004. 150th Anniv of Zsolnay Porcelain Factory, Pecs. Sheet 138×69 mm containing T **1322** and similar vert designs. Multicoloured.

MS4723		160fo.×4, Type **1322**; Vase surmounted by horseman and small decorative vase; Vase with medieval silk design; "Autumn" mocha set	10·00	10·00

1323 Police Launch

2004. Police Day.

4724	**1323**	48fo. multicoloured	75	60

1324 Stars

2004. Hungary's Accession to European Union (5th issue). Sheet 105×71 mm.

MS4725	**1324**	500fo. multicoloured	8·75	8·75

1325 Embroidered Flowers

2004. Enlargement of European Union.

4726		120fo. Type **1325**	1·90	1·60
4727		150fo. New members' flags and stars	2·50	2·10

1326 Mole Rat (*Nannospalax leucodon*)

2004. Fauna. Multicoloured.

4728		48fo. Type **1326**	75	60
4729		65fo. Bearded tit (*Panurus biarmucus*)	1·00	85
4730		90fo. Snake-eyed skink (*Ablepharus kitaibelii fitzingeri*)	1·50	1·20
4731		120fo. Sturgeon (*Huso huso*)	2·00	1·70
MS4732		90×65 mm. 500fo. *Anthaxia hungarica*	8·25	8·25

1327 Walls and Doors (Erzsebet Schaar)

2004. Stamp Day. Art. Multicoloured.

4733		48fo. Type **1327**	75	60
4734		65fo. *Translucent Red Circle* (Tihamer Gyarmathy)	1·00	85
MS4735		71×71 mm. 400fo.+200fo. *Wasp King* (Bela Kondor) (41×32 mm)	9·50	9·50

1328 Hand holding Envelope over Ballot Box

2004. European Elections.

4736	**1328**	150fo. multicoloured	2·50	2·10

1329 People in Countryside

2004. Europa. Holidays.

4737	**1329**	160fo. multicoloured	2·50	2·10

1330 Ball and Turf as Slice of Cake

2004. Centenary of FIFA (Federation Internationale de Football Association).

4738	**1330**	100fo. multicoloured	1·60	1·30

1331 Basilica, Mariazell

2004. Catholics' Day. Sheet 110×160 mm containing T **1331** and similar vert designs. Multicoloured.

MS4739 100fo.×6, Type **1331**; Magna Mater Austriae (Romanesque statue) (Chapel of Grace, Basilica, Mariazell); Madonna (statue); Canopied statue of Mary, Celldomolk; Madonna (painting), Mariazell; Mary of Kiscell, Obuda parish   10·00   10·00

1332 Internet Icons

2004. Information Technology.

4740	**1332**	120fo. multicoloured	1·90	1·60

1333 Theodor Herzl

2004. Death Centenary of Theodor Herzl (writer and Zionist pioneer).

4741	**1333**	150fo. multicoloured	2·50	2·10

A stamp of the same design was issued by Israel and Austria.

1334 Rowers

2004. Olympic Games, Athens 2004. Multicoloured.

4742	90fo. Type **1334**		1·50	1·20
4743	130fo. Ball players		2·10	1·80
4744	150fo. Runners		2·50	2·10

1335 Two Dancers

2004. Third Folkloriada Festival. Showing folk dancers. Multicoloured.

4745	65fo. Type **1335**		1·10	95
4746	65fo. As No. 4745 with colour change		1·10	95
4747	65fo. Back view of dancer		1·10	95
4748	65fo. As No. 4747 with colour change		1·10	95
4749	65fo. Dancer facing right		1·10	95
4750	65fo. Dancer's skirt		1·10	95
4751	65fo. Back view of dancer facing right		1·10	95
4752	65fo. Two dancers (different)		1·10	95
4753	65fo. Dancer's skirt (different)		1·10	95
4754	65fo. Dancer's feet		1·10	95

1336 Rook and A sakkjatek tobbnyire

2004. History of Hungarian Chess. Each stamp either brown and black or flesh and black, the colours alternating to simulate the squares on a chess board (first three words of inscription given).

4755	50fo. Type **1336**		75	60
4756	50fo. A magyaroknak a		75	60
4757	50fo. Bishop and A Magyar tortenelem		75	60
4758	50fo. King and A Magyar sak-kirodalom		75	60
4759	50fo. Queen and A XVIII szazadban		75	60
4760	50fo. Az elso magyar		75	60
4761	50fo. Knight and Az 1839-ben megalakult		75	60
4762	50fo. Rook and A XIX szazad		75	60
4763	50fo. Pawn and A Magyar sakkfeladvanyszerzok		75	60
4764	50fo. Pawn and Harom, a XIX. szazad		75	60
4765	50fo. Pawn and Maroczy Geza 1870		75	60
4766	50fo. Pawn and Ket kivalo sakkozonk		75	60
4767	50fo. Bishop and A levelezesi sakkozas		75	60
4768	50fo. Pawn and A sakkelet megszervezodese		75	60
4769	50fo. Pawn and A ferfi orszagos		75	60
4770	50fo. Pawn and A II. vilaghaboru utan sokaig		75	60
4771	50fo. A noi sakkozas		75	60
4772	50fo. 1958-ban mar a 10		75	60
4773	50fo. Knight and A sakkozok osszefogasanak		75	60
4774	50fo. 1951-ben indult a		75	60
4775	50fo. A XX. szazadnak		75	60
4776	50fo. A II. vilaghaboru utan feladvany		75	60
4777	50fo. A XX. szazadban		75	60
4778	50fo. A XX. szazad		75	60
4779	50fo. A vilag sakkeletet		75	60
4780	50fo. A ket vilaghaboru kozott		75	60
4781	50fo. A haboru utan		75	60
4782	50fo. A ferfi sakkolimpian		75	60
4783	50fo. Pawn and A nemzetek kozti		75	60
4784	50fo. 1957-ben a hollandiai		75	60
4785	50fo. A noi sakkolimpiakon		75	60
4786	50fo. A XIX es XX		75	60
4787	50fo. Sakkirodalom nelkul sem		75	60
4788	50fo. A XX. Szazad magyar		75	60
4789	50fo. Bishop and "A szeles sakkozo"		75	60
4790	50fo. "A Magyar Sakkszovetseg"		75	60
4791	50fo. Pawn and "Barcza Gedeon 1911"		75	60
4792	50fo. "Szabo Laszlo 1917."		75	60
4793	50fo. "Portisch Lajos 1937"		75	60
4794	50fo. "Adorjan Andras '1968-ig"		75	60
4795	50fo. "Sax Gyula 1951"		75	60
4796	50fo. "Ribli Zoltan 1951"		75	60
4797	50fo. "Leko peter1979"		75	60
4798	50fo. "Almasi Zoltan 1976"		75	60
4799	50fo. "Bilek Istvan 1932"		75	60
4800	50fo. Knight and "A ket vila-ghaboru kozti"		75	60
4801	50fo. "Az olimpiakon tobbszor"		75	60
4802	50fo. "Sok kivalo magyar"		75	60
4803	50fo. Pawn and "Polgar Zsuzsa Budapesten 1969"		75	60
4804	50fo. Pawn and "Polgar Judit Budapesten 1976"		75	60
4805	50fo. Pawn and "Polgar Zsofia 1974"		75	60
4806	50fo. Pawn and "Langos Jozsa 1911"		75	60
4807	50fo. "Veroci Zsuzsa 1949"		75	60
4808	50fo. Pawn and "Ivanka Maria 1950"		75	60
4809	50fo. Pawn and "Madl Ildiko 1969"		75	60
4810	50fo. Pawn and "Orszagos bajnoki cimmel"		75	60
4811	50fo. Rook and "Sakkozasunk a XXI."		75	60
4812	50fo. Knight and "A sakkozassal valo kapcsolat"		75	60
4813	50fo. Bishop and "A magyar sakkazas"		75	60
4814	50fo. King and "Minden os-szefoglalo munka"		75	60
4815	50fo. Queen and "A jelen munkaban"		75	60
4816	50fo. "Elek Ferenc 1918—1989"		75	60
4817	50fo. "Katko (Regos) Imre 1904—1948"		75	60
4818	50fo. "grof Pongracz Arnold 1810—1890"		75	60

Nos. 4755/818 were issued in se-tenant sheets of 64 stamps, each stamp bearing an inscription describing part of the history of Hungarian chess.

The stamps were arranged to simulate the "Hungarian Defence" opening gambit with the rows marked either 1—8 vertically or a—h horizontally in the margin.

2004. History of Hungarian Chess. Each stamp either brown and black or flesh and black, the colours alternating to simulate the squares on a chess board (first three words of inscription given).

2004. Hungary's Accession to the European Union (6th issue). Sheet 84×72 mm containing four horiz designs as T **1302**, **1315** and **1321**. Multicoloured.

MS4819 100fo.×4, As Nos. 4692/3; As No. 4714; As No. 4722   7·50   7·50

1337 Istvan Bocskai, Swords and Coins

2004. 400th Anniv of Bocskai's War of Independence.

4820	**1337**	120fo. multicoloured	2·00	1·70

1338 INTOSAI Emblem

2004. 28th International Organization of Supreme Audit Institutions (INTOSAI) Conference, Budapest.

4821	**1338**	150fo. multicoloured	2·50	2·10

2004. Christmas (1st issue). Painting by Erzsebet Udvardi. As T **1227**. Multicoloured.

4822	48fo. As No. 4647		90	70

1339 Cherub

2004. Christmas (2nd issue). Multicoloured.

4823	48fo. Type **1339**		75	60
4824	48fo. Two cherubs		75	60
4825	48fo. Cherub seated with clasped hands		75	60
4826	48fo. Cherub with left hand raised		75	60
4827	48fo. Cherub facing left		75	60
4828	48fo. Cherub seated looking up		75	60

1340 Biscuits

2004. Christmas (3rd issue). Biscuits. Multicoloured.

4829-	48fo.×20 Type **1340** and 19			
4848	other different designs show-ing iced biscuits		7·50	7·50

1341 Green Triangles and Bauble at Right

2004. Christmas (4th issue). Glass Decorations. Multicoloured.

4849	48fo. Type **1341**		75	60
4850	48fo. As No. 4849 but design reversed		75	60
4851	48fo. Bauble at left and blue triangles		75	60
4852	48fo. As No. 4851 but design reversed		75	60
4853	48fo. Bauble at left, red square and green triangles		75	60
4854	48fo. As No. 4853 but design reversed		75	60
4855	48fo. Blue triangle, yellow rectangle, green and blue triangles		75	60
4856	48fo. As No. 4855 but design reversed		75	60
4857	48fo. As Type **1341** but smaller bauble		75	60
4858	48fo. As No. 4857 but with design reversed		75	60

1342 Sandor Csoma (statue), Aurel Stein and Library Hungarian Academy of Science

2004. Hungarian Science. Sandor Korosi Csoma (Tibetan scholar) and Aurel Stein (archaeologist) Commemoration.

4859	**1342**	80fo. multicoloured	1·40	1·10

1343 Pulsatilla and Valley

2004. Natura 2000 (habitat protection).

4860	**1343**	100fo. multicoloured	1·80	1·40

1344 Capricorn

2005. Western Zodiac. Multicoloured.

4861	50fo. Type **1344**		80	65
4862	50fo. Aquarius		80	65
4863	50fo. Pisces		80	65
4864	50fo. Aries		80	65
4865	50fo. Taurus		80	65
4866	50fo. Gemini		80	65
4867	50fo. Cancer		80	65
4868	50fo. Leo		80	65
4869	50fo. Virgo		80	65
4870	50fo. Libra		80	65
4871	50fo. Scorpio		80	65
4872	50fo. Sagittarius		80	65

1345 Seal-point Siamese

2005. Youth Philately. Cats. Sheet 150×50 mm containing T **1345** and similar horiz designs. Multicoloured.

MS4873 100fo. Type **1345**; 100fo. Maine coon; 100fo. White longhair; 100fo.+50fo. Silver tabby   7·50   7·50

The surcharge was for the promotion of philately.

1346 "100" containing Rotary Emblem

2005. Centenary of Rotary International (charitable organization).

4874	**1346**	130fo. multicoloured	2·10	1·80

1347 Rabbit

2005. Easter.

4875	**1347**	50fo. multicoloured	90	70

1348 Weightlifter

2005. Centenary of International Weightlifting Federation.

4876	**1348**	170fo. multicoloured	2·75	2·30

1349 Sandor Iharos

2005. Sandor Iharos (World Champion athlete) Commemoration.

4877	**1349**	90fo. multicoloured	1·50	1·20

1350 Auditorium

2005. Opening of Palace of Arts. Sheet 90×65 mm.
MS4878 **1350** 500fo. multicoloured 8·25 8·25

1351 Figure on Stage

2005. World Theatre Meeting.
4879 **1351** 50fo. multicoloured 90 70

1352 Map and Compass

2005. Corporate Greeting Stamps. Multicoloured.
4880 50fo. Type **1352** 90 70
4881 50fo. Compass at left and map 90 70

1353 Jeno Rejto (writer)

2005. Birth Centenaries. Multicoloured.
4882 90fo. Type **1353** 1·50 1·20
4883 140fo. Attila Jozsef (poet) 2·30 1·90

1354 Police Helicopter

2005. Police Day.
4884 **1354** 85fo. multicoloured 1·40 1·10

1355 "1945", Map and
Dove

2005. 60th Anniv of End of World War II.
4885 **1355** 150fo. multicoloured 2·50 2·10

1356 Hungarian Grey Bull

2005. Traditional Farm Breeds. Multicoloured.
4886 50fo. Type **1356** 90 70
4887 70fo. Hungarian spotted cow 1·10 95
4888 100fo. Racka sheep 1·60 1·30
4889 110fo. Cigaja sheep 1·90 1·60
MS4890 90×65 mm. 500fo. Mangalica
pigs 8·25 8·25

1357 Chicken Paprika
and Dumplings

2005. Europa. Gastronomy. Multicoloured.
4891 160fo. Type **1357** 2·75 2·30
4892 160fo. As No. 4891 but flowers
position changed 2·75 2·30
MS4893 132×70 mm. Nos. 4891/2,
each×2 11·00 11·00

1358 Pope John
Paul II

2005. Pope John Paul II Commemoration. Sheet 110×65 mm.
MS4894 **1358** 500fo. multicoloured 8·25 8·25

1359
Vajdahunyad
Castle

2005. Tourism. Budapest. Sheet 150×86 mm containing T **1359** and similar multicoloured designs.
MS4895 100fo.×5, Type **1359**; Saxlehner Palace; Ethnographic museum (horiz); "Reversed Madonna" stamp and printing block (horiz); Sandor Palace (horiz) 8·25 8·25

1360 Jak Church

2005
4896 **1360** 110fo. multicoloured 1·90 1·60

1361 Pintes Grapes, Zala
Region

2005. Wine Grapes and Regions (7th series). Multicoloured.
4897 120fo. Type **1361** 2·00 1·70
4898 140fo. Kunleany grapes,
Csongrad 2·40 2·00

1362 St. Stephen
(statue)

2005. Centenary of St. Stephen's Basilica, Budapest. Sheet 90×67 mm.
MS4899 **1362** 500fo. multicoloured 8·25 8·25

1363 Soyuz 36 Spacecraft

2005. 25th Anniv of Hungarian Cosmonaut Bertalan Farkas' Spaceflight.
4900 **1363** 130fo. multicoloured 2·30 1·90

2005. Stamp Day. Hungarian Formula 1 Grand Prix. Multicoloured.
4901 50fo. Type **1364** 90 70
4901a 50fo. Hungaroring race track 1·00 85
4902 90fo. Car and chequered flag 1·50 1·20
MS4903 80×60 mm. 500fo.+200fo.
Hungaroring race track 11·50 11·50

1365 St.
Thomas

2005. Holy Crown of Hungary (1st issue). Sheet 90×140 mm containing T **1365** and similar vert designs showing panels from the crown. Multicoloured.
MS4904 80×60 mm. 100fo.×5, Type **1365**; Geza I; Emperor Michael Ducas; Emperor Constantine; Jesus Christ; 500fo. Holy Crown (30×36 mm) 16·00 16·00
See also No. MS4971 and MS5077.

1366 Post Car

2005. Centenary of First Postal Motor Vehicle.
4905 **1366** 50fo. multicoloured 90 70

1367 Recycling Bins

2005. Waste Management.
4906 **1367** 140fo. multicoloured 2·30 1·90

1368 Wrestlers

2005. World Wrestling Championships, Budapest.
4907 **1368** 150fo. multicoloured 2·40 2·00

1369 Woman

2005. Breast Cancer Awareness Campaign.
4908 **1369** 90fo.+50fo. multicoloured 2·30 1·90
No. 4908 is as Type **2342** of USA. The premium was for the benefit of the National Oncology Institute.

1370 Ferenc Farkas

2005. Birth Centenary of Ferenc Farkas (composer).
4909 **1370** 100fo. multicoloured 1·60 1·30

1371 Emblem

2005. World Science Forum, Budapest.
4910 **1371** 120fo. deep green, green and black 2·00 1·70

1372 Star and Three
Wise Men

2005. Christmas (1st issue).
4911 **1372** 50fo. ultramarine and silver 90 70

1373 Candle

2005. Christmas (2nd issue). Multicoloured. Self-adhesive.
4912 50fo. Type **1373** 90 70
4913 50fo. Apple 90 70

4914 50fo. Heart 90 70
4915 50fo. Teddy bear 90 70
Nos. 4912/15 were issued together, se-tenant, forming a composite design.

1374 Pencils as "125"

2005. 125th Anniv of Craft and Design University.
4916 **1374** 90fo. multicoloured 1·50 1·20

1375 Building and Grounds

2005. House of the Future (science museum).
4916a **1375** 100fo. multicoloured 1·80 1·40

1376 Tape Machine and Satellite
Dish

2006. 125th Anniv of News Agency.
4916b **1376** 90fo. multicoloured 1·60 1·30

1377 Maps of Italy on Skis

2006. Winter Olympic Games, Turin.
4917 **1377** 200fo. multicoloured 2·50 2·10

1378 4th-Century
Chapel and Tomb,
Christian Necropolis,
Pecs (Sopiane)

2006. World Heritage Sites. Multicoloured.
4918 52fo. Type **1378** 75 60
4919 90fo. Cliffs and town, Ferto-
Neusiedler Lake (horiz) 1·40 1·10

1379 Boeing 767-200ER (1993)

2006. Aviation. Multicoloured.
4920 120fo. Type **1379** 1·80 1·40
4921 140fo. Lockheed Sirius 8A
(1931) 2·00 1·70

1380 Crucifix

2006. Easter.
4922 **1380** 52fo. multicoloured 75 60

1381 Circle of Stylized Figures and Football

2006. UEFA (Union of European Football Associations) Congress, Budapest.
4923	**1381**	170fo. multicoloured	2·50	2·10

1382 Sandor Legrady

2006. Birth Centenary of Sandor Legrady (artist).
4924	**1382**	75fo. multicoloured	1·10	95

1383

2006. Mrs. Ilona Sasvarine-Paulik (Paralympics table tennis champion) Commemoration.
4925	**1383**	185fo. multicoloured	2·75	2·30

1384 Laslo Detre

2006. Birth Centenary of Laslo Detre (astronomer).
4926	**1384**	185fo. multicoloured	3·25	2·50

1385 Transmitter

2006. Wi-Fi (wireless internet connection).
4927	**1385**	240fo. multicoloured	3·50	3·00

1386 Pink Rose

2006. Greetings Stamps (1st issue). Flowers. Multicoloured.
4928	**1386**	52fo. Type **1386**	75	60
4929		52fo. Cream rose with pink edge	75	60
4930		52fo. Yellow rose	75	60
4931		52fo. Orchid	75	60
4932		52fo. Tulips	75	60
4933		52fo. Gerbera	75	60
4934		52fo. Rose	75	60
4935		52fo. Lily	75	60

See also Nos. 4945/52, 4988/5019 and 5038/72.

1387 Shagya Arab

2006. Hungarian Horses. Multicoloured.
4936		75fo. Type **1387**	1·00	85
4937		90fo. Mezohegyes half-bred	1·30	1·00
4938		140fo. Gidran	2·00	1·70
4939		160fo. Noniusz	2·40	2·00
MS4940	95×70 mm. 200fo.×3, Hucul; Lipizzaner; Kisber half-bred		9·00	9·00

1388 Janos Hunyadi (statue) (Ede Margo)

2006. 550th Anniv of Battle of Belgrade.
4941	**1388**	120fo. multicoloured	1·80	1·40

1389 Ferenc Szisz's Renault Race Car

2006. Youth Welfare. Centenary of Ferenc Szisz's Victory in Inaugural Grand Prix Motor Race.
4942	**1389**	120fo.+50fo. multicoloured	2·50	2·10

1390 Goalkeeper

2006. World Cup Football Championship, Germany.
4943	**1390**	170fo. multicoloured	2·50	2·10

1391 Faces as Flower Petals

2006. Europa. Integration.
4944	**1391**	190fo. multicoloured	3·00	2·40

No. 4944 was issued in sheetlets of four stamps with each stamp rotated at 90 degrees to the previous one, giving a composite design of a flower.

1392 Rings and butterfly

2006. Greetings Stamps (2nd issue). Multicoloured.
4945	**1392**	52fo. Type **1392**	75	60
4946		52fo. Rose and butterfly	75	60
4947		52fo. Dummy	75	60
4948		52fo. Duck	75	60
4949		52fo. Blue booties	75	60
4950		52fo. Pink booties	75	60
4951		90fo. Orange rose	75	60
4952		90fo. Pink flowers	75	60

1393 George Enescu

2006. Composers' 125th Birth Anniversaries. Multicoloured.
4953	**1393**	90fo. Type **1393**	1·30	1·00
4954		90fo. Bela Bartok	1·30	1·00

Stamps of a similar design were issued by Romania.

1394 Base Clef as Swan

2006. MISKOLC International Music Festival.
4955	**1394**	190fo. multicoloured	2·75	2·30

1395 Prudence and Temperance (frescos)

2006. Stamp Day. Multicoloured.
4956	**1395**	52fo. Type **1395**	75	60
4957		52fo. Fortitude and Justice (frescos)	75	60

MS4958	101×71 mm. 400fo.+200fo. Iconostasis, Szentendre Cathedral		8·75	8·75

Nos. 4956/7 were issued together, *se-tenant*, forming a composite design of "The Four Virtues".

1396 *Madonna and Child with the Infant St John* (Esterhazy Madonna) (Raphael)

2006. Centenary of Museum of Art. Multicoloured.
4959	200fo. Type **1396**	3·00	2·50
4960	200fo. *Mary Magdalene* (El Greco)	3·00	2·50
4961	200fo. Equestrian statue (Leonardo da Vinci) (horiz)	3·00	2·50
4962	200fo. *Three Fishing Boats* (Claude Monet) (horiz)	3·00	2·50

1397 Emblem and Falcon

2006. Border Guards.
4963	**1397**	170fo. multicoloured	2·40	2·10

1398 Diving and Synchronised Swimming

2006. European Swimming Championship, Budapest. Multicoloured.
4964	90fo. Type **1398**	1·30	1·10
4965	180fo. Swimmers in open water	2·50	2·20

1399 *Child with Model Aircraft* (Laszlo Feher)

2006. Art. Multicoloured.
4966	120fo. Type **1399**	1·70	1·40
4967	140fo. *Circle Dance* (sculpture) (Istvan Haraszty) (vert)	1·90	1·70
4968	160fo. *Aequilibrium* (tapestry picture) (Zsuzsa Pereli) (vert)	2·20	1·90

1400 Race Car

2006. 20th Anniv of Hungaroring.
4969	**1400**	75fo. multicoloured	1·10	95

1401 Mandrill

2006. 140th Anniv of Budapest Zoological and Botanical Gardens. Sheet 105×67 mm.
MS4970	**1401**	500fo. multicoloured	7·00	7·00

2006. Holy Crown of Hungary (2nd issue). Sheet 141×104 mm containing vert designs as T **1365** showing panels from the crown. Multicoloured.
MS4971	100fo.×7, John; Andrew; Peter; God the Creator; Paul; Philip; Jacob	10·00	10·00

The stamps of **MS**4971 are arranged in the shape of a cross.

1402 Building Facade

2006. 150th Anniv of Consecration of Esztergom Basilica. Sheet 94×69 mm.
MS4972	**1402**	500fo. multicoloured	7·00	7·00

1403 Flag

2006. 50th Anniv of Uprising. Sheet 90×65 mm.
MS4973	**1403**	500fo. multicoloured	7·00	7·00

1404 The Nativity

2006. Christmas.
4974	**1404**	52fo. multicoloured	70	60

1405 Laszlo Papp (boxing gold medallist)

2006. 50th Anniv of Olympic Games, Melbourne. Sheet 100×65 mm.
MS4975	**1405**	500fo. multicoloured	7·00	7·00

1406 Red Cross and Flag

2006. 125th Anniv of Hungarian Red Cross.
4976	**1406**	100fo. multicoloured	1·40	1·20

1407 Laika

2007. 50th Anniv of Launch of First Man-made Satellite.
4977	**1407**	350fo. multicoloured	4·75	4·75

1408 Boy dousing Girl with Scented Water

2007. Easter.
4978	**1408**	62fo. multicoloured	85	70

1409 Couple

2007. Rural Life.
4979	**1409**	62fo. olive and black	85	70
4980	-	95fo. purple and black	1·30	1·10
4981	-	242fo. green and black	3·50	3·00

DESIGNS: 62fo.Type **1409**; 95fo. Woman with fowl; 242fo. Woman cooking over open fire.

1410 Janos Ferencsik (composer)

2007. Anniversaries.

4982	**1410**	107fo. deep lilac, lilac and blue	1·40	1·20
4983	-	135fo. olive, green and black	1·90	1·70

DESIGNS: 107fo.Type **1410** (birth centenary); 135fo. Count Lajos Batthyany (leader of first independent government) (birth bicentenary).

1411 Arms and Building

2007. 140th Anniv of Customs and Finance Guard.

4984	**1411**	180fo. multicoloured	2·40	2·10

1412 Ferenc Molnar (author)

2007. Centenary of The Boys of Paul Street (novel by Ferenc Molnar). Sheet 121×60 mm containing T **1412** and similar vert designs. Multicoloured.

MS4985	160fo. Type **1412**; 160fo.Nemcsek's certificate; 160fo.+30fo. Boy in red shirt fighting; 160fo.+30fo. Boy in green shirt fighting	9·50	9·50

The stamps and margins of **MS**4985 form a composite design, with the two central 160fo.+30fo. stamps forming a design of two boys fighting with sticks.

The premium was for the benefit for Youth Philately.

1413 John Sigismund, Prince of Transylvania

2007. Anniversaries. Multicoloured.

4986	**1413**	210fo. Type **1413** (450th anniv of Diet of Torda)	2·75	2·40
4987	-	230fo. Ferenc Rakoczi II (300th anniv of Diet of Marosvasarhely)	3·25	2·75

1414 Air Balloons

2007. Greetings Stamps (3rd issue). Graduation. Multicoloured.

4988	(62fo.) Belfold Type **1414**	70	60
4989	(62fo.) Belfold Student holding balloon, table of books and air balloon	70	60
4990	(62fo.) Belfold Mortar board, air balloon and student	70	60
4991	(62fo.) Belfold Three students and air balloon	70	60
4992	(62fo.) Belfold Student in basket of air balloon, student holding balloon and two students standing on books	70	60
4993	(62fo.) Belfold Student carrying portfolio	70	60
4994	(62fo.) Belfold Certificate and students standing on books	70	60
4995	(62fo.) Belfold Certificate enlarged and lower part of student's gown	70	60
4996	(62fo.) Belfold Three students on path	70	60
4997	(62fo.) Belfold Table of books, certificate, path and ink well	70	60
4998	(62fo.) Belfold Two students on path	70	60
4999	(62fo.) Belfold Ink well and three books	70	60
5000	(62fo.) Belfold Student holding magnifier facing right	70	60
5001	(62fo.) Belfold Student holding magnifier facing left	70	60
5002	(62fo.) Belfold Certificate enlarged	70	60
5003	(62fo.) Belfold Student carrying portfolio and table of books	70	60
5004	(62fo.) Belfold Table of books, certificate and smaller inkwell	70	60
5005	(62fo.) Belfold Table of books and certificate enlarged	70	60
5006	(62fo.) Belfold Inkwell and student	70	60
5007	(62fo.) Belfold Certificate and student's upper body	70	60
5008	(62fo.) Belfold Sailor suited arm and hand facing right	70	60
5009	(62fo.) Belfold Elbow, hand and elbow facing right	70	60
5010	(62fo.) Belfold Hand and arm facing right	70	60
5011	(62fo.) Belfold Hand on shoulder facing right	70	60
5012	(62fo.) Belfold Hand on shoulder facing left	70	60
5013	(62fo.) Belfold Hand and arm facing left	70	60
5014	(62fo.) Belfold Elbow, hand and elbow facing left	70	60
5015	(62fo.) Belfold Sailor suited arm and hand facing left	70	60
5016	(62fo.) Belfold Quill, ink bottle and book	70	60
5017	(62fo.) Belfold Certificate and mortar board	70	60
5018	(95fo.) Belfold Elsobbsegi Sailor suited arm	1·20	1·00
5019	(95fo.) Belfold Elsobbsegi Rose, certificate and mortar board	1·20	1·00

Nos. 4988/5017 were for use on domestic mail and were initially sold at 62fo.
Nos. 5018/5019 were for use on priority domestic mail and were initially sold at 95fo.

1415 St. Elisabeth tending the Sick

2007. Stamp Day. Saints' Anniversaries Multicoloured.

5021	62fo. Type **1415** (800th birth anniv)	70	60
5022	95fo. St Elizabeth giving alms	1·20	1·00
MS5023	74×60 mm. 500fo.+200fo. St. Emeric at prayer (birth millenary) (40×31 mm)	8·50	8·50

1416 Komondor

2007. Hungarian Dogs. Multicoloured.

5024	62fo. Type **1416**	80	65
5025	150fo. Transylvanian hound	1·90	1·60
5026	180fo. Kuvasz	2·30	1·90
5027	240fo. Pumi	3·00	2·50
MS5028	90×60 mm. 600fo.Vizla	7·25	7·25

1417 Test Card

2007. 50th Anniv of Television Broadcasting.

5029	**1417**	160fo. multicoloured	2·00	1·70

1418 Scouts canoeing

2007. Europa. Centenary of Scouting. Sheet 104×64 mm containing T **1418** and similar square design. Multicoloured.

MS5030	210fo.×4, Type **1418**×2; Scouts and stone commemorating first camp×2	10·50	10·50

The lower stamps and margins of **MS**5030 share a composite background design.

1419 Helmet and Rope

2007. International Cave Rescue Conference, Aggtelek-Josvafo.

5031	**1419**	200fo. multicoloured	2·50	2·10

1420 Building Facade

2007. Centenary of Academy of Music Building.

5032	**1420**	250fo. multicoloured	3·00	2·50

1421 Mystical Betrothal of St Catherine (c 1490)

2007. 50th Anniv of National Art Gallery. Sheet 170×65 mm containing T **1421** and similar multicoloured designs.

MS5033	150fo.×4, Type **1421**; View of Rome (Karoly Marko the elder (1835)); October (Karoly Ferenczy (1903)); Picnic in May (Pal Szinyei Merse (1873)) (50×35 mm)	7·00	7·00

The three vert stamps of **MS**5030 share a composite background design.

1422 Cirfandli Grapes, Pecs Region

2007. Wine Grapes and Regions (8th series). Multicoloured.

5034	95fo. Type **1422**	1·20	1·00
5035	140fo. Ezerfutu grapes, Etyek-Buda	1·70	1·50
5036	260fo. Zenit grapes, Tolna	3·00	2·50

1423 Emblem and Dog

2007. Border Guards.

5037	**1423**	107fo. multicoloured	1·30	1·10

2007. Greetings Stamps (4th issue). Graduation (5038/57). Door Knockers (5058/67). Budapest (5068/5072). As T **1414**. Multicoloured.

5038	(62fo.) Belfold Quill and inkwell	80	65
5039	(62fo.) Belfold Bronze coloured pen with ornate nib	80	65
5040	(62fo.) Belfold Two black pens with gold bands	80	65
5041	(62fo.) Belfold Black pen with gold band and ornate nib	80	65
5042	(62fo.) Belfold Biro facing left	80	65
5043	(62fo.) Belfold Pen top	80	65
5044	(62fo.) Belfold Pen and ink bottle	80	65
5045	(62fo.) Belfold Biro prone	80	65
5046	(62fo.) Belfold Biro facing right	80	65
5048	(62fo.) Belfold Nib and quill pen and feather	80	65
5049	(62fo.) Belfold Black pen and nib	80	65
5050	(62fo.) Belfold Bronze coloured pen with ornate nib prone	80	65
5051	(62fo.) Belfold Nib and quill pen and feather prone facing right	80	65
5052	(62fo.) Belfold Close up of pen top	80	65
5053	(62fo.) Belfold Nib and quill pen and feather prone facing left	80	65
5054	(62fo.) Belfold Ink well, nib and quill	80	65
5055	(62fo.) Belfold Close up of two pens with nibs	80	65
5056	(62fo.) Belfold Top and black pen with gold band	80	65
5057	(62fo.) Belfold Biro in writing position	80	65
5058	(62fo.) Belfold Lion head door knocker on grained door	80	65
5059	(62fo.) Belfold Lion head on peeling turquoise door	80	65
5060	(62fo.) Belfold Bearded man on green streaked door	80	65
5061	(62fo.) Belfold Iron knocker on yellow door	80	65
5062	(62fo.) Belfold Brass lion head on orange brown door	80	65
5063	(62fo.) Belfold Lion head on brown rose door	80	65
5064	(62fo.) Belfold Lion head on blue panelled door	80	65
5065	(62fo.) Belfold Brass door knocker with birds' heads on cream panelled door	80	65
5066	(62fo.) Belfold Horned head with entwined snakes on carved door	80	65
5067	(62fo.) Belfold Filigree door knocker on blue and green streaked door	80	65
5068	(62fo.) Belfold Chain Bridge, Budapest	80	65
5069	(62fo.) Belfold Parliament building, Budapest	80	65
5070	(62fo.) Belfold Millenary Monument, Heroes' Square, Budapest	80	65
5071	(62fo.) Belfold Nagyteteny Castlemuseum, Budapest	80	65
5072	(62fo.) Belfold Fishermen's Bastion, Budapest	80	65

Nos. 5038/5072 were for use on domestic mail and were initially sold at 62fo.

2007. Greetings Stamps (4th issue). My first Stamp. Multicoloured.

MS5072a	Belfold (62fo.)×20, Teething ring×7; Rubber duck×7; Blue booties×3; Pink booties×3	15·00	15·00

1424 Zoltan Kodaly

2007. 125th Birth Anniv of Zoltan Kodaly (composer).

5073	**1424**	200fo. multicoloured	2·40	2·00

1425 Emblem and Athletes

2007. Centenary of University Sports Federation.

5074	**1425**	360fo. multicoloured	4·25	3·50

1426 Flax Flowers

2007. Flowers. Multicoloured. Self-adhesive.

5075	(230f.) Type **1426**	2·75	2·20
5076	(260f.) Anemone	3·00	2·50

No. 5075 was for use on priority mail within Europe and No. 5076 for use on priority mail outside Europe.

2007. Holy Crown of Hungary (3rd issue). Sheet 90×75 mm containing vert designs as T **1365** showing panels from the crown. Multicoloured.

MS5077	Size 20×26 mm. 300fo.×3, Saint Cosmus; Saint George; Archangel Michael	10·50	10·50

1427 Janos Selye

2007. Second World Conference on Stress, Budapest. Birth Centenary of Janos Selye (researcher into stress and its effects).

5078	**1427**	400fo. multicoloured	4·75	4·00

2007. Greetings Stamps. Angels. Multicoloured.

5079a	Belföld (62fo.) As Type **1339**	75	65
5079b	Belföld (62fo.) As Type **1339**	75	65
5079c	Belföld (62fo.) As Type **1339**	75	65
5079d	Belföld (62fo.) As Type **1339**	75	65

5080a	Belföld (62fo.) As No. 4824	75	65
5080b	Belföld (62fo.) As No. 4824	75	65
5080c	Belföld (62fo.) As No. 4824	75	65
5080d	Belföld (62fo.) As No. 4824	75	65
5080e	Belföld (62fo.) As No. 4824	75	65
5081a	Belföld (62fo.) As No. 4825	75	65
5081b	Belföld (62fo.) As No. 4825	75	65
5081c	Belföld (62fo.) As No. 4825	75	65
5082a	Belföld (62fo.) As No. 4826	75	65
5082b	Belföld (62fo.) As No. 4826	75	65
5083a	Belföld (62fo.) As No. 4827	75	65
5083b	Belföld (62fo.) As No. 4827	75	65
5083c	Belföld (62fo.) As No. 4827	75	65
5083d	Belföld (62fo.) As No. 4827	75	65
5084a	Belföld (62fo.) As No. 4828	75	65
5084b	Belföld (62fo.) As No. 4828	75	65

Nos. 5079/84 have been left for 'Greetings Stamps' (As Nos. 4823/8), issued on 27 September 2007, not yet received.

1428 Emblem

2007. World Science Forum, Budapest.
5085 **1428** 230fo. blue and green 2·75 2·20

1429 Flowers and Houses

2007. Christmas. Multicoloured.
5086 62f. Type **1429** 80 65
5087 62f. Shepherds and the Nativity 80 65
5088 62f. The Magi 80 65

Nos. 5086/8 were issued together, se-tenant, forming a composite design of The Birth of Jesus (carpet by Erzsebet Szekeres).

2008. Corporate Greeting Stamps. No value expressed. As T **1352.** Multicoloured.
5089 (70fo.) Map and compass (As Type **1352**) 95 80
5090 (70fo.) Compass at left and map (As No. 4881) 95 80

Type **1430** is vacant.
Nos. 5089/90 were inscribed 'Belfold' and were for use on domestic mail. They were originally on sale for 70fo.

1431 Eggs

2008. Easter.
5091 **1431** 70f. multicoloured 95 80

1432 King Matthias I and Visegrad Palace

2008. Stamp Day. 550th Anniv of King Matthias I's Reign.
5092 70f. Type **1432** 95 80
5093 100f. King Matthias on horse-back, castle and knight 1·30 1·10
MS5094 91×75 mm. 600f.+200f. King Matthias and Queen Beatrix (40×30 mm) 10·50 10·50

1433 Car

2008. Youth Stamps. Transport. Sheet 140×60 mm containing T **1433** and similar vert designs. Multicoloured.
MS5095 150f. Type **1433**; 150f. Ship; 150f.+30f. Train; 150f.+30f. Aircraft 8·75 8·75

The stamps and margins of **MS**5095 form a composite design.

1434 Karoly Knezich

2008. Birth Bicentenary of Karoly Knezich (general).
5096 **1434** 380f. multicoloured 5·00 4·25

1435 Dancer

2008. Hungarian Minorities (1st issue). Roma.
5097 **1435** 260f. multicoloured 3·50 3·00

See also No. 5017.

1436 Water Polo

2008. Olympic Games, Beijing. Designs showing stylized athletes. Multicoloured.
5098 70f. Type **1436** 95 80
5099 100f. Judo 1·30 1·10
5100 170f. Fencing 2·30 1·90

1437 Letter

2008. Europa. The Letter. Sheet 105×65 mm containing T **1437** and similar square design. Multicoloured.
MS5101 100f.×2, Type **1437**×2; 230f.×2, Pen nib×2 8·75 8·75

1438 Hungarian Giant Rabbit

2008. Traditional Farm Breeds. Multicoloured.
5102 145f. Type **1438** 1·90 1·60
5103 150f. Hungarian goat 2·00 1·70
5104 170f. Cikta sheep 2·30 1·90
5105 310f. Hungarian donkey 4·00 3·25
MS5106 90×65 mm. 60f. Water buffalo 8·00 8·00

1439 Dancer

2008. Hungarian Minorities (2nd issue). German.
5107 **1439** 275f. multicolured 3·50 3·00

1440 Crossbill, Lemon Lily and Istvan Chernel (scientist and ornithologist)

2008. Orseg National Park.
5108 **1440** 220f. multicoloured 3·00 2·50

1441 Flags

2008. European Football Championship, Austria and Switzerland.
5109 **1441** 250f. multicloured 3·25 2·75

1442 Cellars and Vineyards

2008. World Heritage Site. Tokaj Wine Region.
5110 **1442** 290f. multicoloured 4·00 3·25

1443 Hand holding Beach Furniture

2008. Tenth Anniv of Holiday Vouchers.
5111 **1443** 70f. multicoloured 95 80

1444 Present Giving (Lili Pota)

2008. Civic Responsibilities. Winning Entry in Children's Drawing Competition.
5112 **1444** 100f.+50f. multicoloured 2·00 1·70

1445 Barber

2008. Youth Stamps. PhilaVillage. Multicoloured.
5113 100fo. Type **1445** 1·30 1·10
5114 100fo. Baker (horiz) 1·30 1·10

2008. Youth Stamps. PhilaVillage. As T **1445.** Multicoloured.
5115 100fo. Photographer 1·30 1·10
5116 100fo. Optician 1·30 1·10

1446 Chapter Initial Ornamented Letter

2008. 650th Anniv of Illuminated Chronicle (attributed to Nicholas, son of Hertul).
5117 **1446** 400fo. multicoloured 5·25 4·50

2008. Youth Stamps. PhilaVillage. As T **1445.** Multicoloured.
5118 100fo. Waiter (vert) 1·30 1·10
5119 100fo. Traffic policeman (horiz) 1·30 1·10

1447 Giraffes and Hippopotamus

2008. 50th Anniv of Debrecen and Veszprem Zoos. Sheet 110×60 mm containing T **1447** and similar horiz design. Multicoloured.
MS5120 260fo.×2, Type **1447**; Camel, lion, zebra and rhinoceros 7·00 7·00

The stamps and margins of **MS**5120 form a composite design.

2008. Holy Crown of Hungary (4th issue). Sheet 90×75 mm containing T **1365** showing panels from the crown. Multicoloured.
MS5121 Size 20×26 mm. 300fo.×3, Saint Damian; Saint Demeter; Archangel Gabriel 12·00 12·00

1448 Orchid

2008. Greetings Stamps. Flowers. Multicoloured.
5122 (70fo.) Type **1448** 95 80
5123 (70fo.) Rose 95 80
5124 (70fo.) Lily 95 80
5125 (70fo.) Tulips 95 80
5126 (70fo.) Gerbera 95 80

Nos. 5122/6 were inscribed 'Belfold' and were for use on domestic mail. They were originally on sale for 70f.

2008. Youth Stamps. PhilaVillage. As T **1445.** Multicoloured.
5127 100fo. School teacher 1·30 1·10
5128 100fo. Museum guide 1·30 1·10

1449 Miklos Zrinyi

2008. 500th Birth Anniv of Miklos Zrinyi (nationalist leader).
5129 **1449** 190f. multicoloured 2·50 2·10

1450 Archangel Gabriel

2008. 150th Birth Anniv of Gyorgy Zala (sculptor).
5130 **1450** 200f. multicoloured 2·75 2·20

1451 New Synagogue, Szeged

2008. Synagogues. Multicoloured.
5131 200f. Type **1451** 2·75 2·20
5132 250f. Jewish Theological Seminary, Budapest 3·25 2·75

1452 Rabbit

2008. Greetings Stamps. Multicoloured.
5133 (70fo.) Type **1452** 95 80
5134 (70fo.) Lion 95 80
5135 (70fo.) Giraffe 95 80
5136 (70fo.) Cat 95 80
5137 (70fo.) Bear 95 80

Nos. 5133/7 were inscribed 'Belfold' and were for use on domestic mail. They were originally on sale for 70f.

2008. Youth Stamps. PhilaVillage. As T **1445.** Multicoloured.
5138 100fo. Station master 1·30 1·10
5139 100fo. Pool life guard 1·30 1·10

1453 The Annunciation

2008. Birth Centenary of Gyorgy Konecsni (artist and stamp designer).
5140 70fo. red 95 80
5141 100fo. blue 1·30 1·10

DESIGNS: 70fo. Type **1453**; 100f. Adoration of the Magi.

1454 Pukas Ferenc

2008. 50th (2002) Anniv of Olympic Games, Helsinki. Sheet 120×70 mm. Phosphor markings.

| MS5142 | **1454** | 60fo. multicoloured | 8·00 | 8·00 |

1455 Ede Teller

2008. Birth Centenary of Ede Teller (physicist).

| 5143 | **1455** | 250fo. multicoloured | 3·25 | 2·75 |

2008. Youth Stamps. PhilaVillage. As T **1445**. Multicoloured.

| 5144 | 100fo. Balloon seller (vert) | 1·30 | 1·10 |
| 5145 | 100fo. Postman (horiz) | 1·30 | 1·10 |

1456 Arms and Building Facade

2008. Bicentenary of Ludovika Academy.

| 5146 | **1456** | 300fo. multicoloured | 4·00 | 3·25 |

1457 Shepherd's Cross (Zoltan Reti)

2009. Easter.

| 5147 | **1457** | 75fo. multicoloured | 1·00 | 50 |

1458 Crocus

2009. Endangered Flora. Multicoloured. (a) Ordinary gum. Inscribed 'BELFOLD'.

| 5148 | (75fo.) Type **1458** | 1·00 | 50 |

(ii) Inscribed 'BELFOLD ELSOBBSEGI'.

| 5149 | (100fo.) Squill | 1·50 | 75 |

(b) Self-adhesive.

| 5150 | (70fo.) As Type **1458** | 1·00 | 50 |

Nos. 5148 and 5150 were for use on domestic mail, No. 5149 was for use on domestic prioirty mail.

1459 St. Francis

2009. 800th Anniv of Franciscan Order.

| 5151 | **1459** | 100fo. multicoloured | 1·50 | 75 |

1460 Bleriot XI and Cliffs at Dover

2009. Centenary of First Flight across English Channel. Multicoloured.

| 5152 | 105fo. Type **1460** | 1·50 | 75 |

| 5153 | 105fo. Louis Bleriot at air display in Hungary | 1·50 | 75 |

Nos. 5152/3 were printed, *se-tenant*, in horizontal strips of two stamps surrounding a central label, the whole forming a composite design.

1461 Reactor

2009. 50th Anniv of Research Reactor, Budapest. Sheet 108×70 mm.

| MS5154 | **1461** | 1000fo. multicoloured | 9·50 | 9·50 |

1462 Ursus maritimus (polar Bear)

2009. Preserve Polar Regions and Glaciers. Multicoloured.

5155	75fo. Type **1462**	1·00	50
5156	130fo. Ovibos moschatus (muskox)	1·30	65
5157	145fo. Uncia uncia (snow leopard)	1·30	65
5158	275fo. Aptenodytes patagonicus (king penguins)	5·75	2·75

MS5159 110×75 mm. 260fo.×2, Polar bear and melting ice; Alopex lagopus (arctic fox) | 5·50 | 5·50

The stamps and margins of **MS**5159 form a composite design.

1463 Mk 48 Series Diesel Locomotive, Zsuzsi Forest Railway

2009. Railways. Multicoloured.

5160	75fo. Type **1463**	1·00	50
5161	100fo. C 50 series diesel locomotive, Hortobagy Fish Pond Railway	1·50	75
5162	125fo. Type MD 40 diesel locomotive, Nagyborzsony Forest Railway	1·60	80
5163	275fo. Morgo steam locomotive, Kiralyret Forest Railway	2·50	1·30

1464 Three Little Pigs

2009. Youth Stamps. 150th Birth Anniv of Elek Benedek (writer). Sheet 140×60 mm containing T **1464** and similar vert designs showing author and characters from his books. Multicoloured.

MS5164 100fo. Type **1464**; 100fo. Diamond Penny; 100fo.+50fo. Elek Benedek; 100fo.+50fo. Puss in Boots | 5·50 | 5·50

The stamps and margins of **MS**5164 form a composite design.

1465 'HAYDN' as Piano Keys

2009. Death Bicentenary of Joseph Haydn (composer).

| 5165 | **1466** | 300fo. multicoloured | 3·50 | 1·75 |

1466 Ferenc Kazinczy

2009. 250th Birth Anniv of Ferenc Kazinczy (writer, language reformist and member of Academy of Science). Sheet 90×65 mm.

| MS5166 | **1466** | 600fo. multicoloured | 6·50 | 6·50 |

1467 Miklos Radnoti

2009. Birth Centenary of Miklos Radnoti (poet).

| 5167 | **1467** | 280fo. multicoloured | 2·75 | 1·40 |

1468 Galileo Galilei

2009. Europa. Astronomy. Sheet 105×65 mm containing T **1468** and similar square design. Multicoloured.

MS5168 100fo.×2, Type **1468**×2; 230fo.×2, Jupiter and moons×2 | 6·50 | 6·50

1469 John Calvin

2009. 500th Birth Anniv of John Calvin (reformer).

| 5169 | **1469** | 200fo. multicoloured | 2·00 | 1·00 |

1470 Donat Banki

2009. 150th Birth Anniv of Donat Banki (engineer and professor).

| 5170 | **1470** | 300fo. multicoloured | 2·75 | 1·40 |

1471 Romanesque Monument and Carvings

2009. Stamp Day. Visegrad Millennary. Multicoloured.

| 5171 | 75fo. Type **1471** | 1·00 | 50 |
| 5172 | 100fo. Gothic fountain and tower | 1·00 | 50 |

MS5173 90×60 mm. 600fo.+200fo. Renaissance courtyard and fountain | 7·50 | 7·50

1472 Virgin and Child (11th–12th century)

2009. 250th Anniv of Finding Ivory Statue of Virgin and Child at Máriabesnyo.

| 5174 | **1472** | 200fo. multicoloured | 2·00 | 1·00 |

1473 St. Stephen and Cathedral, Pecs

2009. Bishopric of Pecs Millenary.

| 5175 | **1473** | 100fo. multicoloured | 1·00 | 50 |

1474 Hand in Hand (Zsuzsanna Flora Szabo)

2009. Winning Design in Children's Drawing Competition. Charity Stamp.

| 5176 | **1474** | 75fo.+50fo. multicoloured | 1·00 | 1·00 |

The premium was for the benefit of Krizis Alap (Crisis foundation).

1475

2009. Greetings Stamps. Pecs. Multicoloured.

5177	Belfold Type **1475**	1·00	50
5178	Belfold Calvary Hill	1·00	50
5179	Belfold City Hall	1·00	50
5180	Belfold Cathedral (detail)	1·00	50
5181	Belfold Red building with portico	1·00	50
5182	Belfold Academy of Science	1·00	50
5183	Belfold Synagogue	1·00	50
5184	Belfold Cathedral	1·00	50
5185	Belfold Lion's head door knocker and door handle	1·00	50
5186	Belfold Klimo Library	1·00	50
5187	Belfold National Theatre	1·00	50
5188	Belfold Zsolnay Fountain (base)	1·00	50
5189	Belfold Decorated roof	1·00	50
5190	Belfold Pavement cafe	1·00	50
5191	Belfold Early Christian necropolis	1·00	50
5192	Belfold Decorated gable	1·00	50
5193	Belfold Pasha Gaz Kasim's Mosque	1·00	50
5194	Belfold Barbican	1·00	50
5195	Belfold Jakovali Hassan's Mosque	1·00	50
5196	Belfold Zsolnay Fountain (detail)	1·00	50

Nos. 5177/96 were inscribed 'Belfold' and were for use on domestic mail. They were originally on sale for 70fo.

1476 '20'

2009. 20th Anniv of Opening of Border between Austria and Hungary.

| 5197 | **1476** | 210fo. multicoloured | 2·20 | 1·10 |

A stamp of a similar design was issued by Austria and Germany.

1477 Rainbow (Jozsef Egry)

2009. Art.

| 5198 | **1477** | 275fo. multicoloured | 2·60 | 1·30 |

1478 Our Lady of the Way (Masa Feszty)

2009. Christmas.

| 5199 | 75fo. multicoloured | 1·00 | 50 |
| 5200 | 100fo. ultramarine and orange-yellow (horiz) | 1·00 | 50 |

DESIGNS: 75fo. Type **1478**; 100fo. Symbols of Christmas.

1479 'BRAILLE' '200'

2009. Birth Bicentenary of Louis Braille (inventor of Braille writing for the blind).

5201	**1479**	200fo. black and chestnut	2·00	1·00

1480 Decorated Canteen

2009. Hungary–Japan Exchange Year. Multicoloured.

5202	260fo. Type **1480**	2·50	1·30
5203	260fo. Mount Fuji	2·50	1·30
5204	260fo. Plumware pot	2·50	1·30
5205	260fo. Macho embroidery	2·50	1·30
5206	260fo. Elizabeth Bridge	2·50	1·30
5207	260fo. Crane and bamboo embroidery	2·50	1·30

Stamps of a similar design were issued by Japan.

1481 Crystal Ware

2009. The Arts. Crystal.

5208	**1481**	300fo. multicoloured	2·75	1·40

1482 Emblem

2009. World Science Forum, Budapest.

5209	**1482**	100fo. multicoloured	1·00	50

1483 Levi Phila

2009. Philaclub. T **1483** and similar horiz designs showing characters from Philaclub (stamp collecting website for young people). Multicoloured.

5210	20fo. Type **1483**	30	15
5211	20fo. Spotty Mouse	30	15
5212	20fo. Bogi Phila	30	15

1484 Jakovali Hassan Mosque

2010. Pecs, European Capital Culture, 2010. Multicoloured.

5213	Belfold Type **1484**	1·00	50
5214	Belfold Calvary Hill	1·00	50
5215	Belfold National Theatre (exterior)	1·00	50
5216	Belfold MTA Headquarters	1·00	50
5217	Belfold Barbican	1·00	50
5218	Belfold Synagogue	1·00	50
5219	Belfold St Francis of Assisi (statue)	1·00	50
5220	Belfold National Theatre (interior)	1·00	50
5221	Belfold Janus Pannonius (statue)	1·00	50
5222	Belfold County Hall	1·00	50
5223	Belfold Postal Palace	1·00	50
5224	Belfold Basilica (left)	1·00	50
5225	Belfold Basilica (right)	1·00	50
5226	Belfold Holy Trinity pinnacle	1·00	50
5227	Belfold Pasha Gaz Kasim's Mosque	1·00	50
5228	Belfold Egyptian Gate	1·00	50
5229	Belfold Early Christian necropolis	1·00	50
5230	Belfold Zsolnay Fountain	1·00	50
5231	Belfold Klimo Library	1·00	50
5232	Belfold Tivadar Kosztka Csontváry (statue)	1·00	50
5233	Belfold Reformed Church	1·00	50

5234	Belfold Ruins, Tettye	1·00	50
5235	Belfold Evangelical Church	1·00	50
5236	Belfold City Hall	1·00	50
5237	Belfold Modern sculpture	1·00	50

Nos. 5224/5 were printed, *se-tenant* in horizontal pairs, the pair forming a composite design of the Basilica. Nos. 5177/96 were inscribed 'Belfold' and were for use on domestic mail. They were originally on sale for 70fo.

1485 Skier

2010. Winter Olympic Games, Vancouver

5238	**1485**	260fo. multicoloured	2·50	1·30

1486 Izidor Kner

2010. 150th Birth Anniv of Izidor Kner (typographer, bookbinder and publisher)

5239	**1486**	295fo. multicoloured	3·00	1·50

1487 Eötvös Loránd University (375th anniv)

2010. Tourism. Multicoloured.

5240	295fo. Type **1487**	3·00	1·50
5241	400fo. Elisabeth Tower, János Hill (centenary)	4·25	2·00

1488 Rabbit and Eggs

2010. Easter

5242	**1488**	80fo. multicoloured	1·00	50

1489 Red Cross

2010. Hungarian Red Cross

5243	**1489**	105fo.+55fo. multicoloured	2·10	1·00

1490 Early and Modern Guards

2010. 250th Anniv of Hungarian Guard Regiment

5244	**1490**	320fo. multicoloured	3·00	1·50

1491 Church of St Ursula and Church of the Virgin Mary

2010. Stamp Day. Alps-Adriatic Stamp Exhibition, Sopron. Multicoloured.

5245	80fo. Type **1491**	1·00	50
5246	105fo. Column of Virgin Mary and Gates of Faith	1·00	50
MS5247	90×62 mm. 500fo.+200fo. Column of Holy Trinity	6·50	6·50

The premium was for the promotion of Philately.

1492 Ferenc Erkel

2010. Birth Bicentenary of Ferenc Erkel (composer, conductor and pianist)

MS5248	**1492**	500fo. multicoloured	4·50	4·50

1493 Deed of Papal Legate Cardinal Gentilis de Monteflorum (first on Hungarian watermarked paper)

2010. 700th Anniv of Use of Paper in Hungary

5249	**1493**	140fo. multicoloured	1·20	60

1494 Cover of *Chroninca az magyaroknak dolgairol*

2010. 500th Birth Anniv of Gaspar Heltai (writer, translator and printer)

5250	**1494**	240fo. multicoloured	2·20	1·10

1495 Gömböc

2010. Expo 2010, Shanghai. Multicoloured.

5251		100fo. Type **1495**	1·00	50

It is reported that there are a further 29 varieties of this stamp showing the Gömböc as it moves.

They are available in sheets of 30 stamps or in booklets with the stamps, perforated on one side only, arranged so that by flicking the edge of the booklet the Gömböc appears to move.

1496 *In Paradise* (Zoltán Réti) (scene 2)

2010. 150th Anniv of *The Tragedy of Man* (play by Imre Mádach). Multicoloured.

MS5252	105fo. Type **1496**; 105fo. *In London* (János Kass) (scene 11); 105fo.+50fo. *In Rome* (Mihály Zichy) (scene 6); 105fo.+50fo. *In Prague* (Zoltán Réti) (scene 8)	1·90	1·90

1497 *Spermophilus citellus*

2010. Fauna and Flora. International Year of Biodiversity. Multicoloured.

5253	80fo. Type **1497**	1·00	50
5254	110fo. *Phyllomorpha laciniata*	1·00	50
5255	215fo *Parus caeruleus*	1·90	85
5256	350fo. *Vipera ursinii rakosiensis*	3·25	1·60
MS5257	90×70 mm. 500fo. *Iris aphylla*	4·50	4·50

1498 Vactor

2010. Europa. Children's Books. *Vackor* (by István Kormos, illustrated by Károly Reich). Multicoloured.

MS5258	150fo.×4, Type **1498**×2; Lying on his back with bird perched on his foot×2	7·50	7·50

1499 Globe as Football

2010. World Cup Football Championships, South Africa

5259	**1499**	325fo. multicoloured	3·00	1·50

(1500)

2010. 20th Anniv of Jozef Antall's Election as Prime Minister. No. **MS**4171 overprinted as T **1500**. Sheet 70×50 mm

MS5260	200fo. on 19fo. multicoloured	1·00	1·00

1501 Frederic Chopin

2010. Birth Bicentenary of Frederic François Chopin (composer)

5261	**1501**	240fo. multicoloured	2·20	1·10

1502 Miklos Barabas

2010. Birth Bicentenary of Miklos Barabas (painter)

5262	**1502**	365fo. multicoloured	3·50	1·75

1503 Athletes

2010. Budapest 2010, World Triathlon Championship

5263	**1503**	280fo. multicoloured	1·00	50

1504 Swimmers

2010. 30th European Swimming League (LEN) Championships, Budapest

5264	**1504**	300fo. multicoloured	1·90	95

1505 Formula 1 and Circuit

2010. 25th Formula 1 Hungarian Grand Prix, Hungaroring Racetrack, Mogyoród

5265	**1505**	230fo. multicoloured	3·25	1·60

1506 Altar, Nagykőrös Synagogue

2010. Synagogues in Hungary. Multicoloured.

5266	110fo. Type **1506**	1·50	75
5267	175fo. Altar, New Synagogue, Szolnok	2·00	1·00

1507 Gymnast
and Seven
Pictograms of
Disciplines

2010. 125th Anniv of Hungarian Gymnastic Federation
| 5268 | **1507** | 140fo. multicoloured | 1·75 | 90 |

1508 Virgin and
Child (detail of
Three Kings,
altarpiece of
Prohászka Ottokár
Ursulite Public
Education Centre
Chapel, Győr by
Erzsébet Udvardi)

2010. Christmas. Multicoloured.
| 5269 | 80fo. Type **1508** | 1·00 | 50 |
| 5270 | 105fo. Angels (detail) (horiz) | 1·50 | 75 |

1509 Termeh Embroidery,
Yazd, Iran

2010. Embroidery. Multicoloured.
| 5271 | 80fo. Type **1509** | 1·00 | 50 |
| 5272 | 240fo. Jazygian embroidery, Hungary | 2·20 | 1·00 |

1523 Holy Crown (detail)

2011. New Fundamental Law. Sheet 105×75 mm
| MS25.4.135295 | **1523** 2011fo. multicoloured | 20·00 | 20·00 |

2011. Greetings Stamps . Multicoloured.
| 5296 | (-) As Type **1392** | 80 | 65 |
| 5297 | (-) As No. **4946** | 80 | 65 |

1535 Bauble and Present

2011. Greetings Stamps. Christmas Baubles . Multicoloured.
| 5319 | (-) Type **1535** | 80 | 65 |
| 5320 | (-) Golden bauble and bell | 80 | 65 |

1536 Nagykarácsony
Church and Nativity

2011. Christmas. 75th Anniv of Nagykarácsony Church. Multicoloured. . Multicoloured.
| 5321 | 90fo. Type **1536** | 1·00 | 1·25 |
| 5322 | 115fo. Roman Catholic church, Vörs and Nativity | 1·80 | 1·50 |

Nos. 5079/84 have been left for 'Greetings Stamps' (As Nos. 4823/8), issued on 27 September 2007, not yet received.

1537 Emblem

2011. World Science Forum, Budapest
| 5323 | **1537** | 270fo. multicoloured | 3·25 | 2·75 |

1538 Saint Martin and
Scenes from his Life

2011. Saint Martin of Tours Commemoration
| 5324 | **1538** | 380fo. multicoloured | 4·50 | 3·50 |

1541 Morning Sunshine

2012. 150th Birth Anniv of Károly Ferenczy (artist)
| 5327 | **1541** | 420fo. multicoloured | |

1542 Weeping Icon of
Theotokos, Máriapócs,
Pantocrator by Ádám Kisleghi
Nagy, Papal Bull establishing
Greek Catholic Church of
Hungary and Iconostasis, Greek
Catholic church, Hajdúdorog

2012. Centenary of the Greek Catholic Diocese of Hajdúdorog
| 5328 | **1542** | 380fo. multicoloured | 4·50 | 3·50 |

1543 Mary
holding
Christ's Body

2012. Easter
| 5329 | **1543** | 105fo. multicoloured | 1·40 | 1·20 |

1544 Puskás Tivadar
Technical School of
Telecommunications

2012. Tourism. Centenaries. Multicoloured.
| 5330 | 180fo. Type **1544** | 2·00 | 1·70 |
| 5331 | 270fo. Hungarian Royal University of Debreczen | 3·25 | 2·75 |

1545 Király Baths,
Budapest

2012. Tourism. Spa Hotels. Multicoloured.
| 5332 | 235fo. Type **1545** | 3·00 | 2·50 |
| 5333 | 260fo. Rudas Baths, Budapest | 3·25 | 2·75 |

1546 Zoltán Várkonyi
(actor and director)

2012. Birth Centenaries. Multicoloured.
| 5334 | 395fo. Type **1546** | 4·60 | 3·60 |
| 5335 | 425fo. Katalin Karády (actor) | 4·75 | 3·75 |

1547 Masat-1

2012. First Hungarian Satellite - Masat -1
| 5336 | **1547** | 310fo. multicoloured | 3·50 | 3·00 |

1548 Rear of Titanic

2012. Centenary of Sinking of Titanic. Multicoloured.
| MS5337 | 800fo.×2, Type **1548**; Front | 15·00 | 15·00 |

1549 World Scout
Jamboree Emblem

2012. Centenary of Hungarian Scout Association. Multicoloured.
| MS5338 | 105fo.×2, Type **1549**; Scout praying and scout salute;105fo.+50fo.×2, Scouts pitching tent; Scouts practising first aid and scout badge | 3·50 | 3·00 |

1550 Aquila heliacal
(Imperial Eagle)

2012. Fauna. Raptors. Multicoloured.
5339	80fo. Type **1550**	1·00	1·25
5340	140fo. Haliaeetus albicilla (White-tailed Sea Eagle)	1·90	1·60
5341	180fo Falco vespertinus (Red-footed Falcon)	2·00	1·70
5342	345fo. Falco cherrug (Saker Falcon)	4·00	3·50

1551 'HU' filled with
Produce

2012. Europa. Visit Hungary. Multicoloured.
| MS5343 | 235fo.×4, Type **1551**×2; 'HU' filled with symbols of culture×2 | 12·00 | 12·00 |

1552 Pándy Sour Cherry

2012. Cultivated Flora. Fruit Trees. Multicoloured.
| 5344 | 185c. Type **1552** | 2·10 | 1·70 |
| 5345 | 230c. Kécske rose apricot | 3·00 | 2·50 |

1553 Raoul Wallenberg

2012. Birth Centenary of Raoul Wallenberg (saviour of thousands of Budapest Jews during WWII)
| 5346 | **1553** | 340fo. multicoloured | 3·75 | 3·25 |

1554
'BELFÖLD'

2012. Greetings Stamps
| 5347 | **1554** | (-) myrtle-green and emerald | 95 | 80 |

1555 Generations (Richárd
Horváth)

2012. Solidarity between Generations
| 5348 | **1555** | 200fo. multicoloured | 2·25 | 1·80 |

1556 Decorated Pots

2012. Cultural Heritage. Filovci Pottery Village. Multicoloured.
| MS5349 | 260fo.×2, Type **1556**; Black jug | 6·75 | 6·75 |

1557 Football

2012. European Football Championships, Poland and Ukraine
| 5350 | **1557** | 270fo. multicoloured | 2·75 | |

1558 Battle Scene
(Chronicon Pictum)

2012. 700th Anniv of Battle of Rozgony
| 5351 | **1558** | 370fo. multicoloured | 4·25 | 3·50 |

1559 Buzzard

2012. Fauna. Buteo buteo (Buzzard). Sheet 90×70 mm
| MS5352 | **1559** 500fo. multicoloured | 7·00 | 7·00 |

1560 Swimming

2012. Olympic Games, London. Multicoloured.
| 5353 | 315fo. Type **1560** | 3·50 | 3·00 |
| 5354 | 360fo. Kayaking | 4·25 | 3·50 |

1561 István Örkény
(writer and chemist)

2012. Birth Centenaries. Multicoloured.
| MS5355 | 105fo.×4, Type **1561**; György (George) Solti (conductor and pianist); Géza Ottlik (writer and literary translator); János Szentágothai (anatomist) | 7·00 | 7·00 |

1562 Embroidery

2012. Stamp Day. Kalocsa. Multicoloured.

5356	80fo. Type **1562**	1·00	1·25
5357	130fo. Paprika	1·90	1·60

MS5357a 92×68 mm. 600fo.+200fo.
Exhibits from Kalocsa Archiepiscopal
Treasury   8·00   8·00

1563 Baja
Synagogue

2012. Synagogues in Hungary. Multicoloured.

5358	300fo. Type **1563**	3·50	3·00
5359	400fo. Kiskunhalas Synagogue	4·60	3·60

1564 Lips as Leaves on
Language Tree

2012. World Congress of Finno-Ugric Peoples, Hungary

5360	**1564**	290fo. multicoloured	3·50	3·00

1567 Statues

2012. 110th Anniv of Hungarian Parliament Building. Multicoloured.

MS5363 200fo.×8, Type **1567**; Coats
of Arms; Speaker's Chair; Alcoves;
Knight on horseback (bas relief);
House of Representatives; National
Coat of Arms with Holy Crown;
House of Magnates   17·00   17·00

1568 *Madonna with Angels*
(Erzsébet Udvardi)

2012. Christmas. Multicoloured.

5364	**1568**	130fo. multicoloured	1·90	1·60

1569 Aerial View of Tihany Abbey (image scaled to 53% of original size)

2012. Benedictine Abbey of Tihany. Sheet 90×70 mm
MS5365 **1569** 600fo. multicoloured   7·50

1570 Mikluš Prison

2013. Košice - European Capital of Culture, 2013. Sheet
90×65 mm
MS5366 **1570** 600fo. multicoloured   7·50   7·50

1571 Miklós Ujvárosi and
Cornflowers

2013. Birth Centenary of Miklós Ujvárosi (botanist)

5367	**1571**	395fo. multicoloured	4·60	3·60

1572 Model Ts and József
Galamb

2013. Centenary of Mass Production of Ford Model T
Car under Direction of József Galamb (designer and
constructor)

5368	**1572**	145fo. multicoloured	1·60	

1573 Wilhelm Richard
Wagner

2013. Birth Bicentenaries of Composers. Multicoloured.

5369	165fo. Type **1537**	2·00	1·70
5370	325fo. Giuseppe Fortunino Francesco Verdi	3·75	3·25

1574 Water
Tower,
Margaret Island

2013. Tourism. 75th Anniv of Budapest's District XIII

5371	**1574**	195fo. multicoloured	2·10	1·70

1575 Easter Egg

2013. Easter. Eggs painted by Csilla Szendrő Bérczi.
Multicoloured.

5372	85fo. Type **1575**	1·00	1·25
5373	85fo. Red spotted and black spotted segments	1·00	1·25
5374	85fo. Scrolled segments	1·00	1·25
5375	85fo. Red spotted and black spotted segments (different)	1·00	1·25
5376	85fo. Scrolled segments (different)	1·00	1·25
5377	85fo. Four eggs as Nos. 5372/6	1·00	1·25
5378	85fo. Four eggs as Nos. 5382/5	1·00	1·25
5379	85fo. Red egg with four segments and flower-like centre	1·00	1·25
5380	85fo. Egg with central diagonal band and leaf-like decoration	1·00	1·25
5381	85fo. Cream spotted segments with red and black bands	1·00	1·25
5382	85fo. Egg with central band with diamond shapes and leaf-like decoration	1·00	1·25
5383	85fo. Cream egg with narrow bands and black and red scrolls	1·00	1·25
5384	110fo. With band inscribed 'halleluja'	1·40	1·20
5385	110fo. With band inscribed 'Krisztus'	1·40	1·20

1577 Széchenyi Thermal
Baths

2013. Tourism. Spa Hotels. Multicoloured.

5387	145fo. Type **1577**	1·90	1·60
5388	165fo. Széchenyi Thermal Baths, interior	2·00	1·70

1578 Competitors

2013. European Judo Championships

5389	**1578**	360fo. multicoloured	4·25	3·50

1579 *Mustela erminea*
(Stoat)

2013. Fauna. Multicoloured.

5390	110fo. Type **1579**	1·80	1·50
5391	140fo. *Sorex minutus* (Pygmy Shrew)	1·90	1·60
5392	230fo. *Lynx lynx*	3·00	2·50
5393	390fo. *Myotis myotis* (Greater Mouse-eared Bat)	4·50	3·50

MS5394 90×65 mm. 600fo. *Erinaceus
roumanicus* (Northern white-breasted Hedgehog)   8·00   8·00

1580 Bishops
Fountain (Jenő Bory)
and Saint Astrik of
Pannonhalma

2013. Stamp Day. HUNFILA2013 – Székesfehérvár
International Stamp Exhibition. Multicoloured.

5395	80fo. Type **1580**	1·00	1·25
5396	130fo. City Hall and Justice (statue) (horiz)	1·90	1·60

MS5397 90×70 mm. 600fo.+200fo.
Cistercian Church of Our Lady   8·00   8·00

1581 Szeged Cathedral

2013. Tourism (2nd issue)

5398	85fo. sepia, deep brown and black	1·00	1·25
5399	325fo. pale green, olive and black	3·50	3·00

Designs: 85fo. Type **1581**; 325fo. Springhouse at Orfű

1582 1914 Csonka Parcel
Delivery Van

2013. Europa. Postal Transport. Multicoloured.
MS5400 235fo.×4, Type **1582**×2; Ford
Transit Connect×2   12·00   12·00

Nos. 5401/2 and Type **1583** are left for Museums, not
yet received.

1584 Krupp V43 (Szili) Electric
Locomotive

2013. Locomotives. Multicoloured.

5403	195fo. Type **1584**	2·25	1·80
5404	445fo. NOHAB M61 diesel locomotive	6·00	6·00

1585 Azeri Peacock (pillow
cover), Transdanubia

2013. Textiles. Cross-stitch Embroidery. Multicoloured.
MS5405 300fo.×2, Type **1585**; Stylized
horse (blanket), Caucasus   10·00   10·00

1586 Poet writing

2012. Birth Centenary of Sándor Weöres (poet, translator
and founder of Béla Pásztor Award for young poets).
Multicoloured.
MS5406 115fo.×2, Type **1586**; Frog
playing flute; 115fo.+50fo.×2, Bobita
Castle   12·00   12·00

1587 Competitors

2013. World Fencing Championships, Budapest.
Centenary of International Fencing Federation

5407	**1587**	300fo. multicoloured	3·25	2·75

1588 Association
Emblem

2013. Centenary of Hungarian Ski Association

5408	**1588**	500fo. multicoloured	7·00	7·00

1589 Competitors

2013. World Wrestling Championships, Papp László
Sports Arena, Budapest

5409	**1589**	360fo. multicoloured	4·25	3·50

1590 Géza Gárdonyi

2013. 150th Birth Anniv of Géza Gárdonyi (writer)

5410	**1590**	425fo. multicoloured	4·75	3·75

1591 Saint Ladilaus (King
of Hungary)

2013. Saints and The Blessed. Multicoloured.
MS5411 600fo.×3, Type **1591**; Saint
Emeric (Prince Emeric); Saint
Stephen (King Stephen I)   15·00   15·00

MS5412 600fo.×3, As Type **1591**;
Saint Emeric (Prince Emeric); Saint
Stephen (King Stephen I)   15·00   15·00

1592 Main Staircase

2013. 110th Anniv of Hungarian Parliament Building (2nd
series). Multicoloured.
MS5413 250fo.×8, Type **1592**; Royal
sceptre; Dome, upper right; Dome,
upper left; Dome, lower right; Dome,
lower left; Dome Hall containing
display of Holy Crown and other
royal accoutrements; King and pages
(statues)   17·00   17·00

1593 *The Source of Art* (fresco),
Academy of Music, Budapest

2013. 150th Birth Anniv of Körösfői Kriesch Aladár (artist)
5414 **1593** 315fo. multicoloured 3·50 3·00

1594 Water and
Summit Emblem

2013. Budapest Water Summit. Sheet 90×90 mm
MS5415 **1594** 365fo. multicoloured 4·50 4·50

1595 *Woman
Gathering a Bundle of
Hay on a Collective
Farm*

2013. Birth Centenary of Endre Ernő Friedmann (Robert
Capa) (journalist and photographer)
5416 **1595** 310fo. black, yellow-brown
and chrome-yellow 3·50 3·00
Nos. 5417/20 and Type **1596** are left for Greetings, not
yet received.

1597 Decorated
Tree

2013. Christmas. Iced Gingerbread. Multicoloured.
5421 85fo. Type **1597** 3·50 3·00
5422 110fo. Shooting star (horiz) 1·40 1·20
5423 140fo. Angel 1·90 1·60

1598 Club Emblem

2013. 125th Anniv of MTK Sports Club
5424 **1598** 400fo. multicoloured 4·60 3·60

1599 Horse

2014. Chinese New Year. Year of the Horse. Multicoloured.
MS5425 110fo.×4, Type **1599**; Horse
galloping, facing left; Horse from
rear; Horse grazing 6·75 6·75

1600 Emblem

2014. 25th Anniv of Hungarian Maltese Charity Service
5426 **1600** 300fo. vermilion, grey
and black 3·50 3·00

No. 5427 and Type **1601** are left for Saints and the
Blessed, not yet received.

1602 Sempla,
Giraffe

2014. Young Animals from Budapest Zoo and Botanical
Gardens. Multicoloured.
MS5428 115fo.×12, Type **1602**; Sid,
Two-toed Sloth; Jakab, Barbary
Sheep; Moira, Orang-utan; Bangita,
Blackbuck; Maszat, Prairie Dog; Maz-
sola, Ground Cuscus; Rozi, Meerkat;
Gizmo, Ring-tailed Lemur; Skipper,
African Penguin; Kiran, Asiatic Lion;
Willo, Wombat 15·00 15·00
Nos. 5429/30 and Type **1603** are left for Birth Cente-
naries, not yet received.

1604 *Pilate condemns
Jesus to Death*

2014. Easter. Paintings by Erzsébet Udvardi.
Multicoloured.
5431 90fo. Type **1604** 1·00 1·25
5432 90fo. Jesus carries his cross 1·00 1·25
5433 90fo. Jesus falls with the cross
for the first time 1·00 1·25
5434 90fo. Jesus meets his mother 1·00 1·25
5435 90fo. Simon of Cyrene helps
Jesus carry the cross 1·00 1·25
5436 90fo. Veronica offers her veil
to Jesus 1·00 1·25
5437 90fo. Jesus falls with the cross
for the second time 1·00 1·25
5438 90fo. Jesus comforts the women
of Jerusalem 1·00 1·25
5439 90fo. Jesus falls under the
weight of the cross for the
third time 1·00 1·25
5440 90fo. Jesus is stripped of his
garments 1·00 1·25
5441 90fo. Jesus is nailed to the cross 1·00 1·25
5442 90fo. Cream spotted segments
with red and black bands 1·00 1·25
5443 90fo. Jesus is taken down from
the cross and laid on his
mother's lap 1·00 1·25
5444 90fo. Jesus is laid in the tomb 1·00 1·25
5445 90fo. The angel announces the
resurrection of Jesus 1·00 1·25
5446 110fo. *Recognition* (30×40 mm.) 1·80 1·50

1605 Wenckheim
Palace,
Szabadkígyós

2014. Birth Bicentenary of Miklós Ybl (architect). Sheet
90×65 mm
MS5447 **1605** 1000fo. multicoloured 15·00 15·00

EXPRESS LETTER STAMPS

E36

1916. Inscr "MAGYAR KIR. POSTA".
E245 **E36** 2f. olive and red 60 60

1916. Optd **KOZTARSASAG**.
E301 2f. olive and red 20 45

1919. Inscr "MAGYAR POSTA".
E349 2f. olive and red 60 60

IMPERIAL JOURNAL STAMPS

J1 J2

1868. Imperf.
J3 **J2** 1k. blue £14000 £9500
J52 **J1** 1k. blue 1·10 55
J53 **J2** 2k. brown 4·25 6·00
No. J3 has the arms at the foot as in Type J **2** but the
corner designs differ.

NEWSPAPER STAMPS

N2 St.
Stephen's
Crown and
Posthorn

1871. Posthorn turned to left. Imperf.
N8 **N2** 1k. red on white £100 47·00

1872. As Type **N2** but with posthorn turned to right.
Imperf.
N14 1k. red 20·00 4·75

N4

1874. Imperf.
N64 **N4** 1k. orange 1·30 45

N9

1900. Imperf.
N136 **N9** (2f.) orange 20 20
N401 **N9** (10f.) blue 40 40
N402 **N9** (20f.) purple 40 40

OFFICIAL STAMPS

O44

1921
O428 **O44** 10f. black and purple 65 40
O429 **O44** 20f. black and brown 65 40
O430 **O44** 60f. black and grey 65 40
O431 **O44** 100f. black and red 65 40
O432 **O44** 250f. black and blue 65 40
O433 **O44** 350f. black and blue 65 40
O434 **O44** 500f. black and brown 65 40
O435 **O44** 1000f. black and brown 65 40

1922. Nos. O429/33 surch (No. O439 optd **KORONA**
only).
O436 15k. on 20f. black and brown 50 40
O437 25k. on 60f. black and grey 50 40
O438 150k. on 100f. black and pink 1·30 65
O439 (350)k. on 350f. black and blue 1·50 65
O440 2000k. on 250f. black and blue 2·50 2·50

1922
O441 5k. brown 40 40
O442 10k. brown 40 40
O443 15k. grey 40 40
O444 25k. orange 40 40
O445 50k. red and brown 50 40
O446 100k. red and bistre 50 40
O447 150k. red and green 25 25
O448 300k. red 25 25
O449 350k. red and violet 25 25
O450a 500k. red and orange 2·10 65
O451 600k. red and bistre 1·30 1·30
O452 1000k. red and blue 2·10 1·30
O453 3000k. red and violet 3·25 65
O454 5000k. red and blue 3·25 1·30

PARCEL POST STAMPS

1954. No. 979 surch.
P1398 **153** 1fo.70 on 1fo.40 green 1·90 65
P1399 **153** 2fo. on 1fo.40 green 2·50 65
P1400 **153** 3fo. on 1fo.40 green 1·90 1·90

POSTAGE DUE STAMPS

D9

1903. Inscr "MAGYAR KIR. POSTA". Figures in centre in
black.
D170 **D9** 1f. green 65 35
D171 **D9** 2f. green 65 35
D172 **D9** 5f. green 60 35
D173 **D9** 6f. green 1·70 70
D174 **D9** 10f. green 1·70 70
D175 **D9** 12f. green 1·20 35
D176 **D9** 20f. green 60 35
D177 **D9** 50f. green 1·20 35
D91 **D9** 100f. green 1·10 1·60

1915. Surch **20**.
D188 **D 9** 20 on 100f. black & grn 1·20 1·70

1915. As Type **D9**, but figures in red.
D190 **D9** 1f. green 10 10
D191 **D9** 2f. green 10 10
D192 **D9** 5f. green 70 25
D193 **D9** 6f. green 10 10
D194 **D9** 10f. green 10 10
D195 **D9** 12f. green 10 10
D196 **D9** 15f. green 10 10
D197 **D9** 20f. green 10 10
D198 **D9** 30f. green 10 10
D349 **D9** 40f. green 25 25
D350 **D9** 50f. green 25 25
D351 **D9** 120f. green 25 25
D352 **D9** 200f. green 25 25
D430 **D9** 2k. green 70 95
D431 **D9** 5k. green 50 50
D432 **D9** 50k. green 50 50

1919. Overprinted **KOZTARSASAG**.
D325 2f. red and green 25 70
D326 3f. red and green 25 70
D327 10f. red and green 25 70
D328 20f. red and green 25 70
D329 40f. red and green 25 70
D324 50f. black and green 5·50 5·00
D330 50f. red and green 25 70

1919. As Type **D9** but inscr "MAGYAR POSTA" and optd
with T **37** and **MAGYAR TANACS KOZTARSASAG**.
Figures in black.
D369 2f. green 1·40 1·40
D370 3f. green 1·40 1·40
D371 10f. green 9·50 9·50
D372 20f. green 1·40 1·40
D373 40f. green 1·40 1·40
D374 50f. green 1·40 1·40

1919. As Type **D9**, but inscr "MAGYAR POSTA". Figures in
Black.
D375 2f. green 30 45
D376 3f. green 30 45
D377 20f. green 30 45
D378 40f. green 30 45
D379 50f. green 30 45

1921. Surch **PORTO** and value. Inscr "MAGYAR KIR
POSTA".
D433 **18** 2½k. on 10f. purple 40 40
D434 **18** 3k. on 15f. purple 40 40
D437 **18** 6k. on 1½k. purple 40 40
D435 **18** 9k. on 40f. purple 40 40
D438 **18** 10k. on 2½k. green 25 25
D436 **18** 12k. on 60f. green 50 40
D439 **18** 15k. on 1½k. purple 25 25
D440 **18** 20k. on 2½k. green 25 25
D441 **18** 25k. on 1½k. purple 25 25
D442 **18** 30k. on 1½k. purple 25 25
D443 **18** 40k. on 2½k. green 25 25
D428 **18** 50k. on 1½k. purple 25 25
D445 **18** 100f. on 15f. purple 25 25
D445 **18** 100k. on 4½k. purple 25 25
D446 **18** 200k. on 4½k. purple 25 25
D447 **18** 300k. on 4½k. purple 40 25
D429 **18** 500f. on 15f. purple 25 25
D448 **18** 500k. on 2k. blue 40 25
D449 **18** 500k. on 3k. brown 40 25
D450 **18** 1000k. on 2k. blue 40 25
D451 **18** 1000k. on 3k. brown 50 40
D452 **18** 2000k. on 2k. blue 65 25
D453 **18** 2000k. on 3k. brown 1·10 40
D454 **18** 5000k. on 5k. brown 1·50 75

D61

1926
D479 **D61** 1f. red 25 15
D480 **D61** 2f. red 30 25
D481 **D61** 3f. red 75 75
D482 **D61** 4f. red 25 25
D483 **D61** 5f. red 5·00 5·00
D486 **D61** 16f. red 50 40
D487 **D61** 32f. red 1·30 65
D489 **D61** 50f. red 3·75 50

D490	D61	80f. red	5·00	1·50
D509	D61	8f. red	50	25
D510	D61	10f. red	65	25
D512	D61	20f. red	1·30	25
D513	D61	40f. red	1·80	40

1927. Nos. 434/36b surch **PORTO** and value.

D491	49	1f. on 500k. light green and green	50	50
D492	49	2f. on 1000k. brown and bistre	50	50
D493	49	3f. on 2000k. blue and deep blue	50	65
D494	49	5f. on 5000k. mauve and purple	1·50	1·90
D495	49	10f. on 10000k. purple and red	1·30	1·50

1931. Surch.

D529	D61	4f. on 5 red	1·00	65
D534	D61	10f. on 16f. red	2·50	2·10
D531	D61	10f. on 80f. red	1·30	65
D532	D61	12f. on 50f. red	1·90	1·00
D533	D61	20f. on 32f. red	1·90	1·30

D84

1934

D569	D84	2f. blue	25	10
D570	D84	4f. blue	25	10
D571	D84	6f. blue	25	10
D572	D84	8f. blue	25	15
D573	D84	10f. blue	30	25
D574	D84	12f. blue	40	40
D575	D84	16f. blue	40	40
D576	D84	20f. blue	40	50
D577	D84	40f. blue	1·10	75
D578	D84	80f. blue	1·90	1·00

D115

1941

D684	D115	2f. brown	10	10
D685	D115	3f. brown	10	10
D686	D115	4f. brown	10	10
D687	D115	6f. brown	10	10
D688	D115	8f. brown	10	10
D689	D115	10f. brown	10	10
D690	D115	12f. brown	15	10
D691	D115	16f. brown	20	10
D692	D115	18f. brown	40	25
D693	D115	20f. brown	20	10
D694	D115	24f. brown	25	15
D695	D115	30f. brown	40	25
D696	D115	36f. brown	40	25
D697	D115	40f. brown	25	20
D698	D115	50f. brown	25	20
D699	D115	60f. brown	40	25

1945. Surch **1945** and value. Blue surface-tinted paper.

D825	10f. on 2f. brown	15	15
D826	10f. on 3f. brown	15	15
D827	20f. on 4f. brown	15	15
D828	20f. on 6f. brown	12·00	12·00
D829	20f. on 8f. brown	15	15
D830	40f. on 12f. brown	15	15
D831	40f. on 16f. brown	15	15
D832	40f. on 18f. brown	15	15
D833	60f. on 24f. brown	15	15
D834	80f. on 30f. brown	15	15
D835	90f. on 36f. brown	15	15
D836	1p. on 10f. brown	15	15
D837	1p. on 40f. brown	15	15
D838	2p. on 20f. brown	15	15
D839	2p. on 50f. brown	15	15
D840	2p. on 60f. brown	15	15
D841	10p. on 3f. brown	25	25
D842	12p. on 8f. brown	40	40
D843	20p. on 24f. brown	65	65

D154 Numeral

1946

D984	D154	4f. red and brown	65	15
D985	D154	10f. red and brown	1·50	15
D986	D154	20f. red and brown	65	15
D987	D154	30f. red and brown	65	15
D988	D154	40f. red and brown	1·00	15
D989	D154	50f. red and brown	2·50	75
D990	D154	60f. red and brown	1·50	25
D991	D154	1fo.20 red and brown	2·50	65
D992	D154	2fo. red and brown	3·75	75

1950

D1114	4fi. purple	15	15
D1115	10fi. purple	15	15
D1116	20fi. purple	1·30	15
D1117	30fi. purple	1·30	15
D1118	40fi. purple	65	15
D1119	50fi. purple	1·30	15
D1120	60fi. purple	1·10	15
D1121	1fo.20 purple	1·60	15
D1122	2fo. purple	3·25	25

D201

1951. Fiscal stamps surch with Arms. **MAGYAR POSTA PORTO** and value.

D1157	D201	8fi. brown	25	25
D1158	D201	10fi. brown	40	40
D1159	D201	12fi. brown	65	65

D215

1951

D1210	D215	4fi. brown	15	15
D1211	D215	6fi. brown	15	15
D1212	D215	8fi. brown	15	15
D1213	D215	10fi. brown	15	15
D1214	D215	14fi. brown	15	15
D1215	D215	20fi. brown	15	15
D1216	D215	30fi. brown	15	15
D1217	D215	40fi. brown	15	15
D1218	D215	50fi. brown	30	15
D1219	D215	60fi. brown	40	15
D1220	D215	1fo.20 brown	50	15
D1221	D215	2fo. brown	90	40

D240

1953. 50th Anniv of First Hungarian Postage Due Stamps.

D1305	D240	4fi. black and green	15	15
D1306	D240	6fi. black and green	15	15
D1307	D240	8fi. black and green	15	15
D1308	D240	10fi. black and green	15	15
D1309	D240	12fi. black and green	15	15
D1310	D240	14fi. black and green	15	15
D1311	D240	16fi. black and green	15	15
D1312	D240	20fi. black and green	15	15
D1313	D240	24fi. black and green	15	15
D1314	D240	30fi. black and green	15	15
D1315	D240	36fi. black and green	15	15
D1316	D240	40fi. black and green	20	15
D1317	D240	50fi. black and green	25	15
D1318	D240	60fi. black and green	40	15
D1319	D240	70fi. black and green	40	15
D1320	D240	80fi. black and green	40	15
D1321	D240	1fo.20 black & green	75	15
D1322	D240	2fo. black and green	1·30	15

D282

1958. Forint values are larger (31×22 mm).

D1498	D282	4fi. black and red	15	15
D1499	D282	6fi. black and red	15	15
D1500	D282	8fi. black and red	15	15
D1501	D282	10fi. black and red	15	15
D1502	D282	12fi. black and red	15	15
D1503	D282	14fi. black and red	15	15
D1504	D282	16fi. black and red	15	15
D1505	D282	20fi. black and red	15	15
D1506	D282	24fi. black and red	15	15
D1507	D282	30fi. black and red	15	15
D1508	D282	36fi. black and red	15	15
D1509	D282	40fi. black and red	15	15
D1510	D282	50fi. black and red	15	15
D1511	D282	60fi. black and red	15	15
D1512	D282	70fi. black and red	15	15
D1513	D282	80fi. black and red	15	15
D1514	-	1fo. brown	15	15
D1515	-	1fo.20 brown	15	15
D1516	-	2fo. brown	25	20
D1517	-	4fo. brown	65	25

D587 Money-order Cancelling Machine

1973. Postal Operations.

D2847	D587	20fi. brown and red	10	10
D2848	-	40fi. blue and red	10	10
D2849	-	80fi. violet and red	25	10
D2850	-	1fo. green and red	35	10
D2851	-	1fo.20 green and red	45	10
D2852	-	2fo. violet and red	80	10
D2853	-	3fo. blue and red	1·00	10
D2854	-	4fo. brown and red	1·00	10
D2855	-	8fo. purple and red	1·50	10
D2856	-	10fo. green and red	1·70	10

DESIGNS—As Type D 587: 40fi. Parcel scales, self-service post office; 80fi. Automatic parcels-registration machine; 1fo. Data-recording machine; 28×22 mm: 1fo. 20, Ilyushin Il-18 mail plane and van; 2fo. Diesel mail train; 3fo. Postman on motor cycle; 4fo. Postman at mailboxes; 8fo. Toshiba automatic sorting machine; 10f. Postman on motor cycle (different).

D944 Foot Messenger

1987. Postal History. Multicoloured.

D3810	1fo. Type D 944	15	10
D3811	4fo. Post rider	50	10
D3812	6fo. Horse-drawn mail coach	75	10
D3813	8fo. Railway mail carriage	1·00	10
D3814	10fo. Mail van	1·30	10
D3815	20fo. Mail plane	2·50	25

SAVINGS BANK STAMP

B17

1916

B199	B17	10f. purple	60	60

SZEGED

The following issues were made by the Hungarian National Government led by Admiral Horthy, which was set up in Szeged in 1919, then under French occupation, and which later replaced the Communist regime established by Bela Kun.

1919. Stamps of Hungary optd **MAGYAR NEMZETI KORMANY Szeged, 1919.** or surch. (a) **War Charity stamps of 1916.**

1	20	10f. (+2f.) red	30	30
2	-	15f. (+2f.) violet	55	55
3	22	40f. (+2f.) lake	1·10	1·60

(b) Harvesters and Parliament Types.

4	18	2f. brown	20	20
5	18	3f. red	20	20
6	18	5f. green	30	30
7	18	6f. blue	8·00	8·00
8	18	15f. violet	30	30
9	18	20f. brown (No. 307)	16·00	27·00
10	18	25f. blue (No. 309)	30	30
11	19	50f. purple	4·25	5·50
12	19	75f. blue	30	30
13	19	80f. green	3·25	3·25
14	19	1k. lake	30	30
15	19	2k. brown	30	30
16	19	3k. grey and violet	30	30
17	19	5k. brown	32·00	38·00
18	19	10k. lilac and brown	32·00	38·00

(c) Nos. 5 and 14 further surch.

19	18	45 on 3f. red	20	20
20	19	10 on 1k. lake	2·20	2·20

(d) Karl and Zita stamps.

21	27	10f. red	30	30
22	27	20f. brown	20	20
23	27	25f. blue	5·50	11·00
24	28	40f. olive	2·20	2·20

The following (Nos. 25/39) are also optd KOZTARSASAG. (e) War Charity stamp.

25	22	40f. (+2f.) lake	3·25	4·25

(f) Harvesters and Parliament Types.

26	18	3f. red	7·50	9·75
27	18	4f. slate	2·20	2·20
28	18	5f. green	4·25	5·50
29	18	6f. blue	3·25	3·25
30	18	10f. red	4·75	4·75
31	18	20f. brown	16·00	22·00
32	18	20 (f) on 2f. bistre	30	30
33	18	40f. olive	30	30
34	19	3k. grey and violet	16·00	22·00

(g) Karl and Zita stamps.

35	27	10f. red	5·50	5·50
36	27	15f. violet	1·60	1·60
37	27	20f. brown	22·00	22·00
38	27	25f. blue	5·50	5·50
39	28	50f. purple	20	30

EXPRESS LETTER STAMPS

1919. No. E245 optd as above.

E41	E18	2f. olive and red	4·25	4·25

NEWSPAPER STAMP

1919. No. N136 optd MAGYAR NEMZETI KORMANY Szeged, 1919.

N40	N9	(2f.) orange	30	30

POSTAGE DUE STAMPS

D42	D9	2f. red and green	65	65
D43	D9	6f. red and green	2·20	2·20
D44	D9	10f. red and green	65	65
D45	D9	12f. red and green	85	85
D46	D9	20f. red and green	65	65
D47	D9	30f. red and green	2·20	2·20

(b) No. E41 surch PORTO and new value.

D48	E18	50f. on 2f. olive and red	65	65
D49	E18	100f. on 2f. olive & red	65	65

Pt. 1

HYDERABAD

A state in India. Now uses Indian stamps.

12 pies = 1 anna; 16 annas = 1 rupee.

1

1869

1	1	1a. green	24·00	9·00

2

1870

2	2	½a. brown	4·00	4·25
3	2	2a. green	85·00	60·00

3

1871

3	3	½a. red	3·75	10
14b	3	1a. grey	2·00	15
15	3	2a. green	4·25	15
16b	3	3a. brown	3·75	1·50
17b	3	4a. grey-green	5·50	3·25
18	3	8a. brown	3·75	4·25
19	3	12a. blue-green	5·00	11·00

(4)

1898. Surch with T **4.**

20	½a. on ½a. on ½a. brown	50	85

5

1900

21	5	¼a. blue	7·00	4·50

6

1905

22	6	¼a. blue	5·50	60
32d	6	¼a.	1·75	10
33	6	¼a. purple	3·25	10
23b	6	½a. red	5·00	25
34	6	½a. blue	4·00	10
26	6	1a. red	8·50	10
27cb	6	2a. lilac	2·25	10
28b	6	3a. orange	3·75	1·25

29c	6	4a. green	2·00	40
30c	6	8a. purple	2·00	1·75
31c	6	12a. green	11·00	6·50

8 Symbol   **9**

1915

35	8	½a. green	2·00	10
58	8	½a. red	3·00	75
36	8	1a. red	4·00	10
37	9	1r. yellow	11·00	12·00

(10)

1930. Surch as T **10.**

38	6	4p. on ¼a. grey	£120	30·00
39	6	4p. on ¼a. purple	1·75	10
40	8	8p. on ½a. green	1·50	10

12 Symbols   **13** The Char Minar

1931

60	12	2p. brown	3·00	3·25
41	12	4p. black	30	10
59	12	6p. red	12·00	10·00
42	12	8p. green	1·25	10
43	13	1a. brown	1·25	10
44	-	2a. violet	3·75	10
45	-	4a. blue	3·25	70
46	-	8a. orange	11·00	4·50
47	-	12a. red	13·00	12·00
48	-	1r. yellow	7·50	50

DESIGNS—HORIZ (32½×21 mm): 2a. High Court of Justice; 4a. Osman Sagar Reservoir; 12a. Bidar College. VERT: 8a. Entrance to Ajanta Caves; 1r. Victory Tower, Daulatabad.

In No. 59 "POSTAGE" is at foot.

19 Unani General Hospital

1937. Inscr "H.E.H. THE NIZAM'S SILVER JUBILEE".

49	19	4p. slate and violet	1·25	3·00
50	-	8p. slate and brown	1·25	3·00
51	-	1a. slate and yellow	1·75	2·00
52	-	2a. slate and green	2·50	5·50

DESIGNS: 8p. Osmania General Hospital; 1a. Osmania University; 2a. Osmania Jubilee Hall.

23 Family Reunion

1945. Victory Commemoration.

53	23	1a. blue	10	10

24 Town Hall

1947. Reformed Legislature.

54	24	1a. black	1·75	1·90

25 Power House, Hyderabad

1947. Inscr as in T **25.**

55	25	1a.4p. green	1·40	2·75
56	-	3a. blue	2·50	6·50
57	-	4a. brown	24·00	24·00

DESIGNS—HORIZ: 3a. Kaktyai Arch, Warangal Fort; 6a. Golkunda Fort.

OFFICIAL STAMPS

(O1)

1873. Optd with Type **O1.**

O2a	2	½a. brown	—	£950
O1	1	1a. green	£150	45·00
O3a		2a. olive		£325

1873. Optd with Type **O1.**

O9a	3	½a. brown	17·00	5·00
O11	3	1a. brown	£350	£140
O12a	3	1a. drab	6·00	4·50
O19	3	1a. black	£130	50
O13a	3	2a. green	13·00	10·00
O20e	3	3a. brown	14·00	7·00
O15a	3	4a. grey	48·00	42·00
O20f	3	4a. green	£600	12·00
O16b	3	8a. brown	90·00	70·00
O17a	3	12a. blue	£110	£160
O20h	3	12a. green		£120

1909. Optd as Type **O1**, or similar smaller opt.

O37e	6	¼a. grey	4·75	40
O38	6	¼a. lilac	4·75	10
O21a	6	½a. red	£225	40
O39d	6	½a. green	6·50	10
O40	6	½a. green	3·50	10
O54	8	½a. red	6·00	8·00
O31	8	1a. red	3·00	15
O41e	8	1a. red	6·00	10
O32b	6	2a. lilac	4·25	1·25
O33b	6	3a. orange	55·00	7·50
O34d	6	4a. green	7·00	15
O35	6	8a. purple	12·00	30
O36	6	12a. green	55·00	5·00

1930. Official stamps surch as T **10.**

O42	6	4p. on ¼a. grey	£750	24·00
O43	6	4p. on ¼a. lilac	4·00	10
O44	8	8p. on ½a. green	3·50	10
O45	8	8p. on ½a. green	45·00	70·00

1934. Optd as Type **O1** but smaller.

O55	12	2p. brown	7·00	12·00
O46	12	4p. black	5·50	10
O56	12	6p. red	11·00	28·00
O47	12	8p. green	2·50	10
O48	13	1a. brown	5·00	10
O49	-	2a. violet (No. 44)	12·00	10
O50	-	4a. blue (No. 45)	8·50	25
O51	-	8a. orange (No. 46)	24·00	70
O52	-	12a. red (No. 47)	28·00	1·75
O53	-	1r. yellow (No. 48)	32·00	3·25

Pt. 11

ICELAND

An island lying S.E. of Greenland. An independent state formerly under the Danish sovereign, now a republic.

1873. 96 skilling = 1 riksdaler.
1876. 100 aurar (singular: eyrir) = 1 krona.

1

1873

1	1	2s. blue	£1100	£2250
5	1	3s. grey	£500	£1500
2	1	4s. red	£180	£1000
3	1	8s. brown	£325	£1100
7	1	16s. yellow	£130	£600

1876

42		3a. yellow	7·75	22·00
27		4a. grey and red	18·00	20·00
13		5a. blue	£350	£700
28		5a. green	3·75	2·75
29a		6a. grey	17·00	18·00
30		10a. red	13·00	2·75
31		16a. brown	70·00	£100
18a		20a. mauve	33·00	£900
32a		20a. blue	44·00	36·00
33		25a. blue and brown	28·00	31·00
19		40a. green	£100	£225
23b		40a. mauve	55·00	44·00
24		50a. red and blue	90·00	£100
25		100a. purple and brown	85·00	£130

(6)

1897. Surch as T **6** with figure **3** under word.

38		3 on 5a. green	£650	£550

1897. Surch as T **6.**

40		3 on 5a. green	£850	£550

10 King Christian IX

1902

43	10	3a. orange	6·00	3·75
44	10	4a. red and grey	3·75	1·70
45	10	5a. green	42·00	1·10
46	10	6a. brown	22·00	10·50
47	10	10a. red	6·00	10
48	10	16a. brown	8·25	11·00
49	10	20a. blue	3·25	4·50
50	10	25a. green and brown	3·75	6·50
51	10	40a. mauve	4·50	6·50
52	10	50a. black and grey	6·00	25·00
53	10	1k. brown and blue	7·25	10·00
54	10	2k. blue and brown	28·00	70·00
55	10	5k. grey and brown	£140	£225

1902. Optd **I GILDI '02–'03.**

67	1	3a. yellow	1·30	2·40
68	1	4a. grey and red	39·00	55·00
69	1	5a. green	1·30	10·00
71	1	6a. grey	1·10	10
73	1	10a. red	1·30	12·00
74	1	16a. brown	25·00	39·00
75	1	20a. blue	1·10	12·00
77	1	25a. blue and brown	1·10	18·00
79	1	40a. mauve	1·10	39·00
80	1	50a. red and blue	3·25	65·00
65	1	100a. purple and brown	55·00	75·00

12 Kings Christian IX and Frederik VIII

1907

81	12	1e. red and green	1·70	1·10
82	12	3a. brown	3·75	1·70
83	12	4a. red and grey	2·00	1·70
84	12	5a. green	90·00	1·10
85	12	6a. grey	85·00	3·25
114	12	10a. red	3·25	1·10
87	12	15a. green and red	6·50	1·10
88	12	16a. brown	8·75	36·00
89	12	20a. blue	8·25	5·50
90	12	25a. green and brown	6·50	11·00
91	12	40a. red	6·50	13·00
92	12	50a. red and grey	6·50	13·00
93	12	1k. brown and blue	25·00	60·00
94	12	2k. green and brown	33·00	70·00
95	12	5k. blue and brown	£190	£325

13 Jon Sigurdsson

1911. Birth Centenary of Jon Sigurdsson (historian and Althing member).

96	13	1e. green	2·20	1·70
97	13	3a. brown	4·50	13·00
98	13	4a. blue	1·70	1·70
99	13	6a. grey	13·00	22·00
100	13	15a. violet	13·00	1·70
101	13	25a. orange	24·00	44·00

1912. As T **13**, but portrait of King Frederik VIII and "JON SIGURDSSON" omitted.

102		5a. green	31·00	11·00
103		10a. red	31·00	11·00
104		20a. blue	44·00	17·00
105		50a. red	8·75	33·00
106		1k. yellow	28·00	70·00
107		2k. red	28·00	70·00
108		5k. brown	£140	£200

15 King Christian X

1920

116	15	1e. red and green	1·10	1·00
117	15	3a. brown	8·25	17·00
184	15	4a. red and grey	2·20	2·20

119	15	5a. green	2·20	2·00
185	15	6a. grey	2·00	4·50
186	15	7a. green	75	1·70
121	15	8a. brown	8·25	2·20
122	15	10a. red	2·40	11·00
133	15	10a. green	3·75	1·80
187	15	10a. brown	£140	1·30
123	15	15a. violet	39·00	1·30
124	15	20a. blue	2·75	18·00
134	15	20a. brown	60·00	1·70
125	15	25a. green and brown	17·00	1·80
135	15	25a. red	17·00	55·00
189	15	30a. green and red	33·00	6·50
127	15	40a. red	42·00	3·25
136	15	40a. blue	75·00	13·00
128	15	50a. red and grey	£200	11·00
191	15	1k. brown and blue	50·00	7·25
130	15	2k. green and brown	£275	33·00
131	15	5k. blue and brown	65·00	17·00
193	15	10k. black and green	£325	£200

1921. Various types surch.

137	10	5a. on 16a. brown	3·75	28·00
138	12	5a. on 16a. brown	2·20	8·25
139	10	10a. on 5a. green	8·25	3·25
140	10	20a. on 25a. green & brn	7·75	8·25
141	12	20a. on 25a. green & brn	5·00	8·25
142	10	20a. on 40a. mauve	8·75	19·00
143	12	20a. on 40a. red	13·00	22·00
144	10	30a. on 50a. grey	33·00	36·00
145	10	50a. on 5k. grey & brown	65·00	50·00
146	15	1k. on 40a. blue	£190	33·00
147	13	2k. on 25a. orange	£170	£130
148	-	10k. on 50a. red (No. 105)	£350	£425
149	-	10k. on 1k. yell (No. 106)	£475	£600
150	10	10k. on 2k. black & brn	90·00	30·00
150a	12	10k. on 5k. black & brn	£450	£550

22 Landing Mails at Vik

1925

151	22	7a. green	55·00	7·25
152	-	10a. brown and blue	55·00	1·10
153	-	20a. red	55·00	1·10
154	-	35a. blue	90·00	8·75
155	22	50a. brown and green	90·00	1·70

DESIGNS: 10a., 35a. Reykjavik and Esjaberg (mountain); 20a. National Museum, Reykjavik.

1928. Air. Optd with airplane.

156	15	10a. red	1·10	11·00
157	-	50a. purple and grey	65·00	£100

24 Discovery of Iceland   **25** Gyrfalcon

1930. Parliament Millenary Celebration.

158	-	3a. violet and lilac (postage)	3·25	8·75
159	24	5a. blue and grey	3·25	8·75
160	-	7a. green and dp green	2·75	8·75
161	-	10a. purple and mauve	8·75	17·00
162	-	15a. dp blue & blue	2·20	10·00
163	-	20a. red and pink	39·00	75·00
164	-	25a. brown and lt brown	6·50	13·00
165	-	30a. green and grey	5·50	13·00
166	-	35a. blue & ultramarine	6·50	13·00
167	-	40a. red, blue and grey	5·50	13·00
168	-	50a. dp brown and brown	70·00	£140
169	-	1k. green and mauve	65·00	£140
170	-	2k. blue and green	70·00	£170
171	-	5k. orange and yellow	44·00	£120
172	-	10k. lake and red	44·00	£120
173	25	10a. blue & dp blue (air)	22·00	65·00

DESIGNS—HORIZ: 3a. Parliament House, Reykjavik; 7a. Encampment at Thingvellir; 10a. Arrival of Ingolf Arnarsson; 15a. Naming the Island; 20a. Chieftains riding to the "Althing" (Parliament); 25a. Discovery of Arnarsson's pillar; 30a. View of Thingvellir; 35a. Queen Aud; 40a. National flag; 50a. Proclamation at Thingvellir; 1k. Map of Iceland; 2k. Winter-bound farmstead; 5k. Woman spinning; 10k. Viking sacrifice to Thor.

26 Snaefellsjokull

1930. Air. Parliamentary Millenary Celebration.

174	26	15a. blue and brown	28·00	50·00
175	-	20a. blue and brown	28·00	50·00

176	-	35a. brown and green	50·00	£100
177	-	50a. blue and green	50·00	£100
178	-	1k. red and green	50·00	£100

DESIGNS: 20a. Old Icelandic fishing boat; 35a. Icelandic pony; 50a. The Gullfoss Falls; 1k. Statue of Arnarsson, Reykjavik.

1931. Air. Optd Zeppelin 1931.

179	15	30a. green and red	39·00	£150
180	15	1k. brown and blue	12·00	£110
181	15	2k. green and brown	55·00	£150

29 Gullfoss Falls

1931

195	29	5a. grey	13·00	1·00
196	29	20a. red	11·00	35
197	29	35a. blue	22·00	14·50
198	29	60a. mauve	13·00	1·30
199	29	65a. brown	2·20	1·10
200	29	75a. blue	90·00	30·00

30 Shipwreck and Breeches-buoy

1933. Philanthropic Associations.

201	30	10a.+10a. brown	1·90	5·50
202	-	20a.+20a. red	1·90	5·50
203	30	35a.+25a. blue	1·90	5·50
204	-	50a.+25a. green	1·90	5·50

DESIGNS: 20a. Children gathering flowers; 50a. Aged fisherman and rowing boat.

1933. Air. Balbo Transatlantic Mass Formation Flight. Optd Hopflug Itala 1933.

205	15	1k. brown and blue	£190	£600
206	15	5k. blue and brown	£650	£1400
207	15	10k. black and green	£1400	£2750

32 Avro 504K Biplane over Thingvellir

1934. Air.

208	32	10a. blue	1·90	3·25
209	32	20a. green	5·00	7·75
210a	-	25a. violet	16·00	18·00
211	-	50a. purple	4·50	7·75
212	-	1k. brown	25·00	33·00
213	-	2k. red	11·50	13·00

DESIGNS: 25a., 50a. Monoplane and Aurora Borealis; 1k., 2k. Monoplane over map of Iceland.

33 Dynjandi Falls

1935

214	33	10a. blue	29·00	35
215	-	1k. green	48·00	35

DESIGN—HORIZ: 1k. Mt. Hekla.

35 Matthias Jochumsson

1935. Birth Centenary of M. Jochumsson (poet).

216	35	3a. green	90	3·75
217	35	5a. grey	17·00	1·30
218	35	7a. green	24·00	2·20
219	35	35a. blue	75	1·30

36 King Christian X

1937. Silver Jubilee of King Christian X.

220	36	10a. green	2·50	24·00
221	36	30a. brown	2·50	10·00
222	36	40a. red	2·50	10·00
MS223		128½×112 mm, 36 15a. violet; 25a. red; 50a. blue (sold at 2k.)	44·00	£275

37 The Great Geyser

1938

224	37	15a. purple	6·25	11·00
225	37	20a. red	25·00	35
226	37	35a. blue	75	1·10
227	-	40a. brown	15·00	28·00
228	-	45a. blue	90	1·10
229	-	50a. green	23·00	1·10
230	-	60a. blue	6·25	1·10
231	-	1k. blue	5·00	45

The frames of the 40a. to 1k. differ from Type **37**.

37b Leif Eiriksson's Statue, Reykjavik

1938. Leif Eiriksson's Day. Sheet 140×100 mm.

MS233b		30a. red (T **37b**), 40a. violet; 60a. green (sold at 2k.)	4·75	24·00

DESIGNS: 40a. Figure from statue; 60a. Part of globe showing Iceland and Vinland (larger).

38 Reykjavik University

1938. 20th Anniv of Independence.

234	38	25a. green	8·25	15·00
235	38	30a. brown	8·25	15·00
236	38	40a. purple	8·25	15·00

1939. Surch 5.

237	35	5 on 35a. blue	90	1·50

40 Trylon and Perisphere

1939. New York World's Fair.

238	40	20a. red	3·75	6·50
239	-	35a. blue	4·50	8·25
240	-	45a. green	4·75	11·00
241	-	2k. black	55·00	£140

DESIGNS: 35a. Viking longship and route to America; 45a., 2k. Statue of Thorfinn Karlsefni, Reykjavik.

41 Atlantic Cod

42 Icelandic Flag

1939

242a	41	1e. blue	50	4·50
243a	-	3a. violet	50	1·10
244a	41	5a. brown	50	45
245	-	7a. green	6·25	10·00
246	42	10a. red and blue	2·50	1·70
247a	-	10a. green	44·00	1·10
248	-	10a. black	40	35
249	-	12a. green	50	90
250a	41	25a. red	31·00	55
251	41	25a. brown	75	45
252	-	35a. red	1·30	65
253	41	50a. green	75	35

DESIGN: 3, 7, 10a. (Nos. 247a/8), 12, 35a. Atlantic herring.

43 Statue of Thorfinn Karlsefni

1939

254	43	2k. grey	3·25	45
255	43	5k. brown	25·00	55
256	43	10k. brown	12·50	2·40

1940. New York World's Fair. Optd 1940.

257	40	20a. red	8·75	28·00
258	-	35a. blue (No. 239)	8·75	28·00
259	-	45a. green (No. 240)	8·75	28·00
260	-	2k. black (No. 241)	£110	£500

1941. Surch 25.

261	35	25a. on 3a. olive	1·00	1·50

46 Statue of Snorri Sturluson (O. Vigeland)

1941. 700th Death Anniv of Snorri Sturluson (historian).

262	46	25a. red	1·30	2·20
263	46	50a. blue	1·90	5·00
264	46	1k. olive	1·90	5·00

47 Jon Sigurdsson (historian and Althing member)

1944. Proclamation of Republic.

265	47	10a. grey	50	90
266	47	25a. brown	50	90
267	47	50a. green	50	90
268	47	1k. black	90	90
269	47	5k. brown	2·50	11·00
270	47	10k. brown	38·00	95·00

48 Grumman G-21 Goose Amphibian over Thingvellir

1947. Air.

271	48	15a. orange	90	1·30
272	-	30a. black	90	1·30
273	-	75a. red	90	1·30
274	-	1k. blue	90	1·30
275	-	1k.80 blue	19·00	14·00
276	-	2k. brown	1·50	2·20
277	-	2k.50 green	31·00	1·10
278	-	3k. green	1·50	2·20
279	-	3k.30 brown	7·50	8·75

DESIGNS—HORIZ: 30a. Consolidated PBY-5 Catalina flying boat over Isafjordur; 75a. Douglas DC-3 over Eyjafjord; 1k.80, Douglas DC-3 over Snaefellsjokull; 2k.50, Consolidated PBY-5 Catalina over Eiriksjokull; 3k. Douglas DC-4 over Reykjavik; 3k.30, Douglas DC-4 over Oraefajokull. VERT: 1k. Grumman G-21 Goose over Sethisfjordur, Strandatindur; 2k. Consolidated PBY-5 Catalina over Hvalfjordur, Thyrill.

For stamps as Type **48** but without airplane, see Nos. 346/8.

50 Mt. Hekla in Eruption

1948. Inscr "HEKLA 1947".

280	50	12a. purple	40	45
281	-	25a. green	1·90	35
282	-	35a. red	50	35
283	50	50a. brown	2·50	35
284	-	60a. blue	8·75	3·75
285	-	1k. brown	15·00	35
286	-	10k. violet	65·00	45

DESIGNS—VERT: 35a., 60a. Mt. Hekla in Eruption (different view). HORIZ: 25a., 1k., 10k. Mt. Hekla.

53 Hospital and Child

1949. Red Cross Fund.

287	53	10a.+10a. green	90	1·30
288	-	35a.+15a. red	90	1·30
289	-	50a.+25a. brown	90	1·30
290	-	60a.+25a. blue	90	1·30
291	-	75a.+25a. blue	90	1·30

DESIGNS: 35a. Nurse and patient; 50a. Nurse arranging patient's bed; 60a. Aged couple; 75a. Freighter and ship's lifeboat.

54 Pony Pack-train

1949. 75th Anniv of U.P.U.

292	54	25a. green	40	55
293	-	35a. red	40	55
294	-	60a. blue	65	1·20
295	-	2k. orange	1·60	1·30

DESIGNS: 35a. Reykjavik; 60a. Map of Iceland; 2k. Almannagja Gorge.

55 "Ingolfur Arnarson" (trawler)

1950

296		5a. brown	40	35
297	55	10a. grey	50	55
298	-	20a. brown	50	55
299	55	25a. red	40	35
300	-	60a. green	19·00	22·00
301	-	75a. orange	75	35
302	-	90a. red	1·50	90
303	-	1k. brown	8·25	35
304	55	1k.25 purple	25·00	45
305	55	1k.50 blue	18·00	55
306	-	2k. violet	31·00	45
307	-	5k. green	44·00	1·30
308	—As T 55	25k. black	£200	17·00

DESIGNS—As T **55**: 5, 90a., 2k. Vestmannaeyjar harbour; 20, 75a., 1k. Tractor; 60a., 5k. Flock of sheep; 25k. Parliament Building, Reykjavik (29½×23½ mm).

56 Bishop Jon Arason

1950. 400th Death Anniv of Bishop Arason.

309	56	1k.80 red	3·75	3·75
310	56	3k.30 green	2·50	3·25

57 Postman, 1776

1951. 175th Anniv of Icelandic Postal Service.

311	57	2k. blue	3·25	2·75
312	-	3k. purple	4·50	3·75

DESIGN: 3k. as 2k. but Saab 90 Scandia aeroplane replaces man.

58 President Bjornsson

1952. Death of S. Bjornsson (first President of Iceland).

313	58	1k.25 blue	3·25	35
314	58	2k.20 green	90	4·50
315	58	5k. blue	10·50	1·70
316	58	10k. brown	45·00	29·00

1953. Netherlands Flood Relief Fund. Surch Hollandshjalp 1953 + 25.

317	-	75a.+25a. orange (No. 301)	1·50	3·75
318	55	1k.25+25a. purple	2·50	3·75

60 "Reykjabok"
(Saga of Burnt
Njal)

1953

319	60	10a. black	25	20
320	-	70a. green	40	30
321	-	1k. red	65	35
322	-	1k.75 blue	31·00	1·70
323	-	10k. brown	14·00	1·30

DESIGNS: 70a. Hand writing on manuscript; 1k. "Stjorn" (15th century manuscript); 1k.75, Books and candle; 10k. Page from "Skardsbok" (14th century law manuscript).

1954. No. 282 surch **5 AURAR** and bars.
| 324 | | 5a. on 35a. red | 50 | 35 |

62 Hannes Hafstein

1954. 50th Anniv of Appointment of Hannes Hafstein as First Native Minister of Iceland. Portraits of Hafstein.
325	62	1k.25 blue	5·00	65
326	-	2k.45 green	25·00	33·00
327	-	5k. red	28·00	3·75

63 Icelandic Wrestling

1955. Icelandic National Sports.
328	63	75a. brown	40	35
329	-	1k.25 blue (Diving)	65	40
330	63	1k.50 red	1·40	35
331	-	1k.75 blue (Diving)	75	35

64 St. Thorlacas

1956. Ninth Centenary of Consecration of First Icelandic Bishop and Skalholt Rebuilding Fund. Inscr as in T **64.**
332	64	75a.+25a. red	40	35
333	-	1k.25+75a. brown	40	55
334	-	1k.75+1k.25 black	1·00	1·70

DESIGNS—HORIZ: 1k.25, Skalholt Cathedral, 1772. VERT: 1k.75, J. P. Vidalin, Bishop of Skalholt, 1698–1720.

65 Skogafoss

1956. Power Plants and Waterfalls.
335	65	15a. blue	40	35
336	-	50a. green	40	35
337	-	60a. brown	3·50	3·75
338	-	1k.50 violet	36·00	35
339	-	2k. brown	2·00	65
340	-	2k.45 black	9·00	10·00
341	-	3k. blue	5·50	1·10
342	-	5k. green	16·00	2·00

DESIGNS—HORIZ: 50a. Ellidaarvirkjun; 60a. Godafoss; 1k.50, Sogsvirkjun; 2k. Dettifoss; 2k.45, Andakilsarvirkjun; 3k. Laxarvirkjun. VERT: 5k. Gullfoss.

67 Map of Iceland

1956. 50th Anniv of Icelandic Telegraph System.
| 343 | 67 | 2k.30 blue | 65 | 1·10 |

67a Whooper Swans

1956. Northern Countries' Day.
| 344 | 67a | 1k.50 red | 65 | 1·00 |
| 345 | 67a | 1k.75 blue | 10·50 | 11·00 |

1957. Designs as T **48** but airplane omitted.
346		2k. green	4·50	35
347		3k. blue	5·00	35
348		10k. brown	6·50	45

DESIGNS—HORIZ: 2k. Snaefellsjokull; 3k. Eiriksjokull; 10k. Oraefajokull.

68 Presidential Residence, Bessastadir

1957
| 349 | 68 | 25k. black | 26·00 | 4·50 |

69 Norwegian Spruce

1957. Reafforestation Campaign.
| 350 | 69 | 35a. green | 40 | 35 |
| 351 | - | 70a. green | 40 | 35 |

DESIGN: 70a. Icelandic birch and saplings.

70 Jonas Hallgrimsson

1957. 150th Birth Anniv of Hallgrimsson (poet).
| 352 | 70 | 5k. black and green | 2·00 | 55 |

71 River Beauty

1958. Flowers. Multicoloured.
| 353 | | 1k. Type **71** | 40 | 35 |
| 354 | | 2k.50 Wild pansy | 50 | 45 |

72 Icelandic Pony

1958
355	72	10a. black	25	20
356	72	1k. red	65	30
357	72	2k.25 brown	80	35

73 Icelandic Flag

1958. 40th Anniv of Icelandic Flag.
| 358 | 73 | 3k.50 red and blue | 2·50 | 65 |
| 359 | 73 | 50k. red and blue | 7·75 | 6·50 |

No. 359 is 23½×26½ mm.

74 Old Government House

1958
| 360 | 74 | 1k.50 blue | 50 | 45 |
| 361 | 74 | 2k. green | 50 | 45 |

| 362 | 74 | 3k. red | 40 | 35 |
| 363 | 74 | 4k. brown | 65 | 55 |

75 Jon Thorkelsson with Children

1959. Death Bicentenary of Jon Thorkelsson (Johannes Thorkillius, Rector of Skalholt).
| 364 | 75 | 2k. green | 65 | 65 |
| 365 | 75 | 3k. purple | 90 | 90 |

76 Vickers Viscount 700 and 1919 Avro 504K Biplane

1959. Air. 40th Anniv of Iceland Civil Aviation.
| 366 | 76 | 3k.50 blue | 90 | 75 |
| 367 | - | 4k.05 green | 1·00 | 1·10 |

DESIGN: 4k.05, Douglas DC-4 and Avro 504K aircraft.

77 Atlantic Salmon

1959
368	77	25a. blue	25	20
369	-	90a. black and brown	40	35
370	-	2k. black	65	35
371	77	5k. green	10·50	1·30
372	-	25k. violet and yellow	16·00	15·00

DESIGNS—VERT: 90a., 2k. Eiders; 25k. Gyr falcon.

78 "The Outcast" (after Jonsson)

1960. World Refugee Year.
| 373 | 78 | 2k.50 brown | 40 | 35 |
| 374 | 78 | 4k.50 blue | 1·00 | 1·10 |

78a Conference Emblem

1960. Europa.
| 375 | 78a | 3k. green | 80 | 55 |
| 376 | 78a | 5k.50 blue | 1·30 | 1·40 |

79 Dandelions

1960. Wild Flowers.
377	-	50a. violet, green and myrtle (Campanulas)	25	20
378	-	1k.20 violet, green and brown (Geraniums)	40	35
379	79	2k.50 yellow, green & brn	40	35
380	-	3k.50 yellow, green and blue (Buttercup)	50	45

See also Nos. 412/15 and 446/7.

80 S. Sigurdsson

1961. 150th Birth Anniv of Jon Sigurdsson (historian and Althing member).
381	80	50a. red	40	35
382	80	3k. blue	1·70	1·10
383	80	5k. purple	65	55

81 Reykjavik Harbour

1961. 175th Anniv of Reykjavik.
| 384 | 81 | 2k.50 blue and green | 65 | 35 |
| 385 | 81 | 4k.50 blue and violet | 1·00 | 55 |

82 Doves

1961. Europa.
| 386 | 82 | 5k.50 multicoloured | 65 | 75 |
| 387 | 82 | 6k. multicoloured | 65 | 90 |

83 B. Sveinsson

1961. 50th Anniv of Iceland University.
388	83	1k. brown	25	20
389	-	1k.40 blue	40	35
390	-	10k. green	1·60	35
MS391 99×50 mm. Nos. 388/90. Imperf 1·30 1·70

DESIGNS—VERT: 1k.40, B. M. Olsen (first Vice-chancellor). HORIZ: 10k. University building.

84 Productivity Institute

1962. Icelandic Buildings.
392	84	2k.50 blue	40	30
393	-	4k. green	50	30
394	-	6k. brown	65	35

DESIGNS: 4k. Fishing Research Institute; 6k. Agricultural Society's Headquarters.

85 Europa "Tree"

1962. Europa.
| 395 | 85 | 5k.50 brown, green & yell | 40 | 35 |
| 396 | 85 | 6k.50 brown, green & yell | 65 | 65 |

86 Cable Map

1962. Opening of North Atlantic Submarine Telephone Communications.
| 397 | 86 | 5k. green, red and lavender | 1·20 | 55 |
| 398 | 86 | 7k. green, red and blue | 65 | 45 |

87 S. Gudmundsson (scholar and curator)

1963. Centenary of National Museum.
| 399 | 87 | 4k. brown and bistre | 65 | 45 |
| 400 | - | 5k.50 brown and olive | 50 | 45 |

DESIGN: 5k.50, Detail from carving on church door, Valth-jofsstad.

88 Herring
Catch

1963. Freedom from Hunger.
401	**88**	5k. multicoloured	90	35
402	**88**	7k.50 multicoloured	40	35

89 View of Akureyri

1963
403	**89**	3k. green	40	45

90 "Co-operation"

1963. Europa.
404	**90**	6k. yellow, ochre and brown	1·00	90
405	**90**	7k. yellow, green and blue	1·00	90

91 Ambulance

1963. Red Cross Centenary.
406	**91**	3k.+50a. multicoloured	65	1·30
407	**91**	3k.50+50a. mult	65	1·30

92 Gullfoss (cargo liner)

1964. 50th Anniv of Iceland Steamship Co.
408	**92**	10k. black, purple and blue	2·50	1·70

93 Scout
Emblem

1964. Icelandic Boy Scouts Commemoration.
409	**93**	3k.50 multicoloured	65	45
410	**93**	4k.50 multicoloured	65	45

94 Arms of
Iceland

1964. 20th Anniv of Icelandic Republic.
411	**94**	25k. multicoloured	3·00	2·40

1964. Wild Flowers. As T 79. Multicoloured.
412		50a. Mountain avens	40	20
413		1k. Glacier buttercup	40	20
414		1k.50 Bogbean	40	20
415		2k. White clover	40	20

95 Europa
"Flower"

1964. Europa.
416	**95**	4k.50 turquoise, cream and brown	80	45

417	**95**	9k. sepia, cream and blue	1·10	70

96 Running

1964. Olympic Games, Tokyo.
418	**96**	10k. black and green	1·40	90

97 Rock Ptarmigan
(summer plumage)

1965. Charity stamps.
419	**97**	3k.50+50a. mult	1·40	2·30
420	-	4k.50+50a. mult	1·40	2·30
DESIGN: 4k.50, Rock ptarmigan in winter plumage.

98 "Sound Waves"

1965. Centenary of I.T.U.
421	**98**	4k.50 green	1·10	60
422	**98**	7k.50 blue	40	35

99 Eruption,
November 1963

1965. Birth of Surtsey Island. Multicoloured.
423		1k.50 Type **99**	80	70
424		2k. Surtsey in April 1964 (horiz)	80	70
425		3k.50 Surtsey in September 1964 (horiz)	95	70

100 Europa "Sprig"

1965. Europa.
426	**100**	5k. green, brown and ochre	2·30	1·40
427	**100**	8k. green, brown & turq	1·40	1·30

101 E. Benediktsson

1965. 25th Death Anniv of Einar Benediktsson (poet).
428	**101**	10k. brown, black and blue	4·00	4·50

102 Girl in
National
Costume

1965
429	**102**	100k. multicoloured	11·00	8·75

103
White-tailed Sea
Eagle

1966. Multicoloured
430		20k. Great northern diver	6·75	5·75
431		50k. Type **103**	13·50	11·50

104 Londrangar

1966. Landscapes (1st series). Multicoloured.
432		2k.50 Type **104**	40	45
433		4k. Myvatn	70	45
434		5k. Bulandstindur	70	45
435		6k.50 Dyrholaey	80	45
See also Nos. 465/8.

105 Europa
"Ship"

1966. Europa.
436	**105**	7k. turquoise blue and red	2·75	1·70
437	**105**	8k. brown, cream and red	2·75	1·70

106 Society Emblem

1966. 150th Anniv of Icelandic Literary Society.
438	**106**	4k. blue	40	35
439	**106**	10k. red	95	60

107 Cogwheels

1967. Europa.
440	**107**	7k. blue, brown and yellow	2·40	1·40
441	**107**	8k. blue, grey and green	2·40	1·40

108 Old and New Maps
of Iceland

1967. World Fair, Montreal.
442	**108**	10k. multicoloured	70	60

109 Trade Symbols

1967. 50th Anniv of Icelandic Chamber of Commerce.
443	**109**	5k. multicoloured	40	35

110 Nest and Eggs of
Ringed Plover

1967. Charity stamps.
444	**110**	4k.+50a. multicoloured	95	1·70
445	-	5k.+50a. multicoloured	95	1·70
DESIGN: 5k. Nest and eggs of rock ptarmigan.

1968. Wild Flowers. As T 79. Multicoloured.
446		50a. Saxifrage	25	25
447		2k.50 Orchid	40	35

111 Europa "Key"

1968. Europa.
448	**111**	9k.50 mauve, black & yell	2·20	1·20

449	**111**	10k. yellow, sepia & green	1·60	1·20

112 Right-hand Traffic

1968. Adoption of Changed Rule of the Road.
450	**112**	4k. brown and yellow	25	25
451	**112**	5k. brown	40	35

113 "Fridriksson
and Boy" (statue
by S. Olafsson)

1968. Birth Cent of Pastor Fridrik Fridriksson (founder of Icelandic Y.M.C.A. and Y.W.C.A.).
452	**113**	10k. black and blue	70	60

114 Library
Interior

1968. 150th Anniv of National Library.
453	**114**	5k. brown and buff	25	25
454	**114**	20k. ultramarine and blue	1·40	1·20

115 Jon
Magnusson
(former Prime
Minister)

1968. 50th Anniv of Independence.
455	**115**	4k. lake	40	35
456	**115**	50k. sepia	4·00	4·50

116 Viking Ships

1969. 50th Anniv of Northern Countries' Union.
457	**116**	6k.50 red	70	60
458	**116**	10k. blue	80	70

117 Colonnade

1969. Europa.
459	**117**	13k. multicoloured	6·00	3·00
460	**117**	14k.50 multicoloured	1·40	1·20

118 Republican
Emblem (after S.
Jonsson)

1969. 25th Anniv of Republic.
461	**118**	25k. multicoloured	1·10	60
462	**118**	100k. multicoloured	8·00	7·00

119 Boeing 727 Airliner

1969. 50th Anniv of Icelandic Aviation.
463	**119**	9k.50 ultramarine & blue	70	60

| 464 | - | 12k. ultramarine and blue | 70 | 60 |

DESIGN: 12k. Canadair CL-44-D4 (inscr "Rolls-Royce 400").

120 Snaefellsjokull

1970. Landscapes (2nd series). Multicoloured.
465	1k. Type **120**	25	25
466	4k. Laxfoss and Baula	25	25
467	5k. Hattver (vert)	40	35
468	20k. Fjardagil (vert)	2·00	70

121 First Court Session

1970. 50th Anniv of Icelandic Supreme Court.
| 469 | **121** | 6k.50 multicoloured | 40 | 35 |

122 Part of "Skardsbok" (14th-cent law manuscript)

1970. Icelandic Manuscripts. Multicoloured.
470	5k. Type **122**	25	25
471	15k. Part of preface to "Flateyjarbok"	80	70
472	30k. Illuminated initial from "Flateyjarbok"	1·40	1·20

123 "Flaming Sun"

1970. Europa.
| 473 | **123** | 9k. yellow and brown | 4·00 | 2·30 |
| 474 | **123** | 25k. brown and green | 6·00 | 3·50 |

124 Nurse tending Patient

1970. 50th Anniv of Icelandic Nurses Assn.
| 475 | **124** | 7k. ultramarine and blue | 40 | 35 |

125 G. Thomsen

1970. 150th Birth Anniv of Grimur Thomsen (poet).
| 476 | **125** | 10k. indigo and blue | 70 | 45 |

126 The Halt (T. B. Thorlaksson)

1970. International Arts Festival, Reykjavik.
| 477 | **126** | 50k. multicoloured | 2·00 | 1·60 |

127 Purple Saxifrage

128 U.N. Emblem and Map

1970. Nature Conservation Year. Multicoloured.
| 478 | 3k. Type **127** | 40 | 35 |
| 479 | 15k. Lakagigar (view) | 1·40 | 1·20 |

1970. 25th Anniv of United Nations.
| 480 | **128** | 12k. multicoloured | 70 | 60 |

129 Flight (A. Jonsson)

1971. "Help for Refugees".
| 481 | **129** | 10k. multicoloured | 95 | 80 |

130 Europa Chain

1971. Europa.
| 482 | **130** | 7k. yellow, red and black | 4·00 | 2·30 |
| 483 | **130** | 15k. yellow, blue and black | 4·00 | 2·00 |

131 Postgiro Emblem

1971. Inauguration of Postal Giro Service.
| 484 | **131** | 5k. blue and light blue | 25 | 25 |
| 485 | **131** | 7k. green and light green | 40 | 35 |

132 Society Emblem

1971. Centenary of Icelandic Patriotic Society.
| 486 | **132** | 30k. lilac and blue | 1·60 | 1·20 |
| 487 | - | 100k. black and grey | 6·75 | 5·75 |

DESIGN: 100k. T. Gunnarsson (president and editor).

133 Freezing Plant and Haddock (*Melanogrammus aeglefinus*)

1971. Icelandic Fishing Industry. Multicoloured.
488	5k. Type **133**	25	25
489	7k. Landing catch and Atlantic cod (*Gadus morhua*)	35	30
490	20k. Canning shrimps and *Pandalus borealis*	1·40	75

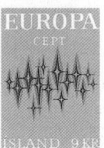

134 Mt. Herdubreid

1972
| 491 | **134** | 250k. multicoloured | 1·10 | 60 |

135 "Communications"

1972. Europa.
| 492 | **135** | 9k. multicoloured | 2·00 | 90 |
| 493 | **135** | 13k. multicoloured | 4·00 | 2·30 |

136 "Municipalities"

1972. Centenary of Icelandic Municipal Laws.
| 494 | **136** | 16k. multicoloured | 70 | 45 |

137 World Map on Chessboard

1972. World Chess Championship, Reykjavik.
| 495 | **137** | 15k. multicoloured | 70 | 45 |

138 Tomatoes

1972. Hot-house Plant Cultivation. Multicoloured.
496	8k. Type **138**	25	25
497	12k. Steam source and valve	40	35
498	40k. Rose cultivation	1·60	1·20

139 Contour Map and Continental Shelf

1972. Iceland's Offshore Claims.
| 499 | **139** | 9k. multicoloured | 40 | 35 |

140 Arctic Tern feeding Young

1972. Charity Stamps.
| 500 | **140** | 7k.+1k. multicoloured | 70 | 1·20 |
| 501 | **140** | 9k.+1k. multicoloured | 70 | 1·20 |

141 Europa "Posthorn"

1973. Europa.
| 502 | **141** | 13k. multicoloured | 6·75 | 2·75 |
| 503 | **141** | 25k. multicoloured | 1·40 | 60 |

142 Postman and 2s. stamp of 1873

1973. Stamp Centenary. Multicoloured.
504	10k. Type **142**	40	35
505	15k. Pony train	40	35
506	20k. Esja (mail steamer)	40	35
507	40k. Mail van	40	35
508	80k. Beech Model 18 mail plane	95	80

143 "The Nordic House", Reykjavik

1973. Nordic Countries' Postal Co-operation.
| 509 | **143** | 9k. multicoloured | 55 | 35 |
| 510 | **143** | 10k. multicoloured | 1·60 | 1·20 |

144 Pres. Asgeirsson

1973. Fifth Death Anniv of Asgeir Asgeirsson (politician).
| 511 | **144** | 13k. red | 55 | 35 |
| 512 | **144** | 15k. blue | 40 | 35 |

145 Exhibition Emblem

1973. "Islandia 73" Stamp Exhibition. Multicoloured.
| 513 | 17k. Type **145** | 55 | 45 |
| 514 | 20k. Exhibition emblem (different) | 40 | 45 |

146 "The Elements"

1973. Centenary of I.M.O.
| 515 | **146** | 50k. multicoloured | 80 | 60 |

147 Ingolfur and High-Seat Pillar (tapestry, J. Briem)

1974. 1100th Anniv of Icelandic Settlement. Multicoloured.
516	10k. Type **147**	40	25
517	13k. *Grimur Geitskor at Thingvellir* (painting) (horiz)	40	25
518	15k. Bishop G. Thorlaksson of Holar	40	25
519	17k. *Snorri Sturluson slaying the King's messenger* (T. Skulason)	40	25
520	20k. Stained glass window from Hallgrimskirkja, Saurbaer	40	25
521	25k. Illuminated "I", from *Flateyjarbok* (manuscript)	40	25
522	30k. *Christ the King* (mosaic altar-piece, Skalholt Cathedral)	1·10	70
523	40k. 18th-century woodcarving	1·40	85
524	60k. *Curing the Catch* (concrete relief by S. Olafsson)	1·40	1·20
525	70k. *Saemunder smiting the Devil Seal* (bronze)	1·40	1·10
526	100k. Altar-cloth, Church of Stafafell (horiz)	1·80	95

148 "Horseman" (17th-century wood-carving)

1974. Europa. Sculptures. Multicoloured.
| 527 | 13k. Type **148** | 40 | 35 |
| 528 | 20k. "Through the Sound Barrier" (bronze, A. Sveinsson) | 1·60 | 95 |

149 Purchasing Stamps

1974. Centenary of Universal Postal Union.
| 529 | **149** | 17k. brown, blue & yellow | 40 | 35 |
| 530 | - | 20k. brown, blue & green | 40 | 35 |

DESIGN: 20k. Postman sorting mail.

150 Village with Erupting Volcano in distance

1975. Volcanic Eruption, Heimaey (1973).
531	**150**	20k. multicoloured	80	50
532	**150**	25k. multicoloured	40	35

151 Autumn Bird (T. Skullason)

1975. Europa. Paintings. Multicoloured.
533	**151**	18k. Type **151**	70	50
534		23k. Sun Queen (J. S. Kjarval) (vert.)	1·40	70

152 Stephan G. Stephansson (poet)

1975. Centenary of Icelandic Settlements in North America.
535	**152**	27k. brown and green	70	35

153 Hallgrimur Petursson (religious poet)

1975. Celebrities.
536	**153**	18k. black and green	40	35
537	-	23k. blue	40	35
538	-	30k. red	40	35
539	-	50k. blue	55	35

PORTRAITS: 23k. Arni Magnusson (historian); 30k. Jon Eiriksson (statesman); 50k. Einar Jonsson (painter and sculptor).

154 Red Cross Flag on Map of Iceland

1975. 50th Anniv of Icelandic Red Cross.
540	**154**	23k. multicoloured	55	50

155 Abstract (N. Tryggvadottir)

1975. International Women's Year.
541	**155**	100k. multicoloured	1·40	60

156 "Bertel Thorvaldsen" (self-statue)

1975. Centenary of Thorvaldsen Society (Charity organization).
542	**156**	27k. multicoloured	95	50

157 "Forestry"

1975. Reafforestation.
543	**157**	35k. multicoloured	70	50

158 Landscape (Asgrimur Jonsson)

1976. Birth Cent of Asgrimur Jonsson (painter).
544	**158**	150k. multicoloured	2·00	1·40

159 Wooden Bowl

1976. Europa. Old Wooden Crafts. Multicoloured.
545	**159**	35k. Type **159**	1·40	95
546		45k. Spinning-wheel (vert)	1·40	1·20

160 Title page of Postal Services Order

1976. Bicent of Icelandic Postal Services.
547	**160**	35k. brown	55	35
548	-	45k. blue	80	50

DESIGN: 45k. Signature appended to Postal Services Order.

161 Iceland 5a. Stamp with Reykjavik Postmark, 1876

1976. Cent of Icelandic Aurar Currency Stamps.
549	**161**	30k. multicoloured	40	35

162 "Workers" and Federation Emblem

1976. 60th Anniv of Icelandic Labour Federation.
550	**162**	100k. multicoloured	1·20	70

163 Water-lilies

1977. Nordic Countries' Co-operation in Nature Conservation and Environment Protection.
551	**163**	35k. multicoloured	95	60
552	**163**	45k. multicoloured	95	60

164 Ofaerufoss, Eldgja

1977. Europa. Multicoloured.
553	**164**	45k. Type **164**	4·00	95
554		85k. Kirkufell from Grundarfjord	2·75	60

165 Harlequin Duck

1977. European Wetlands Campaign.
555	**165**	40k. multicoloured	70	50

166 Co-operative Emblem

1977. 75th Anniv of Federation of Icelandic Co-operative Societies.
556	**166**	60k. blue and light blue	95	60

167 Thermal Spring and Rheumatic Treatment

1977. World Rheumatism Year.
557	**167**	90k. multicoloured	80	60

168 Cairn and Glacier

1977. 50th Anniv of Icelandic Touring Club.
558	**168**	45k. blue	1·10	70

169 Thorvaldur Thoroddsen (geologist)

1978. Famous Icelanders.
559	**169**	50k. green and brown	40	35
560		60k. brown and green	95	60

DESIGN: 60k. Briet Bjarnhedinsdottir (suffragette).

170 Videy Mansion

1978. Europa. Multicoloured.
561	**170**	80k. Type **170**	2·00	60
562		120k. Husavik Church (vert.)	4·00	85

171 Dr. A. Johannesson, Junkers W.34 "Island 1" and Junkers F-13 "Island 2"

1978. 50th Anniv of Domestic Flights.
563	**171**	60k. black and blue	40	35
564	-	100k. multicoloured	70	60

DESIGN: 100k. Fokker F.27 Friendship TF-F1K.

172 Skeidara Bridge

1978. Skeidara Bridge.
565	**172**	70k. multicoloured	40	35

173 Lava Scene near Mt. Hekla (J. Stefansson)

1978
566	**173**	1000k. multicoloured	4·75	3·50

174 Wreck of Sargon and Breeches-buoy

1978. 50th Anniv of National Life-Saving Association of Iceland.
567	**174**	60k. black	40	35

175 "Reykjanesviti" Lighthouse

1978. Centenary of Lighthouses in Iceland.
568	**175**	90k. multicoloured	70	50

176 Halldor Hermannsson

1978. Birth Centenary of Halldor Hermannsson (scholar and librarian).
569	**176**	150k. blue	70	50

177 Old Telephone

1979. Europa. Multicoloured.
570		110k. Type **177**	2·75	60
571		190k. Posthorn and mailbag	4·25	70

178 Bjarni Thorsteinsson (clergyman and composer)

1979. Famous Icelanders.
572	-	80k. purple	25	25
573	**178**	100k. black	25	25
574	-	120k. red	40	35
575	-	130k. brown	55	50
576	-	170k. red	70	50

DESIGNS: 80k. Ingibjorg H. Bjarnason (headmistress and first female member of Althing); 120k. Petur Gudjohnsen (organist); 130k. Sveinbjorn Sveinbjornsson (composer); 170k. Torfhildur Holm (poetess and novelist).

179 Children with Flowers

1979. International Year of the Child.
577　**179**　140k. multicoloured　95　60

180 Icelandic Arms to 1904 and 1904–19

1979. 75th Anniv of Ministry of Iceland.
578　**180**　500k. multicoloured　1·60　95

181 Sigurdsson and I. Einarsdottir

1979. Death Centenaries of Jon Sigurdsson (historian and Althing member) and of his wife, Ingibjorg Einarsdottir.
579　**181**　150k. black　70　60

182 Part of Kringla Leaf (MS of "Heimskringla")

1979. 800th Birth Anniv of Snorri Sturluson (saga writer).
580　**182**　200k. multicoloured　95　60

183 Icelandic Dog

1980. Fauna.
581　**183**　10k. black　25　25
582　–　90k. brown　40　35
583　–　160k. purple　95　35
584　–　170k. black　1·10　60
585　–　190k. brown　40　35
DESIGNS: 90k. Arctic fox; 160k. Greater redfish; 170k. Atlantic puffins; 190k. Common seal.

184 Jon Sveinsson alias Nonni (writer)

1980. Europa.
586　**184**　140k. pink and black　1·40　60
587　–　250k. pink and black　1·40　70
DESIGN: 250k. Gunnar Gunnarsson (writer).

185 Rowan Berries

1980. Year of the Tree.
588　**185**　120k. multicoloured　40　35

186 Sports Complex, Reykjavik

1980. Olympic Games, Moscow.
589　**186**　300k. turquoise　80　60

187 Embroidered Cushion

1980. Nordic Countries' Postal Co-operation. Multicoloured.
590　150k. Carved and painted cabinet door　70　60
591　180k. Type **187**　95　70

188 University Hospital

1980. 50th Anniv of University Hospital.
592　**188**　200k. multicoloured　55　50

189 Loudspeaker

1980. 50th Anniv of State Broadcasting Service.
593　**189**　400k. multicoloured　1·20　60

190 Magnus Stephensen (Chief Justice and publisher)

1981. Famous Icelanders.
594　**190**　170a. blue　70　50
595　–　190a. green　70　50
DESIGN: 190a. Finnur Magnusson (writer and Keeper of Privy Archives).

191 Loftur the Sorcerer

1981. Europa. Illustrations of Icelandic legends. Multicoloured.
596　180a. Type **191**　1·60　95
597　220a. Witch wading the deeps off Iceland　1·60　95

192 Winter Wren

1981. Birds.
598　**192**　50a. brown　20　15
599　–　100a. blue　25　20
600　–　200a. black　40　35
DESIGNS: 100a. Golden plover; 200a. Common raven.

193 Human Jigsaw

1981. International Year for Disabled Persons.
601　**193**　200a. multicoloured　40　35

194 Skyggnir Dish Aerial

1981. 75th Anniv of Icelandic Telephone Service.
602　**194**　500a. multicoloured　1·40　85

195 Hauling the Line (Gunnlaugur Scheving)

1981.
603　**195**　5000a. multicoloured　7·50　4·25

196 Medieval Driftwood crucifix from Alftamyri

1981. Millenary of Missionary Work in Iceland.
604　**196**　200a. lilac　40　35

197 Leaf-bread (star pattern)

1981. Christmas. Multicoloured.
605　200a. Type **197**　80　70
606　250a. Leaf-bread (tree pattern)　80　70

198 Common Northern Whelk

1982. Shells.
607　**198**　20a. red　25　25
608　–　600a. brown　1·10　50
DESIGN: 600a. Iceland scallop.

199 Casting Dais Post into Sea (first Iceland settlement, 874)

1982. Europa. Multicoloured.
609　**199**　350a. Type **199**　6·00　1·20
610　450a. Discovery of Vinland (America), 1000　6·00　1·20

200 Sheep

1982. Domestic Animals.
611　**200**　300a. brown　95　50
612　–　400a. red　70　35
613　–　500a. grey　40　35
DESIGNS: 400a. Cow; 500a. Cat.

201 Co-operative Trading House, Husavik

1982. Centenary of Thingeyjar Co-operative Society.
614　**201**　1000a. black and brown　1·10　50

202 Horseman

1982. Iceland Ponies and Horsemanship.
615　**202**　700a. multicoloured　95　40

203 Holar

1982. Cent of Holar Agricultural College.
616　**203**　1500a. multicoloured　1·40　85

204 "Mount Herdubreid" (Isleifur Konradsson)

1982. Year of the Aged.
617　**204**　800a. multicoloured　95　60

205 T. Sveinsdottir

1982. Famous Icelanders. Thorbjorg Sveinsdottir (midwife and founder of Icelandic Women's Association).
618　**205**　900a. brown　70　50

206 Reynistadur Monastery Seal

1982. "Nordia 84" Stamp Exhibition, Reykjavik (1st issue). Sheet 82×80 mm containing T **206** and similar vert design.
MS619 400a. brown and black; 800a. brown and black (sold at 18k.)　6·75　6·50
DESIGN:—800a. Thingeyrar Monastery seal. See also Nos. **MS**636 and **MS**645.

207 Doves and Opening of The Night was such a Splendid One

1982. Christmas. Multicoloured.
620　**207**　300a. Type **207**　1·10　60
621　350a. Bells and close of The Night was such a Splendid One (composed by Sigvaldi Kaldalons from poem by E. Sigurdsson)　1·20　70

208 Marsh Marigold

1983. Flowers. Multicoloured.
622　**208**　7k.50 Type **208**　55　35
623　8k. Alpine catchfly　1·10　60
624　10k. Marsh cinquefoil　1·60　70
625　20k. Water forgetmenot　3·00　1·20

209 Mount Sulur

1983. Nordic Countries' Postal Co-operation. "Visit the North". Multicoloured.
626　**209**　4k.50 Type **209**　1·10　70
627　5k. Urridafoss Falls　1·40　85

210 Thermal
Area and
Heat-exchange
Plant

1983. Europa. Multicoloured.
| 628 | | 5k. Type **210** | 3·50 | 1·40 |
| 629 | | 5k.50 Thermal area heating houses | 27·00 | 2·20 |

211 Stern Trawler

1983. Fishing Industry.
| 630 | **211** | 11k. blue | 70 | 50 |
| 631 | - | 13k. blue | 1·60 | 85 |
DESIGN: 13k. Line fishing.

212 *Laki Craters* (Finnur Jonsson)

1983. Bicentenary of Skafta Eruption.
| 632 | **212** | 15k. multicoloured | 1·10 | 85 |

213 Skiing

1983. Outdoor Sports. Multicoloured.
| 633 | | 12k. Type **213** | 95 | 60 |
| 634 | | 14k. Jogging | 1·40 | 85 |

214 Aircraft and W.C.Y. Emblem

1983. World Communications Year.
| 635 | **214** | 30k. multicoloured | 2·75 | 1·80 |

215 Seal of
Bishop Magnus
Eyjolfsson

1983. "Nordia 84" Stamp Exhibition, Reykjavik (2nd issue). Sheet 82×80 mm containing T **215** and similar vert design.
MS636 8k. blue and black; 12k. green and black (sold at 30k.) 9·50 9·00
DESIGN: 12k. seal of Bishop Ogmundur Palsson.

216 Virgin Mary
and Child

1983. Christmas. Multicoloured.
| 637 | | 600a. Type **216** | 95 | 50 |
| 638 | | 650a. Visitation of the Angel | 1·10 | 60 |

217 Pres. Eldjarn

1983. First Death Anniv (September) of Kristjan Eldjarn (President, 1968–80).
| 639 | **217** | 6k.50 red | 1·10 | 70 |
| 640 | **217** | 7k. blue | 55 | 35 |

218 Burnet Rose

1984. Flowers. Multicoloured.
| 641 | | 6k. Type **218** | 1·10 | 50 |
| 642 | | 25k. Silverweed | 2·00 | 60 |
See also Nos. 648/9, 657/60 and 717/18.

219 Bridge

1984. Europa. 25th Anniv of European Post and Telecommunications Conference.
| 643 | **219** | 6k.50 deep blue and blue | 2·75 | 1·20 |
| 644 | **219** | 7k.50 dp purple & purple | 1·40 | 1·20 |

220 Map of North
Atlantic by
Abraham Ortelius,
1570

1984. "Nordia 84" Stamp Exhibition, Reykjavik (3rd issue). Sheet 114×76 mm.
MS645 **220** 40k. multicoloured (sold at 60k.) 16·00 15·00

221 Icelandic
Flags

1984. 40th Anniv of Republic.
| 646 | **221** | 50k. multicoloured | 6·75 | 3·50 |

222 I.O.G.T. Lodge,
Akureyri

1984. Centenary of International Order of Good Templars in Iceland.
| 647 | **222** | 10k. green | 95 | 60 |

1984. Flowers. As T **218**. Multicoloured.
| 648 | | 6k.50 Wild azalea | 60 | 35 |
| 649 | | 7k.50 Alpine bearberry | 70 | 50 |

223 Basalt
symbolising
Industries

1984. 50th Anniv of Confederation of Icelandic Employers.
| 650 | **223** | 30k. multicoloured | 1·60 | 1·20 |

224 Bjorn
Bjarnarson
(founder) (after
J. P. Wildenradt)

1984. Centenary of National Gallery.
| 651 | **224** | 12k. black, brown and green | 70 | 60 |
| 652 | - | 40k. black, green and red | 2·75 | 1·40 |
DESIGN: 40k. New gallery building.

225 Virgin and
Child

1984. Christmas.
| 653 | **225** | 600a. blue, lt blue & gold | 80 | 35 |
| 654 | - | 650a. red and gold | 1·10 | 50 |
DESIGN: 650a. Angel with Christmas rose.

226 Text from
Bible

1984. 400th Anniv of Gudbrand's Bible.
| 655 | **226** | 6k.50 red | 80 | 35 |
| 656 | - | 7k.50 purple | 55 | 70 |
DESIGN: 7k.50, Illustration from Bible.

1985. Flowers. As T **218**. Multicoloured.
657		8k. Stone bramble	1·10	35
658		9k. Rock speedwell	1·40	50
659		16k. Sea pea	2·75	60
660		17k. Alpine whitlow-grass	80	60

227 Lady
playing Langspil

1985. Europa. Music Year. Multicoloured.
| 661 | | 6k.50 Type **227** | 3·75 | 95 |
| 662 | | 7k.50 Man playing Icelandic violin | 3·75 | 1·40 |

228 Swedish
Whitebeam

1985. Centenary of Iceland Horticultural Society.
| 663 | **228** | 20k. multicoloured | 1·20 | 70 |

229 Girl and
I.Y.Y. Emblem

1985. International Youth Year.
| 664 | **229** | 25k. multicoloured | 1·50 | 1·10 |

230 Common
Squid

1985. Marine Life.
| 665 | **230** | 7k. purple | 45 | 40 |

| 666 | - | 8k. brown | 55 | 45 |
| 667 | - | 9k. red | 1·50 | 70 |
DESIGNS: 8k. Common spider crab; 9k. Sea anemone.

231 Rev. Hannes
Stephensen (politician)

1985. Famous Icelanders.
| 668 | **231** | 13k. red | 90 | 55 |
| 669 | - | 30k. violet | 2·10 | 95 |
DESIGN: 30k. Jon Gudmundsson (editor and politician).

232 *Flight Yearning*

1985. Birth Centenary of Johannes Sveinsson Kjarval (artist).
| 670 | **232** | 100k. multicoloured | 7·50 | 5·50 |

233 Snow
Scene

1985. Christmas. Multicoloured.
| 671 | | 8k. Type **233** | 1·10 | 40 |
| 672 | | 9k. Snow scene (different) | 1·20 | 70 |

234 Pied Wagtail

1986. Birds. Multicoloured.
673		6k. Type **234**	45	40
674		10k. Pintail	2·30	70
675		12k. Merlin	1·50	70
676		15k. Razorbill	1·40	55
See also Nos. 697/700, 720/1, 726/7, 741/2 and 763/4.

235 Skaftafell National
Park

1986. Europa. Multicoloured.
| 677 | | 10k. Type **235** | 15·00 | 1·40 |
| 678 | | 12k. Jokulsargljufur National Park | 6·00 | 1·60 |

236 Stykkisholmur

1986. Nordic Countries' Postal Co-operation. Twinned Towns. Multicoloured.
| 679 | | 10k. Type **236** | 1·40 | 90 |
| 680 | | 12k. Seydisfjordur | 1·50 | 95 |

237 Head Office, Reykjavik

1986. Centenary of National Bank. Multicoloured.
| 681 | **237** | 13k. green | 1·20 | 80 |
| 682 | - | 250k. brown | 12·00 | 10·00 |
DESIGN: 250k. Reverse of first National Bank 5k. note.

238 First Official Seal

1986. Bicentenary of Reykjavik.
683	**238**	10k. red	75	45
684	-	12k. brown	85	55
685	-	13k. green	90	70
686	-	40k. blue	2·30	1·40

DESIGNS: 12k. "Reykjavik pond, 1856" (illustration from "Journey in the Northern Seas" by Charles Edmond); 13k. Women washing clothes in natural hot water brook, Laugardalur; 40k. City Theatre.

239 Early Telephone Equipment

1986. 80th Anniv of Icelandic Telephone and Telegraph Service. Multicoloured.
687		10k. Type **239**	75	40
688		20k. Modern digital telephone system	1·50	95

240 Hvita River Crossing, 1836 (after Auguste Mayer)

1986. Stamp Day. Sheet 95×67 mm.
MS689 **240** 20k. black (sold at 30k.)   6·75   6·00

241 "Christmas at Peace"

1986. Christmas. Multicoloured.
690		10k. Type **241**	1·40	55
691		12k. "Christmas Night"	75	55

242 "vanur" (ketch) anchored off Olafsvik

1987. 300th Anniv of Olafsvik Trading Station.
692	**242**	50k. purple	3·75	2·00

243 Terminal and Boeing 727 Tail

1987. Opening of Leif Eiriksson Terminal, Keflavik Airport.
693	**243**	100k. multicoloured	6·00	2·75

244 Christ carrying Cross

1987. Europa. Stained Glass Windows by Leifur Breidfoerd, Fossvogur Cemetery Chapel. Multicoloured.
694		12k. Type **244**	2·75	80
695		15k. Soldiers and peace dove	3·50	1·40

245 Rask

1987. Birth Bicentenary of Rasmus Kristjan Rask (philologist).
696	**245**	20k. black	1·50	95

1987. Birds. As T **234**. Multicoloured.
697		13k. Short-eared owl	1·50	70
698		40k. Redwing	2·75	70
699		70k. Oystercatcher	3·75	1·40
700		90k. Mallard	6·00	2·75

246 Girl Brushing Teeth

1987. Dental Protection.
701	**246**	12k. multicoloured	75	55

247 Vulture

1987. National Guardian Spirits. Each red.
702		13k. Type **247**	90	75
703		13k. Dragon	90	75
704		13k. Bull	90	75
705		13k. Giant	90	75

See also Nos. 713/16, 732 and 743/50.

248 Djupivogur Trading Station, 1836 (after Auguste Mayer)

1987. Stamp Day. Sheet 95×67 mm.
MS706 **248** 30k. black (sold at 45k.)   7·50   6·75

249 Christmas Tree

1987. Christmas. Multicoloured.
707		13k. Type **249**	1·10	55
708		17k. "Christmas Light"	1·20	95

250 Steinn Steinarr (poet)

1988. Famous Icelanders. Multicoloured.
709		16k. Type **250**	90	40
710		21k. David Stefansson (writer)	1·40	95

251 Transmission of Messages by Modern Data System

1988. Europa. Communications. Multicoloured.
711		16k. Type **251**	1·50	70
712		21k. Phone pad and globe within envelope (transmission of letters by facsimile machine)	5·25	2·75

1988. National Guardian Spirit. As Nos. 702/5 but values and colour changed.
713		16k. black (Type **247**)	1·10	80
714		16k. black (Dragon)	1·10	80
715		16k. black (Bull)	1·10	80
716		16k. black (Giant)	1·10	80

1988. Flowers. As T **218**. Multicoloured.
717		10k. Tufted vetch	75	40
718		50k. Wild thyme	3·75	1·40

252 Handball

1988. Olympic Games, Seoul.
719	**252**	18k. multicoloured	1·50	70

1988. Birds. As T **234**. Multicoloured.
720		5k. Black-tailed godwit	60	40
721		30k. Long-tailed duck	2·30	1·40

253 Nupsstadur Farm, Fljotshverfi, 1836 (after Auguste Mayer)

1988. Stamp Day. Sheet 95×67 mm.
MS722 **253** 40k. black (sold at 60k.)   6·00   5·50

254 Mother and Baby

1988. 40th Anniv of W.H.O. "Health for All in 2000".
723	**254**	19k. multicoloured	1·50	70

255 Fisherman with Haul of Fish

1988. Christmas. Multicoloured.
724		19k. Type **255**	1·20	70
725		24k. Trawler and buoy	2·00	1·40

1989. Birds. As T **234**. Multicoloured.
726		19k. Red-necked phalarope	1·50	70
727		100k. Snow buntings	7·50	5·50

256 Peysufot (dress costume)

1989. Nordic Countries' Postal Co-operation. Traditional Costumes. Multicoloured.
728		21k. Type **256**	2·10	80
729		26k. Upphlutur (everyday wear)	2·40	1·10

257 Children at Seaside

1989. Europa. Childrens' Toys and Games. Multicoloured.
730		21k. Type **257**	6·75	1·40
731		26k. Girl with hoop and boy with hobby-horse	7·50	1·60

1989. National Guardian Spirit. As No. 703 but colour and value changed.
732		500k. brown (Dragon)	23·00	13·50

258 Mount Skeggi, Arnarfjord

1989. Landscapes. Multicoloured.
733		35k. Type **258**	1·80	70
734		45k. Namaskard thermal spring	2·30	1·10

See also Nos. 757/8 and 765/6.

259 College

1989. Cent of Hvanneyri Agricultural College.
735	**259**	50k. multicoloured	3·00	2·00

260 Seaman throwing Barrels at Whales

1989. Stamp Day. "Nordia 91" Stamp Exhibition, Reykjavik (1st issue). Sheet 114×74 mm containing T **260** and similar vert designs, showing details of the 1539 Carta Marina by Olaus Magnus.
MS736 30k. Type **260**; 30k. Ship harpooning whale; 30k. Sea serpent encircling ship (sold at 130k.)   12·00   11·50

See also Nos. MS760 and MS771.

261 Stefan Stefansson (co-founder) and Flowers

1989. Centenary of Icelandic Natural History Society. Multicoloured.
737		21k. Type **261**	1·20	95
738		26k. Bjarni Saemundsson (first Chairman) and Atlantic cod	1·50	1·10

262 "Virgin and Child"

1989. Christmas. Multicoloured.
739		21k. Type **262**	1·50	70
740		26k. "Three Wise Men"	1·80	1·40

1990. Birds. As T **234**. Multicoloured.
741		21k. European wigeons	2·30	80
742		80k. Pink-footed goose and goslings	5·25	2·75

1990. National Guardian Spirits. As Nos. 702/5 but value and colours changed.
743		5k. green (Type **247**)	45	40
744		5k. green (Dragon)	45	40
745		5k. green (Bull)	45	40
746		5k. green (Giant)	45	40
747		21k. blue (Type **247**)	1·10	95
748		21k. blue (Dragon)	1·10	95
749		21k. blue (Bull)	1·10	95
750		21k. blue (Giant)	1·10	95

263 Gudrun Larusdottir (writer and politician) (after Halldor Petursson)

1990. 110th Birth Anniversaries. Multicoloured.
751		21k. Type **263**	1·50	1·10
752		21k. Ragnhildur Petursdottir (women's educationist) (after Asgrimur Jonsson)	1·50	1·10

264 Posthouse Street, Reykjavik, Post Office and Old Scales

1990. Europa. Post Office Buildings. Multicoloured.

753	21k. Type **264**	4·75	1·40
754	40k. Thoenglabakki 4, Reykjavik, Post Office and modern scales	6·00	2·75

265 Archery

1990. Sport. Multicoloured.

755	21k. Type **265**	1·50	1·10
756	21k. Football	1·50	1·10

1990. Landscapes. As T **258**. Multicoloured.

757	25k. Hvitserkur, Hunafjord	1·50	70
758	200k. Lomagnupur	9·00	4·00

266 Bird, Stars and Map

1990. European Tourism Year.

759	**266**	30k. multicoloured	2·30	1·40

267 Denmark

1990. Stamp Day. "Nordia 91" Stamp Exhibition, Reykjavik (2nd issue). Sheet 114×74 mm containing T **267** and similar vert designs, showing details of the 1539 Carta Marina by Olaus Magnus.

MS760 40k. Type **267**; 40k. Sweden; 40k. Gotland and sailing ship (sold at 170k.)	15·00	14·00

268 Children around Christmas Tree

1990. Christmas. Multicoloured.

761	25k. Type **268**	1·80	70
762	30k. Carol singers	2·30	1·40

1991. Birds. As T **234**. Multicoloured.

763	25k. Slavonian grebes	1·50	55
764	100k. Northern gannets	6·75	1·80

1991. Landscapes. As T **258**. Multicoloured.

765	10k. Mt. Vestrahorn	75	40
766	300k. Kverkfjoll range	13·50	5·50

269 Meteorological Information

1991. Europa. Europe in Space. Multicoloured.

767	26k. Type **269**	9·00	2·00
768	47k. Telecommunications satellite	12·00	3·50

270 Jokulsarlon

1991. Nordic Countries' Postal Co-operation. Tourism. Multicoloured.

769	26k. Type **270**	1·80	95
770	31k. Strokkur hot spring	2·40	1·40

271 Western Iceland

1991. "Nordia 91" Stamp Exhibition (3rd issue). Sheet 114×74 mm containing T **271** and similar vert designs, showing details of the 1539 Carta Marina by Olaus Magnus.

MS771 50k. Type **271**; 50k. Arms and central part of Iceland; 50k. Eastern Iceland, ice floes and compass rose (sold at 215k.)	18·00	17·00

272 Golf

1991. Sports. Multicoloured.

772	26k. Type **272**	1·50	80
773	26k. Glima (wrestling)	1·50	80

273 Pall Isolfsson (composer) (after Hans Muller)

1991. Famous Icelanders. Multicoloured.

774	60k. Ragnar Jonsson (founder of Reykjavik College of Music) (horiz)	2·75	1·40
775	70k. Type **273**	3·25	2·00

274 College Building and Student using Sextant

1991. Cent of College of Navigation, Reykjavik.

776	**274**	50k. multicoloured	3·00	2·00

275 Soloven (mail brigantine)

1991. Stamp Day. Ships. Multicoloured.

777	30k. Type **275**	4·50	2·00
778	30k. Arcturus (cargo liner)	4·50	2·00
779	30k. Gullfoss I (cargo liner)	4·50	2·00
780	30k. Esja II (cargo liner)	4·50	2·00

276 "Light of Christmas"

1991. Christmas. Multicoloured.

781	30k. Type **276**	1·50	80
782	35k. Star	1·80	1·40

277 Skiing

1992. Sport. Multicoloured.

783	30k. Type **277**	2·00	1·40
784	30k. Volleyball	2·00	1·40

278 Map and Santa Maria

1992. Europa. 500th Anniv of Discovery of America by Columbus. Multicoloured.

785	55k. Map and Viking ship (Leif Eriksson)	6·75	2·75
786	55k. Type **278**	6·75	2·75
MS787	85×67 mm. Nos. 785/6	18·00	17·00

279 Agricultural and Industrial Symbols

1992. 75th Anniv of Iceland Chamber of Commerce (30k.) and 50th Anniv of Icelandic Freezing Plants Corporation (35k.). Multicoloured.

788	30k. Type **279**	1·50	95
789	35k. Trawler and Atlantic cod	2·00	1·40

280 River Fnjoska Bridge, Skogar

1992. Bridges. Multicoloured.

790	5k. Type **280**	45	35
791	250k. River Olfusa bridge, Selfoss	11·50	8·00

See also Nos. 804/5.

281 Ford "TT", 1920–26

1992. Postal Vehicles. Multicoloured.

792	30k. Type **281**	3·00	1·40
793	30k. Citroen snowmobile, 1929	3·00	1·40
794	30k. Mail/passenger transport car "RE 231", 1933	3·00	1·40
795	30k. Ford bus, 1946	3·00	1·40

282 Face and Candle reflected in Window

1992. Christmas. Multicoloured.

796	30k. Type **282**	1·50	95
797	35k. Full moon	2·00	1·40

283 Gyr Falcon with Chicks

1992. Endangered Species. The Gyr Falcon. Multicoloured.

798	5k. Type **283**	1·50	70
799	10k. Beating wings	2·30	1·10
800	20k. Eating	3·00	1·60
801	35k. On ground	3·75	2·75

284 Handball

1993. Sport. Multicoloured.

802	30k. Type **284**	1·50	1·10
803	30k. Running	1·50	1·10

1993. Bridges. As T **280**. Multicoloured.

804	90k. River Hvita bridge, Ferjukot	4·50	2·00
805	150k. River Jokulsa a Fjollum bridge, Grimsstadir	7·50	6·00

285 The Blue Lagoon, Svartsengi

1993. Nordic Countries' Postal Co-operation. Tourism. Multicoloured.

806	30k. Type **285**	1·50	1·10
807	35k. Perlan (The Pearl), Reykjavik	1·80	1·40

286 Sailing (Jon Gunnar Arnason)

1993. Europa. Contemporary Art. Multicoloured.

808	35k. Type **286**	3·00	2·00
809	55k. Hatching of the Jet (Magnus Tomasson)	4·50	3·50

287 1933 1k. Balbo Flight Stamp

1993. 60th Anniv of Balbo Transatlantic Mass Formation Flight. Sheet 110×76 mm containing T **287** and similar vert designs. Multicoloured.

MS810 10k. Type **287**; 50k. 1933 5k. Balbo flight stamp; 100k. 1933 10k. Balbo flight stamp (sold at 200k.)	10·50	10·00

288 Junkers "F-13" Seaplane "Sulan" D-483

1993. 65th Anniv of First Icelandic Postal Flight. Multicoloured.

811	30k. Type **288**	3·00	1·40
812	30k. Waco YKS-7 seaplane TF-ORH	3·00	1·40
813	30k. Grumman G-21 Goose amphibian TF-VK	3·00	1·40
814	30k. Consolidated PBY-5 Catalina flying boat "Old Peter" TF-TSP	3·00	1·40

289 Three Wise Men adoring Child

1993. Christmas. Multicoloured.

815	30k. Type **289**	1·50	95
816	35k. Madonna and Child	2·00	1·40

290 Swimming

1994. Sport. Multicoloured.

817	30k. Type **290**	1·50	95
818	30k. Weightlifting	1·50	95

291 Finger Puppets

1994. International Year of the Family.

819	**291**	40k. multicoloured	2·30	1·40

292 St. Brendan visiting Iceland

1994. Europa. St. Brendan's Voyages. Multicoloured.
820		35k. Type **292**	3·00	1·40
821		55k. St. Brendan discovering Faroe Islands	3·75	2·00
MS822		81×76 mm. Nos. 820/1	7·25	7·00

293 Conductor and Instruments

1994. 50th Anniv of Independence. Art and Culture. Multicoloured.
823		30k. Type **293** (44th anniv of Icelandic Symphony Orchestra)	1·50	95
824		30k. Pottery (55th anniv of College of Arts and Crafts)	1·50	95
825		30k. Cameraman and actors (16th anniv of National Film Fund)	1·50	95
826		30k. Ballerina and modern dancers (21st anniv of Icelandic Dance Company)	1·50	95
827		30k. Theatre masks (44th anniv of Icelandic National Theatre)	1·50	95

294 Gisli Sveinsson (President of United Althing, 1944)

1994. 50th Anniv of New Constitution.
828	**294**	30k. multicoloured	2·30	1·40

295 Sveinn Bjornsson (1944–52)

1994. 50th Anniv of Republic. Presidents. Sheet 118×71 mm containing T **295** and similar vert designs. Multicoloured.
MS829		50k. Type **295**; 50k. Asgeir Asgeirsson (1952–68); 50k. Kristjan Eldjarn (1968–80); 50k. Vigdis Finnbogadottir (1980 onwards)	9·75	9·50

296 Children looking at Stamp Album

1994. Stamp Day. Stamp Collecting. Sheet 120×50 mm containing T **296** and similar square designs. Multicoloured.
MS830		30k. Type **296**; 35k. Magnifying glass over stamps; 100k. Girl and elderly man studying globe (sold at 200k.)	13·50	13·00

297 Woman and Stars

1994. Christmas. Multicoloured.
831		30k. Type **297**	1·20	95
832		35k. Man and stars	1·80	1·40

298 Emblem and Airplane

1994. 50th Anniv of I.C.A.O.
833	**298**	100k. multicoloured	5·25	3·50

299 Flag and Salvation Army Members

1995. Anniversaries. Multicoloured.
834		35k. Type **299** (centenary of Salvation Army in Iceland)	2·30	1·40
835		90k. Map of fjord (centenary of Seydisfjordur)	5·25	2·75

300 Geyser

1995. 14th World Men's Handball Championship. Multicoloured.
836		35k. Type **300**	2·30	1·40
837		35k. Stadium	2·30	1·40
838		35k. Volcano	2·30	1·40
839		35k. Entrance to fjord	2·30	1·40

301 Laufas

1995. Nordic Countries' Postal Co-operation. Tourism. Multicoloured.
840		30k. Type **301**	1·50	1·10
841		35k. Fjallsjokull Glacier	2·30	1·40

302 "Spell-broken" (sculpture, Einar Jonsson)

1995. Europa. Peace and Freedom.
842	**302**	35k. multicoloured	2·30	1·60
843	**302**	55k. multicoloured	3·00	2·40

303 Laura (mail ship)

1995. Mail Ships. Multicoloured.
844		30k. Type **303**	1·50	1·10
845		30k. Dronning Alexandrine	1·50	1·10
846		30k. Laxfoss	1·50	1·10
847		30k. Godafoss III	1·50	1·10

304 Redpoll (Acanthis flammea)

1995. European Nature Conservation Year. Birds. Multicoloured.
848		25k. Type **304**	1·50	80
849		250k. Common snipe (Gallinago gallinago)	12·00	10·00

305 Boeing 757

1995. 40th Anniv of Iceland–Luxembourg Air Link.
850	**305**	35k. multicoloured	1·50	1·20

306 Hraunfossar Waterfalls (left detail)

1995. "Nordia 96" Stamp Exhibition, Reykjavik (1st issue). Sheet 105×65 mm containing T **306** and similar horiz design. Multicoloured.
MS851		10k. Type **306**; 150k. Waterfalls (right detail) (sold at 200k.)	12·00	11·50

The stamps form a composite design. See also No. **MS871**.

307 Snowman and Snowwoman

1995. Christmas. Multicoloured.
852		30k. Type **307**	1·50	70
853		35k. Coloured fir trees	2·00	1·40

308 Anniversary Emblem

1995. 50th Anniv of U.N.O.
854	**308**	100k. multicoloured	4·25	3·00

309 Common Cormorant (Phalacrocorax carbo)

1996. Birds. Multicoloured.
855		20k. Type **309**	90	70
856		40k. Barrow's goldeneye (Bucephala islandica)	2·10	1·40

310 Seamen in a Boat (Gunnlaugur Scheving)

1996. Paintings. Multicoloured.
857		100k. Type **310**	4·50	2·75
858		200k. At the Washing Springs (Kristin Jonsdottir)	7·50	5·50

311 Halldora Bjarnadottir (founder of women's societies)

1996. Europa. Famous Women. Multicoloured.
859		35k. Type **311**	2·30	1·60
860		55k. Olafia Johannsdottir (women's rights campaigner and temperance worker)	3·00	2·20

312 1931 Buick

1996. Post Buses. Multicoloured.
861		35k. Type **312**	2·00	1·40
862		35k. 1933 Studebaker	2·00	1·40
863		35k. 1937 Ford	2·00	1·40
864		35k. 1946 Reo	2·00	1·40

313 Running

1996. Olympic Games, Atlanta. Multicoloured.
865		5k. Type **313**	45	25
866		25k. Javelin	90	80
867		45k. Long jumping	1·80	1·60
868		65k. Shot put	2·75	2·40

314 Hospital Ward

1996. Centenary of Order of the Sisters of St. Joseph in Iceland.
869	**314**	65k. black, stone & purple	3·00	2·00

315 School

1996. 150th Anniv of Reykjavik School.
870	**315**	150k. multicoloured	6·00	4·75

316 Godafoss Waterfalls (central detail)

1996. "Nordia 96" Stamp Exhibition, Reykjavik (2nd issue). Sheet 105×65 mm containing T **316** and similar square designs. Multicoloured.
MS871		45k. Type **316**; 65k. Waterfalls (right detail); 90k. Waterfalls (left detail) (sold at 300k.)	15·00	14·00

The stamps form a composite design.

317 Reykjavik Cathedral

1996. Bicentenary of Reykjavik Cathedral.
872	**317**	45k. multicoloured	2·30	1·40

318 Virgin Mary holding Child Jesus (ivory figurine)

1996. Christmas. Exhibits from National Museum of Iceland. Multicoloured.
873		35k. Type **318**	1·50	80
874		45k. Pax depicting Nativity	2·00	1·80

319 Red-breasted Merganser (Mergus serrator)

1997. Ducks. Multicoloured.
875		10k. Type **319**	75	70
876		500k. Green-winged teal (Anas crecca)	20·00	16·00

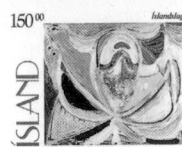

320 *Song of Iceland* (Svavar Gudnason)

1997. Paintings. Multicoloured.
| 877 | 150k. Type **320** | 6·00 | 4·75 |
| 878 | 200k. *The Harbour* (Thorvaldur Skulason) | 9·00 | 6·00 |

321 de Havilland D.H.89A Dragon Rapide

1997. Mail Planes. Multicoloured.
879	35k. Type **321**	2·00	1·40
880	35k. Stinson S.R. 8B Reliant seaplane	2·00	1·40
881	35k. Douglas DC-3 Dakota	2·00	1·40
882	35k. de Havilland D.H.C.6 Twin Otter	2·00	1·40

322 Hurdling

1997. Seventh European Small States' Games. Multicoloured.
| 883 | 35k. Type **322** | 1·50 | 1·10 |
| 884 | 45k. Sailing | 2·30 | 1·60 |

323 *The Deacon of Myrka*

1997. Europa. Tales and Legends. Paintings by Asgrimur Jonsson. Multicoloured.
| 885 | 45k. Type **323** | 2·30 | 1·40 |
| 886 | 65k. Surtla at Blalandseyjar | 3·00 | 2·00 |

324 Printer's Colour Control and Pieces of Type

1997. Centenary of Formation of Icelandic Printers' Association (now part of Union of Icelandic Graphic Workers).
| 887 | **324** | 90k. multicoloured | 3·75 | 3·50 |

325 Stefania Gudmundsdattir and Idno Theatre

1997. Centenary of Reykjavik Theatre.
| 888 | **325** | 100k. multicoloured | 4·50 | 3·50 |

The actress is shown in the role of the Fairy in "New Year's Night" by Indridi Einarsson.

326 Western Islands Eight-oared Fishing Boat

1997. Stamp Day. Icelandic Boats. Sheet 110×76 mm containing T **326** and similar square designs. Each black, brown and chestnut.
MS889 35k. Type **326**; 65k. Engey six-oared sailing boat, 1912; 100k. Egil (Breidafjordur boat), 1904 (sold at 250k.)   13·00   12·00

327 Wise Men

1997. Christmas. Multicoloured.
| 890 | 35k. Type **327** | 1·50 | 1·40 |
| 891 | 45k. Nativity | 2·30 | 1·60 |

328 Mounted Mail Carrier

1997. Rural Post.
| 892 | **328** | 50k. multicoloured | 2·30 | 2·00 |

329 Downhill Skiing

1998. Winter Olympic Games, Nagano, Japan. Multicoloured.
| 893 | 35k. Type **329** | 1·50 | 1·10 |
| 894 | 45k. Cross-country skiing | 2·30 | 1·60 |

330 Sailing Dinghies

1998. Nordic Countries' Postal Co-operation. Sailing. Multicoloured.
| 895 | 35k. Type **330** | 1·50 | 1·10 |
| 896 | 45k. Yachts | 2·30 | 1·60 |

331 Lumpsucker (*Cyclopterus lumpus*)

1998. Fish (1st series). Multicoloured.
897	5k. Type **331**	45	40
898	10k. Atlantic cod (*Gadus morhua*)	75	70
899	60k. Skate (*Raja batis*)	3·00	2·75
900	300k. Atlantic wolffish (*Anarhichas lupus*)	12·00	11·00
MS901	100×68 mm. Nos. 897/900	18·00	17·00

See also Nos. 913/14, 972/3 and 983/4.

332 Children waving Flags

1998. Europa. National Festivals. National Day. Multicoloured.
| 902 | 45k. Type **332** | 2·40 | 2·00 |
| 903 | 65k. Statue of President Jon Sigurdsson and flags | 3·25 | 2·75 |

333 Scolecite

1998. Minerals (1st series). Multicoloured.
| 904 | 35k. Type **333** | 1·60 | 1·40 |
| 905 | 45k. Stilbite | 2·40 | 1·90 |

See also Nos. 933/4.

334 Hospital

1998. Centenary of Founding of Leprosy Hospital, Laugarnes.
| 906 | **334** | 70k. multicoloured | 3·25 | 2·75 |

335 Anniversary Emblem

1998. 125th Anniv of First Iceland Stamps.
| 907 | **335** | 35k. multicoloured | 1·60 | 1·40 |

336 Peat-cutter

1998. Stamp Day. Agricultural Tools. Sheet 110×76 mm containing T **336** and similar square designs.
MS908 35k. green, black and grey; 65k. ochre, black and grey; 100k. blue, black and grey (sold at 250k.)   13·00   12·00
DESIGNS: 65k. Mower; 100k. Grinder.

337 Cat and Houses (Thelma Ingolfsdottir)

1998. Christmas. Multicoloured.
| 909 | 35k. Type **337** | 1·60 | 1·40 |
| 910 | 45k. Two angels (Telma Thrastardottir) | 2·40 | 2·00 |

338 Writing and Hand forming Fist

1998. 50th Anniv of Universal Declaration of Human Rights.
| 911 | **338** | 50k. black, green and red | 2·40 | 2·00 |

339 Leifs

1999. Birth Centenary of Jon Leifs (composer).
| 912 | **339** | 35k. multicoloured | 1·60 | 1·40 |

1999. Fish (2nd series). As T **331**. Multicoloured.
| 913 | 35k. Plaice (*Pleuronectes platessa*) | 1·90 | 1·60 |
| 914 | 55k. Atlantic herring (*Clupea harengus*) | 3·00 | 2·40 |

340 Killer Whale (*Orcinus orca*)

1999. Marine Mammals (1st series). Multicoloured.
915	35k. Type **340**	1·90	1·60
916	45k. Sperm whale (*Physeter macrocephalus*)	2·40	2·00
917	65k. Blue whale (*Balaenoptera musculus*)	3·25	2·75
918	85k. Common porpoise (*Phocoena phocoena*)	4·00	3·50
MS919	100×80 mm. Nos. 915/19	13·00	12·50

See also Nos. 966/9 and 1000/3.

341 Arnold Jung's Steam Locomotive *Minor*, 1892

1999. Transport. Multicoloured.
920	25k. Type **341**	4·75	4·00
921	50k. Type **341**	2·20	1·90
922	75k. "Sigurfari" (fishing cutter)	3·50	3·00

342 Dates and Doves

1999. 50th Anniv of Council of Europe.
| 923 | **342** | 35k. multicoloured | 3·25 | 2·00 |

343 Larch Boletes (*Suillus grevillei*)

1999. Fungi (1st series). Multicoloured.
| 924 | 35k. Type **343** | 1·60 | 1·40 |
| 925 | 75k. Field mushrooms (*Agaricus campestris*) | 3·25 | 2·75 |

See also Nos. 954/5.

344 Skutustadagigar, Lake Myvatn

1999. Europa. Parks and Gardens. Multicoloured.
| 926 | 50k. Type **344** | 2·40 | 2·00 |
| 927 | 75k. Arnarstapi Point | 3·25 | 2·75 |

345 Wheat ("Land Graedsla")

1999. Nature Conservation. Multicoloured.
928	35k. Type **345**	1·60	1·40
929	35k. Rainbow and tree within sun ("Loft")	1·60	1·40
930	35k. Nest with eggs ("Vot Lendis")	1·60	1·40
931	35k. Tree stump ("Skog Raekt")	1·60	1·40
932	35k. Fish and birds ("Stlendur")	1·60	1·40

1999. Minerals (2nd series). As T **333**. Multicoloured.
| 933 | 40k. Calcite | 2·10 | 1·80 |
| 934 | 50k. Heulandite | 2·75 | 2·30 |

346 Facescape (Erro)

1999. Reykjavik, European Cultural City. Multicoloured.
| 935 | 35k. Type **346** | 1·90 | 1·60 |
| 936 | 50k. Cultural symbols | 3·00 | 2·40 |

347 *Danish Sailing Ship off Drangey* (Carl Baagoe)

1999. Stamp Day. Sheet 110×65 mm.
MS937 **347** 200k. brown and black (sold at 250k.)   16·00   15·00

348 *Man cleaning Globe* (Jona Greta Gudmundsdottir)

1999. "Stampin' the Future". Winning Entries in Children's International Painting Competition.
| 938 | **348** | 35k. multicoloured | 2·40 | 1·40 |

349 Goblin (Stiff-legs)

1999. Christmas. Yule Goblins. Multicoloured.
939	35k. Type **349**	1·60	1·40
940	35k. Leaping over rock (Gully-gawk)	1·60	1·40
941	35k. With arm raised (Stubby)	1·60	1·40

942	35k. Licking spoon (Spoon-licker)	1·60	1·40
943	35k. With hand in cooking pot (Pot-scraper)	1·60	1·40
944	35k. With finger in mouth (Bowl-licker)	1·60	1·40
945	35k. Opening door (Door-slammer)	1·60	1·40
946	35k. Drinking from ladle (Skyr-gobbler)	1·60	1·40
947	35k. Carrying sausages (Sausage-swiper)	1·60	1·40
948	35k. Looking through window (Window-peeper)	1·60	1·40
949	50k. With nose raised (Door-sniffer)	2·40	2·00
950	50k. With leg of meat (Meat-hook)	2·40	2·00
951	50k. With candles (Candle-beggar)	2·40	2·00

350 Embroidered Altar Frontal, Holar Cathedral

2000. Millenary of Christianity in Iceland. Multicoloured.

952	40k. Type **350**	2·40	2·00
MS953 70×46 mm. 40k. Family singing hymns (29×39 mm)		2·50	2·40

351 Chanterelle (*Cantharellus cibarius*)

2000. Fungi. Multicoloured.

954	40k. Type **351**	1·90	1·60
955	50k. Shaggy ink cap (*Coprinus comatus*)	2·40	2·00

352 Statue of Thorfinn Karlsefni (early settler) and Globe

2000. Millenary of Discovery of the Americas by Leif Eriksson. Multicoloured.

956	40k. Type **352**	1·80	1·50
957	50k. Viking longship under sail	2·40	2·00
958	75k. Longship on shore	3·25	2·75
959	90k. Leif Eriksson and globe	4·00	3·50
MS960 96×76 mm. Nos. 956/9		13·00	12·00

353 Quill and Profile

2000. New Millennium. Multicoloured.

961	40k. Type **353**	1·80	1·50
962	50k. Family tree, man and computer chip	2·20	1·90

354 Steam Roller

2000. Transport. Multicoloured.

963	40k. Type **354**	2·40	2·00
964	75k. Fire engine	3·25	2·75

355 "Building Europe"

2000. Europa.

965	**355** 50k. multicoloured	3·25	2·75

2000. Marine Mammals (2nd series). As T **340**. Multicoloured.

966	5k. Bottlenose whale (*Hyperoodon ampullatus*)	50	25
967	40k. Atlantic white-sided dolphin (*Lagenorhynchus actus*)	1·90	1·60
968	50k. Humpback whale (*Megaptera novaeangliae*)	2·40	2·00
969	75k. Minke whale (*Balaenoptera acutorostrata*)	3·50	3·00

356 Pansy (*Violea x wittrockiana*)

2000. Summer Flowers (1st series). Multicoloured.

970	40k. Type **356**	1·90	1·60
971	50k. Petunia (*Petunia x hybrida*)	2·40	2·00
See also Nos. 986/7.			

2000. Fish (3rd series). As T **331**. Multicoloured.

972	10k. Haddock (*Melanogrammus aeglefinus*)	65	40
973	250k. Capelin (*Mallotus villosus*)	13·00	12·00

357 Dark Marbled Carpet (*Chioroclysta citrata*)

2000. Butterflies. Multicoloured.

974	40k. Type **357**	1·90	1·60
975	50k. Antler (*Cerapteryx graminis*)	2·40	2·00

358 *Icelandic settlers on the Shore of Lake Winnipeg (Arni Sigurdsson)*

2000. Stamp Day. Sheet 88×73 mm.

MS976 **358** 200k. multicoloured (sold at 250k.)		13·00	12·00

359 Viking Settler's House

2000. Early Dwellings. Multicoloured.

977	45k. Type **359**	1·90	1·60
978	75k. Viking turf houses, Stong Thjorsardal	3·75	3·25

360 Leppaludi

2000. Christmas. Ogres. Multicoloured.

979	40k. Type **360**	2·10	1·80
980	50k. Gryla	2·75	2·30
MS981 105×75 mm. As Nos. 979/80, but 21×36 mm		5·00	4·75

361 Super Puma Helicopter, Fokker 27 Airplane and *Tyr* (ship)

2001. 75th Anniv of Coast Guard Service in Iceland.

982	**361** 20k. multicoloured	2·40	2·00

2001. Fish. As T **331**. Multicoloured.

983	55k. Greenland halibut (*Reinhardtius hippoglossides*)	3·25	2·75
984	80k. Saithe (*Pollachius virens*)	4·00	3·50

362 Man's Face, Tents and Emblem

2001. 50th Anniv of United Nations Commissioner for Refugees.

985	**362** 50k. black and brown	2·40	2·00

363 Marigold (*Calendula officinalis*)

2001. Summer Flowers. Multicoloured.

986	55k. Type **363**	3·00	2·40
987	65k. Livingstone daisy (*Dorotheanthus bellidformis*)	3·25	2·75

364 Dog

2001. Icelandic Sheepdogs. Multicoloured.

988	40k. Type **364**	2·40	2·00
989	80k. Black and white dog	4·00	3·50

365 Olsen-Jonasson Ognin

2001. Airplanes. Multicoloured.

990	55k. Type **365**	3·25	2·75
991	80k. Klemm KL-25E	4·00	3·50

366 Woman's Head and Waterfall

2001. Europa. Water Resources. Multicoloured.

992	55k. Type **366**	2·40	2·00
993	80k. Cupped hands and wave	3·25	2·75

367 Walking

2001. Horses. Multicoloured.

994	40k. Type **367**	1·60	1·40
995	50k. Running walk	2·20	1·90
996	55k. Trotting	2·40	2·00
997	60k. Pacing	3·25	2·75
998	80k. Cantering	4·00	3·50

2001. Domestic Letter Rate. No. 915 optd **Bref 50g**.

999	(35k.) multicoloured	3·00	2·40

2001. Marine Mammals (3rd series). As T **340**. Multicoloured.

1000	5k. Large-beaked dolphin (*Lagenorhynchus albirostris*)	50	25
1001	40k. Fin whale (*Balaenoptera physalus*)	1·60	1·40
1002	80k. Sei whale (*Balaenoptera borealis*)	3·25	2·75
1003	100k. Long-finned pilot whale (*Globicephala melas*)	4·00	3·50

369 Grimsey

2001. Islands (1st series). Multicoloured.

1004	55k. Type **369**	1·90	1·60
1005	55k. Papey	3·00	2·40
See also Nos. 1031/2, 1061/2 and 1094/5.			

370 Esja Mountain

2001. Stamp Day. Sheet 105×48 mm.

MS1006 **370** 250k. multicoloured		13·00	12·00

371 Brautarholt Church, Kjalarnes

2001. Christmas. Multicoloured.

1007	(42k.) Type **371**	1·90	1·60
1008	55k Viomyri Church, Skagafjorour	2·20	1·90

372 Northern Wheatear (*Oenanthe oenanthe*)

2001. Birds (1st series). Multicoloured.

1009	42k. Type **372**	1·60	1·40
1010	250k. Ringed plover (*Charadrius hiaticula*)	11·00	10·00
See also Nos. 1036/7,1055/6 and 1092/3.			

373 Brown Birch Bolete (*Leccinum scabrum*)

2002. Fungi. Multicoloured. (a) Inscr "Bref 20g".

1011	(42k.) Type **373**	1·90	1·60

(b) With face value.

1012	85k. Hedgehog fungus (*Hydnum repandum*)	3·75	3·25

No. 1011 was for use on domestic mail up to 20 grammes.

374 *Stanley* and 2 h.p. Mollerup Engine

2002. Centenary of First Motorboat in Iceland.

1013	**374** 60k. multicoloured	2·50	2·20

375 Mount Snæfell

2002. International Year of the Mountain. Inscr "Bref 20g".

1014	**375** (42k.) multicoloured	2·40	2·00

No. 1014 was for use on domestic mail up to 20 grammes.

376 Laxness

2002. Birth Centenary of Halldor Laxness (writer and Nobel Prize winner).

1015	**376** 100k. multicoloured	4·00	3·50
MS1016 75×45 mm. No. 1015		4·50	4·00

377 "Waterfall" (sculpture, Ruri) and Emblem

2002. Nordic Countries' Postal Co-operation. Modern Art. Multicoloured. (a) Inscr "Bref 20g".

1017	(42k.) Type **377** (50th anniv of Nordic Council)	1·90	1·60

(b) With face value.
1018 60k. "Tension" (sculpture, Hafsteinn Austmann) and emblem 3·25 2·75

No. 1017 was for use on domestic mail up to 20 grammes.

378 Grotta

2002. Lighthouses. Multicoloured.
1019 60k. Type **378** 3·25 2·75
1020 85k. Kogur 4·00 3·50

379 House and Sesselja Sigmundsdottir

2002. Birth Centenary of Sesselja H. Sigmundsdottir (mental health pioneer and environmentalist).
1021 **379** 45k. multicoloured 2·10 1·80

380 Trapeze Artists and Clown

2002. Europa. Circus. Multicoloured.
1022 60k. Type **380** 2·40 2·00
1023 85k. Marionette's head and lion leaping through flaming hoop 3·50 3·00

381 Lobelia (*Lobelia erinus*)

2002. Summer Flowers. Multicoloured.
1024 10k. Type **381** 80 55
1025 200k. Cornflower (*Centaurea cyanus*) 8·75 7·50

382 Arctic Charr (*Salvelinus alpinus*)

2002. Fish from Lake Thingvallavatn. Multicoloured. (a) Inscr "Bref 20g".
1026 (45k.) Type **382** 2·40 2·00

(b) Inscr "Bréf 50g".
1027 (55k.) Brown trout (*Salmo trutta*) (vert) 3·00 2·40

(c) With face value.
1028 60k. Arctic charr (*Salvelinus alpinus*) 3·25 2·75
1029 90k. Arctic charr (*Salvelinus alpinus*) 4·00 3·50
1030 200k. Arctic charr (*Salvelinus alpinus*) 7·25 6·75

No. 1026 was for use on domestic mail up to 20 grammes.
No. 1027 was for use on domestic mail up to 50 grammes.

2002. Islands (2nd series). As T **369**. Multicoloured.
1031 45k. Vigur 1·80 1·50
1032 55k. Flatey 2·20 1·90

383 South Street, Reykjavik, and Mount Keilir (volcano)

2002. Stamp Day. Sheet 85×55 mm.
MS1033 **383** 250k. multicoloured 11·00 10·50

384 Bauble, Flags and Gift

2002. Christmas. Multicoloured.
1034 45k. Type **384** 2·10 1·80
1035 60k. Gifts 2·75 2·30

385 Common Redshank (*Tringa totanus*)

2002. Birds (2nd series). Multicoloured.
1036 50k. Type **385** 2·40 2·00
1037 85k. Grey phalarope (*Phalaropus fulicarius*) 4·00 3·50

386 Modern Policemen

2003. Bicentenary of Icelandic Police Force. Multicoloured.
1038 45k. Type **386** 2·10 1·80
1039 55k. 1803 policeman 2·75 2·30

387 Annual Phlox (*Phlox drummondii*)

2003. Summer Flowers. Multicoloured.
1040 45k. Type **387** 2·10 1·80
1041 60k. Treasure flower (*Gazania x hybrida*) 3·00 2·40

388 Bull and Audhumla (mythological cow)

2003. Icelandic Cattle. Multicoloured.
1042 45k. Type **388** 1·90 1·60
1043 85k. Red-mottled cow 3·75 3·25

389 Map, Raven and Sailing Ship

2003. Nordia 2003 International Stamp Exhibition, Reykjavik. Sheet 86×76 mm
MS1044 **389** 250k. multicoloured 13·00 12·00

390 Saefari

2003. Ferries. Multicoloured.
1045 45k. Type **390** 1·90 1·60
1046 45k. Saevar 1·90 1·60
1047 60k. Herjolfur 2·40 2·00
1048 60k. Baldur 2·40 2·00

391 Church

2003. Centenary of Free Church, Reykjavik.
1049 **391** 200k. multicoloured 8·75 8·00

392 Hen and Cockerel

2003. Icelandic Poultry.
1050 **392** 45k. multicoloured 2·40 2·00

393 Posters

2003. Europa. Poster Art. Multicoloured.
1051 60k. Type **393** 2·40 2·00
1052 85k. Posters (different) 3·25 2·75

394 Friendship (Orn Agustsson)

2006. Winning Entry in Children's Stamp Design Competition.
1053 **394** 45k. multicoloured 2·40 2·00

395 District Officer and Family

2003. 300th Anniv of First Census.
1054 **395** 60k. multicoloured 3·25 2·75

2003. Birds (3rd series). As T **385**. Multicoloured.
1055 70k. Meadow pipit (*Anthus pratensis*) 3·25 2·75
1056 250k. Whimbrel (*Numenius phaeopus*) 10·50 9·50

396 Reindeer (*Rangifer tarandus*)

2003.
1057 **396** 45k. multicoloured 2·40 2·00

397 Barrack converted to House

2003. Stamp Day. Sheet 120×58 mm.
MS1058 **397** 250k. multicoloured 11·00 10·50

398 Girl hanging Baubles on Tree

2003. Christmas. Multicoloured.
1059 45k. Type **398** 1·80 1·50
1060 60k. Boy lighting candles 2·40 2·00

2003. Islands (3rd series). As T **369**.
1061 85k. Heimaey 3·50 3·00
1062 200k. Hrisey 8·00 7·25

399 Marigolds (*Tagetes patula*)

2004. Summer Flowers. Multicoloured.
1063 50k. Type **399** 1·90 1·60
1064 55k. Begonias (*begonia x tuberhybrida*) 2·10 1·80

400 Hannes Hafstein (first minister)

2004. Centenary of Icelandic Home Rule. Multicoloured.
1065 150k. Type **400** 6·00 5·00
MS1066 79×50 mm. No. 1065 6·50 6·00

401 Coot (trawler)

2004
1067 **401** 50k. blue and black 1·90 1·60

402 Snorralaug Thermal Pool

2004. Geo-thermal Energy. Multicoloured.
1068 50k. Type **402** 1·90 1·60
1069 55k. Vent, dome and steam (30×48 mm) 2·10 1·80
1070 60k. Pipeline 2·20 1·90
1071 90k. Turbine 3·75 3·00
1072 250k. Map of Iceland, mid Atlantic ridge and clouds (30×48 mm) 8·75 8·00

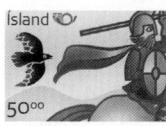

403 Odin

2004. Norse Mythology. Sheet 105×70 mm containing T **403** and similar horiz design (1st issue). Multicoloured.
MS1073 50k. Type **403**; 60k. Sleipnir (Odin's horse) 4·75 4·50

Stamps of a similar theme were issued by Aland Islands, Denmark, Faroe Islands, Finland, Greenland, Norway and Sweden.
See also No. MS1137.

404 Ford Fairlane Victoria, 1956

2004. Cars. Multicoloured.
1074 60k. Type **404** 2·40 2·00
1075 60k. Pobeta, 1954 2·40 2·00
1076 85k. Chevrolet Bel Air, 1955 3·50 3·00
1077 85k. Volkswagen, 1952 3·50 3·00

405 Woman reaching into Barrel of Fish

2004. Centenary of Herring Production.
1078 **405** 65k. multicoloured 2·40 2·00

406 Cyclists

2004. Europa. Holidays. Multicoloured.
1079	65k. Type **406**	2·40	2·00
1080	90k. Four-wheel drive vehicles in snow	3·25	2·75

407 Baby and Emblem

2004. Centenary of Hringurinn (women's charitable organization).
1081	**407**	100k. multicoloured	3·75	3·00

408 Hand holding Light Bulb

2004. Centenary of Electrification.
1082	**408**	50k. multicoloured	1·90	1·60

409 Grisette (*Amanita vaginata*)

2004. Fungi. Multicoloured.
1083	50k. Type **409**	1·90	1·60
1084	60k. *Camarophyllus pratensis*	2·20	1·90

410 Cudell (1901)

2004. Centenary of First Motor Car in Iceland.
1085	**410**	100k. black	3·75	3·00

411 Ground Beetle (*Nebria gyllenhali*)

2004. Insects. Multicoloured.
1086	50k. Type **411**	1·90	1·60
1087	70k. White-tailed bumble bee (*Bombus lucorum*)	2·50	2·20

412 Ship and Hospital Building

2004. Centenary of French Hospital, Faskrudsfirdi.
1088	**412**	60k. multicoloured	2·50	2·00

413 Rock, Hvita River, Bruarhlod

2004. Stamp Day. Sheet 85×55 mm.
MS1089 **413** 250k. multicoloured			12·50	12·00

414 Ptarmigan in Winter Plumage

2004. Christmas. Multicoloured.
1090	45k. Type **414**	1·90	1·60
1091	65k. Reindeer	2·75	2·20

2004. Birds (4th series). As T **385**. Multicoloured.
1092	55k. Sandpiper (*Caladris maritime*)	2·30	1·90
1093	75k. Dunlin (*Caladris alpine*)	3·00	2·50

2005. Islands (4th series). As T **369**.
1094	5k. Videy	55	30
1095	90k. Flatey	4·00	3·25

415 Forest

2005. Centenary of Forestation Programme.
1096	**415**	45k. multicoloured	2·10	1·70

416 Brooch (11th-century)

2005. 60th Anniv of Foundation, and Re-opening (2004) of National Museum. Sheet 105×75 mm containing T **416** and similar vert designs. Multicoloured.
MS1097 100k. Type **416**; 150k. Thor (10th-century statue)		11·50	11·00

417 Field Mouse (*Apodemus sylvaticus*)

2005. Mice. Multicoloured.
1098	45k. Type **417**	2·10	1·70
1099	125k. House mouse (*Mus musculus*)	5·50	4·75

418 Rose

2005. Greetings Stamps. Flowers. Multicoloured.
1100	50k. Type **418**	2·30	1·90
1101	50k. Gerbera	2·30	1·90
1102	50k. Zantedeschia	2·30	1·90
1103	70k. Tulip	3·25	2·50

419 Araneus diadematus

2005. Insect and Spider. Multicoloured.
1104	50k. Type **419**	2·30	2·00
1105	70k. *Musca domestica*	3·25	2·75

420 Vorour PH 4

2005. Old Fishing Boats. Multicoloured.
1106	70k. Type **420**	3·25	2·75

1107	70k. *Karl VE 47*	3·25	2·75
1108	95k. *Sædis IS 67*	4·25	3·75
1109	95k. *Guobjorg NK 74*	4·25	3·75

421 Bridge over Sogid River, Grimsnes

2005. Bridges.
1110	**421**	50k. violet, silver and black	2·30	2·00
1111	-	95k. ultramarine, silver and black	4·25	3·75
1112	-	165k. blue, silver and black	6·00	5·25

DESIGNS: 50k. Type **421**; 95k. Over Lagarfljot river; 165k. Over Jokulsa river, Oxarfjordur.

422 Fish Fillets, Cutlery, Smoked Fish and Water

2005. Europa. Gastronomy. Multicoloured.
1113	70k. Type **422**	3·25	2·75
1114	90k. Cutlery, chillies and fish fillets, smoked fish and flowers	3·75	3·50

423 Fisherman and Red Frances Fly

2005. Salmon Fishing. Multicoloured.
1115	50k. Type **423**	2·50	2·20
1116	60k. Fishing from boat and Laxa Blue fly (vert)	2·75	2·50

424 Vaccinium uliginosum

2005. Berries. Multicoloured.
1117	65k. Type **424**	3·00	2·75
1118	90k. *Fragaria vesca*	4·25	3·75

425 Motorcyclist

2005. Centenary of First Motorcycle.
1119	**425**	50k. multicoloured	2·30	2·00

426 Couple dancing

2005. Centenary of Commercial College.
1120	**426**	70k. multicoloured	3·25	2·75

427 Reykjavik

2005. Stamp Day. Sheet 105×55 mm.
MS1121 **427** 200k. multicoloured			9·50	9·25

428 Apple

2005. Christmas.
1122	**428**	50k. vermilion and gold	2·30	2·00
1123	-	70k. green and gold	3·25	3·00

DESIGNS: 50k. Type **428**; 70k. Pine tree.
Nos. 1122/3 were impregnated with the scent of apples and pine, respectively, which was released when rubbed.

429 Greylag (*Anser anser*)

2005. Birds. Multicoloured.
1124	60k. Type **429**	2·75	2·50
1125	105k. Starling (*Sturnus vulgaris*)	5·00	4·25

430 Dryas octopetala

2006. National Flower.
1126	**430**	50k. multicoloured	2·30	2·00

431 Record Label, Cadillac, Guitar and Dancers

2006. 50th Anniv of Rock and Roll Music in Iceland.
1127	**431**	60k. multicoloured	2·75	2·50

432 Hands, Dove and Barbed Wire

2006. 50th Anniv of First Refugees.
1128	**432**	70k. multicoloured	3·25	2·75

433 1969 14k.50 Europa Stamp (As Type **117**)

2006. 50th Anniv of Europa Stamps. Sheet 80×49 mm containing T **433** and similar horiz design. Multicoloured.
MS1129 150k.×2, Type **433**; 1968 9k.50 Europa stamp (As Type **111**)		13·50	13·00

434 Camera, Programme and First Cinema

2006. Centenary of Cinema in Iceland. Multicoloured.
1130	**434**	50k. Type **434**	2·30	2·00
1131	95k. Faces, projector and tickets	4·50	4·00
1132	160k. Helmeted warrior, clapperboard, popcorn and cameraman	7·25	6·50

435 Landrover (1951)

2006. First Four-wheel Drive Vehicles in Iceland.

1133	70k. Type **435**	3·25	2·75
1134	70k. Willys jeep (1946)	3·25	2·75
1135	90k. Austin Gypsy (1965)	4·00	3·50
1136	90k. Gaz-69 (1955)	4·00	3·50

436 *Mythical Beings*
(Johann Briem)

2004. Norse Mythology (2nd issue). Sheet 105×70 mm.

MS1137 **436** 50k. multicoloured	4·75	4·25

Stamps of a similar theme were issued by Aland Islands, Denmark, Faröe Islands, Greenland, Finland, Norway and Sweden.

437 Faxi

2006. Waterfalls. Multicoloured.

1138	55k. Type **437**	2·75	2·30
1139	65k. Oxararfoss (30×48 mm)	3·25	2·75
1140	75k. Glymur (30×48 mm)	3·75	3·25
1141	95k. Hjalparfoss	4·50	4·00
1142	220k. Skeifarfoss	10·50	10·00

438 Enclosed Heart

2006. Europa. Integration. Ordinary or self-adhesive gum.

1143	**438** 75k. scarlet and black	3·50	3·00
1144	– 95k. blue and black (horiz)	4·50	4·00

DESIGNS: No. 1143, Type **438**; 1144, Arrows, one joining from right.

439 Medal and Athlete

2006. 50th Anniv of First Icelandic Olympic Gold Medal.

1147	**439** 55k. multicoloured	2·75	2·30

440 Iceland outlined
in Cable

2006. Centenary of Telephony in Iceland.

1148	**440** 65k. multicoloured	3·25	2·75

441 *Empetrum
nigrum*

2006. Berries. Multicoloured.

1149	75k. Type **441**	3·50	3·00
1150	130k. *Rubus saxatilis*	6·25	5·50

442 Girdle of Grettir
(trophy)

2006. Centenary of Wrestling (Glima) Tournament. Sheet 80×47 mm.

MS1151 **442** 200k. multicoloured	9·50	9·25

443 Angel

2006. Christmas. Multicoloured.

1152	55k. Type **443**	2·30	2·00
1153	75k. Heart	3·00	2·75

No. 1152 also comes self-adhesive.

444 *Dolchiovespula
norwegica*

2006. Insects. Multicoloured.

1155	65k. Type **444**	2·75	2·30
1156	110k. *Coccinella undecim-punctata*	4·50	4·00

445 *Xerocomus
subtomentosus*

2006. Fungi. Multicoloured.

1157	70k. Type **445**	2·75	2·50
1158	90k. *Kuehneromyces mutablis*	3·75	3·50

446 Emblem

2007. Centenary of Icelandic Women's Society.
Multicoloured.

1159	**446** 60k. multicoloured	2·30	2·00

447 *Jon foseti*

2007. Centenary of *Jon foseti* (first Icelandic deep sea trawler).

1160	**447** 65k. multicoloured	2·50	2·20

448 Eruption

2007. Tenth Anniv of West Nordic Council. Geothermal Power.

1161	**448** 75k. multicoloured	2·75	2·50

449 Volcano erupting

2007. International Polar Year. Sheet 105×70 mm containing T **449** and similar square design. Multicoloured.

MS1162 75k. Type **449**; 95k. Taking radio echo soundings	7·00	6·75

450 Leaves and
Catkins

2007. Centenary of Forestry and Soil Conservation Act. Multicoloured.

1163	10k. Type **450**	55	30
1164	60k. Red leaves	2·75	2·30

451 Figure as Tree

2007. Centenary of National Youth Organization.

1165	**451** 70k. multicoloured	2·75	2·30

452 Face enclosing
Script

2007. 125th Anniv of National Archives.

1166	**452** 80k. multicoloured	3·25	2·75

453 *Hamrafell*

2007. Cargo Ships. Multicoloured.

1167	80k. Type **453**	3·25	2·75
1168	80k. *Trollafoss*	3·25	2·75
1169	105k. *Langjokull*	4·00	3·50
1170	105k. *Akranes*	4·00	3·50

454 Breioamerkurjokull

2007. Glaciers. Multicoloured.

1171	5k. Type **453**	20	15
1172	60k. Langjokull (vert)	2·30	2·00
1173	80k. Hofsjokull	3·25	2·75
1174	115k. Snaefellsjokull	4·25	3·75
1175	300k. Oraefajokull (70×30 mm)	11·50	11·00

455 Dunes and
Grasses

2007. Centenary of Soil Conservation. (a) No Value expressed. Self-adhesive.

1176	**455** (60k.) multicoloured	2·30	2·00

(b) Ordinary gum.

1177	(60k.) multicoloured	2·30	2·00

456 Fleur de Lys

2007. Europa. Centenary of Scouting. Multicoloured. Ordinary or self-adhesive gum.

1178	80k. Type **456**	3·25	2·75
1179	105k. Clover leaf	4·00	3·50

457 'BibLLA' and Dates of
Translations

2007. New Translation of the Bible into Icelandic.

1182	**457** 60k. brown and gold	2·75	2·30

458 *Vaccinium
myrtillus*

2007. Berries. Multicoloured.

1183	120k. Type **458**	5·00	4·50
1184	145k. *Cornus suecica*	6·25	5·50

459 King Frederick
VIII

2007. Centenary of King Frederick VIII's visit to Iceland. Sheet 80×56 mm.

MS1185 250k. brown and gold	11·00	10·50

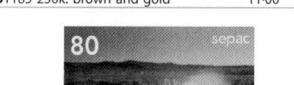

460 Selfoss Waterfall,
Jokulsargljufur

2007. SEPAC (small European mail services) Multicoloured.

1186	80k. Type **460**	3·50	3·00
1187	105k. Selfoss Waterfall, Jokulsar-gljufur (right) (30×27 mm)	5·25	4·75

461 Jonas
Hallgrimsson

2007. Birth Centenary of Jonas Hallgrimsson (poet).

1188	**461** 65k. brown	2·75	2·50

462 *Prionocera turcica*
(cranefly)

2007. Insects. Multicoloured.

1189	70k. Type **462**	3·00	2·75
1190	190k. *Euceraphis punctipennis* (birch aphid)	8·00	7·25

463 Hospital Facade

2007. Centenary of Psychiatric Hospital, Kleppur.

1191	**463** 80k. multicoloured	3·50	3·00

464 Leaf Bread

2007. Christmas. Multicoloured. Self-adhesive.

1192	60k. Type **464**	2·75	2·30
1193	80k. Leaf bread (different)	3·50	3·00

465 Older Couple

2008. Greetings Stamps. Multicoloured.
1194	65k. Type **465**		2·75	2·30
1195	65k. Mother and child		2·75	2·30
1196	75k. Adolescents		3·00	2·75
1197	85k. Couple about to kiss		3·25	3·00

466 Early Students

2008. Centenary of University of Education.
1198	**466**	85k. multicoloured	3·25	3·00

467 'REFILSAUMUR'

2008. Embroidery. Multicoloured.
1199	65k. Type **467**		2·75	2·30
1200	85k. AUGNSAUMUR		3·25	3·00
1201	110k. KROSSSAUMUR		4·25	3·75

468 Ferguson Tractor
TF20

2008. Vintage Agricultural Tools. Multicoloured.
1202	85k. Type **468**		3·25	3·00
1203	85k. IHC Bulldozer		3·25	3·00
1204	110k. Scottish plough (intro-duced by Torfi Bjarnason's agricultural school)		4·50	4·00
1205	110k. Landbaumotor Lanz (turf killer) (used for leveling hay fields)		4·50	4·00

469 Snaefellsnes (home of
9th-century sorcerer Bardur
Snaefellsas)

2008. Norse Mythology. Mythical Places. Sheet 105×70 mm.
MS1206 **469** 20k. multicoloured		4·75	4·25

Stamps of a similar theme were issued by Aland Islands, Denmark, Faroe Islands, Greenland, Finland, Norway and Sweden.

470 Proprio Foot
(intelligent prosthetic foot)

2008. Icelandic Industrial Design. Multicoloured.
1207	65k. Type **470**		1·90	1·70
1208	120k. Marel OptiCut (meat slicer)		3·75	3·25
1209	155k. Wish (fly fishing reel)		4·75	4·25
1210	200k. Gavia (autonomous underwater vehicle)		6·00	5·25

471 Radiator

2008. Centenary of Geothermal Space Heating.
1211	**471**	75k. multicoloured	2·30	2·00

472 Girl skipping

2008. My Stamp
1212	**472**	50g. (75k.) multicoloured	2·30	2·00

473 Buildings

2008. Centenary of HafnarfJorour.
1213	**473**	80k. multicoloured	2·50	2·20

474 Letter as
Paper Boat

2008. Europa. The Letter. Multicoloured. Ordinary or self-adhesve gum.
1214	85k. Type **474**		2·75	2·30
1215	110k. Letter as paper airplane		3·25	3·00

475 Winning Play

2008. Friorik Olafsson—1958 Chess Grandmaster.
1218	**475**	80k. multicoloured	2·50	2·20

476 por (coast guard vessel)

2008. 50th Anniv of Extension of Fishery Zone.
1219	**476**	90k. multicoloured	2·75	2·30

477 Algae, Map and Lake Myvatn

2008. Endangered Species. Aegagropila linnaei (lake ball algae).
1220	**477**	140k. multicoloured	4·00	3·50

478 Satellite Image
of Iceland

2008. International Year of Planet Earth. Sheet 100×55 mm.
MS1221 **478** 215k. multicoloured		6·25	6·00

479 Peace Tower

2008. First Anniv of Peace Tower (John Lennon memorial), Videy.
1222	**479**	120k. multicoloured	3·50	3·00

480 Yule Goblin
Stiff-Legs

2008. Christmas. Children's Design a Stamp Competition, Winning Designs by Heioar Jokull Hafsteinsson and Konrao K. Pormarr. Multicoloured. Self adhesive.
1223	70k. Type **480**		1·90	1·70
1224	90k. Christmas Cat		2·75	2·30

481 Snow-covered Trees

2008. Centenary of Forestry in Vaglaskogur.
1225	**481**	400k. multicoloured	11·50	11·00

2009. Islands (5th series). As T **369**.
1226	75k. Hjorsey		2·10	1·90
1227	90k. Maimey		2·75	2·30

482 Psychodidae (Moth
Fly)

2009. Insects. Multicoloured.
1228	80k. Type **482**		2·30	2·00
1229	120k. Gnaphosa lapponum (field spider)		3·50	3·00

483 Polar Ice

2009. Preserve Polar Regions and Glaciers. Sheet 80×120 mm containing T **483** and similar vert design. Multicoloured.
MS1230 100k. Type **483**; 130k. Iceland		6·75	6·25

484 Hrosshvalur

2009. Legendary Creatures from Folktales. Multicoloured.
1231	80k. Type **484**		2·30	2·00
1232	80k. Skoffin		2·30	2·00
1233	80k. Mushveli		2·30	2·00
1234	80k. Rauokembingur		2·30	2·00
1235	80k. Selamooir		2·30	2·00
1236	80k. Ofuguggi		2·30	2·00
1237	80k. Saeneyti		2·30	2·00
1238	80k. Skeljaskrimsli		2·30	2·00
1239	80k. Uroarkottur		2·30	2·00
1240	80k. Fjorulalli		2·30	2·00

485 Avro 504K

2009. Civil Aviation. Multicoloured.
1241	90k. Type **485**		2·75	2·30
1242	90k. Waco ZKS-7		2·75	2·30
1243	120k. Boeing 757		3·50	3·00
1244	120k. Fokker 50		3·50	3·00

486 Girl and Water

2009. Centenary of Water Works, Reykjavik.
1245	**486**	10k. multicoloured	35	30

487 Athletes

2009. Centenary of Iceland Youth Organization (UMFI) National Sports Tournaments.
1246	**487**	105k. multicoloured	3·00	2·75

488

2009. Europa. Astronomy. Multicoloured. (a) Ordinary or self-adhesive gum.
1247	105k. Type **488**		3·00	2·75
1248	140k. Observatory		4·00	3·50

489 Arch and
Gateway

2009. Centenary of Skruour Garden, Dyrafjorour.
1251	**489**	140k. multicoloured	4·00	3·50

490 Fratercula arctica
(puffin)

2009. Nordia 2009–Nordic Philatelic Exhibition, Reykjavik. Sheet 100×60 mm.
MS1252 **490** 190k. multicoloured		5·75	5·50

491 Gathering Sheep from
the Hills

2009. Sheep Gathering. Multicoloured.
1253	95k. Type **491**		1·90	1·70
1254	160k. Collection pens (vert)		3·25	3·00

492 Skaftafell

2009. SEPAC (small european mail services). Multicoloured.
1255	**492**	120k. Type **492**	2·50	2·20
1256		120k. Skaftafell (right) (30×29 mm)	2·50	2·20

Nos. 1255/6 were printed, se-tenant, each pair forming a composite design of Skaftafell.

493 Heritage Centre

2009. Centenary of National Centre for Cultural Heritage. Sheet 85×57 mm.
MS1257 **493** 150k. multicoloured   4·50   4·25

494 *Sermon on the Mount* (detail) (Gudmundur Einarsson)

2009. Christmas. Multicoloured. Self-adhesive.
1258   (70k.) Type **494**   1·50   1·40
1259   120k. *Holy Mother of God* (Finnur Jónsson)   2·75   2·50

495 *Uria lomvia* (Brunnich's guillemot)

2009. Seabirds. Multicoloured.
1260   110k. Type **495**   2·50   2·30
1261   130k. *Larus hyperboreus* (glaucous gull)   2·75   2·75

496 Thingvellir Church

2009. 150th Anniv of Thingvellir Church.
1262   **496**   190k. multicoloured   4·25   3·75

497 *Phoca vitulina* (harbor seal)

2010. Seals (1st series). Multicoloured.
1263   5k. Type **497**   40   35
1264   220k. *Phoca groenlandica* (harp seal)   5·00   4·50

498 Hanger Tree (Katrín Olina Petursdottir and Michael Young)

2010. Icelandic Design. Furniture. Multicoloured.
1265   75k. Type **498**   1·70   1·60
1266   140k. *Tango* (chair) (Sigurour Gustafsson)   3·00   2·75
1267   155k. MGO 180 dining table (Guorun M. Olafsdottir and Oddgeir Poroarson) (horiz)   3·50   3·25
1268   165k. Dimon sofa (Erla Solveig Oskarsdottir) (horiz)   3·75   3·50

499 Door of Valbjofsstaoir (13th-century)

2010. Icelandic Design. Carving in Wood and Bone. Multicoloured. (a) Ordinary gum.
1269   10k. Type **499**   40   35

1270   (75k.) 17th-century Judge's drinking horn (Brynjolfur Jónsson)   1·70   1·60
1271   200k. *Play in Leaves* (Sigriour Jona Kristjansottir) (vert)   4·25   4·00

  (b) Size 32×28 mm. Self-adhesive.
1272   (75k.) As No. 1269 (drinking horn)   1·70   1·60
Nos. 1270 and 1272 were for use on mail within Iceland up to 50 grams.

500 Man pushing Barrel

2010. Norden by the Sea. Life at the Coast. Sheet 105×70 mm containing T **500** and similar vert design. Multicoloured.
MS1273 75k.×2, Type **500**; Women sorting herrings   3·75   3·50
The stamps and margins of **MS**1273 form a composite design.

501 *Bjarni riddari GK 1*

2010. Trawlers. Multicoloured.
1274   75k. Type **501**   1·70   1·60
1275   75k. *Ingolfur Arnarson RE 201*   1·70   1·60
1276   165k. *Solborg IS 260*   3·50   3·25
1277   165k. *Harobakur EA 3*   3·50   3·25

502 Jónsgarður, Isajörður

2010. Parks. Multicoloured.
1278   90k. Type **502**   1·90   1·80
1279   130k. Helisgerði, Hafnarfjörður   2·75   2·75
1280   285k. Skallagrimsgarður, Borgarnes (horiz)   6·25   5·75

503 Icelandic Pavilion

2010. Expo 2010, Shanghai
MS1281 **503** 130k. multicoloured   3·25   3·00

504 Footballer

2010. Personalised Stamps. Multicoloured.
1282   50g. Type **504**   3·50   3·25
1283   50g. Girl footballer   5·00   4·50
No. 1282 was for mail within Europe, originally on sale for 165k and No. 1283 was for mail outside Europe, originally on sale for 220k.

505 *The Fate of the Gods* (written by Ingunn Asdisardottir and illustrated by Kristin Ragna)

2010. Europa. Children's Books. Multicoloured.

  (a) Ordinary gum
1284   165k. Type **505**   3·50   3·25
1285   220k. *Good Evening* (written and illustrated by Aslaug Jonsdóttir)   5·00   4·50

  (b) Self-adhesive
1286   165k. As Type **505**   3·50   3·25
1287   220k. As Type **1285**   5·00   4·50

506 Lava Flow

2010. Eyjafjallajokull Volcanic Eruption. Multicoloured.
1288   50g. (75k.) Type **506**   1·90   1·80
1289   50g. (165k.) Ash cloud   4·25   3·75
1290   50g. (220k.) Eruption   5·50   5·00
Nos. 1288-90 were for mail weighing up to 50g. No. 1288 was for use on mail within Iceland, No. 1289 for mail within Europe and No.1290 for mail outside Europe.

507 Early Patients

2010. Centenary of Vifilsstaðir Sanatorium
1291   **507**   100g. (90k.) multicoloured   2·30   2·10
No. 1291 was for use on local mail weighing up to 100g.

508 Eagle, Fox and Mouse

2010. International Year of Biodiversity. Multicoloured.
MS1292 90k.×2, Type **508**; Leaping salmon and duck   4·75   4·50

509 Athlete

2010. Youth Olympic Games, Singapore
1293   **509**   165k. multicoloured   4·25   3·75

510 Street Lamp

2010. Centenary of Reykjavik Gas Works
1294   **510**   450k. multicoloured   11·00   10·00

511 Bird and Wreath

2010. Christmas. Multicoloured.
1295   50g. (75k.) Type **511**   1·90   1·80
1296   50g. (165k.) Two birds and wreath   4·25   3·75
Nos. 1295/6 were for mail weighing up to 50g. No. 1295 was for use on mail within Iceland and No. 1296 for mail within Europe.

---

512 Landscape (Isleifur Konráðsson)

2010. Icelandic Visual Art. Multicoloured.
1297   50g. (75k.) Type **512**   1·90   1·80
1298   100g. (90k.) Portrait (Sölvi Helgason) (vert)   2·30   2·10
1299   50g. (165k.) Fisherman in boat (Sigurlaug Jónasdóttir) (vert)   4·25   3·75
1300   50g. (220k.) Dreamscape (Karl Einarsson Dunganon) (vert)   5·50   5·00
Nos. 1297,1299/300 were for mail weighing up to 50g. No. 1297 was for use on mail within Iceland, No. 1299 for mail within Europe and No.1300 for mail outside Europe. No. 1298 was for use on mail weighing up to 100g. within Iceland.

513 '14 DES 1910' and 'ERAÐ ÞREIFA......'

2010. Centenary of *Visir* (newspaper)
1301   **513**   140k. agate and bistre   3·50   3·25

514 *Melanitta nigra* (common scoter)

2011. 50th Anniv of World Wide Fund for Nature. Multicoloured.
1302   50g. (75k.) Type **514**   1·90   1·80
1303   50g. (75k.) *Branta leucopsis* (barnacle goose)   1·90   1·80
1304   50g. (165k.) *Anser albifrons* (white-fronted goose)   4·25   3·75
1305   50g. (165k.) *Anas strepera* (gadwall)   4·25   3·75
Nos. 1302/5 were for mail weighing up to 50g. Nos. 1302/3 were for use on mail within Iceland and Nos. 1304/5 for mail within Europe.

515 *Phoca hispida* (ringed seal)

2011. Seals (2nd series). Multicoloured.
1306   100g. (90k.) Type **515**   2·30   2·10
1307   100g. (220k.) *Halichoerus grypus* (grey seal)   5·75   5·25
Nos. 1306/7 were for mail weighing up to 100g. No. 1306 was for use on mail within Iceland and No. 1307 for mail outside Europe.

516 Moto-Cross

2011. Motor Sports. Multicoloured.
1308   50g. (75k.) Type **516**   1·90   1·80
1309   50g. (75k.) Rallying   1·90   1·80
1310   50g. (165k.) Off-roading   4·25   3·75
1311   50g. (165k.) Drag racing   4·25   3·75
Nos. 1308/11 were for mail weighing up to 50g. Nos. 1308/9 were for use on mail within Iceland and Nos. 1310/11 for mail within Europe.

517 Langanesviti

2011. Lighthouses. Multicoloured.
1312   50g. (75k.) Type **517**   1·90   1·80
1313   50g. (165k.) Stokksnes (vert)   4·25   3·75

518 Tree Rings from Log of Siberian Larch (resources)

2011. Europa. Multicoloured.

	(a) Ordinary gum		
1314	50g. (165k.) Type **518**	4·25	3·75
1315	50g. (220k.) Close-up of leaf (ecosystem)	5·25	5·00

	(b) Self-adhesive		
1316	50g. (165k.) As Type **518**	4·25	3·75
1317	50g. (220k.) As No. 1315	5·25	5·00

No. 1314/17 were for mail weighing up to 50g. Nos. 1314 and 1316 was for use on mail within Europe, Nos. 1315 and 1317 for mail outside Europe.

519 University Building

2011. Centenary of University of Iceland
1318	**519**	50g. (120k.) multicoloured	2·10	1·90

520 Building Façade (image scaled to 42% of original size)

2011. Harpa Reykjavik Concert Hall and Conference Centre.
MS1319 50g.(120k.)×5, Part of structure (black) (28×20 mm); Part of structure (brownish grey) (10×25 mm); Part of structure (grey) (25×47 mm); Part of structure (pink) (17×37 mm); Part of structure (yellow) (50×26 mm)	11·00	10·50

521 Austurvöllur, Reykjavik

2011. Parks. Multicoloured.
1320	100g. (125k.) Type **521**	2·50	2·30
1321	100g. (300k.) Parliament Park (Alþingsgarðurinn)	8·00	7·25

522 Outlines of Athletes and Musicians

2011. Centenary of Melavöllur Stadium
1322	**522**	250g. (155k.) grey, brownish grey and black	3·50	3·25

523 President Jón Sigurðsson

2011. Birth Bicentenary of President Jón Sigurðsson. Each black and bistre.
1323	50g. (120k.) Type **523**	2·10	1·90
1324	1000k. As older man	27·00	24·00
MS1325 100×75 mm.50g. (120k.) as Type **252**; 1000k. As No. 1324		30·00	29·00

524 Snipe

2011. Wetland Conservation
1326	**524**	50g. (120k.) multicoloured	2·50	2·30

525 Saga of Burnt Niall (image scaled to 46% of original size)

2011. The Saga of Burnt Niall (blood feud). Sheet 105×70 mm
MS1327 **525** 100g. (125k.)×3 multicoloured	9·50	9·00

526 Húsavik

2011. Fishing Villages. Sheet 120×81 mm
MS1328 **526** 50g. (345k.) multicoloured	4·50	4·25

527 Snæfellsjökull (Snæfell Glacier)

2011. SEPAC (small European mail services). Snæfellsnes National Park. Multicoloured.
1329	50g. (175k.) Type **527**	4·50	4·00
1330	50g. (165k.) Snæfellsjökull (right) (30×29 mm)	4·50	4·00

528 Hands grasping Candles as Bars

2011. 50th Anniv of Amnesty International
1331	**528**	100g. (300k..) chrome yellow and black	7·50	6·75

529 Sólarlag við Tjornina (Þórarinn B. Þorláksson)

2011. Icelandic Visual Art. The Pioneers. Multicoloured.
1332	50g. (120k.) Type **529**	2·50	2·30
1333	100g. (125k.) *Botnssúlur* (Ásgrímur Jónsson)	3·00	2·75
1334	50g. (175k.) *Útreiðarfólk* (Jón Stefánsson)	4·50	4·00
1335	50g. (230k.) *Fornar slóðir* (Jóhannes Kjarval)	6·00	5·25

Nos. 1332,1334/5 were for mail weighing up to 50g. No. 1332 was for use on mail within Iceland, No. 1334 for mail within Europe and No. 1335 for mail outside Europe.
No. 1333 was for use on mail weighing up to 100g. within Iceland.

530 Flower

2011. Christmas. Multicoloured, background colour given.
1336	50g. (120k.) Type **530**	2·50	2·30
1337	50g. (175k.) Spray of flowers and leaves (blue)	4·50	4·00

Nos. 1336/7 were for mail weighing up to 50g. No. 1336 was for use on mail within Iceland and No. 1337 for mail within Europe.

531 Athletes

2012. Centenary of National Olympic and Sports Association of Iceland
1338	**531**	50g. (120k.) multicoloured	2·50	2·30

532 Silver Chalice (15th-century)

2012. Icelandic Design. Silverwork. Multicoloured.

	(a) Ordinary gum		
1339	50g. (120k.) Type **532**	2·50	2·30
1340	50g. (175k.) Koffur (diadem of gilded silver from headdress of national costume) (designed by painter Sigurður Guðmundsson) (horiz)	4·50	4·00
1341	50g. (230k.) Brum (bowl by Pétur Tryggvi Hjálmarsson)	6·00	5·25

	(b) Self-adhesive		
1342	50g. (120k.) Chalice, As Type **532** but with inscription changed (28×32 mm)	2·50	2·30

No. 1339/42 were for mail weighing up to 50g. No. 1339 and 1342 are for mail within Iceland.
No. 1340 was for use on mail within Europe, No. 1341 was for mail outside Europe.

533 Landmannalaugar

2012. Tourism. Multicoloured.
1343	50g. (175k.) Type **533**	4·50	4·25
1344	50g. (230k.) Lake Hnausapollur	6·00	5·25

534 Waterfall (hydropower)

2012. Green Energy. Multicoloured.
1345	50g. (120k.) Type **534**	2·50	2·30
1346	50g. (120k.) Aluminium	2·50	2·30
1347	50g. (175k.) Escaping steam (geothermal energy)	4·50	4·25
1348	50g. (175k.) Tomatoes	4·50	4·25

535 Shoes (Kron by KronKron)

2012. Icelandic Design. Fashion. Multicoloured.
1349	50g. (120k.) Type **535**	2·50	2·30
1350	100g. (125k.) Dress (Steinunn Sigurdardottir)	2·75	2·50
1351	50g. (175k.) Wool cardigan (Farmers Market)	4·50	4·25
1352	50g. (230k.) Jacket (66° North)	6·00	5·50

536 Rescue, March 9th 2004 (when TF Lif, Coast Guard helicopter, rescued crew of fishing vessel *Baldvin Thorsteinsson* EA 10)

2012. Norden by the Sea. Search and Rescue. Sheet 105×70 mm
MS1353 **536** 250g. (155k.) multicoloured	4·25	4·00

537 Akureyri

2012. 150th Anniv of Akureyi Municipality
1354	**537**	50g. (120k.) multicoloured	2·50	2·30

538 Scarf

2012. Centenary of Scouting in Iceland
1355	**538**	50g. (120k.) multicoloured	2·50	2·30

539 Akureyri Park

2012. Parks. Multicoloured.
1356	500g. (225k.) Type **539**	6·00	5·25
1357	100g. (300k.) Hallargarður Park, Reykjavik	7·75	7·00

540 Geyser and Quick Response Code

2012. Europa. Visit Iceland. Multicoloured.
1358	50g. (175k.) Type **540**	4·50	4·25
1359	50g. (230k.) Northern Lights and QR code	6·00	5·25

541 Athlete

2012. Olympic Games, London
1360	**541**	250g. (580k.) green and black	15·00	13·50

(542)

2012. No. 1219 surch as T 542
1361	B 50g. (103k.) on 90k. multicoloured (As Type **476**)	2·50	2·30

543 *Russula xerampelina*
(Crab Brittlegill)

2012. Fungi
1362 **543** B 50g. (103k.) multicoloured   2·50   2·30

544 Engey Lighthouse

2012. Lighthouses. Multicoloured.
1363 B 50g. (103k.) Type **544**   2·50   2·30
1364 B 50g. (175k.) Kálfshamar (vert)   4·50   4·25

545 *Cystophora cristata*
(Hooded Seal)

2012. Seals (3rd series). Multicoloured.
1365 100g. (475k.) Type **515**   12·50   11·50
1366 1000g. (480k.) *Odobenus
rosmarus* (Walrus)   13·00   12·00

546 Plan of Monastery

2012. Stamp Day. Archeological Excavations at
Skriðuklaustur. 500th Anniv of Consecration of
Skriðuklaustur Church
MS1367 **546** 1500g. (565k.) multi-
coloured   14·50   13·50

547 *Boletus edulis*

2012. Fungi
1368 **547** B 50g. (103k.) multicoloured   2·50   2·30

548 The Sad Prince
(Guðmundur Thorsteinsson
(Muggur))

2012. Icelandic Visual Art. The Second Generation.
Multicoloured.
1369 50g. (120k.) Type **548**   3·00   2·75
1370 100g. (125k.) Stilllife (*Uppstill-
ing*) (Kristín Jónsdóttir)   3·25   2·75
1371 50g. (175k.) From the Westman
Islands (Júlíana Sveinsdóttir)   4·50   4·25
1372 50g. (230k.) Móðurást (Karl
Einarsson Dunganon) (vert)   6·00   5·50

549 Night Troll turning to
Stone at Dawn

2012. Christmas. Multicoloured.
1373 50g. (120k.) Type **549**   3·00   2·75
1374 50g. (175k.) Christmas procession to church   4·50   4·25

550 Hands and
Water Droplets

2013. International Year of Water Cooperation
1375 **550** B50g. (103k.) multicoloured   2·50   2·50

551 Cloth of
Staðarhóls-Páll

2013. 150th Anniv of National Museum
1376 **551** 100g. (125k.) multicoloured   3·25   2·75

552 Waterfall,
Aldeyjarfoss

2013. Tourism. Multicoloured.
1377 50g. (175k.) Type **552**   4·50   4·25
1378 50g. (230k.) Hafursey
palagonite tuff mountain,
Mýrdalssandur   6·00   5·50

553 Ford AA Lorry, 1931

2013. Centenary of Motorised Transport in Iceland.
Multicoloured.
1379 B50g. (103k.) Type **553**   2·50   2·50
1380 B50g. (103k.) Chevrolet dual
purpose vehicle, 1942 - 1943   2·50   2·50
1381 50g. (175k.) Mercedes Benz
bus, 1957   4·50   4·25
1382 50g. (175k.) Bedford fire appli-
ance, 1955   4·50   4·25

554 Puffin
(Sigurdur Oddsson)

2013. Icelandic Design. Graphic Design. Multicoloured.
1383 50g. (120k.) Type **554**   3·00   2·75
1384 250g. (155k.) Sofa with map
back (Ragnar Freyr Pálsson)   3·50   3·25
1385 100g. (300k.) Icelandic hotdog
ingredients (Rán Flygenring)   8·00   7·25
1386 100g. (475k.) Pixelated ponies
(Sigurdur Eggertsson)   12·50   11·50

555 Reykjavík Gay
Parade

2013. Festivals. Multicoloured.
1387 B50g. (103k.) Type **555**   2·50   2·50
1388 B50g. (103k.) Never Been South
music festival, Isafjörður   2·50   2·50
1389 B50g. (103k.) Great Fish Day   2·50   2·50
1390 B50g. (103k.) Smelter music
festival, Borgarfjordur Eystri   2·50   2·50
1391 B50g. (103k.) Vestmannaeyjar
National Holiday   2·50   2·50

556 Northern Lights

557 Northern Lights (image scaled to 43% of original
size)

2013. Nordia 2013 Stamp Exhiibition. Northern Lights.
Multicoloured.
1392 50g. (125k.)×4, Type **556** and
three other designs showing
Northern Lights as T **557**   15·00   15·00

558 Post Van

2013. Europa. Postal Transport. Multicoloured.
1393 50g. (175k.) Type **558**   4·50   4·25
1394 50g. (230k.) Post lorry   6·00   5·50

559 Vattarnes Lighthouse

2013. Lighthouses. Multicoloured.
1395 50g. (120k.) Type **559**   3·00   2·75
1396 100g. (300k.) Skarðsfjara (vert)   8·00   7·25

560 *Capra hircus*

2013. SEPAC (small European mail services). Icelandic
Settlement Goat (*Capra hircus*)
1397 **560** 50g. (175k.) multicoloured   4·50   4·25

561 Skálholt

2013. Stamp Day. Skálholt and Hólar. Multicoloured.
MS1398 500g. (225k.)×2, Type **561**;
Hólar Cathedral   15·00   15·00

562 Surtsey

2013. 50th Anniv of Foundation of Surtsey Island (by
volcanic eruption). UNESCO World Heritage Site
1399 **562** 1500g. (565k.) multicoloured   14·00   13·00

563 Stained Glass

2013. Christmas. Stained Glass Window (by Leifur
Breidfjord), Hallgrímskirkja, Reykjavik. Multicoloured.
1400 B50g. (103k.) Type **563**   2·50   2·50

1401 50g. (120k.) Rose   3·00   2·75
1402 50g. (175k.) Stripes   4·50   4·25

564 *Gjá í Þingvallahrauni*
(Eggert Laxdal)

2013. Icelandic Visual Art. The Landscape Redefined.
Multicoloured.
1403 B50g. (103k.) Type **564**   2·50   2·50
1404 500g. (225k.) *Beinin hennar
Stjörnu* (Finnur Jónsson)   6·00   5·50
1405 250g. (580k.) *Brennisteinsoldur
við Landmannalaugar*
(Guðmundur Einarsson frá
Miðdal)   14·10   13·10
1406 50g. (955k.) *Mt. Herðubreið*
(Sveinn Þórarinsson)   16·00   15·00

565 *Haliaeetus
albicilla*

2014. Birds. White-tailed Eagle (*Haliaeetus albicilla*)
1407 **565** B 50g. (103k.) multicol-
oured   2·50   2·50

564a Front Page

2013. Centenary of *Morgunblaðið* Newspaper
1407a **564a** 50g. (120k.) black   3·00   2·75

566 Symbol of
Statistics

2014. Centenary of Statistics Iceland
1408 **566** 50g. (120k.) multicoloured   3·00   2·75

567 Emblem

2014. Eimskip (Icelandic Steamship Company)
1409 **567** 50g. (175k.) multicoloured   4·50   4·25

568 Sjálfberg
,Munaðarnes, Strandir

2014. Tourism. Multicoloured.
1410 50g. (175k.) Type **568**   4·50   4·25
1411 50g. (230k.) Kvíár glacier,
Öræfajökull, Vatnajökull   6·00   5·25

569 Swimming Pool, Hofsós
(Basalt Architects)

2014. Icelandic Design. Architecture. Multicoloured.
1412 B50g. (112k.) Type **569**   2·50   2·50
1413 50g. (130k.) Akureyri Park Café
(Kollgáta Architects)   3·25   2·75

Iceland (continued)

1414		250g. (155k.) Borgarfjörður Gymnasium (Kurtogpí Architects)	3·75	3·25
1415		50g. (175k.) Footbridge over Hringbraut (Studio Grandi Architects and Efla Engineers)	4·50	4·25

570 Container Ship

2014. Norden by the Sea. Ships. Sheet 105×70 mm
MS1416 **570** 250g. (155k.) multicoloured 4·00 4·00

571 Stone Harp (created by Páll Gudmundsson)

2014. Europa. Musical Instruments. Multicoloured.
1417		50g. (175k.) Type 571	4·50	4·25
1418		50g. (230k.) Electromagnetic harp (created by Ulfur Hansson)	6·00	5·50

572 Pavilion Park

2014. SEPAC (small European mail services). Parks. Multicoloured.
1419		50g. (130k.) Type 572	3·25	2·75
1420		50g. (175k.) Klambratún Park	4·50	4·25

573 Lobster Festival, Höfn, Hornafjörður

2014. Festivals. Multicoloured.
1421		B50g. (112k.) Type 573	2·50	2·50
1422		B50g. (112k.) Herring Adventure, Siglufjörður	2·50	2·50
1423		50g. (130k.) Night of Lights, Reykjanesbær	3·25	2·75
1424		50g. (175k.) Danish Days, Stykkishólmur	4·50	4·25
1425		50g. (230k.) Culture Night, Reykjavík	6·00	5·50

574 Barði NK120

2014. Trawlers and Fishing Vessels. Multicoloured.
1426		B50g. (112k.) Type 574	6·00	5·50
1427		B50g. (112k.) Stálvík SI 1	6·00	5·50
1428		50g. (175k.) Breki VE 61	4·50	4·25
1429		50g. (175k.) Örvar HU 21	4·50	4·25

OFFICIAL STAMPS

1873. As T **1** but inscr "PJON. FRIM." at foot.
O8		4s. green	95·00	£400
O10		8s. mauve	£550	£650

O4

1876
O36	**O4**	3a. yellow	13·00	31·00
O37	**O4**	4a. grey	33·00	44·00
O21b	**O4**	5a. brown	8·75	15·00
O22a	**O4**	10a. blue	70·00	14·50
O23a	**O4**	16a. red	28·00	55·00
O24a	**O4**	20a. green	28·00	44·00
O25	**O4**	50a. mauve	75·00	90·00

1902. As T **10**, but inscr "PJONUSTA".
O81	3a. sepia and yellow	3·75	2·75
O82	4a. sepia and green	4·50	2·20
O83	5a. sepia and brown	3·25	3·75
O84	10a. sepia and blue	3·25	3·75
O85	16a. sepia and red	2·75	14·50
O86	20a. sepia and green	20·00	7·75
O87	50a. sepia and mauve	6·50	11·00

1902. Optd I GILDI '02–'03.
O94	3a. yellow	1·10	2·40
O95	4a. grey	1·10	2·40
O96	5a. brown	90	2·40
O97	10a. blue	75	2·40
O91	16a. red	17·00	65·00
O98	20a. green	90	22·00
O93	50a. mauve	5·50	55·00

1907. As T **12**, but inscr "PJONUSTU".
O99	3a. sepia and yellow	6·50	7·75
O100	4a. sepia and green	3·25	8·25
O101	5a. sepia and brown	10·00	3·75
O102	10a. sepia and blue	2·20	3·00
O103	15a. sepia and blue	4·50	8·25
O104	16a. sepia and red	4·50	28·00
O105	20a. sepia and green	18·00	5·50
O106	50a. sepia and mauve	6·00	10·00

1920. As T **15**, but inscr "PJONUSTU".
O132	3a. black and yellow	4·50	3·75
O133	4a. black and green	1·10	3·25
O134	5a. black and orange	1·10	1·70
O135	10a. black and blue	28·00	1·30
O136	15a. black and blue	75	1·10
O137	20a. black and green	44·00	3·75
O138	50a. black and violet	39·00	2·00
O139	1k. black and red	39·00	2·75
O140	2k. black and blue	6·50	19·00
O141	5k. black and brown	33·00	50·00

1922. Optd **Pjonusta**.
O153	15	20a. on 10a. red	28·00	2·20
O151a	13	2k. red (No. 107)	28·00	55·00
O152	13	5k. brown (No. 108)	£225	£250

1930. Parliamentary Commemoratives of 1930 optd **Pjonustumerki**.
O174	24	3a. violet and lilac (postage)	13·00	39·00
O175	-	5a. blue and grey	13·00	39·00
O176	-	7a. green and dp green	13·00	39·00
O177	-	10a. purple and mauve	13·00	39·00
O178	-	15a. dp blue & blue	13·00	39·00
O179	-	20a. red and pink	13·00	39·00
O180	-	25a. brown & lt brown	13·00	39·00
O181	-	30a. green and grey	13·00	39·00
O182	-	35a. blue & ultramarine	13·00	39·00
O183	-	40a. red, blue and grey	13·00	39·00
O184	-	50a. dp brown & brown	£130	£325
O185	-	1k. green and grey	£130	£325
O186	-	2k. blue and green	£130	£325
O187	-	5k. orange and yellow	£130	£325
O188	-	10k. lake and red	£130	£325
O189	25	10a. blue & dp blue (air)	22·00	£120

1936. Optd **Pjonusta**.
O220	15	7a. green	3·25	22·00
O221	15	10a. red	12·50	2·00
O222	12	50a. red and grey	25·00	28·00

IDAR

A state in Western India. Now uses Indian stamps.

12 pies = 1 anna; 16 annas = 1 rupee.

1 Maharaja Himmat Singh

1939
1c	1	½a. green	22·00	30·00

2 Maharaja Himmat Singh

1944
3	2	½a. green	4·00	85·00
4	2	1a. violet	4·00	70·00
5	2	2a. blue	3·50	£120
6	2	4a. red	4·50	£120

IFNI

Spanish enclave on the Atlantic coast of Northern Morocco ceded in 1860.

By an agreement, made effective on 30 June 1969, Ifni was surrendered by Spain to Morocco.

100 centimos = 1 peseta.

1941. Stamps of Spain optd **TERRITORIO DE IFNI**.
1	181	1c. green (imperf)	8·50	8·00
2	182	2c. brown	8·50	8·00
3	183	5c. brown	1·10	75
4	183	10c. red	4·75	2·75
5	183	15c. green	1·10	70
6	196	20c. violet	1·10	70
7	196	25c. red	1·10	70
8	196	30c. blue	1·10	70
9	196	40c. slate	1·80	65
10	196	50c. slate	9·50	2·40
11	196	70c. blue	9·50	6·75
12	196	1PTA. black	9·50	6·75
13	196	2PTAS. brown	£130	45·00
14	196	4PTAS. red	£375	£200
15	196	10PTS. brown	£1200	£500

3 El Santuario   **4** Nomad Family

1943
16	A	1c. mauve & brown (postage)	20	20
17	B	2c. blue and green	20	20
18	C	5c. blue and purple	20	20
19	A	15c. green and deep green	20	20
20	B	20c. brown and violet	20	20
21	A	40c. violet and purple	25	25
22	B	45c. red and brown	30	30
35	4	50c. black and brown	18·00	85
23	C	75c. blue and indigo	30	30
24	A	1p. brown and red	1·90	1·90
25	B	3p. green and blue	4·50	4·50
26	C	10p. black and brown	45·00	45·00
27	3	5c. brown and purple (air)	20	20
28	D	25c. brown and green	20	20
29	3	50c. blue and indigo	25	25
30	D	1p. blue and violet	25	25
31	3	1p.40 blue and green	25	25
32	D	2p. brown and purple	2·30	2·30
33	3	5p. violet and brown	3·25	3·25
34	D	6p. green and blue	48·00	48·00

DESIGNS: A, Nomadic shepherds; B, Arab rifleman; C, La Alcazaba; D, Airplane over oasis.

1947. Air. Autogyro type of Spain optd **IFNI**.
36	195	5c. yellow	3·25	80
37	195	10c. green	3·25	80

1948. Stamps of Spain optd Territorio de **Ifni**.
45	182	2c. brown (postage)	25	20
46	183	5c. brown	25	20
47	183	10c. red	25	20
39	229	15c. green	4·00	70
48	183	15c. green	25	20
49	196	25c. purple	25	20
50	196	30c. blue	25	20
51	232	40c. brown	25	20
52	232	45c. red	30	20
53	196	50c. grey	25	20
54	232	75c. blue	55	20
55	201	90c. green	55	30
41	196	1PTA. black	35	20
56	201	1p.35 violet	5·25	3·50
57	196	2PTAS. brown	4·00	2·50
58	196	4PTAS. pink	15·00	7·25
59	196	10PTAS. brown	37·00	22·00
60	195	25c. red (air)	60	20
61	195	50c. brown	70	20
62	195	1p. green	70	20
63	195	2p. green	4·00	90
64	195	4p. blue	11·00	4·25
65	195	10p. violet	15·00	8·75

1949. Stamp Day and 75th Anniv of U.P.U. Spanish stamps optd **Territorio de Ifni**.
42	240	50c. brown (postage)	5·75	1·90
43	240	75c. blue	5·75	1·90
44	240	4p. olive (air)	6·25	1·90

8 General Franco

1950. Child Welfare.
66	8	50c.+10c. sepia	55	35
67	8	1p.+25c. blue	18·00	8·25
68	8	6p.50+1p.65 green	6·50	3·75

9 Lope Sancho de Valenzuela

1950. Air. Colonial Stamp Day.
69	9	5p. green	5·25	4·25

10 Woman and Dove

1951. Air. 500th Birth Anniv of Isabella the Catholic.
70	10	5p. red	27·00	9·75

11 General Franco

1951. Gen. Franco's Visit to Ifni.
71	11	50c. orange	55	60
72	11	1p. brown	4·75	1·20
73	11	5p. green	37·00	13·00

12 Fennec Fox

1951. Colonial Stamp Day.
74	12	5c.+5c. brown	1·00	75
75	12	10c.+5c. orange	1·10	80
76	12	60c.+15c. olive	2·10	1·50

13 Mother and Child

1952. Child Welfare.
77	13	5c.+5c. brown	80	60
78	13	50c.+10c. black	80	60
79	13	2p.+30c. blue	3·75	3·00

14 Ferdinand the Catholic

1952. Air. 500th Birth Anniv of Ferdinand the Catholic.
80	14	5p. brown	34·00	9·75

15 Shag

1952. Colonial Stamp Day.
81	**15**	5c.+5c. brown	65	65
82	**15**	10c.+5c. red	70	70
83	**15**	60c.+15c. green	1·40	1·30

16

1952. 400th Death Anniv of Leo Africanus (geographer).
84	**16**	5c. orange	65	65
85	**16**	35c. green	70	70
86	**16**	60c. brown	1·40	1·30

17 Addra Gazelle and Douglas DC-4 Airliner

1953. Air.
87	**17**	60c. green	35	30
88	**17**	1p.20 lake	35	30
89	**17**	1p.60 brown	45	40
90	**17**	2p. blue	3·00	50
91	**17**	4p. myrtle	1·70	70
92	**17**	10p. purple	9·50	3·25

18 Musician

1953. Child Welfare. Inscr "PRO INFANCIA 1953".
93	**18**	5c.+5c. lake	60	60
94	**18**	10c.+5c. purple	60	60
95	**18**	15c. olive	60	60
96	-	60c. brown	70	70

DESIGN: 10c., 60c. Two native musicians.

19 Fish and Jellyfish

1953. Colonial Stamp Day. Inscr "DIA DEL SELLO COLONIAL 1953".
97	**19**	5c.+5c. blue	95	60
98	-	10c.+5c. mauve	95	60
99	**19**	15c. green	95	60
100	-	60c. brown	1·20	70

DESIGN: 10, 60c. Dusky grouper and seaweed.

20 Mediterranean Gull	**21** Asclepiad

1954
101	**20**	5c. orange	20	20
102	**21**	10c. green	20	20
103	-	25c. red	20	20
104	**20**	35c. green	20	20
105	**21**	40c. purple	20	20
106	-	60c. brown	25	20
107	**20**	1p. brown	9·75	1·30
108	**21**	1p.25 red	30	20
109	-	2p. blue	40	20
110	**21**	4p.50 green	55	65

111	-	5p. black	41·00	13·00

DESIGN—VERT: 25, 60c., 2, 5p. Cactus.

22 Woman and Child

1954. Child Welfare. Inscr "PRO-INFANCIA 1954".
112	**22**	5c.+5c. orange	50	50
113	-	10c.+5c. mauve	50	50
114	**22**	15c. green	50	50
115	-	60c. brown	55	55

DESIGN: 10c., 60c. Woman and girl.

23 Lobster

1954. Colonial Stamp Day. Inscr "DIA DEL SELLO COLONIAL 1954".
116	**23**	5c.+5c. brown	80	50
117	-	10c.+5c. violet	80	50
118	**23**	15c. green	80	50
119	-	60c. lake	95	55

DESIGN: 10, 60c. Smooth hammerhead.

24 Ploughman and "Justice"

1955. Native Welfare. Inscr "PRO-INDIGENAS 1955".
120	**24**	10c.+5c. purple	50	50
121	-	25c.+10c. lilac	50	50
122	**24**	50c. olive	55	55

DESIGN: 25c. Camel caravan and "Spain".

25 Eurasian Red Squirrel

1955. Colonial Stamp Day.
123	**25**	5c.+5c. brown	50	50
124	-	15c.+5c. bistre	50	50
125	**25**	70c. green	55	55

DESIGN: 15c. Eurasian red squirrel holding nut.

26 "Senecio antheuphorbium"

1956. Child Welfare. Inscr "PRO-INFANCIA 1956".
126	**26**	5c.+5c. green	50	50
127	-	15c.+5c. brown	50	50
128	**26**	20c. green	50	50
129	-	50c. sepia	55	55

DESIGN: 15c., 50c., "Limoniastrum ifniensis".

27 Arms of Sidi-Ifni and Drummer

1956. Colonial Stamp Day. Inscr "DIA DEL SELLO 1956".
130		5c.+5c. sepia	50	50
131	**27**	15c.+5c. brown	50	50
132	-	70c. green	55	55

DESIGNS—VERT: 5c. Arms of Spain and Bohar reedbucks. HORIZ: 70c. Arms of Sidi-Ifni, shepherd and sheep.

---

28 Feral Rock Pigeons

1957. Child Welfare Fund.
133	**28**	5c.+5c. green and brown	50	50
134	**28**	15c.+5c. brown & ochre	50	50
135	**28**	70c. brown and green	55	55

DESIGN: 15c. Stock pigeons in flight.

29 Golden Jackal

1957. Colonial Stamp Day. Inscr "DIA DEL SELLO 1957".
136	**29**	10c.+5c. brown & purple	50	50
137	-	15c.+5c. green and brown	50	50
138	**29**	20c. brown and green	50	50
139	-	70c. brown and green	55	55

DESIGN—VERT: 15c., 70c., Head of Golden jackal.

30 Barn Swallows and Arms of Valencia and Sidi-Ifni

1958. "Aid for Valencia".
140	**30**	10c.+5c. brown	50	50
141	-	15c.+10c. brown	50	50
142	-	50c.+10c. brown	55	55

31 Basketball

1958. Child Welfare Fund.
143	**31**	10c.+5c. brown	50	50
144	-	15c.+5c. brown	50	50
145	**31**	20c. green	50	50
146	-	70c. green	55	55

DESIGN: 15, 70c. Cycling.

32 Greater Spotted Dogfish

1958. Colonial Stamp Day.
147	**32**	10c.+5c. red	50	50
148	-	25c.+10c. purple	50	50
149	-	50c.+10c. brown	55	55

DESIGNS—VERT: 25c. Black-chinned guitar-fish. HORIZ: 50c. Fishing boats.

33 Ewe and Lamb

1959. Child Welfare Fund.
150	**33**	10c.+5c. brown	50	50
151	-	15c.+5c. brown	50	50
152	-	20c. turquoise	50	50
153	**33**	70c. green	55	55

DESIGNS—VERT: 15c. Native trader with mule; 20c. Mountain goat.

34 Footballer

1959. Colonial Stamp Day. Inscr "DIA DEL SELLO 1959".
154	**34**	10c.+5c. brown	50	50
155	-	20c.+5c. myrtle	50	50
156	-	50c.+20c. olive	55	55

DESIGNS: 20c. Footballers; 50c. Javelin-thrower.

35 Dromedaries

1960. Child Welfare.
157	**35**	10c.+5c. purple	50	50
158	-	15c.+5c. brown	50	50
159	-	35c. green	50	50
160	**35**	80c. green	55	55

DESIGNS: 15c. Wild boar; 35c. Red-legged partridges.

36 White Stork

1960. Birds.
161	**36**	25c. violet	25	25
162	-	50c. brown	25	25
163	-	75c. purple	25	25
164	**36**	1p. red	25	25
165	-	1p.50 turquoise	25	25
166	-	2p. purple	25	25
167	**36**	3p. blue	90	25
168	-	5p. brown	1·60	55
169	-	10p. purple	5·75	2·10

BIRDS—HORIZ: 50c., 1p.50, 5p. Eurasian goldfinches. VERT: 75c., 2, 10p. Eurasian skylarks.

37 Church of Santa Cruze del Mar

1960. Stamp Day. Inscr "DIA DEL SELLO 1960".
170	**37**	10c.+5c. brown	50	50
171	-	20c.+5c. green	50	50
172	**37**	30c.+10c. brown	50	50
173	-	50c.+50c. brown	55	55

DESIGN—HORIZ: 20c., 50c. School building.

38 High Jump

1961. Child Welfare. Inscr "PRO-INFANCIA 1961".
174	**38**	10c.+5c. red	50	50
175	-	25c.+10c. violet	50	50
176	**38**	80c.+20c. turquoise	55	55

DESIGN—VERT: 25c. Football.

39

1961. 25th Anniv of General Franco as Head of State.
177		25c. grey	50	50
178	**39**	50c. brown	50	50
179	-	70c. green	50	50
180	**39**	1p. red	55	55

DESIGNS—VERT: 25c. Map. HORIZ: 70c. Government Building.

40 Camel and Motor Lorry

1961. Stamp Day. Inscr "DIA DEL SELLO 1961".
181	**40**	10c.+5c. lake	50	50
182	-	25c.+10c. plum	50	50
183	**40**	30c.+10c. brown	50	50
184	-	1p.+10c. orange	55	55

DESIGN: 25c., 1p. Freighter at wharf.

41 Admiral Jofre Tenorio

1962. Child Welfare. Inscr "PRO-INFANCIA 1962".

185	41	25c. violet	50	50
186	-	50c. turquoise	50	50
187	41	1p. brown	55	55

DESIGN: 50c. C. Fernandez-Duro (historian).

42 Desert Postman

1962. Stamp Day.

188	42	15c. blue	50	50
189	-	35c. mauve	50	50
190	42	1p. purple	55	55

DESIGN: 35c. Winged letter on hands.

43 "Golden Tower", Seville

1963. Seville Flood Relief.

191	43	50c. green	60	60
192	-	1p. brown	60	60

44 Moroccan Copper and Flower

1963. Child Welfare. Inscr "PRO-INFANCIA 1963".

193		25c. blue	50	50
194	44	50c. green	50	50
195	-	1p. red	55	55

DESIGN: 25c., 1p. Moroccan orange-tips.

45 Child and Flowers

1963. "For Barcelona".

196	45	50c. green	60	60
197	45	1p. brown	60	60

46 Beetle ("Steraspis speciosa")

1964. Stamp Day. Inscr "DIA DEL SELLO 1963".

198	46	25c. blue	50	50
199	-	50c. olive	50	50
200	46	1p. brown	55	55

DESIGN: 50c. Desert locust.

47 Edmi Gazelle

1964. Child Welfare.

201	47	25c. violet	50	50
202	-	50c. grey	50	50
203	47	1p. red	55	55

DESIGN: 50c. Head of roe deer.

48 Cyclists Racing

1964. Stamp Day.

204	48	50c. brown	50	50
205	-	1p. red	50	50
206	48	1p.50 green	55	55

DESIGN: 1p. Motor cycle racing.

49 Port Installation, Sidi Ifni

1965. 25th Anniv of End of Spanish Civil War.

207	-	50c. green	50	50
208	-	1p. red	50	50
209	49	1p.50 blue	55	55

DESIGNS—VERT: 50c. Ifnian; 1p. "Education" (children in class).

50 "Eugaster fernandezi"

1965. Child Welfare.

210	50	50c. purple	50	50
211	-	1p. red ("Halter haltera-tus")	50	50
212	50	1p.50 blue	55	55

51 Arms of Ifni

1965. Stamp Day.

213	-	50c. brown	50	50
214	51	1p. red	50	50
215	-	1p.50 blue	55	55

DESIGN—VERT: 50c., 1p.50, Golden Eagle.

52 de Havilland D.H.9C Biplanes

1966. Child Welfare.

216	-	1p. brown	50	50
217	-	1p.50 blue	50	50
218	52	2p.50 violet	1·90	1·90

DESIGN—VERT: 1p., 1p.50, Douglas DC-8 jetliner over Sidi Ifni.

53 Maid Alice Moth

1966. Stamp Day. Insects.

219	53	10c. green and red	50	50
220	-	40c. brown and deep brown	50	50
221	53	1p.50 violet and yellow	50	50
222	-	4p. blue and purple	55	55

DESIGN: 40c., 4p. African monarch (butterfly).

54 Coconut Palm

1967. Child Welfare.

223	54	10c. green and brown	50	50
224	-	40c. green and brown	50	50
225	54	1p.50 turquoise and sepia	50	50
226	-	4p. sepia and brown	55	55

DESIGN: 40c., 4p. Cactus.

55 Bulk Carrier and Floating Crane

1967. Inauguration of Port Ifni.

227	55	1p.50 brown and green	60	60

56 Skipper

1967. Stamp Day.

228	56	1p. green and blue	55	55
229	-	1p.50 purple and yellow	55	55
230	-	3p.50 red and blue	80	80

FISH—VERT: 1p.50, John Dory, HORIZ: 3p.50, Tub gurnard.

1968. Child Welfare. Signs of the Zodiac. As T 47 of Fernando Poo.

231		1p. mauve on yellow	55	55
232		1p.50 brown on pink	55	55
233		2p.50 violet on yellow	80	80

DESIGNS: 1p., Fishes (Pisces); 1p.50, Ram (Aries); 2p.50, Archer (Sagittarius).

57 Posting Letter

1968. Stamp Day.

234	57	1p. black and yellow	50	50
235	-	1p.50 black, plum and blue	50	50
236	-	2p.50 black, blue and green	55	55

DESIGNS: 1p.50, Dove with letter; 2p.50, Magnifying-glass and stamp.

EXPRESS LETTER STAMPS

1943. As T 4, but view of La Alcazaba inscr "URGENTE".

E35		25c. red and green	1·20	1·20

1949. Express Letter stamp of Spain optd Territorio de Ifni.

E66	E198	25c. red	20	20

Pt. 1

INDIA

A peninsula in the S. of Asia. Formerly consisted of British India and numerous Native States, some of which issued stamps of their own. Divided in 1947 into the Dominion of India and the Dominion of Pakistan. Now a republic within the British Commonwealth.

1852. 12 pies = 1 anna; 16 annas = 1 rupee.
1957. 100 naye paise = 1 rupee.
1964. 100 paisa = 1 rupee.

1

1852. "Scinde Dawk". Imperf.

S1	1	½a. white	£18000	£2500
S2	1	½a. blue	£38000	£9500
S3	1	½a. red	—	£25000

3 **9** **10**

1854. Imperf.

1	3	½a. red	£2500	

2	3	½a. blue	£170	35·00
14	3	1a. red	£140	80·00
31	10	2a. green	£275	42·00
23	9	4a. blue and red	£9000	£550

11

1855. Perf.

75	11	½a. blue	11·00	1·40
59	11	1a. brown	13·00	2·00
41	11	2a. pink	£1000	45·00
63	11	2a. orange	40·00	2·00
46	11	4a. black	£650	5·50
64	11	4a. green	£1000	35·00
73	11	8a. red	65·00	7·50

12

1860. Inscr "EAST INDIA POSTAGE". Various frames.

57	12	8p. mauve	20·00	17·00
77	-	9p. lilac	24·00	24·00
71	-	4a. green	42·00	3·75
81	-	6a. brown	9·00	1·75
72	-	6a.8p. grey	90·00	30·00
82	-	12a. brown	17·00	35·00
79	-	1r. grey	85·00	35·00

14

1866. Optd POSTAGE.

66	14	6a. purple	£2000	£150

23

1882. Inscr "INDIA POSTAGE". Various frames.

84	23	½a. green	9·00	10
86	-	9p. red	2·00	3·75
88	-	1a. purple	10·00	30
90	-	1a.6p. brown	2·00	2·50
91	-	2a. blue	9·00	50
94	-	3a. orange	15·00	2·75
96	-	4a. olive	23·00	2·50
97	-	4a.6p. green	45·00	9·00
99	-	8a. mauve	45·00	2·00
100	-	12a. purple on red	15·00	4·75
101	-	1r. grey	35·00	7·50

1891. No. 97 surch 2½ As.

102		2½a. on 4½a. green	9·00	1·00

37 **38** **40**

1892. As 1882 and some new designs.

111	40	3p. red	40	10
112	40	3p. grey	1·00	2·25
113	23	½a. green	3·75	70
115	-	1a. red	6·50	30
116	-	2a. lilac	11·00	4·00
103	-	2a.6p. brown	8·00	40
118	-	2a.6p. blue	9·50	5·50
106	37	1r. green and red	27·00	2·00
107	38	2r. red and brown	75·00	20·00
108	38	3r. brown and green	65·00	12·00
109	38	5r. blue and violet	80·00	50·00

1898. Surch ¼.

110	23	¼a. on ½a. green	20	1·00

41   **52**

1902. As 1882 and 1892, but portrait of King Edward VII (inscribed "INDIA POSTAGE").

119	41	3p. grey	1·00	10
121	-	½a. green	5·00	20
123	-	1a. red	2·75	10
124	-	2a. violet	9·50	40
125	-	2a. mauve	9·00	40
126	-	2a.6p. blue	8·00	60
127	-	3a. orange	8·00	60
128	-	4a. olive	4·25	70
132	-	6a. bistre	21·00	4·50
133	-	8a. purple	8·50	1·00
135	-	12a. purple on red	16·00	2·00
136	-	1r. green and red	8·50	70
139	52	2r. red and brown	90·00	6·50
140	52	3r. brown and green	65·00	35·00
142	52	5r. blue and violet	£150	45·00
144	52	10r. green and red	£275	45·00
146	52	15r. blue and brown	£325	50·00
147	52	25r. orange and blue	£2250	£1600

1905. No. 121 surch ¼.

148		¼a. on ½a. green	55	10

1906. As Nos. 121 and 123, but inscr "INDIA POSTAGE REVENUE".

149		½a. green	3·25	10
150		1a. red	3·75	10

55   **56**   **57**

58   **59**   **60**

61   **62**   **63**

64   **65**   **66**

67   **70**   **71**

1911. *Two types of 1½a. brown. Type A as illustrated. Type B inscr "1½ As. ONE AND A HALF ANNAS".

201	55	3p. grey	1·25	10
202	56	½a. green	4·00	10
161	57	1a. red	4·50	15
203	57	1a. brown	1·50	10
163	58	1½a. brown (A)*	7·00	75
165	58	1½a. brown (B)*	8·50	8·50
204	58	1½a. red (B)*	8·00	10
166	59	2a. purple	7·50	70
169	59	2a. violet	14·00	1·00
206	70	2a. purple	5·00	10
170	60	2a.6p. blue	3·50	3·50
171	61	2a.6p. blue	4·00	20
207	61	2a.6p. orange	5·50	10
173	62	3a. orange	12·00	45
209	62	3a. blue	16·00	10
210	63	4a. olive	2·50	10
211	71	4a. green	6·00	10
177	64	6a. bistre	4·50	2·50
212	65	8a. mauve	8·50	10
213	66	12a. red	8·50	30
214	67	1r. brown and green	13·00	45
215	67	2r. red and orange	30·00	30
216	67	5r. blue and violet	70·00	1·25
217	67	10r. green and red	£120	8·50
218w	67	15r. blue and olive	30·00	30·00
219	67	25r. orange and blue	£300	60·00

See also Nos. 232, etc.

1921. Surch **NINE PIES** and bar.

192	57	9p. on 1a. red	1·50	30

1922. Surch ¼.

195	56	¼a. on ½a. green	1·25	35

72 de Havilland Hercules

1929. Air.

220w	72	2a. green	5·00	75
221	72	3a. blue	4·50	3·00
222	72	4a. olive	6·50	1·25
223	72	6a. bistre	3·50	1·00
224	72	8a. purple	9·50	1·00
225	72	12a. red	23·00	8·00

73 Purana Qila

1931. Inauguration of New Delhi.

226	73	¼a. green and orange	3·75	6·00
227	-	½a. violet and green	2·75	40
228	-	1a. mauve and brown	1·50	20
229w	-	2a. green and blue	2·00	1·25
230w	-	3a. brown and red	5·00	2·50
231w	-	1r. violet and green	21·00	42·00

DESIGNS: ½a. War Memorial Arch; 1a. Council House; 2a. Viceroy's House; 3a. Secretariat; 1r. Dominion Columns and Secretariat.

79   **80**   **81**

82   **83**

1932.

232	79	½a. green	11·00	10
233	80	9p. green	6·00	10
234	81	1a. brown	7·00	10
235	82	1¼a. mauve	1·50	10
236	70	2a. orange	20·00	6·50
236b	59	2a. orange	3·75	50
237	62	3a. red	17·00	10
238	83	3½a. blue	8·00	20

84 Gateway of India, Bombay

1935. Silver Jubilee

240w	84	½a. black and green	1·50	15
241	-	9p. black and green	3·00	20
242w	-	1a. black and brown	5·00	10
243	-	1¼a. black and violet	1·25	10
244w	-	2½a. black and orange	8·50	1·00
245	-	3½a. black and blue	8·00	10·00
246	-	8a. black and purple	6·50	3·75

DESIGNS—9p. Victoria Memorial, Calcutta; 1a. Rameswaram Temple, Madras; 1¼a. Jain Temple, Calcutta; 2½a. Taj Mahal, Agra; 3½a. Golden Temple, Amritsar; 8a. Pagoda in Mandalay.

91 King George VI   **92** Dak Runner

100 King George VI

1937.

247	91	3p. slate	1·50	10
248	91	½a. brown	9·50	10

249	91	9p. green	8·00	75
250	91	1a. red	1·25	10
251	92	2a. orange	13·00	30
252	-	2a.6p. violet	1·50	20
253	-	3a. green	13·00	30
254	-	3a.6p. blue	11·00	60
255	-	4a. brown	14·00	20
256	-	6a. turquoise	16·00	1·25
257	-	8a. violet	7·50	60
258	-	12a. lake	18·00	1·40
259	100	1r. slate and brown	2·25	15
260	100	2r. purple and brown	13·00	30
261	100	5r. green and blue	45·00	50
262	100	10r. purple and red	30·00	80
263	100	15r. brown and green	£170	95·00
264	100	25r. slate and purple	£250	40·00

DESIGNS—As Type **92**: 2a.6p. Dak bullock cart; 3a. Dak tonga; 3a.6p. Dak camel; 4a. Mail train; 6a. *Strathnaver* (liner); 8a. Mail lorry; 12a. Armstrong Whitworth Ensign 1 mail plane (small head).

100a King George VI   **101** King George VI   **102** King George VI

1940.

265	100a	3p. slate	30	10
266	100a	½a. purple	1·25	10
267	100a	9p. green	1·00	10
268	100a	1a. red	1·75	10
269	101	1a.3p. brown	1·00	10
269b	101	1½a. violet	3·00	30
270	101	2a. orange	1·50	10
271	101	3a. violet	6·00	30
272	101	3½a. blue	1·25	1·00
273	102	4a. brown	1·25	10
274	102	6a. turquoise	4·00	10
275	102	8a. violet	1·50	10
276	102	12a. lake	12·00	1·00
277	-	14a. purple	18·00	2·00

No. 277 is as No. 258, but with large head.

105 "Victory" and King George VI

1946. Victory Commemoration.

278	105	9p. green	1·00	1·50
279	105	1½a. purple	40	30
280	105	3½a. blue	1·25	2·50
281	105	12a. red	2·25	1·50

1946. Surch **3 PIES** and bars.

282	101	3p. on 1a.3p. brown	20	15

DOMINION OF INDIA

303 Douglas DC-4

1947. Independence. Inscr "15TH AUG 1947".

301	-	1½a. green	40	10
302	-	3½a. red, blue and green	3·50	2·25
303	303	12a. blue	5·00	2·75

DESIGNS—VERT: 1½a. Asokan capital. HORIZ: 3½a. Indian national flag.

1948. Air. Inauguration of India–U.K. Service. As T **303**, but showing Lockheed Constellation flying in opposite direction and inscr "AIR INDIA INTERNATIONAL FIRST FLIGHT 8TH JUNE 1948".

304		12a. black and blue	4·75	4·50

305 Mahatma Gandhi

1948. First Anniv of Independence.

305	305	1½a. brown	8·50	1·25
306	305	3½a. violet	14·00	5·00
307	305	12a. green	24·00	8·00
308	-	10r. brown and lake	£375	£130

DESIGN—22½×37 mm: 10r. Profile portrait of Mahatma Gandhi.

307 Ajanta Panel   **308** Konarak Horse   **314** Bhuvanesvara

315 Gol Gumbad, Bijapur   **319** Red Fort, Delhi

322 Satrunjaya Temple, Palitana

1949.

309	307	3p. violet	15	10
310	308	6p. brown	25	10
311	-	9p. green	40	10
312	-	1a. blue (A)	60	10
333	-	1a. blue (B)	8·50	10
313	-	2a. red	1·00	10
333b	-	2½a. lake	3·50	3·25
314	-	3a. orange	2·25	10
315	-	3½a. blue	1·75	5·50
316	314	4a. lake	5·50	45
333c	314	4a. blue	6·00	10
317	315	6a. violet	2·50	30
318	-	8a. turquoise	2·25	10
319	-	12a. blue	8·00	30
320	-	1r. violet and green	42·00	10
321	319	2r. red and violet	28·00	40
322	-	5r. green and brown	65·00	2·75
323	-	10r. brown and blue	£150	25·00
324	322	15r. brown and red	24·00	28·00

DESIGNS—As Type **307**: 9p. Trimurti; 1a. Bodhisattva; 2a. Nataraja. As Type **314**: 2½a, 3½a. Bodh Gaya Temple; 3a. Sanchi Stupa, East Gate. As Type **315**: 8a. Kandarya Mahadeva Temple; 12a. Golden Temple, Amritsar. As Type **319**—VERT: 1r. Victory Tower, Chittorgarh; 10r. Qutb Minar, Delhi. HORIZ: 5r. Taj Mahal, Agra.

1 anna: (A) Left arm of statue outstretched. (B) Reversed—right arm outstretched.

323 Globe and Asokan Capital

1949. 75th Anniv of UPU

325	323	9p. green	5·50	3·25
326	323	2a. red	5·50	3·00
327	323	3½a. blue	6·00	3·00
328	323	12a. purple	9·50	3·00

REPUBLIC OF INDIA

324 Rejoicing Crowds

1950. Inauguration of Republic.

329	324	2a. red	5·50	50
330	-	3½a. blue	9·00	9·00
331	-	4a. violet	9·00	1·50
332	-	12a. purple	15·00	3·00

DESIGNS—VERT: 3½a. Quill, ink-well and verse. HORIZ: 4a. Ear of corn and plough; 12a. Spinning-wheel and cloth.

329 "Stegodon ganesa"

1951. Centenary of Geological Survey.

334	329	2a. black and red	3·50	1·25

330 Torch

1951. First Asian Games, New Delhi.

335	**330**	2a. purple and orange	2·50	1·00
336	**330**	12a. brown and blue	16·00	2·25

331 Kabir

1952. Indian Saints and Poets.

337	**331**	9p. green	2·50	65
338	-	1a. red (Tulsidas)	2·50	20
339	-	2a. orange (Meera)	3·50	50
340	-	4a. blue (Surdas)	16·00	60
341	-	4½a. mauve (Ghalib)	2·00	1·25
342	-	12a. brown (Tagore)	18·00	1·00

332 Locomotives of 1853 and 1953

1953. Centenary of Indian Railways.

343	**332**	2a. black	2·25	10

333 Mount Everest

1953. Conquest of Mount Everest.

344	**333**	2a. violet	2·00	1·00
345	**333**	14a. brown	13·00	25

334 Telegraph Poles of 1851 and 1951

1953. Centenary of Indian Telegraphs.

346	**334**	2a. green	3·00	10
347	**334**	12a. blue	10·00	40

335 Postal Transport, 1854

1954. Indian Stamp Centenary.

348	**335**	1a. purple	2·50	20
349	-	2a. mauve	2·00	10
350	-	4a. brown	10·00	1·50
351	-	14a. blue	4·50	40

DESIGNS: 2, 14a. "Airmail"; 4a. Postal transport, 1954.

338 U.N. Emblem and Lotus

1954. U.N. Day.

352	**338**	2a. turquoise	1·25	10

339 Forest Research Institute

1954. Fourth World Forestry Congress, Dehra Dun.

353	**339**	2a. blue	1·25	10

340 Tractor

344 Woman Spinning

347 "Malaria Control" (Mosquito and Staff of Aesculapius)

1955. Five Year Plan.

354	**340**	3p. mauve	30	10
355	-	6p. violet	30	10
356	-	9p. brown	40	10
357	-	1a. green	45	10
358	**344**	2a. blue	30	10
359	-	3a. green	1·00	20
360	-	4a. red	60	10
361	**347**	6a. brown	2·75	10
362	-	8a. blue	11·00	10
363	-	10a. turquoise	4·00	2·75
364	-	12a. blue	6·00	10
365	-	14a. green	5·00	60
413	-	1r. myrtle	3·75	
367	-	1r.2a. grey	3·00	7·00
368	-	1r.8a. purple	17·00	7·00
369	-	2r. mauve	4·50	10
415	-	5r. brown	9·00	50
371	-	10r. orange	20·00	4·75

DESIGNS—As Type **340**: 6p. Power loom; 9p. Bullock-driven well; 1a. Damodar Valley Dam; 4a. Bullocks; 8a. Chittaranjan Locomotive Works; 12a. Hindustan Aircraft Factory, Bangalore; 1r. Telephone engineer; 2r. Rare Earth Factory, Alwaye; 5r. Sindri Fertiliser Factory; 10r. Steel plant. As Type **344**: 3a. Naga woman hand-weaving. As Type **347**: 10a. Marine Drive, Bombay; 14a. Kashmir landscape; 1r.2a. Cape Comorin; 1r.8a. Mt. Kangchenjunga.

358 Bodhi Tree

1956. Buddha Jayanti.

372	**358**	2a. sepia	2·50	10
373	-	14a. orange	9·00	3·75

DESIGN—HORIZ: 14a. Round parasol and Bodhi tree.

360 Lokmanya Bal Gangadhar Tilak

1956. Birth Centenary of Tilak (journalist).

374	**360**	2a. brown	75	10

361 Map of India

1957. Value in naye paise.

375	**361**	1n.p. green	10	10
376	**361**	2n.p. brown	10	10
377	**361**	3n.p. brown	10	10
402	**361**	5n.p. green	10	10
379	**361**	6n.p. grey	10	10
404	**361**	8n.p. turquoise	1·00	10
405	**361**	10n.p. myrtle	15	10
381	**361**	13n.p. red	1·00	10
407	**361**	15n.p. violet	60	10
408	**361**	20n.p. blue	30	10
409	**361**	25n.p. blue	30	10
410	**361**	50n.p. orange	30	10
411	**361**	75n.p. purple	40	10
412	**361**	90n.p. purple	5·50	10

362 The Rani of Jhansi **363** Shrine

1957. Centenary of Indian Mutiny.

386	**362**	15n.p. brown	1·50	10
387	**363**	90n.p. purple	7·50	1·25

364 Henri Dunant and Conference Emblem

1957. 19th Int Red Cross Conference, New Delhi.

388	**364**	15n.p. grey and red	40	10

365 "Nutrition"

1957. Children's Day.

389	**365**	8n.p. purple	25	25
390	-	15n.p. turquoise	1·00	10
391	-	90n.p. brown	1·00	15

DESIGNS—HORIZ: 15n.p. "Education". VERT: 90n.p. "Recreation".

369 Calcutta University

1957. Centenary of Indian Universities.

392		10n.p. violet	1·25	60
393	**369**	10n.p. grey	1·00	60
394	-	10n.p. brown	1·75	60

DESIGNS—21½×38 mm: No. 392, Bombay University. As Type **369**: No. 394, Madras University.

371 J. N. Tata (founder) and Steel Plant

1958. 50th Anniv of Steel Industry.

395	**371**	15n.p. red	10	10

372 Dr. D. K. Karve

1958. Birth Centenary of Karve (educationist).

396	**372**	15n.p. brown	10	10

373 Westland Wapiti Biplane and Hawker Hunter

1958. Silver Jubilee of Indian Air Force.

397	**373**	15n.p. blue	1·25	25
398	**373**	90n.p. blue	2·75	1·50

375 Bipin Chandra Pal

1958. Birth Centenary of Pal (patriot).

418	**375**	15n.p. green	10	10

376 Nurse with Child Patient

1958. Children's Day.

419	**376**	15n.p. violet	10	10

377 Jagadish Chandra Bose

1958. Birth Centenary of Bose (botanist).

420	**377**	15n.p. turquoise	20	10

378 Exhibition Gate

1958. India 1958 Exhibition, New Delhi.

421	**378**	15n.p. purple	10	10

379 Sir Jamsetjee Jejeebhoy

1959. Death Centenary of Sir Jamsetjee Jejeebhoy (philanthropist).

422	**379**	15n.p. brown	10	10

380 The Triumph of Labour (after Chowdhury)

1959. 40th Anniv of I.L.O.

423	**380**	5n.p. green	10	10

381 Boys awaiting admission to Children's Home

1959. Children's Day.

424	**381**	15n.p. green	10	10

382 "Agriculture"

1959. First World Agriculture Fair, New Delhi.

425	**382**	15n.p. grey	30	10

383 Thiruvalluvar (philosopher)

1960. Thiruvalluvar Commemoration.

426	**383**	15n.p. purple	10	10

384 Yaksha pleading with the Cloud (from the "Meghaduta")

385 Shakuntala writing a letter to Dushyanta (from the "Shakuntala")

1960. Kalidasa (poet) Commemoration.

427	**384**	15n.p. grey	75	10
428	**385**	1r.3n.p. yellow and brown	3·00	1·00

386 S. Bharati (poet)

1960. Subramania Bharati Commemoration.

429	**386**	15n.p. blue	10	10

387 Dr. M. Visvesvaraya

1960. Birth Centenary of Dr. M. Visvesvaraya (engineer).

430	**387**	15n.p. brown and red	10	10

388 "Children's Health"

1960. Children's Day.

431	**388**	15n.p. green	10	10

389 Children greeting U.N. Emblem

1960. UNICEF Day.

432	**389**	15n.p. brown and drab	10	10

390 Tyagaraja

1961. 114th Death Anniv of Tyagaraja (musician).

433	**390**	15n.p. blue	10	10

391 "First Aerial Post" Cancellation

392 Air India Boeing 707 Airliner and Humber Sommer Biplane

1961. 50th Anniv of First Official Airmail Flight, Allahabad–Naini.

434	**391**	5n.p. olive	1·90	30
435	**392**	15n.p. green and grey	1·10	30
436	-	1r. purple and grey	4·25	2·75

DESIGN—As Type **392**: 1r. H. Pecquet flying Humber Sommer plane, and "Aerial Post" cancellation.

394 Shivaji on Horseback

1961. Chatrapati Shivaji (Maratha ruler) Commemoration.

437	**394**	15n.p. brown and green	80	40

395 Motilal Nehru (politician)

1961. Birth Centenary of Pandit Motilal Nehru.

438	**395**	15n.p. brown and orange	30	10

396 Tagore (poet)

1961. Birth Centenary of Rabindranath Tagore.

439	**396**	15n.p. orange and turquoise	80	40

397 All India Radio Emblem and Transmitting Aerials

1961. Silver Jubilee of All India Radio.

440	**397**	15n.p. blue	10	10

398 Prafulla Chandra Ray

1961. Birth Centenary of Prafulla Chandra Ray (social reformer).

441	**398**	15n.p. grey	10	20

399 V. N. Bhatkande

1961. Birth Centenary of V. N Bhatkande (composer) (1960).

442	**399**	15n.p. drab	10	10

400 Child at Lathe

1961. Children's Day.

443	**400**	15n.p. brown	10	20

401 Fair Emblem and Main Gate

1961. Indian Industries Fair, New Delhi.

444	**401**	15n.p. blue and red	10	10

402 Indian Forest

1961. Centenary of Scientific Forestry.

445	**402**	15n.p. green and brown	40	30

403 Pitalkhora: Yaksha

1961. Centenary of Indian Archaeological Survey.

446	**403**	15n.p. brown	50	10
447	-	90n.p. olive and brown	4·00	30

DESIGN—HORIZ: 90n.p. Kalibangan seal.

405 M. M. Malaviya

1961. Birth Centenary of Malaviya (educationist).

448	**405**	15n.p. slate	10	20

406 Gauhati Refinery

1962. Inauguration of Gauhati Oil Refinery.

449	**406**	15n.p. blue	55	20

407 Bhikaiji Cama

1962. Birth Centenary of Bhikaiji Cama (patriot).

450	**407**	15n.p. purple	10	10

408 Village Panchayati and Parliament Building

1962. Inauguration of Panchayati System of Local Government.

451	**408**	15n.p. mauve	10	10

409 D. Saraswati (religious reformer)

1962. Dayanand Saraswati Commemoration.

452	**409**	15n.p. brown	10	10

410 G. S. Vidhyarthi (journalist)

1962. Ganesh Shankar Vidhyarthi Commemoration.

453	**410**	15n.p. brown	10	10

411 Malaria Eradication Emblem

1962. Malaria Eradication.

454	**411**	15n.p. yellow and lake	10	10

412 Dr. R. Prasad

1962. Retirement of President Dr. Rajendra Prasad.

455	**412**	15n.p. purple	30	20

413 Calcutta High Court

1962. Centenary of Indian High Courts.

456	**413**	15n.p. green	50	20
457	-	15n.p. brown (Madras)	50	20
458	-	15n.p. slate (Bombay)	50	20

416 Ramabai Ranade

1962. Birth Centenary of Ramabai Ranade (social reformer).

459	**416**	15n.p. orange	10	30

417 Indian Rhinoceros

1962. Wild Life Week.

460	**417**	15n.p. brown and turquoise	55	15

418 "Passing the Flag to Youth"

1962. Children's Day.

461	**418**	15n.p. red and green	15	20

419 Human Eye within
Lotus Blossom

1962. 19th Int Ophthalmology Congress, New Delhi.
462 **419** 15n.p. brown 45 10

420 S. Ramanujan

1962. 75th Birth Anniv of Srinivasa Ramanujan
(mathematician).
463 **420** 15n.p. brown 70 40

421 S.
Vivekananda

1963. Birth Cent of Vivekananda (philosopher).
464 **421** 15n.p. brown and olive 40 20

1963. Surch. **1r.**
465 **385** 1r. on 1r.3n.p. yellow
and brown 8·00 10

423 Hands
reaching for F.A.O.
Emblem

1963. Freedom from Hunger.
466 **423** 15n.p. blue 3·00 30

424 Henri Dunant
(founder) and
Centenary Emblem

1963. Centenary of Red Cross.
467 **424** 15n.p. red and grey 3·00 40

425 Artillery and Mil Mi-4
Helicopter

1963. Defence Campaign.
468 **425** 15n.p. green 1·50 10
469 - 1r. brown 4·00 65
DESIGN: 1r. Sentry and parachutists.

427 D. Naoroji
(parliamentarian)

1963. Dadabhai Naoroji Commemoration.
470 **427** 15n.p. grey 10 10

428 Annie Besant
(patriot and
theosophist)

1963. Annie Besant Commemoration.
471 **428** 15n.p. green 15 10
No. 471 is incorrectly dated "1837". Mrs. Besant was
born in 1847.

1963. Wild Life Preservation. Animal designs as T **417**.
472 10n.p. black and orange 1·50 1·50
473 15n.p. brown and green 1·75 60
474 30n.p. slate and ochre 3·00 1·50
475 50n.p. orange and green 3·50 80
476 1r. brown and blue 3·00 50
ANIMALS—As Type **417**: 10n.p. Gaur. 25½×35½ mm:
15n.p. Lesser panda; 30n.p. Indian elephant. 35½×25½
mm: 50n.p. Tiger; 1r. Lion.

434 "School Meals"

1963. Children's Day.
477 **434** 15n.p. bistre 10 10

435 Eleanor Roosevelt at
Spinning-wheel

1963. 15th Anniv of Declaration of Human Rights.
478 **435** 15n.p. purple 10 15

436 Dipalakshmi
(bronze)

1964. 26th Int Orientalists Congress, New Delhi.
479 **436** 15n.p. blue 20 15

437 Gopabandhu
Das (social
reformer)

1964. Gopabandhu Das Commemoration.
480 **437** 15n.p. purple 10 10

438 Purandaradasa

1964. 400th Death Anniv of Purandaradasa (composer).
481 **438** 15n.p. brown 15 10

439 S. C. Bose and I.N.A.
Badge

1964. 67th Birth Anniv of Subhas Chandra Bose
(nationalist).
482 **439** 15n.p. olive 50 20
483 - 55n.p. black, orange
and red 75 45
DESIGN: 35n.p. Bose and Indian National Army.

441 Sarojini Naidu

1964. 85th Birth Anniv of Sarojini Naidu (poetess).
484 **441** 15n.p. green and purple 10 10

442 Kasturba
Gandhi

1964. 20th Death Anniv of Kasturba Gandhi.
485 **442** 15n.p. brown 10 10

443 Dr. W. M.
Haffkine
(immunologist)

1964. Haffkine Commemoration.
486 **443** 15n.p. brown on buff 45 10

444 Jawaharlal Nehru
(statesman)

1964. Nehru Mourning Issue.
487 **444** 15p. slate 25 10

445 Sir Asutosh
Mookerjee

1964. Birth Centenary of Sir Asutosh Mookerjee
(education reformer).
488 **445** 15p. brown and olive 10 10

446 Sri Aurobindo

1964. 92nd Birth Anniv of Sri Aurobindo (religious
teacher).
489 **446** 15p. purple 15 10

447 Raja R. Roy (social
reformer)

1964. Raja Rammohun Roy Commemoration.
490 **447** 15n.p. brown 10 10

448 I.S.O. Emblem
and Globe

1964. Sixth Int Organization for Standardisation General
Assembly, Bombay.
491 **448** 15p. red 15 20

449 Jawaharlal
Nehru (from 1r.
commemorative
coin)

1964. Children's Day.
492 **449** 15p. slate 10 10

450 St. Thomas
(after statue,
Ortona
Cathedral, Italy)

1964. St. Thomas Commemoration.
493 **450** 15p. purple 10 30
No. 493 was issued on the occasion of Pope Paul's visit
to India.

451 Globe

1964. 22nd International Geological Congress.
494 **451** 15p. green 40 30

452 J. Tata (industrialist)

1965. Jamsetji Tata Commemoration.
495 **452** 15p. dull purple and
orange 30 20

453 Lala Lajpat Rai

1965. Birth Centenary of Lala Lajpat Rai (social reformer).
496 **453** 15p. brown 20 10

454 Globe and Congress
Emblem

1965. 20th International Chamber of Commerce
Congress, New Delhi.
497 **454** 15p. green and red 15 15

455 Freighter *Jalausha* and
Visakhapatnam

1965. National Maritime Day.
498 **455** 15p. blue 50 30

456 Abraham
Lincoln

1965. Death Centenary of Lincoln.
499   **456**   15p. brown and ochre   15   10

457 I.T.U. Emblem and Symbols

1965. Centenary of I.T.U.
500   **457**   15p. purple   1·00   30

458 "Everlasting Flame"

1965. First Death Anniv of Nehru.
501   **458**   15p. red and blue   15   10

459 I.C.Y. Emblem

1965. International Co-operation Year.
502   **459**   15p. green and brown   1·25   1·25

460 Climbers on Summit

1965. Indian Mount Everest Expedition.
503   **460**   15p. purple   45   20

466 Electric Locomotive   **475** Dal Lake, Kashmir

1965

504	-	2p. brown	10	1·00
505	-	3p. olive	70	4·00
505a	-	4p. brown	10	3·75
506	-	5p. red	10	10
507	-	6p. black	30	4·25
508	-	8p. brown	30	4·25
509	**466**	10p. blue	40	10
510	-	15p. green	6·00	10
511	-	20p. purple	6·00	10
512	-	30p. sepia	15	10
513	-	40p. purple	15	10
514	-	50p. green	20	10
515	-	60p. grey	35	20
516	-	70p. blue	60	20
517	-	1r. brown and plum	60	10
518	**475**	2r. blue and violet	2·00	10
519	-	5r. violet and brown	3·00	90
520	-	10r. black and green	32·00	80

DESIGNS—VERT (as Type **466**): 2p. Bidri vase; 3p. Brass lamp; 5p. "Family Planning"; 6p. Konarak elephant; 8p. Spotted deer ("Chital"); 30p. Indian dolls; 50p. Mangoes; 60p. Somnath Temple. (as Type **475**): 1r. Woman writing a letter (medieval sculpture). HORIZ (as Type **466**): 4p. Coffee berries; 15p. Plucking tea; 20p. Hindustan Aircraft Industries Ajeet jet fighter; 40p. Calcutta G.P.O.; 70p. Hampi Chariot (sculpture). (As Type **475**): 5r. Bhakra Dam, Punjab; 10r. Atomic reactor, Trombay.
See also Nos. 721/38c.

479 G. B. Pant (statesman)

1965. Govind Ballabh Pant Commemoration.
522   **479**   15p. brown and green   10   20

480 V. Patel

1965. 90th Birth Anniv of Vallabhbhai Patel (statesman).
523   **480**   15p. brown   10   30

481 C. Das

1965. 95th Birth Anniv of Chittaranjan Das (lawyer and patriot).
524   **481**   15p. brown   10   10

482 Vidyapati (poet)

1965. Vidyapati Commemoration.
525   **482**   15p. brown   10   10

483 Sikandra, Agra

1966. Pacific Area Travel Assn Conf, New Delhi.
526   **483**   15p. slate   10   10

484 Soldier, Hindustan Aircraft Industries Ajeet Jet Fighters and Cruiser *Mysore*

1966. Indian Armed Forces.
527   **484**   15p. violet   1·75   75

485 Lal Bahadur Shastri (statesman)

1966. Shastri Mourning Issue.
528   **485**   15p. black   80   10

486 Kambar (poet)

1966. Kambar Commemoration.
529   **486**   15p. green   10   10

487 B. R. Ambedkar

1966. 75th Birth Anniv of Dr. Bhim Rao Ambedkar (lawyer).
530   **487**   15p. purple   10   10

488 Kunwar Singh (patriot)

1966. Kunwar Singh Commemoration.
531   **488**   15p. brown   10   10

489 G. K. Gokhale

1966. Birth Centenary of Gopal Krishna Gokhale (patriot).
532   **489**   15p. purple and yellow   10   10

490 Acharya Dvivedi (poet)

1966. Dvivedi Commemoration.
533   **490**   15p. drab   10   10

491 Maharaja Ranjit Singh (warrior)

1966. Maharaja Ranjit Singh Commemoration.
534   **491**   15p. purple   60   30

492 Homi Bhabha (scientist) and Nuclear Reactor

1966. Dr. Homi Bhabha Commemoration.
535   **492**   15p. purple   15   30

493 A. K. Azad (scholar)

1966. Abul Kalam Azad Commemoration.
536   **493**   15p. blue   15   15

494 Swami Tirtha

1966. 60th Death Anniv of Swami Rama Tirtha (social reformer).
537   **494**   15p. blue   30   30

495 Infant and Dove Emblem

1966. Children's Day.
538   **495**   15p. purple   60   20

496 Allahabad High Court

1966. Centenary of Allahabad High Court.
539   **496**   15p. purple   70   30

497 Indian Family

1966. Family Planning.
540   **497**   15p. brown   15   15

498 Hockey Game

1966. India's Hockey Victory in 5th Asian Games.
541   **498**   15p. blue   1·25   60

499 "Jai Kisan"

1967. First Death Anniv of Shastri.
542   **499**   15p. green   30   30

500 Voter and Polling Booth

1967. Indian General Election.
543   **500**   15p. brown   15   15

501 Gurudwara Shrine, Patna

1967. 300th Birth Anniv (1966) of Guru Gobind Singh (Sikh religious leader).
544   **501**   15p. violet   1·25   15

502 Taj Mahal, Agra

1967. International Tourist Year.
545   **502**   15p. brown and orange   30   15

503 Nandalal Bose and *Garuda*

1967. First Death Anniv of Nandalal Bose (painter).
546   **503**   15p. brown   15   15

504 Survey Emblem and Activities

1967. Bicentenary of Survey of India.
547   **504**   15p. lilac   80   40

505 Basaveswara

1967. 800th Anniv of Basaveswara (reformer and statesman).
548 **505** 15p. red   15   15

506 Narsinha
Mehta (poet)

1967. Narsinha Mehta Commemoration.
549 **506** 15p. sepia   15   15

507 Maharana
Pratap

1967. Maharana Pratap (Rajput leader) Commemoration.
550 **507** 15p. brown   20   15

508 Narayana
Guru

1967. Narayana Guru (philosopher) Commemoration.
551 **508** 15p. brown   30   20

509 Pres.
Radhakrishnan

1967. 75th Birth Anniv of Sarvepalli Radhakrishnan (former President).
552 **509** 15p. red   50   15

510 Martyrs' Memorial,
Patna

1967. 25th Anniv of "Quit India" Movement.
553 **510** 15p. lake   15   15

511 Route Map

1967. Centenary of Indo-European Telegraph Service.
554 **511** 15p. black and blue   70   20

512 Wrestling

1967. World Wrestling Championships, New Delhi.
555 **512** 15p. purple and brown   50   20

513 Nehru leading
Naga Tribesmen

1967. Fourth Anniv of Nagaland as a State of India.
556 **513** 15p. blue   15   15

514 Rashbehari
Basu
(nationalist)

1967. Rashbehari Basu Commemoration.
557 **514** 15p. purple   15   20

515 Bugle, Badge and
Scout Salute

1967. 60th Anniv of Scout Movement in India.
558 **515** 15p. brown   1·00   1·00

516 Men embracing
Universe

1968. Human Rights Year.
559 **516** 15p. green   50   30

517 Globe and
Book of Tamil

1968. Int Conf and Seminar of Tamil Studies, Madras.
560 **517** 15p. lilac   60   15

518 U.N. Emblem and
Transport

1968. United Nations Conference on Trade and Development, New Delhi.
561 **518** 15p. blue   60   15

519 Quill and Bow
Symbol

1968. Centenary of *Amrita Bazar Patrika* (newspaper).
562 **519** 15p. sepia and yellow   15   15

520 Maxim
Gorky

1968. Birth Centenary of Maxim Gorky.
563 **520** 15p. plum   15   50

521 Emblem and
Medal

1968. First Triennale Art Exhibition, New Delhi.
564 **521** 15p. orange, blue and
light blue   30   20

522 Letter-box and
"100,000"

1968. Opening of 100,000th Indian Post Office.
565 **522** 20p. red, blue and black   40   15

523 Stalks of Wheat,
Agricultural Institute and
Production Graph

1968. Wheat Revolution.
566 **523** 20p. green and brown   30   15

524 "Self-portrait"

1968. 30th Death Anniv of Gaganendranath Tagore (painter).
567 **524** 20p. purple and ochre   50   15

525 Lakshminath
Bezbaruah

1968. Birth Cent of Lakshminath Bezbaruah (writer).
568 **525** 20p. brown   30   15

526 Athlete's Legs and
Olympic Rings

1968. Olympic Games, Mexico.
569 **526** 20p. brown and grey   15   15
570 **526** 1r. sepia and olive   85   15

527 Bhagat Singh and
Followers

1968. 61st Birth Anniv of Bhagat Singh (patriot).
571 **527** 20p. brown   1·00   1·00

528 Azad Hind
Flag, Swords
and Chandra
Bose (founder)

1968. 25th Anniv of Azad Hind Government.
572 **528** 20p. blue   1·25   15

529 Sister
Nivedita

1968. Birth Cent of Sister Nivedita (social reformer).
573 **529** 20p. green   30   30

530 Marie Curie and
Radium Treatment

1968. Birth Centenary of Marie Curie.
574 **530** 20p. lilac   1·40   1·25

531 Map of the
World

1968. 21st Int Geographical Congress, New Delhi.
575 **531** 20p. blue   15   15

532 Cochin
Synagogue

1968. 400th Anniv of Cochin Synagogue.
576 **532** 20p. blue and red   1·00   40

533 I.N.S. *Nilgiri* (frigate)

1968. Navy Day.
577 **533** 20p. blue   1·75   40

534 Red-billed Blue
Magpie

1968. Birds.
578 **534** 20p. multicoloured   1·25   50
579 —   50p. red, black and
green   1·25   1·50
580 —   1r. blue and brown   2·75   1·00
581 —   2r. multicoloured   2·00   1·50

DESIGNS—HORIZ: 50p. Brown-fronted pied woodpecker; 2r. Yellow-backed sunbird. VERT: 1r. Slaty-headed scimitar babbler.

538 Bankim
Chandra
Chatterjee

1969. 130th Birth Anniv of Chatterjee (writer).
582 **538** 20p. blue   15   20

539 Dr.
Bhagavan Das

1969. Birth Centenary of Das (philosopher).
583 **539** 20p. brown   15   50

540 Dr. Martin Luther King

1969. Martin Luther King Commemoration.
584 **540** 20p. brown   60   20

541 Mirza Ghalib and Letter Seal

1969. Death Centenary of Mirza Ghalib (poet).
585 **541** 20p. sepia, red and flesh   15   15

542 Osmania University

1969. 50th Anniv of Osmania University.
586 **542** 20p. green   15   20

543 Rafi Ahmed Kidwai and Lockheed Constellation Mail Plane

1969. 20th Anniv of "All-up" Airmail Scheme.
587 **543** 20p. blue   1·50   30

544 I.L.O. Badge and Emblem

1969. 50th Anniv of Int Labour Organization.
588 **544** 20p. brown   15   20

545 Memorial, and Hands dropping Flowers

1969. 50th Anniv of Jallianwala Bagh Massacre, Amritsar.
589 **545** 20p. red   15   20

546 K. Nageswara Rao Pantulu (journalist)

1969. Kasinadhuni Nageswara Rao Pantulu Commemoration.
590 **546** 20p. brown   15   20

547 Ardaseer Cursetjee Wadia, and Ships

1969. Ardaseer Cursetjee Wadia (ship-builder) Commemoration.
591 **547** 20p. turquoise   1·00   75

548 Serampore College

1969. 150th Anniv of Serampore College.
592 **548** 20p. plum   15   20

549 Dr. Zakir Husain

1969. President Dr. Zakir Husain Commemoration.
593 **549** 20p. sepia   15   20

550 Laxmanrao Kirloskar

1969. Birth Centenary of Laxmanrao Kirloskar (agriculturist).
594 **550** 20p. black   15   15

551 Gandhi and his Wife

1969. Birth Centenary of Mahatma Gandhi.
595 **551** 20p. brown   70   40
596   -   75p. flesh and drab   1·25 2·00
597   -   1r. blue   1·25   65
598   -   5r. brown and orange   4·50 6·50

DESIGNS AND SIZES—VERT: 75p. Gandhi's head and shoulders (28×38 mm); 1r. Gandhi walking (woodcut) (20×38 mm). HORIZ: 5r. Gandhi with charkha (36×26 mm).

555 *Ajanta* (bulk carrier) and I.M.C.O. Emblem

1969. Tenth Anniv of Inter-Governmental Maritime Consultative Organization.
599 **555** 20p. blue   1·75   40

556 Outline of Parliament Building and Globe

1969. 57th Inter-Parliamentary Conference, New Delhi.
600 **556** 20p. blue   15   20

557 Astronaut walking beside Space Module on Moon

1969. First Man on the Moon.
601 **557** 20p. brown   60   30

558 Gurudwara Nankana Sahib (birthplace)

1969. 500th Birth Anniv of Guru Nanak Dev (Sikh religious leader).
602 **558** 20p. violet   30   20

559 Tiger's Head and Hands holding Globe

1969. Int Union for the Conservation of Nature and Natural Resources Conference, New Delhi.
603 **559** 20p. brown and green   1·00   45

560 Sadhu Vaswani

1969. 90th Birth Anniv of Sadhu Vaswani (educationist).
604 **560** 20p. grey   15   15

561 Thakkar Bapa

1969. Birth Centenary of Thakkar Bapa (humanitarian).
605 **561** 20p. brown   15   20

562 Satellite, Television, Telephone and Globe

1970. 12th Plenary Assembly of Int Radio Consultative Committee.
606 **562** 20p. blue   40   20

563 C. N. Annadurai

1970. First Death Anniv of Conjeevaram Natrajan Annadurai (statesman).
607 **563** 20p. purple and blue   30   15

564 M. N. Kishore and Printing Press

1970. 75th Death Anniv of Munshi Newal Kishore (publisher).
608 **564** 20p. lake   15   20

565 Nalanda College

1970. Centenary of Nalanda College.
609 **565** 20p. brown   60   50

566 Swami Shraddhanand (social reformer)

1970. Swami Shraddhanand Commemoration.
610 **566** 20p. brown   75   60

567 Lenin

1970. Birth Centenary of Lenin.
611 **567** 20p. brown and sepia   40   20

568 New U.P.U. H.Q. Building

1970. New U.P.U. Headquarters Building, Berne.
612 **568** 20p. green, grey and black   15   20

569 Sher Shah Suri (15th century ruler)

1970. Sher Shah Suri Commemoration.
613 **569** 20p. green   30   70

570 V. D. Savarkar and Cellular Jail, Andaman Islands

1970. Vinayak Damodar Savarkar Commemoration.
614 **570** 20p. brown   65   30

571 "UN" and Globe

1970. 25th Anniv of United Nations.
615 **571** 20p. blue   40   20

572 Symbol and Workers

1970. Asian Productivity Year.
616 **572** 20p. violet   20   20

573 Dr. Montessori and I.E.Y. Emblem

1970. Birth Centenary of Dr. Maria Montessori (educationist).
617 **573** 20p. purple   30   30

574 J. N. Mukherjee (revolutionary) and Horse

1970. Jatindra Nath Mukherjee Commemoration.
618 **574** 20p. brown   1·50   30

575 V. S. Srinivasa Sastri

1970. Srinivasa Sastri (educationist) Commemoration.
619 **575** 20p. yellow and purple   30   30

576 I. C. Vidyasagar

1970. 150th Birth Anniv of Iswar Chandra Vidyasagar (educationist).
620 **576** 20p. brown and purple 40 30

577 Maharishi Valmiki

1970. Maharishi Valmiki (ancient author) Commem.
621 **577** 20p. purple 70 30

578 Calcutta Port

1970. Centenary of Calcutta Port Trust.
622 **578** 20p. blue 1·50 70

579 University Building

1970. 50th Anniv of Jamia Millia Islamia University.
623 **579** 20p. green 70 50

580 Jamnalal Bajaj

1970. Jamnalal Bajaj (industrialist) Commemoration.
624 **580** 20p. grey 15 30

581 Nurse and Patient

1970. 50th Anniv of Indian Red Cross.
625 **581** 20p. red and blue 1·00 40

582 Sant Namdeo

1970. 700th Birth Anniv of Sant Namdeo (mystic).
626 **582** 20p. orange 15 30

583 Beethoven

1970. Birth Bicentenary of Beethoven.
627 **583** 20p. orange and black 2·50 70

584 Children examining Stamps

1970. Indian National Philatelic Exhibition, New Delhi.
628 **584** 20p. orange and green 50 10
629 - 1r. brown and ochre 4·00 1·00
DESIGN: 1r. Gandhi commemorative through magnifier.

585 Girl Guide

1970. Diamond Jubilee of Girl Guide Movement in India.
630 **585** 20p. purple 60 30

586 Hands and Lamp (Emblem)

1971. Centenary of Indian Life Insurance.
631 **586** 20p. brown and red 20 30

587 Vidyapith Building

1971. 50th Anniv of Kashi Vidyapith University.
632 **587** 20p. brown 20 30

588 Sant Ravidas

1971. Sant Ravidas (15th-century mystic) Commemoration.
633 **588** 20p. red 1·00 45

589 C. F. Andrews

1971. Birth Centenary of Charles Freer Andrews (missionary).
634 **589** 20p. brown 55 30

590 Acharya Narendra Deo (scholar)

1971. 15th Death Anniv of Acharya Narendra Deo.
635 **590** 20p. green 20 30

591 Crowd and "100"

1971. Centenary of Decennial Census.
636 **591** 20p. brown and blue 50 30

592 Sri Ramana Maharishi (mystic)

1971. 21st Death Anniv of Ramana Maharishi.
637 **592** 20p. orange and brown 30 30

593 Raja Ravi Varma and *Damayanti and the Swan*

1971. 65th Death Anniv of Ravi Varma (artist).
638 **593** 20p. green 75 50

594 Dadasaheb Phalke and Camera

1971. Birth Centenary of Dadasaheb Phalke (cinematographer).
639 **594** 20p. purple 70 40

595 *Abhisarika* (Tagore)

1971. Birth Centenary of Abanindranath Tagore (painter).
640 **595** 20p. grey, yellow and brown 60 30

596 Swami Virjanand (Vedic scholar)

1971. Swami Virjanand Commemoration.
641 **596** 20p. brown 40 40

597 Cyrus the Great and Procession

1971. 2500th Anniv of Charter of Cyrus the Great.
642 **597** 20p. brown 75 55

598 Globe and Money Box

1971. World Thrift Day.
643 **598** 20p. grey 20 30

599 Ajanta Caves Painting

1971. 25th Anniv of UNESCO.
644 **599** 20p. brown 1·75 1·00

600 *Women at Work* (Geeta Gupta)

1971. Children's Day.
645 **600** 20p. red 20 50

607 Refugees

1971. Obligatory Tax. Refugee Relief.

(a) Optd **REFUGEE RELIEF** in Hindi and English.
646 5p. red (No. 506) 70 10

(b) Optd **Refugee Relief**
647 5p. red (No. 506) 4·00 1·50

(c) Optd **REFUGEE RELIEF**
649 5p. red (No. 506) 4·00 2·00

(d) Optd **Refugee Relief**
650c 5p. red (No. 506) 27·00 4·25

(e) Optd **Refugee Relief** in Hindi and English
650d 5p. red (No. 506)

(f) Type **607**
651 **607** 5p. red 50 10
From 15 November 1971 until 31 March 1973 the Indian Government levied a 5p. surcharge on all mail, except postcards and newspapers, for the relief of refugees from the former East Pakistan.

608 C. V. Raman (scientist) and Light Graph

1971. First Death Anniv of Chandrasekhara Venkata Raman.
652 **608** 20p. orange and brown 50 30

609 Visva Bharati Building and Rabindranath Tagore (founder)

1971. 50th Anniv of Visva Bharati University.
653 **609** 20p. sepia and brown 60 60

610 Cricketers

1971. Indian Cricket Victories.
654 **610** 20p. green, myrtle and sage 2·00 65

611 Map and Satellite

1972. First Anniv of Arvi Satellite Earth Station.
655 **611** 20p. purple 45 30

612 Elemental Symbols and Plumb-line

1972. 25th Anniv of Indian Standards Institution.
656 **612** 20p. grey and black 20 50

613 Signal Box Panel

1972. 50th Anniv of Int Railways Union.
657 **613** 20p. multicoloured 1·50 50

614 Hockey-player

1972. Olympic Games, Munich.
658 **614** 20p. violet 2·00 25
659 - 1r.45 45 green and lake 3·00 2·75
DESIGN: 1r.45, Various sports.

615 Symbol of Sri Aurobindo

1972. Birth Centenary of Sri Aurobindo (religious teacher).
660 **615** 20p. yellow and blue 20 30

616 Celebrating Independence Day in front of Parliament

1972. 25th Anniv of Independence. (1st issue).
661 **616** 20p. multicoloured 1·25 30
See also Nos. 673/4.

617 Inter-Services Crest

1972. Defence Services Commemoration.
662 **617** 20p. multicoloured 70 40

618 V. O. Chidambaram Pillai (trade union leader) and Ship

1972. Birth Cent of V. O. Chidambaran Pillai.
663 **618** 20p. blue and brown 75 40

619 Bhai Vir Singh

1972. Birth Centenary of Bhai Vir Singh (poet).
664 **619** 20p. purple 1·00 40

620 T. Prakasam

1972. Birth Centenary of Tanguturi Prakasam (lawyer).
665 **620** 20p. brown 20 40

621 Vemana

1972. 300th Birth Anniv of Vemana (poet).
666 **621** 20p. black 20 40

622 Bertrand Russell

1972. Birth Centenary of Bertrand Russell (philosopher).
667 **622** 1r.45 black 3·25 2·75

623 Symbol of "Asia '72"

1972. "Asia '72" (Third Asian International Trade Fair), New Delhi.
668 **623** 20p. black and orange 15 20
669 - 1r.45 orange and black 70 1·75
DESIGN: 1r.45, Hand of Buddha.

624 V. A. Sarabhai and Rocket

1972. First Death Anniv of Dr. Vikram A. Sarabhai (scientist).
670 **624** 20p. brown and green 20 40

625 Flag of U.S.S.R. and Kremlin Tower

1972. 50th Anniv of U.S.S.R.
671 **625** 20p. red and yellow 30 60

626 Exhibition Symbol

1973. "Indipex '73" Stamp Exhibition (1st issue).
672 **626** 1r.45 mauve, gold & black 45 1·25
See also No. 701/**MS**704.

627 "Democracy"

1973. 25th Anniv of Independence (2nd issue). Multicoloured.
673 20p. Type **627** 20 15
674 1r.45 Hindustan Aircraft Industries Ajeet jet fighters over India Gate (38×20 mm) 1·40 1·60

628 Sri Ramakrishna Paramahamsa (religious leader)

1973. Sri Ramakrishna Paramahamsa Commem.
675 **628** 20p. brown 70 70

629 Postal Corps Emblem

1973. First Anniv of Army Postal Service Corps.
676 **629** 20p. blue and red 40 50

630 Flag and Map of Bangladesh

1973. "Jai Bangla" (Inauguration of 1st Bangladesh Parliament).
677 **630** 20p. multicoloured 20 40

631 Kumaran Asan

1973. Birth Centenary of Kumaran Asan (writer and poet).
678 **631** 20p. brown 50 75

632 Flag and Flames

1973. Homage to Martyrs for Independence.
679 **632** 20p. multicoloured 20 40

633 Dr. Bhim Rao Ambedkar (lawyer)

1973. Ambedkar Commemoration.
680 **633** 20p. green and purple 30 1·25

634 Radha-Kishangarh (Nihal Chand)

1973. Indian Miniature Paintings. Multicoloured.
681 20p. Type **634** 30 35
682 50p. Dance Duet (Aurangzeb's period) 60 1·50
683 1r. Lovers on a Camel (Nasir-ud-din) 80 1·75
684 2r. Chained Elephant (Zain-al-Abidin) 1·10 2·50

635 Mount Everest

1973. 15th Anniv of Indian Mountaineering Foundation.
685 **635** 20p. blue 1·00 1·00

636 Tail of Boeing 747

1973. 25th Anniv of Air-India's International Services.
686 **636** 1r.45 blue and red 4·00 4·00

637 Cross, Church of St. Thomas' Mount, Madras

1973. 19th Death Centenary of St. Thomas.
687 **637** 20p. grey and brown 20 80

638 Michael Madhusudan Dutt (poet–Death Centenary)

1973. Centenaries.
688 **638** 20p. green and brown 1·00 65
689 - 30p. brown 1·25 2·75
690 - 50p. brown 1·50 2·75
691 - 1r. violet and red 1·50 1·50
DESIGNS—HORIZ: 30p. Vishnu Digambar Paluskar (musician, birth cent); 50p. Dr. G. A. Hansen (cent of discovery of leprosy bacillus); 1r. Nicolaus Copernicus (astronomer, 5th birth cent).

639 A. O. Hume

1973. Allan Octavian Hume (founder of Indian National Congress) Commemoration.
692 **639** 20p. grey 20 60

640 Gandhi and Nehru

1973. Gandhi and Nehru Commemoration.
693 **640** 20p. multicoloured 20 40

641 R. C. Dutt

1973. Romesh Chandra Dutt (writer) Commem.
694 **641** 20p. brown 20 40

642 K. S. Ranjitsinhji

1973. K. S. Ranjitsinhji (cricketer) Commemoration.
695 **642** 30p. green 3·50 3·50

643 Vithalbhai Patel

1973. Vithalbhai Patel (lawyer) Commemoration.
696 **643** 50p. brown 30 1·25

644 Sowar of President's Bodyguard

1973. Bicentenary of President's Bodyguard.
697 **644** 20p. multicoloured 1·50 60

645 Interpol Emblem

1973. 50th Anniv of Interpol.
698 **645** 20p. brown 30 40

646 Syed Ahmad Khan (social reformer)

1973. Syed Ahmad Khan Commemoration.
699 **646** 20p. brown 20 1·25

647 Children at Play (Bela Raval)

1973. Children's Day.
700 **647** 20p. multicoloured 20 30

648 Indipex Emblem

1973. "Indipex '73" Philatelic Exhibition, New Delhi (2nd issue). Multicoloured.
701 **648** 20p. Type **648** 20 30
702 1r. Ceremonial elephant and 1½a. stamp of 1947 (vert) 1·25 1·50
703 2r. Common peafowl (vert) 1·50 3·25
MS704 127×127 mm. Nos. 672 and 701/3. Imperf 8·50 9·50

649 Emblem of National Cadet Corps

1973. 25th Anniv of National Cadet Corps.
705 **649** 20p. multicoloured 20 30

650 C. Rajagopalachari (statesman)

1973. Chakravarti Rajagopalachari Commemoration.
706 **650** 20p. brown 20 50

651 "Sun" Mask

1974. Indian Masks. Multicoloured.
707 20p. Type **651** 20 15
708 50p. "Moon" mask 40 60
709 1r. "Narasimha" 65 80
710 2r. "Ravana" (horiz) 70 1·75
MS711 109×135 mm. Nos. 707/10 20·00 15·00

652 Chhatrapati

1974. 300th Anniv of Coronation of Chhatrapati Shri Shivaji Maharaj (patriot and ruler).
712 **652** 25p. multicoloured 1·00 40

653 Maithili Sharan Gupta (poet)

1974. Indian Personalities (1st series).
713 **653** 25p. brown 15 50
714 - 25p. brown 15 50
715 - 25p. brown 15 50
PORTRAITS: No. 714, Jainarain Vyas (politician and journalist); No. 715, Utkal Gourab Madhusudan Das (social reformer).

654 Kandukuri Veeresalingam (social reformer)

1974. Indian Personalities (2nd series).
716 **654** 25p. brown 25 1·00
717 - 50p. purple 55 2·00
718 - 1r. brown 70 1·75
PORTRAITS: 50p. Tipu Sultan; 1r. Max Mueller (Sanskrit scholar).

655 Kamala Nehru

1974. Kamala Nehru Commemoration.
719 **655** 25p. multicoloured 1·00 1·00

656 W.P.Y. Emblem

1974. World Population Year.
720 **656** 25p. purple and brown 20 30

657 Spotted Deer   **657a** Sitar

1974

(a) Vaues expressed with "p" or "Re"
721 - 15p. brown 3·50 1·50
722 **657** 25p. brown 1·75 2·25
723 **657a** 1r. brown and black 2·75 30

(b) Values expressed as numerals only.
724 - 2p. brown 1·25 3·00
725 - 5p. red 70 10
729 - 10p. blue 1·00 15
730 - 15p. brown 1·75 10
731 - 20p. green 20 10
732 - 25p. brown 7·50 2·75
732b - 30p. brown 4·25 55
733 - 50p. violet 6·50 20
734 - 60p. grey 2·75 1·00
735 **657a** 1r. brown and black 3·50 10
736 - 2r. violet and brown 16·00 40
737 - 5r. violet and brown 3·50 1·25
738d - 1·50 1·25
DESIGNS—VERT (as Type **657**): 2p. Bidri vase; 5p. "Family Planning"; 15p. Tiger; 25p. Gandhi; 30p. Indian dolls; 60p. Somnath Temple. HORIZ (as Type **657a**): 10p. Electric locomotive; 20p. Handicrafts toy; 50p. Great egret in flight. (As Type **657a**): 2r. Himalayas; 5r. Bhakra Dam, Punjab; 10r. Atomic reactor, Trombay.
For 30, 35, 50, 60p. and 1r. values as No. 732 see Nos. 968, 979, 1073, 1320 and 1436.

658 President V. Giri

1974. Retirement of President Giri.
739 **658** 25p. multicoloured 20 30

659 U.P.U. Emblem

1974. Centenary of U.P.U.
740 **659** 25p. violet, blue and black 30 10
741 - 1r. multicoloured 50 50
742 - 2r. multicoloured 75 2·00
MS743 – 108×108 mm. Nos. 740/2 9·00 16·00
DESIGNS—1r. Birds and nest, "Madhubani" style. VERT: 2r. Arrows around globe.

660 Woman Flute-player (sculpture)

1974. Centenary of Mathura Museum.
744 **660** 25p. chestnut and brown 75 1·25
745 - 25p. chestnut and brown 75 1·25
DESIGN: No. 745, Vidyadhara with garland.

661 Nicholas Roerich (medallion by H. Dropsy)

1974. Birth Centenary of Professor Roerich (humanitarian).
746 **661** 1r. green and yellow 65 55

662 Pavapuri Temple

1974. 2,500th Anniv of Bhagwan Mahavira's Attainment of Nirvana.
747 **662** 25p. black 60 20

663 Cat (Rajesh Bhatia)

1974. Children's Day.
748 **663** 25p. multicoloured 1·25 70

664 Indian Dancers (Amita Shah)

1974. 25th Anniv of UNICEF in India.
749 **664** 25p. multicoloured 55 45

665 Territorial Army Badge

1974. 25th Anniv of Indian Territorial Army.
750 **665** 25p. black, yellow & green 60 40

666 Krishna as Gopal Bal with Cows (Rajasthan painting on cloth)

1974. 19th International Dairy Congress, New Delhi.
751 **666** 25p. purple and brown 40 40

667 Symbols and Child's Face

1974. Help for Disabled Children.
752　**667**　25p. red and black　60　60

668 Marconi

1974. Birth Centenary of Guglielmo Marconi (radio pioneer).
753　**668**　2r. blue　2·50　1·25

669 St. Francis Xavier's Shrine, Goa

1974. St. Francis Xavier Celebration.
754　**669**　25p. multicoloured　15　40

670 Saraswati (Deity of Language and Learning)

1975. World Hindi Convention, Nagpur.
755　**670**　25p. grey and red　50　40

671 Parliament House, New Delhi

1975. 25th Anniv of Republic.
756　**671**　25p. black, silver and blue　75　50

672 Table-tennis Bat

1975. World Table-tennis Championships, Calcutta.
757　**672**　25p. black, red and green　1·00　30

673 "Equality, Development and Peace"

1975. International Women's Year.
758　**673**　25p. multicoloured　85　45

674 Stylized Cannon

1975. Bicent of Indian Army Ordnance Corps.
759　**674**　25p. multicoloured　1·75　75

675 Arya Samaj Emblem

1975. Centenary of Arya Samaj Movement.
760　**675**　25p. red and brown　50　50

---

676 Saraswati

1975. World Telugu Language Conf, Hyderabad.
761　**676**　25p. black and green　70　30

677 Satellite "Aryabhata"

1975. Launch of First Indian Satellite.
762　**677**　25p. lt blue, blue & purple　1·00　50

678 Blue-winged Pitta

1975. Indian Birds. Multicoloured.
763　　25p. Type **678**　75　25
764　　50p. Asian black-headed oriole　1·75　2·25
765　　1r. Western tragopan (vert)　2·50　2·75
766　　2r. Himalayan monal pheasant (vert)　3·25　5·50

679 Page from *Ramcharitmanas* (manuscript)

1975. Fourth Centenary of *Ramcharitmanas* (epic poem by Goswami Tulsidas).
767　**679**　25p. black, yellow and red　1·00　30

680 Young Women within Y.W.C.A. Badge

1975. Centenary of Indian Y.W.C.A.
768　**680**　25p. multicoloured　75　50

681 *The Creation*

1975. 500th Birth Anniv of Michelangelo. *Creation* Frescoes from Sistine Chapel.
769　**681**　50p. multicoloured　70　1·10
770　–　50p. multicoloured　70　1·10
771　–　50p. multicoloured　70　1·10
772　–　50p. multicoloured　70　1·10
　Nos. 770 and 772 are size 49×34 mm. The four stamps form a composite design.

682 Commission Emblem

1975. 25th Anniv of Int Commission on Irrigation and Drainage.
773　**682**　25p. multicoloured　50　20

---

683 Stylised Ground Antenna

1975. Inauguration of Satellite Instructional Television Experiment.
774　**683**　25p. multicoloured　50　20

684 St. Arunagirinathar

1975. 600th Birth Anniv of St. Arunagirinathar.
775　**684**　50p. purple and black　1·50　1·25

685 Commemorative Text

1975. Namibia Day.
776　**685**　25p. black and red　50　50

686 Mir Anees (poet)　　**687** Memorial Temple to Ahilyabai Holkar (ruler)

1975. Indian Celebrities.
777　**686**　25p. green　30　75
778　**687**　25p. brown　30　75

688 Bharata Natyam

1975. Indian Dances. Multicoloured.
779　　25p. Type **688**　65　20
780　　50p. Orissi　1·00　2·00
781　　75p. Kathak　1·40　2·25
782　　1r. Kathakali　1·60　1·25
783　　1r.50 Kuchipudi　2·50　3·75
784　　2r. Manipuri　2·50　3·75

689 Ameer Khusrau

1975. 650th Death Anniv of Ameer Khusrau (poet).
785　**689**　50p. brown and bistre　1·50　2·25

690 V. K. Krishna Menon

1975. First Death Anniv of V. K. Krishna Menon (statesman).
786　**690**　25p. green　1·00　1·00

---

691 Text of Poem

1975. Birth Bicentenary of Emperor Bahadur Shah Zafar.
787　**691**　1r. black, buff and brown　1·75　1·00

692 Sansadiya Soudha, New Delhi

1975. 21st Commonwealth Parliamentary Conference, New Delhi.
788　**692**　2r. green　2·00　3·00

693 V. Patel

1975. Birth Centenary of Vallabhbhai Patel (statesman).
789　**693**　25p. green　20　60

694 N. C. Bardoloi

1975. Birth Centenary of Nabin Chandra Bardoloi (politician).
790　**694**　25p. brown　50　70

695 *Cow* (Sanjay Nathubhai Patel)

1975. Children's Day.
791　**695**　25p. multicoloured　80　80

696 Original Printing Works, Nasik Road

1975. 50th Anniv of India Security Press.
792　**696**　25p. multicoloured　55　40

697 Gurdwara Sisganj (site of martyrdom)

1975. Tercentenary of the Martyrdom of Guru Tegh Bahadur (Sikh leader).
793　**697**　25p. multicoloured　80　80

698 Theosophical Society Emblem

1975. Centenary of Theosophical Society.
794　**698**　25p. multicoloured　1·00　40

699 Weather Cock

1975. Cent of Indian Meteorological Department.
795   **699**   25p. multicoloured   75   75

700 Early Mail Cart

1975. "Inpex '75" Nat Philatelic Exn, Calcutta.
796   **700**   25p. black and brown   1·00   30
797   -   2r. brown, purple & black   2·50   3·75
DESIGN: 2r. Indian bishop mark, 1775.

701 L. N. Mishra

1976. First Death Anniv of Lalit Narayan Mishra (politician).
798   **701**   25p. brown   40   40

702 Tiger

1976. Birth Cent of Jim Corbett (naturalist).
799   **702**   25p. multicoloured   1·00   1·00

703 Painted Storks

1976. Keoladeo Ghana Bird Sanctuary, Bharatpur.
800   **703**   25p. multicoloured   1·00   1·00

704 Vijayanta Tank

1976. Bicent of 16th Light Cavalry Regiment.
801   **704**   25p. green and brown   1·75   60

705 Alexander Graham Bell

1976. Alexander Graham Bell Commem.
802   **705**   25p. brown and black   1·50   60

706 Muthuswami Dikshitar

1976. Birth Bicentenary of Muthuswami Dikshitar (composer).
803   **706**   25p. violet   70   60

707 Eye and Red Cross

1976. World Health Day. Prevention of Blindness.
804   **707**   25p. brown and red   1·00   75

708 "Industries"

1976. Industrial Development.
805   **708**   25p. multicoloured   30   40

709 Type WDM Diesel Locomotive, 1963

1976. Locomotives. Multicoloured.
806   25p. Type **709**   55   10
807   50p. Rajputra Malwa Railway Class F/1 steam locomotive, 1895   1·50   55
808   1r. Southern Railway Class WP/1 steam locomotive, 1963   2·75   1·25
809   2r. Great Peninsular Railway Class GIP steam locomotive, 1853   3·50   2·50

710 Nehru

1976
810b   **710**   25p. violet   6·00   1·00
811   -   25p. brown   2·00   30
DESIGN: No. 811, Gandhi.
  For these designs in a smaller format see Nos. 732, 968/9, 979/80, 1073/4 and 1320.

713 Spirit of '76 (Willard)

1976. Bicentenary of American Revolution.
812   **713**   2r.80 multicoloured   1·25   1·25

714 K. Kamaraj (politician)

1976. Kumaraswamy Kamaraj Commemoration.
813   **714**   25p. brown   40   20

715 "Shooting"

1976. Olympic Games, Montreal.
814   **715**   25p. violet and red   30   10
815   -   1r. multicoloured   1·00   90
816   -   1r.50 mauve and black   2·00   3·00
817   -   2r.80 multicoloured   1·75   4·25
DESIGNS: 1r. Shot-put; 1r.50, Hockey; 2r.80, Sprinting.

716 Subhadra Kumari Chauhan (poetess)

1976. S. K. Chauhan Commemoration.
818   **716**   25p. blue   20   50

717 Param Vir Chakra Medal

1976. Param Vir Chakra Commemoration.
819   **717**   25p. multicoloured   20   50

718 University Building, Bombay

1976. 60th Anniv of Shreemati Nathibai Damodar Thackersey Women's University.
820   **718**   25p. violet   40   40

719 Bharatendu Harischandra (writer)

1976. Harischandra Commemoration.
821   **719**   25p. brown   30   50

720 S. C. Chatterji

1976. Birth Centenary of Sarat Chandra Chatterji (writer).
822   **720**   25p. black   25   30

721 Planned Family

1976. Family Planning.
823   **721**   25p. multicoloured   20   50

722 Maharaja Agrasen and Coins

1976. Maharaja Agrasen Commemoration.
824   **722**   25p. brown   75   40

723 Swamp Deer

1976. Indian Wildlife. Multicoloured.
825   25p. Type **723**   65   40
826   50p. Lion   1·50   2·25
827   1r. Leopard (horiz)   1·75   2·25
828   2r. Caracal (horiz)   2·00   3·50

724 Hands holding Hearts

1976. Voluntary Blood Donation.
829   **724**   25p. yellow, red and black   1·25   75

725 Suryakant Tripathi ("Nirala")

1976. 80th Birth Anniv of Nirala (poet and novelist).
830   **725**   25p. violet   25   30

726 Loyal Mongoose (H. D. Bhatia)

1976. Children's Day.
831   **726**   25p. multicoloured   70   70

727 Hiralal Shastri (social reformer)

1976. Shastri Commemoration.
832   **727**   25p. brown   30   30

728 Dr. Hari Singh Gour (lawyer)

1976. Dr. Hari Singh Gour Commemoration.
833   **728**   25p. purple   40   40

729 Airbus Industrie A300B4

1976. Inauguration of Indian Airlines' Airbus Service.
834   **729**   2r. multicoloured   2·50   2·25

730 Hybrid Coconut Palm

1976. Diamond Jubilee of Coconut Research.

835	**730**	25p. multicoloured	20	40

731 First Stanza of *Vande Mataram*

1976. Centenary of *Vande Mataram* (patriotic song by B. C. Chatterjee).

836	**731**	25p. multicoloured	1·00	30

732 Globe and Film Strip

1977. Sixth International Film Festival of India, New Delhi.

837	**732**	2r. multicoloured	1·75	2·00

733 Seismograph and Crack in Earth's Crust

1977. Sixth World Conference on Earthquake Engineering, New Delhi.

838	**733**	2r. lilac	2·00	2·00

734 Tarun Ram Phookun

1977. Birth Cent of Tarun Ram Phookun (politician).

839	**734**	25p. grey	20	30

735 Paramahansa Yogananda

1977. Paramahansa Yogananda (religious leader) Commem.

840	**735**	25p. orange	1·25	1·00

736 Asian Regional Red Cross Emblem

1977. First Asian Regional Red Cross Conference, New Delhi.

841	**736**	2r. red, pink and blue	2·00	2·50

737 Fakhruddin Ali Ahmed

1977. Death of President Ahmed.

842	**737**	25p. multicoloured	35	35

738 Emblem of Asian-Oceanic Postal Union

1977. 15th Anniv of Asian–Oceanic Postal Union.

843	**738**	2r. multicoloured	1·75	1·75

739 Narottam Morarjee and *Loyalty* (liner)

1977. Birth Cent of Morarjee (ship owner).

844	**739**	25p. blue	1·25	1·00

740 Makhanlal Chaturvedi (writer and poet)

1977. Chaturvedi Commemoration.

845	**740**	25p. brown	20	50

741 Mahaprabhu Vallabhacharya (philosopher)

1977. Vallabhacharya Commemoration.

846	**741**	1r. brown	75	40

742 Federation Emblem

1977. 50th Anniv of Federation of Indian Chambers of Commerce and Industry.

847	**742**	25p. purple, brown and yellow	20	40

744 "Environment Protection"

1977. World Environment Day.

848	**744**	2r. multicoloured	1·75	1·25

745 Rajya Sabha Chamber

1977. 25th Anniv of Rajya Sabha (Upper House of Parliament).

849	**745**	25p. multicoloured	20	50

746 Lotus

1977. Indian Flowers. Multicoloured.

850		25p. Type 746	30	15
851		50p. Rhododendron (vert)	50	1·25
852		1r. Kadamba (vert)	75	1·00
853		2r. Gloriosa lily	95	2·25

747 Berliner Gramophone

1977. Centenary of Sound Recording.

854	**747**	2r. brown and black	1·75	2·00

748 Coomaraswamy and Siva

1977. Birth Centenary of Ananda Kentish Coomaraswamy (art historian).

855	**748**	25p. multicoloured	60	40

749 Ganga Ram and Hospital

1977. 50th Death Anniv of Sir Ganga Ram (social reformer).

856	**749**	25p. purple	30	30

750 Dr. Samuel Hahnemann (founder of homeopathy)

1977. 32nd Int Homeopathic Congress, New Delhi.

857	**750**	2r. black and green	5·50	2·75

751 Ram Manohar Lohia (politician)

1977. Ram Manohar Lohia Commemoration.

858	**751**	25p. brown	50	30

752 Early Punjabi Postman

1977. "Inpex '77" Philatelic Exn, Bangalore.

859	**752**	25p. multicoloured	50	30
860		2r. grey and red	2·00	2·75

DESIGN: 2r. "Lion and Palm" essay, 1853.

753 Scarlet "Scinde Dawks" of 1852

1977. "Asiana '77" Philatelic Exn, Bangalore.

861	**753**	1r. multicoloured	1·50	1·00
862	-	3r. blue, orange and black	3·00	4·00

DESIGN: 3r. Foreign mail arriving at Ballard Pier, Bombay, 1927.

754 "Mother and Child" (Khajuraho sculpture)

1977. 15th Int Congress of Pediatrics, New Delhi.

863	**754**	2r. blue and brown	4·00	2·75

755 Statue of Kittur Rani Channamma, Belgaum

1977. Kittur Rani Channama (ruler) Commem.

864	**755**	25p. green	1·25	1·00

756 Symbolic Sun

1977. Union Public Service Commission.

865	**756**	25p. multicoloured	45	30

757 Ear of Corn

1977. "Agriexpo '77" Agricultural Exhibition, New Delhi.

866	**757**	25p. green	40	40

758 Cats (Nikur Dilipbhai Mody)

1977. Children's Day. Multicoloured.

867		25p. Type 758	50	30
868		1r. *Friends* (Bhavsar Ashish Ramanlal)	2·25	3·00

759 Jotirao Phooley (social reformer)

1977. Indian Personalities.

869	**759**	25p. olive	30	75
870		25p. brown	30	75

DESIGN: No. 870, Senapti Bapat (patriot).

760 Diagram of
Population Growth

1977. 41st Session of International Statistical Institute,
New Delhi.
871 **760** 2r. turquoise and red   1·75   1·00

761 Kamta Prasad
Guru and Vyakarna
(Hindi Grammar)

1977. Kamta Prasad Guru (writer) Commem.
872 **761** 25p. brown   20   30

762 Kremlin Tower
and Soviet Flag

1977. 60th Anniv of October Revolution.
873 **762** 1r. multicoloured   50   75

763 Climber
crossing a Crevice

1978. Conquest of Kanchenjunga (1977). Multicoloured.
874 25p. Type **763**   20   10
875 1r. Indian flag near summit
(horiz)   80   90

764 "Shikara" on Lake Dal,
Kashmir

1978. 27th Pacific Area Travel Association Conference,
New Delhi.
876 **764** 1r. multicoloured   2·00   1·50

765 Children in Library

1978. Thid World Book Fair, New Delhi.
877 **765** 1r. brown and slate   50   80

766 Mother-
Pondicherry

1978. Birth Centenary of Mother-Pondicherry
(philosopher).
878 **766** 25p. brown and grey   60   40

767 Wheat and
Globe

1978. Fifth International Wheat Genetics Symposium,
New Delhi.
879 **767** 25p. yellow and
turquoise   20   40

768 Nanalal
Dalpatram Kavi
(poet)

1978. Nanalal Dalpatram Kavi Commemoration.
880 **768** 25p. brown   20   40

769 Surjya Sen
(revolutionary)

1978. Surjya Sen Commemoration.
881 **769** 25p. bistre and red   20   30

770 *Two Vaishnavas*
(Jamini Roy)

1978. Modern Indian Paintings. Multicoloured.
882 25p. Type **770**   25   30
883 50p. *The Mosque* (Sailoz
Mookherjea)   45   1·25
884 1r. *Head* (Rabindranath Tagore)   80   1·50
885 2r. *Hill Women* (Amrita Sher Gil)   1·00   2·00

771 *Self-portrait* (Rubens)

1978. 400th Birth Anniv of Peter Paul Rubens.
886 **771** 2r. multicoloured   2·25   3·00

772 Charlie
Chaplin

1978. Charlie Chaplin Commemoration.
887 **772** 25p. blue and gold   1·50   1·00

773 Deendayal
Upadhyaya
(politician)

1978. Deendayal Upadhyaya Commemoration.
888 **773** 25p. brown and orange   40   40

774 Syama Prasad
Mookerjee

1978. Syama Prasad Mookerjee (politician)
Commemoration.
889 **774** 25p. brown   50   50

775 Airavat
(mythological
elephant), Jain
Temple, Gujerat
(Kachchh Museum)

1978. Treasures from Indian Museums. Multicoloured.
890 25p. Type **775**   30   30
891 50p. Kalpadruma (magical tree),
Besnagar (Indian Museum)   40   1·25
892 1r. Obverse and reverse of
Kushan gold coin (National
Museum)   55   1·50
893 2r. Dagger and knife of Emperor Jehangir, Mughal (Salar
Jung Museum)   75   2·00

776 Krishna and Arjuna in
Battle Chariot

1978. Bhagawadgeeta (Divine Song of India)
Commemoration.
894 **776** 25p. gold and red   20   30

777 Bethune College

1978. Centenary of Bethune College, Calcutta.
895 **777** 25p. brown and green   20   30

778 E. V. Ramasami

1978. E. V. Ramasami (social reformer) Commemoration.
896 **778** 25p. black   20   20

779 Uday Shankar

1978. Uday Shankar (dancer) Commem.
897 **779** 25p. brown   20   40

780 Leo Tolstoy

1978. 150th Birth Anniv of Leo Tolstoy (writer).
898 **780** 1r. multicoloured   30   30

781 Vallathol
Narayana Menon

1978. Birth Centenary of Vallathol Narayana Menon
(poet).
899 **781** 25p. purple and brown   20   40

782 *Two Friends* (Dinesh
Sharma)

1978. Children's Day.
900 **782** 25p. multicoloured   20   40

783 Machine Operator

1978. National Small Industries Fair, New Delhi.
901 **783** 25p. green   20   30

784 Sowars of
Skinner's Horse

1978. 175th Anniv of Skinner's Horse (cavalry regiment).
902 **784** 25p. multicoloured   1·25   1·00

785 Mohammad
Ali Jauhar

1978. Birth Centenary of Mohammad Ali Jauhar (patriot).
903 **785** 25p. olive   20   40

786 Chakravarti
Rajagopalachari

1978. Birth Centenary of Chakravarti Rajagopalachari
(first post-independence Governor-General).
904 **786** 25p. brown   35   30

787 Wright
Brothers and Flyer
I

1978. 75th Anniv of Powered Flight.
905   **787**   1r. violet and yellow   1·25   30

788 Ravenshaw College

1978. Centenary of Ravenshaw College, Cuttack.
906   **788**   25p. red and green   20   30

789 Schubert

1978. 150th Death Anniv of Franz Schubert (composer).
907   **789**   1r. multicoloured   1·75   65

790 Uniforms of 1799, 1901 and 1979 with Badge

1979. Fourth Reunion of Punjab Regiment.
908   **790**   25p. multicoloured   1·50   1·00

791 Bhai Parmanand

1979. Bhai Parmanand (scholar) Commemoration.
909   **791**   25p. violet   20   40

792 Gandhi with Young Boy

1979. International Year of the Child.
910   **792**   25p. brown and red   1·00   50
911   –   1r. brown and orange   60   1·50
DESIGN: 1r. India I.Y.C. emblem.

793 Albert Einstein

1979. Birth Centenary of Albert Einstein (physicist).
912   **793**   1r. blue   1·75   1·25

794 Rajarshi Shahu Chhatrapati

1979. Rajarshi Shahu Chhatrapati (ruler of Kolhapur State, and precursor of social reform in India) Commemoration.
913   **794**   25p. purple   20   40

795 Exhibition Logo

1979. "India '80" International Stamp Exhibition (1st issue).
914   **795**   30p. green and orange   20   40

See also Nos. 942/5 and 955/8.

796 Postcards under Magnifying Glass

1979. Centenary of Indian Postcards.
915   **796**   50p. multicoloured   20   40

797 Raja Mahendra Pratap

1979. Raja Mahendra Pratap (patriot) Commemoration.
916   **797**   30p. green   20   40

798 Hilsa, Pomfret and Prawn

1979

920	–	2p. violet	10 1·00
921		5p. blue	1·00 60
921a		5p. blue	20 30
922aw		10p. green	
922b		10p. green	1·00 30
923		15p. green	1·00 40
924a		20p. red	70 30
925a		25p. brown	70 10
925bb		25p. green	1·00 10
926ab		30p. green	2·25 10
927	–	35p. purple	1·75 10
928c		50p. violet	1·50 10
929b		1r. brown	50 10
932a		2r. lilac	50 10
933c		2r.25 red and green	1·25 60
934	–	2r.80 red and green	2·50 2·00
934cca		3r.25 orange and green	1·25 1·25
935c		5r. red and green	1·50 40
936b		10r. purple and green	2·50 1·25

DESIGNS—HORIZ: 2p. Adult education class; 10p. Irrigation canal; 25p. (925a) Chick hatching from egg; 25p. (925bb) Village, wheat and tractor; 30p. Harvesting maize; 50p. Woman dairy farmer, cows and milk bottles. (36×19 mm): 10r. Forest on hillside. VERT (17×20 mm): 15p. Farmer and agricultural symbols; 20p. Mother feeding child; 35p. "Family Welfare". (17×28 mm): 1r. Cotton plant; 2r. Weaving. (20×38 mm): 2r.25, Cashew; 2r.80, Apples; 3r.25, Oranges; 5r. Rubber tapping.
For 75p. in same design as No. 927 see No. 1214.

800 Jatindra Nath Das

1979. 50th Death Anniv of Jatindra Nath Das (revolutionary).
941   **800**   30p. brown   20   60

801 de Havilland Puss Moth

1979. "Air India 80" International Stamp Exhibition (2nd issue). Mail-carrying Aircraft. Multicoloured.
942   30p. Type **801**   50   25
943   50p. Indian Air Force Hindustan Aircraft Industries Chetak helicopter   70   65
944   1r. Indian Airlines Boeing 737 airliner   85   75
945   2r. Air India Boeing 747 airliner   1·10   1·10

---

802 Early and Modern Lightbulbs

1979. Centenary of Electric Lightbulb.
946   **802**   1r. purple   20   30

803 Gilgit Record

1979. International Archives Week.
947   **803**   30p. yellow and brown   20   60

804 Hirakud Dam, Orissa

1979. 50th Anniv and 13th Congress of International Commission on Large Dams.
948   **804**   30p. brown and turquoise   20   30

805 Fair Emblem

1979. India International Trade Fair, New Delhi.
949   **805**   1r. black and red   20   30

806 Child learning to Read

1979. International Children's Book Fair, New Delhi.
950   **806**   30p. multicoloured   20   30

807 Dove with Olive Branch and I.A.E.A. Emblem

1979. 23rd International Atomic Energy Agency Conference, New Delhi.
951   **807**   1r. multicoloured   55   45

808 Hindustan Aircraft Industries HAL-26 Pushpak Light Plane and Rohini-1 Glider

1979. Flying and Gliding.
952   **808**   30p. black, brown and blue   1·40   1·00

809 Gurdwara Baoli Sahib Temple, Goindwal, Amritsar District

1979. 500th Birth Anniv of Guru Amar Das (Sikh leader).
953   **809**   30p. multicoloured   40   60

---

810 Ring of People encircling U.N. Emblem and Cogwheel

1980. Third United Nations Industrial Development Organization General Conference, New Delhi.
954   **810**   1r. multicoloured   20   30

811 Army Post Office and Postmarks

1980. India '80 International Stamp Exhibition (3rd issue).
955   **811**   30p. green   50   30
956   –   50p. brown & deep brown   80   1·25
957   –   1r. red   90   1·00
958   –   2r. brown   90   2·25
DESIGNS: 50p. Money order transfer document, 1879; 1r. Copper prepayment ticket, 1774; 2r. Sir Rowland Hill and birthplace at Kidderminster.

812 Energy Symbols

1980. Institution of Engineers (India) Commem.
959   **812**   30p. gold and blue   20   40

813 Uniforms of 1780 and 1980, Crest and Ribbon

1980. Bicentenary of Madras Sappers.
960   **813**   30p. multicoloured   1·25   1·00

814 Books

1980. Fourth World Book Fair, New Delhi.
961   **814**   30p. blue   30   60

815 Bees and Honey-Comb

1980. Second International Conference on Agriculture.
962   **815**   1r. bistre and brown   1·50   75

816 Welthy Fisher and Saksharta Niketan (Literacy House), Lucknow

1980. Welthy Fisher (teacher) Commemoration.
963 816 30p. blue 40 40

817 Darul-Uloom, Deoband

1980. Darul-Uloom College Commemoration.
964 817 30p. green 30 30

818 Keshub Chunder Sen

1980. Keshub Chunder Sen (religious and social reformer) Commemoration.
965 818 30p. brown 50 60

819 Chhatrapati Shivaji Maharaj

1980. 300th Death Anniv of Chhatrapati Shivaji Maharaj (warrior).
966 819 30p. multicoloured 40 70

820 Table Tennis

1980. Fifth Asian Table Tennis Championships, Calcutta.
967 820 30p. purple 70 70

1980. As Nos. 732 and 810, but 17×20 mm in size.
968 30p. brown (Gandhi) 5·50 2·00
969 30p. violet (Nehru) 3·00 1·00

821 N. M. Joshi

1980. Narayan Malhar Joshi (trade unionist) Commemoration.
970 821 30p. mauve 70 50

822 Ulloor S. Parameswara Iyer

1980. Ulloor S. Parameswara Iyer (poet) Commemoration.
971 822 30p. purple 1·00 50

823 S. M. Zamin Ali

1980. Syed Mohammed Zamin Ali (educationist and poet) Commemoration.
972 823 30p. green 30 50

824 Helen Keller

1980. Birth Centenary of Helen Keller (campaigner for the handicapped).
973 824 30p. black and orange 1·25 55

825 High-jumping

1980. Olympic Games, Moscow. Multicoloured.
974 1r. Type 825 40 40
975 2r.80 Horse-riding 2·00 3·50

826 Prem Chand

1980. Birth Cent of Prem Chand (novelist).
976 826 30p. brown 20 60

827 Mother Teresa and Nobel Peace Prize Medallion

1980. Award of 1979 Nobel Peace Prize to Mother Teresa.
977 827 30p. violet 1·50 1·00

828 Lord Mountbatten

1980. Lord Mountbatten Commemoration.
978 828 2r.80 multicoloured 3·25 3·75

1980. As Nos. 968/9, but new face value.
979 35p. brown 2·75 1·00
980 35p. violet 1·25 60
DESIGNS: No. 979, Gandhi; No. 980, Nehru.

829 Scottish Church College, Calcutta

1980. 150th Anniv of Scottish Church College, Calcutta.
981 829 35p. lilac 20 50

830 Rajah Annamalai Chettiar

1980. Rajah Annamalai Chettiar (banker and educationist) Commemoration.
982 830 35p. lilac 20 30

831 Gandhi marching to Dandi

1980. 50th Anniv of "Dandi March" (Gandhi's defiance of Salt Tax Law).
983 831 35p. black, blue and gold 1·00 1·50
984 - 35p. black, mauve and gold 1·00 1·50
DESIGN: No. 984, Gandhi picking up handful of salt at Dandi.

832 Jayaprakash Narayan

1980. Jayaprakash Narayan (socialist) Commemoration.
985 832 35p. brown 60 70

833 Great Indian Bustard

1980. International Symposium on Bustards, Juipur.
986 833 2r.30 multicoloured 1·50 2·00

834 Arabic Commemorative Inscription

1980. Moslem Year 1400 A.H. Commemoration.
987 834 35p. multicoloured 20 30

835 Girls Dancing (Pampa Paul)

1980. Children's Day.
988 835 35p. multicoloured 1·25 55

836 Dhyan Chand

1980. Dhyan Chand (hockey player) Commemoration.
989 836 35p. brown 1·50 1·00

837 Gold Mining

1980. Cent of Kolar Gold Fields, Karnataka.
990 837 1r. multicoloured 2·00 30

838 M. A. Ansari

1980. Mukhtayar Ahmad Ansari (medical practitioner and politician) Commemoration.
991 838 35p. green 60 50

839 India Government Mint, Bombay

1980. 150th Anniv of India Government Mint, Bombay.
992 839 35p. black, blue and silver 20 30

840 Bride from Tamil Nadu

1980. Brides in Traditional Costume. Multicoloured.
993 1r. Type 840 75 90
994 1r. Rajasthan 75 90
995 1r. Kashmir 75 90
996 1r. Bengal 75 90

841 Mazharul Haque

1981. Mazharul Haque (journalist) Commem.
997 841 35p. blue 20 50

842 St. Stephen's College

1981. Centenary of St. Stephen's College, Delhi.
998 842 35p. red 20 70

843 Gommateshwara

1981. Millenium of Gommateshwara (statue at Shravanabelgola).
999 843 1r. multicoloured 20 30

844 G. V. Mavalankar

1981. 25th Death Anniv of Ganesh Vasudeo Mavalankar (parliamentarian).
1000 844 35p. red 20 40

845 Flame of
Martyrdom

1981. "Homage to Martyrs".
1001 **845** 35p. multicoloured   20   30

846 Heinrich von Stephan
and U.P.U. Emblem

1981. 150th Birth Anniv of Heinrich von Stephan
(founder of U.P.U.).
1002 **846** 1r. brown   80   50

847 Disabled Child being
helped by Able-bodied
Child

1981. International Year for Disabled Persons.
1003 **847** 1r. black and blue   50   30

848 Bhil

1981. Tribes of India. Multicoloured.
1004 **848** 1r. Type 848   50   35
1005   1r. Dandami Maria   50   35
1006   1r. Toda   50   35
1007   1r. Khlamngam Naga   50   35

849 Stylized Trees

1981. Forests Conservation.
1008 **849** 1r. multicoloured   50   30

850 Nilmoni
Phukan

1981. Nilmoni Phukan (poet) Commemoration.
1009 **850** 35p. brown   50   70

851 Sanjay Gandhi

1981. First Death Anniv of Sanjay Gandhi (politician).
1010 **851** 35p. multicoloured   40   70

852 Launch of
"SLV 3" and
Diagram of
"Rohini"

1981. Launch of "SLV 3" Rocket with "Rohini" Satellite.
1011 **852** 1r. black, pink and blue   30   30

853 Games Logo

1981. Asian Games, New Delhi (1st issue). Multicoloured.
1012   1r. Type 853   1·00   65
1013   1r. Games emblem and stylized
               hockey players   1·00   65
    See also Nos. 1026, 1033, 1057, 1059 and 1061/6.

854 Flame of the
Forest

1981. Flowering Trees. Multicoloured.
1014   35p. Type 854   55   15
1015   50p. Crateva   1·00 1·25
1016   1r. Golden shower   1·25   50
1017   2r. Bauhinia   1·60 3·00

855 W. F. D.
Emblem and
Wheat

1981. World Food Day.
1018 **855** 1r. yellow and blue   50   20

856 Stichophthalma
camadeva

1981. Butterflies. Multicoloured.
1019   35p. Type 856   90   20
1020   50p. Cethosia biblis   1·75 1·75
1021   1r. Cyrestis achates (vert) 2·25   70
1022   2r. Teinopalpus imperialis (vert) 2·75 6·00

857 Bellary Raghava

1981. Bellary Raghava (actor) Commemoration.
1023 **857** 35p. green   70   30

858 Regimental
Colour

1981. 40th Anniv of Mahar Regiment.
1024 **858** 35p. multicoloured   1·00   30

859 Toyseller
(Kumari Ruchita
Sharma)

1981. Children's Day.
1025 **859** 35p. multicoloured   75   30

860 Rajghat Stadium

1981. Asian Games, New Delhi (2nd issue).
1026 **860** 1r. multicoloured   1·75   30

861 Kashi Prasad
Jayasawal and
Yaudheya Coin

1981. Birth Centenary of Kashi Prasad Jayasawal (lawyer
and historian).
1027 **861** 35p. blue   50   30

862 Indian and P.L.O. Flags,
and People

1981. Palestinian Solidarity.
1028 **862** 1r. multicoloured   2·25   40

863 I.N.S. Taragiri (frigate)

1981. Indian Navy Day.
1029 **863** 35p. multicoloured   2·25 1·25

864 Henry Heras and Indus
Valley Seal

1981. Henry Heras (historian) Commemoration.
1030 **864** 35p. lilac   45   30

865 Map of South-East
Asia showing Cable Route

1981. Inauguration of I.O.C.O.M. (Indian Ocean
Commonwealth Cable) Submarine Telephone Cable.
1031 **865** 1r. multicoloured   2·25   35

866 Stylized
Hockey-players and
Championship Emblem

1981. World Cup Hockey Championship, Bombay.
1032 **866** 1r. multicoloured   1·25   30

867 Jawaharlal Nehru
Stadium

1981. Asian Games, New Delhi (3rd issue).
1033 **867** 1r. multicoloured   30   20

868 Early and
Modern Telephones

1982. Centenary of Telephone Services.
1034 **868** 2r. black, blue and grey 1·00   75

869 Map of World

1982. International Soil Science Congress, New Delhi.
1035 **869** 1r. multicoloured   30   20

870 Sir J. J.
School of Art

1982. 125th Anniv of Sir J. J. School of Art, Bombay.
1036 **870** 35p. multicoloured   20   20

871 Three Musicians

1982. Birth Centenary (1981) of Picasso.
1037 **871** 2r.85 multicoloured   2·25 1·10

872 Deer
(stone carving),
5th-century
A.D.

1982. Festival of India. Ancient Sculpture. Multicoloured.
1038   2r. Type 872   20   40
1039   3r.05 Kaliya Mardana (bronze
               statue), 9th-century A.D   35   60

873 Radio Telescope, Ooty

1982. Festival of India. Science and Technology.
1040 **873** 3r.05 multicoloured   35   40

874 Robert Koch and
Symbol of Disease

1982. Centenary of Robert Koch's Discovery of Tubercle Bacillus.
| 1041 | 874 | 35p. lilac | 2·25 | 1·00 |

875 Durgabai Deshmukh

1982. First Death Anniv of Durgabai Deshmukh (social reformer).
| 1042 | 875 | 35p. blue | 1·00 | 1·00 |

876 Blue Poppy

1982. Himalayan Flowers. Multicoloured.
1043	35p. Type 876	70	30
1044	1r. Showy inula	1·75	30
1045	2r. Cobra lily	2·25	3·00
1046	2r.85 Brahma kamal	2·75	4·75

877 "Apple" Satellite

1982. First Anniv of "Apple" Satellite Launch.
| 1047 | 877 | 2r. multicoloured | 70 | 1·25 |

878 Bidhan Chandra Roy

1982. Birth Centenary of Bidhan Chandra Roy (doctor and politician).
| 1048 | 878 | 50p. brown | 1·25 | 1·75 |

879 *Sagar Samrat* Oil Rig

1982. 25th Anniv of Oil and Natural Gas Commission.
| 1049 | 879 | 1r. multicoloured | 2·25 | 75 |

880 *Bindu* (S. H. Raza)

1982. Festival of India. Contemporary Paintings. Multicoloured.
| 1050 | 2r. Type 880 | 1·00 | 50 |
| 1051 | 3r.05 *Between the Spider and the Lamp* (M. F. Hussain) | 1·25 | 1·50 |

881 Red Deer Stag, Kashmir

1982. Wildlife Conservation.
| 1052 | 881 | 2r.85 multicoloured | 2·75 | 2·00 |

882 Westland Wapiti Biplane and Mikoyan Gurevich MiG-25 Aircraft

1982. 50th Anniv of Indian Air Force.
| 1053 | 882 | 1r. multicoloured | 6·00 | 1·75 |

883 J. Tata with de Havilland Puss Moth

1982. 50th Anniv of Civil Aviation in India.
| 1054 | 883 | 3r.25 multicoloured | 5·50 | 3·50 |

884 Police Patrol

1982. Police Commemoration Day.
| 1055 | 884 | 50p. green | 60 | 30 |

885 Coins and Economic Symbols

1982. Centenary of Post Office Savings Bank.
| 1056 | 885 | 50p. brown and light brown | 20 | 20 |

886 Wrestling Bout

1982. Asian Games, New Delhi (4th issue).
| 1057 | 886 | 1r. multicoloured | 1·75 | 30 |

887 Troposcatter Communication Link

1982. First Anniv of Troposcatter Communication Link between India and U.S.S.R.
| 1058 | 887 | 3r.05 multicoloured | 30 | 40 |

888 Arjuna shooting Arrow at Fish

1982. Asian Games, New Delhi (5th issue).
| 1059 | 888 | 1r. multicoloured | 1·75 | 30 |

889 *Mother and Child* (Deepak Sharma)

1982. Children's Day.
| 1060 | 889 | 50p. multicoloured | 30 | 30 |

890 Stylized Cyclists

1982. Asian Games, New Delhi (6th issue). Multicoloured.
1061	50p. Type 890	25	10
1062	2r. Javelin-throwing	30	30
1063	2r.85 Discus-throwing	40	45
1064	3r.25 Football	60	55

891 "Enterprise" Dinghies Race

1982. Asian Games, New Delhi (7th issue). Multicoloured.
| 1065 | 2r. Type 891 | 1·25 | 30 |
| 1066 | 2r.85 Rowing | 1·75 | 70 |

892 Chetwode Building

1982. 50th Anniv of Indian Military Academy Dehradun.
| 1067 | 892 | 50p. multicoloured | 30 | 50 |

893 Purushottamdas Tandon

1982. Birth Cent of Purushottamdas Tandon (politician).
| 1068 | 893 | 50p. brown | 30 | 1·00 |

894 Darjeeling Himalayan Railway

1982. Cent of Darjeeling Himalayan Railway.
| 1069 | 894 | 2r.85 multicoloured | 6·50 | 5·50 |

895 Vintage Rail Coach and Silhouette of Steam Locomotive

1982. "Inpex 82" Stamp Exhibition. Multicoloured.
| 1070 | 50p. Type 895 | 1·25 | 1·25 |
| 1071 | 2r. 1854 ½ anna blue stamp and 1947 3½ anna Independence commem (33×44 mm) | 3·00 | 3·50 |

896 Antarctic Camp

1983. First Indian Antarctic Expedition.
| 1072 | 896 | 1r. multicoloured | 4·75 | 2·50 |

1983. As Nos. 968/9, but with new face value.
| 1073 | 50p. brown (Gandhi) | 4·50 | 2·50 |
| 1074a | 50p. blue (Nehru) | 3·25 | 1·00 |

897 Roosevelt with Stamp Collection

1983. Birth Centenary of Franklin D. Roosevelt (American statesman).
| 1075 | 897 | 3r.25 brown | 1·00 | 1·25 |

898 *Siberian Cranes at Bharatpur* (Diane Pierce)

1983. International Crane Workshop, Bharatpur.
| 1076 | 898 | 2r.85 multicoloured | 4·00 | 4·00 |

899 Jat Regiment Uniforms Past and Present

1983. Presentation of Colours to Battalions of the Jat Regiment.
| 1077 | 899 | 50p. multicoloured | 2·50 | 2·00 |

900 Non-aligned Summit Logo

1983. Seventh Non-aligned Summit Conference, New Delhi.
| 1078 | 900 | 1r. lt brown, brown & blk | 25 | 30 |
| 1079 | - | 2r. multicoloured | 75 | 95 |

DESIGN: 2r. Nehru.

901 Shore Temple, Mahabalipuram

1983. Commonwealth Day. Multicoloured.
| 1080 | 1r. Type 901 | 50 | 30 |
| 1081 | 2r. Gomukh, Gangotri Glacier | 50 | 1·50 |

902 Acropolis and Olympic Emblems

1983. Int Olympic Committee Session, New Delhi.
| 1082 | 902 | 1r. multicoloured | 30 | 50 |

903 *St. Francis and Brother Falcon* (statue by Giovanni Collina)

1983. 800th Birth Anniv of St. Francis of Assisi.
| 1083 | 903 | 1r. brown | 1·25 | 50 |

904 Karl Marx and *Das Kapital*

1983. Death Centenary of Karl Marx.
| 1084 | 904 | 1r. brown | 45 | 30 |

905 Darwin and Map of Voyage

1983. Death Centenary (1982) of Charles Darwin (naturalist).
| 1085 | 905 | 2r. multicoloured | 4·00 | 3·50 |

906 Swamp Deer

1983. 50th Anniv of Kanha National Park.

| 1086 | **906** | 1r. multicoloured | 3·00 | 1·25 |

907 Globe and Satellite

1983. World Communications Year.

| 1087 | **907** | 1r. multicoloured | 1·25 | 40 |

908 Simon Bolivar

1983. Birth Bicentenary of Simon Bolivar (South American statesman).

| 1088 | **908** | 2r. multicoloured | 2·50 | 2·50 |

909 Meera Behn

1983. India's Struggle for Freedom (1st series).

1089	50p. red and green	2·00	3·00
1090	50p. brown, green and red	2·00	3·00
1091	50p. multicoloured	1·50	2·25
1092	50p. brown, green and red	15	50
1093	50p. brown, green and orange	15	50
1094	50p. green, yellow and orange	15	50

DESIGNS—VERT: No. 1089, Type **909**; 1090, Mahadev Desai; 1092, Hemu Kalani (revolutionary); 1093, Acharya Vinoba Bhave (social reformer); 1094, Surendranath Banerjee (political reformer). HORIZ (43×31 mm): No. 1091, Quit India Resolution.

See also Nos. 1119/24, 1144/9, 1191/4, 1230/5, 1287/96 and 1345/9.

910 Ram Nath Chopra

1983. Ram Nath Chopra (pharmacologist) Commemoration.

| 1095 | **910** | 50p. red | 75 | 1·50 |

911 Nanda Devi Mountain

1983. 25th Anniv of Indian Mountaineering Federation.

| 1096 | **911** | 2r. multicoloured | 2·75 | 1·25 |

912 Great Indian Hornbill

1983. Centenary of Natural History Society, Bombay.

| 1097 | **912** | 1r. multicoloured | 3·75 | 1·75 |

913 View of Garden

1983. Rock Garden, Chandigarh.

| 1098 | **913** | 1r. multicoloured | 2·00 | 1·50 |

914 Golden Langur

1983. Indian Wildlife. Monkeys. Multicoloured.

| 1099 | 1r. Type **914** | 2·50 | 75 |
| 1100 | 2r. Lion-tailed macaque | 3·50 | 4·75 |

915 Ghats of Varanasi

1983. Fifth General Assembly of World Tourism Organization.

| 1101 | **915** | 2r. multicoloured | 1·50 | 1·00 |

916 Krishna Kanta Handique

1983. Krishna Kanta Handique (scholar).

| 1102 | **916** | 50p. blue | 55 | 70 |

918 Woman and Child (from *Festival* by Kashyap Premsawala)

1983. Children's Day.

| 1103 | **918** | 50p. multicoloured | 30 | 50 |

920 *Udan Khatola*, First Indian Hot Air Balloon

1983. Bicentenary of Manned Flight.. Multicoloured.

| 1104 | 1r. Type **920** | 1·50 | 50 |
| 1105 | 2r. Montgolfier balloon | 2·00 | 2·25 |

921 Tiger

1983. Ten Years of "Project Tiger".

| 1106 | **921** | 2r. multicoloured | 4·00 | 4·00 |

922 Commonwealth Logo

1983. Commonwealth Heads of Government Meeting, New Delhi. Multicoloured.

| 1107 | 1r. Type **922** | 55 | 15 |
| 1108 | 2r. Goanese couple, early 19th century | 95 | 85 |

923 Pratiksha

1983. Birth Centenary of Nanda Lal Bose (artist).

| 1109 | **923** | 1r. multicoloured | 30 | 30 |

925 Lancer in Ceremonial Uniform

1984. Bicentenary of 7th Light Cavalry.

| 1110 | **925** | 1r. multicoloured | 3·75 | 1·75 |

926 Troopers in Ceremonial Uniform and Tank

1984. Presentation of Regimental Guidon to the Deccan Horse.

| 1111 | **926** | 1r. multicoloured | 3·75 | 1·75 |

927 Society Building and Sir William Jones (founder)

1984. Bicentenary of Asiatic Society.

| 1112 | **927** | 1r. green and purple | 30 | 50 |

928 Insurance Logo

1984. Centenary of Postal Life Insurance.

| 1113 | **928** | 1r. multicoloured | 30 | 30 |

929 Hawker Siddeley Sea Harrier

1984. President's Review of the Fleet. Multicoloured.

1114	1r. Type **929**	3·00	3·25
1115	1r. *Vikrant* (aircraft carrier)	3·00	3·25
1116	1r. *Vela* (submarine)	3·00	3·25
1117	1r. *Kashin* (destroyer)	3·00	3·25

Nos. 1114/17 were printed together, *se-tenant*, forming a composite design.

930 I.L.A. Logo and Hemispheres

1984. 12th International Leprosy Congress.

| 1118 | **930** | 1r. multicoloured | 1·00 | 55 |

1984. India's Struggle for Freedom (2nd series). As T **909**.

1119	50p. green, lt green & orange	40	1·25
1120	50p. brown, green and orange	40	1·00
1121	50p. multicoloured	1·00	1·25
1122	50p. multicoloured	1·00	1·25
1123	50p. multicoloured	1·00	1·25
1124	50p. multicoloured	1·00	1·25

DESIGNS: No. 1119, Vasudeo Balvant Phadke (revolutionary); 1120, Baba Kanshi Ram (revolutionary); 1121, Tatya Tope; 1122, Nana Sahib; 1123, Begum Hazrat Mahal; 1124, Mangal Pandey.

932 "Salyut 7"

1984. Indo-Soviet Manned Space Flight.

| 1125 | **932** | 3r. multicoloured | 1·50 | 1·50 |

935 G. D. Birla

1984. 90th Birth Anniv of G. D. Birla (industrialist).

| 1126 | **935** | 50p. brown | 1·00 | 1·50 |

936 Basketball

1984. Olympic Games, Los Angeles. Multicoloured.

1127	50p. Type **936**	90	65
1128	1r. High jumping	75	30
1129	2r. Gymnastics (horiz)	1·00	1·50
1130	2r.50 Weightlifting (horiz)	1·25	2·75

937 Gwalior

1984. Forts. Multicoloured.

1131	50p. Type **937**	80	55
1132	1r. Vellore (vert)	1·10	30
1133	1r.50 Simhagad (vert)	2·00	3·00
1134	2r. Jodhpur	2·25	3·25

938 B. V. Paradkar and Newspaper

1984. B. V. Paradkar (journalist) Commemoration.

| 1135 | **938** | 50p. brown | 1·00 | 1·50 |

939 Dr. D. N. Wadia and Institute of Himalayan Geology, Dehradun

1984. Birth Centenary (1983) of Dr. D. N. Wadia (geologist).

| 1136 | **939** | 1r. multicoloured | 2·00 | 1·00 |

940 Herdsman and Cattle in Forest (H. Kassam)

1984. Children's Day.

| 1137 | **940** | 50p. multicoloured | 1·00 | 1·50 |

941 Indira Gandhi

1984. Prime Minister Indira Gandhi Commemoration (1st issue).

| 1138 | **941** | 50p. black, violet & orange | 2·50 | 2·50 |

See also Nos. 1151, 1167 and 1170.

942 Congress Emblem

1984. 12th World Mining Congress, New Delhi.

| 1139 | **942** | 1r. black and yellow | 2·00 | 30 |

943 Dr. Rajendra Prasad at Desk

1984. Birth Centenary of Dr. Rajendra Prasad (former President).

| 1140 | **943** | 50p. multicoloured | 1·00 | 1·50 |

944 Mrinalini (rose)

1984. Roses. Multicoloured.

| 1141 | 1r.50 Type **944** | | 2·25 | 2·25 |
| 1142 | 2r. Sugandha | | 2·50 | 2·50 |

945 Fergusson College (Gopal Deuskar)

1985. Centenary of Fergusson College, Pune.

| 1143 | **945** | 1r. multicoloured | 1·25 | 65 |

1985. India's Struggle for Freedom (3rd series). As T **909**.

1144	50p. brown, green and orange	80	1·25
1145	50p. brown, green and orange	80	1·25
1146	50p. brown, green and orange	80	1·25
1147	50p. brown, green and orange	80	1·25
1148	50p. blue, green and orange	80	1·25
1149	50p. black, green and orange	80	1·25

DESIGNS—VERT: No. 1144, Narhar Vishnu Gadgil (politician); 1145, Jairamdas Doulatram (journalist); 1147, Kakasaheb Kalelkar (author); 1148, Master Tara Singh (politician); 1149, Ravishankar Maharaj (politician). HORIZ: No. 1146, Jatindra and Nellie Sengupta (politicians).

947 Gunner and Howitzer from Mountain Battery

1985. 50th Anniv of Regiment of Artillery.

| 1150 | **947** | 1r. multicoloured | 4·75 | 1·50 |

948 Indira Gandhi making Speech

1985. Indira Gandhi Commemoration (2nd issue).

| 1151 | **948** | 2r. multicoloured | 4·00 | 4·00 |

949 Minicoy Lighthouse

1985. Centenary of Minicoy Lighthouse.

| 1152 | **949** | 1r. multicoloured | 6·50 | 1·50 |

950 Medical College Hospital

1985. 150th Anniv of Medical College, Calcutta.

| 1153 | **950** | 1r. yellow, brown & purple | 3·50 | 1·00 |

951 Medical College, Madras

1985. 150th Anniv of Medical College, Madras.

| 1154 | **951** | 1r. light brown and brown | 3·50 | 1·00 |

952 Riflemen of 1835 and 1985 and Map of North-East India

1985. 150th Anniv of Assam Rifles.

| 1155 | **952** | 1r. multicoloured | 5·00 | 1·50 |

953 Potato Plant

1985. 50th Anniv of Potato Research in India.

| 1156 | **953** | 50p. deep brown and brown | 1·75 | 2·00 |

954 Baba Jassa Singh Ahluwalia

1985. Death Bicentenary (1983) of Baba Jassa Singh Ahluwalia (Sikh leader).

| 1157 | **954** | 50p. purple | 1·75 | 2·00 |

955 St. Xavier's College

1985. 125th Anniv of St. Xavier's College, Calcutta.

| 1158 | **955** | 1r. multicoloured | 2·00 | 75 |

956 White-winged Wood Duck

1985. Wildlife Conservation. White-winged Wood Duck.

| 1159 | **956** | 2r. multicoloured | 8·00 | 6·00 |

957 "Mahara"

1985. Bougainvillea. Multicoloured.

| 1160 | 50p. Type **957** | | 2·00 | 2·75 |
| 1161 | 1r. "H. B. Singh" | | 2·25 | 1·50 |

958 Yaudheya Copper Coin, c. 200 B.C.

1985. Festival of India (1st issue).

| 1162 | **958** | 2r. multicoloured | 3·25 | 2·50 |

959 Statue of Didarganj Yakshi (deity)

1985. Festival of India (2nd issue).

| 1163 | **959** | 1r. multicoloured | 1·75 | 65 |

962 Swami Haridas

1985. Swami Haridas (philosopher) Commemoration.

| 1164 | **962** | 1r. multicoloured | 2·00 | 1·50 |

963 Stylized Mountain Road

1985. 25th Anniv of Border Roads Organization.

| 1165 | **963** | 2r. red, violet and black | 2·50 | 3·50 |

964 Nehru addressing General Assembly

1985. 40th Anniv of United Nations Organization.

| 1166 | **964** | 2r. multicoloured | 1·40 | 1·25 |

965 Indira Gandhi with Crowd

1985. Indira Gandhi Commemoration (3rd issue).

| 1167 | **965** | 2r. brown and black | 2·75 | 3·25 |

966 Girl using Home Computer

1985. Children's Day.

| 1168 | **966** | 50p. multicoloured | 1·00 | 1·25 |

967 Halley's Comet

1985. 19th General Assembly of International Astronomical Union, New Delhi.

| 1169 | **967** | 1r. multicoloured | 2·25 | 1·50 |

968 Indira Gandhi

1985. Indira Gandhi Commemoration (4th issue).

| 1170 | **968** | 3r. multicoloured | 3·50 | 3·50 |

969 St. Stephen's Hospital

1985. Centenary of St. Stephen's Hospital, Delhi.

| 1171 | **969** | 1r. black and brown | 1·25 | 40 |

971 Map showing Member States

1985. First Summit Meeting of South Asian Association for Regional Co-operation, Dhaka, Bangladesh. Multicoloured.

| 1172 | 1r. Type **971** | | 1·75 | 40 |
| 1173 | 3r. Flags of member nations (44×32 mm) | | 3·50 | 4·50 |

972 Shyama Shastri

1985. Shyama Shastri (composer) Commemoration.

| 1174 | **972** | 1r. multicoloured | 3·00 | 1·50 |

975 Young Runners and Emblem

1985. International Youth Year.
1175 **975** 2r. multicoloured 3·00 1·50

976 Handel and Bach

1985. 300th Birth Annivs of George Frederick Handel and Johann Sebastian Bach (composers).
1176 **976** 5r. multicoloured 5·50 5·50

977 A. O. Hume (founder) and Early Congress Presidents

1985. Centenary of Indian National Congress. Designs showing miniature portraits of Congress Presidents.
1177 **977** 1r. black, orange, green and grey 3·00 3·50
1178 – 1r. black, orange and green 3·00 3·50
1179 – 1r. black, orange and green 3·00 3·50
1180 – 1r. black, orange, green and grey 3·00 3·50

Nos. 1178/80 each show sixteen miniature portraits. The individual stamps can be distinguished by the position of the face value and inscription which are at the top on Nos. 1177/8 and at the foot on Nos. 1179/80. No. 1180 shows a portrait of Prime Minister Rajiv Gandhi in a grey frame at bottom right.

978 Bombay and Duncan Dry Docks, Bombay

1986. 250th Anniv of Naval Dockyard, Bombay.
1181 **978** 2r.50 multicoloured 5·00 5·00

979 Hawa Mahal and Jaipur 1904 2a. Stamp

1986. "INPEX '86" Philatelic Exhibition, Jaipur. Multicoloured.
1182 50p. Type **979** 1·25 1·25
1183 2r. Mobile camel post office, Thar Desert 3·00 3·50

980 I.N.S. *Vikrant* (aircraft carrier)

1986. Completion of 25 Years Service by I.N.S. *Vikrant*.
1184 **980** 2r. multicoloured 7·50 7·00

981 Humber Sommer Biplane and Later Mail Planes

1986. 75th Anniv of First Official Airmail Flight, Allahabad–Naini. Multicoloured.
1185 50p. Type **981** 2·25 2·00
1186 3r. Modern Air India Airbus Industries A300 mail plane and Humber Sommer biplane (37×24 mm) 4·75 7·00

982 Triennale Emblem

1986. Sixth Triennale Art Exhibition, New Delhi.
1187 **982** 1r. purple, yellow & black 1·50 1·00

983 Chaitanya Mahaprabhu

1986. 500th Birth Anniv of Chaitanya Mahaprabhu (religious leader).
1188 **983** 2r. multicoloured 3·25 3·75

984 Main Building, Mayo College

1986. Mayo College (public school), Ajmer, Commemoration.
1189 **984** 1r. multicoloured 2·00 1·00

985 Two Footballers

1986. World Cup Football Championship, Mexico.
1190 **985** 5r. multicoloured 5·50 6·00

1986. India's Struggle for Freedom (4th series). As T **909**.
1191 50p. brown, green and red 1·75 2·25
1192 50p. brown, green and red 1·75 2·25
1193 50p. black, green and orange 1·75 2·25
1194 50p. brown, green and red 1·75 2·25

DESIGNS: No. 1191, Bhim Sen Sachar; 1192, Alluri Seeta Rama Raju; 1193, Sagarmal Gopa; 1194, Veer Surendra Sai.

987 Swami Sivananda

1986. Birth Centenary of Swami Sivananda (spiritual leader).
1195 **987** 2r. multicoloured 3·50 4·25

988 Volleyball

1986. Asian Games, Seoul, South Korea. Multicoloured.
1196 1r.50 Type **988** 2·75 3·25
1197 3r. Hurdling 3·25 4·75

989 Madras G.P.O.

1986. Bicentenary of Madras G.P.O.
1198 **989** 5r. black and red 5·00 6·00

990 Parachutist

1986. 225th Anniv of 8th Battalion of Coast Sepoys (now 1st Battalion Parachute Regiment).
1199 **990** 3r. multicoloured 5·50 6·00

991 Early and Modern Policemen

1986. 125th Anniv of Indian Police. Designs showing early and modern police.
1200 **991** 1r.50 multicoloured 4·25 4·75
1201 – 2r. multicoloured 4·25 4·75

Nos. 1200/1 were printed together, se-tenant, forming a composite design.

992 Hand holding Flower and World Map

1986. International Peace Year.
1202 **992** 5r. multicoloured 5·00 1·75

993 Girl Rock Climber (Sujasha Dasgupta)

1986. Children's Day.
1203 **993** 50p. multicoloured 2·25 2·50

994 Windmill

1986. Science and Technology.
1211 – 35p. red 10 10
1212 – 40p. red 50 10
1213 – 60p. green and red 1·50 10
1214a 75p. 75 60
1215 – 1r. black and red 1·00 10
1217 – 5r. brown and orange 2·50 20
1218 – 20r. brown and blue 2·00 60
1219 **994** 50r. black, blue and mauve 2·75 2·75

DESIGNS—20×17 mm: 35p. Family planning. 37×20 mm: 60p. Indian family; 20r. Bio gas. 17×20 mm: 40p. Television set, dish aerial and transmitter; 75p. "Family" (as No. 927). 20×37 mm: 1r. Petrol pump nozzle (Oil conservation); 5r. Solar energy.

995 Growth Monitoring

1986. 40th Anniv of UNICEF. Multicoloured.
1221 50p. Type **995** 2·00 2·00
1222 5r. Immunization 5·00 6·50

996 Tansen

1986. Tansen (musician and composer) Commem.
1223 **996** 1r. multicoloured 2·50 60

997 Indian Elephant

1986. 50th Anniv of Corbett National Park. Multicoloured.
1224 1r. Type **997** 4·00 1·75
1225 2r. Gharial 4·50 6·50

998 St. Martha's Hospital

1986. Centenary of St. Martha's Hospital, Bangalore.
1226 **998** 1r. blue, orange and black 2·50 2·00

999 Yacht *Trishna* and Route Map

1987. Indian Army Round the World Yacht Voyage, 1985–1987.
1227 **999** 6r.50 multicoloured 4·50 5·00

1000 Map of Southern Africa and Logo

1987. Inauguration of AFRICA Fund.
1228 **1000** 6r.50 black 9·00 6·50

1001 Emblem

1987. 29th Congress of International Chamber of Commerce, New Delhi.
1229 **1001** 5r. violet, blue and red 3·75 2·50

1987. India's Struggle for Freedom (5th series). As T **909**.
1230 60p. brown, green and orange 2·75 30
1231 60p. violet, green and red 30 30
1232 60p. brown, green and red 30 30
1233 60p. blue, green and orange 30 30
1234 60p. brown, green and red 30 30
1235 60p. brown, green and red 30 30
1236 60p. red, green and orange 30 30

DESIGNS: No. 1230, Hakim Ajmal Khan; No. 1231, Lala Har Dayal; No. 1232, M. N. Roy; No. 1233, Tripuraneni Ramaswamy Chowdary; No. 1234, Dr. Kailas Nath Katju; No. 1235, S. Satyamurti; No. 1236, Pandit Hriday Nath Kunzru.

1002 Blast Furnace and Railway Emblem

1987. Cent of South Eastern Railway. Multicoloured.
1237		1r. Type **1002**	50	15
1238		1r.50 Tank locomotive No. 691, 1887 (horiz)	65	35
1239		2r. Electric train on viaduct, 1987	70	60
1240		4r. Steam locomotive, c. 1900 (horiz)	1·00	1·25

1003 Kalia Bhomora Bridge, Tezpur, Assam

1987. Inauguration of Brahmaputra Bridge.
1241	**1003**	2r. multicoloured	1·00	40

1004 Madras Christian College

1987. 150th Anniv of Madras Christian College.
1242	**1004**	1r.50 black and red	1·00	30

1005 Shree Shree Ma Anandamayee

1987. Shree Shree Ma Anandamayee (Hindu spiritual leader) Commemoration.
1243	**1005**	1r. brown	1·00	30

1006 *Rabindranath Tagore* (self-portrait)

1987. Rabindranath Tagore (poet) Commem.
1244	**1006**	2r. multicoloured	1·25	30

1007 Garwhal Rifles Uniforms of 1887

1987. Centenary of Garwhal Rifles Regiment.
1245	**1007**	1r. multicoloured	1·25	20

1008 J. Krishnamurti

1987. J. Krishnamurti (philosopher) Commem.
1246	**1008**	60p. brown	1·00	1·25

1009 Regimental Uniforms of 1887

1987. Centenary of 37th Dogra Regt (now 7th Battalion) (1 Dogra), Mechanised Infantry Regt.
1247	**1009**	1r. multicoloured	1·25	20

1010 Hall of Nations, Pragati Maidan, New Delhi

1987. "India '89" International Stamp Exhibition, New Delhi (1st issue). Multicoloured.
1248		50p. Exhibition logo	10	15
1249		5r. Type **1010**	45	60
MS1250	156×58 mm. Nos. 1248/9 (sold at 8r.)		3·00	3·50

See also Nos. 1264/8, 1333/4, 1341/2 and 1358/61.

1011 "Sadyah-Snata" Sculpture, Sanghol

1987. Festival of India, U.S.S.R.
1251	**1011**	6r.50 multicoloured	2·00	1·00

1012 Flag and Stylized Birds with "40" in English and Hindi

1987. 40th Anniv of Independence.
1252	**1012**	60p. orange, green & bl	20	20

1013 Sant Harchand Singh Longowal

1987. Sant Harchand Singh Longowal (Sikh leader) Commemoration.
1253	**1013**	1r. multicoloured	1·00	20

1014 Guru Ghasidas

1987. Guru Ghasidas (Hindu leader) Commemoration.
1254	**1014**	60p. red	45	20

1015 Thakur Anukul Chandra

1987. Thakur Anukul Chandra (spiritual leader) Commemoration.
1255	**1015**	1r. multicoloured	1·00	20

1016 University of Allahabad

1987. Centenary of Allahabad University.
1256	**1016**	2r. multicoloured	1·25	50

1017 Pankha Offering

1987. Phoolwalon Ki Sair Festival, Delhi.
1257	**1017**	2r. multicoloured	30	50

1018 Chhatrasal on Horseback

1987. Chhatrasal (Bundela ruler) Commemoration.
1258	**1018**	60p. brown	1·25	30

1019 Family and Stylized Houses

1987. International Year of Shelter for the Homeless.
1259	**1019**	5r. multicoloured	2·00	1·00

1020 Map of Asia and Logo

1987. Asia Regional Conference of Rotary International.
1260	**1020**	60p. brown and green	75	25
1261	-	6r.50 multicoloured	2·00	1·00

DESIGN: 6r.50, Oral polio vaccination.

1021 Blind Boy, Braille Books and Computer

1987. Centenary of Service to Blind.
1262	**1021**	1r. multicoloured	75	25
1263	-	2r. deep blue and blue	1·25	75

DESIGN: 2r. Eye donation.

1022 Iron Pillar, Delhi

1987. "India '89" International Stamp Exhibition, New Delhi (2nd issue). Delhi Landmarks. Multicoloured.
1264		60p. Type **1022**	20	15
1265		1r.50 India Gate	25	20
1266		5r. Dewan-e-Khas, Red Fort	65	50
1267		6r.50 Old Fort	80	65
MS1268	100×86 mm. Nos. 1264/7 (sold at 15r.)		8·00	9·50

1023 Tyagmurti Goswami Ganeshdutt

1987. Tyagmurti Goswami Ganeshdutt (spiritual leader and social reformer) Commemoration.
1269	**1023**	60p. red	50	20

1024 "My Home" (Siddharth Deshprabha)

1987. Children's Day.
1270	**1024**	60p. multicoloured	30	20

1025 Chinar

1987. Indian Trees.
1271	**1025**	60p. multicoloured	40	15
1272	-	1r.50 multicoloured	1·25	30
1273	-	5r. black, green & brown	2·00	90
1274	-	6r.50 brown, red & green	3·25	1·25

DESIGNS—HORIZ: 1r.50, Pipal; 6r.50, Banyan. VERT: 5r. Sal.

1026 Logo (from sculpture "Worker and Woman Peasant" by V. Mukhina)

1987. Festival of U.S.S.R., India.
1275	**1026**	5r. multicoloured	1·50	50

1027 White Tiger

1987. Wildlife. Multicoloured.
1276		1r. Type **1027**	1·50	35
1277		5r. Snow leopard (horiz)	4·00	1·25

1028 Execution of Veer Narayan Singh

1987. Veer Narayan Singh (patriot) Commemoration.
1278	**1028**	60p. brown	45	20

1029 Rameshwari Nehru

1987. Rameshwari Nehru (women's rights campaigner) Commemoration.
1279	**1029**	60p. brown	30	20

1030 Father Kuriakose Elias Chavara

1987. Father Kuriakose Elias Chavara (founder of Carmelites of Mary Immaculate) Commemoration.
1280	**1030**	60p. brown	45	20

1031 Dr. Rajah Sir Muthiah Chettiar

1987. Dr. Rajah Sir Muthiah Chettiar (politician) Commemoration.

1281	**1031**	60p. grey	30	20

1032 Golden Temple, Amritsar

1987. 400th Anniv of Golden Temple, Amritsar.

1282	**1032**	60p. multicoloured	1·00	20

1033 Rukmini Devi and Dancer

1987. Rukmini Devi (Bharatanatyam dance pioneer) Commemoration.

1283	**1033**	60p. red	1·00	20

1034 Dr. Hiralal

1987. Dr. Hiralal (historian) Commemoration.

1284	**1034**	60p. blue	50	20

1035 Light Frequency Experiment and Bodhi Tree

1988. 75th Session of Indian Science Congress Association.

1285	**1035**	4r. multicoloured	2·50	1·00

1036 Rural Patient

1988. 13th Asian Pacific Dental Congress.

1286	**1036**	4r. multicoloured	2·00	75

1988. India's Struggle for Freedom (6th series). As T **909**.

1287	60p. black, green and orange	20	40
1288	60p. brown, green and orange	20	40
1289	60p. red, green and orange	20	40
1290	60p. purple, green and orange	20	40
1291	60p. purple, green and red	20	40
1292	60p. black, green and orange	20	40
1293	60p. lilac, green and red	20	40
1294	60p. deep green, green and red	20	30
1295	60p. brown, green and green	20	30
1296	60p. mauve, green and orange	20	30

DESIGNS: No. 1287, Mohan Lal Sukhadia; 1288, Dr. S. K. Sinha; 1289, Chandra Shekhar Azad; 1290, G. B. Pant; 1291, Dr. Anugrah Narain Singh; 1292, Kuladhor Chaliha; 1293, Shivprasad Gupta; 1294, Sarat Chandra Bose; 1295, Baba Kharak Singh; 1296, Sheikh Mohammad Abdullah.

1037 U Tirot Singh

1988. U Tirot Singh (Khasis leader) Commem.

1297	**1037**	60p. brown	45	20

1038 Early and Modern Regimental Uniforms

1988. Bicentenary of 4th Battalion of the Kumaon Regiment.

1298	**1038**	1r. multicoloured	70	20

1039 Balgandharva

1988. Birth Centenary of Balgandharva (actor).

1299	**1039**	60p. brown	30	20

1040 Soldiers and Infantry Combat Vehicle

1988. Presentation of Colours to Mechanised Infantry Regiment.

1300	**1040**	1r. multicoloured	70	20

1041 B. N. Rau

1988. B. N. Rau (constitutional lawyer) Commemoration.

1301	**1041**	60p. black	50	20

1042 Mohindra Government College

1988. Mohindra Government College, Patiala.

1302	**1042**	1r. mauve	50	20

1043 Dr. D. V. Gundappa

1988. Dr. D. V. Gundappa (scholar) Commem.

1303	**1043**	60p. grey	30	20

1044 Rani Avantibai

1988. Rani Avantibai of Ramgarh Commem.

1304	**1044**	60p. mauve	70	20

1045 *Malayala Manorama* Office, Kottayam

1988. Centenary of *Malayala Manorama* (newspaper).

1305	**1045**	1r. black and blue	50	20

1046 Maharshi Dadhichi

1988. Maharshi Dadhichi (Hindu saint) Commemoration.

1306	**1046**	60p. red	30	20

1047 Mohammad Iqbal

1988. 50th Death Anniv of Mohammad Iqbal (poet).

1307	**1047**	60p. gold and red	30	20

1048 Samarth Ramdas

1988. Samarth Ramdas (Hindu spiritual leader) Commemoration.

1308	**1048**	60p. green	30	20

1049 Swati Tirunal Rama Varma

1988. 175th Birth Anniv of Swati Tirunal Rama Varma (composer).

1309	**1049**	60p. mauve	60	20

1050 Bhaurao Patil and Class

1988. Bhaurao Patil (educationist) Commem.

1310	**1050**	60p. brown	50	20

1051 "Rani Lakshmi Bai" (M. F. Husain)

1988. Martyrs from First War of Independence.

1311	**1051**	60p. multicoloured	50	20

1052 Broad Peak

1988. Himalayan Peaks.

1312	**1052**	1r.50 lilac, violet and blue	1·00	30
1313	–	4r. multicoloured	1·50	80
1314	–	5r. multicoloured	2·00	1·00
1315	–	6r.50 multicoloured	3·50	1·50

DESIGNS: 4r. K 2 (Godwin Austen); 5r. Kanchenjunga; 6r.50, Nanda Devi.

1053 Child with Grandparents

1988. "Love and Care for Elders".

1316	**1053**	60p. multicoloured	30	20

1054 Victoria Terminus, Bombay

1988. Centenary of Victoria Terminus Station, Bombay.

1317	**1054**	1r. multicoloured	50	20

1055 Lawrence School, Lovedale

1988. 130th Anniv of Lawrence School, Lovedale.

1318	**1055**	1r. brown and green	1·00	20

1056 Khejri Tree

1988. World Environment Day.

1319	**1056**	60p. multicoloured	50	20

1988. As No. 732, but new face value.

1320	60p. black (Gandhi)	1·75	50

1057 Rani Durgawati

1988. Rani Durgawati (Gondwana ruler) Commemoration.

1322	**1057**	60p. red	70	20

1058 Acharya Shanti Dev

1988. Acharya Shanti Dev (Buddhist scholar) Commemoration.

1323	**1058**	60p. brown	50	20

1059 Y. S. Parmar

1988. Dr. Yashwant Singh Parmar (former Chief Minister of Himachal Pradesh) Commemoration.

1324	**1059**	60p. violet	50	20

1060 Arm pointing at Proclamation in Marathi

1988. 40th Anniv of Independence. Bal Gangadhar Tilak (patriot) Commemoration. Multicoloured.

1325	60p. Type **1060**	1·50	1·00
1326	60p. Battle scene	1·50	1·00

Nos. 1325/6 were printed together, *se-tenant*, forming a composite design showing a painting by M. F. Husain.

1061 Durgadas Rathore

1988. 150th Birth Anniv of Durgadas Rathore (Regent of Marwar).

1327	**1061**	60p. brown	50	20

1062 Gopinath Kaviraj

1988. Gopinath Kaviraj (scholar) Commem.

1328	**1062**	60p. brown	30	20

1063 Lotus and Outline Map of India

1988. Hindi Day.

1329	**1063**	60p. red, green & brown	30	20

1064 Indian Olympic Association Logo

1988. "Sports—1988" and Olympic Games, Seoul.

1330	**1064**	60p. purple	35	20
1331	-	5r. multicoloured	3·25	1·25

DESIGN—HORIZ: 5r. Various sports.

1065 Jerdon's Courser

1988. Wildlife Conservation. Jerdon's Courser.

1332	**1065**	1r. multicoloured	3·00	50

1988. "India '89" International Stamp Exhibition, New Delhi (3rd issue). General Post Offices. As T **1022**. Multicoloured.

1333	4r. Bangalore G.P.O	50	50
1334	5r. Bombay G.P.O	50	50

1066 The Times of India Front Page

1988. 150th Anniv of *The Times of India*.

1335	**1066**	1r.50 black, gold & yell	1·00	50

1067 Maulana Abul Kalam Azad (K. Hebbar)

1988. Birth Centenary of Maulana Abul Kalam Azad (politician).

1336	**1067**	60p. multicoloured	50	20

1068 Nehru

1988. Birth Centenary (1989) of Jawaharlal Nehru (1st issue).

1337	**1068**	60p. black, orange and green	75	30
1338	-	1r. multicoloured	1·25	1·25

DESIGN—VERT: 1r. *Jawaharlal Nehru* (Svetoslav Roerich). See also No. 1393.

1069 Birsa Munda

1988. Birsa Munda (Munda leader) Commem.

1339	**1069**	60p. brown	30	20

1070 Bhakra Dam

1988. 25th Anniv of Dedication of Bhakra Dam.

1340	**1070**	60p. red	75	70

1071 Dead Letter Office Cancellations of 1886

1988. "India '89" International Stamp Exhibition, New Delhi (4th series). Postal Cancellations.

1341	**1071**	60p. brown, black & red	50	40
1342	-	6r.50 brown and black	1·75	1·40

DESIGN: 6r.50, Allahabad–Cawnpore travelling post office handstamp of 1864.

1072 K. M. Munshi

1988. Birth Centenary (1987) of K. M. Munshi (author and politician).

1343	**1072**	60p. green	30	20

1073 Mannathu Padmanabhan

1989. Mannathu Padmanabhan (social reformer) Commemoration.

1344	**1073**	60p. brown	30	20

1989. India's Struggle for Freedom (7th series). As T **909**.

1345	60p. black, green and orange	25	30
1346	60p. orange, green and lilac	25	50
1347	60p. black, green and orange	25	50
1348	60p. brown, green and orange	25	50
1349	60p. brown, green and orange	25	30

DESIGNS: No. 1345, Hare Krishna Mahtab; 1346, Balasaheb Gangadhar Kher; 1347, Raj Kumari Amrit Kaur; 1348, Saifuddin Kitchlew; 1349, Asaf Ali.

1074 Lok Sabha Secretariat

1989. 60th Anniv of Lok Sabha Secretariat (formerly Legislative Assembly Department).

1355	**1074**	60p. green	30	20

1075 Goddess Durga seated on Lion (5th-cent terracotta plaque)

1989. 125th Anniv of Lucknow Museum.

1356	**1075**	60p. deep blue and blue	30	20

1076 Baldev Ramji Mirdha

1989. Birth Centenary of Baldev Ramji Mirdha (nationalist).

1357	**1076**	60p. green	30	20

1077 Girl with Stamp Collection

1989. "India' 89" International Stamp Exhibition, New Delhi (5th issue). Philately.

1358	**1077**	60p. yellow, red and blue	15	10
1359	-	1r.50 grey, yellow and black	20	15
1360	-	5r. red and blue	60	50
1361	-	6r.50 50 black, brown & bl	70	60

DESIGNS: 1r.50, Dawk gharry, c. 1842; 5r. Travancore 1888 2ch. conch shell stamp; 6r.50, Early Indian philatelic magazines.

1078 St. John Bosco and Boy

1989. St. John Bosco (founder of Salesian Brothers) Commemoration.

1362	**1078**	60p. red	30	20

1079 Modern Tank and 19th-century Sowar

1989. 3rd Cavalry Regiment.

1363	**1079**	60p. multicoloured	60	20

1080 Dargah Sharif, Ajmer

1989. Dargah Sharif (Sufi shrine), Ajmer.

1364	**1080**	1r. multicoloured	30	20

1081 Task Force and Indian Naval Ensign

1989. President's Review of the Fleet.

1365	**1081**	6r.50 multicoloured	4·25	1·75

1082 Shaheed Laxman Nayak and Barbed Wire Fence

1989. Shaheed Laxman Nayak Commemoration.

1366	**1082**	60p. brown, grn & orge	30	20

1083 Rao Gopal Singh

1989. Rao Gopal Singh Commemoration.

1367	**1083**	60p. brown	30	20

1084 Sydenham College

1989. 75th Anniv (1988) of Sydenham College, Bombay.

1368	**1084**	60p. black	30	20

1085 Bishnu Ram Medhi

1989. Birth Centenary (1988) of Bishnu Ram Medhi (politician).

1369	**1085**	60p. green, dp grn & red	30	20

1086 Dr. N. S. Hardikar

1989. Birth Centenary of Dr. Narayana Subbarao Hardikar (nationalist).

1370	**1086**	60p. brown	30	20

1087 "Advaita" in Devanagari Script

1989. Sankaracharya (philosopher) Commem.
1371 **1087** 60p. multicoloured   30   20

1088 Gandhi Bhavan, Punjab University

1989. Punjab University, Chandigarh.
1372 **1088** 1r. brown and blue   30   20

1089 Scene from Film "Raja Harischandra"

1989. 75 Years of Indian Cinema.
1373 **1089** 60p. black and yellow   30   20

1090 Cactus and Cogwheels

1989. Centenary of Kirloskar Brothers Ltd (engineering group).
1374 **1090** 1r. multicoloured   1·00   20

1091 Early Class and Modern University Students

1989. Centenary of First D.A.V. College.
1375 **1091** 1r. multicoloured   1·00   20

1092 Post Office, Dakshin Gangotri Base, Antarctica

1989. Opening of Post Office, Dakshin Gangotri Research Station, Antarctica.
1376 **1092** 1r. multicoloured   1·75   35

1093 First Allahabad Bank Building

1989. 125th Anniv (1990) of Allahabad Bank.
1377 **1093** 60p. purple and blue   30   20

1094 Nehru inspecting Central Reserve Police, Neemuch, 1954

1989. 50th Anniv of Central Reserve Police Force (formerly Crown Representative's Police).
1378 **1094** 60p. brown   2·00   30

1095 Dairy Cow

1989. Centenary of Military Farms.
1379 **1095** 1r. multicoloured   1·00   30

1096 Mustafa Kemal Ataturk

1989. 50th Death Anniv (1988) of Mustafa Kemal Ataturk (Turkish statesman).
1380 **1096** 5r. multicoloured   2·50   1·75

1097 Dr. S. Radhakrishnan

1989. Birth Centenary (1988) of Dr. Sarvepalli Radhakrishnan (former President).
1381 **1097** 60p. black   30   20

1098 Football Match

1989. Cent of Mohun Bagan Athletic Club.
1382 **1098** 1r. multicoloured   1·75   30

1099 Dr. P. Subbarayan

1989. Birth Centenary of Dr. P. Subbarayan (politician).
1383 **1099** 60p. brown   30   20

1100 Shyamji Krishna Varma

1989. Shyamji Krishna Varma (nationalist) Commemoration.
1384 **1100** 60p. brown, green & red   30   20

1101 Sayajirao Gaekwad III

1989. 50th Death Anniv of Maharaja Sayajirao Gaekwad III of Baroda.
1385 **1101** 60p. grey   30   20

1102 Symbolic Bird with Letter

1989. "Use Pincode" Campaign.
1386 **1102** 60p. multicoloured   1·00   20

1103 Namakkal Kavignar

1989. Namakkal Kavignar (writer) Commem.
1387 **1103** 60p. black   30   20

1104 Diagram of Human Brain

1989. 18th International Epilepsy Congress and 14th World Congress on Neurology, New Delhi.
1388 **1104** 6r.50 multicoloured   2·25   75

1105 Pandita Ramabai and Original Sharada Sadan Building

1989. Pandita Ramabai (women's education pioneer) Commemoration.
1389 **1105** 60p. brown   30   20

1106 Releasing Homing Pigeons

1989. Orissa Police Pigeon Post.
1390 **1106** 1r. red   75   30

1107 Acharya Narendra Deo

1989. Birth Centenary of Acharya Narendra Deo (scholar).
1391 **1107** 60p. brown, grn & orge   30   20

1108 Acharya Kripalani

1989. Acharya Kripalani (politician) Commemoration.
1392 **1108** 60p. black, green & red   30   20

1109 Nehru

1989. Birth Cent of Jawaharlal Nehru (2nd issue).
1393 **1109** 1r. brown, deep brown and buff   1·25   50

1110 Meeting Logo

1989. Eighth Asian Track and Field Meeting, New Delhi.
1394 **1110** 1r. black, orange & grn   65   20

1111 Sir Gurunath Bewoor

1989. Sir Gurunath Bewoor (former Director-General, Posts and Telegraphs) Commemoration.
1395 **1111** 60p. brown   30   20

1112 Balkrishna Sharma Navin

1989. Balkrishna Sharma Navin (politician and poet) Commemoration.
1396 **1112** 60p. black   30   20

1113 Abstract Painting of Houses

1989. Cent of Bombay Art Society (1988).
1397 **1113** 1r. multicoloured   1·00   20

1114 Lesser Florican

1989. Wildlife Conservation. Lesser Florican.
1398 **1114** 2r. multicoloured   2·50   1·00

1115 Centenary Logo

1989. Centenary of Indian Oil Production.
1399 **1115** 60p. brown   45   20

1116 Dr. M. G. Ramachandran

1990. Dr. M. G. Ramachandran (former Chief Minister of Tamil Nadu) Commemoration.
1400 **1116** 60p. brown   40   20

1117 Volunteers working at Sukhna Lake, Chandigarh

1990. Save Sukhna Lake Campaign.
1401 **1117** 1r. multicoloured 50 20

1118 Gallantry Medals

1990. Presentation of New Colours to Bombay Sappers.
1402 **1118** 60p. multicoloured 1·00 1·75

1119 Indian Chank Shell and Logo

1990. 23rd Annual General Meeting of Asian Development Bank, New Delhi.
1403 **1119** 2r. black, orange & yell 75 30

1120 Penny Black and Envelope

1990. 150th Anniv of the Penny Black.
1404 **1120** 6r. multicoloured 1·75 1·25

1121 Ho Chi-Minh and Vietnamese House

1990. Birth Centenary of Ho Chi-Minh (Vietnamese leader).
1405 **1121** 2r. brown and green 2·00 75

1122 Chaudhary Charan Singh

1990. Third Death Anniv of Chaudhary Charan Singh (former Prime Minister).
1406 **1122** 1r. brown 30 20

1123 Armed Forces' Badge and Map of Sri Lanka

1990. Indian Peace-keeping Operations in Sri Lanka.
1407 **1123** 2r. multicoloured 55 30

1124 Wheat

1990. 60th Anniv of Indian Council of Agricultural Research (1989).
1408 **1124** 2r. black, grn & dp grn 40 30

1125 Khudiram Bose

1990. Khudiram Bose (patriot) Commemoration.
1409 **1125** 1r. orange, green and red 40 20

1126 Life in India (Tanya Vorontsova)

1990. Indo–Soviet Friendship. Children's Paintings. Multicoloured.
1410 Type **1126** 1r. Type **1126** 2·25 2·75
1411 6r.50 St. Basil's Cathedral and Kremlin, Moscow (Sanjay Adhikari) 2·25 2·75
Stamps in similar designs were also issued by U.S.S.R.

1127 K. Kelappan

1990. K. Kelappan (social reformer) Commem.
1412 **1127** 1r. brown 40 20

1128 Girl in Garden

1990. Year of the Girl Child.
1413 **1128** 1r. multicoloured 50 30

1129 Hand guiding Child's Writing

1990. International Literacy Year.
1414 **1129** 1r. multicoloured 50 30

1130 Woman using Water Pump

1990. Safe Drinking Water Campaign.
1415 **1130** 4r. black, red and green 1·50 2·00

1131 Sunder Lal Sharma

1990. 50th Death Anniv of Sunder Lal Sharma (patriot).
1416 **1131** 60p. red 50 50

1132 Kabbadi

1990. 11th Asian Games, Peking. Multicoloured.
1417 1r. Type **1132** 40 20
1418 4r. Athletics 1·50 2·00
1419 4r. Cycling 1·50 2·00
1420 6r.50 Archery 1·75 2·50

1133 A. K. Gopalan

1990. Ayillyath Kuttiari Gopalan (social reformer) Commemoration.
1421 **1133** 1r. brown 50 30

1134 Gurkha Soldier

1990. 50th Anniv of 3rd and 5th Battalions, 5th Gurkha Rifles.
1422 **1134** 2r. black and brown 1·60 1·75

1135 Suryamall Mishran

1990. 75th Birth Anniv of Suryamall Mishran (poet).
1423 **1135** 2r. brown and orange 60 75

1136 Doll and Cat (Subhash Kumar Nagarajan)

1990. Children's Day.
1424 **1136** 1r. multicoloured 60 30

1137 Security Post and Border Guard on Camel

1990. 25th Anniv of Border Security Force.
1425 **1137** 5r. blue, brown & black 4·00 3·00

1138 Hearts and Flowers

1990. Greetings Stamps. Multicoloured.
1426 1r. Type **1138** 30 25
1427 4r. Ceremonial elephants (horiz) 80 1·00

1139 Bikaner

1990. Cities of India. Multicoloured.
1428 4r. Type **1139** 1·25 80
1429 5r. Hyderabad 1·25 85
1430 6r.50 Cuttack 2·25 2·00

1140 Bhakta Kanakadas and Udipi Temple

1990. Bhakta Kanakadas (mystic and poet) Commemoration.
1431 **1140** 1r. red 55 30

1141 Shaheed Minar Monument

1990. 300th Anniv of Calcutta.
1432 **1141** 1r. multicoloured 60 20
1433 – 6r. black, brown and red 3·50 3·00
DESIGN—HORIZ (44×36 mm): 6r. 18th-century shipping on the Ganges.

1142 Dnyaneshwari (poet) and Manuscript

1990. 700th Anniv of Dnyaneshwari (spiritual epic).
1434 **1142** 2r. multicoloured 50 60

1143 Madan Mohan Malaviya (founder) and University

1991. 75th Anniv of Banaras Hindu University.
1435 **1143** 1r. red 40 20

1991. As No. 732 but new face value.
1436 1r. brown (Gandhi) 20 10

1144 Road Users

1991. International Traffic Safety Conference, New Delhi.
1437 **1144** 6r.50 black, blue and red 2·00 2·00

1145 Exhibition
Emblem

1991. Seventh Triennale Art Exhibition, New Delhi.
1438   **1145**   6r.50 multicoloured   1·50   1·75

1146 Jagannath
Sunkersett and
Central Railways
Headquarters

1991. 125th Death Anniv (1990) of Jagannath Sunkersett (educationist and railway pioneer).
1439   **1146**   2r. blue and red   1·25   1·25

1147 Tata Memorial
Centre

1991. 50th Anniv of Tata Memorial Medical Centre.
1440   **1147**   2r. brown and stone   50   75

1148 River Dolphin

1991. Endangered Marine Mammals.
1441   **1148**   4r. brown, blue and
                  green   1·50   1·50
1442   –   6r.50 multicoloured   2·00   2·50
DESIGN: 6r.50, Sea cow.

1149 Drugs

1991. International Conference on Drug Abuse, Calcutta.
1443   **1149**   5r. violet and red   5·00   3·50

1150 Hand, Bomb
Explosion and Dove

1991. World Peace.
1444   **1150**   6r.50 blk, lt brn & brn   2·00   1·75

1151 Remote Sensing
Satellite "IA"

1991. Launch of Indian Remote Sensing Satellite "IA".
1445   **1151**   6r.50 brown and blue   2·00   1·75

1152 Babu
Jagjivan Ram

1991. Babu Jagjivan Ram (politician) Commemoration.
1446   **1152**   1r. brown   50   50

1153 Dr. B. R. Ambedkar
and Demonstration

1991. Birth Centenary of Dr. Bhimrao Ramji Ambedkar (social reformer).
1447   **1153**   1r. brown and blue   50   50

1154 Valar Dance

1991. Tribal Dances. Multicoloured.
1448   2r.50 Type **1154**   60   50
1449   4r. Kayang   80   85
1450   5r. Hozagiri   1·25   1·10
1451   6r.50 Velakali   1·50   2·00

1155 Ariyakudi Ramanuja
Iyengar and Temples

1991. Ariyakudi Ramanuja Iyengar (singer and composer) Commemoration.
1452   **1155**   2r. brown and green   75   1·00

1156 Karpoori
Thakur

1991. Jan Nayak Karpoori Thakur (politician and social reformer) Commemoration.
1453   **1156**   1r. brown   50   50

1157 Emperor Penguins

1991. 30th Anniv of Antarctic Treaty. Multicoloured.
1454   5r. Type **1157**   3·50   3·00
1455   6r.50 Antarctic map and pair of
             Adelie penguins   3·50   3·00
     Nos. 1454/5 were printed together, *se-tenant*, forming a composite design.

1158 Rashtrapati Bhavan
Building, New Delhi

1991. 60th Anniv of New Delhi. Multicoloured.
1456   2r. Type **1158**   2·00   2·25
1457   6r.50 New Delhi monuments   2·00   2·25
     Nos. 1456/7 were printed together, *se-tenant*, forming a composite design.

1159 Sri Ram Sharma
Acharya

1991. Sri Ram Sharma Acharya (social reformer) Commemoration.
1458   **1159**   1r. green and red   75   50

1160 *Shankar awarded
Padma Vibhushan* (cartoon)

1991. Keshav Shankar Pillai (cartoonist) Commemoration.
1459   **1160**   4r. brown   3·00   1·75
1460   –   6r.50 lilac   2·00   2·50
DESIGN—VERT: 6r.50, *The Big Show*.

1161 Sriprakash and Kashi
Vidyapith University

1991. 20th Death Anniv of Sriprakash (politician).
1461   **1161**   2r. brown & light brown   1·00   1·00

1162 Gopinath
Bardoloi

1991. Birth Centenary (1990) of Gopinath Bardoloi (Assamese politician).
1462   **1162**   1r. lilac   1·00   75

1163 Rajiv Gandhi

1991. Rajiv Gandhi (Congress Party leader) Commemoration.
1463   **1163**   1r. multicoloured   1·25   75

1164 Muni Mishrimalji and
Memorial

1991. Birth Centenary of Muni Mishrimalji (Jain religious leader).
1464   **1164**   1r. brown   1·00   75

1165 Mahadevi Verma
(poetess) and "Varsha"

1991. Hindu Writers.
1465   **1165**   2r. black and blue   11·00   9·00
1466   –   2r. black and blue   11·00   9·00
DESIGN: No. 1466, Jayshankar Prasad (poet and dramatist) and scene from *Kamayani*.

1166 Parliament House
and C.P.A. Emblem

1991. 37th Commonwealth Parliamentary Association Conference, New Delhi.
1467   **1166**   6r.50 blue and brown   1·25   1·00

1167 Frog

1991. Greetings Stamps.
1468   **1167**   1r. green and red   2·00   1·50
1469   –   6r.50 red and green   3·00   2·00
DESIGN: 6r.50, Symbolic bird carrying flower.

1168 *Cymbidium
aloifolium*

1991. Orchids. Multicoloured.
1470   1r. Type **1168**   60   15
1471   2r.50 *Paphiopedilum venustum*   80   45
1472   3r. *Aerides crispum*   1·25   65
1473   4r. *Cymbidium bicolour*   1·40   80
1474   5r. *Vanda spathulata*   1·75   1·00
1475   6r.50 *Cymbidium devonianum*   2·50   2·50

1169 Gurkha Soldier in
Battle Dress

1991. 90th Anniv of 2nd Battalion, Third Gurkha Rifles.
1476   **1169**   4r. multicoloured   1·50   1·75

1170 Couple on
Horse (embroidery)

1991. Third Death Anniv of Kamaladevi Chattopadhyaya (founder of All India Handicrafts Board).
1477   **1170**   1r. lake, red and yellow   60   30
1478   –   6r.50 multicoloured   2·00   2·75
DESIGN: 6r.50, Traditional puppet.

1171 Chithira Tirunal and
Temple Sculpture

1991. Chithira Tirunal Bala Rama Varma (former Maharaja of Travancore) Commemoration.
1479   **1171**   2r. violet   1·25   1·25

1172 *Children in
Traditional Costume*
(Arpi Snehalbhai
Shah)

1991. Children's Day.
1480   **1172**   1r. multicoloured   70   30

1173 Mounted Sowar and
Tanks

1991. 70th Anniv (1992) of the 18th Cavalry Regiment.
1481   **1173**   6r.50 multicoloured   2·50   2·75

1174 Kites

1991. India Tourism Year.
1482 **1174** 6r.50 multicoloured 1·00 1·40

1175 Sports on Bricks

1991. International Conference on Youth Tourism, New Delhi.
1483 **1175** 6r.50 multicoloured 1·10 1·50

1176 *Mozart at Piano* (unfinished painting, J. Lange)

1991. Death Bicentenary of Mozart.
1484 **1176** 6r.50 multicoloured 1·75 2·25

1177 Homeless Family

1991. South Asian Association for Regional Co-operation Year of Shelter.
1485 **1177** 4r. brown and ochre 1·00 75

1178 People running on Heart

1991. "Run for Your Heart" Marathon, New Delhi.
1486 **1178** 1r. black, grey and red 50 20

1179 *Sidhartha with an Injured Bird* (Asit Kumar Haldar)

1991. Birth Centenary (1990) of Asit Kumar Haldar (artist).
1487 **1179** 2r. yellow, red and black 1·25 1·25

1180 Bhujangasana

1991. Yoga Exercises. Multicoloured.
1488 **1180** 2r. Type **1180** 60 25
1489 5r. Dhanurasana 1·25 75
1490 6r.50 Ustrasana 1·40 1·00
1491 10r. Utthita trikonasana 2·00 2·50

1181 Y.M.C.A. Logo

1992. Centenary (1991) of National Council of Young Men's Christian Association.
1492 **1181** 1r. red and blue 50 50

1182 Madurai Temple Tower and Hooghly River Bridge

1992. 14th Congress of International Association for Bridge and Structural Engineering, New Delhi.
1493 **1182** 2r. brown, red and blue 10·00 9·00
1494 - 2r. brown, red and blue 10·00 9·00
DESIGN: No. 1494, Gate, Sanchi Stupa and Hall of Nations, New Delhi.

1183 Goat Seal from Harappa Culture, 2500 to 1500 B.C.

1992. Fifth International Goat Conference, New Delhi.
1495 **1183** 6r. blue and brown 8·00 4·50

1184 Early 19th-century Letter with Mail Pouch and National Archives Building, New Delhi

1992. Centenary (1991) of National Archives.
1496 **1184** 6r. multicoloured 10·00 4·75

1185 Krushna Chandra Gajapathi

1992. Krushna Chandra Gajapathi (former Chief Minister of Orissa) Commemoration.
1497 **1185** 1r. lilac 1·00 75

1186 Vijay Singh Pathik

1992. Vijay Singh Pathik (writer) Commem.
1498 **1186** 1r. brown 1·00 75

1187 Hang-gliding

1992. Adventure Sports. Multicoloured.
1499 **1187** 2r. Type **1187** 1·00 30
1500 4r. Windsurfing 2·25 1·00
1501 5r. River rafting 3·25 1·25
1502 11r. Skiing 6·00 7·00

1188 Henry Gidney and Anglo-Indians

1992. 50th Death Anniv of Sir Henry Gidney (ophthalmologist).
1503 **1188** 1r. black and blue 1·50 1·00

1189 Telecommunications Training Centre, Jabalpur

1992. 50th Anniv of Telecommunications Training Centre, Jabalpur.
1504 **1189** 1r. bistre 1·00 40

1190 Sardar Udham Singh

1992. Sardar Udham Singh (patriot) Commemoration.
1505 **1190** 1r. black and brown 1·00 1·00

1191 Men's Discus

1992. Olympic Games, Barcelona. Multicoloured.
1506 **1191** 1r. Type **1191** 60 20
1507 6r. Women's gymnastics 2·00 1·50
1508 8r. Men's hockey 4·00 3·50
1509 11r. Boxing 4·00 4·50

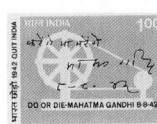

1192 Spinning Wheel Emblem

1992. 50th Anniv of "Quit India" Movement.
1510 **1192** 1r. black and pink 1·75 40
1511 - 2r. black, brown & grey 2·75 3·00
DESIGN: 2r. Mahatma Gandhi and mantra.

1193 Treating Casualty

1992. 50th Anniv of 60th Parachute Field Ambulance.
1512 **1193** 1r. multicoloured 1·50 60

1194 Dr. S. R. Ranganathan and Madras University

1992. Birth Centenary of Shiyali Ramamrita Ranganathan (librarian).
1513 **1194** 1r. blue 2·00 40

1195 Dev Narayan

1992. Phad Scroll Paintings from Rajasthan.
1514 **1195** 5r. multicoloured 2·25 2·00

1196 Hanuman Prasad Poddar

1992. Hanuman Prasad Poddar (editor) Commemoration.
1515 **1196** 1r. green 1·00 1·00

1197 Mikoyan Guerevich MiG-29 Fighter and Ilyushin Il-76 Transport

1992. 60th Anniv of Indian Air Force. Multicoloured.
1516 1r. Type **1197** 18·00 14·00
1517 10r. MiG-27 fighter and Westland Wapiti biplane 18·00 14·00

1198 Lighting Candle

1992. 150th Anniv of Sisters of Jesus and Mary's Arrival in India.
1518 **1198** 1r. blue and grey 50 30

1199 *Sun* (Harshit Prashant Patel)

1992. Children's Day.
1519 **1199** 1r. multicoloured 50 30

1200 Yogiji Maharaj

1992. Birth Centenary of Yogiji Maharaj (Hindu reformer).
1520 **1200** 1r. blue 2·00 60

1201 Army Service Corps Transport

1992. Army Service Corps Commemoration.
1521 **1201** 1r. multicoloured 2·50 75

1202 Stephen Smith and Early Rocket Post Covers

1992. Birth Centenary (1991) of Stephen Smith (rocket mail pioneer).
1522 **1202** 11r. multicoloured 3·50 3·50

1203 Electricity Pylons, Farmers and Crops

1992. 25th Anniv of Haryana State.
1523 **1203** 2r. red, dp green & green 1·00 1·00

1204 Madanlal Dhingra

1992. Madanlal Dhingra (revolutionary) Commemoration.
1524 **1204** 1r. brown, red and green 50 50

1205 Osprey

1992. Birds of Prey. Multicoloured.

1525	2r. Type **1205**	1·25	75
1526	6r. Peregrine falcon	2·25	1·40
1527	8r. Lammergeier	3·50	3·50
1528	11r. Golden eagle	4·50	4·75

1206 Pandit Ravishankar Shukla

1992. Pandit Ravishankar Shukla (social reformer) Commemoration.

1529	**1206**	1r. purple	50	50

1207 William Carey

1993. Bicent of William Carey's Appointment as Baptist Missionary to India.

1530	**1207**	6r. multicoloured	4·00	2·50

1208 Fakirmohan Senapati

1993. Fakirmohan Senapati Commemoration.

1531	**1208**	1r. red	50	50

1209 Workers and C.S.I.R emblem

1993. 50th Anniv of Council of Scientific and Industrial Research.

1532	**1209**	1r. purple	65	50

1210 Parachute Drop and Field Gun

1993. 50th Anniv of 9th Parachute Field Artillery Regiment.

1533	**1210**	1r. multicoloured	1·50	50

1211 Westland Wapiti Biplane

1993. 60th Anniv of No. 1 Squadron, Indian Air Force.

1534	**1211**	1r. multicoloured	1·50	50

1212 Rahul Sankrityayan

1993. Birth Centenary of Rahul Sankrityayan (politician).

1535	**1212**	1r. black, cinnamon and brown	50	50

1213 Parliament Building and Emblem

1993. 89th Inter-Parliamentary Union Conference, New Delhi.

1536	**1213**	1r. black	50	50

1214 Neral Matheran Railway Tank Locomotive, 1905

1993. Mountain Locomotives. Multicoloured.

1537	1r. Type **1214**	70	20
1538	6r. Darjeeling and Himalayan Railway, Class B, 1889	1·40	1·25
1539	8r. Nilgiri Hill Railway, 1914	1·50	2·00
1540	11r. Kalka–Simla Railway, 1934	2·00	3·25

1215 Students and College Building

1993. Centenary of Meerut College.

1541	**1215**	1r. black and brown	50	50

1216 Mahalanobis and Office Block

1993. Prasanta Chandra Mahalanobis Commemoration.

1542	**1216**	1r. brown	1·25	50

1217 Bombay Town Hall

1993. Centenary of Bombay Municipal Corporation.

1543	**1217**	2r. multicoloured	50	50

1218 Abdul Ghaffar Khan and Mountainside

1993. Abdul Ghaffar Khan Commemoration.

1544	**1218**	1r. multicoloured	50	50

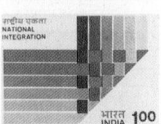

1219 National Integration Emblem

1993. National Integration Campaign.

1545	**1219**	1r. orange and green	35	30

1220 Dadabhai Naoroji and Houses of Parliament, London

1993. Centenary of Dadabhai Naoroji's Election to the House of Commons.

1546	**1220**	6r. multicoloured	4·00	2·75

1221 Swami Vivekananda and Art Institute, Chicago

1993. Centenary of Swami Vivekananda's Chicago Address.

1547	**1221**	2r. orange and grey	1·25	1·25

1222 *Lagerstroemia speciosa*

1993. Flowering Trees.

1548	**1222**	1r. red, green and brown	50	15
1549	–	6r. multicoloured	80	70
1550	–	8r. multicoloured	1·25	1·25
1551	–	11r. multicoloured	1·50	1·75

DESIGNS: 6r. *Cochlospermum religiosum*; 8r. *Erythrina variegata*; 11r. *Thespesia populnea*.

1223 College Building and Emblem

1993. 50th Anniv of College of Military Engineering, Pune.

1552	**1223**	2r. multicoloured	50	50

1224 Dr. Dwaram Venkataswamy Naidu playing Violin

1993. Birth Centenary of Dwaram Venkataswamy Naidu (violinist).

1553	**1224**	1r. red	1·00	75

1225 Children on Elephant

1993. Children's Day.

1554	**1225**	1r. multicoloured	35	20

1226 People with Stress

1993. Heart Care Festival.

1555	**1226**	6r.50 multicoloured	1·50	1·50

1227 Dr. Kotnis performing Operation

1993. Dr. Dwarkanath Kotnis (surgeon) Commemoration.

1556	**1227**	1r. black	1·00	40

1228 Tea Symbol

1993. Indian Tea Production.

1557	**1228**	6r. green and red	3·00	2·00

1229 Papal Seminary Arms and Building

1993. Centenary of Papal Seminary, Pune.

1558	**1229**	6r. multicoloured	5·00	2·00

1230 Meghnad Saha and Eclipse of the Sun

1993. Meghnad Saha (astronomer) Commem.

1559	**1230**	1r. blue	70	70

1231 Speedpost Letter and Arrows circling Globe

1993. Inpex '93 National Stamp Exn, Calcutta. Multicoloura.

1560	1r. Type **1231**	50	20
1561	2r. "Custom-house Wharf, Calcutta" (Sir Charles D'Oyly)	60	70

1232 Dinanath Mangeshkar

1993. Dinanath Mangeshkar Commem.

1562	**1232**	1r. red	75	50

1233 Nargis Dutt

1993. Nargis Dutt Commemoration.

1563	**1233**	1r. red	75	50

1234 S. C. Bose inspecting Troops

1993. 50th Anniv of Indian National Army.

1564	**1234**	1r. green, dp grn & red	1·00	35

1235 Satyendra Nath Bose and Equation

1994. Birth Centenary of Satyendra Nath Bose (scientist).

1565	**1235**	1r. brown	75	50

1236 Dr. Sampurnanand

1994. Dr. Sampurnanand (politician) Commemoration.
1566   **1236**   1r. brown, green and red   75   50

1237 Scene from *Pather Panchali*

1994. Satyajit Ray (film director) Commemoration.
Multicoloured.
1567   6r. Type **1237**   2·75   3·00
1568   11r. Satyajit Ray and Oscar
             (35×35 mm)   3·25   3·50

1238 Dr. Bhatnagar and University Building

1994. Dr. Shanti Swarup Bhatnagar (scientist) Commemoration.
1569   **1238**   1r. blue   75   50

1239 Prajapita Brahma and Memorial

1994. 25th Death Anniv of Prajapita Brahma (social reformer).
1570   **1239**   1r. lilac and blue   75   40

1240 *Window* (K. Subramanyan)

1994. Eighth Triennale Art Exhibition, New Delhi.
1571   **1240**   6r. orange, red and blue   1·25   1·25

1241 Agricultural Products and Tea Garden

1994. Centenary of United Planters' Association of Southern India.
1572   **1241**   2r. multicoloured   1·00   60

1242 Indian Family   **1242a** Sanchi Stupa

1994
1573   **1242**   75p. brown and red   15   10
1574   -   1r. mauve and green   20   10
1575   -   3r. purple   30   10
1576   **1242a**   5r. brown and green   45   20
DESIGNS (as T **1242**)—HORIZ: 1r. Family outside home.
VERT: 3r. Baby and drop of polio vaccine.

1243 Rani Rashmoni on River Bank

1994. Birth Bicentenary of Rani Rashmoni.
1589   **1243**   1r. brown   50   50

1244 Indians releasing Peace Doves

1994. 75th Anniv of Jallianwala Bagh Massacre, Amritsar.
1590   **1244**   1r. black and red   50   30

1245 Chandra Singh Garhwali

1994. 15th Death Anniv of Chandra Singh Garhwali (nationalist).
1591   **1245**   1r. green and orange   50   50

1246 Emblems and National Flag

1994. 75th Anniv of I.L.O.
1592   **1246**   6r. multicoloured   2·00   1·25

1247 Silhouette of Drummer and Logo

1994. 50th Anniv of Indian People's Theatre Association.
1593   **1247**   2r. black, green and gold   1·75   50

1248 Statue of Sepoy

1994. Bicentenary of 4th Battalion, The Madras Regiment.
1594   **1248**   6r.50 multicoloured   1·50   1·25

1249 Institute Building and Emblem

1994. Bicentenary of Institute of Mental Health, Madras.
1595   **1249**   2r. red and blue   75   40

1250 Mahatma Gandhi and Indian Flag

1994. 125th Birth Anniv of Mahatma Gandhi. Multicoloured.
1596   6r. Type **1250**   4·50   3·50
1597   11r. Aspects of Gandhi's life on
             flag (69×34 mm)   5·50   4·50
Nos. 1596/7 were printed together, *se-tenant*, forming
a composite design.

1251 Symbols of Cancer

1994. 16th International Cancer Congress, New Delhi.
1598   **1251**   6r. multicoloured   2·50   1·50

1252 Human Resources Emblem

1994. Human Resource Development World Conference, New Delhi.
1599   **1252**   6r. blue, red and azure   2·50   1·50

1253 "Me and My Pals" (Namarata Amit Shah)

1994. Children's Day.
1600   **1253**   1r. multicoloured   75   30

1254 Family and Emblem

1994. International Year of the Family.
1601   **1254**   2r. multicoloured   50   30

1255 *Taj Mahal* (illustration from Badsha Nama)

1994. Khuda Bakhsh Oriental Public Library, Patna, Commemoration.
1602   **1255**   6r. multicoloured   4·50   1·50

1256 Grey Teal ("Andaman Teal")

1994. Endangered Water Birds. Multicoloured.
1603   1r. Type **1256**   17·00   13·00
1604   6r. Oriental white stork ("East-
             ern White Stork")   23·00   19·00
1605   8r. Black-necked crane   24·00   20·00
·1606   11r. Pink-headed duck   25·00   21·00
   It is reported that Nos. 1603/6 were withdrawn shortly
after issue.

1257 J. R. D. Tata and Aspects of Industrial Symbols

1994. J. R. D. Tata (industrialist) Commemoration.
1607   **1257**   2r. multicoloured   1·00   60

1258 School Building and Computer Class

1994. Centenary of Calcutta Blind School.
1608   **1258**   2r. red, brown and cin-
                  namon   1·25   60

1259 Begum Akhtar

1994. 80th Birth Anniv of Begum Akhtar (singer).
1609   **1259**   2r. multicoloured   12·00   6·00

1260 College Building

1994. 125th Anniv of St. Xavier's College, Bombay.
1610   **1260**   2r. brown and blue   1·00   40

1261 Cavalryman, Infantryman and Dog Handler

1994. 215th Anniv of Remount Veterinary Corps.
1611   **1261**   6r. multicoloured   7·00   3·00

1262 College Building

1994. Bicentenary of College of Engineering, Guindy, Madras.
1612   **1262**   2r. red, brown and black   1·75   50

1263 Righthand Ornament of Bronze Stand

1994. Centenary of Baroda Museum.
1613   **1263**   6r. yellow and brown   8·00   7·00
1614   -   11r. yellow and brown   8·00   7·00
DESIGN: 11r. Bronze Rishabhanatha statue of Buddha on
stand.

1264 "200" and Aspects of Postal Service

1994. Bicentenary of Bombay General Post Office.
1615   **1264**   6r. multicoloured   3·00   2·75

1265 Statue of King Rajaraja Chola

1995. Eighth International Conference Seminar of Tamil Studies, Thanjavur.
1616   **1265**   2r. blue, ultramarine
                  and black   2·25   75

1266 Globe and Emblem

1995. 60th Anniv of National Science Academy.
1617   **1266**   6r. multicoloured   7·00   1·50

1267 Chhotu Ram

1995. Chhotu Ram (social reformer) Commem.
1618   **1267**   1r. brown   1·00   75

1268 Film Reel and Globe

1995. Centenary of Cinema. Multicoloured.
1619   6r. Type **1268**   2·00   2·25
1620   11r. Film reel and early equip-
        ment   2·25   2·50

1269 Symbolic
Hands and
Children

1995. South Asian Association for Regional Cooperation
Youth Year.
1621   **1269**   2r. multicoloured   75   40

1270 Prithviraj
Kapoor and Mask

1995. 50th Anniv of Prithvi Theatre.
1622   **1270**   2r. multicoloured   2·25   60

1271 Field-Marshal
Cariappa

1995. Field-Marshal K. Cariappa Commemoration.
1623   **1271**   2r. multicoloured   1·00   40

1272 Textile
Pattern

1995. "TEX-STYLES INDIA '95" Fair, Bombay.
1624   **1272**   2r. brown, buff and red   65   50

1273 Rafi Ahmed
Kidwai

1995. Birth Centenary (1994) of Rafi Ahmed Kidwai
(politician).
1625   **1273**   1r. brown   50   50

1274 K. L. Saigal, Film Reel
and Gramophone

1995. 90th Birth Anniv of K. L. Saigal (singer).
1626   **1274**   5r. brown, grey and
        black   2·00   1·75

1275 R. S. Ruikar

1995. Birth Centenary of R. S. Ruikar (trade unionist).
1627   **1275**   1r. brown   35   35

1276 Radio Tower, Globe
and Dish Aerial

1995. Centenary of Telecommunications.
1628   **1276**   5r. multicoloured   2·25   1·75

1277 Leaves and
Symbolic Houses

1995. Delhi Development Authority.
1629   **1277**   2r. multicoloured   1·00   35

1278 Handshake

1995. 50th Anniv of United Nations. Multicoloured.
1630   1r. Type **1278**   30   20
1631   6r. Work of U.N. Agencies   70   1·10

1279 Colonnade
on Book Cover

1995. Centenary of Bharti Bhawan Library, Allahabad.
1632   **1279**   6r. black, brown and red   1·40   1·00

1280 Globe showing
South-east Asia

1995. 25th Anniv of Asian-Pacific Postal Training Centre,
Bangkok.
1633   **1280**   10r. multicoloured   2·25   1·75

1281 "75" and
Taurus Formation
Sign

1995. 75th Anniv of Area Army Headquarters, Delhi.
1634   **1281**   2r. multicoloured   75   35

1282 Louis Pasteur
in Laboratory (from
painting by
Edelfelt)

1995. Death Centenary of Louis Pasteur (chemist).
1635   **1282**   5r. black and stone   2·75   2·25

1283 La Martiniere
College, Lucknow

1995. 150th Anniv of La Martiniere College, Lucknow.
1636   **1283**   2r. multicoloured   55   35

1284 Gandhi
in South Africa

1995. India-South Africa Co-operation. 125th Birth Anniv
(1994) of Mahatma Gandhi.
1637   **1284**   1r. red   1·00   1·25
1638   –   2r. red   1·00   1·25
MS1639 68×80 mm. Nos. 1637/8
     (sold at 8r.)   5·00   5·00
DESIGN: 2r. Gandhi wearing dhoti.

1285 Ears of Grain, "50"
and Emblem on Globe

1995. 50th Anniv of F.A.O.
1640   **1285**   5r. multicoloured   2·00   2·00

1286 P. M. Thevar

1995. Pasumpon Muthuramalingam Thevar (social
reformer) Commemoration.
1641   **1286**   1r. red   75   50

1287 W. C.
Rontgen

1995. 150th Birth Anniv of W. C. Rontgen (discoverer of
X-rays).
1642   **1287**   6r. multicoloured   2·50   2·00

1288 Children in
Circle

1995. Children's Day.
1643   **1288**   1r. multicoloured   35   20

1289 Sitar

1995. Communal Harmony Campaign.
1644   **1289**   2r. multicoloured   3·00   1·25

1290 Jat War Memorial,
Bareilly

1995. Bicentenary of Jat Regiments.
1645   **1290**   5r. multicoloured   2·25   2·00

1291 Men of Rajputana
Rifles

1995. 175th Anniv of 5th (Napier's) Battalion, Rajputana
Rifles.
1646   **1291**   5r. multicoloured   2·50   2·00

1292 Sant Tukdoji Maharaj
and Rural Meeting

1995. Sant Tukdoji Maharaj Commemoration.
1647   **1292**   1r. brown   75   50
    Although dated "1993", No. 1647 was not issued until
the date quoted above.

1293 Dr.
Yellapragada
Subbarow

1995. Dr. Yellapragada Subbarow (pharmaceutical
scientist) Commemoration.
1648   **1293**   1r. brown   75   50

1294 Pres. Giani
Zail Singh

1995. First Death Anniv of Pres. Giani Zail Singhn.
1649   **1294**   1r. multicoloured   60   20

1295 Dargah of
Ala Hazrat Barelvi

1995. 75th Death Anniv of Ala Hazrat Barelvi (Moslem
scholar).
1650   **1295**   1r. multicoloured   75   50

1296 Tata Institute
Building

1996. 50th Anniv (1995) of Tata Institute of Fundamental Research.
1651 **1296** 2r. multicoloured 75 50

1297 Kasturba Gandhi

1996. 50th Anniv of the Kasturba Trust.
1652 **1297** 1r. grey, green and red 1·25 30

1298 Sectioned Heart

1996. 100 Years of Cardiac Surgery.
1653 **1298** 5r. multicoloured 2·25 2·00

1299 C. K. Nayudu

1996. Cricketers. Multicoloured.
1654 2r. Type **1299** 95 95
1655 2r. Vinoo Mankad 95 95
1656 2r. Deodhar 95 95
1657 2r. Vijay Merchant 95 95

1300 *Vasant* (Spring) (Ragini Basanti)

1996. Miniature Paintings of the Seasons. Multicoloured.
1658 5r. Type **1300** 1·40 1·75
1659 5r. *Greeshma* (Summer) (Jyestha) 1·40 1·75
1660 5r. *Varsha* (Monsoon) (Rag Megh Malbar) 1·40 1·75
1661 5r. *Hernant* (Winter) (Pausha) 1·40 1·75

1301 Kunjilal Dubey

1996. Kunjilal Dubey Commemoration.
1662 **1301** 1r. brown & chocolate 75 50

1302 Morarji Desai

1996. Birth Centenary of Morarji Desai (former Prime Minister) (1st issue).
1663 **1302** 1r. red 75 75
See also No. 1702.

1303 Blood Pheasant

1996. Himalayan Ecology. Multicoloured.
1664 5r. Type **1303** 1·40 1·75
1665 5r. Markhor (goat) 1·40 1·75
1666 5r. *Meconopsis horridula* (Tsher Gnoin) (plant) 1·40 1·75
1667 5r. *Saussurea simpsoniana* (Sunflower) 1·40 1·75
MS1668 175×105 mm. Nos. 1664/7 (sold at 30r.) 5·00 6·50

1304 S.K.C.G. College Building

1996. Centenary of S.K.C.G. College, Gajapati.
1669 **1304** 1r. brown and cream 75 75

1305 Muhammad Ismail Sahib

1996. Birth Centenary of Muhammad Ismail Sahib (Moslem politician).
1670 **1305** 1r. purple 75 75

1306 Modern Stadium and Ancient Athens

1996. Olympic Games, Atlanta. Multicoloured.
1671 5r. Type **1306** 1·00 1·25
1672 5r. Hand holding Olympic torch 1·00 1·25

1307 Sister Alphonsa

1996. 50th Death Anniv of Sister Alphonsa.
1673 **1307** 1r. black and blue 75 75

1308 "Communications"

1996. 125th Anniv of Videsh Sanchar Nigam Limited (telecommunications company).
1674 **1308** 5r. multicoloured 2·00 1·75

1309 Sir Pherozeshah Mehta

1996. 150th Birth Anniv of Sir Pherozeshah Mehta (politician).
1675 **1309** 1r. blue 1·00 75

1310 Ahilyabai

1996. Death Bicentenary (1995) of Ahilyabai (ruler of Holkar).
1676 **1310** 2r. brown and deep brown 75 75

1311 Chembai Vaidyanatha Bhagavathar

1996. Birth Centenary of Chembai Vaidyanatha Bhagavathar (musician).
1677 **1311** 1r. brown and green 75 75

1312 Red Junglefowl Cockerel

1996. 20th World Poultry Congress, New Delhi.
1678 **1312** 5r. multicoloured 3·00 2·25

1313 Rani Gaidinliu

1996. Rani Gaidinliu (Naga leader) Commemoration.
1679 **1313** 1r. blue 75 75

1314 Nath Pai

1996. 25th Death Anniv of Nath Pai (politician).
1680 **1314** 1r. blue 75 75

1315 Exhibition Logo

1996. INDEPEX '97 International Stamp Exhibition, New Delhi (1st issue).
1681 **1315** 2r. gold and purple 60 60
See also Nos. 1713/16, 1722/5, 1741/4 and 1758/61.

1316 Historic Steam Locomotives

1996. 25th Anniv of National Rail Museum.
1682 **1316** 5r. multicoloured 4·75 2·25

1317 Jananayak Debeswar Sarmah

1996. Birth Centenary of Jananayak Debeswar Sarmah (politician).
1683 **1317** 2r. brown and deep brown 75 75

1318 Monument and Sikh Sentry

1996. 150th Anniv of Sikh Regiment.
1684 **1318** 5r. multicoloured 2·25 2·00

1319 Dr. Salim Ali

1996. Birth Centenary of Salim Ali (ornithologist). Multicoloured.
1685 8r. Type **1319** 4·50 4·50
1686 11r. Painted storks at nest 4·50 4·50
Nos. 1685/6 were printed together, *se-tenant*, with the backgrounds forming a composite design.

1320 "Indian Village" (child's painting)

1996. Children's Day.
1687 **1320** 8r. multicoloured 2·00 2·00

1321 Seeds in a Test-tube

1996. Second International Crop Science Congress.
1688 **1321** 2r. multicoloured 75 55

1322 Regimental Shrine

1996. Bicentenary of 2nd Battalion, Grenadiers.
1689 **1322** 5r. multicoloured 1·75 1·75

1323 Woman writing

1996. Tenth Anniv of South Asian Association for Regional Co-operation (S.A.A.R.C.).
1690 **1323** 11r. multicoloured 1·75 1·75

1324 Abai
Konunbaev

1996. 150th Birth Anniv (1995) of Abai Konunbaev
(Kazakh poet).
1691   **1324**   5r. chestnut, brown
and lilac   1·50   1·50

1325 Buglers in front
of Memorial

1996. 25th Anniv of the Liberation of Bangladesh.
1692   **1325**   2r. multicoloured   65   40

1326 Vivekananda Rock Memoria

1996. 25th Anniv of Vivekananda Rock Memorial,
Kanyakumari.
1693   **1326**   5r. multicoloured   2·75   2·25

1327 Victorian
Doctors performing
Operation

1996. 150th Anniv of Anaesthetics.
1694   **1327**   5r. multicoloured   3·00   1·50

1328 Roorkee University
Buildings

1997. 150th Anniv of Roorkee University.
1695   **1328**   8r. multicoloured   1·50   1·75

1329 Dr.
Vrindavanlal Verma

1997. Dr. Vrindavanlal Verma (writer) Commemoration.
1696   **1329**   2r. red   75   75

1330 Field Post Office

1997. 25th Anniv of Army Postal Service Corps.
1697   **1330**   5r. multicoloured   2·50   1·75

1331 Subhas
Chandra Bose

1997. Birth Centenary of Subhas Chandra Bose
(nationalist).
1698   **1331**   1r. brown   75   75

1332 Jose Marti

1997. Jose Marti (Cuban writer) Commemoration.
1699   **1332**   11r. black and pink   2·00   1·75

1333 Conference Logo

1997. "Towards Partnership between Men and Women in
Politics" Inter-Parliamentary Conference, New Delhi.
1700   **1333**   5r. multicoloured   1·00   1·00

1334 St. Andrew's
Church

1997. St. Andrew's Church, Egmore, Madras
Commemoration.
1701   **1334**   8r. multicoloured   1·50   1·75

1335 Morarji Desai

1997. Birth Centenary of Morarji Desai (former Prime
Minister) (2nd issue).
1702   **1335**   1r. brown and deep
brown   75   75

1336 Shyam Lal
Gupt

1997. Birth Centenary (1996) of Shyam Lal Gupt (social
reformer).
1703   **1336**   1r. cinnamon and brown   75   75

1337 Saint
Dnyaneshwar

1997. 700th Death Anniv (1996) of Saint Dnyaneshwar.
1704   **1337**   5r. multicoloured   1·00   1·25

1338 Parijati Tree

1997. Parijati Tree. Multicoloured.
1705   5r. Type **1338**   1·50   1·50
1706   6r. Parijati flower   1·50   1·50

1339 Monument, Rashtriya
Military College

1997. 75th Anniv of Rashtriya Military College, Dehra
Dun.
1707   **1339**   2r. multicoloured   1·25   75

1340 Ram Manohar
Lohia

1997. Ram Manohar Lohia Commemoration.
1708   **1340**   1r. multicoloured   75   75

1341 Society
Centenary Emblem

1997. Centenary of the Philatelic Society of India.
Multicoloured.
1709   2r. Type **1341**   2·00   2·00
1710   2r. Cover of first "Philatelic
Journal of India", 1897   2·00   2·00

1342 Gyandith
Award Winners

1997. Gyandith Award Scheme.
1711   **1342**   2r. multicoloured   75   1·00

1343 Madhu
Limaye

1997. Madhu Limaye Commemoration.
1712   **1343**   2r. green   75   1·00

1344 Nalanda Monastic
University

1997. INDEPEX '97 International Stamp Exhibition,
New Delhi (2nd issue). Buddhist Cultural Sites.
Multicoloured.
1713   2r. Type **1344**   1·40   1·40
1714   6r. The Bodhi Tree, Bodhgaya 1·40   1·40
1715   10r. Stupa and Pillar, Vaishali 1·40   1·40
1716   11r. Stupa, Kushinagar   1·40   1·40

1345 Pandit
Omkarnath Thakur

1997. Birth Centenary of Pandit Omkarnath Thakur
(musician).
1717   **1345**   2r. black and blue   1·25   1·00

1346 Ram Sewak
Yadav

1997. Ram Sewak Yadav (politician) Commemoration.
1718   **1346**   2r. brown   75   75

1347 Sibnath
Banerjee

1997. Birth Centenary of Sibnath Banerjee (trade
unionist).
1719   **1347**   2r. red and purple   75   75

1348 Rukmini
Lakshmipathi

1997. Rukmini Lakshmipathi (social reformer)
Commemoration.
1720   **1348**   2r. brown   1·50   75

1349 Sri
Basaveswara

1997. Sri Basaveswara (reformer and statesman)
Commemoration.
1721   **1349**   2r. purple   75   75

1350 Gopalpur-on-Sea
Beach

1997. INDEPEX '97 International Stamp Exhibition, New
Delhi (3rd issue). Beaches. Multicoloured.
1722   2r. Type **1350**   50   30
1723   6r. Kovalam   90   75
1724   10r. Anjuna   1·25   1·60
1725   11r. Bogmalo   1·25   1·60

1351 Newspaper
Masthead

1997. 50th Anniv of *Swatantra Bharat* (Hindi daily
newspaper).
1726   **1351**   2r. multicoloured   75   50

1352 Shah Nawaz Khan,
P. K. Sahgal and G. S.
Dhillon

1997. I.N.A. Trials Commemoration.
1727   **1352**   2r. multicoloured   75   75

1353 Sir Ronald Ross (bacteriologist)

1997. Centenary of the Discovery of the Malaria Parasite by Sir Ronald Ross.
1728	**1353**	2r. grey	1·50	1·00

1354 Firaq Gorakhpuri

1997. Birth Centenary (1996) of Firaq Gorakhpuri (poet).
1729	**1354**	2r. brown	75	75

1355 Bhaktivedanta Swami

1997. Birth Centenary (1996) of Bhaktivedanta Swami (philosopher).
1730	**1355**	5r. brown	1·50	1·50

1356 Parachute Regiment Emblem

1997. Bicentenary of 2nd (Maratha) Battalion, Parachute Regiment.
1731	**1356**	2r. multicoloured	1·25	60

1357 Fossil of "Birbalsahnia divyadarshanii"

1997. 50th Anniv of Birbal Sahni Institute of Palaeobotany, Lucknow. Plant Fossils. Multicoloured.
1732		2r. Type **1357**	1·50	1·00
1733		2r. "Glossopteris"	1·50	1·00
1734		6r. "Pentoxylon" (reconstruction)	2·75	1·75
1735		10r. "Williamsonia sewardiana" (model)	3·75	4·00

1358 Swami Brahmanand

1997. Swami Brahmanand (social reformer) Commemoration.
1736	**1358**	2r. grey and stone	75	75

1359 Sir William Jones

1997. 250th Birth Anniv (1996) of Sir William Jones (Sanskrit scholar).
1737	**1359**	4r. multicoloured	1·00	1·25

1360 Lawrence School Building and Crest

1997. 150th Anniv of Lawrence School, Sanawar.
1738	**1360**	2r. multicoloured	1·50	60

1361 V. K. Krishna Menon

1997. Birth Centenary (1996) of V. K. Krishna Menon (politician).
1739	**1361**	2r. red	75	75

1362 Policemen and Globe

1997. 66th General Assembly Session of ICPO Interpol.
1740	**1362**	4r. multicoloured	1·00	1·25

1363 Woman from Arunachal Pradesh

1997. INDEPEX '97 International Stamp Exhibition, New Delhi (4th issue). Women's Costumes. Multicoloured.
1741		2r. Type **1363**	50	50
1742		6r. Gujarat costume	1·10	1·10
1743		10r. Ladakh costume	1·40	1·60
1744		11r. Kerala costume	1·40	1·60

1364 Students in Meditation, Astachai

1997. Centenary of Scindia School, Gwalior. Multicoloured.
1745		5r. Type **1364**	5·00	2·00
1746		5r. Gwalior Fort	5·00	2·00

1365 *Ocimum sanctum*

1997. Medicinal Plants. Multicoloured.
1747		2r. Type **1365**	50	50
1748		5r. *Curcuma longa*	70	80
1749		10r. *Rauvolfia serpentina*	1·00	1·25
1750		11r. *Aloe barbadensis*	1·00	1·25

1366 Sant Kavi Sunderdas

1997. 400th Birth Anniv (1996) of Sant Kavi Sunderdas (Hindu theologian).
1751	**1366**	2r. brown	1·50	1·00

1367 K. Rama Rao

1997. Birth Centenary of K. Rama Rao (parliamentarian and journalist).
1752	**1367**	2r. bistre and brown	1·50	1·00

1368 Jawaharlal Nehru and Child

1997. Children's Day.
1753	**1368**	2r. multicoloured	75	35

1369 Animals on Globe

1997. World Convention on Reverence for All Life, Pune.
1754	**1369**	4r. multicoloured	2·00	1·50

1370 Hazari Prasad Dwivedi

1997. 90th Birth Anniv of Hazari Prasad Dwivedi (scholar).
1755	**1370**	2r. grey	75	75

1371 Mother Teresa

1997. INDEPEX '97 International Stamp Exhibition, New Delhi (5th issue). Mother Teresa Commemoration. Sheet 81×68 mm.
MS1756	**1371**	45r. multicoloured	7·00	7·00

1372 Vallabhbhai Patel and Marchers

1997. 47th Death Anniv of Vallabhbhai Patel (politician).
1757	**1372**	2r. brown	75	75

1373 Head Post Office, Pune

1997. INDEPEX '97 International Stamp Exhibition, New Delhi (6th issue). Post Office Heritage. Multicoloured.
1758		2r. Type **1373**	40	40
1759		6r. River mail barge	60	70
1760		10r. Jal Cooper (philatelist) and cancellations	90	1·25
1761		11r. "Hindoostan" (paddle-steamer)	90	1·25

1374 50th Anniversary Emblem

1997. 50th Anniv of Indian Armed Forces.
1762	**1374**	2r. multicoloured	1·00	60

1375 Dr. Pattabhi Sitaramayya

1997. Dr. Pattabhi Sitaramayya (politician) Commemoration.
1763	**1375**	2r. brown	75	75

1376 Father Jerome d'Souza and Cathedral

1997. Birth Centenary of Father Jerome d'Souza (academic).
1764	**1376**	2r. brown	75	75

1377 Ram Prasad Bismil and Ashfaqullah Khan

1997. 70th Death Anniv of Ram Prasad Bismil and Ashfaqullah Khan (revolutionaries).
1765	**1377**	2r. brown	75	75

1378 Jail Buildings

1997. Cellular Jail, Port Blair.
1766	**1378**	2r. multicoloured	75	60

1379 Sword and Kukri

1998. 50th Anniv of 11th Gorkha Rifles.
1767	**1379**	4r. multicoloured	2·25	1·50

1380 Nahar Singh

1998. 140th Death Anniv of Nahar Singh (Sikh leader).
1768	**1380**	2r. purple	1·00	75

1381 Nanak Singh

1998. Birth Centenary (1997) of Nanak Singh (writer).
1769 **1381** 2r. red   75   75

1382 Rotary International
Emblem

1998. Meeting of Rotary International Council on
Legislation, Delhi.
1770 **1382** 8r. yellow and blue   1·00   1·25

1383 Maharana
Pratap

1998. 400th Death Anniv of Maharana Pratap (Rajput
leader).
1771 **1383** 2r. purple   75   75

1384 V. S.
Khandekar

1998. Birth Centenary of V. S. Khandekar (writer).
1772 **1384** 2r. red   75   75

1385 Elephant
and Dancers

1998. India Tourism Day.
1773 **1385** 10r. multicoloured   2·50   2·25

1386 Jagdish Chandra Jain

1998. Jagdish Chandra Jain (educationist)
Commemoration.
1774 **1386** 2r. brown   75   75

1387 Gandhi as a
Young Man and
Peasants in Fields

1998. 50th Death Anniv of Mahatma Gandhi.
Multicoloured.
1775 2r. Type **1387**   65   75
1776 6r. Woman weaving and Gandhi
          distributing food   85   95
1777 10r. Gandhi collecting salt   1·10   1·25
1778 11r. Gandhi carrying flag   1·10   1·25
   Nos. 1775/8 were printed together, *se-tenant*, with the
backgrounds forming a composite design.

1388 A.
Vedaratnam

1998. Birth Centenary (1997) of A. Vedaratnam (social
reformer).
1779 **1388** 2r. purple   1·00   75

1389 Anniversary
Emblem

1998. 50th Anniv of Universal Declaration of Human
Rights.
1780 **1389** 6r. multicoloured   1·00   1·00

1390 Savitribai Phule

1998. Death Centenary (1997) of Savitribai Phule
(educational reformer).
1781 **1390** 2r. brown   75   75

1391 Sir Syed
Ahmad Khan

1998. Death Centenary of Sir Syed Ahmed Khan (social
reformer).
1782 **1391** 2r. brown   75   75

1392 Barren Landscape
and Living Forest

1998. First Assembly Meeting of Global Environment
Facility, Delhi.
1783 **1392** 11r. multicoloured   2·00   1·75

1393 Ramana Maharshi

1998. Ramana Maharshi (religious leader)
Commemoration.
1784 **1393** 2r. lilac   75   75

1394 College
Arms

1998. 50th Anniv of Defence Services Staff College,
Wellington.
1785 **1394** 6r. red   1·40   1·10

1395 Diesel Train on Viaduct

1998. Completion of Konkan Railway.
1786 **1395** 8r. multicoloured   2·50   2·00

1396 Narayan
Ganesh Goray

1998. Narayan Ganesh Goray (social reformer)
Commemoration.
1787 **1396** 2r. brown   75   75

1397 Dr. Zakir
Husain

1998. Birth Centenary (1997) of Dr. Zakir Husain (former
President of India).
1788 **1397** 2r. brown   75   75

1398 Mohammed
Abdurahiman
Shahib

1998. Mohammed Abdurahiman Shahib (nationalist)
Commemoration.
1789 **1398** 2r. brown   75   75

1399 Lokanayak
Omeo Kumar Das

1998. Lokanayak Omeo Kumar Das (writer)
Commemoration.
1790 **1399** 2r. brown   75   75

1400 Vakkom Abdul
Khader, Satyendra
Chandra Bardhan and
Fouja Singh

1998. Nationalist Martyrs Commemoration.
1791 **1400** 2r. brown and cinnamon   75   75

1401 Bishnu Dey,
Tarashankar
Bandopadhyay
and Ashapurna
Devi

1998. Bangla Jnanpith Literary Award Winners
Commemoration.
1792 **1401** 2r. brown   75   75

1402 Big Ben,
London

1998. 50th Anniv of First Air India International Flight.
1793 5r. Type **1402**   2·00   2·00
1794 6r. Lockheed Super Constel-
          lation airliner, globe and
          Gateway of India, Bombay
          (55×35 mm)   2·00   2·00
   Nos. 1793/4 were printed together, *se-tenant*, forming
a composite design.

1403 Dr. C.
Vijiaraghavachariar

1998. Dr. C. Vijiaraghachariar (lawyer and social
reformer) Commemoration.
1795 **1403** 2r. brown   75   75

1404 Anniversary Logo
and Savings Stream

1998. 50th Anniv of National Savings Organization.
Multicoloured.
1796 5r. Type **1404**   2·25   2·25
1797 6r. Hand dropping coin into jar   2·25   2·25
   Nos. 1796/7 were printed together, *se-tenant*, forming
a composite design.

1405 Bhagawan
Gopinathji

1998. Birth Centenary of Bhagawan Gopinathji (spiritual
leader).
1798 **1405** 3r. brown   75   75

1406 Ardeshir and Pirojsha
Godrej

1998. Centenary of Godrej (industrial conglomerate).
1799 **1406** 3r. green   65   50

1407 Aruna Asaf
Ali

1998. Aruna Asaf Ali (nationalist) Commemoration.
1800 **1407** 3r. brown   75   75

1408 Iswar Chandra
Vidyasagar (educationist)
and College

1998. 125th Anniv of Vidyasagar College, Calcutta.
1801 **1408** 2r. black   75   75

1409 Shivpujan Sahai

1998. Shivpujan Sahai (writer) Commemoration.
1802 **1409** 2r. brown   75   75

1410 Red Fort, Delhi,
and Spinning Wheel

1998. Homage to Martyrs for Independence.
Multicoloured.
1803 3r. Type **1410**   4·75   4·00
1804 8r. Industrial and scientific de-
          velopment in modern India   4·75   4·00

1411 Gostha
Behari Paul

1998. Gostha Paul (footballer) Commemoration.
1805   **1411**   3r. purple   75   75

1412 Youth Hostel
and Logo

1998. 50th Anniv of Youth Hostels Association of India.
1806   **1412**   5r. multicoloured   65   65

1413 Uniforms, Badge
and Tank

1998. Bicentenary of 4th Battalion, Guards' Brigade (1
Rajput).
1807   **1413**   6r. multicoloured   1·40   1·00

1414 Bhai
Kanhaiyaji

1998. Bhai Kanhaiyaji (Sikh social reformer)
Commemoration.
1808   **1414**   2r. red   75   75

1415 Emblem and
Diagram of Head

1998. 20th International Congress of Radiology.
1809   **1415**   8r. multicoloured   1·50   1·50

1416 Dove of
Peace and Boy
reading Book

1998. 26th International Books for Young People
Congress.
1810   **1416**   11r. multicoloured   1·50   1·75

1417 Dr. Tristao
Braganza Cunha

1998. Dr. Tristao Braganza Cunha (nationalist)
Commemoration.
1811   **1417**   3r. brown   75   75

1418 Jananeta
Hijam Irawat
Singh

1998. Jananeta Hijam Irawat Singh (social reformer)
Commemoration.
1812   **1418**   3r. brown   75   75

1419 Women
Aviators and
Bi-plane

1998. Indian Women's Participation in Aviation.
1813   **1419**   8r. blue   1·75   1·40

1420 Acharya Tulsi

1998. First Death Anniv of Acharya Tulsi (Jain religious
leader).
1814   **1420**   3r. brown and orange   70   50

1421 Girl and Bird
reading Book

1998. Children's Day.
1815   **1421**   3r. multicoloured   70   50

1422 I.N.S. *Delhi*
(destroyer)

1998. Navy Day.
1816   **1422**   3r. multicoloured   1·75   1·00

1423 Mounted
Trumpeter

1998. 225th Anniv of President's Bodyguard.
1817   **1423**   3r. multicoloured   1·75   1·00

1424 Sir David
Sassoon and
Library, Bombay

1998. David Sassoon Library and Reading Room
Commemoration.
1818   **1424**   3r. ultramarine and blue   75   75

1425 Regimental Arms
and Soldier

1998. Bicentenary of 2nd Battalion, Rajput Regiment.
1819   **1425**   3r. multicoloured   1·50   1·00

1426 Army Postal Service
Centre, Kamptee

1998. 50th Anniv of Army Postal Service Training Centre.
1820   **1426**   3r. multicoloured   1·25   1·00

1427 Connemara Public
Library, Madras

1998. Centenary (1996) of Connemara Public Library.
1821   **1427**   3r. brown and ochre   70   60

1428 Neem Tree
and Leaves

1998. 50th Anniv of The Indian Pharmaceutical Congress
Association.
1822   **1428**   3r. multicoloured   1·00   60

1429 Baba
Raghav Das

1998. 40th Death Anniv of Baba Raghav Das (social
reformer).
1823   **1429**   2r. violet   75   75

1430 Lt. Indra Lal
Roy D.F.C.

1998. Birth Centenary of Indra Lal Roy (First World War
pilot).
1824   **1430**   3r. multicoloured   1·25   1·00

1431 Sant Gadge Baba

1998. Sant Gadge Baba (social reformer)
Commemoration.
1825   **1431**   3r. lilac, blue and black   60   60

1432 Rudra Veena
(stringed instrument)

1998. Musical Instruments. Multicoloured.
1826   2r. Type **1432**   55   20
1827   6r. Flute   85   60
1828   8r. Pakhawaj (wooden barrel
          drum)   1·25   1·40
1829   10r. Sarod (stringed instrument)   1·40   1·60

1433 *Chicoreus brunneus*
(Murex shell)

1998. Shells. Multicoloured.
1830   3r. Type **1433**   70   70
1831   3r. *Cassis cornuta* (horned
          helmet)   70   70
1832   3r. *Cypraea staphylaea* (cowrie)   70   70
1833   11r. *Lambis lambis* (common
          spider conch)   1·50   1·75

1434 Stylized Police
Officers

1999. 50th Anniv of Indian Police Service.
1834   **1434**   3r. multicoloured   1·25   60

1435 Modern Weapon
Systems

1999. 40th Anniv of Defence Research and Development
Organization.
1835   **1435**   10r. multicoloured   2·75   1·90

1436 Issue of
Orunodoi
(Assamese
newspaper) for
January, 1846

1999. 150th Anniv of Newspapers in Assam.
1836   **1436**   3r. black, yellow and
                        orange   1·00   60

1437 College Building

1999. Centenary of Hindu College, Delhi.
1837   **1437**   3r. blue   60   50

1438 National Defence
Academy and Military
Equipment

1999. 50th Anniv of National Defence Academy,
Khadakwasla.
1838   **1438**   3r. multicoloured   1·60   75

1439 College Building

1999. 175th Anniv of Sanskrit College, Calcutta.
1839   **1439**   3r. brown and ochre   70   60

1440 Patnaik and Tugs

1999. Biju Patnaik (social reformer) Commemoration.
1840   **1440**   3r. brown and green   1·25   1·00

1441 Globe
and Satellite
Dish

1999. 50th Anniv of Press Trust of India.
1841   **1441**   15r. multicoloured   1·40   1·75

1442 "Apsara removing a Thorn from her Foot" (temple statue)

1999. Millenary of the Khajuraho Temples.
1842   **1442**   15r. deep brown, light brown and black   1·40   1·75

1443 Dr. K. B. Hedgewar

1999. Dr. Keshavrao Hedgewar (founder of Rashtriya Swayamsevak Sangha) Commemoration.
1843   **1443**   3r. multicoloured   75   1·00

1444 Terracotta Model Boat from Lothal, 2200 B.C., and Seal

1999. Maritime Heritage. Multicoloured.
1844   3r. Type **1444**   65   70
1845   3r. Ghurab (sailing ship) of Kanhoji Angre, 1700   65   70

1445 Anandpur Sahib Temple

1999. 300th Anniv of the Khalsa Panth (Sikh Order).
1846   **1445**   3r. multicoloured   1·25   75

1446 Bethune College

1999. 150th Anniv of Bethune Collegiate School, Calcutta.
1847   **1446**   3r. green   75   50

1447 Plane, Satellite and Rocket orbiting Globe

1999. Technology Day.
1848   **1447**   3r. multicoloured   65   50

1448 Mumbai Port

1999. 125th Anniv of Mumbai (Bombay) Port Trust.
1849   **1448**   3r. blue   1·00   50

1449 Handshake and Airliner

1999. Mizoram Accord (peace agreement) Commemoration.
1850   **1449**   3r. multicoloured   70   50

1450 Gulzarilal Nanda

1999. Birth Centenary of Gulzarilal Nanda (former Prime Minster).
1851   **1450**   3r. multicoloured   70   70

1451 Jijabai and Chatrapati Shivaji

1999. Jijabai (mother of Chatrapati Shivaji (Maratha leader)) Commemoration.
1852   **1451**   3r. purple   60   50

1452 P. S. Kumaraswamy Raja

1999. P. S. Kumaraswamy Raja (politician) Commemoration.
1853   **1452**   3r. brown and blue   75   75

1453 Balai Chand Mukhopadhyay

1999. Birth Centenary of Balai Chand Mukhopadhyay ("Banaphool") (Bengali writer).
1854   **1453**   3r. blue   75   75

1454 River Sindhu, Ladakh

1999. Sindhu Darshan Festival.
1855   **1454**   3r. multicoloured   75   55

1455 Soldier and Young Girl

1999. 50th Anniv of Geneva Conventions.
1856   **1455**   15r. black and red   1·25   1·75

1456 Sardar Ajit Singh

1999. Heroes of Struggle for Freedom.
1857   **1456**   3r. brown and red   1·00   1·00
1858   -   3r. brown and blue   1·00   1·00
1859   -   3r. blue and red   1·00   1·00
1860   -   3r. purple and drab   1·00   1·00
DESIGNS: No. 1858, Swami Ramanand Teerth; No. 1859, Vishwambhar Dayalu Tripathi; No. 1860, Swami Keshawanand.

1457 Kalki Krishnamurthy

1999. Birth Centenary of Kalki Krishnamurthy (Tamil writer).
1861   **1457**   3r. grey   75   75

1458 Ramdhari Sinha

1999. Ramdhari Sinha "Dinkar" (poet) Commemoration.
1862   **1458**   3r. brown and blue   75   75

1459 Jhaverchand Kalidas Meghani and Graves

1999. Jhaverchand Kalidas Meghani (writer) Commemoration.
1863   **1459**   3r. red and green   75   75

1460 Rambrikish Benipuri and Statue of Horse

1999. Rambrikish Benipuri (writer and journalist) Commemoration.
1864   **1460**   3r. brown and light brown   75   75

1461 Kazi Nazrul Islam

1999. Birth Centenary of Kazi Nazrul Islam (Bengali poet).
1865   **1461**   3r. sepia and yellow   75   75

1462 Arati Gupta

1999. Arati Gupta (swimmer) Commemoration.
1866   **1462**   3r. multicoloured   75   75

1463 Lionesses

1999. Endangered Species. Asiatic Lion. Multicoloured.
1867   3r. Type **1463**   1·00   75
1868   3r. Lions and lionesses lying down   1·00   75
1869   3r. Lioness with cubs   1·00   75
1870   15r. Two lions   1·75   2·25

1464 A. D. Shroff

1999. A. D. Shroff (economist) Commemoration.
1871   **1464**   3r. green and brown   75   75

1465 A. B. Walawalkar and Map

1999. A. B. Walawalkar (railway engineer) Commemoration.
1872   **1465**   3r. purple   1·00   75

1466 Chhaganlal K. Parekh and Medical Staff with Child

1999. Chhaganlal K. Parekh (social reformer) Commemoration.
1873   **1466**   3r. blue and brown   75   55

1467 Dr. T. M. A. Pai and Hospital

1999. 20th Death Anniv of Dr. T. M. A. Pai (educator).
1874   **1467**   3r. chocolate and stone   75   75

1468 Chhau Dance Masks

1999. 125th Anniv of Universal Postal Union. Traditional Arts and Crafts. Multicoloured.
1875   3r. Type **1468**   60   60
1876   3r. Elephant and horseman (Rathva wall painting) (vert)   60   60
1877   3r. Man ploughing (Muria ritual collar)   60   60
1878   15r. Angami ornament (vert)   1·75   2·50

1469 Veerapandia Kattabomman

1999. Death Bicentenary of Veerapandia Kattabomman (ruler of Panchalankuruchi).
1879   **1469**   3r. green   75   75

1470 Ustad Allauddin Khan Saheb (sarod player)

1999. Modern Masters of Indian Classical Music. Multicoloured.
1880   3r. Type **1470**   75   75
1881   3r. Musiri Subramania Iyer (singer)   75   75

1471 Brigadier Rajinder Singh

1999. Birth Centenary of Brigadier Rajinder Singh (First recipient of M.V.C. medal).
1882   **1471**   3r. purple   75   75

1472 Elephant and Rhinoceros

1999. Children's Day.
| 1883 | **1472** | 3r. multicoloured | 75 | 50 |

1473 Dam and Pumping Station

1999. Sri Sathya Sai Water Supply Project.
| 1884 | **1473** | 3r. multicoloured | 1·25 | 70 |

1474 Supreme Court, New Delhi

1999. 50th Anniv of Supreme Court of India.
| 1885 | **1474** | 3r. multicoloured | 65 | 50 |

1475 A. Vaidyanatha Iyer and Temple Tower

1999. March of Progress.
1886	**1475**	3r. red	1·00	85
1887	-	3r. brown and green	1·00	85
1888	-	3r. buff and black	1·00	85
1889	-	3r. brown and green	1·00	85

DESIGNS: No. 1887, Dr. Punjabrao Deshmukh and symbols of agriculture; 1888, Indulal Kanaiyalal Yagnik and newspaper; 1889, Kakkan and machinery.

1476 Aspects of Thermal Power

1999. Centenary of Thermal Power.
| 1890 | **1476** | 3r. chocolate and brown | 65 | 50 |

1477 *Hindustan Times* Front Pages from 1950 and 1999

1999. 75th Anniv of *Hindustan Times* Newspaper.
| 1891 | **1477** | 15r. multicoloured | 1·40 | 2·00 |

1478 Three Faces ("Small Family by Choice")

1999. 50th Anniv of Family Planning Association of India.
| 1892 | **1478** | 3r. multicoloured | 50 | 40 |

1479 Hand inside Flame in front of Cross

1999. 2000th Birth Anniv of Jesus Christ.
| 1893 | **1479** | 3r. multicoloured | 75 | 50 |

1480 Tabo Monastery and Mountains

1999. New Millennium. Unity in Diversity. Multicoloured.
| 1894 | 5r. Type **1480** | | 7·00 | 4·50 |
| 1895 | 10r. Traditional scene | | 7·00 | 4·50 |

1481 Agni II Rocket and Dove

2000. 41st Anniv of Defence Research and Development Organization.
| 1896 | **1481** | 3r. multicoloured | 65 | 50 |

1482 Sunrise

2000. New Millennium.
| 1897 | **1482** | 3r. multicoloured | 40 | 40 |

1483 Stylized Outline of Gandhi as Map of India

2000. 50th Anniv of Republic (1st issue).
| 1898 | **1483** | 3r. black and red | 1·00 | 50 |

1484 Karam Singh and Regimental Badge

2000. 50th Anniv of Republic (2nd issue). Gallantry Award Winners. Multicoloured.
1899	3r. Type **1484**		1·25	1·25
1900	3r. Abdul Hamid and armed jeep		1·25	1·25
1901	3r. Albert Ekka, hand grenades and knife		1·25	1·25
1902	3r. N. J. S. Sekhon and jet fighter		1·25	1·25
1903	3r. M. N. Mulla and warship		1·25	1·25

1485 Batagur Terrapin

2000. Millepex 2000 Stamp Exhibition, Bhubaneshwar. Endangered Species. Multicoloured.
| 1904 | 3r. Type **1485** | | 1·00 | 1·00 |
| 1905 | 3r. Olive Ridley turtle | | 1·00 | 1·00 |

1486 Balwantrai Mehta

2000. Balwantrai Mehta (former Chief Minister of Gujarot) Commemoration.
| 1906 | **1486** | 3r. multicoloured | 75 | 75 |

1487 Dr. Harekrushna Mahatab

2000. Dr. Harekrushna Mahatab (former Chief Minister of Orissa) Commemoration.
| 1907 | **1487** | 3r. multicoloured | 75 | 75 |

1488 Arun Kumar Chanda

2000. Arun Kumar Chanda (trade union leader) Commemoration.
| 1908 | **1488** | 3r. multicoloured | 75 | 75 |

1489 Patna Medical College

2000. 75th Anniv of Patna Medical College.
| 1909 | **1489** | 3r. multicoloured | 75 | 60 |

1490 Dr. Burgula Ramakrishna Rao

2000. Birth Centenary (1999) of Dr. Burgula Ramakrishna Rao (Hyderabad Chief Minister).
| 1910 | **1490** | 3r. brown and yellow | 75 | 75 |

1491 Potti Sriramulu

2000. Potti Sriramulu (Harijan activist) Commemoration.
| 1911 | **1491** | 3r. red | 75 | 75 |

1492 Basawon Sinha

2000. Basawon Sinha (politician) Commemoration.
| 1912 | **1492** | 3r. multicoloured | 75 | 75 |

1493 Siroi Lily

2000. Indepex Asiana 2000 International Stamp Exhibition, Calcutta (1st issue). Flora and Fauna of Manipur and Tripura. Multicoloured.
1913	3r. Type **1493**		55	55
1914	3r. Sangai deer		55	55
1915	3r. Wild guava		55	55
1916	15r. Slow loris		1·40	1·75
MS1917	160×112 mm. Nos. 1913/16		5·00	5·00

See also Nos. 1934/8 and 1966/72.

1494 Maharshi Dayananda Saraswati, Flame and Pages

2000. 125th Anniv of Arya Samaj (philosophical movement).
| 1918 | **1494** | 3r. multicoloured | 1·25 | 80 |

1495 Kankrej Breed

2000. Indigenous Breeds of Cattle. Multicoloured.
1919	3r. Type **1495**	65	65
1920	3r. Kangayam	65	65
1921	3r. Gir	65	65
1922	15r. Hallikar	1·75	2·25

1496 Blackbuck   **1497** Leopard Cat

2000. Wildlife.
1923	**1496**	25p. brown	25	10
1924	-	50p. brown	25	10
1925	-	1r. blue	50	10
1925a	-	2r. purple	25	10
1926	-	3r. violet	25	10
1927	-	4r. red	50	15
1928	**1497**	5r. brown and green	30	20
1929	-	10r. orange, brn & grn	1·00	30
1930	-	15r. red, brn & dp brn	1·00	45
1931	-	20r. yellow and green	1·50	55
1932	-	50r. red, brown & blue	3·75	1·40

DESIGNS—VERT (as Type **1496**): 50p. Nilgiri tahr; 1r. Saras crane ("Saras Crane"); 2r. Rose. As Type **1497**: 4r. Painted stork. (19×37 mm): 20r. Amaltaas (plant); 50r. Asiatic paradise flycatcher (bird) ("Paradise Flycatcher"). HORIZ (as Type **1497**): 3r. Smooth Indian otters. (37×19 mm): 10r. Tiger, Sundarban Reserve; 15r. Butterfly.

1498 Railway Locomotive at Dehradoon Station

2000. Centenary of Doon Valley Railway.
| 1933 | **1498** | 15r. multicoloured | 2·75 | 3·00 |

1499 Rose-coloured Starling ("Rosy Pastor")

2000. "Indepex Asiana 2000" International Stamp Exhibition, Calcutta (2nd issue). Migratory Birds. Multicoloured.
1934	3r. Type **1499**		1·10	1·10
1935	3r. Garganey ("Garganey Teal")		1·10	1·10
1936	3r. Forest wagtail		1·10	1·10
1937	3r. White stork		1·10	1·10
MS1938	157×114 mm. Nos. 1934/7		5·50	5·50

1500 N. T. Rama Rao

2000. Nandamuri Taraka Rama Rao (former Chief Minister of Andhra Pradesh) Commemoration.
| 1939 | **1500** | 3r. multicoloured | 60 | 40 |

1501 Swami
Saraswati

2000. 50th Death Anniv of Swami Sahajanand Saraswati (rural reformer).
1940 **1501** 3r. mauve, brn & stone 75 75

1502 Christian Medical
College and Hospital,
Vellore

2000. Centenary of Christian Medical College and Hospital, Vellore.
1941 **1502** 3r. multicoloured 75 50

1503 Vijaya
Lakshmi Pandit
(diplomat)

2000. Social and Political Leaders. Each including the Indian flag. Multicoloured.
1942 3r. Type **1503** 75 75
1943 3r. Bahadur R. Srinivasan (social reformer) 75 75
1944 3r. Jaglal Choudhary (social reformer) 75 75
1945 3r. Radha Gobinda Baruah (social reformer) 75 75

1504 Mountain, River and
Tree inside Open Book

2000. Centenary of Kodaikanal International School.
1946 **1504** 15r. multicoloured 2·25 2·50

1505 Discus

2000. Olympic Games, Sydney. Multicoloured.
1947 3r. Type **1505** 60 20
1948 6r. Tennis 70 45
1949 10r. Hockey 1·75 1·25
1950 15r. Weightlifting 1·75 2·25

1506 "Oceansat-1"

2000. India's Space Programme. Multicoloured.
1951 3r. Type **1506** 1·00 70
1952 3r. "Insat 3B" in orbit 1·00 70
1953 3r. Astronaut with flag, planets and spacecraft (vert) 2·75 2·75
1954 3r. Earth and spacecraft (vert) 2·75 2·75
Nos. 1953/4 were printed together, *se-tenant*, with the backgrounds forming a composite design.

1507 *Krishna with Gopies*
(Anmana Devi)

2000. Madhubani-Mithila Paintings. Multicoloured.
1955 3r. Type **1507** 65 65
1956 3r. *Flower Girls* (Nirmala Devi) 65 65
1957 3r. *Ball and Sugriva* (Sanjula) (vert) 65 65
1958 5r. Geometrical pattern with sedan chair at foot (vert) 1·75 1·75
1959 10r. Geometrical pattern with elephant at foot (vert) 1·75 1·75

1508 Raj Kumar
Shukla

2000. 125th Birth Anniv of Raj Kumar Shukla (social reformer).
1960 **1508** 3r. brown and buff 10·00 4·50

1509 Dr. Shanker
Dayal Sharma

2000. First Death Anniv of Dr. Shanker Dayal Sharma (former President of India).
1961 **1509** 3r. multicoloured 75 75

1510
Subhas
Chandra
Bose

2000
1962 **1510** 1r. brown 15 10
1963 - 2r. black 20 10
1963*a* - 3r. blue 20 10
DESIGNS: 2r. Vallabhbhai Patel. 3r. Dr. B. R. Ambedkar.

1511 *My Best Friend* (Phuhar
Uppal)

2000. Children's Day.
1964 **1511** 3r. multicoloured 1·00 70

1512 Maharaja Bijli Pasi

2000. Maharaja Bijli Pasi of Bijnor Commemoration.
1965 **1512** 3r. multicoloured 75 75

1513 Ancient Bead Necklace
from Indus Valley

2000. Indepex Asiana 2000 International Stamp Exhibition, Calcutta (3rd issue). Gems and Jewellery. Multicoloured.
1966 3r. Type **1513** 65 65
1967 3r. Gold necklace from Taxila 65 65
1968 3r. Turban ornament from Sarpech 65 65
1969 3r. Navaratna necklace 65 65
1970 3r. Bridal necklace from South India 65 65
1971 3r. Temple necklace from Rajasthan 65 65
MS1972 162×111 mm. Nos. 1966/7 and 1969/70 (sold at 15r.) 4·50 4·50

1514 17th-century
Marakkars Galley

2000. 400th Death Anniv of Admiral Kunjali IV Marakkars.
1973 **1514** 3r. multicoloured 1·25 75

1515 Ustad Hafiz Ali Khan

2000. Ustad Hafiz Ali Khan (musician) Commemoration.
1974 **1515** 3r. multicoloured 75 75

1516 Prithviraj
Chauhan, King of
Delhi

2000. Historical Personalities. Multicoloured.
1975 3r. Type **1516** 1·00 1·25
1976 3r. Raja Bhamashah, Dewan of Mewar 1·00 1·25
1977 3r. Rajarshi Bhagyachandra, King of Manipur 1·00 1·25
1978 3r. General Zorawar Singh of Kashmir (horiz) 1·00 1·25

1517 *St. Aloysius with
Children* (painting)

2001. Centenary of Paintings in St. Aloysius College Chapel, Mangalore.
1979 **1517** 15r. multicoloured 2·25 2·50

1518 Sane Guruji
(writer)

2001. Personalities. Multicoloured.
1980 3r. Type **1518** 55 70
1981 3r. E. M. S. Namboodiripad (Kerala politician) 55 70
1982 3r. Giani Gurmukh Singh Musafir (Punjab politician) 55 70
1983 3r. Prof. N. G. Ranga (social reformer) 55 70

1519 Sheel Bhadra
Yajee

2001. Sheel Bhadra Yajee (patriot) Commemoration.
1984 **1519** 3r. multicoloured 75 75

1520 Jubba Sahni

2001. Personalities. Multicoloured.
1985 3r. Type **1520** 65 75
1986 3r. Yogendra and Baikunth Shukla (patriot) 65 75

1521 Western Railway
Building

2001. Western Railway Building, Churchgate, Mumbai.
1987 **1521** 15r. multicoloured 3·50 3·25

1522 Census
Emblem

2001. Census of India.
1988 **1522** 3r. multicoloured 75 75

1523 *Tarangini* (cadet ship)

2001. International Fleet Review. Multicoloured.
1989 3r. Type **1523** 60 60
1990 3r. *Maratha pal* (sailing ship) 60 60
1991 3r. *Maratha galbat* (sailing ship) 60 60
1992 15r. Fleet Review logo 1·25 1·75

1524 Rocks and Minerals

2001. 150th Anniv of Geological Survey of India.
1993 **1524** 3r. multicoloured 1·00 60

1525 Soldier in
Ceremonial Uniform
and Himalaya Patrol

2001. Bicentenary of 4th Battalion, Maratha Light Infantry.
1994 **1525** 3r. multicoloured 1·50 75

1526 Symbols of
Jain Teaching

2001. 2600th Birth Anniv of Bhagwan Mahavira (Jain teacher).
1995 **1526** 3r. multicoloured 1·00 60

1527 Yuri Gagarin and
Rockets

2001. 40th Anniv of Man's First Space Flight.
1996 **1527** 15r. multicoloured 2·50 2·75

1528 Frederic Chopin

2001. 190th Birth Anniv (2002) of Frederic Chopin (composer).
1997 **1528** 15r. multicoloured 2·75 2·75

1529 Suraj Narain Singh

2001. Suraj Narain Singh (nationalist politician) Commemoration.
1998 **1529** 3r. multicoloured 75 75

1530 B. P. Mandal

2001. B. P. Mandal (former Chief Minister of Bihar) Commemoration.
1999 **1530** 3r. multicoloured 75 75

1531 Samanta Chandra Sekhar, Stars and Gola Yantra (instrument)

2001. Samanta Chandra Sekhar (astronomer) Commemoration.
2000 **1531** 3r. black, vio & grn 1·00 75

1532 Sant Ravidas (Phulan Runi)

2001. Sant Ravidas (philosopher-poet) Commem.
2001 **1532** 3r. multicoloured 75 65

1533 Krishna Nath Sarmah

2001. Personalities. Multicoloured.
2002 4r. Type **1533** 90 1·10
2003 4r. C. Sankaran Nair (lawyer) 90 1·10
2004 4r. Syama Prasad Mookerjee (politician) 90 1·10
2005 4r. U Kiang Nongbah (guerilla leader) 90 1·10

1534 Chandragupta Maurya

2001. Emperor Chandragupta Maurya Commem.
2006 **1534** 4r. multicoloured 75 60

1535 Jhalkari Bai on Horseback

2001. Jhalkari Bai (female warrior from Jhansi) Commemoration.
2007 **1535** 4r. multicoloured 1·00 1·00

1536 Fungia horrida (coral)

2001. Corals. Multicoloured.
2008 4r. Type **1536** 60 40
2009 4r. Acropora digitifera 60 40
2010 15r. Montipora acquituberculata 1·25 1·40
2011 45r. Acropora formosa 3·00 4·00

1537 Dwarka Prasad Mishra

2001. Birth Centenary of Dwarka Prasad Mishra (former Chief Minister of Madhya Pradesh).
2012 **1537** 4r. black and stone 75 75

1538 Chaudhary Brahmparkash

2001. Chaudhary Brahmparkash (former Chief Minister of Delhi) Commemoration.
2013 **1538** 4r. black and blue 75 75

1539 Revolution Monument, Shaheed Park, Ballia

2001. 60th Anniv (2000) of August Revolution, Ballia.
2014 **1539** 4r. multicoloured 75 75

1540 Jagdev Prasad

2001. Jagdev Prasad (journalist and politician) Commemoration.
2015 **1540** 4r. multicoloured 75 75

1541 Rani Avantibai

2001. Rani Avantibai of Ramgarh Commemoration.
2016 **1541** 4r. multicoloured 1·25 75

1542 Rao Tula Ram

2001. Rao Tula Ram of Rewari (patriot) Commemoration.
2017 **1542** 4r. multicoloured 75 75

1543 Chaudhary Devi Lal

2001. Chaudhary Devi Lal (former Deputy Prime Minister) Commemoration.
2018 **1543** 4r. multicoloured 75 75

1544 Satis Chandra Samanta

2001. Satis Chandra Samanta (West Bengal politician) Commemoration.
2019 **1544** 4r. black and stone 75 75

1545 Sivaji Ganesan

2001. Sivaji Ganesan (Tamil actor) Commemoration.
2020 **1545** 4r. multicoloured 75 75

1546 Gandhi on Salt March

2001. "Mahatma Gandhi—Man of the Millennium". Multicoloured.
2021 4r. Type **1546** 1·50 1·25
2022 4r. Mahatma Gandhi 1·50 1·25

1547 Bharathidsan (Tamil poet)

2001. Cultural Personalities. Each black, red and stone.
2023 4r. Type **1547** 50 60
2024 4r. Lachhu Maharaj (choreographer) 50 60
2025 4r. Master Mitrasen (writer) 50 60

1548 Jayaprakash Narayan

2001. Birth Centenary (2002) of Jayaprakash Narayan (socialist).
2026 **1548** 4r. multicoloured 75 75

1549 Monkey in Tree and Crocodile

2001. Stories from "Panchatantra" (Indian fables). Multicoloured.
2027 4r. Type **1549** 55 55
2028 4r. Monkey on crocodile's back (29×39 mm) 55 55
2029 4r. Lion and rabbit 55 55
2030 4r. Lion and rabbit at well (29×39 mm) 55 55
2031 4r. Snake attacking crows' eggs 55 55
2032 4r. Snake attacked by villagers (29×39 mm) 55 55
2033 4r. Geese and tortoise talking 55 55
2034 4r. Tortoise flying with geese (29×39 mm) 55 55

1550 Grocer selling Iodized Salt

2001. Global Iodine Deficiency Disorders Day.
2035 **1550** 4r. multicoloured 1·00 75

1551 Thangal Kunju Musaliar

2001. Thangal Kunju Musaliar (industrialist and philanthropist) Commemoration.
2036 **1551** 4r. black and stone 75 75

1552 Woman self-examining for Breast Cancer

2001. Cancer Awareness Day.
2037 **1552** 4r. multicoloured 75 60

1553 Maharajah Ranjit Singh

2001. Bicentenary of Ranjit Singh's Coronation as Maharajah of the Punjab.
2038 **1553** 4r. multicoloured 1·00 75

1554 Hands clasped around Globe

2001. Children's Day.
2039 **1554** 4r. multicoloured 75 60

1555 Dr. V. Shantaram and Film Scene

2001. Birth Centenary of Dr. V. Shantaram (film director).
2040 **1555** 4r. multicoloured 75 75

1556 Sobha Singh

2001. Birth Centenary of Sobha Singh (painter).
2041 **1556** 4r. multicoloured 1·00 75

1557 Sun Temple, Konark

2001. Centenary of Conservation at Sun Temple, Konark. Multicoloured.
2042 4r. Giant carved wheel, Sun Temple, Konark 75 75
2043 15r. Type **1557** 1·75 2·00

1558 Handshake above Three Symbolic Figures

2001. International Year of Volunteers.
2044 **1558** 4r. multicoloured 70 60

1559 Raj Kapoor and Film Characters

2001. Raj Kapoor (film actor and director) Commemoration.
2045 **1559** 4r. multicoloured 1·25 1·00

1560 Digboi Refinery

2001. Centenary of Digboi Oil Refinery, Assam.
2046 **1561** 4r. multicoloured 1·25 70

1561 Flowers, Fireworks and Christmas Tree

2001. Greetings. Multicoloured.
2047 3r. Type **1561** 70 55
2048 4r. Butterflies and flowers 90 70

1562 Vijaya Raje Scindia

2001. Vijaya Raje Scindia (politician and social reformer) Commemoration.
2049 **1562** 4r. multicoloured 75 75

1563 Kedarnath Temple, Uttaranchal

2001. Inpex-Empirepex 2001 National Stamp Exhibition. Temple Architecture.
2050 **1563** 4r. brown & lt brn 65 65
2051 - 4r. brown & lt brn 65 65
2052 - 4r. brown & lt brn 65 65
2053 - 15r. brown & lt brn 1·75 2·25
DESIGNS: No. 2051, Tryambakeshwar Temple, Maharashtra; 2052, Aundha Nagnath Temple, Maharashtra; 2053, Rameswaram Temple.

1564 Mine Winding Gear and Helmet in Hand

2002. Centenary of Directorate General of Mines Safety.
2054 **1564** 4r. multicoloured 1·00 60

1565 Mount Everest and Climber

2002. Indian Army Expedition to Mt. Everest (2001).
2055 **1565** 4r. multicoloured 1·50 75

1566 Gridhakuta Hills, Rajgir

2002. Bauddha Mahotsav Festival. Multicoloured.
2056 4r. Type **1566** 55 55
2057 4r. Dhamek Stupa, Sarnath 55 55
2058 8r. Mahaparinirvana Temple, Kushinagar 1·25 1·40
2059 15r. Mahabodhi Temple, Bodhgaya 2·00 2·25

1567 Cartoon of Boy reading

2002. Year of Books.
2060 **1567** 4r. multicoloured 70 60

1568 Swami Ramanand (mystic)

2002. Swami Ramanand (mystic) Commemoration.
2061 **1568** 4r. multicoloured 75 1·00

1569 Tank and 19th-century Cannon

2002. Bicentenary of Indian Ordnance Factories.
2062 **1569** 4r. multicoloured 1·50 75

1570 Sido and Kanhu Murmu

2002. Sido and Kanhu Murmu (Santal resistance fighters) Commemoration.
2063 **1570** 4r. multicoloured 1·00 1·00

1571 First Railway Train, 1853

2002. 150th Anniv of Indian Railways.
2064 **1571** 15r. multicoloured 4·00 4·00
MS2065 112×75 mm. No. 2064 5·50 6·50

1572 Kathakali Dancer (India)

2002. 50th Anniv of Diplomatic Relations between India and Japan. Multicoloured.
2066 15r. Type **1572** 2·25 2·25
2067 15r. Kabuki actor (Japan) 2·25 2·25
MS2068 100×70 mm. Nos. 2066/7 5·50 6·50

1573 Central Hall of Parliament, New Delhi

2002. 50th Anniv of Indian Parliament.
2069 **1573** 4r. gold 75 60

1574 Prabodhankar Thackeray

2002. Prabodhankar Thackeray (writer) Commemoration.
2070 **1574** 4r. black 75 1·00

1575 Cotton College, Guwahati

2002. Centenary of Cotton College (2001), Assam.
2071 **1575** 4r. purple and green 70 60

1576 P. L. Deshpande

2002. P. L. Deshpande (writer) Commemoration.
2072 **1576** 4r. multicoloured 75 1·00

1577 Babu Gulabrai

2002. Indian Literary Figures. Multicoloured.
2073 5r. Type **1577** 75 1·00
2074 5r. Pandit Vyas 75 1·00

1578 Brajlal Biyani

2002. Brajlal Biyani (journalist and politician) Commemoration.
2075 **1578** 4r. multicoloured 75 1·00

1579 Sree Thakur Satyananda

2002. Sree Thakur Satyananda Commemoration.
2076 **1579** 5r. multicoloured 75 1·00

1580 Anna Bhau Sathe

2002. Anna Bhau Sathe (Marathi writer) Commemoration.
2077 **1580** 4r. black and grey 75 1·00

1581 Anand Rishiji Maharaj

2002. Tenth Death Anniv of Anand Rishiji Maharaj (Jain spiritual leader).
2078 **1581** 4r. multicoloured 75 1·00

1582 Dr. Vithalrao Vikhe Patil

2002. Dr. Vithalrao Vikhe Patil (co-operative movement pioneer) Commemoration.
2079 **1582** 4r. multicoloured 75 1·00

1583 Sant Tukaram

2002. Sant Tukaram (Marathi poet) Commemoration.
2080 **1583** 4r. multicoloured 1·00 1·00

1584 Bhaurao Krishnarao Gaikwad

2002. Birth Centenary of Bhaurao Krishnarao Gaikwad (social reformer).
2081 **1584** 4r. multicoloured 75 1·00

1585 Ayyan Kali

2002. Social Reformers. Multicoloured.
2082	5r. Type **1585**	65	85
2083	5r. Chandraprabha Saikiani	65	85
2084	5r. Gora	65	85

1586 Ananda Nilayam Vimanam, Tirumala

2002. 700th Anniv of Ananda Nilayam Vimanam Temple Tower, Tirumala.
2085	**1586** 15r. multicoloured	2·50	2·75

1587 Kanika Bandopadhyay

2002. Kanika Bandopadhyay (singer) Commemoration.
2086	**1587** 5r. multicoloured	1·00	1·00

1588 Arya Vaidya Sala, Kottakkal, and Vaidyaratnam Varier (founder)

2002. Centenary of Arya Vaidya Kottakkal Sala (Ayurvedic Medicine), Kottakkal.
2087	**1588** 5r. multicoloured	1·00	1·00

1589 Bhagwan Baba

2002. Bhagwan Baba (mystic and philosopher) Commemoration.
2088	**1589** 5r. multicoloured	1·00	1·00

1590 Bihar Chamber of Commerce Logo

2002. 75th Anniv (2001) of Bihar Chamber of Commerce.
2089	**1590** 4r. multicoloured	80	70

1591 Asiatic Mangrove (*Rhizophora mucronata*)

2002. Eighth Session of U.N. Conference on Climate Change, New Delhi. Mangroves. Multicoloured.
2090	5r. Type **1591**	70	70
2091	5r. Mangrove palm (*Nypa fruticans*)	70	70
2092	5r. Burma mangrove (*Bruguiera gymnorrhiza*)	70	70
2093	15r. Mangrove apple (*Sonneratia alba*)	2·00	2·25
MS2094 192×85 mm. Nos. 2090/3		4·50	5·00

1592 Swami Pranavananda

2002. Swami Pranavananda (social reformer) Commemoration.
2095	**159** 5r. multicoloured	1·25	1·25

1593 Vidhan Bhavan (State Assembly Building) and Samadhi (Buddhist Temple), Nagpur

2002. 300th Anniv of Nagpur.
2096	**1593** 5r. multicoloured	3·25	3·75

1594 *Holi Festival* (Aakash Anand)

2002. Children's Day.
2097	**1594** 5r. multicoloured	1·25	1·50

1595 Cane and Bamboo Ware

2002. Handicrafts. Multicoloured.
2098	5r. Type **1595**	1·00	1·00
2099	5r. Thewa ware (gold leaf work on coloured glass)	1·00	1·00
2100	5r. Patola fabric	1·00	1·00
2101	5r. Dhokra ornaments (metal casting)	1·00	1·00
MS2102 100×100 mm. Nos. 2098/101		5·00	5·50

1596 Santidev Ghose

2002. Santidev Ghose (classical singer) Commemoration.
2103	**1596** 5r. multicoloured	1·25	1·00

1597 Ajoy Kumar Mukherjee (leader) and Newspaper

2002. 60th Anniv of "National Government" of Tamluk (Tamralipta Jatiya Sarkar). Multicoloured.
2104	5r. Type **1597**	3·75	3·75
2105	5r. Matangini Hazra and demonstration	3·75	3·75

1598 Anglo Bengali Inter College, Allahabad

2002. Anglo-Bengali Inter College, Allahabad.
2106	**1598** 5r. multicoloured	75	60

1599 Gurukula Kangri Vishwavidyalaya University, Hardwar

2002. Gurukula Kangri Vishwavidyalaya University, Hardwar Commemoration.
2107	**1599** 5r. multicoloured	1·00	70

1600 Dhirubhai H. Ambani

2002. Dhirubhai H. Ambani (industrialist) Commemoration.
2108	**1600** 5r. multicoloured	1·00	75

1601 T. T. Krishnamachari

2002. T. T. Krishnamachari (Minister of Commerce and Industry, 1952–56, Finance Minister 1963–5) Commemoration.
2109	**1601** 5r. multicoloured	75	1·00

1602 Golconda Fort

2002. Forts of Andhra Pradesh. Multicoloured.
2110	5r. Type **1602**	1·00	1·00
2111	5r. Palace, Chandragiri Fort	1·00	1·00

1603 Hindustan Aircraft Industries HT-2 Trainer, 1951

2003. Centenary of Powered Flight. Aero India 2003. Multicoloured.
2112	5r. Type **1603**	2·25	1·50
2113	5r. Hindustan Aircraft Industries Marut ground attack aircraft, 1961	2·25	1·50
2114	5r. Hindustan Aircraft Industries LCA light combat aircraft, 2001	2·25	1·50
2115	15r. Hindustan Aircraft Industries Dhruv advanced light helicopter	2·75	2·50
MS2116 144×95 mm. Nos. 2112/15		13·00	12·00

1604 Ghantasala

2003. Ghantasala (singer and composer) Commemoration.
2117	**1604** 5r. brown and black	1·00	1·00

1605 S. L. Kirloskar and Cogwheels

2003. Birth Centenary of S. L. Kirloskar (industrialist).
2118	**1605** 5r. multicoloured	75	1·00

1606 Kusumagraj

2003. Kusumagraj (Marathi poet) Commemoration.
2119	**1606** 5r. multicoloured	75	1·00

1607 Sant Eknath

2003. Sant Eknath (saint and poet) Commemoration.
2120	**1607** 5r. multicoloured	75	1·00

1608 Frank Anthony

2003. Tenth Death Anniv of Frank Anthony (politician).
2121	**1608** 5r. multicoloured	75	1·00

1609 Kakaji Maharaj

2003. Kakaji Maharaj (Swaminarayan spiritual leader and philosopher) Commemoration.
2122	**1609** 5r. multicoloured	75	1·00

1610 *Commiphora wightii*

2003. Medicinal Plants of India. Multicoloured.
2123	5r. Type **1610**	3·00	3·00
2124	5r. *Bacopa monnieri*	3·00	3·00
2125	5r. *Emblica officinalis*	3·00	3·00
2126	5r. *Withania somnifera*	3·00	3·00
MS2127 130×80 mm. Nos. 2123/6		11·00	11·00

1611 Durga Das

2003. Durga Das (journalist and newspaper editor) Commemoration.
2128	**1611** 5r. multicoloured	1·00	1·00

1612 Kishore Kumar

2003. "Golden Voices of Yesteryear". Multicoloured.
2129	5r. Type **1612**	70	70
2130	5r. Mukesh	70	70
2131	5r. Mohammed Rafi	70	70
2132	5r. Hemant Kumar	70	70
MS2133 89×105 mm. Nos. 2129/32		4·50	5·50

1613 Mt. Everest

2003. 50th Anniv of Ascent of Mount Everest by Edmund Hilary and Tenzing Norgay. Multicoloured.

2134	15r. Type **1613**	3·25	2·75
MS2135 74×97 mm. 15r. As Type **1613**		4·50	4·50

1614 Muktabai

2003. Muktabai (poet) Commemoration.

2136	**1614**	5r. multicoloured	1·00	1·00

1615 Natesa (12th—Century Bronze from Tanjavur)

2003. Government Museum, Chennai. Multicoloured.

2137	5r. Type **1615**	1·25	1·00
2138	5r. Amravati sculpture (medallion)	1·25	1·00
2139	15r. Museum Theatre (57×28 mm)	2·25	2·50
MS2140 161×73 mm. Nos. 2137/9		6·50	6·50

No. **MS**2140 is also illustrated with other exhibits from the Government Museum.

1616 Vishwanath Kashinath Rajwade

2003. 140th Birth Anniv of Vishwanath Kashinath Rajwade (historian).

2141	**1616**	5r. lilac	75	1·00

1617 Bade Ghulam Ali Khan

2003. Bade Ghulam Ali Khan (singer) Commemoration.

2142	**1617**	5r. multicoloured	1·00	1·00

1618 Three Stylised Children and Rainbow

2003. Autism. Our World of Special Children.

2143	**1618**	5r. multicoloured	1·50	80

1619 Vishal Badri Temple, Badrinath

2003. Temple Architecture. Multicoloured.

2144	5r. Type **1619**	2·25	1·75
2145	5r. Mallikarjunaswamy Temple, Srisailam	2·25	1·75
2146	5r. Tripureswari Temple, Udaipur	2·25	1·75
2147	5r. Jagannath Temple, Puri	2·25	1·75

1620 Janardan Swami

2003. 89th Birth Anniv of Janardan Swami (spiritual leader).

2148	**1620**	5r. brown	75	1·00

1621 Athirapalli Falls

2003. Waterfalls. Multicoloured.

2149	5r. Type **1621**	80	80
2150	5r. Kempty Falls	80	80
2151	5r. Kakolat Falls	80	80
2152	15r. Jog Falls	2·00	2·25
MS2153 134×87 mm. Nos. 2149/52		7·00	8·00

1622 G. Sankara Kurup

2003. Malayalam Jnanpith Literary Award Winners Commemoration. Each black and cream.

2154	5r. Type **1622**	5·50	5·50
2155	5r. S. K. Pottekkatt	5·50	5·50
2156	5r. Thakazhi Sivasankara Pillai	5·50	5·50

1623 Dr. Kota Shivarama Karanth

2003. Dr. Kota Shivarama Karanth (writer and reformer) Commemoration.

2157	**1623**	5r. multicoloured	75	1·00

1624 Narendra Mohan

2003. First Death Anniv of Narendra Mohan (writer and editor of Dainik Jagran).

2158	**1624**	5r. brown and flesh	75	1·00

1625 Govindrao Pansare

2003. 90th Birth Anniv of Govindrao Pansare (martyr).

2159	**1625**	5r. multicoloured	75	1·00

1626 Fish

2003. Greetings Stamps. Multicoloured.

2160	4r. Type **1626**	1·00	1·00
2161	4r. Birds	1·00	1·00
2162	5r. Butterfly	1·00	1·00
2163	5r. Squirrels	1·00	1·00

1627 Satellite Dish, Telegraph Key and Mobile Phone

2003. 150th Anniv of Telecommunications.

2164	**1627**	5r. multicoloured	1·00	70

1628 Bengal Engineer Group memorial, Roorkee and Railroad

2003. Bicentenary of the Benegal Sappers and Miners.

2165	**1628**	5r. multicoloured	1·25	80

1629 Steam Locomotive on the Kalka-Shimla Railway

2003. Centenary of the Kalka-Shimla Railway.

2166	**1629**	5r. multicoloured	1·50	1·00

1630 Python

2003. Snakes. Multicoloured.

2167	5r. Type **630**	1·00	1·00
2168	5r. Bamboo pit viper	1·00	1·00
2169	5r. King cobra	1·00	1·00
2170	5r. Gliding Snake	1·00	1·00
MS2171 169×123 mm. Nos. 2167/70		7·50	8·00

1631 Children

2003. Children's Day.

2172	**1631**	5r. multicoloured	1·25	70

1632 Soldiers of the 2 Guards Battalion

2003. 225th Anniv of the 2 Guards (formerly the 1 Grenadiers).

2173	**1632**	5r. green, vermilion and yellow	1·25	80

1633 Harivansh Rai Bachchan

2003. Harivansh Rai Bachchan (poet) Commemoration.

2174	**1633**	5r. black and brown	75	1·00

1634 Cockerel

2003. Early French and Indian Art. Multicoloured.

2175	22r. Type **1634**	2·25	2·50
2176	22r. Peacock	2·25	2·50
MS2177 116×95 mm. Nos. 2175/6		7·00	8·00

1635 Yashpal

2003. Birth Centenary of Yashpal (revolutionary writer).

2178	**1635**	5r. multicoloured	75	1·00

1636 Cheomseongdae Astronomical Observatory, Gyeongju

2003. 30th Anniv of Diplomatic Relations with South Korea. Multicoloured.

2179	15r. Type **1636**	2·00	2·25
2180	15r. Jantar Mantar astronomical observatory, Jaipur	2·00	2·25

1637 Parliament Building

2003. 200th Session of Rajya Sabha (Council of States).

2181	**1637**	5r. multicoloured	75	65

1638 Mukut Behari Lal Bhargava

2003. Birth Centenary of Mukut Behari Lal Bhargava (politician and lawyer).

2182	**1638**	5r. multicoloured	75	1·00

1639 Swami Swaroopanandji

2003. Birth Centenary of Swami Swaroopanandji (religious leader).

2183	**1639**	5r. multicoloured	2·50	1·00

1640 Actors

2003. 50th Anniv of the Sangeet Natak Akademi. Multicoloured.

2184	5r. Type **1640**	75	75
2185	5r. Dancers	75	75
2186	5r. Musicians	75	75
MS2187 139×82 mm. Nos. 2183/5		4·00	4·50

1641 Lalan Fakir

2003. Folk Music. Multicoloured.

2188	5r. Type **1641**	70	80
2189	5r. Allah Jilai Bai	70	80

1642 Major Somnath Sharma

2003. 80th Birth Anniv of Major Somnath Sharma.
2190 **1642** 5r. multicoloured   75   1·00

1643 Siddavanahalli Nijalingappa

2003. Siddavanahalli Nijalingappa Commemoration (politician and lawyer).
2191 **1643** 5r. multicoloured   75   1·00

1644 Chintaman Dwarkanath Deshmukh

2004. Chintaman Dwarkanath Deshmukh (finance expert) Commemoration.
2192 **1644** 5r. multicoloured   1·25   1·00

1645 Nani Ardeshir Palkhivala

2004. Second Death Anniv of Nani Ardeshir Palkhivala (jurist).
2193 **1645** 5r. multicoloured   75   1·00

1646 Dr. Bhalchandra Digamber Garware

2004. Birth Centenary (2003) of Dr. Bhalchandra Digamber Garware (industrialist).
2194 **1646** 5r. multicoloured   75   1·00

1647 Annamacharya

2004. Annamacharya (saint and composer of devotional songs) Commemoration.
2195 **1647** 5r. multicoloured   75   1·00

1648 9th Battalion of the Madras Regiment, Travancore

2004. Commemoration of the 9th Battalion of the Madras Regiment, Travancore.
2196 **1648** 5r. multicoloured   1·40   1·00

1649 V. Lakshminarayana

2004. V. Lakshminarayana (violinist) Commemoration.
2197 **1649** 5r. multicoloured   1·00   1·00

1650 INS *Tarangini*

2004. Circumnavigation Voyage of INS *Tarangini* (three masted barque).
2198 **1650** 5r. multicoloured   1·25   1·00
MS2199 109×81 mm. No. 2198   6·00   6·50

1651 Illustrated Blocks, Stylised Stairs and Sheaves of Paper

2004. Indian Institute of Social Welfare and Business Management, Kolkata.
2200 **1651** 5r. multicoloured   75   70

1652 Baji Rao Peshwa

2004. Baji Rao Peshwa Commemoration.
2201 **1652** 5r. multicoloured   75   1·00

1653 Siddhar Swamigal

2004. Birth Centenary of Siddhar Swamigal (spiritual leader).
2202 **1653** 5r. multicoloured   75   1·00

1654 Indra Chandra Shastri

2004. 92nd Birth Anniv of Indra Chandra Shastri (philosopher).
2203 **1654** 5r. black, deep green and green   75   1·00

1655 Woodstock School

2004. Woodstock School.
2204 **1655** 5r. multicoloured   75   75

1656 Jyotiprasad Agarwalla

2004. Birth Centenary of Jyotiprasad Agarwalla (2003) (poet and film maker).
2205 **1656** 5r. multicoloured   75   1·00

1657 P. N. Panicker

2004. Reading Day. Ninth Death Anniv of P. N. Panicker (education reformer).
2206 **1657** 5r. multicoloured   75   1·00

1658 Nain Singh

2004. The Great Trigonometrical Survey. Multicoloured.
2207   5r. Type **1658**   75   75
2208   5r. Triangles (40×29 mm)   75   75
2209   5r. Radhanath Sikdar   75   75
MS2210 117×75 mm. Nos. 2207/9   5·00   6·00

1659 Aacharya Bhikshu

2004. Aacharya Bhikshu (philosophical writer and social reformer) Commemoration.
2211 **1659** 5r. multicoloured   75   1·00

1660 Wrestling

2004. Olympic Games, Athens. Multicoloured.
2212   5r. Type **1660**   70   70
2213   5r. Athletics   70   70
2214   15r. Shooting   1·60   1·75
2215   15r. Hockey   1·60   1·75

1661 Kabir (Indian)

2004. Iranian and Indian Poets. T **1661** and similar vert designs. Multicoloured.
2216   15r.   1·75   2·00
2216b   15r. Type **1661**   1·75   2·00
Stamps of the same design were issued by Iran.

1662 Murasoli Maran

2004. 70th Birthday Anniv of Murasoli Maran (writer).
2217 **1662** 5r. multicoloured   75   60

1663 Rajiv Gandhi (President, 1984—89)

2004. 60th Birth Anniv of Rajiv Gandhi and Renewable Energy Day.
2218 **1663** 5r. multicoloured   75   55

1664 S. S. *Vasan*

2004. Birth Centenary of S. S. Vasan (journalist and film producer).
2219 **1664** 5r. multicoloured   75   1·00

1665 Panini

2004. Panini Sanskrit Grammar (c. 500 BC).
2220 **1665** 5r. multicoloured   75   1·00

1666 K. Subrahmanyam

2004. Birth Centenary of K. Subrahmanyam (film maker).
2221 **1666** 5r. multicoloured   75   75

1667 M. C. Chagla

2004. M. C. Chagla (Judge) Commemoration.
2222 **1667** 5r. multicoloured   75   75

1668 Shri N. "Tirupur" Kumaran

2004. Birth Centenary of Tirupur Kumaran (revolutionary).
2223 **1668** 5r. multicoloured   75   75

1669 Early Stamp, Mail Ship and Carriage

2004. 150th Anniv of India Post. Multicoloured.
2224   5r. Type **1669**   1·50   1·25
2225   5r. Airmail stamp and postal runner   1·50   1·25
2226   5r. General Post Office, Calcutta, stamp and pillar box   1·50   1·25
2227   5r. Computer terminal and modern postal services   1·50   1·25
MS2228 222×114 mm. Nos. 2224/7   7·50   8·00

1670 Neerja Bhanot
(Purser, Pan American
World Airways)

2004. Winners of the Ashoka Chakra Bravery Award.
Multicoloured.
| 2229 | 5r. Type **1670** | 2·00 | 1·50 |
| 2230 | 5r. Randhir Prasad Verma (Su-perintendent of Police) | 2·00 | 1·50 |

1671 Guru Dutt

2004. 40th Death Anniv of Guru Dutt (film maker).
| 2231 | **1671** | 5r. multicoloured | 75 | 60 |

1672 Indian Soldiers and Peace Dove

2004. Indian Army in UN Peacekeeping Operations.
| 2232 | **1672** | 5r. multicoloured | 1·00 | 75 |
| MS2233 99×99 mm. No. 2232 | | | 4·00 | 4·50 |

1673 Marudhu
Pandiar Brothers

2004. Marudhu Pandiar Brothers (anti-colonial leaders
and rulers of Sivaganga). Commemoration.
| 2234 | **1673** | 5r. multicoloured | 75 | 1·00 |

1674 Kites

2004. Greetings Stamps. Multicoloured.
| 2235 | 4r. Type **1674** | 55 | 70 |
| 2236 | 4r. Dolls | 55 | 70 |

1675 Dr. S. Roerich

2004. Birth Centenary of Dr. S. Roerich (artist).
| 2237 | **1675** | 5r. multicoloured | 1·00 | 70 |

1676 Tenneti
Viswanatham

2004. 25th Death Anniv of Tenneti Viswanatham
(politician).
| 2238 | **1676** | 5r. multicoloured | 75 | 60 |

1677 Schoolgirls
and Rural Village

2004. Children's Day.
| 2239 | **1677** | 5r. multicoloured | 75 | 60 |

1678 Walchand
Hirachand

2004. 121st Birth Anniv of Walchand Hirachand
(industrialist).
| 2240 | **1678** | 5r. multicoloured | 70 | 50 |

1679 Dula Bhaya
Kag

2004. Birth Centenary (2003) of Dula Bhaya Kag (poet
and nationalist).
| 2241 | **1679** | 5r. multicoloured | 75 | 60 |

1680 Khas Mahal (image scaled to 51% of original size)

2004. Ninth Aga Khan Award for Architecture. Agra Fort.
Multicoloured.
2242	15r. Khas Mahal	2·25	2·50
2243	15r. Agra Fort	2·25	2·50
MS2244 234×105 mm. 15r. Type **1680**; 15r. Agra Fort		6·00	6·50

1681 Bhagat Puran
Singh

2004. Birth Centenary of Bhagat Puran Singh (Sikh
humanitarian and founder of Pingalwara home for
destitute, Amritsar).
| 2245 | **1681** | 5r. multicoloured | 75 | 1·00 |

1682 Sculpture, Nupial
Memorial Complex,
Imphal

2004. Centenary of Nupi Lan ("Women's War") Protest
Movement, Manipur.
| 2246 | **1682** | 5r. multicoloured | 75 | 65 |

1683 Natural and
Mechanical Symbols of
Energy Production

2004. Energy Conservation.
| 2247 | **1683** | 5r. multicoloured | 75 | 65 |

1684 Taj Mahal

2004. Taj Mahal.
| 2248 | **1684** | 15r. multicoloured | 2·25 | 2·25 |
| MS2249 98×143 mm. No. 2248 | | 5·50 | 6·50 |

1685 Script

2004. 50th Anniv of Sahitya Akademi (literature
promotion organization).
| 2250 | **1685** | 5r. multicoloured | 75 | 60 |

1686 Bhaskara
Sethupathy

2004. Bhaskara Sethupathy (ruler of Ramanathapuram
state, 1889–1903) Commem.
| 2251 | **1686** | 5r. multicoloured | 75 | 75 |

1687 Himalayan Sheep
Dog

2005. Indian Breeds of Dogs. Multicoloured.
2252	5r. Type **1687**	80	80
2253	5r. Rampur hound	80	80
2254	5r. Mudhol hound	80	80
2255	15r. Rajapalayam	1·50	1·75

Nos. 2252/3 and 2254/5 were printed together, *se-tenant*, forming a composite background design.

1688 Padampat
Singhania

2005. Birth Centenary of Padampat Singhania
(industrialist).
| 2256 | **1688** | 5r. multicoloured | 75 | 75 |

1689 Rotary Emblem and
Silhouette of Hands

2005. Centenary of Rotary International.
| 2257 | **1689** | 5r. multicoloured | 75 | 75 |

1690 Krishan Kant

2005. Krishan Kant (Vice-President of India 1997–2002)
Commem.
| 2258 | **1690** | 5r. multicoloured | 75 | 75 |

1691 Madhavrao Scindia

2005. Madhavrao Scindia (politician) Commemoration.
| 2259 | **1691** | 5r. multicoloured | 75 | 75 |

1692 Clouded
Leopard

2005. Flora and Fauna of North East India. Multicoloured.
| 2260 | 5r. Type **1692** | 75 | 75 |
| 2261 | 5r. Dillenia indica | 75 | 75 |

2262	5r. Mishmi takin	75	75
2263	5r. Pitcher plant	75	75
MS2264 109×100 mm. Nos. 2260/3		4·50	5·00

1693 Einstein and Theory of
Relativity

2005. International Year of Physics.
| 2265 | **1693** | 5r. multicoloured | 2·50 | 1·00 |

1694 Gandhi leading
Dandi March

2005. 75th Anniv of Dandi March. Multicoloured.
2266	5r. Type **1694**	1·00	1·00
2267	5r. Gandhi and headline "GREAT MARCH FOR LIBERTY BEGINS"	1·00	1·00
2268	5r. Gandhi picking up salt and map showing route	1·00	1·00
2269	5r. Gandhi and declaration	1·00	1·00
MS2270 125×165 mm. Nos. 2265/9		6·00	7·00

Nos. 2266/9 have lilac backgrounds, but stamps from
MS2269 have mauve backgrounds.

1695 Soldiers in Early and
Modern Uniforms

2005. 300 Years of 15 Punjab (Patiala).
| 2271 | **1695** | 5r. multicoloured | 1·00 | 75 |

1696 Nehru and Conference Hall

2005. 50th Anniv of Bandung Conference of African and
Asian Nations, Bandung, Java, Indonesia.
| 2272 | **1696** | 15r. multicoloured | 1·50 | 1·75 |

1697 Narayan Meghaji
Lokhande

2005. Narayan Meghaji Lokhande (campaigner for
worker's rights) Commemoration.
| 2273 | **1697** | 5r. multicoloured | 75 | 75 |

1698 Emblem and
Symbols of Farming
and Industry

2005. Centenary of Co-operative Movement in India.
| 2274 | **1698** | 5r. multicoloured | 75 | 75 |

1699 Family and Bird in
Park and Urban Landscape

2005. World Environment Day. Green Cities.
| 2275 | **1699** | 5r. multicoloured | 1·00 | 75 |

1700 Abdul Qaiyum Ansari

2005. Birth Centenary of Abdul Qaiyum Ansari (nationalist politician).
2276 **1700** 5r. multicoloured 75 75

1701 Dheeran Chinnamalai

2005. Death Bicentenary of Dheeran Chinnamalai (warrior and ruler of Kongu Province).
2277 **1701** 5r. multicoloured 75 75

1702 Seals and Bank Buildings (image scaled to 57% of original size)

2005. Bicentenary of State Bank of India.
2278 **1702** 15r. multicoloured 1·75 2·00

1703 Children planting Flower of Flags

2005. International Day of Peace.
2279 **1703** 5r. multicoloured 75 65

1704 A. M. M. Murugappa Chettiar

2005. 40th Death Anniv of A. M. M. Murugappa Chettiar (industrialist).
2280 **1704** 5r. multicoloured 75 75

1705 Pratap Singh Kairon

2005. 40th Death Anniv of Pratap Singh Kairon (Chief Minister of Punjab, 1956–64).
2281 **1705** 5r. multicoloured 75 75

1706 Dr. T. S. Soundram and Literacy Emblem

2005. Dr. T. S. Soundram (Deputy Minister for Education, 1962) Commemoration.
2282 **1706** 5r. multicoloured 75 75

1707 Victorian Crown Type Letter Box, 1856–7

2005. Letter Boxes. Multicoloured.
2283 5r. Type **1707** 75 75
2284 5r. Hexagonal Penfold letter box, 1866–79 75 75
2285 5r. Two cylindrical letter boxes, from 1879 75 75
2286 5r. Two modern TV type letter boxes 75 75
MS2287 164×118 mm. Nos. 2283/6 4·00 4·50

1708 Kavimani Desiga Vinayagam Pillai

2005. Kavimani Desiga Vinayagam Pillai (Tamil poet) Commemoration.
2288 **1708** 5r. carmine, black and purple 75 75

1709 Vi Kalyanasundarnar

2005. Vi Kalyanasundarnar (nationalist and Tamil scholar) Commemoration.
2289 **1709** 5r. multicoloured 75 75

1710 Ayothidhasa Pandithar

2005. 160th Birth Anniv of Ayothidhasa Pandithar (social reformer).
2290 **1710** 5r. purple 75 75

1711 Prabodh Chandra

2005. Prabodh Chandra (politician) Commemoration.
2291 **1711** 5r. multicoloured 75 75

1712 Festival (Pallavi Majumder)

2005. Children's Day.
2292 **1712** 5r. multicoloured 75 60

1713 Children riding Elephant

2005. 50th Anniv of Children's Film Society.
2293 **1713** 5r. multicoloured 75 75

1714 Map of South Asia and Africa, Ship, Airliner and Buildings

2005. Centenary of PHD Chamber of Commerce and Industry.
2294 **1714** 5r. multicoloured 1·00 75

1715 Globe

2005. World Summit on the Information Society, Tunis.
2295 **1715** 5r. multicoloured 75 75

1716 Kolkata Police Headquarters

2005. 150th Anniv of Kolkata Police Commissionerate.
2296 **1716** 5r. multicoloured 1·50 1·00

1717 Mother and Baby

2005. Newborn Health.
2297 **1717** 5r. ultramarine 75 65

1718 Jawaharlal Darda

2005. Jawaharlal Darda (founder of Lokmat newspaper) Commemoration.
2298 **1718** 5r. multicoloured 75 75

1719 *Udaygiri*, *Kora* and *Delhi*

2005. Builder's Navy.
2299 **1719** 5r. multicoloured 1·25 1·00

1720 M. S. Subbulakshmi

2005. M. S. Subbulakshmi (Carnatic classical singer) Commemoration.
2300 **1720** 5r. multicoloured 75 75

1721 New Railway Carriages

2005. 50th Anniv of Integral Passenger Railway Coach Factory, Chennai.
2301 **1721** 5r. multicoloured 1·50 1·00

1722 Students and Jadavpur University

2005. 50th Anniv of Jadavpur University.
2302 **1722** 5r. multicoloured 75 75

1723 Sepecat Jaguar Fighter and Consolidated B-24 Liberator and English Electric Canberra Bombers

2005. 55th Anniv of 16 Squadron Air Force.
2303 **1723** 5r. multicoloured 1·50 1·00

1724 Park Monument, Pondicherry and Seal

2005. 50th Anniv of De Facto Transfer of Pondicherry by the French to India.
2304 **1724** 5r. multicoloured 75 75

1725 Sweet Rice in Clay Pot, Cattle and Crops

2006. Pongal (Tamil harvest festival).
2305 **1725** 5r. multicoloured 75 75

1726 A. V. Meiyappan Chettiar (founder/film director)

2006. 60th Anniv of AVM Studios.
2306 **1726** 5r. multicoloured 75 1·00

1727 N. M. R. Subbaraman

2006. Birth Centenary of N. M. R. Subbaraman (nationalist and social reformer).
2307 **1727** 5r. multicoloured 75 1·00

1728 Early Soldier and Cavalcade of the Regiment

2006. 150th Anniv of Third Battalion the Sikh Regiment.
2308 **1728** 5r. multicoloured 1·25 1·00

1729 INS *Viraat* (aircraft carrier) and BAE Sea Harrier Fighter Plane

2006. President's Review of the Fleet, Visakhapatnam. Multicoloured.
2309 5r. Type **1729** 1·75 1·50

2310	5r. Talwar and Brahmaputra class frigates and Sea King helicopter		1·75	1·50
2311	5r. Indian Coast Guard offshore patrol ship *Vigraha*, Dornier aircraft and Sandhayak class survey ship		1·75	1·50
2312	5r. Sindhughosh and Sishumar class submarines		1·75	1·50

1730 Thirumuruga Kiruhananda Variyar

2006. Birth Centenary of Thirumuruga Kiruhananda Variyar (Tamil scholar).

2313	**1730**	5r. purple	1·00	1·00

1731 Devaneya Pavanar

2006. 25th Death Anniv of Devaneya Pavanar (Tamil scholar, linguist and author).

2314	**1731**	5r. blue and deep blue	1·00	1·00

1732 Dr. U. V. Swaminatha Iyer

2006. 150th Birth Anniv (2005) of Dr. U. V. Swaminatha Iyer (Tamil scholar and researcher).

2315	**1732**	5r. purple	1·00	1·00

1733 Tamilavel Umamaheswarar

2006. Tamilavel Umamaheswarar (Tamil scholar) Commemoration.

2316	**1733**	5r. grey and black	1·00	1·00

1734 St. Bede's College

2006. Centenary (2004) of St. Bede's College, Shimla.

2317	**1734**	5r. multicoloured	1·00	75

1735 Gemini Ganesan

2006. Gemini Ganesan (actor) Commemoration.

2318	**1735**	5r. brown, grey and black	1·00	1·00

1736 St. John Bosco

1737 M. Singaravelar

2006. 60th Death Anniv of M. Singaravelar (labour leader and social reformer).

2320	**1737**	5r. multicoloured	1·00	1·00

2006. Centenary of Don Bosco Salesians in India.

2319	**1736**	5r. multicoloured	1·00	75

1738 Emblem

2006. World Consumer Rights Day.

2321	**1738**	5r. multicoloured	1·00	75

1739 Institute Building, Researchers and Crops

2006. Centenary of Indian Agricultural Research Institute, Pusa, New Delhi.

2322	**1739**	5r. multicoloured	1·00	75

1740 Tank

2006. 50th Anniv of 62 Cavalry (armoured regiment).

2323	**1740**	5r. multicoloured	1·25	75

1741 . Nati Dance, Himachal Pradesh

2006. Folk Dances. Multicoloured.

2324	15r. Type **1741**		2·00	2·25
2325	15r. Stamna or kouza (pitcher) dance, Cyprus		2·00	2·25
MS2326	146×92 mm. Nos. 2324/5		6·00	7·00

Stamps in similar designs were issued by Cyprus on the same date.

1742 Calcutta Girls' High School

2006. 150th Anniv of Calcutta Girls' High School.

2327	**1742**	5r. multicoloured	1·00	1·00

1743 Pannalal Barupal

2006. Pannalal Barupal (social reformer and MP 1952–77) Commemoration.

2328	**1743**	5r. multicoloured	1·00	1·00

1744 Kurinji Flowers

2006. Kurinji Flowers (*Strobilanthes kunthiranus*).

2329	**1744**	15r. multicoloured	1·75	2·00
MS2330	125×84 mm. No. 2329		3·00	3·50

1745 Pond and Tree in Desert

2006. Rainwater Harvesting.

2331	**1745**	5r. multicoloured	1·00	70

1746 Sri Pratap College, Srinagar

2006. Centenary (2005) of Sri Pratap College, Srinagar.

2332	**1746**	5r. multicoloured	1·00	75

1747 Entrance to Indraprastha Girls' School

2006. Centenary (2004) of Indraprastha Girls' School, Delhi.

2333	**1747**	5r. multicoloured	1·00	75

1748 Vellore Fort

2006. Bicentenary of the Vellore Mutiny.

2334	**1748**	5r. multicoloured	1·25	1·00

1749 Voorhees College, Vellore

2006. Centenary of Voorhees College, Vellore (2005).

2335	**1749**	5r. multicoloured	1·00	75

1750 High Court Buildings at Jammu and Srinagar

2006. High Court of Jammu and Kashmir.

2336	**1750**	5r. multicoloured	1·00	75

1751 Pankaj Kumar Mullick

2006. Birth Centenary of Pankaj Kumar Mullick (singer and composer) (2005).

2337	**1751**	5r. multicoloured	1·00	1·00

1752 Oil Well and Offshore Oil Rig

2006. Oil and Natural Gas Corporation Limited.

2338	**1752**	5r. multicoloured	1·00	60

1753 Ma. Po. Sivagnanam

2006. Birth Centenary of Ma. Po. Sivagnanam (Tamil writer).

2339	**1753**	5r. multicoloured	1·00	1·00

1754 University of Madras

2006. 150th Anniv of University of Madras.

2340	**1754**	5r. multicoloured	1·00	1·00

1755 L. V. Prasad

2006. L. V. Prasad (film director) Commemoration.

2341	**1755**	5r. multicoloured	1·00	1·00

1756 Indian Merchants and Merchant's Chamber Buildings

2006. Centenary (2007) of Indian Merchants' Chamber.

2342	**1756**	5r. multicoloured	1·00	1·00

1757 Early 20th-century Bronze Replica of Equestrian Deity Rao Dev from Bastar, Madhya Pradesh

2006. Ancient Art. Multicoloured.

2343	15r. Type **1757**		1·50	1·75
2344	15r. Ancient bronze horse statue, from Murun city, Mongolia		1·50	1·75
MS2345	110×60 mm. Nos. 2343/4		4·50	5·00

Stamps in similar designs were issued by Mongolia.

1758 Greater Adjutant Stork

2006. Endangered Birds of India. Multicoloured.

2346	5r. Type **1758**		1·00	75
2347	5r. Nilgiri laughing thrush		1·00	75
2348	5r. Manipur bush-quail		1·00	75
2349	5r. Lesser florican		1·00	75
MS2350	109×88 mm. Nos. 2346/9		4·50	5·00

1759 Evolution of Coins in Gwalior Area

2006. Centenary of Madhya Pradesh Chamber of Commerce and Industry, Gwalior.

2351	**1759**	5r. multicoloured	1·00	1·00

1760 Bishwanath Roy

2006. Birth Centenary of Bishwanath Roy (MP 1952–77).

2352	**1760**	5r. multicoloured	1·00	1·00

1761 G. Varadaraj

2006. 70th Birth Anniv of G. Varadaraj (industrialist and educationist).

2353	**1761**	5r. multicoloured	1·00	1·00

1762 Roop Kund

2006. Himalayan Lakes. Multicoloured.

2354	5r. Type **1762**	75	75
2355	5r. Chandra Tal (vert)	75	75
2356	5r. Tsomo Riri	75	75
2357	5r. Sela	75	75
2358	5r. Tsangu	75	75

1763 Lala Deen Dayal and Photographs

2006. Death Centenary of Lala Deen Dayal (pioneer photographer).

2359	**1763**	5r. multicoloured	1·00	1·00

1764 Boy Krishna subduing the Serpent Kaliya

2006. Children's Day. Design showing children's paintings by Keval Thakkar and Shivanna Madvi. Multicoloured.

2360	5r. Type **1764**	65	70
2361	5r. Archer	65	70
MS2362	72×133 mm. As Nos. 2360/1	1·75	2·00

1765 *The Tribune* Newspapers

2006. 125th Anniv of *The Tribune* Newspaper.

2363	**1765**	5r. multicoloured	1·00	75

1766 AIDS Ribbon and Crowd

2006. World AIDS Day.

2364	**1766**	5r. black, scarlet and blue	1·00	1·00

1767 Soldier of British Expeditionary Forces in Persia, 1856

2006. 150th Anniv of Indian Army Field Post Offices. Multicoloured.

2365	5r. Type **1767**	1·50	1·50
2366	5r. Soldier in desert writing letter	1·50	1·50
2367	5r. Soldier reading letter and field post office	1·50	1·50
2368	5r. Mail delivery by helicopter to soldiers in Himalayas	1·50	1·50

Nos. 2365/8 were printed together, *se-tenant*, in horizontal strips of four stamps

1768 Bartholomaeus Ziegenbalg

2006. 300th Anniv of Arrival of Bartholomaeus Ziegenbalg (first Protestant missionary) in India.

2369	**1768**	5r. multicolured	1·00	1·00

1769 Elephant in Forest (sandalwood carving)

2006. Sandalwood.

2370	**1769**	15r. multicoloured	1·75	2·00
MS2371		100×87 mm. No. 2370	2·25	2·50

Nos. 2370/**MS**2371 were embossed with sandalwood powder, giving sandalwood fragrance.

1770 Girl Tightrope Walker

2006. "Stop Child Labour". Multicoloured.

2372	5r. Type **1770**	75	75
2373	5r. Boy labourer with hoe	75	75
2374	5r. Boy serving tea	75	75
2375	5r. Boy in fields carrying heavy basket	75	75

1771 Bimal Roy

2007. Bimal Roy (film director) Commemoration.

2376	**1771**	5r. multicoloured	1·00	1·00

1772 Batsman and Bowler

2007. 70th Anniv of Tamil Nadu Cricket Association.

2377	**1772**	5r. multicoloured	1·50	1·00

1773 "Bhim"

2007. Indian Roses. Multicoloured.

2378	5r. Type **1773**	70	80
2379	5r. "Neelam"	70	80
2380	15r. "Delhi Princess"	1·75	2·00
2381	15r. "Jawahar"	1·75	2·00
MS2382	87×117 mm. Nos. 2378/81	5·00	5·50

Nos. 2378/**MS**2382 have a rose fragrance.

1774 Manoharbhai Patel

2007. Birth Centenary (2006) of Manoharbhai Patel (industrialist and educationist).

2383	**1774**	5r. multicoloured	1·00	1·00

1775 Elephants at Sonepur Fair, Bihar

2007. Fairs of India. Multicoloured.

2384	5r. Type **1775**	75	85
2385	5r. Pushkar Fair, Rajasthan	75	85
2386	5r. Goa Carnival	75	85
2387	5r. Baul singers at Baul Mela, West Bengal	75	85
MS2388	155×97 mm. Nos. 2384/7	3·50	4·00

1776 Two Women

2007. International Women's Day. Paintings by Joyshree Burman. Multicoloured.

2389	5r. Type **1776**	1·00	1·10
2390	5r. Woman holding fan	1·00	1·10
2391	15r. Woman holding peacock	1·40	1·50
2392	15r. Woman and temple	1·40	1·50
MS2393	130×76 mm. Nos. 2389/2	6·50	7·50

1777 Raj Narain

2007. 90th Birth Anniv of Raj Narain (Minister of Health 1977–80).

2394	**1777**	5r. grey, red and black	1·00	1·00

1778 Mehboob Khan and Scene from *Mother India*

2007. Birth Centenary (2006) of Mehboob Khan (film director).

2395	**1778**	5r. multicoloured	1·00	1·00

1779 Dr. R. M. Alagappa Chettiar

2007. 50th Death Anniv of Dr. R. M. Alagappa Chettiar (educationist and industrialist).

2396	**1779**	5r. multicoloured	1·00	1·00

1780 Statue of Prince Siddhartha Gautama

2007. 2550 Years of Mahaparinirvana of the Buddha. Multicoloured.

2397	5r. Type **1780**	70	80
2398	5r. Two images of Buddha and stone carving (horiz)	70	80
2399	5r. Stone meditating Buddha head from Sarnath	70	80
2400	5r. Bronze ascetic Buddha from Myanmar	70	80
2401	5r. Bhumisaparsha Buddha holding nectar of immortality in jar	70	80
2402	5r. Dharma Chakra and other Hinayama symbols (horiz)	70	80
MS2403	219×135 mm. Nos. 2397/402	4·25	4·50

1781 Tiger, Sambar and Chital Deer, Bandhavgarh National Park, Madhya Pradesh

2007. National Parks of India. Multicoloured.

2404	5r. Type **1781**	1·50	1·25
2405	5r. Gaur and elephants, Bandipur National Park, Karnataka	1·50	1·25
2406	5r. Great one-horned rhinoceros, Kaziranga National Park, Assam	1·50	1·25
2407	5r. Leopard, deer and sloth bear, Mudumalai National Park	1·50	1·25
2408	5r. Elephant, Periyar National Park, Kerala	1·50	1·25

1782 Cavalry and Foot Soldiers in Battle at Kanpur

2007. 150th Anniv of First War of Independence. Multicoloured.

2409	5r. Battle at Lucknow	1·25	1·25
2410	15r. Type **1782**	1·75	1·75
MS2411	150×118 mm. Nos. 2409/10	4·50	5·00

1783 Saint Vallalar

2007. Saint Vallalar (Ramalinga Adigal) Commemoration.

2412	**1783**	5r. multicoloured	1·00	1·00

1784 Maraimalai Adigal

2007. Maraimalai Adigal (Tamil scholar) Commemoration.

2413	**1784**	5r. black, yellow and scarlet	1·00	1·00

1785 V. G.
Suryanarayana
Sastriar

2007. Suryanarayana Sastriar (Tamil scholar)
Commemoration.
2414 **1785** 5r. multicoloured   1·00   1·00

1786 Howrah Bridge,
Kolkata

2007. Landmark Bridges of India. Multicoloured.
2415   5r. Type **1786**   1·25   1·00
2416   5r. Mahatma Gandhi Setu,
       Patna   1·25   1·00
2417   5r. Pamban Bridge over Palk
       Strait   1·25   1·00
2418   5r. Vidyasagar Setu, Kolkata   1·25   1·00
MS2419 150×117 mm. Nos. 2415/18   5·50   6·00

1787 J. P. Naik and Ruins of Nalanda
University, Bihar

2007. Birth Centenary of Dr. Jayant Pandurang Naik
(educationist).
2420 **1787** 5r. cinnamon, black
       and blue   1·00   1·00

1788 Rajya Sabha, Upper House of the
Indian Parliament, New Delhi

2007. 53rd Commonwealth Parliamentary Conference.
2421 **1788** 15r. multicoloured   1·60   1·60

1789 S. D. Burman

2007. Birth Centenary (2006) of Sachin Dev Burman
(singer and composer).
2422 **1789** 15r. multicoloured   1·60   1·60

1790 Gandhi expelled
from Train, South Africa,
1893

2007. Centenary of Satyagraha. Multicoloured.
2423   5r. Type **1790**   1·25   1·00
2424   5r. Gandhi, Indian immigrant in
       Transvaal and *Indian Opinion*
       newspaper, 1906   1·25   1·00
2425   5r. Gandhi addressing crowd,
       South Africa, 1906   1·25   1·00
2426   5r. Gandhi leading Dandi
       March, India, 1930   1·25   1·00
MS2427 106×112 mm. As Nos. 2423/6   6·00   6·50

1791 HAL Dhruv Advanced
Light Helicopter

2007. 75th Anniv of the Indian Air Force. Multicoloured.
2428   5r. Type **1791**   1·00   1·00
2429   5r. Beriev (Ilyushin) A-50 'Main-
       stay' (83×31 mm)   1·00   1·00

2430   5r. Westland Wapiti   1·00   1·00
2431   15r. Ilyushin Il-78 'Midas' tanker
       and two Sukhoi Su-30 Mk 1
       (83×31 mm)   1·00   1·00
MS2432 220×122 mm. Nos. 2428/31   7·00   7·50

1792 Parachutist

2007. Fourth CISM Military World Games, Hyderabad and
Mumbai.
2433   5r. Type **1792**   1·00   1·00
2434   5r. Footballer   1·00   1·00
2435   5r. Swimmer   1·00   1·00
MS2436 83×130 mm. Nos. 2433/5   3·25   3·50

1793 Maharashtra Police
Academy

2007. Centenary of Maharashtra Police Academy.
2437 **1793** 5r. multicoloured   1·25   1·00

1794 Children (Swarali V.
Bhakare)

2007. Children's Day. *The Magic of the Night.* Showing
children's paintings. Multicoloured.
2438   5r. Type **1794**   70   70
2439   5r. Night fishermen   70   70
MS2440 120×78 mm. Nos. 2438/9   1·75   2·00

1795 Solar Energy

2007. Renewable Energy. Multicoloured.
2441   5r. Type **1795**   70   85
2442   5r. Wind energy   70   85
2443   5r. Small hydropower (vert)   70   85
2444   5r. Processing plant ('Biomass
       energy') (vert)   70   85
MS2445 123×100 mm. Nos. 2441/4   3·50   4·00
    Nos. 2441/4 commemorate the Silver Jubilee of the
Ministry of New and Renewable Energy.

1796 Veteran with Medals
and Soldiers on
Mountainside

2007. 150th Anniv of the Raising of the First Battalion of
the Fourth Gorkha Rifles.
2446 **1796** 5r. multicoloured   1·25   1·00

1797 Silhouettes

2007. International Day of Disabled Persons.
2447 **1797** 5r. multicoloured   1·00   1·00
    No. 2447 also has Braille inscriptions.

1798 The Daly
College, Indore

2007. 125th Anniv of the Daly College, Indore.
2448 **1798** 5r. multicoloured   1·00   1·00

1799 Wilson
College, Mumbai

2007. 175th Anniv of Wilson College, Mumbai.
2449 **1799** 5r. multicoloured   1·00   1·00

1800 Road leading
into Sunset

2007. Greetings Stamps. Multicoloured.
2450   5r. Type **1800**   70   80
2451   5r. Water lily and fish   70   80
2452   5r. Bird in flight   70   80
2453   5r. Human face, flowers and
       rural houses   70   80
2454   5r. HAPPY NEW YEAR   70   80

1801 S. B. Chavan and
Irrigation Project

2007. Shankarrao Bhaurao Chavan (parliamentarian)
Commemoration.
2455 **1801** 5r. multicoloured   1·00   1·00

1802 Our Lady of Snows Shrine Basilica

2007. 425th Anniv of Our Lady of Snows Shrine Basilica,
Tuticorin.
2456 **1802** 5r. multicoloured   1·00   1·00

1803 Human Profile and Waves

2007. National Water Year.
2457 **1803** 5r. multicoloured   1·00   1·00

1804 Ritwik Ghatak and
Film Scene

2007. Ritwik Ghatak (film director) Commemoration.
2458 **1804** 5r. multicoloured   1·00   1·00

1805 *Papilio mayo*
(Andaman mormon) (male)

2008. Endemic Butterflies of Andaman and Nicobar
Islands. Multicoloured.
2459   5r. Type **1805**   1·25   1·25
2460   5r. *Papilio mayo* (female)   1·25   1·25
2461   5r. *Pachliopta rhodifer* (Anda-
       man club tail) (female)   1·25   1·25
2462   5r. *Pachliopta rhodifer* (male)   1·25   1·25
MS2463 105×83 mm. Nos. 2459/62   5·50   6·50

1806 Dr. B. P. Pal, Roses
and Disease Resistant
Wheat

2008. Birth Centenary (2006) of Dr. Benjamin Peary Pal
(agricultural scientist).
2464 **1806** 5r. multicoloured   1·00   1·00

1807 Dr. D. R.
Gadgil

2008. Dr. D. R Gadgil (economist) Commemoration.
2465 **1807** 5r. multicoloured   1·00   1·00

1808 Damodaram
Sanjeevaiah

2008. 87th Birth Anniv of Damodaram Sanjeevaiah
(parliamentarian).
2466 **1808** 5r. multicoloured   1·00   1·00

1809 Maharshi Bulusu
Sambamurthy

2008. Maharshi Bulusu Sambamurthy (patriot)
Commemoration.
2467 **1809** 5r. multicoloured   1·00   1·00

1810 Madhubala

2008. 75th Birth Anniv of Madhubala (actress).
2468 **1810** 5r. multicoloured   1·25   1·25
MS2469 92×79 mm. No. 2468   1·50   1·50

1811 Asrar-Ul-Haq
'Majaaz'

2008. Birth Centenary (2009) of Asrar-Ul-Haq 'Majaaz'
(Urdu poet).
2470 **1811** 5r. multicoloured   1·00   1·00

1812 Asokan Capitol

2008. Civil Service.
2471 **1812** 5r. multicoloured   1·00   1·00

1813 Steel Production

2008. Centenary of Tata Steel (2007).
2472　**1813**　5r. multicoloured　　1·00　1·00

1814 Jasmine

2008. Jasmine. Multicoloured.
2473　**1814**　5r. Type **1814**　　1·00　1·00
2474　15r. Close-up of jasmine flowers (horiz)　1·50　1·50
MS2475 107×76 mm. Nos. 2473/4　2·75　3·00
Nos. 2473/MS2475 have a jasmine fragrance.

1815 Mosque ('Heritage Restoration')

2008. 30th Anniv of the Aga Khan Foundation. Multicoloured.
2476　**1815**　5r. Type **1815**　　1·25　1·25
2477　15r. Foundation projects ('Social Commitment') (67×38 mm)　1·75　1·75
MS2478 130×96 mm. Nos. 2476/7　3·50　3·75

1816 Shirdi Sai Baba

2008. 90th Death Anniv of Saint Shirdi Sai Baba.
2479　**1816**　5r. multicoloured　　1·00　1·00

1817 Rajesh Pilot as Pilot and Politician

2008. Rajesh Pilot (Rajeshwar Prasad Singh Vidhudi) (parliamentarian) Commemoration.
2480　**1817**　5r. multicoloured　　1·50　1·00

1818 Henning Holck-Larsen

2008. Henning Holck-Larsen (co-founder of Larsen & Toubro engineering firm) Commemoration.
2481　**1818**　5r. multicoloured　　1·00　1·00

1819 Madhav Institute of Technology and Science, Gwalior and Sir Jiwaji Rao Scindia (founder)

2008. 50th Anniv of Madhav Institute of Technology and Science, Gwalior.
2482　**1819**　5r. multicoloured　　1·00　1·00

1820 Maha Bodhi Temple, Bodh Gaya, India

2008. Temples. Multicoloured.
2483　**1820**　15r. Type **1820**　　1·25　1·40
2484　15r. White Horse Temple, Luoyang, China　1·25　1·40
MS2485 100×100 mm. Nos. 2483/4　4·25　4·50

1821 Soldiers of Nabha Akal Infantry, c. 1757

2008. 250th Anniv of 14 Battalion (Nabha Akal) of Punjab Regiment.
2486　**1821**　5r. multicoloured　　1·50　1·00

1822 Damodar Kosambi

2008. Birth Centenary (2007) of Damodar Kosambi (statistician, mathematician and Indologist).
2487　**1822**　5r. multicoloured　　1·50　1·00

1823 Aldabra Giant Tortoise

2008. Aldabra Giant Tortoise. Multicoloured.
2488　**1823**　5r. Type **1823**　　1·25　1·25
2489　15r. Aldabra giant tortoise (front view)　2·00　2·25
No. MS2490 is left for a miniature sheet not yet received.

1824 Olympic Torch and Huanhuan Mascot

2008. Olympic Games, Beijing. Multicoloured.
2491　**1824**　5r. Type **1824**　　75　75
2492　5r. Boxing　　75　75
2493　15r. Shooting　　1·00　1·00
2494　15r. Archery　　1·00　1·00
MS2495 Nos. 2491/4　4·50　4·50

1825 Dornier Fixed Wing Aircraft

2008. 30th Anniv of Indian Coast Guard. Multicoloured.
2496　5r. Type **1825**　　90　90
2497　5r. Advanced light helicopter　90　90
2498　5r. Hovercraft　　90　90
2499　5r. Advanced offshore patrol vessel　90　90
MS2500 157×118 mm. Nos. 2496/9　5·50　6·00

1826 Ustad Bismillah Khan playing Shehnai

2008. Ustad Bismillah Khan (shehnai player) Commemoration.
2501　**1826**　5r. multicoloured　　1·25　1·00

1827 Sir Pitti Theagarayar and Weaver

2008. Sir Pitti Theagarayar (founder of Justice Party and Chairman of Madras Municipality 1920–3) Commemoration.
2502　**1827**　5r. multicoloured　　1·00　1·00

1828 Dr. C. Natesan

2008. Dr. C. Natesan (founder of Justice Party and co-founder of the Dravidian Movement) Commemoration.
2503　**1828**　5r. multicoloured　　1·00　1·00

1829 Dr. T. M. Nair

2008. Dr. Taravat Mahadevan Nair (founder of Justice Party) Commemoration.
2504　**1829**　5r. multicoloured　　1·00　1·00

1830 Bijoya Dashami, Kolkata

2008. Festivals of India. Multicoloured.
2505　5r. Type **1830**　　70　70
2506　5r. Elephant carrying throne of goddess Chamundeshwari in procession, Dussehra, Mysore　70　70
2507　5r. Lamps ('Happy Deepavali') (vert)　70　70
MS2508 160×110 mm. Nos. 2505/7　2·25　2·50
No. 2505 was incorrectly inscribed 'Dussehra'.

2008. Third Commonwealth Youth Games, Pune. Multicoloured.
2509　5r. Type **1831**　　85　85
2510　5r. Wrestling　　85　85
2511　5r. Badminton　　85　85
2512　5r. Hurdling　　85　85
MS2513 135×99 mm. Nos. 2509/12　6·00　6·50

1832 Rural Post Office

2008. Philately Day.
2514　**1832**　5r. multicoloured　　1·00　1·00
A miniature sheet containing the 5r. stamp, No. 1832, was sold for 15r.

1833 Rice Field

2008. Food Safety and Quality Year 2008–9.
2515　**1833**　5r. multicoloured　　1·00　1·00

1834 Tiger Mascot Shera

2008. 19th Commonwealth Games, New Delhi (2010).
2516　**1834**　5r. multicoloured　　1·00　1·00
A miniature sheet containing the 5r. stamp was sold for 15r.

1835 Girl asleep and Dreaming

2008. Children's Day. 'India of My Dreams'. Designs showing children's paintings by Shanker Dinesh Kamath, Anchal Singh and K. Viswanath. Multicoloured.
2517　5r. Type **1835**　　70　70
2518　5r. Group of young people outside church, mosque and temple　70　70
2519　5r. Man, woman and child sat on crescent moon (vert)　70　70
MS2519a 175×127 mm. Nos. 2517/19　4·00　4·50

1836 Saint Alphonsa

2008. Canonisation of St. Alphonsa Muttathupadathu.
2520　**1836**　5r. multicoloured　　1·00　1·00
A miniature sheet containing this 5r. stamp was sold for 15r.

1837 B. N. Reddi

2008. Birth Centenary of Bommireddi Narasimha Reddi (film director).
2521　**1837**　5r. multicoloured　　1·00　1·00

1838 Standard Chartered Bank Building

2008. 150th Anniv of the Standard Chartered Bank.
2522 **1838** 5r. multicoloured 1·00 1·00

1839 Gasworks

2008. 25th Anniv of GAIL (India) Limited (formerly the Gas Authority of India Limited).
2523 **1839** 5r. multicoloured 1·25 1·00

1840 Joachim and Violet Alva

2008. Birth Centenary of Joachim and Violet Alva (nationalists and journalists).
2524 **1840** 5r. multicoloured 1·00 1·00

1841 Marching Cadets and Cadets abseiling on Training Exercise

2008. 60th Anniv of Sardar Vallabhbhai Patel National Police Academy, Hyderabad. Multicoloured.
2525 5r. Type **1841** 75 75
2526 20r. Statue of Sardar Vallabhbhai Patel 1·75 1·75
MS2527 115×78 mm. Nos. 2525/6 3·50 3·75

1842 St. Joseph's Boys High School

2008. 150th Anniv of St. Joseph's Boys High School, Bangalore.
2528 **1842** 5r. multicoloured 1·00 1·00

1843 Buddhadeva Bose

2008. Birth Centenary of Buddhadeva Bose (writer and educationist).
2529 **1843** 5r. multicoloured 1·00 1·00

1844 Jawaharlal Nehru

1844a Homi Jahangir Baba

2008. Builders of Modern India
2530 **1844** 25p. black and claret 10 10
2531 – 50p. blue and grey 10 10
2532 – 1r. black, bistre and brown 10 10
2533 – 2r. purple and deep purple 25 10
2534 – 3r. chocolate, purple and mauve 35 10
2535 **1844a** 4r. multicoloured 50 10
2536 – 5r. black and bistre 60 20
2537 – 5r. reddish brown and brown 60 20
2538 – 10r. red, black and pink 60 60
2539 – 15r. black, grey and mauve 1·75 1·00
2540 – 20r. purple, claret and black 1·90 1·00

2541 50r. black, brown-lilac and claret (11.5.09) 4·25 4·25

DESIGNS—(20×22 mm) No. 2531 E.V. Ramasami; No. 2532 Mahatma Gandhi; No. 2533 Dr. B. R. Ambedkar; No. 2534 Satajit Ray; No. 2536 Indira Gandhi; No. 2537 Rajiv Gandhi. (20×30 mm)—(as T **1844a**) No. 2538 C.V. Raman; No. 2539 J.R.D. Tata; No. 2540 Mother Teresa; No. 2541 Rukmini Devi Arundale (classical music revivalist).

1845 Sunspot and Measurements of Gas Flow

2008. Centenary of the Discovery of the Evershed Effect (the radial flow of gas across the photospheric surface of sunspots).
2542 **1845** 5r. multicoloured 1·00 1·00

1846 Handshake, Map, Warship and Helicopter

2008. Navy Day. 'Reaching Out to Maritime Neighbours'.
2543 **1846** 5r. multicoloured 1·50 1·00

1847 Christmas Star and Sheep

2008. Christmas. Multicoloured.
2544 5r. Type **1847** 75 75
2545 20r. Mary and baby Jesus 1·75 1·75

1848 Dr. Laxmi Mall Singhvi

2008. Dr. Laxmi Mall Singhvi (jurist and constitutional expert) Commemoration.
2546 **1848** 5r. multicoloured 1·00 1·00

1849 Mahatma Gandhi, Abraham Lincoln, Mother Teresa and Martin Luther King

2008. 60th Anniv of the Universal Declaration of Human Rights.
2547 **1849** 5r. multicoloured 1·00 1·00

1850 Indian Institute of Science, Bangalore

2008. Centenary of the Indian Institute of Science, Bangalore. Multicoloured.
2548 5r. Type **1850** 75 75
2549 20r. Scientists and academics including founder Jamsetji Tata and former director C. V. Raman 1·75 1·75
MS2550 130×85 mm. Nos. 2548/9 3·75 4·25

1851 Swami Ranganathananda Maharaj

2008. Birth Centenary of Swami Ranganathananda Maharaj (13th President of Ramakrishna Math and Mission, Kolkata).
2551 **1851** 5r. multicoloured 1·00 1·00

1852 Field Marshal Manekshaw

2008. Field Marshal S. H. F. J. Manekshaw Commemoration.
2552 **1852** 5r. multicoloured 1·00 1·00

1853 T. V. Ramasubbaiyer

2008. Birth Centenary of T. V. Ramasubbaiyer (founder of Tamil newspaper Dinamalar and philanthropist).
2553 **1853** 5r. multicoloured 1·00 1·00

1854 BRAHMOS Missile and Fighter Plane

2008. Tenth Anniv of BRAHMOS Supersonic Cruise Missile. Multicoloured.
2554 5r. Type **1854** 75 50
2555 20r. Warship launching BRAHMOS missile, missiles (on ground) and fighter planes (horiz) 1·75 2·00
MS2556 135×88 mm. Nos. 2554/5 4·00 4·25

1855 Rani Velu Nachchiyar

2008. Rani Velu Nachchiyar (Queen of Sivaganga, 1780–c.1790) Commemoration.
2557 **1855** 5r. multicoloured 1·00 1·00

1856 M. Bhakthavatsalam

2008. M. Bhakthavatsalam (Chief Minister of Madras State 1963–7) Commemoration.
2558 **1856** 5r. multicoloured 1·00 1·00

1857 Thillaiyadi Valliammai

2008. Thillaiyadi Valliammai (anti-Apartheid campaigner in South Africa) Commemoration.
2559 **1857** 5r. multicoloured 1·00 1·00

1858 Sheik Thambi Pavalar

2008. Sheik Thambi Pavalar (Tamil poet) Commemoration.
2560 **1858** 5r. multicoloured 1·00 1·00

1859 A. T. Paneerselvam

2008. A. T. Paneerselvam (Chairman of Indian Banks Association 1997–2000) Commemoration.
2561 **1859** 5r. multicoloured 1·00 1·00

1860 Udumalai Narayana Kavi

2008. Udumalai Narayana Kavi (songwriter) Commemoration.
2562 **1860** 5r. multicoloured 1·00 1·00

1861 Louis Braille and Hands reading Braille

2009. Birth Bicentenary of Louis Braille (inventor of Braille writing for the blind).
2563 **1861** 5r. multicoloured 1·00 1·00
No. 2563 is embossed with Braille characters.

1862 Vaikom Muhammad Basheer

2009. Birth Centenary of Vaikom Muhammad Basheer (Malayalam novelist and short story writer).
2564 **1862** 5r. multicoloured 1·00 1·00

1863 St. Paul's Church, Chennai

2009. 150th Anniv of St. Paul's Church, Chennai.
2565 **1863** 5r. multicoloured 1·00 1·00

1864 Jaisalmer Fort

2009. Heritage Monuments Preservation by INTACH (Indian National Trust for Art and Cultural Heritage). Multicoloured.

2566	5r. Type **1864**	70	85
2567	5r. Mongyu Monastery, Laddakh	70	85
2568	5r. St. Anne Church, Goa	70	85
2569	5r. Qila Mubarak, Patiala	70	85
MS2570	120×76 mm. Nos. 2566/9	3·50	3·75

1865 Bishnu Prasad Rabha

2009. Birth Centenary of Bishnu Prasad Rabha (poet, dramatist, musician, dancer and actor).

2571	**1865**	5r. multicoloured	1·00	1·00

1866 Steel Production

2009. 50th Anniv of SAIL (Steel Authority of India).

2572	**1866**	5r. multicoloured	1·00	1·00

1867 Young Girl running

2009. National Girl Child Day.

2573	**1867**	5r. multicoloured	1·00	1·00

1868 Sant Santaji Jagnade Maharaj

2009. Sant Santaji Jagnade Maharaj Commemoration.

2574	**1868**	5r. multicoloured	1·00	1·00

1869 Maha Kavi Magh

2009. Maha Kavi Magh (Sanskrit poet) Commemoration.

2575	**1869**	5r. multicoloured	1·00	1·00

1870 Family under Umbrella

2009. 125th Anniv of Postal Life Insurance.

2576	**1870**	5r. multicoloured	1·00	1·00

1871 Jainacharya Vallabh Suri

2009. Jainacharya Vallabh Suri (Jain monk) Commemoration.

2577	**1871**	5r. multicoloured	1·00	1·00

1872 Harakh Chand Nahata and Mountain Road

2009. Harakh Chand Nahata (entrepreneur, philanthropist and patron of the arts) Commemoration.

2578	**1872**	5r. multicoloured	1·00	1·00

1873 Medical Council of India

2009. 75th Anniv of the Medical Council of India.

2579	**1873**	5r. multicoloured	1·00	1·00

1874 *Pterospermum acerifolium*

2009. *Pterospermum acerifolium* (flowering tree).

2580	**1874**	5r. multicoloured	1·00	1·00

1875 Baburao Puleshwar Shedmake

2009. Baburao Puleshwar Shedmake (revolutionary) Commemoration.

2581	**1875**	5r. multicoloured	1·00	1·00

1876 Dr. Krishna Kumar Birla

2009. Dr. Krishna Kumar Birla (industrialist) Commemoration.

2582	**1876**	5r. multicoloured	1·00	1·00

1877 Black Pepper

2009. Spices of India. Multicoloured.

2583	5r. Type **1877**	70	80
2584	5r. Cinnamon	70	80
2585	5r. Cardamom	70	80
2586	5r. Clove	70	80
2587	20r. Turmeric, chilly and coriander	1·75	2·00
MS2588	129×129 mm. Nos. 2583/7	5·50	6·50

1878 R. Sankar

2009. Birth Centenary of R. Sankar (former Minister for Education in Kerala).

2589	**1878**	5r. multicoloured	1·00	1·00

1879 Lifeline Express

2009. Lifeline Express (first modern hospital train).

2590	**1879**	5r. multicoloured	1·50	1·00

1880 Soldier of Madras Regiment

2009. 250th Anniv of Madras Regiment.

2591	**1880**	5r. multicoloured	65	65

1881 Rev. J. J. M. Nichols Roy

2009. 125th Birth Anniv of Rev. James Joy Mohan Nichols Roy (political leader of Assam).

2592	**1881**	5r. multicoloured	65	65

1882 Sacred Heart Church

2009. Centenary of Sacred Heart Church, Pudducherry.

2593	**1882**	5r. multicoloured	65	65

1883 Rampur Raza Library

2009. Rampur Raza Library. Multicoloured.

2594	5r. Type **1883**	50	50
2595	5r. Ram and Laxman with Jatayu (from *Valmiki Ramayana* by Sumer Chand) (vert)	50	50
2596	5r. Madonna holding a book (from Jahangir's album) (vert)	50	50
2597	5r. Illustrated page from *Diwan-i-Hafiz* of Akbar's personal collection (vert)	50	50
MS2598	116×145 mm. Nos. 2594/7	2·50	2·50

1884 Petrol Pumps and Oil Refinery

2009. 50th Anniv of Indian Oil Corporation.

2599	**1884**	5r. multicoloured	65	65

1885 Academy Building

2009. 50th Anniv of Lal Bahadur Shastri National Academy of Administration.

2600	**1885**	5r. multicoloured	65	65

1886 Ramcharan Agarwal

2009. Ramcharan Agarwal (nationalist) Commemoration.

2601	**1886**	5r. multicoloured	65	65

1887 The Poet Jayadeva

2009. Jayadeva (Sanskrit poet) and his epic poem *Geetagovinda*. Designs showing Jayadeva (No. 2602) and incarnations of Vishnu. Multicoloured.

2602	5r. Type **1887**	50	50
2603	5r. Kurma the Tortoise	50	50
2604	5r. Varaaha the Boar	50	50
2605	5r. Matsya the Fish	50	50
2606	5r. Vaamana the Dwarf	50	50
2607	5r. Parasuraama	50	50
2608	5r. Narasimha the Man-lion	50	50
2609	5r. Balaraama	50	50
2610	5r. Buddha	50	50
2611	5r. Raama	50	50
2612	5r. Kalki	50	50
MS2613	160×200 mm. Nos. 2602/12	6·25	6·25

1888 St. Joseph's College, Bangalore

2009. St. Joseph's College, Bangalore.

2614	**1888**	5r. multicoloured	65	65

1889 Maharshi Patanjali and Symbols of his Work

2009. Maharshi Patanjali (yogi) Commemoration.

2615	**1889**	5r. multicoloured	65	65

1890 Pingali Venkaiah

2009. Pingali Venkaiah (designer of Indian tricolour) Commemoration.

2616	**1890**	5r. multicoloured	65	65

1891 Howrah Station

2009. Heritage Railway Stations. Multicoloured.

2617	5r. Type **1891**	50	50
2618	5r. Chennai Central Station	50	50
2619	5r. Mumbai CST Station	50	50
2620	5r. Old Delhi Station	50	50

No. **MS**2621 is left for miniature sheet not yet received.

1892 Uttam Kumar

2009. Uttam Kumar (actor) Commemoration.

2622	**1892**	5r. multicoloured	65	65

1893 School Building and Statue

2009. Sacred Heart Matriculation Higher Secondary School, Chennai.
| 2623 | **1893** | 5r. multicoloured | 65 | 65 |

1894 Holy Cross Church

2009. Holy Cross Church, Mapranam.
| 2624 | **1894** | 5r. multicoloured | 65 | 65 |

1895 Dushyant Kumar

2009. Dushyant Kumar (writer) Commemoration.
| 2625 | **1895** | 5r. multicoloured | 65 | 65 |

1896 Barbe's Leaf Monkey

2009. Rare Fauna of the North East. Multicoloured.
2626		5r. Type **1896**	50	50
2627		5r. Marbled cat	50	50
2628		5r. Red panda (horiz)	50	50
MS2629	143×114 mm. Nos. 2626/8		2·75	2·75

1897 Mahatma Gandhi

2009. Mahatma Gandhi and Non Violence.
| 2630 | **1897** | 25r. multicoloured | 2·00 | 2·00 |

1898 Bishop Cotton School and Stained Glass Window

2009. 150th Anniv of Bishop Cotton School, Shimla.
| 2631 | **1898** | 5r. multicoloured | 65 | 65 |

1899 R. K. Narayan

2009. R. K. Narayan (writer) Commemoration.
| 2632 | **1899** | 5r. multicoloured | 65 | 65 |

1900 Dineshnandini Dalmia

2009. Dineshnandini Dalmia (Hindi poet and novelist) Commemoration.
| 2633 | **1900** | 5r. multicoloured | 65 | 65 |

1901 India Post Freighter and Mail Bags

2009. India Post Freighter (aircraft).
| 2634 | **1901** | 5r. multicoloured | 65 | 65 |

1902 Dilwara Temple, near Mount Abu

2009. Heritage Temples. Multicoloured.
| 2635 | | 5r. Type **1902** | 50 | 50 |
| 2636 | | 5r. Ranakpur Temple, near Sadri | 50 | 50 |

No. MS2637 is left for miniature sheet not yet received.

1903 Maharaja Gulab Singh

2009. Maharaja Gulab Singh (founder of Jammu & Kashmir State) Commemoration.
| 2638 | **1903** | 5r. multicoloured | 65 | 65 |

1904 Major General Dewan Misri Chand

2009. Major General Dewan Misri Chand (pioneer aviator) Commemoration.
| 2639 | **1904** | 5r. multicoloured | 65 | 65 |

1905 Old People's Home

2009. Canonization of St. Jeanne Jugan (founder of Order of the Little Sisters of the Poor). T **1905** and similar multicoloured design.
| 2640 | | 5r. Type **1905** | 50 | 50 |
| 2641 | | 20r. St. Jeanne Jugan (29×32 mm) | 1·75 | 1·75 |

Nos. 2640/1 were printed together, se-tenant, in horizontal pairs throughout the sheet, each pair forming a composite design.

1906 Dr. Rajkumar

2009. 80th Birth Anniv of Dr. Rajkumar (actor in Kannada cinema).
| 2642 | **1906** | 5r. multicoloured | 65 | 65 |

1907 Dr. Mahendra Lal Sircar

2009. Dr. Mahendra Lal Sircar (homeopath) Commemoration.
| 2643 | **1907** | 5r. multicoloured | 65 | 65 |

1908 Apollo Hospitals

2009. Apollo Hospitals Group.
| 2644 | **1908** | 5r. multicoloured | 65 | 65 |

1909 Danmal Mathur

2009. Danmal Mathur (pioneer of scout movement in Rajasthan) Commemoration.
| 2645 | **1909** | 5r. multicoloured | 65 | 65 |

1910 Virchand Raghavji Gandhi

2009. Virchand Raghavji Gandhi (Jain scholar) Commemoration.
| 2646 | **1910** | 5r. multicoloured | 65 | 65 |

1911 Kathiawari Horses

2009. Indigenous Horses. T **1911** and similar horiz designs. Multicoloured.
2647		5r. Type **1911**	50	50
2648		5r. Marwari	50	50
2649		5r. Zanskari	50	50
2650		5r. Manipuri	50	50
MS2651	156×88 mm. Nos. 2647/50		2·75	2·75

1912 Rajabhau Khobragade

2009. Rajabhau Khobragade (politician) Commemoration.
| 2652 | **1912** | 5r. multicoloured | 65 | 65 |

1913 Gaurishanker Dalmia

2009. Gaurishanker Dalmia (magazine publisher) Commemoration.
| 2653 | **1913** | 5r. multicoloured | 65 | 65 |

1914 Silhouettes and Emblem

2009. 60th Anniv of the Commonwealth.
| 2654 | **1914** | 5r. multicoloured | 65 | 65 |

1915 Deer drinking from Forest Pool

2009. Children's Day. Showing children's paintings.
| 2655 | | 5r. Type **1915** | 50 | 50 |
| 2656 | | 5r. Tiger | 50 | 50 |

1916 The Silent Valley

2009. 25th Anniv of Silent Valley National Park
| 2657 | **1916** | 5r. multicoloured | 65 | 65 |
| MS2658 | 88×128 mm. No. 2657 | | 1·75 | 1·75 |

1917 Gangetic Dolphin (*Platanista gangetica*)

2009. Dolphin and Whale Shark. Multicoloured.
2659		5r. Type **1917**	50	50
2660		20r. Whale shark (*Rhincodon typus*)	1·75	1·75
MS2661	120×66 mm. Nos. 2657/8		2·25	2·25

Nos. 2659/60 were printed together, se-tenant, forming a composite design.
Similar designs were issued by the Phillipines.

1918 Ganpatrao Govindrao Jadhav

2009. Ganpatrao Govindrao Jadhav (newspaper publisher) Commemoration.
| 2662 | **1918** | 5r. multicoloured | 65 | 65 |

1919 Tamilnadu Police on Parade

2009. 150th Anniv of Tamilnadu Police.
| 2663 | **1919** | 5r. multicoloured | 65 | 65 |

1920 Mandala

2009. Greetings Stamps. Multicoloured.
2664		5r. Type **1920**	50	50
2665		5r. Four white filigree patterns	50	50
2666		5r. Pattern of flowers and hearts	50	50
2667		5r. Floral pattern	50	50
MS2668	108×79 mm. Nos. 2664/7		2·75	2·75

1921 Cavalryman of 1809 and Modern Tank

2009. Bicentenary of 2nd Lancers (Gardner's Horse) Regiment.
| 2669 | **1921** | 5r. multicoloured | 65 | 65 |

1922 Pupils and School Building

2009. Centenary of Convent of Jesus and Mary School, Ambala Cant.
| 2670 | **1922** | 5r. multicoloured | 65 | 65 |

1923 Kalamkari

2009. Traditional Indian Textiles. T **1923** and similar vert designs. Multicoloured.

2671	5r. Type **1923**	50	50
2672	5r. Apa Tani weaves	50	50
2673	5r. Kanchipuram silk	50	50
2674	5r. Banaras silk	50	50
MS2675 160×90 mm. Nos. 2671/4		2·75	2·75

1924 Henry Derozio

2009. Birth Bicentenary of Henry Louis Vivian Derozio (poet).

2676	**1924**	5r. black, brown-purple and yellow-ochre	65	65

1925 Lal Pratap Singh

2009. Lal Pratap Singh (Prince of Kalakankar) Commemoration.

2677	**1925**	5r. multicoloured	65	65

1926 Penguins

2009. Preserve the Polar Regions and Glaciers. T **1926** and similar horiz design. Multicoloured.

2678	5r. Type **1926**	50	50
2679	5r. Polar bear	50	50

1927 Venkataramana Bhagvathar

2009. Venkataramana Bhagvathar (composer of Carnatic music) Commemoration.

2681	**1927**	5r. multicoloured	65	65

1928 Figures forming Triangle

2009. Indian Mathematical Society.

2682	**1928**	5r. multicoloured	65	65

1929 Maharaja Surajmal

2009. Maharaja Surajmal (founder of Kingdom of Bharatpur) Commemoration.

2683	**1929**	5r. multicoloured	65	65

1930 Lok Sabha (Indian Parliament) Building

2010. 20th Conference of Speakers and Presiding Officers of the Commonwealth, New Delhi

2684	**1930**	5r. multicoloured	65	65

1931 Entrance to Reserve Bank

2010. 75th Anniv of the Reserve Bank of India

2685	**1931**	5r. multicoloured	65	65

1932 Voters, Identity Card and Vote

2010. 60th Anniv of the Election Commission of India

2686	**1932**	5r. multicoloured	65	65

1933 Bible and Dove

2010. Bicentenary of the Bible Society of India

2687	**1933**	5r. multicoloured	75	75

1934 P. C. Sorcar

2010. 98th Birth Anniv of Protul Chandra Sorcar (magician)

2688	**1934**	5r. multicoloured	75	75

1935 Insignia (Galley) and 18th-century Sikh and Dogra Soldiers

2010. 300th Anniv of 16 Punjab (2nd Patiala) Regiment

2689	**1935**	5r. multicoloured	75	75

1936 Muthuramalinga Sethupathi

2010. Death Bicentenary (2009) of Muthuramalinga Sethupathi (King of Ramanathapuram).

2690	**1936**	5r. multicoloured	75	75

1937 Special Protection Group surrounding Car

2010. 25th Anniv of Special Protection Group (for Prime Minister of India)

2691	**1937**	5r. multicoloured	75	75

1938 Vallal Pachaiyappa and Temple

2010. Vallal Pachaiyappa (philanthropist) Commemoration

2692	**1938**	5r. multicoloured	75	75

Nos. 2693/704, **MS**2705, T **1939** are left for Astrological Signs, issued 14 April 2010, not yet received.

1939 Pisces

2010. Astrological Signs. Multicoloured.

2693	5r. Type **1939**	50	50
2694	5r. Aries (horiz)	50	50
2695	5r. Taurus (horiz)	50	50
2696	5r. Gemini (horiz)	50	50
2697	5r. Cancer	50	50
2698	5r. Leo	50	50
2699	5r. Virgo	50	50
2700	5r. Libra (horiz)	50	50
2701	5r. Scorpio (horiz)	50	50
2702	5r. Sagittarius (horiz)	50	50
2703	5r. Capricorn	50	50
2704	5r. Aquarius	50	50
MS2705 160×159 mm. Nos. 2693/704		7·75	7·75

1940 Chandra Shekhar

2010. Chandra Shekhar (Prime Minister of India 1990–1) Commemoration.

2706	**1940**	5r. multicoloured	75	75

1941 Kanwar Ram Sahib

2010. 125th Birth Anniv of Kanwar Ram Sahib (spiritual leader and singer)

2707	**1941**	5r. multicoloured	75	75

1942 Velu Thampi

2010. Death Bicentenary (2009) of Velu Thampi (Prime Minister of Travancore 1804–9)

2708	**1942**	5r. multicoloured	75	75

1943 Robert Caldwell and Kannada, Tamil, Malayalam and Telugu Languages

2010. Robert Caldwell (missionary and scholar of South Indian languages) Commemoration.

2709	**1943**	5r. multicoloured	75	75

1944 Dr. Guduru Venkata Chalam and Rice

2010. Birth Centenary (2009) of Dr. Guduru Venkata Chalam (agricultural scientist)

2710	**1944**	5r. multicoloured	75	75

1945 Lucknow Post Office

2010. Indipex 2011 World Philatelic Exhibition, Delhi (1st issue). Postal Heritage. Buildings. Multicoloured.

2711	5r. Type **1945**	55	55
2712	5r. Nagpur Post Office	55	55
2713	5r. Udagamandalam Head Post Office	55	55
2714	5r. Shimla Post Office	55	55
2715	5r. Delhi Post Office	55	55
2716	5r. Cooch Behar Head Post Office	55	55
MS2717 187×144 mm. Nos. 2711/16		4·00	4·00

1946 C. V. Raman Pillai

2010. C. V. Raman Pillai (Malayalam novelist) Commemoration

2718	**1946**	5r. black, cinnamon and stone	75	75

1947 Planting Rice and Owl

2010. International Year of Biodiversity. Multicoloured.

2719	5r. Type **1947**	65	65
2720	20r. Fish, water lilies, crab and goose in wetland	2·10	2·10
MS2721 95×67 mm. Nos. 2719/20		3·25	3·25

No. **MS**2721 forms a composite design.

1948 Deshbandhu Gupta

2010. 110th Birth Anniv of Deshbandhu Gupta (journalist)

2722	**1948**	5r. multicoloured	75	75

1949 Tiger Mascot Shera carrying Queen's Baton

2010. 19th Commonwealth Games, New Delhi (2nd issue). Multicoloured.

2723	5r. Type **1949**	65	65
2724	20r. Hand holding baton and Shera mascot as relay runner	2·10	2·10
MS2725 199×124 mm. Nos. 2723/4		3·25	3·25

1950 Kumaraguruparar Swamigal

2010. Kumaraguruparar Swamigal (saint and Tamil poet) Commemoration

2726   **1950**   5r. black and red-brown   75   75

1951 Emblem (statue of ancient saint and poet Thiruvalluvar)

2010. World Classical Tamil Conference–Kovai–2010, Coimbatore

2727   **1951**   5r. multicoloured   75   75

1952 Sea Harrier and Sea Hawk

2010. 50th Anniv of Indian Naval Air Squadron 300 ('White Tigers')

2728   **1952**   5r. multicoloured   75   75

1953 Pigeons

2010. Pigeons and Sparrows. Multicoloured.

2729   5r. Type **1953**   65   65
2730   5r. Pair of sparrows   65   65
MS2731 100×141 mm. Nos. 2729/30   2·25   2·25

1954 Procession of Statues of Lord Jagannath, Balabhadra and Subhadra in Wooden Chariots

2010. Rath Yatra Festival, Puri

2732   **1954**   5r. multicoloured   75   75
MS2733 127×65 mm. No. 2732   1·75   1·75

1955 Jawaharlal Nehru Stadium

2010. 19th Commonwealth Games, New Delhi (3rd issue). Multicoloured.

2735   5r. Type **1955**   65   65
2736   5r. Talkatora Stadium   65   65
MS2737 164×104 mm. Nos. 2735/6   2·25   2·25

1956 Syed Mohammed Ali Shihab Thangal

2010. First Death Anniv of Syed Mohammed Ali Shihab Thangal (President of Kerala Muslim League, philanthropist and Islamic scholar)

2738   **1956**   5r. multicoloured   75   75

1957 Vethathiri Maharishi

2010. Birth Centenary of Yogiraj Shri Vethathiri Maharishi (spiritual leader and founder-trustee of the World Community Service Centre)

2739   **1957**   5r. multicoloured   75   75

1958 P. Jeevanandham

2010. P. Jeevanandham (Communist leader and social reformer) Commemoration

2740   **1958**   5r. multicoloured   75   75

1959 Omanthur P. Ramaswamy Reddiar

2010. Omanthur P. Ramaswamy Reddiar (Chief Minister of Madras, 1947-9) Commemoration

2741   **1959**   5r. multicoloured   75   75

1960 G. K. Moopanar

2010. G. K. Moopanar (senior Indian National Congress leader) Commemoration

2742   **1960**   5r. multicoloured   75   75

1961 Dr. Y. S. Rajasekhara Reddy

2010. Dr. Yedugiri Sandinti Rajasekhara Reddy (Chief Minister of Andhra Pradesh 2004-9) Commemoration

2743   **1961**   5r. multicoloured   75   75

1962 Brihadeeswarar Temple

2010. Brihadeeswarar Temple

2744   **1962**   5r. multicoloured   75   75

1963 Badminton

2010. 19th Commonwealth Games, Delhi (4th issue). Multicoloured.

2745   5r. Type **1963**   60   60
2746   5r. Archery   60   60
2747   5r. Hockey   60   60
2748   5r. Athlete sprinting   60   60
MS2749 142×72 mm. Nos. 2745/8   2·75   2·75

1964 Indore 1886 ½ a. Stamp and Maharaja Yeshwant Rao Holkar II Stamp

2010. Indipex 2011 World Philatelic Exhibition, Delhi (2nd issue). Indian Postage Stamps. Princely States. Multicoloured.

2750   5r. Type **1964**   60   60
2751   5r. Sirmoor 1899 1r. Raja Shamsher Parkash, 1878 1p. blue and 1894 4a. elephant stamp   60   60
2752   5r. Bamra 1888 Raja Sudhal Deo and 1890 1r. stamps   60   60
2753   5r. Cochin 1898 1 put pink and 1911 3p. Raja Rama Varma I stamps   60   60
MS2754 193×83 mm. Nos. 2750/3   2·75   2·75

1965 The Doon School, Dehradun

2010. 75th Anniv of the Doon School, Dehradun

2755   **1965**   5r. multicoloured   75   75

1966 Sant Shadaram Sahib

2010. Sant Shadaram Sahib Commemoration

2756   **1966**   5r. multicoloured   75   75

1967 Cathedral and John Connon School, Mumbai

2010. 150th Anniv of Cathedral and John Connon School, Mumbai

2757   **1967**   5r. multicoloured   75   75

1968 Kranti Trivedi

2010. First Death Anniv of Kranti Trivedi (Hindi author)

2758   **1968**   5r. multicoloured   75   75

1969 K. A. P. Viswanatham

2010. K. A. P. Viswanatham (Tamil scholar) Commemoration

2759   **1969**   5r. multicoloured   75   75

1970 Two Dolls

2010. Children's Day. Toys

2760   5r. Type **1970**   60   60
2761   5r. Kite   60   60
2762   5r. Spinning tops   60   60
2763   5r. Two dolls (different) (29×39 mm)   60   60
MS2764 117×114 mm. Nos. 2760/3   2·75   2·75

1971 Lakshmipat Singhania

2010. Birth Centenary of Lakshmipat Singhania (industrialist)

2765   **1971**   5r. multicoloured   75   75

1972 Buildings

2010. 150th Anniv of Comptroller and Auditor General of India

2766   **1972**   5r. multicoloured   75   75

1973 C. Subramaniam

2010. Birth Centenary of Chidambaram Subramaniam (Minister for Food and Agriculture 1964-7, led Indian self-sufficiency in wheat)

2767   **1973**   5r. multicoloured   75   75

1974 Kamlapat Singhania

2010. 125th Birth Anniv of Kamlapat Singhania (industrialist)

2768   **1974**   5r. multicoloured   75   75

1975 Veenai Dhanammal (Carnatic musician)

2010. Tamil Musicians. Multicoloured.

2769   5r. Type **1975**   75   75
2770   5r. T. N. Rajarathinam Pillai (Carnatic musician) (vert)   75   75
2771   5r. Thanjavur Balasaraswathi (dancer and musician) (vert)   75   75

1976 Sri Sri Borda

2010. Sri Sri Borda (Amarendranath Chakravarty) (spiritual leader) Commemoration

2772   **1976**   5r. multicoloured   75   75

1977 Prafulla Chandra Chaki

2010. Prafulla Chandra Chaki (revolutionary) Commemoration

2773   **1977**   5r. multicoloured   75   75

1978 Jarabe Tapatio Dance, Mexico

2010. 60th Anniv of Diplomatic Relations between India and Mexico. Dances. Multicoloured.

2774	5r. Type **1978**	55	55
2775	20r. Kalbelia dance, India	2·25	2·25
MS2776	141×96 mm. Nos. 2774/5	3·25	3·25

Similar designs were issued by Mexico.

1979 Tiger in Madhubani Wall Painting

2010. Crafts Museum, New Delhi. Multicoloured.

2777	5r. Type **1979**	65	65
2778	5r. Statues	65	65
MS2779	175×97 mm. Nos. 2777/8	2·25	2·25

1980 Bhausaheb Hiray

2010. Bhausaheb Hiray (educationist) Commemoration

2780	**1980**	5r. multicoloured	75	75

1981 Yashwantrao Balwantrao Chavan

2010. Yashwantrao Balwantrao Chavan (Union Home Minister 1966-70, Union Finance Minister 1970-4, Union Foreign Minister 1974-7, Deputy Prime Minister and Home Minister 1979) Commemoration

2781	**1981**	5r. multicoloured	75	75

1982 Bhai Jeevan Singh

2010. Bhai Jeevan Singh (Sikh General) Commemoration

2782	**1982**	5r. multicoloured	75	75

1983 Central Bank of India

2010. Centenary of Central Bank of India

2783	**1983**	5r. multicoloured	75	75

1984 Jadavpur University, Kolkata

2010. National Council of Education and Dr. Triguna Sen (founder and first Vice Chancellor of Jadavpur University, Union Minister for Education 1967-8, Union Minister for Petroleum 1969) Commemoration. Multicoloured.

2784	5r. Type **1984**	75	75
2785	5r. Dr. Triguna Sen (29×29 mm)	75	75

1985 Immanuel Sekaranar

2010. Immanuel Sekaranar Commemoration

2786	**1985**	5r. multicoloured	75	75

1986 Artwork

2010. Lalit Kala Akademi (National Academy of Art), New Delhi

2787	**1986**	5r. multicoloured	75	75

1987 Emblem and Sunset

2011. Centenary of *Doot* (Gujarati monthly magazine)

2788	**1987**	5r. multicoloured	75	75

1988 Bronze Statue of Krishnadevaraya

2011. Krishnadevaraya (16th-century King of Vijayanagara empire)

2789	**1988**	5r. multicoloured	75	75
MS2790	96×57 mm. No. 2789		1·75	1·75

1989 Chaudhary Ranbir Singh

2011. Chaudhary Ranbir Singh (parliamentarian) Commemoration

2791	**1989**	5r. multicoloured	75	75

1990 Mary Ward (founder of the Institute of the Blessed Virgin Mary) and Loreto Institutions

2011. Loreto Institutions

2792	**1990**	5r. multicoloured	75	75

1991 Corps of Signals

2011. Centenary of the Corps of Signals of the Indian Army

2793	**1991**	5r. multicoloured	75	75

1992 V. Subbiah

2011. V. Subbiah (Communist leader and nationalist) Commemoration

2794	**1992**	5r. multicoloured	75	75

1993 Census-taker and Human Figures

2011. Census of India

2795	**1993**	5r. multicoloured	75	75

1994 V. Venkatasubba Reddiar

2011. V. Venkatasubba Reddiar (independence leader and Chief Minister of Puducherry 1964-8) Commemoration

2796	**1994**	5r. multicoloured	75	75

1995 Pilot Henri Pequet and Newspaper Headline

2011. Indipex 2011 World Philatelic Exhibition, Delhi (3rd issue). Centenary of World's First Official Airmail Flight. Multicoloured.

2797	5r. Type **1995**	60	60
2798	5r. Allahabad Fort and map showing flight path from Al-lahabad to Naini (32×58 mm)	60	60
2799	5r. Pequet's Sommer biplane flying over river Yamuna, 18 February 1911 (32×58 mm)	60	60
2800	5r. Postcard and letter with First Aerial Post cancellations	60	60
MS2801	226×129 mm. Nos. 2797/800	2·75	2·75

1996 Devika Rani

2011. Legendary Heroines of India (actresses). Multicoloured.

2802	5r. Type **1996**	55	55
2803	5r. Nutan	55	55
2804	5r. Kanan Devi	55	55
2805	5r. Savithri	55	55
2806	5r. Meena Kumari	55	55
2807	5r. Leela Naidu	55	55
MS2808	140×126 mm. Nos. 2802/7	4·00	4·00

1997 La Martiniere School for Girls, Kolkata and Bust of Major General Claude Martin (founder)

2011. 175th Anniv of La Martiniere Schools, Kolkata, Lucknow and Lyon

2809	**1997**	5r. multicoloured	75	75

1998 Subhadra Joshi

2011. Subhadra Joshi (social reformer and parliamentarian) Commemoration

2810	**1998**	5r. multicoloured	75	75

1999 Vaju Kotak (founder)

2011. *Chitralekha* (Gujarati magazine)

2811	**1999**	5r. multicoloured	75	75

2000 Umrao Kunwar Ji 'Archana'

2011. Umrao Kunwar Ji 'Archana' (Jain saint) Commemoration

2812	**2000**	5r. multicoloured	75	75

2001 Rabindranath Tagore writing

2011. 150th Birth Anniv of Rabindranath Tagore (poet). Multicoloured.

2813	5r. Type **2001**	65	65
2814	5r. Rabindranath Tagore as young man and painting of flowers	65	65
MS2815	185×58 mm. Nos. 2813/14	2·25	2·25

2002 Indian Elephant

2011. Second Africa - India Forum Summit, Addis Ababa, Ethiopia. Elephants. Multicoloured.

2816	5r. Type **2002**	55	55
2817	25r. African elephant	2·75	2·75
MS2818	172×96 mm. Nos. 2816/17	4·00	4·00

2003 Dr. D. S. Kothari

2011. Dr. D. S. Kothari (educationist) Commemoration

2819	**2003**	5r. multicoloured	75	75

2004 United Theological College, Bangalore

2011. Centenary of United Theological College, Bangalore

2820	**2004**	5r. multicoloured	75	75

2005 Vitthal Sakharam Page

2011. Vitthal Sakharam Page (politician and campaigner for Employment Guarantee Scheme) Commemoration

2821	**2005**	5r. multicoloured	75	75

2006 Kasu Brahmananda Reddy

2011. Kasu Brahmananda Reddy (Chief Minister of Andhra Pradesh 1964-71, Home Minister of India 1974-7) Commemoration

2822	**2006**	5r. multicoloured	75	75

2007 K. M. Mathew

2011. K. M. Mathew (former Chief Editor of *Malayala Manorama* newspaper) Commemoration

2823   **2007**   5r. multicoloured   75   75

2008 Gateway Pillar with Elephant Statues

2011. Rashtrapati Bhavan (President of India's residence)

2824   5r. Type **2008**   60   60
2825   5r. Central dome   60   60
2826   5r. Stone Jali (latticed screen)   60   60
2827   5r. Rashtrapati Bhavan and
            gardens (87×35 mm)   60   60
MS2828 168×131 mm. Nos. 2824/7   2·75   2·75

2009 Pt. K. Santanam

2011. Pandit K. Santanam (nationalist and businessman) Commemoration

2829   **2009**   5r. multicoloured   75   75

2010 Dr. M. S. Aney

2011. Dr. Madhav Shrihari Aney (nationalist politician) Commemoration

2830   **2010**   5r. multicoloured   75   75

2011 Surendranath Jauhar

2011. Surendranath Jauhar (anti colonial campaigner and leader of Delhi ashram) Commemoration

2831   **2011**   5r. multicoloured   75   75

2012 Dev Narayan

2011. Dev Narayan (folk deity of Rajasthan and Malwa)

2832   **2012**   5r. multicoloured   75   75

2013 Tejaji Maharaj

2011. Tejaji Maharaj (folk deity of Rajasthan)

2833   **2013**   5r. multicoloured   75   75

2014 Tripuraneni Gopichand

2011. Tripuraneni Gopichand (Telugu novelist, playwright and scriptwriter) Commemoration

2834   **2014**   5r. multicoloured   75   75

2015 Jaimalji Maharaj

2011. Jaimalji Maharaj (Jain saint) Commemoration

2835   **2015**   5r. multicoloured   40   40

2016 Nurses and Patients

2011. The Trained Nurses Association of India

2836   **2016**   5r. multicoloured   40   40

2017 Chitrapur Math

2011. Chitrapur Math, Shirali village, North Kanara, Karnataka

2837   **2017**   5r. multicoloured   40   40

2018 Soldier and Galley (Regimental Insignia)

2011. 250th Anniv of the Punjab Regiment and 1 Para (SF) (1 Punjab) (formerly 8th Battalion Coast Sepoys)

2838   **2018**   5r. multicoloured   40   40

2019 Microscope

2011. Centenary of Indian Council of Medical Research (formerly Indian Research Fund Association)

2839   **2019**   5r. multicoloured   40   40

2020 Tiger

2011. Children's Day. Winners of Children's Design a Tiger Stamp Competition. Multicoloured.

2840   5r. Type **2020**   40   40
2841   20r. Tiger (sitting)   1·00   1·00
MS2842 100×100 mm. Nos. 2840/1   1·25   1·25

2021 Entrance

2011. 50th Anniv of Grand Lodge of India

2843   **2021**   5r. multicoloured   40   40

2022 Baby before and after Cleft Surgery

2011. The Smile Train - Cleft Surgery

2844   **2022**   5r. multicoloured   40   40

2023 Kavi Pradeep

2011. Kavi Pradeep (Ramchandra Narayanji Dwivedi) (songwriter for Hindi films) Commemoration

2845   **2023**   5r. multicoloured   40   40

2024 Marchers with Indian Flag passing Aguada Fort Lighthouse

2011. 50th Anniv of the Liberation of Goa

2846   **2024**   5r. multicoloured   40   40

2025 Yacht

2011. President's Fleet Review, Mumbai. Multicoloured.

2847   5r. Type **2025**   40   40
2848   5r. Warship   40   40
2849   5r. Submarine   40   40
2850   5r. Fighter airplane   40   40

2026 Woodcarvings

2011. 150th Anniv of the Archaeological Survey of India. Multicoloured.

2851   5r. Type **2026**   40   40
2852   20r. Stonecarvings   1·00   1·00
MS2853 100×65 mm. Nos. 2851/2   3·00   3·00

2027 Chhatrapati Shahuji Maharaj Medical University, Lucknow

2011. Centenary of Chhatrapati Shahuji Maharaj Medical University (formerly King George's Medical College), Lucknow

2854   **2027**   5r. multicoloured   40   40

2028 Srinivasa Ramanujan

2011. 125th Birth Anniv of Srinivasa Ramanujan (mathematician)

2855   **2028**   5r. multicoloured   40   40

2029 Madan Mohan Malaviya

2011. 150th Birth Anniv of Madan Mohan Malaviya (founder of Banaras Hindu University)

2856   **2029**   5r. multicoloured   40   40

2030 Puran Chandra Gupta

2012. Birth Centenary of Puran Chandra Gupta (founder and editor of *Dainiik Jagran* newspaper)

2857   **2030**   5r. multicoloured   40   40

2031 Bhai Jagta Ji

2012. Bhai Jagta Ji (saint of Sewa Panthi order) Commemoration

2858   **2031**   5r. multicoloured   40   40

2032 Shyam Narayan Singh

2012. Shyam Narayan Singh (nationalist and legislator) Commemoration

2859   **2032**   5r. multicoloured   40   40

2033 India International Centre

2012. 50th Anniv of India International Centre, New Delhi

2860   **2033**   5r. multicoloured   40   40

2034 Family, Membership Card and Office Building

2012. 60th Anniv of Employees' State Insurance Corporation

2861   **2034**   5r. multicoloured   40   40

2035 Vasantdada Patil

2012. Vasantdada Patil (former Chief Minister of Maharashtra and Governor of Rajasthan 1985-7) Commemoration

2862   **2035**   5r. multicoloured   40   40

2036 Shyama Charan Shukla

2012. Shyama Charan Shukla (Chief Minister of Madhya Pradesh 1969-72, 1975-7, 1989-90) Commemoration
2863 **2036** 5r. multicoloured 40 40

2037 Aeroplane and Helicopter

2012. Centenary of Civil Aviation. Multicoloured.
2864 5r. Type **2037** 40 40
2865 5r. Flight control room, aircraft and terminal building 40 40
2866 5r. Control tower and aircraft taking off 40 40
2867 20r. Early biplane 1·00 1·00
MS2868 139×69 mm. Nos. 2864/7 1·75 1·75

2038 Students and College Building

2012. 125th Anniv of Isabella Thoburn College, Lucknow
2869 **2038** 5r. multicoloured 40 40

2039 Godiji Temple, Mumbai

2012. Bicentenary of Godiji Temple, Mumbai
2870 **2039** 5r. multicoloured 40 40

2040 R. Venkataraman

2012. Birth Centenary (2010) of Ramaswamy Venkataraman (President of India 1987-92)
2871 **2040** 5r. multicoloured 40 40

2041 Karpoor Chandra 'Kulish'

2012. Karpoor Chandra 'Kulish' (journalist and founder of Hindi newspaper *Rajasthan Patrika*) Commemoration
2872 **2041** 5r. multicoloured 40 40

2042 M. B. Kadadi

2012. M. B. Kadadi (philanthropist and educationist) Commemoration
2873 **2042** 5r. black and chestnut 40 40

2043 Pilgrims at Dargah Sharif Shrine, Ajmer

2012. 800th Urs Festival, Dargah Sharif, Ajmer. Multicoloured.
2874 5r. Type **2043** 40 40
2875 20r. Dargah Sharif sufi shrine, Ajmer 1·00 1·00
MS2876 106×62 mm. Nos. 2874/5 1·50 1·50

2044 Warli Painting, Maharashtra

2012. Shekhawati and Warli Wall Paintings. Brown-red (5r.) or multicoloured (20r.).
2877 5r. Type **2044** 40 40
2878 20r. Shekhawati fresco depicting ridden elephant and horse rider, Rajasthan 1·00 1·00

2045 Rowing

2012. Olympic Games, London. Multicoloured.
2879 5r. Type **2045** 40 40
2880 5r. Windsurfing 40 40
2881 20r. Volleyball 1·00 1·00
2882 20r. Badminton 1·00 1·00
MS2883 108×108 mm. Nos. 2879/82 3·50 3·50

2046 Customs Officer and Launch, Container and Aircraft

2012. 50th Anniv of the Customs Act
2884 **2046** 5r. multicoloured 40 40

2047 Durga Prasad Chaudhary

2012. Durga Prasad Chaudhary (founder of *Dainik Navjyoti* newspaper) Commemoration
2885 **2047** 5r. multicoloured 40 40

2048 Students and Armed Forces Medical College, Pune

2012. 50th Anniv of Armed Forces Medical College, Pune
2886 **2048** 5r. multicoloured 40 40

2049 Husain Ahmad Madani

2012. Husain Ahmad Madani (1879-1957, Islamic scholar and nationalist) Commemoration
2887 **2049** 5r. black and stone 40 40

2050 Motilal Nehru

2012. 150th Birth Anniv of Motilal Nehru (1861-1931, nationalist leader and politician)
2888 **2050** 5r. multicoloured 40 40

2051 Armed Commandos and Himalayan Peaks

2012. 50th Anniv of Indo-Tibetan Border Police (ITBP)
2889 **2051** 5r. multicoloured 40 40

2052 AWACS (Airborne Warning and Control System)

2012. AWACS (Airborne Warning and Control System)
2890 **2052** 5r. multicoloured 40 40

2053 India 1854 4a. Stamp with Head Inverted and 1947 1½a. Independence Stamp

2012. Philately Day. Sheet 85×75 mm
MS2891 **2053** 20r. multicoloured 1·00 1·00

2054 Nicobar Megapode

2012. Endemic Species of Indian Biodiversity Hotspots. Multicoloured.
2892 5r. Type **2054** 40 40
2893 5r. Hoolock Gibbon 40 40
2894 5r. Venated Gliding Frog 40 40
2895 25r. Bugun Liocichla 1·25 1·25
MS2896 102×103 mm. Nos. 2892/5 2·50 2·50

2055 Deepavali

2012. Festival of Lights - Deepavali and Hanukkah. Multicoloured.
2897 5r. Type **2055** 40 40
2898 5r. Hanukkah 40 40
Nos. 2897/8 commemorate the 20th Anniversary of Diplomatic Relations with Israel.
Similar designs were issued by Israel.

2056 T. S. Narayanaswami

2012. Birth Centenary of T. S. Narayanaswami (1911-68, founder of India Cements)
2899 **2056** 5r. multicoloured 40 40

2057 Post Office 2050 (Jai Surya)

2012. Children's Day. Winner of Children's Design a Stamp Competition 'Post Office 2050'
2900 **2057** 5r. multicoloured 40 40

2058 The Scinde Horse

2012. The Scinde Horse (regiment)
2901 **2058** 5r. multicoloured 40 40

2059 Ramgopal Maheshwari

2012. Birth Centenary of Ramgopal Maheshwari (1911-99, Hindi journalist and social reformer)
2902 **2059** 5r. multicoloured 40 40

2060 Silhouettes and Consumer Awareness Campaign Slogan 'JAGO GRAHAK JAGO'

2012. 25th Anniv of Consumer Protection Act
2903 **2060** 5r. multicoloured 40 40

2061 Sri Shivarathri Shivayogi

2012. Sri Shivarathri Shivayogi (10th century saint) Commemoration
2904 **2061** 5r. multicoloured 50 50

2062 Srinivasa Ramanujan and Formula

2012. National Mathematics Day. 125th Birth Anniv of Srinivasa Ramanujan (1887-1920, mathematician)
2905 **2062** 5r. multicoloured 50 50

2063 Mahabalipuram (Mamallapuram) Lighthouse

2012. Lighthouses. Multicoloured.
2906 5r. Type **2063** 50 50
2907 20r. Alleppey (Alappuzha) Lighthouse 1·60 1·60
MS2908 104×85 mm. Nos. 2906/7 2·50 2·50

2064 Boy examining Flower

2013. Centenary of Indian Science Congress Association, Kolkata

2909   **2064**   5r. multicoloured   50   50

2065 Nehru Hospital of the PGIMER, Chandigarh

2013. 50th Anniv of Postgraduate Institute of Medical Education and Research (PGIMER), Chandigarh

2910   **2065**   5r. multicoloured   50   50

2066 Hand holding Torch and Raised Fists

2013. Centenary of Ghadar Movement (anti colonial rebellion)

2911   **2066**   5r. multicoloured   50   50

2067 Uttar Pradesh Legislative Assembly Building, Lucknow

2013. 125th Anniv of Uttar Pradesh Legislature

2912   **2067**   5r. multicoloured   50   50

2068 Scroll

2013. Silk Letter Movement (planned anti colonial revolt, 1913-16)

2913   **2068**   5r. multicoloured   50   50

2069 Swami Vivekananda at Kanyakumari, 1893

2013. 150th Birth Anniv of Swami Vivekananda (1863-1902, Hindu monk and spiritual leader, founder of Ramakrishna Mission). Multicoloured.

2914   5r. Type **2069**   50   50

2915   5r. Swami Vivekananda and World Parliament of Religions, Chicago, 1893   50   50

2916   5r. Swami Vivekananda and Belur Math   50   50

2917   20r. Swami Vivekananda, Dakshineswar Kali Temple and birthplace   1·60   1·60

2070 C. Achyutha Menon

2013. Birth Centenary of C. Achyutha Menon (1913-91, Chief Minister of Kerala 1969-77, Communist Party leader and writer)

2918   **2070**   5r. multicoloured   50   50

2071 Aditya Vikram Birla

2013. Aditya Vikram Birla (1943-95, industrialist) Commemoration

2919   **2071**   5r. multicoloured   50   50

2072 Shrine Basilica, Vailankanni

2013. Shrine Basilica, Vailankanni

2920   **2072**   5r. multicoloured   50   50

2073 Badges

2013. Third Battalion Parachute Regiment (Special Forces)

2921   **2073**   5r. multicoloured   50   50

2074 Officers

2013. 50th Anniv of Officers Training Academy, Chennai

2922   **2074**   5r. multicoloured   50   50

2075 Sahir Ludhianvi

2013. Sahir Ludhianvi (1921-80, Urdu poet and Hindi lyricist) Commemoration

2923   **2075**   5r. multicoloured   50   50

2076 *Malayala Manorama* Newspaper and Office

2013. 125th Anniv of *Malayala Manorama* (Malayalam newspaper)

2924   **2076**   5r. multicoloured   50   50

2077 Jhulelal Sahib

2013. Jhulelal Sahib (community god of Sindhi community)

2925   **2077**   5r. multicoloured   50   50

2078 Shiv Ram Hari Rajguru and Statues of Bhagat Singh, Rajguru and Sukhdev

2013. Shiv Ram Hari Rajguru (1908-31, anti colonial revolutionary) Commmemoration

2926   **2078**   5r. multicoloured   50   50

2079 Srikurmam Temple, Srikakulam

2013. Architectural Heritage of India. Temples. Multicoloured.

2927   5r. Type **2079**   50   50

2928   20r. Arasavalli Temple, Srikakulam   1·60   1·60

MS2929 120×81 mm. Nos. 2927/8   2·50   2·50

2080 Mumbai Post Office

2013. Heritage Buildings. Multicoloured.

2930   5r. Type **2080**   50   50

2931   5r. Agra Head Post Office   50   50

MS2932 120×68 mm. Nos. 2930/1   1·25   1·25

2081 Dr. Babasaheb Ambedkar and Chaitya Boomi, Mumbai

2013. Chaitya Bhoomi, Mumbai (Buddhist place of pilgrimage and memorial to Dr. Ambedkar (architect of the Indian constitution))

2933   **2081**   5r. multicoloured   50   50

2082 Hari Singh Nalwa

2013. Hari Singh Nalwa (1791-1837, Commander-in-Chief of Sikh Army) Commemoration

2934   **2082**   5r. multicoloured   50   50

2083 Ashok Kumar

2013. Centenary of Indian Cinema. Multicoloured.

MS2935 162×110 mm. 5r.×9 Type **2083**; B. N. Sircar; B. R. Chopra; Bhalji Pendharkar; Bhupen Hazarika; Dev Anand; Dhirendranath Ganguly; Durga Khote; Hrishikesh Mukherjee   4·00   4·00

MS2936 162×110 mm. 5r.×9 Majrooh Sultanpuri; Naushad; Nitin Bose; Prithviraj Kapoor; Raichand Boral; Ruby Myers; Sohrab Modi; Tapan Sinha; Yash Chopra   4·00   4·00

MS2937 110×162 mm. 5r.×8 Allu Ramalingiah; Ashok Mehta; Balraj Sahni; Bhanumathi; C. V. Sridhar; Chetan Anand; Kamaal Amrohi; Geeta Dutt   4·00   4·00

MS2938 110×162 mm. 5r.×8 Kannadasan; Madan Mohan; Mehmood; Motilal; Nagesh; O. P. Nayyar; Prem Nazir; R. D. Burman   4·00   4·00

MS2939 110×162 mm. 5r.×8 Raj Khosla; Rajendra Kumar; Rajesh Khanna; S. V. Ranga Rao; Salil Chowdhary; Sanjeev Kumar; Shailendra; Shakeel Badayuni   4·00   4·00

MS2940 110×162 mm. 5r.×8 Shammi Kapoor; Shankar Jaikishan; Smita Patil; Suraiya; Tarachand Barjatya; T. R. Sundaram; Utpal Dutt; Vishnu Vardhan   4·00   4·00

2084 Kiang in Ladakh

2013. Wild Asses of India. Multicoloured.

2941   5r. Type **2082**   50   50

2942   20r. Ghor Khar in Kutch   1·60   1·60

MS2943 138×65 mm. Nos. 2941/2   2·00   2·00

2085 Headquarters Building, Mumbai

2013. 25th Anniv of Securities and Exchange Board of India (SEBI)

2944   **2085**   5r. multicoloured   50   50

2086 Peerzada Ghulam Ahmad Mehjoor

2013. Ghulam Ahmad Mehjoor (1885-1952, Kashmiri poet) Commemoration

2945   **2086**   5r. multicoloured   50   50

2087 Delhi Gymkhana Club

2013. Centenary of Delhi Gymkhana Club

2946   **2087**   5r. multicoloured   50   50

2088 Assembly Building (Niyamasabha Mandiram), Thiruvananthapuram

2013. 125th Anniv of Kerala Legislative Assembly

2947   **2088**   5r. multicoloured   50   50

2089 Raj Bahadur

2013. Raj Bahadur (1912-90, Union Minister 1951-76) Commemoration

2948   **2089**   5r. multicoloured   50   50

2090 Chirita

2013. Asian Pacific Postal Union Congress, New Delhi. Wild Flowers of India. Multicoloured.

2949   5r. Type **2090**   50   50

2950   5r. Kashmir Mallow   50   50

2951   5r. Himalayan Mini Sunflower   50   50

2952   5r. Himalayan Lantern   50   50

2953   5r. Roundleaf Asiabell   50   50

2954   5r. Blue Poppy   50   50

2955   5r. Globe Thistle   50   50

2956   5r. Himalayan Iris   50   50

2957   5r. Himalayan Bellflower   50   50

2958   5r. Cobra Lily   50   50

2959   5r. Bladder Campion   50   50

2960   5r. Rhododendron   50   50

Nos. **MS**2961/3 are left for three miniature sheets not yet received.

2091 Lala Jagat Narain

2013. Lala Jagat Narain (nationalist and journalist) Commemoration
| 2964 | 2091 | 5r. multicoloured | 50 | 50 |

2092 Acharya Gyansagar

2013. Acharya Gyansagar (1891-1973, Jain scholar) Commemoration
| 2965 | 2092 | 5r. multicoloured | 50 | 50 |

2093 Gurajada Venkata Apparao

2013. Gurajada Venkata Apparao (1862-1915, Telugu writer) Commemoration
| 2966 | 2093 | 5r. multicoloured | 50 | 50 |

2094 Pratap Narayan Mishra

2013. Pratap Narayan Mishra (1856-94, writer) Commemoration
| 2967 | 2094 | 5r. multicoloured | 50 | 50 |

2095 Joomdev

2013. Joomdev (1921-96, philanthropist) Commemoration
| 2968 | 2095 | 5r. multicoloured | 50 | 50 |

2096 Gandhi and 1948 12a. First Anniversary of Indian Independence Stamp and 1969 75p. Gandhi Birth Centenary Stamp

2013. Philately Day. Mahatma Gandhi
| MS2969 | 2096 | 20r. multicoloured | 1·60 | 1·60 |

2097 Bhakra Dam

2013. 50th Anniv of Bhakra Dam
| 2970 | 2097 | 5r. multicoloured | 50 | 50 |

2098 Ruchi Ram Sahni

2013. Ruchi Ram Sahni (1863-1948, scientist and educationist) Commemoration
| 2971 | 2098 | 5r. multicoloured | 50 | 50 |

2099 Boys' High School, Allahabad

2013. Boys' High School, Allahabad
| 2972 | 2099 | 5r. multicoloured | 50 | 50 |

2100 Dr. K. M. Munshi (founder) and Bharatiya Vidya Bhavan

2013. 75th Anniv of Bharatiya Vidya Bhavan (educational trust)
| 2973 | 2100 | 5r. multicoloured | 50 | 50 |

2101 Baby

2013. 50th Anniv of Indian Academy of Pediatrics
| 2974 | 2101 | 5r. multicoloured | 50 | 50 |

2102 Emblem

2013. 50th Anniv of Central Bureau of Investigation
| 2975 | 2102 | 5r. multicoloured | 50 | 50 |

2103 Cartoon

2013. 175th Anniv of *The Times of India* (newspaper)
| 2976 | 2103 | 5r. multicoloured | 50 | 50 |

2104 Girl on Swing (Karthik S.)

2013. Children's Day
| 2977 | 2104 | 5r. multicoloured | 50 | 50 |

2105 Sachin Tendulkar

2013. Sachin Tendulkar's 200th Test Match. Multicoloured.
2978	20r. Type 2105		1·60	1·60
2979	20r. Sachin Tendulkar and Tendulkar batting (wearing blue helmet)		1·60	1·60
MS2980	120×76 mm. Nos. 2978/9		3·25	3·25

2106 Sathya Sai Baba

2013. Sathya Sai Baba (1926-2011, spiritual leader) Commemoration
| 2981 | 2106 | 5r. multicoloured | 50 | 50 |

2107 Bureau Logo 'Awake, Day and Night'

2013. 125th Anniv (2012) of Intelligence Bureau
| 2982 | 2107 | 5r. multicoloured | 50 | 50 |

2108 Railway Workshop, Kanchrapara

2013. 150th Anniv of Railway Workshops at Kanchrapara and Jamalpur, Eastern Railway. Multicoloured.
2983	5r. Type 2108		50	50
2984	20r. Railway workshop, Jamalpur		1·60	1·60
MS2985	117×80 mm. Nos. 2983/4		2·00	2·00

OFFICIAL STAMPS

1866. Optd **Service**.
O20	11	½a. blue	75·00	50
O8	12	8p. mauve	45·00	75·00
O23	11	1a. brown	80·00	50
O27	11	2a. orange	16·00	2·25
O13	11	4a. green	£475	£150
O29	-	4a. green (No. 69)	4·00	1·50
O30	11	8a. red	5·00	1·50

1866. Fiscal stamp with head of Queen Victoria surch **SERVICE TWO ANNAS**.
| O15 | 2a. purple | £650 | £475 |

1866. Fiscal stamps optd **SERVICE POSTAGE**.
O19	½a. mauve on lilac	£800	£150
O16	2a. purple	£2500	£1000
O17	4a. purple	£8000	£3000
O18	8a. purple	£7500	£9000

1874. Optd **On H. M. S.** (Queen Victoria).
O31	½a. blue	25·00	20
O32	1a. brown	25·00	20
O33a	2a. orange	80·00	42·00
O34	4a. green (No. 69)	35·00	9·00
O35	11	8a. red	9·00	10·00

1883. Queen Victoria stamps of 1882 and 1892 optd **On H. M. S.**
O37a	40	3p. red	20	10
O39	23	½a. green	2·75	10
O49	23	½a. green	6·00	90
O41	-	1a. purple	1·50	10
O50	-	1a. red	4·75	15
O42	-	2a. blue	15·00	60
O51	-	2a. lilac	55·00	1·50
O44a	-	4a. olive	45·00	50
O46	-	8a. mauve	18·00	50
O48	37	1r. green and red	38·00	40

1902. King Edward VII stamps optd **On H. M. S.**
O54	41	3p. grey	2·50	1·25
O56	-	½a. green (No. 122)	1·50	30
O57	-	1a. red (No. 123)	1·25	10
O59	-	2a. lilac	3·75	10
O60	-	4a. olive	28·00	30
O62	-	6a. bistre	1·75	15
O63	-	8a. mauve	12·00	1·00
O65	-	1r. green and red	4·25	80
O68	52	2r. red and orange	23·00	1·50
O69	52	5r. blue and violet	15·00	1·50
O70	52	10r. green and red	48·00	35·00
O71	52	15r. blue and olive	£130	60·00
O72	52	25r. orange and blue	£275	£100

1906. Nos. 149/50 optd **On H. M. S.**
| O66 | ½a. green | 1·25 | 10 |
| O67 | 1a. red | 2·00 | 10 |

1912. King George V stamps optd **SERVICE**.
O109	55	3p. grey	55	10
O76	56	½a. green	50	10
O80	57	1a. red	1·50	10
O111	57	1a. brown	20	10
O84	59	2a. mauve	1·25	30
O112	70	2a. lilac	30	10
O113	71	4a. green	2·25	20
O132	63	4a. olive	4·75	10
O87	64	6a. bistre	1·50	3·75
O115	65	8a. mauve	7·50	10
O116	66	12a. red	70	2·50
O117	67	1r. brown and green	14·00	1·00
O92	67	2r. red and orange	12·00	13·00
O129	70	2a. red	5·50	2·00
O93	67	5r. blue and violet	32·00	48·00
O94	67	10r. green and red	£110	95·00
O95	67	15r. blue and olive	£190	£200
O96	67	25r. orange and blue	£325	£300

1921. No. O81 surch **NINE PIES**.
| O97 | 57 | 9p. on 1a. red | 1·75 | 1·75 |

1925. Nos. O70/2 surch in words.
O99	52	1r. on 15r. blue and olive	4·25	4·25
O100	52	1r. on 25r. orange & blue	32·00	£100
O101	52	2r. on 10r. green and red	3·75	4·25

1925. Nos. O94/6 surch in words.
O102	67	1r. on 15r. blue and olive	20·00	90·00
O103	67	1r. on 25r. orange & blue	10·00	12·00
O104	67	2r. on 10r. green and red	£4000	

1926. No. O62 surch **ONE ANNA**.
| O105 | 1a. on 6a. bistre | 45 | 30 |

1926. Surch **SERVICE ONE ANNA** and two bars.
O106	58	1a. on 1½a. brown (A)	20	10
O107	58	1a. on 1½a. brown (B)	7·00	4·50
O108	61	1a. on 2a.6p. blue	60	80

1932. Optd **SERVICE**.
O126	79	½a. green	3·75	10
O127	80	9p. green	30	15
O127b	81	1a. brown	5·50	15
O128	82	1a.3p. mauve	30	10
O130b	59	2a. orange	1·25	10
O131	61	2a.6p. orange	60	10

1937. King George VI stamps optd **SERVICE**
O135	91	½a. brown	17·00	1·25
O136	91	9p. green	19·00	1·50
O137	91	1a. red	3·50	10
O138	93	1r. slate and brown	75	50
O139	93	2r. purple and brown	1·75	2·50
O140	93	5r. green and blue	12·00	7·50
O141	93	10r. purple and red	26·00	18·00

1939. King George V stamps surch **SERVICE 1A**.
| O142 | 82 | 1a. on 1¼a. mauve | 15·00 | 20 |

O20 King George VI

1939
O143	O20	3p. slate	60	10
O144	O20	½a. brown	12·00	10
O144b	O20	½a. purple	30	10
O145	O20	9p. green	30	10
O146	O20	1a. red	30	10
O146a	O20	1a.3p. brown	7·00	70
O146b	O20	1½a. violet	65	10
O147	O20	2a. orange	60	10
O148	O20	2½a. violet	2·50	1·25
O149	O20	4a. brown	60	10
O150	O20	8a. violet	90	30

1948. First Anniv of Independence. Optd **SERVICE**.
O150a	305	1½a. brown	90·00	80·00
O150b	305	3½a. violet	£6500	£2750
O150c	305	12a. green	£24000	£8000
O150d	-	10r. brown and red (No. 308)	£160000	

O21 Asokan Capital

1950

O151	O21	3p. violet	15	10
O152	O21	6p. brown	30	10
O153	O21	9p. green	1·25	10
O154	O21	1a. blue	1·25	10
O155	O21	2a. red	2·75	10
O156	O21	3a. red	6·50	2·50
O157	O21	4a. purple	11·00	20
O158	O21	4a. blue	75	10
O159	O21	6a. violet	4·75	2·00
O160	O21	8a. brown	2·50	10
O186	-	1r. violet	15	10
O187	-	2r. red	25	10
O188	-	5r. green	40	75
O189	-	10r. brown	1·00	1·75

The rupee values are larger and with a different frame.

1957. Value in naye paise.

O175	O21	1n.p. slate	10	10
O166	O21	2n.p. violet	10	10
O167	O21	3n.p. brown	20	10
O168	O21	5n.p. green	1·25	10
O169	O21	6n.p. turquoise	40	10
O180	O21	10n.p. green	50	50
O170	O21	13n.p. red	40	10
O182	O21	15n.p. violet	10	10
O183	O21	20n.p. red	70	10
O184	O21	25n.p. blue	10	10
O185	O21	50n.p. brown	70	10

O23

1967

O197	O23	1r. purple	85	10
O200	O23	2p. violet	10	1·00
O201	O23	3p. brown	40	1·25
O202	O23	5p. green	10	10
O203	O23	6p. blue	1·25	1·50
O204	O23	10p. green	10	30
O205	O23	15p. plum	10	30
O206	O23	20p. red	10	30
O207	O23	25p. red	24·00	3·75
O208	O23	30p. blue	10	60
O209	O23	50p. brown	10	60

O25

1971. Obligatory Tax. Refugee Relief. Optd **REFUGEE RELIEF** in English and Devanagari (No. O210) or in English only (No. O211).

O210	-	5p. green	75	60
O213	O25	5p. green	30	40

See note below Nos. 646/51.

O26

1976. Designs redrawn showing face-value in figures only and smaller Capital with Hindi motto beneath as Type **O26**.

O214	O26	2p. blue	20	1·25
O254	O26	5p. green	20	30
O255	O26	10p. green	20	30
O256	O26	15p. purple	20	30
O257	O26	20p. red	20	20
O258	O26	25p. red	20	20
O259	O26	30p. blue	20	20
O260	O26	35p. violet	20	20
O263	O26	60p. brown	20	30
O268	O26	violet (17×19½ mm)	20	20
O269	O26		1·00	1·00
O270	O26	1r. purple (17×19½ mm)	1·00	75
O225b	-	2r. red	40	1·50
O226b	-	5r. green	60	2·25
O227	-	10r. red	1·25	3·50

The 2, 5 and 10r. values are larger.

O28

1982. As 1977 and 1981 issue but with simulated perforations. Imperf.

O231	O28	5p. green	55	1·00
O232	O28	10p. green	70	1·00
O233	O28	15p. purple	70	1·00
O234	O28	20p. red	75	1·00
O235	O28	25p. red	1·50	2·00
O236	O28	35p. violet	85	65
O237	O28	50p. brown	1·50	1·50
O238	O28	1r. brown	1·75	1·50
O239	O28	2r. red	1·75	4·00
O240	O28	5r. green	2·00	5·00
O241	O28	10r. brown	2·50	7·00

O27

1998. Redrawn with face value figures in bottom corners. Size 17 x 19½ mm (Nos. O271/O273) or 16½ x 19 mm (Nos. O273b/O279).

O271	O27	2r. red	1·25	1·00
O272	O27	5r. green	1·75	1·75
O273	O27	brown	2·00	2·00
O273b	O26	50p. brown	10	10
O274	O27	1r. purple	10	10
O275	O27	2r. red	15	10
O276	O27	3r. orange	20	20
O278	O27	5r. green	30	30
O279	O27	10r. brown	60	60

[Pt. 1]

INDIAN CUSTODIAN FORCES IN KOREA

Stamps used by the Indian Forces on custodian duties in Korea in 1953.

12 pies = 1 anna; 16 annas = 1 rupee.

भारतीय
संरक्षा कटक
कोरिया
(K1)

1953. Stamps of India (archaeological series) optd with Type **K1**.

K1	307	3p. violet	3·00	9·50
K2	308	6p. brown	1·50	8·00
K3	-	9p. green	3·00	6·50
K4	-	1a. blue (B)	1·50	4·50
K5	-	2a. red	1·50	4·50
K6	-	2½a. lake	1·50	4·75
K7	-	3a. salmon	1·50	8·00
K8	314	4a. blue	2·25	4·75
K9	315	6a. violet	12·00	9·00
K10	-	8a. green	2·25	16·00
K11	-	12a. blue	2·25	17·00
K12	-	1r. violet and green	8·00	17·00

[Pt. 1]

INDIAN EXPEDITIONARY FORCES, 1914 - 1921

Stamps used by Indian Forces during, and after, the War of 1914–18.

12 pies = 1 anna; 16 annas = 1 rupee.

1914. Stamps of India (King George V) optd **I. E. F.**

E1	55	3p. grey	15	30
E2	56	½a. green	50	30
E3	57	1a. red	1·25	30
E5	59	2a. lilac	1·25	30
E6	61	2a.6p. blue	1·50	3·50
E7	62	3a. orange	1·00	1·50
E8	63	4a. olive	1·00	1·50
E9	65	8a. mauve	1·25	2·50
E11	66	12a. red	2·25	6·00
E13	67	1r. brown and green	3·50	4·00

[Pt. 1]

INDIAN FORCES IN INDO-CHINA

Stamps used by Indian Forces engaged in the International Commission in Indo-China.

1954. 12 pies = 1 anna; 16 annas = 1 rupee.
1957. 100 naye paise = 1 rupee.
1964. 100 paisa = 1 rupee.

अन्तर्राष्ट्रीय आयोग कम्बोज **(N 1)** अन्तर्राष्ट्रीय आयोग लाओस **(N 2)** अन्तर्राष्ट्रीय आयोग वियत नाम **(N 3)**

1954. Stamps of India (archaeological series) overprinted

(a) Optd with Type **N1** for use in Cambodia

N1	307	3p. violet	2·75	14·00
N2	-	1a. blue (B)	1·25	1·00
N3	-	2a. red	1·25	1·00
N4	-	8a. green	1·75	3·50
N5	-	12a. blue	2·00	3·00

(b) Optd with Type **N2** for use in Laos.

N6	307	3p. violet	2·75	14·00
N7	-	1a. blue (B)	1·25	1·00
N8	-	2a. red	1·25	1·00
N9	-	8a. green	1·75	3·00
N10	-	12a. blue	2·00	3·00

(c) Optd with Type **N3** for use in Vietnam.

N11	307	3p. violet	2·75	9·00
N12	-	1a. blue (B)	1·25	1·00
N13	-	2a. red	1·25	1·00
N14	-	8a. green	1·75	3·00
N15	-	12a. blue	2·00	3·00

1957. Map type of India overprinted

(a) Optd with Type **N1** for use in Cambodia

N16	361	2n.p. brown	75	30
N17	361	6n.p. grey	50	30
N18	361	13n.p. red	70	40
N19	361	50n.p. orange	2·25	1·25
N20	361	75n.p. purple	2·25	1·25

(b) Optd with Type **N2** for use in Laos.

N21	361	2n.p. brown	75	30
N22	361	6n.p. grey	50	30
N23	361	13n.p. red	70	40
N24	361	50n.p. orange	2·25	1·25
N25	361	75n.p. purple	2·25	1·25

(c) Optd with Type **N3** for use in Vietnam.

N26	361	2n.p. brown	75	30
N27	361	6n.p. grey	50	30
N28	361	13n.p. red	70	40
N29	361	50n.p. orange	2·25	1·25
N30	361	75n.p. purple	2·25	1·25

1965. Children's Day stamp of India optd **ICC** for use in Laos and Vietnam.

N49	469	15p. slate	1·00	6·00

1968. Nos. 504/6, 509/10, 515 and 517/18, of India optd **ICC** in English and Devanagari, for use in Laos and Vietnam.

N50	-	2p. brown	10	4·25
N51	-	3p. olive	10	4·25
N52	-	5p. red	10	2·50
N53	-	10p. blue	2·25	3·50
N54	467	15p. green	60	3·50
N55	-	60p. grey	35	2·50
N56	-	1r. brown and plum	50	3·50
N57	-	2r. blue and violet	1·25	13·00

[Pt. 1]

INDIAN U.N. FORCE IN CONGO

Stamps used by Indian Forces attached to the United Nations Force in Congo.

100 naye paise = 1 rupee.

1962. Map type of India optd **U.N. FORCE (INDIA) CONGO.**

U1	361	1n.p. turquoise	1·00	5·00
U2	361	2n.p. brown	1·00	2·50
U3	361	5n.p. green	1·00	1·00
U4	361	8n.p. turquoise	1·00	40
U5	361	13n.p. red	1·00	40
U6	361	50n.p. orange	1·00	70

[Pt. 1]

INDIAN U.N. FORCE IN GAZA (PALESTINE)

Stamps used by Indian Forces attached to the United Nations Force in Gaza.

100 paise = 1 rupee.

1965. Children's Day stamp of India optd **UNEF.**

G1	449	15p. slate	3·50	9·50

[Pt. 6]

INDO-CHINA

A French territory in south-east Asia. In 1949 it was split up into the three states of Vietnam, Cambodia and Laos.

1889. 100 centimes = 1 franc.
1918. 100 cents = 1 piastre.

1889. Stamp of French Colonies, "Commerce" type, surch.
(a) **INDO-CHINE 1889 5 R-D.**

1	J	5 on 35c. black on orange	£110	90·00

(b) INDO-CHINE 89 5 R D.

2		5 on 35c. black on orange	17·00	11·00

1892. "Tablet" key-type inscr "INDO-CHINE" in red (1, 5, 15, 25, 50 (No. 27), 75c., 1f.) or blue (others).

6	D	1c. black on blue	2·20	55
7	D	2c. brown on buff	2·50	2·75
8	D	4c. brown on grey	3·00	3·25
23	D	5c. green	4·25	90
10	D	10c. black on lilac	7·25	1·00

24	D	10c. red	7·75	65
11	D	15c. blue	60·00	55
25	D	15c. grey	13·00	45
12	D	20c. red on green	17·00	2·75
13	D	25c. black on pink	32·00	90
26	D	25c. blue	48·00	75
14	D	30c. brown on drab	44·00	9·50
15	D	40c. red on yellow	50·00	14·50
16	D	50c. red on pink	55·00	11·00
27	D	50c. brown on blue	26·00	4·25
17	D	75c. brown on orange	42·00	20·00
18	D	1f. green	70·00	24·00
19	D	5f. mauve on lilac	£120	£120

1903. Surch.

28		5 on 15c. grey	1·70	1·20
29		15c. on 25c. blue	1·80	75

8 "Grasset" type

1904

30	8	1c. green	20	10
31	8	2c. purple on yellow	75	65
32	8	4c. mauve on blue	35	40
33	8	5c. green	3·00	20
34	8	10c. pink	4·50	30
35	8	15c. brown on blue	2·75	30
36	8	20c. red on green	4·25	55
37	8	25c. blue	20·00	35
38	8	30c. brown on cream	9·25	2·30
39	8	35c. black on yellow	34·00	1·20
40	8	40c. black on grey	8·50	90
41	8	50c. brown	12·00	1·80
42	8	75c. red on orange	50·00	24·00
43	8	1f. green	36·00	2·75
44	8	2f. brown on yellow	65·00	28·00
45	8	5f. violet	£200	£150
46	8	10f. red on green	£200	£150

10 Annamite   **11** Cambodian   **12** Cambodian

1907

51	10	1c. black and sepia	1·10	30
52	10	2c. black and brown	55	35
53	10	4c. black and blue	1·40	85
54	10	5c. black and green	4·75	30
55	10	10c. black and red	5·25	30
56	10	15c. black and violet	5·00	45
57	11	20c. black and violet	3·75	3·25
58	11	25c. black and blue	12·00	35
59	11	30c. black and brown	18·00	6·75
60	11	35c. black and green	5·25	55
61	11	40c. black and brown	4·50	2·50
62	11	50c. black and orange	17·00	6·50
63	11	50c. black and red	34·00	2·30
64	12	75c. black and orange	14·00	7·25
65	-	1f. black and red	60·00	11·00
66	-	2f. black and green	32·00	36·00
67	-	5f. black and blue	65·00	60·00
68	-	10f. black and violet	£120	£120

DESIGNS—As Type **12**: 1f. Annamites; 2f. Muong; 5f. Laotian; 10f. Cambodian.

1912. Surch in figures.

69	8	05 on 4c. mauve on blue	4·25	11·00
70	8	05 on 15c. brown on blue	90	10
71	8	05 on 30c. brown on cream	45	2·50
72	8	10 on 40c. black on grey	2·00	3·50
73	8	10 on 50c. brown	1·20	2·75
74	8	10 on 75c. red on orange	4·50	7·00

1914. Red Cross. Surch **5c** and cross.

76	10	5c.+5c. black and green	55	3·25
77	10	10c.+5c. black and red	45	35
78	10	15c.+5c. black and violet	90	3·25

1918. Nos. 75/6 and 78 further surch in figures and words.

79		4c. on 5c.+5c. blk & grn	4·00	14·00
80		6c. on 10c.+5c. black and red	2·30	12·00
81		8c. on 15c.+5c. blk & vio	17·00	40·00

1919. French stamps of "War Orphans" issue surch **INDOCHINE** and value in figures and words.

82	23	10c. on 15c.+10c. grey	2·00	4·00
83	23	16c. on 25c.+15c. blue	9·50	11·00

84	-	24c. on 35c.+25c. violet and grey	9·75	26·00
85	-	40c. on 50c.+50c. brown	13·00	50·00
86	**26**	80c. on 1f.+1f. red	26·00	60·00
87	**26**	4p. on 5f.+5f. blue & blk	£250	£250

1919. Surch in figures and words.

88	**10**	⅖c. on 1c. black and sepia	2·75	30
89	**10**	⅗c. on 2c. black and brown	2·75	1·10
90	**10**	1⅗c. on 4c. black and blue	5·00	75
91	**10**	2c. on 5c. black and green	6·50	20
92	**10**	4c. on 10c. black and red	3·00	30
93	**10**	6c. on 15c. black and violet	7·75	45
94	**11**	8c. on 20c. black and violet	8·00	1·40
95	**11**	10c. on 25c. black and blue	7·25	30
96	**11**	12c. on 30c. black & brown	9·25	90
97	**11**	14c. on 35c. black & green	5·75	65
98	**11**	16c. on 40c. black & brown	6·50	90
99	**11**	18c. on 45c. black & orange	9·25	2·75
100	**11**	20c. on 50c. black and red	20·00	90
101	**12**	30c. on 75c. black & orange	24·00	2·30
102	-	40c. on 1f. black and red	32·00	2·00
103	-	80c. on 2f. black and green	30·00	7·25
104	-	2p. on 5f. black and blue	£110	£110
105	-	4p. on 10f. black and violet	£140	£140

1922. As T 10 and 11 but value in cents or piastres.

115	**10**	⅒c. red and grey	10	1·70
116	**10**	⅕c. black and blue	10	20
117	**10**	⅖c. black and brown	10	90
118	**10**	⅗c. black and mauve	20	1·00
119	**10**	1c. black and brown	1·70	10
120	**10**	2c. black and green	1·10	30
121	**10**	3c. black and violet	90	50
122	**10**	4c. black and orange	2·30	20
123	**10**	5c. black and red	90	10
124	**11**	6c. black and red	1·90	20
125	**11**	7c. black and green	3·75	75
126	**11**	8c. black on lilac	2·30	1·30
127	**11**	9c. black and yellow	2·30	85
128	**11**	10c. black and blue	1·40	30
129	**11**	11c. black and violet	2·50	55
130	**11**	12c. black and brown	90	20
131	**11**	15c. black and orange	1·80	65
132	**11**	20c. black and blue	2·75	90
133	**11**	40c. black and red	4·00	1·80
134	**11**	1p. black and green	9·25	17·00
135	**11**	2p. black & purple on pink	16·00	29·00

22 Ploughman and Tower of Confucius   **23** Bay of Along   **24** Ruins of Angkor

1927

136	**22**	⅒c. olive	10	4·25
137	**22**	⅕c. yellow	35	4·25
138	**22**	⅖c. blue	35	4·00
139	**22**	⅗c. brown	1·10	4·50
140	**22**	1c. orange	1·00	20
141	**22**	2c. green	1·90	55
142	**22**	3c. blue	2·30	20
143	**22**	4c. mauve	2·50	3·50
144	**22**	5c. violet	2·50	20
145	**23**	6c. red	2·30	65
146	**23**	7c. brown	1·40	90
147	**23**	8c. olive	3·00	2·50
148	**23**	9c. purple	2·50	2·50
149	**23**	10c. blue	2·75	45
150	**23**	11c. orange	2·20	4·25
151	**23**	12c. grey	2·20	4·25
152	**24**	15c. brown and red	10·50	11·00
153	**24**	20c. grey and violet	7·50	85
154	-	25c. mauve and brown	7·75	90
155	-	30c. olive and blue	4·25	3·75
156	-	40c. blue and red	8·00	4·50
157	-	50c. grey and green	9·50	2·50
158	-	1p. black, yellow and blue	18·00	7·25
159	-	2p. blue, orange and red	48·00	13·00

DESIGNS—As T **24**: 25, 30c. Wood-carver; 40, 50c. Temple, Thuat-Luong; 1, 2p. Founding of Saigon.

1931. "Colonial Exn" key-types inscr "INDOCHINE" and surch with new value.

160	**F**	4c. on 50c. mauve	3·50	3·75
161	**G**	6c. on 90c. red	3·25	5·50
162	**H**	10c. on 1f.50 blue	5·50	4·50

33 Junk   **36** "Apsara", or dancing Nymph

1931

163	**33**	⅒c. blue	10	2·75
164	**33**	⅕c. red	10	1·20
165	**33**	⅖c. orange	35	6·25
166	**33**	½c. brown	10	1·00
167	**33**	⅗c. violet	20	6·75
168	**33**	1c. brown	10	10
169	**33**	2c. green	30	10
170	-	3c. brown	10	10
171	-	3c. green	13·00	65
172	-	4c. blue	2·75	35
173	-	4c. green	2·00	5·00
174	-	4c. yellow	20	1·10
175	-	5c. purple	50	20
176	-	5c. green	1·00	3·50
177	-	6c. red	35	10
178	-	7c. black	60	50
179	-	8c. red	1·00	1·90
180	-	9c. black on yellow	75	75
181	-	10c. blue	1·10	20
182	-	10c. blue on pink	55	30
183	-	15c. brown	9·75	1·20
184	-	15c. blue	55	35
185	-	18c. blue	1·00	3·50
186	-	20c. red	30	10
187	-	21c. green	45	35
188	-	22c. green	1·00	1·30
189	-	25c. purple	3·50	1·00
190	-	25c. blue	1·10	2·20
191	-	30c. brown	75	20
192	**36**	50c. brown	90	10
193	**36**	60c. purple	85	30
194	**36**	70c. blue	80	75
195	**36**	1p. green	75	30
196	**36**	2p. red	75	30

DESIGNS—As Type **33**: 3c. to 9c. Ruins at Angkor; 10c. to 30c. Worker in rice field.

42 Farman F.190 Mail Plane

1933. Air.

197	**42**	1c. brown	10	1·60
198	**42**	2c. green	10	1·20
199	**42**	5c. green	2·20	2·00
200	**42**	10c. brown	90	45
201	**42**	11c. red	2·30	3·25
202	**42**	15c. blue	4·50	1·40
203	**42**	16c. mauve	90	4·25
204	**42**	20c. green	3·00	1·20
205	**42**	30c. brown	90	60
206	**42**	36c. red	4·75	30
207	**42**	37c. green	1·00	20
208	**42**	39c. green	50	3·00
209	**42**	60c. purple	1·50	1·00
210	**42**	66c. green	2·00	1·00
211	**42**	67c. blue	1·10	3·00
212	**42**	69c. blue	45	7·50
213	**42**	1p. black	1·00	10
214	**42**	2p. orange	90	35
215	**42**	5p. violet	3·00	1·20
216	**42**	10p. red	4·50	1·80
217	**42**	20p. brown	20·00	12·00
218	**42**	30p. brown	25·00	12·50

44 Emperor Bao Dai of Annam

1936. Issue for Annam.

219	**44**	1c. brown	1·60	2·50
220	**44**	2c. green	1·40	2·50
221	**44**	4c. violet	1·10	90
222	**44**	5c. lake	1·30	4·25
223	**44**	10c. red	3·25	4·75
224	**44**	15c. blue	3·00	3·75
225	**44**	20c. red	2·50	6·00
226	**44**	30c. purple	2·30	3·25
227	**44**	50c. green	5·25	5·00
228	**44**	1p. mauve	7·75	7·50
229	**44**	2p. black	9·25	12·00

45 King Sisowath Monivong of Cambodia

1936. Issue for Cambodia.

230	**45**	1c. brown	1·30	2·50
231	**45**	2c. green	1·40	2·75
232	**45**	4c. violet	1·30	2·00
233	**45**	5c. lake	1·40	4·00
234	**45**	10c. red	2·75	4·00
235	**45**	15c. blue	2·50	4·75
236	**45**	20c. red	2·10	4·25
237	**45**	30c. purple	2·75	3·75
238	**45**	50c. green	2·75	4·00
239	**45**	1p. mauve	4·75	3·50
240	**45**	2p. black	3·50	6·25

1937. Int Exn, Paris. As T 58a of Guadeloupe.

241		2c. violet	1·60	2·30
242		3c. green	1·30	2·00
243		4c. red	90	85
244		6c. brown	1·00	45
245		9c. red	1·00	45
246		15c. blue	75	90
MS246a		120×100 mm. 30c. slate-lilac (as T **7**)	10·00	29·00

46 Pres. Doumer

1938. Opening of Trans-Indo-China Railway.

247	**46**	5c. red (postage)	2·00	55
248	**46**	6c. brown	1·60	55
249	**46**	18c. blue	1·60	1·30
250	**46**	37c. orange (air)	55	10

1938. International Anti-cancer Fund. As T 58b of Guadeloupe.

251		18c.+5c. blue	9·25	18·00

1939. New York World's Fair. As T 58c of Guadeloupe.

252		13c. red	75	2·50
253		23c. blue	1·40	2·75

47 Mot Cot Pagoda, Hanoi

1939. San Francisco International Exhibition.

254	**47**	6c. sepia	1·40	1·40
255	**47**	9c. red	75	75
256	**47**	23c. blue	85	2·30
257	**47**	39c. purple	1·80	1·80

1939. 150th Anniv of French Revolution. As T 58d of Guadeloupe.

258		6c.+2c. green & blk (postage)	11·00	23·00
259		7c.+3c. brown and black	11·00	23·00
260		9c.+4c. orange and black	11·00	23·00
261		13c.+10c. red and black	11·00	23·00
262		23c.+20c. blue and black	11·00	23·00
263		39c.+40c. black & orge (air)	25·00	55·00

48 King Sihanouk of Cambodia

1941. Coronation of King of Cambodia. No gum.

264	**48**	1c. orange	1·00	2·30
265	**48**	6c. violet	7·00	9·75
266	**48**	25c. blue	48·00	60·00

49 Processional Elephant

1942. Fetes of Nam-Giao. No gum.

267	**49**	3c. brown	3·00	8·00
268	**49**	6c. red	3·00	7·75

1942. No. 189 surch 10 cents and bars.

269		10c. on 25c. purple	1·80	3·75

51 Hanoi University

1942. University Fund. No gum.

270	**51**	6c.+2c. red	1·10	3·50
271	**51**	15c.+5c. purple	65	3·50

Surch **10c +2 c.**

272		10c.+2c. on 6c.+2c. red	45	6·00

53 Marshal Petain

1942. No gum.

273	**53**	1c. brown	65	3·75
274	**53**	3c. brown	1·80	6·50
275	**53**	6c. red	55	1·20
276	**53**	10c. green	1·50	1·60
277	**53**	40c. blue	90	2·50
278	**53**	40c. grey	1·80	1·30

54 Shield and Sword

1942. National Relief Fund. No gum.

279	**54**	6c.+2c. red and blue	1·40	2·30
280	**54**	15c.+5c. black, red & bl	90	1·40

Surch **10c +2 c.**

281		10c.+2c. on 6c.+2c. red and blue	55	4·50

55 Emperor Bao Dai of Annam   **56** King Sihanouk of Cambodia   **57** Empress Nam-Phaong of Annam

58 King Sisavang-Vong of Laos

1942. No gum.

282	**55**	½c. purple	75	2·50
283	**56**	1c. purple	85	4·75
284	**58**	1c. brown	80	4·25
285	**55**	6c. red	3·00	1·80
286	**56**	6c. red	45	3·50
287	**57**	6c. red	1·70	1·10
288	**58**	6c. red	90	4·00

59 Saigon Fair

1942. Saigon Fair. No gum.

289	**59**	6c. red	75	2·75

60 Alexandre Yersin

1943. No gum.

290	**60**	6c. red	75	4·25
291	**60**	15c. purple	55	1·30
292	-	15c. purple	55	3·50
293	-	20c. red	75	45
294	-	30c. brown	35	20
295	**60**	$1 green	35	20

DESIGNS—HORIZ: Nos. 292, 294, Alexandre de Rhodes; No. 293, Pigneau de Behaire, Bishop of Adran.

63 Do Huu-Vi

1943. Airmen. No gum.

296	**63**	6c.+2c. red	35	4·00
297	-	6c.+2c. red	75	4·50

Surch **10c +2 c.**

298	**63**	10c.+2c. on 6c.+2c. red	45	5·25
299	-	10c.+2c. on 6c.+2c. red	30	2·75

DESIGN—VERT: Nos. 297, 299, Roland Garros.

64 Doudart de Lagree

1943. Sailors. No gum.

300	**64**	1c. brown	20	55
301	**B**	1c. brown	85	1·40
302	**B**	1c. brown	1·80	2·30
303	**B**	5c. brown	45	1·10
304	**C**	6c. red	2·10	1·40
305	**D**	6c. red	1·10	2·75
306	**E**	6c. red	40	3·00
307	**F**	10c. green	85	1·80
308	**64**	15c. purple	35	3·00
309	**F**	20c. red	45	1·20
310	**64**	40c. blue	45	1·00
311	**F**	1p. green	65	2·75

DESIGNS—HORIZ: A, Francis Garnier; B, La Grandiere; C, Courbet; D, Rigault de Genouilly. VERT: E, Chasseloup Laubat; F, Charner.

66 "Family, Homeland and Labour"

1943. Third Anniv of National Revolution. No gum.

312	**66**	6c. red	55	2·75

67 De Lanessan

1944. Governors. No gum.

313	**G**	1c. brown	30	4·50
314	**67**	1c. brown	55	4·00
315	**H**	2c. mauve	20	2·75
316	**J**	4c. orange	75	90
317	**H**	4c. brown	20	30
318	**K**	5c. purple	55	3·25

319	**J**	10c. green	75	90
320	**H**	10c. green	20	2·30
321	**K**	10c. green	20	1·40
322	**G**	10c. green	25	90
323	**67**	15c. purple	1·40	1·70

DESIGNS—HORIZ: G, Van Vollenhoven; J, Auguste Pavie. VERT: H, Paul Doumer; K, Pierre Pasquier.

69 Athlete

1944. Juvenile Sports. No gum.

324	**69**	10c. purple and yellow	45	75
325	**69**	50c. red	55	3·25

70 Orleans Cathedral

1944. Martyr Cities. No gum.

326	**70**	15c.+60c. purple	90	4·50
327	**70**	40c.+1p.10 blue	90	6·50

1945. As T **149** of France surch **INDOCHINE** and values.

328		50c.+50c. on 2f. olive	35	7·00
329		1p.+1p. on 2f. brown	35	6·50
330		2p.+2p. on 2f. grey	55	5·75

1946. Air. Victory. As T **63b** of Guadeloupe.

331		80c. orange	45	85

1946. Air. From Chad to the Rhine. As T **63c** of Guadeloupe.

332		50c. green	90	5·75
333		1p. mauve	90	3·75
334		1p.50 red	90	3·00
335		2p. purple	90	4·75
336		2p.50 blue	90	6·00
337		5p. red	1·40	5·00

1946. Unissued stamps similar to T **24** with portrait of Marshal Petain optd with R F monogram.

338		10c. red	1·00	4·25
339		25c. blue	6·75	8·25

1949. Air. 75th Anniv of U.P.U. As T **39** of French Equatorial Africa.

340		3p. multicoloured	2·75	3·50

OFFICIAL STAMPS

1933. Stamps of 1931 (Nos. 168, etc.) optd **SERVICE**.

O197	1c. sepia	4·00	30
O198	2c. green	5·75	5·25
O199	3c. brown	3·75	2·50
O200	4c. blue	5·75	2·75
O201	5c. purple	3·25	35
O202	6c. red	3·00	3·50
O203	10c. blue	55	30
O204	15c. sepia	4·75	1·20
O205	20c. red	4·25	55
O206	21c. green	2·75	4·25
O207	25c. purple	2·30	3·00
O208	30c. brown	4·25	2·50
O209	50c. sepia	22·00	5·25
O210	50c. purple	1·00	3·25
O211	1p. green	55·00	11·00
O212	2p. red	18·00	16·00

1934. As T **11** but value in "CENTS" or "PIASTRES" and optd **SERVICE**.

O219	1c. brown	1·20	1·00
O220	2c. brown	1·40	1·50
O221	3c. green	4·00	2·00
O222	4c. red	3·00	45
O223	5c. orange	2·20	35
O224	6c. red	10·50	17·00
O225	10c. green	6·25	7·75
O226	15c. blue	4·00	2·30
O227	20c. green	6·50	2·30
O228	21c. violet	23·00	28·00
O229	25c. purple	22·00	22·00
O230	30c. violet	5·00	2·50
O231	50c. mauve	18·00	27·00
O232	60c. grey	30·00	34·00
O233	1p. blue	55·00	40·00
O234	2p. red	70·00	65·00

PARCEL POST STAMPS

1891. Stamp of French Colonies, "Commerce" type, optd **INDO-CHINE TIMBRE COLIS POSTAUX.**

P4	**J**	10c. black on lilac	28·00	7·00

1898. No. 10 optd **Colis Postaux**.

P20	**D**	10c. black on lilac	30·00	60·00

1899. Nos. 10 and 24 optd **TIMBRE COLIS POSTAUX**.

P21	10c. black on lilac	75·00	50·00
P22	10c. red	70·00	35·00

POSTAGE DUE STAMPS

1904. Postage Due stamps of French Colonies optd with value in figures.

D47	**U**	5 on 60c. brown on yellow	12·00	11·00
D48	**U**	5 on 40c. black	60·00	12·00
D49	**U**	10 on 60c. black	60·00	34·00
D50	**U**	30 on 60c. black	60·00	25·00

D13 Annamite Dragon

1908

D69	**D13**	2c. black	1·30	45
D70	**D13**	4c. blue	1·30	55
D71	**D13**	5c. green	1·60	30
D72	**D13**	10c. red	7·50	30
D73	**D13**	15c. violet	4·00	9·50
D74	**D13**	20c. brown	2·20	1·40
D75	**D13**	30c. olive	3·00	7·00
D76	**D13**	40c. purple	9·00	12·00
D77	**D13**	50c. blue	3·75	1·60
D78	**D13**	60c. yellow	21·00	28·00
D79	**D13**	1f. grey	30·00	50·00
D80	**D13**	2f. brown	46·00	40·00
D81	**D13**	5f. red	65·00	60·00

1919. Surch in figures and words.

D106	**D 13**	⅕c. on 2c. black	3·00	5·25
D107	**D 13**	1⅓c. on 4c. blue	2·50	6·00
D108	**D 13**	2c. on 5c. green	5·50	1·80
D109	**D 13**	4c. on 10c. red	6·75	35
D110	**D 13**	6c. on 15c. violet	11·50	3·75
D111	**D 13**	8c. on 20c. brown	16·00	1·80
D112	**D 13**	12c. on 30c. green	16·00	3·25
D113	**D 13**	16c. on 40c. brown	14·50	1·80
D114	**D 13**	20c. on 50c. blue	30·00	7·25
D115	**D 13**	24c. on 60c. yellow	4·75	1·40
D116	**D 13**	40c. on 1f. grey	5·75	3·25
D117	**D 13**	80c. on 2f. brown	48·00	46·00
D118	**D 13**	2p. on 5f. red	75·00	60·00

1922. Type **D13**, but values in cents or piastres.

D136		⅖c. black	10	1·30
D137		⅘c. black and red	20	3·25
D138		1c. black and yellow	45	45
D139		2c. black and green	1·30	65
D140		3c. black and violet	2·00	1·90
D141		4c. black and orange	1·80	1·30
D142		6c. black and olive	1·80	1·60
D143		8c. black on lilac	1·20	90
D144		10c. black and blue	1·70	1·80
D145		12c. blk & orge on grn	1·90	1·70
D146		20c. black & bl on yell	2·00	3·25
D147		40c. blk & red on grey	1·70	2·30
D148		1p. black & pur on pk	5·50	5·50

D28 Mot Cot Pagoda Hanoi   **D29** Annamite Dragon

1927

D160	**D 28**	⅖c. orange and purple	10	2·50
D161	**D 28**	⅘c. black and violet	10	2·50
D162	**D 28**	1c. grey and red	75	4·25
D163	**D 28**	2c. olive and green	1·80	45
D164	**D 28**	3c. blue and purple	90	4·00
D165	**D 28**	4c. brown and blue	1·30	85
D166	**D 28**	6c. red and scarlet	2·75	8·00
D167	**D 28**	8c. violet and brown	2·30	3·25
D168	**D 29**	10c. blue	3·50	2·30
D169	**D 29**	12c. brown	7·75	9·25
D170	**D 29**	20c. red	4·00	2·50
D171	**D 29**	40c. green	5·25	8·00
D172	**D 29**	1p. red	28·00	46·00

D37

1931. All values from 15c. to 50c. are in the same colours.

D197	**D 37**	⅕c. black & red on yell	10	5·75
D198	**D 37**	⅖c. black & red on yell	10	4·75
D199	**D 37**	⅘c. black & red on yell	10	4·75
D200	**D 37**	1c. black & red on yell	10	2·00
D201	**D 37**	2c. black & red on yell	10	65
D202	**D 37**	2,5c. black & red on yell	50	7·25
D203	**D 37**	3c. black & red on yell	45	7·25
D204	**D 37**	4c. black & red on yell	30	3·00
D205	**D 37**	5c. black & red on yell	30	7·25

D206	**D 37**	6c. black & red on yell	35	1·40
D207	**D 37**	10c. black & red on yell	35	1·20
D208	**D 37**	12c. black & red on yell	20	2·30
D209	**D 37**	14c. black & red on yell	90	7·25
D210	**D 37**	18c. black & red on yell	75	7·00
D211	**D 37**	20c. black & red on yell	35	2·30
D212	**D 37**	50c. black & red on yell	90	5·50
D213	**D 37**	1p. blue and red on yell	2·75	8·50

D62

1943

D296	**D62**	1c. red on yellow	55	7·50
D297	**D62**	2c. red on yellow	65	7·75
D298	**D62**	3c. red on yellow	55	7·50
D299	**D62**	4c. red on yellow	30	7·50
D300	**D62**	6c. red on yellow	75	5·75
D301	**D62**	10c. red on yellow	85	6·50
D302	**D62**	12c. blue on pink	30	7·75
D303	**D62**	20c. blue on pink	35	5·50
D304	**D62**	30c. blue on pink	1·40	5·75

Pt. 6, Pt. 17

INDO-CHINESE POST OFFICES IN CHINA

100 centimes = 1 franc.

General Issues

1902. Stamps of Indo-China, "Tablet" key-type, surch **CHINE** and value in Chinese.

15	**D**	1c. black on blue	3·00	2·20
2	**D**	2c. brown on buff	7·50	12·00
17	**D**	4c. brown on grey	4·50	6·50
18	**D**	5c. green	6·00	7·25
5	**D**	10c. red	9·00	9·00
6	**D**	15c. grey	17·00	17·00
20	**D**	20c. red on green	9·50	10·50
21	**D**	25c. black on pink	12·00	22·00
22	**D**	25c. blue	10·00	8·00
23	**D**	30c. brown on drab	8·50	17·00
24	**D**	40c. red on yellow	43·00	70·00
11	**D**	50c. red on pink	£110	£100
25	**D**	50c. brown on blue	11·00	11·50
26	**D**	75c. brown on orange	48·00	65·00
27	**D**	1f. green	60·00	80·00
28	**D**	5f. mauve on lilac	£110	£140

1904. Stamps of Indo-China surch **CHINE** and value in Chinese.

29	**8**	1c. olive	2·00	2·10
30	**8**	2c. red on yellow	2·30	1·80
31	**8**	4c. brown on grey	£1000	£850
32	**8**	5c. green	3·00	1·70
33	**8**	10c. red	3·50	2·75
34	**8**	15c. brown on blue	3·00	2·10
36	**8**	20c. red on green	13·00	37·00
37	**8**	25c. blue	6·50	9·25
38	**8**	40c. black on grey	5·75	6·50
39	**8**	1f. green	£450	£350
40	**8**	2f. brown on yellow	47·00	65·00
41	**8**	10f. red on green	£160	£160

Pt. 4, Pt. 21

INDONESIA

An independent republic was proclaimed in Java and Sumatra on 17 August 1945 and lasted until the end of 1948. During this period the Dutch controlled the rest of the Netherlands Indies, renamed "Indonesia" in September 1948. On 27 December 1949 all Indonesia except New Guinea became independent as the United States of Indonesia which, during 1950, amalgamated with the original Indonesian Republic (Java and Sumatra), a single state being proclaimed on 15 August 1950 as the Indonesian Republic. This was within the Netherlands-Indonesian Union which was abolished on 10 August 1954.

100 cents (or sen) = 1 gulden (or rupiah).

A. DUTCH ADMINISTRATION

1948. Stamps of Netherlands Indies optd **INDONESIA** and bar or bars.

541	**81**	15c. orange	1·60	50
533	**81**	20c. blue	60	50
543	**81**	25c. green	50	50
535	**81**	40c. green	60	50
544	**81**	45c. mauve	1·90	1·40
545	**81**	50c. lake	60	50
536	**81**	80c. red	1·60	50
537a	**81**	1g. green	60	50
538	-	2½g. orange (No. 479)	85·00	16·00
539	**81**	10g. green	£160	50·00
540	**81**	25g. orange	£225	95·00

86

87 Portal to Tjandi Poentadewa Temple

1949. New Currency.

548A	86	1s. grey	60	40
549A	86	2s. purple	95	40
550A	86	2½s. brown	60	40
551A	86	3s. red	95	40
552A	86	4s. green	95	95
553A	86	5s. blue	60	40
554A	86	7½s. green	95	40
555A	86	10s. mauve	60	40
556A	86	12½s. red	3·00	40
557A	87	15s. red	2·75	95
558A	87	20s. black	1·60	40
559A	87	25s. blue	1·60	40
560A	-	30s. red	1·90	40
561A	-	40s. green	1·90	40
562A	-	45s. purple	4·50	7·50
563A	-	50s. brown	2·50	40
564A	-	60s. brown	2·50	3·00
565A	-	80s. red	6·00	60
566A	-	1r. violet	2·20	40
567A	-	2r. green	10·50	40
568A	-	3r. purple	£160	40
569A	-	5r. brown	£110	3·00
570A	-	10r. black	£130	3·00
571A	-	25r. brown	1·30	3·00

DESIGNS—As Type **87**: 30 to 45s. Sculpture from Temple at Bedjoening, Bali; 50 to 80s. Minangkabau house, Sumatra; 21×26 mm: 1 to 3r. Toradja house; 5 to 25r. Detail of Temple of Panahan.

89 Globe and Arms of Berne

1949. 75th Anniv of U.P.U.

572	89	15s. red	1·90	60
573	89	25s. blue	1·90	60

B. REPUBLIC, 1945-48

ISSUES FOR JAVA AND MADURA

1945. Stamps of Netherlands Indies optd **REPOEBLIK INDONESIA.**

J1	46	1c. violet	2·40	3·00
J19	-	2c. red (No. 461)	1·60	2·75
J2	46	2c. purple	5·75	6·75
J4	-	2½c. red (No. 462)	2·50	3·50
J5	-	3c. green (No. 463)	2·50	3·50
J3	46	3½c. grey	70·00	80·00
J6	71	4c. olive	2·50	3·50
J7	71	5c. blue (No. 465)	85·00	95·00

1945. Stamps of Japanese Occupation of Netherlands Indies optd as above.

J8	-	3½s. red (No. 2)	£400	£500
J10	-	3½c. red (No. 5)	50·00	50·00
J9	-	5s. green (No. 3)	29·00	26·00
J11	2	5s. green	85	1·80
J12	-	10c. blue (No. 7)	65	1·30
J13	-	20c. olive (No. 8)	85	1·80
J14	-	40c. purple (No. 9)	1·00	1·90
J15	4	60c. orange	1·30	2·50
J16	-	80s. brown (No. 11)	23·00	26·00

J5 Bull

1945. Declaration of Independence. Inscr "17 AGOESTOES 1945". Perf or imperf.

J23	**J5**	10s. (+ 10s.) brown	7·75	8·75
J24	-	20s. (+ 10s.) brown & red	8·50	9·00

DESIGN—VERT: 20s. Bull and Indonesian flag.

J9 Boat in Storm

1946

J49		5s. blue	90	1·00
J50		20s. brown	95	1·20
J51	**J9**	30s. red	1·00	2·50

DESIGNS: 5s. Road and mountains; 20s. Soldier on waterfront.

J10 Wayang Puppet

1946

J52	**J10**	50s. blue	23·00	21·00
J53	-	60s. red	8·50	£325
J54	-	80s. violet	85·00	£650

DESIGNS: 60s. Kris and flag; 80s. Temple.

J13 Buffalo breaking Chains

J14 Bandung, March, 1946

1946. Perf or imperf.

J55b	**J13**	3s. red	35	50
J56b	**J14**	5s. blue	45	65
J57	-	10s. black	14·50	8·50
J58	-	15s. purple	1·20	1·60
J59b	-	30s. green	2·30	3·00
J60b	-	40s. blue	1·20	1·20
J61cb	**J13**	50s. black	1·00	1·10
J62b	**J14**	60s. lilac	2·30	2·30
J63	-	80s. red	3·25	7·75
J64b	-	100s. red	1·60	1·60
J65b	-	200s. lilac	2·00	3·00
J66b	-	500s. red	11·50	11·50
J67b	-	1000s. green	9·00	11·50

DESIGNS—HORIZ: 10, 15s. Soerabaya, November 1945; 30s. Anti-aircraft gunners; 100s. Ambarawa, November 1945; 200s. Wonokromo Dam, Soerabaya; 1000s. Cavalryman. VERT: 40s. Quay at Tandjong Priok; 80s. Airman; 500s. Mass meeting with flags, Djakarta.

1948. Postage Due Stamps of Netherlands Indies surch **SEGEL 25 sen PORTO.**

J68	D7	25s. on 7½c. orange	31·00	46·00
J69	D7	25s. on 15c. orange	16·00	39·00

Although surcharged for use as postage due stamps the above were employed for ordinary postal use.

J16 "Labour and Transport"

1948. Third Anniv of Independence. Imperf.

J70	**J16**	50s. blue	7·25	7·75
J71	**J16**	100s. red	7·75	8·50

J18 Flag over Waves

1949. Government's Return to Jogjakarta. Perf or Imperf.

J77b	**J18**	100s. red	6·75	11·50
J78b	**J18**	150s. red	9·75	22·00

POSTAGE DUE STAMPS

1948. Nos. J67 and J70/1 optd **DENDA**, or surch also.

JD72	**J16**	50s. blue		50·00
JD73	-	100s. red		50·00
JD74	-	1r. on 50s. blue (A)		50·00
JD75	-	1r. on 50s. blue (B)		50·00
JD76	-	1r. on 1000s. green		50·00

A. Surcharged "RP 1"; B. Surcharged "1—RP".

ISSUES FOR SUMATRA

1946. Stamps of Netherlands Indies surch **Repoeblik Indonesia** and value.

S1	-	15s. on 5c. blue (No. 465)	2·00	2·50
S2	46	20s. on 3½c. grey	16·00	16·00
S3	46	30s. on 1c. violet	14·50	14·50
S4	46	40s. on 2c. purple	50	1·30
S7	-	50s. on 17½c. orange (No. 431)	£100	£100
S9	46	60s. on 2½c. bistre	26·00	26·00
S10	46	80s. on 3c. green	16·00	16·00
S11	-	1r. on 10c. red (No. 429)	20·00	20·00

S9 Ploughing

1946. Freedom Fund.

S17	**S9**	5s. (+25s.) green	1·30	3·00
S18	**S9**	5s. (+25s.) blue	1·00	2·50
S19	-	15s. (+35s.) red	2·50	6·25
S20	-	15s. (+35s.) blue	1·00	2·50
S21	-	40s. (+60s.) orange	1·30	3·00
S22	-	40s. (+60s.) red	1·30	6·50
S23	-	40s. (+60s.) purple	8·25	13·00
S24	-	40s. (+60s.) brown	17·00	46·00

DESIGNS—VERT: 15s. Soldier and flag; 40s. Oil well and factories, Palembang.

S10 Pres. Sukarno

1946

S25	**S10**	40s. (+60s.) red	2·00	4·00

1946. "FONDS KEMERDEKAAN" obliterated by one or two bars.

S27	**S9**	5s. blue	£100	£200
S28	-	40s. red (No. S22)	£100	£120

1946. As Type **S9** but without "FONDS KEMERDEKAAN". Perf or imperf.

S29		2s. red	1·00	9·00
S30		2s. brown	5·25	15·00
S31		3s. green	1·30	7·75
S32		3s. red	6·25	15·00
S33		3s. blue		†
S34		5s. blue	50	5·25
S35		15s. blue	50	2·75
S36		15s. green	6·25	15·00
S37		40s. brown	65	3·25
S38		40s. blue	26·00	46·00

DESIGNS: 2, 3, 5s. As Type S **9**. 15s. Soldier and flag; 40s. Oil well and factories, Palembang.

1947. Fund for Palembang War Victims. Nos. S18, S20 and S23 optd **BPKPP** over triple circle.

S39	**S9**	5s. blue	£120	£140
S40	-	15s. blue	£120	£140
S41	-	40s. brown	£120	£140

S12

1947. Fiscal stamps of Japanese Occupation with blank panels optd in black with **prangko N.R.I.** and value as in Type **S12**.

S42	**S 12**	0f.50 orange	33·00	50·00
S43	**S 12**	1f. orange	26·00	39·00
S44	**S 12**	2f. orange	36·00	50·00
S45	**S 12**	2f.50 orange	27·00	30·00

1947. No. S25 surch with new value and bars.

S46		50s. on 40s. red	7·75	7·75
S47		1f. on 40s. red	11·50	11·50
S48		1f.50 on 40s. red	6·50	6·50
S49		2f.50 on 40s. red	1·30	4·00
S50		3f.50 on 40s. red	1·30	4·00
S51		5f. on 40s. red	1·30	4·00

1947. Surch with ornament and new value.

S63		1s. on 15s. (No. S35)	80	2·50
S64		5s. on 3s. (No. S33)	65	2·50
S65		10s. on 15s. red (as Nos. S35/6)	85	2·50
S52		30s. on 40s. (No. S28)	1·00	2·50
S66		50s. on 3s. (No. S32)	26·00	42·00
S53		50s. on 5s. (No. S34)	9·75	7·25
S59		50s. on 40s. (No. S28)	20·00	26·00
S54		1f. on 5s. (No. S34)	8·50	7·25
S60		1f. on 40s. (No. S28)	65	2·50
S55		1f.50 on 5s. (No. S34)	9·75	9·75
S61		1f.50 on 40s. (No. S28)	5·25	9·00
S62		2f.50 on 40s. (No. S28)	6·50	2·50
S56		1r. on 40s. (No. S37)	80	5·25
S57		2r. on 5s. (No. S34)	1·00	5·25

1947. No. S56 surch **50**.

S58		50(r.) on 1r. on 40s.	80·00	90·00

1947. Air. Surch **Pos Udara** with ornament and new value.

S67		10r. on 40s. (No. S22)	4·00	5·25
S68		20r. on 5s. (No. S34)	2·30	5·25

1947. Stamps of 1946 (Nos. S29/37) surch.

S69		10s. on 15s. blue	20·00	20·00
S70		20s. on 15s. blue	20·00	20·00
S71		30s. on 15s. blue	20·00	10·50
S75		50s. on 5s. blue	£1000	£900
S76		50s. on 15s. blue	£1000	£1000
S77		0f.50 on 15s. blue	£900	£900
S78		1f. on 5s. blue	£200	£200
S79		1f. on 15s. blue	£400	£500
S80		2f.50 on 5s. blue	£1000	£900
S73		2f.50 on 15s. blue	20·00	20·00
S82		2f.50 on 40s. brown	£800	£900
S83		5f. on 15s. blue	£1000	£1000
S74		5f. on 40s. brown	£325	£225
S72		1r. on 2s. red	60·00	60·00
S88		2r. on 3s. green	46·00	90·00
S85		2r.50 on 3s. green	26·00	39·00
S89		5r. on 15s. blue	9·75	16·00
S87		10r. on 3s. green	£100	£100
S91		20r. on 2s. red	£325	£650
S92		50r. on 15s. blue	£450	£650
S93		100r. on 15s. blue	£160	£160
S94		150r. on 40s. red	£200	£200

No. S94 is surcharged on No. S22 with a pen-stroke through "FONDS KEMERDEKAAN".

(S 23) "O.R.I." = "Oeang Repoeblik Indonesia" (Indonesian Republican Money)

1947. Change of Currency. Various stamps optd with Type **S23**. (a) On stamps of Netherlands Indies.

S99	**S12**	1c. red (No. D226)	10·50	11·00
S96	**46**	3c. green (No. 338)	6·25	7·75
S97	**71**	4c. olive (No. 464)	9·50	10·50
S98	-	5c. blue (No. 465)	4·50	7·25
S100	-	15c. red (No. D448)	7·75	9·50

(b) On stamps of Japanese Occupation of Netherlands Indies.

S101		1c. green (No. 15)	1·40	2·00
S102		2c. green (No. 16)	1·40	1·60
S103		3c. blue (No. 17)	1·40	1·60
S104		3½c. red (No. 18)	2·00	2·50
S105		4c. blue (No. 19)	3·25	5·00
S106		5c. orange (No. 20)	2·00	2·50
S107		10c. blue (No. 21)	7·75	8·75
S111	-	10c. red (No. 57)	1·10	1·40
S108		20c. brown (No. 22)	7·75	8·75
S113	-	25c. green (No. 62)	13·00	16·00
S109	**6**	30c. purple (No. 23)	1·40	1·40
S114	-	30c. brown (No. 63)	10·50	11·50
S110	-	50c. brown (No. 25)	2·75	2·75
S115	-	50c. red (No. 66)	13·50	17·00
S116	-	60c. blue (No. 67)	7·25	7·75
S117	-	80c. red (No. 68)	7·25	9·50
S118	-	1g. violet (No. 69)	14·50	16·00

(c) On stamps of Japan.

S119		1s. brown (No. 317)	1·30	2·00
S120		3s. green (No. 319)	1·30	1·60
S121		4s. green (No. 320)	6·50	7·25
S122		6s. orange (No. 322)	2·00	2·50
S123		25s. brn & choc (No. 329)	1·30	1·80
S124		30s. green (No. 330)	3·00	4·50
S125		50s. green & bis (No. 331)	1·30	2·00
S126		1y. brown and chocolate (No. 332)	3·00	4·50

(d) On stamps of Indonesia-Sumatra.

S149	-	1s. on 15s. bl (No. S63)	90	1·80
S136	-	2s. red (No. S29)	3·25	4·00
S137	-	3s. green (No. S31)	8·50	8·50
S138	-	3s. red (No. S32)	1·30	2·20
S132	**S9**	5s. green (No. S17)	3·25	5·25
S133	-	5s. blue (No. S18)	1·20	1·70
S139	-	5s. blue (No. S34)	1·00	1·40
S150	-	10s. on 15s. red (No. S65)	3·00	5·00
S134	-	15s. blue (No. S20)	3·00	5·50
S140	-	15s. blue (No. S35)	1·00	1·40
S141	-	15s. green (No. S36)	5·00	7·25
S127	**46**	20s. on 3½c. grey (No. S2)	8·50	9·75
S128	-	30s. on 1c. violet (No. S3)	8·50	10·50
S146	-	30s. on 40s. red (No. S52)	1·00	1·70
S135	-	40s. red (No. S22)	3·50	4·50
S142	-	40s. brown (No. S37)	90	1·30
S129	**46**	40s. on 2c. purple (No. S4)	4·00	6·50
S151	-	50s. on 5s. blue (No. S53)	2·30	3·00
S152	-	1f.50 on 5s. blue (No. S55)	7·25	9·50
S143	-	1f.50 on 40s. red (No. S48)	8·50	8·50
S147	-	1f.50 on 40s. red (No. S61)	8·50	9·75
S144	-	2f.50 on 40s. red (No. S49)	8·25	9·75
S148	-	2f.50 on 40s. red (No. S62)	8·25	9·75
S145	-	3f.50 on 40s. red (No. S50)	8·25	9·75
S153	-	2r. on 5s. blue (No. S57)	2·10	3·25
S154	-	10r. on 40s. red (No. S67)	9·75	13·00

C. UNITED STATES OF INDONESIA

90 Indonesian
Flag

1950. Inauguration of United States of Indonesia.
574	90	15s. red (20½×26 mm)	2·00	45
575	90	15s. red (18×23 mm)	9·75	2·00

1950. Stamps of 1949 optd **RIS**.
579	86	1s. grey	1·40	1·10
580	86	2s. purple	2·40	3·00
581	86	2½s. brown	1·40	1·10
582	86	3s. red	1·40	85
583	86	4s. green	1·40	1·10
584	86	5s. blue	1·40	1·10
585	86	7½s. green	1·40	1·10
586	86	10s. mauve	1·40	1·10
587	86	12½s. red	1·70	1·10
588	87	20s. black	41·00	49·00
589	87	25s. blue	1·40	1·10
590	-	30s. red	14·00	30·00
591	-	40s. green	1·40	65
592	-	45s. purple	2·75	1·70
593	-	50s. brown	2·40	1·50
594	-	60s. brown	12·00	18·00
595	-	80s. red	5·50	1·70
596	-	1r. violet	3·75	75
597	-	2r. green	£600	£150
598	-	3r. purple	£200	£100
599	-	5r. brown	85·00	28·00
600	-	10r. black	£150	60·00
601	-	25r. brown	35·00	24·00

D. INDONESIAN REPUBLIC

94 Indonesian
Arms

1950. Fifth Anniv of Proclamation of Independence.
602	94	15s. red	3·50	45
603	94	25s. green	4·75	2·00
604	94	1r. sepia	17·00	3·00

95 Maps and
Torch

1951. Asiatic Olympic Games, New Delhi.
605	95	5s.+3s. green	20	10
606	95	10s.+5s. blue	20	10
607	95	20s.+5s. red	20	15
608	95	30s.+10s. brown	55	20
609	95	35s.+10s. blue	4·75	3·75

96   **97** General   **98** "Spirit of
Post-Office,   Indonesia"
Bandung

1951
610	96	1s. grey	65	1·30
611	96	2s. mauve	65	1·10
612	96	2½s. brown	8·75	20
613	96	5s. red	65	20
614	96	7½s. green	65	20
615	96	10s. blue	65	20
616	96	15s. violet	65	20
618	96	20s. red	65	20
619	96	25s. green	65	20
620	97	30s. red	20	10
621	97	35s. violet	1·10	10
622	97	40s. green	20	10
623	97	45s. purple	20	45
624	97	50s. brown	5·25	10
625	98	60s. brown	20	10
626	98	70s. grey	20	10
627	98	75s. blue	20	10
628	98	80s. purple	20	10
629	98	90s. green	20	10

99 President
Sukarno

1951
630	99	1r. violet	45	10
631	99	1r.25 orange	2·75	10
632	99	1r.50 brown	45	10
633	99	2r. green	45	10
634	99	2r.50 brown	45	10
635	99	3r. blue	45	10
636	99	4r. green	45	10
637	99	5r. brown	45	10
638	99	6r. mauve	45	10
639	99	10r. grey	45	10
640	99	15r. stone	45	10
641	99	20r. purple	45	10
642	99	25r. red	1·10	10
643	99	40r. green	1·40	3·75
644	99	50r. violet	2·00	20

101 Sports
Emblem

1951. National Sports Festival.
655	101	5a.+3s. green	65	70
656	101	10s.+5s. blue	65	70
657	101	20s.+5s. orange	65	70
658	101	30s.+10s. sepia	65	70
659	101	35s.+10s. blue	65	1·70

102 Doves

1951. U.N. Day.
660	102	7½s. green	4·75	1·40
661	102	10s. violet	1·40	65
662	102	20s. orange	3·50	1·40
663	102	30s. red	4·75	1·70
664	102	35s. blue	4·75	1·70
665	102	1r. sepia	37·00	5·50

1953. Natural Disasters Relief Fund. Surch **19 53
BENTJANA ALAM +10s.**
666	97	35s.+10s. violet	65	20

104 Melati
Flowers

1953. Mothers' Day and 25th Anniv of Indonesian
Women's Congress.
667	104	50s. green	22·00	1·00

105 Merapi
Volcano in
Eruption

1954. Natural Disasters Relief Fund.
668	105	15s.+10s. green	1·70	2·40
669	105	35s.+15s. violet	1·70	2·00
670	105	50s.+25s. red	1·70	2·00
671	105	75s.+25s. blue	1·70	2·00
672	105	1r.+25s. red	1·70	2·00
673	105	2r.+50s. brown	4·25	2·00
674a	105	3r.+1r. green	20·00	14·00
675a	105	5r.+2r.50 brown	22·00	18·00

106 Girls with
Musical
Instruments

1954. Child Welfare.
676	106	10s.+10s. purple	20	1·00
677	-	15s.+10s. green	20	1·10
678	-	35s.+15s. mauve	20	1·10
679	-	50s.+15s. purple	65	1·10
680	-	75s.+25s. blue	45	4·25
681	-	1r.+25s. red	55	7·50

DESIGNS: 15s. Menangkabau boy and girl performing Umbrella Dance; 35s. Girls playing "Tjongkak"; 50s. Boy on bamboo stilts; 75s. Ambonese boys playing flutes; 1r. Srimpi dancing girl.

107 Globe and
Doves

1955. Asian–African Conference, Bandung.
682	107	15s. black	1·10	1·00
683	107	35s. brown	1·10	1·00
684	107	50s. turquoise	3·25	1·00
685	107	75s. turquoise	2·00	1·00

108 Semaphore
Signaller

1955. National Scout Jamboree.
686	-	15s.+10s. green	55	65
687	108	35s.+15s. blue	55	65
688	-	50s.+25s. red	55	65
689	-	75s.+25s. brown	55	65
690	-	1r.+50s. violet	55	65

DESIGNS: 15s. Indonesian scout badge; 50s. Scouts round campfire; 75s. Scout feeding baby sika deer; 1r. Scout saluting.

109 Proclamation
of Independence

1955. Tenth Anniv of Independence.
691	109	15s. green	1·10	1·00
692	109	35s. blue	1·20	1·00
693	109	50s. brown	6·50	65
694	109	75s. purple	1·20	80

110
Postmaster
Sukarto

1955. Tenth Anniv of Indonesian Post Office.
695	110	15s. brown	1·10	1·00
696	110	35s. red	1·10	1·00
697	110	50s. blue	7·00	2·50
698	110	75s. green	2·75	1·10

111 Electors

1955. First General Indonesian Elections.
699	111	15s. purple	55	65
700	111	35s. green	85	1·10
701	111	50s. red	3·00	1·40
702	111	75s. blue	1·10	65

112 Memorial
Column,
Wreath and
Helmet

1955. Heroes' Day.
703	112	25s. green	75	45
704	112	50s. blue	2·20	1·00
705	112	1r. red	15·00	45

113 Weaving

1956. Blind Relief Fund.
706	113	15s.+10s. green	85	1·00
707	-	35s.+15s. brown	85	1·00
708	-	50s.+25s. red	1·80	2·10
709	-	75s.+50s. blue	85	1·00

DESIGNS—VERT: 35s. Basketwork; 50s. Map reading; 75s. Reading.

114 Torch and
Book

1956. Asian and African Students' Conf, Bandung.
710	114	25s. blue	1·50	55
711	114	50s. red	7·50	1·70
712	114	1r. green	2·75	1·70

115 Lesser
Malay
Chevrotain

1956
713	115	5s. blue	20	10
714	115	10s. brown	20	10
715	115	15s. purple	20	10
716	-	20s. green	20	10
717	-	25s. purple	20	10
718	-	30s. orange	20	10
719	-	35s. blue	20	10
720	-	40s. green	20	10
721	-	45s. purple	2·00	20
722	-	50s. bistre	20	10
723	-	60s. blue	25	10
724	-	70s. red	2·75	45
725	-	75s. sepia	25	10
726	-	80s. red	25	20
727	-	90s. green	25	20

DESIGNS: 20s. to 30s. Hairy-nosed otter; 35s. to 45s. Malayan pangolin; 50s. to 70s. Banteng; 75s. to 90s. Sumatran rhinoceros.

116 Red Cross

1956. Red Cross Fund.
728	116	10s.+10s. red and blue	20	10
729	116	15s.+10s. red & carmine	20	10
730	-	35s.+15s. red and brown	20	15
731	-	50s.+15s. red and green	35	20
732	-	75s.+25s. red & orange	55	45
733	-	1r.+25s. red and violet	75	65

DESIGNS: 35, 50s. Blood transfusion bottle; 75s., 1r. Hands and drop of blood.

117

1956. Bicentenary of Djokjakarta.
734	117	15s. green	2·20	85
735	117	35s. brown	2·20	85
736	117	50s. blue	4·25	1·40
737	117	75s. purple	4·25	1·40

118 Crippled
Child

1957. Cripples' Rehabilitation Fund. Inscr "UNTUK
PENDERITA TJATJAT".
738	-	10s.+10s. blue	20	10
739	-	15s.+10s. brown	20	10
740	-	35s.+15s. red	20	10
741	118	50s.+15s. violet	35	45
742	-	75s.+25s. green	45	55
743	-	1r.+25s. red	65	85

DESIGNS: 10s. One-legged woman painting cloth; 15s. One-handed artist; 35s. One-handed machinist; 75s. Doctor tending cripple; 1r. Man writing with artificial arm.

119 Telegraph Key and Tape

1957. Centenary of Telegraphs in Indonesia.

744	119	10s. red	3·25	85
745	119	15s. blue	75	50
746	119	25s. black	55	20
747	119	50s. red	75	45
748	119	75s. green	85	20

120 Two men with Savings-box

1957. Co-operation Day. Inscr "HARI KOOPERASI".

749	120	10s. blue	60	55
750	-	15s. red	70	55
751	120	50s. green	1·40	1·00
752	-	1r. violet	1·60	1·60

DESIGN: 15s., 1r. "Co-operative Prosperity" (hands holding ear of rice and cotton).

121 Kembodja (*Plumeria acuminata*)

1957. Various Charity Funds. Floral designs. Multicoloured.

753	10s.+10s. Type **121**	2·50	1·60
754	15s.+10s. Tjempakakuning (michelia)	2·00	1·60
755	35s.+15s. Matahari (sunflower)	1·10	1·30
756	50s.+15s. Melati (jasmine)	75	85
757	75s.+50s. Larat (orchid)	75	85

122 Convair CV 340 Airliner

1958. National Aviation Day. Inscr "HARI PENERBANGAN NASIONAL 9-4-1958".

758	122	10s. brown	20	10
759	-	15s. blue	25	10
760	-	35s. orange	45	35
761	122	50s. turquoise	85	55
762	-	75s. slate	1·50	1·50

DESIGNS: 15s. Hiller "Skeeter" helicopter; 35s. Nurtiano Sikumbang trainer; 75s. de Havilland Vampire jet fighter.

123 "Helping Hands"

1958. Indonesian Orphans Welfare Fund Inscr "ANAK PIATU".

763	123	10s.+10s. blue	25	20
764	-	15s.+10s. red	25	20
765	123	35s.+15s. green	25	20
766	-	50s.+25s. drab	25	20
767	123	75s.+50s. brown	25	20
768	-	1r.+50s. brown	25	20

DESIGN: 15s., 50s., 1r. Girl and boy orphans.

124 Thomas Cup

1958. Indonesian Victory in Thomas Cup World Badminton Championships, Singapore.

769	124	25s. red	25	20
770	124	50s. orange	25	20
771	124	1r. brown	55	20

125 Satellite encircling Globe

1958. International Geophysical Year.

785	**125**	10s. pink, green and blue	1·50	85
786	**125**	15s. drab, violet and grey	45	20
787	**125**	35s. blue, sepia and pink	45	20
788	**125**	50s. brown, blue and drab	45	20
789	**125**	75s. lilac, black and yellow	45	20

126 Racing Cyclist

1958. Tour of Java Cycle Race.

790	**126**	25s. blue	65	45
791	**126**	50s. red	1·10	45
792	**126**	1r. grey	65	45

127 "Human Rights"

1958. Tenth Anniv of Declaration of Human Rights.

793	**127**	10s. sepia	25	20
794	-	15s. brown	25	20
795	-	35s. blue	35	20
796	-	50s. bistre	35	20
797	-	75s. green	35	20

DESIGNS: 15s. Hands grasping "Flame of Freedom"; 35s. Native holding candle; 50s. Family acclaiming "Flame of Freedom"; 75s. "Flame" superimposed on figure "10".

128 Babirusa

1959. Animal Protection Campaign.

798	**128**	10s. sepia and olive	25	20
799	-	15s. sepia and brown	40	35
800	-	20s. sepia and green	50	45
801	-	50s. sepia and brown	65	60
802	-	75s. sepia and red	70	65
803	-	1r. black and turquoise	75	70

ANIMALS: 15s. Anoa (buffalo); 20s. Orang-utan; 50s. Javan rhinoceros; 75s. Komodo lizard; 1r. Malayan tapir.

129 Indonesian Scout Badge

1959. Tenth World Scout Jamboree, Manila. Inscr as in T **129**. Badges in red.

804	**129**	10s.+5s. bistre	15	15
805	-	15s.+10s. green	25	15
806	**129**	20s.+10s. violet	25	25
807	-	50s.+25s. olive	25	40
808	**129**	75s.+35s. brown	25	40
809	-	1r.+50s. slate	35	40

DESIGN: 15s., 50s., 1r. Scout badge within compass.

130

1959. Re-adoption of 1945 Constitution.

810	**130**	20s. red and blue	25	20
811	**130**	50s. black and red	25	20
812	**130**	75s. red and brown	25	20
813	**130**	1r.50 black and green	45	25

131 Factory and Girder

1959. 11th Colombo Plan Conference, Djakarta.

814	**131**	15s. black and green	20	10
815	-	20s. black and orange	20	10
816	**131**	50s. black and red	20	10
817	-	75s. black and blue	20	10
818	-	1r.15 black and purple	20	10

DESIGNS: 20, 75s. Cogwheel and diesel train; 1r.15, Forms of transport and communications.

132

1960. Indonesian Youth Conference, Bandung. Inscr "1960".

819	**132**	15s.+5s. sepia and bistre	15	45
820	-	20s.+10s. sepia & green	20	45
821	**132**	50s.+25s. purple & blue	20	45
822	-	75s.+35s. green & bis	20	45
823	-	1r.15+50s. black & red	40	55

DESIGNS: 20s., 75s. Test-tubes in frame; 1r.15, Youth wielding manifesto.

133 Refugee Camp

1960. World Refugee Year. Centres in black.

824	**133**	10s. purple	10	20
825	-	15s. ochre	10	20
826	-	20s. brown	10	20
827	**133**	50s. green	20	20
828	-	75s. blue	40	20
829	-	1r.15 red	40	1·50

DESIGNS: 15s., 75s. Outcast family; 20s., 1r.15, "Care of refugees" (refugee with protecting hands).

134 Tea plants

1960. Agricultural Products.

830		5s. grey	20	10
831		10s. brown	20	10
832		15s. purple	20	10
833		20s. bistre	20	10
834	**134**	25s. green	20	10
835	-	50s. blue	20	10
836	-	75s. red	20	10
837	-	1r.15 red	25	20

DESIGNS: 5s. Oil palm; 10s. Sugar cane; 15s. Coffee plant; 20s. Tobacco plant; 50s. Coconut palm; 75s. Rubber trees; 1r.15, Rice plants.

135 Mosquito

1960. World Health Day.

838	**135**	25s. red	10	10
839	**135**	50s. brown	20	10
840	**135**	75s. green	20	10
841	**135**	3r. orange	50	20

136 Socialist Emblem

1960. Third Socialist Day. Inscr as in T **136**.

842	**136**	10s.+10s. brown & blk	10	20
843	-	15s.+15s. purple & blk	10	20
844	-	20s.+20s. blue and black	20	20
845	-	50s.+25s. black & brn	20	45
846	-	75s.+25s. black & green	20	45
847	-	3r.+50s. black and red	20	65

DESIGNS: 15s. Emblem similar to Type **136** within plants; 20s. Lotus flower; 50s. Boy and girl; 75s. Ceremonial watering of plant; 3r. Mother with children.

137 Pres. Sukarno and Workers Hoeing

1961. National Development Plan.

848	**137**	75s. black	55	20

1961. Flood Relief Fund. Nos. 832/3 and 836 surch BENTJANA ALAM 1961 and premium.

849		15s.+10s. purple	20	15
850		20s.+15s. brown	20	15
851		75s.+25s. red	35	20

139 Bull Race

1961. Tourist Publicity.

852	-	10s. purple	65	55
853	-	15s. grey	65	55
854	**139**	20s. orange	65	55
855	-	25s. red	65	55
856	-	50s. lake	65	55
857	-	75s. brown	65	55
858	-	1r. green	1·10	65
859	-	1r.50 bistre	1·10	65
860	-	2r. blue	1·60	75
861	-	3r. grey	1·60	75

MS862 Three sheets each 140×105 mm containing (a) Nos. 852/3, 859; (b) Nos. 854, 856, 860; (c) Nos. 857/8 and a fourth sheet 105×140 mm. containing Nos. 855, 861 | 24·00 | 24·00

DESIGNS: 10s. Ambonese boat; 15s. Tangkuban Perahu crater; 25s. Daja dancer; 50s. Toradja houses; 75s. Balinese temple; 1r. Lake Toba; 1r.50, Bali dancer; 2r. "Buffalo Hole" (gorge); 3r. Borobudur temple.

140 Stadium

1961. Thomas Cup World Badminton Championships.

863	**140**	75s. lilac and blue	20	15
864	**140**	1r. olive and green	25	15
865	**140**	3r. salmon and blue	45	20

141 "United Efforts"

1961. 16th Anniv of Independence.

866	**141**	75s. violet and blue	20	15
867	**141**	1r.50 green and cream	25	15
868	**141**	3r. red and salmon	55	20

142 Sultan Hasanuddin

1961. National Independence Heroes. Portraits in sepia; inscriptions in black.

869	-	20s. olive	10	45
870	**142**	20s. olive	20	45
871	-	30s. violet	20	45
872	-	40s. brown	20	45
873	-	50s. myrtle	20	45
874	-	60s. turquoise	20	45
875	-	75s. brown	1·20	45
876	-	1r. blue	1·20	45
877	-	1r.25 brown	85	45
878	-	1r.50 green	1·20	45
879	-	2r. red	85	45
880	-	2r.50 red	1·20	45
881	-	3r. slate	1·00	45
882	-	4r. green	1·00	45
883	-	4r.50 purple	55	45
884	-	5r. red	1·20	45
885	-	6r. ochre	1·20	45
886	-	7r.50 blue	1·60	45
887	-	10r. green	1·00	45
888	-	15r. orange	1·00	45

PORTRAITS: 20s. Abdul Muis; 30s. Surjopranoto; 40s. Tengku Tjhik Di Tiro; 50s. Teuku Umar; 60s. K. H. Samanhudi; 75s. Capt. Pattimura; 1r. Raden Adjeng Kartini; 1r.25, K. H. Achmad Dahlan; 1r.50, Tuanku Imam Bondjol; 2r. Si Singamangaradja XII; 2r.50, Mohammed Husni Thamrin; 3r. Ki Hadjar Dewantoro; 4r. Gen. Sudirman; 4r.50, Dr. G. S. S. J. Ratulangie; 5r. Pangeran Diponegoro; 6r. Dr. Setyabudi; 7r.50, H. O. S. Tjokroaminoto; 10r. K. H. Agus Salim; 15r. Dr. Soetomo.

143 Census Emblems

1961. First Indonesian Census.
889	143	75s. purple	65	20

144 Nenas (pineapples)

1961. Charity. Fruits.
890	144	20s.+10s. yellow, red and blue	65	55
891	-	75s.+25s. purple, green and slate	85	65
892	-	3r.+1r. red, yell & grn	1·30	2·00

FRUITS: 75s. Manggis; 3r. Rambutan.

145 Djataju

1962. Ramayana Dancers.
893	145	30s. brown and ochre	55	65
894	-	40s. violet and purple	55	65
895	-	1r. purple and green	85	65
896	-	1r.50 green and pink	85	65
897	-	3r. blue and green	2·75	65
898	-	5r. brown and buff	2·40	65

DANCERS: 40s. Hanoman; 1r. Dasamuka; 1r.50, Kidang Kentjana; 3r. Dewi Sinta; 5r. Rama.

146 Aerial View of Mosque

1962. Construction of Istiqlal Mosque.
899	146	30s.+20s. blue & yellow	55	45
900	-	40s.+20s. red and yellow	55	45
901	146	1r.50+50s. brown & yell	55	45
902	-	3r.+1r. green and yellow	55	45

DESIGN: 40s., 3r. Ground-level view of Mosque.

147 Games Emblem

1962. Fourth Asian Games, Djakarta. Inscr as in T **147**.
903		10s. green and yellow	25	20
904		15s. brown and ochre	25	20
905		20s. lilac and green	45	35
906		25s. red and green	40	35
907		30s. green and buff	40	20
908		40s. ultramarine and blue	45	20
909		50s. brown and drab	50	45
910		60s. mauve and grey	45	40
911		70s. brown and red	45	40
912		75s. brown and orange	45	20
913		1r. violet and blue	50	45
914	**147**	1r.25 blue and mauve	55	50
915	-	1r.50 red and mauve	1·60	55
916	-	1r.75 red and pink	1·10	55
917	**147**	2r. brown and green	85	55

918	-	2r.50 blue and green	1·00	55
919	**147**	3r. black and red	1·00	55
920	-	4r.50 green and red	1·00	55
921	**147**	5r. green and bistre	65	55
922	-	6r. red and brown	75	55
923	-	7r.50 brown and pink	80	55
924	-	10r. ultramarine and blue	1·40	75
925	-	15r. violet and light violet	1·60	1·50
926	-	20r. green and bistre	3·50	1·80

DESIGNS—VERT: 10s. Basketball; 20s. Weightlifting; 40s. Throwing the discus; 50s. Diving; 60s. Football; 70s. Press building; 75s. Boxing; 1r. Volleyball; 1r.50, Badminton; 1r.75, Wrestling; 2r.50, Shooting; 4r.50, Hockey; 6r. Water polo; 7r.50, Tennis; 10r. Table tennis; 15r. Cycling; 20r. "Welcome" monument. HORIZ: 15s. Main stadium; 25s. Hotel Indonesia; 30s. Road improvement.

148 Campaign Emblem

1962. Malaria Eradication.
927	**148**	40s. blue and violet	15	10
928	**148**	1r.50 orange and brown	15	10
929	**148**	3r. green and blue	15	10
930	**148**	6r. violet and black	35	20

On the 1r.50 and 6r. the inscription is at top.

149 National Monument

1962. National Monument.
931	**149**	1r.+50c. brown & black	25	20
932	-	1r.50+50c. green & blue	25	20
933	**149**	3r.+1r. mauve and green	45	20
934	-	6r.+1r.50 blue and red	45	20

DESIGN: 1r.50, 6r. Aerial view of Monument.

150 Atomic Symbol

1962. "Science for Development".
935	**150**	1r.50 blue and yellow	20	20
936	**150**	4r.50 red and yellow	35	45
937	**150**	6r. green and yellow	55	50

151 Phalaenopsis amabilis

1962. Charity. Orchids. Multicoloured.
938		1r.+50s. Vanda tricolor (horiz)	45	20
939		1r.50+50s. Type **151**	45	20
940		3r.+1r. Dendrobium phalaenopsis	45	15
941		6r.+1r.50 "aphiopedilum praestans (horiz)	35	15

152 West Irian Monument, Djakarta

1963. Construction of West Irian Monument.
942	**152**	1r.+50c. green and red	35	10
943	**152**	1r.50+50c. sepia, black and mauve	20	10
944	**152**	3r.+1r. brown and blue	35	10
945	**152**	6r.+1r.50 bistre & grn	35	20

153 Conference Emblem

1963. 12th Pacific Area Travel Association Conference, Djakarta.
946	**153**	1r. blue and green	20	20
947	-	1r.50 blue and olive	20	20
948	**153**	3r. blue and brown	55	20
949	-	6r. blue and orange	55	20

DESIGNS: 1r.50, Prambanan Temple and Mt. Merapi; 6r. Balinese Meru in Pura Taman Ajun.

154 Rice Sheaves

1963. Freedom from Hunger.
950	**154**	1r. yellow and blue	10	10
951	-	1r.50 green and blue	20	10
952	**154**	3r. yellow and red	20	10
953	-	6r. orange and black	35	20

DESIGN—HORIZ: 1r.50, 6r. Tractor; Nos. 950/1 are inscr "CONTRE LA FAIM"; Nos. 952/3, "FREEDOM FROM HUNGER".

155 Lobster

1963. Marine Life. Multicoloured.
954	**155**	1r. Type **155**	55	20
955		1r.50 Kawakawa	55	20
956		3r. River snapper	1·30	55
957		6r. Chinese pomfret	1·30	85

156 Conference Emblem

1963. Asian-African Journalists' Conference.
958	**156**	1r. red and blue	20	10
959	-	1r.50 brown and lavender	20	10
960	-	3r. blue, black and olive	55	20
961	-	6r. salmon and black	75	35

DESIGNS—HORIZ: 1r.50, Pen, emblem and map. VERT: 3r. Pen. Globe and broken chain; 6r. Pen severing chain around Globe.

157 Indonesia, from Atjeh to Merauke

1963. Acquisition of West Irian (West New Guinea).
962	**157**	1r.50 orange, red & black	20	10
963	-	4r.50 blue, green & purple	25	20
964	-	6r. brown, yellow & green	1·30	85

DESIGNS: 4r.50, Parachutist; 6r. Greater bird of paradise.

158 Centenary Emblem

1963. Centenary of Red Cross.
965	**158**	1r. green and red	35	20
966	-	1r.50 red and blue	35	20
967	**158**	3r. grey and red	35	20
968	-	6r. red and bistre	35	20

DESIGN: 1r.50, 6r. Red Cross (inscr in English).

159 Volcano

1963. Bali Volcano Disaster Fund.
969	**159**	4r. (+2r.) red	25	10
970	**159**	6r. (+3r.) green	25	20

160 Bank of Indonesia, Djakarta

1963. National Banking Day.
971	**160**	1r.75 purple and blue	20	20
972	-	4r. green and yellow	20	20
973	**160**	6r. brown and green	20	10
974	-	12r. purple and orange	45	20

DESIGN—VERT: 4r., 12r. Daneswara, God of Prosperity.

161 Athletes with Banners

1963. Games of the New Emerging Forces, Djakarta.
975	**161**	1r.25 sepia and violet	10	10
976	-	1r.75 olive and buff	10	10
977	-	4r. sepia and green	10	10
978	-	6r. sepia and brown	35	20
979	-	10r. sepia and green	35	20
980	-	12r. olive and red	45	20
981	-	25r. ultramarine and blue	65	55
982	-	50r. sepia and red	75	65

DESIGNS: 1r.75, "Pendet" dance; 4r. Conference Hall, Djakarta; 6r. Archery; 10r. Badminton; 12r. Throwing the javelin; 25r. Sailing; 50r. "Ganefo" torch.

162 Papilio blumei

1963. Social Day. Butterflies. Multicoloured.
983		1r.75+50s. Type **162**	45	20
984		4r.+1r. "Charaxes dehaani"	45	20
985		6r.+1r.50 Purple-spotted swallowtail	45	20
986		12r.+3r. "Troides amphrysus"	85	55

163 Pres. Sukarno

1964
987	**163**	6r. blue and brown	25	20
988	**163**	12r. purple and bistre	25	20
989	**163**	20r. orange and blue	25	20
990	**163**	30r. blue and orange	25	20
991	**163**	40r. brown and green	25	20
992	**163**	50r. green and red	25	20
993	**163**	75r. red and violet	25	20
994	**163**	100r. brown and grey	25	20
995	**163**	250r. grey and blue	45	25
996	**163**	500r. gold and red	55	45

164 Lorry and Trailer

1964
997	-	1r. purple	25	20
998	**164**	1r.25 brown	25	20
999	-	1r.75 blue	25	20
1000	-	2r. red	25	20
1001	-	2r.50 blue	25	20
1002	-	4r. green	25	20
1003	-	5r. brown	25	20
1004	-	7r.50 green	25	20
1005	-	10r. orange	25	20
1006	-	15r. blue	25	20
1007	-	25r. blue	45	20
1008	-	35r. brown	45	20

DESIGNS—HORIZ: 1r. Ox-cart; 1r.75, "Hadju Agus Salim" (freighter); 2r. Lockheed Electra airliner; 4r. Cycle-postman; 5r. Douglas DC-3 airliner; 7r.50, Teletypist; 10r. Diesel train; 15r. "Sam Ratulangi" (freighter); 25r. Convair Coronado airliner; 35r. Telephone operator. VERT: 2r.50, Buginese sailing boat.

165 Rameses II, Abu Simbel

1964. Nubian Monuments Preservation. Monuments in brown.

1009	165	4r. drab	45	20
1010	-	6r. blue	45	20
1011	165	12r. pink	45	20
1012	-	18r. green	45	20

DESIGN: 6r., 18r., Trajan's Kiosk, Philae.

166 Various Stamps of Netherlands Indies and Indonesia

1964. Stamp Centenary.

1013	166	10r. multicoloured	1·40	45

167 Indonesian Pavilion at Fair

1964. New York World's Fair.

1014	167	25r. red, blue and silver	65	65
1015	167	50r. red, turquoise & gold	1·60	65

168 Thomas Cup

1964. Thomas Cup World Badminton Championships.

1016	168	25r. gold, red and green	35	45
1017	168	50r. gold, red and blue	45	45
1018	168	75r. gold, red and violet	1·10	1·30

169 *Sandjaja* and *Siliwanghi* (destroyers)

1964. Indonesian Navy.

1019	169	20r. brown and yellow	45	15
1020	-	30r. black and red	55	20
1021	-	40r. blue and green	1·00	1·30

DESIGNS: 30r. *Nanggala* (submarine); 40r. *Matjan Tutul* (torpedo-boat).

170 Pied Fantail

1965. Social Day. Birds.

1022	170	4r.+1r. black, lilac and green	45	35
1023	-	6r.+1r.50 black, buff and green	45	35
1024	-	12r.+3r. black, blue and olive	65	45
1025	-	20r.+5r. yellow, red and purple	65	55
1026	-	30r.+7r.50 black, slate and mauve	1·10	45

BIRDS: 6r. Zebra dove; 12r. Black drongo; 20r. Black-naped oriole; 30r. Java sparrow.

171 Map and Mosque

1965. Afro-Asian Islamic Conf, Bandung.

1027	171	10r. blue and violet	45	15
1028	-	15r. brown and orange	45	15
1029	171	25r. green and brown	65	20
1030	-	50r. purple and red	65	85

DESIGN: 15r., 50r. Mosque and handclasp.

172 Scroll in Hand

1965. Tenth Anniv of First Afro-Asian Conference, Bandung.

1031	172	15r. red and silver	35	15
1032	-	25r. gold, red & turquoise	35	15
1033	172	50r. blue and gold	55	20
1034	-	75r. gold, red and lilac	75	1·10

DESIGN: 25r., 75r. Conference 10th-anniv emblem.

1965. Conf of "New Emerging Forces", Djakarta. T **163** additionally inscr "Conefo". Value, "Conefo" and frame in red; portrait colour given.

1035		1r.+1r. brown	20	15
1036		1r.25+1r.25 red	20	15
1037		1r.75+1r.75 purple	20	15
1038		2r.+2r. green	20	15
1039		2r.50+2r.50 brown	20	15
1040		4r.+3r.50 blue	20	15
1041		6r.+4r. green	20	15
1042		10r.+5r. brown	20	15
1043		12r.+5r.50 orange	20	15
1044		15r.+7r.50 turquoise	20	15
1045		20r.+10r. brown	20	15
1046		25r.+10r. violet	20	15
1047		40r.+15r. purple	20	15
1048		50r.+15r. violet	20	15
1049		100r.+25r. brown	25	20

174 Makara Mask and Rays

1965. Campaign against Cancer.

1050	174	20r.+10r. red and blue	45	20
1051	174	30r.+15r. blue and red	45	20

175 "Happy Family"

1965. The State's Five Principles and 20th Anniv of Republic.

1052	175	10r.+5r. yellow, black and brown	55	35
1053	-	20r.+10r. red, black and yellow	35	35
1054	-	25r.+10r. green, black and red	35	35
1055	-	40r.+15r. black, red and blue	65	35
1056	-	50r.+15r. yellow, black and mauve	65	35

DESIGNS: ("State's Principles"): 20r. "Humanitarianism" (globe and clasped hands); 25r. "Nationalism" (map and garland); 40r. "Democracy" (council meeting); 50r. "Belief in God" (churches and mosques).

177 Samudra Beach Hotel

1965. Tourist Hotels.

1060	177	10r.+5r. blue & turq	25	35
1061	177	25r.+10r. violet, black and green	45	45
1062	177	40r.+15r. brown, black and blue	50	45
1063	-	80r.+20r. pur & orge	75	45

DESIGN: 25r., 80r. Ambarrukmo Palace Hotel.

178 *Gloriosa superba*

1965. Flowers. Multicoloured, Inscr "1965" and with commas and dashes after figures of value.

1064		30r.+10r. Type **178**	1·20	1·40
1065		40r.+15r. Hibiscus tiliaceus	1·20	1·40
1066		80r.+20r. Impatiens balsamina	1·20	1·40
1067		100r.+25r. Lagerstroemia Indica	1·20	1·40

See also Nos. 1108/1116.

1965. Revalued Currency. Optd **'65 Sen.** (a) On Nos. 989/94.

1068	163	(20)s. on 20r.	25	10
1069	163	(30)s. on 30r.	25	20
1070	163	(40)s. on 40r.	25	20
1071	163	(50)s. on 50r.	25	20
1072	163	(75)s. on 75r.	25	3·00
1073	163	(100)s. on 100r.	60	20

(b) On Nos. 1005/7.

1074		(10)s. on 10r.	40	20
1075		(15)s. on 15r.	40	20
1076		(25)s. on 25r.	40	20

180 Pres. Sukarno

1966. Revalued Currency. Inscr "1967" (12r.) or "1966" (others). Values and frames turquoise (12r., 25r.) or chocolate (others); portrait and country name in colour given.

1077	180	1s. blue	25	10
1078	180	3s. olive	25	10
1079	180	5s. red	25	10
1080	180	8s. turquoise	25	10
1081	180	10s. blue	25	10
1082	180	15s. black	25	10
1083	180	20s. green	25	10
1084	180	25s. brown	25	10
1085	180	30s. blue	25	10
1086	180	40s. brown	25	10
1087	180	50s. violet	25	10
1088	180	80s. orange	25	10
1089	180	1r. green	25	10
1090	180	1r.25 brown	25	10
1091	180	1r.50 green	25	10
1092	180	2r. purple	30	20
1093	180	2r.50 slate	30	20
1094	180	5r. orange	45	45
1095	180	10r. olive	45	20
1096	180	12r. orange	45	20
1097	180	25r. violet	45	45

1966. Flowers. As T **178** but inscr "1966" and additionally inscr "sen" instead of commas and dashes. Multicoloured.

1108		10s.+5s. Cassia alata	1·30	1·40
1109		20s.+5s. Barleria cristata	1·30	1·40
1110		30s.+10s. Ixora coccinea	1·30	1·40
1111		40s.+10s. Hibiscus rosa sinensis	1·30	1·40
MS1112	58×78 mm. No. 1111. Imperf		13·00	4·50

1966. National Disaster Fund. Floral designs as T **178** additionally inscr "BENTJANA ALAM NASIONAL 1966". Multicoloured.

1113		15a.+5s. Gloriosa superba	85	90
1114		25a.+5s. Hibiscus tiliaceus	85	90
1115		30s.+10s. Impatiens balsamina	85	90
1116		80s.+20s. Lagerstroemia Indica	85	90

181 Cleaning Ship's Rudder

1966. Maritime Day.

1117	181	20s. green and blue	30	10
1118	-	40s. blue and pink	30	10
1119	-	50s. brown and green	30	10
1120	-	1r. multicoloured	30	10
1121	-	1r.50 green and lilac	30	10
1122	-	2r. red and grey	30	20
1123	-	2r.50 red and mauve	40	20
1124	-	3r. black and green	45	25
MS1125	60×78 mm. No. 1124. Imperf		17·00	19·00

DESIGNS: 40s. Anyer Kidul lighthouse; 50s. Fisherman; 1r. Maritime emblem; 1r.50 Madurese sailing boat; 2r. Quayside; 2r.50 Pearl-diving; 3r. Liner in dry-dock.

182 Gen. A. Yani

1966. Victims of Attempted Communist Coup, 1965. Frames and date in blue.

1126	182	5r. brown	50	25
1127	A	5r. green	50	25
1128	B	5r. purple	50	25
1129	C	5r. olive	50	25
1130	D	5r. grey	50	25
1131	E	5r. violet	50	25
1132	F	5r. purple	50	25
1133	G	5r. green	50	25
1134	H	5r. purple	50	25
1135	I	5r. orange	50	25

PORTRAITS: A, Lt.-Gen. R. Soeprapto; B, Lt.-Gen. M. Harjono; C, Lt.-Gen. S. Parman; D, Maj.-Gen. D. Pandjaitan; E, Maj.-Gen. S. Siswomihardjo; F, Brig.-Gen. Katamso; G, Col. Soegijono; H, Capt. P. Tendean; I, Insp. K. S. Tubun.

183 Python

1966. Reptiles.

1136	183	2r.+25s. brown, green and flesh	25	20
1137	-	3r.+50s. grn, brn & lil	25	20
1138	-	4r.+75s. purple, buff and green	80	20
1139	-	6r.+1r. black, brn & bl	1·00	20

REPTILES: 3r. Chameleon; 4r. Crocodile; 6r. Green turtle.

184 Tjlempung

1967. Musical Instruments.

1140	184	50s. red and black	65	55
1141	-	1r. sepia and red	65	55
1142	-	1r.25 lake and blue	65	55
1143	-	1r.50 green and violet	65	55
1144	-	2r. blue and ochre	65	55
1145	-	2r.50 green and red	65	55
1146	-	3r. green and purple	65	55
1147	-	4r. blue and orange	1·00	55
1148	-	5r. red and blue	1·00	55
1149	-	6r. blue and mauve	80	70
1150	-	8r. lake and green	80	70
1151	-	10r. violet and red	80	55
1152	-	12r. green and violet	1·20	90
1153	-	15r. violet and olive	90	55
1154	-	20r. black and sepia	90	55
1155	-	25r. black and green	1·20	55

INSTRUMENTS: 1r. Sasando; 1r.25, Foi doa; 1r.50, Kultjapi; 2r. Arababu; 2r.50, Genderang; 3r. Katjapi; 4r. Hape; 5r. Gangsa; 6r. Serunai; 8r. Rebab; 10r. Trompet; 12r. Totobuang; 15r. Tamburn; 20r. Kulintang; 25r. Keledi.

185 Pilot and Mikoyan Gurevich MiG-21 Fighter

1967. Aviation Day. Multicoloured.

1156		2r.50 Type **185**	50	45
1157		4r. Convair Coronado airliner and control tower	50	35
1158		5r. Lockheed C-130 Hercules transport aircraft on tarmac	90	45

186 Thomas Cup and Silhouettes

1967. Thomas Cup World Badminton Championships. Multicoloured.

1159		5r. Type **186**	40	25
1160		12r. Thomas Cup on Globe	80	25

187 Balinese Girl

1967. International Tourist Year.

1161	**187**	12r. multicoloured	1·70	1·50
MS1162 85×80 mm. No. 1161 (sold at 15r.)			7·75	8·00

188 Heroes Monument

1967. "Heroes of the Revolution". Monument.

1163	**188**	2r.50 brown and green	25	20
1164	-	5r. purple and drab	65	45
1165	-	7r.50 green and pink	65	45

DESIGNS—HORIZ: 5r. Monument and shrine. VERT: 7r.50, Shrine.

190 Forest Fire

1967. Paintings by Raden Saleh.

1175	**190**	25r. red and green	65	70
1176	-	50r. purple and red	80	70
MS1177 95×63 mm. No. 1175 (sold at 30r.)			9·00	10·00

PAINTING: 50r. *A Fight to the Death.*

191 Flood Victims

1967. National Disaster Fund.

1178	**191**	1r.25+10s. blue & yell	50	55
1179	-	2r.50+25s. blue & yell	50	55
1180	-	4r.+40s. black & orge	50	55
1181	-	5r.+50s. black & orge	50	55
MS1182 95×89 mm. Nos. 1180/1 (sold at 12r.50)			50·00	60·00

DESIGNS: 2r.50, Landslide; 4r. Burning house; 5r. Erupting volcano.

192 Human Rights Emblem

1968. Human Rights Year.

1183	**192**	5r. red, green and blue	50	15
1184	**192**	12r. red, green and drab	50	35

193 Academy Badge

1968. Indonesian Military Academy.

1185	**193**	10r. multicoloured	90	45

194/6 *Sudhana and Manohara at Court of Druma (relief on wall of Borobudur)*

1968. "Save Borobudur Monument".

1186	**194**	2r.50+25s. deep green and green	40	45
1187	**195**	2r.50+25s. deep green and green	40	45
1188	**196**	2r.50+25s. deep green and green	40	45
1189	-	7r.50+75s. green and orange	80	45
MS1190 105×64 mm. Nos. 1186/8 (sold at 12r.50)			50·00	55·00

DESIGN—VERT: 7r.50, Buddhist and statue of Buddha.

197 W.H.O. Emblem and "20"

1968. 20th Anniv of W.H.O.

1191	**197**	2r. purple and yellow	50	45
1192	-	20r. black and green	50	45

DESIGN: 20r. W.H.O. emblem.

198 Diesel Train (1967) and Steam Train (1867)

1968. Centenary (1967) of Indonesian Railways.

1193	**198**	20r. multicoloured	1·20	45
1194	**198**	30r. multicoloured	1·70	1·50

199 Scout with Pick

1968. "Wirakarya" Scout Camp.

1195	**199**	5r.+50s. brown & orge	50	25
1196	-	10r.+1r. grey & brown	1·00	55
1197	-	30r.+3r. brown & grn	1·70	90

DESIGNS—VERT: 10r. Bugler on hillside. HORIZ: (69×29 mm); 30r. Scouts in camp.

200 Butterfly Dancer

1968. Tourism.

1198	**200**	30r. multicoloured	2·30	2·30
MS1199 84×88 mm. No. 1198 (sold at 35r.)			9·00	10·50

202 Observatory and Stars

1968. 40th Anniv of Bosscha Observatory.

1207	**202**	15r. blue, yellow & black	80	45
1208	-	30r. violet and orange	1·20	50

DESIGN—VERT: 30r. Observatory on Globe.

203/4 Yachting

1968. Olympic Games, Mexico.

1209		5r. green, brown & black	15	10
1210	**203**	7r.50 blue, yellow & red	40	25
1211	**204**	7r.50 blue, yellow & red	40	25
1212	-	12r. red, blue and yellow	50	25
1213	-	30r. brown, green & orge	80	35
MS1214 95×65 mm. Nos. 1210/11 (sold at 20r.)			9·00	11·50

DESIGNS:—28½×44½ mm: 5r. Weightlifting; 12r. Basketball. 44½×28½ mm: 30r. Dove and Olympic flame.

Nos. 1210/11 were issued together, se-tenant, forming the composite design illustrated.

205 *Eugenia aquea*

1968. Fruit. Multicoloured.

1215	**205**	7r.50 Type **205**	50	25
1216	-	15r. *Carica papaya*	80	45
1217	-	30r. *Durio zibethinus* (vert)	1·30	70
MS1218 Two sheets (a) 96×62 mm. No. 1216. (b) 62×96 mm. No. 1217 (sold at 55r. the pair)			13·00	17·00

206 I.L.O. Emblem and part of Globe

1969. 50th Anniv of I.L.O.

1219	**206**	5r. red and green	25	10
1220	-	7r.50 green and orange	25	10
1221	**206**	15r. red and violet	40	20
1222	-	25r. red and turquoise	65	35

DESIGN: 7r.50, 25r. I.L.O. emblem.

207 R. Dewi Sartika

1969. National Independence Heroes.

1223	**207**	15r. green and violet	50	25
1224	-	15r. purple and green	50	25
1225	-	15r. blue and red	50	25
1226	-	15r. ochre and red	50	25
1227	-	15r. sepia and blue	50	25
1228	-	15r. lilac and blue	50	25

PORTRAITS: No. 1224, Tjut Nja Din; 1225, Tjut Nja Meuthia; 1226, Sutan Sjahrir; 1227, Dr. F. L. Tobing; 1228, General G. Subroto.

208 Woman with Flower

1969. Women's Emancipation Campaign.

1229	**208**	20r.+2r. red, yellow and green	1·20	55

209 Red Cross "Mosaic"

1969. 50th Anniv of League of Red Cross Societies.

1230	**209**	15r. red and green	70	25
1231	-	20r. red and yellow	80	55

DESIGN: 20r. Hands encircling Red Cross.

210 "Planned" Family and Factory

1969. South-East Asia and Oceania Family Planning Conference.

1232	**210**	10r. orange and green	50	25
1233	-	20r. mauve and green	80	45

DESIGN: 20r. "Planned" family and "National Prosperity".

211 Balinese Mask

1969. Tourism in Bali. Multicoloured.

1234		12r. Type **211**	65	45
1235		15r. Girl with offerings	1·20	55
1236		30r. Cremation rites	1·30	70
MS1237 96×64 mm. No. 1236 (sold at 35r.)			7·00	8·50

212 "Agriculture"

1969. Five-year Development Plan.

1238		5r. blue and green	40	10
1239	**212**	7r.50 yellow and purple	40	10
1240	-	10r. red and blue	40	10
1241	-	12r. red and blue	2·20	90
1242	-	15r. yellow and green	40	10
1243	-	20r. yellow and violet	40	10
1244	-	25r. red and black	40	15
1245	-	30r. black and red	80	20
1246	-	40r. orange and green	90	20
1247	-	50r. brown and orange	1·30	25

DESIGNS: 5r. Religious emblems ("Co-existence"); 10r. Modern family ("Social Welfare"); 12r. Crane and crate ("Overseas Trade"); 15r. Bobbins ("Clothing Industry"); 20r. Children in class ("Education"); 25r. Research worker ("Scientific Research"); 30r. Family and hypodermic syringe ("Health Care"); 40r. Tunas in net ("Fisheries"); 50r. Graph ("Statistics").

213 Dish Aerial

1969. Satellite Communications and Inauguration of Djatiluhur Earth Station. Multicoloured.
1248	15r. Type **213**	80	25
1249	30r. Communications satellite	1·00	80

214 Vickers Vimy Biplane over Borobudur Temple

1969. 50th Anniv of First England–Australia Flight by Ross and Keith Smith.
1253	**214**	75r. purple and red	90	80
1254	–	100r. green and yellow	1·00	80

DESIGNS: 100r. Vickers Vimy and map of Indonesia.

215 Noble Volute

1969. Sea Shells. Multicoloured.
1255	5r.+50c. Type **215**	65	80
1256	7r.50+50c. Common hairy triton	65	80
1257	10r.+1r. Common spider conch	1·00	1·10
1258	15r.+1r.50 Bramble murex	1·00	1·10

216 Indonesian Pavilion

1970. "Expo 70" World Fair, Osaka, Japan.
1259	**216**	5r. yellow, green & brn	80	45
1260	–	15r. red, blue and green	1·20	55
1261	**216**	30r. yellow, blue and red	2·20	90

DESIGN: 15r. Indonesian "Garuda" symbol.

217 Prisoner's Hands and Scales of Justice

1970. "Purification of Justice".
1262	**217**	10r. purple and red	90	50
1263	**217**	15r. purple and green	1·30	55

218 U.P.U. Monument, Berne

1970. Inauguration of New U.P.U. Headquarters Building, Berne.
1264	**218**	15r. red and green	90	55
1265	–	30r. blue and ochre	1·90	1·40

DESIGN: 30r. New Headquarters building.

219 Timor Dancers

1970. "Visit Indonesia Year". Traditional Dancers. Multicoloured.
1266	20r. Type **219**	1·60	80
1267	45r. Bali dancers	2·30	1·40
MS1268 63×97 mm. No. 1267 (sold at 60r.)		11·50	13·50

220 "Productivity" Symbol

1970. Asian Productivity Year.
1269	**220**	5r. red, yellow and green	80	25
1270	**220**	30r. red, yellow and violet	2·10	1·00

221 Independence Monument

1970. 25th Anniv of Independence.
1271	**221**	40r. violet, purple & blue	19·00	8·50

222 Emblems of Post and Giro, and of Telecommunications

1970. 25th Anniv of Indonesian Post and Telecommunications Services.
1272	**222**	10r. brown, yellow & grn	6·50	1·10
1273	–	25r. black, yellow & pink	13·00	1·00

DESIGN: 25r. Telephone dial and P.T.T. worker.

223 U.N. Emblem and Doves

1970. 25th Anniv of United Nations.
1274	**223**	40r. multicoloured	19·00	8·50

224 I.E.Y. Emblem on globe

1970. International Education Year.
1275	**224**	25r. brown, red & yellow	13·00	5·50
1276	–	50r. red, black and blue	26·00	8·50

DESIGNS: 50r. I.E.Y. emblem.

225 *Chrysocoris javanus* (shieldbug)

1970. Insects. Multicoloured.
1277	7r.50+50c. Type **225**	9·00	2·30
1278	15r.+1r.50 *Orthetrum testaceum* (darter)	17·00	11·50
1279	20r.+2r. *Xylocopa flavonigrescens* (carpenter bee)	26·00	8·00

226 Batik handicrafts

1971. "Visit ASEAN (South East Asian Nations Association) Year". Multicoloured.
1280	20r. Type **226**	4·00	2·30
1281	50r. Javanese girl playing angklung (musical instrument) (vert)	6·50	6·25
1282	75r. Wedding group, Minangkabau	16·00	8·50
MS1283 64×97 mm. No. 1281 (sold at 70r.)		80·00	90·00

227 Restoration of Fatahillah Park

1971. 444th Anniv of Djakarta. Multicoloured.
1284	15r. Type **227**	4·00	1·80
1285	65r. Performance at Lenong Theatre	7·75	6·75
1286	80r. Ismail Marzuki Cultural Centre	14·00	5·75
MS1287 121×103 mm. 30r. Djakarta City Hall (sold at 60r.)		39·00	39·00

228 Sita and Rama

1971. International Ramayana Festival.
1288	**228**	30r. multicoloured	4·00	1·40
1289	–	100r. black, blue and red	5·75	3·00

DESIGN: 100r. Rama.

229 Pigeon with Letter, and Workers

1971. Fifth Asian Regional Telecommunications Conf.
1290	**229**	50r. chocolate, brown and buff	3·00	1·70

230 U.P.U. Monument, Berne, and Hemispheres

1971. U.P.U. Day.
1291	**230**	40r. purple, black & blue	2·75	1·70

231 Schoolgirl

1971. 25th Anniv of UNICEF. Multicoloured.
1292	20r. Type **231**	3·50	1·00
1293	40r. Boy with rice-stalks	7·00	2·00

232 Clown Surgeonfish

1971. Fish (1st series). Multicoloured.
1294	15r. Type **232**	7·00	2·10
1295	30r. Moorish idol	14·00	5·75
1296	40r. Emperor angelfish	21·00	8·25

See also Nos. 1318/20, 1343/5, 1390/2 and 1423/5.

233 Microwave Tower

1972. 25th Anniv of E.C.A.F.E.
1297	**233**	40r. blue and turquoise	4·25	1·80
1298	–	75r. multicoloured	5·75	1·90
1299	–	100r. multicoloured	7·00	3·75

DESIGNS—VERT: 40r. E.C.A.F.E. emblem. HORIZ: 100r. Irrigation and highways.

234 Human Heart

1972. World Heart Month.
1300	**234**	50r. multicoloured	3·50	1·40

235 Ancient and Modern Textile Production

1972. 50th Anniv of Textile Technological Institute.
1301	**235**	35r. purple, yellow & orge	3·50	1·40

236 Children reading Books

1972. International Book Year.
1302	**236**	75r. multicoloured	4·25	2·10

237 "Essa 8" Weather Satellite

1972. Space Exploration.
1303	**237**	35r. brown, violet & blue	2·75	1·10
1304	–	50r. blue, black and pink	6·50	6·25
1305	–	60r. black, green & brn	9·25	2·00

DESIGNS: 50r. Astronaut on Moon; 60r. Indonesian "Kartika I" rocket.

238 Hotel Indonesia

1972. Tenth Anniv of Hotel Indonesia.
1306	**238**	50r. green, pale grn & red	3·50	2·00

239 "Silat" (unarmed combat)

1972. Olympic Games, Munich.
1307	**239**	20r. purple, cobalt & blue	2·00	25
1308	–	35r. violet, brown & mve	2·10	65
1309	–	50r. emer, dp grn & grn	4·00	1·10
1310	–	75r. rose, purple and pink	4·25	2·75
1311	–	100r. brown, blue & green	7·00	4·50

DESIGNS: 35r. Running; 50r. Diving; 75r. Badminton; 100r. Olympic stadium.

240 Family and Religious Buildings

1972. Family Planning Campaign. Multicoloured.
1312	30r. Type **240**	2·75	1·10
1313	75r. "Healthy family"	5·75	4·25
1314	80r. "Family of workers"	8·50	5·25

241 Moluccas Dancer

1972. "Art and Culture" (1st series).
1315	**241**	30r. brown, pink & green	2·75	1·10
1316	-	60r. multicoloured	7·00	4·50
1317	-	100r. bl, brn & cinnamon	11·50	5·00

DESIGNS—VERT: 60r. Couple and Toraja traditional house. HORIZ: 100r. West Irian traditional house.
See also 1336/8, 1373/5 and 1401/3.

1972. Fish (2nd series). As T **232**. Multicoloured.
1318	30r. Triangle butterflyfish	10·00	3·25
1319	50r. Royal angelfish	17·00	4·50
1320	100r. Clown triggerfish	20·00	8·25

242 Thomas Cup and Shuttlecock

1972. Thomas Cup Badminton Championships, Djakarta.
1321	**242**	30r. blue and green	1·80	50
1322	-	75r. red and green	2·40	90
1323	-	80r. brown and red	4·00	1·80

DESIGNS: 75r. Thomas Cup and Sports Centre; 80r. Thomas Cup and player.

243 Emblem, Anemometer and "Gatotkaca"

1973. I.M.O. and W.M.O. Weather Organization Centenary.
1324	**243**	80r. multicoloured	3·50	1·40

244 "Health begins at Home"

1973. 25th Anniv of W.H.O.
1325	**244**	80r. blue, orange & green	2·75	1·40

245 Java Mask

1973. Tourism. Indonesian Folk Masks. Multicoloured.
1326	30r. Type **245**	5·75	1·60
1327	60r. Kalimantan mask	11·50	6·25
1328	100r. Bali mask	18·00	3·25

246 Savings Bank and Thrift Plant

1973. Two-Year National Savings Drive.
1329	**246**	25r. black, yellow & bis	90	50
1330	-	30r. green, gold & yellow	1·60	50

DESIGN—HORIZ: 30r. Hand and "City" savings bank.

247 Chess

1973. National Sports Week. Multicoloured.
1331	30r. Type **247**		1·60	1·10
1332	60r. Karate		2·75	1·10
1333	75r. Hurdling (horiz)		5·00	90

248 International Policemen

1973. 50th Anniv of Interpol.
1334	**248**	30r. multicoloured	1·40	65
1335	-	50r. yellow, purple & blk	2·50	1·10

DESIGN—VERT: 50r. Giant temple guard.

1973. "Art and Culture" (2nd series). Weaving and Fabrics. As T **241**. Multicoloured.
1336	60r. Parang Rusak pattern	2·75	3·50
1337	80r. Pagi Sore pattern	7·00	3·75
1338	100r. Merak Ngigel pattern	14·00	7·00

249 "Food Cultivation"

1973. Tenth Anniv of World Food Programme.
1339	**249**	30r. multicoloured	4·25	1·10

250 "Religion"

1973. Family Planning.
1340	**250**	20r. blue, light blue & red	1·00	75
1341	-	30r. black, yellow & brn	2·40	1·10
1342	-	60r. black, yellow & grn	5·00	1·00

DESIGNS: 30r. Teacher and class ("Population Education"); 60r. Family and house ("Health").

1973. Fish (3rd series). As T **232**. Multicoloured.
1343	40r. Powder-blue surgeonfish	2·75	1·60
1344	65r. Melon butterflyfish	11·50	3·25
1345	100r. Blue-ringed angelfish	14·00	5·00

251 Admiral Sudarso and Naval Battle of Arafuru

1974. Naval Day.
1346	**251**	40r. multicoloured	3·00	1·40

252 Bengkulu Costume

1974. Pacific Area Travel Association Conference, Djakarta. Provincial Costumes. Multicoloured.
1347	5r. Type **252**	21·00	1·60
1348	7r.50 Kalimantan. Timor	10·50	1·30
1349	10r. Kalimantan, Tengah	6·50	1·30
1350	15r. Jambi	2·10	1·30
1351	20r. Sulawesi, Tenggara	2·10	1·30
1352	25r. Nusatenggara, Timor	2·10	1·30
1353	27r.50 Maluku	2·10	2·50
1354	30r. Lampung	2·10	2·50
1355	35r. Sumatera, Barat	2·10	1·30
1356	40r. Aceh	2·10	1·30
1357	45r. Nusatenggara, Barat	5·00	1·30
1358	50r. Riau	2·75	3·75
1359	55r. Kalimantan, Barat	4·25	1·30
1360	60r. Sulawesi, Utara	4·25	1·30
1361	65r. Sulawesi, Tengah	4·25	1·30
1362	70r. Sumatera, Selatan	4·25	1·30
1363	75r. Java, Barat	4·25	1·30
1364	80r. Sumatera, Utara	4·25	1·30
1365	90r. Yogyakarta	5·00	5·75
1366	95r. Kalimantan, Selatan	4·25	1·30
1367	100r. Java, Timor	4·25	2·50
1368	120r. Irian, Jaya	8·50	1·60
1369	130r. Java, Tengah	8·50	1·30
1370	135r. Sulawesi, Selatan	10·00	1·30
1371	150r. Bali	10·00	1·30
1372	160r. Djakarta	10·00	2·50

1974. "Art and Culture" (3rd series). Shadow Plays. As T **241**. Multicoloured.
1373	40r. Baladewa	4·25	2·30
1374	80r. Kresna	8·50	4·50
1375	100r. Bima	10·50	4·50

254 Pres. Suharto

1974
1376	**254**	40r. brown, green & blk	1·40	15
1377	**254**	50r. brown, blue & black	3·50	25
1378	**254**	65r. brown, mauve & blk	2·00	1·00
1379	**254**	75r. brown, yellow & blk	3·50	25
1380	**254**	100r. brown, yellow & blk	3·50	25
1381	**254**	150r. brown, green & blk	3·50	25

See also Nos. 1444/7.

255 "Improvement of Living Standards"

1974. World Population Year.
1382	**255**	65r. multicoloured	2·50	90

256 "Welfare"

1974. Family Planning.
1383	**256**	25r. multicoloured	1·40	75
1384	-	40r. blue, black and green	2·10	75
1385	-	65r. ochre, brown & yell	4·25	75

DESIGNS: 40r. Young couple ("Development"); 65r. Arrows ("Religion").

257 Bicycle Postmen

1974. Centenary of U.P.U.
1386	**257**	20r. brown, yellow & grn	4·50	75
1387	-	40r. brown, orange & bl	4·50	1·10
1388	-	65r. brown, yellow & blk	4·50	1·10
1389	-	100r. black, blue and red	4·50	3·00

DESIGNS: 40r. Mail-cart; 65r. Mounted postman; 100r. East Indies galley.

1974. Fish (4th series). As T **232**. Multicoloured.
1390	40r. Sail-finned tang	4·25	75
1391	80r. Blue-girdled angelfish	7·00	3·00
1392	100r. Mandarin fish	10·00	3·75

258 Drilling for Oil

1974. 17th Anniv of Pertamina Oil Complex. Multicoloured.
1393	40r. Type **258**	1·00	50
1394	75r. Oil refinery	1·00	50
1395	95r. Control centre (vert)	1·00	50
1396	100r. Road tanker (vert)	1·00	50
1397	120r. Fokker Fellowship airliner over storage tank farm (vert)	1·60	50
1398	130r. Pipelines and tanker (vert)	1·60	50
1399	150r. Petrochemical storage tanks	1·60	50
1400	200r. Offshore oil rig	1·60	50

1975. "Art and Culture" (4th series). As T **241**.
1401	50r. silver, red and black	2·75	2·30
1402	75r. silver, green and black	4·25	2·30
1403	100r. yellow, blue and black	5·75	2·30

DESIGNS: 50r. Sumatran spittoon; 75r. Sumatran "sirh" dish; 100r. Kalimantan "sirh" dish.

260 "Donorship"

1975. Blood Donors' Campaign.
1404	**260**	40r. red, yellow and green	2·30	1·10

261 Measures and Globe

1975. Centenary of Metre Convention.
1405	**261**	65r. blue, red and yellow	3·00	1·10

262 Women in Public Service

1975. International Women's Year. Multicoloured.
1406	40r. Type **262**	2·10	1·10
1407	100r. I.W.Y. emblem (21×29 mm)	3·50	1·10

263 Dendrobium pakarena

1975. Tourism. Indonesian Orchids. Multicoloured.
1408	40r. Type **263**	5·75	2·00
1409	70r. Aeridachnis bogor	8·50	3·75
1410	85r. Vanda genta	13·00	5·75

264 Stupas and Damaged Temple

1975. UNESCO "Save Borobudur Temple" Campaign. Multicoloured.
1411	25r. Type **264**	4·25	1·30
1412	40r. Buddhist shrines and broken wall	5·00	1·80
1413	65r. Stupas and damaged building (horiz)	10·50	7·00
1414	100r. Buddha and stupas (horiz)	14·00	7·00

265 Battle of Banjarmasin

1975. 30th Anniv of Independence.
1415	**265**	25r. black and yellow	1·30	75
1416	-	40r. black and red	1·70	75
1417	-	75r. black and red	2·10	2·00
1418	-	100r. black and orange	2·75	1·50

DESIGNS: 40r. Battle of Batua; 75r. battle of Margarana; 100r. Battle of Palembang.

266 "Education"

1975. Family Planning. Multicoloured.
1419	20r. Type **266**	1·10	25
1420	25r. "Religion"	1·70	50
1421	40r. "Prosperity"	2·75	90

267 Heroes' Monument, Surabaya

1975. 30th Anniv of Independence War.
| 1422 | 267 | 100r. red and green | 3·50 | 90 |

1975. Fish (5th series). As T **232**. Multicoloured.
1423		40r. Twin-spotted wrasse	2·10	75
1424		75r. Saddleback butterflyfish	7·00	2·30
1425		150r. Dusky batfish (vert)	9·25	4·50

269 Thomas Cup

1976. Indonesian Victory in World Badminton Championships. Multicoloured.
1428		20r. Type **269**	1·30	50
1429		40r. Uber cup	1·40	1·00
1430		100r. Thomas and Uber cups	2·75	1·00

270 Refugees and New Village

1976. World Human Settlements Day. Multicoloured.
1431		30r. Type **270**	1·40	25
1432		50r. Old and restored villages	2·10	70
1433		100r. Derelict and rebuilt houses	2·75	75

271 Early and Modern Telephones

1976. Telephone Centenary.
| 1434 | 271 | 100r. brown, red & yell | 2·10 | 90 |

272 Human Eye

1976. World Health Day. Multicoloured.
| 1435 | | 20r. Type **272** | 70 | 50 |
| 1436 | | 40r. Blind man with stick | 1·40 | 75 |

273 Main Stadium, Montreal

1976. Olympic Games, Montreal.
| 1437 | 273 | 100r. blue | 2·10 | 1·00 |

274 Lake Tondano, Sulawesi

1976. Tourism. Multicoloured.
1438		35r. Type **274**	1·40	75
1439		40r. Lake Kelimutu, Flores	1·60	75
1440		75r. Lake Maninjau, Sumatra	2·00	90

275 "Light Traffic" Station

1976. Inauguration of Domestic Satellite System.
| 1441 | 275 | 20r. multicoloured | 1·10 | 65 |
| 1442 | – | 50r. black and green | 1·40 | 65 |

| 1443 | – | 100r. turquoise, bl & vio | 2·10 | 1·10 |

DESIGNS: 50r. "Master control" station; 100r. "Palapa" satellite.

1976. As T **254** but with background of wavy lines.
1444		200r. brown, blue and green	10·00	25
1445		300r. brown, red and flesh	2·75	25
1446		400r. brown, green and yellow	5·75	50
1447		500r. brown, red and lilac	7·00	1·50

276 Vanda Putri Serang

1976. Orchids. Multicoloured.
1448		25r. Arachnis flos-aeris	2·75	1·80
1449		40r. Type **276**	3·50	1·90
1450		100r. Coelogyne pandurata	5·75	3·75
MS1451 67×90 mm. No. 1448 (sold at 60r.)			£100	£110

277 Stylized Tree

1976. Reafforestation Week.
| 1452 | 277 | 20r. green, blue & brown | 1·40 | 65 |

278 Kelewang Dagger and Sheath (Timor)

1976. Daggers and Sheaths.
1453	278	25r. green, black & brown	1·40	75
1454	–	40r. brown, yellow & orge	2·75	1·40
1455	–	100r. brown, yellow & grn	4·25	3·75
MS1456 94×64 mm. 40r. No. 1454 (sold at 70r.)			26·00	25·00

DESIGNS: 40r. Mandau dagger and sheath (Borneo); 100r. Rencong dagger and sheath (Aceh).

279 Open Book

1976. Books for Children.
| 1457 | 279 | 20r. green, orange & blue | 1·00 | 50 |
| 1458 | – | 40r. violet, red and yellow | 1·80 | 75 |

DESIGN: 40r. Children reading book.

280 UNICEF Emblem

1976. 30th Anniv of UNICEF.
| 1459 | 280 | 40r. blue, turquoise & vio | 2·10 | 75 |

281 Ballot Box

1977. Elections.
1460	281	40r. blue, yellow and grey	2·75	50
1461	–	75r. blue, yellow and pink	3·50	75
1462	–	100r. bistre, red and black	5·75	2·30

DESIGNS: 75r. Ballot box, factory and produce; 100r. Indonesian arrow.

---

282 Scout Emblems and Camp

1977. 11th National Scout Jamboree. Multicoloured.
1463		25r. Type **282**	1·80	80
1464		30r. Emblems, tent and trees	2·00	90
1465		40r. Emblems, tent and flags	2·40	1·90

283 Letter and A.O.P.U. Emblem

1977. 15th Anniv of Asian–Oceanic Postal Union. Multicoloured.
| 1466 | | 65r. Type **283** | 85 | 65 |
| 1467 | | 100r. Stylized carrier pigeon | 2·30 | 90 |

284 Anniversary Emblem

1977. 450th Anniv of Jakarta.
1468	284	20r. blue and red	1·00	70
1469	–	40r. green and blue	1·30	75
1470	–	100r. blue and turquoise	2·40	1·40
MS1471 72×96 mm. No. 1470 (sold at 125r.)			12·00	14·00

DESIGNS: 40; 100r. Similar to Type **284** but with emblem and arms differently arranged.

285 Rose

1977. "Amphilex 77" International Stamp Exhibition, Amsterdam.
1472	285	100r. red, green and black	2·10	75
1473	–	100r. red, green and black	2·10	75
MS1474 Two sheets (sold at 550r.). (a) 71×95 mm. Nos. 1472/3 each ×2. (b) 72×63 mm. 285 100r. scarlet, blue and black			28·00	30·00

DESIGN: No. 1473, Envelope.

286 Sports Pictograms

1977. Ninth National Sports Week.
1475	286	40r. silver, green and red	3·50	2·50
1476		50r. silver, blue and red	5·00	2·75
1477	–	100r. gold, black and red	10·00	6·25

DESIGNS: 50; 100r. Similar to Type **286** but with different pictograms.

287 Trophy

1977. Tenth National Koran Reading Contest.
| 1478 | 287 | 40r. brown, green & yell | 3·50 | 90 |
| 1479 | – | 100r. black, yellow & grn | 4·25 | 1·60 |

DESIGN: 100r. Emblem.

288 Carrier Pigeon and Map

1977. Tenth Anniv of Association of South East Asian Nations. Multicoloured.
1480		25r. Type **288**	1·10	25
1481		35r. Map of ASEAN members	2·75	1·10
1482		50r. Transport and flags of ASEAN members	3·50	1·40

289 Government Officer, Djakarta Region

1977. Economic and Cultural Co-operation with Pakistan.
| 1483 | 289 | 25r. brown, gold & green | 1·30 | 50 |

290 Taeniophyllum sp

1977. Orchids. Multicoloured.
1484		25r. Type **290**	2·75	1·40
1485		40r. Phalaenopsis violacea	3·50	2·75
1486		100r. Dendrobium spectabile	7·75	4·25
MS1487 86×71 mm. As No. 1486 but with blue background (sold at 125r.)			18·00	20·00

291 Child and Mosquito

1977. National Health Campaign.
| 1488 | 291 | 40r. red, green and black | 1·00 | 40 |

292 Proboscis Monkey

1977. Wildlife (1st series). Multicoloured.
1489		20r. Type **292**	1·50	65
1490		40r. Indian elephant	3·50	1·30
1491		100r. Tiger	9·25	2·50
MS1492 94×64 mm. As No. 1491 but colours of country name and values reversed (sold at 125r.)			13·00	15·00

See also Nos. 1515/**MS**1518 and 1558/**MS**1561.

293 Hands holding U.N. Emblem

1978. U.N. Conference on Technical Co-operation among Developing Countries.
| 1493 | 293 | 100r. blue and ultramarine | 2·10 | 1·00 |

294 Mother feeding Baby

1978. Campaign for the Promotion of Breast Feeding.
| 1494 | 294 | 40r. green and red | 70 | 50 |
| 1495 | – | 75r. brown and red | 1·70 | 75 |

DESIGN: 75r. Stylised mother and child.

295 Dome of the Rock

1978. Palestine Welfare.
1496	**295**	100r. multicoloured	2·50	90

296 World Cup Emblem

1978. World Cup Football Championship, Argentina.
1497	**296**	40r. green, black and blue	1·30	50
1498	**296**	100r. mauve, black & bl	2·40	1·10

297 Head and Blood Circulation Diagram

1978. World Health Day.
1499	**297**	100r. blue, black and red	2·10	90

298 Leather Puppets

1978. Puppets from Wayang Museum, Djakarta. Multicoloured.
1500	**298**	40r. Type **298**	3·50	1·10
1501		75r. Wooden puppets	4·25	2·30
1502		100r. Actors wearing masks	9·25	3·75

300 Congress Emblem

1978. 27th Congress of World Confederation of Organizations of the Teaching Profession, Djakarta.
1509	**300**	100r. grey	1·70	75

301 I.A.Y. Emblem

1978. International Anti-Apartheid Year.
1510	**301**	100r. blue and red	1·70	75

302 Couple and Tree

1978. Eighth World Forestry Congress, Djakarta.
1511	**302**	40r. blue and green	30	25
1512		100r. dp green & lt green	1·70	90

DESIGN: 100r. People and trees.

303 Anniversary Emblem

1978. 50th Anniv of Youth Pledge.
1513	**303**	40r. brown and red	1·10	50
1514	**303**	100r. brown, red and pink	1·70	75

1978. Wildlife (2nd series). As T **292**. Multicoloured.
1515	40r. Long-nosed echidna	2·10	65
1516	75r. Sambar	3·50	1·30
1517	100r. Clouded leopard	5·75	1·90

MS1518 Two sheets (sold at 700r.). (a) 94×63 mm. No. 1517. (b) 115×157 mm. No. 1516 and 1517 ×4 but with colours of inscriptions and value reversed   26·00   29·00

304 *Phalaenopsis sri rejeki*

1978. Orchids. Multicoloured.
1519	40r. Type **304**	2·10	75
1520	75r. *Dendrobium macrophyllum*	2·75	1·10
1521	100r. *Cymbidium fynlayso-nianum*	5·75	1·60

MS1522 63×96 mm. As No. 1521 but with some colours changed (sold at 150r.)   10·50   11·50

306 Douglas DC-3 over Volcano

1979. 30th Anniv of Garuda Indonesian Airways. Multicoloured.
1531	40r. Type **306**	1·40	65
1532	75r. Douglas DC-9-30 over village	1·70	75
1533	100r. Douglas DC-10 over temple	3·25	1·80

307 Thomas Cup and Badminton Player

1979. Thomas Cup Badminton Championships, Djakarta.
1534	**307**	40r. pink and turquoise	85	90
1535		100r. brown and pink	1·70	1·40
1536		100r. brown and pink	1·70	1·40

DESIGNS: No. 1535, Player on left side of net hitting shuttlecock; 1536, Player on right side of net.

Nos. 1535/6 were issued together, se-tenant, forming a composite design.

308 *Paphiopedilum lowii*

1979. Orchids. Multicoloured.
1537	60r. Type **308**	1·40	65
1538	100r. *Vanda limbata*	2·75	90
1539	125r. *Phalaenopsis gigantea*	4·25	1·40

MS1540 63×96 mm. No. 1539 (sold at 175r.)   7·75   8·75

See also No. **MS**1548.

309 Family and Houses

1979. Third Five Year Development Plan.
1541	**309**	35r. drab and green	30	15
1542		60r. green and blue	45	20
1543		100r. brown and blue	85	25
1544		125r. brown and green	1·10	40
1545		150r. yellow, orge & red	1·40	40

DESIGNS: 60r. Pylon, dam and fields; 100r. School and clinic; 125r. Loading produce at factory; 150r. Delivering mail.

310/11 Mrs. R. A. Kartini

1979. Birth Centenary of Mrs. R. A. Kartini (pioneer of women's rights).
1546	**310**	100r. brown and green	1·40	65
1547	**311**	100r. green and brown	1·40	65

1979. "Asian–Philatelie '79" International Stamp Exhibition, Dortmund. Sheet 96×119 mm. Multicoloured.

MS1548 250r. Type **308**; 300r. As No. 1538 (sold at 650r.)   13·00   15·00

312 Bureau Emblem

1979. 50th Anniv of International Bureau of Education.
1549	**312**	150r. blue, lt blue & lilac	2·00	75

313 Self Defence

1979. Tenth South East Asia Games, Djakarta.
1550	**313**	60r. yellow, black & grn	1·00	50
1551		125r. orange, grey & blue	1·70	75
1552		150r. yellow, black & red	2·10	1·10

DESIGNS: 125r. Games emblem; 150r. Main stadium, Senayan.

314 Co-operation Emblem

1979. Co-operation Day.
1553	**314**	150r. multicoloured	1·70	65

315 National I.Y.C. Emblem

1979. International Year of the Child.
1554	**315**	60r. black and green	70	25
1555		150r. blue and black	1·40	75

DESIGN: 150r. International I.Y.C. emblem.

316 Exhibition Emblem

1979. Third World Telecommunications Exhibition, Geneva.
1556	**316**	150r. grey, blue & orange	1·70	90

317 Drug Addict

1979. "End Drug Abuse" Campaign.
1557	**317**	150r. black and pink	1·70	90

1979. Wildlife (3rd series). As T **292**. Multicoloured.
1558	60r. Bottle-nosed dolphin	1·40	1·00
1559	125r. Irrawaddy dolphin	4·25	1·40
1560	150r. Leatherback turtle	7·00	1·90

MS1561 94×64 mm. 200r. As No. 1560 (sold at 250r.)   10·50   12·50

318 Pinisi Sailing Ship

1980. Djakarta–Amsterdam Spice Race.
1562	**318**	60r. blue	70	25
1563		125r. brown	1·30	75
1564		150r. purple	2·30	90

MS1565 64×120 mm. 300r. brown   7·00   8·25

DESIGNS—HORIZ: 125, 300r. Schooner made of leaves. VERT: 150r. Madurese sailing boat.

See also No. **MS**1578.

319 Riding the Rapids

1980. Adventure Sports. Multicoloured.
1566	**319**	60r. Type **319**	70	25
1567		125r. Mountaineering (vert)	1·30	90
1568		150r. Hang gliding	2·30	1·40

MS1569 62×76 mm. 300r. Type **319** (sold at 350r.)   7·00   8·25

320 Cigarettes and Heart

1980. Anti-smoking Campaign.
1570	**320**	150r. flesh, black and pink	1·70	75

321 Bouquet

1980. Second Flower Festival, Jakarta. Multicoloured.
1571	**321**	125r. Type **321**	2·10	75
1572		150r. Artificial bouquet	2·50	1·10

See also No. **MS**1579.

322 Conference Building and Globe

1980. 25th Anniv of First Asian–African Conference, Bandung.
1573	**322**	150r. mauve and gold	1·70	75

MS1574 76×104 mm. **322** 300r. magenta and gold (sold at 350r.)   7·00   8·25

323 Danau Poso Statue

1980. Prehistoric Monuments. Multicoloured.
1575	**323**	60r. Type **323**	1·10	50
1576		125r. Elephant stone, Pasemah Village, South Sumatra	1·40	90
1577		150r. Taman Bali sarcophagus	1·70	1·10

1980. "London 1980" International Stamp Exhibition. Two sheets.

MS1578 120×63 mm. 100r. Type **321** 500r. blue   10·00   10·00

MS1579 120×150 mm. 100r. Type **321**; 100r. As No. 1572; 200r. Type **323**; 200r. As No. 1577, each ×2 (sold at 1300r.)   26·00   25·00

324 Discus Thrower

1980. Olympics for the Disabled, Arnhem.
| 1580 | **324** | 75r. brown and orange | 1·40 | 50 |

325 Draughtsman in Wheelchair

1980. 30th Anniv of Disabled Veterans Corps.
| 1581 | **325** | 100r. yellow, blue & blk | 1·30 | 50 |

326 President Suharto

1980
1581a	**326**	10r. olive and green	2·75	25
1582	**326**	12r.50 green & lt green	55	15
1582a	**326**	25r. brown and orange	85	20
1583	**326**	50r. blue and green	70	50
1583a	**326**	55r. red and vermilion	85	20
1584	**326**	75r. brown and yellow	1·10	25
1585a	**326**	100r. blue, violet & mve	2·40	65
1586	**326**	200r. brown and orange	2·75	1·40
1586b	**326**	300r. violet, lilac & gold	2·75	40
1586c	**326**	400r. grey, pink and gold	2·75	40

Nos. 1585a and 1586 exist dated "1980" or "1981", and Nos. 1582a, 1583a and 1586b/c are dated "1983".
See also Nos. 1830/4.

327 People and Map of Indonesia

1980. Population Census.
| 1587 | **327** | 75r. blue and pink | 70 | 25 |
| 1588 | **327** | 200r. blue and yellow | 1·40 | 65 |

328 Ship laying Cable

1980. Inauguration of Singapore–Indonesia Submarine Cable.
| 1589 | **328** | 75r. green, dp grn & orge | 85 | 25 |
| 1590 | **328** | 200r. blue, dp bl & orge | 1·40 | 75 |

329 Immigrants

1980. Indonesian Immigration.
| 1591 | **329** | 12r.50 red and green | 70 | 25 |

330 1946 50s. Stamp

1980. 35th Anniv of Independence.
1592	**330**	75r. cream, black & brn	85	65
1593	-	100r. cream, pur & gold	2·00	75
1594	-	200r. cream, pink and silver	2·75	1·10

DESIGNS—HORIZ: 100r. 1946 15s. stamp. VERT: 200r. 1946 15s. Freedom Fund stamp.

331 Map of A.O.P.U. Members

1980. Tenth Anniv of Asian–Oceanic Postal Union Training School, Bangkok.
| 1595 | **331** | 200r. blue, lt blue & turq | 2·30 | 40 |

332 O.P.E.C. Emblem on Globe

1980. 20th Anniv of Organization of Petroleum Exporting Countries.
| 1596 | **332** | 200r. turquoise, bl & red | 2·30 | 50 |

333 Service Members with Linked Arms

1980. 35th Anniv of Armed Forces. Multicoloured.
| 1597 | | 75r. Indonesians hailing flag | 1·10 | 40 |
| 1598 | | 200r. Type **333** | 1·70 | 65 |

334 Pesquet's Parrot

1980. Parrots. Multicoloured.
1599		75r. Type **334**	3·50	1·10
1600		100r. Chattering lory	4·25	2·30
1601		200r. Rainbow lory	5·75	3·25
MS1602	95×120 mm. 250r. As No. 1601; 350r. Type **334** 400r. As No. 1600		33·00	38·00

335 Dendrobium insigne

1980. Orchids. Multicoloured.
1603		75r. Type **335**	2·10	25
1604		100r. Dendrobium discolor	2·75	1·60
1605		200r. Dendrobium lasianthera	5·75	1·10
MS1606	74×104 mm. 250r. As No. 1604; 350r. As No. 1605		23·00	25·00

336 Von Stephan and U.P.U. Emblem

1981. 150th Birth Anniv of Heinrich von Stephan (U.P.U. founder).
| 1607 | **336** | 200r. blue and deep blue | 2·30 | 1·00 |

337 Jamboree and Scouting Emblems

1981. Sixth Asia–Pacific Scout Jamboree, Cibubur. Multicoloured.
1608		75r. Type **337**	70	50
1609		100r. Scout and Guide map-reading (vert)	2·00	65
1610		200r. Jamboree emblem and tents	2·10	1·40
MS1611	77×63 mm. 150r. As No. 1609		7·00	8·25

338 Ship (relief carving)

1981. Fifth Asian–Oceanic Postal Union Congress, Yogyakarta.
| 1612 | **338** | 200r. blue, black & lt bl | 2·50 | 55 |

339 Child holding Blood Drop

1981. Blood Donors.
1613	**339**	75r. blue, black and red	70	30
1614	-	100r. red and grey	1·40	40
1615	-	200r. red, dp blue & blue	2·00	1·30

DESIGNS: 100r. Hands holding blood drop; 200r. Hands and blood drop.

340 Monuments

1981. International Family Planning Conference.
| 1616 | **340** | 200r. pale blue, brn & bl | 1·80 | 70 |

341 Song of Sritanjung

1981. Traditional Balinese Paintings. Multicoloured.
1617		100r. Type **341**	2·00	55
1618		200r. Song of Sritanjung (different)	2·50	1·30
MS1619	96×96 mm. 400r. and 600r. Birth of the Eagle		18·00	21·00

Nos. 1617/18 were issued together, se-tenant, forming a composite design.

342 Secretariat Building and Emblem

1981. Inauguration of A.S.E.A.N. Secretariat, Djakarta.
| 1620 | **342** | 200r. yellow, orge & pur | 2·30 | 85 |

343 Uber Cup

1981. International Ladies' Badminton Championships, Tokyo.
| 1621 | **343** | 200r. brown, yell & orge | 4·50 | 1·00 |

344 "Tree of Life" (relief from Candi Mendut)

1981. World Environment Day.
| 1622 | **344** | 75r. bistre, grey and black | 1·20 | 30 |
| 1623 | - | 200r. bistre, grey & black | 1·80 | 55 |

DESIGN: 200r. "Yaksha Apacaka".

345 Students reading Koran, Mosque and Emblem

1981. 12th National Koran Reading Contest, Banda Aceh.
| 1624 | **345** | 200r. black, red & yellow | 1·80 | 85 |

346 Blind Man

1981. International Year of Disabled Persons.
| 1625 | **346** | 75r. brown, yellow & bis | 75 | 30 |
| 1626 | - | 200r. blue, brown & grn | 1·80 | 85 |

DESIGN: 200r. Deaf and dumb person.

347 Soekarno-Hatta Monument, Djakarta

1981. Independence Monument.
| 1627 | **347** | 200r. blue, yellow & gold | 2·30 | 70 |

348 Parachute Jumping

1981. National Sports Week, Djakarta.
1628	**348**	75r. red, black and blue	75	30
1629	-	100r. black, blue and red	1·20	1·10
1630	-	200r. brown, green & red	2·30	1·00

DESIGNS—HORIZ: 100r. Scuba diving. VERT: 200r. Horse riding.

349 Food Produce

1981. World Food Day.
| 1631 | **349** | 200r. multicoloured | 3·75 | 1·30 |

350 Arms of Aceh Special Territory

1981. Provincial Arms (1st series).
1632	**350**	100r. yellow, grn & gold	3·75	1·30
1633	-	100r. multicoloured	3·75	1·30
1634	-	100r. multicoloured	3·75	1·30
1635	-	100r. multicoloured	15·00	1·60
1636	-	100r. multicoloured	4·50	3·00

DESIGNS: No. 1633, Bali; No. 1634, Bengkulu; No. 1635, Irian Jaya; No. 1636, Djakarta.
See also Nos. 1643/62 and 1710.

351 Salmon-crested Cockatoo

1981. Cockatoos. Multicoloured.
1637		75r. Type **351**	6·00	1·40
1638		100r. Sulphur-crested cockatoo	6·75	1·60
1639		200r. Palm cockatoo	11·50	5·00
MS1640	73×64 mm. 150r. As No. 1638; 350r. As No. 1639		29·00	31·00

1982. Provincial Arms (2nd series). As T **350**. Multicoloured.
1641		100r. Jambi	1·50	85
1642		100r. Java Barat (West)	1·50	85
1643		100r. Java Tengah (Cent)	1·50	85
1644		100r. Java Timur (East)	1·50	85
1645		100r. Kalimantan Barat (West)	1·50	85
1646		100r. Kalimantan Selatan (South)	1·50	85
1647		100r. Kalimantan Timur (East)	1·50	85
1648		100r. Kalimantan Tengah (Central)	1·50	85
1649		100r. Lampung	1·50	85
1650		100r. Moluccas	1·20	85
1651		100r. Nusa Tenggara Barat (West)	1·20	30
1652		100r. Nusa Tenggara Timur (East)	1·20	30
1653		100r. Riau	1·20	30

1654	100r. Sulawesi Tengah (Central Celebes)	1·20	30
1655	100r. Sulawesi Tenggara (South-east Celebes)	1·20	30
1656	100r. Sulawesi Selatan (South Celebes)	1·40	30
1657	100r. Sumatera Utara (North Celebes)	1·40	30
1658	100r. Sumatera Barat (West)	1·40	30
1659	100r. Sumatera Selatan (South)	1·20	30
1660	100r. Sumatera Utara (North)	1·20	30
1661	100r. Yogyakarta	3·00	30
1662	250r. Republic of Indonesia (45×29 mm)	6·75	1·40

352 Hands enclosing Family

1982. 70th Anniv of Bumiputera Mutual Life Insurance Company.

1663	**352**	75r. yellow, plum & pur	75	30
1664	-	100r. yellow, lt grn & grn	1·50	70
1665	-	200r. multicoloured	2·30	1·10

DESIGNS: 100r. Family in countryside; 200r. Hands supporting industrial activities.

353 Helicopter Rescue

1982. Tenth Anniv of Search and Rescue Institute.

| 1666 | **353** | 250r. multicoloured | 2·40 | 55 |

354 Houses and Ballot Boxes

1982. General Election. Multicoloured.

1667	75r. Type **354**		75	30
1668	100r. Rural houses and ballot boxes		1·20	55
1669	200r. Houses and National arms		2·40	1·30

355 Human Figures, Satellite and Dove

1982. Second U.N. Conference on Exploration and Peaceful Uses of Outer Space, Vienna.

| 1670 | **355** | 150r. blue, violet & black | 1·20 | 70 |
| 1671 | - | 250r. green, light green and deep green | 2·10 | 1·10 |

DESIGN: 250r. Peace dove and text.

356 Thomas Cup

1982. Thomas Cup Badminton Championship, London.

| 1672 | **356** | 250r. multicoloured | 2·75 | 85 |
| MS1673 | 72×95 mm. No. 1672 ×2 | | 11·50 | 13·00 |

357 Footballers

1982. World Cup Football Championship, Spain.

| 1674 | **357** | 250r. multicoloured | 2·75 | 85 |
| MS1675 | 96×72 mm. No. 1674×2 | | 15·00 | 16·00 |

358 Taman Siswa Emblem

1982. 60th Anniv of Taman Siswa (educational organization).

| 1676 | **358** | 250r. yellow, green & red | 2·10 | 55 |

359 Flags forming "15"

1982. 15th Anniv of Association of South-East Asian Nations.

| 1677 | **359** | 150r. orange, red and blue | 2·40 | 85 |

360 President Suharto

1982

1678	**360**	110r. red and orange	75	30
1679	**360**	250r. brown and orange	1·50	30
1680	**360**	275r. green and yellow	2·50	35

Nos. 1678 and 1680 are inscribed "1983".

1982. World Cup Football Championship Result. No. MS1675 optd **ITALIA WORLD CHAMPION**.

| MS1681 | 96×72 mm. 250r. ×2 mult | £130 | £130 |

362 Rothschild's Mynah

1982. Third World National Parks Congress, Bali. Multicoloured.

1682	100r. Type **362**		4·50	70
1683	250r. King bird of paradise		7·50	2·10
MS1684	76×104 mm. 500r. Type **362**	23·00	26·00

363 River Bridge

1982. Five Year Plan.

| 1685 | **363** | 17r.50 brown and green | 90 | 15 |

364 Arfak Parotia

1982. Birds of Paradise. Multicoloured.

1686	100r. Type **364**		3·75	70
1687	150r. Twelve-wired bird of paradise		6·00	1·40
1688	250r. Red bird of paradise		9·00	2·10
MS1689	76×105 mm. 200r. Type **364**; 300r. As No. 1688	38·00	38·00

365 Scouts and Anniversary Emblem

1983. 75th Anniv of Boy Scout Movement.

| 1690 | **365** | 250r. blue, green & violet | 2·75 | 55 |

366 Temple Restoration and Relief

1983. Borobudur Temple.

1691	**366**	100r. green, blue & lt bl	2·30	85
1692	-	150r. lt green, grn & brn	3·00	1·00
1693	-	250r. black, dp brn & brn	9·00	5·00
MS1694	96×64 mm. 500r. multicoloured	27·00	28·00

DESIGNS—VERT: 150r. Temple and statue. HORIZ: 250, 500r. Silhouette of Temple and seated Buddha.

367 President Suharto

1983

| 1695 | **367** | 500r. brown | 2·50 | 70 |

368 Gas Storage Tanks

1983. Seventh International Liquefied Natural Gas Conference, Djarkarta.

| 1696 | **368** | 275r. multicoloured | 2·30 | 55 |

369 Ships and Bird

1983. World Communications Year.

1697	**369**	75r. multicoloured	45	30
1698	-	110r. multicoloured	90	45
1699	-	175r. blue and red	1·50	70
1700	-	275r. blue, dp blue & red	2·30	1·10

DESIGNS: 110r. Satellite and receiving station; 175r. Aircraft and dish aerial, 275r. Globe and letter.

370 Man and Woman reading Koran

1983. 13th National Koran Reading Competition.

| 1701 | **370** | 275r. yellow, green & blk | 2·30 | 1·00 |

371 Eclipse and Map of Indonesia

1983. Total Solar Eclipse.

1702	**371**	110r. brn, dp brn & blk	1·50	45
1703	-	275r. blue, violet & purple	4·50	70
MS1704	96×64 mm. 500r. blue, violet and purple	26·00	26·00

DESIGN: 275, 500r. Map of Indonesia showing path of eclipse.

372 Satellite transmitting to Indonesia

1983. Launching of "Palapa B" Communications Satellite.

| 1705 | **372** | 275r. green, blue & silver | 2·30 | 1·00 |

373 Patient receiving Radiation Treatment

1983. Anti-cancer Campaign.

| 1706 | **373** | 55r.+20r. multicoloured | 1·20 | 85 |
| 1707 | **373** | 75r.+25r. multicoloured | 2·10 | 1·00 |

374 Agricultural Produce

1983. Agricultural Census.

| 1708 | **374** | 110r. grey, green & black | 1·10 | 30 |
| 1709 | - | 275r. red, black and green | 2·00 | 45 |

DESIGN: 275r. Farmer with produce.

1983. Provincial Arms (3rd series). As T **350**. Multicoloured.

| 1710 | 100r. Timor Timur | 3·00 | 30 |

375 Traditional Weaving, Pakistan

1983. Indonesia–Pakistan Economic and Cultural Co-operation. Multicoloured.

| 1711 | 275r. Type **375** | | 2·50 | 1·60 |
| 1712 | 275r. Traditional weaving, Indonesia | | 2·50 | 1·60 |

376 Eruption of Krakatoa

1983. Centenary of Krakatoa Volcanic Eruption. Multicoloured.

| 1713 | 110r. Type **376** | | 90 | 55 |
| 1714 | 275r. Map showing position of Krakatoa | | 2·75 | 85 |

377 Casa-Nurtanio CN-235 Short-haul Passenger Aircraft

1983. Indonesian Aircraft.

| 1715 | **377** | 275r. multicoloured | 2·30 | 1·00 |

1983. World Communications Year. Opening of Philatelic Museum, Djakarta. Sheet 51×84 mm.

| MS1716 | 500r. As No. 1700 | 17·00 | 17·00 |

378 Tiger Barb

1983. Tropical Fish. Multicoloured.

1717	110r. Type **378**		3·50	90
1718	175r. Brilliant rasbora		3·75	1·10
1719	275r. Archerfish		11·50	3·50

1983. "Telecom 83" Exhibition, Geneva. Sheet 75×83 mm. Multicoloured.

MS1720	400r. As No. 1698	17·00	17·00

379 Wilson's Bird of Paradise

1983. Birds of Paradise. Multicoloured.

1721		110r. Type **379**	3·00	70
1722		175r. Black sicklebill	4·50	85
1723		275r. Black-billed sicklebill	7·00	1·80
1724		500r. As No. 1723	10·50	5·00
MS1725	64×95 mm. As No. 1724		38·00	38·00

380 Emblems of Peace and Co-operation

1983. Palestinian Solidarity.

1726	**380**	275r. blue, brown & silver	2·50	55

381 "Stop" Emblem

1984. Anti-poliomyelitis Campaign.

1732	**381**	110r. red, purple and blue	75	30
1733	-	275r. purple, orge & red	2·50	55

DESIGN: 275r. Emblem of Save the Children Fund.

382 Agriculture

1984. Fourth Five Year Plan.

1734	**382**	55r. yellow and blue	30	15
1735	-	75r. green and brown	45	30
1736	-	110r. blue and orange	75	45
1737	-	275r. multicoloured	2·00	1·10

DESIGNS: 75r. Casa-Nurtiano CN-235 airliner (aircraft industry); 110r. Shipbuilding; 275r. Telephone (telecommunications).

383 Manufacturing Plywood

1984. Forestry. Multicoloured.

1738	**383**	75r. Type **383**	1·70	30
1739		110r. Seedling	2·00	35
1740		175r. Measuring tree trunk	2·30	70
1741		275r. Transporting trees	3·00	1·00
MS1742	96×80 mm. Nos. 1740/1		26·00	21·00

384 Children playing with Toys

1984. Children's Day. Multicoloured.

1743		75r.+25r. Type **384**	2·00	30
1744		110r.+25r. Scout camp	1·20	45
1745		175r.+25r. Children on farm	2·75	70
1746		275r.+25r. Scouts and guides in camp	3·00	85

See also No. **MS**1760.

385 Flags of Member Nations

1984. Association of South-East Asian Nations Meeting, Djakarta.

1747	**385**	275r. multicoloured	3·25	1·00

386 Pole Vaulting

1984. Olympic Games, Los Angeles. Multicoloured.

1748		75r. Type **386**	60	15
1749		110r. Archery	75	20
1750		175r. Boxing	90	30
1751		250r. Shooting	2·50	65
1752		275r. Weightlifting	3·25	70
1753		325r. Swimming	5·50	85

387 Horse Dance

1984. Art and Culture. Multicoloured.

1754		75r. Type **387**	1·50	30
1755		110r. "Reog" mask	2·30	45
1756		275r. Lion dance	2·75	70
1757		325r. "Barong" mask	5·25	1·10

388 Thomas Cup (badminton)

1984. National Sports Day. Multicoloured.

1758		110r. Type **388**	1·50	55
1759		275r. Keep-fit exercise	2·30	85

1984. "Filacento" International Stamp Exhibition, The Hague. Two sheets.

MS1760	101×101 mm. No. 1746 ×4 plus two labels	33·00	33·00
MS1761	73×64 mm. No. 1757 plus label	70·00	70·00

1984. "Ausipex 84" International Stamp Exhibition, Melbourne. Sheet 101×76 mm.

MS1762	Nos. 1745/6	45·00	45·00

389 Map and Post Code Zones

1984. Introduction of New Post Code Zones.

1763	**389**	110r. blue, brown & orge	90	55
1764	**389**	275r. orange, blue & brn	2·30	1·30

390 Lauterbach's Bowerbird

1984. Birds. Multicoloured.

1765		75r. Type **390**	4·50	55
1766		110r. Flamed bowerbird	6·75	1·10
1767		275r. Arfak bird of paradise	7·50	4·25
1768		325r. Superb bird of paradise	8·25	2·75
MS1769	76×105 mm. Nos. 1765 and 1768		45·00	45·00

No. **MS**1769 is inscribed for "Philakorea 1984" International Stamp Exhibition.

391 Flag and Fists

1984. Youth Pledge.

1770	**391**	275r. black and red	2·10	1·30

392 Boeing 747-200

1984. 40th Anniv of I.C.A.O.

1771	**392**	275r. red, black and blue	2·30	1·30

393 Tyro and Geological Structure of Seabed

1985. Indonesia–Belanda Expedition.

1772	**393**	50r. blue and brown	1·10	30
1773	-	100r. blue and purple	2·10	45
1774	-	275r. blue and green	2·30	70

DESIGNS: 100r. Tyro (oceanographic survey ship) and map; 275r. Tyro and coral reef.

394 Stylized Birds

1985. International Women's Day.

1775	**394**	100r. mauve and red	3·50	1·10
1776	-	275r. red and brown	5·50	5·00

DESIGN: 275r. Profile silhouettes.

395 Jet Airliner and workers

1985. Fourth Five Year Plan.

1777	**395**	75r. red and brown	75	30
1778	-	140r. grey and brown	1·20	85
1779	-	350r. green and brown	3·00	2·00

DESIGNS: 140r. Children in classroom; 350r. Industrial equipment and buildings.

396 Pres. Suharto

1985

1780	**396**	140r. brown and red	90	30
1781	**396**	350r. mauve and red	2·10	45

397 Conference Building

1985. 30th Anniv of First Asian–African Conference, Bandung.

1786	**397**	350r. multicoloured	2·75	85

398 Globe and Teenagers waving Palm Leaves

1985. International Youth Year.

1787	**398**	75r. yellow, brown & grn	1·10	30
1788	-	140r. blue, green & mve	2·50	45

DESIGN: 140r. Flower on globe supported by teenagers.

399 Profiles

1985. United Nations Women's Decade.

1789	**399**	55r. brown and green	90	45
1790	-	140r. blue, green & brn	1·70	55

DESIGN: 140r. Globe and decade emblems.

400 Housing and Hydro-electricity

1985. 40th Anniv of Indonesian Republic.

1791	**400**	140r. green and red	1·20	30
1792	-	350r. blue, mauve & yell	3·00	70

DESIGN: 350r. Tractor and industrial complex.

401 Sky Diving

1985. National Sports Week, Djakarta. Multicoloured.

1793		55r. Type **401**	60	15
1794		100r. Unarmed combat	1·40	30
1795		140r. High jumping	1·50	45
1796		350r. Sailboards (vert)	2·40	85

402 O.P.E.C. Emblem and Globe

1985. 25th Anniv of Organization of Petroleum Exporting Countries.

1797	**402**	40r. blue, mauve & orge	2·10	55

403 Tanker

1985. Centenary of Indonesian Oil Industry. Multicoloured.

1798		140r. Type **403**	1·10	55
1799		250r. Refinery	2·00	85
1800		350r. Derrick and rigs	2·75	1·70

404 Doves, "40" and U.N. Emblem

1985. 40th Anniv of U.N.O. Multicoloured.

1801	140r. Type **404**	75	30
1802	300r. Bombs and green leaves	2·30	85

405 Javan Rhinoceros

1985. Wildlife.

1803	**405**	75r. brown, green & blue	3·00	55
1804	-	150r. brown, orge & grn	4·50	85
1805	-	300r. brown, blue and red	7·50	1·30

DESIGNS: 150r. Anoa; 300r. Komodo dragon.

406 Emblem

1986. Economic Census. Each orange and violet.

1806	175r. Type **406**	1·20	45
1807	175r. Symbols of economy	1·20	45

407 Baby feeding, Powdered Milk, Syringe and Graph

1986. 40th Anniv of UNICEF.

1808	**407**	75r. multicoloured	1·20	30
1809	-	140r. flesh, brown & pink	1·80	45

DESIGN: 140r. Vaccinating baby.

408 Industry

1986. Fourth Five Year Plan.

1810	**408**	140r. multicoloured	1·10	45
1811	-	500r. yellow, brown & bl	1·50	55

DESIGN: 500r. Agriculture.

409 Thomas Cup and Racket

1986. Thomas (men's) and Uber (women's) Cup Badminton Championships, Djakarta.

1812	**409**	55r. black, yellow & blue	1·20	45
1813	-	150r. red, brown and gold	2·10	55

DESIGN: 150r. Thomas and Uber Cups and shuttlecock.

410 Pinisi Sailing Ship

1986. "Expo 86" World's Fair, Vancouver.

1814	**410**	75r. black, red and yellow	1·10	30
1815	-	150r. multicoloured	2·00	55
1816	-	300r. silver, red & purple	3·00	70

DESIGNS: 150r. Kentongan village drum and "Palapa" satellite; 300r. Indonesian pavilion emblem.

411 Guides on Parade

1986. National Jamboree. Multicoloured.

1817	100r. Type **411**	60	30
1818	140r. Guides cooking over fire	2·40	55
1819	210r. Scouts consulting map (vert)	3·00	1·00

412 "86"

1986. Indonesia Air Show.

1820	**412**	350r. multicoloured	2·75	1·10

413 Tari Legong Kraton

1986. Traditional Dances. Multicoloured.

1821	140r. Type **413**	2·30	30
1822	350r. Tari Barong	3·75	1·00
1823	500r. Tari Kecak	6·00	1·10

414 Woman planting

1986. 19th International Society of Sugar Cane Technologists Congress, Djakarta. Multicoloured.

1824	150r. Type **414**	1·10	30
1825	300r. Cane and sugar spilled from sack	2·50	45

415 Route Map of Cable

1986. Opening of Sea-Me-We Communications Cable.

1826	**415**	140r. green, orange & vio	1·10	45
1827	-	350r. green, yellow & bl	2·50	1·00

DESIGN: 350r. Route map of cable (different).

416 Doves, Wheat and Globe

1986. International Peace Year. Each brown, green and black.

1828	350r. Type **416**	2·10	70
1829	500r. Dove with olive twig flying around globe	2·75	70

1986

1830	**326**	50r. deep brown & brown	40	15
1831	**326**	55r. red and pink	45	15
1832	**326**	100r. ultramarine & blue	75	15
1833	**326**	300r. turq, grn & gold	2·30	15
1834	**326**	400r. green, turq & gold	2·10	30

417 Party Emblems and Buildings

1987. General Election.

1840	**417**	75r. blue, yellow & brn	75	15
1841	-	140r. green, orange & yell	1·10	30
1842	-	350r. blue, yellow & blk	2·30	70

DESIGNS: 140r. Party emblems and arms; 350r. Party emblems, map, wheat and ballot box.

418 Satellite and Globe

1987. Launch of "Palapa B2" Satellite.

1843	**418**	350r. yellow, green & brn	1·70	45
1844	-	500r. multicoloured	2·50	70

DESIGN—VERT: 500r. Rocket and satellite.

419 Boy carving Figures

1987. Fourth Five Year Plan.

1845	**419**	140r. brown, yellow & bl	45	30
1846	-	350.r. violet, grn & orge	1·20	55

DESIGN: 350r. Graph and cattle.

420 Crab and Scanner Unit

1987. Tenth Anniv of Indonesian Cancer Foundation.

1847	**420**	350r.+25r. yellow & bl	2·50	85

421 East Kalimantan Couple

1987. Wedding Costumes (1st series). Multicoloured.

1848	140r. Type **421**	3·00	70
1849	350r. Aceh couple	15·00	9·25
1850	400r. East Timor couple	20·00	2·00

See also Nos. 1891/6, 1955/60, 1992/7 and 2010/15.

422 Weightlifting

1987. 14th South-East Asia Games, Djakarta. Designs showing pictograms.

1851	**422**	140r. yellow, red and blue	75	30
1852	-	250r. blue, yellow and red	1·50	55
1853	-	350r. red, blue and brown	2·30	85

DESIGNS: 250r. Swimming; 350r. Running.

423 Emblems

1987. 460th Anniv of Djakarta and 20th Anniv of Djakarta Fair.

1854	**423**	75r. blue, black & yellow	1·20	30
1855	-	100r. blue, black & yell	2·30	45

DESIGN—VERT: 100r. Emblems (different).

424 Children reading

1987. Children's Day and National Family Planning Co-ordination Board.

1856	**424**	100r. mauve and orange	90	30
1857	-	250r. yellow and blue	1·50	45

DESIGN—VERT: 250r. Globe, baby in cupped hands and dropper.

425 Headquarters, Djakarta

1987. 20th Anniv of Association of South-East Asian Nations.

1858	**425**	350r. multicoloured	2·40	85

426 Emblem

1987. 30th Anniv and Seventh National Congress of Association of Specialists in Internal Diseases.

1859	**426**	300r. red and blue	2·10	30

427 Mount Bromo and Sand Craters

1987. Tourism. Multicoloured.

1860	140r. Type **427**	90	45
1861	350r. Bedugul Lake, Bali	3·25	1·10
1862	500r. Sea gardens, Bunaken Island	4·00	55

428 Woman with Broken Chains, Helmet and Pennant flying from Pen

1987. "Woman's Physical Revolution".

1863	**428**	75r. green, red and yellow	60	30
1864	-	100r. green, yellow & red	1·20	35

DESIGN: 100r. Women with rifles and barbed wire.

429 Giant Gourami

1987. Fish.

1865	**429**	150r. mauve, yellow & bl	2·30	1·10
1866	-	200r. mauve, yellow & bl	3·00	55
1867	-	500r. black, yellow & bl	7·50	70

DESIGNS: 200r. Goldfish; 300r. Walking catfish.

430 Soldiers

1988. 31st Anniv of Veterans Legion.

1868	**430**	250r. green and orange	1·50	30

431 Welder

1988. National Safety and Occupational Health Day.

1869	**431**	350r. blue and green	2·10	85

432 Carved Snake and Frog

1988. Eighth Anniv of National Crafts Council.

1870	**432**	120r. blue and brown	1·40	15
1871	-	350r. blue and brown	2·00	85
1872	-	500r. brown and green	3·50	30

DESIGN: 350r. Cane rocking-chair; 500r. Bamboo goods.

433 Industrial Symbols

1988. Fourth Five Year Plan.

1873	**433**	140r. blue and green	45	30
1874	-	400r. purple and red	1·20	55

DESIGN: 400r. Fishing industry.

434 Indonesian Girls

1988. "Expo 88" World's Fair, Brisbane. Multicoloured.

1875	200r. Type **434**	1·20	30
1876	300r. Indonesian girl	1·80	35
1877	350r. Indonesian girl and boy	2·30	55
MS1878 96×95 mm. Nos. 1875/7. Perf or imperf		18·00	18·00

435
Anniversary
Emblem

1988. 125th Anniv of Red Cross.

1879	**435**	350r. grey, black and red	1·80	45

436
*Dendrobium
none betawi*

1988. Flowers. Multicoloured.

1880	400r. Type **436**	2·30	85
1881	500r. *Dendrobium abang betawi*	2·30	85

437 Running

1988. Olympic Games, Seoul.

1882	**437**	75r. black, brown & gold	90	30
1883	-	100r. black, red and gold	1·80	35
1884	-	200r. black, mve & gold	2·00	85
1885	-	300r. black, green & gold	90	85
1886	-	400r. black, blue and gold	1·20	70
1887	-	500r. black, blue and gold	5·50	85
MS1888 Two sheets, each 72×96 mm. Perf or imperf. (a) Nos. 1882, 1885 and 1887; (b) Nos. 1883/4 and 1886			60·00	60·00

DESIGNS: 100r. Weightlifting; 200r. Archery; 300r. Table tennis; 400r. Swimming; 500r. Tennis.

438 Figures
around
Emblem

1988. Centenary of International Women's Council.

1889	**438**	140r. black and blue	1·20	30

439 Family, Water
and Ear of Wheat

1988. National Farmers' and Fishermen's Week.

1890	**439**	350r. stone and red	2·30	1·00

1988. Wedding Costumes (2nd series). As T **421**. Multicoloured.

1891	55r. Sumatera Barat (West)	45	30
1892	75r. Jambi	30	15
1893	100r. Bengkulu	1·20	15
1894	120r. Lampung	1·70	15
1895	200r. Moluccas	3·00	30
1896	250r. Nusa Tenggara Timur (East)	4·00	1·80

440 President
Suharto

1988

1897	**440**	200r. blue, pink and red	75	30
1898	**440**	700r. mauve, lt grn & grn	2·00	35
1899	**440**	1000r. multicoloured	2·40	45

441 Emblem

1988. 13th Non-Aligned News Agencies Co-ordinating Committee Meeting, Djakarta.

1901	**441**	500r. blue and red	2·30	55

442 Doves and
Envelopes

1988. International Correspondence Week.

1902	**442**	140r. blue and red	2·00	30

1988. "Filacept 88" International Stamp Exhibition, The Hague. Two sheets, each 72×96 mm, each containing design as no. 1630 but colours changed.

MS1903 Two sheets. (a) 200r. 4, black, emerald and rose. (b) 200r. ultramarine, orange and rose plus label — 44·00 — 44·00

443 Means of
Transport and
Communications

1988. Asian–Pacific Transport and Communications Decade.

1904	**443**	350r. blue and black	2·40	1·00

444 Al Mashun Mosque,
Medan

1988. Tourism. Multicoloured.

1905	250r. Type **444**	90	70
1906	300r. Pagaruyung Palace, Batusangkar	1·50	55
1907	500r. Keong Emas Theatre, Djakarta	3·50	65
MS1908 96×57 mm. 1000r. As No. 1906. Perf or imperf	30·00	31·00

See also No. **MS**1954.

445 *Papilio
gigon*

1988. Butterflies. Multicoloured.

1909	400r. Type **445**	3·25	85
1910	500r. *Graphium androcles*	5·75	1·10
MS1911 49×93 mm. 1000r. As No. 1910. Perf or imperf	41·00	41·00

446 *Rafflesia* sp

1989. Flowers. Multicoloured.

1916	200r. Type **446**	1·50	70
1917	1000r. *Amorphophallus titanum*	4·50	1·10
MS1918 50×103 mm. 1000r. As No. 1917	60·00	60·00

447 "40" and Boeing
747

1989. 40th Anniv of Garuda Airline.

1919	**447**	350r. blue and green	3·75	1·10

448 Mother and
Baby

1989. Endangered Animals. The Orang-utan. Multicoloured.

1920	75r. Type **448**	6·00	2·75
1921	100r. Orang-utan in tree	6·00	1·30
1922	140r. Mother and baby in trees	6·00	1·40
1923	500r. Orang-utan	20·00	11·50
MS1924 Two sheets, each 95×125 mm. (a) Nos. 1920/1. (b) Nos. 1922/3	£275	£275

449 Industrial Site

1989. Fifth Five Year Plan.

1925	**449**	55r. violet and green	30	15
1926	-	150r. blue and brown	45	30
1927	-	350r. green and orange	1·10	35

DESIGNS: 150r. Cement works; 350r. Gas plant.

450 Stamp and Map

1989. 125th Anniv of First Netherlands Indies Stamp.

1928	**450**	1000r. green, purple & bl	4·00	30

451 Ki Hadjar
Dewantara and
Graduate

1989. National Education Day.

1929	**451**	140r. red and purple	1·10	30
1930	-	300r. violet and green	1·50	55

DESIGN: 300r. Dewantara (founder of Taman Siswa School), pencil and books.

452 Emblem on
Map

1989. Tenth Anniv of Asia–Pacific Telecommunity.

1931	**452**	350r. purple and green	2·30	1·60

453 Flag and
Cup

1989. Sudirman Cup.

1932	**453**	100r. brown and red	2·75	30

454 Students

1989. Children's Day.

1933	**454**	100r. brown and orange	90	30
1934	-	250r. blue and green	1·70	55

DESIGN: 250r. Youths exercising.

455 Headquarters

1989. Tenth Anniv of Asia–Pacific Integrated Rural Development Centre.

1935	**455**	140r. brown and blue	1·70	30

456 Skull of
"Sangiran 17" and
Hunters

1989. Centenary of Palaeoanthropology in Indonesia.

1936	**456**	100r. black and brown	1·50	30
1937	-	150r. green and red	2·00	35
1938	-	200r. blue and brown	3·00	70
1939	-	250r. violet and brown	3·50	55
1940	-	300r. green and brown	4·50	85
1941	-	350r. blue and brown	5·50	90

DESIGNS—HORIZ: 150r. Skull of "Perning 1" and cavemen; 200r. Skull of "Sangiran 10" and hunter. VERT: 250r. Skull of "Wajak 1"; 300r. Skull of "Sambungmacan 1"; 350r. Skull of "Ngandong 7".

457 Globe and
People

1989. Centenary of Interparliamentary Union.

1942	**457**	350r. green and blue	2·30	1·60

458 Kung Fu

1989. 12th National Games, Djakarta. Multicoloured.

1943	75r. Type **458**	60	20
1944	100r. Tennis	75	30
1945	140r. Judo	90	35
1946	350r. Volleyball	2·30	1·10
1947	500r. Boxing	3·75	45
1948	1000r. Archery	5·25	1·10

459 Taman Burung

1989. Tourism. Multicoloured.

1949	120r. Type **459**	1·50	30
1950	350r. Prangko Museum	2·30	1·10
1951	500r. Istana Anak-Anak (vert)	3·75	1·00
MS1952 100×51 mm. 1500r. As No. 1950	20·00	20·00

460 Trophy

1989. Film Industry.

1953	**460**	150r. ochre and brown	2·00	30

1989. "World Stamp Expo '89" International Stamp Exhibition, Washington D.C. Sheet 102×50 mm. containing designs as Nos. 1905/6. Multicoloured.

MS1954 1500r. Type **444**; 2500r. As No. 1906 — 20·00 — 20·00

1989. Wedding Costumes (3rd series). As T **421**. Multicoloured.

1955	50r. Sumatera Utara (North)	55	15
1956	75r. Sumatera Selatan (South)	60	15
1957	100r. Djakarta	70	20
1958	140r. Sulawesi Utara (North Celebes)	1·40	30
1959	350r. Sulawesi Tengah (Central Celebes)	2·10	1·80
1960	500r. Sulawesi Selatan (South Celebes)	2·75	1·00
MS1961 50×102 mm. 1500r. As No. 1958 Perf or imperf	17·00	17·00

461 Worker wearing
Safety Belt and Flag

1990. Occupational Safety.

1962	**461**	200r. brown and green	1·50	30

462 Benteng Marlborough,
Bengkulu

1990. Tourism. Multicoloured.
1963		200r. Type **462**	1·50	30
1964		400r. National Museum, Djakarta	2·30	70
1965		500r. Baiturrahman Mosque, Banda Aceh	3·00	1·00
MS1966		102×51 mm. 1000r. As No. 1964; As No. 1965	15·00	14·00

463 *Mammilaria fragilis*

1990. Plants. Multicoloured.
1967		75r. Type **463**	75	15
1968		1000r. Bonsai of *Gmelina elliptica*	3·25	85
MS1969		105×50 mm. 1500r. As No. 1968	18·00	17·00

464 Tree-felling
Equipment

1990. Fifth Five Year Plan.
1970	**464**	200r. brown and blue	75	30
1971	-	1000r. black and blue	3·00	2·10

DESIGN: 1000r. Lighthouse and freighter.

465 Arrow pointing to
Indonesia

1990. Visit Indonesia Year (1991) (1st issue). Multicoloured.
1972		100r. Type **465**	75	30
1973		500r. Temple	2·30	70

See also Nos. 1998/2000.

1990. "Stamp World London 90" International Stamp exhibition. Sheet 88×52 mm.
MS1974	**465**	5000r. multicoloured	27·00	26·00

466 Battle and
Disabled Man
using
Soldering-iron

1990. 40th Anniv of Disabled Veterans Corp.
1975	**466**	1000r. orange and green	2·75	1·70

467 Player and
Goalkeeper

1990. World Cup Football Championship, Italy. Multicoloured.
1976		75r. Type **467**	1·10	15
1977		150r. Player tackling	1·50	30
1978		400r. Players competing for high ball	3·25	70
MS1979		98×65 mm. 1500r. As No. 1978	17·00	16·00

468 Lampung
Bridal Pair

1990. National Stamp Exhibition. Sheet 68×95 mm.
MS1980	**468**	2000r. multicoloured	12·00	11·50

No. **MS**1980 also bears inscriptions commemorating various stamp exhibition and label for "Stamp World London 90".

469 U.N. Population
Award

1990. 20th Anniv of Family Planning Movement.
1981	**469**	60r. brown and red	1·10	15

470 Figure with
Pencil and Open
Book

1990. Population Census.
1982	**470**	90r. green and turquoise	1·40	30

471 Children

1990. Children's Day.
1983	**471**	500r. purple and red	2·10	70

472 Soldier
planting Flag

1990. 45th Anniv of Independence. Multicoloured.
1984		200r. Type **472**	1·10	30
1985		500r. Modern building and roads	1·80	85
MS1986		50×105 mm. 1000r. As No. 1985	12·00	11·50

473 Buildings and Cultural
Identities

1990. Indonesia–Pakistan Economic and Cultural Co-operation Organization. Multicoloured.
1987		75r. Type **473**	1·10	30
1988		400r. Dancer (vert)	2·40	85

474 Emblem

1990. 20th Anniv of Asian–Pacific Postal Training Centre.
1989	**474**	500r. blue & ultramarine	2·10	85

475
Anniversary
Emblem

1990. 30th Anniv of Organization of Petroleum Exporting Countries.
1990	**475**	200r. black, grey & orge	1·70	30

476 Houses

1990. Environmental Health.
1991	**476**	1000r. multicoloured	3·25	55

1990. Wedding Costumes (4th series). As T **421**. Multicoloured.
1992		75r. Java Barat (West)	60	15
1993		100r. Java Tengah (Central)	70	20
1994		150r. Yogyakarta	75	25
1995		200r. Java Timur (East)	1·10	30

1996		400r. Bali	1·50	70
1997		500r. Nusa Tenggara Barat (West)	1·70	85

477 Dancer and
House

1991. Visit Indonesia Year (2nd issue). Dancers and Traditional Houses. Multicoloured.
1998		200r. Type **477**	1·80	30
1999		500r. House and dancer with saucers	2·40	1·10
2000		1000r. Dancer and house (different)	4·75	1·00
MS2001		50×100 mm. 1500r. As Type **477**	23·00	21·00

478 Emblem

1991. 16th National Koran Reading Competition, Yogyakarta.
2002	**478**	200r. green and yellow	1·80	30

479 Palace of Sultan
Ternate, Moluccas

1991. Tourism. Multicoloured.
2003		500r. Type **479**	1·80	55
2004		1000r. Bari House, Palembang	2·75	70
MS2005		100×50 mm. As No. 2004	11·50	10·50

No. **MS**2005 also commemorates Flap Exco Meeting Yogyakarta.

480 Steel Mill

1991. Fifth Five Year Plan.
2006	**480**	75r. red and blue	45	15
2007	-	200r. blue and black	60	20

DESIGN—HORIZ: 200r. Computer technology.

481 Damaged
Lungs and
Cigarette
Smoke forming
Skull

1991. Anti-smoking Campaign.
2008	**481**	90r. red and black	2·00	30

482 Hands

1991. 24th Anniv of National Federation for the Welfare of the Mentally Handicapped.
2009	**482**	200r.+25r. black and red	1·80	45

1991. Wedding Costumes (5th series). As T **421**. Multicoloured.
2010		100r. Kalimantan Barat (West)	45	15
2011		200r. Kalimantan Tengah (Central)	1·50	20
2012		300r. Kalimantan Selatan (South)	90	30
2013		400r. Sulawesi Tenggara (South-east Celebes)	1·10	45
2014		500r. Riau	1·50	55
2015		1000r. Irian Jaya	1·80	1·00

483 Tents

1991. National Boy Scout Jamboree, Cibubur.
2016	**483**	200r. blue, black and red	2·10	30

484 Monument

1991. 42nd Anniv of Return of Republican Government to Djokjakarta.
2017	**484**	200r. green and brown	2·00	30

485 Temples
and Family

1991. Farmers' Week.
2018	**485**	500r. yellow and blue	2·75	30

486 Cells

1991. "chemindo '91" Chemistry Congress, Surabaya.
2019	**486**	400r. red and green	2·30	30

487 Weightlifters

1991. Fifth Junior Men's and Fourth Women's Asian Weightlifting Championships, Manado.
2020	**487**	300r. red and black	2·30	30

488 Parachutists

1991. World Parachuting Championships.
2021	**488**	500r. mauve and blue	2·30	30

489 Red Cross
and Hands

1991. 46th Anniv of Indonesian Red Cross.
2022	**489**	200r. red and green	2·10	30

490 Radio
Mast

1991. Eighth International Amateur Radio Union Region III Conference, Bandung.
2023	**490**	300r. blue and yellow	2·30	30

491 Script and
Mosque

1991. Istiqlal Festival, Djakarta.
2024	**491**	200r. black and red	2·30	30

492 Dancer and Inspectors

1991. International Convention on Quality Control Circles, Bali.

2025	**492**	500r. multicoloured	2·75	85

493 Orang-utan

1991. International Conference on Great Apes of the World. The Orang-utan. Multicoloured.

2026	200r. Type **493**	2·10	30
2027	500r. Orang-utan on forest path	2·40	55
2028	1000r. Orang-utan sitting on ground	4·50	1·10
MS2029	50×100 mm. 2500r. As No. 2028	15·00	14·00

494 Model of Jakarta Post Office

1992. Automation of Postal Service. Multicoloured.

2030	200r. Type **494**	75	30
2031	500r. Sorting machine	1·50	55

495 Phalaenopsis ambilis

1992. Flowers. Multicoloured.

2032	200r. Type **495**	90	30
2033	500r. Rafflesia arnoldii	1·70	70
2034	1000r. Jasminum sambac	3·50	85
MS2035	106×50 mm. 2000r. As No. 2034	15·00	14·00

496 Buildings, Ballot Boxes and State Arms

1992. Parliamentary Elections. Multicoloured.

2036	75r. Type **496**	30	20
2037	100r. Ballot boxes and globe	90	30
2038	500r. Ballot boxes and hands holding voting slips	2·00	55

497 Lembah Baliem, Irian Jaya

1992. Visit ASEAN Year. Multicoloured.

2039	300r. Type **497**	90	30
2040	500r. Tanah Lot, Bali	1·80	55
2041	1000r. Lembah Anai, Sumatra Barat	4·00	85
MS2042	100×50 mm. 3000r. As No. 2040	15·00	14·00

498 Road-building

1992. Fifth Five Year Plan.

2043	**498**	150r. purple and green	30	20
2044	-	300r. blue and mauve	1·10	30

DESIGN: 300r. Aircraft.

499 Emblem and Crab

1992. 15th Anniv of Indonesian Cancer Foundation.

2045	**499**	200r.+25r. red & brown	75	30
2046	**499**	500r.+50r. red and blue	1·50	45

500 Weightlifting

1992. Olympic Games, Barcelona. Multicoloured.

2047	75r. Type **500**	45	15
2048	200r. Badminton	60	20
2049	300r. Sports pictograms	1·20	30
2050	500r. Tennis	1·50	45
2051	1000r. Archery	3·75	70
MS2052	751×00 mm. 2000r. As No. 2048; 3000r. As No. 2051	18·00	17·00

501 White-crested Laughing Thrush

1992. Birds. Multicoloured.

2053	100r. Type **501**	45	15
2054	200r. Common golden-backed woodpecker	90	30
2055	400r. Rhinoceros hornbill	1·80	85
2056	500r. Amboina king parrot	2·75	1·00
MS2057	501×00 mm. 3000r. Type **501**	15·00	14·00

502 Busy Street (Tammy Filia)

1992. National Children's Day. Children's paintings. Multicoloured.

2058	75r. Type **502**	30	15
2059	100r. Children with balloons (Cynthia Widiyana Halim)	60	20
2060	200r. Native boats (Dandy Rahmad Adi Kurniawan)	1·20	30
2061	500r. Girl and bird (Intan Sari Dewi Saputro)	2·75	1·40

503 Anniversary Emblem

1992. 25th Anniv of Association of South-East Asian Nations. Multicoloured.

2062	200r. Type **503**	75	30
2063	500r. Map and flags of member nations	2·30	70
2064	1000r. "25" and flags	4·50	85

504 Earth and "Palapa B-4" (satellite)

1992. Communications. Multicoloured.

2065	200r. Type **504**	75	30
2066	500r. "Palapa" satellite (16th anniv of launch)	1·50	70
2067	1000r. Old and modern tel- ephones (modernization of telephone system)	3·75	85

505 Emblem

1992. Tenth Non-Aligned Countries Summit, Djakarta. Multicoloured.

2068	200r. Type **505**	1·10	30
2069	500r. Members' flags and emblem	1·80	85

506 Ngremo Dance, East Java

1992. Traditional Dances (1st series). Multicoloured.

2070	200r. Type **506**	60	30
2071	500r. Gending Sriwijaya dance, South Sumatra	2·75	2·50
MS2072	50×100 mm. 3000r. Type **506**	12·00	11·50

See also Nos. 2122/5, 2166/73, 2211/15, 2292/6, 2366/71 and 2476/81.

507 Anniversary Emblem

1992. 40th Anniv of International Planned Parenthood Federation.

2073	**507**	200r. blue and green	1·50	30

508 Antara Building, Djakarta

1992. 55th Anniv of Antara News Agency.

2074	**508**	500r. black and blue	2·30	30

509 Planting Saplings

1992. National Afforestation.

2075	**509**	500r. multicoloured	2·30	45

1993. No. 1831 surch **50r**.

2076	**326**	50r. on 55r. red and pink	75	15

511 State Arms and Assembly Building

1993. Tenth People's Consultative Assembly. Multicoloured.

2077	300r. Type **511**	90	30
2078	700r. Assembly hall	2·30	55

512 Soldiers and Buildings

1993. Fifth Five Year Plan. Multicoloured.

2079	300r. Type **512**	60	55
2080	700r. Workers and arrow	1·50	1·40
2081	1000r. Runners	2·10	2·00

513 Swarm of Ornithoptera goliath

1993

2082	**513**	1000r. multicoloured	3·00	55

514 Peristiwa Hotel, Yamato, and Adipura Kencana Medal

1993. 700th Anniv of Surabaya (300, 700r.) and "indo tourism 93" (1000r.). Multicoloured.

2083	300r. Type **514**	75	70
2084	700r. Modern city and World Habitat Award, 1992	1·70	1·60
2085	1000r. Candi Bajang Ratu (temple)	2·40	2·30

516 Mascot

1993. "indopex'93" Asian Stamp Exhibition, Surabaya. Nos. 2082/5 optd **indopex'93 surabaya**.

2086	**514**	300r. multicoloured	75	30
2087	-	700r. multicoloured	1·70	70
2088	**513**	1000r. mult (No. 2082)	3·25	1·40
2089	-	1000r. mult (No. 2085)	2·75	1·00
MS2090	**516**	101×50 m. 3500r. multicoloured	9·75	9·25

517 Jasminum sambac

1993. Environmental Protection. Multicoloured.

2091	300r. Type **517**	60	30
2092	300r. Moth orchid (Phalaenopsis amabilis)	60	30
2093	300r. Rafflesia arnoldi (flower)	60	30
2094	700r. Komodo dragon	2·40	70
2095	700r. Asian bonytongue	2·40	70
2096	700r. Java hawk eagle	2·40	70
MS2097	75×105 mm. 1500r. Type **517**; 1500r. As No. 2094	11·50	10·50

Stamps of the same value were issued together, se-tenant, in strips of three stamps, each strip forming a composite design.

518 Scouts making Road

1993. First World Community Development Camp, Lebakharjo. Multicoloured.

2098	300r. Type **518**	60	15
2099	700r. Pres. Suharto greeting girl scout	1·80	30

519 President Suharto

1993

2100	**519**	150r. multicoloured	30	15
2101	**519**	300r. multicoloured	60	20
2102	**519**	700r. multicoloured	1·40	55

On No. 2102 part of the background is a draped flag.

520 Papilio blumei

1993. International Butterfly Conference, Ujungpandang.

2103	**520**	700r. multicoloured	2·30	30
MS2104	50×100 mm. **520** 3000r. multicoloured	11·50	10·50

See also MS2110.

521 Swimming

1993. "Pon XIII" Sports Week, Djakarta. Multicoloured.
2105	150r. Type **521**	30	15
2106	300r. Cycling	60	55
2107	700r. Mascot	1·40	1·30
2108	1000r. High jumping	2·00	1·80
MS2109 51×101 mm. 3500r. As No. 2018		9·00	8·50

1993. "Bangkok 1993" International Stamp Exhibition. Sheet 67×75 mm containing design as T **520** but without top inscription.
MS2110 3000r. multicoloured	11·50	10·50

522 Sigura-Gura Waterfall, North Sumatra

1993. World Tourism Organization Meeting, Bali. Multicoloured.
2111	300r. Type **522**	75	70
2112	700r. Goa Petruk (cave), Central Java	1·70	1·60
2113	1000r. Danau Segara Anak (cove), West Nusa Tenggara (horiz)	2·40	2·30
MS2114 71×75 mm. 5000r. Similar design to Type **522**		8·25	7·75

523 General Soedirman

1993. Armed Forces. Each brown, black and red.
2115	300r. Type **523**	60	30
2116	300r. Lt.-Gen. Oerip Soemohardjo	60	30

Nos. 2115/16 were issued together, *se-tenant*, forming a composite design.

524 Michelia champaca

1993. Flora and Fauna. Multicoloured.
2117	300r. Type **524**	1·40	30
2118	300r. Cananga adorata	1·40	30
2119	300r. Orange-tailed shama (Copsychus pyrrhopygus)	1·40	30
2120	300r. Southern grackle (Gracula religiosa)	1·40	30

525 Plantation

1993. Resettlement Programme.
2121	**525** 700r. multicoloured	1·40	1·30

526 South Sumatran Dancer

1993. Traditional Dances (2nd series). Multicoloured.
2122	300r. Type **526**	1·10	20

2123	700r. West Kalimantan	1·80	30
2124	1000r. Irian Jaya	2·40	45
MS2125 50×101 mm. 3500r. As No. 2124		9·75	9·25

527 Emblems

1994. International Year of the Family.
2126	**527** 300r. multicoloured	75	30

528 Working Women

1994. Sixth Five Year Plan. Multicoloured.
2127	100r. Type **528**	15	10
2128	700r. Graduate and school pupils	1·40	1·30
2129	2000r. Doctor, nurse and children	3·75	3·50

529 Netherlands Indies, Japanese Occupation and Indonesia Stamps

1994. 130th Anniv of First Netherlands Indies Stamps.
2130	**529** 700r. multicoloured	1·50	70

530 Ladige's Rainbowfish

1994. Fish. Multicoloured.
2131	300r. Type **530**	75	30
2132	700r. Boeseman's rainbow fish	2·00	70
MS2133 103×50 mm. 3500r. As No. 2132		8·25	7·75

531 Emblem

1994. National Kidney Foundation.
2134	**531** 300r.+30r. multicoloured	90	45

532 Figure, Globe, and Anniversary Emblem

1994. 75th Anniv of International Red Cross Red Crescent Organization.
2135	**532** 300r. black, red and blue	1·10	30

533 Map and Emblem

1994. Asia–Pacific Ministerial Conference on Women, Djakarta.
2136	**533** 700r. multicoloured	1·50	55

534 Player

1994. 25th Anniv of Bakosurtanal.

1994. World Cup Football Championship, U.S.A.
2137	**534** 150r. multicoloured	30	15
2138	- 300r. multicoloured	60	30
2139	- 700r. blue, red and black	1·40	70
2140	- 1000r. multicoloured	2·30	85
MS2141 109×50 mm. 3500r. multicoloured		8·25	7·75

DESIGNS——VERT: 300r. Striker (mascot). HORIZ: 700r. Emblem; 1000, 3500r. Ball in net .

535 Player and Uber Cup (Women's)

1994. Indonesian Victories in World Team Badminton Championships. Multicoloured.
2142	300r. Type **535**	75	30
2143	300r. Thomas Cup (Men's)	75	30
MS2144 86×92 mm. 1750r. Type **535**; 1750r. As No. 2143		8·25	7·75

Nos. 2142/3 were issued together, *se-tenant*, forming a composite design.

536 Hand holding Scales

1994. National Commission on Human Rights.
2145	**536** 700r. multicoloured	1·50	30

1994. "Philakorea 1994" International Stamp Exhibition, Seoul. Sheet 85×91 mm.
MS2146 3500r. multicoloured	8·25	7·75

537 Vase with Bead Cover

1994. Indonesia–Pakistan Economic and Cultural Co-operation Organization. Multicoloured.
2147	300r. Type **537**	75	45
2148	700r. Blue and white vase	1·50	1·10

538 Skeleton of Quadruped

1994. Centenary of Bogoriense Zoological Museum. Multicoloured.
2149	700r. Type **538**	1·70	1·00
2150	1000r. Outline and skeleton of whale (80×22 mm)	2·40	1·10
MS2151 123×48 mm. 3500r. As No. 2150		9·00	8·50

539 Mascots

1994. 12th Asian Games, Hiroshima, Japan. Multicoloured.
2152	300r. Type **539**	60	45
2153	700r. Hurdling	1·40	1·10

540 Communications and Map

1994. 25th Anniv of Bakosurtanal.
2154	**540** 700r. multicoloured	1·80	55

541 Morus macroura

1994. Flora and Fauna. Multicoloured.
2155	150r. Type **541**	75	30
2156	150r. Oncosperma tiquillaria	75	30
2157	150r. Eucalyptus urophylla	75	30
2158	150r. Moth orchid (Phalaenopsis amabilis)	75	30
2159	150r. Pometia pinnata	75	30
2160	150r. Great argus pheasant (Argusianus argus)	75	30
2161	150r. Blue-crowned hanging parrot (Loriculus pusillus)	75	30
2162	150r. Timor helmeted friarbird (Philemon buceroides)	75	30
2163	150r. Amboina king parrot (Alisterus amboinensis)	75	30
2164	150r. Twelve-wired bird of paradise (Seleucidis melanoleuca)	75	30
MS2165 48×81 mm. 3500r. As No. 2162		12·00	11·50

Nos. 2158 and 2161 are incorrectly inscribed; the correct Latin names are "*Dendrobium phalaenopsis*" and "*Loriculus galgulus*" respectively.

542 Venue

1994. Asia–Pacific Economic Co-operation Summit, Bogor.
2166	**542** 700r. multicoloured	1·50	45

543 Airplane

1994. 50th Anniv of I.C.A.O.
2167	**543** 700r. multicoloured	2·10	45

1994. Traditional Dances (3rd series). As T **506**. Multicoloured.
2168	150r. Mengaup, Jambi	45	15
2169	300r. Topeng, West Java	60	30
2170	700r. Anging Mamiri, South Sulawesi	1·40	45
2171	1000r. Pisok, North Sulawesi	1·80	55
2172	2000r. Bidu, East Nusa Tenggara	3·50	1·70
MS2173 47×87 mm. 3500r. As No. 2169		7·50	7·00

544 Yogyakarta Palace

1995. 20th Anniv of World Tourism Organization. Multicoloured.
2174	300r. Type **544**	45	35
2175	700r. Floating market, Banjarmasin	1·20	1·10
2176	1000r. Pasola (equestrian tradition), Sumba	1·70	1·60

545 Children, President Suharto and First Lady

1995. "Dedication to the Nation".
2177	**545** 700r. multicoloured	1·50	1·10

546 Letter from King of Klungkung, Bali

1995. Sixth Five Year Plan. National Letter Writing Campaign. Multicoloured.
2178	300r. Type **546**	45	35
2179	700r. Carrier pigeon (campaign mascot) and letters	1·40	1·00

547
Schizostachyum brachycladum

1995. Fourth International Bamboo Congress, Ubud, Bali. Multicoloured.

| 2180 | 300r. Type **547** | 45 | 35 |
| 2181 | 700r. *Dendrocalamus asper* | 1·40 | 1·00 |

548 N250 and National Flag

1995. Inaugural Flight of I.P.T.N. N250 Airliner.

| 2182 | **548** | 700r. multicoloured | 1·50 | 1·10 |

549 Anniversary Emblem

1995. 50th Anniv of Indonesian Republic. Multicoloured.

2183	300r. Type **549**	45	35
2184	700r. Boy with national flag	1·40	1·00
MS2185	102×48 mm. 2500r. As No. 2184	8·25	7·50

550 Kota Intan Drawbridge

1995. "Jakarta '95" Asian Stamp Exn. Multicoloured.

| 2186 | 300r. Type **550** | 45 | 35 |
| 2187 | 700r. Fatahillah Jakarta History Museum | 1·40 | 1·00 |

551 *Dewarutji* (cadet barquentine), Pinisi Sailing Ship and Flag

1995. "Sail Indonesia '95." Tall Ships Race and Fleet Review.

| 2188 | **551** | 700r. multicoloured | 1·40 | 85 |
| MS2189 | 91×48 mm. 2500r. multi-coloured | 7·50 | 6·50 |

552 "Mother Love" (Patricia Saerang)

1995. Tenth Asia and Pacific Regional Conference of Rehabilitation International, Indonesia.

| 2190 | **552** | 700r.+100r. mult | 1·70 | 1·20 |

553 Mushaf Istiqlal (illuminated Islamic text)

1995. Istiqlal Festival.

| 2191 | **553** | 700r. multicoloured | 1·20 | 85 |

554 P.T.T. Monument

1995. 50th Anniv of Take-over of P.T.T. Headquarters by Republicans.

| 2192 | **554** | 700r. multicoloured | 1·20 | 85 |

555 Rice

1995. 50th Anniv of F.A.O.

| 2193 | **555** | 700r. multicoloured | 1·20 | 85 |

556 Flags and Emblem

1995. 50th Anniv of U.N.O. Multicoloured.

| 2194 | 300r. Type **556** | 45 | 35 |
| 2195 | 700r. Emblem, Earth and rainbow | 1·40 | 1·00 |

557
Cyrtostachys renda

1995. Flora and Fauna. Multicoloured.

2196	150r. Type **557**	75	35
2197	150r. Tiger (*Panthera tigris*)	75	35
2198	150r. *Bouea macrophylla*	75	35
2199	150r. Javan rhinoceros (*Rhinoceros sondaicus*)	75	35
2200	150r. *Santalum album*	75	35
2201	150r. Komodo dragon (*Varanus komodoensis*)	75	35
2202	150r. *Diospyros celebica*	75	35
2203	150r. Maleo fowl (*Macrocephalon maleo*)	75	35
2204	150r. *Nephelium ramboutan-ake*	75	35
2205	150r. Malay peacock-pheasant (*Polyplectron schleiermacheri*)	75	35
MS2206	48×95 mm. 2500r. as No. 2197	15·00	13·00

558 Yogyakarta Palace

1995. Award of Aga Khan Prize for Architecture to Indonesia. Multicoloured.

| 2207 | 300r. Type **558** | 45 | 35 |
| 2208 | 700r. Surakarta Palace | 1·40 | 1·00 |

559 Hill and Postal Carriers

1995. Birth Bicentenary of Sir Rowland Hill (instigator of postal stamps). Multicoloured.

| 2209 | 300r. Type **559** | 45 | 35 |
| 2210 | 700r. Hill and Indonesian Postal Service emblem | 1·40 | 1·00 |

1995. Traditional Dances (4th series). As T **506.** Multicoloured.

2211	150r. Nguri dance, West Nusa Tenggara	45	35
2212	300r. Muli Betanggai dance, Lampung	60	45
2213	700r. Mutiara dance, Moluccas	1·40	1·00
2214	1000r. Gantar dance, East Kalimantan	1·80	1·30
MS2215	48×81 mm. 2500r. As No. 2211	8·25	7·50

560 Economic Sectors

1996. Economic Census.

| 2216 | **560** | 300r. orange and blue | 45 | 35 |
| 2217 | – | 700r. turquoise & orange | 1·40 | 1·00 |

DESIGN—HORIZ: 700r. Graph of economic activity.

561 Satellite orbiting Earth

1996. Launch of "Palapa-C" Satellite. Multicoloured.

| 2218 | 300r. Type **561** | 75 | 35 |
| 2219 | 700r. Satellite orbiting Earth (triangular) | 1·40 | 1·00 |

562 Mixed Flowers

1996. Greetings Stamps. "Happy Holiday". Inscr "Selamat Hari Raya". Multicoloured.

2220	150r. Type **562**	30	20
2221	300r. Mixed flowers (different)	60	45
2222	700r. Mixed flowers (different)	1·20	85

563 Soemanang Soeriowinoto (Association head, 1946–47 and 1949–50)

1996. 50th Anniv of Indonesian Journalists' Association. Multicoloured.

| 2223 | 300r. Type **563** | 60 | 45 |
| 2224 | 700r. Djamaluddin Adinegoro (head of Indonesian Press Bureau Foundation and founder of Academy of Publicity and Publicity Faculty, Padjadjaran University) | 1·20 | 85 |

564 Tank firing and Map

1996. 47th Anniv of Return of Republican Government to Djokjakarta. Multicoloured.

| 2225 | 700r.+100r. Type **564** | 1·50 | 1·10 |
| 2226 | 700r.+100r. Attack on Palace | 1·50 | 1·10 |

Nos. 2225/6 were issued together, se-tenant, forming a composite design.

565 State House, Bandung

1996. "indonesia 96" International Youth Stamp Exhibition, Bandung. Multicoloured.

2227	300r. Type **565**	75	55
2228	700r. Painted parasols	1·50	1·10
MS2229	99×73 mm. 1250r. Type **565**; 1250r. As No. 2228	7·50	6·50

566 Indonesian Bear Cuscus

1996. Cuscuses. Multicoloured.

2230	300r. Australian spotted cuscus	75	55
2231	300r. Type **566**	75	55
MS2232	98×81 mm. 1250r. As No. 2230; 1250r. As No. 586	4·50	3·75

Nos. 2230/1 were issued together, se-tenant, forming a composite design.

567 Roses

1996. Greetings Stamps. "Congratulations and Best Wishes". Inscr "Selamat dan Sukses". Multicoloured.

2233	150r. Type **567**	30	20
2234	300r. Orchids	60	45
2235	700r. Chrysanthemums	1·20	85

568 Students (Y. Edwin Purwanto)

1996. Compulsory Nine Year Education Programme. Winning Entries in Children's Stamp Design Competition. Multicoloured.

2236	150r. Type **568**	30	20
2237	300r. Children in playground (Andi Pradhana)	60	45
2238	700r. Teacher and pupils (Intan Sari Dewi)	1·20	85

569 Archery

1996. Olympic Games, Atlanta. Multicoloured.

2239	300r. Type **569**	60	45
2240	700r. Weightlifting	1·20	85
2241	1000r. Badminton	2·00	1·40
MS2242	81×48 mm. 2500r. Type **569**	5·25	4·50

中国'96——第9届亚洲国际集邮展览
CHINA'96 — 9th Asian International Philatelic Exhibition
(570)

1996. "China '96" International Stamp Exhibition, Peking. No. MS2232 optd with T **570** in the margin.

| MS2243 | 98×81 mm. 1250r. ×2 multicoloured | 12·00 | 11·00 |

571 Pres. Suharto and Procession

1996. National Youth Kirab. Multicoloured.

| 2244 | 300r. Type **571** | 60 | 45 |
| 2245 | 700r. Pres. Suharto presenting national flag | 1·40 | 1·00 |

572 Nusantara N-2130 Prototype over Soekarno-Hatta Airport

1996. Aviation and Maritime Year. Multicoloured.

| 2246 | 300r. Type **572** | 45 | 35 |
| 2247 | 700r. *Palindo Jaya* (inter-island ferry) | 1·20 | 85 |

573 Scouts climbing over Rope Ladders

1996. National Scout Jamboree, Djakarta. Multicoloured.

2248	150r. Type **573**	45	35
2249	150r. Scouts on ladder and death slide	45	35
2250	150r. Scouts at base of rope ladders	45	35
2251	150r. Girl scouts constructing wooden apparatus	45	35
2252	150r. Scouts on unicycle and climbing frame	45	35
2253	150r. Girl scouts building frame on campsite	45	35
2254	150r. Soldering metal	45	35
2255	150r. Girl at radio taking notes	45	35

Nos. 2248/55 were issued together, se-tenant, Nos. 2248/51 and 2252/5 forming composite designs.

574 Pinisi Prows and Wave

1996. 50th Anniv of Bank BNI. Multicoloured.

| 2256 | 300r. Type **574** | 45 | 35 |
| 2257 | 700r. Pinisi sailing ship | 1·20 | 85 |

575 Mother and Child reading (Salt Iodization Programme)

1996. 50th Anniv of UNICEF. Each brown, green and mauve.

2258	300r. Type **575**	60	45
2259	700r. Giving oral vaccine to children (elimination of polio)	1·20	85
2260	1000r. Children (Children's Rights Convention)	2·00	1·40

576 Ibu Tien Suharto

1996. Ibu Suharto (First Lady) Commemoration.

2261	**576** 700r. multicoloured	1·20	85
MS2262	47×96 mm. **576** 2500r. multicoloured	4·00	3·25

577 Softball

1996. National Sports Week. Multicoloured.

2263	300r. Type **577**	60	45
2264	700r. Hockey	1·20	85
2265	1000r. Basketball	2·00	1·40

1996. "Istanbul '96" Stamp Exhibition, Turkey. Two sheets, each 94×80 mm. each containing one stamp (62×46 mm) featuring composite designs formerly issued in blocks of four.

MS2266	Two sheets (a) 1250r. As Nos. 2248/51; (b) 1250r. As Nos. 2252/5	6·50	5·75

578 Head of Sumatran Rhinoceros

1996. The Sumatran Rhinoceros (*Dicerorhinus sumatrensis*) and the Javan Rhinoceros (*Rhinoceros sondaicus*). Multicoloured.

2267	300r. Type **578**	75	55
2268	300r. Sumatran rhinoceros	75	55
2269	300r. Javan rhinoceros	75	55
2270	300r. Adult and baby Javan rhinoceros	75	55
MS2271	100×47 mm. 1500r. Javan rhinoceros; 1500r. Sumatran rhinoceros	6·75	6·00

579 Flower Arrangement

1996. Greetings Stamps. "Happy New Year". Inscr "Selamat Tahun Baru". Multicoloured.

2272	150r. Type **579**	30	20
2273	300r. Arrangement including red and yellow roses	60	45
2274	700r. Arrangement including white rose and yellow chrysanthemums	1·20	85

580 Coins and Banknotes

1996. 50th Anniv of Financial Day.

2275	**580** 700r. multicoloured	2·30	1·60

581 Sulawesi Hornbill

1996. National Flora and Fauna Day. Multicoloured.

2276	300r. Type **581**	75	55
2277	300r. Irrawaddy dolphin (*Orcaella brevirostris*)	75	55
2278	300r. Black-naped oriole (*Oriolus chinensis*)	75	55
2279	300r. Sun bear (*Helarctos malayanus*)	75	55
2280	300r. Rothschild's mynah (*Leucopsar rothschildi*)	75	55
2281	300r. Lontar palms (*Borassus flabellifer*)	75	55
2282	300r. Black orchid (*Coelogyne pandurata*)	75	55
2283	300r. Michelia (*Michelia alba*)	75	55
2284	300r. Giant aroid lily (*Amorphophallus titanum*)	75	55
2285	300r. Majegau (*Dysoxylum densiflorum*)	75	55
MS2286	Two sheets, each 47×80 mm. (a) 1250r. As No. 2280; (b) 1250r. As No. 2282	7·50	6·50

See also No. MS2287.

1996. "Aseanpex '96" International Stamp Exhibition, Manila, Philippines.

MS2287	**581** 2000r. multicoloured	17·00	14·00

582 Somba Opu Fortress

1996. Eastern Region. Multicoloured.

2288	300r. Divers and sea-bed	60	45
2289	700r. Type **582**	1·20	85

583 School-children at Play

1996. National Movement of Foster Parents. Multicoloured.

2290	150r. Type **583**	45	35
2291	300r. Poor children and photograph of school-child (horiz)	75	55

1996. Traditional Dances (5th series). As T **506**. Multicoloured.

2292	150r. Baksa Kembang dance, South Kalimantan	30	20
2293	300r. Ngarojeng dance, Djakarta	60	45
2294	700r. Rampai dance, Aceh	1·20	85
2295	1000r. Boituka dance, East Timor	1·80	1·30
MS2296	46×75 mm. 2000r. As No. 2293	4·00	3·25

584 Dish Aerial and Control Room

1997. Telecommunications Year. Multicoloured.

2297	300r. Type **584**	60	45
2298	700r. Key pad, communications satellite orbiting Earth and woman using telephone	1·20	85

585 Children shaking Hands ("Happy Birthday")

1997. Greetings Stamps.

2299	**585** 600r. multicoloured	1·10	75
2300	- 600r. black, brn & mve	1·10	75

DESIGN: No. 2300, Heart and ribbons ("Best Wishes").

586 Transport, Ballot Boxes and National Flag

1997. General Election. Multicoloured.

2301	300r. Type **586**	60	45
2302	700r. State arms, map, ballot boxes and buildings	1·20	85
2303	1000r. State arms, ballot boxes, map and city skyline	2·00	1·40

1997. "Hong Kong '97" Stamp Exhibition. Sheet 81×47 mm.

MS2304	2000r. As Type **582** but with addition of postmark	4·50	3·75

587 Pres. Suharto and Wahyu Nusantaraaji

1997. Indonesia's 200,000,000th Citizen.

2305	**587** 700r. multicoloured	1·40	1·00

588 Children with Stamp Collection

1997. 75th Anniv of Indonesian Philatelic Association. Multicoloured.

2306	300r. Type **588**	90	65
2307	700r. Magnifying glass on 1994 150r. Flora and Fauna stamp	1·50	1·10

589 Wage Rudolf Soepratman

1997. Cultural Anniversaries. Multicoloured.

2308	300r. Type **589** (composer of *Indonesia Raya* (national anthem), 60th death anniv (1998))	60	45
2309	700r. Usmar Ismail (film director, 25th death anniv (1996))	1·20	85
2310	1000r. Self-portrait of Affandi (painter, 90th birth anniv)	2·00	1·40
MS2311	47×97 mm. As No. 2310	3·75	3·25

590 Picture Jasper

1997. "Indonesia 2000" International Stamp Exn, Bandung (1st issue). Minerals. Multicoloured.

2312	300r. Type **590**	60	45
2313	700r. Chrysocolla	1·20	85
2314	1000r. Geode	2·00	1·40
MS2315	80×47 mm. 2000r. Banded agate	6·00	5·50

See also Nos. 2403/MS2407, 2529/MS2533 and 2593/MS2597.

591 Black-naped Oriole

1997. "Pacific 97" International Stamp Exhibition, San Francisco. Sheet 49×51 mm.

MS2316	**591** 2000r. multicoloured	5·50	5·00

592 Crowd giving Thumbs Up to "No Smoking" Sign

1997. World "No Smoking" Day. Winning Entry in Students' Design Competition.

2317	**592** 1000r. multicoloured	1·70	1·20

---

593 Fishes and Coral Reef

1997. World Environment Day. Multicoloured.

2318	150r. Type **593**	45	35
2319	300r. Rays and other fishes by brain and other corals	60	45
2320	700r. Two coralfishes amongst corals	1·20	85
MS2321	47×79 mm. 2000r. Coral reef	4·50	4·00

594 Paksi Naga Liman Carriage (built by Pangeran Losari)

1997. Second Indonesian Royal Palace Festival, Cirebon. Multicoloured.

2322	300r. Type **594**	60	45
2323	700r. Singa Barong carriage (built by Ki Nataguna), 1549	1·10	75

595 Venue's Main Gateway

1997. 18th National Koran Reading Contest, Jambi. Multicoloured.

2324	300r. Type **595**	60	45
2325	700r. Al Ikhsaniah Mosque, Olak Kemang, Jambi	1·20	85

596 Co-operatives Monument, Tasikmalaya

597 Pres. Suharto and Dr. Mohammad Hatta (first vice-president)

1997. 50th Anniv of Co-operatives Movement. Multicoloured.

2326	150r. Type **596**	30	20
2327	150r. Co-operatives Monument, Djakarta	30	20
2328	300r. Child's hand clasping adult's hand	60	45
2329	300r. Figure before globe	60	45
2330	700r. Type **597**	1·20	85

598 Hands on Globe

1997. 30th Anniv of Association of South-East Asian Nations. Multicoloured.

2331	300r. Type **598**	60	45
2332	700r. Ears of cereals forming "30th" and globe	1·20	85

599 Games Emblem and Mascot

1997. 19th South-East Asian Games, Djakarta. Multicoloured.

2333	300r. Type **599**	45	35
2334	300r. Torch carrier, flags and emblem	45	35
2335	700r. Running and throwing the discus	1·10	75
2336	700r. Hurdling and sprinting	1·10	75

600 Coach, Bus, Java "International Harvester" Bus and Bullock Cart

1997. National Communications Day. Transport Development. Multicoloured.

2337	300r. Type **600**	45	35
2338	300r. Electric, express, diesel and steam railway locomotives	45	35
2339	700r. Container ship, passenger ship, cargo vessel and lette (Madurese sailing boat)	1·10	75
2340	700r. Seulawah and IPTN CN-235, CN-250 and N-2130 airliners	1·10	75

601 U.P.U. Monument and Mas Soeharto (first head of Indonesian P.T.T.)

1997. 50th Anniv of Indonesian Membership of U.P.U. Multicoloured.

2341	300r. Type **601**	65	45
2342	700r. Heinrich von Stephan (founder of U.P.U.) and monument	1·30	95

602 Assembly Emblem and Building

1997. People's Consultative Assembly General Session.

2343	**602**	700r. multicoloured	1·30	95

603 Village Programme (Army)

1997. Armed Forces Day. Multicoloured.

2344	300r. Type **603**	65	45
2345	300r. Frigates and Jalesveva Jayamahe Monument, Surabaya (Navy)	65	45
2346	300r. "Blue Falcon" acrobatic team (Air Force)	65	45
2347	300r. Rapid Reaction Unit (Police Force)	65	45

604 White Buffalo

1997. "MAKASSAR '97" National Stamp Exhibition, Ujiung Pandeing. Sheet 106×49 mm.

MS2348	**604**	2000r. multicoloured	3·50	3·00

605 Duku Fruit (*Lansium domesticum*)

1997. National Flora and Fauna Day. Multicoloured.

2349	300r. Type **605**	55	40
2350	300r. Salacca of Condet (*Salacca zalacca*)	55	40
2351	300r. Tengawang tungkul (*Shorea stenoptera*)	55	40
2352	300r. Ebony (*Diospyros macrophylla*)	55	40
2353	300r. Fibre orchid (*Diplocaulobium utile*)	55	40
2354	300r. Belida fish (*Chitala lopis*)	55	40
2355	300r. Brahminy kite (*Haliastur indus*)	55	40
2356	300r. Helmeted hornbill (*Rhinoplax vigil*)	55	40

2357	300r. Timor deer (*Cervus timorensis*)	55	40
2358	300r. Anoa (*Bubalus depressicornis*)	55	40
MS2359	98×80 mm. 1250r. As No. 2351; 1250r. As No. 2355	4·25	3·75

606 Oil Field

1997. Association of South-east Asian Nations Council on Petroleum Conference, Djakarta. Multicoloured.

2360	300r. Type **606**	65	45
2361	300r. Oil refinery	65	45
2362	300r. "Eka Putra" (oil tanker)	65	45
2363	300r. Petrol tankers	65	45

607 AIDS Ribbon

1997. World AIDS Day.

2364	**607**	700r.+100r. mult	1·10	80

608 Letter from Foster Son

1997. National Foster Parents Movement.

2365	**608**	700r. multicoloured	95	70

1997. Traditional Dances (6th series). As T **506**. Multicoloured.

2366	150r. Mopuputi Cengke dance, Central Sulawesi	30	25
2367	300r. Mandan Talawang Nyai Balau dance, Central Kalimantan	65	45
2368	600r. Gambyong dance, Central Java	95	70
2369	700r. Cawan dance, North Sumatra	1·10	80
2370	1000r. Legong Keraton dance, Bali	1·40	1·10
MS2371	48×79 mm. As No. 2368	3·25	2·75

609 Baby and Scales

1997. 25th Anniv of Family Welfare Movement.

2372	**609**	700r. multicoloured	95	70

610 Erau Festival, East Kalimantan

1998. Year of Art and Culture. Festivals. Multicoloured.

2373	300r. Type **610**	65	45
2374	700r. Tabot Festival, Bengkulu	95	70

611 Malin Kundang and his Mother

1998. Folk Tales (1st series). Multicoloured. (a) "Malin Kundung".

2375	300r. Type **611**	30	25
2376	300r. Malin returning home and rejecting mother	30	25
2377	300r. Malin's mother praying to God to curse him	30	25
2378	300r. Malin's ship in storm	30	25
2379	300r. Malin turned to stone	30	25

(b) *Sangkuriang*.

2380	300r. Dayang Sumbi weaving	30	25
2381	300r. Dayang Sumbi expelling her son Sanguriang after he killed their dog	30	25
2382	300r. Dayang Sumbi discovering her lover is her son	30	25
2383	300r. Dayang Sumbi creating fake dawn and Sanguriang hurling wooden boat	30	25
2384	300r. Tangkuban Parahu (up-turned boat) Mountain	30	25

(c) *Roro Jonggrang*.

2385	300r. Pengging people attacking Prambanan people	30	25
2386	300r. Bandung Bondowoso proposing to Roro Jonggrang	30	25
2387	300r. Bandung Bondowoso building temples	30	25
2388	300r. Women banging rice-mothers to prematurely announce dawn	30	25
2389	300r. Prambanan Temple and petrified Roro Jonggrang	30	25

(d) *Tengger*.

2390	300r. Roro Anteng and Joko Seger marrying	30	25
2391	300r. Roro and Joko praying to gods for a child	30	25
2392	300r. Volcano erupting	30	25
2393	300r. Raden Kusuma (youngest son) sacrificing himself	30	25
2394	300r. Tengger people giving offerings to volcano	30	25
MS2395	62×64 mm. As No. 2394	2·40	2·00

Nos. 2375/94 were issued together, se-tenant, forming a composite design.

See also Nos. 2489/MS2509, 2572/MS2591, 2679/MS2699, 2761/MS2781, 2838/MS2858, 2942/MS2962 and 3000/MS3020.

612 Djakarta Palace

1997. Presidential Palaces. Multicoloured.

2396	300r. Type **612**	30	25
2397	300r. Bogor Palace	30	25
2398	300r. Cipanas Palace	30	25
2399	300r. Yogyakarta Palace	30	25
2400	300r. Tampak Siring Palace, Bali	30	25

613 Man and Pregnant Woman

1998. 50th Anniv of W.H.O. Multicoloured.

2401	300r. Type **613**	30	25
2402	700r. Mother and child (horiz)	65	45

1998. "Indonesia 2000" International Stamp Exhibition, Bandung (2nd issue). Minerals. As T **590**. Multicoloured.

2403	300r. Chrysopal	30	25
2404	700r. Tektite	50	35
2405	1000r. Amethyst	80	60
MS2406	80×48 mm. 2500r. Petrified wood	2·40	2·10
MS2407	Two sheets. (a) 81×48 mm. 2500r. Opal; (b) 118×133 mm. Nos. 2403/5, each ×2, plus stamps as in No. MS2406 and MS2407a (pair of sheets sold at 35000r.)	30·00	27·00

614 Boys playing Football

1998. World Cup Football Championship, France. Multicoloured.

2408	300r. Type **614**	30	25
2409	700r. Boys and goal-posts	50	35
2410	1000r. Boys challenging for ball	95	70
MS2411	87×57 mm. 2500r. As No. 2411	2·10	1·80

615 Tropical Rainforest

1998. Environmental Protection. Ecophila Stamp Day. Multicoloured.

2412	700r. Type **615**	80	60
2413	700r. Tropical rainforest (different)	80	60

Nos. 2412/13 were issued together, se-tenant, forming a composite design.

616 Fishing Cat

1998. "Juvalex 98" Youth Stamp Exhibition, Luxembourg. Sheet 48×83 mm.

MS2414	**616**	5000r. multicoloured	3·75	3·25

617 School-children and Drug Addict

1998. International Day Against Drug Abuse and Illicit Trafficking. Multicoloured.

2415	700r. Type **617**	65	45
2416	700r. Students campaigning against drugs	65	45

618 Besakih Temple (⅔-size illustration)

1998. Tourism. Multicoloured.

2417	700r. Type **618**	65	45
2418	700r. Taman Ayun Temple (31×23 mm)	65	45
MS2419	77×45 mm. 2500r. Central part of design in Type **618** (41×24 mm)	2·40	2·10

619 Tiger

1998. "Singpex 98" Asian Stamp Exhibition, Singapore. Sheet 102×48 mm.

MS2420	**619**	5000r. multicoloured	4·50	4·00

620 Cattle Wagon and Truck

1998. Railway Rolling Stock. Multicoloured.

2421	300r. Type **620**	50	35
2422	300r. Truck and goods wagon	50	35
2423	300r. Green and yellow passenger carriages	50	35
2424	300r. Passenger carriage and tender	50	35
2425	300r. Class B50 steam locomotive	50	35
2426	300r. Front half of Class D52 steam locomotive	50	35
2427	300r. Back half of Class D52 steam locomotive with tender	50	35
2428	300r. Passenger carriage with two doors	50	35
2429	300r. Observation car	50	35
2430	300r. Goods wagon	50	35
MS2431	76×48 mm. 2500r. Steam locomotive	2·40	2·10

Nos. 2421/30 were issued together, se-tenant, forming a composite design of a train.

621 Pres. Bacharuddin Habibie

1998

2432	**621**	300r. multicoloured	30	25
2433	**621**	700r. multicoloured	65	45
2434	**621**	4500r. multicoloured	2·20	1·60
2435	**621**	5000r. multicoloured	2·50	1·90

622 Fencing

1998. 13th Asian Games, Bangkok, Thailand. Multicoloured.

2436	300r. Type **622**	50	35
2437	700r. Taekwondo	65	45
2438	4000r. Kung fu	2·10	1·50
MS2439	79×100 mm. Nos. 2436/8	3·50	3·00

623 *Baruna Jaya IV* (research ship)

1998. International Year of the Ocean.

2440	**623** 700r. multicoloured	80	60

624 Javan Kingfisher

1998. Fifth Dutch Stamp Dealers' Association Stamp Exhibition, The Hague, Netherlands. Two sheets containing T **624** or similar multicoloured design.

MS2441	Two sheets. (a) 71×46 mm. 5000r. Type **624**; (b) 71×60 mm. 35000r. Javanese wattled lapwing (*Vannelus macropterus*)	21·00	19·00

625 1974 20r. U.P.U. Stamp

1998. World Stamp Day. Multicoloured.

2442	700r. Type **625**	80	60
2443	700r. 1955 15s. Post Office Anniversary stamp	80	60

626 Magpie Goose

1998. Waterfowl (1st series). Multicoloured.

2444	4000r. Type **626**	2·20	1·60
2445	5000r. Spotted whistling duck	2·75	2·00
2446	10000r. Salvadori's duck	5·50	4·00
2447	15000r. Radjah shelduck	7·25	5·25
2448	20000r. White-winged wood duck	11·00	8·25
MS2449	206×115 mm. Nos. 2444/8	30·00	27·00

See also Nos. 2468/**MS**2475 and 2628/9.

627 Djakarta Cathedral

1998. "Italia 98" International Stamp Exhibition, Milan.

MS2450	55×9 mm. **627** 5000r. multicoloured	3·25	2·75

628 State Flag and Jayawijaya Peak

1998. "The Red and White Flag". Multicoloured.

2451	700r. Type **628**	65	45
2452	700r. State flag and Himalayan peak	65	45

629 State Flag

1998. Political Reforms. Multicoloured.

2453	700r. Type **629**	50	35
2454	700r. Dove and State flag	50	35
2455	1000r. Students in front of Parliament building (82×25 mm)	95	70

630 *Stelechocarpus burahol*

1998. Flora and Fauna. Multicoloured.

2456	500r. Type **630**	50	35
2457	500r. Tuberose (*Polianthes tuberosa*)	50	35
2458	500r. Four o'clock (*Mirabilis jalapa*)	50	35
2459	500r. *Mangifera casturi*	50	35
2460	500r. *Ficus minahassae*	50	35
2461	500r. Zebra dove (*Geopelia striata*)	50	35
2462	500r. Red and green junglefowl hybrid (*Gallus varius x G. gallus*)	50	35
2463	500r. Indian elephant (*Elephas maximus*)	50	35
2464	500r. Proboscis monkey (*Nasalis larvatus*)	50	35
2465	500r. Eastern tarsier (*Tarsius spectrum*)	50	35
MS2466	Two sheets. (a) 48×80 mm. 2500r. As No. 2457; (b) 48×92 mm. 2500r. As No. 2464	4·75	4·25

631 Monument at Blitar and Museum, Bogor

1998. 55th Anniv of Formation of Volunteer National Armed Forces (independence fighters).

2467	**631** 700r.+100r. mult	80	60

632 Australian White-eyed Duck

1998. Waterfowl (2nd series). Multicoloured.

2468	250r. Type **632**	50	35
2469	500r. Pacific black duck	65	45
2470	700r. Grey teal	80	60
2471	1000r. Cotton goose	95	70
2472	1500r. Green pygmy goose	1·30	95
2473	2500r. Indian whistling duck	1·60	1·20
2474	3500r. Wandering whistling duck	2·40	1·80
MS2475	45×83 mm. 5000r. Type **632**	4·75	4·25

1998. Traditional Dances (7th series). As T **506**. Multicoloured.

2476	300r. Oreng oreng gae dance, Sulawesi Tenggara (Southeast Celebes)	30	25
2477	500r. Persembahan dance, Bengkulu	50	35
2478	700r. Kipas (fan) dance, Riau	65	45
2479	1000r. Srimpi dance, Yogyakarta	80	60
2480	2000r. Pasambahan, Sumatera Barat (West)	1·30	95
MS2481	48×80 mm. 5000r. As No. 2480	3·50	3·00

633 Water Wheel and Power Lines

1999. Year of Creation and Engineering. Multicoloured.

2482	500r. Type **633**	50	35
2483	700r. Water pipe and pipe network in valley	65	45

634 Throwing the Shot

1999. Seventh Far East and South Pacific Games for Disabled Persons, Bangkok. Multicoloured.

2484	500r. Type **634**	50	35
2485	500r. Medal and wheelchair	50	35

635 Emblem

1999. 50th Anniv of Garuda Indonesia (state airline). Multicoloured.

2486	500r. Type **635**	50	35
2487	700r. Jet engine	65	45
2488	2000r. Pilot, stewardess and airplane	1·30	95

1999. Folk Tales (2nd series). As T **611**. Multicoloured. (a) *Lake Toba.*

2489	500r. Man and yellow fish	50	35
2490	500r. Man proposing to woman	50	35
2491	500r. Woman giving food for father to son Sam and Sam eating it	50	35
2492	500r. Wife turning back into a fish	50	35
2493	500r. Samosir Island and Lake Toba	50	35

(b) *Banjarmasin.*

2494	500r. Rebels and contenders to throne	50	35
2495	500r. Local governors crown Prince Samudera	50	35
2496	500r. Tumenggung sends fleet to Samudera's capital, Bandar Masih	50	35
2497	500r. Samudera and Tumenggung meet on board ship	50	35
2498	500r. Ships in Banjarmasin Harbour	50	35

(c) *Buleleng.*

2499	500r. I Gusti Gede Paseken leaving with guards for Den Bukit	50	35
2500	500r. Forest giant appearing to I Gusti Gede Paseken	50	35
2501	500r. I Gusti Gede Paseken lifting stranded ship	50	35
2502	500r. I Gusti Gede Paseken arriving before King of Den Bukit	50	35
2503	500r. Procession in kingdom of Buleleng	50	35

(d) *Woiram.*

2504	500r. Woiram teaching archery to Woiwallytmang and with wife Donadebu	50	35
2505	500r. Mesan and Mecy looking for shrimps	50	35
2506	500r. Woiram cursing Demontin village	50	35
2507	500r. Woiwallytmang and Mecy clinging to tree trunk	50	35
2508	500r. Woiram's footprints in rock	50	35
MS2509	75×66 mm. 5000r. As No. 2493	3·50	3·00

Nos. 2489/2508 were issued together, *se-tenant*, forming a composite design.

636 Malang Apple

1999. "Surabaya 99" National Stamp Exhibition. Sheet 78×58 mm.

MS2510	**636** 5000r. multicoloured	3·50	3·00

637 Eastern Tarsier

1999. "Australia 99" International Stamp Exhibition, Melbourne. Sheet 60×92 mm.

MS2511	**637** 5000r. multicoloured	3·50	3·00

638 *Ascosparassis heinricherii*

1999. Fungi. Multicoloured. (a) T **638** and similar diamond-shaped designs.

2512	500r. Type **638**	40	30
2513	500r. *Mutinus bambusinus*	40	30
2514	500r. *Mycena* sp.	40	30
2515	700r. *Gloephyllum imponens*	65	45
2516	700r. *Microporus xanthopus*	65	45
2517	700r. *Termitomyces eurrhizus*	65	45
2518	1000r. *Boedijnopeziza insititia*	1·10	80
2519	1000r. *Aseroe rubra*	1·10	80
2520	1000r. *Calostoma orirubra*	1·10	80

(b) As Nos. 2512/14 but rectangular designs, size 31×23 mm.

2521	500r. As No. 2513	80	60
2522	500r. As No. 2512	80	60
2523	500r. As No. 2514	80	60

(c) Sheet 62×92 mm.

MS2524	5000r. *Termitomyces eurrhizus* (different) (24½×41 mm)	3·25	2·75

639 Doctor and Patients outside Surgery

1999. Public Health Care Insurance.

2525	**639** 700r. multicoloured	80	60

640 *Dendrobium abang betawi*

1999. "iBRA 99" International Stamp Exhibition, Nuremberg, Germany. Sheet 63×98 mm.

MS2526	**640** 5000r. multicoloured	3·50	3·00

641 Y2K "Bug"

1999. Millennium Bug (computer programming fault). Multicoloured.

2527	500r. Type **641**	80	60
2528	500r. Robot exploding	80	60

Nos. 2527/8 were issued together, *se-tenant*, forming a composite design.

642 Chrysoprase

1999. "Indonesia 2000" International Stamp Exhibition, Bandung (3rd issue). Gemstones. Multicoloured.

2529	500r. Type **642**	50	35
2530	1000r. Smoky quartz	80	60
2531	2000r. Blue opal	1·40	1·10
MS2532	80×48 mm. 4000r. Silicified coral	3·25	2·75

MS2533 Two sheets. (a) 80×48 mm. 4000r. Javan jade; (b) 122×160 mm. Nos. 2529 ×4, 2530 ×2, 2531 ×2 plus stamps as in Nos. MS2532 and MS2533b   24·00   21·00

643 People carrying Banner

1999. General Election. Multicoloured.
2534		1000r. Type **643**	95	70
2535		1000r. Ballot box and map of Indonesia	95	70

Nos. 2534/5 were issued together, *se-tenant*, forming a composite design.

644 Girl in Blanket and People walking through Water

1999. Environmental Protection. Ecophila Stamp Day. Multicoloured.
2536		500r. Type **644**	30	25
2537		1000r. Boy swimming with duck, plant and berry	95	70
2538		2000r. Elderly woman drinking from jug	1·90	1·40

MS2539 79×46 mm. 3000r. As No. 2537   3·25   2·75

645 Prambanan Temple

1999. "Philexfrance 99" International Stamp Exhibition, Paris. Sheet 59×94 mm.
MS2540 **645** 5000r. multicoloured   4·75   4·25

646 Nurses helping Children

1999. Red Cross.
2541	**646**	1000r. multicoloured	95	70

647 Frans Kaisiepo (Governor of Irian Jaya, 1964)

1999. National Heroes and Heroines.
2542	**647**	500r. brown & cinnamon	40	30
2543	-	500r. brown & cinnamon	40	30
2544	-	500r. brown & cinnamon	40	30
2545	-	500r. brown & cinnamon	40	30

DESIGNS: No. 2543, Maria Walanda Maramis (founder of "PIKAT" (women's education organization, 1917)); 2544, Dr. W. Z. Johannes (founder of Indonesian Christian Party, 1942); 2545, Martha Christina Tijahahu (revolutionary).

648 Rabbit

1999. "CHINA 99" International Stamp Exhibition, Beijing. Sheet 81×60 mm.
MS2546 **648** 5000r. multicoloured   4·75   4·25

649 University Building, 1949

1999. 50th Anniv of Gadjah Mada University, Yogyakarkta. Multicoloured.
2547		500r. Type **649**	40	30
2548		1000r. University facade, 1999	95	70

650 Woman painting Parasol

1999. International Year of the Elderly Person.
2549	**650**	500r. multicoloured	65	45

651 Batik Design, Cirebon

1999. Batik Designs. Different Batik designs. Multicoloured.
2550		500r. Type **651**	80	60
2551		500r. Madura	80	60
2552		500r. Yogyakarta	2·40	1·20
2553		500r. Jambi	2·40	1·20

652 Pillar Box, Postman and Kantoon Post Office (½-size illustration)

1999. 125th Anniv of Universal Postal Union. Multicoloured.
2554		500r. Type **652**	40	30
2555		500r. Modern postal building, motorcycle postman and pillar box	40	30
2556		1000r. Pillar box, left-hand side of Kantoon Post Office and postman on horseback (30×31 mm)	40	30
2557		1000r. Motorcycle postman, modern postal building and pillar box (30×31 mm)	40	30

653 Dog and Puppy

1999. Domestic Animals. Multicoloured.
2558		500r. Type **653**	50	35
2559		500r. Cockerel, hen and chick	50	35
2560		500r. Cat	50	35
2561		500r. Rabbits	50	35
2562		1000r. Feral rock pigeon (20×50 mm)	95	70
2563		1000r. Geese and gosling (20×50 mm)	95	70

MS2564 79×47 mm. 4000r. As No. 2561   3·75   3·25

Nos. 2558/9, 2560/1 and 2562/3 respectively were issued together, *se-tenant*, showing the composite design of a garden.

654 Globe, Diary and Clock Face

1999. New Millennium. Multicoloured.
2565		1000r. Type **654**	95	70
2566		1000r. "2000" and child's face	95	70

MS2567 Two sheets, each 86×57 mm. (a) 20000r. As Type **654**; (b) 20000r. As No. 2566   30·00   27·00

655 Satellite and Fishes

2000. Year of Technology. Multicoloured.
2568		500r. Type **655**	40	30
2569		1000r. Greenhouse and plant	1·20	85

656 University Campus, Salemba

2000. 50th Anniv of University of Indonesia. Multicoloured.
2570		500r. Type **656**	40	30
2571		1000r. University building, Depok	1·20	85

2000. Folk Tales (3rd series). As T **611**. Multicoloured. (a) *Tapak Tuan.*
2572		500r. Dragon finding baby on shore	75	55
2573		500r. Girl meeting other people	75	55
2574		500r. Dragon attacking boat and man	75	55
2575		500r. Man and dragon fighting	75	55
2576		500r. Dead dragon	75	55
		(b) *Batu Ballah.*		
2577		500r. Mak Risah and children	75	55
2578		500r. Children playing	75	55
2579		500r. Mak Risah saddened by her children	75	55
2580		500r. Mak Risah being swallowed by stone	75	55
2581		500r. Mak Risah Rock	75	55
		(c) *Sawerigading.*		
2582		500r. Sariwegading proposing marriage to twin sister	75	55
2583		500r. We Tanriabeng refusing marriage	75	55
2584		500r. Sariwegdaing in stern of boat	75	55
2585		500r. Bow of boat and wedding	75	55
2586		500r. Bulupolole Mountain	75	55
		(d) *7 Putri Kahyangan.*		
2587		500r. Prince hiding wings and angel weeping	75	55
2588		500r. Prince and angel with their children and angel flying away from Earth	75	55
2589		500r. Prince flying on eagle's back to reclaim wife	75	55
2590		500r. Angel refusing to return to Earth	75	55
2591		500r. Prince wearing magical crown	75	55

MS2592 84×61 mm. 5000r. As No. 2576   5·25   4·75

Nos. 2572/91 were issued together, *se-tenant*, forming a composite design.

657 Prehnite

2000. "Indonesia 2000" International Stamp Exhibition, Bandung (4th issue). Gemstones. Multicoloured.
2593		500r. Type **657**	75	55
2594		1000r. Chalcedony	1·20	85
2595		2000r. Volcanic obsidian	2·30	1·70

MS2596 80×48 mm. 5000r. Jasperized limestone   6·25   5·75

MS2597 Two sheets. (a) 80×48 mm. 5000r. Copper jasper; (b) 121×156 mm. No. 2593 ×4, 2594 ×2, 2595 ×2 plus stamps as in MS2596 and MS2597a   31·00   28·00

658 I Brewok (Gun-Gun)

2000. Cartoon Characters. Each black and red.
2598		500r. Type **658**	60	45
2599		500r. "Pak Tuntung" (Basuki)	60	45
2600		500r. "Pak Bei" (Masdi Sunardi)	60	45
2601		500r. "Mang Ohle" (Didin D. Basuni)	60	45
2602		500r. "Panji Koming" (Dwi Koendoro)	60	45

659 Emblem and Weather Chart

2000. 50th Anniv of World Meteorological Organization.
2603	**659**	500r. multicoloured	75	55

660 King Dragon

2000. World Youth Stamp Exhibition and 13th Asian Stamp Exhibition, Bangkok. Sheet 79×49 mm.
MS2604 **660** 5000r. multicoloured 5·75   5·25

661 Cycling

2000. 15th National Sports Week. Multicoloured.
2605		500r. Type **661**	75	55
2606		1000r. Canoeing	1·20	85
2607		2000r. High-jumping	1·90	1·40

662 Coelacanth

2000. "Stamp Show 2000" International Stamp Exhibition, London. Sheet 78×54 mm.
MS2608 **662** 5000r. multicoloured   5·25   4·75

663 Red-footed Booby's on Nest

2000. Environmental Protection. Ecophila Stamp Day. Multicoloured.
2609		500r. Type **663**	60	45
2610		1000r. Monkey	1·30	1·00
2611		2000r. Fishes	2·75	2·00

MS2612 68×52 mm. 4000r. As No. 2610   4·50   4·00

664 Boxing

2000. Olympic Games, Sydney. Multicoloured.
2613		500r. Type **664**	40	30
2614		500r. Judo	40	30
2615		500r. Badminton	75	55
2616		1000r. Weightlifting	75	55
2617		2000r. Swimming	1·50	1·10
2618		2000r. Running	1·50	1·10

MS2619 84×51 mm. 5000r. As No. 2616   5·75   5·25

665 Komodo Dragon

2000. Endangered Species. The Komodo Dragon (*Varanus komodoensis*). Multicoloured.
2620		500r. Type **665**	95	70
2621		500r. Two dragons fighting	95	70
2622		500r. On branch	95	70
2623		500r. Two dragons walking	95	70

MS2624 101×56 mm. 2500r. As Type **665**; 2500r. As No. 2621   7·75   7·00

666 President Abdurrahman Wahid

2000. President and Vice-President. Multicoloured.
2625		1000r. Type **666**	1·20	85
2626		1000r. Vice-President Megawati Soekarnoputri	1·20	85

667 *Rhythmic Gymnastics*

2000. "Olymphilex 2000" Stamp Exhibition, Sydney. Sheet 52×79 mm.
MS2627 **667** 5000r. multicoloured   7·25   6·75

2000. Waterfowl (3rd series). As T **632**. Multicoloured.
2628   800r. Indian whistling duck (*Dendrocygna javanica*)   2·10   1·60
2629   900r. Australian white-eyed duck (*Aythya australis*)   2·50   1·80

668 Couple from D. I. Aceh

2000. Regional Costumes. Showing couples wearing traditional costumes from different regions. Multicoloured.
2630   900r. Type **668**   95   70
2631   900r. Jambi   95   70
2632   900r. Banten   95   70
2633   900r. D. I. Yogyakarta   95   70
2634   900r. Kalimantan Tengah   95   70
2635   900r. Sulawesi Tenggara   95   70
2636   900r. Nusa Tenggara Timur   95   70
2637   900r. Sumatera Utara   95   70
2638   900r. Bengkulu   95   70
2639   900r. D. K. I. Jakarta   95   70
2640   900r. Jawa Timur   95   70
2641   900r. Kalimantan Timur   95   70
2642   900r. Sulawesi Selatan   95   70
2643   900r. Maluku   95   70
2644   900r. Sumatera Barat   95   70
2645   900r. Sumatera Selatan   95   70
2646   900r. Jawa Barat   95   70
2647   900r. Kalimantan Barat   95   70
2648   900r. Sulawesi Utara   95   70
2649   900r. Bali   95   70
2650   900r. Maluku Utara   95   70
2651   900r. Riau   95   70
2652   900r. Lampung   95   70
2653   900r. Jawa Tengah   95   70
2654   900r. Kalimantan Selatan   95   70
2655   900r. Sulawesi Tengah   95   70
2656   900r. Nusa Tenggara Barat   95   70
2657   900r. Irian Jaya   95   70

669 Chairil Anwar (poet)

2000. Personalities. Multicoloured.
2658   900r. Type **669**   95   70
2659   900r. Ibu Sud (children's song writer)   95   70
2660   900r. Bing Slamet (entertainer)   95   70
2661   900r. S. Sudjojono (artist)   95   70
2662   900r. I. Ketut Maria (actor)   95   70
MS2663 62×2 mm. 4000r. Chairil Anwar (different) (vert)   4·50   4·00

670 Hand holding 1989 500r. Endangered Species Stamp

2000. Communications. Multicoloured.
2664   800r. Type **670**   75   55
2665   900r. Satellite, map, television and letter (horiz)   95   70
2666   1000r. Globe and computer monitor   1·20   85
2667   4000r. Airplane, globe and computer   3·50   2·50

671 Pluto

2001. The Solar System. Multicoloured.
2668   900r. Type **671**   95   70
2669   900r. Neptune   95   70
2670   900r. Uranus   95   70
2671   900r. Saturn   95   70
2672   900r. Jupiter   95   70
2673   900r. Mars   95   70
2674   900r. Earth   95   70
2675   900r. Venus   95   70
2676   900r. Mercury   95   70
2677   900r. Sun   95   70
MS2678 120×71 mm. 5000r. Sun (different)   4·75   4·25

2001. Folk Tales (4th series). As T **611**. Multicoloured. (a) *Batang Tuaka.*
2679   900r. Two snakes fighting and Tuaka with stone   75   55
2680   900r. Tuaka selling stone to merchant in Tumasik Port   75   55
2681   900r. Tuaka as a successful merchant with his wife   75   55
2682   900r. Mother cursing Tuaka and his wife   75   55
2683   900r. Tuaka and his wife become birds   75   55

(b) *Si Pitung.*
2684   900r. Si Pitung and gang stealing money from Dutch sympathizers   75   55
2685   900r. Si Pitung's gang leaving money for villagers   75   55
2686   900r. Dutch ruler fighting Si Pitung   75   55
2687   900r. Villagers mourning dead Si Pitung   75   55
2688   900r. Si Pitung Mosque   75   55

(c) *Terusan Nusa.*
2689   900r. Tambing finding and eating dragon's egg   75   55
2690   900r. Tambing turning into dragon   75   55
2691   900r. Dragon (Tambing) eating all the fish in the river   75   55
2692   900r. Tambing dying after eating his own tail   75   55
2693   900r. Empty river   75   55

(d) *Ile Mauraja.*
2694   900r. Raja dreaming   75   55
2695   900r. Raja receiving cotton seeds from bearded man   75   55
2696   900r. Raja and wife   75   55
2697   900r. Snake on bed, burning village and snakes causing upheaval of village   75   55
2698   900r. Mountain formed by village   75   55
MS2699 84×61 mm. 5000r. No. 2686   4·75   4·25

Nos. 2679/98 were issued together, *se-tenant*, forming a composite design.

672 Arsa Wijaya, Bali

2001. Traditional Masks. Showing left (a) or right (b) sides of masks. Multicoloured.
2700   500r. Type **672**   40   30
2701   500r. Arsa Wijaya (b)   40   30
2702   800r. Asmat, Irian Jaya (a)   60   45
2703   800r. Asmat (b)   60   45
2704   800r. Cirebon, Jawa Barat (a)   60   45
2705   800r. Cirebon (b)   60   45
2706   900r. Hudoq, Kalimantan Timur (a)   75   55
2707   900r. Hudoq (b)   75   55
2708   900r. Wayang Wong, Yogyakarta (a)   75   55
2709   900r. Wayang Wong (b)   75   55
MS2710 61×96 mm. 5000r. No. 2706   5·25   4·75

Nos. 2700/1, 2702/3, 2704/5, 2706/7 and 2708/9 were issued together, *se-tenant*, each pair forming a composite design.

673 Beduk

2001. Traditional Instruments. Multicoloured.
2711   900r. Type **673**   95   70
2712   900r. Bende (bronze drum)   95   70
2713   900r. Kentongan (percussion)   95   70
2714   900r. Nafiri (horn)   95   70

674 Bouquet

2001. Greetings Stamps. Multicoloured.
2715   800r. Type **674**   60   45
2716   900r. Rose   75   55
2717   1000r. Bouquet of orange roses and leaves   95   70
2718   1500r. Large white flower and dark green leaf   1·20   85
2719   2000r. Bouquet of yellow flowers with pink bow   1·50   1·10
2720   4000r. Amaryllis flower and ribbon   3·25   2·10
2721   5000r. Table decoration and candles   3·75   2·30
2722   10000r. White flower with yellow centre   7·75   5·75

675 Children and Fish (Surayadi)

2001. World Environment Day. Winning entries in Stamp Design Competition (Nos. 2723, 2725). Multicoloured.
2723   800r. Type **675**   75   55
2724   900r. Boys feeding deer   85   65
2725   1000r. Boy swimming with turtle (Lambok Hutabarat)   95   70
MS2726 82×50 mm. 3000r. As No. 2724   5·75   5·25

676 Youthful Sukarno wearing Turban

2001. Birth Centenary of Dr. Ahmed Sukarno (Bung Karno) (nationalist leader and first president). Multicoloured.
2727   500r. Type **676**   60   45
2728   800r. As young man wearing collar and tie   75   55
2729   900r. Wearing high-necked jacket   95   70
2730   1000r. Wearing uniform with lapel badges   1·20   85
MS2731 138×59 mm. 5000r. Giving speech   5·25   4·75

677 Policeman guiding Children across the Road

2001. Indonesian Police Force. Multicoloured.
2732   1000r. Type **677**   95   70
2733   1000r. Helicopter and women police officers giving directions   95   70

678 Scouts raising Flag

2001. National Scout Jamboree, Banyumas, Java. Multicoloured.
2734   1000r. Type **678**   95   70
2735   1000r. Erecting tent   95   70

Nos. 2734/5 were issued together, *se-tenant*, forming a composite design.

679 Kaki Siapa (blind man's buff)

2001. National Children's Day. Children's Games. Multicoloured.
2736   800r. Type **679**   60   45
2737   900r. Erang Bambu (stilt walking)   75   55
2738   1000r. Dakon (counting game)   95   70
2739   2000r. Kuda Pelepah Pisang (hobby horses)   1·50   1·10

No. 2740 is vacant.

680 Sunflower

2001. Philanippon '01 International Stamp Exhibition. Sheet 93×46 mm.
MS2741 **680** 10000r. multicoloured   9·50   8·50

681 Dr. R. Soeharso (founder) and Operating Theatre

2001. 50th Anniv of Dr. R. Soeharso Orthopaedic Hospital.
2742   **681**   1000r. multicoloured   1·30   1·00

682 Makasaar Post Office

2001. Post Office Architecture. Showing Post Office building. Multicoloured.
2743   800r. Type **682**   95   70
2744   900r. Bandung   95   70
2745   1000r. Balikpapan   95   70
2746   2000r. Padang   75   55

683 Perahu (boat)

2001. Traditional Transport. Multicoloured.
2747   1000r. Type **683**   95   70
2748   1000r. Becak Dayung (tricycle rickshaw)   1·20   85
2749   1000r. Andong (horse-drawn taxi)   1·90   1·40

684 Rose Quartz

2001. Gemstones. Multicoloured.
2750   800r. Type **684**   75   55
2751   900r. Brecciated Jasper   85   65
2752   1000r. Malachite   95   70
MS2753 80×47 mm. 5000r. Diamond   5·25   4·75

685 Children encircling Globe

2001. United Nations Year of Dialogue among Civilizations.
2754   **685**   1000r. multicoloured   95   70

686 *Agestrata dehaan*

2001. Insects. Multicoloured.

2755	800r. Type **686**	75	55
2756	900r. *Mormolyce phyllodes*	85	65
2757	1000r. *Batocera rosenbergi*	95	70
2758	1000r. *Chrysochroa buqueti*	95	70
2759	2000r. *Chalcosoma Caucasus*	2·10	1·60
MS2760	61×90 mm. 5000r. No. 2759	5·25	4·75

2002. Folk Tales (5th series). As T **611**. Multicoloured. (a) *Pulau Kembaro, Sumatera Selatan.*

2761	1000r. Two women	95	70
2762	1000r. Man and woman	95	70
2763	1000r. Boat sinking	95	70
2764	1000r. Man and woman stand-ing in boat	95	70
2765	1000r. Serpent, boat and bridge	95	70

(b) *Nyi Roro Kidul, Jogjakarta.*

2766	1000r. Prabu Siliwangi, Dewi Kaita and harem	95	70
2767	1000r. Dewi Kaita and mother changing	95	70
2768	1000r. Cast out of palace	95	70
2769	1000r. Dewi Kaita changing to Nyi Roro Kidul	95	70
2770	1000r. Sea	95	70

(c) *Aji Tatin, Kalimantan Timur.*

2771	1000r. Palm tree, woman and man with arm outstretched	95	70
2772	1000r. Woman, bird and boat	95	70
2773	1000r. Woman with hand to head	95	70
2774	1000r. Boat breaking	95	70
2775	1000r. Sun and bird	95	70

(d) *Danau Tondano, Sulawesi Utara.*

2776	1000r. Woman seated	95	70
2777	1000r. Man holding spear	95	70
2778	1000r. Man and woman dressed as man	95	70
2779	1000r. Three men under trees	95	70
2780	1000r. Tree and island	95	70
MS2781	108×61 mm. 5000r. No. 2765	5·25	4·75

Nos. 2761/5, 2766/70, 2771/5, 2776/80 respectively were issued together, *se-tenant*, forming a composite design.

687 Player with Shirt over Head

2002. World Cup Football Championships, Japan and South Korea. Multicoloured.

2782	1000r. Type **687**	95	70
2783	1500r. Players in front of goal	1·50	1·10
2784	2000r. Player	2·10	1·60
MS2785	52×80 mm. 5000r. No. 2784	5·75	5·25

688 Outline of Two Women

2002. 25th Anniv of Cancer Foundation.

2786	**688**	1000r. multicoloured	1·30	1·00

689 Aboriginal Man holding Cell Phone

2002. Communications. Multicoloured.

2787	1000r. Type **689**	1·10	80
2788	1000r. Woman holding hand set	1·10	80
2789	1000r. Computer, satellite and disc	1·10	80
2790	1000r. Satellite above globe	1·10	80

690 *Symphyllia radians*

2002. Marine Life. Ecophila. Multicoloured.

2791	1000r. Type **690**	95	70
2792	1000r. *Charonia tritonis*	95	70
2793	1500r. *Acanthaster planci*	1·50	1·10
2794	1500r. Polka dot grouper (*Cromileptes altivelis*)	1·50	1·10
2795	2000r. Blue tang (*Paracanthurus hepatus*)	2·10	1·60
2796	2000r. *Tridacna gigas*	2·10	1·60
MS2797	(a) 97×170 mm. Nos. 2791/5; (b) 60×91 mm. 5000r. No. 2793	14·50	13·00

691 Boy writing and Men dancing

2002. Nanggroe Aceh Province, Darussalam. Multicoloured.

2798	1500r. Type **691**	1·50	1·10
2799	3500r. Mosque	3·75	2·75

692 Family

2002. National Family Day.

2800	**692**	1000r. multicoloured	1·30	1·00

693 Solar Eclipse and Olympiad Emblem

2002. 33rd International Physics Olympiad, Bali. Multicoloured.

2801	1000r. Type **693**	1·10	80
2802	1000r. Colour spectrum and symbols	1·10	80

694 Bird-shaped Kite

2002. Layang-Layang. Kite Flying. Multicoloured.

2803	1000r. Type **694**	1·10	80
2804	1000r. Lion	1·10	80
2805	1000r. Rhomboid	1·10	80
2806	1000r. Winged kite	1·10	80
2807	1000r. Box and glider kites	1·10	80
MS2808	79×49 mm. 5000r. No. 2803	5·25	4·75

Nos. 2803/7 were issued together, se-tenant, forming a composite design.

695 Noni (*Morinda citrifolia*)

2002. Fruit. Multicoloured.

2809	300r. Type **695**	40	30
2810	500r. Mango (*Mangifera indica*)	60	45
2811	1500r. Star fruit (*Averrhoa carambola*)	1·50	1·10
2812	3000r. *Durio zibethinus*	3·00	2·10

696 Tari Pajaga Dancer, Salawesi Selatan

2002. Philakorea 2002 International Stamp Exhibition, Seoul. Sheet 48×80 mm.

MS2813	696 7000r. multicoloured	7·00	6·50

697 Mohammad Hatta

2002. Birth Centenary of Mohammad Hatta (first vice-president). Multicoloured.

2814	1000r. Type **697**	1·10	80
2815	1000r. Wearing high-necked jacket	1·10	80
2816	1500r. Wearing light jacket and dark tie	1·50	1·10
2817	1500r. Wearing light jacket and tie	1·50	1·10
MS2818	137×60 mm. 5000r. Wearing light suit and open neck shirt	7·00	6·50

699 Stylised Flowers (*Hibiscus rosa-sinensis*)

2002. Amphilex 2002 International Stamp Exhibition, Amsterdam. Sheet 92×47 mm.

MS2821	699 7000r. multicoloured	9·25	8·50

700 Soldier

2002. Jogja Panfila 2002 International Stamp Exhibition, Jakarta. Sheet 51×85 mm.

MS2822	700 6000r. multicoloured	8·00	7·25

701 *Cat (Popo Iskander)*

2002. Art. Multicoloured.

2823	1000r. (1) Type **701**	1·20	85
2824	1000r. (2) *Guerrilla Sentry, Seko* (S. Sudjojono)	1·20	85
2825	1500r. (3) *Women and child* (Hendra Gunawan) (vert)	1·70	1·30
2826	1500r. (4) *Gaututkaca, Prigiwa and Prigiwati* (R. Basoeki Abdullah) (vert)	1·70	1·30

702 Hagen's Lanzenotter (*Trimeresurus hageni*)

2002. Flora and Fauna. Multicoloured.

2827	1000r. Type **702**	95	70
2828	1000r. *Rafflesia micropylora*	95	70
2829	1500r. Leopard (*Panthera pardus*)	1·30	1·00
2830	1500r. *Terminalia catappa*	1·30	1·00
2831	2000r. *Papilionanthe hookeriana*	1·70	1·30
2832	2000r. Water monitor (*Varanus salvator*)	1·70	1·30
MS2833	50×83 mm. 3500r. No. 2829 Perf and Imperf	4·50	4·00

Nos. 2827/8, 2829/30 and 2831/2 respectively were is-sued, together, *se-tenant*, forming a composite design.

703 Bull

2002. Espana 2002 International Stamp Exhibition, Salamanca. Sheet 83×50 mm.

MS2834	**703** 7000r. multicoloured	6·25	5·75

704 Buildings, Data Stream and Globe

2002. "LKBN Antara" National News Agency.

2835	**704**	1500r. multicoloured	1·30	1·00

705 Party Food

2003. Greeting Stamps. "Happy Birthday".

2836	1500r. Type **705**	1·50	1·10
2837	1500r. Birthday cake	1·50	1·10

2003. Folk Tales (6th series). As T **611**. Multicoloured. (a) *Danau Ranau.*

2838	1500r. Man holding golden egg and couple near cooking fire	1·10	80
2839	1500r. Men, dragon and weep-ing woman	1·10	80
2840	1500r. Woman riding dragon	1·10	80
2841	1500r. Sleeping woman and dragon holding necklace	1·10	80
2842	1500r. Lake	1·10	80

Nos. 2838/57 were issued together, *se-tenant*, forming a composite design.

(b) *Kongga Owose.*

2843	1500r. Eagle carrying off cow	1·10	80
2844	1500r. Eagle attacking villagers	1·10	80
2845	1500r. Man spearing eagle	1·10	80
2846	1500r. Eagle, injured man, and villagers	1·10	80
2847	1500r. Hills, estuary and rocky coastline	1·10	80

(c) *Putri Gading Cempaku.*

2848	1500r. Woman and man wear-ing tall headdress	1·10	80
2849	1500r. Man looking back at woman	1·10	80
2850	1500r. Men with raised arms and distressed woman	1·10	80
2851	1500r. Man, couple under thatched roof and woman wearing jewelled headdress	1·10	80
2852	1500r. Birds and sandy coastline	1·10	80

(d) *Putri Mandalika Nyale.*

2853	1500r. King and Princess	1·10	80
2854	1500r. Princess and suitors bearing gifts	1·10	80
2855	1500r. Princess and suitors on beach	1·10	80
2856	1500r. Princess in sea	1·10	80
2857	1500r. Fishing	1·10	80
MS2858	106×62 mm. 5000r. No. 2842	4·50	4·00

706 Billiard Player

2003. 22nd South East Asian Games, Vietnam. Multicoloured.

2859	1000r. Type **706**	95	70
2860	1500r. Rowers	1·50	1·10
2861	2500r. Gymnast	2·30	1·70

707 Mount Kerinci

2003. Volcanoes. 50th Anniv of Ascent of Mount Everest (**MS**2867). Volcanoes. Multicoloured.

2862	500r. Type **708**	60	45
2863	1000r. Merapi	95	70
2864	1000r. Krakatau	95	70
2865	1000r. Tambora	95	70
2866	2000r. Ruang	1·90	1·40

MS2867 181×116 mm. Nos. 2862/6, each×2 plus 2 labels — 11·50 — 10·00

708 Moon

2003. Astronomy. Multicoloured.

2868	1000r. Type **708**	75	55
2869	1000r. Earth and Mars	75	55
2870	1000r. Andromeda galaxy	75	55
2871	1500r. Observatory and telescope	1·20	85
2872	1500r. Observatory, Lembang, Java	1·20	85

MS2873 116×67 mm. No. 2872 — 5·00 — 4·50

709 Buildings and Flowers contained in Stylized Banknote

2003. 50th Anniv of Bank Indonesia. Multicoloured.

2874	1000r. Type **709**	95	70
2875	1500r. Teacher, pens and open books	1·30	1·00

710 Sultan Hamengu Buwono IX and Robert Baden-Powell (image scaled to 59% of original size)

2003. Pathfinder Scouts.

2876	**710** 1500r. multicoloured	1·20	85

711 Pillow Fighting on Pole over Water

2003. Traditional Games. Multicoloured.

2877	1000r. Type **711**	75	55
2878	1000r. Pole climbing	75	55
2879	1500r. Sack racing (horiz)	1·20	85
2880	1500r. Teams of three racing on planks (horiz)	1·20	85

712 Dancers

2003. Emmitan Philex 2003 Stamp Exhibition. Seven sheets containing T **712** and similar vert design showing paintings by Srihadi Soedarsono. Multicoloured.

MS2881 107×142 mm. 3000r.×4, Type **712**; Moonlit landscape, each×2 (10th Asean Postal Business Meeting, Surabaya) — 12·50 — 11·00

MS2882 Six sheets, each 107×82 mm. Five sheets (a/e) 3000r.×2, Type **712**; Moonlit landscape (each with different margin colours). (f) 107×82 mm Type **712**; Moonlit landscape. Imperf. Set of 6 sheets — 38·00 — 33·00

713 Woman leading Procession (Mome'Ati, Gorontalo)

2003. Tourism. Multicoloured.

2883	1000r. Type **713**	1·20	85
2884	1000r. Man carried in sedan chair (Jou Uci Sabea, Maluku Utara)	1·20	85
2885	1500r. Boats (Muang Jong, Bangka Belitung)	1·70	1·30
2886	1500r. Seated men (Seba Baduy, Banten)	1·70	1·30

MS2887 113×74 mm. No. 2885 — 5·00 — 4·50

714 Elephant Football, Lampung

2003. Bangkok 2003 International Stamp Exhibition. Sheet 88×25 mm.

MS2888 **714** 8000r. multicoloured — 90 — 90

715 Clasped Hands

2003. Greetings Stamps. Multicoloured.

2889	1000r. Type **715**	1·30	1·00
2890	1500r. Flag and clasped hands	1·50	1·10
2891	1500r. Fish and water lily	1·50	1·10
2892	1500r. Sunflower	1·50	1·10
2893	1500r. Birds	1·50	1·10

716 Anniversary Emblem and Stamps

2003. 75th Anniv of Youth Pledge.

2894	**716** 1500r. multicoloured	1·30	1·00

717 Apis dorsata (bee)

2003. Flora and Fauna. Multicoloured.

2895	1500r. Type **717**	1·20	85
2896	1500r. Freycinetia pseudoinsignis (flower)	1·20	85
2897	1500r. Sia ferox (grasshopper)	1·20	85
2898	1500r. Paphiopedilum mastersianum (orchid)	1·20	85
2899	1500r. Platylomia flavida (insect)	1·20	85
2900	1500r. Osmoxylon palmatum (plant)	1·20	85
2901	1500r. Anaphalis javanica (flower)	1·20	85
2902	1500r. Hierodula vitrea (mantis)	1·20	85
2903	1500r. Saraca declinata (plant)	1·20	85
2904	1500r. Aularches miliaris (insect)	1·20	85
2905	1500r. Butea monosperma (flower)	1·20	85
2906	1500r. Orthetrum testaceum (dragonfly)	1·20	85

MS2907 119×74 mm. 3000r.×2, Nos. 2901 and 2906 — 5·25 — 4·75

718 H. Sutami

2003. Personalities. Each sepia and brown.

2908	2000r. Type **718** (engineer)	1·50	1·10
2909	2000r. R. Roosseno (engineer)	1·50	1·10
2910	2000r. Martinus Putuhena (architect)	1·50	1·10
2911	2000r. Nurtanio Pringgoadisuryo (aviation engineer)	1·50	1·10

719 Styrax benzoin

2004. Flowers. Multicoloured.

2912	1500r. Type **719**	95	70
2913	1500r. Kopsia fruticosa	95	70
2914	1500r. Impatiens tujuhensis	95	70
2915	1500r. Hoya diversifolia	95	70
2916	1500r. Etlingera elatior	95	70
2917	1500r. Dillenia suffruticosa	95	70
2918	1500r. Papilionanthe hookerianum	95	70
2919	1500r. Medinilla speciosa	95	70
2920	1500r. Costus speciosus	95	70
2921	1500r. Melastoma sylvaticum	95	70
2922	1500r. Nelumbo nucifera	95	70
2923	1500r. Begonia robusta	95	70
2924	1500r. Anaphalis longifolia	95	70
2925	1500r. Pisonia grandis	95	70
2926	1500r. Ixora javanica	95	70
2927	1500r. Plumeria acuminate	95	70
2928	1500r. Cassia fistula	95	70
2929	1500r. Calotropis gigantean	95	70
2930	1500r. Dimorphorchis lowii	95	70
2931	1500r. Aeschynanthus radicans	95	70
2932	1500r. Sonneratia caseolaris	95	70
2933	1500r. Rhododendron orbiculatum	95	70
2934	1500r. Passiflora edulis	95	70
2935	1500r. Pterospermum celebricum	95	70
2936	1500r. Quisqualis indica	95	70
2937	1500r. Spathiphyllum commutatum	95	70
2938	1500r. Lilium longifolium	95	70
2939	1500r. Clitoria tematea	95	70
2940	1500r. Pecteilis susannae	95	70
2941	1500r. Grammatophyllum speciosum	95	70

2004. Folk Tales (7th series). As T **611**. Multicoloured. (a) Putri Selaras Pinang Masak.

2942	1500r. Princess	95	70
2943	1500r. Man striking rocks	95	70
2944	1500r. Couple	95	70
2945	1500r. Crowned couple surrounded by cheering crowd	95	70
2946	1500r. Temple	95	70

Nos. 2942/61 were issued together, *se-tenant*, forming a composite design.

(b) Tanjung Lesung.

2947	1500r. Woman and sleeping man	95	70
2948	1500r. Man, horse and dog walking and bathing	95	70
2949	1500r. House, knife, man and turtles	95	70
2950	1500r. Couple and men turning into monkeys	95	70
2951	1500r. Monkey in tree	95	70

2004. (c) Patung Palindo.

2952	1500r. Warrior leading soldiers	95	70
2953	1500r. Battle scene	95	70
2954	1500r. Woman and child, bier, statue and warrior	95	70
2955	1500r. Men toppling statue, fire and battle scene	95	70
2956	1500r. Tilted statue	95	70

(d) Danae Tolire.

2957	1500r. People carrying plants and seated woman	95	70
2958	1500r. Revelry and drunkenness	95	70
2959	1500r. Woman carrying child running from tidal wave	95	70
2960	1500r. Falling woman	95	70
2961	1500r. Lake and mountain	95	70

MS2962 106× 62 mm. 6000r. No. 2950 — 5·75 — 5·25

720 Sail Ship (Maritime Museum, Jakarta)

2004. Museums. Multicoloured.

2963	1500r. Type **720**	95	70
2964	1500r. Dinosaur skeleton (National Geological, Bandgung)	95	70
2965	1500r. Metal artefact (Sri Baduga, Bandgung)	95	70
2966	1500r. Early telephone (Telecommunications, Jakarta)	95	70

721 Voters

2004. Elections. Multicoloured.

2967	1500r. Type **721**	95	70
2968	1500r. Voters placing ballots in ballot box	95	70

722 Gedong Bagoes Oka

2004. Famous Women. Multicoloured.

2969	2500r. Type **722** (teacher and religious reformer)	1·50	1·10
2970	2500r. Ani Idrus (writer and journalist)	1·50	1·10
2971	2500r. Nyonya Meneer (herbal medicine pioneer)	1·50	1·10
2972	2500r. Sandiah (Ibu Kasur) (children's campaigner)	1·50	1·10

723 Swimming

2004. Olympic Games, Athens 2004. Multicoloured.

2973	2500r. Type **723**	1·70	1·30
2974	2500r. High Jump	1·70	1·30
2975	2500r. Hurdling	1·70	1·30

724 Bird, Porpoise and Boat

2004. Marine Preservation. Multicoloured.

2976	1500r. Type **724**	1·20	85
2977	1500r. Shark and turtles	1·20	85

MS2978 103×74 mm. 2500r.×2, Nos. 2976/7 — 3·75 — 3·25

725 Sambal Udang Terung Pipit Kalimantan Barat

2004. Traditional Food. Multicoloured.

2979	1500r. Type **725**	95	70
2980	1500r. Tinotuan Sulawesi Utara	95	70
2981	1500r. Cajebo Sumatera Barat	95	70
2982	1500r. Kare Rajungan Jawa Timur	95	70

726 Kendaraan Presiden R1 Pertama

2004. Presidential Cars. Multicoloured.

2983	2500r. Type **726**	1·50	1·10
2984	2500r. Kendaraan Wakil Presiden R1 Pertama	1·50	1·10

MS2985 105×78 mm. Nos. 2983/4 — 3·75 — 3·25

727 Three Players

2004. Sumsel 2004, Sepaktakraw (ball) Games, Palembang. Multicoloured.

2986	1500r. Type **727**	1·20	85
2987	1500r. Two players	1·20	85

728 *Parkia roxburghii*

2004. Flora and Fauna. Multicoloured.

2988	1500r. Type **728**	95	70
2989	1500r. *Heterometrus cynaneus*	95	70
2990	1500r. *Cinnmomun sintoc* (inscr "sintok")	95	70
2991	1500r. *Scolopendra subspinipes*	95	70
2992	1500r. *Alstonia scholaris*	95	70
2993	1550r. *Gryllotalpa hirsute*	95	70
MS2994	120×75 mm. 3000r.×2, Nos. 2988/9	3·75	3·25

729 Teacher and Pupils

2004. National Teachers' Day. Multicoloured.

2995	1500r. Type **729**	95	70
2996	1500r. Male teacher and pupils	95	70

730 Dancers (*Setagen Rhythm*)

2004. Soerabaija 2004 Stamp Exhibition, Surabaya. Seven sheets containing T **730** and similar horiz designs showing paintings of dancers by Sunaryo. Multicoloured.

MS2997	Three sheets, each 95×94 mm. (a) 5000r. Type **730**; (b) 5000r. *Sebelum Pentas*; (c) 5000r. "*Bercinta*"	14·50	13·00
MS2998	Three sheets, each 95×94 mm. Imperf. (a) 5000r. Type **730**; (b) 5000r. *Sebelum Pentas*; (c) 5000r. *Bercinta*	14·50	13·00
MS2999	128×128 mm. 5000r.×3, Type **730**; *Sebelum Pentas*; *Bercinta*	15·00	14·00

2005. Folk Tales (8th series). As T **611**. Multicoloured. (a) *Lahilote*.

3000	1500r. Man and women bathing	95	70
3001	1500r. Woman and man	95	70
3002	1500r. Women	95	70
3003	1500r. Man, woman and child	95	70
3004	1500r. Invisible foot and footprint	95	70

(b) *Kolam Putri*.

3005	1500r. Older man and young woman on balcony	95	70
3006	1500r. People arguing	95	70
3007	1500r. Castle, cliff, old man, women and fish	95	70
3008	1500r. Old man and deputation	95	70
3009	1500r. Woman and fish	95	70

(c) *Batu Balai*.

3010	1500r. Woman, and man carrying pack	95	70
3011	1500r. Men and ship	95	70
3012	1500r. Couple, small boat and ship	95	70
3013	1500r. Woman begging at couple's feet	95	70
3014	1500r. Rocks and monkey	95	70

(d) *Bulan & Sagu Di Ibuanari*.

3015	1500r. Figure with bow	95	70
3016	1500r. Cutting down trees	95	70
3017	1500r. Climbing steps	95	70
3018	1500r. Falling	95	70

3019	1500r. Trees	95	70
MS3020	106×62 mm. 6000r. No. 3008	3·75	3·25

Nos. 3000/19 were issued together, *se-tenant*, each horizontal strip forming a composite design.

731 "50" and Dove

2005. 50th Anniv of Asia–Africa Conference. Multicoloured.

3021	2500r. Type **731**	1·50	1·10
3022	2500r. Dove, globe and faces	1·50	1·10
MS3023	120×88 mm. As No. 3021	2·30	2·00

732 Face, Map and Flame

2005. National Disaster Fund.

3024	**732** 1500r.+300r. multicoloured	1·30	1·00

The premium was for the benefit of victims of 26 December Tsunami disaster.

733 Stork and Mangroves

2005. Environmental Protection. Multicoloured.

3025	1500r. Type **733**	95	70
3026	1500r. Mangrove tree, roots and fish	95	70
MS3027	77×104 mm. As Nos. 3025/6	1·90	1·70

Nos. 3025/6 were issued together, *se-tenant*, forming a composite design.

734 Nine-masted *Treasure Ship*

2005. 600th Anniv of the Voyages of Zheng He (Ma Sanbao).

3028	**734** 2500r. multicoloured	1·70	1·30
MS3029	110×65 mm. **734** 2500r. multicoloured	4·25	3·75

735 Sayur Tauco

2005. Traditional Foods. Multicoloured.

3030	1500r. Type **735**	95	70
3031	1500r. Soto banjar	95	70
3032	1500r. Nasi timbel	95	70
3033	1500r. Langga roko	95	70

736 Bus, Map and Plug

2005. Energy Conservation. Multicoloured.

3034	1500r. Type **736**	95	70
3035	2000r. Generator, plugs and map	1·20	85
3036	2500r. Map and car	1·50	1·10

737 Ancient Ship (base relief)

2005. Borobudur Ship Expedition (recreating the ancient trading voyages between Indonesia and Africa). Multicoloured.

3037	1500r. Type **737**	95	70
3038	1500r. Reconstructed ship and Buddha head	95	70
MS3039	120×72 mm. As Nos. 3037/8	1·90	1·40

738 President Susilo Bambang Yudhoyono

2005. President and Vice-President. Multicoloured.

3040	1500r. Type **738**	75	55
3041	1500r. Vice-President Jusuf Kalla	75	55
3042	2500r. Type **738**	1·30	1·00
3043	2500r. Vice-President Jusuf Kalla	1·30	1·00
MS3044	122×62 mm. Nos. 3040/1	3·00	2·75

739 Nyawer

2005. National Philatelic Exhibition, Cilegon. Paintings by Sudjana Kerton. Five sheets containing T **739** and similar horiz designs. Multicoloured.

MS3045	133×102 mm. 5000r. Type **739**; 5000r. *Makan Siang*; 5000r. *Wayang Golek*; 8000r. *Tannah Air Indonesia*	12·50	11·50
MS3046	Four sheets, each 115×75 mm. Imperf. (a) 5000r. *Nyawer*. (b) 5000r. *Makan Siang*. (c) 5000r. *Wayang Golek*. (d) 8000r. *Tannah Air Indonesia* Set of 4 sheets	12·50	11·50

740 *Neophocaena phocaenoides*

2005. Fauna and Flora. Multicoloured.

3047	1500r. Type **740**	95	70
3048	1500r. Dugong dugon	95	70
3049	1500r. *Gelidium latifolium*	95	70
3050	1500r. *Halimeda opuntia*	95	70
MS3051	120×74 mm. 1500r.×2, No. 3047; No. 3049	1·90	1·70

2006. Folk Tales (9th series). *Cerita Rakyat*. As T **611**. Multicoloured.

3052	1500r. Bawang, Merah and Bawang Putih	95	70
3053	1500r. Si Kancil	95	70
3054	1500r. Keong Emas	95	70
3055	1500r. Timun Emas	95	70
MS3056	85×120 mm. Nos. 3052/5	3·75	3·25

741 Child and Carriage

2006. Philately Day. Each agate and vermilion (Nos. 3057/70) or multicoloured (Nos. 3071/84).

3057	(1) 1500r. Type **741**	95	70
3058	(2) 1500r. Front wheels and horse	95	70
3059	(3) 1500r. Girl and photos	95	70
3060	(4) 1500r. Kneeling boy and photo of mountains	95	70
3061	(5) 1500r. Seated boy and three photos on floor	95	70
3062	(6) 1500r. Small girl seated	95	70
3063	(7) 1500r. Girl prone	95	70
3064	(8) 1500r. Boy writing	95	70
3065	(9) 1500r. Small boy and crate	95	70
3066	(10) 1500r. Boy making pot	95	70
3067	(11) 1500r. Boy making tall pot	95	70
3068	(12) 1500r. Seated girl and pot with dragons	95	70
3069	(13) 1500r. Small child and decorated pot	95	70
3070	(14) 1500r. Horses	95	70
3071	(15) 1500r. As Type **741**	95	70
3072	(16) 1500r. As No. 3058	95	70

3073	(17) 1500r. As No. 3059	95	70
3074	(18) 1500r. As No. 3060	95	70
3075	(19) 1500r. As No. 3061	95	70
3076	(20) 1500r. As No. 3062	95	70
3077	(21) 1500r. As No. 3063	95	70
3078	(22) 1500r. As No. 3064	95	70
3079	(23) 1500r. As No. 3065	95	70
3080	(24) 1500r. As No. 3066	95	70
3081	(25) 1500r. As No. 3067	95	70
3082	(26) 1500r. As No. 3068	95	70
3083	(27) 1500r. As No. 3069	95	70
3084	(28) 1500r. As No. 3070	95	70

Nos. 3057/8 and 3071/2 were issued in horizontal *se-tenant* pairs, each pair forming a composite design of horse and carriage.

Nos. 3059/64 and 3073/8 were issued in *se-tenant* blocks of six stamps, each block forming a composite design of children and floor map.

Nos. 3065/70 and 3079/84 were also issued in *se-tenant* blocks of six stamps, each block forming a composite design of children and pottery.

742 Emblem, Crowd, Net and Ball

2006. World Cup Football Championship, Germany. Multicoloured. Self-adhesive gum.

3085	(1) 2500r. Type **742**	1·50	1·10
3086	(2) 2500r. Emblem, crowd and ball	1·50	1·10
3087	(3) 2500r. Ball and trophy	1·50	1·10
3088	(4) 2500r. Ball and trophy (different)	1·50	1·10

743 Child

2006. Environmental Protection. Multicoloured.

3089	1500r. Type **743**	95	70
3090	1500r. Flowers, lake and butterfly	95	70
MS3091	105×73 mm. As Nos. 3089/90	3·00	2·75

744 Pempek

2006. Traditional Foods. Multicoloured.

3092	1500r. Type **744**	95	70
3093	1500r. Ayam Betutu	20	20
3094	1500r. Gudeg	20	20
3095	1500r. Aunu Senebre	20	20

745 Kak Mashudi and Campfire Gathering

2006. National Scout Jamboree. 50th Anniv of Asia—Pacific Region Scouts (3097). Multicoloured.

3096	1500r. Type **745**	95	70
3097	1500r. Scouts as jigsaw puzzle	95	70

746 Sultan Agung

2006. Sultans. Multicoloured.

3098	1500r. Type **746**	95	70
3099	1500r. Ma'moen Al Rasyid Perkasa Alamsyah	95	70
3100	1500r. Hasanuddin	95	70
3101	1500r. Adji Mohammed Parikesit	95	70

747 Semar Puppet
(Wayang Golek
traditional theatre),
Java

2006. Puppets. Multicoloured.

3102	2500r. Type **747**	1·50	1·10
3103	2500r. Gasparko puppet, Slovakia	1·50	1·10
MS3104	112×78 mm. As Nos. 3102/3	4·25	4·00

Stamps of a similar design were issued by Slovakia.

747a Singer

2006. Eid ul-Fitr (holiday). Sheet 148×174 mm containing T **747a** and similar horiz designs. Multicoloured.
MS3104a 1500r.×8, Type **747a** (1); Drummer (5); Older woman greeting young woman (2); Man greeting woman (6); Temple (3); Coach (7); Emblem (4); Rickshaw (8) 8·75 8·50

748 *Melipotes carolae*

2006. Newly Discovered Flora and Fauna. Multicoloured.

3105	1500r. Type **748**	95	70
3106	1500r. *Amblyornis flavifrons*	95	70
3107	1500r. *Licuala arbuscula*	95	70
3108	1500r. *Livistona mamberamoensis*	95	70
MS3109	112×78 mm. 2500r.×2, As Nos. 3106/7	3·75	3·50

749 *Panthera pardus*

2006. National Philatelic Exhibition, Bandung 2006. Five sheets, each 123×65 mm containing T **749** and similar horiz design. Multicoloured.
MS3110 2500r.×2, Type **749**; *Bouea macrophylla* 3·00 2·75

The stamps and margins of MS3110 form a composite design.

750 Rattan Basket,
Kalimantan Timur

2006. Crafts. Multicoloured.

3111	1500r. Type **750**	95	70
3112	1500r. Banana leaf pot, Bali	95	70

751 Chinese Zodiac Signs
surrounding Lanterns

2007. Chinese Zodiac. Multicoloured.

3113	1500r. vermilion and lemon	95	70
3114	1500r. vermilion and lemon	95	70

MS3115 Two sheets. (a) 90×90 mm. 6000r. multicoloured. (b) 240×174 mm. 2000r.×12, 6000r. vermilion and lemon 20·00 19·00

DESIGNS: No. 3113 Type **751**; 3114 Zodiac surrounding temple gate. MS3115a As No. 3114 but with temple gate embossed in gold. MS3115b 2000r.×12, Signs of Chinese Zodiac (each 48×32 mm); 6000r. As No. 3114 (96×64 mm). The stamps and margins of No. MS3115b form a composite design.

752 Lion Dance
(China)

2007. Traditional Dances. Multicoloured.

3116	2500r. Type **752**	1·50	1·10
3117	2500r. Dragon dance (Indonesia)	1·50	1·10
MS3118	110×77 mm. Nos. 3116/17	4·25	4·00

Stamps of a similar design were issued by China.

753 Children writing

2007. Literacy. Multicoloured.

3119	1500r. Type **753**	95	70
3120	1500r. Child and adult	95	70

754 Polar Bear's Forehead
and Melting Ice

2007. Environmental Protection. Multicoloured.

3121	1500r. Type **754**	95	70
3122	1500r. Polar bear's lower head and melting ice	95	70
3123	1500r. Burning forest	95	70
3124	1500r. Dead tree	95	70
MS3125	104×74 mm. 2500r.×2, As Nos. 3121/2	3·75	3·50

The stamps and margins of MS3125 form a composite design of a weeping polar bear and melting ice-flows.

755 Young
Footballer and
'SAY NO TO
DRUGS'

2007. International Day against Drug Abuse and Trafficking. Multicoloured.

3126	1500r. Type **755**	95	70
3127	1500r. Young guitarist and 'KATAKAN TIDAK PADA NARKOBA'	95	70

756 Roti Cane and Kari
Kambing

2007. Traditional Foods. Multicoloured.

3128	1500r. Type **756**	95	70
3129	1500r. Gecok	95	70

757 Emblem

2007. Centenary of Scouting. Multicoloured.

3130	1500r. Type **757**	95	70
3131	1500r. Scout	95	70
3132	2500r. As No. 3131	1·50	1·10
3133	2500r. As Type **757**	1·50	1·10

758
*Nepenthes
mirabilis*

2007. Bangkok 2007 International Stamp Exhibition. Two sheets containing T **758** and similar multicoloured design.
MS3134 104×150 mm. VERT: 1500r.×4, Type **758**×4; HORIZ: 1500r.×4, *Nepenthes ampullaria*×4 7·75 7·50
MS3135 107×69 mm. 2500r. Type **758**; 2500r. *Nepenthes ampullaria* 3·50 3·25

759 Fatahillah Museum,
Jakarta

2007. Architecture. 40th Anniv of ASEAN (Association of South-east Asian Nations). Multicoloured.

3136	1500r. Type **759**	95	70
3137	2500r. Secretariat Building, Bandar Seri Begawan, Brunei Darussalam	1·50	1·10
3138	2500r. National Museum, Cambodia	1·50	1·10
3139	2500r. As Type **759**	1·50	1·10
3140	2500r. Traditional house, Laos	1·50	1·10
3141	2500r. Railway Headquarters Building, Malaysia	1·50	1·10
3142	2500r. Yangon Post Office, Union of Myanmar	1·50	1·10
3143	2500r. Malacanang Palace, Manila	1·50	1·10
3144	2500r. National Museum, Singapore	1·50	1·10
3145	2500r. Vimanmek Mansion, Bangkok, Thailand	1·50	1·10
3146	2500r. Presidential Palace, Hanoi, Vietnam	1·50	1·10

Stamps of a similar design were issued by all member countries.

760 Semarang

2007. Mercusuar. Lighthouses. Multicoloured.

3147	1500r. Type **760**	95	70
3148	1500r. Cikoneng	95	70

761 Tiger and Ram

2007. 50th Anniv of Universitas Padjadjaran. Multicoloured.

3149	1500r. Type **761**	95	70
3150	1500r. People	95	70
3151	1500r. Buildings	95	70
3152	1500r. Symbols of education	95	70

Nos. 3147/8 were issued together, *se-tenant*, forming a composite design.

762 *Ornithoptera
aesacus*

2007. Butterflies. Multicoloured.

3153	1500r. Type **762**	95	70
3154	1500r. *Delias kristianiae*	95	70
3155	1500r. *Ornithoptera croesus*	95	70
3156	1500r. *Troides hypolitus*	95	70
MS3157	116×76 mm. 2500r.×2, As No. 3155; As No. 3154	3·75	3·50

2007. Bandung Filex 2007 and Jakarta 2008 International Stamp Exhibitions. Stamps of No. MS3157 surch.
MS3158 5000r.×2, on 2500r.×2 multicoloured 7·00 6·75

764 Ten Pin Bowling

2007. South East Asia Games, Thailand. Multicoloured.

3159	2500r. Type **764**	1·50	1·10
3160	2500r. Futsal	1·50	1·10
3161	2500r. Hammer throwing	1·50	1·10
3162	2500r. Judo	1·50	1·10

765 Prime Minister Djuanda
Kartadiwidjaja and Symbols
of Indonesia

2007. 50th Anniv of Djuanda Declaration. Multicoloured.

3163	1500r. Type **765**	95	70
3164	1500r. Children and islands	95	70
3165	1500r. Djuanda Kartadiwidjaja and archipelago	95	70

766 1600-year-old Inscribed
Stone ('Prasasti Tugu')

2008. Jakarta 2008 International Stamp Exhibition. Sheet 123×165 mm containing T **766** and similar horiz designs. Multicoloured.
MS3166 2500r. Type **766**; 2500r. Vishnu (statue) ('Arca Dewa Vishnu'); 2500r. Inscribed stone ('Prasasti Pradrao'); 2500r. Portugis map of Indonesian Archipelago ('Peta Nusantara Zaman Portugis'); 2500r. Covenant document ('Naskah Perjanjian Sund Kelapa'); 2500r. Portugis vessel ('Kapal Bangsa Portugis'); 10000r. Lion flag ('Bendera Singa Ali') and Fatahillah (national hero) (83×25 mm) 13·50 13·00

See also No. MS3176, MS3195 and MS3221.

767 Rat

2008. New Year. Year of the Rat. Multicoloured.

3167	2000r. Type **767**	1·20	85
3168	2000r. Rat facing left	1·20	85
3169	2000r. Rat washing paws	1·20	85

768 Jerry

2008. Chinese New Year. Tom and Jerry (cartoon characters created by William Hanna and Joseph Barbera). Sheet 144×173 mm containing T **768** and similar horiz designs. Multicoloured.
MS3170 1500r.×6, Type **768**; Tom and Chinese characters; Tom and baubles; Jerry and presents; Jerry and lanterns; Tom with clasped fists 7·75 7·50

769 *Casuarius
casuarius*
(southern
cassowary)

2008. Taipei 2008 International Stamp Exhibition. Sheet 128×82 mm containing T **769** and similar vert design. Multicoloured.
MS3171 5000r.×2, Type **769**; *Crinum asiaticum* 5·75 5·50

The stamps and margins of MS3171 form a composite design.

770 Sailing

2008. Olympic Games, Beijing. Designs showing Barongsai as athlete. Multicoloured.

3172	2500r. Type **770**	1·50	1·10
3173	2500r. Football	1·50	1·10
3174	2500r. Badminton	1·50	1·10
3175	2500r. Weightlifting	1·50	1·10

771 Administrative Building ('Istana Pemerintahan')

2008. Jakarta 2008 International Stamp Exhibition (2nd issue). Sheet 123×165 mm containing T **771** and similar horiz designs. Multicoloured.

MS3176 2500r. Type **771**; 2500r. Finance building ('Gedung Keuangan'); 2500r. Puppet and Batavia (Jakarta) battle ('Penyerangan Batavia oleh Sultan Agung'); 2500r. Battle and puppet ('Penyerangan Batavia oleh Sultan Agung'); 2500r. Signatories to the change from Batavia (Netherlands East Indies) to Jakarta (Indonesia) ('Perubahan Batavia Menjadi Jakarta'); 2500r. Signatories to change to Indonesia and arms ('Penyerahan Kekuasaan Indonesia'); 10000r. Troops seizing prince ('Penangkapan Pangeran Jayawikarta oleh Pasukan Banten') (83×25 mm) .... 13·50 13·00

772 Lake ('Danau Kelimutu')

2008. 50th Anniv of Indonesia—Japan Friendship. Multicoloured.

3177	(1) 2500r. Type **772**	1·30	1·00
3178	(2) 2500r. Mount Fuji	1·30	1·00
3179	(3) 2500r. Buddhist shrine ('Candi Borobudur')	1·30	1·00
3180	(4) 2500r. To-ji temple	1·30	1·00
3181	(5) 2500r. *Rafflesia arnoldi*	1·30	1·00
3182	(6) 2500r. Cherry blossom	1·30	1·00
3183	(7) 2500r. Musical instruments 'Angklung' and 'Gaku-Biwa'	1·30	1·00
3184	(8) 2500r. *Scleropages formosus* (horiz)	1·30	1·00
3185	(9) 2500r. *Nishiki-goi* (horiz)	1·30	1·00
3186	(10) 2500r. ('Danau Kelimutu')	1·30	1·00

Stamps of a similar design were issued by Japan.

773 Scout in Wheelchair

2008. Special Needs Education. Multicoloured.

3187	(1) 1500r. Type **773**	95	70
3188	(2) 1500r. Mixed ability Angklung players	95	70
3189	(3) 1500r. Wheelchair racer	95	70

Nos. 3187/9 are embossed with Braille characters.

773a Hand Shake

2008. Visit of President Soekarno to Cuba.

3189a	**773a** 1500r. multicoloured	95	70

No. 3189a has 2007 imprint and was printed interspersed with stamps size labels showing Pres. Soekarno and Cuban dignatories.

774 Early Demonstrators

2008. Centenary of Nationalism. Multicoloured.

3190	1500r. Type **774**	95	70
3191	1500r. Modern demonstrators	95	70

Nos. 3190/1 were issued together, *se-tenant*, forming a composite design.

775 Cyclists

2008. Environmental Protection. Multicoloured.

3192	1500r. Type **775**	95	70
3193	1500r. Seedling	95	70

No. 3194 has been left for miniature sheet not yet received.

776 Philatelic Agency, Jakarta ('Kantor Filateli Jakarta')

2008. Jakarta 2008 International Stamp Exhibition (3rd issue). Sheet 123×165 mm containing T **776** and similar horiz designs. Multicoloured.

MS3195 2500r. Type **776**; 2500r. National museum ('Museum Nasional'); 2500r. Roller coaster ('Dunia Fantasi'); 2500r. Recreational park ('Taman Mini Indonesia'); 2500r. Traditional procession ('Wisata Seni & Budaya'); 2500r. Jetski and coastline ('Wisata Bahari'); 10000r. Symbols of Jakarta ('Warna Warni Jakarta') (83×25 mm) .... 13·50 13·00

777 Mountain Biker

2008. National Games. Multicoloured.

3196	1500r. Type **777**	95	70
3197	1500r. Bodybuilder	95	70
3198	1500r. Steeplechaser	95	70
3199	1500r. Palaran Stadium	95	70

778 Nasi Lemak

2008. Traditional Foods. Multicoloured.

3200	(1) 1500r. Type **778**	95	70
3201	(2) 1500r. Sate Bandeng	95	70
3202	(3) 1500r. Ayam Cincane	95	70
3203	(4) 1500r. Kaledo	95	70

Nos. 3204/14 have been left for sheet stamps not yet received.

779 Bali

2008. Provincial Emblems. Multicoloured.
MS3215 160×250 mm. 2500r.×11, Type **779**; Gorontalo; Jawa Barat; Jawa Tengan; Kalimantan Barat; Maluku; Nanggroe Aceh Darussalam; Papua; Riau; Sulawesi Barat; Sumatera Barat .... 14·50 14·00

See also Nos. 3304/MS3315. Nos. 3216/20 and T **780** have been left for 'Great Post Road', issued on 27 September 2008, not yet received.

781 Welcome Monument, Jakarta

2008. Jakarta 2008–International Stamp Exhibition. Six sheets (numbered 4a/f), each 101×76 mm, containing T **781** and similar horiz designs (4th issue). Multicoloured.

MS3221	5000r. Type **781**	2·75	2·50
MS3222	5000r. Airliner leaving Soekarno Hatta International Airport	2·75	2·50
MS3223	5000r. Indonesia Stamp Museum	2·75	2·50
MS3224	5000r. 1864 10c. stamp (As Type **1**)	2·75	2·50
MS3225	5000r. *Haliastur indus* (Brahminy kite)	2·75	2·50
MS3226	5000r. Orchestra (80th anniv of Sumpah Pemuda)	2·75	2·50

782 Blue Mosque (Sultan Ahmed Mosque, Istanbul)

2008. Indonesia–Turkey Relations. Multicoloured.

3227	2500r. Type **782**	1·30	1·00
3228	2500r. Istiqlal Mosque, Jakarta	1·30	1·00
3229	2500r. Bosphorus Bridge, Istanbul	1·30	1·00
3230	2500r. Barelang Bridge (connecting Batam, Rempang, and Galang), Indonesia	1·30	1·00
3231	2500r. Whirling dervishes dancing	1·30	1·00
3232	2500r. Saman dance drummers	1·30	1·00
3233	2500r. Tulip, Turkey	1·30	1·00
3234	2500r. Flame of Irian (*Mucana beneetti*), Indonesia	1·30	1·00
3235	2500r. Turkish Van cat	1·30	1·00
3236	2500r. *Prionallurus planiceps* (flat-headed cat)	1·30	1·00

Stamps of a similar design were issued by Turkey.

783 House

2008. Cat Nyak Dhien Commemoration. Multicoloured.

3237	1500r. Type **783**	95	70
3238	1500r. Cat Nyak Dhien	95	70

Nos. 3237/8 were issue together, *se-tenant*, forming a composite design.

784 *Leucopsar rothschildi* (Bali starling), Bali

2008. Provincial Flora and Fauna. Multicoloured.

3239	2500r. Type **784**	1·30	1·00
3240	2500r. *Liza dussumieri* (flat-headed cat), Gorontaio	1·30	1·00
3241	2500r. *Panthera pardus* (leopard), Jawa Barat	1·30	1·00
3242	2500r. *Oriolus chinensis* (black-naped oriole), Jawa Tengah	1·30	1·00
3243	2500r. *Rhinoplax vigil* (helmeted hornbill), Kalimantan Barat	1·30	1·00
3244	2500r. *Alisterus amboinensis* (Moluccan king parrot), Maluku	1·30	1·00
3245	2500r. *Copsychus pyrropygus* (rufous-tailed shama), Nanggroe Aceh Darussalam	1·30	1·00
3246	2500r. *Seleucidis melanoleuca* (twelve-wired bird of paradise), Papua	1·30	1·00
3247	2500r. *Loriculus galgulus* (blue-crowned hanging parrot), Riau	1·30	1·00
3248	2500r. *Aramidopsis plateni* (snoring rail), Sulawesi Barat	1·30	1·00
3249	2500r. *Argusianus argus* (great argus), Sumatera Barat	1·30	1·00

785 Pulau Batubawaikang, Sulawesi Utaro

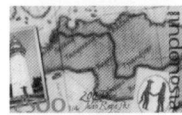

786 Lighthouse and Map

2008. Small Outermost Islands. Multicoloured.

3250	1500r. Type **785**	95	70
3251	1500r. Pulau Sebatik, Kalimantan Timur	95	70
3252	1500r. Pulau Bras, Papua	95	70
3253	1500r. Pulau Damar, Kepulaman Riau	95	70

2008. Bicentenary of Great Post Road. Multicoloured.

3254	2500r. Type **786** (1/4)	35	35
3255	2500r. Map and building (2/4)	35	35
3256	2500r. Map and lighthouse (3/4)	35	35
3257	2500r. Letter (4/4)	35	35
MS3258	152×63 mm. 10000r. As Nos. 3254/6 (125×25 mm)	1·30	1·30

Nos. 3254/7 were issued together, *se-tenant*, forming a composite design.

787 Ox

2009. Chinese New Year. Year of the Ox. Multicoloured.

3259	2000r. Type **787** (1/3)	1·20	85
3260	2000r. Standing facing left (2/3)	1·20	85
3261	2000r. Lying facing right (3/3)	1·20	85
3262	2000r. As Type **787** and symbol	1·20	85
3263	2000r. As No. 3260 and symbol	1·20	85
3264	2000r. As No. 3261 and symbol	1·20	85
MS3265	81×178 mm. 10000r. Ox and symbol	1·30	1·30

788 Emblem

2009. 50th Anniv of Dies Emas Institut Teknologi Bandung. Multicoloured.

3266	1500r. Type **788** (1/4)	95	70
3267	1500r. Students (2/4)	95	70
3268	1500r. '89' and 'Pendidikan Tinggi Teknik di Indonesia' (higher education in engineering) (3/4)	95	70
3269	1500r. Institute arms (4/4)	95	70

789 Flag of Words

2009. General Elections. Multicoloured.

3270	1500r. Type **789** (1/4)	95	70
3271	1500r. tandai pilihan mu (2/4)	95	70
3272	1500r. '1' (mininute) and '5' (years) (3/4)	95	70
3273	1500r. '9 April 2009' and Hand (4/4)	95	70

2009. Preserve Polar Regions and Glaciers. Sheet 162×93 mm containing designs as T **754** and similar horiz design. Multicoloured.
MS3274 2500r.×2, As Type **754**; As No. 3122 .... 3·00 2·75

Type **790** is vacant.

791 Two Oxen

2009. China 2009 International Stamp Exhibition. Sheet 100×67 mm.
MS3275 **791** 10000r. multicoloured .... 6·25 6·00

792 Galilean Telescope

2009. International Year of Astronomy. Multicoloured.

3276	2500r. Type **792** (1/3)	1·50	1·10
3277	2500r. Emblem (2/3)	1·50	1·10
3278	2500r. Galileo Galilei (3/3)	1·50	1·10
MS3279 108×70 mm. 5000r.×3, As Nos. 3276/8		9·50	9·25

Nos. 3276/8 were printed, *se-tenant*, forming a composite design.

793 Orange Fish

2009. World Ocean Conference and Coral Triangle Initiative Summit, Manado, North Salewesi. Designs showing conference emblems and marine life. Multicoloured.

3280	2500r. Type **793** (1/4)	1·50	1·10
3281	2500r. Anemone and shrimp (2/4)	1·50	1·10
3282	2500r. Fish (3/4)	1·50	1·10
3283	2500r. Coral and underwater craft (4/4)	1·50	1·10
MS3284 108×70 mm. 5000r. Turtle		3·00	2·75

794 Polluted and Healthy Environments

2009. Environmental Protection. Winning Designs in National Stamp Design Competition. Multicoloured.

3285	1500r. Type **794** (1/3)	95	70
3286	1500r. Globe, forest, people and factories (2/3)	95	70
3287	1500r. Child holding leaf and parched ground (3/3)	95	70
MS3288 92×61 mm. 5000r. As Type **794**		3·00	2·75

795 Statue, Skyline and Bridge, Surabaya

2009. Inauguration of Suramadu Bridge. Multicoloured.

3289	1500r. Type **795** (1/3)	95	70
3290	1500r. Bridge, central span (2/3)	95	70
3291	1500r. Bridge and water buffalo, Madura (3/3)	95	70
MS3292 165×63 mm. 10000r. As Nos. 3289/91 (124×25 mm)		1·50	1·50

Nos. 3289/91 were printed, *se-tenant*, forming a composite design of the bridge.
The stamp of No. **MS**3292 shows the whole bridge.

796 Ihutilnanga

2009. Traditional Dishes. Multicoloured.

3293	1500r. Type **796** (1/3)	95	70
3294	1500r. Gulai Balak	95	70
3295	1500r. Sate Tambulinas	95	70
3296	1500r. Sambal Goreng Papai	95	70
3297	1500r. Nasi Uduk	95	70
3298	1500r. Ikan Bobara Kuah Asam	95	70

796a Wrinkled Hornbill (Inscr 'Aceros corrigatus')

2009. Birds. Sheet 162×93 mm containing T **801** and similar multicoloured designs.
MS3298a 2500r.×6, Type **796a**; Red-naped trogon *Harpactes kasumba* (horiz); Rufous-collared kingfisher *Actenoides concretus* (horiz); White-winged duck *Asarcornis scutulata* (horiz); Great argus *Argusianus argus* (horiz); Storm's stork *Ciconia stormi* 9·25 9·00

797 Skipping

2009. National Children's Day. Multicoloured.

3299	1500r. Type **797** (1/4)	95	70
3300	1500r. Flying kites (2/4)	95	70
3301	1500r. Hide and seek (3/4)	95	70
3302	1500r. Cycling (4/4)	95	70

Nos. 3299/302 were printed, se-tenant, forming a composite design.

798 Fans

2009. Philakorea 2009 International Stamp Exhibition, Seoul. Sheet 106×106 mm.
MS3303 **798** 10000r. multicoloured 6·25 6·00

799 Banten

2009. Provincial Emblems. Multicoloured.

3304	1500r. Type **799**	95	70
3305	1500r. Jawa Timur	95	70
3306	1500r. Kalimantan Tengah	95	70
3307	1500r. Kalimantan Timur	95	70
3308	1500r. Kepulauan Riau	95	70
3309	1500r. Lampung	95	70
3310	1500r. Nusa Tenggara Timur	95	70
3311	1500r. Papua Barat	95	70
3312	1500r. Sulawesi Tengah	95	70
3313	1500r. Sulawesi Tenggara	95	70
3314	1500r. Sumatera Selatan	95	70
MS3315 160×250 mm. 2500r.×11, As Nos. 3304/3314		15·00	14·00

See also **MS**3215.

JIPEX 2009
(801)

2009. Jipex 2009 International Stamp Exhibition. Birds. Sheet 162×93 mm overprinted as T **801**.
MS3317 2500r.×6, Wrinkled hornbill (Inscr 'Aceros corrigatus'); Red-naped trogon *Harpactes kasumba* (horiz); Rufous-collared kingfisher *Actenoides concretus* (horiz); White-winged duck *Asarcornis scutulata* (horiz); Great argus *Argusianus argus* (horiz); Storm's stork *Ciconia stormi* 9·50 9·25

No. **MS**3317 is as No. **MS**3298a

802 *Rhinoceros sondaicus* (Javan rhinoceros), Banten

2009. Provincial Flora and Fauna. Multicoloured.

3318	2500r. Type **802**	1·50	1·10
3319	2500r. Cockerel, Jawa Timur	1·50	1·10
3320	2500r. *Polyplectron schleirmacheri* (Bornean peacock pheasant), Kalimantan Tengah	1·50	1·10
3321	2500r. *Orcaella brevirostris* (Irrawaddy dolphin), Kalimantan Timur	1·50	1·10
3322	2500r. *Lutjanus sanguineus* (red snapper), Kepulauan Riau	1·50	1·10
3323	2500r. *Elephas maximus* (elephant), Lampung	1·50	1·10
3324	2500r. *Varanus komodoensis* (Komodo dragon), Nusa Tenggara Timur	1·50	1·10
3325	2500r. *Paradisaea rubra* (bird of paradise), Papua Barat	1·50	1·10
3326	2500r. *Macrocephalon maleo* (maleo), Sulawesi Tengah	1·50	1·10
3327	2500r. *Bubalus depressicornis* (lowland anoa), Sulawesi Tenggara	1·50	1·10
3328	2500r. *Notopterus chitala* (clown knifefish), Sumatera Selatan	1·50	1·10

803 Sentosa Island Resort

2009. Tourist Attractions. Multicoloured.

3329	1500r. Type **803**	1·20	85
3330	2500r. Taman Mini Indonesia Park, Jakarta	1·50	1·10
3331	4000r. Merlion and Sentosa Island resort	2·75	2·00
3332	7500r. Singaraja Statue, Bali	4·50	3·50
MS3332a 125×84 mm. Nos. 3329/32		1·20	85

Stamps in a similar design were issued by Singapore.

803a Soltanieh Dome, Western Zanjan Province, Iran

2009. Cultural Heritage. Multicoloured.

3332b	1500r. Type **803a**	2·30	1·70
3332c	3000r. Al-Markaz Mosque, Makassar City, Indonesia	3·00	3·00
MS3332d 148×230 mm. Nos. 3332b/c, each×6		5·75	5·75

804 Tiger

2010. Chinese New Year. Multicoloured.

3333	1500r. Type **804**	1·20	85
3334	1500r. Tiger, facing left	1·20	85
3335	1500r. Tiger, facing right	1·20	85
MS3336 83×98 mm. 5000r. Tiger and kite		3·75	3·50

805 Whitewater Rafting and Emblem

2010. Prisma. Extreme Sports. Multicoloured.

3337	1500r. Type **805**	90	90
3338	1500r. Paragliding (2/5)	90	90
3339	1500r. Rock climbing (3/5)	90	90
3340	1500r. Rope walking (4/5)	90	90
3340a	1500r. 'Flying Fox' (5/5)	90	90

806 Batik

2010. Cultural Heritage.

3341	1000r. Type **806**	75	55
3342	1500r. Hanoman (Wayang puppet) (vert)	1·20	85
3343	2000r. Arjuna (Wayang puppet) (vert)	1·50	1·10
3344	2500r. Kresna (Wayang puppet) (vert)	1·90	1·40
3345	3000r. Keris (knife) (vert)	2·30	1·70
3346	3000r. Gold coloured batik	3·50	2·50
MS3347 98×72 mm. 5000r. Hanoman (As No. 3342, detail) (vert)		3·75	3·50
MS3348 98×72 mm. 5000r.Keris (As No. 3345, larger different background) (vert)		3·75	3·50

807 Player

2010. World Cup Football Championships, South Africa. Multicoloured.

| 3349 | 1500r. Type **807** | 1·20 | 85 |
| 3350 | 1500r. Zakumi (games mascot) | 1·20 | 85 |

| 3351 | 1500r. Games emblem | 1·20 | 85 |
| 3352 | 1500r. Goalkeeper and ball | 1·20 | 85 |

808 Child and Idyllic Environment

2010. Environmental Protection. Multicoloured.

3353	1500r. Type **808**	1·20	85
3354	1500r. Globe, pollution and outstretched arms (impact of environmental destruction)	1·20	85
3355	1500r. Hands enclosing seedling (maintaining biodiversity) (vert)	1·20	85
MSM3356 50×81 mm. 5000r. As No. 3355 (vert)		1·80	1·80

809 Ahmad Dahlan (founder)

2010. Centenary of Muhammadiyah Organization. Multicoloured.

3357	1500r. Type **809**	1·20	85
3358	1500r. Emblem, students and building (education)	1·20	85
3359	1500r. Kauman Yogyakarta Mosque	1·20	85
MS3360 144×211 mm. Nos. 3357/9 each×3		3·75	3·50

810 Lobster Kelapa Muda (West Sulawesi)

2010. Traditional Foods. Multicoloured.

3361	1500r. Type **810**	1·20	85
3362	1500r. Gulai Iga kemba"ang (Bengkulu)	1·20	85
3363	1500r. Ayam Cincane (East Kalimantan)	1·20	85
3364	1500r. Lapis Palaro (North Maluku)	1·20	85
3365	1500r. Sate Udang Pentuk Asam Manis (Jambi)	1·20	85
3366	1500r. Asam Padeh Baung (Riau)	1·20	85
3367	1500r. Lempah Kuning (Bangka Belitung)	1·20	85

811 Badminton

2010. Singapore 2010 Youth Olympic Games. Multicoloured.

| 3368 | 1500r. Type **811** | 1·20 | 85 |
| 3369 | 1500r. Badminton (right) | 1·20 | 85 |

812 Susilo Bambang Yudhoyono

2010. President and Vice President of The Republic of Indonesia. Multicoloured.

3370	2500r. Type **812**	1·70	1·30
3371	2500r. Dr Boediono	1·70	1·30
MS3372 118×78 mm. Nos. 3370/1		3·50	2·50

Nos. 3373/6 and Type **813** are left for Marine Life, issued on 24 October 2010, not yet received.

814 *Haliastur indus* and *Salacca zalacca*

2010. Flora and Fauna. Multicoloured.

| 3377 | 1000r. Type **814** | 75 | 55 |
| 3378 | 1000r. *Geopelia striata* and *Stelechocarpus buranol* | 75 | 55 |

3379	1500r. *Gracula religiosa robusta* and *Canaga odorata*	1·20	85
3380	1500r. *Pantheris tigris sumatrae* and *Cyrtostachys renda*	1·20	85
3381	1500r. *Helarctos malayanus* and *Amorphophallus titanum*	1·20	85
3382	1500r. *Tarsius bancanus saltator* and *Palaquium rostratum*	1·20	85
3383	2000r. *Cervus timorensis* and *Diospyros macrophylla*	1·50	1·10
3384	2500r. *Nasalis larvatus* and *Mangifera casturi*	1·90	1·40
3385	2500r. *Aceros cassidix* and *Barassus flabellifer*	1·90	1·40
3386	2500r. *Tarsius spectrum* and *Ficus minahassae*	1·90	1·40
3387	2500r. *Semiopthera wallacii* and *Syzygium aromaticum*	1·90	1·40
MS3388	149×210 mm. Nos. 3373/83	15·00	14·00

816 Sumatra Utara

2010. Provincial Emblems. Multicoloured.

3391	1500r. Type **816**	1·20	85
3392	1500r. Jambi	1·20	85
3393	1500r. Bengkula	1·20	85
3394	1500r. Banga Belltung	1·20	85
3395	1500r. Jakarta (Jaya Raya)	1·20	85
3396	1500r. Yogyakarta	1·20	85
3397	1500r. Kalimantan Selatan	1·20	85
3398	1500r. Sulawesi Selatan	1·20	85
3399	1500r. Sulawesi Utara	1·20	85
3400	1500r. Maluka Utara	1·20	85
3401	1500r. Nusa Tenggara Barat	1·20	85
MS3402	160×250 mm. 2500r.×11, As Nos. 3391/401	13·00	12·00
MS3403	93×63 mm. 5000r. As No. 3395	3·75	3·50

Nos. 3389/90 and Type **815** are left for 60th Anniv of Diplomatic Relations with Russia, issued on 9 November 2010, not yet received.

817 Rabbit

2011. Chinese New Year. Year of the Rabbit. Multicoloured.

3404	1500r. Type **817**	1·20	85
3405	3000r. Running	2·30	1·70
3406	4000r. Mother and kitten	3·00	2·30
MS3407	124×138 mm. Nos. 3404/6, each×2	13·00	12·00
MS3408	83×102 mm. 5000r. Rex rabbit (head)	3·75	3·50

818 Ritual of Ngaben of Bali

2011. Traditional Ceremonies. Multicoloured.

3409	1500r. Type **818**	1·20	85
3410	1500r. Grebeg Syawal, Yogyakarta	1·20	85
3411	1500r. Pasola -Sumba, Nusa Tenggara	1·20	85
3412	1500r. Tiwah - Dayak, Central Kalimantan	1·20	85

819 Artoindonesianin C

2011. International Year of Chemistry. Multicoloured.

| 3413 | 1500r. Type **819** | 1·20 | 85 |
| 3414 | 2500r. Emblem (vert) | 1·90 | 1·40 |

820 Ulos Hand Woven, North Sumatra

2011. Indonesia 2012 World Stamp Championship and Exhibition, Jakarta. Traditional Textiles. Multicoloured.

| MS3415 | 120×160 mm. 2500r.×8, Type **820**; Tampan Hand Woven, Lampung; Batik Lasem, Central Java; Batik Parang Garuda, DI Yogyakarta; Sasirangan Hand Woven, South Kalimantan; Iban Hand Woven, East Kalimantan; Toraja Hand Woven, South Sulawesi; Sumba Hand Woven, East Nusa Tenggara | 15·00 | 14·00 |
| MS3416 | 83×98 mm. 5000r. Woman weaving | 3·75 | 3·50 |

821 Lapan- TUBSat (Indonesia's first remote sensing satellite)

2011. Space Vehicles. Multicoloured.

| 3417 | 2500r. Type **821** | 1·90 | 1·40 |
| 3418 | 2500r. Roket Pengorbit Satelit 420 (Satellite Orbiting Rocket Number 420) | 1·90 | 1·40 |

822 Girl, Code and Globe plugged into Computer

2011. Healthy and Safe Internet. Multicoloured.

| 3419 | 2500r. Type **822** | 1·90 | 1·40 |
| 3420 | 2500r. Boy, code, laptop, mother and child | 1·90 | 1·40 |

823 Pine Cone, Needles and Trunk of Pine Tree

2011. Environmental Protection. Forests. Multicoloured.

| 3421 | 2500r. Type **823** | 1·90 | 1·40 |
| 3422 | 2500r. Pine marten on trunk of pine tree | 1·90 | 1·40 |

824 Fish and Salad

2011. Fish Consumption Promotion Movement. Multicoloured.

3423	1500r. Type **824**	1·20	85
3424	2000r. Fishmonger's display of fish	1·50	1·10
3425	3000r. Harvesting seaweed	2·30	1·70
3426	5000r. Fisherman and fish	3·75	2·75
MS3427	142×110 mm. Nos. 3423/6	8·75	8·50

2011. Indonesia 2012 World Stamp Championship and Exhibition, Jakarta. Traditional Textiles. Multicoloured.

| MS3427b | 83×98 mm. 5000r. Buffalo chariot | 6·75 | 6·75 |

825 Malaysia's National Monument

2011. Indonesia - Malaysia Relations. Multicoloured.

3428	90s. Type **825**	1·90	1·40
3429	90s. Proclamation Monument, Indonesia	1·90	1·40
3430	90s. Malaysia's first currency issued after Independence	1·90	1·40
3431	90s. ORI (Oeang Republik Indonesia) banknote	1·90	1·40
3432	90s. Malayan Federation 1957 10c. Independence Day stamp	1·90	1·40
3433	90s. Indonesia 1949 Surakarta Military Stamp	1·90	1·40
3434	90s. *Gallus gallus* (red junglefowl)	1·90	1·40
3435	90s. *Gallus varius* (green junglefowl)	1·90	1·40

826 Scout, Flag and Dove

2011. 50th Anniv of Scout Movement in Indonesia. Multicoloured.

3436	2500r. Type **826**	90	90
3437	2500r. Scouts of many races	90	90
3438	2500r. Scouts teaching	90	90
MS3439	81×61 mm. 5000r. As Type **826**	90	90

827 Mohammad Natsir (politician)

2011. Personalities. Multicoloured.

| 3440 | 2500r. Type **827** | 90 | 90 |
| 3441 | 2500r. Sutomo (Bung Tomo) (politician) | 90 | 90 |

828 Lawang Sewu Building, Semarang

2011. Landmarks. Multicoloured.

3442	2500r. Type **828**	90	90
3443	2500r. Monument marking equator, Pontianak	90	90
3444	2500r. Garuda Wisnu Kencana Park, Denpasar	90	90
3445	2500r. Fort Rotterdam, Makassar	90	90
3446	2500r. Ampera Bridge, Palembang	90	90

2011. Indonesia 2012 World Stamp Championship and Exhibition, Jakarta. Traditional Textiles. Multicoloured.

MS3447	120×160 mm. 2500r.×8, 'Songket Malayu'; Mega Mendung Batik; 'Tenun Tolaki'; Papua Batik; 'Songket Mentok'; 'Tenun Sora Langi'; 'Tenun Tanimbar'; Papua Barat Batik	15·00	11·00
MS3448	280×125 mm. 2500r.×8, As Type **820**; Tampan Hand Woven, Lampung; Batik Lasem, Central Java; Batik Parang Garuda, DI Yogyakarta; Sasirangan Hand Woven, South Kalimantan; Iban Hand Woven, East Kalimantan; Toraja Hand Woven, South Sulawesi; Sumba Hand Woven, East Nusa Tenggara (8 stamps as MS3415); 'Tenun Aceh'; Basurek Batik;Madura Batik; 'Tenun Bentenan'; 'Tenun Pandai Sikek'; 'Songket Palembang'; 'Tenun Sambas'; Masambo Batik (8 stamps as MS3427a (not yet received)); 'Songket Malayu'; Mega Mendung Batik; 'Tenun Tolaki'; Papua Batik; 'Songket Mentok'; 'Tenun Sora Langi'; 'Tenun Tanimbar'; Papua Barat Batik(8 stamps as MS3447)	15·00	11·00
MS3449	83×98 mm. 5000r. Hanuman	3·75	3·75

829 Trikora Monument and West Papua

2011. 50th Anniv of Trikora Campaign. Multicoloured.

3450	2500r. Type **829**	1·90	1·40
3451	2500r. Armoured personnel carrier	1·90	1·40
3452	2500r. Disembarkation and naval ship	1·90	1·40
3453	2500r. Fighter aircraft and soldiers	1·90	1·40
MS3454	120×160 mm. Nos. 3450/3	7·00	6·00

830 Sheikh Yusuf of Macassar (founder of Cape Muslim community)

2011. 300 Years of Historic Links between South Africa and Indonesia. Multicoloured.

| 3455 | 2500r. Type **830** | 1·90 | 1·40 |
| 3456 | 2500r. Balla Lompoa Museum | 1·90 | 1·40 |

3457	2500r. Drummer	1·90	1·40
3458	2500r. Hat and sandals	1·90	1·40
3459	2500r. Dancers	1·90	1·40

831 Modo playing Table Tennis

2011. 26th Southeast Asian Games, Jakarta and Palembang. Multicoloured.

3460	2500r. Type **831**	1·90	1·40
3461	2500r. Modi playing badminton	1·90	1·40
3462	2500r. Modo greeting visitors to Jakarta	1·90	1·40
3463	2500r. Modi greeting visitors to Palembang	1·90	1·40
3464	2500r. Modo playing football	1·90	1·40
3465	2500r. Modo demonstrating Pencak Silat	1·90	1·40

832 *Nymphoides indica* (waterlily)

2011. Flora and Fauna. Multicoloured.

3466	2500r. Type **832**	1·90	1·40
3467	2500r. *Leptophryne cruentata* (Fire toad)	1·90	1·40
MS3468	137×65 mm. Nos. 3466/7	4·00	3·00

833 'Kelenteng Sam Poo Kong'

2011. China 2011, Asian International Stamp Exhibition, Wuxi. Sheet 96×65 mm

| MS3469 | **833** 10000r. multicoloured | 7·50 | 5·50 |

834 Dragon and Mythical Beasts

2012. Chinese New Year. Year of the Dragon. Multicoloured.

3470	2500r. Type **834**	1·90	1·40
3471	2500r. Dragon, pagoda and phoenix (green)	1·90	1·40
3472	2500r. Dragon, facing left, and pagoda (grey)	1·90	1·40
MS3473	124×138 mm. Nos. 3470/2, each×2	3·75	2·75
MS3474	83×102 mm. 5000r. Dragon (head)	3·75	2·75

Nos. 3475/80 and Type **835** are left for PONXVIII, not yet received.

836 Anniversary Emblem

2012. 50th Anniv of Asian Pacific Postal Union

| 3481 | **836** | 5000r. multicoloured | 3·75 | 2·75 |

EXPRESS LETTER STAMPS

E189 "Garuda" Bird

1967. Inscr "1967".

| E1166 | **E189** | 10r. purple and blue | 80 | 25 |
| E1167 | **E189** | 15r. purple and orange | 1·40 | 70 |

1968. As Nos. E1166/7 but dated "1968".

E1202	10r. purple and blue	80	25
E1203	15r. purple & orange	90	35
E1204	20r. purple and yellow	90	35
E1205	30r. purple and green	1·70	70
E1206	40r. purple & lt pur	90	35

1969. As Nos. E1166/7 but dated "1969".

E1250	20r. purple and yellow		65	20
E1251	30r. purple and green		70	20
E1252	40r. purple & lt pur		80	25

POSTAGE DUE STAMPS

1950. Postage Due stamps of Netherlands Indies surch **BAJAR PORTO** and new value.

D576	2½s. on 50c. (No. D499)		1·50	1·00
D577	5s. on 100c. (No. D501)		3·75	1·50
D578	10s. on 75c. (No. D500)		8·75	2·10

D100

1951

D645	D100	2½s. orange	20	75
D646	D100	5s. orange	20	10
D647	D100	10s. orange	20	10
D648	D100	15s. red	20	20
D773	D100	15s. orange	35	75
D649	D100	20s. blue	20	20
D774	D100	20s. orange	35	75
D650	D100	25s. olive	35	35
D775	D100	25s. orange	35	75
D651	D100	30s. brown	35	35
D776	D100	30s. orange	35	75
D652	D100	40s. green	35	35
D777	D100	50s. orange	2·00	75
D778	D100	50s. green	15	10
D779	D100	100s. orange	1·10	75
D780	D100	100s. brown	15	10
D781	D100	250s. blue	35	10
D782	D100	500s. yellow	15	10
D783	D100	750s. lilac	35	10
D784	D100	1000s. salmon	25	20
D654	D100	1r. green	2·20	2·00

D176

1965. Provisional issue for use on parcels.

D1057	D176	25r. black on yellow	65	

1966

D1058	D100	50r. red	10	10
D1059	D100	100r. lake	20	20

1966. As Type **D100**, but with coloured network background incorporating "1966".

D1098	5s. green and yellow		40	35
D1099	10s. red and blue		40	35
D1100	20s. blue and pink		40	35
D1101	30s. sepia and red		40	35
D1102	40s. violet and bistre		40	35
D1103	50s. olive and mauve		40	15
D1104	100s. lake and green		40	15
D1105	200s. green and pink		40	15
D1106	500s. yellow and blue		40	15
D1107	1000s. red and yellow		40	25

1967. As Nos. 1098/1107 but dated "1967".

D1168	50s. green and lilac		25	20
D1169	100s. red and green		25	20
D1170	200s. green and pink		25	20
D1171	500s. brown and blue		80	45
D1172	1000s. mauve and yellow		80	45
D1173	15r. orange and grey		1·60	70
D1174	25r. violet and grey		3·75	2·50

1973. As Type **D100** but inscr "BAYAR PORTO" and dated "1973".

D1320a	25r. violet and grey		1·10	15

1974. As Type **D100** but inscr "BAYAR PORTO" and dated "1974".

D1346	65r. green and yellow		2·75	65
D1347	125r. purple and pink		5·75	1·90

1975. As Type **D100** but inscr "BAYAR PORTO" and dated "1975".

D1401	25r. violet and drab		2·10	1·40

D268

1976

D1426	D268	25r. violet and drab	70	75
D1427	D268	65r. green and stone	1·40	1·50

1978. Various stamps surch **BAYAR PORTO** and value.

D1503	25r. on 1r. sepia and red (No. 1141)		70	65
D1504	50r. on 2r. blue and ochre (No. 1144)		70	65

D1505	100r. on 4r. blue and orange (No. 1147)		1·40	1·30
D1506	200r. on 5r. red and blue (No. 1148)		2·75	2·40
D1507	300r. on 10r. violet and red (No. 1151)		4·00	3·50
D1508	400r. on 15r. violet and olive (No. 1153)		4·25	3·75

1978. Nos. 1145 and 1152 surch **BAYAR PORTO** and value.

D1523	40r. on 2r.50 green and red		2·10	1·90
D1524	40r. on 12r. green and violet		2·10	1·90
D1525	65r. on 2r.50 green and red		2·75	2·50
D1526	65r. on 12r. green and violet		4·25	3·75
D1527	125r. on 2r.50 green & red		2·10	1·90
D1528	125r. on 12r. green & violet		2·10	1·90
D1529	150r. on 2r.50 green & red		2·75	2·50
D1530	150r. on 12r. green & violet		4·25	3·75

1980. Dated "1980".

D1599	D268	25r. mauve and drab	30	25
D1600	D333a	50r. green and lilac	70	65
D1601	D333a	75r. purple and pink	1·10	1·00
D1602	D 268	125r. mauve & pink	1·70	1·50

1981. Dated "1981".

D1641	25r. purple & stone		30	30
D1642	50r. green and lilac		60	55
D1643	75r. purple and pink		90	85
D1644	125r. purple & grn		1·80	1·70

1982. Dated "1982".

D1645	125r. purple & pink		2·30	55

D333a

1983. Dated "1983".

D1728	200r. lilac and blue		90	30
D1729	300r. green & yell		1·10	45
D1730	400r. green & buff		1·40	55
D1731	500r. brown & pink		1·80	85

1984. Dated "1984".

D1772	25r. purple & stone		1·10	45
D1773	50r. green and lilac		1·10	55
D1774	500r. deep brown and brown		6·00	70

1988. Dated "1988".

D1912	1000r. pur & grey		1·40	1·00
D1913	2000r. red & mauve		2·75	2·00
D1914	3000r. red & yellow		4·75	2·75
D1915	5000r. green & blue		8·25	3·75

Pt. 1

INDORE (HOLKAR STATE)

A state in C. India. Now uses Indian stamps.

12 pies = 1 anna; 16 annas = 1 rupee.

1 Maharaja Tukoji Rao Holkar II

1886

2	1	½a. mauve	7·50	3·25

2 Type I

1889. No gum. Imperf.

4	2	½a. black on pink	5·00	3·75

3 Maharaja Shivaji Rao Holkar

1889

5	3	¼a. orange	3·50	1·50
6a	6	½a. purple	4·50	25
7	3	1a. green	7·00	2·25
8	3	2a. red	12·00	2·75

4 Maharaja Tukoji Holkar III

1904

9	5	¼a. orange	2·00	10
10	5	½a. red	15·00	10
11	5	1a. green	4·25	10
12	5	2a. brown	17·00	1·00
13	5	3a. violet	42·00	7·00
14a	5	4a.	12·00	1·40

The ¼a. is inscr "HOLKAR".

पाव आना.
(6)

1905. No. 6a. surch as T **6**.

15	3	¼a. on ½a. purple	12·00	28·00

7 Maharaja Yeshwant Rao Holkar II

1928

16	7	¼a. orange	1·75	20
17	7	½a. purple	4·25	20
18	7	1a. green	5·00	10
19	7	1¼a. green	7·00	2·25
20	7	2a. brown	14·00	3·75
21	7	2a. green	15·00	2·25
22	7	3a. violet	6·00	11·00
23	7	3a. blue	25·00	
24	7	3½a. violet	7·00	15·00
25	7	4a. blue	15·00	5·50
26	7	4a. yellow	45·00	2·50
27	7	8a. grey	12·00	4·50
28	7	8a. orange	38·00	28·00
29	7	12a. red	5·00	10·00
30	-	1r. black and blue	16·00	18·00
31	-	2r. black and red	85·00	90·00
32	-	5r. black and brown	£140	£150

The rupee values are larger, 23×28 mm.

1940. Surch diagonally in words.

33		¼a. on 5r. (No. 32)	26·00	1·75
34		½a. on 2r. (No. 31)	32·00	3·25
35	7	1a. on 1¼a. green (No. 19)	42·00	1·00

9 Maharaja Yeshwant Rao Holkar II

1940

36	9	¼a. orange	2·25	20
37	9	½a. red	7·00	10
38	9	1a. green	11·00	20
39	9	1¼a. green	21·00	3·00
40	9	2a. blue	16·00	1·00
41	9	4a. yellow	21·00	15·00

The rupee values are larger, 23×28 mm.

OFFICIAL STAMPS

1904. Optd **SERVICE**.

S1	5	¼a. orange	2·00	2·00
S2	5	½a. red	75	10
S3	5	1a. green	25	25
S4	5	2a. brown	35	35
S5	5	3a. violet	3·25	5·50
S6	5	4a. blue	8·50	2·25

Pt. 9

INHAMBANE

A district of Mozambique, which used its own stamps from 1895 to 1920.

1895. 1000 reis = 1 milreis.
1913. 100 centavos = 1 escudo.

1895. 700th Birth Anniv of St. Anthony. Optd **CENTENARIO DE S. ANTONIO Inhambane MDCCCXCV.** (a) "Embossed" key-type inscr "PROVINCIA DE MOCAMBIQUE".

1	Q	5r. black	55·00	40·00
2	Q	10r. green	55·00	40·00
3	Q	20r. brown	80·00	60·00
4	Q	40r. brown	80·00	40·00
5	Q	50r. blue	80·00	40·00
6	Q	200r. violet	£110	90·00
7	Q	300r. orange	£110	90·00

12	R	50r. blue	80·00	60·00
16	R	75r. red	£130	£100
13	R	80r. green	85·00	70·00
14	R	100r. brown on yellow	£300	£275
17	R	150r. red on rose	£130	£100

1903. "King Carlos" key type inscr "INHAMBANE".

18	S	2½r. grey	70	65
19	S	5r. orange	75	65
20	S	10r. green	80	75
21	S	15r. green	2·10	1·50
22	S	20r. lilac	2·10	1·50
23	S	25r. red	2·10	1·50
24	S	50r. brown	5·00	2·10
25	S	65r. blue	23·00	16·00
26	S	75r. purple	3·25	2·10
27	S	100r. blue on blue	3·25	2·10
28	S	115r. brown on pink	8·50	7·50
29	S	130r. brown on yellow	8·50	7·50
30	S	200r. purple on pink	8·50	7·50
31	S	400r. blue on yellow	14·00	11·50
32	S	500r. black on blue	25·00	17·00
33	S	700r. grey on yellow	32·00	23·00

1905. No. 25 surch **50 REIS** and bar.

34		50r. on 65r. blue	7·25	5·50

1911. 1903 issue optd **REPUBLICA**.

35		2½r. grey	55	50
36		5r. orange	55	50
37		10r. green	65	50
38		15r. green	65	50
39		20r. lilac	1·20	90
40		25r. red	1·20	90
41		50r. brown	65	50
42		75r. purple	90	65
43		100r. blue on blue	90	65
44		115r. brown on pink	1·20	90
45		130r. brown on yellow	2·75	2·10
46		200r. purple on pink	1·80	1·20
47		400r. blue on yellow	2·75	2·10
48		500r. black on blue	3·00	2·10
49		700r. black on yellow	3·50	2·75

1913. Surch **REPUBLICA INHAMBANE** and value on "Vasco da Gama" stamps. (a) Portuguese Colonies.

50		¼c. on 2½r. green	1·80	1·40
51		½c. on 5r. red	1·80	1·40
52		1c. on 10r. purple	1·80	1·40
53		2½c. on 25r. green	1·80	1·40
54		5c. on 50r. blue	2·10	1·40
55		7½c. on 75r. brown	3·25	2·75
56		10c. on 100r. brown	3·25	2·75
57		15c. on 150r. bistre	3·25	3·00

(b) Macao.

58		¼c. on ½a. green	2·30	1·90
59		½c. on 1a. red	2·30	1·90
60		1c. on 2a. purple	2·30	1·90
61		2½c. on 4a. green	2·30	1·90
62		5c. on 8a. blue	2·30	1·90
63		7½c. on 12a. brown	4·00	3·25
64		10c. on 16a. brown	3·25	2·10
65		15c. on 24a. bistre	3·25	2·10

(c) Timor.

66		¼c. on ½a. green	2·30	1·90
67		½c. on 1a. red	2·30	1·90
68		1c. on 2a. purple	2·30	1·90
69		2½c. on 4a. green	2·30	1·90
70		5c. on 8a. blue	2·30	1·90
71		7½c. on 12a. brown	4·00	3·25
72		10c. on 16a. brown	3·25	2·10
73		15c. on 24a. bistre	3·25	2·10

1914. No. 34 optd **REPUBLICA**.

74		50r. on 65r. blue	4·25	2·20

1914. "Ceres" key type inscr "INHAMBANE".

75	U	¼c. olive	1·20	75
76a	U	½c. black	3·50	2·50
77	U	1c. green	1·30	75
78	U	1½c. brown	1·30	75
79	U	2c. red	1·30	75
80	U	2½c. violet	60	55
81	U	5c. blue	80	75
82	U	7½c. brown	2·20	1·60
83	U	8c. grey	2·20	1·60
84	U	10c. red	2·20	1·80
85	U	15c. red	2·75	2·10
86	U	20c. green	2·75	2·10
87	U	30c. brown on green	3·75	2·30
88	U	40c. brown on red	3·75	2·30
89	U	50c. orange on pink	7·00	4·75
90	U	1e. green on blue	7·00	4·75

ININI

A territory in French Guiana, in the N.E. of S. America, separately administered from 1930 but reunited with Fr. Guiana in 1946.

100 centimes = 1 franc.

1931. Stamps of French Guiana optd **TERRITOIRE DE L'ININI** (Type 20) or **Territoire de l'ININI** (others).

1	20	1c. green and lilac	20	7·25
2	20	2c. green and red	20	6·50
3	20	3c. green and violet	55	8·50
4	20	4c. mauve and brown	45	7·75
5	20	5c. orange and blue	35	8·25
6	20	10c. brown and mauve	15	6·75
7	20	15c. orange and brown	15	7·00
8	20	20c. green and blue	75	7·50
9	20	25c. brown and red	85	8·00
10	21	30c. green and deep green	3·50	9·75
11	21	30c. brown and green	35	8·50
12	21	35c. green and blue	2·75	8·75
13	21	40c. grey and brown	65	9·25
14	21	45c. brown and olive	1·50	8·75
15	21	50c. grey and blue	65	7·50
16	21	55c. red and blue	3·50	14·50
17	21	60c. green and red	65	9·00
18	21	65c. green and red	3·00	11·00
19	21	70c. green and blue	2·00	9·25
20	21	75c. blue and black	5·25	11·00
21	21	80c. blue and black	2·10	9·25
22	21	90c. red and carmine	4·75	10·50
23	21	90c. brown and mauve	2·75	9·25
24	21	1f. brown and mauve	23·00	44·00
25	21	1f. red	3·50	9·25
26	21	1f. blue and black	90	9·25
27	22	1f.25 green and brown	3·25	10·00
28	22	1f.25 red	2·20	9·25
29	22	1f.40 mauve and brown	1·00	9·50
30	22	1f.50 light blue and blue	1·00	8·25
31	22	1f.60 green and brown	1·30	9·50
32	22	1f.75 brown and red	50·00	60·00
33	22	1f.75 blue and deep blue	3·00	9·75
34	22	2f. red and green	1·00	8·25
35	22	2f.25 blue	1·20	10·00
36	22	2f.50 brown and red	1·30	10·00
37	22	3f. mauve and red	2·20	8·25
38	22	5f. green and violet	1·40	8·75
39	22	10f. blue and green	1·40	8·75
40	22	20f. green and blue	2·00	10·50

1939. New York World's Fair. As T **58c** of Guadeloupe.

51		1f.25 red	6·00	19·00
52		2f.25 blue	6·00	19·00

1939. 150th Anniv of French Revolution. As T **58d** of Guadeloupe.

53		45c.+25c. green and black	12·00	32·00
54		70c.+30c. brown and black	12·00	32·00
55		90c.+35c. orange and black	12·00	32·00
56		1f.25+1f. red and black	12·00	32·00
57		2f.25+2f. blue and black	12·00	32·00

POSTAGE DUE STAMPS

1932. Postage Due Stamps of French Guiana optd **TERRITOIRE DE L'ININI.**

D41	D23	5c. blue and deep blue	10	6·25
D42	D23	10c. blue and brown	45	7·00
D43	D23	20c. red and green	45	7·50
D44	D23	30c. red and brown	45	7·50
D45	D23	50c. brown and mauve	1·70	9·50
D46	D23	60c. brown and red	2·00	9·50
D47	D 24	1f. brown and blue	2·50	12·50
D48	D 24	2f. green and red	3·25	12·50
D49	D 24	3f. grey and mauve	4·25	19·00

IONIAN ISLANDS

A group of islands off the W. coast of Greece, placed under the protection of Gt. Britain in 1815 and ceded to Greece in 1864.

12 pence = 1 shilling; 20 shillings = 1 pound.

1

1859. Imperf.

1	1	(½d.) orange	£140	£750
2	1	(1d.) blue	35·00	£300
3	1	(2d.) red	28·00	£300

IRAN

A State of W. Asia.

1868. 20 shahis (or chahis) = 1 kran; 10 krans = 1 toman.
1932. 100 dinars = 1 rial.

NOTE.—The word "English" in the descriptive headings to various Persian issues is to be taken as referring to the lettering or figures and not to the language which is often French.

1

1868. Imperf or roul.

1		1(sh.) violet	£200	
1c		1(sh.) grey	£450	
15		1(sh.) black	23·00	38·00
2		2(sh.) green	85·00	
16		2(sh.) blue	90·00	55·00
35		2(sh.) black	£300	£1500
3		4(sh.) blue	£140	
17		4(sh.) red	£190	60·00
4		8(sh.) red	80·00	
8		8(sh.) green	70·00	42·00
13		1(kr.) yellow	£1200	
18		1kr. red	£375	46·00
38		1kr. red on yellow	£1600	80·00
19		4kr. yellow	£600	30·00
36		4kr. blue	£200	80·00
40		5kr. violet	£275	75·00
41		5kr. gold	£550	£190
39		1to. bronze on blue	£42000	£5000

3 Nasred-Din

1876. Perf.

20	3	1(sh.) black and mauve	50·00	12·00
24	3	2(sh.) black and green	16·00	5·00
25	3	5(sh.) black and pink	25·00	4·00
30	3	10(sh.) black and blue	37·00	9·75

4 Nasred-Din

1879. Perf.

45	4	1(sh.) black and red	36·00	6·75
46	4	2(sh.) black and yellow	50·00	4·25
47a	4	5(sh.) black and green	55·00	2·50
48a	4	10(sh.) black and mauve	£325	21·00
49c	4	1(kr.) black and brown	£110	2·30
50c	4	5(kr.) black and blue	46·00	70

5   6

1881.

56	5	5c. mauve	25·00	5·25
57a	5	10c. red	25·00	5·00
61a	5	25c. green	£200	10·50
62	6	50c. black, yellow and orange	£325	9·75
69	6	50c. black	80·00	25·00
63	6	1f. black and blue	80·00	3·50
64	6	5f. black and red	65·00	7·25
65	6	10f. black, yellow and red (30½×36 mm)	£120	12·00

1882. As T **5** and **6.**

66		5s. green	25·00	1·60
68		10s. black, yellow and orange	49·00	4·00

10   11

1885.

70	10	1c. green	12·50	1·20
71	10	2c. red	12·50	1·20
72	10	5c. blue	21·00	80
73	11	10c. brown	12·50	1·20

74	11	1k. grey	29·00	2·10
75	11	5k. purple	£500	29·00

1885. Surch **OFFICIEL** and value in English and Persian.

81	–	3 on 5s. green (No. 66)	£100	25·00
76	–	6 on 5s. green (No. 66)	£100	22·00
83	–	6 on 10s. (No. 68)	£100	25·00
84	6	8 on 50c. black	£100	25·00
78	6	12 on 50c. black	£100	22·00
79	–	18 on 10s. (No. 68)	£100	22·00
80	6	1t. on 5f. black and red	£100	22·00

13   14

1889.

85	13	1c. pink	2·10	40
86	13	2c. blue	2·10	40
87	13	5c. mauve	1·20	40
88	13	7c. brown	8·25	80
89	14	10c. black	1·60	40
90	14	1k. orange	3·00	40
91	14	2k. red	29·00	4·00
92	14	5k. green	21·00	4·00

15   16

1891.

93A	15	1c. black	2·10	80
94A	15	2c. brown	2·10	80
95A	15	5c. blue	2·10	25
96B	15	7c. grey	£250	9·75
97A	15	10c. red	2·10	40
98	15	14c. orange	2·10	1·20
99A	16	1k. green	21·00	2·10
100A	16	2k. orange	£550	21·00
101A	16	5k. orange	6·50	16·00

17   18

1894.

102	17	1c. mauve	80	25
103	17	2c. green	80	25
104	17	5c. blue	80	25
105	17	8c. brown	80	25
106	18	10c. yellow	1·10	80
107	18	16c. pink	21·00	41·00
108	18	1k. pink and yellow	2·50	80
109	18	2k. brown and blue	3·25	1·10
110	18	5k. violet and silver	4·00	1·60
111	18	10k. pink and gold	12·50	8·25
112	18	50k. green and gold	25·00	9·00

See also Nos. 116/24.

1897. Surch in English and Persian in frame.

113	17	5c. on 8c. brown	21·00	3·25
114	18	1k. on 5k. violet and silver	25·00	12·50
115	18	2k. on 5k. violet and silver	41·00	21·00

21
Muzaffered-Din

1898. Chahi values on white or green paper.

116	17	1c. grey	1·20	25
117	17	2c. brown	1·20	25
118	17	3c. purple	1·20	25
119	17	4c. red	1·20	25
120	17	5c. yellow	3·25	25
121	17	8c. orange	3·25	80
154	17	10c. blue	4·00	1·60
123	17	12c. red	2·50	80
124	17	16c. green	5·25	80
125	21	1k. blue	5·00	80
157	21	1k. red	21·00	8·25
126	21	2k. pink	4·00	1·60
158	21	2k. green	25·00	1·60
127	21	3k. yellow	4·00	1·60
159	21	3k. brown	25·00	12·50
128	21	4k. grey	4·00	1·60

160	21	4k. red	25·00	12·50
129	21	5k. green	4·00	1·60
161	21	5k. brown	25·00	12·50
130	21	10k. orange	12·50	6·50
162	21	10k. blue	£100	12·50
131	21	50k. mauve	25·00	16·00
163	21	50k. brown	80·00	12·50

(21a)

1899. Optd with control mark of various scroll devices as T **21a.**

132	17	1c. grey	4·00	1·20
133	17	2c. brown	4·00	1·20
134	17	3c. purple	4·00	1·20
135	17	4c. red	4·00	1·20
136	17	5c. yellow	4·00	80
137	17	8c. brown	4·00	1·50
138	17	10c. blue	4·00	80
139	17	12c. red	12·50	1·00
140	17	16c. green	21·00	1·60
141	21	1k. blue	21·00	80
142	21	2k. pink	25·00	2·50
143	21	3k. yellow	25·00	3·00
144	21	4k. grey	25·00	3·00
145	21	5k. green	25·00	3·00
146	21	10k. orange	£100	3·00
147	21	50k. mauve	80·00	6·50

(22)

1900. Optd with T **22** across two stamps.

164	17	1c. grey	29·00	12·50
165	17	2c. brown	37·00	16·00
166	17	3c. purple	60·00	41·00
167	17	4c. red	65·00	41·00
168	17	5c. yellow	16·00	8·25
169	17	10c. blue	£250	80·00
170	17	12c. red	65·00	41·00

Prices quoted in this issue are for pairs.

1901. Surch in various ways in English and Persian.

176		5 on 8c. brown	41·00	2·50
179	21	12c. on 1k. red	80·00	41·00
180	21	5k. on 50k. brown	£160	41·00

(24)

1902. Surch with T **24.**

177	17	5c. on 10c. blue	41·00	16·00
178	17	5c. on 1k. red	41·00	16·00

1902. Optd **PROVISOIRE 1319** in ornamental frame.

181	17	1c. grey	16·00	1·60
182	17	2c. brown	16·00	1·60
183	17	3c. purple	16·00	1·60
184	17	4c. red	16·00	80
185	17	5c. yellow	33·00	2·50
197	17	5 on 8c. brown (No. 176)	80·00	41·00
186	17	8c. orange	49·00	4·00
187	17	10c. blue	41·00	5·00
188	17	12c. red	75·00	10·50
198	21	12c. on 1k. (No. 179)	80·00	41·00
189	21	16c. green	£120	25·00
190	21	1k. red	£600	£500
191	21	2k. green		29·00
192	21	3k. brown		45·00
193	21	4k. red		49·00
194	21	5k. brown		55·00
199	21	5k. on 50k. (No. 180)	£160	41·00
195	21	10k. blue		55·00
196	21	50k. brown		60·00

28   (29)

1902. Inscr "CHAHIS" or "KRANS" in capital letters. Optd with T **29.**

200	28	1c. grey	31·00	2·10
201	28	2c. brown	55·00	2·30
202	28	3c. purple	60·00	2·10
203	28	5c. red	31·00	2·10
204	28	10c. yellow	60·00	2·10
205	28	12c. blue	75·00	3·00

206	28	1k. mauve	£110	3·50
207	28	2k. green	£110	7·00
208	28	10k. blue	£130	65·00
209	28	50k. red	£550	£425

1902. Surch **5 KRANS** in English and Persian.

210		5k. on 5k. yellow	£140	41·00

1902. Optd **PROVISOIRE 1319** in ornamental frame.

211		1c. grey	£120	80·00
212		2c. brown	£120	80·00
213		3c. green	£140	90·00
214		5c. red	80·00	65·00
215		12c. blue	£160	£120

34

1902. Inscr "Chahis" or "Krans" in lower case letters.

227	34	1c. grey	16·00	1·60
228	34	2c. brown	16·00	1·60
229	34	3c. green	16·00	1·60
230	34	5c. red	16·00	80
231	34	10c. yellow	33·00	2·50
232	34	12c. blue	49·00	4·00
233	34	1k. mauve	41·00	5·00
234	34	2k. green	75·00	10·50
235	34	10k. blue	£120	25·00
236	34	50k. red	£600	£500

1902. Surch **5 KRANS** without T **29** opt.

237		5k. on 5k. yellow	£140	41·00

1903. Optd **PROVISOIRE 1903** and lion in frame, but without Arms opt (T **29**).

239	28	1c. grey		11·50
240	28	2c. brown		11·50
241	28	5c. red		7·50
242	28	10c. yellow		23·00
243	28	12c. blue		38·00
244	28	1k. mauve		46·00

38   **39** Muzaffered-Din

1903

246	38	1c. lilac	1·60	25
247	38	2c. grey	1·60	25
248	38	3c. green	1·60	25
249	38	5c. red	1·60	25
250	38	10c. brown	2·50	1·20
251	38	12c. blue	3·25	50
252	39	1k. purple	9·75	40
253	39	2k. blue	16·00	1·00
254	39	5k. brown	25·00	1·60
255	39	10k. red	25·00	3·25
256	39	20k. orange	29·00	4·00
257	39	30k. green	49·00	9·75
258	39	50k. green	£325	80·00

See also Nos. 298/303.

1903. Surch in both English and Persian except those marked* which are surch in English only.

272	38	"1 CHAHI" on 3c. green	12·50	8·25
287	38	"1 CHAI" on 3c. green	29·00	12·50
288	39	1c. on 1k. purple	29·00	12·50
273	38	2c. on 3c. green	12·50	8·25
289	39	2c. on 5k. brown	33·00	21·00
277	38	3c. on 10c. brown	16·00	80
278	38	6c. on 10c. brown	16·00	80
279	39	9c. on 1k. purple	29·00	3·25
274	39	12c. on 10k. red	60·00	33·00
275	39	2t. on 50k. green*	£140	80·00
280	39	3t. on 50k. green	£120	49·00
276	39	3t. on 50k. green*	£160	£100
281	39	3t. on 50k. green	£120	49·00

50

1906. Optd **PROVISOIRE** and lion. Imperf or perf.

292	50	1c. violet	4·00	80
293	50	2c. grey	6·25	4·00
294	50	3c. green	4·00	80
295	50	6c. red	6·25	80
296	50	10c. brown	49·00	37·00
297	50	13c. blue	29·00	8·25

52 Shah Muhammad Ali Mirza

1907

298	38	1ch. violet on blue	1·60	35
299	38	2ch. grey on blue	1·60	35
300	38	3ch. green on blue	1·60	35
301	38	6ch. red on blue	1·60	35
302	38	9ch. yellow on blue	1·60	40
303	38	10ch. sepia on blue	2·50	1·20
305	52	13c. blue	3·25	1·60
306	52	26c. brown	5·00	1·20
307	52	1k. red	4·00	1·60
308	52	2k. green	10·50	1·20
309	52	3k. blue	11·50	80
311	52	4k. ochre	12·50	2·50
312	52	5k. brown	12·50	2·50
313	52	10k. pink	16·00	2·50
314	52	20k. brown	16·00	8·25
315	52	30k. purple	16·00	12·50
316	–	50k. red and gold	80·00	21·00

The 50k. is larger with the head facing the other way.

(54)

1909. Nos. 298/315 optd as T **54.** Imperf.

320	38	1ch. on 1ch. violet on blue	£120	80·00
321	38	1ch. on 2ch. grey on blue	£120	80·00
322	38	1ch. on 3ch. green on blue	£120	80·00
323	38	1ch. on 6ch. red on blue	£120	80·00
324	38	1ch. on 9ch. yellow on blue	£120	80·00
325	38	1ch. on 10ch. brown on bl	£120	80·00
326	52	2ch. on 13ch. blue	£120	80·00
327	52	2ch. on 26ch. brown	£120	80·00
328	52	2ch. on 1kr. red	£120	80·00
329	52	2ch. on 2kr. green	£120	80·00
330	52	2ch. on 3kr. blue	£120	80·00
331	52	2ch. on 4kr. yellow	£120	80·00
333	52	2ch. on 5kr. brown	£120	80·00
334	52	2ch. on 10kr. pink	£120	80·00
335	52	2ch. on 20kr. black	£120	80·00
336	52	2ch. on 30kr. purple	£120	80·00

56

1909

337	56	1c. purple and orange	1·60	25
338	56	2c. purple and violet	1·60	25
339	56	3c. purple and green	1·60	25
340	56	6c. purple and red	1·60	25
341	56	9c. purple and grey	2·75	35
342	56	10c. maroon and purple	2·75	35
343	56	13c. purple and blue	5·25	50
344	56	26c. purple and green	5·25	65
345	56	1k. brown, violet and silver	5·25	1·10
346	56	2k. brown, green and silver	21·00	1·60
347	56	3k. brown, grey and silver	21·00	2·10
348	56	4k. brown, blue and silver	25·00	3·25
349	56	5k. sepia, brown and gold	29·00	4·00
350	56	10k. brown, orange and gold	£100	10·50
351	56	20k. brown, green and gold	£120	12·50
352	56	30k. brown, red and gold	£200	15·00

Stamps of this issue offered at very low prices are reprints.

For stamps as Type 56 but with curved inscriptions, see Nos. O836 etc.

1911

361	57	1c. orange and green	65	25
362	57	2c. brown and red	65	25
363	57	3c. green and grey	65	25
364	57	3c. green and brown	65	1·10
365	57	5c. red and green	1·10	80
366	57	6c. red and grey	1·10	25
367	57	6c. red and green	65	25
368	57	9c. lilac and brown	1·10	25
369	57	10c. brown and red	2·10	25
370	57	12c. blue and green	2·50	25
371	57	13c. blue and violet	12·50	2·10
372	57	24c. green and purple	7·00	25
373	57	26c. brown and blue	5·25	25
374	57	1k. red and blue	21·00	7·50
375	57	2k. purple and green	10·50	60
376	57	3k. black and lilac	14·00	60
377	57	4k. black and gold	49·00	16·00
378	57	5k. blue and red	29·00	1·10
379	57	10k. pink and brown	£180	4·00
380	57	20k. buff and brown	£200	8·25
381	57	30k. green and red	£300	9·75

1911. Various stamps optd **Relais** in English and Persian.

382	56	2ch. purple and violet	80·00	41·00
386	57	2ch. brown and red	80·00	41·00
383	56	3ch. purple and green	80·00	41·00
387	57	3ch. green and grey	80·00	41·00
384	56	6ch. purple and red	80·00	41·00
388	57	6ch. red and grey	80·00	41·00
385	56	13ch. purple and blue	80·00	60·00
388a	57	13ch. blue and violet	£100	60·00

1912. Optd **Officiel** in English and Persian.

389		1c. orange and green	16·00	2·50
390		2c. brown and red	16·00	2·50
391		3c. green and grey	16·00	2·50
392		6c. red and grey	16·00	2·50
393		9c. lilac and brown	16·00	2·50
394		10c. brown and red	25·00	2·50
395		13c. blue and violet	25·00	4·00
396		26c. green and blue	60·00	5·75
397		1k. red and blue	49·00	8·25
398		2k. purple and green	60·00	8·25
399		3k. black and lilac	80·00	8·25
400		5k. blue and red	£120	12·50
401		10k. pink and brown	£250	25·00
402		20k. buff and brown	£250	25·00
403		30k. green and red	£325	33·00

1914. Surch with new value and **1914** in English and Persian.

412		1c. on 13c. blue and violet	12·50	1·60
413		3c. on 26c. green and blue	12·50	3·25

1915. Surch with new value in frame and **1915** in English and Persian.

414		1c. on 5c. red and brown	12·50	1·60
415b		2c. on 5c. red and brown	12·50	1·60
416		6c. on 12c. blue and green	16·00	1·60

1915. Surch with new value in English and Persian.

417	56	5c. on 1k. (No. 345)	21·00	4·00
418	56	12c. on 13c. (No. 343)	25·00	5·75

 ۱۳۳۳

(65)

1915. Optd with T **65** ("1333").

419		1c. purple and orange	12·50	2·10
420		2c. purple and violet	12·50	2·10
421		3c. purple and green	12·50	2·10
422		6c. purple and red	12·50	2·10
423		9c. purple and grey	12·50	2·50
424		10c. purple and mauve	41·00	4·00
425		1k. brown, violet and silver	60·00	4·00

66 The Imperial Crown   **67** King Darius on his Throne

1915. Coronation of Shah Ahmed.

426	66	1c. blue and red	25	1·60
427	66	2c. red and blue	25	1·60
428	66	3c. green	25	1·60
429	66	5c. red	25	2·10
430	66	6c. red and green	25	1·60
431	66	9c. violet and brown	25	1·60

57 Ahmed Mirza

1911

432	66	10c. brown and green	25	1·60
433	66	12c. blue	25	1·60
434	66	24c. sepia and brown	25	4·00
435	67	1k. black, brown and silver	65	4·00
436	67	2k. red, blue and silver	65	4·00
437	67	3k. brown, lilac and silver	75	4·00
438	67	5k. grey, brown and silver	75	5·75
439	–	1t. black, violet and gold	75	8·25
440	–	2t. brown, green and gold	80	8·25
441	–	3t. red, crimson and gold	80	8·25
442	–	5t. grey, blue and gold	80	8·25

DESIGNS: 1t. to 5t. Gateway of the Palace of Persepolis.

۱۳۳۴

(69)

1915. Optd with T **69** ("1334").

477	56	1k. brown, violet and silver	41·00	16·00
478	56	10k. brown, orange and gold	41·00	16·00
479	56	20k. brown, green and gold	£160	65·00
480	56	30k. brown, red and gold	£160	65·00

1917. Surch with value in English only.

481	57	12c. on 1k. red and blue	£800	£600
482	57	24c. on 1k. red and blue	£500	£325

۱۳۳۵

(73)

1917. Optd with T **73** ("1335") or surch also with new value in English and Persian.

483	56	1c. purple and orange	£250	£160
484	56	1c. on 2c. (No. 338)	16·00	2·50
485	56	1c. on 9c. (No. 341)	21·00	3·25
486	56	1c. on 10c. (No. 342)	16·00	2·50
490	57	1c. on 10c. brown and red	25·00	1·20
487	56	3c. on 9c. purple and grey	21·00	3·25
491	57	3c. on 10c. brown and red	25·00	1·20
488	56	3c. on 26c. (No. 344)	25·00	4·00
489	56	5c. on 13c. (No. 343)	23·00	3·75
492	57	5c. on 1k. red and blue	30·00	6·50
493	57	6c. on 10c. brown and red	45·00	15·00
494	57	6c. on 12c. blue and green	49·00	12·50

۱۳۳۶

(78)

1918. Optd with T **78** ("1336").

507	56	2k. brown, green and silver	41·00	8·25

1918. Surch as T **78** and new value in English and Persian.

508		24c. on 4k. (No. 348)	49·00	8·25
509		10k. on 5k. (No. 349)	80·00	12·50

1918. Coronation issue of 1915 optd **Novembre 1918** (date also in Persian).

510	67	2k. red, blue and silver	8·25	8·25
511	67	3k. brown, lilac and silver	8·25	8·25
512	67	5k. grey, brown and silver	8·25	8·25
513	–	1t. black, violet and gold	12·50	12·50
514	–	2t. brown, green and gold	12·50	12·50
515	–	3t. red, crimson and gold	12·50	12·50
516	–	5t. grey, blue and gold	12·50	16·00

(82)

1918. Surch as T **82** and new value in English and Persian.

517	57	3c. on 12c. blue and green	33·00	1·20
518	57	6c. on 10c. brown and red	21·00	1·20
519	57	6c. on 1k. red and blue	21·00	1·20

1918. Optd with bottom line of T **82** ("1337").

520	56	2k. brown, green and silver	80·00	55·00
521	56	3k. brown, grey and silver	49·00	12·50
522	56	4k. brown, blue and silver	80·00	41·00
523	56	5k. sepia, brown and gold	£120	49·00

524	56	10k. brown, orange and gold	£150	49·00
525	56	20k. brown, green and gold	£400	£160
526	56	30k. brown, red and gold	£120	80·00

84 Ahmed Mirza

1919. Type **84** surch Provisoire 1919 and value in English and Persian.

527	84	1c. yellow	12·50	80
528	84	3c. green	12·50	80
529	84	5c. purple	25·00	2·50
530	84	6c. violet	5·00	80
531	84	12c. blue	49·00	8·25

1919. Surch **1919** and value in English and Persian.

532	13	2k. on 5c. mauve	6·25	6·25
533	13	3k. on 5c. mauve	6·25	6·25
534	13	4k. on 5c. mauve	6·25	6·25
535	13	5k. on 5c. mauve	6·25	6·25
536	15	10k. on 10c. red	16·00	16·00
537	15	20k. on 10c. red	16·00	16·00
538	15	30k. on 10c. red	16·00	16·00
539	15	50k. on 14c. orange	16·00	2·50

1921. Surch **6-CHAHIS** in English and Persian.

539a	57	6c. on 12c. blue and green	£160	12·50

1921. Coup d'Etat of Reza Khan. Coronation issue of 1915 optd **21. FEV. 1921** in English and Persian.

540	66	3c. green	12·50	
541	66	5c. red	12·50	
542	66	6c. red and green	12·50	
543	66	10c. brown and green	12·50	
544	66	12c. blue	12·50	
545	67	1k. black, brown and silver	16·00	
546	67	2k. red, blue and silver	16·00	
547	67	5k. grey, brown and silver	16·00	
548	-	2t. brown, green and gold	21·00	
549	-	3t. red, crimson and gold	25·00	
550	-	5t. grey, blue and gold	25·00	

1922. Surch with value in English only.

551	57	10c. on 6c. brown & green	£100	33·00
552	57	1k. on 12c. blue and green	£100	33·00

1922. Surcharged with value in English only over **BENADERS**.

553		10c. on 6c. brown & green	£100	33·00
554		1k. on 12c. blue and green	£100	33·00

1922. Optd **CONTROLE 1922** in English and Persian.

555		1c. orange and green	3·25	25
556		2c. brown and red	3·25	25
557		3c. green and grey	3·25	25
558		3c. green and brown	3·50	25
559		5ch. red and brown	60·00	21·00
560		6c. brown and green	4·00	25
561		9c. lilac and brown	4·00	25
562		10c. brown and red	5·00	25
563		12c. blue and green	9·75	10
564		24c. green and purple	12·50	80
565		1k. red and blue	12·50	80
566		2k. purple and green	33·00	80
567		3k. black and lilac	37·00	50
568		4k. blue and black	49·00	16·00
569		5k. blue and red	41·00	1·60
570		10k. red and brown	£200	4·00
571		20k. yellow and brown	£200	5·75
572		30k. green and red	£325	8·25

1922. Surch in English and Persian.

573		3c. on 12c. (No. 563)	37·00	1·60
574		6c. on 24c. (No. 564)	37·00	1·60
575		10c. on 20k. (No. 571)	60·00	8·25
576		1k. on 30k. (No. 572)	80·00	12·50

92 Ahmed Mirza

1924

577	92	1c. orange	2·75	25
578	92	2c. red	2·75	25
579	92	3c. brown	2·75	25
580	92	6c. sepia	2·75	25
581	92	9c. green	5·25	80
582	92	10c. violet	5·25	35
583	92	12c. red	5·25	40
584	92	1k. blue	5·25	1·10
585	92	2k. red and blue	5·25	1·60
586	92	3k. purple and violet	15·00	1·60
587	92	5k. sepia and red	16·00	16·00
588	92	10k. violet and sepia	21·00	21·00
589	92	20k. sepia and green	25·00	25·00
590	92	30k. black and orange	33·00	33·00

1924. Surch **p. re. 1924** and value in English and Persian.

591	84	1c. brown	2·10	1·10
592	84	2c. grey	2·10	1·10
593	84	3c. red	2·10	1·10
594	84	6c. orange	4·00	1·60

1925. Surch **p. re. 1925** and value in English and Persian.

595		2c. green	2·50	50
596		3c. red	2·50	50
597		6c. blue	2·50	50
598		9c. brown	8·25	50
599		10c. grey	16·00	2·50
600		1k. green	33·00	5·75
601		2k. mauve	80·00	21·00

94   **95** "Provisional Pahlavi Government, 31 Oct 1925"

1925. Deposition of Shah Ahmed and Provisional Government of Riza Khan Pahlavi. Fiscal stamps as T **94** (various frames) optd with T **95**.

602	94	1c. red	5·75	3·25
603	94	2c. yellow	5·75	3·25
604	94	3c. green	5·75	3·25
605	94	5c. grey	25·00	12·50
606	94	10c. red	12·50	4·00
607	94	1k. blue	12·50	8·25

(96)

1926. Optd with T **96**.

608	92	1c. orange	2·50	1·20
609	92	2c. red	2·50	1·60
610	92	3c. brown	3·25	1·20
611	92	6c. sepia	60·00	60·00

1926. Optd **Regne de Pahlavi 1926** in English and Persian.

612A	56	1c. purple and orange	5·75	25
613A	56	2c. purple and violet	5·75	25
614A	56	3c. purple and green	5·75	25
615A	56	6c. purple and red	5·75	25
616A	56	9c. purple and grey	5·75	25
617A	56	10c. maroon and purple	5·75	40
618A	56	13c. purple and blue	12·50	40
619A	56	26c. purple and green	25·00	40
620A	56	1k. brown, violet and silver	12·50	40
621A	56	2k. brown, green and silver	25·00	50
622A	56	3k. brown, grey and silver	60·00	50
623A	56	4k. brown, blue and silver	£400	8·25
624A	56	5k. sepia, brown and gold	£120	7·00
625A	56	10k. brown, orange and gold	£325	8·75
626A	56	20k. brown, green and gold	£475	9·75
627A	56	30k. brown, red and gold	£400	12·50

98 Riza Shah Pahlavi   **99** Riza Shah Pahlavi

1926

628	98	1c. green	3·25	25
629	98	2c. blue	3·25	25
630	98	3c. green	3·25	25
631	98	6c. red	4·00	25
632	98	9c. red	8·25	40
633	98	10c. brown	16·00	4·00
634	98	12c. orange	16·00	2·50
635	98	15c. blue	21·00	1·60
636	99	1k. blue	33·00	8·25
637	99	2k. mauve	£120	33·00

1927. Air. Optd with airplane and **POSTE AERIENNE** in English and Persian.

642	56	1c. purple and orange	1·60	80
643	56	2c. purple and violet	1·60	80
644	56	3c. purple and green	1·60	80
645	56	6c. purple and red	1·60	80
646	56	9c. purple and grey	3·25	80
647	56	10c. maroon and purple	5·00	80
648	56	13c. purple and blue	6·50	2·10
649	56	26c. purple and green	6·50	2·10
650	56	1k. brown, violet and silver	6·50	2·10
651	56	2k. brown, green and silver	6·50	2·10
652	56	3k. brown, grey and silver	21·00	8·25
653	56	4k. brown, blue and silver	33·00	12·50
654	56	5k. sepia, brown and gold	33·00	8·25
655	56	10k. brown, orange and gold	£450	£160
656	56	20k. brown, green and gold	£300	£160
657	56	30k. brown, red and gold	£300	£160

1928. Air. Fiscal stamps surch with Junkers F-13 airplane, **Poste aerien** and new value in French and Persian.

657a	94	3k. brown	£100	33·00
657b	94	5k. brown	25·00	8·25
657c	94	1t. violet	25·00	8·25
657d	94	2t. green	25·00	8·25
657e	94	3t. green	29·00	12·50

102

1929. Air. Fiscal stamps as T **102** (various frames) surch with Junkers F-13 airplane, **Poste aerienne** and value in French and Persian.

658	102	1c. purple	80	50
659	102	2c. blue	80	25
660	102	3c. red	80	25
661	102	5c. brown	80	25
662	102	10c. green	80	25
663	102	1k. violet	1·60	80
664	102	2k. orange	4·00	1·60
665	102	3k. brown (22×30 mm)	80·00	21·00
666	102	5k. brown (22×33 mm)	16·00	4·00
667	102	10k. violet (21×31 mm)	21·00	8·25
668	102	20k. green (21×31 mm)	25·00	8·25
669	102	30k. green (21×31 mm)	33·00	12·50

104 Riza Shah Pahlavi

1929

670	104	1c. red and green	1·60	25
671	104	2c. blue and red	1·20	25
672	104	3c. green and red	1·20	25
673	104	6c. green and brown	1·60	25
674	104	9c. red and blue	2·50	35
675	104	10c. brown and green	3·25	35
676	104	12c. violet and black	5·00	40
677	104	15c. blue and yellow	5·75	40
678	104	24c. lake and olive	5·75	40
679	104	1k. black and blue	8·25	1·20
680	104	2k. violet and orange	70·00	90
681	104	3k. red and green	85·00	90
682	104	5k. green and brown	36·00	2·20
683	104	1t. red and blue	36·00	4·50
684	104	2t. black and red	42·00	27·00
685	-	3t. violet and gold	75·00	30·00

DESIGN: 3t. Shah enthroned (28½×39 mm).

106 Riza Shah Pahlavi and Elburz Mts

1930. Air.

686	106	1c. blue and yellow	40	40
687	106	2c. black and blue	40	40
688	106	3c. violet and olive	40	40
689	106	4c. blue and violet	40	40
690	106	5c. red and green	40	40
691	106	6c. green and red	40	40
692	106	8c. violet and grey	40	40
693	106	10c. red and blue	40	40
694	106	12c. orange and grey	40	40
695	106	15c. olive and brown	40	40
696	106	1k. red and blue	4·00	2·10
697	106	2k. blue and black	4·00	2·10
698	106	3k. green and brown	3·50	2·00
699	106	5k. black and red	3·75	2·75
700	106	1t. purple and orange	18·00	3·50
701	106	2t. brown and green	18·00	7·50
702	106	3t. green and purple	£130	48·00

107

1931

703	107	1c. blue and brown	2·50	25
704	107	2c. black and red	2·50	25
705	107	3c. brown and mauve	2·50	25
706	107	6c. violet and red	2·50	25
707	107	9c. red and blue	8·25	40
708	107	10c. grey and red	8·25	80
709	107	11c. red and blue	20·00	60
710	107	12c. mauve and blue	14·00	40
711	107	16c. red and black	28·00	90
712	107	27c. blue and black	46·00	95
713	107	1k. blue and red	40·00	1·20

108 Riza Shah Pahlavi   **109**

1933. New Currency.

714	108	5d. brown	1·20	25
715	108	10d. blue	1·20	25
716	108	15d. grey	1·20	25
717	108	30d. green	1·20	25
718	108	45d. blue	1·20	25
719	108	50d. mauve	1·20	25
720	108	60d. green	3·25	40
721	108	75d. brown	5·75	65
722	108	90d. red	6·50	80
723	109	1k. black and red	16·00	80
724	109	1r.20 red and black	18·00	45
725	109	1r.50 blue and yellow	22·00	45
726	109	2r. brown and blue	28·00	50
727	109	3r. green and mauve	36·00	75
728	109	5r. red and brown	£180	10·50

110 "Justice"   **112** Cement Works, Chah-Abdul-Azim

1935. Tenth Anniv of Riza Khan's Advent to Power.

729	110	5d. green and brown	1·20	40
730	-	10d. grey and orange	1·20	40
731	-	15d. blue and red	1·60	40
732	-	30d. green and black	1·60	40
733	-	45d. lake and olive	2·50	40
734	112	75d. brown and green	4·00	80
735	-	90d. red and blue	18·00	50
736	-	1r. violet and brown	28·00	4·25
737	-	1r.50 blue and purple	40·00	6·50

DESIGNS: 10d. Ruins of Persepolis (40×26 mm); 15d. "Education" (23×33 mm); 30d. De Havilland Tiger Moth biplanes over Teheran Aerodrome (38×25 mm); 45d. Sakhtessar Sanatorium, Mazanderan (40×27 mm); 90d. Gunboat "Palang" (38×24 mm); 1r. Railway bridge over R. Karun (42×29 mm); 1r.50, Post and Customs House, Teheran (42×27 mm).

1935. Optd **POSTES IRANIENNES.** (a) Stamps of 1929.

738	104	1c. red and green	90·00	23·00
739	104	2c. blue and red	38·00	30·00
740	104	3c. green and red	55·00	38·00
741	104	6c. green and brown	38·00	1·50
742	104	9c. red and blue	19·00	9·50
743	104	1t. red and blue	38·00	3·75

744	104	2t. black and red	38·00	30·00
745	-	3t. violet and gold	90·00	49·00

(b) Stamps of 1931.

746	107	1c. blue and brown	90·00	30·00
747	107	2c. black and red	10·00	4·00
748	107	3c. brown and mauve	5·00	4·50
749	107	6c. violet and red	22·00	14·00
750	107	9c. red and blue	22·00	14·00
751	107	11c. red and blue	1·00	15
752	107	12c. mauve and blue	65·00	25·00
753	107	16c. red and black	16·00	15
754	107	27c. blue and black	21·00	15

(c) Stamps of 1933.

755	108	5c. brown	90	10
756	108	10d. blue	10	10
757	108	15d. grey	90	10
758	108	30d. green	90	10
759	108	45d. blue	90	10
760	108	50d. mauve	1·60	10
761	108	60d. green	2·50	20
762	108	75d. brown	5·25	60
763	108	90d. red	6·00	75
764	109	1r. black and red	15·00	75
765	109	1r.20 red and black	19·00	75
766	109	1r.50 blue and green	23·00	75
767	109	2r. brown and blue	30·00	75
768	109	3r. green and mauve	38·00	1·10
769	109	5r. red and brown	1·90	19·00

1935. Air. Air stamps of 1930 optd **Iran**.

770	106	1c. blue and yellow	40	40
771	106	2c. black and blue	40	40
772	106	3c. violet and olive	40	40
773	106	4c. blue and violet	40	40
774	106	5c. red and green	40	40
775	106	6c. green and red	40	40
776	106	8c. violet and grey	40	40
777	106	10c. red and blue	40	40
778	106	12c. orange and blue	40	40
779	106	15c. olive and brown	40	40
780	106	1k. red and blue	6·75	6·75
781	106	2k. blue and black	23·00	6·25
782	106	3k. green and brown	4·75	4·50
783	106	5k. black and red	5·00	4·75
784	106	1t. purple and orange	£100	70·00
785	106	2t. brown and green	14·50	10·50
786	106	3t. green and purple	70·00	30·00

116

1935. Rial values are larger, 22×31 mm.

787	116	5d. violet	1·10	25
788	116	10d. purple	1·10	25
789	116	15d. blue	1·10	25
790	116	30d. green	1·50	25
791	116	45d. orange	1·50	25
792	116	50d. brown	1·90	30
793	116	60d. blue	4·50	40
794	116	75d. red	4·50	55
795	116	90d. red	9·00	1·10
796	116	1r. purple	15·00	75
797	116	1r.50 blue	19·00	1·50
798	116	2r. green	30·00	75
799	116	3r. brown	34·00	1·00
800	116	5r. grey	£160	70·00

117 Riza Shah Pahlavi

1936. Rial values are larger, 23×31 mm.

801	117	5d. violet	40	15
802	117	10d. mauve	40	15
803	117	15d. blue	75	25
804	117	30d. green	75	25
805	117	45d. red	90	25
806	117	50d. brown	1·10	25
807	117	60d. brown	1·10	25
808	117	75d. red	1·50	25
809	117	90d. red	1·90	25
810	117	1r. green	11·50	40
811	117	1r.50 blue	11·50	40
812	117	2r. blue	15·00	40
813	117	3r. purple	19·00	75
814	117	5r. green	30·00	90
815	117	10r. blue and brown	£150	15·00

117a

1938. 60th Birthday of Shah. Perf or imperf.

815a	117a	5d. blue	1·10	75
815b	117a	10d. red	1·10	75
815c	117a	30d. blue	1·10	75
815d	117a	60d. brown	1·10	75
815e	117a	90d. red	3·50	1·50
815f	117a	1r. violet	7·50	
815g	117a	1r.50 blue	7·50	3·75
815h	117a	2r. red	7·50	3·75
815i	117a	5r. mauve	30·00	15·00
815j	117a	10r. red	55·00	45·00

118 Riza Shah Pahlavi

1938. Rial values are larger, 23×31 mm.

816	118	5d. violet	40	15
817	118	10d. mauve	40	15
818	118	15d. blue	50	15
819	118	30d. blue	50	15
820	118	45d. red	55	15
821	118	50d. brown	90	15
822	118	60d. orange	90	20
823	118	75d. red	1·60	20
824	118	90d. red	2·40	20
825	118	1r. green	7·25	15
826	118	1r.50 blue	9·25	20
827	118	2r. blue	11·50	25
828	118	3r. purple	20·00	35
829	118	5r. green	33·00	60
830	118	10r. blue and brown	£110	8·00

119 Princess Fawzieh and Crown Prince

1939. Royal Wedding.

831	119	5d. brown	20	25
832	119	10d. violet	30	25
833	119	30d. green	70	30
834	119	90d. red	10·00	55
835	119	1r.50 blue	15·00	1·10

120 Railway Bridge over Karun River

123 Mohammed Riza Pahlavi

1942

850	120	5d. violet	1·10	15
851	120	5d. orange	40	15
852	-	10d. mauve	1·10	15
853	-	10d. green	40	15
854	-	20d. violet	1·50	15
855	-	20d. mauve	75	15
856	-	25d. red	19·00	3·75
857	-	25d. violet	3·75	40
858	-	35d. green	1·10	25
859	-	50d. blue	1·90	25
860	-	50d. green	1·10	15
861	-	70d. brown	1·10	30
862	-	75d. purple	9·00	30
863	-	75d. red	7·50	30
864	-	1r. red	7·50	25
865	-	1r. purple	7·50	25
866	-	1r.50 red	7·50	25
867	123	2r. blue	11·50	25
868	-	2r. green	9·00	25
869	-	2r.50 blue	11·50	25
870	-	3r. green	75·00	75
871	-	3r. purple	30·00	30
872	-	5r. green	£140	7·50
873	-	5r. blue	19·00	40
874	123	10r. black and orange	38·00	2·30
875	123	10r. black and brown	15·00	75
876	123	20r. violet and brown	£375	38·00
877	123	20r. black and orange	75·00	3·00
878	123	30r. green and black	£900	38·00
879	123	30r. black and green	34·00	3·75
880	123	50r. red and blue	£110	19·00
881	123	50r. black and purple	38·00	7·50
882	123	100r. black and red	£275	38·00
883	123	200r. black and blue	£275	38·00

DESIGNS—HORIZ: 10d. Vereshk Railway Bridge, N. Iran; 20d. Granary, Ahwaz; 25d. Steam train on Karj Bridge; 50d. Ministry of Justice; 70d. School building. VERT: 35d. Museum; 75d. Side view of museum; 1 to 5r. Full-face portrait of Mohammed Riza Pahlavi.

124 Lion and Bull, Persepolis

1948. Fund to rebuild Avicenna's Tomb at Hamadan (1st issue).

899	124	50d.+25d. green	15	25
900	-	1r.+50d. red	30	40
901	-	2½r.+1¼r. blue	60	55
902	-	5r.+2½r. violet	1·30	1·10
903	-	10r.+5r. purple	2·30	1·50

DESIGNS—VERT: 1r. Persian Warrior, Persepolis. HORIZ: 2½r. Palace of Darius, Persepolis; 5r. Tomb of Cyrus, Pasargades; 10r. King Darius enthroned.
See also Nos. 909/13, 930/4, 939/43 and 1024/28.

126 National Flag

1949. Iran's War Effort.

904	126	25d. multicoloured	1·90	75
905	-	50d. violet	1·90	1·00
906	-	1r.50 red	9·00	1·20
907	-	2r.50 blue	11·50	1·50
908	-	5r. green	38·00	2·40

DESIGNS—HORIZ: 50d. Bandar Shahpur (port); 1r.50, Lorries on winding road; 2r.50, Vereshk Railway Bridge; 5r. Mohammed Riza Pahlavi and map of Iran.

127 King Ardashir II

128 King Ardashir I and Ahura Mazda

1949. Fund to rebuild Avicenna's Tomb (2nd issue).

909	127	50d.+25d. green	95	95
910	-	1r.+50d. red	95	95
911	-	2½r.+1¼r. blue	1·00	1·00
912	-	5r.+2½r. plum	1·50	1·50
913	128	10r.+5r. green	2·00	1·80

DESIGNS—VERT: 1r. King Narses. HORIZ: 2½r. King Shapur I and Emperor Valerian; 5r. Arch of Ctesiphon.

129 Mohammed Riza Pahlavi and Post and Customs House, Teheran

130 Old G.P.O., Teheran

131 Mohammed Riza Pahlavi

1949

914	-	5d. green and red	45	25
915	-	10d. brown and blue	45	25
916	-	20d. blue and violet	45	40
917	-	25d. blue and brown	45	25
918	-	50d. blue and green	90	25
919	-	75d. red and brown	1·70	40
920	-	1r. green and violet	2·30	25
921	-	1r.50 red and green	2·30	25
922	129	2r. brown and red	3·50	40
923	-	2r.50 blue	3·50	40
924	-	3r. orange and blue	4·50	15
925	-	5r. violet and red	7·25	15
926	130	10r. green and red	24·00	55
927	130	20r. red and black	£400	13·00
928	131	30r. blue and brown	43·00	6·75
929	131	50r. blue and red	43·00	6·75

DESIGNS—HORIZ: All show buildings. In the dinar values, portrait is to right of stamp, and in rial values, to left; 5d. Ramsar Hotel, Darband, Caspian Sea; 10d. Zayende River Bridge; 20d. Bank Melli Iran building; 25d. Old Royal Palace, Isfahan; 50d. Chaharbagh School, Isfahan; 75d. Railway Square; 1r. Justice Ministry; 1r.50, Shah Mosque, Teheran; 2r.50, Parliament Building; 3r. The Great Gate, Isfahan; 5r. Isfahan.

132 Tomb of Ali Abarquh

1949. Fund to rebuild Avicenna's Tomb (3rd issue).

930	132	50d.+25d. green	1·10	1·10
931	-	1r.+50d. brown	1·10	1·10
932	-	2½r.+1¼r. blue	1·10	1·10
933	-	5r.+2½r. red	2·30	2·30
934	-	10r.+5r. olive	2·30	2·30

DESIGNS—VERT: 1r. Jami Mosque, Isfahan. HORIZ: 2½r. Tomb tower, Hamadan; 5r. Jami Mosque, Ardistan; 10r. Seljuk coin.

134 Allegory

1950. 75th Anniv of U.P.U.

935	-	50d. lake	27·00	25·00
936	134	2r.50 blue	33·00	33·00

DESIGN—HORIZ: 50d. Hemispheres and doves.

135 Riza Shah Pahlavi and Mausoleum

1950. Interment of Riza Shah Pahlavi at Shah Abdul Azim.

937	135	50d. brown	13·00	5·25
938	135	2r. black	27·00	7·75

136 Tomb of Baba Afzal, Kashan

1950. Fund to Rebuild Avicenna's Tomb (4th issue).

939	136	50d.+25d. green	1·50	1·50
940	-	1r.+50d. blue	1·50	1·50
941	-	2½r.+1¼r. purple	1·50	1·50
942	-	5r.+2½r. red	2·30	2·30
943	-	10r.+5r. grey	2·30	2·30

DESIGNS—VERT: 1r. Gorgan vase; 2½r. Ghazan Tower, Bistam. HORIZ: 5r. Masjid-i Gawhar Shad Mosque, Meshed; 10r. Niche in wall of Mosque at Rezaieh.

139 Flag and Book

1950. Second Economic Conference of Islamic Countries.

944	139	1r.50+1r. multicoloured	22·00	9·25

140 Mohammed Riza Pahlavi in Military School Uniform

1950. Shah's 31st Birthday. Portraits of Shah at different ages, framed as T 140.

945	140	25d. black and red	5·75	1·20
946	-	50d. black and orange	5·75	1·20
947	-	75d. black and brown	26·00	6·00
948	-	1r. black and green	15·00	4·50
949	-	2r.50 black and blue	23·00	5·25
950	-	5r. black and red	38·00	7·50

PORTRAITS—Shah in uniform: 50d. Naval cadet; 75d. Boy Scout; 1r. Naval officer; 2r.50, Army officer-cadet; 5r. Army general.

142 Memorial

1950. Fourth Anniv of Re-establishment of Control in Azerbaijan.

951	-	10d.+5d. brown	7·50	3·75
952	142	50d.+25d. purple	8·25	3·75
953	-	1r.+50d. purple	17·00	5·00
954	-	1r.50+75d. red and green	17·00	9·75
955	-	2r.50+1r.25 blue	18·00	12·00
956	-	3r.+1r.50 blue	24·00	9·75

DESIGNS—VERT: 10d. Shah and map; 1r.50, Map and battle scene; 2r.50, Shah and flags. HORIZ: 1r. Troops marching; 3r. Cavalry parade.

143 Shah and Queen Soraya

1951. Royal Wedding. T 143 and similar portraits.

959	143	5d. purple	5·75	1·10
960	143	25d. orange	5·75	1·10
961	143	50d. green	7·50	1·50
962	-	1r. brown	7·50	1·50
963	-	1r.50 red	7·50	1·70
964	-	2r.50 blue	7·50	1·70

DESIGNS: 1r. to 2r.50, As T 143 but portraits centrally placed.

144 Farabi

1951. Millenary of Death of Farabi (philosopher).

965	144	50d. red	7·50	1·10
966	144	2r.50 blue	1·70	1·10

145 Mohammed Riza Pahlavi
146 Mohammed Riza Pahlavi

1951

967	145	5d. red	40	25
968	145	10d. violet	40	25
969	145	20d. sepia	40	25
970	145	25d. blue	40	25
971	145	50d. green	1·10	25
972	145	50d. deep green	23·00	25
973	145	75d. red	1·10	25
974	146	1r. green	1·10	25
975	146	1r. turquoise	1·10	25
976	146	1r.50 red	1·70	25
977	146	2r. brown	1·70	25
978	146	2r.50 blue	1·70	25
979	146	3r. orange	5·25	25
980	146	5r. green	7·50	40
981	146	10r. olive	29·00	30
982	146	20r. brown	17·00	90
983	146	30r. blue	12·00	1·30
984	146	50r. black	31·00	1·80

147 Coran Gate, Shiraz

1951. 600th Death Anniv of Saadi (Muslih-ad-Din) (poet).

985	147	25d.+25d. green	3·00	1·70
986	-	50d.+50d. green	3·50	2·00
987	-	1r.50+50d. blue	11·50	6·75

DESIGNS—HORIZ: 50d. Tomb of Saadi. VERT: (as T 144): 1r.50, Saadi.

150 Shah and Lockheed Super Constellation over Mosque

1952. Air.

988	-	50d. green	75	25
989	150	1r. red	90	25
990	150	2r. blue	75	25
991	150	3r. sepia	1·10	25
992	150	5r. lilac	1·10	25
993	150	10r. red	1·90	30
994	150	20r. violet	3·00	45
995	150	30r. olive	4·50	75
996	150	50r. brown	11·50	1·50
997	150	100r. sepia	70·00	3·75
998	150	200r. green	55·00	7·50

DESIGN: 50d. Shah and Lockheed Super Constellation airplane over Mt. Demavend.

151 Oil Well and Mosque

1953. Discovery of Oil at Qum. (a) Postage.

999	151	50d. bistre and green	1·50	25
1000	-	1r. bistre and mauve	1·50	30
1001	151	2r.50 bistre and blue	2·30	40
1002	-	5r. bistre and brown	3·75	1·50

(b) Air. With Lockheed Super Constellation airplane.

1003	151	3r. bistre and violet	11·50	5·75
1004	-	5r. bistre and brown	23·00	11·50
1005	151	10r. bistre and green	30·00	30·00
1006	-	20r. bistre and purple	60·00	60·00

DESIGN: 1r., 5r. (2), 20r. As Type 151 but horiz.

153 Power Station Boiler Plant

1953. Second Anniv of Nationalization of Oil Industry.

1007	153	50d. green	2·30	40
1008	-	1r. red	2·30	40
1009	-	2r.50 blue	4·50	75
1010	-	5r. orange	4·50	1·10
1011	-	10r. lilac	9·00	1·90

DESIGNS—HORIZ: 1r. Crude oil stabilizer; 5r. Pipe-lines; 10r. View of Abadan. VERT: 2r.50, Super fractionaters.

154 Family and U.N. Emblem

1953. United Nations Day.

1012	154	1r. green and turquoise	90	30
1013	154	2r.50 blue and light blue	1·70	60

155 Gymnast

1953. Ancient Persian Sports.

1014	155	1r. green	3·75	75
1015	-	2r.50 blue	11·50	1·50
1016	-	3r. grey	15·00	1·90
1017	-	5r. ochre	17·00	9·00
1018	-	10r. violet	45·00	3·75

DESIGNS—HORIZ: 2r.50, Archer; 3r. Mountaineers. VERT: 5r. Polo-player (Persian Sports Club Badge); 10r. Lion-hunter.

156 Iranian Roach
157 Machinery

1954. Nationalization of Fishing Industry.

1019	156	1r. multicoloured	3·75	75
1020	-	2r.50 multicoloured	23·00	3·00
1021	-	3r. multicoloured	11·50	1·50
1022	157	5r. green	11·50	4·50
1023	-	10r. multicoloured	38·00	9·00

DESIGNS—HORIZ: As Type 156: 2r.50, Clupeid; 10r. Sturgeon. As Type 157: 3r. Refrigeration machinery.

158 Hamadan
159 Avicenna

1954. Fund to Rebuild Avicenna's Tomb (5th issue).

1024	158	50d.+25d. green	1·50	1·50
1025	159	1r.+½r. brown	1·50	1·50
1026	-	2½r.+1¼r. blue	1·50	1·50
1027	-	5r.+2½r. red	2·30	2·30
1028	-	10r.+5r. olive	3·00	3·00

DESIGNS—VERT: As Type 159: 2½r. Qabus tower, Gargan. HORIZ: As Type 158: 5r. Old tomb of Avicenna; 10r. New tomb of Avicenna.

160 Shah in Military Uniform

1954

1029	160	5d. brown	20	15
1062	160	5d. violet	60	45
1030	160	10d. violet	20	15
1063	160	10d. red	60	25
1031	160	25d. red	20	15
1064	160	25d. brown	60	25
1032	160	50d. brown	20	15
1065	160	50d. red	60	25
1066	-	1r. green	60	25
1034	-	1r.50 red	45	15
1067	-	1r.50 brown	38·00	3·00
1035	-	2r. brown	65	15
1068	-	2r. green	1·10	25
1069	-	2r.50 blue	1·70	30
1037	-	3r. green	2·50	20
1070	-	3r. brown	3·00	25
1038	-	5r. green	5·25	50
1071	-	5r. purple	5·25	25
1039	-	10r. lilac	11·00	1·00
1072	-	10r. blue	9·00	40
1040	-	20r. blue	13·50	3·75
1073	-	20r. green	19·00	1·50
1041	-	30r. brown	8·50	4·25
1074	-	30r. orange	95·00	15·00
1042	-	50r. orange	15·00	2·40
1075	-	50r. brown	70·00	17·00
1043	-	100r. violet	£400	29·00
1044	-	200r. yellow	£120	11·00

DESIGN: 1r. to 200r. Shah in naval uniform.

161 Hands breaking Chain

1954. First Anniv of Return of Shah. Multicoloured.

1045	2r. Type 161	3·75	75
1046	3r. Hand holding torch and Iranian flag	6·00	1·50
1047	5r. Man clasping Iranian flag	9·00	2·30

SIZES: 3r. (19½×27½ mm); 5r. (20½×28½ mm).

162 Nurse and Child

1954. U.N. Day.

1048	162	2r. orange and purple	2·75	55
1049	162	3r. orange and violet	2·00	1·20

163 Felling Trees

1954. Fourth World Forestry Congress. Inscr "4eme congres mondial forestier".

1050	163	1r. green and brown	14·50	11·00
1051	-	2r.50 blue and green	18·00	13·00
1052	-	5r. brown and lavender	29·00	24·00
1053	-	10r. lake and blue	38·00	33·00

DESIGNS: 2r.50, Man carrying logs; 5r. Man operating circular saw; 10r. Ancient Persian galley.

164

1955. National Costumes.

1054	164	1r. multicoloured	4·50	1·50
1055	-	2r. multicoloured	6·00	1·90
1056	-	2r.50 multicoloured	7·50	2·30
1057	-	3r. multicoloured	6·75	2·75
1058	-	5r. multicoloured	15·00	5·00

DESIGNS—2r. Male costume; 2r.50, 3r., 5r. Female costumes.

165 Parliament Building

1955. 50th Anniv of Constitution.

1059		2r. green and purple	1·90	75
1060		3r. blue	7·50	1·50
1061	165	5r. orange and green	6·00	3·00

DESIGNS—HORIZ: 2r. Gateway of Parliament Building. VERT: 3r. Winged Statue.

167 U.N. Emblem and Hemispheres

1955. United Nations Day.

1077	167	1r. orange and red	1·10	40
1078	167	2r.50 light blue and blue	1·10	75

168 Wrestlers

1955. International Success of Iranian Wrestlers.

1079	168	2r.50 multicoloured	3·50	1·50

169 Hospital Buildings

1956. Opening of Nemazi Hospital, Shiraz. Multicoloured.

1080	-	50d. (24×33½ mm)	2·30	45
1081	169	1r. (36×24½ mm)	3·00	75
1082	-	2r.50 (24×33½ mm)	5·75	2·75
1083	-	5r. (36×23 mm)	12·00	5·25
1084	-	10r. (24×33½ mm)	23·00	7·50

DESIGNS: 50d. Hospital garden; 2r.50, Spear thrower; 5r. Koran gate, Shiraz; 10r. Poet Hafiz and his tomb.

170

1956. Tenth Anniv of National Olympic Committee.
| 1085 | 170 | 5r. lilac | 30·00 | 15·00 |

171 Tusi's Tomb, Maragheh

1956. 700th Death Anniv of Nasir ed-Din Tusi, 1201–74 (astronomer and scientist).
1086	171	1r. orange	2·75	75
1087	–	2r.50 blue (Astrolabe)	4·50	90
1088	–	5r. lilac and sepia (Portrait)	10·50	1·10

172 Reveille

1956. National Scout Jamboree.
| 1089 | 172 | 2r.50 blue & ultramarine | 7·50 | 3·75 |
| 1090 | – | 5r. mauve and lilac | 9·00 | 5·75 |

DESIGN: 5r. Shah in scout's uniform and badge.

173

1956. World Health Organization.
| 1091 | 173 | 6r. mauve | 2·30 | 75 |

174 U.N. Emblem and Young People

1956. United Nations Day.
| 1092 | 174 | 1r. green | 1·10 | 40 |
| 1093 | – | 2r.50 blue and green | 1·90 | 75 |

DESIGN: 2r.50, U.N. emblem and scales of justice.

175 Telecommunications Centre, Teheran

1956. Centenary of Persian Telegraphs.
| 1094 | 175 | 2r.50 green and blue | 6·00 | 2·30 |
| 1095 | – | 6r. mauve and pink | 7·50 | 3·50 |

DESIGN: 6r. Telegraph poles and mosque.

176 Shah and Pres. Mirza

1956. Visit of President of Pakistan.
| 1096 | 176 | 1r. multicoloured | 2·30 | 75 |

177 Mohammed Riza Pahlavi

1956
1097	177	5d. red and rose	55	1·00
1098	177	10d. violet and blue	55	1·00
1099	177	25d. brown and sepia	75	40
1100	177	50d. olive and sepia	75	15
1101	177	1r. green and brown	75	25
1102	177	1r.50 brown and mauve	75	25
1103	177	2r. red and mauve	75	25
1104	177	2r.50 blue & ultramarine	40	25
1105	177	3r. bistre and brown	1·10	25
1106	177	5r. red	1·10	25
1132	177	6r. blue and light blue	1·90	25
1133	177	10r. turquoise and green	3·00	30
1134	177	20r. olive and green	4·50	45
1135	177	30r. sepia and blue	7·50	2·30
1136	177	50r. brown and sepia	15·00	5·00
1137	177	100r. red & bright purple	£150	7·50
1138	177	200r. bistre and violet	£110	23·00

178 Mohammed Riza Pahlavi

1956
1122	178	5d. plum and violet	30	2·00
1123	178	10d. mauve and purple	30	2·00
1124	178	25d. orange and red	60	40
1125	178	50d. green and grey	45	25
1126	178	1r. turquoise and green	45	25
1127	178	1r.50 purple and mauve	60	25
1128	178	2r. turquoise and blue	1·90	25
1129	178	2r.50 turquoise and blue	1·90	25
1130	178	3r. red and rose	1·90	25
1131	178	5r. violet and blue	1·90	25
1107	178	6r. mauve and lilac	1·50	25
1108	178	10r. green and blue	3·75	25
1109	178	20r. blue and green	45·00	40
1110	178	30r. orange and red	55·00	7·50
1111	178	50r. sage and green	19·00	3·75
1112	178	100r. red and purple	£350	30·00
1113	178	200r. violet and purple	£150	34·00

179 Lord Baden-Powell

1957. Birth Centenary of Lord Baden-Powell (founder of Boy Scout movement).
| 1114 | 179 | 10r. brown and green | 6·00 | 3·00 |

180 Steam Express Train and Mosque

1957. Inauguration of Teheran–Meshed Railway. Multicoloured.
1115		2r.50 Track and signal	7·50	1·10
1116		5r. Diesel train and map (horiz)	9·00	1·90
1117		10r. Type 180	18·00	6·00

181 President Gronchi and Shah

1957. Visit of President of Italy.
| 1118 | 181 | 2r. grey, green and red | 3·75 | 90 |
| 1119 | – | 6r. blue, green and red | 5·25 | 1·50 |

DESIGN: 6r. Plaque and flags between ruins of Persepolis and Colosseum.

183 Queen Soraya and Ramsar Hotel

1957. Sixth Medical Congress, Ramsar.
| 1120 | 183 | 2r. green and blue | 3·00 | 75 |

184 Shah and King Faisal II of Iraq

1957. Visit of King of Iraq.
| 1121 | 184 | 2r. blue, red and green | 3·75 | 75 |

185 Globes within Laurel Sprays

1957. Int Cartographical Conf, Teheran.
| 1140 | 185 | 10r. multicoloured | 6·00 | 1·50 |

186 "Flight"

1957. Air. United Nations Day.
| 1141 | 186 | 10r. red and mauve | 2·30 | 75 |
| 1142 | 186 | 20r. purple and violet | 4·50 | 90 |

187 "The Weightlifter"

1957. International Weightlifting Championships.
| 1143 | 187 | 10r. blue, green and red | 3·75 | 1·10 |

188 Radio Mast and Buildings

1958. 30th Anniv of Iranian Broadcasting Service.
| 1144 | 188 | 10r. sepia, buff and blue | 3·75 | 1·50 |

189 Oil Derrick and "Bowl of Flames"

1958. 50th Anniv of Iranian Oil Industry.
| 1145 | 189 | 2r. brown, yellow and grey | 3·00 | 75 |
| 1146 | 189 | 10r. brown, yellow & blue | 6·00 | 1·50 |

190 Exhibition Emblem

1958. Brussels International Exhibition.
| 1147 | 190 | 2r.50 red | 70 | 25 |
| 1148 | 190 | 6r. red | 1·20 | 25 |

191 Steam Train on Viaduct

1958. Inaug of Teheran–Tabriz Railway.
| 1149 | 191 | 6r. lilac | 15 | 40 |
| 1150 | – | 8r. green | 20 | 10 |

DESIGN: 8r. Steam express train and route map.

192 Mohammed Riza Pahlavi

1958
1162	192	5d. violet	40	25
1163	192	5d. brown	40	25
1164	192	10d. red	40	25
1165	192	10d. green	40	25
1166	192	10d. turquoise	40	25
1167	192	25d. red	40	25
1168	192	25d. orange	40	25
1169	192	50d. blue	40	25
1170	192	50d. red	75	40
1171	192	1r. green	40	25
1172	192	1r. violet	1·10	25
1232	192	2r. brown	3·00	25
1176	192	3r. brown	3·00	25
1177	192	6r. blue	3·00	25
1179	192	8r. purple	3·75	25
1180	192	8r. brown	3·75	25
1181	192	10r. black	3·75	40
1182	192	14r. blue	3·00	90
1183	192	14r. green	3·75	25
1185	192	20r. green	6·00	60
1186	192	30r. red	7·50	75
1187	192	30r. brown	6·75	40
1188	192	50r. purple	60·00	2·30
1189	192	50r. blue	11·50	75
1190	192	100r. orange	15·00	3·00
1191	192	100r. green	45·00	1·50
1192	192	200r. green	55·00	4·50
1193	192	200r. mauve	£225	9·00

193 U.N. Emblem and Map of Persia

1958. United Nations Day.
| 1194 | 193 | 6r. blue and light blue | 90 | 30 |
| 1195 | 193 | 10r. violet and green | 1·50 | 40 |

194 Clasped Hands

1958. Tenth Anniv of Declaration of Human Rights.
| 1196 | 194 | 6r. brown and chocolate | 75 | 40 |
| 1197 | 194 | 8r. olive and green | 1·10 | 45 |

195 Rudagi playing Lyre

1958. 1100th Birth Anniv of Rudagi (poet and musician).
1198	195	2r.50 blue	4·50	90
1199	–	5r. violet	7·50	1·50
1200	195	10r. sepia	19·00	3·00

DESIGN: 5r. Rudagi meditating.

196

1959. Red Cross Commemoration.
| 1201 | 196 | 1r. multicoloured | 1·20 | 60 |
| 1202 | 196 | 6r. multicoloured | 1·80 | 75 |

197 Wrestlers

1959. World Wrestling Championships.
1203 **197** 6r. multicoloured 9·00 2·30

198 Torch of Freedom

1959. United Nations Day.
1204 **198** 6r. red, brown and bistre 1·10 40

199 Shah and President Khan

1959. Visit of President of Pakistan.
1205 **199** 6r. multicoloured 5·75 75

200 I.L.O. Emblem

1959. 40th Anniv of I.L.O.
1206 **200** 1r. blue and light blue 90 40
1207 **200** 5r. brown and light
              brown 1·40 55

201 Pahlavi Foundation
         Bridge, Khorramshahr

1960. Opening of Pahlavi Foundation Bridge, Khorramshahr.
1208 **201** 1r. blue and brown 1·10 25
1209 -   5r. green and blue 1·90 40
DESIGN: 5r. Close-up view of bridge.

202 "Uprooted Tree
         and Columns"

1960. World Refugee Year.
1210 **202** 1r. blue 45 25
1211 -   6r. black and green 60 25
DESIGN: 6r. "Uprooted tree" and columns.

203 Insecticide
         Sprayer

1960. Anti-Malaria Campaign.
1212 1r. black & red on yellow 1·10 25
1213 **203** 2r. blue, black & light bl 1·50 40
1214 -   3r. black and red on
              green 3·00 75
DESIGNS (30×37 mm): 1r., 3r. Different views of mosquito crossed out in red.

204 Polo Player

1960. "Olympic Games Week".
1215 **204** 1r. purple 85 40
1216 -   6r. violet and blue 2·10 75
DESIGN: 6r. Archer.

205 Shah and King Hussein

1960. Visit of King of Jordan.
1217 **205** 6r. multicoloured 5·00 75

206 Scout
         Emblem within
         Flower

1960. Third National Scout Jamboree.
1218 **206** 1r. green 45 25
1219 -   6r. ochre, sepia and blue 1·00 55
DESIGN: 6r. Scout camp, Persepolis.

207 Shah and Queen Farah

1960. Royal Wedding.
1220 **207** 1r. green 2·75 40
1221 **207** 5r. blue 5·00 75

208 UN Emblem

1960. 15th Anniv of U.N.O.
1222 **208** 6r. sepia, blue and bistre 75 25

209 Shah and Queen
         Elizabeth II

1961. Visit of Queen Elizabeth II.
1223 **209** 1r. brown 1·50 40
1224 **209** 6r. blue 2·30 75

210 Girl playing
         Pan-pipes

1961. International Music Congress, Teheran.
1225 **210** 1r. stone and brown 60 40
1226 -   6r. slate 1·40 60
DESIGN—(24×39½ mm): 6r. Safiaddin Anmavi (musician).

211 Royal Family

1961. Birth of Crown Prince.
1227 **211** 1r. purple 1·90 75
1228 **211** 6r. blue 5·75 2·30

212 U.N. Emblem
         and Birds

1961. United Nations Day.
1236 **212** 2r. red and blue 75 25
1237 **212** 6r. violet and blue 90 30

213 Tree-planting

1962. Afforestation Week.
1238 **213** 2r. blue, cream and
              green 60 25
1239 **213** 6r. green, blue & ultram 75 30

214 Worker

1962. Workers' Day.
1240 **214** 2r. multicoloured 60 25
1241 **214** 6r. multicoloured 90 30

215 Family on
         Map

1962. Social Insurance.
1242 **215** 2r. violet, black & yellow 60 25
1243 **215** 6r. blue, black & lt blue 90 30

216 Sugar Plantation

1962. Sugar Cane Production.
1244 **216** 2r. green, blue & ultram 60 25
1245 **216** 6r. blue, cream & ultram 1·00 40

217 Karaj Dam

1962. Inauguration of Karaj Dam.
1246 **217** 2r. green and brown 1·10 25
1247 **217** 6r. blue and ultramarine 1·50 40

218 Sefid Rud Dam

1962. Inauguration of Sefid Rud Dam.
1248 **218** 2r. buff, blue and myrtle 1·20 25
1249 -   6r. black, blue and
              brown 1·50 55
DESIGN: 6r. Distant view of dam.

219 U.N. Emblem

1962. 15th Anniv of UNESCO.
1250 **219** 2r. black, green and red 75 25
1251 **219** 6r. blue, green and red 1·50 40

220 Arrow piercing
         Mosquito

1962. Malaria Eradication.
1252 **220** 2r. black and green 40 25
1253 -   6r. blue and red 75 25
1254 -   10r. ultramarine and
              blue 1·50 30
DESIGNS—VERT (29½×34½ mm): 6r. Mosquito and insecticide-sprayer. HORIZ (As Type **220**): 10r. Globe and campaign emblem.

221   **222** Shah and Palace of
Mohammed   Darius, Persepolis
Riza Pahlavi

1962
1255a **221** 5d. green 90 25
1256 **221** 10d. brown 1·00 55
1257 **221** 25d. blue 1·00 40
1336 **221** 50d. turquoise 75 25
1337 **221** 1r. orange 75 25
1338 **221** 2r. violet 55 25
1339 **221** 5r. brown 3·00 55
1340 **222** 6r. blue 6·00 1·00
1341 **222** 8r. green 3·50 25
1342 **222** 10r. blue 3·00 25
1265a **222** 11r. green 1·40 25
1266a **222** 14r. violet 1·90 25
1345 **222** 20r. brown 5·00 1·90
1346 **222** 50r. red 6·00 1·90

223 Oil Pipelines

1962. Second Petroleum Symposium of Economic Commission for Asia and the Far East.
1269 **223** 6r. brown and blue 1·20 25
1270 **223** 14r. brown and grey 2·30 45

224 Hippocrates and
         Avicenna

1962. W.H.O. Medical Congress, Teheran.
1271 **224** 2r. blue, brown and
              cream 1·90 40
1272 **224** 6r. blue, sage and green 2·30 55

225 New Houses

1962. United Nations Day.
1273 **225** 6r. blue and indigo 1·20 25
1274 -   14r. green and blue 1·70 40
DESIGN—HORIZ: 14r. Laying foundation stone.

226 "Bouquet for the Crown Prince"

1962. Crown Prince's Birthday.
1275	**226**	6r. blue	3·75	75
1276	**226**	14r. green	7·50	1·50

227 Persian Gulf Map

1962. Persian Gulf Seminar.
1277	**227**	6r. blue, pink & pale blue	1·00	25
1278	**227**	14r. blue, flesh and pink	1·50	40

228 Hilton Hotel, Teheran

1963. Opening of Royal Teheran Hilton Hotel.
1279	**228**	6r. blue	2·30	30
1280	**228**	14r. brown	3·75	45

229 Refugees

1963. Earthquake Relief Fund.
1281	**229**	14r.+6r. blue, brn & grn	1·70	75

230 Mohammed Riza Shah Dam

1963. Inaug of Mohammed Riza Shah Dam.
1282	**230**	6r. multicoloured	2·75	30
1283	**230**	14r. multicoloured	4·50	60

231 Worker with Pickaxe

1963. Workers' Day.
1283a	**231**	2r. black and yellow	85	25
1283b	**231**	6r. black and blue	1·50	30

232 Bird and Globe

1963. Freedom from Hunger.
1284	**232**	2r. ultramarine, bl & bis	1·10	25
1285	-	6r. black, bistre and blue	1·70	30
1286	-	14r. bistre and green		70

DESIGNS: 6r. Globe and ears of wheat (stylized); 14r. Globe encircled by scroll, and campaign emblem.

233 Shah and Scroll

1963. Agrarian Reform Act.
1287	**233**	6r. green and blue	3·75	1·10
1288	**233**	14r. green and yellow	5·75	1·90

234 Shah and King Frederick

1963. Visit of King of Denmark.
1289	**234**	6r. blue and indigo	2·75	55
1290	**234**	14r. brown and sepia	3·75	1·00

235 Flags of Iran and India; Ibn Sina Mosque, Teheran, and Taj Mahal, India

1963. Visit of President Radhakrishnan of India.
1291	**235**	6r. multicoloured	2·75	40
1292	**235**	14r. multicoloured	3·75	75

236 Shahnaz Dam

1963. Inauguration of Shahnaz Dam.
1293	**236**	6r. ultramarine, bl & grn	2·75	40
1294	**236**	14r. green, blue and buff	2·75	60

237 Centenary Emblem

1963. Red Cross Centenary.
1295	**237**	6r. multicoloured	2·75	40
1296	**237**	14r. grey, red and buff	3·50	60

238 Shah and Queen Juliana

1963. Visit of Queen of the Netherlands.
1304	**238**	6r. blue and ultramarine	3·00	40
1305	**238**	14r. green and black	4·50	60

240 Students in Class

1963. Formation of Literacy Teaching Corps.
1306	**240**	6r. multicoloured	3·50	55
1307	**240**	14r. multicoloured	5·00	55

241 Pres. De Gaulle and View of Teheran

1963. Visit of President of France.
1308	**241**	6r. ultramarine and blue	3·50	55
1309	**241**	14r. brown and ochre	4·25	60

242 Plant, Route Map and Emblem

1963. Opening of Chemical Fertilizer Plant, Shiraz.
1310	**242**	6r. black, yellow and red	3·50	55
1311	-	14r. black, blue & yellow	4·25	1·00

DESIGN—HORIZ: 14r. Fertilizer plant and emblem.

243 Pres. Lubke and Shah Mosque, Isfahan

1963. Visit of President of German Federal Republic.
1312	**243**	6r. blue and violet	3·50	55
1313	**243**	14r. brown and grey	4·25	1·00

244 U.N. Emblem

1963. United Nations Day.
1314	**244**	8r. multicoloured	1·90	55

245 Aircraft crossing U.N. Emblem

1963. Iranian Air Force in Congo.
1315	**245**	6r. multicoloured	1·90	55

246 Crown Prince Riza

1963. Children's Day.
1316	**246**	2r. brown	1·40	25
1317	**246**	6r. blue	2·40	55

247 Chairman Brezhnev

1963. Visit of Chairman of Soviet Presidium.
1318	**247**	5r. multicoloured	2·40	30
1319	**247**	11r. multicoloured	4·50	60

248 Ataturk's Mausoleum

1963. 25th Death Anniv of Kemal Ataturk.
1320	**248**	4r. brown, grey and green	2·40	25
1321	-	5r. black, red and yellow	2·40	25

DESIGN: 5r. Kemal Ataturk.

249 Scales of Justice and Globe

1963. 15th Anniv of Declaration of Human Rights.
1322	**249**	6r. black, blue and green	1·90	30
1323	**249**	14r. black, cream & brn	2·75	40

250 Mother and Child

1963. Mothers Day.
1324	**250**	2r. multicoloured	1·70	25
1325	**250**	4r. multicoloured	2·40	55

251 Cogwheel and Map

1963. Industrial Development.
1326	**251**	8r. blue, cream & turq	3·00	40

252 Hand with Document (Profit- sharing)

1964. Six-Point Reform Law.
1327	**252**	2r. brown, violet and blue	3·00	10
1328	-	4r. brown and grey	3·00	10
1329	-	6r. multicoloured	3·00	15
1330	-	8r. multicoloured	3·00	1·00
1331	-	10r. red, green & dp grn	3·00	1·20
1332	-	12r. brown and red	6·50	1·50

DESIGNS: 4r. Factory and documents on scales (Sale of Shares to Workers); 6r. Worker on Globe (Education Corps); 8r. Tractor (Land reform); 10r. Trees (Nationalization of forests); 12r. Silhouettes within gateway (Votes for Women).

253 U.N. Emblem

1964. 20th Economic Commission for Asia and the Far East Session, Teheran.
1347	**253**	14r. black and green	2·30	40

254 Blossom

1964. New Year Greetings.
1348	**254**	50d. orange, sepia & grn	40	25
1349	**254**	1r. orange, black and blue	40	25

255 Weather Vane

1964. World Meteorological Day.
1350	**255**	6r. violet and blue	1·10	25

256 "Tourism"

1964. First Anniv of Iranian Tourist Organization (INTO).
1351	**256**	6r. green, violet and black	2·00	40
1352	-	11r. orange, brown & blk	2·75	55

DESIGN: 11r. Winged beasts, column and INTO emblem.

257 Rudagi (blind poet)

1964. Opening of Blind Institute.
| 1353 | **257** | 6r. blue | 1·90 | 40 |
| 1354 | **257** | 8r. brown | 3·50 | 55 |

258 Sculptured Head

1964. "7000 Years of Persian Art" Exhibition.
1355	**258**	2r. blue and grey	3·50	1·00
1356	–	4r. ultramarine and blue	7·25	1·40
1357	–	6r. yellow and brown	7·25	1·40
1358	–	10r. green and yellow	9·00	1·40

DESIGNS—HORIZ. 4r. Sumerian war chariot on map. VERT: 6r. Golden cup with lion decorations; 10r. Sculptured head of man.

259 Shah and Emperor Haile Selassie

1964. Visit of Emperor of Ethiopia.
| 1359 | **259** | 6r. ultramarine and blue | 2·75 | 40 |

260 Congress Emblem

1964. Second Iranian Dental Assn Congress.
| 1360 | **260** | 2r. red, deep blue & blue | 1·10 | 30 |
| 1361 | – | 4r. multicoloured | 1·50 | 40 |

DESIGN: 4r. "2 IDA" in symbolic form.

261 Bark Beetle under Lens

1964. Inauguration of Plant Parasites and Diseases Research Institute.
| 1362 | | 2r. brown, red and buff | 2·30 | 25 |
| 1363 | **261** | 6r. indigo, brown & blue | 3·00 | 30 |

DESIGN: 2r. Microscope, plants and research centre.

262 Plaque

1964. Mehregan Festival.
| 1364 | **262** | 8r. red and yellow | 1·90 | 75 |

263 Eleanor Roosevelt

1964. Eleanor Roosevelt Commemoration.
| 1365 | **263** | 10r. blue and violet | 1·90 | 75 |

264 Clasped Hands and U.N. Emblem

1964. United Nations Day.
| 1366 | **264** | 6r. multicoloured | 1·10 | 25 |
| 1367 | – | 14r. red, blue and orange | 1·70 | 40 |

DESIGN: 14r. U.N. and "Bird" emblems.

265 Gymnast

1964. Olympic Games, Tokyo.
| 1368 | **265** | 4r. sepia, turquoise & brn | 1·20 | 40 |
| 1369 | – | 6r. red and blue | 1·70 | 40 |

DESIGN—Diamond (39×39 mm): 6r. Polo.

266 Crown Prince Riza

1964. Children's Day.
1370	**266**	1r. green and brown	1·10	30
1371	**266**	2r. red and blue	1·90	45
1372	**266**	6r. blue and red	3·00	60

267 Conference and U.N. Emblems

1964. Petro-Chemical Conf and Gas Seminar.
| 1373 | **267** | 6r. multicoloured | 75 | 40 |
| 1374 | **267** | 8r. multicoloured | 1·50 | 40 |

268 Shah and King Baudouin

1964. Visit of King of Belgium.
| 1375 | **268** | 6r. black, orange & yell | 1·50 | 40 |
| 1376 | **268** | 8r. black, orange & green | 2·30 | 75 |

269 Rhazes

1964. 1100th Birth Anniv of Rhazes (Zakariya Ar-Razi, alchemist).
| 1377 | **269** | 2r. multicoloured | 1·50 | 40 |
| 1378 | **269** | 6r. multicoloured | 2·30 | 45 |

270 Shah and King Olav

1965. Visit of King of Norway.
| 1379 | **270** | 2r. mauve and purple | 1·90 | 40 |
| 1380 | **270** | 4r. green and olive | 2·75 | 55 |

271 Crown, Map and Star

1965. Six-Point Reform Law.
| 1381 | **271** | 2r. orange, black and blue | 1·10 | 25 |

272 Woman and U.N. Emblem

1965. 18th Session of United Nations Commission on Status of Women, Teheran.
| 1382 | **272** | 6r. black, blue & lt blue | 60 | 25 |
| 1383 | **272** | 8r. blue, red and light red | 90 | 25 |

273 Festival Plant

1965. New Year Festival.
| 1384 | **273** | 50d. multicoloured | 40 | 25 |
| 1385 | **273** | 1r. multicoloured | 40 | 25 |

274 Pres. Bourguiba and Minarets

1965. Visit of President of Tunisia.
| 1386 | **274** | 4r. multicoloured | 1·00 | 40 |

275 Map of Oil Pipelines

1965. 14th Anniv of Nationalization of Oil Industry.
| 1387 | | 6r. multicoloured | 1·50 | 25 |
| 1388 | **275** | 14r. multicoloured | 2·30 | 55 |

276 I.T.U. Emblem and Symbols

1965. Centenary of I.T.U.
| 1389 | **276** | 14r. red and grey | 1·20 | 40 |

277 I.C.Y. Emblem

1965. International Co-operation Year.
| 1390 | **277** | 10r. green and blue | 2·30 | 40 |

278 Boeing 727-100 and Airline Emblem

1965. Inauguration of Jet Services by Iranian National Airlines.
| 1391 | **278** | 14r. multicoloured | 2·30 | 40 |

279 "Co-operation" (Hands holding Book)

1965. First Anniv of Regional Development Co-operation Plan. Multicoloured.
| 1392 | | 2r. Type **279** | 40 | 25 |
| 1393 | | 4r. Globe and flags of Turkey, Iran and Pakistan (40½×24½ mm) | 70 | 25 |

280 Moot Emblem and Arabesque Pattern

1965. Middle East Rover (Scout) Moot.
| 1394 | **280** | 2r. multicoloured | 70 | 25 |

281 Gateway of Parliament Building

1965. 60th Anniv of Iranian Constitution.
| 1397 | **281** | 2r. brown and mauve | 40 | 25 |

282 Congress Emblem

1965. Iranian Dental Congress.
| 1398 | **282** | 6r. blue, mauve and silver | 60 | 25 |

283 Teacher and Class

1965. World Eradication of Illiteracy Congress, Teheran. Multicoloured.
1399		2r. Type **283**	40	25
1400		5r. Globe showing alphabets (25×30 mm)	40	25
1401		6r. UNESCO emblem and symbols (diamond, 36×36 mm)	75	30
1402		8r. Various scripts (35×23 mm)	75	25
1403		14r. Shah and multi-lingual inscriptions (41×52 mm)	1·50	30

284 Shah Riza Pahlavi

1965. 25th Anniv (actually 24th) of Shah's Accession.
| 1404 | **284** | 1r. red and grey | 1·50 | 25 |
| 1405 | **284** | 2r. red and yellow | 1·50 | 40 |

285 Congress Emblem

1965. 14th Medical Congress.
| 1406 | **285** | 5r. ultramarine, bl & gold | 55 | 25 |

286 President Jonas

1965. Visit of President of Austria.
| 1407 | 286 | 6r. blue and brown | 1·10 | 25 |

287 Plaque

1965. Mehregan Festival.
| 1408 | 287 | 4r. multicoloured | 60 | 25 |

See also No. 1464.

289 U.N. Emblem and "Flowers"

1965. United Nations Day.
| 1409 | 289 | 5r. multicoloured | 55 | 25 |

290 Emblem and "Arches"

1965. Iranian Industrial Exhibition, Teheran.
| 1410 | 290 | 3r. multicoloured | 55 | 25 |

291 Crown Prince Riza

1965. Children's Day.
| 1411 | 291 | 2r. chocolate, brn & gold | 1·10 | 45 |

292 "Weightlifting"

1965. World Weightlifting Championships, Teheran.
| 1412 | 292 | 10r. mauve, violet & blue | 60 | 25 |

293 Open Book

1965. Book Week.
| 1416 | 293 | 8r. multicoloured | 60 | 25 |

294 Shah and King Faisal

1965. Visit of King of Saudi Arabia.
| 1417 | 294 | 4r. brown and bistre | 1·50 | 40 |

295 Scales of Justice

1965. Human Rights Day.
| 1418 | 295 | 14r. multicoloured | 15 | 25 |

296 Tractor (Land Reform)

1966. Third Anniv of Shah's White Revolution (Parliamentary Assent to Shah's Reform Plan).
1419	296	1r. brown and yellow	25	25
1420	-	2r. green and light green	25	25
1421	-	3r. brown and silver	25	25
1422	-	4r. violet and light violet	40	25
1423	-	5r. lake and red	55	25
1424	-	6r. brown and bistre	75	25
1425	-	7r. ultramarine and blue	75	25
1426	-	8r. ultramarine and blue	1·10	25
1427	-	9r. brown & light brown	1·10	25

DESIGNS: 2r. Trees (Nationalization of Forests); 3r. Cog-wheel emblem (Sale of shares to workers); 4r. Cylinders (Profit-sharing); 5r. Parliament gateway (Votes for Women); 6r. Blackboard and pupils (Education Corps); 7r. Staff of Aesculapius (Medical Corps); 8r. Scales (Justice); 9r. Girders (Construction Corps).

297 Mohammed Riza Pahlavi

1966
1428	297	5d. green	25	25
1429	297	10d. brown	25	25
1430	297	25d. blue	25	25
1431	297	50d. turquoise	55	25
1432	297	1r. orange	55	25
1433	297	2r. violet	40	25
1434	297	4r. brown	5·75	75
1435	297	5r. sepia	1·00	25
1436	298	6r. blue	90	25
1437	298	8r. green	90	25
1438	298	10r. blue	1·50	25
1439	298	11r. green	1·50	25
1440	298	14r. violet	2·00	25
1441	298	20r. brown	11·50	55
1442	298	50r. red	5·00	1·50
1443	298	100r. blue	15·00	2·40
1444	298	200r. brown	12·00	4·25

299 Nurse taking Oath

1966. Nurses' Day.
| 1445 | 299 | 5r. blue and deep blue | 55 | 40 |
| 1446 | 299 | 5r. mauve and red | 55 | 40 |

300 Narcissus

1966. New Year Festival.
| 1447 | 300 | 50d. multicoloured | 25 | 25 |
| 1448 | 300 | 1r. multicoloured | 1·50 | 40 |

See also Nos. 1530/3.

301 Oil Rigs

1966. Inauguration of Six New Oil Companies in Persian Gulf.
| 1449 | 301 | 14r. black, purple & blue | 55 | 15 |

302 Radar Aerial

1966. C.E.N.T.O. (Iran, Pakistan and Turkey) Telecommunications Organization.
1450	302	2r. green	25	25
1451	-	4r. orange and blue	25	25
1452	-	6r. grey and purple	30	25
1453	-	8r. indigo and blue	40	30
1454	-	10r. brown and ochre	55	30

DESIGNS—VERT: 4r. Aerial and radio "waves"; 6r. "CENTO" and emblem; 8r. Emblem and "waves"; 10r. Bowl aerial and "waves".

303 W.H.O. Building

1966. Inaug of W.H.O. Headquarters, Geneva.
| 1455 | 303 | 10r. black, blue & yellow | 55 | 30 |

304 Globe Emblem and Motto

1966. Conference of International Women's Council, Teheran.
| 1456 | 304 | 6r. multicoloured | 40 | 30 |
| 1457 | 304 | 8r. multicoloured | 55 | 30 |

305 UNESCO Emblem

1966. Air. 20th Anniv of UNESCO.
| 1458 | 305 | 14r. multicoloured | 90 | 25 |

306 Ruins of Persepolis, Map and Globe

1966. Int Iranology Congress, Teheran.
| 1459 | 306 | 14r. multicoloured | 90 | 40 |

307 Medical Emblem

1966. 15th Medical Congress, Teheran.
| 1460 | 307 | 4r. gold, blue & ultram | 40 | 30 |

308 Parliament Gateway

1966. 55th Interparliamentary Union Conference, Teheran.
| 1461 | 308 | 6r. green, blue and red | 25 | 25 |
| 1462 | - | 8r. green, blue and mauve | 40 | 25 |

DESIGN: 8r. Senate Building.

309 President Sunay

1966. Visit of President of Turkey.
| 1463 | 309 | 6r. brown and violet | 40 | 25 |

1966. Mehregan Festival. Plaque design similar to T **287** but vert (30×40 mm).
| 1464 | | 6r. brown and bistre | 45 | 30 |

310 Farmers

1966. Rural Courts of Justice.
| 1465 | 310 | 5r. brown and bistre | 1·10 | 55 |

311 U.N. Emblem

1966. U.N. Day and 21st Anniv of U.N.O.
| 1466 | 311 | 6r. brown and black | 40 | 30 |

312 Crown Prince

1966. Children's Day.
| 1467 | 312 | 1r. blue | 60 | 55 |
| 1468 | 312 | 2r. violet | 1·00 | 55 |

313 I.W.O. Emblem

1966. Iranian Women's Organization.
| 1469 | 313 | 5r. blue, black and gold | 30 | 25 |

314 Strip of Film

1966. First Children's Film Festival, Teheran.
| 1470 | 314 | 4r. black, purple & violet | 40 | 25 |

315 Counting on the Fingers

1966. National Census.
| 1471 | 315 | 6r. brown and grey | 30 | 25 |

316 Cover of Book

1966. Book Week.
| 1472 | 316 | 8r. brown, ochre and blue | 40 | 25 |

317 Riza Shah Pahlavi

1966. Riza Shah Pahlavi Commemoration.

1473	317	1r. brown	1·90	40
1474	317	1r. blue	1·90	40
1475	–	2r. blue	1·90	40
1476	–	2r. green	1·90	40

Nos. 1475/6 show Riza Shah Pahlavi bare-headed.

318 E.R.O.P.A. Emblem and Map

1966. Fourth General Assembly of Public Administrators Organization (E.R.O.P.A.).

1477	318	8r. brown and green	45	30

319 Shah with Farmers

1967. Fifth Anniv of Land Reform Laws.

1485	319	6r. brown, yellow & bis	90	25

320 Torch and Stars

1967. Fourth Anniv of Shah's White Revolution.

1486	320	2r. multicoloured	1·00	55
1487	–	6r. multicoloured	1·70	55

DESIGN: 6r. Shah acknowledging greetings.

321 Golden "Bull"

1967. Museum Week. Multicoloured.

1488	3r. Type 321	75	25
1489	5r. Golden "leopard"	1·00	40
1490	8r. Capital with rams' heads	1·30	55

322 Planting a Tree

1967. Tree-planting Week.

1491	322	8r. green and brown	30	25

323 Goldfish

1967. New Year Festival.

1492	323	1r. blue, red and brown	25	25
1493	–	8r. ultramarine, bl & red	1·10	30

DESIGN—35×27 mm: 8r. Barn swallows.

324 Microscope, Horses and Emblem

1967. Second Veterinary Congress.

1494	324	5r. red, black and grey	40	25

325 Pres. Arif and Mosques

1967. Visit of President of Iraq.

1495	325	6r. green and blue	40	30

---

326 U.N. Emblem and Fireworks

1967. U.N. Stamp Day.

1496	326	5r. multicoloured	40	25

327 Map showing Pipeline Routes

1967. Nationalization of Oil Industry.

1497	327	6r. multicoloured	1·00	25

328 Fencing

1967. Int Youth Fencing Championships, Teheran.

1498	328	5r. yellow and violet	55	25

329 Shah and King Bhumibol

1967. Visit of King of Thailand.

1499	329	6r. brown and light brown	1·10	25

330 Emblem, Old and Young Couples

1967. 15th Anniv of Social Insurance Scheme.

1500	330	5r. blue and bistre	30	25

331 Skiing

1967. Olympic Committee Meeting, Teheran.

1501	331	3r. brown and black	40	25
1502	–	6r. multicoloured	60	30
1503	–	8r. brown and blue	90	40

DESIGNS: 6r. Olympic "shield"; 8r. Wrestling.

332 "LIONS" and Lions Head

1967. 50th Anniv of Lions International. Multicoloured.

1504	3r. Type 332	55	25
1505	7r. Lions emblem (36×42 mm)	1·00	25

333 President Stoica

1967. Visit of President of Rumania.

1506	333	6r. blue and orange	30	25

---

334 I.T.Y. Emblem

1967. International Tourist Year.

1507	334	3r. blue and red	30	25

335 Iranian Pavilion

1967. World Fair, Montreal.

1508	335	4r. red, gold and brown	40	25
1509	335	10r. brown, gold and red	55	25

336 First Persian Stamp

1967. Stamp Centenary.

1510	336	6r. purple, blue & lt blue	55	25
1511	336	8r. purple, myrtle & green	60	25

337 Globe and Schoolchildren

1967. Campaign Against Illiteracy.

1512	337	3r. violet and blue	25	25
1513	337	5r. brown and yellow	30	25

338 "Musician"

1967. International Musical Education in Oriental Countries Conference, Teheran.

1514	338	14r. purple and brown	75	55

339 "Helping Hand"

1967. First "S.O.S." Children's Village in Iran.

1515	339	8r. brown and yellow	3·00	2·30

340 Winged Ram

1967. First Shiraz Arts Festival, Persepolis.

1516	340	8r. brown and bistre	60	25

341 U.N. Emblem

1967. United Nations Day.

1517	341	6r. blue and bistre	40	25

---

342 Shah Mohammed Riza Pahlavi and Empress Farah

1967. Coronation of Shah and Empress Farah.

1518	342	2r. brown, blue and silver	85	25
1519	342	10r. violet, blue and silver	90	55
1520	342	14r. multicoloured	2·30	75

343 Crown Prince Riza

1967. Children's Day.

1521	343	2r. violet and silver	90	25
1522	343	8r. brown and silver	1·20	25

344 Pres. G. Traikov

1967. Visit of President of Bulgaria.

1523	344	10r. brown and violet	40	25

345 Scout Emblem and Neckerchiefs

1967. Boy Scouts Co-operation Week.

1524	345	8r. brown and green	75	30

346 "Co-operation" (linked hands)

1967. Co-operation Year.

1525	346	6r. multicoloured	30	25

347 Shaikh Sabah

1968. Visit of Shaikh of Kuwait.

1526	347	10r. green and blue	40	25

348 Shah and Text of Reform Plan

1968. Fifth Anniv of Shah's White Revolution.

1527	348	2r. green, sepia and flesh	40	25
1528	348	8r. violet, green and blue	1·20	25
1529	348	14r. brown, blue & mve	1·50	40

1968. New Year Festival. As T 300. Multicoloured.

1530	1r. Almond blossom	25	25
1531	2r. Red tulips	25	25
1532	2r. Yellow tulips	25	25
1533	6r. Festival dancer	75	25

349 Oil Technician and Rig

1968. National Oil Industry.
1534 349   14r. black, yellow & green   60   25

350 W.H.O. Emblem

1968. 20th Anniv of W.H.O.
1535 350   14r. orange, blue & pur   60   25

351 Ancient Chariot (sculpture)

1968. Fifth World Congress of Persian Archaeology and Art, Teheran.
1536 351   8r. multicoloured   40   25

352 Shah and King Hassan

1968. Visit of King of Morocco.
1537 352   6r. violet and flesh   1·10   25

353 Human Rights Emblem

1968. Human Rights Conference, Teheran.
1538 353   8r. red and green   25   25
1539   —   14r. ultramarine and blue   55   25
DESIGN: 14r. As Type 353, but rearranged, and inscr "INTERNATIONAL CONFERENCE ON HUMAN RIGHTS—TEHERAN 1968".

354 Footballer

1968. Asian Football Cup Finals, Teheran.
1540 354   8r. multicoloured   25   25
1541 354   10r. multicoloured   55   25

355 Oil Refinery

1968. Inauguration of Teheran Oil Refinery.
1542 355   14r. multicoloured   75   25

356 Empress Farah in Guides' Uniform

1968. Iranian Girl Guides "Great Camp".
1543 356   4r. blue and purple   1·20   25
1544 356   6r. brown and red   2·00   55

357 Mosquito Emblem

1968. Eighth International Tropical Medicine and Malaria Congresses, Teheran.
1545 357   6r. purple and black   40   25
1546 357   14r. green and purple   55   25

358 Allegory of Literacy

1968. World Illiteracy Eradication Campaign Day.
1547 358   6r. blue, brown and lilac   30   25
1548 358   14r. green, brown & yell   45   25

359 "Horseman" and "Flower"

1968. Second Shiraz Arts Festival, Persepolis.
1549 359   14r. multicoloured   60   25

360 Police Emblem on Map

1968. Police Day.
1550 360   14r. multicoloured   1·00   25

361 Interpol Emblem

1968. 37th Interpol General Assembly.
1551 361   10r. purple, black & blue   55   25

362 U.N. Emblem and Dove

1968. United Nations Day.
1552 362   14r. ultramarine and blue   75   25

363 Empress Farah

1968. First Anniv of Coronation. Multicoloured.
1553 363   6r. Type 363   5·25   2·75
1554   8r. Shah Mohammed Riza Pahlavi   6·00   3·75
1555   10r. Family group   7·50   4·50

364 Imperial Crown and Bulls' Heads Capital (festival emblem)

1968. National Festival of Art and Culture, Teheran.
1556 364   14r. multicoloured   75   25

365 "Landscape"

1968. Children's Day. Children's Paintings. Multicoloured.
1557 365   2r. Type 365   25   25
1558   3r. "Boat and House" (35×29 mm)   25   25
1559   5r. "Flowers" (35×29 mm)   30   25

366 Hands supporting Globe

1968. Insurance Day.
1560 366   4r. blue and grey   25   25
1561   —   5r. multicoloured   25   25
1562   —   8r. multicoloured   25   25
1563   —   10r. multicoloured   45   25
DESIGNS: 5r. Factory aflame ("Fire risk"); 8r. Urban workers ("Life"); 10r. Insurance Institute emblem and transport ("Travel insurance").

367 Emblem and Human Figures

1968. 20th Anniv of Declaration of Human Rights.
1564 367   8r. purple, ultram & bl   30   25

368 Justice, Construction Corps and Medical Corps

1969. Sixth Anniv of Shah's White Revolution. Each green, brown and lilac.
1565 368   2r. Type 368   1·00   25
1566   4r. Working conditions, civil engineering and irrigation   1·00   25

1567   6r. Land reform, nationalization of forests and sale of shares to workers   1·20   25
1568   8r. Profit-sharing, votes for women and education corps   1·90   25
Nos. 1565/8, each showing symbols of three of the reforms, were issued, se-tenant, forming a composite design of a rosette.

369 Shah Mohammed Riza Pahlavi

1969. 10,000th Day of Shah's Reign.
1569 369   6r. brown, red and blue   1·50   25

370 Eurasian Goldfinch

1969. New Year Festival. Multicoloured.
1570 370   1r. Type 370   25   25
1571   2r. Common pheasant   45   25
1572   8r. Roses   1·50   25

371 Scales of Justice and "Blindfold Globe"

1969. 15th FIDA (Female Jurists) Convention, Teheran.
1573 371   6r. black and blue   55   25

372 Symbols of I.L.O.

1969. 50th Anniv of I.L.O.
1574 372   10r. violet and blue   55   25

373 Wrestling "Throw"

1969. Third Aryamehr Cup International Wrestling Championships.
1575 373   10r. multicoloured   1·10   45

374 "Flower and Birds"

1969. World Handicrafts Day.
1576 374   10r. multicoloured   75   25

375 Mask and Cord

1969. "Philia 1969". Outdoor Course for Scout Patrol Leaders.
1577 375   6r. multicoloured   1·00   25

376 Mughal Miniature (Pakistan)

1969. Fifth Anniv of Regional co-operation for Development. Miniatures. Multicoloured.

1578	25r. Type **376**	2·00	55
1579	25r. *Kneeling Figure* (Safavi, Iran)	2·00	55
1580	25r. *Suleiman the Magnificent and Court* (Ottoman, Turkey)	2·00	55

377 Astronauts on Moon

1969. First Man on the Moon.

1581	**377**	24r. brown, blue and buff	5·75	1·90

378 "Education"
(quotation from Shah's Declaration)

1969. Education Reform Conference.

1582	**378**	10r. red, green and buff	60	25

379 Oil Rig

1969. Tenth Anniv of Iranian–Italian Marine Drilling Project.

1583	**379**	8r. multicoloured	1·00	25

380 Festival Emblem

1969. Third Shiraz Arts Festival.

1584	**380**	6r. multicoloured	30	25
1585	**380**	8r. multicoloured	40	25

381 Thumb-print and Cross

1969. International Anti-illiteracy Campaign.

1586	**381**	4r. multicoloured	30	25

382 Shah, Persepolis and U.P.U. Emblem

1969. 16th U.P.U. Congress, Tokyo.

1587	**382**	10r. multicoloured	2·30	55
1588	**382**	14r. multicoloured	2·30	55

383 Fair Emblem

1969. Second International Asian Trade Fair, Teheran. Multicoloured.

1589	8r. Type **383**	30	25
1590	14r. As T **383**, but inscr "ASIA 69"	40	25
1591	20r. Emblem and sections of globe (horiz)	55	30

384 "Justice"

1969. Rural Courts of Justice Day.

1592	**384**	8r. brown and green	60	25

385 U.N. Emblem

1969. 25th Anniv of United Nations Day.

1593	**385**	2r. blue and pale blue	40	25

386 Festival Emblem

1969. National Festival of Art and Culture, Teheran.

1594	**386**	2r. multicoloured	60	25

387 "In the Garden"

1969. Children's Week. Children's Drawings. Multicoloured.

1595	1r. Type **387**	25	25
1596	2r. "Three Children" (horiz)	25	25
1597	5r. "Mealtime" (horiz)	55	25

388 Global Emblem

1969. National Association of Parents and Teachers Congress, Teheran.

1598	**388**	8r. brown and blue	40	25

389 Earth Station

1969. Opening of First Iranian Satellite Communications Earth Station.

1599	**389**	6r. brown and ochre	40	25

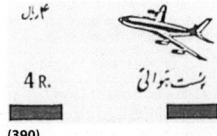
(390)

1969. Air. 50th Anniv of First England–Australia Flight. No. 1281 surch as T **390**.

1600	**229**	4r. on 14r.+6r.	2·00	60
1601	**229**	10r. on 14r.+6r.	2·00	60
1602	**229**	14r. on 14r.+6r.	2·00	60

391 Mahatma Gandhi

1969. Birth Centenary of Mahatma Gandhi.

1603	**391**	14r. brown and grey	5·25	1·00

392 Globe and Flags

1969. 50th Anniv of League of Red Cross Societies. Multicoloured.

1604	2r. Type **392**	60	25
1605	6r. Red Cross emblems on Globe	90	25

393 Shah and Reform Symbols

1970. Seventh Anniv of Shah's White Revolution.

1606	**393**	1r. multicoloured	1·00	40
1607	**393**	2r. multicoloured	1·00	40

394 Pansies

1970. New Year Festival. Multicoloured.

1608	1r. Type **394**	25	25
1609	8r. New Year table (40×26 mm)	1·50	30

395 Nationalization Decree

1970. 20th Anniv of Oil Industry Nationalization. Multicoloured.

1610	2r. Type **395**	1·10	25
1611	4r. Laying pipeline	1·20	30
1612	6r. Part of Kharg Island plant	1·40	40
1613	8r. Ocean terminal, Kharg Island (vert)	1·70	45
1614	10r. Refinery, Teheran	1·90	55

396 "EXPO" Emblem

1970. EXPO 70 World Fair, Osaka, Japan.

1615	**396**	4r. blue and mauve	30	25
1616	**396**	10r. violet and blue	45	25

397 Dish Aerial and Satellite

1970. Asian Plan Communications Committee Meeting, Teheran.

1617	**397**	14r. multicoloured	75	25

398 New U.P.U. H.Q.

1970. New U.P.U. Headquarters Building, Berne.

1618	**398**	2r. sepia, mauve & green	55	25
1619	**398**	4r. sepia, mauve and lilac	75	25

399 A.P.Y. Emblem

1970. Asian Productivity Year.

1620	**399**	8r. multicoloured	40	25

400 Stork carrying Baby

1970. 50th Anniv of Midwifery School.

1621	**400**	8r. blue and brown	60	25

401 Tomb of Cyrus the Great

1970. 2500th Anniv of Persian Empire (1st issue). Achaemenian Era.

1622	**401**	6r. violet, red and grey	75	25
1623	-	8r. green, black and pink	1·50	55
1624	-	10r. brown, red & yellow	1·90	60
1625	-	14r. brown, black & blue	2·30	1·00

DESIGNS—HORIZ: 10r. Religious ceremony (Median bas-relief); 14r. Achaemenian officers (bas-relief). VERT: 8r. Columns, Palace of Apadana.

　See also Nos. 1629/32, 1633/6, 1640/2, 1658/61, 1664/7, 1674/7 and 1679/82.

402 Saiful Malook Lake (Pakistan)

1970. Sixth Anniv of Regional Co-operation for Development. Multicoloured.

1626	2r. Type **402**	75	25
1627	2r. Seeyo-Se-Pol Bridge, Isfahan (Iran) (62×46 mm)	75	25
1628	2r. View from Fethiye (Turkey)	75	25

1970. 2500th Anniv of Persian Empire (2nd issue). Achaemenian Era. Designs as T **401**.

1629	2r. gold, deep green and green	1·00	40
1630	6r. gold, violet and green	1·20	40
1631	8r. gold, blue and orange	1·70	55
1632	14r. red, black and blue	2·00	1·10

DESIGNS—VERT: 2r. Eagle amulet; 6r. "Lion" goblet; 8r. Winged ibex statue. HORIZ: 14r. Tapestry.

1970. 2500th Anniv of Persian Empire (3rd issue). Coins of Sassanid and Parthian Eras. Designs as T **401**. Multicoloured, frames in gold.

1633	1r. Queen Buran dirham	1·00	40

1634	2r. Mithridates I dirham	1·20	40
1635	6r. Shapur I dirham	1·70	45
1636	8r. Ardeshir I dirham	1·70	55

405 Candle and Globe Emblem

1970. World Literacy Day.

| 1637 | **405** | 1r. multicoloured | 25 | 25 |
| 1638 | **405** | 2r. multicoloured | 25 | 25 |

406 Isfahan Tile

1970. International Architects' Congress, Isfahan.

| 1639 | **406** | 6r. multicoloured | 40 | 25 |

1970. 2500th Anniv of Persian Empire (4th issue). Achaemenian and Sassanid Eras. Designs as T **401**.

1640	2r. multicoloured	1·20	40
1641	6r. brown, blue and lilac	1·70	55
1642	8r. green, red and lilac	1·70	1·40

DESIGNS—VERT: 2r. Sassanid arch and art. HORIZ: 6r. Achaemenian mounted courier; 8r. Seal of Darius I.

408 Councils Emblem

1970. First Congress of Provincial Councils.

| 1643 | **408** | 2r. violet and blue | 25 | 25 |

409 Dove and U.N. Emblem

1970. United Nations Day.

| 1644 | **409** | 2r. ultramarine, pur & bl | 30 | 25 |

410 "1970" and I.A.T.A. Emblem

1970. Air. 26th International Air Transport Association General Meeting, Teheran.

| 1645 | **410** | 14r. multicoloured | 4·50 | 55 |

411 Festival Emblem

1970. National Festival of Art and Culture, Teheran.

| 1646 | **411** | 2r. multicoloured | 40 | 25 |

412 "Goatherd and Goats"

1970. Children's Week. Children's Drawings. Multicoloured.

| 1647 | 50d. Type **412** | 25 | 25 |

| 1648 | 1r. "Family picnic" | 25 | 25 |
| 1649 | 2r. "Mosque" | 40 | 25 |

413 Shah Mohammed Riza Pahlavi

1971. Eighth Anniv of Shah's White Revolution.

| 1650 | **413** | 2r. multicoloured | 2·30 | 75 |

414 Common Shelduck

1971. International Wetland and Waterfowl Conference, Ramsar. Multicoloured.

1651	1r. Type **414**	1·10	40
1652	2r. Ruddy shelduck	1·40	60
1653	8r. Greater flamingo (vert)	2·30	75

415 Riza Shah Pahlavi

1971. 50th Anniv of Rise of Pahlavi Dynasty.

| 1654 | **415** | 6r. multicoloured | 3·50 | 75 |

416 Red Junglefowl

1971. New Year Festival. Birds. Multicoloured.

1655	1r. Type **416**	60	25
1656	2r. Barn swallow at nest	1·00	30
1657	6r. Hoopoe	2·75	40

417 Stone Bull's Head, Persepolis

1971. 2500th Anniv of Persian Empire (5th issue). Age of Cyrus the Great. Multicoloured.

1658	4r. Type **417**	1·50	25
1659	5r. Winged lion ornament	1·70	25
1660	6r. Persian Archer (bas-relief)	1·70	25
1661	8r. Imperial audience (bas-relief)	2·30	55

418 Prisoners' Rehabilitation

1971. Rehabilitation Week.

| 1662 | **418** | 6r. multicoloured | 1·70 | 25 |
| 1663 | **418** | 8r. multicoloured | 3·00 | 25 |

1971. 2500th Anniv of Persian Empire (6th issue). Art of Ancient Persia. As T **417**.

1664	1r. multicoloured	1·00	25
1665	2r. black and brown	1·50	25
1666	2r. brown, black and purple	1·50	25
1667	10r. black, blue and brown	1·50	25

DESIGNS—VERT: No. 1664, "Harpist" (mosaic); 1667, Bronze head of Parthian prince. HORIZ: No. 1665, "Shapur I hunting" (ornamental plate); 1666, "Investiture of Ardashir I" (bas-relief).

420 Badshahi Mosque, Lahore (Pakistan)

1971. Seventh Anniv of Regional Co-operation for Development. Multicoloured.

1668	2r. Type **420**	40	25
1669	2r. Selimiye Mosque, Edirne, Turkey (vert)	40	25
1670	2r. Chaharbagh School, Isfahan (Iran) (vert)	40	25

421 Shiraz Arts

1971. Fifth Shiraz Arts Festival, Persepolis.

| 1671 | **421** | 2r. multicoloured | 70 | 25 |

422 "Book-reading"

1971. World Literacy Day.

| 1672 | **422** | 2r. multicoloured | 55 | 25 |

423 Kings Abdullah and Hussein II

1971. 50th Anniv of Hashemite Kingdom of Jordan.

| 1673 | **423** | 2r. multicoloured | 55 | 25 |

424 National Steel Foundry

1971. 2500th Anniv of Persian Empire (7th issue). Modern Iran. Multicoloured.

1674	1r. Type **424**	1·00	25
1675	2r. Shahyad Aryamehr Memorial	1·00	40
1676	3r. Senate Building, Teheran	1·00	40
1677	11r. Shah Abbas the Great Dam	2·30	75

425 Ghatur Railway Bridge

1971. Inaug of Iran–Turkey Railway Link.

| 1678 | **425** | 2r. multicoloured | 1·00 | 55 |

426 Shah Mohammed Riza Pahlavi

1971. 2500th Anniv of Persian Empire (8th issue). Pahlavi Era. Multicoloured.

1679	1r. Type **426**	3·50	1·50
1680	2r. Riza Shah Pahlavi	3·50	1·50
1681	5r. Proclamation tablet of Cyrus the Great (horiz)	3·50	1·50
1682	10r. Pahlavi Crown	5·00	1·50

427 Racial Equality Year Emblem

1971. Racial Equality Year.

| 1683 | **427** | 2r. multicoloured | 25 | 25 |

428 Shah Mohammed Riza Pahlavi

1971

1684	**428**	5d. purple	25	25
1685	**428**	10d. red	25	25
1686	**428**	50d. green	25	25
1687	**428**	1r. green	30	25
1688	**428**	2r. brown	30	25
1689	**428**	6r. green	1·10	25
1690	**428**	8r. violet	1·50	1·10
1691	**428**	10r. purple	1·40	30
1692	**428**	11r. green	5·00	1·10
1693	**428**	14r. blue	6·50	55
1694	**428**	20r. mauve	6·00	60
1695	**428**	50r. ochre	5·25	1·20

Nos. 1689/95 are larger, 27×37 mm.
See also Nos. 1715/26b and 1846/50.

429 "Waiters at a Banquet"

1971. Children's Week. Children's Drawings. Multicoloured.

1696	2r. Type **429**	25	25
1697	2r. "Persepolis Ruins" (vert)	25	25
1698	2r. "Persian Archer" (vert)	25	25

430 UNESCO Emblem

1971. 25th Anniv of UNESCO.

| 1699 | **430** | 6r. blue and purple | 40 | 25 |

431 Congress Emblem and Livestock

1971. Fourth Iranian Veterinary Congress.

| 1700 | **431** | 2r. red, black and grey | 40 | 25 |

432 I.L.O. Emblem and Globe

1971. Seventh Asian International Labour Organization Regional Conference, Teheran.

| 1701 | **432** | 2r. orange, blue and black | 40 | 15 |

433 Bird feeding Young

1971. 25th Anniv of UNICEF.

| 1702 | **433** | 2r. multicoloured | 15 | 10 |

434 Shah Mohammed Riza Pahlavi

1972. Ninth Anniv of Shah's White Revolution.

1703	**434**	2r. multicoloured	3·00	1·00
MS1704	80×94 mm. **434** 20r. multicoloured. Imperf		11·50	7·50

435 Chukar Partridge

1972. New Year Festival. Birds. Multicoloured.

1705	1r. Type **435**	40	25
1706	1r. Pin-tailed sandgrouse	40	25
1707	2r. Swee waxbill and red-cheeked cordon-bleu	2·30	25

436 Human Heart

1972. World Heart Day.

1708	**436**	10r. multicoloured	1·70	25

437 Winged Ibex Symbol

1972. International Film Festival, Teheran.

1709	**437**	6r. gold and blue	75	25
1710	-	8r. multicoloured	1·50	25

DESIGN: 8r. Symbolic spectrum.

438 Scarlet Roses

1972. Roses. Multicoloured.

1711	1r. Type **438**	30	25
1712	2r. Yellow roses	60	25
1713	5r. Red rose	75	25

1972. As Nos. 1684/95, but with bistre frames and inscriptions.

1715	**428**	5d. purple	25	25
1716	**428**	10d. brown	25	25
1717	**428**	50d. green	25	25
1718	**428**	1r. green	25	25
1719	**428**	2r. brown	55	25
1720	**428**	6r. green	85	25
1721	**428**	8r. violet	85	25
1722	**428**	10r. purple	1·00	25
1723	**428**	11r. blue	1·40	75
1724	**428**	14r. blue	5·25	60
1725	**428**	20r. mauve	8·25	55
1726	**428**	50r. blue	3·50	1·00
1726a	**428**	100r. violet	5·00	2·00
1726b	**428**	200r. black	10·50	3·50

Nos. 1720/26b are larger, 27×37 mm.

439 "U.I.T." Emblem

1972. World Telecommunications Day.

1726c	**439**	14r. multicoloured	2·40	55

440 Fisherman (Cevat Dereli, Turkey)

1972. Eighth Anniv of Regional Co-operation for Development. Paintings. Multicoloured.

1727	5r. Type **440**	1·40	30
1728	5r. *Iranian Woman* (Behzad, Iran)	1·40	30
1729	5r. *Will and Power* (A. R. Chughtai, Pakistan)	1·40	30

441 Floral Patterns

1972. Sixth Shiraz Arts Festival.

1730	**441**	6r. black, red and green	1·10	25
1731	**441**	8r. black and purple	1·50	25

442 Pens

1972. World Literacy Day.

1732	**442**	1r. multicoloured	25	25
1733	**442**	2r. multicoloured	40	25

443 "10" and Dental Emblem

1972. Tenth Annual Congress of Iranian Dental Association.

1734	**443**	1r. multicoloured	25	25
1735	**443**	2r. multicoloured	45	25

444 A.B.U. Emblem within "9"

1972. Ninth General Assembly of Asian Broadcasting Union, Teheran.

1736	**444**	6r. multicoloured	75	25
1737	**444**	8r. multicoloured	1·50	25

445 3ch. stamp of 1910 on Cover

1972. World Stamp Day.

1738	**445**	10r. multicoloured	2·30	25

446 Chess

1972. Olympic Games, Munich. Iranian Sports. Multicoloured.

1739	1r. Type **446**	2·00	1·50
1740	2r. Hunting	2·00	55
1741	3r. Archery	2·40	55
1742	5r. Horse-racing	2·50	75
1743	6r. Polo	2·75	75
1744	8r. Wrestling	2·75	90
MS1745	177×106 mm. Nos. 1739/44. Imperf	19·00	11·50

447 Communications Emblem

1972. United Nations Day.

1746	**447**	10r. multicoloured	2·00	25

448 "Children in Garden"

1972. Children's Week. Children's Drawings. Multicoloured.

1747	2r. Type **448**	40	25
1748	2r. "At the Theatre"	75	25
1749	6r. "Children at play" (horiz)	1·40	25

449 Festival Emblem

1972. National Festival of Art and Culture, Teheran.

1750	**449**	10r. multicoloured	5·00	30

450 Family Planning Emblem

1972. Family Planning Campaign.

1751	**450**	1r. multicoloured	25	25
1752	**450**	2r. multicoloured	30	25

451 Scouting Emblem

1972. 20th Anniv of Scouting in Iran.

1753	**451**	2r. multicoloured	55	25

452 Cuneiform Seal

1973. "Origins of Writing" (1st issue). Impressions from ancient seals. Multicoloured. Background colours given.

1754	**452**	1r. blue	60	25
1755	-	1r. yellow	60	25
1756	-	1r. mauve	60	25
1757	-	2r. orange	60	25
1758	-	2r. green	60	25
1759	-	2r. buff	60	25

See also Nos. 1774/9 and 1822/7.

453 Open Books in Space

1973. International Book Year. Multicoloured.

1760	2r. Type **453**	75	25
1761	6r. Illuminated manuscript	1·10	25

454 "Twelve Reforms"

1973. Tenth Anniv of Shah's White Revolution. Multicoloured.

1762	1r. Type **454**	25	25
1763	2r. Pyramid of 12 balls	25	25
1764	6r. As Type **454** but size 71×92 mm.	1·70	75
MS1765	71×92 mm. 10r. Design as 2r	2·75	75

455 Long-spined Seabream (*Sparus spinifer*)

1973. New Year Festival. Fish. Multicoloured.

1766	1r. Type **455**	60	25
1767	1r. Purple tang (*Acanthurus sp.*)	60	25
1768	2r. Two-banded seabream (*Anisotremus sp.*)	90	30
1769	2r. Sergeant major (*Abdufef*)	90	30
1770	2r. Black-spotted snapper (*Lutyanus fulniflamma*)	90	30

456 W.H.O. Emblem

1973. 25th Anniv of W.H.O.

1771	**456**	10r. multicoloured	1·20	25

457 "Footballers"

1973. 15th Asian Youth Football Tournament, Teheran.

1772	**457**	14r. multicoloured	1·40	25

458 Railway Track encircling Globe

1973. International Railway Conference, Teheran.

1773	**458**	10r. blue, black & mauve	1·20	40

459 Ancient Aryan Script

1973. "Origins of Writing". Multicoloured.

1774	1r. Type **459**	55	25

1775	1r. Achaemenian priest and text	55	25
1776	1r. Kharochtani tablet	55	25
1777	2r. Parthian medallion (Arsacid)	90	25
1778	2r. Parthian coin (Mianeh)	90	25
1779	2r. Gachtak inscribed medallion (Dabireh)	90	25

460 Orchid

1973. Flowers. Multicoloured.

1780	**460**	1r. Type **460**	25	25
1781		2r. Hyacinth	55	25
1782		6r. Wild rose	1·20	25

461 Carved Head, Tomb of Antiochus I (Turkey)

1973. Ninth Anniv of Regional Co-operation for Development. Multicoloured.

1783		2r. Type **461**	40	25
1784		2r. Statue, Lut excavations (Iran)	40	25
1785		2r. Street in Moenjodaro (Pakistan)	40	25

462 Shah and Oil Installations

1973. Full Independence for Iranian Oil Industry.

1786	**462**	5r. black and blue	1·40	40

463 Soldiers and "Sun"

1973. 20th Anniv of Gen. Zahedi's Uprising.

1787	**463**	2r. multicoloured	30	25

464 Sportswomen and Globe

1973. Seventh International Women's Congress on Physical Education and Sport, Teheran.

1788	**464**	2r. multicoloured (blue background)	25	25
1789	**464**	2r. multicoloured (green background)	25	25

466 Shahyad Monument and Rainbow

1973. Cent of World Meteorological Organization.

1792	**466**	5r. multicoloured	75	25

467 Wrestling

1973. World Wrestling Championships, Teheran.

1793	**467**	6r. multicoloured	70	30

468 Alphabetic "Sun"

1973. World Literacy Day.

1794	**468**	2r. multicoloured	25	25

469 Globe wearing Earphones

1973. Int Audio-visual Exhibition, Teheran.

1795	**469**	10r. multicoloured	60	25

470 Al-Biruni

1973. Birth Millenary of Abu al-Rayhan al-Biruni (mathematician and philosopher).

1796	**470**	10r. black and brown	1·10	40

471 C.I.S.M. Badge and Emblem

1973. 25th Anniv of International Military Sports Council (C.I.S.M.).

1797	**471**	8r. multicoloured	60	25

472 Crown Prince Cup

1973. Crown Prince Cup Football Championship.

1798	**472**	2r. brown, black and lilac	40	25

473 Interpol Emblem

1973. 50th Anniv of International Criminal Police Organization (Interpol).

1799	**473**	2r. multicoloured	25	25

474 Curves on Globe

1973. 25th Anniv of World Mental Health Federation.

1800	**474**	10r. multicoloured	55	25

475 U.P.U. Emblem, Post-horn and Letter

1973. World Post Day.

1801	**475**	6r. orange and blue	55	25

476 Emblems within Honeycomb

1973. Fifth Anniv of United Nations Volunteers.

1802	**476**	2r. multicoloured (brown background)	25	25
1803	**476**	2r. multicoloured (green background)	25	25

477 Festival Emblem and "People"

1973. National Festival of Art and Culture, Teheran.

1804	**477**	2r. multicoloured	40	25

478 Bosphorus Bridge

1973. 50th Anniv of Turkish Republic. Multicoloured.

1805		2r. Type **478**	75	25
1806		8r. Meeting of Kemal Ataturk and Reza Shah Pahlavi	1·20	25

479 "House and Garden"

1973. Children's Week. Children's Drawings. Multicoloured.

1807		2r. Type **479**	30	25
1808		2r. "Collecting Fruit"	30	25
1809		2r. "Caravan" (horiz)	30	25

480 Ear of Grain and Cow

1973. Tenth Anniv of World Food Programme.

1810	**480**	10r. multicoloured	1·00	25

481 Cylinder of Cyrus and Red Cross Emblems

1973. 22nd Int Red Cross Conference, Teheran.

1811	**481**	6r. multicoloured	55	25

482 IATA Emblem

1973. Tourist Managers Congress, Teheran.

1812	**482**	10r. multicoloured	55	25

483 Emblem, Film and Flags

1973. International Film Festival, Teheran.

1813	**483**	2r. multicoloured	25	25

484 Flame Emblem

1973. 25th Anniv of Declaration of Human Rights.

1814	**484**	8r. multicoloured	40	25

485 Harp Emblem

1973. "Art of Music" Festival.

1815	**485**	10r. red, green and black	55	25
1816	–	10r. ultram, bl & pur	55	25

DESIGN: No. 1816, Musical symbols.

486 Reform Symbols

1974. 11th Anniv of Shah's White Revolution. Multicoloured.

1817		1r. Type **486**	25	25
1818		1r. Tractor, factory in cogwheel, women and parliament gate	25	25
1819		2r. Girders, hose and worker	25	25
1820		2r. Rod of Aesculapius, scales and road passing house	25	25
MS1821	76×102 mm. 20r. Symbols from Nos. 1817/20 arranged in four panels. Imperf	3·25	1·20

487 Pir Amooz Ketabaty Script

1974. "Origins of Writing" (3rd issue). Multicoloured.
1822		1r. Din Dabireh Avesta	75	30
1823		1r. Mo Eghely Ketabaty	75	30
1824		1r. Type **487**	75	30
1825		2r. Pir Amooz, Naskh style	75	30
1826		2r. Pir Amooz, decorative	75	30
1827		2r. Pir Amooz, decorative and architectural	75	30

488 Chicken, Cow and Syringe

1974. Fifth Iranian Veterinary Congress.
1828	**488**	6r. multicoloured	40	25

490 Scarce Swallowtail

1974. Nawrooz and Spring Festivals. Butterflies. Multicoloured, background colours given.
1841	**490**	1r. mauve	75	25
1842	-	1r. purple	75	25
1843	-	2r. green	1·10	40
1844	-	2r. brown	1·10	40
1845	-	2r. blue	1·10	40

DESIGNS: No. 1842, Swallowtail; 1843, Peacock; 1844, Painted lady; 1845, Cardinal.

1974. As Nos. 1684/95, but colours changed.
1846	**428**	50d. blue and orange	45	25
1847	**428**	1r. blue and green	60	25
1848	**428**	2r. blue and red	85	25
1849	**428**	10r. blue and green	6·00	25
1850	**428**	20r. blue and mauve	3·50	1·10

Nos. 1849/50 are larger, 27×37 mm.

491 Mevlana

1974. 700th Death Anniv of Jalal-udin Mevlana (poet).
1851	**491**	2r. multicoloured	55	25

492 Palace of Forty Columns, Isfahan

1974. Ninth Near- and Middle-East Medical Congress, Isfahan.
1852	**492**	10r. multicoloured	55	25

493 Asiatic Wild Ass

1974. International Game and Wild Life Protection Congress, Teheran. Multicoloured.
1853		1r. Type **493**	40	25
1854		2r. Great bustard	55	25
1855		6r. Fawn and fallow deer	1·20	40
1856		8r. Caucasian black grouse	2·00	40

494 Gymnastics

1974. Seventh Asian Games, Teheran (1st series). Multicoloured.
1857		1r. Type **494**	55	25
1858		1r. Table tennis	55	25
1859		2r. Boxing	1·00	25
1860		2r. Hurdling	1·00	25
1861		6r. Weightlifting	1·50	25
1862		8r. Handball	2·40	25

See also Nos. 1874/9, 1890/3 and 1909.

495 Lion of St. Mark's

1974. UNESCO "Save Venice" Campaign. Multicoloured.
1863		6r. Type **495**	55	25
1864		8r. Merchants at the Doge's court	1·00	40

496 Chain Link

1974. Farm Co-operatives' Day.
1865	**496**	2r. multicoloured	25	25

497 Shah and Douglas DC-9-80 Super Eighty

1974. Air.
1866	**497**	4r. black and orange	40	25
1867	**497**	10r. black and blue	1·50	25
1868	**497**	12r. black and brown	1·50	40
1869	**497**	14r. black and green	1·70	40
1870	**497**	20r. black and mauve	2·30	55
1871	**497**	50r. black and blue	5·75	1·40

498 De Havilland D.H.9A, 1924

1974. 50th Anniv of Imperial Iranian Air Force. Multicoloured.
1872	**498**	10r. Type **498**	1·50	40
1873		10r. McDonnell Douglas F-4D Phantom II fighter of 1974	1·50	40

499 Tennis (men's doubles)

1974. Seventh Asian Games, Teheran (2nd series). Multicoloured.
1874		1r. Type **499**	55	25
1875		1r. Swimming	55	25
1876		2r. Wrestling	75	25
1877		2r. Hockey	75	25
1878		4r. Volleyball	1·10	40
1879		10r. Tennis (women's singles)	2·00	55

500 Mazanderan Costume

1974. Regional Costumes. Multicoloured.
1880		2r. Type **500**	1·40	55
1881		2r. Bakhtiari	1·40	55
1882		2r. Turkoman	1·40	55
1883		2r. Ghasgai	1·40	55
1884		2r. Kirmanshah (Kurdistan)	1·40	55
1885		2r. Sanandadj (Kurdistan)	1·40	55

501 Gold Cup

1974. Iranian Football Championships.
1886	**501**	2r. yellow, brown & green	30	25

502 Iranian Carpet

1974. Tenth Anniv of Regional Co-operation for Development. Multicoloured.
1887		2r. Pakistani carpet (diamond) centre	45	25
1888		2r. Turkish carpet (striped)	45	25
1889		2r. Type **502**	45	25

503 Rifle-shooting

1974. Seventh Asian Games, Teheran (3rd series). Multicoloured.
1890		2r. Type **503**	75	25
1891		2r. Fencing	75	25
1892		2r. Football	75	25
1893		2r. Cycling	75	25

504 Persian King

1974. Eighth Shiraz Arts Festival, Persepolis.
1894	**504**	2r. multicoloured	30	25

505 Games Emblem

1974. Seventh Asian Games, Tehran (4th issue). Two sheets, each 74×95 mm, containing single stamps as T **505**. Multicoloured.
MS1895		(a) 10r. Type **505**; (b) 10r. Plan of Games area	4·50	2·30

506 Petrochemical Works, Khark

1974
1896	**506**	5d. green and brown	30	25
1897	-	10d. orange and brown	30	25
1898	-	50d. green and brown	30	25
1899	-	1r. blue and brown	30	25
1900	-	2r. purple and brown	30	25
1901	-	6r. brown and blue	55	25
1902	-	8r. turquoise and blue	55	25
1903	-	10r. purple and blue	75	40
1904	-	14r. green and blue	13·50	60
1905	-	20r. red and blue	3·50	55
1906	-	50r. violet and blue	4·25	1·10

DESIGNS—As T **506**: 10d. Railway bridge, Ghatur; 50d. Dam, Farahnaz; 1r. Oil Refinery; 2r. Radio telescope. 37×27 mm: 6r. Steelworks, Aryamehr; 8r. Tabriz University; 10r. Shah Abbas Kabir Dam; 14r. Teheran Opera House; 20r. Shahyad Square; 50r. Aryamehr Stadium.
See also Nos. 1939/49.

507 Family within Hands

1974. State Education and Health Services. Multicoloured.
1907		2r. Type **507**	25	25
1908		2r. Children, pen and book within hands	25	25

508 Aryamehr Stadium, Teheran

1974. Seventh Asian Games, Teheran (4th series).
1909	**508**	6r. multicoloured	1·00	25

509 Plan of Hasanlu

1974. Second International Architectural Congress, Shiraz.
1910	**509**	8r. multicoloured	40	25

510 Charioteer

1974. Centenary of U.P.U. Multicoloured.
1911		6r. Type **510**	85	40
1912		14r. U.P.U. emblem and letters	1·20	40

511 Road through Park

1974. Opening of Farahabad Park, Teheran. Multicoloured.
1913		1r. Type **511**	25	25
1914		2r. Recreation pavilion	25	25

512 Festival Emblem

1974. National Festival of Art and Culture, Teheran.
1915 **512** 2r. multicoloured 30 25

513 Crown Prince in Aircraft

1974. Air. Crown Prince's Birthday.
1916 **513** 14r. multicoloured 1·10 40

514 Destroyer *Palang*

1974. Navy Day.
1917 **514** 10r. multicoloured 90 25

515 Scarecrow

1974. Children's Week. Children's Drawings. Multicoloured.
1918 2r. Type **515** 25 25
1919 2r. Girl at spinning wheel (horiz) 25 25
1920 2r. New Year picnic (horiz) 25 25

516 Winged Bull Emblem

1974. Third International Film Festival, Teheran.
1921 **516** 2r. multicoloured 25 25

517 W.P.Y. Emblem

1974. World Population Year.
1922 **517** 8r. multicoloured 55 25

518 Gold Butterfly Brooch

1974. 14th Wedding Anniv of Shah and Empress Farah. Multicoloured.
1923 6r. Type **518** 45 25
1924 8r. Gold diadem 70 30

519 Angel with Banner

1975. International Women's Year.
1925 **519** 2r. orange, blue and red 25 25

520 Emblems of Agriculture, Industry and the Arts

1975. 12th Anniv of Shah's White Revolution.
1926 **520** 2r. multicoloured 25 25

521 Tourism Year Emblem

1975. South Asia Tourism Year.
1927 **521** 6r. multicoloured 25 25

522 Farabi's Initial

1975. 1100th Birth Anniv of Abu-Nasr al-Farabi (philosopher).
1928 **522** 2r. multicoloured 25 25

523 Ornament

1975. New Year Festival. Multicoloured.
1929 1r. Type **523** 25 25
1930 1r. Blossoms and tree 25 25
1931 1r. Arabesque and patterns 25 25

524 Nasser Khosrov

1975. Birth Millenary of Nasser Khosrov (poet).
1932 **524** 2r. black, red and bistre 25 25

525 Persian Warriors

1975. 70th Anniv of Rotary International. Multicoloured.
1933 2r. Type **525** 1·50 60
1934 10r. Charioteer (horiz) 3·50 90

526 Biochemical Emblem

1975. Fifth Biochemical Symposium.
1935 **526** 2r. multicoloured 25 25

527 "Co-operative Peoples"

1975. Co-operatives Day.
1936 **527** 2r. multicoloured 25 25

528 Ancient Signal-beacons

1975. World Telecommunications Day. Multicoloured.
1937 6r. Type **528** 40 25
1938 8r. Telecommunications satellite 55 30

1975. As Nos. 1896/1906 but colours changed.
1939 **506** 5d. orange and turquoise 30 25
1940 - 10d. purple and turquoise 30 25
1941 - 50d. mauve and turquoise 30 25
1942 - 1r. blue and turquoise 30 25
1943 - 2r. brown and turquoise 30 25
1944 - 6r. violet and brown 40 40
1945 - 8r. red and brown 2·00 30
1946 - 10r. green and brown 1·50 25
1947 - 14r. mauve and brown 6·00 25
1948 - 20r. turquoise and brown 3·00 40
1949 - 50r. blue and brown 2·75 75

529 "Iran Air" Boeing 747SP

1975. "Iran Air's" First Teheran–New York Flight.
1950 **529** 10r. multicoloured 60 40

530 Environmental Emblem

1975. World Environment Day.
1951 **530** 6r. multicoloured 30 25

531 Dam and Reservoir

1975. 25th Anniv of International Commission on Irrigation and Drainage.
1952 **531** 10r. multicoloured 40 25

532 Party Emblem

1975. Formation of Resurgence Party.
1953 **532** 2r. multicoloured 25 25

533 Saluting Hand

1975. Second National Girl Scout Camp, Teheran.
1954 **533** 2r. multicoloured 25 25

534 Festival Motif

1975. Festival of Tus (honouring poet Firdausi).
1955 **534** 2r. multicoloured 25 25

535 Iranian Tile

1975. 11th Anniv of Regional Co-operation for Development. Multicoloured.
1956 2r. Type **535** 30 25
1957 2r. Pakistani camel-skin vase (vert) 30 25
1958 2r. Turkish porcelain vase (vert) 30 25

536 Parliament Gateway

1975. 70th Anniv of Iranian Constitution.
1959 **536** 10r. multicoloured 40 25

537 Stylized Column

1975. Ninth Shiraz Arts Festival.
1960 **537** 8r. multicoloured 55 25

538 Flags over Globe

1975. International Literacy Symposium, Persepolis.
1961 **538** 2r. multicoloured 25 25

539 Stylized Globe

1975. Third International Trade Fair, Teheran.
1962 **539** 2r. multicoloured 25 25

540 Envelope on World Map

1975. World Post Day.
1963 **540** 14r. multicoloured 75 25

541 Festival Emblem

1975. National Festival of Art and Culture, Teheran.
1964 **541** 2r. multicoloured 25 25

542 Face within Film

1975. International Festival of Children's Films, Teheran.
1965   **542**   6r. multicoloured   30   25

543 "Mother's Face"

1975. Children's Week. Multicoloured.
1966   2r. Type **543**   25   25
1967   2r. "Young Girl"   25   25
1968   2r. "Our House" (horiz)   25   25

544 "Sound Film"

1975. Fourth International Film Festival, Teheran.
1969   **544**   8r. multicoloured   45   25

545 Reform Symbols

1976. 13th Anniv of Shah's White Revolution. Multicoloured.
1970   2r. Type **545**   25   25
1971   2r. Symbols representing "People"   25   25
1972   2r. Five reform symbols   25   25

546 Motor Cycle Patrol

1976. Highway Police Day. Multicoloured.
1973   2r. Type **546**   75   30
1974   6r. Bell Model 205 Iroquois police helicopter (horiz)   1·10   45

547 Football Cup

1976. Third International Football Cup.
1975   **547**   2r. multicoloured   25   25

548 Candlestick

1976. New Year. Multicoloured.
1976   1r. Type **548**   25   25
1977   1r. Incense burner   25   25
1978   1r. Rosewater jug   25   25

549 Early and Modern Telephones

1976. Telephone Centenary.
1979   **549**   10r. multicoloured   60   25

550 Human Eye

1976. World Health Day.
1980   **550**   6r. multicoloured   30   10

551 Nurse holding Child

1976. 30th Anniv of Social Services Organization. Multicoloured.
1981   2r. Type **551**   30   25
1982   2r. Workshop apprentices   30   25
1983   2r. Handclasp (help the aged) (vert)   30   25

552 Linked Men on Map

1976. Tenth Anniv of Iranian Co-operative Movement.
1984   **552**   2r. multicoloured   30   25

553 Sound Waves and Headphones

1976. World Telecommunications Day.
1985   **553**   14r. multicoloured   55   25

554 "Patriotism"

1976. National Resistance Organization.
1986   **554**   2r. multicoloured   30   25

555 Nasser-Khosrow and Landmarks on Map

1976. Tourism Day and Birth Anniv of Nasser-Khosrow "The Great Iranian Tourist".
1987   **555**   6r. multicoloured   40   25

556 Riza Shah Pahlavi

1976. 12th Anniv of Regional Co-operation for Development. Multicoloured.
1988   2r. Type **556**   45   25
1989   6r. Mohammed Ali Jinnah (Pakistan)   60   25
1990   8r. Kemal Ataturk (Turkey)   75   25

557 Olympic Flame and Emblem

1976. Olympic Games, Montreal.
1991   **557**   14r. multicoloured   75   25

558 Riza Shah Pahlavi in Coronation Dress

1976. 50th Anniv of Pahlavi Dynasty. Multicoloured.
1992   2r. Riza Shah Pahlavi and Mohammed Riza Pahlavi (horiz)   75   30
1993   6r. Type **558**   1·50   40
1994   14r. Mohammed Riza Pahlavi in Coronation dress   2·30   45

559 Festival Emblem

1976. Tenth Shiraz Arts Festival.
1995   **559**   10r. multicoloured   55   25

560 Conference Emblem

1976. Tenth Asia–Pacific Scout Conference, Teheran.
1996   **560**   2r. multicoloured   25   25

561 Radiation Treatment

1976. Campaign against Cancer.
1997   **561**   2r. multicoloured   30   25

562 Target and Presentation to Policewoman

1976. Police Day.
1998   **562**   2r. multicoloured   30   25

563 Shah in Coronation Dress

1976. 35th Anniv of Shah's Reign. Sheet 75×100 mm.
MS1999 **563** 20r. multicoloured   6·00   3·75

564 U.P.U. Emblem and Iranian Stamp on Envelope

1976. International Post Day.
2000   **564**   10r. multicoloured   1·00   25

565 Crown Prince presenting Cup

1976. Society of Village Culture Houses.
2001   **565**   6r. multicoloured   30   25

566 Mohammed Riza Pahlavi, Riza Shah Pahlavi and Steam Train

1976. Railway Day.
2002   **566**   8r. multicoloured   2·00   40

567 Festival Emblem

1976. National Festival of Art and Culture, Teheran.
2003   **567**   14r. multicoloured   55   25

568 Census Symbols

1976. National Census.
2004   **568**   2r. multicoloured   25   25

569 Flowers and Birds

1976. Children's Week. Multicoloured.

2005	2r. Type **569**		40	25
2006	2r. Flowers and bird		40	25
2007	2r. Flowers and butterfly		40	25

570
Mohammed Ali
Jinnah
(Quaid-i-Azam)

1976. Birth Centenary of Mohammed Ali Jinnah (first Governor-General of Pakistan).

2008	**570**	10r. multicoloured	45	25

571 Tractor (Land reform)

1977. 14th Anniv of Shah's White Revolution. Shah's head and frame in gold.

2009	**571**	5d. green and pink	25	25
2010	-	10d. green and brown	25	25
2011	-	50d. blue and orange	25	25
2012	-	1r. blue and mauve	25	25
2013	-	2r. green and orange	25	25
2014	-	3r. red and blue	40	25
2015	-	5r. lilac and green	40	25
2016	-	6r. purple, brown & black	55	25
2017	-	8r. purple, blue and black	55	25
2018	-	10r. blue, green and black	1·40	25
2019	-	12r. brown, lilac & black	1·10	25
2020	-	14r. red, orange and black	1·40	75
2021	-	20r. orange, grey & black	3·00	55
2022	-	30r. green, blue and black	3·00	60
2023	-	50r. red, yellow and black	4·50	60
2024	-	100r. blue, mauve & blk	4·50	1·10
2025	-	200r. violet, green & blk	9·00	1·90

DESIGNS—21×28 mm: 10d. Trees (Nationalization of forests); 50d. Banknotes (Profit-sharing); 1r. Factory workers (Sale of shares to workers); 2r. Parliament gate (Votes for women); 3r. Teacher and pupils (Education corps); 5r. Doctor examining patient (Medical corps). 36×27 mm: 6r. Bulldozer (Civil engineering); 8r. Scales (Justice); 10r. Dam (Irrigation); 12r. Building site (Construction corps); 14r. Clock and receptionist (Working conditions); 20r. Screen and students (Adult literacy); 30r. Sound waves (Telecommunications); 50r. Students and pupils (Education); 100r. Baby in hands (Child care); 200r. Elderly couple (Care of the aged).

572 Man in Guilan Costume

1977. New Year Festival. Multicoloured.

2026	1r. Type **572**	25	25
2027	2r. Women in Guilan costume	25	25

573 Circuit Diagram

1977. World Telecommunications Day.

2028	**573**	20r. multicoloured	90	25

574 Riza Shah Dam

1977. Inauguration of Riza Shah Dam.

2029	**574**	5r. multicoloured	40	25

575 Olympic Rings

1977. Olympic Day.

2030	**575**	14r. multicoloured	70	25

576 Turkish "Human Face" Vase

1977. 13th Anniv of Regional Co-operation for Development. Multicoloured.

2031	**576**	5r. Type **576**	30	25
2032		5r. Pakistani toy bullock cart	30	25
2033		5r. Iranian buff earthenware	30	25

577 Flowers on Map of Asia

1977. Second Asia–Pacific Jamboree, Nishapur.

2034	**577**	10r. multicoloured	70	25

578 Map and Emblem

1977. Ninth Asian Electronics Conference, Teheran.

2035	**578**	3r. multicoloured	25	25

579 "Tree" in Farsi Script

1977. Teachers' Day.

2036	**579**	10r. multicoloured	30	25

580 Globe and Envelope

1977. Centenary of Iran's Admission to U.P.U.

2037	**580**	14r. multicoloured	45	25

581 "Tree and Lions"

1977. Popular Arts Festival.

2038	**581**	5r. multicoloured	40	25

582 Festival Emblem

1977. National Festival of Art and Culture, Teheran.

2039	**582**	20r. multicoloured	60	25

583 "Two Horsemen" (Persian miniature)

1977. Children's Week. Multicoloured.

2040		3r. Type **583**	25	25
2041		3r. "Lover and his mistress"	25	25
2042		3r. "Five people round a bed"	70	70

584 Seminar Emblem

1977. First Regional Seminar on Education and Welfare of the Deaf.

2043	**584**	5r. multicoloured	30	25

585 A. M. Iqbal

1977. Birth Centenary of Allama Mohammad Iqbal (Pakistani poet).

2044	**585**	5r. multicoloured	45	25

586 Bronze Head from Nigeria

1977. "Art of Black Africa" Exhibition, Teheran.

2045	**586**	20r. multicoloured	3·00	55

587 Ruins at Persepolis

1978

2059	**587**	1r. brown and gold	30	25
2060	-	2r. green and gold	30	25
2061	-	3r. purple and gold	55	25
2062	-	5r. green and gold	70	25
2063	-	9r. brown and gold	1·40	60
2064	-	10r. blue and gold	4·50	70
2065	-	20r. red and gold	1·70	60
2066	-	25r. blue and gold	19·00	9·00
2067	-	30r. red and gold	2·75	60
2068	-	50r. green and gold	4·50	3·50
2069	-	100r. blue and gold	11·50	9·00
2070	-	200r. violet and gold	15·00	15·00

DESIGNS: 30×23 mm: 2r. Khajou Bridge, Isfahan; 3r. Shah Mosque, Isfahan; 5r. Imam Riza Shrine, Meshed. 35×26 mm: 9r. Warrior frieze, Persepolis; 10r. Djameh Mosque, Isfahan; 20r. Bas-relief, Persepolis; 25r. Shaikh Lotfollah Mosque, Isfahan; 30r. Ruins, Persepolis (different); 50r. Ali Ghapou Palace, Isfahan; 100r. Stone relief, Tagh Bastan; 200r. Relief, Naqsh Rostam.

588 Mohammad Riza Pahlavi

1978. 15th Anniv of Shah's White Revolution.

2071	**588**	20r. multicoloured	3·50	1·00

589 Animals (carpet)

1978. Inauguration of Persian Carpets Museum, Teheran. Multicoloured.

2072		3r. Type **589**	25	25
2073		5r. Court scene	45	25
2074		10r. Floral pattern	60	30

590 Costume of Mazandera Province

1978. New Year Festival. Multicoloured.

2075	3r. Type **590**	25	25
2076	5r. Woman in costume of Mazandera Province	40	25

591 Riza Shah Pahlavi and Crown Prince inspecting Girls' School

1978. Birth Centenary of Riza Shah Pahlavi. Multicoloured.

2077	3r. Type **591**	40	25
2078	5r. Riza Shah Pahlavi and Crown Prince at inauguration of Trans-Iranian Railway	60	30
2079	10r. Riza Shah Pahlavi and Crown Prince at Palace of Persepolis	1·10	40
2080	14r. Shah handing Crown Prince officer's diploma	1·50	60

592 Satellite and Receiving Station

1978. Tenth Anniv of Admission to International Telecommunications Union.

2081	**592**	20r. multicoloured	1·00	25

593 Microwave Antenna

1978. World Telecommunications Day.

2082	**593**	15r. multicoloured	60	25

594 Welfare Legion Emblem

1978. Tenth Anniv of Universal Welfare Legion.

2083	**594**	10r. multicoloured	60	25

595 Pink Roses

1978. 14th Anniv of Regional Co-operation for Development. Roses. Multicoloured.

2084	5r. Type **595**	55	25
2085	10r. Salmon rose	60	25
2086	15r. Red roses	85	40

596 Rhazes and
Pharmaceutical Equipment

1978. Pharmacists' Day.
2087 **596** 5r. multicoloured 55 25

597 Girl Guides and
Aryamehr Arch

1978. 23rd World Girl Guides Conference, Teheran.
2088 **597** 5r. multicoloured 45 25

598 Riza Shah Pahlavi

1978. 50th Anniv of Bank Melli Iran. Multicoloured.
2089 3r. Type **598** 1·20 40
2090 5r. Mohammed Riza Pahlavi 1·50 55

599 Young Girl and Bird

1978. Children's Week.
2091 **599** 3r. multicoloured 75 30

600 U.P.U. Emblem over
Map of Iran

1978. World Post Day.
2092 **600** 14r. multicoloured 1·20 40

601 Classroom and
Communications Equipment

1978. 50th Anniv of Communications Faculty.
2093 **601** 10r. multicoloured 1·00 40

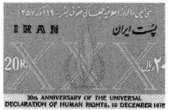

602 Human Rights
Emblem

1978. 30th Anniv of Human Rights Declaration.
2094 **602** 20r. multicoloured 3·00 55

603 Rose

1979. New Year Festival. Multicoloured.
2095 2r. Type **603** 40 25
2096 3r. Man in Khurdistan costume 75 25
2097 5r. Woman in Khurdistan costume 1·10 25

604 Revolutionary Crowd

1979. Islamic Revolution. Multicoloured.
2098 3r. Type **604** 1·50 30

2099 5r. Hands holding flower, gun and torch 1·10 30
2100 10r. Protest march 1·10 55
2101 20r. Bloodied hands releasing dove (vert) 2·40 60

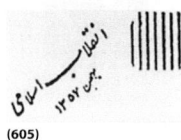

(605)

1979. Designs as T **587** optd with T **605**. (a) Nos. 1945/6.
2102 8r. red and brown 3·00 1·00
2103 10r. green and brown 1·50 1·50

(b) Nos. 2063/4, 2068/70 and unissued 15r. and 19r. stamps.
2104 9r. brown and gold 38·00 7·50
2105 10r. turquoise and gold 1·70 1·00
2106 15r. mauve and gold 1·70 1·00
2107 19r. green and gold 1·70 1·00
2108 50r. green and gold 5·00 2·00
2109 100r. blue and gold 7·50 3·00
2110 200r. violet and gold 9·00 6·00

DESIGNS—HORIZ (36×26 mm): 15r. Rock carvings, Naqsh Rostam; 19r. Chehel Sotoon Palace, Isfahan.

606 Tulip
formed from
"Allah" and
"Islamic
Republic"

1979. Islamic Republic.
2111 **606** 5r. multicoloured 1·20 40

607 Iranian Goldsmith (Kamal el Mol)

1979. 15th Anniv of Regional Co-operation for Development. Paintings. Multicoloured.
2112 5r. Type **607** 3·00 30
2113 5r. Turkish Harvest (Namik Ismail) 2·30 30
2114 5r. Pakistan Village Scene (Allah Baksh) 2·30 30

608 "Telecom 79"

1979. Third World Telecommunications Exhibition, Geneva.
2115 **608** 20r. gold, black and red 6·00 25

609 Tulip rising
from Blood of
Revolutionary

1979. International Year of the Child. Children's Paintings. Multicoloured.
2116 2r. Type **609** 85 55
2117 3r. Children greeting the rising sun (vert) 1·10 55
2118 5r. Children with banners 1·50 55

610 Persian
Rug

1979
2119 **610** 50d. brown and orange 25 25
2120 **610** 1r. blue and light blue 25 25

2121 **610** 2r. red and yellow 25 25
2122 **610** 3r. blue and mauve 25 25
2123 **610** 5r. olive and green 25 25
2124 **610** 10r. black and pink 40 25
2125 **610** 20r. brown and grey 55 25
2126 **610** 50r. violet and grey 1·40 55
2127 **610** 100r. black and green 3·75 1·10
2128 **610** 200r. blue and stone 4·25 2·30
Nos. 2126/8 are larger, 27×37 mm.

611 Globe in
Envelope

1979. World Post Day.
2134 **611** 10r. multicoloured 3·00 40

612 Kashani and
Astrolabe

1979. 550th Death Anniv of Ghyath-al-din Jamshid Kashani (mathematician and astronomer).
2135 **612** 5r. black and brown 1·50 40

613 Kaaba, Mecca

1980. 1400th Anniv of Hegira (1st issue). Multicoloured.
2136 3r. Type **613** 25 25
2137 5r. Koran and globe (vert) 25 25
2138 10r. Pilgrim and Kaaba 55 25
See also Nos. 2148/51.

614 Flag and
Revolutionaries

1980. First Anniv of Islamic Revolution. Multicoloured.
2139 1r. Type **614** (28×40 mm) 25 25
2140 3r. Dagger and dripping blood (28×40 mm) 40 25
2141 5r. Open window and rising sun (28×40 mm) 60 30
2432 1r. As No. 2139 but 24×35 mm 25 25
2433 3r. As No. 2140 but 24×36 mm 35 35
2435 5r. As No. 2141 but 24×36 mm 45 45

615 Dehkhoda

1980. Birth Centenary of Dehkhoda (compiler, Iranian encyclopedia).
2142 **615** 10r. multicoloured 30 25

616 Female
Costume of
East Azerbaijan

1980. New Year Festival. Multicoloured.
2143 3r. Type **616** 25 25
2144 5r. Male costume of East Azerbaijan 25 25

617 M.
Mossadegh

1980. Birth Centenary of Dr. Mohammed Mossadegh (statesman).
2145 **617** 20r. multicoloured 60 25

618 Morteza
Mottahari

1980. First Death Anniv of Prof. Morteza Mottahari.
2146 **618** 10r. black and red 55 25

619 Telephone

1980. World Telecommunications Day.
2147 **619** 20r. black, green and red 55 25

620 Mosque Interior

1980. 1400th Anniv of Hegira (2nd issue). Multicoloured.
2148 50d. Type **620** 25 25
2149 1r. Crowd with banner 25 25
2150 3r. Al-Biruni, Farabi and Avicenna 40 25
2151 5r. Mosque and Kaaba 30 25

621 Dr. Ali Shariati

1980. Dr. Ali Shariati (educator) Commemoration.
2152 **621** 5r. multicoloured 30 25

622 Kaaba and
Banner

1980. Birth Anniv of Hazrat Mehdi (Shi'ite Imam).
2153 **622** 5r. green, red and black 30 25

623 Ayatollah
Teleghani

1980. Ayatollah Teleghani Commemoration.
2154 **623** 5r. multicoloured 30 25

624 O.P.E.C.
Emblem and Globe

1980. 20th Anniv of Organization of Petroleum Exporting Countries. Multicoloured.

2155		5r. Type **624**	30	25
2156		10r. Figures supporting O.P.E.C. emblem	60	25

625 Hands breaking Star of David around Dome of the Rock

1980. "Let us Liberate Jerusalem".

2157	**625**	5r. multicoloured	25	25
2158	**625**	20r. multicoloured	85	25

626 Tulip and Feizieh Theological College

1981. Second Anniv of Islamic Revolution. Multicoloured.

2159		3r. Type **626** (dated "1981" at right)	25	25
2160		5r. Tulip (in red), drops of blood and "Martyr" in Persian script	40	25
2161		20r. Open tulip (in red) and crest of Republic	60	25
2434		3r. As No. 2159 but dated at left	35	35
2436		5r. As No. 2160 but orange tulip	45	45
2441		20r. As No. 2161 but orange tulip	70	70

627 Male Costume of Lorestan

1981. New Year Festival. Multicoloured.

2162		5r. Type **627**	25	25
2163		10r. Female costume, Lorestan	30	25

628 I.T.U. and W.H.O. Emblems with Ribbons forming Caduceus

1981. World Telecommunications Day.

2164	**628**	5r. orange, black & green	25	25

630 Militia Training

1981

2165	**630**	50d. black and brown	25	25
2166	-	1r. purple and green	25	25
2167	-	2r. brown and blue	25	25
2168	-	3r. black and green	25	25
2169	-	5r. blue and brown	25	25
2170	-	10r. ultramarine and blue	30	25
2171	-	20r. black and red	60	25
2172	-	50r. black and mauve	1·40	40
2173	-	100r. black and brown	25	25
2174	-	200r. blue and black	4·50	1·20

DESIGNS—As Type **630**: 1r. Man and boy at school desk (Literacy campaign); 2r. Digging irrigation ditch. 37×27 mm: 3r. Massed prayers; 20r. Woman with rifle; 50r. Worker at lathe; 100r. Pilgrims around Kaaba. 27×37 mm: 5r. Revolutionary Guards emblem and crowd; 10r. Arabic tapestry; 200r. Niche in Mosque illuminated by sun.

631 Ayatollah Kashani

1981. Birth Centenary of Ayatollah Kashani.

2175	**631**	15r. purple and green	45	25

632 Armed Forces

1981. Islamic Iranian Army.

2176	**632**	5r. multicoloured	40	25

633 Carrier Pigeon flying over Gun Barrels

1981. U.P.U. Day.

2177	**633**	20r. black and blue	55	25

634 Inscription

1981. Millenary of "Nabj al-Blagah" (sacred book).

2178	**634**	25r. green, blue and black	60	25

635 Victims of Bomb at Islamic Party's Headquarters

1981. Iranian Bomb and War Victims, Commemoration.

2179	**635**	3r. black and red	25	25
2180	-	5r. brown & deep brown	25	25
2181	-	10r. multicoloured	25	25

DESIGNS: 5r. President Rajai and Prime Minister Bahomar (bomb victims); 10r. Dr. Chamran (killed in Iran–Iraq War).

636 Ayatollah Tabatabaie

1981. Death Centenary of Ayatollah Ghazi Tabatabaie.

2182	**636**	5r. brown, green and gold	25	25

637 Hand writing on Board

1982. Literacy Campaign.

2183	**637**	5r. blue and gold	25	25

638 Text "God is Great" over Map of Iran

1982. Third Anniv of Islamic Revolution. Multicoloured.

2184		5r. Type **638**	25	25
2185		10r. Dove forming tulip	25	25
2186		20r. "God is Great" over Globe	55	25

639 Banner around Globe

1982. Islamic Unity Week.

2187	**639**	25r. multicoloured	1·00	25

640 Manacled Hands reaching towards Christ

1982. Glorification of Christ's Birth.

2188	**640**	20r. multicoloured	55	25

641 Male Costume of Khuzestan

1982. New Year Festival. Multicoloured.

2189		3r. Type **641**	25	25
2190		5r. Female costume of Khuzestan	45	45

642 National Flag

1982. Third Anniv of Islamic Republic.

2191	**642**	30r. black, red and green	90	25

643 Ayatollah Sadr

1982. Second Death Anniv of Ayatollah Sadr.

2192	**643**	50r. multicoloured	1·00	40

644 Ayatollahs Madani and Dastghib

1982. Ayatollahs Sayed Assadollah Madani and Sayed Abdolhossein Dastghib Commemoration.

2193	**644**	50r. red, black and gold	1·00	40

645 Hand holding Cogwheels

1982. Labour Day.

2194	**645**	100r. multicoloured	2·30	75

646 Geometric Pattern

1982. World Telecommunications Day.

2195	**646**	100r. multicoloured	2·30	75

647 Symbolic Design

1982. Mab'as Festival.

2196	**647**	32r. multicoloured	1·00	40

648 Rifles and Clenched Fist

1982. 19th Anniv of 1963 Islamic Rising.

2197	**648**	20r. black, red and silver	70	30

649 Lieutenant Islambuli

1982. Lieutenant Khaled Islambuli (assassin of Pres. Sadat of Egypt) Commemoration.

2198	**649**	2r. multicoloured	40	25

650 Ayatollah Beheshti

1982. First Death Anniv of Ayatollah Mohammed Hossein Beheshti.

2199	**650**	10r. multicoloured	40	25

651 Soldiers, Tanks and Hand holding Banner

1982. Victims of War against Iraq Commemoration.

2200	**651**	5r. multicoloured	25	25

652 Dome of the Rock

1982. World Jerusalem Day.

2201	**652**	1r. multicoloured	25	25

653 Pilgrims around Kaaba

1982. Pilgrimage to Mecca.

2202	**653**	10r. multicoloured	30	25

654 Globe and Letters

1982. World U.P.U. Day.

| 2203 | 654 | 30r. multicoloured | 75 | 25 |

655 Bloodied Hand releasing Dove

1983. Fourth Anniv of Islamic Revolution.

| 2204 | 655 | 30r. multicoloured (crowd in brown) | 75 | 25 |
| 2445 | 655 | 30r. multicoloured (crowd in orange) | 1·00 | 1·00 |

656 Casting Vote

1983. Fourth Anniv of Islamic Republic.

| 2205 | 656 | 10r. red, black and green | 30 | 25 |

657 "Enlightenment"

1983. Teachers' Day.

| 2206 | 657 | 5r. multicoloured | 25 | 25 |

658 Microwave Antenna and "83"

1983. World Communications Year.

| 2207 | 658 | 20r. blue, mauve & brown | 60 | 25 |

659 Assembly

1983. First Session of Islamic Consultative Assembly.

| 2208 | 659 | 5r. multicoloured | 25 | 25 |

660 Doves and Crowd

1983. 20th Anniv of 1963 Islamic Rising.

| 2209 | 660 | 10r. multicoloured | 30 | 25 |

661 Map of Persian Gulf and burning Oil Wells at Nowruz

1983. Ecology Week.

| 2210 | 661 | 5r. black, red and blue | 55 | 25 |

662 Sadooghi

1983. Ayatollah Mohammad Sadooghi Commem.

| 2211 | 662 | 20r. black and red | 60 | 25 |

663 Hands holding Rifle over Dome of the Rock

1983. World Jerusalem Day.

| 2212 | 663 | 5r. yellow, brown & blue | 25 | 25 |

664 Rajai and Bahomar

1983. Government Week (death anniv of Pres. Rajai and Prime Minister Dr. Bahomar).

| 2213 | 664 | 3r. orange and blue | 25 | 25 |

665 Cartridges and Text

1983. War Week.

| 2214 | 665 | 5r. green and red | 25 | 25 |

666 Stamps and Map of Iran around Globe

1983. World U.P.U. Day.

| 2215 | 666 | 10r. multicoloured | 40 | 25 |

667 Esfahani

1983. Fourth Death Anniv of Ayatollah Ashrafi Esfahani.

| 2216 | 667 | 5r. multicoloured | 25 | 25 |

668 Mirza Kuchik Khan

1983. Religious and Political Personalities.

2217	-	1r. black and pink	25	25
2218	668	2r. black and orange	25	25
2219	-	3r. black and blue	25	25
2220	-	5r. black and red	25	25
2221	-	10r. black and green	30	25
2222	-	20r. black and purple	60	25
2223	-	30r. black and brown	90	30
2224	-	50r. black and blue	1·50	55
2225	-	100r. black and red	2·30	90
2226	-	200r. black and green	4·50	1·50

DESIGNS: 1r. Sheikh Mohammed Khiabani; 3r. Seyd Modjtaba Navab Safavi; 5r. Seyd Jamal-ed-Din Assadabadi; 10r. Seyd Hassah Modaress; 20r. Sheikh Fazel Assad Nouri; 30r. Mirza Mohammad Hossein Naieni; 50r. Sheikh Mohammed Hossein Kashef; 100r. Seyd Hassan Shirazi; 200r. Mirza Reza Kermani.

669 Sword severing "Right of Veto" Hand

1983. United Nations Day.

| 2228 | 669 | 32r. multicoloured | 1·10 | 40 |

670 Storming the U.S. Embassy, Hostage and burning American Flag

1983. Fourth Anniv of Storming of United States Embassy.

| 2229 | 670 | 28r. multicoloured | 85 | 55 |

671 Avicenna and Globe

1983. International Medical Seminar, Teheran.

| 2230 | 671 | 3r. purple and blue | 55 | 25 |

672 Young and Old Soldiers

1983. Preparation Day.

| 2231 | 672 | 20r. green, black and red | 60 | 25 |

673 Fist with Gun and Dove

1983. Saddam's Crimes Conference.

| 2232 | 673 | 5r. black and mauve | 25 | 25 |

674 Dr. Mohammad Mofatteh

1983. Fourth Death Anniv of Dr. Mohammed Mofatteh.

| 2233 | 674 | 10r. mauve, black & gold | 40 | 25 |

675 Light shining on Globe

1983. Mohammed's Birth Anniv.

| 2234 | 675 | 5r. blue, brown and green | 25 | 25 |

676 Tulips and Flag

1984. Fifth Anniv of Islamic Revolution.

| 2235 | 676 | 10r. multicoloured | 75 | 25 |

677 Nurse tending Wounded Soldier

1984. Nurses' Day.

| 2240 | 677 | 20r. multicoloured | 45 | 25 |

678 Soldier in Wheelchair

1984. Invalids' Day.

| 2241 | 678 | 5r. multicoloured | 25 | 25 |

679 Lotus gebelia

1984. New Year Festival. Flowers. Multicoloured.

2242		3r. Type 679	25	25
2243		5r. Tulipa chrysantha	30	25
2244		10r. "lycyrrhiza glabra	45	25
2245		20r. "atthiola alyssifolia	90	25

680 Malcolm Little (founder of Union of Moslem Mosques and Organization for African–American Unity)

1984. Struggle Against Racial Discrimination.

| 2246 | 680 | 5r. multicoloured | 25 | 25 |

681 Flag around Globe

1984. Fifth Anniv of Islamic Republic.

| 2247 | 681 | 5r. multicoloured | 25 | 25 |

682 Well-fed and Starving Children

1984. World Health Day.

| 2248 | 682 | 10r. multicoloured | 40 | 25 |

683 Harb

1984. 22nd Death Anniv of Sheikh Ragheb Harb.

| 2249 | 683 | 5r. black, red and green | 25 | 25 |

684 Family holding Red Crescent Banner

1984. World Red Cross and Red Crescent Day.
2250   **684**   5r. multicoloured   25   25

685 Transmitter

1984. World Telecommunications Day.
2251   **685**   20r. black, blue and red   60   40

686 Ghotb

1984. 19th Death Anniv of Seyyed Ghotb.
2252   **686**   10r. black, gold & orange   40   25

687 Kaaba and Destruction of Images

1984. Conquest of Mecca.
2253   **687**   5r. multicoloured   25   25

688 Jerusalem, Map of Israel and Koran

1984. World Jerusalem Day (5r.) and Fetr Feast (10r.). Multicoloured.
2254   5r. Type **688**   25   25
2255   10r. Crowd around mosque   40   25

689 Choga Zanbil, Susa

1984. Preservation of Cultural Heritage. Multicoloured.
2256   5r. Type **689**   25   25
2257   5r. Emamzadeh Hossein shrine, Qazvin (Arabic date at left)   25   25
2258   5r. Imam Mosque, Isfahan   25   25
2259   5r. Ark Fortress, Tabriz   25   25
2260   5r. Prophet Daniel's Mausoleum, Susa (with conical tower)   25   25

691 Crowd around Kaaba

1984. Feast of Sacrifices.
2261   **691**   10r. multicoloured   30   25

692 Spirit Nebula

1984. Tenth International Trade Fair, Teheran.
2262   **692**   10r. blue and red   30   25

---

693 Rifle and Cartridges on Flower

1984. War Week.
2263   **693**   5r. multicoloured   25   25

694 Stylized Pigeon and U.P.U. Emblem

1984. World Universal Postal Union Day.
2264   **694**   20r. multicoloured   60   40

695 Khomeini

1984. Seventh Death Anniv of Haj Seyyed Mostafa Khomeini.
2265   **695**   5r. multicoloured   25   25

696 Tabatabaie

1984. Ghazi Tabatabaie Commemoration.
2266   **696**   5r. black, gold and red   25   25

697 Saadi

1984. 800th Birth Anniv of Saadi (poet) Congress.
2267   **697**   10r. multicoloured   55   25

698 Clasped Hands, Mosque and Koran

1984. Mohammed's Birth Anniv and Unity Week.
2268   **698**   5r. multicoloured   25   25

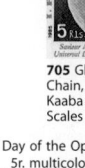

699 Doves as Petals

1985. Sixth Anniv of Islamic Revolution (1st issue).
2269   **699**   40r. multicoloured (tulip emblem in red)   1·10   75
2446   **699**   40r. multicoloured (tulip emblem in mauve)   1·30   1·30

See also No. 2277.

---

700 Sapling and Forest

1985. Tree Planting Day. Multicoloured.
2270   3r. Type **700**   25   25
2271   5r. Sapling growing near forest   25   25

701 Crown Imperial ("Fritillaria imperialis")

1985. New Year Festival. Multicoloured.
2272   5r. Type **701**   40   25
2273   5r. Pilewort (Ranunculus ficarioides)   40   25
2274   5r. Saffron crocus (Crocus sativus)   40   25
2275   5r. Primula heterochroma   40   25

702 Procession of Women with Flags

1985. Women's Day and Birth Anniv of Fatima.
2276   **702**   10r. multicoloured   40   25

703 Tulip and Ballot Box

1985. Sixth Anniv of Islamic Republic (2nd issue).
2277   **703**   20r. multicoloured   55   30

704 Koran

1985. Mab'as Festival.
2278   **704**   10r. multicoloured   40   25

705 Globe, Chain, Banner, Kaaba and Scales

1985. World Day of the Oppressed.
2279   **705**   5r. multicoloured   25   25

706 I.T.U. Emblem and Telephone Handsets

1985. World Telecommunications Day.
2280   **706**   20r. multicoloured   55   30

---

707 Soldier saluting and Bridge

1985. Liberation of Khorramshahr.
2281   **707**   5r. multicoloured   25   25

708 Fist, Rifles and Qum Theological College

1985. 22nd Anniv of 1963 Islamic Rising.
2282   **708**   10r. multicoloured   55   25

709 Decorated Plates and Vases

1985. World Handicrafts Day.
2283   **709**   20r. multicoloured   60   40

710 Map of Israel and Dome of the Rock

1985. World Jerusalem Day.
2284   **710**   5r. multicoloured   25   25

711 Arabic Script

1985. Fetr Feast.
2285   **711**   5r. blue, red and black   25   25

712 Organization Emblem

1985. Fourth Anniv of Islamic Propagation Organization.
2286   **712**   5r. brown, green & black   25   25

713 Abdolhossein Amini and the Koran

1985. Ayatollah Sheikh Abdolhossein Amini (theologian) Commemoration.
2287   **713**   5r. multicoloured   25   25

714 Pilgrims around Holy Kaaba

1985. Pilgrimage to Mecca.

2288	**714**	10r. multicoloured	40	25

715 Two Swords Pattern

1985. Preservation of Cultural History. Ancient Ceramic Plates from Nishabur. Multicoloured.

2289	**715**	Type **715**	25	
2290		5r. Plate with border of Farsi script	25	25
2291		5r. Stylized bird pattern	25	25
2292		5r. Four leaves and knot pattern	25	25

716 Revolutionaries and Mosque

1985. 50th Anniv of Rising in Goharshad Mosque, Meshed.

2293	**716**	10r. multicoloured	40	25

717 Health Services

1985. Government and People Week. Multicoloured.

2294		5r. Envelope, crane and mechanical digger	25	25
2295		5r. Factory, cogwheel and ear of wheat	25	25
2296		5r. Type **717**	25	25
2297		5r. Literacy campaign emblem on book	25	25

718 Red Tulips dripping Blood

1985. Seventh Anniv of "Bloody Friday" Riots.

2298	**718**	10r. multicoloured	40	25

719 O.P.E.C. Emblem and "25"

1985. 25th Anniv of Organization of Petroleum Exporting Countries.

2299	**719**	5r. yellow and brown	25	25
2300	-	5r. blue and green	25	25

DESIGN: No. 2300, O.P.E.C. emblem and world map.

720 Dead Iranian

1985. Fifth Anniv of Iran–Iraq War. Multicoloured.

2301		5r. Type **720**	25	25
2302		5r. Dome of mosque and text "Ashura"	25	25
2303		5r. White doves with map of Iran under a hail of bombs	25	25
2304		5r. Oasis and exploding rifle	25	25

721 Symbolic Design

1985. Death Millenary of Ash-Sharif Ar-Radi (writer).

2305	**721**	20r. blue, gold & ultram	60	40

722 Envelopes and Posthorn

1985. World U.P.U. Day.

2306	**722**	20r. multicoloured	60	40

723 Emblem

1985. World Standards Day.

2307	**723**	20r. multicoloured	60	40

724 Seedling and Ear of Wheat in Hand

1985. Agricultural Training and Extension Year.

2308	**724**	5r. multicoloured	25	25

725 Seal of U.S. Embassy

1985. Sixth Anniv of Storming of United States Embassy.

2309	**725**	40r. multicoloured	1·40	75

726 Kaaba, Mosque and Clasped Hands

1985. Mohammed's Birth Anniv and Unity Week.

2310	**726**	10r. multicoloured	40	25

727 Rose growing from Pen Nib and Tulip

1985. High Council of Cultural Revolution Anniv.

2311	**727**	5r. multicoloured	25	25

728 Profiles and Symbols of Learning

1985. International Youth Year. Multicoloured.

2312		5r. Type **728**	25	25
2313		5r. Profiles and symbols of war	25	25
2314		5r. Profiles and symbols of industry and agriculture	25	25
2315		5r. Profiles and sports pictograms	25	25

729 Ezzeddin Al-Qassam

1985. 50th Death Anniv of Ezzeddin Al-Qassam.

2316	**729**	20r. brown, red and silver	60	40

730 Bayonets, Map and Clenched Fists

1985. Afghan Resistance to Occupation.

2317	**730**	40r. multicoloured	1·30	85

731 Mirza Taqi Khan Amir Kabir

1986. 135th Death Anniv of Mirza Taqi Khan Amir Kabir.

2318	**731**	5r. multicoloured	1·20	25

732 Tulips and Crowd destroying Statue

1986. Seventh Anniv of Islamic Revolution.

2319	**732**	20r. multicoloured	60	40

733 Sulayman Khater and Dome of the Rock

1986. 40th Death Anniv of Sulayman Khater.

2320	**733**	10r. black, blue and red	40	25

734 Woman, Child and Crowd

1986. Women's Day and Birth Anniv of Fatima.

2321	**734**	10r. multicoloured	40	25

735 "Papaver orientale"

1986. New Year Festival. Flowers. Multicoloured.

2322		5r. Type **735**	30	25
2323		5r. "Anemone coronaria"	30	25
2324		5r. "Papaver bracteatum"	30	25
2325		5r. "Anemone biflora"	30	25

736 Fist and Text

1986. "2000th Day of Sacred Defence" (Iran–Iraq war).

2326	**736**	5r. green and red	25	25

737 Rose, Globe and Coloured Bands

1986. Struggle against Racial Discrimination.

2327	**737**	5r. multicoloured	25	25

738 Iranian Flag and Map

1986. Seventh Anniv of Islamic Republic.

2328	**738**	10r. multicoloured	40	25

739 Dome

1986. Mab'as Festival.

2329	**739**	40r. multicoloured	1·20	75

740 Insignia

1986. Army Day.

2330	**740**	5r. multicoloured	25	25

741 Dead Soldier and Wrecked Helicopter

1986. Sixth Anniv of United States Landing at Tabas.

2331	**741**	40r. orange, green & blk	1·20	75

742 Text

1986. World Day of the Oppressed. Birth Anniv of Imam Mahdi.
2332 **742** 10r. black, red and gold   40   25

743 Symbolic Design

1986. Teachers' Day.
2333 **743** 5r. multicoloured   25   25

744 Antennae and Radio Waves

1986. World Communications Day.
2334 **744** 20r. black, silver and blue   60   40

745 Soldier and Tanks

1986. International Children's Day.
2335 **745** 15r. multicoloured   45   25
2336 - 15r. black, blue & mauve   45   25
DESIGN: No. 2336, Boy and text.

746 Qum Theological College and Sun Rays

1986. 23rd Anniv of 1963 Islamic Rising.
2337 **746** 10r. multicoloured   40   25

747 Dome of the Rock, Map of Israel and Barbed Wire

1986. World Jerusalem Day.
2338 **747** 10r. multicoloured   40   25

748 Crowd at Prayer

1986. Fetr Festival.
2339 **748** 10r. multicoloured   75   25

749 Baluchi Needle Work

1986. World Handicrafts Day. Multicoloured.
2340 **749** 10r. Type 749   40   30
2341 - 10r. Master craftswomen at work   40   30
2342 - 10r. Carpet   40   30
2343 - 10r. Engraved copper vase   40   30

750 Linked Hands around Map on Globe

1986. Solidarity with South African People.
2344 **750** 10r. multicoloured   40   25

751 Dr. Beheshti, Doves and Explosion

1986. Fifth Anniv of Bomb Explosion at Islamic Party Headquarters, Teheran.
2345 **751** 10r. multicoloured   40   25

752 Ayatollah Mohammad Taqi Shirazi and Map

1986. Iraqi Muslim Rising.
2346 **752** 20r. multicoloured   60   40

753 Shrine, Meshed

1986. Birth Anniv of Imam Riza.
2347 **753** 10r. multicoloured   40   25

754 Crowd around Kaaba, Flag and Clenched Fists

1986. Feast of Sacrifices.
2348 **754** 10r. multicoloured   40   25

755 Soltanieh Mosque

1986. Preservation of Cultural Heritage. Multicoloured.
2349 **755** 5r. Type 755   25   25
2350 - 5r. Mausoleum of Sohel Ben Ali, Astaneh   25   25

2351 5r. Bam fortress   25   25
2352 5r. Gateway of Blue Mosque, Tabriz   25   25

756 "Eid-ul-Ghadir" in Arabic

1986. Ghadir Festival.
2353 **756** 20r. light green, green and black   60   40

757 Graph, Roof and People

1986. Population and Housing Census.
2354 **757** 20r. multicoloured   60   30

758 Missile Boat *Paykan* in Fist below Bombs

1986. Sixth Anniv of Iran-Iraq War. Multicoloured.
2355 **758** 10r. blue, black and red   40   25
2356 - 10r. red and black   40   25
2357 - 10r. yellow, black and red   40   25
2358 - 10r. blue, black and red   40   25
2359 - 10r. green, black and red   40   25
DESIGNS: No. 2356, Khorramshahr; 2357, Howeizah; 2358, Siege of Abadan; 2359, Susangard.

759 Wrestling

1986. Tenth Asian Games, Seoul. Multicoloured.
2360 15r. Type 759   40   25
2361 15r. Rifle shooting   40   25

760 Bird with Envelopes as Wings on Globe

1986. World Universal Postal Union Day.
2362 **760** 20r. multicoloured   60   40

761 Emblem

1986. 40th Anniv of UNESCO.
2363 **761** 45r. blue, black and red   1·20   70

762 Allameh Tabatabaie

1986. Fifth Death Anniv of Allameh Tabatabaie.
2364 **762** 10r. green, gold and black   30   25

763 Sun behind Dome and Minaret

1986. Mohammed's Birth Anniv and Unity Week.
2365 **763** 10r. multicoloured   30   25

764 Militiamen with Flags

1986. "Mobilization of the Oppressed" Week.
2366 **764** 5r. multicoloured   25   25

765 Guerrilla Fighters

1986. Afghan Resistance to Occupation.
2367 **765** 40r. multicoloured   1·20   40

766 Nurse tending Boy

1987. Nurses' Day.
2368 **766** 20r. multicoloured   60   40

767 Emblem and Tulip on Globe

1987. Fifth Islamic Theology Conference, Teheran.
2369 **767** 20r. multicoloured   60   40

768 Emblems of Revolution

1987. Eighth Anniv of Islamic Revolution.
2370 **768** 20r. multicoloured (38×58 mm)   60   40
2444 **768** 20r. multicoloured (24×37 mm)   70   70

769 Emblem and Crowd

1987. Eighth Anniv of Revolutionary Committees.
2371 **769** 10r. yellow, blue and red 30 25

770 Woman and Soldiers

1987. Women's Day and Birth Anniv of Fatima.
2372 **770** 10r. multicoloured 30 25

771 Airbus Industrie A300 Aircraft and Banner around Globe

1987. 25th Anniv of Iranair.
2373 **771** 30r. multicoloured 90 55

772 Ayatollah Naeini

1987. 50th Death Anniv of Ayatollah Mirza Mohammad Hossein Naeini.
2374 **772** 10r. multicoloured 30 25

773 Flag Irises

1987. New Year Festival. Flowers. Multicoloured.
2375 5r. Type **773** 40 25
2376 5r. Tulips 40 25
2377 5r. Dutch irises 40 25
2378 5r. Roses 40 25

774 Arabic Text and Arched Window

1987. Mab'as Festival.
2379 **774** 45r. lt green, grn & gold 1·40 75

775 Flag as Star on Map

1987. Eighth Anniv of Islamic Republic.
2380 **775** 20r. multicoloured 60 30

776 Soldiers with Flag

1987. Revolutionary Guards' Day. Birth Anniv of Imam Hossein.
2381 **776** 5r. multicoloured 25 25

777 Emblems on Map and Dome of the Rock

1987. Commemoration of Lebanese Hizbollah Dead.
2382 **777** 10r. red, green and grey 30 25

778 Child and Vaccination Dropper

1987. World Health Day. Multicoloured.
2383 3r. Syringe and children 25 25
2384 5r. Type **778** 30 25

779 Stars around Holy Kaaba

1987. World Day of the Oppressed. Birth Anniv of Imam Mahdi.
2385 **779** 20r. multicoloured 60 30

780 Worker with Rifle and Koran, Factory and Cogwheel

1987. International Labour Day.
2386 **780** 5r. multicoloured 25 25

781 Ayatollah Mottahari, Candle and Book

1987. Teachers' Day.
2387 **781** 5r. red, yellow and blue 25 25

782 Map in Telephone Dial

1987. World Telecommunications Day.
2388 **782** 20r. violet and blue 70 30

783 12th-century Ceramic Lidded Pot, Rey

1987. International Museums Day.
2389 **783** 20r. chestnut, brn & grey 60 30
2390 - 20r. brown, black & grn 60 30
DESIGN: No. 2390, Sassanian silver-gilt flower vase.

784 Dove, Globe and Dome of the Rock dripping Blood onto Star

1987. World Jerusalem Day.
2391 **784** 20r. multicoloured 60 30

785 Qum Theological College, Crown and Bayonets

1987. 24th Anniv of 1963 Islamic Rising.
2392 **785** 20r. multicoloured 60 30

786 Blown Glass

1987. World Crafts Day. Multicoloured.
2393 5r. Type **786** 25 25
2394 5r. Khatam marquetry 25 25
2395 5r. Ceramic ware 25 25
2396 5r. Ceramic master-craftsman 25 25

787 Factory, Freighter and Dam

1987. Campaign against Tax Evasion.
2397 **787** 10r. gold, black and silver 40 25

788 Figures in Cupped Hand

1987. Welfare Week.
2398 **788** 15r. multicoloured 45 25

789 Crowd around Mosque

1987. Feast of Sacrifices.
2399 **789** 12r. turquoise, sil & blk 45 25

790 Design from Mosque Tile

1987. Ghadir Festival.
2400 **790** 18r. gold, green and black 55 30

791 Hands clasped over National Emblem

1987. Islamic Banking Week.
2401 **791** 15r. brown, blue and gold 45 25

792 Typical Persian Calligraphy

1987. First Iranian Calligraphers' Cultural and Artistic Congress.
2402 **792** 20r. multicoloured 60 30

793 Blood running from Heart as Globe, Mosque and Kaaba

1987. Commemoration of Pilgrims killed at Mecca.
2403 **793** 8r. multicoloured 40 25

794 Toothbrushes as Mouths

1987. 25th Anniv of Iranian Dentists Association.
2404 **794** 10r. multicoloured 40 25

795 Dove with Globe as Eye

1987. International Peace Day.
2405 **795** 20r. bronze and blue 60 30

796 Rifleman and Armed Launch

1987. Seventh Anniv of Iran–Iraq War.
2406 **796** 25r. green, blue and black 75 40
2407 - 25r. red, black and blue 75 40
DESIGN: No. 2407, Rifleman and soldiers.

797 Open Book
on Crossed
Pistols

1987. Police Day.
2408   **797**   10r. multicoloured   30   25

798 People in
Cupped Hands

1987. Int Social Security Co-operation Week.
2409   **798**   15r. black, blue and gold   45   25

799 Dove with
Envelopes as Tail on
Globe

1987. World Post Day. Multicoloured.
2410   15r. Type **799**   45   25
2411   15r. Dr. M. Ghandi (Postal Minis-
        ter) commemoration   45   25

800 American Flag,
Great Seal and
Capitol

1987. Sixth Anniv of Storming of United States Embassy.
2412   **800**   40r. multicoloured   1·20   60

801 Tree
growing from
Open Book

1987. First Teheran Book Fair.
2413   **801**   20r. multicoloured   60   30

802 Clasped Hands

1987. Mohammed's Birth Anniv and Unity Week.
2414   **802**   25r. brown, flesh & green   60   40

803 Ayatollah
Modarres

1987. 50th Death Anniv of Ayatollah Seyyed Hassan
Modarres.
2415   **803**   10r. brown and ochre   30   25

804 Djameh
Mosque, Urmia

1987. Mosques.
2415a   -   1r. orange and silver   10   10
2416   **804**   2r. mauve and silver   15   15
2416a   -   3r. green and silver   10   10
2417   -   5r. red and silver   25   25
2594   -   10r. blue and silver   1·10   15
2419   -   20r. violet and silver   60   25
2420   -   30r. red and silver   1·20   30
2421   -   40r. blue and silver   1·50   40
2422   -   50r. brown and silver   1·10   60
2423   -   100r. green and silver   1·90   1·10
2602   -   200r. black and silver   3·50   2·00
2604   -   500r. green and silver   11·50   5·00
DESIGNS—HORIZ: 1r. Djameh Mosque, Schuschter; 3r.
Djameh Mosque, Kerman; 5r. Qazvin; 10r. Veramin; 20r.
Saveh; 40r. Shiraz; 100r. Hamadan. VERT: 30r. Natanz; 50r.
Isfahan; 200r. Dizful; 500r. Yezd.

805 Open Book, Profiles and
Ear of Wheat

1987. Agricultural Training and Extension Week.
2426   **805**   10r. multicoloured   30   25

806 Guerrilla Fighters on Map

1987. Afghan Resistance to Occupation.
2427   **806**   40r. multicoloured   1·10   60

807 Crowd with Banners

1988. Tenth Anniv of Qum Uprising.
2428   **807**   20r. multicoloured   60   40

808 Bombs
and Pencils

1988. Iranian Schools Victims' Commemoration.
2429   **808**   10r. multicoloured   30   25

809 Takhti and Mountain

1988. Victory of Gholamreza Takhti in World Freestyle
Wrestling Championships.
2430   **809**   15r. multicoloured   40   25

810 Woman
carrying armed
Man

1988. Women's Day and Birth Anniv of Fatima.
2431   **810**   20r. multicoloured   55   30

811 Text

1988. Ninth Anniv of Islamic Revolution.
2447   **811**   40r. multicoloured   1·30   1·30

812 Crowd burning Statue

1988. Tenth Anniv of Tabriz Uprising.
2448   **812**   25r. multicoloured   55   40

813 Tree in Hand

1988. Tree Day.
2449   **813**   15r. multicoloured   40   30

814 Anthemis
hyalina

1988. New Year Festival. Flowers. Multicoloured.
2450   10r. Type **814**   30   25
2451   10r. Common mallows   30   25
2452   10r. Violets   30   25
2453   10r. Echium amaenum   30   25

815 Hand putting
Ballot Paper into Box

1988. Ninth Anniv of Islamic Republic.
2454   **815**   20r. multicoloured   60   40

816 Calligraphy

1988. World Day of the Oppressed. Birth Anniv of Imam
Mahdi.
2455   **816**   20r. brown and blue   60   40

817 Shahid Mottahari
Mosque and
Theology School,
Teheran

1988. Preservation of Cultural Heritage. Multicoloured.
2456   **817**   10r. Type **817**   30   25
2457   10r. Colonnade of Tarikhaneh
       Mosque, Damghan   30   25
2458   10r. Gateway of Sepahdari
       Mosque and Theology
       School, Arak (horiz)   30   25
2459   10r. Agha Bozorg Mosque and
       Theology School, Kashan
       (courtyard with pool) (horiz)   30   25

818 Bomb, Gas Cloud
and Victims

1988. Halabja Chemical Attack Victims' Commemoration.
2460   **818**   20r. multicoloured   60   40

819 Map, Dome of
the Rock and
Palestinian

1988. Palestinian "Intifida" Movement. Each brown, red
and black.
2461   **819**   10r. Type **819**   40   25
2462   10r. Man with rounded beard   40   25
2463   10r. Man wearing crew-necked
       jumper   40   25
2464   10r. Man with long pointed
       beard   40   25
2465   10r. Crowd and hand holding
       stone   40   25

820 Satellite and
Telephone Handset

1988. World Telecommunications Day.
2466   **820**   20r. blue and green   60   40

821 Ceramic Vase

1988. International Museum Day. Multicoloured.
2467   10r. Type **821**   30   25
2468   10r. Iran Bastan Museum porch   30   25
2469   10r. 14th-century Tabriz silk rug   30   25
2470   10r. 7th-century B.C. gold ring,
       Arjan, Behbahan   30   25

822 Miners pushing
Coal Truck

1988. Mining Day.
2471   **822**   20r. multicoloured   75   40

823 Children playing
by River

1988. International Children's Day.
2472   **823**   10r. multicoloured   40   25

824 Bleeding Dove
and Broken Bayonets

1988. 25th Anniv of 1963 Islamic Rising.
2473	**824**	10r. multicoloured	40	25

825 Glim Weaving

1988. World Handicrafts Day. Multicoloured.
2474	10r. Type **825**	30	25
2475	10r. Miniature of horsemen	30	25
2476	10r. Glim weaver (horiz)	30	25
2477	10r. Straw basket (horiz)	30	25

826 Child in Flower

1988. Child Health Campaign.
2478	**826**	20r. blue, green and black	40	25

827 Symbols of
Industry and
Agriculture

1988. Campaign Against Tax Evasion.
2479	**827**	20r. gold, blue and silver	40	25

828 Balkhi

1988. Allameh Balkhi (Afghan revolutionary writer) Commemoration.
2480	**828**	20r. black, red and silver	40	25

829 Blood raining on
Holy Kaaba

1988. First Anniv of Death of Mecca Pilgrims. Multicoloured.
2481	10r. Type **829**	25	25
2482	10r. Holy Kaaba and blood-stained robe	25	25

830 Missile hitting
Airplane

1988. Destruction of Iranair Passenger Airplane.
2483	**830**	45r. multicoloured	1·10	55

831 Seyyed Ali
Andarzgou

1988. Tenth Death Anniv of Seyyed Ali Andarzgou (revolutionary).
2484	**831**	20r. blue, black & brown	45	25

832 Central
Bank, Teheran

1988. Islamic Banking Week.
2485	**832**	20r. grey, brown and gold	45	25

833 Carrying away
Victim

1988. Tenth Anniv of "Bloody Friday" Riots.
2486	**833**	25r. green, purple and red	60	40

834 Weightlifting

1988. Olympic Games, Seoul. Multicoloured.
2487	10r. Type **834**	30	25
2488	10r. Men's gymnastics	30	25
2489	10r. Judo	30	25
2490	10r. Football	30	25
2491	10r. Wrestling	30	25

835 Plant

1988. Agricultural Census.
2492	**835**	30r. yellow, black & grn	60	40

836 Iranians and
Rifle

1988. Eighth Anniv of Iran–Iraq War.
2493	**836**	20r. multicoloured	40	25

837 Envelopes around Globe

1988. World Post Day.
2494	**837**	20r. green, black and blue	40	25

838 Child's Face and
Profiles

1988. Parents' and Teachers' Co-operation Week.
2495	**838**	20r. multicoloured	40	25

839 Clasped Hands
and Emblem

1988. Mohammed's Birth Anniv and Unity Week.
2496	**839**	10r. multicoloured	25	25

840 Fist and
Shattered Eagle

1988. Seventh Anniv of Storming of United States Embassy.
2497	**840**	45r. multicoloured	1·00	55

841 Tree as
Umbrella

1988. Insurance Day.
2498	**841**	10r. multicoloured	25	25

842 Tomb of Hafiz

1988. International Hafiz (writer) Congress, Shiraz.
2499	**842**	20r. blue, gold and mauve	55	25

843 Agricultural
Symbols on Open
Book

1988. Agricultural Training and Extension Week.
2500	**843**	15r. multicoloured	40	25

844 Parvin Etessami
(writer)

1988. Iranian Celebrities of Science, Art and Literature. Multicoloured.
2501	10r. Type **844**	30	25
2502	10r. Qaem Maqam Farahani (writer)	30	25
2503	10r. Kamal al-Molk (artist)	30	25
2504	10r. Jalal al-Ahmad (writer)	30	25
2505	10r. Dr. Mohammad Mo'in (writer)	30	25

845 Map and Armed
Afghan

1988. Afghan Resistance to Occupation.
2506	**845**	40r. multicoloured	1·00	55

846 Satellite, Envelopes
and Dish Aerial

1989. Asian and Pacific Transport and Communications Decade. Multicoloured.
2507	20r. Type **846**	60	40
2508	20r. Air transport	60	40
2509	20r. Road and rail transport	60	40
2510	20r. Shipping	60	40

847 Tulips and
Script

1989. Air. Tenth Anniv of Islamic Revolution.
2511	**847**	40r. mauve, gold & black	1·00	55
2512	**847**	50r. violet, gold and black	1·30	75

848 Sun illuminating
Koran

1989. Mab'as Festival.
2513	**848**	20r. multicoloured	40	30

849 Hands
protecting Tree

1989. Tree Day.
2514	**849**	20r. multicoloured	40	30

850 *Cephalanthera kurdica*

1989. New Year Festival. Flowers. Multicoloured.

2515		10r. Type **850**	25	25
2516		10r. *Dactylorhiza romana*	25	25
2517		10r. *Comperia comperiana*	25	25
2518		10r. *Orchis mascula*	25	25

851 Wind Gauge and Wheat

1989. World Meteorological Day. Multicoloured.

2519		20r. Type **851**	45	30
2520		30r. Wind gauge, airplane and weather ship	90	40

852 State Arms

1989. Tenth Anniv of Islamic Republic.

2521	**852**	20r. multicoloured	40	30

853 Refinery

1989. Commissioning of First Phase of Abadan Oil Refinery.

2522	**853**	20r. multicoloured	55	30

854 Mottahari

1989. Teachers' Day. 10th Death Anniv of Ayatollah Mottahari.

2523	**854**	20r. multicoloured	40	30

855 Dome of the Rock and Barbed Wire

1989. World Jerusalem Day.

2524	**855**	30r. multicoloured	85	45

856 Satellite, Globe and Dish Aerial

1989. World Telecommunications Day.

2525	**856**	20r. multicoloured	55	30

857 Jar

1989. International Museums Day. 6th-century Gurgan Artefacts.

2526	**857**	20r. yellow, blue & black	45	30
2527	-	20r. blue, black & mauve	45	30

DESIGN: No. 2527, Flagon.

858 Armed Men, Tent and Family with Sheep

1989. Nomads' Day.

2528	**858**	20r. multicoloured	40	25

859 Man engraving Vase

1989. World Crafts Day. Multicoloured.

2529		20r. Type **859**	40	30
2530		20r. Engraved copper vase	40	30
2531		20r. Engraved copper plate (vert)	40	30
2532		20r. Engraved copper wall-hanging (vert)	40	30

860 Khomeini and Crowd

1989. Ayatollah Khomeini Commemoration.

2533	**860**	20r. orange, black and blue (postage)	45	25
2534	-	70r. blk, vio & gold (air)	1·30	75

DESIGN—HORIZ: 70r. Ayatollah Khomeini.

861 Pasteur, Avicenna and Hand holding Quill

1989. Philexfrance 89 International Stamp Exhibition, Paris. Each black, blue and brown, background colour given.

2535	**861**	30r. blue	60	40
2536	**861**	50r. brown	85	60

862 Map and Satellite

1989. Tenth Anniv of Asia–Pacific Telecommunity.

2537	**862**	30r. orange, black & blue	60	40

863 Araghi

1989. Tenth Death Anniv of Mehdi Araghi.

2538	**863**	20r. orange and purple	40	25

864 Shahryar and Monument

1989. Mohammed Hossein Shahryar (poet) Commemoration.

2539	**864**	20r. multicoloured	40	25

865 U.N. Security Council Document

1989. Ninth Anniv of Iran–Iraq War.

2540	**865**	20r. multicoloured	40	25

866 Khomeini addressing Crowd

1989. Ayatollah Khomeini.

2541	-	1r. multicoloured	30	25
2542	-	2r. multicoloured	15	15
2543	**866**	3r. multicoloured	30	25
2544	-	5r. multicoloured	30	15
2545	-	10r. multicoloured	70	15
2546	-	20r. multicoloured	40	15
2547	-	30r. multicoloured	60	40
2548	-	40r. multicoloured	75	60
2549	-	50r. multicoloured	90	60
2550	-	70r. multicoloured	1·30	75
2551	-	100r. ultram, bl & grn	1·90	1·10
2552	-	200r. brown, yell & grn	3·50	1·70
2553	-	500r. multicoloured	8·25	4·50
2554	-	1000r. multicoloured	17·00	9·00

DESIGNS: 1r. Rose and courtyard; 2r. Khomeini as young man; 5r. Khomeini going into exile; 10r. Khomeini's return from exile; 20r. Khomeini making speech; 30r. Boy kissing Khomeini; 40r. Ayatollahs; 50r. Khomeini; 70r. Meeting in house; 100r. Arabic inscription; 200r. Microphones and chair; 500r. Qum Mosque and roses; 1000r. Sun's rays.

867 Pigeon carrying Letter

1989. World Post Day.

2561	**867**	20r. multicoloured	40	25

868 Multi-pointed Star in Window Arch

1989. Mohammed's Birth Anniv and Unity Week.

2562	**868**	10r. multicoloured	25	15

869 U.S. Emblem and Crowd in Dove

1989. Eighth Anniv of Storming of United States Embassy.

2563	**869**	40r. orange, black & blue	75	45

870 Iranian and Launch with Machine Gun

1989. Tenth Anniv of People's Militia.

2564	**870**	10r. multicoloured	40	25

871 Mehdi Elahi Ghomshei

1989. Iranian Celebrities of Science, Art and Literature.

2565	**871**	10r. red, black and gold	25	15
2566	-	10r. green, black and gold	25	15
2567	-	10r. yellow, black & gold	25	15
2568	-	10r. green, black and gold	25	15
2569	-	10r. mauve, black & gold	25	15

DESIGNS: No. 2566, Grand Ayatollah Seyyed Hossein Boroujerdi; 2567, Grand Ayatollah Sheikh Abdulkarim Haeri; 2568, Dr. Abdulazim Gharib; 2569, Seyyed Hossein Mirkhani.

872 Guiding Child's Hand

1990. International Literacy Year.

2570	**872**	20r. multicoloured	40	25

873 Book as Profiles forming Flower

1990. Identity Cards.

2571	**873**	10r. multicoloured	25	15

874 Drinking Vessel

1990. Cultural Heritage.

2572	**874**	20r. black and orange	40	25
2573	-	20r. black and green	40	25

DESIGN: No. 2563, Vase with stem.

875 Crowd

1990. 11th Anniv of Islamic Revolution.
2574 **875** 50r. multicoloured 90 60

876 Emblem

1990. Int Koran Recitation Competition.
2575 **876** 10r. black, blue and green 25 15

877 Soldier in Wheelchair

1990. Invalids' Day.
2576 **877** 10r. multicoloured 25 15

878 Figures encircling Tree

1990. Tree Day.
2577 **878** 20r. multicoloured 40 25

879 *Coronilla varia*

1990. New Year Festival. Flowers. Multicoloured.
2578 10r. Type **879** 25 15
2579 10r. *Astragalus cornucaprae* 25 15
2580 10r. *Astragalus obtusifolius* 25 15
2581 10r. *Astragalus straussii* 25 15

880 Crowd and Ballot Box

1990. 11th Anniv of Islamic Republic.
2582 **880** 30r. multicoloured 60 40

881 Flower growing from Globe

1990. World Health Day.
2583 **881** 40r. multicoloured 75 45

882 Khomeini

1990. First Death Anniv of Ayatollah Khomeini.
2584 **882** 50r. multicoloured 1·10 60

883 Turkoman Jewellery

1990. World Handicrafts Day. Multicoloured.
2585 20r. Type **883** 40 25
2586 50r. Gilded-steel bird 90 60

884 Crayons

1990. International Children's Day.
2587 **884** 20r. multicoloured 45 25

885 Seismograph on Map and Red Crescent Camp

1990. Aid for Earthquake Victims.
2588 **885** 100r. multicoloured 1·80 1·10

886 P.O.W. and Roses

1990. Returned Prisoners of War.
2589 **886** 250r. multicoloured 4·50 2·75

887 Ayatollah Khomeini and Dome of the Rock

1990. World Jerusalem Day.
2590 **887** 100r. multicoloured 2·00 1·10

888 Arabic Script

1990. International Congress on Abu-I Kasim Mansur Firdausi (poet). 16 sheets as T **888**, each 60× 75 mm. Multicoloured (except T **888**).
MS2591 16 sheets. (a) 100r. black, gold and silver (Type **888**); (b) Arabic script in cartouches within floral frame; (c) 100r. Arabic script in rectangles; (d) 100r. Portrait of Firdausi; (e) 100r. Statue of Firdausi, Tehran; (f) 100r. Tomb, Tuss; (g) 200r. Shackled man and miners; (h) 200r. Assault on man; (i) 200r. Hunters in forest; (j) 200r. Horesman riding through flames; (k) 200r. Phoenix, boy and archer; (l) 200r. Domestic scene; (m) 200r. White elephant trampling fallen men; (n) 200r. Archer in cage surrounded by birds; (o) 200r. Sleeping archer, demon and horse; (p) 200r. Horesmen greeting each other 70·00 70·00

The 200r. values illustrate Firdausi's works.

889 Flowers, Crowd and Khomeini

1991. 12th Anniv of Islamic Revolution.
2605 **889** 100r. multicoloured 2·00 1·10

890 11th-century Gold Jug

1991. International Museum Day. Multicoloured.
2606 50r. Type **890** 90 60
2607 50r. 14th-century silver-inlaid brass basin 90 60

891 Flowers and Fists

1991. 11th Anniv of Iran–Iraq War.
2608 **891** 100r. multicoloured 1·80 1·10

892 Museum

1991. Inauguration of Post Museum, Teheran.
2609 **892** 200r. brown and black 3·50 25

893 Headset on Globe

1991. World Telecommunications Day (1990).
2610 **893** 50r. multicoloured 90 60

894 *Iris spuria*

1991. New Year Festival. Irises. Multicoloured.
2611 20r. Type **894** 75 45
2612 20r. *Iris lycotis* 40 25
2613 20r. *Iris demawendica* 40 25
2614 20r. *Iris meda* 40 25

895 Map, Dome of the Rock and Hosseini

1991. Tenth Death Anniv of Saleh Hosseini.
2615 **895** 30r. red and black 1·00 40

896 Light Beam on Mountains

1991. Mab'as Festival.
2616 **896** 100r. multicoloured 1·80 1·10

897 Revolutionaries

1991. 25th Death Anniv (1990) of Revolutionaries.
2617 **897** 50r. brown and orange 1·10 60

898 Arabic Script

1991. World Day of the Oppressed. Birth Anniv of Mahdi.
2618 **898** 50r. multicoloured 1·20 60

899 Crowd, Flag and Ballot Box

1991. 12th Anniv of Islamic Republic.
2619 **899** 20r. multicoloured 60 25

900 Map and Bayonets

1991. World Jerusalem Day.
2620 **900** 100r. multicoloured 1·80 1·10

901 Mother
and Child

1991. Women's Day and Birth Anniv of Fatima.
2621 **901** 50r. multicoloured   90   60

902
Boroujerdi

1991. 30th Death Anniv of Ayatollah Boroujerdi.
2622 **902** 200r. black and green   3·50 2·30

903 Disasters

1991. International Decade for Natural Disaster
Reduction.
2623 **903** 100r. multicoloured   2·30 1·30

904 Book, Candle and Dr. Mottahari

1991. Teachers' Day.
2624 **904** 50r. yellow, orange & blk   90   60

906 Mausoleum,
Meshed

1991. World Telecommunications Day.
"Telecommunications and Safety of Human Life".
2625 **905** 100r. multicoloured   1·80 1·10

905 Rays striking
Globe

1991. Birth Anniv of Imam Riza. Multicoloured.
2626 **905** 10r. Type **906**   25   15
2627 **905** 30r. Tombstone   60   40

907 Khomeini

1991. Second Death Anniv of Ayatollah Khomeini.
2628 **907** 100r. multicoloured   1·80 1·10

908 Karbala Shrine

1991. Iraqi Attack on Shi'ite Shrine, Karbala.
2629 **908** 70r. multicoloured   1·20   75

909 Nisami

1991. 900th Birth Anniv of Nisami (writer) International
Congress, Tabris.
2630 **909** 50r. multicoloured   1·00   60

910 Archway

1991. 1330th Death Anniv of Ali ibn Ali Talib (Caliph).
2631 **910** 50r. multicoloured   90   60

911 Hands
reaching through
Parched Earth to
Blood Drop

1991. Blood Donation.
2632 **911** 50r. multicoloured   90   60

912 Heart as Tree
and Cardiograph

1991. World Health Day.
2633 **912** 100r. multicoloured   1·80 1·10

913 Nedjefi

1991. Marashi Nedjefi Commemoration.
2634 **913** 30r. multicoloured   60   40

914 Doves flying from Cage

1991. First Anniv of Return of Prisoners of War.
2635 **914** 100r. multicoloured   1·80 1·10

915 Engraved
Brassware

1991. World Crafts Day. Multicoloured.
2636 **915** 40r. Type **915**   75   45
2637 **915** 40r. Gilded samovar   75   45

916 Ayatollah Lari

1991
2638 **916** 30r. multicoloured   60   40

917 Fist and Roses
in Cartouche

1991. 11th Anniv of Iran–Iraq War.
2639 **917** 20r. multicoloured   40   25

918 Islamic Symbols

1991. Islamic Unity Week.
2640 **918** 30r. multicoloured   60   40

919 13th-century
Kashan Ewer

1991. International Museum Day. Multicoloured.
2641 **919** 20r. Type **919**   40   25
2642 **919** 40r. 13th-century Kashan ewer
             with bird's head lip   75   45

920 Gharib

1991. Dr. Mohammed Gharib.
2643 **920** 100r. black and blue   1·80 1·10

921 Banners

1991. Liberation of Khorramshahr.
2644 **921** 30r. multicoloured   70   40

922 Stamped Envelope

1991. World Post Day.
2645 **922** 70r. multicoloured   1·30   75

923 Khaju-Ye Kermani

1991. International Congress on Khaju-Ye Kermani
(writer).
2646 **923** 30r. multicoloured   75   40

924 Globe and
Seismograph

1991. First International Seismology and Earthquake
Engineering Conference.
2647 **924** 100r. multicoloured   1·80 1·10

925 Cogwheel,
Grain, Tree,
Figures and
Globe

1991. World Food Day.
2648 **925** 80r. multicoloured   1·40   85

926 Conference
Emblem

1991. Palestinian Peoples Conference.
2649 **926** 40r. gold and violet   90   45

927 Green
Woodpecker and
Flower Decoration

1991. First Asian Biennial Exhibition of Children's Book
Illustrations.
2650 **927** 100r. multicoloured   2·30 1·10

928 Script and
Emblem

1991. Children's Book Fair, Teheran.
2651 **928** 20r. multicoloured   70   25

929 Festival Award

1991. Roshd International Educational Film Festival.
2652 **929** 50r. multicoloured   90   60

930 Meeting Emblem

1991. Seventh Ministerial Meeting of Group of 77.
2653	**930**	30r. green and violet	70	40

931 Militia Members

1991. People's Militia Week.
2654	**931**	30r. multicoloured	70	40

932 Child throwing Stone at Star of David

1991. World Children's Day.
2655	**932**	50r. multicoloured	90	60

933 Globe and Doves

1991. World Tourism Day.
2656	**933**	200r. black, mauve & bl	3·50	1·80

934 Emblems

1991. World Standards Day.
2657	**934**	100r. multicoloured	1·80	1·10

935 Trees, Hand, Water and Wheat

1991. Agricultural Training Week.
2658	**935**	70r. multicoloured	1·30	75

936 Araf Hosseini

1992
2659	**936**	50r. multicoloured	90	40

937 Sadegh Ghanji

1992
2660	**937**	50r. multicoloured	90	40

938 Revolutionary Scenes

1992. 13th Anniv of Islamic Revolution. Multicoloured.
2661		30r. Type **938**	75	25
2662		50r. Revolutionary scenes (different)	90	40

939 Members' Flags

1992. Economic Co-operation Organization Summit, Teheran.
2663	**939**	200r. multicoloured	3·25	1·70

940 Seyd Abbas Musawi (Hezbollah Secretary-General) and Dome of the Rock

1992. World Jerusalem Day.
2664	**940**	200r. multicoloured	3·50	1·80

941 Planets, Satellite, Globe and Mobile Dish Aerial

1992. World Meteorological Day.
2665	**941**	100r. multicoloured	1·30	90

942 Badshahi Mosque, Lahore, Pakistan

1992. South and West Asia Postal Union. Multicoloured.
2666		50r. Type **942**	75	45
2667		50r. Imam's Mosque, Isfahan	75	45
2668		50r. St. Sophia's, Istanbul, Turkey	75	45

943 Ayatollah Khomeini Voting

1992. 13th Anniv of Islamic Republic.
2669	**943**	50r. multicoloured	1·20	45

944 Embraer Bandeirante and Crates

1992. Establishment of Postal Air Service.
2670	**944**	60r. multicoloured	1·10	55

945 Hands holding Trees

1992. National Resources Week.
2671	**945**	100r. multicoloured	1·80	90

946 Tulips

1992. New Year Festival. Flowers. Multicoloured.
2672		20r. Type **946**	45	30
2673		20r. Rose	45	30
2674		40r. Orange blossom	75	40
2675		40r. Yellow jasmine	75	40

947 Members' Flags

1992. Economic Co-operation Organization.
2676	**947**	20r. multicoloured	45	30

948 Morse Apparatus

1992. World Telecommunications Day. Multicoloured.
2677		20r. Type **948**	45	30
2678		20r. Telegraph poles and wires	45	30
2679		20r. Old wall and candlestick telephones	45	30
2680		40r. Dish aerials	85	40
2681		40r. Satellite and Earth	85	40

Nos. 2677/81 were issued together, se-tenant, forming a composite design.

949 Sabzevari

1992. Science, Art and Literature. Multicoloured.
2682		50r. Type **949**	75	45
2683		50r. Madjlessi (in turban)	75	45
2684		50r. Arabic script by Mir Emad	75	45
2685		50r. Samani (in fez)	75	45

950 Emblem

1992. 21st Near East Regional Conference Session of F.A.O., Teheran.
2686	**950**	40r. green, blue and black	75	40

951 Globe, Equipment and Charts

1992. International Surveying and Mapping Conf.
2687	**951**	40r. multicoloured	75	40

952 Palm Trees

1992. Second Anniv of Unification of Yemen.
2688	**952**	50r. multicoloured	90	45

953 Dome of the Rock, Oasis and Child

1992. World Children's Day.
2689	**953**	50r. multicoloured	90	45

954 Khomeini

1992. Third Death Anniv of Ayatollah Khomeini.
2690	**954**	100r. multicoloured	1·50	85

955 Diagram of Wind Tunnel Test, Section of Spine and Robot Hand

1992. International Engineering Applications of Mechanics Conference, Teheran.
2691	**955**	50r. multicoloured	1·10	45

956 Building and Books

1992. Hajia Nosrat Baygom Amin Mo'in (lawyer) Commemoration.
2692	**956**	20r. multicoloured	55	25

957 Emblem and Iranian Flag

1992. Sixth Non-aligned News Agencies Pool Conference, Teheran.
2693	**957**	100r. multicoloured	1·40	85

958 ESCAP Emblem

1992. Meeting of Economic and Social Commission for Asia and the Pacific Industry and Technology Ministers.
2694	**958**	100r. green, gold & black	1·40	85

959 Drugs in Hand

1992. World Anti-drugs Day.
2695	**959**	100r. multicoloured	1·40	70

960 Ceramic Bowl, Neyshabour City

1992. International Museum Day. Multicoloured.
2696		40r. Type **960**	75	30
2697		40r. Ceramic vessel, Shahroud City	75	30

961 Khomeini winding Turban

1992. Prayers of Ayatollah Khomeini (1st series). Multicoloured.
2698		50r. Type **961**	90	45
2699		50r. Mosque and Khomeini	90	45
2700		50r. Khomeini	90	45
See also Nos. 2701/2 and 2703.

962 Arabic Script

1992. Prayers of Ayatollah Khomeini (2nd series).
2701	**962**	50r. turquoise and blue	75	40
2702	-	50r. yellow and green	75	40
DESIGN: No. 2702, Arabic script (different).

963 Kaaba

1992. Prayers of Ayatollah Khomeini (3rd series).
2703	**963**	50r. multicoloured	85	40

964 Tanker

1992. 25th Anniv of Iranian Shipping Lines.
2704	**964**	200r. multicoloured	2·75	1·70

965 Arabic Script

1992. Mohammed's Birth Anniv and Unity Week.
2705	**965**	40r. multicoloured	75	30

966 Soldiers and Sun

1992. 12th Anniv of Iran–Iraq War. Multicoloured.
2706		20r. Type **966**	40	15
2707		40r. Soldier on riverbank (horiz)	45	30

967 Patient and Doctor

1992. International History of Medicine in Islam and Iran Congress. Multicoloured.
2708		20r. Type **967**	40	15
2709		40r. Medical instruments	45	30
Nos. 2708/9 were issued together, *se-tenant*, forming a composite design.

968 Foundry and Steel Products

1992. Steel Industry. Multicoloured.
2710		20r. Type **968**	40	25
2711		70r. Steel products and steel works	85	40
Nos. 2710/11 were issued together, *se-tenant*, forming a composite design.

969 Isfahan

1992. World Tourism Day. Multicoloured.
2712		20r. Type **969**	40	25
2713		20r. Mazandaran	40	25
2714		30r. Bushehr	55	30
2715		30r. Hormozgan	55	30

970 Map and Flags

1992. International Trade Fair.
2716	**970**	200r. multicoloured	2·75	1·40

971 Early Post Office Service

1992. World Post Day.
2717	**971**	30r. brown and violet	60	40

972 Starving Child and Food Distribution

1992. World Food Day.
2718	**972**	100r. multicoloured	1·50	60

973 Child drawing

1992. International Children's and Youth Photographic Festival.
2719	**973**	40r. multicoloured	75	40

974 Flames and Child's Face

1992. Bosnia and Herzegovina.
2720	**974**	40r. multicoloured	75	40

975 Storming Embassy, Doves and Crow

1992. Multicoloured.
2721		100r. Type **975** (11th anniv of storming of U.S. Embassy)	1·40	60
2722		100r. Soldiers, crows and doves (Students' Day)	1·40	60
2723		100r. Ayatollah Khomeini, crows and doves (13th anniv of Khomeini's return from exile)	1·40	60
Nos. 2721/3 were issued together, *se-tenant*, forming a composite design.

976 Emblem

1992. 17th Annual Meeting of Islamic Development Bank Board of Governors.
2724	**976**	20r. multicoloured	40	25

977 Flags and Dish Aerials on Maps

1992. Azerbaijan–Iran Telecommunications Co-operation.
2725	**977**	40r. multicoloured	75	40

978 Star

1992. Tenth Anniv of Islamic University.
2726	**978**	200r. green & deep green	2·30	1·10

979 Soldiers in Armed Motor Boat

1992. People's Militia Week.
2727	**979**	40r. multicoloured	75	40

980 Shahryar

1992. International Congress on Mohammed Hossein Shahryar (poet).
2728	**980**	80r. multicoloured	90	45

981 "Heaven and Hell"

1992. Women's Day and Birth Anniv of Fatima.
2729	**981**	70r. multicoloured	85	40

982 Oil Derrick

1992. Oil Industry. Multicoloured.
2730		100r. Type **982**	1·10	60
2731		100r. Drilling	1·10	60

983 Arabic Script and Hand holding Pen

1992. Literacy Campaign.
2732	**983**	80r. multicoloured	90	45

984 Ayatollah Mirza Abolhassan Sharani

1993. Celebrities. Multicoloured.
2733		20r. Type **984**	40	25
2734		20r. Prof. Mahmoud Hessabi and formula	40	25
2735		20r. Mohit Tabatabaie and books	40	25
2736		20r. Mehrdad Avesta and Arabic script	40	25

985 Narcissi

1993. Flowers. Multicoloured.
2737		20r. Type **985**	30	25
2738		30r. Blue and yellow irises	45	30
2738a		35r. Tulips	60	40
2739		40r. White irises	30	25
2740		50r. Jasmine	60	40
2741		60r. Viburnum berries	1·10	45
2742		70r. Pansies	1·30	70
2743		75r. Antirrhinums	1·30	70
2745		100r. Martagon lilies	1·10	75
2746		120r. Petunias	1·80	85
2747		150r. Hyacinths	1·50	1·10
2749		200r. Roses	2·30	1·10
2750		500r. Convolvulus	5·25	1·10
2751		1000r. Poppies	10·50	7·25

986 Wings and Koran

1993. Mab'as Festival.
2752	**986**	200r. multicoloured	2·30	1·40

987 Rainbow and Emblem

1993. Programming Day.

| 2753 | 987 | 100r. multicoloured | 1·70 | 60 |

988 Man in
Wheelchair tying
Girl's Ribbon

1993. Invalids' Day. Multicoloured.

| 2754 | 20r. Type **988** | 40 | 25 |
| 2755 | 40r. Medal winner in wheelchair | 60 | 40 |

Nos. 2754/5 were issued together, *se-tenant*, forming a composite design.

989 Fatima
Mosque, Qom

1993. Preservation of Cultural Heritage. Multicoloured.

| 2756 | 40r. Type **989** | 60 | 40 |
| 2757 | 40r. Interior of mosque | 60 | 40 |

990 Hands reaching
towards Sun

1993. World Day of the Oppressed. Birth Anniv of Mahdi.

| 2758 | 990 | 60r. multicoloured | 75 | 40 |

991 National Flag

1993. 14th Anniv of Islamic Revolution. Multicoloured.

2759	20r. Type **991**	85	25
2760	20r. Flag and soldiers	85	25
2761	20r. Guerrillas	85	25
2762	20r. Oil derricks, harvesters and crowd	85	25
2763	20r. Ayatollah Khomeini in motorcade and on arrival in Iran	85	25

Nos. 2759/63 were issued together, *se-tenant*, forming a composite design.

992 Volleyball

1993. First Islamic Countries Women's Games. Multicoloured.

2764	40r. Type **992**	90	40
2765	40r. Basketball	90	40
2766	40r. Gold medal	90	40
2767	40r. Swimming	90	40
2768	40r. Running	90	40

Nos. 2764/8 were issued together, *se-tenant*, forming a compostite design.

993 Ansari

1993. Congress on Sheikh Morteza Ansari.

| 2769 | 993 | 40r. multicoloured | 50 | 30 |

994 World Map as Tree
Foliage and Rainbow

1993. Tree Day.

| 2770 | 994 | 70r. multicoloured | 90 | 55 |

995 Burning Tank
and Man with
Sling

1993. World Jerusalem Day.

| 2771 | 995 | 20r. multicoloured | 25 | 15 |

996 Butterfly
and Tulip

1993. New Year Festival. Flowers and Butterflies. Multicoloured.

2772	20r. Type **996**	40	25
2773	20r. Butterfly and narcissus	40	25
2774	40r. Butterfly, tulips and rose	60	40
2775	40r. Butterfly and roses	60	40

997 Grass and
Goldfish in Bowl

1993. Fetr Feast.

| 2776 | 997 | 100r. multicoloured | 2·50 | 1·40 |

998 Open Music Book

1993. 14th Anniv of Islamic Republic.

| 2777 | 998 | 40r. multicoloured | 60 | 40 |

999 Door and Landscape

1993. International Birth Millenary of Sheikh Mofeed Congress.

| 2778 | 999 | 80r. multicoloured | 1·10 | 60 |

1000 Emblem

1993. 13th Asian and Pacific Labour Ministers' Conference, Teheran.

| 2779 | 1000 | 100r. multicoloured | 1·40 | 75 |

1001 Globe

1993. Int Congress for Advancement of Science and Technology in Islamic World.

| 2780 | 1001 | 50r. multicoloured | 90 | 45 |

1002 Mirror Box

1993. International Museum Day.

| 2781 | 1002 | 40r. multicoloured | 75 | 30 |

1003 Khomeini

1993. Fourth Death Anniv of Ayatollah Khomeini.

| 2782 | 1003 | 20r. multicoloured | 60 | 15 |

1004 Girl on Swing

1993. World Children's Day.

| 2783 | 1004 | 50r. multicoloured | 85 | 40 |

1005 Knitted Socks

1993. World Crafts Day.

| 2784 | 1005 | 70r. multicoloured | 1·10 | 55 |

1006 Family at
Window

1993. World Population Day.

| 2785 | 1006 | 30r. multicoloured | 60 | 25 |

1007 Football

1993. Student Games. Multicoloured.

2786	20r. Type **1007**	30	15
2787	40r. Judo and wrestling	75	30
2788	40r. Long jumping, weightlifting, badminton and basketball	75	30

1008 Butterfly and Film Frame

1993. International Children's and Youths' Film Festival, Isfahan.

| 2789 | 1008 | 60r. multicoloured | 90 | 45 |

1009 Postal Messenger

1993. World Post Day.

| 2790 | 1009 | 60r. multicoloured | 90 | 45 |

1010 Stars and
Birds

1993. Third International Biennial Children's Book Illustrations Exhibition, Teheran. Multicoloured.

2791	30r. Type **1010**	70	30
2792	30r. Moon and girl in boat	70	30
2793	30r. Cherub blowing trumpet	70	30
2794	30r. Trees and clouds	70	30

Nos. 2791/4 were issued together, *se-tenant*, forming a composite design.

1011 Khaje
Nassireddin Tussy

1993. 719th Death Anniv of Khaje Nassireddin Tussy (scientist).

| 2795 | 1011 | 30r. multicoloured | 60 | 30 |

1012 Militia Member

1993. People's Militia Week. Multicoloured.

| 2796 | 50r. Type **1012** | 75 | 30 |
| 2797 | 50r. Woman tying headband for Militia member | 75 | 30 |

1013 Ayatollah
Golpayegani

1993. Ayatollah Golpayegani Commem.

| 2798 | 1013 | 300r. multicoloured | 3·50 | 1·70 |

1014 Hopscotch Grid
drawn in Blood

1993. Support for Moslems of Bosnia and Herzegovina. Multicoloured.

2799	40r. Type **1014**	90	30
2800	40r. Youth giving "V" sign	90	30
2801	40r. Woman and mosque	90	30

1015 Flags

1994. Invalids' Day and Birthday of Abalfazil el Abbas.

| 2802 | 1015 | 80r. multicoloured | 1·10 | 60 |

1016 Trees and Ploughed
Field in Book

1994. Agricultural Week.
2803 **1016** 60r. multicoloured   1·10   60

1017 Electrification
of Villages

1994. 15th Anniv of Islamic Revolution. Multicoloured.
2804 40r. Type **1017**   75   45
2805 40r. Ayatollah Khomeini and
       workers with flag   75   45
2806 40r. Fishing and new roads   75   45
2807 40r. Harvesting wheat and
       weaving   75   45
   Nos. 2804/7 were issued together, *se-tenant*, forming a
composite design.

1018 Dome of the
Rock

1994. Congress on Islamic Law.
2808 **1018** 60r. multicoloured   70   40

1019 Doctor, Gymnast,
Camera, Paintbrush, Book
and Student

1994. Youth Welfare.
2809 **1019** 30r. multicoloured   75   40

1020 Palestinian and Peaceful
Scene

1994. World Jerusalem Day.
2810 **1020** 50r. multicoloured   75   40

1021
Black-crowned
Night Heron

1994. New Year Festival. Birds. Multicoloured.
2811 40r. Type **1021**   90   45
2812 40r. Eurasian bittern   90   45
2813 40r. Chukar partridges (horiz)   90   45
2814 40r. Common pheasants (horiz)   90   45

1022 Ball and
Rectangles

1994. 25th Annual Mathematics Conference.
2815 **1022** 30r. multicoloured   75   40

1023 Book and Roses

1994. 15th Anniv of Islamic Republic.
2816 **1023** 40r. multicoloured   75   40

1024 Child and Roses

1994. World Health Day.
2817 **1024** 100r. multicoloured   1·40   70

1025 Delvari, Cavalrymen
and Ship

1994. 80th Death Anniv of Raiss Ali Delvari
(revolutionary).
2818 **1025** 50r. multicoloured   75   40

1026 I.Y.F.
Emblem

1994. International Year of the Family.
2819 **1026** 50r. multicoloured   60   30

1027 Old Telephone
System and Computer
Operator

1994. World Telecommunications Day.
2820 **1027** 50r. multicoloured   60   30

1028 Marlik
Gold Cup

1994. International Museum Day.
2821 **1028** 40r. multicoloured   60   25

1029 Kufic
Enamelled Pot

1994. Cultural Preservation.
2822 **1029** 40r. multicoloured   60   25

1030 Khomeini

1994. Fifth Death Anniv of Ayatollah Khomeini.
2823 **1030** 30r. multicoloured   40   25

1031 Motahhari

1994. 15th Death Anniv of Ayatollah Motahhari.
2824 **1031** 30r. multicoloured   40   25

1032 Rose-water
Sprinkler

1994. World Crafts Day. Multicoloured.
2825 60r. Type **1032**   70   40
2826 60r. Silk weaving, Khorassan   70   40

1033 Games Emblem

1994. Islamic Countries' University Student Games.
2827 **1033** 60r. multicoloured   60   40

1034 Mosaic and
Rose

1994. Mohammed's Birth Anniv and Unity Week.
2828 **1034** 30r. multicoloured   40   25

1035 Cameraman

1994. 14th Anniv of Iran–Iraq War.
2829 **1035** 70r. multicoloured   75   45

1036 Envelope

1994. World Post Day.
2830 **1036** 50r. multicoloured   60   30

1037 Allegory of
Woman

1994. Women's Day and Birth Anniv of Fatima.
2831 **1037** 70r. multicoloured   75   45

1038 Soldier

1994. People's Militia Week.
2832 **1038** 30r. multicoloured   40   25

1039 Book

1994. Book Week.
2833 **1039** 40r. multicoloured   45   25

1040 Arms, Map and
Town

1994. Support for Moslems of Bosnia and Herzegovina.
Multicoloured.
2834 80r. Type **1040**   1·00   55
2835 80r. Commander Adnan (de-
       ceased) and family   1·00   55

1041 Araki

1995. Second Death Anniv of Grand Ayatollah
Mohammad Ali Araki (Shia leader).
2836 **1041** 100r. multicoloured   1·10   60

1042 Arabic Script

1995. World Day of the Oppressed. Birth Anniv of Mahdi.
2837 **1042** 50r. multicoloured   60   30

1043 Flag, Dome
and Man

1995. Revolutionaries (1st series). Multicoloured.
2838 50r. Type **1043**   60   30
2839 50r. Man in patterned shirt   60   30
2840 50r. Man with full beard wear-
       ing grey shirt   60   30
2841 50r. Man in jacket and sweater
       looking to right   60   30
   See also Nos. 2874/7, 2909/16, 2953/6, 3029/32 and
3034/7.

1044 Crowd, National Flag and Ayatollah Khomeini

1995. 16th Anniv of Islamic Revolution.
2842 **1044** 100r. multicoloured 1·10 60

1045 Dome of the Rock

1995. World Jerusalem Day.
2843 **1045** 100r. multicoloured 1·10 60

1046 Hand holding Tree

1995. Tree Day.
2844 **1046** 50r. multicoloured 60 30

1047 Hyacinths

1995. New Year Festival. Multicoloured.
2845 50r. Type **1047** 70 40
2846 50r. Pansies 70 40
2847 50r. Grass and bow 70 40
2848 50r. Tulips, bow and goldfish bowl 90 55

1048 Diesel Goods Train on Bridge

1995. Inauguration of Bafq–Bandar Abbas Railway.
2849 **1048** 100r. multicoloured 1·10 90

1049 Phoenix rising from Tulips

1995. 16th Anniv of Islamic Republic.
2850 **1049** 100r. multicoloured 1·10 60

1050 Shapes

1995. Press Festival.
2851 **1050** 100r. multicoloured 1·10 60

1051 Khomeini

1995. Ayatollah Ahmad Khomeini Commem.
2852 **1051** 50r. multicoloured 60 30

1052 Arabic Script

1995. Invalids' Day.
2853 **1052** 80r. multicoloured 90 45

1053 Yezd Mosque and Vaziri

1995. Ayatollah Ali Vaziri Commemoration.
2854 **1053** 100r. multicoloured 1·10 60

1054 Telecommunications

1995. World Telecommunications Day.
2855 **1054** 100r. multicoloured 1·10 60

1055 Khomeini

1995. Sixth Death Anniv of Ayatollah Khomeini.
2856 **1055** 100r. multicoloured 1·10 60

1056 Immunizing Baby

1995. 50th Anniv of U.N.O. Multicoloured.
2857 100r. Type **1056** 1·10 60
2858 100r. Child laughing 1·10 60
2859 100r. Cereals and world map 1·10 60
2860 100r. Woman reading 1·10 60

1057 Ashtiany

1995. Iqbal Ashtiany (historian) Commem.
2861 **1057** 100r. multicoloured 1·10 60

1058 Dam Workers

1995. Government Week.
2862 **1058** 100r. multicoloured 1·10 60

1059 Man with Gun and Book

1995. People's Militia Week.
2863 **1059** 100r. multicoloured 1·10 60

1060 Envelopes and Globe forming Flower

1995. World Post Day.
2864 **1060** 100r. multicoloured 1·10 60

1061 Cypher

1995. Prophet Mohammed Commemoration.
2865 **1061** 100r. multicoloured 1·10 60

1062 Tondgoyan

1995. M. J. Tondgoyan (oil minister) Commem.
2866 **1062** 100r. multicoloured 1·10 60

1063 Shaghaghi

1996. Fathi Shaghaghi (Islamic Jihad Secretary-General) Commemoration.
2867 **1063** 100r. multicoloured 1·10 60

1064 Crowd, Flowers and Ayatollah Khomeini

1996. 17th Anniv of Islamic Revolution.
2868 **1064** 100r. multicoloured 1·10 60

1065 Dome of the Rock

1996. World Jerusalem Day.
2869 **1065** 100r. multicoloured 1·10 60

1066 Common Cardinal

1996. New Year Festival. Birds. Multicoloured.
2870 100r. Type **1066** 1·70 90
2871 100r. Budgerigar 1·70 90
2872 100r. Golden oriole 1·70 90
2873 100r. European roller 1·70 90

1996. Revolutionaries (2nd series). As T **1043**. Multicoloured.
2874 100r. Colonel-pilot Abbas Babaiy 1·10 60
2875 100r. Officer-pilot Ali Akbar Sharoudi 1·10 60
2876 100r. Commandant Mohammad Ebrahim Hemmat 1·00 55
2877 100r. Commandant Mohammad Boroudjerdi 1·10 60

1067 Ayatollah Khomeini, Ballot Box and Crowd

1996. 17th Anniv of Islamic Republic.
2878 **1067** 200r. multicoloured 2·10 1·40

1068 Open Book, Flowers and Birds

1996. International Book Fair, Teheran.
2879 **1068** 85r. multicoloured 1·00 60

1069 Diesel Locomotive in Tunnel, Imam Riza's Shrine, Meshed, and Horses

1996. Meshed–Sarakhs–Tajan International Railway.
2880 **1069** 200r. multicoloured 2·10 1·10

1070 Camel Train and Prisoner tied to Stake

1996. Day of Prisoners of War and Missing in Action.
2881 **1070** 200r. multicoloured 2·30 1·10

1071 Khomeini

1996. Seventh Death Anniv of Ayatollah Khomeini.
2882 **1071** 200r. multicoloured 2·30 1·10

1072 Carpet

1996. World Crafts Day.
2883 **1072** 200r. multicoloured   2·30   1·10

1073 Emblem

1996. Third Posts and Telecommunications Ministerial Conference, Teheran.
2884 **1073** 200r. multicoloured   2·30   1·10

1074 Zouqeblateyne Mosque

1996. Mohammed's Birth Anniv and Unity Week. Multicoloured.
2885   200r. Type **1074**   2·30   1·10
2886   200r. Tomb of Imam Hossein (dome with flag flying to right)   2·30   1·10
2887   200r. Prophet's Mosque (dome without flag)   2·30   1·10
2888   200r. Tomb of Imam Riza (dome with flag flying to left)   2·30   1·10
2889   200r. Qaba Mosque (with four corner minarets)   2·30   1·10

1075 Teheran Underground

1996. Government Week. Multicoloured.
2890   200r. Type **1075**   2·30   1·10
2891   200r. Ispahan iron works   2·30   1·10
2892   200r. Merchant fleet   2·30   1·10
2893   200r. Bandar-e-Imam oil refinery   2·30   1·10
2894   200r. Boumehen Earth Station   2·30   1·10

1076 Ardabily and Mosque Interior

1996. Allameh Moghaddas Ardabily Commem.
2895 **1076** 200r. multicoloured   2·30   1·10

1077 Artillery Position and Soldier praying

1996. 16th Anniv of Iran–Iraq War.
2896 **1077** 200r. multicoloured   2·30   1·10

1078 Cogs and Equipment

1996. World Standards Day.
2897 **1078** 200r. multicoloured   1·90   1·00

1079 Harvesting and Man working on "Globe" Rick

1996. World Food Summit, Rome.
2898 **1079** 200r. multicoloured   1·90   1·00

1080 Men, Houses and Women

1996. National Population and Housing Census.
2899 **1080** 200r. multicoloured   1·90   1·00

1081 Wrestlers

1996. Second World University Wrestling Championship, Teheran.
2900 **1081** 500r. multicoloured   4·50   2·75

1082 Ayatollah Khomeini embracing Youth

1997. 18th Anniv of Islamic Revolution. Multicoloured.
2901   200r. Type **1082**   1·90   1·00
2902   200r. Banner of Khomeini above crowd   1·90   1·00
2903   200r. Khomeini waving   1·90   1·00
2904   200r. Khomeini returning from exile in France   1·90   1·00
2905   200r. Soldiers   1·90   1·00

1083 Hands holding Tree

1997. Tree Day.
2906 **1083** 200r. multicoloured   1·90   1·00

1084 Rainbow and National Flag

1997. 18th Anniv of Islamic Republic.
2907 **1084** 200r. multicoloured   1·90   1·00

1085 Water Droplet falling to "Globe" Pool in Cupped Hands

1997. Eighth International Rainwater Catchment Systems Conference.
2908 **1085** 200r. multicoloured   1·90   1·00

1997. Revolutionaries (3rd series). As T **1043**. Multicoloured.
2909   100r. Alireza Mowahhed Danesh (blue flag, white turban)   90   45
2910   100r. Mohammad Reza Dastwareh (orange flag, white turban)   90   45
2911   100r. Abbas Karimi (blue flag, full-face without glasses)   90   45
2912   100r. Nasser Kazemi (orange flag, white vest with red trim)   90   45
2913   100r. Youssef Kolahdouz (blue flag, three-quarter face)   90   45
2914   100r. Yadollah Kolhar (orange flag, full-face)   90   45
2915   100r. Fazlollah Mahallati (blue flag, full-face with glasses)   90   45
2916   100r. Abdollah Meyssami (orange flag, green vest and coat)   90   45

1086 Satellite, Letter, Globe and Computer

1997. Post, Telecommunications and Productivity.
2917 **1086** 200r. multicoloured   1·50   75

1087 Khomeini

1997. Eighth Death Anniv of Ayatollah Khomeini.
2918 **1087** 200r. multicoloured   1·50   75

1088 Teheran Underground Railway Map and Tunnel

1997. National Achievements. Multicoloured.
2919   40r. Type **1088**   30   15
2920   50r. Cornfield and silo   40   25
2921   65r. Medals from Student Scientific Olympiads   40   25
2922   70r. Steelworks, Mobarakeh   55   30
2923   100r. Modern communications systems   75   40
2924   130r. Harbour and tanker   60   30
2925   150r. Oil refinery, Bandar Abbas   90   60
2926   200r. Martyr Radja-ee dam   1·20   75
2927   350r. Martyr Radja-ee power station   2·10   1·40
2928   400r. Foreign Ministry building   2·40   1·50
2929   500r. Child receiving oral vaccination   3·00   2·00
2930   650r. Koran Printing House and Koran   3·75   2·75
2931   1000r. Imam Khomeini International Airport, Teheran   60   30
2932   2000r. Tomb of Imam Khomeini, Teheran   5·25   2·75

1089 Flora and Fauna

1997. Tenth Anniv of Montreal Protocol (on reduction of use of chlorofluorocarbons).
2933 **1089** 200r. multicoloured   1·20   75

1090 Crowd with Flags and Banners

1997. 17th Anniv of Iran–Iraq War.
2934 **1090** 200r. multicoloured   1·20   75

1091 Allama Mohammad Iqbal (Pakistani poet)

1997. Iranian–Pakistani Culture. Multicoloured.
2935   200r. Type **1091**   1·20   75
2936   200r. Jalal-ad-din Moulana Rumi (Persian mystic)   1·20   75

1092 Airplane, Letters and Computer

1997. World Post Day.
2937 **1092** 200r. multicoloured   1·20   75

1093 Frasheri and Etehemberg Mosque, Tirana

1997. 150th Birth Anniv (1996) of Naim Frasheri (Albanian writer).
2938 **1093** 200r. multicoloured   1·20   75

1094 Calligraphy

1997. Eighth Islamic Summit, Teheran. Illustrated pages from the Koran. Each green, gold and red.
2939   300r. Type **1094**   1·80   1·20
2940   300r. Page with rose at bottom left   1·80   1·20
2941   300r. Page with rose on right-hand side   1·80   1·20
2942   300r. Page with rose at top left-hand corner   1·80   1·20
2943   300r. Summit emblem   1·80   1·20

1095 Games Emblem

1997. Second Islamic Countries Women's Games, Teheran.
2944 **1095** 200r. multicoloured   1·20   75

1096 Dome of the Rock

1998. World Jerusalem Day.
2945 **1096** 250r. multicoloured   1·50   1·10

1097 State Flags and Poppies

1998. 19th Anniv of Islamic Revolution. Multicoloured.
2946 200r. Type **1097**   1·30   85
2947 200r. Harvesting grain   1·30   85
2948 200r. Soldiers with flags   1·30   85
2949 200r. Crowd with banner of Khomeini   1·30   85
2950 200r. Ayatollah Khomeini   1·30   85
    Nos. 2946/50 were issued together, *se-tenant*, forming a composite design.

1098 Tree and Town

1998. Tree Day.
2951 **1098** 200r. multicoloured   1·30   85

1099 Flower Arrangement and Gifts

1998. New Year Festival.
2952 **1099** 200r. multicoloured   1·30   85

1998. Revolutionaries (4th series). As T **1043**. Multicoloured.
2953 100r. Man in open-necked shirt   70   60
2954 100r. Man in vest and jacket (three-quarter face) 70 60
2955 100r. Man in vest and jacket (profile)   70   60
2956 100r. Man in crew-neck jumper and jacket 70   60

1100 M. Shahryar (poet)

1998
2957 **1100** 200r. multicoloured   1·30   1·10

1101 Khomeini

1998. Ninth Death Anniv of Ayatollah Khomeini.
2958 **1101** 200r. multicoloured   1·30   1·10

1102 Map and Emblem

1998. Second South and West Asia Postal Union Congress.
2959 **1102** 250r. multicoloured   1·50   1·40

1103 Player, Ball and Stadium

1998. World Cup Football Championship, France.
2960 **1103** 500r. multicoloured   3·25   3·00

1104 Globe and Headset

1998. World Telecommunications Day.
2961 **1104** 200r. multicoloured   1·30   1·10

1105 Silver Vessel

1998. World Handicrafts Day.
2962 **1105** 200r. multicoloured   1·30   1·10

1106 State Flag as Dove, Birds and Flowers

1998. First Anniv of Presidential Election.
2963 **1106** 200r. multicoloured   1·30   1·20

1107 Khomeini voting

1998. 19th Anniv of Islamic Republic.
2964 **1107** 250r. multicoloured   1·50   1·10

1108 Handshake, Rainbow and Doves

1998. Co-operation Day.
2965 **1108** 250r. multicoloured   1·50   1·40

1109 Arabic Script

1998. "1000th Friday of Public Prayer".
2966 **1109** 250r. blue, gold and black   1·50   1·40

(1110)

1998. Mosques. Nos. 2415a and 2416a surch as T **1110**.
2967 **1110** 200r. on 1r. orange and silver 1·20   1·10
2968 **1110** 200r. on 3r. green and silver   1·20   1·10

1111 Globe and Shark's Fin

1998. International Year of the Ocean.
2969 **1111** 250r. multicoloured   1·50   1·40

1112 Arabic Script

1998. Sacred Defence Week.
2970 **1112** 250r. multicoloured   1·50   1·40

1113 Envelope and Clouds as World Map

1998. World Post Day.
2971 **1113** 200r. multicoloured   1·20   1·10

1114 Wrestlers

1998. World Wrestling Championship, Iran.
2972 **1114** 250r. multicoloured   1·40   1·20

1115 Rosebud in Hand

1998. Children's Cancer Relief.
2973 **1115** 250r. multicoloured   1·10   1·10

1116 Navigation Instrument

1999. Museum Exhibit.
2974 **1116** 250r. multicoloured   1·50   1·40

1117 Khomeini

1999. 20th Anniv of Islamic Revolution.
2975 **1117** 250r. multicoloured   1·30   1·10

(1118)

1999. Flowers. Nos. 2738/a surch as T **1118**.
2976 200r. on 35r. multicoloured   1·10   1·00
2977 900r. on 30r. multicoloured   4·50   4·25

(1119)

1999. International Book Fair, Teheran. No. 2879 surch as T **1119**.
2978 250r. on 85r. multicoloured   1·30   1·20

1120 Flag and Emblem

1999. 20th Anniv of Islamic Republic.
2979 **1120** 250r. multicoloured   1·30   1·10

1121 Emblem

1999. Ghadir Khom Religious Festival.
2980 **1121** 250r. multicoloured 1·30 1·20

1122 Harbour

1999. Ayatollah Khomeini Charity Fund. Multicoloured.
2981 250r. Type **1122** 1·20 1·10
2982 250r. Houses 1·20 1·10

1123 Soldier, Tank, Ship and Aircraft

1999. Army Day.
2983 **1123** 250r. multicoloured 1·10 1·00

1124 Sadra al-Din Shirazi

1999. Sadra al-Din Shirazi (philosopher) Commem.
2984 **1124** 250r. multicoloured 1·30 1·20

1125 Khomeini

1999. Tenth Death Anniv of Ayatollah Khomeini.
2985 **1125** 250r. multicoloured 1·30 1·20

1126 Parliament Building and Khomeini

1999. 20th Anniv of Iranian Parliament.
2986 **1126** 250r. multicoloured 1·30 1·20

1127 Emblem and Map

1999. Organization of Islamic Conference Interparliamentary Union Congress, Tehran.
2987 **1127** 250r. multicoloured 1·30 1·20

1128 Emblem and Dome

1999. Unity Week.
2988 **1128** 250r. multicoloured 1·10 1·10

1129 Tapestry

1999. World Handicrafts Day.
2989 **1129** 250r. multicoloured 1·10 1·10

1130 River Kingfisher

1999. Birds. Multicoloured.
2990 100r. Hoopoe 1·50 1·40
2991 150r. Type **1130** 75 70
2992 200r. Robin 45 40
2993 250r. Crested lark 1·10 1·10
2994 300r. Red-backed shrike 1·50 1·40
2995 350r. Roller 1·40 1·40
2996 400r. Blue tit 90 85
2997 500r. Bee eater 2·75 2·40
2998 1000r. Redwing 3·75 3·50
2999 2000r. Twite 7·50 7·25
2999a 3000r. Whitethroat 11·50 11·00
2999b 4500r. Collar dove 11·50 11·00

1131 Moon partially covering Sun

1999. Solar Eclipse. Multicoloured.
3000 250r. Type **1131** 1·10 1·10
3001 250r. Moon passing in front of Sun 1·10 1·10
3002 250r. Full solar eclipse 1·10 1·10
3003 250r. Sun appearing from right-hand side of Moon 1·10 1·10
3004 250r. Sun appearing 1·10 1·10

1132 Letters, Globe and Letter Box

1999. 125th Anniv of Universal Postal Union.
3005 **1132** 250r. multicoloured 1·20 1·10

1133 Chinese Girl

1999. International Children's Day. Showing children from different cultures. Multicoloured.
3006 150r. Type **1133** 75 70
3007 150r. Indian girl 75 70
3008 150r. Native American girl 75 70
3009 150r. Arabian boy 75 70
3010 150r. Iranian girl 75 70
3011 150r. Mexican boy 75 70
3012 150r. Eskimo boy 75 70
3013 150r. African girl 75 70
3014 150r. Russian boy 75 70
3015 150r. European girl 75 70

1134 Winged Egg

1999. International Children's Book Illustrations Exhibition. Multicoloured.
3016 250r. Type **1134** 1·20 1·10
3017 250r. Decorated egg 1·20 1·10
3018 250r. Egg decorated with white crescent 1·20 1·10
3019 250r. Egg decorated with flowers 1·20 1·10

1135 Ayatollah Mohammed Taghi

1999. Ayatollah Mohammed Taghi Commemoration.
3020 **1135** 250r. multicoloured 1·20 1·10

1136 Ayatollah Khomeni

2000. 21st Anniv of Islamic Revolution.
3021 **1136** 300r. multicoloured 1·50 1·40

2000. Flowers. Nos. 2741, 2743, 2746 surch **250 R.**
3022 250r. on 60r. multicoloured 1·40 1·20
3023 250r. on 75r. multicoloured 1·40 1·20
3024 250r. on 120r. multicoloured 1·40 1·20

1138 Bee Eaters

2000. New Year Festival.
3025 **1138** 300r. multicoloured 2·30 1·50

1139 Inscription

2000. National Archives Day.
3026 **1139** 300r. multicoloured 1·80 1·80

1140 Books, Cogs, Chimneys and Hand holding Torch

2000. 70th Anniv of Science and Technology University.
3027 **1140** 300r. multicoloured 1·70 1·50

1141 Mofatteh and Building

2000. Ayatollah Mofatteh Commemoration.
3028 **1141** 300r. multicoloured 1·70 1·50

1142 Khalil Motahar Nia

2000. Revolutionaries (5th series). Multicoloured.
3029 150r. Type **1142** 1·70 1·50
3030 150r. Haschem Etemadi (pink shirt) 1·70 1·50
3031 150r. Madjid Sepassi (green shirt) 1·70 1·50
3032 150r. Mahmud Sotoudeh (blue T-shirt and shirt) 1·70 1·50

1143 Mother and Baby

2000. International Breast-feeding Week.
3033 **1143** 300r. multicoloured 1·70 1·60

1144 Hadj Reza Habubollahi

2000. Revolutionaries (6th series). Multicoloured.
3034 150r. Type **1144** 85 75
3035 150r. Hassan Agharebparast (shirt with epaulettes) 85 75
3036 150r. Mostafa Ravani Pou (white turban) 85 75
3037 150r. Mohsen Safavi (wearing glasses) 85 75

1145 Books and Educational Symbols

2000. University Anniversary.
3038 **1145** 300r. multicoloured 1·70 1·50

1146 Stylized Bird

2000. Eighth Asian-Pacific Postal Union Congress, Tehran.
3039 **1146** 300r. blue, mauve and black 1·70 1·50

1147 Satellite and Dish

2000. International World Space Week. Multicoloured.
3040 **1147** 500r. Type **1147** 2·00 1·80
3041 500r. Satellite and dish (different) 2·00 1·80

1148 Birds, Flowers and Calligraphy

2001. Eid-ul Ghadir.
3042	**1148**	500r. multicoloured	2·00	1·90

1149 Flowers, Calligraphy and Sun

2001. Year of Imam Ali.
3043	**1149**	500r. multicoloured	2·00	1·90

1150 Red-headed Bunting

2001. New Year Festival. Multicoloured.
3044	**1150**	300r. Type **1150**	1·20	1·10
3045		300r. Hawfinch (vert)	1·20	1·10

1151 Mosque and Mohamed Al Dorra and Father

2001. Intifada.
3046	**1151**	350r. multicoloured	1·40	1·20

1152 Chaffinch

2001. Belgica 2001 International Stamp Exhibition, Brussels. Multicoloured.
3047	**1152**	350r. Type **1152**	1·40	1·30
3048		350r. Waxwing	1·40	1·30
3049		350r. Gate to Melli Bagh National Garden (vert)	1·40	1·30

1153 Mount Fuji, Japan

2001. Philanippon '01 International Stamp Exhibition, Tokyo. Multicoloured.
3050	**1153**	250r. Type **1153**	1·10	90
3051		250r. Mount Damavand, Iran	1·10	90

1154 Flag, Globe and Iranian Buildings

2001. World Tourism Day.
3052	**1154**	500r. multicoloured	2·10	1·90

1155 Police Helicopters and Vehicles

2001. Police Week. Multicoloured.
3053	**1155**	250r. Type **1155**	1·10	1·00
3054		250r. Flag, boats and Policeman	1·10	1·00

Nos. 3053/4 were issued together, *se-tenant*, forming a composite design.

1156 Children encircling Globe

2001. United Nations Year of Dialogue among Civilizations. Multicoloured.
3055	**1156**	250r. Type **1156**	1·10	90
3056		250r. European and Asian faces (horiz)	1·10	90

1157 Ball and Dove

2001. Third Islamic Women's Games, Tehran.
3057	**1157**	250r. multicoloured	1·10	90

1158 Koran and Flowers

2001. Koran.
3058	**1158**	500r. multicoloured	2·10	1·90

1159 P 232 *Tabarza*

2001. Navy Day. Multicoloured.
3059	**1159**	500r. Type **1159**	2·10	2·00
3060		500r. Frigate	2·10	2·00
3061		500r. Helicopter and hovercraft	2·10	2·00
3062		500r. Submarine	2·10	2·00

1160 Bees on Honeycomb

2001. Bee-keeping.
3063	**1160**	500r. multicoloured	2·10	2·00

1161 Hands enclosing Face

2001. 50th Anniv of United Nations High Commissioner for Refugees.
3064	**1161**	500r. blue, black and mauve	2·10	2·00

1162 Vehicle, Roadways and Bridge

2001. Transportation Day. Multicoloured.
3065	**1162**	350r. Type **1162**	1·40	1·20
3066		350r. Bridge, vehicles and buildings	1·40	1·20

Nos. 3065/6 were issued together, *se-tenant*, forming a composite design.

1163 Locomotive

2001. Tehran Subway. Multicoloured.
3067	**1163**	500r. Type **1163**	1·70	1·50
3068		500r. Locomotive right view	1·70	1·50

1164 Samand Saloon Car

2002. First Iranian Manufactured Car. Multicoloured.
3069	**1164**	500r. Type **1164**	1·50	1·40
3070		500r. Grey car (horiz)	1·50	1·40

1165 Globe as Plant Pot containing Tree

2002. Tree Planting Day.
3071	**1165**	500r. multicoloured	1·50	1·40

1166 Squacco Heron (*Ardeola ralloides*)

2002. New Year Festival. Multicoloured.
3072	**1166**	500r. Type **1166**	1·40	1·10
3073		500r. Hoopoe (*Upupa epops*)	1·40	1·10
3074		500r. Blue tit (*Parus caeruleus*)	1·40	1·10
3075		500r. Alexandrine parakeet (*Psittacula eupatria*)	1·40	1·10

1167 Imam Hossein's Wounded Horse returning to Kerbala (image scaled to 50% of original size)

2002. Death of Imam Hossein (grandson of Mohamed). Sheet 99×76 mm. Imperf.
MS3076	**1167**	400r. multicoloured	1·10	1·10

1168 Chestnut Tiger (*Danaus sita*)

2002. Butterflies. Multicoloured.
3077	**1168**	400r. Type **1168**	1·10	1·00
3078		400r. Comma (*Polygonia c-album*)	1·10	1·00
3079		400r. Blue argus (*Precis orithya*)	1·10	1·00
3080		400r. Painted lady (*Vanessa cardui*)	1·10	1·00
3081		400r. *Papilio maacki*	1·10	1·00

1169 Caspian

2002. Horses. Multicoloured.
3082	**1169**	400r. Type **1169**	1·10	1·00
3083		400r. Kurd	1·10	1·00
3084		400r. Turkoman	1·10	1·00
3085		400r. Arab	1·10	1·00

1170 *Hyoscyamus muticus*

2002. Philakorea 2002 International Stamp Exhibition, Seoul. Flowers. Multicoloured.
3086	**1170**	400r. Type **1170**	1·10	1·00
3087		400r. *Fritillaria* ("Frittillaria")	1·10	1·00
3088		400r. *Calotropis procera*	1·10	1·00
3089		400r. *Ranuculus*	1·10	1·00

1171 Ayatollah Khomeini

2002. Birth Centenary of Ayatollah Khomeini.
3090	**1171**	400r. multicoloured	1·00	90

1172 Child and Dome of the Rock

2002. Jerusalem Day.
3091	**1172**	400r. multicoloured	1·00	90

1173 Iranian Decorated Pots

2002. Centenary of Brazil—Iran Diplomatic Relations. Multicoloured.
3092	**1173**	400r. Type **1173**	1·00	90
3093		400r. Marajoara pots, Brazil	1·00	90

1174 Emblem

2002. Second Biennial Exhibition of Contemporary Islamic Painting.
3094	**1174**	400r. multicoloured	1·00	90

1175 Smelting Pot and Mill

2003. 31st Anniv of Esfahan Steel Mill.
3095	**1175**	400r. multicoloured	1·00	90

1176 Grumman F-14A Tomcat

2003. Air Force Day. Multicoloured.
3096	300r. Type **1176**		70	60
3097	400r. Northrop F-5E Tiger II		90	85
3098	500r. F-14A Tomcat and missile carrier		1·10	1·10
3099	600r. Macdonell Douglas F-5E Phantom II		1·40	1·30
3100	700r. Mikoyan Mig-29		1·60	1·60

1177 Sheep

2003. New Year Festival. Multicoloured.
3101	1000r. Type **1177**		2·30	2·10
3102	1000r. Goitered gazelle male		2·30	2·10
3103	1000r. Goitered gazelle female		2·30	2·10
3104	1000r. Red deer		2·30	2·10

1178 Mosque, Isfahan

2003. Buildings.
3105	400r. Type **1178**		90	75
3106	400r. Bell Tower, Xi'an		90	75

Stamps of the same design were issued by People's Republic of China.

1179 Family enclosed in House of Books

2003. Book, Children and Family.
3107	**1179**	500r. multicoloured	75	70

1180 Zygaena

2003. Butterflies. Multicoloured.
3108	100r. Type **1180**		15	15
3109	200r. Issoria lathonia		30	30
3110	250r. Utethesia pulchella		40	40
3111	300r. Argynnis paphia		45	45
3112	500r. Polygonia egea		75	75
3113	600r. Papilio machaon		90	90
3113a	650r. Colias aurorina		90	55
3114	1000r. Inachis Io		1·50	1·50
3115	2000r. Papilio demoleus		3·00	3·00
3115a	2100r. Papilio demolerus		2·75	1·60
3116	3000r. Euphydryas aurinia		4·50	4·50
3118	4400r. Danaus melanippus		6·25	6·25
3119	5500r. Colias auriona		8·00	8·00

1181 Emblem

2003. 50th Anniv of Social Security.
3125	**1181**	600r. multicoloured	75	70

1182 Revolutionaries

2003.
3126	**1182**	600r. multicoloured	90	75

1183 Mohammed Ali Rajai and Arabic Script

2003. Government Week.
3127	**1183**	600r. multicoloured	90	75

1184 Caspian Seal (*Phoca caspia*)

2003. Preservation of the Caspian Sea. Multicoloured.
3128	600r. Type **1184**		90	75
3129	600r. Beluga (*Huso huso*)		90	75
MS3130	130×97 mm. Nos. 3128/9 each×2		3·75	3·75

Stamps of a similar design were issued by Russia.

1185 Hand holding Apple

2003.
3131	**1185**	500r. multicoloured	75	70

1186 Computer and Satellite

2003. World Post Day. Multicoloured.
3132	600r. Type **1186**		85	75
3133	600r. Post lorries and airplanes		85	75
3134	600r. Seated man holding letter and lorry		85	75
3135	600r. Post rider and statues		85	75

1187 Asiatic Cheetah

2003. Endangered Species. Asiatic Cheetah (*Acinonyc jubatus*). Multicoloured.
3136	500r. Type **1187**		75	70
3137	500r. Adult and cub		75	70

3138	500r. Two adults		75	70
3139	500r. Adult with open mouth		75	70

1188 Minaret

2003. Fetr Feast.
3140	**1188**	600r. multicoloured	85	75

1189 City Walls

2004. Bam Earthquake. Sheet 136×101 mm containing T **1189** and similar horiz designs. Multicoloured.
MS3141	500r.×4, Type **1189**; Ruins; Medical staff and patients; Rescue workers		3·00	3·00

1190 Emblem

2004. 25th Anniv of Republic.
3142	**1190**	600r. multicoloured	90	75

1191 Hossein Rezazadeh

2004. Hossein Rezazadeh, Champion Weightlifter.
3143	**1191**	1200r. multicoloured	1·80	1·60

1192 Postman and Customer

2004. Obtaining ISO 9001–2000 Certification (quality control).
3144	**1192**	600r. multicoloured	90	75

1193 Goldfish (*Carassius auratus*)

2004. New Year. Ornamental Fish. Multicoloured.
3145	100r. Type **1193**		15	10
3146	200r. *Carrasius auratus* with grey tail		30	25
3147	300r. Guppy (*Poecilia reticulate*)		45	40
3148	400r. Siamese fighting fish (*Betta splendens*)		60	55
3149	500r. *Carassius auratus* large facing left		75	70
3150	600r. *Carassius auratus* with raised fin		90	85

1194 Clown Triggerfish (*Balistoides conspicillum*)

2004. Saltwater Fish. Sheet 137×166 mm containing T **1194** and similar horiz designs. Multicoloured.
MS3151	250r. Type **1194**; 350r. *Acanthurus glaucopareius*; 450r. Lionfish (*Pteois volitans*); 550r. Sail-finned tang (*Zebrasoma veliferum*); 650r. Regal angelfish (*Pygoplites diacanthus*); 750r. Jigsaw triggerfish (*Pseudobalistes fuscus*)		4·50	4·50

1195 National Team Members

2004. Centenary of FIFA (Federation Internationale de Football Association).
3152	**1195**	600r. multicoloured	90	85

1196 Camera, Hand and Page

2004. Reporters Day.
3153	**1196**	650r. multicoloured	60	55

1197 Taekwondo

2004. Olympic Games, Athens. Multicoloured.
3154	650r. Type **1197**		60	45
3155	650r. Weightlifting		60	45
3156	650r. Wrestling		60	45
3157	650r. Judo		60	45

1198 Kabir

2004. Iranian and Indian Poets. Multicoloured.
3158	600r. Type **1198** (Indian)		55	45
3159	600r. Khajeh Shamseddin Mohammad Hafez Shirazi (Hafez) (Iranian)		55	45

Stamps of the same design were issued by India.

1199 Memorial, Hamedan

2004. Avicina International Conference, Bu-Ali Sina University, Hamedan. Multicoloured.
3160	650r. Type **1199**		60	50
3161	650r. Abu Ali al-Husain ibn Abdallah ibn Sina (Avicina) (poet)		60	50

1200 Chacma Baboon (*Papio ursinus*)

2004. World Stamp Collecting Championship, Singapore. Sheet 138×101 mm containing T **1200** and similar horiz designs. Multicoloured.
MS3162 500r.×4, Type **1200**; Chimpanzee (*Pan troglodytes*); Two chimpanzees; Mandrill (*Mandrillus sphinx*)   3·75   3·75

1201 Tabby Shorthair

2004. Cats. Sheet 168×136 mm containing T **1201** and similar vert designs. Multicoloured.
MS3163 500r.×6, Type **1201**; Silver tabby longhair; Bi-colour longhair; Persian; Silver tabby shorthair; Tabby and white shorthair   5·25   5·25

1202 Volleyball Players

2004. Paralympics, Athens.
3164   **1202**   650r. multicoloured   60   55

1203 Airplanes and Missiles

2004. 24th Anniv of Iran–Iraq War.
3165   **1203**   650r. multicoloured   60   55

1204 Emblem

2004. 70th Anniv of Tehran University.
3166   **1204**   650r. multicoloured   60   55

1205 Mullah

2004. Multicoloured.
3167   **1205**   500r. Type **1205**   45   40
3168   500r. Man with moustache   45   40
3169   500r. Man facing right   45   40
3170   500r. Man facing left   45   40

1206 Damavand Mountain, Iran

2004. Mountains. Multicoloured.
3171   650r. Type **1206**   60   55
3172   650r. Bolivar Peak, Venezuela   60   55
Stamps of a similar design were issued by Venezuela.

1207 Hand

2004. Biennial International Islamic Poster Exhibition. Multicoloured.
3173   500r. Type **1207**   45   40
3174   500r. Bird on nest   45   40
3175   500r. Slingshot   45   40
3176   500r. Moon   45   40

1208 Tomb

2004. Imam Reza Commemoration. Designs showing parts of shrine. Multicoloured.
3177   500r. Type **1208**   45   40
3178   500r. Roof   45   40
3179   500r. Facade   45   40
3180   500r. Doorway   45   40

1209 Ali Daei

2005. Ali Daei (world all-time leading goal scorer in international matches).
3181   **1209**   650r. multicoloured   60   60

1210 Scene from *Where is the Friend's Home* (by Abbas Kiarostami)

2005. Film Museum, Iran. Scenes from Iranian films. Multicoloured.
3182   **1210**   500r. Type **1210**   45   45
3183   500r. "The Children of Heaven" (by Majid Majidi)   45   45
3184   500r. Museum building   45   45
3185   500r. "The Cow" (Dariush Mehrjui)   45   45

1211 Antonov-140

2005. Aircraft. Multicoloured.
3186   **1211**   850r. Type **1211**   75   75
3187   850r. Iran-140   75   75
Stamps of a similar design were issued by Ukraine.

1212 Persepolis

2005. World Expo 2005, Aichi, Japan. Sheet 127×99 mm containing T **1212** and similar horiz designs. Multicoloured.
MS3188 650r.×4, Type **1212**; Yazd ventilation wind towers; Desert architecture; Cyrus the Great's Cylinder (First World Charter of Human Rights)   2·30   2·30

1213 Operating Theatre and University Building

2005. 70th Anniv of Tehran University of Medical Sciences.
3189   **1213**   650r. multicoloured   60   60

1214 Officer and Crowd

2005. Police Week.
3190   **1214**   650r. multicoloured   60   60

1215 Rumi and Dervish Dancers

2005. 800th Birth Anniv (2007) of Mevlana Celaleddin (Rumi) (poet and philosopher).
3191   **1215**   650r. multicoloured   60   60
A stamp of a similar design was issued by Syria, Turkey and Afghanistan.

1216 La Granja de San Ildefonso Garden, Segovia

2005. Gardens. Multicoloured.
3192   650r. Type **1216**   60   60
3193   650r. Bagh-e-Shahzadeh, Kerman   60   60
Stamps of a similar design were issued by Spain.

No. 3194 and Type **1217** have been left for 'Wheat Self-Sufficiency', issued on 4 January 2006, not yet received.

1218 (image scaled to 36% of original size)

2006. Centenary of Constitution Revolution. Sheet 135×102 mm as T **1218**. Multicoloured.
MS3195 650r.×4 Type **1218**   6·50   6·50
The stamps and margins of MS3195 form a composite background design.

1219 16th-century Map of Persian Gulf

2006. History of Persian Gulf. Maps. Sheet 135×102 mm containing T **1219** and similar horiz designs. Multicoloured.
MS3196 650r.×4 Type **1219**; Persian Sea, 1966; Arab peninsula, 1952; 18th-century map of Persia by Scoteri Motthaei   6·50   6·50
The stamps of MS3196 form a composite background design.

1220 Trophy, Players and Emblem

2006. World Cup Football Championship, Germany.
3197   **1220**   650r. multicoloured   1·90   1·90

1221 Abbas Schafii

2006. Personalities. Multicoloured.
3198   650r. Type **1221**   1·70   1·70
3199   650r. Alameh Mohammad Reza Hakimi   1·70   1·70
3200   650r. Mohammad Hossein Gandji   1·70   1·70
3201   650r. Almeh Mohmmad Hassan Amoli   1·70   1·70

1222 Members Flags and Map

2006. ECO (Economic Cooperation Organization) Postal Authorities Conference, Ankara.
3202   **1222**   650r. multicoloured   1·90   1·90

1223 Parliamentary Association Emblem

2006. General Assembly of Association of Asian Parliaments. Sheet 135×102 mm containing T **1223** and similar horiz designs. Multicoloured.
MS3203 650r.×4 Type **1223**; Dove; Assembly building; Islamic Consultative Assembly emblem   6·75   6·75
The stamps of MS3203 form a composite background design.

1224 Flag and Flowers

2006. 27th Anniv of Basji.
3204   **1224**   650r. multicoloured   2·00   2·00

1225 Chehel Sotun Palace

670   Iran

2006. Isfahan. Sheet 135×102 mm containing T **1225** and similar horiz design. Multicoloured.
MS3205 650r.×4 Type **1225**; Imam
Mosque; Aliqapu Palace; Khajo
Bridge   6·50   6·50
The stamps and margins of **MS**3205 form a composite background design.

1226 Ahmad Kazemi

2007. First Death Anniv of Ahmad Kazemi (commander). Multicoloured.
3206   650r. Type **1226**   1·75   1·75
3207   650r. Ahmad Kazemi encircled
by other senior officers killed
in accident   1·75   1·75

1227 Emblems and Dove

2007. Nuclear Power.
3208   **1227**   650r. multicoloured   2·00   2·00

1228 Minarets and Dome

2007. Shrine of Lady Fatima Masuma (Fatima al-Masumeh), Qum.
3209   **1228**   650r. multicoloured   2·00   2·00

1229 Dancer

2007. New Year. Multicoloured.
3210   650r. Type **1229**   1·75   1·75
3211   650r. Symbols of New Year   1·75   1·75

1229a Emblem

2007. Communications and Public Relations Day.
3211a **1229a** 650r. multicoloured   1·75   1·75

1230 Persian Gulf

2007
3212   **1230**   300r. multicoloured   1·00   1·00

1231 Sick Children

2007. Tenth Anniv of Ratification of Chemical Weapons Convention (CWC).
3213   **1231**   650r. multicoloured   2·00   2·00

1232 Emblem

2007. Physics Olympiad, Isfahan.
3214   **1232**   650r. multicoloured   2·00   2·00

2007. As Type **1230**.
3214a 4400r. multicoloured   11·25   11·25

1233 K. K. Sarughy

2007. K. K. Sarughy Commemoration.
3215   **1233**   650r. multicoloured   2·00   2·00

1234 Engine

2007. Design and Production of First Iranian Engine.
3216   **1234**   650r. multicoloured   2·00   2·00

1235 Sayyid Musa al-Sadr

2007. Sayyid Musa al-Sadr (Imam Moussa Sadar) (politician and philosopher) Commemoration.
3218   **1235**   650r. multicoloured   2·00   2·00

2007. As Type **1230**.
3219   200r. multicoloured   1·00   1·00

1236 Siberian Cranes

2007. Siberian Crane (*Grus leucogranus*). Multicoloured.
3220   650r. Type **1236**   1·70   1·70
3221   650r. Two cranes (different)   1·70   1·70
3222   650r. Cranes on land   1·70   1·70
3223   650r. Crane preparing to fly   1·70   1·70

1237 Archway

2007. Great Messenger Year (PBUH). Sheet 137×101 mm containing T **1237** and similar horiz designs. Multicoloured.
MS3224 650r.×4, Type **1237**; Script;
Coliseum, Rome; Pyramids   6·50   6·50

1238 Posting Letter

2007. World Post Day.
3225   **1238**   650r. multicoloured   2·00   2·00

2007. As Type **1230**.
3225a 2100r. multicoloured   5·25   5·25

1239 Jamkaran Mosque, Qum

2007
3226   **1239**   650r. multicoloured   2·00   2·00

2007. As Type **1230**.
3226a 650r. multicoloured   2·00   2·00

1240 Swans flying

2007. Anniversary of Prisoners of War Return. Sheet 138×99 mm containing T **1240** and similar horiz designs. Multicoloured.
MS3227 650r.×4, Type **1240**; Cleric;
Returnees waving from bus; Motor-
cyclists and bus carrying returnees 6·50   6·50

2008. As Type **1230**.
3228   5500r. multicoloured   14·00   14·00

2008. As Type **1230**.
3229   2000r. multicoloured   3·00   3·00

2008. As Type **1230**.
3230   1000r. multicoloured   1·50   1·50

1241 Navvab Safavi

2008. Mojtaba Mir-Lowhi (Navvab Safavi) (founder of Fadayan-e Islam (Iranian Islamic fundamentalist society)) Commemoration.
3231   **1241**   650r. multicoloured   2·00   2·00

1242 Falsafi

2008. Birth Centenary of Mohammad Taqi Falsafi (Falsafi) (preacher).
3232   **1242**   650r. multicoloured   2·00   2·00

1243 Fibre Optic Cable, Satellite and Computer Language (0,1)

2008. Information Technology, Development Infrastructure.
3233   **1243**   650r. multicoloured   2·00   2·00

1244 Mevlana

2008. 800th Birth Anniv of Mawlana Jalal-ad-Din Muhammad Rumi (Mevlana or Rumi) (philosopher and writer).
3234   **1244**   650r. multicoloured   2·00   2·00
No. 3235 and Type **1245** are vacant.

1246 Emad Moghnie

2008
3236   **1246**   650r. multicoloured   2·00   2·00

1247 Symbols of New Year

2008. New Year.
3237   **1247**   650r. multicolured   2·00   2·00

1248 Shrine Complex (Illustration reduced. Actual size 63×24 mm)

2008. H. H. Abdulazim's Holy Shrine (hadith–teller (oral tradition)).
3238   **1248**   650r. multicoloured   2·00   2·00

1249 Fish in Water

2008. Children and Youth Art Festival. Water.
3239   **1249**   650r. multicoloured   2·00   2·00

1250 City and Mountains

2008. Tenth Anniv of Islamic City Councils.
3240   **1250**   650r. multicoloured   2·00   2·00

1250a Sheikh Hashem Ghazvini

2008. Sheikh Hashem Ghazvini Commemoration.
3240a **1250a** 650r. multicoloured   2·00   2·00

1251 Emblem

2008. 1100th Death Anniv of Thiqat al-Islam Kulayni.
3241 **1251** 650r. multicoloured   2·00   2·00

1251a La Kasbah des Oudayas, Morocco and Script

2008. Iran—Morocco Issue. Multicoloured.
3241a **1251a** 650r. Type **1251a**   2·00   2·00
3241b 650r. Falak Ol Aflak Castle, Iran   2·00   2·00
Stamps of a similar design were issued by Morocco.

2008. As Type **1230**.
3242 500r. multicoloured   1·50   1·50

1252 Engraved Copper Cup (Mansour Hafezparast)

2008. World Handicraft Day. Multicoloured.
3243 650r. Type **1252**   2·00   2·00
3244 650r. Mina Vase (Hossein Bagher Esmaili)   2·00   2·00

1253 Javid-al-Asar Motevasselian

2008
3245 **1253** 650r. multicoloured   2·00   2·00

1254 Khan-Tengri Peak, Kyrgyzstan

2008. Mountains. Multicoloured.
3246 650r. Type **1254**   2·00   2·00
3247 650r. Sabalan Peak, Iran   2·00   2·00
Stamps of a similar design were issued by Kyrgyzstan.

1255 17th-century Gold Medallion, Iran

2008. Jewellery. Multicoloured.
3248 650r. Type **1255**   2·00   2·00
3249 650r. 4th/ 5th-century gold buckle, Kazakhstan   2·00   2·00
Stamps of a similar design were issued by Kazakhstan.

2008. As Type **1230**.
3250 100r. multicoloured   1·00   1·00

2008. As Type **1230**.
3251 400r. multicoloured   1·30   1·30

1255a Symbols of Protest

2008. International Day of Al-Quds (Ghods).
3251a **1255a** 650r. multicoloured   2·00   2·00

1256 Symbols of Post

2008. 20th Anniv of Iran Post Company.
3252 **1256** 1200r. multicoloured   3·75   3·75

1257 Emblem

2008. 80th Anniv of Melli Iran Bank.
3253 **1257** 650r. multicoloured   2·00   2·00

2008. As Type **1230**.
3254 250r. multicoloured   2·00   2·00

1257a Emblem

2008. National Day of Exports.
3254a **1257a** 650r. multicoloured   6·00   6·00

1258 M. R. Pourkian

2008. Martyrs.
3255 **1258** 650r. multicoloured   2·00   2·00

1259 Emblem

2008. National Day of Consumers Rights.
3256 **1259** 650r. multicoloured   2·00   2·00

1260 Emblem

2008. 28th Anniv of Security Services.
3257 **1260** 650r. multicoloured   2·00   2·00

1260a Gijack, Badahshon

2008. Musical Instruments. Multicoloured.
3257a 650r. Type **1260a**   6·00   6·00
3257b 650r. Dotar (Inscr 'Dotaar'), Khorasan   6·00   6·00
Stamps of a similar design were issued by Tadjikistan.

1261 Ruins

2008. Zabol.
3258 **1261** 650r. multicoloured   2·00   2·00

1262 Sheikh Kharaghani

2009. Sheikh Abul Hasan Kharaghani Commemoration.
3259 **1262** 650r. multicoloured   2·00   2·00

1263 Crying Woman, Corpse and Flames

2009. Gaza.
3260 **1263** 1200r. multicoloured   3·75   3·75

1264 Ayatollah Khomeini

2009. 30th Anniv of Revolution.
3261 **1264** 650r. multicoloured   2·00   2·00

2009. As Type **1230**
3262 3000r. As Type **1230**   8·00   8·00

1265 Abbas Karimi, Reza Cheragi and Mohammed Hemat

2009. Martyrs.
3263 **1265** 650r. multicoloured   2·00   2·00

1266 Launch

2008. First Iranian Satellite. Multicoloured.
3264 1300r. Type **1266**   4·00   4·00
3265 1300r. In orbit   4·00   4·00

1267 Emblem growing from Map

2009. Tenth Economic Co-operation Organization Conference, Tehran.
3266 **1267** 1300r. multicoloured   4·00   4·00

1268 Symbols of New Year

2009. New Year.
3267 **1268** 1300r. multicoloured   4·00   4·00

1269 Hand holding Apple and Dove

2009. Nurses' Day.
3268 **1269** 1300r. multicoloured   4·00   4·00

1270 Mother and Child

2009. Mothers' Day.
3269 **1270** 1100r. multicoloured   3·50   3·50

1270a (image scaled to 38% of original size)

2009. Trenchless Trench Makers. Sheet 134×103 mm as T **1270a**
MS3271a 650r.×4, Type **1270a**   7·50   7·50

1271 *Chaetodontoplus seplentrionalis*

2009. Fish. As T **1271**
3270   **1271**   1000r. multicoloured   3·50   3·50

1272 *Haliaeetus albicilla* (white-tailed eagle)

2009. Raptors. Multicoloured.
3271   2000r. Type **1272**   5·00   5·00
3272   2000r. *Pandion haliaetus* (osprey)   5·00   5·00
   Nos. 3271/2 were printed, se-tenant, each pair forming a composite design.
   Stamps of a similar design were issued by Portugal.

1273 *Porphyrio porphyrio* (purple swamphen), Flags and *Cyanolimnas cervai* (Zapata rail) (image scaled to 30% of original size)

2009. Convention on Wetlands of International Importance (Ramsar Convention).
3273   **1273**   1500r. multicoloured   2·75   2·75
   A stamp of a similar design was issued by Cuba.

1274 *Eretmochelys imbricata*

2009. Conservation of Marine Turtles. Sheet 139×101 containing T **1274** and similar horiz designs. Multicoloured.
MS3274 650r. Type **1274**; 1000r. *Eretmochelys imbricata* (different); 1500r. *Chelonia mydas*; 1850r. *Chelonia mydas* (different)   8·25   8·25
   The stamps and margins of No. **MS**3274 form a composite design.

2009. Fish. As T **1271**. Multicoloured.
3275   7500r. *Premnas biaculeatus*   15·00   15·00

2009. Fish. As T **1271**. Multicoloured.
3276   200r. *Holacanthus ciliaris*   1·00   1·00

1275 Emblem

2009. Book Week.
3277   **1275**   1200r. bright bottle green, deep rose-red and black   3·75   3·75

1276 Document

2009. Rob'e Rashidi Endowment Document.
3278   **1276**   1200r. multicoloured   3·75   3·75

1276b Figures

2009. Ghadir Khom Festival
3278a   **1276b**   1200r. multicoloured   3·50   3·50

2009. Fish. As T **1271**. Multicoloured.
3279   6400r. *Paracanthurus hepatus*   8·75   8·75

1276a Ayatollah Mohammad Mofateh

2009. 30th Death Anniv of Ayatollah Mohammad Mofateh (philosopher)
3279a   **1276a**   1200r. multicoloured   3·75   3·75

1277 Emblem

2009. 60th Anniv of Universal Declaration of Human Rights.
3280   **1277**   1200r. multicoloured   3·75   3·75

2009. Fish. As T **1271**. Multicoloured.
3281   500r. *Centropyge bicolor*   1·70   1·70

1278 Soltanieh Dome, Western Zanjan Province, Iran

2009. Cultural Heritage. Multicoloured
3282   2000r. Type **1278**   3·00   3·00
3283   2000r. Al-Markaz Mosque, Makassar City, Indonesia   3·00   3·00
   Stamps of a similar design were issued by Indonesia.

1279 Post Van

2010. World Post Day. Multicoloured.
3284   1200r. Type **1279**   3·75   3·75
3285   1200r. Children encircling globe and envelopes as kites   3·75   3·75
   Nos. 3284/5 were printed, se-tenant, each pair forming a composite design.

1280 Marveh Sherbini

2010. Martyr.
3286   **1280**   1300r. multicoloured   4·25   4·25

1281 Emblem

2010. Rural Information and Communications Technology Day
3287   **1281**   1000r. multicoloured   1·50   1·50

1282 Emblem

2010. Islamic Human Rights and Human Dignity Day
3288   **1282**   1200r. multicoloured   4·25   4·25

1282a Space Technology Day

2010. Space Technology Day. Multicoloured.
3288a   1200r. Type **1282a**   3·75   3·75
3288b   1200r. Kavoshgar 2 rocket   3·75   3·75
3288c   1400r. Tolou satellite   4·00   4·00
3288d   1600r. Mesbah satellite   4·25   4·25
3288e   1800r. Ground station   4·50   4·50

2010. Fish
3289   3100r. *Chaetodon semilarvatus*   7·50   7·50
   Horiz design as Type **1271**

1282b Maragheh Observatory

2010. International Year of Astronomy (2009). Multicoloured.
2389a   1000r. Type **1282b**   3·50   3·50
3289a   1200r. Diagram from *Al-Tafhim li Awa'il Sana'at al-Tanjim* (by Iranian scientist, Abu-Rayhan al-Biruni)   3·75   3·75
3289c   1300r. Armillary sphere   3·75   3·75
3289d   1500r. Taqi al Din and astronomers (16th-century painting)   4·25   4·25

1282d Emblem

2010. Global Celebration of Nowruz
3289f   **1282d**   2000r. multicoloured   5·75   5·75

1283 Protestors

2010. 22 Khordad (12 June 2011). Anniversary of Disputed Elections
3290   **1283**   1300r. multicoloured   3·25   3·25

2010. Fish
3291   250r. *Euxiphipops xanthometopon* (inscr 'xanthometapon')   1·50   1·50
   Horiz design as Type **1271**

2010. Fish
3292   300r. *Pomacanthus maculosus*   1·70   1·70
   Horiz design as Type **1271**

1284 Molla Sadra

2010. Sadr ad-Din Muhammad Shirizi (Molla Sadra) (Shia philosopher, theologian and leader of 17th-century cultural renaissance) Commemoration

2010. Fish
3294   5000r. *Pomacanthus navarchus* (inscr 'Pomaconthus')   4·50   4·50
   Horiz design as Type **1271**

2010. Fish
3295   4000r. *Pomacanthus chrysurus*   5·50   5·50
   Horiz design as Type **1271**

1285 Khajah Abdullah Ansari (inscr 'Khaje Abdullah Ansari')

2010. Abu Ismaïl Abdullah ibn Abi-Mansour Mohammad (Khajah Abdullah Ansari) (Sufi writer and philosopher) Commemoration
3296   **1285**   200r. multicoloured   2·75   2·75

1285a Minar-e-Pakistan (minaret), Iqbal Park, Lahore

2010. Architecture. Multicoloured.
3296a   2000r. Type **1285a**   5·50   5·50
3296b   2000r. Milad Tower, Tehran   5·50   5·50

2010. Fish
3297   2000r. *Chaetodon larvatus*   2·75   2·75
   Horiz design as Type **1271**

1285b Sedjil Missile

2010. Defence Industry Day. Multicoloured.
3297a   1000r. Type **1285b**; 1500r. Saegheh Aircraft; 2000r. Mersad Radar Systems; 2500r. Ghadir Submarine   19·00   10·00

1286 Jamaran (destroyer)
and Ayatollah Khamenei

2010. Ships
3298	**1286**	2000r. multicoloured	2·75	2·75

2010. Fish
3299		100r. *Chaetodon mesoleucos*	1·00	1·00

Horiz design as Type **1271**

1286a Soldier

2010. Martyrs of Defence
3299a	**1286a**	2000r. multicoloured	5·75	5·75

1286b Aircraft

2010. World Post Day. Multicoloured.
MS3299b 1000r. Type **1286b**; 1100r.
Coins (Financial Post); 1300r. Mail
lorry (Pishtaz Post); 1400r.
Shopping trolley full of presents and @;1500r.
'username@post.ir'; 1700r. Mail man
driving motor scooter; 2000r. UPU
emblem   25·00   25·00

1287 Shah e Cheragh Mosque

2010. Shah e Cheragh Mausoleum and Mosque, Shiraz. Multicoloured.
3300		1200r. Type **1287**	3·50	3·50
3301		1300r. Shah e Cheragh shrine	3·50	3·50

1288 Compass, Tag
and Emblem

2010. Congress of 1400 Martyred Engineers
3302	**1288**	2000r. multicoloured	3·75	2·75

1288a Embroidery, Jazygia,
Hungary

2010. Textiles. Multicoloured.
3302a		2000r. Type **1288a**	5·50	5·50
3302b		2000r. Termeh hand woven cloth, Yazd, Iran	5·50	5·50

1289 Book and
Flowers

2010. Book Week
3303	**1289**	2000r. multicoloured	2·75	2·75

1290 Haj Sheikh
Abbas Qomi

2010. 70th Death Anniv of Haj Sheikh Abbas Qomi (Sheikh Abbass Qumi) (scholar and compiler of Mafatih-al-Janan)
3304	**1290**	2000r. multicoloured	2·75	2·75

2010. Fish
3305		400r. *Chaetodon rafflesi*	1·50	1·50

Horiz design as Type **1271**.

1291 Anniversary
Emblem

2011. 73rd Anniv of Maskan Bank
3306	**1291**	2000r. multicoloured	5·75	5·75

1292 Flag, Clasped
Hands, Map and @

2010. Electronic Communication of People and Government
3307	**1292**	2000r multicoloured	5·75	5·75

1293 Ayatollah
Khomeini

2011. 32nd Anniv of Islamic Revolution. Multicoloured.
3308		1000r. Type **1293**	1·50	1·50
3309		1000r. Candle, Khomeini and leaves	1·50	1·50
3310		1000r. Flowers, three candles and Khomeini	1·50	1·50
3311		1000r. Multicoloured birds and Khomeini facing left	1·50	1·50

2011. Fish
3312		350r. *Pomacanthus annularis*	1·50	1·50

Horiz design as Type **1271**.

1293a Cherry Tree

2011. Nature Day. Multicoloured.
3312a		1100r. Type **1293a**	3·00	3·00

3312b	1200r. Birch and willow trees in parkland		3·25	3·25
3312c	1300r. Stream in wooded valley		3·50	3·50
3312d	1400r. Snow covered trees		4·25	4·25

1293b Flowers and Wheat

2011. New Year. Multicoloured.
MS3312e 1250r.×4, Type **1293b**; Candle and mirror; Goldfish bowl and apples; Koran on stand   14·00   14·00

1294 Ayatollah
Taleghani

2011. Birth Centenary of Ayatollah Taleghani
3313	**1294**	2500r. multicoloured	7·75	7·75

1295 Bowl of Decorated Eggs in
Grass (meadow)

2011. New Year 1390. Nowruz. Multicoloured.
MS3314 1000r. Bowl of Coins; 1100r.
Type **1295**; 1300r. Bowl of sumac;
1400r. Bowl of apples; 1500r. Bowl of
Garlic; 1700r. Bowl of oleaster; 2000r.
Hyancinth and book   14·00   14·00

1296 Open Book and Doves

2011. Convergence of Monotheistic Religions
3315	**1296**	2000r. multicoloured	7·75	7·75

2011. Fish
3316		3000r. *Chaetodon auriga*	5·75	5·75

Horiz design as Type **1271**.

1297 Filigree Vase

2011. World Craft Day. Multicoloured.
3317		2000r. Type **1297**	5·50	5·50
3318		2000r. Engraved cup with lid	5·50	5·50

1298 Ayatollah
Mohammad Fazel
Lankarani

2011. Fourth Death Anniv of Ayatollah Mohammad Fazel Lankarani
3320	**1298**	2000r. multicoloured	5·00	5·00

No. 3321 is now left for Bridges. Javadieh Bridge, issued on 5 July 2011, not yet received.

No. 3322 is now left for Bridges. Khajoo Bridge, issued on 20 July 2011, not yet received.

1300 Two Green Pheasants (image scaled to 55% of original size)

2011. PhilaNippon '11 International Stamp Exhibition. Sheet 132×74 mm
MS3323 **1300** 5000r. multicoloured   12·00   12·00

Nos. 3324/5 are for stamps, not yet received.

1301 Early and Modern
Treatment of Cattle

2011. National Veterinary Day
3326	**1301**	2200r. multicoloured	6·00	6·00

1301a
Shams-i-Tabrizi

2011. Shams-i-Tabrizi (Persian Muslim, who is credited as spiritual instructor of Mewlānā Jalāl ad-Dīn (Rumi)) Commemoration
3327	**1301a**	2200r. multicoloured	6·00	6·00

No. 3328 is for a stamp not yet received.

1302 Emblem

2011. Population and Housing Census, 2011
3329	**1302**	2200r. multicoloured	6·00	6·00

1296a Veresk Bridge

2011. Bridges
3316a	**1296a**	20000r. multicoloured	20·00	19·00

2011. Bridges
3319		10000r. Jahanara Bridge	17·00	17·00

2011. Bridges
3321		20700r. Javadieh Bridge	21·00	21·00

2011. Bridges
3346		14800r. Khajoo Bridge	18·00	18·00

1300a Karimkhani Citadel,
Shiraz (prospective UNESCO
World Heritage Site)

2011. Architecture. Multicoloured.
MS3324 2200r.×2, Type **1300a**; Kryzhachok (Belarus)   10·00   10·00

1300b Team Members

2011. Iran 16th Asian Senior Men's Volleyball Champions. Sheet 100×72 mm
MS3325 **1300b** 3400r. multicoloured   6·50   6·50

1301b Parcel

2011. World Post Day
3328   **1301b** 2000r. multicoloured   5·00   5·00

1303 Open Book

2011. Book Week
3330   **1303** 2200r. multicoloured   6·00   6·00

1304 Moving from Dark to Light (image scaled to 55% of original size)

2011. Directing to Good Revival Week. Sheet 133×73 mm
MS3331 **1304** 2200r. multicoloured   6·50

1305 Emblem

2011. Islamic Awakening
3332   **1305** 2200r. multicoloured   6·00   6·00

1306 Long-eared Owl (*Asio otus*)

2011. Owls. Multicoloured.
3333   600r. Type **1306**   1·60   1·60
3334   1100r. Spotted Owlet (*Athene brama*)   3·50   3·50
3335   1600r. Pallid Scops Owl (*Otus brucei*)   4·75   4·75
3336   2200r. Brown Fish Owl (*Ketupa zeylonensis*)   6·00   6·00
MS3337 133×97 mm. Nos. 3333/6   19·00   19·00

1307 Tomb of Sheikh Safi-e-din Ardebili

2012. Culture and Civilization
3338   **1307** 2200r. multicoloured   6·00   6·00

1308 Fires and Falling Statue

2012. 33rd Anniv of Islamic Revolution. Multicoloured.
MS3339 2200r.×3, Type **1308**; Ayatollah Khomeini   15·00

1309 Gold Fish, Fan and Writing Materials

2012. New Year 1391. Nowruz. Multicoloured.
3340   2200r. Type **1309**   6·00   6·00
3341   2200r. Flowers, fruit and lamp   6·00   6·00
MS3342 13372 mm. Nos. 3340/4   11·00   11·00

1310 Ayatollah Khomeini

2012. Iran Day
3343   **1310** 2200r. multicoloured   6·00   6·00

1311 Emblem

2012. International Book Fair, Tehran
3344   **1311** 2200r. multicoloured   6·00   6·00

1312 Ayatollah Bahjat

2012. Grand Ayatollah Mohammad Taqi Bahjat Foumani (Ayatollah Bahjat) Commemoration
3345   **1312** 2200r. multicoloured   6·00   6·00

2012. Bridges
3346   9000r. Mardogh Bridge   16·00   16·00

1313 Rugs

2012. World Craft Day. Multicoloured.
MS3347 2000r.×4, Type **1313**; Drugget; Gabe; Jajim   16·00   16·00

1314 Script, Bird and Koran

2012. Ramadan
3348   **1314** 2200r. multicoloured   6·00   6·00

1315 Globe and Dove

2012. Non-Aligned Movement Summit, Tehran
3349   **1315** 2200r. multicoloured   6·00   6·00

2012. Bridges
3350   15700r. Bahrami Bridge   18·50   18·50

1316 Mohammad Hussein Falmideh

2012. Dedication and Sacrifice. Multicoloured.
MS3351 2200r.×2, Type **1316**; Railway track and figure holding torch (Riz Ali Khajavi (farmer who prevented rail crash))   11·00   11·00

1317 Bunker and Soldier writing Letter

2012. World Post Day. Sheet 99×66 mm
MS3352 **1317** 3400r. multicoloured   7·00   7·00

2012. Bridges
3353   200r. Broken Bridge   1·00   1·00

2012. Bridges
3354   8000r. Qishlaq Bridge   15·50   15·50

1318 Tiles, Book and Script

2012. Book Week
3355   **1318** 2200r. multicoloured   6·00   6·00

2012. Bridges
3356   1000r. Khosro Abad Bridge   2·00   2·00

2013. Bridges
3357   5000r. Kalantari Bridge   11·50   11·50

2013. Bridges
3358   3000r. Kantoon Bridge   6·25   6·25

2013. Bridges
3359   500r. Zamankhan Bridge   1·50   1·50

2013. Bridges
3360   100r. Inscr 'Earthen Bridge'   60   60

1319 Avicenna and Canon

2013. Culture and Civilization. Millenary of Avicenna's *Canon Of Medicine*
3361   **1319** 3000r. multicoloured   6·25   6·25

2013. Bridges
3362   800r. Yaqubie Bridge   1·90   1·90

2013. Bridges
3363   4000r. Ghotoor Bridge   9·00   9·00

2013. Bridges
3364   20000r. Tinoj Bridge   20·00   19·00

NEWSPAPER POSTAGE DUE STAMPS

1909. Optd **Imprimes** in English and Persian.
N319   **38**   2ch. grey on blue   26·00   5·25

OFFICIAL STAMPS

1902. Stamp of 1898 surch **Service** and value in English and Persian.
O224   **21**   5c. on 1k. red   21·00   21·00
O225   **21**   10c. on 1k. red   21·00   21·00
O226   **21**   12c. on 1k. red   25·00   25·00

1903. Stamps of 1903 optd **Service**.
O259   **38**   1c. lilac   1·60   25
O260   **38**   2c. grey   1·60   25
O261   **38**   3c. green   1·60   25
O262   **38**   5c. red   1·60   25
O263   **38**   10c. brown   3·25   25
O264   **38**   12c. blue   5·00   25
O265   **39**   1k. purple   5·00   80
O266   **39**   2k. blue   5·00   1·30
O267   **39**   5k. brown   12·50   1·60
O268   **39**   10k. red   12·50   2·10
O269   **39**   20k. orange   41·00   5·00
O270   **39**   30k. green   49·00   12·50
O271   **39**   50k. green   £160   65·00

1905. Nos. 275/6 and 280/1 optd **Service**.
O283   2t. on 50k. green (275)   £100   41·00
O285   2t. on 50k. green (280)   £100   41·00
O284   3t. on 50k. green (276)   £100   41·00
O286   3t. on 50k. green (281)   £100   41·00

(O57)

1911. Stamps of 1909 optd **Service** and with Type **O57**.
O353   **56**   1c. purple and orange   5·75   3·25
O354   **56**   2c. purple and violet   5·75   3·25
O355   **56**   3c. purple and green   5·75   3·25
O356   **56**   6c. purple and red   5·75   3·25
O357   **56**   9c. purple and grey   9·75   6·50
O358   **56**   10c. purple and mauve   9·75   6·50
O359   **56**   1k. brown, violet & silver   2·50   21·00
O360   **56**   2k. brown, green & silver   6·50   49·00

1915. Coronation stamps of 1915 optd **SERVICE** in English and Persian.
O460   **66**   1c. blue and red   1·80   1·80
O461   **66**   2c. red and blue   1·80   1·80
O462   **66**   3c. green   1·80   1·80
O463   **66**   5c. red   1·80   1·80
O464   **66**   6c. red and green   1·80   1·80
O465   **66**   9c. violet and brown   1·80   1·80
O466   **66**   10c. brown and green   1·80   1·80
O467   **66**   12c. blue   2·10   2·10
O468   **66**   24c. chocolate and brown   3·00   3·00
O469   **67**   1k. black, brown & silver   5·00   5·00
O470   **67**   2k. red, blue and silver   5·25   5·25
O471   **-**   3k. sepia, lilac and silver   5·25   5·25
O472   **67**   5k. grey, sepia and silver   5·25   5·25
O473   **-**   1t. black, violet and gold   7·50   7·50
O474   **-**   2t. brown, green and gold   7·50   7·50
O475   **-**   3t. red, crimson and gold   9·75   9·75
O476   **-**   5t. grey, blue and gold   10·50   10·50

O120

1941
O836   **O120**   5d. violet   3·00   25
O837   **O120**   10d. mauve   3·00   25
O838   **O120**   25d. red   3·00   25
O839   **O120**   50d. black   3·00   25
O840   **O120**   75d. red   4·50   45
O841   **O120**   1r. green   6·00   45
O842   **O120**   1r.50 blue   7·50   1·10
O843   **O120**   2r. blue   9·00   1·10
O844   **O120**   3r. purple   11·50   1·10
O845   **O120**   5r. green   23·00   1·50
O846   **O120**   10r. blue and brown   £225   3·50
O847   **O120**   20r. mauve and blue   £300   11·50
O848   **O120**   30r. green and violet   £375   90·00
O849   **O120**   50r. brown and blue   £750   £150
The rial values are larger (23×30 mm).

O489 Red Lion and Sun Emblem

1974
O1829   **O489**   5d. violet and mauve   25   25
O1830   **O489**   10d. mauve and blue   25   25
O1831   **O489**   50d. orange & green   25   25
O1832   **O489**   1r. blue and gold   30   25
O2046   **O489**   1r. black and gold   25   25
O1833   **O489**   2r. green and orange   55   25
O2047   **O489**   2r. brown and grey   25   25
O2048   **O489**   3r. blue and orange   30   25
O2049   **O489**   5r. green and pink   40   25
O1834   **O489**   6r. green and yellow   55   25
O2050   **O489**   6r. black and blue   55   40
O1835   **O489**   8r. blue and yellow   70   25
O2051   **O489**   8r. red and green   55   40
O1836   **O489**   10r. blue and mauve   3·00   25

No.	Type	Description		
O2052	O489	10r. turquoise & grn	55	25
O1837	O489	11r. purple and blue	1·40	25
O2053	O489	11r. blue and yellow	1·10	45
O1838	O489	14r. red and blue	1·40	60
O2054	O489	14r. green and grey	1·10	45
O2055	O489	15r. red and mauve	2·30	90
O1839	O489	20r. blue and orange	2·40	55
O2056	O489	20r. purple and yellow	2·30	45
O2057	O489	30r. brown & orange	2·75	1·10
O1840	O489	50r. brown and green	6·50	1·70
O2058	O489	50r. black and gold	6·00	1·10

The 6r. to 50r. are larger, 23×37 mm.

PARCEL POST STAMPS

1915. Coronation stamps of 1915 optd **COLIS POSTAUX** in English and Persian.

No.	Type	Description		
P443	66	1c. blue and red	2·10	2·10
P444	66	2c. red and blue	2·10	2·10
P445	66	3c. green	2·10	2·10
P446	66	5c. red	2·10	2·10
P447	66	6c. red and green	2·10	2·10
P448	66	9c. violet and brown	2·10	2·10
P449	66	10c. brown and green	2·10	2·10
P450	66	12c. red	2·10	2·10
P451	66	24c. chocolate and brown	3·00	3·00
P452	67	1k. black, brown & silver	5·00	5·00
P453	67	2k. red, blue and silver	5·00	5·00
P454	67	3k. sepia, lilac and silver	5·00	5·00
P455	67	5k. grey, sepia and silver	5·25	5·25
P456	-	1t. black, violet and gold	7·50	7·50
P457	-	2t. brown, green and gold	7·50	7·50
P458	-	3t. red, crimson and gold	9·75	9·75
P459	-	5t. grey, blue and gold	10·50	10·50

P192

1958

No.	Type	Description		
P1151	P192	50d. drab	45	25
P1152	P192	1r. red	60	25
P1153	P192	2r. blue	60	25
P1154	P192	3r. myrtle	60	25
P1478	P192	5r. violet	3·75	25
P1479	P192	10r. brown	3·75	25
P1480	P192	20r. orange	6·00	45
P1481	P192	30r. mauve	7·50	25
P1482	P192	50r. lake	9·00	1·20
P1483	P192	100r. yellow	30·00	2·30
P1484	P192	200r. green	45·00	5·25

The word "IRAN" with a black frame is printed in reverse on the back of the above stamps and is intended to show through the stamps when attached to parcels.

POSTAL TAX STAMPS

1950. Hospitals Fund.

No.	Type	Description		
T1139	T142a	50d. red and green	3·00	75
T1396	T142a	2r. red and lilac	1·90	55

T142a Red Lion and Sun Emblem (8 lines to each ray)

1976. As T 142a but with five lines to each ray.

No.	Description		
T2007	50d. red and green	1·90	25
T2008	2r. red and blue	1·90	1·90

[Pt 1., Pt. 19]

IRAQ

A country W. of Persia, formerly under Turkish dominion, then under British mandate after the 1914–18 War. An independent kingdom since 1932 until 14 July 1958, when the king was assassinated and a republic proclaimed.

1917. 16 annas = 1 rupee.
1931. 1000 fils = 1 dinar.

1918. Stamps of Turkey (Pictorial issue, Nos. 501/514) surch **IRAQ IN BRITISH OCCUPATION** and value in Indian currency.

No.	Description		
1	¼a. on 5pa. purple	50	1·00
2	½a. on 10pa. green	70	20
3	1a. on 20pa. red	50	10
17	1½a. on 5pa. purple	4·00	1·25
5	2½a. on 1pi. blue	1·25	1·40
6	3a. on 1½pi. grey and red	1·50	25
7	4a. on 1¾pi. brown and grey	1·50	25
8	6a. on 2pi. black and green	2·00	1·75
9	8a. on 2½pi. green and orange	3·50	2·00
10	12a. on 5pi. lilac	2·00	6·00

No.	Description		
11	1r. on 10pi. brown	2·50	1·40
12	2r. on 25pi. green	10·00	3·00
13	5r. on 50pi. red	28·00	30·00
14	10r. on 100pi. blue	£100	17·00

2 Sunni Mosque, Muadhdham
4 Winged Cherub

3 Gufas on the Tigris

1923

No.	Type	Description		
41	2	½a. green	3·00	10
42	-	1a. brown	6·00	10
43	4	1½a. red	2·25	10
44	-	2a. buff	2·75	15
45	-	3a. blue	4·50	15
46	-	4a. violet	5·00	30
47	-	6a. blue	2·00	30
48	-	8a. bistre	4·50	30
49	3	1r. brown and green	27·00	1·50
50	2	2r. black	24·00	8·00
51	2	2r. bistre	80·00	3·25
52	-	5r. orange	50·00	13·00
53	-	10r. red	60·00	21·00

DESIGNS—30×24 mm: 1a. Gufas on the Tigris; 2a. Bull from Babylonian wall-sculpture; 6a., 10r. Shiah Mosque, Kadhimain. 34×24 mm: 3a. Arch of Ctesiphon. 24×30 mm: 4, 8a., 5r. Tribal Standard, Dulaim Camel Corps.

10 King Faisal I

1927

No.	Type	Description		
78	10	1r. brown	15·00	1·00

11 King Faisal I
12

1931

No.	Type	Description		
80	11	½a. green	2·75	30
81	11	1a. brown	2·25	30
82	11	1½a. red	2·75	50
83	11	2a. orange	2·25	10
84	11	3a. blue	2·25	20
85	11	4a. purple	2·50	3·75
86	11	6a. blue	2·50	80
87	11	8a. green	2·50	3·75
88	12	1r. brown	45·00	3·75
89	12	2r. brown	15·00	8·50
90	12	5r. orange	45·00	55·00
91	12	10r. red	£130	£160
92	10	25r. violet	£1400	£1700

1932. Nos. 80/92 and 46 surch in "Fils" or "Dinar".

No.	Type	Description		
106	11	2f. on ½a. green	50	10
107	11	3f. on ½a. green	50	10
108	11	4f. on 1a. brown	3·00	25
109	11	5f. on 1a. brown	75	10
110	11	8f. on 1½a. red	1·00	50
111	11	10f. on 2a. orange	50	10
112	11	15f. on 3a. blue	1·50	1·00
113	11	20f. on 4a. purple	2·75	2·75
114	-	25f. on 4a. violet (No. 46)	4·50	8·00
115	11	30f. on 6a. blue	6·00	1·00
116	11	40f. on 8a. green	3·50	7·00
117	12	75f. on 1r. brown	4·75	7·00
118	12	100f. on 2r. brown	8·00	4·00
119	12	200f. on 5r. orange	45·00	45·00
120	12	½d. on 10r. red	£110	£160
121	10	1d. on 25r. violet	£250	£375

1932. As Types 10/12 but value in FILS or DINAR.

No.	Type	Description		
138	11	2f. blue	50	20
139	11	3f. green	50	10
140	11	4f. purple	1·00	10
141	11	5f. green	50	10
142	11	8f. red	2·25	10
143	11	10f. yellow	1·75	10
144	11	15f. blue	1·75	10
145	11	20f. orange	3·75	50
146	11	25f. mauve	4·00	50
147	11	30f. olive	4·00	15

No.	Type	Description		
148	11	40f. violet	3·25	1·00
149	12	50f. brown	4·50	20
150	12	75f. red	11·00	4·25
151	12	100f. green	14·00	1·25
152	12	200f. red	25·00	3·75
153	10	½d. blue	80·00	60·00
154	10	1d. purple	£180	£150

16 King Ghazi
17

1934

No.	Type	Description		
172	16	1f. violet	50	35
173	16	2f. blue	35	35
174	16	3f. green	35	35
175	16	4f. purple	35	35
176	16	5f. green	35	35
177	16	8f. red	60	35
178	16	10f. yellow	70	35
179	16	15f. blue	70	35
180	16	20f. orange	70	35
181	16	25f. mauve	1·40	45
182	16	30f. green	1·10	35
183	16	40f. violet	1·20	35
184	16	50f. brown	3·00	35
185	17	75f. blue	2·40	45
186	17	100f. green	3·50	55
187	17	200f. red	6·00	1·20
188	-	½d. blue	16·00	12·50
189	-	1d. red	70·00	20·00

DESIGN—23×27½ mm: ½, 1d. Portrait as in Types 16/17 but different frame.

19 Mausoleum of Sitt Zubaidah
21 Lion of Babylon
22 Spiral Tower of Samarra

1941

No.	Type	Description		
208	19	1f. purple	35	35
209	19	2f. brown	35	35
210	-	3f. green	35	35
211	-	4f. violet	35	35
212	-	5f. red	35	35
213	21	8f. red	85	35
214	21	8f. yellow	35	35
215	21	10f. yellow	16·00	3·25
216	21	10f. red	85	35
217	21	15f. blue	1·40	35
218a	21	15f. black	1·40	55
219	21	20f. black	5·00	65
220	21	20f. brown	70	35
221	22	25f. purple	35	35
222	22	30f. orange	35	35
223b	22	40f. brown	1·40	55
224b	-	50f. blue	3·00	65
225a	-	75f. mauve	1·80	65
226	-	100f. olive	2·10	1·20
227	-	200f. orange	7·25	1·10
228	-	½d. blue	21·00	5·50
229a	-	1d. green	45·00	13·50

DESIGNS—HORIZ: 3f., 4f., 5f. King Faisal's Mausoleum (24×20 mm); ½d., 1d. Mosque of the Golden Dome, Samarra (24×21 mm). VERT: 50f., 75f. as Type 22, but larger (21×24 mm); 100f., 200f. Oil Wells (20×22 mm).

26 King Faisal II

1942

No.	Type	Description		
255	26	1f. brown and violet	40	40
256	26	2f. brown and blue	40	40
257	26	3f. brown and green	40	40
258	26	4f. sepia and brown	40	40
259	26	5f. brown and green	40	40
260	26	6f. brown and red	40	40
261	26	10f. brown and pink	40	40
262	26	12f. brown and green	40	40

27

1948

No.	Type	Description		
271	27	1f. blue	60	10
272	27	2f. brown	35	10
273	27	3f. green	35	10

No.	Type	Description		
274	27	3f. red	11·50	2·50
275	27	4f. lilac	35	10
276	27	5f. red	35	10
277	27	5f. green	12·00	5·00
278	27	6f. mauve	2·30	15
279	27	8f. brown	5·50	90
280	27	10f. red	50	10
281	27	12f. green	50	10
282	27	14f. green	3·00	35
283	27	15f. black	9·00	2·50
284	27	16f. red	2·75	1·00
285	27	20f. blue	95	15
286	27	25f. purple	1·10	15
287	27	28f. blue	3·00	65
288	27	30f. orange	1·10	15
289	27	40f. brown	2·75	90
290	27	50f. blue	9·00	1·70
291	27	60f. blue	1·80	90
292	27	75f. mauve	1·80	90
293	27	100f. green	7·75	1·70
294	27	200f. orange	6·00	1·70
295	27	½d. blue	16·00	5·50
296	27	1d. green	65·00	21·00

MS297 161×179 mm. Nos. 273, 280, 284 and 292/4. Perf or imperf £140 £275
The 50f. to 1d. are larger (22½×27½ mm).

29 Vickers Viking "Al Mahfoutha" over Basrah Aerodrome

1949. Air.

No.	Type	Description		
330	29	3f. green	35	35
331	-	4f. purple	35	35
332	-	5f. brown	35	35
333	29	10f. red	4·75	1·70
334	-	20f. blue	2·10	80
335	-	35f. orange	2·10	80
336	-	50f. green	3·25	1·30
337	-	100f. violet	8·50	2·75

MS338 235×165 mm. Nos. 330/7
DESIGNS—As Type 29: 4, 20f. "Al Mahfoutha" over Kut Barrage; 5, 35f. "Al Mahfoutha" over Faisal II Bridge. 31×22½ mm: 50, 100f. "Al Mahfoutha" over Dhiyala Railway Bridge.

31 King Faisal I and Equestrian Statue

1949. 75th Anniv of U.P.U.

No.	Type	Description		
339		20f. blue	3·00	2·00
340	31	40f. orange	4·25	2·00
341	-	50f. violet	10·00	7·25

DESIGNS: 20f. King Ghazi and mounted postman; 50f. King Faisal II, globe and wreath.

32 King Faisal II

1953. Coronation of King Faisal II.

No.	Type	Description		
342	32	3f. red	1·40	1·50
343	32	14f. brown	3·00	1·50
344	32	28f. blue	8·50	2·00
MS345		134×138 mm. Nos. 342/4	£120	£325

33

1954

No.	Type	Description		
346	33	1f. blue	70	10
347	33	2f. brown	25	10
348	33	3f. lake	25	10
349	33	4f. violet	25	10
350	33	5f. green	35	10
351	33	6f. mauve	35	10
352	33	8f. brown	35	10
353	33	10f. blue	25	10
354	33	15f. black	1·90	1·50
355	33	16f. red	3·00	2·50
356	33	20f. olive	1·40	10
357	33	25f. purple	1·40	10
358	33	30f. red	1·40	10
359	33	40f. brown	1·70	55
360	33	50f. blue	2·20	80

361	33	75f. mauve	3·50	90
362	33	100f. olive	6·75	90
363	33	200f. salmon	11·00	1·90

The 50f. to 200f. are larger (22×28 mm).

(35)

1955. Abrogation of Anglo–Iraqi Treaty. Optd with T 35.

380		3f. lake	1·30	55
381		10f. blue	1·40	55
382	27	28f. blue	2·40	1·10

36 King Faisal II

1955. Sixth Arab Engineers' Conference, Baghdad.

383	36	3f. red	1·10	45
384	36	10f. blue	1·80	65
385	36	28f. blue	2·75	1·70

37 King Faisal II and Globe

1956. Third Arab Postal Union Conference, Baghdad.

386	37	3f. red	1·40	65
387	37	10f. blue	1·90	65
388	37	28f. blue	2·75	1·50

38 King Faisal II and Power Loom

1957. Development Week.

389	38	1f. blue and buff	60	20
390	-	3f. multicoloured	60	20
391	-	5f. multicoloured	70	20
392	-	10f. multicoloured	1·10	20
393	-	40f. multicoloured	2·20	90

DESIGNS: 3f. Irrigation dam; 5f. Residential road, Baghdad; 10f. Cement kiln; 40f. Tigris Bridge.

39 King Faisal II and Exhibition Emblem

1957. Agricultural and Industrial Exn, Baghdad.

394	39	10f. brown and cream	1·20	1·20

(40)

1957. Silver Jubilee of Iraqi Red Crescent Society. No. 388 optd with T 40.

395	37	28f. blue	5·50	2·50

41 King Faisal II

1957

396	41	1f. blue	35	55
397	41	2f. brown	35	55
398	41	3f. red	35	55
399	41	4f. violet	35	55
400	41	5f. green	85	85
401	41	6f. red	85	85
402	41	8f. brown	1·70	1·20
403	41	10f. blue	1·70	1·20

42 King Faisal II and Tanks

1958. Army Day.

411	42	8f. grey and green	1·20	1·20
412	-	10f. black and brown	1·60	1·60
413	-	20f. brown and blue	1·60	1·60
414	-	30f. violet and red	2·30	1·80

DESIGNS—As T 42: King Faisal II and: 10f. Platoon marching; 20f. Mobile artillery unit and De Havilland D.H.112 Venom jet fighters. 22½×27½ mm: 30f. King Faisal II (full-length portrait).

1958. Development Week. As T 38, inscr "1958".

415		3f. green, drab and violet	50	35
416		5f. multicoloured	70	55
417		10f. multicoloured	1·90	1·10

DESIGNS—VERT: 3f. Sugar beet and refining plant. HORIZ: 5f. Building and pastoral scene; 10f. Irrigation dam.

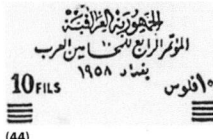

(44)

1958. Optd with T 43. (a) On No. 189.

418	1d. purple	34·00	34·00

(b) On T 27.

418a	1f. blue	43·00	13·50
419	12f. olive	95	35
420	14f. olive	1·20	35
421	16f. red	16·00	4·50
422	28f. blue	1·60	80
423	60f. blue	4·25	80
424	½d. blue	27·00	6·25
425	1d. green	50·00	22·00

(c) On T 33.

426	1f. blue	85	35
427	2f. brown	85	35
428	4f. violet	85	35
429	5f. green	85	35
430	6f. mauve	85	35
431	8f. brown	85	35
432	10f. blue	90	35
433	15f. black	1·20	35
434	16f. red	3·00	65
435	20f. olive	1·40	80
436	25f. purple	95	45
437	30f. red	1·40	45
438	40f. brown	1·40	35
439	50f. blue	6·75	3·75
440	75f. mauve	5·00	1·10
441	100f. olive	6·00	3·75
442	200f. salmon	18·00	7·25

Nos. 439/42 are larger (22×28 mm).

(d) On T 41.

443	1f. blue	4·00	90
444	2f. brown	85	35
445	3f. red	85	35
446	4f. violet	90	35
447	5f. green	85	35
448	6f. red	85	35
449	8f. brown	85	65
450	10f. blue	85	35
451	20f. green	85	35
452	25f. purple	1·80	1·00
453	30f. red	2·10	35
454	40f. brown	5·50	1·90
455	50f. purple	4·00	90
456	75f. purple	4·00	1·70
457	100f. orange	5·50	1·70
458	200f. blue	14·50	3·00

Nos. 455/8 are larger (22½×27½ mm).

43 "Iraqi Republic"

1958. Arab Lawyers Conf, Baghdad. Surch with T 44.

506	36	10f. on 28f. blue	2·10	1·20

45 Republican Soldier and Flag

1959. Army Day.

507	45	3f. blue	50	20
508	45	10f. olive	95	45
509	45	40f. violet	1·80	90

45a Orange Tree

1959. Afforestation Day.

510	45a	10f. orange and green	95	35

(46)

1959. International Children's Day. Surch with T 46.

511	37	10f. on 28f. blue	1·60	80

47 Worker and Buildings

1959. First Anniv of Revolution. Inscr "14TH JULY 1958".

512	47	10f. blue and ochre	70	65
513	-	30f. green and ochre	1·40	90

DESIGN—HORIZ: 30f. Revolutionaries brandishing weapons.

48 Harvesters

1959. Agricultural Reform.

514	48	10f. black and green	70	20

49 Republican Emblem

1959

515	49	1f. multicoloured	25	15
516	49	2f. multicoloured	25	15
517	49	3f. multicoloured	25	15
518	49	4f. multicoloured	25	15
519	49	5f. multicoloured	25	15
520	49	10f. multicoloured	25	15
521	49	15f. multicoloured	70	15
522	49	20f. multicoloured	70	15
523	49	30f. multicoloured	70	35
524	49	40f. multicoloured	1·30	45
525	49	50f. multicoloured	5·00	1·10
526	49	75f. multicoloured	2·10	55
527	49	100f. multicoloured	3·00	1·10
528	49	200f. multicoloured	5·50	1·10
529	49	500f. multicoloured	9·00	3·50
530	49	1d. multicoloured	21·00	9·00

(50)

1959. "Health and Hygiene". Optd with T 50.

531	10f. multicoloured	1·20	65

51 Gen. Kassem and Military Parade

1960. Army Day.

532	51	10f. lake and green	70	70
533	-	16f. red and blue	1·20	90
534	-	30f. olive, brown and buff	1·20	90
535	-	40f. violet and buff	1·70	1·10
536	-	60f. buff, chocolate & brn	2·40	1·30

DESIGNS—Gen. Kassem and: HORIZ: 16f. Infantry on manoeuvres; 60f. Partisans. VERT: 30f. Anti-aircraft gun-crew; 40f. Oilfield guards on parade.

52 Gen. Kassem

1960. Gen. Kassem's Escape from Assassination.

537	52	10f. violet	70	45
538	52	30f. green	1·30	65

53 Al Rasafi (poet)

1960. Al Rasafi Commemoration. Optd 1960 in English and Arabic.

539	53	10l. red	3·50	1·80

See also No. 732.

54 Gen. Kassem at Tomb of Unknown Soldier

1960. Second Anniv of Revolution.

540	-	6f. gold, olive and orange	85	65
541	54	10f. orange, green and blue	85	65
542	54	16f. orange, violet and blue	1·10	1·10
543	-	18f. gold, blue and orange	1·10	1·10
544	-	30f. gold, brown and orange	1·40	1·20
545	54	60f. orange, sepia and blue	3·00	1·90

DESIGN—VERT: 6f., 18f., 30f. Symbol of Republic.

55 Gen. Kassem, Flag and Troops

1961. Army Day.

546	55	3f. multicoloured	35	15
547	55	6f. multicoloured	35	15
548	55	10f. multicoloured	70	15
549	-	20f. black, yellow and green	85	35
550	-	30f. black, yellow & brown	85	45
551	-	40f. black, yellow and blue	1·20	80

DESIGN: 20, 30, 40f. Kassem and triumphal arch.

56 Gen. Kassem with Children

1961. World Children's Day. Main design brown; background colours given.

558	56	3f. yellow	85	55
559	56	6f. blue	1·20	55
560	56	10f. pink	1·70	55
561	56	30f. lemon	1·70	55
562	56	50f. green	3·00	90

57 Gen. Kassem saluting

1961. Third Anniv of Revolution.

563	-	1f. multicoloured	35	10
564	-	3f. multicoloured	35	10
565	**57**	5f. multicoloured	35	10
566	-	6f. multicoloured	35	10
567	-	10f. multicoloured	50	35
568	**57**	30f. multicoloured	95	65
569	**57**	40f. multicoloured	1·20	65
570	-	50f. multicoloured	2·10	1·30
571	-	100f. multicoloured	6·75	3·25

DESIGN: 1, 3, 6, 10, 50, 100f. Gen. Kassem and Iraqi flag.

58 Gen. Kassem and Army Emblem

1962. Army Day.

572		1f. multicoloured	35	35
573		3f. multicoloured	35	35
574		6f. multicoloured	35	35
575	**58**	10f. black, gold and lilac	60	35
576	**58**	30f. black, gold and orange	1·20	65
577	**58**	50f. black, gold and green	2·10	1·30

DESIGN—VERT: 1, 3, 6f. Gen. Kassem saluting and part of speech.

مؤتمر
العالم الاسلامي
بغـداد
٥١٣٨١–١٩٦٢م
(59)

1962. Fifth Islamic Congress. Optd with T **59**.

578	**49**	3f. multicoloured	35	35
579	**49**	10f. multicoloured	35	35
580	**49**	30f. multicoloured	1·20	65

60 Gen. Kassem, Flag and Handclasp

1962. Fourth Anniv of Revolution. Flag in green and gold.

581	**60**	1f. orange and sepia	10	10
582	**60**	3f. green and sepia	10	10
583	**60**	6f. brown and black	10	10
584	**60**	10f. lilac and sepia	60	55
585	**60**	30f. red and sepia	85	55
586	**60**	50f. grey and sepia	1·70	1·00

61 Fanfare

1962. Millenary of Baghdad. Multicoloured.

603		3f. Type **61**	60	35
604		6f. Al Kindi (philosopher)	60	35
605		10f. Map of old "Round City" of Baghdad	95	45
606		40f. Gen. Kassem and flag	2·75	1·20

62 Republican Emblem

1962. Aerogramme Stamps.

607	**62**	14f. black and green	2·40	85
608	**62**	35f. black and red	3·25	1·30

Nos. 607/8 were originally issued only attached to aerogramme forms covering the old imprinted King Faisal II stamps, but later appeared in sheets.

63 Campaign Emblem

1962. Malaria Eradication.

609	**63**	3f. multicoloured	35	35
610	**63**	10f. multicoloured	85	35
611	**63**	40f. multicoloured	1·40	65

64 Gen. Kassem and Tanks

1963. Army Day.

612	**64**	3f. black and yellow	10	10
613	**64**	5f. sepia and purple	10	10
614	**64**	6f. black and green	10	10
615	**64**	10f. black and blue	35	35
616	**64**	10f. black and pink	35	35
617	**64**	20f. black and blue	85	45
618	**64**	40f. black and mauve	1·40	80
619	**64**	50f. sepia and blue	2·10	1·60

65 Gufas on the Tigris

1963

620	**65**	1f. green	85	35
621	-	2f. violet	85	35
622	**65**	3f. black	85	35
623	-	4f. black and yellow	85	35
624	-	5f. purple and green	95	35
625	-	10f. red	1·30	35
626	-	15f. brown and yellow	2·10	35
627	-	20f. violet	2·20	35
628	-	30f. orange	1·40	45
629	-	40f. green	2·40	35
630	-	50f. brown	10·00	80
631	-	75f. black and green	5·00	55
632	-	100f. purple	5·50	65
633	-	200f. brown	10·00	65
634	-	500f. blue	14·50	3·00
635	-	1d. purple	19·00	5·50

DESIGNS: 2f., 500f. Spiral tower of Samarra; 4f., 15f. Sumerian Harp; 5f., 75f. Republican emblem; 10f., 50f. Lion of Babylon; 20f., 40f. Koranic school of Abbasid period; 30f., 200f. Mosque and minarets; 100f., 1d. Winged bull of Kharsabad.

66 Shepherd with Sheep

1963. Freedom from Hunger.

636	**66**	3f. black and green	35	35
637	-	10f. mauve and brown	85	35
638	-	20f. brown and blue	1·40	90

MS639 175×120 mm. Nos. 636/8 (sold at 50f.) | 7·25 | 7·25

DESIGNS: 10f. Harvester; 20f. Trees.

67 Centenary Emblem

1963. Red Cross Centenary.

640	**67**	3f. violet and red	35	35
641	**67**	10f. blue and red	70	35
642	-	30f. blue and red	1·30	80

DESIGN—HORIZ: 30f. Hospital.

68 Helmet, Rifle and Flag

1964. Army Day.

643	**68**	3f. sepia, green and blue	35	35
644	**68**	10f. sepia, green and pink	70	35
645	**68**	30f. sepia, green and yellow	1·30	80

69 Revolutionaries and Flag

1964. First Anniv of 14th Ramadan Revolution. Flag in red, green and black.

646	**69**	10f. violet	70	35
647	**69**	30f. brown	1·30	80

MS648 125×75 mm. Nos. 646/7 in new colours (sold at 50f.) | 8·50 | 6·75

See also No. **MS**746.

70 Shamash (Sun-God) and Hammurabi

1964. 15th Anniv of Declaration of Human Rights.

649	**70**	6f. olive and purple	70	55
650	**70**	10f. violet and orange	1·30	55
651	**70**	30f. green and blue	2·10	90

DESIGN: 10f. U.N. Emblem and Scales of Justice.

71 Soldier raising Flag on Map of Iraq

1964. Sixth Anniv of Revolution.

652	-	3f. orange, grey and black	35	35
653	**71**	10f. red, black and green	35	35
654	**71**	20f. red, black and green	70	35
655	-	30f. orange, grey and black	1·40	80

DESIGN—HORIZ: 3f., 30f. Soldier "protecting" people and factories with outstretched arm.

72 Soldier, Civilians and Star Emblem

1964. First Anniv of 18 November Revolution.

656	**72**	5f. orange and brown	50	35
657	**72**	10f. orange and blue	50	35
658	**72**	50f. orange and violet	1·40	55

73 Musician

1964. International Arab Music Conf, Baghdad.

659	**73**	3f. multicoloured	1·30	35
660	**73**	10f. multicoloured	1·30	35
661	**73**	30f. multicoloured	1·80	1·20

74 Conference Emblem and Map

1964. Ninth Arab Engineer's Conf, Baghdad.

662	**74**	10f. green and mauve	85	35

75 A.P.U. Emblem

1964. Tenth Anniv of Arab Postal Union's Permanent Office.

663	**75**	3f. blue and red	35	15
664	**75**	10f. slate and purple	60	15
665	**75**	30f. blue and orange	1·60	65

76 Soldier, Civilians and Flag

1965. Army Day.

666	**76**	5f. multicoloured	35	15
667	**76**	15f. multicoloured	50	35
668	**76**	30f. multicoloured	1·60	80

MS669 110×83 mm. Stamps similar to No. 668 but without value shown together with stamps-size portrait of Pres. Arif. Imperf. (sold at 60f.) | 10·00 | 10·00

77 Cogwheel and Factory

1965. First Arab Ministers of Labour Conf, Baghdad.

670	**77**	10f. multicoloured	70	35

78 Oil Tanker

1965. Inauguration of Deep Sea Terminal for Tankers.

671	**78**	10f. multicoloured	1·30	55

79 Armed Soldier with Flag

1965. Second Anniv of 14th Ramadan Revolution.

672	**79**	10f. multicoloured	70	20

80 Tree

1965. Tree Week.

673	**80**	6f. multicoloured	35	35
674	**80**	20f. multicoloured	1·60	35

81 Federation Emblem

1965. Arab Insurance Federation. Sun in gold.

675	81	3f. ultramarine and blue	35	35
676	81	10f. black and grey	35	40
677	81	30f. red and pink	1·30	90

82 Dagger of Deir Yassin, Palestine

1965. Deir Yassin Massacre.

678	82	10f. drab and black	1·30	45
679	82	20f. brown and blue	2·40	65

83 "Threat of Disease"

1965. World Health Day.

680	83	3f. multicoloured	60	35
681	83	10f. multicoloured	70	35
682	83	20f. multicoloured	1·70	90

84 I.T.U. Emblem and Symbols

1965. Centenary of I.T.U.

683	84	10f. multicoloured	95	20
684	84	20f. multicoloured	2·10	65
MS685		139×95 mm. Nos. 683/4. Imperf or perf	22·00	17·00

85 Flag and Map

1965. First Anniv of Iraq–U.A.R. Pact.

686	85	10f. multicoloured	60	20

85a Lamp and Burning Library

1965. Reconstitution of Algiers University Library.

687	85a	5f. red, green and black	50	35
688	85a	10f. green, red and black	85	35

86 Revolutionary and Flames

1965. 45th Anniv of 1920 Rebellion.

689	86	5f. multicoloured	35	20
690	86	10f. multicoloured	60	20

87 Mosque

1965. Mohammed's Birthday.

691	87	10f. multicoloured	85	80
MS692		110×75 mm. No. 691 (sold at 50f.)	9·00	9·00

88 Factory and Ear of Wheat

1965. Seventh Anniv of 14 July Revolution.

693	88	10f. multicoloured	60	60

89 I.C.Y. Emblem

1965. Air. International Co-operation Year.

694	89	5f. black and brown	85	35
695	89	10f. brown and green	1·30	35
696	89	30f. black and blue	3·50	1·30

90 Fair Emblem

1965. Baghdad Fair.

697	90	10f. multicoloured	50	20

91 Pres. Arif (photo by Studio Jean)

1965. Second Anniv of 18 November Revolution.

698	91	5f. blue and orange	50	35
699	91	10f. sepia and blue	70	35
700	91	50f. blue and mauve	3·00	1·10

92 Census Graph

1965. National Census.

701	92	3f. black and purple	50	20
702	92	5f. red and brown	50	20
703	92	15f. bistre and blue	2·20	75

93 Hawker Siddeley Trident 1E Airliner

1965. Air. Inauguration of Hawker Siddeley Trident 1E Aircraft by Iraqi Airways.

704	93	5f. multicoloured	50	50
705	93	10f. multicoloured	50	50
706	93	40f. multicoloured	5·25	1·00

94 Date Palms

1965. Second F.A.O. Dates Conference, Baghdad.

707	94	3f. multicoloured	50	35
708	94	10f. multicoloured	1·20	35
709	94	15f. multicoloured	2·20	1·00

95 Army Memorial

1966. 45th Anniv of Army Day.

710	95	2f. multicoloured	60	35
711	95	5f. multicoloured	60	35
712	95	40f. multicoloured	2·40	90

96 "Eagle" and Flag

1966. Third Anniv of 14th Ramadan Revolution.

713	96	5f. multicoloured	35	35
714	96	10f. multicoloured	85	35

96a Arab League Emblem

1966. Arab Publicity Week.

715	96a	5f. green, brown & orange	60	20
716	96a	15f. blue, purple and olive	60	20

97 Footballers

98 Footballer's Legs, and Iraq Football Union Emblem (image scaled to 43% of original size)

1966. Arab Football Cup, Baghdad. Multicoloured.

717		2f. Type **97**	60	35
718		5f. Goalkeeper with ball	60	35
719		15f. Type **97**	1·80	90
MS720		116×70 mm. 50f. Type **98**	9·00	11·00

99 Excavator

1966. Labour Day.

721	99	15f. multicoloured	35	20
722	99	25f. black, silver and red	60	20

100 Queen Nefertari

1966. Nubian Monuments Preservation.

723	100	5f. yellow, black and olive	50	35
724	100	15f. yellow, brown & blue	50	35
725	–	40f. brown, chestnut & red	2·75	1·90

DESIGN—HORIZ: (41×32 mm): 40f. Rock temples, Abu Simbel.

101 President Arif

1966. Eighth Anniv of 14 July Revolution.

726	101	5f. multicoloured	50	35
727	101	15f. multicoloured	70	35
728	101	50f. multicoloured	2·40	1·30

102

1966. Mohammed's Birthday.

729	102	5f. multicoloured	25	10
730	102	15f. multicoloured	35	10
731	102	30f. multicoloured	1·90	1·60

1966. As No. 539 but without opt.

732	53	10f. red	12·00	12·00

103 Iraqi Museum, Statue and Window

1966. Inauguration of Iraqi Museum, Baghdad. Multicoloured.

733		15f. Type **103**	1·40	35
734		50f. Gold headdress	2·20	1·00
735		80f. Sumerian head (vert)	4·50	1·50

104 Revolutionaries

1966. Third Anniv of 18 November Revolution.

736	104	15f. multicoloured	85	65
737	104	25f. multicoloured	1·30	1·30

105 "Magic Carpet"

1966. Air. Meeting of Arab International Tourist Union, Baghdad. Multicoloured.

738		2f. White stork emblem (27½×39 mm)	35	35
739		5f. Type **105**	35	35

| 740 | | 15f. As 2f. | 50 | 50 |
| 741 | | 50f. Type **105** | 1·90 | 80 |

106 UNESCO Emblem

1966. 20th Anniv of UNESCO.

| 742 | **106** | 5f. brown, black and blue | 25 | 10 |
| 743 | **106** | 15f. green, black and red | 70 | 35 |

107 Soldier and Rocket-launchers

1967. Army Day.

| 744 | **107** | 15f. ochre, brown & yellow | 60 | 20 |
| 745 | **107** | 20f. ochre, brown and lilac | 85 | 35 |

1967. Fourth Anniv of Revolution of 14th Ramadan. No. MS648 with original inscriptions obliterated "4th" in place of "1st" and sheet value amended to 70fils.

MS746 125×75 mm. Nos. 646/7. Imperf (sold at 70f.) — 9·75 9·75

108 Oil Refinery

1967. Sixth Arab Petroleum Congress, Baghdad. Multicoloured.

747		5f. Congress emblem (vert)	35	20
748		15f. Type **108**	50	20
749		40f. Congress emblem (vert)	1·10	90
750		50f. Type **108**	2·40	1·20

109 "Spider's Web" Emblem

1967. Hajeer Year (1967).

| 751 | **109** | 5f. multicoloured | 35 | 20 |
| 752 | **109** | 15f. multicoloured | 50 | 35 |

110 Worker holding Cogwheel

1967. Labour Day.

| 753 | **110** | 10f. multicoloured | 35 | 10 |
| 754 | **110** | 15f. multicoloured | 50 | 20 |

111

1967. Mohammed's Birthday.

| 755 | **111** | 5f. multicoloured | 50 | 35 |
| 756 | **111** | 15f. multicoloured | 60 | 35 |

112 Flag and Hands with Clubs

1967. 47th Anniv of 1920 Rebellion.

| 757 | **112** | 5f. multicoloured | 50 | 10 |
| 758 | **112** | 15f. multicoloured | 70 | 10 |

113 Um Qasr Port

1967. Ninth Anniv of 14 July Revolution and Inaug of Um Qasr Port. Multicoloured.

759		5f. Type **113**	35	20
760		10f. Freighter at quayside	85	35
761		15f. As 10f.	1·40	35
762		40f. Type **113**	2·75	1·30

114 Costume

1967. Iraqi Costumes.

765	**114**	2f. multicoloured (postage)	35	35
766	-	5f. multicoloured	35	35
767	-	10f. multicoloured	95	35
768	-	15f. multicoloured	1·20	65
769	-	20f. multicoloured	1·60	65
770	-	25f. multicoloured	1·70	80
771	-	30f. multicoloured	2·10	80
772	-	40f. multicoloured (air)	1·80	90
773	-	50f. multicoloured	2·75	1·30
774	-	80f. multicoloured	3·50	1·70

DESIGNS: 5f. to 80f. Different costumes.

115 Pres. Arif and Map

1967. Fourth Anniv of 18 November Revolution. Multicoloured.

| 775 | | 5f. President Arif | 50 | 35 |
| 776 | | 15f. Type **115** | 1·10 | 55 |

116 Ziggurat of Ur

1967. International Tourist Year. Multicoloured.

777		2f. Type **116** (postage)	35	35
778		5f. Statues of Nimroud	35	35
779		10f. Babylon (arch)	60	35
780		15f. Minaret of Mosul (vert)	70	35
781		25f. Arch of Ctesiphon	85	35
782		50f. Statue, Temple of Hatra (vert) (air)	3·75	55
783		80f. Spiral Minaret of Samarra (vert)	4·25	80
784		100f. Adam's Tree (vert)	4·00	1·00
785		200f. Aladdin ("Aladdin's Cave") (vert)	9·00	4·00
786		500f. Golden Mosque of Kadhimain	43·00	25·00

117 Guide Emblem and Saluting Hand

1967. Iraqi Scouts and Guides. Multicoloured.

787		2f. Type **117**	1·80	45
788		5f. Guides by camp-fire	2·20	55
789		10f. Scout emblem and saluting hand	2·40	80
790		15f. Scouts setting up camp	2·40	1·00

MS791 120×48 mm. Nos. 787/90. Imperf (sold at 50f.) 12·00 12·00

118 Soldiers Drilling

1968. Army Day.

| 792 | **118** | 5f. brown, green and blue | 50 | 20 |
| 793 | **118** | 15f. indigo, olive and blue | 95 | 35 |

119 White-cheeked Bulbul

1968. Iraqi Birds. Multicoloured.

794	**119**	5f. Type **119**	85	35
795		10f. Hoopoe	1·10	35
796		15f. Jay	1·60	35
797		25f. Peregrine falcon	2·40	55
798		30f. White stork	3·25	55
799		40f. Black partridge	3·75	90
800		50f. Marbled teal	5·25	1·50

120 Battle Scene

1968. Fifth Anniv of 14th Ramadan Revolution.

| 801 | **120** | 15f. orange, black and blue | 4·25 | 1·10 |

121 Symbols of "Labour"

1968. Labour Day.

| 802 | **121** | 15f. multicoloured | 50 | 35 |
| 803 | **121** | 25f. multicoloured | 85 | 35 |

122 Football

1968. 23rd International Military Sports Council Football Championship. Multicoloured.

804		2f. Type **122**	50	35
805		5f. Goalkeeper in mid air (vert)	50	35
806		15f. Type **122**	60	35
807		25f. As 5f.	3·50	1·00

MS808 59×61 mm. 70f. Championship shield. Imperf 11·00 12·00

123 Soldier with Iraqi Flag

1968. Tenth Anniv of 14 July Revolution.

| 809 | **123** | 15f. multicoloured | 60 | 20 |

124 Anniversary and W.H.O. Emblems

1968. 20th Anniv of W.H.O.

810		5f. multicoloured	35	20
811	-	10f. multicoloured	35	20
812	**124**	15f. red, blue and black	70	20
813	-	25f. red, green and black	95	45

DESIGN—VERT: 5, 10f. Combined anniversary and W.H.O. emblems.

125 Human Rights Emblem

1968. Human Rights Year.

| 814 | **125** | 10f. red, yellow and blue | 50 | 35 |
| 815 | **125** | 25f. red, yellow and green | 50 | 35 |

MS816 55×75 mm. **125** 100f. scarlet, lemon and mauve. Imperf. 7·25 7·25

126 Mother and children

1968. UNICEF Commemoration.

| 817 | **126** | 15f. multicoloured | 60 | 35 |
| 818 | **126** | 25f. multicoloured | 1·70 | 45 |

MS819 56×76 mm. **126** 100f. multicoloured. Imperf 11·00 7·75

127 Army Tanks

1969. Army Day.

| 820 | **127** | 25f. multicoloured | 4·25 | 2·00 |

128 Agricultural Scene

1969. Sixth Anniv of 14th Ramadan Revolution.

| 821 | **128** | 15f. multicoloured | 70 | 35 |

129 Mosque and Worshippers

1969. Hajeer Year.

| 822 | **129** | 15f. multicoloured | 70 | 70 |

130 Emblem of Iraqi Veterinary Medical Association

1969. First Arab Veterinary Union Conf, Baghdad.

| 823 | **130** | 10f. multicoloured | 85 | 45 |
| 824 | **130** | 15f. multicoloured | 1·30 | 45 |

131 Mahseer

1969. Multicoloured. (a) Postage. Fish.

825		2f. Type **131**	2·10	45
826		3f. Sharpey's barbel	2·20	45
827		10f. Silver pomfret	2·40	45
828		100f. Pike barbel	7·75	4·00

(b) Air. Fauna.

829		2f. Striped hyena	50	35
830		3f. Leopard	50	35
831		5f. Mountain gazelle	50	35
832		10f. Head of Arab horse	60	45
833		200f. Arab horse	14·50	7·75

132 Kaaba, Mecca

1969. Mohammed's Birthday.

834	132	15f. multicoloured	85	35

133 I.L.O. Emblem

1969. 50th Anniv of I.L.O.

835	133	5f. yellow, blue and black	25	10
836	133	15f. yellow, green & black	25	10
837	133	50f. yellow, red and black	1·90	1·20
MS838 75×55 mm. 133 100f. multicoloured. Imperf			7·25	7·25

134 Weightlifting

1969. Olympic Games, Mexico (1968). Multicoloured.

839		3f. Type **134**	70	35
840		5f. High jumping	70	35
841		10f. As Type **134**	85	45
842		35f. As 5f.	1·60	1·10
MS843 91×116 mm. Nos. 839/42. Imperf (sold at 100f.)			13·50	13·50

135 Arms of Iraq and "Industry"

1969. 11th Anniv of 14 July Revolution.

844	135	10f. multicoloured	50	35
845	135	15f. multicoloured	70	35

136 Rebuilding Roads

1969. Anniv of 17 July Revolution and Inaug of Baghdad International Airport. Mult.

846	136	10f. Type **136**	70	45
847		15f. Type **136**	70	45
848		20f. Airport building	2·20	55
849		200f. President Bakr (vert)	21·00	10·00

137 Ear of Wheat and Fair Emblem

1969. Sixth International Baghdad Fair.

850	137	10f. brown, gold and green	85	35
851	137	15f. red, gold and blue	1·10	45

138 Floating Crane "Antara"

1969. 50th Anniv of Port of Basra. Multicoloured.

852	138	15f. Type **138**	60	35
853		20f. Harbour tender "Al-Walid"	85	55
854		30f. Pilot boat "Al-Rashid"	1·30	65
855		35f. Dredger "Hillah"	2·10	1·10
856		50f. Survey ship "Al-Fao"	6·00	3·00

139 Radio Beacon and Outline of Palestine

1969. Tenth Anniv of Iraqi News Agency.

857	139	15f. multicoloured	1·40	45
858	139	50f. multicoloured	3·75	90

140 Emblem, Book and Hands

1969. Campaign Against Illiteracy.

859	140	15f. multicoloured	35	20
860	140	20f. multicoloured	70	45

141 Ross and Keith Smith's Vickers Vimy Biplane

1969. Air. 50th Anniv of First England–Australia Flight.

861	141	15f. multicoloured	3·25	1·50
862	141	35f. multicoloured	5·00	3·50
MS863 81×100 mm. Nos. 861/2 (sold at 100f.). Imperf			18·00	16·00

142 Newspaper Headline

1969. Centenary of Iraqi Press.

864	142	15f. black, orange & yell	70	45

143 Soldier and Map

1970. Army Day.

865	143	15f. multicoloured	95	45
866	143	20f. multicoloured	1·90	90

144 Iraqis supporting Wall

1970. Seventh Anniv of 14th Ramadan Revolution.

867	144	10f. multicoloured	25	20
868	144	15f. multicoloured	60	20

عيدنوروز
1970

(145)

1970. New Year ("Nawrooz"). Nos. 891/6 optd with T 145.

869		2f. multicoloured	50	35
870		3f. multicoloured	50	35
871		5f. multicoloured	50	35
872		10f. multicoloured	95	35
873		15f. multicoloured	1·20	35
874		50f. multicoloured	3·25	1·70

146 Map of Arab Countries, and Slogans

1970. 23rd Anniv of Al-Baath Party. Multicoloured.

875		15f. Type **146**	50	35
876		15f. Type **146**	85	65
877		50f. Iraqis acclaiming Party	2·40	90
MS878 115×76 mm. 150f. As 50f. Imperf			14·50	14·50

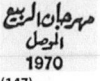

(147)

1970. Mosul Spring Festival. Nos. 891/6 optd with T 147.

879		2f. multicoloured	70	70
880		3f. multicoloured	70	70
881		5f. multicoloured	70	70
882		10f. multicoloured	70	70
883		15f. multicoloured	1·60	1·10
884		50f. multicoloured	3·50	1·30

148 Iraqis celebrating Labour Day

1970. Labour Day.

885	148	10f. multicoloured	50	35
886	148	15f. multicoloured	60	45
887	148	35f. multicoloured	1·90	90

149 Kaaba, Mecca, Broken Statues and Koran

1970. Mohammed's Birthday.

888	149	15f. multicoloured	50	20
889	149	20f. multicoloured	50	35

150 Poppies

1970. Spring Festival. Flowers. Multicoloured.

891		2f. Type **150**	60	35
892		3f. Narcissi	60	35
893		5f. Tulip	60	35
894		10f. Carnations	85	45
895		15f. Roses	1·40	65
896		50f. As 10f.	4·25	1·80

1970 ١٩٧٠

عيد الصحافة

(151)

1970. Press Day. No. 864 optd with T 151.

896a	142	15f. black, orange & yell	70	70

152 Revolutionaries

1970. 50th Anniv of Revolution of 1920.

897	152	10f. black and green	25	20
898	152	15f. black and gold	50	20
899	–	35f. black and orange	1·20	55
MS900 119×71 mm. 100f. Designs as Nos. 897 and 899 but without face values. Imperf.			7·25	7·25

DESIGN: 35f. Revolutionary and rising sun.

153 Bomb-burst and Broken Chain

1970. 12th Anniv of 14 July Revolution.

901	153	15f. multicoloured	35	20
902	153	20f. multicoloured	60	20

154 Hands and Map of Iraq

1970. Second Anniv of 17 July Revolution.

903	154	15f. multicoloured	35	20
904	154	25f. multicoloured	70	35

155 Pomegranates

1970. Fruit. Multicoloured.

905		3f. Type **155**	50	20
906		5f. Grapefruit	50	20
907		10f. Grapes	50	20
908		15f. Oranges	1·40	45
909		35f. Dates	4·25	2·20

The Latin inscriptions on Nos. 906/7 are transposed.

156 Kaaba, Mecca

1970. Hajeer Year.

910	156	15f. multicoloured	35	20
911	156	25f. multicoloured	70	35

الدورة السابعة

970 – ٩٧٠

(157)

1970. Seventh Int Baghdad Fair. Optd with T 157.

912	137	10f. brown, gold and green	4·25	2·20
913	137	15f. red, gold and blue	4·25	2·20

158 Arab League Flag and Map

1970. 25th Anniv of Arab League.

914	158	15f. purple, green and olive	35	10
915	158	35f. red, green and grey	70	55

159 Euphrates Bridge

1970. Air. National Development. Multicoloured.

916	159	10f. Type **159**	2·40	65
917	159	15f. Type **159**	3·50	1·60
918		1d. Pres. Bakr and banknotes (37×27 mm)	70·00	28·00

160 I.E.Y. Emblem

1970. International Education Year.

919	160	5f. multicoloured	35	20
920	160	15f. multicoloured	60	35

1970. 25th Anniv of United Nations. No. MS639 optd 1945 UNITED NATIONS 1970 together with other inscriptions and with face values of the stamps in the miniature sheet obliterated.

MS921 175×120 mm. 50f.			9·00	9·00

161 Baghdad Hospital and Society Emblem

1970. 50th Anniv of Iraq Medical Society.
922	**161**	15f. multicoloured	35	20
923	**161**	40f. multicoloured	1·60	80

162 Union Emblem

1970. Air. Tenth Arab Telecommunications Union Conference, Baghdad.
924	**162**	15f. multicoloured	35	10
925	**162**	25f. multicoloured	70	55

163 Sugar Beet

1970. 12th Anniv of Mosul Sugar Refinery. Multicoloured.
926		5f. Type **163**	35	10
927		15f. Sugar refinery (horiz)	60	20
928		30f. Type **163**	2·10	90

164 O.P.E.C. Emblem

1970. Tenth Anniv of Organization of Petroleum Exporting Countries (O.P.E.C.).
929	**164**	10f. blue, bistre and purple	95	45
930	**164**	40f. blue, bistre and green	3·75	1·60

165 Soldiers, Tank and Aircraft

1971. 50th Anniv of Army Day.
931	**165**	15f. black, mauve and gold	70	35
932	-	40f. multicoloured	4·00	1·30

MS933 124×91 mm. Nos. 931/2. Imperf (sold at 100f.) 11·50 11·50

DESIGN—42×35 mm: 40f. Soldiers and map of Middle East.

166 "Revolutionary Army"

1971. Eighth Anniv of 14th Ramadan Revolution.
934	**166**	15f. multicoloured	60	35
935	**166**	40f. multicoloured	1·80	65

167 Pilgrims and Web

1971. Hajeer Year.
936	**167**	10f. multicoloured	35	20
937	**167**	15f. multicoloured	60	35

168 Pres. Bakr with Torch

1971. First Anniv of 11th March Manifesto.
938	**168**	15f. multicoloured	95	55
939	**168**	100f. multicoloured	4·00	1·90

169 Boatman in Marshland

1971. Tourism Week. Multicoloured.
940		5f. Type **169**	60	35
941		10f. Stork over Baghdad	1·10	35
942		15f. Landscape ("Summer Resorts")	1·30	55
943		100f. "Return of Sinbad"	6·75	3·00

170 Blacksmith taming Serpent

1971. New Year ("Nawrooz").
944	**170**	15f. multicoloured	1·20	45
945	**170**	25f. multicoloured	2·30	90

1971. World Meteorological Day. Nos. 780 and 783 optd **W.M. DAY 1971** in English and Arabic.
946	15f. multicoloured (postage)	3·75	1·30
947	80f. multicoloured (air)	8·50	5·50

172 Emblem and Workers

1971. 24th Anniv of Al-Baath Party. Multicoloured.
948		15f. Type **172**	1·10	55
949		35f. Type **172**	1·80	1·10
950		250f. As Type **172** but central portion of design only (42×42 mm)	14·50	14·50

On No. 950 the circular centre is also perforated.

مهرجان الربيع

1971

(173)

1971. Mosul Spring Festival. Nos. 765/6 and 770 optd with T **173**.
951	**114**	2f. multicoloured	60	35
952	-	5f. multicoloured	60	35
953	-	25f. multicoloured	2·75	1·20

174 Worker and Farm-girl

1971. Labour Day.
954	**174**	15f. multicoloured	50	35
955	**174**	40f. multicoloured	1·80	45

175 Muslim at Prayer

1971. Mohammed's Birthday.
956	**175**	15f. multicoloured	85	35
957	**175**	100f. multicoloured	3·00	1·90

176 Revolutionaries, and Hands with Broken Chains

1971. 13th Anniv of 14 July Revolution.
958	**176**	25f. multicoloured	70	35
959	**176**	50f. multicoloured	1·80	80

177 Rising Sun and "Prosperity"

1971. Third Anniv of 17 July Revolution.
960	**177**	25f. multicoloured	85	45
961	**177**	70f. multicoloured	2·75	1·00

182 Bank Emblem

1971. 30th Anniv of Rafidain Bank.
989	**182**	10f. multicoloured	70	75
990	**182**	15f. multicoloured	1·20	1·20
991	**182**	25f. multicoloured	2·30	2·30
992	**182**	65f. multicoloured	12·00	10·00
993	**182**	250f. multicoloured	30·00	29·00

Nos. 992/3 are larger, 42×42 mm.

التعداد الزراعي العام

١٩٧١/١٠/١٥

(183)

1971. Agricultural Census. Nos. 905, 908/9 optd with T **183**.
994	3f. multicoloured	2·75	2·75
995	15f. multicoloured	2·75	2·75
996	35f. multicoloured	2·75	2·75

184 Football

1971. Fourth Pan-Arab Schoolboy Games, Baghdad. Multicoloured.
997		15f. Type **184**	35	35
998		25f. Throwing the discus and running	95	45
999		35f. Table tennis	1·20	1·00
1000		70f. Gymnastics	5·00	1·70
1001		95f. Volleyball and basketball	8·50	3·00

MS1002 195×146 mm. Nos. 997/1001. Imperf (sold at 200f.) 24·00 24·00

70 Fils

يوم الطالب
٢٣ تشرين الثاني
١٩٦١ – ١٩٧١
٧ فلسا

(185)

1971. Students' Day. Nos. 892/3 surch and 895 optd as T **185**.
1003	**185**	15f. multicoloured	2·10	45
1004		25f. on 5f. multicoloured	3·25	1·50
1005		70f. on 3f. multicoloured	11·50	3·75

186 Society Emblem

1971. Air. 20th Anniv of Iraqi Philatelic Society.
1006	**186**	25f. multicoloured	1·70	1·20
1007	**186**	70f. multicoloured	5·00	3·00

1971. 25th Anniv of UNICEF. Nos. 817/18 optd **25th Anniversary 1971**.
1008	**126**	15f. multicoloured	4·00	1·50
1009	**126**	25f. multicoloured	9·75	4·50

188 Schoolchildren on Zebra Crossing

1971. Second Traffic Week.
1010	**188**	15f. multicoloured	2·10	1·00
1011	**188**	25f. multicoloured	4·00	1·90

189 A.P.U. Emblem

1971. 25th Anniv of Founding of Arab Postal Union at Sofar Conference.
1012	**189**	25f. brown, yellow & grn	60	35
1013	**189**	70f. red, yellow and blue	2·30	90

190 Racial Equality Year Symbol

1971. Racial Equality Year.
1014	**190**	25f. multicoloured	35	20
1015	**190**	70f. multicoloured	1·40	1·20

191 Soldiers with Flag and Torch

1972. Army Day.
1016	**191**	25f. multicoloured	1·40	80
1017	**191**	70f. multicoloured	5·50	3·00

192 Workers

1972. Ninth Anniv of 14th Ramadan Revolution.
1018	**192**	25f. multicoloured	3·00	65
1019	**192**	95f. multicoloured	5·00	3·00

193 Mosque and Crescent

1972. Hajeer Year.

1020	**193**	25f. multicoloured	50	20
1021	**193**	35f. multicoloured	95	55

المؤتمر التاسع للاتحاد الوطني
لطلبة العراق
٢٥ شباط – ٢ آذار ١٩٧٢
(194)

1972. Air. Ninth Iraqi Students' Union Congress. Nos. 916/17 optd with T 194.

1022	**159**	10f. multicoloured	3·00	2·75
1023	**159**	15f. multicoloured	3·00	2·75

195 Dove, Olive Branch and Manifesto

1972. Second Anniv of 11 March Manifesto.

1024	**195**	25f. blue, lt blue & black	1·70	45
1025	**195**	70f. purple, mauve & blk	5·00	1·50

196 Observatory and Weather Balloon on Isobar Map

1972. World Meteorological Day.

1026	**196**	25f. multicoloured	2·40	65
1027	**196**	35f. multicoloured	4·25	1·90

197 Cogwheel Emblem

1972. Iraqi Chamber of Commerce.

1028	**197**	25f. multicoloured	70	35
1029	**197**	35f. multicoloured	1·30	55

198 Oil Rig and Flame

1972. Inauguration of North Rumaila Oilfield.

1030	**198**	25f. multicoloured	1·80	35
1031	**198**	35f. multicoloured	2·40	1·20

199 Party Emblem

1972. 25th Anniv of Al Baath Party. Multicoloured.

1032	**199**	10f. Type **199**	50	20
1033		25f. Emblem and inscription	1·10	55
1034	**199**	35f. Type **199**	1·20	65
1035		70f. As 25f.	3·75	2·75

SIZES—HORIZ: 25f., 70f. 51×27 mm.

200 Mountain Scene

1972. New Year ("Nawrooz").

1036	**200**	25f. mauve, yellow & blue	1·70	35
1037	**200**	70f. brown, yellow & blue	5·50	1·90

201 Congress "Quills" Emblem

1972. Third Arab Journalists Congress.

1038	**201**	25f. orange, black & grn	70	20
1039	**201**	35f. blue, black and green	2·40	1·50

202 Federation Emblem

1972. Fourth Anniv of Iraqi Women's Federation.

1040	**202**	25f. multicoloured	70	45
1041	**202**	35f. multicoloured	2·40	1·70

204 Hand holding Spanner

1972. Labour Day.

1046	**204**	25f. multicoloured	60	20
1047	**204**	35f. multicoloured	1·10	55

205 Kaaba, Mecca

1972. Mohammed's Birthday.

1048	**205**	25f. black, gold and green	70	20
1049	**205**	35f. black, gold and violet	2·40	1·70

206 Shooting for Goal

1972. Air. 25th International Military Sports Council Football Championship, Baghdad. Multicoloured.

1050		10f. Type **206**	70	35
1051		20f. Players in goalmouth	1·60	35
1052		25f. Type **206**	1·60	35
1053		35f. As 20f.	5·50	1·00
MS1054	77×64 mm. 100f. Olympic and C.I.S.M. emblems. Imperf		24·00	24·00

207 Soldiers and Artillery

1972. 14th Anniv of 14 July Revolution.

1055	**207**	35f. multicoloured	1·20	45
1056	**207**	70f. multicoloured	3·75	1·50

208 "Spirit of Revolution"

1972. Fourth Anniv of 17 July Revolution.

1057	**208**	25f. multicoloured	1·60	80
1058	**208**	95f. multicoloured	4·25	3·50

209 Scout Badge and Camp Scene

1972. Tenth Jamboree and Conference of Arab Scouts, Mosul.

1059	**209**	20f. multicoloured	3·00	1·50
1060	**209**	25f. multicoloured	4·25	1·70

210 Guide Badge and Camp

1972. Fourth Conference and Camp of Arab Guides, Mosul.

1061	**210**	10f. multicoloured	2·10	90
1062	**210**	45f. multicoloured	6·00	1·70

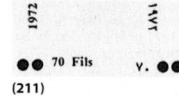

(211)

1972. Third Traffic Week. Nos. 1010/11 surch or optd as T 211.

1063	**188**	25f. multicoloured	7·75	3·25
1064	**188**	70f. on 15f. mult	10·00	8·25

(212)

1972. Festival of Palm Trees and Feast of Dates. Nos. 707 and 709 surch as T 212.

1065	**94**	25f. on 3f. multicoloured	5·00	3·00
1066	**94**	70f. on 15f. multicoloured	13·50	7·75

213 "Strong Man" Statuette

1972. Air. World Body-building Championships and Asian Congress, Baghdad. Multicoloured.

1067		25f. Type **213**	1·80	90
1068		70f. Ancient warriors and modern Strong Man	4·75	3·00

214 Bank Building

1972. 25th Anniv of Central Bank of Iraq.

1069	**214**	25f. multicoloured	1·10	55
1070	**214**	70f. multicoloured	3·25	1·30

216 International Railway Union Emblem

1972. 50th Anniv of Int Railway Union.

1073	**216**	25f. multicoloured	2·20	80
1074	**216**	45f. multicoloured	6·00	4·00

1973. Various "Faisal" definitives with portrait obliterated with 3 bars. (a) 1954 issue.

1075	**33**	10f. blue	4·25	1·30
1076	**33**	15f. black	4·25	1·30
1077	**33**	25f. purple	4·25	1·30

(b) 1957 issue.

1078	**41**	10f. blue	4·25	1·30
1079	**41**	15f. black	4·25	1·30
1080	**41**	25f. purple	4·25	1·30

المؤتمر الدولي
للتاريخ/١٩٧٣
(219)

1973. International History Congress. Nos. 780, 783 and 786 optd with T 219.

1094		15f. multicoloured (postage)	12·00	4·50
1095		80f. multicoloured (air)	24·00	8·25
1096		500f. multicoloured	80·00	80·00

220 Iraqi Oil Workers

1973. First Anniv of Nationalization of Iraqi Oil Industry.

1097	**220**	25f. multicoloured	2·75	1·00
1098	**220**	70f. multicoloured	11·50	3·75

221 Harp

1973.

1099	**221**	5f. black and orange	25	10
1100	**221**	10f. black and brown	25	10
1101	**221**	20f. black and mauve	35	15
1102	–	25f. black and blue	60	20
1103	–	35f. black and green	70	35
1104	–	45f. black and blue	70	35
1105	–	50f. yellow and green	1·10	35
1106	–	70f. yellow and violet	1·40	65
1107	–	95f. yellow and brown	2·40	1·00

DESIGNS: 25, 35, 45f. Minaret of Mosul; 50, 70, 95f. Statue of a Goddess.

225a Iraqis and Flags

1973. July Festivals.

1122	**225a**	25f. multicoloured	95	45
1123	**225a**	35f. multicoloured	1·90	55

1973. International Journalists' Conference. Nos. 857/8 optd **I.O.J. SEPTEMBER 26-29. 1973**.

1124	**139**	15f. multicoloured	4·00	4·00
1125	**139**	50f. multicoloured	5·50	5·50

227 Interpol H.Q., Paris

1973. 50th Anniv of International Criminal Police Organization (Interpol).

1126	**227**	25f. multicoloured	1·40	80
1127	**227**	70f. multicoloured	7·25	4·75

228 Flags and Fair Emblems

1973. Tenth Baghdad International Fair.

1128	**228**	10f. multicoloured	60	35
1129	**228**	20f. multicoloured	1·10	45
1130	**228**	55f. multicoloured	2·40	1·20

229 W.M.O. Emblem

1973. Cent of World Meteorological Organization.

1148	**229**	25f. black, green & orge	95	20
1149	**229**	35f. black, green & mve	3·00	1·50

230 Arab Flags and Map

1973. 11th Session of Arab States' Civil Aviation Council, Baghdad.

1150	**230**	20f. multicoloured	60	20
1151	**230**	35f. multicoloured	1·90	1·20

المجلس التنفيذي

بغداد/١٩٧٣

(232)

1973. Sixth Executive Council Meeting of Arab Postal Union, Baghdad. No. 665 optd with T **232**.

1153	**75**	30f. blue and orange	6·75	4·00

233 Human Rights Emblem

1973. 25th Anniv of Declaration of Human Rights.

1154	**233**	25f. multicoloured	35	35
1155	**233**	70f. multicoloured	1·20	65

234 Shield and Military Activities

1974. 50th Anniv of Military College.

1156	**234**	25f. multicoloured	60	35
1157	**234**	35f. multicoloured	2·10	1·30

236 U.P.U. Emblem

1974. Centenary of Universal Postal Union.

1159	**236**	25f. multicoloured	1·20	35
1160	**236**	35f. multicoloured	1·20	55
1161	**236**	70f. multicoloured	2·20	1·30

237 Allegory of Nationalization

1974. Second Anniv of Nationalization of Iraqi Oil Industry.

1162	**237**	10f. multicoloured	60	20
1163	**237**	25f. multicoloured	1·20	35
1164	**237**	70f. multicoloured	3·50	2·75

238 Festival Theme

1975. July Festivals.

1165	**238**	20f. multicoloured	50	20
1166	**238**	35f. multicoloured	1·40	65

239 National Front Emblem and Heads

1975. First Anniv of Progressive National Front.

1167	**239**	20f. multicoloured	85	45
1168	**239**	50f. multicoloured	2·10	1·00

240 Cement Plant

1975. 25th Anniv of Iraqi Cement Industry.

1169	**240**	20f. multicoloured	60	35
1170	**240**	25f. multicoloured	85	45
1171	**240**	70f. multicoloured	1·90	1·50

1975. Surch.

1172	**155**	10f. on 3f. multicoloured	4·75	2·75
1173	-	25f. on 3f. mult (No. 892)	13·50	9·00

242 W.P.Y. Emblem

1975. World Population Year (1974).

1174	**242**	25f. green and blue	85	20
1175	**242**	35f. blue and mauve	1·40	80
1176	**242**	70f. violet and olive	4·25	1·80

243 Festival Emblems

1975. July Festivals.

1177	**243**	5f. multicoloured	35	20
1178	**243**	10f. multicoloured	35	35
1179	**243**	35f. multicoloured	2·40	1·00

244 Map and Emblems

1975. Tenth Anniv of Arab Labour Organization.

1180	**244**	25f. multicoloured	70	20
1181	**244**	35f. multicoloured	1·20	80
1182	**244**	45f. multicoloured	1·30	90

245 "Equality, Development, Peace"

1975. International Women's Year.

1183	**245**	10f. multicoloured	60	35
1184	**245**	35f. multicoloured	1·20	90
1185	**245**	70f. multicoloured	5·00	1·80

MS1186 100×83 mm. 100f. multi-coloured As T **245**, but face value outside design. Imperf ... 12·00 12·00

246 Diyala Barrage

1975. 25th Anniv of International Commission on Irrigation and Drainage.

1187	**246**	3f. multicoloured	25	10
1188	**246**	25f. multicoloured	95	35
1189	**246**	70f. multicoloured	3·75	1·80

247 Company Seal

1975. 25th Anniv of National Insurance Company, Baghdad.

1190	**247**	20f. multicoloured	1·10	35
1191	**247**	25f. multicoloured	1·30	55

MS1192 71×71 mm. **247** 100f. multi-coloured. Imperf ... 9·00 9·00

248 Court Musicians

1975. International Music Conference, Baghdad.

1193	**248**	25f. multicoloured	85	35
1194	**248**	45f. multicoloured	2·10	1·20

250 Telecommunications Centre

1975. Opening of Telecommunications Centre.

1203	**250**	5f. multicoloured	25	20
1204	**250**	10f. multicoloured	35	20
1205	**250**	60f. multicoloured	2·40	1·50

251 Diesel Train

1975. 15th Taurus Railway Conference, Baghdad. Multicoloured.

1206	**251**	25f. Type **251**	6·75	1·10
1207		30f. Diesel locomotive	10·00	4·50
1208		35f. Tank locomotive and train	13·50	4·50
1209		50f. Steam locomotive	19·00	11·00

252 Goddess (statue)

1976

1210	**252**	5f. multicoloured	10	10
1211	**252**	10f. multicoloured	10	10
1212	**252**	15f. multicoloured	35	10
1213	-	20f. multicoloured	35	15
1214	-	25f. multicoloured	60	20
1215	-	30f. multicoloured	85	20
1216	-	35f. multicoloured	1·10	35
1217	-	50f. multicoloured	1·60	35
1218	-	75f. multicoloured	2·20	80

DESIGNS: 20, 25, 30f. Two females forming column; 35, 50, 75f. Head of bearded man.

253 Soldier and Symbols of Industry and Agriculture

1976. Arab Day.

1219	**253**	5f. multicoloured	25	10
1220	**253**	25f. multicoloured on silver	70	20
1221	**253**	50f. mult on gold	2·10	80

254 Crossed-out Thumbprint

1976. Arab Literacy Day.

1222	**254**	5f. multicoloured	35	35
1223	**254**	15f. multicoloured	60	35
1224	**254**	35f. multicoloured	2·10	1·30

255 Iraq Earth Station

1976. 13th Anniv of Revolution of 14th Ramadan.

1225	**255**	10f. multicoloured	50	35
1226	**255**	25f. multicoloured on silver	1·40	55
1227	**255**	75f. mult on gold	6·00	2·20

256 Early and Modern Telephones

1976. Telephone Centenary.

1228	**256**	35f. multicoloured	1·60	55
1229	**256**	50f. multicoloured	3·25	90
1230	**256**	75f. multicoloured	5·00	1·30

257 Map and Emblem

1976. 20th International Arab Trade Unions Conf.

1231	**257**	5f. mult (postage)	50	20
1232	**257**	10f. multicoloured	50	20
1233	**257**	75f. multicoloured (air)	4·25	1·90

258 Iraqi Family on Map

1976. Police Day.

1234	**258**	5f. multicoloured	25	10
1235	**258**	15f. multicoloured	60	20
1236	**258**	35f. multicoloured	3·00	1·30

259 "Strategy" Pipeline

1976. Fourth Anniv of Oil Nationalisation.

1237	**259**	25f. multicoloured	2·10	20
1238	**259**	75f. multicoloured	4·75	2·20
MS1239	80×90 mm. 150f. multicoloured. Imperf		36·00	36·00

DESIGN—35×33 mm.: 150f. President Bakr embracing Prime Minister.

260 Human Eye

1976. Air. World Health Day. "Foresight Prevents Blindness".

1240	**260**	25f. blue and black	50	20
1241	**260**	35f. green and black	70	20
1242	**260**	50f. orange and brown	1·40	80

261 "Agriculture, Industry and Construction"

1976. July Festivals.

1243	**261**	15f. multicoloured	50	35
1244	**261**	35f. multicoloured	1·40	90

262 Basketball

1976. Olympic Games, Montreal. Multicoloured.

1245	**262**	25f. Type **262**	60	20
1246		35f. Volleyball	95	65
1247		50f. Wrestling	1·40	1·10
1248		75f. Boxing	2·75	1·80
MS1249	121×91 mm. 100f. Rifle-shooting. Imperf		8·50	8·50

263 Bishop Capucci, Wounded Dove and Map of Palestine

1976. Second Anniv of Bishop Capucci's Arrest.

1250	**263**	25f. multicoloured	85	20
1251	**263**	35f. multicoloured	95	45
1252	**263**	75f. multicoloured	3·25	1·70

264 River Kingfisher

1976. Birds. Multicoloured.

1253	**264**	5f. Type **264**	3·50	1·00
1254		10f. Turtle dove	3·50	1·00
1255		15f. Pin-tailed sandgrouse	4·25	1·00
1256		25f. Blue rock thrush	7·75	1·20
1257		50f. Purple heron and grey heron	12·00	1·80

See also Nos. O1258/62.

265 Emblem within "15"

1976. 15th Anniv of Iraqi Students' Union.

1263	**265**	30f. multicoloured	85	35
1264	**265**	70f. multicoloured	3·00	1·20

266 Children with Banner

1976. 30th Anniv of UNESCO. "Children's Books". Multicoloured.

1265	**266**	10f. Type **266**	35	35
1266		25f. Children in garden	2·75	55
1267		75f. Children with Iraqi flag	4·75	1·70

267 Tanker *Rumaila* and Emblem

1976. Fourth Anniv of First Iraqi Oil Tanker and First Anniv of Basrah Petroleum Co Nationalisation. Multicoloured.

1268	**267**	10f. Type **267**	85	35
1269	**267**	15f. Type **267**	1·20	45
1270		25f. Oil jetty and installations	2·75	90
1271		50f. As 25f.	3·75	1·60

268 Islamic Design with Inscriptions

1977. Birthday of Prophet Mohammed.

1272	**268**	25f. multicoloured	95	35
1273	**268**	35f. multicoloured	1·40	45

269 Dove Emblem

1977. Peace Day.

1274	**269**	25f. multicoloured	50	20
1275	**269**	30f. multicoloured	85	45

270 Dahlia

1977. Flowers. Multicoloured.

1276		5f. Type **270**	35	35
1277		10f. *Lathyrus odoratus*	60	35
1278		35f. *Chrysanthemum coronarium*	1·60	45
1279		50f. *Verbena hybrida*	3·00	90

271 "V" Emblem with Doves

1977. 30th Anniv of Al-Baath Party. Multicoloured.

1280		25f. Type **271**	70	20
1281		75f. Human figures as a flame	2·40	1·30
MS1282	80×60 mm. 100f. Dove with olive-branch. Imperf		7·25	7·25

272 A.P.U. Emblem and Flags

1977. 25th Anniv of Arab Postal Union.

1283	**272**	25f. multicoloured	50	20
1284	**272**	35f. multicoloured	95	55

273 1st May Emblem

1977. Labour Day.

1285	**273**	10f. multicoloured	25	10
1286	**273**	30f. multicoloured	70	20
1287	**273**	35f. multicoloured	95	80

274 First Stage of Lift

1977. Eighth Asian Weightlifting Championships, Baghdad. Multicoloured.

1288		25f. Type **274**	1·10	65
1289		75f. Press-up stage of lift	3·00	1·60
MS1290	60×80 mm. 100f. Championships emblem. Imperf		10·00	10·00

275 Dome of the Rock

1977. Palestinian Welfare.

1291	**275**	5f. multicoloured	4·00	65

276 Arabian Garden

1977. Arab Tourism Year. Multicoloured.

1292		5f. Type **276**	35	35
1293		10f. Town view with minarets (horiz)	35	35
1294		30f. Country stream	1·20	35
1295		50f. Oasis (horiz)	3·50	2·20

277 Dove and Ear of Wheat

1977. July Festivals.

1296	**277**	25f. multicoloured	70	20
1297	**277**	30f. multicoloured	95	45

278 Map of Middle East and North Africa

1977. U.N. Conference on Desertification.

1298	**278**	30f. multicoloured	95	55
1299	**278**	70f. multicoloured	3·00	1·10

279 Emblem

1977. Census Day.

1300	**279**	20f. multicoloured	35	20
1301	**279**	30f. multicoloured	95	20
1302	**279**	70f. multicoloured	1·80	1·00

280 Abstract Calligraphic Emblem

1977. Al-Mutanabby Festival.

1303	**280**	25f. multicoloured	35	10
1304	**280**	50f. multicoloured	85	55

281 Kamal Jumblatt and Political Caricatures

1977. Kamal Jumblatt (Lebanese socialist) Commemoration.

1305	**281**	20f. multicoloured	50	35
1306	**281**	30f. multicoloured	70	35
1307	**281**	70f. multicoloured	1·60	80

282 Hajeer Year Emblem

1977. Hajeer Year.

1308	282	30f. multicoloured	50	20
1309	282	35f. multicoloured	70	35

283 Girl, Boy and National Flag Ribbon

1978. Youth Day.

1310	283	10f. multicoloured	25	10
1311	283	15f. multicoloured	25	20
1312	283	35f. multicoloured	70	45

284 Hand placing Coin in Box

1978. Sixth Anniv of Postal Savings Bank.

1313	284	15f. multicoloured	50	15
1314	284	25f. multicoloured	70	20
1315	284	35f. multicoloured	1·30	55

285 Transmitting and Receiving Equipment

1978. Tenth World Telecommunications Day and First Anniv of Iraqi Microwave Network.

1316	285	25f. multicoloured	60	20
1317	285	35f. multicoloured	60	20
1318	285	75f. multicoloured	1·30	80

286 Map and Flags

1978. First Conference of Arabian Gulf Postal Ministers.

1319	286	25f. multicoloured	70	20
1320	286	35f. multicoloured	1·20	65

287 Silver Coins

1978. Ancient Iraqi Coins.

1321	287	1f. black, silver & yellow	20	10
1322	-	2f. black, gold and blue	20	10
1323	-	3f. black, silver & orange	20	10
1324	-	4f. black, gold and green	25	20
1325	-	5f. black, gold and green	3·00	2·75

DESIGNS—HORIZ: 2f. Two gold coins; 3f. Two silver coins; 4f. Two gold coins. VERT: 75f. Gold coin.

288 Flower Emblem

1978. July Festivals.

1326	288	25f. multicoloured	50	20
1327	288	35f. multicoloured	70	35
MS1328		80×60 mm. 100f. multicoloured (horiz)	7·75	7·75

DESIGN: 100f. Flame and emblem.

289 Nurse, Hospital and Sick Child

1978. Global Eradication of Smallpox.

1329	289	25f. multicoloured	35	10
1330	289	35f. multicoloured	85	35
1331	289	75f. multicoloured	2·40	1·20

290 Altharthar–Euphrates Canal

1978

1332	290	5f. multicoloured	25	20
1333	290	10f. multicoloured	25	20
1334	290	15f. multicoloured	25	20
1335	290	25f. multicoloured	25	20
1336	290	35f. multicoloured	50	20
1337	290	50f. multicoloured	95	45

See also Nos. O1338/41.

291 I.M.C.O. Emblem

1978. World Maritime Day.

1342	291	25f. multicoloured	70	35
1343	291	75f. multicoloured	1·80	65

292 Workers in the Countryside

1978. Tenth Anniv of People's Work Groups.

1344	292	10f. multicoloured	35	20
1345	292	25f. multicoloured	70	20
1346	292	35f. multicoloured	1·30	80

293 Fair Emblem

1978. Baghdad International Fair.

1347	293	25f. multicoloured	25	20
1348	293	35f. multicoloured	35	20
1349	293	75f. multicoloured	2·30	1·10

294 Map, Rule and Emblem

1978. World Standards Day.

1350	294	25f. multicoloured	25	10
1351	294	35f. multicoloured	35	20
1352	294	75f. multicoloured	2·10	1·10

295 Conference Chamber

1978. Ninth Arab Summit Conference, Baghdad.

1353	295	25f. multicoloured	35	20
1354	295	35f. multicoloured	50	20
1355	295	75f. multicoloured	1·60	1·10

296 Congress Emblem

1978. Fourth Congress of Association of Thoracic and Cardiovascular Surgeons of Asia.

1356	296	25f. multicoloured	50	20
1357	296	75f. multicoloured	1·40	90

297 Pilgrims and Kaaba

1978. Pilgrimage to Mecca.

1358	297	25f. multicoloured	50	20
1359	297	35f. multicoloured	70	35

298 Map and Symbol

1978. U.N. Conference for Technical Co-operation among Developing Countries.

1360	298	25f. multicoloured	35	20
1361	298	50f. multicoloured	85	35
1362	298	75f. multicoloured	1·30	80

299 Hands holding Emblem

1978. International Year to Combat Racism.

1363	299	25f. multicoloured	50	20
1364	299	50f. multicoloured	95	35
1365	299	75f. multicoloured	2·75	80

300 Globe and Human Rights Emblem

1978. 30th Anniv of Declaration of Human Rights.

1366	300	25f. multicoloured	60	20
1367	300	75f. multicoloured	2·10	1·50

301 Candle and Emblem

1979. Police Day.

1368	301	10f. multicoloured	50	35
1369	301	25f. multicoloured	50	35
1370	301	35f. multicoloured	85	35

302 Open Book, Pencil and Flame

1979. Anniv of Application of Compulsory Education Law.

1371	302	15f. multicoloured	25	20
1372	302	25f. multicoloured	50	20
1373	302	35f. multicoloured	1·20	35

303 School, Teacher and Assyrian Relief

1979. Teachers' Day.

1374	303	10f. multicoloured	25	20

1375	303	15f. multicoloured	25	20
1376	303	50f. multicoloured	1·20	65

304 Clenched Fist, Pencil and Book

1979. National Literacy Campaign.

1377	304	15f. multicoloured	35	35
1378	304	25f. multicoloured	60	35
1379	304	35f. multicoloured	95	35

305 World map, Koran and Symbols of Arab Achievements

1979. The Arabs.

1380	305	35f. multicoloured	70	20
1381	305	75f. multicoloured	2·10	90

306 Girl playing Flute

1979. Mosul Spring Festival.

1382	306	15f. multicoloured	50	35
1383	306	25f. multicoloured	70	35
1384	306	35f. multicoloured	1·40	55

307 Iraqi Map and Flag with U.P.U. Emblem

1979. 50th Anniv of Admission to Universal Postal Union.

1385	307	25f. multicoloured	85	35
1386	307	35f. multicoloured	85	35
1387	307	75f. multicoloured	2·10	90

308 Championship Emblem with Sea and Sky

1979. Fifth Arabian Gulf Football Championship.

1388	308	10f. multicoloured	25	20
1389	308	25f. multicoloured	50	20
1390	308	50f. multicoloured	1·20	65

309 Child with Globe and Candle

1979. International Year of the Child.

1391	309	25f. multicoloured	95	45
1392	309	75f. multicoloured	2·40	1·50
MS1393		68×80 mm. 100f. multicoloured (vert)	31·00	28·00

DESIGN: 100f. Two children and U.N. emblem.

310 Flower and Branch

1979. July Festivals.

1394	310	15f. multicoloured	25	20
1395	310	25f. multicoloured	50	20
1396	310	35f. multicoloured	70	35

311 Children supporting Globe

1979. 50th Anniv of International Bureau of Education.

1397	311	25f. multicoloured	70	35
1398	311	50f. multicoloured	1·30	65
1399	311	100f. multicoloured	2·20	1·30

312 Jawad Selim (sculptor)

1979. Writers and Artists. Multicoloured.

1400		25f. Type 312	60	35
1401		25f. S. al-Hosari (philosopher)	60	35
1402		25f. Mustapha Jawad (historian)	60	35

313 The Kaaba, Mecca

1979. Pilgrimage to Mecca.

1403	313	25f. multicoloured	60	35
1404	313	50f. multicoloured	1·10	45

314 Figure "20" and Globe

1979. 20th Anniv of Iraqi News Agency.

1405	314	25f. multicoloured	60	20
1406	314	50f. multicoloured	1·30	35
1407	314	75f. multicoloured	1·70	55

315 Wave Pattern and Television Screen

1979. World Telecommunications Exhibition and Radio Conference, Geneva.

1408	315	25f. multicoloured	60	20
1409	315	50f. multicoloured	95	45
1410	315	75f. multicoloured	1·70	80

316 Clenched Fists and Refugee

1979. Palestinian Solidarity Day.

1411	316	25f. multicoloured	1·10	35
1412	316	50f. multicoloured	2·10	55
1413	316	75f. multicoloured	3·00	1·00

317 Ahmed Hassan Al-Bakir

1979. Inaug of Pres. Saddam Hussain. Multicoloured.

1414		25f. Type 317	50	35
1415		35f. Pres. Hussain taking the oath	70	35
1416		75f. Type 317	1·30	55
1417		100f. As No. 1415	5·00	2·75

318 Boy with Violin

1979. Activities of Vanguards (youth organization). Multicoloured.

1418		10f. Type 318	35	35
1419		15f. Boys on building site	35	35
1420		25f. Boys on assault course and in personal combat	50	35
1421		35f. Vanguards emblem	60	35

319 Wind-speed Indicator and Thermometer

1980. World Meteorological Day.

1422	319	15f. multicoloured	25	20
1423	319	25f. multicoloured	35	20
1424	319	35f. multicoloured	85	35

320 Lighting Cigarette and Cancerous Lungs

1980. World Health Day. Anti-smoking Campaign.

1425	320	25f. multicoloured	50	35
1426	320	35f. multicoloured	60	35
1427	320	75f. multicoloured	2·40	65

321 Festivals Emblem

1980. July Festivals.

1428	321	25f. multicoloured	50	35
1429	321	35f. multicoloured	60	35
MS1430 60×80 mm. 100f. Pres. Hussain (27×44 mm)			7·25	7·25

322 Hurdling

1980. Olympic Games, Moscow. Multicoloured.

1431		15f. Type 322	35	35
1432		20f. Weightlifting (vert)	60	45
1433		30f. Boxing	1·10	55
1434		35f. Football (vert)	2·10	1·00
MS1435 79×60 mm. 100f. Wrestling (37×29 mm)			12·00	12·00

323 *Rubus sanctus*

1980. Fruit. Multicoloured.

1436		5f. Type 323	35	20
1437		15f. Peaches	60	20
1438		20f. Pears	85	20
1439		25f. Apples	1·10	20
1440		35f. Plums	1·40	45

324 Conference Emblem and Arabic Text

1980. World Tourism Conference, Manila.

1441	324	25f. multicoloured	50	20
1442	324	50f. multicoloured	1·10	35
1443	324	100f. multicoloured	2·10	1·10

325 A.P.U. Emblem Posthorn and Map

1980. 11th Congress of Arab Postal Union, Baghdad.

1444	325	10f. multicoloured	35	35
1445	325	30f. multicoloured	60	35
1446	325	35f. multicoloured	85	35

326 O.P.E.C. Emblem and Globe

1980. 20th Anniv of Organization of Petroleum Exporting Countries.

1447	326	30f. multicoloured	95	35
1448	326	75f. multicoloured	2·10	1·00

327 African Monarch

1980. Butterflies. Multicoloured.

1449		10f. Swallowtail	2·20	35
1450		15f. Type 327	2·75	65
1451		20f. Red admiral	3·50	90
1452		30f. Clouded yellow	6·00	1·50

328 Mosque and Ka'aba

1980. 1400th Anniv of Hegira.

1453	328	15f. multicoloured	35	20
1454	328	25f. multicoloured	70	20
1455	328	35f. multicoloured	85	45

329 Riflemen and Dome of the Rock on Map of Israel

1980. Palestinian Solidarity Day.

1456	329	25f. multicoloured	70	20
1457	329	35f. multicoloured	1·10	35
1458	329	75f. multicoloured	2·20	1·00

330 Soldier and Rocket

1981. 60th Anniv of Army Day.

1459	330	5f. multicoloured	35	20
1460	330	30f. multicoloured	70	20
1461	330	75f. multicoloured	1·90	90

331 "8" and Flags forming Torch

1981. 18th Anniv of 14th Ramadan Revolution.

1462	331	15f. multicoloured	35	20
1463	331	30f. multicoloured	60	20
1464	331	35f. multicoloured	85	35

332 Map of Arab States tied with Ribbon

1981. The Arabs.

1465	332	5f. multicoloured	25	20
1466	332	25f. multicoloured	60	20
1467	332	35f. multicoloured	85	35

333 Pres. Hussain and Modern Military Equipment

1981. Saddam's Battle of Qadisiya.

1468	333	30f. multicoloured	60	20
1469	333	35f. multicoloured	70	35
1470	333	75f. multicoloured	1·30	65
MS1471 80×59 mm. 100f. Pres. Hussain, military equipment and flag (37×29 mm)			6·00	6·00

334 I.T.U. and W.H.O. Emblems and Ribbons forming Caduceus

1981. World Telecommunications Day.

1472	334	25f. multicoloured	70	35
1473	334	50f. multicoloured	1·40	55
1474	334	75f. multicoloured	2·40	1·10

335 Mil Mi-24 Helicopters attacking Ground Forces

1981. 50th Anniv of Air Force. Multicoloured.

1475		5f. Type 335 (postage)	25	20
1476		10f. Antonov An-2 biplane trainer	50	20
1477		15f. "SAM-15" missile	60	20
1478		120f. de Havilland Dragon Rapide biplane and Mikoyan Gurevich MiG-21 jet fighters (vert) (air)	5·00	2·75

336 Map and
Flower enclosing
Ballot Box

1981. First Anniv of National Assembly Election.
1479	336	30f. multicoloured	60	20
1480	336	35f. multicoloured	70	20
1481	336	45f. multicoloured	1·20	45

337 Festivals Emblem

1981. July Festivals.
1482	337	15f. multicoloured	35	10
1483	337	25f. multicoloured	50	20
1484	337	35f. multicoloured	85	20

338 Basket Weaver

1981. Popular Industries. Multicoloured.
1485	5f. Type 338	25	20
1486	30f. Copper worker	70	20
1487	35f. Potter	95	35
1488	50f. Weaver (horiz)	1·20	45

339 Saddam
Hussain
Gymnasium

1981. Modern Buildings. Multicoloured.
1489	336	45f. Type 339	95	35
1490	50f. Palace of Conferences	95	35
1491	120f. As 50f.	2·75	1·80
1492	150f. Type 339	3·50	2·00

340 Pilgrims

1981. Pilgrimage to Mecca.
1493	340	25f. multicoloured	70	15
1494	340	45f. multicoloured	1·30	45
1495	340	50f. multicoloured	1·30	45

341 Harvesting

1981. World Food Day.
1496	341	30f. multicoloured	70	20
1497	341	45f. multicoloured	1·30	55
1498	341	75f. multicoloured	1·90	1·00

343 Teacher with
Deaf Child

1981. International Year of Disabled Persons.
1501	343	30f. multicoloured	60	35
1502	343	45f. multicoloured	95	45
1503	343	75f. multicoloured	1·30	80

344 Medal and
Map

1981. Martyr's Day.
1504	344	45f. multicoloured	60	45
1505	344	50f. multicoloured	70	55
1506	344	120f. multicoloured	1·90	1·30

See also Nos. O1507/9.

345 *Ibn Khaldoon*
(freighter)

1981. Fifth Anniv of United Arab Shipping Company.
| 1507 | 345 | 50f. multicoloured | 1·60 | 65 |
| 1508 | 345 | 120f. multicoloured | 4·25 | 2·00 |

346 Woman and
Symbols of
Technology

1982. Iraqi Women's Day.
1509	346	25f. multicoloured	70	20
1510	346	45f. multicoloured	1·20	55
1511	346	50f. multicoloured	1·20	65

347 President
Hussain, "7" and
"Flowers"

1982. 35th Anniv of Al-Baath Party. Multicoloured.
1512	25f. Type 347	60	20
1513	30f. Rainbow and "7 7 7"	60	20
1514	45f. Type 347	95	55
1515	50f. As 30f.	95	55

MS1516 99×53 mm. 150f. Pres. Hussain, globe and Arabic "7" (27×39 mm). Imperf   4·75   4·75

348 A.P.U. Emblem
and Globe

1982. 30th Anniv of Arab Postal Union.
1517	348	25f. multicoloured	70	20
1518	348	45f. multicoloured	1·20	45
1519	348	50f. multicoloured	1·20	45

349 White Storks

1982. Mosul Spring Festival. Multicoloured.
1520	349	25f. Type 349	1·40	20
1521	30f. Doll	85	20
1522	349	45f. Type 349	1·40	65
1523	50f. As 30f.	1·30	55

350 World Map, Factories
and "1"

1982. Labour Day.
1524	350	25f. multicoloured	60	10
1525	350	45f. multicoloured	85	45
1526	350	50f. multicoloured	95	55

351 Geometric Figure and
I.T.U. Problem

1982. World Telecommunications Day.
1527	351	5f. multicoloured	20	10
1528	351	45f. multicoloured	95	45
1529	351	100f. multicoloured	2·20	1·20

352 Oil Gusher

1982. Tenth Anniv of Oil Nationalization. Multicoloured.
1530	5f. Type 352	35	15
1531	25f. Type 352	70	20
1532	45f. Bronze sculpture of bull and horse flanking couple holding model of oil rig	1·40	55
1533	50f. As 45f.	1·70	55

353 Nuclear Power
Emblem and Lion

1982. First Anniv of Attack on Iraqi Nuclear Reactor. Multicoloured.
1534	30f. Type 353	70	35
1535	45f. Bomb aimed at egg	1·20	35
1536	50f. Type 353	1·30	55
1537	120f. As No. 1535	2·40	1·70

354 Footballers

1982. World Cup Football Championship, Spain. Multicoloured.
1538	5f. Type 354	60	35
1539	45f. Three footballers	95	45
1540	50f. Type 354	1·00	55
1541	100f. As 45f.	1·90	1·20

MS1542 85×60 mm. 150f. Two footballers (horiz)   4·25   4·25

355 President
Hussain and
Fireworks

1982. July Festivals.
1543	355	25f. multicoloured	35	20
1544	355	45f. multicoloured	85	35
1545	355	50f. multicoloured	85	45

356 Green Lizard

1982. Reptiles. Multicoloured.
1546	356	25f. Type 356	2·75	90
1547	30f. Asp	2·75	90
1548	45f. Two green lizards	3·50	1·20
1549	50f. "Natrix tessellata"	3·75	1·80

357 Pandit Nehru
(India)

1982. Seventh Non-Aligned Countries Conference, Baghdad. Multicoloured.
1550	50f. Type 357	1·10	45
1551	50f. Josef Tito (Yugoslavia)	1·10	45
1552	50f. Abdul Nasser (Egypt)	1·10	45
1553	50f. Kwame Nkrumah (Ghana)	1·10	45
1554	100f. President Hussain (Iraq)	2·40	1·20

358 Microscope and
Bacilli

1982. Cent of Discovery of Tubercule Bacillus.
1555	358	20f. multicoloured	85	20
1556	358	50f. multicoloured	1·60	45
1557	358	100f. multicoloured	2·75	1·10

359 U.P.U. Building, Berne

1982. U.P.U. Day.
1561	359	5f. multicoloured	25	15
1562	359	45f. multicoloured	85	45
1563	359	100f. multicoloured	2·20	1·10

360 Drums

1982. Musical Instruments. Multicoloured.
1564	5f. Type 360	35	15
1565	10f. Stringed board instrument	35	20
1566	35f. Bowed instruments	1·10	35
1567	100f. Mandolin	3·50	1·20

361 Mosque and Minaret,
Mecca

1982. Prophet Mohammed's Birthday. Multicoloured.
1568	25f. Type 361	35	20
1569	30f. Courtyard of mosque	50	20
1570	45f. Type 361	70	45
1571	50f. As No. 1569	85	45

362 Flowers

1982. Flowers. Multicoloured.
1572	10f. Type 362	35	20
1573	20f. Flowers (different)	60	20
1574	30f. Type 362	70	35
1575	40f. As No. 1573	1·20	55

1576	50f. Type **362**	1·40	65
1577	100f. As No. 1573	3·00	1·30

1983. Nos. 1489/51 surch.

1578	60f. on 50f. Palace of Conferences	1·60	45
1579	70f. on 45f. Type **339**	2·10	65
1580	160f. on 120f. Palace of Conferences	5·00	2·20

364 President Hussain

1983. July Festivals.

1583	**364**	30f. multicoloured	60	35
1584	**364**	60f. multicoloured	1·30	55
1585	**364**	70f. multicoloured	1·70	80

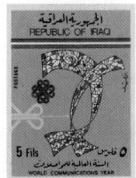

365 Emblem and Interlocked Bands

1983. World Communications Year. Multicoloured.

1586		5f. Type **365**	20	10
1587		25f. Hexagons of primary colours	35	20
1588		60f. Type **365**	1·30	65
1589		70f. As No. 1587	1·40	80
MS1590	80×60 mm. 200f. Emblem. Imperf		5·00	5·00

366 Horseman and Map

1983. Battle of Thiqar. Multicoloured.

1591	20f. Type **366**	35	20
1592	50f. Eagle swooping on pyre	95	45
1593	60f. Type **366**	1·20	55
1594	70f. As No. 1592	1·30	65

367 Fair Emblem and Silhouette of Baghdad

1983. Baghdad International Fair.

1595	**367**	60f. multicoloured	95	55
1596	**367**	70f. multicoloured	1·20	65
1597	**367**	160f. multicoloured	2·75	1·80

368 Pres. Hussain within Figure "9"

1983. Ninth Al-Baath Party Congress. Multicoloured.

1598	**368**	30f. Type **368**	50	35
1599		60f. Eagle, torch, map and book	95	55
1600	**368**	70f. Type **368**	1·20	65
1601		100f. As No. 1599	1·80	90

369 Fishermen hauling Boat

1983. Paintings. Multicoloured.

1602	60f. Type **369**	1·70	65
1603	60f. *Festive crowd*	1·70	65
1604	60f. *Hanging decorations*	1·70	65
1605	70f. *Crowd*	1·90	1·00
1606	70f. *Bazaar*	1·90	1·00

370 Dove and Victim

1983. Massacre of Palestinians in Sabra and Shatila Refugee Camps, Lebanon. Multicoloured.

1607	10f. Type **370**	35	20
1608	60f. Type **370**	1·30	55
1609	70f. Dove and clasped fist shedding blood and victims	1·60	65
1610	160f. As No. 1609	3·50	1·90

371 Apartment Building

1983. Buildings.

1611	**371** 60f. lt green, black & grn	95	55
1612	- 70f. purple, black & grey	1·20	65
1613	- 160f. purple, blk & grey	3·00	1·50
1614	**371** 200f. green, black & olive	3·50	1·90

DESIGNS: 70, 160f. Apartment building (different).
See also Nos. O1615/16.

372 President Hussain

1983. Fourth Anniv of President Hussain as Party and State Leader.

1617	**372**	60f. multicoloured	95	45
1618	**372**	70f. multicoloured	1·30	65
1619	**372**	250f. multicoloured	4·25	2·50

373 Congress Emblem

1984. 25th International Military Medicine and Pharmacy Congress.

1620	**373**	60f. multicoloured	1·10	55
1621	**373**	70f. multicoloured	1·30	65
1622	**373**	200f. multicoloured	3·50	1·90

374 President Hussain and Flowers

1984. Pres. Saddam Hussain's 47th Birthday. Multicoloured.

1623	60f. Type **374**	85	45
1624	70f. Pres. Hussain in army uniform	95	55
1625	160f. As No. 1623	2·75	1·80
1626	200f. Type **374**	3·25	2·10
MS1627	81×61 mm. 250f. Pres. Hussain and rose (horiz)	5·00	5·00

375 Boxing

1984. Olympic Games, Los Angeles. Multicoloured.

1628	50f. Type **375**	95	65
1629	60f. Hurdling, weightlifting and wrestling	1·20	65
1630	70f. Type **375**	1·40	80
1631	100f. As No. 1629	2·10	1·20
MS1632	80×60 mm. 200f. Footballers (30×40 mm)	4·75	4·75

376 Pres. Hussain and Horses' Heads

1984. Battle of Qadisiya. Multicoloured.

1633	50f. Type **376**	70	45
1634	60f. President Hussain and symbolic representation of battle	95	55
1635	70f. Type **376**	1·10	65
1636	100f. As No. 1634	1·70	90
MS1637	80×60 mm. 200f. Shield and eagle (30×40 mm)	4·75	4·75

377 Flag as Ribbon and Two Domes

1984. Martyr's Day. Multicoloured.

1638	50f. Type **377**	60	45
1639	60f. Woman holding rifle and medal	85	45
1640	70f. Type **377**	95	55
1641	100f. As No. 1639	1·30	90

378 Text

1985. Fifth Anniv of President Hussain's Visit to Al-Mustansiriyah University.

1646	378 60f. red and blue	70	45
1647	378 70f. red and green	85	55
1648	378 250f. red and black	3·25	1·90

379 Pres. Hussain and Jet Fighters

1985. 54th Anniv of Iraqi Air Force. Multicoloured.

1649	10f. Type **379**	35	10
1650	60f. Fighter airplanes trailing flag and "54" (horiz)	1·70	90
1651	70f. As No. 1650	1·90	90
1652	160f. Type **379**	4·75	2·20
MS1653	80×60 mm. 200f. As No. 1650	6·00	6·00

380 Pres. Hussain within Flower

1985. 48th Birthday of President Saddam Hussain. Multicoloured.

1654	30f. Type **380**	50	35

1655	60f. Pres. Hussain, candle and flowers	85	45
1656	70f. Type **380**	95	55
1657	100f. As No. 1655	1·40	80
MS1658	87×60 mm. 200f. "28", flowers and text	4·25	4·25

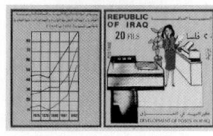

381 Graph and Modern Office

1985. Posts and Telecommunications Development. Multicoloured.

1659	20f. Type **381**	50	20
1660	50f. Dish aerial and graph	95	45
1661	60f. Type **381**	95	45
1662	70f. As No. 1660	1·20	65

382 Arms at Crossroads, and Building

1985. Saddam's Battle of Qadisiya. Multicoloured.

1663	10f. Type **382**	25	20
1664	20f. Pres. Hussain and emblem of Al-Baath Party	35	20
1665	60f. Type **382**	1·20	55
1666	70f. As No. 1664	1·30	90
MS1667	80×60 mm. 200f. Peace dove and soldiers (27×43 mm)	4·00	4·00

383 Solar Energy Research Centre

1985.

1668	**383**	10f. multicoloured	25	10
1669	**383**	50f. multicoloured	1·20	55
1670	**383**	100f. multicoloured	2·40	1·20

384 Disabled Children

1985. UNICEF Child Survival Campaign. Multicoloured.

1671	10f. Type **384**	15	10
1672	15f. Toddler and baby	25	20
1673	50f. Type **384**	95	45
1674	100f. As No. 1672	1·90	1·10

385 Hand holding Quill

1985. Death Millenary of Al-Sharif Al-Radhi (poet).

1675	**385**	10f. multicoloured	35	10
1676	**385**	50f. multicoloured	70	45
1677	**385**	100f. multicoloured	1·60	1·00

386 U.N. Emblem

1985. 40th Anniv of U.N.O.

1678	**386**	10f. multicoloured	20	10
1679	**386**	40f. blue, black & yellow	70	35
1680	**386**	100f. multicoloured	1·80	1·00

387 World Map

1985. Palestinian Solidarity Day.
1681	387	10f. multicoloured	35	15
1682	387	50f. multicoloured	1·20	55
1683	387	100f. multicoloured	2·75	1·20

389 I.Y.Y. Emblem and Soldier with Flag

1985. Martyr's Day.
1684	388	10f. multicoloured	25	20
1685	388	40f. multicoloured	60	35
1686	388	100f. multicoloured	1·70	1·00

388 Flag, Man and Blood Vessels as Roots

1985. International Youth Year. Multicoloured.
1687	389	40f. Type **389**	60	35
1688	389	50f. Young couple, flag and I.Y.Y. emblem	85	45
1689	389	100f. Type **389**	1·80	1·00
1690	389	200f. As No. 1688	3·50	2·75
MS1691 80×60 mm. 250f. Cogwheel, flag, rifle and symbols of agriculture, industry and science (29×44 mm)			5·00	5·00

390 Pres. Hussain and Soldier in "6"

1986. Army Day. Multicoloured.
1692	390	10f. Type **390**	25	20
1693	390	40f. Pres. Hussain, cogwheel, "6" and missiles (horiz)	85	35
1694	390	50f. Type **390**	1·10	45
1695	390	100f. As No. 1693	2·30	1·20
MS1696 80×60 mm. 200f. Pres. Hussain, "6" in star and rifle (51×36 mm)			5·00	5·00

391 Pen as Knife in Sheet of Text

1986. Iraqi Prisoners of War Commemoration. Multicoloured.
1697	391	30f. Type **391**	50	35
1698	391	70f. Dove, cherub holding flag and three prisoners	95	55
1699	391	100f. Type **391**	1·40	90
1700	391	200f. As No. 1698	3·25	1·80
MS1701 110×80 mm. 250f. As Nos. 1699/1700			5·50	5·50

392 Pres. Hussain with Children

1986. 49th Birthday of President Saddam Hussain. Multicoloured.
1702	392	30f. Type **392**	60	35
1703	392	50f. Pres. Hussain and doves holding flag	95	45
1704	392	100f. Type **392**	1·90	90
1705	392	150f. As No. 1703	2·75	1·20
MS1706 80×60 mm. 250f. Pres. Hussain, flag and flowers			5·00	5·00

393 Worker, Globe and Cogwheel

1986. Labour Day. Multicoloured.
1707	393	10f. Type **393**	35	35
1708	393	40f. Candle in cogwheel	95	35
1709	393	100f. Type **393**	1·80	90
1710	393	150f. As No. 1708	2·75	1·20

394 Pres. Hussain and "30 July 17"

1986. July Festivals and Seventh Anniv of Pres. Hussain's State Leadership. Multicoloured.
1711	394	20f. Type **394**	35	20
1712	394	30f. Pres. Hussain and "17 1986"	50	20
1713	394	100f. Type **394**	1·60	90
1714	394	150f. As No. 1712	2·40	1·50
MS1715 80×60 mm. 250f. Pres. Hussain within laurel wreath and text			5·00	5·00

395 Pres. Hussain and Jet Fighter

1986. 55th Anniv of Iraqi Air Force. Multicoloured.
1716	395	30f. Type **395**	95	35
1717	395	50f. Pres. Hussain and jet fighters	1·80	45
1718	395	100f. Type **395**	3·50	1·90
1719	395	150f. As No. 1717	5·50	2·50
MS1720 80×60 mm. 250f. Air Force Medal. Imperf			6·75	6·75

396 Refinery

1986. Oil Nationalization Day. Multicoloured.
1721	396	10f. Type **396**	15	10
1722	396	40f. Derrick and pipeline within flag (vert)	70	20
1723	396	100f. Type **396**	1·90	1·00
1724	396	150f. As No. 1722	2·75	1·80

397 Arab Warrior

1986. First Battle of Qadisiya. Multicoloured.
1725	397	20f. Type **397**	50	10
1726	397	60f. Pres. Hussain and battle scene	1·10	55
1727	397	70f. Type **397**	1·20	65
1728	397	100f. As No. 1726	2·10	90

398 Pres. Hussain, Battlefield and Cheering Soldiers

1986. Saadam's Battle of Qadisiya. Multicoloured.
1729	398	30f. Type **398**	1·20	35
1730	398	40f. Pres. Hussain within flag "swords" and symbols of ancient and modern warfare (horiz)	1·60	55
1731	398	100f. Type **398**	3·25	1·60
1732	398	150f. As No. 1730	5·50	2·20
MS1733 80×60 mm. 250f. Pres. Hussain, soldiers and flag "swords". Imperf			6·00	6·00

399 Pres. Hussain

1986
1734	399	30f. multicoloured	85	20
1735	399	50f. multicoloured	1·20	35
1736	399	100f. multicoloured	2·40	90
1737	399	150f. multicoloured	3·25	1·10
1738	399	250f. multicoloured	6·00	1·90
1739	399	350f. multicoloured	8·50	2·50

401 Women

1986. Iraqi Women's Day. Multicoloured.
1744	401	30f. Type **401**	60	35
1745	401	50f. Woman and battle scenes (horiz)	85	45
1746	401	100f. Type **401**	1·80	1·00
1747	401	150f. As No. 1745	3·00	1·50

402 Flag and Treble Clef forming Dove

1986. International Peace Year. Multicoloured.
1748	402	50f. Type **402**	85	35
1749	402	100f. Globe, dove with flag and hand holding rifle and olive branch	1·60	80
1750	402	150f. Type **402**	2·30	1·50
1751	402	As No. 1749	3·25	1·90
MS1752 80×60 mm. 200f. I.P.Y. emblem, flag and dove and fist on map. Imperf			3·25	3·25

403 Freighter *Al Alwah* and Map

1987. Tenth Anniv of United Arab Shipping Company. Multicoloured.
1753	403	50f. Type **403**	70	35
1754	403	100f. Container ship *Khaled Ibn Al Waleed*	1·40	80
1755	403	150f. Type **403**	2·30	1·10
1756	403	250f. As No. 1754	3·50	1·90
MS1757 100×90 mm. 200f. *Khaled Ibn Al Waleed* at wharf. Imperf			4·25	4·25

404 Activities on Tree

1987. 40th Anniv of UNICEF. Multicoloured.
1758	404	20f. Type **404**	35	35
1759	404	40f. Doves and "40" containing children and UNICEF emblem (horiz)	50	45
1760	404	90f. Type **404**	1·20	1·10
1761	404	100f. As No. 1759	1·30	1·20

405 Pres. Hussain in "6"

1987. Army Day. Multicoloured.
1762	405	20f. Type **405**	35	35
1763	405	40f. Pres. Hussain and military scenes	50	45
1764	405	90f. Type **405**	1·20	1·10
1765	405	100f. As No. 1763	1·30	1·20

406 Torch, Cogwheel, Wheat and Map

1987. 40th Anniv of Al-Baath Party. Multicoloured.
1766	406	20f. Type **406**	35	35
1767	406	40f. Pres. Hussain, map and flag as "7"	50	45
1768	406	90f. Type **406**	1·20	1·10
1769	406	100f. As No. 1767	1·30	1·20

407 Pres. Hussain

1987. 50th Birthday of President Saddam Hussain. Multicoloured.
1770	407	20f. Type **407**	35	35
1771	407	40f. Anniversary dates, flowers and Pres. Hussain	50	45
1772	407	90f. Type **407**	1·20	1·10
1773	407	100f. As No. 1771	1·30	1·20

408 Pres. Hussain, Civilians, Soldiers and buried Soldier

1987. July Festivals and Eighth Anniv of Pres. Hussain's State Leadership. Multicoloured.
1774	408	20f. Pres. Hussain and flag (horiz)	35	35
1775	408	40f. Type **408**	50	45
1776	408	90f. As No. 1174	1·20	1·10
1777	408	100f. Type **408**	1·30	1·20

409 Symbolic Family on Graph

1987. Census. Multicoloured.

1778	20f. Type **409**	35	20
1779	30f. People on graph	50	35
1780	50f. As No. 1779	70	35
1781	500f. Type **409**	6·75	4·75

410 Pres. Hussain in "6" and Troops

1988. Army Day. Multicoloured.

1782	20f. Type **410**	35	35
1783	30f. Soldier and medal (horiz)	35	35
1784	50f. Type **410**	70	35
1785	150f. As No. 1783	2·10	80

411 "8" and Pres. Hussain

1988. 18th Anniv of People's Army (1786, 1788) and 25th Anniv of Eighth February Revolution (others). Multicoloured.

1786	20f. Type **411**	50	35
1787	30f. Pres. Hussain and eagle on "8" (vert)	60	35
1788	50f. Type **411**	85	45
1789	150f. As No. 1787	2·75	90

412 Flag as "V" and Lyre

1988. Art Day. Multicoloured.

1790	20f. Type **412**	50	35
1791	30f. Pres. Hussain, rifle as torch, clef and dove on film strip	60	45
1792	50f. Type **412**	85	45
1793	100f. As No. 1791	1·70	55
MS1794	60×80 mm. 150f. Musical notes, lute and keyboard. Imperf	3·00	3·00

413 Rally and Ears of Wheat

1988. 41st Anniv of Al-Baath Party. Multicoloured.

1795	20f. Type **413**	50	35
1796	30f. Flowers and "7 April 1947–1988"	60	45
1797	50f. Type **413**	85	45
1798	150f. As No. 1796	2·75	80

414 Emblem

1988. Regional Marine Environment Day. Multicoloured.

1799	20f. Type **414**	60	35
1800	40f. Fishes (horiz)	60	45
1801	90f. Type **414**	1·60	55
1802	100f. As No. 1800	1·70	55

415 Pres. Hussain

1988. 51st Birthday of President Saddam Hussain. Multicoloured.

1803	20f. Type **415**	50	35
1804	30f. Pres. Hussain and hands holding flowers	60	45
1805	50f. Type **415**	85	45
1806	100f. As No. 1804	1·70	65
MS1807	90×100 mm. 150f. Pres. Hussain and flowers within flag as heart. Imperf	2·75	2·75

416 Emblem

1988. 40th Anniv of W.H.O. Multicoloured.

1808	20f. Type **416**	50	35
1809	40f. Red crescent protecting line of people (vert)	60	45
1810	90f. Type **416**	1·60	55
1811	100f. As No. 1809	1·70	55

417 Bomb and Open Book showing School, Child and Wreath

1988. Bilat Al-Shuhada School Bomb Victims. Multicoloured.

1812	20f. Type **417**	50	35
1813	40f. Explosion and girl (horiz)	60	45
1814	90f. Type **417**	1·70	55
1815	100f. As No. 1813	1·70	55
MS1816	80×60 mm. 150f. Child's severed head in clawed hand (49×39 mm)	2·50	2·50

418 Hand holding Flash of Lightning

1988. July Festivals and Ninth Anniv of President Hussain's State Leadership. Multicoloured.

1817	50f. Type **418**	85	45
1818	90f. Sun, map and Pres. Hussain	1·60	55
1819	100f. Type **418**	1·70	55
1820	150f. As No. 1818	2·40	65
MS1821	90×70 mm. 250f. Pres. Hussain and flag. Imperf	4·25	4·25

419 Pres. Hussain and al-Sail al-Kabir Miqat

1988. President Hussain's Pilgrimage to Mecca.

1822	419	90f. multicoloured	1·60	55
1823	419	100f. multicoloured	1·70	80
1824	419	150f. multicoloured	2·75	80

420 Mosul

1988. Tourism. Multicoloured.

1825	50f. Type **420**	1·20	35
1826	100f. Basrah	1·80	80
1827	150f. Baghdad (vert)	3·75	1·30

421 Pres. Hussain and Soldiers

1988. "Victorious Iraq".

1828	421	50f. multicoloured	6·00	5·50
1829	421	100f. multicoloured	11·50	10·50
1830	421	150f. multicoloured	17·00	16·00

422 Emblem

1988. Navy Day. Multicoloured.

1831	50f. Type **422**	1·30	45
1832	90f. Missile boats	2·40	65
1833	100f. Type **422**	2·75	80
1834	150f. As No. 1832	3·75	1·20
MS1835	90×70 mm. 250f. Emblem and Pres. Hussain decorating officers. Imperf	7·75	7·75

423 Map and Hands holding Flag

1988. Liberation of Fao City.

1836	423	100f. multicoloured	2·75	80
1837	423	150f. multicoloured	3·75	1·20
MS1838	60× 80 mm. 500f. multicoloured. Imperf	16·00	16·00

DESIGN: 100f. Pres. Hussain and document.

424 Missile Launch from Winged Map

1988. Iraq Missile Research.

1839	424	100f. multicoloured	1·70	55
1840	424	150f. multicoloured	2·75	90
MS1841	80×60 mm. 500f. multicoloured. Imperf	8·50	8·50

DESIGN: 500f. President Hussain, map and missiles.

425 Boxer and Hodori (mascot)

1988. Olympic Games, Seoul. Multicoloured.

1842	100f. Type **425**	2·75	80
1843	150f. Games emblem	3·75	1·20
MS1844	100×90 mm. 500f. Pres. Hussain presenting football trophy. Imperf	16·00	16·00

426 Dancers and Golden Cow

1988. Second Babylon International Festival.

1845	426	100f. multicoloured	1·70	55
1846	426	150f. multicoloured	2·40	80
MS1847	60×80 mm. 500f. multicoloured. Imperf	8·50	8·50

DESIGN: 500f. Medallion and laurel wreath.

427 Crescent and Camel Train

1988. Mohammed's Birth Anniv.

1848	427	100f. multicoloured	1·70	65
1849	427	150f. multicoloured	2·40	1·00
1850	427	1d. multicoloured	17·00	6·75

428 Hand holding Candle

1988. Martyr's Day.

1851	428	100f. multicoloured	1·30	55
1852	428	150f. multicoloured	2·40	1·00
1853	428	500f. multicoloured	8·50	3·00

انتـه مرالعراق
١٩٨٨/٨/٨

429 "Victory"

1988. Nos. 1738/9 optd with T **429**.

1854	399	250f. multicoloured	6·00	1·90
1855	399	350f. multicoloured	8·50	2·75

430 Family on Pedestrian Crossing

1989. Police Day.

1856	430	50f. multicoloured	85	45
1857	430	100f. multicoloured	1·70	55
1858	430	150f. multicoloured	2·40	1·00

431 Children and Money

1989. Postal Savings Bank. (a) Size 32×32 mm.

1859	431	50f. multicoloured	2·20	1·00

(b) Size 24×25 mm. With or without Arabic opt.

1860a	100f. multicoloured	35	35
1861a	150f. multicoloured	50	45

DESIGN: 100, 150f. Motif as Type **431** but with inscriptions differently arranged and inscr "REPUBLIC OF IRAQ".

432 Members' Flags and Leaders

1989. Formation of Arab Co-operation Council (Egypt, Iraq, Jordan and Yemen Arab Republic). Multicoloured.

1862	100f. Type **432**	1·70	55
1863	150f. Leaders in formal pose	2·40	90

433 Dates

1989. First Anniv of Liberation of Fao City.

1864	433	100f. multicoloured	1·60	55
1865	433	150f. multicoloured	2·20	55
MS1866	60×80 mm. 250f. multicoloured. Imperf	3·75	3·75

DESIGN: 250f. Calendar.

434 Pres. Hussain

1989. 52nd Birthday of President Saddam Hussain.
1867	434	100f. multicoloured	1·60	55
1868	434	150f. multicoloured	2·20	55

MS1869 60×80 mm. 250f. multicoloured. Imperf — 3·75 3·75
DESIGN: 250f. Hussain and laurel branches.

435 Khairalla

1989. General Adnan Khairalla Commem.
1870	435	50f. multicoloured	1·10	45
1871	435	100f. multicoloured	2·10	55
1872	435	150f. multicoloured	3·00	1·00

436 Hussain laying Mortar

1989. Completion of Basrah Reconstruction Project.
1873	436	100f. multicoloured	2·10	55
1874	436	150f. multicoloured	3·00	1·00

437 Crane and Buildings

1989. Start of Reconstruction of Fao City.
1875	437	100f. multicoloured	2·10	55
1876	437	150f. multicoloured	3·00	1·00

438 "Women"

1989
1877	438	100f. multicoloured	1·20	45
1878	438	150f. multicoloured	1·80	65
1879	438	1d. multicoloured	12·00	4·50
1880	438	5d. multicoloured	60·00	19·00

439 Pres. Hussain

1989. July Festivals and Tenth Anniv of President Hussain's State Leadership.
1881	439	50f. multicoloured	85	45
1882	439	100f. multicoloured	1·70	55
1883	439	150f. multicoloured	2·75	90

440 Flag and Victory Signs

1989. Victory Day.
1884	440	100f. multicoloured	1·70	55
1885	440	150f. multicoloured	2·75	90

MS1886 70×90 mm. 250f. multicoloured. Imperf — 5·00 5·00
DESIGN: 250f. Hussain, palm, Boeing 737 airliner and container ship *Khawla*.

441 Children, Heart and Bride

1989. Iraqi Family.
1887	441	50f. multicoloured	1·10	45
1888	441	100f. multicoloured	2·10	85
1889	441	150f. multicoloured	6·00	2·50

442 Najaf

1989. Tourism. Multicoloured.
1890		100f. Type **442**	2·20	65
1891		100f. Arbil	2·20	65
1892		100f. Marsh Arab punt and Ziggurat of Ur	2·20	65

443 Map and Means of Transport

1989. Fifth Session of Arab Ministers of Transport Council, Baghdad. Multicoloured.
1893		50f. Type **443**	1·40	65
1894		100f. Sun, means of transport and map	3·00	90
1895		150f. Means of transport and members' flags (vert)	4·50	1·30

444 City and Pres. Hussain placing Final Stone

1989. Completion of Fao City Reconstruction.
1896	444	100f. multicoloured	1·80	55
1897	444	150f. multicoloured	2·75	90

445 Anniversary Emblem

1989. 30th Anniv of Iraqi News Agency.
1898	445	50f. multicoloured	70	45
1899	445	100f. multicoloured	1·40	55
1900	445	150f. multicoloured	2·20	90

446 Emblem

1989. First Anniv of Declaration of Palestinian State. Multicoloured.
1901		25f. Type **446**	35	35
1902		50f. Crowd of children	85	45
1903		100f. Type **446**	1·70	55
1904		150f. As No. 1902	2·75	80

447 Pansies

1989. Flowers. Multicoloured.
1905		25f. Type **447**	50	45
1906		50f. Antirrhinums	95	45
1907		100f. "Hibiscus trionum"	1·80	55
1908		150f. Mesembryanthemums	3·00	90

MS1909 90×110 mm. As Nos. 1905/8 but larger (26½×36 mm) — 11·00 11·00

448 Map and Emblem

1989. Centenary of Interparliamentary Union.
1910	448	25f. multicoloured	50	35
1911	448	100f. multicoloured	1·70	55
1912	448	150f. multicoloured	2·75	90

449 Sun, Flag, Doves and Mosque Domes

1989. Martyr's Day.
1913	449	50f. multicoloured	85	45
1914	449	100f. multicoloured	1·60	55
1915	449	150f. multicoloured	2·20	90

450 Dove, Red Crescent and Pres. Hussain

1989. Iraqi Red Crescent Society.
1916	450	100f. multicoloured	85	45
1917	450	150f. multicoloured	2·30	90
1918	450	500f. multicoloured	7·75	2·75

451 Members' Flags on Map

1990. First Anniv of Arab Co-operation Council.
1919	451	50f. multicoloured	1·30	65
1920	451	100f. multicoloured	3·25	1·20

MS1921 80×60 mm. 451 250f. multicoloured. Imperf — 9·00 9·00

452

1990. Arab League Summit Conference, Baghdad. Nos. 1906 and 1908 optd with T **452**.
1922		50f. multicoloured	1·40	1·10
1923		150f. multicoloured	4·50	2·75

453 Doves and Flag as Flame

1990. Second Anniv of Liberation of Fao City.
1924	453	50f. multicoloured	70	65
1925	453	100f. multicoloured	1·60	1·50

(454)

1992. No. 1291 surch with T **454**.
1927		100f. on 5f. multicoloured	3·50	3·50

455 Children and Currency

1993. Postal Savings.
1928	455	100f. multicoloured	35	35
1929	455	150f. multicoloured	50	45
1930	455	250f. multicoloured	85	80

(456)

1993. No. O1742 surch with T **456**.
1931		1d. on 100f. multicoloured	10·00	10·00

(457)

1993. No. 1901 surch with T **457**.
1932		10d. on 25f. multicoloured	36·00	36·00

458 Satellite and Receiver

1993. Re-construction. Multicoloured.
1933		250f. Type **458**	95	90
1934		500f. Bridge over Tigris river	1·80	1·70
1935		750f. Power transformers	2·75	2·50
1936		1d. Damaged and restored buildings	3·50	3·25

459 Ibn Khaldoon (trading vessel)

1993
1937	459	2d. multicoloured	3·00	2·75
1938	459	5d. multicoloured	7·75	7·25

(460) (461)

(461a) (461b)

(461c) (461d)

(462) (462a) (463)

(463a) (464) (464a)

(464b) (464c)

(465) (466)

(466a) (467)

1994. No. 1291 surch with T **460/467**.

1939	500f. on 5f. multicoloured (T **460**)		2·40	2·40
1940	1d. on 5f. multicoloured (T **461**)		2·40	2·40
1941	1d. on 5f.multicoloured (T **461a**)		3·50	3·50
1942	1d. on 5f. multicoloured (T **461b**)		7·75	7·75
1943	1d. on 5f. multicoloured (T **461c**)		3·50	3·50
1944	1d. on 5f. multicoloured (T **461d**)		3·50	3·50
1945	2d. on 5f. multicoloured (T **462**)		4·25	4·25
1946	2d. on 5f. multicoloured (T **462a**)		4·25	4·25
1947	3d. on 5f. multicoloured (T **463**)		2·40	2·40
1948	3d. on 5f. multicoloured (T **463a**)		2·40	2·40
1950	5d. on 5f. multicoloured (T **464**)		2·40	2·40
1951	5d. on 5f. multicoloured (T **464a**)		3·50	3·50
1952	5d. on 5f. multicoloured (T **464b**)		5·00	5·00
1953	5d. on 5f. multicoloured (T **464c**)		5·00	5·00
1954	10d. on 5f. multicoloured (T **465**)		5·00	5·00
1955	25d. on 5f. multicoloured (T **466**)		10·00	10·00
1957	25d. on 5f. multicoloured (T **466a**)		17·00	17·00
1958	50d. on 5f. multicoloured (T **467**)		34·00	34·00

ميلاد القائد
٩٤/٤/٢٨
❋ ٥ دينار ❋
(472)

ميلاد القائد
٩٤/٤/٢٨
● ٥ دينار ●
(473)

1994. 57th Birth Anniv of Pres. Hussein. No. 1739 surch with T **472/473**.

1967	5d. on 350f. multicoloured (T **472**)		7·25	7·25
1968	5d. on 350f. multicoloured (T **473**)		7·25	7·25

474 Alqaid Bridge

1994

1969	**474**	1d. multicoloured	1·40	1·40
1970	**474**	3d. multicoloured	4·25	4·25

عيد النصر
٩٩٤/٨/٨
❋ ٥ دينار ❋
(475)

1994. Victory Day. No. 1739 surch with T **475**.

1971	5d. on 350f. multicoloured		5·75	5·75

١٩٩٥/١/٢
(476)

1995. 20th Anniv of World Tourism Organization. No. 1878 surch with T **476**.

1972	5d. on 150f. multicoloured (Arabic inscription)		4·75	4·75
1973	5d. on 150f. multicoloured (English inscription)		4·75	4·75

477 Baghdad Clock

1995. Multicoloured.

1974	**477**	7d. blue and black	3·00	3·00

MS1975 86×110 mm. 25d. As No. 1974 but with design enlarged. Imperf | 14·50 | 14·50

478 Saddam Tower (television transmitter)

1995

1976	**478**	2d. multicoloured	1·20	1·20
1977	**478**	5d. multicoloured	2·75	2·75

479 Pres. Hussein

1995. 58th Birth Anniv of Pres. Hussein. Two sheets. Imperf.
MS1978 (a) 60×78 mm. 25d. Type **479**; (b) 78×60 mm. 25d. President and child (horiz) Set of 2 sheets | 31·00 | 31·00

480 Woman and River Basin

1995. Completion of "Saddam River" (canal between Iraq and Persian Gulf).

1979	**480**	4d. red and blue	4·50	4·50
1980	**480**	4d. ochre and blue	4·50	4·50

MS1981 106×86m. **480** 25d. multicoloured | 16·00 | 16·00

481 Barbed Wire, Tower, Woman and Child

1995

1982	**481**	10d. blue and red	3·50	3·50

MS1983 85×110 mm. **481** 25d. multicoloured | 17·00 | 17·00

❋ ٢٥ دينار ❋
(482)

1995. No. 1739 surch with T **482**.

1984	25d. on 350f. multicoloured		1·40	1·40
1985	250d. on 350f. multicoloured		9·00	9·00
1986	350d. on 350f. multicoloured		22·00	22·00
1987	1000d. on 350f. multicoloured		43·00	43·00

(483)   (484)

(485)   (486)

1995. Nos. 1930 surch as T **483/486**.

1988	**483**	50d. on 250f. multicoloured	3·00	3·00
1989	**484**	500d. on 250f. multicoloured	29·00	29·00
1990	**485**	2500d. on 250f. multicoloured	£110	90·00
1991	**485**	5000d. on 250f. multicoloured	£250	£180

يوم الاستفتاء
١٩٩٥/١٠/١٥
❋ ٢٥ دينار ❋
(487)

Referendum
15/10/1995
❋ 25 Dinars ❋
(488)

1995. Referendum Day. No. 1739 surch with T **487/488**.

1992	25d. on 350f. multicoloured		3·50	3·50
1993	25d. on 350f. multicoloured		3·50	3·50

❋ ٢٥ دينار ❋

(489)

1996. No. 1297 surch with T **489** (overprint on overprint).

1994	25d. on 100f. on 5f multicoloured		5·50	5·50

٢٥ دينار
(490)

(490a)

(490b)

1996. Nos. 1859/61 surch with T **490/490a/490b**.

1995	25d. on 100f. multicoloured (T **490**)		1·40	1·40
1996	25d. on 150f. multicoloured (T **490a**)		1·40	1·40
1997	50d. on 50f. multicoloured (T **490b**) (32×32 mm)		3·00	3·00

مائة دينار
(491)

1996. No. O1616 surch with T **491**.

1998	100d. on 70f. yellow, black and flesh		6·00	6·00

492 Flag, Doves and Flames

1996. Sheet 86×62 mm. Imperf.
MS1999 **492** 100d. multicoloured | 13·50 | 13·50

١٠٠ دينار
(493)

1996. No. 1878 surch with T **493**.

2000	100d. on 150f. multicoloured		6·00	6·00

(494)   (495)

1996. Nos. 1989/91 surch with T **494/495** (overprint on overprint).

2001	**494**	25d. on 500d. on 250f. multicoloured	5·50	5·50
2002	**494**	25d. on 5000d. on 250f. multicoloured	5·50	5·50
2003	**495**	50d. on 2500d. on 250f. multicoloured	11·00	11·00

(496)   (497)

1996. Un-issued stamps surch with T **496/497**.

2004	**496**	25d. on 10f. multicoloured	42·00	42·00
2005	–	25d. on 25f. multicoloured	2·40	2·40
2006	**497**	50d. on 10f. multicoloured	70·00	70·00
2007	–	50d. on 50f. multicoloured	3·50	3·50

DESIGNS: Nos. 2004/7 School children in classroom.

٥٠ ١٠٠ دنلمر
(498)

1996. No. 1906 surch with T **498**.

2008	100d. on 50f. Antirrhinums		6·75	6·75

٢٥ دينان
(499)

1996. No. 1930 surch with T **499**.

2009	25d. on 250f. multicoloured		1·40	1·40

❋ مائة دينار ❋
(500)

1996. No. O1645 surch with T **500**.

2010	100d. on 60f. multicoloured		6·25	6·25

٢٥ دينار   مائة دينار
(501/a)

1996. Nos. 1572/7 surch as T **501/a**.

2011	**501**	25d. on 10f. multicoloured	2·30	2·30
2012	**501**	25d. on 30f. multicoloured	2·30	2·30
2013	**501**	25d. on 50f. multicoloured	2·30	2·30
2014	**501a**	100d. on 20f. multicoloured	9·75	9·75
2015	**501a**	100d. on 40f. multicoloured	9·75	9·75
2016	**501a**	100d. on 100f. multicoloured	9·75	9·75

١٠٠ دينار
(502)

1996. No. 1924 surch with T **502**.

2017	100d. on 50f. multicoloured		6·00	6·00

يوم العلم
٢٥ دينار
(503)

1997. No. 1933 surch as T **503**.

2018	25d. on 250f. multicoloured		1·40	1·40

504 Geometric Design

1997

2019	**504**	25d. emerald, black and rosine	1·20	1·20
2020	**504**	100d. emerald, blue and vermilion	6·00	6·00

اليوبيل الذهبي
لميلاد الحزب القائد
١٩٩٧
❋ ٢٥ دينار ❋
(505)

1997. 50th Anniv of Baath Party. No. 1920 surch with T **505**.

2021	25d. on 100f. multicoloured		2·20	2·20

يوم البريد
١٩٩٧/٤/٢١
❋ ٢٥ دينار ❋
(506)

1997. 45th Anniv of Arab Post Union. No. 1878 surch with T **506**.

2022	25d. on 150f. multicoloured		5·00	5·00

507 Pres. Hussein

1997. Second Anniv of Referendum.
| 2023 | **507** | 25d. multicoloured | 1·80 | 1·80 |
| 2024 | **507** | 100d. multicoloured | 7·25 | 7·25 |

MS2025 96×81 mm. 250d. President Saddam Hussein and map. Imperf 12·00 12·00

508 Pres. Hussein, Water and Plants

1997. Completion of Al Qaid Water Project. Multicoloured. (a) Sheet stamps. (i) Ordinary gum.
| 2026 | 25d. Type **508** | 70 | 70 |

(ii) Self-adhesive gum.
| 2027 | 100d. As No. 2026 | 3·00 | 3·00 |

(b) Miniature Sheets. Ordinary gum.
MS2028 Two sheets. (a) 79×91 mm. 250d. As No. 2026; (b) 75×92 mm. 250d. Pres. Hussein and pipeline Set of 2 sheets 14·50 14·50

509 Saladin and Pres. Hussein

1998. Jerusalem Day. Self-adhesive.
| 2029 | **509** | 25d. multicoloured | 70 | 70 |
| 2030 | **509** | 100d. multicoloured | 3·00 | 3·00 |

MS2031 88×75 mm. **509** 250d. multicoloured. Imperf 7·25 7·25

510 Zinnias

1998. Kurdish New Year. Two sheets containing T **510** and similar vert design. Imperf.
MS2032 (a) 71×93 mm. 250d. Type **510**; (b) 68×93 mm. 250d. Iris Set of 2 sheets 22·00 22·00

511 Goalkeeper and Players (image scaled to 58% of original size)

1998. World Cup Football Championships, France (1st issue). Two sheets containing T **511** and similar multicoloured design. Imperf.
MS2033 (a) 72×85 mm. 250d. Type **511**; (b) 84×62 mm. 250d. Two players (vert) Set of 2 sheets 17·00 17·00
See also Nos. 2061/2.

512 Emblem (image scaled to 57% of original size)

1998. 25th Anniv of Arab Police Security Chiefs' Conference. Sheet 93×67 mm. Imperf.
MS2034 **512** 250d. multicoloured 7·25 7·25

513 *Chamomile recuita*

1998. Flora. Multicoloured. (a) Ordinary gum.
2035	25d. Type **513**	35	35
2036	50d. *Helianthus annuus*	60	60
2037	1000d. *Carduus nutans*	10·00	10·00

(b) Self-adhesive gum.
| 2038 | 25d. Type **513** | 1·90 | 1·90 |

514 Pres. Hussain and Map

1998. Arab Languages Day. Multicoloured.
| 2039 | 25d. Type **514** | 60 | 60 |
| 2040 | 100d. Map and emblem | 2·30 | 2·30 |

515 Mosque Outline, Calligraphy and Dove

1998. Martyrs Day. Multicoloured.
| 2041 | 25d. Type **515** | 50 | 50 |
| 2042 | 100d. Calligraphy and banner | 1·90 | 1·90 |

MS2043 94×74 mm. 250d. Emblem 5·00 5·00

516 *Precis orithya*

1998. Butterflies. Multicoloured.
| 2044 | 100d. Type **516** | 3·50 | 3·50 |
| 2045 | 150d. *Anthocharis euphome* | 5·50 | 5·50 |

517 Ishtar Gate, Babylon

1999. Tower of Babylon and Borsippa Ziggurat Conference. Multicoloured.
| 2046 | 25d. Type **517** | 50 | 50 |
| 2047 | 50d. Ishtar Gate (different) | 95 | 95 |

MS2048 71×90 mm. 250d. Ziggurat, Borsippa 7·25 7·25

518 Tower and Dam

1999. Dams on the Tigris River. Multicoloured.
| 2049 | 25d. Type **518** | 60 | 60 |
| 2050 | 100d. Dam, flowers, fruit and pylon | 2·30 | 2·30 |

MS2051 71×93 mm. 250d. As No. 2050. Imperf 7·25 7·25

519 Pres. Hussain

1999. 62nd Birthday of Pres. Hussain. Multicoloured.
2052	25d. Type **519**	25	25
2053	50d. With flag in background	50	50
2054	100d. With tree in background	1·30	1·30
2055	500d. Wearing uniform facing right	4·50	4·50
2056	1000d. Wearing uniform facing left	9·00	9·00
2057	5000d. Seated with clasped hands (horiz)	46·00	46·00

520 Emblem and Pres. Hussain

1999. Saddamiya al Therthar. Multicoloured.
| 2058 | 25d. Type **520** | 60 | 60 |
| 2059 | 100d. Flowers, tower and gateway | 2·10 | 2·10 |

MS2060 93×71 mm. 250d. Emblem, tower and Pres. Hussain. Imperf 7·25 7·25

521 Two Players

1999. World Cup Football Championships, France (2nd issue). Multicoloured.
| 2061 | 25d. Type **521** | 95 | 95 |
| 2062 | 100d. Goalkeeper and players (horiz) | 3·50 | 3·50 |

522 Bees (*Apis mellifica*)

1999. Apiculture.
| 2063 | **522** | 25d. multicoloured | 1·20 | 1·20 |
| 2064 | | 50d. As Type **522** | 2·75 | 2·75 |

523 Dome of the Rock

1999. Jerusalem Day. Multicoloured.
2065	25d. Type **523**	35	35
2066	50d. Dome and map (horiz)	60	60
2067	100d. Dome, flag and shield	1·20	1·20
2068	150d. Dome and Pres. Hussain (horiz)	1·90	1·90

MS2069 93×71 mm. 250d. As No. 2068. Imperf 5·50 5·50

524 Flags and Pres. Hussain

1999. Victory Day. Multicoloured.
| 2070 | 25d. Type **524** | 60 | 60 |
| 2071 | 50d. Pres. Hussain and crowd | 1·10 | 1·10 |

MS2072 93×71 mm. 250d. Eagle's head and Pres. Hussain. Imperf 5·50 5·50

525 Pres. Hussain and Flowers

2000. 63rd Birthday of Pres. Hussain. Multicoloured.
| 2073 | 25d. Type **525** | 50 | 50 |
| 2074 | 100d. Pres. Hussain and "28" (horiz) | 95 | 95 |

MS2075 93×71 mm. 500d. Pres. Hussain wearing coat with fur collar. Imperf 9·75 9·75

526 Men and Women holding Tools (detail)

2000. Nasb al-Hurriyyah (sculpture by Jawad Salim). Multicoloured.
2076	25d. Type **526**	50	50
2077	25d. Women and child carrying corn	50	50
2078	25d. Men and broken fence	50	50
2079	25d. Grieving women	50	50
2080	25d. Men with raised arms	50	50

527 Pres. Hussain

2000. Victory Day. Multicoloured.
| 2081 | 25d. Type **527** | 95 | 95 |
| 2082 | 50d. Flag and guns | 1·90 | 1·90 |

MS2083 72×92 mm. 255d. As No. 2081. Imperf 5·50 5·50

528 Mallards (*Anas platyrhynchos*)

2000. Birds. Multicoloured.
2084	25d. Type **528**	50	50
2085	50d. House sparrow (*Passer domesticus*)	1·10	1·10
2086	100d. Purple swamphen (*Porphyrio porphyrio*)	3·50	3·50

MS2087 92×71 mm. 500d. Goldfinch (*Carduelis carduelis*). Imperf 11·00 11·00

529 Emblem

2000. 430th Birth Anniv of Mohammed. Multicoloured.
| 2088 | 25d. Type **529** | 85 | 85 |
| 2089 | 50d. Emblem (different) | 1·70 | 1·70 |

530 Flag, Pres. Hussain and Voting Cards

2000. Fifth Anniv of Referendum. Multicoloured.

2090	25d. Type **530**		35	35
2091	50d. Pres. Hussain wearing uniform (horiz)		85	85

MS2092 93×72 mm. 250d. Pres. Hussain wearing traditional clothes. Imperf ..... 5·50 5·50

531 Emblem

2000. 1200th Anniv of Baytol Hikma.

2093	**531**	50d. multicoloured	60	60
2094	**531**	100d. multicoloured	1·20	1·20

532 Woman carrying Child

2001. Tenth Anniv of Al-Amiriyah. Multicoloured.

2095	25d. Type **532**		60	60
2096	50d. National colours and doves		1·20	1·20

MS2097 93×71 mm. 250d. As No. 2095. Imperf ..... 4·25 4·25

533 Inscribed Tablet and Statuette

2001. 5000th Anniv of Writing in Mesopotamia. Multicoloured.

2098	25d. Type **533**		25	25
2099	50d. Sumerian script and figures		60	60
2100	75d. As No. 2098		85	85
2101	100d. As No. 2099		1·10	1·10
2102	150d. Figure wearing skirt (statue)		1·70	1·70
2103	250d. As No. 2102		3·00	3·00

534 Arabic Script as Torch Flame and Crowd

2001. 54th Anniv of Al Baath Party. Multicoloured.

2104	25d. Type **534**		35	35
2105	50d. Michael Aflaq (founder) and Pres. Hussain		60	60
2106	100d. Map of Arab states		1·20	1·20

535 Pres. Hussain

2001. 13th Anniv of Cessation of Hostilities. Multicoloured.

2107	25d. Type **535**		35	35
2108	100d. Pres. Hussain, soldier and map (horiz)		1·20	1·20

536 Pres. Hussain

2001. 64th Birthday of Pres. Hussain

2109	25d. Type **536**		25	25
2110	50d. Wearing dark suit (horiz)		50	50
2111	100d. Seated with children (horiz)		95	95

MS2112 90×69 mm. 250d. With children carrying flowers. Imperf ..... 4·75 4·75

537 *Barbus sharpeyi*

2001. Fish. Multicoloured.

2113	25d. Type **537**		35	35
2114	50d. *Barbus esocinus*		70	70
2115	100d. *Barbus xanthopterus*		1·40	1·40
2116	150d. *Pampus argenteus*		2·30	2·30

538 Gazelle (*Gazella subgutturosa*)

2001. Fauna. Multicoloured.

2117	100d. Type **538**		95	95
2118	250d. Hare (*Lepus europaeus*) (vert)		2·40	2·40
2119	500d. Dromedary (*Camelus dromedaries*)		4·75	4·75

MS2120 92×70 mm. 1000d. Horse, gazelle, sheep and camel. Imperf ..... 9·75 9·75

539 Hawk and Flags

2001. Tenth Anniv of Um Al Marik.

2121	**539**	25d. multicoloured	25	25
2122	**539**	100d. multicoloured	1·10	1·10

540 National Colours joining Maps of Palestine and Iraq

2001. Al Asqa Intifada. Multicoloured.

2123	25d. Type **540**		35	35
2124	25d. Dome of the Rock, flag and man carrying gun (vert)		35	35
2125	50d. Dome of the Rock, leaves and man with raised arms (vert)		70	70

MS2126 Two sheets, each 89×67 mm. (a) 250d. Mohammed Dorra and father; (b) 250d. Tank and protester. Imperf Set of 2 sheets ..... 6·00 6·00

541 Drilling Rig and Workers

2001. 29th Anniv of Nationalization of Oil Industry. Multicoloured.

2127	25d. Type **541**		35	35
2128	50d. Flaming tower, processing plant and oil		70	70

542 World Map and Footballers

2001. Under 20 Junior World Cup Football Championships, Argentina. Multicoloured.

2129	25d. Type **542**		35	35
2130	50d. Player and trophy (vert)		70	70

543 Sick Child

2001. Tenth Anniv of Gulf War. Multicoloured.

2131	25d. Type **543**		60	60
2132	25d. Woman and children		60	60
2133	50d. Flag and family (horiz)		1·20	1·20

MS2134 70×92 mm. 250d. As No. 2131. Imperf ..... 4·25 4·25

544 Soldiers and Flag

2002. Army Day. Multicoloured.

2135	25d. Type **544**		60	60
2136	50d. Statue of soldiers (vert)		1·20	1·20
2137	100d. Soldier (vert)			

MS2138 70×90 mm. 250d. As No. 2135. Imperf ..... 4·25 4·25

545 Aircraft, Flames and Girl

2002. 11th Anniv of Gulf War.

2139	**545**	100d. multicoloured	1·90	1·90

546 Pres. Hussain wearing Hat

2002. Jerusalem Day.

2140	**546**	25d. multicoloured	35	35
2141	**546**	50d. multicoloured	60	60
2142	**546**	100d. multicoloured	1·20	1·20

547 Flags and Fist

2002. 39th Anniv of 8 February. Multicoloured.

2143	50d. Type **547**		60	60
2144	100d. Sumerians, Saladin and modern crowd (horiz)		1·20	1·20

548 Aircraft Sights

2002. 11th Anniv of Al-Amiriyah.

2145	**548**	25d. multicoloured	35	35
2146	**548**	50d. multicoloured	60	60

549 Orange Roses

2002. Flowers. Multicoloured.

2147	25d. Type **549**		35	35
2148	50d. Pink and red roses		60	60
2149	150d. Carnations, anemone and narcissi		1·80	1·80

MS2150 73×91 mm. 250d. Bouquet. Imperf ..... 3·50 3·50

550 Web and Mosques

2002. Hajeer New Year. Multicoloured.

2151	25d. Type **550**		35	35
2152	50d. Crescent moon and mosque (vert)		60	60
2153	75d. Web and doves		95	95

551 Envelope

2002. Post Day. Multicoloured.

2154	50d. Type **551**		70	70
2155	100d. Aircraft, ship and train		1·40	1·40

MS2156 70×91 mm. 250d. Envelope and globe. Imperf ..... 5·50 5·50

552 Pres. Hussain as Boy

2002. 65th Birth Anniv of Pres. Hussain. Multicoloured.

2157	25d. Type **552**		35	35
2158	50d. As young man		60	60
2159	75d. With flag at left		95	95
2160	100d. With flag at right		1·20	1·20

MS2161 Two sheets, each 74×91 mm. (a) 250d. Wearing traditional clothes; (b) 250d. Surrounded by flowers. Imperf Set of 2 sheets ..... 7·25 7·25

553 Trophy and Player

2002. World Cup Football Championships, Japan and South Korea. Multicoloured.

2162	50d. Type **553**		60	60
2163	100d. Player chasing ball		1·20	1·20
2164	150d. Player kicking ball		1·80	1·80

MS2165 69×91 mm. 250d. Championship emblem and trophy enclosing players. Imperf ..... 4·75 4·75

554 Soldier, Child and Woman

2002. Second Anniv of Al Asqa Intifada.

2166	**554**	5000d. multicoloured	36·00	36·00

555 Sheikh Maruf Mosque

2002. Mosques. Multicoloured.
2167	25d. Type **555**	35	35
2168	50d. Al- Mouiz	70	70
2169	75d. Um Al Marik	1·10	1·10

556 Stylized Eagle, Flag and Pres. Hussain

2002. Victory Day. Multicoloured.
2170	25d. Type **556**	35	35
2171	50d. As No. 2149	60	60
MS2172	70×91 mm. 150d. Eagle's head. Imperf	3·50	3·50

557 Reed Boats and Coracle

2002. Traditional Watercraft. Multicoloured.
2173	150d. Type **557**	1·80	1·80
2174	250d. Galley	3·00	3·00
2175	500d. Sail boat	6·00	6·00

558 Jameel Sidqi Al-Zahawi

2002. Writers. Multicoloured.
2176	25d. Type **558**	35	35
2177	50d. Abdul Musin Al-Qadumi	60	60
2178	75d. Badr Shaker Al-Sayab	95	95
2179	100d. Ma'rouf Al-Rasafi	1·20	1·20
MS2180	71×91 mm. 150d. Badr Shaker Al-Sayab and rose. Imperf	3·50	3·50

559 Hands holding Flowers and Pres. Hussain

2002. Referendum. Multicoloured.
2181	100d. Type **559**	1·20	1·20
2182	150d. Fist and ballot box	1·80	1·80
MS2183	70×92 mm. 250d. As No. 2181. Imperf	3·25	3·25

560 Woman Spinning

2002. Baghdad Day. Multicoloured.
2184	25d. Type **560**	35	35
2185	50d. Street performer and children	60	60
2186	75d. Two women talking (horiz)	95	95
MS2187	91×71 mm. 250d. Musicians. Imperf	6·00	6·00

561 Oryx leucoryx

2003. Fauna. Multicoloured.
2188	25d. Type **561**	35	35
2189	50d. *Acinonyx jubatus* (vert)	60	60
2190	75d. *Panthera leo* (vert)	95	95
2191	100d. *Castor fiber*	1·20	1·20
2192	150d. *Equus hemionus*	1·80	1·80
MS2193	69×93 mm. 250d. As No. 2188. Imperf	6·00	6·00

562 Emblem

2003. Tenth Anniv of Saddam University.
2194	**562**	50d. multicoloured	60	60
2195	**562**	100d. multicoloured	1·20	1·20

563 Coracle

2004. Transportation. Multicoloured.
2196	50d. Type **563**	50	50
2197	100d. Horse-drawn cab	95	95
2198	250d. Tram	1·60	1·60
2199	500d. Skiff carrying reeds	3·50	3·50
2200	5000d. Camel train. Perf or imperf	26·00	26·00

564 Woman and Flowers

2006. New Year.
2201	**564**	250d. multicoloured	1·60	1·60

565 Women and Map

2006. Installation of Interim Government, 30 June 2004. Multicoloured.
2202	100d. Type **565**	95	95
2203	250d. Map and hands enclosing sun	3·50	3·50

566 Bust wearing Headdress

2006. Iraqi Civilization. Multicoloured.
2204	100d. Type **566**	95	95
2205	150d. Golden bull	1·40	1·40
2206	200d. Carved bull with human head	1·90	1·90
MS2207	80×61 mm. 250d. Tiled mosaic animals. Imperf	2·40	2·40

567 Football

2006. Olympic Games, Athens (2004). Multicoloured.
2208	100d. Type **567**	95	95
2209	150d. Athletics	1·40	1·40
MS2210	100×70 mm. 500d. Sportsmen. Imperf	2·40	2·40

568 Two Women (Akram Shukri)

2006. Paintings. Multicoloured.
2211	100d. Type **568**	95	95
2212	150d. Abstract (Hafidh Al Duroubi)	1·40	1·40
2213	200d. Horseman (Faiq Hassan)	1·90	1·90
MS2214	88×70 mm. 250d. Abstract (different) Imperf	2·40	2·40

569 Anemone

2007. Flowers. Multicoloured. Self-adhesive.
2215	250d. Type **569**	2·40	2·40
2216	750d. *Viola mamola*	7·25	7·25
2217	1000d. *Atropa belladonna*	9·75	9·75
MS2218	88×70 mm. Nos. 2215/17	18·00	18·00

570 Papilio demodocus

2007. Butterflies. Multicoloured.
2219	100d. Type **570**	55	55
2220	250d. Inscr 'Precis orithua'	1·20	1·20
2221	500d. Inscr 'Ciotas croceus'	2·30	2·30
MS2222	81×60 mm. 1000d. *Papilio demodocus* (different)	4·25	4·25

572 Rug Maker

2007. Artisans. Multicoloured. Self-adhesive.
2224	250d. Type **572**	1·30	1·30
2225	350d. Blanket maker	1·80	1·80
2226	500d. Basket maker	2·40	2·40
MS2227	106×60 mm. Nos. 2224/6	7·75	7·75

No. 2223 and Type **571** have been left for 'Singers', issued on 23 April 2007, not yet received.

573 Women and Children (Actual size 111×80 mm)

2007. Folklore. Sheet 111×80 mm.
MS2228	**573**	1000d. multicoloured	4·50	4·50

574 Anniversary Emblem

2007. 65th Anniv (2006) of Rafidain Bank.
2229	**574**	100d. multicoloured	55	55
2230	**574**	150d. multicoloured	90	90
2231	**574**	250d. multicoloured	1·20	1·20
2232	**574**	500d. multicoloured	2·30	2·30

575 Ducks

2007. Birds. Multicoloured.
2233	150d. *Anser anser* (greylag goose)	1·10	1·10
2234	250d. *Merops superciliosus* (olive beeeater)	1·20	1·20
2235	500d. *Pterocles alchata* (pin-tailed sandgrouse)	2·40	2·40
MS2236	80×83 mm. 1500d. Type **575**. Imperf	7·00	7·00

576 Mohammad Alqubanchi (singer)

2007. Theatre Personalities. Multicoloured. Self-adhesive.
(a) Size 30×40 mm.
2237	250d. Type **576**	1·20	1·20
2238	500d. Haqi Al Shibly (theatre manager) (horiz)	2·30	2·30
2239	750d. Nadhum Al Ghazali (singer) (horiz)	3·50	3·50
2240	1000d. Munir Bashir (musician) (horiz)	4·50	4·50

(b) Size 30×42 mm.
2241	250d. As Type **576**	1·30	1·30
2242	500d. As No. 2238 (horiz)	2·40	2·40
2243	700d. As No. 2239 (horiz)	3·50	3·50
2244	1000d. As No. 2240 (horiz)	4·50	4·50

577 Clasped Hands, Girl holding Map and Ship

2008. National Reconciliation. Multicoloured.
2245	250d. Type **577**	1·20	1·20
2246	500d. Symbols of conflict (40×40 mm)	2·30	2·30
2247	750d. Child holding rifle (40×40 mm)	3·25	3·25

578 Flags Intertwined

2008. 50th Anniv of Iraq–China Diplomatic Relations
2248	**578**	500d. multicoloured	2·30	2·30

579 Buraq and Statue

2008. Wasit Poetry Competition
2249	**579**	5000d. multicoloured	22·00	22·00

580 Graves and grieving Woman

2008. Collective Cemeteries. Multicoloured.
2251		250d. Type **580**	1·20	1·20
2252		500d. Bones	2·30	2·30

581 Gateway, Female and Animal Statues

2009. Campaign to Regain Iraqi Antiques. Multicoloured.
2253		250d. Type **581**	1·20	1·20
2254		500d. Gateway, two statues and head	2·30	2·30
2255		750d. Gateway, head and plaque	3·50	3·50

It is reported that an imperforate miniature sheet, value 1000d. (Baghdad at Night), two perforated stamps value 250d., 1000d. (Calligraphy) and a imperforated miniature sheet, value 1500d. (Calligraphy), were printed but not issued due to poor printing quality.

582 Cooling Towers, Crayfish, Geese and Trees

2009. Environmental Protection.
2256	**582**	1000d. multicoloured	4·50	4·50

583 Boats and Wildfowl

2009. International Campaign to Reclaim Marshes.
2257	**583**	10000d. multicoloured	4·50	4·50

584 Couple

2009. International Children's Day. Children's Paintings. Multicoloured.
2258		50d. Type **584**	35	35
2259		50d. Two girls	35	35
2260		50d. Family	35	35
2261		50d. Mother and daughter	35	35
2262		50d. Three girls	35	35
MS2263	80×60 mm. 500d. Mother cradling baby. Imperf		2·40	2·40

585 Emblem and Goalkeeper

2009. FIFA Confederations Cup, South Africa. Multicoloured.
2264		100d. Type **585**	55	55
2265		250d. Emblem and player	1·20	1·20

2266		500d. Emblem and player with leg extended	2·40	2·40
MS2267	80×80 mm. 750d. Emblem		3·50	5·50

586 Musicians and Seated Men

2009. Tourism Week. Multicoloured
2268		250d. Type **586**	1·20	1·20
2269		250d. Market, draughtsman and apothecary	1·20	1·20
2270		250d. Women	1·20	1·20
2271		250d. Men working	1·20	1·20
MS2272	90×60 mm. 500d. Horsemen. Imperf		2·40	2·40

Nos. 2268/9 and 2270/1, respectively, were printed, se-tenant, each pair forming a composite design.

587 Emblem

2009. al-Quds—2009 Capital of Arab Culture. Multicoloured.
2273		250d. Type **587**	1·20	1·20
MS2274	60×80 mm. 750d. As Type **587**. Imperf		3·50	3·50

588 Amo Baba

2009. Emmanuel Baba Dawud (Amo Baba) (football coach) Commemoration. Multicoloured.
2275		250d. Type **588**	1·20	1·20
2276		500d. As older man	2·30	2·30

589 Steam Locomotive

2010. National Railways. Multicoloured.
2277		250d. Type **589**	1·20	1·20
2278		500d. Diesel locomotive	2·30	2·30
2279		750d. Green steam locomotive	3·25	3·25
MS2280	80×80 mm. 1000d. As No. 2278 design enlarged. Imperf		4·50	4·50

589a Stylized Figures and Palm Tree

2010. Elections.
2280a	**589a**	250d. multicoloured	1·20	1·20
2280b		500d. multicoloured	2·30	2·30
2280c		1000d. multicoloured	4·50	4·50

590 Girl Scouts

2010. Arabian Brotherhood Scout Day. Multicoloured.
2281		250d. Type **590**	1·20	1·20
2282		250d. Boy bugler	1·20	1·20
2283		250d. Girls on parade	1·20	1·20
2284		250d. Boys saluting flag	1·20	1·20
MS2285	80×60 mm. 1000d. Parading scouts enclosed in knot. Imperf		4·50	4·50

591 Envelope and Letterbox

2010. Post Day. Multicoloured.
2286		250d. Type **591**	1·20	1·20
2287		500d. Envelope and dove	2·30	2·30

592 Pterodactyls

2010. Pre-Historic Animals. Multicoloured.
2288		250d. Type **592**	1·20	1·20
2289		250d. Pterodactyls and trees	1·20	1·20
2290		250d. Archaeopteryx, flight-less birds and Brachiosaurus	1·20	1·20
2291		250d. Tyranosaurus rex, Iguanadon and Archaeopteryx in flight	1·20	1·20
2292		250d. Albertosaurus and Stegosaurus	1·20	1·20
2293		250d. Stegosaurus, Brontosaurus and Ankylosaurus	1·20	1·20
2294		250d. Ankylosaurus and early crocodiles	1·20	1·20
2295		250d. Spinosaurus	1·20	1·20
MS2296	104×78 mm. 500d. Deinonychus. Imperf		2·30	2·30

Nos. 2288/95 were printed, se-tenant, forming a composite design.

593 Throwing Ball

2010. World Cup Football Championships, South Africa. Multicoloured.
2297		250d. Type **593**	1·20	1·20
2298		500d. Player celebrating	2·30	2·30
2299		750d. Player wearing green shorts and ball	3·50	3·50
2300		1000d. Player wearing red shorts and ball	4·50	4·50
MS2301	125×70 mm. 1000d. Emblem and players. Imperf		4·50	4·50

594 Koran

2010. National Campaign for the Koran. Multicoloured.
2302		250d. Type **594**	1·20	1·20
MS2303	90×70 mm. 500d. Koran (different). Imperf		2·30	2·30

595 Young Couple

2010. United Nations International Year of Youth. Multicoloured.
2304		250d. Type **595**	1·20	1·20
2305		250d. Two faces in profile and hand holding candle	1·20	1·20

596 Anniversary Emblem and Symbols of Iraq

2010. 50th Anniv of Organization of Petroleum Exporting Countries (OPEC). Multicoloured.
2306		250d. T **596** and similar vert design.	1·20	1·20
2307		500d. Ishtar Gate, Samorra Mosque, Al-Najaf and Shedu (human-headed winged bull)	2·30	2·30

597 Kirkuk Citadel

2010. Kirkuk–Iraqi City of Culture
2308	**597**	1000d. multicoloured	4·50	4·50

598 Child holding Adult's Hand

2010. United Nations Convention on the Rights of the Child. Multicoloured.
2309		500d. Type **598**	2·30	2·30
2310		750d. Boy writing on blackboard	3·50	3·50
2311		1000d. Children on carousel	4·00	4·00

599 Coccinella septempunctata

2011. International Year of Biodiversity. Multicoloured.
2312		250d. Type **599**	1·90	1·90
2313		500d. Egretta alba (great egret) (inscr 'Great White Heron')	3·75	3·75
2314		750d. Persian gazelle (horiz)	5·75	5·75
2315		1000d. Ophisops elegans (snake-eyed lizard) (horiz)	8·50	8·50
MS2316	151×75 mm. 1000d. Ducks (108×25 mm). Imperf		8·50	8·50

600 Goalkeeper and Ball

2011. Asia Cup Football Championships, Qatar. Multicoloured.
2318		250d. Type **600**	1·90	1·90
2319		500d. Player and ball facing left	3·75	3·75
2320		750d. Player and ball facing right	5·75	5·75
2321		1000d. Player with right knee raised and ball	7·75	7·75
2322		60×60 mm. 1000d. Two players and central emblem. Imperf	8·50	8·50

601 *Metapenaeus affinis*

2011. Biodiversity of Shatt al Arab and Northern Gulf. Multicoloured.

2323	250d.	1·90	1·90
2324	500d. *Torpedo panthera*	3·75	3·75
2325	750d. *Eupagurus prideaux* (inscr 'Eupagurus prideauxl')	5·75	5·75
2326	1000d. Carp		
MS2327	80×60 mm. 1000d. Lionfish. Imperf	8·50	8·50

602 Child, Seedling and Desert

2011. National Day to Control Desertification. Multicoloured.

2328	750d. Type **602**	5·25	5·25
2329	1000d. Hands holding seedling and desert	7·75	7·75

603 Lungs, Diseased and Healthy Tissue

2011. International Day of TB Awareness

2330	**603** 250d. multicoloured	3·00	3·00
2331	**603** 500d. multicoloured	3·00	3·00

604 Babylon

2011. Archaeology. Multicoloured.

2332	250d. Type **604**	1·90	1·90
2333	500d. Hatra	3·75	3·75
2334	750d. Ziggurat of Ur	5·75	5·75
2335	1000d. Nineveh	7·75	7·75
MS2336	60×80 mm. 1000d. Spiral Minaret. Imperf	7·75	7·75

605 Abd al-Wahhab Al-Bayati

2011. Personalities. Poets. Multicoloured.

2337	250d. Type **605**	1·70	1·70
2338	500d. Muhammad Mahdi Al-Jawahiri	3·50	3·50
2339	750d. Nazik Al-Malaika	5·75	5·75

OBLIGATORY TAX

28a King Faisal II

28b

28c "Tax 2 Fils Save Palestine"

28d "Tax Save Palestine"

28e "Save Palestine" (size varies)

28g "Tax 10 Fils Save Palestine" (size varies)

28h "Tax 5 Fils Save Palestine"

1949. Aid for Palestine. (a) Nos. O300 and 278 surch as T **28c**.

T324	27	2f. on 3f. green	36·00	20·00
T325	27	2f. on 6f. mauve	48·00	19·00

(b) Nos. O299 and O303 optd as T **28d** but smaller.

T326		2f. brown	29·00	12·50
T327		5f. red	60·00	29·00

(c) No. O234 optd with T **28d**.

T328	20	5f. red	30·00	7·25

(d) Revenue stamp surch in Arabic (="2 Fils Save Palestine") as bottom two lines of T **28c**.

T329	28a	2f. on 5f. blue	19·00	10·00

(e) Revenue stamps optd with T **28e**.

T330	28a	5f. blue	9·75	1·60
T332	28b	10f. orange		55·00
T335	28a	10f. orange	29·00	12·50

(f) Revenue stamp surch as T **28g**.

T336	28b	10f. on 20f. green	85·00	36·00

(h) No. 278 surch with T **28h**.

T337	27	5f. on 6f. mauve	60·00	21·00

113a (113b)

1968. Flood Relief.

T763	113a	5f. brown	60	35

1968. Defence Fund. Optd with Type **113b**.

T764	5f. brown	60	60

(164a) (215)

1970. Obligatory Tax. Defence Fund. Nos. 620 and 625/9 surch with Type T **164a**.

T931	65	5f. on 1f. green	5·50	6·25
T932	-	5f. on 10f. red	5·50	6·25
T933	-	5f. on 15f. brown & yell	5·50	6·25
T934	-	5f. on 20f. violet	5·50	6·25
T935	-	5f. on 30f. orange	5·50	6·25
T936	-	5f. on 40f. green	5·50	6·25

1973. Obligatory Tax. Defence Fund. Nos. 607/8 surch with Type **215**.

T1071	62	5f. on 14f. black & grn	9·75	9·75
T1072	62	5f. on 35f. black and red	9·75	9·75

(223) (231)

1973. Nos. 738, 765, 777, 787 and 891 optd similar to Type **215** (No. T1119) or as Type **223** (others).

T1117	-	5f. on 2f. multicoloured	12·00	12·00
T1118	114	5f. on 2f. multicoloured	12·00	12·00
T1119	116	5f. on 2f. multicoloured	12·00	12·00
T1120	117	5f. on 2f. multicoloured	12·00	12·00
T1121	150	5f. on 2f. multicoloured	12·00	12·00

1973. No. 1099 optd with Type **231**.

T1152	221	5f. black and orange	8·50	5·50

235 Soldier

1974. Defence Fund.

T1158	235	5f. black, yellow & brn	7·25	4·00

OFFICIAL STAMPS

1920. Issue of 1918 (surch Turkish stamps) optd ON STATE SERVICE.

O33		½a. on 10pa. green	1·00	1·00
O20		1a. on 20pa. red	7·50	1·00
O35		1½a. on 5pa. brown	2·75	1·00

O22		2½a. on 1pi. blue	7·50	8·00
O23		3a. on 1½pi. black and pink	27·00	1·00
O36		4a. on 1¾pi. brown and blue	2·00	3·00
O25		6a. on 2pi. black and green	40·00	9·00
O8		8a. on 2½pi. green and brown	3·25	2·00
O27		12a. on 5pi. purple	30·00	22·00
O28		1r. on 10pi. red	42·00	12·00
O29		2r. on 25pi. green	42·00	20·00
O30		5r. on 50pi. red	80·00	60·00
O31		10r. on 100pi. blue	£120	£150

1923. Nos. 41/50 and 52/3 optd ON STATE SERVICE in English only.

O54	2	½a. green	1·50	1·75
O55	3	1a. red	1·75	30
O56	3	1½a. red	1·75	30
O57	-	2a. buff	2·00	55
O58	-	3a. blue	2·50	1·50
O59	-	4a. violet	4·25	45
O60	-	6a. blue	3·75	1·25
O61	-	8a. bistre	4·00	4·25
O62	4	1r. brown and green	16·00	3·75
O63	2	2r. black	32·00	14·00
O64	-	5r. orange	75·00	50·00
O65	-	10r. red	£170	70·00

1924. Nos. 41/9 and 51/3 optd ON STATE SERVICE in English and Arabic.

O66	2	½a. green	1·50	10
O67	-	1a. brown	1·25	10
O68	3	1½a. red	1·25	30
O69	-	2a. buff	1·50	10
O70	-	3a. blue	2·00	10
O71	-	4a. violet	4·00	30
O72	-	6a. blue	1·75	20
O73	-	8a. bistre	3·75	35
O74	4	1r. brown and green	17·00	3·50
O75	2	2r. bistre	40·00	3·75
O76	-	5r. orange	80·00	50·00
O77	-	10r. red	£140	42·00

1927. Optd ON STATE SERVICE in English and Arabic.

O79	10	1r. brown	13·00	2·75

1931. Optd ON STATE SERVICE in English and Arabic.

O93	11	½a. green	65	2·75
O94	11	1a. brown	2·50	10
O95	11	1½a. red	4·50	27·00
O96	11	2a. orange	80	10
O97	11	3a. blue	85	1·25
O98	11	4a. purple	1·00	45
O99	11	6a. blue	5·50	29·00
O100	11	8a. green	5·50	29·00
O101	12	1r. brown	22·00	27·00
O102	12	2r. brown	35·00	80·00
O103	12	5r. orange	48·00	£160
O104	12	10r. red	£180	£275
O105	10	25r. violet	£1400	£1800

1932. Official stamps of 1924 and 1931 surch in "Fils" or "Dinar".

O122	11	3f. on ½a. green	7·00	3·50
O123	11	4f. on 1a. brown	2·50	10
O124	11	5f. on 1a. brown	2·50	10
O125	4	8f. on 1½a. red	13·00	50
O126	11	10f. on 2a. orange	4·50	10
O127	11	15f. on 3a. blue	4·25	7·00
O128	11	20f. on 4a. purple	4·75	4·25
O129	11	25f. on 4a. purple	4·75	2·00
O130	-	30f. on 6a. bl (No. O72)	13·00	1·75
O131	-	40f. on 8a. green	4·00	3·50
O132	12	50f. on 1r. brown	16·00	4·25
O133	12	75f. on 1r. brown	7·50	10·00
O134	2	100f. on 2r. bistre	40·00	3·50
O135	-	200f. on 5r. orange (No. O76)	26·00	26·00
O136	-	½d. on 10r. red (No. 77)	£130	£160
O137	10	1d. on 25r. violet	£275	£425

1932. Issue of 1932 optd ON STATE SERVICE in English and Arabic.

O155	11	2f. blue	1·50	10
O156	11	3f. green	1·50	10
O157	11	4f. purple	1·50	10
O158	11	5f. green	1·50	10
O159	11	8f. red	1·50	10
O160	11	10f. yellow	2·25	10
O161	11	15f. blue	2·50	10
O162	11	20f. orange	2·50	15
O163	11	25f. mauve	2·50	15
O164	11	30f. olive	3·50	20
O165	11	40f. violet	4·50	30
O166	12	50f. brown	3·25	20
O167	12	75f. blue	2·50	1·00
O168	12	100f. green	11·00	3·25
O169	12	200f. red	27·00	6·50
O170	10	½d. brown	24·00	40·00
O171	10	1d. purple	£130	£150

1934. Issue of 1934 optd ON STATE SERVICE in English and Arabic.

O190	16	1f. violet	1·80	65
O191	16	2f. blue	1·80	20

O192	16	3f. green	85	20
O193	16	4f. purple	1·80	20
O194	16	5f. green	1·60	20
O195	16	8f. red	6·00	35
O196	16	10f. yellow	35	20
O197	16	15f. blue	13·50	2·00
O198	16	20f. orange	1·30	20
O199	16	25f. mauve	27·00	7·75
O200	16	30f. green	6·00	35
O201	16	40f. violet	7·75	55
O202	17	50f. brown	1·30	90
O203	17	75f. blue	9·00	1·10
O204	17	100f. green	2·40	1·30
O205	17	200f. red	6·75	3·25
O206	-	½d. blue (No. 188)	17·00	25·00
O207	-	1d. red (No. 189)	65·00	75·00

1941. Issue of 1941 optd ON STATE SERVICE in English and Arabic.

O230	19	1f. purple	35	20
O231	19	2f. brown	35	20
O232	-	3f. green (No. 210)	35	20
O233	-	4f. violet (No. 211)	35	20
O234	-	5f. red (No. 212)	35	20
O235	21	8f. red	1·20	20
O236	21	8f. yellow	35	20
O237	21	10f. yellow	9·00	55
O238	21	10f. red	95	20
O239	21	15f. blue	9·00	1·00
O240	21	15f. black	1·60	45
O241	21	20f. black	2·75	45
O242	21	20f. green	85	20
O244	22	25f. purple	1·40	45
O246a	22	30f. orange	60	45
O248a	22	40f. brown	60	35
O249c	-	50f. blue (No. 224)	1·60	90
O250	-	75f. mauve (No. 225)	1·60	35
O251	-	100f. olive (No. 226)	3·25	45
O252	-	200f. orange (No. 227)	4·25	1·10
O253	-	½d. blue (No. 228)	16·00	6·75
O254	-	1d. green (No. 229)	27·00	12·50

1942. Issue of 1942 optd ON STATE SERVICE in English and Arabic.

O263	26	1f. brown and violet	50	45
O264	26	2f. brown and blue	50	45
O265	26	3f. brown and green	50	45
O266	26	4f. sepia and brown	50	45
O267	26	5f. brown and green	60	55
O268	26	6f. brown and red	60	55
O269	26	10f. brown and pink	85	80
O270	26	12f. brown and green	1·10	1·00

1948. Issue of 1948 optd ON STATE SERVICE in English and Arabic.

O298	27	1f. blue	25	45
O299	27	2f. brown	25	55
O300	27	3f. green	25	55
O301	27	3f. red	4·25	1·30
O302	27	4f. lilac	25	45
O303	27	5f. red	25	65
O304	27	5f. green	4·75	1·30
O305	27	6f. mauve	25	55
O306	27	8f. brown	25	55
O307	27	10f. red	25	45
O308	27	12f. green	35	45
O309	27	14f. green	2·40	45
O310	27	15f. black	5·50	8·25
O311	27	16f. red	4·25	45
O312	27	20f. blue	35	20
O313	27	25f. purple	35	20
O314	27	28f. blue	1·30	45
O315	27	30f. orange	35	35
O316	27	40f. brown	70	55
O317	27	50f. blue	1·10	45
O318	27	60f. blue	85	35
O319	27	75f. mauve	1·90	45
O320	27	100f. green	1·90	1·30
O321	27	200f. orange	3·00	1·30
O322	27	½d. blue	27·00	20·00
O323	27	1d. green	36·00	42·00

1955. Issue of 1954 optd ON STATE SERVICE in English and Arabic.

O364	33	1f. blue	20	15
O365	33	2f. brown	20	15
O366	33	3f. lake	20	15
O367	33	4f. violet	35	15
O368	33	5f. green	35	15
O369	33	6f. mauve	35	15
O370	33	8f. brown	35	15
O371	33	10f. red	35	15
O372	33	16f. red	31·00	31·00
O373	33	20f. olive	60	35
O374	33	25f. purple	3·25	1·50
O375	33	30f. red	1·40	35
O376	33	40f. brown	60	35
O377	33	50f. blue	3·25	1·00
O378	-	60f. purple	21·00	7·25
O379	-	100f. olive	46·00	20·00

No. O378 does not exist without opt.

1958. Issue of 1957 optd **ON STATE SERVICE** in English and Arabic.

O404	41	1f. blue	6·00	2·20
O405	41	2f. brown	7·25	4·75
O406	41	3f. red	9·00	3·25
O407	41	4f. violet	11·00	2·20
O408	41	5f. green	6·00	2·20
O409	41	6f. red	6·00	3·25
O410	41	10f. blue	6·00	1·90

1958. Official stamps optd with T **43**. (a) Nos. O251/2.

O459		100f. green		
O459a		200f. orange	13·50	7·25

(b) Nos. O298 etc.

O460	27	1f. blue	48·00	45·00
O461	27	2f. brown	48·00	45·00
O462	27	3f. green	48·00	45·00
O463	27	3f. red	48·00	45·00
O464	27	4f. lilac	48·00	45·00
O465	27	5f. red	48·00	45·00
O466	27	5f. green	48·00	45·00
O467	27	6f. mauve	48·00	45·00
O468	27	8f. brown	48·00	45·00
O470	27	12f. green	1·40	1·00
O471	27	14f. green	1·70	1·10
O472	27	15f. black	1·20	65
O473	27	16f. red	5·00	2·75
O474	27	25f. purple	4·50	2·75
O475	27	28f. blue	2·75	2·10
O476	27	40f. brown	1·80	1·30
O477	27	60f. blue	6·75	3·25
O478	27	75f. mauve	3·25	2·50
O479	27	200f. orange	3·75	3·25
O480	27	½d. blue	23·00	7·75
O481	27	1d. green	36·00	16·00

(c) Nos. O364 etc.

O482	33	1f. blue	85	35
O483	33	2f. brown	85	35
O484	33	3f. red	85	35
O485	33	4f. violet	85	35
O486	33	5f. green	90	35
O487	33	6f. mauve	85	55
O488	33	8f. brown	70	35
O489	33	10f. blue	90	35
O490	33	16f. red	10·00	9·00
O491	33	20f. green	85	35
O492	33	25f. purple	85	35
O493	33	30f. red	90	55
O494	33	40f. brown	1·30	55
O495	-	50f. blue	1·30	65
O496	-	60f. purple	1·30	80
O497	-	100f. green	3·00	80

(d) Nos. O404 etc.

O498	41	1f. blue	35	35
O499	41	2f. brown	35	35
O500	41	3f. red	60	35
O501	41	4f. violet	35	35
O502	41	5f. green	35	35
O503	41	6f. red	35	35
O504	41	8f. brown	85	20
O505	41	10f. blue	95	20

No. O504 does not exist without opt T **43**.

1961. Nos. 515, etc. optd **On State Service** in English and Arabic.

O552	49	1f. multicoloured	50	50
O553	49	2f. multicoloured	50	50
O554	49	4f. multicoloured	50	50
O555	49	5f. multicoloured	60	50
O556	49	10f. multicoloured	1·10	80
O557	49	50f. multicoloured	18·00	13·50

1962. Nos. 515, etc. optd **ON STATE SERVICE** in English and Arabic.

O587	1f. multicoloured		50	50
O588	2f. multicoloured		50	50
O589	3f. multicoloured		50	50
O590	4f. multicoloured		50	50
O591	5f. multicoloured		50	50
O592	10f. multicoloured		50	50
O593	15f. multicoloured		50	50
O594	20f. multicoloured		50	50
O595	30f. multicoloured		60	50
O596	40f. multicoloured		60	50
O597	50f. multicoloured		70	50
O598	75f. multicoloured		1·20	55
O599	100f. multicoloured		1·30	90
O600	200f. multicoloured		4·75	1·90
O601	500f. multicoloured		17·00	7·75
O602	1d. multicoloured		34·00	16·00

1971. Various stamps optd or surch **Official** in English and Arabic. (a) Costumes. Nos. 768 and 770/4.

O962	15f. multicoloured (postage)		2·40	90
O963	25f. multicoloured		16·00	3·75
O964	30f. multicoloured		16·00	3·75
O965	40f. multicoloured (air)		6·75	1·90
O966	50f. multicoloured		8·50	1·90
O967	80f. multicoloured		7·75	1·90

(b) International Tourist Year. Nos. 778 and 780/2.

O969	5f. multicoloured (postage)		8·50	45
O970	15f. multicoloured		8·50	80
O971	25f. multicoloured		12·00	2·10
O972	50f. multicoloured (air)		7·75	5·00

(c) Birds. No. 798.

O1178	30f. multicoloured		8·50	5·50

(d) 20th Anniv of W.H.O. Nos. 811/13.

O973	-	10f. multicoloured	11·50	4·50
O974	124	15f. red, blue and black	11·50	4·50
O975	124	25f. red, green and black	11·50	4·50

(e) Human Rights Year. Nos. 814/15.

O976	125	10f. red, yellow and blue	7·25	65
O977	125	25f. red, yellow & green	7·25	1·20

(f) UNICEF. Nos. 817/18.

O978	126	15f. multicoloured	7·25	55
O979	126	25f. multicoloured	7·25	1·50

(g) Army Day. No. 820.

O980	127	25f. multicoloured	16·00	4·50

(h) Fish and Fauna. Nos. 825/7, 829/30 and 832.

O981	10f. multicoloured (postage)		9·00	5·50
O982	15f. on 3f. multicoloured		9·00	5·50
O983	25f. on 2f. multicoloured		9·00	5·50
O984	10f. multicoloured (air)		9·00	5·50
O985	15f.+3f. multicoloured		9·00	5·50
O986	25f.+2f. multicoloured		9·00	5·50

(i) Fruits. Nos. 906/9.

O987	5f. multicoloured		7·25	5·00
O988	10f. multicoloured		7·25	5·00
O989	15f. multicoloured		7·25	5·00
O990	35f. multicoloured		7·25	5·00

(j) Arab Football Cup, Baghdad. No. 717.

O991	97	2f. multicoloured	8·50	5·50

(k) 50th Anniv of I.L.O. No. 836.

O992	133	15f. yellow, green & blk	8·50	5·50

1972. Nos. 625/8 optd **Official** in English and Arabic.

O1042	10f. red		11·00	11·00
O1043	15f. brown and yellow		11·00	11·00
O1044	20f. violet		11·00	11·00
O1045	30f. orange		11·00	11·00

1973. Various stamps with portrait obliterated by 3 bars. (i) 1948 issue.

O1081	27	25f. purple (No. O313)	9·00	2·10
O1082	27	50f. blue (No. O317)	9·00	7·75

(ii) 1955 issue.

O1083	33	25f. purple (No. O374)	9·00	2·10
O1084	-	50f. blue (No. O377)	9·00	7·75

(iii) Similar to 1958 issue (T **41**) but size 22½×27½ mm.

O1085		50f. purple	9·00	7·75

(O218) (size varies)   **(O237a)**

1973. "Faisal" stamps with portrait obliterated. (a) Optd with 3 bars and Type **O218**.

O1086	33	10f. blue	5·50	5·50
O1087	41	15f. black	5·50	5·50

(b) Optd with Type **O218** only.

O1090	33	15f. black	5·50	1·10
O1091	41	15f. black	5·50	1·10
O1092	33	25f. purple	5·50	1·10
O1093	41	25f. purple	5·50	1·10
O1096	27	25f. purple	21·00	7·75

1973. No. 1097 optd Official in English and Arabic.

O1099	220	25f. multicoloured	5·50	1·60

1973. Nos. 1099/1107 optd **OFFICIAL** in English and Arabic.

O1108	221	5f. black and orange	50	45
O1109	221	10f. black and brown	50	45
O1110	221	20f. black and mauve	85	45
O1111	-	25f. black and blue	1·70	1·70
O1112	-	35f. black and green	1·70	65
O1113	-	45f. black and blue	1·70	80
O1114	-	50f. yellow and green	2·30	90
O1115	-	70f. yellow and violet	2·30	1·20
O1116	-	95f. yellow and brown	3·50	1·60

1973. Various "Faisal" Official stamps optd **ON STATE SERVICE** in English and Arabic, with portrait obliterated by "leaf" motif similar to that used in Type **O218**. (a) 1948 issue.

O1130a	27	12f. olive	2·30	45
O1131	27	14f. olive	2·30	65
O1132	27	15f. black	2·30	65
O1133	27	16f. red	4·50	1·10
O1134	27	28f. blue	9·00	1·60
O1134a	27	30f. orange	9·00	1·30
O1134b	27	40f. brown	9·00	1·90
O1135	27	60f. blue	9·00	6·75
O1136	27	100f. green	30·00	10·50

O1137	27	½d. blue	80·00	28·00
O1138	27	1d. green	£160	£160

(b) 1955 issue.

O1139	33	3f. lake	2·30	80
O1140	33	6f. mauve	2·30	80
O1141	33	8f. brown	2·30	80
O1142	33	16f. red	23·00	23·00
O1142a	33	20f. green	2·30	80
O1142b	33	30f. red	2·30	1·30
O1142c	33	40f. brown	2·30	2·30
O1143	-	60f. purple	2·30	2·30
O1144	-	100f. green	41·00	11·00

(c) 1958 issue.

O1145	41	3f. lake	7·25	1·60
O1146	41	6f. mauve	7·25	1·60
O1147	41	8f. brown	7·25	1·60
O1147a	41	30f. red	7·25	1·60

1974. No. T1158 optd with Type **O237a**.

O1165	235	5f. black, yellow & brn	4·25	4·25

O **249** Eagle Emblem

1975

O1195	O249	5f. multicoloured	50	50
O1196	O249	10f. multicoloured	50	50
O1197	O249	15f. multicoloured	60	60
O1198	O249	20f. multicoloured	85	85
O1199	O249	25f. multicoloured	1·20	1·20
O1200	O249	30f. multicoloured	1·40	1·40
O1201	O249	50f. multicoloured	2·30	2·30
O1202	O249	100f. multicoloured	4·50	4·50

1976. Nos. 1253/7 additionally inscr "OFFICIAL" in English and Arabic.

O1258	264	5f. multicoloured	1·90	1·00
O1259	-	10f. multicoloured	1·90	1·10
O1260	-	15f. multicoloured	1·90	1·10
O1261	-	25f. multicoloured	5·00	1·90
O1262	-	50f. multicoloured	8·50	3·00

1978. As T **290**, but additionally inscr "OFFICIAL" in English and Arabic.

O1338	5f. multicoloured		50	50
O1339	10f. multicoloured		50	50
O1340	15f. multicoloured		60	50
O1341	25f. multicoloured		1·20	50

O **342** Entrance to Baghdad University

1981

O1499	O342	45f. multicoloured	85	55
O1500	O342	50f. multicoloured	95	65

1982. As Nos. 1504/6, additionally inscr "OFFICIAL" in English and Arabic.

O1507	45f. multicoloured		1·90	55
O1508	50f. multicoloured		1·90	65
O1509	120f. multicoloured		4·75	1·70

1983. Nos. O1499/1500 surch.

O1581	60f. on 45f. mult		3·50	65
O1582	70f. on 50f. mult		4·25	1·00

1983. Design as T **371**.

O1615	60f. yellow, black and pink		1·20	65
O1616	70f. yellow, black and pink		1·30	90

DESIGN: Nos. O1615/16, Aerial view of building.

1984. Multicoloured.. Multicoloured..

O1642	20f. Type **377**		50	50
O1643	30f. Type **377**		50	50
O1644	50f. As No. 1639		70	55
O1645	60f. As No. 1639		70	55

O **400** Pres. Hussain

1986

O1740	O400	30f. multicoloured	85	20
O1741	O400	50f. multicoloured	1·20	30
O1742	O400	100f. multicoloured	2·30	90
O1743	O400	150f. multicoloured	3·00	2·20

Nos. O1740/3 are inscribed "POSTAGE".

IRELAND

Ireland (Eire) consisting of Ireland less the six counties of Ulster, became the Irish Free State in 1922 and left the British Empire in 1949 when it became an independent republic.

1949. 12 pence = 1 shilling; 20 shillings = 1 pound.
1971. 100 (new) pence = 1 pound (Punt).
2002. 100 cents = 1 euro.

Rialtar Sealadac na hÉireann 1922

(1) "Provisional Government of Ireland, 1922"

1922. Stamps of Great Britain optd with T **1** (date in thin figures and no full point).

1	105	½d. green	2·25	40
2	104	1d. red	3·50	60
4b	104	2½d. blue	2·50	4·00
5	106	3d. violet	6·00	6·50
6	106	4d. green	6·00	23·00
7	107	5d. brown	6·00	8·50
8b	108	9d. black	17·00	19·00
9	108	10d. blue	11·00	65·00
17	109	2s.6d. brown	60·00	85·00
19	109	5s. red	90·00	£170
21	109	10s. blue	£180	£375

On Nos. 17, 19 and 21 the overprint is in four lines instead of five.

Rialtar Sealadac na hÉireann 1922.

(2)

1922. Stamps of Great Britain optd with T **2** (date in thick figures followed by full point).

47	105	½d. green	1·00	2·00
31	104	1d. red	3·25	50
10	105	1½d. brown	3·00	1·75
12	106	2d. orange	9·00	50
35	104	2½d. blue	7·00	28·00
36a	106	3d. violet	5·00	2·00
37	106	4d. green	4·50	10·00
38	107	5d. brown	5·50	11·00
39a	107	6d. purple	8·50	4·25
40	108	9d. black	14·00	27·00
41	108	9d. green	6·00	50·00
42	108	10d. blue	29·00	75·00
43	108	1s. brown	14·00	14·00

Saorstát Éireann 1922

5 "Irish Free State, 1922"

1922. Stamps of Great Britain optd with T **5**.

52		½d. green	2·00	30
53	104	1d. red	2·50	50
54	105	1½d. brown	3·50	8·50
55	106	2d. orange	1·50	1·00
56	104	2½d. blue	7·50	12·00
57	106	3d. violet	4·75	11·00
58	106	4d. green	4·75	12·00
59	107	5d. brown	5·50	4·75
60	107	6d. purple	3·75	2·00
61	108	9d. green	9·00	5·50
62	108	10d. blue	23·00	75·00
63	108	1s. brown	8·00	11·00
86	109	2s.6d. brown	50·00	60·00
87	109	5s. red	80·00	£100
88	109	10s. blue	£190	£225

6 "Sword of Light"   **7** Map of Ireland   **8** Arms of Ireland

9 Celtic Cross

1922

71	6	½d. green	3·00	90
112	7	1d. red	50	10
73	7	1½d. purple	3·50	2·00
114	7	2d. green	50	10
75	8	2½d. brown	5·00	3·75
116	9	3d. blue (18½×22½ mm)	85	10

227	9	3d. blue (17×21 mm)	40	15
117	8	4d. blue	55	10
118	6	5d. violet (18½×22½ mm)	1·00	10
228	6	5d. violet (17×21 mm)	30	15
119b	6	6d. purple	1·25	20
119c	6	8d. red	80	1·50
120	8	9d. violet	1·50	80
121	9	10d. brown	75	80
121b	9	11d. red	2·25	3·25
82	6	1s. blue	16·00	4·50

12 Daniel O'Connell

1929. Centenary of Catholic Emancipation

89	12	2d. green	70	45
90	12	3d. blue	4·25	11·00
91	12	9d. violet	4·25	5·00

13 Shannon Barrage

1930. Completion of Shannon Hydro-electric Scheme.

92	13	2d. deep brown	1·25	55

14 Reaper

1931. Bicentenary of Royal Dublin Society.

93	14	2d. blue	1·00	30

15 The Cross of Cong

1932. International Eucharistic Congress.

94	15	2d. green	2·50	30
95	15	3d. blue	3·75	6·50

16 Adoration of the Cross

1933. "Holy Year".

96	16	2d. green	2·25	15
97	16	3d. blue	4·00	2·50

17 Hurler

1934. 50th Anniv of Gaelic Athletic Assn.

98	17	2d. green	2·00	55

1937

123b	18	2s.6d. green	1·50	3·25
124ca	18	5s. red	4·00	9·50
125ba	18	10s. blue	4·00	16·00

19 Ireland and New Constitution

1937. Constitution Day.

105	19	2d. red	2·00	20
106	19	3d. blue	5·00	3·75

For similar stamps see Nos. 176/7.

20 Father Mathew

1938. Centenary of Temperance Crusade.

107	20	2d. black	2·50	50
108	20	3d. blue	12·00	6·50

21 George Washington, American Eagle and Irish Harp

1939. 150th Anniv of U.S. Constitution and Installation of First U.S. President.

109	21	2d. red	2·75	1·00
110	21	3d. blue	4·00	5·50

1941. 25th Anniv of Easter Rising (1916). Provisional issue. Optd with two lines of Irish characters between the dates "**1941**" and "**1916**".

126	7	2d. orange	2·00	1·00
127	9	3d. blue	27·00	11·00

24 Volunteer and G.P.O., Dublin

1941. 25th Anniv of Easter Rising (1916). Definitive issue

128	24	2½d. black	3·25	1·25

25 Dr. Douglas Hyde

1943. 50th Anniv of Gaelic League.

129	25	½d. green	1·25	70
130	25	2½d. purple	2·00	10

26 Sir William Rowan Hamilton

1943. Centenary of Announcement of Discovery of Quaternions.

131	26	½d. green	75	70
132	26	2½d. brown	2·25	20

27 Bro. Michael O'Clery

1944. Death Tercentenary of Michael O'Clery (Franciscan historian) (commemorating the "Annals of the Four Masters").

133	27	½d. green	10	10
134	27	1s. brown	1·25	10

28 Edmund Ignatius Rice

1944. Death Centenary of Edmund Rice (founder of Irish Christian Brothers).

135	28	2½d. slate	1·75	45

29 "Youth sowing Seeds of Freedom"

1945. Death Centenary of Thomas Davis (founder of Young Ireland Movement).

136	29	2½d. blue	2·00	75
137	29	6d. purple	7·00	8·00

30 "Country and Homestead"

1946. Birth Centenaries of Michael Davitt and Charles Parnell (land reformers).

138	30	2½d. red	2·50	25
139	30	3d. blue	3·50	4·25

31 Angel Victor over Rock of Cashel

1948. Air. Inscr "VOX HIBERNIAE".

140	31	1d. brown	3·00	5·50
141	-	3d. blue	3·00	3·50
142	-	6d. purple	1·00	2·50
142b	-	8d. lake	8·50	9·00
143	-	1s. green	1·00	2·00
143a	31	1s.3d. orange	8·50	1·50
143b	31	1s.5d. blue	4·00	2·00

DESIGNS: 3d., 8d. Angel Victor over Lough Derg; 6d. Over Croagh Patrick; 1s. Over Glendalough.

35 Theobald Wolfe Tone

1948. 150th Anniv of Insurrection.

144	35	2½d. purple	1·00	10
145	35	3d. violet	3·25	4·25

36 Leinster House and Arms of Provinces

1949. International Recognition of Republic.

146	36	2½d. brown	2·00	10
147	36	3d. blue	6·50	4·25

37 J. C. Mangan

1949. Death Centenary of James Clarence Mangan (poet).

148	37	1d. green	1·50	35

38 Statue of St. Peter, Rome

1950. Holy Year.

149	38	2½d. violet	1·00	40
150	38	3d. blue	8·00	12·00
151	38	9d. brown	8·00	15·00

39 Thomas Moore

1952. Death Centenary of Thomas Moore (poet).

152	39	2½d. purple	1·00	10
153	39	3½d. olive	1·75	4·25

40 Irish Harp

1953. "An Tostal" (Ireland at Home) Festival.

154	40	2½d. green	1·75	35
155	40	1s.4d. blue	19·00	29·00

41 Robert Emmet

1953. 150th Death Anniv of Emmet (patriot).

156	41	3d. green	3·00	15
157	41	1s.3d. red	45·00	10·00

42 Madonna and Child (Della Robbia)

1954. Marian Year.

158	42	3d. blue	1·00	10
159	42	5d. green	2·00	3·25

43 Cardinal Newman (first Rector)

1954. Centenary of Founding of Catholic University of Ireland.

160	43	2d. purple	2·00	10
161	43	1s.3d. blue	16·00	6·50

44 Statue of Commodore Barry

1956. Barry Commemoration.

162	44	3d. lilac	1·00	10
163	44	1s.3d. blue	4·50	8·00

45 John Redmond

1957. Birth Centenary of John Redmond (politician).

164	45	3d. blue	1·00	10
165	45	1s.3d. purple	9·00	15·00

46 Thomas O'Crohan

1957. Birth Cent of Thomas O'Crohan (author).

166	46	2d. purple	1·00	20
167	46	5d. violet	1·25	4·50

47 Admiral Brown

1957. Death Cent of Admiral William Brown.

168	47	3d. blue	3·00	20
169	47	1s.3d. red	25·00	17·00

48 Father Wadding (Ribera)

1957. Death Tercentenary of Father Luke Wadding (theologian).

170	**48**	3d. blue	2·00	10
171	**48**	1s.3d. lake	15·00	8·50

49 Tom Clarke

1958. Birth Centenary of Thomas J. ("Tom") Clarke (patriot).

172	**49**	3d. green	2·00	10
173	**49**	1s.3d. brown	4·00	11·00

50 Mother Mary Aikenhead

1958. Death Centenary of Mother Mary Aikenhead (foundress of Irish Sisters of Charity).

174	**50**	3d. blue	2·00	10
175	**50**	1s.3d. red	11·00	8·00

1958. 21st Anniv of Irish Constitution.

176	**19**	3d. brown	1·00	10
177	**19**	5d. green	1·00	4·50

51 Arthur Guinness

1959. Bicentenary of Guinness Brewery.

178	**51**	3d. purple	3·00	10
179	**51**	1s.3d. blue	12·00	10·00

52 "The Flight of the Holy Family"

1960. World Refugee Year.

180	**52**	3d. purple	40	10
181	**52**	1s.3d. sepia	60	3·75

53 Conference Emblem

1960. First Anniv of Europa.

182	**53**	6d. brown	5·50	1·00
183	**53**	1s.3d. violet	19·00	20·00

54 Dublin Airport, de Havilland Dragon Mk 2 EI-ABI "Iolar" and Boeing 720 EI-ALA

1961. Silver Jubilee of Aer Lingus Airlines.

184	**54**	6d. blue	1·75	3·75
185	**54**	1s.3d. green	2·25	5·50

55 St Patrick

1961. 15th Death Centenary of St. Patrick.

186	**55**	3d. blue	1·00	10
187	**55**	8d. purple	2·75	5·50
188	**55**	1s.3d. green	2·75	1·60

56 John O'Donovan and Edugen O'Curry

1962. Death Centenaries of O'Donovan and O'Curry (scholars).

189	**56**	3d. red	30	10
190	**56**	1s.3d. purple	1·25	2·25

57 Europa "Tree"

1962. Europa.

191	**57**	6d. red	70	1·00
192	**57**	1s.3d. turquoise	80	1·50

58 Campaign Emblem

1963. Freedom from Hunger.

193	**58**	4d. violet	50	10
194	**58**	1s.3d. red	2·75	2·75

59 "Co-operation"

1963. Europa.

195	**59**	6d. red	1·00	75
196	**59**	1s.3d. blue	3·25	3·75

60 Centenary Emblem

1963. Centenary of Red Cross.

197	**60**	4d. red and grey	40	10
198	**60**	1s.3d. red, grey and green	1·10	2·00

61 Wolfe Tone

1964. Birth Bicentenary of Wolfe Tone (revolutionary).

199	**61**	4d. black	50	10
200	**61**	1s.3d. blue	1·90	2·00

62 Irish Pavilion at Fair

1964. New York World's Fair.

201	**62**	5d. multicoloured	50	10
202	**62**	1s.5d. multicoloured	2·00	2·00

63 Europa "Flower"

1964. Europa.

203	**63**	8d. green and blue	1·50	1·25
204	**63**	1s.5d. brown and orange	6·00	3·25

64 "Waves of Communications"

1965. Centenary of I.T.U.

205	**64**	3d. blue and green	30	10
206	**64**	8d. black and green	1·25	1·60

65 W. B. Yeats (poet)

1965. Birth Centenary of Yeats.

207	**65**	5d. black, brown and green	30	10
208	**65**	1s.5d. black, green & brown	2·25	1·75

66 I.C.Y. Emblem

1965. International Co-operation Year.

209	**66**	3d. blue	60	10
210	**66**	10d. brown	1·00	3·25

67 Europa "Sprig"

1965. Europa.

211	**67**	8d. black and red	1·50	1·00
212	**67**	1s.5d. purple and turquoise	7·00	3·50

68 James Connolly

1966. 50th Anniv of Easter Rising.

213	**68**	3d. black and blue	75	10
214	-	3d. black and bronze	75	10
215	-	5d. black and olive	75	10
216	-	5d. black, orange and green	75	10
217	-	7d. black and brown	75	2·25
218	-	7d. black and green	75	2·25
219	-	1s.5d. black and turquoise	75	1·50
220	-	1s.5d. black and green	75	1·50

DESIGNS: No. 214, Thomas J. Clarke; No. 215, P. H. Pearse; No. 216, "Marching to Freedom"; No. 217, Eamonn Ceannt; No. 218, Sean MacDiarmada; No. 219, Thomas MacDonagh; No. 220, Joseph Plunkett.

76 Roger Casement

1966. 50th Death Anniv of Roger Casement (patriot).

221	**76**	5d. black	15	10
222	**76**	1s. brown	40	50

77 Europa "Ship"

1966. Europa.

223	**77**	7d. green and orange	1·00	40
224	**77**	1s.5d. green and grey	2·00	1·60

78 Interior of Abbey (from lithograph)

1966. 750th Anniv of Ballintubber Abbey.

225	**78**	5d. brown	10	10
226	**78**	1s. black	20	25

79 Cogwheels

1967. Europa.

229	**79**	7d. green, gold and cream	60	50
230	**79**	1s.5d. red, gold and cream	1·90	1·75

80 Maple Leaves

1967. Canadian Centennial.

231	**80**	5d. multicoloured	10	10
232	**80**	1s.5d. multicoloured	20	1·00

81 Rock of Cashel (from photo by Edwin Smith)

1967. International Tourist Year.

233	**81**	7d. sepia	15	20
234	**81**	10d. blue	15	40

82 1c. Fenian Stamp Essay

1967. Centenary of Fenian Rising.

235	**82**	5d. black and green	10	10
236	-	1s. black and pink	20	30

DESIGN: 1s.24c. Fenian Stamp Essay.

84 Jonathan Swift

1967. 300th Birth Anniv of Jonathan Swift.

237	**84**	3d. black and grey	10	10
238	-	1s.5d. brown and blue	20	30

DESIGN: 1s.5d. Gulliver and Lilliputians.

86 Europa Key

1968. Europa.

239	**86**	7d. red, gold and brown	50	50
240	**86**	1s.5d. blue, gold and brown	75	1·00

87 St Mary's Cathedral, Limerick

1968. 800th Anniv of St. Mary's Cathedral, Limerick.

241	**87**	5d. blue	10	10
242	**87**	10d. green	20	60

88 Countess Markievicz

1968. Birth Centenary of Countess Markievicz (patriot).

243	**88**	3d. black	10	10
244	**88**	1s.5d. indigo and blue	20	90

89 James
Connolly

1968. Birth Centenary of James Connolly (patriot).

| 245 | 89 | 6d. brown and chocolate | 20 | 75 |
| 246 | 89 | 1s. green, lt green & myrtle | 20 | 10 |

90 Stylized Dog (brooch) **92** Winged Ox (Symbol of St. Luke)

1968

247	90	½d. orange	10	30
248	90	1d. green	15	10
249	90	2d. ochre	50	10
250	90	3d. blue	35	10
251	90	4d. red	30	10
252	90	5d. green	1·25	1·00
253	90	6d. brown	30	10
254	-	7d. brown and yellow	45	4·00
255	-	8d. brown and chestnut	45	3·25
256	-	9d. blue and green	50	10
257	-	10d. brown and violet	1·50	3·25
258	-	1s. chocolate and brown	40	10
259	-	1s.9d. black and turquoise	4·00	3·00
260	92	2s.6d. multicoloured	1·75	30
261	92	5s. multicoloured	3·00	3·50
262	92	10s. multicoloured	4·75	4·75

DESIGNS—As Type **90**: 7d., 8d., 9d., 10d., 1s., 1s.9d., Stag. As Type **92**: 10s Eagle (Symbol of St. John The Evangelist). See also Nos. 287, etc.

94 Human
Rights Emblem

1968. Human Rights Year.

| 263 | 94 | 5d. yellow, gold and black | 15 | 10 |
| 264 | 94 | 7d. yellow, gold and red | 15 | 40 |

95 Dail Eireann Assembly

1969. 50th Anniv of Dail Eireann (1st National Parliament).

| 265 | 95 | 6d. green | 15 | 10 |
| 266 | 95 | 9d. blue | 15 | 30 |

96 Colonnade

1969. Europa.

| 267 | 96 | 9d. grey, ochre and blue | 1·00 | 1·10 |
| 268 | 96 | 1s.9d. grey, gold and red | 1·25 | 1·75 |

97 Quadruple I.L.O. Emblems

1969. 50th Anniv of I.L.O.

| 269 | 97 | 6d. black and grey | 20 | 10 |
| 270 | 97 | 9d. black and yellow | 20 | 25 |

98 "The Last Supper and Crucifixion" (Evie Hone Window, Eton Chapel)

1969. Contemporary Irish Art (1st issue).

| 271 | 98 | 1s. multicoloured | 30 | 1·50 |

See also Nos. 280, 306, 317, 329, 362, 375, 398, 408, 452, 470 and 498.

99 Mahatma Gandhi

1969. Birth Centenary of Mahatma Gandhi.

| 272 | 99 | 6d. black and green | 50 | 10 |
| 273 | 99 | 1s.9d. black and yellow | 75 | 90 |

100 Symbolic Bird in Tree

1970. European Conservation Year.

| 274 | 100 | 6d. bistre and black | 20 | 10 |
| 275 | 100 | 9d. violet and black | 25 | 80 |

101 "Flaming Sun"

1970. Europa.

276	101	6d. violet and silver	55	10
277	101	9d. brown and silver	90	1·25
278	101	1s.9d. grey and silver	1·75	2·00

102 *Sailing Boats* (Peter Monamy)

1970. 250th Anniv of Royal Cork Yacht Club.

| 279 | 102 | 4d. multicoloured | 15 | 10 |

103 *Madonna of Eire* (Mainie Jellett)

1970. Contemporary Irish Art (2nd issue).

| 280 | 103 | 1s. multicoloured | 15 | 20 |

104 Thomas MacCurtain

1970. 50th Death Annivs of Irish Patriots.

281	104	9d. black, violet and grey	1·00	25
282	104	9d. black, violet and grey	1·00	25
283	104	2s.9d. black, blue and grey	1·75	2·50
284	-	2s.9d. black, blue and grey	1·75	5·00

DESIGN: Nos. 282 and 284, Terence MacSwiney.

106 Kevin Barry

1970. 50th Death Anniv of Kevin Barry (patriot).

| 285 | 106 | 6d. green | 30 | 10 |
| 286 | 106 | 1s.2d. blue | 40 | 1·10 |

1971. Decimal Currency. As Nos. 247/62 but with face values in new currency, without "p", and some colours changed.

287	90	½p. green	10	10
340	90	1p. blue	10	10
289	90	1½p. red	15	50
341	90	2p. green	10	10
291	90	2½p. brown	15	10
342	90	3p. brown	10	10
293	90	3½p. orange	25	10
294	90	4p. violet	20	10
295	-	5p. brown and olive	1·00	20
344	90	5p. green	60	10
296	-	6p. grey and brown	3·50	1·25
346	90	6p. grey	20	10
347	-	7p. blue and green	70	35
348	90	7p. green	35	10
297	-	7½p. mauve and brown	50	1·40
349	-	8p. brown and deep brown	60	50
350	90	8p. green	30	10
351	-	9p. black and green	70	30
352	90	9p. green	30	10
352a	90	9½p. red	35	20
353	92	10p. multicoloured	1·25	30
354	-	10p. black and lilac	70	10
354a	90	10p. mauve	70	10
355	-	11p. black and red	45	1·00
299b	92	12p. multicoloured	60	1·50
355a	-	12p. black and green	55	10
355b	90	12p. green	30	10
355c	-	13p. brown	40	1·75
356	92	15p. multicoloured	55	40
356a	90	15p. blue	40	10
356b	-	16p. black and green	40	1·00
356c	92	17p. multicoloured	50	1·40
478	90	18p. red	45	50
479	90	19p. blue	55	2·00
357	92	20p. multicoloured	50	15
480	90	22p. blue	65	10
481	90	24p. brown	1·25	1·25
482	90	26p. green	1·50	40
483	90	29p. mauve	2·00	3·00
358	-	50p. multicoloured	1·00	30
359	-	£1 multicoloured	1·75	30

DESIGNS—As Type **90**: 5p. (295); 6p. (296); 7p. (347); 7½p., 8p., 9p. (351) 10p. (354), 11p., 12p. (No. 355a), 13p., 16p. Stag. As Type **92**: 50p., £1, Eagle (symbol of St. John the Evangelist).

107 "Europa Chain"

1971. Europa.

| 302 | 107 | 4p. brown and green | 75 | 10 |
| 303 | 107 | 6p. black and blue | 2·75 | 2·75 |

108 J. M. Synge

1971. Birth Centenary of J. M. Synge (playwright).

| 304 | 108 | 4p. multicoloured | 15 | 10 |
| 305 | 108 | 10p. multicoloured | 60 | 80 |

109 *An Island Man* (Jack B. Yeats)

1971. Contemporary Irish Art (3rd issue). Birth Centenary of J. B. Yeats (artist).

| 306 | 109 | 6p. multicoloured | 55 | 55 |

110 Racial Harmony Symbol

1971. Racial Equality Year.

| 307 | 110 | 4p. red | 20 | 10 |
| 308 | 110 | 10p. black | 50 | 75 |

111 "Madonna and Child" (statue by J. Hughes)

1971. Christmas.

| 309 | 111 | 2½p. black, gold and green | 10 | 10 |
| 310 | 111 | 6p. black, gold and blue | 65 | 65 |

112 Heart

1972. World Health Day.

| 311 | 112 | 2½p. gold and brown | 30 | 15 |
| 312 | 112 | 12p. silver and grey | 1·10 | 1·75 |

 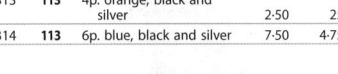

113 "Communications"

1972. Europa.

| 313 | 113 | 4p. orange, black and brown | 2·50 | 25 |
| 314 | 113 | 6p. blue, black and silver | 7·50 | 4·75 |

114 Dove and Moon

1972. Patriot Dead 1922–1923.

| 315 | 114 | 4p. multicoloured | 10 | 10 |
| 316 | 114 | 6p. yellow, green & dp grn | 65 | 50 |

115 *Black Lake* (Gerard Dillon)

1972. Contemporary Irish Art (4th issue).

| 317 | 115 | 3p. multicoloured | 60 | 35 |

116 "Horseman" (Carved Slab)

1972. 50th Anniv of Olympic Council of Ireland.

| 318 | 116 | 3p. yellow, black and gold | 15 | 10 |
| 319 | 116 | 6p. pink, black and gold | 55 | 60 |

117 Madonna and Child (from *Book of Kells*)

1972. Christmas.
320	**117**	2½p. multicoloured	10	10
321	**117**	4p. multicoloured	25	10
322	**117**	12p. multicoloured	1·00	1·00

118 2d. Stamp of 1922

1972. 50th Anniv of 1st Irish Postage Stamp.
| 323 | **118** | 6p. grey and green | 60 | 60 |
| MS324 | 72×104 mm. No. 323×4 | | 3·75 | 7·50 |

119 Celtic Head Motif

1973. Entry into European Communities.
| 325 | **119** | 6p. multicoloured | 45 | 70 |
| 326 | **119** | 12p. multicoloured | 65 | 90 |

120 Europa "Posthorn"

1973. Europa.
| 327 | **120** | 4p. blue | 1·75 | 10 |
| 328 | **120** | 6p. black | 3·75 | 3·25 |

121 *Berlin Blues II* (W. Scott)

1973. Contemporary Irish Art (5th issue).
| 329 | **121** | 5p. blue and black | 40 | 30 |

122 Weather Map

1973. Centenary of I.M.O./W.M.O.
| 330 | **122** | 3½p. multicoloured | 30 | 10 |
| 331 | **122** | 12p. multicoloured | 1·10 | 2·00 |

123 Tractor ploughing

1973. World Ploughing Championships, Wellington Bridge.
| 332 | **123** | 5p. multicoloured | 15 | 10 |
| 333 | **123** | 7p. multicoloured | 1·00 | 50 |

124 *Flight into Egypt* (Jan de Cock)

1973. Christmas.
| 334 | **124** | 3½p. multicoloured | 15 | 10 |
| 335 | **124** | 12p. multicoloured | 1·10 | 1·50 |

125 Daunt Island Lightship and *Mary Stanford* (Ballycotton Lifeboat), 1936

1974. 150th Anniv of R.N.L.I.
| 336 | **125** | 5p. multicoloured | 30 | 30 |

126 "Edmund Burke" (statue by J. H. Foley)

1974. Europa.
| 337 | **126** | 5p. black and blue | 1·50 | 10 |
| 338 | **126** | 7p. black and green | 5·00 | 2·50 |

127 *Oliver Goldsmith* (statue by J. H. Foley)

1974. Death Bicentenary of Oliver Goldsmith (writer).
| 360 | **127** | 3½p. black and yellow | 25 | 10 |
| 361 | **127** | 12p. black and green | 75 | 1·00 |

128 *Kitchen Table* (Norah McGuiness)

1974. Contemporary Irish Art (6th issue).
| 362 | **128** | 5p. multicoloured | 35 | 30 |

129 Rugby Players

1974. Centenary of Irish Rugby Football.
| 363 | **129** | 3½p. green | 50 | 10 |
| 364 | **129** | 12p. multicoloured | 2·00 | 2·75 |

130 U.P.U. "Postmark"

1974. Centenary of Universal Postal Union.
| 365 | **130** | 5p. green and black | 25 | 10 |
| 366 | **130** | 7p. blue and black | 35 | 55 |

131 *Madonna and Child* (Bellini)

1974. Christmas.
| 367 | **131** | 5p. multicoloured | 15 | 10 |
| 368 | **131** | 15p. multicoloured | 60 | 90 |

132 "Peace"

1975. International Women's Year.
| 369 | **132** | 8p. purple and blue | 25 | 75 |
| 370 | **132** | 15p. blue and green | 50 | 1·25 |

133 *Castletown Hunt* (R. Healy)

1975. Europa.
| 371 | **133** | 7p. grey | 2·00 | 15 |
| 372 | **133** | 9p. green | 5·50 | 2·50 |

134 Putting

1975. Ninth European Amateur Golf Team Championship, Killarney.
| 373 | **134** | 6p. multicoloured | 75 | 45 |
| 374 | **134** | 9p. multicoloured | 1·50 | 1·50 |
No. 374 is similar to Type **134** but shows a different view of the putting green.

135 "Bird of Prey" (sculpture by Oisin Kelly)

1975. Contemporary Irish Art (7th issue).
| 375 | **135** | 15p. brown | 75 | 75 |

136 Nano Nagle (founder) and Waifs

1975. Bicentenary of Presentation Order of Nuns.
| 376 | **136** | 5p. black and blue | 20 | 10 |
| 377 | **136** | 7p. black and brown | 30 | 30 |

137 Tower of St. Anne's Church, Shandon

1975. European Architectural Heritage Year.
378	**137**	5p. brown	20	10
379	**137**	6p. multicoloured	40	85
380	-	7p. blue	40	10
381	-	9p. multicoloured	40	80
DESIGN: Nos. 380/1, Interior of Holycross Abbey, Co. Tipperary.

138 St. Oliver Plunkett (commemorative medal by Imogen Stuart)

1975. Canonization of Oliver Plunkett.
| 382 | **138** | 7p. black | 15 | 10 |
| 383 | **138** | 15p. brown | 55 | 45 |

139 *Madonna and Child* (Fra Filippo Lippi)

1975. Christmas.
384	**139**	5p. multicoloured	15	10
385	**139**	7p. multicoloured	20	10
386	**139**	10p. multicoloured	75	60

140 James Larkin (from a drawing by Sean O'Sullivan)

1975. Birth Centenary of James Larkin (Trade Union Leader).
| 387 | **140** | 7p. green and grey | 20 | 10 |
| 388 | **140** | 11p. brown and yellow | 40 | 55 |

141 Alexander Graham Bell

1976. Centenary of Telephone.
| 389 | **141** | 9p. multicoloured | 20 | 10 |
| 390 | **141** | 15p. multicoloured | 45 | 50 |

142 1847 Benjamin Franklin Essay

1976. Bicentenary of American Revolution.
391	-	7p. blue, red and silver	20	10
392	-	8p. blue, red and silver	25	1·10
393	**142**	9p. blue, orange and silver	25	10
394	**142**	15p. red, grey and silver	45	75
MS395	95×75 mm. Nos. 391/4		2·75	8·00
DESIGNS: 7p. Thirteen Stars; 8p. Fifty Stars.

143 Spirit Barrel

1976. Europa. Irish Delft. Multicoloured.
| 396 | 9p. Type **143** | | 1·25 | 20 |
| 397 | 11p. Dish | | 3·25 | 1·60 |

144 *The Lobster Pots, West of Ireland* (Paul Henry)

1976. Contemporary Irish Art (8th issue).
| 398 | **144** | 15p. multicoloured | 60 | 60 |

145 Radio Waves

1976. 50th Anniv of Irish Broadcasting Service.
| 399 | **145** | 9p. blue and green | 20 | 10 |

172 George
Bernard Shaw

1980. Europa. Personalities. Multicoloured.

459	12p. Type **172**	1·25	50
460	13p. Oscar Wilde (29×40 mm)	2·00	2·50

173 Stoat

1980. Wildlife. Multicoloured.

461	12p. Type **173**	25	40
462	15p. Arctic hare	25	15
463	16p. Red fox	25	80
464	25p. Red deer	35	1·60
MS465	73×97 mm. Nos. 461/4	1·00	2·75

174 Playing
Bodhran and
Whistle

1980. Traditional Music and Dance. Multicoloured.

466	12p. Type **174**	15	10
467	15p. Playing Uilleann pipes	20	15
468	25p. Dancing	35	1·10

175 Sean O'Casey

1980. Commemorations.

469	12p. multicoloured	20	10
470	25p. black, buff and brown	35	1·00

DESIGNS AND COMMEMORATIONS: 12p. Type **175** (playwright) (birth centenary); 25p. *Gold Painting No. 57* (P. Scott) (Contemporary Irish Art (11th issue)).

176 *Nativity Scene*
(painting by
Geraldine McNulty)

1980. Christmas.

471	**176**	12p. multicoloured	15	10
472	**176**	15p. multicoloured	20	10
473	**176**	25p. multicoloured	40	1·25

177 Boyle Air-pump,
1659

1981. Irish Science and Technology. Multicoloured.

474	12p. Type **177**	20	10
475	15p. Ferguson tractor, 1936	25	10

476	16p. Parsons turbine, 1884	30	90
477	25p. Holland submarine, 1878	35	1·25

178 *The Legend of
the Cock and the Pot*

1981. Europa. Folklore. Paintings by Maria Simonds-Gooding.

491	**178**	18p. black, yellow and red	1·25	10
492	-	19p. black, orange & yellow	2·25	1·50

DESIGN: 19p. *The Angel with the Scales of Judgement.*

179 Cycling

1981. 50th Anniv of "An Oige" (Irish Youth Hostel Association). Multicoloured.

493	15p. Type **179**	25	40
494	18p. Hill-walking (horiz)	25	10
495	19p. Mountaineering (horiz)	25	95
496	30p. Rock-climbing	40	95

180 Jeremiah
O'Donovan Rossa

1981. 150th Birth Anniv of Jeremiah O'Donovan Rossa (politician). Multicoloured.

497	**180**	15p. multicoloured	40	30

181 *Railway Embankment*
(W. J. Leech)

1981. Contemporary Irish Art (12th issue).

498	**181**	30p. multicoloured	1·00	70

182 James Hoban and
White House

1981. 150th Death Anniv of James Hoban (White House architect).

499	**182**	18p. multicoloured	50	30

183 *Arkle* (steeplechaser)

1981. Famous Irish Horses. Multicoloured.

500	18p. Type **183**	50	1·00
501	18p. *Boomerang* (show- jumper)	50	1·00
502	22p. *King of Diamonds* (Draught horse)	50	30
503	24p. *Ballymoss* (flat-racer)	50	70
504	36p. *Coosheen Finn* (Connemara pony)	60	1·00

184 *Nativity* (F. Barocci)

1981. Christmas.

505	**184**	18p. multicoloured	25	10
506	**184**	22p. multicoloured	30	10
507	**184**	36p. multicoloured	80	1·50

185 Eviction Scene

1981. Anniversaries. Multicoloured.

508	18p. Type **185**	50	25
509	22p. Royal Dublin Society emblem	50	30

ANNIVERSARIES: 18p. Centenary of Land Law (Ireland) Act. 22p. Royal Dublin Society (organization for the advancement of agriculture, industry, art and science), 250th Anniv.

186 Upper Lake, Killarney
National Park

1982. 50th Anniv of Killarney National Park. Multicoloured.

510	18p. Type **186**	40	20
511	36p. Eagle's Nest	85	1·60

187 *The
Stigmatization of St.
Francis* (Sassetta)

1982. Religious Anniversaries.

512	**187**	22p. multicoloured	50	15
513	-	24p. brown	75	85

DESIGNS AND ANNIVERSARIES: 22p. Type **187** (St. Francis of Assisi (founder of Franciscan order) (500th birth anniv); 24p. Francis Makemie (founder of American Presbyterianism) and old Presbyterian Church, Ramelton, Co. Donegal (300th anniv of ordination).

188 The Great
Famine,
1845–50

1982. Europa. Historic Events.

514	**188**	26p. black and stone	3·50	50
515	-	29p. multicoloured	4·50	5·00

DESIGN—HORIZ: 29p. The coming of Christianity to Ireland.

189 Padraic O.
Conaire (writer)
(birth centenary)

1982. Anniversaries of Cultural Figures.

516	**189**	22p. black and blue	25	30
517	-	26p. black and brown	55	30
518	-	29p. black and blue	65	1·75

519	-	44p. black and grey	65	1·60

DESIGNS AND ANNIVERSARIES: 26p. James Joyce (writer) (birth centenary); 29p. John Field (musician) (birth centenary); 44p. Charles Kickham (writer) (death centenary).

190 Porbeagle Shark

1982. Marine Life. Multicoloured.

520	22p. Type **191**	60	1·25
521	22p. Common European oyster	60	1·25
522	26p. Atlantic salmon	70	30
523	29p. Dublin Bay prawn	70	1·75

191 *St. Patrick*
(Galway hooker)

1982. Irish Boats. Multicoloured.

524	22p. Type **191**	60	1·25
525	22p. Currach (horiz)	60	1·25
526	26p. *Asgard II* (cadet brigantine) (horiz)	70	30
527	29p. Howth 17 foot yacht	70	1·75

192 *Irish House of Commons*
(painting by Francis
Wheatley)

1982. Bicentenary of Grattan's Parliament and Birth Centenary of Eamon de Valera. Multicoloured.

528	22p. Type **192**	35	1·25
529	26p. Eamon de Valera (vert)	40	40

193 "Madonna and
Child" (sculpture)

1982. Christmas.

530	**193**	22p. multicoloured	30	90
531	**193**	26p. multicoloured	30	35

194
Aughnanure
Castle

1983. Irish Architecture.

532	-	1p. blue	10	10
533	-	2p. green	20	10
534	-	3p. black	20	10
535	-	4p. red	20	10
536	-	5p. brown	30	10
537	-	6p. blue	30	15
538	-	7p. green	30	1·25
539	-	10p. black	30	10
540	-	12p. brown	30	1·75
541	**194**	15p. green	45	35
542	**194**	20p. purple	50	45
543	**194**	22p. blue	50	10
544	-	23p. green	85	1·25
544a	-	24p. brown	1·25	35
545	-	26p. black	75	10
545c	-	28p. red	75	45
546	-	29p. green	70	1·00
547	-	30p. black	70	30
547c	-	37p. brown	2·50	3·00
547d	-	37p. blue	1·00	2·75
547e	-	39p. red	2·50	2·75
548	-	44p. black and grey	1·00	70
548b	-	46p. green and grey	6·50	2·00
549	-	50p. blue and grey	1·75	65
550	-	£1 brown and grey	4·50	3·75
550b	-	£1 blue and grey	5·00	1·25

550c	-	£2 green and black	6·50	5·50
551	-	£5 red and grey	12·00	6·00

DESIGNS—HORIZ: (As T **194**): 1 to 5p. Central Pavilion, Dublin Botanic Gardens; 6 to 12p. Dr. Steevens' Hospital, Dublin; 28 to 37p. St. MacDara's Church. (37×21 mm); 46p., £1 (No. 550) Cahir Castle; 50p., £2 Casino Marino. £5 Central Bus Station, Dublin. VERT: (As T **194**): 23 to 26p., 39p. Cormac's Chapel. (21×37 mm); 44p., £1 (No. 550b) Killarney Cathedral.

195 Ouzel Gallery Goblet

1983. Bicentenaries of Dublin Chamber of Commerce (22p.) and Bank of Ireland (26p.). Multicoloured.

552		22p. Type **195**	30	90
553		26p. Bank of Ireland building (horiz)	35	35

196 Padraig O. Siochfhradha (writer and teacher)

1983. Anniversaries. Multicoloured.

554		26p. Type **196** (birth cent)	50	75
555		29p. Young Boys' Brigade member (centenary)	90	1·50

197 Neolithic Carved Pattern, Newgrange Tomb

1983. Europa.

556	**197**	26p. black and yellow	2·50	50
557		29p. black, brown & yellow	7·00	5·50

DESIGN: 29p. Sir William Rowan Hamilton's formulae for the multiplication of quaternions.

198 Kerry Blue Terrier

1983. Irish Dogs. Multicoloured.

558		22p. Type **198**	65	35
559		26p. Irish wolfhound	70	45
560		26p. Irish water spaniel	70	45
561		29p. Irish terrier	75	2·25
562		44p. Irish setters	1·25	2·50
MS563		142×80 mm. Nos. 558/62	6·00	8·00

199 Animals (Irish Society for the Prevention of Cruelty to Animals)

1983. Anniversaries and Commemorations.

564	**199**	22p. multicoloured	50	1·00
565	-	22p. multicoloured	50	1·00
566	-	26p. multicoloured	50	60
567	-	26p. multicoloured	50	60
568	-	44p. blue and black	75	2·00

DESIGNS—VERT: No. 565, Sean MacDiarmada (patriot) (birth cent); 567, *St. Vincent de Paul in the Streets of Paris* (150th anniv of Society of St. Vincent de Paul); 568, *Andrew Jackson* (Frank McKelvey) (President of the United States). HORIZ: No. 566, "100" (Centenary of Industrial Credit Company).

---

200 Postman with Bicycle

1983. World Communications Year. Multicoloured.

569		22p. Type **200**	1·10	75
570		29p. Dish antenna	90	2·00

201 Weaving

1983. Irish Handicrafts. Multicoloured.

571		22p. Type **201**	60	50
572		26p. Basket making	60	35
573		29p. Irish crochet	65	1·25
574		44p. Harp making	1·25	2·50

202 *La Natividad* (R. van der Weyden)

1983. Christmas.

575	**202**	22p. multicoloured	40	30
576	**202**	26p. multicoloured	60	30

203 Dublin and Kingstown Railway Steam Locomotive "Princess"

1984. 150th Anniv of Irish Railways. Multicoloured.

577		23p. Type **203**	75	1·25
578		26p. Great Southern Railways steam locomotive *Macha*	75	35
579		29p. Great Northern Railway steam locomotive No. 87 *Kestrel*	85	1·75
580		44p. Two-car electric train Coras Iompair Eireann	1·10	2·25
MS581		129×77 mm. Nos. 577/80	3·75	5·00

204 *Sorbus hibernica*

1984. Irish Trees. Multicoloured.

582		22p. Type **204**	55	70
583		26p. *Taxus baccata fastigiata*	60	30
584		29p. *Salix hibernica*	70	1·75
585		44p. *Betula pubescens*	1·00	2·50

205 St. Vincent's Hospital, Dublin

1984. 150th Anniv of St. Vincent's Hospital and Bicentenary of Royal College of Surgeons. Multicoloured.

586		26p. Type **205**	75	30
587		44p. Royal College and logo	1·25	1·50

206 C.E.P.T. 25th Anniversary Logo

1984. Europa.

588	**206**	26p. blue, dp blue and black	2·50	50
589	**206**	29p. lt green, green and black	5·00	4·25

207 Flags on Ballot Box

1984. Second Direct Elections to European Assembly.

590	**207**	26p. multicoloured	1·00	70

208 John McCormack

1984. Birth Centenary of John McCormack (tenor).

591	**208**	22p. multicoloured	50	70

209 Hammer-throwing

1984. Olympic Games, Los Angeles.

592	**209**	22p. mauve, black and gold	35	80
593	-	26p. violet, black and gold	40	65
594	-	29p. blue, black and gold	60	1·25

DESIGNS: 26p. Hurdling; 29p. Running.

210 Hurling

1984. Cent of Gaelic Athletic Association. Multicoloured.

595		22p. Type **210**	50	90
596		26p. Irish football (vert)	60	90

211 Galway Mayoral Chain

1984. Anniversaries. Multicoloured.

597		26p. Type **211** (500th anniv of mayoral charter)	35	50
598		44p. St. Brendan (from 15th-cent Bodleian manuscript) (1500th birth anniv) (horiz)	75	1·50

212 Hands passing Letter

1984. Bicentenary of Irish Post Office.

599	**212**	26p. multicoloured	60	70

213 *Virgin and Child* (Sassoferrato)

1984. Christmas. Multicoloured.

600		17p. Christmas star (horiz)	45	80
601		22p. Type **213**	45	1·25
602		26p. Type **213**	65	40

214 "Love" and Heart-shaped Balloon

1985. Greetings Stamps. Multicoloured.

603		22p. Type **214**	50	75
604		26p. Bouquet of hearts and flowers (vert)	60	75

215 Dunsink Observatory (bicentenary)

1985. Anniversaries. Multicoloured.

605		22p. Type **215**	60	50
606		26p. *A Landscape at Tivoli, Cork, with Boats* (Nathaniel Grogan) (800th anniv of City of Cork) (horiz)	60	30
607		37p. Royal Irish Academy (bicentenary)	80	1·75
608		44p. Richard Crosbie's balloon flight (bicentenary of first aeronautic flight by an Irishman)	1·00	1·75

216 *Polyommatus icarus*

1985. Butterflies. Multicoloured.

609		22p. Type **216**	1·50	1·00
610		26p. *Vanessa atalanta*	1·50	70
611		28p. *Gonepteryx rhamni*	1·75	3·00
612		44p. *Eurabyas aurinia*	2·00	3·25

217 Charles Villiers Stanford (composer)

1985. Europa. Irish Composers. Multicoloured.

613		26p. Type **217**	2·50	50
614		37p. Turlough Carolan (composer and lyricist)	5·50	6·00

218 George Frederick Handel

1985. European Music Year. Composers. Multicoloured.

615		22p. Type **218**	1·25	2·50
616		22p. Guiseppe Domenico Scarlatti	1·25	2·50
617		26p. Johann Sebastian Bach	1·50	50

219 U.N. Patrol of Irish Soldiers, Congo, 1960

1985. Anniversaries. Multicoloured.

618		22p. Type **219** (25th anniv of Irish Participation in U.N. Peace-keeping Force)	55	80
619		26p. Thomas Ashe (patriot) (birth cent) (vert)	55	60
620		44p. Bishop George Berkeley (James Lathan) (philosopher, 300th birth anniv) (vert)	85	3·00

220 Group of Young People

1985. International Youth Year. Multicoloured.
621	22p. Type **220**	55	50
622	26p. Students and young workers (vert)	55	50

221 Visual Display Unit

1985. Industrial Innovation. Multicoloured.
623	22p. Type **221**	50	75
624	26p. Turf cutting with hand tool and with modern machinery	50	55
625	44p. *The Key Man* (Sean Keating) (150th anniv of Institution of Engineers of Ireland)	1·00	2·50

222 Lighted Candle and Holly

1985. Christmas. Multicoloured.
626	22p. Type **222**	50	50
627	22p. *Virgin and Child in a Landscape* (Adrian van Ijsenbrandt)	80	2·00
628	22p. *The Holy Family* (Murillo)	80	2·00
629	22p. *The Adoration of the Shepherds* (Louis le Nain) (horiz)	80	25

No. 626 was only issued in sheetlets of 16 sold at £3, providing a discount of 52p. off the face value of the stamps.

224 Stylized Love Bird with Letter

1986. Greetings Stamps. Multicoloured.
630	22p. Type **224**	75	90
631	26p. Heart-shaped pillar-box	75	90

225 Hart's Tongue Fern

1986. Ferns. Multicoloured.
632	24p. Type **225**	70	70
633	28p. Rusty-back fern	80	70
634	46p. Killarney fern	1·25	2·10

226 "Harmony between Industry and Nature"

1986. Europa. Protection of the Environment. Multicoloured.
635	28p. Type **226**	6·00	50
636	39p. *Vanessa atalanta* (butterfly) and tractor in field ("Preserve hedgerows") (horiz)	18·00	6·00

227 Boeing 747-200 over Globe showing Aer Lingus Routes

1986. 50th Anniv of Aer Lingus (airline). Multicoloured.
637	28p. Type **227**	1·50	75
638	46p. de Havilland Dragon Mk 2 EI-ABI *Iolar* (first airplane)	2·25	3·00

228 Grand Canal at Robertstown

1986. Irish Waterways. Multicoloured.
639	24p. Type **228**	1·50	1·00
640	28p. Fishing in County Mayo (vert)	1·60	1·00
641	30p. Motor cruiser on Lough Derg	1·75	2·50

229 *Severn* (19th-century paddlesteamer)

1986. 150th Anniv of British and Irish Steam Packet Company. Multicoloured.
642	24p. Type **229**	75	1·00
643	28p. *Leinster* (modern ferry)	85	60

230 Kish Lighthouse and Bell JetRanger III Helicopter

1986. Irish Lighthouses. Multicoloured.
644	24p. Type **230**	1·50	75
645	30p. Fastnet Lighthouse	2·50	2·75

231 J. P. Nannetti (first president) and Linotype Operator (Dublin Council of Trade Unions centenary)

1986. Anniversaries and Commemorations.
646	**231**	24p. multicoloured	50	90
647	-	28p. black and grey	60	80
648	-	28p. multicoloured	60	80
649	-	30p. multicoloured	70	1·00
650	-	46p. multicoloured	80	1·75

DESIGNS:—VERT: No. 647, Arthur Griffith (statesman); 649, Clasped hands (International Peace Year). HORIZ: No. 648, Woman surveyor (Women in Society); 650, Peace dove (International Peace Year).

232 William Mulready and his Design for 1840 Envelope

1986. Birth Bicentenaries of William Mulready (artist) (24p.) and Charles Bianconi (originator of Irish mail coach service) (others). Multicoloured.
651	24p. Type **232**	70	70
652	28p. Bianconi car outside Hearns Hotel, Clonmel (vert)	85	55
653	39p. Bianconi car on the road	1·40	1·75

233 *Adoration of the Shepherds* (Francesco Pascucci)

1986. Christmas. Multicoloured.
654	21p. Type **233**	1·10	1·40
655	28p. *Adoration of the Magi* (Frans Francken III) (vert)	65	60

234 *Butterfly and Flowers* (Tara Collins)

1987. Greetings Stamps. Children's Paintings. Multicoloured.
656	24p. Type **234**	75	1·25
657	28p. *Postman on Bicycle delivering Hearts* (Brigid Teehan) (vert)	1·25	1·25

235 Cork Electric Tram

1987. Irish Trams. Multicoloured.
658	24p. Type **235**	65	65
659	28p. Dublin standard tram No. 29	70	85
660	30p. Howth (Great Northern Railway) tram	80	2·00
661	46p. Galway horse tram	1·25	2·25
MS662	131×85 mm. Nos. 658/61	3·75	5·25

236 Ships from Crest (Bicentenary of Waterford Chamber of Commerce)

1987. Anniversaries.
663	**236**	24p. black, blue and green	70	60
664	-	28p. multicoloured	70	60
665	-	30p. multicoloured	70	2·00
666	-	39p. multicoloured	75	1·75

DESIGNS—HORIZ: 28p. Canon John Hayes and symbols of agriculture and development (birth centenary and 50th anniv of Muintir na Tire programme); 39p. Mother Mary Martin and International Missionary Training Hospital, Drogheda (50th anniv of Medical Missionaries of Mary). VERT: 30p. *Calceolaria burbidgei* and College crest (300th anniv of Trinity College Botanic Gardens, Dublin).

237 Bord na Mona Headquarters and "The Turf Cutter" (sculpture, John Behan), Dublin

1987. Europa. Modern Architecture. Multicoloured.
667	28p. Type **237**	3·00	60
668	39p. St. Mary's Church, Cong	6·50	6·50

238 Kerry Cow

1987. Irish Cattle. Multicoloured.
669	24p. Type **238**	80	75
670	28p. Friesian cow and calf	95	60
671	30p. Hereford bullock	1·00	2·25
672	39p. Shorthorn bull	1·10	2·25

239 Fleadh Nua, Ennis

1987. Festivals. Multicoloured.
673	24p. Type **239**	75	70
674	28p. Rose of Tralee International Festival	80	60
675	30p. Wexford Opera Festival (horiz)	1·50	2·00
676	46p. Ballinasloe Horse Fair (horiz)	1·50	2·00

240 Flagon (1637), Arms and Anniversary Ornament (1987) (350th anniv of Dublin Goldsmiths' Company)

1987. Anniversaries and Commemorations.
677	**240**	24p. multicoloured	80	80
678	-	24p. grey and black	80	80
679	-	28p. multicoloured	80	80
680	-	46p. multicoloured	1·40	1·10

DESIGNS—VERT: 24p. (No. 678) Cathal Brugha (patriot); 46p. Woman chairing board meeting (Women in Society). HORIZ: 28p. Arms of Ireland and inscription (50th anniv of Constitution).

241 Scenes from *The Twelve Days of Christmas* carol)

1987. Christmas. Multicoloured.
681	21p. Type **241**	60	1·00
682	24p. The Nativity (detail, late 15th-century Waterford Vestments) (vert)	75	1·00
683	28p. Figures from Neapolitan crib, c. 1850 (vert)	75	80

242 Acrobatic Clowns spelling "LOVE"

1988. Greetings Stamps. Multicoloured.
684	24p. Type **242**	75	60
685	28p. Pillar box and hearts (vert)	75	65

243 *Robert Burke* (Sidney Nolan) and Map of Burke and Wills Expedition Route

1988. Bicent of Australian Settlement. Multicoloured.
686	24p. Type **243**	1·00	60
687	46p. *Eureka Stockade* (mural detail, Sidney Nolan)	1·25	1·75

244 Past and Present Buildings of Dublin

1988. Dublin Millennium.
688	**244**	28p. multicoloured	45	55

245 Showjumping

1988. Olympic Games, Seoul. Multicoloured.
689		28p. Type **245**	1·00	1·40
690		28p. Cycling	1·00	1·40

246 William T. Cosgrave (statesman)

1988. Anniversaries and Events.
691	**246**	24p. grey and black	45	45
692	-	30p. multicoloured	80	1·00
693	-	50p. multicoloured	1·00	1·90

DESIGNS—HORIZ: 30p. Members with casualty and ambulance (50th anniv of Order of Malta Ambulance Corps). VERT: 50p. Barry Fitzgerald (actor) (birth centenary).

247 Air Traffic Controllers and Airbus Industrie A320

1988. Europa. Transport and Communications. Multicoloured.
694		28p. Type **247**	2·25	55
695		39p. Globe with stream of letters from Ireland to Europe	3·25	3·50

248 *Sirius* (paddle-steamer)

1988. Transatlantic Transport Anniversaries. Multicoloured.
696		24p. Type **248** (150th anniv of regular transatlantic steamship services)	1·00	50
697		46p. Short S.20 seaplane *Mercury* G-ADHJ and Short S.21 flying boat G-ADHK *Maia* (Short Mayo composite aircraft) in Foynes Harbour (50th anniv of first commercial transatlantic flight)	1·75	3·00

249 Cottonweed

1988. Endangered Flora of Ireland. Multicoloured.
698		24p. Type **249**	70	55
699		28p. Hart's saxifrage	80	55
700		46p. Purple milk-vetch	1·00	2·75

250 Garda on Duty

1988. Irish Security Forces. Multicoloured.
701		28p. Type **250**	70	1·10
702		28p. Army unit with personnel carrier	70	1·10
703		28p. Navy and Air Corps members with *Eithne* (helicopter patrol vessel)	70	1·10
704		28p. Army and Navy reservists	70	1·10

251 Computer and Abacus

1988. Anniversaries. Multicoloured.
705		24p. Type **251** (Institute of Chartered Accountants in Ireland centenary)	40	40
706		46p. *Duquesa Santa Ana* off Donegal (400th anniv of Spanish Armada) (horiz)	1·25	1·25

252 President Kennedy (James Wyeth)

1988. 25th Death Anniv of John F. Kennedy (American statesman).
707	**252**	28p. multicoloured	1·00	80

253 St. Kevin's Church, Glendalough

1988. Christmas. Multicoloured.
708		21p. Type **253**	80	1·00
709		24p. The Adoration of the Magi	50	60
710		28p. The Flight into Egypt	60	45
711		46p. The Holy Family	1·00	2·75

The designs of Nos. 709/11 are from a 15th-century French *Book of Hours*.

254 Spring Flowers spelling "Love" in Gaelic

1989. Greetings Stamps. Multicoloured.
712		24p. Type **254**	75	55
713		28p. The Sonnet (William Mulready) (vert)	75	55

255 Italian Garden, Garinish Island

1989. National Parks and Gardens. Multicoloured.
714		24p. Type **255**	90	55
715		28p. Lough Veagh, Glenveagh National Park	1·10	55
716		32p. Barnaderg Bay, Connemara National Park	1·25	1·25
717		50p. St. Stephen's Green, Dublin	1·75	1·75

256 "Silver Stream", 1908

1989. Classic Irish Cars. Multicoloured.
718		24p Type **256**	50	55
719		28p Benz "Comfortable", 1898	50	55
720		39p "Thomond", 1929	1·25	1·50
721		46p Chambers' 8 h.p. model, 1905	1·50	1·50

257 Ring-a-ring-a-roses

1989. Europa. Children's Games. Multicoloured.
722		28p. Type **257**	75	75
723		39p. Hopscotch	1·00	2·25

258 Irish Red Cross Flag (50th anniv)

1989. Anniversaries and Events.
724	**258**	24p. red and black	55	60
725		28p. blue, black and yellow	1·60	1·10

DESIGN: 28p. Circle of twelve stars (third direct elections to European Parliament).

259 Saints Kilian, Totnan and Colman (from 12th-century German manuscript)

1989. 1300th Death Anniv of Saints Kilian, Totnan and Colman.
726	**259**	28p. multicoloured	45	1·10

260 19th-century Mail Coach passing Cashel

1989. Bicentenary of Irish Mail Coach Service.
727	**260**	28p. multicoloured	1·50	75

261 Crest and 19th-century Dividers (150th anniv of Royal Institute of Architects of Ireland)

1989. Anniversaries and Commemorations.
728	-	24p. grey and black	65	55
729	**261**	28p. multicoloured	65	55
730	-	30p. multicoloured	1·75	2·25
731	-	46p. brown	3·00	3·25

DESIGNS—VERT: 24p. Sean T. O'Kelly (statesman) (drawing by Sean O'Sullivan); 46p. Jawaharlal Nehru (birth centenary). HORIZ: 30p. Margaret Burke-Sheridan (soprano) (portrait by De Gennaro) and scene from *La Boheme* (birth centenary).

262 *NCB Ireland* rounding Cape Horn" (Des Fallon)

1989. First Irish Entry in Whitbread Round the World Yacht Race.
732	**262**	28p. multicoloured	1·50	1·25

263 Willow/Red Grouse

1989. Game Birds. Multicoloured.
733	**263**	24p. Type **263**	1·00	55
734		28p. Northern lapwing	1·00	55
735		39p. Eurasian woodcock	1·25	2·50
736		46p. Common pheasant	1·25	2·50
MS737		128×92 mm. Nos. 733/6	5·00	7·00

264 *The Annunciation*

1989. Christmas. Multicoloured.
738		21p. Children decorating crib	75	75
739		24p. Type **264**	75	60
740		28p. *The Nativity*	80	55
741		46p. *The Adoration of the Magi*	1·60	2·50

265 Logo (Ireland's Presidency of the European Communities)

1990. European Events. Multicoloured.
742		30p. Type **265**	1·00	60
743		50p. Logo and outline map of Ireland (European Tourism Year)	2·25	3·00

266 Dropping Messages from Balloon

1990. Greetings Stamps.
744	**266**	26p. multicoloured	1·50	1·25
745		30p. red, buff and brown	1·50	1·25

DESIGN: 30p. Heart and "Love" drawn in lipstick.

267 Silver Kite Brooch

1990. Irish Heritage.
746	**267**	1p. black and blue	10	10
747	**267**	2p. black and orange	10	10
748	-	4p. black and violet	15	30
749	-	5p. black and green	20	10
750	-	10p. black and orange	30	25
751	-	20p. black and yellow	50	40
752	-	26p. black and violet	1·50	65
809	-	28p. black and orange	1·75	3·00
754	-	30p. black and blue	1·25	1·50
810	-	32p. black and green	50	80
756	-	34p. black and yellow	1·25	1·25
757	-	37p. black and green	1·50	2·25
758	-	38p. black and violet	1·50	2·25
758b	-	40p. black and blue	1·50	1·50
759	-	41p. black and orange	1·50	2·25
760	-	44p. brown and yellow	2·50	3·00
760a	-	45p. black and violet	3·25	2·00
761	-	50p. black and yellow	1·75	2·25
762	-	52p. black and blue	3·25	3·50
763	-	£1 black and yellow	3·25	2·25
764	-	£2 black and green	4·50	3·25
765	-	£5 black and brown	10·00	9·00

DESIGNS: 4, 5p. Dunamase food vessel; 26, 28p. Lismore crozier; 34, 37, 38, 40p. Gleninsheen collar; 41, 44p. Silver thistle brooch; 45, 50, 52p. Brighter boat. 22×38 mm: £5 St. Patrick's Bell Shrine. HORIZ: 10p. Derrinboy armlets; 20p. Gold dress fastener; 30p. Enamelled latchet brooch; 32p. Brighter collar. 38×22 mm: £1 Ardagh Chalice; £2 Tara brooch.

For 32p. value as No. 755 but larger, 29×24 mm, and self-adhesive, see No. 823.

268 Posy of Flowers

1990. Greetings Stamps. Multicoloured.
766	**268**	26p. Type **268**	2·00	2·50
767		26p. Birthday presents	2·00	2·50

768	30p. Flowers, ribbon and horseshoe	2·00	2·50
769	30p. Balloons	2·00	2·50

269 Player heading Ball

1990. World Cup Football Championship, Italy. Multicoloured.

770	30p. Type **269**	1·50	2·00
771	30p. Tackling	1·50	2·00

270 Battle of the Boyne, 1690

1990. 300th Anniv of the Williamite Wars (1st issue). Multicoloured.

772	30p. Type **270**	1·75	1·75
773	30p. Siege of Limerick, 1690	1·75	1·75

See also Nos. 806/7.

271 1990 Irish Heritage 30p. Stamp and 1840 Postmark

1990. 150th Anniv of the Penny Black. Multicoloured.

774	30p. Type **271**	90	90
775	50p. Definitive stamps of 1922, 1969, 1982 and 1990	1·25	2·25

272 General Post Office, Dublin

1990. Europa Post Office Buildings. Multicoloured.

776	30p. Type **272**	1·00	60
777	41p. Westport Post Office, County Mayo	1·75	3·00

273 Medical Missionary giving Injection

1990. Anniversaries and Events.

778	**273**	26p. multicoloured	80	40
779	-	30p. black	1·00	2·75
780	-	50p. multicoloured	1·00	1·75

DESIGNS—VERT: 30p. Michael Collins (statesman) (birth centenary). HORIZ: 50p. Missionaries working at water pump (Irish missionary service).

274 Narcissus "Foundling" and Japanese Gardens, Tully

1990. Garden Flowers. Multicoloured.

781	26p. Type **274**	60	55
782	30p. *Rosa x hibernica* and Mulahide Castle gardens	70	80
783	41p. Primula "Rowallane Rose" and Rowallane garden	1·25	2·50
784	50p. *Erica erigena* "Irish Dusk" and Palm House, National Botanical Gardens	1·50	2·75

275 *Playboy of the Western World* (John Synge)

1990. Irish Theatre. Multicoloured.

785	30p. Type **275**	1·25	1·75
786	30p. *Juno and the Pay-cock* (Sean O'Casey)	1·25	1·75
787	30p. *The Field* (John Keane)	1·25	1·75
788	30p. *Waiting for Godot* (Samuel Beckett)	1·25	1·75

276 Nativity

1990. Christmas. Multicoloured.

789	26p. Child praying by bed	75	80
790	26p. Type **276**	60	60
791	30p. Madonna and Child	90	90
792	50p. Adoration of the Magi	1·75	3·50

277 Hearts in Mail Sack and Postman's Cap

1991. Greetings Stamps. Multicoloured.

793	26p. Type **277**	85	1·00
794	30p. Boy and girl kissing	90	1·00

278 Starley "Rover" Bicycle, 1886

1991. Early Bicycles. Multicoloured.

795	26p. Type **278**	90	60
796	30p. Child's horse tricycle, 1875	1·00	1·00
797	50p. "Penny Farthing", 1871	1·75	2·50
MS798	113×72 mm. Nos. 795/7	3·25	4·00

279 "Cuchulainn" (statue by Oliver Sheppard) and Proclamation

1991. 75th Anniv of Easter Rising.

799	**279**	32p. multicoloured	1·00	1·40

280 Scene from *La Traviata* (50th anniv of Dublin Grand Opera Society)

1991. "Dublin 1991 European City of Culture". Multicoloured.

800	28p. Type **280**	1·00	1·00
801	32p. City Hall and European Community emblem	1·10	1·60
802	44p. St. Patrick's Cathedral (800th anniv)	90	1·60
803	52p. Custom House (bicent) (41×24 mm)	1·00	1·60

281 "Giotto" Spacecraft approaching Halley's Comet

1991. Europa. Europe in Space. Multicoloured.

804	32p. Type **281**	1·00	1·00
805	44p. Hubble Telescope orbiting Earth	1·50	3·00

282 Siege of Athlone

1991. 300th Anniv of the Williamite Wars (2nd issue). Multicoloured.

806	28p. Type **282**	1·25	1·75
807	28p. Generals Ginkel and Sarsfield (signatories of Treaty of Limerick)	1·25	1·75

283 *John A. Costello* (statesman)

1991. Anniversaries.

811	**283**	28p. black	1·25	70
812	-	32p. multicoloured	1·40	1·00
813	-	52p. multicoloured	1·75	2·00

DESIGNS—VERT: 28p. Type **283** (birth cent) (drawing by Sean O'Sullivan); 32p. *Charles Stewart Parnell* (Sydney Hall) (death cent); HORIZ: 52p. Meeting of United Irishmen.

284 Player on 15th Green, Portmarnock (Walker Cup)

1991. Golf Commemorations. Multicoloured.

814	28p. Type **284**	1·00	75
815	32p. Logo and golfer of 1900 (cent of Golfing Union of Ireland) (vert)	1·25	1·00

285 Wicklow Cheviot

1991. Irish Sheep. Multicoloured.

816	32p. Type **285**	1·00	80
817	38p. Donegal Blackface	1·40	1·75
818	52p. Galway (horiz)	2·00	3·50

286 Boatyard

1991. Fishing Fleet. Multicoloured.

819	28p. Type **286**	70	65
820	32p. Traditional inshore trawlers	80	80
821	44p. Inshore lobster pot boat	1·60	2·50
822	52p. *Veronica* (fish factory ship)	1·90	2·75

1991. As No. 755, but larger, 27×21 mm. Self-adhesive.

823a	32p. black and bright green	1·00	1·25

287 The Annunciation

1991. Christmas.

827	-	28p. multicoloured	1·00	1·00
828	**287**	28p. blue, green and black	1·00	65
829	-	32p. red and black	1·10	75
830	-	52p. multicoloured	2·00	3·25

DESIGNS: No. 827, Three Kings; No. 829, The Nativity; No. 830, Adoration of the Kings.

288 Multicoloured Heart

1992. Greetings Stamps. Multicoloured.

831	28p. Type **288**	1·00	95
832	32p. "LOVE" at end of rainbow (vert)	1·10	1·10

289 Healthy Family on Apple

1992. "Healthy Living" Campaign.

833	**289**	28p. multicoloured	1·25	1·00

290 Boxing

1992. Olympic Games, Barcelona. Multicoloured.

834	32p. Type **290**	75	90
835	44p. Sailing	1·00	2·25
MS836	130×85 mm. Nos. 834/5×2	4·75	6·00

291 *Mari* (cog) and 14th-century Map

1992. Irish Maritime Heritage. Multicoloured.

837	32p. Type **291**	1·00	90
838	52p. *Ovoca* (trawler) and chart (vert)	1·50	2·75

292 Chamber Logo and Commercial Symbols

1992. Bicentenary of Galway Chamber of Commerce and Industry.

839	**292**	28p. multicoloured	1·00	1·00

293 Cliffs and Cove

1992. Greetings Stamps. Multicoloured.

840	28p. Type **293**	90	1·10
841	28p. Meadow	90	1·10
842	32p. Fuchsia and honeysuckle	90	1·10
843	32p. Lily pond and dragonfly	90	1·10

294 Fleet of Columbus

1992. Europa. 500th Anniv of Discovery of America by Columbus. Multicoloured.

844	32p. Type **294**	1·25	90
845	44p. Columbus landing in the New World	2·00	3·00

295 Irish Immigrants

1992. Irish Immigrants in the Americas. Multicoloured.

846	52p. Type **295**	1·75	1·75
847	52p. Irish soldiers, entertainers and politicians	1·75	1·75

296 Pair of Pine Martens

1992. Endangered Species. Pine Marten. Multicoloured.

848	28p. Type **296**	1·00	70
849	32p. Marten on branch	1·00	80
850	44p. Female with kittens	1·60	1·50
851	52p. Marten catching great tit	2·00	2·50

297 The Rotunda and New Rooms (James Malton)

1992. Dublin Anniversaries. Multicoloured.

852	28p. Type **297**	70	65
853	32p. Trinity College Library (27×44 mm)	1·00	1·00
854	44p. *Charlemont House*	1·10	2·00
855	52p. Trinity College main gate (27×44 mm)	1·40	2·25

ANNIVERSARIES: 28, 44p. Bicentenary of Publication of Malton's *Views of Dublin*; 32, 52p. 400th anniv of Founding of Trinity College.

298 European Star and Megalithic Dolmen

1992. Single European Market.

856	**298** 32p. multicoloured	55	80

299 Farm Produce

1992. Irish Agriculture. Multicoloured.

857	32p. Type **299**	1·25	1·25
858	32p. Dairy and beef herds	1·25	1·25
859	32p. Harvesting cereals	1·25	1·25
860	32p. Market gardening	1·25	1·25

Nos. 857/60 were printed together, se-tenant, forming a composite design.

300 The Annunciation (from illuminated manuscript)

1992. Christmas. Multicoloured.

861	28p. Congregation entering church	80	65
862	28p. Type **300**	80	65
863	32p. *Adoration of the Shepherds* (Da Empoli)	1·10	1·00
864	52p. *Adoration of the Magi* (Rottenhammer)	1·40	1·50

301 Queen of Hearts

1993. Greetings Stamps. Multicoloured.

865	28p. Type **301**	90	75
866	32p. Hot air balloon trailing hearts (horiz)	1·00	85

302 *Evening at Tangier* (Sir John Lavery)

1993. Irish Impressionist Painters. Multicoloured.

867	28p. Type **302**	70	60
868	32p. *The Goose Girl* (William Leech)	75	65
869	44p. *La Jeune Bretonne* (Roderic O'Conor) (vert)	75	1·75
870	52p. *Lustre Jug* (Walter Osborne) (vert)	80	2·40

303 Bee Orchid

1993. Irish Orchids. Multicoloured.

871	28p. Type **303**	90	60
872	32p. O'Kelly's orchid	1·10	80
873	38p. Dark red helleborine	1·60	2·25
874	52p. Irish lady's tresses	1·90	2·75
MS875	130×71 mm. Nos. 871/4	5·00	6·00

304 *Pears in a Copper Pan* (Hilda van Stockum)

1993. Europa. Contemporary Art. Multicoloured.

876	32p. Type **304**	75	75
877	44p. *Arrieta Orzola* (Tony O'Malley)	1·10	1·10

305 Cultural Activities

1993. Centenary of Conradh Na Gaeilge (cultural organization). Multicoloured.

878	32p. Type **305**	85	75
879	52p. Illuminated manuscript cover (vert)	1·50	1·50

306 Diving

1993. Centenary of Irish Amateur Swimming Association. Multicoloured.

880	32p. Type **306**	1·00	1·50
881	32p. Swimming	1·00	1·50

307 Nurse with Patient and Hospital Buildings

1993. Anniversaries and Events. Multicoloured.

882	28p. Type **307** (250th anniv of Royal Hospital, Donnybrook)	1·25	60
883	32p. College building and crest (bicentenary of St. Patrick's College, Carlow) (vert)	80	60
884	44p. Map of Neolithic field system, Ceide (opening of interpretative centre)	1·75	1·60
885	52p. Edward Bunting (musicologist) (150th death anniv) (25×42 mm)	1·75	2·00

308 Great Northern Railways Gardner at Drogheda

1993. Irish Buses. Multicoloured.

886	28p. Type **308**	85	70
887	32p. C.I.E. Leyland Titan at College Green, Dublin	1·00	70
888	52p. Horse-drawn omnibus at Old Baal's Bridge, Limerick	1·75	2·50
889	52p. Char-a-banc at Lady's View, Killarney	1·75	2·50

309 The Annunciation

1993. Christmas. Multicoloured.

890	28p. The flight into Egypt (vert)	80	80
891	28p. Type **309**	80	55
892	32p. Holy Family	90	70
893	52p. Adoration of the shepherds	2·00	2·50

310 Biplane skywriting "Love"

1994. Greetings Stamps. Multicoloured.

894	28p. Type **310**	90	75
895	32p. Couple within heart (vert)	1·00	85

311 Smiling Sun

1994. Greetings Stamps. Multicoloured.

896	32p. Type **311**	1·00	1·50
897	32p. Smiling daisy	1·00	1·50
898	32p. Smiling heart	1·00	1·50
899	32p. Smiling rose	1·00	1·50

1994. "Hong Kong '94" International Stamp Exhibition. Chinese New Year ("Year of the Dog").

MS900	137×74 mm. Nos. 896/8	4·50	6·50

312 Stylized Logo of Macra na Feirme (50th anniv)

1994. Anniversaries and Events.

901	**312** 28p. gold and blue	75	65
902	– 32p. multicoloured	1·00	75
903	– 38p. multicoloured	2·50	2·25
904	– 52p. black, cobalt and blue	1·75	2·50

DESIGNS—38×35 mm: 32p. *The Taking of Christ* (Caravaggio) (loan of painting to National Gallery). 37½×27 mm: 38p. Sir Horace Plunkett with 19th-century milk carts and modern tankers (centenary of Irish Co-operative Organization Society); 52p. Congress emblem (centenary of Irish Congress of Trade Unions).

313 St. Brendan visiting Iceland

1994. Europa. St. Brendan's Voyages. Multicoloured.

905	32p. Type **313**	75	70
906	44p. Discovering Faroe Islands	1·50	2·00
MS907	82×76 mm. Nos. 905/6	2·75	4·00

314 First Meeting of Dail, 1919

1994. Parliamentary Anniversaries. Multicoloured.

908	32p. Type **314** (75th anniv)	90	1·00
909	32p. European Parliament (4th direct elections)	90	1·00

315 Irish and Argentine Footballers

1994. Sporting Anniversaries and Events. Multicoloured.

910	32p. Type **315**	80	1·25
911	32p. Irish and German footballers	80	1·25
912	32p. Irish and Dutch women's hockey match (horiz)	2·00	1·25
913	52p. Irish and English women's hockey match (horiz)	2·25	2·50

ANNIVERSARIES AND EVENTS: Nos. 910/11, World Cup Football Championship, U.S.A.; 912, Women's Hockey World Cup, Dublin; 913, Centenary of Irish Ladies' Hockey Union.

316 *Arctia caja*

1994. Moths. Multicoloured

(a) Size 37×26 mm

914	28p. Type **316**	65	60
915	32p. *Calamia tridens*	75	70
916	38p. *Saturnia pavonia*	90	1·10
917	52p. *Deilephila elpenor*	1·50	2·00
MS918	120×71 mm. Nos. 914/17	3·50	4·00

(b) Size 34×22 mm. Self-adhesive.

919	32p. *Calamia tridens*	1·25	1·75
920	32p. Type **316**	1·25	1·75
921	32p. *Deilephila elpenor*	1·25	1·75
922	32p. *Saturnia pavonia*	1·25	1·75

317 Statue of Edmund Rice and Class

1994. Anniversaries and Events. Multicoloured.

923	28p. St. Laurence Gate, Drogheda (44×27 mm)	1·50	1·60
924	32p. Type **317**	1·50	1·60
925	32p. Edmund Burke (politician)	1·50	1·60
926	52p. Vickers FB-27 Vimy and map (horiz)	1·50	1·75
927	52p. Eamonn Andrews (broadcaster)	1·50	1·75

ANNIVERSARIES AND EVENTS: No. 923, 800th anniv of Drogheda; 924, 150th death anniv of Edmund Rice (founder of Irish Christian Brothers); 925, 927, The Irish abroad; 926, 75th anniv of Alcock and Brown's first trans-atlantic flight.

318 George Bernard Shaw (author) and *Pygmalion* Poster

1994. Irish Nobel Prize Winners. Multicoloured.
928	28p. Type **318**	60	90
929	28p. Samuel Beckett (author) and pair of boots	60	90
930	32p. Sean MacBride (human rights campaigner) and peace doves	70	90
931	52p. William Butler Yeats (poet) and poem	1·10	2·00

319 *The Annunciation* (ivory plaque)

1994. Christmas. Multicoloured.
932	28p. Nativity	70	60
933	28p. Type **319**	80	60
934	32p. *Flight into Egypt* (wood carving)	90	70
935	52p. *Nativity* (ivory plaque)	1·40	2·00

320 Tree of Hearts

1995. Greetings Stamps. Multicoloured.
936	32p. Type **320**	1·10	1·25
937	32p. Teddy bear holding balloon	1·10	1·25
938	32p. Clown juggling hearts	1·10	1·25
939	32p. Bouquet of flowers	1·10	1·25

1995. Chinese New Year ("Year of the Pig").
MS940	137×74 mm. Nos. 936, 938/9	4·50	4·50

321 West Clare Railway Steam Locomotive No. 1 *Kilkee* at Kilrush Station

1995. Transport. Narrow Gauge Railways. Multicoloured.
941	28p. Type **321**	85	60
942	32p. County Donegal Railway tank locomotive No. 2 *Blanche* at Donegal Station	1·10	90
943	38p. Cork and Muskerry Railway tank locomotive No. 1 *City of Cork* on Western Road, Cork	1·40	1·75
944	52p. Cavan and Leitrim Railway tank locomotive No. 3 *Lady Edith* on Arigna Tramway	1·90	2·50
MS945	127×83 mm. Nos. 941/4	4·75	5·50

322 English and Irish Rugby Players

1995. World Cup Rugby Championship, South Africa. Multicoloured.
946	32p. Type **322**	1·00	75
947	52p. Australian and Irish players	1·40	1·75
MS948	108×77 mm. £1 Type **322**	3·00	3·50

323 Peace Dove and Skyscrapers

1995. Europa. Peace and Freedom. Multicoloured

(a) Size 38×26 mm. Ordinary gum
949	32p. Type **323**	85	75
950	44p. Peace dove and map of Europe and North Africa	1·40	2·00

(b) Size 34½×23 mm. Self-adhesive.
951	32p. Type **323**	90	90
952	32p. As No. 950	90	90

324 Soldiers of the Irish Brigade and Memorial Cross

1995. 250th Anniv of Battle of Fontenoy.
953	**324**	32p. multicoloured	1·25	80

A similar stamp was issued by Belgium.

325 Irish Brigade, French Army, 1745

1995. Military Uniforms. Multicoloured.
954	28p. Type **325**	70	60
955	32p. Tercio Irlanda, Spanish army in Flanders, 1605	80	75
956	32p. Royal Dublin Fusiliers, 1914	80	75
957	38p. St. Patrick's Battalion, Papal Army, 1860	1·10	1·25
958	52p. 69th Regiment, New York State Militia, 1861	1·60	1·75

326 Guglielmo Marconi and Original Radio Transmitter

1995. Centenary of Radio. Multicoloured.
959	32p. Type **326**	1·50	1·75
960	32p. Traditional radio dial	1·50	1·75

327 Bartholomew Mosse (founder) and Hospital Building

1995. Anniversaries. Multicoloured.
961	28p. Type **327** (250th anniv of Rotunda Hospital)	1·40	70
962	32p. St. Patrick's House, Maynooth College (bicent) (25×41 mm)	80	80
963	32p. Laurel wreath and map of Europe (50th anniv of end of Second World War)	80	80
964	52p. Geological map of Ireland (150th anniv of Geological Survey of Ireland) (32½×32½ mm)	1·25	1·50

328 Natterjack Toad

1995. Reptiles and Amphibians. Multicoloured

(a) Size 40×27 mm. Ordinary gum.
965	32p. Type **328**	1·00	1·25
966	32p. Common lizards	1·00	1·25
967	32p. Smooth newts	1·00	1·25
968	32p. Common frog	1·00	1·25

(b) Size 37×25 mm. Self-adhesive.
969	32p. Type **328**	1·25	1·75
970	32p. Common lizard	1·25	1·75
971	32p. Smooth newts	1·25	1·75
972	32p. Common frog	1·25	1·75

Nos. 965/8 were printed together, *se-tenant*, with the backgrounds forming a composite design.

329 *Crinum moorei*

1995. Bicentenary of National Botanic Gardens, Glasnevin. Flowers. Multicoloured.
973	32p. Type **329**	1·50	70
974	38p. *Sarracenia x moorei*	1·25	1·50
975	44p. *Solanum crispum* 'Glasnevin'	1·25	2·50

330 Anniversary Logo and Irish United Nations Soldier

1995. 50th Anniv of United Nations. Multicoloured.
976	32p. Type **330**	80	70
977	52p. Emblem and "UN"	1·25	1·40

331 *Adoration of the Shepherds* (illuminated manuscript) (Benedetto Bardone)

1995. Christmas. Multicoloured.
978	28p. Adoration of the Magi	1·10	65
979	28p. Type **331**	80	65
980	32p. *Adoration of the Magi* (illuminated manuscript) (Bardone)	1·00	70
981	52p. *The Holy Family* (illuminated manuscript) (Bardone)	1·75	2·75

332 Zig and Zag on Heart

1996. Greetings Stamps. Multicoloured.
982	32p. Type **332**	1·25	75
983	32p. Zig and Zag waving	2·50	2·50
984	32p. Zig and Zag in space suits	2·50	2·50
985	32p. Zig and Zag wearing hats	2·50	2·50

1996. Chinese New Year ("Year of the Rat").
MS986	130×74 mm. Nos. 982, 984/5	3·00	3·00

333 Wheelchair Athlete

1996. Olympic and Paralympic Games, Atlanta. Multicoloured.
987	28p. Type **333**	70	65
988	32p. Running	80	80
989	32p. Throwing the discus	80	80
990	32p. Single kayak	80	80

334 Before the Start, Fairyhouse Race Course

1996. Irish Horse Racing. Multicoloured.
991	28p. Type **334**	70	65
992	32p. Steeplechase, Punch-estown	80	80
993	32p. On the Flat, The Curragh	80	80
994	38p. Steeplechase, Galway	1·25	1·25
995	52p. After the race, Leopard-stown	1·50	1·50

335 Irish and French Coloured Ribbons merging

1996. "L'Imaginaire Irlandais" Festival of Contemporary Irish Arts, France.
996	**335**	32p. multicoloured	1·00	1·00

336 Louie Bennett (suffragette)

1996. Europa. Famous Women

(a) Size 40×29 mm. Ordinary gum
997	**336**	32p. violet	80	70
998		44p. green	1·10	1·25

(b) Size 37×25 mm. Self-adhesive.
999	**336**	32p. violet	1·10	1·25
1000	-	32p. green	1·10	1·25

DESIGN: Nos. 998, 1000, Lady Augusta Gregory (play-wright).

337 Newgrange Passage Tomb (Boyne Valley World Heritage Site)

1996. Anniversaries and Events.
1001	**337**	28p. brown and black	1·00	60
1002		32p. multicoloured	1·10	90

DESIGN: 32p. Children playing (50th anniv of UNICEF).

1996. CHINA '96. Ninth Asian International Stamp Exhibition, Peking. Sheet 120×95 mm, containing Nos. 992/3.
MS1003	32p. Steeplechase, Punches-town; 32p. On the Flat, The Curragh	11·00	11·00

338 Stanley Woods

1996. Isle of Man Tourist Trophy Motor Cycle Races. Irish Winners. Multicoloured.
1004	32p. Type **338**	80	70
1005	44p. Artie Bell	1·25	1·50
1006	50p. Alec Bennett	1·50	1·75
1007	52p. Joey and Robert Dunlop	1·50	1·75
MS1008	100×70 mm. 50p. As 52p.	1·75	2·00

339 Michael Davitt (founder of The Land League)

1996. Anniversaries and Events. Multicoloured.
1009	28p. Type **339** (150th birth anniv)	80	60
1010	32p. Presidency logo (Ireland's Presidency of European Union) (horiz)	80	70

| 1011 | 38p. Thomas McLaughlin (hydro-electric engineer) and Ardnacrusha Power Station (birth centenary) (horiz) | 1·25 | 1·10 |
| 1012 | 52p. Mechanical peat harvester (50th anniv of Bord na Mona) (horiz) | 1·75 | 1·75 |

340 *Ciara* (coastal patrol vessel)

1996. 50th Anniv of Irish Naval Service. Multicoloured.

1013	32p. Type **340**	80	70
1014	44p. *Cliona* (corvette)	1·40	1·50
1015	52p. *M-1* (motor torpedo boat) (vert)	1·50	1·60

341 Blind Woman with Child

1996. People with Disabilities. Multicoloured.

| 1016 | 28p. Type **341** | 1·25 | 1·25 |
| 1017 | 28p. Man in wheelchair playing bowls | 1·25 | 1·25 |

342 Green-winged Teal

1996. Freshwater Ducks. Multicoloured.

1018	32p. Type **342**	1·00	70
1019	38p. Common shoveler	1·10	1·25
1020	44p. European wigeon	1·25	1·75
1021	52p. Mallard	1·60	2·00
MS1022	127×85 mm. Nos. 1018/21	4·50	5·50

343 Man of Aran

1996. Centenary of Irish Cinema. Multicoloured.

1023	32p. Type **343**	85	1·10
1024	32p. *My Left Foot*	85	1·10
1025	32p. *The Commitments*	85	1·10
1026	32p. *The Field*	85	1·10

344 Visit of the Magi

1996. Christmas. Designs from 16th-century *Book of Hours* (Nos. 1028/30). Multicoloured.

1027	28p. The Holy Family	75	60
1028	28p. Type **344**	60	60
1029	32p. The Annunciation	80	75
1030	52p. The Shepherds receiving new of Christ's birth	1·40	1·60

345 Black-billed Magpie ("Magpie")

1997. Birds. Multicoloured

(a) Ordinary gum. Size 23×26 mm or 26×23 mm.

1031	1p. Type **345**	10	60
1032	2p. Northern gannet ("Gannet") (vert)	15	60
1033	4p. Corn crake (vert)	20	40
1034	5p. Wood pigeon (horiz)	20	80

1035	10p. River kingfisher ("Kingfisher") (vert)	40	1·00
1036	20p. Northern lapwing ("Lapwing") (vert)	65	1·00
1037	28p. Blue tit (horiz)	2·50	50
1038	30p. Blackbird (vert)	85	1·00
1039p	30p. Goldcrest (vert)	1·25	1·25
1040	30p. Common stonechat ("Stonechat") (vert)	1·25	1·25
1041	30p. As No. 1036	1·25	1·25
1042	30p. As No. 1032	1·25	1·25
1043	30p. As No. 1033	1·25	1·25
1044	30p. Type **345**	1·25	1·25
1045	30p. As No. 1035	1·25	1·25
1046	30p. Peregrine falcon (vert)	1·25	1·25
1047	30p. Barn owl (vert)	1·25	1·25
1048	30p. European robin ("Robin") (vert)	1·25	1·25
1049	30p. Song thrush (vert)	1·25	1·25
1050	30p. Winter wren ("Wren") (vert)	2·50	3·25
1051	30p. Pied wagtail (vert)	2·50	3·25
1052	30p. Atlantic puffin ("Puffin") (vert)	1·25	1·25
1053	32p. As No. 1048	2·25	55
1054	35p. As No. 1040	1·00	1·50
1055p	40p. Ringed plover (horiz)	1·50	1·00
1056	44p. As No. 1052	3·50	2·25
1057ac	45p. As No. 1049	1·50	1·50
1058ac	50p. Northern sparrow hawk ("European Sparrow Hawk") (horiz)	2·25	1·25
1059	52p. As No. 1047	4·00	2·00

(b) Size 26×47 mm or 47×26 mm.

1060	£1 White-fronted goose ("Greenland White-fronted Goose") (vert)	2·00	1·60
1061	£2 Northern pintail ("Pintail") (horiz)	3·75	3·50
1062	£5 Common shelduck ("Shelduck") (vert)	8·50	9·00

(c) Size 17×21 mm or 21×17 mm.

1080	4p. Corn crake	1·25	2·00
1081	5p. Wood pigeon	80	1·00
1082	30p. Blackbird	1·60	1·60
1083	30p. Goldcrest	1·00	1·75
1084	32p. European robin ("Robin")	1·00	1·50
1085	32p. Peregrine falcon	1·50	1·50

(d) Size 24×29 mm. Self-adhesive.

1086	30p. Goldcrest	1·00	1·10
1087	30p. Blackbird	1·00	1·10
1088	32p. Peregrine falcon	2·50	4·00
1089	32p. European robin ("Robin")	2·50	4·00

346 Pair of Doves

1997. Greetings Stamps. Multicoloured.

1100	32p. Type **346**	85	50
1101	32p. Cow jumping over moon	1·10	1·25
1102	32p. Pig going to market	1·10	1·25
1103	32p. Cockerel	1·10	1·25

1997. "HONG KONG '97" International Stamp Exhibition. Chinese New Year ("Year of the Ox").

| MS1104 | 124×74 mm. Nos. 1101/3 | 2·75 | 2·75 |

347 Troops on Parade

1997. 75th Anniv of Irish Free State. Multicoloured.

1105	28p. Page from the *Annals of the Four Masters*, quill and 1944 ½d. O'Clery stamp	75	55
1106	32p. Type **347**	1·00	1·25
1107	32p. The Dáil, national flag and Constitution	1·00	1·25
1108	32p. Athlete, footballer and hurling player	1·00	1·25
1109	32p. Singer, violinist and bodhran player	1·00	1·25
1110	32p. Stained glass window and 1929 9d. O'Connell stamp	1·00	1·00
1111	32p. 1923 2d. map stamp and G.P.O., Dublin	1·00	1·00
1112	52p. Police personnel and Garda badge	1·50	2·00
1113	52p. The Four Courts and Scales of Justice	1·50	2·00
1114	52p. Currency, blueprint and food-processing plant	1·50	2·00
1115	52p. Books, palette and Seamus Heaney manuscript	1·50	2·00

| 1116 | 52p. Air Lingus Boeing 737 and 1965 1s.5d. air stamp | 1·50 | 1·50 |
| MS1117 | 174×209 mm. As Nos. 1105/16, but each with face value of 32p. | 12·00 | 15·00 |

348 Grey Seals

1997. Marine Mammals. Multicoloured.

1118	28p. Type **348**	75	60
1119	32p. Bottle-nosed dolphins	85	80
1120	44p. Harbour porpoises (horiz)	1·25	1·40
1121	52p. Killer whale (horiz)	1·40	1·50
MS1122	150×68 mm. As Nos. 1118/21	6·00	6·00

349 Dublin Silver Penny of 997

1997. Millenary of Irish Coinage.

| 1123 | **349** 32p. multicoloured | 65 | 65 |

350 The Children of Lir

1997. Europa. Tales and Legends. Multicoloured

(a) Size 38×28 mm. Ordinary gum.

| 1124 | 32p. Type **350** | 75 | 60 |
| 1125 | 44p. Oisin and Niamh | 1·10 | 2·00 |

(b) Size 36×25 mm. Self-adhesive.

| 1126 | 32p. Type **350** | 1·50 | 70 |
| 1127 | 32p. Oisin and Niamh | 1·50 | 70 |

351 Emigrants waiting to board Ship

1997. 150th Anniv of The Great Famine.

1128	**351** 28p. blue, red and stone	1·00	70
1129	– 32p. orange, blue & stone	1·25	70
1130	– 52p. brown, blue & stone	1·75	3·00

DESIGNS: 32p. Family and dying child; 52p. Irish Society of Friends soup kitchen.

1997. "Pacific '97" International Stamp Exhibition, San Francisco. Sheet 100×70 mm, containing No. 1061. Multicoloured.

| MS1131 | £2 Pintail (48×26 mm) | 4·75 | 6·50 |

352 Kate O'Brien (novelist) (birth centenary)

1997. Anniversaries. Multicoloured.

1132	28p. Type **352**	85	1·00
1133	28p. St. Columba crossing to Iona (stained glass window) (1400th death anniv)	85	1·00
1134	32p. *Daniel O'Connell* (J. Haverty) (politician) (150th death anniv) (27×49 mm)	95	70
1135	52p. *John Wesley* (N. Hone) (founder of Methodism) (250th anniv of first visit to Ireland)	1·75	2·50

353 The Baily Lighthouse

1997. Lighthouses. Multicoloured.

1136	32p. Type **353**	1·40	1·40
1137	32p. Tarbert	1·40	1·40
1138	38p. Hookhead (vert)	1·40	1·10
1139d	50p. The Fastnet (vert)	1·40	2·00

354 Commemorative Cross

1997. Ireland–Mexico Joint Issue. 150th Anniv of Mexican St. Patrick's Battalion.

| 1140 | **354** 32p. multicoloured | 55 | 60 |

355 Dracula and Bat

1997. Centenary of Publication of Bram Stoker's *Dracula*. Multicoloured.

1141	28p. Type **355**	60	55
1142	32p. Dracula and female victim	65	60
1143	38p. Dracula emerging from coffin (horiz)	80	90
1144	52p. Dracula and wolf (horiz)	1·10	1·75
MS1145	150×90 mm. As Nos. 1141/4	3·25	3·75

356 *The Nativity* (Kevin Kelly) **357** Christmas Tree

1997. Christmas. Multicoloured

(a) Stained-glass Windows. Ordinary gum.

| 1146 | 28p. Type **356** | 70 | 55 |
| 1147 | 32p. *The Nativity* (Sarah Purser and A. E. Child) | 80 | 65 |

(b) Self-adhesive.

| 1148 | 52p. *The Nativity* (A. E. Child) | 1·50 | 1·75 |
| 1149 | 28p. Type **357** | 80 | 80 |

358 Holding Heart

1998. Greetings Stamps (1st series). Designs based on the "love is ..." cartoon characters of Kim Casali. Multicoloured.

1150	32p. Type **358**	1·10	50
1151	32p. Receiving letter	1·10	1·25
1152	32p. Sitting on log	1·10	1·25
1153	32p. With birthday presents	1·10	1·25

See also Nos. 1173/6.

1998. Chinese New Year ("Year of the Tiger").

| MS1154 | 124×73 mm. Nos. 1151/3 | 4·50 | 5·50 |

359 Lady Mary Heath and Avro Type 581 Avian II over Pyramids

1998. Pioneers of Irish Aviation. Multicoloured.

1155	28p. Type **359**	60	55
1156	32p. Col. James Fitzmaurice and Junkers W.33 *Bremen* over Labrador	65	60
1157	44p. Captain J. P. Saul and Fokker F.VIIa/3m *Southern Cross*	1·25	1·25
1158	52p. Captain Charles Blair and Sikorsky V-S 44 (flying boat)	1·50	1·50

360 Show-jumping

1998. Equestrian Sports. Multicoloured.

1159	30p. Type **360**	90	60
1160	32p. Three-day eventing	95	65
1161	40p. Gymkhana	1·00	1·40
1162	45p. Dressage (vert)	1·00	1·40
MS1163	126×84 mm. Nos. 1159/62	3·50	4·00

361 Figure of "Liberty"

1998. Bicentenary of United Irish Rebellion. Multicoloured.

1164	30p. Type **361**	1·00	1·00
1165	30p. United Irishman	1·00	1·00
1166	30p. French soldiers	1·00	1·00
1167	45p. Wolfe Tone	1·00	1·25
1168	45p. Henry Joy McCracken	1·00	1·25

362 Gathering of the Boats, Kinvara

1998. Europa. Festivals. Multicoloured

(a) Size 39×27 mm.

1169	30p. Type **362**	1·50	80
1170	40p. Puck Fair, Killorglin	1·50	95

(b) Size 34×23 mm. Self-adhesive.

1171	30p. Type **362**	1·50	90
1172	30p. Puck Fair, Killorglin	1·50	90

1998. Greetings Stamps (2nd series). As Nos. 1105/8, but with changed face value. Multicoloured.

1173	30p. As No. 1153	70	95
1174	30p. As No. 1152	70	95
1175	30p. As No. 1151	70	95
1176	30p. Type **358**	70	95

363 Cyclists rounding Bend

1998. Visit of "Tour de France" Cycle Race to Ireland. Multicoloured.

1177	30p. Type **363**	85	85
1178	30p. Two cyclists ascending hill	85	85
1179	30p. "Green jersey" cyclist and other competitor	85	85
1180	30p. "Yellow jersey" (race leader)	85	85

364 Voter and Local Councillors of 1898

1998. Democracy Anniversaries. Multicoloured.

1181	30p. Type **364** (cent of Local Government (Ireland) Act)	60	60
1182	32p. European Union flag and harp symbol (25th anniv of Ireland's entry into European Community)	65	65
1183	35p. Woman voter and suffragettes, 1898 (cent of women's right to vote in local elections)	75	75
1184	45p. Irish Republic flag (50th anniv of Republic of Ireland Act)	1·00	1·25

365 *Asgard II* (cadet brigantine)

1998. *Cutty Sark* International Tall Ships Race, Dublin. Multicoloured

(a) Ordinary gum.

1185	30p. Type **365** (26×38 mm)	1·00	1·00
1186	30p. U.S.C.G. *Eagle* (cadet barque) (26×38 mm)	1·00	1·00
1187	45p. *Boa Esperanza* (replica caravel) (38×26 mm)	1·25	1·00
1188	£1 *Royalist* (training brigantine) (38×26 mm)	2·00	2·75

(b) Self-adhesive.

1189	30p. *Boa Esperanza* (34×23 mm)	85	1·00
1190	30p. Type **365** (23×34 mm)	85	1·00
1191	30p. U.S.C.G. *Eagle* (23×34 mm)	85	1·00
1192	30p. *Royalist* (34×23 mm)	85	85

366 Ashworth Pillbox (1856)

1998. Irish Postboxes. Multicoloured.

1193	30p. Type **366**	75	1·00
1194	30p. Irish Free State wallbox (1922)	75	1·00
1195	30p. Double pillarbox (1899)	75	1·00
1196	30p. Penfold pillarbox (1866)	75	1·00

367 Mary Immaculate College, Limerick (centenary)

1998. Anniversaries. Multicoloured.

1197	30p. Type **367**	75	60
1198	40p. Newtown School, Waterford (bicent) (vert)	1·00	1·50
1199	45p. Trumpeters (50th anniv of Universal Declaration of Human Rights)	1·10	1·75

1998. "Portugal '98" International Stamp Exhibition, Lisbon. Sheet 101×71 mm, containing design as No. 1187.

MS1200	£2 "Boa Esperanza" (caravel) (horiz)	4·50	5·50

368 Cheetah

1998. Endangered Animals. Multicoloured.

1201	30p. Type **368**	1·00	1·25
1202	30p. Scimitar-horned oryx	1·00	1·25
1203	40p. Golden lion tamarin (vert)	1·10	1·25
1204	45p. Tiger (vert)	1·40	1·50
MS1205	150×90 mm. As Nos. 1201/4	3·50	4·25

369 The Holy Family   **370** Choir Boys

1998. Christmas. Multicoloured.

(a) Ordinary gum.

1206	30p. Type **369**	70	60
1207	32p. Shepherds	75	65
1208	45p. Three Kings	1·00	1·75

(b) Self-adhesive.

1209	30p. Type **370**	80	80

371 Puppy and Heart

1999. Greetings Stamps. Pets. Multicoloured.

1210	30p. Type **371**	80	50
1211	30p. Kitten and ball of wool	80	1·00
1212	30p. Goldfish	80	1·00
1213	30p. Rabbit with lettuce leaf	80	1·00

1999. Chinese New Year ("Year of the Rabbit").

MS1214	124×74 mm. Nos. 1211/13	3·75	4·00

372 Micheal Mac Liammoir

1999. Irish Actors and Actresses.

1215	**372**	30p. black and brown	65	60
1216	-	45p. black and green	1·00	1·10
1217	-	50p. black and blue	1·00	1·25

DESIGNS: 45p. Siobhan McKenna, 50p. Noel Purcell.

373 Irish Emigrant Ship

1999. Ireland–U.S.A. Joint Issue. Irish Emigration.

1218	**373** 45p. multicoloured	1·25	1·00

374 *Polly Woodside* (barque)

1999. Maritime Heritage. Multicoloured.

1219	30p. Type **374**	55	60
1220	35p. *Ilen* (schooner)	65	70
1221	45p. R.N.L.I. Cromer class lifeboat (horiz)	80	85
1222	£1 *Titanic* (liner) (horiz)	2·00	2·50
MS1223	150×90 mm. No. 1222×2	3·25	4·00

1999. Ireland—Australia Joint Issue. "Polly Woodside" (barque). Sheet 137×72 mm. Multicoloured.

MS1224	45c. Type **603** of Australia; 30p. Type **374** (No. MS1224 was sold at 52p. in Ireland)	1·25	1·75

No. **MS**1224 includes the "Australia '99" emblem on the sheet margin and was postally valid in Ireland to the value of 30p.

The same miniature sheet was also available in Australia.

375 Sean Lemass

1999. Birth Centenary of Sean Lemass (politician).

1225	**375** 30p. black and green	1·40	1·00

376 European Currency Emblem

1999. Introduction of Single European Currency.

1226	**376** 30p. multicoloured	75	65

The face value of No. 1226 is shown in both Irish and euro currency.

377 European Flags

1999. 50th Anniv of Council of Europe.

1227	**377** 45p. multicoloured	1·00	1·00

378 Whooper Swans, Kilcolman Nature Reserve

1999. Europa. Parks and Gardens. Multicoloured

(a) Size 36×26 mm. Ordinary gum.

1228	30p. Type **378**	90	50
1229	40p. Fallow deer, Phoenix Park	1·00	1·75

(b) Size 34×23 mm. Self-adhesive.

1230	30p. Type **378**	1·50	2·25
1231	30p. Fallow deer, Phoenix Park	1·50	2·25

379 Father James Cullen and St. Francis Xavier Church, Dublin

1999. Centenary of Pioneer Total Abstinence Association.

1232	**379** 32p. brown, bistre and black	75	65

380 Elderly Man and Child using Computer

1999. International Year of Older Persons.

1233	**380** 30p. multicoloured	70	65

381 Postal Van, 1922

1999. 125th Anniv of Universal Postal Union.

1234	**381** 30p. green and deep green	1·40	1·25
1235	-	30p. multicoloured	1·40	1·25

DESIGN: No. 1235, Modern postal lorries.

382 Danno Keeffe

1999. Gaelic Athletic Association "Millennium Football Team". Multicoloured

(a) Size 37×25 mm. Ordinary gum.

1236	30p. Type **382**	65	70
1237	30p. Enda Colleran	65	70
1238	30p. Joe Keohane	65	70
1239	30p. Sean Flanagan	65	70
1240	30p. Sean Murphy	65	70
1241	30p. John Joe Reilly	65	70
1242	30p. Martin O'Connell	65	70
1243	30p. Mick O'Connell	65	70
1244	30p. Tommy Murphy	65	70
1245	30p. Sean O'Neill	65	70
1246	30p. Sean Purcell	65	70
1247	30p. Pat Spillane	65	70
1248	30p. Mikey Sheehy	65	70
1249	30p. Tom Langan	65	70
1250	30p. Kevin Heffernan	65	70

(b) Size 33×23 mm. Self-adhesive.

1251	30p. Type **382**	1·50	2·50
1252	30p. Enda Colleran	55	80

1253	30p. Joe Keohane	1·50	2·50
1254	30p. Sean Flanagan	55	80
1255	30p. Sean Murphy	1·50	2·50
1256	30p. John Joe Reilly	45	60
1257	30p. Martin O'Connell	45	60
1258	30p. Mick O'Connell	1·50	2·50
1259	30p. Tommy Murphy	55	80
1260	30p. Sean O'Neill	45	60
1261	30p. Sean Purcell	55	80
1262	30p. Pat Spillane	55	80
1263	30p. Mikey Sheehy	55	80
1264	30p. Tom Langan	55	80
1265	30p. Kevin Heffernan	45	60

383 Douglas DC-3

1999. Commercial Aviation. Multicoloured.

1266	30p. Type **383**	65	50
1267	32p. Pilatus-Britten BN-2 Norman Islander	75	55
1268	40p. Boeing 707	80	1·40
1269	45p. Lockheed Constellation	90	1·50

384 Mammoth

1999. Extinct Irish Animals. Multicoloured

(a) Size 26×38 mm (vert) or 38×26 mm (horiz). Ordinary gum.

1270	30p. Type **384**	70	70
1271	30p. Giant deer	70	70
1272	45p. Wolves (horiz)	90	1·25
1273	45p. Brown bear (horiz)	90	1·25
MS1274	150×63 mm. Nos. 1270/3	2·75	3·00

(b) Size 33×23 mm (horiz) or 22×34 mm (vert). Self-adhesive.

1275	30p. Brown bear (horiz)	70	85
1276	30p. Type **384**	70	85
1277	30p. Wolves (horiz)	70	85
1278	30p. Giant deer	70	85

385 Holy Family

1999. Christmas. Children's Nativity Plays. Multicoloured

(a) Size 35×25 mm. Ordinary gum.

1279	30p. Type **385**	60	50
1280	32p. Visit of the Shepherds	65	55
1281	45p. Adoration of the Magi	1·25	1·50

(b) Size 16×26 mm. Self-adhesive.

1282	30p. Angel	70	50

386 Grace Kelly (American actress)

1999. New Millennium (1st issue). Famous People of the 20th Century. Multicoloured.

1283	30p. Type **386**	1·75	2·00
1284	30p. Jesse Owens (American athlete)	1·75	2·00
1285	30p. John F. Kennedy (former American President)	1·75	2·00
1286	30p. Mother Teresa (missionary)	1·75	2·00
1287	30p. John McCormack (tenor)	1·75	2·00
1288	30p. Nelson Mandela (South African statesman)	1·75	2·00

See also Nos. 1289/94, 1300/5, 1315/20, 1377/82 and 1383/88.

387 Ruined Castle (Norman Invasion, 1169)

2000. New Millennium (2nd issue). Irish Historic Events. Multicoloured.

1289	30p. Type **387**	1·75	2·00
1290	30p. Flight of the Earls, 1607	1·75	2·00
1291	30p. Opening of Irish Parliament, 1782	1·75	2·00
1292	30p. Eviction (formation of the Land League)	1·75	2·00
1293	30p. First four Irish Prime Ministers (Irish Independence)	1·75	2·00
1294	30p. Irish soldier and personnel carrier (U.N. Peace-keeping)	1·75	2·00

388 Frog Prince

2000. Greetings Stamps. Mythical Creatures. Multicoloured.

1295	30p. Type **388**	1·00	60
1296	30p. Pegasus	1·00	1·25
1297	30p. Unicorn	1·00	1·25
1298	30p. Dragon	1·00	1·25

2000. Chinese New Year ("Year of the Dragon").
| MS1299 | 124×74 mm. Nos. 1296/8 | 3·00 | 3·00 |

389 Revd. Nicholas Callan (electrical scientist)

2000. New Millennium (3rd issue). Discoveries. Multicoloured.

1300	30p. Type **389**	1·75	2·00
1301	30p. Birr Telescope	1·75	2·00
1302	30p. Thomas Edison (inventor of light bulb)	1·75	2·00
1303	30p. Albert Einstein (mathematical physicist)	1·75	2·00
1304	30p. Marie Curie (physicist)	1·75	2·00
1305	30p. Galileo Galilei (astronomer and mathematician)	1·75	2·00

390 *Jeanie Johnston* (emigrant ship)

2000. Completion of *Jeanie Johnston* Replica.
1306	**390**	30p. multicoloured	70	50

391 "Building Europe"

2000. Europa

(a) 25½×36½ mm
1307	**391**	32p. multicoloured	80	55

(b) 22×34 mm. Self-adhesive.
1308	30p. multicoloured	75	50

DENOMINATION. From No. 1309 to 1465 some Irish stamps are denominated both in Irish pounds and in euros.

392 Oscar Wilde

2000. Death Centenary of Oscar Wilde (writer). Multicoloured.

1309	30p. Type **392**	1·40	1·40
1310	30p. *The Happy Prince*	1·40	1·40
1311	30p. Lady Bracknell from *The Importance of being Earnest*	1·40	1·40
1312	30p. *The Picture of Dorian Gray*	1·40	1·40
MS1313	150×190 mm. £2 Type **392**	3·25	4·00

A further 30p. exists in a design similar to Type **392**, but 29×29 mm, printed in sheets of 20, each stamp having a se-tenant half-stamp size label attached at right inscribed "Oscar". These sheets could be personalized by the addition of a photograph in place of the inscription on the labels. Such stamps are not listed as they were not available at face value, the sheets of 20 containing the "Oscar" labels being sold for £10.

393 Ludwig van Beethoven (German composer)

2000. New Millennium (4th issue). The Arts. Multicoloured.

1315	30p. Type **393**	1·40	1·50
1316	30p. Dame Ninette de Valois (ballet director)	1·40	1·50
1317	30p. James Joyce (author)	1·40	1·50
1318	30p. *Mona Lisa* (Leonardo da Vinci)	1·40	1·50
1319	30p. *Lady Lavery* (Sir John Lavery)	1·40	1·50
1320	30p. William Shakespeare (playwright)	1·40	1·50

394 Running

2000. Olympic Games, Sydney. Multicoloured.

1321	30p. Type **394**	70	70
1322	30p. Javelin throwing	70	70
1323	50p. Long jumping	1·00	1·25
1324	50p. High jumping	1·00	1·25

395 *Space Rocket over Flowers* (Marguerite Nyhan)

2000. "Stampin' the Future" (children's stamp design competition). Multicoloured.

1325	30p. Type **395**	60	50
1326	32p. *Tree, rocket and hands holding globe in '2000'* (Kyle Staunton) (horiz)	70	55
1327	45p. *People holding hands on globe* (Jennifer Branagan) (horiz)	90	1·10
1328	45p. *Colony on Moon* (Diarmuid O'Ceochain) (horiz)	90	1·10

396 Tony Reddin

2000. "Hurling Team of the Millennium". Multicoloured

(a) Size 36×27 mm

1329	30p. Type **396**	60	70
1330	30p. Bobby Rackard	60	70
1331	30p. Nick O'Donnell	60	70
1332	30p. John Doyle	60	70

1333	30p. Brian Whelahan	60	70
1334	30p. John Keane	60	70
1335	30p. Paddy Phelan	60	70
1336	30p. Lory Meagher	60	70
1337	30p. Jack Lynch	60	70
1338	30p. Jim Langton	60	70
1339	30p. Mick Mackey	60	70
1340	30p. Christy Ring	60	70
1341	30p. Jimmy Doyle	60	70
1342	30p. Ray Cummins	60	70
1343	30p. Eddie Keher	60	70

(b) Size 33×23 mm. Self-adhesive.

1344	30p. Type **396**	60	1·00
1345	30p. Jimmy Doyle	60	1·00
1346	30p. John Doyle	60	1·00
1347	30p. Paddy Phelan	60	1·60
1348	30p. Jim Langton	60	1·60
1349	30p. Lory Meagher	60	1·00
1350	30p. Eddie Keher	60	1·00
1351	30p. Mick Mackey	60	1·00
1352	30p. Brian Whelahan	60	1·00
1353	30p. John Keane	60	1·00
1354	30p. Bobby Rackard	60	1·00
1355	30p. Nick O'Donnell	60	1·00
1356	30p. Jack Lynch	60	1·00
1357	30p. Ray Cummins	60	1·00
1358	30p. Christy Ring	60	1·00

397 Peacock Butterfly

2000. Butterflies. Multicoloured.

1359	30p. Type **397**	80	50
1360	32p. Small tortoiseshell	85	55
1361	45p. Silver-washed fritillary	1·25	1·75
1362	50p. Orange-tip	1·40	2·50
MS1363	150×90 mm. Nos. 1359/62	3·75	4·50

2000. Military Aviation. Multicoloured.

(a) Size 37×26 mm.

1364	30p. Hawker Hurricane Mk IIC	1·25	1·50
1365	30p. Bristol F.2B Mk II	1·25	1·50
1366	45p. de Havilland DH.115 Vampire T 55	1·50	1·75
1367	45p. Eurocopter S.E. 3160 Alouette III (helicopter)	1·50	1·75

(b) Size 33×22 mm. Self-adhesive.

1368	30p. Bristol F.2B Mk II	1·25	1·25
1369	30p. Hawker Hurricane Mk IIC	1·25	1·25
1370	30p. de Havilland DH.115 Vampire T.55	1·25	1·25
1371	30p. Eurocopter SE. 3160 Alouette III	1·25	1·25

398 Tractor ploughing Field

2000. Centenary of An Roinn Talmhaiochta (Department of Agriculture).
1372	**398**	50p. multicoloured	1·00	1·10

399 The Nativity

2000. Christmas. Multicoloured

(a) Size 24×27 mm.

1373	30p. Type **399**	65	25
1374	32p. Three Magi	75	55
1375	45p. Shepherds	1·00	1·50

(b) Size 24×29 mm. Self-adhesive.

1376	30p. Flight into Egypt	90	50

400 Storming the Bastille, Paris, 1789

2000. New Millennium (5th issue). World Events. Multicoloured.

1377	30p. Type **400**	1·75	2·00
1378	30p. Early railway	1·75	2·00
1379	30p. Returning troop ship, 1945	1·75	2·00
1380	30p. Suffragettes	1·75	2·00
1381	30p. Destruction of the Berlin Wall, 1989	1·75	2·00
1382	30p. Internet communications	1·75	2·00

2001. New Millennuim (6th issue). Epic Journeys. As T **400**. Multicoloured.

1383	30p. Marco Polo	2·00	2·00
1384	30p. Captain James Cook	2·00	2·00
1385	30p. Burke and Wills expedition crossing Australia, 1860	2·00	2·00
1386	30p. Ernest Shackleton in Antarctica	2·00	2·00
1387	30p. Charles Lindbergh and Ryan NYP Special *Spirit of St. Louis*	2·00	2·00
1388	30p. Astronaut on Moon	2·00	2·00

401 Goldfish

2001. Greetings Stamps. Pets

(a) As Type **401**. Multicoloured.

1389	30p. Type **401**	80	50

(b) Designs smaller, 20×30 mm. Self-adhesive.

1390	30p. Lizard	1·00	1·10
1391	30p. Frog	1·00	1·10
1392	30p. Type **401**	1·00	1·10
1393	30p. Snake	1·00	1·10
1394	30p. Tortoise	1·00	1·10

2001. Chinese New Year ("Year of the Snake").

MS1395 124×75 mm. As Nos. 1391 and 1393/4, but larger, 28×39 mm	2·50	2·50

402 Television Presenter and Audience

2001. Irish Broadcasting.

1396	**402**	30p. multicoloured	70	50
1397	-	32p. black, ultramarine and blue	80	55
1398	-	45p. black, brown and orange	1·00	1·10
1399	-	50p. brown, yellow and green	1·00	1·25

DESIGNS: 32p. Radio sports commentators; 45p. Family around radio; 50p. Play on television set.

403 Archbishop Narcissus Marsh and Library Interior

2001. Literary Anniversaries. Multicoloured.

1400	30p. Type **403** (300th anniv of Marsh's Library)	60	50
1401	32p. Book of Common Prayer, 1551 (450th anniv of first book printed in Ireland)	65	1·00

404 Bagpipe Player

2001. 50th Anniv of Comhaltas Ceoltoiri Eireann (cultural organization). Multicoloured.

1402	30p. Type **404**	70	1·00
1403	30p. Bodhran player	70	1·00
1404	45p. Young fiddler and Irish dancer (horiz)	1·00	1·50
1405	45p. Flautist and singer (horiz)	1·00	1·50

405 Jordan Formula 1 Racing Car

2001. Irish Motorsport. Multicoloured.

(a) As Type **405**

1406	30p. Type **405**	75	50
1407	32p. Hillman Imp on Tulip Rally	80	55
1408	45p. Mini Cooper S on Monte Carlo Rally	1·25	80
1409	£1 Mercedes SSK, winner of 1930 Irish Grand Prix	2·00	2·50
MS1410 150×90 mm. £2 Type **405**		3·75	4·25

(b) Designs smaller, 33½×22½ mm. Self-adhesive.

1411	30p. Type **405**	90	1·00
1412	30p. Hillman Imp on Tulip Rally	1·40	1·75
1413	30p. Mini Cooper S on Monte Carlo Rally	1·40	1·75
1414	30p. Mercedes SSK, winner of 1930 Irish Grand Prix	1·40	1·75

406 Peter Lalor (leader at Eureka Stockade) and Gold Licence

2001. Irish Heritage in Australia. Multicoloured.

1415	30p. Type **406**	60	60
1416	30p. Ned Kelly (bush ranger) and "Wanted" poster	60	60
1417	45p. Family leaving for Australia and immigrant ship	1·25	1·25
1418	45p. Irish settler and life in gold camp	1·25	1·25
MS1419 150×90 mm. £1 As No. 1416		2·25	2·50

407 Children playing in River

2001. Europa; Water Resources. Multicoloured.

(a) Size 36½×26½ mm

1420	30p. Type **407**	1·25	50
1421	32p. Man fishing	1·50	75

(b) Designs smaller, 33×22 mm. Self-adhesive.

1422	30p. Type **407**	90	90
1423	30p. As 32p	90	90

408 Blackbird

2001. Dual Currency Birds. Vert designs as Nos. 1038, 1050, 1053, 1056/7 and 1060 (some with different face values) showing both Irish currency and euros as in T **408**. Multicoloured.

(a) Ordinary gum.

1424	30p./38c. Type **408**	1·50	1·00
1425	32p./41c. European robin ("Robin")	1·60	1·00
1426	35p./44c. Atlantic puffin ("Puffin")	1·75	1·75
1427	40p./51c. Winter wren ("Wren")	2·00	2·50
1428	45p./57c. Song thrush	2·25	2·50
1429	£1/€1.27 White-fronted goose ("Greenland White-fronted Goose") (23×44 mm)	5·50	7·00

(b) Designs as Nos. 1038/9, but 25×30 mm. Self-adhesive.

1430	30p./38c. Type **408**	1·50	1·50
1431	30p./38c. Goldcrest	1·50	1·50

409 Irish Pikeman

2001. 400th Anniv of Battle of Kinsale. Nine Years War. Multicoloured.

1432	30p. Type **409**	90	1·00
1433	30p. English cavalry	90	1·00
1434	32p. Spanish pikeman	1·00	80
1435	45p. Town of Kinsale	1·40	1·50

410 Ruffian 23 Yachts

2001. Yachts. Multicoloured.

(a) Size 26×37½ mm.

1436	30p. Type **410**	70	60
1437	32p. Howth 17 yacht	75	65
1438	45p. 1720 Sportsboat yacht	1·10	1·25
1439	45p. Glen class cruising yacht	1·10	1·25

(b) Self-adhesive. Size 22×34 mm.

1440	30p. Type **410**	1·00	1·00
1441	30p. Howth 17 yacht	1·00	1·00
1442	30p. Glen class cruising yacht	1·00	1·00
1443	30p. 1720 Sportsboat yacht	1·00	1·00

411 Padraic Carney (footballer)

2001. Gaelic Athletic Association Hall of Fame 2001 (1st series). Multicoloured

(a) Size 36½×27 mm.

1444	30p. Type **411**	90	90
1445	30p. Frank Cummins (hurler)	90	90
1446	30p. Jack O'Shea (footballer)	90	90
1447	30p. Nicky Rackard (hurler)	90	90

(b) Self-adhesive. Size 33½×22½ mm.

1448	30p. Type **411**	70	70
1449	30p. Frank Cummins (hurler)	70	70
1450	30p. Jack O'Shea (footballer)	70	70
1451	30p. Nicky Rackard (hurler)	70	70

See also Nos. 1550/3.

2001. "Belgica 2001" International Stamp Exhibition, Brussels. No. **MS**1410 with "Belgica 2001" added to the sheet margin.

MS1452 150×90 mm. £2 Type **405**	4·00	4·25

See also Nos. 1550/3.

412 Blackbird

2001. Birds. Vert designs as Nos. 1038/9, 1048 and 1049, but 24×29 mm, each showing a letter in place of face values as T **412**. Multicoloured. Self-adhesive.

1453	(N) Type **408**	1·40	80
1454	(N) Goldcrest	1·40	80
1455	(E) Robin	1·60	70
1456	(W) Song thrush	1·75	80

Nos. 1453/6 were intended to cover the changeover period to euros. Nos. 1453/4 were sold for 30p, No. 1455 for 32p. and No. 1456 for 45p.

413 Perch

2001. Freshwater Fish. Multicoloured.

1457	30p. Type **413**	75	50
1458	30p. Arctic charr	80	85
1459	32p. Pike	80	85
1460	45p. Common bream	1·10	1·25

414 "Out of Bounds" (sculpture by Eilis O'Connell)

2001. 50th Anniv of Government Support for Arts.

1461	**414**	50p. multicoloured	1·25	1·40

415 The Nativity (Richard King)

2001. Christmas. Paintings by Richard King. Multicoloured.

(a) Size 25½×36½ mm

1462	30p. Type **415**	70	50
1463	32p. *The Annunciation*	75	55
1464	45p. *Presentation in the Temple*	1·10	1·25

(b) Size 25×30 mm. Self-adhesive.

1465	30p. *Madonna and Child*	1·10	50

416 Black-billed Magpie ("Magpie")

2002. New Currency. Birds, as Nos. 1031/62, and new designs, with face values in cents and euros, as T **416**

(a) Ordinary gum. (i) Size 23×26 mm or 26×23 mm.

1466	1c. Type **416**	10	50
1467	2c. Northern gannet ("Gannet")	10	50
1468	3c. Blue tit (horiz)	15	50
1469	4c. Corn crake	20	50
1470	5c. Woodpigeon (horiz)	20	50
1470a	7c. Common stonechat	1·25	75
1471	10c. River kingfisher ("Kingfisher")	30	55
1472	20c. Northern lapwing ("Lapwing")	55	1·00
1473	38c. Blackbird	1·00	75
1474	41c. Chaffinch	70	60
1475	41c. Goldcrest	2·25	2·75
1476	44c. European robin ("Robin")	1·00	65
1477	47c. Kestrel (horiz)	1·25	70
1477a	48c. Peregrine falcon	1·00	70
1477b	48c. Pied wagtail	2·50	3·00
1478	50c. Grey heron (horiz)	1·25	90
1479	51c. Roseate tern (horiz)	1·25	75
1480	55c. Oystercatcher (horiz)	1·25	1·50
1481	57c. Western curlew ("Curlew")	1·25	80
1482	60c. Jay (horiz)	1·25	1·25
1482a	60c. Atlantic puffin (horiz)	1·75	1·00
1482b	65c. Song thrush	1·50	1·00
1482c	75c. Ringed plover (horiz)	2·75	1·10
1482d	95c. Sparrowhawk (horiz)	2·75	1·40

(ii) Size 47×26 mm or 26×47 mm.

1483	€1 Barnacle goose (horiz)	2·00	1·40
1484	€2 White-fronted goose ("Greenland White-fronted Goose")	3·25	3·00
1485	€5 Northern pintail ("Pintail") (horiz)	7·50	7·00
1486	€10 Common shelduck ("Shelduck")	16·00	18·00

(iii) Size 20×23 mm.

1486a	4c. Corncrake	80	1·50
1487	10c. River kingfisher ("Kingfisher")	2·50	3·25
1488	36c. Wren	2·75	3·50
1489	38c. Blackbird	70	1·00
1490	41c. Chaffinch	70	80
1490a	48c. Peregrine falcon	75	90

(b) Self-adhesive. Size 24×29 mm.

1491	38c. Blackbird	70	70
1492	38c. Goldcrest	70	70
1493	41c. Chaffinch	90	90
1494	41c. Goldcrest	90	90
1495	44c. Robin	95	95
1495b	(–) Peregrine falcon	1·75	1·75
1495c	(–) Pied wagtail	1·75	1·75
1495d	48c. Peregrine falcon	1·00	1·00
1495e	48c. Pied wagtail	1·00	1·00
1496	50c. Puffin	1·25	1·25
1497	57c. Song thrush	1·10	1·10
1497b	60c. Atlantic puffin	1·40	1·40
1497c	65c. Song thrush	1·75	1·75

Nos. 1495b/c were sold for 48c.

417 Reverse of Irish €1 Coin, 2002

2002. Introduction of Euro Currency. Irish Coins. Multicoloured.

1506	38c. Type **417**	75	50
1507	41c. Reverse of 50p. coin, 1971–2001	80	60
1508	57c. Reverse of 1d. coin, 1928–71	1·10	1·25

418 Teddy Bear

2002. Greetings Stamps. Toys. Multicoloured

(a) Design 25×37 mm.

1509	38c. Type **418**	70	50

(b) Designs 20×27 mm. Self-adhesive.

1510	38c. Type **418**	80	80
1511	38c. Rag doll	80	80
1512	38c. Rocking horse	80	80
1513	38c. Train	80	80
1514	38c. Wooden blocks	80	80

2002. Chinese New Year ("Year of the Horse").
MS1515 124×74 mm. As Nos. 1511/13, but 25×37 mm ... 2·75 2·75

419 Around the Camp Fire

2002. 75th Anniv of Scouting Ireland CSI. Multicoloured.

1516	41c. Type **419**	75	75
1517	41c. Setting up camp	75	75
1518	57c. Scouts canoeing	1·10	1·25
1519	57c. Scouts on hill walk	1·10	1·25

420 *Arkle*

2002. 250th Anniv of Steeplechasing in Ireland. Irish Steeplechasers. Multicoloured.

1520	38c. Type **420**	1·00	1·00
1521	38c. *L'Escargot*	1·00	1·00
1522	38c. *Dawn Run*	1·00	1·00
1523	38c. *Istabraq*	1·00	1·00

421 Badger

2002. Irish Mammals. Multicoloured.

1524	41c. Type **421**	75	60
1525	50c. Otter	90	70
1526	57c. Red squirell (vert)	1·10	1·25
1527	€1 Hedgehog (vert)	1·75	1·90
MS1528	150×67 mm. €5 As 50c.	7·00	8·50

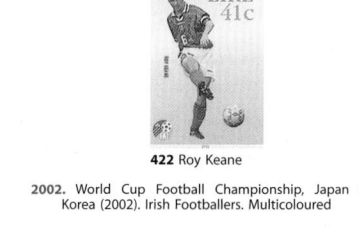

422 Roy Keane

2002. World Cup Football Championship, Japan and Korea (2002). Irish Footballers. Multicoloured

(a) Size 29×40 mm or 40×29 mm.

1529	41c. Packie Bonner (horiz)	1·00	75
1530	41c. Type **422**	1·00	75
1531	41c. Paul McGrath	1·00	75
1532	41c. David O'Leary	1·00	75

(b) Size 25×37 mm or 37×35 mm. Self-adhesive.

1533	41c. Packie Bonner (horiz)	1·00	1·00
1534	41c. Type **422**	1·00	1·00
1535	41c. Paul McGrath	1·00	1·00
1536	41c. David O'Leary	1·00	1·00

423 Clown

2002. Europa. Circus. Multicoloured

(a) Size 40×29 mm. Ordinary gum

1537	41c. Type **423**	70	70
1538	44c. Girl on horse	70	70

(b) Self-adhesive. Size 37×25 mm.

1539	41c. Type **423**	70	70
1540	41c. As No. 1538	70	70

424 Padre Pio

2002. Canonisation of St. Pio de Pietrelcina (Padre Pio).

1541	**424**	41c. multicoloured	75	70

425 Brian Boru leading Army

2002. 1000th Anniv of Declaration of Brian Boru as High King of Ireland. Multicoloured.

1542	41c. Type **425**	75	60
1543	44c. Leading fleet	75	60
1544	57c. Receiving surrender of the O'Neills	90	80
1545	£1 Decreeing primacy of bishopric of Armagh in the Irish Church	1·75	1·90

426 *Before the Start* (J. B. Yeats)

2002. 140th Anniv of National Gallery of Ireland (2004) (1st issue). Paintings. Multicoloured.

1546	41c. Type **426**	70	1·00
1547	41c. *The Conjuror* (Nathaniel Hone)	70	1·00
1548	41c. *The Colosseum and Arch of Constantine, Rome* (Giovanni Panini)	70	1·00
1549	41c. *The Gleaners* (Jules Breton)	70	1·00

See also Nos. 1606/9 and 1700/3.

2002. Gaelic Athletic Association Hall of Fame 2002 (2nd series). As T **411**.

1550	41c. Peter McDermott (footballer)	1·00	1·00
1551	41c. Jimmy Smyth (hurler)	1·00	1·00
1552	41c. Matt Connor (footballer)	1·00	1·00
1553	41c. Seanie Duggan (hurler)	1·00	1·00

427 Archbishop Thomas Croke

2002. Death Centenary of Archbishop Croke (first patron of Gaelic Athletic Association).

1554	**427**	44c. multicoloured	80	70

428 U2

2002. Irish Rock Legends. Multicoloured.

1555	41c. Type **428**	1·40	1·25
1556	41c. Phil Lynott	1·40	1·25
1557	57c. Van Morrison	1·60	2·00

1558	57c. Rory Gallagher	1·60	2·00

MS1559 Four sheets, each 150×90 mm.
(a) €2 Type **428**. (b) €2 No. 1556. (c)
€2 No. 1557. (d) €2 No. 1558 ... 9·00 13·00

429 "Adoration of the Magi"

2002. Christmas. Illustrations from *Les Tres Riches Heures du Duc de Berry* (medieval book of hours). Multicoloured

(a) Size 30×41 mm.

1560	41c. Type **429**	70	60
1561	44c. "The Annunciation to the Virgin Mary"	75	60
1562	57c. "The Annunciation to the Shepherds"	1·00	1·10

(b) Size 25×30 mm. Self-adhesive.

1563	41c. "The Nativity"	1·00	60

430 Labrador Puppies

2003. Greetings Stamps. Baby Animals. Multicoloured

(a) 29×40 mm.

1564	41c. Type **430**	80	65

(b) Designs 24×29 mm. Self-adhesive.

1565	41c. Type **430**	80	80
1566	41c. Chicks	80	80
1567	41c. Kids	80	80
1568	41c. Kittens	80	80
1569	41c. Baby rabbits	80	80

2003. Chinese New Year ("Year of the Goat"). Designs as Nos. 1566/8, but 29×40 mm.
MS1570 124×74 mm. 50c. Chicks; 50c.
Kids; 50c. Kittens ... 3·75 4·50

431 St. Patrick

2003. St. Patrick's Day. Multicoloured

(a) Size 29×40 mm.

1571	41c. Type **431**	80	60
1572	50c. St. Patrick's Day Parade passing St. Patrick's Cathedral, Dublin	95	1·00
1573	57c. St. Patrick's Day Parade, New York	1·10	1·25

(b) Size 25×26 mm. Self-adhesive.

1574	41c. St. Patrick	85	90
1575	50c. St. Patrick's Day Parade passing St. Patrick's Cathedral, Dublin	85	1·00
1576	57c. St. Patrick's Day Parade, New York	95	1·25

432 Seven-spotted Ladybird

2003. Irish Beetles. Multicoloured.

1577	41c. Type **432**	90	65
1578	50c. Great diving beetle	1·00	70
1579	57c. Leaf beetle	1·25	80
1580	€1 Green tiger beetle	2·25	2·50
MS1581	150×68 mm. €2 Type **432**	3·75	4·50

433 Dingle Peninsula ("IRELAND for HOLIDAYS")

2003. Europa. Poster Art. Posters by Paul Henry. Multicoloured.

1582	41c. Type **433**	80	65
1583	57c. Connemara ("IRELAND THIS YEAR")	95	1·10

434 "2003" and EYPD Logo

2003. European Year of People with Disabilities.

1584	**434**	41c. multicoloured	80	65

435 Athletes waving to Crowd

2003. 11th Special Olympics World Summer Games, Dublin. Multicoloured.

1585	41c. Type **435**	75	45
1586	50c. Swimmer	80	60
1587	57c. Athlete on starting block	95	65
1588	€1 Athlete running	2·25	3·25

436 Napier

2003. Centenary of Gordon Bennett Race in Ireland. Racing cars of 1903. Multicoloured

(a) Ordinary gum. Size 39×29 mm.

1589	41c. Type **436**	80	1·00
1590	41c. Mercedes	80	1·00
1591	41c. Mors	80	1·00
1592	41c. Winton	80	1·00

(b) Self-adhesive. Size 36×25 mm.

1593	41c. As No. 1592	80	90
1594	41c. As No. 1591	80	90
1595	41c. As No. 1590	80	90
1596	41c. Type **436**	80	90

437 Henry Ford and Model T Ford, 1908–28

2003. Centenary of the Ford Motor Company.

1597	**437**	41c. multicoloured	80	65

438 Harry Ferguson flying first Irish Monoplane, 1909

2003. Centenary of Powered Flight. Multicoloured.

1598	41c. Type **438**	80	60
1599	50c. Alcock and Brown's Vickers FB.27 Vimy over Galway after first transatlantic flight, 1919	1·10	80
1600	57c. *Wright Flyer I*, 1903	1·25	1·50
1601	57c. Lillian Bland's biplane, 1910	1·25	1·50
MS1602	150×90 mm. €5 As No. 1600	8·50	10·00

439 Robert Emmet

2003. Centenary of Rebellion of 1803. Multicoloured.

1603	41c. Type **439**	80	60
1604	50c. Thomas Russell	1·10	1·10
1605	57c. Anne Devlin	1·40	1·60

2003. 140th Anniv of National Gallery of Ireland (2004) (2nd issue). Paintings. As T **426** but vert. Multicoloured.

1606	48c. *Self-portrait as Timanthes* (James Barry)	1·00	1·25
1607	48c. *Man writing a Letter* (Gabriel Metsu)	1·00	1·25
1608	48c. *Woman reading a Letter* (Gabriel Metsu)	1·00	1·25
1609	48c. *Woman seen from the Back* (Jean-Antoine Watteau)	1·00	1·25

440 Frank O'Connor

2003. Birth Centenary of Frank O'Connor (writer).

1610	**440** 50c. multicoloured	1·00	1·00

441 E. T. S. Walton

2003. Birth Centenary of E. T. S. Walton (Nobel Prize for Physics, 1951).

1611	**441** 57c. cream, black and brown	1·00	1·00

442 Admiral William Brown (founder of the Argentine Navy)

2003. Irish Mariners. Multicoloured

(a) Ordinary gum. Size 40×29 mm.

1612	48c. Type **442**	1·25	1·25
1613	48c. Commodore John Barry (Commanding Officer of US Navy, 1794–1803)	1·25	1·25
1614	57c. Captain Robert Halpin (Commander of cable ship *Great Eastern*)	1·40	1·40
1615	57c. Captain Richard Roberts (captain of *Sirius*, first scheduled passenger steamship London to New York voyage)	1·40	1·40
MS1616	150×90 mm. €5 Commodore John Barry	8·00	8·50

(b) Self-adhesive. Size 36×21 mm.

1617	48c. Commodore John Barry	1·10	1·40
1618	48c. Admiral William Brown	1·10	1·40
1619	48c. Captain Robert Halpin	1·10	1·40
1620	48c. Captain Richard Roberts	1·10	1·40

443 Pope John Paul II

2003. 25th Anniv of the Election of Pope John Paul II. Multicoloured.

1621	48c. Type **443**	1·25	90
1622	50c. Pope in St. Peter's Square, Rome	1·40	95
1623	57c. Making speech at United Nations	1·50	1·40

444 Angel

2003. Christmas. Multicoloured

(a) Ordinary gum.

1624	48c. Flight into Egypt (32×32 mm)	90	80
1625	50c. Type **444**	95	80
1626	57c. Three Kings	1·10	1·25

(b) Self-adhesive. Size 29×24 mm.

1627	48c. Nativity	1·00	70

445 Boyne Bridge

2004. Ireland's Presidency of European Union.

1628	**445** 48c. multicoloured	1·50	1·00

446 "Monkeys in Love"

2004. Greetings Stamps. Animals. Multicoloured

(a) Ordinary gum. Size 29×39 mm.

1629	48c. Type **446**	1·50	1·25
MS1630	124×74 mm. 60c. Type **446**; 60c. "Jolly Panda"; 60c. "Cute Koalas"	3·50	3·75

(b) Self-adhesive. Size 24×29 mm.

1631	48c. Type **446**	1·00	1·00
1632	48c. "Jolly Panda"	1·00	1·00
1633	48c. "Cute Koalas"	1·00	1·00
1634	48c. "Happy Hippo"	1·00	1·00

447 St. Patrick and Stained Glass Window from Church of the Holy and Undivided Trinity, Magheralin, Co. Down

2004. St. Patrick's Day.

1635	**447** 65c. multicoloured	1·50	1·50

448 Abbey Theatre Logo

2004. Centenary of Abbey Theatre, Dublin.

1636	**448** 48c. multicoloured	1·10	1·10

449 Expedition Members, Dogs and *Endurance* trapped in Ice

2004. 90th Anniv of Shackleton's Antarctic Expedition. Multicoloured.

1637	48c. Type **449**	1·75	1·50
1638	48c. Two crew members, huskies and bow of *Endurance*	1·75	1·50

1639	65c. Crew member looking out of tent	2·50	2·25
1640	65c. Crew members and tented camp on ice	2·50	2·25
MS1641	149×90 mm. €1 As No. 1639; €1 As No. 1640	5·50	5·50

450 Flags, Football and Globe

2004. Centenary of FIFA (Federation Internationale de Football Association).

1642	**450** 60c. multicoloured	1·40	1·40

451 Map of Europe showing Acceding Countries

2004. Enlargement of the European Union.

1643	**451** 65c. multicoloured	2·25	1·40

452 Tufted Duck

2004. Ducks. Multicoloured.

1644	48c. Type **452**	1·00	70
1645	60c. Red-breasted merganser	1·50	1·25
1646	65c. Gadwall	1·50	1·25
1647	€1 Garganey	2·50	2·00
MS1648	150×90 mm. Nos. 1644/7	6·00	6·00

453 Ross Castle, Co. Kerry

2004. Europa. Holidays. Multicoloured.

1649	48c. Type **453**	1·25	70
1650	65c. Cliffs of Moher, Co. Clare	1·50	1·50

454 Emblem

2004. Tenth Anniv of UN International Year of the Family.

1651	**454** 65c. scarlet, yellow and green	1·25	1·50

455 Frog (Daire Lee)

2004. Winning Entries in Children's Painting Competition. Multicoloured.

1652	48c. Type **455**	90	70
1653	60c. *Marmalade Cat* (Cian Colman)	1·25	1·25
1654	65c. *Ralleshin Dipditch* (Daire O'Rourke)	1·25	1·25
1655	€1 *Fish on a Dish* (Ailish Fitzpatrick) (horiz)	1·90	2·00

456 "James Joyce" (Tullio Pericoli)

2004. Centenary of "Leopold Bloom's Adventure" (from Ulysses by James Joyce). Multicoloured.

1656	48c. Type **456**	80	70
1657	65c. James Joyce	1·10	1·40

457 College Entrance

2004. 426th Anniv of Irish College, Paris.

1658	**457** 65c. multicoloured	1·00	1·00

458 LUAS Tram

2004. Introduction of LUAS Tram System, Dublin. Multicoloured.

1659	48c. Type **458**	65	70
1660	48c. People accessing LUAS tram	65	70

459 Javelin Thrower and Olympic Flame

2004. Olympic Games, Athens. Multicoloured.

1661	48c. Type **459**	1·25	70
1662	60c. Discobolus (sculpture, Myron) and Olympic flame	1·50	1·60

460 Two Camogie Players and O'Duffy Cup

2004. Centenary of Camogie (Gaelic game for women). Multicoloured.

1663	48c. Type **460**	95	1·10
1664	48c. Two players and Camogie emblem	95	1·10

461 Common Dog-violet

2004. Wild Flowers. Multicoloured

(a) Ordinary gum. (i) 23 x 26 mm

1665	1c. Bloody crane's-bill	10	10
1666	2c. Irish orchid	10	10
1667	3c. Yellow flag	10	10
1668	4c. Type **461**	10	15
1669	5c. Dandelion	10	15
1670	7c. Fly orchid	15	20
1671	10c. Mountain avens	15	20
1672	12c. Autumn gorse	15	20
1673	20c. Thrift	30	35
1674	25c. Common knapweed	35	40
1675	48c. Daisy	65	70
1676	48c. Primrose	65	70
1677	50c. Biting stonecrop	70	75
1678	55c. Large-flowered butterwort	1·20	1·20
1679	60c. Hawthorn	80	85
1680	65c. Bluebell	90	95

1681	75c. Navelwort	1·00	1·10
1682	78c. Black bog-rush	1·80	1·80
1683	82c. Sea aster	1·20	1·30
1684	90c. Viper's bugloss	1·20	1·30
1685	95c. Purple loosestrife	2·20	2·20

(ii) 26×47 mm (€1, €2) or 47×26 mm (others).

1686	€1 Foxglove	1·40	1·50
1687	€2 Lords-and-ladies	2·75	3·00
1688	€5 Dog-rose	6·75	7·00
1689	€10 Spring Gentian	13·50	14·00

(b) Booklet stamps. Ordinary gum. Size 20×23 mm

1690	5c. Dandelion	45	
1691	25c. Common knapweed	1·00	1·25
1692	55c. Large-flowered butterwort	1·40	1·40

(c) Size 23×29 mm

1693	48c. Daisy	65	65
1694	48c. Primrose	65	65
1695 -	(N) Large-flowered butterwort	1·75	1·75
1696 -	(N) Blue-eyed grass	1·75	1·75
1697 -	55c. Large-flowered butterwort	1·25	1·25
1698 -	75c. Navelwort	1·70	1·70
1699 -	78c. Black bog-rush	1·75	1·75
1699b -	82c. Sea aster	1·80	1·80

(d) Size 20×24 mm. Self-adhesive

1699c	(N) Yellow horned-poppy	1·75	1·75
1699d	55c. Large-flowered butterwort	1·75	1·75
1699e	82c. Sea aster	2·40	2·40

2004. 140th Anniv of National Gallery of Ireland (3rd issue). As T 426. Multicoloured.

1700	48c. "The House Builders" (Walter Osborne)	80	80
1701	48c. "Kitchen Maid with the Supper at Emmaus" (Diego Velazquez)	80	80
1702	48c. "The Lamentation over the Dead Christ" (Nicolas Poussin)	80	80
1703	48c. "The Taking of Christ" (Caravaggio)	80	80

462 William Butler Yeats

2004. Irish Winners of Nobel Prize for Literature. Multicoloured.

1704	(N) Type 462	1·00	1·00
1705	(N) George Bernard Shaw	1·00	1·00
1706	(N) Samuel Beckett	1·00	1·00
1707	(N) Seamus Heaney	1·00	1·00

Nos. 1706 were inscribed "N" and sold for 48c. each. Stamps of similar designs were issued by Sweden.

463 George Fox (Founder of The Society of Friends ("Quakers"))

2004. 350th Anniv of Quakers in Ireland.

1708	463 60c. multicoloured	1·00	1·00

464 Patrick Kavanagh

2004. Birth Centenary of Patrick Kavanagh (poet).

1709	464 48c. green and dull green	1·00	75

465 The Holy Family

2004. Christmas. Multicoloured.

(a) Ordinary gum

1710	48c. Type 465	85	50
1711	60c. The flight into Egypt	1·10	1·25
1712	65c. The Adoration of the Magi	1·25	1·40

(b) Size 24×29 mm. Self-adhesive.

1713	48c. The Holy Family	1·00	70

466 Lovebirds

2005. Love, Greetings and Chinese New Year (Year of the Rooster). Multicoloured

(a) Ordinary gum.

1714	48c. Type 466	1·00	1·00
MS1715	130×74 mm. 60c. Rooster; 60c. Type 466; 60c. Owl	4·00	4·00

(b) Self-adhesive. Designs 30×25 mm.

1716	48c. Rooster	1·50	1·50
1717	48c. Stork	1·50	1·50
1718	48c. Type 466	1·00	1·00
1719	48c. Owl	1·25	1·25

467 St. Patrick

2005. St. Patrick's Day.

1720	467 65c. multicoloured	1·25	1·25

468 Landscape, Co. Wicklow (Evie Hone)

2005. Female Artists. Multicoloured.

1721	48c. Type 468	85	95
1722	48c. Seabird and Landmarks (Nano Reid)	85	95
1723	65c. Three Graces (Gabriel Hayes) (vert)	1·10	1·25
1724	65c. Threshing (Mildred Anne Butler) (vert)	1·10	1·25

469 Statue, City Hall and Churches

2005. Cork—European Capital of Culture 2005. Multicoloured.

1725	48c. Type 469	80	80
1726	48c. Court House and Shandon Steeple (clock tower)	80	80

Nos. 1725/6 were printed together, se-tenant, forming a composite design showing Patrick's Bridge and a montage of landmark buildings and monuments of the city of Cork.

470 William Rowan Hamilton (birth bicentenary)

2005. UNESCO World Year of Physics. Multicoloured.

1727	48c. Type 470	85	70
1728	60c. UNESCO Headquarters, Paris, trees and reflections of sunlight	1·10	1·25
1729	65c. Albert Einstein (50th death anniv)	1·25	1·40

471 201 Class Diesel Locomotive pulling "Enterprise Express" Train

2005. 150th Anniv of Dublin–Belfast Railway. Multicoloured.

1730	48c. Type 471	1·00	1·00
1731	48c. V Class 3 steam locomotive No. 85, Merlin, arriving at Amiens Street (now Connolly) Station, Dublin, c. 1951	1·00	1·00
1732	60c. Q Class steam locomotive No. 131 crossing Boyne Valley viaduct, Drogheda	1·40	1·40
1733	65c. Modern "Enterprise Express" leaving Belfast Central Station	1·40	1·40
MS1734	150×90 mm. Nos. 1730/3	4·25	4·50

472 Red Deer Stags, Killarney National Park, Ireland

2005. Biosphere Reserves. Multicoloured.

1735	48c. Type 472	70	70
1736	65c. Saskatoon Berries and Osprey, Waterton Lakes National Park, Alberta, Canada	1·40	1·50
MS1737	150×90 mm. Nos. 1735/6	2·00	2·50

Stamps in similar designs were issued by Canada.

473 Lamb, Cabbage, Carrots and Potato (ingredients of Irish Stew)

2005. Europa. Gastronomy. Multicoloured.

1738	48c. Type 473	75	70
1739	65c. Oysters	1·00	1·25

474 Small Copper

2005. Butterflies. Multicoloured.

1740	48c. Type 474	75	70
1741	60c. Green hairstreak	95	90
1742	65c. Painted lady	1·00	1·10
1743	€1 Pearl-bordered fritillary	1·90	2·25
MS1744	150×67 mm. €5 As No. 1742	7·50	9·00

475 Dunbrody

2005. Cutty Sark International Tall Ships Race, Waterford. Multicoloured.

1745	48c. Type 475	85	70
1746	60c. Tenacious	1·00	1·10
1747	65c. USCG Eagle	1·10	1·25

476 Glendalough, Co. Wicklow

2005. Round Towers of Ireland. Each black.

1748	48c. Type 476	75	85
1749	48c. Ardmore, Co. Waterford	75	85
1750	48c. Clones, Co. Monaghan	75	85
1751	48c. Kilmacduagh, Co. Galway	75	85

Nos. 1748/51 commemorate the 75th Anniversary of the Monuments of Ireland Act.

477 Bees on Honeycomb

2005. Apimondia 2005 (international bee-keeping conference and exhibition), Dublin.

1752	477 65c. multicoloured	1·25	1·25

478 Eamonn Darcy, Christy O'Connor Jnr and Philip Walton holding Ryder Cup

2005. Ireland and the Ryder Cup (golf tournament). Multicoloured.

1753	48c. Type 478	1·25	1·25
1754	48c. Darren Clarke, Paul McGinley and Padraig Harrington with Ryder Cup	1·25	1·25
1755	60c. Harry Bradshaw, Ronan Rafferty and Christy O'Connor Snr	1·50	1·50
1756	65c. The K Club, Straffan, Co. Kildare (venue of 2006 Ryder Cup)	1·50	1·50

479 Erskine Childers

2005. Birth Centenary of Erskine Childers (President of Ireland 1973–4).

1757	479 48c. multicoloured	75	75

480 An Garda Siochana on Overseas Duty

2005. 50th Anniv of Ireland's Membership of United Nations. Multicoloured.

1758	48c. Type 480	1·00	1·00
1759	48c. Irish Army medical aid in East Timor	1·00	1·00
1760	60c. F. H. Boland (signatory of Ireland's membership), 1955	1·25	1·25
1761	65c. Member of Irish Defence Force in classroom, Lebanon	1·25	1·25

481 "Arthur Griffith" (Leo Whelan) and Title Page of Essay

2005. Centenary of Arthur Griffith's Essays The Resurrection of Hungary: A Parallel for Ireland.

1762	481 48c. multicoloured	75	75

482 Nativity

2005. Christmas. Multicoloured

(a) Ordinary gum.

1763	48c. Type 482	80	50
1764	60c. Choir of angels with harp	1·10	1·25
1765	65c. Choir of angels with tambourine and trumpet	1·25	1·50

(b) Size 24×29 mm. Self-adhesive.

1766	48c. Type 482	85	80

483 Patrick Gallagher (founder) and Templecrone Co-operative Store

2006. Centenary of the Templecrone Co-operative Agricultural Society ("The Cope").

| 1767 | **483** | 48c. multicoloured | 85 | 85 |

484 Red Setter and Couple Embracing

2006. Love, Greetings and Chinese New Year of the Dog. Multicoloured.

(a) Ordinary gum.

| 1768 | | 48c. Type **484** | 1·00 | 85 |
| **MS**1769 | | 130×74 mm. 65c. Two Chinese crested dogs; 65c. As No. 1768.; 65c. Golden labrador | 5·00 | 5·00 |

(b) Self-adhesive. Size 29×24 mm.

1770		48c. Two Chinese crested dogs	1·75	1·75
1771		48c. Golden Labrador	1·75	1·75
1772		48c. Type **484**	1·75	1·75
1773		48c. Red setter puppy	1·75	1·75

485 St. Patrick lights the Paschal Fire at Slane (Sean Keating)

2006. St. Patrick's Day.

| 1774 | **485** | 65c. multicoloured | 1·75 | 1·25 |

486 Sessile Oak (*Quercus petraea*)

2006. Trees of Ireland. Multicoloured.

1775		48c. Type **486**	60	85
1776		60c. Yew (*Taxus baccata*)	1·10	1·10
1777		75c. Ash (*Fraxinus excelsior*)	1·40	1·40
1778		€1 Strawberry-tree (*Arbutus unedo*)	1·75	2·00
MS1779		150×90 mm. Nos. 1775/8	6·50	6·50

487 St. Hubert, Church of Ireland, Carnalway, Co. Kildare

2006. 75th Death Anniv of Harry Clarke (stained glass artist).

| 1780 | **487** | 48c. multicoloured | 1·00 | 85 |

488 General Post Office, Dublin

2006. 90th Anniv of the Easter Rising.

| 1781 | **488** | 48c. multicoloured | 1·00 | 85 |

489 Children waving Irish and EU Flags (Katie McMillan)

2006. Europa. Winning Entries in Children's Stamp Design Competition. Multicoloured.

| 1782 | | 48c. Type **489** | 1·25 | 60 |
| 1783 | | 75c. Flags of EU members in flowers (Sarah Naughter) | 1·60 | 2·25 |

490 EU Flag

2006. Tenth Anniv of European Union Flag.

| 1784 | **490** | 48c. multicoloured | 1·00 | 85 |

491 Interior of University Church (Dr. Thomas Ryan)

2006. 150th Anniv of University Church, St. Stephen's Green, Dublin.

| 1785 | **491** | 48c. multicoloured | 1·00 | 75 |

492 Mairtin O Cadhain (Irish language writer) (birth centenary)

2006. Celtic Scholars. Multicoloured.

| 1786 | | 48c. Type **492** | 1·00 | 1·00 |
| 1787 | | 48c. Johann Caspar Zeus (Celtic languages researcher) (birth bicentenary) | 1·00 | 1·00 |

493 Pebbles and Typewriter Keyboard

2006. 50th Anniv of the Department of the Gaeltacht.

| 1788 | **493** | 48c. multicoloured | 1·00 | 75 |

494 Emblem

2006. Tenth Anniv of TG4 (Teilifíse Gaeilge 4) Television Channel.

| 1789 | **494** | 48c. multicoloured | 1·00 | 75 |

495 St. David (ferry), 1906

2006. Centenary of the Rosslare–Fishguard Ferry Service. Multicoloured.

1790		48c. Type **495**	1·50	1·50
1791		48c. *Stena Lynx* (ferry), 2006	1·50	1·50
MS1792		150×90 mm. Nos. 1790/1	3·00	3·00

496 *The Battle of the Somme* (36th Ulster Division)" (J. P. Beadle)

2006. 90th Anniv of the Battle of the Somme.

| 1793 | **496** | 75c. multicoloured | 3·00 | 2·50 |

497 Guide Dog

2006. 30th Anniv of Irish Guide Dogs for the Blind.

| 1794 | **497** | 48c. multicoloured | 1·75 | 1·25 |

498 Golf Ball on Tee

2006. Ryder Cup Golf Tournament, K Club, Straffan, Co. Kildare (1st issue). Multicoloured

(a) Ordinary gum

1795		48c. Type **498**	1·40	1·40
1796		48c. Golf ball in the rough	1·40	1·40
1797		48c. Golf ball in bunker	1·40	1·40
1798		48c. Golf ball at edge of green	1·40	1·40
MS1799		150×90 mm. Nos. 1795/8	5·00	5·00

(b) Self-adhesive. Size 24×29 mm.

1800		48c. Type **498**	1·40	1·40
1801		48c. As No. 1796	1·40	1·40
1802		48c. As No. 1797	1·40	1·40
1803		48c. As No. 1798	1·40	1·40

See also No. **MS**1808.

499 *Ronnie Delany* (Dr. Thomas Ryan)

2006. 50th Anniv of Ronnie Delany's Gold Medal for 1500 Metres at Olympic Games, Melbourne.

| 1804 | **499** | 48c. multicoloured | 1·00 | 75 |

500 Michael Cusack

2006. Death Centenary of Michael Cusack (founder of Gaelic Athletic Association).

| 1805 | **500** | 48c. multicoloured | 1·00 | 75 |

501 *Michael Davitt* (Sir William Orpen)

2006. Death Centenary of Michael Davitt (founder of Irish National Land League).

| 1806 | **501** | 48c. multicoloured | 1·00 | 75 |

502 RTE National Symphony Orchestra

2006. 25th Anniv of National Concert Hall, Dublin.

| 1807 | **502** | 48c. multicoloured | 1·00 | 75 |

503 Teeing Off

2006. Ryder Cup Golf Tournament, K Club, Straffan, Co. Kildare (2nd issue). Sheet 140×102 mm containing T **503** and similar horiz design. Multicoloured. Self-adhesive.

| **MS**1808 | | 75c. Type **503**; 75c. In bunker | 4·50 | 5·00 |

504 River Barrow at Graiguenamanagh, Co. Kilkenny

2006. Inland Waterways. Multicoloured.

1809		75c. Type **504**	1·60	1·90
1810		75c. Belturbet Marina, River Erne, Co. Cavan	1·60	1·90
1811		75c. Lock-keepers cottage on Grand Canal, Cornalour, Co. Offaly	1·60	1·90
1812		75c. River Shannon at Meelick Quay	1·60	1·90

505 The Chieftains

2006. Irish Music (1st series). Multicoloured.

1813		48c. Type **505**	1·25	1·00
1814		48c. The Dubliners	1·25	1·00
1815		75c. The Clancy Brothers and Tommy Makem	1·75	2·00
1816		75c. Altan	1·75	2·00
MS1817		150×90 mm. Nos. 1813/16	5·50	6·50

See also Nos. 1919/23.

506 Madonna and Child   **507** *The Nativity* (Simon Bening)

2006. Christmas. Multicoloured

(a) Ordinary gum.

| 1818 | | 48c. Type **506** | 1·00 | 50 |
| 1819 | | 75c. Shepherd with lamb | 1·75 | 2·25 |

(b) Self-adhesive. Size 22×30 mm.

| 1820 | | 48c. Type **507** | 1·25 | 60 |

2006. Belgica 2006 International Stamp Exhibition, Brussels. No. MS1817 with Belgica '06 emblem and "16–20 November, 2006" added to the sheet margin.

| **MS**1821 | | 150×90 mm. Nos. 1813/16 | 5·50 | 6·50 |

2006. MonacoPhil 2006 International Stamp Exhibition. No. MS1817 with MonacoPhil 2006 emblem and "1–3 December, 2006" added to the sheet margin.

| **MS**1822 | | 150×90 mm. Nos. 1813/16 | 5·50 | 6·50 |

508 Franciscan and Door to Auditorium of Irish College

2007. 400th Anniv of the Irish Franciscan College, Louvain, Belgium.
1823 **508** 75c. multicoloured — 1·75 2·25

509 Father Luke Wadding

2007. 350th Death Anniv of Father Luke Wadding (theologian).
1824 **509** 75c. multicoloured — 1·75 2·25

510 Linked Hands

2007. Weddings (1st issue). Chalk-surfaced paper. Self-adhesive.
1825 **510** (N) multicoloured — 1·00 70

No. 1825 is inscribed "N" and was sold for 48c. each. See also Nos. 1862, 1880 and 1929.

511 Cartoon Stamp and Heart

2007. Greetings Stamps. Multicoloured. Self-adhesive.
1826 (48c.) Type **511** — 1·10 70
1827 (48c.) Birthday cake — 1·10 70

Nos. 1826/7 are inscribed "N" and sold for 48c. each.

512 Two Pigs

2007. Chinese New Year ("Year of the Pig").
1828 **512** 75c. multicoloured — 1·75 2·25
MS1829 130×74 mm. 75c.×2 Type **512**; 75c. As Type **512** but green background — 5·25 6·75

513 Shamrock

2007. St. Patrick's Day.
1830 **513** 75c. multicoloured — 2·00 2·50

514 Hugh O'Neill, Earl of Tyrone

2007. 400th Anniv of the Flight of the Earls. Multicoloured.
1831 48c. Type **514** — 1·00 1·25
1832 48c. Rory O'Donnell, Earl of Tyrconnell — 1·00 1·25
MS1833 150×90 mm. Nos. 1831/2 — 2·25 2·50

Nos. 1831/2 were printed together, se-tenant, forming a composite background design showing Lough Swilly and map of Europe.

515 Trim Castle, Co. Meath

2007. Castles. Multicoloured.
1834 55c. Type **515** — 1·50 1·50

1835 55c. Dunluce Castle, Co. Antrim — 1·50 1·50
1836 55c. Lismore Castle, Co. Waterford — 1·50 1·50
1837 55c. Portumna Castle, Co. Galway — 1·50 1·50
MS1838 150×90 mm. Nos. 1834/7 — 5·50 5·50

516 EU Flag, Signatures and Palazzo dei Conservatori, Rome

2007. 50th Anniv of the Treaty of Rome.
1839 **516** 55c. multicoloured — 1·25 1·25

517 Girl Scout at Campsite, c. 2007

2007. Europa. Centenary of Scouting. Multicoloured.
1840 55c. Type **517** — 1·50 75
1841 78c. Boy scout camping, c. 1907 — 2·00 2·50

518 Jupiter

2007. The Planets (1st series). Multicoloured.
1842 55c. Type **518** — 1·40 1·50
1843 55c. Neptune — 1·40 1·50
1844 78c. Saturn — 1·90 2·25
1845 78c. Uranus — 1·90 2·25
MS1846 150×90 mm. Nos. 1842/5 — 6·00 6·75

Nos. 1842/3 and 1844/5 were printed together, se-tenant, forming a composite design showing Planet Earth.

519 St. Charles of Mount Argus, Dublin

2007. Canonisation of Blessed Charles of Mount Argus.
1847 **519** 55c. multicoloured — 1·25 1·25

520 Anniversary Emblem

2007. 50th Anniv of the IPA (Institute of Public Administration).
1848 **520** 55c. multicoloured — 1·25 1·25

521 RTE National Symphony Orchestra

2007. RTE Performing Groups. Multicoloured. Ordinary or self-adhesive gum.
1849 55c. Type **521** — 1·40 1·50
1850 55c. RTE Concert Orchestra — 1·40 1·50
1851 55c. RTE Vanbrugh Quartet — 1·40 1·50
1852 55c. RTE Philharmonic Choir — 1·40 1·50
1853 55c. RTE Cor na nOg children's choir — 1·40 1·50

---

522 Society Seal and Gandon Facade of King's Inns Building

2007. 400th Anniv of Revival of the Honourable Society of King's Inns.
1859 **522** 55c. multicoloured — 1·25 1·25

523 Bound Books containing Records in Registry of Deeds

2007. 300th Anniv of the Registry of Deeds Act.
1860 **523** 78c. multicoloured — 1·75 1·75

524 Girls Choir from Colaiste Iosagain, Co. Dublin

2007. Centenary of the National Anthem.
1861 **524** 55c. multicoloured — 1·25 1·25

2007. Weddings (2nd issue). As T **510** but new value. Self-adhesive.
1862 55c. As Type **510** — 1·25 1·25

525 Skuldelev 2 (Viking longship)

2007. Voyage of the Havhingsten fra Glendalough (replica of Viking longship Skuldelev 2) from Denmark to Dublin. Multicoloured.
1863 55c. Type **525** — 1·25 1·25
MS1864 150×90 mm. €3 Havhingsten fra Glendalough (replica Viking longship) — 6·75 7·50

526 Paul O'Connell

2007. Rugby World Cup, France. Multicoloured.
1865 55c. Type **526** — 1·40 1·25
1866 78c. Irish players in lineout, Croke Park, 2007 — 2·25 2·50
MS1867 Two sheets, each 150×90 mm. (a) No. 1865. (b) No. 1866 Set of 2 sheets — 3·00 3·50

527 'Fat Cat'

2007. Celtic Cats. Multicoloured.
1868 55c. Type **527** — 1·25 1·50
1869 55c. Celtic Tigress — 1·25 1·50
1870 78c. Cool Cats — 2·00 2·25
1871 78c. Kilkenny Cat — 2·00 2·25
MS1872 150×90 mm. As Nos. 1868/71 but 18×18 mm — 6·00 6·75

---

528 Fr. Joseph Mullooly in 4th-century Basilica, San Clemente, Rome

2007. 150th Anniv of Archaeological Discoveries, San Clemente, Rome.
1873 **528** 55c. multicoloured — 1·25 1·25

529 James Fintan Lalor

2007. Birth Bicentenary of James Fintan Lalor (nationalist and journalist).
1874 **529** 55c. multicoloured — 1·25 1·25

530 Giant Elk Antlers

2007. 150th Anniv of the Natural History Museum, Dublin.
1875 **530** 55c. multicoloured — 1·25 1·25

531 The Presentation in the Temple

2007. Christmas. Multicoloured

(a) Ordinary gum.
1876 55c. Type **531** — 1·25 75
1877 78c. The Three Magi — 2·00 3·50

(b) Self-adhesive. Size 24×29 mm.
1878 55c. The Adoration of the Shepherds — 1·25 1·25

532 Charles Wesley (The Lily Portrait)

2007. 300th Birth Anniv of Charles Wesley (founder of Methodism and hymn writer).
1879 **532** 78c. multicoloured — 1·90 2·25

533 Bride and Groom Embracing

2008. Weddings (3rd issue). Self-adhesive.
1880 **533** 55c. multicoloured — 1·25 1·40

534 Rat and Candle

2008. Chinese New Year ('Year of the Rat').
1881 **534** 78c. multicoloured — 2·00 2·25
MS1882 130×74 mm. No. 1881×3 — 5·75 6·50

535 Liam Whelan and Munich Memorial Clock, Old Trafford, Manchester

2008. 50th Anniv of the Munich Air Disaster.
| 1883 | **535** | 55c. multicoloured | 2·00 | 1·40 |

536 Juggling Frog

2008. Greetings Stamps. Multicoloured. Self-adhesive.
| 1884 | | 55c. Trumpeting elephant | 2·00 | 2·25 |
| 1885 | | 55c. Type **536** | 1·40 | 1·40 |

537 St. Patrick (line engraving by Leonard Gaultier)

2008. St. Patrick's Day.
| 1886 | **537** | 78c. multicoloured | 2·00 | 2·25 |

No. 1886 is based on a drawing made in 1619 by Thomas Messingham.

538 Logo

2008. European Year of Intercultural Dialogue.
| 1887 | **538** | 55c. multicoloured | 1·40 | 1·40 |

539 *Hugh Lane* (Antonio Mancini)

2008. Centenary of Hugh Lane Gallery, Dublin.
| 1888 | **539** | 55c. multicoloured | 1·40 | 1·40 |

540 *West of Ireland Landscape*

2008. Paul Henry Landscape Paintings. Multicoloured.
1889		55c. Type **540** (signature at left)	1·75	1·75
1890		55c. *West of Ireland Landscape* (rocks in foreground, signature at right)	1·75	1·75
1891		55c. *A Connemara Village* (signature at left)	1·75	1·75
1892		55c. *A Connemara Village* (signature at right)	1·75	1·75

Nos. 1889/92 commemorate the 50th death anniversary of Paul Henry.

541 Logo of Irish League of Credit Unions (ILCU)

2008. 50th Anniv of the Credit Union Movement in Ireland.
| 1893 | **541** | 55c. multicoloured | 1·50 | 1·50 |

542 World Map showing Africa and Asia (Mohammed Rahman)

2008. International Year of Planet Earth. Showing children's plasticine models of Planet Earth. Multicoloured. Self-adhesive.
| 1894 | | 55c. Type **542** | 1·50 | 1·50 |
| 1895 | | 55c. World map showing the Americas and Atlantic Ocean (Conor Reid) | 1·40 | 1·40 |

543 '50'

2008. 50th Anniv of the Institute of Creative Advertising and Design (ICAD).
| 1896 | **543** | 55c. multicoloured | 1·50 | 1·50 |

544 RMS *Leinster*

2008. 90th Anniv of the Sinking of RMS *Leinster*.
| 1897 | **544** | 55c. multicoloured | 2·00 | 1·50 |

545 Boy writing Letter

2008. Europa. The Letter. Multicoloured.
| 1898 | | 55c. Type **545** | 1·50 | 1·50 |
| 1899 | | 82c. Girl writing letter | 2·00 | 2·00 |

546 Aughrim, Co. Wicklow (2007 winner)

2008. 50th Anniv of the Tidy Towns Competition.
| 1900 | **546** | 55c. multicoloured | 1·50 | 1·50 |

547 Lt. Col. McCarthy, Comdt. Higgins, Capt. Lavelle, Comdt. Coughlan and Capt. Henderson

2008. 50th Anniv of the First Irish Defence Forces Mission to the UN.
| 1901 | **547** | 55c. multicoloured | 2·00 | 1·50 |

548 Colm Meaney in *Kings*

2008. Filmed in Ireland. Multicoloured.
1902		55c. Type **548**	1·50	1·50
1903		55c. Brid Ni Neachtain in *Cre Na Cille*	1·50	1·50
1904		82c. Cillian Murphy in *The Wind that Shakes the Barley*	2·10	2·10
1905		82c. Pat Shortt in *Garage*	2·10	2·10
MS1906	150×90 mm. Nos. 1902/5		7·25	8·00

549 Rowing

2008. Olympic Games, Beijing. Multicoloured.
1907		55c. Type **549**	1·50	1·50
1908		82c. Shot-putt	2·00	2·00
MS1909	150×90 mm. As Nos. 1907/8 optd 'Olympex 2008'		3·50	4·00

549a Lock-keeper's Cottage on Grand Canal, Cornalaur, Co. Offaly

2008. Inland Waterways. Multicoloured.
1909a		55c. Type **549a**	1·60	1·60
1909b		55c. Belturbet Marina, River Erne, Co. Cavan	1·60	1·60
1909c		55c. River Barrow at Graiguenamanagh, Co. Kilkenny	1·60	1·60
1909d		55c. River Shannon, Meelick Quay	1·60	1·60

550 Parasol (*Macrolepiota procera*)

2008. Fungi. Multicoloured.
1910		55c. Type **550**	1·50	1·50
1911		55c. Orange birch bolete (*Leccinum versipelle*)	1·50	1·50
1912		82c. Pink waxcap (*Hygrocybe calyptriformis*)	2·00	2·00
MS1913	150×67 mm. 95c. Scarlet elfcup (*Sarcoscypha austriaca*)		3·50	4·00

551 HMS *Agamemnon* and USS *Niagra* laying Cable, 1858

2008. 150th Anniv of the First Transatlantic Cable Message.
| 1914 | **551** | 82c. multicoloured | 2·75 | 2·75 |

552 'STATE PENSIOON'

2008. Centenary of the Old Age Pensions Act.
| 1915 | **552** | 55c. multicoloured | 1·50 | 1·50 |

553 Open Books forming Star

2008. Centenary of the National University of Ireland.
| 1916 | **553** | 55c. multicoloured | 1·50 | 1·50 |

554 Padraic Mac Piarais and Cullenswood House, Ranelagh, Dublin, 1908–10

2008. Centenary of Opening of Scoil Eanna (bilingual Irish/English school). Showing founder and school premises. Multicoloured.
| 1917 | | 55c. Type **554** | 1·50 | 1·50 |
| 1918 | | 55c. Padraic Mac Piarais and The Hermitage, Rathfarnham, 1910–35 | 1·50 | 1·50 |

555 Planxty

2008. Irish Music (2nd series). Multicoloured.
1919		55c. Type **555**	1·75	1·75
1920		55c. De Dannan	1·75	1·75
1921		82c. Tulla Ceili Band	2·25	2·25
1922		82c. The Bothy Band	2·25	2·25
MS1923	150×90 mm. Nos. 1919/22		7·25	8·00

556 Irish Dancer

2008. Traditional Dances. Multicoloured.
| 1924 | | 55c. Type **556** | 1·50 | 1·50 |
| **MS**1925 | 150×90 mm. No. 1924; 82c. Flamenco dancer | | 4·00 | 4·50 |

Stamps in a similar design were issued by Spain.

557 The Flight into Egypt

2008. Christmas. Multicoloured

    (a) Ordinary gum.
| 1926 | | 55c. Type **557** | 1·75 | 1·50 |
| 1927 | | 82c. The Annunciation | 2·25 | 2·50 |

    (b) Self-adhesive. Size 25×30 mm.
| 1928 | | 55c. Infant Jesus in manger | 1·50 | 1·50 |

558 Pair of Wedding Rings

2009. Weddings (4th issue). Self-adhesive.
| 1929 | **558** | 55c. multicoloured | 1·60 | 1·60 |

Éire 55c
Louis Braille (1809–1852)

559 Eye

2009. Birth Bicentenary of Louis Braille (inventor of Braille writing for the blind).
| 1930 | **559** | 55c. black | 2·25 | 1·60 |

No. 1930 has 'Eire' and '55c' in Braille.

560 Ox

2009. Chinese New Year ('Year of the Ox').
| 1931 | **560** | 82c. multicoloured | 2·50 | 2·50 |
| **MS**1932 | 130×74 mm. No. 1931×3 | | 7·25 | 8·00 |

561 *St. Patrick Climbs Croagh Patrick* (Margaret Clarke)

2009. St. Patrick's Day.
1933 **561** 82c. multicoloured 2·50 2·50

562 Little Girl posting Card, helped by her Father

2009. Greetings Stamps. Multicoloured. Self-adhesive.
1934 55c. Type **562** 1·60 1·60
1935 55c. Girl with opened birthday card and dog 1·60 1·60

563 *Charles Darwin* (pen and ink drawing, Harry Furniss)

2009. Birth Bicentenary of Charles Darwin (naturalist and evolutionary theorist).
1936 **563** 82c. multicoloured 2·40 2·40

564 Scene from *The Playboy of the Western World* (Sean Keating)

2009. Death Centenary of John Millington Synge (writer).
1937 **564** 55c. multicoloured 1·60 1·60

565 *Irish Times* Clock

2009. 150th Anniv of *The Irish Times* (newspaper).
1938 **565** 55c. multicoloured 1·60 1·60

566 Girl writing Letter

2009. 25th Anniv of An Post. Multicoloured. Self-adhesive

(a) Size 25×30 mm.
1939 55c. Type **566** 2·00 2·00
1940 55c. Girl posting letter 2·00 2·00
1941 55c. Postman emptying pillar box 2·00 2·00
1942 55c. Woman at post office counter 2·00 2·00
1943 55c. An Post van and lorry 2·00 2·00
1944 55c. Flying letters 2·00 2·00
1945 55c. Postman with trolley 2·00 2·00
1946 55c. Postman with mail 2·00 2·00
1947 55c. Seán Kelly cycling team sponsored by An Post 2·00 2·00
1948 55c. G.P.O., Dublin 2·00 2·00

(b) Size 20×24 mm.
1949 55c. As Type **566** 1·60 2·00
1950 55c. As No. 1940 1·60 2·00
1951 55c. As No. 1941 1·60 2·00
1952 55c. As No. 1942 1·60 2·00
1953 55c. As No. 1943 1·60 2·00
1954 55c. As No. 1944 1·60 2·00
1955 55c. As No. 1945 1·60 2·00
1956 55c. As No. 1946 1·60 2·00
1957 55c. As No. 1947 1·60 2·00
1958 55c. As No. 1948 1·60 2·00

567 *Self-portrait*, 1969

2009. Birth Centenary of Francis Bacon (artist). Multicoloured.
1959 55c. Type **567** 1·60 1·60
MS1960 150×90 mm. 82c. Francis Bacon's studio 2·40 2·75

568 James Larkin (union organiser) addressing Crowd, c. 1908

2009. Centenary of IT&GWU (Irish Transport and General Workers Union).
1961 **568** 55c. multicoloured 1·60 1·60

569 *Green Dragon* (Irish entry)

2009. Volvo Ocean Race. Multicoloured.
1962 55c. Type **569** 1·60 1·60
MS1963 150×90 mm. €3 *Green Dragon* and other yachts (27×47 mm) 8·75 9·50

570 Crab Nebula

2009. Europa. Astronomy. Multicoloured.
1964 55c. Type **570** 1·60 1·60
1965 82c. Brown dwarf 2·40 2·40

571 CEPT Logo, '50', Telephone Dial and Pillar Box

2009. 50th Anniv of CEPT (European Conference of Postal and Telecommunications Administration).
1966 **571** 82c. multicoloured 2·25 2·25

572 'Aberann Conan' (Glen of Imaal terrier)

2009. European Dog Show, Dublin.
1967 **572** 55c. multicoloured 1·50 1·50

573 Castle and St. John's Bridge, Kilkenny City

2009. 400th Anniv of City Status for Kilkenny.
1968 **573** 55c. multicoloured 1·75 1·50

574 *Anthony Trollope* (from albumen print by Julia Margaret Cameron, 1864)

2009. Anthony Trollope (novelist) Commemoration.
1969 **574** 82c. multicoloured 2·25 2·25

575 *Augustine Birrell* (Sir Leslie Ward)

2009. Centenary of the Birrell Land Act (Irish Land Act).
1970 **575** 82c. multicoloured 2·25 2·25

576 *Wolfgang Amadeus Mozart* (Josef Grassi) and Overture of Opera *Don Giovanni*

2009. Classical Composers. Each showing composer and score. Multicoloured.
1971 55c. Type **576** 1·60 1·60
1972 55c. *George Frideric Handel* (Thomas Hudson, 1736) and last folio from opera *Susanna*, 1748 1·60 1·60
1973 82c. *Joseph Haydn* (John Carl Rossler, 1799) and Symphony No. 95 2·25 2·25
1974 82c. *Frederic Chopin* (Ary Scheffer) and Ballade Number 2 in F 2·25 2·25
MS1975 150×90 mm. Nos. 1971/4 7·50 8·00

577 Arthur Guinness (founder)

2009. 250th Anniv of the Guinness Brewery.
1976 **577** 82c. multicoloured 2·40 2·40

578 'Plantation of Ulster 1609' in Irish

2009. 400th Anniv of the Plantation of Ulster. Multicoloured.
1977 55c. Type **578** 1·60 1·60
1978 55c. 'PLANTATION of ULSTER 1609' in English 1·60 1·60

579 Brian Friel

2009. Modern Irish Playwrights. Multicoloured.
1979 55c. Type **579** 1·90 1·90
1980 55c. Frank McGuinness 1·90 1·90
1981 55c. Tom Murphy 1·90 1·90

580 Irish Bluet (*Coenagrion lunulatum*)

2009. Dragonflies. Multicoloured.
1982 55c. Type **580** 1·75 1·90
1983 55c. Large red damselfly (*Pyrrhosoma nymphula*) 1·75 1·90
1984 82c. Four-spotted chaser (*Libellula quadrimaculata*) (horiz) 2·75 3·00
MS1985 150×65 mm. 95c. Banded demoiselle (*Calopteryx splendens*) (60×26 mm) 2·75 3·00

581 Nativity

2009. Christmas. Illustrations from the Gospel Book, Gamaghiel Monastery, Khizan (1986/7) or the Rosarium of King Philip II of Spain (1988). Multicoloured designs showing illustrations

(a) Ordinary gum.
1986 55c. Type **581** 1·60 1·00
1987 82c. Annunciation 2·40 3·00

(b) Size 25×30 mm. Self-adhesive.
1988 55c. *Virgin and Child* (Simon Bening) 1·60 1·60

The images on Nos. 1986/7 come from the *Gospel Book* from the Monastery of Gamaghiel, Khizan, and on No. 1988 from the Rosarium of Philip II, King of Spain.

582 Dr. Douglas Hyde

2010. 150th Birth Anniv of Douglas Hyde (first President of Ireland 1938–45).
1989 **582** 55c. multicoloured 1·50 1·50

583 Pair of Stylised 'Lovebirds'

2010. Weddings (5th issue). Self-adhesive.
1990 **583** 55c. multicoloured 1·75 1·75

584 Boy Astronaut and Heart

2010. Greetings Stamps. Multicoloured.
1991 55c. Type **584** 1·75 1·75
1992 55c. Girl astronaut riding rocket and birthday cake 1·75 1·75

585 Tiger (18th century Tibetan painting)

2010. Chinese New Year. Year of the Tiger.
1993 **585** 82c. multicoloured 2·25 2·25
MS1994 150×90 mm. No. 1993×3 7·00 7·50

586 St. Patrick (stained glass window, St. Patrick's Cathedral, Co. Armagh)

2010. St. Patrick's Day.
1995   586   82c. multicoloured   2·25   2·25

587 Gaisce Symbol and Aras an Uachtarain (President's official residence)

2010. 25th Anniv of Gaisce the President's Award.
1996   587   55c. multicoloured   1·60   1·60

588 Women playing Golf, Baking, Exercising and Painting

2010. Centenary of Irish Countrywoman's Association.
1997   588   55c. multicoloured   1·50   1·50

589 Monasterboice Cross, Co. Louth

2010. Ireland Series—High Crosses. Each black.
1998   55c. Type **589**   1·75   1·75
1999   55c. Carndonagh Cross, Co. Donegal   1·75   1·75
2000   55c. Drumcliffe Cross, Co. Sligo   1·75   1·75
2001   55c. Ahenny Cross, Co. Tipperary   1·75   1·75

590 The Happy Prince (Oscar Wilde)

2010. Europa. Multicoloured.
2002   55c. Type **590**   2·00   2·00
2003   82c. *Gulliver's Travels* (Jonathan Swift)   2·00   2·00

591 Máirtín Ó Direáin and Aran Islands

2010. Birth Centenary of Máirtín Ó Direáin (poet)
2004   591   55c. multicoloured   1·50   1·50

592 The Breton Girl, 1906

2010. 150th Birth Anniv of Roderic O'Conor (artist). Multicoloured.
2005   55c. Type **592**   1·50   1·50
2006   55c. *Self-portrait*, 1928   1·50   1·50

593 Mother Teresa

2010. International Humanitarians. Multicoloured.
2007   55c. Type **593**   1·50   1·50
2008   55c. Henry Dunant (founder of Red Cross) and Battle of Solferino   1·50   1·50

594 Top and Skirt (Paul Costelloe)

2010. Irish Fashion Designers. Multicoloured.
2009   55c. Type **594**   1·50   1·50
2010   55c. Dark blue jacket (Louise Kennedy)   1·50   1·50
2011   55c. Olive-brown crocheted coat (Lainey Keogh)   1·50   1·50
2012   82c. Black dress with ruffled skirt (John Rocha)   2·25   2·25
2013   82c. Black hat with white ribbons (Philip Treacy)   2·25   2·25

595 Mountain Avens (*Dryas octopetala*)

2010. Irish Wild Flowers. Multicoloured.
2015   55c. Type **595**   1·60   1·60
2016   55c. Spring gentian (*Gentiana verna*)   1·60   1·60
2017   55c. Bloody cranes-bill (*Geranium sanguineum*)   1·60   1·60
2018   55c. Common knapweed (*Centaurea nigra*)   1·60   1·60

596 Buzzard (*Buteo buteo*)

2010. Birds of Prey. Multicoloured.
2019   55c. Type **596**   1·50   1·50
2020   55c. Golden eagle (*Aquila chrysaetos*)   1·50   1·50
2021   82c. Peregrine falcon (*Falco peregrinus*)   2·25   2·25
2022   95c. Merlin (*Falco columbarius*)   2·75   2·75
MS2023 150×90 mm. Nos. 2019/22   8·00   8·00

597 Anneli Alhanko and Per-Arthur Segerström in Romeo and Juliet

2010. Czeslaw Slania (engraver and stamp designer) Commemoration
2024   597   55c. black and light brown   2·00   1·60
Stamps in a similar design were issued by Sweden.

598 Oliver Murphy (founding member) and Shane Barker

2010. 50th Anniv of the Irish Wheelchair Association
2025   598   55c. multicoloured   1·60   1·60

599 Green Tiger Beetle (*Cicindela campestris*)

2010. Irish Animals and Marine Life (1st series). Multicoloured.
2026   55c. Type **599**   1·60   1·60
2027   55c. Golden eagle (*Aquila chrysaetos*)   1·60   1·60
2028   55c. Tompot blenny (*Parablennius gattorugine*)   1·60   1·60
2029   55c. Red squirrel (*Sciurus vulgaris*)   1·60   1·60
2030   55c. Common octopus (*Octopus vulgaris*)   1·60   1·60
2031   55c. Hermit crab (*Pagurus bernhardus*)   1·60   1·60
2032   55c. Sea slug (*Lomanotus genei*)   1·60   1·60
2033   55c. Bottlenose dolphin (*Tursiops truncates*)   1·60   1·60

600 The Miami Showband

2010. Legendary Showbands. Multicoloured.
2034   55c. Type **600**   1·50   1·50
2035   55c. The Drifters Showband   1·50   1·50
2036   82c. The Royal Showband   2·40   2·40
2037   82c. The Freshmen   2·40   2·40
MS2038 150×90 mm. Nos. 2034/7   7·75   7·50

601 Early Patrolman

2010. Centenary of Automobile Association Ireland
2039   601   55c. multicoloured   1·50   1·50

602 John MacKenna

2010. Bicentenary of Chilean Independence. Multicoloured.
2040   82c. Type **602**   1·75   1·75
2041   82c. Bernardo O'Higgins   1·75   1·75
Stamps in similar designs were issued by Chile.

603 The Nativity (St. Brigid's Church, Dangan, Co. Roscommon)   **604** Robin

2010. Christmas. Multicoloured.

    (a) Sheet stamps. Ordinary gum
2042   55c. Type **603**   1·60   1·60
2043   82c. Annunciation (Church of Our Lady of Perpetual Help, Aughrim, Co. Roscommon)   2·00   2·00

    (b) Booklet stamp. Self-adhesive. Size 30×25 mm.
2044   604   55c. multicoloured   1·60   1·60

    (c) 'Stamps on a roll'. Designs as Nos. 2042/3 but 55×24 mm. Self-adhesive
2045   55c. As Type **603**   1·75   1·75
2046   82c. As No. 2043   2·00   2·00

605 Couple Sharing Umbrella

2011. Weddings (6th issue)
2047   605   55c. multicoloured   1·60   1·60

606 Couple sharing Umbrella

2011. Greetings Stamps. Multicoloured.
2048   55c. Type **606**   1·60   1·60
2049   55c. Balloons   1·60   1·60

607 USA and Ireland Flags and Entrance to American Chamber of Commerce, Dublin

2011. 50th Anniv of the American Chamber of Commerce, Ireland
2050   607   55c. multicoloured   1·75   1·75

608 Cearbhall Ó Dálaigh

2011. Birth Centenary of Cearbhall Ó Dálaigh (President of Ireland 1974–6)
2051   608   55c. multicoloured   1·75   1·75

609 St. Patrick (stone carving from St. Patrick's College Chapel, Maynooth)

2011. St. Patrick's Day.
2052   609   82c. multicoloured   2·50   2·50

610 'VOTES FOR WOMEN'

2011. Women's Rights. Multicoloured.
2053   55c. Type **610**   1·75   1·75
2054   82c. 'EQUALITY'   2·00   2·00

611 Boxing Match

2011. Centenary of the Irish Amateur Boxing Association
2055 **611** 55c. multicoloured 1·50 1·50

612 Tulip Tree, Knockabbey Gardens

2011. Europa. Forests. Multicoloured.
2056 55c. Type **612** 1·60 1·60
2057 82c. River Walk, Avondale Forest Park 2·50 2·50

613 Ceramic (Deirdre McLoughlin)

2011. Year of Craft. Multicoloured.
2058 55c. Type **613** 1·60 1·60
2059 55c. Glass artwork (Róisín de Buitléar) 1·60 1·60
2060 55c. Jewellery(Inga Reed) 1·60 1·60
2061 55c. Slippers (Helen McAllister) 1·60 1·60
2062 55c. Wooden pot (Liam Flynn) 1·60 1·60

614 Ballycroy National Park

2011. Ireland's National Parks. Multicoloured.
2063 55c. Type **614** 1·60 1·60
2064 55c. The Burren National Park 1·60 1·60
2065 55c. Connemara National Park 1·60 1·60
2066 82c. Glenveagh National Park 2·50 2·50
2067 82c. Killarney National Park 2·50 2·50
2068 82c. Wicklow Mountains National Park 2·50 2·50
MS2069 150×90 mm. Nos. 2063/6 4·50 4·50
MS2070 150×90 mm. Nos. 2066/8 7·00 7·00

615 Hermit Crab (*Pagurus bernhardus*)

2011. Irish Animals and Marine Life. Multicoloured.
2071 55c. Type **615** 1·60 1·60
2071c 82c. Common frog (*Rana temporaria*) (1.5.12) 2·50 2·50

616 Candle wrapped with Barbed Wire

2011. 50th Anniv of Amnesty International
2072 **616** 55c. greenish yellow, black and yellow-green 1·60 1·60

2011. Irish Animals and Marine Life (2nd series). As T **599**. Multicoloured.
2073 55c. Beadlet anemone (*Actinia equina*) 1·60 1·60
2074 55c. Squat lobster (*Munida rugosa*) 1·60 1·60
2075 55c. Cuckoo wrasse (*Labrus mixtus*) 1·60 1·60
2076 55c. Common frog (*Rana temporaria*) 1·60 1·60
2077 55c. Green huntsman spider (*Micrommata virescens*) 1·60 1·60
2078 55c. Elephant hawk-moth (*Deilephila elpenor*) 1·60 1·60
2079 55c. Goldfinch (*Carduelis carduelis*) 1·60 1·60
2080 55c. Red deer stag (*Cervus elaphus*) 1·60 1·60

617 House with Solar Panels

2011. Renewable Energy. Multicoloured.
2081 55c. Type **617** 1·60 1·60
2082 55c. Ardnacrusha hydro electric power station 1·60 1·60
2083 55c. Wind turbines 1·60 1·60
2084 55c. Wave energy 1·60 1·60
2085 55c. Field of rape (Biofuel) 1·60 1·60

618 Coloured Horse

2011. The Irish Horse. Multicoloured.
2086 55c. Type **618** 1·60 1·60
2087 55c. Irish draught horse 1·60 1·60
2088 55c. Thoroughbred 1·60 1·60
2089 55c. Connemara pony 1·60 1·60
MS2090 150×90 mm. Nos. 2086/9 6·25 6·25

619 Golfers

2011. Solheim Cup Women's Golf Tournament, Killeen Castle, Co. Meath
2091 **619** 55c. multicoloured 1·75 1·75

2011. Irish Animals and Marine Life (3rd series). As T **599**.
2092 55c. Red squirrel (*Sciurus vulgaris*) 1·75 1·75
2093 55c. Bottlenose dolphin (*Tursiops truncatus*) 1·75 1·75

620 Brian O'Nolan (painting by Micheál Ó Nualláin)

2011. Birth Centenary of Brian O'Nolan (Flann O'Brien) (novelist)
2094 **620** 55c. multicoloured 1·75 £175

621 Flight into Egypt

622 Baubles

2011. Christmas. Multicoloured.
(a) Booklet stamp
2095 55c. Type **621** 1·75 1·75
(b) 'Stamps on a roll'. Two phosphor bars
2096 55c. Type **622** 1·75 1·75
2097 82c. Star tree decorations 2·50 2·50

623 *The Late Late Show* Presenter Gay Byrne

2011. 50th Anniv of the First RTÉ (Radio Telefís Éireann) Broadcast. Multicoloured.
2098 55c. Type **623** 1·75 1·75

2099 55c. Children's TV presenter Emma O'Driscoll on set of *Hubble* 1·75 1·75
2100 55c. Newsreader Anne Doyle 1·75 1·75

624 Bride and Groom

2012. Weddings (7th issue)
2101 **624** 55c. multicoloured 1·60 1·60

625 Wrapped Present

2012. Greetings Stamps. Multicoloured.
2102 55c. Type **625** 1·60 1·60
2103 55c. Candles 1·60 1·60

626 Logo

2012. Ireland's Chairmanship of the OSCE (Organisation for Security and Co-operation in Europe)
2104 **626** 55c. multicoloured 1·60 1·60

627 St. Patrick (from icon painting by Ekaterina Platoshechkina)

2012. St. Patrick's Day
2105 **627** 82c. multicoloured 2·50 2·50

628 Dancer from Fabulous Beast Dance Theatre

2012. Contemporary Arts - Dance. Multicoloured.
2106 55c. Type **628** 1·60 1·60
2107 55c. Two dancers from Dance Theatre of Ireland 1·60 1·60
2108 55c. Male dancer (wearing white) from Irish Modern Dance Theatre 1·60 1·60
2109 55c. Underwater dancer from CoisCéim Dance Theatre 1·60 1·60

629 Thomas Andrews (shipbuilder) and *Titanic* under Construction

2012. Centenary of the Sinking of RMS *Titanic*. Multicoloured.
2110 55c. Type **629** 1·60 1·60
2111 55c. Father Browne (photographer) and *Titanic* 1·60 1·60
2112 82c. Captain Edward Smith and *Titanic* 2·50 2·50
2113 82c. Molly Brown and *Titanic* 2·50 2·50

630 Bram Stoker

2012. Death Centenary of Bram Stoker (author of *Dracula*). Multicoloured.
2114 55c. Type **630** 1·60 1·60
2115 55c. Count Dracula and victim 1·60 1·60
MS2116 150×90 mm. Nos. 2114/15 3·25 3·25

631 Small Skellig, Co. Kerry

2012. Europa. Visit Ireland. Multicoloured.
2117 55c. Type **631** 1·60 1·60
2118 82c. Ha'penny Bridge, Dublin 2·50 2·50

632 The Chalice and Host

2012. 50th International Eucharistic Congress, Dublin. Multicoloured.
2119 55c. Type **632** 1·60 1·60
2120 82c. The Monstrance and the Blessed Sacrament 2·50 2·50

633 Yachts in Volvo Ocean Race

2012. Volvo Ocean Race. Multicoloured.
2121 55c. Type **633** 1·60 1·60
MS2122 151×90 mm. €3 Two yachts (27×48 mm) 7·50 7·50

634 Rescuing Baby from Fire

2012. 150th Anniv of Dublin Fire Brigade. Multicoloured.
2123 55c. Type **634** 1·60 1·60
2124 55c. Fighting chemical fire 1·60 1·60
2125 55c. Rescuing trapped person from crashed car 1·60 1·60
2126 55c. Water rescue 1·60 1·60

635 The Conference Centre, Dublin and Molecular Structure of DNA

2012. Significant Science Milestones. Multicoloured.
2127 55c. Type **635** (Euroscience Open Forum and Dublin City of Science 2012) 1·60 1·60
2128 55c. Robert Boyle (chemist) and his formula (350th anniv of the formulation of Boyle's Law) 1·60 1·60
MS2129 150×90 mm. Nos. 2127/8 3·25 3·25

636 Medal
Ceremony

2012. Olympic Games, London. Multicoloured.
| 2130 | 55c. Type **636** | 1·60 | 1·60 |
| 2131 | 82c. 'EIRE IRELAND LONDON 2012' in vertical columns | 2·50 | 2·50 |

2012. Irish Animals and Marine Life (3rd series). Multicoloured.
2132	55c. Pike (*Esox lucius*)	1·60	1·60
2133	55c. Green crab (*Carcinus maenas*)	1·60	1·60
2134	55c. Spiny seahorse (*Hippocampus guttulatus*)	1·60	1·60
2135	55c. Fireworks anemone (*Pachycerianthus multiplicatus*)	1·60	1·60
2136	55c. Kestrel (*Falco tinnunculus*)	1·60	1·60
2137	55c. Raft spider (*Dolomedes fimbriatus*)	1·60	1·60
2138	55c. Irish hare (*Lepus timidus hibernicus*)	1·60	1·60
2139	55c. Smooth newt (*Lissotriton vulgaris*)	1·60	1·60

637 The Children of Lir

2012. Myths and Legends. Multicoloured.
2140	55c. Type **637**	1·60	1·60
2141	55c. Deirdre of the Sorrows	1·60	1·60
2142	82c. Fionn Mac Cunhaill and the Salmon of Knowledge	2·50	2·50
2143	82c. Cú Chulainn	2·50	2·50

638 Girl

2012. 50th Anniv of Barnardos in Ireland
| 2144 | **638** | 55c. multicoloured | 1·60 | 1·60 |

639 Candle   **640** *The Adoration of the Shepherds* (Girolamo Troppa)

2012. Christmas. Multicoloured.
(a) Booklet stamp
| 2145 | 55c. Type **639** | 1·60 | 1·60 |

(b) "Stamps on a roll"
| 2146 | 55c. Type **640** | 1·60 | 1·60 |
| 2147 | 82c. *The Adoration of the Magi* (Jan Brueghel the Elder) | 2·50 | 2·50 |

641 Irish EU
Presidency Logo

2013. Ireland's Presidency of the European Union, January to June 2013
| 2148 | **641** | 55c. greenish blue and bright yellow-green | 1·60 | 1·60 |

642 Elements of The Gathering's Logo forming Map of Ireland

643 St. Patrick's Day Parade

2013. The Gathering Ireland 2013
| 2149 | **642** | 82c. multicoloured | 2·50 | 2·50 |

2013. St. Patrick's Day
| 2150 | **643** | 82c. multicoloured | 2·50 | 2·50 |

644 Bride and Groom lighting Candle

2013. Weddings (8th issue)
| 2151 | **644** | (55c.) multicoloured | 1·60 | 1·60 |
No. 2151 was inscr 'N' and was originally sold for 55c.

645 Girl carrying Giant Birthday Card

2013. Greetings Stamps. Paintings by Cathy Dineen. Multicoloured.
| 2152 | (55c.) Type **645** | 1·60 | 1·60 |
| 2153 | (55c.) Boy holding birthday card and balloon | 1·60 | 1·60 |
Nos. 2152/3 were both inscr 'N' and originally sold for 55c.

646 Daffodil

2013. 50th Anniv of the Irish Cancer Society
| 2154 | **646** | (55c.) multicoloured | 1·60 | 1·60 |
No. 2154 was inscr 'N' and was originally sold for 55c.

2013. Irish Animals and Marine Life. Multicoloured.
2155	60c. Golden Eagle (*Aquila chrysaetos*) (25×30 mm)	1·60	1·60
2156	60c. Red Deer (*Cervus elaphus*) (25×30 mm)	1·60	1·60
2157	60c. Goldfinch (*Carduelis carduelis*)	1·60	1·60
2158	90c. Beadlet Anemone (*Actinia equina*) (horiz)	2·50	2·50

647 *Doors and Sunlight* (Stephen McKenna)

2013. Contemporary Arts - Visual Arts (1st issue). Multicoloured.
2159	60c. Type **647**	1·60	1·60
2160	60c. *Ghost Ship* (Dorothy Cross)	1·60	1·60
2161	60c. *The Fall* (Amanda Coogan) (performance art)	1·60	1·60
2162	60c. *Smoke Tree* (John Gerrard) (virtual sculpture)	1·60	1·60

648 Postmen pushing Trolley and on Bicycle

2013. Europa. Postal Vehicles. Multicoloured.
| 2163 | 60c. Type **648** | 1·60 | 1·60 |
| 2164 | 90c. Postman with Anpost van | 2·50 | 2·50 |

649 Story about Dublin by Eoin Moore

2013. Dublin UNESCO City of World Literature
| 2165 | **649** | 60c. black and lemon | 1·60 | 1·60 |

650 Pres. John F. Kennedy with Second Cousin Mary Ann Ryan at his Great Grandfather's Birthplace, Dunganstown, New Ross

2013. 50th Death Anniv of Pres. John F. Kennedy (1917-63, US President 1960-3). Pres. Kennedy's Visit to Ireland, June 1963. Multicoloured.
| 2166 | 60c. Type **650** | 1·60 | 1·60 |
| 2167 | 90c. Pres. Kennedy and Taoiseach Sean Lemass laying wreath for leaders of Easter Rising, Arbour Hill | 2·50 | 2·50 |

651 Container Ship

2013. Port of Cork. Multicoloured.
2168	60c. Type **651**	1·60	1·60
2169	60c. Yachts in Clipper Round the World Race, 2010	1·60	1·60
2170	90c. Cunard liner *Queen Elizabeth*	2·50	2·50
MS2171	150×90 mm. Nos. 2168/70	5·50	5·50

2013. Irish Animals and Marine Life (4th series). Multicoloured.
2172	60c. Cushion Star	1·60	1·60
2173	60c. Red Tube Worm	1·60	1·60
2174	60c. European Eel	1·60	1·60
2175	60c. Common Seal	1·60	1·60
2176	60c. Natterjack Toad	1·60	1·60
2177	60c. Red Fox	1·60	1·60
2178	60c. Great Spotted Woodpecker	1·60	1·60
2179	60c. Black-legged Kittiwake	1·60	1·60

652 Jim Larkin (founder of ITGWU) and Bloody Sunday Riot, 31 August 1913

2013. Centenary of the General Lockout. Multicoloured.
2180	60c. Type **652**	1·60	1·60
2181	60c. James Connolly and original Irish Transport and General Workers Union headquarters	1·60	1·60
2182	60c. Countess Markievicz (distributed food for workers) and children outside tenement buildings	1·60	1·60

653 Helicopter

2013. Irish Defence Forces. Multicoloured.
2183	60c. Type **653**	1·60	1·60
2184	60c. Troops performing medivac drill	1·60	1·60
2185	60c. Ships of Irish Naval Service	1·60	1·60
2186	60c. UN tank and soldier	1·60	1·60

654 Dongdong Zheng in Garda Uniform

2013. Ireland - An Integrated Society. Multicoloured.
2187	60c. Type **654**	1·60	1·60
2188	60c. Luas Revenue Protection Officer Sammy Akorede	1·60	1·60
2189	90c. Christian Tshibangu in hurling match	2·50	2·50
2190	90c. Anna Gąciarz in marketing	2·50	2·50

655 Volunteers, Waterford, c. 1915

2013. Irish Volunteer Force
| 2191 | **655** | 60c. multicoloured | 1·60 | 1·60 |

656 Glucksman Gallery, University College, Cork

2013. Contemporary Public Buildings. Multicoloured.
2192	60c. Type **656**	1·60	1·60
2193	60c. Cork Institute of Technology	1·60	1·60
2194	90c. Fingall County Hall, Swords	2·50	2·50
2195	90c. Croke Park Stadium	2·50	2·50
MS2196	150×90 mm. Nos. 2192/5	7·50	7·50

657 Nativity (stained glass window), Black Abbey Church, Kilkenny   **658** Robin

2013. Christmas. Multicoloured.
(a) Booklet stamp
| 2197 | 60c. Type **657** | 1·60 | 1·60 |

(b) 'Stamps on a roll'.
| 2198 | 60c. Type **658** | 1·60 | 1·60 |
| 2199 | 90c. Sprig of holly | 2·50 | 2·50 |

659 Robot and Alien

2014. Greetings Stamps. Multicoloured.
| 2200 | 60c. Type **659** | 1·60 | 1·60 |
| 2201 | 60c. Adult and child robots with birthday cake | 1·60 | 1·60 |

660 Red Rose

2014. Love and Marriage
| 2202 | **660** | 60c. multicoloured | 1·60 | 1·60 |

2014. St. Patrick's Day
| 2203 | **661** | 90c. multicoloured | 2·50 | 2·50 |

662 Brendan Behan

2014. 50th Death Anniv of Brendan Behan (writer)
| 2204 | **662** | 60c. grey, black and olive-grey | 1·60 | 1·60 |

2014. Contemporary Arts - Visual Arts (2nd issue). Multicoloured.
2205	60c. *Maesta* (Sean Scully)	1·60	1·60
2206	60c. *Light Receiver* (sculpture) (Eilis O'Connell)	1·60	1·60
2207	60c. *Patterned Behaviour* (Diana Copperwhite)	1·60	1·60
2208	60c. *Chaplet* (Alice Maher)	1·60	1·60

663 Cumann na mBan Members in Nationalist Funeral Procession, 1914

2014. Centenary of Cumann na mBan (nationalist women's association)

2209	**663**	60c. multicoloured	1·60	1·60

664 Irish Citizen Army at Croydon House, Dublin

2014. Centenary of the Irish Citizen Army

2210	**664**	60c. multicoloured	1·60	1·60

665 Waterford Kite Brooch (c. 1090) and Map of Waterford City

2014. Viking Heritage. Multicoloured.

2211		60c. Type **665**	1·60	1·60
2212		60c. 10th-century Viking sword and portion of the *Annals of the Four Masters*	1·60	1·60

666 The Irish Bodhrán (drum)

2014. Europa. National Musical Instruments. Multicoloured.

2213		60c. Type **666**	1·60	1·60
2214		90c. The Irish Harp	2·50	2·50

POSTAGE DUE STAMPS

D1

1925

D1	**D1**	½d. green	12·00	16·00
D6	**D1**	1d. red	1·50	70
D7	**D1**	1½d. orange	4·00	9·50
D8	**D1**	2d. green	2·75	70
D9	**D1**	3d. blue	5·00	4·00
D10	**D1**	5d. violet	6·00	2·25
D11	**D1**	6d. plum	6·00	3·50
D12	**D1**	8d. orange	9·00	17·00
D13	**D1**	10d. purple	8·50	8·50
D14	**D1**	1s. green	8·50	11·00

1971. Decimal Currency. Colours changed.

D15		1p. brown	30	60
D16		1½p. green	40	1·50
D17		3p. stone	60	2·00
D18		4p. orange	60	1·25
D19		5p. blue	60	3·00
D20		7p. yellow	40	3·75
D21		8p. red	40	3·00

D2

1980

D25	**D2**	1p. green	30	70
D26	**D2**	2p. blue	30	70
D27	**D2**	4p. green	40	70
D28	**D2**	6p. flesh	40	80
D29	**D2**	8p. blue	40	85
D30	**D2**	18p. green	75	1·25
D31	**D2**	20p. red	2·25	6·00
D32	**D2**	24p. green	75	2·00
D33	**D2**	30p. violet	3·00	7·50
D34	**D2**	50p. pink	3·75	7·50

D3

1988

D35	**D3**	1p. black, red and yellow	10	60
D36	**D3**	2p. black, red and brown	10	60
D37	**D3**	3p. black, red and purple	15	60
D38	**D3**	4p. black, red and violet	15	60
D39	**D3**	5p. black, red and blue	15	60
D40	**D3**	17p. black, red and green	40	65
D41	**D3**	20p. black, red and blue	55	80
D42	**D3**	24p. black, red and green	60	85
D43	**D3**	30p. black, red and grey	80	1·25
D44	**D3**	50p. black, red and grey	1·25	1·75
D45	**D3**	£1 black, red and brown	1·75	2·25

Pt. 1

ISLE OF MAN

An island in the Irish Sea to the north-west of England. Man became a possession of the English Crown during the Middle Ages, but retains its own Assembly.

Regional issues from 1958 to 1971 are listed at end of "GREAT BRITAIN".

Isle of Man had an independent postal administration from 1973.

100 pence = 1 pound.

5 Castletown

17 Manx Cat

1973. Multicoloured.

12		½p. Type **5**	10	10
13		1p. Port Erin	10	10
14		1½p. Snaefell	10	10
15		2p. Laxey	10	10
16		2½p. Tynwald Hill	10	10
17		3p. Douglas Promenade	10	10
18		3½p. Port St. Mary	10	10
19		4p. Fairy Bridge	10	10
20		4½p. As 2½p.	20	15
21		5p. Peel	15	10
22		5½p. As 3p.	20	15
23		6p. Cregneish	20	15
24		7p. As 2p.	20	15
25		7½p. Ramsey Bay	20	20
26		8p. As 7½p.	25	25
27		9p. Douglas Bay	20	20
28		10p. Type **17**	35	20
29		11p. Monk's Bridge, Ballasalla	35	30
30		13p. Derbyhaven	40	35
31		20p. Manx loaghtyn ram	50	50
32		50p. Manx shearwater	1·20	1·30
33		£1 Viking longship	2·50	2·50

SIZES: Nos. 13/27 and 29/30 as Type **4**; Nos. 31/3 as Type **5**.

23 Viking Landing on Man, A.D. 938

1973. Inauguration of Postal Independence.

34	**23**	15p. multicoloured	35	35

24 No. 1 *Sutherland*, 1873

1973. Cent of Steam Railway. Multicoloured.

35		2½p. Type **24**	15	10
36		3p. No. 4 *Caledonia*, 1885	15	15
37		7½p. No. 13 *Kissack* 1910	25	25
38		9p. No. 3 *Pender*, 1873	25	25

28 Leonard Randles, First Winner, 1923

1973. Golden Jubilee of Manx Grand Prix. Multicoloured.

39		3p. Type **28**	10	15
40		3½p. Alan Holmes, Double Winner, 1957	15	15

30 Princess Anne and Capt. Mark Phillips

1973. Royal Wedding.

41	**30**	25p. multicoloured	70	70

31 Badge, Citation and Sir William Hillary (founder)

1974. 150th Anniv of Royal National Lifeboat Institution. Multicoloured.

42		3p. Type **31**	10	10
43		3½p. Wreck of *St. George*, 1830	15	15
44		8p. R.N.L.B. *Manchester and Salford*, 1868–87	25	25
45		10p. R.N.L.B. *Osman Gabriel*	30	30

35 Stanley Woods, 1935

1974. Tourist Trophy Motorcycle Races (1st issue). Multicoloured.

46		3p. Type **35**	15	15
47		3½p. Freddy Frith, 1937	15	15
48		8p. Max Deubel and Emil Horner, 1961	40	45
49		10p. Mike Hailwood, 1961	40	45

See also Nos. 63/6.

39 Rushen Abbey and Arms

1974. Historical Anniversaries. Multicoloured.

50		3½p. Type **39**	20	20
51		4½p. Magnus Haraldson rows King Edgar on the Dee	20	20
52		8p. King Magnus and Norse fleet	40	40
53		10p. Bridge at Avignon and bishop's mitre	40	40

COMMEMORATIONS: Nos. 50 and 53, William Russell, Bishop of Sodor and Man, 600th death anniv; Nos. 51/2, 1000th anniv of rule of King Magnus Haraldson.

43 Churchill and Bugler Dunne at Colenso, 1899

1974. Birth Centenary of Sir Winston Churchill. Multicoloured.

54		3½p. Type **43**	20	20
55		4½p. Churchill and Government Buildings, Douglas	20	20
56		8p. Churchill and Manx ack-ack crew	40	40
57		20p. Churchill as Freeman of Douglas	40	40
MS58		121×91 mm. Nos. 54/7	1·00	1·00

47 Cabin School and Names of Pioneers

1975. Manx Pioneers in Cleveland, Ohio. Multicoloured.

59		4½p. Type **47**	10	10
60		5½p. Terminal Tower Building, J. Gill and R. Carran	10	15
61		8p. Clague House Museum, and Robert and Margaret Clague	15	20
62		10p. S.S. *William T. Graves* and Thomas Quayle	25	40

51 Tom Sheard, 1923

1975. Tourist Trophy Motor-cycle Races (2nd issue). Multicoloured.

63		5½p. Type **51**	10	10
64		7p. Walter Handley, 1925	15	15
65		10p. Geoff Duke, 1955	15	15
66		12p. Peter Williams, 1973	25	20

55 Sir George Goldie and Birthplace

1975. 50th Death Anniv of Sir George Goldie. Multicoloured.

67		5½p. Type **55**	10	10
68		7p. Goldie and map of Africa (vert)	15	15
69		10p. Goldie as President of Geographical Society (vert)	15	15
70		12p. River scene on the Niger	25	25

59 Title Page of Manx Bible

1975. Christmas and Bicentenary of Manx Bible. Multicoloured.

71		5½p. Type **59**	20	20
72		7p. Rev. Philip Moore and Ballaugh Old Church	20	20
73		11p. Bishop Hildesley and Bishops Court	40	40
74		13p. John Kelly saving Bible manuscript	40	40

63 William Christian listening to Patrick Henry

1976. Bicent of American Independence. Multicoloured.

75		5½p. Type **63**	10	10
76		7p. Conveying the Fincastle Resolutions	15	15
77		13p. Patrick Henry and William Christian	30	30
78		20p. Christian as an Indian fighter	35	35
MS79		153×89 mm. Nos. 75/8	90	1·00

67 First Horse Tram, 1876

1976. Cent of Douglas Horse-Trams. Multicoloured.

80		5½p. Type **67**	20	20
81		7p. "Toast-rack" tram, 1890	20	20
82		11p. Horse-bus, 1895	40	40
83		13p. Royal tram, 1972	40	40

71 Barrose
Beaker

1976. Europa. Ceramic Art. Multicoloured.

84	5p. Type **71**	20	10
85	5p. Souvenir teapot	20	10
86	5p. Laxey jug	20	10
87	10p. Cronk Aust food vessel (horiz)	25	10
88	10p. Sansbury bowl (horiz)	25	10
89	10p. Knox urn (horiz)	25	10

77 Diocesan
Banner

1976. Christmas and Centenary of Mothers' Union. Multicoloured.

90	6p. Type **77**	10	10
91	7p. Onchan banner	15	15
92	11p. Castletown banner	25	25
93	13p. Ramsey banner	30	30

81 Queen Elizabeth II

1977. Silver Jubilee. Multicoloured.

94	6p. Type **81**	15	10
95	7p. Queen Elizabeth and Prince Philip (vert)	20	20
96	25p. Queen Elizabeth (different)	60	60

84 Carrick Bay from "Tom-the-Dipper"

1977. Europa. Landscapes. Multicoloured.

97	6p. Type **84**	15	30
98	10p. View from Ramsey	25	35

86 F. A. Applebee, 1912

1977. Linked Anniversaries. Multicoloured.

99	6p. Type **86**	15	15
100	7p. St. John's Ambulance Brigade at Governor's Bridge, 1938	20	20
101	11p. Scouts operating the scoreboard	35	35
102	13p. John Williams, 1976	40	40

The events commemorated are: 70th anniv of Manx TT races; 70th anniv of Boy Scouts; Centenary of St. John's Ambulance Brigade.

90 Old Summer House, Mount Morrison, Peel

1977. Bicentenary of First Visit of John Wesley. Multicoloured.

103	6p. Type **90**	15	15
104	7p. Wesley preaching in Castletown Square	20	20
105	11p. Wesley preaching outside Braddan Church	35	35
106	13p. New Methodist Church, Douglas	40	40

Nos. 104/5 are larger, 38×26 mm.

94 Short Type 184 Seaplane and H.M.S. *Ben-My-Chree*, 1915

1978. 60th Anniv of Royal Air Force. Multicoloured.

107	6p. Type **94**	15	15
108	7p. Bristol Scout C and H.M.S. *Vindex*, 1915	20	20
109	11p. Boulton Paul P.82 Defiant over Douglas Bay, 1941	35	35
110	13p. SEPECAT Jaguar over Ramsey, 1977	40	40

98 Watch Tower, Langness

1978. Multicoloured.

111	½p. Type **98**	10	10
112	1p. Jurby Church (horiz)	10	10
113	6p. Government Buildings	30	30
114	7p. Tynwald Hill (horiz)	35	35
115	8p. Milner's Tower	25	25
116	9p. Laxey Wheel	35	35
117a	10p. Castle Rushen (horiz)	35	35
118	11p. St. Ninian's Church	40	40
119	12p. Tower of Refuge (horiz)	40	25
120a	13p. St. German's Cathedral (horiz)	30	25
121a	14p. Point of Ayre Lighthouse (horiz)	30	25
122a	15p. Corrin's Tower (horiz)	30	25
123	16p. Douglas Head Lighthouse (horiz)	75	75
124	20p. Fuchsia	90	90
125	25p. Manx cat	80	90
126	50p. Red-billed chough ("Chough")	1·25	1·25
127	£1 Viking warrior	2·50	2·50
128	£2 Queen Elizabeth II	4·50	4·50

Nos. 124/7 are larger, 25×31 mm and No. 128, 38×48 mm.

115 Queen Elizabeth in Coronation Regalia

1978. 25th Anniv of Coronation.

132	**115**	25p. multicoloured	75	75

116 Wheel-headed Cross-slab

1978. Europa. Celtic and Norse Crosses. Multicoloured.

133	6p. Type **116**	15	10
134	6p. Celtic wheelcross	15	15
135	6p. Keeil Chiggyrt Stone	15	10
136	11p. Olaf Liotulfson Cross	25	15
137	11p. Odd's and Thorleif's Crosses	25	15
138	11p. Thor Cross	25	15

122 J. K. Ward and Ward Library, Peel

1978. Anniversaries and Events. Multicoloured.

139	6p. Type **122**	15	15
140	7p. Swimmer, cyclist and walker (42×26 mm)	20	20
141	11p. American bald eagle, Manx arms and maple leaf (42×26 mm)	35	35

142	13p. Lumber camp, Three Rivers, Quebec	40	40

ANNIVERSARIES AND EVENTS: 6, 13p. James Kewley Ward (Manx pioneer in Canada) commemoration; 7p. Commonwealth Games, Edmonton; 11p. 50th anniv of North American Manx Association.

126 Hunt the Wren

1978. Christmas.

143	**126**	5p. multicoloured	20	20

127 P. M. C. Kermode and "Nassa kermodei"

1979. Centenary of Natural History and Antiquarian Society. Multicoloured.

144	6p. Type **127**	15	15
145	7p. Peregrine falcon	20	20
146	11p. Fulmar	35	35
147	13p. *Epitriptus cowini* (fly)	40	40

131 Postman, 1859

1979. Europa. Communications. Multicoloured.

148	6p. Type **131**	15	15
149	11p. Postman, 1979	40	45

133 Viking Longship Emblem

135 Viking Raid at Garwick

1979. Millennium of Tynwald. Multicoloured.

150	3p. Type **133**	10	10
151	4p. "Three Legs of Man" emblem	10	10
152	6p. Type **135**	15	15
153	7p. 10th-century meeting of Tynwald	20	20
154	11p. Tynwald Hill and St. John's Church	35	35
155	13p. Procession to Tynwald Hill	40	40

The 4p. value is as Type **34** and the remainder as Type **35**.

139 Queen and Court on Tynwald Hill

1979. Royal Visit. Multicoloured.

156	7p. Type **139**	20	20
157	13p. Queen and procession from St. John's Church to Tynwald Hill	35	35

141 *Odin's Raven*

1979. Voyage of *Odin's Raven*.

158	**141**	15p. multicoloured	50	50

142 John Quilliam seized by the Press Gang

1979. 150th Death Anniv of Captain John Quilliam. Multicoloured.

159	6p. Type **142**	15	15
160	8p. Steering H.M.S. *Victory*, Battle of Trafalgar	20	15
161	13p. Captain John Quilliam and H.M.S. *Spencer*	35	35
162	15p. Captain John Quilliam (member of the House of Keys)	40	40

146 Young Girl with Teddybear and Cat

1979. Christmas. Int Year of the Child. Multicoloured.

163	5p. Type **146**	25	25
164	7p. Father Christmas with young children	40	40

148 Conglomerate Arch, Langness

1980. 150th Anniv of Royal Geographical Society. Multicoloured.

165	7p. Type **148**	15	15
166	8p. Braaid Circle	20	20
167	12p. Cashtal-yn-Ard	35	35
168	13p. Volcanic rocks at Scarlett	40	40
169	15p. Sugar-loaf Rock	45	45

153 *Mona's Isle I*

1980. 150th Anniv of Isle of Man Steam Packet Company. Multicoloured.

170	7p. Type **153**	15	15
171	8p. *Douglas I*	20	20
172	11½p. H.M.S. *Mona's Queen II* sinking U-boat	35	35
173	12p. H.M.S. *King Orry III* at surrender of German fleet, 1918	35	35
174	13p. *Ben-My-Chree II*	40	40
175	15p. *Lady of Mann II*	45	45
MS176	180×125 mm. Nos. 170/5	1·70	1·70

No. **MS**176 was issued to commemorate "London 1980" International Stamp Exhibition.

159 Stained Glass Window, T. E. Brown Room, Manx Museum

1980. Europa. Personalities. Thomas Edward Brown (poet and scholar) Commemoration. Multicoloured.

177	7p. Type **159**	15	15
178	13½p. Clifton College, Bristol	40	40

161 King Olav V and *Norge* (Norwegian royal yacht)

1980. Visit of King Olav of Norway, August 1979.

179	**161**	12p. multicoloured	30	30
MS180	125×157 mm. Nos. 158 and 179		75	75

No. **MS**180 also commemorates the "NORWEX 80" Stamp Exhibition, Oslo.

162 Winter Wren and View of Calf of Man

1980. Christmas and Wildlife Conservation Year. Multicoloured.
181	6p. Type **162**	15	10
182	8p. European robin and view of Port Erin Marine Biological Station	30	35

164 William Kermode and Brig *Robert Quayle*, 1819

1980. Kermode Family in Tasmania Commemoration. Multicoloured.
183	7p. Type **164**	15	15
184	9p. *Mona Vale*, Van Diemen's Land, 1834	20	20
185	13½p. Ross Bridge, Tasmania	30	30
186	15p. *Mona Vale*, Tasmania (completed 1868)	40	40
187	17½p. Robert Quayle Kermode and Parliament Buildings, Tasmania	45	45

169 Peregrine Falcon

1980. Multicoloured
188	1p. Type **169**	20	20
189	5p. Loaghtyn ram	30	30

171 Luggers passing Red Pier, Douglas

1981. Centenary of Royal National Mission to Deep Sea Fishermen. Multicoloured.
190	8p. Type **171**	15	15
191	9p. Peel Lugger *Wanderer* rescuing survivors from *Lusitania*	20	20
192	18p. Nickeys leaving Port St. Mary	40	40
193	20p. Nobby entering Ramsey Harbour	45	45
194	22p. Nickeys *Sunbeam* and *Zebra* at Port Erin	50	50

176 "Crosh Cuirn" Superstition

1981. Europa. Folklore. Multicoloured.
195	8p. Type **176**	20	20
196	18p. "Bollan Cross" superstition	50	50

178 Lt. Mark Wilks (Royal Manx Fencibles) and Peel Castle

1981. 150th Death Anniv of Colonel Mark Wilks. Multicoloured.
197	8p. Type **178**	15	15
198	20p. Ensign Mark Wilks and Fort St. George, Madras	45	45
199	22p. Governor Mark Wilks and Napoleon, St. Helena	50	50
200	25p. Col. Mark Wilks (Speaker of the House of Keys) and estate, Kirby	60	60

182 Miss Emmeline Goulden (Mrs. Pankhurst) and Mrs. Sophia Jane Goulden

1981. Centenary of Manx Women's Suffrage.
201	**182** 9p. black, grey and stone	30	30

183 Prince Charles and Lady Diana Spencer

1981. Royal Wedding.
202	**183** 9p. black, blue and light blue	15	20
203	**183** 25p. black, blue and pink	75	80
MS204	130×183 mm. Nos. 202/3×2	2·00	2·00

184 Douglas War Memorial, Poppies and Commemorative Inscription

1981. 60th Anniv of The Royal British Legion. Multicoloured.
205	8p. Type **184**	15	15
206	10p. Major Robert Cain (war hero)	20	20
207	18p. Festival of Remembrance, Royal Albert Hall	40	40
208	20p. T.S.S. *Tynwald* at Dunkirk, May 1940 and Supermarine Spitfire	45	45

188 Nativity Scene (stained glass window, St. George's Church)

1981. Christmas. Multicoloured.
209	7p. Type **188**	15	15
210	9p. Children from Special School performing nativity play (48×30 mm)	40	40

190 Joseph and William Cunningham (founders of Isle of Man Boy Scout Movement) and Cunningham House Headquarters

1982. 75th Anniv of Boy Scout Movement and 125th Birth Anniv of Lord Baden-Powell. Multicoloured.
211	9p. Type **190**	15	15
212	10p. Baden-Powell visiting Isle of Man, 1911	20	20
213	19½p. Baden-Powell and Scout emblem (40×31 mm)	45	45
214	24p. Scouts and Baden-Powell's last message	60	60
215	29p. Scout salute, handshake, emblem and globe	80	80

195 *The Principals and Duties of Christianity* (Bishop T. Wilson) (first book printed in Manx, 1707)

1982. Europa. Historic Events. Multicoloured.
216	9p. Type **195**	25	25
217	19½p. Landing at Derbyhaven (visit of Thomas, 2nd Earl of Derby, 1507)	50	50

197 Charlie Collier (first TT race (single cylinder) winner) and Tourist Trophy Race, 1907

1982. 75th Anniv of Tourist Trophy Motorcycle Racing. Multicoloured.
218	9p. Type **197**	15	15
219	10p. Freddie Dixon (Sidecar and Junior TT winner) and Junior TT Race, 1927	20	20
220	24p. Jimmie Simpson (TT winner and first to lap at 60, 70 and 80 mph) and Senior TT, 1932	60	60
221	26p. Mike Hailwood (winner of fourteen TT's) and Senior TT, 1961	60	60
222	29p. Jock Taylor (Sidecar TT winner, 1978, 1980 and 1981) and Sidecar TT (with Benga Johansson), 1980	80	80

202 *Mona I*

1982. 150th Anniv of Isle of Man Steam Packet Company Mail Contract. Multicoloured.
223	12p. Type **202**	30	25
224	19½p. *Manx Maid II*	45	45

204 Three Wise Men bearing Gifts

1982. Christmas. Multicoloured.
225	8p. Type **204**	20	20
226	11p. Christmas snow scene (vert)	40	40

206 Princess Diana with Prince William

1982. 21st Birthday of Princess of Wales and Birth of Prince William. Sheet 100×83 mm.
MS227	**206** 50p. multicoloured	1·50	1·50

207 Opening of Salvation Army Citadel, and T. H. Cannell, J.P.

1983. Centenary of Salvation Army in Isle of Man. Multicoloured.
228	10p. Type **207**	15	15
229	12p. Early meeting place and Gen. William Booth	25	25
230	19½p. Salvation Army band	45	45
231	26p. Treating lepers and Lt.-Col. Thomas Bridson	65	60

211 Atlantic Puffins ("Puffins")

227 *Queen Elizabeth II* (Ricardo Macarron)

1983. Sea Birds. Multicoloured.
232	1p. Type **211**	30	30
233	2p. Northern gannets ("Gannets")	30	30
234	5p. Lesser black-backed gulls	60	40

235	8p. Great cormorants ("Cormorants")	60	40
236	10p. Black-legged kittiwakes ("Kittiwakes")	60	35
237	11p. Shags	60	35
238	12p. Grey herons ("Herons")	70	40
239	13p. Herring gulls	70	40
240	14p. Razorbills	70	40
241	15p. Greater black-backed gulls ("Great Black-backed Gulls")	80	50
242	16p. Common shelducks ("Shelducks")	80	50
243	18p. Oystercatchers	80	50
244	20p. Arctic terns	1·00	70
245	25p. Common guillemots ("Guillemots")	1·20	75
246	50p. Common redshank ("Redshanks")	1·70	1·50
247	£1 Mute swans	2·50	2·75
248	£5 Type **227**	9·00	8·50

Nos. 244/7 are larger, 39×26 mm.

228 Design Drawings by Roger Casement for the Great Laxey Wheel (image scaled to 58% of original size)

1983. Europa. The Great Laxey Wheel.
249	**228** 10p. black, blue and buff	25	20
250	– 20½p. multicoloured	50	55

DESIGN: 20½p. Roger Casement and the Great Laxey Wheel.

230 Nick Keig (international yachtsman) and Trimaran *Three Legs of Man III*

1983. 150th Anniv of King William's College. Multicoloured.
251	10p. Type **230**	20	20
252	12p. King William's College, Castletown	25	25
253	28p. Sir William Bragg (winner of Nobel Prize for Physics) and spectrometer	60	60
254	31p. General Sir George White, V.C. and action at Charasiah	70	70

234 New Post Office Headquarters, Douglas

1983. World Communications Year and Tenth Anniv of Isle of Man Post Office Authority. Multicoloured.
255	10p. Type **234**	20	20
256	15p. As Type **234** but inscr "POST OFFICE DECENNIUM 1983"	40	40

236 Shepherds

1983. Christmas. Multicoloured.
257	9p. Type **236**	20	20
258	12p. Three Kings	30	30

238 *Manx King* (full-rigged ship)

1984. The Karran Fleet. Multicoloured.
259	10p. Type **238**	20	20
260	13p. *Hope* (barque)	30	30
261	20½p. *Rio Grande* (brig)	45	45
262	28p. *Lady Elizabeth* (barque)	65	65
263	31p. *Sumatra* (barque)	70	70
MS264	103×94 mm. 28p. As No. 262; 31p. *Lady Elizabeth* (as shown on Falkland Islands No. 417) (sold at 60p.)	2·20	2·20

No. **MS**264 was issued to commemorate links between the Isle of Man and the Falkland Islands.

244 C.E.P.T. 25th Anniversary Logo

1984. Europa.

265	**244**	10p. orange, brown and light orange	30	25
266	**244**	20½p. blue, deep blue and light blue	50	50

245 Railway Air Services de Havilland D.H.84 Dragon Mk 2 G-ACXI of Railway Air Service

1984. 50th Anniv of First Official Airmail to the Isle of Man and 40th Anniv of International Civil Aviation Organization. Multicoloured.

267	11p. Type **245**	25	25
268	13p. West Coast Air Services de Havilland D.H. 86A Dragon Express G-ADJV *Ronaldsway*	40	40
269	26p. B.E.A. Douglas DC-3 G-AGZB	70	70
270	28p. B.E.A. Vickers Viscount 800	70	70
271	31p. Britten-Norman BN-2 Islander G-AXXH of Telair	80	80

250 Window from Glencrutchery House, Douglas

1984. Christmas. Stained-glass Windows. Multicoloured.

272	10p. Type **250**	30	30
273	13p. Window from Lonan Old Church	60	60

252 William Cain's Birthplace, Ballasalla

1984. William Cain (civic leader, Victoria) Commemoration. Multicoloured.

274	11p. Type **252**	25	20
275	22p. The *Anna* leaving Liverpool, 1852	50	50
276	26p. Early Australian railway	60	60
277	30p. William Cain as Mayor of Melbourne, and Town Hall	70	70
278	33p. Royal Exhibition Building, Melbourne	75	75

257 Queen Elizabeth II and Commonwealth Parliamentary Association Badge

1984. Links with the Commonwealth. 30th Commonwealth Parliamentary Association Conference. Multicoloured.

279	14p. Type **257**	35	35
280	33p. Queen Elizabeth II and Manx emblem	65	65

259 Cunningham House Headquarters and Mrs. Willie Cunningham and Mrs. Joseph Cunningham (former Commissioners)

1985. 75th Anniv of Girl Guide Movement. Multicoloured.

281	11p. Type **259**	30	25

282	14p. Princess Margaret, Isle of Man standard and guides	35	35
283	29p. Lady Olave Baden-Powell opening Guide Headquarters, 1955	70	70
284	31p. Guide uniforms from 1910 to 1985	75	75
285	34p. Guide handclasp, salute and early badge	85	85

264 Score of Manx National Anthem

1985. Europa. European Music Year.

286	**264**	12p. black, light brown and brown	30	15
287	-	12p. black, light brown & brown	30	15
288	-	22p. black, light blue & blue	80	25
289	-	22p. black, light blue & blue	80	25

DESIGNS: No. 287, William H. Gill (lyricist); 288, Score of hymn "Crofton"; 289, Dr. John Clague (composer).

268 Charles Rolls in 20 h.p. Rolls-Royce (1906 Tourist Trophy Race)

1985. Century of Motoring. Multicoloured.

290	12p. Type **268**	25	15
291	12p. W. Bentley in 3 litre Bentley (1922 Tourist Trophy Race)	25	15
292	14p. F. Gerrard in E.R.A. (1950 British Empire Trophy Race)	25	15
293	14p. Brian Lewis in Alfa Romeo (1934 Mannin Moar Race)	25	15
294	31p. Jaguar "XJ-SC" ("Roads Open" car, 1984 Motor Cycle TT Races)	60	40
295	31p. Tony Pond and Mike Nicholson in Vauxhall "Chevette" (1981 Rothmans International Rally)	60	40

274 Queen Alexandra and Victorian Sergeant with Wife

1985. Centenary of Soldiers', Sailors' and Airmen's Families Association. Association Presidents. Multicoloured.

296	12p. Type **274**	20	20
297	15p. Queen Mary and Royal Air Force family	40	40
298	29p. Earl Mountbatten and Royal Navy family	75	75
299	34p. Prince Michael of Kent and Royal Marine with parents, 1982	1·00	1·00

278 Kirk Maughold (birthplace)

1985. Birth Bicentenary of Lieutenant-General Sir Mark Cubbon (Indian administrator). Multicoloured.

300	12p. Type **278**	35	35
301	22p. Lieutenant-General Sir Mark Cubbon (vert)	65	65
302	45p. Memorial statue, Bangalore, India (vert)	1·25	1·25

281 St. Peter's Church, Onchan

1985. Christmas. Manx Churches. Multicoloured.

303	11p. Type **281**	30	25
304	14p. Royal Chapel of St. John, Tynwald	40	35
305	31p. Bride Parish Church	1·00	90

284 Swimming

1986. Commonwealth Games, Edinburgh. Multicoloured.

306	12p. Type **284**	20	15
307	15p. Race walking	25	30
308	31p. Rifle-shooting	90	95
309	34p. Cycling	1·00	95

No. 309 also commemorates the 50th anniversary of Manx International Cycling Week.

288 Viking Necklace and Peel Castle

1986. Centenary of Manx Museum. Multicoloured.

310	12p. Type **288**	20	15
311	15p. Meayll Circle, Rushen	25	20
312	22p. Skeleton of Great Deer and Manx Museum (vert)	65	50
313	26p. Viking longship model (vert)	80	60
314	29p. Open Air Museum, Cregneash	90	60

293 Viking Longship

1986. Manx Heritage Year.

315	**293**	2p. multicoloured	40	40
316	-	10p. black, green and grey	35	35

DESIGN: 10p. Celtic cross logo.

295 *Usnea articulata* (lichen) and *Neotinea intacta* (orchid), The Ayres

1986. Europa. Protection of Nature and the Environment. Multicoloured.

317	12p. Type **295**	35	35
318	12p. Hen harrier, Calf of Man	35	35
319	22p. Manx stoat, Eary Cushlin	90	90
320	22p. *Stenobothus stigmaticus* (grasshopper), St. Michael's Isle	90	90

299 Ellanbane (home of Myles Standish)

1986. "Ameripex '86" International Stamp Exhibition, Chicago. Captain Myles Standish of the *Mayflower*. Multicoloured.

321	12p. Type **299**	20	20
322	15p. Mayflower crossing the Atlantic, 1620	25	25
323	31p. Pilgrim Fathers landing at Plymouth, 1620	90	90
324	34p. Captain Myles Standish	95	95
MS325	100×75 mm. Nos. 323/4	2·10	2·10

No. **MS**325 also commemorates the 75th anniversary of the World Manx Association.

303 Prince Andrew in Naval Uniform and Miss Sarah Ferguson

1986. Royal Wedding. Multicoloured.

326	15p. Type **303**	30	30
327	40p. Engagement photograph	1·60	1·60

305 Prince Philip (from photo by Karsh)

1986. Royal Birthdays. Multicoloured.

328	15p. Type **305**	30	30
329	15p. Queen Elizabeth II (from photo by Karsh)	30	30
330	34p. Queen Elizabeth and Prince Philip (from photo by Karsh) (48×35 mm)	1·10	1·10

Nos. 328/30 also commemorate "Stockholmia '86" International Stamp Exhibition, Sweden and the 350th anniversary of the Swedish Post Office.

308 European Robins on Globe and "Peace and Goodwill" in Braille

1986. Christmas and International Peace Year. Multicoloured.

331	11p. Type **308**	30	30
332	14p. Hands releasing peace dove	30	30
333	31p. Clasped hands and "Peace" in sign language	80	80

311 North Quay

1987. Victorian Douglas. Multicoloured.

334	2p. Type **311**	10	10
335	3p. Old Fishmarket	10	10
336	10p. The Breakwater	25	25
337	15p. Jubilee Clock	30	30
338	31p. Loch Promenade	90	90
339	34p. Beach	1·00	1·00

317 *The Old Fishmarket and Harbour, Douglas*

1987. Paintings by John Miller Nicholson. Multicoloured.

340	12p. Type **317**	30	30
341	26p. *Red Sails at Douglas*	70	60
342	29p. *The Double Corner, Peel*	90	80
343	34p. *Peel Harbour*	1·00	1·00

321 Sea Terminal, Douglas

1987. Europa. Architecture. Multicoloured.

344	12p. Type **321**	45	85
345	12p. Tower of Refuge, Douglas	45	85
346	22p. Gaiety Theatre, Douglas	65	1·25
347	22p. Villa Marina, Douglas	65	1·25

325 Supercharged "BMW" 500cc Motor Cycle, 1939

1987. 80th Anniv of Tourist Trophy Motor Cycle Races. Multicoloured.

348	12p. Type **325**	45	30
349	15p. Manx "Kneeler" Norton 350cc, 1953	50	40
350	29p. MV Agusta 500cc 4, 1956	90	80
351	31p. Guzzi 500cc V8, 1957	90	80

352	34p. Honda 250cc 6, 1967	1·00	1·00
MS353	150×140 mm. Nos. 348/52	3·00	3·50

Nos. 348/**MS**353 also commemorate the Centenary of the St. John Ambulance Brigade and No. **MS**353 carries the logo of "Capex '87" International Stamp Exhibition, Toronto, on its margin.

330 Fuchsia and Wild Roses

1987. Wild Flowers. Multicoloured.

354	16p. Type **330**	50	40
355	29p. Field scabious and ragwort	90	80
356	31p. Wood anemone and celandine	90	1·00
357	34p. Violets and primroses	1·00	1·20

334 Stirring the Christmas Pudding

1987. Christmas. Victorian Scenes. Multicoloured.

358	12p. Type **334**	50	50
359	15p. Bringing home the Christmas tree	70	70
360	31p. Decorating the Christmas tree	90	90

337 Russell Brookes in Vauxhall "Opel" (Manx Rally winner, 1985)

1988. Motor Sport. Multicoloured.

361	13p. Type **337**	75	40
362	26p. Ari Vatanen in Ford "Escort" (Manx Rally winner, 1976)	1·20	1·20
363	31p. Terry Smith in Repco "March 761" (Hill Climb winner, 1980)	1·40	1·50
364	34p. Nigel Mansell in Williams/Honda (British Grand Prix winner, 1986 and 1987)	1·60	1·70

341 Horse Tram Terminus, Douglas Bay Tramway

356a Queen Elizabeth II taking Salute at Trooping the Colour

1988. Manx Railways and Tramways. Multicoloured.

365	1p. Type **341**	10	10
366	2p. Snaefell Mountain Railway	10	10
367	3p. Marine Drive Tramway	10	10
367c	4p. Douglas Cable Tramway	20	10
368	5p. Douglas Head Incline Railway	20	20
369	10p. Douglas & Laxey Coast Electric Tramway car at Maughold Head	30	30
370	13p. As 4p.	50	50
371	14p. Manx Northern Railway No. 4, Caledonia, at Gob-y-Deigan	50	50
372	15p. Laxey Mine Railway Lewin locomotive Ant	50	50
373	16p. Port Erin Breakwater Tramway locomotive Henry B. Loch	50	50
374	17p. Ramsey Harbour Tramway	50	50
375	18p. Locomotive No. 7, Tynwald, on Foxdale line	55	55
375a	18p. T.P.O. Special leaving Douglas, 3 July 1991	70	70
376	19p. Baldwin Reservoir Tramway steam locomotive No. 1, Injebreck	60	60
377	20p. I.M.R. No. 13, Kissack, near St. Johns	60	60
377a	21p. As 14p.	60	60

377b	23p. Double-deck horse tram, Douglas	80	80
378	25p. I.M.R. No. 12, Hutchinson, leaving Douglas	60	60
379	50p. Groudle Glen Railway locomotive Polar Bear	1·30	1·20
380	£1 I.M.R. No. 11, Maitland, pulling Royal Train, 1963	2·50	2·50
380a	£2 Type **356a**	5·00	5·00

357 Laying Isle of Man–U.K. Submarine Cable

1988. Europa. Transport and Communications. Multicoloured.

381	13p. Type **357**	50	45
382	13p. Flex Services (cable ship)	50	45
383	22p. Earth station, Braddan	75	75
384	22p. "INTELSAT 5" satellite	75	75

Nos. 381/2 and 383/4 were each printed together, se-tenant, Nos. 381/2 forming a composite design.

361 Euterpe (full-rigged ship) off Ramsey, 1863

1988. Manx Sailing Ships. Multicoloured.

385	16p. Type **361**	45	40
386	29p. Vixen (topsail schooner) leaving Peel for Australia, 1853	90	90
387	31p. Ramsey (full-rigged ship) off Brisbane, 1870	90	90
388	34p. Star of India (formerly Euterpe) (barque) off San Diego, 1976	1·10	1·10
MS389	110×85 mm. Nos. 385 and 388	1·90	2·00

Nos. 386/7 also commemorate the Bicent of Australian Settlement.

365 "Magellanica"

1988. 50th Anniv of British Fuchsia Society. Multicoloured.

390	13p. Type **365**	40	25
391	16p. "Pink Cloud"	45	35
392	22p. "Leonora"	65	60
393	29p. "Satellite"	90	90
394	31p. "Preston Guild"	1·00	1·00
395	34p. "Thalia"	1·10	1·20

371 Long-eared Owl

1988. Christmas. Manx Birds. Multicoloured.

396	12p. Type **371**	40	30
397	15p. European robin	60	65
398	31p. Grey partridge	1·20	1·20

374 Ginger Cat

1989. Manx Cats. Multicoloured.

399	16p. Type **374**	50	30
400	27p. Black and white cat	90	85
401	30p. Tortoiseshell and white cat	1·20	1·00
402	40p. Tortoiseshell cat	1·50	1·30

378 Tudric Pewter Clock, c. 1903

1989. 125th Birth Anniv of Archibald Knox (artist and designer). Multicoloured.

403	13p. Type **378**	20	20
404	16p. Celtic Cross watercolour	30	25
405	23p. Silver cup and cover 1902–03	50	50
406	32p. Gold and silver brooches from Liberty's Cymric range (horiz)	1·20	1·00
407	35p. Silver jewel box, 1900 (horiz)	1·40	1·00

383 William Bligh and Old Church, Onchan

1989. Bicentenary of the Mutiny on the Bounty. Multicoloured.

408	13p. Type **383**	30	20
409	16p. Bligh and loyal crew cast adrift	35	30
410	23p. Pitcairn Islands 1989 Settlement Bicentenary 90c., No. 345	1·00	1·00
411	27p. Norfolk Island 1989 Bicentenary 39c., No. 461	1·00	1·00
412	30p. Midshipman Peter Heywood and Tahiti	60	60
413	32p. H.M.S. Bounty anchored off Pitcairn Island	70	70
414	35p. Fletcher Christian and Pitcairn Island	80	80
MS415	110×85 mm. Nos. 410/11 and 414	3·75	3·75

390 Skipping and Hopscotch

1989. Europa. Children's Games. Multicoloured.

416	13p. Type **390**	45	40
417	13p. Wheelbarrow, leapfrog and piggyback	45	40
418	23p. Completing model house and blowing bubbles	70	75
419	23p. Girl with doll and doll's house	70	75

Nos. 416/17 and 418/19 were printed together, se-tenant, forming composite designs.

394 Atlantic Puffin

1989. Sea Birds. Multicoloured.

420	13p. Type **394**	55	55
421	13p. Black guillemot	55	55
422	13p. Great cormorant ("Cormorant")	55	55
423	13p. Black-legged kittiwake ("Kittiwake")	55	55

398 Red Cross Cadets learning Resuscitation

1989. 125th Anniv of International Red Cross and Centenary of Noble's Hospital, Isle of Man.

424	**398** 14p. multicoloured	40	30
425	– 17p. grey and red	60	35
426	– 23p. multicoloured	75	85
427	– 30p. multicoloured	1·00	1·10
428	– 35p. multicoloured	1·20	1·20

DESIGNS: 17p. Anniversary logo; 23p. Signing Geneva Convention, 1864; 30p. Red Cross ambulance; 35p. Henri Dunant (founder).

403 Mother with Baby, Jane Crookall Maternity Home

1989. Christmas. 50th Anniv of Jane Crookall Maternity Home and 75th Anniv of St. Ninian's Church, Douglas. Multicoloured.

429	13p. Type **378**	50	45
430	16p. Mother with child	60	60
431	34p. Madonna and Child	1·10	1·20
432	37p. Baptism, St. Ninian's Church	1·20	1·40

407 "the Isle of Man Express going up a Gradient"

1990. Isle of Man Edwardian Postcards. Multicoloured.

433	15p. Type **407**	35	35
434	19p. A way we have in the Isle of Man	60	50
435	32p. Douglas-waiting for the male boat	1·10	1·10
436	34p. The last toast rack home, Douglas Parade	1·50	1·50
437	37p. The last Isle of Man boat	1·60	1·60

412 Modern Postman

1990. Europa. Post Office Buildings. Multicoloured.

438	15p. Type **412**	55	30
439	15p. Ramsey Post Office, 1990 (40×26 mm)	55	30
440	24p. Postman, 1890	90	40
441	24p. Douglas Post Office, 1890 (40×26 mm)	90	40

416 Penny Black

1990. 150th Anniv of the Penny Black.

442	**416**	1p. black, buff and gold	15	15
443	–	19p. gold, black and buff	60	50
444	–	32p. multicoloured	1·20	1·10
445	–	34p. multicoloured	1·40	1·30
446	–	37p. multicoloured	1·50	1·40
MS447	100×71 mm. £1 black, gold and buff (50×60 mm)		4·25	4·00

DESIGNS: 19p. Wyon Medal, 1837; 32p. Wyon's stamp essay; 34p. Perkins Bacon engine-turned essay, 1839; 37p. Twopence Blue, 1840; £1 Block of four Penny Black stamps lettered IM-JN.

No. **MS**447 also commemorates "Stamp World London 90" International Stamp Exhibition.

422 Queen Elizabeth the Queen Mother

1990. 90th Birthday of Queen Elizabeth the Queen Mother.

448	**422**	90p. multicoloured	3·00	3·00

423 Hawker Hurricane Mk I, Bristol Type 142 Blenheim Mk 1, Dornier Do-17 inflames and Home Defence

1990. 50th Anniv of Battle of Britain. Multicoloured.

449	15p. Type **423**	35	20
450	15p. Supermarine Spitfire with Westland Lysander Mk I rescue aircraft and Supermarine Watrus Flying boat	35	20
451	24p. Rearming Hawker Hurricanes Mk I fighters and Supermarine Spitfire	80	25
452	24p. Ops room and scramble	80	25
453	29p. Civil Defence personnel	1·00	30
454	29p. Barrage balloons	1·00	30

429 Churchill with
Freedom of Douglas
Casket

1990. 25th Death Anniv of Sir Winston Churchill.
Multicoloured.

455	19p. Type **429**	45	45
456	32p. Churchill and London blitz	1·00	1·00
457	34p. Churchill and searchlights over Westminster	1·20	1·20
458	37p. Churchill with R.A.F. Hawker Hurricane Mk I fighters	1·20	1·20

433 Boy on
Toboggan and
Girl posting
Letter

1990. Christmas. Multicoloured.

459	14p. Type **433**	40	40
460	18p. Girl on toboggan and skaters	50	50
461	34p. Boy with snowman	1·20	1·20
462	37p. Children throwing snowballs	1·50	1·50
MS463	123×55 mm. As Nos. 459/62, but face values in black	3·00	3·75

437 Henry Bloom
Noble and Orphans
(Marshall Wane)

1991. Manx Photography.

464	**437**	17p. brown, grey and black	35	35
465	-	21p. brown and ochre	50	50
466	-	26p. brown, stone and black	65	65
467	-	31p. brown, lt brown & blk	90	90
468	-	40p. multicoloured	1·10	1·10

DESIGNS: 21p. Douglas (Frederick frith); 26p. Studio portrait of three children (Hilda Newby); 31p. Castital yn Ard (Christopher Killip); 40p. Peel Castle (Colleen Corlett).

442 Lifeboat *Sir William
Hillary*, Douglas

1991. Manx Lifeboats. Multicoloured.

469	17p. Type **442**	45	45
470	21p. *Osman Gabriel*, Port Erin	55	55
471	26p. *Ann and James Ritchie*, Ramsey	90	90
472	31p. *The Gough Ritchie*, Port St. Mary	1·20	1·20
473	37p. *John Batstone*, Peel	1·40	1·40

No. 469 is inscribed "HILARY" and No. 471 "JAMES & ANN RITCHIE", both in error.

447 "Intelsat"
Communications
Satellite

1991. Europa. Europe in Space. Multicoloured.

474	17p. Type **447**	70	20
475	17p. "Ariane" rocket launch and fishing boats in Douglas harbour	70	20
476	26p. Weather satellite and space station	1·00	30
477	26p. British Aerospace ATP over Ronaldsway Airport, Manx Radio transmitter and Space shuttle launch	1·00	30

Nos. 474/5 and 476/7 were each printed together, *se-tenant*, each pair forming a composite design.

451 Oliver Godfrey with
Indian 500cc at Start, 1911

1991. 80th Anniv of Tourist Trophy Mountain Course.
Multicoloured.

478	17p. Type **451**	50	40
479	21p. Freddie Dixon on Douglas "banking" sidecar, 1923	65	60
480	26p. Bill Ivy on Yamaha 125cc, 1968	80	80
481	31p. Giacomo Agostini on MV Agusta 500cc, 1972	1·20	1·10
482	37p. Joey Dunlop on RVF Honda 750cc, 1985	1·50	1·50
MS483	149×144 mm. Nos. 478/82	4·00	4·00

1991. Ninth Conference of Commonwealth Postal
Administration, Douglas. Sheet 119×77 mm.
Multicoloured.

MS484	Nos. 367c and 377a, each ×2	1·90	2·00

LAXEY HAND-CART

456 Laxey Hand-cart,
1920

1991. Fire Engines. Multicoloured.

485	17p. Type **456**	45	40
486	21p. Horse-drawn steamer, Douglas, 1909	65	65
487	30p. Merryweather "Hatfield" pump, 1936	85	90
488	33p. Dennis "F8" pumping appliance, Peel, 1953	1·20	1·20
489	37p. Volvo turntable ladder, Douglas, 1989	1·40	1·50

461 Mute Swans, Douglas
Harbour

1991. Swans. Multicoloured.

490	17p. Type **461**	40	20
491	17p. Black swans, Curraghs Wildlife Park	40	20
492	26p. Whooper swans, Bishop's Dub, Ballaugh	1·10	30
493	26p. Tundra ("Bewick's") swans, Eairy Dam, Foxdale	1·10	30
494	37p. Coscoroba swans, Curraghs Wildlife Park	1·20	30
495	37p. Whooper ("Trumpeter") swans, Curraghs Wildlife Park	1·20	40

The two designs of each value were printed together, *se-tenant*, forming a composite design.

467 The Three
Kings

1991. Christmas. Paper Sculptures. Multicoloured.

496	16p. Type **467**	45	35
497	20p. Mary with manger	65	70
498	26p. Shepherds with sheep	85	85
499	37p. Choir of angels	1·10	1·10

471 North African and Italian
Campaigns, 1942–43

1992. 50th Anniv of Parachute Regiment. Multicoloured.

502	23p. Type **471**	70	25
503	23p. D-Day, 1944	70	25
504	28p. Arnhem, 1944	80	30
505	28p. Rhine crossing, 1945	80	30
506	39p. Operations in Near, Middle and Far East, 1945–68	1·20	40
507	39p. Liberation of Falkland Islands, 1982	1·20	40

477 Queen
Elizabeth II at
Coronation, 1953

1992. 40th Anniv of Accession. Multicoloured.

508	18p. Type **477**	45	40
509	23p. Queen visiting Isle of Man, 1979	60	60
510	28p. Queen in evening dress	70	70
511	33p. Queen visiting Isle of Man, 1989	1·20	1·40
512	39p. Queen arriving for film premiere, 1990	1·40	1·40

482 Brittle-stars

1992. Centenary of Port Erin Marine Laboratory.
Multicoloured.

513	18p. Type **482**	40	35
514	23p. Phytoplankton	60	55
515	28p. Atlantic herring	60	60
516	33p. Great scallop	1·20	1·20
517	39p. Dahlia anemone and delesseria	1·50	1·50

487 The Pilgrim
Fathers embarking at
Delfshaven

1992. Europa. 500th Anniv of Discovery of America by
Columbus. Multicoloured.

518	18p. Type **487**	40	20
519	18p. *Speedwell* leaving Delfshaven	40	30
520	28p. *Mayflower* setting sail for America	75	30
521	28p. *Speedwell* anchored at Dartmouth	75	30

The two designs for each value were printed together, *se-tenant*, in horizontal pairs forming composite designs.

491 Central Pacific
Locomotive *Jupiter*, 1869

1992. Construction of the Union Pacific Railroad, 1866–
69. Multicoloured.

522	33p. Type **491**	90	35
523	33p. Union Pacific locomotive No. 119, 1869	90	35
524	39p. Union Pacific locomotive No. 844, 1992	1·20	40
525	39p. Union Pacific locomotive No. 3985, 1992	1·20	40
MS526	105×78 mm. £1.50 Golden Spike ceremony, 10 May 1869 (60×50 mm)	4·25	4·50

496 *King Orry V* in Douglas Harbour

1992. Manx Harbours. Multicoloured.

527	18p. Type **496**	45	45
528	23p. Castletown	55	55
529	37p. Port St. Mary	1·20	1·20
530	40p. Ramsey	1·40	1·40

500 *Saint Eloi* in 1972 (image scaled to 44% of original size)

1992. "Genova '92" International Thematic Stamp
Exhibition. Sheet 111×68 mm, containing T **500** and
similar horiz design. Multicoloured.

MS531	18p. "King Orry V" in 1992 (as in Type **496**); £1 Type **500**	3·25	3·50

501 Stained
Glass Window,
St. German's
Cathedral, Peel

1992. Christmas. Manx Churches. Multicoloured.

532	17p. Type **501**	50	50
533	22p. Reredos, St. Matthew the Apostle Church, Douglas	75	75
534	28p. Stained glass window, St. George's Church, Douglas	1·00	1·00
535	37p. Reredos, St. Mary of the Isle Catholic Church, Douglas	1·00	1·00
536	40p. Stained glass window, Trinity Methodist Church, Douglas	1·50	1·50

506 Mansell on Lap of
Honour, British Grand Prix,
1992

1992. Nigel Mansell's Victory in Formula 1 World Motor
Racing Championship. Multicoloured.

537	20p. Type **506**	80	80
538	24p. Mansell in French Grand Prix, 1992	1·00	1·00

508 H.M.S. *Amazon*
(frigate)

523a Manx Red
Ensign

523b Queen
Elizabeth II
(hologram)

1993. Ships. Multicoloured.

539	1p. Type **508**	10	10
540	2p. *Fingal* (lighthouse tender)	10	10
541	4p. *Sir Winston Churchill* (cadet schooner)	10	10
542	5p. *Dar Mlodziezy* (full-rigged cadet ship)	10	10
543	20p. *Tynwald I* (paddle-steamer)	40	25
544	21p. *Ben Veg* (freighter)	50	50
545	22p. *Waverley* (paddle-steamer)	50	50
546	23p. Royal Yacht *Britannia*	55	55
547	24p. *Francis Drake* (ketch)	50	35
548	25p. *Royal Viking Sky* (liner)	60	60
549	26p. *Lord Nelson* (cadet barque)	65	65
550	27p. *Europa* (liner)	65	65
551	30p. *Snaefell V* (ferry) leaving Ardrossan	75	75
552	35p. *Seacat* (catamaran ferry)	85	85
553	40p. *Lady of Man I* (ferry) off Ramsey	1·00	90
554	50p. *Mona's Queen II* (paddle ferry) leaving Fleetwood	1·20	1·10
555	£1 *Queen Elizabeth 2* (liner) and *Mona's Queen V* (ferry) off Liverpool	2·50	2·40
556	£2 Type **523a**	3·75	4·00

| 557 | £5 Type **523b** | 10·00 | 12·00 |

For 4, 20 and 24p. in smaller size, 21×18 mm, see Nos. 687/93.

524 No. 1 Motor Car and No. 13 Trailer at Groudle Glen Hotel

1993. Cent of Manx Electric Railway. Multicoloured.

559	20p. Type **524**	60	60
560	24p. No. 9 Tunnel Car and No. 19 Trailer at Douglas Bay Hotel	90	90
561	28p. No. 19 Motor Car and No. 59 Royal Trailer Special at Douglas Bay	1·00	1·00
562	39p. No. 33 Motor Car, No. 45 Trailer and No. 13 Van at Derby Castle	1·40	1·40

528 *Sir Hall Caine* (statue) (Bryan Kneale)

1993. Europa. Contemporary Art. Works by Bryan Kneale. Multicoloured.

563	20p. Type **528**	40	20
564	20p. *The Brass Bedstead* (painting)	40	20
565	28p. Abstract bronze sculpture	75	30
566	28p. *Polar Bear Skeleton* (drawing)	75	30

532 Graham Oates and Bill Marshall (1933 International Six Day Trial) on Ariel Square Four

1993. Manx Motor Cycling Events. Multicoloured.

567	20p. Type **532**	35	35
568	24p. Sergeant Geoff Duke (1947 Royal Signals Display Team) on Triumph 3T Twin	45	45
569	28p. Denis Parkinson (1953 Senior Manx Grand Prix) on Manx Norton	70	60
570	33p. Richard Swallow (1991 Junior Classic MGP) on Aermacchi	90	90
571	39p. Steve Colley (1992 Scottish Six Day Trial) on Beta Zero	1·00	95
MS572	165×120 mm. Nos. 567/71	4·50	4·50

537 *Inachis io* (Peacock)

1993. Butterflies. Multicoloured.

573	24p. Type **537**	75	65
574	24p. *Argynnis aglaja* (Dark green fritillary)	75	65
575	24p. *Cynthia cardui* (Painted lady)	75	65
576	24p. *Celastrina argiolus* (Holly blue)	75	65
577	24p. *Vanessa atalanta* (Red admiral)	75	65

542 Children decorating Christmas Tree

1993. Christmas. Multicoloured.

578	19p. Type **542**	50	50
579	23p. Girl with snowman	60	60
580	28p. Boy opening presents	70	70
581	39p. Girl with teddy bear	1·10	1·10
582	40p. Children with toboggan	1·10	1·10

547 White-throated Robin

1994. Calf of Man Bird Observatory. Multicoloured.

583	20p. Type **547**	50	20
584	20p. Black-eared wheatear	50	20
585	24p. Goldcrest	80	25
586	24p. Northern oriole	80	25
587	30p. River kingfisher ("Kingfisher")	1·00	30
588	30p. Hoopoe	1·00	30
MS589	100×71 mm. £1 Black-billed magpie (51½×61 mm)	3·00	3·50

No. **MS**589 also commemorates the "Hong Kong '94" philatelic exhibition.

554 Gaiety Theatre, Douglas

1994. Manx Tourism Centenary. Multicoloured.

590	24p. Type **554**	60	60
591	24p. Sports	60	60
592	24p. Artist at work and yachts racing	60	60
593	24p. TT Races and British Aerospace Hawk T.1 of Red Arrows display team	60	60
594	24p. Musical instruments	60	60
595	24p. Laxey Wheel and Manx cat	60	60
596	24p. Tower of Refuge, Douglas, with bucket and spade	60	60
597	24p. Cyclist	60	60
598	24p. Tynwald Day and classic car	60	60
599	24p. Santa Mince Pie train, Groudle Glen	60	60

564 *Eubranchus tricolor* (sea slug)

1994. Europa. Discoveries of Edward Forbes (marine biologist). Multicoloured.

600	20p. Type **564**	40	20
601	20p. *Loligo forbesii* (common squid)	40	20
602	20p. Edward Forbes and signature	40	20
603	30p. *Solaster moretonis* (fossil starfish)	75	30
604	30p. *Adamsia carciniopados* (anenome) on hermit crab	75	30
605	30p. *Solaster endeca* (starfish)	75	30

570 Maj-Gen. Bedell Smith and Naval Landing Force including *Ben-my-Chree IV* (ferry)

1994. 50th Anniv of D-Day. Multicoloured.

606	4p. Type **570**	10	10
607	4p. Admiral Ramsay and naval ships including *Victoria* and *Lady of Man* (ferries)	10	10
608	20p. Gen. Montgomery and British landings	50	20
609	20p. Lt-Gen. Dempsey and 2nd Army landings	50	20
610	30p. Air Chief Marshal Leigh-Mallory and U.S. paratroops and aircraft	75	30
611	30p. Air Chief Marshal Tedder and British paratroops and aircraft	75	30
612	41p. Lt-Gen. Bradley and U.S. 1st Army landings	85	45
613	41p. Gen. Eisenhower and American landings	85	45

578 Postman Pat, Jess and Ffinlo at Sea Terminal, Douglas

1994. Postman Pat visits the Isle of Man. Multicoloured.

614	1p. Type **578**	15	15
615	20p. Laxey Wheel	60	60
616	24p. Cregneash	80	80
617	30p. Manx Electric Railway trains	90	90
618	36p. Peel Harbour	1·10	1·10
619	41p. Douglas Promenade	1·20	1·20
MS620	110×85 mm. £1 Postman Pat (25×39 mm)	2·20	2·20

585 Cycling

1994. Centenary of International Olympic Committee. Multicoloured.

621	10p. Type **585**	35	25
622	20p. Downhill skiing	55	50
623	24p. Swimming	70	65
624	35p. Hurdling	95	1·00
625	48p. Centenary logo	1·60	1·80

590 Santa Train to Santon

1994. Christmas. Father Christmas in the Isle of Man. Multicoloured.

626	19p. Type **590**	60	60
627	23p. Father Christmas and Postman Pat on mini tractor, Douglas (vert)	80	80
628	60p. Father Christmas and majorettes in sleigh, Port St. Mary	2·00	2·00

593 Foden Steam Wagon, Highway Board Depot, Douglas

1995. Steam Traction Engines. Multicoloured.

629	20p. Type **593**	60	60
630	24p. Clayton & Shuttleworth and Fowler engines pulling dead whale	70	70
631	30p. Wallis and Steevens engine at Ramsey Harbour	85	85
632	35p. Marshall engine with threshing machine, Ballarhenny	1·10	1·10
633	41p. Marshall convertible steam roller	1·20	1·20

598 Car No. 2 and First Train, 1895

1995. Centenary of Snaefell Mountain Railway. Multicoloured.

634	20p. Type **598**	70	70
635	24p. Car No. 4 in green livery and Car No. 3 in Laxey Valley	80	80
636	35p. Car No. 6 and Car No. 5 in 1971	1·10	1·10
637	42p. Goods Car No. 7 and *Caledonia* steam locomotive pulling construction train	1·20	1·20
MS638	110×87 mm. £1 Passenger car and Argus char-a-banc at Bungalow Hotel (60×37 mm)	3·50	3·50

603 Peace Doves forming Wave and Tower of Refuge, Douglas Bay

1995. Europa. Peace and Freedom. Multicoloured.

| 639 | 20p. Type **603** | 60 | 75 |
| 640 | 30p. Peace dove breaking barbed wire | 1·00 | 1·00 |

605 Spitfire, Tank and Medals

1995. 50th Anniv of End of Second World War. Multicoloured.

641	10p. Type **144**	30	15
642	10p. Hawker Typhoon, anti-aircraft gun and medals	30	15
643	20p. Auro Type **683** Lancaster, H.M.S. *Biter* (escort carrier) and medals	55	25
644	20p. Grumman TBM Avenger aircraft, jungle patrol and medals	55	25
645	24p. Celebrations in Parliament Square	70	25
646	24p. V.E. Day bonfire	70	25
647	40p. Street party	1·10	50
648	40p. King George VI and Queen Elizabeth on Isle of Man in July 1945	1·10	50

613 Reg Parnell in Maserati "4 CLT", 1951

1995. 90th Anniv of Motor Racing on Isle of Man. Multicoloured.

649	20p. Type **613**	65	60
650	24p. Stirling Moss in Frazer Nash, 1951	80	75
651	30p. Richard Seaman in Delage, 1936	90	85
652	36p. Prince Bira in ERA R2B "Romulus", 1937	1·10	1·00
653	41p. Kenelm Guinness in Sunbeam 1, 1914	1·20	1·20
654	42p. Freddie Dixon in Riley, 1934	1·20	1·50
MS655	103×73 mm. £1 John Napier in Arrol Johnston, 1905 (47×58 mm)	3·75	3·75

620 Thomas the Tank Engine and Bertie Bus being Unloaded

1995. 50th Anniv of *Thomas the Tank Engine* Stories by Revd. Awdry. "Thomas the Tank Engine's Dream". Multicoloured.

656	20p. Type **620**	65	60
657	24p. Mail train	80	75
658	30p. Bertie and engines at Ballasalla	90	85
659	36p. *Viking* the diesel engine, Port Erin	1·10	1·10
660	41p. Thomas and railcar at Snaefell summit	1·20	1·10
661	45p. Engines racing past Laxey Wheel	1·50	1·20

626 *Amanita muscaria*

1995. Fungi. Multicoloured.

662	20p. Type **626**	60	60
663	24p. *Boletus edulis*	70	70
664	30p. *Coprinus disseminatus*	70	70
665	35p. *Pleurotus ostreatus*	90	90
666	45p. *Geastrum triplex*	1·50	1·50

MS667 100×71 mm. £1 Shaggy ink cap and bee orchid (50×59 mm)   3·00   3·00

No. MS667 is inscribed "Singapore World Stamp Exhibition 1st–10th September 1995" on the sheet margin.

632 St. Catherine's Church, Port Erin

1995. Christmas. Multicoloured.

668	19p. Type **632**		55	55
669	23p. European robin on holly branch		70	70
670	42p. St. Peter's Church and wild flowers		1·50	1·50
671	50p. Hedgehog hibernating under farm machinery		1·70	1·70

636 Langness Lighthouse

1996. Lighthouses. Multicoloured.

672	20p. Type **636**		50	50
673	24p. Point of Ayre lighthouse (horiz)		60	60
674	30p. Chicken Rock lighthouse		90	90
675	36p. Calf of Man lighthouse (horiz)		1·00	1·00
676	41p. Douglas Head lighthouse		1·10	1·10
677	42p. Maughold Head lighthouse (horiz)		1·20	1·20

642 White Manx Cat and Celtic Interlaced Ribbons

1996. Manx Cats. Multicoloured.

678	20p. Type **642**		50	50
679	24p. Cat and Union Jack ribbons		60	60
680	36p. Cat on rug in German colours, mouse and Brandenburg Gate		90	90
681	42p. Cat, U.S.A. flag and Statue of Liberty		1·10	1·10
682	48p. Cat, map of Australia and kangaroo		1·20	1·20

MS683 100×71 mm. £1.50 Cat with kittens (51×61 mm)   4·00   4·00

See also No. MS712.

648 Douglas Borough Arms

1996. Centenary of Douglas Borough. Self-adhesive.

684	**648**	(20p.) multicoloured	70	1·00

1996. Ships. As Nos. 541, 543 and 547, but smaller, 21×18 mm. Multicoloured.

687	4p. *Sir Winston Churchill* (cadet schooner)		20	15
689	20p. *Tynwald I* (paddle-steamer), 1846		60	70
693	24p. *Francis Drake* (ketch)		90	90

The 20p. and 24p. show the positions of the face value and Queen's head reversed.

665 Princess Anne (President, Save the Children Fund) and Children

1996. Europa. Famous Women. Multicoloured.

701	24p. Type **665**		70	75
702	30p. Queen Elizabeth II and people of the Commonwealth		90	1·00

667 Alec Bennett

1996. Tourist Trophy Motorcycle Races. Irish Winners. Multicoloured.

703	20p. Type **667**		60	60
704	24p. Stanley Woods		75	75
705	45p. Artie Bell		1·00	1·00
706	60p. Joey and Robert Dunlop		1·75	1·75

MS707 100×70 mm. £1 R.A.F. Red Arrows display team (vert)   3·00   3·00

672 National Poppy Appeal Trophy

1996. 75th Anniv of Royal British Legion. Multicoloured.

708	20p. Type **672**		65	55
709	24p. Manx War Memoial, Braddan		70	60
710	42p. Poppy appeal collection box		1·10	1·20
711	75p. Royal British Legion badge		2·00	2·00

1996. "Capex '96" International Stamp Exhibition, Toronto.
No. MS683 additionally inscribed with "CAPEX '96" exhibition logo on sheet margin.

MS712 100×71 mm. £1.50 Cat with kittens (51×61 mm)   6·00   6·50

676 UNICEF Projects in Mexico

1996. 50th Anniv of UNICEF. Multicoloured.

713	24p. Type **676**		50	30
714	24p. Projects in Sri Lanka		50	30
715	30p. Projects in Colombia		60	60
716	30p. Projects in Zambia		60	60
717	42p. Projects in Afghanistan		80	80
718	42p. Projects in Vietnam		80	80

682 Labrador

1996. Dogs. Multicoloured.

719	20p. Type **682**		60	55
720	24p. Border collie		70	65
721	31p. Dalmatian		1·00	90
722	38p. Mongrel		1·10	1·10
723	43p. English setter		1·50	1·50
724	63p. Alsatian		2·00	2·00

MS725 100×71 mm. £1.20 Labrador guide dog and working Border collie (38×50 mm)   3·75   3·75

689 *Snowman and Pine Trees* (David Bennett)

1996. Christmas. Children's Paintings. Multicoloured.

726	19p. Type **689**		55	50
727	23p. *Three-legged Father Christmas* (Louis White)		70	65
728	50p. *Family around Christmas Tree* (Robyn Whelan)		1·60	1·60
729	75p. *Father Christmas in Sleigh* (Claire Bradley)		2·10	2·20

693 Primroses and Cashtyl ny Ard

1997. Spring in Man. Multicoloured.

730	20p. Type **693**		50	50
731	24p. Lochtan sheep and lambs		70	70
732	43p. Daffodils, mallard and ducklings		1·10	1·10
733	63p. Dabchick with young and frog on lily pad		1·60	1·60

697 Barn Owl

1997. Owls. Multicoloured.

734	20p. Type **697**		65	60
735	24p. Short-eared owl		80	75
736	31p. Long-eared owl		1·00	90
737	36p. Little owl		1·20	1·10
738	43p. Snowy owl		1·40	1·50
739	56p. Eurasian tawny owl		1·60	1·70

MS740 100×71 mm. £1.20 Long-eared owl (different) (51×60 mm)   4·00   4·25

No. MS740 includes the "HONG KONG '97" International Stamp Exhibition logo on the sheet margin.

704 Moddey Dhoo, Peel Castle

1997. Europa. Tales and Legends. Multicoloured.

741	21p. Type **704**		55	55
742	25p. Fairies in tree and cottage		65	65
743	31p. Fairies at Fairy Bridge		85	85
744	36p. Giant Finn Macooil and Calf of Man		1·10	1·10
745	37p. The Buggane of St. Trinian's		1·10	1·10
746	43p. Fynoderee and farm		1·40	1·40

Nos. 742/3 include the "EUROPA" emblem.

710 Sopwith Tabloid

1997. Manx Aircraft. Multicoloured.

747	21p. Type **710**		30	25
748	21p. Grumman Tiger (1996 Schneider Trophy)		30	25
749	25p. BAe ATP (15th anniv of Manx Airlines)		35	25
750	25p. BAe 146-200 (15th anniv of Manx Airlines)		35	25
751	31p. Boeing 757-200 (largest aircraft to land on Isle of Man)		70	35
752	31p. Farman biplane (1st Manx flight, 1911)		70	35
753	36p. Supermarine Spitfire		75	40
754	36p. Hawker Hurricane		75	40

Nos. 747/8, 749/50, 751/2 and 753/4 respectively were each printed together, *se-tenant*, the backgrounds forming composite of Isle of Man.

No. 752 is inscribed "EARMAN BIPLANE" in error.

718 14th Hole, Ramsey Golf Club

1997. Golf. Multicoloured.

755	21p. Type **718**		50	50
756	25p. 15th Hole, King Edward Bay Golf and Country Club		60	60
757	43p. 17th Hole, Rowany Golf Club		1·10	1·10
758	50p. 8th Hole, Castletown Golf Links		1·50	1·50

MS759 100×71 mm. £1.30 Golf ball (circular, diameter 39 mm)   3·50   3·50

No. MS759 includes the "Pacific '97" International Stamp Exhibition logo on the sheet margin.

1997. Return of Hong Kong to China. Sheet 130×90 mm, containing No. 546. Multicoloured.

MS760 23p. Royal Yacht "Britannia"   1·75   1·95

724 Steve Colley

1997. F.I.M. "Trial de Nations" Motorcycle Team Trials. Multicoloured.

761	21p. Type **724**		55	50
762	25p. Steve Saunders (vert)		65	60
763	37p. Sammy Miller (vert)		1·20	1·00
764	44p. Don Smith		1·50	1·20

728 Angel and Shepherd

1997. Christmas. Multicoloured.

765	20p. Type **728**		65	55
766	24p. Angel and King		75	70
767	63p. The Nativity (54×39 mm)		1·80	1·80

731 Engagement of Princess Elizabeth and Lieut. Philip Mountbatten, 1947

1997. Golden Wedding of Queen Elizabeth and Prince Philip. Multicoloured (except No. 768).

768	50p. Type **731** (brown and gold)		1·00	1·00
769	50p. Wedding photograph, 1947		1·00	1·00
770	50p. At Ascot, 1952		1·00	1·00
771	50p. Golden Wedding photograph, 1997		1·00	1·00

MS772 100×72 mm. £1 Queen Elizabeth and Prince Philip at Peel, 1989 (47×58 mm)   3·00   3·00

738 Shamrock   **753** Queen Elizabeth II and Queen Elizabeth the Queen Mother

1998. Flowers. Multicoloured.

773	1p. Bearded iris		10	10
774	2p. Daisy		10	10
775	4p. Type **738**		10	10
776	5p. Silver Jubilee rose		10	15
777	10p. Oriental poppy		20	25
778	20p. Heath spotted orchid		40	30
779	21p. Cushag		40	45
780	22p. Gorse		45	50
781	25p. Princess of Wales rose		50	40
782	26p. Dog rose		50	40
783	30p. Fuchsia "Lady Thumb"		60	60
784	50p. Daffodil		1·00	1·00
785	£1 Spear thistle		2·00	2·00
790	£2.50 Type **753**		5·00	4·75

756 Viking Figurehead

1998. Viking Longships. Multicoloured.

793	21p. Type **756**		55	50
794	25p. Viking longship at sea		75	75
795	31p. Viking longship on beach		90	90
796	75p. Stern of ship		2·20	2·50

MS797 100×71 mm. £1 Viking ship at Peel Castle   3·00   3·00

761 Bottle-nosed Dolphins

1998. UNESCO International Year of the Ocean. Multicoloured.

798	10p. Type **761**	30	30
799	21p. Basking shark	50	50
800	25p. Front view of basking shark	65	65
801	31p. Minke whale	75	75
802	63p. Killer whale and calf	1·60	1·60

766 Locomotive No. 12 *Hutchinson*

1998. 125th Anniv of Isle of Man Steam Railway. Multicoloured.

803	21p. Type **766**	60	50
804	25p. Locomotive No. 10 *G. H. Wood*	70	60
805	31p. Locomotive No. 11 *Maitland*	90	80
806	63p. Locomotive No. 4 *Loch*	1·60	1·60
MS807	119×54 mm. 25p. Pillar box and train at Douglas Station; £1 Locomotive No. 1 *Sutherland*	3·00	3·00

771 Purple Helmets Display Team

1998. Isle of Man T.T. Races and 50th Anniv of Honda (manufacturer). Multicoloured.

808	21p. Type **771**	45	45
809	25p. Joey Dunlop	55	55
810	31p. Dave Molyneux	70	65
811	43p. Naomi Taniguchi	1·10	1·00
812	63p. Mike Hailwood	1·50	1·50

776 Princess Diana wearing Protective Clothing, Angola

1998. Diana, Princess of Wales Commemoration. Multicoloured.

813	25p. Type **776**	50	30
814	25p. Receiving award from United Cerebral Palsy Charity, New York, 1995	50	30
815	25p. With children, South Korea, 1992	50	30
816	25p. Wearing blue jacket, July 1993	50	30

780 Tynwald Day Ceremony

1998. Europa. Festivals. Multicoloured.

817	25p. Type **780**	50	45
818	30p. Traditional dancers, Tynwald Fair	1·10	1·20

782 Father Christmas at North Pole

1998. Christmas. "A Very Special Delivery". Multicoloured.

819	20p. Type **782**	40	30
820	24p. Father Christmas checking list	50	45
821	30p. Flying over Spring Valley sorting office	75	75

822	43p. Passing through Baldrine village	95	95
823	63p. Father Christmas delivering presents	1·40	1·40

787 Large Oval Pillar Box, Kirk Onchan

1999. Local Post Boxes. Multicoloured.

824	10p. Type **787**	25	25
825	20p. Wall box, Ballaterson	45	45
826	21p. King Edward VII pillar box, Laxey Station	50	50
827	25p. Wall box, Spaldrick	85	85
828	44p. Small oval pillar box, Derby Road, Douglas	1·50	1·50
829	63p. Wall box, Baldrine Station	1·75	1·75

793 Cottage, Ballaglass Glen

1999. Europa. Parks and Gardens. Multicoloured.

830	25p. Type **793**	70	70
831	30p. Glen Maye Waterfall	1·00	1·00

795 *Ann and James Ritchie*, Ramsey

1999. 175th Anniv of Royal National Lifeboat Institution. Multicoloured.

832	21p. Type **795**	50	50
833	25p. *Sir William Hillary*, Douglas	55	55
834	37p. *Ruby Clery*, Peel	80	80
835	43p. *Herbert and Edith* (inshore lifeboat), Port Erin	90	90
836	43p. 1974 150th Anniv 8p. stamp	1·00	1·00
837	56p. *Gough Ritchie II*, Port St. Mary	1·20	1·20
838	56p. 1991 Manx Lifeboats 21p. stamp	1·50	1·50
MS839	100×70 mm. £1 *Sir William Hillary* (founder) (37×50 mm)	4·00	4·00

No. **MS839** includes the "Australia '99" World Stamp Exhibition emblem on the sheet margin.

803 Winter

1999. Centenary of Yn Cheshaght Ghailckagh (Manx Gaelic Society). The Seasons. Multicoloured.

840	22p. Type **803**	60	60
841	26p. Spring	65	65
842	50p. Summer	1·10	1·10
843	63p. Autumn	1·60	1·60

Nos. 840/3 are inscribed "Ellan Vannin", the Manx name for the Isle of Man.

807 Queen Victoria (image scaled to 28% of original size)

1999. British Monarchs of the 20th Century. Sheet 170×75 mm, containing T **179** and similar horiz designs. Multicoloured.

MS844	26p. Type **807**; 26p. King Edward VII; 26p. King George V; 26p. King Edward VIII; 26p. King George VI; 26p. Queen Elizabeth II	4·00	4·00

808 Tilling-Stevens Double-deck Bus, 1922

1999. Manx Buses. Multicoloured.

845	22p. Type **808**	50	50
846	26p. Thornycroft BC single-deck, 1928	55	55
847	28p. Cumberland ADC 416 single-deck, 1927	65	65
848	37p. Straker-Squire single-deck, 1914	1·25	1·25
849	38p. Thornycroft A2 single-deck, 1927	1·50	1·50
850	40p. Leyland Lion LT9 single-deck, 1938	1·75	1·75

814 Miss Sophie Rhys-Jones

1999. Royal Wedding. Multicoloured.

851	22p. Type **814**	60	60
852	26p. Leaving St. George's Chapel, Windsor	60	60
853	39p. Prince Edward	1·10	1·10
854	44p. Miss Sophie Rhys-Jones and Prince Edward (horiz)	1·50	1·50
855	53p. In landau (horiz)	1·75	1·75

1999. "Philexfrance 99" International Stamp Exhibition, Paris. No. **MS807** additionally inscribed with "Philexfrance" exhibition logo on sheet margin.

MS856	119×54 mm. 25p. Pillar box and train at Douglas Station; £1 Locomotive No. 1 *Sutherland*	8·00	8·00

819 St. Luke's Church, Baldwin

1999. Christmas. Churches. Multicoloured.

857	21p. Type **819**	45	45
858	25p. St. Mark's Chapel, Malew	60	60
859	30p. St. German's Parish Church and Cathedral, Peel	70	70
860	64p. Kirk Christ Church, Rushen	1·50	1·50

823 *Massachusetts*, 1967

1999. Legends of Music. The Bee Gees (pop group). Designs showing compact discs. Multicoloured.

861	22p. Type **823**	60	50
862	26p. *Words*, 1968	70	65
863	29p. *I've Gotta Get a Message to You*, 1968	75	75
864	37p. *Ellan Vannin*, 1998	90	90
865	38p. *You Win Again*, 1987	90	90
866	66p. *Night Fever*, 1978	1·50	1·70
MS867	Two sheets, each 119×108 mm. (a) 60p. *Immortality*, 1998 (circular, 40 mm diam). (b) 90p. *Stayin' Alive*, 1978 (circular, 40 mm diam) Set of 2 sheets	8·00	10·00

831 Sky at Sunset over Calf of Man (image scaled to 28% of original size)

1999. New Millennium. Sheet 169×74 mm, containing T **184** and similar vert designs. Multicoloured.

MS868	50p. Type **831**; 50p. Sky at dawn over Maughold Head; £2 Constellations over Man at start of new millennium	8·00	8·00

832 Harrison's Chronometer, 1735, and Map

2000. "The Story of Time". Multicoloured.

869	22p. Type **832**	50	55
870	26p. Daniels' chronometer, 2000, and clock face	55	60
871	29p. Harrison's chronometer, 1767, map and clock	65	70
872	34p. Mudge's chronometer, 1769, and steam locomotives	90	90
873	38p. Arnold's chronometer, 1779, and map of Africa	1·20	1·20
874	44p. Earnshaw's chronometer, 1780, and map of Caribbean	1·50	1·50

838 Duke and Duchess of York on Wedding Day, 1923

2000. "Queen Elizabeth the Queen Mother's Century". Multicoloured (except 26p. and 30p.).

875	22p. Type **838**	50	55
876	26p. Queen Elizabeth with Princess Elizabeth, 1940 (brown and black)	55	60
877	30p. King George VI and Queen Elizabeth visiting troops, 1944 (brown and black)	65	70
878	44p. Queen Mother and Queen Elizabeth, 1954	95	80
879	52p. Queen Mother with Prince Charles, 1985	1·00	1·00
880	64p. Queen Mother, 1988	1·10	1·10
MS881	100×70 mm. £1 Queen Mother visiting Isle of Man (74×49 mm)	2·50	2·50

845 Barn Swallow ("Swallow")

2000. Endangered Species. Song Birds. Multicoloured.

882	22p. Type **845**	50	55
883	26p. Spotted flycatcher	55	60
884	64p. Eurasian sky lark ("Sky Lark")	80	80
885	77p. Yellowhammer	1·00	1·00

2000. "The Stamp Show 2000" International Stamp Exhibition, London. As No. **MS881**, but with "The Stamp Show 2000" multicoloured logo added to the bottom sheet margin.

MS886	100×70 mm. £1 Queen Mother visiting Isle of Man (74×49 mm)	5·00	5·00

849 Lieut. John Quilliam and Admiral Lord Nelson, Battle of Trafalgar

2000. Isle of Man at War. Multicoloured.

887	22p. Type **849**	50	55
888	26p. Ensign Caesar Bacon and Duke of Wellington, Battle of Waterloo	55	60
889	36p. Col. Thomas Leigh Goldie and Earl of Cardigan, Crimea	75	80
890	48p. Bugler John Dunne and Sir Robert Baden Powell, Boer War	1·00	1·10
891	50p. George Kneale and Viscount Kitchener of Khartoum, First World War	1·10	1·20
892	77p. First Officer Alan Watterson and Sir Winston Churchill, Second World War	1·50	1·60
MS893	170×75 mm. 60p. Two Supermarine Spitfires (40×29 mm); 60p. Spitfire on ground (40×29 mm), Battle of Britain	2·75	2·75

856 Prince William as Child (image scaled to 28% of original size)

2000. 18th Birthday of Prince William. Sheet 170×75 mm, containing T **189** and similar vert designs. Multicoloured.

MS894	22p. Type **856**; 26p. With Queen Mother; 45p. Prince William; 52p. With Prince Charles and Prince Harry; 56p. Wearing ski-suit	5·00	4·50

857 Ballet Shoes and Painted Ceiling

2000. Centenary of Gaiety Theatre, Douglas. Multicoloured.

895	22p. Type **857**	50	55
896	26p. Comedy mask and box decoration	55	60
897	36p. Drama mask and statue	75	80
898	45p. Pantomime dame with wig and mosaic	95	1·00
899	52p. Opera glasses and decoration	1·10	1·20
900	65p. Top hat with cane and painted ceiling	1·40	1·50

863 Map of Great Britain, Union Jack and Liner

2000. "BT Global Challenge" Round the World Yacht Race. Each showing spinnaker of Isle of Man. Multicoloured.

901	22p. Type **863**	50	55
902	26p. Sydney Opera House, Australian flag and map	55	60
903	36p. New Zealand map and flag	75	80
904	40p. Map of Buenos Aires and waterfront	85	90
905	44p. U.S. flag, map of Boston and harbour	95	1·00
906	65p. South African flag, map and Table Mountain	1·40	1·50

869 Sailing and Holiday Tours Poster, 1925

2000. 170th Anniv of Steam Packet Company. Tourism posters. Multicoloured.

907	22p. Type **869**	50	55
908	26p. "Isle of Man for Happy Holidays"	55	60
909	36p. Woman in swim suit standing on Isle of Man, 1929	75	80
910	45p. Stewardess and ferry	1·50	1·50
911	65p. "Isle of Man for Holidays 1931" and ferry	1·90	2·00

874 Girl with Christingle Candle

2000. Christmas and Europa. Multicoloured.

912	21p. Type **874**	45	50
913	25p. Children dancing around Christmas tree	55	60
914	36p. "Building Europe"	75	80
915	45p. Girl hugging teddy bear	1·50	1·50
916	65p. Children with stars	1·90	2·00

879 Wyon Medal, Penny Black and Queen Victoria

2001. Death Centenary of Queen Victoria. Multicoloured.

917	22p. Type **879**	50	55
918	26p. Great Exhibition medal and Albert Tower, Ramsey	55	60
919	34p. Silver coin and *Great Britain* (early steamship)	75	80
920	39p. Manx coin of 1839, *Oliver Twist* and St. Thomas' Church, Douglas	1·10	1·20
921	40p. Silver coin of 1887, arrival of first train at Vancouver and Jubilee lamp standard	1·10	1·20
922	52p. Silver coin of 1893, Joe Mylchreest at Kimberley diamond mine and Foxdale Clock Tower	1·60	1·70

885 St. Patrick and Snakes (image scaled to 44% of original size)

2001. Chinese New Year ("Year of the Snake"). Sheet 110×85 mm.

MS923	**885** £1 multicoloured	3·00	3·50

No. **MS923** includes the "Hong Kong 2001" logo on the sheet margin.

886 White-tailed Bumble Bee

2001. Insects. Multicoloured.

924	22p. Type **886**	50	55
925	26p. Seven-spot ladybird	55	60
926	29p. Lesser mottled grasshopper	80	90
927	59p. Manx robber fly	1·50	1·60
928	66p. Elephant hawkmoth	1·90	2·00

891 Letter-carrier, 1805

2001. Postal Uniforms. Multicoloured.

929	22p. Type **891**	50	55
930	26p. Postman, 1859	55	60
931	36p. Postman, 1910	75	80
932	39p. Postman, 1933	1·10	1·20
933	40p. Postman, 1983	1·10	1·20
934	66p. Postman, 2001	1·90	2·00

897 1967–70 Great Britain ½d. Machin (image scaled to 28% of original size)

2001. 75th Birthday of Queen Elizabeth II. Sheet 170×75 mm, containing T **897** and similar vert designs showing stamps. Multicoloured.

MS935	29p. Type **897**; 34p. 1952–54 Great Britain 6d. Wilding; 37p. 1971 Isle of Man 2½p. Regional; 50p. 1958–68 Isle of Man 4d. Regional	3·75	4·00

898 Joey Dunlop on Rea Yamaha, Parliament Square, 1977 TT Races

2001. Joey Dunlop (motorcycle champion) Commemoration. Each incorporating different portraits. Multicoloured.

936	22p. Type **898**	50	55
937	26p. At Governor's, 1983 TT Races	55	60
938	36p. Leaving Ramsey, 1988 TT Races	75	80
939	45p. On Honda motorbike, 1991	95	1·00
940	65p. On 250cc Honda at Ballaspur, 1999	1·40	1·50
941	77p. On the Mountain	1·60	1·70

904 The Manx Derby, 1627 (Johnny Jonas)

2001. Horse Racing Paintings. Multicoloured.

942	22p. Type **904**	50	55
943	26p. *Post Haste* (Johnny Jonas)	55	60
944	36p. *Red Rum* (Hamilton-Rennick)	85	80
945	52p. *Hyperion* (Sir Alfred Munnings)	1·50	1·60
946	63p. *Isle of Man* (Johnny Jonas)	1·70	1·70

909 Beef

2001. Europa. Local Dishes prepared by Kevin Woodford. Multicoloured.

947	22p. Type **909**	50	55
948	26p. Queenies with salmon caviar	55	60
949	36p. Seafood	75	80
950	45p. Lamb	1·20	1·20
951	50p. Kipper tart	1·30	1·50
952	66p. Lemon tart with raspberries	1·90	2·00

The 26p. and 36p. show the inscription "EUROPA 2001" at bottom right.

915 Castletown Police Station

2001. The Architecture of Mackay Hugh Bailie Scott. Multicoloured.

953	22p. Type **915**	50	55
954	26p. "Leafield" (semi-detached house)	55	60
955	37p. "The Red House" (Bailie Scott's home)	80	85
956	40p. "Ivydene" (detached house)	1·00	1·10
957	80p. Onchan Village Hall	2·40	2·10

Nos. 953/7 are inscribed "HUGH MACKAY" in error.

2001. "Hafnia 01" International Stamp Exhibition, Denmark. No. **MS935** additionally inscr with "Hafnia 01" logo in red on sheet margin.

MS958	170×75 mm. 29p. Type **897**; 34p. 1952–54 Great Britain 6d. Wilding; 37p. 1971 Isle of Man 2½p. Regional; 50p. 1958–68 Isle of Man 4d. Regional	6·50	7·00

920 Royal Refreshments at Glasgow

2001. Golden Jubilee (1st issue). "The Daily Life of the Queen—An Artist's Diary" (paintings by Michael Noakes). Multicoloured.

959	22p. Type **920**	50	55
960	26p. Queen on visit to Lancaster	55	60
961	39p. Queen with labradors, Sandringham	85	90
962	40p. Queen meeting Scottish Korean War veterans	85	90
963	45p. Queen at desk, Sandringham	95	1·00
964	65p. Queen with bouquet, Oxford	1·90	2·00

See also Nos. 970/4.

926 Christmas Tree Wall Decoration

2001. Christmas. Decorations by Isle of Man Floreat Workshop. Multicoloured.

965	21p. Type **926**	45	50
966	25p. Traditional wreath	55	60
967	37p. Table decoration	1·00	1·10
968	45p. Topiary tree	1·20	1·30
969	65p. Contemporary wreath	1·90	2·00

931 The Coronation, 1953 (Terence Cuneo)

2002. Golden Jubilee (2nd issue). Royal Paintings. Multicoloured.

970	50p. Type **931**	80	60
971	50p. *Queen Elizabeth II as Colonel-in-Chief of Grenadier Guards on Imperial, 1962* (T. Cuneo)	80	60
972	50p. *Queen Elizabeth II in Evening Dress, 1981* (June Mendoza)	80	60
973	50p. "Queen Elizabeth II in Garter Robes, 2000" (Chen Yan Ning)	80	60
974	50p. *The Royal Family in the White Drawing Room, Buckingham Palace* (John Wonnacott)	80	60
MS975	110×85 mm. £1 Sculpture of Queen Elizabeth II by David Cregeen (40×61 mm)	2·50	2·50

937 Cycling

2002. 17th Commonwealth Games, Manchester. Each showing photographic montages. Multicoloured.

976	22p. Type **937**	45	50
977	26p. Running	50	55
978	29p. Javelin and high jump	60	65
979	34p. Swimming	70	75
980	45p. Decathlon	1·00	1·10
981	45p. Wheelchair racing	1·10	1·20

943 *Queen Elizabeth the Queen Mother* (Johnny Jonas)

2002. Queen Elizabeth the Queen Mother Commemoration.

982	**943** £3 multicoloured	6·00	6·25

944 Ireland v Czech Republic

2002. World Cup Football Championship, Japan and Korea (2002). Multicoloured.

983	22p. Type **944**	45	50
984	26p. England v Greece	50	55
985	39p. Italy v Belgium	80	85
986	40p. France v Portugal	80	85
987	66p. England v Brazil	1·20	1·40
988	68p. France v Japan	1·40	1·50

950 Monk's Bridge, Ballasalla (Toni Onley)

2002. Watercolours by Toni Onley. Multicoloured.

989	22p. Type **950**	45	50
990	26p. *Laxey*	50	55
991	37p. *Langness Lighthouse*	75	80
992	45p. *King William's College*	1·10	1·20
993	65p. *The Mull Circle and Bradda Head*	1·50	1·60

2002. Golden Jubilee Celebrations. Nos. **MS**975 additionally inscribed "THE ISLE OF MAN CELEBRATES THE JUBILEE 4th JUNE 2002" in purple on the sheet margin.

MS994 110×85 mm. £1 Sculpture of Queen Elizabeth II by David Cregeen (40×61 mm) .... 6·50 6·50

955 Magenta Flower on Yellow Background

2002. Memories of the Isle of Man. Multicoloured.

995	22p. Type **955**	45	50
996	26p. Green flower on pink background	50	55
997	29p. Purple flower on green background	60	65
998	52p. Maroon flower on brown background	1·00	1·10
999	63p. Red flower on blue background	1·20	1·40
1000	77p. Orange flower on yellow background	1·50	1·60

961 Manx Milestone (Mrs. B. Trimble)

2002. Photography – The People's Choice. Designs showing competition winners. Multicoloured. Ordinary or self-adhesive gum.

1001	23p. Type **961**	30	25
1002	23p. Plough horses (Miss D. Flint)	30	25
1003	23p. Manx emblem (Ruth Nicholls)	30	25
1004	23p. Loaghtan sheep (Diana Burford)	30	25
1005	23p. Fishing fleet, Port St. Mary (Phil Thomas)	30	25
1006	23p. Peel (Michael Thompson)	30	25
1007	23p. Daffodils (Michael Thompson)	30	25
1008	23p. Millennium sword (Mr. F. K. Smith)	30	25
1009	23p. Peel Castle (Kathy Brown)	30	25
1010	23p. Snaefell Railway (Joan Burgess)	30	25
1011	27p. Laxey Wheel (Kathy Brown)	35	30
1012	27p. Sheep at Druidale (John Hall)	35	30
1013	27p. Carousel at Silverdale (Colin Edwards)	35	30
1014	27p. Grandma (Stephanie Corkhill)	35	30
1015	27p. Manx rock (Ruth Nicholls)	35	30
1016	27p. T.T. riders at Signpost (Neil Brew)	35	30

1017	27p. Groudle Railway (Albert Lowe)	35	30
1018	27p. Royal cascade (Brian Speedie)	35	30
1019	27p. St. Johns (John Hall)	35	30
1020	27p. Niarbyl cottages with poppies (Cathy Galbraith)	35	30

981 Father Christmas

2002. Christmas. Entertainment. Multicoloured.

1041	22p. Type **981**	45	50
1042	26p. Virgin Mary and Jesus	50	55
1043	37p. Clown	75	80
1044	47p. Bandsman playing cymbals	95	1·00
1045	68p. Fairy	1·40	1·50

MS1046 123×55 mm. £1.30 "CHRISTMAS" and festive characters (103×40 mm) .... 3·00 3·25

The 37p. value includes the "EUROPA" emblem.

987 Dish Aerial and Peel Castle

2003. Isle of Man Involvement in Space Exploration. Multicoloured.

1047	23p. Type **987**	45	50
1048	23p. Dish aerial, Tromode Teleport	45	50
1049	27p. Camp on Moon and lunar vehicle	55	60
1050	27p. Astronaut exploring lunar surface	55	60
1051	37p. *Sea Launch Odyssey* (marine launch platform)	75	80
1052	37p. *Sea Launch Commander* (assembly command ship)	75	80
1053	42p. Loral Telstar 1 satellite	85	90
1054	42p. Loral Telstar 8 satellite	85	90

MS1055 110×85 mm. 75p. Phobos and American spaceship (30×36 mm); 75p. Mars, astronauts and transfer vehicle (30×36 mm) .... 4·00 4·00

Nos. 1047/8, 1049/50, 1051/2 and 1053/4 were each printed together, as horizontal *se-tenant* pairs, in sheets of 8 with enlarged illustrated right margins.

996 Delivery Handcart (1900–45)

2003. Post Office Vehicles. Multicoloured.

1056	23p. Type **996**	45	50
1057	27p. Morris Z van (1942)	55	60
1058	37p. Morris L diesel van (1960s)	1·00	1·10
1059	42p. DI BSA Bantam telegraph delivery motorbikes	1·10	1·20
1060	89p. Ford Escort 55 van	2·20	2·40

1001 Queen Elizabeth II wearing St. Edward's Crown

2003. 50th Anniv of Coronation. Multicoloured.

1061	50p. Type **1001** (26×57 mm)	70	75
1062	50p. The Ring (23×28 mm)	70	75
1063	50p. The Orb (23×28 mm)	70	75
1064	50p. Royal Sceptre and Rod of Equity and Mercy (23×28 mm)	70	75
1065	50p. Queen Elizabeth II wearing Imperial State Crown (26×57 mm)	70	75
1066	50p. State Coach (81×27 mm)	70	75

1007 de Havilland D.H. 83 Fox Moth and Saunders Roe (Saro) Cloud (amphibian)

2003. Centenary of Powered Flight. Each showing two aircraft. Multicoloured.

1067	23p. Type **1007**	45	50
1068	27p. de Havilland D.H. 61 Giant Moth and D.H. 80 Puss Moth	60	60
1069	37p. Avro Type 652 Anson and Boeing B-17 Flying Fortress	70	80
1070	40p. Eurofighter EF-2000 Typhoon and Avro Type **698** Vulcan	70	85
1071	67p. Handley Page Herald and Bristol Wayfarer	80	1·50
1072	89p. Aerospatiale Concorde and projected Airbus Industrie A380	1·20	1·90

1012a Avro Lancaster attacking Mohne Dam (image scaled to 28% of original size)

2003. 60th Anniv of Attack on German Dams by No. 617 ("Dambusters") Squadron. Sheet 170×75 mm.

MS1073 **1012a** £2 multicoloured .... 4·50 4·25

1013 Prince William

2003. 21st Birthday of Prince William of Wales.

1074	**1013**	42p. black and grey	1·00	90
1075	–	47p. black and grey	1·25	1·00
1076	–	52p. black and grey	2·00	1·50
1077	–	68p. black and grey	2·50	2·00

DESIGNS: 47p. to 68p. Showing recent photographs.

2003. Trilaterale Ticino Exhibition, Locarno, Switzerland. No. **MS**1073 additionally inscr with "Ticino 2003" logo in blue on sheet margin.

MS1078 £2 multicoloured .... 4·75 4·75

1017 *Manx Gold* (Agatha Christie)

2003. "The Manx Bookshelf". Book covers. Multicoloured.

1079	23p. Type **1017**	45	50
1080	27p. *Quatermass and the Pit* (Nigel Kneale)	55	60
1081	30p. *Flashman at the Charge* (George MacDonald Fraser)	60	65
1082	38p. *The Eternal City* (Hall Caine)	75	80
1083	40p. *Peveril of the Peak* (Sir Walter Scott)	1·00	1·10
1084	53p. *Emma's Secret* (Barbara Taylor Bradford)	1·20	1·30

The 38p. value includes the "EUROPA 2003" emblem.

1023 King Henry VII and Henry Tudor crowned by Sir Thomas Stanley on Bosworth Battlefield

2003. 400th Anniv of End of the Tudor Reign. Multicoloured.

1085	23p. Type **1023**	45	50
1086	27p. King Henry VIII and Manx church (Dissolution of the Monasteries)	55	60
1087	38p. Queen Elizabeth I and globe showing route of Drake's circumnavigation	75	80

1088	40p. King Henry VIII, Cardinal Wolsey and Hampton Court Palace	80	85
1089	47p. Queen Mary I and Tudor rose	95	1·00
1090	67p. Queen Elizabeth I and ships of Spanish Armada	1·40	1·50

1029 Henry Bloom Noble and Orphanage Boys

2003. Centenary of Henry Bloom Noble Trust. Multicoloured.

1091	23p. Type **1029**	40	25
1092	23p. Nurse and Ramsey Cottage Hospital	40	25
1093	23p. Children and Children's Home	40	25
1094	23p. Bathers at Noble's Baths	40	25
1095	23p. Scout and Headquarters	40	25
1096	27p. Noble's Hospital, c. 1912	45	30
1097	27p. Villa Marina	45	30
1098	27p. Noble's Park	45	30
1099	27p. St. Ninian's Church	45	30
1100	27p. Noble's Library	45	30

Nos. 1091/1100 also come self-adhesive.

1039 Boy tying Scarf on Snowman

2003. Christmas. The Snowman by Raymond Briggs. Multicoloured.

1111	22p. Type **1039**	45	50
1112	26p. Snowman (wearing black hat and scarf)	50	55
1113	38p. Boy and Snowman holding hands	75	80
1114	47p. Snowman (wearing brown hat and scarf)	95	1·00
1115	68p. Boy flying with Snowman	1·40	1·50

1044 Aragorn

2003. Making of The Lord of the Rings Film Trilogy: The Return of the King. Multicoloured.

1116	23p. Type **1044**	45	50
1117	27p. Gimli	55	60
1118	30p. Gandalf	60	65
1119	38p. Legolas on horseback	1·00	90
1120	42p. Gollum	1·50	1·00
1121	47p. Frodo and Sam	2·00	2·00
1122	68p. Legolas drawing bow	3·00	3·50
1123	85p. Aragorn on horseback	3·50	3·00

MS1124 120×78 mm. £2 The Ring (44×40 mm) .... 5·00 5·50

1053 *Maitland* (Simon Hall)

2004. Bicentenary of Running of First Steam Locomotive. Paintings of steam locomotives by named artists. Multicoloured.

1125	23p. Type **1053**	75	75
1126	27p. *Evening Star* (Terence Cuneo)	90	90
1127	40p. *Pen-y-Darren* Tramroad Locomotive (Terence Cuneo)	1·30	1·30
1128	57p. *Duchess of Hamilton* (Craig Tiley)	1·80	1·80
1129	61p. *City of Truro* (B. J. Freeman)	2·00	2·00
1130	90p. *Mallard* (Terence Cuneo)	3·00	3·00

1059 Troops on Landing
Craft and Tanks going Ashore

2004. 60th Anniv of D-Day. Multicoloured.

1131	23p. Type **1059**	50	25
1132	23p. Troops leaving landing craft and tanks going ashore	50	25
1133	27p. Troops leaving landing craft	60	30
1134	27p. Landing craft and troops wading ashore	60	30
1135	47p. *Lady of Mann* (ferry used as landing craft carrier)	1·00	50
1136	47p. *Ben-my-Chree* (ferry used as landing craft carrier)	1·00	50
1137	68p. Consolidated B-24 Liberators (bombers) and North American P-51 Mustang (fighter)	1·20	70
1138	68p. Airspeed AS 51 Horsa gliders (troop carriers)	1·20	70
MS1139	170×75 mm. 50p. Winston Churchill; 50p. Troops and aircraft; 50p. Military vehicles on street; 50p. Soldiers with France guidebook	6·50	6·50

Nos. 1131/2, 1133/4, 1135/6 and 1137/8 were each printed together, *se-tenant*, each pair forming a composite design.

1068 Lesser
Celandine

2004. Bicentenary of Royal Horticultural Society. Wild Flowers. Multicoloured.

1140	25p. Type **1068**	85	85
1141	28p. Red campion	95	95
1142	37p. Devil's-bit scabious	1·20	1·20
1143	40p. Northern harebell	1·30	1·30
1144	68p. Wood anemone	2·20	2·20
1145	85p. Common spotted orchid	2·75	2·75

1074 In *No Limit*,
1936

2004. Birth Centenary of George Formby (entertainer). Showing scenes from film *No Limit*. Multicoloured.

1146	25p. Type **1074**	80	80
1147	28p. Pushing motorcycle	90	90
1148	40p. Riding in TT race	1·30	1·30
1149	47p. With Florence Desmond	1·40	1·40
1150	50p. On motorcycle	1·70	1·70
1151	74p. Goerge Formby in close-up	2·40	2·40

1080 Johnny Weismuller
(swimmer), Paris, 1924

2004. Olympic Games, Athens. Olympic Legends. Multicoloured.

1152	25p. Type **1080**	85	85
1153	28p. Jesse Owens (athlete), Berlin, 1936	95	95
1154	43p. John Mark carrying Olympic Flame, London, 1948	1·40	1·40
1155	55p. Fanny Blankers-Koen (sprinter), London, 1948	1·80	1·80
1156	91p. Steve Redgrave and Coxless Four (Gold Medallists), Sydney, 2000	3·00	3·00

1085 Celtic
Islanders and Viking
Invaders

2004. Manx National Heritage. *The Story of Mann*. Multicoloured. Ordinary or self-adhesive gum.

1157	(25p.) Type **1085**	1·00	25

1158	(25p.) Fisherman ("Ships and the Sea")		
		1·00	25
1159	(25p.) Miner and Laxey Wheel ("Laxey Miners")	1·00	25
1160	(25p.) Soldier with Longbow and Castle ("Kings and Lords of Mann")	1·00	25
1161	(25p.) Woman with Spinning Wheel ("Farmers and Crofters")	1·00	25
1162	(28p.) Calf of Man	1·20	30
1163	(28p.) Peel Castle	1·20	30
1164	(28p.) Laxey Wheel	1·20	30
1165	(28p.) Castle Rushen	1·20	30
1166	(28p.) Cregneash	1·20	30

Nos. 1157/61 and 1167/71 are inscribed "IOM" and were initially sold at 25p. Nos. 1162/6 and 1172/6 are inscribed "UK" and were initially sold at 28p.

1095 Laxey Wheel (image scaled to 40% of original size)

2004. 150th Anniv of the Great Laxey Wheel. Sheet 120×78 mm.

MS1177	**1095** £2 multicoloured	6·50	6·50

1096 *Maughold Church*

2004. The Isle of Man Watercolours by Alfred Heaton Cooper. Multicoloured.

1178	25p. Type **1096**	80	80
1179	28p. *Port St. Mary*	90	90
1180	40p. *Ballaugh Old Church*	1·30	1·30
1181	41p. *Douglas Bay (A Midsummer's Night)*	1·30	1·30
1182	43p. *Point of Ayre*	1·40	1·40
1183	74p. *Peel Harbour and Castle*	2·40	2·40

The 28p. and 40p. values include the 'EUROPA 2004' emblem.

2004. Sindelfingen International Stamp Exhibition, Sindelfingen, Germany. No. **MS**1177 additionally inscribed with "Sindelfingen" logo on the sheet margin.

MS1184	£2 multicoloured	6·50	6·50

1102 Robin on Flower Pot

2004. Robins—Winter's Friends. Multicoloured.

1185	25p. Type **1102**	80	80
1186	28p. Robin at foot of tree	90	90
1187	40p. Robin perched on branch	1·30	1·30
1188	47p. Robin on window ledge	1·50	1·50
1189	68p. Robin on snowy logs	2·30	2·30
MS1190	148×200 mm. Nos. 1185/9	13·50	13·50

1107 Harry Potter
(Daniel Radcliffe), Ron
Weasley (Rupert Grint)
and Hermione Granger
(Emma Watson)

2004. *Harry Potter and the Prisoner of Azkaban* (film). Multicoloured.

1191	25p. Type **1107**	80	80
1192	28p. Snowy Owl delivering Owl Post	90	90
1193	39p. Harry Potter and White Stag	1·30	1·30
1194	40p. Hogwarts Express	1·30	1·30
1195	49p. Rubeus Hagrid (Robbie Coltrane)	1·60	1·60
1196	55p. Purple Triple-decker Bus	1·80	1·80
1197	57p. Dementor and Harry Potter flying	1·90	1·90

1115 The Nile Campaign

2005. 200th Anniv of the Battle of Trafalgar. Multicoloured.

1199	25p. Type **1115**	50	55
1200	25p. The Battle of Copenhagen	50	55
1201	28p. Emma, Horatia and Nelson	55	60
1202	28p. Band of Brothers	55	60
1203	50p. Prepare for Battle	1·00	1·10
1204	50p. Victory in Sight	1·00	1·10
1205	65p. The Fall of Nelson	1·30	1·40
1206	65p. The Death of Nelson	1·30	1·40
MS1207	170×75 mm. £1 Lieut. John Quilliam and Admiral Lord Nelson (No. 887); £1 Steering HMS *Victory* (No. 160)	4·00	4·25

1124 Two Couples by
Waterside

2005. 60th Anniv of the End of World War II. Multicoloured.

1208	26p. Type **1124**	45	30
1209	26p. Group celebrating in the street	45	30
1210	26p. Man trying on hat	50	30
1211	29p. Civil Service personnel	50	30
1212	60p. King George VI and Winston Churchill on balcony of Buckingham Palace	1·25	70
1213	60p. King George VI and Queen Elizabeth in carriage	1·25	70
1214	65p. Servicemen	1·25	70
1215	65p. War graves	1·25	70
MS1216	170×75 mm. £1 The Manx Regiment; £1 Royal visit, 1945	4·50	4·50

1133 *Mona's Isle* (Samuel
Walters)

2005. 175th Anniv of Steam Packet Company. Multicoloured.

1217	26p. Type **1133**	45	30
1218	26p. *Viking* (Norman Wilkinson)	45	30
1219	29p. *King Orry* (Robert Lloyd)	50	30
1220	29p. *Mona's Queen* (Arthur Burgess)	50	30
1221	40p. *Ben-my-Chree* (John Nicholson)	75	45
1222	40p. *King Orry* (Robert Lloyd)	75	45
1223	66p. *Ben-my-Chree* (Robert Lloyd)	1·25	70
1224	66p. *Lady of Mann* (Robert Lloyd)	1·25	70

1141 Bill Ivy and Phil Read

2005. 50th Anniv of Yamaha. Multicoloured.

1225	26p. Type **1141**	50	55
1226	29p. Joey Dunlop and Ray McCullough	60	65
1227	40p. Steve Hislop	80	85
1228	42p. Carl Fogarty	85	90
1229	68p. David Jefferies	1·40	1·50
1230	78p. John McGuinness	1·60	1·70

1147 Paul Harris (founder)

2005. Centenary of Rotary International and Europa. Gastronomy (42p.). Multicoloured.

1231	26p. Type **1147**	50	55
1232	29p. Planting tree, children grouped and child drinking	60	65
1233	40p. Child being immunised and boy with leg braces and crutches	80	85
1234	42p. Food preparations	85	90
1235	64p. Supply truck, children with volunteer and loading cases	1·30	1·40
1236	68p. Child having eye test, group under Rotary banner and family	1·40	1·50

The 42p. value includes the "EUROPA 200" emblem.

1153 Guttin' Herrin'

2005. Time to Remember. Multicoloured. Ordinary or self-adhesive gum.

1237	26p. Type **1153**	45	30
1238	26p. Pickin' spuds	45	30
1239	26p. J. C. Kelly, Master Butcher	45	30
1240	26p. Winkles, Foxdale	45	30
1241	26p. Palace Ballroom	45	30
1242	29p. Land Army	50	30
1243	29p. Farmyard, Glen Maye	50	30
1244	29p. Eva Kane, Summer Season Stars	50	30
1245	29p. Donkey rides	50	30
1246	29p. Alfie Gilmour, "Give us a go Mister!"	50	30

1163 Obelisk in St. Peter's Square (image scaled to 28% of original size)

2005. 20th World Youth Day. Sheet 170×75 mm, containing T **1163** and similar vert design. Multicoloured.

MS1257	42p. Type **1163**; £1.50 St. Peter's Basilica	4·00	4·00

1164 Harry Potter
(Daniel Radcliffe)

2005. Harry Potter and the *Goblet of Fire* (film). Multicoloured.

1258	26p. Type **1164**	65	55
1259	29p. Harry Potter, Hermione, Ron Weasley and Goblet of Fire	70	65
1260	33p. Trophy	80	70
1261	64p. Hungarian Horntail Dragon	1·50	1·40
1262	68p. Hogwarts Coat of Arms	1·60	1·50
1263	75p. Murcus, Chieftainess of the Merpeople	1·75	1·60

1170 Arrival of Nelson's funeral procession at St. Paul's Cathedral, London (image scaled to 28% of original size)

2005. Death Bicentenary of Admiral Lord Nelson. Sheet 170×75 mm.

MS1264	£1 Type **1170** together with £1 stamp from Gibraltar No. **MS**1145	4·50	4·50

The same miniature sheet was also issued by Gibraltar.

1171 Mary and
Jesus

2005. Christmas. Stained-glass Windows from Manx Churches. Multicoloured.

1265	26p. Type **1171**	50	55
1266	29p. Angel with the Crown of Glory	60	65
1267	42p. Shepherds worshipping Christ Child	85	90

| 1268 | 60p. Nativity | 1·20 | 1·30 |
| 1269 | 68p. Three Kings | 1·40 | 1·50 |

Nos. 1265/7 are from St. German's Cathedral, Peel and Nos. 1268/9 from Kirk Christ, Rushen.

1176 Princess Elizabeth aged Five with Duke and Duchess of York and Princess Margaret, 1931

2006. 80th Birthday of Queen Elizabeth II (1st issue). Multicoloured.

1270	20p. Type **1176**	40	30
1271	20p. Princess Elizabeth wearing ATS uniform, c. 1944	40	30
1272	20p. Queen Elizabeth wearing diadem, 1952	40	30
1273	20p. With Princes Philip, Andrew, Edward, Charles and Princess Anne, 1972	40	30
1274	80p. With Prince Philip at Balmoral on Silver Wedding Anniversary, 1972	1·60	1·00
1275	80p. With regalia in Throne Room, Buckingham Palace, 2001	1·60	1·00
1276	80p. With Prince William on Buckingham Palace balcony	1·60	1·00
1277	80p. With crowd at Aylesbury, Berkshire on Golden Jubilee tour, 2002	1·60	1·00

See also No. MS1294.

1184 Jurby Chalice and Jurby Church

2006. Manx Study—Isle of Man Natural History and Antiquarian Society. Multicoloured.

1278	26p. Type **1184**	50	55
1279	29p. Viking period gold pin head and Peel Castle	60	65
1280	64p. Fragment of early Neolithic bowl and Meayll Hill, Rushen	1·30	1·40
1281	68p. Manx stoat and Cronk Sumark late iron age hill fort	1·40	1·50
1282	78p. Hen harrier and South Barrule Hill, Malew	1·60	1·70
1283	97p. Fossil ammonite, Scarlett Point and Castletown	1·90	2·00

1190 Peregrine Falcon

2006. Manx Bird Atlas. Multicoloured. Ordinary or self-adhesive gum.

1284	28p. Type **1190**	55	35
1285	28p. Puffin	55	35
1286	28p. Manx Shearwater	55	35
1287	28p. Chough	55	35
1288	28p. Guillemot	55	35
1289	31p. Whinchat	60	40
1290	31p. Hen harrier	60	40
1291	31p. Goldcrest	60	40
1292	31p. Grey wagtail	60	40
1293	31p. Wren	60	40

1200 Queen Elizabeth II at Tynwald Ceremony, 2003 (image scaled to 40% of original size)

2006. 80th Birthday of Queen Elizabeth II (2nd issue). Sheet 120×78 mm, containing T 1200 and similar vert design. Multicoloured.

| MS1294 | £1 Type **1200**; £1 Queen in 1972, Manx Cross in background | 4·00 | 4·25 |

1201 West German Player

2006. World Cup Football Championship, Germany. 40th Anniv of England's World Cup Victory. Multicoloured.

1295	28p. Type **1201**	55	60
1296	31p. West German team	60	65
1297	44p. Bobby Moore (England captain) with trophy and Alf Ramsey (manager)	90	95
1298	72p. Bobby Moore holding trophy aloft	1·40	1·50
1299	83p. West German players	1·70	1·80
1300	94p. Victorious England team	1·90	2·00

1207 1977 10p. View from Ramsey Stamp (image scaled to 28% of original size)

2006. 50th Anniv of First Europa Stamp. Sheet 170×75 mm containing T 1207 and similar horiz design showing Isle of Man Europa stamps. Multicoloured.

| MS1301 | 42p. Type **1207**; 83p. 1990 15p. Ramsey Post Office Stamp | 2·50 | 2·75 |

1208 Letitia Tyler (First Lady 1841–2)

2006. Manx Links with Washington. Multicoloured.

1302	28p. Type **1208**	55	60
1303	31p. Joseph Gurney "Czar" Cannon (Speaker of House of Representatives 1903–11)	60	65
1304	45p. Matthew Quay (Civil War hero and Republican Party National Committee chairman)	90	95
1305	50p. Mary Clemmer (19th-century journalist)	1·00	1·10
1306	76p. Ewan Clague (economist)	1·50	1·60
1307	83p. Henry "Marse" Watterson (advisor to Pres. Roosevelt)	1·70	1·80

Nos. 1302/7 were issued to coincide with the Washington 2006 Stamp Exhibition.

1214 Peel P50

2006. Peel Cars. Multicoloured.

1308	28p. Type **1214**	55	60
1309	31p. Trident	60	65
1310	38p. Viking Sport	75	80
1311	41p. BMC GRP Mini	1·00	85
1312	54p. Manxcar	1·50	1·20
1313	94p. P1000	2·00	2·00

1220 Ewan Christian

2006. 150th Anniv of National Portrait Gallery, London. Multicoloured.

1314	28p. Type **1220**	55	60
1315	31p. Dame Agatha Christie (John Gay)	60	65
1316	38p. Sir Hall Caine (Harry Furniss)	75	80
1317	41p. William Bligh (John Condé, after John Russell)	80	85
1318	44p. Lady Maria Callcott (Sir Thomas Lawrence)	90	95
1319	54p. John Martin (Henry Warren)	1·10	1·20

| 1320 | 64p. Sir John Betjeman (Stephen Hyde) | 1·30 | 1·40 |
| 1321 | 96p. Sir Edward Elgar (Herbert Lambert) | 1·90 | 2·00 |

1228 Christmas Tree and Gifts

2006. Christmas. Trees. Multicoloured. (a) Ordinary gum.

1322	28p. Type **1228**	55	60
1323	31p. Tree with Three Legs of Mann decoration at top	60	65
1324	41p. Tree with four tiers of white decorations	80	85
1325	44p. Monkey-puzzle tree and Three Legs of Mann symbols	90	95
1326	72p. Tree with three tiers of yellow Three Legs of Mann decorations	1·40	1·50
1327	94p. Tree with brown Three Legs of Mann decorations	1·90	2·00

Nos. 1323, 1325 and 1329 include the "EUROPA 2006" emblem.

(b) Size 28×39 mm. Self-adhesive.

| 1328 | 28p. Type **1228** | 55 | 60 |
| 1329 | 31p. As No. 1323 | 60 | 65 |

1234 Benjamin Bunny (image scaled to 28% of original size)

2006. The Tales of Beatrix Potter. Sheet 170×75 mm containing T 1234 and similar multicoloured designs.

| MS1330 | 170×75 mm. 28p. Type **1234**; 50p. Jemima Puddle-duck (horiz); 72p. Peter Rabbit (horiz); 75p. Jeremy Fisher (vert) | 4·50 | 4·75 |

2006. Belgica '06 International Stamp Exhibition, Brussels. Sheet 148×210 mm Multicoloured.

| MS1331 | Nos. 1284/93 | 8·50 | 10·00 |

1235 Steve Hislop

2007. Centenary of Isle of Man TT Motor Cycle Races. Multicoloured.

1332	(31p.) Type **1235**	65	50
1333	(31p.) Joey Dunlop (cobalt)	65	50
1334	(31p.) David Jefferies (violet)	65	50
1335	(31p.) Dave Molyneux (black)	65	50
1336	(31p.) John McGuinness (orange)	65	50
1337	(44p.) Stanley Woods (magenta)	85	80
1338	(44p.) Geoff Duke (green)	85	80
1339	(44p.) Bob McIntyre (lilac)	85	80
1340	(44p.) Giacomo Agostini (scarlet)	85	80
1341	(44p.) Mike Hailwood (red)	85	80

Nos. 1332/6 are inscribed "UK" and were sold at 31p. each. Nos. 1337/41 are inscribed "E" and were sold at 44p. each.

1245 Scouts hiking near South Barrule

2007. Centenary of Scouting. Multicoloured.

1342	28p. Type **1245**	65	65
1343	31p. Scout Investiture on Douglas Beach	75	75
1344	44p. Backpacking below Cronk-ny-Arrey-Laa	1·00	1·00
1345	72p. Manx Scouts on parade at St. Johns	1·70	1·70
1346	83p. Sea kayaking off Laxey Beach	2·00	2·00

| 1347 | £1 Manx Scouts operating the TT scoreboard | 2·40 | 2·40 |
| MS1348 | 135×85 mm. 50p. Two scouts at camp, 1913 (horiz); £1.50 Scout camp with bell tent and open fire, 1913 (42×56 mm) | 4·75 | 4·75 |

1252 Wedding, 1947

2007. Diamond Wedding of Queen Elizabeth and Prince Philip. Multicoloured.

1349	60p. Type **1252**	1·25	1·00
1350	60p. Queen Elizabeth II and Duke of Edinburgh, c. 1955	1·25	1·00
1351	60p. Queen Elizabeth (wearing pink blouse) and Duke of Edinburgh, c. 1965	1·25	1·00
1352	60p. Queen Elizabeth (wearing red) and Duke of Edinburgh, c. 1977	1·25	1·00
1353	60p. Queen Elizabeth (wearing green dress) and Duke of Edinburgh, c. 1997	1·25	1·00
1354	60p. Queen Elizabeth (wearing pale mauve) and Duke of Edinburgh, c. 2002	1·25	1·00

1258 Headland, Cornaa

2007. Watercolour Paintings by Norman Sayle. Multicoloured. (a) Ordinary gum.

1355	28p. Type **1258**	65	65
1356	28p. Headland, Sound	65	65
1357	31p. St Marks Church	75	75
1358	31p. Castletown Harbour Moonlight	75	75
1359	42p. Bridge House, Castletown	1·00	1·00
1360	44p. Winter Sun	1·00	1·00
1361	65p. In Ancient Times	1·50	1·50
1362	75p. Bracken Mountain	1·70	1·70

(b) Self-adhesive.

1363	28p. Type **1258**	85	85
1364	28p. As No. 1356	85	85
1365	31p. As No. 1357	95	95
1366	31p. As No. 1358	95	95

1266 King John granting Royal Charter

2007. 800th Anniv of the Royal Charter of Liverpool. Multicoloured.

1367	31p. Type **1266**	70	70
1368	48p. Liverpool Cathedral and Liverpool Metropolitan Cathedral	1·10	1·10
1369	54p. Statue of Capt. Noel Chavasse ("Liverpool war heroes")	1·30	1·30
1370	74p. St. George's Hall	1·70	1·70
1371	80p. Port of Liverpool	1·90	1·90
1372	£1 The Wall of Fame	2·30	2·30

1272 Susan Constant and Map showing Voyage from England to Virginia, 1607

2007. 400th Anniv of Jamestown, Virginia, USA. Multicoloured.

1373	28p. Type **1272**	65	65
1374	31p. Capt. Christopher Newport and Susan Constant, Godspeed and Discovery on the James River	75	75
1375	44p. James Fort and James River, 1607	1·00	1·00
1376	54p. Algonquin Princess Pocahontas and Capt. John Smith	1·30	1·30
1377	78p. Jamestown settlement, 1607	1·90	1·90
1378	90p. Powhatan village	2·20	2·20

1278 James Brown (image scaled to 28% of original size)

2007. 800 Years of Trade between Liverpool and the Isle of Man. Sheet 170×75 mm containing T **1278** and similar horiz designs. Multicoloured.

MS1379	25p. Type **1278**; 40p. Joseph Cunningham and holiday camp, c. 1895; 80p. William Gill and first landing stage at Liverpool, c. 1857; 80p. Dalrymple Maitland and *Liverpool Echo* newspaper	5·50	6·00

2007. TT Race Winners. Sheet 180×235 mm.

MS1379a	Nos. 1332/41	11·50	12·00

2007. 21st World Scout Jamboree, Chelmsford, England. No. **MS1348** additionally inscr with jamboree emblem on the margin.

MS1380	135×85 mm. 50p. Two scouts at camp, 1913; £1.50 Scout camp with bell tent and open fire, 1913 (42×56 mm)	5·00	5·50

1279 Map by John Speed, 1605

2007. Maps of the Isle of Man. Multicoloured.

1381	28p. Type **1279**	65	65
1382	31p. Map by Captain Greenville Collins, 1693	75	75
1383	44p. Map published by John Drinkwater based on trigonometrical survey, 1826	1·10	1·10
1384	48p. Ordnance Survey County series map, 1870	1·10	1·10
1385	75p. Six-inch series map based on National Grid, 1975	1·80	1·80
1386	88p. 1:100,000 map, 2006	2·10	2·10

1285 Captain John Ross and *Victory* trapped in Ice

2007. International Polar Year (1st issue). Voyage of the Victory to the North Pole, 1829–33. Multicoloured.

1387	28p. Type **1285**	65	65
1388	31p. Flares from *Victory* guide returning exploration parties	70	70
1389	55p. *Victory's* crew hunting with Inuit	1·30	1·30
1390	75p. Hunted musk ox	1·80	1·80
1391	90p. Crew on 300 mile trek after abandoning *Victory*	2·10	2·10
1392	117p. Crew in whaleboats rescued by whaler *Isabella*	2·75	2·75

1291 'Ben-my-Chree' Log Cabin, Tagish Lake, British Columbia (image scaled to 28% of original size)

2007. International Polar Year. T **1291** and similar multicoloured designs.

MS1393	50p. Type **1291**; 50p. Graham 'Jimmy' Oates taking motorcycle and sidecar along railroad track to Hudson Bay, 1932 (vert); 75p. Kermode bear (subspecies of Grizzly bear) (vert); 75p. Dog sled and Hudson Bay Post Office, 1931–61	6·00	6·50

1292 Ploughing

2007. European Vintage Ploughing Championships, Isle of Man. Multicoloured.

1394	28p. Type **1292**	65	65
1395	31p. Ploughing with grey tractor	70	70
1396	48p. Horse-drawn plough	1·10	1·10
1397	71p. Hand plough	1·70	1·70

1398	90p. Ploughing with red tractor	2·10	2·10
1399	£1.27 Ploughing with blue tractor	3·00	3·00

No. 1396 is inscr 'sepac'.

1298 Angel playing Trumpet

2007. Christmas. *Hark the Herald Angels Sing.* Multicoloured. Self-adhesive.

1400	28p. Type **1298**	65	65
1401	31p. Angel playing lute	75	75
1402	69p. Angel wearing crown	1·60	1·60
1403	78p. Angel with harp	1·80	1·80
1404	£1.24 Angel with hands clasped in prayer	3·00	3·00

1303 *Queen Elizabeth 2*

2008. Cunard Ocean Liners. Sheet 170×75 mm. Multicoloured.

1405	**1303** £1 Type **1303**	3·00	3·50
1405a	**1303** £1 *Queen Mary 2*	3·00	3·50
1405b	**1303** £1 *Queen Victoria*	3·00	3·50

1306 H.P. 0/400 and Bristol F2B Fighter

2008. 90th Anniv of Royal Air Force. Multicoloured.

1406	31p. Type **1306**	60	60
1407	31p. Avro 504N and Westland Wapiti	60	60
1408	31p. Hawker Hurricane and Short S25 Sunderland	60	60
1409	90p. Gloster Meteor and Westland Whirlwind	1·70	1·70
1410	90p. Hawker Hunter and E.E. Canberra	1·70	1·70
1411	90p. Harrier and Lockheed Hawker Siddeley C-130 Hercules	1·70	1·70

1312 The Pagan Lady of Peel

2008. The Viking Age on the Isle of Man. Multicoloured.

1412	28p. Type **1312**	65	65
1413	31p. Ship burial	75	75
1414	44p. Godred Crovan ('King Orry')	1·00	1·00
1415	54p. Gautr Bjornsson the sculptor	1·30	1·30
1416	69p. Sigurd the dragon slayer	1·60	1·60
1417	£1.24 Coming of Christianity	3·00	3·00

1318 Isle of Man Bank £1 Note, 1956

2008. Bank Notes of the Isle of Man. Multicoloured. (a) Ordinary gum.

1418	30p. Type **1318**	70	70
1419	31p. Isle of Man Govt £10 note, 1972	75	75
1420	44p. Manx Bank (1882–1900) £1 note	1·00	1·00
1421	56p. Isle of Man Govt 50p decimal note, 1969	1·40	1·40
1422	85p. Isle of Man Govt £50 note, 1983	2·00	2·00
1423	114p. Parr's Bank £1 note, 1918	2·75	2·75

(b) Self-adhesive.

1424	30p. As Type **1318**	80	1·00

1324 Archery (image scaled to 28% of original size)

2008. Olympic Games, Beijing. Sheet 170×75 mm containing T **1324** and similar square designs. Multicoloured.

MS1425	1p. Type **1324**; 2p. Showjumping; 3p. Cycling; 94p. Hand holding Olympic torch	2·40	3·00

1325 Cornish Flag

2008. Interceltique. Designs showing flags of Celtic countries. Multicoloured.

1426	20p. Type **1325**	45	45
1427	30p. Isle of Man flag	70	70
1428	31p. Scottish flag	70	70
1429	48p. Breton flag	1·10	1·10
1430	50p. Irish flag	1·20	1·20
1431	56p. Flag of Asturias	1·30	1·30
1432	72p. Welsh flag	1·70	1·70
1433	£1.13 Flag of Galicia	2·75	2·75
MS1434	174×210 mm. Nos. 1426/33	9·75	9·75

Nos. 1428 and 1430 include the 'EUROPA' emblem.

1333 Reg Parnell in Maserati 4CLT

2008. British Motor Racing. Multicoloured.

1435	20p. Type **1333**	45	45
1436	30p. Mike Hawthorn	70	70
1437	70p. Tony Brooks in Vanwall	1·60	1·60
1438	81p. Roy Salvadori in Aston Martin	1·90	1·90
1439	94p. Stirling Moss at Pit Stop	2·20	2·20
1440	£1.22 Jim Clark in Lotus-Climax 25 R4	3·00	3·00
MS1441	170×75 mm. 50p.×6 Aston Martin DB4 GT Zagato, 1961; Ferrari 250 LM, Le Mans, 1965; Ferrari 250 GTO, Goodwood Revival, 1962; Ford GT 40, Goodwood Festival of Speed, 1965; Mercedes-Benz 300 SLR, Mille Miglia Road Race, Italy, 1955; Shelby Cobra, Goodwood Revival, 1964 (all 40×29 mm)	7·00	7·00

1340 Miss M. L. Wood (founder of Manx Music Festival)

2008. New Manx Worthies. Showing characters from book. Multicoloured.

1442	31p. Type **1340**	60	60
1443	31p. Harry Kelly (last native Manx speaker) and cottage at Cregneash Folk Museum	60	60
1444	31p. Sir Frank Gill (telephony and communications engineer) and phone box	60	60
1445	31p. Ramsey Gelling Johnson (second deemster (Manx judge), 1947–54)	60	60
1446	31p. John Nicholson (artist and designer of Manx stamps, currency notes and gold coinage)	60	60
1447	50p. Dr. Dorothy Pantin (Island's first woman doctor and first medical supervisor of Jane Crookall Maternity Home)	1·00	1·00
1448	50p. Richard Costain (founder of construction company)	1·00	1·00
1449	50p. Sir William Percy Cowley (first deemster and Clerk of the Rolls, 1947–58)	1·00	1·00
1450	50p. Revd Fred Cubbon (philanthropist)	1·00	1·00
1451	50p. William Henry Gill (author, musician and collector of Manx folk music)	1·00	1·00

2008. Olympex Olympic Stamp Expo, Beijing. No. **MS1425** additionally inscr with 'Beijing 2008' emblem and 'OLYMPEX, THE OLYMPIC EXPO' on the bottom margin.

MS1452	1p. Type **1324**; 2p. Showjumping; 3p. Cycling; 94p. Hand holding Olympic torch	2·40	2·75

2008. Team GB Olympic Cyclists. Sheet 145×208 mm. Multicoloured.

MS1453	3p. Cycling; 94p. Hand holding Olympic torch	2·40	2·75

No. **MS1453** contains 3p. and 94p. designs as in **MS1425**.

1350 Orange-tip Butterfly (*Anthocharis cardamines*)

2008. A Walk in the Ballaugh Curragh. Multicoloured.

1454	30p. Type **1350**	70	70
1455	31p. Curlew (*Numenius arquata*)	75	75
1456	50p. Birch bracket fungus (*Piptoporus betulinus*)	1·20	1·20
1457	70p. Large red damselfly (*Pyrrhosoma nymphula*)	1·70	1·70
1458	82p. Marsh cinquefoil (*Potentilla palustris*)	1·90	1·90
1459	£1.38 Royal fern (*Osmunda regalis*)	3·25	3·25

1356 Second Lt. Roy F. Corlett, 1916

2008. 90th Anniv of the End of World War I. Manx Soldiers and their Letters Home. Multicoloured.

1460	30p. Type **1356**	70	70
1461	31p. Second Lt. John W. Lewis, 1916	70	70
1462	44p. Pte. Joseph Killey	1·00	1·00
1463	56p. Lt. Col. W. A. W. Crellin, 1917	1·30	1·50
1464	81p. Lance Cpl. Tom Quilliam, 1918	1·90	2·00
1465	94p. Pte. Robert Oates, 1914	2·20	2·50
MS1466	110×70 mm. £2 Manx National War Memorial, St. John's	4·75	5·00

1363 Christmas Cards and Postman on Bicycle

2008. Christmas. Illustrations from *The Jolly Christmas Postman* by Janet and Allan Ahlberg. T **277** and similar horiz designs. Multicoloured.

1467	28p. Type **1363**	65	65
1468	31p. Postman icing biscuits and giant biscuit tin	75	75
1469	48p. Offering postman mince pies and decorating Christmas tree	1·10	1·10
1470	50p. Postman holding card and Toy Town	1·20	1·20
1471	56p. Postman on bicycle and winter landscape	1·30	1·30
1472	£1.56 Postman relaxing at home	3·50	3·50

1369 Fairey Barracuda II

2009. Centenary of Naval Aviation. Multicoloured.

1473	30p. Type **1369**	70	70
1474	31p. Blackburn Buccaneer S.2	70	70
1475	72p. Fairey Flycatcher	1·75	1·75
1476	85p. EH101 Merlin Helicopter	2·00	2·00
1477	98p. BAe Sea Harrier FRS.1	2·25	2·25
1478	£1.36 Sea Scout SS.24 Airship	3·00	3·00

1375 McLaren Mercedes Race Car

2009. Lewis Hamilton, Formula One World Champion, 2008. Muliticoloured.

1479	30p. Type **1375**	70	70
1480	31p. Celebrating with champagne	70	70
1481	56p. Crossing finishing line	1·25	1·25
1482	85p. Seated in Race Car	2·00	2·00
1483	98p. Race car	2·25	2·25
1484	£1.42 With arms raised in triumph	3·25	3·25

1381 Henry VIII

2009. 500th Anniv of the Accession of King Henry VIII.. Multicoloured.

1485	50p. Type **1381**	1·25	1·25
1486	50p. Catherine of Aragon	1·25	1·25
1487	50p. Anne Boleyn	1·25	1·25
1488	50p. Jane Seymour	1·25	1·25
1489	50p. Anne of Cleves	1·25	1·25
1490	50p. Catherine Howard	1·25	1·25
1491	50p. Catherine Parr	1·25	1·25
1492	50p. Hampton Court	1·25	1·25

1389 Ballakilley Farm

2009. Mills and Millers. Photographs by Chris Kilip. Multicoloured. (a) Ordinary gum.

1493	32p. Type **1389**	70	70
1494	32p. Grenaby Farm	70	70
1495	33p. Mr. Cubbon	70	70
1496	33p. Glenmoar Mill	70	70
1497	50p. Golden Meadow Mill	1·25	1·25
1498	50p. Bernie Mylcraine	1·25	1·25
1499	78p. Golden Meadow Mill	1·75	1·75
1500	78p. Loughtan Farm	1·75	1·75

(b) Self-adhesive.

1501	32p. multicoloured	70	70
1502	32p. multicoloured	70	70
1503	33p. multicoloured	70	70
1504	33p. multicoloured	70	70

1397 Peonies

2009. China World Stamp Exhibition and Peony Festival, Luoyang. Multicoloured; colour of right-hand border given.

1505	**1397**	10p. multicoloured (gold)	25	25
1506	**1397**	10p. multicoloured (green)	25	25
1507	**1397**	10p. multicoloured (rose)	25	25
1508	**1397**	10p. multicoloured (blue)	25	25
1509	**1397**	10p. multicoloured (mauve)	25	25
1510	**1397**	10p. multicoloured (red)	25	25
1511	**1397**	10p. multicoloured (blue)	25	25
1512	**1397**	10p. multicoloured (yellow)	25	25

1398 Boot Print and *Sunrise over Antares* (Apollo 14 lunar module)

1404 *On the Rim* (John Young and Charlie Duke at North Ray Crater, 1972) (image scaled to 44% of original size)

2009. 40th Anniv of First Manned Moon Landing. Paintings by Alan Bean. Multicoloured.

1513	33p. Type **1398**	1·00	1·00
1514	50p. *Clan MacBean* (Alan Bean) arrives on the Moon and *Documenting the Sample*	1·50	1·50
1515	56p. *Pete and Me* (Pete Conrad taking photograph)	1·50	1·50
1516	81p. *Headed for the Last Parking Lot* (Gene Cernan and lunar roving vehicle)	2·00	2·00
1517	105p. *The Eagle* (Apollo 11 lunar module) *is Headed Home* and *In the Beginning*	2·50	2·50
1518	135p. *Ceremony on the Plain at Hadley* and *The Hoer* (Jim Irwin digging trench)	3·00	3·00
MS1519	109×84 mm. **1404** £2.50 multicoloured (vert)	6·00	6·00

1405 Naomi Taniguchi, 1959

2009. 50th Anniv of Honda Motorcycles in World Championship Racing. Multicoloured.

1520	32p. Type **1405**	70	70
1521	33p. Mike Hailwood, 1960s	75	75
1522	56p. Alex George, 1970s	1·25	1·25
1523	62p. Joey Dunlop, 1980s	1·60	1·60
1524	90p. Steve Hislop, 1990s	2·40	2·40
1525	£1.77 John McGuinness, 2000s	3·75	3·75

1411 W. G. Grace at Lord's, 1895; MCC Ashes Trophy and Urn; England v. Australia, Lord's, 2005 (image scaled to 28% of original size)

2009. The Ashes. England v. Australia 2009. Sheet 170×75 mm.

MS1526	**1411** £1×3 multicoloured	7·00	7·00

1412 Barry, Maurice and Robin Gibb as Boys

2009. 50th Anniv of the Bee Gees (pop group). Multicoloured.

1527	32p. Type **1412**	75	75
1528	33p. *Children of the World* album cover	75	75
1529	50p. *Bee Gees* album cover	1·25	1·25
1530	54p. *Still Waters* album	1·25	1·25
1531	56p. *One Night Only* album	1·25	1·25
1532	62p. *This is Where I Came In* album	1·60	1·60
1533	78p. Bee Gees *Number Ones* ac lbum	1·75	1·75
1534	£1.28 Bee Gees *The Studio Albums 1967–8*	3·00	3·00

2009. 40th Anniv of First Manned Moon Landing (2nd issue). As Type **1404**. No. **MS**1519 additionally inscr with '40th anniversary man on the moon' emblem on the bottom right margin

MS1534a	As Type **1404**. £2.50 *On the Rim* (John Young and Charlie Duke at North Ray Crater, 1972) (Alan Bean)	6·00	6·00

1420 Brown Hare

2009. Country File. Paintings by Jeremy Paul. Multicoloured.

1535	32p. Type **1420**	75	75
1536	33p. Hedgehogs	75	75
1537	54p. Pheasants	1·25	1·25
1538	90p. Barn owl	2·40	2·40
1539	92p. Cockerel	2·40	2·40
1540	£1.58 *On the Hill*	3·50	3·50
MS1541	148×210 mm. Nos. 1535/40	11·00	11·00

1426 Bridge

2009. Watercolour Paintings by Archibald Knox. Multicoloured.

1542	32p. Type **1426**	75	75
1543	33p. *Willows and Blue Mountain*	75	75
1544	56p. *Kew*	1·25	1·25
1545	62p. *Eairy Beg*	1·60	1·60
1546	81p. *Leaning Trees*	1·90	1·90
1547	182p. *Old Laxey*	4·25	4·25

1432 Captain James Teare and SS *Ellan Vannin*; SS *Ellan Vannin* in Ramsey Harbour (image scaled to 28% of original size)

2009. Centenary of Sinking of the SS Ellan Vannin (steam packet). Sheet 170×75 mm.

MS1548	**1432** £1.50×2 multicoloured	7·00	7·00

1433 Father Christmas putting Present into Stocking

2009. Christmas. Father Christmas. Multicoloured. (a) Ordinary gum.

1549	30p. Type **1433**	70	70
1550	33p. Writing list	75	75
1551	56p. Carrying sack of toys	1·25	1·25
1552	62p. Carrying wrapped present	1·60	1·60
1553	81p. With Archbishop's Staff, Mitre and Robes	1·75	1·75
1554	90p. With Christmas pudding and wine goblet	2·40	2·40

(b) Self-adhesive gum.

1555	30p. As Type **1433**	70	70
1556	33p. Writing list	75	75

1439 Woman walking in Lane

2010. Island Life. Multicoloured. (a) Ordinary gum.

1557	32p. Type **1439**	75	75
1558	(32p.) Angler	75	75
1559	(32p.) Yachtsman	75	75
1560	(32p.) Climber	75	75
1561	(33p.) Children riding ponies	75	75
1562	(33p.) Apple picking	75	75
1563	(33p.) Unloading kayak	75	75
1564	(33p.) Motorcyclist	75	75
1565	56p. Children on rocky shore	1·25	1·25
1566	90p. Horses ploughing at Cregneash National Folk Museum	2·40	2·40

(b) Self-adhesive.

1567	(32p.) AS Type **1439**	75	75
1568	(32p.) Angler	75	75
1569	(32p.) Yachtsman	75	75
1570	(32p.) Climber	75	75
1571	(33p.) Children riding ponies	75	75
1572	(33p.) Apple picking	75	75
1573	(33p.) Unloading kayak	75	75
1574	(33p.) Motorcyclist	75	75

Nos. 1557/60 and 1567/70 were inscribed 'IOM RATE' and sold for 32p. each.

Nos. 1561/4 and 1571/4 were inscribed 'UK RATE' and sold for 33p. each.

1449 Two Rainbows

1457 Manx Guide Leaders (£1.50); Trefoil Guild Members planting Tree, 1985 (£1.50) (image scaled to 28% of original size)

2010. Centenary of Girlguiding. Multicoloured.

1575	32p. Type **1449**	75	75
1576	32p. Company of rainbows and leaders	75	75
1577	33p. Brownies holding badges	75	75
1578	33p. Five brownies	75	75
1579	56p. Girl guide	1·25	1·25
1580	56p. Guides and leaders on parade	1·25	1·25
1581	£1 Senior section members	2·25	2·25
1582	£1 Queen Elizabeth II meeting guide leaders	2·25	2·25
MS1583	170×75 mm. **1457** £1.50×2	7·00	7·00

Nos. 1577 and 1579 include the 'EUROPA' emblem.

1458 Messerschmitt BF109 and Defiant

1464 1981 60th Anniversary of Royal British Legion 20p. Stamp and Ship crowded with Evacuated Troops, Dunkirk, 1940 (£1.50); 1990 50th Anniversary of Battle of Britain Pair of 24p. Stamps and Aircrew running for Planes (£1.50) (image scaled to 28% of original size)

2010. 70th Anniv of the Battle of Britain. Multicoloured.

1584	70p. Type **1458**	1·60	1·60
1585	70p. Spitfire and Messerschmitt BF109	1·60	1·60
1586	70p. Junkers Ju87 and Hurricane	1·60	1·60
1587	70p. Messerschmitt BF110 and Hurricane	1·60	1·60
1588	70p. Blenheim I and Junkers 88	1·60	1·60
1589	70p. Heinkel III and Spitfire	1·60	1·60
MS1590	170×75 mm. **1464** £1.50 multicoloured; £1.50 multicoloured	7·00	7·00

MS1590 also commemorates the 70th anniversary of Operations Dynamo and Ariel (evacuation of troops from Dunkirk).

1465 King George V and Queen Mary at Grand Hall, Douglas, 1920 and Cast of Great Britain 1d. George V Stamp

2010. Centenary of Accession of King George V. Multicoloured.

1591	55p. Type **1465**	1·25	1·25
1592	60p. King George V and Queen Mary, Isle of Man, 1920 and Cape of Good Hope tete-beche pairs of 1861 1d. 'Hope' stamps	1·50	1·50

1593	67p. King George V and Queen Mary arriving at Queen's Pier, Ramsey, 1920 and Great Britain 1910 2d. Tyrian plum stamp	1·60	1·60
1594	96p. King George V and Queen Mary with Nurses, Ramsey, and Oil Rivers Protectorate 1893 20s. on 1s. stamp	2·50	2·50
1595	97p. King George V planting Tree at Bishopscourt, 1920 and George V ½d. green stamp	2·50	2·50
1596	£1.10 King George V and Queen Mary at Castletown and Mauritius 1847 2d. deep blue stamp	3·00	3·00

1471 Model T Speedster, 1915

2010. 50th Anniv of Model T Ford Register. Multicoloured.

1597	35p. Type **1471**	80	80
1598	36p. Model T coupe, 1926	85	85
1599	60p. Model T 7cwt van, 1923	1·50	1·50
1600	74p. Model T town car, 1912	1·75	1·75
1601	97p. Model T charabanc, 1922	2·25	2·25
1602	172p. Model T tourer, 1912	4·00	4·00

1477 Lord Derby Halfpenny, 1709 and Castle Rushen

2010. History of Manx Coins. Multicoloured.

1603	35p. Type **1477**	60	60
1604	36p. Matthew Boulton 'Cartwheel' Copper Penny, 1798 and Soho Mint, Birmingham	65	65
1605	55p. Victorian Manx Farthing, 1839 and View of Douglas	90	90
1606	60p. Revestment Act Bicentenary Gold Coin, 1965 and Manx Flag over Castle Rushen, c. 1760	1·00	1·00
1607	67p. Decimal 5p. Coin, 1971 and Tower of Refuge	1·25	1·25
1608	£1.87 £5 Coin, 2010 and Laxey Wheel	6·50	6·50

1483 Steam Locomotive Caledonia with Trailer No. 57 at Snaefell Summit, 1995

2010. Isle of Man Railways and Tramways. Multicoloured.

1609	35p. Type **1483**	65	65
1610	36p. Steam Locomotive *Sutherland* and Manx Electric Railway Car No. 1, Laxey Station, 1998	70	70
1611	55p. Steam Locomotive *Caledonia* with MER Trailer No. 58 at Bulgham	95	95
1612	88p. Steam Locomotive *Loch* with Trailers No. 57 and 58 at Skinscoe on MER Line	1·25	1·25
1613	£1.32 Manx Electric Railway Car No. 33 at Keristal on Steam Railway Line	1·40	1·40
1614	£1.46 Steam Locomotives No. 4 *Loch* and No. 11 *Maitland*, 1993	6·50	6·50
MS1615	150 x 210 mm. Nos. 1609/14 and three stamp-size labels	11·00	11·00

2010. Girlguiding UK Centenary Camp.

MS1616	170x75 mm. **1457** £1.50x2 multicoloured	7·00	7·00

No. **MS**1583 additionally inscr with 'GIRLGUIDING UK CENTENARY CAMP Harewood House 31 July - 7 August 2010' and emblem on the upper left sheet margin

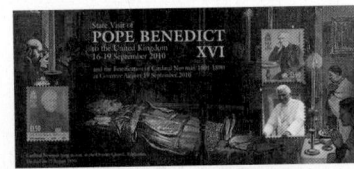

1489 Cardinal Newman (image scaled to 28% of original size)

1490 *Three-Legged Postman* (Bertram), 1940

2010. Isle of Man Internment Art History (1st series). Multicoloured.

1618	35p. Type **1490**	90	90
1619	36p. *Peveril Camp, Peel* (Herbert Kaden), 1940	95	95
1620	55p. *Life at Palace Camp, Douglas* (Imre Goth), 1941	1·40	1·40
1621	67p. *Douglas, Isle of Man* (linocut) (Hermann Fechenbach), 1941	1·90	1·90
1622	132p. *Violinist at Onchan Camp* (Ernst Eisenmayer), 1941	2·75	2·75
1623	172p. *Portrait of Klaus E. Hinrichsen* (Kurt Schwitters), 1941	4·00	4·00

1496 Nativity (image scaled to 28% of original size)

2010. Friends and Heroes (animated TV series). The Christmas Story. Sheet 170x75 mm. Multicoloured.

MS1624	**1496** £1x3 'Jesus is born'; 'Shepherds hear first'; 'The Magi see a star'	7·00	7·00

1497 Old Braddan Church

2010. Christmas. 'Let it Snow'. Multicoloured.

1625	35p. Type **1497**	70	70
1626	36p. The Braaid	75	75
1627	60p. The Dhoon Glen	1·75	1·75
1628	88p. The Dhoon Beach	2·10	2·10
1629	97p. Cronk my Arree Laa	2·40	2·40
1630	£1.46 St. Patrick's Isle in Snow	3·25	3·25

1503 Prince William (image scaled to 28% of original size)

2010. Engagement of Prince William and Miss Catherine Middleton. Sheet 170x75 mm

MS1631	**1503** £1.50x2 multicoloured	7·00	7·00

1504 Queen Elizabeth II, 1953

2011. Queen Elizabeth II and Prince Philip: 'Lifetime of Service'. Multicoloured.

1632	35p. Type **1504**	90	90
1633	36p. Queen and Prince Philip, Diamond Wedding Anniversary, November 2007, Broadlands, Romsey	95	95
1634	55p. Princess Elizabeth and Prince Philip on Honeymoon at Broadlands, 1949	1·50	1·50
1635	60p. On Buckingham Palace Balcony after Trooping the Colour, 1971	1·75	1·75
1636	£1.14 Watching Golden Jubilee Parade, London, June 2002	2·50	2·50
1637	£1.46 Prince Philip, 1953	3·25	3·25
MS1638	110x70 mm. £3 multicoloured (21 Apr)	7·25	7·25
MS1639	175x164 mm. Nos. 1632/7 and three stamp-size labels	11·00	11·00

1511 'School Days'

2011. Genealogy. Multicoloured.

1640	35p. Type **1511**	90	90
1641	35p. 'Baptisms'	90	90
1642	36p. 'Weddings'	95	95
1643	36p. 'Working Life'	95	95
1644	67p. 'Family Album'	1·75	1·75
1645	67p. 'Emigration'	1·75	1·75
1646	£1.10 'Memorials'	2·40	2·40
1647	£1.10 'Family Tree'	2·40	2·40

1519 Wall Butterfly (*Lasiommata megera*)

2011. The Isle of Man Butterfly Collection. Multicoloured.

(a) Ordinary gum

1648	37p. Type **1519**	90	90
1649	37p. Small Tortoiseshell (*Aglais urticae*)	90	90
1650	38p. Dark Green Fritillary (*Argynnis aglaja*)	1·00	1·00
1651	38p. Common Blue (*Polyommatus icarus*)	1·00	1·00
1652	58p. Comma (*Polygonia c-album*)	1·50	1·50
1653	58p. Green-veined White (*Pieris napi*)	1·50	1·50
1654	115p. Red Admiral (*Vanessa atalanta*)	2·40	2·40
1655	115p. Speckled Wood (*Pararge aegeria*)	2·40	2·40
MS1656	210x250 mm. Nos. 1648, 1650, 1652 and 1654, each ×4	22·00	22·00

(b) Self-adhesive

1657	37p. As No. 1649	90	90

1527 Senior TT Stanley Woods v. Jimmy Guthrie, 1935

2011. TT2011 Centenary of the Mountain Course. Greatest TT Races of All Time. Multicoloured.

1658	38p. Type **1527**	90	90
1659	38p. Senior TT Mike Hailwood v. Giacomo Agostini, 1967	90	90
1660	38p. Senior TT Tom Herron v. John Williams, 1976	90	90
1661	38p. Sidecar TT Race A George O'Dell v. Dick Greasley, 1977	90	90
1662	38p. Classic TT Alex George v. Mike Hailwood, 1979	90	90
1663	68p. Senior TT Steve Hislop v. Carl Fogarty, 1992	1·60	1·60
1664	68p. Formula 1 TT Joey Dunlop v. David Jefferies, 2000	1·60	1·60
1665	68p. Senior TT John McGuinness v. Cameron Donald, 2008	1·60	1·60
1666	68p. Sidecar TT Klaus Klaffenbock v. John Holden, 2010	1·60	1·60
1667	68p. Superstock TT Ian Hutchinson v. Ryan Farquhar, 2010	1·60	1·60
MS1668	110x85 mm. £3 Senior TT Steve Hislop v. Carl Fogarty, 1992	7·25	7·25

1538 Miss Catherine Middleton; Prince William (image scaled to 28% of original size)

2011. Royal Wedding

1668a	**1537**a £1 multicoloured	2·25	2·25
1668b	**1537**b £1 multicoloured	2·25	2·25
MS1669	170x75 mm. **1538** £1x2 multicoloured	4·75	4·75

1539 The Southern Hundred, 1955

2011. Cartoons by Harold 'Dusty' Miller. Multicoloured.

1670	37p. Type **1539**	90	90
1671	38p. "I'm staking my claim on the sands at Douglas", early 1950s	90	90
1672	68p. Over the Water – "I must get me a bigger horse", 1955	1·60	1·60
1673	76p. Will Uncle Sam provide the 'Third Leg'?, 1940	1·90	1·90
1674	110p. Bob a Job Week, 1954	2·75	2·75
1675	165p. 'Well Councillor – did you vote for evening meetings?'	4·00	4·00

1545 Manx Cats holding Coat of Arms

2011. Tales of the Tailless (Manx Cats). Multicoloured.

1676	37p. Type **1545**	90	90
1677	38p. Three Manx Cats and Coat of Arms	90	90
1678	58p. Tabby Manx Cat on Wall	1·50	1·50
1679	76p. Tabby Manx Cat	1·90	1·90
1680	115p. Manx Cats and Coat of Arms	2·40	2·40
1681	165p. Manx Cat on Quayside standing on Coat of Arms	4·00	4·00

1551 South Lancashire Brigade on Peel Harbour, August 1908

2011. Isle of Man Internment (2nd series). Postal History of Knockaloe Camp. Multicoloured.

1682	37p. Type **1551**	90	90
1683	37p. Postcard with King Edward VII 1/2d. Stamp with 1908 Knockaloe Camp Cancellation	90	90
1684	38p. Knockaloe Camp (from postcard designed by internee, 1915)	90	90
1685	38p. Alien's Detention Camp Letter with Pair of King George V Profile Head 1/2d. Stamps, cancelled 1914	90	90
1686	58p. Easter Postcard published by Knockaloe Camp Printer's Workshop and Peace Dove	1·50	1·50
1687	58p. King George V 3d. Registered Envelope with 1915 Knockaloe Camp Cancellation	1·50	1·50
1688	£1.15 Knockaloe Camp (from postcard designed and printed with camp)	2·75	2·75
1689	£1.15 Letter with Internee Produced Stamp (for internal camp mail)	2·75	2·75
MS1690	171x76 mm. 50p. multicoloured; 50p. multicoloured; £1 multicoloured; £1 multicoloured	7·25	7·25

1560 Narcissus (image scaled to 39% of original size)

2011. Narcissus. Sheet 124×184 mm

MS1691 **1560**	5p.×2, 10p.×2, 35p.×2 multicoloured	2·50	2·50

No. **MS**1691 was released to commemorate the 27th Asian International Stamp Exhibition, Wuxi, Jiangsu, China.

1562 Games Mascot Tosha; Badminton; Boxing; Rugby 7; Cycling; Gymnastics; Athletics; Swimming (image scaled to 28% of original size)

2011. Fourth Commonwealth Youth Games, Isle of Man. Sheet 170×76 mm

MS1697 **1562**	38p.×8 multicoloured	7·25	7·25

1563 Robin

2011. Birds in Winter. Multicoloured.

	(a) Ordinary gum		
1698	(37p.) Type **1563**	90	90
1699	(38p.) Redwing	90	90
1700	58p. Goldfinches	1·40	1·40
1701	68p. Siskins	1·75	1·75
1702	76p. Waxwings	1·90	1·90
1703	£2 Long-tailed Tits	4·75	4·75
	(b) Self-adhesive		
1704	(37p.) As Type **1563**	90	90
1705	(38p.) As No. 1699	90	90

Nos. 1698 and 1704 were inscr 'IOM' and originally sold for 37p.
Nos. 1699 and 1705 were inscr 'UK' and originally sold for 38p.
No. 1700 was inscr 'sepac'.
No. 1701/a include the 'EUROPA' emblem.

1569 Triumph Herald Sailboat

2011. Top Gear Challenges. Multicoloured.

	(a) Ordinary gum		
1706	37p. Type **1569**	90	90
1707	38p. Citroen Grand Design	90	90
1708	58p. Polar Hilux	1·40	1·40
1709	68p. Hammerhead Eagle i-Thrust	1·75	1·75
1710	£1.10 Robin Reliant Space Shuttle	2·40	2·40
1711	£1.82 Caravan Airship	4·25	4·25
	(b) Self-adhesive		
MS1712	209×237 mm. As No. 1710×5	2·40	2·40
MS1713	210×238 mm. As No. 1711×5	4·25	4·25

1575 Sailing

1582 Cycling (image scaled to 40% of original size)

2012. Olympic Games, London. Multicoloured.

1714	37p. Type **1575**	90	90
1715	38p. Cycling	90	90
1716	58p. Swimming	1·40	1·40
1717	68p. Tennis	1·75	1·75
1718	76p. Rowing	1·90	1·90
1719	£1 Athletics	2·40	2·40
1720	£1.15 Shooting	2·50	2·50

MS1721	120×78 mm. **1582** £3 multicoloured	8·00	8·00
MS1722	210×230 mm. Nos. 1714/20, each ×2	23·00	23·00

1583 Queen Elizabeth II in 1990

1589 Queen Elizabeth II, c. 2005 (image scaled to 44% of original size)

2012. Diamond Jubilee (1st issue). Multicoloured.

1723	37p. Type **1583**	90	90
1724	38p. Queen Elizabeth II Trooping the Colour, 1979	90	90
1725	58p. Queen Elizabeth II at Film Premiere, 1955	1·40	1·40
1726	68p. Queen Elizabeth II in Tuvalu, 1982	1·75	1·75
1727	£1.10 Queen Elizabeth II, 1968	2·40	2·40
1728	£1.82 Queen Elizabeth II at the Derby, Epsom, 2008	4·25	4·25
MS1729	174×164 mm. Nos. 1723/8 and three stamp-size labels	11·50	11·50
MS1730	110×70 mm. **1589** £3 multicoloured	7·25	7·25

1590 Frost Arbory (oil on canvas), 1931

2012. Paintings by William Hoggatt. Multicoloured.

1731	38p. Type **1590**	90	90
1732	38p. A Colby Mill (watercolour), 1954	90	90
1733	38p. Landing the Catch, Port St. Mary (watercolour), c. 1913	90	90
1734	38p. Early Spring (oil on canvus), 1910	90	90
1735	38p. Port Erin Bay (oil on canvus), 1937	90	90

1595 Titanic

2012. Centenary of the Sinking of the Titanic. Multicoloured.

1736	37p. Type **1595**	90	90
1737	38p. Interior of Titanic	90	90
1738	68p. Captain Edward Smith, Lifebelt and Letter	1·75	1·75
1739	76p. Lifebelt and Titanic sinking	2·00	2·00
1740	£1.15 Survivors in Lifeboats	2·40	2·40
1741	£1.65 Passengers and Titanic	4·00	4·00
MS1742	210×297 mm. Nos. 1736/8 and Nos. 1739/41×2	25·00	25·00

Nos. 1736/8 and 1739/41 were each printed together, se-tenant, as horizontal strips of three, each strip forming a composite background design.

1601 Castletown Harbour Lighthouse

2012. Harbour Lights. Minor Lighthouses of the Isle of Man. Multicoloured.

1743	1p. Type **1601**	10	10
1744	68p. Douglas Harbour Lighthouse	1·75	1·75
1745	75p. Peel Harbour Lighthouse	2·00	2·00
1746	£1 Laxey Harbour Lighthouse	2·40	2·40
1747	£1.30 Ramsey Harbour Lighthouse	2·50	2·50
1748	£1.60 Port St. Mary Harbour Lighthouse	4·00	4·00

1607 Goss China Manx Cottage

2012. The Kelly Collection of Manx Memorabilia. Multicoloured.

1749	(38p.) Type **1607**	90	90
1750	(41p.) Crown Devon Model of Early Manx Racing Car	95	95
1751	58p. Royal Doulton Spittoon showing Postman at Maughold	1·10	1·10
1752	68p. Willow Art China Model of Three-legged Manx Dog "Prince Toby Orry"	1·75	1·75
1753	£1.10 China Plate showig Cat "Ginger-Manx of Glen Orry", 1962	2·40	2·40
1754	£1.82 Enamelled Silver Freemasons Founder's Jewel showing Tower of Refuge, Douglas Bay	4·25	4·25

1613 Thames Diamond Jubilee Pageant (image scaled to 28% of original size)

2012. Diamond Jubilee (2nd issue). Thames Diamond Jubilee Pageant. Multicoloured.

MS1755	170×75mm. **1613** 50p. Gloriana (royal rowbarge); 50p. Lifeboat from TSS Lady of Mann; 50p. Vital Spark (replica Viking longboat); £1.50 Royal Barge Spirit of Chartwell (85×29 mm)	7·25	7·25
MS1756	210×298 mm. 50p.×3 Gloriana (royal rowbarge); 50p.×3 Lifeboat from TSS Lady of Mann; 50p.×3 Vital Spark (replica Viking longboat); £1.50×3 Royal Barge Spirit of Chartwell (85×29 mm) and nine stamp-size labels	20·00	20·00
MS1757	210×298 mm. Nos. 1632/4, each ×2, 1635×3, 1636×2, 1637 and £3 multicoloured (as stamp within **MS**1638) and 12 stamp-size labels (4 June)	25·00	25·00
MS1758	210×296 mm. Nos. 1723/6, each ×2, 1727/8, £3 multicoloured (as stamp within **MS**1730) and 18 stamp-size labels (5 June)	22·00	22·00

1614 Mark Cavendish celebrating Win in Scratch Race, 2006 Commonwealth Games

2012. Victories of Mark Cavendish (cyclist). Multicoloured.

1759	38p. Type **1614**	90	90
1760	41p. Winning Scheldeprijs Vlaanderen, Belgium, 2007	95	95
1761	65p. Winning Milan – San Remo Classic, Italy, 2009	1·50	1·50
1762	71p. Wearing Green Jersey at end of Tour de France, Paris, 2011	1·60	1·60
1763	80p. Winning World Road Race Championships, Copenhagen, September 2011	1·90	1·90
1764	105p. Wearing Medal and Rainbow Jersey of World Road Race Champion	2·40	2·40
1765	116p. At Kuurne-Brussels-Kuurne Race, 2012	2·50	2·50
MS1766	210×296 mm. Nos. 1759/62, each ×2, 1763 and 1764/5, each ×2, and seven stamp-size labels	16·00	16·00

1621 Colletes succinctus

2012. Bee Fauna of the Isle of Man. Multicoloured.

	(a) Ordinary gum		
1767	38p. Type **1621**	90	90
1768	41p. Epeolus variegatus	95	95
1769	£1 Osmia rufa	2·40	2·40
1770	£1.05 Halictus rubicundus	2·40	2·40
1771	£1.30 Bombus monticola	2·50	2·50
1772	£1.47 Apis mellifera	3·25	3·25
	(b) Self-adhesive		
1773	38p. Colletes succinctus	90	90
1774	41p. Epeolus variegates	95	95

1629 AW FK.8 B5773 (1918)

2012. Centenary of the Royal Flying Corps. Multicoloured.

1775	38p. Type **1629**	90	90
1776	41p. MS Type L 3253 (1915)	95	95
1777	65p. DH.2 5964 (1916)	1·50	1·50
1778	80p. Sopwith Camel B5648 (1918)	1·90	1·90
1779	£1.37 RAF BE.2C 4359 (1917)	2·75	2·75
1780	£1.91 Short S.32 402 (1912)	4·25	4·25

1635 Terra Nova at the ice foot of Cape Evans, 5 January 1911; Memorial Cairn erected at Site of Scott's Tent, 1912 (image scaled to 28% of original size)

2012. Centenary of Captain Robert Scott's South Pole Expedition, 1910-13. Sheet 170×75 mm

MS1781 **1635**	£1.50×2 black, grey and lavender	7·25	7·25

1636 Ramsey Christmas Lights

2012. Christmas Scenes. 'A Time Gone By.' Paintings by Michael Starkey. Multicoloured.

	(a) Ordinary gum		
1782	38p. Type **1636**	90	90
1783	41p. Glen Auldyn	95	95
1784	71p. Castletown Police Station	1·60	1·60
1785	£1.05 Sulby Glen	2·40	2·40
1786	£1.16 Martin's Sweet Shop, Ramsey	2·50	2·50
1787	£1.73 Lake Lane, Peel	4·00	4·00
	(b) Self-adhesive		
1788	38p. As Type **1636**	90	90
1789	41p. As No. 1783	95	95

1642 Knight

2013. The Chronicles of Man and the Lewis Chessmen. Multicoloured.

1790	38p. Type **1642**	90	90
1791	41p. King	95	95
1792	71p. Warder	1·60	1·60
1793	80p. Bishop	1·90	1·90
1794	130p. Queen	2·75	2·75
1795	191p. Pawn	4·25	4·25

1648 Queen Victoria

1654 Coronation Photograph (image scaled to 44% of original size)

2013. 60th Anniv of the Coronation. 'A Celebration of Coronation Commemoratives' (Coronation memorabilia). Multicoloured.

1796	38p. Type **1648**	90	90
1797	41p. King Edward VII and Queen Alexandra	95	95
1798	65p. Souvenir of Visit of King George V and Queen Mary to Manchester, 1913	1·50	1·50
1799	£1.05 King George VI , Queen Elizabeth, Princess Elizabeth and Princess Margaret	2·40	2·40
1800	£1.37 Arms and Photo of Queen Elizabeth II	2·75	2·75
1801	£1.73 Queen Elizabeth II and Duke of Edinburgh (Coronation souvenir)	4·00	4·00
MS1802 110×70 mm. **1654** £3 multicoloured (21 Apr)		7·25	7·25

1655 Year of the Snake (image scaled to 28% of original size)

2013. Chinese New Year. Year of the Snake. Multicoloured.
MS1803 171×75 mm. **1655** 5p. Multicoloured coiled snake; 20p. Chinese letter containing fish; 20p. Chinese letter containing two cranes; 20p. Chinese letter containing deer; 20p. Chinese letter containing magpie and flowers; £2.15 Coiled yellow snake with flower and foliage pattern ..... 7·25 7·25

MS1804 170×211 mm. 5p. Multicoloured coiled snake×16; 20p. Chinese letter containing fish; 20p. Chinese letter containing deer; 20p. Chinese letter containing two cranes; 20p. Chinese letter containing magpie and flowers ..... 4·00 4·00

1656 Early and Modern Uniforms

2013. 150th Anniv of the Isle of Man Constabulary. Multicoloured.

1805	38p. Type **1656**	90	90
1806	41p. Early Police Motorbikes and Modern Car and Motorcycle ('Vehicles')	95	95
1807	71p. German Shepherd Dogs tracking Suspect and in Training and Springer Spaniel Sniffer Dog	1·60	1·60
1808	80p. Control Room Computers and Police with Radios ('Communications')	1·90	1·90
1809	£1.47 Police Constable at Door and Police talking to Children ('Community')	3·25	3·25
1810	£1.82 Early and Current Police Stations	4·25	4·25

1662 Fire Engine (image scaled to 29% of original size)

2013. Isle of Man Fire and Rescue Service. Sheet 170×75 mm
MS1811 **1662** £3 multicoloured ..... 7·25 7·25

1663 Three Legs of Man wearing Armour

2013. The Three Legs of Man. Multicoloured.

(a) Ordinary gum

1812	5p. Type **1663**	10	10
1813	10p. Arms with Three Legs of Man	25	25
1814	40p. Three Legs of Man with Crown	95	95
1815	42p. Three Legs of Man in Stained Glass Window	95	95
1816	69p. Three Legs of Man wearing Spurs	1·60	1·60
1817	73p. Arms with Three Legs of Man, Peregrine Falcon, Raven and Crown	1·60	1·60
1818	£1.19 Symbolic Three Legs of Man	2·50	2·50
1819	£2 Three Legs of Man on Wall, Douglas	4·25	4·25

(b) Self-adhesive

1820	40p. As No. 1814	95	95
1821	42p. As No. 1815	95	95

1671 Robin's Reign, 1970

2013. Robin Gibb (singer and songwriter) Commemoration. Album Covers. Multicoloured.

1822	2p. Type **1671**	10	10
1823	40p. How Old are you?, 1983	95	95
1824	42p. Secret Agent, 1984	95	95
1825	50p. Walls Have Ears, 1985	1·25	1·25
1826	69p. Magnet, 2003	1·60	1·60
1827	73p. Robin Gibb Live, 2005	1·60	1·60
1828	120p. Titanic Requiem (composed with R. J. Gibb, performed by Royal Philharmonic Orchestra), 2012	2·50	2·50
1829	178p. 50 St. Catherine's Drive	4·00	4·00
MS1830 211×298 mm. Nos. 1822/5 and Nos. 1826/9×2		25·00	25·00

1679 Dubs Steam Locomotive Caledonia, Douglas Station, July 2009

2013. Isle of Man Railways. 140th Anniv of the Isle of Man Steam Railway and 120th Anniv of the Manx Electric Railway Douglas to Groudle Line. Modern Isle of Man Railways Posters. Multicoloured.

1831	40p. Type **1679**	95	95
1832	42p. Manx Electric Railway Tramcar No. 6 at Halfway House Crossing, August 2012	95	95
1833	69p. Beyer Peacock Steam Locomotive No. 10 G. H. Wood leaving Douglas Station, July 2009	1·60	1·60
1834	119p. Manx Electric Railway Tramcar No. 5, Baldrine, September 2012	2·50	2·50
1835	160p. Beyer Peacock Steam Locomotive No. 13 Kissack, Ellenbrook, July 2012	3·75	3·75
1836	161p. Manx Electric Railway Tramcar No. 7 arriving at Laxey Station, May 2012	3·75	3·75

1685 Eugène Christophe, 1919

2013. Centenary of the Tour de France (cycle race). Multicoloured.

1837	1p. Type **1685**	10	10

1838	40p. Mark Cavendish, 2011	95	95
1839	42p. Brian Robinson, 1960	95	95
1840	69p. Miguel Indurain, 1992	1·60	1·60
1841	73p. Jacques Anquetil, 1963	1·60	1·60
1842	108p. Eddy Merckx, 1970	2·40	2·40
1843	119p. Bernard Hinault, 1979	2·50	2·50
1844	120p. Bradley Wiggins, 2012	2·50	2·50

1693 The Last Flight of Concorde, 2003

2013. 225th Anniv of the *Times* of London. Newspaper Headlines. Multicoloured.

1845	40p. Type **1693**	95	95
1846	42p. England win the World Cup, 1966	95	95
1847	73p. Isle of Man Postal Independence, 1973	1·60	1·60
1848	108p. Queen Elizabeth II's State Visit to China, 1986	2·40	2·40
1849	141p. President Kennedy Assassinated in Dallas, 1963	3·25	3·25
1850	179p. Man Lands on the Moon, 1969	4·25	4·25

1699 Murals from St. Thomas' Church, Douglas (image scaled to 28% of original size)

2013. St. Thomas' Church Murals by John Miller Nicholson. Multicoloured.
MS1851 170×76 mm. **1699** £1 Angels; £2 Saints ..... 7·25 7·25

1700 Lion

2013. Big Cats by Jeremy Paul. Multicoloured.

1852	40p. Type **1700**	95	95
1853	42p. Snow Leopard	95	95
1854	69p. Tiger	1·60	1·60
1855	120p. Cheetah	2·50	2·50
1856	160p. Leopard	3·75	3·75
1857	161p. Jaguar	3·75	3·75

1706 Baboon; Rhinoceros; Giraffes; Kudu (image scaled to 28% of original size)

2013. A Journey through Africa with Jeremy Paul. Sheet 170×75 mm
MS1858 **1706** 75p.×4 multicoloured ..... 7·25 7·25

1707 Girl posting Letter (Christmas 1990)

2013. A Christmas Stamp Gallery. Designs adapted from previous Christmas Stamps. Multicoloured.

(a) Ordinary gum

1859	40p. Type **1707**	95	95
1860	42p. The Three Kings ('Love Came Down at Christmas' 1991)	95	95
1861	73p. Angel with the Crown of Glory (Stained Glass Windows, 2005)	1·60	1·60
1862	108p. Robin (Christmas 1988)	2·40	2·40
1863	119p. St. Catherine's Church, Port Erin ('Winter in Mann', 1995)	2·50	2·50
1864	178p. Christmas Tree and Gifts (Christmas Trees, 2006)	4·25	4·25

(b) Self-adhesive

1865	40p. As Type **1707**	95	95
1866	42p. As No. 1860	95	95

1713 Visual Arts

2014. Island of Culture 2014

1867	(40p.) Type **1713**	95	95
1868	(40p.) Drama	95	95
1869	(42p.) Literature	95	95
1870	(42p.) Film	95	95
1871	(73p.) Music	1·60	1·60
1872	(£1.19) Craft	2·50	2·50
1873	(£1.19) Dance	2·50	2·50
1874	(£1.19) Design	2·50	2·50

Nos. 1867/8 were inscr 'IOM' and originally sold for 40p., Nos. 1869/70 were inscr 'UK' and sold for 42p., No. 1871 was inscr 'EU' and sold for 73p. and Nos. 1872/4 were inscr 'ROR' and sold for £1.19.

1721 Winter Berries and Flowers (image scaled to 37% of original size)

2014. Winter Flora. Sheet 130×90 mm. Multicoloured.
MS1875 **1721** 75p.×4 Ivy berries; Fir cones; Hellebore flowers; Rose hips ..... 7·25 7·25

1722 Communications

2014. Centenary of World War I (1st issue). Life in the Trenches. Multicoloured.

1876	40p. Type **1722**	95	95
1877	42p. Sappers	95	95
1878	69p. Trenches	1·60	1·60
1879	£1.08 Horses	2·40	2·40
1880	£1.41 Christmas Truce	3·25	3·25
1881	£1.60 Officers' Dugout	3·75	3·75

1728 Trench Art (image scaled to 44% of original size)

MS1882 110×70 mm. **1728** £3 Detail from German Christmas card produced in Knockaloe Internment Camp, 1917 ..... 7·25 7·25

1729 Four Red Arrows

2014. 50th Display Season of Royal Air Force Red Arrows. Multicoloured.

1883	40p. Type **1729**	95	95
1884	42p. Red Arrows flying in Formation	95	95
1885	69p. Two Red Arrows	1·60	1·60
1886	73p. Two Red Arrows	1·60	1·60
1887	108p. Four Red Arrows	2·40	2·40
1888	265p. View from Cockpit	6·25	6·25

POSTAGE DUE STAMPS

D1

1973

D1	D1	½p. red, black and yellow	1·50	1·10
D2	D1	1p. red, black and brown	50	60
D3	D1	2p. red, black and green	15	20
D4	D1	3p. red, black and grey	20	20
D5	D1	4p. red, black and pink	30	35
D6	D1	5p. red, black and blue	30	35
D7	D1	10p. red, black and violet	40	40
D8	D1	20p. red, black and green	75	60

D2

1975

D9	D2	½p. yellow, black and red	10	10
D10	D2	1p. brown, black and red	10	10
D11	D2	4p. lilac, black and red	10	15
D12	D2	7p. blue, black and red	15	20
D13	D2	9p. grey, black and red	25	30
D14	D2	10p. mauve, blk & red	25	20
D15	D2	50p. orange, blk & red	90	90
D16	D2	£1 green, black and red	1·50	1·60

D3

1982

D17	D3	1p. multicoloured	10	10
D18	D3	2p. multicoloured	10	10
D19	D3	5p. multicoloured	10	10
D20	D3	10p. multicoloured	20	25
D21	D3	20p. multicoloured	40	45
D22	D3	50p. multicoloured	90	1·10
D23	D3	£1 multicoloured	1·60	2·10
D24	D3	£2 multicoloured	3·25	4·25

D4

1992

D25	D4	£5 multicoloured	8·00	8·50

Pt. 19

ISRAEL

The former British Mandate over Palestine was ended by the partition plan approved by the United Nations General Assembly on 29 November 1947, and on 14 May 1948 the new state of Israel was proclaimed.

1948. 1000 prutot (mils) = 1 Israeli pound.
1960. 100 agorot = 1 Israeli pound.
1980. 100 agorot = 1 shekel.

"**TABS**". All Israeli stamps (except the Postage Dues) exist with descriptive sheet margin attached. These so-called "Tabs" are popular and in some cases scarce. Prices are for stamps without "tab". Separate prices for stamps with "tabs" are given in Stanley Gibbons Catalogue, Part 19 (Middle East).

1 Palm Tree and Baskets with Dates   **2** Silver Shekel and Pomegranates

1948. Ancient Jewish Coins. Perf or roul.

1	1	3m. orange	1·20	45
2	-	5m. green	1·20	45
3a	-	10m. mauve	7·00	3·50
4	-	15m. red	1·70	45
5	-	20m. blue	3·50	85
6	-	50m. brown	23·00	4·00
7	2	250m. green	60·00	23·00
8	2	500m. red on buff	£225	£100
9	2	1000m. blue on blue (36×24 mm)	£475	£200

DESIGNS ON COINS: 5m. Vine leaf; 10m. Ritual jar; 15m. Bunch of grapes; 20m. Ritual cup; 50m. Tied palm branches and lemon.
See also Nos. 21/6, 40/51 and 90/93.

3 "Flying Scroll" Emblem

1948. Jewish New Year.

10	3	3m. brown and blue	95	60
11	3	5m. green and blue	95	60
12	3	10m. red and blue	1·20	95
13	3	20m. blue and light blue	4·75	2·10
14	3	65m. brown and red	26·00	11·50

4 Road to Jerusalem

1949. Inauguration of Constituent Assembly.

15	4	250pr. brown and grey	3·25	2·50

5 National Flag

1949. Adoption of New National Flag.

16	5	20pr. blue	1·50	70

1949. First Anniv of Israeli Postage Stamps. Sheet containing stamp similar to T **8** in block of four.

MS16a	75×95 mm. 10pr. claret		£170	95·00

6 Petah Tiqwa Well

1949. 70th Anniv of Founding of Petah Tiqwa.

17	6	40pr. brown and green	19·00	3·00

7 Air Force Badge

1949. Jewish New Year.

18	7	5pr. blue	1·50	60
19	-	10pr. green	1·50	60
20	-	35pr. brown	11·50	7·00

BADGES: 10pr. Navy; 35pr. Army.

8 Ancient Jewish Coin

1949. Second Jewish Coins issue. Inscr at left of Six or Eight characters.

21	8	3pr. grey	25	25
22	-	5pr. violet (as No. 2)	25	25
23	-	10pr. green (as No. 3)	25	25
24	-	15pr. red (as No. 4)	45	25
25	-	30pr. blue	80	45
26	-	50pr. brown (as No. 6)	2·75	95

DESIGN: 30p.r. Ritual vessel.
For designs with larger inscription at left, see Nos. 40/51 and 90/93.

10 Stag and Globe

1950. Israel's Membership and 75th Anniv of U.P.U.

27	10	40pr. violet	1·70	95
28	10	80pr. red	2·10	1·20

11 Landing of Immigrants

1950. Second Anniv of Independence.

29	11	20pr. brown	4·75	2·30
30	11	40pr. green	19·00	10·50

DESIGN: 40pr. Line of immigrant ships.

12 Library and Book

1950. 25th Anniv of Founding of Hebrew University, Jerusalem.

31	12	100pr. green	70	70

13 Eagle

1950. Air.

32	-	5pr. blue	95	60
33	-	30pr. grey	60	60
34	-	40pr. green	60	60
35	-	50pr. brown	60	60
36	13	100pr. red	29·00	19·00
37	-	250pr. blue	3·50	2·30

DESIGNS—VERT: 5pr. Doves pecking grapes; 30pr. Eagle; 40pr. Ostrich; 50pr. Dove. HORIZ: 250pr. Dove with olive branch.

14 Star of David and Fruit

1950. Jewish New Year.

38	14	5pr. violet and orange	25	25
39	14	15pr. brown and green	1·20	1·20

1950. Third Jewish Coins issue. Inscr at left of 13 characters.

40	-	3pr. grey	25	25
41	-	5pr. violet	25	25
42	-	10pr. green	25	25
43	-	15pr. red	25	25
44	-	20pr. orange	25	25
45	-	30pr. blue	25	25
46	-	35pr. green	80	45
47	-	40pr. brown	30	30
48	-	45pr. mauve	30	30
49	-	50pr. brown	35	30
50	-	60pr. red	30	30
51	-	85pr. blue	80	45

DESIGNS ON COINS: 3, 20pr. Palm tree and baskets with dates; 5, 35pr. Vine leaf; 10, 40pr. Ritual jar; 15, 45pr. Bunch of grapes; 30, 60pr. Ritual vessel; 50, 85pr. Tied palm branches and lemon.
For further designs with value at right, see Nos. 90/93.

16 Runner and Track

1950. Third Maccabiah (sports meeting).

52	16	80pr. green and olive	5·75	3·00

17 The Negev (after R. Rubin)

1950. Opening of Post Office at Elat.

53	17	500pr. brown & light brown	21·00	14·00

19 Memorial Tablet

1951. 40th Anniv of Founding of Tel Aviv.

54	19	40pr. brown	1·00	70

20 "Supporting Israel"

1951. Independence Bonds Campaign.

55	20	80pr. red	70	70

21 Metsudat Yesha

1951. Third Anniv of State of Israel.

56	21	15pr. brown	35	35
57	-	40pr. blue (Hakastel)	1·00	1·00

22 Tractor   **23** Ploughing and Savings Stamp

1951. 50th Anniv of Jewish National Fund.

58	22	15pr. brown	25	25
59	-	25pr. green	25	25
60	23	80pr. blue	2·30	1·60

DESIGN—As Type **22**: 25pr. Stylized tree.

24 Dr. T. Herzl

1951. 23rd Zionist Congress.

61	24	80pr. green	70	60

25 Carrier Pigeons

1951. Jewish New Year.

62	25	5pr. blue	25	10
63	-	15pr. red	25	10
64	-	40pr. violet	35	35

DESIGNS: 15pr. Woman and dove; 40pr. Scroll of the Law.

26 Menora and Emblems

1952

64a	26	1000pr. black and blue	28·00	17·00

26a Haifa Bay, Mt. Carmel and City Seal

1952. Air. National Stamp Exn ("TABA").

64b	-	100pr. blue and black	1·20	80
64c	26a	120pr. purple and black	1·60	1·20

DESIGN: 100pr. Haifa Bay and City Seal.

27 Thistle and Yad Mordechai

1952. Fourth Anniv of Independence.

65	**27**	30pr. brown and mauve	35	25
66	-	60pr. slate and blue	60	35
67	-	110pr. brown and red	1·20	80

DESIGNS: 60pr. Cornflower and Deganya; 110pr. Anemone and Safed.

28 New York Skyline and Z.O.A. Building

1952. Opening of American Zionist Building, Tel Aviv.

68	**28**	220pr. grey and blue	1·40	70

29 Figs

1952. Jewish New Year.

69	**29**	15pr. yellow and green	45	25
70	-	40pr. yellow, blue and violet	70	45
71	-	110pr. grey and red	1·00	95
72	-	220pr. green, brown & orge	1·50	1·20

FLOWERS: 40pr. Lily ("Rose of Sharon"); 110pr. Dove; 220pr. Nuts.

30 Dr. C. Weizmann (from sketch by R. Errell)

1952. Death of First President.

73	**30**	30pr. blue	35	25
74	**30**	110pr. black	1·00	80

31

1952. 70th Anniv of Bet Yaakov Lechu Venelcha Immigration Organization.

75	**31**	110pr. buff, green and brown	1·00	70

32 Douglas DC-4 Airliner over Tel Aviv Yafo

1953. Air.

76	-	10pr. deep green and green	45	30
77	-	70pr. violet and lilac	45	30
78	-	100pr. deep green and green	45	30
79	-	150pr. brown and orange	45	30
80	-	350pr. red and pink	70	70
81	-	500pr. deep blue and blue	1·50	1·20
81a	-	750pr. deep brown & brown	25	25
82	**32**	1000pr. deep green & green	5·75	4·75
82a	-	3000pr. purple	60	60

DESIGNS—HORIZ: 10pr. Olive tree; 70pr. Sea of Galilee; 100pr. Shaar Hogay on road to Jerusalem; 150pr. Lion Rock, Negev; 350pr. Bay of Elat. VERT: 500pr. Tanour Falls, near Metoulla; 750pr. Lake Hula; 3000pr. Tomb of Meir Baal Haness.

33 Anemones and Arms

1953. Fifth Anniv of Independence.

83	**33**	110pr. red, green and blue	60	35

35 Maimonides (philosopher)

1953. Seventh Int Congress of History of Science.

84	**35**	110pr. brown	2·00	80

36 Holy Ark, Petah-Tikvah

1953. Jewish New Year.

85	-	20pr. blue	15	15
86	**36**	45pr. red	25	25
87	-	200pr. violet	1·00	70

DESIGNS: 20pr. Holy Ark, Jerusalem; 200pr. Holy Ark, Zefat.

37 Hand holding Globe/ Football

1953. Fourth Maccabiah.

88	**37**	110pr. brown and blue	70	35

38 Exhibition Emblem

1953. "Conquest of the Desert" Exhibition.

89	**38**	200pr. multicoloured	70	35

39 Ancient Jewish Coin

1954. Fourth Jewish Coins issue.

90	**39**	80pr. bistre	15	15
91	-	95pr. green	25	15
92	-	100pr. brown	25	15
93	-	125pr. blue	35	15

DESIGNS ON COINS: 95pr. Wheat; 100pr. Gate; 125pr. Lyre.

40 Gesher and Narcissus

1954. Sixth Anniv of Independence.

94	-	60pr. blue, red and grey	10	10
95	**40**	350pr. brown, yellow & grn	70	45

DESIGN: 60pr. Yehiam and helichrysum.

41 Dr. T. Z. Herzl

1954. 50th Death Anniv of Herzl (founder of World Zionist Movement).

96	**41**	160pr. sepia, buff and blue	60	35

43

1954. Jewish New Year.

97	**43**	25pr. sepia	20	20

44 19th century Mail Coach and P.O.

1954. National Stamp Exhibition.

98	**44**	60pr. black, yellow and blue	10	10
99	-	200pr. black, red and green	60	60

DESIGN: 200pr. Mail van and G.P.O., 1954.

45 Baron Edmond de Rothschild

1954. 20th Death Anniv of De Rothschild (financier).

100	**45**	300pr. turquoise	60	35

46 Lamp of Knowledge

1955. 50th Anniv of Teachers' Association.

101	**46**	250pr. blue	45	35

47 Parachutist and Barbed Wire

1955. Jewish Mobilization during Second World War.

102	**47**	120pr. black and turquoise	35	25

48 Menora and Olive Branches

1955. Seventh Anniv of Independence.

103	**48**	150pr. orange, black & grn	60	35

49 Immigrants and Ship

1955. 20th Anniv of Youth Immigration Scheme.

104	**49**	5pr. black and blue	10	10
105	-	10pr. black and red	10	10
106	-	25pr. black and green	10	10
107	-	30pr. black and orange	10	10
108	-	60pr. black and violet	10	10
109	-	750pr. black and brown	1·40	80

DESIGNS: 10pr. Immigrants and Douglas DC-3 airplane; 25pr. Boy and calf; 30pr. Girl watering flowers; 60pr. Boy making pottery; 750pr. Boy using theodolite.

50 Musicians playing Timbrel and Cymbals

1955. Jewish New Year.

110	**50**	25pr. green and orange	10	10
111	-	60pr. grey and orange	10	10
112	-	120pr. blue and yellow	10	10
113	-	250pr. brown and orange	45	35

DESIGNS—Musicians playing: 60pr. Ram's horn; 120pr. Tuba; 250pr. Harp.

51 Ambulance

1955. 25th Anniv of Magen David Adom (Jewish Red Cross).

114	**51**	160pr. green, black and red	25	25

52 "Reuben"

1955. Twelve Tribes of Israel.

115A	**52**	10pr. green	10	10
116A	-	20pr. mauve	10	10
117A	-	30pr. blue	10	10
118A	-	40pr. brown	10	10
119A	-	50pr. blue	10	10
120A	-	60pr. bistre	10	10
121A	-	80pr. violet	10	10
122A	-	100pr. red	10	10
123A	-	120pr. olive	20	10
124A	-	180pr. mauve	70	35
125A	-	200pr. green	35	15
126A	-	250pr. grey	45	20

EMBLEMS: 20pr. "Simeon" (castle); 30pr. "Levi" (High Priest's breastplate); 40pr. "Judah" (lion); 50pr. "Dan" (scales); 60pr. "Naphtali" (gazelle); 80pr. "Gad" (tents); 100pr. "Asher" (tree); 120pr. "Issachar" (sun and stars); 180pr. "Zebulun" (ship); 200pr. "Joseph" (sheaf of wheat); 250pr. "Benjamin" (wolf).

53 Professor Einstein

1956. Einstein Commemoration.

127	**53**	350pr. brown	45	35

54 Technion

1956. 30th Anniv of Israel Institute of Technology, Haifa.

128	**54**	350pr. green and black	35	35

55 "Eight Years of Independence"

1956. Eighth Anniv of Independence.

129	**55**	150pr. multicoloured	25	15

56 Oranges

1956. Fourth International Congress of Mediterranean Citrus Fruit Growers.

130	**56**	300pr. multicoloured	35	35

57 Musican playing Lyre

1956. Jewish New Year. Musicians playing instruments.

131	**57**	30pr. brown and blue	10	10
132	-	50pr. violet and orange	10	10
133	-	150pr. turquoise and orange	20	20

INSTRUMENTS—VERT: 50pr. Sistrum. HORIZ: 150pr. Double oboe.

58 Insignia of "Haganah"

1957. Defence Fund.

134	**58**	80pr.+20pr. green	10	10
135	**58**	150pr.+50pr. red	10	10
136	**58**	350pr.+50pr. blue	20	20

59 Airplane sky-writing Figure "9"

1957. Ninth Anniv of Independence.

137	**59**	250pr. black, blue & lt blue	35	25

60 Bezalel Museum and Candelabrum

1957. 50th Anniv of Bezalel Museum, Jerusalem.

138	**60**	400pr. multicoloured	25	25

61 Seal of Tamach and Horse

1957. Jewish New Year. Ancient Hebrew Seals.

139	**61**	50pr. black & brn on blue	10	10
140	-	160pr. black & grn on buff	10	10
141	-	300pr. black & red on pink	20	10

DESIGNS: 160pr. Seal of Shema and lion; 300pr. Seal of Netanyahuv Ne'avadyahu and gazelle.

61a Part of Ancient "Bet Alpha" Synagogue Floor Mosaic

1957. First Israeli International Stamp Exhibition. Sheet containing four triangular stamps, which together form the complete centre-piece of floor mosaic.

MS141a 103×105 mm. 100pr. Type **61a**; 200, 300, 400pr. (similar)   70   70

---

62 Throwing the Hammer

1958. 25th Anniv of Maccabiah Games.

142	**62**	500pr. red and bistre	35	25

63 Ancient Hebrew Ship

1958. Israel Merchant Marine Commemoration.

143	**63**	10pr. red, blue and brown	10	10
144	-	20pr. brown and green	10	10
145	-	30pr. grey and red	20	10
146	-	1000pr. green and blue	45	45

DESIGNS—As T **63**: 20pr. Immigration ship *Nirit*; 30pr. Freighter *Shomron*. 57×22 ½ mm: 1000pr. Liner "Zion".

64 Menora and Olive Branch

1958. Tenth Anniv of Independence.

147	**64**	400pr. green, black and gold	35	35

65 Dancing Children forming "10"

1958. First World Conference of Jewish Youth, Jerusalem.

148	**65**	200pr. green and orange	35	25

66 Convention Centre, Jerusalem, and Exhibition Emblem

1958. Tenth Anniv (of Israel) Exn, Jerusalem.

149	**66**	400pr. orange and lilac on cream	35	35

67 Wheat

1958. Jewish New Year.

150	**67**	50pr. brown and ochre	10	10
151	-	60pr. black and yellow	10	10
152	-	160pr. purple and violet	10	10
153	-	300pr. green and apple	35	35

DESIGNS: 60pr. Barley; 160pr. Grapes; 300pr. Figs. See also Nos. 166/8.

68 Ancient Stone

1958. Tenth Anniv of Declaration of Human Rights.

154	**68**	750pr. black, yellow & blue	45	35

---

69 Post Office Emblem

1959. Tenth Anniv of Israel Postal Services.

155	**69**	60pr. black, red and olive	10	10
156	-	120pr. black, red and olive	20	20
157	-	250pr. black, red and olive	30	20
158	-	500pr. black, red and olive	35	35

DESIGNS—HORIZ: 120pr. Mail van. VERT: 250pr. Radio-telephone equipment; 500pr. "Telex" dial and keyboard.

70 Sholem Aleichem

1959. Birth Cent of Sholem Aleichem (writer).

159	**70**	250pr. brown and green	30	25

71 Tel Aviv

1959. 50th Anniv of Tel Aviv.

160	**71**	120pr. multicoloured	35	25

72 Anemone

1959. 11th Anniv of Independence. Multicoloured.

161		60pr. Type **72**	10	10
162		120pr. Cyclamen	10	10
163		300pr. Narcissus	10	10

See also Nos. 188/9, 211/13 and 257/9.

73 C. N. Bialik

1959. 25th Anniv of Chaim Bialik (poet).

164	**73**	250pr. olive and orange	35	25

74 Bristol 175 Britannia Airliner and Wind-sock

1959. Tenth Anniv of Civil Aviation in Israel.

165	**74**	500pr. multicoloured	45	35

1959. Jewish New Year. As T **67**.

166		60pr. red and brown	20	20
167		200pr. green and deep green	35	25
168		350pr. orange and brown	45	35

DESIGNS: 60pr. Pomegranates; 200pr. Olives; 350pr. Dates.

76 E. Ben-Yehuda

1959. Birth Centenary of Ben-Yehuda (pioneer of Hebrew language).

169	**76**	250pr. deep blue and blue	35	35

---

77 Merhavya Settlement

1959. 50th Anniv of Merhavya and Deganya Settlements. 75th Anniv of Yesud Ha-Maala Settlement.

170	**77**	60pr. green and yellow	10	10
171	-	120pr. brown & light brown	35	25
172	-	180pr. green and blue	60	45

DESIGNS: 120pr. Yesud Ha-Maala; 180pr. Deganya.

78 Ancient Jewish Coin

1960. New currency. Values in black.

173	**78**	1a. bistre on pink	10	10
174	**78**	3a. red on pink	10	10
175	**78**	5a. slate on pink	15	10
176	**78**	6a. green on blue	15	10
176a	**78**	7a. grey on blue	15	10
177	**78**	8a. mauve on blue	15	10
178	**78**	12a. blue on blue	20	10
179	**78**	18a. orange	20	10
180	**78**	25a. blue	30	20
181	**78**	30a. red	35	20
182	**78**	50a. lilac	45	45

79 Tiberias

1960. Air.

183	-	15a. black and lilac	35	25
184	-	20a. black and green	45	35
184a	-	25a. black and orange	70	60
184b	-	30a. black and turquoise	1·20	1·20
184c	-	35a. black and green	1·50	1·20
184d	-	40a. black and lilac	3·00	2·30
184e	-	50a. black and olive	1·20	1·20
185	**79**	65a. black and blue	3·00	3·00
185a	-	I£1 black and pink	6·50	6·50

DESIGNS—VERT: 15a. Old town, Zefat; 20a. Tower, Ashqelon; 25a. Akko Tower and boats; 30a. View of Haifa from Mt. Carmel. HORIZ: 35a. Ancient synagogue, Capernaum; 40a. Kefar Hittim—Tomb of Jethro; 50a. City walls, Jerusalem. I£1, Old city, Yafo (Jaffa).

80 Operation "Magic Carpet"

1960. World Refugee Year.

186	**80**	25a. brown	35	35
187		50a. green	35	35

DESIGN: 50a. Resettled family.

1960. 12th Anniv of Independence. Flowers as T **72**.

188		12a. multicoloured	45	35
189		32a. yellow, green and brown	70	35

DESIGNS: 12a. *Pancratium maritimum*; 32a. *Oenothera drummondi*.

81 Atomic Symbol and Reactor Building

1960. Inauguration of Atomic Reactor.

190	**81**	50a. red, black and blue	1·00	60

83 King Saul

1960. Jewish New Year. Centres multicoloured.

191	**83**	7a. green	35	25
192	-	25a. brown	70	45
193	-	40a. blue	95	45

DESIGNS: 25a. King David; 40a. King Solomon.

84 Dr. Theodor Herzl

1960. Birth Centenary of Dr. Theodor Herzl (founder of World Zionist Movement).

| 194 | 84 | 25a. sepia and cream | 60 | 60 |

85 Postal Courier, Prague, 1741

1960. "TAVIV" National Stamp Exhibition, Tel Aviv.

| 195 | 85 | 25a. black and grey | 1·90 | 1·20 |

MS195a 192×135 mm. No. 195 but in brown and green   46·00   46·00

No. MS195a was only sold at the stamp exhibition.

86 Henrietta Szold

1960. Birth Centenary of Henrietta Szold (founder of Youth Immigration Scheme).

| 196 | 86 | 25a. violet and blue | 45 | 35 |

87 Badges of First Zionist Congress and Jerusalem

1960. 25th Zionist Congress, Jerusalem.

| 197 | 87 | 50a. light and deep blue | 1·60 | 70 |

88 Ram (Aries)

89 The Twelve Signs

1961. Signs of the Zodiac.

198	88	1a. green	20	10
199	-	2a. red	20	10
200	-	6a. blue	20	10
201	-	7a. brown	20	10
202	-	8a. myrtle	20	10
203	-	10a. orange	20	10
204	-	12a. violet	35	20
205	-	18a. mauve	60	45
206	-	20a. olive	35	25
207	-	25a. purple	60	35
208	-	32a. black	80	65
209	-	50a. turquoise	95	75
210	89	I£1 blue, gold and indigo	2·30	2·00

DESIGNS—As Type **88**: 2a. Bull (Taurus); 6a. Twins (Gemini); 7a. Crab (Cancer); 8a. Lion (Leo); 10a. Virgin (Virgo); 12a. Scales (Libra); 18a. Scorpion (Scorpio); 20a. Archer (Sagittarius); 25a. Goat (Capricorn); 32a. Waterman (Aquarius); 50a. Fishes (Pisces).

1961. 13th Anniv of Independence. Flowers as T **72**.

211		7a. yellow, brown and green	25	20
212		12a. green, purple and mauve	45	45
213		32a. red, green and blue	65	50

FLOWERS: 7a. Myrtle; 12a. Squill; 32a. Oleander.

91 Throwing the Javelin

1961. Seventh "Hapoel" Sports Association Int Congress, Ramat Gan.

| 214 | 91 | 25a. multicoloured | 70 | 60 |

92 "A Decade of Israel Bonds"

1961. Tenth Anniv of Israel Bond Issue.

| 215 | 92 | 50a. blue | 80 | 70 |

93 Samson

1961. Jewish New Year. Heroes of Israel. Centres multicoloured.

216	93	7a. red	45	35
217	-	25a. grey	60	45
218	-	40a. lilac	70	60

HEROES: 25a. Yehuda Maceabi; 40a. Bar Kochba.

94 Bet Hamidrash (synagogue), Medzibozh (Russia)

1961. Death Bicentenary of Rabbi Baal Shem Tov (founder of Hassidism movement).

| 219 | 94 | 25a. sepia and yellow | 60 | 45 |

95 Fir Cone

1961. Afforestation Achievements.

| 220 | 95 | 25a. yellow, black and green | 1·30 | 1·00 |
| 221 | - | 30a. multicoloured | 1·40 | 1·20 |

DESIGN: 30a. Symbol of afforestation.

96 Musical Instruments

1961. 25th Anniv of Israel Philharmonic Orchestra.

| 222 | 96 | 50a. multicoloured | 2·30 | 2·30 |

97 Bay of Elat

1962. Air.

| 223 | 97 | I£3 multicoloured | 20·00 | 15·00 |

1962. As Nos. 198, 201 and 208 but colours changed and surch.

224	88	3a. on 1a. mauve	20	20
225	-	5a. on 7a. grey	20	20
226	-	30a. on 32a. green	20	20

99 Symbolic Flame

1962. Heroes and Martyrs Day.

| 227 | 99 | 12a. yellow, red and black | 45 | 35 |
| 228 | - | 55a. multicoloured | 1·40 | 1·20 |

DESIGN: 55a. Nazi "Yellow Star" and candles.

100 Sud Aviation Vatour IIA Bomber

1962. 14th Anniv of Independence.

| 229 | 100 | 12a. blue | 85 | 85 |
| 230 | - | 30a. green | 1·50 | 1·30 |

DESIGN: 30a. Flight of Vatour IIA bombers.

101 Mosquito and Malaria Graph

1962. Malaria Eradication.

| 231 | 101 | 25a. bistre, red and black | 60 | 45 |

102 Rosh Pinna

1962. 80th Anniv of Rosh Pinna.

| 232 | 102 | 20a. green and yellow | 60 | 45 |

103 Fair Flags

1962. Near East International Fair, Tel Aviv.

| 233 | 103 | 55a. multicoloured | 1·00 | 85 |

104 "The wolf also shall dwell with the lamb ..."

1962. Jewish New Year. Illustrating quotations from the Book of Isaiah.

234	104	8a. black, red and olive	45	40
235	-	28a. black, purple & olive	1·00	60
236	-	43a. black, orange & olive	1·50	1·20

DESIGNS: 28a. "And the leopard shall lie down with the kid ..."; 43a. "And the suckling child shall play on the hole of the asp ...".

105 Boeing 707 Jetliner

1962. El Al Airline Commemoration.

| 237 | 105 | 55a. indigo, lilac and blue | 1·30 | 1·20 |

MS237a 195×36 mm. **105** 55a. indigo, lilac and blue (sold at I£1)   4·75   4·75

106 Pennant Coralfish

1962. Red Sea Fish (1st series). Multicoloured.

238		3a. Type **106**	20	20
239		6a. Racoon butterflyfish	20	20
240		8a. Indian Ocean lionfish	35	25
241		12a. Royal angelfish	45	30

See also Nos. 265/8.

107 Symbolic Cogwheels

1962. 25th Anniv of United Jewish Appeal.

| 242 | 107 | 20a. blue, silver and red | 70 | 60 |

108 J. Korczak (child educator)

1962. Janusz Korczak Commemoration.

| 243 | 108 | 30a. sepia and grey | 70 | 60 |

109 Houbara Bustard

1963. Air. Birds.

244	-	5a. pink, brown and violet	20	15
245	-	20a. turquoise, brn & red	35	25
246	-	28a. black, brown & green	35	25
247	-	30a. multicoloured	35	25
248	-	40a. multicoloured	50	25
249	-	45a. multicoloured	80	60
250	109	55a. orange, black & turq	80	60
251	-	70a. bistre, brown & black	95	80
252	-	I£1 orange, black and red	1·00	80
253	-	I£3 multicoloured	3·25	3·25

DESIGNS—HORIZ: 5a. Sinai rosefinch; 20a. White-throated kingfisher; 28a. Mourning wheatear. VERT: 30a. European bee eater; 40a. Graceful prinia; 45a. Palestine sunbird; 70a. Eurasian scops owl; I£1 Purple heron; I£3, White-tailed sea eagle.

110 Bird in the Hand

1963. Freedom from Hunger.

| 254 | 110 | 55a. grey and black | 1·20 | 1·20 |

111 Construction at Daybreak

1963. 25th Anniv of Stockade and Tower Settlements.

| 255 | 111 | 12a. brown, black & yell | 45 | 45 |
| 256 | - | 30a. purple, black and blue | 70 | 70 |

DESIGN: 30a. Settlement at night.

1963. 15th Anniv of Independence. Flowers. As T **72**.

257		8a. multicoloured	40	40
258		30a. yellow, rose and pink	1·20	1·20
259		37a. multicoloured	2·00	1·00

FLOWERS: 8a. White lily; 30a. Bristly hollyhock; 37a. Sharon tulip.

112 Compositor

1963. Centenary of Hebrew Press.

| 260 | 112 | 12a. purple and buff | 1·30 | 1·00 |

No. 260 comes in sheets of 16 (4×4) with overall background of replica of front page of first issue of Hebrew newspaper "Halbanon".

113 "And the sun beat upon the head of Jonah ..."

1963. Jewish New Year. Illustrating quotations from the Book of Jonah. Multicoloured.

261	8a. Type **113**	45	45
262	30a. "And there was a mighty tempest in the sea" (horiz)	1·30	1·30
263	55a. "And Jonah was in the belly of the fish" (horiz)	2·40	2·40

114 Hoe clearing Thistles

1963. 80th Anniv of Israeli Agricultural Settlements.

| 264 | **114** | 37a. multicoloured | 1·20 | 85 |

1963. Red Sea Fish (2nd series). As T **106**. Multicoloured.

265	2a. Undulate triggerfish	20	20
266	6a. Radial lionfish	30	30
267	8a. Catalufa	40	40
268	12a. Emperor angelfish	60	45

115 Shalom

1963. Maiden Voyage of Liner Shalom.

| 269 | **115** | I£1 blue, turquoise & pur | 9·75 | 7·25 |

116 "Old Age and Survivors"

1964. Tenth Anniv of National Insurance. Multicoloured.

270	12a. Type **116**	1·50	70
271	25a. Nurse and child within hands ("Maternity")	2·40	1·30
272	37a. Family within hand ("Large families")	3·00	1·50
273	50a. Hand with arm and crutch ("Employment injuries")	5·00	2·40

117 Pres. Ben-Zvi

1964. First Death Anniv of President Izhak Ben-Zvi.

| 274 | **117** | 12a. brown | 35 | 35 |

118 "Terrestrial Spectroscopy"

1964. 16th Anniv of Independence. Israel's Contribution to Science. Multicoloured.

275	8a. Type **118**	40	40
276	35a. Macromolecules of living cell	1·20	1·00
277	70a. Electronic computer	2·40	2·10

119 Running

1964. Olympic Games, Tokyo.

278	**119**	8a. black and red	15	15
279	-	12a. black and mauve	25	25
280	-	30a. red, black and blue	30	30
281	-	50a. red, purple and green	45	45

DESIGNS: 12a. Throwing the discus; 30a. Basketball; 50a. Football.

120 3rd Century Glass Vessel

1964. Jewish New Year. Showing glass vessels in Haaretz Museum, Tel Aviv. Multicoloured.

282	8a. Type **120**	15	15
283	35a. 1st-2nd century vessel	45	40
284	70a. 1st century vessel	70	45

121 Congress Emblem

1964. Sixth Israel Medical Assn's World Congress.

| 285 | **121** | I£1 multicoloured | 1·20 | 1·00 |

122 Exodus (immigrant ship)

1964. "Year of the Blockade-Runners".

| 286 | **122** | 25a. black, blue & turq | 45 | 40 |

123 Eleanor Roosevelt

1964. 80th Birth Anniv of Eleanor Roosevelt.

| 287 | **123** | 70a. purple | 60 | 60 |

124 Olympics Symbols and Knight

1964. 16th Chess Olympics.

| 288 | **124** | 12a. brown | 45 | 30 |
| 289 | - | 70a. green | 2·10 | 1·50 |

DESIGN: 70a. Olympics symbol and rook.

125 "African–Israeli Friendship"

1964. "TABAI" National Stamp Exn, Haifa.

| 290 | **125** | 57a. multicoloured | 2·10 | 1·20 |

MS290a 125×81 mm. No. 290 (I£1)   2·75   2·75

No. **MS**290a was only sold at the stamp exhibition.

126 Masada

1965. Masada.

291	**126**	25a. green	45	30
292	-	36a. blue	70	45
293	-	I£1 brown	1·00	75

DESIGNS—HORIZ: 36a. "Northern Palace", lower section. VERT: I£1, "Northern Palace" aerial view.

127 Ashdod

1965. Civic Arms (1st series).

294		1a. brown (Lod)	20	20
295		2a. mauve (Qiryat Shmona)	20	20
296		5a. black (Petah Tiqwa)	20	20
297		6a. violet (Nazareth)	20	20
298		8a. orange (Beer Sheva)	20	20
299		10a. green (Bet Shean)	20	20
300		12a. purple (Tiberias)	20	20
301	**127**	15a. green	20	20
302	-	20a. red (Elat)	20	20
303	-	25a. blue (Akko)	40	20
304	-	35a. purple (Dimona)	40	20
305	-	37a. green (Zefat)	1·40	1·20
305a		40a. brown (Mizpe Ramon)	60	40
306		50a. blue (Rishon Le Zion)	60	40
306a		55a. red (Ashqelon)	60	40
307	-	70a. brown (Jerusalem)	1·00	75
307a		80a. red (Rosh Pinna)	1·40	1·20
308	-	I£1 green (Tel Aviv-Yafo)	1·20	1·00
309	-	I£3 mauve (Haifa)	1·50	1·40

Nos. 307, 308/9 are 22½×27 mm in size.
See also Nos. 413/24.

128 Fair Emblem

1965. Second International Book Fair, Jerusalem.

| 310 | **128** | 70a. black, blue and green | 45 | 45 |

129 Hands reaching for barbed wire

1965. 20th Anniv of Concentration Camps Liberation.

| 311 | **129** | 25a. black, yellow and grey | 60 | 45 |

130 "National Water Supply"

1965. 17th Anniv of Independence.

| 312 | **130** | 37a. brown, dp blue & bl | 40 | 40 |

131 Potash Works, Sedom

1965. Dead Sea Industrial Development. Multicoloured.

| 313 | 12a. Potash Works, Sedom | 35 | 10 |
| 314 | 50a. Type **131** | 75 | 45 |

The two stamps form one composite design when placed side by side.

132 "Syncom" Satellite and Telegraph Pole

1965. I.T.U. Centenary.

| 315 | **132** | 70a. violet, black and blue | 70 | 45 |

133 "Co-operation"

1965. International Co-operation Year.

| 316 | **133** | 36a. multicoloured | 45 | 40 |

134 "Light"

1965. Jewish New Year. "The Creation". Multicoloured.

317	6a. Type **134**	20	20
318	8a. "Heaven"	20	20
319	12a. "Earth"	20	20
320	25a. "Stars"	40	40
321	35a. "Birds and Beasts"	60	60
322	70a. "Man"	1·00	1·00

135 Foxy Charaxes

1965. Butterflies and Moths. Multicoloured.

323	2a. Type **135**	15	15
324	6a. Southern swallowtail	30	30
325	8a. Oleander hawk moth	30	30
326	12a. Sooty orange-tip	40	40

136 War of Independence Memorial

1966. Memorial Day.

| 327 | **136** | 40a. brown and black | 40 | 40 |

137 Flags

1966. 18th Anniv of Independence. Multicoloured.

328	12a. Type **137**	10	10
329	30a. Fireworks	15	15
330	80a. Dassault Mirage IIICJ jet fighters and warships	30	30

138 Knesset Building

1966. Inaug of Knesset Building, Jerusalem.

| 331 | **138** | I£1 blue | 85 | 75 |

139 Scooter
Rider

1966. Road Safety. Multicoloured.

332	2a. Type **139**	10	10
333	5a. Cyclist	10	10
334	10a. Pedestrian on crossing	10	10
335	12a. Child with ball	10	10
336	15a. Motorist in car	20	20

140 Spice
Box

1966. Jewish New Year. Religious Ceremonial Objects. Multicoloured.

337	12a. Type **140**	20	20
338	15a. Candlesticks	20	20
339	35a. Kiddush cup	20	20
340	40a. Torah pointer	20	20
341	80a. Hanging lamp	45	45

141 Panther (bronze)

1966. Israel Museum Exhibits. Multicoloured.

342	15a. Type **141**	1·50	1·50
343	30a. Synagogue menora (stone)	2·00	2·00
344	40a. Phoenician sphinx (ivory)	2·40	2·40
345	55a. Earring (gold)	3·00	3·00
346	80a. Miniature capital (gold)	3·50	3·50
347	I£1.15 Drinking horn (gold) (vert)	6·50	6·50

142 Levant
Postman and
Mail Coach

1966. Stamp Day.

348	**142** 12a. green and brown	10	10
349	- 15a. mauve, brown & grn	15	15
350	- 40a. blue and mauve	30	30
351	- I£1 brown and blue	60	45

DESIGNS: 15a. Turkish postman and camels; 40a. Palestine postman and steam locomotive. I£1, Israeli postman and Boeing 707 jetliner.

143 "Fight
Cancer and Save
Life"

1966. Cancer Research.

352	**143** 15a. green and red	35	35

144 Akko (Acre)

1967. Ancient Israeli Ports.

353	**144** 15a. purple	30	15
354	- 40a. green	45	40
355	- 80a. blue	70	60

PORTS: 40a. Caesarea; 80a. Yafo (Jaffa).

145 Book and
Crowns

1967. Shulhan Arukh ("Book of Wisdom").

356	**145** 40a. multicoloured	45	45

146 War of Independence
Memorial

1967. Memorial Day.

357	**146** 55a. silver, blue & turq	60	45

147 Taylorcraft Auster
AOP.5 Reconnaissance
Plane

1967. Independence Day. Military Aircraft.

358	**147** 15a. blue and green	20	20
359	- 30a. brown and orange	40	40
360	- 80a. violet and turquoise	60	60

AIRCRAFT: 30a. Dassault Mystere IVA jet fighter; 80a. Dassault Mirage IIICJ jet fighters.

148 Freighter *Dolphin* in
Straits of Tiran

1967. Victory in Arab–Israeli War.

361	15a. black, yellow and red	10	10
362	**148** 40a. green	20	20
363	- 80a. violet	20	20

DESIGNS—VERT: 15a. Sword emblem of "Zahal" (Israeli Defence Forces). HORIZ: 80a. "Wailing Wall", Jerusalem.

149 Law
Scroll

1967. Jewish New Year. Scrolls of the Torah (Mosaic Law), and similar designs.

364	**149** 12a. multicoloured	15	15
365	- 15a. multicoloured	15	15
366	- 35a. multicoloured	30	30
367	- 40a. multicoloured	30	30
368	- 80a. multicoloured	30	30

150 "Welcome
to Israel"

1967. International Tourist Year. Each with "Sun" emblem. Multicoloured.

369	**150** 30a. Type **150**	20	20
370	- 40a. "Air hostess"	30	30
371	- 80a. "Orange" child	30	30

151 Lord Balfour

1967. 50th Anniv of Balfour Declaration.

372	- 15a. green	20	20
373	**151** 40a. brown	30	30

DESIGN: 15a. Dr. C. Weizmann.

152 Ibex

1967. Israeli Nature Reserves. Multicoloured.

374	12a. Type **152**	10	10
375	18a. Caracal	25	25
376	60a. Dorcas gazelle	40	40

153 Diamond

1968. Air. Israeli Exports.

377	- 10a. multicoloured	15	15
378	- 30a. multicoloured	15	15
379	- 40a. multicoloured	15	15
380	- 50a. multicoloured	40	40
381	- 55a. multicoloured	40	40
382	- 60a. multicoloured	45	40
383	- 80a. multicoloured	45	40
384	- I£1 multicoloured	70	60
385	- I£1.50 multicoloured	70	60
386	**153** I£3 violet and green	1·20	1·00

DESIGNS: 10a. Draped curtains ("Textiles"); 30a. "Stamps"; 40a. Jar and necklace ("Arts and Crafts"); 50a. Chick and egg ("Chicks"); 55a. Melon, avocado and strawberries ("Fruits"); 60a. Gladioli ("Flowers"); 80a. Telecommunications equipment ("Electronics"). I£1, Atomic equipment ("Isotopes"). I£1.50, Models ("Fashion").

154 Beflagged
Football

1968. Pre-Olympic Football Tournament.

387	**154** 80a. multicoloured	40	40

155 "Immigration"

1968. Independence Day. Multicoloured.

388	**155** 15a. Type **155**	10	10
389	80a. "Settlement"	30	30

156 Rifles
and Helmet

1968. Memorial Day.

390	**156** 55a. multicoloured	35	35

157 Zahal
Emblem

1968. Independence Day (Zahal–Israel Defence Forces).

391	**157** 40a. multicoloured	35	35

158 Resistance
Fighter (detail
from Warsaw
Monument)

1968. 25th Anniv of Warsaw Ghetto Rising.

392	**158** 60a. bistre	50	40

159 Moshe
Sharett

1968. 27th Zionist Congress, Jerusalem.

393	**159** I£1 sepia	40	40

160 Candle and
Cell Bars

1968. Fallen Freedom Fighters.

394	**160** 80a. black, grey and brown	40	40

161 Jerusalem

1968. Jewish New Year.

395	**161** 12a. multicoloured	20	20
396	- 15a. multicoloured	40	40
397	- 35a. multicoloured	45	45
398	- 40a. multicoloured	60	60
399	- 60a. multicoloured	75	75

DESIGNS: Jerusalem—views of the Old City (12, 15, 35a.) and of the New City (40, 60a.).

162 Scout Badge
and Knot

1968. 50th Anniv of Jewish Scout Movement.

400	**162** 30a. multicoloured	25	25

163 "Lions' Gate",
Jerusalem (detail)

1968. "Tabira" Stamp Exhibition, Jerusalem.

401	**163** I£1 brown	35	35
MS402	122×75 mm. No. 401 (sold at I£1.50)	3·50	3·75

164 A. Mapu

1968. Death Cent of Abraham Mapu (writer).

403	**164** 30a. olive	35	25

165 Paralytics playing Basketball

1968. International Games for the Paralysed.
404	**165**	40a. green and light green	35	25

166 Elat

1969. Israeli Ports.
405	**166**	30a. mauve	75	75
406	-	60a. brown (Ashdod)	1·00	1·00
407	-	I£1 green (Haifa)	1·20	1·20

167 "Worker" and I.L.O. Emblem

1969. 50th Anniv of I.L.O.
408	**167**	80a. green and lilac	40	40

168 Israeli Flag at Half-mast

1969. Memorial Day.
409	**168**	55a. gold, blue and violet	40	40

169 Army Tank

1969. Independence Day. Multicoloured.
410	**169**	15a. Type **169**	20	20
411		80a. "Elat" (destroyer)	40	40

170 Flaming Torch

1969. Eighth Maccabiah.
412	**170**	60a. multicoloured	60	60

171 Arms of Hadera

1969. Civic Arms (2nd series).
413		2a. green (Type **171**)	30	30
414		3a. purple (Herzliyya)	40	40
415		5a. orange (Holon)	45	45
416		15a. red (Bat Yam)	60	60
417		18a. blue (Ramla)	70	70
418		20a. brown (Kefar Sava)	70	70
419		25a. blue (Giv'atayim)	85	85
420		30a. mauve (Rehovot)	40	40
421		40a. violet (Netanya)	1·00	1·00
422		50a. blue (Bene Beraq)	1·50	1·50
423		60a. green (Nahariyya)	1·00	1·00
424		80a. green (Ramat Gan)	2·10	2·10

172 Building the Ark

1969. Jewish New Year, showing scenes from "The Flood". Multicoloured.
425		12a. Type **172**	10	10
426		15a. Animals going aboard	15	15
427		35a. Ark afloat	25	25
428		40a. Dove with olive branch	30	30
429		60a. Ark on Mt. Ararat	30	30

173 *King David* (Chagall)

1969. "King David".
430	**173**	I£3 multicoloured	2·00	2·00

174 Atomic "Plant"

1969. 25th Anniv of Weizmann Institute of Science.
431	**174**	I£1.15 multicoloured	1·50	1·50

175 Dum Palms, Emeq He-Arava

1970. Nature Reserves.
432	**175**	2a. olive	10	10
433	-	3a. blue	10	10
434	-	5a. red	10	10
435	-	6a. green	10	10
436	-	30a. violet	20	20

DESIGNS: 3a. Tahana Waterfall, Nahal Iyon; 5a. Nahal Baraq Canyon, Negev; 6a. Ha-Masreq, Judean Hills; 30a. Soreq Cave, Judean Hills.

176 Immigrant "Aircraft"

1970. 20th Anniv of Operation "Magic Carpet" (Immigration of Yemenite Jews).
437	**176**	30a. multicoloured	40	30

177 Joseph Trumpeldor

1970. 50th Anniv of Defence of Tel Hay.
438	**177**	I£1 violet	1·00	1·00

178 Prime Minister Levi Eshkol

1970. Levi Eshkol Commemoration.
439	**178**	15a. multicoloured	35	35

179 Ze'ev Jabotinsky (commander)

1970. 50th Anniv of Defence of Jerusalem.
440	**179**	80a. green and cream	45	45

180 Camel and Diesel Train

1970. Opening of Dimona–Oron Railway.
441	**180**	80a. multicoloured	1·00	1·00

181 Mania Schochat (author)

1970. 60th Anniv of "Ha-Shomer".
442	**181**	40a. purple and cream	40	40

182 Scene from *The Dybbuk*

1970. 50th Anniv of Habimah National Theatre.
443	**182**	I£1 multicoloured	75	75

183 Memorial Flame

1970. Memorial Day.
444	**183**	55a. black, red and violet	45	45

184 *Orchis laxifloris*

1970. Independence Day. Israeli Wild Flowers. Multicoloured.
445		12a. Type **184**	30	30
446		15a. *Iris mariae*	45	40
447		80a. *Lupinus pilosus*	75	70

185 C. Netter (founder)

1970. Centenary of Miqwe Yisrael Agricultural College. Multicoloured.
448	**185**	40a. Type **185**	70	45
449		80a. College building and gate	1·20	75

186 I.A.I. Arava Transport Airplane

1970. Israeli Aircraft Industry.
450	**186**	I£1 silver, violet and blue	60	45

187 Yachts

1970. World "420" Class Sailing Championships. Multicoloured.
451	**187**	15a. Type **187**	40	40
452		30a. Yacht with spinnaker	45	40
453		80a. Yachts turning around buoy	70	60

188 Keren Hayesod

1970. 50th Anniv of Keren Hayesod.
454	**188**	40a. multicoloured	40	40

189 Old Synagogue, Cracow

1970. Jewish New Year. Multicoloured.
455		12a. Type **189**	10	10
456		15a. Great Synagogue, Tunis	10	10
457		35a. Portuguese Synagogue, Amsterdam	20	20
458		40a. Great Synagogue, Moscow	20	20
459		60a. Shearith Israel Synagogue, New York	30	30

190 Jewish "Bird" heading for Sun

1970. "Operation Ezra and Nehemiah" (Exodus of Iraqi Jews to Israel).
460	**190**	80a. multicoloured	40	40

191 Mother and Child

1970. 50th Anniv of Women's International Zionist Organization (W.I.Z.O.).
461	**191**	80a. yellow, green & silver	70	60

192 Tel Aviv Post Office, 1920

1970. "Tabit" Stamp Exhibition, Tel Aviv, and 50th Anniv of Tel Aviv Post Office.

462	**192**	I£1 multicoloured	45	45

MS463 115×70 mm. No. 462 (sold at I£1.50)   3·50   3·50

193 Histadrut Emblem

1970. 50th Anniv of "Histadrut" (General Federation of Labour).

464	**193**	35a. multicoloured	30	30

194 Landscape with Bridge (C. Pissaro)

1970. Paintings in Tel Aviv Museum. Multicoloured.

465		85a. Jewish Wedding (J. Israels)	30	30
466		I£1 Type **194**	45	45
467		I£2 Flowers in a Vase (F. Leger)	75	75

195 Inn of the Ghosts (Cameri Theatre)

1971. Israeli Theatre. Multicoloured.

468		50a. Type **195**	40	40
469		50a. Samson and Delilah (National Opera Company)	40	40
470		50a. A Psalm of David (I.N.B.A.L. Dance Theatre)	40	40

196 Fallow Deer

1971. Nature Reserves. Animals of Biblical Times. Multicoloured.

471		2a. Type **196**	20	20
472		3a. Asiatic wild ass	20	20
473		5a. Arabian oryx	20	20
474		78a. Cheetah	45	20

197 "Haganah" Emblem

1971. Memorial Day.

475	**197**	78a. multicoloured	45	45

198 Jaffa Gate

1971. Independence Day. Gates of Jerusalem (1st series). Multicoloured.

476		15a. Type **198**	45	45
477		18a. New Gate	60	60
478		35a. Damascus Gate	75	75
479		85a. Herod's Gate	1·30	1·30

MS480 93× mm. As Nos. 476/9, but each in 28×28 format (sold for I£2)   5·75   5·75

See also 527/**MS**531.

---

199 Gymnastics

1971. Ninth "Hapoel" Games. Multicoloured.

481		50a. Type **199**	30	30
482		50a. Basketball	30	30
483		50a. Running	30	30

200 "... and he wrote upon the tables ..."

1971. Feast of Weeks ("Shavuot"). Illuminated verses from the Bible. Multicoloured.

484		50a. Type **200**	45	45
485		85a. "The first of the firstfruits ..."	70	60
486		I£1. 50 "... and ye shall observe the feast ..."	1·00	85

See also Nos. 488/92.

201 "Sun over the Emeq"

1971. 50th Anniv of Settlements in the "Emeq" (Yezreel Valley).

487	**201**	40a. multicoloured	35	35

1971. Jewish New Year. Feast of the Tabernacles ("Sukkot"). Illuminated Verses from the Bible. As T **200**. Multicoloured.

488		15a. "You shall rejoice in your feast"	20	20
489		18a. "You shall dwell in booths ..."	20	20
490		20a. "That I made the people ..."	30	30
491		40a. "... gathered in the produce"	30	30
492		65a. "... I will give you your rains ..."	30	30

202 Kinneret

1971. Landscapes (1st series).

493		3a. blue	45	45
494		5a. green	30	30
495		15a. orange	30	30
496	**202**	18a. purple	1·70	1·70
497		20a. green	1·00	1·00
498		22a. blue	2·10	2·10
498a		25a. red	45	45
499		30a. mauve	40	40
500		35a. purple	1·00	1·00
501		45a. blue	40	40
502		50a. green	60	60
503		55a. green	60	60
504		65a. brown	1·20	1·20
505		70a. red	60	60
505apa		80a. blue	5·00	5·00
506		88a. blue	2·20	2·20
507		95a. red	2·20	2·20
508		I£1.10 brown	1·70	1·70
508a		I£1.30 blue	1·00	1·00
508b		I£1.70 brown	45	45
509pa		I£2 brown	3·00	3·00
510pa		I£3 violet	9·50	9·50
510a		I£10 brown	2·50	2·40

DESIGNS—As T **202**: 3a. Judean desert; 5a. Gan Ha-Shelosha; 15a. Negev desert; 20a. Tel Dan; 22a. Yafo; 25a. Arava; 30a. En Avedat; 35a. Brekhat Ram; 45a. Mt. Hermon; 50a. Rosh Pinna; 55a. Natanya; 65a. Plain of Zebulun; 70a. Engedi; 80a. Beach at Elat; 88a. Akko (Acre); 95a. Hamifratz Hane'Elam; I£1.10, Aqueduct near Acre; I£1.30, Zefat; I£1.70, Nazerat Illit; I£2, Coral Island; I£3, Haifa. 28×27 mm: I£10, Elat.

See also Nos. 682/4a.

---

203 "Agricultural Research"

1971. 50th Anniv of Volcani Institute of Agricultural Research.

511	**203**	I£1 multicoloured	45	45

204 Hebrew Text

1971. Educational Development. Multicoloured.

512		15a. Type **204**	20	20
513		18a. Mathematical formulae	20	20
514		20a. Engineering symbols	20	20
515		40a. University degree abbreviations	20	20

205 The Scribe (sculpture, B. Schatz)

1972. Jewish Art.

516	**205**	40a. brown, copper & blk	30	30
517	–	55a. multicoloured	30	30
518	–	70a. multicoloured	45	45
519	–	85a. black and yellow	60	60
520	–	I£1 multicoloured	60	60

DESIGNS—VERT: 55a. Sarah (A. Pann); 85a. Old Jerusalem (woodcut, J. Steinhardt); I£1; Resurrection (A. Kahana). HORIZ: 70a. Zefat (M. Shemi).

206 The Flight from Egypt

1972. Passover Feast ("Pesah"). Multicoloured.

521		18a. Type **206**	40	40
522		45a. Baking unleavened bread	45	45
523		95a. "Seder" table	70	70

207 "Let My People Go"

1972. Campaign for Jewish Immigration.

524	**207**	55a. multicoloured	2·40	2·40

208 Bouquet

1972. Memorial Day.

525	**208**	55a. multicoloured	40	40

---

209 Jethro's Tomb

1972. "Nebi Shuaib" (Jethro's Tomb) (Druse shrine).

526	**209**	55a. multicoloured	40	40

1972. Independence Day. Gates of Jerusalem (2nd series). As T **198**. Multicoloured.

527		15a. Lion's Gate	75	60
528		18a. Golden Gate	1·00	70
529		45a. Dung Gate	1·00	75
530		55a. Zion Gate	1·20	85

MS531 93×93 mm. As Nos. 527/530, but each in format 28×28 mm (sold for I£2)   5·75   5·75

210 Ghetto Entrance

1972. 400th Death Anniv of Rabbi Yizhaq Luria ("Ari").

532	**210**	70a. multicoloured	3·00	3·00

211 Book Year Texts

1972. International Book Year.

533	**211**	95a. black, red and blue	60	60

212 Dish Aerial

1972. Opening of Satellite Earth Station.

534	**212**	I£1 multicoloured	40	40

213 Ancona Ark

1972. Jewish New Year. Holy Arks from Italy.

535	**213**	15a. brown and yellow	20	20
536	–	45a. green, gold & lt green	30	30
537	–	70a. red, blue and yellow	45	45
538	–	95a. purple and gold	70	70

DESIGNS: 45a. Soragna Ark; 70a. Padua Ark; 95a. Reggio Emilia Ark.

214 Menora Emblem

1972. 25th Anniv of State of Israel.

539	**214**	I£1 blue, purple and silver	30	30

215 Hanukka Lamp (Morocco, 18th–19th century)

1972. Festival of Lights ("Hanukka"). Ceremonial Lamps. Multicoloured.

540	12a. Type **215**	20	20
541	25a. 18th-century Polish lamp	20	20
542	70a. 17th-century German silver lamp	40	40

216 Pendant

1973. Immigration of North African Jews.

543	**216**	18a. multicoloured	30	30

217 Horse and Rider

1973. Children's Drawings. Multicoloured.

544	2a. Type **217**	10	10
545	3a. Balloon ride (17×48 mm)	10	10
546	55a. Party-time	30	30

218 "Reuben" Window

1973. "Tribes of Israel" Stained-glass Windows by Chagall, Hadassah Synagogue, Jerusalem. Multicoloured.

547	I£1 "Levi"	1·00	1·00
548	I£1 "Simeon"	1·00	1·00
549	I£1 Type **218**	1·00	1·00
550	I£1 "Issachar"	1·00	1·00
551	I£1 "Zebulun"	1·00	1·00
552	I£1 "Judah"	1·00	1·00
553	I£1 "Asher"	1·50	1·50
554	I£1 "Gad"	1·50	1·50
555	I£1 "Dan"	1·50	1·50
556	I£1 "Benjamin"	1·50	1·50
557	I£1 "Joseph"	1·50	1·50
558	I£1 "Naphtali"	1·50	1·50

219 Flame of Remembrance

1973. Memorial Day.

559	**219**	65a. multicoloured	40	40

220 Skeletal Hand

1973. Holocaust (Persecution of European Jews 1933–45) Memorial.

560	**220**	55a. blue	30	30

221 Signatures of Declaration of Independence

1973. Independence Day.

561	**221**	I£1 multicoloured	40	40

MS562 65×147 mm. No. 561 (sold for I£1.50)　1·70　1·70

222 Star of David and Runners

1973. Ninth Maccabiah.

563	**222**	I£1.10 multicoloured	30	30

223 Isaiah

1973. Jewish New Year. Prophets of Israel.

564	18a. Type **223**	10	10
565	65a. Jeremiah	15	15
566	I£1.10 Ezekiel	20	20

224 Jews in Boat, and Danish Flag

1973. 30th Anniv of Rescue of Danish Jews.

567	**224**	I£5 black, red and brown	1·20	1·00

225 Institute Emblem and Cogwheel

1973. 50th Anniv of "Technion" Israel Institute of Technology.

568	**225**	I£1.25 multicoloured	30	30

226 Collectors within "Stamp"

1973. "Jerusalem 73" International Stamp Exhibition. Multicoloured.

569	20a. Type **226**	10	10
570	I£1 Collectors within "Stamp" (different)	20	20

MS571 Three sheets, each 121×75 mm. (a) I£1 250m. stamp of 1948; (b) I£2 500m. stamp of 1948; (c) I£3 1000m. stamp of 1948　5·25　5·25

227 Soldier with Prayer Shawl

1974. Memorial Day.

572	**227**	I£1 black and blue	30	30

228 Quill and Bottle of Ink

1974. 50th Anniv of Hebrew Writers' Association.

573	**228**	I£2 black and gold	40	40

229 Woman in Blue (M. Kisling)

1974. Jewish Art. Multicoloured.

574	I£1.25 Type **229**	30	30
575	I£2 Mother and Child (bronze, C. Orloff)	40	30
576	I£3 Girl in Blue (C. Soutine)	40	40

See also Nos. 604/6.

230 Spanner

1974. 50th Anniv of Young Workers' Movement.

577	**230**	25a. multicoloured	20	20

231 Lady Davis Technical Centre, Tel Aviv

1974. "Architecture in Israel" (1st series).

578	**231**	25a. grey	10	10
579	-	60a. blue	20	20
580	-	I£1.45 brown	20	20

DESIGNS: 60a. Elias Sourasky Library, Tel Aviv University. I£1.45, Mivtahim Rest-home, Zikhron Yaaqov.
See also Nos. 596/8.

232 Istanbuli Synagogue

1974. Jewish New Year. Rebuilt Synagogues in Jerusalem's Old City. Multicoloured.

581	25a. Type **232**	10	10
582	70a. Emtzai Synagogue	15	15
583	I£1 Raban Yohanan Ben Zakai Synagogue	20	20

233 Arrows on Globe

1974. Centenary of U.P.U. Multicoloured.

584	25a. Type **233**	15	15
585	I£1.30 Dove "postman" (27×27 mm)	30	30

234 David Ben Gurion (statesman)

1974. Ben Gurion Memorial.

586	**234**	25a. brown	15	15
587	**234**	I£1.30 green	30	30

236 Child with Plant, and Rainbow

1975. Arbor Day. Multicoloured.

588	1a. Type **236**	10	10
589	35a. Bird in tree	10	10
590	I£2 Child with plant and sun	25	25

237 Hebrew University, Jerusalem

1975. 50th Anniv of Hebrew University, Jerusalem.

591	**237**	I£2.50 multicoloured	40	40

238 Welding

1975. "Occupational Safety". Multicoloured.

592	30a. Type **238**	10	10
593	80a. Tractor-driving	15	15
594	I£1.20 Telegraph line main-tenance	20	20

239 Harry S. Truman

1975. Truman Commemoration.

595	**239**	I£5 brown	60	60

1975. "Architecture in Israel" (2nd series). As T **231**.

596	80a. brown	20	20
597	I£1.30 green	25	25
598	I£1.70 brown	30	30

DESIGNS: 80a. Hebrew University Synagogue, Jerusalem. I£1.30, Museum, Yad Mordechai. I£1.70, City Hotel, Bat Yam.

240 Memorial

1975. Memorial Day.

599	**240**	I£1 red, black and mauve	35	35

241 Text and Poppy

1975. Fallen Soldiers' Memorial.
600 **241** I£1.45 black, red and grey | 35 | 35

242 Hurdling

1975. Tenth Hapoel Games. Multicoloured.
601 25a. Type **242** | 20 | 20
602 I£1.70 Cycling | 25 | 25
603 I£3 Volleyball | 30 | 30

1975. Jewish Art. As T **229**. Multicoloured.
604 I£1 *Hanukka* (M. D. Oppenheim) | 30 | 30
605 I£1.40 *The Purim Players* (J. Adler) (horiz) | 40 | 40
606 I£4 *Yom Kippur* (M. Gottlieb) | 45 | 45

243 Old People

1975. Gerontology.
607 **243** I£1.85 multicoloured | 30 | 30

244 Gideon

1975. Jewish New Year. Judges of Israel. Multicoloured.
608 35a. Type **244** | 10 | 10
609 I£1 Deborah | 20 | 20
610 I£1.40 Jephthah | 30 | 30

245 Zalman Shazar

1975. First Death Anniv of Zalman Shazar (President 1963–73).
611 **245** 35a. black and silver | 30 | 30

246 Emblem of Pioneer Women

1975. 50th Anniv of Pioneer Women's Organization.
612 **246** I£5 multicoloured | 35 | 35

247 New Hospital Buildings

1975. Return of Hadassah Hospital to Mt. Scopus.
613 **247** I£4 multicoloured | 40 | 40

248 Pratincole

1975. Protected Wild Birds. Multicoloured.
614 I£1.10 Type **248** | 30 | 30
615 I£1.70 Spur-winged plover | 40 | 40
616 I£2 Black-winged stilt | 45 | 45

---

249 "Air Pollution"

1975. "Environmental Quality". Multicoloured.
617 50a. Type **249** | 15 | 15
618 80a. "Water pollution" | 20 | 20
619 I£1.70 "Noise pollution" | 30 | 30

250 Star of David

1975
620 **250** 75a. blue and red | 40 | 40
621 **250** I£1.80 blue and grey | 45 | 45
622 **250** I£1.85 blue and brown | 40 | 40
623 **250** I£2.45 blue and green | 40 | 40
623a **250** I£2.70 blue and mauve | 60 | 60
623b **250** I£4.30 blue and red | 30 | 30
624 **250** I£5.40 blue and bistre | 1·20 | 1·20
625 **250** I£8 blue and turquoise | 85 | 85

251 Symbolic "Key"

1976. 70th Anniv of Bezalel Academy of Arts and Design, Jerusalem.
626 **251** I£1.85 multicoloured | 40 | 40

252 "Border Settlements"

1976. Jewish Border Settlements.
627 **252** I£1.50 multicoloured | 40 | 40

253 "In the days of Ahasuerus ..."

1976. "Purim" Festival. Multicoloured.
628 40a. Type **253** | 10 | 10
629 80a. "He set the royal crown ..." | 15 | 15
630 I£1.60 "Thus shall it be done ..." | 20 | 20
MS631 127×86 mm. Nos. 628/30 | 95 | 95

254 Monument to the Fallen

1976. Memorial Day.
632 **254** I£1.85 multicoloured | 40 | 40

255 Dancers of Meron (R. Rubin)

1976. Lag Ba-Omer Festival.
633 **255** I£1.30 multicoloured | 60 | 45

---

256 "200" Flag

1976. Bicentenary of American Revolution.
634 **256** I£4 multicoloured | 60 | 60

257 Diamond ("Industry")

1976. "Netyanya 76" National Stamp Exhibition. Sheet 112×75 mm, containing T **257** and similar vert designs. Multicoloured.
MS635 I£1 Type **257**; I£2 Sailing ("sport"); I£4 Beach umbrella ("tourism") | 1·70 | 1·70

258 High Jump

1976. Olympic Games, Montreal.
636 **258** I£1.60 black and red | 40 | 40
637 - I£2.40 black and blue | 40 | 40
638 - I£4.40 black and mauve | 45 | 45
DESIGNS: I£2.40, Swimming. I£4.40, Gymnastics.

259 Multiple Tent Emblems

1976. Camping.
639 **259** I£1.60 multicoloured | 30 | 30

260 "Truth"

1976. Jewish New Year. Multicoloured.
640 45a. Type **260** | 45 | 45
641 I£1.50 "Judgement" | 45 | 45
642 I£1.90 "Peace" | 45 | 45

261 Excavated Byzantine House

1976. Archaeology in Jerusalem (1st series). Multicoloured.
643 **261** I£1.30 Type **261** | 30 | 30
644 I£2.40 Arch of 2nd Temple | 45 | 45
645 I£2.80 Staircase to 2nd Temple | 60 | 60

262 Pawn

1976. 22nd Chess Olympiad, Haifa. Multicoloured.
646 I£1.30 Type **262** | 60 | 60
647 I£1.60 Rook | 60 | 60

1976. Archaeology in Jerusalem (2nd series). As T **261**. Multicoloured.
648 70a. City Wall, First Temple period | 20 | 20
649 I£5 Omayyad palace | 1·00 | 1·00

263 Clearing Ground

1976. Pioneers.
650 **263** 5a. brown and gold | 10 | 10
651 - 10a. lilac and gold | 10 | 10
652 - 60a. red and gold | 15 | 15
653 - I£1.40 blue and gold | 20 | 20
654 - I£1.80 green and gold | 20 | 20
DESIGNS—HORIZ: 10a. Building breakwater. I£1.40, Ploughing. I£1.80, Ditch-clearing. VERT: 60a. Road construction.

264 "Grandfather's Carrot"

1977. Voluntary Service.
655 **264** I£2.60 multicoloured | 45 | 45

265 By the Rivers of Babylon

1977. Drawings of E. M. Lilien.
656 **265** I£1.70 brown, grey & black | 40 | 35
657 - I£1.80 black, stone & brn | 40 | 35
658 - I£2.10 green, lt green & blk | 45 | 45
PAINTINGS—VERT: I£1.80, *Abraham*. HORIZ: I£2.10, *May Our Eyes Behold*.

266 Jew and Arab shaking Hands

1977. Children's Drawings on Peace. Multicoloured.
659 50a. Type **266** | 15 | 15
660 I£1.40 Arab and Jew holding hands | 30 | 30
661 I£2.70 Peace dove, Jew and Arab | 45 | 45

267 Parachute Troops Memorial

1977. Memorial Day.
662 **267** I£3.30 multicoloured | 65 | 65

268 Embroidery showing Sabbath Loaves

1977. Sabbath.
663 **268** I£3 multicoloured | 45 | 45

269 Trumpet

1977. Ancient Musical Instruments. Multicoloured.

664	I£1.50 Type **269**	30	30
665	I£2 Lyre	30	30
666	I£5 "Jingle" (cymbals)	35	35

270 Fencing

1977. Tenth Maccabiah Games.

667	**270**	I£1 grey, blue and black	30	30
668	-	I£2.50 grey, red and black	35	35
669	-	I£3.50 grey, green & black	45	45

DESIGNS: I£2.50, Putting the shot. I£3.50, Judo.

271 Petah Tiqwa

1977. Centenary of Petah Tiqwa.

670	**271**	I£1.50 multicoloured	35	35

272 American Zionist Emblem

1977. Zionist Organization of America Convention.

671	**272**	I£4 multicoloured	60	60

273 Page of 16th-cent Book "Kohelet Yaakov"

1977. 400th Anniv of Hebrew Printing at Zefat.

672	**273**	I£4 black, gold and red	75	45

274 Sarah

1977. Jewish New Year. Matriarchs of Israel. Multicoloured.

673	70a. Type **274**	10	10
674	I£1.50 Rebekah	15	15
675	I£2 Rachel	30	30
676	I£3 Leah	35	35

See also Nos. 728/30.

275 Police

1977. National Police Force. Multicoloured.

677	I£1 Type **275**	20	20
678	I£1 Civil Guard	20	20
679	I£1 Frontier Guard	20	20

276 Helmet and Model Settlement

1977. "Nahal" Pioneering Fighting Youth.

680	**276**	I£3.50 multicoloured	45	45

---

277 Accelerator Building, Weizmann Institute

1977. Inauguration of Koffler Accelerator.

681	**277**	I£8 blue and black	80	80

278 Caesarea

1977. Landscapes (2nd series).

682	**278**	10a. blue	95	95
683b	-	I£1 bistre	1·10	1·10
684	-	I£20 green and orange	2·30	2·20
684a	-	I£50 multicoloured	2·75	2·50

DESIGNS—As T **278**: I£1, Arava. 29×27 mm: I£20, Rosh Pinna. 27½×36½ mm: I£50, Soreq Cave.

279 *Mogul* Steam Locomotive, 1892

1977. Railways in the Holy Land. Multicoloured.

685	65a. Type **279**	30	25
686	I£1.50 Steam locomotive	35	35
687	I£2 4-6-0 Class P steam locomotive	35	35
688	I£2.50 Diesel locomotive	45	35
MS689	112×75 mm. Nos. 685/8	2·50	2·50

280 Blood-stained Scallop (*Gloripallium pallium*)

1977. Red Sea Shells. Multicoloured.

690	I£2 Type **280**	25	25
691	I£2 Pacific grinning tun (*Malea pomum*)	25	25
692	I£2 Isabelle cowrie (*Cypraea isabella*)	25	25
693	I£2 Camp Pitar venus (*Lioconcha castrensis*)	25	25

281 *The Marriage Parties* (Dutch Ketubah)

1978. Illuminated Jewish Marriage Contracts (Ketubah). Multicoloured.

694	75a. Type **281**	15	15
695	I£3.90 Moroccan Ketubah	35	30
696	I£6 Jerusalem Ketubah	45	40

282 *A Street in Jerusalem* (H. Gliksberg)

1978. Jewish Art.

697	**282**	I£3 multicoloured	30	25
698		I£3.80 black, yellow & grey	35	35
699		I£4.40 multicoloured	45	45

DESIGNS: I£3.80, *Thistles* (L. Krakauer).I£4.40, *An Alley in Zefat* (M. Levanon).

---

283 Eliyahu Golomb (leader of Hagana)

1978. Historical Personalities (1st series).

700	**283**	I£2 green and yellow	35	35
701	-	I£2 blue and stone	35	35
702	-	I£2 purple and stone	35	35
703	-	I£2 brown and stone	35	35
704	-	I£2 black and grey	35	35

DESIGNS: No. 701, David Raziel (Irgun commander); 702, Yitzhak Sadeh (nationalist and military commander); 703, Dr. Moshe Sneh (Zionist politician); 704, Abraham Stern (underground fighter).

See also Nos. 721/2, 725/6, 732/3, 738/40, 763/5, 809/11 and 831/3.

284 Children's Flower Paintings (from mural, Petah Tikvah Museum)

1978. Memorial Day.

705	**284**	I£1.50 multicoloured	10	10
706	-	I£1.50 multicoloured	10	10
707	-	I£1.50 multicoloured	10	10
708	-	I£1.50 multicoloured	10	10
709	-	I£1.50 multicoloured	10	10
710	-	I£1.50 multicoloured	10	10
711	-	I£1.50 multicoloured	10	10
712	-	I£1.50 multicoloured	10	10
713	-	I£1.50 multicoloured	10	10
714	-	I£1.50 multicoloured	10	10
715	-	I£1.50 multicoloured	60	45
716	-	I£1.50 multicoloured	60	45
717	-	I£1.50 multicoloured	60	45
718	-	I£1.50 multicoloured	60	45
719	-	I£1.50 multicoloured	60	45

Nos. 705/19 issued together form a composite design, each showing a different portion of the Memorial Wall.

1978. Historical Personalities (2nd series). As T 283.

721	I£2 blue and stone	70	70
722	I£2 brown and grey	70	70

DESIGNS: No. 721, Dr. Chaim Weizmann (first president of Israel); No. 722, Dr. Theodor Herzl (founder of Zionism).

286 Y.M.C.A. Building Jerusalem

1978. Centenary of Jerusalem Y.M.C.A.

723	**286**	I£5.40 multicoloured	60	60

287 Verse of National Anthem

1978. Centenary of Publication of "Hatiqwa" (Jewish National Anthem).

724	**287**	I£8.40 silver, dp blue & bl	75	75

1978. Historical Personalities (3rd series). As T 283.

725	I£2 purple and cream	70	70
726	I£2 green and cream	70	70

DESIGNS: No. 725, Rabbi Ouziel; No. 726, Rabbi Kook.

288 Family Groups

1978. Social Welfare.

727	**288**	I£5.10 multicoloured	60	60

1978. Jewish New Year, Patriarchs of Israel. As T 274. Multicoloured.

728	I£1.10 Abraham	30	30
729	I£5.20 Isaac	35	35
730	I£6.60 Jacob	45	45

289 Star of David, Young Tree and Globe showing U.S.A.

1978. United Jewish Appeal.

731	**289**	I£8.40 multicoloured	75	75

1978. Historical Personalities (4th series). As T 283.

732	I£2 purple and stone	20	20
733	I£2 blue and grey	20	20

DESIGNS: No. 732, David Ben-Gurion (first Prime Minister); No. 733, Ze'ev Jabotinsky (Zionist leader).

290 Shaare Zedek Medical Centre, New and Old Buildings

1978. Opening of New Shaare Zedek Medical Centre, Jerusalem.

734	**290**	I£5.40 multicoloured	20	10

291 Indian Silver and Enamelled Vase

1978. Institute for Islamic Art, Jerusalem. Multicoloured.

735	I£2.40 Type **291**	15	10
736	I£3 13th-century Persian pottery chess rook (elephant with howdah)	30	30
737	I£4 Syrian Mosque lamp	35	35

1978. Historical Personalities (5th series). As T 283.

738	I£2 black and stone	20	20
739	I£2 blue and grey	20	20
740	I£2 black and stone	20	20

DESIGNS: No. 738, Menahem Ussishkin (president of Jewish National Fund); No. 739, Berl Katzenelson (pioneer of Zionist socialism); No. 740, Dr. Max Nordau (journalist).

292 *Iris lortetii*

1978. Wild Irises. Multicoloured.

741	I£1.10 Type **292**	30	30
742	I£5.40 *Iris haynei*	45	45
743	I£8.40 *Iris nazarena*	60	60

293 Agricultural Mechanization

1979. Technological Achievements. Multicoloured.

744	I£1.10 Type **293**	10	10
745	I£2.40 Sea water desalination	25	15
746	I£4.30 Electronics	25	15
747	I£5 Chemical fertilizers	25	15

294 Jewish Brigade Flag

1979. Yishuv Volunteers serving in Second World War.

748	294	I£5.10 yellow, blue & dp bl	60	60

295 "Good from Evil"

1979. "Salute to the Righteous among Nations".

749	295	I£5.40 multicoloured	60	60

296 Prayer for Peace in Western Wall

1979. Signing of Egyptian–Israeli Peace Treaty.

750	296	I£10 multicoloured	60	60
MS751		119×78 mm. No. 750. Imperf	95	95

297 Naval Memorial, Ashdod

1979. Memorial Day.

752	297	I£5.10 multicoloured	45	45

298 Weightlifting

1979. 11th Hapoel Games. Multicoloured.

753	I£1.50 Type 298	30	25
754	I£6 Tennis	45	45
755	I£11 Gymnastics	75	70

299 "50" and Rotary Emblem

1979. 50th Anniv of Rotary in Israel.

756	299	I£7 multicoloured	60	60

300 Rabbi Joshua Ben Hananiah (blacksmith)

1979. Jewish New Year. The "Hazal" (sages and craftsmen). Multicoloured.

757	I£1.80 Type 300	25	10
758	I£8.50 Rabbi Meir Ba'al Ha-Nes (scribe)	35	25
759	I£13 Rabbi Johanan the Sandal-maker	45	45

301 Tiberias Hot Springs

1979. Health Resorts. Multicoloured.

760	I£8 Type 301	30	25
761	I£12 Dead Sea Hot Spring	60	60

302 "Searchlight Beam"

1979. 50th Anniv of Jewish Agency.

762	302	I£10 blue, grey & turquoise	45	45

1979. Historical Personalities (6th series). As T **283**.

763	I£7 purple and grey	30	25
764	I£9 blue	30	25
765	I£13 black and stone	45	45

DESIGNS: I£7, Dr. Arthur Ruppin ("father of Zionist settlement"). I£9, Joseph Trumpeldor (founder of Zion Mule Corps and Jewish Legion). I£13, Aaron Aaronsohn (botanist).

303 Arab and Jew before Jerusalem

1979. Children Paint Jerusalem. Multicoloured.

766	I£1.80 Type 303	10	10
767	I£4 Jewish, Christian and Muslim citizens of Jerusalem (horiz)	25	15
768	I£5 Worshippers at the Western Wall (horiz)	25	15

304 Boy sliding down Rainbow

1979. International Year of the Child.

769	304	I£8.50 multicoloured	45	45

305 Cog with Star of David

1980. Centenary of Organization for Rehabilitation through Training.

770	305	I£13 multicoloured	75	75

306 Scolymus maculatus

1980. Thistles. Multicoloured.

771	50a. Type 306	25	10
772	I£5.50 Echinops viscosus	40	30
773	I£8.50 Cynara syriaca	45	35

307 "The Road of Courage" Monument

1980. Memorial Day.

774	307	I£12 multicoloured	45	45

308 Symbolical Human Figure with Blood-drop

1980. 50th Anniv of Magden David Adom (voluntary medical corps).

775	308	I£2.70 red, grey and black	25	15
776	-	I£13 multicoloured	35	35
MS777		124×64 mm. Nos. 775/776 ×2	4·00	4·00

DESIGN: I£13, Mobile intensive care unit and graph.

309 Sabbath Lamp, Netherlands, 18th-century

1980. Jewish New Year. Sabbath Lamps. Multicoloured.

778	I£4.30 Type 309	15	25
779	I£20 Germany, 18th-century	60	45
780	I£30 Morocco, 19th-century	75	60

310 Yizhak Gruenbrum

1980. Tenth Death Anniv of Yizhak Gruenbaum (Zionist and politician).

781	310	I£32 brown	1·10	1·10

311 Tree and Flowers

1980. Renewal of Jewish Settlement in Gush Etzion.

782	311	I£19 multicoloured	65	65

312 Haifa

1980. "Hafia 80" National Stamp Exhibition. Sheet 100×84 mm containing T **312** and similar vert design showing details of 17th-century engraving of Hafia. Multicoloured.

MS783		2s. Type 312; 3s. Hafia (different) (sold at 7s.50)	3·50	3·50

313 "Shekel"

1980.

784	313	5a. green and emerald	35	35
785	313	10a. red and mauve	35	35
786	313	20a. turquoise and blue	35	35
787	313	30a. violet & deep violet	35	35
788	313	50a. orange and red	45	35
789a	313	60a. green and purple	45	35
790	313	70a. blue and black	1·10	1·10
791	313	90a. violet and brown	1·40	1·40
792	313	1s. mauve and green	65	65
793	313	1s.10 green and red	60	60
794	313	1s.20 blue and red	60	60
795	313	2s. green and purple	80	80
796	313	2s.80 brown and green	80	80
797a	313	3s. red and blue	2·30	2·30
798	313	3s.20 grey and red	95	80
799b	313	4s. purple and mauve	1·70	1·70
800	313	4s.20 blue and violet	95	80
801a	313	5s. green and black	95	80
802pa	313	10s. brown & dp brown	13·50	12·00

314 Golda Meir

1981. Golda Meir (former Prime Minister). Commemoration.

803	314	2s.60 purple	60	60

315 Landscape (Anna Ticho)

1981. Paintings of Jerusalem. Multicoloured.

804	50a. Type 315	25	15
805	1s.50 View of City (Joseph Zaritsky) (vert)	45	35
806	2s.50 Landscape (Mordechai Ardon)	60	45

316 Hand putting Coin into Light Bulb

1981. Energy. Multicoloured.

807	2s.60 Type 316	45	45
808	4s.20 Hand squeezing energy from the sun	65	50

317 A. H. Silver (Zionist)

1981. Historical Personalities (7th series).

809	-	2s. blue	60	60
810	-	2s.80 green	60	60
811	317	3s.20 ochre and black	60	60

DESIGNS—As T **283**: 2s. Shmuel Yosef Agnon (writer); 2s.80, Moses Montefiore (Zionist).

318 Biq'at
Ha-yarden
Memorial

1981. Memorial Day.

| 812 | **318** | 1s. multicoloured | 35 | 35 |

319 Board
Sailing

1981. 11th Maccabiah Games. Multicoloured.

813	80a. Type **319**	35	30
814	4s. Basketball	60	50
815	6s. High jump	75	70

320 "Family
Tree"

1981. The Jewish Family Heritage.

| 816 | **320** | 3s. multicoloured | 65 | 65 |

321 Moses
and the
Burning
Bush

1981. Jewish New Year. Moses. Multicoloured.

817	70a. Type **321**	15	15
818	1s. Moses and Aaron petition-ing Pharoah for Israelites' freedom	30	25
819	3s. Israelites crossing the Red Sea	60	50
820	4s. Moses with the Tablets	65	60

322 Rosa
damascena

1981. Roses. Multicoloured.

821	90a. Type **322**	25	25
822	3s.50 Rosa phoenicia	60	60
823	4s.50 Rosa hybrida	75	75

323 Ha-Shiv'a Interchange

1981. Ha-Shiv'a Motorway Interchange.

| 824 | **323** | 8s. multicoloured | 80 | 80 |

324 Balonea
Oak

1981. Trees. Multicoloured.

825	3s. Type **324**	45	40
826	3s. Wild strawberry	45	40
827	3s. Judas tree	45	40

325 Elat Stone

1981. Precious Stones. Multicoloured.

828	2s.50 Type **325**	35	25
829	5s.50 Star sapphire	65	60
830	7s. Emerald	80	70

1982. Historical Personalities (8th series). As T **283**.

831	7s. multicoloured	75	70
832	8s. brown, stone and black	75	70
833	9s. blue and grey	75	70

DESIGNS: 7s. Perez Bernstein (politician); 8s. Rabbi Arye Levin; 9s. Joseph Gedaliah Klausner (writer, editor and President of Hebrew Language Academy).

327 Child crossing Road

1982. Road Safety.

| 834 | **327** | 7s. multicoloured | 80 | 80 |
| MS835 | 127×79 mm. No. 834 (sold at 10s.) | 3·25 | 3·25 |

328
Armoured
Brigade
Memorial,
En Zetim

1982. Memorial Day.

| 836 | **328** | 1s.50 multicoloured | 35 | 35 |

329 Landscape (Aryeh Lubin)

1982. Israeli Art. Multicoloured.

837	7s. Type **329**	75	75
838	8s. Landscape (Sionah Tagger) (vert)	95	80
839	15s. Pastorale (Israel Paldi)	1·60	1·60

330 Emblem
and Flowers

1982. 40th Anniv of Gadna (Youth Corps).

| 840 | **330** | 5s. multicoloured | 1·00 | 1·00 |

331
Agricultural
Products

1982

841	**331**	40a. blue and green	95	95
842	**331**	80a. blue and mauve	95	95
843	**331**	1s.40 green and red	60	60
844	**331**	6s. mauve and red	1·10	1·10
845	**331**	7s. red and green	45	45
846	**331**	8s. green and red	45	45
847	**331**	9s. green and brown	1·90	1·90
848	**331**	15s. red and green	9·25	9·25
849	**331**	30s. purple and red	4·00	4·00
850	**331**	50s. bistre and red	2·75	2·75
851	**331**	100s. black and green	5·50	5·50
852	**331**	500s. red and black	7·00	7·00

332 Joshua and
Israelites setting out
for Canaan

1982. Jewish New Year. Joshua. Multicoloured.

860	1s.50 Type **332**	30	25
861	5s.50 Priests carrying Ark of the Covenant over River Jordan	35	35
862	7s.50 The fall of the walls of Jericho	45	40
863	9s.50 The suspension of twilight during the battle against the five kings of Amorite	60	45

333 Rosh Pinna

1982. Centenaries of Rosh Pinna and Rishon Le Zion Settlements. Multicoloured.

| 864 | 2s.50 Type **333** | 45 | 45 |
| 865 | 3s.50 Rishon Le Zion | 45 | 45 |

See also Nos. 868/9, 905/6 and 967.

334 Symbolic
Figures on Star
of David

1982. 70th Anniv of Hadassah (Women's Zionist Organization of America).

| 866 | **334** | 12s. multicoloured | 1·10 | 1·10 |

335 Branch

1982. No value expressed.

| 867 | **335** | (–) brown and orange | 60 | 60 |

No. 867 was initially sold at 1s.70 but this value was subsequently increased several times.

1982. Centenaries of Zikhron Yaaqov and Mazkeret Batya. As T **333**. Multicoloured.

| 868 | 6s. Zikhron Yaaqov | 75 | 75 |
| 869 | 9s. Mazkeret Batya | 95 | 95 |

336 Flower

1982. Council for a Beautiful Israel.

| 870 | **336** | 17s. multicoloured | 1·40 | 1·40 |

1982. Beer Sheva 82" National Stamp Exhibition. Sheet 130×78 mm.

| MS871 | No. 870 (sold at 25s.) | 3·25 | 3·25 |

337 Eliahu Bet
Tzuri

1982. "Martyrs of the Struggle for Israel's Independence".

872	**337**	3s. grey, black and brown	30	30
873	-	3s. grey, black and olive	30	30
874	-	3s. grey, black and blue	30	30
875	-	3s. grey, black and olive	30	30
876	-	3s. grey, black and brown	30	30
877	-	3s. grey, black and blue	30	30
878	-	3s. grey, black and brown	30	30
879	-	3s. grey, black and olive	30	30
880	-	3s. grey, black and blue	30	30
881	-	3s. grey, black and olive	30	30
882	-	3s. grey, black and brown	30	30
883	-	3s. grey, black and olive	30	30
884	-	3s. grey, black and blue	30	30
885	-	3s. grey, black and brown	30	30
886	-	3s. grey, black and olive	30	30
887	-	3s. grey, black and blue	30	30
888	-	3s. grey, black and olive	30	30
889	-	3s. grey, black and brown	30	30
890	-	3s. grey, black and olive	30	30
891	-	3s. grey, black and brown	30	30

DESIGNS: No. 873, Hannah Szenes; 874, Shlomo Ben Yosef; 875, Yosef Lishanski; 876, Naaman Belkind; 877, Eliezer Kashani; 878, Yechiel Dresner; 879, Dov Gruner; 880, Mordechai Alkachi; 881, Eliahu Hakim; 882, Meir Nakar; 883, Avshalom Haviv; 884, Ya'akov Weiss; 885, Meir Feinstein; 886, Moshe Barazani; 887, Eli Cohen; 888, Samuel Azaar; 889, Dr. Moshe Marzouk; 890, Shalom Sa-lih; 891, Yosef Basri.

338 Honey Bee,
Honeycomb and Flowers

1983. Bee-keeping.

| 892 | **338** | 30s. multicoloured | 2·30 | 2·30 |

339 Sweets in
Ashtray

1983. Anti-smoking Campaign.

| 893 | **339** | 7s. multicoloured | 60 | 60 |

340 Golan Settlement

1983. Settlements. Multicoloured.

894	8s. Type **340**	75	70
895	15s. Galil settlement	95	95
896	20s. Yehuda and Shomeron settlements	1·10	1·00

341 84th
Division "of
Steel" Memorial,
Besor (Israel
Godowitz)

1983. Memorial Day.

| 897 | **341** | 3s. multicoloured | 45 | 45 |

342 Star of David

1983. 35th Anniv of Independence.

898	342	25s. multicoloured	2·10	2·10
MS899		120×84 mm. No. 898. Imperf	3·75	3·75

343 Running

1983. 12th Hapoel Games.

900	343	6s. multicoloured	60	60

344 Missile and Blueprint

1983. 50th Anniv of Israel Military Industries.

901	344	12s. multicoloured	80	80

345 The Last Way (Iosef Kuzhovsky)

1983. Babi Yar Massacre.

902	345	35s. multicoloured	1·90	1·90

346 Yosef Glazman

1983. 40th Anniv of Warsaw and Vilna Ghettos Uprising. Sheet 120×86 mm containing T **346** and similar square designs. Multicoloured.

MS903	10s. Type **346**; 10s. Commemorative text; 10s. Mordechai Anielewicz (sold at 45s.)	5·00	5·00

347 Raoul Wallenberg

1983. Raoul Wallenberg (Swedish diplomat) Commemoration.

904	347	14s. stone and brown	1·40	1·40

1983. Centenary of Yesud Ha-Maala and Nes Ziyyona. As T **333**. Multicoloured.

905	11s. Yesud Ha-Maala	75	75
906	13s. Nes Ziyyona	75	75

348 Ohel Moed Synagogue, Tel Aviv

1983. Jewish New Year. Synagogues. Multicoloured.

907	3s. Type **348**	30	30
908	12s. Yeshurun Synagogue, Jerusalem	45	45
909	16s. Ohel Aharon Synagogue, Haifa	80	80
910	20s. Khalaschi Synagogue, Beer Sheva	95	95

349 Afula Landscape

1983. Afula Urban Centre, Jezreel Valley.

911	349	15s. multicoloured	1·00	1·00

350 Promenade, Tel Aviv

1983. "Tel Aviv 83" Stamp Exhibition. Sheet 142×88 mm containing T **350** and similar vert design. Multicoloured.

MS912	30s. Type **350**; 50s. Promenade (sold at 120s.)	10·50	10·50

351 Israeli Aircraft Industry Kfir-C2 Jet Fighter

1983. Military Equipment. Multicoloured.

913	8s. Type **351**	30	25
914	18s. "Reshef" (missile vessel)	45	45
915	30s. "Merkava" battle tank	75	70

352 Rabbi Meir Bar-Ilan

1983. 34th Death Anniv of Rabbi Meir Bar-Ilan (Zionist leader).

916	352	9s. blue and green	45	45

353 "Aliya" ("immigration")

1983. 50th Anniv of Jewish Immigration from Germany.

917	353	14s. red, gold and blue	45	45

354 Michael Halperin

1984. 65th Death Anniv of Michael Halperin (nationalist).

918	354	7s. brown, stone & dp brn	35	35

355 Yigal Allon

1984. Fourth Death Anniv of Yigal Allon (politician).

919	355	15s. blue, green and black	35	35

356 Uri Zvi Grinberg

1984. Third Death Anniv of Uri Zvi Grinberg (poet).

920	356	16s. brown and red	35	35

357 Hevel Ha-Besor

1984. Settlements. Multicoloured.

921	12s. Type **357**	35	35
922	17s. Arava	45	45
923	40s. Hevel Azza	95	95

358 Alexander Zaid Monument (David Polus)

1984. Sculptures.

924	358	15s. stone, black and blue	45	45
925	-	15s. stone, black & brown	45	45
926	-	15s. green, black and grey	45	45

DESIGNS: No. 925, Tel Hay Memorial (Abraham Melnikov); 926, Dov Gruner monument (Chana Orloff).

359 Oliphant House, Dalyat Al Karmil (memorial to Druse Community)

1984. Memorial Day.

927	359	10s. multicoloured	30	30

360 Worker with Flag

1984. 50th Anniv of National Labour Federation.

928	360	35s. multicoloured	60	60

361 Leon Pinsker

1984. 93rd Death Anniv of Leon Pinsker (Zionist leader).

929	361	20s. lilac and purple	35	35

362 Stars and Hearts

1984. 70th Anniv of American Jewish Joint Distribution Committee.

930	362	30s. red, blue and black	45	45

363 Dove on Olympic Podium

1984. Olympic Games, Los Angeles.

931	363	80s. multicoloured	1·00	1·00
MS932		119×80 mm. 363 240s. multicoloured	9·25	9·25

364 General Charles Orde Wingate

1984. 40th Death Anniv of Gen. Charles Orde Wingate (military strategist).

933	364	20s. grey, black and green	35	35

365 Hannah

1984. Jewish New Year. Women in the Bible. Multicoloured.

934	15s. Type **365**	35	30
935	70s. Ruth	75	70
936	100s. Huldah the prophetess	95	85

366 Nahalal (first Moshav)

1984. Moshavim (Co-operative Workers' Settlements).

937	366	80s. multicoloured	80	80

367 David Wolffsohn

1984. 70th Death Anniv of David Wolffsohn (president of Zionist Organization).

938	367	150s. brown, blue & black	1·70	1·70

368 Apartment to Let (Leah Goldberg, illus Shemuel Katz)

1984. Children's Books. Multicoloured.
939	20s. Type **368**	30	30
940	30s. *Why is the Zebra wearing pyjamas?* (O. Hille, illus Alona Frankel) (28×28 mm)	35	35
941	50s. *Across the Sea* (Haim Nahman Bialik, illus Nahum Gutman)	45	45

369 Bread and Wheat

1984. World Food Day.
| 942 | **369** | 200s. multicoloured | 1·40 | 1·40 |

370 Isaac Herzog

1984. 25th Death Anniv of Isaac Herzog (Israel's first Chief Rabbi).
| 943 | **370** | 400s. multicoloured | 2·50 | 2·50 |

371 Lappet-faced Vulture

1985. Biblical Birds of Prey (1st series). Multicoloured.
944	100s. Type **371**	95	95
945	200s. Bonelli's eagle	1·40	1·40
946	300s. Sooty falcon	2·30	2·30
947	500s. Griffon vulture	3·75	3·75
MS948 120×82 mm. As Nos. 944/7 but smaller (33×23 mm)		14·00	14·00

See also Nos. 1015/**MS**1019.

372 Golani Brigade Monument and Museum

1985. Memorial Day.
| 949 | **372** | 50s. multicoloured | 45 | 45 |

373 Bleriot XI

1985. Aviation in the Holy Land. Multicoloured.
950	50s. Type **373** (landing by Jules Vedrines, 1913)	35	35
951	150s. Short S.17 Kent flying boat *Scipio* (Imperial Airways regular flights via Palestine, 1931–42)	75	75
952	250s. de Havilland D.H.82A Tiger Moth (foundation of Palestine Flying Club, 1934)	1·20	1·20
953	300s. Short S.16 Scion II (international flights by Palestine Airways, 1937–40)	1·40	1·40

374 Zivia and Yitzhak Zuckerman

1985. Zivia and Yitzhak Zuckerman (Polish Jewish freedom fighters) Commemoration.
| 954 | **374** | 200s. brown, grey & black | 1·10 | 1·10 |

376 Dome of the Rock

1985. "Israphil 85" International Stamp Exhibition, Tel Aviv. Three sheets containing various designs.
MS956 Three sheets. (a) 120×80 mm. 200s. Type **376**; 200s. Western wall; 200s. Church of the Holy Sepulchre; (b) 120×80 mm. 350s. 16th-century relief; 350s. 18th-century relief; 350s. 12–13th century relief (each 25×39 mm); (c) 79×120 mm. 800s. Adam and Eve with serpent (30×30 mm) (sold at 1200s) ..... 24·00 24·00

377 Ark of the Covenant

1985. Jewish New Year. Tabernacle Furnishings. Multicoloured.
957	100s. Type **377**	45	40
958	150s. The table	45	40
959	200s. Candlestick	60	50
960	300s. Incense altar	80	80

378 "Medals"

1985. International Youth Year.
| 961 | **378** | 150s. multicoloured | 45 | 45 |

379 Basketball

1985. 12th Maccabiah Games. Multicoloured.
962	400s. Type **379**	95	95
963	500s. Tennis	1·40	1·20
964	600s. Windsurfing	1·90	1·70

380 Recanati

1985. 40th Death Anniv of Leon Yehuda Racanati (founder of Palestine Discount Bank).
| 965 | **380** | 200s. brown, grey and blue | 60 | 60 |

381 *Dizengoff* (after J. Steinhardt and M. Sima)

1985. 49th Death Anniv of Meir Dizengoff (founder and Mayor of Tel Aviv).
| 966 | **381** | 500s. black, brown & silver | 1·70 | 1·70 |

1985. Centenary of Gedera. As T **333**. Multicoloured.
| 967 | 600s. Gedera | 1·40 | 1·40 |

382 Kibbutz Members

1985. The Kibbutz.
| 968 | **382** | 900s. multicoloured | 2·20 | 2·20 |

383 Dr. Theodor Herzl

1986
969	**383**	1a. blue and red	65	65
970	**383**	2a. blue and red	75	75
971	**383**	3a. blue and bistre	95	95
972	**383**	5a. blue and turquoise	1·10	1·10
973	**383**	10a. blue and orange	1·70	1·70
974a	**383**	20a. blue and purple	7·00	7·00
975a	**383**	30a. blue and yellow	7·00	7·00
976a	**383**	50a. blue and violet	3·75	3·75

384 Corinthian Capital, 1st Century B.C.

1986. Jerusalem Archaeology.
977	-	40a. green, orange & blk	3·25	3·25
978	-	60a. brown, violet & blk	3·25	2·75
979	-	70a. green, brown & blk	3·25	2·75
980	-	80a. purple, bistre & blk	3·75	3·25
981	-	90a. yellow, lilac & black	3·00	2·30
982	**384**	1s. brown, green & black	3·75	3·75
983a	-	2s. blue, green and black	11·50	11·50
984	-	3s. mauve, blue and black	5·50	5·50
987	-	10s. green, blue and black	10·00	10·00

DESIGNS—As T **384**: 40a. Relief, 1st century B.C. (Second Temple); 60a. Byzantine capital, 6th century A.D.; 3s. Archaic Ionic capital, 1st century B.C. (Second Temple). 32×23 mm: 70a. Relief from palace of Umayyid Caliphs, 8th century A.D.; 80a. Crusader capital from Church of Ascension, Mount of Olives, 12–13th centuries; 90a. Relief from Suleiman's Wall, 16th century A.D.; 2s. Insignia of Sayif addin Attaz from Mameluke Academy, 14th century A.D.; 10s. Frieze from burial cave entrance, end of Second Temple period.

385 *Balanophyllia coccinea*

1986. Red Sea Corals. Multicoloured.
991	30a. Type **385**	1·10	1·10
992	40a. *Goniopora*	1·20	1·20
993	50a. *Dendronephthya*	1·40	1·40

386 Sketches of Rubinstein (Pablo Picasso)

1986. Birth Cent (1987) of Arthur Rubinstein and Fifth International Rubinstein Piano Competition.
| 994 | **386** | 60a. multicoloured | 1·70 | 1·70 |

387 Microphone and Map

1986. 50th Anniv of Broadcasting from Jerusalem.
| 995 | **387** | 70a. multicoloured | 1·40 | 1·40 |

388 Negev Bridge Monument, Beer Sheva

1986. Memorial Day.
| 996 | **388** | 20a. multicoloured | 75 | 75 |

389 El-Jazzar Mosque, Akko

1986. Id Al-Fitr (end of Ramadan).
| 997 | **389** | 30a. emerald, green & ol | 75 | 75 |

390 Hebrew Union College, Cincinnati

1986. "Ameripex '86" International Stamp Exhibition, Chicago. Jewish Institutes of Higher Learning. Multicoloured.
998	50a. Type **390**	1·30	1·30
999	50a. Yeshiva University, New York	1·30	1·30
1000	50a. Jewish Theology Seminary, New York	1·30	1·30
MS1001 100×70 mm. 75a. ×3 As Nos. 998/1000 but smaller (35×22 mm) (sold at 3s.)		9·25	9·25

391 Nabi Sabalan's Tomb, Hurfeish

1986. Feast of Nabi Sabalan (Druse feast).
| 1002 | **391** | 40a. multicoloured | 95 | 95 |

392 Graffiti on Wall

1986. Anti-racism Campaign.
| 1003 | **392** | 60a. multicoloured | 1·50 | 1·50 |

393 Sprinzak

1986. Birth Centenary (1985) of Joseph Sprinzak (first Speaker of Knesset).
| 1004 | **393** | 80a. blue, green and black | 1·50 | 1·50 |

394 Airport through Cabin Windows

1986. 50th Anniv of Ben Gurion Airport.
| 1005 | **394** | 90a. multicoloured | 1·90 | 1·90 |

395 Gates of Heaven, with Jerusalem above, opening to Power of Prayer

1986. Jewish New Year. Pages from *Worms Mahzor* (prayer book). Multicoloured.

1006	20a. Type **395** (prayers for Yom Kippur)		1·10	1·10
1007	40a. Man weighing shekel for Temple (prayer for Sheqalim, first special Sabbath)		1·20	1·20
1008	90a. Roses (illustration of liturgical poem)		1·60	1·60

396 David Ben Gurion

1986. Birth Centenary of David Ben Gurion (Prime Minister, 1948–53 and 1955–63).

1009	**396**	1s. bistre, brown & black	2·00	2·00

397 Map of Holy Land by Gerard de Jode, 1578

1986. "Netanya 86" National Stamp Exhibition. Sheet 126×80 mm.

MS1010	**397**	2s. multicoloured (sold at 3s.)	10·50	10·50

398 Satellite and Isobars over Map

1986. 50th Anniv of Meteorological Service.

1011	**398**	50a. multicoloured	1·40	1·40

399 Basilica of the Annunciation, Nazareth

1986. Christmas.

1012	**399**	70a. multicoloured	2·10	2·10

400 Bronislaw Huberman (violinist and founder)

1986. 50th Anniv of Israel Philharmonic Orchestra.

1013	**400**	1s.50 brown, blk & yell	4·00	4·00
1014	-	1s.50 grey, black & yell	4·00	4·00

DESIGN: No. 1014, Arturo Toscanini (conductor of Orchestra's first concert, 1936).

401 Hume's Owl

1987. Biblical Birds of Prey (2nd series). Owls. Multicoloured.

1015	30a. Desert eagle owl		95	95
1016	40a. Pallid striated scops owl		1·40	1·40
1017	50a. Barn owl		1·90	1·70
1018	80a. Type **401**		3·25	3·00
MS1019	102×82 mm. As Nos. 1015/18 but smaller (31×23 mm) (sold at 3s.)		10·50	10·50

402 Six-Day War Memorial, Ammunition Hill, Jerusalem

1987. Memorial Day.

1020	**402**	30a. multicoloured	1·10	1·10

403 Emblem

1987. 13th Hapoel Games.

1021	**403**	90a. multicoloured	2·20	2·20

404 1952 120pr. "TABA" Stamp

1987. "Hafia 87" National Stamp Exhibition. Sheet 111×77 mm.

MS1022	**404**	2s.70 multicoloured (sold at 4s.)	11·50	11·50

405 Street Cleaner

1987. "A Clean Environment".

1023	**405**	40a. multicoloured	1·10	1·10

406 Saluki

1987. World Dog Show. Dogs of Israeli Origin. Multicoloured.

1024	40a. Type **406**		1·70	1·60
1025	50a. Sloughi		1·70	1·60
1026	2s. Canaan dog		4·00	4·00

407 Radio Operators and Globe

1987. Israel Radio Amateurs.

1027	**407**	2s.50 multicoloured	6·00	6·00

408 Altneuschul Synagogue, Prague

1987. Jewish New Year. Synagogue Models in Museum of the Diaspora, Tel Aviv (1st issue). Multicoloured.

1028	30a. Type **408**		75	75
1029	50a. Main Synagogue, Aleppo, Syria		1·30	1·30
1030	60a. Israelite Temple, Florence		1·70	1·70

See also Nos. 1054/6.

409 Rabbi Amiel

1987. 104th Birth Anniv of Rabbi Moshe Avigdor Amiel (Chief Rabbi of Tel Aviv).

1031	**409**	1s.40 multicoloured	3·50	3·50

410 Family

1987. 75th Anniv of Kupat Holim Health Insurance Institution.

1032	**410**	1s.50 multicoloured	3·50	3·50

411 Camp (Christopher Costigan, 1835, and Thomas Howard Molyneux, 1847)

1987. Holy Land Explorers. Multicoloured.

1033	30a. Type **411**		1·00	95
1034	50a. Map of River Jordan (William Francis Lynch, 1848)		1·20	1·00
1035	60a. Men in canoe (John MacGregor, 1868–9)		1·60	1·60
MS1036	106×75 mm. 40a. Type **411**; 50a. As No. 1034; 80a. As No. 1035; but each smaller (22×35 mm) (sold at 2s.50)		7·00	7·00

412 Rosen

1987. Birth Centenary of Pinhas Rosen (lawyer and politician).

1037	**412**	80a. multicoloured	1·70	1·70

413 Computers in Industry

1988. Centenary of Israeli Industry. Multicoloured.

1038	10a. Type **413**		65	45
1039	80a. Genetic engineering		2·30	1·70
1040	1s.40 Medical engineering		2·75	1·90

414 Corked Tap

1988. "Save Water".

1041	**414**	40a. multicoloured	1·10	1·10

415 Kangaroos holding Birthday Cake

1988. Bicentenary of Australian Settlement.

1042	**415**	1s. multicoloured	2·75	2·75

416 Sunflower

1988. No value expressed.

1043	**416**	(30a.) green and yellow	1·10	1·10

417 Hebrew Year 5748

1988. Memorial Day.

1044	**417**	40a. multicoloured	1·10	1·10
MS1045	86×70 mm. As No. 1044 but smaller (33×25 mm) (sold at 60a.)		4·75	4·75

418 Anne Frank and House, Amsterdam

1988. 43rd Death Anniv of Anne Frank (concentration camp victim).

1046	**418**	60a. multicoloured	1·90	1·90

419 Jerusalem

1988. "Independence 40" National Stamp Exhibition, Jerusalem.

1047	**419**	1s. light brown and brown	2·30	2·30
MS1048	68×85 mm. 2s. cinnamon and brown		11·50	11·50

DESIGN. 34×25 mm. 2s. Jerusalem (detail of No. 1047).

420 1963 37a. Kibbutzim Stamp (Settling)

1988. "40th Anniv of Independence" Exhibition, Tel Aviv. Sheet 118×88 mm containing T **420** and similar horiz designs showing stamps. Multicoloured.

MS1049	20a.×9 Type **420**; 1965 50a. Potash Works (Industry); 1956 300pr. Oranges (Agriculture); 1955 25pr. Youth Immigration (Immigrant absorption); 1981 8s. Ha-Shiv'a motorway interchange (Construction); 1964 Cancer Research (Health); 1972 40a. Educational Development (Education) (sold at 2s.40)		11·50	11·50

421 Ein Zin Nature Reserve

1988. Nature Reserves in the Negev. Multicoloured.

1050	40a. Type **421**		1·00	80
1051	60a. She' zaf		1·40	1·30
1052	70a. Ramon		1·60	1·40

422 Jerusalem Lodge

1988. Centenary of B'nai B'rith in Jerusalem.

1053	**422**	70a. multicoloured	1·60	1·60

1988. Jewish New Year. Synagogue Models in Museum of the Diaspora, Tel Aviv (2nd issue). As T **408**. Multicoloured.

1054	35a. 12th-century Kai-Feng Fu Synagogue, China		1·00	1·00
1055	60a. 17th-century Zabludow Synagogue, Poland		1·10	1·10
1056	70a. 18th-century Touro Synagogue, Newport, Rhode Island		1·20	1·20

423 Havivah Reik

1988. Jewish World War II Underground Fighters. Multicoloured.

1057	**423**	40a. multicoloured	95	95
1058	-	1s.65 dp blue, blue & blk	3·75	3·75

DESIGN: 1s.65, Enzo Hayyim Sereni.

424 Dayan

1988. Seventh Death Anniv of Moshe Dayan (soldier and politician).

1059	**424**	40a. multicoloured	4·00	4·00

425 Burning Illustration of German Synagogue

1988. 50th Anniv of "Kristallnacht" (Nazi pogrom).

1060	**425**	80a. multicoloured	2·30	2·30

426 Menorah and Soldiers

1988. 74th Anniv of Formation of Jewish Legion.

1061	**426**	2s. dp brown, brn & bis	4·75	4·75

427 Avocado (fruit-growing)

1988. Agricultural Achievements in Israel. Multicoloured.

1062		50a. Type **427**	1·10	1·10
1063		60a. Easter lily (plant breeding)	1·40	1·40
1064		90a. Plants and drip-pipe (irrigation systems)	1·70	1·70

428 Red Sea

1989. Tourism. Multicoloured.

1065		40a. Type **428**	75	75
1066		60a. Dead Sea	95	95
1067		70a. Mediterranean	1·10	1·10
1068		1s.70 Sea of Galilee	2·30	2·30

429 Rabbi Maimon

1989. 114th Birth Anniv of Rabbi Judah Leib Maimon (writer).

1069	**429**	1s.70 multicoloured	3·50	3·50

430 "Rashi" in Rashi Script

1989. 950th Birth Anniv of Rashi (Rabbi Solomon Ben Isaac of Troyes) (scholar).

1070	**430**	4s. cream and brown	7·00	7·00

431 Airforce Memorial, Har Tayassim

1989. Memorial Day.

1071	**431**	50a. multicoloured	95	95

432 Child

1989. 20th Anniv of Israel United Nations Children's Fund National Committee.

1072	**432**	90a. multicoloured	1·70	1·70

433 Games Emblem

1989. 13th Maccabiah Games.

1073	**433**	80a. multicoloured	1·40	1·40

434 Smoira

1989. Birth Centenary (1988) of Moshe Smoira (first President of Israel's Supreme Court).

1074	**434**	90a. blue	2·20	2·20

435 Tree of Liberty

1989. Bicentenary of French Revolution. Sheet 120×80 mm.

MS1075	**435**	3s.50 multicoloured	17·00	17·00

436 Garganey

1989. Ducks. Multicoloured.

1076		80a. Type **436**	1·90	1·70
1077		80a. Mallard	1·90	1·70
1078		80a. Green-winged teal ("Teal")	1·90	1·70
1079		80a. Common shelduck ("Shelduck")	1·90	1·70

437 Printed Circuit and Pencil

1989. 13th International Council of Graphic Design Associations Congress.

1080	**437**	1s. multicoloured	2·10	2·10

438 Lion Design (Ukraine, 1921)

1989. Jewish New Year. Paper-cuts. Multicoloured.

1081		50a. Type **438**	75	70
1082		70a. Hand design (Morocco, 1800s)	95	95
1083		80a. Stag design (Germany, 1818)	1·40	1·00

439 Founders of Safa Brurah

1989. Centenaries of Safa Brurah ("Clear Language") and Hebrew Language Committee (precursors of Hebrew Language Council).

1084	**439**	1s. multicoloured	1·70	1·70

440 Rabbi Alkalai

1989. 11th Death Anniv of Rabbi Hai Alkalai (Zionist).

1085	**440**	2s.50 multicoloured	4·00	4·00

441 "Stag"

1989. "Tevel 89" Youth Stamp Exhibition.

1086	**441**	50a. multicoloured	1·70	1·70

442 Postal Authority Emblem

1989. First Stamp Day.

1087	**442**	1s. multicoloured	1·10	1·10

443 "See You Again"

1989. Greetings Stamps. No value expressed. Multicoloured.

1088		(–) Type **443**	3·75	3·50
1089		(–) Patched heart ("With Love")	3·75	3·50
1090		(–) Flower ("Good Luck")	3·75	3·50

See also Nos. 1111/13 and 1128/30.

1989. "World Stamp Expo 89" International Stamp Exhibition, Washington D.C. Sheet 99×64 mm containing design as Nos. 1076/9 but smaller 27×22 mm.

MS1091		80a.×4 multicoloured (sold at 5s.)	11·50	11·50

444 Rebab and Carpet

1990. The Bedouin in Israel.

1092	**444**	1s.50 multicoloured	2·20	2·20

445 Traditional Dancing

1990. Circassians in Israel.

1093	**445**	1s.50 multicoloured	2·75	2·75

446 Photograph Album and Orange

1990. Centenary of Rehovot Settlement.

1094	**446**	2s. multicoloured	3·25	3·25

447 Artillery Corps Monument, Zikhron Yaaqov

1990. Memorial Day.

1095	**447**	60a. multicoloured	1·00	1·00

448 Ruins of Gamla, Yehudiyya

1990. Nature Reserves (1st series). Multicoloured.

1096		60a. Type **448**	95	70
1097		80a. Huleh	1·30	80
1098		90a. Mt. Meron	1·50	1·20

See also Nos. 1200/2.

449 School, Deganya Kibbutz (Richard Kauffmann)

1990. Architecture.

1099b		75a. Type **449**	37·00	37·00
1100		1s.10 Dining hall, Tel Yosef Kibbutz (Leopold Krahauer)	1·40	95
1101		1s.20 Engel House, Tel Aviv (Ze'ev Rechter)	1·40	95
1102		1s.40 Weizmann House, Rehovot (Erich Mendelsohn)	1·90	1·10
1103		1s.60 National Institutions Building, Jerusalem (Yohanan Ratner)	1·70	1·40

450 Roads to Jerusalem

1990. "Stamp World London 90" International Stamp Exhibition. Stained Glass Windows by Mordecai Ardon in National and University Library illustrating Book of Isiah. Sheet 151×67 mm containing T **450** and similar vert design. Multicoloured.

MS1110		1s.50 Type **450**; 1s.50 Weapons beaten into ploughshares (sold at 4s.50)	17·00	17·00

1990. Greetings Stamps. As Nos. 1088/90 but with value.

1111		55a. As No. 1090	4·75	4·75
1112		80a. Type **443**	5·00	5·00
1113		1s. As No. 1089	5·25	5·25

451 Badges

1990. 70th Anniv of Formation of Hagana (underground military organization).

1114	**451**	1s.50 multicoloured	2·75	2·75

452 Dancers

1990. Eighth International Folklore Festival, Haifa. Multicoloured.

1115		1s.90 Type **452**	3·50	3·50
1116		1s.90 Dancers and accordion player	3·50	3·50

Nos. 1115/16 were printed together, *se-tenant*, forming a composite design.

453 19th-century Austro-Hungarian Spice Box

1990. Jewish New Year. Silver Spice Boxes. Multicoloured.

1117		55a. Type **453**	1·10	80
1118		80a. 19th-century Italian box	1·20	95
1119		1s. German painted and gilt box by Matheus Wolf, 1700	1·40	1·20

454 People forming Star of David

1990. Absorption of Immigrants.

1120	**454**	1s.10 multicoloured	1·70	1·70

455 Ancient and Modern Means of Communication

1990. Electronic Mail.

1121	**455**	1s.20 green, black & yell	1·70	1·70

456 Abraham's well (after 17th-century engraving)

1990. "Beer Sheva 90" National Stamp Exhibition. Sheet 90×86 mm.

MS1122	**456**	3s. multicoloured (sold at 4s.)	8·75	8·75

457 Basketball

1990. Computer Games. Multicoloured.

1123		60a. Type **457**	95	70
1124		60a. Chess	95	70
1125		60a. Racing cars	95	70

458 Tel Aviv-Yafo Post Office and 1948 20m. Stamp

1990. Stamp Day.

1126	**458**	1s.20 multicoloured	3·00	3·00

459 Jabotinsky

1990. 50th Death Anniv of Ze'ev Jabotinsky (Zionist leader).

1127	**459**	1s.90 multicoloured	2·20	2·20

1991. Greetings Stamps. No value expressed. As T **443**. Multicoloured.

1128		(–) Birthday cake ("Happy Birthday")	3·50	3·25
1129		(–) Champagne bottle ("Greetings")	3·50	3·25
1130		(–) Envelopes ("Keep in Touch")	3·50	3·25

Nos. 1128/30 were sold at the current inland letter rate.

460 Sarah Aaronsohn (intelligence agent)

1991. Anniversaries. Multicoloured.

1131		1s.30 Type **460** (birth centenary (1990))	1·10	95
1132		1s.30 Rahel Bluwstein (poet, 60th death anniv)	1·10	95
1133		1s.30 Lea Goldberg (writer and translator, 80th birth anniv)	1·10	95

461 Eucalyptus Tree and Hadera

1991. Centenary of Hadera.

1134	**461**	2s.50 multicoloured	2·75	2·75

462 Karate

1991. 14th Hapoel Games. Multicoloured.

1135		60a. Type **462**	1·70	95
1136		90a. Table tennis	95	95
1137		1s.10 Football	1·10	1·00

463 Intelligence Services Memorial, Centre for Special Studies, Tel Aviv

1991. Memorial Day.

1138	**463**	65a. multicoloured	1·00	1·00

464 First (Diesel) Power Station, Tel Aviv

1991. Inauguration of Rutenberg Power Station. Multicoloured.

1139		70a. Type **464**	95	80
1140		90a. Yarden Hydro-electric Station, Naharayim	1·20	1·00
1141		1s.20 Rutenberg coal fired power station, Ashqelon	1·60	1·30

465 Rabbi Shimon Hakham (co-founder) and Armon Building

1991. Centenary (1990) of Bukharim Quarter of Jerusalem.

1142	**465**	2s.10 multicoloured	2·30	2·30

466 Cover bearing Israeli, Palestine and Turkish Stamps

1991. Tel Aviv Postal and Philatelic Museum Project. Sheet 120×89 mm.

MS1143	**466**	3s.40 multicoloured	9·25	9·25

467 Ram's Head and Man blowing Shofar

1991. Festivals. Multicoloured.

1144		65a. Type **467** (Jewish New Year)	75	70
1145		1s. "Penitence Cock", father blessing children and men blowing shofars (Day of Atonement)	1·20	1·00
1146		1s.20 Family in booth (Festival of Tabernacles)	1·30	1·20

468 Front Page of First Edition

1991. 150th Anniv of "Jewish Chronicle" (weekly newspaper).

1147	**468**	1s.50 black, blue and red	1·90	1·90

469 Colonists and Baron Maurice de Hirsch (founder)

1991. Centenary of Jewish Colonization Association.

1148	**469**	1s.60 multicoloured	2·10	2·10

470 *Haifa, 1898* (Gustav Bauernfreind)

1991. "Haifa 91" Israel—Poland Stamp Exhibition. Sheet 104×62 mm.

MS1149	**470**	3s. multicoloured	9·25	9·25

471 Cancelled 1948 5m. Stamp

1991. Stamp Day.

1150	**471**	70a. multicoloured	95	95

472 Rahel Yanait Ben-Zvi (Zionist)

1991. Personalities. Multicoloured.

1151		1s. Type **472**	1·40	1·20
1152		1s.10 Dona Gracia Nasi (supporter of 16th-century Jewish settlement in Tiberias)	1·50	1·30

473 Runner

1991. Olympic Games, Barcelona.

1153	**473**	1s.10 multicoloured	1·50	1·50

474 Flame and Hebrew Script

1991. 51st Anniv of Lehi (resistance organization).

1154	**474**	1s.50 multicoloured	1·90	1·90

475 Southern Wing of Acre Prison

1991. 60th Anniv of Etzel (resistance organization).

1155	**475**	1s.50 black, red and grey	1·90	1·90

476 Mozart and Score of *Don Giovanni*

1991. Death Bicentenary of Wolfgang Amadeus Mozart (composer).

1156	**476**	2s. multicoloured	3·00	2·50

477 Anemone

1992. No value expressed.

1157	**477**	(–) red and green	2·20	2·20

No. 1157 was sold at the current inland letter rate, initially 75a.

478 Hanna Rovina (actress)

1992. Personalities. Multicoloured.
1158	80a. Type **478**		1·10	1·10
1159	1s.30 Rivka Guber (teacher and writer)		1·40	1·40

479 Trees

1992. Sea of Galilee. Multicoloured.
1160	85a. Type **479**		2·30	1·90
1161	85a. Sailboard		2·30	1·90
1162	85a. Fishes		2·30	1·90

480 Palmah Emblem

1992. 51st Anniv of Palmah (resistance organization).
1163	**480**	1s.50 gold, blue & mauve	1·90	1·90

481 Samaritans praying on Mount Gerizim

1992. The Samaritans.
1164	**481**	2s.60 multicoloured	3·25	3·25

482 Border Guard Memorial, Eiron Junction (Yechiel Arad)

1992. Memorial Day.
1165	**482**	85a. multicoloured	1·10	1·10

483 Azulai

1992. 186th Death Anniv of Rabbi Hayyim Joseph David Azulai (scholar).
1166	**483**	85a. multicoloured	1·90	1·90

484 Hayyim

1992. 83rd Death Anniv of Rabbi Joseph Hayyim Ben Elijah.
1167	**484**	1s.20 multicoloured	1·90	1·90

485 "Almanach Perpetuum" and Models of Columbus's Ships

1992. 500th Anniv of Discovery of America by Columbus.
1168	**485**	1s.60 multicoloured	2·10	2·10

486 Bedridden Patient and Map

1992. 500th Anniv of Expulsion of Jews from Spain. Sheet 140×71 mm containing T **486** and similar horiz designs showing details of map by Abraham Cresques. Multicoloured.
MS1169	80a. Type **486**; 1s.10 Doctor and map; 1s.40 Writer-philosopher and map	8·25	8·25

487 Diesel Trains, Greasing of Wheels and Blueprint of Baldwin Engine

1992. Centenary of Jaffa–Jerusalem Railway. Multicoloured.
1170	85a. Type **487**		80	70
1171	1s. Scottish steam locomotive, track plan at Lod, electric signalling board at Tel Aviv, semaphore arms and points at Lod		95	80
1172	1s.30 Diesel locomotive, interior and exterior of passenger carriages, Palestine Railways ticket and 1926 timetable		1·20	1·00
1173	1s.60 Diesel train, drawing of facade of Jerusalem station, platform at Lod, Jaffa station in 1900 and points at Bar-Giora station		1·30	1·20
MS1174	140×71 mm. 4 ×50a. As Nos. 1170/3		8·25	8·25

488 Cover of *Or-HaHayyim* ("Light of Life") (Rabbi Hayyim Benatar, 250th (1993) anniv)

1992. Death Anniversaries.
1175	**488**	1s.30 lilac, green & gold	1·20	1·20
1176	-	3s. lilac, green and gold	2·30	2·30

DESIGN: 3s. 19th-century drawing of Bet-El Yeshiva, Jerusalem (Rabbi Shalom Sharabi, 215th anniv).

489 Leopard

1992. Zoo Animals. Multicoloured.
1177	50a. Type **489**		60	45
1178	50a. Indian elephant		60	45
1179	50a. Chimpanzee		60	45
1180	50a. Lion		60	45

490 *Parables* (Yitzhak ben Shlomo ibn Sahula) (1st edition, Brescia, 1491)

1992. Jewish New Year. Centenary of Jewish National and University Library, Jerusalem. Multicoloured.
1181	85a. Type **490**		95	75
1182	1s. Mahzor (prayer book) (15th-century manuscript by Leon ben Yehoshua de Rossi)		1·00	80
1183	1s.20 Draft of translation by Martin Buber of Leviticus 25: 10-13		1·10	1·00

491 Court Building

1992. Inauguration of New Supreme Court Building.
1184	**491**	3s.60 multicoloured	3·75	3·50

492 Wallcreeper

1992. Songbirds. Multicoloured.
1185	10a. Type **492**		30	25
1186	20a. Tristram's grackle		30	25
1187	30a. Pied wagtail ("White")		35	30
1188	50a. Palestine sunbird		45	45
1189	85a. Sinai rosefinch		50	50
1190	90a. Barn swallows ("Swallow")		75	40
1191	1s. Trumpeter finches		75	40
1192	1s.30 Graceful prinia ("Graceful Warbler")		95	70
1193	1s.50 Black-eared wheatear		1·10	95
1194	1s.70 White-eyed bulbuls ("Common Bulbul")		1·60	1·30

493 *Judah Released*

1992. 75th Anniv of First All-Hebrew Film. Scenes from films. Multicoloured.
1195	80a. Type **493** (first Hebrew film)		1·40	1·30
1196	2s.70 *Oded the Wanderer* (first Hebrew feature film)		2·10	1·90
1197	3s.50 *This is the Land* (first Hebrew talking film)		2·75	2·30

494 European Community Emblem on Graph

1992. Stamp Day. European Single Market.
1198	**494**	1s.50 multicoloured	1·50	1·50

495 Begin

1993. First Death Anniv of Menahem Begin (Prime Minister, 1977–83).
1199	**495**	80a. multicoloured	95	80

1993. Nature Reserves (2nd series). As T **448**. Multicoloured.
1200	1s.20 Hof Dor		1·40	95
1201	1s.50 Nahal Ammud		1·20	1·00
1202	1s.70 Nahal Ayun		1·40	1·30

496 Shrine of the Bab

1993. Baha'i World Centre, Haifa.
1203	**496**	3s.50 multicoloured	2·75	2·50

497 Medical Corps Memorial, Carmel, Haifa (Akiva Lomnitz)

1993. Memorial Day.
1204	**497**	80a. multicoloured	80	75

498 "The Eye's Memory"

1993. Illustration of Scientific Concepts. Exhibits from the Israel National Museum of Science, Haifa (Nos. 1205/6) or the Bernard M. Bloomfield Science Museum, Jerusalem (others).
1205	80a. Type **498**		95	80
1206	80a. Colour mixing		95	80
1207	80a. Waves		95	80
1208	80a. Floating balls (principle of lift)		95	80

499 Prisoner

1993. 50th Anniv of Uprisings in the Ghettos and Concentration Camps.
1209	**499**	1s.20 black, yellow & bl	1·20	1·00

500 Hurbat Rabbi Yehuda Hassid Synagogue, Jerusalem

1993. 45th Anniv of Independence.
1210	**500**	3s.60 multicoloured	3·50	3·25

501 Giulio Racah

1993. Physicists. Multicoloured.
1211	80a. Type **501**		80	75
1212	1s.20 Aharon Katchalsky-Katzir		1·10	1·00

502 *Family using Crossing* (Lior Abohovsky)

1993. Road Safety. Children's Paintings. Multicoloured.
1213	80a. Type **502**		90	80
1214	1s.20 *Vehicles and road signs* (Elinor Paz)		1·20	1·10
1215	1s.50 *Road signals on "man"* (Moran Dadush)		1·40	1·20

503 Poppy

1993. Anti-drugs Campaign.
1216	**503**	2s.80 multicoloured	2·50	2·50

504 Passing Baton

1993. 14th Maccabiah Games.
1217	**504**	3s.60 multicoloured	3·75	3·75

505 Tree

1993. International Day of the Elderly.
1218	**505**	80a. multicoloured	80	75

506 Ear of Wheat

1993. Jewish New Year. Multicoloured.
1219		80a. Type **506**	80	70
1220		1s.20 Grapes	1·10	90
1221		1s.50 Olives	1·60	1·30

507 Environmental Concerns

1993. Environment Year.
1222	**507**	1s.20 multicoloured	1·10	1·00

508 Emblems

1993. 150th Anniv of B'nai B'rith (cultural and social organization).
1223	**508**	1s.50 multicoloured	1·10	1·00

509 *Immigrant Ship* (Marcel Janco)

1993. "Telafila 93" Israel—Rumania Stamp Exhibition, Tel Aviv. Sheet 60×90 mm.
MS1224	**509**	3s.60 multicoloured	7·00	7·00

510 Talmudic Oil Lamp

1993. Festival of Hanukka. Multicoloured.
1225		90a. Type **510**	80	75
1226		1s.30 Hanukka lamp in shape of building	1·20	1·00
1227		2s. "Lighting the Hanukka Lamp" (illustration from the "Rothschild Miscellany")	1·80	1·50

511 Cover of First Issue

1993. Stamp Day. Centenary (1992) of "Miniature World" (children's magazine).
1228	**511**	1s.50 multicoloured	1·50	1·30

512 Yellow-banded Borer (*Chlorophorus varius*)

1994. Beetles. Multicoloured.
1229		85a. Type **512**	1·30	1·10
1230		85a. Copper beetle (*Potosia cuprea*)	1·30	1·10

1231		85a. Pied ground beetle (*Graphopterus serrator*)	1·30	1·10
1232		85a. Seven-spotted ladybird (*Coccinella septempunctata*)	1·30	1·10

513 Man carrying Car ("Exercise Regularly")

1994. Health and Well-being. Multicoloured.
1233		85a. Type **513**	80	70
1234		1s.30 Blowing soap bubbles ("Don't Smoke")	1·10	1·00
1235		1s.60 Inspecting food through magnifying glass ("Eat Sensibly")	1·40	1·30

514 Haffkine

1994. 64th Death Anniv of Dr. Mordecai Haffkine (bacteriologist).
1236	**514**	3s.85 multicoloured	3·25	2·75

515 Communications, Electronics and Computer Corps Memorial, Yehud (Claude Grundman)

1994. Memorial Day.
1237	**515**	85a. multicoloured	80	75

516 Assuta Private Hospital (Yosef Neufeld)

1994. International Style Architecture in Tel Aviv. Each grey, blue and green.
1238		85a. Type **516**	1·00	90
1239		85a. Co-operative workers' housing (flats with separate balconies) (Arieh Sharon)	1·00	90
1240		85a. Citrus House (Karl Rubin)	1·00	90

517 Battered Child

1994. "No to Violence" Campaign.
1241	**517**	3s.85 black and red	2·75	2·50

518 Saul Adler

1994. Birth Centenary (1995) of Saul Adler (scientist).
1242	**518**	4s.50 multicoloured	3·00	3·00

519 Inflating Balloon

1994. Ayalon Valley International Hot-Air Balloon Race. Multicoloured.
1243		85a. Type **519**	1·00	90
1244		85a. Balloons in air	1·00	90
1245		85a. Balloon hovering over target (cross on ground)	1·00	90

520 Chemistry Class at Bialystok and Physical Education at Wolyn

1994. 75th Anniv of Tarbut Schools (Hebrew schools in Eastern Europe).
1246	**520**	1s.30 multicoloured	1·00	90

521 Israeli Team at Munich Games, 1972, and National Committee Emblem

1994. Centenary of Int Olympic Committee.
1247	**521**	2s.25 multicoloured	1·60	1·40

522 The Little Prince (book character) and Saint-Exupery

1994. 50th Death Anniv of Antoine de Saint-Exupery (writer and pilot).
1248	**522**	5s. multicoloured	3·50	3·25

523 *Adam and Eve* (Itai Cohen)

1994. Jewish New Year. Entries in the "Children and Young People draw the Bible" exhibition. Multicoloured.
1249		85a. Type **523**	75	65
1250		1s.30 *Jacob's Dream* (Moran Sheinberg)	90	75
1251		1s.60 *Moses in the Bulrushes* (Carmit Crspi)	1·30	1·10
MS1252		65×90 mm. 4s. *Parting of the Red Sea* (Avital Kaisar) (39×50 mm)	4·50	4·50

524 Jewish and Arab Houses merging

1994. Israeli–Palestinian Peace Process.
1253	**524**	90a. multicoloured	1·80	1·60

525 Silicat Brick Factory, Tel Aviv (Fourth Aliya, 1924–28)

1994. Aliyot (immigration of Jews to Israel). Multicoloured.
1254		1s.40 Settlers and booklet distributed in Poland to encourage Jews to settle the Valley of Jezreel (Third Aliya, 1919–23)	80	70
1255		1s.70 Type **525**	1·10	90

526 Road to Peace

1994. Signing of Israel–Jordan Peace Treaty.
1256	**526**	3s.50 multicoloured	2·50	2·30

527 Ford Model "T" Converted Car, 1920s

1994. Public Transport. Multicoloured.
1257		90a. Type **527**	80	70
1258		1s.40 "White Super" bus, 1940s	1·10	90
1259		1s.70 Leyland "Royal Tiger" bus, 1960s	1·30	1·10

528 Hanukka Lamp from Mazagan, Morocco

1994. Festival of Hanukka.
1260	**528**	1s.50 multicoloured	1·20	1·10

529 Computerized Post Office Counter

1994. Stamp Day. Computerization of the Post Office.
1261	**529**	3s. multicoloured	1·90	1·60

530 Breaking Dreyfus's Sword

1994. Centenary of "The Dreyfus Affair" (conviction for treason of French Army Captain Alfred Dreyfus).
1262	**530**	4s.10 multicoloured	3·00	2·50

531 "Serpentine" (Itzhak Danziger), Yarkon Park, Tel Aviv

1995. Outdoor Sculptures. Multicoloured.
1263		90a. Type **531**	75	80
1264		1s.40 "Stabile" (Alexander Calder), Mount Herzl, Jerusalem	1·10	1·00
1265		1s.70 Hall of Remembrance Gate (David Palombo), Yad Vashem, Jerusalem	1·30	1·10

532 Score from *Schelomo*, Solomon (after Dore) and Ernest Bloch

1995. Composers (1st series). Multicoloured.
1266		4s.10 Type **532**	3·00	2·50
1267		4s.10 Score from *Jeremiah*, Jeremiah (after Gustave Dore) and Leonard Bernstein	3·00	2·50

See also Nos. 1272/3, 1330 and 1338.

533 Ordnance Corps Memorial, Netanya

1995. Memorial Day.
1268 533 1s. multicoloured 90 90

534 Liberation of Dachau Concentration Camp

1995. 50th Anniv of End of Second World War.
1269 **534** 1s. multicoloured 1·30 1·10
MS1270 140×70 mm. 2s.50 As No. 1269 but larger (50×39 mm) 5·00 5·00

535 U.N. Projects

1995. 50th Anniv of U.N.O.
1271 535 1s.50 multicoloured 1·60 1·60

1995. Composers (2nd series). As T 532. Multicoloured.
1272 2s.40 Arnold Schoenberg and scene from *Moses and Aaron* 1·90 1·80
1273 2s.40 Darius Milhaud and score and scene from opera *David* 1·90 1·80

536 Soldier teaching Children Hebrew

1995. Jewish Brigade of Second World War. Sheet 95×65 mm.
MS1274 536 2s.50 multicoloured 5·00 5·00

537 Canoeist

1995. 15th Hapoel Games.
1275 537 1s. multicoloured 2·10 2·10

538 Box Kite and Cody "War" Kite

1995. Kites. Multicoloured.
1276 1s. Type 538 75 65
1277 1s. Bird-shaped, hexagonal "Tiara" and rhombic "Eddy" kites 75 65
1278 1s. Multiple rhombic and triangular "Deltic" aerobatic kites 75 65
Nos. 1276/8 were printed together, *se-tenant*, forming a composite design.

539 Stars in a Bucket (Anda Amir-Pinkerfeld, illus. Hava Nathan)

1995. Children's Books. Designs illustrating poems. Multicoloured.
1279 1s. Type 539 90 75
1280 1s.50 Hurry, Run, Dwarfs (Miriam Yallan-Stekelis, illus. Tirzah Tanny) 1·30 1·00
1281 1s.80 Daddy's Big Umbrella (Levin Kipnis, illus. Pazit Meller-Dushi) 1·40 1·10

540 Zim Israel (container ship)

1995. 50th Anniv of Zim Navigation Company.
1282 540 4s.40 multicoloured 3·50 3·25

541 Elijah's Chair (German, 1768)

1995. Jewish New Year. Multicoloured.
1283 1s. Type 541 (circumcision) 1·10 90
1284 1s.50 Velvet bag for prayer shawl (Moroccan, 1906) (Bar-Mitzvah) 1·60 1·40
1285 1s.80 Marriage stone (from Bingen Synagogue, Germany, 1700) 1·80 1·50

542 King David playing Harp (mosaic pavement, Gaza Synagogue)

1995. 3000th Anniv of City of David (Jerusalem). Multicoloured.
1286 1s. Type 542 1·00 90
1287 1s.50 Illustration of Jerusalem from 19th-century map by Rabbi Pinie 1·50 1·30
1288 1s.80 Aerial view of Knesset (parliament) 1·60 1·40

543 Sheep (Menashe Kadishman)

1995. 75th Anniv of Veterinary Services.
1289 543 4s.40 multicoloured 3·75 3·50

544 Rabin

1995. Yitzhak Rabin (Prime Minister) Commem.
1290 544 5s. multicoloured 3·75 3·50

545 Putting out Fire

1995. 70th Anniv of Fire and Rescue Service. Multicoloured.
1291 1s. Type 545 80 75
1292 1s. Cutting crash victim out of car 80 75

546 Miniature Silver Menorah (Zusia Ejbuszyc)

1995. Festival of Hanukka.
1293 546 1s.50 multicoloured 1·30 1·10

547 Flying Model Plane

1995. Stamp Day.
1294 547 1s.80 multicoloured 1·30 1·10

548 Film Stars

1995. Centenary of Motion Pictures.
1295 548 4s.40 multicoloured 2·75 2·50
The stars depicted are the Marx Brothers, Simone Signoret, Peter Sellers, Danny Kaye and Al Jolson.

549 Illustration from Jerusalem From 19-century Map of Rabbi Pinie

1995. 3000th Anniv of City of David (Jerusalem) (2nd issue) and "Jerusalem 3000" Israeli—European Stamp Exhibition. Sheet 140×70 mm containing T 549 and similar horiz designs. Multicoloured.
MS1296 1s. King David playing Harp (mosaic pavement, Gaza Synagogue); 1s.50 Type 549; 1s.80 Aerial view of Knesset (Parliament) 7·50 7·50
The stamps in No. MS1296 depict the same motifs as No. 1286/8 but with differences in inscriptions.

550 Cycling

1996. Sport. Multicoloured.
1301 1s.05 Type 550 90 75
1302 1s.10 Show jumping 90 75
1303 1s.80 Water skiing 1·30 1·10
1304 1s.90 Paragliding 1·50 1·20
1305 2s. Volleyball 1·60 1·20
1306 2s.30 Whitewater rafting 1·80 1·30
1307 3s. Bat and ball 1·90 1·40
1308 5s. Archery 2·75 2·40
1309 10s. Abseiling 5·25 4·50

551 "Temple and Walls of Jerusalem"

1996. 3000th Anniv of City of David (Jerusalem) (3rd issue). Third-century Murals from Dura-Europos Synagogue, Syria. Sheet 141×71 mm containing T 551 and similar vert designs. Multicoloured.
MS1310 1s.05 Type 551; 1s.60, Torah Ark niche; 1s.90 Prophet Samuel anointing David as King 8·75 8·75

552 Cow and Computer

1996. 70th Anniv of Israel Dairy Cattle Breeders' Association.
1311 552 4s.65 multicoloured 3·75 3·50

1996. "China 96" International Stamp Exhibition, Peking. Birds. Sheet 128×89 mm containing designs as Nos. 1185/94 but face values and colours changed.
MS1312 30a.×10 multicoloured 13·00 13·00

553 Abraham Shlonsky (poet)

1996. Modern Hebrew Writers. Multicoloured.
1313 40a. Type 553 40 40
1314 40a. Joseph Brenner (novelist and essayist) 40 40
1315 40a. Judah Gordon (poet) 40 40
1316 40a. Haim Hazaz (novelist) 40 40
1317 40a. Devorah Baron (novelist) 40 40
1318 40a. Yehuda Burla (novelist) 40 40
1319 40a. Micha Berdyczewski (novelist and historian) 40 40
1320 40a. Yaakov Shabtai (novelist) 40 40
1321 40a. Isaac Peretz (novelist) 40 40
1322 40a. Nathan Alterman (poet) 40 40
1323 40a. Saul Tchernichowsky (poet) 40 40
1324 40a. Amir Gilboa (poet) 40 40
1325 40a. Yokheved Bat-Miriam (poet) 40 40
1326 40a. Mendele Sefarim (novelist) 40 40

554 Fallen Policemen Monument, National Police Academy, Kiryat Ata (Yosef Assa)

1996. Memorial Day.
1327 554 1s.05 multicoloured 3·75 3·75

555 Circuit Boards

1996. 75th Anniv of Manufacturers' Association.
1328 555 1s.05 multicoloured 2·30 2·30

556 Emblem and Old Photographs

1996. Centenary of Metulla.
1329 556 1s.90 multicoloured 3·75 3·75

1996. Composers (3rd series). As T 532. Multicoloured.
1330 4s.65 Gustav Mahler, score from *Resurrection Symphony* and creation of light 7·50 7·50

557 Plant growing in Cracked Earth

1996. 50th Anniv of the 11 Negev Settlements.
1331 557 1s.05 multicoloured 1·80 1·60

558 Fencing

1996. Olympic Games, Atlanta. Multicoloured.
1332 1s.05 Type 558 1·50 1·30
1333 1s.60 Pole vaulting 1·80 1·50
1334 1s.90 Wrestling 2·00 1·80

559 Jaffa Orange Tree and Citrus Fruit

1996. Israeli Fruit Production. Multicoloured.
1335 1s.05 Type 559 1·30 1·10
1336 1s.60 Grape vine, avocado, date, sharon fruit and mango 1·50 1·30
1337 1s.90 Star fruit plant and exotic fruit 1·80 1·60

1996. Composers (4th series). As T 532. Multicoloured.
1338 4s.65 Felix Mendelssohn, Prophet Elijah (after Albrecht Durer) and score from oratorio *Elijah* 4·00 3·75

560 Road Systems

1996. 75th Anniv of Public Works Department.
1339 560 1s.05 multicoloured 1·60 1·40

561 New Year

1996. Jewish Festivals. Paintings by Sahar Pick. Multicoloured.

1340	1s.05 Type **561**	1·30	1·10
1341	1s.60 Booth decoration (Festival of Tabernacles)	1·60	1·40
1342	1s.90 Pulpit (Simchat Torah Festival)	1·90	1·60

1996. Centenary of First Zioist Congress, Basel, Switzerland. Multicoloured.

1343	4s.65 Type **562**	4·00	3·50

MS1344 70×97 mm. 5s. Casino, Basel (venue) (39×50 mm)   9·25   9·25

563 Lighted Candles

1996. Festival of Hanukkah. Self-adhesive.

1345	**563**	2s.50 multicoloured	2·10	2·00

564 Bird and Fighter Aircraft

1996. Coexistence between Man and Animals. Multicoloured.

1346	1s.10 Type **564**	1·20	1·00
1347	1s.75 Dog, people and cat	1·40	1·20
1348	2s. Dolphins and diver	1·70	1·50

565 Ahad Ha'am

1996. Centenary of First Edition of "Ha-Shilo'ah" (periodical) and 140th Birth Anniv of Ahad Ha'am (editor and Zionist).

1349	**565**	1s.15 multicoloured	1·30	1·20

566 Shavit Rocket, Earth and "Ofeq-3" (satellite)

1996. Stamp Day. Space Research.

1350	**566**	2s.05 multicoloured	2·30	2·10

567 Equal Opportunities Emblem

1996. Equal Opportunities for Disabled People.

1351	**567**	5s. multicoloured	3·50	3·25

568 Woman, Ethiopia

1997. Traditional Costumes of Jewish Communities Abroad. Multicoloured.

1352	1s.10 Type **568**	1·30	1·20
1353	1s.70 Man, Kurdistan	1·90	1·70
1354	2s. Woman, Salonica	2·30	2·10

569 Alexander Graham Bell demonstrating Telephone

1997. "Hong Kong 97" International Stamp Exhibition. Inventors' 150th Birth Anniversaries. Sheet 90×56 mm containing T **569** and similar vert design.

MS1355 1s.50 Type **569**; 2s. Thomas Edison and lightbulb   6·50   6·50

570 Windmills, Don Quixote and Sancho Panza (Ya'acov Farkas (Ze'ev))

1997. 450th Birth Anniv of Miguel de Cervantes (writer).

1356	**570**	3s. multicoloured	2·30	2·10

571 Logistics Corps Memorial, Hadir

1997. Memorial Day.

1357	**571**	1s.10 multicoloured	1·00	95

572 Ark of the Torah, Old–New Synagogue (east side)

1997. Jewish Monuments in Prague. Multicoloured.

1358	1s.70 Type **572**	1·70	1·50
1359	1s.70 Grave of Rabbi Loew (chief Rabbi of Prague), Old Jewish Cemetery	1·70	1·50

573 Rabbi Elijah (Mario Sermoneta)

1997. Death Bicentenary of Vilna Gaon (Rabbi Elijah ben Solomon).

1360	**573**	2s. multicoloured	1·50	1·40

574 *Exodus* in Haifa Port

1997. Clandestine Immigration, 1934–48.

1361	**574**	5s. multicoloured	3·00	2·75

575 Ben Ezra Synagogue, Cairo

1997. "Pacific 97" International Stamp Exhibition, San Francisco. Sheet 90×60 mm containing T **575** and similar square design. Multicoloured.

MS1362 2s. Type **575** (centenary of discovery of Cairo Hebrew archives); 3s. Qumran and the Dead Sea, Prof E. Sukenik and Shrine of Dead Sea Scrolls)   6·50   6·50

576 Classroom (Navit Mangashsa)

1997. Winning Entry in "Hello First Grade!" Stamp Drawing Competition.

1363	**576**	1s.10 multicoloured	1·20	1·00

577 Drunk Driver

1997. Road Safety. Multicoloured.

1364	1s.10 Type **577** ("Don't Drink and Drive")	1·20	1·00
1365	1s.10 Car sinking in water ("Keep in Lane")	1·20	1·00
1366	1s.10 Car hitting bird ("Keep your Distance")	1·20	1·00

578 Ice Skating

1997. 15th Maccabiah Games.

1367	**578**	5s. multicoloured	4·25	3·50

579 Abraham and Tamarisk Tree

1997. Festival of Sukkot. The Visiting Patriarchs (1st series). Paintings from the Sukkah of Rabbi Loew Immanuel of Szeged, Hungary. Multicoloured.

1368	1s.10 Type **579**	1·00	80
1369	1s.70 Abraham preparing to sacrifice Isaac	1·50	1·10
1370	2s. Jacob dreaming of angels on ladder to heaven	1·90	1·40

See also Nos. 1453/6.

580 Mt. Scopus (Jerusalem) and Choirs

1997. Music and Dance Festivals. Multicoloured.

1371	1s.10 Type **580** (Zimriya World Assembly of Choirs, Hebrew University)	1·20	1·00
1372	2s. Fireworks over Karmiel and dancers (Dance Festival)	1·50	1·40
1373	3s. Zefat and klezmers (Hassidic musicians) (Klezmer Festival)	2·10	1·50

581 *The Night of 29th November* (Ya'acov Eisenscher)

1997. 50th Anniv of U.N. Resolution on Establishment of State of Israel.

1374	**581**	5s. multicoloured	3·00	2·50

582 Sketch by Pushkin of Himself and Onegin

1997. Translation into Hebrew by Arbraham Shlonsky of *Eugene Onegin* (poem) by Aleksandr Pushkin. Sheet 75×60 mm.

MS1375 **582** 5s. multicoloured   3·75   3·75

583 National Flag and Srulik with Flower

1997. 50th Anniv (1998) of State of Israel. (1st issue). No value expressed. (a) Size 18×23½ mm.

1376	**583**	(–) multicoloured	1·20	95

(b) Size 17½×21½ mm.

1377	(–) multicoloured	1·20	95

See also No. 1395.

584 Norseman Aircraft, Soldier, Missile Corvette and Cannon "Napoleon-Chick"

1997. 50th Anniv of Arrival in Israel of Machal (overseas volunteers) (1377) and Gachal (overseas recruits) (1378). Multicoloured.

1378	1s.15 Type **584**	95	80
1379	1s.80 Infantry soldier and Holocaust survivors	1·20	80

585 Bezalel (spinning-top)

1997. Festival of Hanukka. Museum Exhibits. Multicoloured.

1380	1s.80 Type **585** (Eretz Israel Museum, Tel Aviv)	1·20	1·20
1381	2s.10 Coin of Bar-Kokhba during war against the Romans (Israel Museum, Jerusalem)	1·40	1·00

586 Children leaving Airliner

1997. Chabad Children of Chernobyl Organization (for evacuation of Jewish children from irradiated areas of Europe to Israel).

1382	**586**	2s.10 multicoloured	1·40	1·20

587 Julia Set Fractal

1997. Stamp Day.

1383	**587**	2s.50 multicoloured	1·70	1·50

588 Photograph of Soldiers of Palmach Battalion and Civilians (Zefat)

1998. 50th Anniv of War of Independence. Battle Fronts. Multicoloured.

1384	1s.15 Type **588**	95	80
1385	1s.15 "Castel Conquered" (Arieh Navon) superimposed on armoured vehicles (Jerusalem)	95	80
1386	1s.15 Soldiers raising flag (Elat)	95	80
MS1387 140×70 mm. 1s.50, 2s.50, 3s. showing enlarged details of Nos. 1383/5		8·25	8·25

589 Herzog

1998. 80th Birth Anniv of Chaim Herzog (President 1983–93).

| 1388 | **589** | 5s.35 multicoloured | 3·00 | 2·75 |

590 Franz Kafka (writer)

1998. Jewish Contribution to World Culture (1st series). Multicoloured.

1389	90a. Type **590**	70	60
1390	90a. George Gershwin (composer)	70	60
1391	90a. Lev Davidovich Landau (physicist)	70	60
1392	90a. Albert Einstein (physicist and mathematician)	70	60
1393	90a. Leon Blum (writer)	70	60
1394	90a. Elizabeth Rachel Felix (actress)	70	60

See also Nos. 1436/41.

591 Declaration Ceremony, 1948

1998. 50th Anniv of State of Israel (2nd issue).

| 1395 | **591** | 1s.15 multicoloured | 80 | 70 |

592 Olive Branch

1998. Memorial Day.

| 1396 | **592** | 1s.15 multicoloured | 80 | 70 |

593 Swearing In Ceremony in 1948 and Badge entwined with Medal Ribbons

1998. 50th Anniv of Defence Forces.

| 1397 | **593** | 5s.35 multicoloured | 3·00 | 2·75 |

594 Giorgio Perlasca, Aristides de Sousa Mendes, Charles Lutz, Sempo Sugihara and Selahattin Ulkumen (diplomats) (image scaled to 53% of original size)

1998. Holocaust Memorial Day. Righteous Among the Nations (non-Jews who risked their lives to save Jews during the Holocaust).

| 1398 | **594** | 6s. multicoloured | 4·25 | 4·25 |

595 Kitten

1998. Children's Pets. Multicoloured.

1399	60a. Type **595**	60	45
1400	60a. Puppy	60	45
1401	60a. Crimson rosella	60	45
1402	60a. Goldfish	60	45
1403	60a. Hamster	60	45
1404	60a. Rabbit	60	45

Nos. 1399/1404 were issued together in se-tenant sheetlets of six stamps and six triangular labels bearing the emblem of "Israel 98" International Stamp Exhibition, each label with an adjacent stamp completing a square. The complete sheetlet forms a composite design.

596 Srulik at Post Office Counter

1998. Inauguration of Postal and Philatelic Museum, Tel Aviv. Sheet 142×72 mm containing T **596** and similar horiz designs showing illustrations by K. Gardosh. Multicoloured.

| **MS**1405 1s.50 Type **596**; 2s.50 Srulik viewing stamp through magnifying glass; 3s. Srulik posting letter | | 7·00 | 7·00 |

597 Drawing of Temple Entrance

1998. "Israel 98" International Stamp Exhibition, Tel Aviv (1st issue). King Solomon's Temple. Sheet 92×66 mm containing T **597** and similar square design. Multicoloured.

| **MS**1406 2s. Type **597**; 3s. Inscribed ivory pomegranate | | 5·25 | 5·25 |

598 de Havilland D.H.89 Dragon Rapide

1998. Aircraft of War of Independence. Multicoloured.

1407	2s.20 Type **598**	1·20	1·00
1408	2s.20 Supermarine Spitfire	1·20	1·00
1409	2s.20 Boeing B-17 Flying Fortress	1·20	1·00

599 Woman's Head (mosaic from Zippori)

1998. "Israel 98" International Stamp Exhibition, Tel Aviv (2nd issue). Sheet 90×60 mm.

| **MS**1410 599 5s. multicoloured | | 5·25 | 5·25 |

600 "Amos" Satellite, Immigration, Grapes, Dove and Lion's Gate, Jerusalem

1998. "Israel Jubilee" Exhibition, Tel Aviv.

| 1411 | **600** | 5s.35 multicoloured | 2·75 | 2·30 |

601 Holding Hands (Nitzan Shupak)

1998. "Living in a World of Mutual Respect" Elementary Education Programme.

| 1412 | **601** | 1s.15 multicoloured | 70 | 60 |

602 Birds (Hechal Yitshak Synagogue, Moshav Yonatan)

1998. Jewish New Year. Synagogue Curtains. Multicoloured.

1413	1s.15 Type **602**	65	50
1414	1s.80 Lions (Ohal Chanah Synagogue, Neve Tsuf)	95	80
1415	2s.20 Leaves (Hatzvi Israel Synagogue, Jerusalem)	1·30	1·00

603 Hebron

1998. Jewish Life in Eretz Israel (1st series). Showing sections from Holy Cities Wall Plaque. Multicoloured.

| 1416 | 1s.80 Type **603** | 1·00 | 85 |
| 1417 | 2s.20 Jerusalem | 1·30 | 1·00 |

See also Nos. 1430/1.

604 State Flag

1998. Self-adhesive.

1418	**604**	1s.15 blue and deep blue	95	80
1419	**604**	2s.15 blue and green	1·40	1·20
1420	**604**	3s.25 blue and mauve	2·10	1·70
1421	**604**	5s.35 blue and yellow	3·50	3·00

605 Hanukka Lamp showing Mattathias (Boris Schatz)

1999. Festival of Hanukka.

| 1426 | **605** | 2s.15 multicoloured | 1·20 | 1·20 |

606 *Hyacinthus orientalis*

1999. Wild Hyacinths. No value expressed.

| 1427 | **606** | (1s.15) green and lilac | 60 | 45 |

607 The Knesset, Menorah and Knesset Stone Wall (des. Danny Karavan)

1999. 50th Anniv of the Knesset (Parliament).

| 1428 | **607** | 1s.80 multicoloured | 95 | 80 |

608 Manuscript

1999. 380th Birth Anniv of Rabbi Shalem Shabazi (Yemeni poet).

| 1429 | **608** | 2s.20 multicoloured | 1·20 | 1·00 |

1999. Jewish Life in Eretz Israel (2nd series). As T **603**, showing sections from Holy Cities Wall Plaque. Multicoloured.

| 1430 | 1s.15 Zefat | 75 | 65 |
| 1431 | 5s.35 Tiberias | 2·50 | 2·30 |

609 Part of £1 Share Certificate

1999. Centenary of Jewish Colonial Trust.

| 1432 | **609** | 1s.80 multicoloured | 95 | 80 |

610 Yemeni Woman

1999. Traditional Costumes of Jewish Communities (1st series). Multicoloured.

| 1433 | 2s.15 Type **610** | 1·20 | 1·00 |
| 1434 | 3s.25 Woman wearing sari, India | 1·60 | 1·50 |

See also Nos. 1457/8.

611 Reconstruction of Ship

1999. "Australia 99" International Stamp Exhibition, Melbourne. Excavation of Ancient Ship, Sea of Galilee. Sheet 100×63 mm containing T **611** and similar square design. Multicoloured.

| **MS**1435 3s. Type **611**; 5s. Remains of ship | | 4·75 | 4·75 |

1999. Jewish Contribution to World Culture (2nd series). As T **590**. Multicoloured.

1436	90a. Emile Durkheim (sociologist)	60	45
1437	90a. Paul Ehrlich (medical researcher)	60	45
1438	90a. Rosa Luxemburg (revolutionary)	60	45
1439	90a. Norbert Wiener (mathematician)	60	45
1440	90a. Sigmund Freud (psychologist)	60	45
1441	90a. Martin Buber (philosopher)	60	45

612 Memorial to Bedouin Soldiers, Rish Lakish

1999. Memorial Day.

| 1442 | **612** | 1s.20 multicoloured | 70 | 60 |

613 Flags of U.N., Israel and Other States

1999. 50th Anniv of Israel's Admission to United Nations.

| 1443 | **613** | 2s.30 multicoloured | 1·00 | 95 |

614 Holtzberg

1999. 75th Birth Anniv of Simcha Holtzberg.

| 1444 | **614** | 2s.50 multicoloured | 1·20 | 1·00 |

615 *My Favourite Room* (detail)

1999. 50th Death Anniv of James Ensor (artist).

| 1445 | **615** | 2s.30 multicoloured | 1·20 | 1·00 |

616 Ouza the Goose

1999. Lovely Butterfly (children's television programme). Multicoloured.

1446	1s.20 Type **616**	70	60
1447	1s.20 Nooly the chick and Shabi the snail	70	60
1448	1s.20 Batz the tortoise and Pingi the penguin	70	60

617 *Church of the Holy Sepulchre, Jerusalem* (F. Geyer)

1999. Paintings of Christian Pilgrimage Sites. Multicoloured.

1449	3s. Type **617**	1·60	1·50
1450	3s. *Mary's Well, Nazareth* (W. H. Bartlett)	1·60	1·50
1451	3s. *The River Jordan* (E. Finden after A. W. Callcott)	1·60	1·50

618 Illustration from Nehemia Emshel's Manuscript of *Musa-Nameh* by Shahin (poet)

1999. 205th Death Anniv of Rabbi Or Sharga from Persia.

1452	**618**	5s.60 multicoloured	2·30	2·10

1999. Festival of Sukkot. The Visiting Patriarchs (2nd series). As T **579**, showing paintings from the Sukkah of Rabbi Loew Immanuel of Szeged, Hungary. Multicoloured.

1453	1s.20 Joseph interpreting Pharaoh's dreams	75	65
1454	1s.90 Moses and the burning bush	1·00	85
1455	2s.30 Aaron and Holy Ark	1·40	1·20
1456	5s.60 David playing harp	2·50	2·30

1999. Traditional Costumes of Jewish Communities (2nd series). As T **610**. Multicoloured.

1457	2s.30 Woman from Seus region, Morocco	1·20	1·00
1458	3s.40 Man from Bukhara	1·70	1·40

619 Family and Part of 1948 250m. Stamp

1999. Stamp Day.

1459	**619**	5s.35 multicoloured	2·30	2·10

620 18th-century Ceramic Urn showing Funeral Procession

1999. Jewish Culture in Slovakia. Multicoloured.

1460	1s.90 Type **620**	95	75
1461	1s.90 18th-century urn showing visit to a sick man	95	75

621 View over Town from Arch of Columns

1999. 50th Anniv of Kiryat Shemona.

1462	**621**	1s.20 multicoloured	70	60

622 *The Street of the Jews in Old Jerusalem* (Ludwig Blum)

1999. 50th Anniv of Proclamation of Jerusalem as Capital.

1463	**622**	3s.40 multicoloured	1·70	1·50

623 Sali

1999. 15th Death Anniv of Admor (Rabbi) Israel Abihssira Sidna "Baba Sali".

1464	**623**	4s.40 multicoloured	2·00	1·70

624 *Children and Aliens holding Hands* (Renana Barak)

2000. "Stampin' the Future" Children's Painting Competition. Multicoloured.

1465	1s.20 Type **624**	75	65
1466	1s.90 *Man and robot* (Tal Engelsten)	95	80
1467	2s.30 *Futuristic street scene* (Asia Aizenshteyn)	1·20	1·00
1468	3s.40 *Alien's and child's heads* (Ortal Hasid)	1·70	1·50

625 Globe, Joggers and Skiers

2000. Year 2000. Multicoloured.

1469	1s.40 Type **625** (quality of life)	80	70
1470	1s.90 Da Vinci's "Proportion of Man", ear of corn and scientist (biotechnology)	95	80
1471	2s.30 Computer, satellite dish and website address (information technology)	1·20	1·00
1472	2s.80 Moon's surface, astronaut and globe (space research)	1·50	1·20

626 *The Little Mermaid*

2000. 125th Death Anniv of Hans Christian Andersen (writer). Illustrations by Samuel Katz. Multicoloured.

1473	1s.20 Type **626**	75	60
1474	1s.90 *The Emperor's New Clothes*	1·10	95
1475	2s.30 *The Ugly Duckling*	1·40	1·20

627 *All Apostles Church, Capernaum*

2000. Paintings of Christian Pilgrimage Sites (2nd series). Depicting paintings by Zina Roitman. Multicoloured.

1476	1s.40 Type **627**	80	70
1477	1s.90 *St. Andrew's Church, Jerusalem*	1·10	95
1478	2s.30 *The Church of the Visitation, Ein Kerem*	1·40	1·20

628 Fort Shuni (Zina Roitman)

2000. Buildings and Historical Sites.

1479	**628**	2s.30 multicoloured	1·20	1·20

629 King Hussein

2000. King Hussein of Jordan Commemoration.

1480	**629**	4s.40 multicoloured	2·30	2·30

630 Monument to Jewish Volunteers in British Army, Jerusalem

2000. Memorial Day.

1481	**630**	1s.20 multicoloured	85	80

631 Fox yawning

2000. Endangered Species. Blanford's Fox. Multicoloured.

1482	1s.20 Type **631**	70	60
1483	1s.20 Fox watching mourning wheater (bird)	70	60
1484	1s.20 Fox	70	60
1485	1s.20 Three foxes	70	60

632 Mobile Telephone

2000. International Communications Day.

1486	**632**	2s.30 multicoloured	1·00	95

633 Cross, Crescent and Menorah

2000. "The Holy Land".

1487	**633**	3s.40 multicoloured	2·20	2·00

634 Bach (bust) and Manuscript of Juara Chaconne for Violin Solo

2000. 250th Death Anniv of Johann Sebastian Bach (composer).

1488	**634**	5s.60 multicoloured	2·75	2·30

635 Fortified Stone Building (Zina Roitman)

2000. Buildings and Historical Sites.

1489	**635**	1s.20 multicoloured	50	45

636 Couscous

2000. Traditional Foods. Multicoloured.

1490	1s.40 Type **636**	85	70
1491	1s.90 Stuffed carp	1·20	95
1492	2s.30 Falafel	1·50	1·20

637 Olympic Rings and Koala

2000. Olympic Games, Sydney.

1493	**637**	2s.80 multicoloured	1·70	1·50

638 King Hassan II

2000. First Death Anniv of King Hassan II of Morocco.

1494	**638**	4s.40 multicoloured	2·30	1·90

639 Young Boy and Girl

2000. Festivals. New Year Cards. Multicoloured.

1495	1s.20 Type **639**	70	60
1496	1s.90 Young woman holding Zionist flag	95	85
1497	2s.30 Man presenting flowers to woman	1·20	95

640 Adam and Eve

2000. Dental Health Campaign.

1498	**640**	2s.20 multicoloured	1·50	1·40

641 Menorah and Interior of Synagogue

2000. Dohany Synagogue, Budapest.

1499	**641**	5s.60 multicoloured	3·50	3·25

642 Revivim Observatory, Negev (Zina Roitman)

2000. Buildings and Historical Sites.

1500	**642**	2s.20 multicoloured	1·30	1·00

643 Struthiomymus running

2000. Dinosaurs. Multicoloured.

1501	2s.20 Type **643**	1·30	1·20
1502	2s.20 Head of Struthiomymus	1·30	1·20
1503	2s.20 Struthiomymus standing by tree	1·30	1·20

644 Robot (*I, Robot*) (Isaac Asimov)

2000. Science Fiction Novels. Multicoloured.

1504	2s.80 Type **644**	1·40	1·10
1505	3s.40 Time travel machine (*The Time Machine*) (H. G. Wells)	1·60	1·30
1506	5s.60 Space rocket (*Journey to the Moon*) (Jules Verne)	2·75	2·20

645 Open Book

2000. Aleppo Codex (earliest known manuscript of the Bible).

1507	**645**	4s.40 multicoloured	2·40	2·20

646 Tof

2001. Hebrew Alphabet. Designs each showing a different Hebrew letter. Multicoloured.

1508	10a. Type **646**	10	10
1509	10a. Shin	10	10
1510	10a. Reish	10	10
1511	10a. Kuf	10	10
1512	10a. Tzadi Kekufa	10	10
1513	10a. Pay Kekufah	10	10
1514	10a. Ayin	10	10
1515	10a. Samech	10	10
1516	10a. Nun	10	10
1517	10a. Mem	10	10
1518	10a. Lamed	10	10
1519	10a. Chof Kefufa	10	10
1520	10a. Yud	10	10
1521	10a. Tes	10	10
1522	10a. Ches	10	10
1523	10a. Zayin	10	10
1524	10a. Vov	10	10
1525	10a. Heh	10	10
1526	10a. Daled	10	10
1527	10a. Gimel	10	10
1528	10a. Beis	10	10
1529	10a. Aleph	10	10
1530	10a. Tzade Peshuta	10	10
1531	10a. Pay Peshuta	10	10
1532	10a. Chof Peshuta	10	10
1533	10a. Mem Stumah	10	10
1534	10a. Vov	10	10
1535	1s. Aleph and Beis	60	45

647 Pupils in front of School (Yavne'el)

2001. Village Centenaries. Multicoloured.

1536	2s.50 Type **647**	1·30	1·00
1537	4s.70 Farmers, horses and cart (Kefar Tavor)	2·30	1·70
1538	5s.90 Cart full of flowers (Menahamiya)	2·75	1·90

648 Segera Spring, Ilaniyya

2001. Buildings and Historical Sites.

1539	**648**	3s.40 multicoloured	2·00	1·70

649 Prairie Gentian

2001. Flowers. Multicoloured.

1540	1s.20 Type **649**	80	65
1541	1s.20 Barberton daisy	80	65
1542	1s.20 Star of Bethlehem	80	65
1543	1s.20 Florists calla	80	65

650 Lesser Kestrel

2001. Endangered Species. Multicoloured.

1544	1s.20 Type **650**	75	60
1545	1s.70 Kuhl's pipstrelle	95	70
1546	2s.10 Roe deer	1·20	80
1547	2s.50 Greek tortoise	1·30	95

651 Jerusalem (detail of ceramic tile, Ze'ev Rabin)

2001. "Jerusalem 2001" International Stamp Exhibition. Sheet 131×67 mm.

MS1548	**651**	10s. multicoloured	6·50	6·50

652 Monument for the Fallen Nahal Soldiers, Pardes Hanna

2001. Memorial Day.

1549	**652**	1s.20 multicoloured	1·20	1·00

653 Marquise Diamonds

2001. "Belgica 2001" International Stamp Exhibition, Brussels. Diamonds. Sheet 117×70 mm containing T **653** and similar vert designs. Multicoloured.

MS1550	1s.40 Type **653**; 1s.70 Round diamond; 4s.70 Square diamond	7·50	7·50

654 Sha'ar HaGay Inn

2001. Buildings and Historical Sites.

1551	**654**	2s. multicoloured	1·20	95

655 Mausoleum and Terraces

2001. Shrine of the Bab, Haifa.

1552	**655**	3s. multicoloured	2·10	1·40

656 Prayer Shawl and Tassel

2001. Karaite Jews.

1553	**656**	5s.60 multicoloured	3·50	2·75

657 Hebron

2001. Ceramic Tiles. Showing tiles from facade of Ahad Ha'am Municipal Boys School, Tel Aviv. Multicoloured.

1554	1s.20 Type **657**	75	60
1555	1s.40 Jaffa	95	70
1556	1s.90 Haifa	1·40	80
1557	2s.30 Tiberias	1·50	95

658 "and me? I want to ride in a hot air balloon" (Eyar Shteiman)

2001. "PHILA NIPPON 01" International Stamp Exhibition, Tokyo. Winning Entries in Children's Painting Competition. Sheet 120×75 mm containing T **658** and similar vert designs. Multicoloured.

MS1558	1s.20 Type **658**; 1s.40 "I wish I had a kitten" (Rony Schechter-Malve); 2s. "My dream is to be a vet" (Dana Srebrnik); 4s.70 "to swim with dolphins" (Hila Malka)	6·50	6·50

659 Clasped Hands and Hikers

2001. Israeli Council of Youth Movements.

1559	**659**	5s.60 multicoloured	3·75	3·50

660 Soldier and Peace Dove

2001. Festivals. New Year Cards. Multicoloured.

1560	1s.20 Type **660**	95	70
1561	1s.90 Two women	1·40	80
1562	2s.30 Boy carrying flowers	1·50	95

661 Rustaveli

2001. 32nd Anniv of the Translation into Hebrew of *The Knight in a Tiger's Skin* (poem by Shota Rustaveli).

1563	**661**	3s.40 multicoloured	2·30	2·10

---

662 Field, Leaves and Sky

2001. Centenary of Jewish National Fund.

1564	**662**	5s.60 multicoloured	3·50	3·00

663 Amichai

2001. First Death Anniv of Yehuda Amichai (poet).

1565	**663**	5s.60 multicoloured	2·30	3·00

664 Sunshade on Beach

2001. Coastal Conservation.

1566	**664**	10s. multicoloured	5·75	4·75

665 Flags reflected in Helmet Visor

2001. First Israeli Astronaut.

1567	**665**	1s.20 multicoloured	70	60

666 Child Painting (Yaffa Dahan)

2001. 50th Anniv of Association for Rehabilitation of the Handicapped (AKIM).

1568	**666**	2s.20 multicoloured	1·40	1·20

667 *Heinrich Heine* (painting, Moritz Daniel Oppenheim)

2001. 145th Death Anniv of Heinrich Heine (poet and satirist).

1569	**667**	4s.40 multicoloured	3·25	2·75

668 "Israel" in Braille

2001. Centenary of Institute for the Blind, Jerusalem.

1570	**668**	5s.60 multicoloured	3·75	3·25

669 Lily

2002. Flowers

1571	**669**	1s.20 multicoloured	70	60

670 Hat and Rattle (Adar)

2002. Months of the Year. Multicoloured. Ordinary or self-adhesive gum.

1572	1s.20 Type **670**	70	60
1573	1s.20 Almond twig, flowers and fruit (Shevat)	70	60
1574	1s.20 Grapefruit and anemones (Tevet)	70	60
1575	1s.20 Spinning top and candles (Kislev)	70	60
1576	1s.20 Autumn leaves (Heshvan)	70	60
1577	1s.20 Ram's horn and pomegranates (Tishrei)	70	60
1578	1s.20 Cup, unleavened bread and flowers (Nisan)	70	60
1579	1s.20 Bow, arrows and oleanders (Iyyar)	70	60
1580	1s.20 Sickle and grains (Sivian)	70	60
1581	1s.20 Sunflower and shells (Tammuz)	70	60
1582	1s.20 Couple wearing wedding dress and grapes (Av)	70	60
1583	1s.20 Torah, cotton and figs (Elul)	70	60

671 Field Mushroom

2002. Fungi. Multicoloured.

1596	1s.90 Type **671** (*Agaricus campestri*) (inscr "campester")	1·20	95
1597	2s.20 Fly agaric (*Amanita muscaria*)	1·30	1·00
1598	2s.80 Granulated boletus (*Suillus granulatus*)	1·60	1·40

672 "Ladino" in Rashi Script

2002. Judaic Languages. Multicoloured.

1599	2s.10 Type **671** (Ladino (Judeo-Spanish))	1·40	1·20
1600	2s.10 Peacock (Yiddish)	1·40	1·20

673 Military Police Memorial And Eternal Flame, Bet Lid

2002. Memorial Day.

1601	**673** 1s.20 multicoloured	65	50

674 Heinrich Graetz

2002. Historians. Multicoloured.

1602	2s.20 Type **674**	1·40	1·20
1603	2s.20 Simon Dubnow	1·40	1·20
1604	2s.20 Benzion Dinur	1·40	1·20
1605	2s.20 Yitzhak Baer	1·40	1·20

See also No. 1686/8.

675 King and Torah

2002. Hakel Ceremony.

1606	**675** 4s.70 multicoloured	2·75	2·20

676 "50" and Wheels

2002. 50th Anniv of ILAN (Israel foundation for handicapped children).

1607	**676** 5s.90 multicoloured	3·50	3·00

677 Cable Cars, Menara

2002. Tourism. Cable Cars. Multicoloured.

1608	2s.20 Type **677**	1·20	95
1609	2s.20 Rosh Haniqra	1·20	95
1610	2s.20 Haifa	1·20	95
1611	2s.20 Massada	1·20	95

678 Fish Fossil

2002. Geology. Sheet 115×70 mm containing T **678** and similar vert designs. Multicoloured.

MS1612	2s.20 Type **678**; 3s.40, Copper mineral; 4s.40 Ammonite	6·50	6·50

679 Hatsar Kinneret

2002. Buildings and Historical Sites.

1613	**679** 3s.30 multicoloured	1·50	1·20

680 Rechavam Ze'evy

2002. First Death Anniv of Rechavam Ze'evy (Minister for tourism).

1614	**680** 1s.20 multicoloured	80	70

681 Grape Scissors and Grapes

2002. Festivals. Wine. Multicoloured.

1615	1s.20 Type **681**	70	50
1616	1s.90 Cork screw and cork	1·00	70
1617	2s.30 Wine glass and bottle	1·20	80

682 Golden Eagle

2002. Birds of Jordan Valley. Multicoloured.

1618	2s.20 Type **682**	1·30	95
1619	2s.20 Black stork	1·30	95
1620	2s.20 Crane	1·30	95

683 Kadoorie School

2002. Buildings and Historical Sites.

1621	**683** 4s.60 multicoloured	2·30	1·70

684 Baruch Spinoza

2002. 370th Birth Anniv of Baruch (Benedictus) Spinoza.

1622	**684** 5s.90 multicoloured	3·50	3·00

685 Menorah Candlestick

2002. Menorah Candlestick.

1623	**685** 20a. red	25	10
1624	**685** 30a. brown	25	10
1625	**685** 40a. green	25	10
1626	**685** 50a. olive	25	20
1627	**685** 1s. violet	50	40
1628	**685** 1s.30 blue	65	50

See also 1918a/c and 1953a.

686 Abba Ahimeir

2002. Political Journalists. Multicoloured.

1630	1s.20 Type **686**	70	50
1631	3s.30 Israel Eldad	1·70	1·30
1632	4s.70 Moshe Beilinson	2·50	2·30
1633	5s.90 Rabbi Binyamin (Yehshua Radler-Feldman)	3·50	3·25

687 Marbles

2002. Stamp Day. Children's Toys. Multicoloured.

1634	2s.20 Type **687**	1·20	95
1635	2s.20 Top	1·20	95
1636	2s.20 Five stones	1·20	95
1637	2s.20 Yo-yo	1·20	95

688 Students

2003. Yeshivot Hahesder (college).

1638	**688** 1s.20 multicoloured	70	60

689 "11 September 2001" (Michael Gross)

2003.

1639	**689** 2s.30 multicoloured	1·30	95

690 Glider (1902)

2003. Centenary of Powered Flight. Multicoloured.

1640	2s.30 Type **690**	1·00	75
1641	3s.30 Engine and Wright brothers	1·50	1·00
1642	5s.90 Orville Wright flying *Wright Flier*	2·75	1·70

691 Memorial Monument, Mount Herzl

2003.

1643	**691** 4s.70 multicoloured	2·40	2·00

692 Burnt-out Vehicle

2003. Memorial Day.

1644	**692** 1s.20 multicoloured	60	45

693 Opened Box

2003. Greetings Stamps (1st issue). Multicoloured.

1645	(1s.20) Type **693**	80	70
1646	(1s.20) Boy and growing heart	80	70
1647	(1s.20) Married couple	80	70

See also Nos. 1655/7.

694 Ya'akov Meridor

2003. 90th Birth Anniv of Ya'akov Meridor (soldier and politician).

1648	**694** 1s.90 multicoloured	85	70

695 Star of David

2003. Holocaust Memorial Day.

1649	**695** 2s.20 multicoloured	1·00	85

696 Ya'akov Dori

2003. 30th Death Anniv of Ya'akov Dori (Chief of Staff 1948—50).

1650	**696** 2s.20 multicoloured	1·00	85

...

697 Sheikh Ameen Tarif

2003. Tenth Death Anniv of Sheikh Ameen Tarif (Druze (religious sect) leader).
1651 **697** 2s.80 multicoloured 1·20 75

698 Soldier

2003. Jewish Immigration from Yemen, 1881.
1652 **698** 3s.30 multicoloured 1·60 1·30

699 Paper Airplane and Computer Circuit Board

2003. 50th Anniv of Israel Aircraft Industries.
1653 **699** 3s.30 multicoloured 1·60 1·30

700 "55"

2003. 55th Anniv of Israel.
1654 **700** 5s.90 multicoloured 3·00 2·50

2003. Greetings Stamps (2nd issue). As T **693**. Multicoloured.
1655 (1s.20) Flowers 80 70
1656 (1s.20) Air balloon 80 70
1657 (1s.20) Boy holding teddy bear 80 70

701 Prague Jewish Community Flag (15th-century)

2003. Development of Israel State Flag. Multicoloured.
1658 1s.90 Type **701** 95 75
1659 2s.30 Ness Ziona (Jewish settlement) (1891) 1·00 85
1660 4s.70 Draft design from *Der Judenstaat* (Theodor Herzl) (1896) 2·00 1·40
1661 5s.90 State flag (1948) 2·75 2·20

702 Coast, Ruined Castle and Houses (Atlit)

2003. Village Centenaries. Multicoloured.
1662 3s.30 Type **702** 1·70 1·40
1663 3s.30 Tractor, crops and houses (Givat-Ada) 1·70 1·40
1664 3s.30 Houses and bungalow amongst trees (Kfar-Saba) 1·70 1·40

703 Olives

2003. Olive Oil Production. Multicoloured.
1665 1s.30 Type **703** 70 60
1666 1s.90 Mill stone and wheel 85 70
1667 2s.30 Oil 1·20 80

704 Teddy Bear and Page of Testimony

2003. 50th Anniv of Vad Yashem (Holocaust remembrance organization). Multicoloured.
1668 2s.20 Type **704** 1·10 80
1669 2s.20 Rail tracks and list of forced labourers 1·10 80

705 Deer and flowers (Karakashian-Balian studio, c.1940)

2003. Armenian Ceramics in Jerusalem. Sheet 120×65 mm containing T **705** and similar circular designs showing ceramic patterns. Multicoloured.
MS1670 2s.30 Type **705**; 3s.30 Bird (Stepan Karakshian, c. 1980); 4s.70 Tree of life (Marie Balian, c. 1990) 8·75 8·75

2003. No value expressed. As T **600**. Self-adhesive.
1671 **600** (1s.30) green and lilac 70 60

706 Yehoshua Hankin

2003. 58th Death Anniv of Yehoshua Hankin (Zionist pioneer).
1672 **706** 6s.20 multicoloured 4·00 3·75

707 Boy riding Bicycle

2003. Philately Day. Children and Wheels. Multicoloured.
1673 1s.30 Type **707** 80 60
1674 1s.30 Girl on roller skates 80 60
1675 1s.30 Girl pushing scooter 80 60
1676 1s.30 Boy on skateboard 80 60

708 Leibowitch Family and Administrative Building, Zikhron Ya'akov

2003. First and Second Aliya (immigration to Eretz Yisrael). Multicoloured.
1677 2s.10 Type **708** (1st Aliya) 1·50 95
1678 6s.20 Young men (2nd Aliya) 3·50 2·30

709 Aharon David Gordon

2003. Personalities. Multicoloured.
1679 3s.30 Type **709** (land purchase pioneer) (81st death anniv) 2·50 1·70
1680 4s.90 Emile Habiby (writer) (82nd death anniv) 3·50 2·50

710 Two-banded Anemonefish (*Amphirion Bicinctus*)

2003. Fish. Multicoloured.
1681 1s.30 Type **710** 70 50
1682 1s.30 Butterfly perch (*Pseudanthias squamipinnis*) 70 50
1683 1s.30 *Pseudochromis fridmani* 70 50
1684 1s.30 Crown butterflyfish (*Chaetodon paucifasciatus*) 70 50
MS1685 118×77 mm. Nos. 1681/4 3·00 3·00

2004. Historians. As T **674**. Multicoloured.
1686 2s.40 Emanuel Ringelblum 95 80
1687 3s.70 Jacob Talmon 1·50 1·20
1688 6s.20 Jacob Herzog 2·50 1·80

711 Menachem Begin and Building

2004. Menachem Begin Heritage Centre, Jerusalem.
1689 **711** 2s.50 multicoloured 1·10 85

712 Ilan Ramon

2004. First Death Anniv of Ilan Ramon (astronaut on Columbia Space Shuttle).
1690 **712** 2s.60 multicoloured 1·10 85

713 Memorial Garden, Mount Herzl

2004. Memorial Day.
1691 **713** 1s.30 multicoloured 55 45

714 Saraya Clock Tower, Safed

2004. Ottoman Clock Towers. Multicoloured.
1692 1s.30 Type **714** 45 30
1693 1s.30 Khan El-Umdan, Acre 45 30
1694 1s.30 El-Jarina Mosque, Haifa 45 30
1695 1s.30 Jaffa Gate, Jerusalem 45 30
1696 1s.30 Clock Square, Jaffa 45 30
1697 3s.10 No. 1692 90 55
1698 3s.70 No. 1693 1·10 70
1699 5s.20 No. 1694 1·50 95
1700 5s.50 No. 1695 1·60 1·10
1701 7s. No. 1696 2·00 1·40

715 Football and Israel—USA Match, 1948

2004. Centenary of FIFA (Federation Internationale de Football Association).
1702 **715** 2s.10 multicoloured 75 55

716 Football

2004. 50th Anniv of UEFA (Union of European Football Associations).
1703 **716** 6s.20 multicoloured 2·10 1·90

717 Candlestick, Ornamental Panel and Synagogue Facade

2004. Centenary of the Great Synagogue, Rome. Multicoloured.
1704 2s.10 Type **717** 75 55
1705 2s.10 Synagogue (different) 75 55
Stamps of the same design were issued by Italy.

718 Judo and Israeli Silver Medal (Barcelona, 1992)

2004. Olympic Games 2004, Athens. Multicoloured.
1706 1s.50 Type **718** 55 40
1707 2s.40 Wind surfing and Israeli bronze medal (Atlanta, 1996) 75 55
1708 6s.90 Kayaking and Israeli bronze medal (Sydney, 2000) 2·10 1·50

719 Theodor Herzl

2004. Death Centenary of Theodor Herzl (writer and Zionist pioneer).
1709 **719** 2s.50 multicoloured 85 65
A stamp of the same design was issued by Austria.

720 Anniversary Emblem

2004. 50th Anniv of National Insurance Institute.
1710 **720** 7s. multicoloured 2·30 1·90

721 Ear of Corn

2004. Bread. Multicoloured.
1711 1s.50 Type **721** 60 45
1712 2s.40 Grinding stones 80 60
1713 2s.70 Bread in oven 90 70

722 Building Facade and Test Tubes

2004. Centenary (2005) of Herzliya Hebrew High School.
1714 **722** 2s.20 multicoloured 75 55

723 Parachutist

2004. Children's Adventure Stories. Illustrations from book covers. Multicoloured.

1715		2s.20 Type **723** ("Eight on the Trail of One" by Yemima Avidar-Tchernovitz)	55	40
1716		2s.50 Children and donkey ("Hasamba" by Igal Moss-insohn)	1·00	55
1717		2s.60 Faces ("Our Gang" by Pucho)	1·10	60

724 Building and David Ben-Gurion

2004. Ben-Gurion Heritage Institute.

1718	**724**	2s.50 multicoloured	65	45

725 Airport Buildings

2004. Ben Gurion Airport.

1719	**725**	2s.70 multicoloured	90	65

726 Post Woman and Envelope

2004. Telabul 2004 International Stamp Exhibition, Tel Aviv. Design a Stamp Competition Winner.

1720	**726**	1s.30 multicoloured	45	25

727 Ottoman Period Austrian Mailbox

2004. Stamp Day. Mailboxes. Multicoloured.

1721		2s.10 Type **727**	50	30
1722		2s.20 British Mandate period	55	35
1723		3s.30 Modern	1·70	1·30

728 "20, 50, 100, 200"

2004. 50th Anniv of Bank of Israel.

1724	**728**	6s.20 multicoloured	2·10	1·50

729 Brown Bear

2005. Biblical Animals. Multicoloured.

1725		1s.30 Type **729**	35	25
1726		1s.30 Ostrich	35	25
1727		2s.20 Nile crocodile	65	45
1728		2s.20 Wolf	65	45

MS1729 110×72 mm. 1s.30 No. 1726; 2s.10 Type **729**; 2s.30 No. 1728; 2s.80 No. 1727 ... 4·75 4·75

730 Tunnel and Spoon

2005. Ancient Water Systems. Multicoloured.

1730		2s.10 Type **730** (Hazor) (9th—8th century BC)	55	35
1731		2s.20 Top of shaft (Megiddo) (10th century)	65	45
1732		3s.30 Aqueduct (Caesarea) (BC)	1·70	1·30
1733		6s.20 Tunnel and pool (Heze-kiah's Tunnel) (8th century)	2·10	1·50

731 Last of Kin Monument (Micha Ullman)

2005. Memorial Day.

1734	**731**	1s.50 multicoloured	45	30

732 Hebrew Kindergarten, Rishon Le-Zion

2005. Educational Institutions. Multicoloured.

1735		2s.10 Type **732**	55	35
1736		6s.20 Lemel Elementary School, Jerusalem	2·10	1·50

733 University Buildings

2005. 50th Anniv of Bar-Ilan University.

1737	**733**	2s.20 multicoloured	65	45

734 Family and Soldiers

2005. National Reserve Force.

1738	**734**	2s.20 multicoloured	65	45

735 Jewish Partisans

2005. 60th Anniv of End of World War II. Multicoloured.

1739		3s.30 Type **735**	1·20	80
1740		3s.30 Jewish soldiers with Allied Forces	1·20	80

736 Pope John Paul II

2005. Pope John Paul II Commemoration.

1741	**736**	3s.30 multicoloured	1·20	80

737 Emblem

2005. Maccabiah 2005 Sports Festival.

1742	**737**	3s.30 multicoloured	1·20	80

738 Gagea Commutate

2005. No value expressed. Ordinary or self-adhesive gum.

1743	**738**	(1s.30) multicoloured	35	25
1743a	**738**	(1s.50) multicoloured	35	20

739 Agrippas Street (Arie Aroch)

2005. Art. Multicoloured.

1744		2s.20 Type **739**	65	45
1745		4s.90 "Tablets of the Covenant" (Moshe Castel)	1·60	1·20
1746		6s.20 "The Rift in Time" (Moshe Kupferman)	2·10	1·50

740 Maimonides as Eagle and Map of Mediterranean

2005. 800th Death Anniv of Maimonides (Rabbi Moses Ben Maimon) (Jewish scholar).

1747	**740**	8s.20 multicoloured	2·75	2·10

741 Sack of Grain (Order of Zeraim)

2005. Mishnah (laws). Multicoloured.

1748		1s.30 Type **741**	35	25
1749		2s.10 Zodiac and wine goblet (Order of Moed)	55	35
1750		2s.30 Two rings (Order of Nashim)	65	50

742 Elderly hand holding Stick and Stethoscope (geriatrics)

2005. Medicine. Multicoloured.

1751		1s.40 Type **742**	40	30
1752		2s.20 Wheelchair user and dumb-bell (rehabilitation)	65	45
1753		2s.20 Child holding teddy bear and thermometer (pae-diatrics)	65	45
1754		6s.20 Bi-coloured face and tablet (mental health)	2·10	1·50

743 Yitzhak Rabin

2005. Yitzhak Rabin Centre.

1755	**743**	2s.20 multicoloured	65	45

744 Albert Einstein

2005. International Year of Physics. Centenary of Publication of "Special Theory of Relativity" by Albert Einstein.

1756	**744**	3s.30 multicoloured	1·20	80

745 Wall

2005. Priestly Blessing.

1757	**745**	6s.20 multicoloured	2·10	1·50

746 Israeli and German Flags

2005. 40th Anniv of Diplomatic Relations with Germany.

1758	**746**	2s.20 multicoloured	65	45

A stamp of the same design was issued by Germany.

747 Childhood is Happiness (Lya Kasif)

2005. International Convention on the Rights of the Child. Winning Designs in Children's Painting Competition. Multicoloured.

1759		1s.30 Type **747**	35	25
1760		1s.30 A Warm Home (Menahem Mendel Albo)	35	25
1761		1s.30 Indifference Hurts (Irina Rogozinsky)	35	25

748 Moshe Halevy (director)

2005. Theatre Personalities. Multicoloured.

1762		2s.20 Type **748**	65	45
1763		2s.20 Joeseph Millo (actor and director)	65	45
1764		6s.20 Shai K Ophir (Isaiah Gold-stein) (actor and director)	2·10	1·50
1765		6s.20 Nissim Aloni (playwright and director)	2·10	1·50

2005. Stamp Day. International Year of Physics. Sheet 84×59 mm.

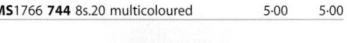

MS1766	**744**	8s.20 multicoloured	5·00	5·00

749 Symbols of Industry

2005. 85th Anniv of Manufacturers' Association.

1767	**749**	1s.50 multicoloured	45	35

750 Emblem

2006. Inauguration of Israel Post Ltd (1 March 2006).
1768 **750** 1s.50 multicoloured 45 35

751 *Desert Bloom* (Yael Bildner)

2006. Winning Designs in Jewish–American Children's Design-a-Stamp Competition. Multicoloured.
1769 1s.50 Type **751** 45 35
1770 2s.40 *Harmony* (Michela Janower) 70 55
1771 3s.60 *Together in Israel* (Jessica Deautsch) 1·30 90
1772 7s.40 *Colours in Israel* (Marissa Galin) 2·50 1·80

752 Rebbe

2006. Chabad–Lubavitch Chassism (religious movement).
1773 **752** 2s.50 multicoloured 75 60

753 Ezer Weizman

2006. First Death Anniv of Ezer Weizman (president 1993–2000).
1774 **753** 7s.40 multicoloured 2·50 1·80

754 Latrun Memorial

2006. Memorial Day.
1775 **754** 1s.50 multicoloured 45 35

755 Aquilegia

2006. Flowers. Multicoloured.
1776 1s.50 Type **755** 45 35
1777 1s.50 Tulip 45 35

756 Uranus

2006. Solar System. Jerusalem 2006 National Stamp Exhibition. Multicoloured. Ordinary or self adhesive gum.
1778 2s.50 Type **756** 75 60
1779 2s.50 Saturn 75 60
1780 2s.50 Jupiter 75 60
1781 2s.50 Neptune and Pluto 75 60
1782 2s.50 Earth and Mars 75 60
1783 2s.50 Mercury and Venus 75 60

757 Symbols of Art and Science

2006. 50th Anniv of Tel Aviv University.
1790 **757** 3s.60 multicoloured 1·30 90

758 Postal Emblem

2006. Israeli Post. Sheet 92×67 mm. Imperf.
MS1791 **758** 5s.90 multicoloured 3·00 3·00

759 Mosaic

2006. Third-century Mosaic, Megiddo. Jerusalem 2006 National Stamp Exhibition. Sheet 62×74 mm.
MS1792 **759** 10s. multicoloured 6·00 6·00

760 Jacob Saul Eliachar

2006. Rabbis. Multicoloured.
1793 1s.50 Type **760** 45 35
1794 2s.20 Samuel Salant 65 45
1795 2s.40 Jacob Meir 70 55

761 Moroccan Khamsa

2006. Khamsa (protective amulets). Multicoloured.
1796 1s.50 Type **761** 45 35
1797 2s.50 Tunisian 75 60
1798 7s.40 Iranian 2·50 1·80

762 Rabbis, Children and Star of David

2006. Centenary of Religious Zionist Education.
1799 **762** 3s.60 multicoloured 1·30 90

2006. Mishnah (laws). As T **741**. Multicoloured.
1800 1s.50 Bull (Order of Nezikin) 45 35
1801 2s.20 Pigeon (Order of Kodashim) 65 45
1802 2s.40 Hand washing vessel (Order of Tohorot) 70 55

763 Man on Wheel

2006. Centenary of Bezalel Academy of Arts and Design.
1803 **763** 2s.50 emerald 75 60
1804 **763** 2s.50 ultramarine 75 60
1805 **763** 2s.50 orange 75 60

764 Abba Eban

2006. Abba Eban (politician and diplomat) Commemoration.
1806 **764** 7s.30 multicoloured 2·75 2·00

765 *Coriandrum sativum*

2006. Medicinal Plants. Multicoloured.
1807 1s.50 Type **765** 50 40
1808 2s.50 *Micromeria fructicosa* 85 65
1809 3s.30 *Mentha piperita* 1·30 90

766 Oriental Style Fabric, 1882—1948

2006. Fashion in Israel. Designs showing fabric. Multicoloured.
1810 1s.50 Type **766** 50 40
1811 2s.50 Ethnic style, 1948–73 85 65
1812 3s.30 International style, 1973–90 1·30 90
1813 7s.30 Technological style, 1990—2006 2·75 2·20

767 Atlit

2006. Crusader Sites in Israel. Multicoloured.
1814 2s.50 Type **767** 85 65
1815 2s.50 Caesarea 85 65
1816 2s.50 Montfort 85 65
1817 2s.50 Belvoir 85 65

768 Lazarus Ludwig Zamenhof (creator)

2006. 120th Anniv of Esperanto (international constructed language).
1818 **768** 3s.30 multicoloured 1·00 90

769 Ma Pit'om

2007. 40th Anniv of Educational Television. Multicoloured. Ordinary or self-adhesive gum.
1819 2s.50 Type **769** 85 65
1820 2s.50 Krovim 65 65
1821 2s.50 No Secrets 65 65

770 Negev

2007. Development of Negev and Galilee. Multicoloured.
1825 2s.50 Type **770** 85 65
1826 3s.30 Galilee 1·30 90

771 Physical Education in Schools

2007. Physical Education and Sport in Israel. Multicoloured.
1827 2s.90 Type **771** 1·00 80
1828 3s.00 Wingate Institute for Sport 1·10 85
1829 7s.30 Sport for All 2·75 2·20

772 Givati Brigade Memorial

2007. Memorial Day.
1830 **772** 1s.50 multicoloured 50 40

773 Founding Members

2007. 120th Anniv of Neve-Tzedek. Sheet 125×72 mm containing T **773** and similar vert designs. Multicoloured.
MS1831 2s.20 Type **773**; 3s.30 Neve-Tzedek; 5s.80 Intellectuals 6·00 6·00

774 Scouts

2007. Centenary of Scouting.
1832 **774** 2s.50 multicoloured 85 65

775 Sederot (southern Israel)

2007. Urban Development in Israel. Multicoloured.
1833 2s.50 Type **775** 85 65
1834 3s.30 Aqiva (central Israel) 1·30 90
1835 7s.30 Migdal Ha'emeq (northern Israel) 2·75 2·20

776 Circle of Stylized Figures

2007. 40th Anniv of Reunification of Jerusalem.
1836 **776** 1s.50 multicoloured 50 40

777 Figure and Jigsaw

2007. Volunteer Organizations.
1837 **777** 1s.50 multicoloured 50 40

778 Ballet Dancers

2007. Dance. Multicoloured.

1838	2s.20 Type **778**		70	50
1839	2s.20 Ethnic		70	50
1840	2s.20 Folk		70	50
1841	2s.20 Modern		70	50

779 Prison Officers

2007. National Prison Service.

1842	**779**	2s.50 multicoloured	85	65

780 Dining Hall, Knights Hospitaller's Compound, Acre

2007. UNESCO World Heritage Sites. Multicoloured.

1843	3s.30 Type **780**		1·30	90
1844	5s. Zina Dizengoff Circle, Tel Aviv		1·50	1·10
1845	5s.80 Mosaic floor, Western Palace, Masada		2·00	1·50

781 Beach and 'Israel' (in Hebrew)

2007. Personalised Stamp. No value expressed.

1846	**781**	(1s.50) multicoloured	50	40

782 Jael (killed Sisera to deliver Israel from the troops of King Jabin.)

2007. Women from the Bible. Multicoloured.

1847	1s.50 Type **782**		50	40
1848	2s.20 Esther (risked her life to save her adoptive father and the Jewish people)		70	50
1849	2s.40 Miriam (sister of Moses)		80	60

783 Horsemen

2007. Centenary of Hashomer (The Watchmen) (early Jewish defence organization).

1850	**783**	3s.30 multicoloured	1·20	90

784 Soldiers and Reservists

2007. National Reserve Force.

1851	**784**	7s.30 multicoloured	2·75	2·20

785 Rabbi Chalom Messas

2007. Rabbi Chalom Messas (Moroccan Jewish Halachic scholar) Commemoration.

1852	**785**	7s.30 multicoloured	2·75	2·20

786 Zina Dizengff Circle (As No. 1844)

2007. Centenary (2009) of Tel Aviv. Sheet 96×70.

MS1853	10s. multicoloured		6·00	6·00

787 Bay Leaves

2007. Herbs. Multicoloured.

1854	1s.55 Type **786**		50	40
1855	2s.25 Wild thyme		75	55

788 Mother and Child

2007. Family Love. Multicoloured.

1856	1s.55 Type **788**		50	40
1857	2s.25 Brother and sister		70	50
1858	3s.55 Father and child		1·40	1·00

789 Otter, Catfish and Cranes

2007. Hula Nature Reserve. Multicoloured. Ordinary or self-adhesive gum.

1859	2s.25 Type **789**		70	50
1860	2s.25 Terrapins, iris and pelicans		70	50
1861	2s.25 Water buffalo, duck, warbler and jungle cat		70	50

Nos. 1859/61 were issued together, *se-tenant*, forming a composite design.

790 Dove

2007. Noah's Ark. Sheet 159×93 mm containing T **790** and similar horiz designs. Multicoloured.

MS1865 2s.25×6, Type **790**; Noah, family, Ark and animals; Elephants; Peacocks, bears and tiger; Lions and wolves; Wolf, leopards and kangaroos ...... 6·75 6·75

The stamps and margins of **MS**1865 form a composite design of the Ark and animals on dry land.

791 1927 Western Electric Projector, Pianist and Screen showing The Jazz Singer

2007. Stamp Day. Israeli Cinema. Multicoloured.

1866	4s.50 Type **791**		1·50	1·10

2007.

1867	4s.60 1937 BTH projector and wide-screen showing The Robe		1·50	1·10

792 Rabbi Itzhak Kaduri

2007. Rabbi Itzhak Kaduri Commemoration.

1868	**792**	8s.15 multicoloured	3·00	2·40

793 Israel Rokach

2008. Israel Rokach (mayor of Tel Aviv 1936–1953) Commemoration.

1869	**793**	2s.25 multicoloured	70	50

794 'Shema Servant of Jeroboam' Seal and Tel Hazor ('The Biblical Tels')

2008. World Heritage Sites. Multicoloured.

1870	2s.25 Type **794**		70	50
1871	3s.40 Camel figurine and Nabatean temple ('The Incense Route')		1·30	90

795 Members of Ahuzat-Bayit Association

2008. Ahuzat-Bayit Land Lottery (the founding of Tel Aviv).

1872	**795**	4s.50 multicoloured	1·50	1·20

796 Barbed Wire becoming Flowers

2008. International Holocaust Remembrance Day.

1873	**796**	4s.60 multicoloured	1·50	1·20

797 Symbols of Water

2008. 70th Anniv of Mekorot–National Water System.

1874	**797**	5s.80 multicoloured	2·00	1·50

798 Akiva Weiss

2008. 140th Birth Anniv of Akiva Aryeh Weiss (chairman of Ahuzat–Bayit association).

1875	**798**	8s.15 multicoloured	3·00	2·40

799 Fireworks and Emblem

2008. 60th Anniv of Independence.

1876	**799**	1s.55 multicoloured	50	40

800 Srulik (created by Dosh (cartoonist))

2008. The Israeli. Multicoloured. Ordinary or self-adhesive gum.

1877	(1s.55) Type **800**		50	40

801 Hemerocallis Flower

2008. Memorial Day.

1879	**801**	1s.55 multicoloured	50	40

802 Women and Corn (Paul Kor) (1952)

2008. Independence Day Posters. Multicoloured.

1880	2s.55 Type **802**		85	65
1881	2s.55 Heart as Landscape (Hila Biran) (2006)		85	65
1882	2s.55 Boy watering flowers (Amram Prat) (1965)		85	65
1883	2s.55 Star of David as ship containing immigrants (Assaf Berg) (1989)		85	65
1884	2s.55 Lions supporting tulips as menorah (Kopel Gurwin) (1968)		85	65
1885	2s.55 Landscape with steeples, mosques, synagogues and water towers (Assaf Berg) (1979)		85	65

803 Israeli Flag and World Map as Clasped Hands

2008. 50th Anniv of Export Institute.

1886	**803**	2s.80 multicoloured	1·00	80

804 Rose

2008. Flowers. Multicoloured.

1887	1s.55 Type **804**		50	40
1888	1s.55 Cyclamen persicum		50	40

Nos. 1887/8 were impregnated with floral scent.

805 Emblem

2008. 120th Anniv of 'Hatikva' (hope) (song now national anthem). Sheet 140×85 mm.
MS1889 **805** 110s. multicoloured   7·25   7·25

806 Girl with Telescope (Israel's 60th) (Daniel Hazan)

2008. 60th Anniv of Independence. Children's Drawings. Multicoloured.
1890   2s.25 Type **806**   70   50
1891   2s.25 Script (Israel is my Home) (Yuval Sulema and Eden Vilker)   70   50
1892   2s.25 House and script (I Love Israel) (Etai Epstein)   70   50

2008. Hula Nature Reserve. Children's self-adhesive stamps. As Type **789**. Multicoloured.
1892a   2s.25 As No. 1861 (water buffalo)   70   50
1892b   2s.25 As No. 1859 (otter)   70   50
1892c   2s.25 As No. 1860 (terrapins)   70   50

2008. Noah's Ark. Children's self-adhesive stamps. As Type **790**. Multicoloured.
1892d   2s.25 As Type **790**   70   50
1892e   2s.25 Noah, family, Ark and animals   70   50
1892f   2s.25 Elephants   70   50
1892g   2s.25 Peacocks, bears and tiger   70   50
1892h   2s.25 Lions and wolves   70   50
1892i   2s.25 Wolf, leopards and kangaroos   70   50

807 First Concert

2008. Centenary of Tel-Aviv (2009). Sheet 150×85 mm containing T **807** and similar horiz designs showing drawings of Ahuzat Bayit (Tel-Aviv) by Nahum Gutman.
MS1893 3s.50 Type **807**; 4s.50 First Lamp Post; 5s.50 Dr Hisin (physician) riding his donkey   8·50   8·50

808 Circle of Stylized Figures (As Type **776**)

2008. Jerusalem of Gold (song by Naomi Shemer). Sheet 110×70 mm.
MS1894 **808** 18s. multicoloured   11·00   11·00

809 Seashore, Neve Dekalim, Greenhouses, Tomatoes and Children

2008. Gush Katif.
1895   **809** 1s.55 multicoloured   50   40

810 Swimming

2008. Olympic Games, Beijing. Multicoloured.
1896   1s.55 Type **810**   50   40
1897   1s.55 Rhythmic gymnastics   50   40
1898   2s.25 Tennis   70   50
1899   2s.25 Sailing, Laser Radial   70   50

811 Capernaum-Tabgha Promenade, Sea of Galilee

2008. Promenades. Multicoloured.
1900   4s.50 Type **811**   1·50   1·10
1901   4s.60 Armon Hanatziv Promenade, Jerusalem   1·50   1·10
1902   8s.15 Rishom Promenade, Netanya   3·00   2·40

812 *Artemisia arborescens*

2008. Herbs. Multicoloured.
(a) Ordinary gum
1903   1s.60 Type **812**   1·00   75
1904   (2s.90) *Salvia fruticosa*   1·50   1·10
(b) Size 24×18 mm. Self-adhesive
1905   (2s.90) As No. 1904   1·50   1·10

813 Aden

2008. Torah Crowns. Designs showing crowns. Multicoloured.
1906   1s.60 Type **813**   55   45
1907   3s.80 Turkey   1·50   1·10
1908   3s.80 Poland   1·50   1·10

814 Rabbi Samuel Mohilewer

2008. Pioneers of Zionism. Multicoloured.
1909   2s.30 Type **814**   75   55
1910   8s.50 Rabbi Zevi Hirsch Kalischer   3·25   2·50

815 Air France DC3, Envelope and Haifa

2008. 60th Anniv of France—Israel Relations. 60th Anniv of First Flight from Israel to France. Multicoloured.
1911   1s.60 Type **1765**   55   45
1912   3s.80 Paris, envelope and aircraft   1·50   1·10
Stamps of a similar design were issued by France.

816 Families and Calculations

2008. 2008 Census.
1913   **816** 1s.60 multicoloured   55   45

817 Bar Kokhba Letter

2008. Stamp Day. Ancient Letters. Multicoloured.
1914   1s.60 Type **817**   55   45
1915   2s.30 Lachish letter   75   55
1916   8s.50 Letter from Ugarit   3·25   2·50

818 Microphone

2008. 50th (2010) Anniv of Galei Zahal (IDF Broadcasting Service).
1917   **818** 2s.30 multicoloured   75   55

819 Young People enclosed in Frame

2008. Taglit–Birthright Israel (young adults educational tour of Israel).
1918   **819** 5s.60 multicoloured   2·00   1·50

819a Menorah

2009. Menorah. Self-adhesive.
1918a   **819a** 30a. olive-brown   25   15
1918b   **819a** 50a. brown-olive   45   35
1918c   **819a** 1s. deep reddish violet   90   70
See also 1953a and Nos. 1623 etc

820 Grapes

2009. Fruit. No Value Expressed. Multicoloured.
1919   (1s.60) Type **820**   55   45
1920   (1s.60) Lemon   55   45
1921   (1s.60) Avocado   55   45
1922   (1s.60) Orange   55   45
1923   (1s.60) Pomegranate   55   45

821 Coastal Scenes

2009. Centenary of Tel Aviv. Multicoloured.
1924   1s.60 Type **821**   55   45
1925   2s.30 White City (World Heritage Site of Bauhaus style buildings)   75   55
1926   3s.80 Parks and gardens   1·50   1·10

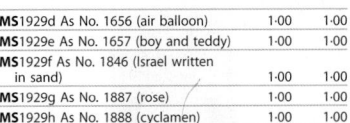

822 Mountain Biking

2009. Extreme Sports. Multicoloured.
1927   4s.40 Type **822**   1·60   1·30
1928   5s.40 Sky diving   2·00   1·60
1929   5s.60 Surfing   2·30   1·80

2009. Children's Sheets. Eight sheets, each 148×200 mm containing various vert designs.
MS1929a As No. 1645 (open box)   1·00   1·00
MS1929b As No. 1646 (boy growing heart)   1·00   1·00
MS1929c As No. 1655 (flowers)   1·00   1·00
MS1929d As No. 1656 (air balloon)   1·00   1·00
MS1929e As No. 1657 (boy and teddy)   1·00   1·00
MS1929f As No. 1846 (Israel written in sand)   1·00   1·00
MS1929g As No. 1887 (rose)   1·00   1·00
MS1929h As No. 1888 (cyclamen)   1·00   1·00

823 Yossi Banai

2009. Israeli Music. Multicoloured.
1930   1s.60 Type **823**   8·75   6·50
1931   1s.60 Meir Ariel   8·75   6·50
1932   1s.60 Sasha Argov   8·75   6·50
1933   1s.60 Zohar Argov   8·75   6·50
1934   1s.60 Naomi Shemer   8·75   6·50
1935   1s.60 Yair Rosenblum   8·75   6·50
1936   1s.60 Ehud Manor   8·75   6·50
1937   1s.60 Arik Lavie   8·75   6·50
1938   1s.60 Uzi Hitman   8·75   6·50
1939   1s.60 Ofra Haza   8·75   6·50
1940   1s.60 Moshe Wilensky   8·75   6·50
1941   1s.60 Shoshana Damari   8·75   6·50
Nos. 1930/3 and 1936/9 were printed se-tenant, each strip or pair sharing a composite background design, surrounding a block of four stamp size labels, each showing part of a disc.

824 Jacob's Staff (tool for mapping stars invented by Gersonides)

2009. Astronomy. Multicoloured.
1942   2s.30 Type **824**   1·20   90
1943   3s.80 Gravitational Lensing   2·10   1·60
1944   8s.50 Laser Interferometer Space Antenna   4·75   3·50

825 Memorial Day Badge

2009. Memorial Day.
1945   **825** 1s.60 multicoloured   1·00   75

826 *Berek Joselewicz* (Juliusz Kossak)

2009. Polish Year in Israel. Sheet 70×90 mm.
MS1946 **826** 6s.10 multicoloured   3·25   3·25

827 Heart

2009. Love. No value expressed
1947   **827** (1s.60) multicoloured   1·00   75

828 Floating Tourist and Ibex

2009. Dead Sea–Lowest Place on Earth.
1948   **828** 2s.30 multicoloured   1·30   1·00

829 Globe as Kettle

2009. Global Warming. Multicoloured.
1949	2s.30 Type **829**		1·20	90
1950	2s.30 Globe melting in frypan (61×31 mm)		1·20	90
1951	2s.30 Solar powered house		1·20	90

830 Athletes

2009. 18th Maccabiah (games).
1952	**830**	5s.60 multicoloured	3·00	2·30

831 Harpist

2009. 50th Anniv of International Harp Contest, Israel.
1953	**831**	8s.50 multicoloured	4·50	3·25

2009. Menorah. Self-adhesive.
1953a	**819a**	40a. slate-green	1·00	1·00

See also Nos. 1918a/c and Nos. 1623 etc.

832 Honeybee and Flower

2009. Honey. Multicoloured.
1954	1s.60 Type **832**		1·30	1·00
1955	4s.60 Honeycomb		2·20	1·70
1956	6s.70 Pouring honey		3·50	2·50

833 Woman with Dog

2009. Animal Assisted Therapy. Multicoloured. (a) Ordinary gum.
1957	2s.40 Type **833**		1·30	95
1958	2s.40 Girl with dolphin		1·30	95
1959	2s.40 Girl with horse		1·30	95

(b) Self-adhesive.
1960	2s.40 As Type **833**		1·30	95
1961	2s.40 As No. 1958		1·30	95
1962	2s.40 As No. 1959		1·30	95

834 Instant Messaging Software

2009. Virtual Communication. Multicoloured.
1963	2s.40 Type **834**		1·30	95
1964	5s.30 USB flash drive		2·75	1·80
1965	6s.50 Voice over internet protocol		3·75	2·75

835 Child playing Doctor

2009. 75th Anniv of Leumit Health Fund.
1966	**835**	8s.80 multicoloured	4·50	3·75

836 Stage

2009. Death Centenary of Avram Goldfaden (founder of first Yiddish theatre (1876), Iasi, Romania).
1967	**836**	4s..60 multicoloured	2·20	1·70

837 Jaffa

2009. Stamp Day. Lighthouses. Multicoloured.
1968	4s.60 Type **837**		2·20	1·70
1969	6s.70 Tel Aviv		3·75	2·75
1970	8s.80 Ashdod		4·75	3·50

838 Amphora

2009. Marine Archaeology. Multicoloured.
1971	2s.40 Type **838**		80	60
1972	2s.40 Figurines		80	60
1973	3s.60 Weaponry		1·60	1·20
1974	5s. Anchors		2·30	1·80

2009. Fruit. As T **820**. No Value Expressed. Multicoloured. Self-adhesive.
1975	(1s.60) As Type **820**		90	65
1976	(1s.60) Lemon (As No. 1920)		90	65
1977	(1s.60) Avocado (As No. 1921)		90	65
1978	(1s.60) Orange (As No. 1922)		90	65
1979	(1s.60) Pomegranate (As No. 1923)		90	65

839 Date Palm and Peppers

2010. 50th Anniv of Settling the Arava.
1980	**839**	1s.60 multicoloured	5·00	3·75

840 *Carduelis carduelis* (gold finch)

2010. Birds. Multicoloured.
1981	2s.40 Type **840**		1·40	1·10
1982	2s.40 *Upupa epops* (hoopoe) (national bird)		1·40	1·10
1983	2s.40 *Prinia gracilis* (graceful prinia)		1·40	1·10

Nos. 1981/3 were printed, *se-tenant*, forming a composite design.

841 Child and Dove

2010. 50th Anniv of Lions, Israel.
1984	**841**	4s.60 multicoloured	1·00	75

842 Child's and Camp Inmate's Arms

2010. Holocaust Remembrance Day.
1985	**842**	6s.70 multicoloured	3·75	2·75

843 Gymnasts and Students, Alliance School, Tehran, May 1936

2010. 150th Anniv of Alliance Iraelite Universelle.
1986	**843**	8s.80 multicoloured	5·00	3·75

844 Flower and Rocks

2010. Memorial Day
1987	**844**	1s.60 multicoloured	95	70

845 Monument, Jerusalem

2010. Living Memorial Plaza (designed by Eliezer Weishoff) (tribute to World Trade Centre victims)
1988	**845**	2s.40 multicoloured	1·40	1·00

846 Drip Irrigation (agriculture)

2010. Expo 2010, Shanghai. Multicoloured.
1989	2s.40 Type **846**		1·40	1·00
1990	2s.40 Intel chips and processors (information technology)		1·40	1·00
1991	2s.40 Pill camera (medicine)		1·40	1·00

847 Theodor Herzl

2010. 150th Birth Anniv of Theodor Binyamin Ze'ev Herzl (zionist pioneer). Multicoloured.
MS1992 3s.70 Type **847**; 4s.60 Builders, houses and tents; 6s.70 Modern Israelis
		25·00	25·00

848 Figures forming Maple Leaf and Star of David

2010. 60th Anniv of Israel–Canada Diplomatic Relations
1993	**848**	4s.60 bright rose-red, blue and dull yellow-green	2·75	2·10

A similar design was issued Canada.

849 Alice in Wonderland

2010. Europa. Multicoloured.
MS1994	4s.60×3, Type **849**; *Peter Pan*; *Gulliver's Travels*		9·00	9·00

850 Oboe and Zorna

2010. Musical Instruments of the Middle East. Multicoloured.
1995	1s.70 Type **850**		85	65
1996	1s.70 Rebab and violin		85	65
1997	1s.70 Darbuka (inscr 'Darbouka') and drum		85	65
1998	1s.70 Qanun and piano		85	65
1999	1s.70 Oud and guitar		85	65

851 Water Tower (security), Orange (agriculture) and Mill Wheel (industry)

2010. Centenary of Kibbutz
2000	**851**	2s.50 multicooured	1·50	1·10

852 Shmulikipod (Shmuel the Hedgehog) (Noga Yudkowitz)

2010. Story Gardens, Holon. Multicoloured.
2001	2s.50 Type **852**		1·40	1·00
2002	2s.50 *Where is Pluto* (Dorit Levinstein)		1·40	1·00
2003	2s.50 *Soul Bird* (David Gerstein)		1·40	1·00

853 Tikun Clali Assembly at Rabi Nachman's Gravesite, Uman, Ukraine

2010. Death Bicentenary of Rabbi Nachman of Breslev (Hasidic philosopher)
2004	**853**	3s.70 multicoloured	2·10	1·60

854 Simon Wiesenthal in Star of David

2010. Simon Wiesenthal (holocaust survivor and pursuer of war criminals) Commemoration
2005	**854**	5s. multicoloured	3·00	2·00

855 Dinghies

2010. International 420 Sailing World Championship, 2010, Haifa
2006	**855**	9s. multicoloured	5·25	4·00

856 Wine Glass ('Happy Holidays')

2010. Greetings Stamps. Multicoloured.

(a) Ordinary gum

2007	(1s.70) As Type **856**		1·00	75
2008	(1s.70) Script and pen ('With compliments')		1·00	75

(b) Booklet stamps. Self-adhesive

2009	(1s.70) As Type **856**		1·00	75
2010	(1s.70) As No. 2008		1·00	75

857 Two Chicks

201. Domestic Animals and their Young. Multicoloured.

2011	1s.70 Type **857**	60	45
2012	1s.70 Hen	60	45
2013	1s.70 Kitten and ball of wool	60	45
2014	1s.70 Cat	60	45
2015	1s.70 Rabbit kitten	60	45
2016	1s.70 Rabbit	60	45

858 Ram's Horn Shofar

2010. Festivals. Shofars. Multicoloured.

2017	1s.70 Type **858**	1·40	1·00
2018	4s.20 Yemeni shofar made from Kudu horn	2·20	1·60
2019	6s.10 Ram's horn shofar (different)	3·25	2·40

859 Clasped Hands

2010. 50th Anniv of Tzevet (Israel Defence Forces Veterans' Association)

2020	**859**	2s.50 multicoloured	1·40	1·00

860. Early Apartments and Windmill

2010. 150th Anniv of First Habitations outside Jerusalem Old City Walls

2021	**860**	3s.70 multicoloured	2·00	1·40

861 Woman with Dog and City Street Scene

2010. Urban Renaissance

2022	**861**	8s.90 multicoloured	5·00	3·75

862 Church of All Nations and Garden of Gethsemane, Jerusalem

2010. Visit of Pope Benedict XVI to Israel, May 2009

2023	**862**	4s.20 multicoloured	2·50	1·90

A stamp of a similar design was issued by Vatican City.

863 Star of David

2010. National Flag

2024	**863**	(1s.70) pale dull ultramarine and black	1·40	1·00

864 Jonah and the Whale (inscr 'Fish')

2010. Bible Stories

2025	1s.70 Type **864**		1·00	75
2026	1s.70 Samson and the Lion		1·00	75
2027	1s.70 Adam and Eve		1·00	75
MS2028	100×70 mm. 6s. Parting of the Red Sea (30×40 mm)		4·75	4·75

865 Farmer picking Sabra Fruit

2010. 50th Anniv of ASIFA (Association Internationale du Film d'Animation), France and 25th Anniv of ASIFA, Israel. Multicoloured.

(a) Sheet stamps. Ordinary gum

2029	1s.70 Type **865**		1·00	75
2030	1s.70 Farmer smiling, grasping fruit, girl with clasped hands		1·00	75
2031	1s.70 Farmer squashing fruit, girl reaching forward		1·00	75
2032	1s.70 Farmer squashing fruit, girl reaching forward		1·00	75
2033	1s.70 Farmer facing forward		1·00	75
2034	1s.70 Farmer facing left, opening hands, girl with hands between gloves		1·00	75
2035	1s.70 Girl taking fruit, farmer with open hands		1·00	75
2036	1s.70 Girl eating fruit		1·00	75
2037	1s.70 Girl with both hands to mouth		1·00	75
2038	1s.70 Girl with both hands to mouth, farmer looking worried		1·00	75
2039	1s.70 Girl with eyes closed, farmer looking worried		1·00	75
2040	1s.70 Girl smiling, farmer looking worried		1·00	75
2041	1s.70 Farmer laughing		1·00	75
2042	1s.70 Farmer looking over left shoulder at sabra cactus		1·00	75
2043	1s.70 Girl with hands behind back, farmer turning towards cactus		1·00	75

(b) Booklet stamps. Self-adhesive.

2044	1.70 As Type **865**		1·00	75
2045	1.70 As No. 2030		1·00	75
2046	1.70 As No. 2031		1·00	75
2047	1.70 As No. 2032		1·00	75
2048	1.70 As No. 2033		1·00	75
2049	1.70 As No. 2034		1·00	75
2050	1.70 As No. 2035		1·00	75
2051	1.70 As No. 2036		1·00	75
2052	1.70 As No. 2037		1·00	75
2053	1.70 As No. 2038		1·00	75
2054	1.70 As No. 2039		1·00	75
2055	1.70 As No. 2040		1·00	75
2056	1.70 As No. 2041		1·00	75
2057	1.70 As No. 2042		1·00	75
2058	1.70 As No. 2043		1·00	75

866 Armon Cinema, Haifa

2010. Stamp Day. Cinemas. Multicoloured.

2059	4s.20 Type **866**		2·20	1·70
2060	9s. Zion Cinema, Jerusalem		5·00	4·25

867 Ubiquitin (protein destructor) (Aaron Ciechanover, Avram Hershko and Irwin Rose's Nobel Prize in Chemistry, 2004)

2011. International Year of Chemistry. Multicoloured.

2061	4s.20 Type **867**		2·00	1·40
2062	6s.10 Ribosome (protein constructor) (Venkatraman Ramakrishnan, Thomas A. Steitz and Ada E. Yonath's Nobel Prize in Chemistry, 2009)		3·25	2·50

868 Leopard

2011. Endangered Species. Persian Leopard (*Panthera pardus saxicolor*). Multicoloured.

2063	1s.70 Type **868**		1·00	75
2064	1s.70 Leaping		1·00	75
2065	1s.70 Drinking		1·00	75
2066	1s.70 Mother and cub		1·00	75

869 Ceasarea

2011. Herod's Building Projects. Multicoloured.

2067	1s.70 Type **869**		1·00	75
2068	1s.70 Masada		1·00	75
2069	2s.50 Jerusalem		1·50	1·00
2070	2s.50 Herodian		1·50	1·00

870 Plant with Hebrew Language as Roots and Soil

2011. Hebrew Language

2071	**870**	3s.70 multicoloured	1·60	1·20

871 Baby and Laptop showing Health Care Providers

2011. Centenary of Clalit Health Services

2072	**871**	9s. multicoloured	5·50	4·25

872 Papilio machaon syriacus

2011. Butterflies. Multicoloured.

(a) Ordinary gum

2073	(1s.70) Type **872**		1·00	75
2074	(1s.70) Vanessa atalanta		1·00	75
2075	(1s.70) Anaphaeis aurota		1·00	75
2076	(1s.70) Apharitis acamas		1·00	75
2077	(1s.70) Danaus chrysippus		1·00	75

2078	(1s.70) Polyommatus icarus zelleri		1·00	75

(b) Self-adhesive

2078a	(1s.70) As Type **872**		1·00	75
2078b	(1s.70) Vanessa atalanta		1·00	75
2078c	(1s.70) Anaphaeis aurota		1·00	75
2078d	(1s.70) Apharitis acamas		1·00	75
2078e	(1s.70) Danaus chrysippus		1·00	75
2078f	(1s.70) Polyommatus icarus zelleri		1·00	75

873 Crowd

2011. Aliyah of Ethiopian Jewry

2079	**873**	2s.50 multicoloured	1·50	1·00

874 Country Road

2011. Memorial Day

2080	**874**	4s.20 multicoloured	2·20	1·70

875 Sea of Galilee

2011. Tourism. Multicoloured.

2081	4s.20 Type **875**		2·20	1·70
2082	6s. Tower and fort, Jerusalem		3·00	2·75
2083	6s.10 Fish (Red Sea)		3·25	3·00

876 Stylised Figures circling Globe

2011. 50th Anniv of Mount Carmel Training Centre, Haifa

2084	**876**	5s. multicoloured	2·30	1·80

877 Ephraim Katzir

2011. Ephraim Katzir (Ephraim Katchalski) (president 1973–1978, biophysicist and politician) Commemoration

2085	**877**	9s. multicoloured	5·50	4·25

878 Rabbi Goren

2011. Rabbi Shlomo Goren (scholar and soldier) Commemoration

2086	**878**	1s.70 multicoloured	1·00	75

879 Sea of Galilee Beach

2011. Tourism. Beaches. Multicoloured.

2087	1s.70 Type **879**		1·00	75
2088	1s.70 Sea of Galilee beach, right		1·00	75
2089	1s.70 Caesarea beach, left		1·00	75
2090	1s.70 Caesarea beach, right		1·00	75
2091	1s.70 Tel-Aviv beach, left		1·00	75
2092	1s.70 Tel-Aviv beach, right		1·00	75
2093	1s.70 Dead Sea beach, left		1·00	75

2094	1s.70 Dead Sea beach, right		1·00	75
2095	1s.70 Eilat beach, left		1·00	75
2096	1s.70 Eilat beach, right		1·00	75

880 Irrigating with Reclaimed Water

2011. Israeli Achievements - Agriculture. Multicoloured.

2097	2s.50 Type **880**		1·50	1·10
2098	2s.50 Improving Tomatoes through Breeding		1·50	1·10
2099	2s.50 Growing Crops with Saline Water		1·50	1·10

881 Clown Doctor and Child

2011. Clown Care (programme in hospitals and medical centres involving visits from specially trained clowns)

2100	**881**	9s. multicoloured	5·00	4·25

882 Arik Einstein and Shalom Hanoch in Concert

883 Player and Album Covers (image scaled to 30% of original size)

2011. Israeli Music - Albums. Multicoloured.

2101	1s.70 Type **882**		1·00	75
2102	1s.70 Shlomo Artzi - *Ways*		1·00	75
2103	1s.70 The Israel Andalusian Orchestra Hosts Jo Amar		1·00	75
2104	1s.70 Kaveret - *Poogy Tales*		1·00	75
2105	1s.70 Lehakat Tsliley Ha'ud		1·00	75
2106	1s.70 Corinne Allal - *Antarctica*		1·00	75
2107	1s.70 Lamb on green field and tree (HaKeves HaShisha Asar)		1·00	75
2108	1s.70 Boy seated on crossing bar watching train pass (Yehuda Poliker - *Ashes and Dust*)		1·00	75
2109	1s.70 Stylized face (Ehud Banai and the Refugees)		1·00	75
2110	1s.70 Yehoram Gaon - *The Middle of the Road*		1·00	75
2111	1s.70 The Doodaim		1·00	75
2112	1s.70 Woman seated outside radio shack (The Idan Raichel Project - *Out of the Depths*)		1·00	75

Nos. 2101/12 from a composite design.

884 Apple and Honey

2011. Festivals. Rosh Hashanah Feast. Multicoloured.

2113	1s.70 Type **884**		1·00	75
2114	4s. Fish head		2·00	1·50
2115	5s.90 Pomegranate		3·00	2·20

885 Tag

2011. Children's Games. Multicoloured.

(a) Ordinary gum

2116	2s.60 Type **885**		1·50	1·00
2117	2s.60 Hopscotch		1·50	1·00
2118	2s.60 Hide and seek		1·50	1·00

(b) Self-adhesive

2119	2s.60 As Type **885**		1·50	1·00
2120	2s.60 As No. 2117		1·50	1·00
2121	2s.60 As No. 2118		1·50	1·00

886 Emblem

2011. Israel - Organisation for Economic Co-operation and Development (OECD) Member

2122	**886**	9s.30 multicoloured	5·75	4·50

887 Avi Cohen

2011. Israeli Football Legends. Multicoloured.

2123	1s.70 Type **887** (Maccabi Tel Aviv, Liverpool and national team player)		1·00	75
2124	1s.70 Nahum Stelmach (Hapoel Petach Tikva player and national team player and captain)		1·00	75
2125	1s.70 Eli Fuchs (Maccabi Tel Aviv player and national team player and captain)		1·00	75
2126	1s.70 Natan Panz (Maccabi Tel Aviv, Beitar and national team player)		1·00	75
2127	1s.70 Avi Ran (Maccabi Haifa and national team goalkeeper)		1·00	75
2128	1s.70 Menachem Ashkenazi (international referee)		1·00	75
2129	1s.70 Jerry Beit Halevi (Maccabi Tel Aviv player and manager)		1·00	75
2130	1s.70 Shmuel Ben-Dror (Maccabi Avshalom Petach Tikva player and captain of national team)		1·00	75
2131	1s.70 Ya'akov Grundman (Bnei Yehuda Tel Aviv player and national team player and manager)		1·00	75
2132	1s.70 Ya'akov Hodorov (Hapoel Tel Aviv and national team goalkeeper)		1·00	75

888 Hartmann 2-8-2 Steam Engine and Train in Jezreel Valley

2011. The Valley Railway (Rakevet HaEmek) (Hebrew nickname for Haifa branch line of Hijaz Railway)

2133	**888**	2s.60 multicoloured	1·50	1·00

889 Love Message on Stylized Tree

2011. Rescue Forces.

2134	**889**	3s.90 scarlet and apple-green	1·60	1·20

890 '75' and Violin

2011. 75th Anniv of Israel Philharmonic Orchestra

2135	**890**	4s. multicoloured	1·75	1·20

891 Script

2012. Death Bicentenary of Rabbi Shneur Zalman of Liadi (founder of Chabad Hasidism and a leader of Czarist Russia's Jewish community)

2136	**891**	1s.70 multicoloured	1·00	75

892 Candle

2012. In Memory. No Value Expressed

2137	**892**	(1s.70) multicoloured	1·00	75

893 'Nano-parachute' (detector of airborne toxins) and Schematic of Building Façade

2012. Centenary of Technion - Israel Institute of Technology

2138	**893**	2s.60 multicoloured	1·50	1·00

894 Reuven – Carnelian

2012. Jewels of the Choshen - The High Priest's Breastplate (1st issue). Multicoloured.

2139	2s.60 Type **894**		1·50	1·00
2140	2s.60 Shimon - Topaz		1·50	1·00
2141	2s.60 Levi - Emerald		1·50	1·00
2142	2s.60 Yehuda - Turquoise		1·50	1·00

895 Bracha Zefira (singer)

2012. Pioneering Women. Multicoloured.

2143	4s. Type **895**		2·10	1·50
2144	5s.90 Batia Makov (pioneer of the First Aliyah)		2·40	2·00

896 Accusing Finger of Gideon Hausner (Attorney General and trial prosecutor) (Miron Sima)

2012. 50th Anniv of Execution of Adolf Eichman (war criminal)

2145	**896**	9s.30 multicoloured	5·20	4·00

897 Waxwing

2012. Peace Birds. 20th Anniv of Israel - China Diplomatic Relations. Multicoloured.

2146	2s. Type **897**		1·10	90
2147	3s. White dove		2·00	1·70

898 Child and Balloon (image from song Mi Shechalam (He Who Dreamt) (by Didi Menusiand Yochanan Zarai)

2012. Memorial Day

2148	**898**	1s.70 multicoloured	1·00	75

899 Girl with Balloon (*A Tale of Five Balloons* (Miriam Roth and Ora Eyal))

2012. Children's Books. Multicoloured.

2149	2s. Type **899**		1·10	90
2150	2s. Whale and script (*Caspion the Little Fish* (Paul Kor))		1·10	90
2151	2s. *Itamar Walks on Walls* (David Grossman and Ora Eyal)		1·10	90
2152	2s. *The Lion that Loved Strawberries* (Tirtza Atar and Danny Kerman)		1·10	90
2153	2s. Lion and giraffe (*Raspberry Juice* (Haya Shenhav and Tamara Rikman))		1·10	90
2154	2s. *The Absent-Minded Guy from Kefar Azar* (Leah Goldberg)		1·10	90
2155	2s. Children eating sweetcorn (*Hot Sweet Corn* (Miriam Roth and Ora Eyal))		1·10	90
2156	2s. *Come to Me, Nice Butterfly* (Fania Bergstein and Ilse Kantor)		1·10	90

900 Hehalutz, 1919, Jaffa

2012. Renaissance of Jewish Seamanship. Multicoloured.

2157	3s. Type **900**		2·00	1·70
2158	3s. *Sarah A*, 1936, Haifa		2·00	1·70
2159	3s. *Har Zion*, 1936, Tel-Aviv		2·00	1·70

2012. Jewels of the Choshen - The High Priest's Breastplate (2nd issue). Multicoloured.

2160	3s. Issachar - Lazurite		2·00	1·70
2161	3s. Zevulun - Quartz		2·00	1·70
2162	3s. Dan - Zircon		2·00	1·70
2163	3s. Naftali - Amethyst		2·00	1·70

901 The Western Wall

2012. Chain of Generations Visitor Centre, Western Wall

2164	**901**	9s.30 multicoloured	6·00	4·50

902 High Jump

2012. Olympic Games, London. Multicoloured.

2165	2s. Type **902**		1·10	90
2166	2s. Gymnastics		1·10	90

2167	4s.50 Taekwondo	2·30	1·70

2012. Jewels of the Choshen - The High Priest's Breastplate (3rd issue). Multicoloured.

2168	3s. Gad - Agate	2·00	1·70
2169	3s. Asher - Aquamarine	2·00	1·70
2170	3s. Yosef - Onyx	2·00	1·70
2171	3s. Binyamin - Jasper	2·00	1·70

903 Teddy Kollek

2012. Teddy Kollek (Mayor of Jerusalem (1965–1993)) Commemoration

2172	**903** 9s.40 multicoloured	6·00	4·50

904 Tashlikh, Rosh Hashanah

2012. Festivals. The Month of Tishrei. Multicoloured.

2173	2s. Type **904**	1·10	85
2174	4s.20 Kol Nidrei Prayer, Yom Kippur	1·85	1·60
2175	6s.20 Bearing the Lulav, Sukkot	2·75	2·50

905 Rosh Hanika

2012. Tourism. Visit Israel. Multicoloured.

(a) Sheet stamps. Ordinary gum

2176	3s. Type **905**	1·60	1·20
2177	3s. Old Jaffa, port and Tel-Aviv	1·60	1·20
2178	3s. Solomon's Pillars, Timna	1·60	1·20

(b) Booklet stamps. Self-adhesive

2179	3s. As Type **905**	1·60	1·20
2180	3s. As No. 2177	1·60	1·20
2181	3s. As No. 2178	1·60	1·20

906 Mount Everest and Dead Sea

2012. Highest and Lowest Places on Earth. Israel - Nepal Diplomatic Relations

2182	**906** 5s. multicoloured	2·30	1·80

907 Anniversary Emblem

2012. 50th Anniv of International Police Association, Israel

2183	**907** 4s.20 multicoloured	1·85	1·60

908 Hands moulding Star of David

2012. Senior Citizens' Contribution to Israel

2184	**908** 9s.40 multicoloured	5·25	4·50

909 Symbols of Organization

2012. Centenary of Hadassah - Women's Zionist Organization of America

2185	**909** 6s.20 multicoloured	2·75	2·50

910 Hunukkah

2012. Festivals of Lights. 20th Anniv of Israel - India Diplomatic Relations. Multicoloured.

2186	2s. Type **910**	1·10	85
2187	2s. Deepavali	1·10	85

911 Mediterranean Spur-thighed Tortoise (*Testudo graeca*)

2012. Wildlife Conservation. Israeli Wildlife Hospital. Multicoloured.

2188	3s. Type **911**	1·60	1·20
2189	3s. Mountain Gazelle fawn (*Gazella gazella gazella*)	1·60	1·20
2190	3s. Imperial Eagle (*Aquila heliaca*)	1·60	1·20

912 Off-shore Drilling Platform

2012. Energy Resources in Israel

2191	**912** 4s.20 multicoloured	1·85	1·60

913 High Priest wearing Breastplate

2012. Jewels of the Choshen - The High Priest's Breastplate (4th issue). Sheet 85×150 mm

MS2192	**913** 5s. multicoloured	3·00	3·00

914 Bible and National Flag

2012. 50th Anniv of Koren Jerusalem Bible

2193	**914** 9s.50 multicoloured	5·25	4·50

915 Light Pink Duplex Bloom

2013. Gerberas. Multicoloured.

(a) Ordinary gum

2194	20a. Type **915**	20	10
2195	30a. Orange crested bloom	30	20
2196	40a. White single (flower structure) bloom	40	30
2197	50a. Yellow single (flower structure) bloom	50	40
2198	1s. Dark pink duplex bloom	75	45

(b) Self-adhesive

2199	20a. As Type **915**	20	10
2200	50a. As No. 2197	50	40
2201	1s. As No. 2198	75	45

916 Symbols of Arad

2013. 50th Anniv of Arad

2202	**916** 2s. multicoloured	1·10	85

917 Man-made Lake

2013. Water - The Source of Life

2203	**917** 3s. multicoloured	1·50	1·00

918 School Buildings

2013. Centenary of Hebrew Reali School

2204	**918** 4s.20 multicoloured	1·85	1·60

919 Symbols of International Movement

2013. Israel Customs Directorate

2205	**919** 9s.50 multicoloured	5·25	4·50

920 *Torgos tracheliotos* (Lappet-faced Vulture) and *Neophron percnopterus* (Egyptian Vulture)

2013. Taking Vultures under our Wing

2206	**920** 3s. multicoloured	1·50	1·00

921 Service Personnel (illustrating *The Silver Platter* (poem by Natan Alterman))

2013. Memorial Day - The Silver Platter

2207	**921** 2s. multicoloured	1·10	85

2013. Taking Vultures under our Wing (2nd issue). Multicoloured.

2208	3s. *Gyps fulvus* (Griffon Vulture)	1·50	1·00
2209	3s. *Gypaetus barbatus* (Bearded Vulture)	1·50	1·00

922 Percutaneous Heart Valve (transcatheter aortic valve replacement (TAVR))

2013. Israeli Achievements - Cardiology. Multicoloured.

2210	3s. Type **922**	1·50	1·10
2211	4s.20 Stent	1·85	1·60
2212	5s. Implantable defibrillator	2·30	1·80

923 Pawel Frenkel

2013. Flags Over the Ghetto - 70th Anniv of Warsaw Uprising

2213	**923** 9s.50 multicoloured	5·25	4·50

924 Horseman (statue, Australian Soldier Park)

2013. Australian Light Horse Brigade and Battle of Beersheba, 1917. 95th Anniv of Israel - Australia Relations. Multicoloured.

2214	2s. Type **924**	1·10	85
2215	6s.10 Bridge and horsemen (re-enactment of battle)	2·75	2·50

925 Hang-glider

2013. Israel National Trail. Multicoloured.

MS2216	2s.x10, Type **925**; Deer sniffing girl's nose; Windsurfer and Scoutmaster; Picnic, father and son hiking and cable car; Woman leaning against ruin and quad bike; Abseiling, reading, cliffs and camping; Cyclist and pedalo; Ostrich, ladder, girl in tree and antelope; Dolphin and tower; Off-road vehicle, dog and sitting under palm trees	10·00	10·00

926 Austrian Post Carriage and Jaffa Gate, Jerusalem

2013. Postal Vehicles in Eretz Israel. Multicoloured.

MS2217	2s. Type **926**; 3s. Mail sorting train car, operated by Mandatory Railway; 5s. 'The Red Van' (early post van)	7·00	7·00

927 Blue Shirt with White String (Hashomer Hatzair uniform) and '100'

2013. Centenary of Hashomer Hatzair Movement (first Zionist youth movement)

2218	**927** 3s. multicoloured	1·00	

928 Athletes

2013. 19th Maccabiah (games)

2219	**928** 3s. multicoloured	1·50	1·00

929 Yitzhak Shamir

2013. Yitzhak Shamir (Icchak Jeziernicky) (prime minister 1983/4 and 1986/92) Commemoration

2220	**929**	9s.50 multicoloured	6·00	6·00

930 Dorcas Gazelle (*Gazella dorcas*)

2013. Endangered Species. Animals from Arctic to Desert. Sheet 90×70 mm

MS2221	**930**	7s. multicoloured	4·50	4·50

931 Buba Zehava (Doll)

2013. Israeli Music - Children's Songs. Multicoloured.

2222	2s. Type **931**		1·10	85
2223	2s. I Wanted You To Know		1·10	85
2224	2s. What Do the Does Do?		1·10	85
2225	2s. A Brave Clock		1·10	85
2226	2s. I Am Always Me		1·10	85
2227	2s. Merry Choir		1·10	85
2228	2s. Brave Danny		1·10	85
2229	2s. Horse Rider		1·10	85
2230	2s. My Dad		1·10	85
2231	2s. The Post Van		1·10	85
2232	2s. The Prettiest Girl in Kindergarten		1·10	85
2233	2s. Why Does the Zebra Wear Pajamas?		1·10	85

932 Etrog Box, Bezalel, Jerusalem

2013. Festivals - Etrog (citrus fruit) Boxes. Multicoloured.

2234	2s. Type **932**		1·10	85
2235	3s.90 Shallow oval Etrog box, Austria		1·60	1·20
2236	5s.70 Bird-shaped Etrog box, Iraq		2·50	2·00

933 Young People

2013. 80th Anniv of Betar - World Zionist Youth Movement

2237	**933**	3s.10 multicoloured	1·50	1·00

934 Missiles

2013. Israel Military Industries

2238	**934**	9s.60 multicoloured	5·50	5·00

OFFICIAL STAMPS

כול שרות

(O18)

1951. As Nos. 41 etc, but colours changed. Optd with Type **O18**.

O54	5pr. mauve		25	15
O55	15pr. red		25	15
O56	30pr. blue		40	35
O57	40pr. brown		50	35

POSTAGE DUE STAMPS

דמי דאר

(D3)

1948. As T **1**, optd with Type **D3**.

D10	**1**	3m. orange on yellow	3·75	2·50
D11	**1**	5m. green on yellow	5·25	4·00
D12	**1**	10m. mauve on yellow	13·00	9·00
D13	**1**	20m. blue on yellow	38·00	30·00
D14	**1**	50m. brown on yellow	£140	£110

D9

1949

D27	**D9**	2pr. orange	35	25
D28	**D9**	5pr. violet	60	35
D29	**D9**	10pr. green	60	25
D30	**D9**	20pr. red	70	25
D31	**D9**	30pr. blue	95	45
D32	**D9**	50pr. brown	1·60	1·40

D30

1952

D73	**D30**	5pr. brown	15	10
D74	**D30**	10pr. violet	15	10
D75	**D30**	20pr. purple	30	15
D76	**D30**	30pr. black	15	10
D77	**D30**	40pr. green	15	10
D78	**D30**	50pr. sepia	15	10
D79	**D30**	60pr. violet	15	10
D80	**D30**	100pr. red	30	25
D81	**D30**	250pr. blue	45	25

Pt. 8

ITALIAN COLONIES

100 centesimi = 1 lira

GENERAL ISSUES

1932. As Garibaldi stamps of Italy, but inscr "POSTE COLONIALI ITALIANE".

1	-	10c. green (postage)	4·00	9·25
2	**128**	20c. red	4·00	8·00
3	-	25c. green	4·00	8·00
4	**128**	30c. green	4·00	9·25
5	-	50c. red	4·00	8·00
6	-	75c. red	4·00	14·00
7	-	1l.25 blue	4·00	15·00
8	-	1l.75 +25c. blue	9·25	28·00
9	-	2l.55 +50c. sepia	9·25	40·00
10	-	5l.+1l. blue	9·25	50·00
11	**130**	50c. red (air)	4·75	13·00
12	-	80c. green	5·25	14·00
13	**130**	1l.+25c. sepia	8·75	29·00
14	-	2l.+50c. sepia	8·75	29·00
15	-	5l.+1l. sepia	8·75	37·00

1932. Dante stamps of Italy (colours changed) optd **COLONIE ITALIANE**.

18	-	10c. slate (postage)	1·20	2·30
19	-	15c. sepia	1·20	2·30
20	-	20c. green	1·20	2·30
21	-	25c. green	1·20	2·30
22	-	30c. brown	1·20	2·30
23	-	50c. blue	1·20	1·20
24	-	75c. red	2·30	3·50
25	-	1l.25 blue	2·30	7·00
26	-	1l.75 violet	2·30	11·50
27	-	2l.75 orange	2·30	23·00
28	-	5l.+2l. olive	2·30	29·00
29	**124**	10l.+2l.50 blue	2·30	40·00
30	**125**	50c. slate (air)	2·30	7·00
31	-	1l. blue	2·30	7·00
32	-	3l. green	4·00	14·00
33	-	5l. sepia	4·00	18·00
34	**125**	7l.70 +2l. red	4·00	29·00
35	-	10l.+2l.50 orange	4·00	35·00
36	**127**	100l. sepia and green	24·00	90·00

No. 36 is inscribed instead of overprinted.

9 Ploughing

10 Savoia Marchetti S-55X Flying Boat

1933. 50th Anniv of Foundation of Colony of Eritrea.

37	**9**	10c. brown (postage)	11·50	16·00
38	-	20c. purple	11·50	16·00
39	-	25c. green	11·50	16·00
40	**9**	50c. violet	11·50	16·00
41	-	75c. red	11·50	18·00
42	-	1l.25 blue	11·50	21·00
43	**9**	2l.75 red	20·00	35·00
44	-	5l.+2l. green	35·00	75·00
45	-	10l.+2l. brown	35·00	85·00
46	-	50c. brown (air)	14·50	15·00
47	-	1l. black	14·50	15·00
48	**10**	3l. red	23·00	29·00
49	**10**	5l. brown	23·00	29·00
50	-	7l.70+2l. green	29·00	70·00
51	**10**	10l.+2l.50 blue	29·00	70·00
52	-	50l. violet	29·00	70·00

DESIGNS—VERT: (Postage): 20, 75c., 5l. Camel transport; 25c., 1l.25, 10l. Lioness with star on left shoulder (Arms). HORIZ: (Air): 50c., 1l., 7l. 70, Eagle; 50l. Savoia Marchetti S-55X flying boat over map of Eritrea.

11 Agricultural Implements

13 Macchi Castoldi MC-72 Seaplane

1933. Tenth Anniv of Fascist March on Rome. (a) Postage.

53	**11**	5c. orange	8·75	11·50
54	-	25c. green	8·75	11·50
55	-	50c. violet	8·75	11·50
56	**11**	75c. red	8·75	18·00
57	-	1l.25 blue	8·75	18·00
58	-	1l.75 red	8·75	18·00
59	**11**	2l.75 blue	8·75	28·00
60	-	5l. black	16·00	32·00
61	-	10l. blue	16·00	46·00
62	-	25l. olive	24·00	65·00

DESIGNS—HORIZ: 50c., 1l.75, 10l. Tractor. VERT: 25c., 1l.25, 5l. Arab and camel; 25l. Soldier.

(b) Air.

63	**13**	50c. brown	10·50	14·00
64	-	75c. purple	10·50	14·00
65	**13**	1l. sepia	10·50	14·00
66	-	3l. green	10·50	32·00
67	**13**	10l. violet	10·50	32·00
68	-	12l. blue	10·50	46·00
69	-	20l. green	22·00	55·00
70	-	50l. blue	35·00	55·00

DESIGNS—HORIZ: 75c., 3, 12l. Savoia Marchetti S-71 airplane. VERT: 20l. Pilot swinging propeller; 50l. Propeller.

15

1934. 15th Milan Exhibition.

71	**15**	20c. red	1·50	7·00
72	**15**	30c. green	1·50	7·00
73	**15**	50c. black	1·50	7·00
74	**15**	1l.25 blue	1·50	11·50

16 Hailing Marina Fiat MF.5 Flying Boat

1934. Air. Honouring the Duke of the Abruzzi (explorer).

75	**16**	25l. black	43·00	£160

17 Scoring a Goal

1934. World Football Championship.

76	**17**	10c. green (postage)	40·00	46·00
77	**17**	50c. violet	75·00	46·00
78	**17**	1l.25 blue	75·00	£120
79	-	5l. brown	£100	£325
80	-	10l. blue	£100	£325

DESIGN—VERT: 5, 10l. Fascist salute before kick-off.

18 Marina Fiat MF.5 Flying Boat over Stadium

81	**18**	50c. brown (air)	22·00	46·00
82	**18**	75c. purple	22·00	46·00
83	-	5l. black	70·00	£100
84	-	10l. red	70·00	£100
85	**18**	15l. red	70·00	£100
86	-	25l. green	70·00	£225
87	-	50l. green	70·00	£225

DESIGNS—VERT: 5, 10, 25l. "Saving a goal". HORIZ: 50l. Giant football and Marina Fiat MF.5 flying boat.

EXPRESS STAMPS

1932. Air. As Garibaldi stamps of Italy.

E16	**E131**	2l.25+1l. blk & vio	9·25	29·00
E17	**E131**	4l.50+1l.50 grn & brn	9·25	40·00

Pt. 8

ITALIAN EAST AFRICA

Italian Empire in East Africa comprising Eritrea, Ethiopia and Italian Somaliland, constituted by Royal Decree of 1 June 1936. Occupied by British Forces 1942–43 (see BRITISH OCCUPATION OF ITALIAN COLONIES (MIDDLE EAST FORCES) in Volume 1).

100 centesimi = 1 lira.

1 Grant's Gazelle   **2** R. Nile Statue and Lake Tsana

1938

1	**1**	2c. red	1·70	1·70
2	**A**	5c. brown	1·70	30
3	**B**	7½c. violet	2·30	4·50
4	**2**	10c. brown	4·50	30
5	**C**	15c. green	1·70	90
6	**B**	20c. red	1·70	30
7	**D**	25c. green	3·50	30
8	**1**	30c. brown	3·00	1·20
9	**A**	35c. blue	3·50	9·25
10	**B**	50c. violet	1·20	30
11	**C**	75c. red	3·50	70
12	**D**	1l. green	3·00	30
13	**A**	1l.25 blue	4·00	65
14	**2**	1l.75 orange	35·00	30
15	**A**	2l. red	4·00	70
16	**2**	2l.55 brown	20·00	31·00
17	**1**	3l.70 violet	60·00	70·00
18	**C**	5l. blue	14·50	5·25
19	**A**	10l. red	20·00	21·00
20	**2**	20l. green	38·00	35·00

DESIGN—VERT: A, Italian eagle and Lion of Judah; B, Profile of King Emmanuel III; C, Soldier implanting Fascist emblem. HORIZ: D, Shadows on road.

5 Mussolini Monument and Mt. Amba Aradam

1938. Air.

21	**E**	25c. green	5·75	4·50
22	**5**	50c. brown	90·00	35
23	**F**	60c. red	3·00	11·50
24	**E**	75c. brown	5·75	3·50
25	**G**	1l. blue	1·70	35
26	**5**	1l.50 violet	3·00	1·20
27	**F**	2l. blue	3·00	2·30
28	**E**	3l. red	4·50	9·25
29	**G**	5l. brown	46·00	29·00
30	**5**	10l. purple	14·50	14·00
31	**E**	25l. blue	38·00	35·00

DESIGNS—HORIZ: E, Savoia Marchetti S-73 airplane, rock sculpture of eagle and Mt. Amba Aradam; F, Savoia Marchetti S-73 airplane over Lake Tsana. VERT: G, Bateleur.

9 Statue of Augustus

1938. Birth Bimillenary of Augustus the Great.

36	**9**	5c. brown (postage)	1·20	2·30
37	-	10c. red	1·20	1·70
38	**9**	25c. green	1·20	1·70
39	-	50c. violet	1·20	1·20
40	**9**	75c. red	1·20	4·50
41	-	1l.25 blue	1·20	11·50

DESIGN: 10c., 50c., 1l.25, Statue of Goddess of Abundance.

10 Eagle and Serpent

42	10	50c. brown (air)	1·70	3·50
43	10	1l. violet	1·70	6·00

11 Ethiopian Canoe

1940. Naples Exhibition.

44	11	5c. brown (postage)	60	1·40
45	-	10c. orange	60	1·40
46	-	25c. green	1·70	2·30
47	11	50c. violet	1·70	1·40
48	-	75c. red	1·70	7·00
49	-	1l.25 blue	1·70	7·00
50	-	2l.+75c. red	1·70	20·00

DESIGNS—VERT: 10c, 75c., 2l. Soldier; 25c., 1l.25, Allegory of Italian Conquest of Ethiopia.

51		50c. grey (air)	1·60	5·75
52		1l. violet	1·60	5·75
53		2l.+75c. blue	2·00	
54		5l.+2l. brown	2·00	

DESIGNS—VERT: 50c., 2l. Savoia Marchetti S-66 flying boat over tractor. HORIZ: 1l., 5l. Savoia Marchetti S.M.83 airplane over city.

15 Hitler and Mussolini

1941. Axis Commemoration.

55	15	5c. yellow (postage)	2·30	
56	15	10c. brown	2·30	
57	15	20c. black	4·00	
58	15	25c. green	4·00	
59	15	50c. purple	4·00	
60	15	75c. red	4·00	
61	15	1l.25 blue	4·00	
62	15	1l. blue (air)	£120	
63	15	1l. blue	9·25	

In No. 62 the "l lira" tablet is in the centre; in No. 63 it is in the lower left corner.

EXPRESS LETTER STAMPS

E7 Plough and Native Huts

1938. Air.

E32	E7	2l. blue	8·00	11·50
E33	E7	2l.50 brown	8·00	17·00

E8 King Victor Emmanuel III

1938

E34	E8	1l.25 green	8·00	11·50
E35	E8	2l.50 red (inscr "EX-PRESS")	8·00	23·00

POSTAGE DUE STAMPS

1941. Nos. D395/407 of Italy optd A.O.I.

D64	D141	5c. brown	1·70
D65	D141	10c. blue	1·70
D66	D141	20c. red	3·75
D67	D141	25c. green	3·75
D68	D141	30c. orange	7·50
D69	D141	40c. brown	7·50
D70	D141	50c. violet	7·50
D71	D141	60c. blue	12·50
D72	D142	1l. orange	35·00
D73	D142	2l. green	35·00
D74	D142	5l. violet	60·00
D75	D142	10l. blue	35·00
D76	D142	20l. red	35·00

Pt. 3

ITALIAN OCCUPATION OF CEPHALONIA AND ITHACA

Two of the Greek Ionian Islands off the W. coast of Greece, under Italian occupation in 1941.

100 lepta = 1 drachma.

PRICES. Prices are for unsevered pairs. Single stamps from several pairs are worth 1/3 unused and 1/2 used prices.

1941. Stamps of Greece optd ITALIA Occupazione Militare Italiana isole Cefalonia e Itaca across a pair of stamps. (a) On postage stamps of 1937.

1	86	5l. blue and brown	32·00	32·00
2	-	10l. brown and blue	32·00	32·00
3	-	20l. green and black	32·00	32·00
4	-	40l. black and green	32·00	32·00
5	-	50l. black and brown	32·00	32·00
6	-	80l. brown and violet	46·00	46·00
7	89	1d. green	£450	£300
8	89a	1d.50 green	£225	£130
9	-	2d. blue	35·00	44·00
10	-	5d. red	£120	50·00
11	-	6d. brown	£120	50·00
12	-	7d. brown	£120	50·00
13	89	8d. blue	£300	£140
14	-	10d. brown	£120	60·00
15	-	15d. green	£225	£100
16	-	25d. blue	£300	£150
17	89a	30d. red	£1300	£700

(b) On air stamps of 1938 and 1935.

18	D20	50l. brown (No. 521)	75·00	£200
19	79	1d. red	85·00	£150
20a	-	2d. blue	29·00	46·00
21	-	5d. mauve	60·00	80·00
22	-	7d. blue	70·00	£120
23	-	25d. red	£350	£450
24	-	30d. green	£425	£600
25	-	50d. mauve	£2250	£3250
26a	-	100d. brown	£1400	£2250

(c) On Charity Tax stamps.

27	D20	10l. red (No. C498)	37·00	46·00
28	C96	10l. red	46·00	40·00
29	C96	50l. green (No. C525)	35·00	29·00
30	C96	50l. green (No. C554)	£900	£1000
31	C96	1d. blue (No. C526)	90·00	85·00

Pt. 3

ITALIAN OCCUPATION OF CORFU

One of the Greek Ionian Islands situated off the coast of Albania temporarily occupied by Italy during a dispute with Greece in 1923. For later Occupation Issues see ITALIAN OCCUPATION OF CORFU AND PAXOS below.

100 centesimi = 1 lira.
100 lepta = 1 drachma.

1923. Stamps of Italy optd CORFU.

1	37	5c. green	9·75	10·50
2	37	10c. red	9·75	10·50
3	37	15c. grey	9·75	10·50
4	41	20c. orange	9·75	10·50
5	39	30c. brown	9·75	10·50
6	39	50c. mauve	9·75	10·50
7	39	60c. blue	9·75	10·50
8	34	1l. brown and green	9·75	10·50

1923. Stamps of Italy surch CORFU and value.

9	37	25l. on 10c. red	£100	46·00
10	39	60l. on 25c. blue	29·00	
11	39	70l. on 30c. brown	29·00	
12	39	1d.20 on 50c. mauve	50·00	46·00
13	34	2d.40 on 1l. brown & green	50·00	46·00
14	34	4d.75 on 2l. green & orange	23·00	

Pt. 3

ITALIAN OCCUPATION OF CORFU AND PAXOS

Greek Ionian Islands occupied by Italy in 1941.

100 lepta = 1 drachma.

1941. Stamps of Greece optd CORFU. (a) On postage stamps of 1937.

1	86	5l. blue and brown	7·00	4·50
2	-	10l. brown and blue	3·50	3·50
4	-	20l. green and black	3·50	3·50
5	-	40l. black and green	3·50	4·00
6	-	50l. black and brown	3·50	3·50
7	-	80l. brown and violet	3·50	5·75
8	89	1d. green	15·00	14·00
9	89a	1d.50 green	11·50	11·50
10	-	2d. blue	9·25	6·25
11	89	3d. brown	11·50	9·25

12	-	5d. red	9·25	7·00
13	-	6d. olive	9·25	9·25
14	-	7d. brown	14·00	9·25
15	89	8d. blue	29·00	25·00
16	-	10d. brown	£700	£250
17	-	15d. green	35·00	28·00
18	-	25d. blue	25·00	28·00
19	89a	30d. red	£130	£100
20	89	100d. red	£425	£250

(b) On air stamps of 1938 and 1935.

22	D20	50l. brown (No. 521)	14·00	10·50
23	79	1d. red	£1000	£350
24	79	2d. blue	17·00	7·50
25	79	5d. mauve	21·00	12·50
26	79	7d. blue	21·00	12·50
27	79	10d. brown	£1200	£500
28	79	10d. orange	80·00	50·00
29	79	25d. red	£130	65·00
30	79	30d. green	£160	85·00
31	79	50d. mauve	£140	80·00
32	79	100d. brown	£1700	£850

(c) On Charity Tax stamps of 1939.

33	C96	10l. red	3·00	5·75
34	C96	50l. green	3·50	5·75
35	C96	1d. blue	46·00	35·00

(d) On Postage Due stamps of 1902 and 1913.

D36	D20	10l. red	4·50	4·50
D37	D20	25l. blue	5·75	4·50
D38	D20	80l. purple	£1600	£400
D39	D20	1d. blue	£2250	£900
D40	D20	2d. red	11·50	11·50
D41	D20	5d. blue	29·00	29·00
D42	D20	10d. green	23·00	23·00
D43	D20	15d. brown	29·00	23·00
D44	D20	25d. red	29·00	23·00
D45	D20	50d. orange	29·00	23·00
D46	D20	100d. green	£900	£600

Pt. 3

ITALIAN OCCUPATION OF IONIAN ISLANDS

A group of islands off the W. coast of Greece, placed under the protection of Gt. Britain in 1815 and ceded to Greece in 1864. Under Italian occupation in 1941. For use in all islands except Kithyra.

100 lepta = 1 drachma.

1941. Stamps of Italy optd ISOLE JONIE. (a) On postage stamps of 1929.

1	98	5c. brown	90	3·50
2	-	10c. brown	90	3·50
3	99	20c. red	90	3·50
4	-	25c. green	90	3·50
5	103	30c. brown	90	3·50
6	103	50c. violet	90	3·50
7	-	75c. red	90	3·50
8	-	1l.25 blue	90	5·50

(b) On air stamp of 1930.

9	110	50c. brown	1·20	4·50

(c) On Postage Due stamps of 1934.

D10	D141	10c. brown	2·30	5·75
D11	D141	20c. red	2·30	5·75
D12	D141	30c. orange	2·30	5·75
D13	D142	1l. orange	2·30	5·75

Pt. 8

ITALIAN POST OFFICES IN CHINA

Italian Military Posts in China, including Peking and Tientsin, now closed.

100 centesimi = 1 lira. 100 cents = 1 dollar.

Stamps of Italy overprinted or surcharged.

A. PEKING

1917. Surch PECHINO and value.

1	37	2c. on 5c. green	£225	£170
3	37	4c. on 10c. pink	£450	£275
4	41	6c. on 15c. grey	£900	£575
5	41	8c. on 20c. on 15c. grey	£4500	£2500
6	41	8c. on 20c. orange	£7500	£2750
7	39	20c. on 50c. violet	£46000	£28000
8	34	40c. on 1l. brown and green	£200000	£36000

1917. Optd Pechino.

9	30	1c. brown	19·00	19·00
10	31	2c. brown	19·00	19·00
11	37	5c. green	8·00	16·00
12	37	10c. pink	8·00	16·00
13	41	20c. orange	£200	£160
14	39	25c. blue	8·00	19·00
15	39	50c. violet	8·50	21·00
16	34	1l. brown and green	16·00	35·00
17	34	5l. blue and pink	32·00	50·00
18	34	10l. green and pink	£200	£400

1918. Surch Pechino and value.

19	30	½c. on 1c. brown	£130	£150
20	31	1c. on 2c. brown	7·00	15·00
21	37	2c. on 5c. green	7·00	15·00
22	37	4c. on 10c. pink	7·00	15·00
23	41	8c. on 20c. orange	27·00	25·00
24	39	10c. on 25c. blue	6·50	18·00
25	39	20c. on 50c. violet	16·00	25·00
26	34	40c. on 1l. brown and green	£225	£275
27	34	2 dollari. on 5l. blue and pink	£400	£700
30	34	2 DOLLARI. on 5l. blue and pink	£90000	£65000

EXPRESS LETTER STAMPS

1917. Express Letter stamp optd Pechino or surch 12 CENTS also.

E19	E41	30c. blue and pink	14·00	37·00
E28	E41	12c. on 30c. bl & pink	90·00	£250

POSTAGE DUE STAMPS

1917. Postage Due stamps optd Pechino.

D19	D12	10c. mauve and orange	5·00	14·00
D20	D12	20c. mauve and orange	5·00	14·00
D21	D12	30c. mauve and orange	5·00	14·00
D22	D12	40c. mauve and orange	12·50	17·00

1918. Surch Pechino and value.

D28	D12	4c. on 10c. mve & orge	£90000	£70000
D29	D12	8c. on 20c. mve & orge	30·00	55·00
D30	D12	12c. on 30c. mve & orge	90·00	£150
D31	D12	16c. on 40c. mve & orge	£350	£600

B. TIENTSIN

1917. Surch TIENTSIN and value.

31	37	2c. on 5c. green	£450	£400
32	37	4c. on 10c. pink	£800	£500
33	41	6c. on 15c. grey	£1700	£1200

Prices for the above are for stamps with surcharge inverted.

1917. Optd Tientsin.

34	30	1c. brown	14·00	32·00
35	31	2c. brown	14·00	32·00
36	37	5c. green	7·00	16·00
37	37	10c. pink	7·00	16·00
38	41	20c. orange	£160	£190
39	39	25c. blue	8·00	21·00
40	39	50c. violet	8·00	21·00
41	34	1l. brown and green	14·00	32·00
42	34	5l. blue and pink	22·00	55·00
43	34	10l. green and pink	£200	£400

1918. Surch Tientsin and value.

44	30	½c. on 1c. brown	£130	£150
45	31	1c. on 2c. brown	7·00	15·00
46	37	2c. on 5c. green	7·00	15·00
47	37	4c. on 10c. pink	7·00	15·00
48	41	8c. on 20c. orange	27·00	30·00
49	39	10c. on 25c. blue	14·00	27·00
50	39	20c. on 50c. violet	16·00	30·00
51	34	40c. on 1l. brown and green	£160	£275
52	34	2 Dollari. on 5l. blue and pink	£425	£700
54	34	2 dollari. on 5l. blue and pink	£11000	£9000

EXPRESS LETTER STAMPS

1917. Express Letter stamp optd Tientsin or surch 12 CENTS also.

E53	E41	12c. on 30c. blue & pink	85·00	£250
E44	E41	30c. blue and pink	14·00	37·00

POSTAGE DUE STAMPS

1917. Postage Due stamps optd Tientsin.

D44	D12	10c. mauve and orange	5·00	14·00
D45	D12	20c. mauve and orange	5·00	14·00
D46	D12	30c. mauve and orange	5·00	14·00
D47	D12	40c. mauve and orange	12·50	14·00

1918. Surch Tientsin and value.

D53	D12	4c. on 10c. mve & orge	£4000	£5000
D54	D12	8c. on 20c. mve & orge	32·00	65·00
D55	D12	12c. on 30c. mve & orge	£120	£160
D56	D12	16c. on 40c. mve & orge	£475	£600

ITALIAN POST OFFICES IN CRETE

Italian P.O.s in Crete, now closed.

1900. 40 paras = 1 piastre.
1906. 100 centesimi = 1 lira.

Stamps of Italy surcharged or overprinted.

1900. Surch **1 PIASTRA 1.**

1	27	1pi. on 25c. blue	16·00	85·00

1901. Surch **LA CANEA 1 PIASTRA 1.**

2	33	1pi. on 25c. blue	8·00	16·00

1906. 1901 stamps optd **LA CANEA.**

3	30	1c. brown	2·75	4·25
4	31	2c. brown	2·75	4·25
5	31	5c. green	3·75	4·25
6	33	10c. red	£300	£190
7	33	15c. on 20c. orange	5·25	4·25
8	33	25c. blue	13·50	17·00
9	33	40c. brown	13·50	17·00
10	33	45c. green	13·50	17·00
11	33	50c. mauve	13·50	17·00
12	34	1l. brown and green	80·00	80·00
13	34	5l. blue and pink	£425	£350

1907. 1906 stamps optd **LA CANEA.**

14	37	5c. green	2·75	3·25
15	37	10c. red	2·75	3·25
16	41	15c. black	6·50	5·25
17	39	25c. blue	6·50	10·50
18	39	40c. brown	35·00	43·00
19	39	50c. violet	6·50	10·50

EXPRESS LETTER STAMP

1906. Express Letter stamp optd **LA CANEA.**

E1	E35	25c. red	10·50	24·00

ITALIAN POST OFFICES IN THE TURKISH EMPIRE

The following were in use in P.O.s in Alexandria, Assab, La Goletta, Massawa, Susa, Tripoli and Tunis and also at Consular post offices at Buenos Aires and Montevideo.

Currency: Italian and Turkish

Stamps of Italy overprinted and surcharged.

A. GENERAL ISSUES.

1874. 1863 type, slightly altered, optd **ESTERO.**

1	4	1c. green	35·00	46·00
2	5	2c. brown	40·00	50·00
3	6	5c. grey	£1200	65·00
4	6	10c. orange	£2750	£100
10	6	10c. blue	£600	40·00
5	10	20c. blue	£2500	£500
11	10	20c. orange	£11000	35·00
6	6	30c. brown	9·25	31·00
7	6	40c. red	9·25	31·00
8	6	60c. mauve	23·00	£225
9	7	2l. red	£250	£900

1881. 1879 type, slightly altered, optd **ESTERO.**

12	12	5c. green	29·00	25·00
13	12	10c. red	14·50	21·00
14	12	20c. orange	14·50	17·00
15	12	25c. blue	14·50	25·00
16	12	50c. mauve	32·00	£120

B. OFFICES IN TURKISH EMPIRE.
(a) Albania

1902. Surch **ALBANIA** and value.

18	31	10pa. on 5c. green	5·50	4·50
24	31	10pa. on 5c. green	55·00	80·00
25	37	20pa. on 10c. red	43·00	40·00
19	33	35pa. on 20c. orange	8·25	9·25
20	33	40pa. on 25c. blue	18·00	9·25
26	33	80pa. on 50c. mauve	43·00	40·00

1902. Surch with figures of value repeated twice and currency in words thus, **20 Para 20.**

21	31	10pa. on 5c. green	12·00	4·50
27	37	10pa. on 5c. green	3·75	5·75
28	37	20pa. on 10c. red	3·75	5·75
22	33	35pa. on 20c. orange	7·50	7·00
23	33	40pa. on 25c. blue	38·00	17·00
29	33	80pa. on 50c. mauve	80·00	60·00

(b) General Offices in Europe and Asia

1908. Surch with figures of value repeated twice and currency in words thus, **30 Para 30.**

32	41	30pa. on 15c. grey	3·50	4·50
30	39	40pa. on 25c. blue	4·25	4·50
31	39	80pa. on 50c. mauve	7·25	5·75

EXPRESS LETTER STAMPS

1908. Express Letter stamps surch **LEVANTE** and new value.

E33	E35	1pi. on 25c. red	4·00	5·75
E34	E41	60pa. on 30c. blue & red	7·00	8·00

C. INDIVIDUAL OFFICES IN EUROPE AND ASIA.
(a) Constantinople.

1908. Surch in one line with figure of value and currency in words.

40	37	10pa. on 5c. green	16·00	23·00
41	37	20pa. on 10c. pink	16·00	23·00
46	34	20pi. on 5l. blue and pink	£6500	£3750
47	41	30pa. on 15c. grey	9·75	11·50
43	39	1pi. on 25c. blue	16·00	25·00
44	39	2pi. on 50c. mauve	£100	£120
45	34	4pi. on 1l. brown and green	£14000	£1300

1908. Surch in two lines with figures of value repeated twice and currency in words.

48	34	4pi. on 1l. brown and green	75·00	£120
51	34	20pi. on 5l. blue and pink	70·00	£100

1909. Surch **Costantinopoli** (10pa. to 2pi.) or **COSTANTINOPOLI** (4 to 40pi.) and value in figures twice repeated and currency in words.

52	37	10pa. on 5c. green	3·00	3·50
53	37	20pa. on 10c. pink	3·00	3·50
54	41	30pa. on 15c. grey	3·00	3·50
55	39	1pi. on 25c. blue	3·00	3·50
56	39	2pi. on 50c. mauve	3·75	5·75
57	34	4pi. on 1l. brown and green	5·00	5·75
58	34	20pi. on 5l. blue and pink	75·00	70·00
59	34	40pi. on 10l. green and pink	7·00	40·00

1921. Surch with value in figures and currency in words thus, **4 PIASTRE.**

60	37	1pi. on 5c. green	£225	£450
61	37	2pi. on 15c. grey	9·25	17·00
62	41	4pi. on 20c. orange	80·00	£100
63	39	5pi. on 25c. blue	80·00	£100
64	39	10pi. on 60c. red	4·00	11·50

1921. Surch with value in figures and currency in words thus, **PARA 20.**

65	30	10pa. on 1c. brown	3·50	4·50
66	31	20pa. on 2c. brown	3·50	4·50
67	37	30pa. on 5c. green	6·25	8·00
68	37	1pi. 20 on 15c. grey	9·75	4·50
69	41	3pi. on 20c. orange	14·00	25·00
70	39	3pi. 30 on 25c. blue	5·25	4·50
71	39	7pi. 20 on 60c. red	8·75	8·00
72	34	15pi. on 1l. brown and green	46·00	65·00

1922. Surch **COSTANTINOPOLI** and value in figures once only after currency in words.

73	37	20pa. on 5c. green	23·00	40·00
74	37	1pi. 20 on 15c. grey	3·00	4·50
75	39	3pi. on 30c. brown	3·00	4·50
76	39	3pi. 30 on 40c. brown	3·00	4·50
77	34	7pi. 20 on 1l. brown & green	3·00	4·50

1922. Surch **Piastre 3,75** in two lines.

78	39	3,75pi. on 25c. blue	4·75	4·75

1922. Para values surch in one line thus **30 PARA** and piastre values with **PIASTRE** over new value except Nos. 81, 86, 98 and 99 where the figures of value are above.

79	37	30pa. on 2c. brown	4·00	7·75
80	37	30pa. on 5c. green	9·50	24·00
81	41	1,50pi. on 20c. orange	4·00	7·25
82	39	1,50pi. on 25c. blue	4·00	9·50
83	39	3,75pi. on 40c. brown	6·00	12·00
84	39	4,50pi. on 50c. mauve	13·00	30·00
85	39	7,50pi. on 60c. red	12·00	22·00
86	39	15pi. on 85c. brown	20·00	42·00
87	34	18,75pi. on 1l. brown & grn	12·00	42·00
98	34	45pi. on 5l. blue and red	£180	£120
99	34	90pi. on 10l. olive and red	£140	£250

1922. Para values surch in two lines and piastre values with **PIASTRE** under new value.

90	37	30pa. on 5c. green	3·25	4·75
91	37	1½pi. on 10c. red	3·25	4·75
92	39	3pi. on 25c. blue	24·00	9·50
93	39	3¾pi. on 40c. brown	5·50	6·00
94	39	4½pi. on 50c. mauve	85·00	48·00
95	39	7½pi. on 85c. brown	11·00	14·50
96	34	7½pi. on 1l. brown and green	13·00	19·00
97	34	15pi. on 1l. brown and green	£120	£180

1923. Surch **COSTANTINOPOLI** and value in figures once only after currency in words.

100	37	30pa. on 5c. green	3·00	3·50
101	39	1pi. 20 on 25c. blue	3·00	3·50
103	39	4pi. 20 on 50c. mauve	3·00	3·50
104	39	7pi. 20 on 60c. red	3·00	4·75
105	39	15pi. on 85c. brown	3·00	3·75
106	34	18pi. 30 on 1l. brown and green	4·25	4·75
107	34	45pi. on 5l. blue and pink	6·50	12·00
108	34	90pi. on 10l. green & pink	6·50	14·50

EXPRESS LETTER STAMPS

1922. Express Letter stamps surch **15 PIASTRE.**

E90	E41	15pi. on 1l.20 on 30c. blue and red	38·00	85·00
E100	E41	15pi. on 30c. blue and red	£500	£900

1923. Express Letter stamp surch **COSTANTINOPOLI 15 PIASTRE.**

E109		15pi. on 1l.20 blue and red	10·00	42·00

POSTAGE DUE STAMPS

1922. Postage Due stamps optd **Costantinopoli.**

D100	D12	10c. mauve and orange	85·00	£150
D101	D12	30c. mauve and orange	85·00	£150
D102	D12	60c. mauve and orange	85·00	£150
D103	D12	1l. mauve and blue	85·00	£150
D104	D12	2l. mauve and blue	£1600	£2500
D105	D12	5l. mauve and blue	£700	£950

Nos. D100/5 bear a control cachet applied over blocks of four so that a quarter of the circle falls in a corner of each stamp.

(b) Durazzo

1909. Surch **Durazzo** (10pa. to 2pi.) or **DURAZZO** (4 to 40pi.) and value.

109	37	10pa. on 5c. green	2·20	4·75
110	37	20pa. on 10c. pink	2·20	4·75
111	41	30pa. on 15c. grey	55·00	7·25
112	39	1pi. on 25c. blue	3·00	7·25
113	39	2pi. on 50c. mauve	3·00	7·25
114	34	4pi. on 1l. brown and green	6·00	7·25
115	34	20pi. on 5l. blue and pink	£325	£300
116	34	40pi. on 10l. green & pink	24·00	£140

1915. No. 111 of Durazzo surch **CENT. 20.**

116a	41	20c. on 30pa. on 15c. grey	7·75	42·00

(c) Janina

1909. Surch **Janina** (10pa. to 2pi.) or **JANINA** (4 to 40pi.) and value.

117	37	10pa. on 5c. green	2·40	3·50
118	37	20pa. on 10c. pink	2·40	3·50
119	41	30pa. on 15c. grey	2·40	3·50
120	39	1pi. on 25c. blue	2·40	3·50
121	39	2pi. on 50c. mauve	2·40	3·50
122	34	4pi. on 1l. brown and green	6·00	6·00
123	34	20pi. on 5l. blue and pink	£350	£400
124	34	40pi. on 10l. green & pink	26·00	£130

(d) Jerusalem

1909. Surch **Gerusalemme** (10pa. to 2pi.) or **GERUSALEMME** (4 to 40pi.) and value.

125	37	10pa. on 5c. green	11·00	18·00
126	37	20pa. on 10c. pink	11·00	18·00
127	41	30pa. on 15c. grey	11·00	24·00
128	39	1pi. on 25c. blue	11·00	18·00
129	39	2pi. on 50c. mauve	30·00	55·00
130	34	4pi. on 1l. brown and green	42·00	85·00
131	34	20pi. on 5l. blue and pink	£1300	£1200
132	34	40pi. on 10l. green & pink	65·00	£475

(e) Salonica

1909. Surch **Salonicco** (10pa. to 2pi.) or **SALONICCO** (4 to 40pi.) and value.

133	37	10pa. on 5c. green	2·75	4·75
134	37	20pa. on 10c. pink	2·75	4·75
135	41	30pa. on 15c. grey	3·50	4·75
136	39	1pi. on 25c. blue	3·50	4·75
137	39	2pi. on 50c. mauve	3·50	4·75
138	34	4pi. on 1l. brown and green	6·00	9·50
139	34	20pi. on 5l. blue and pink	£650	£650
140	34	40pi. on 10l. green & pink	36·00	£120

(f) Scutari

1909. Surch **Scutari di Albania** (4pa. to 2pi.) or **SCUTARI DI ALBANIA** (4 to 40pi.) and value.

141	31	4pa. on 2c. brown	3·50	8·50
142	37	10pa. on 35c. green	1·60	3·50
143	37	20pa. on 10c. pink	1·60	3·50
144	41	30pa. on 15c. grey	32·00	8·50
145	39	1pi. on 25c. blue	1·60	4·75
146	39	2pi. on 50c. mauve	2·50	6·00
147	34	4pi. on 1l. brown and green	3·00	7·25
148	34	20pi. on 5l. blue and pink	42·00	60·00
149	34	40pi. on 10l. green & pink	95·00	£200

1916. No. 144 of Scutari surch **CENT. 20.**

150	41	20c. on 30pa. on 15c. grey	8·50	36·00

(g) Smyrna

1909. Surch **Smirne** (10pa. to 2pi.) or **SMIRNE** (4 to 40pi.) and value.

151	37	10pa. on 5c. green	1·60	2·40
152	37	20pa. on 10c. pink	1·60	2·40
153	41	30pa. on 15c. grey	3·50	6·50
154	39	1pi. on 25c. blue	3·50	7·25
155	39	2pi. on 50c. mauve	4·25	7·25
156	34	4pi. on 1l. brown and green	5·50	12·00
157	34	20pi. on 5l. blue and pink	£250	£275
158	34	40pi. on 10l. green & pink	34·00	£130

(h) Valona

1909. Surch **Valona** (10pa. to 2pi.) or **VALONA** (4 to 40pi.) and value.

159	37	10pa. on 5c. green	2·10	3·50
160	37	20pa. on 10c. pink	2·10	3·50
161	41	30pa. on 15c. grey†	28·00	11·00
167	41	30pa. on 15c. grey†	7·25	19·00
162	39	1pi. on 25c. blue	3·75	6·00
163	39	2pi. on 50c. mauve	3·75	7·25
164	34	4pi. on 1l. brown and green	4·25	7·25
165	34	20pi. on 5l. blue and pink	70·00	90·00
166	34	40pi. on 10l. green & pink	90·00	£200

†On No. 161 the surcharge is **Para**, on No. 167 **PARA.**

1916. No. 167 of Valona surch **CENT. 20.**

168		20c. on 30pa. on 15c. grey	3·50	24·00

D. OFFICES IN AFRICA.
(a) Benghazi

1901. Surch **BENGASI 1 PIASTRA 1.**

169	33	1pi. on 25c. blue	75·00	£200
170	39	1pi. on 25c. blue	75·00	£200

(b) Tripoli

1909. Optd **Tripoli di Barberia** (1 to 50c.) or **TRIPOLI DI BARBERIA** (1, 2l.).

171	30	1c. brown	7·00	5·75
173	31	2c. brown	4·00	5·75
174	37	5c. green	£170	17·00
175	37	10c. red	5·25	4·50
176	41	15c. grey	7·50	9·25
177	39	25c. blue	5·25	9·25
178	39	40c. brown	10·50	11·50
179	39	50c. violet	15·00	14·00
180	34	1l. brown and green	£170	£130
181	34	5l. blue and pink	60·00	£275

EXPRESS LETTER STAMPS

1909. Express Letter stamps optd **TRIPOLI DI BARBERIA.**

E182	E35	25c. pink	15·00	16·00
E183	E41	30c. blue and pink	12·50	23·00

ITALY

A Republic in S. Europe on the Mediterranean and Adriatic Seas. Originally a kingdom formed by the union of various smaller kingdoms and duchies that issued their own stamps.

1862. 100 centesimi = 1 lira.
2002. 100 cents = 1 euro.

1 King Victor
Emmanuel II

1862. Head embossed. Imperf (15c.) or perf (others).

1	1	10c. bistre	£11000	£400
5	1	15c. black	£100	65·00
2a	1	20c. blue	27·00	48·00
3	1	40c. red	£375	£250
4	1	80c. yellow	80·00	£2250

For stamps of this type imperf, see Sardinia Nos. 27 etc.

3

1863. Imperf.
7	3	15c. blue	9·50	17·00

4   5   6

7   10

1863. Perf.
8	4	1c. green	10·50	5·25
9	5	2c. brown	43·00	3·25
10	6	5c. grey	£2250	5·25
11	6	10c. brown	£3750	7·50
21	6	10c. blue	£7500	8·50
12	6	15c. blue	£3000	4·25
20a	10	20c. blue	£900	1·60
22a	10	20c. orange	£5500	5·25
13	6	30c. brown	17·00	21·00
14	6	40c. red	£7000	10·50
15	6	60c. mauve	26·00	26·00
16	7	2l. red	37·00	£150

1865. Surch C 20 20 C and curved bar.
17	6	20c. on 15c. blue	£900	5·25

1878. Official stamps surch 2 C and wavy bars.
23	O11	2c. on 2c. red	£200	37·00
24	O11	2c. on 5c. red	£225	48·00
25	O11	2c. on 20c. red	£900	5·25
26	O11	2c. on 30c. red	£800	17·00
27	O11	2c. on 1l. red	£700	5·25
28	O11	2c. on 2l. red	£700	13·00
29	O11	2c. on 5l. red	£900	19·00
30	O11	2c. on 10l. red	£700	24·00

12 King Umberto I

1879. Corners vary for each value.
31	12	5c. green	12·00	1·60
32	12	10c. red	£600	2·10
33	12	20c. orange	£550	1·60
34	12	25c. blue	£950	10·50
35	12	30c. brown	£190	£2500
36	12	50c. mauve	27·00	27·00
37	12	2l. orange	70·00	£400

13 Arms of Savoy   14

1889. Figures in four corners. Various frames.
38	13	5c. green	£1000	3·25
39	14	40c. brown	15·00	24·00
40	14	45c. green	£2500	10·50
41	14	60c. mauve	19·00	41·00
42	14	1l. brown and orange	19·00	21·00
43	14	5l. red and green	43·00	£1100

1890. Surch Cmi. 2 or Cmi 20.
44	12	2c. on 5c. green	27·00	65·00
45	12	20c. on 30c. brown	£500	14·00
46	12	20c. on 50c. mauve	£600	60·00

1890. Parcel Post stamps surch Valevole per le stampe Cmi. 2 and bars.
47	P13	2c. on 10c. grey	7·50	8·50
48	P13	2c. on 20c. blue	7·50	8·50
49	P13	2c. on 50c. pink	85·00	70·00
50	P13	2c. on 75c. green	7·50	8·50
51	P13	2c. on 1l.25 orange	65·00	48·00
52	P13	2c. on 1l.75 brown	29·00	75·00

21   22   23

24   25   26

27   29

1891
53	21	1c. brown	12·00	8·50
54	22	2c. brown	12·00	4·25
55	23	5c. green	£750	2·75
56	24	5c. brown	43·00	2·10
57	25	10c. red	10·50	2·75
58a	26	20c. orange	10·50	2·75
59	27	25c. blue	10·50	5·25
60	27	45c. olive	10·50	5·25
61	29	5l. red and blue	£100	£250

30   31   33 King Victor Emmanuel III

34 King Victor Emmanuel III

1901. Designs vary.
62	30	1c. brown	1·30	30
63	31	2c. brown	1·30	45
64	31	5c. green	90·00	65
65	33	10c. red	£130	1·40
66	33	20c. orange	24·00	1·40
67	33	25c. blue	£180	3·50
68	33	40c. brown	£800	10·50
69	33	45c. green	12·50	65
70	33	50c. violet	£950	19·00
71	34	1l. brown and green	6·50	65
72	34	5l. blue and pink	36·00	8·50
85	34	10l. green and pink	95·00	37·00

See also Nos. 171s, 181, 185 and 186/7.

1905. Surch C. 15.
73	33	15c. on 20c. orange	95·00	2·75

37   39   41

1906
75	37	5c. green	1·20	55
76	37	10c. red	1·20	35
90	41	15c. grey	43·00	1·40
77	39	25c. blue	1·90	50
78	39	40c. brown	3·75	50
79	39	50c. violet	1·70	50

See also Nos. 104 etc, 171d/h and 171j/r.

42 Garibaldi

1910. 50th Anniv of Plebiscite in Naples and Sicily.
81	42	5c.(+5c.) green	27·00	32·00
82	42	15c.(+5c.) red	55·00	70·00

43

1910. National Plebiscite of Southern States, 1860.
83	43	5c.(+5c.) pink	£190	£160
84	43	15c.(+5c.) green	£300	£275

45   46

1911. Jubilee of Italian Kingdom.
86	45	2c.(+3c.) brown	12·00	7·00
87	46	5c.(+5c.) green	24·00	37·00
88	-	10c.(+5c.) red	35·00	60·00
89	-	15c.(+5c.) grey	41·00	85·00

DESIGNS: Symbolic of the Genius of Italy (10c.) and the Glory of Rome (15c.).

50

1912. Re-erection of Campanile of St. Mark, Venice.
91	50	5c. black	10·50	16·00
92	50	15c. brown	41·00	70·00

1913. Surch 2 2.
93	46	2 on 5c. green	2·40	7·50
94	-	2 on 10c. red (No. 88)	2·40	7·50
95	-	2 on 15c. grey (No. 89)	2·40	7·50

53 Banner of United Italy   54 Italian Eagle and Arms of Savoy

1915. Red Cross Society. No. 98 is surch 20.
96	53	10c.+5c. red	4·25	12·00
97	54	15c. grey	7·00	12·00
98	54	20 on 15c.+5c. grey	14·00	55·00
99	54	20c.+5c. orange	19·00	65·00

1916. Surch CENT. 20.
100	41	20c. on 15c. grey	24·00	1·60

1917. Air. Express Letter stamp optd ESPERIMENTO POSTA AEREA MAGGIO 1917 TORINO=ROMA=ROMA=TORINO.
102	E35	25c. red	21·00	48·00

1917. Air. Express Letter stamp surch IDROVOLANTE NAPOLI-PALERMO NAPOLI 25 CENT 25.
103	E59	25c. on 40c. violet	22·00	55·00

1917
104	37	15c. grey	1·40	65
105	41	20c. orange	5·25	55
178	39	20c. orange	2·75	1·30
179	39	20c. green	1·10	30
180	39	20c. purple	3·25	55
181	34	25c. green and light green	2·20	55
182	39	25c. green	11·00	16·00
106	39	30c. brown	3·25	1·10
183	39	30c. grey	4·00	30
107	39	55c. purple	18·00	17·00
108	39	60c. red	3·50	70
109	39	60c. blue	8·50	55·00
184	39	60c. orange	8·75	85
185	34	75c. red and carmine	6·50	55
110	39	85c. brown	10·50	8·50
186	34	1l.25 blue and ultramarine	9·50	55
111	34	2l. green and orange	34·00	9·00
187	34	2l.50 green and orange	75·00	9·00

See also Nos. 171a/c and 171i.

59 Ancient Seal of Republic of Trieste

1921. Union of Venezia Giulia with Italy.
112	59	15c. red and black	4·75	48·00
113	59	25c. red and blue	4·75	48·00
114	59	40c. red and brown	4·75	48·00

60

1921. 600th Death Anniv of Dante.
115	60	15c. red	6·50	32·00
116	-	25c. green	6·50	32·00
117	-	40c. brown	6·50	32·00

DESIGNS: 25c. Woman with book; 40c. Dante.

62 "Victory"

1921. Victory of 1918.
118	62	5c. green	1·60	4·25
119	62	10c. red	1·60	16·00
120	62	15c. grey	4·75	27·00
121	62	25c. blue	1·60	16·00

1922. Ninth Italian Philatelic Congress. Trieste. Optd IX CONGRESSO FILATELICO ITALIANO TRIESTE 1922.
122	37	10c. red	£400	£400
123	37	15c. grey	£275	£300
124	39	25c. blue	£275	£350
125	39	40c. brown	£425	£400

64

1922. 50th Death Anniv of Mazzini.
126	64	25c. purple	7·50	34·00
127	-	40c. purple	27·00	43·00
128	-	80c. blue	7·50	60·00

DESIGNS—VERT: 40c. Mazzini. HORIZ: 80c. Tomb of Mazzini.

66

1923. Tercentenary of Propagation of the Faith.
129	66	20c. orange and green	4·75	£110
130	66	30c. orange and red	4·75	£110
131	66	50c. orange and violet	4·75	£110
132	66	1l. orange and blue	4·75	£110

The portraits and arms in the corners at right vary for each value.

1923. Surch in words and figures. (15c. surch DIECI only).
133	39	7½c. on 85c. brown	60	2·10
135	39	10c. on 1c. brown	55	55
136	31	10c. on 2c. brown	55	55
137	37	10c. on 15c. grey	45	55
138	39	20c. on 25c. blue	45	55
139	33	25c. on 45c. olive	45	16·00
140	39	25c. on 60c. blue	2·10	1·60
141	39	30c. on 50c. mauve	55	55
142	39	30c. on 55c. purple	75	55
143	39	50c. on 40c. brown	3·25	1·10
144	39	50c. on 55c. purple	32·00	17·00
145	34	1l.75 on 10l. olive and red	21·00	37·00

73   74

75

1923. First Anniv of Fascist March on Rome.
146	73	10c. green	4·75	6·50
147	73	30c. violet	4·75	6·50
148	73	50c. red	8·50	10·50
149	74	1l. blue	10·00	14·00
150	74	2l. brown	10·00	21·00
151	75	5l. black and blue	24·00	70·00

76

1923. Fascist "Black Shirt" Fund.

152	76	30c.+30c. brown	41·00	£120
153	76	50c.+50c. mauve	41·00	£120
154	76	1l.+1l. grey	41·00	£120

77

1923. 50th Death Anniv of A. Manzoni (writer).

155	77	10c. black and red	9·50	80·00
156	-	15c. black and green	9·50	80·00
157	-	30c. black	9·50	80·00
158	-	50c. black and brown	9·50	80·00
159	-	1l. black and blue	£120	£350
160	-	5l. black and purple	£850	£3000

DESIGNS: 10c. to 50c. Scenes from Manzoni's "I Promessi Sposi"; 1l. Manzoni's home, Milan; 5l. Portrait of Manzoni.

1924. Victory stamps surch LIRE UNA between stars.

161	62	1l. on 5c. green	48·00	£275
162	62	1l. on 10c. red	27·00	£275
163	62	1l. on 15c. grey	48·00	£275
164	62	1l. on 25c. blue	27·00	£275

1924. Trade Propaganda. Optd CROCIERA ITALIANA 1924.

165	37	10c. red	3·00	27·00
166	39	30c. brown	3·00	27·00
167	39	50c. violet	3·00	27·00
168	39	60c. blue	16·00	90·00
169	39	85c. brown	8·50	90·00
170	34	1l. brown and green	70·00	£400
171	34	2l. green and orange	60·00	£400

Used on an Italian cruiser which visited South America for trade propaganda.

1924. Previous issues with attached advertising labels (imperf between stamp and label). Colour of label given.

171a	15c. (104) + Columbia (blue)	65·00	55·00
171b	15c. (104) + Bitter Campari (blue)	4·50	22·00
171c	15c. (104) + Cordial Campari (black)	4·50	22·00
171d	25c. (77) + Coen (green)	£275	60·00
171e	25c. (77) + Piperno (brown)	£1800	£950
171f	25c. (77) + Tagliacozzo (brown)	£900	£900
171g	25c. (77) + Abrador (blue)	£140	£130
171h	25c. (77) + Reinach (brown)	£120	95·00
171i	30c. (106) + Columbia (green)	37·00	60·00
171j	50c. (79) + Coen (blue)	£1800	£110
171k	50c. (79) + Columbia (red)	26·00	21·00
171l	50c. (79) + De Montel (blue)	4·50	21·00
171m	50c. (79) + Piperno (green)	£2250	£325
171n	50c. (79) + Reinach (blue)	£120	70·00
171o	50c. (79) + Singer (red)	4·50	9·00
171p	50c. (79) + Tagliacozzo (green)	£2750	£650
171q	50c. (79) + Siero Casali (blue)	29·00	48·00
171r	50c. (79) + Tantal (red)	£425	£190
171s	1l. (71) + Columbia (blue)	£900	£950

81 Church of St. John Lateran

1924. Holy Year (1925).

172	-	20c.+10c. brown & green	3·50	13·50
173	81	30c.+15c. brown & choc	3·50	13·50
174	-	50c.+25c. brown & violet	3·50	13·50
175	-	60c.+30c. brown and red	3·50	37·00
176	-	1l.+50c. purple and blue	3·50	37·00
177	-	5l.+2l.50 purple and red	13·50	95·00

DESIGNS: 20c. Church of St. Maria Maggiore; 50c. Church of St. Paul; 60c. St. Peter's; 1l. Pope opening Holy Door; 5l. Pope shutting Holy Door.

82

1925. Royal Jubilee.

188B	82	60c. red	1·20	1·20
189B	82	1l. blue	2·20	1·20
190A	82	1l.25 blue	4·50	2·50

83 Vision of St. Francis

1926. 700th Death Anniv of St. Francis of Assisi.

191	83	20c. green	65	1·10
194B	-	30c. black	75	1·10
192	-	40c. violet	1·10	1·60
193	-	60c. red	1·10	1·60
195B	-	1l.25 blue	1·40	1·20
196	-	5l.+2l.50 brown	14·00	£120

DESIGNS—HORIZ: 40c. St. Damian's Church and Monastery, Assisi; 60c. St. Francis's Monastery, Assisi; 1l.25, Death of St. Francis, from fresco in Church of the Holy Cross, Florence. VERT: 30c., 5l. St. Francis (after Luca della Robbia).

88

1926. Air.

197	88	50c. red	4·75	12·00
198	88	60c. grey	4·75	12·00
199	88	80c. brown and purple	48·00	95·00
200	88	1l. blue	9·00	12·00
201	88	1l.20 brown	21·00	£120
202	88	1l.50 orange	20·00	33·00
203	88	5l. green	50·00	£120

89 Castle of St. Angelo

1926. First National Defence issue.

204	89	40c.+20c. black & brown	3·75	16·00
205	-	60c.+30c. brown and red	3·75	16·00
206	-	1l.25+60c. black & grn	3·75	43·00
207	-	5l.+2l.50 black and blue	6·50	£160

DESIGNS: 60c. Aqueduct of Claudius; 1l.25, Capitol; 5l. Porta del Popolo.

See also Nos. 219/22 and 278/81.

90 Volta

1927. Death Centenary of Volta.

208	90	20c. red	1·10	1·30
209	90	50c. green	2·10	1·10
210	90	60c. purple	4·25	5·25
211	90	1l.25 blue	7·50	8·50

91

1927

212	91	1l.75 brown	5·25	55
213	91	1l.85 black	1·20	1·60
214	91	2l.55 red	8·50	14·00
215	91	2l.65 purple	9·50	70·00
216	91	50c. grey and brown	4·25	55

No. 216 is smaller (17½×21½ mm).

1927. Air. Surch.

217	88	50c. on 60c. grey	19·00	60·00
218	88	80c. on 1l. blue	48·00	£200

1928. Second National Defence issue. As Nos. 204/7.

219	89	30c.+10c. black and violet	8·00	28·00
220	-	50c.+20c. black and olive	9·00	32·00
221	-	1l.25+50c. black & blue	27·00	80·00
222	-	5l.+2l. black and red	55·00	£300

92

1928

223	92	7½c. brown	4·50	15·00
224	92	15c. orange	5·50	45
225	92	35c. grey	8·00	14·00
226	92	50c. mauve	16·00	30

93 Emmanuele Filiberto   **94** Soldier of First World War and Statue   **95** Statue, Turin (Maroghetti)

1928. 400th Birth Anniv of Emmanuele Filiberto, Duke of Savoy, and Tenth Anniv of Victory in World War.

227a	93	20c. blue and brown	2·20	6·75
228a	93	25c. green and red	2·20	6·75
229a	93	30c. brown and green	4·50	11·00
230	94	50c. red and blue	2·20	1·20
231	94	75c. red and pink	3·50	5·25
232	95	1l.25 black and blue	3·50	5·25
233	94	1l.75 green and blue	5·75	16·00
234	93	5l. green and mauve	17·00	£110
235	94	10l. black and pink	35·00	£250
236	95	20l. green and mauve	75·00	£850

96 King Victor Emmanuel II

1929. 50th Death Anniv of King Victor Emmanuel II. Veterans' Fund.

237	96	50c.+10c. green	4·50	10·50

97 Fascist Arms of Italy   **98** Romulus, Remus and Wolf   **99** Julius Caesar

103 King Victor Emmanuel III

1929. Imperial Series.

238	97	2c. orange	1·10	35
239	98	5c. brown	20	20
240	99	7½c. violet	20	20
241	-	10c. brown	20	20
242	-	15c. green	20	20
243	99	20c. red	20	20
244	-	25c. green	20	20
245	103	30c. brown	20	20
246	-	35c. blue	20	20
247	103	50c. violet	20	20
248	-	75c. red	20	20
249	99	1l. violet	30	20
250	-	1l.25 blue	20	20
251	-	1l.75 orange	20	20
252	-	2l. red	20	20
253	98	2l.55 green	20	60
254	98	3l.70 violet	30	1·20
255	98	5l. red	25	20
256	-	10l. violet	2·40	3·00
257	99	20l. green	4·50	15·00
258	-	25l. black	11·00	44·00
259	-	50l. violet	16·00	60·00

DESIGNS—As Type 99: 10c., 1l.75, 25l. Augustus the Great; 15c., 35c., 2l., 10l. Italia (Woman with castle on her head); 25c., 75c., 1l.25, 50l. Profile of King Victor Emmanuel III.

For stamps as above but without Fascist emblems, see Nos. 633 etc., and for stamps with integral label for armed forces see Nos. 563/74.

104 Bramante Courtyard

1929. 1400th Anniv of Abbey of Montecassino.

260	104	20c. orange	1·70	2·20
261	-	25c. green	1·70	2·20
262	-	50c.+10c. brown	2·40	17·00
263	-	75c.+15c. red	3·50	28·00
264	104	1l.25+25c. blue	4·50	32·00

265	-	5l.+1l. purple	13·00	90·00
266	-	10l.+2l. green	18·00	£225

DESIGNS—HORIZ: 25c. "Death of St. Benedict" (fresco); 50c. Monks building Abbey; 75c., 5l. Abbey of Montecassino. VERT: 10l. St. Benedict.

109

1930. Marriage of Prince Umberto and Princess Marie Jose.

267	109	20c. orange	1·10	80
268	109	50c.+10c. brown	2·20	4·25
269	109	1l.25+25c. blue	3·50	14·00

110 Pegasus   **113**

1930. Air.

270	-	25c. green	20	25
271	110	50c. brown	20	25
272	-	75c. brown	20	25
273	-	80c. orange	20	25
274	-	1l. violet	20	25
275	113	2l. blue	20	20
276	110	5l. green	75	1·10
277	110	10l. red	1·10	5·25

DESIGNS—As Type 110: 25c., 80c. Wings; 75c., 1l. Angel.

1930. Third National Defence issue. Designs as Nos. 204/7.

278	89	30c.+10c. violet & green	1·20	24·00
279	-	50c.+10c. blue and green	2·50	18·00
280	-	1l.25+30c. green & blue	8·00	60·00
281	-	5l.+1l.50 choc & brn	14·00	£225

114 Ferrucci on Horseback   **117** Francesco Ferrucci

1930. 400th Death Anniv of Francesco Ferrucci.

282	114	20c. red (postage)	1·20	1·60
283	-	25c. green	2·20	1·10
284	-	50c. violet	1·20	80
285	-	1l.25 blue	11·00	7·25
286	-	5l.+2l. orange	20·00	£160
287	117	50c. violet (air)	2·20	13·00
288	117	1l. brown	2·20	19·00
289	117	5l.+2l. purple	8·75	£150

DESIGNS—HORIZ: 25c., 50c., 1l.25, Ferrucci assassinated by Maramaldo. VERT: 5l. Ferrucci in helmet.

119 Jupiter sending forth Eagle

1930. Birth Bimillenary of Virgil.

290	-	15c. brown (postage)	1·40	2·10
291	-	20c. orange	1·40	2·10
292	-	25c. green	1·60	2·10
293	-	30c. purple	2·75	4·50
294	-	50c. violet	1·40	1·40
295	-	75c. red	2·75	7·50
296	-	1l.25 blue	2·75	7·50
297	-	5l.+1l.50 brown	75·00	£275
298	-	10l.+2l.50 olive	75·00	£325
299	119	50c. brown (air)	10·50	25·00
300	-	1l. orange	10·50	25·00
301	119	7l.70+1l.30 purple	50·00	£300
302	119	9l.+2l. brown	65·00	£375

DESIGNS (scenes from "Aeneid" or "Georgics"): 15c. Helenus and Anchises; 20c. The passing legions; 25c. Landing of Aeneas; 30c. Earth's bounties; 50c. Harvesting; 75c. Rural life; 1l.25, Aeneas sights Italy; 5l. A shepherd's hut; 10l. Turnus, King of the Rutuli.

120 Savoia Marchetti S-55A Flying Boats

1930. Air. Transatlantic Mass Formation Flight.

303	120	7l.70 blue and brown	£800	£1800

121 St. Antony's
Installation as a Franciscan

1931. 700th Death Anniv of St. Antony of Padua.

304	121	20c. purple	3·25	1·60
305	-	25c. green	2·10	1·60
306	-	30c. brown	4·50	2·40
307	-	50c. violet	3·50	1·20
308	-	75c. lake	12·00	12·00
309	-	1l.25 blue	17·00	9·00
310	-	5l.+2l.50 olive	50·00	£200

DESIGNS—HORIZ: 25c. Sermon to the Fishes; 30c. Hermitage of Olivares; 50c. Basilica of the Saint at Padua; 75c. Death of St. Antony; 1l.25, St. Antony liberating prisoners. VERT: 5l. Vision of St. Antony.

123 Tower of
the Marzocco

1931. 50th Anniv of Naval Academy, Leghorn.

311	123	20c. red	5·50	2·40
312	-	50c. violet	5·50	1·20
313	-	1l.25 blue	16·00	7·50

DESIGNS—HORIZ: 50c. Cadet ship "Amerigo Vespucci"; 1l.25, Cruiser "Trento".

124 Dante (1265–1321)   **125** Leonardo da Vinci's
Drawing *Flying Man*

127 Leonardo
da Vinci

1932. Dante Alighieri Society. (a) Postage.

314		10c. brown	2·10	2·10
315	-	15c. green	2·10	1·10
316	-	20c. red	2·10	1·10
317	-	25c. green	2·10	1·10
318	-	30c. brown	3·25	2·10
319	-	50c. violet	1·10	1·10
320	-	75c. red	6·75	6·75
321	-	1l.25 blue	2·10	4·50
322	-	1l.75 orange	5·50	6·75
323	-	2l.75 green	22·00	34·00
324	-	5l.+2l. red	34·00	£180
325	124	10l.+2l.50 olive	48·00	£250

DESIGNS—10c. Giovanni Boccaccio (writer); 15c. Niccolo Machiavelli (statesman); 20c. Fra Paolo Sarpi (philosopher); 25c. Vittorio Alfieri (poet); 30c. Ugo Foscolo (writer); 50c. Giacomo Leopardi (poet); 75c. Giosue Carducci (poet); 1l.25, Carlo Botta (historian); 1l.75, Torquato Tasso (poet); 2l.75, Francesco Petrarch (poet); 5l. Ludovico Ariosto (poet).

(b) Air.

326	125	50c. brown	2·10	6·50
327	-	1l. violet	3·25	7·50
328	-	3l. red	5·50	28·00
329	-	5l. green	5·50	33·00
330	125	7l.70+2l. blue	7·75	90·00
331	-	10l.+2l.50 grey	11·00	£150
332	127	100l. green and blue	41·00	£475

DESIGN—HORIZ: 1, 3, 5, 10l. Leonardo da Vinci.

128 Garibaldi and Victor   **130** Caprera
Emmanuel

1932. 50th Death Anniv of Garibaldi.

333		10c. blue (postage)	3·25	2·10
334	128	20c. brown	3·25	1·20
335	-	25c. green	3·25	2·10
336	128	30c. orange	3·25	3·25

337	-	50c. violet	2·10	85
338	-	75c. red	17·00	8·75
339	-	1l.25 blue	24·00	5·50
340	-	1l.75+25c. blue	29·00	£100
341	-	2l.55+50c. brown	29·00	£140
342	-	5l.+1l. lake	29·00	£150

DESIGNS—HORIZ: 10c. Garibaldi's birthplace, Nice; 25c., 50c. "Here we make Italy or die"; 75c. Death of Anita (Garibaldi's wife); 1l.25, Garibaldi's tomb; 1l.75, Quarto Rock. VERT: 2l.55, Garibaldi's statue in Rome; 5l. Garibaldi.

343	130	50c. lake (air)	4·50	8·75
344	-	80c. green	4·50	16·00
345	130	1l.+25c. brown	5·50	34·00
346	-	2l.+50c. blue	6·75	50·00
347	-	5l.+1l. green	10·00	65·00

DESIGNS—VERT: 80c. The Ravenna hut; 2l. Anita; 5l. Garibaldi.

132 Agriculture

1932. Tenth Anniv of Fascist March on Rome. (a) Postage.

350	132	5c. sepia	1·10	1·10
351	-	10c. sepia	1·10	1·10
352	-	15c. green	1·10	1·10
353	-	20c. red	1·10	65
354	-	25c. green	1·10	85
355	-	30c. sepia	2·10	3·25
356	-	35c. blue	5·50	11·00
357	-	50c. violet	2·10	60
358	-	60c. brown	5·50	7·75
359	-	75c. red	3·25	4·50
360	-	1l. violet	6·75	6·75
361	-	1l.25 blue	3·25	2·10
362	-	1l.75 orange	7·75	2·10
363	-	2l.55 green	29·00	46·00
364	-	2l.75 green	30·00	46·00
365	-	5l.+2l.50 red	70·00	£325

DESIGNS—10c. Fascist soldier; 15c. Fascist coastguard; 20c. Italian youth; 25c. Tools forming a shadow of the Fasces; 30c. Religion; 35c. Imperial highways; 50c. Equestrian statue of Mussolini; 60c. Land reclamation; 75c. Colonial expansion; 1l. Marine development; 1l.25, Italians abroad; 1l.75, Sport, 2l.55, Child Welfare; 2l.75. "O.N.D." Recreation; 5l. Caesar's statue.

(b) Air.

366		50c. brown	3·25	11·00
367		75c. brown	10·00	34·00

DESIGNS: 50c. Savoia Marchetti S-55A flying boat over Eagle (front of Air Ministry Building, Rome); 75c. Aerial view of Italian cathedrals.

134 Airship *Graf Zeppelin*

1933. Air. LZ-127 *Graf Zeppelin* issue.

372	134	3l. green and black	13·00	£110
373	-	5l. brown and green	19·00	£130
374	-	10l. blue and red	19·00	£275
375	-	12l. orange and blue	28·00	£400
376	-	15l. black and brown	28·00	£500
377	-	20l. blue and brown	28·00	£600

DESIGNS (all with airship): 3l. S. Paola Gate and tomb of Consul Caius Cestius; 5l. Appian Way and tomb of Cecilia Metella; 10l. Portion of Mussolini Stadium; 12l. S. Angelo Castle; 15l. Forum Romanum; 20l. Empire Way, Colosseum and Baths of Domitian.

135 Italian Flag / King Victor Emmanuel III / "Flight"
(image scaled to 44% of original size)

136 Italian Flag / King Victor Emmanuel III / Rome–
Chicago (image scaled to 44% of original size)

1933. Air. Balbo Transatlantic Mass Formation Flight by Savoia Marchetti S-55X Flying Boats.

378	135	5l.25+19l.75 red, green and blue	£180	£2250
379	136	5l.25+44l.75 red, green and blue	£180	£2250

The first part of the illustration in each group is of the Registered Air Express label and has an abbreviation of one of the pilots' names overprinted on it; the second part is the stamp for Ordinary Postage and the third is the actual Air Mail stamp.

137 Athlete

1933. International University Games, Turin.

380	137	10c. brown	60	1·20
381	137	20c. red	60	1·20
382	137	50c. violet	1·20	65
383	137	1l.25 blue	2·40	7·00

138 Dome of   **139** St. Peter's and Church
St. Peter's   of the Holy Sepulchre

1933. "Holy Year". (a) Postage.

384	138	20c. red	3·50	1·30
385	-	25c. green	4·50	2·20
386	-	50c. violet	3·50	1·20
387	138	1l. 25 blue	4·50	6·75
388	-	2l.55+2l.50 black	10·50	£225

DESIGNS: 25, 50c. Angel with Cross; 2l.55, Cross with Doves of Peace.

(b) Air.

389	139	50c.+25c. brown	1·30	17·00
390	139	75c.+50c. purple	3·50	29·00

1934. Air. Rome-Buenos Aires Flight. Surch with airplane, **1934 XII PRIMO VOLO DIRETTO ROMA = BUENOS-AYRES TRIMOTORE "LOMBARDI MAZZOTTI"**, value and fasces.

391	113	2l. on 2l. yellow	8·50	70·00
392	113	3l. on 2l. green	8·50	£120
393	113	5l. on 2l. red	8·50	£250
394	113	10l. on 2l. violet	8·50	£350

141 Anchor of
the
*Emmanuele
Filiberto*

1934. Tenth Anniv of Annexation of Fiume.

395	141	10c. brown (postage)	5·25	4·25
396	141	20c. red	45	1·40
397	-	50c. violet	45	1·40
398	-	1l.25 blue	55	6·75
399	-	1l.75+1l. brown	1·40	40·00
400	-	2l.55+2l. purple	1·40	65·00
401	-	2l.75+2l.50 olive	1·40	70·00

DESIGNS: 50c. Gabriele d'Annunzio; 1l.25, St. Vito's Tower barricaded; 1l.75, Hands supporting crown of historical monuments; 2l.55, Victor Emmanuel III's arrival in the "Brindisi" (cruiser); 2l.75, Galley, gondola and battleship.

402		25c. green (air)	45	4·25
403	-	50c. brown	45	3·25
404	-	75c. brown	45	11·00
405	-	1l.+50c. purple	45	17·00
406	-	2l.+1l.50 blue	45	25·00
407	-	3l.+2l. black	1·10	25·00

DESIGNS—Marina Fiat MF.5 flying boat over: 25, 75c. Fiume Harbour; 50c., 1l. War Memorial; 2l. Three Venetian lions; 3l. Roman Wall.

142 Antonio
Pacinotti

1934. 75th Anniv of Invention of Pacinotti's Dynamo.

411	142	50c. violet	60	65
412	142	1l.25 blue	1·20	3·00

143

1934. World Cup Football Championship, Italy.

413	143	20c. red (postage)	17·00	10·50
414	-	25c. green	15·00	3·25
415	-	50c. violet	17·00	1·60
416	-	1l.25 blue	36·00	17·00
417	-	5l.+2l.50 brown	95·00	£425

DESIGNS—VERT: 5l. Players heading the ball. HORIZ: 25c., 50c., 1l.25, Two footballers.

418		50c. red (air)	9·00	27·00
419	-	75c. blue	9·00	32·00
420	-	5l.+2l.50 olive	40·00	£250
421	-	10l.+5l. brown	55·00	£350

DESIGNS—HORIZ: 50c. Marina Fiat MF.5 flying boat over Mussolini Stadium, Turin; 5l. Marina Fiat MF.5 flying boat over Stadium, Rome. VERT: 75c. Savoia Marchetti S-55X flying boat over footballer; 10l. Marina Fiat MF.5 flying boat over Littoral Stadium, Bologna.

145 Luigi
Galvani

1934. First Int Congress of Electro-radio-biology.

422	145	30c. brown on buff	90	1·20
423	145	75c. red on pink	1·30	3·50

146 Military
Symbol

1934. Military Medal Centenary.

424	146	10c. brown (postage)	1·20	2·20
425	-	15c. green	1·20	5·50
426	-	20c. red	1·20	2·20
427	-	25c. green	2·20	2·20
428	-	30c. brown	4·50	9·00
429	-	50c. violet	2·20	1·20
430	-	75c. red	13·50	13·50
431	-	1l.25 blue	14·50	9·00
432	-	1l.75+1l. red	19·00	60·00
433	-	2l.55+2l. purple	21·00	80·00
434	-	2l.75+2l. brown	33·00	85·00

DESIGNS—VERT: 25c. Mountaineers; 1l.75, Cavalry. HORIZ: 15c., 50c. Barbed-wire cutter; 20c. Throwing hand-grenade; 30c. Cripple wielding crutch; 75c. Artillery; 1l.25, Soldiers cheering; 2l.55, Sapper; 2l.75, First Aid.

435		25c. green (air)	2·30	5·75
436	-	50c. grey	2·30	9·00
437	-	75c. brown	2·30	11·00
438	-	80c. blue	2·30	13·50
439	-	1l.+50c. brown	4·50	36·00
440	-	2l.+1l. blue	5·50	42·00
441	-	3l.+2l. black	9·00	50·00

DESIGNS—HORIZ: 25, 80c. Italian "P" Type airship under fire; 50, 75c. Marina Fiat MF.5 flying boat and Naval launch; 1l. Caproni Ca 101 airplane and troops in desert; 2l. Pomilio PC type biplane and troops. VERT: 3l. Marina Fiat MF.5 flying boat over Unknown soldier's tomb.

148 King Victor Emmanuel
III

1934. Air. Rome–Mogadiscio Flight and King's visit to Italian Somaliland.

444	148	1l. violet	2·30	50·00
445	148	2l. blue	2·30	65·00
446	148	4l. brown	6·00	£200
447	148	5l. green	6·00	£275
448	148	8l. red	26·00	£375
449	148	10l. brown	30·00	£475

149 Man with Fasces

1935. University Contests. Inscr "LITTORIALI".

450	149	20c. red	1·20	1·20
451	-	30c. brown	3·50	5·75
452	-	50c. violet	1·20	70

DESIGNS: 30c. Eagle and soldier. 50c. Standard-bearer and bayonet attack.

150

1935. National Militia. Inscr "PRO OPERA PREVID. MILIZIA".

453	150	20c.+10c. red (postage)	10·00	13·50
454	-	25c.+15c. green	10·00	19·00
455	-	50c.+30c. violet	10·00	27·00
456	-	1l.25+75c. blue	10·00	44·00
457	-	50c.+50c. brown (air)	11·00	40·00

DESIGNS: 25c. Roman standards; 50c. Soldier and cross; 50c.+50c. Wing over Globe; 1l.25, Soldiers and arch.

152 Symbol of Flight   **153** Leonardo da Vinci

1935. International Aeronautical Exn, Milan.

458	152	20c. red	9·00	2·30
459	152	30c. brown	27·00	7·75
460	153	50c. violet	34·00	1·40
461	153	1l.25 blue	39·00	9·00

154 Vincenzo Bellini   **155** "Music"

1935. Death Centenary of Bellini (composer).

462	154	20c. red (postage)	7·25	4·00
463	154	30c. brown	10·50	11·50
464	154	50c. violet	10·50	1·30
465	154	1l.25 blue	12·00	14·50
466	-	1l.75+1l. orange	39·00	£180
467	-	1l.75+2l. olive	55·00	£200

DESIGNS—VERT: 2l.75, Bellini's villa. HORIZ: 1l.75, Hands at piano.

468	155	25c. brown (air)	2·40	11·50
469	155	50c. brown	2·40	6·75
470	155	60c. red	6·00	19·00
471	-	1l.+1l. violet	12·00	£120
472	-	5l.+2l. green	20·00	£200

DESIGNS: 1l. Angelic musicians; 5l. Mountain landscape (Bellini's birthplace).

156 "Commerce" and Industrial Map of Italy

1936. 17th Milan Fair. Inscr as in T 156.

473	156	20c. red	60	65
474	-	30c. brown	60	1·40
475	-	50c. violet	60	65
476	156	1l.25 blue	1·80	3·50

DESIGN—HORIZ: 30c., 50c. Cog-wheel and plough.

157 "Fertility"

1936. 2000th Birth Anniv of Horace.

477	157	10c. green (postage)	6·00	1·40
478	-	20c. red	3·50	1·20
479	-	30c. brown	7·25	2·50
480	-	50c. violet	7·25	1·00
481	-	75c. red	14·50	11·50
482	-	1l.25+1l. blue	31·00	£120
483	-	1l.75+1l. red	39·00	£130
484	-	2l.55+1l. blue	44·00	£190

DESIGNS—HORIZ: 20c., 1l.25, Landscape; 75c. Capitol; 2l.55, Dying gladiator. VERT: 30c. Ajax defying lightning; 50c. Horace; 1l.75, Pan.

485	-	25c. green (air)	3·50	10·00
486	-	50c. brown	5·00	10·00
487	-	60c. red	6·75	18·00
488	-	1l.+1l. violet	14·50	£140
489	-	5l.+2l. green	22·00	£225

DESIGNS—HORIZ: 25c. Savoia Marchetti S-55A flying boat; 50c., 1l. Caproni Ca 101 airplane over lake; 60c. Eagle and oak tree; 5l. Rome.

159   **160**

1937. Child Welfare. Inscr as in T 159/160.

490	159	10c. brown (postage)	3·50	1·30
491	160	20c. red	3·50	1·30
492	159	25c. green	3·50	2·30
493	-	30c. sepia	3·50	3·50
494	160	50c. violet	3·50	65
495	-	75c. red	9·00	11·50
496	160	1l.25 blue	11·50	11·50
497	-	1l.75+75c. orange	48·00	£140
498	-	2l.75+1l.25 green	33·00	£160
499	160	5l.+3l. blue	44·00	£200

DESIGNS—As Type 159: 30c., 1l.75, Boy between Fasces; 75c., 2l.75, "Bambino" (after della Robbia).

500	-	25c. green (air)	9·00	11·50
501	-	50c. brown	9·00	9·00
502	-	1l. violet	9·00	11·50
503	-	2l.+1l. blue	14·50	£110
504	-	3l.+2l. orange	20·00	£170
505	-	5l.+2l. green	22·00	£200

DESIGNS—As Type 160: 25c., 1l., 3l. Little child with rifle. As Type 159: 50c., 2l., 5l. Children's heads.

163 Naval Memorial   **164** Augustus the Great

1937. 2000th Birth Anniv of Augustus the Great.

506	163	10c. green (postage)	3·50	1·10
507	-	15c. brown	3·50	1·40
508	-	20c. red	3·50	1·10
509	-	25c. green	3·50	1·10
510	-	30c. brown	3·50	2·20
511	-	50c. violet	3·50	65
512	-	75c. red	5·50	5·50
513	-	1l.25 blue	9·00	6·75
514	-	1l.75+1l. purple	50·00	£130
515	-	2l.55+2l. black	55·00	£160

DESIGNS—VERT: 15c. Military trophies; 20c. Reconstructing temples of Rome; 25c. Census (with reference to birth of Jesus Christ); 30c. Statue of Julius Caesar; 50c. Election of Augustus as Emperor; 75c. Head of Augustus (conquest of Ethiopia); 1l.25, Constructing new fleet; 1l.75, Building Altar of Peace; 2l.55, The Capitol.

516	-	25c. purple (air)	7·00	12·00
517	-	50c. brown	7·00	9·50
518	-	80c. brown	16·00	13·50
519	-	1l.+1l. blue	37·00	£110
520	164	5l.+1l. violet	50·00	£170

DESIGNS—HORIZ: 25c. "Agriculture"; 50c. Prosperity of the Romans; 80c. Horses of the Sun Chariot; 1l. Staff and map of ancient Roman Empire.

165 Gasparo Spontini (composer)

1937. Famous Italians.

521	165	10c. sepia	1·30	1·30
522	-	20c. red	1·30	1·30
523	-	25c. green	1·30	1·30
524	-	30c. brown	1·30	2·40
525	-	50c. violet	1·30	1·30
526	-	75c. red	2·50	5·50
527	-	1l.25 blue	3·50	5·50
528	165	1l.75 orange	3·50	5·50
529	-	2l.55+2l. green	16·00	£130
530	-	2l.55+2l. brown	19·00	£160

DESIGNS—20c., 2l.55, Antonio Stradivarius (violin maker); 25, 50c. Giacomo Leopardi (poet); 30, 75c., Giovanni Battista Pergolesi (composer); 1l.25, 2l.75, Giotto di Bondone (painter and architect).

166 Marconi

1938. Guglielmo Marconi (telegraphy pioneer) Commemoration.

531	166	20c. red	2·75	1·20
532	166	50c. violet	1·20	65
533	166	1l.25 blue	2·75	5·50

167 Founding of Rome   **168** Victor Emmanuel III

1938. Second Anniv of Proclamation of Italian Empire.

534	167	10c. brown (postage)	2·20	1·10
535	-	20c. red	2·20	1·10
536	-	25c. green	2·20	1·10
537	-	30c. brown	2·20	2·20
538	-	50c. violet	2·20	1·10
539	-	75c. red	3·25	3·25
540	-	1l.25 blue	6·75	3·25
541	-	1l.75 violet	9·00	4·50
542	-	2l.75 green	24·00	44·00
543	-	5l. red	41·00	55·00

DESIGNS—VERT: 20c. Emperor Augustus; 25c. Dante; 30c. Columbus; 50c. Leonardo da Vinci; 75c. Garibaldi and Victor Emmanuel II; 1l.25, Italian Unknown Warrior's Tomb; 1l.75, "March on Rome"; 2l.75, Wedding ring on map of Ethiopia; 5l. Victor Emmanuel III.

544	168	25c. green (air)	3·25	6·75
545	-	50c. brown	3·25	6·75
546	-	1l. violet	4·50	11·00
547	-	2l. blue	5·50	33·00
548	168	3l. red	9·00	39·00
549	-	5l. green	10·00	65·00

DESIGNS—HORIZ: 50c., 1l. Dante: 2, 5l. Leonardo da Vinci.

169 Steam Locomotive and ETR 200 Express Train

1939. Centenary of Italian Railways.

550	169	20c. red	1·30	65
551	169	50c. violet	1·30	65
552	169	1l.25 blue	2·40	4·50

170 Hitler and Mussolini   **171** Hitler and Mussolini

1941. Italo-German Friendship.

553	170	10c. brown	1·30	2·20
554	170	20c. orange	1·30	2·20
555	170	25c. green	1·30	2·20
556	171	50c. violet	2·20	2·20
557	171	75c. red	5·75	6·75
558	171	1l.25 blue	7·00	11·00

172 Roman Cavalry

1941. 2000th Birth Anniv of Livy (Latin historian).

559	172	20c.+10c. red	45	1·70
560	172	30c.+15c. brown	45	2·20
561	-	50c.+25c. violet	55	2·20
562	-	1l.25+1l. blue	65	2·75

DESIGN: 50c., 1l.25, Roman legionary.

1942. War Propaganda. Nos. 244/5 and 247 with attached labels (imperf between stamp and label) to encourage war effort.

563		25c. green (Navy)	50	1·40
564	-	25c. green (Army)	50	1·40
565	-	25c. green (Air Force)	50	1·40
566	-	25c. green (Militia)	50	1·40
567	-	30c. brown (Navy)	50	5·50
568	-	30c. brown (Army)	50	5·50
569	-	30c. brown (Air Force)	50	5·50
570	-	30c. brown (Militia)	50	5·50
571	-	50c. violet (Navy)	60	1·40
572	-	50c. violet (Army)	60	1·40
573	-	50c. violet (Air Force)	60	1·40
574	-	50c. violet (Militia)	60	1·40

173 Galileo teaching at Padua

1942. Death Tercentenary of Galileo.

575	173	10c. red and orange	60	60
576	-	25c. green and olive	60	60
577	-	50c. violet and purple	65	60
578	-	1l.25 blue and grey	65	4·00

DESIGNS: Galileo at Venice (25c.) and at Arcetri, near Florence (1l.25), 50c. Portrait of Galileo.

174 Rossini

1942. 150th Birth Anniv of Rossini (composer).

579	-	25c. green	30	65
580	-	30c. brown	30	65
581	174	50c. violet	35	65
582	174	1l. blue	35	2·20

DESIGN: 25c., 30c. Rossini Monument, Pescaro.

175

1943. Allied Military Government issue.

583	175	15c. orange	85	1·70
584	175	25c. bistre	85	1·70
585	175	30c. grey	1·10	1·70
586	175	50c. violet	1·10	1·70
587	175	60c. yellow	1·10	1·70
588	175	1l. green	1·10	1·70
589	175	2l. red	1·10	4·00
590	175	5l. blue	1·70	7·75
591	175	10l. brown	1·70	9·00

1943. Allied Military Government issue. Stamps of 1929 optd GOVERNO MILITARE ALLEATO.

592	99	20c. red	1·10	4·50
593	99	35c. blue	7·75	30·00
594	103	50c. violet	40	2·20

187 Romulus, Remus and Wolf (after Pollaiuolo)

1944

619	187	50c. purple	30	2·20

1944. As issue of 1929, but with Fascist emblems removed.

633	-	10c. brown (Augustus the Great)	2·20	1·20
640	99	20c. red	65	55
620	103	30c. brown	55	30
621	103	50c. violet	1·10	3·25
635	-	50c. violet (Italia)	80	30
636	-	60c. orange (Italia)	80	60
641	103	60c. green	65	55
637	99	1l. violet	80	30
643	-	1l.20 brown (Italia)	65	55

638	-	2l. red (Italia)	2·20	1·20
645	**98**	5l. red	3·25	55
646	-	10l. violet (Italia)	13·50	9·00

1945. Stamps of Italy surch **L. 2,50** (No. 629) and stamps of Italian Social Republic surch **POSTE ITALIANE** and new value (Nos. 627/8).

627		1l.20 on 20c. red (No. 102)	10	10
628		2l. on 25c. green (No. 103)	55	40
629		2l.50 on 1l.75 orange (No. 251)	55	40

193 "Work, Justice and Family"　　**195** Planting a Sapling　　**196** "Peace"

197 "Work, Justice and Family"

1945

647	-	10c. brown	20	15
648	**193**	20c. brown	20	15
649	-	25c. blue	20	15
650	**195**	40c. grey	20	20
651	-	50c. violet	20	20
652	-	60c. green	30	65
653	-	80c. red	20	15
654	**195**	1l. green	30	15
655	-	1l.20 brown	40	65
656	-	2l. brown	35	35
657	-	3l. red	35	15
658	-	4l. red	60	15
659	**193**	5l. blue	1·30	20
660	**195**	6l. violet	13·50	20
661	-	8l. green	9·00	35
662	-	10l. grey	2·20	30
663	**193**	10l. red	44·00	20
664	**195**	15l. blue	18·00	20
665	-	20l. purple	11·00	20
666	**196**	25l. green	39·00	35
667	-	30l. blue	£600	60
668	**196**	50l. purple	20·00	30
669	**197**	100l. red	£550	4·50

DESIGNS: 10, 50, 80c., 8, 10l. (662) Hammer breaking chain ("Freedom"); 25c., 1l.20, 3, 4, 20, 30l. Flaming torch ("Enlightenment"); 60c., 2l. Gardener tying sapling to stake.

198 Clasped Hands and Caproni Campini N-1 Jet

1945. Air.

670	**198**	1l. grey	55	20
671	-	2l. blue	55	20
672	**198**	3l.20 red	55	35
673	-	5l. green	55	20
674	**198**	10l. red	55	20
675	-	25l. blue	17·00	13·50
676	-	25l. brown	55	20
677	**198**	50l. green	44·00	22·00
678	**198**	50l. violet	55	20

DESIGN: 2, 5, 25l. Barn swallows in flight.

200 Amalfi

1946. Mediaeval Italian Republics.

679	**200**	1l. sepia	20	20
680	-	2l. blue	20	20
681	-	3l. green	20	20
682	-	4l. orange	30	20
683	-	5l. violet	30	20
684	-	10l. red	30	20
685	-	15l. blue	2·40	1·30
686	-	20l. brown	70	45

DESIGNS—VERT: 2l. Lucca; 3l. Siena; 4l. Florence. HORIZ: 5l. Pisa; 10l. Genoa; 15l. Venice; 20l. "The Oath of Pontida".

1947. Air. Surch LIRE 6-.

687	**198**	6l. on 3l.20 orange	45	30

202 Wireless Mast

1947. Air. 50th Anniv of Radio.

688	**202**	6l. violet	30	20
689	-	10l. red	30	20
690	-	20l. orange	1·30	1·20
691	**202**	25l. blue	2·00	1·40
692	-	35l. blue	3·25	2·75
693	-	50l. purple	4·50	4·00

DESIGNS: 10, 35l. Ship's aerial; 20, 50l. Heinkel He 70 Blitz wireless-equipped airplane.

204 Douglas DC-2 over Rome

1948. Air.

911	**204**	100l. green	75	40
912	**204**	300l. mauve	90	75
913	**204**	500l. blue	1·90	1·90
914	**204**	1000l. brown	3·75	3·25

For No. 911 in smaller size see No. 1297.

205 St. Catherine giving her Cloak to a Beggar　　**206** St. Catherine carrying the Cross

1948. 600th Birth Anniv of St. Catherine of Siena.

698	**205**	3l. blue and green (postage)	35	30
699	-	5l. blue and violet	35	30
700	-	10l. violet and brown	5·00	2·40
701	-	30l. grey and bistre	28·00	24·00
702	**206**	100l. violet and brown (air)	£140	65·00
703	-	200l. blue and bistre	85·00	28·00

DESIGNS—All show St. Catherine. VERT: 5l. Carrying the Cross; 10l. Extending her arms to Italy; 30l. Dictating "The Dialogue" to a Disciple. HORIZ: 200l. Extending her arms to Italy.

207 "Proclamation of New Constitution"

1948. Proclamation of New Constitution.

704	**207**	10l. violet	1·80	1·20
705	**207**	30l. blue	6·75	3·50

208 Rising at Palermo

1948. Centenary of Revolution of 1848.

706	**208**	3l. brown	1·50	80
707	-	4l. purple	1·50	80
708	-	5l. blue	4·75	95
709	-	6l. green	3·00	1·40
710	-	8l. brown	2·75	1·40
711	-	10l. red	4·50	65
712	-	12l. green	17·00	4·75
713	-	15l. black	34·00	95
714	-	20l. red	80·00	12·00
715	-	30l. blue	19·00	3·50
716	-	50l. violet	£200	8·50
717	-	100l. blue	£225	30·00

DESIGNS: 4l. Rising at Padua; 5l. Concession of Statute, Turin; 6l. Storming Porta Tosa, Milan; 8l. Proclamation of Venetian Republic; 10l. Defence of Vicenza; 12l. Hero of Curtatone; 15l. Hero of Goito; 20l. Austrian retreat from Bologna; 30l. Fighting at Brescia; 50l. Garibaldi; 100l. Goffredo Mameli (party patriot) on death bed, July 1849.

209 Alpinist and Bassano Bridge

1948. Rebuilding of Bassano Bridge.

718	**209**	15l. green	6·00	3·00

210 Gaetano Donizetti

1948. Death Centenary of Donizetti (composer).

719	**210**	15l. brown	3·00	2·50

211 Exhibition Grounds

1949. 27th Milan Fair.

720	**211**	20l. sepia	18·00	6·50

212

1949. 25th Biennial Art Exhibition. Venice.

721	**212**	5l. red and flesh	1·20	30
722	-	15l. green and cream	8·50	3·00
723	-	20l. brown and buff	16·00	35
724	-	50l. blue and yellow	£120	3·00

DESIGNS: 15l. Clock bell-ringers, St. Mark's Column and Campanile; 20l. Emblem of Venice and "Bucentaur" (state gallery); 50l. Winged lion on St. Mark's Column.

213 Globes and Forms of Transport

1949. 75th Anniv of U.P.U.

725	**213**	50l. blue	£120	12·00

214 Vascello Castle

1949. Centenary of Roman Republic.

726	**214**	100l. brown	£500	£160

215 Worker and Ship

1949. European Recovery Plan.

727	**215**	5l. green	12·00	7·25
728	**215**	15l. violet	55·00	26·00
729	**215**	20l. brown	£130	30·00

216 Statue of Mazzini

1949. Honouring Giuseppe Mazzini (founder of "Young Italy").

730	**216**	20l. black	22·00	7·75

217 V. Alfieri

1949. Birth Bicentenary of Vittorio Alfieri (poet).

731	**217**	20l. brown	15·00	6·50

218 San Giusto Cathedral

1949. First Trieste Free Election.

732	**218**	20l. lake	28·00	26·00

219 Staff of Aesculapius and Globe

1949. Second World Health Congress, Rome.

733	**219**	20l. violet	70·00	21·00

220 A. Palladio and Vicenza Basilica

1949. 400th Anniv of Completion of Palladio's Basilica at Vicenza.

734	**220**	20l. violet	24·00	13·00

221 Lorenzo de Medici

1949. 500th Birth Anniv of Lorenzo de Medici "The Magnificent".

735	**221**	20l. blue	22·00	4·50

222 Galleon and Exhibition Buildings

1949. 13th Levant Fair, Bari.

736	**222**	20l. red	15·00	4·50

223 Voltaic Pile　　**224** Count Alessandro Volta

1949. 150th Anniv of Volta's Discovery of the Electric Cell.

737	**223**	20l. red	13·00	3·25
738	**224**	50l. blue	£190	55·00

225 Holy Trinity Bridge, Florence

1949. Rebuilding of Holy Trinity Bridge, Florence.

739	**225**	20l. green	23·00	4·50

226 Caius Valerius Catullus

1949. Death Bimillenary of Catullus (poet).
740 **226** 20l. blue 26·00 4·50

227 Domenico Cimarosa

1949. Birth Bicentenary of Cimarosa (composer).
741 **227** 20l. violet 21·00 3·25

228 Entrance to Exhibition

1950. 28th Milan Fair.
742 **228** 20l. brown 7·75 3·25

229 Car and Flags

1950. 32nd Int Automobile Exhibition, Turin.
743 **229** 20l. violet 22·00 3·25

230 Statue of Perseus

1950. Fifth General UNESCO Conference, Florence.
744 **–** 20l. green 19·00 2·50
745 **230** 55l. blue £120 21·00
DESIGN—HORIZ: 20l. Pitti Palace, Florence.

231 St. Peter's Basilica

1950. Holy Year.
746 **231** 20l. violet 19·00 1·30
747 **231** 55l. blue £150 3·75

232 Gaudenzio Ferrari

1950. Honouring Gaudenzio Ferrari (painter).
748 **232** 20l. green 38·00 3·75

233 Town Hall, Florence, Statue of Columbus and Wireless Mast

1950. International Radio Conf, Florence.
749 **233** 20l. violet 32·00 15·00
750 **233** 55l. blue £375 £190

234 L. Muratori

1950. Death Bicentenary of Ludovico Muratori (historian).
751 **234** 20l. brown 14·00 3·25

235 Guido D'Arezzo

1950. Ninth Death Cent of D'Arezzo (musician).
752 **235** 20l. green 44·00 3·75

236 Galleon

1950. 14th Levant Fair, Bari.
753 **236** 20l. brown 23·00 3·25

237 Marzotto and Rossi

1950. Pioneers of Wool Industry.
754 **237** 20l. blue 7·75 2·20

238 Tobacco Plant and Factory

1950. European Tobacco Conference, Rome.
755 **238** 5l. green and mauve 5·25 3·25
756 **–** 20l. green and brown 7·75 1·70
757 **–** 55l. brown and blue £140 36·00
DESIGNS: 20l. Plant; 55l. Girl and plant.

239 Seal of Academy

1950. Bicentenary of Academy of Fine Arts, Venice.
758 **239** 20l. lt brown and brown 10·50 3·25

240 A. Righi

1950. Birth Centenary of Augusto Righi (physicist).
759 **240** 20l. black and buff 10·50 3·25

241 Blacksmith

1950. Provincial Occupations. As T **241**.
760 **241** 50c. blue 25 30
762 **–** 2l. brown 40 30
881 **–** 1l. violet 25 15
763 **–** 5l. black 1·30 25
764 **–** 6l. brown 40 30
765 **–** 10l. green 7·00 25
766 **–** 12l. green 7·75 25
883 **–** 15l. blue 1·90 15
768 **–** 20l. violet 41·00 25
769 **–** 25l. brown 7·75 25
770 **–** 30l. purple 5·25 30
771 **–** 35l. red 31·00 85
772 **–** 40l. brown 1·30 30
773 **–** 50l. violet 60·00 25
774 **–** 55l. blue 3·75 30
775 **–** 60l. red 11·50 1·00
776 **–** 65l. green 3·25 45
777 **–** 100l. brown £130 65
778 **–** 200l. brown 38·00 5·75

DESIGNS: 1l. Motor mechanic; 2l. Stonemason; 5l. Potter; 6l. Girls embroidering and water-carrying; 10l. Weaver; 12l. Fisherman at tiller; 15l. Boat builder; 20l. Fisherman trawling; 25l. Girl packing oranges; 30l. Girl carrying grapes; 35l. Gathering olives; 40l. Carter and wagon; 50l. Shepherd; 55l. Ploughman; 60l. Ox-cart; 65l. Girl harvester; 100l. Women handling maize; 200l. Woodcutter.

242 First Tuscan Stamp

1951. Centenary of First Tuscan Stamp.
779 **242** 20l. red and purple 5·25 1·90
780 **242** 55l. blue and ultramarine 70·00 60·00

243 Car and Flags

1951. 33rd International Motor Show, Turin.
781 **243** 20l. green 28·00 4·50

244 Peace Hall, Rome

1951. Consecration of Hall of Peace, Rome.
782 **244** 20l. violet 19·00 4·50

245 Westland W.81 Helicopter over Fair   **246** Fair Building

1951. 29th Milan Fair.
783 **245** 20l. brown 26·00 3·25
784 **246** 55l. blue £140 90·00

247 Allegory

1951. Tenth International Textile Art and Fashion Exhibition, Turin.
785 **247** 20l. violet 46·00 5·25

248 Columbus disembarking

1951. 500th Birth Anniv of Columbus.
786 **248** 20l. green 38·00 5·25

249 Gymnastics Symbols

1951. Int Gymnastic Festival, Florence.
787 **249** 5l. red and brown 60·00 £600
788 **249** 10l. red and green 60·00 £600
789 **249** 15l. red and blue 60·00 £600

250 Montecassino Abbey restored

1951. Restoration of Montecassino Abbey.
790 **250** 20l. green 13·00 3·25
791 **–** 55l. blue £130 75·00
DESIGN: 55l. Abbey in ruins, 1944.

251 Perugino

1951. 500th Birth Anniv of Perugino (painter).
792 **251** 20l. brown and sepia 8·25 5·25

252 Modern Art

1951. Triennial Art Exhibition, Milan.
793 **252** 20l. black and green 15·00 3·75
794 **–** 55l. pink and blue 75·00 65·00
DESIGN—HORIZ: 55l. Jug and symbols.

253 Cyclist and Globe

1951. World Cycling Championship.
795 **253** 25l. black 23·00 4·50

254 Galleon and Hemispheres

1951. 15th Levant Fair, Bari.
796 **254** 25l. blue 15·00 3·75

255 "Jorio's Daughter"

1951. Birth Centenary of Francesco Paolo Michetti (painter).
797 **255** 25l. brown 13·00 3·75

256 T **1** of Sardinia and Arms of Cagliari

1951. Sardinian Postage Stamp Centenary.
798	**256**	10l. black and sepia	4·50	3·75
799	-	25l. green and red	5·75	3·25
800	-	60l. red and blue	28·00	26·00

DESIGNS: 25l. 20c. stamp and arms of Genoa; 60l. 40c. stamp and arms of Turin.

257 "Industry and Commerce"

1951. Third Industrial and Commercial Census.
| 801 | **257** | 10l. green | 2·50 | 2·30 |

258 Census in Ancient Rome

1951. Ninth National Census.
| 802 | **258** | 25l. black | 11·50 | 2·30 |

259 G. Verdi and Roncole Church

1951. 50th Death Anniv of Giuseppe Verdi (composer).
803	-	10l. green and purple	7·00	3·25
804	**259**	25l. brown and chocolate	13·00	3·25
805	-	60l. blue and green	80·00	26·00

DESIGNS: 10l. Verdi, Theatre Royal and Cathedral, Parma; 60l. Verdi, La Scala Opera House and Cathedral, Milan.

260 Mountain Forest

1951. Forestry Festival. Inscr "FESTA DEGLI ALBERI".
| 806 | **260** | 10l. green and olive | 4·50 | 3·75 |
| 807 | - | 25l. green | 13·00 | 2·50 |

DESIGN—HORIZ: 25l. Tree and wooded hills.

261 V. Bellini

1952. 150th Birth Anniv of Bellini (composer).
| 808 | **261** | 25l. black | 9·00 | 1·90 |

262 Royal Palace, Caserta

1952. Bicentenary of Construction of Caserta Palace by Vanvitelli.
| 809 | **262** | 25l. bistre and green | 11·50 | 1·90 |

263

1952. First Int Sports Stamps Exhibition, Rome.
| 810 | **263** | 25l. brown and black | 3·25 | 1·50 |

264 Motor-boat Pavilion

1952. 30th Milan Fair.
| 811 | **264** | 60l. blue | 90·00 | 22·00 |

265 Leonardo da Vinci

1952. 500th Birth Anniv of Leonardo da Vinci.
812	**265**	25l. orange	75	65
813	-	60l. blue	11·00	10·50
814	**265**	80l. red	29·00	95

DESIGN—(inscr "LEONARDO DA VINCI 1452–1952"): 60l. "The Virgin of the Rocks".

267 Campaniles and First Stamps

1952. Modena and Parma Stamp Centenary.
| 815 | **267** | 25l. black and brown | 1·90 | 1·80 |
| 816 | **267** | 60l. indigo and blue | 18·00 | 17·00 |

268 Hand, Torch and Globe

1952. Overseas Fair, Naples.
| 817 | **268** | 25l. blue | 3·75 | 1·50 |

269 Lion of St. Mark

1952. 26th Biennial Art Exhibition, Venice.
| 818 | **269** | 25l. black and cream | 5·25 | 1·50 |

270 Emblem of Fair

1952. 30th Padua Fair.
| 819 | **270** | 25l. red and blue | 7·00 | 1·90 |

271 San Giusto Cathedral and Flag

1952. Fourth Trieste Fair.
| 820 | **271** | 25l. green, red and brown | 5·25 | 1·90 |

272 Caravel and Bari Fair

1952. 16th Levant Fair, Bari.
| 821 | **272** | 25l. green | 2·50 | 1·50 |

273 Girolamo Savonarola

1952. Fifth Birth Cent of Savonarola (reformer).
| 822 | **273** | 25l. violet | 8·25 | 1·90 |

274 Savoia Marchetti S.M.95C over Colosseum

1952. First Civil Aeronautics Law Conf, Rome.
| 823 | **274** | 60l. blue and ultramarine | 29·00 | 27·00 |

275 Alpine Climbing Equipment

1952. Alpine Troops National Exhibition.
| 824 | **275** | 25l. black | 1·90 | 1·00 |

276 Army, Navy and Air Force Symbols

277 Sailor, Soldier and Airman

1952. Armed Forces Day.
825	**276**	10l. green	30	20
826	**277**	25l. sepia and brown	1·00	40
827	-	60l. black and blue	18·00	7·00

DESIGN—As Type **277**: 60l. Airplane, motor torpedo boat and tank.

278 Cardinal Massaia and Map

1952. Centenary of Mission to Ethiopia.
| 828 | **278** | 25l. deep brown & brown | 3·25 | 2·75 |

279 V. Gemito

1952. Birth Centenary of Gemito (sculptor).
| 829 | **279** | 25l. brown | 1·90 | 1·30 |

280 A. Mancini

1952. Birth Centenary of Mancini (painter).
| 830 | **280** | 25l. myrtle | 1·90 | 1·30 |

281

1952. Centenary of Martyrdom of Belfiore.
| 831 | **281** | 25l. blue and black | 4·50 | 1·30 |

282 Antonello da Messina

1953. Antonello Exhibition, Messina.
| 832 | **282** | 25l. red | 3·75 | 1·30 |

283 Cars Racing

1953. 20th "Mille Miglia" Car Race.
| 833 | **283** | 25l. violet | 2·50 | 1·30 |

284 Bee and Medals

1953. Creation of Orders of Meritorious Labour.
| 834 | **284** | 25l. violet | 2·20 | 1·30 |

285 Arcangelo Corelli

1953. Birth Tercentenary of Corelli (composer).
| 835 | **285** | 25l. brown | 2·20 | 1·30 |

286 Coin of Syracuse

1953. (a) Size 17×21 mm.
887	**286**	1l. black	25	15
888	**286**	5l. grey	25	15
889	**286**	6l. brown	25	15
890	**286**	10l. red	25	15
891	**286**	12l. green	25	15
892	**286**	13l. purple	25	15
893	**286**	15l. grey	25	15
894	**286**	20l. brown	25	15
895	**286**	25l. violet	50	15
896	**286**	30l. brown	45	15
897	**286**	35l. red	30	15
898	**286**	40l. mauve	1·30	25
899	**286**	50l. green	95	20
900	**286**	60l. blue	40	25
901	**286**	70l. green	50	25
902	**286**	80l. brown	40	25
903	**286**	90l. brown	1·00	25
1008	**286**	100l. brown	90	40
905	**286**	130l. red and grey	40	30
1009	**286**	200l. blue	1·00	15

(b) Size 22½×28 mm.
| 904 | | 100l. brown | 32·00 | 30 |
| 846 | | 200l. blue | 13·00 | 75 |

See also Nos. 1202/19b.

287 St. Clare of Assisi

1953. 700th Death Anniv of St. Clare.
| 847 | **287** | 25l. red and brown | 1·30 | 90 |

288 Mountains and Reservoirs

1953. Mountains Festival.
848	**288**	25l. green	3·00	75

289 "Agriculture"

1953. International Agricultural Exn, Rome.
849	**289**	25l. brown	1·90	40
850	**289**	60l. blue	9·50	4·25

290 Rainbow over Atlantic

1953. Fourth Anniv of Atlantic Pact.
851	**290**	25l. turquoise and orange	9·00	30
852	**290**	60l. blue and mauve	21·00	5·75

291 L. Signorelli

1953. 500th Birth Anniv of Signorelli (painter).
853	**291**	25l. green and brown	1·50	65

292 A. Bassi

1953. Sixth Int Microbiological Congress, Rome.
854	**292**	25l. brown and black	1·30	65

293 Capri

1953. Tourist Series.
855	-	10l. brown and sepia	40	40
856	-	12l. black and grey	65	50
857	-	20l. brown and orange	90	20
858	-	25l. green and blue	3·25	25
859	-	35l. brown and buff	3·75	1·00
860	**293**	60l. blue and green	6·75	1·90

DESIGNS—VERT: 10l. Siena; 25l. Cortina d'Ampezzo. HORIZ: 12l. Rapallo; 20l. Gardone; 35l. Taormina.

294 Lateran Palace

1954. 25th Anniv of Lateran Treaty.
861	**294**	25l. brown and sepia	90	30
862	**294**	60l. blue and bright blue	5·75	4·50

295 Television Aerial and Screen

1954. Introduction of Television in Italy.
863	**295**	25l. violet	2·50	30
864	**295**	60l. turquoise	11·50	6·50

296 "Everyone Must Contribute to the Public Expense"

1954. "Encouragement to Taxpayers".
865	**296**	25l. violet	3·25	65

297 Vertical Flight Trophy

1954. First Experimental Helicopter Mail Flight, Milan–Turin.
866	**297**	25l. green	1·90	90

298 Golden Eagle and Campanile

1954. Tenth Anniv of Resistance Movement.
867	**298**	25l. black and brown	75	65

299 A. Catalani

1954. Birth Centenary of Catalani (composer).
868	**299**	25l. green	75	65

300 Marco Polo, Lion of St. Mark, Venice, and Dragon Pillar, Peking

1954. Seventh Birth Centenary of Marco Polo.
869	**300**	25l. brown	90	65
870	**300**	60l. green	8·25	7·75

301 Cyclist, Car and Landscape

1954. 60th Anniv of Italian Touring Club.
871	**301**	25l. green and red	1·30	65

302 St. Michael the Archangel (after Guido Reni)

1954. International Police Congress, Rome.
872	**302**	25l. red	65	30
873	**302**	60l. blue	2·50	3·00

303 Pinocchio

1954. 64th Death Anniv of Carlo Lorenzini (Collodi) (writer).
874	**303**	25l. red	1·30	65

304 Amerigo Vespucci

1954. Fifth Birth Cent of Vespucci (explorer).
875	**304**	25l. purple	75	50
876	**304**	60l. blue	4·50	4·50

305 Madonna (Perugino)

1954. Termination of Marian Year.
877	**305**	25l. brown and buff	75	65
878	-	60l. black and cream	3·50	3·25

DESIGN: 60l. Madonna's head (Michelangelo).

306 Silvio Pellico

1955. Death Centenary of Pellico (dramatist).
879	**306**	25l. blue and violet	75	65

308 "The Nation Expects a Faithful Declaration of Your Income"

1955. "Encouragement to Taxpayers".
907	**308**	25l. lilac	2·50	40

309

1955. Fourth World Petroleum Congress.
908	**309**	25l. green	65	40
909	-	60l. red	1·70	2·20

DESIGN: 60l. Oil derricks and globe.

310 A. Rosmini

1955. Death Cent of Rosmini (theologian).
910	**310**	25l. brown	1·50	40

311 Girolamo Fracastoro (physician) and Roman Arena, Verona

1955. International Medical Conf, Verona.
915	**311**	25l. brown and black	1·00	40

312 Basilica of St. Francis

1955. Bicentenary of Elevation of Basilica of St. Francis of Assisi to Papal Chapel.
916	**312**	25l. black and cream	65	40

313 Scholar and Drawing-board

1955. Centenary of "Montani" Institute, Fermo.
917	**313**	25l. green	65	40

314 "The Harvester"

1955. 50th Anniv of Int Agricultural Institute.
918	**314**	25l. brown and red	50	40

315 F.A.O. Building, Rome

1955. Tenth Anniv of F.A.O.
919	**315**	60l. violet and black	2·10	1·50

316 G. Matteotti

1955. 70th Birth Anniv of Giacomo Matteotti (politician).
920	**316**	25l. red	1·50	40

317 B. Grassi

1955. 30th Death Anniv of Grassi (biologist).
921	**317**	25l. green	65	40

318 St. Stephen giving Alms to the Poor

1955. Fifth Death Cent of Fra Angelico (painter).
922	**318**	10l. black and cream	25	20
923	-	25l. blue and cream	40	30

DESIGN—HORIZ: 25l. St. Lawrence giving goods of the Church to the poor.

319 G. Pascoli

1955. Birth Centenary of Pascoli (poet).
924 **319** 25l. black   65   40

320 G. Mazzini

1955. Air. 150th Birth Anniv of Mazzini (founder of "Young Italy").
925 **320** 100l. green   3·25 1·90

321 "Italia" Ski-jump

1956. Seventh Winter Olympic Games, Cortina d'Ampezzo.
926 **321** 10l. green and orange   15   25
927   -   12l. black and yellow   15   40
928   -   25l. purple and orange   50   25
929   -   60l. blue and orange   4·00 3·50
DESIGNS: 12l. Snow Stadium; 25l. Ice Stadium; 60l. Skating Arena, Misurina.

1956. Air. Italian President's Visit to U.S.A. and Canada.
Surch **1956 Visita del Presidente della Repubblica negli U.S.A. e nel Canada L. 120.**
930 **198** 120l. on 50l. mauve   2·50 2·75

323 Coach and Steam Train

1956. 50th Anniv of Simplon Tunnel.
931 **323** 25l. green   11·50 1·30

324

1956. Tenth Anniv of Republic.
932 **324** 10l. grey and blue   30   30
933 **324** 25l. carmine and red   65   30
934 **324** 60l. light blue and blue   7·00 7·75
935 **324** 80l. orange and brown   13·00   85

325 Count Avogadro

1956. Death Centenary of Avogadro (physicist).
936 **325** 25l. black   40   40

326

1956. Europa.
937 **326** 25l. deep green and green 2·50   20
938 **326** 60l. deep blue and blue   17·00 1·70

327

1956. Int Astronautical Congress, Rome.
939 **327** 25l. blue   65   40

---

328 The Globe

1956. First Anniv of Admission to U.N.
940 **328** 25l. red and green on pink   40   25
941 **328** 60l. green and red on green 65   40

---

329 Savings Bank, Books and Certificates

1956. 80th Anniv of Post Office Savings Bank.
942 **329** 25l. blue and slate   40   40

330 Ovid

1957. Birth Bimillenary of Ovid (poet).
943 **330** 25l. black and olive   50   40

331 St. George (after Donatello)

1957
944a **331** 500l. green   £190 3·25
945a **331** 1000l. red   15·00 1·00

332 Antonio Canova

1957. Birth Bicentenary of Canova (sculptor).
946 **332** 25l. brown   25   25
947   -   60l. slate   45   75
948   -   80l. blue   50   25
DESIGNS—VERT: 60l. Hercules and Lica. HORIZ: 80l. Pauline Borghese (bust).

333 Traffic Lights at Crossroads

1957. Road Safety Campaign.
949 **333** 25l. red, black and green   50   40

334 "Europa" Flags

1957. Europa. Flags in national colours.
950 **334** 25l. blue   1·30   25
951 **334** 60l. blue   10·50 1·30

---

335 Giosue Carducci

1957. 50th Death Anniv of Carducci (poet).
954 **335** 25l. sepia   65   40

336 Filippino Lippi (after self-portrait)

1957. 500th Birth Anniv of Filippino Lippi (painter).
955 **336** 25l. brown   40   40

337 Cicero (bust)

1957. Death Bimillenary of Cicero (statesman).
956 **337** 25l. red   40   40

338 Garibaldi (after M. Lorusso)

1957. 150th Birth Anniv of Garibaldi.
957 **338** 15l. grey   25   20
958   -   110l. lilac   65   40
DESIGN—HORIZ: 110l. Statue of Garibaldi on horseback (after Romanelli).

339 St. Domenico Savio and Youths

1957. Death Centenary of St. Domenico Savio.
959 **339** 15l. black and violet   40   30

340 St. Francis of Paola

1957. 450th Death Anniv of St. Francis of Paola.
960 **340** 25l. black   40   30

341 Dams, Peasant and Map of Sardinia

1958. Inaug of Flumendosa–Mulargia Irrigation Scheme, Sardinia.
961 **341** 25l. turquoise   40   30

---

342 Statue of the Holy Virgin and Lourdes Basilica

1958. Centenary of Apparition of Virgin Mary at Lourdes.
962 **342** 15l. purple   25   15
963 **342** 60l. blue   40   25

343 "The Constitution"

1958. Tenth Anniv of Constitution.
964 **343** 25l. green and brown   25   15
965   -   60l. sepia and blue   25   15
966   -   110l. sepia and brown   25   15
DESIGNS—VERT: 60l. Oak tree with new growth. HORIZ: 110l. Montecitorio Palace, Rome.

344 Exhibition Emblem and Ancient Roman Road

1958. Brussels International Exhibition.
967 **344** 60l. yellow and blue   40   30

345 Rodolfo's Attic (La Boheme)

1958. Birth Centenary of Puccini (operatic composer).
968 **345** 25l. blue   40   30

346 The Prologue (I Pagliacci)

1958. Birth Centenary of Leoncavallo (operatic composer).
969 **346** 25l. red and indigo   40   30

347 Ave Maria (after Segantini)

1958. Birth Centenary of Giovanni Segantini (painter).
970 **347** 110l. green on cream   75   40

348 Fattori in his Studio (self-portrait)

1958. 50th Death Anniv of Giovanni Fattori (painter).
971 **348** 110l. brown   75   40

349 Federal Palace, Brasilia and Arch of Titus, Rome

1958. Visit of Pres. Gronchi to Brazil.

972	349	175l. green	1·30	1·90

349a "Europa"

1958. Europa.

973	349a	25l. blue and red	65	50
974	349a	60l. red and blue	1·90	1·30

350 Naples ½ grano stamp of 1858

1958. First Naples Postage Stamps Centenary.

975	350	25l. brown	40	25
976	-	60l. brown and sepia	40	25

DESIGN: 60l. Naples 1 grano stamp of 1858.

351 Winged Horse (sculpture in Sorrento Cathedral)

1958. Visit of Shah of Iran.

977	351	25l. sepia and lavender	25	20
978	351	60l. blue and pale blue	1·00	1·30

352 E. Torricelli

1958. 350th Birth Anniv of Evangelista Torricelli (physicist).

979	352	25l. red	90	75

353 Triumphs of Julius Caesar (after fresco by Mantegna)

1958. 40th Anniv of Victory in World War I.

980	353	15l. green	25	20
981	-	25l. slate	25	20
982	-	60l. red	40	25

DESIGNS—HORIZ: 25l. Arms of Trieste, Rome and Trento. VERT: 60l. Memorial bell of Rovereto.

354 Eleonora Duse

1958. Birth Centenary of Eleonora Duse (actress).

983	354	25l. blue	40	30

355 "Drama"

1958. Tenth Anniv of "Premio Italia" (international contest for radio and television plays).

984	355	25l. black, blue and red	25	20
985	-	60l. black and blue	40	30

DESIGN: 60l. "Music" (radio mast and grand piano).

356 Sicily 5gr. stamp of 1859.

1959. First Sicilian Postage Stamps Centenary.

986		25l. turquoise	25	20
987	356	60l. orange	40	30

DESIGN: 25l. Sicily 2gr. stamp of 1859.

357 Capitol, Quirinal Square Obelisk and Dome of St. Peter's

1959. 30th Anniv of Lateran Treaty.

988	357	25l. blue	40	30

358 N.A.T.O. Emblem and Map

1959. Tenth Anniv of N.A.T.O.

989	358	25l. blue and yellow	25	20
990	358	60l. blue and green	40	30

359 Arms of Paris and Rome

1959. Rome-Paris Friendship.

991	359	15l. red, brown and blue	25	20
992	359	25l. red, brown and blue	40	30

360 Olive Branch growing from shattered Tree

1959. Int War Veterans' Assn Convention, Rome.

993	360	25l. green	40	30

361 Lord Byron Monument

1959. Unveiling of Lord Byron Monument, Rome.

994	361	15l. green	40	30

362 C. Prampolini

1959. Birth Centenary of Camillo Prampolini (politician).

995	362	15l. red	10·00	65

363 Quirinal Square Obelisk, Rome

1959. Olympic Games Propaganda. Roman Monuments and Ruins. Inscr "ROMA MCMLX".

996	363	15l. sepia and orange	25	20
997	-	25l. sepia and blue	25	25
998	-	35l. sepia and buff	25	25
999	-	60l. sepia and mauve	40	40
1000	-	110l. sepia and yellow	65	25

DESIGNS—VERT: 25l. Tower of City Hall, Quirinal Hill. HORIZ: 35l. Baths of Caracalla; 60l. Arch of Constantine (Colosseum); 110l. Basilica of Massentius.

364 Victor Emmanuel II, Garibaldi, Cavour and Mazzini

1959. Centenary of Second War of Independence.

1001	364	15l. black	15	15
1002	-	25l. red and brown	20	20
1003	-	35l. violet	25	25
1004	-	60l. blue	40	30
1005	-	110l. lake	50	40

DESIGNS—VERT: 25l. Italian camp after the Battle of Magenta (after painting by Fattori); 110l. Battle of Magenta (after painting by Induno). HORIZ: 35l. Battle of San Fermo (after painting by Trezzini); 60l. Battle of Palestro.
The 25l. is also a Red Cross commemorative.

365 Workers' Monument and I.L.O. Building, Geneva

1959. 40th Anniv of I.L.O.

1006	365	25l. violet	25	20
1007	365	60l. brown	65	40

366 Romagna 8b. Stamp of 1859

1959. Romagna Postage Stamps Centenary.

1010	366	25l. brown and black	25	20
1011	-	60l. green and black	40	25

DESIGN: 60l. Romagna 20b. stamp of 1859.

366a "Europa"

1959. Europa.

1012	366a	25l. green	25	25
1013	366a	60l. blue	40	40

367

1959. Stamp Day.

1014	367	15l. red, black and grey	40	30

368 The Fire of Borgo (after Raphael)

1960. World Refugee Year.

1015	368	25l. red	25	20
1016	368	60l. purple	40	30

369 Garibaldi's Message to Sicilians

1960. Cent of Garibaldi's Expedition to Sicily.

1017	369	15l. brown	20	15
1018	-	25l. red	20	15
1019	-	60l. blue	40	30

DESIGNS—VERT: 25l. Garibaldi meeting King Victor Emmanuel II near Naples (after Matania). HORIZ: 60l. Embarkation of volunteers at Quarto, near Genoa (after T. van Elven).

370 The Discus Thrower (after Miron)

1960. Olympic Games. Inscr as in T **370**.

1020		5l. brown	25	15
1021		10l. blue and orange	25	15
1022		15l. blue	25	15
1023		25l. sepia and lilac	25	20
1024	370	35l. red	25	20
1025	-	60l. sepia and green	25	20
1026	-	110l. purple	45	25
1027	-	150l. brown and blue	2·20	2·75
1028	-	200l. green	1·80	40

DESIGNS—VERT: 5l. Games emblem; 15l. Starting the Race (statue); 110l. Pugilist at rest (after Apollonius); 200l. The Apoxiomenos (after Lisippos). HORIZ: 10l. Olympic Stadium, Rome; 25l. Cycling Stadium, Rome; 60l. Sports Palace, Rome; 150l. Little Sports Palace.

371 Vittorio Bottego (after Ettore Ximenes)

1960. Birth Centenary of Vittorio Bottego (explorer).

1029	371	30l. brown	40	30

371a Conference Emblem

1960. Europa.

1030	371a	30l. brown and green	25	20
1031	371a	70l. orange and blue	40	30

372 Caravaggio

1960. 350th Death Anniv of Caravaggio (painter).

1032	372	25l. brown	40	30

373 Coach and Posthorn

1960. Stamp Day.

1033	373	15l. sepia and red	40	30

374 Michelangelo

1961. Works of Michelangelo. Frescoes on ceiling of Sistine Chapel. (a) Size 17×20½ mm.

1034	-	1l. black	25	15
1035	-	5l. orange	25	15
1036	-	10l. red	25	15
1037	-	15l. purple	25	15
1038	-	20l. green	25	15
1039	-	25l. brown	25	15
1040	-	30l. purple	25	25
1041	-	40l. red	25	15
1042	-	50l. green	25	15
1043	-	55l. brown	25	30
1044	-	70l. blue	25	15
1045	-	85l. green	25	15
1046	-	90l. mauve	30	60
1047	-	100l. violet	30	15
1048	-	115l. blue	30	30
1049	-	150l. brown	65	25
1050	374	200l. blue	1·30	50

(b) Size 22×26½ mm.

1051		500l. green	6·50	65
1052		1000l. red	5·75	7·75

DESIGNS: 1, 5, 10, 115, 150l. Ignudo (different versions); 15l. Joel; 20l. Libyan Sibyl; 25l. Isaiah; 30l. Erythraean Sibyl; 40l. Daniel; 50l. Delphic Sibyl; 55l. Cumaean Sibyl; 70l. Zachariah; 85l. Jonah; 90l. Jeremiah; 100l. Ezekiel; 500l. Adam; 1000l. Eve.

375 Douglas DC-8 crossing Atlantic Ocean

1961. Visit of President Gronchi to S. America.

1053	375	170l. blue (Argentina)	5·75	5·75
1054	375	185l. green (Uruguay)	6·50	6·50
1055	375	205l. violet (Peru)	19·00	19·00

The countries indicated are shown in deep colours on the map.

376 Pliny the Younger

1961. 19th Birth Cent of Pliny the Younger.

1056	376	30l. brown and buff	40	30

377 Ippolito Nievo

1961. Birth Centenary of Ippolito Nievo (poet).

1057	377	30l. blue and red	40	30

378 St. Paul in Ship (from 15th-century Bible of Borso d'Este)

1961. 19th Cent of St. Paul's Arrival in Rome.

1058	378	30l. multicoloured	25	25
1059	378	70l. multicoloured	50	50

379 Cannon and Gaeta Fortress

1961. Cent of Italian Unification and Independence.

1060	379	15l. brown and blue	25	20
1061	-	30l. brown and blue	25	25
1062	-	40l. brown and blue	65	50
1063	-	70l. mauve and brown	90	65
1064	-	115l. blue and brown	3·75	25
1065	-	300l. red, brown & green	10·50	11·00

DESIGNS: 30l. Carignano Palace, Turin; 40l. Montecitorio Palace, Rome; 70l. Vecchio Palace, Florence; 115l. Madama Palace, Rome; 300l. Capitals, "Palace of Work", Int. Exn. of Work, Turin.

380 Doves

1961. Europa.

1066	380	30l. red	25	20
1067	380	70l. green	40	30

381 G. Romagnosi

1961. Birth Bicent of Romagnosi (philosopher).

1068	381	30l. green	40	30

382 Imprint of 50c. Provisional Postal Franked Paper of Sardinia, 1819

1961. Stamp Day.

1069	382	15l. mauve and black	40	30

383 The Sweet-burning Lamp from Pascoli's La Poesia (after wood-eng by P. Morbiducci)

1962. 50th Death Anniv of G. Pascoli (poet).

1070	383	30l. red	25	20
1071	383	70l. blue	40	30

384 Pacinotti's Dynamo (diagram)

1962. 50th Death Anniv of Antonio Pacinotti (physicist).

1072	384	30l. black and red	25	20
1073	384	70l. black and blue	40	65

385 St. Catherine (after 15th-century woodcut)

1962. Fifth Centenary of Canonization of St. Catherine of Siena.

1074	-	30l. violet	25	20
1075	385	70l. black and red	65	65

DESIGN: 30l. St. Catherine (after A. Vanni).

386 Camera Lens

1962. 30th Anniv of International Cinematograph Art Fair. Venice.

1076	386	30l. black and blue	25	20
1077	-	70l. black and red	40	65

DESIGN: 70l. Lion of St. Mark.

387 Cyclist being paced

1962. World Cycling Championships.

1078	387	30l. black and green	30	20
1079	-	70l. blue and black	40	40
1080	-	300l. black and red	6·50	6·50

DESIGNS: 70l. Cyclists road-racing; 300l. Cyclists on track.

388 Europa "Tree"

1962. Europa.

1081	388	30l. red and carmine	70	25
1082	388	70l. ultramarine and blue	75	65

389 Balzan Medal

1962. International Balzan Foundation.

1083	389	70l. red and green	1·20	50

390 Campaign Emblem

1962. Malaria Eradication.

1084	390	30l. violet	25	20
1085	390	70l. blue	65	65

391 10c. Stamp of 1862 and 30l. Stamp of 1961

1962. Stamp Day.

1086	391	15l. multicoloured	40	30

392 The Pentecost (from Codex Syriacus)

1962. Ecumenical Council, Vatican City.

1087	392	30l. orange & bl on cream	25	20
1088	392	70l. blue & orge on cream	40	40

393 Statue of Cavour (statesman)

394 Pico della Mirandola (scholar)

1962. Centenary of Court of Accounts.

1089	393	30l. green	40	30

1963. Fifth Birth Cent of G. Pico della Mirandola.

1090	394	30l. violet	40	30

395 D'Annunzio

1963. Birth Centenary of Gabriele D'Annunzio (author and soldier).

1091	395	30l. green	40	30

396 "Sowing" (bas-relief after G. and N. Pisano)

1963. Freedom from Hunger.

1092	396	30l. sepia and red	25	20
1093	-	70l. sepia and blue	50	65

DESIGN: 70l. "Harvesting" (bas-relief after G. and N. Pisano).

397 Monviso, Italian Alps, Ice-axe and Rope

1963. Italian Alpine Club Centenary.

1094	397	115l. sepia and blue	40	30

398 "I.N.A." Lighthouse

1963. 50th Anniv of Italian National Insurance Corporation.

1095	398	30l. black and green	40	30

399 Posthorn and Globe

1963. Paris Postal Conference Centenary.

1096	399	70l. blue and green	40	30

400 Three-dimensional Emblem

1963. Red Cross Centenary.

1097	400	30l. red and purple	25	20
1098	400	70l. red and blue	65	65

401 "World Tourism"

1963. U.N. Tourism Conference, Rome.
| 1099 | 401 | 15l. blue and olive | 40 | 25 |
| 1100 | 401 | 70l. brown and blue | 50 | 50 |

402 "Co-operation"

1963. Europa.
| 1101 | 402 | 30l. brown and red | 25 | 25 |
| 1102 | 402 | 70l. green and brown | 75 | 40 |

403 "Naples"

1963. Fourth Mediterranean Games, Naples. Inscr "NAPOLI 1963".
| 1103 | 403 | 15l. ochre and blue | 25 | 20 |
| 1104 | - | 70l. orange and green | 40 | 30 |

DESIGN: 70l. Greek "Olympic" vase.

404 Mascagni and Costanzi Theatre

1963. 150th Birth Anniv of Verdi (1105) and Birth Centenary of Mascagni (1106) (composers).
| 1105 | | 30l. brown and green | 40 | 40 |
| 1106 | 404 | 30l. green and brown | 40 | 40 |

DESIGN: No. 1105, Verdi and La Scala Opera House.

405 G. Belli

1963. Death Centenary of Giuseppe Belli (poet).
| 1107 | 405 | 30l. brown | 40 | 30 |

406 Stamp "Flower"

1963. Stamp Day.
| 1108 | 406 | 15l. red and blue | 40 | 30 |

407 Galileo Galilei

1964. 400th Birth Anniv of Galileo Galilei.
| 1109 | 407 | 30l. brown | 25 | 25 |
| 1110 | 407 | 70l. black | 40 | 40 |

408 Nicodemus (from Michelangelo's *Pieta*)

1964. 400th Death Anniv of Michelangelo.
| 1111 | 408 | 30l. sepia (postage) | 25 | 25 |
| 1112 | - | 185l. black (air) | 65 | 65 |

DESIGN: 185l. Michelangelo's *Madonna of Bruges*.

410 Carabinieri on Parade

1964. 150th Anniv of Carabinieri (military police).
| 1113 | 410 | 30l. red and blue | 25 | 20 |
| 1114 | - | 70l. brown | 40 | 30 |

DESIGN: 70l. *The Charge at Pastrengo (1848)* (De Albertis).

411 G. Bodoni

1964. 150th Death Anniv (1963) of Giambattista Bodoni (type-designer and printer).
| 1115 | 411 | 30l. red | 40 | 30 |

412 Europa "Flower"

1964. Europa.
| 1116 | 412 | 30l. purple | 25 | 20 |
| 1117 | 412 | 70l. blue | 50 | 40 |

413 European Buildings

1964. Seventh European Municipalities' Assembly.
1118	413	30l. brown and green	25	20
1119	413	70l. brown and blue	40	30
1120	413	500l. red	2·75	2·50

414 Victor Emmanuel Monument, Rome

1964. War Veterans' Pilgrimage to Rome.
| 1121 | 414 | 30l. brown | 25 | 20 |
| 1122 | 414 | 70l. blue | 40 | 30 |

415 G. da Verrazzano and Verrazano Narrows Bridge

1964. Opening of Verrazano Narrows Bridge, New York.
| 1123 | 415 | 30l. black and brown (postage) | 40 | 30 |
| 1124 | 415 | 130l. black and green (air) | 65 | 40 |

This American bridge is designated "Verrazano" with one "z".

416 Italian Stamps

1964. Stamp Day.
| 1125 | 416 | 15l. brown and bistre | 40 | 30 |

417 Prisoners of War

1965. 20th Anniv of Resistance.
1126	417	10l. black	25	20
1127	-	15l. black, red and green	25	20
1128	-	30l. purple	25	20
1129	-	70l. blue	25	20
1130	-	115l. red	25	20
1131	-	130l. brown, green & red	25	20

DESIGNS—VERT: 15l. Servicemen and casualty ("Liberation Army"); 70l. Alpine soldiers ("Resistance in the mountains"). HORIZ: 30l. Gaunt hands and arms on swastika ("Political and Racial Persecution"); 115l. Patriots with banners ("Resistance in the Towns"); 130l. Ruined building and torn flags ("Martyred Cities").

418 I.T.U. Emblem, Meucci and Marconi

1965. I.T.U. Centenary.
| 1132 | 418 | 70l. red and green | 40 | 30 |

419 "Flying Dutchman" Dinghies

1965. World Sailing Championships, Alassio and Naples.
1133	419	30l. black and red	20	15
1134	-	70l. black and blue	25	20
1135	-	500l. black and blue	90	75

DESIGNS—VERT: 70l. "5.5 S.1" class yachts. HORIZ: 500l. "Lightning" dinghies.

420 Mont Blanc and Tunnel

1965. Opening of Mont Blanc Road Tunnel.
| 1136 | 420 | 30l. black | 40 | 30 |

421 A. Tassoni and Episode from his *Secchia Rapita*

1965. 400th Birth Anniv of Alessandro Tassoni (poet).
| 1137 | 421 | 40l. multicoloured | 40 | 30 |

422 Europa "Sprig"

1965. Europa.
| 1138 | 422 | 40l. green and orange | 25 | 20 |
| 1139 | 422 | 90l. green and blue | 45 | 25 |

423 *Hell* (Codex, Vatican Library)

1965. 700th Birth Anniv of Dante.
1140	423	40l. multicoloured	25	15
1141	-	90l. multicoloured	25	20
1142	-	130l. multicoloured	25	25
1143	-	500l. green	65	90

DESIGNS—VERT: 90l. *Purgatory* (codex, Marciana Library, Venice); 500l. Head of Dante (bronze, Naples Museum). HORIZ: 130l. *Paradise* (codex, British Museum).

424 House and Savings-bank

1965. Savings Day.
| 1144 | 424 | 40l. multicoloured | 40 | 30 |

425 Douglas DC-6B passing Control-tower

1965. Night Airmail Service.
| 1145 | 425 | 40l. red and blue | 25 | 20 |
| 1146 | - | 90l. multicoloured | 40 | 30 |

DESIGN: 90l. Sud Aviation SE 210 Caravelle jetliner within airmail envelope "border".

426 Map of "Highway to the Sun"

1965. Stamp Day.
| 1147 | 426 | 20l. multicoloured | 40 | 30 |

427 Two-man Bobsleigh

1966. World Bobsleigh Championships, Cortina d'Ampezzo.
| 1148 | 427 | 40l. red, blue and grey | 25 | 20 |
| 1149 | - | 90l. violet and blue | 40 | 30 |

DESIGN: 90l. Four-man bobsleigh.

428 Skier carrying Torch

1966. University Winter Games, Turin.
1150	428	40l. black and red	25	15
1151	-	90l. violet and red	25	20
1152	-	500l. brown and red	75	75

DESIGNS—VERT: 90l. Ice skating; 500l. Ice hockey.

429 B. Croce

1966. Birth Centenary of Benedetto Croce (philosopher).
| 1153 | 429 | 40l. sepia | 40 | 30 |

430 Arms of Cities of Venezia

1966. Centenary of Union of Venezia and Italy.
| 1154 | 430 | 40l. multicoloured | 40 | 30 |

431 Pine, Palatine Hill, Rome

1966. "Trees and Flowers". Multicoloured.
1155	**431**	20l. Type **431**	25	20
1156		25l. Apples	25	20
1157		40l. Carnations	25	20
1158		50l. Irises	25	20
1159		90l. Anthemis (Golden Marguerite)	25	20
1160		170l. Olive tree, Villa Adriana, Tivoli	25	20
1241		55l. Cypresses (26×35½ mm)	40	25
1242		180l. Broom (26×35½ mm)	65	40

432 "Visit Italy"

1966. Tourist Propaganda.
1161	**432**	20l. multicoloured	40	30

433 Capital "I"

1966. 20th Anniv of Republic.
1162	**433**	40l. multicoloured	25	20
1163	**433**	90l. multicoloured	40	30

434 Battle Scene

1966. Centenary of Battle of Bezzecca.
1164	**434**	90l. olive	40	30

435 *Singing Angels* (from copper panel on altar of St. Antony's Basilica, Padua)

1966. Fifth Death Centenary of Donatello.
1165	**435**	40l. multicoloured	40	30

436 Europa "Ship"

1966. Europa.
1166	**436**	40l. violet	25	20
1167	**436**	90l. blue	40	30

437 *Madonna in Maesta* (after Giotto)

1966. Giotto's 700th Birth Anniv.
1168	**437**	40l. multicoloured	40	30

438 Filzi, Battisti, Chiesa and Sauro

1966. 50th Death Annivs of World War I Heroes.
1169	**438**	40l. green and slate	40	30

439 Postal Emblem

1966. Stamp Day.
1170	**439**	20l. multicoloured	40	30

440 Compass and Globe

1967. Centenary of Italian Geographical Society.
1171	**440**	40l. blue and black	40	30

441 Toscanini

1967. Birth Centenary of Arturo Toscanini (orchestral conductor).
1172	**441**	40l. buff and blue	40	30

442 Campidoglio, Rome

1967. Tenth Anniv of Rome Treaties.
1173	**442**	40l. brown and black	25	25
1174	**442**	90l. purple and black	40	30

443 Cogwheels

1967. Europa.
1175	**443**	40l. purple and pink	25	20
1176	**443**	90l. blue and cream	40	30

444 Brown Bear (Abruzzo Park)

1967. Italian National Parks. Multicoloured.
1177		20l. Ibex (Gran Paradiso Park) (vert)	25	20
1178		40l. Type **444**	25	20
1179		90l. Red deer stag (Stelvio Park)	25	20
1180		170l. Tree (Circeo Park) (vert)	40	30

445 Monteverdi

1967. 400th Death Anniv of Claudio Monteverdi (composer).
1181	**445**	40l. brown and chestnut	40	30

446 Racing Cyclists

1967. 50th Tour of Italy Cycle Race. Designs showing cyclists.
1182	**446**	40l. multicoloured	25	20
1183	-	90l. multicoloured	30	25
1184	-	500l. multicoloured	1·90	1·30

447 Pirandello and Stage

1967. Birth Centenary of Luigi Pirandello (dramatist).
1185	**447**	40l. multicoloured	40	30

448 Stylized Mask

1967. Two Worlds Festival, Spoleto.
1186	**448**	20l. black and green	25	20
1187	**448**	40l. black and red	40	30

449 Coded Addresses

1967. Introduction of Postal Codes.
1188	**449**	20l. black, blue & yellow	25	20
1189	**449**	25l. black, red and yellow	40	30
1190	**449**	40l. black, purple & yell	25	20
1191	**449**	50l. black, green & yellow	40	30

450 Pomilio PE Type Biplane and Postmark

1967. 50th Anniv of First Airmail Stamp.
1192	**450**	40l. black and blue	40	30

451 St. Ivo's Church, Rome

1967. 300th Death Anniv of Francesco Borromini (architect).
1193	**451**	90l. multicoloured	40	30

452 U. Giordano and Music from "Andrea Chenier"

1967. Birth Centenary of Umberto Giordano (composer).
1194	**452**	20l. brown and black	40	30

453 *The Oath of Pontida* (from painting by Adolfo Cao)

1967. 800th Anniv of Oath of Pontida.
1195	**453**	20l. brown	40	30

454 I.T.Y. Emblem

1967. International Tourist Year.
1196	**454**	20l. black, blue and yellow	25	20
1197	**454**	50l. black, blue & orange	40	30

455 Lions Emblem

1967. 50th Anniv of Lions International.
1198	**455**	50l. multicoloured	40	30

456 Sentry

1967. 50th Anniv of Stand on the Piave.
1199	**456**	50l. multicoloured	40	30

457 E. Fermi (scientist) and Reactor

1967. 25th Anniv of First Nuclear Chain Reaction.
1200	**457**	50l. black and brown	40	30

458 Stamp and Dove

1967. Stamp Day.
1201	**458**	25l. multicoloured	40	30

1968. As Nos. 887, etc (1952), size 16×20 mm.
1202	286	1l. black	20	15
1203	286	5l. slate	20	15
1204	286	6l. brown	20	15
1205	286	10l. red	20	15
1206	286	15l. violet	20	15
1207	286	20l. sepia	20	15
1208	286	25l. violet	20	15
1209	286	30l. brown	20	15
1210	286	40l. purple	20	15
1211	286	50l. olive	20	15
1212	286	55l. violet	20	20
1213	286	60l. blue	20	20
1214	286	70l. green	20	20
1215	286	80l. brown	20	20
1215a	286	90l. brown	20	15
1216	286	100l. brown	20	15
1216a	286	120l. blue and green	25	20
1216b	286	125l. purple and brown	65	40
1217	286	130l. red and grey	40	25
1217a	286	150l. violet	25	20

1217b	**286**	170l. green and brown	50	40
1218	**286**	180l. purple and grey	75	40
1218a	**286**	200l. blue	65	25
1219	**286**	300l. green	1·00	45
1219a	**286**	350l. orange, red & yell	75	25
1219b	**286**	400l. red	90	40

459 Scouts around
Campfire

1968. Italian Boy Scouts.

| 1220 | **459** | 50l. multicoloured | 60 | 40 |

460 Europa "Key"

1968. Europa.

| 1221 | **460** | 50l. green and pink | 25 | 20 |
| 1222 | **460** | 90l. brown and blue | 40 | 30 |

461 "Tending the
Sick"

1968. 400th Birth Anniv of Luigi Gonzaga (St. Aloysius).

| 1223 | **461** | 25l. violet and brown | 40 | 30 |

462 Boito and
Mephistopheles

1968. 50th Death Anniv of Arrigo Boito (composer and
librettist).

| 1224 | **462** | 50l. multicoloured | 40 | 30 |

463 F. Baracca and *Aerial
Combat* (abstract by G.
Balla)

1968. 500th Death Anniv of Francesco Baracca (airman of
World War I).

| 1225 | **463** | 25l. multicoloured | 40 | 30 |

464
Giambattista
Vico (300th
Birth Anniv)

1968. Italian Philosophers' Birth Annivs.

| 1226 | **464** | 50l. blue | 40 | 30 |
| 1227 | - | 50l. black | 40 | 30 |

DESIGN: No. 1227, Tommaso Campanella (400th birth anniv).

465 Cycle Wheel
and Stadium

1968. World Road Cycling Championships.

| 1228 | **465** | 25l. blue, pink and
brown | 25 | 20 |
| 1229 | - | 90l. indigo, red and blue | 40 | 30 |

DESIGN: 90l. Cyclists and Imola Castle.

466 *St. Mark's Square, Venice*
(Canaletto)

1968. Death Bicentenary of Canaletto (painter).

| 1230 | **466** | 50l. multicoloured | 40 | 30 |

467 Rossini

1968. Death Centenary of Gioacchino Rossini (composer).

| 1231 | **467** | 50l. red | 40 | 30 |

468 Mobilization

1968. 50th Anniv of Victory in World War I. Multicoloured.

1232	20l. Type **468**		20	15
1233	25l. Trench warfare		20	15
1234	40l. Naval forces		25	15
1235	50l. Air Force		25	25
1236	50l. Battle of Vittorio Veneto		25	20
1237	180l. Tomb of Unknown Soldier		40	30

469 "Conti
Correnti Postali"

1968. 50th Anniv of Postal Cheque Service.

| 1238 | **469** | 50l. multicoloured | 40 | 30 |

470 Tracking Equipment
and Buildings

1968. Space Telecommunications Centre, Fucino.

| 1239 | **470** | 50l. multicoloured | 40 | 30 |

471 "Postal
Development"

1968. Stamp Day.

| 1240 | **471** | 25l. red and yellow | 40 | 30 |

472
Commemorative
Medal

1969. Centenary of State Audit Department.

| 1243 | **472** | 50l. black and pink | 40 | 30 |

473 Colonnade

1969. Europa.

| 1244 | **473** | 50l. multicoloured | 25 | 20 |
| 1245 | **473** | 90l. multicoloured | 40 | 30 |

474
Machiavelli

1969. 500th Birth Anniv of Niccolo Machiavelli
(statesman).

| 1246 | **474** | 50l. multicoloured | 40 | 30 |

475 I.L.O. Emblem

1969. 50th Anniv of I.L.O.

| 1247 | **475** | 50l. black and green | 25 | 20 |
| 1248 | **475** | 90l. black and red | 40 | 30 |

476 Postal Emblem

1969. 50th Anniv of Italian Philatelic Federation.

| 1249 | **476** | 50l. multicoloured | 40 | 30 |

477 Sondrio-Tirano
Mailcoach of 1903

1969. Stamp Day.

| 1250 | **477** | 25l. blue | 40 | 30 |

478 Skiing

1970. World Skiing Championships, Val Gardena.
Multicoloured.

| 1251 | 50l. Type **478** | | 25 | 20 |
| 1252 | 90l. Dolomites | | 40 | 30 |

479 *Galatea* (detail of
fresco by Raphael)

1970. 450th Death Anniv of Raphael. Multicoloured.

| 1253 | 20l. Type **479** | | 25 | 20 |
| 1254 | 50l. *Madonna of the Goldfinch* | | 40 | 30 |

480 Symbols of Flight

1970. 50th Anniv of Rome–Tokyo Flight by A. Ferrarin.

| 1255 | **480** | 50l. multicoloured | 25 | 20 |
| 1256 | **480** | 90l. multicoloured | 40 | 30 |

481 "Flaming Sun"

1970. Europa.

| 1257 | **481** | 50l. yellow and red | 25 | 25 |
| 1258 | **481** | 90l. yellow and red | 40 | 40 |

482 Erasmo da
Narni (from
statue by
Donatello)

1970. 600th Birth Anniv of Erasmo da Narni "Il
Gattamelata" (condottiere).

| 1259 | **482** | 50l. green | 40 | 30 |

483 Running

1970. World University Games, Turin. Multicoloured.

| 1260 | 20l. Type **483** | | 25 | 20 |
| 1261 | 180l. Swimming | | 50 | 40 |

484 Dr. Montessori and
children

1970. Birth Centenary of Dr. Maria Montessori
(educationist).

| 1262 | **484** | 50l. multicoloured | 40 | 30 |

485 Map and Cavour's
Declaration

1970. Centenary of Union of Rome and Papal States with
Italy.

| 1263 | **485** | 50l. multicoloured | 40 | 30 |

486 Loggia of Campanile,
St. Mark's Square, Venice

1970. 400th Death Anniv of Jacopo Tatti, "Il Sansovino"
(architect).

| 1264 | **486** | 50l. brown | 40 | 30 |

487 *Garibaldi at Dijon*
(engraving)

1970. Centenary of Garibaldi's Participation in Franco-
Prussian War.

| 1265 | **487** | 20l. grey and blue | 25 | 20 |
| 1266 | **487** | 50l. purple and blue | 40 | 30 |

488 U.N. Emblem
within Tree

1970. 25th Anniv of United Nations.

| 1267 | **488** | 25l. green, black &
brown | 25 | 20 |
| 1268 | **488** | 90l. yellow, black and
blue | 50 | 40 |

489 Rotary Emblem

1970. 65th Anniv of Rotary International.

| 1269 | **489** | 25l. ultramarine, yell & bl | 25 | 20 |
| 1270 | **489** | 90l. ultramarine, yell & bl | 40 | 30 |

490 Telephone Dial and
"Network"

1970. Completion of Telephone Trunk-dialling System.
1271	**490**	25l. green and red	25	20
1272	**490**	90l. blue and red	40	30

491 Urban Complex and Tree

1970. Nature Conservation Year.
1273	**491**	20l. red and green	25	20
1274	**491**	25l. grey and green	40	30

492 Electric Locomotive *Tartaruga*

1970. Stamp Day.
1275	**492**	25l. black	40	30

493 The Adoration (F. Lippi)

1970. Christmas. Multicoloured.
1276		25l. Type **493** (postage)	30	30
1277		150l. *The Adoration of the Magi* (Gentile da Fabriano) (44×35 mm) (air)	40	40

494 Saverio Mercadante

1970. Death Centenary of Saverio Mercadante (composer).
1278	**494**	25l. violet and grey	40	30

495 "Mercury" (part of Cellini's *Perseus with the Head of Medusa*)

1971. 400th Death Anniv of Benvenuto Cellini (goldsmith and sculptor).
1279	**495**	50l. blue	40	30

496 Bramante's "Little Temple", St. Peter's Montorio, Rome

1971
1280	**496**	50l. black and brown	40	30

497 Adenauer, Schuman and De Gasperi

1971. 20th Anniv of European Coal and Steel Community.
1281	**497**	50l. brown, black & grn	25	20
1282	**497**	90l. brown, black and red	40	30

498 Europa Chain

1971. Europa.
1283	**498**	50l. red	30	20
1284	**498**	90l. purple	60	40

499 Mazzini

1971. 25th Anniv of Republic.
1285	**499**	50l. multicoloured	25	20
1286	**499**	90l. multicoloured	40	30

500 Canoeist in Slalom

1971. World Canoeing Slalom and Free Descent Championships, Merano. Multicoloured.
1287		25l. Type **500**	25	20
1288		90l. Canoeist making free descent	40	30

501 Three Sports

1971. Youth Games.
1289	**501**	20l. black, green & brn	25	20
1290	-	50l. black, violet & orge	40	30

DESIGN: 50l. Four other sports.

502 Alitalia Emblem

1971. 25th Anniv of Alitalia State Airline. Multicoloured.
1291		50l. Type **502**	25	15
1292		90l. Emblem and Globe	30	20
1293		150l. Tailplane of Boeing 747	40	25

503 Grazia Deledda

1971. Birth Cent of Grazia Deledda (writer).
1294	**503**	50l. black and brown	40	30

504 Boy in "Savings" Barrel

1971. Postal Savings Bank.
1295	**504**	25l. multicoloured	25	20
1296	**504**	50l. multicoloured	40	30

1971. Air. As No. 911 but smaller, 20×36 mm.
1297	**204**	100l. green	40	30

505 UNICEF Emblem and Paper Dolls

506 Liner *Tirrenia*

1971. Stamp Day.
1303	**506**	25l. green	40	30

507 The Nativity

1971. Christmas. Miniatures from *Matilda's Evangelarium*, Nonantola Abbey, Modena. Multicoloured.
1304		25l. Type **507**	25	20
1305		90l. *The Adoration of the Magi*	40	30

508 G. Verga and Sicilian Cart

1972. 50th Death Anniv of Giovanni Verga (writer).
1306	**508**	25l. multicoloured	25	20
1307	**508**	50l. multicoloured	40	30

509 G. Mazzini

1972. Death Cent of Giuseppe Mazzini (statesman).
1308	**509**	25l. green and black	15	15
1309	**509**	90l. grey and black	25	25
1310	**509**	150l. red and black	40	30

510 Stylized Flags

1972. 50th International Fair, Milan.
1311	**510**	25l. green and black	15	15
1312	-	50l. red and black	25	20
1313	-	90l. blue and black	40	25

DESIGNS: 50l. "Windows, stand and pavilions" (abstract); 90l. Abstract general view of Fair.

511 "Communications"

1972. Europa.
1314	**511**	50l. multicoloured	50	30
1315	**511**	90l. multicoloured	1·00	40

512 Alpine Soldier

1972. Centenary of Alpine Corps. Multicoloured.
1316		25l. Type **512**	20	15
1317		50l. Soldier's hat	30	20
1318		90l. Soldier and mountains	45	25

513 Brenta Mountains

1971. 25th Anniv of UNICEF. Multicoloured.
1301		25l. Type **505**	25	20
1302		90l. Children acclaiming UNICEF emblem	40	30

1972. Centenary of Tridentine Alpinists Society. Multicoloured.
1319		25l. Type **513**	20	15
1320		50l. Alpinist	30	25
1321		180l. Mt. Crozzon	40	35

514 Diagram of Conference Hall

1972. 60th Interparliamentary Union Conference, Rome.
1322	**514**	50l. multicoloured	25	20
1323	**514**	90l. multicoloured	40	30

515 St. Peter Damiani (miniature, after G. di Paolo)

1972. 900th Death Anniv of St. Peter Damiani.
1324	**515**	50l. multicoloured	40	30

516 The Three Graces (Canova)

1972. 150th Death Anniv of Antonio Canova (sculptor).
1325	**516**	50l. green	40	30

517 Initial and First Verse (Foligno edition)

1972. 500th Anniv of *The Divine Comedy*. Multicoloured.
1326		50l. Type **517**	25	15
1327		90l. Initial and first verse (Mantua edition) (vert)	45	25
1328		180l. Initial and first verse ("Jesino" edition)	50	30

518 "Angel"

1972. Christmas. Multicoloured.
1329		20l. Type **518**	15	15
1330		25l. "Holy Child in Crib" (horiz)	30	25
1331		150l. "Angel" (looking to left)	40	40

519 Postal Coach

1972. Stamp Day.
1332	**519**	25l. red	40	30

520 L. B. Alberti (from bronze by M. de Pasti, Louvre)

1972. 500th Death Anniv of Leon B. Alberti (writer and savant).
1333	**520**	50l. blue and yellow	40	30

521 L. Perosi

1972. Birth Centenary of Lorenzo Perosi (composer and priest).

1334	**521**	50l. brown and yellow	25	20
1335	**521**	90l. black and green	40	30

522 Don Orione

1972. Birth Centenary of Don Orione (child-welfare pioneer).

1336	**522**	50l. blue and turquoise	25	20
1337	**522**	90l. green and yellow	40	30

523 Oceanic Survey

1973. Centenary of Military Marine Institute of Hydrography.

1338	**523**	50l. multicoloured	40	30

524 Grand Staircase, Royal Palace, Caserta

1973. Death Bicentenary of Luigi Vanvitelli (architect).

1339	**524**	25l. green	40	30

525 Schiavoni Shore

1973. "Save Venice" Campaign. Multicoloured.

1340		20l. Type **525**	25	20
1341		25l. *The Tetrarchs* (sculpture) (vert)	25	15
1342		50l. *The Triumph of Venice* (V. Carpaccio)	25	15
1343		90l. Bronze horses, St. Mark's Basilica (vert)	25	20
1344		300l. Piazzetta S. Marco	1·00	90

526 Fair Theme

1973. 75th Int Agricultural Fair, Verona.

1345	**526**	50l. multicoloured	40	30

527 Title-page of *Diverse Figure*

1973. 300th Death Anniv of Salvator Rosa (painter and poet).

1346	**527**	25l. black and orange	40	30

528 Formation of Fiat G-91 PAN Acrobatic Jet Aircraft

1973. 50th Anniv of Military Aviation. Multicoloured.

1349		20l. Type **528** (postage)	25	20
1350		25l. Formation of Savoia Marchetti S-55X flying boats	25	20
1351		50l. Fiat G-91Y jet fighters on patrol	25	20
1352		90l. Fiat CR-32 biplanes performing aerobatics	25	25
1353		180l. Caproni Campini N-1 jet airplane	25	30
1354		150l. Lockheed F-104S Starfighter over Aeronautical Academy, Pozzuoli (air)	40	30

529 Football and Pitch

1973. 75th Anniv of Italian Football Association. Multicoloured.

1355		25l. Type **529**	40	30
1356		90l. Players in goalmouth	90	75

530 A. Manzoni (after F. Hayez)

1973. Death Centenary of Alessandro Manzoni (writer and politician).

1357	**530**	25l. brown and black	40	30

531 Palladio's "Rotunda", Vicenza

1973. Andrea Palladio Commemoration.

1358	**531**	90l. multicoloured	40	30

532 Spring and Cogwheels

1973. 50th Anniv of Italian State Supplies Office.

1359	**532**	50l. multicoloured	40	30

533 Europa "Posthorn"

1973. Europa.

1360	**533**	50l. gold, lilac and yellow	25	20
1361	**533**	90l. gold, green & yellow	40	30

534 "Catcher" and Baseball Field

1973. First Intercontinental Baseball Cup. Multicoloured.

1362		25l. Type **534**	25	20
1363		90l. "Striker" and baseball field	40	30

535 Carnival Setting

1973. Viareggio Carnival.

1364	**535**	25l. multicoloured	40	30

536 *Argenta Episode*

1973. 50th Death Anniv of Don Giovanni Minzoni (military chaplain).

1365	**536**	50l. multicoloured	40	30

537 G. Salvemini

1973. Birth Centenary of Gaetano Salvemini (political historian).

1366	**537**	50l. multicoloured	40	30

538 Farnese Palace, Caprorola

1973. 400th Birth Anniv of "Vignola" (Jacopa Barozzi—architect).

1367	**538**	90l. purple and yellow	40	30

539 *St. John the Baptist*

1973. 400th Birth Anniv of Caravaggio (painter).

1368	**539**	25l. black and yellow	40	30

540 Leaning Tower of Pisa

1973. Tourism.

1369	**540**	50l. multicoloured	40	30

541 Botticelli

1973. Italian Painters (1st series).

1370	**541**	50l. brown and red	25	20
1371	-	50l. blue and brown	25	20
1372	-	50l. green and emerald	25	20
1373	-	50l. black and red	25	20
1374	-	50l. brown and blue	25	20

PAINTERS: No. 1371, Piranesi; No. 1372, Veronese; No. 1373, Verrocchio; No. 1374, Tiepolo.

See also Nos. 1392/6, 1456/61, 1495/9 and 1518/22.

542 Immacolatella Fountain, Naples

1973. Italian Fountains (1st series). Multicoloured.

1375		25l. Type **542**	25	20
1376		25l. Trevi Fountain, Rome	25	20
1377		25l. Pretoria Fountain, Palermo	25	20

See also Nos. 1418/20, 1453/5, 1503/5, 1529/31, 1570/2 and 1618/20.

543 Angels

1973. Christmas. Sculptures by A. di Duccio.

1378	**543**	20l. black and green	20	15
1379	-	25l. black and blue	20	15
1380	-	150l. black and yellow	25	25

DESIGNS: 25l. "Virgin and Child"; 150l. "Angels" (different).

544 Map and Emblems

1973. 50th Anniv of Italian Rotary.

1381	**544**	50l. blue, green and red	40	30

545 Sud Aviation Super Caravelle 12

1973. Stamp Day.

1382	**545**	25l. blue	40	30

546 Military Medal for Valour

1973. 150th Anniv of Holders of the Gold Medal for Military Valour Organisation.

1383	**546**	50l. multicoloured	40	30

547 Caruso as Duke of Mantua in Verdi's *Rigoletto*

1973. Birth Centenary of Enrico Caruso (operatic tenor).

1384	**547**	50l. red	40	30

548 *Christ crowning King Roger* (Martorana Church, Palermo)

1974. Norman Art in Sicily. Mosaics.

1385	**548**	20l. blue and yellow	25	20
1386	-	50l. red and green	40	30

DESIG: 50l. "King William offering Church to the Virgin Mary" (Monreale Cathedral).

549 Pres. L. Einaudi

1974. Birth Centenary of Luigi Einaudi (President 1948–55).

| 1387 | **549** | 50l. green | 40 | 30 |

550 G. Marconi in Headphones

1974. Birth Centenary of Guglielmo Marconi (radio pioneer).

| 1388 | **550** | 50l. brown and green | 25 | 20 |
| 1389 | – | 90l. multicoloured | 40 | 30 |

DESIGN: 90l. Marconi and world map.

551 *David* (Bernini)

1974. Europa. Sculptures. Multicoloured.

| 1390 | | 50l. Type **551** | 50 | 25 |
| 1391 | | 90l. "Spirit of Victory" (Michelangelo) | 75 | 30 |

1974. Italian Painters (2nd series). As T **541**.

1392		50l. blue and green	25	20
1393		50l. brown and blue	25	20
1394		50l. black and red	25	20
1395		50l. brown and yellow	25	20
1396		50l. blue and brown	25	20

PORTRAITS: No. 1392, Borromini; No. 1393, Carriera; No. 1394, Giambellino (Giovanni Bellini); No. 1395, Mantegna; No. 1396, Raphael.

552 Guards from Lombardy-Venetia (1848), Sardinian Marines (1815) and Tebro Battalion (1849)

1974. Bicentenary of Italian Excise Guards. Uniforms. Multicoloured.

1397		40l. Sardinian chasseurs, 1774 and 1795, and Royal Fusilier of 1817	20	20
1398		50l. Type **552**	25	20
1399		90l. Lieutenant (1866), Sergeant-major of Marines (1892) and guard (1880)	35	25
1400		180l. Helicopter pilot, naval and alpine guards of 1974	50	45

553 Feather Headdress

1974. 50th Anniv of National Bersaglieri Association. Multicoloured.

| 1401 | | 40l. Type **553** | 25 | 20 |
| 1402 | | 50l. Bersaglieri emblem on rosette | 40 | 30 |

554 Running

1974. European Athletics Championships, Rome. Multicoloured.

| 1403 | | 40l. Type **554** | 25 | 20 |
| 1404 | | 50l. Pole vaulting | 40 | 30 |

555 Francesco Petrarch

1974. 600th Death Anniv of Francesco Petrarch (poet and scholar).

| 1405 | **555** | 40l. multicoloured | 25 | 20 |
| 1406 | – | 50l. blue, yellow & brown | 40 | 30 |

DESIGN: 50l. Petrarch at work in his study.

556 Portofino

1974. Tourist Publicity (1st series). Multicoloured.

| 1407 | | 40l. Type **556** | 25 | 20 |
| 1408 | | 40l. Gradara | 25 | 20 |

See also Nos. 1442/4, 1473/5, 1513/14, 1515/17, 1543/5, 1596/9, 1642/5, 1722/5, 1762/5, 1806/9, 1845/8, 1877/80, 1917/20, 1963/6, 1992/5, 2031/4, 2088/91, 2115/18, 2165/8, 2212/15, 2248/51, 2315/16, 2365/8, 2425/8, 2486/9, 2550/3, 2661/4, 2752/5, 2872/4, 2940/2, 3004/6, 3158/61, 3218/21, 3277/80, 3357/60 and 3410/14.

557 Tommaseo's Statue, Sebenico

1974. Death Centenary of Niccolo Tommaseo (writer).

| 1409 | **557** | 50l. green and pink | 40 | 30 |

558 Giacomo Puccini

1974. 50th Death Anniv of Giacomo Puccini (composer).

| 1410 | **558** | 40l. multicoloured | 40 | 30 |

559 Cover Engraving of Ariosto's *Orlando Furioso*

1974. 500th Birth Anniv of Ludovico Ariosto (poet).

| 1411 | **559** | 50l. blue and red | 40 | 30 |

560 Commemoration Tablet (Quotation from Varrone's "Menippean Satire")

1974. 2000th Death Anniv of Marco Varrone (Varrone Reatino) (author).

| 1412 | **560** | 50l. lake, red and yellow | 40 | 30 |

---

561 *The Month of October* (detail from 15th-century mural)

1974. 14th International Wine Congress.

| 1413 | **561** | 50l. multicoloured | 40 | 30 |

562 "U.P.U." and Emblem

1974. Centenary of Universal Postal Union. Multicoloured.

| 1414 | | 50l. Type **562** | 25 | 20 |
| 1415 | | 90l. "U.P.U." emblem and letters | 40 | 30 |

563 *The Triumph of St. Thomas Aquinas* (detail—F. Traini)

1974. 700th Death Anniv of St. Thomas Aquinas.

| 1416 | **563** | 50l. multicoloured | 40 | 30 |

564 Detail of Bas-relief, Ara Pacis

1974. Centenary of Italian Order of Advocates.

| 1417 | **564** | 50l. black, green & brown | 40 | 30 |

1974. Italian Fountains (2nd series). As T **542**. Multicoloured.

1418		40l. Oceanus Fountain, Florence	25	20
1419		40l. Neptune Fountain, Bologna	25	20
1420		40l. Maggiore Fountain, Perugia	25	20

565 *The Adoration* (Presepe di Greccio)

1974. Christmas.

| 1421 | **565** | 40l. multicoloured | 40 | 30 |

566 Pulcinella

1974. Children's Comic Characters. Multicoloured.

1422		40l. Type **566**	20	15
1423		50l. Clowns	25	20
1424		90l. Pantaloon from Bisognosi	40	30

567 *God admonishing Adam* (Jacopo della Quercia (sculptor) (1374–1438))

1974. Italian Artists' Anniversaries (1st series).

| 1425 | **567** | 90l. violet | 40 | 30 |
| 1426 | – | 90l. multicoloured | 40 | 30 |

DESIGN: No. 1426, Uffizi Gallery, Florence (Giorgio Vasari (architect and painter) (1511–1574)).

See also Nos. 1445/6, 1480/2, 1523/4, 1564/5, 1593/4, 1699/1700, 1731/2, 1774/5, 1824/5, 1885/6, 1949/50 and 1987.

568 *Angel with Tablet*

1975. Holy Year. Multicoloured.

1427		40l. Type **568**	25	20
1428		50l. Angel with column	25	20
1429		90l. Bridge of the Holy Angels, Rome (49×40 mm)	25	20
1430		150l. Angel with crown of thorns	25	20
1431		180l. Angel with cross	40	30

569 *Pitti Madonna*

1975. 500th Birth Anniv of Michelangelo.

1432	**569**	40l. green	25	20
1433	–	50l. brown	25	20
1434	–	90l. red	25	20

DESIGNS: 50l. Sculptured niche, Vatican Palace; 90l. Detail from fresco "Flood of the Universe" (Sistine Chapel).

570 *The Four Days of Naples* (M. Mazzacurati)

1975. 30th Anniv of Italian Resistance Movement. Resistance Monuments. Multicoloured.

1435		70l. Type **570**	20	15
1436		100l. *Martyrs of the Ardeatine Caves* (F. Coccia)	25	20
1437		150l. *The Resistance Fighters of Cuneo* (U. Mastroianni)	50	40

571 *The Flagellation of Christ* (Caravaggio)

1975. Europa. Paintings. Multicoloured.

| 1438 | | 100l. Type **571** | 65 | 40 |
| 1439 | | 150l. *The Appearance of the Angel to Agar and Ishmael in the Desert* (Tiepolo) | 90 | 45 |

572 Globe and Emblems

1975. International Women's Year.

| 1440 | **572** | 70l. multicoloured | 40 | 30 |

573 "San Marco III" (satellite) and "Santa Rita" (marine launching pad)

1975. Italian Space Project.

1441	573	70l. multicoloured	40	30

1975. Tourist Publicity (2nd series). As T **556**. Multicoloured.

1442	150l. Cefalu	40	30
1443	150l. Isola Bella	40	30
1444	150l. Montecatini Terme	40	30

1975. Italian Artists' Annivs (2nd series). As T **567**. Multicoloured.

1445	90l. *Flora* (Guido Reni (1575–1642))	30	20
1446	90l. *Artist and Model* (Armando Spadini (1883–1925))	30	20

574 Cover Engraving from Palestrina's *Primo Libro delle Messe*

1975. 450th Birth Anniv of Giovanni Pierluigi da Palestrina (composer).

1447	574	100l. purple and brown	40	30

575 Boat in Harbour

1975. Italian Emigration.

1448	575	70l. multicoloured	30	30

576 Notoriat Emblem

1975. Centenary of Unification of Italian Laws.

1449	576	100l. mauve, stone & blue	30	30

577 Railway Steam Locomotive Driving-wheels

1975. 21st International Railway Congress, Bologna.

1450	577	70l. multicoloured	40	30

578 D'Acquisto's Sacrifice (Vittorio Pisani)

1975. 32nd Death Anniv of Salvo d'Acquisto (carabiniere who sacrificed himself to save 22 hostages).

1451	578	100l. multicoloured	50	40

579 Symbolised Head representing Files

1975. Centenary of State Archives Unification.

1452	579	100l. multicoloured	40	30

1975. Italian Fountains (3rd series). As T **542**. Multicoloured.

1453	70l. Rosello Fountain, Sassari	30	25
1454	70l. 99 Channel Fountain, L'Aquila	30	25
1455	70l. Piazza Fountain, Milan	30	25

1975. Italian Composers. As T **541**.

1456	100l. blue, pink and red	30	20
1457	100l. blue, green & deep green	30	20
1458	100l. green, brown & dp brn	30	20
1459	100l. brown, red and lake	30	20
1460	100l. purple, grey and green	30	20
1461	100l. black, lt yellow & yellow	30	20

DESIGNS: No. 1456, Ferruccio Busoni; 1457, Alessandro Scarlatti; 1458, Francesco Cilea; 1459, Antonio Vivaldi; 1460, Franco Alfa; No. 1461, Gaspare Spontini.

581 *Annunciation to the Shepherds*

1975. Christmas. Alatri Cathedral Carvings. Multicoloured.

1462	70l. Type **581**	25	20
1463	100l. *The Nativity*	25	20
1464	150l. *Annunciation to the Kings*	40	25

582 Children on Horseback

1975. Stamp Day. Children's Stories. Multicoloured.

1465	70l. Type **582**	25	20
1466	100l. *The Magic Orchard* (vert)	25	20
1467	150l. *Church Procession*	40	25

583 *Boccaccio* (from fresco by A. del Castagno)

1975. 600th Death Anniv of Giovanni Boccaccio. Multicoloured.

1468	100l. Type **583**	25	20
1469	150l. Cover engraving from Boccaccio's *Fiammetta*	30	25

584 Entrance to State Advocate's Office

1976. Centenary of State Advocate's Office.

1470	584	150l. multicoloured	40	30

585 "Italia 1976" Emblem

1976. "Italia 76" International Stamp Exhibition, Milan (1st issue).

1471	585	150l. red, green and black	25	20
1472	-	180l. multicoloured	30	25

DESIGN: 180l. Exhibition Hall, Milan.
See also Nos. 1487/91.

1976. Tourist Publicity (3rd series). As T **556**. Multicoloured.

1473	150l. Fenis Castle, Aosta	40	30
1474	150l. Forio Ischia	40	30
1475	150l. Itria Valley	40	30

586 Majolica Plate

1976. Europa. Italian Crafts. Multicoloured.

1476	150l. Type **586**	65	25
1477	180l. Vase in form of woman's head	1·00	40

587 Republican Flags

1976. 30th Anniv of Republic. Multicoloured.

1478	100l. Type **587**	30	20
1479	150l. Statesmen	40	25

588 *Fortitude* (Giacomo Serpotta) (1656–1732)

1976. Italian Artists' Annivs (3rd series).

1480	588	150l. blue	40	30
1481	-	150l. multicoloured	40	30
1482	-	150l. black and red	40	30

DESIGNS: No. 1481, *Woman at Table* (Umberto Boccioni (1882–1916)); 1482, *Gunner's Letter from the Front* (Filippo Tommaso Marinetti (1876–1944)).

589 *The Dragon*

1976. 450th Death Anniv of Vittore Carpaccio (painter).

1483	589	150l. red	50	40
1484	-	150l. red	50	40

DESIGN: No. 1484, "St. George".
Nos. 1483/4 form Carpaccio's *St. George and the Dragon*.

590 *Flora*

1976. 400th Death Anniv of Titian.

1485	590	150l. red	40	30

591 St. Francis (13th-century fresco)

1976. 750th Death Anniv of St. Francis of Assisi.

1486	591	150l. brown & lt brown	40	30

592 "Cursus Publicus" Post Cart

1976. "Italia 76" International Stamp Exhibition, Milan (2nd issue).

1487	592	70l. black, grey and blue	15	15
1488	-	100l. black, grey & yellow	30	20
1489	-	150l. black, grey & brown	45	25
1490	-	200l. multicoloured	60	40
1491	-	400l. multicoloured	75	65

DESIGNS: 100l. Emblem of Royal Sardinian Posts; 150l. 19th-century "Lion's head" letterbox; 200l. Early cancelling machine; 400l. Modern letter-coding machine.

593 Girl with Protective Umbrella and Animals

1976. Stamp Day. Nature Protection. Multicoloured.

1492	40l. Type **593**	15	10
1493	100l. "Protective scarf"	30	15
1494	150l. Doctor with bandaged tree	35	20

1976. Italian Painters (3rd series). As T **541**.

1495	170l. green, yellow and red	45	25
1496	170l. black, turquoise & green	45	25
1497	170l. black, purple and mauve	45	25
1498	170l. brown, lavender & violet	45	25
1499	170l. black and brown	45	25

DESIGNS: No. 1495, Carlo Dolci; 1496, Lorenzo Ghiberti (sculptor); 1497, Domenico Ghirlandaio; 1498, Giovanni Piazzetta; 1499, *Sassoferrato* (Giovanni Salvi).

594 *The Visit* (S. Lega)

1976. 150th Birth Anniv of Silvestro Lega (painter).

1500	594	170l. multicoloured	45	30

595 *Adoration of the Magi* (Bartolo di Fredi)

1976. Christmas. Multicoloured.

1501	70l. Type **595**	30	20
1502	120l. *The Nativity* (Taddao Gaddi)	45	30

1976. Italian Fountains (4th series). As T **542**. Multicoloured.

1503	170l. Antique Fountain, Gallipoli	50	25
1504	170l. Erbe Madonna Fountain, Verona	50	25
1505	170l. Fountain of Palazzo Doria, Gerona	50	25

596 Net of Serpents obscuring the Sun

1977. Campaign against Drug Abuse. Multicoloured.

1506	120l. Type **596**	35	25
1507	170l. "Addict" and poppy	45	30

597 Igniting Explosives

1977. 300th Birth Anniv of Pietro Micca (national hero).

1508	597	170l. multicoloured	45	30

598 "Globe" and
Cross

1977. Salesian Missionaries. Multicoloured.
| 1509 | 70l. Type **598** | 30 | 20 |
| 1510 | 120l. St. John Bosco and "United people" | 45 | 30 |

599 Article 53 of the
Italian Constitution

1977. "Encouragement to Taxpayers".
| 1511 | **599** | 120l. black, brn & stone | 30 | 25 |
| 1512 | **599** | 170l. black, olive & green | 45 | 30 |

1977. Europa. As T **556** but with C.E.P.T. emblem.
Multicoloured.
| 1513 | 170l. Mount Etna | 90 | 25 |
| 1514 | 200l. Castel del Monte | 2·20 | 40 |

1977. Tourist Publicity (4th series). As T **556**.
Multicoloured.
1515	170l. Canossa Castle	45	25
1516	170l. Castellana Grotto	45	25
1517	170l. Fermo	45	25

1977. Famous Italians. As T **541**.
1518	70l. brown, green & dp green	30	25
1519	70l. black, blue and green	30	25
1520	70l. brown, yellow & lt brown	30	25
1521	70l. blue, pink and red	30	25
1522	70l. black, brown & dp brown	30	25
DESIGNS: No. 1518, Filippo Brunelleschi (architect); 1519, Pietro Aretino (satirist); 1520, Carlo Goldoni (dramatist); 1521, Luigi Cherubini (composer); 1522, Edoardo Bassini (surgeon).

1977. Italian Artists' Anniversaries (4th series). As T **567**
Multicoloured.
| 1523 | 170l. *Winter* (G. Arcimboldi (c. 1527–93)) | 60 | 25 |
| 1524 | 170l. *Justice* (Andrea Delitio (15th century)) | 60 | 25 |

601 Paddle-steamer *Ferdinando
Primo*

1977. Italian Ship-building (1st series). Multicoloured.
1525	170l. Type **601**	60	25
1526	170l. Sail corvette *Carracciolo*	60	25
1527	170l. Liner *Saturnia*	60	25
1528	170l. Hydrofoil missile boat *Sparviero*	60	25
See also Nos. 1552/5, 1621/4 and 1691/4.

1977. Italian Fountains (5th series). As T **542**.
Multicoloured.
1529	120l. Pacassi Fountain, Gorizia	45	40
1530	120l. Fraterna Fountain, Isernia	45	40
1531	120l. Palma Fountain, Palmi	45	40

602 Handball

1977. Stamp Day. "Leisure Time". Multicoloured.
1532	120l. Type **602**	35	20
1533	120l. Catching butterflies	35	20
1534	120l. Kites	35	20

603 "Pulse"

1977. "Give Blood". Multicoloured.
| 1535 | 70l. Type **603** | 45 | 25 |
| 1536 | 120l. "Transfusion" | 60 | 30 |

604 Quintino Sella
and 1863 1l.
Stamps

1977. 150th Birth Anniv of Quintino Sella (statesman).
| 1537 | **604** | 170l. green and brown | 60 | 40 |

605 Dina Galli

1977. Birth Centenary of Dina Galli (actress).
| 1538 | **605** | 170l. multicoloured | 60 | 40 |

606 *Adoration of the Shepherds*
(P. Testa)

1977. Christmas.
| 1539 | **606** | 70l. black and green | 30 | 20 |
| 1540 | - | 120l. black and green | 45 | 30 |
DESIGN: 120l. *The Adoration of the Shepherds* (J. Caraglio).

607 La Scala
Opera House

1978. Bicentenary of La Scala Opera House.
| 1541 | 170l. Type **607** | 45 | 25 |
| 1542 | 200l. Theatre interior | 75 | 40 |

1978. Tourist Publicity (5th series). As T **556**.
Multicoloured.
1543	70l. Gubbio	30	20
1544	200l. Udine	60	40
1545	600l. Paestum	1·50	1·00

608 Dusky Grouper

1978. Environmental Protection. Mediterranean Fauna.
Multicoloured.
1546	170l. Type **608**	75	30
1547	170l. Leathery turtle	75	30
1548	170l. Mediterranean monk seal	75	30
1549	170l. Audouin's gull	75	30

609 Maschio Angioino
Castle, Naples

1978. Europa. Multicoloured.
| 1550 | 170l. Type **609** | 95 | 40 |
| 1551 | 200l. Pantheon, Rome | 1·10 | 50 |

1978. Italian Ship-building (2nd series). As T **601**.
Multicoloured.
1552	170l. Brigantine *Fortuna*	65	25
1553	170l. Cruiser *Benedetto Brin*	65	25
1554	170l. Frigate *Lupo*	65	25
1555	170l. Container ship *Africa*	65	25

610 Matilde
Serao (writer)

1978. Famous Italians.
1556	**610**	170l. black and red	45	25
1557	-	170l. brown and blue	45	25
1558	-	170l. blue and pale blue	45	25
1559	-	170l. black and green	45	25
1560	-	170l. brown and green	45	25
1561	-	170l. blue and red	45	25
DESIGNS: No. 1557, Vittorino da Feltre (scientist); No. 1558, Victor Emmanuel II; No. 1559, Pope Pius IX; No. 1560, Marcello Malpighi (biologist); No. 1561, Antonio Meucci (telephone pioneer).
See also Nos. 1600/4.

611 First and Last
Paragraphs of
Constitution

1978. 30th Anniv of Constitution.
| 1562 | **611** | 170l. multicoloured | 45 | 30 |

612 Telephone
Wires and Lens

1978. Photographic Information.
| 1563 | **612** | 120l. grey, blue and green | 35 | 30 |

1978. Italian Artists' Annivs (5th series). As T **567**.
Multicoloured.
| 1564 | 170l. *The Ivy* (Tranquillo Cremona, 1837–78) | 1·50 | 65 |
| 1565 | 520l. *The Cook* (Bernardo Strozzi, 1581–1644) | 3·75 | 1·30 |

613 The Holy Shroud of Turin

1978. 400th Anniv of Translation of the Holy Shroud from Savoy to Turin.
| 1566 | **613** | 220l. yellow, black & red | 80 | 40 |

614 Volleyball
Players

1978. World Volleyball Championships.
| 1567 | **614** | 80l. black, red and blue | 45 | 25 |
| 1568 | - | 120l. black, blue & orge | 75 | 40 |
DESIGN: 120l. Players with ball.

615 Detail from *St.
Peter distributing
Ananias's Silver*

1978. 550th Death Anniv of Tommaso Guidi (Masaccio).
| 1569 | **615** | 170l. blue | 45 | 30 |

1978. Italian Fountains (6th series). As T **542**.
Multicoloured.
1570	120l. Neptune Fountain, Trento	45	25
1571	120l. Fountain of Fortune, Fano	45	25
1572	120l. Cavallina Fountain, Genzano di Lucania	45	25

616 Madonna and
Child (Giorgione)

1978. Christmas.
| 1573 | **616** | 80l. red and brown | 30 | 20 |
| 1574 | - | 120l. multicoloured | 45 | 30 |
DESIGN—HORIZ (48×27 mm): 120l. *Adoration of the Magi* (Giorgione).

617 "Flowers"

1978. Stamp Day. United Europe. Multicoloured.
1575	120l. Type **617**	45	25
1576	120l. Flags and ribbon	45	25
1577	120l. Figures raising globe inscribed "E"	45	25

618

1978
1578	**618**	1500l. multicoloured	3·00	25
1579	**618**	2000l. multicoloured	4·00	25
1580	**618**	3000l. multicoloured	6·25	40
1581	**618**	4000l. multicoloured	8·25	40
1582	**618**	5000l. multicoloured	11·00	85
1583	**618**	10000l. multicoloured	17·00	1·90
1584	**618**	20000l. multicoloured	33·00	7·75

619 State Polygraphic
Institute

1979. 50th Anniv of State Polygraphic Institute.
Multicoloured.
| 1588 | 170l. Type **619** | 45 | 25 |
| 1589 | 220l. Printing press | 60 | 40 |

620 *St. Francis washing
the Feet of a Leper*
(Maestro di Francesco
Bardi)

1979. Leprosy Relief.
| 1590 | **620** | 80l. multicoloured | 35 | 25 |

621 Cyclist
carrying Bicycle

1979. World Cyclo-cross Championships.
| 1591 | **621** | 170l. multicoloured | 45 | 25 |
| 1592 | **621** | 220l. multicoloured | 60 | 40 |

1979. Italian Artists' Annivs (6th series). As T **567**.
Multicoloured.
| 1593 | 170l. *Annunciation* (Antonella da Messina c. 1430–79) | 75 | 40 |
| 1594 | 520l. *Field with Haystack* (Ardengo Soffici 1879–1964) | 1·50 | 70 |

622 Albert Einstein

1979. Birth Centenary of Albert Einstein (physicist).

1595	622	120l. purple, grey & bl	45	30

1979. Tourist Publicity (6th series). As T 556. Multicoloured.

1596		70l. Asiago	30	20
1597		90l. Castelsardo, Sardinia	45	25
1598		170l. Orvieto	60	40
1599		220l. Scilla	85	50

1979. Famous Italians. As T 610.

1600		170l. brown, blue and black	45	25
1601		170l. green, yellow and violet	45	25
1602		170l. blue and pink	45	25
1603		170l. brown and ochre	45	25
1604		170l. mauve, brown and green	45	25

DESIGNS: No. 1600, Carlo Maderno (architect); No. 1601, Lazzaro Spallanzani (biologist); No. 1602, Ugo Foscolo (author); No. 1603, Massimo Bontempelli (writer); No. 1604, Francesco Severi (mathematician).

623 Morse Telegraph Apparatus

1979. Europa. Multicoloured.

1605		170l. Type 623	2·40	40
1606		220l. Carrier pigeon with message tube	2·75	50

624 Flags of Member States forming "E"

1979. First Direct Elections to European Parliament.

1607	624	170l. multicoloured	45	25
1608	624	220l. multicoloured	60	40

625 Head of Aeneas (bas-relief, Ara Pacis, Rome)

1979. 70th World Rotary Congress, Rome.

1609	625	220l. multicoloured	75	40

626 Ball in Basket (poster)

1979. 21st European Basketball Championships.

1610	626	80l. multicoloured	30	20
1611	-	120l. lake, black & yellow	60	30

DESIGN: 120l. Two players.

627 Doctor examining Patient with Stomach Ailment (woodcut from Giovanni da Cuba's Hortus Sanitatus)

1979. Prevention of Digestive Illnesses.

1612	627	120l. multicoloured	60	40

628 Emblem, Ribbon "3" and Milan Cathedral

1979. Third World Machine Tool Exhibition, Milan.

1613	628	170l. multicoloured	45	25
1614	628	220l. multicoloured	60	30

629 Ottorino Respighi and Appian Way, Rome

1979. Birth Centenary of Ottorino Respighi (composer).

1615	629	120l. multicoloured	60	40

630 Woman with Telephone and Morse Key

1979. Third World Telecommunications Exhibition, Geneva.

1616	630	170l. black and red	60	25
1617	-	220l. grey and green	85	50

DESIGN: 220l. Woman with early telephone and communications satellite.

1979. Italian Fountains (7th series). As T 542. Multicoloured.

1618		120l. Melograno Fountain, Issogne	60	40
1619		120l. Bollente Fountain, Acqui Terme	60	40
1620		120l. Grand Fountain, Viterbo	60	40

1979. Italian Ship-building (3rd series). As T 601. Multicoloured.

1621		170l. Full-rigged ship Cosmos	65	25
1622		170l. Cruiser Dandolo	65	25
1623		170l. Ferry Deledda	65	25
1624		170l. Submarine Carlo Fecia di Cossato	65	25

631 Sir Rowland Hill and Penny Black

1979. Death Centenary of Sir Rowland Hill.

1625	631	220l. multicoloured	60	40

632 Christmas Landscape

1979. Christmas.

1626	632	120l. multicoloured	45	30

633 Children under Umbrella (Group IIB, Varapodio School)

1979. Stamp Day. International Year of the Child. Drawings by Schoolchildren. Multicoloured.

1627		70l. Children of different races holding hands (L. Carra) (horiz)	20	20
1628		120l. Type 633	35	25
1629		150l. Children with balloons (V. Fedon) (horiz)	45	30

634 Solar Energy (alternative sources)

1980. Energy Conservation. Multicoloured.

1630		120l. Type 634	30	20
1631		170l. Oil well (reduction of consumption)	45	30

635 St. Benedict (detail, fresco by Sodoma in Monastery of Monteoliveto Maggiore)

1980. 1500th Birth Anniv of St. Benedict of Nursia (founder of Benedictine Order).

1632	635	220l. blue	75	45

636 Royal Palace, Naples

1980. "Europa 80" International Stamp Exhibition, Naples.

1633	636	220l. multicoloured	60	40

637 Antonio Pigafetta (navigator) and Vitoria

1980. Europa. Multicoloured.

1634		170l. Type 637	1·40	30
1635		220l. Antonio lo Surdo (geophysicist)	2·00	50

638 St. Catherine (reliquary bust)

1980. 600th Death Anniv of St. Catherine of Siena.

1636	638	170l. multicoloured	60	40

639 Red Cross Flags

1980. First International Exhibition of Red Cross Stamps in Italy.

1637	639	70l. multicoloured	35	25
1638	639	80l. multicoloured	45	30

640 Philae Temples

1980. Italian Work for the World (1st series). Preservation of Philae Temples, Egypt. Multicoloured.

1639		220l. Type 640	50	25
1640		220l. Right hand view of temples	50	25

Nos. 1639/40 were issued together se-tenant, forming a composite design.

See also Nos. 1720/1, 1758/9, 1780/1, 1830/1, 1865/6 and 1937/40.

641 Footballer

1980. European Football Championship, Italy.

1641	641	80l. multicoloured	3·00	2·40

1980. Tourist Publicity (7th series). As T 556. Multicoloured.

1642		80l. Erice	30	25
1643		150l. Ravello	45	30
1644		200l. Roseto degli Abruzzi	75	40
1645		670l. Salsomaggiore Terme	1·50	1·00

642 Cosimo I with his Artists (Vasari)

1980. "Florence and Tuscany of the Medicis in 16th Century Europe" Exhibition. Multicoloured.

1646		170l. Type 642 (ceiling medallion, Palazzo Vecchio, Florence)	35	25
1647		170l. Armillary sphere	35	25

643 Fonte Avellana Monastery

1980. Millenary of Fonte Avellana Monastery.

1648	643	200l. dp green, grn & brn	60	40

644 Castel Sant' Angelo, Rome

1980. Castles. (a) Size 22×27 mm.

1649	644	5l. blue and red	30	15
1650	-	10l. brown and ochre	30	15
1651	-	20l. brown and blue	30	15
1652	-	30l. orange and blue	30	15
1653	-	40l. brown and blue	30	15
1654	-	50l. multicoloured	30	15
1655	-	60l. green and mauve	30	15
1656	-	70l. multicoloured	30	15
1657	-	80l. multicoloured	30	15
1658	-	90l. multicoloured	30	15
1659	-	100l. multicoloured	30	15
1660	-	120l. blue and pink	30	15
1661	-	150l. violet and brown	45	15
1662	-	170l. black and yellow	1·00	15
1663	-	180l. blue and pink	1·70	1·40
1664	-	200l. multicoloured	1·10	20
1665	-	250l. multicoloured	1·00	20
1666a	-	300l. multicoloured	75	15
1667	-	350l. brown, blue & grn	1·20	20
1667a	-	380l. multicoloured	1·50	40
1668	-	400l. blue, green & brn	1·20	20
1669	-	450l. multicoloured	1·50	25
1670	-	500l. blue, brown & grn	1·20	20
1670a	-	550l. multicoloured	1·70	40
1671	-	600l. black and green	1·30	20
1671a	-	650l. multicoloured	1·70	65
1672	-	700l. multicoloured	1·50	25
1673	-	750l. brown, green & bl	1·70	65
1674	-	800l. brown, grn & mve	1·60	25
1675	-	850l. multicoloured	2·00	75
1676	-	900l. multicoloured	1·70	25
1677	-	1000l. multicoloured	1·90	40
1678	-	1400l. brown, blue & vio	3·00	65

(b) Size 16×21 mm.

1679		30l. mauve	45	25
1680b		50l. blue	20	20
1680c		100l. brown	35	25
1681		120l. brown	60	30
1682		170l. violet	1·20	75
1683	-	220l. violet and blue	4·00	2·50
1684		300l. light green and green	85	65
1685		400l. brown and green	85	65
1686a		450l. green	1·00	70

1687	500l. blue	1·50	1·00
1687a	600l. green	1·90	1·30
1688	650l. mauve	1·30	1·00
1689	750l. violet	1·50	1·20
1690	800l. red	1·90	1·30

DESIGNS: 10l. *Sforzesco Castle, Milan*; 20l. *Castel del Monte, Andria*; 30l. (1652), *L'Aquila Castle*; 30l. (1679), 100l. (1680c), *Santa Severa Castle*; 40l. *Ursino Castle, Catania*; 50l. (1654), *Rocca di Calascio, L'Aquila*; 50l. (1680b), *Scilla*; 60l. *Norman Tower, San Mauro*; 70l. *Aragonese Castle, Reggio Calabria*; 80l. *Sabbionara, Avio*; 90l. *Isola Capo Rizzuto*; 100l. (1659), *Aragonese Castle, Ischia*; 120l. (1660), *Estense Castle, Ferrara*; 120l. (1681), *Lombardia Enna*; 150l. *Miramare, Trieste*; 170l. (1662), *Ostia*; 170l. (1682), 650l. (1688), *Serralunga d'Alba*; 180l. *Castel Gavone, Finale Ligure*; 200l. (1664), *Cerro al Volturno*; 200l. (1683), *Svevo Angioina Fortress, Lucera*; 250l. *Rocca di Mondavio, Pesaro*; 300l. (1666a), *Norman Castle, Svevo, Bari*; 300l. (1684), 500l. (1687), *Norman Castle, Melfi*; 350l. *Mussomeli*; 380l. *Rocca di Vignola, Modena*; 400l. (1668), *Emperor's Castle, Prato*; 400l. (1685), 750l. (1689), *Venafro*; 450l. (1669), *Bosa*; 450l. (1686a) *Piobbico Castle, Pesaro*; 500l. (1670), *Rovereto*; 550l. *Rocca Sinibalda*; 600l. *Scaligero Castle, Sirmione*; 650l. (1671a), *Montecchio*; 700l. *Ivrea*; 750l. (1673), *Rocca di Urbisaglia*; 800l. *Rocca Maggiore, Assisi*; 850l. *Castello di Arechi, Salerno*; 900l. *Castello di Saint-Pierre, Aosta*; 1000l. *Montagnana, Padua*; 1400l. *Calloresco Castle, Vasto*.

1980. Italian Ship-building (4th series). As T **601**. Multicoloured.

1691	200l. Corvette *Gabbiano*	1·70	65
1692	200l. Destroyer *Audace*	1·70	65
1693	200l. Barque *Italia*	1·70	65
1694	200l. Pipe-layer *Castoro Sei*	1·70	65

645 Filippo Mazzei

1980. 250th Birth Anniv of Filippo Mazzei (writer and American revolutionary).

| 1695 | **645** | 320l. multicoloured | 1·00 | 40 |

646 Villa Foscari
Malcontenta, Venice

1980. Italian Villas (1st series). Multicoloured.

1696	80l. Type **646**	75	40
1697	150l. Barbaro Maser, Treviso	1·30	40
1698	170l. Godi Valmarana, Vicenza	1·50	40

See also Nos. 1737/9, 1770/2, 1811/14, 1853/6, 1893/6 and 1943/7.

1980. Italian Artists Anniversaries (7th series). As T **567**. Multicoloured.

| 1699 | 520l. *Saint Barbara* (Jacopo Palma, the Elder (1480–1528)) | 1·50 | 90 |
| 1700 | 520l. *Apollo and Daphne* (Gian Lorenzo Bernini (1598–1680)) | 1·50 | 90 |

647 *Nativity* (Federico Brandani)

1980. Christmas.

| 1701 | **647** | 120l. green and brown | 45 | 30 |

648 "My Town" (Treviso)

1980. Stamp Day. Paintings by Schoolchildren entitled "My Town". Multicoloured.

1702	70l. Type **648**	30	20
1703	120l. Sansepolcro	45	25
1704	170l. Sansepolcro (different)	75	50

649 Daniele Comboni and
African Village

1981. 150th Birth Anniv and Death Centenary of Daniele Comboni (missionary).

| 1705 | **649** | 80l. brown, indigo and blue | 45 | 30 |

650 Alcide de
Gasperi

1981. Birth Centenary of Alcide de Gasperi (politician).

| 1706 | **650** | 200l. green | 45 | 30 |

651 Landscape
outlined by Person
in Wheelchair

1981. International Year of Disabled Persons.

| 1707 | **651** | 300l. multicoloured | 75 | 50 |

652 Anemone

1981. Flowers (1st series). Multicoloured.

1708	200l. Type **652**	75	50
1709	200l. Oleander	75	50
1710	200l. Rose	75	50

See also Nos. 1753/5 and 1797/9.

653 Human Chess
Game, Marostica

1981. Europa. Multicoloured.

| 1711 | 300l. Type **653** | 3·00 | 75 |
| 1712 | 300l. "Il Palio" horse race, Siena | 3·00 | 75 |

654 St. Rita of
Cascia

1981. 600th Birth Anniv of St. Rita of Cascia.

| 1713 | **654** | 600l. multicoloured | 2·20 | 1·30 |

655 Ciro
Menotti

1981. 150th Death Anniv of Ciro Menotti (patriot).

| 1714 | **655** | 80l. black and brown | 45 | 30 |

656 Agusta A.109 Helicopter

1981. Italian Aircraft (1st series). Multicoloured.

| 1715 | 200l. Type **656** | 60 | 40 |
| 1716 | 200l. Partenavia P.68B Victor-PART airplane | 60 | 40 |

| 1717 | 200l. Aeritalia G.222 transport | 60 | 40 |
| 1718 | 200l. Aermacchi MB 339 jet trainer | 60 | 40 |

See also Nos. 1748/51 and 1792/5.

657 Fertile and
Barren Soil

1981. Water Conservation.

| 1719 | **657** | 80l. multicoloured | 45 | 30 |

1981. Italian Work for the World (2nd series). As T **640**.

| 1720 | 300l. blue | 1·10 | 65 |
| 1721 | 300l. red | 1·10 | 65 |

DESIGNS: No. 1720, Sao Simao, Brazil; No. 1721, High Island, Hong Kong.

1981. Tourist Publicity (8th series). As T **556**. Multicoloured.

1722	80l. Matera	30	60
1723	150l. Riva del Garda	60	1·40
1724	300l. Santa Teresa di Gallura	85	65
1725	900l. Tarquinia	2·50	1·50

658 Naval Academy and
Badge

1981. Centenary of Naval Academy, Livorno. Multicoloured.

1726	80l. Type **658**	30	15
1727	150l. Aerial view of Academy	45	60
1728	200l. "Amerigo Vespucci" (cadet ship) and sailor using sextant	60	40

659 Spada Palace, Rome,
and Decorative Motif from
Grand Hall

1981. 150th Anniv of Council of State.

| 1729 | **659** | 200l. brown, green & blue | 60 | 40 |

660 Running

1981. World Cup Light Athletics Championships, Rome.

| 1730 | **660** | 300l. multicoloured | 1·00 | 65 |

1981. Italian Artists' Annivs (8th series). As T **567**. Multicoloured.

| 1731 | 200l. *Harbour* (Carlo Carra (1881–1966)) | 60 | 40 |
| 1732 | 200l. *Nightfall* (Giuseppe Ugonia (1881–1944)) | 60 | 40 |

661 Riace Bronze

1981. Riace Bronzes (ancient Greek statues). Multicoloured.

| 1733 | 200l. Type **661** | 75 | 45 |
| 1734 | 200l. Riace bronze (different) | 75 | 45 |

662 *Virgil* (Treviri mosaic)

1981. Death Bimillenary of Virgil (poet).

| 1735 | **662** | 600l. multicoloured | 1·90 | 75 |

663 *Still-life* (Gregorio
Sciltian)

1981. World Food Day.

| 1736 | **663** | 150l. multicoloured | 60 | 40 |

1981. Italian Villas (2nd series). As T **646**. Multicoloured.

1737	100l. Villa Campolieto, Ercolano	30	25
1738	200l. Villa Cimbrone, Ravello	60	40
1739	300l. Villa Pignatelli, Naples	1·20	50

664 *Adoration of the Magi*
(Giovanni da Campione d'Italia)

1981. Christmas.

| 1740 | **664** | 200l. dp blue, brown & bl | 60 | 40 |

665 Pope John
XXIII

1981. Birth Centenary of Pope John XXIII.

| 1741 | **665** | 200l. multicoloured | 85 | 40 |

666 Envelopes forming
Railway Track

1981. Stamp Day.

1742	**666**	120l. green, red and black	45	60
1743	-	200l. multicoloured	75	70
1744	-	300l. multicoloured	1·20	75

DESIGNS—VERT: 200l. Caduceus, chest, envelopes and cherub blowing posthorn. HORIZ: 300l. Letter seal.

667 *St. Francis
receiving the
Stigmata* (Pietro
Cavaro)

1982. 800th Birth Anniv of St. Francis of Assisi.

| 1745 | **667** | 300l. brown and blue | 85 | 40 |

668 Paganini
(after Ingres)

1982. Birth Bicentenary of Niccolo Paganini (composer and violinist).

1746	**668**	900l. multicoloured	2·50	1·70

669 Skeletal Hand
lighting Cigarette "Bomb"

1982. Anti-smoking Campaign.

1747	**669**	300l. multicoloured	75	40

1982. Italian Aircraft (2nd series). As T **656**. Multicoloured.

1748		300l. Panavia (inscr "Aeritalia") MRCA Tornado jet fighter	1·60	65
1749		300l. Savoia SIAI 260 Turbo I-FAIR trainer	1·60	65
1750		300l. Piaggio P-166 DL-3 Turbo I-PIAE	1·60	65
1751		300l. Nardi NH 500 helicopter	1·60	65

670 Church of
Santo Spirito o del
Vespro, Palermo

1982. 700th Anniv of Sicilian Vespers (uprising).

1752	**670**	120l. red, blue and purple	45	30

1982. Flowers (2nd series). As T **652**. Multicoloured.

1753		300l. Camellias	1·30	1·00
1754		300l. Carnations	1·30	1·00
1755		300l. Cyclamen	1·30	1·00

671 Coronation of
Charlemagne, 799

1982. Europa.

1756	**671**	200l. brown, black & blue	3·00	1·20
1757	-	450l. multicoloured	3·75	1·00

DESIGN: 450l. Stars and signatures to Treaty of Rome, 1957.

1982. Italian Work for the World (3rd series). As T **640**. Multicoloured.

1758		450l. Radio communication across Red Sea	1·30	40
1759		450l. Automatic letter sorting	1·30	40

672 Garibaldi

1982. Death Centenary of Giuseppe Garibaldi.

1760	**672**	200l. multicoloured	1·20	90

673 Bridge Game,
Pisa

1982. Folk Customs (1st series).

1761	**673**	200l. multicoloured	75	50

See also Nos. 1804, 1850, 1875/6, 1914, 1972, 2004, 2028 and 2092.

1982. Tourist Publicity (9th series). As T **556**. Multicoloured.

1762		200l. Frasassi Grotto	75	85
1763		200l. Fai della Paganella	75	85
1764		450l. Rodi Garganico	1·50	90
1765		450l. Temples of Agrigento	1·50	90

674 Coxless Four

1982. World Junior Rowing Championships.

1766	**674**	200l. multicoloured	75	50

675 Ducal Palace, Urbino,
Montefeltro and Palazzo
dei Consoli, Gubbio

1982. 500th Death Anniv of Federico da Montefeltro, Duke of Urbino.

1767	**675**	300l. multicoloured	60	45

676 Footballer holding
aloft World Cup

1982. Italy's World Cup Football Victory.

1768	**676**	1000l. multicoloured	3·00	2·20

677 Seating Plan

1982. 69th Interparliamentary Union Conference.

1769	**677**	450l. multicoloured	1·00	65

1982. Italian Villas (3rd series). As T **646**. Multicoloured.

1770		150l. Temple of Aesculapius, Villa Borghese, Rome	85	70
1771		250l. Villa D'Este, Tivoli	1·50	65
1772		350l. Villa Lante, Bagnaia, Viterbo	3·00	1·90

678 Francis of Taxis

1982. Commemoration of Establishment of First Public Postal System in Europe.

1773	**678**	300l. red, blue & verm	85	50

1982. Italian Artists' Annivs (9th series). As T **567**. Multicoloured.

1774		300l. *Portrait of Antonietta Negroni Prati Morosini as a Child* (Francesco Hayez (1791–1882))	1·10	65
1775		300l. *The Fortuneteller* (Giovanni Piazzetta (1682–1754))	1·10	65

679 Tree, Chair and Bed
(Maria di Pastena)

1983. Stamp Day. Timber in Human Life. Drawings by Schoolchildren. Multicoloured.

1776	**679**	150l. Type **679**	60	40
1777		250l. Tree with timber products in branches (Lucia Andreoli)	85	65
1778		350l. Forest (Marco Gallea)	1·20	85

680 Microscope

1983. Cancer Control.

1779	**680**	400l. multicoloured	1·40	65

1983. Italian Work for the World (4th series). Automobile Industry. As T **640**. Multicoloured.

1780		400l. Factories on globe	1·30	60
1781		400l. Assembly line	1·30	60

681 Academy
Emblem

1983. 400th Anniv of Accademia della Crusca (Florentine Academy of Letters).

1782	**681**	400l. red, brown and blue	1·00	65

682 Shooting

1983. World Biathlon Championships, Antholz.

1783	**682**	200l. multicoloured	1·00	65

683 Gabriele
Rossetti

1983. Birth Centenary of Gabriele Rossetti (poet).

1784	**683**	300l. blue and brown	1·00	65

684 Guicciardini
(after G.
Bugiardini)

1983. 500th Birth Anniv of Francesco Guicciardini (lawyer and diplomat).

1785	**684**	450l. brown	1·50	90

685 Saba and Trieste

1983. Birth Centenary of Umberto Saba (poet).

1786	**685**	600l. multicoloured	1·70	1·00

686 Pope Pius XII

1983. 25th Death Anniv of Pope Pius XII.

1787	**686**	1400l. blue	4·25	2·50

687 Pope and
St. Paul's
Basilica

1983. Holy Year. Multicoloured.

1788	**687**	250l. Type **687**	75	50
1789		300l. Pope John Paul II and Basilica of Santa Maria Maggiore	85	40
1790		400l. Pope and St. John's Basilica	1·20	50
1791		500l. Pope and St. Peter's Cathedral.	1·50	65

1983. Italian Aircraft (3rd series). As T **656**. Multicoloured.

1792		400l. Savoia SIAI 211 I-SUE	1·40	65
1793		400l. Agusta A.129 Mangusta helicopter	1·40	65
1794		400l. Caproni C22J glider I-CAVJ	1·40	65
1795		400l. Aeritalia/Aermacchi AM-X jet fighter	1·40	65

688 Launch of
Ship

1983. Labour Day.

1796	**688**	1200l. blue	3·25	1·90

1983. Flowers (3rd series). As T **652**. Multicoloured.

1797		200l. Gladiolus	1·50	1·00
1798		200l. Mimosa	1·50	1·00
1799		200l. Rhododendron	1·50	1·00

689 Galileo (after O. Leoni)
and Telescope

1983. Europa. Multicoloured.

1800	**689**	400l. Type **689**	13·00	1·90
1801		500l. Archimedes (marble bust) and screw	13·00	1·40

690 Moneta and Doves

1983. 150th Birth Anniv of Ernesto Teodoro Moneta (Nobel Peace Prize winner).

1802	**690**	500l. multicoloured	1·50	1·00

691 Quadriga,
Globe and V.D.U.

1983. Third International Juridical Information Congress, Rome.

1803	**691**	500l. multicoloured	1·50	1·00

1983. Folk Customs (2nd series). As T **673**. Multicoloured.

1804		300l. Ceri procession, Gubbio	1·30	75

692
Elevation of
Host

1983. 20th National Eucharistic Congress, Milan.

1805	**692**	300l. multicoloured	1·00	65

1983. Tourist Publicity (10th series). As T **556**. Multicoloured.

1806		250l. Alghero	1·20	1·30
1807		300l. Bardonecchia	1·50	1·30
1808		400l. Riccione	2·20	1·50
1809		500l. Taranto	3·00	1·30

693 Frescobaldi

1983. 400th Birth Anniv of Girolamo Frescobaldi (composer).

1810	**693**	400l. green, blue & brn	1·00	65

1983. Italian Villas (4th series). As T **646**. Multicoloured.

1811	250l. Villa Fidelia, Spello	1·50	2·50
1812	300l. Villa Imperiale, Pesaro	1·50	60
1813	400l. Michetti Convent, Francavilla al Mare	1·90	60
1814	500l. Villa di Riccia	2·50	65

694 Francesco de Sanctis

1983. Death Centenary of Francesco de Sanctis (writer).

1815	**694**	300l. multicoloured	1·10	65

695 Madonna of the Chair

1983. Christmas. 500th Birth Anniv of Raphael (artist). Multicoloured.

1816	250l. Type **695**	75	50
1817	400l. Sistine Madonna	1·50	45
1818	500l. Madonna of the Candles	2·20	45

696 Chain of Letters (Roberta Rizzi)

1983. Stamp Day. Drawings by School Children. Multicoloured.

1819	200l. Type **696**	1·00	90
1820	300l. Space postman delivering letter (Maria Grazia Federico) (vert)	1·60	75
1821	400l. Steam train leaving envelope and globe (Paolo Bucciarelli)	1·70	75

697 Battered Road Sign

1984. Road Safety. Multicoloured.

1822	300l. Type **697**	1·20	90
1823	400l. Crashed car and policeman	1·50	1·00

1984. Italian Artists Anniversaries (10th series). As T **567**. Multicoloured.

1824	300l. Races at Bois de Boulogne (Giuseppe de Nittis (1846–84))	1·20	65
1825	400l. Paul Guillaume (Amedeo Modigliani (1884–1920))	1·70	90

698 Maserati "Biturbo"

1984. Italian Motor Industry (1st series). Multicoloured.

1826	450l. Type **698**	2·50	90
1827	450l. Iveco "190.38 Special" lorry	2·50	90
1828	450l. Same Trattori "Galaxy" tractor	2·50	90
1829	450l. Alfa "33"	2·50	90

See also Nos. 1867/70 and 1933/6.

699 Glassblower, Glasses and Jug

1984. Italian Work for the World (5th series). Ceramic and Glass Industries. Multicoloured.

1830	300l. Ceramic plaque and furnace	1·00	40
1831	300l. Type **699**	1·00	40

700 European Parliament Building, Strasbourg

1984. Second European Parliament Direct Elections.

1832	**700**	400l. multicoloured	1·50	90

701 State Forest Corps Hughes 500 Helicopter

1984. Nature Protection. Forests. Multicoloured.

1833	450l. Type **701**	3·50	95
1834	450l. Forest animals and burning cigarette	3·50	95
1835	450l. River and litter	3·50	95
1836	450l. Wildlife and building construction	3·50	95

702 Ministry of Posts and Telecommunications, Rome

1984. "Italia '85" International Stamp Exhibition, Rome (1st issue). Multicoloured.

1837	450l. Type **702**	1·50	50
1838	550l. Appian Way	2·20	65

See also Nos. 1857/9, 1862/4, 1871/3 and 1898/1911.

703 G. di Vittorio, B. Buozzi and A. Grandi

1984. 40th Anniv of Rome Pact (foundation of Italian Trade Unions).

1839	**703**	450l. multicoloured	1·70	95

704 Bridge

1984. Europa. 25th Anniv of European Post and Telecommunications Conference.

1840	**704**	450l. multicoloured	11·50	2·50
1841	**704**	550l. multicoloured	14·50	6·50

705 Symposium Emblem

1984. Int Telecommunications Symposium, Florence.

1842	**705**	550l. multicoloured	2·20	1·30

706 Horse-race

1984. Centenary of Italian Derby. Multicoloured.

1843	250l. Type **706**		2·20	1·90
1844	400l. Horse-race (different)		3·25	1·30

1984. Tourist Publicity (11th series). As T **556**. Multicoloured.

1845	350l. Campione d'Italia	2·50	2·50
1846	400l. Chianciano Terme	2·00	1·30
1847	450l. Padula	2·30	1·30
1848	550l. Syracuse	2·75	1·50

1984. Folk Customs (3rd series). As T **673**. Multicoloured.

1850	400l. Procession of Shrine of Santa Rosa, Viterbo	1·70	1·00

708 Harvester, Thresher and Medieval Fields Map

1984. Farming Communities. Multicoloured.

1851	250l. Type **708**	1·20	65
1852	350l. Hand oil press, cart and medieval fields map	1·30	75

1984. Italian Villas (5th series). As T **646**. Multicoloured.

1853	250l. Villa Caristo, Stignano	1·70	1·30
1854	350l. Villa Doria Pamphili, Genoa	2·20	1·00
1855	400l. Villa Reale, Stupinigi	2·50	1·20
1856	450l. Villa Mellone, Lecce	3·00	1·30

709 Etruscan Bronze of Warrior

1984. "Italia '85" International Stamp Exhibition, Rome (2nd issue). Multicoloured.

1857	550l. Type **709**	1·60	65
1858	550l. Exhibition emblem	1·60	65
1859	550l. Etruscan silver-backed mirror	1·60	65

710 Dish Aerial, Globe and Punched Tape

1985. Information Technology.

1860	**710**	350l. multicoloured	1·50	65

711 Man helping Old Woman

1985. Problems of Elderly People.

1861	**711**	250l. multicoloured	1·00	75

712 Venus in her Chariot (fresco, Raphael)

1985. "Italia '85" International Stamp Exhibition, Rome (3rd issue). Multicoloured.

1862	600l. Type **712**	1·50	50
1863	600l. Exhibition emblem	1·50	50
1864	600l. Warriors (detail of fresco, Baldassare Peruzzi)	1·50	50

713 Plate, Vase and Pot

1985. Italian Work for the World (6th series). Ceramics. Multicoloured.

1865	600l. Type **713**	1·70	50
1866	600l. Decorated plate	1·70	50

1985. Italian Motor Industry (2nd series). As T **698**. Multicoloured.

1867	450l. Fiat "Uno"	4·00	70
1868	450l. Lamborghini "Countach LP500"	4·00	70
1869	450l. Lancia "Thema"	4·00	70
1870	450l. Fiat Abarth "100 Bialbero"	4·00	70

714 St. Mary of Peace Church, Rome

1985. "Italia '85" International Stamp Exhibition, Rome (4th issue). Baroque Art. Multicoloured.

1871	250l. Type **714**	80	55
1872	250l. Exhibition emblem	80	55
1873	250l. Fountain obelisk and Saint Agnes's Church, Rome	80	55

715 Pope Sixtus V

1985. 400th Anniv of Election of Pope Sixtus V.

1874	**715**	1500l. multicoloured	4·25	2·50

1985. Folk Customs (4th series). As T **673**. Multicoloured.

1875	250l. March of the Turks, Potenza	1·50	85
1876	350l. Republican regatta, Amalfi	1·90	85

1985. Tourist Publicity (12th series). As T **556**. Multicoloured.

1877	350l. Bormio	1·50	1·40
1878	400l. Castellammare di Stabia	1·50	65
1879	450l. Stromboli	1·60	75
1880	600l. Termoli	3·50	1·30

716 European Otter

1985. Nature Protection. Multicoloured.

1881	500l. Type **716**	4·00	70
1882	500l. Primulas	4·00	70
1883	500l. Fir tree	4·00	70
1884	500l. Black-winged stilts	4·00	70

1985. Anniversaries of Italian Artists (11th series). As T **567**. Multicoloured.

1885	350l. Madonna (Giambattista Salvi (1609–85))	1·70	1·40
1886	400l. The Pride of Work (Mario Sironi (1885–1961))	1·90	1·30

717 Aureliano Pertile and Giovanni Martinelli (singers)

1985. Europa. Music Year. Multicoloured.

1887	500l. Type **717**		11·50	1·30

1888 600l. Vicenzo Bellini and Johann Sebastian Bach (composers) 14·50 2·50

718 San Salvatore Abbey

1985. 950th Anniv of San Salvatore Abbey, Mt. Amiata.
1889 718 450l. multicoloured 2·20 90

719 Cyclists

1985. World Cycling Championships, Bassano del Grappa.
1890 719 400l. multicoloured 2·20 50

720 U.N. and Congress Emblems and Globe

1985. Seventh United Nations Crime Prevention Congress, Milan.
1891 720 600l. multicoloured 3·00 50

721 Profile and Emblem

1985. International Youth Year.
1892 721 600l. multicoloured 3·00 50

1985. Villas (6th series). As T 646. Multicoloured.
1893 300l. Villa Nitti, Maratea 2·20 85
1894 400l. Villa Aldrovandi Mazzacorati, Bologna 3·00 50
1895 500l. Villa Santa Maria, Pula 3·50 60
1896 600l. Villa de Mersi, Villazzano 4·25 65

722 State Emblems of Italy and Vatican City and Medallion (Mario Soccorsi)

1985. Ratification of the Modification of 1929 Lateran Concordat.
1897 722 400l. multicoloured 2·20 50

723 Parma Town Hall and 1857 25c. Stamp

724 Basel 1845 2¼r. Stamp

1985. "Italia '85" International Stamp Exhibition. Rome (5th issue). Multicoloured. (a) As T 723.
1898 300l. Type 723 75 65
1899 300l. Naples New Castle and 1858 2g. stamp 75 65
1900 300l. Palermo Cathedral and Sicily 1859 ½g. stamp 75 65
1901 300l. Modena Cathedral and 1852 15c. stamp 75 65
1902 300l. Piazzo Navona, Rome, and Papal States 1852 7b. stamp 75 65
1903 300l. Palazzo Vecchio, Florence, and Tuscany 1851 2c. stamp 75 65
1904 300l. Turin and Sardinia 1861 3l. stamp 75 65
1905 300l. Bologna and Romagna 1859 6b. stamp 75 65

1906 300l. Palazzo Litta, Milan, and Lombardy and Venetia 1850 15c. stamp 75 65

(b) As T 724.
1907 500l. Type 724 2·20 70
1908 500l. Japan 1871 48m. stamp 2·20 70
1909 500l. United States 1847 10c. stamp 2·20 70
1910 500l. Western Australia 1854 1d. stamp 2·20 70
1911 500l. Mauritius 1848 2d. stamp 2·20 70

(c) Sheet 86×56 mm. Imperf.
MS1912 4000l. Sardinia 1851 5c. stamp and Great Britain "Penny Black" 8·00 7·75

725 Skiers

1986. Cross-country Skiing.
1913 725 450l. multicoloured 1·70 65

1986. Folk Customs (5th series). As T 673. Multicoloured.
1914 450l. Le Candelore, Catania 1·70 65

726 Amilcare Ponchielli and Scene from La Gioconda

1986. Composers. Multicoloured.
1915 2000l. Type 726 (death centenary) 5·75 1·00
1916 2000l. Giovan Battista Pergolesi (250th death anniv) 5·75 1·00

727 Acitrezza

1986. Tourist Publicity (13th series). Multicoloured.
1917 350l. Type 727 1·20 70
1918 450l. Capri 1·50 1·00
1919 550l. Merano 1·90 65
1920 650l. San Benedetto del Tronto 2·20 70

728 Heart-shaped Tree (life)

1986. Europa. Multicoloured.
1921 650l. Type 728 7·25 65
1922 650l. Star-shaped tree (poetry) 7·25 65
1923 650l. Butterfly-shaped tree (colour) 7·25 65
1924 650l. Sun-shaped tree (energy) 7·25 65

729 "Eyes"

1986. 25th International Ophthalmology Congress, Rome.
1925 729 550l. multicoloured 1·70 65

730 Italian Police

1986. European Police Meeting, Chianciano Terme.
1926 730 550l. multicoloured 2·50 1·50
1927 730 650l. multicoloured 3·00 1·80

731 Battle Scene

1986. 120th Anniv of Battle of Bezzecca.
1928 731 550l. multicoloured 2·20 90

732 Figure with Flag

1986. National Independence Martyrs' Day.
1929 732 2000l. multicoloured 6·50 2·50

733 Bersagliere and Helmets

1986. 150th Anniv of Turin Bersaglieri Corps (alpine troops).
1930 733 450l. multicoloured 2·20 90

734 Dish Aerial, Transmitter and "Messages"

1986. Telecommunications.
1931 734 350l. multicoloured 1·00 65

735 Varallo

1986. Holy Mountain of Varallo.
1932 735 2000l. green and blue 6·00 2·50

1986. Italian Motor Industry (3rd series). As T 698. Multicoloured.
1933 450l. Alfa Romeo "AR 8 Turbo" 3·75 85
1934 450l. Innocenti "650 SE" 3·75 85
1935 450l. Ferrari "Testarossa" 3·75 85
1936 450l. Fiatallis "FR 10B" 3·75 85

736 Clothes and Woman (fashion)

1986. Italian Work for the World (7th series). Multicoloured.
1937 450l. Type 736 3·00 65
1938 450l. Man and clothes (fashion) 3·00 65
1939 650l. Olivetti personal computer, keyboard and screen 4·25 65
1940 650l. Breda steam turbine 4·25 65

737 Airplane flying through "40"

1986. 40th Anniv of Alitalia (national airline). Multicoloured.
1941 737 550l. Type 737 1·90 75
1942 650l. Airplane and landing lights 2·20 1·00

1986. Italian Villas (7th series). As T 646. Multicoloured.
1943 350l. Villa Necker, Trieste 1·20 85
1944 350l. Villa Borromeo, Cassana d'Adda 1·20 85
1945 450l. Villa Palagonia, Bagheria 1·50 85

1946 550l. Villa Medicea, Poggio a Caiano 1·70 85
1947 650l. Issogne Castle 2·00 85

738 Madonna and Child (bronze sculpture by Donatello)

1986. Christmas.
1948 738 450l. bistre 1·70 75

1986. Anniversaries of Italian Artists (12th series). As T 567.
1949 450l. black and orange 2·50 50
1950 550l. multicoloured 3·00 65
DESIGNS: 450l. Drawing of woman (Andrea del Sarto (1486–1531)); 550l. Daphne at Pavarola (Felice Casorati (1883–1963)).

739 Lockheed C130 Hercules Transport dropping Squares in National Colours onto Globe

1986. International Peace Year. Multicoloured.
1951 550l. Type 739 1·90 1·00
1952 650l. Airplane, Cross and people (commemoration of Italian airmen killed on mission to Kindu, Congo) 2·20 1·30

740 Engraving 1862 Stamp

1986. Stamp Day. Francesco Maria Matraire (engraver).
1953 740 550l. multicoloured 2·20 90

741 Woven Threads (Marzotto Textile Industry)

1987. Italian Industry.
1954 741 700l. multicoloured 2·20 1·30
1955 - 700l. blue and turquoise 2·20 1·30
DESIGN: No. 1955, Clouds and flame (Italgas Gas Corporation).

742 River Volturno

1987. Nature Protection. Rivers and Lakes. Multicoloured.
1956 500l. Type 742 3·00 50
1957 500l. Lake Garda 3·00 50
1958 500l. Lake Trasimeno 3·00 50
1959 500l. River Tirso 3·00 50

743 Gramsci

1987. 50th Death Anniv of Antonio Gramsci (politician).
1960 743 600l. grey, black and red 1·90 90

744 Church of the Motorway of the Sun, Florence (Giovanni Michelucci)

1987. Europa. Architecture. Multicoloured.
1961	600l. Type **744**	7·25	1·30
1962	700l. Termini station, Rome (Nervi)	8·75	1·70

1987. Tourist Publicity (14th series). As T **556**. Multicoloured.
1963	380l. Verbania Pallanza	1·50	75
1964	400l. Palmi	1·60	1·00
1965	500l. Vasto	1·90	75
1966	600l. Villacidro	2·20	75

745 View of Naples on Football

1987. S.S.C. Naples, National Football Champion, 1986–87.
1967	**745**	500l. multicoloured	4·25	2·50

746 *The Absinthe Drinker* (Edgar Degas)

1987. Anti-alcoholism Campaign.
1968	**746**	380l. multicoloured	2·20	65

747 Liguori and Gulf of Naples

1987. Death Bicentenary of St. Alfonso Maria de Liguori (co-founder of Redemptorists).
1969	**747**	400l. multicoloured	1·90	90

748 Emblem and Olympic Stadium, Rome

1987. World Light Athletics Championships, Rome (1970) and "Olymphilex '87" Stamp Exhibition, Rome (1971).
1970	700l. Type **748**	1·90	1·30
1971	700l. International Olympic Committee building, Foro Italico, Rome	1·90	1·30

1987. Folk Customs (6th series). As T **673**. Multicoloured.
1972	380l. Joust, Foligno	1·90	1·00

749 Piazza del Popolo, Ascoli Piceno

1987. Piazzas (1st series). Multicoloured.
1973	380l. Type **749**	1·20	1·00
1974	500l. Piazza Giuseppe Verdi, Palermo	1·50	40
1975	500l. Piazza San Carlo, Turin	1·90	65
1976	700l. Piazza dei Signori, Verona	2·30	1·00

See also Nos. 2002/3 and 2023/4.

750 *The Adoration in the Manger* (St. Francis's Basilica, Assisi)

1987. Christmas. Frescoes by Giotto. Multicoloured.
1977	500l. Type **750**	1·90	75
1978	600l. *Epiphany* (Scrovegni Chapel, Padua)	2·30	1·00

751 Battle Scene

1987. 120th Anniv of Battle of Mentana.
1979	**751**	380l. multicoloured	1·60	1·00

752 *Christ Pantocrator* (mosaic, Monreale Cathedral)

1987. Artistic Heritage. Multicoloured.
1980	500l. Type **752**	2·50	70
1981	500l. San Carlo Theatre, Naples (18th-century engraving)	2·50	70

753 College and 1787 and 1987 Uniforms

1987. Bicentenary of Nunziatella Military Academy, Naples.
1982	**753**	600l. multicoloured	2·20	1·30

754 Marco de Marchi (philatelist) and Milan Cathedral

1987. Stamp Day.
1983	**754**	500l. multicoloured	2·50	1·30

755 Man chipping Flints

1988. "Homo aeserniensis".
1984	**755**	500l. multicoloured	1·50	90

756 Lyceum

1988. E.Q. Visconti Lyceum, Rome.
1985	**756**	500l. multicoloured	1·50	90

See also Nos. 2019, 2109 and 2127.

757 Statue, Bosco and Boy

1988. Death Centenary of St. John Bosco (founder of Salesian Brothers).
1986	**757**	500l. multicoloured	1·50	90

1988. Anniversaries of Italian Artists (13th series). As T **567**. Multicoloured.
1987	650l. *Archaeologists* (Giorgio de Chirico (1888–1978))	3·00	1·90

758 15th-Century Soncino Bible

1988. 500th Anniv of First Printing of Bible in Hebrew.
1988	**758**	550l. multicoloured	1·70	1·30

759 St. Valentine, Epileptics and Wave Patterns

1988. Anti-epilepsy Campaign.
1989	**759**	500l. multicoloured	1·60	1·00

760 ETR 450 High Speed Train in Station

1988. Europa. Transport and Communications. Multicoloured.
1990	650l. Type **760**	5·75	1·90
1991	750l. Map and keyboard operator (electronic postal systems)	7·25	2·50

1988. Tourist Publicity (15th series). As T **556**. Multicoloured.
1992	400l. Castiglione della Pescaia	1·20	95
1993	500l. Lignano Sabbiadoro	1·40	85
1994	650l. St. Domenico's Church, Noto	1·70	1·00
1995	750l. Vieste	2·20	1·30

761 Golfer on Ball

1988. Golf.
1996	**761**	500l. multicoloured	1·50	90

762 Stadium and Mascot

1988. World Cup Football Championship, Italy (1990) (1st issue).
1997	**762**	3150l. multicoloured	6·50	5·25

See also Nos. 2049 and 2052/87.

763 Milan Cathedral on Football

1988. A. C. Milan. National Football Champion, 1987–88.
1998	**763**	650l. multicoloured	1·50	1·00

764 Horse's Head

1988. Artistic Heritage. Pergola Bronzes. Multicoloured.
1999	500l. Type **764**	1·60	90
2000	650l. Bust of woman	2·00	1·30

765 Student (bas-relief)

1988. 900th Anniv of Bologna University.
2001	**765**	500l. violet	1·50	90

1988. Piazzas (2nd series). As T **749**. Multicoloured.
2002	400l. Piazza del Duomo, Pistoia	1·60	90
2003	550l. Piazza del Unita d'Italia, Trieste	2·00	1·00

1988. Folk Customs (7th series). As T **673**. Multicoloured.
2004	500l. Candle procession, Sassari	2·00	1·00

766 Emblem and Appian Way

1988. "Roma 88" Int Gastroenterology and Digestive Endoscopy Congress.
2005	**766**	750l. multicoloured	2·20	1·30

767 *Ossessione* (Luchino Visconti, 1942)

1988. Italian Films. Scenes from and Advertising Posters of named Films. Multicoloured.
2006	500l. Type **767**	1·60	1·70
2007	650l. *Ladri di Biciclette* (Vittorio de Sica, 1948)	2·20	2·00
2008	2400l. *Roma Citta Aperta* (Roberto Rossellini, 1945)	7·25	2·50
2009	3050l. *Riso Amaro* (Giuseppe de Santis, 1949)	10·00	4·50

768 Bird (aluminium)

1988. Italian Industry. Multicoloured.
2010	750l. Type **768**	2·00	1·20
2011	750l. Oscilloscope display (electronics)	2·00	1·20
2012	750l. Banknote engraving, 1986 tourism stamp and medals (60th anniv of State Polygraphic Institute)	2·00	1·20

769 *Holy Family* (Pasquale Celommi)

1988. Christmas (1st issue).
2013	**769**	650l. multicoloured	2·50	1·30

See also No. 2015.

770 Borromeo and Plague Victims

1988. 450th Birth Anniv of St. Carlo Borromeo, Archbishop of Milan.
| 2014 | 770 | 2400l. multicoloured | 5·75 | 3·25 |

771 "Nativity" (bas-relief)

1988. Christmas (2nd issue).
| 2015 | 771 | 500l. green and brown | 2·20 | 1·00 |

772 Edoardo Chiossone (stamp designer) and Japanese 1879 2s. "Koban" Stamp

1988. Stamp Day.
| 2016 | 772 | 500l. multicoloured | 1·50 | 90 |

773 AIDS Virus

1989. Anti-AIDS Campaign.
| 2017 | 773 | 650l. multicoloured | 1·70 | 65 |

774 1907 Itala Car and Route Map

1989. Re-enactment of 1907 Peking–Paris Car Rally.
| 2018 | 774 | 3150l. multicoloured | 7·25 | 6·50 |

1989. Giuseppe Parini Lyceum, Milan. As T 756.
| 2019 | | 650l. multicoloured | 2·20 | 1·00 |

776 Fresco, Ragione Palace, Padua

1989. Artistic Heritage.
| 2020 | 776 | 500l. multicoloured | 1·60 | 1·00 |
| 2021 | – | 650l. blue | 2·20 | 1·00 |

DESIGN: 650l. Crypt, Basilica of St. Nicolas, Bari.

777 Stylized Yachts

1989. World Sailing Championships, Alassio, Naples and Porto Cervo.
| 2022 | 777 | 3050l. multicoloured | 8·00 | 5·25 |

1989. Piazzas (3rd series). As T 749. Multicoloured.
| 2023 | | 400l. Piazza di Spagna, Rome | 1·20 | 85 |

| 2024 | | 400l. Piazza del Duomo, Catanzaro | 1·20 | 85 |

778 Leap-frog (Luca Rizzello)

1989. Europa. Children's Games. Multicoloured.
2025	778	500l. Type 778	3·00	1·20
2026		650l. Girl dressing up (Serena Forcuti) (vert)	4·25	1·20
2027		750l. Sack race (Adelise Lahner)	5·00	1·20

1989. Folk Customs (8th series). As T 673. Multicoloured.
| 2028 | | 400l. Spello flower paintings | 1·50 | 65 |

779 Cloisters

1989. Pisa University.
| 2029 | 779 | 500l. violet | 1·60 | 90 |

780 Parliamentary Emblem as Tree on Map

1989. Third Direct Elections to European Parliament.
| 2030 | 780 | 500l. multicoloured | 2·20 | 1·30 |

No. 2030 is also inscribed with the European Currency Unit rate of 0.31 ECU.

1989. Tourist Publicity (16th series). As T 556. Multicoloured.
2031		500l. Grottammare	1·70	1·20
2032		500l. Spotorno	1·70	1·20
2033		500l. Pompeii	1·70	1·20
2034		500l. Giardini Naxos	1·70	1·20

781 1889 5c. Savoy Arms Stamp

1989. Centenary of Ministry of Posts and Telecommunications. Multicoloured.
| 2035 | | 500l. Type 781 | 1·70 | 2·50 |
| 2036 | | 2400l. Globe within posthorn | 5·75 | 2·50 |

782 Ball and Club Emblem

1989. Inter Milan, National Football Champion, 1988–89.
| 2037 | 782 | 650l. multicoloured | 1·90 | 75 |

783 Stylized Chamber

1989. Centenary of Interparliamentary Union.
| 2038 | 783 | 750l. multicoloured | 2·20 | 1·30 |

784 Phrygian Cap

1989. Bicentenary of French Revolution.
| 2039 | 784 | 3150l. multicoloured | 7·25 | 5·75 |

785 Corinaldo Wall

1989. Artistic Heritage. 550th Birth Anniv of Francesco di Giorgio Martini (architect).
| 2040 | 785 | 500l. multicoloured | 1·70 | 1·30 |

786 Chaplin in Film Scenes

1989. Birth Centenary of Charlie Chaplin (film actor and director).
| 2041 | 786 | 750l. black and brown | 2·30 | 1·30 |

787 Inauguration of Naples–Portici Line (left-hand detail, S Fergola)

1989. 150th Anniv of Naples–Portici Railway. Multicoloured.
| 2042 | 787 | 550l. Type 787 | 1·30 | 40 |
| 2043 | | 550l. Right-hand detail | 1·30 | 40 |

Nos. 2042/3 were printed together, *se-tenant*, forming a composite design.

788 Castelfidardo, Accordion and Stradella

1989. Italian Industry. Multicoloured.
| 2044 | 788 | 450l. Type 788 | 1·30 | 75 |
| 2045 | | 450l. Books (Arnoldo Mondadori Publishing House) | 1·30 | 75 |

789 Madonna and Child

1989. Christmas. Details of *Adoration of the Magi* (Correggio). Multicoloured.
| 2046 | 789 | 500l. Type 789 | 1·40 | 40 |
| 2047 | | 500l. Magi | 1·40 | 40 |

Nos. 2046/7 were printed together, *se-tenant*, forming a composite design.

790 Emilio Diena (stamp dealer)

1989. Stamp Day.
| 2048 | 790 | 500l. black, brown & blue | 1·50 | 90 |

791 Monument (Mario Ceroli) and Football Pitch

1989. World Cup Football Championship, Italy (1990) (2nd issue).
| 2049 | 791 | 450l. multicoloured | 2·20 | 90 |

792 Old Map (left half) with Route superimposed

1990. Columbus's First Voyages, 1474–84. Multicoloured.
| 2050 | | 700l. Type 792 | 1·60 | 70 |
| 2051 | | 700l. Right half of map | 1·60 | 70 |

Nos. 2050/1 were printed together, *se-tenant*, forming a composite design.

793 Italy

1990. World Cup Football Championship, Italy (3rd issue). Designs showing finalists' emblems or playing venues. Multicoloured.
2052		450l. Type 793	75	1·00
2053		450l. U.S.A.	75	1·00
2054		450l. Olympic Stadium, Rome	75	1·00
2055		450l. Comunale Stadium, Florence	75	1·00
2056		450l. Austria	75	1·00
2057		450l. Czechoslovakia	75	1·00
2058		600l. Argentina	85	85
2059		600l. U.S.S.R.	85	85
2060		600l. San Paolo Stadium, Naples	85	85
2061		600l. New Stadium, Bari	85	85
2062		600l. Cameroun	85	85
2063		600l. Rumania	85	85
2064		650l. Brazil	1·00	70
2065		650l. Costa Rica	1·00	70
2066		650l. Delle Alpi Stadium, Turin	1·00	70
2067		650l. Ferraris Stadium, Genoa	1·00	70
2068		650l. Sweden	1·00	70
2069		650l. Scotland	1·00	70
2070		700l. United Arab Emirates	1·20	50
2071		700l. West Germany	1·20	50
2072		700l. Dall'Ara Stadium, Bologna	1·20	50
2073		700l. Meazza Stadium, Milan	1·20	50
2074		700l. Colombia	1·20	50
2075		700l. Yugoslavia	1·20	50
2076		800l. Belgium	1·50	1·00
2077		800l. Uruguay	1·50	1·00
2078		800l. Bentegodi Stadium, Verona	1·50	1·00
2079		800l. Friuli Stadium, Udine	1·50	1·00
2080		800l. South Korea	1·50	1·00
2081		800l. Spain	1·50	1·00
2082		1200l. England	2·20	1·30
2083		1200l. Netherlands	2·20	1·30
2084		1200l. Sant'Elia Stadium, Cagliari	2·20	1·30
2085		1200l. La Favorita Stadium, Palermo	2·20	1·30
2086		1200l. Ireland	2·20	1·30
2087		1200l. Egypt	2·20	1·30

See also No. 2104.

1990. Tourist Publicity (17th series). As T 556. Multicoloured.
2088		600l. San Felice Circeo	1·20	70
2089		600l. Castellammare del Golfo	1·20	70
2090		600l. Montepulciano	1·20	70
2091		600l. Sabbioneta	1·20	70

1990. Folk Customs (9th series). As T 673. Multicoloured.
| 2092 | | 600l. Avelignesi horse race, Merano | 1·90 | 1·00 |

794 National Colours

1990. Death Centenary of Aurelio Saffi.
| 2093 | 794 | 700l. multicoloured | 1·50 | 90 |

795 Giovanni Giorgi (inventor)

1990. 55th Anniv of Invention of Giorgi/MKSA System of Electrotechnical Units.
2094 **795** 600l. multicoloured   1·50   1·00

796 Flags, Globe and Workers (after *The Four States* (Pellizza da Volpedo))

1990. Centenary of Labour Day.
2095 **796** 600l. multicoloured   1·50   1·00

797 Ball on Map

1990. S. S. C. Naples, National Football Champion, 1989–90.
2096 **797** 700l. multicoloured   1·70   1·30

798 Piazza San Silvestro Post Office, Rome

1990. Europa. Post Office Buildings. Multicoloured.
2097 700l. Type **798**   4·25   1·00
2098 800l. Fondaco Tedeschi post office, Venice   5·75   1·50

799 Paisiello

1990. 250th Birth Anniv of Giovanni Paisiello (composer).
2099 **799** 450l. multicoloured   1·20   75

800 Globe, Open Book and Bust of Dante

1990. Centenary of Dante Alighieri Society.
2100 **800** 700l. multicoloured   1·50   1·00

801 Byzantine Mosaic, Ravenna

1990. Artistic Heritage. Multicoloured.
2101 450l. Type **801**   1·00   85
2102 700l. *Christ and Angels* (detail of Rachis altar, Friuli) (Lombard art)   1·70   1·30

ITALIA 600
802 Malatestiana Temple, Rimini

1990. 40th Anniv of Malatestiana Religious Music Festival.
2103 **802** 600l. multicoloured   1·50   90

1990. West Germany, Winner of World Cup Football Championship. As No. 2071 but value changed and additionally inscr "CAMPIONE DEL MONDO".
2104 600l. multicoloured   2·10   1·30

803 *Still Life*

1990. Birth Cent of Giorgio Morandi (painter).
2105 **803** 750l. black   1·90   1·00

804 Ancient and Modern Wrestlers

1990. World Greco-Roman Wrestling Championships, Rome.
2106 **804** 3200l. multicoloured   6·50   2·50

805 *New Life* (Emidio Vangelli)

1990. Christmas. Multicoloured.
2107 600l. Type **805**   1·20   65
2108 750l. *Adoration of the Shepherds* (fresco by Pellegrino in St. Daniel's Church, Friuli)   1·70   65

806 Catania University

1990. Architecture.
2109 –   600l. multicoloured   1·20   75
2110 **806** 750l. blue and ultra-marine   1·90   1·00
DESIGN—As T **756**: 600l. Bernardino Telesio High School, Cosenza.

807 Corrado Mezzana (stamp designer, self-portrait)

1990. Stamp Day.
2111 **807** 600l. multicoloured   1·50   90

808 Holy Family

1991. "The Living Tableau", Rivisondoli.
2112 **808** 600l. multicoloured   1·50   90

809 Fair Emblem

1991. "EuroFlora '91" Fair, Genoa.
2113 **809** 750l. multicoloured   1·50   90

---

810 Emblem

1991. 750th Anniv of Siena University.
2114 **810** 750l. gold, black and blue   1·50   90

1991. Tourist Publicity (18th series). As T **556**. Multicoloured.
2115 600l. Cagli   1·30   1·00
2116 600l. La Maddalena   1·30   1·00
2117 600l. Roccaraso   1·30   1·00
2118 600l. Sanremo   1·30   1·00

811 European Community Flag

1991. Europa Youth Meeting, Venice.
2119 **811** 750l. multicoloured   1·50   90
   No. 2119 is also valued in ECUs (European Currency Unit).

812 City and Columbus's Fleet

1991. 500th Anniv (1992) of Discovery of America by Christopher Columbus (1st issue). Multicoloured.
2120 750l. Type **812**   1·50   65
2121 750l. Map, Columbus, seal and King and Queen of Spain   1·50   65
   Nos. 2120/1 were printed together, *se-tenant*, forming a composite design.
   See also Nos. 2151/4 and **MS**2158.

813 Belli and View of Rome

1991. Birth Bicentenary of Giuseppe Gioachino Belli (poet).
2122 **813** 600l. brown and blue   1·50   1·00

814 St Gregory's Church, Rome

1991. Artistic Heritage.
2123 **814** 3200l. multicoloured   6·50   2·10

815 "DRS" Satellite

1991. Europa. Europe in Space. Multicoloured.
2124 750l. Type **815**   5·00   1·30
2125 800l. "Hermes" spaceship and "Columbus" space station   5·75   1·40

816 Sta Maria Maggiore Church, Lanciano

1991. Artistic Heritage.
2126 **816** 600l. brown   1·50   1·00

1991. D. A. Azuni Lyceum, Sassari. As T **756**.
2127 600l. multicoloured   1·50   1·00

817 Football and Genoa Lantern

1991. Sampdoria, National Football Champion, 1990–91.
2128 **817** 3000l. multicoloured   5·75   4·50

818 Hands and Ball

1991. Centenary of Basketball.
2129 **818** 500l. multicoloured   1·50   75

819 Children and Butterflies

1991. United Nations Conference on Rights of the Child. Multicoloured.
2130 600l. Type **819**   1·30   65
2131 750l. Child with balloon on man's shoulders   1·90   1·00

820 *Youth and Gulls* (sculpture, Pericle Fazzini)

1991. Artistic Heritage. Multicoloured.
2132 **820** 600l. yellow, blue & black   1·50   1·30
2133 –   3200l. multicoloured   5·75   3·00
DESIGN: 3200l. Palazzo Esposizioni, Turin (Pier Luigi Nervi (birth centenary)).

821 Winged Sphinx

1991. Egyptian Museum, Turin.
2134 **821** 750l. gold, green & yellow   1·90   1·30

822 Luigi Galvani (physiologist) and Experimental Equipment

1991. 100 Years of Radio (1st issue).
2135 **822** 750l. multicoloured   1·90   1·30
Galvani carried out experiments in electricity.
See also Nos. 2148, 2203, 2241 and 2321/2.

823 Mozart at
Spinet

1991. Death Bicentenary of Wolfgang Amadeus Mozart
(composer).
| 2136 | **823** | 800l. multicoloured | 2·00 | 1·30 |

824 Bear

1991. Nature Protection. Multicoloured.
2137	500l.	Type **824**	1·70	90
2138	500l.	Peregrine falcon	1·70	90
2139	500l.	Deer	1·70	90
2140	500l.	Marine life	1·70	90

825 The Angel of
Life (Giovanni
Segantini)

1991. Christmas.
| 2141 | **825** | 600l. multicoloured | 1·50 | 90 |

826 Giulio and Alberto Bolaffi
(stamp catalogue publishers)

1991. Stamp Day.
| 2142 | **826** | 750l. multicoloured | 1·50 | 1·00 |

827 Signature and National Flag

1991. Birth Cent of Pietro Nenni (politician).
| 2143 | **827** | 750l. multicoloured | 1·50 | 1·00 |

828 Runners

1992. 22nd European Indoor Light Athletics
Championships, Genoa.
| 2144 | **828** | 600l. multicoloured | 1·70 | 1·00 |

829 Neptune
Fountain, Florence

1992. 400th Death Anniv of Bartolomeo Ammannati
(architect and sculptor).
| 2145 | **829** | 750l. multicoloured | 1·50 | 1·00 |

830 Statue of
Marchese Alberto V
of Este (founder)
and University

1992. 600th Anniv (1991) of Ferrara University.
| 2146 | **830** | 750l. multicoloured | 1·50 | 1·00 |

831 Pediment

1992. Naples University.
| 2147 | **831** | 750l. multicoloured | 1·50 | 1·00 |

1992. 100 Years of Radio (2nd issue). As T **822.**
Multicoloured.
| 2148 | | 750l. Alessandro Volta (physi-
cist) and Voltaic pile | 1·90 | 1·00 |

Volta formulated the theory of current electricity and
invented an electric battery.

832 Emblem and
Venue

1992. "Genova '92" International Thematic Stamp
Exhibition (1st issue).
| 2149 | **832** | 750l. multicoloured | 1·50 | 1·00 |
See also Nos. 2170/5.

833 Medal of Lorenzo
(Renato Beradi)

1992. 500th Death Anniv of Lorenzo de Medici, "The
Magnificent".
| 2150 | **833** | 750l. multicoloured | 1·50 | 1·00 |

834 Columbus before
Queen Isabella

1992. 500th Anniv of Discovery of America by Columbus
(2nd issue). Multicoloured.
2151	500l.	Type **834**	1·20	75
2152	500l.	Columbus's fleet	1·20	75
2153	500l.	Sighting land	1·20	75
2154	500l.	Landing in the New World	1·20	75

835 Scenes from
Life of St. Maria
Filippini (altar,
Montefiascone
Cathedral)

1992. 300th Anniv of Maestre Pie Filippini Institute.
| 2155 | **835** | 750l. multicoloured | 1·50 | 1·00 |

836 Columbus
Monument, Genoa
(G. Giannetti)

1992. Europa. 500th Anniv of Discovery of America by
Columbus. Multicoloured.
| 2156 | | 750l. Type **836** | 4·75 | 1·30 |
| 2157 | | 850l. Emblem of "Colombo '92"
exhibition, Genoa | 5·75 | 1·30 |

837 Columbus presenting
Natives

1992. 500th Anniv of Discovery of America by Columbus
(3rd issue). Six sheets each 113×93 mm containing
horiz designs as T **837** reproducing scenes from
United States 1893 Columbian Exposition issue.
MS2158 Six sheets (a) 50l. green
(Type **837**); 300l. blue (Columbus
announcing discovery); 4000l. mauve
(Columbus in chains). (b) 100l. lilac
(Columbus welcomed at Barcelona);
800l. red (Columbus restored to
favour); 3000l. green (Columbus
describing third voyage). (c) 200l.
blue (Columbus sighting land); 900l.
blue (Columbus's fleet); 1500l. red
(Queen Isabella pledging jewels).
(d) 400l. brown (Columbus soliciting
aid of Queen Isabella); 700l. red
(Columbus at La Rabida); 1000l. blue
(Recall of Columbus). (e) 500l. brown
(Landing of Columbus); 600l. green
(Santa Maria); 2000l. red (Portraits
of Queen Isabella and Columbus).
(f) 5000l. green (America, Columbus
and Liberty) Set of 6 sheets   44·00   38·00

838 Seascape and Cyclists

1992. 75th "Tour of Italy" Cycle Race. Multicoloured.
| 2159 | | 750l. Type **838** | 1·60 | 65 |
| 2160 | | 750l. Mountains and cyclists | 1·60 | 65 |
Nos. 2159/60 were issued together, se-tenant, forming
a composite design.

839 Ball, Team
Badge and
Stylization of
Milan Cathedral

1992. A.C. Milan, National Football Champion, 1991–92.
| 2161 | **839** | 750l. green, red and
black | 1·60 | 1·00 |

840 Viareggio

1992. Seaside Resorts. Multicoloured.
| 2162 | | 750l. Type **840** | 1·50 | 1·00 |
| 2163 | | 750l. Rimini | 1·50 | 1·00 |

841 Nuvolari

1992. Birth Centenary of Tazio Nuvolari (racing driver).
| 2164 | **841** | 3200l. multicoloured | 7·00 | 3·75 |

1992. Tourist Publicity (19th series). As T **556.**
Multicoloured.
2165		600l. Arcevia	1·30	1·00
2166		600l. Braies	1·30	1·00
2167		600l. Maratea	1·30	1·00
2168		600l. Pantelleria	1·30	1·00

842 Adoration of the Shepherds
(detail)

1992. 400th Death Anniv of Jacopo da Ponte (painter).
| 2169 | **842** | 750l. multicoloured | 1·90 | 1·30 |

843 Columbus's
House, Genoa

1992. "Genova '92" International Thematic Stamp
Exhibition (2nd issue). Multicoloured.
| 2170 | | 500l. Type **843** | 1·10 | 60 |
| 2171 | | 600l. Departure of Columbus's
fleet from Palos, 1492 | 1·30 | 60 |
| 2172 | | 750l. Route map of Columbus's
first voyage | 1·60 | 60 |
| 2173 | | 850l. Columbus sighting land | 1·90 | 70 |
| 2174 | | 1200l. Columbus landing on
San Salvador | 3·00 | 1·30 |
| 2175 | | 3200l. Columbus, Man
(Leonardo da Vinci), Fury
(Michelangelo) and Raphael's
portrait of Michelangelo | 5·75 | 3·25 |

844 Woman's
Eyes and
Mouth

1992. Stamp Day. Ordinary or self-adhesive gum.
| 2176 | **844** | 750l. multicoloured | 1·50 | 65 |

845 Map of Europe and
Lions Emblem

1992. 75th Anniv of Lions International and 38th Europa
Forum, Genoa.
| 2178 | **845** | 3000l. multicoloured | 5·75 | 3·25 |

846 European Community
Emblem and Members'
Flags

1992. European Single Market (1st issue).
| 2179 | **846** | 600l. multicoloured | 1·50 | 1·00 |
See also Nos. 2182/93.

847 Woman with Food
Bowl

1992. International Nutrition Conference, Rome.
| 2180 | **847** | 500l. multicoloured | 1·10 | 65 |

848 Caltagirone Crib

1992. Christmas.
| 2181 | **848** | 600l. multicoloured | 1·50 | 1·00 |

849 Buildings on
Flag of Italy

1993. European Single Market (2nd issue). Designs differing in flag of country and language of inscription. Multicoloured.

2182	750l. Type **849**	1·90	60
2183	750l. Belgium	1·90	60
2184	750l. Denmark	1·90	60
2185	750l. France	1·90	60
2186	750l. Germany	1·90	60
2187	750l. Greece	1·90	60
2188	750l. Ireland	1·90	60
2189	750l. Luxembourg	1·90	60
2190	750l. Netherlands	1·90	60
2191	750l. Portugal	1·90	60
2192	750l. United Kingdom	1·90	60
2193	750l. Spain	1·90	60

850 Russian and Italian
Alpine Veterans

1993. 50th Anniv Meeting of Veterans of Battle of Nikolayevka.

2194	**850**	600l. multicoloured	1·70	1·00

851 Mezzettino,
Colombina and
Arlecchino

1993. Death Bicentenary of Carlo Goldoni (dramatist). Multicoloured.

2195	500l. Type **851**	1·20	90
2196	500l. Arlecchino and portrait of Goldoni	1·20	90

852 *Africa* (mosaic,
Roman villa, Piazza
Armerina)

1993. Artistic Heritage.

2197	**852**	750l. multicoloured	1·90	1·30

853 Wedge stopping
Heart-shaped Cog

1993. National Health Day. Campaign against Heart Disease.

2198	**853**	750l. multicoloured	1·50	90

854 Tabby

1993. Domestic Cats. Multicoloured.

2199	600l. Type **854**	1·30	75
2200	600l. White Persian	1·30	75
2201	600l. Devon rex (vert)	1·30	75
2202	600l. Maine coon (vert)	1·30	75

1993. 100 Years of Radio (3rd issue). As T **822**. Multicoloured.

2203	750l. Temistocle Calzecchi Onesti (physicist) and apparatus for detecting electromagnetic waves	1·70	90

855 *The Piazza*

1993. Death Bicentenary of Francesco Guardi (artist).

2204	**855**	3200l. multicoloured	7·25	3·75

856 Horace

1993. 2000th Death Anniv of Horace (Quintus Horatius Flaccus) (poet).

2205	**856**	600l. multicoloured	1·50	75

857 Cottolengo
and Small House
of the Divine
Providence, Turin

1993. St. Giuseppe Benedetto Cottolengo Commemoration.

2206	**857**	750l. multicoloured	1·90	1·30

858 *Carousel
Horses* (Lino
Bianchi Barriviera)

1993. Europa. Contemporary Art. Multicoloured.

2207	750l. Type **858**	1·90	1·20
2208	850l. *Dynamism of Coloured Shapes* (Gino Severini)	2·20	1·30

859 *Medal*
(Giuseppe
Romagnoli)

1993. 400th Anniv of San Luca National Academy.

2209	**859**	750l. multicoloured	1·70	1·30

860 Emblem

1993. "Family Fest '93" International Conference, Rome.

2210	**860**	750l. multicoloured	1·70	1·30

861 Player and
Club Badge

1993. Milan, National Football Champion, 1992–93.

2211	**861**	750l. multicoloured	1·70	1·30

862 Carloforte

1993. Tourist Publicity (20th series). Multicoloured.

2212	600l. Type **862**	1·50	65
2213	600l. Palmanova	1·50	65
2214	600l. Senigallia	1·50	65
2215	600l. Sorrento	1·50	65

See also Nos. 2248/51 and 2315/18.

863 Canoeing

1993. World Canoeing Championships, Trentino.

2216	**863**	750l. multicoloured	1·70	1·30

864 Observatory

1993. Centenary of Regina Margherita Observatory.

2217	**864**	500l. multicoloured	1·50	75

865 Staircase, St.
Salome's
Cathedral, Veroli

1993. Artistic Heritage.

2218	**865**	750l. multicoloured	1·70	1·00

866 Soldier, Boy
with Rifle and
German Helmet

1993. Second World War 50th Anniversaries (1st issue). Multicoloured.

2219	750l. Type **866** (the Four Days of Naples)	1·70	90
2220	750l. Menorah, people in railway truck and Star of David (deportation of Roman Jews)	1·70	90
2221	750l. Seven Cervi brothers (execution)	1·70	90

See also Nos. 2259/61.

867 Carriage

1993. The Taxis Family in Postal History. Multicoloured.

2222	750l. Type **867**	1·50	65
2223	750l. Taxis arms	1·50	65
2224	750l. Gig	1·50	65
2225	750l. 17th-century postal messenger	1·50	65
2226	750l. 18th-century postal messenger	1·50	65

868 Head Office, Rome

1993. Centenary of Bank of Italy. Multicoloured.

2227	750l. Type **868**	4·25	1·00
2228	1000l. 1000 lire banknote (first note issued by Bank)	5·75	1·30

869 Colonies Express
Letter Stamp Design

1993. Stamp Day. Centenary of First Italian Colonies Stamps.

2229	**869**	600l. red and blue	1·50	75

870 Tableau
Vivant, Corchiano

1993. Christmas. Multicoloured.

2230	600l. Type **870**	1·60	85
2231	750l. *The Annunciation* (Piero della Francesca)	2·00	70

871 17th-century Map of
Foggia

1993. Treasures from State Archives and Museums (1st series). Multicoloured.

2232	600l. Type **871** (Foggia Archives)	1·50	90
2233	600l. *Concert* (Bartolomeo Manfredi) (Uffizi Gallery, Florence)	1·50	90
2234	750l. View of Siena from 15th-century illuminated manuscript (Siena Archives) (vert)	1·70	1·00
2235	850l. *The Death of Adonis* (Sebastiano del Piombo) (Uffizi Gallery)	2·00	1·00

See also Nos. 2266/9, 2306/9 and 2346/9.

872 Ringmaster
and Bareback
Riders

1994. The Circus. Multicoloured.

2236	600l. Type **872**	1·50	65
2237	750l. Clowns	1·70	75

873 Mother and Child
inside House

1994. "The Housewife, a Presence that Counts".

2238	**873**	750l. multicoloured	2·00	65

874 *Bread* (Dario
Piazza)

1994. Paintings of Italian Food. Multicoloured.

2239	500l. Type **874**	1·20	75
2240	600l. *Italian Pasta in the World* (Erminia Scaglione)	1·50	65

1994. 100 Years of Radio (4th issue). As T **822**. Multicoloured.

2241	750l. Augusto Righi (physicist) and his Hertzian oscillator	2·10	90

875 Boxer

1994. Dogs. Multicoloured.
2242	600l. Type **875**	1·50	70
2243	600l. Dalmatian	1·50	70
2244	600l. Maremma sheepdog	1·50	70
2245	600l. German shepherd	1·50	70

876 *The Risen Christ* (statue)

1994. Procession of "The Risen Christ", Tarquinia.
2246	**876**	750l. multicoloured	2·20	90

877 Pacioli in Study

1994. 500th Anniv of Publication of "Summary of Arithmetic, Geometry, Proportion and Proportionality" by Fra' Luca Pacioli.
2247	**877**	750l. multicoloured	2·20	90

1994. Tourist Publicity (21st series). As T **862**. Multicoloured.
2248	600l. Odescalchi Castle, Santa Marinella	1·50	65
2249	600l. St. Michael's Abbey, Monticchio	1·50	65
2250	600l. Orta San Giulio	1·50	65
2251	600l. Cathedral, Messina	1·50	65

878 Kossuth

1994. Death Centenary of Lajos Kossuth (Hungarian statesman).
2252	**878**	3750l. multicoloured	8·00	3·25

879 Women's High-diving

1994. World Water Sports Championships. Multicoloured.
2253	600l. Type **879**	1·90	65
2254	750l. Water polo	2·00	75

880 Club Badge, Football and Colours

1994. Milan, National Football Champion, 1993–94.
2255	**880**	750l. multicoloured	2·20	90

881 Camillo Golgi (cytologist) and Golgi Cells

1994. Europa. Discoveries. Italian Nobel Prize winners. Multicoloured.
2256	750l. Type **881** (medicine, 1906)	2·30	75

2257	850l. *Giulio Natta* (chemist) and diagram of polymer structure (chemistry, 1963)	2·75	90

882 *Goddess of Caldevigo* (bronze statuette, 5th century B.C.)

1994. "Ancient Peoples of Italy" Archaeological Exhibition, Rimini.
2258	**882**	750l. multicoloured	2·20	90

883 Destruction of Montecassino

1994. Second World War 50th Anniversaries (2nd issue). Multicoloured.
2259	750l. Type **883**	1·90	65
2260	750l. Bound prisoners (Ardeatine Caves Massacre)	1·90	65
2261	750l. Family (Marzabotto Massacre)	1·90	65

884 Washing of Feet

1994. 22nd National Eucharistic Congress, Siena.
2262	**884**	600l. multicoloured	1·70	90

885 *Ariadne, Venus and Bacchus*

1994. Artistic Heritage. 400th Death Anniv of Tintoretto (artist).
2263	**885**	750l. multicoloured	2·20	90

886 *Piazza del Duomo during the Plague, 1630* (attr Cigoli)

1994. 750th Anniv of Arciconfraternita della Misericordia, Florence.
2264	**886**	750l. multicoloured	2·20	90

887 *"E", European Union Emblem and Parliament*

1994. European Parliament Elections.
2265	**887**	600l. multicoloured	1·70	75

1994. Treasures from State Archives and Museums (2nd series). As T **871**. Multicoloured.
2266	600l. Frontispiece of notary's register, 1623–24 (Catania Archives)	1·30	60
2267	600l. *Death of Patroclus* (Attic vase, 5th century B.C.) (Agrigento Archaeological Museum) (vert)	1·30	60

2268	750l. *Galata and his Wife* (statue) (National Roman Museum) (vert)	1·60	65
2269	850l. Civic seal, 1745 (Campobasso Archives) (vert)	1·90	90

888 Olympic Rings and Pierre de Coubertin (founder)

1994. Centenary of Int Olympic Committee.
2270	**888**	850l. multicoloured	2·30	90

889 Vesuvius and "G 7"

1994. Group of Seven (industrialized countries) Summit, Naples.
2271	**889**	600l. blue, ultram & grn	1·50	65

890 Church of the Holy House and *Madonna and Child*

1994. 700th Anniv of Shrine of the Nativity of the Virgin, Loreto.
2272	**890**	500l. multicoloured	1·80	90

891 Pietro Miliani (papermaker) (after Francesco Rosaspina)

1994. Stamp Day. Multicoloured.
2273	600l. Type **891**	1·50	75
2274	750l. Paper and Watermark Museum (former St. Dominic's Monastery), Fabriano	1·80	75

892 Frederick II (sculpture, Bitonto Cathedral)

1994. 800th Birth Anniv of Frederick II, Holy Roman Emperor.
2275	**892**	750l. multicoloured	2·00	65

893 St. Mark's Basilica

1994. 900th Anniv of Dedication of St. Mark's Basilica, Venice.
2276	**893**	750l. multicoloured	2·30	1·30
MS2277	80×115 mm. No. 2276 together with No. 1491 of San Marino		4·25	3·75

894 *The Annunciation* (Melozzo da Forli)

1994. Christmas. Multicoloured.
2278	600l. Type **894**	1·70	60
2279	750l. *Sacred Conversation* (detail, Lattanzio da Rimini)	3·50	75

895 Club Emblem on Globe

1994. Centenary of Italian Touring Club.
2280	**895**	600l. multicoloured	1·80	65

896 Headquarters, Rome

1994. 75th Anniv of Credit for Businesses and Public Works.
2281	**896**	750l. multicoloured	4·00	90

897 New Emblem

1994. Incorporation of Italian Post. Size 34×26 mm.
2282	–	600l. red and silver	1·80	60
2283	**897**	750l. black, green and red	2·30	75
2284	**897**	750l. red	2·30	75

DESIGN—VERT: 600l. Palazzo Querini Dubois, Venice (restored with Post Office help).
For 750 and 850l. values, size 26×17 mm, see Nos. 2343/4.

898 Gentile

1994. 50th Death Anniv of Giovanni Gentile (philosopher).
2285	**898**	750l. multicoloured	2·30	90

899 Rainbow, Dove, Olive Tree and Flood

1995. For Flood Victims.
2286	**899**	750l.+2250l. multicoloured	10·50	6·50

900 Skater

1995. World Speed Skating Championships, Baselga di Pine.
2287	**900**	750l. multicoloured	2·30	90

901 First Issue of
*La Domenica del
Corriere*

1995. 50th Death Anniv of Achille Beltrame (painter).
2288 **901** 500l. multicoloured 1·80 75

902 Rice

1995. Italian Food. Multicoloured.
2289 500l. Type **902** 1·70 70
2290 750l. Olives and olive oil 2·30 65

903 Grey Herons

1995. Birds. Multicoloured.
2291 600l. Type **903** 1·50 90
2292 600l. Griffon vultures ("Grifone") 1·50 90
2293 600l. Golden eagles ("Aquila Reale") 1·50 90
2294 600l. White-winged snow finches ("Fringuello Alpino") 1·50 90

904 Anniversary Emblem

1995. 50th Anniv of U.N.O.
2295 **904** 850l. black, blue and gold 2·50 90

905 Detail of Monument
(Giuseppe Grande)

1995. Centenary of Monument to the Fallen of the Five Days of Milan (1848 uprising).
2296 **905** 750l. multicoloured 1·80 75

906 Princess Mafalda of
Savoy and Concentration
Camp

1995. 50th Anniv of End of Second World War. Multicoloured.
2297 750l. Type **906** 1·80 40
2298 750l. DUKW at Anzio 1·80 40
2299 750l. Teresa Gullace and scene of her death 1·80 40
2300 750l. Florence Town Hall and Military Medal 1·80 40
2301 750l. Vittorio Veneto Town Hall and Military Medal 1·80 40
2302 750l. Cagliari Town Hall and Military Medal 1·80 40
2303 750l. Battle of Mount Lungo 1·80 40
2304 750l. Martin B-26 Maraudes parachuting supplies in the Balkans 1·80 40
2305 750l. Light cruisers of the Eighth Division in Atlantic 1·80 40

1995. Treasures from State Archives and Museums (3rd series). As T **871**. Multicoloured.
2306 500l. Illuminated letter "P" from statute of Pope Innocent III (Rome Archives) (vert) 1·20 75
2307 500l. *Port of Naples* (detail, Bernardo Strozzi) (St. Martin National Museum, Naples) 1·20 75

2308 750l. Illuminated letter "I" showing the Risen Christ from 1481 document (Mantua Archives) (vert) 1·70 90
2309 850l. *Sacred Love and Profane Love* (Titian) (Borghese Museum and Gallery, Rome) 2·00 1·00

907 Emblem

1995. Centenary of Venice Biennale.
2310 **907** 750l. blue, gold & yellow 2·00 75

908 Santa Croce
Basilica, Florence

1995. Artistic Heritage.
2311 **908** 750l. brown 2·00 75

909 Soldiers and
Civilians
celebrating

1995. Europa. Peace and Freedom. Multicoloured.
2312 750l. Type **909** (50th anniv of end of Second World War in Europe) 2·50 75
2313 850l. Mostar Bridge, (Bosnia) and Council of Europe emblem 2·75 90

910 Players

1995. Centenary of Volleyball.
2314 **910** 750l. blue, orange & grn 2·30 75

1995. Tourist Publicity (22nd series). As T **862**. Multicoloured.
2315 750l. Alatri 2·20 75
2316 750l. Nuoro 2·20 75
2317 750l. Susa 2·20 75
2318 750l. Venosa 2·20 75

911 Experiment
demonstrating X-rays

1995. Centenary of Discovery of X-rays by Wilhelm Rontgen.
2319 **911** 750l. multicoloured 1·80 75

912 Player and
Club Badge

1995. Juventus, National Football Champion, 1994–95.
2320 **912** 750l. multicoloured 2·30 90

913 Villa Griffone (site of
Marconi's early
experiments)

1995. 100 Years of Radio (5th issue). Centenary of First Radio Transmission. Multicoloured.
2321 750l. Type **913** 2·00 65
2322 850l. Guglielmo Marconi and transmitter (36×21 mm) 2·30 75

914 St. Antony,
Holy Basilica
(Padua) and Page
of Gospel

1995. 800th Birth Anniv of St. Antony of Padua. Multicoloured.
2323 750l. Type **914** 2·00 65
2324 850l. St. Antony holding Child Jesus (painting, Vieira Lusitano) (horiz) 2·30 75

915 Durazzo Pallavicini,
Pegli

1995. Public Gardens (1st series). Multicoloured.
2325 750l. Type **915** 2·00 50
2326 750l. Boboli, Florence 2·00 50
2327 750l. Ninfa, Cisterna di Latina 2·00 50
2328 750l. Parco della Reggia, Caserta 2·00 50
See also Nos. 2439/42.

916 Milan
Cathedral and Eye
(congress emblem)

1995. Tenth European Ophthalmological Society Congress, Milan.
2329 **916** 750l. multicoloured 1·80 75

917 *Sailors' Wives*

1995. Birth Centenary of Massimo Campigli (painter).
2330 **917** 750l. multicoloured 2·50 1·00

918 Dome of Santa Maria
del Fiore (Florence),
Galileo and Albert
Einstein

1995. 14th World Relative Physics Conference, Florence.
2331 **918** 750l. blue, brown & black 1·80 75

919 Rudolph
Valentino in *The
Son of the Sheik*

1995. Centenary of Motion Pictures.
2332 **919** 750l. black, blue and red 2·00 90
2333 - 750l. multicoloured 2·00 90
2334 - 750l. multicoloured 2·00 90
2335 - 750l. multicoloured 2·00 90
DESIGNS: No. 2333, Toto in *The Gold of Naples*; 2334, Frederico Fellini's "*Cabiria Nights*; 2335, Poster (by Massimo Geleng) for *Cinecitta 95* film festival.

920 Wheatfield and
Anniversary Emblem

1995. 50th Anniv of F.A.O.
2336 **920** 850l. multicoloured 2·50 90

921 St. Albert's Stone
Coffin (detail) and Basilica

1995. 900th Anniversaries of Pontida Basilica and Death of St. Albert of Prezzate.
2337 **921** 1000l. brown and blue 2·75 1·00

922 Athletes

1995. First World Military Games, Rome.
2338 **922** 850l. multicoloured 2·50 90

923 Globe and Means of
Communication

1995. 50th Anniv of Ansa News Agency.
2339 **923** 750l. multicoloured 2·30 75

924 Crib (Stefano da
Putignano), Polignano
Cathedral

1995. Christmas. Multicoloured.
2340 750l. Type **924** 3·00 65
2341 850l. *Adoration of the Wise Men* (detail, Fra Angelico) 3·50 75

925 Renato Mondolfo
(philatelist) and Trieste
1949 20l. Stamp

1995. Stamp Day.
2342 **925** 750l. multicoloured 1·80 40

1995. First Anniv of Incorporation of Italian Post. Size 26×17 mm.
2343 **897** 750l. red 1·70 50
2344 **897** 850l. black, green and red 2·20 75

926 Collage representing Marinetti's Works

1996. 120th Birth Anniv of Filippo Marinetti (writer and founder of Futurist movement).
2345 **926** 750l. multicoloured 2·30 75

1996. Treasures from State Archives and Museums (4th series). As T **871**. Multicoloured.
2346		750l. Arms (Georgofili Academy, Florence)	2·20	75
2347		750l. Illuminated letter showing St. Luke and his ox from Constitution of 1372 (Lucca Archives) (vert)	2·20	75
2348		850l. Inkwells, pen and manuscript of Gabriele d'Annunzio (writer) (Il Vittoriale, Gardone Riviera)	2·50	90
2349		850l. *Life of King Modus and Queen Racio* from 1486 miniature (Turin Archives)	2·50	90

927 *Sarah and the Angel* (fresco, Archbishop's Palace, Udine)

1996. 300th Birth Anniv of Giambattista Tiepolo (painter).
2350 **927** 1000l. multicoloured 3·00 1·30

928 White Wine

1996. Italian Wine Production. Multicoloured.
2351		500l. Type **928**	1·80	65
2352		750l. Red wine	2·75	75

929 Marco Polo and Palace in the Forbidden City

1996. 700th Anniv (1995) of Marco Polo's Return from Asia and "China '96" International Stamp Exhibition, Peking.
2353 **929** 1250l. multicoloured 3·75 1·90

930 Milan Cathedral (left detail)

1996. "Italia 98" International Stamp Exhibition, Milan (1st issue). Multicoloured.
2354	**930**	750l. Type **930**	2·00	65
2355		750l. Cathedral (right detail)	2·00	65

Nos. 2354/5 were issued together, *se-tenant*, forming a composite design of the Cathedral.
See also Nos. **MS**2412, 2518, 2523, 2528/30 and 2531.

931 Quill pen and Satellite (50th Anniv of National Federation of Italian Press)

1996. Anniversaries.
2356	**931**	750l. multicoloured	2·00	75
2357	-	750l. blue, pink and black	2·00	75

DESIGN—HORIZ: No. 2357, Globe (centenary of *La Gazetta dello Sport* (newspaper)).

932 Postman and Emblem

1996. International Museum of Postal Images, Belvedere Ostrense.
2358 **932** 500l. multicoloured 1·50 65

933 Uniforms of Different Periods

1996. Centenary of Academy of Excise Guards.
2359 **933** 750l. multicoloured 2·20 75

934 Truck and Route Map

1996. Trans-continental Drive, Rome–New York.
2360 **934** 4650l. multicoloured 12·50 5·25

935 Carina Negrone (pilot) and Biplane

1996. Europa. Famous Women. Multicoloured.
2361		750l. Type **935**	2·30	75
2362		850l. Adelaide Ristori (actress)	2·75	90

936 Fishes, Sea and Coastline from St. Raphael to Genoa

1996. 20th Anniv of Ramoge Agreement on Environmental Protection of the Mediterranean.
2363 **936** 750l. multicoloured 2·30 75

937 Celestino V and Town of Fumone

1996. 700th Death Anniv of Pope Celestino V.
2364 **937** 750l. multicoloured 2·30 75

938 St Anthony's Church, Diano Marina

1996. Tourist Publicity (23rd series). Multicoloured.
2365		750l. Type **938**	2·20	75
2366		750l. Pienza Cathedral	2·20	75
2367		750l. Belltower of St. Michael the Archangel's Church, Monte Sant'Angelo	2·20	75
2368		750l. Prehistoric stone dwelling, Lampedusa	2·20	75

939 Abbey and Relief from 12th-century Ivory Reliquary

1996. 500th Anniv of Reconsecration of Farfa Abbey.
2369 **939** 1000l. black, yell & orge 3·00 1·00

940 Fair Entrance and Mt. Pellegrino

1996. Mediterranean Fair, Palermo.
2370 **940** 750l. multicoloured 2·20 90

941 State Arms

1996. 50th Anniv of Italian Republic.
2371 **941** 750l. multicoloured 2·20 90

942 Rider and Emblem

1996. 50th Anniv of Production of Vespa Motor Scooters.
2372 **942** 750l. multicoloured 2·75 90

943 Views of Messina and Venice

1996. 40th Anniv of Founding Meetings of European Economic Community, Messina and Venice.
2373 **943** 750l. multicoloured 2·30 1·00

944 Athlete on Starting Block and 1896 Athletes

1996. Centenary of Modern Olympic Games and Olympic Games, Atlanta. Multicoloured.
2374		500l. Type **944**	1·20	75
2375		750l. Throwing the discus and view of Atlanta (vert)	1·80	90
2376		850l. Gymnast, stadium and basketball player	2·20	1·00
2377		1250l. 1896 stadium, Athens, and 1996 stadium, Atlanta (vert)	3·00	1·20

945 *Acanthobrahmaea europaea*

1996. Butterflies. Multicoloured.
2378		750l. Type **945**	2·20	90
2379		750l. *Melanargia arge*	2·20	90
2380		750l. *Papilio hospiton*	2·20	90
2381		750l. *Zygaena rubicundus*	2·20	90

946 *Prima Comunione*

1996. Italian Films (1st series).
2382	**946**	750l. black, red and blue	2·00	90
2383	-	750l. multicoloured	2·00	90
2384	-	750l. multicoloured	2·00	90

DESIGNS: No. 2383, Poster for "Cabiria"; 2384, "Scusate il Ritardo".
See also Nos. 2453/5 and 2528/30.

947 Santa Maria del Fiore

1996. 700th Anniv of Cathedral of Santa Maria del Fiore, Florence.
2385 **947** 750l. blue 2·30 90

948 Player, Shield and Club Badge

1996. Milan, National Football Champion, 1995–96.
2386 **948** 750l. multicoloured 3·00 90

949 Choppy (congress mascot)

1996. 13th International Prehistoric and Protohistoric Sciences Congress.
2387 **949** 850l. multicoloured 2·50 1·00

950 Games Emblem and Pictograms

1996. Mediterranean Games, Bari (1997).
2388 **950** 750l. multicoloured 2·30 90

951 Fair Entrance

1996. Levant Fair, Bari.
2389 **951** 750l. multicoloured 2·30 90

952 Rejoicing
Crowd and Club
Badge

1996. Juventus, European Football Champion, 1995–96.
2390 **952** 750l. multicoloured   2·50   90

953 Pertini

1996. Birth Centenary of Alessandro Pertini (President 1978–85).
2391 **953** 750l. multicoloured   2·30   90

954 Montale and
Hoopoe

1996. Birth Centenary of Eugenio Montale (poet).
2392 **954** 750l. brown and blue   2·30   90

955 The
Annunciation

1996. 400th Birth Anniv of Pietro Berrettini da Cortona (artist).
2393 **955** 500l. multicoloured   2·20   90

956 Tex Willer (Galep)

1996. Stamp Collecting. Strip Cartoons. Multicoloured.
2394 750l. Type **956**   2·50   90
2395 850l. Corto Maltese (Hugo
      Pratt)   2·75   1·00

957 Vortex and
"Stamps"

1996. Stamp Day.
2396 **957** 750l. multicoloured   2·20   90

958 Bell Tower
and Former
Benedictine Abbey
(seat of faculty)

1996. Universities.
2397 **958** 750l. brown   1·80   90
2398 –   750l. blue   1·80   90
2399 –   750l. green   1·80   90

DESIGNS—VERT: No. 2397. Type **958** (centenary of Faculty of Agriculture, Perugia University); 2398, Former St. Matthew's Cathedral (seat of Medical School), Salerno University. HORIZ: No. 2399, Athenaeum, Sassari University.

959 Emblem

1996. World Food Summit, Rome.
2400 **959** 850l. green and black   2·20   1·00

960 Madonna of
the Quail (Antonio
Pisanello)

1996. Christmas. Multicoloured.
2401 750l. Type **960**   2·30   75
2402 850l. Father Christmas and
      toys (horiz)   2·75   90

961 "UNESCO" and
Globe

1996. 50th Anniversaries of UNESCO and UNICEF.
2403 750l. Type **961**   2·30   75
2404 850l. UNICEF emblem on kite,
      baby and globe   2·75   90

962 Headquarters,
Rome

1996. 70th Anniv of National Statistics Institute.
2405 **962** 750l. multicoloured   2·30   90

963 Bookcase

1996. 50th Anniv of Strega Prize.
2406 **963** 3400l. multicoloured   8·50   3·50

964 Hall of the
Tricolour, Reggio
Emilia

1997. Bicentenary of First Tricolour (now national flag), Cisalpine Republic.
2407 **964** 750l. multicoloured   2·00   90

965 Tower Blocks
and Skier

1997. World Alpine Skiing Championships, Sestriere. Multicoloured.
2408 750l. Type **965**   2·00   90
2409 850l. Olympic colours forming
      ski run and ski   2·20   1·00

966 Ferraris, Early Motor
and Ferraris National
Electrotechnology
Institute, Turin

1997. Death Centenary of Galileo Ferraris (physicist).
2410 **966** 750l. multicoloured   2·00   90

967 Loi

1997. Fifth Death Anniv of Emanuela Loi (bodyguard killed in Mafia car bombing).
2411 **967** 750l. multicoloured   2·00   90

968 1819 Letter
and Handstamps
of Italian States

1997. "Italia '98" International Stamp Exhibition, Milan (2nd issue). Sheet 150×80 mm containing T **968** and similar vert designs. Multicoloured.
MS2412 750l. Bologna 1910 cancellation aerogramme from Balboa flight and postcard with 1917 25c. airmail stamp (Aerophilately); 750l. Cancellations used for the signing of the Rome Treaty (forming European Economic Community), Rome Olympic Games and Holy Year, 1952 Leonardo da Vinci 80l. stamp and 1931 inauguration of Milan railway station postcard (Thematic Philately); 750l. Type **968** (Postal History); 750l. *Democratica*, Italian stamp catalogue and L'Italia Filatelica (stamp review) (Philatelic Literature)   8·75   5·25

969 Statue of
Marcus Aurelius

1997. 40th Anniv of Treaty of Rome (foundation of European Economic Community).
2413 **969** 750l. multicoloured   2·00   90

970 St.
Germiniano (after
Bartolomeo
Schedoni) holding
Modena Cathedral

1997. 1600th Death Anniv of St. Germiniano (patron saint of Modena).
2414 **970** 750l. multicoloured   2·00   90

971 Baptism of
St. Ambrose
and Hand of
God recalling
him to City

1997. 1600th Death Anniv of St. Ambrose, Bishop of Milan.
2415 **971** 1000l. multicoloured   2·50   1·30
      The illustrations are taken from reliefs by Volvinio on the Golden Altar in St. Ambrose's Cathedral, Milan.

972 Statue of Minerva,
Central Square, Rome
University

1997. Universities.
2416 **972** 750l. red   1·80   65
2417 –   750l. blue   1·80   65
DESIGN: No. 2417, Palace of Bo, Padua University.

973 St. Peter's Cathedral
and Colosseum within
"Wolf suckling Romulus
and Remus"

1997. 2750th Anniv of Foundation of Rome.
2418 **973** 850l. multicoloured   2·20   90

974 Pre-Roman Walls,
Gela

1997
2419 **974** 750l. multicoloured   2·00   90

975 First Page
of Prison
Notebook and
Signature

1997. 60th Death Anniv of Antonio Gramsci (politician).
2420 **975** 850l. multicoloured   3·00   1·00

976 Teracotta
Relief and
Cloisters

1997. 500th Anniv of Consecration of Pavia Church.
2421 **976** 1000l. multicoloured   3·25   1·30

977 Shoemaker's
Workshop

1997. Europa. Tales and Legends. Multicoloured.
2422 800l. Type **977** ("He who
      becomes the Property of
      Others works for his Soup")   2·20   75
2423 900l. Street singer (19th-
      century copper etching)   2·50   90

978 Detail of 1901
Poster for *Tosca*
and Theatre

1997. Centenary of Teatro Massimo, Palermo.
2424 **978** 800l. multicoloured   2·20   75

979 St. Sebastian's Church, Acireale

1997. Tourist Publicity (24th series). Multicoloured.

2425	800l. Type 979	2·00	75
2426	800l. Cicero and his tomb, Formia	2·00	75
2427	800l. St. Mary of the Assumption, Positano	2·00	75
2428	800l. St. Vitale's Basilica, Ravenna	2·00	75

980 Books and Marble Floor

1997. Tenth Book Salon, Turin.

2429	**980**	800l. multicoloured	2·20	1·00

981 Queen Paola and Castel Sant'Angelo, Rome

1997. 60th Birthday of Queen Paola of Belgium.

2430	**981**	750l. multicoloured	2·00	90

982 Palazzo della Civilta del Lavoro and Fair Pavilions

1997. Rome Fair.

2431	**982**	800l. multicoloured	2·20	1·00

983 Orvieto Cathedral

1997

2432	**983**	450l. violet	1·40	65

984 Morosini in Via Tasso Prison, 1944

1997. 53rd Death Anniv of Father Giuseppe Morosini.

2433	**984**	800l. multicoloured	2·20	1·00

985 Player, Club Emblem and Football

1997. Juventus, National Football Champion, 1996–97.

2434	**985**	800l. multicoloured	3·00	1·00

986 Chamois and *Iris marsica*

1997. 75th Anniv of Abruzzo National Park.

2435	**986**	800l. multicoloured	2·20	1·00

987 Towers and Fair Complex

1997. Bologna Fair.

2436	**987**	800l. multicoloured	2·20	1·00

988 Pennant and Ships' Bows

1997. Centenary of Italian Naval League.

2437	**988**	800l. multicoloured	2·20	1·00

989 Runner, High Jumper and Gymnast

1997. 13th Mediterranean Games, Bari.

2438	**989**	900l. multicoloured	2·40	1·20

1997. Public Gardens (2nd series). As T **915**. Multicoloured.

2439	800l. Orto Botanico, Palermo	2·20	1·00
2440	800l. Villa Sciarra, Rome	2·20	1·00
2441	800l. Cavour, Santena	2·20	1·00
2442	800l. Miramare, Trieste	2·20	1·00

990 Cogwheel and Robot Arm (industry)

1997. Italian Work. Multicoloured.

2443	800l. Type **990**	2·20	1·00
2444	900l. Cereals, fruit trees, grapes and sun (agriculture) (horiz)	2·50	1·20

991 Globe and the *Matthew*

1997. 500th Anniv of John Cabot's Discovery of North America.

2445	**991**	1300l. multicoloured	3·50	2·50

992 Verri

1997. Death Bicentenary of Pietro Verri (illuminist).

2446	**992**	3600l. multicoloured	8·75	5·25

993 *Madonna of the Rosary* (Pomarancio il Vecchio)

1997. Painters' Anniversaries. Multicoloured.

2447	450l. Type **993** (400th death anniv)	1·60	65
2448	650l. *The Miracle of Ostia* ((detail, Paolo Uccello) (600th birth anniv)) (26×37 mm)	2·40	1·00

994 Procession

1997. Varia Festival, Palmi.

2449	**994**	800l. multicoloured	2·20	1·00

995 Basketball

1997. University Games, Sicily. Multicoloured.

2450	450l. Type **995**	1·40	75
2451	800l. High jumping	2·00	90

996 Rosmini

1997. Birth Bicentenary of Antonio Rosmini (philosopher).

2452	**996**	800l. multicoloured	2·10	1·00

1997. Italian Films (2nd series). As T **946**.

2453	800l. multicoloured	2·10	1·00
2454	800l. black, blue and red	2·10	1·00
2455	800l. multicoloured	2·10	1·00

DESIGNS: No. 2453, Pietro Germi in *Il Ferroviere*; 2454, Anna Magnani in *Mamma Roma*; 2455, Ugo Tognazzi in *Amici Miei*.

997 Open Book and Beach, Viareggio

1997. Viareggio-Repaci Prize.

2456	**997**	4000l. multicoloured	9·25	5·25

998 Venue and Bell Tower

1997. International Trade Fair, Bolzano.

2457	**998**	800l. multicoloured	3·00	40

999 Bronze Head (500 BC)

1997. Museum Exhibits. Multicoloured.

2458	450l. Type **999** (National Museum, Reggio Calabria)	1·20	65
2459	650l. *Madonna and Child with Two Vases of Roses* (Ercole de Roberti) (National Picture Gallery, Ferrara)	1·60	75

2460	800l. Miniature of poet Sordello da Goito (Arco Palace Museum, Mantua)	2·10	1·00
2461	900l. *St. George and the Dragon* (Vitale di Bologna) (National Picture Gallery, Bologna)	2·50	1·30

1000 Pope Paul VI and Door of Death, St. Peter's Cathedral, Rome

1997. Birth Centenary of Pope Paul VI.

2462	**1000**	4000l. blue	11·50	5·25

1001 Portello Pavilion (venue) and Milan Cathedral

1997. Milan Fair.

2463	**1001**	800l. multicoloured	2·30	1·00

1002 War-ravaged and Reconstructed Cities

1997. 50th Anniv of European Recovery Programme ("Marshall Plan").

2464	**1002**	800l. multicoloured	2·30	1·00

1003 Nativity (crib, St Francis's Church, Leonessa)

1997. Christmas. Multicoloured.

2465	800l. Type **1003**	2·30	1·00
2466	900l. *Nativity* (painting, Sta. Maria Maggiore, Spelo)	2·75	1·20

1004 Production Plant and Merloni

1997. Birth Centenary of Aristide Merloni (entrepreneur).

2467	**1004**	800l. multicoloured	2·30	1·00

1005 Cavalcaselle and Drawings

1997. Death Centenary of Giovanni Battista Cavalcaselle (art historian).

2468	**1005**	800l. multicoloured	2·30	1·00

1006 Magnifying Glass and Fleur-de-lis

1997. Stamp Day.
2469   **1006**   800l. multicoloured   2·30   1·00

1007 Refugees aboard
Toscana (steamer)

1997. 50th Anniv of Exodus of Italian Inhabitants from
Istria, Fiume and Dalmatia.
2470   **1007**   800l. multicoloured   2·30   1·00

1008 Arms of State Police
and Badge of Traffic
Police

1997. 50th Anniv of Traffic Police.
2471   **1008**   800l. multicoloured   2·30   1·00

1009 Map of Italy
in Column and
Flag

1998. 50th Anniv of Constitution.
2472   **1009**   800l. black, red & green   2·30   1·00

1010 *Hercules and the*
Hydra

1998. 500th Death Anniv of Antonio del Pollaiolo
(painter).
2473   **1010**   800l. multicoloured   2·30   1·00

1011 Bertolt Brecht

1998. Writers' Birth Centenaries.
2474   **1011**   450l. multicoloured   1·20   65
2475   –   650l. multicoloured   1·80   75
2476   –   800l. multicoloured   2·30   1·00
2477   –   900l. blue, green & black   2·75   1·30
DESIGNS—HORIZ: 650l. Federico Garcia Lorca (poet); 800l.
Curzio Malaparte. VERT: 900l. Leonida Repaci.

1012 Fair Complex

1998. Verona Fair.
2478   **1012**   800l. multicoloured   2·30   1·00

1013 Memorial Tablet in
Casale Montferrato
Synagogue

1998. 150th Anniv of Granting of Full Citizen Rights to
Italian Jews.
2479   **1013**   800l. multicoloured   2·30   1·00

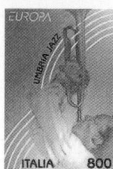

1014 Trombonist

1998. Europa. National Festivals. Multicoloured.
2480   800l. Type **1014** (Umbria Jazz
      Festival)   2·30   1·00
2481   900l. Boy holding animal (Gif-
      foni Film Festival)   2·75   1·30

1015 "The Last Supper"

1998. 500th Anniv of Completion of *The Last Supper*
(mural) by Leonardo da Vinci.
2482   **1015**   800l. brown   2·30   1·00

1016 Costumes
designed by
Bernardo
Buontalenti for First
Opera in Florence

1998. Italian Theatre. Multicoloured.
2483   800l. Type **1016** (400th anniv
      of opera)   2·30   1·00
2484   800l. Gaetano Donizetti (com-
      poser, 150th death anniv)
      (horiz)   2·30   1·00

1017 Turin
Cathedral and
Holy Shroud

1998. 500th Anniv of Turin Cathedral. Display of the Holy
Shroud.
2485   **1017**   800l. multicoloured   2·30   1·00

1018 Otranto Castle

1998. Tourist Publicity (25th series). Multicoloured.
2486   800l. Type **1018**   2·30   1·00
2487   800l. Mori Fountain and Orsini
      Tower. Marino   2·30   1·00
2488   800l. Valfederia Chapel, Livigno   2·30   1·00
2489   800l. Marciana Marina, Elba   2·30   1·00

1019 Cagliari Cathedral,
Drummer and Fair
Building

1998. International Sardinia Fair, Cagliari.
2490   **1019**   800l. multicoloured   2·30   1·00

1020 *Charge of*
the Carabinieri at
Pastrengo
(Sebastiano de
Albertis)

1998. 150th Anniv of Battle of Pastrengo.
2491   **1020**   800l. multicoloured   2·30   1·00

1021 Flags

1998. Padua Fair.
2492   **1021**   800l. multicoloured   2·30   1·00

1022 Player and
Club Badge

1998. Juventus, National Football Champion, 1997–98.
2493   **1022**   800l. multicoloured   2·30   1·00

1023 Turin Polytechnic

1998. Universities.
2494   **1023**   800l. blue   2·30   1·00

1024 Emblem

1998. World Food Programme.
2495   **1024**   900l. multicoloured   2·75   1·20

1025 Santa Maria de
Pesio Carthusian
Monastery

1998. Artistic Heritage.
2496   **1025**   800l. multicoloured   2·30   1·00

1026 Ammonites and
Pergola

1998. Fourth International "Fossils, Evolution, Ambience"
Congress, Pergola.
2497   **1026**   800l. multicoloured   2·30   1·00

1027 Flag at
Half-mast

1998. "The Forces of Order, the Fallen".
2498   **1027**   800l. multicoloured   2·30   1·00

1028 Endoscope
and Globe

1998. Sixth World General Endoscopic Surgery Congress,
Rome.
2499   **1028**   900l. multicoloured   2·75   1·20

1029 First Parliamentary
Chamber

1998. National Museums. Multicoloured.
2500   800l. Type **1029** (Italian Risorgi-
      mento Museum, Turin)   2·30   1·00
2501   800l. Statue of an ephebus
      (Athenian youth), Temple
      of Concord and column of
      Temple of Vulcan (Regional
      Archaeology Museum, Agri-
      gento) (vert)   2·30   1·00
2502   800l. Sculpture by Umberto
      Boccioni and Palazzo Venier
      dei Leoni (venue) (Peggy
      Guggenheim Collection,
      Venice)   2·30   1·00

1030 Fair Complex
and Basilica

1998. Vicenza Trade Fair.
2503   **1030**   800l. multicoloured   2·30   1·00

1031 Leopardi (after Luigi
Lolli) and Palazzo
Leopardi, Recanati

1998. Birth Bicentenary of Giacomo Leopardi (poet).
2504   **1031**   800l. brown and black   2·30   1·00

1032 Young
Etruscan Girl
(detail of tomb
painting)

1998. Women in Art.
2505   **1032**   100l. black, green & sil   45   25
2506   –   450l. multicoloured   1·50   40
2507   –   650l. multicoloured   2·20   50
2508   –   800l. brown and black   2·75   65
2509   –   1000l. blue, brn & blk   3·50   75
DESIGNS: 450l. Detail of*"Herod's Banquet and the Dance of
Salome* (fresco by Filippo Lippi in Prato Cathedral); 650l.
Profile of a Woman (Antonio del Pollaiuolo); 800l. *Lady
with a Unicorn* (detail, Raphael); 1000l. *Constanza Buon-
arelli* (bust by Gian Lorenzo Bernini).
     For these designs but with face values in euros added,
see Nos. 2537/41.

1033 Pitch, Pitcher and
Batter

1998. 33rd World Cup Baseball Championship, Florence.
2510   **1033**   900l. multicoloured   2·75   1·20

1034 Columbus and
Vespucci

1998. 500th Anniversaries of Landing of Christopher
Columbus in Venezuela and of Amerigo Vespucci's
Explorations.
2511   **1034**   1300l. multicoloured   3·50   1·50

1035 Emblem

1998. 50th International Stamp Fair, Riccione.
2512	**1035**	800l. multicoloured	2·30	1·00

1036 Mother Teresa and Child

1998. First Death Anniv of Mother Teresa (founder of Missionaries of Charity). Multicoloured.
2513	800l. Type **1036**	2·30	1·00
2514	900l. Mother Teresa (vert)	2·75	1·20

1037 Father Pio and Monastery Church, San Giovanni Rotondo

1998. 30th Death Anniv of Father Pio da Pietrelcina (Capuchin friar who bore the stigmata).
2515	**1037**	800l. blue	2·30	1·00

1038 Titus Arch, Rome, and Sicilian Mosaic of Rider

1998. World Equestrian Championships, Rome.
2516	**1038**	4000l. multicoloured	11·50	4·50

1039 Telecommunications College, Rome

1998. Universities.
2517	**1039**	800l. blue	2·30	1·00

1040 Pope John Paul II and his Message

1998. "Italia 98" International Stamp Exhibition, Milan (3rd issue). Stamp Day.
2518	**1040**	800l. multicoloured	2·75	1·00

1041 *Giuseppe Garibaldi* (aircraft carrier)

1998. Armed Forces Day. Multicoloured.
2519	800l. Type **1041** (Navy)	2·30	1·00
2520	800l. Eurofighter EF-2000 Typhoon (75th anniv of Air Force)	2·30	1·00
2521	800l. Carabiniere (vert)	2·30	1·00
2522	800l. Battle of El-Alamein at night (Army) (vert)	2·30	1·00

1042 *Dionysus* (bronze statue)

1998. "Italia 98" International Stamp Exhibition, Milan (4th issue). Art Day.
2523	**1042**	800l. multicoloured	2·30	1·00

1043 Ferrari competing in Race, 1931

1998. "Italia 98" International Stamp Exhibition, Milan (5th issue). Birth Centenary of Enzo Ferrari (car designer). Sheet 160×110 mm containing T **1043** and similar horiz designs. Multicoloured.
MS2524	800l. Type **1043**; 800l. Formula 1 Ferrari, 1952; 800l. Ferrari GTO, 1963; 800l. Formula 1 Ferrari, 1998	14·00	11·50

1044 Hand releasing Birds

1998. 50th Anniv of Universal Declaration of Human Rights.
2525	**1044**	1400l. multicoloured	4·25	1·40

1045 Cogwheels and *Proportions of Man* (Leonardo da Vinci)

1998. Europa Day. Ordinary or self-adhesive gum.
2526	**1045**	800l. multicoloured	3·00	1·00

1998. "Italia 98" International Stamp Exhibition, Milan (6th issue). Cinema Day. As T **946**. Multicoloured.
2528	450l. *Ti Conosco Mascherino* (dir. Eduardo de Filippo)	1·80	90
2529	800l. *Fantasmia a Roma* (Antonio Pietrangeli)	3·00	65
2530	900l. *Il Signor Max* (Mario Camerini)	3·50	85

1046 Satellite Dish, Type, Book and "Internet"

1998. "Italia 98" International Stamp Exhibition, Milan (7th issue). Communications Day.
2531	**1046**	800l. multicoloured	2·30	1·00

1047 Arrows circling Letter

1998. "Italia 98" International Stamp Exhibition, Milan (8th issue). Post Day. Sheet 130×90 mm.
MS2532	**1047**	4000l. multicoloured	12·50	10·50

1048 Epiphany (sculpture, St. Mark's Church, Seminara)

1998. Christmas.
2533	**1048**	800l. blue	2·30	1·20
2534	-	900l. brown	2·75	1·20

DESIGN—HORIZ: 900l. "Adoration of the Shepherds" (drawing, Giulio Romano).

1049 Ecstasy of St. Teresa

1998. 400th Birth Anniv of Gian Lorenzo Bernini (sculptor).
2535	**1049**	900l. multicoloured	2·75	1·20

1050 Royal Decree and Waldensian Emblem

1998. 150th Anniv of Toleration of the Waldenses (religious sect).
2536	**1050**	800l. multicoloured	2·30	1·00

DENOMINATION. From No. 2537 Italian stamps are denominated both in lira and in euros. As no coins or notes for the latter were in circulation until 2002, the catalogue continues to use the lira value.

1999. As Nos. 2505/9, but with face value in euros added.
2537	100l. black, green and silver	90	50
2538	450l. multicoloured	1·60	65
2539	650l. multicoloured	2·30	75
2540	800l. brown and black	2·75	90
2541	1000l. blue, brown and black	3·50	1·00

1051 Space Concept–Wait

1999. Birth Centenary of Lucio Fontana (artist).
2542	**1051**	450l. blue and black	1·60	65

1052 La Sila National Park, Calabria

1999. Europa. Parks and Gardens. Multicoloured.
2543	800l. Type **1052**	2·75	1·00
2544	900l. Tuscan Archipelago National Park (horiz)	3·00	1·20

1053 Holy Door, St. Peter's Cathedral

1999. Holy Year 2000.
2545	**1053**	1400l. multicoloured	4·00	1·30

1054 St. Egidius's Church, Cellere

1999. Artistic Heritage.
2546	**1054**	800l. brown	2·30	1·00

1055 Holy Year 2000 and 11th-century Bells

1999. Museums. Multicoloured.
2547	800l. Type **1055** (History of Campanology Museum, Agnone)	2·30	1·00
2548	800l. Lake with Swan (stained glass) (Casina delle Civette Museum, Rome)	2·30	1·00
2549	800l. Renaissance majolica dish (International Ceramics Museum, Faenza) (vert)	2·30	1·00

1056 Earth Pyramids, Segonzano

1999. Tourist Publicity (26th series). Multicoloured.
2550	800l. Type **1056**	2·30	1·00
2551	800l. Marmore Waterfall, Terni	2·30	1·00
2552	800l. Cathedral, Lecce	2·30	1·00
2553	800l. Lipari	2·30	1·00

1057 Audience Chamber

1999. Constitutional Court.
2554	**1057**	800l. multicoloured	2·30	1·00

1058 Fire Engine at Fire

1999. Fire Brigade.
2555	**1058**	800l. multicoloured	2·30	1·00

1059 Cadet and Academy

1999. Modena Military Academy.
2556	**1059**	800l. multicoloured	2·30	1·00

1060 Players and Airplane

1999. 50th Anniv of Death in Aircrash of Grand Turin Football Team. Multicoloured.
2557	800l. Type **1060**	2·30	1·00
2558	900l. Superga Basilica, club arms and names of victims	2·75	1·20

1061 Council Seat, Strasbourg

1999. 50th Anniv of Council of Europe.
2559 **1061** 800l. multicoloured   2·30 1·00

1062 Players and Club Emblem

1999. Milan, National Football Champion, 1998–99.
2560 **1062** 800l. multicoloured   2·75 1·00

1063 Ballot Box and Parliament Chamber, Strasbourg

1999. 20th Anniv of First Direct Elections to European Parliament.
2561 **1063** 800l. multicoloured   2·30 1·00

1064 Coppi

1999. 80th Birth Anniv of Fausto Coppi (racing cyclist).
2562 **1064** 800l. multicoloured   2·30 1·00

1065 "P"

1999. Priority Mail stamp. Self-adhesive.
2563 **1065** 1200l. black and gold   4·00 1·50
See also Nos. 2591 and 2660.

1066 First Fiat Car (advertising poster)

1999. Centenary of Fiat (motor manufacturer).
2564 **1066** 4800l. multicoloured   11·50 5·25

1067 "Our Lady of the Snow"

1999. Centenary of Erection of Statue of "Our Lady of the Snow" on Mt. Rocciamelone.
2565 **1067** 800l. multicoloured   2·30 1·00

1068 Pimentel and St. Elmo Castle, Naples

1999. Death Bicentenary of Eleonora de Fonseca Pimentel (writer and revolutionary).
2566 **1068** 800l. multicoloured   2·30 1·00

1069 Canoes

1999. 30th World Speed Canoeing Championships.
2567 **1069** 900l. multicoloured   2·75 1·20

1070 Goethe in the Rome Countryside (Johann Tischbein)

1999. 250th Birth Anniv of Johann Wolfgang Goethe (poet and playwright).
2568 **1070** 4000l. multicoloured   10·50 4·50

1071 Cyclist and Stopwatch

1999. World Cycling Championships, Treviso and Verona.
2569 **1071** 1400l. multicoloured   4·50 1·50

1072 Child with Rucksack

1999. Stamp Day.
2570 **1072** 800l. multicoloured   2·30 1·00

1073 Architectural Drawing of Basilica

1999. Re-opening of Upper Basilica of St. Francis of Assisi.
2571 **1073** 800l. multicoloured   2·30 1·00

1074 Parini (after Francesco Rosaspina)

1999. Death Bicentenary of Giuseppe Parini (poet).
2572 **1074** 800l. blue   2·30 1·00

1075 Volta (bust by Giovan Commolli) and Voltaic Pile

1999. Bicentenary of Invention of Electrochemical Battery by Alessandro Volta.
2573 **1075** 3000l. multicoloured   8·00 3·25

1076 Forms and U.P.U. Emblem

1999. 125th Anniv of Universal Postal Union.
2574 **1076** 900l. multicoloured   2·75 1·20

1077 Mameli with 1948 and 1949 100l. Stamps

1999. 150th Death Anniv of Goffredo Mameli (poet and patriot) and 150th Anniv of Roman Republic.
2575 **1077** 1500l. multicoloured   3·75 1·90

1078 Man and Town

1999. "The Stamp Our Friend". Multicoloured.
2576   450l. Type **1078**   1·30 50
2577   650l. Campaign emblem   1·50 75
2578   800l. Schoolchildren   2·10 1·00
2579   1000l. Windmill (toy)   2·50 1·30

1079 First World War Soldiers (after postcard)

1999. Centenary of Generation of '99.
2580 **1079** 900l. multicoloured   2·75 1·20

1080 Santa Claus

1999. Christmas. Multicoloured.
2581   800l. Type **1080**   2·50 1·00
2582   1000l. "Nativity" (Dosso Dossi)   3·50 1·30

1081 Peutinger Tablet (medieval map showing pilgrim route by C. Celtes and Conrad Peutinger)

1999. Holy Year 2000. Multicoloured.
2583   1000l. Type **1081**   2·75 1·20
2584   1000l. 18th-century pilgrim's stamp   2·75 1·20
2585   1000l. 13th-century bas-relief of pilgrims (facade of Fidenza Cathedral)   2·75 1·20

1082 Urbino State Art Institute

1999. Schools and Universities.
2586 **1082** 450l. black   1·20 50
2587   650l. brown   1·60 65
DESIGN: 650l. Pisa High School.

1083 Leopard bitten by Tarantula

1999. Birth Centenary of Antonio Ligabue (artist).
2588 **1083** 1000l. multicoloured   2·75 1·30

1084 Robot's Hand meeting Man's Hand (after Michelangelo)

1999. Year 2000.
2589 **1084** 4800l. multicoloured   11·50 5·25

1085 Child looking at Aspects of Earth

2000. New Millennium. "The Past and the Future". Sheet 110×80 mm containing T **1085** and similar horiz design. Multicoloured.
MS2590 2000l. Type **1085**; 2000l. Astronaut looking at Moon   11·50 9·50

2000. Priority Mail Stamp. As T **1065** but different colour. Self-adhesive.
2591   1200l. black, yellow and gold   4·50 1·50

1086 Tosca and Scenery

2000. Centenary of the First Performance of Tosca (opera).
2592 **1086** 800l. multicoloured   2·75 1·20

1087 St. Paul (statue) and Holy Door, St. Peter's Basilica, Rome

2000. Holy Year 2000.
2593 **1087** 1000l. multicoloured   3·50 1·50

1088 Players

2000. Six Nations Rugby Championship.
2594 **1088** 800l. multicoloured   2·75 1·10

1089 Painting

2000. Fifth Conference on Breast Diseases. Multicoloured.
2595   800l. Type **1089**   2·20 90
2596   1000l. Painting (different)   3·25 1·30

1090 "Enigma of an Autumn Afternoon"

2000. New Millennium (1st issue). Art and Science. Sheet 111×80 mm containing T **1090** and similar horiz design showing paintings by Giorgio de Chirico. Multicoloured.

MS2597 800l. Type **1090** (art); 800l. *The Inevitable Temple* (science)   6·00   4·50

See also Nos. **MS2613** and **MS2623**.

1091 Skier and Trophy

2000. World Cup Skiing Championships.
2598   **1091**   4800l. multicoloured   13·50   5·50

1092 Lamp (Achillle and Pier Giacomo Castiglioni), Chair (Carlo Batroli), Coffee Pot (Aldo Rossi) and Bookcase (Ettore Softsass Jr.)

2000. Italian Design. Sheet 154×138 mm containing T **1092** and similar horiz designs. Multicoloured.
MS2599 800l. Type **1092**; 800l. Armchair (Mario Bellini), corkscrew (Alessandro Mendini), table lamp (Vico Magistretti) and suspended lamp (Alberto Meda and Paolo Rizzatto); 800l. Chair (Gio Ponti), bean bag (Gatti Paolini Teodoro), pasta set (Massimo Morozzi) and standard uplighter (Tobia Scarpa); 800l. White standard uplighter (Pietro Chiesa), hostess trolley (Joe Columbo), chair (Cini Boeri and Tomu Katayanagi) and sideboard (Lodovico Acerbis and Giotto Stoppino); 800l. Easy chairs (Gaetano Pesce), chair (Enzo Mari), clothes horse (De Pas d'Urbino Lomazzi) and mobile filing cabinet (Antonio Citterio and Oliver Loew); 800l. Chair (Marco Zanuso), anglepoise lamp (Michele de Lucchi and Giancarlo Fassina), ice bucket (Bruno Munari) and stool (Anna Castelli Ferrieri)   15·00   11·00

1093 *Adoration of the Magi* (Domenico Ghirlandaio)

2000. Holy Year 2000. Multicoloured.
2600   450l. Type **1093**   1·60   45
2601   650l. *Baptism of Christ* (Paolo Caliari Veronese) (vert)   2·20   65
2602   800l. *The Last Supper* (Ghirlandaio) (vert)   2·75   90
2603   1000l. *Regret of Christ's Death* (Giotto di Bondone)   3·25   1·10
2604   1200l. *The Resurrection* (Piero della Francesca) (vert)   3·75   1·30

1094 Library and Emblem

2000. 150th Anniv of La Civiltà Cattolica Foundation (collection of Church publications).
2605   **1094**   800l. multicoloured   2·75   1·10

1095 Courtyard

2000. 150th Anniv of St. Joseph's College, Rome.
2606   **1095**   800l. multicoloured   2·75   1·10

1096 Terre di Franciacorta, Erbrusco

2000. Tourist Publicity (27th series). Multicoloured.
2607   800l. Type **1096**   2·75   1·10
2608   800l. Dunarobba fossil forest, Avigliano Umbro   2·75   1·10
2609   800l. View of Ercolano   2·75   1·10
2610   800l. Beauty Island, Taormina   2·75   1·10

1097 Cyclist

2000. Centenary of International Cycling Union.
2611   **1097**   1500l. multicoloured   4·00   1·70

1098 Christ carrying Cross

2000. Papier-mache Figurines, Caltanisetta.
2612   **1098**   800l. multicoloured   2·75   1·10

1099 Landscape (Gilorgione)

2000. New Millennium (2nd issue). Countryside and City. Sheet 110×80 mm containing T **1099** and similar horiz design. Multicoloured.
MS2613 800l. Type **1099**; 800l. *Perspective of an Ideal Town* (Piero della Francesca)   6·00   4·00

1100 Piccinni

2000. Death Bicentenary of Niccolo Piccinni (composer).
2614   **1100**   4000l. multicoloured   11·00   4·50

1101 "Building Europe"

2000. Europa.
2615   **1101**   800l. multicoloured   2·75   1·10

1102 Sardinia 1851 5, 20 and 40c. Stamps

2000. Museum of Posts and Telecommunications. Multicoloured.
2616   800l. Type **1102**   2·75   1·10
2617   800l. Reconstruction of radio and telegraph cabin aboard Elettra (Marconi's steam yacht)   2·75   1·10

1103 Footballer and Pitch

2000. Lazio, National Football Champion, 1999–2000.
2618   **1103**   800l. multicoloured   2·75   1·10

1104 Cathedral Facade

2000. 700th Anniv of Monza Cathedral.
2619   **1104**   800l. multicoloured   2·75   1·10

1105 Globe and Ears of Corn

2000. United Nations World Food Programme.
2620   **1105**   1000l. multicoloured   3·25   1·30

1106 Statue

2000. Centenary of the Jesus the Redeemer Monument, Nuoro.
2621   **1106**   800l. multicoloured   2·75   1·10

1107 Bridge, Parana River, Argentina

2000. 120th Anniv of Italian Water Board.
2622   **1107**   800l. multicoloured   2·75   1·10

1108 Profiles

2000. New Millennium (3rd issue). Technology and Space. Sheet 110×80 mm containing T **1108** and similar horiz design. Multicoloured.
MS2623 800l. Type **1108**; 800l. Symbolic man   6·00   3·25

1109 Child with Ladder to Moon (Giacomo Chiesa)

2000. "Stampin' the Future". Winning Entry in Children's International Painting Competition.
2624   **1109**   1000l. multicoloured   4·00   1·70

1110 Archer

2000. World Archery Championship, Campagna.
2625   **1110**   1500l. multicoloured   5·50   2·20

1111 Cyclist and Globe

2000. World Junior Cycling Championships.
2626   **1111**   800l. multicoloured   3·25   1·30

1112 Fair Attractions

2000. Millenary of St. Orso.
2627   **1112**   1000l. multicoloured   3·50   1·40

1113 *Madonna and Child* (Crivelli)

2000. 570th Birth Anniv of Carlo Crivelli (artist).
2628   **1113**   800l. multicoloured   3·25   1·30

1114 Internal Organs

2000. 18th International Transplantation Society Congress, Rome.
2629   **1114**   1000l. multicoloured   3·50   1·40

1115 Athlete and Stadium

2000. Olympic Games, Sydney. Multicoloured.
2630   800l. Type **1115**   3·00   1·20
2631   1000l. "Discus Thrower" (statue) and Sydney Harbour   4·00   1·70

1116 *War*

2000. New Millennium (4th issue). War and Peace. Frescoes by Taddeo Zuccan. Sheet 110×80 mm containing T **1116** and similar vert design. Multicoloured.
MS2632 800l. Type **1116**; 800l. "Peace"   6·00   4·50

1117 Battle Scene (Jacques Debreville)

2000. Bicentenary of Marengo.
2633 **1117** 800l. multicoloured   3·25   1·30

1118 Figures in Evening Dress and City Skyline

2000. New Year.
2634 **1118** 800l. multicoloured   3·25   1·30

1119 Child holding Magnifying Glass

2000. Stamp Day.
2635 **1119** 800l. multicoloured   3·25   1·30

1120 Monti and Sick Child

2000. Death Centenary of Father Luigi Monti.
2636 **1120** 800l. multicoloured   3·25   1·30

1121 Salieri

2000. 250th Birth Anniv of Antonio Salieri (composer).
2637 **1121** 4800l. multicoloured   16·00   5·50

1122 Disabled Athletes

2000. Paralympic Games, Sydney.
2638 **1122** 1500l. multicoloured   5·50   2·20

1123 Emblem, Chaos Model and Globe in Container

2000. World Mathematics Year.
2639 **1123** 800l. multicoloured   3·25   1·30

1124 Couple and Globe

2000. Volunteers.
2640 **1124** 800l. multicoloured   3·25   1·30

1125 Quill, Text and Bust of Bruno (Pietro Masulli)

2000. 400th Death Anniv of Giordano Bruno (writer and philosopher).
2641 **1125** 800l. multicoloured   3·25   1·30

1126 *Madonna of the Rose Garden*

2000. 600th Birth Anniv of Luca della Robbia (artist).
2642 **1126** 800l. multicoloured   3·25   1·30

1127 Arms of Academy

2000. 250th Anniv of Roveretana degli Agiati Academy.
2643 **1127** 800l. multicoloured   3·25   1·30

1128 Martino and Map of Europe

2000. Birth Centenary of Gaetano Martino (politician).
2644 **1128** 800l. multicoloured   3·25   1·30

1129 *Perseus with the Head of Medusa* (bronze statue)

2000. 500th Birth Anniv of Benvenuto Cellini (goldsmith and sculptor).
2645 **1129** 1200l. multicoloured   5·00   2·00

1130 Young Woman

2000. New Millennium (5th series). Meditation and Expression. Sheet 110×80 mm containing T **1130** and similar horiz design. Multicoloured.
MS2646 800l. Type **1130**; 800l. Dancing
figures   6·50   3·25

1131 Camerino University

2000. Universities. Each blue.
2647 **1131** 800l. Type **1131**   2·50   1·00
2648 1000l. Calabria University   3·25   1·30

1132 Snowflakes and Globe

2000. Christmas. Multicoloured.
2649 800l. Type **1132**   2·75   1·10
2650 1000l. Crib, Matera Cathedral   4·00   1·70

1133 Snowboarding

2001. World Snowboarding Championships, Madonna di Campiglio.
2651 **1133** 1000l. multicoloured   3·25   1·30

1134 *The Annunciation* (detail, Botticelli)

2001. "Italy in Japan 2001" (cultural and scientific event).
2652 **1134** 1000l. multicoloured   3·25   1·30

1135 Vincenzo Bellini (composer, birth bicentenary)

2001. Composers' Anniversaries. Sheet 87×180 mm containing T **1135** and similar vert designs. Multicoloured.
MS2653 800l. Type **1135**; 800l. Domenico Cimarosa (death bicentenary); 800l. Gasparo Luigi Pacifico Spontini (150th death anniv); 800l. Giuseppe Verdi (death centenary)   11·00   9·00

1136 St. Rose and Angels (Francesco Podesti di Ancona)

2001. 750th Death Anniv of St. Rose of Viterbo.
2654 **1136** 800l. multicoloured   3·25   1·30

1137 Racing Car

2001. Ferrari, Formula One Constructor's Championship Winner (2000). Sheet 110×81 mm.
MS2655 **1137** 5000l. multicoloured   16·00   13·50

1138 Abbey of Santa Maria in Sylvis, Sesto al Reghena

2001
2656 **1138** 800l. blue   2·75   1·10

1139 Lombardy and Venetia 1850 5c. Stamp (151st anniv)

2001. Stamp Anniversaries. Multicoloured.
2657 800l. Type **1139**   3·25   1·30
2658 800l. Sardinia 1851 5c. stamp
     (150th anniv)   3·25   1·30
2659 800l. Tuscany 1851 1q. stamp
     (150th anniv)   3·25   1·30

2001. Priority Mail Stamp. As T **1065** but central "P" larger, 12×12 mm. Self-adhesive.
2660 1200l. black, yellow and gold   4·75   1·90

1140 Bridge, Comacchio

2001. Tourist Publicity (28th series). Multicoloured.
2661 800l. Type **1140**   2·75   1·10
2662 800l. Diamante   2·75   1·10
2663 800l. Pioraco   2·75   1·10
2664 800l. Stintino   2·75   1·10

1141 Campanula

2001. World Day to Combat Desertification and Drought. Multicoloured.
2665 450l. Type **1141**   1·40   55
2666 650l. Marmosets   2·20   80
2667 800l. White storks   3·25   1·00
2668 1000l. Desert and emblem   4·00   1·20

1142 Map of Italy and Tractors

2001. Confederation General of Italian Agriculture.
2669 **1142** 800l. multicoloured   2·50   1·00

1143 Castle and Emblem

2001. Millenary of Gorzia City.
2670 **1143** 800l. multicoloured   2·75   1·10

1144 Water pouring from Vase

2001. Europa. Water Resources.
2671 **1144** 800l. multicoloured   4·00   1·70

1145 Profiles

2001. European Union.
2672 **1145** 800l. multicoloured   2·75   1·10

1146 Medals

2001. Centenary of Order of Merit for Labour.
| 2673 | **1146** | 800l. multicoloured | 2·75 | 1·10 |

1147 Rose and Workers' Silhouettes

2001. National Day for Victims of Industrial Accidents.
| 2674 | **1147** | 800l. multicoloured | 2·75 | 1·10 |

1148 Child with Stamp and Magnifying Glass (Rita Vergari)

2001. Day for Art and Student Creativity. Multicoloured.
2675		800l. Type **1148**	2·75	1·10
2676		800l. People standing on rainbow (Lucia Catena)	2·75	1·10
2677		800l. Painting with eye (Luigi di Cristo)	2·75	1·10
2678		800l. Colours and profile (Barbara Grilli)	2·75	1·10

1149 St. Peter healing with his Shadow

2001. 600th Birth Anniv of Tommaso de Giovanni di Simone Guidi "Masaccio" (painter).
| 2679 | **1149** | 800l. multicoloured | 2·75 | 1·10 |

1150 Madonna and Child (Piero della Francesca)

2001. 500th Death Anniv of Giovanni della Rovere.
| 2680 | **1150** | 800l. multicoloured | 2·75 | 1·10 |

1151 Emblem

2001. 50th Anniv of Panathlon International (sports organization).
| 2681 | **1151** | 800l. multicoloured | 2·75 | 1·10 |

1152 Guaita Tower, Mt. Titano

2001. 1700th Anniv of San Marino.
| 2682 | **1152** | 800l. multicoloured | 2·75 | 1·10 |

1153 Footballer and Net

2001. A S Roma, National Football Champion, 2000–1.
| 2683 | **1153** | 800l. multicoloured | 2·75 | 1·10 |

1154 Motorboat and Bell UH1 Iroquois Helicopter

2001. Harbour Master's Office.
| 2684 | **1154** | 800l. multicoloured | 2·75 | 1·10 |

1155 Quasimodo

2001. Birth Centenary of Salvatore Quasimodo (writer).
| 2685 | **1155** | 1500l. multicoloured | 4·50 | 1·80 |

1156 Octagonal Hall, Domus Aurea, Rome

2001
| 2686 | **1156** | 1000l. brown | 2·75 | 1·10 |

1157 Bookcase (Piero Lissoni and Patricia Urquiola) and Chair (Anna Bartolli)

2001. Italian Design. Sheet 155×137 mm containing T **1157** and similar horiz designs. Multicoloured.
| MS2687 | 800l. Type **1157**; 800l. Chair (Monica Graffeo) and table lamp (Rodolfo Dordoni); 800l. Lamp (Ferruccio Laviani) and sofa (Massimo Iosa Ghini); 800l. Armchair (Anna Gili) and side table (Miki Astori); 800l. Vertical storage unit (Marco Ferreri) and double seat (M. Cananzi and R. Semprini); 800l. Stool (Stefano Giovannoni) and flexible-necked lamp (Massimiliano Datti) | 16·00 | 13·50 |

1158 The Fourth State (detail, Guiseppe Pellizza da Volpedo)

2001
| 2688 | **1158** | 1000l. brown | 4·00 | 1·70 |

1159 Stone Age Man and Pick

2001. Archaeological Museum, Alto Adige.
| 2689 | **1159** | 800l. multicoloured | 2·75 | 1·10 |

1160 Schoolchildren

2001. Youth Philately.
| 2690 | **1160** | 800l. multicoloured | 2·75 | 1·10 |

1161 Fermi

2001. Birth Centenary of Enrico Fermi (physicist).
| 2691 | **1161** | 800l. multicoloured | 2·75 | 1·10 |

1162 Pavia University

2001. Universities.
2692	**1162**	800l. blue	2·75	1·10
2693	-	800l. brown	2·75	1·10
2694	-	800l. turquoise	2·75	1·10

DESIGNS—VERT: No. 2693 Bari, University. HORIZ: 2694, School of Science, Rome.

1163 Latinas and Messenger

2001. Unione Latina (Romance language speaking countries).
| 2695 | **1163** | 800l. black, yellow and blue | 2·75 | 1·10 |

1164 Exhibits

2001. National Archaeological Museum, Taranto.
| 2696 | **1164** | 1000l. multicoloured | 3·25 | 1·30 |

1165 International Fund for Agricultural Development Emblem

2001. World Food Day. Each stamp featuring The Seed (sculpture) by Roberto Joppolo. Multicoloured.
2697		800l. Type **1165**	2·75	1·10
2698		800l. Plants and woman hoeing (50th anniv of Food and Agriculture Organization Summit Conference, Rome) (50×29 mm)	2·75	1·10
2699		800l. World Food Programme emblem	2·75	1·10

1166 Enthroned Christ with Angels (painting on wood)

2001
| 2700 | **1166** | 800l. multicoloured | 2·75 | 1·10 |

1167 Madonna and Child (painting from triptych)

2001. 500th Anniv of "Madonna and Child, Angels, St. Francis, St. Thomas Aquinas and two Donors" (triptych, Macrino d'Alba).
| 2701 | **1167** | 800l. multicoloured | 2·75 | 1·10 |

1168 Dawn of Peace (collage, San Vito dei Normani Primary School)

2001. Christmas. Multicoloured.
| 2702 | | 800l. Type **1168** | 2·75 | 1·10 |
| 2703 | | 1000l. "Nativity" (painting, St. Mary Major Basilica) | 3·25 | 1·30 |

1169 Fabric

2001. Italian Silk Industry. Sheet 140×92 mm. Self-adhesive gum. Imperf.
| MS2704 | **1169** | 5000l. multicoloured | 19·00 | 13·50 |

No. **MS**2704 was printed on fabric mounted on silk jacquard. A peel-off plastic backing featured instructions for use. If required, the address could be written in the blank area at the bottom right of the sheet.

2002. Women in Art

		(a) No Watermark		
2705		1c. multicoloured	55	20
2706		2c. multicoloured	55	20
2707		3c. multicoloured	55	20
2708		5c. multicoloured	55	20
2709		10c. multicoloured	55	20
2710		20c. multicoloured	1·40	45
2711		23c. multicoloured	1·60	55

		(b) W **307**		
2715		41c. brown, grey and black	2·20	90
2716		45c. purple, blue and black	2·50	1·00
2717		50c. turquoise, red and black	2·75	1·10
2718		65c. blue and red	3·50	1·40
2719		70c. violet and green	4·50	1·80
2720		77c. brown, green and black	4·75	1·90
2721		85c. purple and black	5·00	2·00
2722		90c. green and red	5·50	2·20

DESIGNS: 1c. Ebe (detail, painting, Antonia Canova); 2c. Profile (5th-century B.C. coin, Syracuse); 3c. Woman's head (detail from mural, Piero della Francesca); 5c. As No. 2505, Lucera); 10c. Head (3rd-century B.C. sculpture, G. Fiorelli civic museum, Lucera); 20c. Portrait of a Lady (Correggio); 23c. As No. 2506; 41c. As No. 2508; 45c. Venere di Urbino (Tiziano Vecellio); 50c. Portrait of a young girl (detail, painting, Francesco Mazzola); 65c. San Giorgio e la Principessa di Trebisonda (detail by Antonis Pisano); 70c. Wettuno a Venezia (detail by Giambattista Foggini, sculpture); 77c. Spring (detail, painting, Botticelli); 85c. Costigiana (detail, by Vittore (arpaccio)); 90c. Venere e Marte legati de Amore (detail, by Paolo Calieri).

1170 "Ducato" (Venetian coin), 1285

2002. European Coins. Multicoloured.
2725	41c.	Type **1170**	2·75	1·10
2726	41c.	"Genovino" (Genoa) and "Fiorino" (Florence), 1252	2·75	1·10
2727	41c.	Flags of E.U. forming Euro symbol	2·75	1·10
2728	41c.	1946 lira coin transforming into euro coin	2·75	1·10

2002. Priority Mail Stamps. Designs as No. 2660 but with face values in euros only. Multicoloured, background colour given. Self-adhesive gum.
2729	62c.	yellow	4·00	1·10
2730	77c.	blue	5·50	1·70
2731	€1	lavender	6·75	2·20
2732	€1.24	green	8·25	2·75
2733	€1.86	pink	11·00	4·25
2734	€4.13	lilac	25·00	9·25

1171 Woman's Head and State Arms

2002. Woman's Head and State Arms
2735	**1171**	€1 multicoloured	6·75	2·20
2736		€1.24 multicoloured	8·25	2·75
2737		€1.55 multicoloured	11·00	4·00
2738		€2.17 multicoloured	13·50	5·00
2739		€2.35 multicoloured	16·00	5·25
2740		€2.58 multicoloured	18·00	6·00
2741		€2.80 multicoloured	18·00	6·50
2742		€3 multicoloured	19·00	6·75
2743		€3.62 multicoloured	22·00	8·25
2744		€6.20 multicoloured	41·00	13·50

1172 Escriva

2002. Birth Centenary of Josemaria Escriva de Balaguer (founder of Opus Dei (religious organization)).
2745	**1172**	41c. multicoloured	2·75	1·10

1173 Luigi Bocconi and University Building

2002. Centenary of Bocconi University.
2746	**1173**	41c. brown and stone	2·75	1·10

The University was established with an endowment from Ferinando Bocconi in memory of his son Luigi.

1174 1852 5c. Stamp

2002. 150th Anniv of First Stamp of Parma. Fluorescent paper.
2747	**1174**	41c. multicoloured	2·75	1·10

1175 Mountain Peak

2002. International Year of Mountains.
2748	**1175**	41c. multicoloured	2·75	1·10

1176 Emblem and Olympic Rings

2002. Winter Olympic Games, Turin (2006).
2749	**1176**	41c. multicoloured	2·75	1·10

1177 Queen Elena

2002. 50th Death Anniv of Queen Elena of Savoy.
2750	**1177**	41c.+21c. multicoloured	3·50	1·40

1178 Sculpture (Arnolfo di Cambio)

2002. 700th Death Anniv of Arnolfo di Cambio (sculptor).
2751	**1178**	41c. mauve	2·75	1·10

1179 Venaria Reale

2002. Tourist Publicity (29th series). Multicoloured.
2752	41c.	Type **1179**	2·75	1·10
2753	41c.	Capo d'Orlando	2·75	1·10
2754	41c.	San Gimignano	2·75	1·10
2755	41c.	Sannicandro di Bari	2·75	1·10

1180 Santa Maria delle Grazie Sanctuary

2002.
2756	**1180**	41c. brown	2·75	1·10

1181 Police Officers, Computer Screen and Patrol Car

2002. 150th Anniv of State Police Force.
2757	**1181**	41c. multicoloured	2·75	1·10

1182 Ricci and World Map

2002. 450th Birth Anniv of Matteo Rici (missionary).
2758	**1182**	41c. multicoloured	2·75	1·10

1183 Circus Performers

2002. Europa. Circus.
2759	**1183**	41c. multicoloured	4·00	1·70

1184 Sailing Ship and Student

2002. Francesco Morosini Naval Military School, Venice.
2760	**1184**	41c. multicoloured	2·75	1·10

1185 Vittorio de Sica (film director, birth centenary)

2002. Cinema Anniversaries. Multicoloured.
2761	41c.	Type **1185**	2·75	1·10
2762	41c.	Text and clouds (birth centenary (1901) of Cesare Zavattini (screen writer))	2·75	1·10

1186 Football Player and Emblem

2002. Juventus, National Football Champions, 2001–2002.
2763	**1186**	41c. multicoloured	3·25	1·30

1187 Falcone and Boresellino

2002. Tenth Death Anniv of Giovanni Falcone and Paolo Borsellino (judges).
2764	**1187**	62c. multicoloured	3·50	1·40

1188 Emblems and Member Flags

2002. Russia's Membership of North Atlantic Treaty Organization (N.A.T.O.).
2765	**1188**	41c. multicoloured	2·75	1·10

1189 Kayaking

2002. World Kayaking Championship, Valsesia.
2766	**1189**	52c. multicoloured	3·50	1·40

1190 Modena 1853 1 lira Arms of Este Stamp

2002. 150th Anniv of Modena (Italian State) Stamps.
2767	**1190**	41c. multicoloured	2·75	1·10

1191 Arms

2002. Italian Military Involvement in Peace Missions.
2768	**1191**	41c. multicoloured	2·75	1·10

1192 Binda

2002. Birth Centenary of Alfredo Binda (cyclist).
2769	**1192**	41c. multicoloured	2·75	1·10

1193 Santo

2002. Canonization of Father Padre Pio Santo.
2770	**1193**	41c. multicoloured	2·75	1·10

1194 Divisione Acqui (monument, Mario Salazzari)

2002. "Divisione Acqui" (World War II resistance group on Cephalonia).
2771	**1194**	41c. multicoloured	2·75	1·10

1195 Crucifixion (Arezzo Basilica)

2002.
2772	**1195**	€2.58 multicoloured	15·00	5·50

1196 Building Facade

2002. Bicentenary of Ministry of Interior.
2773	**1196**	41c. multicoloured	2·75	1·10

1197 Maria Goretti

2002. Death Centenary of Saint Maria Goretti.
2774	**1197**	41c. multicoloured	2·75	1·10

1198 Mazarin

2002. 400th Birth Anniv of Cardinal Jules Mazarin (minister to Louis XIV of France).
2775 1198 41c. multicoloured 2·75 1·10

1199 National Colours encircling Globe

2002. "Italians in the World".
2776 1199 52c. multicoloured 3·25 1·30

1200 Monument (Vincenzo Gasperetti)

2002. Monument to the Victims of Massacre at Sant' Anna di Stazzema.
2777 1200 41c. multicoloured 2·75 1·10

1201 Jacket (Krizia)

2002. Italian Design. Sheet 157×137 mm, containing T **1201** and similar vert designs. Multicoloured.
MS2778 41c. Type **1201**; 41c. Brassiere (Dolce & Gabbana); 41c. Drawing of dress (Gianfranco Ferre); 41c. Drawing of suit (Giorgio Armani); 41c. Dress (Laura Biagiotti); 41c. Shoes (Prada) 16·00 12·00

1202 Cathedral and Tower, Pisa

2002. UNESCO World Heritage Sites. Multicoloured.
2779 41c. Type **1202** 2·75 1·10
2780 52c. Aeolian Islands 3·25 1·30

Stamps of a similar design were issued by the United Nations.

1203 Dalla Chiesa

2002. 20th Anniv of Assassination of Carlo Alberto Dalla Chiesa (police chief and prefect of Palermo).
2781 1203 41c. multicoloured 2·75 1·10

1204 Teatro della Concordia, Monte Castello di Vibio, Perugia

2002
2782 1204 41c. multicoloured 2·75 1·10

1205 Yacht

2002. 12th Prada Classic Yacht Challenge, Imperia.
2783 1205 41c. multicoloured 2·75 1·10

1206 Papal States 1852 5b. Stamp

2002. 150th Anniv of First Papal States Stamp.
2784 1206 41c. multicoloured 2·75 1·10

1207 Cross, City Museum, Santa Giulia, Brescia

2002. Museum Exhibits. Multicoloured.
2785 41c. Type **1207** 2·75 1·10
2786 41c. Busts, Museo Nazionale, Palazzo Altemps, Rome (horiz) 2·75 1·10

1208 Orchid

2002. Flora and Fauna. Multicoloured.
2787 23c. Type **1208** 1·60 55
2788 52c. European lynx 2·50 1·00
2789 77c. Stag beetle 5·00 1·80

1209 Emblem

2002. World Food Day.
2790 1209 41c. multicoloured 2·75 1·10

1210 Corps Member and Emblem

2002. State Forestry Corps.
2791 1210 41c. multicoloured 2·75 1·10

1211 Gnocchi and Children

2002. Birth Centenary of Carlo Gnocchi (founder of rehabilitation centres for disabled children).
2792 1211 41c. multicoloured 2·75 1·10

1212 Microscope and Emblem

2002. "Telethon 2002" (campaign to combat muscular dystrophy and genetic disease).
2793 1212 41c. multicoloured 2·75 1·10

1213 The Holy Family

2002. Christmas. Multicoloured.
2794 41c. Type **1213** 2·75 1·10
2795 62c. Child and Christmas tree 4·00 1·70

1214 "Nike di Samotracia" (statue) and Athlete

2002. Women in Sport.
2796 1214 41c. multicoloured 2·75 1·10

1215 Flags of Championship Winners and Football

2002. 20th-century World Cup Football Champions. Multicoloured.
2797 52c. Type **1215** 3·50 1·40
2798 52c. Italian footballer 3·50 1·40

1216 Magnifying Glass, Stamps and Children

2002. Stamp Day. Philately in Schools.
2799 1216 62c. multicoloured 4·00 1·70

1217 Vittorio Orlando

2002. 50th Death Anniv of Vittorio Emanuele Orlando (politician).
2800 1217 41c. multicoloured 2·75 1·10

1218 Event Emblem

2003. "Tarvisio 2003" (winter sports competition).
2801 1218 52c. multicoloured 3·00 1·20

1219 Family and Scales

2003. The Italian Republic on Stamps.
2802 1219 62c. multicoloured 3·50 1·40

1220 Cyclist carrying Cycle

2003. World Cyclo-cross Championship, Monopoli.
2803 1220 41c. multicoloured 2·75 1·10

1221 Building and Tandem

2003. 150th Anniv (2002) of Fratelli Alinari (photographic company).
2804 1221 77c. multicoloured 4·75 1·80

1222 Jigsaw Puzzle

2003. European Year of the Disabled.
2805 1222 41c. multicoloured 2·75 1·10

1223 Skiers

2003. World Nordic Skiing Championship, Val di Fiemme.
2806 1223 41c. multicoloured 2·75 1·10

1224 Couple, Flower and Emblem

2003. National Civil Service.
2807 1224 62c. multicoloured 3·75 1·60

1225 Knights on Horseback

2003. 500th Anniv of the Barletta Challenge (battle between 13 French and 13 Italian knights).
2808 1225 41c. multicoloured 2·75 1·10

1226 Building Facade

2003. Torquato Tasso Grammar School (gymnasium).
2809 1226 41c. multicoloured 2·75 1·10

1227 "Encounter by the Golden Door" (Giotto)

2003
2810 1227 41c. multicoloured 2·75 1·10

1228 Gian Rinaldo Carli and Building

2003. Gian Rinaldo Carli Grammar School (gymnasium).
2811   **1228**   41c. multicoloured   2·75   1·10

1229 Academy Emblem

2003. 400th Anniv of "Accademia dei Lincei" (academy of lynxes) (scientific society).
2812   **1229**   41c. multicoloured   2·75   1·10

1230 Foils and Fencers

2003. World Junior Fencing Championships, Trapani.
2813   **1230**   41c. multicoloured   2·75   1·10

1231 Sestri Levante

2003. Tourist Publicity (30th series). Multicoloured.
2814   **1231**   41c. Type **1231**   2·75   1·10
2815   41c. Lanciano   2·75   1·10
2816   41c. Procida   2·75   1·10

1232 Golfer

2003. Centenary of Roma Acquasanta Golf Course.
2817   **1232**   77c. multicoloured   4·50   1·80

1233 Minerva (statue) and Building Facade

2003. 700th Anniv of La Sapienza University, Rome.
2818   **1233**   41c. multicoloured   2·75   1·10

1234 Pasta

2003. National Pasta Museum, Rome.
2819   **1234**   41c. multicoloured   2·75   1·10

1235 Guido Carli and University Building

2003.   Guido Carli-LUISS (international liberal social studies) University.
2820   **1235**   €2.58 multicoloured   16·00   6·75

1236 Woman in Blue Dress

2003. Europa. Poster Art. Posters by Marcello Dudovich. Multicoloured.
2821   41c. Type **1236**   3·25   1·30
2822   52c. Woman in white dress 3·50   1·40

1237 Buildings and Text

2003. 50th Anniv of State Archives.
2823   **1237**   41c. multicoloured   2·20   1·10

1238 Logo and St. Peter of Verona

2003. Centenary of Veronafil Exhibition.
2824   **1238**   41c. multicoloured   2·20   1·10

1239 Aldo Moro

2003. 25th Death Anniv of Aldo Moro (politician).
2825   **1239**   62c. multicoloured   3·50   1·80

1240 Antonio Meucci

2003.   Antonio   Meucci   (telephone   pioneer) Commemoration. Sheet 90×70 mm.
MS2826 **1240** 52c. multicoloured   3·50   2·75

1241 Padre E. Barsanti and F. Matteucci (motor pioneers)

2003. 150th Anniv of Invention of Internal Combustion Engine.
2827   **1241**   52c. multicoloured   2·75   1·40

1243 Flags of Italy and European Union

2003. Italian Presidency of the European Union.
2829   **1243**   41c. multicoloured   2·20   1·10

1244 Ezio Vanoni

2003. Birth Centenary of Ezio Vanoni (politician).
2830   **1244**   €2.58 multicoloured   16·00   8·25

1245 The Ascension of Mary

2003. 300th Birth Anniv of Corrado Giaquinto (artist).
2831   **1245**   77c. multicoloured   4·50   2·75

1246 Eugenio Balzan

2003. 50th Death Anniv of Eugenio Balzan (journalist).
2832   **1246**   41c. multicoloured   2·20   1·10

1247 Diana and Atteone (detail, fresco, Sanvitale Castle)

2003.   500th Birth Anniv of Francesco Mazzola (Parmigianino) (artist).
2833   **1247**   41c. multicoloured   2·20   1·10

1248 Player and Club Emblem

2003. Juventus, National Football Champions, 2002–3.
2834   **1248**   41c. multicoloured   2·20   1·10

1249 San Silvestro Abbey, Nonantola

2003.
2835   **1249**   41c. multicoloured   2·20   1·10

1250 Mario Calderara

2003. Centenary of First Powered Flight. Italian Aviation. Multicoloured.
2836   52c. Type **1250** (first Italian pilot)   3·00   1·50
2837   52c. Mario Cobianchi (pilot) 3·00   1·50
2838   52c. Gianni Caproni (aircraft designer)   3·00   1·50
2839   52c. Alessandro Marchetti (aircraft designer)   3·00   1·50
MS2840 105×146 mm. Nos. 2836/9   12·00   9·50

1251 Giovanni Giolitti

2003. 75th Death Anniv of Giovanni Giolitti (prime minister 1892–3 and 1903–14).
2841   **1251**   41c. multicoloured   2·20   1·10

1252 Still Life (Giorgio Morandi)

2003. Europhalia 2003 Italy Festival. Italian Presidency of European Union. Multicoloured.
2842   41c. Type **1252**   2·20   1·10
2843   52c. Cistalia 202 (1947)   3·00   1·50
Stamps of the same design were issued by Belgium.

1253 Attilio Vallecchi (founder) and Leonardo

2003.   Centenary of First Publication of Leonardo. Centenary of Vallecchi Publishing House.
2844   **1253**   41c. multicoloured   2·20   1·10

1254 Family enclosed in Atom Model

2003. The Family.
2845   **1254**   77c. multicoloured   4·50   2·75

1255 Maesta (detail) (Duccio di Buoninsegna)

2003. Extension to Metropolitan Opera House, Sienna.
2846   **1255**   41c. multicoloured   2·20   1·10

1256 Vittorio Alfieri

2003. Death Bicentenary of Vittorio Alfieri (writer).
2847   **1256**   41c. multicoloured   2·20   1·10

1242 Post and Telegraph Building (Angiolo Mazzoni)

2003
2828   **1242**   41c. blue   2·20   1·10

1257 Ugo La Malfa and Chamber of Deputies Assembly Hall

2003. Birth Centenary of Ugo La Malfa (politician).
2848 **1257** 62c. multicoloured 3·50 1·80

1258 Bernando Ramazzini and Frontispiece of *De morbis aertifcum diatriba*

2003. 370th Birth Anniv of Bernando Ramazzini (medical pioneer).
2849 **1258** 41c. multicoloured 2·20 1·10

1259 Building Facade

2003. 120th Anniv of Confediliizia Institute, Rome.
2850 **1259** $2.58 multicoloured 14·00 9·00

1260 *Nativity* (Gian Paolo Cavagna)

2003. Christmas. Multicoloured.
2851 41c. Type **1260** 2·20 1·40
2852 62c. Poinsettia 3·50 2·20

1261 *Forme Grido Viva l'Italia*

2003. 40th Death Anniv of Giacomo Balla (artist). Multicoloured.
2853 41c. Type **1261** 2·20 1·40
2854 52c. Linee—*Forza del Pugno di Boccioni* 3·00 1·90

1262 Pencil and Sharpener

2003. Stamp Day.
2855 **1262** 41c. multicoloured 2·20 1·40

2004. Priority Mail Stamps. Designs as No. 2660. Multicoloured, background colour given. Self-adhesive gum.
2856 60c. orange 3·25 2·10
2856a 62c. yellow 3·75 2·40
2856b 80c. red 4·50 2·75
2856c £1 violet 8·25 5·25
2857 €1.40 green 9·50 6·00
2857a €1.50 grey 10·50 6·50
2858 €2 green 12·50 7·75
2859 €2.20 cannine 13·00 8·00
No. 2856/9 were issued with an attached label inscribed "postaprioritaria Priority Mail".

1263 "50" enclosing Test Screen

2004. 50th Anniv of Television.
2860 **1263** 41c. blue and grey 2·20 1·40
2861 62c. multicoloured 3·50 2·20
DESIGN: 62c. "50" enclosed in colour blocks.

1264 Giorgio La Pira and Script

2004. Birth Centenary of Giorgio La Pira (politician).
2862 **1264** 41c. cinnamon, blue and red 2·20 1·40

1265 Tower, Map and Compass

2004. Genoa–European Capital of Culture, 2004.
2863 **1265** 45c. multicoloured 2·50 1·50

1266 Santa Maria Assunta Church, Pragelato

2004. Winter Olympic Games, Turin (2006) (1st series). Multicoloured.
2864 23c. Type **1266** 1·20 75
2865 45c. San Pietro Apostolo church, Bardonecchia 2·50 1·50
2866 62c. 28th-century fountain, Sauze d'Oulx 3·25 2·10
2867 65c. Mole Antonelliana, Turin 3·50 2·20
See also Nos. 2926/9.

1267 Petrarch

2004. 700th Birth Anniv of Francesco Petrarca (Petrarch) (poet).
2868 **1267** 45c. multicoloured 2·50 1·50

1268 Mortar, Pestle, Museum Building and Liquorice Sticks

2004. Giorgio Amarelli Liquorice Museum.
2869 **1268** 45c. multicoloured 2·50 1·50

1269 Heart-shaped Seat Belt Buckle and Map covered with Traffic Signs

2004. Road Safety. Multicoloured.
2870 60c. Dashboard and traffic signs (horiz) 3·25 2·10
2871 62c. Type **1269** 3·50 2·20

1270 Vignola

2004. Tourist Publicity (31st series). Multicoloured.
2872 45c. Type **1270** 2·50 1·50
2873 45c. Viterbo 2·50 1·50
2874 45c. Egadi Islands 2·50 1·50

1271 Casa del Fascio

2004. Birth Centenary of Guiseppe Terragni (architect).
2875 **1271** 85c. multicoloured 4·75 3·00

1272 Sakate Temple, Bangkok

2004. Bangkok and Rome. Sheet 140×70 mm containing T **1272** and similar horiz design. Multicoloured.
MS2876 65c.×2, Type **1272**; Colosseum, Rome 7·00 4·50
Stamps of a similar design were issued by Thailand.

1273 St. George and Crowd

2004. 1700th Anniv of Martyrdom of St. George.
2877 **1273** €2.80 multicoloured 15·00 9·50

1274 Case

2004. Europa. Holidays. Multicoloured.
2878 45c. Type **1274** 2·50 1·50
2879 62c. Open case 3·50 2·20

1275 Sheep and Castle, Bologna

2004. Tratturo Magno (drovers' way). Sheet 90×70 mm.
MS2880 **1275** 45c. multicoloured 3·75 2·40

1276 Synagogue Facade

2004. Centenary of the Great Synagogue, Rome. Multicoloured.
2881 60c. Type **1276** 3·25 2·10
2882 62c. Candlestick, ornamental panel and synagogue (vert) 3·50 2·20
Stamps of the same design were issued by Israel.

1277 Football, Player and Emblem

2004. A. C. Milan, National Football Champions, 2004.
2883 **1277** 45c. multicoloured 2·50 1·50

1278 Giacomo Puccini

2004. 50th Anniv of Puccini Festival, Torre del Lago.
2884 **1278** 60c. multicoloured 3·25 2·10

1279 Courtyard and Emblem

2004. 600th Anniv of Turin University.
2885 **1279** 45c. brown 2·50 1·50

1280 Achille Varzi, Motorcycle and Racing Cars

2004. Birth Centenary of Achille Varzi (motorcyclist and racing driver).
2886 **1280** 45c. multicoloured 2·50 1·50

1281 Arms and Policemen

2004. Prison Police.
2887 **1281** 45c. multicoloured 2·50 1·50

1282 Ice Pick and Mountain Peak

2004. 50th Anniv of First Assent of K2 (mountain).
2888 **1282** 65c. blue, black and ultramarine 3·25 2·10

1283 Statuette and Map

2004. Regions. Multicoloured.
2889 45c. Type **1283** (Abruzzo) 2·50 1·50
2890 45c. Troglodyte settlement and map (Basilicata) 2·50 1·50
2891 45c. Medieval map (Liguria) 2·50 1·50
2892 45c. Roman mosaic (Emilia Romagna) 2·50 1·50

1284 Stained Glass
Window

2004. 500th Anniv of the Apparition of Madonna di
Tirano.
2893 **1284** 45c. multicoloured 2·50 1·50

1285 St. Nilo and Abbey
Buildings

2004. Death Millenary Nilo di Rossano and Millenary of
Foundation of Grottaferrata Abbey.
2894 **1285** 45c. multicoloured 2·50 1·50

1286 Map and Stylized Building
Façade

2004. Florence State Archive.
2895 **1286** 45c. multicoloured 2·50 1·50

1287 Flower

2004. Lace Making. Self-adhesive. Textile. Imperf.
2896 **1287** €2.80 blue and cream 15·00 9·50

1288 Hands

2004. 40th Anniv of "Lega del Filo d'Oro" (humanitarian
organization for deaf blind people).
2897 **1288** 45c. multicoloured 2·50 1·50

1289 Institute Buildings

2004. Vittorio Emanuele III Technical Institute.
2898 **1289** 45c. multicoloured 2·50 1·50

1290 Luigi
Guanella

2004. Luigi Guanella Commemoration (priest and
humanitarian).
2899 **1290** 45c. multicoloured 2·50 1·50

1291 Piazza dell'Unita,
Trieste

2004. 50th Anniv of Return of Trieste to Italy.
2900 **1291** 45c. multicoloured 2·50 1·50

1292 Emblem

2004. Information and Military Emergency Service.
2901 **1292** 60c. multicoloured 3·25 2·10

1293 Stars and Map of
Europe

2004. Constitution of Europe Treaty.
2902 **1293** 62c. multicoloured 3·50 2·20

1294 Nativity

2004. Christmas. Multicoloured.
2903 45c. Type **1294** 2·50 1·50
2904 62c. Decorated tree (vert) 3·50 2·20

1295 Map of Arsenal

2004. 900th Anniv of Venice Arsenal.
2905 **1295** €2.80 multicoloured 13·50 9·50

1296 St. Lucia

2004. 1700th Anniv of Martyrdom of St. Lucia.
2906 **1296** 45c. multicoloured 2·50 1·50

1297 Hands reading Braille

2004. Louis Braille System of Reading and Writing for the
Blind.
2907 **1297** 45c. multicoloured 2·50 1·50
No. 2907 was embossed with Braille letters.

1298 Boy holding
Stamp

2004. Stamp Day.
2908 **1298** 45c. multicoloured 2·50 1·50

1299 Emblem and
Water

2004. Tenth "Sport for All" Congress.
2909 **1299** 65c. multicoloured 3·50 2·20

1300 University Building

2004. Libera Universita Maria SS. Assunta (LUMSA)
(university), Rome.
2910 **1300** 45c. multicoloured 2·50 1·50

1301 Woman's
High-heeled Shoe

2004. Made in Italy. Shoes. Sheet 90×114 mm containing
T **1301** and similar vert designs. Multicoloured.
2911- 45c.×4 Type **1301**; Man's laced
2914 shoe; Man's loafer; Trainers 7·50 2·40

1302 Club Emblem
and Italy

2005. Centenary of Automobile Club d'Italia (ACI).
2915 **1302** 45c. multicoloured 2·50 1·50

2005
2916 **1171** €1 multicoloured 5·50 3·50

1303 Luigi
Calabresi

2005. Luigi Calabresi (Milanese police officer)
Commemoration.
2917 **1303** 45c. multicoloured 2·50 1·50

1304 Refugees

2005. Memorial Day for the Exodus from Istria, Fiume
and Dalmazia.
2918 **1304** 45c. multicoloured 2·50 1·50

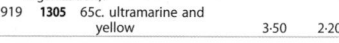

1305 Emblem

2005. Centenary of Rotary International (charitable
organization).
2919 **1305** 65c. ultramarine and
yellow 3·50 2·20

1306 Badge and Soldiers

2005. Sassari Brigade.
2920 **1306** 45c. multicoloured 2·50 1·50

1307 "Q"

2005. Quadrennial Exhibition, Rome.
2921 **1307** 45c. multicoloured 2·50 1·50

1308 Bronzes of Riace
(Greek statues)

2005. Regions. Multicoloured.
2922 45c. Type **1308** (Calabria) 2·50 1·50
2923 45c. Ship (bas relief) and
Miramare castle, Trieste (Fruili
Venezia Guila) 2·50 1·50
2924 45c. Woman's head (fresco,
Pompeii), (Campania) 2·50 1·50
2925 45c. Certosa, Pavia (Lombardy) 2·50 1·50

1309 San Maurizio
Church, Pinerolo

2005. Winter Olympic Games, Turin (2006) (2nd series).
Multicoloured.
2926 23c. Type **1309** 1·40 85
2927 45c. San Giovanni Battista
church, Cesana Torinese,
San Sicario 2·50 1·50
2928 60c. Neve and Gliz (Games'
mascots) 3·25 2·10
2929 62c. Hotel, Sestriere 3·50 2·20

1310 Pavia (engraving by
Gerolamo de Sanctis), Black
Hole Diagram, Year Emblem
and Feynman Diagram

2005. International Year of Physics.
2930 **1310** 85c. multicoloured 4·75 3·00

1311 Pavilions

2005. Inauguration of Milan International Fair Complex,
Pero.
2931 **1311** 45c. multicoloured 2·50 1·50

1312 "100" and Steam

2005. Centenary of State Railways.
2932 **1312** 45c. multicoloured 2·50 1·50

1313 Early and
Modern Soldiers

2005. National Army.
| 2933 | **1313** | 45c. multicoloured | 2·50 | 1·50 |

1314 Stars and
Grain

2005. Europa. Gastronomy. Multicoloured.
| 2934 | **1314** | 45c. Type **1314** | 2·50 | 1·50 |
| 2935 | | 62c. Grapes, wine glass and stars | 3·50 | 2·20 |

1315 Saint Ignazio

2005. Saint Ignazio of Laconi Commemoration.
| 2936 | **1315** | 45c. multicoloured | 2·50 | 1·50 |

1316 Association
Emblem

2005. 60th Anniv of Confcommercio (trade association).
| 2937 | **1316** | 60c. silver, steel blue and gold | 3·25 | 2·10 |

1317 School Building

2005. Tommaso Campanella Grammar School, Reggio Calabria.
| 2938 | **1317** | 45c. multicoloured | 2·50 | 1·50 |

1318 Building Facade

2005. Saint Giuseppe of Copertino Basilica, Osimo.
| 2939 | **1318** | 45c. indigo | 2·50 | 1·50 |

1319 Asolo

2005. Tourist Publicity (32nd series). Multicoloured.
2940		45c. Type **1319**	2·50	1·50
2941		45c. Rocchetta a Volturno	2·50	1·50
2942		45c. Amalfi	2·50	1·50

1320 Gerardo Maiella and
St. Gerardo Maiella Church,
Materdomini

2005. 250th Death Anniv of Gerardo Maiella (priest).
| 2943 | **1320** | 45c. multicoloured | 2·50 | 1·50 |

1321 Player and
Club Emblem

2005. Juventus, National Football Champions, 2004–5.
| 2944 | **1321** | 45c. multicoloured | 2·50 | 1·50 |

1322 Emblems and Map

2005. 20th Anniv of Ratification Italy–Vatican Concordat (abolishing Catholicism as state religion). Multicoloured.
| 2945 | | 45c. Type **1322** | 2·50 | 1·50 |
| 2946 | | €2.80 Emblems, manuscript and pen | 15·00 | 9·50 |
Stamps of the same design were issued by Vatican City.

1323 Almerico da Schio
and Dirigible

2005. Centenary of First Italian Dirigible.
| 2947 | **1323** | €3 multicoloured | 16·00 | 10·50 |

1324 Mascot and Emblem

2005. European Youth Olympic Festival, Lignano.
| 2948 | **1324** | 62c. multicoloured | 3·50 | 2·20 |

1325 Tunnel containing
Flower

2005. International Day against Drugs.
| 2949 | **1325** | 45c. multicoloured | 2·50 | 1·50 |

1326 Emblem

2005. Institute for Marine Security (I.P.SE.MA.).
| 2950 | **1326** | 45c. green, ultramarine and silver | 2·50 | 1·50 |

1327 Leo
Longanesi

2005. Birth Centenary of Leo Longanesi (writer and artist).
| 2951 | **1327** | 45c. blue | 2·50 | 1·50 |

1328 Alberto Ascari and
Race Car

2005. 50th Death Anniv of Alberto Ascari (World Champion race driver 1952–53).
| 2952 | **1328** | €2.80 multicoloured | 15·00 | 9·50 |

1329 Emblem and Team
Aermacchi MB-339 PAN

2005. Frecce Tricolori (Italian Air Force acrobatic display team). Multicoloured.
| 2953 | **1329** | 45c. Type **1329** | 2·50 | 1·50 |
| 2954 | | 60c. Aermacchi MB-339 PAN (different) | 3·25 | 2·10 |

1330 Pietro
Savorgnan di Brazza

2005. Death Centenary of Pietro Paolo Savorgnan di Brazza (explorer).
| 2955 | **1330** | 45c. multicoloured | 2·50 | 1·50 |

1331 Guido Gonella

2005. Birth Centenary of Guido Gonella (politician).
| 2956 | **1331** | 45c. multicoloured | 2·50 | 1·50 |

1332 Space Craft and Mars

2005. Mars Exploration Programme. Self-adhesive.
| 2957 | **1332** | 80c. multicoloured | 4·50 | 2·75 |

1333 Raised Arms

2005. 50th Anniv of Intercultura (voluntary service organization).
| 2958 | **1333** | 60c. multicoloured | 3·25 | 2·10 |

1334 Yacht and Trapani Bay

2005. America's Cup Yacht Race, Trapani. Sheet 96×80 mm.
| MS2959 | **1334** | €2.80 multicoloured | 15·00 | 9·50 |

1335 "F"

2005. Stamp Day.
| 2960 | **1335** | 45c. multicoloured | 2·50 | 1·50 |

1336 Heart as
Flower

2005. Italian Organ Donors Association (AIDO).
| 2961 | **1336** | 60c. multicoloured | 3·25 | 2·10 |

1337 Castle

2005. National Association (ANCI).
| 2962 | **1337** | 45c. multicoloured | 2·50 | 1·50 |

1338 *Disputation in the
Synagogue* (detail)

2005. Restoration of Frescoes by Filippo Lippi, Prato Cathedral. Multicoloured.
| 2963 | | 45c. Type **1338** | 2·50 | 1·50 |
| 2964 | | €1.50 *Saint's Funeral* (detail) | 8·25 | 5·25 |

1339 *The Annunciation*
(Beato Angelico)

2005. Christmas. Multicoloured.
| 2965 | | 45c. Type **1339** | 2·50 | 1·50 |
| 2966 | | 62c. Family (vert) | 3·50 | 2·20 |

1340 Alcide de
Gasperi

2005. Alcide de Gasperi (politician) Commemoration.
| 2967 | **1340** | 62c. multicoloured | 3·50 | 2·20 |

1341 "Humanity" Medal

2005. Birth Bicentenary of Giuseppe Mazzini (nationalist).
2968 **1341** 45c. multicoloured   2·50   1·50

1342 Civil Protection Department Emblem

2005. Civil Protection and Italian Red Cross. Multicoloured.
2969   45c. Type **1342**   2·50   1·50
2970   45c. Globe and Red Cross emblem   2·50   1·50

1343 "50" and UN Emblem

2005. 50th Anniv of United Nations Membership.
2971 **1343** 70c. multicoloured   3·75   2·40

1344 Pope John Paul II

2005. Pope John Paul II Commemoration and Election of Pope Benedict XVI. Multicoloured.
2972   45c. Type **1344**   2·50   1·50
2973   65c. Pope Benedict XVI   3·50   2·20

1345 Royal Palace

2005. 60th Anniv of Re-constitution of Caserta Province.
2974 **1345** 45c. multicoloured   2·50   1·50

1346 Stylized Submarine

2005. Re-location of Submarine Enrico Toti to National Museum of Sciences and Technology, Milan.
2975 **1346** 62c. grey and deep grey   3·50   2·20

1347 Egg Timer

2006. Greetings Stamps. 18th Birthday Greetings. Multicoloured, background colour given.
2976   45c. Type **1347** (pink)   2·50   1·50
2977   45c. As No. 2976 (blue)   2·50   1·50

1348 Calciatori (footballers) Sticker Album Emblem

2006. Panini SpA (sticker manufacturer and publisher).
2978 **1348** €2.80 multicoloured   15·00   9·50

1349 First Magazine Cover

2006. 50th Anniv of *Quattroruote* (motoring magazine founded by G. Mazzochi).
2979 **1349** 62c. multicoloured   3·50   2·20

1350 Alessandro Tassoni State High School, Modena

2006. Schools and Universities.
2980 **1350** 45c. multicoloured   2·50   1·50
2981 -   45c. multicoloured   2·50   1·50
2982 -   45c. multicoloured   2·50   1·50
2983 -   45c. yellow, slate and ultramarine   2·50   1·50
DESIGNS: Type **1350**; No. 2981 Agostino Nifo State High School, Sessa Aurunca; 2982 Ernesto Cairoloi State High School, Varese; 2983 Carlo Bo University, Urbino.

1351 Biathlon

2006. Winter Olympic Games, Turin. Each blue, new blue and light blue.
2984   23c. Type **1351**   1·40   85
2985   45c. Figure skating   2·50   1·50
2986   65c. Ice hockey   3·50   2·20
2987   70c. Curling   3·75   2·40
2988   85c. Bob sledding   4·75   3·00
2989   90c. Alpine skiing   5·00   3·00
2990   €1 Olympic flame (detail)   5·50   3·50
2991   €1.30 Luge   7·00   4·50
2992 $1.70 Three medals   9·25   5·75
MS2993 149×102 mm. Nos. 2984/92   41·00   34·00
The stamps and margins of **MS**2993 form a composite design.

1352 1879 5c., 1863 15c., 1901 10c. and 1930 20c. Stamps

2006. Il Regno d'Italia Philatelic Exhibition, Palazzo Montecitorio (chamber of deputies).
2994 **1352** 60c. multicoloured   3·25   2·10

1353 Society Emblem

2006. 80th Anniv of Society for the Preservation of Italian Culture in Dalmatia.
2995 **1353** 45c. blue and vermilion   2·50   1·50

1354 *Camera degli Sposi* (The Wedding Chamber) (Andrea Mantegna)

2006. 500th Death Anniv of Andrea Mantegna (artist).
2996 **1354** 45c. multicoloured   2·50   1·50

1355 Emblem

2006. Centenary of International Congress on Occupational Health. 28th Congress on Occupational Health, Milan.
2997 **1355** 60c.+30c. multicoloured   5·00   3·00
The premium was for the benefit of Breast Cancer charities.

1356 Emblem

2006. Winter Paralympic Games, Turin.
2998 **1356** 60c. multicoloured   3·25   2·10

1357 Ice Cream Seller

2006. Made in Italy. Multicoloured.
2999   60c. Type **1357**   3·25   2·10
3000   €2.80 Marble statue and quarry   15·00   9·50

1358 Football Team with Faces forming Notes

2006. 25th Anniv of National Association of Singers.
3001 **1358** 45c. multicoloured   2·50   1·50

1359 *Cavour* (aircraft carrier)

2006. Navy.
3002 **1359** 60c. multicoloured   3·25   2·10

1360 Swiss and Italian Flags and Tunnel

2006. Centenary of Simplon Tunnel.
3003 **1360** 62c. multicoloured   3·50   2·20

1361 Lake Como

2006. Tourist Publicity (33rd series). Multicoloured.
3004   45c. Type **1361**   2·50   1·50
3005   45c. Marina di Pietrasanta   2·50   1·50
3006   45c. Temple of Serapis, Pozzuoli   2·50   1·50

1362 Three Dimensional Diagram of Mountain Range

2006. Centenary of International Day of Mountains.
3007 **1362** 60c. multicoloured   3·25   2·10

1363 St. Mary Incaldana (icon), Basilica Minore, St. Mary Incaldana, Modragone.

2006. Cultural Heritage.
3008 **1363** 45c. multicoloured   2·50   1·50

1364 Stylized Vote Papers and Ballot Box

2006. First Vote cast by Italian Citizens Resident Abroad.
3009 **1364** 62c. multicoloured   3·50   2·20

1365 Palazzo Mentcitorio, Rome and Palazzo Pubblico, San Marino

2006. Le Due Repubbliche (two republics) Philatelic Exhibition. Multicoloured.
3010   62c. Type **1365**   3·50   2·20
MS3011 121×90 mm. 62c.×2, Type **1365**; Type **584** of San Marino   8·25   6·00
No. **MS**3011 is identical to **MS**2084 of San Marino.

1366 Instructor and Pupils

2006. 70th Anniv of Ski School, Cervina.
3012 **1366** 45c. multicoloured   2·50   1·50

1367 *Madonna of Humility* (Gentile da Fabriano), Museo Nazionale di San Matteo, Pisa.

2006. Cultural Heritage.
3013 **1367** €2.80 multicoloured   15·00   10·50

1368 Man at Window (poster) (Raymond Savignac) (1956)

2006. 50th Anniv of *Il Giorno* Newspaper. Photo.
3014 **1368** 45c. multicoloured   2·50   1·50

1369 Court Chamber

2006. 50th Anniv of Constitutional Court.
3015 **1369** 45c. indigo   2·50   1·50

1370 Enrico Mattei

2006. Birth Centenary of Enrico Mattei (entrepreneur).
3016 **1370** 45c. multicoloured   2·50   1·50

1371 Statue (Emanuele Filiberto), Royal Castle, Racconigi (Piedmont)

2006. Regions. Multicoloured.
3017   45c. Type **1371**   2·50   1·50
3018   45c. David (statue) (Michelangelo) and landscape (Tuscany)   2·50   1·50
3019   45c. Sarcophagus of the bride and groom (Sarcofago degli Sposi) and Etruscan necropolis, Cerveteri (Lazio)   2·50   1·50
3020   45c. Basilica of St Nicholas, Bari, outline of Puglia and Tremiti Islands. (Puglia)   2·50   1·50

1372 *La Targa Florio* (Margaret Bradley)

2006. Centenary of Targa Florio (automobile endurance race), Palermo.
3021 **1372** 60c. multicoloured   3·25   2·10

1373 Christopher Columbus

2006. 500th Death Anniv of Christopher Columbus.
3022 **1373** 62c. multicoloured   3·50   2·20

1374 Young People of Many Nations

2006. Europa. Integration. Multicoloured.
3023   45c. Type **1374**   2·50   1·50
3024   62c. Backview   3·50   2·20

1375 Coliseum and Emblem

2006. International Military Sports Council General Meeting, Rome.
3025 **1375** 45c. multicoloured   2·50   1·50

1376 Emblem

2006. International Team Chess Championship, Turin.
3026 **1376** 62c. multicoloured   3·50   2·20

1377 Assembly Chamber and National Colours

2006. 60th Anniv of Elected Constituent Assembly.
3027 **1377** 60c. multicoloured   3·25   2·10

1378 Nilde Iotti (politician)

2006. 60th Anniv of Women's Suffrage.
3028 **1378** 60c. multicoloured   3·25   2·10

1379 Emblem

2006. World Bridge Championship.
3029 **1379** 65c. multicoloured   3·50   2·20

1380 Arms and Map

2006. Test Firing Range, Salto di Quirra (Poligono Interforze del Salto di Quirra (PISQ)), Sardinia.
3030 **1380** 60c. multicoloured   3·25   2·10

1381 Headquarters

2006. Centenary of Guardia di Finanza Cadets Corps and General Headquarters. Multicoloured.
3031   60c. Type **1381**   3·25   2·10
3032   60c. Cadet and building facade (horiz)   3·25   2·10

1382 Stage, Walls and Sea

2006. 50th Anniv of Greek Theatre, Tindari.
3033 **1382** €1.50 multicoloured   8·25   5·25

1383 Bridge across Map of Italy

2006. 50th Anniv of Autostrada del Sole.
3034 **1383** 60c. multicoloured   3·25   2·10

1384 Devastation

2006. 26th Anniv of Bombing of Bologna Railway Station.
3035 **1384** 60c. multicoloured   3·25   2·10

1385 Emblem

2006. 40th Anniv of Union of Italian Philatelic Journalists.
3036 **1385** 60c. multicoloured   4·00   2·50

1386 St Gregory

2006. St Gregory Commemoration.
3037 **1386** 60c. multicoloured   3·25   2·10

1387 Flag and Fans

2006. Italy—2006 World Cup Football Champions.
3038 **1387** €1 multicoloured   5·50   3·50

1388 Face and Figure Outlines

2006. Victims of Terrorism.
3039 **1388** 60c. multicoloured   3·25   2·10

1389 Ettore Majorana and Atomic Symbol

2006. Birth Centenary of Ettore Majorana (physicist).
3040 **1389** 60c. multicoloured   3·25   2·10

1390 St Francis Xavier

2006. Saints' Anniversaries. Multicoloured.
3041   60c. Type **1390** (500th birth anniv)   3·25   2·10
3042   60c. St Ignatius Loyola (450th death anniv)   3·25   2·10

1391 Fencers

2006. World Fencing Championship, Turin.
3043 **1391** 65c. multicoloured   3·50   2·20

1392 Boy, Stamps and Globe

2006. Philately Day.
3044 **1392** 60c. multicoloured   3·25   2·10

1393 Blind-folded Woman

2006. 500th Anniv of National Lottery.
3045 **1393** 60c. multicoloured   3·25   2·10

1394 Emblem

2006. National System of Environment Protection.
3046 **1394** 65c. multicoloured   3·50   2·20

1395 Luchino Visconti

2006. Birth Centenary of Luchino Visconti (film maker).
3047 **1395** 60c. multicoloured   3·25   2·10

1396 Dino Buzzati

2006. Birth Centenary of Dino Buzzati (writer).
3048 **1396** 60c. multicoloured   3·25   2·10

1397 Adoration of the Magi (Jacopo Bassano)

2006. Christmas.
3049 **1397** 60c. magenta   3·25   2·10
3050   –   65c. multicoloured (vert)   3·50   2·20
DESIGNS: 60c. Type **1397**; 65c. Decorated tree.

1398 Vittoriano Building, Rome and Tomb of the Unknown Warrior

2006. In Memory of the Fallen in Nassiriya.
3051   **1398**   60c. multicoloured   3·25   2·10

1399 St. Evasio Cathedral, Casale Monferrato

2007. Cultural Heritage.
3052   **1399**   60c. cerise   3·25   2·10

1400 Maria Montessori and Children

2007. Centenary of Montessori Nursery Schools.
3053   **1400**   60c. multicoloured   3·25   2·10

1401 Milvio Bridge, River Tiber and Building Facade

2007. 50th Anniv of National School for Public Administration.
3054   **1401**   65c. multicoloured   3·50   2·20

1402 Parma Cathedral and Baptistery

2007. Cultural Heritage.
3055   **1402**   60c. olive   3·25   2·10

1403 Arturo Toscanini

2007. 50th Death Anniv of Arturo Toscanini (conductor).
3056   **1403**   60c. multicoloured   3·25   2·10

1404 St. Francis of Paola crossing Straits of Medina (Benedetto Luti)

2007. 500th Death Anniv of St. Francis of Paola.
3057   **1404**   60c. multicoloured   3·25   2·10

1405 Ferrante Gonzaga triumphing over Envy (statue, Leone Leoni)

2007. 500th Birth Anniv of Ferrante Gonzaga (soldier).
3058   **1405**   €1 multicoloured   5·50   3·50

1406 Foundation Office

2007. 20th Anniv of Fondazione Antonio Genovesi Salerno.
3059   **1406**   60c. multicoloured   3·25   2·10

1407 Refugees and Map of Sardinia

2007. 60th Anniv of Borgata Giuliana di Fertilia, Alghero (immigration of Italian speaking refugees from Istria and Dalmatia to Sardinia).
3060   **1407**   60c. multicoloured   3·25   2·10

1408 Father Lodovico Acernese

2007. Father Lodovico Acernese (founder of Congregation of the Franciscan Immaculatine Sisters) Commemoration.
3061   **1408**   23c. multicoloured   1·40   85

1409 Giosue Carducci

2007. Death Centenary of Giosue Carducci (1906—Nobel Prize for Literature winner).
3062   **1409**   60c. multicoloured   3·25   2·10

1410 Brescia University

2007
3063   **1410**   60c. multicoloured   3·25   2·10

1411 Stylized Woman and Child

2007. European Year of Equal Opportunities.
3064   **1411**   60c. multicoloured   3·25   2·10

1412 "Scipione Maffei" State High School

2007
3065   **1412**   60c. multicoloured   3·25   2·10

1413 Nicolo Carosio

2007. Birth Centenary of Nicolo Carosio (sports commentator).
3066   **1413**   65c. multicoloured   3·50   2·20

1414 Rialto Bridge and Gondola

2007. Venice–UNESCO World Heritage Site.
3067   **1414**   60c. black   3·25   2·10

1415 Mareccio Castle and Castell del Buonconsiglio (Trentino-Aldo Adige)

2007. Regions. Multicoloured.
3068   60c. Type **1415**   3·25   2·10
3069   60c. Asceli Piceno and "Bronzi Dorati da Cartoceto di Pergola" (statues) (Marche)   3·25   2·10
3070   60c. Orvieto Cathedral and "Annunciation" (mosaic) (Umbria)   3·25   2·10
3071   60c. Beach, flamingo and bronze statue (Sardinia)   3·25   2·10

1416 Circuit Board

2007. International Electro-technical Commission.
3072   **1416**   €1.50 multicoloured   8·25   5·25

1417 '50', Stylized Piazza del Campidoglio and Stars

2007. 50th Anniv of Treaty of Rome. Sheet 120×96 mm containing T **1417** and similar vert design. Multicoloured.
MS3073 60c. Type **1417**; 65c. 'INSIEME', stylized Piazza del Campidoglio and stars   7·50   5·25
The stamps of **MS**3073 form a composite design.

1418 Bishop's Castle, Brunico-Bruneck

2007. Tourist Publicity (34th series). Multicoloured.
3074   60c. Type **1418**   3·25   2·10
3075   60c. Castle, Gaeta   3·25   2·10
3076   60c. Medieval Castle, Massafra   3·25   2·10
3077   60c. Eraclea Minoa Amphitheatre, Cattolica Eraclea   3·25   2·10

1419 Giuseppe di Lampedusa and Il Gattopardo

2007. 50th Death Anniv of Giuseppe Tomasi de Lampedusa (writer).
3078   **1419**   60c. multicoloured   3·25   2·10

1420 Forum

2007. Rome–Capital City.
3079   **1420**   60c. multicoloured   3·25   2·10

1421 Scouts and Canoe

2007. Europa. Centenary of Scouting. Multicoloured.
3080   60c. Type **1421**   3·25   2·10
3081   65c. Scouts and campfire   3·50   2·20
MS3082 97×120 mm. Nos. 3080/1   7·50   5·25

1422 Duccio Galimberti

2007. Birth Centenary of Duccio Galimberti (resistance organiser).
3083   **1422**   60c. multicoloured   3·25   2·10

1423 Statues and Building Facade

2007. 50th Anniv of National Higher School for Economics and Finance.
3084   **1423**   €2.80 multicoloured   15·00   9·50

1424 Director, Camera and Building Facade

2007. 70th Anniv of Cinecitta Film Studios, Rome.
3085   **1424**   65c. multicoloured   3·50   2·20

1425 Polirone Monastery, Mantua

2007. Cultural Heritage.
3086   **1425**   60c. indigo   3·25   2·10

1426 Malatesta Castle, Montefiore

2007. Cultural Heritage.
3087   **1426**   60c. brown   3·25   2·10

1427 Stele enclosing Musical Score

2007. Folk Music Project.
3088 **1427** 60c. multicoloured 3·25 2·10

1428 Lamborghini Emblem

2007. Made in Italy. Lamborghini Miura.
3089 **1428** 85c. multicoloured 4·75 3·00

1429 Player, Ball and Emblem

2007. Inter Football Club, Italian Football Champions– Serie A 2007
3090 **1429** 60c. multicoloured 3·25 2·10

1430 Chianca Dolmen, Apulia

2007. Cultural Heritage.
3091 **1430** 60c. chestnut 3·25 2·10

1431 Luigi Ganna

2007. 50th Death Anniv of Luigi Ganna (cyclist, winner of first Giro d'Italia–1909).
3092 **1431** 60c. multicoloured 3·25 2·10

1432 Altiero Spinelli

2007. Birth Centenary of Altiero Spinelli (federalist).
3093 **1432** 60c. multicoloured 3·25 2·10

1433 Dancer and Rose Window, Spoleto Cathedral

2007. Festival dei Due Mondi (Festival of the Two Worlds) (annual music and opera festival), Spoleto.
3094 **1433** 60c. multicoloured 3·25 2·10

1434 Basilica, San Vincenzo in Galliano, Cantu

2007. Cultural Heritage. Birch wood. Self-adhesive.
3095 **1434** €2.80 brown 15·00 9·50
No. 3095 was printed on wooden sheets.

1435 Fiat 500

2007. Made in Italy.
3096 **1435** 60c. multicoloured 3·25 2·10

1436 Giuseppe Garibaldi

2007. Birth Bicentenary of Giuseppe Garibaldi (soldier and nationalist).
3097 **1436** 65c. multicoloured 3·50 2·20

1437 Maurizio Poggiali and Tornado Fighter Airplane

2007. Tenth Death Anniv of Maurizio Poggiali (poet and pilot).
3098 **1437** 60c. multicoloured 3·25 2·10

1438 Caver, Stalactites, Stalagmites and Bat (club emblem)

2007. Speleological Club of Rome.
3099 **1438** €1.40 multicoloured 7·75 4·75

1439 Primo Carnera

2007. 40th Death Anniv of Primo Carnera (boxer).
3100 **1439** 60c. multicoloured 3·25 2·10

1440 Cloister, 'Marco Foscarini' Boarding School for Classical Studies

2007. Schools. Multicoloured.
3101 60c. Type **1440** 3·25 2·10
3102 60c. S.Pio V 3·25 2·10
3103 60c. Salerno Medical College 3·25 2·10

1441 Donkeys

2007. Italian Protected Donkey Breeds.
3104 **1441** 60c. multicoloured 3·25 2·10

1442 Player

2007. European Senior Women's Basketball Championship.
3105 **1442** 65c. multicoloured 3·50 2·20

1443 Sacra di San Michele (abbey), Sant'Ambrogio di Torino

2007. Cultural Heritage.
3106 **1443** 60c. Indian red 3·25 2·10

1444 Concetto Marchesi

2007. 50th Death Anniv of Concetto Marchesi (Latin scholar, politician and writer).
3107 **1444** 60c. multicoloured 3·25 2·10

1445 Il Vignola and Scala Regia (royal stairs), Palazzo Farnese, Caprarola

2007. 400th Birth Anniv of Jacopo Barozzi da Vignola (Il Vignola) (architect).
3108 **1445** €2.80 multicoloured 15·00 9·50

1446 Children and Grandparents

2007. Grandparents Day.
3109 **1446** 60c. multicoloured 3·25 2·10

1447 Stamps as Figure

2007. Stamp Day.
3110 **1447** 60c. multicoloured 3·25 2·10

1448 *Cupid and Pscyche* (sculpture)

2007. 250th Birth Anniv of Antonio Canova (artist).
3111 **1448** €1.50 black 8·25 5·25

1449 Beniamino Gigli

2007. Entertainment Personalities' Anniversaries. Sheet 151×100 mm containing T **1449** and similar vert designs. Multicoloured.
MS3112 60c.×3, Type **1449** (tenor) (50th death anniv); Maria Callas (soprano) (30th death anniv); Amedeo Nazzari (actor) (birth centenary) 10·50 7·25

1450 Giuseppe di Vittorio

2007. 50th Death Anniv of Giuseppe di Vittorio (trade unionist and politician).
3113 **1450** 60c. multicoloured 3·25 2·10

1451 Anniversary Emblem

2007. Centenary of Mondadori (publishers).
3114 **1451** 60c. vermilion, black and gold 3·25 2·10

1452 *Madonna and Child* (Giovan Battista Cima Conegliano)

2007. Christmas (1st issue).
3115 **1452** 60c. olive 3·25 2·10

1453 Snow-covered House and Trees

2007. Christmas (2nd issue).
3116 **1453** 65c. multicoloured 3·50 2·20

1454 Soldier carrying Child

2007. Italy's Election as Temporary Member of UN Security Council.
3117 **1454** 85c. multicoloured 4·75 3·00

1455 Maritime and History Museum

2007. Fiume (now Croatian city of Rijeka).
3118 **1455** 65c. multicoloured 3·50 2·20

1456 '60'

2008. 60th Anniv of Constitution.
3119　**1456**　60c. multicoloured　3·25　2·10

1457 Nurses

2008. Centenary of Italian Red Cross Volunteer Nursing Corps.
3120　**1457**　60c. multicoloured　3·25　2·10

1458 Amintore Fanfani

2008. Birth Centenary of Amintore Fanfani (politician).
3121　**1458**　€1 multicoloured　5·50　3·50

1459 Building Facade

2008. Bicentenary of Italian Stock Exchange.
3122　**1459**　65c. blue, light blue and brown　3·50　2·20

1460 Typewriter and Factory Building

2008. Centenary of Olivetti Typewriter Factory, Ivrea.
3123　**1460**　60c. multicoloured　3·25　2·10

1461 Villa Reale, Monza

2008. Death Bicentenary of Giuseppe Piermarini (architect).
3124　**1461**　€1.40 blue and ultramarine　7·75　4·75

1462 Wheat, Cogwheels, Coin and Villa Lubin (headquarters), Rome

2008. 50th Anniv of National Council of Economics and Labour.
3125　**1462**　€1.50 multicoloured　8·25　5·25

1463 Dorando Pietri winning Olympic Marathon, London, 1908

2008. Dorando Pietri (marathon runner) Commemoration.
3126　**1463**　60c. multicoloured　3·25　2·10

1464 Disc and Diver

2008. *Nel blu dipinto de blu* (song). Sheet 96×79 mm.
MS3127　**1464**　60c. multicoloured　3·50　2·20

1465 Anna Magnani

2008. Birth Centenary of Anna Magnani (actor).
3128　**1465**　60c. multicoloured　3·25　2·10

1466 Emblem and La Scala Opera House, Milan

2008. Bicentenary of Ricordi Publishing House.
3129　**1466**　60c. black and grey　3·25　2·10

1467 Congress Centre, Rome

2008. Italia 2009 International Festival of Philately. Multicoloured.
3130　**1467**　60c. Type **1467**　3·25　2·10
3131　　65c. Colosseum　3·50　2·20

1468 Building Facade

2008. Carlo Combi High School, Capodistria.
3132　**1468**　60c. multicoloured　3·25　2·10

1469 Edmundo de Amicis

2008. Death Centenary of Edmundo de Amicis (writer).
3133　**1469**　60c. green and black　3·25　2·10

1470 Self Portrait

2008. Artistic and Cultural Heritage. Bernadino di Betto (Pintoricchio) (artist) Commemoration.
3134　**1470**　60c. multicoloured　3·25　2·10

1471 Madonna supported by Members of Confraternita di Santa Maria di Loreto

2008. Folklore. Feast of 'La Madonna che scappa in piazza', Sulmona.
3135　**1471**　60c. multicoloured　3·25　2·10

1472 Early Rowers

2008. 120th Anniv of National Rowing Federation.
3136　**1472**　65c. multicoloured　3·50　2·20

1473 *La Conferma della Regola* (from *The Life of Saint Francis* series of paintings by Giotto di Bondone)

2008. 700th Anniv of the Franciscan Order.
3137　**1473**　60c. multicoloured　3·25　2·10

1474 Imperial Forum

2008. Rome–Capital City.
3138　**1474**　60c. multicoloured　3·25　2·10

1475 Newsletter No. 1

2008. Centenary of National Press Federation.
3139　**1475**　60c. grey and black　3·25　2·10

1476 *The Flight* (bronze statue) (Pasquale Basile) (campaign emblem)

2008. UNESCO International Decade of Education for Sustainable Development.
3140　**1476**　€1.40 multicoloured　7·75　4·75

1477 *Giovannino Guareschi* (Arturo Coppola)

2008. Birth Centenary of Giovannino Guareschi (journalist, cartoonist and humorist).
3141　**1477**　60c. multicoloured　3·25　2·10

1478 Ludovico Geymonat

2008. Birth Centenary of Ludovico Geymonat (mathematician, historian and philosopher of science).
3142　**1478**　60c. multicoloured　3·25　2·10

1479 Post Box and Envelopes

2008. Europa. The Letter. Multicoloured.
3143　　60c. Type **1479**　3·25　2·10
3144　　65c. Brown post-box and envelopes　3·50　2·20

1480 Design for Bassano Bridge (Ponte Degli Alpini)

2008. 500th Birth Anniv of Andrea Palladio (architect).
3145　　60c. brown, blue and black　3·25　2·10
3146　　65c. chestnut and green　3·50　2·20
DESIGNS: 60c. Type **1480**; 65c. Palladian Basilica, Vincenza.

1480a Pope Sixtus V receiving Rule of Order from St Francis

2008. 400th Death Anniv of St Francis Caracciolo (Ascanio Pisquizio) (co-founder of Congregation of Minor Clerks Regular).
3146a　**1480a**　60c. multicoloured　3·25　2·10

1481 Savoy Castle, Gressoney Saint Jean and Mount Cervino (Aosta Valley)

2008. Regions. Multicoloured.
3147　　60c. Type **1481**　3·25　2·10
3148　　60c. *Salome with the Head of John the Baptist* (Titian) and Lagoon City (Veneto)　3·25　2·10
3149　　60c. Romanesque Fraterna Fountain, Piazza Celestino V (Molise)　3·25　2·10
3150　　60c. Baroque cathedral facade (Sicily)　3·25　2·10

1482 School Building

2008. Guastalla Boarding School.
3151　**1482**　60c. blue　3·25　2·10

1483 Motorcyclist riding Ducati Desmosedici GP7

2008. Ducatti Motorcycle.
3152 **1483** 60c. multicoloured   3·25   2·10

1484 Giacomo
Puccini

2008. 150th Birth Anniv of Giacomo Puccini.
3153 **1484** €1.50 multicoloured   8·25   5·25

1485 Player wearing
Centenary Shirt and
Emblem of 16th Victory

2008. Inter Football Club, Italian Football Champions–
Serie A 2008.
3154 **1485** 60c. multicoloured   3·25   2·10

1486 Torch Relay Runner
on Globe

2008. Olympic Games, Beijing. Stylized ceramic plates.
Multicoloured.
3155   60c. Type **1486**   3·25   2·10
3156   85c. Greek and Asian athletes   4·75   3·00

1487 Tommaso Landolfi

2008. Birth Centenary of Tommaso Landolfi (writer).
3157 **1487** 60c. multicoloured   3·25   2·10

1488 Dolomite Mountains, Tre
Cime di Lavaredo

2008. Tourist Publicity (35th series). Multicoloured.
3158 **1488** 60c. Type **1488**   3·25   2·10
3159   60c. Mt. Epomeo and port,
          Casamicciola Terme   3·25   2·10
3160   60c. Medieval tower and
          Introdacqua village   3·25   2·10
3161   60c. Mamuthones   3·25   2·10

1489 Stigmas and Flowers of
Crocus sativus

2008. Made in Italy. Zafferano dell'Aquila (saffron from
L'Aquila).
3162 **1489** 60c. multicoloured   3·25   2·10

1490 Ingredients

2008. Made in Italy. Spaghetti all'amatriciana Festival.
3163 **1490** 60c. multicoloured   3·25   2·10

1491 Bell Tower, Treviglio

2008. Cultural Heritage.
3164 **1491** 60c. indigo   3·25   2·10

1492 Dante Alighieri High
School, Gorizia

2008. Universities and Schools. Multicoloured.
3165   60c. Type **1492**   3·25   2·10
3166   60c. Statue of San Ercolano and
          griffin (images from official
          seal), University of Perugia   3·25   2·10

1493 Cesare Pavese
and Script

2008. Birth Centenary of Cesare Pavese (writer).
3167 **1493** 65c. black, vermilion
                and blue   3·50   2·20

1494 *Alberico Gentili*
(sculpture by Giuseppe
Guastalla)

2008. 400th Birth Anniv of Alberico Gentili (jurist; regius
professor of civil law, University of Oxford and one
of the first writers on public international law).
3168 **1494** 65c. multicoloured   3·50   2·20

1495 Malatestiana Library,
Cesena

2008. Cultural Heritage.
3169 **1495** 60c. black   3·25   2·10

1496 Emblem

2008. Union Cycliste Internationale Road World
Championships, Varese.
3170 **1496** 60c. multicoloured   3·25   1·90

1497 Stamps as
Map of Italy

2008. Stamp Day.
3171 **1497** 60c. multicoloured   3·25   2·10

1498 Mouth of Truth (1st–
century mask, Church of
Santa Maria, Rome)

2008. Italia–2009 International Stamp Exhibition.
Multicoloured. (a) Ordinary gum.
3172 **1498** 85c. Type **1498**   4·75   3·00

          (b) Self-adhesive.
3173 **1498** €2.80 Mouth of Truth   15·00 10·50

1499 Traffic
Policeman

2008. Local Police Force.
3174 **1499** 60c. multicoloured   3·25   2·10

1500 *Les Gracques*
(sculpture) (Eugene
Guillaume)

2008. 2500th Anniv of Roman Republic's People's Tribune.
3175 **1500** 60c. multicoloured   3·25   2·10

1501 *Madonna and
Child Enthroned with
Two Angels* (Lorenzo
di Credi)

2008. Christmas. Multicoloured. (a) Ordinary gum.
3176   60c. Type **1501**   3·25   2·10

          (b) Self-adhesive.
3177   €2.80 Wreath   15·00 10·50

1502 Val d' Orcia

2008. World Heritage Sites.
3178   –   60c. green and mauve   3·25   2·10
3179   –   €2.80 blue   15·00 10·50
DESIGNS: 60c. Type **1502**; €2.80 Historical Centre, Urbino.

1503 Epicentre

2008. Centenary of Messina Earthquake.
3180 **1503** 60c. multicoloured   3·25   2·10

1504 Cover of First Issue

2008. Centenary of Corriere dei Piccoli (weekly magazine
for children).
3181 **1504** 60c. multicoloured   3·25   2·10

1505 Charles Darwin

2009. Birth Bicentenary of Charles Robert Darwin
(naturalist and evolutionary theorist).
3182 **1505** 65c. multicoloured   3·50   2·20

1506 Moonlight

2009. *Tintarella di Luna* (song). Sheet 96×80 mm.
MS3183 **1506** 60c. multicoloured   3·50   2·20

1507 Father Oreste
Benzi, Carlo Valenzi
and Vincenzo
Muccioli

2009. National Conference on Drugs, Trieste.
3184 **1507** 60c. multicoloured   3·25   2·10

1508 Stamps and Exhibition
Visitors (pink background)

2009. Italia 2009–International Stamp Exhibition, Rome.
Multicoloured.
3185   60c. Type **1508**   3·25   2·10
3186   €1 Stamps and exhibition visi-
          tors (blue-grey background)   5·50   3·50

1509 Rock Engraving, Camonica
Valley

2009. Cultural Heritage.
3187 **1509** €2.80 brown   15·00   9·50

1510 Don Primo Mazzolari

2009. 50th Death Anniv of Don Primo Mazzolari (writer
and partisan).
3188 **1510** 60c. multicoloured   3·25   2·10

1511 Soldiers

2009. 350th Anniv of Grenadier Corps of Sardinia.
3189   **1511**   60c. multicooured   3·25   2·10

1512 Plazza di Spagna

2009. Rome–Capital City.
3190   **1512**   60c. multicoloured   3·25   2·10

1513 Indro
Montanelli and
Typewriter

2009. Birth Centenary of Indro Montanelli (journalist).
3191   **1513**   60c. multicoloured   3·25   2·10

1514 Necklace

2009. Made in Italy. 125th Anniv of Bvlgari (jewellery maker).
3192   **1514**   60c. multicoloured   3·25   2·10

1515 Swiss and Italian
Flags

2009. Centenary of Italian Chamber of Commerce for Switzerland.
3193   **1515**   60c. multicoloured   3·25   2·10

1516 Division Arms

2009. 40th Anniv of Carabinieri Division for Protection of Cultural Heritage.
3194   **1516**   60c. multicoloured   3·25   2·10

1517 Map and Stylized
Athletes

2009. Mediterranean Games.
3195   **1517**   60c. multicoloured   3·25   2·10

1518 European Parliament
Headquarters, Strasbourg
and Stars

2009. European Parliamentary Elections.
3196   **1518**   60c. multicoloured   3·25   2·10

1519 Italian Galileo
Telescope, La Palma, Canary
Islands

2009. Europa. Astronomy. Multicoloured.
3197   60c. Type **1519**   3·25   2·10
3198   65c. Satellite *AGILE* and Earth   3·50   2·20

1520 Early Cyclist

2009. Centenary of Giro d'Italia (cycle race).
3199   **1520**   60c. multicoloured   3·25   2·10

1521 Johann von Goethe
and Dnate Alighieri (logo)

2009. 50th Anniv of Academy of Italian–German Studies, Merano.
3200   **1521**   60c. multicoloured   3·25   2·10

1522 Alfa Romeo 6C 1500
Gran Sport

2009. Mille Miglia (thousand miles (open-road endurance race which took place from 1927 to 1957)).
3201   **1522**   60c. multicoloured   3·25   2·10

1523 Carrying
'Ingegno' of
Sant'Antonio Abate

2009. Festival of Mysteries, Campobasso.
3202   **1523**   60c. multicoloured   3·25   2·10

1524 Santa Maria Madre di Dio in
Rieti Cathedral

2009. Cultural Heritage.
3203   **1524**   60c. black   3·25   2·10

1525 Giovanni
Palatucci

2009. Birth Centenary of Giovanni Palatucci (police chief).
3204   **1525**   60c. multicoloured   3·25   2·10

1526 Gilera VT 317
(reconstruction of first
motorbike made by Gilera)

2009. Centenary of Gilera (motorcycle manufacturer).
3205   **1526**   60c. multicoloured   3·25   2·10

1527 1859 ½g. Stamp of
Sicily (As Type 1) and
Handstamp

2009. 150th Anniv of First Stamps in Sicily.
3206   **1527**   60c. multicoloured   3·25   2·10

1528 Player

2009. Baseball World Cup. Sheet 80×60 mm.
MS3207 **1528** 60c. multicoloured   3·50   2·20

1529 Saint John
Leonardi

2009. 400th Death Anniv of Saint John Leonardi (San Giovanni Leonardi) (founder of Clerks Regular of the Mother of God of Lucca).
3208   **1529**   60c. multicoloured   3·25   2·10

1530 Player

2009. Italian Football Championship (Inter 2009).
3209   **1530**   60c. multicoloured   3·25   2·10

1531 Ham and San Daniele
del Friuli

2009. Made in Italy. San Daniele Ham.
3210   **1531**   60c. multicoloured   3·25   2·10

1532 St. Marks Square

2009. St. Marks Square (SMS) Venice Project
3211   **1532**   60c. black and indigo   3·25   2·10

1533 Envelope

2009. Posta Italiana (Italian Mail). Self adhesive.
3212   **1533**   60c. multicoloured   3·25   2·10
3213   **1533**   €1.40 multicoloured   7·75   4·75
3214   **1533**   €1.50 multicoloured   8·00   5·00
3215   **1533**   €2 multicoloured   10·50   6·50

1534 Women

2009. 65th Anniv of Insurrection of Women of Carrara.
3216   **1534**   €1.50 multicoloured   8·25   5·25

1535 Summit
Emblem

2009. G8 Summit, L'Aquila.
3217   **1535**   65c. multicoloured   3·50   2·20

1536 Piazza Sant'Agostino and
Ligurian Coast, Verezzi

2009. Tourist Publicity (36th series). Multicoloured.
3218   60c. Type **1536**   3·25   2·10
3219   60c. Lighthouse and Port Giglio,
       Giglio Island   3·25   2·10
3220   60c. Headland and typical
       vegetation, Costa degli Dei–
       Capo Vaticano   3·25   2·10
3221   60c. Narrow lava walls,
       Alcantara Gorges   3·25   2·10

1537 Vintage
Advertising Poster

2009. 150th Anniv of *La Nazione* Newspaper, Florence.
3222   **1537**   60c. multicoloured   3·25   2·10

1538 Freestyle Swimmer

2009. 13th World Aquatics Championships, Italy.
3223   **1538**   €1.50 steel blue   8·25   5·25

1539 Living and
Burnt Forest

2009. Measures to Prevent and Fight Fires.
3224   **1539**   60c. multicoloured   3·25   2·10

1540 '30' enclosing
Dove

2009. 30th (2010) Meeting for Friendship Among Peoples, Rimini.
3225   **1540**   60c. bright emerald   3·25   2·10

1541 *Ufficiali e tromba dei Cavalleggeri di Montebello* (Antonio Cervi)

2009. 150th Anniv of Lancieri di Montebello Cavalry Regiment.
3226 **1541** 60c. multicoloured   3·25   2·10

1542 *San Gennaro* (Francesco Solimena)

2009. Artistic and Cultural Heritage. Museum of Treasure of San Gennaro, Naples.
3227 **1542** 60c. multicoloured   3·25   2·10

1543 Library and Picture Gallery Building, Milan and *Portrait of a Lady* (Giovanni Ambrogio de Predis)

2009. Artistic and Cultural Heritage. Ambrosian Academy Library and Picture Gallery, Milan.
3228 **1543** €1.40 black   7·75   4·75

1544 *Emilio Alessandrini*

2009. 30th Death Anniv of Emilio Alessandrini (magistrate).
3229 **1544** 60c. multicoloured   3·25   2·10

1545 Cross and Map of Europe

2009. Patron Saints of Europe. Sheet 126×126 mm containing T **1545** and similar horiz design. Multicoloured.
MS3230 60c. Type **1545**; 65c. As Type
     1545 with colours reversed   7·50   5·25

1546 Early and Modern Front Page

2009. 120th Anniv of *L'Union Sarda* Newspaper.
3231 **1546** 60c. multicloured   3·25   2·10

1547 Luigi Sturzo

2009. 50th Death Anniv of Luigi Sturzo (Catholic priest and politician).
3232 **1547** €1.50 salmon-pink and bistre-brown   8·25   5·25

1548 Norberto Bobbio

2009. Birth Centenary of Norberto Bobbio (philosopher of law and political sciences and historian of political thought).
3233 **1548** 65c. multicoloured   3·50   2·20

1549 Fathers Giovanni Minozzi and Giovanni Semeria

2009. Father Giovanni Semeria and Father Giovanni Minozzi (founders of Opera Nazionale per il Mezzogiorno d'Italia (poverty and war orphans charity)) Commemoration.
3234 **1549** 60c. multicoloured   3·25   2·10

1550 Envelopes surrounding School

2009. Stamp Day.
3235 **1550** 60c. multicoloured   3·25   2·10

1551 Dante and Virgil and Three Wild Beasts (from 15th-century *Codex Urbinate Latino 365*, Vatican Apostolic Library)

2009. Italia 2009 International Stamp Exhibition, Rome. Italian Language.
3236 **1551** 60c. multicoloured   3·50   2·20
    A stamp of a similar design was issued by San Marino and Vatican City.

1552 Gino Bartali (cyclist, twice winner of Giro d'Italia)

2009. Italia 2009. Sports Day. Multicoloured.
3237 60c. Type **1552**   3·25   2·10
3238 65c. Valentino Mazzola (footballer, captain of Grande Torino)   3·50   2·10
3239 €1.40 Michele Alboreto beside a Ferrari F1 156/85 (1997–24 Hours of Le Mans and 2001–12 Hours of Sebring winner)   7·75   4·75

1553 Flags as Pen and Ink

2009. 130th Anniv of Italy–Bulgaria Diplomatic Relations. Sheet 101×71 mm.
MS3240 **1553** 65c. multicoloured   3·75   2·50

1554 *Coccobill* (Benito Franco Jacovitti)

2009. Italia 2009. Collectors' Day. Italian Comics. Sheet 80×120 mm containing T **1554** and similar horiz designs. Multicoloured.
MS3241 €1×3, Type **1554**; *Diabolik* (Angela and Luciana Giussani); *Lupo Alberto* (Guido Silvestri (Silver))   17·00   12·00

1555 *The Adoration of the Shepherds* (Domenico Piola)

2009. Christmas (1st issue).
3242 **1555** 60c. multicoloured   3·25   2·10

1556 Bauble, Star and Moon

2009. Christmas (2nd issue). Self-adhesive.
3243 **1556** 60c. multicoloured   3·25   2·10

1557 *Luciano Pavarotti* (tenor)

2009. Italia 2009. Music Day. Multicoloured.
3244 65c. Type **1557**   3·50   2·20
3245 €1 Mino Reitano (singer and actor)   5·50   3·50
3246 €1.50 Nino Rota (musician and composer)   8·25   5·25

1558 Pont du Gard, France

2009. Italia 2009. Europe Day. Multicoloured. Self-adhesive.
3247 65c. Type **1558**   3·50   2·20
3248 65c. Hadrian's Wall, Great Britain   3·50   2·20
3249 65c. Odeon of Patras, Greece   3·50   2·20
3250 65c. Porta Nigra, Trier, Germany   3·50   2·20
3251 65c. Aqueduct of Segovia, Spain   3·50   2·20

1559 *Guantanamera* (sculpture) (Giacomo Manzù)

2009. Art. Italian Masters of the 20th Century. Multicoloured.
3252 60c. Type **1559**   3·25   2·10
3253 65c. *The Bear Dance* (Gino Severini)   3·50   2·20
3254 85c. *Donna e Ambiente* (Federico De Pistoris)   4·75   3·00

2009. Posta Italiana (Italian Mail). Self adhesive.
3255 **1533** €3.30 multicoloured   16·00   13·50

1560 Giorgio Perlasca

2010. Birth Centenary of Giorgio Perlasca (saviour of Jews during World War II and recipient of Righteous among the Nations).
3256 **1560** 60c. multicoloured   3·25   2·10

1561 Basilica Santa Maria di Collemaggio

2010. Artistic and Cultural Heritage. Romanesque Art. Sheet 96 mm×80mm
MS3257 **1561** 60c. multicoloured   3·50   2·50

1562 Corsa alla Stella and Componidori (Farmers' and Carpenters' Guilds) and Cathedral of Santa Maria Assunta (Sa Sartiglia, Oristano)

2010. Folklore Customs. Multicoloured.
3258 60c. Type **1562**   3·25   2·10
3259 60c. Float and Acireale Cathedral (Acireale carnival)   3·25   2·10

1563 Skier

2010. Winter Olympic Games, Vancouver
3260 **1563** 85c. multicoloured   4·75   3·00

1564 Basketball Players

2010. Youth Olympic Games, Singapore
3261 **1564** 85c. multicoloured   4·75   3·00

1565 Ennio Flaiano

2010. Birth Centenary of Ennio Flaiano
3262 **1565** 60c. multicoloured   3·25   2·10

1566 Mario Pannunzio

2010. Birth Centenary of Mario Pannunzio (writer and journalist)
3263 **1566** 60c. multicoloured   3·25   2·10

1567 Basilica of Madonna dei Miracoli, Motta di Livenza, Treviso

2010. Artistic and Cultural Heritage
3264 **1567** 60c. multicoloured   3·25   2·10

1568 Massimo D'Azeglio (first provincial president) and Palazzo Isimbardi

2010. 150th Anniv of Milan Province
3265 **1568** 60c. multicoloured   3·25   2·10

1569 24 HP (1910)

2010. Made in Italy. Multicoloured.
3266   60c. Type **1569**   3·25   2·10
3267   60c. Modern hatchback   3·25   2·10
Nos. 3266/7 were printed, *se-tenant*, forming a composite design

1570 Sepoltura del Cristo e tre angeli che reggono il Sudario (Burial of Christ with three angels holding up the Shroud) (Gerolamo della Rover)

2010. Ostension of Turin Shroud
3268 **1570** 60c. multicoloured   3·25   2·10

1571 L'imbarco di Garibaldi a Quarto (Garibaldi sets sail from Quarto) (V. Azzola)

2010. 150th Anniv of the Expedition of the Thousand. Multicoloured.
MS3269 60c. Type **1571**; 65c. *Lo sbarco a Marsala. 11 maggio 1860* (Landing at Marsala. 11th May 1860); 85c. *La Battaglia di Calatafimi* (Battle of Calatafimi) (Remigio Legat); €1 *L'incontro di Teano tra Giuseppe Garibaldi e Vittorio Emanuele II* (Meeting in Teano between Giuseppe Garibaldi and Vittorio Emanuele II) (Pietro Aldi)   18·00   13·50

1572 Centenary Emblem

2010. Centenary of Confindustria
3270 **1572** €1.40 multicoloured   7·75   4·75

1573 Viaduct

2010. Centenary of Rhaetian Railway
3271 **1573** 65c. multicoloured   3·50   2·20

1574 Pinocchio (Jacovitti after Carlo Collodi)

2010. Europa. Multicoloured.
3272   60c. Type **1574**   3·25   2·10
3273   65c. Geronimo Stilton (Elisabetta Dami)   3·50   2·20
No. 3274 and Type **1575** are vacant

1576 Sr. Maria Domenica Brun Barbantini (founder) and Sisters caring for the Sick

2010. 180th (2009) Anniv of Congregation of the Sister Servants of the Sick of St. Camillus
3275 **1576** 60c. multicoloured   3·25   2·10

1577 Gardens

2010. Hanbury Botanic Gardens, Ventimiglia
3276 **1577** 60c. multicoloured   3·25   2·10

1578 Isole Tremiti

2010. Tourist Publicity (37th series). Multicoloured.
3277   60c. Type **1578**   3·25   2·10
3278   60c. Todi   3·25   2·10
3279   60c. Viggiano   3·25   2·10
3280   60c. Courmayeur   3·25   2·10

1579 ENIT (national tourist agency) Poster, 1955

2010. Tourism
3281 **1579** 60c. multicoloured   3·25   2·10

1580 Camillo Benso

2010. Birth Bicentenary of Camillo Benso, Count of Cavour.
3282 **1580** 60c. multicoloured   3·25   2·10

1581 Anniversary Emblem

2010. Centenary of Assonime (Association of Italian Joint Stock Companies)
3283 **1581** 60c. multicoloured   3·25   2·10

1582 Inter Milan Player, Number 18 (number of times Inter Milan has won championship) and the Club Crest

2010. Inter Milan, Italian Football Champions–Serie A 2010
3284 **1582** 60c. multicoloured   3·25   2·10

1583 Emblem

2010. Made in Italy. Centenary of Federacciai (iron and steel casting plant), Bagnoli
3285 **1583** €3.30 black   18·00   13·50

2010. Posta Italiana (Italian Mail)
3286   5c. As Type **1533** (30×25 mm)   25   15
3287   10c. As Type **1533** (30×25 mm)   55   35
3288   20c. As Type **1533** (30×25 mm)   1·10   70
See also 3212/15, 3255, 3350 and 3457

1584 Giovanni Schiaparelli, Map and Mars

2010. Death Centenary of Giovanni Virginio Schiaparelli (astronomer)
3289 **1584** 65c. multicoloured   3·50   2·20

1585 Pope Benedict XVI, Cathedral of San Panfilo of Sulmona and Pope Celestine V (statue)

2010. Celestian Jubilee Year
3290 **1585** 60c. multicoloured   3·25   2·10

1586 *David with the Head of Goliath*

2010. 400th Death Anniv of Michelangelo Merisi da Caravaggio (artist)
3291 **1586** 60c. multicoloured   3·25   2·10

1587 Ettore Paratore and 3rd-century Mosaic Trionfo di Dioniso (Triumph of Dionysius),

2010. 50th Anniv of Plautus Festival, Sarsina
3292 **1587** 65c. multicoloured   3·50   2·20

1588 Amphitheatre

2010. Artistic and Cultural Heritage. Samnite Theatre in Pietrabbondante
3293 **1588** 60c. reddish-brown   3·25   2·10

1589 Joe Petrosino, Brooklyn Bridge and Statue of Liberty

2010. 150th Birth Anniv of Giuseppe (Joe) Petrosino (New York City policeman who was a pioneer in the fight against organized crime)
3294 **1589** 85c. multicoloured   4·75   3·00

1590 17th Olympic Games Emblem, Torch Bearer and Tripod containing Olympic Flame

2010. 50th Anniv of Rome 1960, Olympic Games
3295 **1590** 60c. multicoloured   3·25   2·10

1591 Fire Brigade Members and Cortina d'Ampezzo (event venue)

2010. First National Gathering of Italian Fire Brigades
3296 **1591** 60c. multicoloured   3·25   2·10

1592 Italian Flag, National Acrobatic Team in Arrow Formation

2010. 50th Anniv National Air Force Acrobatic Team
3297 **1592** 60c. multicoloured   3·25   2·10

1593 Piazzale di Porta Pia, Monumento al Bersagliere and Porta Pia Gate in Aurelian Walls

2010. Rome as Capital City
3298 **1593** 60c. multicoloured   3·25   2·10

1594 Players

2010. Sport. Men's World Volleyball Championships
3299 **1594** 85c. deep dull blue ... 4·75 3·00

1595 19th-century Coral Bracelet

2010. Made in Italy. Torre del Greco Coral Jewellery
3300 **1595** 60c. multicoloured ... 3·25 2·10

1596 Frecciarossa High Speed Train

2010. Turin–Salerno High Speed Rail Line
MS3301 **1596** 60c. multicoloured ... 3·50 2·50

1597 Front *Page of Corriere delle Marche* (previous title), 5 October 1860, Map of Area and *Corriere Adriatico* Front Page

2010. 150th Anniv of *Corriere Adriatico* Newspaper
3302 **1597** 60c. multicoloured ... 3·25 2·10

1598 People, Italian Flag and European Union Flag

2010. Anti-trust Authority
3303 **1598** €1.40 multicoloured ... 7·75 4·75

1599 Building Façade

2010. School of Oenology (study of wine and winemaking), Conegliano, Treviso
3304 **1599** 60c. multicoloured ... 3·25 2·10

1600 Leonardo Sciascia

2010. Leonardo Sciascia (writer) Commemoration
3305 **1600** 60c. black ... 3·25 2·10

1601 Players, Emblem and Anniversary Emblem

2010. Sport. Centenary of Italian Tennis Federation
3306 **1601** 60c. multicoloured ... 3·25 2·10

1602 Self Portrait

2010. Artistic and Cultural Heritage. Birth Centenary of Pietro Annigoni (artist)
3307 **1602** 60c. multicoloured ... 3·25 2·10

1603 Federico Fellini

2010. Italian Cinema 2010. Each black and green.
MS3308 60c.×3, Type **1603**; Vittorio Gassman; Alberto Sordi ... 10·50 7·75

1604 *Adoration of the Magi* (Sandro Botticelli)

2010. Christmas (1st issue)
3309 **1604** 60c. multicoloured ... 3·25 2·10

1605 Magnifying Glass and 'FILATELIA'

2010. Stamp Day
3310 **1605** 60c. multicoloured ... 3·25 2·10
Type **1606** is vacant.

1607 'NATALE' carried by Toy Train

2010. Christmas (2nd issue)
3311 **1607** 65c. multicoloured ... 3·50 2·20

1608 19th-century Jaquard Fabric, featuring 'F' (company logo)

2010. Made in Italy
3312 **1608** 60c. multicoloured ... 3·25 2·10

1609 Mario Mazzuca and Rugby Players

2010. Sport. Birth Centenary of Mario Mazzuca (rugby player and sports manager)
3313 **1609** 60c. multicoloured ... 3·25 2·10

1610 Biscuit Tin, Biscuits and Poster

2010. Made in Italy
3314 **1610** 60c. multicoloured ... 3·25 2·10

1611 Pinot di Franciacorta, 1961

2010. Made in Italy
3315 **1611** 60c. multicoloured ... 3·25 2·10

1612 Anniversary Emblem

2011. 150th Anniv of Re-unification of Italy. Multicoloured.

(a) Sheet stamp. Self-adhesive
3316 60c. Type **1612** ... 3·25 2·10

(b) Miniature sheet. Ordinary gum
MS3317 80×60 mm. 60c. Colours of Italian flag crossed through by two waving green and red ribbons (40×30 mm) ... 3·50 2·40

1613 Battle of the Oranges, Palazzo Comunale, Piazza Vittorio Emanuele. and Mugnaia, (heroic female figure, symbol of the Carnival)

2011. Folklore Customs
3318 **1613** 60c. multicoloured ... 3·25 2·10

1614 Antonio Fogazzaro

2011. Death Centenary of Antonio Fogazzaro (writer)
3319 **1614** 60c. multicoloured ... 3·25 2·10

1615 Three Women

2011. International Women's Day
3320 **1615** 75c. multicoloured ... 4·00 2·50

1616 'TERRITORIO' (land registry)

2011. Taxation Agencies. Multicoloured.
MS3321 60c.×4, Type **1616**,' DOGANE' (customs); 'DEMANIO' (state property); 'ENTRATE' (revenue) ... 13·50 12·00

1617 Palazzo Montecitorio, Rome, (current seat of the Italian Parliament) and Palazzo Carignano, Turin, (seat of the first Italian Parliament)

2011. 150th Anniv of Proclamation of Kingdom of Italy. Sheet 80×60 mm
MS3322 **1617** 60c. multicoloured ... 3·50 3·00

1618 Flaminio Obelisk, Santa Maria dei Miracoli Church and Santa Maria in Montesanto Church, Piazza del Popolo, Rome

2011. 150th Anniv of Unification of Italy. Sheet 96×80 mm
MS3323 **1618** €1.50 multicoloured ... 9·00 7·75

1619 Parmigiano Reggiano

2011. Made in Italy. Cheeses. Multicoloured.
3324 60c. Type **1619** ... 3·25 2·10
3325 60c. Gorgonzola ... 3·25 2·10
3326 60c. Mozzarella ... 3·25 2·10
3327 60c. Ragusano ... 3·25 2·10

1620 World Theatre Day Poster (Interaction) and '27 marzo 2011'

2011. World Theatre Day
3328 **1620** 60c. multicoloured ... 3·25 2·10

1621 1863 15c. Stamp (As No. 7)

2011. Philatelic Exhibition. 'Quel magnifico biennio 1859-1861'
3329 **1621** 60c. multicoloured ... 3·25 2·10

1622 Yuri Gagarin

2011. 50th Anniv of First Manned Space Flight
3330 **1622** 75c. multicoloured ... 4·00 2·50

1623 *Roma dalle Quadrighe del Vittoriano: dal Quirinale al Colosseo* (Marcella Morlacchi)

2011. Rome as Capital City
3331 **1623** 60c. multicoloured ... 3·25 2·10

1624 Emilio Salgari

2011. Death Centenary of Emilio Salgari (Journalist and writer)
3332 **1624** 60c. multicoloured   3·25   2·10

1625 Pope John Paul II

2011. Beatification of Pope John Paul II
3333 **1625** 60c. multicoloured   3·25   2·10

1626 Forest, Squirrel and Fungi

2011. Europa. Forests. Multicoloured.
3334 60c. Type **1626**   3·25   2·10
3335 75c. Trees, bird, flower and leaf   4·00   2·50

1627 Emblem

2011. 50th Anniv of Amnesty International
3336 **1627** 60c. multicoloured   3·25   2·10

1628 *Gli emigranti* (The Emigrants) (Angiolo Tommasi)

2011. Museum of Italian Emigration
3337 **1628** 60c. multicoloured   3·25   2·10

1629 *Count Camillo Benso di Cavour* and *Les Congres de Paris* (lithograph)

2011. 150th Anniv of Re-unification of Italy (3rd issue). Personalities. Multicoloured.
MS3338 60c. Type **1629**   3·50   3·00
MS3339 60c. *Carlo Cattaneo* and *I remember the days 5, 1848 in Port Victoria*
                                             3·50   3·00
MS3340 60c. *Giuseppe Garibaldi and The Entry of Garibaldi into Naples September 7, 1860*
                                             3·50   3·00
MS3341 60c. *Roscioni Vincenzo Vincenzo Gioberti* and *Event to Celebrate Joy of Neapolitan Pius IX and Gioberti*
                                             3·50   3·00
MS3342 60c. *Clara Maffei, Cristina Trivulzio Belgiojoso* and *The Sharpshooter Lombard's Death and Spearmen carrying badly Wounded at Villa Luciano Manara*
                                             3·50   3·00
MS3343 60c. *Giuseppe Mazzini, frontispiece of Young Italy* (magazine) and flag with 'Union, Strength and Freedom!'
                                             3·50   3·00
MS3344 60c. *Carlo Pisacane* and *The Death of Carlo Pisacane*
                                             3·50   3·00

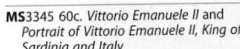

MS3345 60c. *Vittorio Emanuele II* and *Portrait of Vittorio Emanuele II, King of Sardinia and Italy*
                                             3·50   3·00

1630 Anita and Giuseppe Garibaldi, and Three Towers on Mount Titano

2011. 150th Anniv of Re-unification of Italy (4th issue). Sheet 80×60 mm
MS3346 **1630** €1.50 multicoloured   8·25   7·75

1631 Arms of Savoia Family, with Royal Crown; Heraldic Emblem of Italian Navy, with Turreted Naval Crown, and Naval Pennant with Heraldic Emblem

2011. 150th Anniv of Re-unification of Italy (5th issue). 150th Anniv of Italian Navy. Multicoloured.
MS3347 60c.×4, Type **1631**; Naval Academy of Livorno; *Amerigo Vespucci* (training ship); Arms of Italian Sailors' Union and National Association of Italian Sailors
                                            13·50   12·00

1632 Referee holding Yellow Card and Players

2011. Centenary of Italian Referees' Association
3348 **1632** 60c. multicoloured   3·25   2·10

1633 Carlo Dapporto

2011. Birth Centenary of Carlo Dapporto (actor)
3349 **1633** 60c. multicoloured   3·25   2·10

2011. Posta Italiana (Italian Mail)
3350 75c. As Type **1533** (30×25 mm)   4·00   2·50
   See also 3212/15, 3255, and 3457

1634 Botanic Garden of Padua

2011. Gardens. Multicoloured.
3351 60c. Type **1634**   3·25   2·10
3352 60c. Giardino di Flora Appenninica (Garden of Apennine Flora of Capracotta)
                                             3·25   2·10

1635 Benedictine Abbey of the Santissima Trinità

2011. Artistic and Cultural Heritage. Benedictine Abbey of the Santissima Trinità
3353 **1635** 60c. black   3·25   2·10

1636 Award Emblem

2011. Made in Italy. ADI Compasso d'Oro (Industrial Design Association Golden Compass) Award
3354 **1636** 60c. multicoloured   3·25   2·10

1637 Ruins of Hadrian's Villa

2011. Artistic and Cultural Heritage. Hadrian's Villa, Tivoli
3355 **1637** 60c. multicoloured   3·25   2·10

1637a Eté en Italie Poster

2011. Tourism. Eté en Italie (Summer in Italy) Poster, 1955
3356 **1637a** 60c. multicoloured   3·25   2·10

1638 Tarvisio

2011. Tourist Publicity (38th series). Multicoloured.
3357 60c. Type **1638**   3·25   2·10
3358 60c. Sepino   3·25   2·10
3359 60c. Bosa   3·25   2·10
3360 60c. Riviera del Conero-Sirolo   3·25   2·10

1639 *San Luca dipinge la Vergine* (St. Luke Painting the Virgin)

2011. Artistic and Cultural Heritage. 500th Birth Anniv of Giorgio Vasari (artist). Sheet 120×144 mm
MS3361 **1639** €1.40 multicoloured   8·25   7·75

1640 Renewal of the Oath of Allegiance

2011. Folklore Customs. Mastrogiurato of Lanciano (Chieti)
3362 **1640** 60c. multicoloured   3·25   2·10

1641 Arms of Milan, Figure 18 (championships won by team) and Rossoneri (Red and Blacks) Player kicking Ball

2011. AC Milan, Italian Football Champions–Serie A 2011
3363 **1641** 60c. multicoloured   3·25   2·10

1642 Inter (FC Internazionale) Arms, Trophy and Football

2011. Inter Milan, National Football Champions, 2010-2011. 150th Anniv of Re-unification of Italy
3364 **1642** 60c. multicoloured   3·25   2·10

1643 Anglers and Fish

2011. Sport. Fishing World Championship, Italia 2011
3365 **1643** 60c. multicoloured   3·25   2·10

1644 Archer and Target

2011. European Field Archery Championships
3366 **1644** 75c. multicoloured   4·00   2·50

1645 Eucharist (tapestry after Peter Paul Rubens)

2011. 25th National Eucharistic Congress
3367 **1645** 60c. multicoloured   3·25   2·10

1646 Arch of Trajan

2011. Artistic and Cultural Heritage. Arch of Trajan, Benevento
3368 **1646** 60c. black   3·25   2·10

1647 Molecular Structure, Test Tubes and Emblem of Italian Chemistry Society

2011. International Year of Chemistry
3369 **1647** €1.40 multicoloured   7·75   4·75

1648 Gallery of Palazzo Spada, Rome (seat of Council of State)

2011. Council of State
3370	**1648**	60c. black	3·25	2·10

1649 Emblem

2011. 50th Anniv of Organisation for Economic Cooperation and Development (OECD)
3371	**1649**	60c. multicoloured	3·25	2·10

1650 Hug

2011. European Year of Volunteering
3372	**1650**	75c. multicoloured	4·00	2·50

1651 Marzotto Wool Mill and Rolls of Wool

2011. Made in Italy. 175th Anniv of Marzolto Wool Mill
3373	**1651**	60c. multicoloured	3·25	2·10

1652 Italo Svevo

2011. 150th Birth Anniv of Aron Ettore Schmitz (Italo Svevo) (writer and businessman)
3374	**1652**	60c. multicoloured	3·25	2·10

1653 Saint Pius and the Equestrian Order of the Holy Sepulchre of Jerusalem (Painting of tapestry, destroyed in WWII) (Mario Albertella)

2011. Equestrian Order of the Holy Sepulchre of Jerusalem
3375	**1653**	60c. multicoloured	3·25	2·10

1654 Battle of Pastrengo

2011. 150th Anniv of Re-unification of Italy (5th issue). Battles. Multicoloured.
MS3376	60c.×3 Type **1654**; *Battle of Soferino*, 1839 (Adolphe Yvon); *Battle of Volturno*, 1860 (Giovanni Fattori)	10·50	8·50
MS3377	60c.×3 *Battle of Bezzecca*, 1866; *Breach of Porta Pia*, 1870 (Charles Ademollo); *Battle of Isonzo*, 1915 - 1917	10·50	8·50

1655 Soldier and Globe

2011. Italian Military Missions Abroad
3378	**1655**	75c. multicoloured	4·00	2·50

1656 1965 500l. Stamp showing Dante, 2007 Special Cancellation with Profile of Poet, 2009 Special Cancellation with Dante's Inferno and 1938 Envelope franked with Stamps depicting Poet

2011. Stamp Day
3379	**1656**	60c. multicoloured	3·25	2·10

1657 Palazzo della Zecca, Medal (created by Attilio Motti) and New Mint Building

2011. Centenary of Palazzo della Zecca dell'Italia Unita (headquarters of Italian Mint), Rome
3380	**1657**	60c. multicoloured	3·25	2·10

1658 Oldest Examples of Postal Savings Account

2011. Postal Savings. Multicoloured.
3381		60c. Type **1658**	3·25	2·10
3382		75c. Modern postal savings accounts and postal card booklet.	4·00	2·50

1659 Hill planted with Olive Trees, Demijohn and Vintage Fratelli Carli Lorry

2011. Made in Italy. Centenary of Fratelli Carli (olive oil retailers)
3383	**1659**	60c. multicoloured	3·25	2·10

1660 *Madonna and Child with Pomegranate* (16th-century unknown artist)

2011. Christmas (1st issue)
3384	**1660**	60c. multicoloured	3·25	2·10

1660a Reindeer above Snow-covered House

2011. Christmas (2nd issue)
3385	**1660a**	75c. multicoloured	3·25	2·10

1661 Official Emblem

2011. Year of Russian Culture and Language in Italy and of Italian Culture and Language in Russia
3386	**1661**	75c. multicoloured	4·00	2·50

1662 Headquarters of Italian National Olympic Committee, Rome

2012. Sport. Birth Centenary of Guilio Onesti (Italian sports manager and member of International Olympic Committee)
3387	**1662**	60c. multicoloured	3·25	2·10

1663 Italia Turrita ((allegory of Italy) from medal by Pio Tailetti), holding Reverse of 1863 Vittorio Emanuele II Silver One Lira Coin

2012. 150th Anniv of Unification of National Monetary System. Lira
MS3388	60c.×3, multicoloured; olive-grey, grey and black; grey and black	10·50	8·50

Designs: 60c.×3, Type **1663**; Anniversary emblem including reverse of 1946 lira coin (first issued by Republic of Italy); reverse of 1862 Vittorio Emanuele II silver one lira coin

1664 Aglianico del Vulture Superiore

2012. Wine. Multicoloured.
3389	60c. Type **1664**	3·25	2·10
3389a	60c. Cannellino di Frascati	3·25	2·10
3389b	60c. Barolo	3·25	2·10
3389c	60c. Greco di Tufo	3·25	2·10
3389d	60c. Brunello di Montalcino	3·25	2·10
3389e	60c. Montepulciano d'Abruzzo Colline Teramane	3·25	2·10
3389f	60c. Colli Orientali del Friuli Picolit	3·25	2·10
3389g	60c. Montefalco Sagrantino	3·25	2·10
3389h	60c. Prosecco Conegliano Valdobbiadene	3·25	2·10
3389i	60c. Vernaccia di Serrapetrona	3·25	2·10
3389j	60c. Cerasuolo di Vittoria	3·25	2·10
3389k	60c. Vermentino di Gallura	3·25	2·10
3389l	60c. Moscato di Scanzo	3·25	2·10
3389m	60c. Romagna DOCG Albana	3·25	2·10
3389n	60c. Primitivo di Manduria Dolce Naturale	3·25	2·10

1665 Fracchia (torch) carried on Carts during Procession held on Good Friday, Bell Tower of Collegiate Church and Our Lady of Sorrows (statue)

2012. Folklore Customs. Fracchie in San Marco, Lamis
3390	**1665**	60c. multicoloured	3·25	2·10

1666 Giovanni Pascoli and Script

2012. Death Centenary of Giovanni Pascoli (writer)
3391	**1666**	60c. multicoloured	3·25	2·10

1667 Anniversary Emblem

2012. Centenary of Italian Association of Foundations and Savings Banks (Associazione di Fondazioni e di Casse di Risparmio) (Acri)
3392	**1667**	60c. light green and scarlet vermilion	3·25	2·10

1668 Barbanera and First Almanac (single sheet printed 1762 in Foligno)

2012. 250th Anniv of Barbanera's Almanac of Foligno
3393	**1668**	60c. multicoloured	3·25	2·10

1669 Bottle of Balsamic Vinegar and Barrels

2012. Made in Italy. Balsamic Vinegar of Modena
3394	**1669**	60c. multicoloured	3·25	2·10

1670 Early Postal Workers

2012. 150th Anniv of Italian Postal Service. Multicoloured. (blue).
3395	60c. Type **1670**	3·25	2·10
3396	60c. Postal worker riding camel	3·25	2·10
3397	60c. Loading post onto aircraft	3·25	2·10
3398	60c. Postal vehicles in semi-circle	3·25	2·10
3399	60c. Collecting mail from box at rear of tram	3·25	2·10
3400	60c. Woman using early computer	3·25	2·10
3401	60c. Modern postal worker riding scooter	3·25	2·10
3402	60c. Modern Post Office	3·25	2·10

3403 60c. Modern postal workers
using computers   3·25   2·10

1671 Sunflowers and
Ruined Temple viewed
through Train Window

2012. Europa. Visit Italy. Multicoloured.
3404 60c. Type **1671**   3·25   2·10
3405 75c. Silhouette of dance, part
of ancient capital and coastal
village   4·00   2·50

1672 Sales Room of Officina
Profumo **1673**

2012. Made in Italy. 400th Anniv of Officina Profumo - Farmaceutica di Santa Maria Novella (pharmacy), Florence
3406 **1672** 75c. multicoloured   4·00   2·50
No. 3407 and Type **1673** are vacant, awaiting stamps

1673 Trani Cathedral

2013. Artistic and Cultural Heritage. Trani Cathedral. Rita Morena.
3407 **1673** 60c. black   3·25   2·10

1674 Luigi Einaudi

2012. Luigi Einaudi (politician, economist and president of Italian Republic 1948 - 1955) Commemoration
3408 **1674** 60c. multicoloured   3·25   2·10

1675 *Battaglia di Cavalieri*

2012. Artistic and Cultural Heritage. Birth Centenary of Aligi Sassau
3409 **1675** 60c. multicoloured   3·25   2·10

1676 Maiori

2012. Tourist Publicity (39th series). Multicoloured.
3410 60c. Type **1676**   3·25   2·10
3411 60c. Ustica   3·25   2·10
3412 60c. Baveno   3·25   2·10
3413 60c. Montecassino   3·25   2·10
3414 60c. 1955 ENIT(national tourist
board) poster (26×37 mm)   3·25   2·10

1677 Juventus Stadium,
Tricolour Sheild and
Juventus Crest

2012. Sport. Juventus - Series A Italian Football Champions
3415 **1677** 60c. multicoloured   3·25   2·10

1678 Expo Emblem **1679**
1680

2012. Milano 2015 Universal Expo
3416 **1678** 60c. multicoloured   3·25   2·10
Nos. 3417/18 and Type **1679/80** are vacant, awaiting stamps.

1679 Building Façade

2013. Artistic and Cultural Heritage. Terme di Bonifacio VIII Spa Complex, Fiuggi
3417 **1679** €1.50 black

1680 Fermo Cathedral

2012. Artistic and Cultural Heritage. Fermo Cathedral
3418 **1680** 60c. black

1681 *Garibaldi sbarca a
Marsala* (Girolamo Induno)
and First Page of *Roma*

2012. 150th Anniv of *Roma* Newspaper
3419 **1681** 60c. multicoloured   2·10

1682 Battle Scene (detail of
fresco by Giulio Romano)

2012. Battle of Milvian Bridge. Sheet 100×75 mm
MS3420 **1682** €1.40 multicoloured   8·25   7·75

1683 Giovanni
Falcone, Paolo
Borsellino, Rosario
Livatino and
Anti-Mafia
Investigation
Department
Emblem

2012. 20th Anniv of Anti-Mafia Investigation Department
3421 **1683** 60c. multicoloured   3·25   2·10

1684 Stylized Man

2012. Italian Congress of Surgeons, 2012
3422 **1684** 60c. green and bright
scarlet   3·25   2·10

1685 Triton Fountain, Vegetation
and Palazzo Riario-Corsini

2012. Parks and Gardens. Multicoloured.
3423 75c. Type **1685**   4·00   2·50
3424 75c. Catinia Botanic Gardens 4·00   2·50

1686 Count Camillo Benso
di Cavour (statue by
Antonio Rossetti)

2012. 150th Anniv of Court of Auditors
3425 **1686** 60c. grey-olive   3·25   2·10

1687 Art Nouveau Water
Tower (symbol of Cusano
Milanino) and Original
Design for City (modelled
on those built in Britain)

2012. Centenary of Cusano Milanino (first garden city in Italy)
3426 **1687** 60c. multicoloured   3·25   2·10

1688 Interior of Basilica of St.
Peter , Pope Benedict XVI, Pope
Paul VI and John XXIII

2012. 50th Anniv of Second Vatican Ecumenical Council
3427 **1688** 60c. multicoloured   3·25   2·10
No. 3428 and Type **1689** are vacant, awaiting stamps.

1690 Consultation

2012. Stamp Day. Green and black (3430) or multicoloured (others).
3429 60c. Type **1690**   3·25   2·10
3430 60c. Decree   3·25   2·10
3431 60c. Design   3·25   2·10
3432 60c. Descision as to design 3·25   2·10
3433 60c. Production   3·25   2·10

1691 *Il Presepe con i Santi
Giovanni Battista e
Bartolomeo* (The Nativity
with Saints John the
Baptist and Bartholomew)
(Antonio del Massaro)

2012. Christmas (1st issue)
3434 **1691** 60c. multicoloured   3·25   2·10

1692 Tree of Stars

2012. Christmas (2nd issue)
3435 **1692** 60c. multicoloured   3·25   2·10

1693 Products

2012. Made in Italy. Centenary of Fratelli Guzzini (kitchen utensils retailer)
3436 **1693** 60c. multicoloured   3·25   2·10

1694 Ceramic Plate
depicting Artemis (painted
by Carlo Antonio Grue)
(Castelli)

2012. Made in Italy. Ceramics. Multicoloured.
3437 60c. Type **1694**   3·25   2·10
3438 60c. Staircase of Santa Maria
del Monte (Caltagirone)   3·25   2·10
3439 60c. Blue ceramic tiles   3·25   2·10
3440 60c. Two cermaic stoves (Castel-
lamonte)   3·25   2·10
3441 60c. Ceramic plate depicting
bird (Squillace)   3·25   2·10

1695 Pope John Paul I blessing
the Faithful and Detail of St
Peter's Basilica

2012. Birth Cent of Pope John Paul I
3442 **1695** 60c. multicoloured   3·25   2·10

1696 Brera Observatory
and Galaxy M51

2012. Observatories. 250th Anniv of Brera Observatory Milan (3343) or Bicentenary of Capodimonte Observatory, Naples (3444). Multicoloured.
3443 60c. Type **1696**   3·25   2·10
3444 60c. Capodimonte Observatory
and Galaxy ARP273   3·25   2·10

1697 L. C. Farini

2012. Birth Bicentenary of Luigi Carlo Farini (physician, statesman and historian)
3445 **1697** 60c. multicoloured   3·25   2·10

1698 Quota 33 part of Italian El Alamein War Memorial and Emblem of Folgore Parachute Brigade

2012. 'Folgore' Parachute Brigade. 70th Anniv of Battle of El Alamein
3446 **1698** €1.40 multicoloured 7·75 4·75

1699 Emblems

2012. 81st General Assembly of International Criminal Police Organization (INTERPOL)
3447 **1699** 60c. multicoloured 3·25 2·10

1700 Anniversary Emblem

2012. 50th Anniv of Italian National Electricity Company (ENEL)
3448 **1700** 60c. multicoloured 3·25 2·10

1701 Wheelchair with Digger Bucket knocking down Flight of Stairs

2012. Elimination of Architectural Barriers to Disabled People
3449 **1701** 60c. multicoloured 3·25 2·10

1702 Primo Levi

2012. 25th Death Anniv of Primo Levi (writer)
3450 **1702** 75c. multicoloured 4·00 2·50

1703 Emblem

2012. 50th Anniv of Carabinieri NAS (Carabinieri Command for Protection of Health (Core Commodities and Health))
3451 **1703** 60c. multicoloured 3·25 2·10

1704 Procession bearing Flaming Torches

2012. Folklore Customs. Ndocciata of Agnone (fire festival)
3452 **1705** 60c. multicoloured 3·25 2·10

1705 Emblem

2012. European Union's Nobel Peace Price
3453 **1705** 75c. multicoloured 4·00 2·50

1706 Masks and Prendigetto (container used to catch sweets thrown from floats)

2013. Folklore Customs. Fano Carnival
3454 **1706** 60c. multicoloured 3·25 2·10

1707 Skiers

2013. Sport. Nordic World Ski Championships, Val di Fiemme
3455 **1707** 85c. multicoloured 4·00 2·50

1708 Float with Papier Mâché Figures

2013. Folklore Customs. Termini Imerese Carnival
3456 **1708** 70c. multicoloured 4·00 2·50

2013. Posta Italiana (Italian Mail)
3457 25c. As Type 1533 (30×25 mm) 1·10 85
See also 3212/15, 3255, 3350

1709 Anna Maria Luisa dè Medici

2013. 270th Death Anniv of Anna Maria Luisa dè Medici (patron of the arts)
3458 **1709** €3.60 multicoloured 19·00 12·50

1710 Saint John the Baptist preaching, with Self-portrait of the Artist (detail)

2013. Artistic and Cultural Heritage. 400th Birth Anniv of Mattia Preti (artist)
3459 **1710** 70c. multicoloured 4·00 2·50

2013. Posta Italiana (Italian Mail)
3460 70c. As Type 1533 4·00 2·50
See also 3212/15, 3255, 3350 and 3457

1711 Stamp Designs by Paolo Paschetto

2013. Artistic and Cultural Heritage. 50th Death Anniv of Paolo Paschetto (designer of emblem of Italian Republic)
3461 **1711** 70c. multicoloured 4·00 2·50

1712 Gabriele D'Annunzio

2013. 150th Birth Anniv of Gabriele d'Annunzio (writer, soldier and politician)
3462 **1712** 70c. multicoloured 4·00 2·50

1713 Stylized Arena

2013. Centenary of Opera Festival of Arena of Verona. Sheet 60×80 mm
MS3463 **1713** €1.90 multicoloured 10·50 6·50

1714 Emblem

2013. 90th Anniv National Air Force
3464 **1714** 70c. ultramarine, scarlet-vermilion and emerald 4·00 2·50

1715 Castel Trauttmansdorff Gardens, Merano

2013. Parks and Gardens. Multicoloured.
3465 70c. Type 1715 4·00 2·50
3466 70c. Cinque Terre National Park 4·00 2·50
3467 70c. Botanic Garden Museum, Bari 4·00 2·50

1716 Pope Sylvester meeting Emperor Constantine (fresco, Oratory of Saint Sylvester, Santi Quattro Coronati Basilica, Rome)

2013. 1700th Anniv of Edict of Milan. Sheet 100×72 mm
MS3468 **1716** €1.90 multicoloured 10·50 6·50

1717 Pope Francis

2013. Enthronement of Pontificate of Pope Francis
3469 **1717** 70c. multicoloured 4·00 2·50

1718 University Façade

2013. 150th Anniv of Polytechnic University of Milan
3470 **1718** 70c. dull scarlet and brownish grey 4·00 2·50

1719 Early and Modern Post Motorcycles

2013. Europa. Postal Transport. Multicoloured.
3471 70c. Type 1719 4·25 4·00
3472 85c. Early and modern postvan 4·75 4·60
No. 3473 and Type 1720 are left for Theatre of Bologna, not yet received.

1721 Headquarters Façade

2013. State Police Headquarters, Rome
3474 **1721** 70c. multicoloured 4·00 2·50

1722 Amphora-shaped Drop Earrings (Etruscan art, 3rd – 2nd century B.C.)

2013. Made in Italy. Goldsmithing. Multicoloured.
3475 70c. Type 1722 4·00 2·50
3476 70c. François I's salt cellar depicting Neptune and the Earth (sculpted by Benvenuto Cellini, 1543) 4·00 2·50
3477 70c. Star-shaped buckle (14th century) 4·00 2·50
3478 70c. *The Golden Sphere* ((detail) Leonardo Montalbano, 1640) 4·00 2·50
3479 70c. Palermo brooch with marine Venus (19th century, by engraver Antonio Berini and Manifattura Castellani) 4·00 2·50

1723 Dinghies

2013. Sport. Centenary of 12 Foot Dinghy Sailboat
3480 **1723** 70c. multicoloured 4·00 2·50

1724 Two Submarines and Submerged Conning Tower

2013. International Submariner Association Congress, Catania
3481 **1724** 70c. multicoloured 4·25 4·00

1725 Vintage Italian Alpine Club Poster

2013. 150th Anniv of Italian Alpine Club
3482   **1725**   70c. multicoloured   4·25   4·00

1726 Emblem

2013. Italian Medicines Agency
3483   **1726**   70c. multicoloured   4·00

1727 Giovanni Boccaccio

2013. 700th Birth Anniv of Giovanni Boccaccio (writer and Renaissance humanist)
3484   **1727**   70c. steel blue   4·25   4·00

1728 Map (detail)

1729 Map (image scaled to 25% of original size)

2013. 550th Anniv of San Marino. Multicoloured.
MS3485 70c.×4, Type **1728**; three similar designs showing part of map as T **1729**   15·00   15·00

1730 Camaldoli Hermitage

2013. Artistic and Cultural Heritage. Camaldoli Hermitage. Antonio Ciaburro.
3486   **1730**   70c. multicoloured   4·25   4·00

2013. Posta Italiana (Italian Mail)
3487   **1730**   85c. As Type **1533**   4·75   4·50
3488   €1.90 As Type **1533**   7·00   6·50
3489   €3.60 As Type **1533** (21.9.14)   9·00   8·50
    See also 3212/15, 3255, 3350, 3457 and 3460

1731 Competitors

2013. Sport. UCI World Road Championships
3490   **1731**   70c. multicoloured   4·25   4·00

1732 Giuseppe Verdi

2013. Birth Bicentenary of Giuseppe Verdi
3491   **1732**   70c. multicoloured   4·25   4·00

1733 *Vittoria Olimpica* (detail)

2013. Artistic and Cultural Heritage. Birth Centenary of Emilio Greco (sculptor)
3492   **1733**   70c. black   4·25   4·00

1734 Aglianico del Taburno

2013. Wine. Multicoloured.
3493   70c. Type **1734**   4·25   4·00
3494   70c. Alta Langa   4·25   4·00
3495   70c. Amarone della Valpolicella   4·25   4·00
3496   70c. Barbera d'Asti   4·25   4·00
3497   70c. Bardolino Superiore   4·25   4·00
3498   70c. Castel del Monte Bombino Nero   4·25   4·00
3499   70c. Cesanese del Piglio   4·25   4·00
3500   70c. Colli Bolognesi Classico Pignolette   4·25   4·00
3501   70c. Morellino di Scansano   4·25   4·00
3502   70c. Oltrepò Paqvese Metodo Classico   4·25   4·00
3503   70c. Ramandolo   4·25   4·00
3504   70c. Sfursat di Valtellina   4·25   4·00
3505   70c. Torgiano Rosso Riserva   4·25   4·00
3506   70c. Castelli di Jesi Verdicchio Reseva   4·25   4·00
3507   70c. Vino Nobile di Montepulciano   4·25   4·00

1735 Envelope (mailed 18 December, 1860 from Florence to Paris (Rothschild Envelope) franked by Provisional Government of Tuscany) and ½ Tornese Stamp (issued in Naples in December 1860)

2013. Stamp Day. Multicoloured.
3508   70c. Type **1735**   4·25   4·00
3509   70c. First postcard issued by Kingdom of Italy January 1, 1874, depicting King Victtor Emanue ll   4·25   4·00
3510   70c. Two 15 cents stamps showing Garibaldi (Types **42** and **43**), celebrating the 50th anniv of Southern States plebiscite   4·25   4·00
3511   70c. Three AIR stamps (Types **135/a/b**) issued for Balbo Transatlantic Mass Formation Flight (1933) and registered envelope addressed to the Mayor of Chicago   4·25   4·00
3512   70c. 'Catalogue of Victory' (1923) and 'E-World' magazine   4·25   4·00

1736 Player

2013. Sport. Juventus - Series A Italian Football Champions
3513   **1736**   70c. multicoloured   4·25   4·00

1737 Table of Pi Numbers Geometrical Constructions and the Letter Pi (π) (Archimedes' constant)

2013. Archimedean Year
3514   **1737**   70c. multicoloured   4·25   4·00

1738 *St Joseph with Child* (Guido Reni)

2013. Christmas (1st issue)
3515   **1738**   70c. multicoloured   4·25   4·00
    No. 3516 and Type **1739** are left for Christmas (2nd issue), not yet received.

1740 Theatre Façade

2013. Artistic and Cultural Heritage. Social Theatre of Como
3517   **1740**   70c. black   4·25   4·00

1741 Auditorium

2013. Artistic and Cultural Heritage. 'La Fenice' Theatre, Venice
3518   **1741**   70c. multicoloured   4·25   4·00

1742 Civita di Bagnoregio

2013. 25th Anniv of Civita Association
3519   **1742**   70c. blue and black   4·25   4·00

1743 Ponza

2013. Tourist Publicity (40th series)
3520   70c. Type **1743**   4·25   4·00
3521   70c. Scanno   4·25   4·00
3522   70c. San Leo   4·25   4·00
3523   70c. Tropea   4·25   4·00

1744 Symbols of Tourism

2013. Tourism. ENIT Manifesto
3524   **1744**   70c. multicoloured   4·25   4·00

1745 Rita Levi-Montalcini

2013. Rita Levi-Montalcini (winner of Nobel Prize for Medicine, 1986) Commemoration
3525   **1745**   70c. multicoloured   4·25   4·00

1746 Giuseppe Belli

2013. 150th Birth Anniv of Giuseppe Gioachino Belli (writer)
3526   **1746**   85c. multicoloured   4·75   4·50

1747 Cola di Rienzo (statue)

2013. 700th Birth Anniv of Cola di Rienzo (politician and Tribune of Rome)
3527   **1747**   70c. deep green and black   4·25   4·00

1748 Aerial View of City

2013. Artistic and Cultural Heritage. Renaissance City Walls of Lucca
3528   **1748**   70c. black   4·25   4·00

1749 Ruins of Alba Fucens

2013. Artistic and Cultural Heritage. Archaeological Site of Alba Fucens
3529   **1749**   70c. multicoloured   4·25   4·00

1750 Nardò Cathedral Façade

2013. Artistic and Cultural Heritage. Nardò Cathedral
3530   **1750**   70c. black   4·25   4·00

1751 Colonnade in Medieval Church Complex

2013. Artistic and Cultural Heritage. Monumental Complex of Santa Sofia, Benevento

3531	1751	70c. multicoloured	4·25	4·00

1752 Mole Antonelliana

2013. Artistic and Cultural Heritage. Mole Antonelliana, Turin

3532	1752	70c. black	4·25	4·00

1753 Text

2013. Made in Italy. 50th Anniv of Adnkronos (news agency)

3533	1753	70c. multicoloured	4·25	4·00

CONCESSIONAL LETTER POST

CL93 Arms of Savoy and Fasces

1928

CL227	CL93	10c. blue	8·50	65

CL109 Arms and Fasces

1930

CL267	CL109	10c. brown	20	25

1945. No. CL267, surch with Royal Arms (obliterating fasces) and new value.

CL647		40c. on 10c. brown	1·20	1·40

1945. As Type CL109, but Arms redrawn without fasces.

CL648		10c. brown	60	1·10
CL649		1l. brown	9·00	4·50

CL201 Italia

1947

CL687	CL201	1l. green	2·20	55
CL688	CL201	8l. red	44·00	55

CL220 Italia

1948

CL734	CL220	15l. violet	£180	25
CL916	CL220	20l. green	65	50
CL917	CL220	30l. green	65	40
CL918	CL220	35l. brown	65	40
CL919	CL220	110l. blue	65	40
CL920	CL220	270l. mauve	1·00	75
CL921	CL220	300l. green & pink	75	65
CL922	CL220	370l. brown & orge	90	65

CONCESSIONAL PARCEL POST

CP288

1953

CP918	CP288	40l. orange	1·90	50
CP919	CP288	50l. blue	1·90	50
CP920	CP288	60l. violet	7·75	1·90
CP921	CP288	70l. green	65·00	6·75
CP850	CP288	75l. sepia	£200	3·75
CP923	CP288	80l. brown	65	25
CP924	CP288	90l. lilac	65	25
CP851	CP288	110l. red	£225	5·25
CP926	CP288	110l. yellow	65	25
CP927	CP288	120l. green	65	25
CP928	CP288	140l. black	65	25
CP929	CP288	150l. red	65	40
CP930	CP288	180l. red	50	40
CP931	CP288	240l. slate	75	40
CP932	CP288	500l. brown	1·90	65
CP933	CP288	600l. turquoise	2·20	65
CP934	CP288	900l. blue	2·20	65

Unused prices are for the complete pair. Used prices are for the left half; right halves are worth more.

CP707

1984

CP1849	CP707	3000l. blue and red	7·25	5·25

EXPRESS LETTER STAMPS

E35

1903. For inland letters.

E73	E35	25c. red	55·00	1·60
E113	E35	50c. red	2·10	2·10
E129	E35	60c. red	5·25	1·10
E178	E35	70c. red	75	55
E179	E35	1l.25 blue	75	30

E41 King Victor Emmanuel III

1908. For foreign letters.

E80	E41	30c. blue and pink	1·60	4·25
E180	E41	2l. blue and pink	4·75	65·00
E181	E41	2l.50 blue and pink	3·50	6·00

E59

1917. Surch **25** and bars.

E112	E59	25c. on 40c. violet	40·00	90·00

1921. Surch with new value.

E118	E41	L.1.20 on 30c. blue and pink	1·60	21·00
E173	E41	L.1.60 on 1l.20 blue and pink	1·90	65·00

1922. Surch in words and figures.

E122	E35	60c. on 50c. red	37·00	2·75
E172	E35	70c. on 60c. red	1·30	1·20

E131 "Garibaldi" (statue), Savoia Marchetti S-55A Flying Boat and "Anita Garibaldi" (statue)

1932. Air. 50th Death Anniv of Garibaldi.

E348	E131	2l.25+1l. violet and red	12·00	65·00
E349	E131	4l.50+1l.50 brown and green	12·00	65·00

E132 King Victor Emmanuel III

1932

E350	E132	1l.25 green	25	30
E351	E132	2l.50 orange	35	4·75

1932. Tenth Anniv of March on Rome. As T **132.** (a) For inland letters. Inscribed "ESPRESSO".

E368		1l.25 green	2·10	2·10

(b) For foreign letters. Inscribed "EXPRES".

E369		2l.50 orange	6·75	£170

DESIGNS: 1l.25, Roman road; 2l.50, Flags and head of Mussolini.

E133 Savoia Marchetti S-55A Flying Boat

1933. Air.

E370	E133	2l. black	25	3·50
E371	E133	2l.25 black	5·00	£180

1934. Air. Tenth Anniv of Annexation of Fiume. Inscr as in T **141.**

E408		2l.+1l.25 blue	1·40	32·00
E409		2l.25+1l.25 green	2·10	27·00
E410		4l.50+2l. red	2·10	27·00

DESIGN: Foundation of Fiume.

1934. Air. Military Medal Centenary. Inscr as in T **146.**

E442		2l.+1l.25 brown	6·75	44·00
E443		4l.50+2l. red	11·00	44·00

DESIGN—HORIZ: 2l., 4l.50, Caproni Ca 101 airplane over triumphal arch.

E192 Italia

1945

E647	E192	5l. red	55	1·30

E200 Winged Foot of Mercury

1945

E679	E200	5l. red	30	20
E680	-	10l. blue	85	55
E681	-	15l. red	5·50	20
E682	E200	25l. orange	65·00	20
E683	E200	30l. violet	8·25	2·40
E915	E200	50l. purple	11·50	40
E685	-	60l. red	90·00	20

DESIGN: 10, 15, 60l. Horse and torch bearer.

E209 Rising at Naples

1948. Centenary of 1848 Revolution.

E718	E209	35l. violet	£200	28·00

E341 Etruscan Horses

1958

E961	E341	75l. purple	40	25
E1220	E341	150l. green	25	20
E1221	E341	250l. blue & light blue	40	30
E1222	E341	300l. brown & lt brn	50	40

MILITARY POST STAMPS

1943. Stamps of Italy optd **P.M.** (a) Postage stamps of 1929 (Nos. 239/56).

M583		5c. brown	55	2·20
M584		10c. brown	55	2·20
M585		15c. green	55	2·20
M586		20c. red	55	2·20
M587		25c. green	55	2·20
M588		30c. brown	55	2·20
M589		50c. violet	55	2·20
M590		1l. violet	3·25	22·00

M591		1l.25 blue	55	4·00
M592		1l.75 orange	55	4·00
M593		2l. red	55	4·00
M594		5l. red	55	5·50
M595		10l. violet	3·25	33·00

(b) Air stamps of 1930 (Nos. 271/7).

M596		50c. brown	55	2·20
M597		1l. violet	55	3·25
M598		2l. blue	55	17·00
M599		5l. green	3·50	22·00
M600		10l. red	3·50	28·00

(c) Air Express stamp of 1933 (No. E370).

M601		2l. black	3·50	39·00

(d) Express Letter stamp of 1932 (No. E350).

M602		1l.25 green	45	5·50

NEWSPAPER STAMPS

N2

1862. Imperf.

N5	N2	2c. yellow	60·00	£130

For similar stamps in black, see Sardinia.

OFFICIAL STAMPS

O11

1875

O21	O11	2c. red	2·75	4·75
O22	O11	5c. red	2·75	4·75
O23	O11	20c. red	1·60	2·10
O24	O11	30c. red	1·90	3·25
O25	O11	1l. red	4·75	19·00
O26	O11	2l. red	24·00	43·00
O27	O11	5l. red	95·00	£200
O28	O11	10l. red	£170	£160

1934. Air. Optd **SERVIZIO DI STATO.**

O450	148	10l. grey	£1100	£14000

PARCEL POST STAMPS

P13 King Umberto I

1884. Various frames.

P38	P13	10c. grey	£200	£110
P39	P13	20c. blue	£375	£190
P40	P13	50c. pink	21·00	16·00
P41	P13	75c. green	21·00	16·00
P42	P13	1l.25 orange	37·00	36·00
P43	P13	1l.75 brown	41·00	£150

The left-hand portion of the following parcel post stamps is affixed to the packet-card, the right-hand portion to the receipt. Unused prices are for the complete pair and used prices for the half-stamp. Unsevered stamps in used condition are usually from cancelled-to-order material and are worth more than the half-stamp.

P53

1914

P96	P53	5c. brown	4·25	10·50
P97	P53	10c. blue	4·25	10·50
P98	P53	20c. black	19·00	10·50
P99	P53	25c. red	21·00	10·50
P100	P53	50c. orange	32·00	25·00
P101	P53	1l. violet	37·00	10·50
P102	P53	2l. green	43·00	13·00
P103	P53	3l. yellow	55·00	32·00
P104	P53	4l. grey	65·00	43·00
P105	P53	10l. purple	£120	48·00
P106	P53	12l. brown	£225	£350
P107	P53	15l. olive	£190	£350
P108	P53	20l. purple	£130	£350

1923. Surch with figures on left half and words and figures on right half.

P146		30c. on 5c. brown	1·30	17·00
P147		60c. on 5c. brown	1·30	17·00
P148		1l.50 on 5c. brown	4·50	£120
P149		3l. on 10l. purple	4·50	65·00

P92

1927

P217	**P92**	5c. brown	1·30	2·20
P218	**P92**	10c. blue	1·30	2·20
P219	**P92**	25c. red	1·30	2·20
P220	**P92**	30c. blue	1·30	3·50
P221	**P92**	50c. orange	1·30	2·20
P222	-	60c. red	1·30	3·50
P223	**P92**	1l. violet	1·30	3·50
P224	**P92**	2l. green	1·30	3·50
P225	**P92**	3l. bistre	1·30	7·75
P226	**P92**	4l. black	1·30	7·75
P227	**P92**	10l. purple	3·75	37·00
P228	**P92**	20l. purple	5·25	48·00

The value in the right-hand portion of the 60c. is in figures.

1945. Optd with ornamental device obliterating Fascist emblems in centre.

P647		5c. brown	2·75	9·00
P648		10c. blue	3·00	9·00
P649		25c. red	3·00	9·00
P650		30c. blue	39·00	31·00
P651		50c. orange	3·00	5·50
P652	-	60c. red	3·00	5·50
P653	**P92**	1l. violet	3·00	5·50
P654	**P92**	2l. green	3·00	5·50
P655	**P92**	3l. bistre	3·00	5·50
P656	**P92**	4l. black	3·00	5·50
P657	**P92**	10l. purple	41·00	55·00
P658	**P92**	20l. purple	70·00	£100

1946. As Type **P92**, but without fasces between stamps.

P679	1l. mauve	3·25	5·50
P680	2l. green	2·20	5·50
P681	3l. orange	4·50	9·00
P682	4l. black	6·75	9·00
P683	10l. purple	£110	55·00
P684	20l. purple	£170	£190

P201

1946

P687a	**P201**	25c. blue	55	30
P688	**P201**	50c. brown	90	30
P689	**P201**	1l. brown	1·10	30
P690	**P201**	2l. blue	2·75	80
P691	**P201**	3l. orange	1·10	30
P692	**P201**	4l. grey	16·00	6·00
P910	**P201**	5l. purple	25	15
P911	**P201**	10l. purple	25	15
P912	**P201**	20l. purple	25	15
P914	**P201**	40l. violet	25	15
P915	**P201**	50l. red	25	15
P916	**P201**	60l. violet	25	15
P917	**P201**	100l. blue	25	15
P918	**P201**	140l. red	40	25
P919	**P201**	150l. green	30	20
P920	**P201**	200l. green	40	20
P921	**P201**	280l. yellow	70	40
P922	**P201**	300l. purple	50	30
P923	**P201**	400l. black	75	50
P924	**P201**	500l. brown	2·00	65
P925	**P201**	600l. brown	1·50	75
P926	**P201**	700l. blue	3·00	1·30
P927	**P201**	800l. orange	3·75	1·30
P1348	**P201**	30l. purple	25	25

P298

1954

P928a	**P298**	1000l. blue	1·70	1·00
P929	**P298**	2000l. red and brown	6·00	5·75

PNEUMATIC POST LETTERS

PE53

1913

PE96	**PE53**	10c. brown	3·25	21·00
PE97	**PE53**	15c. lilac	4·25	27·00
PE191	**PE53**	15c. pink	4·50	13·50
PE192	**PE53**	15c. purple	4·50	13·50
PE193	**PE53**	20c. purple	19·00	43·00
PE98	**PE53**	30c. blue	21·00	£130
PE194	**PE53**	35c. red	21·00	£250
PE195	**PE53**	40c. red	28·00	£225

1924. Surch.

PE165	15c. on 10c. brown	4·75	27·00
PE166	15c. on 20c. purple	12·00	48·00
PE167	20c. on 20c. brown	9·50	43·00
PE168	20c. on 15c. lilac	12·00	27·00
PE169	35c. on 40c. red	22·00	£225
PE170	40c. on 30c. blue	13·00	£190

PE134 Galileo Galilei

1933

PE372	-	15c. purple	45	1·60
PE373	**PE134**	35c. red	45	2·75

DESIGN: 15c. Dante Alighieri.

1945. As Type **PE134**, but inscr "ITALIA" instead of "REGNO D'ITALIA".

PE679		60c. brown (Dante)	65	3·25
PE680	**PE134**	1l.40 blue	65	3·25

PE204 Minerva

1947

PE694	**PE204**	3l. purple	10·00	9·75
PE695	**PE204**	5l. blue	65	30
PE961	**PE204**	10l. red	40	25
PE962	**PE204**	20l. blue	40	25

POSTAGE DUE STAMPS

D3

1863. Imperf.

D6B	**D3**	10c. yellow	£2250	£275

FOOTNOTE: Our price for mint stamps is for stamps without gum. Stamps with gum are worth considerably more.

D11

1869. Perf.

D21	**D11**	10c. brown	£5500	80·00

D12

1870

D22	**D12**	1c. mauve and orange	6·50	16·00
D23	**D12**	2c. mauve and orange	17·00	30·00
D24	**D12**	5c. mauve and orange	1·70	1·10
D25	**D12**	10c. mauve and orange	1·70	1·10
D26	**D12**	20c. mauve and orange	19·00	1·10
D27	**D12**	30c. mauve and orange	5·25	1·40
D28	**D12**	40c. mauve and orange	5·25	3·75
D29	**D12**	50c. mauve and orange	5·25	1·30
D30		60c. mauve and orange	£275	5·25
D31		60c. brown and orange	37·00	16·00
D32		1l. brown and blue	£6500	27·00
D33		1l. mauve and blue	34·00	1·60
D34		2l. brown and blue	£6500	43·00
D35		2l. mauve and blue	65·00	8·50
D36		5l. brown and blue	£550	48·00
D37		5l. mauve and blue	£225	37·00
D38		10l. brown and blue	£9000	48·00
D39		10l. mauve and blue	£225	9·50

D13

1884

D40	**D13**	50l. green	95·00	85·00
D73	**D13**	50l. yellow	£110	60·00
D41	**D13**	100l. red	95·00	43·00
D74	**D13**	100l. blue	85·00	21·00

(D 20)

1890. Surch over numeral as Type **D20**.

D47	**D12**	10(c.) on 2c. (D23)	£140	43·00
D48	**D12**	20(c.) on 1c. (D22)	£600	32·00
D49	**D12**	30(c.) on 2c. (D23)	£1900	16·00

D141   **D142**

1934. With Fascist emblems.

D395	**D141**	5c. brown	65	70
D396	**D141**	10c. blue	65	70
D397	**D141**	20c. red	65	70
D398	**D141**	25c. green	65	70
D399	**D141**	30c. orange	65	70
D400	**D141**	40c. brown	65	4·25
D401	**D141**	50c. violet	65	70
D402	**D141**	60c. blue	65	10·50
D403	**D142**	1l. orange	65	70
D404	**D142**	2l. green	65	70
D405	**D142**	5l. violet	2·10	1·10
D406	**D142**	10l. blue	3·75	6·00
D407	**D142**	20l. red	6·00	17·00

D191   **D192**

1945. Fascist emblems removed.

D630	**D191**	5c. brown	2·75	3·25
D631	**D191**	10c. blue	80	1·20
D632	**D191**	20c. red	2·75	1·20
D633	**D191**	25c. green	80	1·20
D634	**D191**	30c. orange	80	1·20
D635	**D191**	40c. black	80	1·20
D636	**D191**	50c. violet	80	1·20
D637	**D191**	60c. blue	80	3·25
D685	**D192**	1l. orange	1·70	60
D639	**D192**	2l. green	80	1·20
D640	**D192**	5l. violet	80	1·20
D641	**D192**	10l. blue	80	1·20
D642	**D192**	20l. red	4·50	4·50

D201

1947

D690	**D201**	1l. orange	35	15
D691	**D201**	2l. green	65	15
D692	**D201**	3l. red	2·75	2·20
D693	**D201**	4l. brown	2·75	1·40
D924	**D201**	5l. violet	25	20
D694	**D201**	6l. blue	11·00	2·40
D696	**D201**	8l. mauve	37·00	4·00
D926	**D201**	10l. blue	25	20
D698	**D201**	12l. brown	12·00	2·40
D927	**D201**	20l. purple	25	20
D928	**D201**	25l. red	25	20
D929	**D201**	30l. purple	25	20
D930	**D201**	40l. brown	25	20
D931	**D201**	50l. green	25	20
D932	**D201**	100l. orange	25	20
D935	**D201**	500l. red and blue	1·90	65
D936	**D201**	500l. purple and blue	1·20	65
D937	**D201**	900l. mve, blk & grn	2·30	65
D938	**D201**	1500l. orange & brown	3·25	1·30

PUBLICITY ENVELOPE STAMPS

1921. Optd **B.L.P.**

B129	37	10c. red	£160	£110
B137	37	15c. grey	£375	£500
B138	41	20c. orange	£400	£500
B132	39	25c. blue	£160	£120
B140	39	30c. brown	£275	£200
B115	39	40c. brown	£110	27·00
B134	39	50c. violet	£850	£750
B135	39	60c. red	£3000	£2500
B141	39	85c. brown	£350	£500
B136	34	1l. brown and green	£4500	£3000

ITALIAN SOCIAL REPUBLIC

Following the surrender of Italy on 3 September 1943, and his rescue from imprisonment on 12 September, Mussolini proclaimed the Italian Social Republic at Salo on 23 September 1943. From this town on Lake Garda the Republican government administered those parts of Italy, north of the Gustav Line, which were under German occupation.

1944. Stamps of Italy optd **G. N. R.** (a) Postage. (i) Nos. 239 and 241/59.

1	**98**	5c. brown	3·75	7·00
2	-	10c. brown	3·75	7·00
3	-	15c. green	3·75	7·00
4	**99**	20c. red	3·75	11·50
5	-	25c. green	3·75	7·00
6	**103**	30c. brown	3·75	7·00
7	-	35c. blue	£170	£225
8	**103**	50c. violet	3·75	11·50
9	-	75c. red	3·75	7·00
10	**99**	1l. violet	3·75	7·00
11	-	1l.25 blue	3·75	7·00
12	-	1l.75 red	13·00	40·00
13	-	2l. red	13·00	40·00
14	**98**	2l.55 green	65·00	£300
15	**98**	3l.70 violet	50·00	£200
16	**98**	5l. red	11·50	46·00
17	-	10l. violet	£120	£300
18	**99**	20l. green	£325	£650
19	-	25l. black	£900	£1800
20	-	50l. violet	£700	£1800

(ii) War Propaganda issue. Nos. 563/74.

21		25c. green (Navy)	10·50	23·00
22		25c. green (Army)	10·50	23·00
23		25c. green (Air Force)	10·50	23·00
24		25c. green (Militia)	10·50	23·00
25		30c. brown (Navy)	10·50	46·00
26		30c. brown (Army)	10·50	46·00
27		30c. brown (Air Force)	10·50	46·00
28		30c. brown (Militia)	10·50	46·00
29		50c. violet (Navy)	10·50	23·00
30		50c. violet (Army)	10·50	23·00
31		50c. violet (Air Force)	10·50	23·00
32		50c. violet (Militia)	10·50	23·00

(b) Air. Nos. 270/7.

33	-	25c. green	19·00	60·00
34	**110**	50c. brown	5·25	11·50
35	-	75c. brown	26·00	80·00
36	-	80c. red	65·00	£170
37	-	1l. violet	5·25	11·50
38	**113**	2l. green	£120	£250
39	**110**	5l. green	£110	£350
40	**110**	10l. red	£1400	£3000

REPUBBLICA SOCIALE ITALIANA
(4)   **(5)**

1944. Stamps of Italy. (a) Optd with T **4**.

57		25c. green (No. 244)	50	2·40
60		75c. red (No. 248)	50	3·00

(b) Optd with T **5**.

58	**103**	30c. brown	50	2·40
61	-	1l.25 blue (No. 250)	50	3·00
77	-	50l. violet (No. 259)	£450	£3250

(c) Optd **REPUBBLICA SOCIALE ITALIANA**.

59	**103**	50c. violet	50	2·40

1944. War Propaganda stamps. Nos. 563/74 optd with T **4** (25c.), T **5** (30c.) or **REPUBBLICA SOCIALE ITALIANA** (50c.).

64A		25c. green (Navy)	60	3·50
65A		25c. green (Army)	60	3·50
66A		25c. green (Air Force)	60	3·50
67A		25c. green (Militia)	60	3·50
68A		30c. brown (Navy)	60	7·00
69A		30c. brown (Army)	60	7·00
70A		30c. brown (Air Force)	60	7·00
71A		30c. brown (Militia)	60	7·00
72A		50c. violet (Navy)	60	2·30
73A		50c. violet (Army)	60	2·30
74A		50c. violet (Air Force)	60	2·30
75A		50c. violet (Militia)	60	2·30

Prices are for examples overprinted on the stamp part only; items overprinted twice (on stamp and label) are worth more.

10 Loggia dei Mercanti, Bologna

11 Loggia dei Mercanti, Bologna

12 Basilica de St. Lorenzo, Rome

13 Basilica de St. Lorenzo, Rome

1944. Inscr "REPUBBLICA SOCIALE ITALIANA".

106		5c. brown	25	35
107		10c. brown	25	30
102	**10**	20c. red	30	90

108	11	20c. red	25	30
103	12	25c. green	30	90
109	13	25c. green	25	30
110	-	30c. brown	25	30
111	-	50c. violet	25	30
112	-	75c. red	1·30	9·25
113	-	1l. violet	25	30
114	-	1l.25 blue	65	14·00
115	-	3l. green	65	60·00

DESIGN: 5c. St. Ciriaco's Church, Ancona; 10c., 1l. Montecassino Abbey; 30c., 75c. Drummer; 50c. Fascist allegory; 1l.25, 3l. St. Mary of Grace, Milan.

17 Bandiera Brothers

1944. Death Centenary of Attilio and Emilio Bandiera (revolutionaries).

117	17	25c. green	25	1·20
118	17	1l. violet	25	1·20
119	17	2l.50 red	25	9·25

CONCESSIONAL LETTER POST

Following the surrender of Italy on 3 September 1943, and his rescue from imprisonment on 12 September, Mussolini proclaimed the Italian Social Republic at Salo on 23 September 1943. From this town on Lake Garda the Republican government administered those parts of Italy, north of Gustav Line, which were under German Oeccupation.

1944. Concessional Letter Post stamp of Italy optd as T **5** but smaller.

CL76	**CL109**	10c. brown	30	1·20

EXPRESS LETTER STAMPS

1944. Express stamps of Italy optd **G. N. R.**

E41	**E132**	1l.25 green (postage)	19·00	46·00
E42	**E132**	2l.50 red	£275	£700
E43	**E133**	2l. black (air)	£1100	£1500

REPUBBLICA SOCIALE ITALIANA

(E7)

1944. Express stamps of Italy optd with Type **E7**.

E62	**E132**	1l.25 green	50	90
E63	**E132**	2l.50 orange	50	14·00

E16 Palermo Cathedral

1944

E116	**E16**	1l.25 green	25	1·20

PARCEL POST STAMPS

1944. Parcel Post stamps of Italy optd **REP. SOC. ITALIANA** on left-hand side and Fascist Emblem on right.

P77	**P92**	5c. brown	3·75	40·00
P78	**P92**	10c. blue	3·75	40·00
P79	**P92**	25c. green	3·75	40·00
P80	**P92**	30c. blue	3·75	40·00
P81	**P92**	50c. orange	3·75	40·00
P82	**P92**	60c. red	3·75	£120
P83	**P92**	1l. violet	3·75	40·00
P84	**P92**	2l. green	£375	£1600
P85	**P92**	3l. bistre	7·75	£350
P86	**P92**	4l. black	19·00	£375
P87	**P92**	10l. purple	£170	£1800
P88	**P92**	20l. purple	£450	£2750

The unused and used prices are for unsevered stamps.

POSTAGE DUE STAMPS

1944. Postage Due stamps of Italy optd **G. N. R.**

D44	**D141**	5c. brown	26·00	65·00
D45	**D141**	10c. blue	26·00	65·00
D46	**D141**	20c. red	26·00	40·00
D47	**D141**	25c. green	26·00	40·00
D48	**D141**	30c. orange	26·00	65·00
D49	**D141**	40c. brown	26·00	40·00
D50	**D141**	50c. violet	90·00	£325
D51	**D141**	60c. blue	£500	£1300
D52	**D142**	1l. orange	38·00	46·00
D53	**D142**	2l. green	50·00	90·00
D54	**D142**	5l. violet	£250	£550
D55	**D142**	10l. blue	£150	£375
D56	**D142**	20l. red	£150	£375

1944. Postage Due stamps of Italy optd with small Fascist emblems.

D89	**D141**	5c. brown	2·50	6·00

D90	**D141**	10c. blue	2·50	6·00
D91	**D141**	20c. red	2·50	6·00
D92	**D141**	25c. green	2·50	6·00
D93	**D141**	30c. orange	2·50	10·50
D94	**D141**	40c. brown	2·50	11·50
D95	**D141**	50c. violet	2·50	4·50
D96	**D141**	60c. blue	13·00	23·00
D97	**D142**	1l. orange	2·50	4·50
D98	**D142**	2l. green	6·50	17·00
D99	**D142**	5l. violet	38·00	£130
D100	**D142**	10l. blue	£110	2·50
D101	**D142**	20l. red	£110	£250

Pt. 6, Pt. 13

IVORY COAST

A French colony in W. Africa on the Gulf of Guinea incoporated in French West Africa in 1944. In 1958 it became an autonomous republic within the French Community, and in 1960 it became fully independent.

100 centimes = 1 franc.

1892. "Tablet" key-type inscr "COTE D'IVOIRE" in blue (Nos. 2, 3, 5, 14, 7, 9/11) or red (others).

1	D	1c. black on blue	2·00	3·75
2	D	2c. brown on buff	2·20	2·20
3	D	4c. brown on grey	3·25	3·50
4a	D	5c. green on green	22·00	9·75
5	D	10c. black on lilac	17·00	12·00
6	D	15c. blue	50·00	9·25
7	D	20c. red on green	11·00	17·00
8	D	25c. black on pink	18·00	3·75
9	D	30c. brown on drab	55·00	55·00
10	D	40c. red on yellow	20·00	23·00
11	D	50c. red on pink	55·00	65·00
12	D	75c. brown on yellow	7·75	30·00
13	D	1f. green	60·00	28·00
14	D	10c. red	£110	£120
15	D	15c. grey	4·50	2·75
16	D	25c. blue	38·00	55·00
17	D	50c. brown on blue	17·00	11·00

1904. Surch in figures and bars.

18		0.05 on 30c. brown	80·00	£100
19		0.10 on 75c. brown on yellow	14·00	34·00
20		0.15 on 1f. olive	25·00	36·00

1906. "Faidherbe", "Palms" and "Balay" key-types inscr "COTE D'IVOIRE" in blue (10c., 5f.) or red (others).

22	I	1c. grey	2·50	35
23	I	2c. brown	1·00	90
24	I	4c. brown on blue	55	1·10
25	I	5c. green	3·75	1·20
26	I	10c. pink	7·50	90
27	J	20c. black on blue	5·75	6·00
28	J	25c. blue	3·00	1·80
29	J	30c. brown on pink	11·00	14·50
30	J	35c. black on yellow	7·25	2·30
32	J	45c. brown on green	10·00	13·00
33	J	50c. violet	11·50	17·00
34	J	75c. green on orange	11·00	34·00
35	K	1f. black on blue	34·00	70·00
36	K	2f. blue on pink	50·00	85·00
37	K	5f. red on yellow	80·00	£120

1912. Surch in figures.

38A	D	05 on 15c. grey	1·20	1·50
39A	D	05 on 30c. brown on drab	2·30	8·75
40A	D	10 on 40c. red on yellow	1·10	7·75
41A	D	10 on 50c. brown on blue	2·00	5·50
42A	D	10 on 75c. brown on orange	3·75	13·50

7 River Scene

1913

43	7	1c. violet and purple	20	55
44	7	2c. black and brown	10	1·50
45	7	4c. purple and violet	35	1·70
46	7	5c. green and light green	3·00	1·30
61	7	5c. brown and chocolate	35	80
47	7	10c. pink and red	2·30	2·30
62	7	10c. green and light green	80	2·10
63	7	10c. pink on blue	50	80
48	7	15c. red and orange	1·00	1·20
49	7	20c. grey and black	1·60	1·10
50	7	25c. blue and ultramarine	13·50	4·50
64	7	25c. violet and black	2·50	20
51	7	30c. brown and chocolate	3·25	4·25
65	7	30c. pink and red	3·00	6·50
66	7	30c. red and blue	35	70
67	7	30c. green and olive	1·20	2·30

52	7	35c. orange and violet	2·30	4·50
53	7	40c. green and grey	2·30	1·40
54	7	45c. brown and red	1·70	2·50
68	7	45c. purple and red	8·00	19·00
55	7	50c. violet and black	5·50	5·25
69	7	50c. blue and ultramarine	1·00	2·50
70	7	50c. blue and green	1·50	30
71	7	60c. violet on pink	1·00	6·50
72	7	65c. green and red	2·10	8·25
56	7	75c. pink and brown	2·00	1·00
73	7	75c. ultramarine and blue	8·00	12·00
74	7	85c. black and purple	1·10	9·25
75	7	90c. carmine and red	11·50	46·00
57	7	1f. black and yellow	2·00	35
76	7	1f.10 brown and green	5·75	23·00
77	7	1f.50 blue and light blue	6·50	6·75
78	7	1f.75 mauve and blue	22·00	13·50
58	7	2f. blue and brown	3·50	1·40
79	7	3f. mauve on pink	5·00	2·30
59	7	5f. brown and blue	7·00	6·25

1915. Surch **5c** and red cross.

60		10c.+5c. pink and red	1·40	2·75

1934. Surch with new value twice.

80		50 on 45c. purple and red	6·00	7·00
81		50 on 75c. ultramarine & blue	3·50	3·75
82		50 on 90c. pink and red	3·75	3·75
83		60 on 75c. violet on pink	65	90
84		65 on 15c. red and orange	1·40	7·25
85		85 on 75c. pink and brown	1·40	8·00

1922. Surch in figures and bars.

86		25c. on 2f. blue and brown	1·10	7·50
87		25c. on 5f. brown and blue	65	7·75
88		90c. on 75c. pink and red	85	4·50
89		1f.25 on 1f. ultram & blue	30	5·50
90		1f.50 on 1f. blue & light blue	1·40	1·70
91		3f. on 5f. green and red	3·25	6·00
92		10f. on 5f. mauve and blue	8·25	38·00
93		20f. on 5f. red and green	11·00	55·00

1931. "Colonial Exhibition" key-types inscr "COTE D'IVOIRE".

94	E	40c. black and green	2·50	6·00
95	F	50c. black and mauve	3·75	8·75
96	G	90c. black and red	1·80	5·25
97	H	1f.50 black and blue	6·00	18·00

1933. Stamps of Upper Volta optd **Cote d'Ivoire** or surch also.

98	3	2c. brown and violet	35	3·25
99	3	4c. black and yellow	70	3·00
100	3	5c. indigo and blue	1·50	7·00
101	3	10c. blue and pink	2·30	2·30
102	3	15c. brown and blue	1·40	7·25
103	3	20c. brown and green	2·50	3·00
104	-	25c. brown and yellow	2·30	3·25
105	-	30c. deep green and green	2·40	3·75
106	-	45c. brown and blue	10·50	14·00
107	-	65c. indigo and blue	3·50	11·00
108	-	75c. black and violet	3·25	4·75
109	-	90c. red and mauve	3·00	6·50
110	6	1f. brown and green	2·75	4·25
111		1f.25 on 40c. black and pink	90	1·20
112	6	1f.50 ultramarine and blue	2·00	1·60
113		1f.75 on 50c. black & green	3·25	1·20

12 Baoule Woman

1936

114	12	1c. red	30	3·25
115	12	2c. blue	55	3·50
116	12	3c. green	90	6·25
117	12	4c. brown	70	2·75
118	12	5c. violet	75	1·80
119	12	10c. blue	35	1·60
120	12	15c. red	55	55
121	-	20c. blue	70	1·30
122	-	25c. red	65	85
123	-	30c. green	1·70	3·25
124	-	30c. brown	30	5·75
125	12	35c. green	2·30	4·75
126	-	40c. red	35	65
127	-	45c. brown	1·60	4·25
128	-	45c. green	2·00	7·75
129	-	50c. purple	55	20
130	-	55c. violet	1·80	5·00

131	-	60c. red	2·30	6·25
132	-	65c. brown	1·90	2·50
133	-	70c. brown	1·50	5·75
134	-	75c. violet	1·90	1·70
135	-	80c. brown	1·20	3·25
136	-	90c. red	7·00	16·00
137	-	90c. green	1·00	3·25
138	-	1f. green	3·25	65
139	-	1f. red	3·25	2·50
140	-	1f. violet	1·70	4·00
141	-	1f.25 red	1·70	1·80
142	-	1f.40 blue	1·70	6·25
143	-	1f.50 blue	1·50	5·00
144	-	1f.50 grey	4·50	7·25
145	-	1f.60 brown	1·20	5·75
146	-	1f.75 red	2·50	3·00
147	-	1f.75 blue	2·50	5·00
148	-	2f. blue	1·00	30
149	-	2f.50 blue	1·90	5·00
150	-	2f.50 red	2·00	2·50
151	-	3f. green	1·30	55
152	-	5f. brown	1·10	75
153	-	10f. violet	1·70	85
154	-	20f. red	3·25	3·25

DESIGNS—HORIZ: 20c. to 30c. and 40c. to 55c. Mosque at Bobo-Dioulasso; 60c. to 1f.60, Coastal scene. VERT: 1f.75, to 20f. Comoe Rapids.

12a Commerce

1937. International Exhibition, Paris.

155	**12a**	20c. violet	1·50	5·25
156	**12a**	30c. green	90	5·00
157	**12a**	40c. red	1·00	3·75
158	**12a**	50c. brown and blue	75	5·00
159	**12a**	90c. red	90	2·75
160	**12a**	1f.50 blue	1·60	3·00
MS160a	120×100 mm. 3f. brown (as T **4**)		7·25	50·00

16 General Binger

1937. 50th Anniv of Gen. Binger's Exploration.

161	**16**	65c. brown	45	55

16a Pierra and Marie Curie

1938. International Anti-cancer Fund.

162	**16a**	1f.75+50c. blue	3·75	17·00

16b

1939. Death Centenary of Rene Caillie (explorer).

163		90c. orange	65	1·50
164	**16b**	2f. violet	90	1·60
165	**16b**	2f.25 blue	1·00	2·30

16c

1939. New York World's Fair.

166	**16c**	1f.25 red	1·40	4·00
167	**16c**	2f.25 blue	1·50	4·25

16d Storming the Bastille

1939. 150th Anniv of French Revolution.

168	**16d**	45c.+25c. green and black	7·25	14·50

169	**16d**	70c.+30c. brown and black	7·25	14·50
170	**16d**	90c.+35c. orange and black	7·25	14·50
171	**16d**	1f.25+1f. red and black	7·25	14·50
172	**16d**	2f.25+2f. blue and black	7·25	14·50

1940. Air.

173	**16e**	1f.90 blue	50	3·50
174	**16e**	2f.90 red	1·10	5·00
175	**16e**	4f.50 green	75	1·50
176	**16e**	4f.90 olive	85	3·75
177	**16e**	6f.90 orange	1·00	2·75

16e Twin-engine Airliner over Jungle

1941. National Defence Fund. Surch **SECOURS NATIONAL** and value.

178		+1f. on 50c. (No. 129)	3·50	5·75
178a		+2f. on 80c. (No. 135)	18·00	40·00
178b		+2f. on 1f.50 (No. 143)	19·00	44·00
178c		+3f. on 2f. (No. 148)	21·00	40·00

16f Pirogue

1942. Marshal Petain issue.

178d	**16f**	1f. green	75	2·40
178e	**16f**	2f.50 blue	75	3·00

16g Weighting Baby

1942. Air. Colonial Child Welfare Fund.

178f	–	1f.50+3f.50 green	75	3·75
178g	–	2f.+6f. brown	75	4·50
178h	**16g**	3f.+9f. red	75	4·00

DESIGNS: 49×28 mm. 1f.50. Maternity Hospital; 2f. Dispensary.

1942. Air Imperial Fortnight.

178i	**16h**	1f.20+1f.80 blue and red	65	4·50

16h "Vocation"

1942. Air. As T **27** of French Sudan, but inscr "COTE D'IVOIRE".

179		50f. olive and green	2·30	4·00

REPUBLIC

17 African Elephant

1959

180	**17**	10f. black and green	2·75	1·20
181	**17**	25f. brown and bistre	1·10	35
182	**17**	30f. olive and turquoise	1·90	2·30

18 Place Lapalud, Abidjan

1959. Air.

183	**18**	100f. brown, green & choc	4·00	1·40
184	–	200f. brown, myrtle & turq	9·25	5·00

185	–	500f. turquoise, brn & grn	9·50	5·25

DESIGNS: 200f. Houphouet-Boigny railway bridge, Abidjan; 500f. Ayame Barrage.

19 Pres. Houphouet-Boigny

1959. First Anniv of Republic.

186	**19**	25f. brown	2·00	1·20

20 Bete Mask

1960. Native Masks.

187	**20**	50c. chocolate and brown	25	4·00
188	–	1f. violet and red	90	2·50
189	–	2f. green and blue	90	2·30
190	–	4f. red and green	1·20	2·75
191	–	5f. brown and red	1·30	1·30
192	–	6f. blue and purple	1·40	2·50
193	–	45f. purple and green	2·75	1·60
194	–	50f. blue and brown	3·25	1·30
195	–	85f. green and red	4·75	3·25

DESIGNS—VERT: MASKS OF: 1f. Guere; 2f. Guere (different type); 45f. Bete (different type); 50f. Gouro; 85f. Gouro (different type). HORIZ: 4f. Baole; 5f. Senoufo; 6f. Senoufo (different type).

1960. Tenth Anniv of African Technical Co-operation Commission. As T **4** of Malagasy.

196		25f. violet and turquoise	2·30	1·70

21 Conseil de l'Entente Emblem

1960. First Anniv of Conseil de l'Entente.

197	**21**	25f. multicoloured	1·50	2·50

21a "World Peace"

1961. First Anniv of Independence.

198	**21a**	25f. black, green & brown	85	50

22 *Thoningia sanguigna*

1961

199	–	5f. red, yellow and green	85	30
200	–	10f. yellow, red and blue	50	30
201	–	15f. purple, green & orange	1·60	50
202	**22**	20f. yellow, red and brown	90	50
203	–	25f. yellow, red and green	90	50
204	–	30f. red, green and black	1·10	75
205	–	70f. yellow, red and green	3·25	1·60
206	–	85f. multicoloured	4·75	1·90

FLOWERS: 5f. *Plumeria rubra*; 10f. *Haemanthus cinnabarinus*; 15f. *Bougainvillea spectabilis*; 25f. *Eulophia cucullata*; 30f. *Newbouldia laevis*; 70f. *Mussaenda erythrophylla*; 85f. *Strophantus sarmentosus*.

---

23 Mail-carriers

1961. Stamp Day.

207	**23**	25f. brown, blue and green	85	65

24 Ayame Dam

1961

208	**24**	25f. sepia, blue and green	85	50

25 Swimming

1961. Abidjan Games. Inscr as in T **25**.

209	**25**	5f. sepia, green and blue (postage)	35	10
210	–	20f. brown, green and grey	50	30
211	–	25f. brown, green and blue	85	50
211a	–	100f. blk, red & bl (air)	4·00	2·10

DESIGNS: 20f. Basketball; 25f. Football; 100f. High-jumping.

26 Palms

1962. 17th Session of African Technical Co-operation Commission, Abidjan.

212	**26**	25f. multicoloured	85	50

1962. Air. "Air Afrique" Airline. As T **32** of Mauritania.

213		50f. blue, brown and chestnut	1·60	90

1962. Malaria Eradication. As T **11a** Malagasy Republic.

214		25f.+5f. green	1·00	1·00

27 Fort Assinie

1962. Postal Centenary.

215	**27**	85f. multicoloured	2·50	1·50

28 Village, Man Region

1962. Air.

216	–	200f. sepia, purple & green	6·25	2·75
217	**28**	500f. green, purple & black	11·00	5·00

DESIGN—VERT: 200f. Street Scene, Odienne.

28a

1962. First Anniv of Union of African and Malagasy.

218	**28a**	30f. red	1·10	95

29 U.N. Headquarters and Emblem

1962. Air. Second Anniv of Admission to U.N.

219	**29**	100f. multicoloured	2·40	1·30

30 Bouake Arms and Cotton Exhibit

1963. Bouake Fair.

220	**30**	50f. sepia, brown and green	90	50

30a

1963. Freedom from Hunger.

221	**30a**	25f.+5f. violet, brown & pur	1·30	1·30

31 Map of Africa

1963. Conference of African Heads of State, Addis Ababa.

222	**31**	30f. green and blue	1·10	95

32 Sassandra Bay

1963. Air.

223	–	50f. green, brown and blue	1·70	60
224	**32**	100f. brown, blue & myrtle	2·75	1·40
225	–	200f. turquoise, grn & brn	5·00	2·40

DESIGNS: 50f. Moosou Bridge; 200f. River Comoe.

1963. Air. African and Malagasian Posts and Telecommunications Union. As T **20a** of Malagasy Republic.

226		85f. multicoloured	1·90	1·30

33 Hartebeest

1963. "Tourism and Hunting".

227	–	1f. multicoloured	50	10
228	–	2f. multicoloured	50	30
229	–	4f. multicoloured	45	35
230	–	5f. multicoloured	45	35
247	–	5f. green, yellow and brown	70	30
231	**33**	10f. brown, green and grey	70	30
248	–	10f. brown, green & purple	1·80	50
232	–	15f. black, green and brown	1·00	50
249	–	15f. brown, green & purple	2·75	50
233	–	20f. brown, green and red	1·40	50
234	–	25f. brown, green & yellow	1·90	75
235	–	45f. purple, green & turq	4·00	1·60
236	–	85f. brown and brown	5·50	2·10
MS236a		170×100 mm. Nos. 231, 233 and 235/6	27·00	26·00

DESIGNS—HORIZ: 1f. Yellow-backed duiker; 4f. Beecroft's hyrax; 5f. (No. 247) African manatee; 10f. (No. 248) Pygmy hippopotamus; 15f. (No. 232) Giant forest hog; 20f. Warthog; 45f. Hunting dogs. VERT: 2f. Potto; 5f. (No. 230) Water chevrotain; 15f. (No. 249) Royal antelope; 25f. Bongo; 50f. Western black and white colobus.

1963. Air. First Anniv of "Air Afrique" and "DC-8" Service Inauguration. As T **87** of Mauritania.

237		25f. multicoloured	85	35

34 Scales of
Justice, Globe
and UNESCO
Emblem

1963. 15th Anniv of Declaration of Human Rights.
238 **34** 85f. black, blue and
orange   1·70   90

35 Rameses II and
Nefertari, Abu
Simbel

1964. Air. Nubian Monuments Preservation.
239 **35** 60f. black, brown
and red   2·30   1·30

36 Map of
Africa

1964. Inter-African National Education Ministers'
Conference, Abidjan.
240 **36** 30f. red, green and blue   85   50

37 Weather
Balloon

1964. World Meteorological Day.
241 **37** 25f. multicoloured   95   60

38 Doctor
tending Child

1964. National Red Cross Society.
242 **38** 50f. multicoloured   1·50   70

39 Arms of the Ivory Coast

1964. Air.
243 **39** 200f. gold, blue and
green   4·25   1·80

40 Globe and
Athletes

1964. Olympic Games, Tokyo.
244 **40** 35f. brown, green and
violet   1·40   65
245   -   65f. ochre, brown and
blue   2·50   1·30
DESIGN—HORIZ: 65f. Wrestling and Globe.

41 Symbolic Tree

1964. First Anniv of European–African Convention.
246 **41** 30f. multicoloured   1·00   45

41a
"Co-operation"

1964. French, African and Malagasy Co-operation.
250 **41a** 25f. brown, red and
green   85   45

42 Pres. Kennedy

1964. Air. Pres. Kennedy Commemoration.
251 **42** 100f. brown and grey   2·75   2·00

43 Korhogo Mail-carriers,
1914

1964. Stamp Day.
252 **43** 85f. sepia, brown and
blue   2·40   1·40

44 Pottery

1965. Native Handicrafts.
253 **44** 5f. black, red and green   35   20
254   -   10f. black, purple and
green   45   25
255   -   20f. blue, chocolate
& brn   80   30
256   -   25f. brown, red and olive   85   50
DESIGNS: 10f. Wood-carving; 20f. Ivory-carving; 25f. Weaving.

45 Mail coming ashore

1965. Stamp Day.
257 **45** 30f. multicoloured   1·00   70

46 I.T.U. Emblem and
Symbols

1965. I.T.U. Centenary.
258 **46** 85f. blue, red and green 1·90   1·30

47 Abidjan Railway
Station

1965.
259 **47** 30f. multicoloured   1·20   70

48 Pres. Houphouet-
Boigny and Map

1965. Fifth Anniv of Independence.
260 **48** 30f. multicoloured   85   50

49 Hammerkop

1965. Birds.
261   -   1f. green, yellow and
violet   55   20
262   -   2f. multicoloured   60   25
263   -   5f. purple, red and olive   85   50
264 **49** 10f. brown, black &
purple   85   30
265   -   15f. red, grey and green   1·10   35
266   -   30f. brown, green and
lake   1·60   65
267   -   50f. blue, black and
brown   3·00   1·00
268   -   75f. red, green and
orange   5·50   1·80
269   -   90f. multicoloured   6·00   3·25
BIRDS—HORIZ: 1f. Yellow-bellied green pigeon; 2f. Spur-
winged goose; 30f. Namaqua dove; 50f. Lizard buzzard.
VERT: 5f. Stone partridge; 15f. White-breasted guineafowl;
75f. Yellow-billed stork; 90f. Latham's francolin.

50 Lieupleu Rope-bridge

1965. Air.
270 **50** 100f. brown, green &
lt grn   2·75   1·60
271   -   300f. purple, flesh and
blue   7·25   3·75
DESIGN: 300f. Street in Kong.

51 Steam Mail Train, 1906

1966. Stamp Day.
272 **51** 30f. green, black and
purple   2·50   1·20

52 "Maternity"

1966. World Festival of Negro Arts, Dakar.
273 **52** 5f. black and green   35   20
274   -   10f. black and violet   50   30
275   -   20f. black and orange   1·60   80
276   -   30f. black and red   2·00   1·00
DESIGNS—CARVED WORK: 10f. Pomade box; 20f. Drums;
30f. "Ancestor".

53 Ivory Hotel

1966. Inauguration of Ivory Hotel.
277 **53** 15f. multicoloured   65   35

54 Tractor Cultivation

1966. Sixth Anniv of Independence.
278 **54** 30f. multicoloured   85   55

54a

1966. Air. Inauguration of Douglas DC-8F Air Services.
279 **54a** 30f. grey, black and
green   85   50

55 Open-air Class

1966. National School of Administration.
280 **55** 30f. black, blue and lake 85   50

56 Inoculating Cattle

1966. Campaign for Prevention of Cattle Plague.
281 **56** 30f. brown, green and
blue   1·00   60

57 UNESCO.
"Waves"
enveloping
"Man"

1966. 20th Anniv of UNESCO.
282 **57** 30f. violet and blue   85   55
283   -   30f. black, brown and
blue   85   55
DESIGN: No. 283, Distributing food parcels to children.

58 Bouake Hospital

1966.
284 **58** 30f. multicoloured   85   55

59 "Air Afrique"
Headquarters

1966. Air.
285 **59** 500f. blue, ochre and
green   10·50   4·75

60 Sikorsky S-43 Amphibian (30th anniv)

1967. Stamp Day.
286	**60**	30f. blue, brown & turq	2·75	1·30

61 Cutting Pineapples

1967. Fruits.
287	**61**	20f. purple, brown & green	50	40
288	–	30f. red, brown and green	70	50
289	–	100f. brown, olive and blue	3·00	1·20

DESIGNS: 30f. Cutting palm-nuts; 100f. Cutting bananas.

62 "African Mythology"

1967. 35th Pen Club Int Congress, Abidjan.
290	**62**	30f. black, green and lake	85	55

63 "Improvement of Rural Housing"

1967. Seventh Anniv of Independence.
291	**63**	30f. multicoloured	85	40

64 Lions Emblems

1967. 50th Anniv of Lions International.
292	**64**	30f. multicoloured	1·10	65

64a

1967. Air. Fifth Anniv of U.A.M.P.T.
293	**64a**	100f. red, blue and violet	2·75	1·30

64b

1967. Fifth Anniv of West African Monetary Union.
294	**64b**	30f. black, green and mauve	65	35

65 African Man and Woman

1967. 20th Anniv of Recognition Days.
295	**65**	90f. multicoloured	1·90	90

See also No. 342.

66 Senoufo Village

1968. Air.
296	**66**	100f. brown, yellow & green	2·75	1·20
297	–	500f. brown, blue and green	10·50	4·25

DESIGN: 500f. Tiegba lake village.

67 Tabou Radio Station, 1912

1968. Stamp Day.
298	**67**	30f. green, brown & turq	1·00	55

68 Cotton Loom

1968. Industries.
299	**68**	5f. black, red and green	35	10
300	**68**	10f. brown, green and slate	60	10
301	–	15f. black, blue and red	1·30	70
302	–	20f. blue and purple	95	55
303	–	30f. brown, green and blue	95	70
304	–	50f. black, green and mauve	1·60	90
305	–	70f. chocolate, blue & brn	2·10	1·10
306	–	90f. black, purple and blue	2·75	1·60

DESIGNS—HORIZ: 5f. Palm-oil works; 30f. Flour mills; 50f. Cocoa-butter extraction machine; 90f. Timber sawmill and logs. VERT: 15f. Oil refinery, Abidjan; 20f. Raw cotton and reeling machine; 70f. Soluble-coffee plant.
See also Nos. 335/7.

69 Canoeing

1968. Olympic Games, Mexico.
307	**69**	30f. brown, blue and green	90	45
308	–	100f. purple, ultram & blue	2·40	95

DESIGN: 100f. 100 m sprint.

70 Sacrificial Offering

1968. Eighth Anniv of Independence.
309	**70**	30f. multicoloured	85	40

71 Doctor inoculating Patient

1968. 20th Anniv of W.H.O.
310	**71**	30f. chocolate, brown & bl	85	50

72 Impala in Forest

1968. Fauna and Flora Protection.
311	**72**	30f. brown, green and blue	3·50	1·10

73 Museum and Carved Screen

1968. Opening of Abidjan Museum.
312	**73**	30f. brown, red and blue	85	40

74 Human Rights Emblem and "Justice" Totems

1968. Human Rights Year.
313	**74**	30f. orange, purple and blue	85	40

74a Grand Bassam (Achalme)

1969. Air. "Philexafrique" Stamp Exhibition, Abidjan, Ivory Coast (1st issue).
314	**74a**	100f. multicoloured	4·75	4·75

74b Aerial View of San Pedro village and stamp of 1936

1969. Air. "Philexafrique" Stamp Exn, Abidjan, Ivory Coast (2nd issue).
315	**74b**	50f. red, blue and green	2·75	2·75
316	–	100f. blue, brown and orange	4·25	4·25
317	–	200f. slate, blue and brown	6·00	6·00
MS318	161×100 mm. Nos. 315/17		16·00	16·00

DESIGNS—HORIZ: 200f. Chambers of Agriculture and Industry building, Abidjan, and 5f. stamp of 1913. VERT: 100f. Chief's costume and 5f. stamp of 1936.

75 Ville de Maranhao (mail steamer) at Grand-Bassam

1969. Stamp Day.
319	**75**	30f. purple, blue and green	1·30	60

76 Ivory Hotel

1969. Opening of Ivory Hotel.
320	**76**	30f. blue, red and green	1·00	50

77 Man on Horseback (statuette)

1969. Ivory Coast Art Exn, Vevey, Switzerland.
321	**77**	30f. black, purple and red	1·00	65

78 Hertzian-wave Radio Station, Man

1969. Ninth Anniv of Independence.
322	**78**	30f. green, brown and blue	1·00	50

79 Bank Emblem

1969. Fifth Anniv of African Development Bank.
323	**79**	30f. brown, green and lake	60	40

80 Arms of Bouake

1969. Coats of Arms.
324	**80**	10f. multicoloured	35	10
325	–	15f. multicoloured	40	20
326	–	30f. black, gold and green	60	20

ARMS: 15f. Abidjan; 30f. Ivory Coast Republic. See also Nos. 402/3 and 432/6.

81 Game Fishing

1969. Int SKAL Tourist Assn Congress, Abidjan.
327	**81**	30f. blue, purple and violet	2·75	55
328	–	100f. multicoloured	3·50	1·40

DESIGN: 100f. Assinie Holiday Village.

81a

1969. Tenth Anniv of Aerial Navigation Security Agency for Africa and Madagascar (A.S.E.C.N.A.).
329	**81a**	30f. red	80	45

82 Man Waterfall

1970. Air.
330	**82**	100f. blue, green and brown	3·00	1·30
331	–	200f. red, green and emerald	3·75	1·60

DESIGN: 200f. Mt. Niangbo.

83 University Hospital Centre, Abidjan

1970. "Ten Years of Higher Education".
332	**83**	30f. indigo, green and blue	80	50

84 Telegraphist and Gabriel Dadie (Postal administrator)

1970. Stamp Day.
333 **84** 30f. black, green and red 60 40

85 Abidjan University

1970. Third A.U.P.E.L.F. (Association of French Speaking Universities). General Assembly, Abidjan.
334 **85** 30f. purple, green and blue 80 50

86 Safety-match Manufacture

1970. Industrial Expansion.
335 **86** 5f. brown, blue & chocolate 35 30
336 - 20f. red, green and grey 50 30
337 - 50f. brown, blue and green 1·30 40
DESIGNS: 20f. Textile-printing; 50f. Ship-building.

87 Dish Aerial and Television Class

1970. World Telecommunications Day.
338 **87** 40f. green, drab and red 1·00 55

87a

1970. New U.P.U. Headquarters Building, Berne.
339 **87a** 30f. brown, green and purple 1·00 50

88 Wild Life

1970. 25th Anniv of United Nations.
340 **88** 30f. brown, green and blue 2·75 1·30

89 Coffee Plant

1970. Tenth Anniv of Independence (1st issue).
341 **89** 30f. green, brown & orange 1·00 50
See also Nos. 344/9.

90 African Man and Woman

1970. Fifth P.D.C.I. (Ivory Coast Democratic Party) Congress.
342 **90** 40f. multicoloured 1·00 50

91 Power Station

1970. Thermal Power Plant, Vridi.
343 **91** 40f. brown, blue and green 1·60 45

92 Pres. Houphouet-Boigny and De Gaulle

1970. Tenth Anniv of Independence (2nd issue). Embossed on silver (300f. values) or gold foil.
344 300f. Type **92** (postage) 16·00 16·00
345 300f. Ivory Coast Arms 13·00 13·00
346 1000f. Type **92** 46·00 47·00
347 1000f. As No. 345 44·00 44·00
348 300f. Pres. Houphouet-Boigny and African elephants (air) 13·00 13·00
349 1200f. As No. 348 44·00 44·00

93 Mail Bus, 1925

1971. Stamp Day.
350 **93** 40f. purple, green & brown 1·80 50

94 Port of San Pedro

1971. Air.
351 **94** 100f. red, blue and green 1·90 80
352 - 500f. green, blue and brown 10·50 5·00
DESIGN: 500f. African Riviera coastline.

95 Desjardin's Marginella

1971. Marine Life.
353 1f. brown, blue and green 45 10
354 5f. red, lilac and blue 55 35
355 10f. red, blue and green 80 30
356 **95** 15f. brown, purple and blue 95 35
357 - 15f. brown, violet and red 1·30 40
358 - 20f. red and yellow 1·60 45
359 - 20f. lake, purple and red 1·90 65
360 - 25f. brown, black and lake 1·10 25
361 - 35f. red, yellow and green 2·30 80
362 - 40f. brown, blue and green 3·75 1·30
363 - 40f. red, turquoise & brown 2·50 75
364 - 45f. brown, green & emer 4·50 1·70
365 - 50f. green, red and violet 4·50 1·30
366 - 65f. blue, green and brown 3·25 1·60
DESIGNS—HORIZ: 1f. African pelican's-foot; 5f. Neptunus validus; 20f. (No. 359) Digitate carrier shell; 25f. Butterfly cone; 40f. (No. 362) Garter cone; 45f. Bubonion conch; 65f. Rat cowrie. VERT: 10f. Hermodice carunculata; 15f. (No. 357) Fanel moon; 20f. (No. 358) Goniaster cuspidatus; 35f. Polycheles typhiops; 40f. (No. 363) African fan scallop; 50f. Enoplometopus callistas.

96 Telegraph Station, Grand Bassam, 1891

1971. World Telecommunications Day.
367 **96** 100f. brown, green and blue 1·90 85

97 Treichville Swimming Pool

1971. Air.
368 **97** 100f. multicoloured 2·75 95

98 Tool-making

1971. Technical Training and Instruction.
369 **98** 35f. blue, red and green 80 45

99 African Telecommunications Map

1971. Pan-African Telecommunications Network.
370 **99** 45f. yellow, red and purple 80 45

100 Bondoukou Market

1971. 11th Anniv of Independence.
371 **100** 35f. brown, blue and grey (postage) 85 50
372 - 200f. black and blue on gold (air) 4·00 2·20
No. 372 has a similar design to Type **100** but in smaller format, size 38×27 mm.

101 Children of Three Races

1971. Racial Equality Year. Multicoloured.
373 40f. Type **101** 80 30
374 45f. Children around Globe 80 30

101a Headquarters and Ivory Coast Arms

1971. Tenth Anniv of U.A.M.P.T.
375 **101a** 100f. multicoloured 1·90 90
U.A.M.P.T. = African and Malagasy Posts and Telecommunications Union.

102 Gaming Table

1971. National Lottery.
376 **102** 35f. multicoloured 1·00 40

103 Technicians working on Power Cables

1971. Electricity Works Centre, Akovai-Santai.
377 **103** 35f. multicoloured 1·50 55

104 Lion of St. Mark's

1972. Air. UNESCO. "Save Venice" Campaign. Multicoloured.
378 100f. Type **104** 3·00 1·40
379 200f. St. Mark's Square 5·25 2·75

105 Cogwheel and Students

1972. Technical Instruction Week.
380 **105** 35f. blue, brown and red 60 45

106 Heart Emblem

1972. World Heart Month.
381 **106** 40f. blue, red and green 80 45

107 Child learning to write

1972. International Book Year.
382 - 35f. brown, orange & grn 60 25
383 **107** 40f. black, orange & green 85 45
DESIGN—HORIZ: 35f. Students and open book.

108 Gouessesso Tourist Village

1972. Air.
384 **108** 100f. brown, green & blue 2·75 1·20
385 - 200f. green, brown & blue 4·00 1·60
386 - 500f. brown, bistre & blue 9·75 5·00
DESIGNS: 200f. Jacqueville Lake; 500f. Mosque of Kawara.

109 Regional Postal Training Centre, Abidjan

1972. Stamp Day.
387 **109** 40f. bistre, green & purple 1·00 50

110 Aerial Mast, Abobo Hertzian Centre

1972. World Telecommunications Day.
388 **110** 40f. red, blue and green 1·40 50

112 Computer Operator

1972. Development of Information Services.
| 393 | 112 | 40f. blue, brown and green | 1·40 | 50 |

113 Odienne

1972. 12th Anniv of Independence.
| 394 | 113 | 35f. brown, green and blue | 80 | 50 |

114 Africans and 500f. Coin

1972. Tenth Anniv of West African Monetary Union.
| 395 | 114 | 40f. grey, purple and brown | 80 | 45 |

115 Diamond and Mine

1972. Development of the Diamond Industry.
| 396 | 115 | 40f. blue, grey and brown | 3·00 | 1·40 |

116 Lake-dwellings, Bletankoro

1972. Air.
| 397 | 116 | 200f. purple, green & blue | 3·75 | 1·70 |
| 398 | - | 500f. brown, green & blue | 10·00 | 5·00 |

DESIGN: 500f. Kossou Dam.

117 Louis Pasteur and Institute

1972. Inauguration of Pasteur Institute, Abidjan.
| 399 | 117 | 35f. blue, green and brown | 1·00 | 50 |

118 Satellite Earth Station

1972. Air. Opening of Satellite Earth Station, Akakro.
| 400 | 118 | 200f. brown, green & blue | 4·00 | 1·60 |

119 Child pumping Water

1972. "Conserve Water" Campaign.
| 401 | 119 | 35f. black, green and red | 1·00 | 45 |

See also No. 414.

1973. Coats of Arms. As T **80**. Multicoloured.
| 402 | | 5f. Arms of Daloa | 40 | 10 |
| 403 | | 10f. Arms of Gagnoa | 40 | 10 |

See also Nos. 432/6.

120 Dr. G. A. Hansen

1973. Centenary of Hansen's Identification of Leprosy Bacillus.
| 404 | 120 | 35f. brown, blue & purple | 1·00 | 45 |

121 Pearly Razorfish

1973. Fish.
405	-	15f. blue and green	1·20	60
406	-	20f. red and brown	2·20	75
406a	-	25f. red and green	3·25	80
406b	-	35f. red and green	2·50	1·10
407	121	50f. red, blue and black	3·75	1·40

FISHES: 15f. Grey triggerfish; 20f. West African goatfish; 25f. African hind; 35f. Bigeye.

122 Child and Emblem

1973. Establishment of first S.O.S. Children's Village in Africa.
| 408 | 122 | 40f. black, red and green | 1·00 | 60 |

123 National Assembly Building

1973. 112th Interparliamentary Council Session, Abidjan.
| 409 | 123 | 100f. multicoloured | 1·10 | 50 |

124 Classroom and Shop

1973. "Commercial Action" Programme.
| 410 | 124 | 40f. multicoloured | 60 | 25 |

125 "Women's Work"

1973. Technical Instruction for Women.
| 411 | 125 | 35f. multicoloured | 80 | 45 |

126 Scouts helping with Food Cultivation

1973. 24th World Scouting Congress, Nairobi, Kenya.
| 412 | 126 | 40f. multicoloured | 1·00 | 50 |

127 Party Headquarters

1973. New Party Headquarters Building, Yamoussokro.
| 413 | 127 | 35f. multicoloured | 60 | 30 |

128 Children at Dry Pump

1973. Pan-African Drought Relief.
| 414 | 128 | 40f. sepia, brown and red | 1·00 | 40 |

129 The Judgment of Solomon (Nandjui Legue)

1973. Air. Sixth World Peace and Justice Conf.
| 415 | 129 | 500f. multicoloured | 12·00 | 5·00 |

129a

1973. U.A.M.P.T.
| 416 | 129a | 100f. black, red and violet | 1·80 | 80 |

130 "Arrow-heads"

1973. Abidjan Museum.
| 417 | 130 | 5f. black, red and brown | 40 | 20 |

131 Ivory Coast 1c. Stamp of 1892

1973. Stamp and Post Day.
| 418 | 131 | 40f. black, orange & green | 1·00 | 50 |

132 Motorway Junction

1973. Motorway Projects. Indenie Interchange, Abidjan.
| 419 | 132 | 35f. black, green and blue | 80 | 45 |

133 Map of Africa and Emblem

1973. 18th General Assembly of International Social Security Association.
| 420 | 133 | 40f. brown, ultram & bl | 60 | 25 |

134 "Elephants" Ticket

1973. Travel-Agents Assns' Seventh World Congress.
| 421 | 134 | 40f. multicoloured | 60 | 25 |

136 Kong Mosque

1974
| 426 | 136 | 35f. brown, blue and green | 80 | 50 |

137 Grand-Lahou Post Office

1974. Stamp Day.
| 427 | 137 | 35f. brown, green and blue | 80 | 50 |

138 Converging Columns

1974. "Formation Permanente".
| 428 | 138 | 35f. multicoloured | 60 | 30 |

139 Sassandra Bridge

1974. Air.
| 429 | 139 | 100f. brown and green | 1·80 | 80 |
| 430 | 139 | 500f. black and green | 11·00 | 3·75 |

140 Map of Member Countries

1974. 15th Anniv of Conseil de l'Entente.
| 431 | 140 | 40f. multicoloured | 60 | 25 |

141 Arms of Ivory Coast

1974
432	141	35f. gold, green and brown	65	10
433	141	40f. gold, green and blue	75	10
434	141	60f. gold, green and red	80	25
435	141	65f. gold, lt green & green	80	25
436	141	70f. gold, green and blue	1·00	35

142 View of Factory

1974. Air. Vridi Soap Factory, Abidjan.
| 437 | 142 | 200f. multicoloured | 3·00 | 1·50 |

143 Pres. Houphouet-Boigny

1974
| 438 | 143 | 25f. brown, orange & grn | 50 | 25 |

144 W.P.Y. Emblem

1974. World Population Year.
| 439 | 144 | 40f. blue and green | 80 | 25 |

145
Cotton-picking

1974. Cotton Production (1st series).
440	145	50f. multicoloured	1·00	50

See also Nos. 456/7.

146 Pres.
Houphouet-
Boigny

1974
889	146	5f. brown, mauve and red	10	10
890	146	10f. brown, blue and green	10	10
891	146	20f. lt brown, brown & red	10	10
892	146	25f. brown, mauve & blue	30	10
893	146	30f. lt brown, brown & red	30	10
441	146	35f. brown, green & orge	70	10
894	146	40f. brown, orange & grn	35	10
895	146	50f. brown, purple and red	45	10
443	146	60f. brown, red and blue	80	35
444	146	65f. brown, blue and red	80	35
896	146	90f. brown, red and purple	75	25
897	146	125f. brown, red & purple	1·20	25
898	146	155f. brown, blue and lilac	1·20	55

147 U.P.U. Emblem   **148** Flag and
U.P.U. Emblems

1974. Centenary of U.P.U.
445	147	40f. green, blue and brown (postage)	75	25
446	148	200f. multicoloured (air)	4·25	2·30
447	148	300f. multicoloured	5·25	3·25

149 Raoul
Follereau

1974. Follereau (leprosy pioneer) Commem.
448	149	35f. red, yellow and green	1·70	70

150 Civic Service Emblem

1974. 14th Anniv of Independence.
449	150	35f. multicoloured	60	25

151 Library Building and
Students

1975. First Anniv of Inauguration of National Library.
450	151	40f. multicoloured	60	25

153 Coffee Flower

1975. 52nd International Seedcrushers Association
Congress, Abidjan.
451	152	40f. black and green	60	25

152 Congress
Emblem

1975. Coffee Production. Multicoloured.
452		5f. Type **153**	30	10
453		10f. Coffee-berries	50	25

154 Sassandra Wharf

1975
454	154	100f. brown, green & blue	2·00	1·20

155 Postal Sorters

1975. Stamp Day.
455	155	40f. multicoloured	1·00	50

156 Cotton Flower

1975. Cotton Production (2nd series). Multicoloured.
456		5f. Type **156**	35	35
457		10f. Cotton bolls	60	35

157 Marie Kore and I.W.Y. Emblem

1975. International Women's Year.
458	157	45f. brown, blue and green	80	35

158 Dabou Fort

1975
459	158	50f. violet, blue and green	80	50

159 Abidjan Harbour

1975. 25th Anniv of Abidjan Port. Multicoloured.
460		35f. Type **159**	1·00	50

MS461 151×100 mm. 35f. Type **159**;
40f. Grand-Bassam wharf (vert); 100f.
Proposed Locodjiro extension   8·75   8·75

160 Cocoa Tree

1975
462	160	35f. multicoloured	1·60	50

161 Rural Activities

1975. Promotion of Rural Development.
463	161	50f. mauve, violet & black	80	50

162 Railway Bridge over the
N'Zi, Dimbokro

1975. 15th Anniv of Independence.
464	162	60f. multicoloured	3·50	1·00

164 Baoule Mask

1976. Mothers' Day.
465	163	65f. multicoloured	1·70	60

163 *Mother* (statue)

1976. Ivory Coast Art. Multicoloured.
466		20f. Type **164** (postage)	50	25
467		25f. Senoufo statuette	50	30
468		150f. Chief Abron's chair	2·75	1·20
469		200f. Akans royal symbols: fly swatter and panga (air)	4·50	1·80

165 Early and
Modern Telephones

1976. Telephone Centenary.
470	165	70f. blue, brown and black	1·00	60

166 Effigy, Map and
Carrier Pigeon

1976. 20th Anniv of Stamp Day and Ivory Coast Philatelic
Club.
471	166	65f. multicoloured	80	50

167 "Smiling Trees"
and Cat

1976. Nature Protection.
472	167	65f. multicoloured	1·00	45

168 Children
Reading

1976. Literature for Children.
473	168	65f. multicoloured	1·00	50

169 Throwing the
Javelin

1976. Olympic Games, Montreal. Multicoloured.
474		60f. Type **169**	85	50
475		65f. Running (horiz)	85	50

170 Mohammed Ali
Jinnah

1976. Birth Centenary of Mohammed Ali Jinnah (first
Governor-General of Pakistan).
476	170	50f. multicoloured	55·00	11·00

171 Cashew-nut

1976
477	171	65f. multicoloured	1·70	60

172 Houphouet-Boigny Bridge,
Abidjan

1976. Third African Roads Conference, Abidjan.
478	172	60f. multicoloured	80	45

173 John Paul Jones (after Peale)
and detail of *First Salute to the
Stars and Stripes* (E. Moran)

1976. Bicentenary of American Revolution. Multicoloured.
479		100f. Type **173**	1·30	25
480		125f. Comte de Rochambeau, grenadier and flag	1·70	45
481		150f. Admiral D'Estaing, French marine and French warships	2·00	50

482	175f. Marquis de Lafayette (after Peale), grenadier and flag	2·00	55
483	200f. Thomas Jefferson (after Peale), militiaman and Declaration of Independence	2·50	70

MS484 101×76 mm. 500f. George Washington (after Stuart), officer and flag   6·25   2·75

174 Independence Motif

1976. 16th Anniv of Independence.

485	**174**	60f. multicoloured	80	50

175 Ife Bronze Mask

1977. Second World Festival of Negro Arts, Lagos.

486	**175**	65f. multicoloured	1·00	60

176 Baoule Handbells

1977. Musical Instruments (1st series).

487	**176**	5f. brown and green	30	25
488	–	10f. black and red	30	25
489	–	20f. black and violet	45	25

DESIGNS: 10f. Senoufo xylophone; 20f. Dida tom-tom. See also Nos. 603/4.

177 Unloading Mail from Douglas DC-8

1977. Stamp Day.

490	**177**	60f. multicoloured	1·00	50

178 *Charaxes jasius epijasius*

1977. Butterflies (1st series). Multicoloured.

491		30f. *Epiphora rectifascia boolana*	3·25	1·70
492	**178**	60f. Type **178**	17·00	13·00
493		65f. *Imbrasia arata*	5·50	3·00
494		100f. *Palla decius*	7·75	5·25

See also Nos. 546/9 and 585/7.

179 Tingrela Mosque

1977. Air.

495	**179**	500f. brown, green & blue	6·75	3·75

180 Chateau Sassenage, Grenoble

1977. Tenth Anniv of International French Language Council.

496	**180**	100f. multicoloured	1·40	60

181 Wright Brothers and Wright Type A Biplane

1977. History of Flying. Multicoloured.

497		60f. Type **181**	90	35
498		75f. Louis Bleriot crossing English Channel	1·00	25
499		100f. Ross Smith and Vickers Vimy aircraft	1·30	25
500		200f. Charles Lindbergh and *Spirit of St. Louis*	2·75	65
501		300f. Concorde	4·50	1·40

MS502 116×91 mm. 500f. Lindbergh and *Spirit of St. Louis* (different)   6·50   2·40

182 Santos Dumont's *Ville de Paris*

1977. History of the Airship. Multicoloured.

503		60f. Type **182** (air)	80	25
504		65f. Launch of LZ-1	80	25
505		150f. *Schwaben*	1·90	50
506		200f. *Bodensee*	2·75	70
507		300f. *Graf Zeppelin* over Egypt	4·00	1·30

MS508 92×104 mm. 500f. *Graf Zeppelin* over New York (air)   7·00   2·40

183 Congress Emblem

1977. 17th International Congress of Administrative Sciences in Africa.

509	**183**	60f. green and emerald	65	35

184 Pres. Houphouet-Boigny

1977

510	**184**	35f. black, mauve & brown	95	20
511	**184**	40f. black, orange & green	3·50	70
512	**184**	45f. black, green & orange	4·25	95
513	**184**	60f. black, purple & brown	5·00	95
514	**184**	65f. black, orange & green	5·50	1·50

185 Container Ship *Yamoussoukro*

1977. Yamoussoukro Container Port.

515	**185**	65f. multicoloured	2·20	80

186 Hand holding Symbols of Development   **187** *Strophantus hispidus*

1977. 17th Anniv of Independence.

516	**186**	60f. black, orange & green	80	50

1977. Flowers (1st series). Multicoloured.

517		5f. Type **187**	55·00	10·00
518		20f. *Anthurium cultorum*	55·00	10·00
519		60f. *Arachnis flos-aeris*	55·00	5·50
520		65f. *Renanthera storiei*	55·00	5·50

See also Nos. 571/3, 622/5, 678/80, 791c/e, 827a/b and 873e/f.

188 Presidents Giscard d'Estaing and Houphouet-Boigny

1978. Visit of President Giscard d'Estaing of France.

521	**188**	60f. multicoloured	1·00	35
522	**188**	65f. multicoloured	1·00	45
523	**188**	100f. multicoloured	1·70	80

MS524 159×120 mm. 500f. multicoloured   9·00   9·00

189 St. George and the Dragon

1978. 400th Birth Anniv of Peter Paul Rubens (artist). Multicoloured.

525		65f. Type **189**	75	25
526		150f. *Head of a Child*	1·80	60
527		250f. *The Annunciation*	2·75	90
528		300f. *The Birth of Louis XIII*	3·75	1·30

MS529 96×115 mm. 500f. *Madonna and Child*   5·75   2·40

190 Members of the Royal Guard

1978. Images of History.

530	**190**	60f. red, black and blue	1·00	45
531	–	65f. black, blue and red	1·00	45

DESIGN: 65f. Figures of traditional cosmology.

191 Rural Post Office

1978. Stamp Day.

532	**191**	60f. multicoloured	80	50

192 Microwave Antenna

1978. Telecommunications Day.

533	**192**	60f. multicoloured	80	50

193 S. A. Arrhenius and Equipment (Chemistry, 1903)

1978. Nobel Prize Winners. Multicoloured.

534	**193**	60f. Type **193**	65	10
535		75f. Jules Bordet (Medicine, 1920)	80	25
536		100f. Andre Gide (Literature, 1947)	1·00	30
537		200f. John Steinbeck (Literature, 1962)	2·00	65
538		300f. UNICEF. (Peace, 1965)	3·50	1·00

MS539 119×81 mm. 500f. Max Planck (physics, 1914)   5·50   1·80

194 Player kicking Ball

1978. World Cup Football Championship, Argentina. Multicoloured.

540		60f. Football and player (horiz)	60	10
541	**194**	65f. Type **194**	80	25
542		100f. Football and player (different) (horiz)	1·00	50
543		150f. Goalkeeper (horiz)	1·80	60
544		300f. Football "sun" and player	3·00	95

MS545 102×77 mm. 500f. Football as globe showing South America   5·50   1·80

1978. Butterflies (2nd series). As T **178**. Multicoloured.

546		60f. *Miniodes discolor*	3·00	90
547		65f. *Charaxes lactetinctus*	3·00	90
548		100f. *Papilio zalmoxis*	4·75	1·70
549		200f. *Papilio antimachus*	7·50	3·25

195 Banded Cricket

1978. Insects (1st series). Multicoloured.

550		10f. Type **195**	70	30
551		20f. "Nepa cinerea" (water scorpion)	1·10	40
552		60f. Horned tree-hopper	2·20	80
553		65f. "Goliathus cassicus" (beetle)	3·25	1·00

See also Nos. 600/2.

196 Passengers in Train

1978. Educational Television. Multicoloured.

554		60f. Figures emerging from television screen	75	30
555	**196**	65f. Type **196**	75	30

197 Astragale (oil exploration ship)

1978. First Anniv of Discovery of Oil in Ivory Coast. Multicoloured.

556	**197**	60f. Type **197**	1·30	45
557		65f. Ram, map of Ivory Coast and gold goblets	1·30	45

MS558 89×110 mm. 500f. Ram, map of Ivory Coast and President holding goblets   10·50   10·50

1978. Air. "Philexafrique" Stamp Exhibition, Gabon (1st issue) and International Stamp Fair, Essen, West Germany. As T **203a** of Mauritania. Multicoloured.

559	100f. Common pheasant and Bavaria 1849 1k. stamp	3·50	2·40
560	100f. African elephant and Ivory Coast 1965 90f. stamp	3·50	2·40

See also Nos. 588/9.

198 National Assembly Building, Paris

1978. Centenary of Paris U.P.U. Congress.

561	**198**	200f. multicoloured	1·90	80

199 African with Ballot Box

200 Ribbon of Flags

1978. 18th Anniv of Independence.

562	**199**	60f. multicoloured	1·00	50

1978. Technical Co-operation among Developing Countries. Multicoloured.

563	60f. Type **200**	80	30
564	65f. Ribbon of flags forming arrows	80	30

201 Ploughing

1979. Agriculture.

565	**201**	100f. multicoloured	1·50	50

202 King Hassan and Pres Houphouet-Boigny

1979. Visit of King Hassan of Morocco.

566	**202**	60f. multicoloured	2·20	75
567	**202**	65f. multicoloured	3·50	1·10
568	**202**	500f. multicoloured	17·00	7·25

203 Isis

1979. UNESCO. Campaign for Preservation of Nubian Monuments.

569	**203**	200f. silver, green & turq	2·30	1·20
570		500f. gold, brown & orge	5·50	3·00

DESIGN: 500f. Gold medal.

204 Loranthus sp.

1979. Flowers (2nd series). Multicoloured.

571	30f. Type **204**	90	50
572	60f. Vanda josephine	1·30	60
573	65f. Renanthera storiei	1·60	80

205 Sable Antelopes

1979. Endangered Animals (1st series). Multicoloured.

574	5f. Type **205**	50	30
575	20f. Yellow-backed duiker	80	45
576	50f. Pygmy hippopotamus	1·50	40
577	60f. Aardvark	2·75	1·00

See also Nos. 613/18.

206 Children and Globe

1979. International Year of the Child. Multicoloured.

578	60f. Type **206**	60	35
579	65f. Child on dove	75	45
580	100f. Type **206**	1·30	80
581	500f. As 65f.	5·25	3·00

207 Travelling Post Office

1979. Stamp Day.

582	**207**	60f. multicoloured	1·00	30

208 Korhogo Cathedral

1979. 75th Anniv of Arrival of Holy Fathers.

583	**208**	60f. multicoloured	80	45

209 Crying Child

1979. Tenth Anniv of S.O.S. Children's Village.

584	**209**	65f. multicoloured	80	50

210 Euphaedra xypete

1979. Butterflies (3rd series). Multicoloured.

585	60f. Type **210**	1·80	60
586	65f. Pseudacraea bois duvali	2·00	65
587	70f. Auchenisa schausi	3·00	90

211 Carved Figure and Antelope

1979. "Philexafrique", Stamp Exhibition, Gabon (2nd issue).

588	**211**	70f. multicoloured	2·50	2·00
589	-	70f. green, turquoise & red	2·50	2·00

DESIGN: No. 589, U.P.U. emblem, antenna, ship and truck.

212 Astronaut Greeting Boy

1979. Tenth Anniv of Moon Landing. Multicoloured.

590	60f. Type **212**	95	60
591	65f. Trajectory between Earth and Moon (horiz)	95	60
592	70f. Type **212**	1·50	75
593	150f. As 65f.	2·75	1·80

213 A4 Pacific (4-6-2) Locomotive and Great Britain £1 stamp, 1878

1979. Death Centenary of Sir Rowland Hill. Multicoloured.

594	60f. Type **213**	55	20
595	75f. Steam locomotive and Ivory Coast 45c. stamp, 1936	75	25
596	100f. Diesel locomotive No. 105, U.S.A. and Hawaiian 13c. "missionary" stamp, 1852	1·30	45
597	150f. Steam locomotive No. 1, Japan and Japanese 20s. stamp, 1872	1·50	50
598	300f. Class BB 15000 electric locomotive, France and French 15c. stamp, 1850	3·00	85
MS599	105×78 mm. 500f. Locomotive, Concorde and Ivory Coast 35c. stamp, 1936	7·25	2·40

214 Delta sp.

1979. Insects (2nd series). Multicoloured.

600	30f. Type **214**	6·00	2·00
601	60f. Mantis religiosa (vert)	9·50	3·00
602	65f. Locusta migratorius	10·50	3·00

215 Harp

1979. Musical Instruments (2nd series). Multicoloured.

603	100f. Type **215**	30·00	9·50
604	150f. Senoufo funeral horns	40·00	14·00

216 "Telecom 79"

1979. Third World Telecommunications Exhibition, Geneva.

605	**216**	60f. grey, orange and blue	80	35

217 Carved Head

1979. Culture Days.

606	**217**	65f. multicoloured	80	30

218 Boxing

1979. Pre-Olympic Year. Multicoloured.

607	60f. Type **218**	60	25
608	65f. Running	70	25
609	100f. Football	1·20	45
610	150f. Cycling	1·50	60
611	300f. Wrestling	3·00	1·00
MS612	117×85 mm. 500f. Gymnastics (horse)	5·50	1·70

See also Nos. 642/**MS**646.

219 Jentink's Duiker

1979. Endangered Animals (2nd series). Multicoloured.

613	40f. Type **219**	1·80	25
614	60f. Olive colobus	2·00	45
615	75f. African manatees	2·75	45
616	100f. Temminck's giant squirrel	4·00	65
617	150f. Pygmy hippopotamus	5·75	85
618	300f. Chimpanzee	10·50	1·80

220 Raoul Follereau and Institute

1979. Raoul Follereau d'Adzope Institute.

619	**220**	60f. multicoloured	1·30	50

221 Post, Adze and Plant

1979. 19th Anniv of Independence.

620	**221**	60f. multicoloured	1·00	25

222 Concorde and Map of Africa

1979. 20th Anniv of ASECNA (African Air Safety Organization).

621	**222**	60f. multicoloured	80	30

222a Coelancanth

1979. Fish (1st series). Multicoloured.

621a	60f. Lionfish	£120	7·75
621b	65f. Type **222a**	£120	7·75

See also Nos. 629/31 and 666/8.

223 Clerodendron thomsonae

1980. Flowers (3rd series). Multicoloured.

622	5f. Type **223**	10	10

623		10f. *La Boule de Feu* (horiz)	30	10
624		50f. *Costus incanusiamus*	85	25
625		60f. *Ficus elastica*	95	30

224 Elephant, Map and Rotary Emblem

1980. 75th Anniv of Rotary International.

626	**224**	65f. multicoloured	80	35

225 Seal

1980. International Archives Day.

627	**225**	65f. multicoloured	80	50

226 Boys with Stamp Album

1980. Stamp Day.

628	**226**	65f. brown and turquoise	1·00	25

1980. Fish (2nd series). As T 222a. Multicoloured.

629		60f. Emperor snapper	2·75	60
630		65f. Guinean fingerfish (vert)	2·75	95
631		100f. Banded gourami	3·50	1·30

228 Missionary and Church, Aboisso

1980. 75th Anniv of Settlement of Holy Fathers at Aboisso.

632	**228**	60f. multicoloured	1·00	50

229 Hands protecting Child from Cigarettes

1980. Anti-Smoking Campaign.

633	**229**	60f. multicoloured	1·00	25

230 Pope John-Paul II and President Houphouet-Boigny

1980. Papal Visit.

634	**230**	65f. yellow, brn & dp brn	2·30	90

231 *Le Belier* Express Train, Abidjan–Bouake

1980. Railways. Multicoloured.

635		60f. Type **231**	75	25
636		65f. Abidjan Station, 1904	75	45
637		100f. Steam train, 1908	1·30	60
638		150f. Steam goods train, 1940	1·80	90

232 Headquarters Building, Dakar

1980. First Anniv of West African Central Bank.

639	**232**	60f. multicoloured	80	45

233 Cobra

1980. Animals. Multicoloured.

640		60f. Type **233**	1·40	35
641		150f. Toad	3·25	1·20

234 Gymnastics   **235** World Tourism Conference Emblem

1980. Air. Olympic Games, Moscow. Multicoloured.

642		75f. Type **234**	95	25
643		150f. Ring exercise	1·60	45
644		250f. Vaulting horse (horiz)	2·75	80
645		350f. Bar exercise	3·75	1·30
MS646		106×80 mm. 500f. Floor exercise (horiz)	5·00	1·70

1980. Tourism. Multicoloured.

647		60f. Village scene	60	35
648		65f. Type **235**	60	25

1980. Insects (3rd series). As T 214. Multicoloured.

649		60f. *Ugada limbata* (25×35 mm)	3·50	1·60
650		60f. *Forticula auricularia* (36×26 mm)	1·60	1·00
651		65f. *Mantis religiosa* (26×32 mm)	3·50	1·60
652		200f. Grasshopper (35×25 mm)	6·00	2·50

236 Hands breaking Chains, Map and President

1980. President Houphouet-Boigny's 75th Birthday.

653	**236**	60f. mult (postage)	1·30	55
654	-	65f. multicoloured	1·50	65
655	-	70f. multicoloured	1·80	85
656	**236**	150f. multicoloured	4·00	2·10
657	-	300f. multicoloured	7·00	3·50
658	-	2000f. silver (air)	20·00	20·00
659	-	3000f. gold	31·00	31·00

DESIGNS—SQUARE: 70f. Presidential speech on map in national colours. HORIZ (44×29 mm): 65f., 300f. President and symbols of progress. VERT (35×45 mm): 2000f., 3000f. President Houphouet-Boigny.

237 Map of Ivory Coast

1980. Seventh P.D.C.I.–R.D.A. Congress.

660	**237**	60f. green, orange & black	80	25
661	**237**	65f. green, orange & black	80	25

238 "Sotra" (ferry)

1980. New Lagoon Transport.

662	**238**	60f. multicoloured	1·00	50

239 Abidjan

1980. 20th Anniv of Independence.

663	**239**	60f. multicoloured	80	25

240 Conference Emblem

1980. Fifth General Conference of African Universities Association, Yamoussoukro.

664	**240**	60f. multicoloured	80	35

241 Map of Africa and Posthorn

1980. Fifth Anniv of African Posts and Telecommunications Union.

665	**241**	150f. multicoloured	1·50	50

241a Red-billed Dwarf Hornbill

1980. Birds. Multicoloured.

665a		60f. Superb starling	80·00	4·75
665b		65f. Type **241a**	80·00	4·75
665c		65f. South African crowned crane	80·00	4·75
665d		100f. Saddle-bill stork	80·00	14·50

242 Rio Grande Cichlid

1981. Fish (3rd series). Multicoloured.

666		60f. Type **242**	90	55
667		65f. Red-tailed black shark	90	55
668		200f. Green pufferfish	2·75	1·50

243 Post Office, Grand Lahou

1981. Stamp Day.

669	**243**	60f. multicoloured	80	25

244 Mask

1981. 25th Anniv of Ivory Coast Philatelic Club.

670	**244**	65f. black, lt brown & brn	80	25

245 Red Cross Aircraft, Satellite and Globe (Telecommunications and Health)

1981. World Telecommunications Day.

671	**245**	30f. multicoloured	35	10
672	**245**	60f. multicoloured	90	35

246 "Viking" landing on Mars

1981. Conquest of Space. Multicoloured.

673		60f. Type **246**	60	20
674		75f. Space Shuttle on launch pad	80	25
675		125f. Space Shuttle erecting experiment	1·30	55
676		300f. Space Shuttle performing experiment	2·75	1·30
MS677		103×78 mm. 500f. Space Shuttles constructing framework in space	5·50	1·70

1981. Flowers (4th series). Multicoloured.

678		50f. Type **247**	1·50	55
679		60f. Sugar cane flowers	2·10	80
680		100f. "Heliconia ivoirea"	3·00	1·40

See also Nos. 791c/e, 827a/b and 873e/f.

248 Prince Charles, Lady Diana Spencer and Coach

1981. Royal Wedding.

681	**248**	80f. multicoloured	80	25
682	-	100f. multicoloured	1·00	45
683	-	125f. multicoloured	1·30	60
MS684		104×80 mm. 500f. multicoloured	5·25	1·80

DESIGNS: 100f. to 500f. Showing Prince Charles, Lady Diana Spencer and coaches.

249 Map formed of Flag

1981

684a	**249**	5f. multicoloured	10	10
684aa	**249**	10f. multicoloured	30	10
684ab	**249**	20f. multicoloured	35	10
684b	**249**	25f. multicoloured	30	10
684c	**249**	30f. multicoloured	35	10
684ca	**249**	35f. multicoloured	45	10
684d	**249**	40f. multicoloured	50	10
684e	**249**	50f. multicoloured	50	10
685	**249**	80f. multicoloured	75	25
686	**249**	100f. multicoloured	1·00	50
687	**249**	125f. multicoloured	1·30	60

250 Goalkeeper

1981. World Cup Football Championship, Spain (1982). Multicoloured.

688	70f. Type **250**		60	25
689	80f. Saving a goal		80	50
690	100f. Diving for ball (vert)		1·00	55
691	150f. Goalmouth scene		1·50	85
692	350f. Fighting for ball (vert)		3·50	1·60
MS693 103×78 mm. 500f. Goalmouth scene			5·25	3·75

251 Association Emblem

1981. West Africa Rice Development Association.

694	**251**	80f. multicoloured	1·00	35

252 Post Office

1981. Stamp Day.

695	**252**	70f. multicoloured	60	25
696	**252**	80f. multicoloured	75	45
697	**252**	100f. multicoloured	95	50

253 Hands with and without Fruit, and F.A.O. Emblem

1981. World Food Day.

698	**253**	100f. multicoloured	1·00	50

254 Felice Nazarro

1981. 75th Anniv of French Grand Prix Motor Race. Multicoloured.

699	15f. Type **254**		30	10
700	40f. Jim Clark		50	25
701	80f. Fiat, 1907		1·00	50
702	100f. Auto Union, 1936		1·30	60
703	125f. Ferrari, 1961		1·50	75
MS704 121×95 mm. 500f. Monaco Grand Prix, 1933			6·25	2·30

255 Symbols of Economic Growth

1981. 21st Anniv of Independence.

705	**255**	50f. multicoloured	50	25
706	**255**	80f. multicoloured	80	50

256 "Queue de Cheval"

1982. Hairstyles. Multicoloured.

707	80f. Type **256**		1·30	60
708	100f. "Belier"		2·10	85
709	125f. "Cheri regarde mon visage"		2·75	1·10

257 Bingerville Post Office, 1902

1982. Stamp Day.

710	**257**	100f. multicoloured	1·00	50

258 Rotary Emblem on Map of Africa

1982. Rotary International Conference, Abidjan.

711	**258**	100f. blue and gold	1·00	55

259 George Washington

1982. Celebrities' Anniversaries. Multicoloured.

712	80f. Type **259** (250th birth anniv)		80	30
713	100f. Auguste Piccard (20th death anniv)		1·00	50
714	350f. Goethe (150th death anniv)		3·50	1·30
715	450f. Princess of Wales (21st birthday)		4·25	1·70
MS716 80×104 mm. 500f. Princess of Wales (different)			4·50	1·90

260 Hexagonal Pattern and Telephone

1982. World Telecommunications Day.

717	**260**	80f. multicoloured	80	30

261 Presidents Mitterand and Houphouet-Boigny

1982. Visit of President Mitterand of France.

718	**261**	100f. multicoloured	1·40	60

262 Dr. Koch, Bacillus and Microscope

1982. Cent of Discovery of Tubercle Bacillus.

719	**262**	30f. multicoloured	50	25
720	**262**	80f. multicoloured	1·30	70

263 Scouts in Dinghy

1982. 75th Anniv of Boy Scout Movement. Multicoloured.

721	80f. Type **263**		80	25
722	100f. Dinghy (horiz)		1·30	35
723	150f. Leaning into wind		1·50	60
724	350f. Hauling sail		3·50	1·20
MS725 65×81 mm. 500f. Yachts			5·75	1·80

264 Aerial View of Coastline

1982. Tenth Anniv of U.N. Environmental Programme.

726	**264**	40f. multicoloured	50	25
727	**264**	80f. multicoloured	90	50

265 Congress Emblem

1982. First League of Ivory Coast Secretaries Congress, Abidjan.

728	**265**	80f. multicoloured	80	30
729	**265**	100f. multicoloured	1·00	45

247 *Amorphophallus* sp.

1982. Birth of Prince William of Wales. Nos. 681/**MS**684 optd **NAISSANCE ROYALE 1982**.

730	**247**	80f. multicoloured	85	35
731	-	100f. multicoloured	1·00	50
732	-	125f. multicoloured	1·20	60
MS733 104×80 mm. 500f. multicoloured			4·50	4·50

267 Child with Dove

1982. Picasso Paintings. Multicoloured.

734	80f. Type **267**		75	35
735	100f. *Self-portrait*		1·10	35
736	185f. *Les Demoiselles d'Avignon*		2·50	60
737	350f. *The Dream*		4·25	1·20
738	500f. *La Colombe de l'Avenir* (horiz)		6·00	1·70

268 Post Office Counter, Abidjan 17

1982. World U.P.U. Day. Multicoloured.

739	80f. Type **268**		95	45
740	100f. Postel 2001 Building, Abidjan (vert)		1·20	45
741	350f. Counter clerks at Abidjan 17 Post Office		3·50	1·40

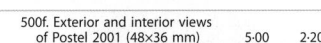

742	500f. Exterior and interior views of Postel 2001 (48×36 mm)		5·00	2·20

249 Map formed of Flag

1982. World Cup Football Championship Results. Nos. 688/92 optd.

743	70f. Type **249**		60	25
744	80f. Saving a goal		80	50
745	100f. Diving for ball (vert)		1·00	50
746	150f. Goalmouth scene		1·50	85
747	350f. Fighting for ball (vert)		3·50	1·60
MS748 103×78 mm. 500f. Goalmouth scene			5·25	5·25

DESIGNS: 70f. **1966 VAINQUEUR GRAND-BRETAGNE**; 80f. **1970 VAINQUEUR BRESIL** 100f. **1974 VAINQUEUR ALLEMAGNE** (REA) (vert); 150f. **1978 VAINQUEUR ARGENTINE**; 350f. **1982. VAINQUEUR ITALIE** (vert); 500f. **ITALI-ALLEMAGNE (RFA) 3 1**.

270 President Houphouet-Boigny with Farming Implements and Agricultural Produce

1982. 22nd Anniv of Independence.

749	**270**	100f. multicoloured	1·00	50

271 Emblem and Map of Member Countries

1982. 20th Anniv of West African Monetary Union.

750	**271**	100f. brown, blue & dp bl	1·00	55

272 Man Waterfall

1982. Landscapes. Multicoloured.

751	**272**	80f. Type **272**	11·00	1·20
752		80f. Wooded savanna	14·50	65
753	**272**	500f. Type **272**	39·00	5·50

273 Child and S.O.S. Village

1983. S.O.S. Children's Village.

754	**273**	125f. multicoloured	1·40	60

274 Long-tailed Pangolin

1983. Animals. Multicoloured.

755	**274**	35f. Type **274**	50	25
756		90f. Bush pig (horiz)	1·00	45
757		100f. Eastern black-and-white colobus	1·30	50
758		125f. African buffalo (horiz)	1·40	60

275 Post Office, Grand Bassam, 1903

1983. Stamp Day.
759	**275**	100f. multicoloured	1·00	50

276 Montgolfier Balloon, 1783

1983. Bicentenary of Manned Flight. Multicoloured.
760	100f. Type **276**		1·00	35
761	125f. Charles's hydrogen balloon, 1783		1·40	45
762	150f. Balloon *Armand Barbes* (Paris siege post, 1870) (horiz)		1·70	55
763	350f. Balloon *Double Eagle II* over Atlantic		4·25	1·20
764	500f. Advertising airship (horiz)		6·25	1·80

277 *Descent from the Cross*

1983. Easter. Multicoloured.
765	100f. Type **277**		1·00	25
766	125f. *The Resurrection of Christ* (horiz)		1·20	45
767	350f. *The Raising of the Cross* (horiz)		3·25	1·10
768	400f. *The Piercing of the Lance*		4·00	1·30
769	500f. *Descent from the Cross*		4·50	1·60

278 Safe containing U.N. Emblem

1983. 25th Anniv of U.N. Economic Commission for Africa.
770	**278**	100f. multicoloured	1·00	50

279 African Fish Eagle

1983. Birds. Multicoloured.
771	100f. Type **279**		1·50	60
772	125f. Grey parrot (horiz)		2·00	55
773	150f. Violet turaco (horiz)		3·00	85

280 Swimming

1983. Air. Pre-Olympic Year. Multicoloured.
774	100f. Type **280**		95	30
775	125f. Diving		1·20	50
776	350f. Backstroke		3·25	1·20
777	400f. Butterfly stroke		3·75	1·40
MS778	116×90 mm. 500f. water polo		5·75	1·80

281 Forest destroyed by Fire

1983. Ecology in Action. Multicoloured.
779	25f. Type **281**		60	35
780	100f. Animals running from fire		1·70	70
781	125f. Protected animals		2·30	95

282 Flali Dance

1983. Traditional Dances. Multicoloured.
782	50f. Type **282**		45	25
783	100f. Mask dance		95	45
784	125f. Stilt dance		1·40	50

283 Hotel Ivoire

1983. 20th Anniv of Hotel Ivoire, Abidjan.
785	**283**	100f. multicoloured	1·00	50

284 Rally Car and Route

1983. World and African Car Rally Championships.
786	**284**	100f. multicoloured	1·30	60

285 *Christ and St. Peter*

1983. Christmas. Paintings by Raphael. Multicoloured.
787	100f. Type **285**		1·00	40
788	125f. Study for St. Joseph		1·30	55
789	350f. *Virgin of the House of Orleans*		3·50	1·30
790	500f. *Virgin of the Blue Diadem*		4·50	1·70

286 President Houphouet-Boigny

1983. 23rd Anniv of Independence.
791	**286**	100f. multicoloured	1·00	50

286a Telegraphist, Dish Aerial and National Postal Sorting Centre

1983. World Communications Year. Multicoloured.
791a	100f. Cable-laying, Postel 2001 building, Abidjan, and telephonists		75·00	4·75
791b	125f. Type **286a**		75·00	6·50

1983. Flowers (5th series). As T **247**. Multicoloured.
791c	100f. Pineapple flowers		£200	
791d	125f. *Heliconia rostrata*		49·00	12·00
791e	150f. *Rose de Porcelaine*		49·00	12·00

287 Arrow piercing Television Screen

1984. First Audio-Visual Forum.
792	**287**	100f. black and green	1·00	50

288 Competition Emblem

1984. Africa Cup Football Competition.
793	**288**	100f. multicoloured	95	45
794	-	200f. orange, green & blk	1·80	85

DESIGN: 200f. Maps of Africa and Ivory Coast shaking hands.

289 Spider

1984. Multicoloured.
795	100f. Type **289**		1·70	70
796	125f. "Polistes gallicus" (wasp)		2·00	95

290 Abidjan Post Office, 1934

1984. Stamp Day.
797	**290**	100f. multicoloured	1·00	45

291 Swimming

1984. Air. Olympic Games, Los Angeles. Multicoloured.
798	100f. Type **291**		1·00	30
799	125f. Cross-country		1·30	45
800	185f. Pistol shooting		1·70	55
801	350f. Fencing		3·50	1·10
MS802	104×80 mm. 500f. Equestrian		6·00	1·80

292 Lions Club Badge

1984. Third Lions Multi District 403 Convention. Multicoloured.
803	100f. Type **292**		1·00	50
804	125f. As Type **292** but with badge at right		1·50	75

293 Telecommunications Stations on Map of Ivory Coast

1984. World Telecommunications Day.
805	**293**	100f. multicoloured	1·10	50

294 Flags, Agriculture and Symbols of Unity and Growth

1984. 25th Anniv of Council of Unity.
806	**294**	100f. multicoloured	95	45
807	**294**	125f. multicoloured	1·30	50

295 First Government House, Grand-Bassam

1984. Old Buildings (1st series). Multicoloured.
808	100f. Type **295**		1·00	45
809	125f. Palace of Justice, Grand-Bassam		1·30	50

See also Nos. 873a/c.

296 Eklan Board

1984. Eklan. Multicoloured.
810	100f. Type **296**		1·30	40
811	125f. Two Eklan players		1·30	60

297 *La Gazelle* Express Train, Abidjan–Ouagadougou

1984. Transport. Multicoloured. (a) Locomotives.
812	100f. Type **297**		1·20	40
813	125f. Steam locomotive, 1931, France		1·80	50
814	350f. Type 10 steam locomotive, Belgium		4·25	1·20
815	500f. Class GT2 Mallet steam locomotive		6·00	1·70

(b) Ships.
816	100f. Container Ship		1·00	35
817	125f. Cargo liner		1·30	50
818	350f. *Queen Mary* (liner)		3·75	1·10
819	500f. "France" (liner)		6·00	1·60

298 Envelope, Map and Symbols of Postal Service

1984. Stamp Day.
820	**298**	100f. multicoloured	1·30	55

299 Emblem

1984. Tenth Anniv of West African Economic Community.
821	**299**	100f. multicoloured	95	50

300 Book Cover

1984. 90th Anniv (1982) of Ivory Coast Postage Stamps.

822	**300**	125f. multicoloured	1·30	85

301 Map Outline, People and Flag

1984. 24th Anniv of Independence.

823	**301**	100f. multicoloured	95	50

302 G. Tiacoh (400 m silver)

1984. Air. Olympic Games Medallists. Multicoloured.

824	100f. Type **302**		1·10	25
825	150f. C. Lewis (100 and 200 m gold)		1·60	45
826	200f. A. Babers (400 m gold)		2·20	80
827	500f. J. Cruz (800 m gold)		4·75	1·50

1984. Flowers (6th series). As T **247**. Multicoloured.

827a	100f. *Allamanda cathartica*		55·00	12·00
827b	125f. Baobab flowers		55·00	12·00

302a Serval

1984. Animals. Multicoloured.

827c	100f. Bushbuck		49·00	12·00
827d	150f. Type **302a**		49·00	12·00

302b Valtur Club, Assouinde

1984

827e	50f. Type **302b**		43·00	7·75
827f	100f. Azagni Canal		43·00	8·75

303 Virgin and Child (Correggio)

1985. Air. Christmas. Multicoloured.

828	100f. Type **303**		1·10	50
829	200f. *Virgin and Child* (Andrea del Sarto)		2·10	90
830	400f. *Virgin and Child* (Jacopo Bellini)		4·00	1·90

Nos. 829/30 are wrongly inscribed "Le Correge" (Correggio).

304 Map, Hands, Emblem and Dove

1985. African Conference of Rotary International, Abidjan.

831	**304**	100f. multicoloured	1·00	50
832	**304**	125f. multicoloured	1·20	55

305 "Le Babou" (Dan costume)

1985. Traditional Costumes. Multicoloured.

833	90f. Type **305**		1·30	40
834	100f. Avikam post-natal dress		1·30	60

305a Hadada Ibis

1985. Birds. Multicoloured.

834a	25f. Marabou stork		£120	15·00
834b	100f. African jacana		£120	15·00
834c	350f. Type **305a**		£120	15·00

306 River Steamer "Adjame"

1985. Stamp Day.

835	**306**	100f. multicoloured	1·60	80

308 Emblem

1985. Seventh Conference of District 18 of Zonta International, Abidjan.

836	**308**	125f. multicoloured	1·20	45

309 Airplane, Van and Industrial Landscape

1985. "Philexafrique" Stamp Exhibition, Lome, Togo (1st issue). Multicoloured.

837	200f. Type **309**		2·30	1·60
838	200f. Sports and agriculture		2·30	1·60

See also Nos. 864/5.

310 Red-breasted Mergansers

1985. Air. Birth Bicentenary of John J. Audubon (ornithologist). Multicoloured.

839	100f. Type **310**		1·00	50
840	150f. American white pelican (vert)		1·60	70
841	200f. American wood stork (vert)		2·75	90
842	350f. Velvet scoters		3·75	1·60

311 Chemical Plant, Senegal

1985. 20th Anniv of African Development Bank.

843	100f. Type **311**		1·00	40
844	125f. Tree seedlings, Gambia		1·30	60

312 Profiles within Map and IYY Emblem

1985. International Youth Year.

845	**312**	125f. multicoloured	1·20	60

313 Presidential Guard Shoulder Flash

1985. 25th Anniv of National Armed Forces.

846	**313**	100f. gold and purple	95	40
847	-	100f. gold and blue	95	40
848	-	125f. gold and black	1·30	60
849	-	200f. gold and brown	2·20	85
850	-	350f. silver and blue	3·25	1·50

DESIGNS: Shoulder flashes of—No. 847, F.A.N.C.I. (army); 848, Air Force; 849, Navy; 850, Gendarmerie.

314 Ivory Coast Arms

1985. Postal Convention with Sovereign Military Order of Malta. Multicoloured.

851	125f. Type **314**		1·20	60
852	350f. Sovereign Military Order of Malta arms		3·25	1·90

315 Footballers

1985. World Cup Football Championship, Mexico. Multicoloured.

853	100f. Type **315**		95	40
854	150f. Footballers (different)		1·30	65
855	200f. Footballers (different)		1·70	80
856	350f. Footballers (different)		3·50	1·40
MS857	106×82 mm. 500f. Footballers (different)		4·50	1·70

316 Pope and Abidjan Cathedral

1985. Visit of Pope John Paul II.

858	**316**	100f. multicoloured	1·60	80

317 Vaccinating Baby

1985. UNICEF Child Survival Campaign. Multicoloured.

859	100f. Type **317**		95	50
860	100f. Mother breast-feeding baby while child plays		95	50
861	100f. Mother spoon-feeding child		95	50
862	100f. Mother giving child a drink (oral rehydration)		95	50

318 Rainbow, U.N. Emblem and Joined Hands

1985. 40th Anniv of U.N.O. and 25th Anniv of Ivory Coast Membership.

863	**318**	100f. multicoloured	95	40

319 Footballers and Children with Injured Animal

1985. Air. "Philexafrique" International Stamp Exhibition, Lome, Togo (2nd issue). Multicoloured.

864	250f. Type **319**		3·50	2·20
865	250f. Dish aerial, rocket and container ship		3·50	2·20

320 City Skyline

1985. "Expo 85" World's Fair, Tsukuba, Japan.

866	**320**	125f. multicoloured	1·30	55

321 Young Duiker

1985. World Wildlife Fund. Banded Duiker. Multicoloured.

867	50f. Type **321**		2·50	40
868	60f. Duiker in front of bushes		3·75	60
869	75f. Two duikers		6·25	1·00
870	100f. Duiker (different)		8·25	1·50

322 Children on Open Ground

1985. "Return to the Earth".

871	**322**	125f. multicoloured	1·30	55

323 Woman spinning Cotton

1985. Rural Handicrafts. Multicoloured.

872	125f. Type **323**		1·30	55
873	155f. Man painting on cotton cloth		1·70	75

323a Samatiguila Mosque

1985. Old Buildings (2nd series). Multicoloured.

873a	100f. Bondoukou Market		29·00	8·00
873b	125f. Type **323a**		29·00	8·00
873c	200f. Samory House, Bondoukou		29·00	8·00

1985. Flowers (7th series). As T **247**. Multicoloured.

873d	100f. *Amorphophallus staudtii*		32·00	9·50
873e	125f. Crinum		32·00	9·50
873f	200f. *Triphyophyllum peltotum*		32·00	9·50

324 Edmond Halley and Computer Picture of Comet

1986. Air. Appearance of Halley's Comet. Multicoloured.

874	125f. Type **324**	1·20	45
875	155f. Sir William Herschel and Uranus	1·50	65
876	190f. Space telescope and comet	1·70	80
877	350f. "MS T-5" space probe and comet	3·25	1·40
878	440f. "Skylab" and Kohoutek's comet	3·75	1·80

325 "Millettia takou"

1986. Plants. Multicoloured.

879	40f. Omphalocarpum elatum	45	20
880	50f. Momordica charantia	55	25
881	125f. Type **325**	1·30	65
882	200f. Costus afer	2·00	1·00

326 Vase from We

1986. Traditional Kitchenware and Tools. Multicoloured.

883	20f. Type **326**	20	10
884	30f. Baoule vase	30	10
885	90f. Baoule dish	1·00	35
886	125f. Dan knife (vert)	1·30	50
887	440f. Baoule pottery jug (vert)	4·25	2·00

327 Institute Building

1986. Tenth Anniv of Institute for Higher Technical and Professional Education.

888	**327**	125f. multicoloured	1·30	55

329 Cable Ship Stephan, 1910

1986. Stamp Day.

899	**329**	125f. multicoloured	1·70	55

330 Footballers

1986. Air. World Cup Football Championship, Mexico.

900	**330**	90f. multicoloured	80	35
901	-	125f. multicoloured	1·30	45
902	-	155f. multicoloured	1·50	65
903	-	440f. multicoloured	4·00	1·80
904	-	500f. multicoloured	4·50	2·10

MS905 104×83 mm. 600f. multicoloured   5·50   2·00

DESIGNS: 125f. to 600f. Different football scenes.

---

331 Emblem

1986. 25th Anniv of National Youth and Sports Institute.

906	**331**	125f. green and orange	1·30	55

332 Endlicher's Bichir

1986. Fish. Multicoloured.

907	5f. Type **332**	15	15
908	125f. Daget's squeaker	1·30	70
909	150f. West African lung-fish	1·70	80
910	155f. Ivory Coast squeaker	1·80	80
911	440f. Electric catfish	5·00	2·30

333 Sacred Tom-tom

1986. Enthronement of King of the Agni. Multicoloured.

912	50f. Type **333**	45	45
913	350f. King being carried	3·50	2·00
914	440f. King and his Court	4·50	2·75

334 Baoule Village, Aoulo

1986. Rural Dwellings (1st series). Multicoloured.

915	125f. Type **334**	1·20	60
916	155f. Avikam village, Eva	1·50	85
917	350f. Lobi village, Soukala	3·25	1·80

See also Nos. 938/9, 990 and 1012.

336 Rocky Coastline

1986

921	**335**	50f. red	45	20
924	**335**	125f. green	1·30	30
926	**335**	155f. red	1·50	30
927	**335**	195f. blue	1·80	30

335 Ivory Coast Arms

1986. Coastal Landscapes. Multicoloured.

930	125f. Type **336**	1·50	80
931	155f. Sandy beach	2·00	1·00

337 Fishery Lake

1986. Oceanographic Research Centre. Multicoloured.

932	125f. Type **337**	1·20	60
933	155f. Fishermen hauling in net	1·50	85

---

338 Pres. Houphouet-Boigny, Rainbow and Dove

1986. International Peace Year.

934	**338**	155f. multicoloured	1·50	75

339 Bull

1986. Research and Development. Multicoloured.

935	125f. Type **339**	1·60	90
936	155f. Rice (IDSA 6)	1·60	90

340 Pres. Houphouet-Boigny and Symbols of Development

1986. 26th Anniv of Independence.

937	**340**	155f. multicoloured	1·50	75

341 Guesseple Dan Village

1987. Rural Dwellings (2nd series). Multicoloured.

938	190f. Type **341**	2·00	1·20
939	550f. M'Bagui Senoufo village	5·50	3·00

342 Postman, 1918

1987. Stamp Day.

940	**342**	155f. multicoloured	1·50	85

343 Elephant and Cockerel

1987. 25th Anniv of French–Ivory Coast Cultural Friendship. Jean Mermoz College. Multicoloured.

941	40f. Type **343**	45	25
942	155f. Children's faces in dove	1·50	70

344 Child running to Adult

1987. World Red Cross Day.

943	**344**	195f.+5f. multicoloured	2·30	1·80

345 "Soling" Class Yachts

1987. Air. Olympic Games, Seoul (1988) (1st issue). Sailing. Multicoloured.

944	155f. Type **345**	1·50	65
945	195f. Windsurfers	2·00	80
946	250f. "470" class dinghies	2·75	95
947	550f. Windsurfer	5·50	2·20

MS948 104×80 mm. 650f. "470" class yachts (51×30 mm)   7·25   2·50

See also Nos. 959/MS963.

346 Excavations (Krah N'Guessan)

1987. Paintings. Multicoloured.

949	195f. Type **346**	2·00	1·20
950	500f. Ceremonial Cortege (Santoni Gerard)	4·50	3·00

347 Airplane and Van

1987. World Post Day. International Express Post.

951	**347**	155f. multicoloured	1·50	1·00
952	**347**	195f. multicoloured	1·80	1·20

348 Map and Forms of Communication

1987. 100 Years of International Mail and Communications Exchanges.

953	**348**	155f. multicoloured	1·50	85

349 Tower Block reflecting Symbols of Progress

1987. 27th Anniv of Independence.

954	**349**	155f. multicoloured	1·50	85

350 Baby in Aloe Plant on Map

1988. Lions International. "For the Life of a Child".

955	**350**	155f. multicoloured	1·50	85

351 Bereby Post Office, 1900

1988. Stamp Day.

956	**351**	155f. multicoloured	1·50	80

352 Heart

1988. 15th Francophone Cardiological Congress, Abidjan.
957   **352**   195f. red and black   2·30   1·50

353 Man working
Soil

1988. Tenth Anniv of International Agricultural
Development Fund.
958   **353**   195f. multicoloured   2·00   1·00

354 Gymnastics (rings)

1988. Air. Olympic Games, Seoul (2nd issue).
Multicoloured.
959   100f. Type **354**   95   45
960   155f. Women's handball   1·50   65
961   195f. Boxing   2·00   90
962   500f. Gymnastics (parallel bar)   4·50   2·00
MS963 102×78 mm. 500f. Gymnastics
(fixed bar) (51×39 mm)   10·00   2·40

355 Stone
Sculpture with
Deep Nostrils

1988. Archaeological Research. Stone Sculptures from
Niangoran-Bouah Collection.
964   **355**   5f. brown and flesh   10   10
965   -   10f. brown and green   10   10
966   -   30f. brown and green   30   10
967   -   155f. brown and yellow   1·60   80
968   -   195f. brown and green   2·40   1·00
DESIGNS: 10f. Sculpture with full lips; 30f. Sculpture with
large nose; 155f. Sculpture with triangular mouth; 195f.
Sculpture with sunken eyes.

356 Healthy Youth and
Drug Addict

1988. First International Drug Abuse and Illegal
Trafficking Day.
969   **356**   155f. multicoloured   1·50   1·00

357 The Couple (K. J.
Houra)

1988. Paintings by Local Artists. Multicoloured.
970   20f. Type **357**   30   10
971   30f. *The Canary of Gentleness*
(Monne Bou) (horiz)   30   10
972   150f. *The Eternal Dancer* (Monne
Bou)   1·40   80
973   155f. *The Termite Hill* (Mathilde
Moro)   1·50   85
974   195f. *The Sun of Independence*
(Michel Kodjo)   2·00   1·00

358 Emblem

1988. 25th Anniv of Organization of African Unity.
975   **358**   195f.+5f. multicoloured   1·80   1·70

359 Collector with Album

1988. World Post Day.
976   **359**   155f. multicoloured   1·50   85

360 Emblem

1988. 28th Anniv of Independence. Forestry Year.
Multicoloured.
977   40f. Type **360**   50   25
978   155f. "To each his tree"   1·90   85
979   155f. "Stop fires"   1·90   90

361 Marie Therese
Houphouet-Boigny and
Emblem

1988. First Anniv of N'Daya International.
980   **361**   195f.+5f. multicoloured   2·10   1·90

362 Money Cowries
and Bones

1989. History of Money (1st series).
981   **362**   50f. multicoloured   80   25
982   -   195f. black, grey and
blue   2·30   1·20
DESIGN: 195f. Bank of Senegal notes.
See also Nos. 1004/5, 1019/21 and 1053.

363 Voltaic Bracelets

1989. Traditional Jewellery. Multicoloured.
983   **363**   90f. Type **363**   1·00   60
984   155f. Dan ankle bracelets   1·80   1·20

364 Stamp used as
Money   **365** "Old Man
and Child"

1989. Stamp Day.
985   **364**   155f. multicoloured   1·70   95

1989. Carvings by Christian Lattier. Multicoloured.
986   40f. Type **365**   45   25
987   155f. "Saxophone Player"   1·80   95
988   550f. "Panther" (horiz)   5·00   2·75

366 Map and Tractor

1989. 30th Anniv of Council of Unity.
989   **366**   75f. multicoloured   1·00   45

367 Sirikukube Dan

1989. Rural Dwellings (3rd series).
990   **367**   155f. multicoloured   1·50   85

368 Congress Venue and Pres.
Houphouet-Boigny

1989. International Peace Congress, Yamoussoukro.
991   **368**   195f. multicoloured   1·80   95

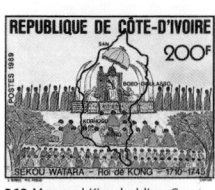

369 Map and King holding Court

1989. Anniversaries. Multicoloured.
992   200f. Type **369** (279th anniv
of accession of King Sekou
Watara of Kong)   3·00   1·80
993   200f. Bastille and detail of
Declaration of Rights of
Man (bicentenary of French
Revolution)   3·00   1·80

370 Nile Monitor

1989. Reptiles. Multicoloured.
994   25f. Type **370**   30   15
995   100f. Nile crocodile   1·30   80

371 Globe and Emblem

1989. World Post Day.
996   **371**   195f. multicoloured   1·80   85

372 Telephone Kiosks and
Mail Boxes

1989. 30th Anniv of West African Posts and
Telecommunications Association.
997   **372**   155f. multicoloured   1·50   85

373 Milan

1989. Air. World Cup Football Championship (1990)
Preliminary Rounds. Multicoloured.
998   195f. Type **373**   2·00   75
999   300f. Genoa   2·75   1·10
1000   450f. Turin   3·75   1·70
1001   550f. Bologna   5·50   1·90

374 Crowd and
Handclasp

1989. 29th Anniv of Independence.
1002   **374**   155f. multicoloured   1·50   80

375 Emblem

1990. Tenth Anniv of Pan-African Postal Union.
1003   **375**   155f. multicoloured   1·40   75

376 West African Bank
25f. Banknote

1990. History of Money (2nd series).
1004   **376**   155f. black and green   1·50   80
1005   195f. black and orange   2·30   1·20
DESIGN: 195f. Banknotes, 1917–44.
See also Nos. 1019/21 and 1053.

377 *Afrique* (steam
packet)

1990. Stamp Day.
1006   **377**   155f. multicoloured   1·80   85

378 Envelopes on
Map

1990. 20th Anniv of Multinational Postal Training School,
Abidjan.
1007   **378**   155f. multicoloured   1·50   75

379 Footballers

1990. Air. World Cup Football Championship, Italy.
Designs showing match scenes. Multicoloured.
1008   155f. Type **379**   1·50   55
1009   195f. Brazil v. West Germany   2·00   75
1010   500f. England v. Russia   4·50   1·90
1011   600f. England v. Netherlands   6·25   2·30

1990. Rural Dwellings (4th series). As T **367**.
Multicoloured.
1012   155f. Malinke village   1·40   55

380 Teacher writing Letters
on Blackboard

1990. International Literacy Year.
1013   **380**   195f. multicoloured   1·80   85

381 Cathedral

1990. Consecration of Our Lady of Peace Cathedral, Yamoussoukro. Multicoloured.

1014	155f. Type **381**	1·50	80
1015	195f. Aerial view	2·30	1·20

382 Pres. Houphouet-Boigny and Pope

1990. Third Visit of Pope John Paul II.

1016	**382** 500f. multicoloured	5·00	2·75

383 Postman delivering to Village

1990. World Stamp Day.

1017	**383** 195f. multicoloured	3·25	1·60

384 Modern Building and Road Network

1990. 30th Anniv of Independence.

1018	**384** 155f. multicoloured	1·60	85

1991. History of Money (3rd series). As T **376**.

1019	40f. black and yellow	45	25
1020	155f. black and green	1·50	85
1021	195f. black and mauve	2·00	1·30

DESIGNS: 40, 155f. West African Bank 100f. and 5f. notes, 1942; 195f. Issuing Institute for French West Africa and Togo 50f. and 500f. notes.

385 Communications

1991. Stamp Day. Multicoloured.

1022	150f. Type **385**	1·40	50

386 Suzanne Lenglen

1991. Centenary of French Open Tennis Championships. Tennis players. Multicoloured.

1023	200f. Type **386**	2·00	1·50
1024	200f. Helen Wills Moody	2·00	1·50
1025	200f. Simone Mathieu	2·00	1·50
1026	200f. Maureen Connolly	2·00	1·50
1027	200f. Francoise Durr	2·00	1·50
1028	200f. Margaret Court	2·00	1·50
1029	200f. Chris Evert	2·00	1·50
1030	200f. Martina Navratilova	2·00	1·50
1031	200f. Steffi Graf	2·00	1·50
1032	200f. Henri Cochet	2·00	1·50
1033	200f. Rene Lacoste	2·00	1·50
1034	200f. Jean Borotra	2·00	1·50

1035	200f. Donald Budge	2·00	1·50
1036	200f. Marcel Bernard	2·00	1·50
1037	200f. Ken Rosewall	2·00	1·50
1038	200f. Rod Laver	2·00	1·50
1039	200f. Bjorn Borg	2·00	1·50
1040	200f. Yannick Noah	2·00	1·50

387 Europe

1991. Steam Packets. Multicoloured.

1041	50f. Type **387**	50	25
1042	550f. Asie	5·00	3·00

1991. Various stamps surch.

1043	-	150f. on 155f. mult (987)	1·50	45
1044	**367**	150f. on 155f. mult	1·50	45
1045	-	150f. on 155f. black and green (1020)	1·50	60
1046	-	200f. on 195f. black and mauve (1021)	2·00	80

389 Post and Savings Society's Emblem and Letter-box

1991. World Post Day. Multicoloured.

1047	50f. Type **389**	50	25
1048	100f. S.I.P.E. emblem and globe	95	50

390 We Drum

1991. Drums.

1049	**390**	5f. purple and lilac	10	10
1050	-	25f. red and pink	25	10
1051	-	150f. green and turquoise	1·60	1·00
1052	-	200f. green and brown	1·90	1·40

DESIGNS: 25f. Krou drum, Soubre; 150f. Nafana drum, Sinematiau; 200f. Akye drum, Alepe.

1991. History of Money (4th series). As T **376**.

1053	100f. black and mauve	1·00	65

DESIGN: 100f. French West Africa and Togo banknotes.

391 Government Buildings

1991. 31st Anniv of Independence.

1054	**391** 150f. multicoloured	1·60	70

392 Orchid

1991. Orchids.

1055	**392**	150f. mauve, green & blk	1·50	45
1056	-	200f. red, emerald & grn	2·00	80

DESIGNS—HORIZ: 200f. Different orchid.

393 Footballer and Cup

1992. Ivory Coast Victory in African Nations Football Cup Championship, Senegal. Multicoloured.

1057	20f. Type **393**	1·00	85
1058	150f. Elephants supporting cup with their trunks (vert)	1·60	1·30

394 African Civet

1992. Animals in Abidjan Zoo.

1059	**394**	5f. brown, red and green	10	10
1060	-	40f. brown, green & orge	45	10
1061	-	150f. brown, green & red	1·80	75
1062	-	500f. brown, grn & ochre	4·75	3·00

DESIGNS: 40f. African palm civet; 150f. Bongo; 500f. Leopard.

395 World Map

1992. World Post Day.

1063	**395** 150f. blue and black	1·40	80

396 1892 "Tablet" and 1962 Postal Centenary Stamps

1992. Stamp Day. Centenary of First Ivory Coast Stamps. Multicoloured.

1064	150f. Type **396**	1·50	95
1065	150f. 1961 Independence and 1991 World Post Day stamps	1·50	95
MS1066	290×104 mm. As Nos. 1064/5 but each size 78×45 mm	35·00	33·00

397 Tomb Entrance

1992. Tourism, Funerary Monuments.

1067	**397**	5f. red, green and blue	10	10
1068	-	50f. brown, green & blue	60	25
1069	-	150f. brown, blue & green	1·50	80
1070	-	400f. green, blue and red	3·75	1·80

DESIGNS (tombs): 50f. Angels, lions and figures; 150f. Drummer, angel, sentry and animals; 400f. Angels, figures and tree.

398 Dove, Flag and Head of Statue of Liberty

1992. 32nd Anniv of Independence. Multicoloured.

1071	30f. Type **398**	35	35
1072	150f. Crowd waving flags, Statue of Liberty and map	1·70	80

399 Runners and Flags

1992. International Marathon. Multicoloured.

1073	150f. Type **399**	1·20	50
1074	200f. Runners and landmarks	2·00	70

400 Emblem and Map

1992. First Anniv of Ity Gold Mine.

1075	**400** 200f. multicoloured	2·00	75

400a Dent de Man

1992. Tourist Sites. Multicoloured.

1075a	10f. Hotel complex		
1075b	25f. Type **400a**		
1075c	100f. Holiday village (horiz)		
1075d	200f. Tourist map		

400b Building and Emblem

1992. First World Conference on Environmental Protection. Multicoloured.

1075e	150f. Tree (vert)		
1075f	200f. Type **400b**		

401 Girl with Stockbook and Collectors swapping Stamp

402 Argemone mexicana

1993. Stamp Day. Youth Philately. Multicoloured.

1076	50f. Type **401**	50	25
1077	50f. Girl pointing at stamps	50	25
1078	150f. Boy perusing album and girls viewing exhibition display	1·70	80

1993. Medicinal Plants. Multicoloured.

1079	5f. Type **402**	25	10
1080	20f. Hibiscus esculentus	30	10
1081	200f. Cassia alata	2·20	1·30

403 Presidential Decree establishing Colony

1993. Centenary of Ivory Coast.

1082	**403** 25f. black and green	30	10
1083	-	100f. blue and black	1·10	65
1084	-	500f. black and brown	5·00	3·00

DESIGNS: 100f. Louis Binger (first Governor) and Felix Houphouet-Boigny (President); 500f. Factory.

404 Calyptrochilum emarginatum

1993. Orchids. Multicoloured.

1085	10f. Type **404**	10	10
1086	50f. Plectrelminthus caudathus	45	25
1087	150f. Eulophia guineensis	1·50	95

405 Heading Ball

1993. World Cup Football Championship, U.S.A. (1994). Multicoloured.

1088	150f. Type **405**	1·00	45
1089	200f. Players jumping	2·00	80
1090	300f. Player dribbling ball past opponent	2·75	1·80
1091	400f. Ball ricocheting off players	3·75	2·30

406 19th-century Map of Ivory Coast

1993. World Post Day.

1092	406	30f. red, black and blue	45	30
1093		200f. multicoloured	2·00	1·30

DESIGN: 200f. Bouake post office.

407 Abstract Design

1993. African Plastic Arts Biennale, Abidjan.

1094	407	200f. multicoloured	1·30	70

408 Map of Mining Centre

1993. 33rd Anniv of Independence.

1095	408	200f. multicoloured	2·00	95

409 Boigny and Modern Developments

1994. Felix Houphouet-Boigny (President, 1960–93) Commemoration. Multicoloured.

1096	409	150f. Type 409	80	25
1097		150f. Boigny, tractor, ploughing with oxen and container ship	80	25
1098		150f. Boigny and Our Lady of the Peace Cathedral, Yamoussoukro	80	25
1099		200f. Type 409	1·10	45
1100		200f. As No. 1097	1·10	45
1101		200f. As No. 1098	1·10	45
MS1102		195×81 mm. 500f. Type 409; 500f. As No. 1097; 500f. As No. 1098	9·00	9·00

410 Raoul Follereau and Globe

1994. 50th Anniv (1992) of World Anti-leprosy Campaign.

1103	410	150f. multicoloured	1·10	50

411 Globe, Satellites and Flags

1994. First Meeting of Regional African Satellite Communications Organization Board of Directors, Abidjan.

1104	411	150f. multicoloured	80	40

412 Country-woman with Basket on Back

1994. Multicoloured, colour of frame given.

1105	412	5f. orange	10	10
1106	412	25f. blue	10	10
1107	412	30f. bistre	10	10
1108	412	40f. green	10	10
1109	412	50f. brown	20	10
1110	412	75f. purple	35	10
1111	412	150f. green	75	45
1112	412	180f. purple	95	35
1115	412	280f. grey	1·30	65
1116	412	300f. violet	1·40	75

413 "Christ"

1994. Stained Glass Windows by Pierre Fakhoury from Our Lady of Peace Cathedral, Yamoussoukro. Multicoloured.

1120	413	25f. Type 413	25	10
1121		150f. "The Fisher of Men"	1·00	60
1122		200f. "Madonna and Child"	1·20	80
MS1123		103×85 mm. 600f. Our Lady of Peace Cathedral, Yamoussoukro (28×42 mm)	4·50	4·50

414 Modern Developments

1994. 34th Anniv of Independence. The Family.

1124	414	150f. multicoloured	80	45

415 Green Mamba

1995. Snakes. Multicoloured.

1125		10f. Royal python	10	10
1126		20f. Green bush snake	10	10
1127		100f. Type 415	50	25
1128		180f. Common puff adder	1·10	65
1129		500f. Rhinoceros viper	2·40	1·50

416 Women collecting Water

417 Lentinus tuberregium

1995. 50th Anniversaries. Multicoloured.

1130		100f. Type 416 (F.A.O.)	70	25
1131		280f. Dove on globe (U.N.O.)	1·90	70

1995. Fungi. Multicoloured.

1132		30f. Type 417	45	25
1133		50f. Chinese mushroom	80	70
1134		180f. Dictyophora indusiata	2·40	95
1135		250f. Termite mushroom	2·75	1·90

418 Laboratory Worker and Pasteur

1995. Death Centenary of Louis Pasteur (chemist).

1136	418	280f. multicoloured	1·50	80

419 GSR Emblem on Butterfly Wing

1995. School Philatelic Clubs. Multicoloured.

1137		50f. Type 419	45	25
1138		180f. LBP emblem on butterfly wing	1·40	75

420 Palla

1995. Butterflies. Multicoloured.

1139		180f. Type 420	2·10	75
1140		280f. Mocker swallowtail	3·00	1·00
1141		550f. Emperor swallowtail	4·25	1·70

421 Motor Vehicles and Handcart

1996. Abidjan Transport. Multicoloured.

1142		180f. Type 421	1·10	60
1143		280f. Catching bus	1·60	95

422 African Bonytongue

1996. Fish. Multicoloured.

1144		50f. Type 422	30	25
1145		180f. Western grunter	1·00	60
1146		700f. Guinean butter catfish	4·00	2·30

423 Cyrtorchis arcuata

424 Boxing

1996. Flowers. Multicoloured.

1147		40f. Type 423	25	25
1148		100f. Eulophia horsfalii	65	35
1149		180f. Eulophidium maculatum	1·40	95
1150		200f. Ansellia africana	1·50	85

1996. Centenary of Modern Olympic Games and Olympic Games, Atlanta. Multicoloured.

1151		200f. Type 424	1·10	60
1152		280f. Running	1·60	1·00
1153		400f. Long jumping	2·20	1·30
1154		500f. National Olympic Committee arms and pictograms	2·75	1·80

425 Huntsmens' Sticks, Birifor

1996. Ceremonial Sticks.

1155	425	180f. black and green	1·10	60
1156		200f. black and orange	1·10	70
1157		280f. black and lilac	1·60	1·00

DESIGNS: 200f. Lobi chief's stick from Bindam; 280f. Lobi chief's stick from Gboberi.

426 Sacred Lotus

1997. Water Plants. Multicoloured.

1158		50f. Type 426	30	25
1159		180f. White lotus	1·10	60
1160		280f. Cape Blue water-lily	1·60	1·00
1161		700f. White water-lily	4·00	2·40

427 Pres. Houphouet-Boigny and Cathedral

1997. Our Lady of Peace Cathedral, Yamoussoukro. Multicoloured.

1162		180f. Type 427	1·10	80
1163		200f. Interior of church	1·10	80
1164		280f. Pope John Paul II and elevated view of cathedral	1·60	1·00

428 Pearl Necklace

1997. Traditional Necklaces. Each lilac and black.

1165		50f. Type 428	30	25
1166		100f. Necklace of small pearls	55	45
1167		180f. Broken necklace of pearls	1·10	70

429 Stone Head

1997. Stone Heads from Gohitafla. Multicoloured.

1168		100f. Type 429	55	25
1169		180f. Stone head (full-face)	1·10	70
1170		500f. Stone head (side-view)	2·75	1·50

430 Pulley

1997. Wooden Weaving Tools.

1171	430	180f. multicoloured	1·10	50
1172		280f. black, grn & dp grn	1·60	75
1173		300f. black, bl & ultram	1·60	75

DESIGNS—VERT: 280f. Combing frame. HORIZ: 300f. Shuttle.

431 Manatees

1997. Endangered Species. Multicoloured.

1174		180f. Type 431	1·60	95
1175		280f. Jentink's duiker	1·60	95
1176		400f. Waterbuck	2·20	1·30

432 Goalkeeper

1998. World Cup Football Championship, France. Multicoloured.

1177		180f. Type 432	1·10	65
1178		280f. Player composed of flags of competing nations (vert)	1·60	90
1179		400f. Match scene showing trajectory of ball	2·20	1·30
1180		500f. Players and ball as mascot (vert)	2·75	1·30

433 *Agaricus bingensis*

1998. Fungi. Multicoloured.
1181	50f. Type **433**	55	35
1182	180f. *Lactarius gymnocarpus*	1·30	95
1183	280f. *Termitomyces letestui*	2·10	1·30

434 *Hutchinsonia barbata*

1998. Plants. Multicoloured.
1184	40f. Type **434**	35	10
1185	100f. *Synsepalum aubrevillei*	75	50
1186	180f. *Cola lorougnonis*	1·10	70

435 *Tapa Woman*

1998. Traditional Costumes. Multicoloured.
1187	180f. Type **435**	1·10	60
1188	280f. Raphia woman	1·60	90

436 *Steam Locomotive, South Africa, 1918*

1999. Railways of Africa. Multicoloured.
1189	180f. Type **436**	1·10	65
1190	280f. Beyer Peacock 15th Class Garratt type steam locomotive, 1925 (wrongly inscr "Garret")	1·60	1·00
MS1191	110×80 mm. 500f. Cecil Rhodes	3·00	3·00

437 *Man carrying Parcel*

1999. 40th Anniv of Rural Development Council.
1192	**437** 180f.+20f. mult	1·10	75

438 *Emblem and Carved Heads*

1999. 125th Anniv of Universal Postal Union. Multicoloured.
1193	180f.+20f. Type **438**	1·10	65
1194	280f. Emblem and forms of transport	1·60	1·00

439 *African Elephants*

1999. "PHILEX FRANCE '99" International Stamp Exhibition, Paris. Animals in Abidjan Zoo. Multicoloured.
1195	180f.+20f. Type **439**	1·50	1·10
1196	250f. African buffaloes	1·50	1·10
1197	280f. Chimpanzees	1·70	1·10
1198	400f. Savanna monkey	2·30	1·30

440 *Ancistrochilus rothschildianus*

1999. Flowers. Multicoloured.
1199	100f. Type **440**	55	35
1200	180f.+20f. *Brachycorythis pubescens*	1·60	1·10
1201	200f. *Bulbophyllum barbigerum*	1·60	1·10
1202	280f. *Habenaria macrandra*	1·80	1·10

441 *Rock and Trees*

1999. Rock Formations, Ahouakro. Multicoloured.
1203	180f.+20f. Type **441**	1·30	65
1204	280f. Two rocks	1·60	95
1205	400f. Large rock (vert)	2·20	1·40

442 *France 1849 20c. Ceres Stamp*

1999. 150th Anniv of First French Stamp.
1206	**442** 280f. multicoloured	2·00	1·20

443 *African Golden Oriole (Oriolus auratus)*

1999. Birds. Multicoloured.
1207	50f. Type **443**	35	25
1208	180f.+20f. Variable sunbird (*Nectarinia venusta*)	1·30	95
1209	280f. Madagascar green pigeon (*Treron australis*)	2·00	1·20
1210	300f. Grey parrot (*Psittacus erithacus*)	2·00	1·20

444 *Wahrindi (Synodontis schall)*

1999. Fish. Multicoloured.
1211	100f. Type **444**	65	35
1212	180f.+20f. Gunther's krib (*Chromidotilapia guntheri*)	1·30	95
1213	280f. Grass-eater perch (*Distichodus rostratus*)	2·00	1·20

445 *School Children and "EDUCATION"*

1999. New Millennium. Multicoloured.
1214	100f. Type **445**	55	30
1215	180f.+20f. Fruit and "AGRICULTURE"	1·10	65
1216	200f. Factory and "INDUSTRIE"	1·10	65
1217	250f. Computer and "INFORMATIQUE"	1·40	85
1218	280f. Dove and "PAIX"	1·40	90
1219	400f. Mask and "CULTURE"	1·60	1·30

446 *Wambele*

2000. Traditional Masks. Multicoloured.
1220	50f. Type **446**	30	25
1221	180f.+20f. Dje	1·10	70
1222	400f. Korobla (vert)	2·00	1·30

447 *Blighia sapida*

2000. Native Plants. Multicoloured.
1223	30f. Type **447**	25	20
1224	180f.+20f. *Ricinodendron heudelotti*	1·20	75
1225	300f. *Telfaira occidentalis*	1·50	1·00
1226	400f. *Napoleonaea vogelii*	2·00	1·40

448 *Pres. Robert Guei, Map, Elephant and Dove*

2000. 40th Anniv of Independence.
1227	**448** 180f.+20f. mult	1·10	80
1228	**448** 400f. multicoloured	2·20	1·40

449 *Cacao*

2000
1229	**449** 5f. multicoloured	10	10
1230	**449** 10f. multicoloured	10	10
1231	**449** 20f. multicoloured	10	10
1232	**449** 25f. multicoloured	10	10
1233	**449** 30f. multicoloured	10	10
1234	**449** 40f. multicoloured	15	15
1235	**449** 50f. multicoloured	20	15
1236	**449** 100f. multicoloured	45	15
1237	**449** 180f.+20f. mult	85	30
1238	**449** 300f. multicoloured	1·30	50
1239	**449** 350f. multicoloured	1·50	50
1240	**449** 400f. multicoloured	1·70	50
1241	**449** 600f. multicoloured	2·50	75

450 *Emblem*

452 *Braided Hairstyle*

2000. 30th Anniv of National Lottery.
1242	**450** 180f.+20f. mult	1·10	80
1243	**450** 400f. multicoloured	2·20	1·60

451 *Football*

2000. Olympic Games, Sydney. Multicoloured.
1244	180f.+20f. Type **451**	1·10	70
1245	400f. Kangaroo holding rugby ball and Sydney Opera House	2·20	1·50
1246	600f. Athletics	3·25	2·10
1247	750f. Olympic stadium and bird	4·25	3·00

2000. Hairstyles. Multicoloured.
1248	180f.+20f. Type **452**	1·10	70
1249	300f. Braid in hair	1·60	1·10
1250	400f. Twisted hair on head	2·20	1·50
1251	500f. Braided into loops	2·75	1·70

453 *Mandela*

2000. Tenth Anniv of Release of Nelson Mandela.
1252	**453** 300f. multicoloured	1·60	1·10

454 *"Queen Pokou"*

2000. Statues. Multicoloured.
1253	180f.+20f. Type **454**	1·10	75
1254	400f. "Akwaba"	2·20	1·40
1255	600f. "Invocation of the Spirits"	3·25	2·10

455 *Refugees*

2000. 50th Anniv of United Nations Commissioner for Refugees.
1256	**455** 400f. multicoloured	2·20	1·60

456 *Buffalo*

2001. Abokouamekro National Park. Multicoloured.
1257	50f. Type **456**	35	20
1258	100f. Rhinoceros and calf	55	30
1259	180f.+20f. Rhinoceros	1·10	80
1260	400f.+20f. Buffalo under trees	2·50	1·40

457 *Carved Wooden Poles*

2001. Exhibits in National Museum, Abidjan. Multicoloured.
1261	100f. Type **457**	45	10
1262	180f.+20f. Blolo Bian	85	35
1263	300f.+20f. Botoumo	1·40	60
1264	400f.+20f. Odi Oka	1·80	80

458 *Maps and Flag*

2001. 41st Anniv of Independence.
1265	**458** 180f.+20f. multicoloured	90	85

459 *Player heading Ball*

2001. World Cup Football Championship (2002), Japan and South Korea. Multicoloured.
1266	180f.+20f. Type **459**	95	70
1267	400f.+20f. Players legs	1·50	1·20
1268	600f.+20f. Players tackling	3·00	2·10
1269	700f. Players tackling	3·25	2·40

460 Children encircling Globe

2001. United Nations Year of Dialogue among Civilisations.
1270	460	400f.+20f. multicoloured	1·80	1·70

461 National Flag

2001. First Anniv of Second Republic.
1271	461	180f.+20f. multicoloured	90	85

462 Cloth

2001. Traditional Crafts. Korhogo Cloth. Multicoloured.
1272		100f. Type **462**	45	10
1273		180f.+20f. Animals and birds	95	35
1274		400f.+20f. Man decorating cloth (vert)	1·90	80

463 Emblem, Map of Africa and Dancers

2001. 23rd UPU Congress (2004), Abidjan.
1275	463	180f.+20f. multicoloured	90	35
1276	463	400f.+20f. multicoloured (26×37 mm)	1·90	80
1277	463	600f.+20f. multicoloured (36×49 mm)	2·75	1·10

464 Heart enclosing Couple and Cupid

2002. St. Valentine's Day. Self-adhesive.
1278	464	180f.+20f. multicoloured	95	35

465 Airplane, Flags and Globe

2002. 40th Anniv of Jean Mermoz International College. Multicoloured.
1279		180f.+20f. Type **465**	90	35
1280		400f.+20f. As No. 1279 but with title banner changed	1·90	75

466 Football and Emblems

2002. World Cup Football Championships, Japan and South Korea. Multicoloured.
1281		180f.+20f. Type **466**	1·00	35
1282		300f.+20f. Players tackling (36×28 mm)	1·70	55

1283		400f.+20f. As No. 1281 but with colours changed	2·20	75
1284		600f.+20f. Trophy enclosing two players (28×36 mm)	3·25	1·10
MS1285		96×96 mm (circular) 500f. No. 1283	2·50	2·50

467 Elephants

2002. Decentralization.
1286	467	400f.+20f. multicoloured	1·90	75

468 Flags and Palace de Culture Building

2003. 20th Anniv of Ivory Coast—People's Republic of China Diplomatic Relations.
1288	468	180f. multicoloured	80	25
1289	468	400f. multicoloured	1·80	75
1290	468	650f. multicoloured	3·00	1·20

469 Alingue Bia

2003. Carved Columns, Museum of Civilization. Multicoloured.
1291		20f. Type **469**	10	10
1292		100f. Lalie	45	20
1293		180f.+20f. Tre Ni Tre	85	35
1294		300f.+20f. Golikple-Kple	1·40	55

470 People pointing to AIDS Virus

2003. Anti-AIDS Campaign. Multicoloured.
1295		180f.+20f. Type **470**	90	30
1296		400f.+20f. Combating virus (38×38 mm) (circular)	1·80	70

MILITARY FRANK STAMP

MF59

1967. No value indicated.
MF1	MF59	(–) multicoloured	2·75	2·75

OFFICIAL STAMPS

O135 Arms of Ivory Coast

1973. No value indicated. Multicoloured. Background colours given.
O422	O135	(–) green and turquoise	65	25
O423	O135	(–) yellow and orange	1·00	50
O424	O135	(–) pink and mauve	1·40	80
O425	O135	(–) violet and blue	3·75	1·60

Nos. O422/5 represent the following face values. No. O422, 35f. No. O423, 75f. No. O424, 100f. No. O425, 250f.

PARCEL POST STAMPS

1903. Postage Due stamps of French Colonies optd. (a) **Cote d'Ivoire COLIS Postaux.**
P18	U	50c. purple	55·00	65·00
P20	U	1f. pink on buff	60·00	55·00

(b) **Colis Postaux.**
P19	50c. purple	£3250	£3250
P21	1f. pink on buff	£3250	£3250

(c) **Cote d'Ivoire Colis Postaux.**
P22	50c. purple	£140	£140
P23	1f. pink on buff	£100	£110

1903. Postage Due stamps of French Colonies surch. (a) **Cote d'Ivoire Colis Postaux** and new value.
P24	50c. on 15c. green	30·00	19·00
P25	50c. on 60c. brown on buff	60·00	55·00
P26	1f. on 5c. blue	24·00	26·00
P27	1f. on 10c. brown	29·00	40·00
P30	4f. on 60c. brown on buff	£130	£130

(b) **Colis Postaux Cote d'Ivoire** and new value.
P35	4f. on 5c. blue	£250	£250
P28	4f. on 15c. green	£130	£130
P29	4f. on 30c. pink	£130	£130
P36	8f. on 15c. green	£250	£250

1904. Postage Due stamps of French Colonies optd. (a) **C. P. Cote d'Ivoire.**
P31	50c. purple	42·00	70·00
P32	1f. pink on buff	24·00	65·00

(b) **Cote d'Ivoire C.P.**
P33	50c. purple	55·00	55·00
P34	1f. pink on buff	65·00	65·00

1905. Postage Due stamps of French Colonies surch **Cote d'Ivoire C. P.** and new value.
P39	2f. on 1f. pink on buff	£225	£225
P40	4f. on 1f. pink on buff	£225	£225
P41	8f. on 1f. pink on buff	£500	£550

POSTAGE DUE STAMPS

1906. "Natives" key-type inscr "COTE D'IVOIRE".
D38	L	5c. green	1·40	90
D39	L	10c. purple	1·20	1·40
D40	L	15c. blue on blue	3·50	2·30
D41	L	20c. black on yellow	2·00	2·75
D42	L	30c. red on cream	6·50	6·75
D43	L	50c. violet	2·75	5·50
D44	L	60c. black on buff	7·25	60·00
D45	L	1f. black on pink	18·00	55·00

1915. "Figure" key-type inscr "COTE D'IVOIRE".
D60	M	5c. green	10	4·00
D61	M	10c. red	10	1·60
D62	M	15c. grey	10	2·50
D63	M	20c. brown	35	4·75
D64	M	30c. blue	20	4·75
D65	M	50c. black	20	5·00
D66	M	60c. orange	45	5·50
D67	M	1f. violet	55	6·00

1927. Surch in figures.
D94		"2 F." on 1f. purple	45	7·00
D95		"3 F." on 1f. purple	45	7·50

D21 Guere Mask

1960. Values in black.
D196	D21	1f. violet	1·10	5·50
D197	D21	2f. green	1·10	5·50
D198	D21	5f. yellow	1·30	5·75
D199	D21	10f. blue	1·50	6·50
D200	D21	20f. mauve	2·00	13·00

D30 Mask

1962
D220	D30	1f. blue and orange	15	15
D221	-	2f. red and black	30	25
D222	-	5f. green and red	40	40
D223	-	10f. purple and green	80	80
D224	-	20f. black and violet	1·40	1·40

DESIGNS: 2f. to 20f. Various native masks from Bingerville Art School.

D70 Baoule Weight

1968. Designs showing different types of weights.
D309	D70	5f. multicoloured	15	15
D310	-	10f. multicoloured	30	25
D311	-	15f. multicoloured	80	80
D312	-	20f. multicoloured	1·00	95
D313	-	30f. multicoloured	1·50	1·40

D111 "Animal" Weight

1972. Gold Weights and Measures.
D389	D111	20f. brown and violet	95	90
D390	-	40f. brown and red	1·30	1·30
D391	-	50f. purple and orange	2·00	1·90
D392	-	100f. brown and green	3·75	3·50

DESIGNS: 40f. "Dagger"; 50f. "Bird"; 100f. "Triangle".

APPENDIX

The following stamps have either been issued in excess of postal needs, or have not been available to the public in reasonable quantities at face value. Such stamps may later be given full listings if there is evidence of regular postal use. Miniature sheets and imperforate stamps are excluded from this listing.

2005
Otters.250f.; 400f.; 650f.; 1000f.
Football World Cup, Germany, 2006. 3000f. x 2
Olympic Games, Beijing, 2008. 3000f. x 2
Death Centenary of Jules Verne. 3000f. x 4
Michael Schumacher-Formula I World Champion 3000f. x 2

Pt. 1

JAIPUR

A state of Rajasthan, India. Now uses Indian stamps.

12 pies = 1 anna; 16 annas = 1 rupee.

1 Chariot of the Sun God, Surya

1904. Chariot of the Sun God
3	2	½a. blue	4·75	9·00
4	2	1a. red	8·00	17·00
5	2	2a. green	10·00	17·00

3 Chariot of the Sun God, Surya

1904
9	3	¼a. olive	2·25	2·25
10a	3	½a. blue	3·50	1·50
11a	3	1a. red	6·50	1·50
12	3	2a. green	10·00	3·00
13	3	4a. brown	13·00	3·50
14	3	8a. violet	9·50	2·75
15a	3	1r. yellow	40·00	16·00

This set was issued engraved in 1904 and surface-printed in 1913.

4 Chariot of the Sun God, Surya

1911. No gum.
17	4	¼a. olive	40	2·25
18	4	½a. blue	50	2·25
20	4	1a. red	50	2·25
21a	4	2a. green	2·00	8·00

३ आना

(5)

1926. Surch with T **5**.
32	3	3a. on 8a. on 8a. violet	4·50	5·50
33	3	3a. on 1r. on 1r. yellow	5·00	9·50

6 Chariot of the Sun God, Surya

7 Maharaja Sawai Man Singh II

1931. Investiture of Maharaja. Centres in black.

40	6	¼a. red	6·00	4·50
58	7	¼a. red	75	50
41	7	½a. violet	75	20
59	7	¾a. red	13·00	6·50
42	-	1a. blue	18·00	15·00
60	7	1a. blue	16·00	9·00
43	-	2a. orange	16·00	14·00
61	7	2a. orange	17·00	8·00
44	-	2½a. red	48·00	70·00
62	7	2½a. red	8·00	3·50
45	-	3a. green	32·00	60·00
63	7	3a. green	4·75	2·00
46	-	4a. green	40·00	85·00
64	7	4a. green	75·00	£275
47	-	6a. blue	12·00	75·00
65	7	6a. blue	12·00	55·00
48	-	8a. brown	29·00	£130
66	7	8a. brown	48·00	£200
49	-	1r. olive	90·00	£550
67	7	1r. bistre	20·00	£250
50	-	2r. green	£100	£600
51	-	5r. purple	£110	£700

DESIGNS:—VERT: 1a. (No. 42), Elephant and banner; 2a. (No. 43), Sowar in armour; 2½a. (No. 44), Common peafowl; 8a. (No. 48), Sireh-Deorhi Gate. HORIZ: 3a. (No. 45), Bullock carriage; 4a. (No. 46), Elephant carriage; 6a. (No. 47), Albert Museum; 1r. (No. 49), Chandra Mahal; 2r. Amber Palace; 5r. Maharajas Sawai Jai Singh and Man Singh.

1932. As T 7, but inscr "POSTAGE & REVENUE". Portrait in black.

52	1a. blue	5·50	3·25
53	2a. brown	9·00	3·50
54	4a. green	4·75	20·00
55	8a. brown	6·00	28·00
56	1r. bistre	40·00	£275
57	2r. green	£140	£800

1936. Nos. 57 and 51 surch One Rupee.

68	1r. on 2r. green	14·00	£180
69	1r. on 5r. purple	18·00	£130

1938. No. 41 surch in native characters.

70	7	¼a. on ½a. on ½a. violet	22·00	23·00

1948. No. 41 surch 3 PIES and bars.

71	7	3p. on ½a. on ½a. violet	22·00	38·00

21 Palace Gate

1947. Silver Jubilee of Maharaja's Accession to the Throne. Inscr as in T 21.

72	21	¼a. brown and green	3·00	7·00
73	-	½a. green and violet	50	4·50
74	-	¾a. black and red	3·50	10·00
75	-	1a. brown and blue	1·50	4·75
76	-	2a. violet and red	1·25	7·00
77	-	3a. green and black	3·75	12·00
78	-	4a. blue and brown	1·25	7·00
79	-	8a. red and brown	1·50	7·00
80	-	1r. purple and green	5·50	75·00

DESIGNS: ¼a. Palace Gate; ¾a. Map of Jaipur; 1a. Observatory; 2a. Wind Palace; 3a. Coat of Arms; 4a. Amber Fort Gate; 8a. Chariot of the Sun; 1r. Maharaja's portrait between State flags.

OFFICIAL STAMPS

1929. Optd SERVICE. No gum (except for No. O6a).

O1a	3	¼a. bistre	5·50	4·50
O2	3	½a. blue	2·75	40
O3c	3	1a. red	4·00	1·25
O5	3	2a. green	4·00	75
O6a	3	4a. brown (with gum)	4·50	1·75
O7	3	8a. violet	18·00	70·00
O8	3	1r. orange	45·00	£550

1931. Stamps of 1931–32 optd SERVICE.

O23	7	¼a. red	50	10
O13	7	½a. violet	40	10
O24	7	¾a. red	2·00	50
O14	-	1a. blue (No. 42)	£650	7·00
O18	-	1a. blue (No. 52)	8·00	15
O25	7	1a. blue	7·00	30
O15	-	2a. orange (No. 43)	8·00	8·00
O19	-	2a. brown (No. 53)	12·00	15
O26	7	2a. orange	5·00	3·25
O27	7	2½a. red	14·00	£110
O16	-	4a. green (No. 46)	80·00	65·00
O20	-	4a. green (No. 54)	£450	17·00
O28	7	4a. green	8·50	7·50
O21	-	8a. brown (No. 55)	18·00	1·75
O29	7	8a. brown	4·75	9·50
O22	-	1r. bistre (No. 56)	55·00	40·00
O30	7	1r. bistre	35·00	

1932. No. O5 surch in native characters.

O17	3	½a. on 2a. on 2a. green	£275	5·00

1947. Official stamps surch.

O33	7	3p. on ½a. on ½a. violet	10·00	19·00
O32	7	9p. on 1a. on 1a. blue	3·75	3·75

1948. No. O13 surch in native characters.

O34		¾a. on ½a. on ½a. violet	28·00	24·00

For later issues see RAJASTHAN.

Pt. 1

JAMAICA

An island in the W. Indies. Part of the Br. Caribbean Federation from 3 January 1958, until 6 August 1962 when Jamaica became an independent state within the Commonwealth.

1860. 12 pence = 1 shilling; 20 shillings = 1 pound.
1969. 100 cents = 1 dollar.

8

1860. Portrait as T 8. Various frames.

7	8	½d. red	20·00	3·50
16a	8	½d. green	2·75	10
8	8	1d. blue	£100	75
18a	8	1d. red	65·00	1·00
9	8	2d. red	£100	70
20a	8	2d. grey	£100	65
21a	8	3d. green	2·50	2·25
11	8	4d. orange	£325	12·00
22b	8	4d. brown	2·00	35
23a	8	6d. yellow	3·00	3·50
52a	8	6d. lilac	10·00	29·00
24	8	1s. brown	9·00	6·00
25	8	2s. red	32·00	30·00
26	8	5s. lilac	65·00	90·00

See also Nos. 47a etc.

11

1889.

27	11	1d. purple and mauve	10·00	20
28a	11	2d. green	22·00	8·00
29	11	2½d. purple and blue	8·50	50

1890. No. 22a surch TWO PENCE HALF-PENNY.

30	8	2½d. on 4d. orange	40·00	17·00

13 Llandovery Falls, Jamaica

1900.

31	13	1d. red	11·00	20
32	13	1d. black and red	10·00	20

14 Arms of Jamaica

1903.

33	14	½d. grey and green	1·75	30
34	14	1d. grey and red	4·25	10
35	14	2½d. grey and blue	8·00	30
42	14	2½d. blue	5·00	1·25
36	14	5d. grey and yellow	15·00	23·00
44	14	6d. purple	14·00	19·00
45	14	5s. grey and violet	55·00	55·00

16

1906.

38b	16	½d. green	3·00	20
40	16	1d. red	1·50	10

1908. Queen Victoria portraits as 1860.

47a	3d. purple on yellow	2·00	1·50
49	4d. black on yellow	15·00	55·00
50	4d. red on yellow	1·50	4·50
54	1s. black on green	10·00	8·50
56	2s. purple on blue	12·00	6·00

17

1911.

57	17	2d. grey	8·00	13·00

1912. As T 17, but King George V.

92	½d. green	3·50	10
58	1d. red	1·50	10
59	1½d. orange	1·50	40
60	2d. grey	2·25	15
61a	2½d. blue	80	1·00
62	3d. purple on yellow	50	45
63	4d. black and red on yellow	50	2·75
64a	6d. purple and mauve	1·00	1·00
65	1s. black on green	2·25	2·00
66	2s. purple and blue on blue	24·00	35·00
67	5s. green and red on yellow	80·00	£100

1916. Optd WAR STAMP. in one line (with full point).

68	16	½d. green	20	35
69a	-	3d. purple on yellow (62)	2·50	22·00

See also Nos. 76/77a.

1916. Optd WAR STAMP. in two lines.

73	16	½d. green	2·00	30
74	-	1½d. orange (No. 59)	20	10
75	-	3d. purple on yellow (No. 62)	2·25	1·40

1919. Optd WAR STAMP in one line (no full point).

76	15	½d. green	20	15
77b	-	3d. purple on yellow (No. 62)	5·00	1·25

23 Jamaica Exhibition, 1891

24 Arawak Woman preparing Cassava

27 Return of War Contingent, 1919

34

1919.

94a	23	½d. green and olive	50	50
79	24	1d. red and orange (A)*	1·75	1·75
95	24	1d. red and orange (B)*	1·50	10
96	-	1½d. orange	3·00	45
81	-	2d. blue and green	1·00	4·00
82a	27	2½d. blue	1·50	1·75
99a	-	3d. green and blue	3·00	20
100	-	4d. brown and green	1·25	30
101a	-	6d. black and blue	13·00	1·00
102a	-	1s. orange	1·75	65
103	-	2s. blue and brown	3·25	65
104	-	3s. violet and orange	18·00	9·00
105	-	5s. blue and bistre	30·00	25·00
106	34	10s. green	55·00	70·00

DESIGNS:—HORIZ (41½×26 mm): 1½d. War Contingent embarking, 1915; 6d. Port Royal, 1853. (27×22 mm): 3d. Landing of Columbus, 1494. VERT (22×29 mm): 2d. King's House, Spanish Town; 4d. Cathedral, Spanish Town. (25×30 mm): 1s. Statue of Queen Victoria, Kingston; 2s. Admiral Rodney Memorial, Spanish Town; 3s. Sir Charles Metcalfe Monument; 5s. Jamaican scenery.
*Two types of the 1d. (A) Without and (B) with "POSTAGE & REVENUE" at foot.

37

1923. Child Welfare. Designs as T 37.

107	37	½d.+½d. black and green	1·25	5·50
107b	-	1d.+½d. black and red	3·50	12·00
107c	-	2½d.+½d. black and blue	22·00	19·00

41

1929. Various frames.

108	41	1d. red	14·00	20
109	41	1½d. brown	8·50	15
110	41	9d. maroon	8·50	1·00

43 Coco Palms at Don Christopher's Cove   **45** Priestman's River, Portland

1932.

111	43	2d. black and green	35·00	3·75
112	-	2½d. turquoise and blue	6·50	1·50
113	45	6d. black and purple	35·00	5·00

DESIGN:—As T 43: 2½d. Wag Water River, St. Andrew.

1935. Silver Jubilee. As T 14a of Kenya, Uganda and Tanganyika.

114	1d. blue and red	50	15
115	1½d. blue and black	60	1·50
116	6d. green and blue	13·00	20·00
117	1s. grey and purple	8·00	20·00

1937. Coronation. As T 14b of Kenya, Uganda and Tanganyika.

118	1d. red	30	15
119	1½d. grey	65	30
120	2½d. blue	1·00	70

46 King George VI   **47** Coco Palms at Don Christopher's Cove

48 Bananas   **52** Bamboo Walk

1938.

121	46	½d. green	1·75	10
121b	46	½d. orange	3·00	30
122	46	1d. red	1·25	10
122a	46	1d. green	4·00	10
123	46	1½d. brown	1·25	10
124d	47	2d. black and green	1·25	10
125	-	2½d. green and blue	8·50	2·75
126	48	3d. blue and green	1·00	1·50
126b	48	3d. green and blue	4·50	1·25
126c	48	3d. green and red	5·50	30
127	-	4d. brown and green	1·00	10
128a	48	6d. black and purple	2·25	10
129	-	9d. red	1·00	50
130	-	1s. green and brown	14·00	20
131	52	2s. blue and brown	35·00	1·00
132ba	-	5s. blue and brown	11·00	3·00
133	-	10s. green	11·00	11·00
133a	-	£1 brown and violet	60·00	38·00

DESIGNS:—As Type 47: 2½d. Wag Water River, St. Andrew. As Type 48: 4d. Citrus grove; 9d. Kingston Harbour; 1s. Sugar industry; £1 Tobacco growing and cigar making. As previous issues, but with portrait of King George VI: 6d. As Type 45; 5s. As No. 102c; 10s. As Type 34.

54 Courthouse, Falmouth   **56** Institute of Jamaica

1945. New Constitution.

134	54	1½d. brown	30	30
135a	-	2d. green	30	50
136	56	3d. blue	30	50
137	-	4½d. black	1·00	30
138	-	2s. brown	1·50	50
139	-	5s. blue	4·00	1·00
140	56	10s. green	3·25	2·25

DESIGNS:—VERT (as Type 54): 2s. "Labour and Learning". HORIZ (as Type 54): 2d. Kings Charles II and George VI. (As Type 56): 4½d. House of Assembly; 5s. Scroll, flag and King George VI.

59a Houses of Parliament, London

1946. Victory.

| 141a | 59a | 1½d. brown | 65 | 4·50 |
| 142a | 59a | 3d. blue | 65 | 8·50 |

59b King George VI and Queen Elizabeth

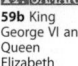

59c

1948. Silver Wedding.

| 143 | 59b | 1½d. brown | 30 | 10 |
| 144 | 59c | £1 red | 28·00 | 75·00 |

59d Hermes, Globe and forms of Transport

59e Hemispheres, Jet-powered Vickers Viking Airliner and Steamer

59f Hermes and Globe

59g U.P.U. Monument

1949. U.P.U.

145	59d	1½d. brown	20	15
146	59e	2d. green	1·25	5·25
147	59f	3d. blue	50	1·50
148	59g	6d. purple	50	2·50

59h University Arms   **59i** Princess Alice

1951. Inauguration of B.W.I. University College.

| 149 | 59h | 2d. black and brown | 30 | 50 |
| 150 | 59i | 6d. black and purple | 70 | 30 |

60 Scout Badge and Map of Caribbean   **61** Scout Badge and Map of Jamaica

1952. First Caribbean Scout Jamboree.

| 151 | 60 | 2d. blue, green and black | 30 | 10 |
| 152 | 61 | 6d. green, red and black | 70 | 60 |

61a Queen Elizabeth II

1953. Coronation.

| 153 | 61a | 2d. black and green | 1·50 | 10 |

1953. Royal Visit. As T **47** but with portrait of Queen Elizabeth II and inscr "ROYAL VISIT 1953".

| 154 | | 2d. black and green | 55 | 10 |

63 H.M.S. *Britannia* (ship of the line) at Port Royal

1955. Tercentenary Issue.

155	63	2d. black and green	85	10
156	-	2½d. black and blue	15	35
157	-	3d. black and claret	15	30
158	-	6d. black and red	30	20

DESIGNS: 2½d. Old Montego Bay; 3d. Old Kingston; 6d. Proclamation of Abolition of Slavery, 1838.

67 Coconut Palms   **75** Blue Mountain Peak

71 Mahoe   **79** Arms of Jamaica

1956

159	67	½d. black and red	10	10
160	-	1d. black and green	10	10
161	-	2d. black and green	15	10
162	-	2½d. black and blue	75	50
163	71	3d. green and brown	20	10
164	-	4d. green and blue	40	10
165	-	5d. red and green	40	2·50
166	-	6d. black and red	3·75	10
167	75	8d. blue and orange	2·50	10
168	-	1s. green and blue	2·50	10
169	-	1s.6d. blue and purple	1·25	10
170	-	2s. blue and green	16·00	3·25
171	79	3s. black and blue	3·50	3·75
172	-	5s. black and red	4·50	7·50
173	-	10s. black and green	35·00	22·00
174	-	£1 black and purple	35·00	22·00

DESIGNS—As Type **67**: 1d. Sugar cane; 2d. Pineapples; 2½d. Bananas. As Type **71**: 4d. Bread-fruit; 5d. Ackee; 6d. Streamertail. As Type **75**: 1s. Royal Botanic Gardens, Hope; 1s.6d. Rafting on the Rio Grande; 2s. Fort Charles. As Type **79** but vert: 10s., £1 Arms without portrait.

80a Federation Map

1958. British Caribbean Federation.

175	80a	2d. green	80	10
176	80a	5d. blue	1·25	3·50
177	80a	6d. red	1·25	40

81 Bristol Britannia 312 flying over *City of Berlin*, 1860   **83** 1s. Stamps of 1860 and 1956

1960. Centenary of Jamaica Postage Stamps.

178	81	2d. blue and purple	75	10
179	-	6d. red and olive	75	50
180	83	1s. brown, green and blue	75	55

DESIGN—As Type **81**: 6d. Postal mule-cart and motor-van.

1962. Independence. (a) Nos. 159/74 optd **INDEPENDENCE** and **1962** (3d. to 2s.) or 1962 1962 (others).

205	74	½d. black and red	10	15
182	-	1d. black and green	10	10
183	-	2½d. black and blue	10	1·00
184	75	3d. green and brown	10	10
185	-	5d. red and olive	20	60
186	-	6d. black and red	3·25	10
187	76	8d. blue and orange	20	10
188	-	1s. green and blue	20	10
189	-	2s. blue and olive	1·00	1·50
190	77	3s. black and blue	1·00	1·50
191	-	10s. black and green	4·50	4·25
192	-	£1 black and purple	4·50	5·50

86 Military Bugler and Map

(b) As T **86** inscr "INDEPENDENCE".

193	86	2d. multicoloured	2·25	10
194	86	4d. multicoloured	1·50	10
195	-	1s.6d. black and red	5·50	85
196	-	5s. multicoloured	11·00	7·50

DESIGNS: 1s.6d. Gordon House and banner; 5s. Map, factories and fruit.

89 Kingston Seal, Weightlifting, Boxing, Football and Cycling

1962. Ninth Central American and Caribbean Games, Kingston.

197	89	1d. sepia and red	20	10
198	-	6d. sepia and blue	20	10
199	-	8d. sepia and bistre	20	10
200	-	2s. multicoloured	30	90

DESIGNS: 6d. Diver, sailing, swimming and water polo; 8d. Javelin, discus, pole-vault, hurdles and relay-racing; 2s. Kingston coat of arms and athlete.

93 Farmer and Crops

1963. Freedom from Hunger.

| 201 | 93 | 1d. multicoloured | 25 | 10 |
| 202 | 93 | 8d. multicoloured | 1·25 | 60 |

94 Red Cross Emblem

1963. Cent of Red Cross.

| 203 | 94 | 2d. red and black | 15 | 10 |
| 204 | 94 | 1s.6d. red and blue | 50 | 1·50 |

95 Carole Joan Crawford ("Miss World 1963")

1964. "Miss World 1963" Commem.

214	95	3d. multicoloured	10	10
215	-	1s. multicoloured	15	10
216	-	1s.6d. multicoloured	20	50
MS216a 153×101 mm. Nos. 214/16.				
		Imperf	1·40	2·75

96 "Lignum vitae"   **103** Gypsum Industry

1964

217	96	1d. blue, green and brown	10	10
218	-	1½d. multicoloured	15	10
219	-	2d. red, yellow and green	15	10
220	-	2½d. multicoloured	1·00	60
221	-	3d. yellow, black & green	15	10
222	-	4d. ochre and violet	50	10
223	-	6d. multicoloured	2·25	10
224	-	8d. multicoloured	2·50	1·50
225	103	9d. blue and bistre	1·50	10
226	-	1s. black and brown	20	10
227	-	1s.6d. black, blue & buff	4·00	15
228	-	2s. brown, black and blue	2·75	10
229b	-	3s. blue and green	35	65
230	-	5s. black, ochre and blue	1·25	1·25
231	-	10s. multicoloured	1·25	1·25

| 232 | - | £1 multicoloured | 2·50 | 1·00 |

DESIGNS—HORIZ (As T **96**): 1½d. Ackee (fruit); 2½d. Land shells; 3d. National flag over Jamaica; 4d. Antillean murex (sea shell); 6d. *Papilio homerus* (butterfly); 8d. Streamertail. VERT (As T **96**): 2d. Blue Mahoe (tree). HORIZ (As T **103**): 1s. National Stadium; 1s.6d. Palisadoes International Airport; 2s. Bauxite mining; 3s. Blue marlin (sport fishing); 5s. Exploration of sunken city, Port Royal; £1 Queen Elizabeth II and national flag. VERT (As T **96**): 10s. Arms of Jamaica.

114 Scout Badge and Alligator

1964. Sixth Inter-American Scout Conf, Kingston.

233	-	3d. red, black and pink	10	10
234	-	8d. blue, olive and mauve	15	25
235	114	1s. gold, blue and light blue	20	45

DESIGNS—VERT (25½×30 mm): 3d. Scout belt; 8d. Globe, scout hat and scarf.

115 Gordon House, Kingston

1964. Tenth Commonwealth Parliamentary Conference, Kingston.

236	115	3d. black and green	10	10
237	-	6d. black and red	30	10
238	-	1s.6d. black and blue	50	30

DESIGNS: 6d. Headquarters House, Kingston; 1s.6d. House of Assembly, Spanish Town.

118 Eleanor Roosevelt

1964. 16th Anniv of Declaration of Human Rights.

| 239 | 118 | 1s. black, red and green | 10 | 10 |

119 Guides' Emblem on Map

1965. Golden Jubilee of Jamaica Girl Guides' Association. Inscr "1915–1965".

| 240 | 119 | 3d. yellow, green and black | 10 | 10 |
| 241 | - | 1s. yellow, black and green | 20 | 40 |

DESIGN—TRIANGULAR (61½×30½ mm): 1s. Guide emblems.

121 Uniform Cap

1965. Centenary of Salvation Army. Multicoloured.

| 242 | | 3d. Type **121** | 30 | 10 |
| 243 | | 1s.6d. Flag-bearer and drummer (vert) | 70 | 50 |

123 Paul Bogle, William Gordon and Morant Bay Court House

1965. Centenary of Morant Bay Rebellion.

244	123	3d. brown, blue and green	10	10
245	123	1s.6d. brown, green & blk	20	15
246	123	3s. brown, red and black	30	1·25

124 Abeng-blower, "Telstar", Morse Key and I.T.U. Emblem

1965. Centenary of I.T.U.

247	**124**	1s. black, slate and red	40	20

1966. Royal Visit. Nos. 221, 223, 226/7 optd **ROYAL VISIT MARCH 1966.**

248	3d. yellow, black and green	15	10
249	6d. multicoloured	2·25	50
250	1s. black and brown	55	10
251	1s.6d. black, blue and buff	2·50	3·00

126 Sir Winston Churchill

1966. Churchill Commemoration.

252	**126**	6d. black and green	65	30
253	**126**	1s. brown and blue	85	80

127 Statue of Athlete and Flags

1966. Eighth British Empire and Commonwealth Games.

254	**127**	3d. multicoloured	10	10
255	-	6d. multicoloured	60	10
256	-	1s. multicoloured	10	10
257	-	3s. gold and blue	35	45
MS258	128×103 mm. Nos. 254/7. Imperf		4·00	8·00

DESIGNS: 6d. Racing cyclists; 1s. National Stadium, Kingston; 3s. Games emblem.

131 Bolivar's Statue and Flags of Jamaica and Venezuela

1966. 150th Anniv of "Jamaica Letter".

259	**131**	8d. multicoloured	20	10

132 Jamaican Pavilion

1967. World Fair, Montreal.

260	**132**	6d. multicoloured	10	15
261	**132**	1s. multicoloured	10	15

133 Sir Donald Sangster (Prime Minister)

1967. Sangster Memorial Issue.

262	**133**	3d. multicoloured	10	10
263	**133**	1s.6d. multicoloured	20	20

134 Traffic Duty

1967. Centenary of Constabulary Force. Multicoloured.

264	3d. Type **134**	40	10

265	1s. Personnel of the Force (56½×20½ mm)	40	10
266	1s.6d. Badge and Constables of 1867 and 1967	50	75

1968. M.C.C.'s West Indies Tour. As Nos. 445/7 of Guyana.

267	6d. multicoloured	50	65
268	6d. multicoloured	50	65
269	6d. multicoloured	50	65

137 Sir Alexander and Lady Bustamante

1968. Labour Day.

270	**137**	3d. red and black	10	15
271	**137**	1s. olive and black	10	15

138 Human Rights Emblem over Map of Jamaica

1968. Human Rights Year. Multicoloured.

272	3d. Type **138**	10	10
273	1s. Hands cupping Human Rights emblem	20	10
274	3s. Jamaican holding "Human Rights"	60	1·50

141 I.L.O. Emblem

1969. 50th Anniv of I.L.O.

275	**141**	6d. yellow and brown	10	10
276	**141**	3s. green and brown	30	45

142 Nurse and Children being Weighed and Measured

1969. 20th Anniv of W.H.O. Multicoloured.

277	6d. Type **142**	10	15
278	1s. Malaria eradication (horiz)	10	15
279	3s. Trainee nurse	20	1·25

1969. Decimal Currency. Nos. 217, 219, 221/3 and 225/32 surch **C-DAY 8th September 1969** and value.

280	**95**	1c. on 1d. blue, grn & brn	10	10
281	-	2c. on 2d. red, yellow & grn	10	10
282	-	3c. on 3d. yellow, black and green	10	10
283	-	4c. on 4d. ochre and violet	1·25	10
284	-	5c. on 6d. multicoloured	1·25	10
285	**103**	8c. on 9d. blue and bistre	10	10
286	-	10c. on 1s. black & brown	10	10
287	-	15c. on 1s.6d. black, blue and buff	50	90
288	-	20c. on 2s. brown, blk & bl	1·50	1·50
289	-	30c. on 3s. blue & green	2·50	3·00
290	-	50c. on 5s. black, ochre and blue	1·25	3·00
291	-	$1 on 10s. multicoloured	1·25	6·50
292	-	$2 on £1 multicoloured	2·25	6·50

146 *The Adoration of the Kings* (detail, Foppa)

1969. Christmas. Paintings. Multicoloured.

293	2c. Type **146**		20	40
294	5c. *Madonna, Child and St. John* (Raphael)		25	40
295	8c. *The Adoration of the Kings* (detail, Dosso Dossi)		25	40

149 Half Penny, 1869

1969. Centenary of First Jamaican Coins.

296	**149**	3c. silver, black and mauve	15	25
297	-	15c. silver, black and green	10	10

DESIGN: 15c. One penny, 1869.

151 George William Gordon

1970. National Heroes. Multicoloured; background colours given.

298	**151**	1c. mauve	10	10
299	-	3c. blue	10	10
300	-	5c. grey	10	10
301	-	10c. red	15	10
302	-	15c. green	30	25

PORTRAITS: 3c. Sir Alexander Bustamante; 5c. Norman Manley; 10c. Marcus Garvey; 15c. Paul Bogle.

156 *Christ appearing to St. Peter* (Carracci)

1970. Easter. Centres multicoloured; frame colours given.

303	**156**	3c. red	10	10
304	-	10c. green	10	10
305	-	20c. grey	20	60

DESIGNS: 10c. *Christ Crucified* (Antonello); 20c. Easter lily.

1970. No. 219 surch **2c.**

306	2c. on 2d. red, yellow & green		20	20

160 *Lignum vitae*

1970. Decimal Currency. Designs as Nos. 217, 219, 221/23, 225/32, but with values inscr as T **160** in new currency.

307	**160**	1c. blue, green and brown	75	2·00
308	-	2c. red, yell & grn (as 2d.)	30	10
309	-	3c. yell, blk & grn (as 3d.)	50	1·00
310	-	4c. ochre and violet (as 4d.)	2·75	30
311	-	5c. multicoloured (as 6d.)	3·00	65
312	**103**	8c. blue and yellow	2·25	10
313	-	10c. black & brown (as 1s.)	60	20
314	-	15c. black, blue and buff (as 1s.6d.)	2·75	3·00
315	-	20c. brown, black and blue (as 2s.)	1·25	3·00
316	-	30c. blue and green (as 3s.)	4·00	6·50
317	-	50c. black, ochre and blue (as 5s.)	1·75	3·75
318	-	$1 multicoloured (as 10s.)	1·00	5·50
319	-	$2 multicoloured (as £1)	1·50	4·00

161 Cable Ship *Dacia*

1970. Centenary of Telegraph Service.

320	**161**	3c. yellow, black and red	25	10
321	-	10c. black and green	35	10
322	-	50c. multicoloured	80	1·00

DESIGNS: 10c. Bright's cable gear aboard *Dacia*; 50c. Morse key and chart.

164 Bananas, Citrus, Sugar-Cane and Tobacco

1970. 75th Anniv of Jamaican Agricultural Society.

323	**164**	2c. multicoloured	25	60
324	**164**	10c. multicoloured	45	10

165 Locomotive *Projector* (1845)

1970. 125th Anniv of Jamaican Railways.

325	3c. Type **165**		30	10
326	15c. Steam locomotive No. 54 (1944)		65	30
327	50c. Diesel locomotive No. 102 (1967)		1·25	1·75

168 Church of St. Jago de la Vega

1971. Centenary of Disestablishment of Church of England in Jamaica.

328	**168**	3c. multicoloured	10	10
329	**168**	10c. multicoloured	10	10
330	**168**	20c. multicoloured	30	30
331	-	30c. multicoloured	30	1·25

DESIGN: 30c. Emblem of Church of England in Jamaica.

169 Henry Morgan and Ships

1971. Pirates and Buccaneers. Multicoloured.

332	3c. Type **169**		75	10
333	15c. Mary Read, Anne Bonny and trial pamphlet		1·00	15
334	30c. Pirate schooner attacking merchantman		1·75	1·25

170 1s. Stamp of 1919 with Frame Inverted

1971. Tercentenary of Post Office.

335	-	3c. black and brown	15	20
336	-	5c. black and green	20	20
337	-	8c. black and violet	20	10
338	-	10c. brown, black and blue	20	10
339	-	20c. multicoloured	35	45
340	**170**	50c. brown, black and grey	50	2·00

DESIGNS—HORIZ: 3c. Drummer packet letter, 1705; 5c. Pre-stamp inland letter, 1793; 8c. Harbour St. P.O., Kingston, 1820; 10c. Modern stamp and cancellation; 20c. British stamps used in Jamaica, 1859.

171 Satellite and Dish
Aerial

1972. Opening of Jamaican Earth Satellite Station.

341	171	3c. multicoloured	15	10
342	171	15c. multicoloured	30	15
343	171	50c. multicoloured	65	1·25

172 Causeway,
Kingston Harbour

1972. Multicoloured.

344		1c. Pimento (vert)	10	10
345		2c. Red ginger (vert)	10	10
346		3c. Bauxite Industry	10	10
347		4c. Type **172**	10	10
348		5c. Oil refinery	10	10
349		6c. Senate Building, University of the West Indies	10	10
350		8c. National Stadium	30	10
351		9c. Devon House	10	10
352		10c. Air Jamaica Hostess and Vickers VC-10	20	10
353		15c. Old Iron Bridge, Spanish Town (vert)	2·00	10
354		20c. College of Arts, Science and Technology	30	15
355		30c. Dunn's River Falls (vert)	65	15
356		50c. River rafting	1·75	40
357		$1 Jamaica House	75	75
358		$2 Kings House	1·00	1·50

Designs for 8c. to $2 are larger, 35×27 or 27×35 mm.

1972. Tenth Anniv of Independence Nos. 346, 352 and 356 optd **TENTH ANNIVERSARY INDEPENDENCE 1962–1972.**

359	3c. multicoloured	30	30
360	10c. multicoloured	30	10
361	50c. multicoloured	75	2·25

175 Arms of
Kingston

1972. Centenary of Kingston as Capital.

362	175	5c. multicoloured	15	10
363	175	30c. multicoloured	35	35
364	-	50c. multicoloured	60	2·25

DESIGN—HORIZ: 50c. design similar to Type **175**.

176 Mongoose on Map

1973. Centenary of Introduction of the Small Indian Mongoose.

365	176	8c. green, yellow and black	15	10
366	-	40c. dp blue, blue & black	35	65
367	-	60c. pink, salmon & black	60	1·25
MS368	165×95 mm. Nos. 365/7		1·10	4·00

DESIGNS: 40c. Mongoose and rat; 60c. Mongoose and chicken.

177 Euphorbia punicea

1973. Flora. Multicoloured.

369		1c. Type **177**	10	30
370		6c. Hylocereus triangularis	15	20
371		9c. Columnea argentea	15	20
372		15c. Portlandia grandiflora	25	20
373		30c. Samyda pubescens	40	60
374		50c. Cordia sebestena	60	1·40

178 Broughtonia sanguinea

1973. Orchids. Multicoloured.

375		5c. Type **178**	40	10
376		10c. Arpophyllum jamaicense (vert)	50	10
377		20c. Oncidium pulchellum (vert)	1·00	25
378		$1 Brassia maculata	2·50	3·25
MS379	161×95 mm. Nos. 375/8		4·00	5·50

179 Mary, 1808–15

1974. Mail Packet Boats. Multicoloured.

380		5c. Type **179**	75	10
381		10c. Queensbury, 1814–27	75	10
382		15c. Sheldrake, 1829–34	1·00	40
383		50c. Thames I, 1842	2·00	2·50
MS384	133×159 mm. Nos. 380/3 (sold at 90c.)		2·75	5·00

180 "Journeys"

1974. National Dance Theatre Company. Multicoloured.

385		5c. Type **180**	10	10
386		10c. "Jamaican Promenade"	10	10
387		30c. "Jamaican Promenade" (different)	30	30
388		50c. "Misa Criolla"	50	80
MS389	161×102 mm. Nos. 385/8 (sold at $1)		1·50	2·50

181 U.P.U. Emblem and
Globe

1974. Centenary of U.P.U.

390	181	5c. multicoloured	10	10
391	181	9c. multicoloured	10	10
392	181	50c. multicoloured	35	80

182 Senate Building and Sir
Hugh Wooding

1975. 25th Anniv of University of West Indies. Multicoloured.

393		5c. Type **182**	10	10
394		10c. University Chapel and Princess Alice	10	10
395		30c. Type **182**	20	25
396		50c. As 10c.	35	60

183 Commonwealth
Symbol

1975. Heads of Commonwealth Conf. Multicoloured.

397		5c. Type **183**	10	10
398		10c. Jamaican coat of arms	10	10
399		30c. Dove of Peace	15	30
400		50c. Jamaican flag	30	2·25

184 Jamaican Kite
Swallowtail

1975. Butterflies (1st series), showing the family "Papilionidae". Multicoloured.

401		10c. Type **184**	55	20
402		20c. Orange swallowtail (Papilo thoas)	1·10	1·10
403		25c. False androyeus swallow-tail (Papilo thersites)	1·25	2·00
404		30c. Homerus swallowtail (Papilo homerus)	1·40	2·75
MS405	134×179 mm. Nos. 401/4 (sold at 95c.)		5·50	7·50

See also Nos. 429/32 and 443/6.

185 Koo Koo or
Actor Boy

1975. Christmas. Belisario prints of "John Canoe" Festival (1st series). Multicoloured.

406		8c. Type **185**	15	10
407		10c. Red Set-girls	15	10
408		20c. French Set-girls	50	20
409		50c. Jaw-bone or House John Canoe	95	2·50
MS410	138×141 mm. Nos. 406/9 (sold at $1)		1·75	3·50

See also Nos. 421/3.

186 Bordone Map, 1528

1976. 16th Century Maps of Jamaica.

411	186	10c. brown, lt brown & red	25	10
412	-	20c. multicoloured	45	25
413	-	30c. multicoloured	70	85
414	-	50c. multicoloured	95	2·75

DESIGNS: 20c. Porcacchi map, 1576; 30c. De Bry map, 1594; 50c. Langenes map, 1598.
See also Nos. 425/8.

187 Olympic Rings

1976. Olympic Games, Montreal.

415	187	10c. multicoloured	15	10
416	187	20c. multicoloured	30	20
417	187a	25c. multicoloured	30	25
418	187a	50c. multicoloured	45	2·25

187a Map of the Caribbean

1976. West Indian Victory in World Cricket Cup.

419		10c. Type **187a**	50	50
420		25c. Prudential Cup	75	1·75

1976. Christmas. Belisario Prints (2nd series). As T **185**. Multicoloured.

421		10c. Queen of the Set-girls	10	10
422		20c. Band of the Jaw-bone John Canoe	25	10
423		50c. Koo Koo (actor-boy)	45	2·00
MS424	110×140 mm. Nos. 421/3 (sold at 90c.)		70	2·00

1977. 17th Cent Maps of Jamaica. As T **186**.

425		9c. multicoloured	30	40
426		10c. red, brown and buff	30	10
427		25c. black, blue and light blue	70	60
428		40c. black, blue and green	80	2·25

DESIGNS: 9c. Hickeringill map, 1661; 10c. Ogilby map, 1671; 25c. Visscher map, 1680; 40c. Thornton map, 1689.

1977. Butterflies (2nd series). As T **184**. Multicoloured.

429		10c. False barred sulphur (Eurema elathea)	35	10
430		20c. Bronze wing (Dynamine egaea)	75	55
431		25c. Jamaican harlequin (Chlo-syne pantoni)	1·00	1·50
432		40c. Mimic (Hypolimnas misippus)	1·50	5·00
MS433	139×120 mm. Nos. 429/32 (sold at $1.05)		4·50	7·00

188 Map, Scout
Emblem and
Streamertail

1977. Sixth Caribbean Scout Jamboree, Jamaica.

434	188	10c. multicoloured	65	10
435	188	20c. multicoloured	1·00	25
436	188	25c. multicoloured	1·00	35
437	188	50c. multicoloured	1·50	1·75

189 Trumpeter

1977. 50th Anniv of Jamaica Military Band. Multicoloured.

438		9c. Type **189**	15	10
439		10c. Clarinet players and oboe player	15	10
440		20c. Two kettle drummers and clarinetist (vert)	40	35
441		25c. Double-bass player and trumpeter (vert)	55	65
MS442	120×137 mm. Nos. 438/41 (sold at 75c.)		2·50	4·50

1978. Butterflies (3rd series). As T **184**. Multicoloured.

443		10c. Jamaican hairstreak (Cal-lophrys crethona)	50	10
444		20c. Malachite (Siproeta stelenes)	85	20
445		25c. Common long-tailed skip-per (Urbanus proteus)	95	65
446		50c. Troglodyte (Anaea troglodyta)	2·00	3·25
MS447	100×125 mm. Nos. 443/6 (sold at $1.15)		4·50	6·00

190 Half-figure
with Canopy

1978. Arawak Artefacts (1st series).

448	190	10c. brown, yellow & black	10	10
449	-	20c. brown, mauve & black	15	10
450	-	50c. brown, green & black	35	35
MS451	135×90 mm. Nos. 448/50 (sold at 90c.)		60	1·25

DESIGNS: 20c. Standing figure; 50c. Birdman.
See also Nos. 479/83.

191 Norman
Manley (statue)

1978. 24th Commonwealth Parliamentary Conference. Multicoloured.

452		10c. Type **191**	15	10
453		20c. Sir Alexander Bustamante (statue)	25	15

454	25c. City of Kingston Crest		35	20
455	40c. Gordon House Chamber, House of Representatives		35	65

192 Band and Banner

1978. Christmas. Centenary of Salvation Army. Multicoloured.

456	10c. Type **192**		30	10
457	20c. Trumpeter		35	20
458	25c. Banner		35	30
459	50c. William Booth (founder)		60	2·00

193 "Negro Aroused" (sculpture by Edna Manley)

1978. International Anti-Apartheid Year.

460	**193**	10c. multicoloured	30	20

194 Tennis, Montego Bay

1979. Multicoloured.

461	1c. Type **194**		70	75
462	2c. Golf, Tryall, Hanover		2·25	2·75
463	4c. Horse riding, Negril Beach		50	2·25
464	5c. Old waterwheel, Tryall, Hanover		1·25	30
465	6c. Fern Gully, Ocho Rios		1·50	2·50
466	7c. Dunn's River Falls, Ocho Rios		50	30
467	8c. Jamaican tody		1·00	1·25
468	10c. Jamaican mango		1·00	20
469	12c. Yellow-billed amazon		1·00	2·00
470	15c. Streamertail		1·00	30
471	35c. White-chinned thrush		1·50	30
472	50c. Jamaican woodpecker		1·75	30
473	65c. Rafting, Martha Brae Trelawny		1·75	2·75
474	75c. Blue Marlin fleet, Port Antonio		2·00	2·25
475	$1 Scuba diving, Ocho Rios		2·00	2·25
476	$2 Sailing boats, Montego Bay		2·00	65
477	$5 Arms and map of Jamaica (37×27 mm)		1·00	1·75

1979. Tenth Anniv of Air Jamaica. No. 352 optd **TENTH ANNIVERSARY AIR JAMAICA 1st APRIL 1979.**

478	10c. multicoloured		50	50

197 Grinding Stone, c. 400 B.C.

1979. Arawak Artefacts (2nd series). Multicoloured.

479	5c. Type **197**		10	10
480	10c. Stone implements, c. 500 B.C. (horiz)		10	10
481	20c. Cooking pot, c. 300 A.D. (horiz)		10	15
482	25c. Serving boat, c. 300 A.D. (horiz)		10	20
483	50c. Storage jar fragment, c. 300 A.D.		25	60

198 1962 1s.6d. Independence Commemorative Stamp

1979. Death Centenary of Sir Rowland Hill.

484	**198**	10c. black, brown and red	15	10
485	-	20c. yellow and brown	15	15
486	-	25c. mauve and blue	20	20
487	-	50c. multicoloured	25	70
MS488	146×94 mm. No. 485 (sold at 30c.)		30	85

DESIGNS: 20c. 1920 1s. with frame inverted; 25c. 1860 6d. stamp; 50c. 1968 3d. Human Rights Year commemorative.

199 Group of Children

1979. Christmas. International Year of the Child. Multicoloured.

489	10c. Type **199**		10	10
490	20c. Doll (vert)		10	10
491	25c. "The Family" (painting by child)		15	15
492	50c. "House on the Hill" (painting by child)		25	40

200 Date Tree Hall, 1886 (original home of Institute)

1980. Centenary of Institute of Jamaica. Multicoloured.

493	5c. Type **200**		10	10
494	15c. Institute building, 1980		15	10
495	35c. Microfilm reader (vert)		25	20
496	50c. Hawksbill turtle and green turtle		45	85
497	75c. Jamaican owl (vert)		1·75	3·00

201 Don Quarrie (200 m, 1976)

1980. Olympic Games, Moscow. Jamaican Olympic Gold Medal Winners. Multicoloured.

498	15c. Type **201**		40	15
499	35c. Arthur Wint (4×400 m Relay, 1952)		45	80
500	35c. Leslie Laing (4×400 m Relay, 1952)		45	80
501	35c. Herbert McKenley (4×400 m Relay, 1952)		45	80
502	35c. George Rhoden (4×400 m, 1952)		45	80

202 Parish Church

1980. Christmas. Churches (1st series). Multicoloured.

503	15c. Type **202**		10	10
504	20c. Coke Memorial Church		10	10
505	25c. Church of the Redeemer		15	10
506	$5 Holy Trinity Cathedral		1·00	2·00
MS507	120×139 mm. Nos. 503/6 (sold at $5.70)		1·25	3·25

See also No. 537/9 and 570/2.

203 Blood Cup Sponge

1981. Marine Life (1st series). Multicoloured.

508	20c. Type **203**		15	10
509	45c. Tube sponge (horiz)		25	35
510	60c. Black coral		35	45
511	75c. Tyre reef (horiz)		40	75

See also Nos. 541/5.

204 Brown's Hutia (or Indian Coney)

1981. Brown's Hutia (or Indian Coney).

512	20c. Hutia facing right		15	30
513	20c. Type **204**		15	30
514	20c. Hutia facing left and eating		15	30
515	20c. Hutia family		15	30

205 White Orchid

1981. Royal Wedding. Multicoloured.

516	20c. Type **205**		10	10
517	45c. Royal Coach		10	10
518	60c. Prince Charles and Lady Diana Spencer		25	20
519	$5 St. James' Palace		70	85
MS520	98×85 mm. No. 519		1·00	1·75

206 Blind Man at Work

1981. International Year for Disabled Persons. Multicoloured.

521	20c. Type **206**		20	15
522	45c. Painting with the mouth		40	40
523	60c. Deaf student communicating with sign language		50	75
524	$1.50 Basketball players		2·25	2·50

207 W.F.D. Emblem on 1964 1½d. Definitive

1981. World Food Day. Stamps on Stamps.

525	**207**	20c. multicoloured	45	15
526	-	45c. black, red and orange	80	40
527	-	$2 black, blue and green	2·25	1·40
528	-	$4 black, green and brown	3·25	2·50

DESIGNS—VERT (As T **207**): 45c. 1922 1d. value. HORIZ (40×26 mm): $2 As 1938 3d. but with W.F.D. emblem replacing King's head; $4 As 1938 1s. but with W.F.D. emblem replacing King's head.

208 *Survival* (song title)

1981. Bob Marley (musician) Commemoration. Song Titles. Multicoloured.

529	1c. Type **208**		70	1·10
530	2c. *Exodus*		70	1·10
531	3c. *Is this Love*		70	1·10
532	15c. *Coming in from the Cold*		3·25	30
533	20c. *Positive Vibration*		3·25	30
534	60c. *War*		4·00	3·00
535	$3 *Could you be Loved*		6·50	12·00
MS536	134×110 mm. $5.25 Bob Marley		8·50	4·75

No. 533 is incorrectly inscribed "OSITIVE VIBRATION".

209 Webb Memorial Baptist Church

1981. Christmas. Churches (2nd series). Multicoloured.

537	10c. Type **209**		10	10
538	45c. Church of God in Jamaica		30	15
539	$5 Bryce United Church		1·75	2·50
MS540	120×168 mm. Nos. 537/9		3·50	3·50

210 Gorgonian Coral

1982. Marine Life (2nd series). Multicoloured.

541	20c. Type **210**		45	10
542	45c. Hard sponge and diver (horiz)		65	25
543	60c. American manatee (horiz)		90	55
544	75c. Plume worm (horiz)		1·00	65
545	$3 Coral banded shrimp (horiz)		2·50	1·75

211 Cub Scout

1982. 75th Anniv of Boy Scout Movement. Multicoloured.

546	20c. Type **211**		50	15
547	45c. Scout camp		85	40
548	60c. "Out of Many, One People"		1·10	90
549	$2 Lord Baden-Powell		1·75	2·50
MS550	80×130 mm. Nos. 546/9		5·00	6·00

212 *Lignum vitae* (national flower)

1982. 21st Birthday of Princess of Wales.

551	20c. Type **212**		35	20
552	45c. Carriage ride		50	35
553	60c. Wedding		70	60
554	75c. *Saxifraga longifolia*		1·25	2·75
555	$2 Princess of Wales		1·60	3·00
556	$3 *Viola gracilis major*		1·60	3·50
MS557	106×75 mm. $5 Honeymoon photograph		1·40	2·50

1982. Birth of Prince William of Wales. Nos. 551/6 optd **ROYAL BABY 21.6.82.**

558	20c. Type **212**		20	20
559	45c. Carriage ride		30	35
560	60c. Wedding		40	60
561	75c. *Saxifraga longifolia*		70	2·25
562	$2 Princess of Wales		75	2·75
563	$3 *Viola gracilis major*		1·00	2·50
MS564	106×75 mm. $5 Honeymoon photograph		1·50	3·50

213 Prey Captured

1982. Jamaican Birds (1st series). Jamaican Lizard Cuckoo. Multicoloured.

565	$1 Type **213**		1·40	1·60
566	$1 Searching for prey		1·40	1·60
567	$1 Calling prior to prey search		1·40	1·60
568	$1 Adult landing		1·40	1·60
569	$1 Adult flying in		1·40	1·60

See also Nos. 642/5 and 707/10.

1982. Christmas. Churches (3rd series). As T **209**. Multicoloured.

570	20c. United Pentecostal Church		70	10
571	45c. Disciples of Christ Church		1·25	25
572	75c. Open Bible Church		2·00	3·75

214 Queen
Elizabeth II

1983. Royal Visit. Multicoloured.
573	$2 Type **214**	3·00	3·50
574	$3 Coat of arms	4·00	6·00

215 Folk Dancing

1983. Commonwealth Day. Multicoloured.
575	20c. Type **215**	15	15
576	45c. Bauxite mining	35	35
577	75c. World map showing position of Jamaica	45	45
578	$2 Coat of arms and family	60	1·40

216 General Cargo Ship at Wharf

1983. 25th Anniv of International Maritime Organization. Multicoloured.
579	15c. Type **216**	75	30
580	20c. *Veendam* (cruise liner) at Kingston	1·00	40
581	45c. *Astronomer* (container ship) entering port	1·75	85
582	$1 Tanker passing International Seabed Headquarters Building	2·75	5·00

217 Norman Manley and Sir Alexander Bustamante

1983. 21st Anniv of Independence.
583	**217**	15c. multicoloured	15	50
584	**217**	20c. multicoloured	15	60
585	**217**	45c. multicoloured	30	85

218 Ship-to-Shore Radio

1983. World Communications Year. Multicoloured.
586	20c. Type **218**	90	15
587	45c. Postal services	1·75	40
588	75c. Telephone communications	1·90	3·50
589	$1 T.V. via satellite	2·00	4·00

219 Racing at Caymanas (Sidney McLaren)

1983. Christmas. Paintings. Multicoloured.
590	15c. Type **219**	15	10
591	20c. *Seated Figures* (Karl Parboosingh)	15	10
592	75c. *The Petitioner* (Henry Daley) (vert)	50	65
593	$2 *Banana Plantation* (John Dunkley) (vert)	1·25	4·00

220 Sir Alexander Bustamante

1984. Birth Centenary of Sir Alexander Bustamante. Multicoloured.
594	20c. Type **220**	90	1·60
595	20c. Birthplace, Blenheim	90	1·60

221 de Havilland Gipsy Moth Seaplane

1984. Seaplanes and Flying Boats. Multicoloured.
596	25c. Type **221**	1·50	20
597	55c. Consolidated Commodore flying boat	2·00	85
598	$1.50 Sikorsky S-38A flying boat	3·25	4·00
599	$3 Sikorsky S-40 flying boat *American Clipper*	4·00	6·00

222 Cycling

1984. Olympic Games, Los Angeles. Multicoloured.
600	25c. Type **222**	2·00	50
601	55c. Relay running	60	30
602	$1.50 Start of race	1·75	4·50
603	$3 Finish of race	2·25	5·00
MS604	135×105 mm. Nos. 600/3 (sold at $5.40)	7·50	8·50

1984. Nos. 465 and 469 surch.
605	5c. on 6c. Fern Gully, Ocho Rios	15	40
606	10c. on 12c. Yellow-billed amazon	1·10	60

224 Head of Jamaican Boa Snake

1984. Endangered Species. Jamaican Boa Snake. Multicoloured.
607	25c. Type **224**	6·00	40
608	55c. Boa snake on branch over tree	7·00	80
609	70c. Snake with young	8·00	4·00
610	$1 Snake on log	9·00	5·00
MS611	133×97 mm. As Nos. 607/10 but without W.W.F. emblem (sold at $2.60)	6·00	7·00

225 Locomotive "Enterprise" (1845)

1984. Railway Locomotives (1st series). Multicoloured.
612	25c. Type **225**	1·50	30
613	55c. Tank locomotive (1880)	1·75	70
614	$1.50 Kitson-Meyer tank locomotive (1904)	2·75	3·00
615	$3 Super-heated locomotive No. 40 (1916)	4·00	5·50

See also Nos. 634/7.

226 "Accompong Madonna" (Namba Roy)

1984. Christmas. Sculptures. Multicoloured.
616	20c. Type **226**	30	10

617	25c. "Head" (Alvin Marriott)	35	10
618	55c. "Moon" (Edna Manley)	80	65
619	$1.50 "All Women are Five Women" (Mallica Reynolds (Kapo))	1·90	4·00

227 Brown Pelicans flying

1985. Birth Bicentenary of John J. Audubon (ornithologist). Brown Pelican. Multicoloured.
620	20c. Type **227**	1·00	20
621	55c. Diving for fish	1·50	40
622	$2 Young pelican taking food from adult	2·50	3·25
623	$5 *Brown Pelican* (John J. Audubon)	3·75	6·50
MS624	100×100 mm. Nos. 620/3 (sold at $7.85)	6·00	8·00

228 The Queen Mother at Belfast University

1985. Life and Times of Queen Elizabeth the Queen Mother. Multicoloured.
625	25c. With photograph album, 1963	50	10
626	55c. With Prince Charles at Garter Ceremony, Windsor Castle, 1983	70	15
627	$1.50 Type **228**	1·25	1·75
628	$3 With Prince Henry at his christening (from photo by Lord Snowdon)	2·25	3·25
MS629	91×74 mm. $5 With the Queen, Prince Philip and Princess Anne at Ascot	2·75	1·75

229 Maps and Emblems

1985. International Youth Year and Fifth Pan-American Scout Jamboree.
630	**229**	25c. multicoloured	1·50	10
631	**229**	55c. multicoloured	1·75	25
632	**229**	70c. multicoloured	2·00	1·50
633	**229**	$4 multicoloured	4·00	10·00

1985. Railway Locomotives (2nd series). As T **225**. Multicoloured.
634	25c. Baldwin steam locomotive No. 16	1·25	30
635	55c. Rogers locomotive	1·75	35
636	$1.50 Locomotive *Projector*, 1845	2·75	3·50
637	$4 Diesel locomotive No. 102	3·75	6·50

230 *The Old Settlement* (Ralph Campbell)

1985. Christmas. Jamaican Paintings. Multicoloured.
638	20c. Type **230**	10	10
639	55c. *The Vendor* (Albert Huie) (vert)	15	15
640	75c. *Road Menders* (Gaston Tabois)	20	35
641	$4 *Woman, must I not be about my Father's business?* (Carl Abrahams) (vert)	1·10	2·25

1986. Jamaican Birds (2nd series). As T **213**. Multicoloured.
642	25c. Chestnut-bellied cuckoo	50	10
643	55c. Jamaican becard	65	30
644	$1.50 White-eyed thrush	85	2·00
645	$5 Rufous-tailed flycatcher	1·75	4·75

230a Princess Elizabeth and Princess Margaret, 1939

1986. 60th Birthday of Queen Elizabeth II. Multicoloured.
646	20c. Type **230a**	35	10
647	25c. With Prince Charles and Prince Andrew, 1962	35	10
648	70c. Queen visiting War Memorial, Montego Bay, 1983	40	30
649	$3 On state visit to Luxembourg, 1976	60	1·50
650	$5 At Crown Agents Head Office, London, 1983	75	2·25

231 Bustamante Children's Hospital

1986. "Ameripex '86" International Stamp Exhibition, Chicago. Multicoloured.
651	25c. Type **231**	70	15
652	55c. Air Jamaica Boeing 737 airliner and map of holiday resorts	2·25	40
653	$3 Norman Manley Law School	1·25	4·00
654	$5 Bauxite and agricultural exports	7·50	9·50
MS655	85×106 mm. Nos. 651/4 (sold at $8.90)	10·50	12·00

231a Prince Andrew and Miss Sarah Ferguson, Ascot, 1985

1986. Royal Wedding. Multicoloured.
656	20c. Type **231a**	15	10
657	$5 Prince Andrew making speech, Fredericton, Canada, 1985	1·00	1·90

232 Richard "Shrimpy" Clarke

1986. Jamaican Boxing Champions. Multicoloured.
658	45c. Type **232**	20	15
659	70c. Michael McCallum	30	30
660	$2 Trevor Berbick	70	1·75
661	$4 Richard "Shrimpy" Clarke, Michael McCallum and Trevor Berbick	1·25	3·00

1986. Nos. 472/3 surch.
662	5c. on 50c. Jamaican woodpecker	3·00	3·00
663	10c. on 65c. Rafting, Martha Brae Trelawny	1·75	2·50

234 *Heliconia wagneriana*

1986. Christmas. Flowers (1st series). Multicoloured.
664	20c. Type **234**	10	10
665	25c. *Heliconia psittacorum* (horiz)	10	10
666	55c. *Heliconia rostrata*	20	30
667	$5 *Strelitzia reginae* (horiz)	1·60	5·00

See also Nos. 703/6 and 739/42.

235 Crown Cone

1987. Sea Shells. Multicoloured.

668	35c. Type **235**	45	15
669	75c. Measled cowrie	65	60
670	$1 Atlantic trumpet triton	75	90
671	$5 Rooster-tail conch	1·50	4·50

236 Norman Manley **237** Arms of Jamaica

1987. Portraits.

672A	**236**	1c. red and pink	10	75
673A	**236**	2c. red and pink	10	75
674A	**236**	3c. green and stone	10	75
675A	**236**	4c. green & light green	10	75
676A	**236**	5c. blue and grey	30	40
677A	**236**	6c. blue and grey	20	75
678A	**236**	7c. violet and mauve	50	75
679A	**236**	8c. mauve and pink	20	10
680A	**236**	9c. sepia and brown	50	10
681aB	-	10c. red and pink	20	30
682A	-	20c. orange and flesh	20	30
683A	-	30c. green & light green	40	10
684B	-	40c. deep green & green	60	50
685A	-	50c. green and grey	30	40
685cB	-	55c. bistre and cream	75	40
686A	-	60c. blue and light blue	30	20
687A	-	70c. violet & light violet	30	20
688A	-	80c. violet and lilac	50	30
689A	-	90c. brown & lt brown	60	75
690A	**237**	$1 brown and cream	30	20
690cB	**237**	$1.10 brown and cream	70	40
691AB	**237**	$2 orange and cream	1·00	70
692aB	**237**	$5 green and stone	65	80
693A	**237**	$10 blue and azure	70	1·75
693cB	**237**	$25 violet and lilac	1·50	1·75
693dB	**237**	$50 mauve and lilac	2·50	3·00

DESIGN: 10c. to 90c. Sir Alexander Bustamante.
The 5, 20, 40, 50, 90c. and $1 exist with or without imprint date at foot.

238 Jamaican Flag and Coast at Sunset

1987. 25th Anniv of Independence. Multicoloured.

694	55c. Type **238**	1·50	60
695	70c. Jamaican flag and inscription (horiz)	1·50	2·75

239 Marcus Garvey

1987. Birth Centenary of Marcus Garvey (founder of Universal Negro Improvement Association). Each black, green and yellow.

696	25c. Type **239**	1·25	2·00
697	25c. Statue of Marcus Garvey	1·25	2·00

240 Salvation Army School for the Blind

1987. Cent of Salvation Army in Jamaica. Multicoloured.

698	25c. Type **240**	1·50	30

699	55c. Col. Mary Booth and Bramwell Booth Memorial Hall	1·50	30
700	$3 Welfare Service lorry, 1929	4·75	5·50
701	$5 Col. Abram Davey and S.S. "Alene", 1887	6·00	8·50
MS702	100×80 mm. Nos. 698/701 (sold at $8.90)	15·00	15·00

1987. Christmas. Flowers (2nd series). As T **234**. Multicoloured.

703	20c. Hibiscus hybrid	15	10
704	25c. *Hibiscus elatus*	15	10
705	$4 *Hibiscus cannabinus*	2·00	3·75
706	$5 *Hibiscus rosasinensis*	2·25	3·75

1988. Jamaican Birds (3rd series). As T **213**. Multicoloured.

707	45c. Chestnut-bellied cuckoo, black-billed amazon and Jamaican euphonia	1·75	2·50
708	45c. Black-billed amazon, jamaican white-eyed vireo, rufous-throated solitaire and yellow elaenia	1·75	2·50
709	$5 Snowy plover, little blue heron and great blue heron (white phase)	4·25	5·50
710	$5 Black-necked stilt, snowy egret, snowy plover and black-crowned night heron	4·25	5·50

The two designs of each value were printed together, *se-tenant*, each pair forming a composite design.

243 Blue Whales

1988. Marine Mammals. Multicoloured.

711	20c. Type **243**	2·00	70
712	25c. Gervais's whales	2·00	70
713	55c. Killer whales	3·00	80
714	$5 Common dolphins	5·00	10·00

243a Jackie Hendriks

1988. West Indian Cricket. Each showing portrait, cricket equipment and early belt buckle. Multicoloured.

715	25c. Type **243a**	1·50	40
716	55c. George Headley	1·60	40
717	$2 Michael Holding	3·50	3·00
718	$3 R. K. Nunes	3·75	4·75
719	$4 Allan Rae	4·00	5·00

244 Jamaican Red Cross Workers with Ambulance

1988. 125th Anniv of Int Red Cross. Multicoloured.

720	55c. Type **244**	75	30
721	$5 Henri Dunant (founder) in field hospital	2·75	4·25

245 Boxing

1988. Olympic Games, Seoul. Multicoloured.

722	25c. Type **245**	40	10
723	45c. Cycling	2·50	70
724	$4 Athletics	2·50	3·25
725	$5 Hurdling	2·50	3·25
MS726	127×87 mm. Nos. 722/5 (sold at $9.90)	7·00	7·00

246 Bobsled Team Members and Logo

1988. Jamaican Olympic Bobsled Team. Multicoloured.

727	25c. Type **246**	50	1·25

728	25c. Two-man bobsled	50	1·25
729	$5 Bobsled team members (different) and logo	2·50	4·00
730	$5 Four-man bobsled	2·50	4·00

1988. Hurricane Gilbert Relief Fund. Nos. 722/5 surch + **25c HURRICANE GILBERT RELIEF FUND.**

731	25c.+25c. Type **245**	10	20
732	45c.+45c. Cycling	20	30
733	$4+$4 Athletics	1·10	2·25
734	$5+$5 Hurdling	1·10	2·50

248 Nurses and Firemen

1988. Year of the Worker. Multicoloured.

735	25c. Type **248**	2·00	30
736	55c. Woodcarver	45	30
737	$3 Textile workers	1·00	3·00
738	$5 Workers on fish farm	1·25	3·50

1988. Christmas. Flowers (3rd series). As T **234**. Multicoloured.

739	25c. *Euphorbia pulcherrima*	70	10
740	55c. *Spathodea campanulata* (horiz)	85	15
741	$3 *Hylocereus triangularis*	2·00	2·00
742	$4 *Broughtonia sanguinea* (horiz)	2·00	2·00

249 Old York Castle School

1989. Bicent of Methodist Church in Jamaica.

743	**249**	25c. black and blue	30	10
744	-	45c. black and red	35	10
745	-	$5 black and green	3·00	5·50

DESIGNS: 45c. Revd. Thomas Coke and Parade Chapel, Kingston; $5 Father Hugh Sherlock and St. John's Church.

250 *Syntomidopsis variegata*

1989. Jamaican Moths (1st series). Multicoloured.

746	25c. Type **250**	50	10
747	55c. *Himantoides perkinsae*	80	30
748	$3 *Arctia nigriplaga*	1·50	3·50
749	$5 *Sthenognatha toddi*	1·90	4·25

See also Nos. 758/61 and 790/3.

251 Arawak Fisherman with Catch

1989. 500th Anniv (1992) of Discovery of America by Columbus (1st issue). Multicoloured.

750	25c. Type **251**	20	10
751	70c. Arawak man smoking	45	30
752	$5 King Ferdinand and Queen Isabella inspecting caravels	3·25	4·50
753	$10 Columbus with chart	6·50	9·50
MS754	150×200 mm. Nos. 750/3 (sold at $16.15)	17·00	17·00

See also Nos. 774/7 and 802/7.

252 Girl Guide

1990. 75th Anniv of Girl Guide Movement in Jamaica. Multicoloured.

755	45c. Type **252**	1·50	30
756	55c. Guide leader	1·50	30
757	$5 Brownie, guide and ranger	6·00	9·00

1990. Jamaican Moths (2nd series). As T **250**. Multicoloured.

758	25c. *Eunomia rubripunctata*	85	35
759	55c. "*erigonia jamaicensis*"	1·25	35
760	$4 *Uraga haemorrhoa*	2·50	4·50
761	$5 *Empyreuma pugione*	2·50	4·50

1990. "EXPO '90" International Garden and Greenery Exhibition, Osaka. Nos. 758/61 optd **EXPO '90** and logo.

762	25c. *Eunomia rubripunctata*	85	35
763	55c. *Perigonia jamaicensis*	1·25	35
764	$4 *Uraga haemorrhoa*	2·50	4·50
765	$5 *Empyreuma pugione*	2·50	4·50

254 Teaching English

1990. International Literacy Year. Multicoloured.

766	55c. Type **254**	75	25
767	$5 Teaching maths	4·75	6·50

255 To the Market

1990. Christmas. Children's Paintings. Multicoloured.

768	20c. Type **255**	60	10
769	25c. House and Garden	60	10
770	80c. Jack and Jill	80	15
771	70c. Market	1·00	40
772	$1.50 Lonely	1·75	3·50
773	$5 Market Woman (vert)	3·50	7·00

256 Map of First Voyage, 1492

1990. 500th Anniv (1992) of Discovery of America by Columbus (2nd issue). Multicoloured.

774	25c. Type **256**	1·50	40
775	45c. Map of second voyage, 1493	1·75	40
776	$5 Map of third voyage, 1498	5·50	6·00
777	$10 Map of fourth voyage, 1502	8·00	10·00
MS778	126×99 mm. 25, 45c., $5, $10 Composite map of Caribbean showing routes of voyages	15·00	17·00
MS779	148×207 mm. Nos. 774/7. Imperf	17·00	19·00

257 Weather Balloon, Dish Aerial and Map of Jamaica

1991. 11th World Meteorological Congress, Kingston.

780	**257**	50c. multicoloured	50	20
781	**257**	$10 multicoloured	6·50	9·50

258 Bust of Mary Seacole

1991. International Council of Nurses Meeting of National Representatives.

782	**258**	50c. multicoloured	85	30
783	-	$1.10 multicoloured	1·75	2·25
MS784	89×60 mm. $8 agate, brown and ochre (sold at $8.20)	3·75	7·50

DESIGNS: $1.10 Mary Seacole House; $8 Hospital at Scutari, 1854.

259 Jamaican Iguana

1991. 50th Anniv of Natural History Society of Jamaica. Jamaican Iguana. Multicoloured.

785	$1.10 Type **259**	80	1.00
786	$1.10 Head of iguana looking right	80	1.00
787	$1.10 Iguana climbing	80	1.00
788	$1.10 Iguana on rock looking left	80	1.00
789	$1.10 Close-up of iguana's head	80	1.00

1991. Jamaican Moths (3rd series). As T **250**. Multicoloured.

790	50c. *Urania sloanus*	65	20
791	$1.10 *Phoenicoprocta jamaicensis*	90	60
792	$1.40 *Horama grotei*	1·10	90
793	$8 *Amplypterus gannascus*	3·25	6·00

1991. "Phila Nippon '91" International Stamp Exhibition, Tokyo. Nos. 790/3 optd **PHILA NIPPON 91** and emblem.

794	50c. *Urania sloanus*	1·00	20
795	$1.10 *Phoenicoprocta jamaicensis*	1·40	65
796	$1.40 *Horama grotei*	1·50	1·00
797	$8 *Amplypterus gannascus*	5·00	8·00

261 Doctor Bird

1991. Christmas. Children's Paintings. Multicoloured.

798	50c. Type **261**	80	10
799	$1.10 Road scene	1·25	25
800	$5 Children and house	4·00	3·50
801	$10 Cows grazing	7·00	9·00

262 Indians threatening Ships

1991. 500th Anniv (1992) of Discovery of America by Columbus (3rd issue). Multicoloured.

802	50c. Type **262**	65	15
803	$1.10 Spaniards setting dog on Indians	75	30
804	$1.40 Indian with gift of pineapple	75	30
805	$25 Columbus describes Jamaica with crumpled paper	8·50	12·00
MS806	125×102 mm. Nos. 802/5 (sold at $28.20)	9·00	12·00
MS807	210×150 mm. Nos. 802/5. Imperf	10·00	12·00

263 Compasses and Square Symbol

1992. 250th Anniv of First Provincial Grand Master of English Freemasonry in Jamaica. Multicoloured.

808	50c. Type **263**	70	30
809	$1.10 Symbol in stained glass window	90	40
810	$1.40 Compasses and square on book	90	40
811	$25 Eye in triangle symbol	9·00	12·00
MS812	140×80 mm. Nos. 808/11 (sold at $28.50)	15·00	16·00

264 Ship in Flooded Street

1992. 300th Anniv of Destruction of Port Royal. Multicoloured.

813	50c. Type **264**	55	40
814	$1.10 Church tower falling	70	45
815	$1.40 Houses collapsing	70	45
816	$25 Inhabitants falling into fissure	9·00	12·00
MS817	116×75 mm. $5 Contemporary broadsheet of earthquake	7·00	8·00

265 Credit Union Symbol

1992. 50th Anniv of Credit Union Movement.

818	**265**	50c. blue, emerald & green	1·00	50
819	-	$1.40 multicoloured	1·75	1·75

DESIGN: $1.40, O'Hare Hall.

266 Jamaican Flag and Beach Scene

1992. 30th Anniv of Independence.

820	**266**	50c. multicoloured	10	10
821	**266**	$1.10 multicoloured	20	20
822	**266**	$25 multicoloured	2·75	6·00

267 *Rainbow* (Cecil Baugh)

1993. Art Ceramics and Pottery. Multicoloured.

823	50c. Type **267**	20	10
824	$1.10 *Yabba Pot* (Louisa Jones)	30	20
825	$1.40 *Sculptured Vase* (Gene Pearson)	30	20
826	$25 *Lidded Form* (Norma Harrack)	4·50	6·50

268 Girls' Brigade Parade

1993. Centenary of Girls' Brigade. Multicoloured.

827	50c. Type **268**	90	50
828	$1.10 Brigade members	1·00	1·10

269 Cadet, Armoured Car and Emblem

1993. 50th Anniv of Jamaica Combined Cadet Force. Multicoloured.

829	50c. Type **269**	40	20
830	$1.10 Cadet and Britten Norman Islander aircraft (horiz)	60	40
831	$1.40 Cadet and patrol boats	60	40
832	$3 Cadet and emblem (horiz)	80	2·00

270 Constant Spring Golf Course

1993. Golf Courses. Multicoloured.

833	50c. Type **270**	45	10
834	$1.10 Type **270**	65	20
835	$1.40 Half Moon	70	20
836	$2 As $1.40	1·00	90
837	$3 Jamaica Jamaica	1·10	1·25
838	$10 As $3	2·50	3·50
MS839	66×71 mm. $25 Tryall (vert) (sold at $28)	5·75	6·00

271 Norman Manley

1994. Birth Centenary of Norman Manley.

840	**271**	$25 multicoloured	2·00	2·75
841	**271**	$50 multicoloured	2·50	4·25

1994. "Hong Kong '94" International Stamp Exhibition. No. **MS**839 optd **HONG KONG '94** and emblem.

MS842	66×71 mm. $25 Tryall	6·00	6·50

273 Flags of Great Britain and Jamaica

1994. Royal Visit. Multicoloured.

843	$1.10 Type **273**	65	10
844	$1.40 Royal Yacht *Britannia*	1·50	30
845	$25 Queen Elizabeth II	3·00	4·00
846	$50 Queen Elizabeth and Prince Philip	5·00	8·00

274 Douglas DC-9

1994. 25th Anniv of Air Jamaica. Multicoloured.

847	50c. Type **274**	35	25
848	$1.10 Douglas DC-8	35	25
849	$5 Boeing 727	75	75
850	$50 Airbus A300	3·50	6·50

275 Giant Swallowtail

1994. Giant Swallowtail Butterfly Conservation. Multicoloured.

851	50c. Type **275**	40	25
852	$1.10 With wings closed	40	25
853	$10 On flower	1·60	2·25
854	$25 With wings spread	2·75	5·00
MS855	56×61 mm. $50 Pair of butterflies	5·50	7·00

276 "Royal Botanical Gardens" (Sidney McLaren)

1994. Tourism. Multicoloured.

856	50c. Type **276**	55	20
857	$1.10 Blue Mountains	85	30
858	$5 Tourist in hammock and water sports	3·00	3·75
MS859	105×80 mm. $25 Carolina parakeets; $25 Silhouetted scuba diver; $25 Carolina parakeet and foliage; $25 Tourist raft	6·00	7·50

277 Jamaican Red Poll Calf

1994. Jamaican Red Poll Cattle. Multicoloured.

860	50c. Type **277**	10	10
861	$1.10 Red Poll heifer	10	10
862	$25 Red Poll cow	1·25	2·25
863	$50 Red Poll bull	2·50	4·50

278 Refuse Collectors

1994. Christmas. Children's Paintings. Multicoloured.

864	50c. Type **278**	10	10
865	90c. Hospital ward	10	10
866	$1.10 House	10	10
867	$50 Landscape	3·75	6·00

279 Jamaican Band-tailed Pigeon ("Ring-tailed Pigeon")

1995. Jamaican Wild Birds. Multicoloured.

868	50c. Type **279**	65	40
869	90c. Yellow-billed amazon ("Yellow-billed parrot")	80	40
870	$1.10 Black-billed amazon ("Black-billed parrot")	80	40
871	$50 Jamaican owl ("Brown owl")	5·50	7·00
MS872	47×62 mm. $50 Streamertail	4·75	7·00

For No. **MS**872 additionally inscribed for "Singapore '95" see No. **MS**888.

280 Graph, National Flag and Logo

1995. 25th Anniv of Caribbean Development Bank.

873	**280**	50c. green, black and yellow	10	10
874	**280**	$1 green, black and yellow	10	10
875	-	$1.10 multicoloured	10	10
876	-	$50 multicoloured	2·75	5·50

DESIGNS—HORIZ: $1.10, Industry, agriculture and commerce; $50 Jamaican currency.

281 *Song of Freedom*

1995. 50th Birth Anniv of Bob Marley (reggae singer). Record covers. Multicoloured.

877	50c. Type **281**	40	15
878	$1.10 *Fire*	55	20
879	$1.40 *Time will Tell*	60	25
880	$3 *Natural Mystic*	1·10	1·00
881	$10 *Live at Lyceum*	2·00	3·00
MS882	105×57 mm. $100 *Legend*	8·00	9·00

282 Queen Elizabeth the Queen Mother

1995. 95th Birthday of Queen Elizabeth the Queen Mother. Sheet 81×95 mm.

MS883	**282** $75 multicoloured	4·50	5·50

283 Michael Manley

1995. Recipients of the Order of the Caribbean Community. Multicoloured.

884	50c. Type **283**		15	15
885	$1.10 Sir Alister McIntyre		20	10
886	$1.40 Sir P. Telford Georges		20	10
887	$50 Dame Nita Barrow		6·50	8·50

1995. "Singapore '95" International Stamp Exhibition. No. **MS**872 additionally inscr with exhibition emblem on sheet margin.

MS888	47×62 mm. $50 Streamertail	3·75	5·00

284 Dish Aerial and Landrover, Balkans

1995. 50th Anniv of United Nations. Multicoloured.

889	50c. Type **284**		30	20
890	$1.10 Antonov An-32 aircraft, Balkans		55	25
891	$3 Bedford articulated road tanker, Balkans		70	90
892	$5 Fairchild C-119 Flying Boxcar, Korea		80	1·40
MS893	100×70 mm. $50 U.N.T.A.G. vehicles, Namibia		2·25	3·50

285 Landing of Indian Immigrants

1996. 150th Anniv of Indian Immigration to Jamaica. Multicoloured.

894	$2.50 Type **285**		25	15
895	$10 Indian musicians and traditional dancers		75	1·25

286 Jamaican Flag and UNICEF Emblem

1996. 50th Anniv of UNICEF.

896	**286**	$2.50 multicoloured	65	20
897	**286**	$8 multicoloured	1·25	1·25
898	**286**	$10 multicoloured	1·25	1·50

287 Brown's Hutia

1996. Endangered Species. Brown's Hutia ("Jamaican Hutia"). Multicoloured.

899	$2.50 Type **287**		15	10
900	$10 Hutia on rock		50	65
901	$12.50 Female with young		60	1·00
902	$25 Head of hutia		1·25	2·25

288 High Altar, Church of St. Thomas the Apostle

1997. 300th Anniv of Kingston Parish Church. Multicoloured.

903	$2 Type **288**		35	10
904	$8 Church of St. Thomas the Apostle		1·10	80
905	$12.50 "The Angel" (wood carving by Edna Manley) (vert)		1·75	2·25
MS906	106×76 mm. $60 St. Thomas the Apostle at sunset (42×56 mm)		3·50	4·50

No. 903 is inscribed "ALTER" in error.

289 Child's Face and UNESCO Emblem

1998. Tenth Anniv of Chernobyl Nuclear Disaster.

907	**289**	$55 multicoloured	3·25	3·75

289a Map of Caribbean

1997. 50th Anniv of Caribbean Integration Movement and 18th CARICOM Heads of Government Conference. Multicoloured.

907a	$2.50 Type **289a**		5·50	5·50
907b	$8 Coastal scenery		6·50	2·25
907c	$10 As $8		7·00	2·25

290 Coelia triptera

1997. Orchids. Multicoloured.

908A	$1 Type **290**		20	30
909A	$2 Oncidium pulchellum (horiz)		30	30
910A	$2.50 Oncidium triquetum		30	20
911A	$3 Broughtonia negrilensis		40	30
912A	$4.50 Oncidium gauntlettii (horiz)		50	40
913A	$5 Encyclia fragans (horiz)		50	30
914A	$8 Broughtonia sanguinea (horiz)		80	30
915A	$12 Phaius tankervilleae		1·00	60
916B	$25 Cochleanthes flabelliformis (horiz)		1·75	2·00
917A	$50 Broughtonia sanguinea (three varieties) (horiz)		1·40	1·50

291 Diana, Princess of Wales

1998. Diana, Princess of Wales Commemoration. Multicoloured.

918	**291**	$20 Type **291**	1·00	1·25
MS919	70×100 mm. $80 Princess Diana and Mother Teresa (42×55 mm)		4·50	5·50

292 University Chapel, Mona

1998. 50th Anniv of University of West Indies. Multicoloured.

920	$8 Type **292**		40	40
921	$10 Philip Sherlock Centre for Creative Arts, Mona		40	40
922	$50 University arms (vert)		2·25	3·75

293 Flags of Jamaica and CARICOM

1998. 25th Anniv of Caribbean Community.

923	**293**	$30 multicoloured	2·50	2·50

294 Jamaican Footballer

1998. World Cup Football Championship, France. Multicoloured.

924	$10 Type **294**		65	40
925	$25 Jamaican team (horiz)		1·50	1·50
926	$100 As $25		5·00	7·00

295 Coral Reef

1998. Christmas. International Year of the Ocean. Multicoloured.

927	$10 Type **295**		1·00	40
928	$30 Fishing boats, Negril		2·50	1·25
929	$50 Black spiny sea urchin		3·50	4·00
930	$100 Composite design as Nos. 927/9 (22×41 mm)		7·00	10·00

296 Michael Collins (astronaut)

1999. 30th Anniv of First Manned Landing on Moon. Multicoloured.

931	$7 Type **296**		40	25
932	$10 Service module docking with lunar module		50	40
933	$25 Buzz Aldrin on Moon's surface		1·00	1·40
934	$30 Command module in Earth orbit		1·10	1·50
MS935	90×80 mm. $100 Earth as seen from Moon (circular, 40 mm diam)		3·50	4·75

297 Lesley Ann Masterton and Fong-Yee (polo)

1999. Jamaican Sporting Personalities. Multicoloured.

936	$5 Type **297**		75	35
937	$10 Lawrence Rowe, Collie Smith and Alfred Valentine (cricket)		1·25	55
938	$20 Vivalyn Latty-Scott (women's cricket) (vert)		1·75	1·25
939	$25 Lindy Delapenha (football) (vert)		1·75	1·25
940	$30 Joy Grant-Charles (netball) (vert)		1·75	1·75
941	$50 Percy Hayles, Gerald Gray and Bunny Grant (boxing)		1·90	4·00
MS942	110×90 mm. $100 Lindy Delapenha and Joy Grant-Charles (56×42 mm)		4·50	6·00

298 Spey (mail ship), 1891

1999. 125th Anniv of Universal Postal Union. Multicoloured.

943	$7 Type **298**		1·00	30
944	$10 Jamaica Planter (mail ship), 1936		1·25	50
945	$25 Lockheed Constellation (aircraft), 1950		2·25	2·75
946	$30 Airbus A-310 (aircraft), 1999		2·25	3·00

299 Airbus A-310

1999. 30th Anniv of Air Jamaica. Multicoloured.

947	$10 Type **299**		1·25	50
948	$25 A-320		2·00	2·25
949	$30 A-340		2·25	2·50

300 Shih Tzu

1999. Dogs. Multicoloured.

950	$7 Type **300**		1·25	65
951	$10 German shepherd		1·50	65
952	$30 Doberman pinscher		3·25	3·75

301 Nelson Mandela Park

1999. Parks and Gardens. Multicoloured.

953	$7 Type **301**		40	35
954	$10 St. William Grant Park		50	35
955	$25 Seaview Park		1·25	1·50
956	$30 Holruth Park		1·50	2·00

302 The Prophet (sculpture)

2000. Birth Centenary of Edna Manley (artist). Multicoloured.

957	$10 Type **302**		45	35
958	$25 Horse of the Morning		1·10	90
959	$30 The Angel		1·40	1·25
960	$100 Edna Manley		4·50	7·50
MS961	128×159 mm. Nos. 957/60		7·00	10·00

303 Lennox Lewis

2000. Lennox Lewis, World Heavyweight Boxing Champion. Multicoloured.

962	$10 Holding W.B.C. Championship belt		30	45
963	$10 In ring with right arm raised		30	45
964	$10 Holding W.B.C. belt above head		30	45
965	$25 Taking punch on chin		75	1·00
966	$25 Type **303**		75	1·00
967	$25 In corner		75	1·00
968	$30 With W.B.C. belt after fight		95	1·10
969	$30 Holding all four belts		95	1·10
970	$30 With belts in front of skyscraper		95	1·10

304 Ferrari Racing Car 125 S, 1947

2000. Birth Centenary (1998) of Enzo Ferrari (car designer). Racing cars. Multicoloured.

971	$10 Type **304**		60	70
972	$10 375 F1, 1950		60	70
973	$10 312 F1, 1966		60	70
974	$25 DINO 166 P, 1965		1·10	1·50
975	$25 312 P, 1971		1·10	1·50
976	$25 F1 90, 1990		1·10	1·50

305 Queen Elizabeth the Queen Mother

2000. Queen Elizabeth the Queen Mother's 100th Birthday. Multicoloured, background colours given.

977	**305**	$10 lavender	70	35
978	-	$25 green	90	90
979	-	$30 mauve	1·60	1·40
980	-	$50 blue	2·50	4·00

DESIGNS: $25 to $50, Various recent photographs.

306 *The Runner*, Jamaican Flag and Olympic Rings

2000. Olympic Games, Sydney. Each showing *The Runner* (sculpture by Alvin Marriot), Jamaican flag and Olympic Rings. Multicoloured.

981		$10 Type **306**	80	35
982		$25 Head and shoulders	1·40	90
983		$30 With flag at top (vert)	1·75	1·40
984		$50 With flag in centre (vert)	2·75	4·00

307 Bull Thatch Palm

2000. Native Trees. Multicoloured.

985		$10 Type **307**	80	35
986		$25 Blue mahoe	1·75	1·25
987		$30 Silk cotton	2·00	1·75
988		$50 Yellow poui	3·00	5·00
MS989	112×70 mm. $100 Lignum Vitae (horiz)		7·50	8·50

308 *Madonna and Child* (Osmond Watson)

2000. Christmas. Jamaican Religious Paintings. Multicoloured.

990		$10 Type **308**	55	35
991		$20 *Boy in the Temple* (Carl Abrahams) (horiz)	90	90
992		$25 *Ascension* (Carl Abrahams)	1·10	1·10
993		$30 *Jah Lives* (Osmond Watson)	1·25	1·40

309 Children of the Commonwealth

2001. 25th Anniv of Commonwealth Day.

994	**309**	$30 multicoloured	1·50	1·75

310 Andrew Mowatt (founder)

2001. Centenary of Jamaica Burial Scheme Society.

995	**310**	$15 multicoloured	1·25	1·25

311 *Falmouth Market* (lithograph)

2001. Birth Bicentenary of Adolphe Duperly (pioneer photographer). Multicoloured.

996		$15 Type **311**	1·00	50
997		$40 *Ferry Inn, Spanish Town Road* (lithograph)	2·25	2·25
998		$45 *Coke Chapel, Kingston* (lithograph)	2·25	2·25
999		$60 *King Street, Kingston* (lithograph)	3·00	3·50
MS1000	103×170 mm. Nos. 996/9		9·00	10·00

312 Poinsettia in Church Window

2001. Christmas.

1001	**312**	$15 multicoloured	1·00	50
1002	**312**	$30 multicoloured	2·00	1·40
1003	**312**	$40 multicoloured	2·25	2·25

2002. Golden Jubilee. As T **219** of Falkland Islands.

1004		$15 agate, blue and gold	1·00	50
1005		$40 multicoloured	2·25	2·25
1006		$45 black, blue and gold	2·25	2·25
1007		$60 multicoloured	3·00	3·50
MS1008	162×95 mm. Nos. 1004/7 and $30 multicoloured		8·00	8·50

DESIGNS—HORIZ: $15 Princess Elizabeth in orchard, 1941; $40 Queen Elizabeth wearing pearls and striped dress; $45 Queen Elizabeth in evening dress, 1953; $60 Queen Elizabeth visiting Gloucester, 1995. VERT (38×51 mm): $30 Queen Elizabeth after Annigoni.

Designs as Nos. 1004/7 in No. **MS**1008 omit the gold frame around each stamp and the "Golden Jubilee 1952–2002" inscription.

313 Queen Elizabeth and Jamaican Royal Standard

2002. Royal Visit. Multicoloured.

1009	**313**	$15 Type **313**	1·00	50
1010		$45 Queen Elizabeth in evening dress and Jamaican coat of arms	2·50	2·75

314 Sir Philip Sherlock

2002. Birth Centenary of Sir Philip Sherlock (historian).

1011	**314**	$40 mauve, magenta and blue	1·50	1·60

315 Female Dancers

2002. 40th Anniv of National Dance Theatre Company.

1012	**315**	$15 multicoloured	1·25	1·00

316 P.A.H.O. Centenary Logo

2002. Centenary of Pan American Health Organization.

1013	**316**	$40 multicoloured	2·25	1·75

317 *Masquerade* (Osmond Watson)

2002. Christmas. Local Works of Art. Multicoloured.

1014		$15 Type **317**	1·00	45
1015		$40 *John Canoe in Guanaboa Vale* (Gaston Tabois) (horiz)	2·00	1·50
1016		$45 *Mother and Child* (carving by Kapo)	2·00	1·75
1017		$60 *Hills of Papine* (carving by Edna Manley) (horiz)	2·75	2·75

318 Dancers

2002. 40th Anniv of Independence. Multicoloured.

1018		$15 Type **318**	1·00	45
1019		$40 Independence Day celebrations	2·25	1·75
1020		$60 Welder and fish processing worker	3·50	4·50

319 Kingston in Early 1800s

2002. Bicentenary of Kingston. Multicoloured.

1021		$15 Type **319**	1·00	1·25
1022		$15 Wharf and statue of Queen Victoria, early 1900s	1·00	1·25
1023		$15 Horse-drawn cab, early 1900s, and modern street scene	1·00	1·25

Nos. 1021/3 were printed together, *se-tenant*, as horizontal strips of 3 throughout the sheet, forming a montage.

320 Queen Elizabeth II in St. Edward's Chair flanked by Bishops of Durham and Bath & Wells

2003. 50th Anniv of Coronation. Multicoloured.

1024		$15 Type **320**	1·00	45
1025		$45 Coronation Coach in procession	2·50	3·00
MS1026	95×115 mm. $50 As $45; $100 As Type **320**		6·00	7·50

Nos. 1024/5 have scarlet frame; stamps from **MS**1026 have no frame and country name in mauve panel.

321 "30" as Key

2003. 30th Anniv of CARICOM.

1027	**321**	$40 multicoloured	2·25	2·00

322 Jamaican Stripe-headed Tanager

2003. Bird Life International. (1st series). Jamaican Birds. Multicoloured.

1028		$15 Type **322**	1·25	65
1029		$40 Crested quail dove (horiz)	2·00	1·75
1030		$45 Jamaican tody (horiz)	2·00	1·75
1031		$60 Blue mountain vireo	2·75	3·50
MS1032	175×80 mm. $30 Jamaican blackbird nestlings (34×30 mm); $30 Searching for food in bromeliad (30×34 mm); $30 Singing from perch (30×34 mm); $30 Singing from perch (34×30 mm); $30 With insect in beak (34×30 mm)		8·50	9·00

See also Nos. 1040/9.

323 Sailing ships and Map of Kingston Harbour

2003. Maritime History. Multicoloured.

1033		$40 Type **323**	2·25	2·25
1034		$40 Passengers on cruise ship and sailing ships	2·25	2·25
1035		$40 *Sugar Refiner* (cargo ship)	2·25	2·25

Nos. 1033/5 were printed together, *se-tenant*, forming a composite design.

324 Baby Jesus

2003. Christmas. Multicoloured.

1036		$15 Type **324**	85	35
1037		$30 Close-up of Baby Jesus	1·60	65
1038		$60 Holy Family	2·75	3·25

325 Toussaint L'Ouverture

2004. Bicentenary of Haitian Revolution.

1039	**325**	$40 multicoloured	2·25	1·75

326 Yellow-billed Amazon

2004. Bird Life International (2nd series). Caribbean Endemic Birds Festival. Multicoloured.

1040		$10 Type **326**	90	90
1041		$10 Jamaican oriole	90	90
1042		$10 Orangequit	90	90
1043		$10 Yellow-shouldered grassquit	90	90
1044		$10 Jamaican woodpecker	90	90
1045		$10 Streamertail ("Red-billed Streamertail")	90	90
1046		$10 Jamaican mango	90	90
1047		$10 White-eyed thrush	90	90
1048		$10 Jamaican lizard cuckoo	90	90
1049		$10 Arrow-headed warbler	90	90

327 Water Lilies

2004. World Environment Day. Sheet 195×85 mm containing T **327** and similar horiz designs. Multicoloured.
MS1050 $10 Type **327**; $10 Hawksbill turtle; $10 Tube sponge; $10 Man in canoe, Parottee pond; $40 Vase sponge and Star coral; $40 Sea fan and black and white crinoid; $40 Glassy sweeper; $40 Giant sea anemone ... 6·00 7·00

328 Hurdling

2004. Olympic Games, Athens. Multicoloured.
1051	$30 Type **328**	1·00	65
1052	$60 Running	2·00	1·75
1053	$70 Swimming	2·00	1·90
1054	$90 Badminton and shooting	2·75	3·50

329 Two Jamaican Players and Opponent (blue strip)

2004. Centenary of FIFA (Federation Internationale de Football Association). Multicoloured.
1055	$10 Type **329**	55	30
1056	$30 Two Jamaican players and opponent (white top)	1·25	70
1057	$45 Two Jamaican players and opponent (blue top)	1·75	1·50
1058	$50 Two Jamaican players and opponent (white strip)	1·75	2·50

330 Ambassador John Pringle and Round Hill Hotel

2004. Centenary of the Jamaica Hotel Law. Multicoloured.
MS1059 152×114 mm. $40 Type **330** (bottom left panel in pink or blue, three of each) ... 8·00 9·00
MS1060 152×114 mm. $40 Abe Issa and Tower Isle Hotel; $40 John Issa and Tower Isle Hotel (both with bottom right panels in green, light green or carmine, two of each) ... 8·00 9·00
MS1061 152×114 mm. $40 Ralph Lauren and Doctors Cave Beach, Montego Bay (with left-hand panel in dark blue, blue or azure, two of each) ... 8·00 9·00

331 White Sorrel

2004. Christmas.
1062	**331**	$10 multicoloured	65	20
1063	-	$20 multicoloured	1·25	40
1064	-	$50 multicoloured (horiz)	2·75	2·75
1065	-	$60 multicoloured (horiz)	2·75	2·75
DESIGNS: $20 to $60 All showing white sorrel.

332 Mary Morris Knibb and Mizpah Moravian Church

2004. 250th Anniv of the Moravian Church in Jamaica. Multicoloured.
1066	90c. Type **332**	10	40
1067	$10 Reverend W. O'Meally and Mizpah Moravian Church	65	30
1068	$50 Bishop S. U. Hastings and Redeemer Moravian Church	3·25	3·50

333 Ackee, Lychee and Pak Choy

2005. 150th Anniv of Chinese Population in Jamaica. Multicoloured.
1069	$30 Type **333**	1·25	60
1070	$60 Old Chinatown	2·50	2·00
1071	$90 Entrance to Chinese Benevolent Association Headquarters, Kingston	4·00	4·50

334 Rose Hall Great House, St James

2005. Buildings (1st series). Multicoloured. (a) Ordinary gum.
1072	90c. Type **334**	10	20
1073	$5 Holy Trinity Cathedral	20	20
1074	$30 Atrium of the National Commercial Bank, New Kingston	1·10	90
1075	$60 The Court House, Falmouth	2·25	2·50

(b) Self-adhesive.
1076	$5 Holy Trinity Cathedral	20	30
1077	$30 As No. 1074	1·10	1·10
1078	$60 As No. 1075	2·25	2·75
See also Nos. 1105/12.

335 CEPT Emblem

2005. 50th Anniv of the European Philatelic Corporation (Europa). Each showing the CEPT emblem, each with a different colour "stamp frame". Multicoloured.
1079	$60 Type **335**	1·60	1·25
1080	$70 Yellow frame	1·75	1·75
1081	$100 Blue frame	2·50	3·50
MS1082 120×70 mm. Nos. 1079/81 ... 5·25 6·00

336 Gun Captain holding Powder Cartridge

2005. Bicentenary of the Battle of Trafalgar (1st issue). Multicoloured.
1083	$20 Type **336**	1·00	70
1084	$30 Admiral Nelson (vert)	1·40	75
1085	$50 British 12 Pounder cannon	1·60	1·25
1086	$60 HMS Africa (vert)	2·25	1·75
1087	$70 HMS Leviathan (vert)	2·40	2·50
1088	$90 HMS Victory	3·00	4·00
MS1089 120×79 mm. $200 HMS Africa at Port Royal (44×44 mm) ... 8·00 9·00
No. 1088 contains traces of powdered wood from HMS Victory. See also Nos. 1092/4.

337 Rotary Emblem

2005. Centenary of Rotary International.
| 1090 | **337** | $30 multicoloured | 1·50 | 1·50 |

338 Pope John Paul II

2005. Pope John Paul II Commemoration.
| 1091 | **338** | $30 multicoloured | 1·50 | 1·50 |

339 HMS Victory

2005. Bicentenary of the Battle of Trafalgar (2nd issue). Multicoloured.
1092	$50 Type **339**	1·75	1·10
1093	$90 Ships engaged in battle (horiz)	3·00	3·25
1094	$100 Admiral Lord Nelson	3·00	3·25

340 Mary Seacole and Herbal Remedies and Medicines

2005. Birth Bicentenary of Mary Seacole (nursing pioneer). Multicoloured.
1095	$30 Type **340**	80	55
1096	$50 Mary Seacole and Seacole Hall, Mona Campus, University of the West Indies	1·25	1·10
1097	$60 Mary Seacole and Crimean War soldiers, 1854–6	1·75	1·40
1098	$70 Mary Seacole and her British Crimean, Turkish Medjidie, French Legion of Honour and Jamaican Order of Merit medals	1·75	2·00

341 AIDS Emblem and Montage of Faces

2005. World AIDS Day.
| 1099 | **341** | $30 multicoloured | 1·00 | 1·00 |

342 Poinsettia Flowers and Star

2005. Christmas. Multicoloured (background colours given).
1100	**342**	$20 claret and scarlet	70	40
1101	**342**	$30 violet and scarlet	95	55
1102	**342**	$50 scarlet and emerald	1·50	1·00
1103	**342**	$80 green and scarlet	2·50	3·25

343 Jessie Ripoll (Mother Claver) (founder)

2005. 125th Anniv of Alpha.
| 1104 | **343** | $30 multicoloured | 75 | 75 |

2006. Buildings (2nd series). As T **334**. Multicoloured. Ordinary or self-adhesive gum.
1105	$10 Courthouse, Morant Bay	45	30
1106	$15 Spanish Town Square, St. Catherine	65	40
1107	$20 Mico College	80	50
1108	$25 Jamaica College	90	60
1109	$50 Devon House, St. Andrew	1·75	1·25
1110	$70 Ward Theatre	2·25	2·50

| 1111 | $90 Vale Royal, St. Andrew | 2·75 | 3·00 |
| 1112 | $100 Falmouth Post Office | 2·75 | 3·00 |

344 Nestlings

2006. Endangered Species. Black-billed Amazon (*Amazona agilis*). Square designs. Multicoloured.
1121	$5 Type **344**	65	50
1122	$10 In close-up	85	50
1123	$30 In captivity	2·25	1·75
1124	$50 Pair in native forest	3·00	3·50

345 *Blakea trinervia* (cup and saucer)

2006. Christmas. Flowers. Multicoloured.
1125	$20 Type **345**	1·25	70
1126	$30 *Guaiacum officinale* (Lignum Vitae)	1·75	90
1127	$50 *Neocogniauxia monophylla* (vert)	2·25	1·75
1128	$60 *Dendrophylax funalis* (ghost orchid) (vert)	2·50	3·00

346 Courtney Walsh (fast bowler 1984–2001)

2007. ICC Cricket World Cup. Multicoloured.
1129	$30 Type **346**	1·75	1·10
1130	$30 Collie Smith (cricketer 1955–9)	1·75	1·10
1131	$40 New Sabina Park Stadium, Kingston (horiz)	1·90	1·25
1132	$50 Type **346**	2·25	1·75
1133	$60 Trelawny Multi-purpose Sports Complex (horiz)	2·50	3·00
MS1134 118×92 mm. $200 ICC Cricket World Cup trophy ... 8·50 9·00

347 Emblem

2007. Bicentenary of the Abolition of the Transatlantic Trade in Africans.
| 1135 | **347** | $30 multicoloured | 1·00 | 75 |

348 Scout and Jamaican Flag

2007. Centenary of Scouting. Multicoloured.
1136	$5 Type **348**	35	25
1137	$10 Early Jamaican scouts	50	25
1138	$30 Scout leaders	1·25	75
1139	$70 Scouts with Jamaican flag	2·75	3·50
MS1140 90×65 mm. $50 Scout parade (vert); $100 Lord Baden-Powell (vert) ... 4·00 4·50

349 *Tolumnia triquetra*

2007. 'The Christmas Collection 2007'. Flowers. Multicoloured.

1141	$20	Type **349**	80	35
1142	$30	*Broughtonia negrilensis* (horiz)	1·25	50
1143	$50	*Broughtonia sanguinea* (horiz)	2·00	1·50
1144	$60	*Spathelia sorbifolia*	2·25	2·50

350 Asafa Powell

2008. Olympic Games, Beijing. Designs showing athletes. Multicoloured.

1145	$20	Type **350**	75	40
1146	$30	Aleen Bailey and Veronica Campbell-Brown	1·25	1·40
1147	$30	Sherone Simpson and Tayna Lawrence	1·25	1·40
1148	$60	Veronica Campbell-Brown	2·50	2·75

Nos. 1146/7 were printed together, *se-tenant*, forming a composite design showing athletes with medals.

351 Anniversary Emblem

2008. 50th Anniv of University of Technology, Jamaica.

1149	**351**	$30 multicoloured	1·00	65
MS1150	95×70 mm. **351**	$30 multicoloured	1·00	1·25

352 Keyboard

2008. Centenary of ABRSM (Associated Board of the Royal Schools of Music) Examinations in Jamaica. Multicoloured.

1151	$30	Type **352**	1·25	60
1152	$70	Violin	2·50	3·00

353 Fern Fronds

2008. Christmas. Ferns. Multicoloured.

1153	$20	Type **353**	80	50
1154	$30	Curled single fern leaf	1·25	60
1155	$50	Close-up of fern frond	2·00	1·50
1156	$60	Fern frond	2·25	2·50

354 George Headley

2009. Birth Centenary of George Headley (cricketer). Multicoloured.

1157	$10	Type **354**	25	15
1158	$30	George Headley at wicket	75	50
1159	$200	Statue of George Headley	4·25	4·00
MS1160	110×95 mm.	$250 Statue of George Headley at Sabina Park, Kingston (42×56 mm)	5·50	5·50

355 Angel and Two Children

2009. Christmas. Multicoloured.

1161	$20	Type **355**	70	50
1162	$30	Madonna and infant Jesus	75	50
1163	$50	Madonna (horiz)	1·50	1·10

356 NDTC Singers

2010. Christmas. Multicoloured.

1164	$40	Type **356**	95	50
1165	$60	Kingston College Chapel Choir	1·00	50
1166	$120	The University Singers	2·75	1·40
1167	$160	The Jamaican Folk Singers	4·75	2·40

2011. Royal Wedding. Multicoloured.

MS1168	$400	Prince William and Miss Catherine Middleton	9·25	9·25

357 Negril Lighthouse

2011. Lighthouses. Multicoloured.

1169	$20	Type **357**	60	50
1170	$50	Morant Point Lighthouse	1·25	1·00
1171	$60	Lover's Leap Lighthouse (vert)	1·40	1·25
1172	$200	Galina Lighthouse (vert)	3·25	3·00

358 Hummingbird Emblem

2012. 50th Anniv of Independence. Multicoloured.

1173	$60	Type **358**	1·40	1·25
1174	$120	Arms of Jamaica (vert)	2·75	1·40

359 Veronica Campbell-Brown (gold, 200 metres)

2013. Jamaican Olympic Medallists, Beijing, 2008. Multicoloured.

1175	$60	Type **359**	1·40	1·25
1176	$60	Melanie Walker (gold, 400 metres hurdles)	1·40	1·25
1177	$60	Women's 100 metres medal winners Shelly-Ann Fraser (centre, gold) and Kerron Stewart and Sherone Simpson (dead heated for silver)	1·40	1·25
1178	$60	Record breaking men's 4×100 metres relay team of Usain Bolt, Michael Frater, Asafa Powell and Nesta Carter	1·40	1·25
1179	$60	Usain Bolt (100 and 200 metres record holder)	1·40	1·25

360 Night Blooming Cereus

2013. Christmas. Multicoloured.

1180	$20	Type **360**	45	45
1181	$60	Coffee berries and flowers	1·40	1·25
1182	$120	Century Palm	2·75	1·40
1183	$160	Cactus bloom	3·25	3·00

OFFICIAL STAMPS

1890. Optd **OFFICIAL**.

O3	**8**	½d. green	10·00	1·75
O4	**11**	1d. red	8·00	1·25
O5	**11**	2d. grey	26·00	1·25

Pt. 1

JAMMU AND KASHMIR

A state in the extreme N. of India.

12 pies = 1 anna; 16 annas = 1 rupee.

1 (½a.)

1866. Imperf.

20	**1**	½a. green	£225	£400
26	**1**	½a. red	60·00	95·00
41	**1**	½a. black	50·00	£100
44	**1**	½a. blue	£110	£450
48	**1**	½a. yellow	£250	
15	**1**	1a. black	£475	
21	**1**	1a. green	£250	£450
24	**1**	1a. yellow	£1700	
27	**1**	1a. red	80·00	£325
34	**1**	1a. blue	60·00	£425
8	**1**	4a. red	£150	£200
16	**1**	4a. black	£450	
19	**1**	4a. blue	£400	
25	**1**	4a. yellow	£1000	
37	**1**	4a. green	£225	

Prices for the circular stamps (Nos. 5/48) are for cut-square examples. Cut-to-shape examples are worth from 10% to 20% of these prices, according to condition.

4

1867

58	**4**	½a. blue	£400	£160
60	**4**	½a. red	16·00	9·00
64	**4**	½a. orange	£190	£250
68	**4**	½a. green	£3500	£1800
69a	**4**	½a. black	£275	£325
55	**4**	1a. blue	£1500	26·00
61	**4**	1a. red	35·00	20·00
65	**4**	1a. orange	£5000	£3000
69	**4**	1a. green	£5500	£3000
69b	**4**	1a. black	£4500	£3250

The characters denoting the value are in the upper part of the inner circle and contains three ½a. and one 1a. values.

8 (¼a.)

1867. Imperf.

90	**8**	¼a. black	8·00	8·00
91	**8**	½a. blue	10·00	4·50
93	**8**	1a. blue	£7000	£3500
94	**8**	1a. orange	28·00	20·00
97	**8**	2a. yellow	35·00	38·00
99	**8**	4a. green	90·00	75·00
101	**8**	8a. red	95·00	80·00

12 (¼a.)

1878. Imperf or perf.

139	**12**	⅛a. yellow	3·00	3·50
125	**12**	¼a. red	7·00	7·50
130a	**12**	¼a. blue	£1400	£900
131	**12**	¼a. orange	24·00	28·00
142	**12**	¼a. brown	2·75	1·75
105	**12**	½a. violet	26·00	22·00
126	**12**	½a. red	2·50	2·50
132	**12**	½a. orange	30·00	24·00
143	**12**	½a. blue	17·00	
106	**12**	1a. mauve	46·00	42·00
127	**12**	1a. red	4·75	6·00
133	**12**	1a. orange	42·00	26·00
148	**12**	1a. grey	2·50	2·50
150	**12**	1a. green	2·75	2·75
108	**12**	2a. violet	48·00	50·00
110	**12**	2a. blue	£110	£110
128	**12**	2a. red	6·00	8·00
134	**12**	2a. orange	35·00	26·00
152	**12**	2a. red on yellow	6·00	2·75
153	**12**	2a. red on green	7·50	9·00
129	**12**	4a. red	22·00	17·00
135	**12**	4a. orange	75·00	80·00
156	**12**	4a. green	6·50	6·50
130	**12**	8a. red	24·00	20·00
136	**12**	8a. orange	£110	£110
159	**12**	8a. blue	17·00	16·00
161a	**12**	8a. lilac	17·00	32·00

OFFICIAL STAMPS

1878. Imperf or perf.

O6	¼a. black	3·25	3·25
O7	½a. black	50	1·75
O8	1a. black	1·50	2·25
O9	2a. black	2·75	3·25
O10	4a. black	2·75	3·25
O11	8a. black	4·25	2·75

Pt. 18

JAPAN

An empire of E. Asia, consisting of numerous islands.

1871. 100 mon = 1 sen.
1872. 10 rin = 1 sen; 100 sen = 1 yen.

1 (48 mon)

1871. Imperf.

1	**1**	48m. brown	£250	£375
3	**1**	100m. blue	£225	£300
5	**1**	200m. red	£375	£325
15b	**1**	500m. green	£550	£550

1872. Perf.

17	**1**	½s. brown	90·00	£130
19	**1**	1s. blue	£325	£325
21	**1**	2s. red	£475	£500
22	**1**	5s. green	£650	£650

5   **12**

1872. Various sizes. Design details differ.

34	**5**	½s. brown	20·00	25·00
66	**5**	½s. grey	24·00	22·00
35	**5**	1s. blue	80·00	46·00
67	**5**	1s. brown	38·00	24·00
36	**5**	2s. red	£170	60·00
74	**5**	2s. yellow	£120	16·00
46	**5**	4s. red	£140	33·00
68	**5**	4s. green	£140	30·00
75	**12**	5s. green	£200	£110
57	**12**	6s. brown	£180	75·00
69	**12**	6s. orange	£110	27·00
58	**5**	10s. green	£160	65·00
70	**5**	10s. blue	£190	30·00
59	**5**	20s. violet	£325	£100
71	**5**	20s. red	£150	21·00
60	**5**	30s. black	£375	£100
72	**5**	30s. violet	£190	70·00

13 Bean Goose

1875

61	**13**	12s. red	£375	£160
62	-	15s. lilac (Pied Wagtail)	£375	£160
63	-	45s. red (Northern Goshawk)	£475	£190

20   **21**   **22**

23   **24**

1876

77	20	1s. black	45·00	5·00
78	20	1s. brown	15·00	2·00
113c	20	1s. green	15·00	1·20
79	20	2s. grey	90·00	12·50
102f	20	2s. violet	70·00	2·50
114f	20	2s. red	22·00	1·00
95	20	3s. orange	75·00	30·00
117	20	3s. red	25·00	1·00
82a	20	4s. blue	50·00	6·25
103	20	4s. green	50·00	5·00
118h	20	4s. bistre	17·00	75
83b	21	5s. brown	55·00	2·00
115g	21	5s. blue	32·00	2·00
116	20	5r. grey	3·50	30
104	21	6s. orange	£190	90·00
105	21	8s. brown	37·00	3·00
119	21	8s. violet	37·00	3·00
86d	21	10s. blue	50·00	2·50
120h	21	10s. brown	25·00	75
87e	21	12s. red	£225	£170
88	22	15s. green	£150	12·50
121h	22	15s. violet	60·00	1·00
89	22	20s. blue	£160	£150
122h	22	20s. orange	75·00	3·00
123h	23	25s. green	£110	3·00
90	22	30s. mauve	£250	£110
111	22	45s. red	£500	£600
112	22	50s. red	£225	17·00
124h	22	50s. brown	£120	6·00
125h	24	1y. red	£150	6·00

25 Imperial Crest and Cranes

1894. Emperor's Silver Wedding.

126	25	2s. red	37·00	3·50
127	25	5s. blue	50·00	15·00

26 Prince Kitashirakawa   **27** Prince Arisugawa

1896. China War.

128	26	2s. red	32·00	4·00
129	27	2s. red	32·00	4·00
130	26	5s. blue	75·00	4·00
131	27	5s. blue	75·00	4·00

Both 2s. have an oval medallion, and both 5s. a circular one.

28   **29**   **30**

31   **32** Empress Jingu

1899

132	28	5r. grey	14·00	15·00
133	28	½s. grey	7·50	25
134	28	1s. brown	10·00	25
135b	28	1½s. blue	30·00	1·20
136	28	1½s. violet	22·00	60
137	28	2s. green	20·00	25
138	28	3s. purple	20·00	30
139	28	3s. red	25·00	25
140	28	4s. red	20·00	2·50
141	28	5s. yellow	30·00	30
142	29	6s. red	50·00	5·00

143	29	8s. olive	65·00	6·00
144	29	10s. blue	25·00	25
145	29	15s. violet	25·00	35
146	29	20s. orange	50·00	30
147	30	25s. green	£110	1·50
148	30	50s. brown	£110	2·00
149	31	1y. red	£150	2·50
183	32	5y. green	£600	6·00
184	32	10y. violet	£900	10·00

33 Rice Cakes used at Japanese Weddings

1900. Prince Imperial Wedding.

152	33	3s. red	36·00	1·10

34 Symbols of Korea and Japan

1905. Amalgamation of Japanese and Korean Postal Services.

153	34	3s. red	£130	23·00

35 Gun and Japanese Flag

1906. Triumphal Military Review of Russo-Japanese War.

154	35	1½s. blue	55·00	7·00
155	35	3s. red	£110	29·00

36   **37**   **38**

1914

167e	36	½s. brown	5·00	25
168e	36	1s. orange	6·50	25
232	36	1½s. blue	6·50	25
170e	36	2s. green	9·00	25
298	36	3s. red	3·00	45
172e	37	4s. red	25·00	2·50
300	37	5s. violet	11·00	30
174e	37	6s. brown	40·00	7·50
302	37	7s. orange	14·00	30
175e	37	8s. grey	32·00	22·00
176e	37	10s. blue	22·00	25
236	37	13s. brown	14·00	35
178e	37	20s. red	£130	2·00
179e	37	25s. olive	22·00	2·50
180e	38	30s. brown	35·00	1·50
238	38	30s. orange and green	40·00	60
181e	38	50s. brown	50·00	2·20
239	38	50s. brown and blue	17·00	90
309	38	1y. green and brown	£150	1·10

40 Ceremonial Cap   **42** Hall of Ceremony

1915. Emperor's Coronation.

185	40	1½s. grey and red	4·00	85
186	-	3s. violet and brown	5·25	1·20
187	42	4s. red	23·00	15·00
188	42	10s. blue	55·00	25·00

DESIGN—As T **40**: 3s. Imperial throne.

43 Mandarin Duck   **44** "Kammuri" (ceremonial headband)

1916. Investiture of Prince Hirohito as Heir Apparent.

189	43	1½s. green, red and yellow	4·25	1·60
190	43	3s. red and yellow	8·00	1·90
191	44	10s. blue	£950	£400

45 Dove of Peace   **46** Dove of Peace

1919. Restoration of Peace.

192	45	1½s. brown	3·50	1·40
193	46	3s. green	4·75	2·20
194	45	4s. red	11·50	7·00
195	46	10s. blue	34·00	20·00

1919. Air. First Tokyo–Osaka Airmail Service. Optd with airplane.

196	36	1½s. blue	£375	£150
197	36	3s. red	£650	£450

48 7th-century Censor

1920. First Census.

198	48	1½s. purple	8·25	6·00
199	48	3s. red	9·50	6·00

49 Meiji Shrine

1920. Dedication of Meiji (Emperor Mutsuhito) Shrine.

200	49	1½s. violet	4·00	2·00
201	49	3s. red	4·00	2·00

50 Postal and National Flags   **51** Dept. of Communications, Tokyo

1921. 50th Anniv of Japanese Post.

202	50	1½s. red and green	3·25	1·90
203	51	3s. brown	4·50	2·50
204	51	4s. red and pink	55·00	44·00
205	51	10s. blue	£300	£200

52 Warships "Katori" and "Kashima"

1921. Return of Crown Prince from European Tour.

206	52	1½s. violet	4·00	2·20
207	52	3s. olive	3·50	2·20
208	52	4s. red	48·00	33·00
209	52	10s. blue	70·00	40·00

53 Mt. Fuji and Sika Deer

1922

266	53	4s. orange	15·00	55
293	53	4s. green	4·50	1·10
211	53	8s. red	34·00	9·75
267	53	8s. green	22·00	35
303	53	8s. bistre	19·00	2·20
268	53	20s. purple	95·00	55
305	53	20s. brown	22·00	70

54 Mt. Niitaka

1923. Crown Prince's visit to Taiwan.

213	54	1½s. yellow	20·00	23·00
214	54	3s. violet	25·00	12·50

55   **56**

1923. Imperf.

215	55	½s. grey	4·75	5·00
216	55	1½s. blue	7·25	2·20
217	55	2s. brown	8·25	2·20
218	55	3s. red	3·75	1·40
219	55	4s. green	38·00	34·00
220	55	5s. violet	19·00	2·20
221	55	8s. red	55·00	44·00
222	56	10s. brown	50·00	2·20
223	56	20s. blue	80·00	2·75

58 Empress Jingu

1924

224	58	5y. green	£300	4·50
225	58	10y. violet	£475	3·25

59 Cranes   **60** Phoenix

1925. Imperial Silver Wedding.

226	59	1½s. purple	2·20	1·70
227a	60	3s. brown and silver	4·00	3·50
228	59	8s. red	32·00	23·00
229b	60	20s. green and silver	70·00	60·00

61a Yomei Gate, Tosho Shrine, Nikko

1926

241	-	2s. green	3·00	15
242	61a	6s. red	14·00	50
243	-	10s. blue	14·00	15
304	-	10s. red	12·50	30

DESIGNS: 2s. Mt. Fuji; 10s. Nagoya Castle.

62 Baron Maeshima   **63** Globe

1927. 50th Anniv of Membership of U.P.U.

244	62	1½s. purple	3·75	2·20
245	62	3s. olive	5·00	2·20
246	62	6s. red	90·00	65·00
247	63	10s. blue	£130	65·00

64 Phoenix   **65** Ceremonial Shrines

1928. Emperor's Enthronement.

248	64	1½s. green on yellow	1·00	90
249	65	3s. purple on yellow	1·00	85
250	64	6s. red on yellow	5·50	3·25
251	65	10s. blue on yellow	5·75	4·00

66 Shrine of Ise

1929. 58th Vicennial Removal of Shrine of Ise.

255	66	1½s. violet	2·20	1·60
256	66	3s. red	2·75	2·20

67
Nakajima-built
Fokker F.VIIb/3m
over Lake Ashi,
Hakone

1929. Air.

257	67	8½s. brown	65·00	50·00
258	67	9½s. red	17·00	11·00
259	67	16½s. green	20·00	20·00
260	67	18s. blue	19·00	8·25
261	67	33s. black	55·00	11·00

68 Map of
Japan

1930. Third Census.

262	68	1½s. purple	3·75	1·90
263	68	3s. red	4·25	2·40

Although Type **68** is inscr "Second Census", this was actually the third census.

69 Meiji Shrine

1930. Tenth Anniv of Meiji Shrine Dedication.

264	69	1½s. green	2·75	2·20
265	69	3s. orange	4·00	2·75

1934. Air. Establishment of Communications Commemoration Day. Sheet containing Nos. 258/61.

MS271 110×100 mm		£1300	£1800

70 Insignia of
Red Cross
Society

1934. 15th Int Red Cross Conference, Tokyo.

272	70	1½s. green	2·30	1·80
273	-	3s. violet	2·75	3·00
274	70	6s. red	13·50	13·00
275	-	10s. blue	16·00	12·50

DESIGN—HORIZ: 3s.; 10s. Red Cross Society Buildings, Tokyo.

72 Cruiser *Hiyei*
and Pagoda,
Liaoyang

73 Akasaka Palace,
Tokyo

1935. Visit of Emperor of Manchukuo.

276	72	1½s. green	1·80	1·60
277	73	3s. brown	3·00	1·80
278	72	6s. red	10·50	8·75
279	73	10s. blue	14·00	11·00

74 Mt. Fuji
(after Kazan
Watanabe)

1935. New Year's Greetings.

280	74	1½s. red	18·00	35

75c Mt. Fuji from Mishima

1936. Fuji-Hakone National Park.

281	-	1½s. brown	4·00	6·75
282	-	3s. green	7·25	11·50
283	-	6s. red	16·00	22·00
284	75c	10s. blue	18·00	25·00

DESIGNS: Mt. Fuji (1½s.); from Lake Ashi (3s.); from Lake Kawaguchi (6s.).

76 Dove of Peace   **77** Shinto Shrine
Port Arthur

1936. 30 Years of Occupation of Kwantung.

285	76	1½s. violet	18·00	22·00
286	77	3s. brown	22·00	27·00
287	-	10s. green	£200	£250

DESIGN—HORIZ: 10s. Govt. House, Kwantung.

78 Imperial Diet

1936. Inauguration of New Houses of the Imperial Diet, Tokyo.

288	78	1½s. green	2·00	2·00
289	-	3s. purple	2·30	2·30
290	-	6s. red	7·75	8·75
291	78	10s. blue	15·00	11·00

DESIGN: 3, 6s. Grand Staircase.

80 Wedded
Rocks,
Futami Bay

1936. New Year's Greetings.

292	80	1½s. red	8·00	35

82
Goshuinsen
(16th-cent
trading ship)

83 General
Nogi

84 Lake
Taisho,
Kamikochi

85 Mitsubishi
B5N1 and
Map

86 Kamatari
Fujiwara

87 Plum Tree

1937. Imperf or perf (424), perf (others). Without gum (424), with or without gum (392, 394, 396), with gum (others).

313	82	½s. violet	1·30	80
314	-	1s. brown	3·50	70
392b	83	2s. red	65	60
316	-	3s. green	1·00	10
394	83	3s. brown	1·10	15
317	-	4s. green	1·30	10
318	84	5s. blue	2·30	10
396	-	5s. purple	40	20
319	-	6s. orange	4·75	2·10
320	-	7s. green	1·20	45
398	-	7s. red	1·20	50
321	-	8s. violet	1·50	60
322	-	10s. red	7·00	20
323	85	12s. blue	1·00	1·00
324	-	14s. red and brown	1·30	45
325	-	20s. blue	1·60	10
326	-	25s. light brown and brown	1·20	30
327	-	30s. blue	3·50	20
328	-	50s. green and bistre	1·60	20
329	-	1y. light brown and brown	6·25	80
424	86	5y. green	6·25	80
331	87	10y. purple	32·00	1·60

DESIGNS: 1s. Rice harvesting; 3s. Hydro-electric Power Station; 4, 5s. (No. 396), 7s. (No. 398), Admiral Togo; 6s. Garambi Lighthouse, Taiwan; 7s. (No. 320), Diamond Mountains, Korea; 8s. Meiji Shrine; 10s. Yomei Gate, Tosho Shrine, Nikko; 14s. Inner Gate, Kasuga Shrine; 20s. Mt. Fuji and cherry blossom; 25s. Horyu Temple; 30s. Torii, Itsukushima Shrine at Miyajima; 50s. Temple of Golden Pavilion, Kyoto; 1y. Great Buddha, Kamakura.

88
Nakajima-built
Douglas DC-2
Airliner

1937. Aerodrome Fund.

336	88	2s.+2s. red	2·75	1·80
337	88	3s.+2s. violet	2·75	2·10
338	88	4s.+2s. green	3·50	1·90

89 New
Year's
Emblem

1937. New Year's Greetings.

339	89	2s. red	13·00	20

90 Nantai
Volcano

92 Shinkyo Bridge

91 Kegon Falls   **93** Hiuchi Volcano

1938. Nikko National Park.

340	90	2s. orange	80	95
341	91	4s. green	80	95
342	92	10s. red	9·50	8·25
343	93	20s. blue	9·75	8·50
MS344 128×182 mm. Nos. 340/3 (sold at 50s.)			70·00	80·00

94 Daisen Volcano and
Meadow

95 Yashima Plateau and
Estuary

96 Abuto Kwannon Shrine

97 Tomo Bay

1939. Daisen and Setonaikai National Parks.

345	94	2s. brown	60	80
346	95	4s. green	5·00	2·75
347	96	10s. red	10·00	10·50
348	97	20s. blue	10·00	10·50
MS349 127×180 mm. Nos. 345/8 (sold at 50s.)			44·00	50·00

98 Mt. Kuju and Village

99 Naka Volcano

100 Naka Crater

101 Volcanic Cones of Mt. Aso

1939. Aso National Park.

350	98	2s. brown	60	1·10
351	99	4s. green	3·50	6·50
352	100	10s. red	23·00	27·00
353	101	20s. blue	33·00	22·00
MS354 127×181 mm. Nos. 350/3 (sold at 50s.)			£140	£160

102 Globe

1939. 75th Anniv of Membership of International Red Cross Union.

355	102	2s. brown	1·90	2·00
356	-	4s. green	2·20	2·50
357	102	10s. red	12·50	15·00
358	-	20s. blue	12·50	15·00

DESIGN: 4s., 20s. Count Tsunetami Sano.

104 Golden Bird   **105** Mt. Takachiho

106 Sake Jar
and Ayu

107 Kashiwara
Shrine

1940. 2600th Anniv of Japanese Empire.

359	104	2s. orange	1·10	1·60
360	105	4s. green	55	85
361	106	10s. red	5·25	7·75
362	107	20s. blue	1·60	2·50

108 Mt. Hokuchin

109 Mt. Asahi   **110** Sounkyo
Gorge, Kobako

111 Tokachi Range

1940. Daisetsu-zan National Park.

363	108	2s. brown	60	1·10
364	109	4s. green	3·25	5·50
365	110	10s. red	10·50	11·50
366	111	20s. blue	13·00	11·50
MS367 127×181 mm. Nos. 363/6 (sold at 50s.)			£300	£325

112 Mt. Shimmoe

113 Takachiho Peak

114 Kirishima Shrine

115 Lake Roku-Kwannon

1940. Kirishima National Park, Kyushu.

368	112	2s. brown	60	1·10
369	113	4s. green	1·30	2·20
370	114	10s. red	9·75	11·50
371	115	20s. blue	12·50	11·50

MS372 127×181 mm. Nos. 368/71 (sold at 50s.) £300 £375

116 Ceremonial Shrine (after Y. Araka)

117 "Loyalty and Filial Piety"

1940. 50th Anniv of Promulgation of Imperial Re-script on Education.

373	116	2s. violet	1·10	1·90
374	117	4s. green	1·50	2·40

118 Mt. Daiton

119 Central Peak, Mt. Niitaka

120 Buddhist Temple, Mt. Kwannon

121 View of Mt. Niitaka

1941. Daiton and Niitaka-Arisan National Parks.

375	118	2s. brown	1·30	1·30
376	119	4s. green	2·75	2·75
377	120	10s. red	8·25	10·00
378	121	20s. blue	11·50	11·50

MS379 128×182 mm. Nos. 375/8 (sold at 90s. together with No. MS384) £130 £150

122 Seisui Precipice, East Taiwan Coast   **124** Taroko Gorge, Taiwan

123 Mt. Tsugitaka

125 Mt. Taroko, Source of R. Takkiri

1941. Tsugitaka and Taroko National Parks.

380	122	2s. brown	1·30	1·30
381	123	4s. green	2·75	2·75
382	124	10s. red	8·25	9·75
383	125	20s. blue	11·50	13·50

MS384 128×182 mm. Nos. 380/3 (sold at 90s. together with No. MS379) £100 95·00

陥落　シンガポール
+1
(126)

1942. Surrender of Singapore. Surch as T **126**.

385	83	2s.+1s. red	1·10	2·00
386	-	4s.+2s. green (No. 317)	1·10	2·00

127 Kenkoku Shrine

129 Orchids and Crest of Manchukuo

1942. Tenth Anniv of Establishment of Manchukuo.

387	127	2s. brown	55	85
388	-	5s. olive	85	1·30
389	127	10s. red	1·90	3·75
390	129	20s. blue	4·00	5·75

DESIGN—VERT: 5s. Boys of Japan and Manchukuo.

130 Girl War-worker

135 "The Enemy will Surrender"

140 Garambi Lighthouse, Taiwan

141 Garambi Lighthouse, Taiwan

1942. Imperf (418/19, 421), imperf or perf (400, 420), perf (others). With or without gum (398, 420), without gum (400, 418/19, 421), with gum (others).

391	130	1s. brown	15	15
393	-	2s. green	80	80
395	-	4s. green	30	30
397	-	6s. blue	65	65
399	-	10s. red and pink	95	10
400	135	10s. grey	5·25	5·25
418	135	10s. blue	45·00	
419	-	10s. orange	60	35
401	-	15s. blue	4·00	2·30
402	-	17s. violet	1·20	25
420	-	20s. blue	80	30
404	-	27s. red	1·20	1·10
405	-	30s. green	4·00	2·00
421	-	30s. blue	2·20	70
406	140	40s. purple	60	15
407	141	40s. purple	2·40	2·10

DESIGNS: 2s. Shipbuilding; 4s. Hyuga Monument and Mt. Fuji; 6s. War-worker; 10s. (No. 399) Palms and map of Greater East Asia; 10s. (No. 419) 20s. Mt. Fuji; 15s. Air-man; 17s., 27s. Yasukuni Shrine; 30s. (2) Myajima Shrine.

142 Class C59 Steam Locomotive No. 28

1942. 70th Anniv of First National Railway.

408	142	5s. green	3·75	6·00

143 Tanks in action at Bataan

1942. First Anniv of Declaration of War.

409	143	2s.+1s. brown	1·60	2·75
410	-	5s.+2s. blue	2·40	3·75

DESIGN: 5s. Attack on Pearl Harbor.

144 Yasukuni Shrine

1944. 75th Anniv of Yasukuni Shrine.

411	144	7s. green	80	1·30

145 Kwantung Shrine and Map of Kwantung Peninsula

1944. Dedication of Kwantung Shrine.

412	145	3s. brown	3·75	11·50
413	145	7s. grey	4·00	11·50

146 Sun and Cherry Blossom

149 Torii of Yasukuni Shrine

1945. Imperf or perf and with or without gum (422), imperf without gum (others).

415	146	3s. red	50	40
416	-	5s. green	40	30
422	-	50s. brown	85	30
423	149	1y. olive	1·90	95

DESIGNS: 5s. Sunrise and Kawasaki Ki-61 Hien fighter; 50s. Coal miners.

150 Pagoda of Horyu Temple, Nara

153 Kiyomizu Temple, Kyoto

154 Noh Mask

1946. Imperf or perf (30s., 50, 100y.), imperf (others). With or without gum (30s., 5, 50, 100y.), without gum (others).

426	-	15s. green	60	55
427	150	30s. violet	1·00	30
428a	-	1y. blue	1·70	30
429	-	1y.30 bistre	4·50	1·40
430	-	1y.50 grey	4·00	80
431	153	2y. red	3·25	30
432	-	5y. mauve	10·50	1·10
433b	154	50y. brown	£100	1·50
434a	-	100y. purple	£100	1·30

DESIGNS: 15s. Baron H. Maeshima; 1y. Mt. Fuji, after Hokusai; 1y.30, Snow and white-fronted geese (after Hokusai); 1y.50, Kintai Bridge, Iwakuni; 5y. Veil-tailed gold-fish; 100y. Plum tree.

For 30s., 1y.20, 4y. and 10y. as Nos. 427, 429 and 434a but with Japanese characters reading in reverse order, see Nos. 441, 445/6 and 449.

156 Mediaeval Postman's Bell

157 Baron Maeshima

1946. 75th Anniv of Government Postal Service.

436	156	15s. orange	6·00	6·00
437	157	30s. green	8·00	8·00
438	-	50s. red	4·00	4·00
439	-	1y. blue	4·00	4·00

MS440 183×125 mm. Nos. 436/9 (sold at 3y.). Imperf. No gum. £170 £190

DESIGNS—As Type **156**: 50s. First Japanese Postage Stamp; 1y. Symbols of communication.

160   **161** Baron Maeshima

163 National Art

1947. As issues of 1946 but with Japanese characters in reverse order and new designs. Imperf without gum (449), perf with gum (others).

441	150	30s. violet	6·00	6·00
442	160	35s. green	95	65
443	-	45s. mauve	1·40	1·20
444	161	1y. brown	5·00	75
445	150	1y.20 green	2·50	70
446	-	4y. blue (as No. 429)	6·75	30
447	-	5y. blue	10·00	20
448	163	10y. violet	11·00	15
449	-	10y. purple (as No. 434a)	46·00	2·10

DESIGNS—VERT: 45s. Numeral; 5y. Whaling.
For similar designs, but without the chrysanthemum emblem, see Nos. 467/70.

164 Mother and Child

165 Roses and Wisteria

1947. Inauguration of New Constitution.

451	164	50s. red	65	70
452	165	1y. blue	95	90

MS453 128×180 mm. Nos. 451/2 (sold at 3y.). Imperf. No gum. 10·50 12·00

1947. "Know Your Stamps" Exhibition, Tokyo, 1947. May Sheet containing No. 445 in block of fifteen.
MS454 237×76 mm (sold at 18y.). £200 £180

166 National Products

1947. Re-opening of Private Foreign Trade.

455	166	1y.20 brown	4·00	2·10
456	166	4y. blue	8·00	2·75

1947. "Know Your Stamps" Exhibition, Kyoto, August 1947. Sheet containing No. 431 in block of five. Imperf. No gum.
MS457 115×69 mm (sold at 10y.). 33·00 38·00

167 Lily of the Valley

1947. Relief of Ex-convicts Day.

458	167	2y. green	6·50	3·25

1947. 75th Anniv of Japanese Railway Service. Imperf. No gum.
MS459 115×72 mm. 168 4y. blue (sold at 5y.) 23·00 23·00

169 Hurdling

1947. Second National Athletic Meeting. Kanazawa. Each mauve.

460	1y.20 Type **169**	13·00	12·00
461	1y.20 Diving	13·00	12·00
462	1y.20 Throwing the discus	13·00	12·00
463	1y.20 Volleyball	13·00	12·00

1947. Philatelic Week. Sheet containing No. 428a in strip of five. No gum.
MS464 114×71 mm 5·50 6·75

170

1947. Community Chest.

465	170	1y.20+80s. red	2·00	1·80

1947. Philatelic Exhibition, Sapporo, November 1947. Sheet containing No. 422 in block of five. Imperf. No gum.
MS466 114×71 mm. (sold at 2y.50) — 18·00 / 20·00

172 Kiyomizu Temple, Kyoto   **173** National Art

1948. Designs without chrysanthemum.

467	-	1y.50 blue	4·50	65
468	172	2y. red	12·00	30
469	-	3y.80 brown	12·00	7·75
470	173	10y. violet	23·00	25

DESIGNS: 1y.50, 3y.80, Numeral types.

1948. Philatelic Exhibition, Osaka. Sheet containing No. 432 twice with two Japanese characters in centre below stamps. Imperf. No gum.
MS472 114×71 mm. — 18·00 / 22·00

1948. Philatelic Exhibition, Nagoya. Sheet as last but three Japanese characters in centre below stamps.
MS473 114×71 mm. — 21·00 / 23·00

174 Stylized Tree

1948. Encouragement of Afforestation.
474 | 174 | 1y.20 green — 1·60 / 1·60

1948. Philatelic Exhibition, Mishima, April, 1948. Sheet No. MS473 optd at top, bottom and sides with Japanese characters and flowers in green.
MS475 114×71 mm. — £110 / 46·00

1948. Death Centenary of Hokusai Katsushika (painter). Sheet No. MS464 optd at top and bottom with Japanese characters in purple.
MS476 114×71 mm. — 37·00 / 28·00

175 Sampans, Seto Inland Sea

1948. Sheets Commemorating Various Exhibitions. Each sheet contains two stamps as T 175 (2y. red), with coloured borders and inscriptions. Imperf. No gum.
(a) Communications Exhibition, Tokyo, April 27 to May 4 1948.
MS477 113×71 mm. Green border — 21·00 / 11·50

(b) Newspaper and Postage Stamp Exhibition, Aomori City.
MS478 113×71 mm. Blue border — 28·00 / 20·00

(c) Communications Exhibition, Fukushima.
MS479 113×71 mm. Turquoise — 28·00 / 20·00

176 Boy and Girl reading

1948. Re-organization of Educational System.
480 | 176 | 1y.20 red — 1·60 / 1·40

177 Horse Race

1948. 25th Anniv of Japanese Horse Racing Laws.
481 | 177 | 5y. brown — 3·50 / 2·00

178 Swimmer

1948. Third National Athletic Meeting, Yawata.
482 | 178 | 5y. blue — 4·75 / 2·40

179 Distillery Towers

1948. Tenth Anniv of Govt. Alcohol Monopoly.
483 | 179 | 5y. brown — 4·50 / 2·75

1948. Philatelic Exhibition, Kumamoto. Sheet containing two copies of Nos. 467 and 469. Imperf. Nogum. Imperf. No gum.
MS484 114×71 mm — 46·00 / 38·00

180 Nurse   **181** Varied Tit Feeding Young

1948. Red Cross and Community Chest.

485	180	5y.+2y.50 red	12·50	12·50
486	181	5y.+2y.50 green	12·50	12·50

MS487 128×90 mm. T 181 (both 5y.+5y.). Imperf. No gum. — 95·00 / 80·00

182 Farm Girl   **183** Harpooning   **184** Miner

185 Girl plucking Tea   **186** Girl Printer   **187** Mill Girl

188 Mt. Hodaka   **189** Tree Planting

190 Postman   **191** Blast-Furnace   **192** Constructing Class C62 Steam Locomotive

1948

488	182	2y. green and light green	3·25	10
489	183	3y. turquoise	7·75	20
490	184	5y. bistre	18·00	1·50
491	185	5y. green	60·00	8·00
492	186	6y. orange	12·00	15
493	184	8y. brown	13·00	10
494	187	15y. blue	4·75	20
495	188	16y. blue	12·50	6·50
496	189	20y. green	50·00	20
497	190	30y. blue	60·00	20
506	191	100y. red	£650	1·40
507	192	500y. blue	£550	1·60

1948. Philatelic Exhibition, Nagano. Sheet comprising No. 494. Imperf. No gum.
MS508 114×71 mm — 60·00 / 44·00

193 Baseball

1948. Third National Athletic Meeting, Fukuoke.

509	193	5y. green	13·50	6·75
510	-	5y. green (bicycle race)	13·50	6·75
511	-	5y. green (sprinter)	13·50	6·75
512	-	5y. green (high jumper)	13·50	6·75

1948. Commemorating the Shikoku Travelling Philatelic Exhibition, November 1948. Sheet containing two copies of No. 490. Imperf. No gum.
MS513 115×72 mm — 70·00 / 55·00

194 Beauty Looking Back (Moronobu Hishikawa)

1948. Philatelic Week.
514 | 194 | 5y. brown — 95·00 / 49·00

1948. Postal Service Exhibition, Kanazawa and Takaoka. Sheet containing No. 514. Imperf. No gum.
MS515 71×115 mm. — 65·00 / 39·00

195 Girl playing with Shuttlecock

1948. New Year's Greetings.
516 | 195 | 2y. red — 6·50 / 6·00

196 Skater   **197** Ski Jumper

1949. Fourth National Athletic Meeting. (a) Suwa City.
517 | 196 | 5y. violet — 3·75 / 2·30

(b) Sapporo, Hokkaido.
518 | 197 | 5y. blue — 4·50 / 2·30

198 "Koan Maru" (ferry) in Beppu Harbour

1949
519 | 198 | 2y. blue and red — 1·60 / 1·20
520 | 198 | 5y. blue and green — 6·75 / 1·70

199 Exhibition Grounds

1949. Foreign Trade Fair, Yokohama. Perf or imperf.
521 | 199 | 5y. red — 4·25 / 2·75

200 Seto Inland Sea

1949. Matsuyama, Okayama and Takamatsu Exhibitions.

522	200	10y. red (Matsuyama)	37·00	23·00
523	200	10y. pink (Okayama)	30·00	21·00
524	200	10y. claret (Takamatsu)	55·00	26·00

201 Stylized Trees

1949. Encouragement of Afforestation.
525 | 201 | 5y. green — 12·50 / 2·40

202 Shishi-Iwa (Lion Rock)

203 Mt. Omine

204 Doro-Hatcho River Pool

205 Hashikui-Iwa

1949. Yoshino-Kumano National Park.

526	202	2y. brown	1·70	1·00
527	203	5y. green	5·50	1·60
528	204	10y. red	21·00	12·00
529	205	16y. blue	10·00	5·50

MS530 126×182 mm. Nos. 526/9. No gum. (sold at 40y.) — 50·00 / 37·00

206 Boy

1949. Children's Day.
531 | 206 | 5y. purple and buff — 7·50 / 2·40

1949. Children's Exhibition, Inuyama. Sheet containing No. 531 in block of ten. Imperf.
MS532 143×90 mm. — £400 / £375

207 Radio Mast

1949. Electrical Communications Week. Sheet containing T 207.
MS533 71×108 mm. 20y. blue — £140 / £120

208 Observatory Tower

1949. 75th Anniv of Central Meteorological Observatory, Tokyo.
534 | 208 | 8y. green — 4·50 / 2·20

209 Radio Mast, Pigeon and Globe

1949. Establishment of Joint Ministries of Postal and Electrical Communications.
535 | 209 | 8y. blue — 4·50 / 2·20

210 Park in Autumn

211 Park in Spring

212 Park in Summer

213 Park in Winter

1949. Fuji-Hakone National Park.

536	**210**	2y. brown	4·50	1·10
537	**211**	8y. green	4·75	1·60
538	**212**	14y. red	2·20	65
539	**213**	24y. blue	7·50	80
MS540	127×180 mm. Nos. 536/9 (sold at 55y.)		47·00	47·00

214 Woman holding Rose

1949. Establishment of Memorial City at Hiroshima.

541	**214**	8y. brown	10·50	2·75

215 Doves

1949. Establishment of International Cultural City at Nagasaki.

542	**215**	8y. green	6·25	2·75

216 Swimmer

1949. Fourth National Athletic Meeting, Yokohama.

543	**216**	8y. blue	5·25	2·10

217 Boy Scout

1949. First National Scout Jamboree, Tokyo.

544	**217**	8y. brown	8·75	2·75

218 Symbolical of Writing and Printing

1949. Press Week.

545	**218**	8y. blue	6·75	2·75

219 Map of Japan and Letters

220 Globe and Forms of Transport

1949. 75th Anniv of U.P.U.

546	**219**	2y. green	3·50	2·10
547	**220**	8y. red	4·50	2·10
548	**219**	14y. red	12·50	9·00

549	**220**	24y. blue	17·00	10·00
MS550	115×70 mm. Nos. 546/7. Imperf.			
	No gum		5·75	6·75

221 Throwing the Javelin

1949. Fourth National Athletic Meeting, Tokyo. Each brown.

551	8y. Type **221**		8·50	3·50
552	8y. Dinghy sailing		8·50	3·50
553	8y. Relay racing		8·50	3·50
554	8y. Tennis		8·50	3·50

222 Telescope

1949. 50th Anniv of Establishment of Latitude Observatory, Mizusawa.

555	**222**	8y. green	4·75	2·10

223 "Moon and Brent Geese" (after Hiroshige)

1949. Postal Week.

556	**223**	8y. violet	£140	50·00

224 Dr. H. Noguchi   A   B   C   D

E   F   G   H   I   J

K   L   M   N   O   P

Q   R

1949. Various portraits as illustrated, in frame as T **224**.

557	A	8y. green	11·50	1·40
558	B	8y. green	4·75	1·40
559	C	8y. green	4·75	1·40
560	D	8y. green	4·50	1·40
561	E	8y. violet	12·50	4·50
562	F	8y. purple	4·50	1·40
563	G	8y. green	11·50	2·75
564	H	8y. violet	11·50	2·75
565	I	8y. red	18·00	2·75
566	J	8y. red	30·00	3·00
567	K	8y. brown	18·00	3·00
568	L	8y. blue	14·00	3·00
569	M	10y. green	60·00	5·50
570	N	10y. purple	12·50	1·80
571	O	10y. red	4·50	1·60
572	P	10y. grey	6·00	1·60
573	Q	10y. brown	5·50	1·60
574	R	10y. blue	6·00	1·60

PORTRAITS: A, Hideyo Noguchi (bacteriologist); B, Y. Fukuzawa (educationist); C, Soseki Natsume (novelist); D, Shoyo Tsubouchi (dramatist); E, Danjuro Ichikawa (actor); F, Jo Niijima (religious leader); G, Hogai Kano (painter); H, Kanzo Uchimura (religious leader); I, Mme. Higuchi (author); J, Ogai Mori (doctor); K, S. Masaoka (poet); L, S. Hishida (painter); M, A. Nishi (scholar); N, K. Ume (lawyer); O, H. Kimura (astrophysicist); P, I. Nitobe (statesman); Q, T. Torada (physicist); R, Tenshin Okakura (writer).

225 Green Pheasant and Pampas Grass

1950. Air.

575	**225**	16y. grey	41·00	27·00
576	**225**	34y. purple	70·00	24·00
577	**225**	59y. red	95·00	17·00
578	**225**	103y. orange	65·00	21·00
579	**225**	144y. olive	70·00	30·00

226 Tiger (after Maruyama Okyo)

1950. New Year's Greetings.

580	**226**	2y. red	9·75	2·75

227 Microphones of 1925 and 1950

1950. 25th Anniv of Japanese Broadcasting System.

582	**227**	8y. blue	4·50	2·10

228 Dove

1950. First Anniv of Joint Ministries of Postal and Electrical Communications.

583	**228**	8y. green	4·25	1·60

229 Lake Akan and Mt. O-Akani

230 Lake Kutcharo

231 Mt. Akan-Fuji

232 Lake Mashu

1950. Akan National Park.

584	**229**	2y. brown	1·60	1·20
585	**230**	8y. green	3·25	1·80
586	**231**	14y. red	15·00	6·75
587	**232**	24y. blue	16·00	7·75
MS588	127×181 mm. Nos. 584/7 (sold at 55y.)		50·00	49·00

233 Gymnast on Rings

1950. Fifth National Athletic Meeting.

589	**233**	8y. red	32·00	17·00
590	-	8y. red (Pole vaulting)	32·00	17·00
591	-	8y. red (Football)	32·00	17·00
592	-	8y. red (Horse jumping)	32·00	17·00

234 Tahoto Pagoda, Ishiyama Temple   **235** Baron Maeshima   **236** Long-tailed Cock

237 Kannon Bosatsu (detail of wall painting, Horyu Temple)   **238** Himeji Castle

239 Phoenix Temple, Uji   **240** Buddhisattva Statue, Chugu Temple

1950. With noughts for sen after value.

593	**234**	80s. red	2·30	2·10
594	**235**	1y. brown	3·00	45
595	**236**	5y. green and brown	6·75	20
596	**237**	10y. lake and mauve	13·50	15
597	**238**	14y. brown	55·00	44·00
598	**239**	24y. blue	44·00	23·00
599	**240**	50y. brown	£160	1·00

For designs without noughts see Nos. 653 etc and for designs additionally inscr "NIPPON" see Nos. 1041/59.

1950. Miniature sheets, each 76×50 mm and each containing one of stamps from the above issue.

MS600	80s. carmine	10·50	14·00
MS601	14y.brown	75·00	85·00
MS602	24y. blue	47·00	60·00
MS603	50y. brown	£300	£350

241 Girl and Rabbit

1951. New Year's Greetings.

604	**241**	2y. red	8·00	1·10

For 50y. in this design dated "1999" see No. 2565.

242 Skiing, Mt. Zao

1951. Tourist Issue. Mt. Zao.

606	**242**	8y. olive	18·00	3·75
607		24y. blue	20·00	8·75

DESIGN—HORIZ: 24y. Two skiers on Mt. Zao.

243 Nihon-Daira   **244** Mt. Fuji from Nihon Daira

1951. Tourist Issue. Nihon-Daira.

608	**243**	8y. green	18·00	3·75
609	**244**	24y. blue	£130	35·00

1951. 80th Anniv of Japanese Postal Service. Sheet containing No. 594 in block of four.

MS610	86×64 mm	25·00	22·00

245 Child's Head

1951. Children's Charter.

611	**245**	8y. brown	30·00	4·50

246 Hot Springs, Owaki Valley **247** Lake Ashi

1951. Tourist Issue. Hakone Spa.

612	246	8y. brown	11·00	3·00
613	247	24y. blue	9·25	4·50

248 Senju Waterfall **249** Ninai Waterfall

1951. Tourist Issue. Akame Waterfalls.

614	248	8y. green	13·00	3·00
615	249	24y. blue	12·00	4·50

250 Waka-no-Ura **251** Tomo-ga-Shima

1951. Tourist Issue. Coastal Resorts.

616	250	8y. brown	9·25	3·00
617	251	24y. blue	8·75	4·50

252 Oirase River

253 Lake Towada

254 View from Kankodai

255 Hakkoda Mountains

1951. Towada National Park.

618	252	2y. brown	3·00	1·10
619	253	8y. green	11·00	1·60
620	254	14y. red	12·50	6·75
621	255	24y. blue	14·00	7·75

MS622 128×182 mm. Nos. 618/21 (sold at 55y.) 47·00 47·00

256 Uji River **257** Uji Bridge

1951. Tourist Issue. Uji River.

623	256	8y. brown	9·75	3·00
624	257	24y. blue	9·00	4·50

258 Douglas DC-4 Airliner over Horyuji Pagoda **259** Douglas DC-4 Airliner and Mt. Tate

1951. Air. With noughts for sen after numerals of value.

625	258	15y. violet	5·75	4·50
626	258	20y. blue	38·00	2·75

627	258	25y. green	37·00	50
628	258	30y. red	29·00	45
629	258	40y. black	9·75	50
630	259	55y. black	£250	46·00
631	259	75y. red	£180	25·00
632	259	80y. mauve	37·00	5·75
633	259	85y. black	60·00	21·00
634	259	125y. brown	20·00	5·75
635	259	160y. green	46·00	6·25

For similar designs, but without noughts after numerals of value, see Nos. 671/81.

260 Chrysanthemum **261** Japanese Flag

1951. Peace Treaty.

636	260	2y. brown	2·75	1·40
637	261	8y. red and blue	8·00	3·75
638	260	24y. green	25·00	8·75

262 Oura Catholic Church, Nagasaki **263** Gateway, Sofuku Temple

1951. Tourist Issue. Nagasaki.

639	262	8y. red	13·00	3·00
640	263	24y. blue	9·75	4·50

264 Lake Marunuma **265** Lake Sugenuma

1951. Tourist Issue.

641	264	8y. purple	17·00	2·75
642	265	24y. green	8·25	4·50

266 Shosenkyo Valley **267** Nagatoro Bridge

1951. Tourist Issue. Shosenkyo.

643	266	8y. red	12·50	3·00
644	267	24y. blue	13·50	4·50

268 Putting the Shot

1951. Sixth National Athletic Meeting.

645	268	2y. brown	4·50	2·50
646	-	2y. blue (Hockey)	4·50	2·50

269 Noh Mask

1952. New Year's Greetings.

647	269	5y. red	14·00	1·10

270 Ship's Davit and Southern Cross

1952. 75th Anniv of U.P.U. Membership.

649	270	5y. violet	7·75	1·80
650	-	10y. green	20·00	4·50

DESIGN: 10y. Earth and Ursa Major. Inscr "1952".

271 Red Cross and Lily

1952. 75th Anniv of Japanese Red Cross.

651	271	5y. red	6·00	2·00
652	-	10y. green and red (Nurse)	14·00	4·00

272 Akita Dog **273** Small Cuckoo **274** Tahoto Pagoda, Ishiyama Temple

275 Mandarins **276** Japanese Serow **277** Chuson Temple

278 Veil-tailed Goldfish **279** Yomei Gate, Tosho Shrine, Nikko **280** *Marimo* (water plant) and Sockeye Salmon

281 Great Purple **282** Fishing with Japanese Cormorants **283** "Bridge and Irises" (from lacquered box)

1952. Without noughts after numerals of value.

653	235	1y. brown	55	10
654	272	2y. black	10	10
655	273	3y. turquoise	15	10
656	274	4y. purple and red	2·50	10
657	275	5y. brown and blue	15	10
658	276	8y. brown and light brown	10	10
659	237	10y. red and mauve	5·50	10
660	238	14y. green	7·50	2·40
661	277	20y. green	1·50	10
662	239	24y. violet	18·00	4·50
663	239	30y. purple	43·00	80
664	278	35y. orange	12·00	10
665	279	45y. blue	5·25	10
666	240	50y. brown	6·50	10
667	280	55y. green, black and blue	18·00	80
668	281	75y. multicoloured	9·75	80
669	282	100y. red	35·00	10
670	283	500y. purple	85·00	15

For 1, 2, 3, 50, 55 and 75y. in same designs, but inscr "NIPPON", see Nos. 1041, 1582a, 1226, 1058/60, 1232 and 1064.

1952. Air. As Nos. 625/35 but without noughts after numerals of value.

671	258	15y. violet	2·10	95
672	258	20y. blue	60·00	1·30
673	258	25y. green	1·20	10
674	258	30y. red	4·50	10
675	258	40y. black	5·50	25
676	259	55y. blue	90·00	6·75
677	259	75y. red	£160	16·00
678	259	80y. mauve	£120	4·50
679	259	85y. black	5·00	2·75
680	259	125y. brown	10·00	3·75
681	259	160y. green	43·00	4·50

---

284 Mt. Yari **285** Kurobe Valley

286 Mt. Shirouma

287 Mt. Norikura

1952. Chubu-Sangaku National Park.

682	284	5y. brown	7·00	1·20
683	285	10y. green	33·00	4·00
684	286	14y. red	8·50	7·75
685	287	24y. blue	14·00	7·75

MS686 129×182 mm. Nos. 682/5 but imperf. No gum (sold at 60y.) £130 £120

288 Central Hall

1952. 75th Anniv of Tokyo University.

687	288	10y. green	21·00	3·50

289 Wrestlers

1952. Seventh National Athletic Meeting.

688	-	5y. blue (Mountaineer)	8·00	2·40
689	289	5y. brown	8·00	2·40

290 Mt. Azuma-Kofuji

291 Mt. Asahi

292 Mt. Bandai

293 Mt. Gessan

1952. Bandai-Asahi National Park.

690	290	5y. brown	5·50	1·00
691	291	10y. olive	17·00	2·75
692	292	14y. red	6·75	4·50
693	293	24y. blue	14·00	7·50

MS694 128×181 mm. Nos. 690/3 but imperf. No gum (sold at 60y.) £150 95·00

294 "Kirin" and Chrysanthemums **295** Flag of Crown Prince

1952. Investiture of Crown Prince Akihito.

695	294	5y. orange and brown	3·00	1·20
696	294	10y. orange and green	3·00	2·50
697	295	24y. blue	18·00	8·75

MS698 130×130 mm. Nos. 695/7.
Imperf. No gum (sold at 50y.)   £120   £350

296 Dancing Doll

1953. New Year's Greetings.
699	**296**	5y. red	9·50	1·10

297 First Japanese Electric Lamp

1953. 75th Anniv of Electric Lamp in Japan.
701	**297**	10y. brown	9·00	3·00

299 Kintai Bridge

1953. Tourist Issue. Kintai Bridge.
702	–	10y. brown	9·25	3·00
703	**299**	24y. blue	8·50	4·50

DESIGN—VERT: 10y. Kintai Bridge (after Hiroshige).

300 Lake Shikotsu (½-size illustration)

301 Mt. Yotei (½-size illustration)

1953. Shikotsu-Toya National Park.
704	**300**	5y. blue	2·75	80
705	**301**	10y. green	8·75	1·60

MS706 148×105 mm. Nos. 704/5 but imperf. No gum (sold at 20y.)   50·00   47·00

302 Great Buddha, Kamakura

1953. Air.
707	**302**	70y. brown	4·00	15
708	**302**	80y. blue	5·75	15
709	**302**	115y. olive	2·75	20
710	**302**	145y. turquoise	18·00	2·10

303 Wedded Rocks, Futami Bay (½-size illustration)

304 Nakiri Coast (½-size illustration)

1953. Ise Shima National Park.
711	**303**	5y. red	2·50	80
712	**304**	10y. blue	5·50	1·60

MS713 148×105 mm. Nos. 711/2 but imperf. No gum (sold at 2y.)   39·00   21·00

305 "Ho-o" (Happy Phoenix)

1953. Return of Crown Prince from Overseas Tour.
714	**305**	5y. lake	4·25	1·60
715	–	10y. blue	7·50	2·75

DESIGN: 10y. Manchurian crane in flight.

306 Judo

1953. Eighth National Athletic Meeting, Matsuyama.
716	**306**	5y. green	7·25	2·10
717	–	5y. black	7·25	2·10

DESIGN: 5y. Rugby footballers.

307 Tokyo Observatory

1953. 75th Anniv of Tokyo Observatory.
718	**307**	10y. blue	13·00	3·00

308 Mt. Unzen (½-size illustration)

309 Mt. Unzen (½-size illustration)

1953. Unzen National Park.
719	**308**	5y. red	2·75	80
720	**309**	10y. blue	6·00	1·60

MS721 148×105 mm. Nos. 719/20 but imperf. No gum (sold at 20y.)   39·00   21·00

310 Wooden Horse

1953. New Year's Greetings.
722	**310**	5y. red	7·25	80

311 Ice Skaters

1954. World Speed Skating Championships, Sapporo.
724	**311**	10y. blue	6·50	2·75

312

1954. International Trade Fair, Osaka.
725	**312**	10y. red	5·50	2·10

313 Wrestlers

1954. Int Free-style Wrestling Championship.
726	**313**	10y. green	4·50	2·00

314 Mt. Asama (½-size illustration)

315 Mt. Tanigawa (½-size illustration)

1954. Jo-Shin-Etsu Kogen National Park.
727	**314**	5y. sepia	3·00	80
728	**315**	10y. turquoise	5·50	1·60

MS729 148×108 mm. Nos. 727/8 but imperf. No gum (sold at 20y.)   39·00   21·00

316 Archery

1954. Ninth National Athletic Meeting, Sapporo.
730	**316**	5y. green	6·25	2·00
731	–	5y. brown (Table tennis)	6·25	2·00

317 Telegraph Table

1954. 75th Anniv of Japan's Membership of I.T.U.
732	**317**	5y. purple	2·75	1·30
733	–	10y. blue	7·50	2·30

DESIGN—HORIZ: 10y. I.T.U. Monument.

1954. Philatelic Week. Sheet 150×50 mm containing ten of No. 659 (arranged as one row of 6 and one row of 4 (with printed label at each end).
MS734 10y. lake and mauve   £200   £190

318 Tumbler

1954. New Year's Greetings.
735	**318**	5y. red and black	7·25	80

319 Tama Gorge   **320** Chichibu Mountains

1955. Chichibu-Tama National Park.
737	**319**	5y. blue	2·00	80
738	**320**	10y. lake	2·50	1·10

MS739 148×105 mm. Nos. 737/8 but imperf. No gum (sold at 20y.)   39·00   21·00

321 Paper Carp

1955. 15th International Chamber of Commerce Congress, Tokyo.
740	**321**	10y. multicoloured	7·25	2·40

322 Bentenzaki Peninsula   **323** Jodoga Beach

1955. Rikuchu-Kaigan National Park.
741	**322**	5y. green	1·70	65
742	**323**	10y. red	2·50	1·10

MS743 147×104 mm. Nos. 741/2 but imperf. No gum (sold a20y.)   37·00   21·00

324 Gymnastics

1955. Tenth National Athletic Meeting, Kanagawa.
744	**324**	5y. red	4·00	1·60
745	–	5y. blue (Running)	4·00	1·60

---

325 *Girl Playing Glass Flute* (Utamaro)

1955. Philatelic Week.
746	**325**	10y. multicoloured	16·00	12·00

326 "Kokeshi" Dolls

1955. New Year's Greetings.
747	**326**	5y. green and red	2·75	40

327 Table Tennis

1956. World Table Tennis Championships.
749	**327**	10y. brown	2·00	1·10

328 Judo

1956. World Judo Championships.
750	**328**	10y. purple and green	2·20	1·10

329 Children and Paper Carps

1956. International Children's Day.
751	**329**	5y. black and blue	1·70	80

330 Osezaki Lighthouse (½-size illustration)

331 Kujuku Island (½-size illustration)

1956. 25th Anniv of National Park Law. Saikai National Park.
752	**330**	5y. brown	1·30	65
753	**331**	10y. indigo and blue	1·70	1·10

MS754 147×104 mm. Nos. 752/3 but imperf. No gum (sold at 20y.)   31·00   20·00

332 Imperial Palace, and Modern Buildings

1956. Fifth Centenary of Tokyo.
755	**332**	10y. purple	2·75	1·20

333 Sakuma Dam

1956. Completion of Sakuma Dam.
756   **333**   10y. blue   2·75   1·20

334 Basketball

1956. 11th National Athletic Meeting, Kobe.
757   **334**   5y. green   1·60   80
758   -   5y. purple (Long
            jumping)   1·60   80

335 *Ebizo Ichikawa*
(actor) (after Sharaku)

1956. Philatelic Week.
759   **335**   10y. black, orange and
            grey   13·50   9·75

336 Mt. Manaslu and
Mountaineer

1956. Conquest of Mt. Manaslu.
760   **336**   10y. multicoloured   4·50   2·40

337 View of Yui (after
Hiroshige) and Type EF 58
Electric Locomotive No. 4

1956. Electrification of Tokaido Railway Line.
761   **337**   10y. black, green &
            brown   7·25   2·40

338 Cogwheel, Valve
and Freighter "Nissyo
Maru"

1956. Floating Machinery Fair.
762   **338**   10y. blue   1·10   1·00

339 Whale
(float)

1956. New Year's Greetings.
763   **339**   5y. multicoloured   1·70   30

340 U.N.O. Emblem

1957. First Anniv of Japan's Admission into U.N.
765   **340**   10y. red and blue   1·00   80

341 I.G.Y.
Emblem,
Emperor
Penguin and
Antarctic
Research Vessel
Soya

1957. International Geophysical Year.
766   **341**   10y. blue, yellow and
            black   1·00   65

342 Atomic
Reactor

1957. Completion of Atomic Reactor at Tokai-Mura.
767   **342**   10y. violet   60   30

343 Gymnast

1957. 12th National Athletic Meeting, Shizuoka.
768   **343**   5y. blue   55   35
769   -   5y. red (Boxing)   55   35

344 *Girl Bouncing Ball*
(after Harunobu)

1957. Philatelic Week.
770   **344**   10y. multicoloured   2·10   2·40

345 Ogochi Dam

1957. Completion of Ogochi Dam.
771   **345**   10y. blue   50   40

346 Japan's First Blast
Furnace and Modern
Plant

1957. Centenary of Japanese Iron Industry.
772   **346**   10y. purple and orange   35   30

347 "Inu-hariko"
(toy dog)

1957. New Year's Greetings.
773   **347**   5y. multicoloured   35   30

348 Kan-Mon Tunnel

1958. Opening of Kan-Mon Undersea Tunnel.
775   **348**   10y. multicoloured   50   25

349 *Lady returning from
Bath-house* (after
Kiyonaga)

1958. Philatelic Week.
776   **349**   10y. multicoloured   80   25

350 Statue of Ii Naosuke,
"Powhattan" (1858
paddle-steamer) and
Modern Liner

1958. Centenary of Opening of Ports to Traders.
777   **350**   10y. red and blue   40   25

351 National
Stadium, Tokyo

1958. Third Asian Games, Tokyo. Inscr as in T **351.**
Multicoloured.
778   5y. Type **351**   25   20
779   10y. Flame and Games emblem   50   40
780   14y. Runner breasting tape   40   30
781   24y. High-diver   50   40

352 Emigration Ship *Kasato
Maru* and South American
Map

1958. 50th Anniv of Japanese Emigration to Brazil.
782   **352**   10y. multicoloured   40   20

353 Dado-Okesa   **354** Mt. Yahiko and
Dancer on Sado Island   Echigo Plain

1958. Sado-Yahiko Quasi-National Park.
783   **353**   10y. multicoloured   1·10   40
784   **354**   10y. multicoloured   1·30   60

355 Stethoscope

1958. International Congresses of Chest Diseases and
Bronchoesophagology, Tokyo.
785   **355**   10y. turquoise   40   25

356 *Old Kyoto Bridge*
(after Hiroshige)

1958. International Correspondence Week.
786   **356**   24y. multicoloured   3·50   90
     The design is taken from the series of 53 woodcuts,
showing stages of the Tokaido Road. Others from this series are shown on Nos. 810, 836, 878 and 908.

357 Badminton
Player

1958. 13th National Athletic Meeting, Toyama.
787   **357**   5y. purple   45   25
788   -   5y. blue (Weightlifting)   45   25

358 Yukichi
Fukuzawa
(founder) and
Keio University

1958. Centenary of Keio University.
789   **358**   10y. red   50   25

359 Children Skipping
across Globe

1958. International Child and Social Welfare Conferences,
Tokyo.
790   **359**   10y. green   50   25

360 "Flame of
Freedom"

1958. Tenth Anniv of Declaration of Human Rights.
791   **360**   10y. multicoloured   45   25

361 Ebisu with
Madai
Seabream (toy)

1958. New Year's Greetings.
792   **361**   5y. multicoloured   65   20

362 Map of
Kojima Bay and
Tractor

1959. Completion of Kojima Bay Reclamation Project.
794   **362**   10y. purple and ochre   40   25

363 Karst Plateau   **364** Akiyoshi
                        Cavern

1959. Akiyoshidai Quasi-National Parks.
795   **363**   10y. multicoloured   2·00   25
796   **364**   10y. multicoloured   3·50   25

365 Map of
Asia

1959. Asian Congress Commemorating 2500th Anniv of
Buddha's Death.
797   **365**   10y. red   50   25

366 Crown Prince
Akihito and Princess
Michiko

1959. Imperial Wedding.
798   -   5y. violet and purple   35   15
799   **366**   10y. purple and brown   90   25
800   -   20y. sepia and brown   1·20   25
801   **366**   30y. deep green and
            green   3·75   35
MS802   127×88 mm. Nos. 798/9 but
     imperf. No gum (sold at 20y.)   7·00   5·25
DESIGN: 5, 20y. Ceremonial fan.

367 *Ladies reading poems* (from *Ukiyo Genji* after Eishi)

1959. Philatelic Week.
803	**367**	10y. multicoloured	4·75	2·00

368 Graduated Glass and Scales

1959. Ratification of Adoption of Metric System in Japan.
804	**368**	10y. sepia and blue	40	15

369 Stretcher-party with Casualty

1959. Red Cross.
805	**369**	10y. red and green	50	15

370 Mt. Fuji from Lake Motosu

1959. National Parks Day.
806	**370**	10y. green, purple and blue	80	15

371 Ao Caves, Yabakei   **372** Japanese Cormorant with Hita and Mt. Hiko background

1959. Yaba-Hita-Hikosan Quasi-National Parks.
807	**371**	10y. multicoloured	1·40	40
808	**372**	10y. multicoloured	1·40	40

373 Nagoya and Golden Dolphin

1959. 350th Anniv of Nagoya.
809	**373**	10y. gold, black and blue	1·10	15

374 *Kuwana* (after Hiroshige)

1959. International Correspondence Week.
810	**374**	30y. multicoloured	12·00	1·60

375 Flying Manchurian Crane and I.A.T.A. Emblem

1959. 15th International Air Transport Association Meeting, Tokyo.
811	**375**	10y. blue	80	40

376 Throwing the Hammer

1959. 14th National Athletic Meeting, Tokyo.
812	**376**	5y. blue	1·00	30
813	-	5y. brown (Fencer)	1·00	30

377 Open Book showing portrait of Shoin Yoshida

1959. Death Centenary of Shoin Yoshida (educator) and National Parents/Teachers Assn Convention.
814	**377**	10y. brown	70	30

378 Halves of Globe

1959. 15th Session of Contracting Parties to G.A.T.T.
815	**378**	10y. brown	70	30

379 Rice-eating Rat of Kanazawa (toy)

1959. New Year's Greetings.
816	**379**	5y. multicoloured	1·80	25

380 Yukio Ozaki and Clock Tower Memorial Hall

1960. Completion of Ozaki Memorial Hall, Tokyo.
818	**380**	10y. purple and brown	70	30

381 Deer

1960. 1250th Anniv of Transfer of Capital to Nara.
819	**381**	10y. olive	90	30

382 Godaido Temple, Matsushima   **383** Bridge of Heaven (sandbank), Miyazu Bay

384 Miyajima from the Sea

1960. "Scenic Trio".
820	**382**	10y. turquoise and brown	2·20	60
821	**383**	10y. green and blue	3·00	60
822	**384**	10y. green and violet	3·00	60

385 Takeshima-Gamagori Causeway

1960. Mikawa Bay Quasi-National Park.
823	**385**	10y. multicoloured	1·25	20

386 Ise (from Satake picture scroll *Thirty-six Immortal Poets*)

1960. Philatelic Week.
824	**386**	10y. black, red and brown	4·50	2·75

387 *Kanrin Maru* (barque) crossing the Pacific

1960. Centenary of Japanese–American Treaty.
825	**387**	10y. sepia and green	80	30
826	-	30y. black and red	2·20	45

DESIGN: 30y. Pres. Buchanan receiving Japanese mission.

388 Japanese Crested Ibis

1960. 12th Int Bird Preservation Congress, Tokyo.
827	**388**	10y. red, pink and grey	90	45

389 Radio Waves around Globe

1960. 25th Anniv of Japanese Overseas Broadcasting Service, "Radio Japan".
828	**389**	10y. red	70	30

390 Abashiri Flower Gardens

1960. Abashiri Quasi-National Park.
829	**390**	10y. multicoloured	1·70	45

391 Cape Ashizuri

1960. Ashizuri Quasi-National Park.
830	**391**	10y. multicoloured	1·70	45

392 Rainbow linking Hawaii and Japan

1960. 75th Anniv of Japanese Emigration to Hawaii.
831	**392**	10y. multicoloured	1·10	30

393 Douglas DC-8 and Farman H.F.III Biplane

1960. 50th Anniv of Japanese Aviation.
832	**393**	10y. brown and grey	80	30

394 Seat Plan of the Diet

1960. 49th Inter-Parliamentary Union Conference. Inscr "49TH INTER-PARLIAMENTARY CONFERENCE TOKYO 1960".
833	**394**	5y. orange and blue	70	25
834	-	10y. brown and blue	1·00	30

DESIGN: 10y. "Clear Day with Southern Breeze" (from "36 Views of Mt. Fuji" by Hokusai Katsushika).

1960. Visit of Crown Prince Akihito and Princess Michiko to the United States. Sheet containing Nos. 825/6.
MS835	120×76 mm		39·00	31·00

395 *Kambara* (after Hiroshige)

1960. International Correspondence Week.
836	**395**	30y. multicoloured	25·00	5·50

396 Okayama Observatory

1960. Opening of Okayama Astrophysical Observatory.
837	**396**	10y. violet	1·10	25

397 "Kendo" (Japanese fencing)

1960. 15th National Athletic Meeting, Kumamoto.
838	**397**	5y. blue	80	30
839	-	5y. purple (Vaulting)	80	30

398 Lieut. Shirase and Map of Antarctica

1960. 50th Anniv of 1st Japanese Antarctic Expedition.
840	**398**	10y. black and brown	1·10	25

399 Red Beko and Golden Bekokko (Japanese toys)

1960. New Year's Greetings.
841	**399**	5y. multicoloured	1·10	25

400 Diet Building and Stars

1960. 70th Anniv of Diet.
843	**400**	5y. violet and black	70	25
844	-	10y. red	1·00	25

DESIGN: 10y. Opening ceremony of first session of Diet.

401 Narcissus

1961. Japanese Flowers. Flowers in natural colours. Background colours given.
845	10y. purple (T **401**)	6·00	1·10
846	10y. brown (Plum blossom)	2·50	1·10
847	10y. bistre (Camellia)	1·80	1·10
848	10y. grey (Cherry blossom)	1·80	1·10
849	10y. sepia (Peony)	1·40	1·00
850	10y. grey (Iris)	75	85
851	10y. turquoise (Lily)	60	50
852	10y. blue (Morning glory)	60	50
853	10y. sage (Bellflower)	60	50
854	10y. orange (Gentian)	60	50

| 855 | | 10y. blue (Chrysanthemum) | 60 | 50 |
| 856 | | 10y. slate (Camellia) | 60 | 50 |

402 Pearl-divers at Shirahama

1961. Minami-Boso Quasi-National Park.

| 857 | **402** | 10y. multicoloured | 1·00 | 30 |

403 Hirase's Slit Shell · **404** Nanten · **405** Cherry Blossoms

406 Engaku Temple · **407** Yomei Gate, Tosho Shrine, Nikko · **408** Noh Mask

409 Copper Pheasant · **410** "The Wind God" · **411** Manchurian Cranes

412 "Kalavinka" (legendary bird)

1961

858	**403**	4y. red and brown	15	10
859	**404**	6y. red and green	15	10
860	**405**	10y. mauve and purple	35	10
861	**406**	30y. violet	6·25	10
862	**407**	40y. red	7·50	10
863	**408**	70y. black and ochre	3·00	10
864	**409**	80y. brown and red	1·50	10
865	**410**	90y. green	42·00	30
866	**411**	100y. grey, black and pink	15·00	10
867	**412**	120y. violet	14·50	75

For 70, 80, 90, 100, and 120y. in different colours and additionally inscr "NIPPON" see Nos. 1065/6, 1068, 1234/6 and 1238.

413 Baron Maeshima

1961. 90th Anniv of Japanese Postal Service.

| 868 | **413** | 10y. green and black | 2·00 | 25 |

414 *Dancing Girl* (from 17th-century screen)

1961. Philatelic Week.

| 869 | **414** | 10y. multicoloured | 2·00 | 1·60 |

415 Lake Biwa

1961. Lake Biwa Quasi-National Park.

| 870 | **415** | 10y. multicoloured | 1·10 | 30 |

416 Rotary Emblem and "Peoples of the World"

1961. 52nd Rotary International Convention.

| 871 | **416** | 10y. orange and black | 50 | 25 |

417 "Benefits Irrigation"

1961. Inauguration of Aichi Irrigation Scheme.

| 872 | **417** | 10y. blue and purple | 50 | 30 |

418 Globe showing Longitude 135° E. and Sun

1961. 75th Anniv of Japanese Standard Time.

| 873 | **418** | 10y. red, black and ochre | 70 | 25 |

419 Parasol Dancer, Tottori Beach

1961. San'in Kaigan Quasi-National Park.

| 874 | **419** | 10y. multicoloured | 1·40 | 30 |

420 Komagatake Volcano

1961. Onuma Quasi-National Park.

| 875 | **420** | 10y. multicoloured | 1·40 | 30 |

421 Gymnast

1961. 16th National Athletic Meeting, Akita.

| 876 | **421** | 5y. green | 80 | 30 |
| 877 | – | 5y. blue (Rowing) | 80 | 30 |

422 *Hakone* (after Hiroshige)

1961. International Correspondence Week.

| 878 | **422** | 30y. multicoloured | 9·75 | 6·25 |

423 Throwing the Javelin

1961. Olympic Games, Tokyo, 1964 (1st issue).

879	**423**	5y.+5y. brown	1·30	1·60
880	–	5y.+5y. green	1·30	1·60
881	–	5y.+5y. red	1·30	1·60

DESIGNS: No. 880, Wrestling; 881, Diver (Woman).
See also Nos. 899/901, 909/11, 935/7, 949/52, 969/72 and 981/5.

424 Library and Book

1961. Opening of National Diet Library.

| 882 | **424** | 10y. blue and gold | 50 | 30 |

425 Tiger (Izumo toy)

1961. New Year's Greetings.

| 883 | **425** | 5y. multicoloured | 90 | 10 |

426 Mt. Fuji from Lake Aishi · **427** Minokake-Iwa, Irozaki

428 Mt. Fuji from Mitsutoge · **429** Mt. Fuji from Osezaki

1962. Fuji-Hakone-Izu National Park.

885	**426**	5y. green	1·00	30
886	**427**	5y. blue	90	30
887	**428**	10y. brown	1·40	45
888	**429**	10y. black	1·80	55

430 Omishima Island

1962. Kitanagato-Kaigan Quasi-National Park.

| 889 | **430** | 10y. multicoloured | 80 | 30 |

431 Doll Festival

1962. National Festivals. Multicoloured.

890		10y. Type **431**	1·70	60
891		10y. Children and decorated tree ("Star Festival")	60	30
892		10y. Three children ("Seven-Five-Three Festival")	60	30
893		10y. Children throwing beans ("Spring Festival")	50	30

432 *Dancer* (after N. Kano)

1962. Philatelic Week.

| 894 | **432** | 10y. multicoloured | 2·00 | 1·60 |

433 Sakurajima Volcano

1962. Kinkowan Quasi-National Park.

| 895 | **433** | 10y. multicoloured | 60 | 30 |

434 Mount Kongo

1962. Kongo-Ikoma Quasi-National Park.

| 896 | **434** | 10y. multicoloured | 60 | 30 |

435 Suigo View

1962. Suigo Quasi-National Park.

| 897 | **435** | 10y. multicoloured | 80 | 30 |

436 *Hakucho* (swan) Express Train emerging from Tunnel

1962. Opening of Hokuriku Railway Tunnel.

| 898 | **436** | 10y. brown | 3·00 | 40 |

1962. Olympic Games, Tokyo, 1964 (2nd issue). Sports. As T **423**.

899		5y.+5y. red	80	1·10
900		5y.+5y. green	80	1·10
901		5y.+5y. purple	80	1·10

SPORTS: No. 899 Judo; 900, Water-polo; 901, Gymnastics (female).

437 Scout's Hat on Map

1962. Asian Scout Jamboree, Mt. Fuji.

| 902 | **437** | 10y. black, bistre and red | 40 | 30 |

438 Mt. Shibutsu and Ozegahara Swamp · **439** Smoking Summit of Mt. Chausu, Nasu

440 Lake Chuzenji and Mt. Nantai · **441** Senryu-kyo Narrows, Shiobara

1962. Nikko National Park.

903	**438**	5y. turquoise	40	25
904	**439**	5y. lake	40	25
905	**440**	10y. purple	60	25
906	**441**	10y. olive	60	25

442 Wakato Suspension Bridge

1962. Opening of Wakato Suspension Bridge.

| 907 | **442** | 10y. red | 1·10 | 45 |

443 *Nihonbashi* (after Hiroshige)

1962. International Correspondence Week.

| 908 | **443** | 40y. multicoloured | 8·25 | 5·50 |

1962. Olympic Games, Tokyo, 1964 (3rd issue). Sports. As T **423**.

909		5y.+5y. green	70	55
910		5y.+5y. lilac	70	55
911		5y.+5y. red	70	55

SPORTS: No. 909, Basketball; 910, Rowing; 911, Fencing.

444 Rifle-shooting

1962. 17th National Athletic Meeting, Okayama.

912	**444**	5y. purple	40	30
913	–	5y. blue	40	30

DESIGN: No. 913, Softball.

445
Hare-bell
(Nogomi
toy)

1962. New Year's Greetings.

914	**445**	5y. multicoloured	60	10

For 50y. in this design dated "1999" see No. 2566.

446 Mt. Ishizuchi and
Kamega Forest

1963. Ishizuchi Quasi-National Park.

916	**446**	10y. multicoloured	50	30

447 "Five Towns"

1963. Amalgamation of Five Towns as Kita-Kyushu.

917	**447**	10y. brown	40	25

448 Frosted Foliage, Fugen Peak **449** Amakusa Islands and Mt. Unzen

1963. Unzen-Amakusa National Park.

918	**448**	5y. blue	40	25
919	**449**	10y. red	40	25

450 Midorigaike (Green Pond) **451** Hakusan Mountains

1963. Hakusan National Park.

920	**450**	5y. brown	30	25
921	**451**	10y. green	30	25

452 Great Rocks, Keya

1963. Genkai Quasi-National Park.

922	**452**	10y. multicoloured	50	10

453 Globe and Emblem

1963. Freedom from Hunger.

923	**453**	10y. green	40	25

454 Portrait of
Heihachiro Honda
(anon-Yedo period)

1963. Philatelic Week.

924	**454**	10y. multicoloured	1·20	70

455 Centenary Emblem
and World Map

1963. Centenary of Red Cross.

925	**455**	10y. multicoloured	40	25

456 Globe and
Leaf

1963. Fifth International Irrigation and Drainage Commission Congress, Toyko.

926	**456**	10y. blue	40	25

457 Mt. Ito, Asahi Range **458** Mt. Bandai across Lake Hibara

1963. Bandai-Asahi National Park.

927	**457**	5y. green	40	30
928	**458**	10y. brown	50	30

459 Purple Jay

1963. Japanese Birds. Multicoloured.

929		10y. Type **459**	1·20	70
930		10y. Rock ptarmigan	60	30
931		10y. Eastern turtle dove	60	30
932		10y. White stork	60	30
933		10y. Japanese bush warbler	60	30
934		10y. Siberian meadow bunting	60	30

1963. Olympic Games, Tokyo, 1964 (4th issue). Sports. As T **423**.

935		5y.+5y. blue	60	30
936		5y.+5y. brown	60	30
937		5y.+5y. brown	60	30

SPORTS: No. 935, Dinghy sailing; 936, Boxing; 937, Volleyball.

460 Road Junction, Ritto, Shiga

1963. Opening of Nagoya–Kobe Expressway.

938	**460**	10y. green, black & orange	40	10

461 Girl Scout
and Flag

1963. Asian Girl Scout Camp, Nagano.

939	**461**	10y. multicoloured	40	25

462 Mt. Washiu **463** Whirlpool at Naruto

1963. Seto Inland Sea National Park.

940	**462**	5y. brown	40	25
941	**463**	10y. green	50	25

464 Lake Shikaribetsu **465** Mt. Kurodake

1963. Daisetsuzan National Park.

942	**464**	5y. blue	40	25
943	**465**	10y. purple	50	25

466 Antenna

1963. 14th International Scientific Radio Union Conference, Tokyo.

944	**466**	10y. multicoloured	40	25

467 Great Wave off
Kanagawa (from 36 Views
of Mt. Fuji by Hokusai
Katsushika)

1963. International Correspondence Week.

945	**467**	40y. multicoloured	6·75	2·30

The design is taken from the series of 36 woodcuts showing Mt. Fuji. Others from this series are shown as Nos. 989, 1010, 1075, 1100, 1140 and 1185.

468 Athletes

1963. "Pre-Olympic" Athletic Meeting, Tokyo.

946	**468**	10y. multicoloured	40	25

469 Wrestling

1963. 18th National Athletic Meeting, Yamaguchi.

947	**469**	5y. brown	40	25
948	–	5y. green	40	25

DESIGN: No. 948, Free-style gymnastics.

1963. Olympic Games, Tokyo, 1964 (5th issue). Sports. As T **423**.

949		5y.+5y. blue	50	25
950		5y.+5y. olive	50	25
951		5y.+5y. black	50	25
952		5y.+5y. purple	50	25

SPORTS: No. 949, Cycling; 950, Show jumping; 951, Hockey; 952, Pistol-shooting.

470 Hachijo Island

1963. Izu Islands Quasi-National Park.

953	**470**	10y. multicoloured	50	25

471 Kai and
Iwai Dragon
Toys

1963. New Year's Greetings.

954	**471**	5y. multicoloured	60	25

472 Wakasa Bay

1964. Wakasa Bay Quasi-National Park.

956	**472**	10y. multicoloured	50	25

473 View from Horikiri
Pass and Agave Plant

1964. Nichinan-Kaigan Quasi-National Park.

957	**473**	10y. multicoloured	40	25

474 Uji Bridge **475** View of Toba

1964. Ise-Shima National Park.

958	**474**	5y. brown	40	25
959	**475**	10y. purple	50	45

476 Festival
Float and Mt.
Norikura
(Tokayama
Festival) **477** "Yamaboko"
Shrine (Gion
Festival)

478 Warriors on Horseback
(Soma Horse Festival)

479 Festival Scene (Chichibu
Festival)

1964. Regional Festivals.

960	**476**	10y. multicoloured	40	25
961	**477**	10y. multicoloured	40	25
962	**478**	10y. multicoloured	40	15
963	**479**	10y. multicoloured	50	15

480 Prince Niou playing for Lady
Nakanokimi (detail of Takayoshi
Yadorigi croll illustrating Tale of
Genji by Lady Murasaki)

1964. Philatelic Week.

964	**480**	10y. multicoloured	60	30

481 Himeji Castle

1964. Rebuilding of Himeji Castle.

965	**481**	10y. brown	50	30

482 Handball

1964. 19th National Athletic Meeting, Niigata.

966	**482**	5y. green	40	25
967	–	5y. red (Gymnastics)	40	25

483 Cross-section of
Cable

1964. Opening of Japan–U.S. Submarine Telephone Cable.

968	**483**	10y. multicoloured	40	25

1964. Olympic Games, Tokyo (6th issue). Sports. As T **423**.

969		5y.+5y. violet	50	25
970		5y.+5y. blue	50	25
971		5y.+5y. lake	50	25
972		5y.+5y. olive	50	25

SPORTS: No. 969, Modern pentathlon; 970, Canoeing; 971, Football; 972, Weightlifting.

484 Nihonbashi
Bridge

1964. Opening of Tokyo Expressway.

973	**484**	10y. green, silver and black	40	25

1964. Olympic Games, Tokyo (12th issue). Set of six miniature sheets each 135×60 mm containing stamps as indicated below.

MS974	Nos. 879/81	9·25	9·75
MS975	Nos. 899/901	6·00	6·75
MS976	Nos. 909/11	4·50	5·00
MS977	Nos. 935/7	11·00	12·00
MS978	Nos. 949/52	11·00	12·00
MS979	Nos. 969/72	11·00	12·00

485 "Coins"

1964. Int Monetary Fund Convention, Tokyo.
| 980 | **485** | 10y. gold and red | 40 | 25 |

486 Olympic Flame

1964. Olympic Games, Tokyo (7th issue). Inscr "1964". Multicoloured.
981	5y. Type **486**		30	25
982	10y. Main stadium (horiz)		40	25
983	30y. Fencing hall (horiz)		80	30
984	40y. Indoor stadium (horiz)		1·00	30
985	50y. Komazawa hall (horiz)		1·10	30
MS986	93×144 mm. Nos. 981/5		6·00	6·25

487 "Agriculture"

1964. Reclamation of Hachirogata Lagoon.
| 987 | **487** | 10y. gold and purple | 60 | 25 |

488 Hikari (light) Express Train

1964. Inauguration of Tokyo–Osaka Shinkansen Railway Line.
| 988 | **488** | 10y. blue and black | 90 | 15 |

489 Tokaido Highway (from 36 Views of Mt. Fuji by Hokusai Katsushika)

1964. International Correspondence Week.
| 989 | **489** | 40y. multicoloured | 2·00 | 60 |

490 Straw Snake

1964. New Year's Greetings.
| 990 | **490** | 5y. multicoloured | 50 | 25 |

491 Mt. Daisen and Akamatsu Pond   **492** Jodo-ga-Ura (Paradise Islands) of Oki

1965. Daisen-Oki National Park.
| 992 | **491** | 5y. blue | 30 | 25 |
| 993 | **492** | 10y. brown | 40 | 25 |

493 Niseko-Annupuri Mountains

1965. Niseko Shakotan Otaru Quasi-National Park.
| 994 | **493** | 10y. multicoloured | 40 | 25 |

494 Radar Station

1965. Completion of Meteorological Radar Station, Mt. Fuji.
| 995 | **494** | 10y. multicoloured | 40 | 25 |

495 Kiyotsu Gorge   **496** Mt. Myoko across Lake Nojiri

1965. Jo-Shin-Etsu Kogen National Park.
| 996 | **495** | 5y. brown | 30 | 25 |
| 997 | **496** | 10y. purple | 40 | 25 |

497 Postal Museum

1965. Inauguration of Postal Museum, Ote-machi, Tokyo, and Stamp Exhibition.
| 998 | **497** | 10y. green | 40 | 15 |

498 The Prelude (after Shoen Uyemura)

1965. Philatelic Week.
| 999 | **498** | 10y. multicoloured | 50 | 25 |

499 Children at Play

1965. Inaug of National Children's Gardens.
| 1000 | **499** | 10y. multicoloured | 50 | 10 |

500 Tree within "Leaf"

1965. Reafforestation.
| 1001 | **500** | 10y. multicoloured | 40 | 25 |

501 Globe and Symbols

1965. Centenary of I.T.U.
| 1002 | **501** | 10y. multicoloured | 40 | 25 |

502 Mt. Naka Crater   **503** Aso Peaks

1965. Aso National Park.
| 1003 | **502** | 5y. red | 30 | 25 |
| 1004 | **503** | 10y. green | 40 | 25 |

504 I.C.Y. Emblem and Doves

1965. International Co-operation Year.
| 1005 | **504** | 40y. multicoloured | 90 | 10 |

505 Meiji Maru (cadet ship) and Japanese Gulls

1965. 25th Maritime Day.
| 1006 | **505** | 10y. multicoloured | 60 | 25 |

506 "Blood Donation"

1965. Campaign for Blood Donors.
| 1007 | **506** | 10y. multicoloured | 40 | 25 |

507 Atomic Power Station, Tokyo

1965. Ninth International Atomic Energy Authority Conference, Tokyo.
| 1008 | **507** | 10y. multicoloured | 40 | 25 |

508 "Population"

1965. Tenth National Census.
| 1009 | **508** | 10y. multicoloured | 40 | 25 |

509 Water at Misaka (from 36 Views of Mt. Fuji by Hokusai Katsushika)

1965. International Correspondence Week.
| 1010 | **509** | 40y. multicoloured | 1·30 | 70 |

510 Emblems and Plan of Diet

1965. 75th Anniv of National Suffrage.
| 1011 | **510** | 10y. multicoloured | 40 | 25 |

511 Walking

1965. 20th National Athletic Meeting, Gifu.
| 1012 | **511** | 5y. green | 40 | 30 |
| 1013 | – | 5y. brown (Gymnastics) | 40 | 30 |

512 Outline of Face, and Baby

1965. International Conferences of Otology, Rhinology and Laryngology (ICORL) and Pediatrics (ICP), Tokyo.
| 1014 | **512** | 30y. multicoloured | 70 | 25 |

513 Mt. Iwo   **514** Mt. Rausu

1965. Shiretoko National Park.
| 1015 | **513** | 5y. turquoise | 30 | 25 |
| 1016 | **514** | 10y. blue | 40 | 25 |

515 Antarctic Map, Research Vessel Fuji and Aurora Australis

1965. Antarctic Expedition of 1965.
| 1017 | **515** | 10y. multicoloured | 50 | 10 |

516 "Straw Horse"

1965. New Year's Greetings.
| 1018 | **516** | 5y. multicoloured | 60 | 30 |

517 Telephone Switchboard (1890) and Modern Dial

1965. 75th Anniv of Japanese Telephone Service.
| 1020 | **517** | 10y. multicoloured | 40 | 25 |

518 Spiny Lobster

1966. Fishery Products. Multicoloured.
1021	10y. Type **518**	40	15
1022	10y. Golden carp	40	15
1023	10y. Madai seabream	40	15
1024	10y. Skipjack tuna	40	15
1025	10y. Ayu	40	15
1026	15y. Japanese eel	50	15
1027	15y. Chub mackerel	50	15
1028	15y. Chum salmon	50	15
1029	15y. Buri	80	15
1030	15y. Tiger pufferfish	80	25
1031	15y. Japanese common squid	1·00	30
1032	15y. Horned turban (shellfish)	1·40	30

NIPPON. From this point onwards all stamps are additionally inscribed "NIPPON".

519 Pleasure Garden, Mito   **519a** Pleasure Garden and Manchurian Cranes, Okayama

519b Kerokuen Garden, Kanazawa

1966. Famous Japanese Gardens.
1033	**519**	10y. green, black & gold	40	10
1034	**519a**	15y. black, red and blue	50	10
1035	**519b**	15y. black, green & sil	50	10

520 Crater of Mt. Zao

1966. Zao Quasi-National Park.
1036 520 10y. multicoloured 40 25

521 Muroto Cape   **522** Senba Cliffs, Anan

1966. Muroto-Anan Kaigan Quasi-National Park.
1037 521 10y. multicoloured 40 25
1038 522 10y. multicoloured 40 25

523 A.I.P.P.I. Emblem

1966. General Assembly of Int Association for Protection of Industrial Property (A.I.P.P.I.).
1039 523 40y. multicoloured 1·20 25

524 "Butterflies" (after T. Fujishima)

1966. Philatelic Week.
1040 524 10y. multicoloured 90 30

525 Goldfish   **526** Chrysanthemums   **527** Fuji (wisteria)

528 Hydrangea   **529** Golden Hall, Chuson Temple   **530** Watasenia scintillans (squid)

531 Yomei Gate, Tosho Shrine, Nikko   **532** Mizubasho   **533** Konponchudo Hall, Enryaku Temple

534 Ancient Clay Horse   **535** Garden of Katsura Palace   **536** Onjo Bosatsu (relief from bronze lantern, Todai Temple)

537 Kongo-Rikishi Statue, Todai Temple Nara

1966. Inscr "NIPPON".
1041 235 1y. bistre 15 10
1047 525 7y. orange and green 25 20
1049 526 15y. yellow and blue 1·80 20
1050 526 15y. yellow and blue 35 20
1052 527 20y. green and violet 2·10 20
1053 528 25y. blue and green 80 10
1054 529 30y. gold and blue 1·30 15
1055 530 35y. black, brown & blue 2·50 20
1056 531 40y. green and brown 80 10
1057 532 45y. multicoloured 80 20

1058 240 50y. red 12·50 20
1059 240 50y. mauve 1·10 20
1060 280 55y. green, black and blue 1·20 10
1061 533 60y. green 1·30 20
1062 534 65y. brown 20·00 20
1063 534 65y. orange 1·40 20
1064 281 75y. multicoloured 1·40 20
1065 410 90y. brown and gold 2·75 20
1066 411 100y. grey, black and red 2·00 10
1067 535 110y. brown 2·00 20
1068 412 120y. red 3·50 20
1069 536 200y. green 7·25 20
1070 537 500y. purple 8·00 25

No. 1050 is as T **526** but with white figures of value. See also Nos. 1226/49.

538 U.N. and UNESCO Emblems

1966. 20th Anniv of UNESCO.
1071 538 15y. multicoloured 40 25

539 Pacific Ocean

1966. 11th Pacific Science Congress, Tokyo.
1072 539 15y. multicoloured 40 25

540 Amakusa Bridges

1966. Completion of Amakusa Bridges.
1073 540 15y. multicoloured 40 25

541 Family and Emblem

1966. 50th Anniv of Post Office Life Insurance Office.
1074 541 15y. multicoloured 40 25

542 Sekiya on the Sumida (from 36 Views of Mt. Fuji by Hokusai Katsushika)

1966. International Correspondence Week.
1075 542 50y. multicoloured 2·20 85

543 Rotary Cobalt Radiator

1966. Ninth International Cancer Congress, Tokyo.
1076 543 7y.+3y. black & orge 30 25
1077 — 15y.+5y. multicoloured 40 25
DESIGN—VERT: 15y. Detection by X-rays.

544 Triple Jump

1966. 21st National Athletic Meeting, Oita.
1078 544 7y. red 40 25
1079 — 7y. blue (Clay-pigeon shooting) 40 25

545 National Theatre Building

1966. Inauguration of Japanese National Theatre. Multicoloured.
1080 15y. Type **545** 40 25
1081 25y. "Kabuki" performance (48×33½ mm) 1·10 40
1082 50y. "Bunraku" puppet act (33½×48 mm) 1·30 60

546 Rice Year Emblem

1966. International Rice Year.
1083 546 15y. black, ochre and red 40 25

547 Ittobori Sheep (sculpture)

1966. New Year's Greetings.
1084 547 7y. multicoloured 60 30

548 Satellite "Intelsat 2", Earth and Moon

1967. Inauguration of International Commercial Satellite Communications in Japan.
1086 548 15y. brown and blue 40 10

549 Douglas DC-8 and Flight Route

1967. Inauguration of Round-the-World Air Service.
1087 549 15y. multicoloured 40 10

550 Literature Museum

1967. Opening of Japanese Modern Literature Museum, Meguro-ku, Tokyo.
1088 550 15y. multicoloured 40 25

551 Lakeside (after S. Kuroda)

1967. Philatelic Week.
1089 551 15y. multicoloured 50 30

552 Port of Kobe

1967. Fifth International Association of Ports and Harbours Congress, Tokyo.
1090 552 50y. multicoloured 1·30 40

553 Emblem of Welfare Service

1967. 50th Anniv of Welfare Commissioner Service.
1091 553 15y. gold and agate 50 10

554 Pedestrian Road Crossing

1967. 20th Anniv of Road Safety Campaign.
1092 554 15y. multicoloured 40 25

555 Mts. Kita and Koma   **556** Mts. Akashi, Hijiri and Higashi

1967. Southern Alps National Park.
1093 555 7y. blue 30 10
1094 556 15y. purple 40 10

557 Protein Molecules

1967. Seventh Int Biochemistry Congress, Tokyo.
1095 557 15y. multicoloured 40 25

558 Gymnast

1967. "Universiade 1967" (Sports Meeting), Tokyo. Multicoloured.
1096 15y. Type **558** 40 25
1097 50y. Universiade "U" emblem (25×35½ mm) 1·30 40

559 Paper Lantern   **560** Mt. Fuji (after T. Yokoyama)

1967. International Tourist Year.
1098 559 15y. multicoloured 60 30
1099 560 50y. multicoloured 2·40 1·70

561 Kajikazawa in Kai Province (from 36 Views of Mt. Fuji by Hokusai Katsushika)

1967. International Correspondence Week.
1100 561 50y. multicoloured 3·00 80

562 Athlete

1967. 22nd National Athletic Meeting, Saitama.
1101 562 15y. multicoloured 1·00 30

563 Buddha, Koryu Temple, Kyoto

564 Kudara Kannon (Budda), Horyu Temple, Nara

565 Horyu Temple, Nara

1967. National Treasures. Asuka Period.

1102	**563**	15y. multicoloured	60	40
1103	**564**	15y. multicoloured	60	40
1104	**565**	50y. multicoloured	2·50	1·00

See also Nos. 1113/15, 1120/2, 1134/6, 1152/4, 1170/2 and 1177/80.

566 Motor Expressway

1967. 13th World Road Congress, Tokyo.

1105	**566**	50y. multicoloured	1·30	30

567 Mt. Kumotori   **568** Lake Chichibu

1967. Chichibu-Tama National Park.

1106	**567**	7y. olive	30	10
1107	**568**	15y. violet	40	10

569 "Noborizaru" (Miyazaki toy)

1967. New Year's Greetings.

1108	**569**	7y. multicoloured	60	30

570 Mt. Sobo   **571** Takachiho Gorge

1967. Sobo-Katamuki Quasi-National Park.

1110	**570**	15y. multicoloured	40	10
1111	**571**	15y. multicoloured	40	10

572 Boy and Girl and Cruise Liner *Sakura Maru*

1968. Youth Goodwill Cruise to mark Meiji Centenary.

1112	**572**	15y. violet, yellow & blue	30	10

573 Asura Statue, Kofuku Temple, Nara   **574** Gakko Bosatsu, Todai Temple, Nara

575 *Srimaha devi* (painting), Yakushi Temple, Nara

1968. National Treasures. Nara Period (710–784).

1113	**573**	15y. multicoloured	50	30
1114	**574**	15y. multicoloured	60	30
1115	**575**	50y. multicoloured	2·20	1·40

576 Mt. Yatsugatake and Cattle   **577** Mt. Tateshina and Lake

1968. Yatsugatake-Chushin Kogen Quasi-National Park.

1116	**576**	15y. multicoloured	50	30
1117	**577**	15y. multicoloured	50	30

578 *Dancer in a Garden* (after Bakusen Tsuchida)

1968. Philatelic Week.

1118	**578**	15y. multicoloured	80	30

579 View of Rishiri Island from Rebun Island

1968. Rishiri-Rebun Quasi-National Park.

1119	**579**	15y. multicoloured	40	25

580 Lacquer Casket   **582** Fugen Bosatsu (painting of Bodishattva Samantabhadva)

581 *The Origin of Shigisan* (painting in Chogo-sonshi Temple)

1968. National Treasures. Heinan Period (794–1185).

1120	**580**	15y. multicoloured	50	40
1121	**581**	15y. multicoloured	60	40
1122	**582**	50y. multicoloured	4·75	2·00

583 Centenary Tower and Star

1968. Hokkaido Centenary.

1123	**583**	15y. multicoloured	40	25

584 Biro Trees and Pacific Sunrise

1968. Return of Ogasawara Islands to Japan.

1124	**584**	15y. multicoloured	40	25

585 "Map of Japan" in Figures

1968. Postal Codes Campaign.

1125	**585**	7y. red, brown & grn (I)	1·50	30
1126	–	7y. red, brown & grn (II)	1·50	30
1127	**585**	15y. mauve, vio & bl (I)	1·50	30
1128	–	15y. mauve, vio & bl (II)	1·50	30

(II) Inscr reading "Postal code also on your address" measures 12 mm.

586 River Kiso   **587** Inuyama Castle and View

1968. Hida-Kisogawa Quasi-National Park.

1129	**586**	15y. multicoloured	40	10
1130	**587**	15y. multicoloured	40	10

588 Federation Emblem and "Sun"

1968. Int Youth Hostel Conference, Tokyo.

1131	**588**	15y. multicoloured	40	25

589 Humans forming Emblem   **590** Baseball "Pitcher"

1968. 50th All-Japan High School Baseball Championships, Koshi-en, Tokyo.

1132	**589**	15y. multicoloured	1·20	40
1133	**590**	15y. multicoloured	1·20	40

591 *Minamoto Yoritomo* (Jingo Temple Collection)   **593** Red-braided Armour (Kasuga Grand Shrine Collection)

592 Emperor Nijo escaping from Black Palace (from *Tale of Heiji* picture scroll)

1968. National Treasures. Kamakura Period (1185–1334).

1134	**591**	15y. multicoloured	60	40
1135	**592**	15y. multicoloured	60	40
1136	**593**	50y. multicoloured	3·00	1·60

594 Mt. Iwate   **595** Lake Towada

1968. Towada-Hachimantai National Park.

1137	**594**	7y. brown	30	10
1138	**595**	15y. green	40	10

596 Gymnastics

1968. 23rd National Athletic Meeting.

1139	**596**	15y. multicoloured	50	30

597 *Fujimihara in Owari Province* (from *36 Views of Mt. Fuji* by Hokusai Katsushika)

1968. International Correspondence Week.

1140	**597**	50y. multicoloured	1·90	95

598 Centenary Emblem and Sail Warship "Shohei Maru", 1868   **599** *Arrival of the Imperial Carriage in Tokyo* (after Tomone Kobori)

1968. Centenary of Meiji Era.

1141	**598**	15y. multicoloured	40	25
1142	**599**	15y. multicoloured	40	25

600 Old and New Kannonzaki Lighthouses

1968. Centenary of Japanese Lighthouses.

1143	**600**	15y. multicoloured	50	10

601 Ryo's Dancer and State Hall

1968. Completion of Imperial Palace.

1144	**601**	15y. multicoloured	60	30

602 Mt. Takachiho   **603** Mt. Motobu, Yaku Island

1968. Kirishima-Yaku National Park.

1145	**602**	7y. violet	60	30
1146	**603**	15y. orange	60	30

604 "Niwatori" (Yamagata toy)

1968. New Year's Greetings.

1147	**604**	7y. multicoloured	60	30

605 Human Rights Emblem and Dancers

1968. Human Rights Year.

1149	**605**	50y. multicoloured	1·10	30

606 Siberian Chipmunk with Nuts

1968. Savings Promotion.

1150	**606**	15y. sepia and green	70	25

607 Coastal Scenery

1969. Echizen-Kaga-Kaigan Quasi-National Park.

1151	**607**	15y. multicoloured	60	30

608 Silver Pavilion, Jisho Temple, Kyoto

609 Pagoda, Anraku Temple, Nagano

610 *Winter Landscape* (Sesshu)

1969. National Treasures. Muromachi Period.

1152	**608**	15y. multicoloured	50	30
1153	**609**	15y. multicoloured	50	30
1154	**610**	50y. multicoloured	2·20	1·40

611 Mt. Chokai, from Tobishima

1969. Chokai Quasi-National Park.

1155	**611**	15y. multicoloured	50	10

612 "Expo" Emblem and Globe

613 *Cherry Blossom* (from mural Chichakuin Temple, Kyoto)

1969. "EXPO 70" World Fair, Osaka (1st issue).

1156	**612**	15y.+5y. mult	60	45
1157	**613**	50y.+10y. mult	1·60	1·20

See also Nos. 1193/**MS**1196 and 1200/**MS**1203.

614 Mt. Koya from Jinnogamine

615 Mt. Gomadan and Rhododendrons

1969. Koya-Ryujin Quasi-National Park.

1158	**614**	15y. multicoloured	40	25
1159	**615**	15y. multicoloured	40	25

616 *Hair* (Kokei Kobayashi)

1969. Philatelic Week.

1160	**616**	15y. multicoloured	60	40

617 Woman and Child crossing "Roads"

1969. Road Safety Campaign.

1161	**617**	15y. green, blue and red	40	25

618 Sakawagawa Bridge

1969. Completion of Tokyo–Nagoya Expressway.

1162	**618**	15y. multicoloured	50	30

619 Museum Building

1969. Opening of National Museum of Modern Art, Tokyo.

1163	**619**	15y. multicoloured	40	25

620 Nuclear-powered Freighter *Mutsu* and Atomic Symbol

1969. Launching of Japan's 1st Nuclear Ship "Mutsu".

1164	**620**	15y. multicoloured	50	10

621 Cable Ship *KDD Maru* and Map

1969. Opening of Japanese Ocean Cable.

1165	**621**	15y. multicoloured	50	10

622 Symbol and Cards

1969. Postal Codes Campaign.

1166	**622**	7y. red and green	30	25
1167	-	15y. red and blue	80	25

DESIGN: 15y. Symbol, postbox and code numbers.

624 Lions Emblem and Rose

1969. 52nd Lions Int Convention, Tokyo.

1168	**624**	15y. multicoloured	60	30

625 Hotoke-ga-ura (coast)

1969. Shimokita-Hanto Quasi-National Park.

1169	**625**	15y. multicoloured	60	30

626 Himeji Castle, Hyogo Prefecture

627 *Pinewoods* (T. Hasegawa)

628 *The Japanese Cypress* (artist unknown)

1969. National Treasures. Momoyama Period.

1170	**626**	15y. multicoloured	60	30
1171	**627**	15y. black and drab	60	30
1172	**628**	50y. multicoloured	1·10	55

629 Harano-fudo Waterfalls

630 Mt. Nagisan

1969. Hyonosen-Ushiroyama-Nagisan Quasi-National Park.

1173	**629**	15y. multicoloured	40	25
1174	**630**	15y. multicoloured	40	25

631 Mt. O-akan   **632** Mt. Iwo

1969. Akan National Park.

1175	**631**	7y. blue	30	25
1176	**632**	15y. sepia	40	25

633 *Choben* (T. Ikeno)

634 *The Red-plum Tree* (K. Ogata)

635 *The White-plum Tree* (K. Ogata)

636 *Japanese Pheasant* Incense-burner (after Ninsei)

1969. National Treasures. Edo Period.

1177	**633**	15y. multicoloured	60	45
1178	**634**	15y. multicoloured	60	45
1179	**635**	15y. multicoloured	60	45
1180	**636**	50y. multicoloured	2·40	1·40

637 Globe and Doves

638 *Woman Reading a Letter* (Utamaro Kitagawa)

639 *Reading a Letter* (Harunobu Suzuki)

640 *Miyako Dennai* (Sharaku Toshusai)

1969. 16th U.P.U. Congress, Tokyo.

1181	**637**	15y. multicoloured	40	25
1182	**638**	30y. multicoloured	1·00	80
1183	**639**	50y. multicoloured	1·60	95
1184	**640**	60y. multicoloured	1·60	95

641 *Mishima Pass* (from **36 Views of Mt. Fuji** by Hokusai Katsushika)

1969. International Correspondence Week.

1185	**641**	50y. multicoloured	1·30	80

642 Rugby Football

1969. 24th National Athletic Meeting.

1186	**642**	15y. multicoloured	60	30

643 Cape Kitayama   **644** Goishi Coast

1969. Rikuchu-Kaigan National Park.

1187	**643**	7y. blue	30	25
1188	**644**	15y. red and salmon	40	25

645 Worker in Safety Helmet

1969. 50th Anniv of I.L.O.

1189	**645**	15y. multicoloured	40	30

646 Guardian Dog, Hokkeji Temple

1969. New Year's Greetings.

1190	**646**	7y. multicoloured	60	30

647 Peasants, Tsushima Island

1970. Iki-Tsushima Quasi-National Park.

1192	**647**	15y. multicoloured	50	10

648 View of Fair and Firework Display

1970. "EXPO 70" World Fair, Osaka (2nd issue). Multicoloured.

1193	7y. Type **648**		30	25
1194	15y. Earth and cherry blossom garland		30	25
1195	50y. "Irises" (Korin Ogata) (48×33 mm)		50	25
MS1196 144×93 mm. Nos. 1193/5			3·50	3·75

651 *Woman with Drum* (Saburosuke Okada)

1970. Philatelic Week.

1197	**651**	15y. multicoloured	40	25

652 Cherry Blossom, Mt. Yoshino   **653** Waterfall, Nachi

1970. Yoshino-Kumano National Park.

1198	**652**	7y. black and pink	30	25
1199	**653**	15y. dp green, green & bl	40	25

654 Kanto (lantern) Festival   **655** Japanese Pavilions

656 *Flowers of Autumn* (detail, Hoitsu Sakai)

1970. "EXPO 70" World Fair, Osaka (3rd issue).

1200	**654**	7y. multicoloured	30	25
1201	**655**	15y. multicoloured	30	25
1202	**656**	50y. multicoloured	80	45
MS1203 144×93 mm. Nos. 1200/2			2·50	2·50

657 Houses and Code Symbol

1970. Postal Codes Campaign.

1204	**657**	7y. violet and green	40	10
1205	**657**	15y. purple and blue	60	10

658 Utaemon Nakamura VI as Hanako in *Musume Dojoji*   **659** Danjuro Ichikawa XI as Sukeroku in *Sukeroku*

660 *Kanjincho*

1970. Japanese Theatre "Kabuki".

1206	**658**	15y. multicoloured	30	25

1207	**659**	15y. multicoloured	30	25
1208	**660**	50y. multicoloured	1·00	40

See also Nos. 1250/2, 1284/6 and 1300/2.

661 Girl Scout saluting

1970. 50th Anniv of Japanese Girl Scouts.

1209	**661**	15y. multicoloured	50	10

662 Festival Drummer and Kinoura Coastline   **663** Mt. Tate from Himi Shore

1970. Noto-Hanto Quasi-National Park.

1210	**662**	15y. multicoloured	40	25
1211	**663**	15y. multicoloured	40	25

664 "Sunflower" and U.N. Emblem

1970. Fourth U.N. Congress on Prevention of Crime and Treatment of Offenders, Kyoto.

1212	**664**	15y. multicoloured	40	25

665 Mt. Myogi   **666** Mt. Arafune

1970. Myogi-Arafune-Sakukuogen Quasi-National Park.

1213	**665**	15y. multicoloured	40	25
1214	**666**	15y. multicoloured	40	25

667 *Tokyo Post Office* (woodcut, Hiroshige III)

1970. International Correspondence Week.

1215	**667**	50y. multicoloured	1·10	40

668 Show Jumping, Mt. Iwate and Paulownia Flowers

1970. 25th National Athletic Meeting, Iwate.

1216	**668**	15y. multicoloured	60	30

669 *Hodogaya Stage* (print, Hiroshige III)

1970. Centenary of Telegraph Service.

1217	**669**	15y. multicoloured	60	30

670 U.N. Emblem within "Tree"

1970. 25th Anniv of U.N.O. Multicoloured.

1218	15y. Type **670**		40	25

1219	50y. U.N. emblem, New York H.Q. and flags		1·00	30

672 Competition Emblem

1970. 19th International Vocational Training Competition, Chiba City.

1220	**672**	15y. multicoloured	40	25

673 Diet Building and Doves

1970. 80th Anniv of Japanese Diet.

1221	**673**	15y. multicoloured	60	30

674 "Wild Boar" (folk-handicraft)

1970. New Year's Greetings.

1222	**674**	7y. multicoloured	60	30

675 Ski Jumping

1971. Winter Olympic Games, Sapporo (1972) (1st issue). Multicoloured.

1224	15y.+5y. Type **675**		50	40
1225	15y.+5y. Ice-hockey (horiz)		50	20

See also Nos. 1280/MS1283.

677 Mute Swan   **678** Sika Deer   **679** *Allomyrina dichotomus*

680 Pine Tree (T. Kano)   **682** Golden Eagle   **684** "Ho-o" (Phoenix), Byodoin Temple, Uji

692 Statue of Kissho, Joruri Temple

1971. Inscr "NIPPON".

1226	**273**	3y. green	30	10
1227	**677**	5y. blue	20	10
1228	**678**	10y. brown and green	20	10
1229	**679**	12y. brown	35	10
1230	**680**	20y. brown and green	35	15
1231	**528**	25y. blue and green	40	15
1232	**240**	50y. green	90	10
1233	-	60y. green and yellow	1·10	15
1234	**408**	70y. black and orange	1·40	15
1235	**409**	80y. brown and red	1·40	15
1236	**410**	90y. brown and orange	1·80	15
1237	**682**	90y. black and red	1·80	15
1238	**412**	120y. brown and green	1·70	10
1239	-	140y. purple and mauve	2·40	15
1240	**684**	150y. turquoise & green	3·00	15
1240a	-	150y. brown and red	2·75	15
1241	-	200y. red	3·75	10
1242	-	200y. brown	3·25	10

1243	-	200y. red	1·80	10
1244	-	250y. blue	3·25	15
1245	-	300y. blue	5·00	15
1246	-	350y. brown	5·00	15
1247	-	400y. red	5·50	15
1248	-	500y. green	4·25	10
1249	**692**	1000y. multicoloured	11·00	60
MS1249a 51×102 mm. No. 1249			15·00	13·00

DESIGNS: 60y. Narcissi; 140y. Noh mask of aged man; 200y. (No. 1241), Onjo Bosatsu (relief); Todai Temple; 200y. (Nos. 1242/3), Warrior (statuette); 250y. Komainu (guardian dog), Katori Shrine; 300y. Buddha, Kofuku Temple; 350y. Goddess of Mercy, Yaluski Temple, Nara; 400y. Tentoki (demon); 500y. Buddhist deity.

No. 1231 is Type **528**, redrawn. The inscription and face value are smaller, but the main difference is in the position of the leaves. On No. 1053 they touch the left edge of the design, but on No. 1231 they are completely clear of it.

No. 1241 is as Type **536** but smaller, 18×22 mm.

For 210y. as Nos. 1242/3 and 360y. as No. 1246, see Nos. 1600 and 1604.

693 "Gen-jo-raku"   **694** "Ko-cho"

695 "Tai-hei-raku"

1971. Japanese Theatre "Gagaku".

1250	**693**	15y. multicoloured	30	25
1251	**694**	15y. multicoloured	30	25
1252	**695**	50y. multicoloured	1·00	40

696 Voter and Diet Building

1971. 25th Anniv of Women's Suffrage.

1253	**696**	15y. multicoloured	40	30

697 Pine Trees and Maple Leaves

1971. National Afforestation Campaign.

1254	**697**	7y. black, violet & green	30	10

698 *Tsukiji-akashicho* (K. Kaburagi)

1971. Philatelic Week.

1255	**698**	15y. multicoloured	40	25

699 *Posting a Letter* (K. Dogishi)   **700** *Postman* (K. Kasai)

701 *Railway Post Office* (S. Onozaki)

1971. Centenary of Japanese Postal Services.

1256	**699**	15y. multicoloured	40	10
1257	**700**	15y. black and brown	40	10
1258	**701**	15y. multicoloured	40	10

702 Great Tit

1971. 25th Bird Week.

1259	**702**	15y. multicoloured	50	10

703 Adelie Penguins

1971. Tenth Anniv of Antarctic Treaty.

1260	**703**	15y. multicoloured	1·00	30

705 Kuzyuku-shima

704 Goto-Wakamatsu-Seto

1971. Saikai National Park.

1261	**704**	7y. green	40	30
1262	**705**	15y. brown	40	30

706 Postal Code Numerals

1971. Postal Code Campaign.

1263	**706**	7y. red and green	30	10
1264	**706**	15y. red and blue	50	25

707 Scout Bugler

1971. 13th World Scout Jamboree, Asagiri.

1265	**707**	15y. multicoloured	50	10

708 Rose Emblem

1971. 50th Anniv of Family Conciliation System.

1266	**708**	15y. multicoloured	40	30

709 Tokyo Horse Tram (Yoshimura)

1971. International Correspondence Week.

1267	**709**	50y. multicoloured	1·10	25

710 Emperor's Standard

1971. European Tour by Emperor Hirohito and Empress Nagako. Multicoloured.

1268		15y. Type **710**	40	30
1269		15y. "Beyond the Sea" (drawing by Empress Nagako)	40	30
MS1270		141×111 mm. Nos. 1268/9. Imperf	2·00	1·60

712 Tennis

1971. 26th National Athletic Meeting.

1271	**712**	15y. multicoloured	40	30

713 Child's Face and "100"

1971. Centenary of National Family Registration System.

1272	**713**	15y. multicoloured	40	30

714 Dragon (G. Hashimoto)

1971. Centenary of Government Printing Works, Tokyo. Multicoloured.

1273		15y. Type **714**	50	25
1274		15y. *Tiger* (from same drawing as above)	50	25

716 Mt. Yotei from Lake Toya   **717** Mt. Showa-Shinzan

1971. Shikotsu-Toya National Park.

1275	**716**	7y. green and olive	30	25
1276	**717**	15y. blue and brown	40	25

718 Takarabune ("Treasure Ship")

1971. New Year's Greetings.

1277	**718**	7y. multicoloured	30	25
1278	**718**	10y. multicoloured	40	25

719 Skiing

1972. Winter Olympic Games, Sapporo (2nd issue). Multicoloured.

1280		20y. Type **719**	40	25
1281		20y. Bobsleighing	40	25
1282		50y. Figure skating (pair) (52×36 mm)	90	30
MS1283		145×94 mm. Nos. 1280/2	2·00	1·60

722 "Kumagai-jinya"

723 "Nozaki-mura"

724 "Awa-no-Naruto"

1972. Japanese Theatre. "Banraku" Puppet Theatre.

1284	**722**	20y. multicoloured	30	25
1285	**723**	20y. multicoloured	30	25
1286	**724**	50y. multicoloured	1·00	40

725 *Hikari* Express Train

1972. Centenary of Japanese Railways (1st issue) and Opening of Sanyo Shinkansen Line.

1287	**725**	20y. multicoloured	50	10

See also Nos. 1305/6.

727 Fishing, Taishakukyo Valley   **726** Hiba Mountains

1972. Hiba-Dogo-Taishaku Quasi-National Park.

1288	**726**	20y. multicoloured	40	25
1289	**727**	20y. multicoloured	40	25

728 Adult with Human Heart

1972. World Heart Month.

1290	**728**	20y. multicoloured	40	30

729 *Rising Balloon* (Gakuryo Nakamura)

1972. Philatelic Week.

1291	**729**	20y. multicoloured	40	30

730 Courtesy Gate, Shuri

1972. Return of Ryukyu Islands to Japan.

1292	**730**	20y. multicoloured	40	30

731 Japanese Camellia

1972. National Afforestation Campaign.

1293	**731**	20y. yellow blue & green	40	30

732 Mt. Kurikoma and Kokeshi Doll

733 Naruko-kyo Gorge and Kokeshi Doll

1972. Kurikoma Quasi-National Park.

1294	**732**	20y. multicoloured	40	30
1295	**733**	20y. multicoloured	40	30

734 Envelope and Code Symbol

1972. Postal Codes Campaign (5th issue).

1296	**734**	10y. black, purple & blue	30	10
1297	-	20y. red and green	30	10

DESIGN: 20y. Mail-box and code symbol.

736 Mt. Hodaka

737 Mt. Tate

1972. Chubu Sangaku National Park.

1298	**736**	10y. violet and mauve	40	30
1299	**737**	20y. blue and brown	40	30

738 "Tamura"   **739** "Aoi-no-ue"

740 "Hagoromo"

1972. Japanese Theatre. "Noh".

1300	**738**	20y. multicoloured	30	25
1301	**739**	20y. multicoloured	30	25
1302	**740**	50y. multicoloured	1·00	40

741 "Profiles of Schoolchildren"

1972. Centenary of Japanese Educational System.

1303	**741**	20y. multicoloured	40	30

742 *Eitai Bridge* (Hiroshige III)

1972. International Correspondence Week.

1304	**742**	50y. multicoloured	1·00	25

743 *Inauguration of Railway Service* (Hiroshige III)

1972. Centenary of Japanese Railways (2nd issue). Multicoloured.

1305		20y. Type **743**	70	10
1306		20y. Class C-62 steam locomotive No. 2	70	10

745 Kendo (Japanese Fencing)

1972. 27th National Athletic Meeting, Kagoshima.

1307	**745**	10y. multicoloured	40	30

746 Scout and Cub

1972. 50th Anniv of Japanese Boy Scouts.

1308	**746**	20y. multicoloured	50	10

747 *Harbour and Bund, Yokohama* (Hiroshige III)

1972. Centenary of Japanese Customs Service.
1309 **747** 20y. multicoloured   50   10

748 *Plum Blossoms* Plate (K. Ogata)

1972. New Year's Greetings.
1310 **748** 10y. multicoloured   40   25

749 Mt. Tsurugi   **750** River Yoshino, Oboke Valley

1973. Tsurugi-San Quasi-National Park.
1312 **749** 20y. multicoloured   40   25
1313 **750** 20y. multicoloured   40   25

751 Mt. Takao   **752** Minoo Falls and Japanese Macaques

1973. Meiji-no-mori Quasi-National Park.
1314 **751** 20y. multicoloured   50   10
1315 **752** 20y. multicoloured   50   10

753 "Dragon" (East Wall)   **754** "Male Figures" (East Wall)

755 "Female Figures" (West Wall)

1973. Asuka Archaeological Conservation Fund. Takamatsuzuka Kofun Tomb Murals.
1316 **753** 20y.+5y. multicoloured   40   30
1317 **754** 20y.+5y. multicoloured   40   30
1318 **755** 50y.+10y. multicoloured   1·30   1·00

756 Phoenix Tree

1973. National Afforestation Campaign.
1319 **756** 20y. multicoloured   40   30

757 *Sumiyoshimode* (R. Kishida)

1973. Philatelic Week.
1320 **757** 20y. multicoloured   50   30

758 Mt. Kama   **759** Rock Outcrops, Mt. Haguro

1973. Suzuka Quasi-National Park.
1321 **758** 20y. multicoloured   40   30
1322 **759** 20y. multicoloured   40   30

760 Chichi-jima Island Beach   **761** Coral Reef, Minami-jimi Island

1973. Ogasawara Islands National Park.
1323 **760** 10y. blue   30   10
1324 **761** 20y. purple   40   10

762 Postal Code Symbol and Tree

1973. Postal Codes Campaign.
1325 **762** 10y. gold and green   30   10
1326 **–** 20y. lilac, red and blue   40   10
DESIGN: 20y. Postman and symbol.

765 Waterfall, Sandan-kyo Gorge   **764** Mt. Shinnyu

1973. Nishi-Chugoku-Sanchi Quasi-National Park.
1327 **764** 20y. multicoloured   40   30
1328 **765** 20y. multicoloured   40   30

766 Valley of River Tenryu   **767** Oriental Scops Owl and Woodland Path, Mt. Horaiji

1973. Tenryu-Okumikowa Quasi-National Park.
1329 **766** 20y. multicoloured   70   10
1330 **767** 20y. blue, green and silver   70   10

768 Cock (J. Ito)

1973. International Correspondence Week.
1331 **768** 50y. multicoloured   1·20   10

769 Sprinting

1973. 28th National Athletic Meeting. Chiba.
1332 **769** 10y. multicoloured   40   30

770 Kan-Mon Bridge

1973. Opening of Kan-Mon Suspension Bridge.
1333 **770** 20y. multicoloured   50   10

771 Hanasaka-jijii and his Dog   **772** Hanasaka-jijii finds the Gold

773 Hanasaka-jijii and Tree in Blossom

1973. Japanese Folk Tales (1st series). "Hanasaki-jijii".
1334 **771** 20y. multicoloured   40   15
1335 **772** 20y. multicoloured   40   15
1336 **773** 20y. multicoloured   40   15
See also Nos. 1342/4, 1352/4, 1358/60, 1362/4, 1378/80 and 1387/9.

774 Lantern

1973. New Year's Greetings.
1337 **774** 10y. multicoloured   30   10

775 Niju-bashi Bridge

1974. Imperial Golden Wedding. Multicoloured.
1339   20y. Type **775**   40   30
1340   20y. Imperial Palace   40   30
MS1341 145×89 mm. Nos. 1339/40   1·60   1·20

777 The Crane Damsel

1974. Japanese Folk Tales (2nd series). *Tsuru-Nyobo*. Multicoloured.
1342   20y. Type **777**   40   10
1343   20y. Manchurian Crane "weaving"   40   10
1344   20y. Manchurian Cranes in flight   40   10

780 *A Reefy Coast* (Hyakusui Hirafuku)

1974. International Ocean Exposition, Okinawa (1975) (1st issue).
1345 **780** 20y.+5y. multicoloured   50   40
See also Nos. 1401/3.

781 Marudu Falls   **782** Seascape

1974. Iriomote National Park.
1346 **781** 20y. multicoloured   50   10
1347 **782** 20y. multicoloured   50   10

783 Iriomote Cat

1974. Nature Conservation (1st series).
1348 **783** 20y. multicoloured   50   25
See also Nos. 1356, 1361, 1372, 1377, 1381, 1405, 1419, 1422, 1430, 1433/4, 1449, 1457, 1469, 1470, 1475, 1490, 1497 and 1502.

784 *Finger* (Shinsui Ito)

1974. Philatelic Week.
1349 **784** 20y. multicoloured   40   30

785 Nambu Red Pine

1974. National Afforestation Campaign.
1350 **785** 20y. multicoloured   40   30

786 Supreme Court Building

1974. Completion of Supreme Court Building, Tokyo.
1351 **786** 20y. brown   40   30

787 *Sailing in a Wooden Bowl*   **788** *Conquering the Goblins*

789 *Wielding the Little Magic Mallet*

1974. Japanese Folk Tales (3rd series). *The Dwarf*.
1352 **787** 20y. multicoloured   40   30
1353 **788** 20y. multicoloured   40   30
1354 **789** 20y. multicoloured   40   30

790 "Uniform Rivalry" (detail after Kunimasa Baido)

1974. Centenary of Japanese Police System.
1355 **790** 20y. multicoloured   40   30

1974. Nature Conservation (2nd series). As T **783**. Multicoloured.
1356   20y. European otter (*Lutra lutra*)   50   25

792 World
Blood Donation

1974. International Red Cross Day.
| 1357 | **792** | 20y. multicoloured | 50 | 10 |

793 *Discovery of Kaguya Hime*   **794** *Kaguya Hime as Young Woman*

795 *The Ascent to Heaven*

1974. Japanese Folk Tales (4th series). "Kaguya Hime".
1358	**793**	20y. multicoloured	40	30
1359	**794**	20y. multicoloured	40	30
1360	**795**	20y. multicoloured	40	30

1974. Nature Conservation (3rd series). As T **783**. Multicoloured.
| 1361 | | 20y. Ryukyu rabbit (*Pentalagus furnessi*) | 50 | 25 |

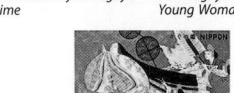

797 *Old Men in front of Yahata Shrine*   **798** *Old Man dancing with Demons*

799 *Old Man with Two Warts*

1974. Japanese Folk Tales (5th series). *Kobutori-Jiisan.*
1362	**797**	20y. multicoloured	40	30
1363	**798**	20y. multicoloured	40	30
1364	**799**	20y. multicoloured	40	30

800 Map of World

1974. 61st Inter-Parliamentary Union Congress, Tokyo. Multicoloured.
| 1365 | | 20y. Type **800** | 30 | 10 |
| 1366 | | 50y. "Aizen"—Mandarins in pond (Kawabata) (48×33 mm) | 90 | 25 |

802 *Pine and Northern Goshawk* (detail, Sesson)

1974. International Correspondence Week.
| 1367 | **802** | 50y. brown and purple | 1·00 | 25 |

803 U.P.U. Emblem

1974. Centenary of U.P.U. Multicoloured.
| 1368 | | 20y. Type **803** | 40 | 10 |
| 1369 | | 50y. *Tending a Cow* (fan-painting—Sotatsu Tawaraya) (50×29 mm) | 90 | 25 |

---

805 Footballers

1974. 29th National Athletic Meeting.
| 1370 | **805** | 10y. multicoloured | 40 | 30 |

806 Shii-take Mushrooms

1974. Ninth International Scientific Congress on Cultivation of Edible Fungi.
| 1371 | **806** | 20y. multicoloured | 50 | 10 |

1974. Nature Conservation (4th series). As T **783**. Multicoloured.
| 1372 | | 20y. Bonin Islands flying fox (*Pteropus pselaphon*) | 80 | 30 |

808 Class D51 Locomotive   **809** Class C57 Locomotive

1974. Railway Steam Locomotives (1st series).
| 1373 | **808** | 20y. multicoloured | 65 | 10 |
| 1374 | **809** | 20y. multicoloured | 65 | 10 |

See also Nos. 1382/3, 1385/6, 1395/6 and 1398/9.

810
"Kugikakushi" (ornamental nail-covering) in the form of a daffodil

1974. New Year's Greetings.
| 1375 | **810** | 10y. multicoloured | 40 | 25 |

1975. Nature Conservation (5th series). As T **783**. Multicoloured.
| 1377 | | 20y. Short-tailed albatrosses (*Diomedea albatrus*) (vert) | 1·00 | 10 |

812 *Taro releasing Tortoise*   **813** *Sea-God's Palace*

814 *Taro and Pandora's Box*

1975. Japanese Folk Tales (6th series). *Urashima Taro.*
1378	**812**	20y. multicoloured	40	10
1379	**813**	20y. multicoloured	40	10
1380	**814**	20y. multicoloured	40	10

1975. Nature Conservation (6th series). As T **783**. Multicoloured.
| 1381 | | 20y. Manchurian cranes (*Grus japonensis*) (vert) | 1·00 | 25 |

816 Class C58 Locomotive   **817** Class D52 Locomotive

1975. Railway Steam Locomotives (2nd series).
| 1382 | **816** | 20y. multicoloured | 80 | 25 |
| 1383 | **817** | 20y. multicoloured | 80 | 25 |

---

818 *Sight and Hearing* (Shiko Munakata)

1975. 50th Anniv of Japanese Broadcasting Corporation.
| 1384 | **818** | 20y. multicoloured | 40 | 25 |

819 Class 8620 Locomotive No. 68622   **820** Class C11 Locomotive

1975. Railway Steam Locomotives (3rd series).
| 1385 | **819** | 20y. multicoloured | 80 | 25 |
| 1386 | **820** | 20y. multicoloured | 80 | 25 |

821 *Old Man feeding Mouse*   **822** *Old Man holding Mouse's Tail*

823 *Mice giving Feast to Old Man*

1975. Japanese Folk Tales (7th series). *Nezumi No Jodo.*
1387	**821**	20y. multicoloured	40	25
1388	**822**	20y. multicoloured	40	25
1389	**823**	20y. multicoloured	40	25

824/5 Matsuura Screen

1975. Philatelic Week.
| 1390 | **824** | 20y. multicoloured | 40 | 25 |
| 1391 | **825** | 20y. multicoloured | 40 | 25 |

Nos. 1390/1 were issued together, *se-tenant*, forming the composite design shown.

827 Oil Rigs

1975. Ninth World Petroleum Congress, Tokyo.
| 1394 | **827** | 20y. multicoloured | 40 | 25 |

828 Class 9600 Locomotive No. 69820   **829** Class C51 Locomotive No. 225

1975. Railway Steam Locomotives (4th series).
| 1395 | **828** | 20y. multicoloured | 80 | 25 |
| 1396 | **829** | 20y. multicoloured | 80 | 25 |

830 Plantation

1975. National Land Afforestation Campaign.
| 1397 | **830** | 20y. multicoloured | 40 | 25 |

---

831 Class 7100 Locomotive *Benkei*, 1880   **832** Class 150 Locomotive, 1872

1975. Railway Steam Locomotives (5th series).
| 1398 | **831** | 20y. black and buff | 80 | 25 |
| 1399 | **832** | 20y. black and yellow | 80 | 25 |

833 Woman's Head and I.W.Y. Emblem

1975. International Women's Year.
| 1400 | **833** | 20y. multicoloured | 40 | 25 |

834 Okinawa Dance

1975. International Ocean Exposition, Okinawa (2nd issue). Multicoloured.
1401		20y. Type **834**	40	25
1402		30y. Bingata textile pattern	60	25
1403		50y. "Aquapolis and Globe" emblem (48×34 mm)	90	30
MS1404		144×94 mm. Nos. 1401/3	2·00	1·60

1975. Nature Conservation (7th series). As T **783**. Multicoloured.
| 1405 | | 20y. Bonin Island honey-eater ("*Apalopteron familiare*) | 1·00 | 25 |

838 *Kentoshisen* (7th–9th centuries)   **839** *Kenminsen* (7th–9th centuries)

1975. Japanese Ships (1st series).
| 1406 | **838** | 20y. red | 70 | 25 |
| 1407 | **839** | 20y. brown | 70 | 25 |

See also Nos. 1409/10, 1420/1, 1423/4, 1428/9 and 1431/2.

840 Apple

1975. Centenary of Apple Cultivation in Japan.
| 1408 | **840** | 20y. multicoloured | 40 | 25 |

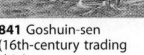

841 *Goshuin-sen* (16th-century trading ship)   **842** *Tenchi-maru* (state barge), 1630

1975. Japanese Ships (2nd series).
| 1409 | **841** | 20y. green | 70 | 25 |
| 1410 | **842** | 20y. blue | 70 | 25 |

843 *Green Peafowl* (after K. Ogata)

1975. International Correspondence Week.
| 1411 | **843** | 50y. multicoloured | 1·20 | 30 |

844 United States Flag

1975. American Tour by Emperor Hirohito and Empress Nagako. Multicoloured.

1412	**844**	20y. Type **844**	40	25
1413		20y. Japanese flag	40	25
MS1414	146×93 mm. Nos. 1412/3		1·90	1·50

846 Savings Box

1975. Centenary of Japanese Post Office Savings Bank.

1415	**846**	20y. multicoloured	40	25

847 Weightlifting

1975. 30th National Athletic Meeting.

1416	**847**	10y. multicoloured	40	25

848 "Tatsu-guruma" (toy)

1975. New Year's Greetings.

1417	**848**	10y. multicoloured	60	25

1976. Nature Conservation (8th series). As T **783**. Multicoloured.

1419		50y. Ryukyu robin (*Erithacus komadori*)	1·20	25

850 Sengoku-bune (fishing boat)   **851** Shohei Maru (sail warship)

1976. Japanese Ships (3rd series).

1420	**850**	50y. blue	1·00	25
1421	**851**	50y. violet	1·00	25

1976. Nature Conservation (9th series). As T **783**. Multicoloured.

1422		50y. Tortoise (*Goemyda spengleri*)	1·00	10

853 Taisei Maru (cadet ship)   **854** Tenyo Maru (liner)

1976. Japanese Ships (4th series).

1423	**853**	50y. black	1·00	25
1424	**854**	50y. brown	1·00	25

855 Section of Hikone Folding Screen

1976. Philatelic Week. Multicoloured.

1425		50y. Type **855**	70	25
1426	-	50y. Similar to Type **855**	70	25

NOTE: The two stamps form a composite design of the *Hikone Folding Screen*.

---

857 Cedar Forest, Plum Blossom, and Mt. Tsukuba

1976. National Land Afforestation Campaign.

1427	**857**	50y. multicoloured	70	10

858 Asama Maru (liner)   **859** Kinai Maru (cargo liner)

1976. Japanese Ships (5th series).

1428	**858**	50y. green	1·00	25
1429	**859**	50y. brown	1·00	25

1976. Nature Conservation (10th series). As T **783**. Multicoloured.

1430		50y. Green tree frog (*Racophorus arboreus*) (vert)	1·10	25

861 Kamakura Maru (container ship)   **862** "Nissei Maru" (oil tanker)

1976. Japanese Ships (6th series).

1431	**861**	50y. blue	1·00	25
1432	**862**	50y. blue	1·00	25

1976. Nature Conservation (11th and 12th series). As T **783**. Multicoloured.

1433		50y. Tokyo bitterling (*Tanakia tanago*)	1·10	25
1434		50y. Three-spined sticklebacks (*Gasterosteus aculeatus*)	1·10	25

865 Kite and Rooks (detail, Yosa Buson)

1976. International Correspondence Week.

1435	**865**	100y. multicoloured	1·90	25

866 Gymnastics

1976. 31st National Athletic Meeting.

1436	**866**	20y. multicoloured	40	25

867 KDD Maru (cable ship) laying cable

1976. Opening of Sino-Japanese Cable.

1437	**867**	50y. multicoloured	1·00	25

868 Man-zai-raku (classical dance)

1976. Golden Jubilee of Emperor's Accession.

1438	**868**	50y. multicoloured	70	25
1439	-	50y. red, gold and black	70	25
MS1440	144×93 mm. Nos. 1438/9		1·90	1·50

DESIGN: No. 2439, Coronation coach.

---

870 Children at First Kindergarten

1976. Centenary of First Kindergarten. Tokyo.

1441	**870**	50y. multicoloured	70	25

871 Family Group

1976. 50th Anniv (1977) of Health Insurance System.

1442	**871**	50y. multicoloured	70	25

872 Bamboo Snake

1976. New Year's Greetings.

1443	**872**	20y. multicoloured	50	25

873 East Pagoda, Yakushi Temple

1976. National Treasures (1st series). Multicoloured.

1445		50y. Type **873**	1·20	30
1446		100y. Deva King, Todai Temple (33×48 mm)	2·20	45

See also Nos. 1447/8, 1452/3, 1463/4, 1471/2, 1480/1 and 1486/9.

875 Golden Pavilion, Toshodai Temple

1977. National Treasures (2nd series). Multicoloured.

1447		50y. Type **875**	1·20	30
1448		100y. Illustration from *Heike Nokyo Sutra* (33×48 mm)	2·40	45

1977. Nature Conservation (13th series). As T **783**. Multicoloured.

1449		50y. Horseshoe crabs (*Tachypleus tridentatus*)	1·00	10

878 Figure Skating   **879** Figure Skating

1977. World Figure Skating Championships, Tokyo.

1450	**878**	50y. multicoloured	70	25
1451	**879**	50y. multicoloured	70	25

880 Detail of Picture Scroll (attr. Toba Sojo Kakuyu)

---

881 Wood Carving of Buddhist Saint (attr. Jocho) Byodoin Temple, Uji

1977. National Treasures (3rd series).

1452	**880**	50y. multicoloured	80	25
1453	**881**	100y. dp brn, brn & grn	2·00	30

882 Forest in Sunshine

1977. National Land Afforestation Campaign.

1454	**882**	50y. multicoloured	1·00	10

883/4 Women Weavers (part)

1977. Philatelic Week.

1455	**883**	50y. multicoloured	70	25
1456	**884**	50y. multicoloured	70	25

Nos. 1455/6 were issued in *se-tenant* pairs, forming a composite design.

1977. Nature Conservation (14th series). As T **783**. Multicoloured.

1457		50y. Mikado swallowtail (*Graphium doson*) (vert)	1·00	25

886 Nurses

1977. 16th Congress of the International Council of Nurses.

1458	**886**	50y. multicoloured	70	25

887 Central Part of Nuclear Reactor

1977. Reaching of Critical Mass by Joyo Fast-Breeder Reactor, Oarai Town.

1459	**887**	50y. multicoloured	70	25

888 Carrier Pigeons and Mail Box with U.P.U. Emblem   **889** U.P.U. Emblem and World Map

1977. Centenary of Japan's Admission to U.P.U.

1460	**888**	50y. multicoloured	70	25
1461	**889**	100y. multicoloured	1·80	30
MS1462	144×93 mm. Nos. 1460/1		2·40	1·90

890 Illustration from *Picture Scroll of Lady Murasaki's Diary*

891 Statue of Seitaka Doji

1977. National Treasures (4th series).

1463	890	50y. multicoloured	70	25
1464	891	100y. brown, deep brown and light brown	1·80	30

892 Green Cross (safety emblem) and Workmen

1977. National Safety Week. Multicoloured.

1465	50y. Type 892	1·10	25
1466	50y. Worker and high-rise building	1·10	25
1467	50y. Unloading freight	1·10	25
1468	50y. Machine-worker	1·10	25

1977. Nature Conservation (15th series). As T **783**. Multicoloured.

1469	50y. Firefly (*Luciola cruciata*)	1·00	10

1977. Nature Conservation (16th series). As T **783**. Multicoloured.

1470	50y. Cicada (*Euterpnosia chibensis*)	1·00	10

898 Drawing of Han Shan by Kao   **899** Matsumoto Castle

1977. National Treasures (5th series).

1471	898	50y. multicoloured	70	25
1472	899	100y. multicoloured	1·80	30

900 Map and Child on Telephone

1977. Opening of Okinawa–Luzon–Hong Kong Submarine Cable.

1473	900	50y. multicoloured	70	10

901 Surgeon

1977. 27th Congress of International Society of Surgeons.

1474	901	50y. multicoloured	70	15

1977. Nature Conservation (17th series). As T **783**. Multicoloured.

1475	50y. Dragonfly (*Boninthemis insularis*) (vert)	1·00	25

903 Horn-shaped Speaker and Telegraph Key

1977. 50th Anniv of Amateur Radio League.

1476	903	50y. multicoloured	70	10

904 Racing Cyclist and Mt. Iwaki

1977. 32nd National Athletic Meeting.

1477	904	20y. multicoloured	40	30

905 *Kacho-zu* (Nobuharu Hasegawa)

1977. International Correspondence Week.

1478	905	100y. multicoloured	2·00	25

906 Long-necked Dinosaur and Museum

1977. Centenary of National Science Museum.

1479	906	50y. multicoloured	2·00	30

907 Detail, Folding Screen, Chishakuin Temple, Kyoto

908 Kiyomizu-dera Temple

1977. National Treasures (6th series).

1480	907	50y. multicoloured	70	25
1481	908	100y. brown, green & bl	1·70	30

909 Toy Horse

1977. New Year's Greetings.

1482	909	20y. multicoloured	50	10

910 Underground Train, 1927   **911** Underground Train No. 1101, 1977

1977. 50th Anniv of Japanese Underground Railway.

1484	910	50y. multicoloured	1·00	25
1485	911	50y. multicoloured	1·00	25

912 Genji's Carriage at Sumiyoshi Shrine (scene on folding screen (Sotatsu Tawaraya) from *Tale of Genji* by Lady Murasaki)

913 Inkstone Case (Koetsu Honami)

1978. National Treasures (7th series).

1486	912	50y. multicoloured	70	25
1487	913	100y. multicoloured	1·70	30

914 *Noryozu* (Morikage Kusumi)

915 Yomei Gate, Tosho Shrine, Nikko

1978. National Treasures (8th series).

1488	914	50y. multicoloured	70	25
1489	915	100y. multicoloured	1·70	30

916 "Primula sieboldi"

1978. Nature Conservation (18th series).

1490	916	50y. multicoloured	90	25

917 *Seated Woman With Flower* (hanging scroll)   **918** *Dancing Woman* (hanging scroll)

1978. Philatelic Week. "Kanbun Bijinzu" Genre Paintings.

1491	917	50y. multicoloured	70	30
1492	918	50y. multicoloured	70	30

919 Rotary Emblem and Mt. Fuji (from *36 Views of Mt. Fuji* by Hokusai Katsushita)

1978. Rotary International Convention, Tokyo.

1493	919	50y. multicoloured	1·00	10

920 Congress Emblem

1978. 23rd Int Ophthalmological Congress.

1494	920	50y. multicoloured	70	10

921 Passenger Terminal Buildings

1978. Opening of Narita Airport, Tokyo.

1495	921	50y. multicoloured	80	10

922 Cape Ashizuri, Rainbow and Cedar Trees

1978. National Afforestation Campaign.

1496	922	50y. multicoloured	70	10

923 *Pinguicula ramosa*

1978. Nature Conservation (19th series).

1497	923	50y. multicoloured	90	25

924 *Karashishi* (attr. Sotatsu Tawaraya) and Lions Emblem

1978. 61st Lions International Convention, Tokyo.

1498	924	50y. multicoloured	1·00	10

925/6 *Grand Champion Raigoyo Hidenoyama in the Ring* (Toyokuni III)

927 *Drum Tower of Ekoin Temple, Ryogoku* (Hiroshige)

1978. Sumo (Japanese Wrestling) Pictures (1st series).

1499	925	50y. multicoloured	70	30
1500	926	50y. multicoloured	70	30
1501	927	50y. multicoloured	70	30

Nos. 1499/500 were issued together, *se-tenant*, forming the composite design illustrated.
See also Nos. 1505/7, 1513/15, 1519/21 and 1523/5.

928 *Dicentra peregrina*

1978. Nature Conservation (20th series).

1502	928	50y. multicoloured	90	25

929 Keep Fit Exercise

1978. 50th Anniv of Radio Gymnastic Exercises.

1503	929	50y. multicoloured	1·60	10

930 Chamber of
Commerce and Industry
Building and Centenary
Emblem

1978. Centenary of 1st Chambers of Commerce, Tokyo
and Osaka.
1504 **930** 50y. multicoloured   70   10

931/2 "Dohyoiri" wrestlers Tanikaze
and Onogawa (Shunsho Katsukawa)

933 Jinmaku
versus Raiden
(Shunnei
Katsukawa)

1978. Sumo Pictures (2nd series).
1505 **931** 50y. multicoloured   70   30
1506 **932** 50y. multicoloured   70   30
1507 **933** 50y. multicoloured   70   30
   Nos. 1505/6 were issued together *se-tenant*, forming
the composite design illustrated.

934 Statues on
Tokyo Securities
Exchange Building

1978. Centenary of Tokyo and Osaka Stock Exchanges.
1508 **934** 50y. brown, purple & grn   70   10

935 Copper
Pheasant (detail of
door painting attr.
Sanraku Kano)

1978. International Correspondence Week.
1509 **935** 100y. multicoloured   2·50   25

936 Mt. Yari and
Softball Players

1978. 33rd National Athletic Meeting.
1510 **936** 20y. multicoloured   40   30

937 Artificial
Joint

1978. 14th Congress of International Society of
Orthopaedic and Traumatic Surgeons, Kyoto.
1511 **937** 50y. blue, ultram & silver   70   15

938 Refracting
Telescope and
Stars

1978. Centenary of Tokyo Astronomical Observatory.
1512 **938** 50y. multicoloured   70   10

939/40 The then Heroic Champion's
Sumo Wrestling (detail, Toyokuni III)

941 Children's
Charming Sumo
Play (Utamaro
Kitagawa)

1978. Sumo Pictures (3rd series).
1513 **939** 50y. multicoloured   70   30
1514 **940** 50y. multicoloured   70   30
1515 **941** 50y. multicoloured   70   30
   Nos. 1513/14 were issued together *se-tenant*, forming
the composite design illustrated.

942 Sheep
Bell (folk toy)

1978. New Year's Greetings.
1516 **942** 20y. multicoloured   50   10

943 Family and
Human Rights
Emblem

1978. 30th Anniv of Declaration of Human Rights.
1518 **943** 50y. multicoloured   70   10

944/5 Great Sumo Wrestlers crossing
Ryogoku Bridge (Toyokuni III)

946 "Yumitori
Ceremony at
Grand
Fund-raising
Tournament"
(Kunisada II)

1979. Sumo Pictures (4th series).
1519 **944** 50y. multicoloured   70   30
1520 **945** 50y. multicoloured   70   30
1521 **946** 50y. multicoloured   70   30
   Nos. 1519/20 were issued together *se-tenant*, forming
the composite design illustrated.

947 Hands
protecting Children

1979. Education for the Handicapped.
1522 **947** 50y. multicoloured   70   25

948/9 Takekuma versus Iwamigata
(Kuniyoshi Utagawa)

950 Daidozan's
Dohyoiri (Sharaku
Toshusai)

1979. Sumo Pictures (5th series).
1523 **948** 50y. multicoloured   70   30
1524 **949** 50y. multicoloured   70   30
1525 **950** 50y. multicoloured   70   30
   Nos. 1523/4 were issued together *se-tenant*, forming
the composite design illustrated.

951 Telephone
Dial and
Pushbuttons

1979. Telephone Automation Completion.
1526 **951** 50y. multicoloured   70   10

952 Drawing by
Leonardo da
Vinci

1979. Centenary of Western Medicine in Japan.
1527 **952** 50y. multicoloured   70   10

953 Standing   **954** Standing
Beauties (Kaigetsudo   Beauties (Kaigetsudo
School)   School)

1979. Philatelic Week.
1528 **953** 50y. multicoloured   70   25
1529 **954** 50y. multicoloured   70   25

955 Mt.
Horaiji and
Maple Leaves

1979. National Afforestation Campaign.
1530 **955** 50y. multicoloured   70   10

956 Goddess of   **957** The Princess of
Maternal Mercy   the Sea God (Aoki
(Kano Hogai)   Shigeru)

1979. Modern Japanese Art (1st series).
1531 **956** 50y. multicoloured   90   25
1532 **957** 50y. multicoloured   80   25
   See also Nos. 1533/4. 1544/5, 1550/1, 1558/9, 1567/8,
1574/5, 1610/11, 1618/19, 1628/9, 1650/1, 1656/7,
1675/6, 1689/90, 1693/4 and 1697/8.

958 Fire Dance   **959** Leaning Figure
(Gyosha Hayami)   (Tetsugoro Yorozu)

1979. Modern Japanese Art (2nd series).
1533 **958** 50y. multicoloured   1·20   25
1534 **959** 50y. multicoloured   1·20   25

960 Quarantine Officers

1979. Centenary of Quarantine System.
1535 **960** 50y. multicoloured   1·00   10

961 Girl with   **962** Hakata Doll
Letter

1979. Letter writing Day.
1536 **961** 20y. multicoloured   40   25
1537 **962** 50y. multicoloured   70   25

963 Baseball
Pitcher and Ball

1979. 50th National Inter-City Amateur Baseball
Tournament.
1538 **963** 50y. multicoloured   70   15

964 Girl collecting Stars   **965** Boy catching Toy
                                Insects

1979. International Year of the Child.
1539 **964** 50y. multicoloured   1·00   15
1540 **965** 50y. multicoloured   1·00   15
MS1541 144×93 mm. Nos. 1539/40   2·40   1·90

966 The Moon   **967** Evening Glow
over the Castle   (Uko Nakamura
Ruins (Bansui Doi   and Shin
and Rentaro Taki)   Kusakawa)

1979. Japanese Songs (1st series).
1542 **966** 50y. multicoloured   70   25
1543 **967** 50y. multicoloured   70   25

See also Nos. 1552/3, 1556/7, 1561/2, 1565/6, 1572/3, 1580/1, 1616/17 and 1620/1.

968 *Black Cat*
(Shunso Hishida)

969 *Kinyo* (Sotaro
Yasui)

1979. Modern Japanese Art (3rd series).

1544	**968**	50y. multicoloured	1·10	25
1545	**969**	50y. multicoloured	1·10	25

970 *Steep
Mountains and the
Dark Dale* (Okyo
Maruyama)

1979. International Correspondence Week.

1546	**970**	100y. multicoloured	2·50	25

971 *Long
Distance Runner*

1979. 34th National Athletic Meeting, Miyazaki.

1547	**971**	20y. multicoloured	70	10

972 *"ITU" and
Globe*

**1979. Centenary of Admission to International
Telecommunications Union.**

1548	**972**	50y. multicoloured	70	10

973 *Woman and
Embryo*

**1979. Ninth International Obstetrics and Gynaecology
Convention, Tokyo.**

1549	**973**	50y. multicoloured	70	25

974 *Nude* (Kagaku
Murakami)

975 *Harvest* (Asai Chu)

1979. Modern Japanese Art (4th series).

1550	**974**	50y. multicoloured	70	25
1551	**975**	50y. multicoloured	50	10

976 *Maple Leaves*
(Tatsuyuki Takano and
Teiichi Okano)

977 *Birthplace*
(Tatsuyuki Takano
and Teiichi Okano)

1979. Japanese Songs (2nd series).

1552	**976**	50y. multicoloured	50	10
1553	**977**	50y. multicoloured	50	10

978 *"Happy
Monkeys"*
(folk toy)

1979. New Year's Greeting.

1554	**978**	20y. multicoloured	50	10

979 *Winter Scene* (anon)   **980** *Mount Fuji* (anon)

1980. Japanese Songs (3rd series).

1556	**979**	50y. multicoloured	1·00	25
1557	**980**	50y. multicoloured	1·00	25

981 *Salmon* (Yuichi
Takahashi)

982 *Hall of the
Supreme* Buddha
(Kokei Kobayashi)

1980. Modern Japanese Art (5th series).

1558	**981**	50y. multicoloured	1·20	25
1559	**982**	50y. multicoloured	1·20	25

983 *Scales*

1980. Centenary of Government Auditing Bureau.

1560	**983**	50y. multicoloured	70	10

984 *Spring Brook*
(Tatsuyuki Takano and
Teiichi Okano)

985 *Cherry Blossoms*
(anon)

1980. Japanese Songs (4th series).

1561	**984**	50y. multicoloured	70	25
1562	**985**	50y. multicoloured	70	25

986 *Scenes of
Outdoor Play in Spring*
(Sukenobu
Nishikawa)

987 *Scenes of Outdoor
Play in Spring*
(Sukenobu Nishikawa)

1980. Philatelic Week.

1563	**986**	50y. multicoloured	70	25
1564	**987**	50y. multicoloured	70	25

988 *Sea* (Ryuha Hayashi
and Takeshi Inoue)

989 *Misty
Moonlight Night*
(Tatsuyuki Takano
and Teiichi Okano)

1980. Japanese Songs (5th series).

1565	**988**	50y. multicoloured	70	25
1566	**989**	50y. multicoloured	70	25

990 *Maiko Girls* (Seiki
Kuroda)

991 *Mother and Child*
(Shoen Uemura)

1980. Modern Japanese Art (6th series).

1567	**990**	50y. multicoloured	70	25
1568	**991**	50y. multicoloured	70	25

992 *Nippon
Maru I*

1980. 50th Anniv of Training Cadet Ships *Nippon Maru I*
and *Kaio Maru.*

1569	**992**	50y. multicoloured	1·20	10

993 *Mount
Gozaisho and
Cedars*

1980. National Afforestation Campaign.

1570	**993**	50y. multicoloured	80	30

994 *Acrobatic
Performances on
a Ladder at New
Year's Parade of
Yayosu Fire
Brigades*
(Hiroshige III)

1980. Centenary of Fire Fighting System.

1571	**994**	50y. multicoloured	80	30

995 *The Sun* (Taksuyuki
Takano and Teiichi
Okano)

996 *Memories of
Summer* (Shoko
Ema and Yoshinao
Nakata)

1980. Japanese Songs (6th series).

1572	**995**	50y. multicoloured	80	25
1573	**996**	50y. multicoloured	80	25

997 *Black Fan*
(Takeji Fujishima)

998 *The Dance 'Are
Yudachi ni* (Seiho
Takeuchi)

1980. Modern Japanese Art (7th series).

1574	**997**	50y. multicoloured	80	25
1575	**998**	50y. multicoloured	80	25

999 *Teddy
Bear holding
Letter*

1000 *Knotted
Letter*

1980. Letter Writing Day.

1576	**999**	20y. multicoloured	50	30
1577	**1000**	50y. multicoloured	1·00	25

1001 *Luehdorfia japonica*

1980. 16th International Congress of Entomology, Kyoto.

1578	**1001**	50y. multicoloured	90	30

1002 *Map
on Three- dimensional
Graph*

**1980. 24th International Geographical Congress and 10th
International Cartographic Conference, Tokyo.**

1579	**1002**	50y. multicoloured	80	30

1003 *Red Dragonfly*
(Rofu Miki and Kosaku
Yamada)

1004 *Song by the
Sea* (Kokui
Hayashi and
Tamezo Narita)

1980. Japanese Songs (7th series).

1580	**1003**	50y. multicoloured	80	25
1581	**1004**	50y. multicoloured	80	25

1005 *Integrated Circuit*

**1980. Eighth World Computer Congress and Third World
Conference on Medical Informatics, Tokyo.**

1582	**1005**	50y. multicoloured	80	30

1006 *Akita
Dog*

1007 *Adonis*

1008 *Lily*

1009
Camellia

1010 *Small
Cabbage
Whites on
Rape
Blossom*

1011
*Japanese
Babylonia*

1012 Noble Scallops

 1013 Flowering Cherry

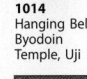 **1014** Hanging Bell, Byodoin Temple, Uji

 1015 Yoka Star Shell

 1016 Precious Wentletrap

1017 Flautist, Horyu Temple

 1018 Deer (from lacquer writing box)

 1019 Mirror with Figures

1020 Heart-shaped Earthen Figurine

 1021 Silver Crane, Kasuga Taisha Shrine, Nara

1022 Miroku Bosatsu, Horyu Temple

1023 Dainichi Buddha, Chuson Temple

 **1024** Keiki Doji, Kongobu Temple

 1025 Komoku Ten, Todai Temple, Nara

 1026 Lady Maya, Horyu Temple

 1027 Tea Jar with Wisteria Decoration (Ninsei Nonomura)

1028 Miroku Bosatsu

1980. 41y. and 62y. perf or imperf (self-adhesive), others perf.

1582a	1006	2y. blue	10	10
1583	1007	10y. yellow, grn & brn	20	15
1584	1008	20y. yellow, blue & grn	30	15
1585	1009	30y. multicoloured	55	20
1586	1010	40y. multicoloured	50	15
1587	1011	40y. multicoloured	85	25
1588	1012	41y. multicoloured	70	20
1589	1013	50y. multicoloured	80	15
1590	1014	60y. green and black	70	10
1591	1015	60y. multicoloured	1·00	10
1592	1016	62y. multicoloured	1·10	20
1593	1017	70y. blue and yellow	1·30	30
1594	1018	70y. yellow, black & bl	80	15
1594a	1018	72y. yellow, black & bl	80	15
1595	1019	80y. green and black	1·50	10
1596	1020	90y. yellow, blk & grn	1·60	10
1597	1021	100y. black, blue and ultramarine	90	10
1598	1022	170y. purple and bistre	2·00	15
1599	1022	175y. brown, grn & bis	1·90	15
1600	-	210y. orange and lilac (as No. 1242)	2·30	15
1601	1023	260y. brown and red	3·00	15
1602	1024	300y. brown	3·50	10
1603	1025	310y. brown and violet	3·50	10
1604	-	360y. purple and pink (as No. 1246)	4·00	25
1605	1026	410y. orange and blue	6·50	30
1606	1027	410y. multicoloured	6·75	15
1607	1028	600y. yellow, purple and lilac	7·00	15

 1031 Manchurian Cranes (door painting, Motooki Watanabe)

1980. International Correspondence Week.

1608	1031	100y. multicoloured	1·90	30

 1032 Archery and Mt. Nantai

1980. 35th National Athletic Meeting, Tochigi.

1609	1032	20y. multicoloured	40	25

 1033 Woman (sculpture, Morie Ogiwara)

 1034 Woman of the Kurofune-ya (Yumeji Takehisa)

1980. Modern Japanese Art (8th series).

1610	1033	50y. multicoloured	80	25
1611	1034	50y. multicoloured	80	25

 1035 "Energy"

1980. 35th World Congress of Junior Chambers of Commerce, Osaka.

1612	1035	50y. multicoloured	80	30

 1036 Diet Building and Doves

1980. 90th Anniv of Japanese Diet.

1613	1036	50y. multicoloured	1·00	10

 1037 Toy Rooster

1980. New Year's Greetings.

1614	1037	20y. multicoloured	50	10

 1038 Komori-Uta (nursery song)

 1039 Coconut (Toson Shimazaki and Toraji Ohaka)

1981. Japanese Songs (8th series).

1616	1038	60y. multicoloured	80	25
1617	1039	60y. multicoloured	80	25

 1040 Power Station in the Snow (Shiskanosuke Oka)

 1041 Nukada-no-Okimi of Asuka in Spring (Yukihiko Yasuda)

1981. Modern Japanese Art (9th series).

1618	1040	60y. multicoloured	1·10	30
1619	1041	60y. multicoloured	1·10	30

 1042 Spring has Come (Tatsuyuki Takano and Teiichi Okano)

 1043 Cherry Blossoms (Hagoromo Takeshima and Rentaro Taki)

1981. Japanese Songs (9th series).

1620	1042	60y. multicoloured	1·10	25
1621	1043	60y. multicoloured	1·10	25

 1044 Port Island and Exposition Emblem

1981. Kobe Port Island Exposition, Kobe City.

1622	1044	60y. multicoloured	1·00	30

 1045 Cereal, Tree and Fish on "100"

1981. Centenary of Agricultural, Forestry and Fishery Promotion.

1623	1045	60y. multicoloured	1·20	10

 1046/7 Yugao (Lady of the Evening Roses) and Genji

1981. Philatelic Week. Details of Harunobu Suzuki's Illustrations of *Tale of Genji* by Lady Murasaki.

1624	1046	60y. multicoloured	1·00	30
1625	1047	60y. multicoloured	1·00	30

Nos. 1624/5 were issued together, *se-tenant*, forming a composite design.

 1048 Pagodas at Nara and Double Cherry Blossom

1981. National Afforestation Campaign.

1626	1048	60y. multicoloured	1·00	30

 1049 Container Ship and Crane

1981. 12th International Port and Harbour Association Conference.

1627	1049	60y. multicoloured	1·00	10

 1050 N's Family (Narashinge Koide)

 1051 Bamboo Shoots (Heihachiro Fukuda)

1981. Modern Japanese Art (10th series).

1628	1050	60y. multicoloured	80	25
1629	1051	60y. multicoloured	80	25

 1052 Stylized Debris Barriers

1981. Centenary of Land Erosion Control.

1630	1052	60y. multicoloured	1·00	25

 1053 Human Figure and Dose Response Chart

1981. Eighth International Congress of Pharmacology, Tokyo.

1631	1053	60y. multicoloured	1·00	30

 1054 Girl writing Letter

1055 Boy with Pencil and Stamp

1981. Letter Writing Day.

1632	1054	40y. multicoloured	70	30
1633	1055	60y. multicoloured	1·00	25

 1056 Japanese Crested Ibis

1981. 50th Anniv of National Parks.

1634	1056	60y. multicoloured	1·10	30

 1057 Electric Plug and dripping Tap

 1058 Energy Recycling

1981. Energy Conservation.

1635	1057	40y. dp blue, lilac & bl	80	30
1636	1058	60y. multicoloured	1·20	25

 1059 Oura Cathedral, Nagasaki

1060 Hyokei Hall, Tokyo

1981. Modern Western-style Architecture (1st series).

1637	1059	60y. multicoloured	1·00	30
1638	1060	60y. multicoloured	1·00	30

See also Nos. 1648/9, 1654/5, 1658/9, 1669/70, 1680/1, 1695/6, 1705/6, 1710/11 and 1732/3.

1061 Bluebird and I.Y.D.P. Emblem

1981. International Year of Disabled Persons.
1639	**1061**	60y.+10y. mult	1·20	30

1062 Globe in Brain

1981. International Neurological Conferences, Kyoto.
1640	**1062**	60y. multicoloured	80	10

1063 Convention Emblem

1981. International Federation of Postal, Telegram and Telephone Workers' Unions World Convention, Tokyo.
1641	**1063**	60y. multicoloured	1·00	30

1064 Eastern Turtle Doves (Sanraku Kano)

1981. International Correspondence Week.
1642	**1064**	130y. multicoloured	2·50	30

1065 48m. Stamp 1871

1981. "Philatokyo '81" International Stamp Exhibition, Tokyo. Multicoloured, frame colour of stamp within design given.
1643	**1065**	60y. brown	90	30
1644	-	60y. blue	90	30
1645	-	60y. red	90	30
1646	-	60y. green	90	30

DESIGNS: No. 1644, 100m. stamp, 1871; 1645, 200m. stamp, 1871; 1646, 500m. stamp, 1871.

1069 Badminton and Lake Biwa

1981. 36th National Athletic Meeting, Shiga.
1647	**1069**	40y. multicoloured	70	25

1070 Former Kaichi School Matsumoto　　**1071** Doshisha Chapel, Kyoto

1981. Modern Western-style Architecture (2nd series).
1648	**1070**	60y. multicoloured	1·00	30
1649	**1071**	60y. multicoloured	1·00	30

1072 Portrait of Reiko (Ryusei Kishida)　**1073** Ichiyo (Kiyokata Kaburagi)

1981. Modern Japanese Art (11th series).
1650	**1072**	60y. multicoloured	80	30
1651	**1073**	60y. multicoloured	80	30

1074 Clay Dog (folk toy)

1981. New Year's Greetings.
1652	**1074**	40y. multicoloured	70	10

1075 St John's Church, Inuyama　**1076** Military Exercise Hall, Sapporo Agricultural School

1982. Modern Western-style Architecture (3rd series).
1654	**1075**	60y. multicoloured	1·00	30
1655	**1076**	60y. multicoloured	1·00	30

1077 Yoritomo in a Cave (Seison Maeda)

1078 Posters on a Terrace (Yuzo Saeki)

1982. Modern Japanese Art (12th series).
1656	**1077**	60y. multicoloured	80	30
1657	**1078**	60y. multicoloured	80	30

1079 Bank of Japan, Kyoto Branch (now museum)　**1080** Saiseikan Hospital, Yamagata

1982. Modern Western-style Architecture (4th series).
1658	**1079**	60y. multicoloured	1·00	30
1659	**1080**	60y. multicoloured	1·00	30

1081 Gorilla and Greater Flamingo

1982. Ueno Zoo. Centenary. Multicoloured.
1660	60y. Type **1081**	90	25
1661	60y. Lion and king penguins	90	25
1662	60y. Giant panda and Indian elephants	90	25
1663	60y. Giraffe and common zebras	90	25

1085/6 Enjoying Snow Landscape of Matsuchi-yama (Torii Kiyonaga)

1982. Philatelic Week.
1664	**1085**	60y. multicoloured	90	30
1665	**1086**	60y. multicoloured	90	30

Nos. 1664/5 were issued together se-tenant forming the composite design illustrated.

1087 Lion

1982. Tenth Anniv of Return of Okinawa (Ryukyu Islands).
1666	**1087**	60y. multicoloured	90	25

1088 Arbor Festival Emblem and Blue and White Fly-catcher

1982. National Afforestation Campaign.
1667	**1088**	60y. multicoloured	1·20	25

1089 Noh Mask

1982. 16th World Dermatology Congress, Tokyo.
1668	**1089**	60y. multicoloured	90	25

1090 Divine Gate of Oyama Shrine, Kanazawa　**1091** Former Iwasaki Mansion, Taito-ku, Tokyo (now Training Institute)

1982. Modern Western-style Architecture (5th series).
1669	**1090**	60y. multicoloured	90	25
1670	**1091**	60y. multicoloured	90	25

1092 Class 1290 Locomotive Zenko, 1881　**1093** Yamabiko (echo) Express Train

1982. Opening of Tohoku–Shinkansen Railway Line.
1671	**1092**	60y. multicoloured	1·10	25
1672	**1093**	60y. multicoloured	1·10	25

1094 Gull and Balloon with Letter　**1095** Bird carrying Letter to Fairy

1982. Letter Writing Day.
1673	**1094**	40y. multicoloured	90	30
1674	**1095**	60y. multicoloured	1·30	25

1096 Garment Patterned with Irises (Saburosuke Okada)　**1097** Buddhisattva Kannon on Potalaka Island (Tessai Tomioka)

1982. Modern Japanese Art (13th series).
1675	**1096**	40y. multicoloured	90	25
1676	**1097**	60y. multicoloured	90	25

1098 Wreath (condolences)　**1099** Folded Paper Crane (congratulations)　**1100** Pine, Plum and Bamboo Blossom (congratulations)

1982. Special Correspondence Stamps.
1677	**1098**	60y. multicoloured	1·20	30
1678	**1099**	60y. multicoloured	1·20	30
1679	**1100**	70y. multicoloured	1·40	30

For other values see Nos. 1722/3, 2013/16 and 2289/92.

1101 Hokkaido Prefectural Building, Sapporo　**1102** Saigo Tsugumichi Mansion, Meguro (now in Inuyama)

1982. Modern Western-style Architecture (6th series).
1680	**1101**	60y. multicoloured	1·40	40
1681	**1102**	60y. multicoloured	1·40	40

1103 16th-century Portuguese Galleon and World Map

1982. 400th Anniv of Christian Boys' Delegation to Europe.
1682	**1103**	60y. multicoloured	1·20	25

1104 T'ien T'an in the Clouds (Ryuzaburo Umehara)

1982. Tenth Anniv of Restoration of Diplomatic Relations with China.
1683	**1104**	60y. multicoloured	1·00	30

1105 Table Tennis and Monument of the Meet

1982. 37th National Athletic Meeting, Matsue.
1684	**1105**	40y. multicoloured	70	30

1106 Amusement (wooden doll by Goyo Hirata)

1982. International Correspondence Week.
1685	**1106**	130y. multicoloured	1·90	30

1107 Bank of Japan near Eitaibashi in Snow (Yasuji Inoue)

1982. Centenary of Central Bank System.
1686	**1107**	60y. multicoloured	1·00	30

1108 Asahi (rising sun) Express Train   **1109** ED 16 Electric Locomotive No. 8

1982. Opening of Joetsu–Shinkansen Railway Line.
1687	**1108**	60y. multicoloured	1·10	25
1688	**1109**	60y. multicoloured	1·10	25

1110 Srimhadevi (Shiko Munakata)   **1111** Saltimbanque (Seiji Togo)

1982. Modern Japanese Art (14th series).
1689	**1110**	60y. multicoloured	90	25
1690	**1111**	60y. multicoloured	90	25

1112 Kintaro on a Wild Boar (clay Tsutsumi doll)

1982. New Year Greetings.
1691	**1112**	40y. multicoloured	70	25

1113 Snowstorm (Shinsui Ito)   **1114** Spiraea and Calla in a Perrian Vase (Zenzaburo Kojima)

1983. Modern Japanese Art (15th series).
1692	**1113**	60y. multicoloured	75	10
1693	**1114**	60y. multicoloured	90	25

1115 Fujimura Memorial Hall, Kofu (formerly Mutsuzawa School)   **1116** Porch of Sakuranomiya Public Hall, Osaka

1983. Modern Western-style Architecture (7th series).
1695	**1115**	60y. multicoloured	90	25
1696	**1116**	60y. multicoloured	90	25

1117 Selflessness (Taikan Yokoyama)   **1118** Aged Monkey (wood carving, Koun Takamura)

1983. Modern Japanese Art (16th series).
1697	**1117**	60y. multicoloured	1·00	30
1698	**1118**	60y. multicoloured	1·00	30

1119 Museum and Japanese Characters representing History, Folklore and Antiquity

1983. Opening of National Museum of History and Folklore.
1699	**1119**	60y. multicoloured	1·00	30

1120/1 Women working in the Kitchen (Utamaro Kitagawa)

1983. Philatelic Week.
1700	**1120**	60y. multicoloured	1·00	30
1701	**1121**	60y. multicoloured	1·00	30

Nos. 1695/6 were issued together, *se-tenant*, forming the composite design illustrated.

1122 Hiba arborvitae, Japanese Black Fritillary and Hakusan Mountains

1983. National Afforestation Campaign.
1702	**1122**	60y. multicoloured	1·00	30

1123 Colt and Racehorse

1983. 50th Nippon Derby.
1703	**1123**	60y. multicoloured	1·20	25

1124 Rabbit and Empty Can

1983. Islands Clean-up Campaign.
1704	**1124**	60y. multicoloured	1·20	25

1125 Hohei-kan House (Wedding Hall), Sapporo   **1126** Glover House, Nagasaki

1983. Modern Western-style Architecture (8th series).
1705	**1125**	60y. multicoloured	90	25
1706	**1126**	60y. multicoloured	90	25

1127 First Issue and Nihonbashi Bulletin Board

1983. Centenary of "Government Journal".
1707	**1127**	60y. multicoloured	1·00	30

1128 Boy with Letter   **1129** Fairy with Letter

1983. Letter Writing Day.
1708	**1128**	40y. multicoloured	70	30
1709	**1129**	60y. multicoloured	1·00	25

1130 59th Bank, Hirosaki   **1131** Auditorium of Gakushuin Elementary School (now in Narita)

1983. Modern Western-style Architecture (9th series).
1710	**1130**	60y. multicoloured	90	25
1711	**1131**	60y. multicoloured	90	25

1132 Theatre and Noh Player

1983. Opening of National Noh Theatre, Tokyo.
1712	**1132**	60y. multicoloured	1·00	30

1133 Okinawa Rail

1983. Endangered Birds (1st series). Multicoloured.
1713	60y. Type **1133**	1·50	30
1714	60y. Blakiston's fish owl (*Ketupa blakistoni*) (horiz)	1·50	30

See also Nos. 1724/5, 1729/30, 1735/6 and 1742/3.

1135 Chi-kyu (paper doll by Juzo Kagoshima)

1983. International Correspondence Week.
1715	**1135**	130y. multicoloured	1·90	40

1136 Naginata Player and Myogi Mountains

1983. 38th National Athletic Meeting, Gumman.
1716	**1136**	40y. multicoloured	70	30

1137 Ferris Wheel   **1138** Children supporting Globe

1983. World Communications Year.
1717	**1137**	60y. multicoloured	1·00	30
1718	**1138**	60y. multicoloured	1·00	30

1139 Park and Monument

1140 Congress Emblem and Mouth Mirror

1983. Opening of Showa Memorial National Park.
1719	**1139**	60y. multicoloured	1·00	25

1983. 71st World Dental Congress, Tokyo.
1720	**1140**	60y. multicoloured	1·00	30

1141 Shirase

1983. Maiden Voyage of Antarctic Research Ship "Shirase".
1721	**1141**	60y. multicoloured	2·50	25

1983. Special Correspondence Stamps.
1722	**1098**	60y. multicoloured	80	30
1723	**1099**	40y. multicoloured	80	30

1983. Endangered Birds (2nd series). As T **1133**. Multicoloured.
1724	60y. Pryer's woodpecker "Sapheopipo noguchii"	1·40	25
1725	60y. Canada goose (*Branta canadensis leucopareia*) (horiz)	1·40	25

1144 Mouse riding a Small Hammer (folk toy)

1983. New Year's Greetings.
1726	**1144**	40y. multicoloured	70	25

1145 Human Rights Emblem

1983. 35th Anniv of Declaration of Human Rights.
1728	**1145**	60y. multicoloured	70	25

1984. Endangered Birds (3rd series). As T **1133**. Multicoloured.
1729	60y. Japanese marsh warbler (*Megalurus pryeri pryeri*) (horiz)	1·00	30
1730	60y. Crested serpent eagle (*Spilornis cheela perplexus*)	1·50	25

1148 Exhibition Emblem and Mascot

1984. "Expo '85" International Science and Technology Exhibition, Tsukuba (1985).
1731	**1148**	60y.+10y. mult	1·50	25

1149 Bank of Japan Head Office   **1150** Hunter House, Kobe

1984. Modern Western-style Architecture (10th series).
1732	**1149**	60y. multicoloured	90	25
1733	**1150**	60y. multicoloured	90	25

1151 Japanese-style Cake and Bamboo Tea Whisk

1984. 20th Confectionery Fair, Tokyo.
1734	**1151**	60y. multicoloured	1·00	30

1984. Endangered Birds (4th series). As T **1133**. Multicoloured.

1735		60y. Black wood pigeon (*Columba janthina nitens*)	1·50	25
1736		60y. Spotted greenshank (*Tringa guttifer*) (horiz)	1·50	25

1154 Bunraku Puppet and Theatre

1984. Opening of National Bunraku Theatre, Osaka.

1737	**1154**	60y. multicoloured	1·40	40

1155 *Otani Oniji as Edobeh* (Toshusai Sharaku)   **1156** *Iwai Hanshiro IV as Shigenoi* (Toshusai Sharaku)

1984. Philatelic Week.

1738	**1155**	60y. multicoloured	1·00	30
1739	**1156**	60y. multicoloured	1·00	30

1157 Kaikozu Tree and Sakura Volcano

1984. National Afforestation Campaign.

1740	**1157**	60y. multicoloured	1·00	30

1158 "Himawari" Weather Satellite and Chart

1984. Centenary of National Weather Forecasts.

1741	**1158**	60y. multicoloured	1·00	25

1984. Endangered Birds (5th series). As T **1133**. Multicoloured.

1742		60y. White-backed woodpecker (*Dendrocopos leucotos owstoni*) (horiz)	1·50	25
1743		60y. Peregrine falcon (*Falco peregrinus fruitii*)	1·50	25

1161 Doves

1984. Federation of UNESCO Clubs and Associations World Congress, Sendai.

1744	**1161**	60y. multicoloured	1·20	25

1162 Birds in Tree   **1163** Bird and Flowers

1984. Letter Writing Day.

1745	**1162**	40y. multicoloured	90	30
1746	**1163**	60y. multicoloured	1·30	25

1164 *Fire and Wind* (Motomi Hagimoto)   **1165** *Bonds* (Noboru Kanda)

1984. Disaster Prevention Week.

1747	**1164**	40y. multicoloured	70	30
1748	**1165**	60y. black and yellow	1·00	25

1166 *Leontopodium fauriei*

1984. Alpine Plants (1st series). Multicoloured.

1749		60y. Type **1166**	1·00	30
1750		60y. *Lagotis glauca* (horiz)	1·00	30

See also Nos. 1752/3, 1769/70, 1775/6, 1802/3, 1813/14 and 1827/8.

1168 Basho's Crossroads, Sendai

1984. Sixth International Virology Congress, Sendai.

1751	**1168**	60y. multicoloured	90	25

1984. Alpine Plants (2nd series). As T **1166**. Multicoloured.

1752		60y. Globe flower (*Trollius riederianus*)	1·00	30
1753		60y. *Primula cuneifolia*	1·00	30

1171 Logo

1984. Electronic Mail.

1754	**1171**	500y. multicoloured	14·50	6·25

1172 *Serenity* (doll by Ryujo Hori)

1984. International Correspondence Week.

1755	**1172**	130y. multicoloured	1·90	30

1173 Silver Pavilion, Jisho Temple

1984. 17th International Internal Medicine Congress, Kyoto City.

1756	**1173**	60y. multicoloured	90	25

1174 Hockey and East Pagoda of Yakushi Temple

1984. 39th National Athletic Meeting, Nara.

1757	**1174**	40y. multicoloured	70	30

1175 Birds in Tree   **1176** Flowers

1177 Chrysanthemums Design   **1178** Leaf and Bird Design

1984. Traditional Crafts (1st series). Kutani Porcelain Plates and Nishijin Silk Weavings.

1758	**1175**	60y. multicoloured	90	25
1759	**1176**	60y. multicoloured	90	25
1760	**1177**	60y. multicoloured	90	25
1761	**1178**	60y. multicoloured	90	25

See also Nos. 1771/4, 1787/90, 1795/8, 1805/8, 1820/3 and 1829/32.

1179 Eiji Sawamura (pitcher)

1984. 50th Anniv of Japan Tokyo Baseball Club. Multicoloured.

1762		60y. Type **1179**	90	25
1763		60y. Masaru Kageura (striker)	90	25
1764		60y. Ball, birds and Matsutaro Shoriki (founder)	90	25

1182 Workers' Profiles and Symbols

1984. Centenary of Technical Education.

1765	**1182**	60y. multicoloured	1·20	25

1183 Bamboo Ox (Sakushu folk toy)

1984. New Year's Greetings.

1766	**1183**	40y. multicoloured	1·10	30

1984. Endangered Birds (6th series). Sheet 93×120 mm. As Nos. 1714 and 1743.

MS1768		60y. blue (as No. 1714); 60y. purple (as No. 1730); 60y. black (as No. 1743)	6·00	4·00

1984. Alpine Plants (3rd series). As T **1166**. Multicoloured.

1769		60y. *Rhododendron aureum*	1·00	30
1770		60y. *Oxytropis nigrescens* (horiz)	1·00	30

1186 Dolls   **1187** Doll with Cat

1188 Bird and Flower Design   **1189** Birds and Chrysanthemums Design

1985. Traditional Crafts (2nd series). Edo Kimekomi Dolls and Okinawa Bingata Cloth.

1771	**1186**	60y. multicoloured	1·00	30
1772	**1187**	60y. multicoloured	1·00	30
1773	**1188**	60y. multicoloured	1·00	30
1774	**1189**	60y. multicoloured	1·00	30

1985. Alpine Plants (4th series). As T **1166**. Multicoloured.

1775		60y. *Dryas octopetala* (horiz)	1·00	30
1776		60y. *Draba japonica*	1·00	30

1192 Theme Pavilion and Symbol Tower

1985. "EXPO '85" World Fair, Tsukuba. Multicoloured.

1777		40y. Type **1192**	80	30
1778		60y. Geometric city	90	30
MS1779		144×93 mm. Nos. 1777/8	3·25	2·50

1194 University Buildings, Chiba City, and Transmitter

1985. Inauguration of University of the Air.

1780	**1194**	60y. multicoloured	1·00	25

1195 Aerial and Communication Lines

1985. Privatization of Nippon Telegraph and Telephone Corporation.

1781	**1195**	60y. multicoloured	1·00	25

1196 Map of Japan (after Teixeira's Map in Ortelius's *Atlas*, 1595)

1985. World Import Fair, Nagoya.

1782	**1196**	60y. multicoloured	1·20	25

1197 Korekiyo Takahashi (proposer of Patent Laws)

1985. Centenary of Industrial Patents System.

1783	**1197**	60y. multicoloured	90	25

1198 *Winter in the North* (Yumeji Takehisa)   **1199** *Toward the Morning Light* (Yumeji Takehisa)

1985. Philatelic Week.

1784	**1198**	60y. multicoloured	90	30
1785	**1199**	60y. multicoloured	90	30

1200 Mt. Aso and Gentian

1985. National Afforestation Campaign.

1786	**1200**	60y. multicoloured	1·20	25

1201 Hawk   **1202** Ducks

1203 Bowl   **1204** Plate

1985. Traditional Crafts (3rd series). Yew Wood Carvings and Arita Porcelain.

1787	**1201**	60y. multicoloured	1·00	30
1788	**1202**	60y. multicoloured	1·00	30
1789	**1203**	60y. multicoloured	1·00	30
1790	**1204**	60y. multicoloured	1·00	30

1205/6 *Cherry Trees at Night* (Taikan Yokoyama)

1985. 50th Anniv of Radio Japan (overseas broadcasting station).

| 1791 | **1205** | 60y. multicoloured | 1·00 | 30 |
| 1792 | **1206** | 60y. multicoloured | 1·00 | 30 |

Nos. 1791/2 were issued together, se-tenant, forming the composite design illustrated.

1207 Maeshima and *Tokyo Post Office* (Hiroshige III)

1985. 150th Birth Anniv of Baron Hisoka Maeshima (first Postmaster-General).

| 1793 | **1207** | 60y. multicoloured | 90 | 25 |

1208 Bridge

1985. Opening of Great Naruto Bridge.

| 1794 | **1208** | 60y. multicoloured | 90 | 25 |

1209 Weaving   **1210** Weaving

1211 Dish   **1212** Panel

1985. Traditional Crafts (4th series). Ojiya Linen Weavings and Kamakura Lacquered Wood Carvings.

1795	**1209**	60y. multicoloured	90	30
1796	**1210**	60y. multicoloured	90	30
1797	**1211**	60y. multicoloured	90	30
1798	**1212**	60y. multicoloured	90	30

1213 Silhouette of Laurel and Couple

1985. International Youth Year.

| 1799 | **1213** | 60y. multicoloured | 90 | 25 |

1214 Owl with Letter   **1215** Girl holding Bird, Letter and Cat

1985. Letter Writing Day.

| 1800 | **1214** | 40y. multicoloured | 70 | 30 |
| 1801 | **1215** | 60y. multicoloured | 1·00 | 30 |

1985. Alpine Plants (5th series). As T **1166**. Multicoloured.

| 1802 | | 60y. Gentian (*Gentiana nipponica*) | 1·00 | 30 |
| 1803 | | 60y. *Callianthemum insigne* | 1·00 | 30 |

1218 Logo

1985. Electronic Mail.

| 1804 | **1218** | 500y. multicoloured | 9·25 | 95 |

1219 Noh Theatre Actor   **1220** Mother with Child

1221 Tea Kettle with Fish Design   **1222** Tea Kettle

1985. Traditional Crafts (5th series). Hakata Clay Figurines and Nambu Iron Ware.

1805	**1219**	60y. multicoloured	90	30
1806	**1220**	60y. multicoloured	90	30
1807	**1221**	60y. multicoloured	90	30
1808	**1222**	60y. multicoloured	90	30

1223 Hideki Yukawa (physicist) and Meson Field

1985. 50th Anniv of Yukawa's Meson Theory.

| 1809 | **1223** | 60y. multicoloured | 90 | 25 |

1224 Gymnasts

1985. University Games, Kobe.

| 1810 | **1224** | 60y. multicoloured | 90 | 25 |

1225 Competitor filing Test Piece

1985. 28th International Vocational Training Competition, Osaka.

| 1811 | **1225** | 40y. multicoloured | 80 | 30 |

1226 *Hibiscus syriacus* (national flower of S. Korea)

1985. 20th Anniv of Japan–South Korea Diplomatic Relations.

| 1812 | **1226** | 60y. multicoloured | 1·00 | 30 |

1985. Alpine Plants (6th series). As T **1166**. Multicoloured.

| 1813 | | 60y. *Viola crassa* (horiz) | 1·00 | 30 |
| 1814 | | 60y. *Campanula chamissonis* | 1·00 | 30 |

1229 Tunnels and Section through Mt. Tanigawa

1985. Opening of North-bound Kan-Etsu Tunnel.

| 1815 | **1229** | 60y. multicoloured | 90 | 25 |

1230 *Seisen* (doll by Goyo Hirata)

1985. International Correspondence Week.

| 1816 | **1230** | 130y. multicoloured | 1·90 | 30 |

1231 Youth helping African Farmer

1985. 20th Anniv of Japanese Overseas Co-operation Volunteers.

| 1817 | **1231** | 60y. multicoloured | 90 | 25 |

1232 Honey Bee on Strawberry Blossom

1985. 30th International Bee-keeping Congress, Nagoya.

| 1818 | **1232** | 60y. multicoloured | 1·20 | 25 |

1233 Handball Player and Mt. Daisen

1985. 40th Int Athletic Meeting, Tottori.

| 1819 | **1233** | 40y. multicoloured | 1·10 | 40 |

1234 Table   **1235** Bowl

1236 Lantern on Column   **1237** Lantern

1985. Traditional Crafts (6th series). Wajima Lacquerware and Izumo Sandstone Lanterns.

1820	**1234**	60y. multicoloured	90	30
1821	**1235**	60y. multicoloured	90	30
1822	**1236**	60y. multicoloured	90	30
1823	**1237**	60y. multicoloured	90	30

1238 Osaka Papier-mache Tiger

1985. New Year's Greetings.

| 1824 | **1238** | 40y. multicoloured | 70 | 25 |

1239 Cabinet Emblem and Official Seal

1985. Cent of Cabinet System of Government.

| 1826 | **1239** | 60y. multicoloured | 90 | 25 |

1986. Alpine Plants (7th series). As T **1166**. Multicoloured.

| 1827 | | 60y. *Diapensia lapponica* | 1·00 | 30 |
| 1828 | | 60y. *Pedicularis apodochila* | 1·00 | 30 |

1242 Fan with Tree Design   **1243** Fan with Flower Design

1244 Flask with Fish Pattern   **1245** Tea Caddy

1986. Traditional Craft (7th series). Kyoto Fans and Tobe Porcelain.

1829	**1242**	60y. multicoloured	90	30
1830	**1243**	60y. multicoloured	90	30
1831	**1244**	60y. multicoloured	90	30
1832	**1245**	60y. multicoloured	90	30

1246 Gothic Style Finial and "Golden Norm"

1986. Centenary of Architecture Institute, Shiba, Tokyo.

| 1833 | **1246** | 60y. multicoloured | 1·00 | 30 |

1247 Standing Lady   **1248** Seated Lady

1986. Philatelic Week. Details of *South of Hateruma* by Kaigetsu Kikuchi.

| 1834 | **1247** | 60y. multicoloured | 1·00 | 30 |
| 1835 | **1248** | 60y. multicoloured | 1·00 | 30 |

1249 Phoenix and Enthronement Hall, Kyoto Palace   **1250** Imperial Palace Ridge Decoration

1986. 60th Anniv of Emperor Hirohito's Accession.

1836	**1249**	60y. multicoloured	1·00	30
1837	**1250**	60y. multicoloured	1·00	30
MS1838	144×93 mm. Nos. 1836/7		2·50	1·90

1251 *Mt. Fuji in Early Morning* (Yukihiko Yasuda)

1986. 12th Economic Summit of Industrialized Countries, Tokyo.

| 1839 | **1251** | 60y. multicoloured | 1·00 | 30 |

1252 Bull-headed
Shrike in Reeds

1986. National Afforestation Campaign.
1840 **1252** 60y. multicoloured 1·20 25

1253 Capsule, Tablets
and Structure of
Toluene

1986. Centenary of Japanese Pharmacopoeia.
1841 **1253** 60y. multicoloured 90 25

1254 Map and
Clock

1986. Centenary of Japanese Standard Time.
1842 **1254** 60y. multicoloured 1·00 30

1255 Bird on
Chair and
Letter on
Table

1986. Letter Writing Day. Multicoloured.
1843 40y. Type **1255** 90 25
1844 60y. Girl holding rabbit and
letter 1·30 25

1257 Yataro Iwasaki,
Makoto Kondo and
Cadet Ship *Nippon Maru*
II

1986. 110th Anniv of Merchant Navy Education.
1846 **1257** 60y. multicoloured 1·20 25

1258 Asian
Apollo (*Parnassius
eversmanni*)

1986. Insects (1st series). Multicoloured.
1847 60y. Type **1258** 1·50 30
1848 60y. Shieldbug (*Poecilocoris
lewisi*) 1·50 30
1849 60y. Longhorn beetle (*Rosalia
batesi*) 1·50 30
1850 60y. *Epiophlebia superstes* 1·50 30
See also Nos. 1854/7, 1861/4, 1869/72, 1878/**MS**1882
and 1911/12.

1262 *Folkways in
Twelve Months*
(detail, Shunsho
Katsukawa)

1986. 52nd International Federation of Library
Associations General Conference, Tokyo.
1851 **1262** 60y. multicoloured 1·00 30

1263 Electron
Microscope

1986. 11th International Electron Microscopy Congress,
Kyoto.
1852 **1263** 60y. multicoloured 1·00 30

1264 Couple and
Conference Emblem

1986. 23rd International Social Welfare Conference,
Tokyo.
1853 **1264** 60y. multicoloured 1·00 30

1986. Insects (2nd series). As T **1258**. Multicoloured.
1854 60y. Dragonflies (*Sympetrum
pedemonatanum*) 1·50 30
1855 60y. Weevil (*Damaster
blaptoides*) 1·50 30
1856 60y. Stag beetle ("Dorcus
hopei) 1·50 30
1857 60y. Wonderful hair-streak
(*Thermozephyrus ataxus*) 1·50 30

1269 *Ohmori
Miyage* (shiso doll,
Juzoh Kagoshima)

1986. International Correspondence Week.
1858 **1269** 130y. multicoloured 2·00 30

1270 Gymnast and
Mt. Fuji

1986. 41st National Athletic Meeting, Yamanashi.
1859 **1270** 40y. multicoloured 70 25

1271 *Flowers in Autumn
and Girl in Rakuhoku*

1986. Fifth World Ikebana Convention, Kyoto.
1860 **1271** 60y. multicoloured 1·00 30

1986. Insects (3rd series). As T **1258**. Multicoloured.
1861 60y. *Elcysma westwoodii* (moth) 1·50 30
1862 60y. *Rhyothemis variegata* 1·50 30
1863 60y. Cicada (*Tibicen japonicus*) 1·50 30
1864 60y. *Chrysochroa holstii* 1·50 30

1276 Stylized
Dove

1986. International Peace Year. Multicoloured.
1865 40y. Type **1276** 70 30
1866 60y. Circle of children (horiz) 1·00 30

1278 *Rabbits
making Rice
Cake*
(Nagoya clay
model)

1986. New Year's Greetings.
1867 **1278** 40y. multicoloured 1·10 40
For 50y. in this design dated "1999" see No. 2567.

1987. Insects (4th series). As T **1258**. Multicoloured.
1869 60y. *Cheirotonus jambar* 1·50 30
1870 60y. Chestnut tiger (*Parantica
sita*) 1·50 30
1871 60y. *Anotogaster sieboldii* 1·50 30
1872 60y. Stag beetle (*Lucanus
maculifemoratus*) 1·50 30

1283 Characters for
"Toki" (Registry) and Map

1987. Centenary of Land Registration.
1873 **1283** 60y. multicoloured 1·00 30

1284 Basho
Matsuo (after
Haritsu Ogawa)

1285 *Departing
Spring* (Senju)

1286 Kegon Falls

1287 *Sunlight*
(Toshu Shrine)

1987. *Narrow Road to a Far Province* (travel diary) by
Basho Matsuo (1st series).
1874 **1284** 60y. multicoloured 1·00 30
1875 **1285** 60y. multicoloured 1·00 30
1876 **1286** 60y. multicoloured 1·00 30
1877 **1287** 60y. multicoloured 1·00 30
In this series, each pair of stamps (except Nos. 1874/5)
illustrates one "haiku" (17-syllable poem) from the diary.
The full text of the "haiku" is printed on one stamp and
given in calligraphy on the other with appropriate illustrations. Each "haiku" was written at a particular point in
the journey (given in brackets in the caption to the second stamp of each pair).
See also Nos. 1896/9, 1906/9, 1925/8, 1932/5, 1945/8,
1962/5, 1973/6, 1982/5 and 2000/3.

1987. Insects (5th series). As T **1258**. Multicoloured.
1878 60y. Owl-fly (*Ascaraphus
ramburi*) 1·50 30
1879 60y. Cockchafer (*Polyphylla
laticollis*) 1·50 30
1880 60y. Leaf butterfly (*Kallima
inachus*) 1·50 30
1881 60y. *Calopteryx cornelia* 1·50 30
MS1882 143×93 mm. multicoloured.
40y. Orange-tip (*Anthocaris cardamines*); 40y. Great purple (*Sasakia
charonda*); 60y. Asian apollo (*Parnassius eversmanni*); 60y. Chestnut tiger
(*Parantica sita*) 5·50 4·25

1294 Wind
Orchid

1295 Lobster-root

1987. 12th International Orchid Conference, Tokyo.
1883 **1294** 60y. multicoloured 1·00 30
1884 **1295** 60y. multicoloured 1·00 30

1296 Early Mail Sorting
Carriage

1987. Ending of Railway Mail Carriage Contracts.
1885 60y. Type **1296** 1·20 30
1886 60y. Loading mail sacks (detail
of scroll painting by Beisen
Kubota) 1·20 30

1298 Class 860 Tank
Locomotive No. 137,
1893

1987. Privatization of Japan Railways. Multicoloured.
1887 60y. Type **1298** 1·10 25
1888 60y. Maglev MLU 002 1·10 25

1300 Nudibranchs

1987. Centenary of Marine Biology Studies in Japan.
1889 **1300** 60y. multicoloured 1·00 30

1301 *Woman
with a Comb*

1987. Philatelic Week. Paintings by Goyo Hashiguchi.
Multicoloured.
1890 60y. Type **1301** 1·00 30
1891 60y. *Woman putting on make-up* 1·00 30

1303 Map and Emblem

1987. 20th Annual General Meeting of Asian
Development Bank.
1892 **1303** 60y. multicoloured 1·00 30

1304 Black-billed
Magpie and
Forested Coastline

1987. National Afforestation Campaign.
1893 **1304** 60y. multicoloured 1·00 30

1305 Yatsuhashi Gold
Lacquer and Nacre
Inkstone Case (Kohrin
Ogata)

1306 Hikone Castle

1987. National Treasures (1st series).
1894 **1305** 60y. multicoloured 1·00 40
1895 **1306** 110y. multicoloured 1·80 55
See also Nos. 1900/1, 1929/30, 1949/50, 1968/9,
1980/1, 2006/7 and 2017/18.

1307 European
Cuckoo

1308 Horse and
River (Nasu)

1309 *In the Shade
of the Willow*

1310 Paddy Field
(Ashino)

1987. *Narrow Road to a Far Province* by Basho Matsuo
(2nd series).
1896 **1307** 60y. multicoloured 1·50 30
1897 **1308** 60y. multicoloured 1·50 30

1898	1309	60y. multicoloured	1·50	30
1899	1310	60y. multicoloured	1·50	30

1311 Golden Turtle Reliquary for Buddha's Ashes (Tashodai Temple)
1312 Inuyama Castle

1987. National Treasures (2nd series). Multicoloured.

1900	1311	60y. multicoloured	1·00	40
1901	1312	110y. multicoloured	1·80	55

1313 Flowers in Envelope

1987. Letter Writing Day. Multicoloured.

1902	40y. Type 1313	90	30
1903	60y. Elephant holding letter in trunk	1·30	45

1315 Flood Barrier across Rivers

1987. Centenary of Modern Flood Control of Rivers Kiso, Nagara and Ibi.

1905	1315	60y. multicoloured	1·00	25

1316 Chestnut Blossoms
1317 Chestnut Leaves (Sukagawa)

1318 Transplanting Rice
1319 Fern Leaves (Dyeing Stone, Shinobu)

1987. *Narrow Road to a Far Province* by Basho Matsuo (3rd series).

1906	1316	60y. multicoloured	1·00	30
1907	1317	60y. multicoloured	1·00	30
1908	1318	60y. multicoloured	1·00	30
1909	1319	60y. multicoloured	1·00	30

1320 Temple of Emerald Buddha and Cherry Blossom

1987. Centenary of Japan–Thailand Friendship Treaty.

1910	1320	60y. multicoloured	1·00	30

1987. Insects (6th series). As T 1258. Multicoloured.

1911	40y. Orange-tip (*Anthocaris cardamines*)	2·00	1·60
1912	40y. Great purple (*Sasakia charonda*)	2·00	1·60

1321 *Gensho Kanto* (Ryujo Hori)

1987. International Correspondence Week. Multicoloured.

1913	130y. Type 1321	2·00	40
1914	150y. *Utage-no-Hana* (Goyo Hirata)	2·20	45

1323 *Three Beauties* (detail, Toyokuni Utagawa)

1987. 13th International Certified Public Accountants Congress, Tokyo.

1915	1323	60y. multicoloured	1·00	30

1324 Lion's Head Public Water Tap

1987. Centenary of Yokohama Waterworks.

1916	1324	60y. multicoloured	1·00	30

1325 Basketball Players and Shuri Gate, Naha

1987. 42nd National Athletic Meeting, Okinawa.

1917	1325	40y. multicoloured	30	25

1326 Playing Card with Queen holding Bird and King smoking

1987. Sixth International Smoking and Health Conference, Tokyo.

1918	1326	60y. multicoloured	1·00	30

1327 Dish Aerial, Kashima Station

1987. International Telecommunications Conference, Tokyo.

1919	1327	60y. multicoloured	1·00	25

1328 Nijo Castle

1987. World Historic Cities Conference, Kyoto.

1920	1328	60y. multicoloured	1·00	30

1329 *Family in Tree* (Takahiro Nagahama)

1987. International Year of Shelter for the Homeless. Multicoloured.

1921	40y. Type 1329	90	30
1922	60y. *Houses* (Yoko Sasaki)	1·30	25

1331 Kurashiki Papier-mache Dragon

1987. New Year's Greetings.

1923	1331	40y. multicoloured	70	25

1332 Sweet Flags
1333 Sweet Flags and Birds (Sendai)

1334 *Recollecting the Past*
1335 *Summer Grasses* (Hiraizumi)

1988. *Narrow Road to a Far Province* by Basho Matsuo (4th series).

1925	1332	60y. multicoloured	1·00	30
1926	1333	60y. multicoloured	1·00	30
1927	1334	60y. multicoloured	1·00	30
1928	1335	60y. multicoloured	1·00	30

1336 Kongo Samma-in Pagoda, Mt. Koya
1337 Ekoh-Doji, Kongobu Temple

1988. National Treasures (3rd series).

1929	1336	60y. multicoloured	1·00	40
1930	1337	110y. multicoloured	1·80	55

1338 Class ED 79 Locomotive *Sea of Japan* leaving Tunnel and Map

1988. Opening of Seikan (Aomori–Hakodate) Railway Tunnel.

1931	1338	60y. multicoloured	1·20	25

1339 Safflower
1340 Willow Trees (Obanazawa)

1341 Risshaku (or Mountain) Temple
1342 Pine Trees (Risshaku Temple)

1988. *Narrow Road to a Far Province* by Basho Matsuo (5th series).

1932	1339	60y. multicoloured	1·00	40
1933	1340	60y. multicoloured	1·00	40
1934	1341	60y. multicoloured	1·00	40
1935	1342	60y. multicoloured	1·00	40

1343/4 South Bisan Section from Kagawa Side

1345/6 Shimotsui Section from Okayama Side

1988. Opening of Seto Great Road and Rail Bridge.

1936	1343	60y. multicoloured	1·40	40
1937	1344	60y. multicoloured	1·40	40
1938	1345	60y. multicoloured	1·40	40
1939	1346	60y. multicoloured	1·40	40

Nos. 1936/7 and 1938/9 were printed together, *se-tenant,* each pair forming the composite design illustrated.

1347 *Long Undergarment* (Kotondo Torii)

1988. Philatelic Week. Multicoloured.

1940	60y. Type 1347	1·40	40
1941	60y. *Kimono Sash* (Kotondo Torii)	1·40	40

1349 Detail of Biwa Plectrum Guard

1988. "Silk Road" Exhibition, Nara.

1943	1349	60y. multicoloured	1·40	45

1350 Yashima, Small Cuckoo and Olive Tree

1988. National Afforestation Campaign.

1944	1350	60y. multicoloured	1·50	45

1351 River Mogami
1352 Irises in the Rain (Oishida)

1353 Moon Mountain
1354 Moon Mountain (Gassan)

1988. *Narrow Road to a Far Province* by Basho Matsuo (6th series).

1945	1351	60y. multicoloured	1·00	30
1946	1352	60y. multicoloured	1·00	30
1947	1353	60y. multicoloured	1·00	30
1948	1354	60y. multicoloured	1·00	30

1355 Morodo Shrine, Itsukushima

1356 Kozakura-gawa Braided Armour

1988. National Treasures (4th series).

1949	**1355**	60y. multicoloured	1·00	30
1950	**1356**	100y. multicoloured	1·70	40

1357 Mt. Sakura

1988. International Conference on Volcanoes, Kagoshima.

1951	**1357**	60y. multicoloured	1·00	30

1358 Cat with Letter

1988. Letter Writing Day. Multicoloured.

1952	40y. Type **1358**		90	30
1953	40y. Crab with letter (34×25 mm)		1·20	40
1954	60y. Fairy with letter		1·40	40
1955	60y. Girl and letter (25×32 mm)		90	30

Nos. 1952 and 1954 exist both perforated with ordinary gum and imperforate with self-adhesive gum.

1362 Ohana (Kinosuke puppet, Japan)

1988. International Puppetry Festival, Nagoya, Iida and Tokyo. Multicoloured.

1956	60y. Type **1362**		90	25
1957	60y. Stick puppet of girl (Czechoslovakia)		90	25
1958	60y. Shadow puppet (China)		90	25
1959	60y. Knight (Italy)		90	25

1366 Peonies

1988. Tenth Anniv of Japanese–Chinese Treaty of Peace and Friendship. Multicoloured.

1960	60y. Type **1366**		1·50	25
1961	60y. Ton-ton (giant panda)		1·50	25

1368 Mimosa Flowers

1369 Lagoon and Grass (Kisagata)

1370 Rough Sea

1371 Waves (Ichiburi)

1988. *Narrow Road to a Far Province* by Basho Matsuo (7th series).

1962	**1368**	60y. multicoloured	1·00	30
1963	**1369**	60y. multicoloured	1·00	30
1964	**1370**	60y. multicoloured	1·00	30
1965	**1371**	60y. multicoloured	1·00	30

1372 Nagoya and Egg

1988. 18th International Poultry Congress, Nagoya.

1966	**1372**	60y. multicoloured	1·00	30

1373 Globe and "Rehabilitation" in Braille

1988. 16th Rehabilitation International World Congress, Tokyo.

1967	**1373**	60y. multicoloured	90	25

1374 Nakatsuhime-no-mikoto, Yakushi Temple

1375 Murou Temple

1988. National Treasures (5th series).

1968	**1374**	60y. multicoloured	1·00	30
1969	**1375**	100y. multicoloured	1·70	40

1376 *Kimesaburo Iwai as Chiyo* (Kunimasa Utagawa)

1988. International Correspondence Week. Multicoloured.

1970	80y. Type **1376**		1·10	40
1971	120y. *Komazo Ichikawa III as Ganryu Sasaki* (Toyokuni Utagawa)		1·80	40

1378 Gymnast and Temple of the Golden Pavilion

1988. 43rd National Athletic Meeting, Kyoto.

1972	**1378**	40y. multicoloured	60	25

1379 Rice

1380 Ariso Sea (Kurikara Pass)

1381 Sun

1382 Autumn Wind and Sun (Kanazawa)

1988. *Narrow Road to a Far Province* by Basho Matsuo (8th series).

1973	**1379**	60y. multicoloured	1·00	30
1974	**1380**	60y. multicoloured	1·00	30
1975	**1381**	60y. multicoloured	1·00	30
1976	**1382**	60y. multicoloured	1·00	30

1383 Mexican State Arms

1988. Centenary of Japan–Mexico Friendship and Trade Treaty.

1977	**1383**	60y. multicoloured	1·00	40

1384 Snake (Shimotsuke clay bell)

1988. New Year's Greetings.

1978	**1384**	40y. multicoloured	1·00	25

1385 Figures on Globe

1988. 40th Anniv of Declaration of Human Rights.

1979	**1385**	60y. multicoloured	90	25

1386 Gold-plated Silver Pot with Hunting Design, Todai Temple

1387 Bronze Figure of Yakushi (Buddha of Medicine), Horyu Temple

1989. National Treasures (6th series).

1980	**1386**	60y. multicoloured	1·00	30
1981	**1387**	100y. multicoloured	1·70	40

1388 Nata Temple

1389 Pampas Grass (Natadera)

1390 Moonlight, Kehi Shrine

1391 Moon and Pine Trees (Tsuruga)

1989. *Narrow Road to a Far Province* by Basho Matsuo (9th series).

1982	**1388**	60y. multicoloured	1·00	30
1983	**1389**	60y. multicoloured	1·00	30
1984	**1390**	60y. multicoloured	1·00	30
1985	**1391**	60y. multicoloured	1·00	30

1989. Letter Writing Day (1988).

1986	40y. As Type **1354**		1·10	85
1987	60y. As No. 1954		1·40	1·10

1989. *Narrow Road to a Far Province* by Basho Matsuo (10th series). Ten sheets, each 112×72 mm.

MS1988 10 sheets. (a) Nos. 1874/5; (b) Nos. 1876/7; (c) Nos. 1896/7; (d) Nos. 1898/7; (e) Nos. 1906/7; (f) Nos. 1908/9; (g) Nos. 1925/6; (h) Nos. 1927/8; (i) Nos. 1932/3; (j) Nos. 1934/5   29·00   23·00

1392 Globe and Exhibition Site

1989. "Fukuoka '89" Asian–Pacific Exhibition, Fukuoka.

1989	**1392**	60y. multicoloured	1·00	25
1996	**1392**	62y. multicoloured	1·00	45

1393 *Russian Ladies sight-seeing at Port* (detail, Yoshitora) and Art Gallery

1989. "Space and Children" Exhibition, Yokohama.

1990	**1393**	60y. multicoloured	90	25
1997	**1393**	62y. multicoloured	90	45

1394 Bonsai Japanese White Pine

1989. World Bonsai Convention, Omiya.

1993	**1394**	62y. multicoloured	90	25

1395 Lute-player

1989. Philatelic Week. Details of *Awa Dance* (painting) by Tsunetomi Kitano. Multicoloured.

1994	62y. Type **1395**		90	25
1995	62y. Dancer		90	25

1397 *Dutch East Indiaman entering Harbour* (Nagasaki woodblock print)

1989. "Holland Festival '89".

1998	**1397**	62y. multicoloured	1·00	25

1398 Chikura Communication Tower and Cable Route

1989. Opening of Third Trans-Pacific Submarine Telephone Cable (Japan–Hawaii).

1999	**1398**	62y. multicoloured	1·40	30

1399 Beach in Autumn

1400 Bush Clover (Ironohama)

1401 Poker-drop Venuses

1402 Wedded Rocks, Futami Bay (Ohgaki)

1989. *Narrow Road to a Far Province* by Basho Matsuo (11th series).

2000	**1399**	62y. multicoloured	1·00	30
2001	**1400**	62y. multicoloured	1·00	30
2002	**1401**	62y. multicoloured	1·00	30
2003	**1402**	62y. multicoloured	1·00	30

1403 Mt. Tsurugi, Lime and Bay Trees

1989. National Afforestation Campaign.
2004 **1403** 62y. multicoloured 90 25

1404 Children in Bird and Flower "Balloon"

1989. International Garden and Greenery Exposition, Osaka (1990) (1st issue).
2005 **1404** 62y.+10y. mult 1·50 30
See also Nos. 2035/6.

1405 Saddle Fitting from Burial Mound, Konda | **1406** *Beetle Wings* Zushi, Horyu Temple

1989. National Treasures (7th series).
2006 **1405** 62y. multicoloured 90 25
2007 **1406** 100y. multicoloured 1·60 30

1407 *Crystal of Light and Auspicious Clouds*

1989. World Design Exposition, Nagoya. Multicoloured.
2008 41y. Type **1407** 60 25
2009 62y. "design" 90 25

1409 Bird as Vase holding Envelope

1989. Letter Writing Day. Multicoloured.
2010 41y. Type **1409** 70 45
2011 62y. Mother Rabbit reading letter 1·90 1·50

1989. *Narrow Road to a Far Province* by Basho Matsuo (12th series). Ten sheets, each 112×72 mm.
MS2012 10 sheets. (a) Nos. 1945/6; (b) Nos. 1947/8; (c) Nos. 1963/4; (d) Nos. 1965/6; (e) Nos. 1973/4; (f) Nos. 1975/6; (g) Nos. 1982/3; (h) Nos. 1984/5; (i) Nos. 2000/2001; (j) Nos. 2002/3 29·00 23·00

1989. Special Correspondence Stamps.
2013 **1098** 41y. multicoloured 60 30
2014 **1099** 41y. multicoloured 90 30
2015 **1099** 62y. multicoloured 1·00 30
2016 **1100** 72y. multicoloured 1·20 30

1411 Gold Stamp | **1412** Bronze Mirror

1989. National Treasures (8th series).
2017 **1411** 62y. multicoloured 90 25
2018 **1412** 100y. multicoloured 1·60 30

1413 Bouquet of Orchids and Stephanotis

1989. Sixth Interflora World Congress, Tokyo.
2019 **1413** 62y. multicoloured 90 60

1414 Wheelchair Race

1989. Far East and South Pacific Games for the Disabled, Kobe.
2020 **1414** 62y. multicoloured 90 60

1415 Narrators and Drummers

1989. "Europalia 89 Japan" Festival, Belgium. Details of "Okuni Theatre" (painting on folding screen). Multicoloured.
2021 62y. Type **1415** 90 25
2022 70y. Okuni (actress) 1·00 30

1417 New Emperor and Kaoru playing Go (*Yadorigi* scroll)

1989. International Correspondence Week. Details of Takayoshi Picture Scrolls illustrating *Tale of Genji* by Lady Murasaki. Multicoloured.
2023 80y. Type **1417** 1·00 30
2024 120y. Yugao's granddaughters playing Go ("Takekawa scroll") 1·80 45

1419 Ear of Rice and Paddy Field

1989. Seventh Asian/African Conference of Int Irrigation and Drainage Commission.
2025 **1419** 62y. multicoloured 90 25

1420 Shinzan (first winner of all five major races)

1989. 100th Tenno Sho Horse Race.
2026 **1420** 62y. multicoloured 1·00 30

1421 Hot-air Balloons

1989. Ninth Hot Air Balloon World Championship, Saga City.
2027 **1421** 62y. multicoloured 1·00 25

1422 Conductor

1989. 50th Anniv of Japanese Copyright Control Act.
2028 **1422** 62y. multicoloured 90 25

1423 Yawata Wooden Horse

1989. New Year's Greetings.
2029 **1423** 41y. multicoloured 1·00 25

1424 Hamamatsu Papier-mache Horse

1989. New Year Lottery Stamp.
2030 **1424** 62y. multicoloured 1·00 60
Each stamp carries a lottery number.

1425 Type 10000

1990. Electric Railway Locomotives (1st series).
2031 **1425** 62y. purple, lilac & grn 1·10 25
2032 - 62y. multicoloured 1·10 25
DESIGN: No. 2032, Type EF 58 No. 38, 1946.
See also Nos. 2033/4, 2039/40, 2089/90 and 2101/2.

1990. Electric Railway Locomotives (2nd series). As T **1425**. Multicoloured.
2033 62y. Type ED 40 No. 12, 1919 1·10 25
2034 62y. Type EH 10 No. 8, 1954 1·10 25

1429 Fairies on Flower

1990. "Expo 90" International Garden and Greenery Exposition, Osaka. Multicoloured.
2035 41y.+4y. Type **1429** 70 55
2036 62y. Bicycle under tree 1·00 30

1431 *Women gazing at the Stars* (Chou Ohta)

1990. Philatelic Week.
2037 **1431** 62y. multicoloured 80 30
MS2038 60×77 mm. No. 2037 2·00 1·60

1990. Electric Railway Locomotives (3rd series). As T **1425**. Multicoloured.
2039 62y. Type EF 53, 1932 1·10 25
2040 62y. Type ED 70, 1957 1·10 25

1434 Sweet Briar (Hokkaido) | **1435** Apple Blossom (Aomori) | **1436** "Paulownia tomentosa" (Iwate)

1437 Japanese Bush Clover (Miyagi) | **1438** Butterbur Flower (Akita) | **1439** Safflower (Yamagata)

1440 Rhododendron (Fukushima) | **1441** Rose (Ibaraki) | **1442** Yashio Azalea (Tochigi)

1443 Japanese Azalea (Gunma) | **1444** Primrose (Saitama) | **1445** Rape (Chiba)

1446 Cherry Blossom (Yamanashi) | **1447** Gold-banded Lily (Kanagawa) | **1448** Cherry Blossom (Tokyo)

1449 Gentian (Nagano) | **1450** Tulip (Niigata) | **1451** Tulip (Toyama)

1452 Fritillaria (Ishikawa) | **1453** Narcissi (Fukui) | **1454** Chinese Milk Vetch (Gifu)

1455 Azalea (Shizuoka) | **1456** Rabbit-ear Iris (Aichi) | **1457** Iris (Mie)

1458 Rhododendron (Shiga) | **1459** Weeping Cherry Blossom (Kyoto) | **1460** Japanese Apricot and Primrose (Osaka)

1461 Marguerites (Hyogo) | **1462** Double Cherry Blossom (Nara) | **1463** Japanese Apricot (Wakayama)

1464 Pear Blossom (Tottori) | **1465** Peony (Shimane) | **1466** Peach Blossom (Okayama)

1467 Japanese Maple (Hiroshima) | **1468** Summer Orange Blossom (Yamaguchi) | **1469** Sudachi Orange Blossom (Tokushima)

1470 Olive Blossom (Kagawa)　**1471** Mandarin Orange Blossom (Ehime)　**1472** "Myrica rubra" (Kochi)

1473 Japanese Apricot (Fukuoka)　**1474** Laurel (Saga)　**1475** Unzen Azalea (Nagasaki)

1476 Gentian (Kumamoto)　**1477** Japanese Apricot (Oita)　**1478** Crinum (Miyazaki)

1479 Rhododendron (Kagoshima)　**1480** Coral Tree (Okinawa)

1990. Prefecture Flowers.

2041	**1434**	62y. multicoloured	2·50	1·90
2042	**1435**	62y. multicoloured	80	60
2043	**1436**	62y. multicoloured	80	60
2044	**1437**	62y. multicoloured	80	60
2045	**1438**	62y. multicoloured	80	60
2046	**1439**	62y. multicoloured	80	60
2047	**1440**	62y. multicoloured	80	60
2048	**1441**	62y. multicoloured	80	60
2049	**1442**	62y. multicoloured	80	60
2050	**1443**	62y. multicoloured	80	60
2051	**1444**	62y. multicoloured	80	60
2052	**1445**	62y. multicoloured	80	60
2053	**1446**	62y. multicoloured	80	60
2054	**1447**	62y. multicoloured	80	60
2055	**1448**	62y. multicoloured	80	60
2056	**1449**	62y. multicoloured	2·50	1·90
2057	**1450**	62y. multicoloured	80	60
2058	**1451**	62y. multicoloured	80	60
2059	**1452**	62y. multicoloured	80	60
2060	**1453**	62y. multicoloured	80	60
2061	**1454**	62y. multicoloured	1·00	80
2062	**1455**	62y. multicoloured	1·30	1·00
2063	**1456**	62y. multicoloured	80	60
2064	**1457**	62y. multicoloured	80	60
2065	**1458**	62y. multicoloured	2·00	1·60
2066	**1459**	62y. multicoloured	2·00	1·60
2067	**1460**	62y. multicoloured	80	60
2068	**1461**	62y. multicoloured	80	60
2069	**1462**	62y. multicoloured	1·30	1·00
2070	**1463**	62y. multicoloured	1·00	80
2071	**1464**	62y. multicoloured	80	60
2072	**1465**	62y. multicoloured	80	60
2073	**1466**	62y. multicoloured	80	60
2074	**1467**	62y. multicoloured	80	60
2075	**1468**	62y. multicoloured	80	60
2076	**1469**	62y. multicoloured	1·00	80
2077	**1470**	62y. multicoloured	3·25	2·50
2078	**1471**	62y. multicoloured	1·60	1·20
2079	**1472**	62y. multicoloured	1·30	1·00
2080	**1473**	62y. multicoloured	80	60
2081	**1474**	62y. multicoloured	80	60
2082	**1475**	62y. multicoloured	80	60
2083	**1476**	62y. multicoloured	80	60
2084	**1477**	62y. multicoloured	80	60
2085	**1478**	62y. multicoloured	80	60
2086	**1479**	62y. multicoloured	80	60
2087	**1480**	62y. multicoloured	80	60

1481 Mt. Unzen and Unzen Azalea

1990. National Afforestation Campaign.

2088	**1481**	62y. multicoloured	80	30

1990. Electric Railway Locomotives (4th series). As T **1425**. Multicoloured.

2089		62y. Type EF 55, 1936	1·10	25
2090		62y. Type ED 61 No. 13, 1958	1·10	25

1484 Fritillary on Thistle

1990. Winning Entries in Postage Stamp Design Contest. Multicoloured.

2091		62y. Type **1484**	1·40	25
2092		70y. "Communication"	1·60	30

1486 17th-century Ottoman Tile

1990. Century of Japan–Turkey Friendship.

2093	**1486**	62y. multicoloured	80	30

1487/91 Folding Screen (image scaled to 45% of original size)

1492 Ponies (Kayo Yamaguchi)

1990. The Horse in Culture (1st series).

2094	**1487**	62y. multicoloured	1·50	25
2095	**1488**	62y. multicoloured	1·50	25
2096	**1489**	62y. multicoloured	1·50	25
2097	**1490**	62y. multicoloured	1·50	25
2098	**1491**	62y. multicoloured	1·50	25
2099	**1492**	62y. multicoloured	1·50	25

Nos. 2094/8 were printed together, *se-tenant*, forming a composite design showing a 17th-century folding screen painting.

See also Nos. 2106/8, 2113/14, 2132/4 and 2135/6.

1493 Emblem and Landscape

1990. 38th International Youth Hostel Federation Congress. Muikamachi and Kashiwazaki.

2100	**1493**	62y. multicoloured	90	30

1990. Electric Railway Locomotives (5th series). As T **1425**. Multicoloured.

2101		62y. Type ED 57, 1941	1·10	25
2102		62y. Type EF 30 Nos. 3 and 6, 1961	1·10	25

1496 Bluebird and Heart　**1497** Fairy on Horse

1990. Letter Writing Day.

2103	**1496**	41y. multicoloured	70	30
2104	**1497**	62y. multicoloured	1·00	25
MS2105	72×93 mm. No. 2104		1·50	1·20

For similar design to No. 2104, see No. 2157.

1500 A Horse (Suisho Nishiyama)

1990. The Horse in Culture (2nd series). Multicoloured.

2106		62y. 16th-century lacquered saddle	1·50	25
2107		62y. 16th-century lacquered stirrups	1·50	25
2108		62y. Type **1500**	1·50	25

1501 Origami Polyhedron

1990. Int Mathematicians Congress, Kyoto.

2109	**1501**	62y. multicoloured	80	30

1502 Track Race

1990. World Cycling Championships. Maebashi and Tochigi Prefecture.

2110	**1502**	62y. multicoloured	80	30

1503 Ogai Mori (translator) and Passage from Goethe's *Faust*

1990. Eighth International Association for Germanic Studies Congress, Tokyo.

2111	**1503**	62y. blue, yellow & brn	80	30

1504 "Ji" (character) and Rosetta Stone

1990. International Literacy Year.

2112	**1504**	62y. multicoloured	80	30

1505 Kurabeuma Race (detail of Kimono)　**1506** Kettei (Shodo Sasaki)

1990. The Horse in Culture (3rd series).

2113	**1505**	62y. multicoloured	80	30
2114	**1506**	62y. multicoloured	80	30

1507 Peaceful Landscape

1990. International Decade for Natural Disaster Reduction Conference, Yokohama.

2115	**1507**	62y. multicoloured	80	30

1508 Animals at Dance

1990. International Correspondence Week. Details from *Choju-jinbutsu-giga* Picture Scroll. Multicoloured.

2116		80y. Type **1508**	1·20	40
2117		120y. Dancing frogs	1·80	40

1510 Midwife, Mother and Baby

1990. 22nd International Confederation of Midwives Congress, Kobe City.

2118	**1510**	62y. multicoloured	80	40

1511 Letter Bearer (detail, Harunobu Suiendo)

1990. "Phila Nippon '91" International Stamp Exhibition, Tokyo (1st issue).

2119	**1511**	100y. multicoloured	1·40	45
MS2120	94×90 mm. No. 2119		2·00	1·60

See also Nos. 2170/MS2171.

1512 Hand reading Braille

1990. Centenary of Japanese Braille.

2121	**1512**	62y. multicoloured	80	30

1513 "Justice" (Supreme Court bronze statue, Katsuzo Entsuba)

1990. Centenary of Modern Judiciary System.

2122	**1513**	62y. multicoloured	80	30

1514 Chinese Phoenix (detail from dais of Emperor's enthronement seat)

1990. Enthronement of Emperor. Multicoloured.

2123		62y. Type **1514**	1·00	30
2124		62y. Pattern from robe of Manzai Raku dancers	1·00	30
MS2125	144×93 mm. Nos. 2123/4		3·00	2·30

1516 Stained Glass Window (Diet building)

1990. Centenary of Diet.

2126	**1516**	62y. multicoloured	80	30

1517 Sheep (Nogomi ceramic bell)

1990. New Year's Greetings.

2127	**1517**	41y. multicoloured	1·00	25

1519
Tsuneishi-Hariko
Papier-mache
Ram

1990. New Year Lottery Stamps. Multicoloured.
2128		41y. Sheep (Tosa ceramic bell)	70	55
2129		62y. Type **1519**	1·00	80

Each stamp carries a lottery number.

1520 Dr. Nishina
and Radio
Isotope

1990. Birth Centenary of Dr. Yoshio Nishina (physicist) and 50th Anniv of First Japanese Cyclotron (radio isotope generator).
2130	**1520**	62y. multicoloured	80	30

1521 "Lady using
Telephone"
(Senseki
Nakamura)

1990. Centenary of Telephone Service in Japan.
2131	**1521**	62y. multicoloured	80	30

1522/3 Horse-drawn Post Carriages (details of scroll painting by Beisen Kubota)

1991. The Horse in Culture (4th series).
2132	**1522**	62y. multicoloured	1·00	30
2133	**1523**	62y. multicoloured	1·00	30
2134	**1524**	62y. multicoloured	1·00	30

Nos. 2132/3 were issued together, se-tenant, forming the composite design illustrated.

1525 *Spring Warmth* (Kogetsu Saigo)   **1526** *Senju in Musashi Province* (from *36 Views of Mt. Fuji* by Hokusai Katsushika)

1991. The Horse in Culture (5th series).
2135	**1525**	62y. multicoloured	80	30
2136	**1526**	62y. multicoloured	80	30

1527 Figure
Skating

1991. Winter Universiade, Sapporo and Furano. Multicoloured.
2137		41y. Type **1527**	80	40

2138		62y. Short-track speed skating (horiz)	90	40

1529 Bouquet

1991. New Postal Life Insurance System.
2139	**1529**	62y. multicoloured	80	60

1530 *Glory of the Earth* (Komei Bekki)

1991. "Ceramic World Shigaraki '91" Exn.
2140	**1530**	62y. multicoloured	80	30

1531 *Beauty looking Back* (Moronobu Hishikawa)

1991. Philatelic Week. 120th Anniv of First Japanese Stamps.
2141		62y. Type **1531**	90	30
2142		62y. *The Prelude* (Shuho Yamakawa)	90	30
MS2143	93×77 mm. Nos. 2141/2		2·50	2·00

1533 Weeping
Cherry Blossom
and Phoenix
Hall, Byodoin
Temple

1991. National Afforestation Campaign.
2144	**1533**	41y. multicoloured	60	30

1534 Early
Leveller and
Standard Datum
Repository, Tokyo

1991. Centenary of Standard Datum of Levelling.
2145	**1534**	62y. multicoloured	80	30

1535 Flowers

1991. Winning Entries in Postage Stamp Design Contest.
2146	**1535**	41y. multicoloured	60	30
2147	-	62y. multicoloured	80	30
2148	-	70y. brown, blue & blk	1·10	30
2149	-	100y. multicoloured	1·60	40

DESIGNS—HORIZ: 62y. Couple in traditional dress; 100y. Butterfly. VERT: 70y. "World Peace".

1539 Japanese Snipe (*Gallinago hardwickii*)

1991. Water Birds (1st series). Multicoloured.
2150	**1539**	62y. Type **1539**	1·50	80
2151		62y. Brown booby (*Sula leucogaster*)	1·50	80

See also Nos. 2162/3, 2179/80, 2184/5, 2198/9, 2241/2, 2247/8 and 2251/2.

1541 Kikugoro Onoe VI in Title Role of *Spirit of the Lion*   **1542** Utaemon Nakamura VI as Princess Yaegaki in *24 Examples of Filial Piety*

1991. Kabuki Theatre (1st series).
2152	**1541**	62y. green, gold & black	1·00	30
2153	**1542**	100y. multicoloured	1·70	40

See also Nos. 2164/5, 2172/3, 2181/2, 2186/7 and 2190/1.

1543 "Solidarity"
in Sign Language
and Congress
Emblem

1991. 11th World Federation of the Deaf International Congress, Tokyo.
2154	**1543**	62y.+10y. mult	1·00	30

The premium was assigned to programmes for helping the deaf.

1544 Crystal Structure

1991. International Conf on Materials and Mechanism of Superconductivity, Kanazawa.
2155	**1544**	62y. multicoloured	80	30

1545 Girl sitting on Morning Glory   **1546** Fairy on Horse

1991. Letter Writing Day.
2156	**1545**	41y. multicoloured	70	30
2157	**1546**	62y. multicoloured	1·00	30
MS2158	72×93 mm. No. 2157		1·10	85

For design similar to No. 2157 but with central motif drawn larger, see No. 2104.

1547 High
Jumping

1991. Third World Athletics Championships, Tokyo. Multicoloured.
2159		41y. Type **1547**	60	30
2160		62y. Putting the shot	80	30

1549 Map and
Computer Image of
Hokkaido

1991. International Symposium on Environmental Change and Geographic Information Systems, Asahikawa, Hokkaido.
2161	**1549**	62y. multicoloured	80	30

1991. Water Birds (2nd series). As T **1539**. Multicoloured.
2162		62y. Japanese gull (*Larus crassirostris*)	1·50	80
2163		62y. Little grebe (*Podiceps ruficollis*)	1·50	80

1552 Koshiro Matsumoto VII as Benkei in *The Subscription List*   **1553** Danjuro Ichikawa XI as Danjo in *Tweezers*

1991. Kabuki Theatre (2nd series).
2164	**1552**	62y. black, grey & gold	1·00	30
2165	**1553**	100y. multicoloured	1·70	40

1554 Nobles watching
burning Oten Gate

1991. International Correspondence Week. Details from *Ban Dainagon Picture Scrolls* by Mitsunaga Tokiwa. Multicoloured.
2166		80y. Type **1554**	1·00	30
2167		120y. Arrest of Yoshio Tomo (arsonist)	1·60	45

1556 *Clear Day
with Southern
Breeze* (from *36
Views of Mt. Fuji* by
Hokusai
Katsushika) and
Seismographic
Wave

1991. Earthquake and Natural Disaster Countermeasures Conference. Tokyo.
2168	**1556**	62y. multicoloured	85	30

1557 Tea Utensils
and Flower

1991. 800th Anniv of Introduction of Green Tea into Japan.
2169	**1557**	62y. multicoloured	85	30

1558 *Saucy Girl*
(from *A Selection
of Beautiful
Women* by
Kunisada
Utagawa)

1991. "Phila Nippon '91" International Stamp Exhibition, Tokyo (2nd issue).
2170	**1558**	62y. multicoloured	95	30
MS2171	93×77 mm. No. 2170 ×2		2·00	2·00

1559 Baigyoku Nakamura III as the Ogiya Courtesan Yugiri in *Yoshida-ya*   **1560** Ganjiro Nakamura III as Jihei Kamiya in *Shinju-Ten no Amijima*

1991. Kabuki Theatre (3rd series). Works by Chikamatsu Monzaemon.
2172	**1559**	62y. black, pur & gold	1·00	30
2173	**1560**	100y. multicoloured	1·80	40

1561 Boy building Toy Town

1991. 30th Anniv of Administrative Councillors System.

2174	**1561**	62y. multicoloured	85	25

1562 Ishikawa Papier-mache Monkey

1991. New Year's Greetings. Multicoloured.

2175	41y. Type **1562**		65	30
2176	62y. Obata monkey		85	30

1565 Obata Monkey

1991. New Year Lottery Stamps. Multicoloured.

2177	41y.+3y. Ishikawa papier-mache monkey	85	60
2178	62y.+3y. Type **1565**	1·20	85

Each stamp carries a lottery number.

1992. Water Birds (3rd series). As T **1539**. Multicoloured.

2179	62y. Tufted puffin (*Lunda cirrhata*)	1·60	70
2180	62y. Hooded cranes (*Grus monacha*)	1·60	70

1568 Kichiemon Nakamura I as Jiro Naozane Kumagai in *Chronicle of Two Boys in Battle of Ichinotani* by Munesuke Namiki

1569 Nizaemon Kataoka XIII as Old Man in *Kotobuki Shiki Sambaso*

1992. Kabuki Theatre (4th series).

2181	**1568**	62y. multicoloured	1·00	30
2182	**1569**	100y. multicoloured	1·80	40

1570 Orchid and Chimpanzees

1992. Eighth Conference of Parties to Convention on International Trade in Endangered Species, Kyoto City.

2183	**1570**	62y. multicoloured	1·30	40

1992. Water Birds (4th series). As T **1539**. Multicoloured.

2184	62y. Whooper swan (*Cygnus cygnus*)	1·60	35
2185	62y. Painted-snipe (*Rostratula benghalensis*)	1·50	35

1573 Enjaku Jitsukawa II as Ishikawa-Geomon in *Two-Storey Gate—Pawlonia* by Gohei Namiki

1574 Hakuo Matsumoto I as Oishi-Kuranosuke in *Loyal Retainers in Genroku* by Seika Mayama

1992. Kabuki Theatre (5th series).

2186	**1573**	62y. multicoloured	1·00	35
2187	**1574**	100y. multicoloured	1·80	40

1575 *Flowers on Chair* (Hoshun Yamaguchi)

1992. Philatelic Week.

2188	**1575**	62y. multicoloured	85	35

1576 Shuri Castle

1992. 20th Anniv of Return of Okinawa (Ryukyu Islands).

2189	**1576**	62y. multicoloured	1·30	25

1577 Baiko Onoe VII as the Wisteria Maiden

1578 Shoroku Onoe II as Goro Soga and Kanzaburo Nakamura XVII as Juro Soga in *Kotobuki-Soga-taimen*

1992. Kabuki Theatre (6th series).

2190	**1577**	62y. multicoloured	1·00	35
2191	**1578**	100y. multicoloured	1·80	40

1579 "ADEOS" Observation Satellite

1992. International Space Year. Multicoloured.

2192	62y. Type **1579**	85	25
2193	62y. "BS-3" broadcasting satellite and space station	85	25

Nos. 2192/3 were printed together, *se-tenant*, forming a composite design.

1581 Bird delivering Letter to Flower

1992. Letter Writing Day. Multicoloured.

2194	41y. Type **1581**	75	25
2195	62y. Bird delivering letter to dog	1·00	60
MS2196	76×93 mm. No. 2195	3·25	2·75

1583 Ammonite, Map and Stratigraphic Plan

1992. 29th Int Geological Congress, Kyoto.

2197	**1583**	62y. multicoloured	85	40

1992. Water Birds (5th series). As T **1539**. Multicoloured.

2198	62y. White-faced shearwater (*Calonectris leucomelas*)	1·60	60
2199	62y. Ruddy kingfisher ("Halcyon coromanda")	1·60	60

1586 Canoeing

1992. 47th National Athletic Meeting, Yamagata.

2200	**1586**	41y. multicoloured	75	25

1587 Japanese Jar (Ninsei Nonomura)

1588 Chinese Vase (Tang dynasty)

1992. 20th Anniv of Restoration of Diplomatic Relations with China.

2201	**1587**	62y. multicoloured	85	35
2202	**1588**	62y. multicoloured	85	35

1589 Nobles arriving at Taiken Gate

1590 Fujiwarano Nobuyori giving Audience

1992. International Correspondence Week. Details from *Tale of Heiji* Shinzei Picture Scroll.

2203	**1589** 80y. multicoloured	1·20	35
2204	**1590** 120y. multicoloured	1·90	35

1591 "Friends" (Tomoko Komoto)

1992. Third Stamp Design Competition Winners. Multicoloured.

2205	62y. Type **1591**	85	35
2206	70y. "Gaiety on Christmas Night" (Brat Anca)	95	35

1593 "Kyo" Ideograph, Mt. Fuji, Sun and Waves

1992. 30th International Co-operative Alliance Congress, Tokyo.

2207	**1593**	62y. multicoloured	85	35

1594 Takakazu Seki (mathematician, 350th birth)

1595 Akiko Yosano (poet, 50th death)

1992. Anniversaries.

2208	**1594**	62y. multicoloured	1·10	35
2209	**1595**	62y. multicoloured	1·10	35

1596 Certified Public Tax Accountants' Assn Emblem

1992. 50th Anniv of Tax Accountants Law.

2210	**1596**	62y. multicoloured	85	35

1597 Papier-mache and Clay Cock

1992. New Year's Greetings. Multicoloured.

2211	41y. Type **1597**	75	35
2212	62y. Tsuyazaki clay cock on drum	1·10	35

1600 Tsuyazaki Clay Cock on Drum

1992. New Year Lottery Stamps. Multicoloured.

2213	41y.+3y. Papier-mache and clay cock	85	70
2214	62y.+3y. Type **1600**	1·20	95

Each stamp carries a lottery number.

1601 *Orthetrum albistylum* (dragonfly)

1601a *Oxycetonia jucunda* (beetle)

1602 Mikado Swallowtail

1603 Ladybirds

1603a Honey Bee

1603b *Lycaena phleas* (copper butterfly)

1604 Mandarin

1605 Japanese White-Eye

1606 Eastern Turtle Dove

1606a Great Tit

1607 Varied Tit

1608 Greater Pied Kingfisher

1609 Pacific Black Duck

1609a Little Ringed Plover

1609b Bull-headed Shrike

1610 Northern Bullfinch

1610a Masked Hawfinch

1610b Jay

1611 Orchids

1612 Wild Pink

1613 Adder's Tongue Lily

1614 Day-flowers

1615 Iris

1616 Violets

1617 Praying Mantis, Chrysanthemums and Hibiscus (after Hatsu Sakai)

1618 "Pine and Hawk" (Sesson Shukei)

1992. Fauna and Flora

2215	**1601**	9y. yellow, black & bl	20	20
2215a	**1601a**	10y. multicoloured	20	20
2216	**1602**	15y. brown, light green and green	30	25
2217	**1603**	18y. green, grey and red	65	55
2217a	**1603a**	20y. multicoloured	45	45
2217b	**1603b**	30y. multicoloured	75	35
2218	**1604**	41y. orge, dp bl & bl	95	25
2219	**1605**	50y. yellow, bl & blk	1·60	55
2220	**1606**	62y. orge, dp bl & bl	1·10	45
2220a	**1606a**	70y. multicoloured	1·20	45
2221	**1607**	72y. orange, bl & grn	2·40	95
2222	**1608**	80y. blue, stone and green	2·50	55
2223	**1609**	90y. brown, yell & bl	3·00	60
2223a	**1609a**	110y. multicoloured	2·20	70
2223b	**1609b**	120y. multicoloured	2·75	95
2224	**1610**	130y. multicoloured	2·40	45
2224a	**1610a**	140y. multicoloured	3·25	1·10
2224b	**1610b**	160y. multicoloured	3·75	1·10
2225	**1611**	190y. multicoloured	3·50	70
2226	**1612**	270y. multicoloured	5·50	90
2227	**1613**	350y. mauve, lilac and green	7·00	1·20
2228	**1614**	390y. multicoloured	7·50	80
2229	**1615**	420y. violet, light green and green	8·75	1·40
2230	**1616**	430y. multicoloured	8·00	1·60
2231	**1617**	700y. multicoloured	13·00	5·25
2232	**1618**	1000y. multicoloured	15·00	5·25

The 41, 50, 62 and 80y. also exist imperforate with self-adhesive gum.

1993. Water Birds (6th series). As T **1539**. Multicoloured.

2241	62y. River kingfisher (*Alcedo atthis*)	1·80	45
2242	62y. Cattle egret (*Bubulcus ibis*)	1·80	45

1623 Super Giant Slalom

1993. World Alpine Skiing Championships, Shizukuishi (nr. Morioka). Multicoloured.

2243	41y. Type **1623**	75	35
2244	62y. Downhill	1·10	35

1625 Poppies (after Hochu Nakamura)

1993. Seasonal Flowers (1st series). Multicoloured.

2245	41y. Type **1625**	1·10	45
2246	62y. Cherry Blossoms (after Haitsu Sakai) (25×35 mm)	1·70	45

See also Nos. 2258/9, 2269/70 and 2287/8.

1993. Water Birds (7th series). As T **1539**. Multicoloured.

2247	62y. White-fronted geese (*Anser albifrons*)	1·80	45
2248	62y. Japanese white-naped cranes (*Grus vipio*)	1·80	45

No. 2247 is wrongly inscribed "Ansner".

1629 "In the Studio" (Nanpu Katayama)

1993. Philatelic Week.

2249	**1629** 62y. multicoloured	95	35

1630 Coral Trees and Reef, Minnajima Island

1993. National Afforestation Campaign.

2250	**1630** 41y. multicoloured	1·20	45

1993. Water Birds (8th series). As T **1539**. Multicoloured.

2251	62y. Baikal teal (*Anas formosa*)	1·30	1·10
2252	62y. White-tailed sea eagle (*Haliaeetus albicilla*)	1·30	1·10

1635 "Mandarin Duck in Nest" and "Gardenia in Nest"

1993. Wedding of Crown Prince Naruhito and Masako Owada. Multicoloured.

2253	62y. "Mandarin Duck in Nest" (pattern of groom's jacket) (vert)	1·10	45
2254	62y. "Gardenia in Nest" (pattern of bride's robe) (vert)	1·10	45
2255	70y. Type **1635**	1·20	45

1636 Manchurian Crane with Chicks

1993. Fifth Meeting of Ramsar Convention for the Preservation of Wetlands, Kushiro (Hokkaido).

2256	62y. Type **1636**	1·10	45
2257	62y. Head of Manchurian crane	1·10	45

1993. Seasonal Flowers (2nd series) As T **1615**. Multicoloured.

2258	41y. Lily (after Kiitsu Suzuki)	75	25
2259	62y. Thistle (after Shiko Watanabe) (25×35 mm)	1·10	45

1640 Stylized Ideographs for "Commercial Registration"

1641 Puppy reading Letter under Tree

1993. Centenary of Commercial Registration System.

2260	**1640** 62y. multicoloured	1·10	45

1993. Letter Writing Day. Multicoloured.

2261	41y. Type **1641**	95	35
2262	62y. Man pointing at flying letter (23×27 mm)	1·30	45
MS2263	72×93 mm. No. 2262	1·40	1·10

1643 Heart, Clouds and Flowers

1993. World Federation for Mental Health Congress, Chiba City.

2264	**1643** 62y. multicoloured	1·10	45

1644 *Glaucidium palmatum*

1993. 15th International Botanical Congress, Yokohama. Multicoloured.

2265	62y. Type **1644**	1·10	45
2266	62y. *Sciadopitys verticillata*	1·10	45

1646 Swimming

1993. 48th National Athletic Meeting, Kagawa Prefecture. Multicoloured.

2267	41y. Type **1646**	85	35
2268	41y. Karate	85	35

1993. Seasonal Flowers (3rd series). As T **1615**. Multicoloured.

2269	41y. *Chinese Bell-flowers* (Korin Ogata)	75	25
2270	62y. Chrysanthemums (detail of *Cranes and Plants in Spring and Autumn*, Kiitsu Suzuki) (25×35 mm)	1·20	45

1650 *Arrival of Portuguese* (folding screen)

1993. 450th Anniv of First Portuguese Visit to Japan. Multicoloured.

2271	62y. Type **1650**	1·10	45
2272	62y. Jesuit mother-of-pearl inlaid host box	1·10	45

1652 Ki no Tsurayuki (Agetatami Scrolls)

1993. International Correspondence Week. Picture Scrolls of the *Thirty-six Immortal Poets*.

2273	80y. Type **1652**	1·40	55
2274	120y. Kodai no Kimi (Satake Scrolls)	2·10	80

1654 Sprinter

1993. Tenth International Veterans' Athletic Championships, Miyazaki.

2275	**1654** 62y. multicoloured	1·10	45

1655 Prince Naruhito and Princess Masako

1993. Wedding of Crown Prince Naruhito and Masako Owada (2nd issue). Sheet 90×93 mm.

MS2276	**1655** 62y. multicoloured	2·40	1·90

1656 Toson Shimazaki (writer, 50th death)

1993. Anniversaries. Multicoloured.

2277	62y. Type **1656**	1·10	45
2278	62y. Umetaro Suzuki (scientist, 50th death)	1·10	45
2279	62y. Kazan Watanabe (after Chinzan Tsubaki) (artist, birth bicentenary)	1·10	45

1659 Shibahara Clay Dog

1993. New Year's Greetings. Multicoloured.

2280	41y. Type **1659**	95	35
2281	62y. Kosen clay tosa dog	1·10	45

1662 Kosen Clay Tosa Dog

1993. New Year Lottery Stamps. Multicoloured.

2282	41y. Shibahara clay dog	1·10	90
2283	62y. Type **1662**	1·20	95

1663 Rice Flowers

1993. Centenary of Agricultural Research Centre, Nishigahara.

2284	**1663** 62y. multicoloured	1·10	45

1664 Man and Bird (Soichiro Asaba)

1993. 45th Anniv of Declaration of Human Rights. Stamp design contest winning entries.

2285	62y. Type **1664**	1·10	45
2286	70y. Symbols (Armand Clotagatilde)	1·20	45

1994. Seasonal Flowers (4th series). As T **1625**. Multicoloured.

2287	50y. *Plum Blossom* (after Korin Ogata)	85	35
2288	80y. *Winter Camellia* (after Hoitsu Sakai) (26×35 mm)	1·40	60

1994. Special Correspondence Stamps. As Nos. 1677/9 but values changed.

2289	**1098**	50y. multicoloured	1·50	45
2290	**1099**	50y. multicoloured	85	35
2291	**1099**	80y. multicoloured	1·40	60
2292	**1100**	90y. multicoloured	1·60	60

1668 Ladies' Figure Skating

1994. World Figure Skating Championships, Chiba City. Multicoloured.

2293	**1668**	50y. Type **1668**	85	35
2294		50y. Ice dancing	85	35
2295		80y. Men's figure skating	1·40	60
2296		80y. Pairs figure skating	1·40	60

1672 *Irises* (Heihachiro Fukuda)

1994. Philatelic Week.

2297	**1672**	80y. multicoloured	2·40	60

1673 "Love" (Chieko Kitajima)

1994. International Year of the Family. Winning Entries in Stamp Design Contest. Multicoloured.

2298	**1673**	50y. Type **1673**	1·20	35
2299		50y. "Happiness Flower" (Shigenobu Nagaishi)	1·20	35
2300		80y. "Family flowering at Home" (Junichi Mineta)	3·75	1·30
2301		80y. "Family in Flight" (Soichiro Asaba)	1·70	60

1677 White Stork, Marguerites and Camphor Tree

1994. National Afforestation Campaign.

2302	**1677**	50y. multicoloured	1·50	60

1678 Houses by the Waterside

1994. International Conference on Reduction of Natural Disasters, Yokohama.

2303	**1678**	80y. multicoloured	1·40	60

1679 Pylon and Monju Building

1994. Achievement of Initial Criticality (self-sustaining reaction) in Monju Nuclear Fast Breeder Reactor, Tsuruga.

2304	**1679**	80y. multicoloured	2·40	60

1680 Wildlife

1994. Environment Day.

2305	**1680**	80y. multicoloured	2·40	60

1681 Envelope "Ship" and Man

1994. Letter Writing Day. Multicoloured.

2306	**1681**	50y. Type **1681**	1·10	35
2307		80y. Giraffe carrying envelope	1·40	60
MS2308	72×93 mm. No. 2307		1·50	1·20

1683 Emblem in Eye

1994. Tenth Int AIDS Conference, Yokohama.

2309	**1683**	80y. multicoloured	1·40	60

1684 Baron Maeshima (Postal Minister) and 1871 48 mon "Dragon" Stamp

1994. History of Stamps (1st series). First Japanese Issue. Multicoloured, frame colour of "Dragon" stamp given.

2310	**1684**	80y. brown	1·40	60
2311	-	80y. blue	1·40	60
2312	-	80y. red	1·40	60
2313	-	80y. green	1·40	60

DESIGNS: No. 2311, 100mon "Dragon" stamp; 2312, 200mon "Dragon" stamp; 2313, 500mon "Dragon" stamp. The central portion of the stamp portrayed varies according to value.

See also Nos. 2339/42, 2345/6, 2363/4, 2382/5 and 2416/19.

1685/6 Airport and Boeing 747 bearing Airport Code

1994. Opening of Kansai International Airport, Osaka. Multicoloured.

2314	**1685**	80y. Type **1685**	1·40	60
2315	**1686**	80y. Type **1686**	1·40	60
2316		80y. Airplane approaching Airport	1·40	60

Nos. 2314/15 form the composite design shown.

1688 Dish Aerial and Satellite

1994. I.T.U. Plenipotentiary Conference, Kyoto.

2317	**1688**	80y. multicoloured	1·40	55

1689 Kickball

1994. 12th Asian Games, Hiroshima. Multicoloured.

2318	**1689**	50y. Type **1689**	85	35
2319		80y. Steeplechase	1·40	55
2320		80y. Synchronized swimming	1·40	55

1692 Sugoroku

1994. International Correspondence Week. Details of *House of Entertainment* (folding screen). Multicoloured.

2321	**1692**	90y. Type **1692**	1·60	60
2322		110y. Shogi	1·90	80
2323		130y. Go	2·20	90

1695 Handball

1994. 49th National Athletic Meeting, Aichi.

2324	**1695**	50y. multicoloured	85	35

1696 Michio Miyagi (composer)

1994. Birth Anniversaries. Multicoloured.

2325	**1696**	80y. Type **1696**	1·40	55
2326		80y. Gyoshu Hayami (painter) and "Moths"	1·40	55

1698 Fujiwara no Michinaga and Insulin Crystals

1994. 15th International Diabetes Federation Congress, Kobe.

2327	**1698**	80y. multicoloured	1·40	55

Fujiwara no Michinaga (966–1028) was the earliest known Japanese diabetic.

1699/1703 *Viewing Maple Leaves at Takao* (folding screen, Hideyori Kano) (image scaled to 45% of original size)

1704 *Yokuryuchi Pool, Shugakuin Imperial Villa* (Kenji Kawai)

1705 *Rock Garden, Ryoan Temple* (Eizo Kato)

1994. 1200th Anniv of Kyoto. Paintings.

2328	**1699**	80y. multicoloured	1·40	55
2329	**1700**	80y. multicoloured	1·40	55
2330	**1701**	80y. multicoloured	1·40	55
2331	**1702**	80y. multicoloured	1·40	55
2332	**1703**	80y. multicoloured	1·40	55

2333	**1704**	80y. multicoloured	1·40	55
2334	**1705**	80y. multicoloured	1·40	55

Nos. 2328/32 were issued together, *se-tenant*, forming the composite design illustrated.

1706 Izumo Papier-mache Boar

1994. New Year's Greetings. Multicoloured.

2335	**1706**	50y. Type **1706**	85	35
2336		80y. Boar (Takayama soft toy)	1·40	55

1709 Boar (Takayama soft toy)

1994. New Year's Greetings. Lottery Stamps. Multicoloured.

2337		50y.+3y. Izumo Papier-mache boar	95	35
2338		80y.+3y. Type **1709**	1·50	60

Each stamp carries a lottery number.

1710 5r. Stamp and Eduardo Chiossone (designer)

1994. History of Stamps (2nd series). "Koban" issue of 1876–88. Multicoloured, colour of featured stamp given.

2339	**1710**	80y. grey	1·40	55
2340		80y. brown	1·40	55
2341		80y. red	1·40	55
2342		80y. blue	1·40	55

FEATURED STAMPS: No. 2340, 1s. stamp (Type **20**); 2341, 12s. stamp (Type **21**); 2342, 20s. stamp (Type **22**).

1711 Himeji Castle Tower   **1712** *Himeji Castle* (Masami Takahashi)

1994. World Heritage Sites (1st series).

2343	**1711**	80y. multicoloured	1·40	55
2344	**1712**	80y. multicoloured	1·40	55

See also Nos. 2347/8, 2373/4 and 2400/1.

1713 2s. Stamp and Postal Delivery by Hand-drawn Cart

1995. History of Stamps (3rd series). 1894 Emperor's Silver Wedding issue and paintings by Shinsai Shibata.

2345	**1713**	80y. Type **1713**	1·40	55
2346		80y. 5s. stamp and postal delivery by horse-drawn carriage	1·40	55

1715 "Kannon Bosatsu" (wall painting, Kondo Hall)

1716 Kondo Hall, Horyu Temple

1995. World Heritage Sites (2nd series). Multicoloured.

2347	**1715**	80y. multicoloured	1·40	55
2348	**1716**	110y. multicoloured	1·90	80

1717 Emblem and National Flowers

1995. Centenary of Japan–Brazil Treaty of Friendship. Multicoloured.

2349	80y. Type **1717**		1·40	55
2350	80y. Emblem and sports		1·40	55

1719 Unebi and Nijo Mountains and Tile from Palace

1720 Remembering Times Past (Saburosuke Okada)

1995. 1300th Anniv of Fujiwara Palace, Kashihara.

2351	**1719**	50y. multicoloured	85	35
2352	**1720**	80y. multicoloured	1·40	55

1721 Dissection (Seison Maeda)

1995. Modern Anatomy Education.

2353	**1721**	80y. multicoloured	1·40	55

1722 "National Census" and "16"

1995. 16th National Census.

2354	**1722**	80y. multicoloured	1·40	55

1723 Volunteer teaching Bangladeshi Woman to Read

1995. 30th Anniv of Japanese Overseas Co-operation Volunteers Service.

2355	**1723**	80y. multicoloured	1·40	55

1724 Visitor to Art Studio (Keika Kanashima)

1995. Philatelic Week.

2356	**1724**	80y.+20y. mult	1·80	1·50

The premium was for the Osaka/Kobe and Awaji earthquake victims' fund.

1725 Auspicious Clouds

1726 Reeds (mourning)

1727 Water Lily (mourning)

1728 Cloud, "Wind" and Pine Bark Pattern

1729 Daphniphyllum macropodum

1995. Special Correspondence Stamps.

2357	**1725**	50y. multicoloured	85	35
2358	**1726**	50y. multicoloured	1·20	35
2359	**1727**	80y. multicoloured	1·70	55
2360	**1728**	80y. multicoloured	1·40	55
2361	**1729**	90y. multicoloured	1·60	60

1730 Maple and Shrine Island, Akiteline

1995. National Afforestation Campaign.

2362	**1730**	50y. multicoloured	85	35

1731 8½s. Stamp and First Airmail Flight from Osaka to Tokyo

1995. History of Stamps (4th series). 1929 First Airmail issue. Multicoloured.

2363	110y. Type **1731**		1·90	80
2364	110y. 18s. stamp and loading freight onto airplane		1·90	80

1733 Hearts forming Flower

1995. Greetings Stamps. Multicoloured. Self-adhesive.

2365	80y. Type **1733**		1·40	55
2366	80y. Child with balloon		1·40	55
2367	80y. Flower and pencil		1·40	55
2368	80y. Star, sun and moon		1·40	55
2369	80y. Child with dog		1·40	55

1738 Postman

1995. Letter Writing Day. Multicoloured.

2370	50y. Type **1738**		85	35
2371	80y. Ostrich		1·40	55
MS2372	72×93 mm. No. 2371		1·50	1·20

1740 Cedar

1995. World Heritage Sites (3rd series). Yaku Island. Multicoloured.

2373	80y. Type **1740**		1·40	55
2374	80y. Sika deer		1·40	55

1742 Friends, One and All (Yuki Ogawa)

1743 Atomic Bomb Dome, Hiroshima (Nobuya Nagata)

1744 Light of Peace (Nobuo Suenaga)

1995. 50th Anniv of End of Second World War. Stamp Design Contest Winners.

2375	**1742**	50y. multicoloured	85	35
2376	**1743**	80y. multicoloured	1·40	55
2377	**1744**	80y. multicoloured	1·40	55

1745 Marathon Runners

1995. 18th International University Games, Fukuoka.

2378	**1745**	80y. multicoloured	1·40	55

1746 Radio-controlled Aircraft

1995. World Aeromodel Championships, Kasaoka. Multicoloured.

2379	50y. Type **1746**		85	35
2380	80y. Radio-controlled helicopter		1·40	55

1748 Horse, Cow and Labrador

1995. World Veterinary Congress, Yokohama.

2381	**1748**	80y. multicoloured	1·40	1·10

1749 5y. Stamp and Cherub and Tokyo Mailbox

1995. History of Stamps (5th series). Industries issue of 1948–49. Multicoloured.

2382	80y. Type **1749**		1·30	55
2383	80y. 50y. stamp and mail van		1·30	55
2384	80y. 90y. stamp and mail van		1·30	55
2385	80y. 10y. stamp and cherub on Tokyo mailbox		1·30	55

1753 Judo (Makuhari, Chiba)

1995. World Sports Championships. Multicoloured.

2386	80y. Type **1753**		1·30	55
2387	80y. Gymnastics (Sabae, Fukui)		1·30	55

1755 Shell Matching Game (from New Year's Amusements)

1995. International Correspondence Week. Details of paintings on folding screens. Multicoloured.

2388	90y. Type **1755**		1·40	1·10
2389	110y. Battledore and Shuttlecock (from Twelve Months)		1·70	1·40
2390	130y. Playing Cards (from Matsuura Folding Screen)		2·10	1·70

1758 Cyclists

1995. 50th Anniv of National Athletic Meeting, Fukushima.

2391	**1758**	50y. multicoloured	95	45

1759 Patchwork Hearts (Tomoko Suzuki)

1995. 50th Anniversaries of U.N.O. (2392) and UNESCO (2393). Multicoloured.

2392	80y. Type **1759**		1·30	1·10
2393	80y. Children with Heart Balloon (Yukino Ikeda)		1·30	1·10

1761 Tadataka Ino (cartographer, 250th birth)

1995. Anniversaries. Multicoloured.

2394	80y. Type **1761**		1·30	55
2395	80y. Kitaro Nishida (philosopher, 50th death)		1·30	55

1763 Tsutsumi Clay Rat on Cayenne Pepper

1995. New Year's Greetings. Multicoloured.

2396	50y. Type **1763**		75	25
2397	80y. Satsuma papier-mache rat in rice store		1·30	55

1766 Satsuma
Papier-mache
Rat in Rice Store

1995. New Year's Lottery Stamps. Multicoloured.
2398	50y.+3y. Tsutsumi clay rat on turnip	1·10	90
2399	80y.+3y. Type **1766**	1·50	1·20

Each stamp carries a lottery number.

1767 Beech
Forest

1995. World Heritage Sites (4th series). Shirakami Mountains. Multicoloured.
2400	80y. Type **1767**	1·30	55
2401	80y. Black woodpecker	1·30	55

1769 Obi
Material showing
Choson Dynasty
Boxes (Keisuke
Serizawa)

1995. 30th Anniv of Resumption of Japan–Korea Diplomatic Relations.
2402	**1769** 80y. multicoloured	1·30	55

1770 Siebold

1996. Birth Bicentenary of Philipp Franz von Siebold (physician and Japanologist).
2403	**1770** 80y. multicoloured	1·40	55

1771 Twined
Ropes

1996. 50th Anniv of Labour Relations Commissions.
2404	**1771** 80y. multicoloured	1·20	45

1772 Turtle and
Crane

1996. Senior Citizens.
2405	**1772** 80y. multicoloured	1·20	45

1773 Driving to
Diet for
Promulgation of
Constitution, 1946

1774 Signing San
Francisco Peace
Treaty, 1951

1775 Return of
Okinawa, 1972

1996. 50 Post-war Years (1st series).
2406	**1773**	80y. mauve, lilac & gold	2·20	1·10
2407	**1774**	80y. dp grn, grn & gold	2·20	1·10
2408	**1775**	80y. indigo, blue and gold	2·20	1·10

See also Nos. 2420/1, 2429/30, 2443/4 and 2449/54.

1776 Woman and
Diet Building

1996. 50th Anniv of Women's Suffrage.
2409	**1776** 80y. multicoloured	1·20	45

1777 *Window*
(Yukihiko Yasuda)

1996. Philatelic Week.
2410	**1777** 80y. multicoloured	1·20	45

1778 Mother and
Child

1996. 50th Anniv of UNICEF.
2411	**1778** 80y. multicoloured	1·50	55

1779 Children
and Sun

1996. Child Welfare Week.
2412	**1779** 80y. multicoloured	1·50	55

1780 Narcissus
Flycatcher

1996. Bird Week. Multicoloured.
2413	80y. Type **1780**	1·30	55
2414	80y. Binoculars and bird feeding nestlings	1·30	55

1782 Cherry
Blossom and
Tokyo Buildings

1996. National Afforestation Campaign.
2415	**1782** 50y. multicoloured	95	45

1783 1991
Design

1784 1949
Design

1996. History of Stamps (6th series). Philatelic Week Issues.
2416	**1783** 80y. brown, ochre and lilac	1·20	45
2417	**1783** 80y. multicoloured	1·20	45
2418	**1784** 80y. deep lilac and lilac	1·20	45
2419	**1784** 80y. multicoloured	1·20	45

1785 Olympic
Flame (Olympic
Games, Tokyo,
1964)

1786 Sun Tower
("EXPO 70" World
Fair, Osaka)

1996. 50 Post-war Years (2nd series).
2420	**1785** 80y. multicoloured	1·50	45
2421	**1786** 80y. multicoloured	1·50	45

1787/8 *Oirase no Keiryu* (Chikkyo Ono)

1996. Centenary of Modern River Control Systems.
2422	**1787** 80y. multicoloured	1·30	1·10
2423	**1788** 80y. multicoloured	1·30	1·10

Nos. 2422/3 were issued together, *se-tenant*, forming the composite design illustrated.

1789 Emblem

1790 *Nippon
Maru II* (cadet
ship)

1996. Marine Day.
2424	**1789** 50y. multicoloured	95	45
2425	**1790** 80y. multicoloured	1·30	45

1791 Cat

1996. Letter Writing Day. Multicoloured.
2426	50y. Type **1791**	95	80
2427	80y. Toy horse	1·30	1·10
MS2428	72×93 mm. No. 2427	1·50	1·20

1793 *Hikari*
Express Train and
Motorway

1794 Woman
and Modern
Appliances

1996. 50 Post-war Years (3rd series). Modern Life.
2429	**1793** 80y. multicoloured	1·50	1·20
2430	**1794** 80y. multicoloured	1·50	1·20

1795 Kenji
Miyazawa (writer,
centenary)

1996. Birth Anniversaries. Multicoloured.
2431	80y. Type **1795**	1·50	1·20
2432	80y. Hokiichi Hanawa (scholar and editor, 250th)	1·50	1·20

1797 Archer

1996. 51st National Athletic Meeting, Hiroshima.
2433	**1797** 50y. multicoloured	85	70

1798 Paper-chain
People around
Red Feather
(donor pin)

1996. 50th Anniv of Community Chest.
2434	**1798** 80y. multicoloured	1·50	1·20

1799 Piano Keys
and Double Clef

1996. International Music Day.
2435	**1799** 80y. multicoloured	1·50	1·20

1800 *Water Mill in Onden*

1801 Flowers

1803 Flowers

1805 Flowers

1996. International Correspondence Week. Paintings from *36 Views of Mt. Fuji* by Hokusai Katsushika (2436, 2438, 2440) and details of paintings on folding screen by Kohrin Ogata (others).
2436	**1800**	90y. multicoloured	1·30	1·10
2437	**1801**	90y. multicoloured	1·30	1·10
2438	–	110y. multicoloured	1·80	1·50
2439	**1803**	110y. multicoloured	1·80	1·50
2440	–	130y. multicoloured	2·10	1·70
2441	**1805**	130y. multicoloured	2·10	1·70

DESIGNS—As T **1800**: No. 2438; *Fine Day with a South Wind*; 2440, *Lake in Sosyu Hakone*.

1806 Congress Emblem and Squirrel

1996. 18th Int Savings Banks Congress, Tokyo.
2442 **1806** 80y. multicoloured   1·50   1·20

1807 Mobile Telephone, Fibre-optic Cable and Communications Satellite

1808 Satellite Photograph of Earth

1996. 50 Post-war Years (4th series). Telecommunications and Environmental Protection.
2443 **1807** 80y. multicoloured   1·50   1·20
2444 **1808** 80y. multicoloured   1·50   1·20

1809 Okinawa Papier-mache Fighting Bull

1996. New Year's Greetings. Multicoloured.
2445 50y. Type **1809**   95   80
2446 80y. Child on bull (Takamatsu wedding doll)   1·40   1·10

1812 Child on Bull (Takamatus Wedding Doll)

1996. New Year Lottery Stamps. Multicoloured.
2447 50y.+3y. Okinawa papier-mache fighting bull   1·10   90
2448 80y.+3y. Type **1812**   1·50   1·20
Each stamp carries a lottery number.

1813 Yujiro Ishihara (actor) as Youth

1814 Ishihara smoking Pipe

1815 Hibari Misora (actress' and singer) in *Kanashiki Kuchibue*

1816 Misora singing

1817 Osamu Tezuka (cartoonist) and Cartoon Characters

1818 Self-portrait and Astroboy

1997. 50 Post-war Years (5th series). Entertainers.
2449 **1813** 80y. black, brn & gold   1·20   45
2450 **1814** 80y. multicoloured   1·20   45
2451 **1815** 80y. black, blue & gold   1·20   45
2452 **1816** 80y. multicoloured   1·20   45
2453 **1817** 80y. multicoloured   1·20   45
2454 **1818** 80y. multicoloured   1·20   45

1819 Emblem

1997. Winter Olympic Games, Nagano (1998). Multicoloured.
2455 80y.+10y. Type **1819**   1·60   1·30
2456 80y.+10y. Snowlets (mascots)   1·60   1·30

1821 *Daigo* (Togyu Okumura)

1997. Philatelic Week.
2457 **1821** 80y. multicoloured   1·50   60

1822 Main Court Room

1997. 50th Anniv of Supreme Court.
2458 **1822** 80y. multicoloured   1·50   60

1823 Parachutist

1824 Waving to Mechanical Doll

1825 Stamp Lover

1826 Helicopter Postman

1827 With Love Letter

1997. Greetings Stamps. Doraemon (cartoon character). Self-adhesive gum.
2459 **1823** 80y. multicoloured   1·30   90
2460 **1824** 80y. multicoloured   1·30   90
2461 **1825** 80y. multicoloured   1·30   90
2462 **1826** 80y. multicoloured   1·30   90
2463 **1827** 80y. multicoloured   1·30   90

1828 Mexican Mythological Figures (Luis Nishizawa)

1997. Centenary of Japanese Emigration to Mexico.
2464 **1828** 80y. multicoloured   1·50   60

1829 Zao Crater Lake and Bush Clover

1997. National Afforestation Campaign.
2465 **1829** 50y. multicoloured   85   35

1830 House's Seal and Diet Building

1997. 50th Anniv of House of Councillors.
2466 **1830** 80y. multicoloured   1·50   60

1831 "Happy Balloon" (Orville Isaac)

1832 "Bird Friends" (Haruka Kumiya)

1833 "Message from Rainbow Forest" (Anna Romanovskaya)

1834 "Greetings" (Yumi Kiryu)

1997. Letter Writing Day.
2467 **1831** 50y. multicoloured   95   80
2468 **1832** 70y. multicoloured   1·20   95
2469 **1833** 80y. multicoloured   1·40   1·10
2470 **1834** 90y. multicoloured   1·50   1·20
MS2471 72×93 mm. No. 2469   1·80   1·30

1835 Bird with Letter and Owl on Blackboard

1997. 50th Anniv of High School Part-time and Correspondence Courses.
2472 **1835** 50y. multicoloured   85   35

1836 Stylized Worker

1997. 50th Anniv of Labour Standards Law.
2473 **1836** 80y. multicoloured   1·50   60

1837 *Pacific Ocean and Mt. Osorno* (after Hokusai Katsushika)

1997. Centenary of Japan–Chile Relations.
2474 **1837** 80y. multicoloured   1·50   60

1838 Mopi (mascot) and Synchronized Swimmers

1997. 52nd National Athletic Meeting, Osaka.
2475 **1838** 50y. multicoloured   85   35

1839 *Hodogaya* (from *53 Stations of Tokaido*)

1840 Woodpecker and Flower

1842 Foliage

1844 Snow-covered Tree

1997. International Correspondence Week. Paintings by Hiroshige Ando (Nos. 2476, 2478, 2480) and details from *The Four Seasons* by Hoitsu Sakai (others). Multicoloured.
2476 90y. Type **1839**   1·40   60
2477 90y. Type **1840**   1·40   60
2478 110y. "Kameyama" (from "53 Stations of Tokaido")   1·70   70
2479 110y. Type **1842**   1·70   70
2480 130y. "Snow View from Sumida River Revetment" (from "Edo Scenic Sites: Snow, Moon and Flower")   2·10   90
2481 130y. Type **1844**   2·10   90

1845 Auditorium, Takeru (opera character) and Ballerina

1997. Inaug of New National Theatre. Tokyo.
2482 **1845** 80y. multicoloured   1·50   60

1846 *Iihi Tabidachi* (Shinji Tanimura)

1847 *Tsuki no Sabaku* (Masao Kato and Suguru Sasaki)

1997. Favourite Songs (1st series).
2483 **1846** 50y. multicoloured   95   45
2484 **1847** 80y. multicoloured   1·40   60
See also Nos. 2497/8, 2499/2500, 2522/3, 2527/8, 2531/2, 2558/9, 2568/9 and 2578/9.

1848 Rohan Kouda (writer, 130th anniv)

1997. Birth Anniversaries. Multicoloured.
2485 80y. Type **1848**   1·50   60
2486 80y. Hiroshige Ando (after Toyo Kuni III) (painter, bicentenary)   1·50   60

1850 Miharu
Hariko Paper
Tiger

1997. New Year's Greetings. Multicoloured.
2487	50y. Type **1850**		95	80
2488	80y. Hakata Hariko paper tiger		1·40	1·10

1853 Hakata
Hariko Paper
Tiger

1997. New Year Lottery Stamps. Multicoloured.
2489	50y.+3y. Miharu Hariko paper tiger		1·10	90
2490	80y.+3y. Type **1853**		1·50	1·20

Each stamp carries a lottery number.

1854 *Yotsutake,
Ryukyu Dance*
(Taiji Hamada)

1997. 25th Anniv of Return of Okinawa (Ryukyu Islands).
2491	**1854**	80y. multicoloured	1·50	60

1855 Former Shibuya
House, Yamagata

1856 Tomizawa House

1997. Traditional Houses (1st series).
2492	**1855**	80y. multicoloured	1·50	60
2493	**1856**	80y. multicoloured	1·50	60

See also Nos. 2513/14, 2529/30, 2539/40 and 2570/2.

1857 *Mother Sea*
(Bokunen Naka)

1858 *Mother
Earth* (Bokunen
Naka)

1997. United Nations Framework Convention on Climate Change, Kyoto.
2494	**1857**	80y. multicoloured	1·50	60
2495	**1858**	80y. multicoloured	1·50	60

1859 Drying
Harvested Rice

1997. 50th Anniv of Agricultural Insurance System.
2496	**1859**	80y. multicoloured	1·50	60

1860 *Sunayama*
(Hakushu Kitahara
and Shinpei
Nakayama)

1861 *Jingle Bells*
(Shoji Miyazawa
and J. Pierpont)

1997. Favourite Songs (2nd series).
2497	**1860**	50y. multicoloured	95	45
2498	**1861**	80y. multicoloured	1·40	60

1862
Shabondama (Ujo
Noguchi and
Shinpei
Nakayama)

1863 *Kitaguni no
Haru* (Haku Ide
and Minoru Endo)

1998. Favourite Songs (3rd series).
2499	**1862**	50y. multicoloured	95	45
2500	**1863**	80y. multicoloured	1·40	60

1864 Hollyhock

1998. Winter Paralympics, Nagano. Multicoloured.
2501	50y. Type **1864**		1·40	60
2502	80y. Ice sledge hockey		1·70	70

1866 Miyama
Gentian
("Gentiana
nipponica")

1871
Snow-boarding

1998. Winter Olympic Games, Nagano. Multicoloured.
2503	50y. Type **1866**		95	80
2504	50y. Marsh marigold (*Caltha palustris*)		95	80
2505	50y. Black lily (*Fritillaria camtschaensis*)		95	80
2506	50y. Peony (*Paeonia japonica*)		95	80
2507	50y. Adder's tongue lily (*Erythronium japonicum*)		95	80
2508	80y. Type **1871**		1·30	1·10
2509	80y. Curling		1·30	1·10
2510	80y. Speed skating		1·30	1·10
2511	80y. Cross-country skiing		1·30	1·10
2512	80y. Alpine skiing		1·30	1·10

1876 Former Baba
House, Nagano

1877 Naka House

1998. Traditional Houses (2nd series).
2513	**1876**	80y. multicoloured	1·50	60
2514	**1877**	80y. multicoloured	1·50	60

1878 Fireman
and Ambulance

1879 Fireman and
Fire Engine

1998. 50th Anniv of Japanese Fire Service.
2515	**1878**	80y. multicoloured	1·50	60
2516	**1879**	80y. multicoloured	1·50	60

The firemen in the designs are taken from paintings of actors by Kunichika Toyohara.

1880 Puppy

1998. Greetings Stamps. Self-adhesive. Multicoloured.
2517	80y. Type **1880**		1·20	95

2518	80y. Kitten		1·20	95
2519	80y. Budgerigars		1·20	95
2520	80y. Pansies		1·20	95
2521	80y. Rabbit		1·20	95

1885
Medaka-no-Gakko
(Shigeru Chaki
and Yoshinao
Nakada)

1886 *Aoi
Sanmyaku* (Yaso
Saijo and Ryoichi
Hattori)

1998. Favourite Songs (4th series).
2522	**1885**	50y. multicoloured	95	45
2523	**1886**	80y. multicoloured	1·40	60

1887 *Poppies* (Kokei
Kobayashi)

1998. Philatelic Week.
2524	**1887**	80y. multicoloured	1·50	60

1888 *Liberty Leading the
People* (Eugene Delacroix)

1998. Year of France in Japan.
2525	**1888**	110y. multicoloured	1·80	1·10

1889 Trout and
Japanese
Azalea

1998. National Afforestation Campaign.
2526	**1889**	50y. multicoloured	85	35

1890 *Wild Roses*
(Sakufu Kondo
and Franz
Schubert)

1891 *Hill abloom
with Tangerine
Flowers* (Minoru
Uminuma and
Shogo Kato)

1998. Favourite Songs (5th series).
2527	**1890**	50y. multicoloured	95	45
2528	**1891**	80y. multicoloured	1·40	60

1892 Kowata Residence,
Shinji

1893 Kamihaga
Residence, Uchiko

1998. Traditional Houses (3rd series).
2529	**1892**	80y. multicoloured	1·50	60
2530	**1893**	80y. multicoloured	1·50	60

1894 *This Road*
(Hakusyu Kitahara
and Kousaku
Yamada)

1895 *I'm a Boy of
the Sea* (anon)

1998. Favourite Songs (6th series).
2531	**1894**	50y. multicoloured	95	45
2532	**1895**	80y. multicoloured	1·40	60

1896 Boy writing

1998. Letter Writing Day. Multicoloured.
2533	50y. Type **1896**		95	45
2534	50y. Girl with letter		95	45
2535	80y. Girl holding pen		1·50	60
2536	80y. Boy holding pen		1·50	60
2537	80y. Boy and girl reading letters (horiz)		1·50	60
MS2538	93×72 mm. No. 2537		1·80	1·50

1901 Kamio Residence,
Oita

1902 Nakamura
Residence, Okinawa

1998. Traditional Houses (4th series).
2539	**1901**	80y. multicoloured	1·50	60
2540	**1902**	80y. multicoloured	1·50	60

1903 FJ Class
Dinghy Racing

1998. 53rd National Athletic Meeting, Kanagawa.
2541	**1903**	50y. multicoloured	85	35

1904 *Sketch of Maple Leaf*
(detail)

1905 *Parakeet in Oak Tree*

1907 *Coloured Chicken in
Snow-laden Bamboo*

1909 *Parakeet in Rose Bush*

**1998. International Correspondence Week. Paintings by
Shakuchu Ito. Multicoloured.**
2542	90y. Type **1904**		1·50	1·20
2543	90y. Type **1905**		1·50	1·20
2544	110y. *Drake and Duck in Snow* (detail)		1·80	1·50
2545	110y. Type **1907**		1·80	1·50
2546	130y. *Butterfly in the Peonies* (detail)		2·10	1·70
2547	130y. Type **1909**		2·10	1·70

1910 Serving

1911 Receiving

1912 Set and Attack

1913 Blocking

1998. World Volleyball Championships, Japan.

2548	**1910**	80y. multicoloured	1·50	60
2549	**1911**	80y. multicoloured	1·50	60
2550	**1912**	80y. multicoloured	1·50	60
2551	**1913**	80y. multicoloured	1·50	60

1914 Bakin Takizawa (writer, 150th death anniv)

1915 Yoshie Fujiwara (opera singer, birth centenary)

1998. Anniversaries.

2552	**1914**	80y. multicoloured	1·50	60
2553	**1915**	80y. multicoloured	1·50	60

1916 Sahara Papier-mache Rabbit making Rice Cake

1998. New Year's Greetings. Multicoloured.

2554		50y. Type **1916**	95	45
2555		80y. Yamagata papier-mache rabbit on ball	1·40	60

1919 Yamagata Papier-mache Rabbit on Ball

1998. New Year's Lottery Stamps. Multicoloured.

2556		50y.+3y. Sahara papier-mache rabbit making rice cake	1·10	90
2557		50y.+3y. Type **1919**	1·50	1·20

Each stamp carries a lottery number.

1920 The Apple Song (Hachiro Sato and Tadashi Manjome)

1921 The Toy Cha-Cha-Cha (Akiyuki Nasaka and Osamu Yoshioka)

1998. Favourite Songs (7th series).

2558	**1920**	50y. multicoloured	95	45
2559	**1921**	80y. multicoloured	1·40	60

1922 Tango Dancers (Goro Sasaki)

1998. Centenary of Friendship Treaty between Japan and Argentina.

2560	**1922**	80y. multicoloured	1·50	60

1923 "Family" (Chakou Wiam)

1924 "Heart Tree" (Atsuko Niizato)

1925 "Hito" (Shozo Somekawa)

1926 "Happiness" (Mary Carmel Mulloor)

1998. 50th Anniv of Universal Declaration of Human Rights.

2561	**1923**	50y. multicoloured	95	45
2562	**1924**	70y. multicoloured	1·30	55
2563	**1925**	80y. multicoloured	1·40	60
2564	**1926**	90y. multicoloured	1·70	70

1998. 50th Anniv of New Year's Greetings Stamps. Previous issues now dated "1999".

2565	**241**	50y. mauve	95	45
2566	**445**	50y. multicoloured	95	45
2567	**1278**	50y. multicoloured	95	45

1927 Flowing like a River (Yasushi1 Akimoto and Akira Mitake)

1928 Song of the Four Seasons (Toyohisa Araki)

1999. Favourite Songs (8th series).

2568	**1927**	50y. multicoloured	1·20	55
2569	**1928**	80y. multicoloured	1·80	80

1929 Iwase Residence, Nishi-Akao

1930/1 Ogimachi Houses, Shirakawa

1999. Traditional Houses (5th series).

2570	**1929**	80y. multicoloured	1·50	60
2571	**1930**	80y. multicoloured	1·50	60
2572	**1931**	80y. multicoloured	1·50	60

Nos. 2571/2 were issued together, *se-tenant*, forming the composite design illustrated.

1932 The Kaen-daiko Drum (Shinsho Kokontei V)

1933 Toku the Boatman (Bunraku Katsura VIII)

1934 Mr. Kobee, the Faultfinder (Ensho Sanyutei VI)

1935 Time Noodles (Kosan Yanagiya V)

1936 Once in a Hundred Years (Beicho Katsura III)

1999. Comic Stories.

2573	**1932**	80y. multicoloured	1·30	90
2574	**1933**	80y. multicoloured	1·30	90
2575	**1934**	80y. multicoloured	1·30	90
2576	**1935**	80y. multicoloured	1·30	90
2577	**1936**	80y. multicoloured	1·30	90

1937 Sukiyaki (Rokusuke Ei and Hachidai Nakamura)

1938 Early Spring (Kazumasa Yoshimaru and Akira Nakada)

1999. Favourite Songs (9th series).

2578	**1937**	50y. multicoloured	95	45
2579	**1938**	80y. multicoloured	1·50	60

1939 Kitten

1999. Greetings Stamps. Multicoloured. Self-adhesive.

2580		80y. Type **1939**	1·50	90
2581		80y. Roses	1·50	90
2582		80y. Puppy (47×37 mm)	1·50	90
2583		80y. Brown rabbit	1·50	90
2584		80y. Grey and white rabbit (41×38 mm)	1·50	90

1944 Body Parts and Staff of Asclepius

1999. 25th General Assembly of Japan Medical Congress.

2585	**1944**	80y. multicoloured	1·70	60

1945/6 Hare playing on the field in Spring (Insho Domoto)

1999. Philatelic Week.

2586	**1945**	80y. multicoloured	1·50	60
2587	**1946**	80y. multicoloured	1·50	60

Nos. 2586/7 were issued together, *se-tenant*, forming the composite design illustrated.

1947 Nazca Lines, Llama and Machu Picchu Ruins

1999. 100 Years of Japanese Emigration to Peru.

2588	**1947**	80y. multicoloured	1·50	60

1948 Amagi Alpine Rose and Mount Fuji

1999. National Afforestation Campaign.

2589	**1948**	50y. multicoloured	1·10	70

1949 Tholos, Delphi

1999. Centenary of Japan–Greece Treaty of Commerce and Navigation.

2590	**1949**	80y. multicoloured	1·50	60

1950 Demon Dancer (Ouro Carnival), Lake Titicaca and Andean Condor

1999. 100 Years of Japanese Emigration to Bolivia.

2591	**1950**	80y. multicoloured	1·50	60

1951 Houses and Paddy Fields

1999. 50th Anniv of Land Improvement Law.

2592	**1951**	80y. multicoloured	1·50	60

1952 "Hill where Camellias Bloom" (detail of statue, Naoki Tominaga) and "Hope" (detail of stained glass window, Louis Fransen)

1999. 50th Anniv of Family Court.

2593	**1952**	80y. multicoloured	1·50	60

1953 Primroses

1999. 50th Anniv of Rehabilitation Support Programme.

2594	**1953**	80y. multicoloured	1·50	60

1954 Rickshaw, 1899

1999. Centenary of Patent Attorney System.
| 2595 | **1954** | 80y. multicoloured | 1·50 | 60 |

1955 Masaakira Tomii, Kenjiro Ume and Nobushige Hozumi (drafters)

1999. Centenaries of Civil (1998) and Commercial (1999) Laws.
| 2596 | **1955** | 80y. multicoloured | 1·50 | 60 |

1956 Sayo-chan, Saku-chan and Ken-chan (originator, developer and inspector) (Takashi Yanase)

1999. Centenary of Japanese Copyright System.
| 2597 | **1956** | 80y. multicoloured | 1·50 | 60 |

1957 Children and Envelope

1999. Letter Writing Day. 50th Anniv of Japanese Association of Pen Friend Clubs.
2598	**1957**	50y. multicoloured	1·10	70
2599	-	50y. multicoloured	1·10	70
2600	-	50y. multicoloured	1·10	70
2601	-	50y. multicoloured	1·10	70
2602	-	80y. blue, black & yell	1·50	95
2603	-	80y. multicoloured	1·50	95
2604	-	80y. black, blue & yell	1·50	95
2605	-	80y. black, red & yellow	1·50	95
2606	-	80y. multicoloured	1·50	95
2607	-	80y. black, yellow & bl	1·50	95
2608	-	80y. multicoloured	1·50	95
2609	-	80y. black and red	1·50	95
2610	-	80y. black, yellow & grn	1·50	95
2611	-	80y. green, black & yell	1·50	95

DESIGNS: As T **1957**—No. 2599, Bear and crayon; 2600, Girl with pen; 2601, Clown jumping from envelope; 2604, Boy and star; 2606, Miffie and Barbara; 2610, Girl with letter. 52×27 mm—2602, Giraffes. 35×27 mm—2603, Kite. 29×29 mm—2605, Girl with pencil; 2609, Girl; 2611, Ducklings. 38×38 mm—2607, Boy playing trumpet. 27×36 mm—2608, Girl playing cello.

1971 Doves and Hearts

1999. Greetings Stamps.
2613		50y. Type **1971**	95	60
2614	-	80y. Japanese character	1·50	1·10
2615	-	90y. Manchurian crane and leaves	1·70	1·30

1974 *Wagahai wa Neko de Aru* (novel by Natsume Soseki)

1976 Yosano Akiko (poet)

1978 Tram, Tokyo, 1903

1980 "Haikara" (western-style fashion)

1982 Moving Casualties, Russo–Japanese War, 1904–05

1999. The Twentieth Century (1st series). The 1900s. Multicoloured.
2616	50y. Type **1974**	1·30	95
2617	50y. "Bochan" (novel by Natsume Soseki)	1·30	95
2618	80y. Type **1976**	1·50	1·10
2619	80y. Denkikan Cinema, Asakusa	1·50	1·10
2620	80y. Type **1978**	1·50	1·10
2621	80y. Kawakami Otojirou and Sadayakko (actor couple)	1·50	1·10
2622	80y. Type **1980**	1·50	1·10
2623	80y. Sumo wrestlers (opening of Sumo Ring, Ryogoku, Tokyo, 1909)	1·50	1·10
2624	80y. Type **1982**	1·50	1·10
2625	80y. Military hospital, Russo–Japanese War	1·50	1·10

See also Nos. 2627/36, 2664/53, 2677/86, 2687/96, 2697/2706, 2707/16, 2717/26, 2739/48, 2759/68, 2771/80, 2798/807, 2808/17, 2819/28, 2832/41, 2850/59 and 2861/70.

1984 Golfer and Gentian

1999. 54th National Sports Festival, Kumamoto.
| 2626 | **1984** | 50y. multicoloured | 1·10 | 60 |

1985/6 Biplane *Kaishiki No. 1* and Airship *Yamadashiki No. 1* (first Japanese built aircraft)

1987 Children singing (School Song Book, 1910)

1989 Dr. Noguchi Hideyo (discovery of Oroya Fever germ, 1926)

1991 Kanaguri Shizo and Mishima Yahiko at Opening Parade, Olympic Games, Stockholm, 1912

1993 Matsui Sumako as Kachucha in *Resurrection* (play by Shimamura Hogetsu), 1914

1999. The Twentieth Century (2nd series). Multicoloured.
2627	50y. Type **1985**	1·30	95
2628	50y. Type **1986**	1·30	95
2629	50y. Type **1987**	1·50	1·10
2630	80y. Explorer and dog (Shirase Antarctic Expedition, 1910)	1·50	1·10
2631	80y. Type **1989**	1·50	1·10
2632	80y. Wolf (extinction of indigenous wolves, 1905)	1·50	1·10
2633	80y. Type **1991**	1·50	1·10
2634	80y. Dancers (formation of Takarazuka Musical Company, 1913)	1·50	1·10
2635	80y. Type **1993**	1·50	1·10
2636	80y. Mother and children (first sale of milk caramel in Japan, 1913)	1·50	1·10

Nos. 2627/8 were issued together, *se-tenant*, forming the composite design illustrated.

1995 Stork on Elephant

1999. International Year of the Elderly.
| 2637 | **1995** | 80y. multicoloured | 1·50 | 80 |

1996 *Sea Route in Kazusa Area* (from *36 Views of Mt. Fuji* by Hokusai Katsushika)

1998 *Rain beneath the Mountain Top* (from *36 Views of Mt. Fuji*)

1999 *Chrysanthemums and a Horsefly*

2000 "Under the Fukagawa Mannen Bridge" (from *36 Views of Mt. Fuji*)

1999. International Correspondence Week. 125th Anniv of Universal Postal Union. Multicoloured.
2638	90y. Type **1996**	1·60	95
2639	90y. Confederate Roses and a Sparrow	1·60	95
2640	110y. Type **1998**	2·20	1·10
2641	110y. Type **1999**	2·20	1·10
2642	130y. Type **2000**	2·40	1·30
2643	130y. *Peonies and a Butterfly*	2·40	1·30

2002 Couple in Junk (Takehisa Yumeji)

2004/5 Inauguration of Tokyo Railway Station, 1914

2006 Navy Cadets (Start of First World War, 1914)

2008 Akutagawa Ryunosuke and Title Page of *Rashomon* (first book of poetry, published 1915)

2010 Yoshino Sakuzo (political scientist) (Taisho Democracy)

1999. The Twentieth Century (3rd series). Multicoloured.
2644	50y. Type **2002**	1·30	95
2645	50y. Takehisa Yumeji (artist)	1·30	95
2646	80y. Type **2004**	1·50	1·10
2647	80y. Type **2005**	1·50	1·10
2648	80y. Type **2006**	1·50	1·10
2649	80y. "Yohatsu" (western-style hair)	1·50	1·10
2650	80y. Type **2008**	1·50	1·10
2651	80y. Princess and Clouds (postal life assurance, 1916)	1·50	1·10
2652	80y. Type **2010**	1·50	1·10
2653	80y. Farmers (rice riots, 1918)	1·50	1·10

Nos. 2646/7 were issued together, *se-tenant*, forming the composite design illustrated.

2012 Yokohama Bay Stars Mascot (Central League)

2013 Chunichi Dragon Mascot (Central League)

2014 Seibu Lions Mascot (Pacific League)

2015 Nippon Ham Fighters Mascot (Pacific League)

2016 Yomiuri Giants Mascot (Central League)

2017 Yakult Swallows Mascot (Central League)

2018 Orix Blue Wave Mascot (Pacific League)

2019 Fukuoka Daiei Hawks Mascot (Pacific League)

2020 Hiroshima Toyo Carp Mascot (Central League)

2021 Hanshin Tigers Mascot (Central League)

2022 Kintetsu Buffaloes Mascot (Pacific League)

2023 Chiba Lotte Marines Mascot (Pacific League)

1999. Professional Japanese Baseball Clubs. Self-adhesive.

2654	**2012**	80y. multicoloured	1·50	1·10
2655	**2013**	80y. multicoloured	1·50	1·10
2656	**2014**	80y. multicoloured	1·50	1·10
2657	**2015**	80y. multicoloured	1·50	1·10
2658	**2016**	80y. multicoloured	1·50	1·10
2659	**2017**	80y. multicoloured	1·50	1·10
2660	**2018**	80y. multicoloured	1·50	1·10
2661	**2019**	80y. multicoloured	1·50	1·10
2662	**2020**	80y. multicoloured	1·50	1·10
2663	**2021**	80y. multicoloured	1·50	1·10
2664	**2022**	80y. multicoloured	1·50	1·10
2665	**2023**	80y. multicoloured	1·50	1·10

2024 Rainbow, Buildings and Mt. Fuji

1999. 50th Anniv of Japanese Science Council.

2666	**2024**	80y. multicoloured	1·50	95

2025 Katsushika Hokusai (artist, 150th death anniv)

2026 Uemera Shoen (artist, 50th death anniv)

2027 Kawabata Yasunari (author, birth centenary)

1999. Anniversaries.

2667	**2025**	80y. multicoloured	1·50	95
2668	**2026**	80y. multicoloured	1·50	95
2669	**2027**	80y. multicoloured	1·50	95

2028 Paulownia and Bamboo Embroidery (Manzairaku costume)

1999. Tenth Anniv of Accession of Emperor Akihito. Multicoloured.

2670	80y. Type **2028**	1·00	20
2671	80y. Chinese phoenix embroidery (Engiraku costume)	1·60	1·10
MS2672	144×93 mm. As Nos. 2670/1	3·50	3·00

2030 Karatsuyama ningyo Folk Toy

1999. New Year's Greetings. Multicoloured.

2673	50y. Type **2030**	1·30	80
2674	80y. Tsuneishihariko doll	2·10	1·10

2033 Tsuneishihariko Doll

1999. New Year's Lottery Stamps. Multicoloured.

2675	50y.+3y. Karatsuyama ningyo folk toy	1·20	95
2676	80y.+3y. Type **2033**	1·80	1·50

Each stamp carries a lottery number.

2034 Onoe Matsunosuke (silent film star, 1925)

2035 Bandoh Tsumasaburo (silent film star, 1925)

2036 Runners (first Hakone relay marathon, 1920)

2038 Ruined Building (Great Kanto earthquake, 1923)

2040 Adventures of Sho-chan (comic illustrated by Katsuichi Kabashima, 1923)

2042 Baseball Players (opening of Koshien Stadium, 1924)

1999. The Twentieth Century (4th series). Multicoloured.

2677	50y. Type **2034**	1·30	95
2678	50y. Type **2035**	1·30	95
2679	80y. Type **2036**	1·50	1·10
2680	80y. Gramophone (*Gondola Song*, 1920)	1·50	1·10
2681	80y. Type **2038**	1·50	1·10
2682	80y. Easygoing Dad (comic strip character by Yutaka Aso, 1923)	1·50	1·10
2683	80y. Type **2040**	1·50	1·10
2684	80y. Manchurian crane (protected species, 1924)	1·50	1·10
2685	80y. Type **2042**	1·50	1·10
2686	80y. Couple wearing western-style clothes	1·50	1·10

2044 Underground Train (opening of Tokyo Underground, 1927)

2046 Arashi Chozaburo in Title Role (*Kurama Tengu* (film), 1927)

2048 Tsuruta Yoshiyuki (swimmer) (Gold Medal winner, Olympic Games, Amsterdam, 1928)

2050 2nd August Track and Field Programme (Olympic Games, Amsterdam)

2052 Man (emergence of cafes for social gatherings)

2000. The Twentieth Century (5th series). Multicoloured.

2687	50y. Type **2044**	1·30	95
2688	50y. Platform (opening of Tokyo Underground)	1·30	95
2689	80y. Type **2046**	1·50	1·10
2690	80y. Man doing gymnastics (first radio broadcast of gymnastic exercises, 1928)	1·50	1·10
2691	80y. Type **2048**	1·50	1·10
2692	80y. Oda Mikio (athlete) (Gold medal winner, Olympic Games, Amsterdam)	1·50	1·10
2693	80y. Type **2050**	1·50	1·10
2694	80y. Hitomi Kinue (athlete) (Silver medal winner, Olympic Games, Amsterdam)	1·50	1·10
2695	80y. Type **2052**	1·50	1·10
2696	80y. Cover of Horoki (novel by Hayashi Fumiko)	1·50	1·10

2054/5 Datsun Model 10, 1932 and Toyota Model AA, 1936 (mass production of domestic cars)

2056 Eruption of Mt. Asama, 1929

2058 Couple wearing Western Clothes (importing of western fashion)

2060 Kabutoyama (winner of first Japanese Derby, 1932)

2062 Woman (release of *Longing for Your Shadow* (song by Koga Masao), 1931)

2000. The Twentieth Century (6th series). Multicoloured.

2697	50y. Type **2054**	1·30	95
2698	50y. Type **2055**	1·30	95
2699	80y. Type **2056**	1·50	1·10
2700	80y. Kobayashi Takiji (author) (*Crab Cannery Ship* published in *War Banner* paper) (25×32 mm)	1·50	1·10
2701	80y. Type **2058**	1·50	1·10
2702	80y. Kuro (comic strip character by Tagawa Suiha, 1931) (27×33 mm)	1·50	1·10
2703	80y. Type **2060**	1·50	1·10
2704	80y. Matsumidori (winner of 14th Derby) (27×33 mm)	1·50	1·10
2705	80y. Type **2062**	1·50	1·10
2706	80y. Prime Minister's Residence (assassinations of Prime Minister Tsuyoshi Inukai, 1932, and of Finance Minister Takahashi Korekiyo and Lord Keeper of the Privy Seal Saito Makoto, 1936) (25×35 mm)	1·50	1·10

Nos. 2697/8 were issued together, *se-tenant*, forming the composite design illustrated.

2064/5 D51 Steam Locomotive, 1936

2066 Otsuki Fumihiko (first edition of *Daigenkai* (dictionary compiled by Otsuki Fumihiko and Otsuki Joden), 1932)

2071 Chuken Hachiko and Statue (erection of statue of Chuken Hachiko, Shikuya Station, 1934)

2069/70 Players (formation of Tokyo Baseball Club, 1934)

2000. The Twentieth Century (7th series). Multicoloured.

2707	50y. Type **2064**	1·30	95
2708	50y. Type **2065**	1·30	95
2709	80y. Type **2066**	1·50	1·10
2710	80y. Woman (release of *Tokyo Ondo* (song by Nakayama Shimpei), 1933) (25×33 mm)	1·50	1·10
2711	80y. Enomoto Kenichi (actor) (25×33 mm)	1·50	1·10
2712	80y. Type **2069**	1·50	1·10
2713	80y. Type **2070**	1·50	1·10
2714	80y. Type **2071**	1·50	1·10
2715	80y. Yoshikawa Eiji (author) (*Miyamoto* (story) first published in 1935) (27×33 mm)	1·50	1·10
2716	80y. Silver-banded black pigeon (declared extinct, 1936) (27×33 mm)	1·50	1·10

Nos. 2707/8 and 2712/13 respectively were issued together, *se-tenant*, forming the composite design illustrated.

2074/5 Mitsubishi Twin-engined Transport and Ki-15 Prototype Type 97 *Kamikaze* Airplanes

2076 Helen Keller's First Visit to Japan, 1937

2078 Yamamoto Yuzo (author) (*Robo No Ishi* (novel) first published in 1937)

2080 Yokozuna Futabayama (sumo wrestler) (victory in 69 consecutive matches, 1936–39)

2082 Birds (release of *Dareka Kokyo wo Omowazaru* (song by Koga Masao))

2000. The Twentieth Century (8th series). Multicoloured.

2717	50y. Type **2074**	1·30	95
2718	50y. Type **2075**	1·30	95
2719	80y. Type **2076**	1·50	1·10
2720	80y. Woman with bag and civilian in national uniform (wartime clothing, 1937–40) (25×33 mm)	1·50	1·10
2721	80y. Type **2078**	1·50	1·10
2722	80y. Tanaka Kinuyo and Uehara Ken (actors) in *Aizenkatsura* (film), 1938 (25×33 mm)	1·50	1·10
2723	80y. Type **2080**	1·50	1·10
2724	80y. Sawamura Eiji (baseball player) (27×33 mm)	1·50	1·10
2725	80y. Type **2082**	1·50	1·10
2726	80y. Woodblock carving (Munakata Shiko) (25×34 mm)	1·50	1·10

Nos. 2717/18 were issued together, *se-tenant*, forming the composite design illustrated.

2084/5 Children and Flowers

2086/7 Faces and Building

2088 Girl as Butterfly with Book

2089 Two Faces and Building

2000. Children's Book Day.

2727	**2084**	80y. multicoloured	1·60	1·10
2728	**2085**	80y. multicoloured	1·60	1·10
2729	**2086**	80y. multicoloured	1·60	1·10
2730	**2087**	80y. multicoloured	1·60	1·10
2731	**2088**	80y. multicoloured	1·60	1·10
2732	**2089**	80y. multicoloured	1·60	1·10

Nos. 2727/8 and 2929/30 respectively were issued together, *se-tenant*, forming the composite designs illustrated.

2090 Hanaoka Seisyu (surgeon) and Korean Morning Glory

2000. Cent of Japanese Surgical Society Congress.

2733	**2090**	80y. multicoloured	1·80	1·10

2091/2 *Liefde* (17th-century merchant ship), Dutchman and Nagasaki

2000. 400th Anniv of Japan–Netherlands Cultural Relations.

2734	**2091**	80y. multicoloured	1·80	1·10
2735	**2092**	80y. multicoloured	1·80	1·10

Nos. 2734/5 were issued together, *se-tenant*, forming a composite design.

2093/4 *Ryukozu* (Hashimoto Gaho)

2000. Philatelic Week.

2736	**2093**	80y. multicoloured	1·80	1·10
2737	**2094**	80y. multicoloured	1·80	1·10

Nos. 2736/7 were issued together, *se-tenant*, forming the composite design illustrated.

2095 Japanese White-eye, Plum Tree and Kuju Mountain Range

2000. National Afforestation Campaign.

2738	**2095**	50y. multicoloured	1·10	60

2096 Golden Bat (comic strip character by Suzuki Ichiro)

2098 Vice-Consul Sugihara Chiune (issued visas to Jews from Consulate in Lithuania), 1940

2100 Airplane over Pearl Harbor (outbreak of Second World War in the Pacific, 1941)

2102 Mt. Showashin- zan (formed by volcanic activity of Mt. Usu, 1944)

2104 Statue (atomic bomb on Nagasaki, 9 August 1945)

2000. The Twentieth Century (9th series). Multicoloured.

2739	50y. Type **2096**	1·60	1·10
2740	50y. Golden Bat (27×36 mm)	1·60	1·10
2741	80y. Type **2098**	1·80	1·30
2742	80y. Children (Kokumin Gakko school system, 1941) (25×33 mm)	1·80	1·30
2743	80y. Type **2100**	1·80	1·30
2744	80y. Takamura Kotaro (poet) (*Dotei* (collected poems) awarded First Imperial Art Academy Prize, 1942) (26×35 mm)	1·80	1·30
2745	80y. Type **2102**	1·80	1·30
2746	80y. Damaged buildings (atomic bomb on Hiroshima, 6 August 1945) (27×33 mm)	1·80	1·30
2747	80y. Type **2104**	1·80	1·30
2748	80y. Lieut-General Umezu, Chief of the Imperial General Staff signing Surrender (end of Second World War, 1945)	1·80	1·30

2106 Bean Goose

2109 *Girl playing Glass Flute* (Kitagawa Utamaro)

2111 Roses and Pansies

2113 Girl with Pen and Boy with Letter

2000. "Phila Nippon '01" International Stamp Exhibition, Tokyo. Multicoloured. Self-adhesive.

2749	80y. Type **2106**	1·80	1·30
2750	80y. White wagtail (25×34 mm)	1·80	1·30
2751	80y. Northern goshawk (25×35 mm)	1·80	1·30
2752	80y. Type **2109**	1·80	1·30
2753	80y. Ichikawa Ebizo (actor) (Toshusai Sharaku) (25×48 mm)	1·80	1·30
2754	80y. Type **2111**	1·80	1·30
2755	80y. Puppy and kitten (24×42 mm)	1·80	1·30
2756	80y. Type **2113**	1·80	1·30
2757	80y. Children and letter (31×43 mm)	1·80	1·30
2758	80y. Girl with letter and boy with pen (31×40 mm)	1·80	1·30

2116 Astro Boy (comic strip character by Tezuka Osamu, 1951) on cover of *Shonen* (magazine), July, 1951

2118 Cover of Music Score and Apples (release of *Song of Apples* (song by Sato Hachiro and Manjoume Tadashi), 1945)

2120 Mother and Child (promulgation of new constitution, 1947)

2122 Dr. Yukawa Hideki and Atoms (winner of Nobel Prize for Physics, 1949)

2124 Kishi Keiko and Sata Keiji (actors) in *Kimino Na Wa* (film), 1953

2000. The Twentieth Century (10th series). Multicoloured.

2759	50y. Type **2116**	1·60	1·10
2760	50y. Astro Boy from cover of *Shonen*, August, 1961 (26×36 mm)	1·60	1·10
2761	80y. Type **2118**	1·80	1·30
2762	80y. Sazae San (comic strip by Hasegawa Machiko) (25×34 mm)	1·80	1·30
2763	80y. Type **2120**	1·80	1·30
2764	80y. Trophy (new world records set by Furuhashi Hironoshin (swimmer), 1949) (25×34 mm)	1·80	1·30
2765	80y. Type **2122**	1·80	1·30

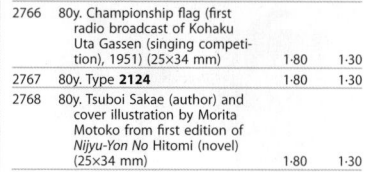

2000.

2766	80y. Championship flag (first radio broadcast of Kohaku Uta Gassen (singing competition), 1951) (25×34 mm)	1·80	1·30
2767	80y. Type **2124**	1·80	1·30
2768	80y. Tsuboi Sakae (author) and cover illustration by Morita Motoko from first edition of *Nijyu-Yon No* Hitomi (novel) (25×34 mm)	1·80	1·30

2126 Flowers

2127 Flowers and Sea

2000. Kyushu–Okinawa Summit.

2769	**2126**	80y. multicoloured	1·80	1·30
2770	**2127**	80y. multicoloured	1·80	1·30

2128 Tokyo Tower Entrance Ticket, 1958

2131/2 Kurosawa Akira (film director) and Scene from *Seven Samurai*, 1954

2133 Rikidozan (wrestler) and Championship Belt

2136 Prince Shotoku (issue of 10,000 yen banknote, 1958)

2000. The Twentieth Century (11th series). Multicoloured.

2771	**2128**	50y. multicoloured	1·60	1·10
2772	–	50y. multicoloured (27×35 mm)	1·60	1·10
2773	–	80y. multicoloured (25×35 mm)	1·80	1·30
2774	**2131**	80y. multicoloured	1·80	1·30
2775	**2132**	80y. multicoloured	1·80	1·30
2776	**2133**	80y. multicoloured	1·80	1·30
2777	–	80y. multicoloured (28×36 mm)	1·80	1·30
2778	–	80y. multicoloured (25×33 mm)	1·80	1·30
2779	**2136**	80y. brown and stone	1·80	1·30
2780	–	80y. multicoloured (25×33 mm)	1·80	1·30

DESIGNS: No. 2772, Tokyo Tower (construction completed in 1958); 2773, Early radio and television sets (regular television broadcasts, 1953); 2777, Rikidozan; 2778, *Godzilla* (release of film, 1954); 2780, Influence of Taiyozoku Fashion on Youth Culture (release of *Taiyo No Kisetsu* (film), 1956).

Nos. 2774/5 were issued together, *se-tenant*, forming the composite design illustrated.

2138/9 Sunflowers

2000. 50th Anniv of Crime Prevention Campaign.

2781	**2138**	80y. multicoloured	1·80	1·30
2782	**2139**	80y. multicoloured	1·80	1·30

Nos. 2781/2 were issued together, *se-tenant*, forming the composite design.

2140 Girl with
Pen

2000. Letter Writing Day. Multicoloured.

2783	50y. Type **2140**	1·70	1·20
2784	50y. House and birds (25×33 mm)	1·70	1·20
2785	50y. Clown and envelope (25×33 mm)	1·70	1·20
2786	50y. Boy with dog (25×33 mm)	1·70	1·20
2787	80y. Girl and dog in balloon basket (27×36 mm)	2·10	1·50
2788	80y. Apple tree (30×30 mm)	2·10	1·50
2789	80y. Parrots holding letter (22×34 mm)	2·10	1·50
2790	80y. Bicycle (28×40 mm)	2·10	1·50
2791	80y. Girl and boy holding dove (29×35 mm)	2·10	1·50
2792	80y. Girl, letter and hedgehog (27×40 mm)	2·10	1·50
2793	80y. Girl playing harp (28×35 mm)	2·10	1·50
2794	80y. Boy playing recorder (27×35 mm)	2·10	1·50
2795	80y. Boy playing cello (23×39 mm)	2·10	1·50
2796	80y. Boy carrying pen (27×36 mm)	2·10	1·50
MS2797	72×93 mm. Nos. 2784 and 2791	3·25	2·75

2154/5 Taro and Giro (left at Showa
Base, 1958)

2156 Commemorative Cake Box (marriage of Prince Akihito, 1959)

2158 Stars and Music Score (release of *Sukiyaki* (song by Ei Rokusuke and Nakamura Hachidai), 1960)

2160 Doll and Music Score (release of *Hello, My Baby* (song by Ei Rokusuke and Nakamura Hachidai)), 1963)

2162 Official Poster of Olympic Games, Tokyo, 1964

2000. The Twentieth Century (12th series). Multicoloured.

2798	50y. Type **2154**	1·80	1·30
2799	50y. Type **2155**	1·80	1·30
2800	80y. Type **2156**	2·10	1·50
2801	80y. Meteorological chart showing the Isewan typhoon, 1959 (25×33 mm)	2·10	1·50
2802	80y. Type **2158**	2·10	1·50
2803	80y. Shiba Ryotaro (author) (serialization of *Ryomaga Yuku* (novel), 1962 (25×33 mm)	2·10	1·50
2804	80y. Type **2160**	2·10	1·50
2805	80y. Tokyo–Osaka High Speed Bullet Train Service, 1964 (25×33 mm)	2·10	1·50
2806	80y. Type **2162**	2·10	1·50
2807	80y. Official poster of Olympic Games, Tokyo (28×36 mm)	2·10	1·50

Nos. 2798/9 were issuesd together, *se-tenant*, forming the composite design illustrated.

2164/5 Characters from *Hyokkori Hyotan-jima* (launch of children's television programme, 1964)

2166 Television, Car and Air Conditioning Unit, 1960

2168 Baltan (character from *Ultraman*)

2170 Kawabata Yasunari and Oe Kenzaburo (winners of the Nobel Prize for Literature)

2172 Tower of the Sun (sculpture, Okamoto Taro) (World's Fair, Osaka, 1970)

2000. The Twentieth Century (13th series). Multicoloured.

2808	50y. Type **2164**	1·80	1·30
2809	50y. Type **2165**	1·80	1·30
2810	80y. Type **2166**	2·10	1·50
2811	80y. Ultraman (launch of *Ultraman* television series, 1966) (27×33 mm)	2·10	1·50
2812	80y. Type **2168**	2·10	1·50
2813	80y. Guitars (formation of pop bands following 1966 tour by The Beatles) (25×33 mm)	2·10	1·50
2814	80y. Type **2170**	2·10	1·50
2815	80y. Atsumi Taro (actor) in *Otokowa Tsuraiyo* (film) (25×34 mm)	2·10	1·50
2816	80y. Type **2172**	2·10	1·50
2817	80y. Youths and music score (release of *Children Who Didn't Know the War* (song), by Kitayama Osamu and Sugita Jiro, 1971) (25×33 mm)	2·10	1·50

Nos. 2808/9 were issued together, *se-tenant*, forming the composite design illustrated.

2174 Naruse Jinzo (founder of Women's University), Yoshioka Yayoi (founder of Women's Medical College, Tokyo) and Tsuda Umeko (founder of Tsuda College)

2000. Centenary of Private Higher Education for Women.

2818	**2174** 80y. multicoloured	2·10	1·30

2175 Oh Sadaharu (baseball player) swinging Bat, 1964

2177 Wall Painting (discovery of wall paintings at Takamatsu Zuka, 1972)

2179 Pandas (gift from China to Japan, 1972)

2181 Lady Oscar (character from *Belubara*, 1972) (cartoon by Ikeda Riyoko)

2183 Cliffs and Music Score (release of *Erimo Misaki* (song) by Okamoto Osami and Yoshida Takuro, 1974)

2000. The Twentieth Century (14th series). Multicoloured.

2819	50y. Type **2175**	1·80	1·30
2820	50y. Nagashima Shigeo (baseball player) running, 1962	1·80	1·30
2821	80y. Type **2177**	2·10	1·50
2822	80y. Wall painting (from Takamatsu Zuka)	2·10	1·50
2823	80y. Type **2179**	2·10	1·50
2824	80y. Shureimon Gate (return to Japan of administrative rights over Okinawa, 1972)	2·10	1·50
2825	80y. Type **2181**	2·10	1·50
2826	80y. Ozawa Seiji (conductor)	2·10	1·50
2827	80y. Type **2183**	2·10	1·50
2828	80y. Futuristic space shuttle (cartoon series *Uchu Senkan Yamato* by Matsumoto Reiji, 1974)	2·10	1·50

2185 *Okabe*

2000. International Correspondence Week. Paintings from *53 Stations of the Tokaido* by Ando Hiroshige. Multicoloured.

2829	90y. Type **2185**	2·20	1·60
2830	110y. *Maisaka*	2·75	2·20
2831	130y. *Okazaki*	3·25	2·50

2188 Gundam (cartoon character) (launch of *Kidosenshi Gundam*, television programme, 1979)

2190 Guitar and Music Score (release of *Jidai* (song by Nakajima Miyuki), 1975)

2192 Microphones and Musical Notes (introduction of Karaoke, 1977)

2194 Alien Space Ship and Music Score (release of *UFO* (song by Aku Yu and Tokura Shunichi), 1979)

2196 Keyboard and Musical Notes (popularity of synthesizer music, 1970s)

2000. The Twentieth Century (15th series). Multicoloured.

2832	50y. Type **2188**	1·80	1·30
2833	50y. Amuro (cartoon character from *Kidosenshi Gundam*)	1·80	1·30
2834	80y. Type **2190**	2·10	1·50
2835	80y. Fish and music score (release of *Oyoge! Taiyaki-kun* (song by Takada Hiroo and Sase Juichi), 1975)	2·10	1·50
2836	80y. Type **2192**	2·10	1·50
2837	80y. Flowers and music score (release of *Cosmos* (song by Sada Masashi), 1977)	2·10	1·50
2838	80y. Type **2194**	2·10	1·50
2839	80y. People crossing field (launch of *San Nen B Gumi Kinpachi Sensi* (television series), 1979)	2·10	1·50
2840	80y. Type **2196**	2·10	1·50
2841	80y. Woman and snow-covered house (launch of *Oshine* (television drama), 1983)	2·10	1·50

2198 Nagaoka Hantaro (physicist, 50th death anniv) and Atomic Models

2199 Nakaya Ukichiro (physicist, birth centenary) and Snow Crystal

2200 Nakamura Teijo (haiku poet, birth centenary) and Text

2000. Anniversaries.

2842	**2198** 80y. multicoloured	2·10	1·50
2843	**2199** 80y. multicoloured	2·10	1·50
2844	**2200** 80y. multicoloured	2·10	1·50

2201 Jindaiji (snake-shaped clay bell)

2000. New Year's Greetings. Multicoloured.

2845	50y. Type **2201**	1·30	90
2846	80y. Sasano (carved wooden toy snake)	2·10	1·50

2204 Sasano (carved wooden toy snake)

2000. New Year's Lottery Stamps. Multicoloured.

2847	50y.+3y. Jindaiji (snake-shaped clay bell)	1·40	1·20
2848	80y.+3y. Type **2204**	2·20	1·80

Each stamp carries a lottery number.

2205/6 Characters from *Go! Anpanman* (launch of children's television programme, 1988)

2207 Trains on Trial and Inaugural Runs (opening of Seikan Tunnel, 1988)

2209 Rebuilt Watchtower (excavation of ruins at Yoshinogari Iseki, 1989)

2211/12 "J-Boy" (mascot) and Football (Inception of J-League Football, 1993)

2213 *Tonkomeisya* (detail of painting, Hirayama Ikuo) (World Heritage Site, 1987)

2000. The Twentieth Century (16th series). Multicoloured.

2849	50y. Type **2205**		1·80	1·30
2850	50y. Type **2206**		1·80	1·30
2851	80y. Type **2207**		2·10	1·50
2852	80y. Halley's Comet (first appearance for 76 years, 1986)		2·10	1·50
2853	80y. Type **2209**		2·10	1·50
2854	80y. Misora Hibari (singer) (recipient of National Medal of Honor, 1989)		2·10	1·50
2855	80y. Type **2211**		2·10	1·50
2856	80y. Type **2212**		2·10	1·50
2857	80y. Type **2213**		2·10	1·50
2858	80y. "Ikarugano Sato Cyoyo Horyuji" (detail of painting, Hirayama Ikuo) (World Heritage Site, 1998)		2·10	1·50

Nos. 2849/50 and 2855/6 were respectively issued together, *se-tenant*, forming the composite design illustrated.

2215 Central Tower and Mosaic Marble Floors (detail)

2000. 110th Anniv of Diet (Japanese Parliament).

2859	**2215**	80y. multicoloured	2·10	1·50

2216 Emblem, Nagano Olympic Games, 1998

2218 Crown Prince Noruhito and Princess Masako (wedding, 1993)

2220 Lap-top Computer and Mobile Phone (increased use of wireless telecommunications)

2222 Doi Takao (Japanese astronaut) outside Spaceship

2224 *Mother Earth* (Bokunan Naka) (United Nations Framework Convention on Climate Change, Kyoto, 1997)

2000. The Twentieth Century (17th series). Multicoloured.

2860	50y. Type **2216**		1·80	1·30
2861	50y. "Snowlets" (Nagano Olympic mascots)		1·80	1·30
2862	80y. Type **2218**		2·10	1·50
2863	80y. Phoenix, map of Hanshin-Awaji and collapsed bridge (Hanshin-Awaji earthquake, 1995)		2·10	1·50
2864	80y. Type **2220**		2·10	1·50

2865	80y. Launch of space shuttle *Endeavor* (inclusion of first Japanese astronaut on N.A.S.A. mission, 1992)		2·10	1·50
2866	80y. Type **2222**		2·10	1·50
2867	80y. Footballer (Japanese participation in World Cup Football Championship, France, 1998)		2·10	1·50
2868	80y. Type **2224**		2·10	1·50
2869	80y. Official poster of Nagano Olympic Games		2·10	1·50

2226/7 Manchurian Cranes (*"Grus japonensis"*, Matazo Kayama)

2001. "Internet Expo 2001 Japan" (virtual Internet fair).

2870	**2226**	80y. multicoloured	1·70	1·40
2871	**2227**	80y. multicoloured	1·70	1·40

Nos. 2870/1 were issued together, *se-tenant*, forming a composite design.

2228 Heliotrope, Flax and Emblem

2001. United Nations Year of Volunteers.

2872	**2228**	80y. multicoloured	1·70	1·40

2229 "Gyoseishoshi" (Japanese calligraphy) and Computer

2001. 50th Anniv of Gyoseishoshi Lawyer System (specialist administrative lawyers).

2873	**2229**	80y. multicoloured	1·70	1·40

2230 Shinkyo Bridge, Futarasan Shrine

2231 Main Sanctuary, Futarasan Shrine

2232 Karamon Gate, Toshugu Shrine

2233 Kirin (mythical winged horse) (painting), Toshugu Shrine

2234 Wind God (statue), Rinnoji Temple

2235 Thunder God (statue), Rinnoji Temple

2236 Peacock, Toshugu Shrine

2237 Sleeping Cat, Toshugu Shrine

2238/9 Rinnoji Temple

2001. World Heritage Sites (1st series). Shrines and Temples, Nikko.

2874	**2230**	80y. multicoloured	1·70	1·40
2875	**2231**	80y. multicoloured	1·70	1·40
2876	**2232**	80y. multicoloured	1·70	1·40
2877	**2233**	80y. multicoloured	1·70	1·40
2878	**2234**	80y. multicoloured	1·70	1·40
2879	**2235**	80y. multicoloured	1·70	1·40
2880	**2236**	80y. multicoloured	1·70	1·40
2881	**2237**	80y. multicoloured	1·70	1·40
2882	**2238**	80y. multicoloured	1·70	1·40
2883	**2239**	80y. multicoloured	1·70	1·40

Nos. 2883/4 were issued together, *se-tenant*, forming the composite design illustrated.

See also Nos. 2887/96, 2906/15, 2960/9, 2985/94, 2997/3006, 3020/9, 3045/54, 3060/9, 3083/92 and 3107/16.

2240 Emblem

2241 *The Annunciation* (detail, Botticelli)

2242 *The Annunciation* (detail, Botticelli)

2001. "Italy in Japan 2001" (cultural and scientific event).

2884	**2240**	80y. multicoloured	1·70	1·40
2885	**2241**	110y. multicoloured	2·40	1·90
2886	**2242**	110y. multicoloured	2·40	1·90

Nos. 2885/6 were issued together in *se-tenant* pairs featuring two separate panels of the painting.

2243/4 Marodo Shrine

2245 Main Sanctuary

2246 Lion Dog (statue)

2247 Marodo Shrine and Pagoda

2248 Traditional Dance Mask

2249 Horse (statue)

2250 Buildings

2251 Treasure Pagoda

2252 Oomoto Shrine

2001. World Heritage Sites (2nd series). Itsukushima Shrine.

2887	**2243**	80y. multicoloured	1·70	1·40
2888	**2244**	80y. multicoloured	1·70	1·40
2889	**2245**	80y. multicoloured	1·70	1·40
2890	**2246**	80y. multicoloured	1·70	1·40
2891	**2247**	80y. multicoloured	1·70	1·40
2892	**2248**	80y. multicoloured	1·70	1·40
2893	**2249**	80y. multicoloured	1·70	1·40
2894	**2250**	80y. multicoloured	1·70	1·40
2895	**2251**	80y. multicoloured	1·70	1·40
2896	**2252**	80y. multicoloured	1·70	1·40

Nos. 2888/9 were issued together, *se-tenant*, forming the composite design illustrated.

2253 Emblem

2001. Centenary of Japanese Dermatological Association. Multicoloured, colour of triangle beneath face value given.

2897	**2253**	80y. pink	1·70	1·40
2898	**2253**	80y. flesh	1·70	1·40
2899	**2253**	80y. yellow	1·70	1·40
2900	**2253**	80y. green	1·70	1·40
2901	**2253**	80y. blue	1·70	1·40

2254 *Woman posting Letter* (Nakamura Senseki)

2001. Philatelic Week. Centenary of Red Cylindrical Letter Boxes (designed by Taraya Takashhichi and Nakamura Koji).

2902	**2254**	80y. multicoloured	1·70	1·40

2255 "Ato, Nik and Kaz" (mascots)

2256 "Kaz"

2257 "Nik"

2001. World Cup Football Championship, Japan and South Korea (2002).

2903	**2255**	80y.+10y. mult	2·20	1·80
2904	**2256**	80y.+10y. mult	2·20	1·80
2905	**2257**	80y.+10y. mult	2·20	1·80

2258 Hosodono, Maidono and Tsuchinoya Halls, Kamowakeikazuchi Shrine

2259 Roman Gate, Kamowakeikazazuchi Shrine

2260 East Main Hall, Kamomioya Shrine

2261 Guardian Dog (statue), Kamomioya Shrine

2262 Pagoda and South Great Gate, Toji Temple

2263 Fukuu Joju Nyorai (statue), Toji Temple

2264 Pagoda and West Gate, Kiyomizudera Temple

2265 Main Hall, Kiyomizudera Temple

2266 "Nyorin Kannon" (painting), Toji Temple

2267 Daiitoku Myoo (statue), Toji Temple

2001. World Heritage Sites (3rd series). Temples and Shrines, Kyoto.

2906	**2258**	80y. multicoloured	1·70	1·40
2907	**2259**	80y. multicoloured	1·70	1·40
2908	**2260**	80y. multicoloured	1·70	1·40
2909	**2261**	80y. multicoloured	1·70	1·40
2910	**2262**	80y. multicoloured	1·70	1·40
2911	**2263**	80y. multicoloured	1·70	1·40
2912	**2264**	80y. multicoloured	1·70	1·40
2913	**2265**	80y. multicoloured	1·70	1·40
2914	**2266**	80y. multicoloured	1·70	1·40
2915	**2267**	80y. multicoloured	1·70	1·40

2268 Flowers and Pigeons

2001. 50th Anniv of Membership of United Nations Educational, Scientific and Cultural Organization.

2916	**2268**	80y. multicoloured	1·70	1·40

2269 Swimming

2001. Ninth International Swimming Federation Championships, Fukuoka. Multicoloured.

2917	**2269**	80y. Type **2269**	1·70	1·40
2918	**2270**	80y. Synchronized swimming	1·70	1·40

2919	**2271**	80y. Diving	1·70	1·40
2920	**2272**	80y. Water polo	1·70	1·40

Nos. 2917/20 were issued together, *se-tenant*, the backgrounds forming a composite design.

2273 Rabbits

2001. Letter Writing Day. Multicoloured.

2921	**2273**	50y. Type **2273**	1·30	1·10
2922		50y. Girl and pencil (28×36 mm)	1·30	1·10
2923		50y. Boy holding envelope (28×36 mm)	1·30	1·10
2924		50y. Girl with ribbons (28×36 mm)	1·30	1·10
2925		80y. Bird in tree (30×30 mm)	1·70	1·40
2926		80y. Girl holding rabbit (27×36 mm)	1·70	1·40
2927		80y. Boy holding pen (27×36 mm)	1·70	1·40
2928		80y. Girl with envelope and dog (27×26 mm)	1·70	1·40
2929		80y. Girl and flowers (27×36 mm)	1·70	1·40
2930		80y. Flowers and bird with envelope (30×30 mm)	1·70	1·40
2931		80y. Birds and roof (27×36 mm)	1·70	1·40
2932		80y. Rabbit and flowers (22×33 mm)	1·70	1·40
2933		80y. Boy and rabbit (27×33 mm)	1·70	1·40
2934		80y. Chicks, hen and pig (27×39 mm)	1·70	1·40

MS2935	72×93 mm. Nos. 2923 and 2932		3·25	3·00

2287 Ootani Oniji as Edobei (Toshusai Sharaku)

2288 Iwai Hanshiro IV as Shigenoi (Toshusai Shakuru)

2289 Sakata Hangoro as Fujikwa Mizuemon (Toshusai Shakuru)

2290 Segawa Kikunojo as Oshizu, Tanabe Bunzo's Wife (Toshusai Shakuru)

2291 Ichikawa Omezo as Yakko Ippei (Toshusai Shakuru)

2292 Beauty looking Back (Hishikawa Moronobu)

2293 Girl playing Glass Flute (Kitagawa Utamaro)

2294 Fuzoku Higashino Nishiki, returning from the Bath-house in the Rain (Torii Kiyonaga)

2295 Iwai Kumesaburo as Chiyo (Utagawa Kunimasa)

2296 Ichikawa Komazo III as Sasaski Ganryu (Utagawa Toyokuni)

2297 Iwai Hanshiro IV as Shigenoi (Toshusai Shakuru)

2298 Ootani Oniji as Edobei (Toshusai Shakuru)

2299 Mandarin Duck

2300 Japanese White-Eye

2301 Girl and Boy holding Envelopes

2302 Iwai Kumesaburo as Chiyo (Utagawa Kunimasa)

2303 Ichikawa Komazo III as Sasaki Ganryu (Utagawa Toyokuni)

2304 Eastern Turtle Dove

2305 Greater Pied Kingfisher

2306 1871 48m. Stamp

2001. "PHILA NIPPON '01" International Stamp Exhibition, Tokyo. (a) Ordinary gum.

2936	**2287**	50y. multicoloured	1·40	1·10
2937	**2288**	50y. multicoloured	1·40	1·10
2938	**2289**	50y. multicoloured	1·40	1·10
2939	**2290**	50y. multicoloured	1·40	1·10
2940	**2291**	50y. multicoloured	1·40	1·10
2941	**2292**	80y. multicoloured	1·70	1·40
2942	**2293**	80y. multicoloured	1·70	1·40
2943	**2294**	80y. multicoloured	1·70	1·40
2944	**2295**	80y. multicoloured	1·70	1·40
2945	**2296**	80y. multicoloured	1·70	1·40

(b) Self-adhesive gum.

2946	**2297**	50y. multicoloured	1·50	1·20
2947	**2298**	50y. multicoloured	1·50	1·20
2948	**2299**	50y. multicoloured	1·50	1·20
2949	**2300**	50y. multicoloured	1·50	1·20
2950	**2301**	50y. multicoloured	1·50	1·20
2951	**2302**	80y. multicoloured	1·80	1·50
2952	**2303**	80y. multicoloured	1·80	1·50
2953	**2304**	80y. multicoloured	1·80	1·50
2954	**2305**	80y. multicoloured	1·80	1·50
2955	**2306**	80y. multicoloured	1·80	1·50

2307 Fly Casting and Discus

2001. Sixth World Games, Akita. Multicoloured.

2956	**2307**	50y. Type **2307**	1·30	1·10
2957		50y. Aerobics and billiards	1·30	1·10
2958		80y. Water skiing and life saving	1·70	1·40
2959		80y. Tug of war and body building	1·70	1·40

2311 Konpon Chudo Hall, Enryakuji Temple

2312 Eternal Flame, Enryakuji Temple

2313 Ninai-do Hall, Enryakuji Temple

2316 Pagoda, Daigoji Temple

2314/15 Sanbo-in Temple Garden, Daigoji Temple

2317 Palace, Ninnaji Temple

2318 Pagoda, Ninnaji Temple

2319 Phoenix Hall, Byodoin Temple

2320 Bodhisattva floating on Clouds (statue), Byodoin Temple

2001. World Heritage Sites (4th series). Temples, Kyoto.

2960	**2311**	80y. multicoloured	1·70	1·40
2961	**2312**	80y. multicoloured	1·70	1·40
2962	**2313**	80y. multicoloured	1·70	1·40
2963	**2314**	80y. multicoloured	1·70	1·40
2964	**2315**	80y. multicoloured	1·70	1·40
2965	**2316**	80y. multicoloured	1·70	1·40
2966	**2317**	80y. multicoloured	1·70	1·40
2967	**2318**	80y. multicoloured	1·70	1·40
2968	**2319**	80y. multicoloured	1·70	1·40
2969	**2320**	80y. multicoloured	1·70	1·40

Nos. 2963/4 were issued together, *se-tenant*, forming the composite design illustrated.

2321 War Memorial Opera House and Flowers

2001. 50th Anniv of San Francisco Peace Treaty.

2970	**2321**	80y. multicoloured	2·20	1·80

Japan

2322 Hara

2001. International Correspondence Week. Paintings from "53 Stations of Tokaido" by Ando Hiroshige. Multicoloured.

2971	90y. Type **2322**	2·50	2·00
2972	110y. "Oiso"	3·00	2·40
2973	130y. "Sakanoshita"	3·25	2·75

2325 Boy with Birds and Insects

2001. "Let's Keep our Towns Safe" (national community safety campaign). Multicoloured.

2974	80y. Type **2325**	1·80	1·50
2975	80y. Girl with bird and animals	1·80	1·50

2327 Man catching Disc

2001. First National Sports Games for the Disabled, Sendai City and Miyagi-gun. Multicoloured.

2976	80y. Type **2327**	1·80	1·50
2977	80y. Wheelchair race	1·80	1·50

2329 Norinaga Motoori (writer and scholar, death bicentenary)

2330 Gidayu Takemoto (jojuri chanter and puppeteer, 350th birth) and Illustration from *Sonezaki Shinju*

2001. Anniversaries.

2978	**2329**	80y. multicoloured	1·80	1·50
2979	**2330**	80y. multicoloured	1·80	1·50

2331 Horse carrying Rice

2001. New Years Greeting's. Multicoloured.

2980	50y. Type **2331**	1·30	1·10
2981	80y. Red horse of Kira	1·70	1·40

2334 Red Horse of Kira (sedge handicraft)

2001. New Year's Lottery Stamps. Multicoloured.

2982	50y.+3y. Horse carrying rice	1·40	1·10
2983	80y.+3y. Type **2334**	1·80	1·50

Each stamp carries a lottery number.

2335 Television Camera, Television Set and Radio Microphone

2001. 50th Anniv of Commercial Broadcasting.

2984	**2335**	80y. multicoloured	1·70	1·40

2336 Ujikami Shrine

2337 Kaeru Mata (main shrine), Ujikami Shrine

2338 Path to Kozanji Temple

2339 Sekisuiin, Kozanji Temple

2340 Kasumijima Garden, Saihoji Temple

2341 Kojokan Garden, Saihoji Temple

2342/3 Garden, Tenryuji Temple

2344 Golden Temple, Rokuonji Temple

2345 Golden Temple in Winter

2001. World Heritage Sites (5th series). Temples and Shrines, Kyoto.

2985	**2336**	80y. multicoloured	1·70	1·40
2986	**2337**	80y. multicoloured	1·70	1·40
2987	**2338**	80y. multicoloured	1·70	1·40
2988	**2339**	80y. multicoloured	1·70	1·40
2989	**2340**	80y. multicoloured	1·70	1·40
2990	**2341**	80y. multicoloured	1·70	1·40
2991	**2342**	80y. multicoloured	1·70	1·40
2992	**2343**	80y. multicoloured	1·70	1·40
2993	**2344**	80y. multicoloured	1·70	1·40
2994	**2345**	80y. multicoloured	1·70	1·40

Nos. 2985/94 were issued together in sheetlets of ten stamps, Nos. 2991/2 forming the composite design illustrated, with descriptions of each stamp in Japanese in the illustrated margin.

2346 Upraised Hand

2002. 50th Anniv of Legal Aid System.

2995	**2346**	80y. multicoloured	1·70	1·40

2347 Horse-shaped Fiddle Head

2002. 30th Anniv of Japan—Mongolia Diplomatic Relations.

2996	**2347**	80y. multicoloured	1·70	1·40

2348 Silver Pavilion in Snow, Jishoji Temple

2349 Silver Pavilion

2350 Hojo Garden, Ryoanji Temple

2351 Hojo Garden in Winter

2352 Karamon Gate, Honganji Temple

2353 Hiunkaku, Honganji Temple

2354 Shoin, Honganji Temple

2355 Ninomaru Palace, Nijo Castle

2356 *Hawk on Pine* (detail, painting), Nijo Castle

2357 *Hawk on Pine* (detail)

2002. World Heritage Sites (6th series). Temples, Kyoto.

2997	**2348**	80y. multicoloured	1·70	1·40
2998	**2349**	80y. multicoloured	1·70	1·40
2999	**2350**	80y. multicoloured	1·70	1·40
3000	**2351**	80y. multicoloured	1·70	1·40
3001	**2352**	80y. multicoloured	1·70	1·40
3002	**2353**	80y. multicoloured	1·70	1·40
3003	**2354**	80y. multicoloured	1·70	1·40
3004	**2355**	80y. multicoloured	1·70	1·40
3005	**2356**	80y. multicoloured	1·70	1·40
3006	**2357**	80y. multicoloured	1·70	1·40

2358 Bell and Mythical Lion-dog

2002. 50th Anniv of Japan Lions (charitable organization).

3007	**2358**	80y. multicoloured	1·60	1·30

2359 Men's Singles Skater

2002. World Figure Skating Championships, Nagano. Multicoloured.

3008	80y. Type **2359**	1·60	1·30
3009	80y. Pairs skaters	1·60	1·30

2361 Taj Mahal, India

2362 Artefact and Ruins, Moenjodaro, Pakistan

2363 Sigiriya, Sri Lanka

2364 Terracotta Panel and Ruins, Paharpur, Bangladesh

2002. 50th Anniv of Japan–South East Asia Diplomatic Relations.

3010	**2361**	80y. multicoloured	1·60	1·30
3011	**2362**	80y. multicoloured	1·60	1·30
3012	**2363**	80y. multicoloured	1·60	1·30
3013	**2364**	80y. multicoloured	1·60	1·30

2365 Two Horsemen

2002. Philately Week. (Kamo folding screen). Multicoloured.

3014	80y. Type **2365**	1·60	1·30
3015	80y. Horseman and spectator	1·60	1·30

2367 *Hikawa-Maru* (passenger ship)

2002. 50th Anniv of Japan–U.S.A. Fulbright Exchange Programme.

3016	**2367**	80y. multicoloured	1·60	1·30

2368 Ship and Irises

2002. 30th Anniv of Return of Okinawa.

3017	**2368**	80y. multicoloured	1·60	1·30

2369 Stylized Football Pitch

2002. World Cup Football Championships, Japan and South Korea. Multicoloured.

3018	80y. Type **2369**	1·60	1·30
3019	80y. FIFA World Cup Trophy	1·60	1·30

2371 Great Buddha Hall, Todaiji Temple

2372 Southern Gate, Todaiji Temple

DESIGNS: No. 2383, House and flowers (28×34 mm); 2384, Young boy and fence (25×34 mm); 2385, Ladybird and caterpillar (28×25 mm); 2386, Farmer and sheep (30×25 mm); 2387, Cow (32×25 mm); 2388, Girl and flowers (30×41 mm); 2389, Boy with football (22×35 mm); 2390, Girl carrying Tennis racquet (22×35 mm); 2391, Mother and child (28×36 mm); 2392, Man riding bicycle (28×36 mm); 2393, Girl and vase (27×27 mm); 2394, Van and car (27×27 mm).

2406 Basketball Players

2002. World Wheelchair Basketball Championship, Japan.

3056	**2406**	80y. multicoloured	1·60	1·30

2420 Naval Ships and Flags

2002. Fleet Review.

3070	**2420**	80y. multicoloured	1·60	1·30

2373 Great Buddha (detail), Todaiji Temple

2374 Virupaksu (statue), Todaiji Temple

2407 Boeing 777 and Douglas DC-7

2002. 50th Anniv of Japanese Civil Aviation.

3057	**2407**	80y. multicoloured	1·60	1·30

2375 Lotus Hall, Todaiji Temple

2376 Five-storied Pagoda, Kofukuji Temple

2377 Northern Octagonal Hall, Kofukuji Temple

2378 Ashura (statue), Kofukuji Temple

2408 "Shitoka" (Denj Lin)

2409 "Generyucho" (Wang Chuan Feng)

2002. 30th Anniv of Japan–China Diplomatic Relations.

3058	**2408**	80y. multicoloured	1·60	1·30
3059	**2409**	80y. multicoloured	1·60	1·30

2410/11 Houses, Ogimachi, Shirakawa-Mura

2379 Buddha Head, Kofukuji Temple

2380 Ryutoki Demon (statue), Kofukuji Temple

2002. World Heritage Sites (7th series). Temples, Nara.

3020	**2371**	80y. multicoloured	1·60	1·30
3021	**2372**	80y. multicoloured	1·60	1·30
3022	**2373**	80y. multicoloured	1·60	1·30
3023	**2374**	80y. multicoloured	1·60	1·30
3024	**2375**	80y. multicoloured	1·60	1·30
3025	**2376**	80y. multicoloured	1·60	1·30
3026	**2377**	80y. multicoloured	1·60	1·30
3027	**2378**	80y. multicoloured	1·60	1·30
3028	**2379**	80y. multicoloured	1·60	1·30
3029	**2380**	80y. multicoloured	1·60	1·30

Nos. 3020/9 were issued in sheetlets of ten stamps, with descriptions of each stamp in Japanese in the illustrated margin.

2412 House and Flowers, Ogimachi

2413 Houses, Ogimachi

2414 Houses covered in Snow, Ogimachi

2415 Aerial View, Ainokura, Taira-Mura

2416 House, Ainokura

2417 Houses, Ainokura

2418 House, Ainokura

2419 House covered in Snow, Ainokura

2002. World Heritage Sites (9th series). Ogimachi and Ainokura Communitites.

3060	**2410**	80y. multicoloured	1·60	1·30
3061	**2411**	80y. multicoloured	1·60	1·30
3062	**2412**	80y. multicoloured	1·60	1·30

3063	**2413**	80y. multicoloured	1·60	1·30
3064	**2414**	80y. multicoloured	1·60	1·30
3065	**2415**	80y. multicoloured	1·60	1·30
3066	**2416**	80y. multicoloured	1·60	1·30
3067	**2417**	80y. multicoloured	1·60	1·30
3068	**2418**	80y. multicoloured	1·60	1·30
3069	**2419**	80y. multicoloured	1·60	1·30

Nos. 3060/9 were issued in sheetlets of ten stamps, Nos. 3060/1 forming the composite design illustrated, with descriptions of each stamp in Japanese in the illustrated margin.

2421 *Yui*

2002. International Correspondence Week. Paintings from "53 Stations of Tokaido" by Ando Hiroshige. Multicoloured.

3071	90y. Type **2421**		1·80	1·50
3072	110y. *Shono*		2·40	2·00
3073	130y. *Tozuka*		2·75	2·40

2424 Stylized People

2002. Asian and Pacific Decade of Disabled Persons Conference.

3074	**2424**	80y. multicoloured	1·60	1·30

2395 Covered Passageway, Kasuga Taisha Shrine

2396 Middle Gate, Kasuga Taisha Shrine

2397 Deer, Kasuga-yama Forest

2398 Zen Meditation Hall, Gango-ji Temple

2399 Pagoda, Gango-ji Temple

2400 East and West Pagodas, Yakushi-ji Temple

2401 Buddha of Healing, Yakushi-ji Temple

2402 Golden Hall, Toshodai-ji Temple

2403 Standing Image of the Thousand Handed Goddess of Mercy, Toshodai-ji Temple

2404 Suzakumon Gate, Heijo Imperial Palace

2002. World Heritage Sites (8th series). Temples.

3045	**2395**	80y. multicoloured	1·60	1·30
3046	**2396**	80y. multicoloured	1·60	1·30
3047	**2397**	80y. multicoloured	1·60	1·30
3048	**2398**	80y. multicoloured	1·60	1·30
3049	**2399**	80y. multicoloured	1·60	1·30
3050	**2400**	80y. multicoloured	1·60	1·30
3051	**2401**	80y. multicoloured	1·60	1·30
3052	**2402**	80y. multicoloured	1·60	1·30
3053	**2403**	80y. multicoloured	1·60	1·30
3054	**2404**	80y. multicoloured	1·60	1·30

Nos. 3045/54 were issued in sheetlets of ten stamps, with descriptions of each stamp in Japanese in the illustrated margin.

2405 Stylized Human and Flowers

2002. 12th World Psychiatry Congress.

3055	**2405**	80y. multicoloured	1·60	1·30

2002. National Letter Writing Day.

3030	**2381**	50y. multicoloured	1·20	95
3031	-	50y. multicoloured	1·20	95
3032	-	50y. multicoloured	1·20	95
3033	-	50y. multicoloured	1·20	95
3034	-	80y. multicoloured	1·60	1·30
3035	-	80y. lemon, black and blue	1·60	1·30
3036	-	80y. multicoloured	1·60	1·30
3037	-	80y. multicoloured	1·60	1·30
3038	-	80y. multicoloured	1·60	1·30
3039	-	80y. multicoloured	1·60	1·30
3040	-	80y. multicoloured	1·60	1·30
3041	-	80y. multicoloured	1·60	1·30
3042	-	80y. multicoloured	1·60	1·30
3043	-	80y. multicoloured	1·60	1·30
MS3044 72×94 mm. Nos. 3031 and 3040			3·25	3·00

2381 Girl carrying Envelope

2425 Masaoka Shiki (writer, death centenary)

2426 Three Women (Torii Kiyonaga (artist, 250th birth))

2427 Tanakadate Aikitu (geophysicist, 50th death)

2002. Anniversaries.

3075	**2425**	80y. multicoloured	1·60	1·30
3076	**2426**	80y. multicoloured	1·60	1·30
3077	**2427**	80y. multicoloured	1·60	1·30

2428 Sheep (earthenware Dorei figure)

2002. New Year's Greetings. Multicoloured.

3078	50y. Type **2428**		1·30	1·10
3079	80y. Sheep with Gem (Edo folk toy)		1·60	1·30

2430 Sheep holding Fan (Aizunakayugawa doll)

2002. New Year Lottery Stamps. Multicoloured.

3081	50y.+3y. Type **2430**	1·40	1·10
3082	80y.+3y. Sheep (Oku Hariko doll)	1·70	1·40

Each stamp carries a lottery number.

2432 Stone Lion, Shou Dynasty Royal Mausoleum

2433 Stone Gate, Sonohyan'utaki Sanctuary

2434 Cherry Blossom, Nakijinjou castle

2435 Stone Gate, Zakimijou Castle

2436 Katsurenjou Castle Walls

2437 Second Citadel, Nakagusukujou Castle

2438 "Kankaimon", Shurijou Castle Gate

2439 Main Hall, Shurijou Castle

2440 "Shikina'en" (royal garden)

2441 Seifautaki Sanctuary

2002. World Heritage Sites (10th series).

3083	**2432** 80y. multicoloured	1·60	1·30
3084	**2433** 80y. multicoloured	1·60	1·30
3085	**2434** 80y. multicoloured	1·60	1·30
3086	**2435** 80y. multicoloured	1·60	1·30
3087	**2436** 80y. multicoloured	1·60	1·30
3088	**2437** 80y. multicoloured	1·60	1·30
3089	**2438** 80y. multicoloured	1·60	1·30
3090	**2439** 80y. multicoloured	1·60	1·30
3091	**2440** 80y. multicoloured	1·60	1·30
3092	**2441** 80y. multicoloured	1·60	1·30

2442 Kabuki Screen showing Izumo no Okuni in Costume

2443 Actors from *Shibaraku* and *Tsuchigumo*

2003. 400th Anniv of First Kabuki Theatre Performance.

3093	**2442** 80y. multicoloured	1·70	1·40
3094	**2443** 80y. multicoloured	1·70	1·40

2444 Television Company Emblem and Street Television Set

2003. 50th Anniv of Japanese Television. Multicoloured.

3095	80y. Type **2444**	1·70	1·40
3096	80y. "Hyokkori Hyotan-Jima" (puppet) and early television set	1·70	1·40

2446 Heart

2003. Greetings Stamps. Multicoloured. Self-adhesive.

3097	80y. Type **2446**	1·70	1·40
3098	80y. Dog wearing party clothes	1·70	1·40
3099	80y. Snowman	1·70	1·40
3100	80y. Bird on cake	1·70	1·40
3101	80y. Cranes and turtle	1·70	1·40
3102	80y. Roses	1·70	1·40
3103	80y. Reindeer	1·70	1·40
3104	80y. Cat	1·70	1·40
3105	80y. Cats in car	1·70	1·40
3106	80y. Cherry blossom	1·70	1·40

2456 Genbaku Dome (atomic bomb memorial)

2003. World Heritage Sites (11th series). Peace Stamp Design Competition Winners. Multicoloured.

3107	80y. Type **2456**	1·70	1·40
3108	80y. Hiroshima Prefectural Hall	1·70	1·40
3109	80y. "La Paix" (Jean-Paul Veret LeMarinier)	1·70	1·40
3110	80y. "Taika" (peace) (Pakalkaite Joskaude)	1·70	1·40
3111	80y. "Universal Shrine of Peace" (Issac M. Oriville)	1·70	1·40
3112	80y. "A Prayer for Peace" (Keiji Sugita)	1·70	1·40
3113	80y. "The Radiance of Life" (Shigenobu Nagaishi)	1·70	1·40
3114	80y. "An Encounter" (Natsuki Nakatani)	1·70	1·40
3115	80y. Rainbow-coloured Dove (Makoto Oooka)	1·70	1·40
3116	80y. "Rabbit" (Shiho Kobayashi)	1·70	1·40

2466 Posuton

2003. Postal Services Mascots. Self-adhesive. Multicoloured.

3117	50y. Aichan	1·60	1·30
3118	50y. Kanchan boy	1·60	1·30
3118a	50y. Posuton	1·60	1·30
3118b	50y. Yuchan	1·60	1·30
3119	50y. Kanchan girl	1·60	1·30
3120	50y. Posuton	1·60	1·30
3121	50y. Type **2466**	1·60	1·30
3122	80y. Aichan	1·60	1·30
3123	80y. Kanchan girl	1·60	1·30
3124	80y. Posuton	1·60	1·30
3125	80y. Yuchan	1·60	1·30
3126	80y. Kanchan boy	1·60	1·30

2476 Yellow Flower

2003. Inauguration of Japan Post (public postal corporation). Designs from *Birds and Flowers of the Four Seasons* (folding screen by Sakai Hoitsu). Multicoloured. Self-adhesive.

3127	80y. Type **2476**	1·70	1·40
3128	80y. Primula	1·70	1·40
3129	80y. Violets and quince	1·70	1·40
3130	80y. Horsetail	1·70	1·40
3131	80y. White wisteria	1·70	1·40
3132	80y. Flowering cherry and swallow	1·70	1·40
3133	80y. Hydrangea	1·70	1·40
3134	80y. Magnolia	1·70	1·40
3135	80y. Water lily and moorhen	1·70	1·40
3136	80y. Peonies and butterfly	1·70	1·40

2486 Tree and Sheep

2003. Philately Week. (Batik folding screen).

3137	**2486** 80y. multicoloured	1·70	1·40

2487 Map of Edo (folding screen)

2003. 400th Anniv of Edo Shogunate (1st issue). Multicoloured.

3138	80y. Type **2487**	1·70	1·40
3139	80y. Hon-maru (fresco, Edo Castle)	1·70	1·40
3140	80y. Domarugusoku Helmet and Armour	1·70	1·40
3141	80y. Hatsune maki-e Lacquer Box(detail)	1·70	1·40
3142	80y. 24 91 "Chujo" (Noh mask)	1·70	1·40

See also Nos. 3143/8 and 3159/64.

2492 Nihonbashi Bridge (53 Stations of Tokaido)

2003. 400th Anniv of Edo Shogunate (2nd issue). Multicoloured.

3143	80y. Type **2492**	1·50	1·20
3144	80y. Fireman's Haori (coat)	1·50	1·20
3145	80y. *Beauty Spots in Edo* (folding screen)	1·50	1·20
3146	80y. Kyoho-Bina Girl Doll	1·50	1·20
3147	80y. Kyoho-Bina Boy Doll	1·50	1·20
3148	80y. Danjuro Ichikawa (actor) as Goro Takenuki	1·50	1·20

2498 Omar Ali Saifuddien Mosque, Brunei Darussalam

2499 Angkor Wat, Cambodia

2500 Borobudur Temple, Indonesia

2501 That Luang, Laos

2502 Sultan Abdul Samad Building, Malaysia

2503 Shwedagon Pagoda, Myanmar

2504 Rice Terraces, Cordilleras, Philippines

2505 Merlion (legendary beast), Singapore

2506 Wat Phra Kaeo, Thailand

2507 Van Mieu, Vietnam

2003. ASEAN—Japan Exchange Year (Association of Southeast Asian Nations and Japan co-operation).

3149	**2498** 80y. multicoloured	1·70	1·40
3150	**2499** 80y. multicoloured	1·70	1·40
3151	**2500** 80y. multicoloured	1·70	1·40
3152	**2501** 80y. multicoloured	1·70	1·40
3153	**2502** 80y. multicoloured	1·70	1·40
3154	**2503** 80y. multicoloured	1·70	1·40
3155	**2504** 80y. multicoloured	1·70	1·40
3156	**2505** 80y. multicoloured	1·70	1·40
3157	**2506** 80y. multicoloured	1·70	1·40
3158	**2507** 80y. multicoloured	1·70	1·40

2508/9 Powhatan

2003. 400th Anniv of Edo Shogunate (3rd issue). Multicoloured.

3159	80y. Type **2508**	1·70	1·40
3160	80y. Type **2509**	1·70	1·40
3161	80y. Bakumatsu Fusoku Zukan (detail, screen)	1·70	1·40
3162	80y. Dutch East India Company plate	1·70	1·40
3163	80y. European Woman (detail, painting)	1·70	1·40
3164	80y. Wind-up Clock (Hisahige Tanaka)	1·70	1·40

2514 Bear playing Guitar (28½×36 mm)

2003. Letter Writing Day. Multicoloured.

3165	50y. Type **2514**	1·40	1·10
3166	50y. Monkey (28½×36 mm)	1·40	1·10
3167	50y. Crocodile playing Accordion (28½×36)	1·40	1·10
3168	50y. Cat holding Camera and Envelope (28½×36 mm)	1·40	1·10
3169	80y. Hippo holding Flowers (29×40 mm)	1·70	1·40
3170	80y. Parrot (28×37 mm)	1·70	1·40
3171	80y. Owl (30×30 mm)	1·70	1·40
3172	80y. Seated Bear holding Envelope (28×40 mm)	1·70	1·40
3173	80y. Elephant (28×37 mm)	1·70	1·40
3174	80y. Giraffe (29×40 mm)	1·70	1·40
3175	80y. Rabbit holding Envelope and Flowers (41×24 mm)	1·70	1·40
3176	80y. Lion carrying Lantern (28×37 mm)	1·70	1·40
3177	80y. Goat holding Envelope (28×37 mm)	1·70	1·40
3178	80y. Gorilla (28×37)	1·70	1·40
MS3179	72×94 mm. Nos. 3170 and 3165	4·25	4·00

2528 *Kawaski*

2529 *Miya*

2530 *Otsu*

2003. International Correspondence Week. Paintings from *53 Stations of Tokaido* by Ando Hiroshige.

3180	**2528**	90y. multicoloured	2·10	1·80
3181	**2529**	110y. multicoloured	2·40	2·00
3182	**2530**	130y. multicoloured	2·75	2·40

2531 *Byakko (White Tiger of the West)*

2003. Cultural Heritage. Wall Paintings, Kitora Tumulus, Nara Prefecture. Multicoloured.

| 3183 | | 80y.+10y. Type **2532** | 1·60 | 1·30 |
| 3184 | | 80y.+10y. Suzaku (Red Bird of the South) | 1·60 | 1·30 |

2533 Mokichi Saito (writer, 150th death)

2534 Shibasaburo Kitasato (scientist, 150th birth)

2003. Anniversaries.

| 3185 | **2533** | 80y. multicoloured | 1·70 | 1·40 |
| 3186 | **2534** | 80y. multicoloured | 1·70 | 1·40 |

2535 *Flowers and Butterflies, Amami Forest (painting, Isson Tanaka)*

2003. 50th Anniv of Return of Amami Islands to Japan.

| 3187 | **2535** | 80y. multicoloured | 1·70 | 1·40 |

2536 Monkey (Iyo Ittobori wood carving)

2003. New Year's Greetings. Multicoloured.

| 3188 | **2536** | 50y. Type **2536** | 1·30 | 1·10 |
| 3189 | | 80y. The Successful Monkey (Edo folk toy) | 1·60 | 1·30 |

2539 The Successful Monkey (Edo folk toy)

2003. New Year Lottery Stamps. Multicoloured.

| 3191 | | 50y.+3y. Monkey (Iyo Ittobori wood carving) | 1·40 | 1·10 |
| 3192 | | 80y.+3y. Type **2539** | 1·70 | 1·40 |

Each stamp carries a lottery number.

2540 Tetsuwan Atom (flying down)

2003. Science, Technology and Animation (1st issue). Multicoloured.

3193		80y. Type **2540**	1·80	1·50
3194		80y. Tetsuwan Atom (with raised arm)	1·80	1·50
3195		80y. Tetsuwan Atom (upside down)	1·80	1·50
3196		80y. Yumihiki Doji (Edo mechanical doll)	1·80	1·50
3197		80y. Nagaoka Hantaro (physicist)	1·80	1·50
3198		80y. H-II Rocket	1·80	1·50
3199		80y. Morph 3 Robot	1·80	1·50
3200		80y. Tetsuwan Atom (flying up)	1·80	1·50

See also Nos. 3202/8; 3224/31; 3232/9, 3264/71, 3286/93 and 3305/12.

2548 Super Jetter 1

2549 Wadokei (clock)

2550 Otomo-go (vintage car)

2551 KAZ (modern car)

2552 Stratospheric Balloon

2553 Super Jetter 2

2554 Super Jetter 3

2555 Super Jetter 4

2004. Science, Technology and Animation (2nd issue).

3201	**2548**	80y. multicoloured	1·80	1·50
3202	**2549**	80y. multicoloured	1·80	1·50
3203	**2550**	80y. multicoloured	1·80	1·50
3204	**2551**	80y. multicoloured	1·80	1·50
3205	**2552**	80y. multicoloured	1·80	1·50
3206	**2553**	80y. multicoloured	1·80	1·50
3207	**2554**	80y. multicoloured	1·80	1·50
3208	**2555**	80y. multicoloured	1·80	1·50

 2556 Hello Kitty
 2557 Hello Kitty
 2558 Hello Kitty
2559 Hello Kitty
2560 Hello Kitty
2561 Hello Kitty
 2562 Hello Kitty
2563 Hello Kitty
 2564 Hello Kitty
2565 Hello Kitty
 2566 Hello Kitty
 2567 Hello Kitty
 2568 Hello Kitty
 2569 Hello Kitty
 2570 Hello Kitty

2004. Greetings Stamps. Hello Kitty. Self-adhesive.

3209	**2556**	50y. multicoloured	1·30	1·10
3210	**2557**	50y. multicoloured	1·30	1·10
3211	**2558**	50y. multicoloured	1·30	1·10
3212	**2559**	50y. multicoloured	1·30	1·10
3213	**2560**	50y. multicoloured	1·30	1·10
3214	**2561**	50y. multicoloured	1·30	1·10
3215	**2562**	50y. multicoloured	1·30	1·10
3216	**2563**	50y. multicoloured	1·30	1·10
3217	**2564**	50y. multicoloured	1·30	1·10
3218	**2565**	50y. multicoloured	1·30	1·10
3219	**2566**	80y. multicoloured	1·80	1·50
3220	**2567**	80y. multicoloured	1·80	1·50
3221	**2568**	80y. multicoloured	1·80	1·50
3222	**2569**	80y. multicoloured	1·80	1·50
3223	**2570**	80y. multicoloured	1·80	1·50

2571 Marvellous Melmo 1

2573 Wooden Microscope

2572 Hanaoka Seishu

2574 Takamine Jokichi

2575 Drug Delivery System

2576 Marvellous Melmo 2

2577 Marvellous Melmo 3

2578 Marvellous Melmo 4

2004. Science, Technology and Animation (3rd issue).

3224	**2571**	80y. multicoloured	1·80	1·50
3225	**2572**	80y. multicoloured	1·80	1·50
3226	**2573**	80y. multicoloured	1·80	1·50
3227	**2574**	80y. multicoloured	1·80	1·50
3228	**2575**	80y. multicoloured	1·80	1·50
3229	**2576**	80y. multicoloured	1·80	1·50
3230	**2577**	80y. multicoloured	1·80	1·50
3231	**2578**	80y. multicoloured	1·80	1·50

2579 Kagaku Ninja-Tai Gatchman 1

2580 Perpetual Motion Machine

2581 OHSUMI (satellite) 2502 Conducting Polymer

2583 Eye (Tissue/Organ Reproductive Medicine)

2584 Kagaku Ninja-Tai Gatchman 2

2585 Kagaku Ninja-Tai Gatchman 3

2586 Kagaku Ninja-Tai Gatchman 4

2004. Science, Technology and Animation (4th issue).

3232	**2579**	80y. multicoloured	1·80	1·50
3233	**2580**	80y. multicoloured	1·80	1·50
3234	**2581**	80y. multicoloured	1·80	1·50
3235	**2582**	80y. multicoloured	1·80	1·50
3236	**2583**	80y. multicoloured	1·80	1·50
3237	**2584**	80y. multicoloured	1·80	1·50
3238	**2585**	80y. multicoloured	1·80	1·50
3239	**2586**	80y. multicoloured	1·80	1·50

2587 Morizo and Kiccoro (official mascots) in Orbit

2005. EXPO 2005 World Exhibition, Aichi, Japan. Multicoloured.

| 3240 | | 80y.+10y. Type **2587** | 1·90 | 1·60 |

3241 80y.+10y. Morizo and Kiccoro holding hands — 1·90 1·60

2589 Uchuno sakura gohiki no saru zu (Mori Sosen)

2004. Philately Week.
3242 2589 80y. multicoloured — 1·80 1·50

2590 Ten Point and Tosho Boy (22nd Arima Memorial Stakes)

2004. 50th of Japan Racing Association. Multicoloured.
3243 80y. Type 2590 — 1·80 1·50
3244 80y. Narita Brian (61st Tokyo Yushun (Japanese Derby)) — 1·80 1·50

2592 Police Car

2004. 50th Anniv of Police Law. Multicoloured.
3245 80y. Type 2592 — 1·80 1·50
3246 80y. Police motorcyclist — 1·80 1·50
Nos. 3245/6 were issued together, se-tenant, forming a composite design.

2594 Donkichi holding Pencil

2003. Letter Writing Day. Multicoloured.
3247 50y. Type 2594 — 1·30 1·10
3248 50y. Hime (25×33 mm) — 1·30 1·10
3249 50y. Shochan (25×33 mm) — 1·30 1·10
3250 50y. Owl (33×36 mm) — 1·30 1·10
3251 80y. Pigeon carrying envelope (33×34 mm) — 1·80 1·50
3252 80y. Squirrel with wings (33×36 mm) — 1·80 1·50
3253 80y. Stork (30×30 mm) — 1·80 1·50
3254 80y. Hime with wings (27×36 mm) — 1·80 1·50
3255 80y. Donkichi (27×37 mm) — 1·80 1·50
3256 80y. Kuriko (27×37 mm) — 1·80 1·50
3257 80y. Goddess (28×40 mm) — 1·80 1·50
3258 80y. Shochan with wings (28×36 mm) — 1·80 1·50
3259 80y. Squirrel holding envelope and flowers (28×29 mm) — 1·80 1·50
3260 80y. Rabbit (30×30 mm) — 1·80 1·50
MS3261 72×94 mm. Nos. 3247 and 3256 — 3·25 3·00

2608 Athens 2004 Emblem

2004. Olympic Games, Athens. Multicoloured.
3262 2608 80y. — 1·60 1·30
3263 80y. Olympic Rings, Flame and Olympia Ruins — 1·60 1·30

2610 Majinga Z 4

2611 Model Steam Engine

2612 KS Steel

2613 Shinkai 6500

2614 Fuel Cell

2615 Majinga Z 1

2616 Majinga Z 2

2617 Majinga Z 3

2004. Science, Technology and Animation (5th issue).
3264 2610 80y. multicoloured — 1·70 1·40
3265 2611 80y. multicoloured — 1·70 1·40
3266 2612 80y. multicoloured — 1·70 1·40
3267 2613 80y. multicoloured — 1·70 1·40
3268 2614 80y. multicoloured — 1·70 1·40
3269 2615 80y. multicoloured — 1·70 1·40
3270 2616 80y. multicoloured — 1·70 1·40
3271 2617 80y. multicoloured — 1·70 1·40

2618 Mount Fuji (Frederic Harris)

2004. 150th Anniv of America—Japan Relations. Multicoloured.
3272 80y. Type 2618 — 1·70 1·40
3273 80y. Cafe (Yasuo Kuniyoshi) — 1·70 1·40

2620 Medical Symbols as Figure

2004. World Medical Association (WMA) General Assembly, Tokyo.
3274 2620 80y. multicoloured — 1·70 1·40

2621 Hirarsukai

2004. International Correspondence Week. Paintings from 53 Stations of Tokaido by Utagawa Hiroshige. Multicoloured.
3275 90y. Type 2621 — 1·90 1·60
3276 110y. Yokkaichi — 2·50 2·10
3277 130y. Tsuchiyama — 3·00 2·50

2624 Lafcadio Hearn (Koizumi Yakumo) (writer) (death centenary)

2004. Anniversaries. Multicoloured.
3278 80y. Type 2624 — 1·60 1·30
3279 80y. Isamu Noguchi (sculptor) (birth centenary) — 1·60 1·30
3280 80y. Koga Masao (composer) (birth centenary) — 1·60 1·30

2627 Rooster (Hita-Dorei (clay bell))

2004. New Year's Greetings.
3281 50y. Type 2627 — 1·10 90
3282 80y. Rooster (Shimotsuke-Dorei (clay bell)) — 1·60 1·30

2630 Rooster (Shimotsuke-Dorei (clay bell))

2004. New Year Lottery Stamps. Multicoloured.
3284 50y.+3y. Rooster (Hita-Dorei (clay bell)) — 1·20 95
3285 80y.+3y. Type 2630 — 1·70 1·40
Each stamp carries a lottery number.

2631 Doraemon 4

2632 Hiraga Gennai

2633 Mechanical "netsuke"

2634 Television Set

2635 Plastic Optical Fibre (POF)

2636 Doraemon 1

2637 Doraemon 2

2638 Doraemon 3

2004. Science, Technology and Animation (6th issue). Multicoloured.
3286 2631 80y. multicoloured — 1·60 1·30
3287 2632 80y. multicoloured — 1·60 1·30
3288 2633 80y. multicoloured — 1·60 1·30
3289 2634 80y. multicoloured — 1·60 1·30
3290 2635 80y. multicoloured — 1·60 1·30
3291 2636 80y. multicoloured — 1·60 1·30

3292 2637 80y. multicoloured — 1·60 1·30
3293 2638 80y. multicoloured — 1·60 1·30

2639 "tori" (Tensho style) (Toda Teizan)

2640 "tori" (Kinbun style) (Seki Masato)

2641 "tori" (Kinbun style) (Onchi Shunyou)

2642 "tori" (Tensho style) (Funamoto Hou'un)

2643 "tori" (Kana style) (Koyama Yasuko)

2644 "tori" (Sousho style) (Watanabe Kan'ou)

2645 "tori" (Kobun style) (Inamuru un'dou)

2646 "tori" (Reisho style) (Oono Kouken)

2647 "tori" (Kokotsumoji style) (Oohira Santou)

2648 "tori" (Kobun style) (Noguchi Hakutei)

2004. Greetings Stamps. Eto Calligraphy.
3294 2639 80y. multicoloured — 1·60 1·30
3295 2640 80y. multicoloured — 1·60 1·30
3296 2641 80y. multicoloured — 1·60 1·30
3297 2642 80y. multicoloured — 1·60 1·30
3298 2643 80y. multicoloured — 1·60 1·30
3299 2644 80y. multicoloured — 1·60 1·30
3300 2645 80y. multicoloured — 1·60 1·30
3301 2646 80y. multicoloured — 1·60 1·30
3302 2647 80y. multicoloured — 1·60 1·30
3303 2648 80y. multicoloured — 1·60 1·30

2649 "Nangicho" (bird of suffering)

2005. International Conference on Disaster Reduction.
3304 2649 80y. multicoloured — 1·60 1·30

2650 Douglas 747 and Flowers

2005. Opening of Chubu International Airport.
3304a 2650 80y. multicoloured — 1·60 1·30

2651 Time Bokan 1   **2652** Circular Loom (invented by Toyoda Sakichi)

2653 Shinkansen (bullet train)   **2654** Micro-machine

2655 International Space Station   **2656** Time Bokan 2

2657 Time Bokan 3   **2658** Time Bokan 4

2005. Science, Technology and Animation (7th issue).

3305	**2651**	80y. multicoloured	1·60	1·30
3306	**2652**	80y. multicoloured	1·60	1·30
3307	**2653**	80y. multicoloured	1·60	1·30
3308	**2654**	80y. multicoloured	1·60	1·30
3309	**2655**	80y. multicoloured	1·60	1·30
3310	**2656**	80y. multicoloured	1·60	1·30
3311	**2657**	80y. multicoloured	1·60	1·30
3312	**2658**	80y. multicoloured	1·60	1·30

2659/60 Mammoth and Globe

2005. EXPO 2005, World Exposition, Aichi.

3313	**2659**	80c. multicoloured	1·60	1·30
3314	**2660**	80c. multicoloured	1·60	1·30

Nos. 3313/14 were issued together, *se-tenant*, forming a composite design.

2661 Daikei-shiyu-zu (giant hen and rooster)

2005. Philately Week.

3315	**2661**	80c. multicoloured	1·60	1·30

2662 Children

2005. Centenary of Rotary International.

3316	**2662**	80c. multicoloured	1·60	1·30

2663 Mt. Hodakadake   **2664** *Anemone narcissiflora*   **2665** Mt. Yarigatake

2666 *Aquilegia flabellate*

2005. Centenary of Japanese Alpine Club.

3317	**2663**	50c. multicoloured	1·30	1·10
3318	**2664**	50c. multicoloured	1·30	1·10
3319	**2665**	50c. multicoloured	1·30	1·10
3320	**2666**	50c. multicoloured	1·30	1·10

2667 Rayquaza   **2668** Gonbe

2669 Pikachu   **2670** Rizadon

2671 Mew

2005. Heroes and Heroines of Animation (1st issue). Pocket Monsters.

3321	**2667**	50y. multicoloured	1·30	1·10
3322	**2668**	50y. multicoloured	1·30	1·10
3323	**2669**	80y. multicoloured	1·60	1·30
3324	**2670**	80y. multicoloured	1·60	1·30
3325	**2671**	80y. multicoloured	1·60	1·30

See also Nos. 3341/50, 3389/98, 3404/13, 3536/45, 3572/81 and 3692/3701.

2672 Squirrel holding Nut

2005. Letter Writing Day. Multicoloured.

3326		50y. Type **2672**	1·30	1·10
3327		50y. Rabbit	1·30	1·10
3328		50y. Owl	1·30	1·10
3329		50y. Kuriko carrying envelope	1·30	1·10
3330		80y. Pigeon carrying envelope	1·60	1·30
3331		80y. Donkichi	1·60	1·30
3332		80y. Castle	1·60	1·30
3333		80y. Shochan	1·60	1·30
3334		80y. White rabbit	1·60	1·30
3335		80y. Kuriko	1·60	1·30
3336		80y. Hime	1·60	1·30
3337		80y. Violet	1·60	1·30
3338		80y. Squirrel	1·60	1·30
3339		80y. Fox	1·60	1·30
MS3340	72×94 mm. Nos. 3327 and 3333		3·00	2·75

2686 Gundum W   **2687** Hiiro

2688 Freedom Gundam and Kira Yamato   **2689** Justice Gundam and Arthrun Zala

2690 Amuro Ray   **2691** Gundum

2692 Zaku   **2693** Char Aznable

2694 Kamille   **2695** Z Gundum

2005. Heroes and Heroines of Animation (2nd issue). Mobile Suit Gundam.

3341	**2686**	50y. multicoloured	1·20	95
3342	**2687**	50y. multicoloured	1·20	95
3343	**2688**	80y. multicoloured	1·60	1·30
3344	**2689**	80y. multicoloured	1·60	1·30
3345	**2690**	80y. multicoloured	1·60	1·30
3346	**2691**	80y. multicoloured	1·60	1·30
3347	**2692**	80y. multicoloured	1·60	1·30
3348	**2693**	80y. multicoloured	1·60	1·30
3349	**2694**	80y. multicoloured	1·60	1·30
3350	**2695**	80y. multicoloured	1·60	1·30

Nos. 3341/2, Nos. 3343/4, Nos. 3345/6, Nos. 3347/8 and Nos. 3349/50, respectively, were issued together, *se-tenant*, forming a composite design.

2696 Ono No Komachi (poet) (painting) (Tosa Mitsuoki)   **2697** Fujiwara no Teika (poet) (painting) (Kano Tanyu)

2005. Literary Anniversaries.

3351	**2696**	80y. multicoloured (1100th anniv of Kokinshu)	1·60	1·30
3352	**2697**	80y. multicoloured (800th anniv of Shinkokinshu)	1·60	1·30

2698/9 Globe, Satellite and Rocket

2005. International Astronautical Congress, Fukuoka.

3353	**2698**	80y. multicoloured	1·60	1·30
3354	**2699**	80y. multicoloured	1·60	1·30

Nos. 3353/4 were issued together, *se-tenant*, forming a composite design.

2700 Mariko

2701 Minakuchi

2702 Shinagawa

2005. International Correspondence Week. Paintings from *53 Stations of Tokaido* by Utagawa Hiroshige.

3355	**2700**	90y. multicoloured	1·70	1·40
3356	**2701**	110y. multicoloured	1·90	1·60
3357	**2702**	130y. multicoloured	2·20	1·80

2703 Cyclamen (*Arai Sonoko*)

2005. Greetings Stamps. Self-adhesive.

3358		50y. Type **2703**	1·20	95
3359		50y. Flower Fairy (Nagata Moe)	1·20	95
3360		50y. Bear (Sugita Yutaka)	1·20	95
3361		50y. Gorilla (Murakami Tsutomu)	1·20	95
3362		50y. Snowman (Koide Masaki)	1·20	95
3363		80y. Father Christmas (Koide Masaki) (27×38 mm)	1·60	1·30
3364		80y. Poinsettias and Candle (Arai Sonoko) (27×38 mm)	1·60	1·30
3365		80y. Angel, Presents and Tree (Nagata Moe) (27×38 mm)	1·60	1·30
3366		80y. Hamster (Sugita Yutaka) (27×38 mm)	1·60	1·30
3367		80y. Cat (Murakami Tsutomu) (27×38 mm)	1·60	1·30

2713 Akita Dog

2005. New Year's Greetings. Multicoloured.

3368		50y. Type **2713**	1·20	95
3369		80y. Dog (Sadowara (clay))	1·60	1·30
MS3370	94×72 mm. Nos. 3368/9		2·75	2·40

2716 Dog (Sadowara (clay))

2005. New Year Lottery Stamps. Multicoloured.

3371		50y.+3y. Akita Dog	1·30	1·10
3372		80y.+3y. Type **2716**	1·70	1·40

Each stamp carries a lottery number.

2717 "inu" (Tensho style) (Ooi Kintei)   **2718** "inu" (Kinbun style) (Takagiwa Suihou)

2719 "inu"
(pictograph)
(Kaneko Takyoshi)

2720 "inu"
(phonetic letters)
(Yonemoto Ikkou)

2721 "inu"
(Tensho style)
(Kishimoto Tarou)

2722 "inu"
(Tensho style in
half moon)
(Tsujimoto
Daiwun)

2723 "inu"
(symbolic
characters) (Seki
Masato)

2724 "inu"
(semi-cursive
style) (Tanaka
Touwun)

2725 "inu"
(semi-cursive
style) (Katou
Shoudou)

2726 "inu"
(Koukotsumoji
style) (Kobayashi
Hougyu)

2005. Greetings Stamps. Eto Calligraphy.

3373	**2717**	80y. multicoloured	1·60	1·30
3374	**2718**	80y. multicoloured	1·60	1·30
3375	**2719**	80y. multicoloured	1·60	1·30
3376	**2720**	80y. multicoloured	1·60	1·30
3377	**2721**	80y. multicoloured	1·60	1·30
3378	**2722**	80y. multicoloured	1·60	1·30
3379	**2723**	80y. multicoloured	1·60	1·30
3380	**2724**	80y. multicoloured	1·60	1·30
3381	**2725**	80y. multicoloured	1·60	1·30
3382	**2726**	80y. multicoloured	1·60	1·30

2727 Beethoven

2005. Germany in Japan. Multicoloured.

3383	80y. Type **2727**	1·60	1·30
3384	80y. Karl Benz driving Benz Patent Motorwagen, 1886	1·60	1·30
3385	80y. Male Japanese musician (Meissen)	1·60	1·30
3386	80y. Female Japanese musician (Meissen)	1·60	1·30
3387	80y. Equestrian acrobat (Meissen)	1·60	1·30
3388	80y. Harlequin (Meissen)	1·60	1·30

2733/4 Tetsuro and Maetel

2735/6 Claire and The Conductor

2737/8 Freija and Maetel and Tetsuro
and Moriki Yutaka

2739/40 Emeraldas and Count Mecha
and Herlock

2741/2 Maetel and Galaxy Express 999

2006. Heroes and Heroines of Animation (3rd issue). Galaxy Express 999.

3389	**2733**	80y. multicoloured	1·60	1·30
3390	**2734**	80y. multicoloured	1·60	1·30
3391	**2735**	80y. multicoloured	1·60	1·30
3392	**2736**	80y. multicoloured	1·60	1·30
3393	**2737**	80y. multicoloured	1·60	1·30
3394	**2738**	80y. multicoloured	1·60	1·30
3395	**2739**	80y. multicoloured	1·60	1·30
3396	**2740**	80y. multicoloured	1·60	1·30
3397	**2741**	80y. multicoloured	1·60	1·30
3398	**2742**	80y. multicoloured	1·60	1·30

Nos. 3389/90, 3391/2, 3393/4, 3395/6 and 3397/8, respectively, were issued together, *se-tenant*, each pair forming a composite design.

2743 Rabbit and
Bird (Hirosawa Yo)

2006. International Exchanges and Friendship. Winning Entries in Design a Stamp Competition. Multicoloured.

3399	80y. Type **2743**	1·60	1·30
3400	80y. Children kissing (Ogasawara Maki)	1·60	1·30
3401	80y. Bears exchanging Fish (Mori Kiyotaka)	1·60	1·30
3402	80y. Dog and bear (Kobayashi Ryota)	1·60	1·30
3403	80y. Animals on globe (Takanami Suzuka)	1·60	1·30

2748/9 Shrunken Detective and
Detective Conan

2750/1 Shin'ichi and Conan and Ran

2752/3 Doctor Agasa and Ayumi and
Mitsuhiko and Genta

2754/5 Haibara Ai and Conan

2756/7 Mysterious Thief Kid and
Shin'ichi and Conan

2006. Heroes and Heroines of Animation (4th issue). Detective Conan.

3404	**2748**	80y. multicoloured	1·60	1·30
3405	**2749**	80y. multicoloured	1·60	1·30
3406	**2750**	80y. multicoloured	1·60	1·30
3407	**2751**	80y. multicoloured	1·60	1·30
3408	**2752**	80y. multicoloured	1·60	1·30
3409	**2753**	80y. multicoloured	1·60	1·30
3410	**2754**	80y. multicoloured	1·60	1·30
3411	**2755**	80y. multicoloured	1·60	1·30
3412	**2756**	80y. multicoloured	1·60	1·30
3413	**2757**	80y. multicoloured	1·60	1·30

Nos. 3404/5, 3406/7, 3408/9, 3410/11 and 3412/13 respectively, were issued together, *se-tenant*, each pair forming a composite design.

2758 Morning
Glory

2006. Philatelic Week. Paintings by Maruyama Oukyo. Multicoloured.

3414	80y. Type **2758**	1·50	1·20
3415	80y. Puppies	1·50	1·20

2760
Australian
Flag and
Uluru (Ayers
Rock)

2006. Japan—Australia Exchange Year—2006. Multicoloured.

3416	80y. Type **2760**	1·50	1·20
3417	80y. Kangaroo	1·50	1·20
3418	80y. Sydney Opera House	1·50	1·20
3419	80y. Flag and Sydney Opera House	1·50	1·20
3420	80y. Fish (Great Barrier Reef)	1·50	1·20
3421	80y. Heart Reef	1·50	1·20
3422	80y. Golden wattle	1·50	1·20
3423	80y. Bottle bush	1·50	1·20
3424	80y. Koalas	1·50	1·20
3425	80y. Kookabura	1·50	1·20

Nos. 3416/17 3418/19 and 3424/5 respectively were issued together, *se-tenant*, forming composite designs.

2770/1 Kumano Hongu-taisha Shrine

2772
Nachinoootaki
Waterfall

2773 Kumano
Hongu-taisha
Shrine

2774 Fire Festival,
Nachi

2775 Nyoirin-dou
Main Hall,
Seigantoji Temple

2776 Kongobuji
Temple Gate

2777
Kongaradouji
(wooden statue),
Kongobuji Temple

2778 Zaou-dou
Main Hall,
Kinpusenji
Temple

2779
Zaou-gongen
(wooden statue),
Kinpusenji
Temple

2006. World Heritage.

3426	**2770**	80y. multicoloured	1·50	1·20
3427	**2771**	80y. multicoloured	1·50	1·20
3428	**2772**	80y. multicoloured	1·50	1·20
3429	**2773**	80y. multicoloured	1·50	1·20
3430	**2774**	80y. multicoloured	1·50	1·20
3431	**2775**	80y. multicoloured	1·50	1·20
3432	**2776**	80y. multicoloured	1·50	1·20
3433	**2777**	80y. multicoloured	1·50	1·20
3434	**2778**	80y. multicoloured	1·50	1·20
3435	**2779**	80y. multicoloured	1·50	1·20

2780 Fairy on
Flower

2006. Greetings Stamps. Multicoloured. Self-adhesive.

3436	50y. Type **2780** (23×27 mm)	1·10	90
3437	50y. Church bell (23×27 mm)	1·10	90
3438	50y. Bouquet (23×27 mm)	1·10	90
3439	50y. Dolphin (23×27 mm)	1·10	90
3440	50y. Humming bird (23×27 mm)	1·10	90
3441	80y. Pink orchid (23×27 mm)	1·50	1·20
3442	80y. Fairy and flowers (25×37 mm)	1·50	1·20
3443	80y. Oranges and blossom (25×37 mm)	1·50	1·20
3444	80y. Parrot (25×37 mm)	1·50	1·20
3445	80y. Orange flowers (25×37 mm)	1·50	1·20

2790 *Iseno-taifu*
(Koyama Yasuko)

2791
*Goptokudaijino-
sadaijin*
(Mitsuoka Keiso)

2792
*Ooshikouchino-
mitsune* (Miyazaki
Shikou)

2793
*Yamabeno-
akahito*
(Matsumoto Eiko)

2794
Suouno-naishi
(Miyake Soushu)

2795 *Double Cherry Blossoms (Koyama Yasuko)*

2796 *"Iseno-taifu" (Koyama Yasuko)*

2797 *A Wan Morning Moon (Mitsuoka Keiso)*

2798 *Goptokudaijino-sadaijin (Mitsuoka Keiso)*

2799 *White Chrysanthemums (Miyazaki Shikou)*

2800 *Ooshikouchino-mitsune (Miyazaki Shikou)*

2801 *Mt. Fuji (Matsumoto Eiko)*

2802 *Yamabeno-akahito (Matsumoto Eiko)*

2803 *Spring Night (Miyake Soushu)*

2804 *Suouno-naishi (Miyake Soushu)*

2006. Letter Writing Day. Multicoloured. Sizes Nos. 3446/50 25×30 mm. and Nos. 3451/60 28×39 mm.

3446	**2790**	50y. multicoloured	1·10	90
3447	**2791**	50y. multicoloured	1·10	90
3448	**2792**	50y. multicoloured	1·10	90
3449	**2793**	50y. multicoloured	1·10	90
3450	**2794**	50y. multicoloured	1·10	90
3451	**2795**	80y. multicoloured	1·50	1·20
3452	**2796**	80y. multicoloured	1·50	1·20
3453	**2797**	80y. multicoloured	1·50	1·20
3454	**2798**	80y. multicoloured	1·50	1·20
3455	**2799**	80y. multicoloured	1·50	1·20
3456	**2800**	80y. multicoloured	1·50	1·20
3457	**2801**	80y. multicoloured	1·50	1·20
3458	**2802**	80y. multicoloured	1·50	1·20
3459	**2803**	80y. multicoloured	1·50	1·20
3460	**2804**	80y. multicoloured	1·50	1·20

2805 *World and Flowers*

2006. Letter Writing Week. 50th Anniv of Accession to United Nations. Multicoloured.

3461		90y. Type **2805**	1·70	1·40
3462		110y. World, mountain and flowers	1·90	1·60

2807 *Vanda "Miss Joaquim"*

2808 *Mokara "Lion's Gold"*

2809 *Vanda "Mimi Palmer"*

2810 *Renanthera Singaporean*

2811 *Heron and Hollyhocks (detail) (Flowers and Birds of Four Seasons) (Sakai Hoitsu)*

2812 *Iris and Moorhen (detail) (Flowers and Birds of Four Seasons) (Sakai Hoitsu)*

2006. Greetings Stamps. 40th Anniv of Japan—Singapore Diplomatic Relations. Self-adhesive.

3463	**2808**	50y. multicoloured	1·10	90
3464	**2810**	50y. multicoloured	1·10	90
3465	**2807**	80y. multicoloured	1·50	1·20
3466	**2809**	80y. multicoloured	1·50	1·20
3467	**2811**	90y. multicoloured	1·70	1·40
3468	**2812**	110y. multicoloured	1·90	1·60

Stamps of a similar design were issued by Singapore.

2813 *Tange Sazen*

2814 *Carmen Comes Home*

2815 *Ugetsu Monogatari*

2816 *Tokyo Story*

2817 *Seven Samurai*

2818 *A Night in Hawaii*

2819 *Unknown*

2820 *Guitar o Motta Wataridori*

2821 *Miyamoto Musashi*

2822 *Kyupora no Aru Machi*

2823 *Sailor-fuku to Kikanju*

2824 *Otoko.wa Tsuraiyo*

2825 *Kamata Koshin-kyoku*

2826 *Yomigaeru Kinro*

2827 *MacArthur's Children*

2828 *HANA-BI*

2829 *Paradise Lost*

2830 *Gamera*

2831 *Twilight Samurai*

2832 *Godzilla*

2006. Japanese Cinema.

3469	**2813**	80y. multicoloured	1·50	1·20
3470	**2814**	80y. multicoloured	1·50	1·20
3471	**2815**	80y. multicoloured	1·50	1·20
3472	**2816**	80y. multicoloured	1·50	1·20
3473	**2817**	80y. multicoloured	1·50	1·20
3474	**2818**	80y. multicoloured	1·50	1·20
3475	**2819**	80y. multicoloured	1·50	1·20
3476	**2820**	80y. multicoloured	1·50	1·20
3477	**2821**	80y. multicoloured	1·50	1·20
3478	**2822**	80y. multicoloured	1·50	1·20
3479	**2823**	80y. multicoloured	1·50	1·20
3480	**2824**	80y. multicoloured	1·50	1·20
3481	**2825**	80y. multicoloured	1·50	1·20
3482	**2826**	80y. multicoloured	1·50	1·20
3483	**2827**	80y. multicoloured	1·50	1·20
3484	**2828**	80y. multicoloured	1·50	1·20
3485	**2829**	80y. multicoloured	1·50	1·20
3486	**2830**	80y. multicoloured	1·50	1·20
3487	**2831**	80y. multicoloured	1·50	1·20
3488	**2832**	80y. multicoloured	1·50	1·20

2833 *Autumn Flowers and Ox Cart*

2834 *Autumn Flowers and Ox Cart*

2006. 50th Anniv of International Ikebana Convention.

3489	**2833**	80y. multicoloured	1·50	1·20
3490	**2834**	80y. multicoloured	1·50	1·20

2835 *Treasured Boar*

2006. New Year's Greetings. Multicoloured.

3491		50y. Type **2835**	1·10	90
3492		80y. Zodiac boar	1·50	1·20

2838 *Zodiac Boar*

2006. New Year Lottery Stamps. Multicoloured.

3494		50y.+3y. Treasured boar	1·20	95
3495		80y.+3y. Type **2838**	1·60	1·30

Each stamp carries a lottery number.

2839 *Squirrel (Sugita Yutaka)*

2006. Greetings Stamps. Multicoloured. Self-adhesive.

3496		50y. Type **2839**	1·10	90
3497		50y. Bell (Arai Sonoko)	1·10	90
3498		50y. Clown (Nagata Moe)	1·10	90
3499		50y. Polar bear (Watanabe Hiroshi)	1·10	90
3500		50y. Bear Santa Claus (Murakami Tsutomu)	1·10	90
3501		80y. Cat Santa Claus (Murakami Tsutomu)	1·50	1·20
3502		80y. Cyclamen (Nagata Moe)	1·50	1·20
3503		80y. Snowman (Koide Masaki)	1·50	1·20
3504		80y. Reindeer (Watanabe Hiroshi)	1·50	1·20
3505		80y. Wreath (Arai Sonoko)	1·50	1·20

2849 *Semi-cursive Style (Minagawa Gashu)*

2850 *Kinbun Style (Usuda Tousen)*

2851 *Reisho Style (Hayashi Shouen)*

2852 *Former Japanese Cursive (Yamazaki Kyouko)*

2853 *Kinbun Style (Sugano Seihou)*

2854 *Kinbun Style (Seki Masato)*

2855 *Inscribed on Kanae (Youhida Seiso)*

2856 *Kinbun Style (Nakano Hokumei)*

2857 Tensho Style (Sadamasa Shoutou)   **2858** Reisho Style (Kamigori Aichiku)

2006. Greetings Stamps. Eto Calligraphy.

3506	**2849**	80y. multicoloured	1·50	1·20
3507	**2850**	80y. multicoloured	1·50	1·20
3508	**2851**	80y. multicoloured	1·50	1·20
3509	**2852**	80y. multicoloured	1·50	1·20
3510	**2853**	80y. multicoloured	1·50	1·20
3511	**2854**	80y. multicoloured	1·50	1·20
3512	**2855**	80y. multicoloured	1·50	1·20
3513	**2856**	80y. multicoloured	1·50	1·20
3514	**2857**	80y. multicoloured	1·50	1·20
3515	**2858**	80y. multicoloured	1·50	1·20

2859/60 Research Ship and Pilatus PC-6 Turbo Porter Research Airplane

2861/2 Penguins

2863/4 Research Ship and Penguins and Penguins

2865/6 Sled Dog and Sled Dog standing

2867/8 Ship and Scientist and Tracked Vehicle

2869 Tracked Vehicle   **2870** Research Airplane

2871 Research Ship and Sled Team   **2872** Seal

2873 Penguin

2874 Two Penguins

2875 Sled Dog

2876 Penguin Chicks

2877 Penguin and Chick

2878 Sled Dog

2007. 50th Anniversary of the Japanese Antarctic Research Expedition. (a) Ordinary gum.

3516	**2859**	80y. multicoloured	1·50	1·20
3517	**2860**	80y. multicoloured	1·50	1·20
3518	**2861**	80y. multicoloured	1·50	1·20
3519	**2862**	80y. multicoloured	1·50	1·20
3520	**2863**	80y. multicoloured	1·50	1·20
3521	**2864**	80y. multicoloured	1·50	1·20
3522	**2865**	80y. multicoloured	1·50	1·20
3523	**2866**	80y. multicoloured	1·50	1·20
3524	**2867**	80y. multicoloured	1·50	1·20
3525	**2868**	80y. multicoloured	1·50	1·20

(b) Self-adhesive.

3526	**2869**	80y. multicoloured	1·60	1·30
3527	**2870**	80y. multicoloured	1·60	1·30
3528	**2871**	80y. multicoloured	1·60	1·30
3529	**2872**	80y. multicoloured	1·60	1·30
3530	**2873**	80y. multicoloured	1·60	1·30
3531	**2874**	80y. multicoloured	1·60	1·30
3532	**2875**	80y. multicoloured	1·60	1·30
3533	**2876**	80y. multicoloured	1·60	1·30
3534	**2877**	80y. multicoloured	1·60	1·30
3535	**2878**	80y. multicoloured	1·60	1·30

Nos. 3516/17, 3518/19, 3520/1, 3522/3 and 3524/5 respectively were issued together, *se-tenant*, each pair forming a composite design.

Nos. 3526/35 were issued together forming a composite design.

2879/80 Evangelion Unit 01 and Ikari Shinji

2881/2 Ayanami Rei and Evangelion Unit 00

2883/4 Soryu Asuka Langley and Evangelion Unit 02

2885/6 Ayanami Rei and Soryu Asuka Langley and Katsuragi Misato

2887/8 Nagisa Kaworu and Sachiel, the Third Angel

2007. Heroes and Heroines of Animation (5th issue). Neon Genesis Evangelion.

3536	**2879**	80y. multicoloured	1·50	1·20
3537	**2880**	80y. multicoloured	1·50	1·20
3538	**2881**	80y. multicoloured	1·50	1·20
3539	**2882**	80y. multicoloured	1·50	1·20
3540	**2883**	80y. multicoloured	1·50	1·20
3541	**2884**	80y. multicoloured	1·50	1·20
3542	**2885**	80y. multicoloured	1·50	1·20
3543	**2886**	80y. multicoloured	1·50	1·20
3544	**2887**	80y. multicoloured	1·50	1·20
3545	**2888**	80y. multicoloured	1·50	1·20

Nos. 3536/7, 3538/9, 3540/1, 3542/3 and 3544/5, respectively, were issued together, *se-tenant*, forming a composite design.

2889 Honden, Yoshino Mikumari Shrine

2890 Romon Soshoku, Yoshino Mikumari Shrine

2891 Omine-Okugake-Michi

2892 Honden, Kumano Hayatama-taisha Shrine

2893 Honden, Kumano Hayatama-taisha Shrine

2894 Kumano-Fusumino-Okami-Zazo, Kumano Hayatama-taisha Shrine

2895 Kumano Sankei-Michi Nakahechi   **2896** Statue, Kumano Sankei-Michi Nakahechi

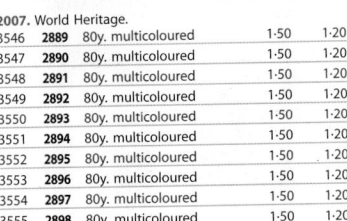

2897 Tahoto, Kongo-Sanmaiin Temple   **2898** Kyozo, Kongo-Sanmaiin Temple

2007. World Heritage.

3546	**2889**	80y. multicoloured	1·50	1·20
3547	**2890**	80y. multicoloured	1·50	1·20
3548	**2891**	80y. multicoloured	1·50	1·20
3549	**2892**	80y. multicoloured	1·50	1·20
3550	**2893**	80y. multicoloured	1·50	1·20
3551	**2894**	80y. multicoloured	1·50	1·20
3552	**2895**	80y. multicoloured	1·50	1·20
3553	**2896**	80y. multicoloured	1·50	1·20
3554	**2897**	80y. multicoloured	1·50	1·20
3555	**2898**	80y. multicoloured	1·50	1·20

2899 *Running Boar* ((detail) 'Inoshishi-Zu')

2007. Philately Week. Paintings by Mori Ippo. Multicoloured.

3556	80y. Type **2899**	1·30	85
3557	80y. Sparrow ((detail) 'Sakura-Ni-suzume-Zu')	1·30	85
3558	80y. Cherry Tree ((detail) 'Sakura-Ni-suzume-Zu')	1·30	85
3559	80y. Flock of Birds ((detail) 'Guncho')	1·30	85
3560	80y. Great Tits ((detail) 'Hagi-Ni-Shijukara-Zu')	1·30	85
3561	80y. Sleeping Boar ((detail) 'Inoshishi-Zu')	1·30	85

2905 Taj Mahal

2007. Japan–India Friendship Year. Multicoloured.

3562	80y. Type **2905**	1·30	85
3563	80y. Camels	1·30	85
3564	80y. Bengal Tiger	1·30	85
3565	80y. Peacock	1·30	85
3566	80y. Buddhist Monastery, Sanchi	1·30	85
3567	80y. Goddess (statue), Sanchi	1·30	85
3568	80y. Woman ((detail) Indian miniature painting)	1·30	85
3569	80y. Woman ((detail) Indian calico print)	1·30	85
3570	80y. Bharat Natyam	1·30	85
3571	80y. Kathakali	1·30	85

2915/6 Conan and Lana

2917/8 Lana and Conan (different)

2919/20 Monsley and Lepka

2921/2 Jimsy, Umaso and Dyce

2923/4 Dr. Lao and Grandpa

2007. Heroes and Heroines of Animation (6th issue). Future Boy Conan.

3572	**2915**	80y. multicoloured	1·30	85
3573	**2916**	80y. multicoloured	1·30	85
3574	**2907**	80y. multicoloured	1·30	85
3575	**2918**	80y. multicoloured	1·30	85
3576	**2919**	80y. multicoloured	1·30	85

3577	2920	80y. multicoloured	1·30	85
3578	2921	80y. multicoloured	1·30	85
3579	2922	80y. multicoloured	1·30	85
3580	2923	80y. multicoloured	1·30	85
3581	2924	80y. multicoloured	1·30	85

Nos. 3572/3, 3574/5, 3576/7, 3578/9 and 3580/1 were issued together, *se-tenant*, forming a composite design.

2925/6 Lake and Mountains and Lake and Mountains (different)

2007. World Heritage. Shiretoko. Multicoloured.

3582	80y. Type **2925**	1·30	85
3583	80y. Type **2926**	1·30	85
3584	80y. Blakiston's fish owl	1·30	85
3585	80y. Sea ice and Mount Rausu	1·30	85
3586	80y. Chishima cherry blossom	1·30	85
3587	80y. Brown bear	1·30	85
3588	80y. Harbour seal	1·30	85
3589	80y. Yezo deer	1·30	85
3590	80y. Sea eagle	1·30	85
3591	80y. Viola kitmiana	1·30	85

Nos. 3582/3 were issued together, in *se-tenant*, pairs, forming a composite design.

2935 Kino Tsurayuki   **2936** Empress Jito

2937 Sarumaru Dayu   **2938** Minamotono Kanemasa

2939 Nijoinno Sanuki   **2940** Plum Blossom

2941 Kino Tsurayuki   **2942** Mount Kagu

2943 Empress Jito   **2944** Deer

2945 Sarumaru Dayu   **2946** Plovers

2947 Minamotono Kanemasa   **2948** Stone in Sea

2949 Nijoinno Sanuki

2007. Letter Writing Day.

3592	2935	50y. multicoloured	1·30	85
3593	2936	50y. multicoloured	1·30	85
3594	2937	50y. multicoloured	1·30	85
3595	2938	50y. multicoloured	1·30	85
3596	2939	50y. multicoloured	1·30	85
3597	2940	80y. multicoloured	1·30	85
3598	2941	80y. multicoloured	1·30	85
3599	2942	80y. multicoloured	1·30	85
3600	2943	80y. multicoloured	1·30	85
3601	2944	80y. multicoloured	1·30	85
3602	2945	80y. multicoloured	1·30	85
3603	2946	80y. multicoloured	1·30	85
3604	2947	80y. multicoloured	1·30	85
3605	2948	80y. multicoloured	1·30	85
3606	2949	80y. multicoloured	1·30	85

2950 Tamesue Dai   **2951** Ikeda Kumiko

2952 Kanemaru Yuzo   **2953** Suetsugu Shingo

2954 Fukushi Kayoko   **2955** Naito Masato

2956 Daigo Naoyuki   **2957** Narisako Kenji

2958 Sawano Daichi   **2959** Murofushi Koji

2007. International Association of Athletics Federations' World Championships, Osaka.

3607	2950	80y. multicoloured	1·30	85
3608	2951	80y. multicoloured	1·30	85
3609	2952	80y. multicoloured	1·30	85
3610	2953	80y. multicoloured	1·30	85
3611	2954	80y. multicoloured	1·30	85
3612	2955	80y. multicoloured	1·30	85
3613	2956	80y. multicoloured	1·30	85

3614	2957	80y. multicoloured	1·30	85
3615	2958	80y. multicoloured	1·30	85
3616	2959	80y. multicoloured	1·30	85

2960 Maple Leaves and Bamboo   **2961** Cherry Blossoms   **2962** Ratchaphruek Flower

2963 Rhynchostylis gigantean   **2964** Elephant   **2965** Flower

2966 Thai Dancer   **2967** Wat Phra Keo

2968 Elephant (Toshogu Shrine)   **2969** Elephant (Toshogu Shrine)

2007. 120th Anniv of Japan—Thailand Diplomatic Relations. Self-adhesive.

3617	2960	80y. multicoloured	1·30	85
3618	2961	80y. multicoloured	1·30	85
3619	2962	80y. multicoloured	1·30	85
3620	2963	80y. multicoloured	1·30	85
3621	2964	80y. multicoloured	1·30	85
3622	2965	80y. multicoloured	1·30	85
3623	2966	80y. multicoloured	1·30	85
3624	2967	80y. multicoloured	1·30	85
3625	2968	80y. multicoloured	1·30	85
3626	2969	80y. multicoloured	1·30	85

2970 Hodogaya

2007. International Correspondence Week. Paintings from *53 Stations of Tokaido* by Utagawa Hiroshige. Multicoloured.

3627	90y. Type **2970**	1·40	90
3628	110y. *Arai*	1·50	1·00
3629	130y. *Kusatsu*	1·70	1·10

2973 Maejima Hisoka (founder of modern post office)

2007. Establishment of Japan Post Corporation. Multicoloured.

3630	80y. Type **2973**	1·30	85
3631	80y. Early Post Office	1·30	85
3632	80y. Mail cart	1·30	85
3633	80y. Early customers	1·30	85
3634	80y. Early customers queuing	1·30	85
3635	80y.18 71 100mon Stamp (As Type **2**)	1·30	85
3636	80y. Sunflower	1·30	85
3637	80y. Leaves and blossom	1·30	85
3638	80y. Chrysanthemums	1·30	85
3639	80y. Maple leaves	1·30	85
3640	80y. Maple leaves (different)	1·30	85
3641	80y. Roses	1·30	85
3642	80y. Bird and flowers	1·30	85

3643	80y. Peonies	1·30	85
3644	80y. Irises	1·30	85
3645	80y. Hydrangeas	1·30	85

2989 Computer Programming   **2990** Computer Programming

2991 Plastering   **2992** Plastering

2993 Cooking   **2994** Cooking

 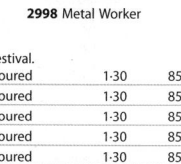

2995 Flower Arranging   **2996** Flower Arranging

2997 Metal Worker and Car   **2998** Metal Worker

2007. International Skills Festival.

3646	2989	80y. multicoloured	1·30	85
3647	2990	80y. multicoloured	1·30	85
3648	2991	80y. multicoloured	1·30	85
3649	2992	80y. multicoloured	1·30	85
3650	2993	80y. multicoloured	1·30	85
3651	2994	80y. multicoloured	1·30	85
3652	2995	80y. multicoloured	1·30	85
3653	2996	80y. multicoloured	1·30	85
3654	2997	80y. multicoloured	1·30	85
3655	2998	80y. multicoloured	1·30	85

2999 Two Rats sitting on Straw Bag

2007. New Year's Greetings. Multicoloured.

3656	50y. Type **2999**	60	10
3657	50y. Rat ('Junishi Shofuku Dorei')	60	10

3002 Rat ('Junishi Shofuku Dorei') ('Fukutoku Junishi Dorei')

2007. New Year Lottery Stamps. Multicoloured.

3658	50y.+3y. Two Rats sitting on Straw Bag ('Fukutoku Junishi Dorei')	60	10

3659	80y.+3y. Type 3002		1·30	85

Each stamp carries a lottery number.

3003 '08 NEW YEAR'

2007. New Year's Greetings. Multicoloured.

3660	3003	50y. multicoloured	70	10
3661	3003	50y. multicoloured	70	10

3004 Church (Tsutomu Murakami)

2007. Greetings Stamps. Multicoloured. Self-adhesive.

3662		50y. Type 3004	60	10
3663		50y. Swans (Moe Nagata)	60	10
3664		50y. Santa Claus (Tsutomu Murakami)	60	10
3665		50y. Flowers (Sonoko Arai)	60	10
3666		50y. Kitten (Ken Kuroi)	60	10
3667		80y. Santa Claus and Reindeer (Murakami Tsutomu)	1·30	85
3668		80y. Hellebore (Nagata Moe)	1·30	85
3669		80y. Snowman	1·30	85
3670		80y. Strawberries	1·30	85
3671		80y. Snowman	1·30	85

Nos. 3662/6 are 29×29 mm. and Nos. 3667/71 are 27×33 mm.

3014 'Rat' Kinbun Style (Seki Masato)

3015 'Rat' Reisho Style (Dairaku Kasersu)

3016 'Boshi' Reisho Style (Goto Chiskusei)

3017 'Rat' (Ishitobi Hakuko)

3018 'Rat' Sosho Style (Yahagi Shunkei)

3019 'Rat' Shoden Style (Yoshikawa Juichi)

3020 'Rat' Tensho Style (Hatsumi Kazuo)

3021 'Ne' Kana Style (Uchiyama Reiko)

3022 'Rat' Zhou Dynasty (Mizushima Sanyo)

3023 'Rat' Kinbun Style (Nakagawa Kyoji)

2007. Greetings Stamps. Eto Calligraphy.

3672	3014	80y. multicoloured	1·30	85
3673	3015	80y. multicoloured	1·30	85
3674	3016	80y. multicoloured	1·30	85
3675	3017	80y. multicoloured	1·30	85
3676	3018	80y. multicoloured	1·30	85

3677	3019	80y. multicoloured	1·30	85
3678	3020	80y. multicoloured	1·30	85
3679	3021	80y. multicoloured	1·30	85
3680	3022	80y. multicoloured	1·30	85
3681	3023	80y. multicoloured	1·30	85

3024 Mount Fuji

3025 Mount Fuji in Spring

3026 Mount Fuji in Summer

3027 Mount Fuji in Autumn

3028 Mount Fuji in Winter

3029 Bamboo Grove

3030 Somei-Yoshino Cherry Blossom

3031 *Hydrangea macrophylla*

3032 Maple Leaves

3033 Narcissus

2008. Yokoso! Japan Weeks (experiencing Japan).

3682	3024	80y. multicoloured	1·30	85
3683	3025	80y. multicoloured	1·30	85
3684	3026	80y. multicoloured	1·30	85
3685	3027	80y. multicoloured	1·30	85
3686	3028	80y. multicoloured	1·30	85
3687	3029	80y. multicoloured	1·30	85
3688	3030	80y. multicoloured	1·30	85
3689	3031	80y. multicoloured	1·30	85

3690	3032	80y. multicoloured	1·30	85
3691	3033	80y. multicoloured	1·30	85

3034/5 Hanasaka Jisan

3036/7 Kaguya Hime

3038/9 Kasajizo

3040/1 Momotaro

3042/3 Tsuru no Ongaeshi

2008. Heroes and Heroines of Animation (7th issue). Manga Nippon Mukashi Banashi.

3692	3034	80y. multicoloured	1·30	85
3693	3035	80y. multicoloured	1·30	85
3694	3036	80y. multicoloured	1·30	85
3695	3037	80y. multicoloured	1·30	85
3696	3038	80y. multicoloured	1·30	85
3697	3039	80y. multicoloured	1·30	85
3698	3040	80y. multicoloured	1·30	85
3699	3041	80y. multicoloured	1·30	85
3700	3042	80y. multicoloured	1·30	85
3701	3043	80y. multicoloured	1·30	85

Nos. 3692/3, 3694/5, 3696/7, 3698/9 and 3700/1, respectively, were issued together, *se-tenant*, each pair forming a composite design.

3044/5 Sun and Saturn

3046/7 Galaxy and *Suzaku* X-Ray Astronomy Satellite

3048/3049 *Hayabusa* Space Probe and Asteroid and Earth

3050/3051 National Astronomical Observatory Subaru Telescope and Galaxy

3052/3053 Mars and National Astronomical Observatory Nobeyama 45 mm Radio Telescope

2008. Centenary of National Astronomical Society.

3702	3044	80y. multicoloured	1·30	85
3703	3045	80y. multicoloured	1·30	85
3704	3046	80y. multicoloured	1·30	85
3705	3047	80y. multicoloured	1·30	85
3706	3048	80y. multicoloured	1·30	85
3707	3049	80y. multicoloured	1·30	85
3708	3050	80y. multicoloured	1·30	85
3709	3051	80y. multicoloured	1·30	85
3710	3052	80y. multicoloured	1·30	85
3711	3053	80y. multicoloured	1·30	85

Nos. 3702/3, 3704/5, 3706/7, 3708/9 and 3710/11, respectively, were issued together, *se-tenant*. each pair forming a composite design.

3054 Bird Cherry

2008. Philately Week. Multicoloured.

3712		80y. Type 3054	1·40	90
3713		80y. Peony and butterfly	1·40	90
3714		80y. Egrets	1·40	90
3715		80y. Grapes and rat	1·40	90
3716		80y. Seabirds	1·40	90

3059 Boats

2008. Hometowns. Multicoloured.

3717		80y. Type 3059	1·40	90
3718		80y. Bus stop	1·40	90
3719		80y. Fishing	1·40	90
3720		80y. Railway	1·40	90
3721		80y. Beach	1·40	90
3722		80y. Jetty and boats	1·40	90
3723		80y. Children	1·40	90
3724		80y. Waterside houses	1·40	90
3725		80y. Postal delivery	1·40	90
3726		80y. Railway station	1·40	90

3069/3070 Hideyo Noguchi (bacteriologist), Microscope and Map of Africa

2008. First Hideyo Noguchi Africa Prize. 80th Death Anniv of Hideyo Noguchi

3727	3069	80y. multicoloured	1·40	90
3728	3070	80y. multicoloured	1·40	90

Nos. 3727/8 were issued together *se-tenant* forming a composite design.

3071/3072 Visa Stamp, Beans and Migrant Ship

3073/3074 Christ the Redeemer and Rio de Janeiro Port

3075/3076 Iguazu Falls

3077/3078 Salvador Historical Buildings

3079/3080 Brazilian Morpho and Toucan

2008. Japan—Brazil Exchange Year.

3729	**3071**	80y. multicoloured	1·40	90
3730	**3072**	80y. multicoloured	1·40	90
3731	**3073**	80y. multicoloured	1·40	90
3732	**3074**	80y. multicoloured	1·40	90
3733	**3075**	80y. multicoloured	1·40	90
3734	**3076**	80y. multicoloured	1·40	90
3735	**3077**	80y. multicoloured	1·40	90
3736	**3078**	80y. multicoloured	1·40	90
3737	**3079**	80y. multicoloured	1·40	90
3738	**3080**	80y. multicoloured	1·40	90

3081 Anne Shirley   **3082** Anne's House

3083/3084 Mathew Cuthbert and Anne

3085/3086 Anne and Diana Barry

3087/3088 Teenage Anne and Gilbert Blythe

3089/3090 Mathew, Anne and Marilla Cuthbert

2008. International Correspondence Week. Centenary of *Anne of Green Gables* (written by Lucy Maud Montgomery).

3739	**3081**	80y. multicoloured (38×28 mm)	1·40	90
3740	**3082**	80y. multicoloured (38×28 mm)	1·40	90
3741	**3083**	80y. multicoloured (29×36 mm)	1·40	90
3742	**3084**	80y. multicoloured (29×36 mm)	1·40	90
3743	**3085**	80y. multicoloured (29×36 mm)	1·40	90
3744	**3086**	80y. multicoloured (29×36 mm)	1·40	90
3745	**3087**	80y. multicoloured (29×36 mm)	1·40	90
3746	**3088**	80y. multicoloured (29×36 mm)	1·40	90
3747	**3089**	80y. multicoloured (29×36 mm)	1·40	90
3748	**3090**	80y. multicoloured (29×36 mm)	1·40	90

Nos. 3741/2, 3743/4, 3745/6 and 3747/8, respectively, were issued together, *se-tenant*, each pair forming a composite design.

Stamps of a similar design to Nos. 3739/40 were issued by Canada.

3091 Keri Lake   **3092** Mount Fuji

3093 Buddhist Shrine, Borobudur   **3094** To-ji Temple

3095 *Rafflesia arnoldi*   **3096** Cherry Blossom

3097 Angklung (Musical instrument)   **3098** Gaku-Biwa (Musical instrument)

3099 *Scleropages formosus* (horiz)   **3100** *Nishiki-goi* (horiz)

2008. 50th Anniv of Japan—Indonesia Friendship.

3749	**3091**	80y. multicoloured	1·40	90
3750	**3092**	80y. multicoloured	1·40	90
3751	**3093**	80y. multicoloured	1·40	90
3752	**3094**	80y. multicoloured	1·40	90
3753	**3095**	80y. multicoloured	1·40	90
3754	**3096**	80y. multicoloured	1·40	90
3755	**3097**	80y. multicoloured	1·40	90
3756	**3098**	80y. multicoloured	1·40	90
3757	**3099**	80y. multicoloured (38×28 mm)	1·40	90
3758	**3100**	80y. multicoloured (38×28 mm)	1·40	90

Stamps of a similar design were issued by Indonesia.

3101 Cranes

2008. 60th Anniv of Local Government, Hokkaido. Multicoloured.

3759	80y. Type **3101**	1·40	90
3760	80y. Goryokaku Fort multicoloured (28×34 mm)	1·40	90
3761	80y. Autumn Landscape (28×34 mm)	1·40	90
3762	80y. *Clione limacina* (sea angel) (28×34 mm)	1·40	90
3763	80y. Canal (28×34 mm)	1·40	90

3106 Mt. Yotei

3107 Shiraneaoi Flowers

3108 Peak

3109 Squirrel

3110 Toya Lake

3111 Blossom

3112 Fukidashi Park

3113 Rowan Berries

3114 Lake and Peak

3115 Fox Cub

2008. G8 Summit, Hokkaido.

3764	**3106**	80y. multicoloured	1·40	90
3765	**3107**	80y. multicoloured	1·40	90
3766	**3108**	80y. multicoloured	1·40	90
3767	**3109**	80y. multicoloured	1·40	90
3768	**3110**	80y. multicoloured	1·40	90
3769	**3111**	80y. multicoloured	1·40	90
3770	**3112**	80y. multicoloured	1·40	90
3771	**3113**	80y. multicoloured	1·40	90
3772	**3114**	80y. multicoloured	1·40	90
3773	**3115**	80y. multicoloured	1·40	90

3116 *Murasaki Shikibu*   **3117** *Fujiwara*

3118 *Murasaki Shikibu*   **3119** *Tsutomu Hiroshi Dainagon*

3120 *Murasaki Shikibu*

3121/3122 *Moon, Cloud and Murasaki Shikibu*

3123/3124 *Twigs and Fujiwara*

3125/3126 *Cliff, Tree and Murasaki Shikibu*

3127/3128 *Waterfall and Tsutomu Hiroshi Dainagon*

3129/3130 *Trees and Murasaki Shikibu*

2008. Letter Writing Day.

3774	3116	50y. multicoloured		
		(25×30 mm)	85	60
3775	3117	50y. multicoloured		
		(25×30 mm)	85	60
3776	3118	50y. multicoloured		
		(25×30 mm)	85	60
3777	3119	50y. multicoloured		
		(25×30 mm)	85	60
3778	3120	50y. multicoloured		
		(25×30 mm)	85	60
3779	3121	80y. multicoloured		
		(28×38 mm)	1·40	90
3780	3122	80y. multicoloured		
		(28×38 mm)	1·40	90
3781	3123	80y. multicoloured		
		(28×38 mm)	1·40	90
3782	3124	80y. multicoloured		
		(28×38 mm)	1·40	90
3783	3125	80y. multicoloured		
		(28×38 mm)	1·40	90
3784	3126	80y. multicoloured		
		(28×38 mm)	1·40	90
3785	3127	80y. multicoloured		
		(28×38 mm)	1·40	90
3786	3128	80y. multicoloured		
		(28×38 mm)	1·40	90
3787	3129	80y. multicoloured		
		(28×38 mm)	1·40	90
3788	3130	80y. multicoloured		
		(28×38 mm)	1·40	90

3131/3132 Dear Daniel and Hello Kitty

3133/3134 Hello Kitty and Dear Daniel

3135/3136 Dear Daniel and Hello Kitty

3137/3138 Hello Kitty and Dear Daniel

3139/3140 Dear Daniel and Hello Kitty

3141 Hello Kitty and Dear Daniel   3142 Hello Kitty

3143 Hello Kitty

3144 Dear Daniel

3145 Dear Daniel and Hello Kitty

3146 Hello Kitty

3147 Hello Kitty

3148 Dear Daniel

3149 Hello Kitty and Dear Daniel

3150 Hello Kitty

2008. Greetings Stamps. Hello Kitty. Self adhesive.

3789	3131	50y. multicoloured		
		(28×28 mm)	85	60
3790	3132	50y. multicoloured		
		(28×28)	85	60
3791	3133	50y. multicoloured		
		(28×28 mm)	85	60
3792	3134	50y. multicoloured		
		(28×28 mm)	85	60
3793	3135	50y. multicoloured		
		(28×28 mm)	85	60
3794	3136	50y. multicoloured		
		(28×28 mm)	85	60
3795	3137	50y. multicoloured		
		(28×28 mm)	85	50
3796	3138	50y. multicoloured		
		(28×28 mm)	85	60
3797	3139	50y. multicoloured		
		(28×28 mm)	85	60
3798	3140	50y. multicoloured		
		(28×28 mm)	85	60
3799	3141	80y. multicoloured		
		(45×28 mm)	1·40	90
3800	3142	80y. multicoloured		
		(45×28 mm)	1·40	90
3801	3143	80y. multicoloured		
		(45×28 mm)	1·40	90
3802	3144	80y. multicoloured		
		(45×28 mm)	1·40	90
3803	3145	80y. multicoloured		
		(45×28 mm)	1·40	90
3804	3146	80y. multicoloured		
		(34×34 mm (circular))	1·40	90
3805	3147	80y. multicoloured		
		(34×34 mm (circular))	1·40	90
3806	3148	80y. multicoloured		
		(34×34 mm (circular))	1·40	90
3807	3149	80y. multicoloured		
		(34×34 mm (circular))	1·40	90
3808	3150	80y. multicoloured		
		(40×28 mm (oval))	1·40	90

Nos. 3789/90, 3791/2, 3793/4, 3795/6 and 3797/8 were issued together, *se-tenant*, each pair forming a composite design.

3151/3152 Woman (Utamaro Kitagawa) and *One Hundred Views of Edo* (Hiroshige Utagawa)

3153/3154 *One Hundred Views of Edo* (Hiroshige Utagawa) and Man

3155/3156 Woman (Utamaro Kitagawa) and *One Hundred Views of Edo* (Hiroshige Utagawa)

3157/3158 *One Hundred Views of Edo* (Hiroshige Utagawa) and Man

3159/3160 Woman (Utamaro Kitagawa) and *One Hundred Views of Edo* (Hiroshige Utagawa)

2008. Paintings.

3809	3151	80y. multicoloured	1·40	90
3810	3152	80y. multicoloured	1·40	90
3811	3153	80y. multicoloured	1·40	90
3812	3154	80y. multicoloured	1·40	90
3813	3155	80y. multicoloured	1·40	90
3814	3156	80y. multicoloured	1·40	90
3815	3157	80y. multicoloured	1·40	90
3816	3158	80y. multicoloured	1·40	90
3817	3159	80y. multicoloured	1·40	90
3818	3160	80y. multicoloured	1·40	90

3161 Temple of Heaven   3162 Huangshan Lingfeng Peak

3163 Painting, Dunhuang Caves   3164 Horyuji Pagoda

3165/3166 Mandarin Ducks

3167 *Water Fish Seasons* (plum blossom, Spring)   3168 *Water Fish Seasons* (water lily, Summer)

3169 *Water Fish Seasons* (leaves, Autumn)   3170 *Water Fish Seasons* (daffodils, Winter)

2008. 30th Anniv of Japan—China Treaty.

3819	3161	80y. multicoloured	1·40	90
3820	3162	80y. multicoloured	1·40	90
3821	3163	80y. multicoloured	1·40	90
3822	3164	80y. multicoloured	1·40	90
3823	3165	80y. multicoloured	1·40	90
3824	3166	80y. multicoloured	1·40	90
3825	3167	80y. multicoloured	1·40	90
3826	3168	80y. multicoloured	1·40	90
3827	3169	80y. multicoloured	1·40	90
3828	3170	80y. multicoloured	1·40	90

Nos. 3823/4 were issued together, *se-tenant*, the pair forming a composite design.

3171/2 Ingram and Noa Izumi

3173/4 Isao Ohta and Ingram 2

3175/6 Shinobu Nagumo and Ingram 3

3177/8 Type Zero and Asuma Shinohara

3179/80 Ingram and Two Division

2008. Heroes and Heroines of Animation (8th issue). Patlabor, The Mobile Police.

3829	3171	80y. multicoloured	1·40	90
3830	3172	80y. multicoloured	1·40	90
3831	3173	80y. multicoloured	1·40	90
3832	3174	80y. multicoloured		
3833	3175	80y. multicoloured	1·40	90
3834	3176	80y. multicoloured	1·40	90
3835	3177	80y. multicoloured	1·40	90
3836	3178	80y. multicoloured	1·40	90
3837	3179	80y. multicoloured	1·40	90
3838	3180	80y. multicoloured	1·40	90

Nos. 3829/30, 3831/2, 3833/4, 3835/6 and 3837/8, respectively, were issued together, *se-tenant*, each pair forming a composite design.

3181 Statues and Temple

2008. Tourism. Arashiyama and Sagano, Kyoto. Multicoloured.

3839	80y. Type 3181	1·40	90
3840	80y. Gateway	1·40	90
3841	80y. Autumn colour	1·40	90
3842	80y. Grove in autumn	1·40	90
3843	80y. Boddhisattvas	1·40	90
3844	80y. Small Temple	1·40	90
3845	80y. Pagoda	1·40	90
3846	80y. Sagano train	1·40	90
3847	80y. Hozu River boat tour	1·40	90
3848	80y. Togetsukyo Bridge	1·40	90

3191 Houses

2008. Hometowns. Multicoloured.

3849	80y. Type 3191	1·40	90
3850	80y. Wedding	1·40	90
3851	80y. Lake	1·40	90
3852	80y. Planting	1·40	90
3853	80y. Gardening	1·40	90
3854	80y. Boats on lake	1·40	90
3855	80y. Crops, farm and forest	1·40	90
3856	80y. Weeding, buildings and train	1·40	90
3857	80y. Roadside stall	1·40	90
3858	80y. River valley	1·40	90

3201 Musicians

3202 Seated Group

3203 Cradling Child

3204 Man and Woman

3205 Woman reading

3206 Serenade

3207 Man and Woman behind Decorated Screens

3208 Women

3209 Woman and Two Men

3210 Woman cradling Child

2008. Tale of Genji (Murasaki Shikibu) (11th century).

3859	3201	80y. multicoloured	1·80	1·30
3860	3202	80y. multicoloured	1·80	1·30
3861	3203	80y. multicoloured	1·80	1·30
3862	3204	80y. multicoloured	1·80	1·30
3863	3205	80y. multicoloured	1·80	1·30
3864	3206	80y. multicoloured	1·80	1·30
3865	3207	80y. multicoloured	1·80	1·30
3866	3208	80y. multicoloured	1·80	1·30
3867	3209	80y. multicoloured	1·80	1·30
3868	3210	80y. multicoloured	1·80	1·30

3211/12 Kiyomizu Temple

3213/14 Flowers

3215/16 Kodaiji Temple

3217 Steps

3218 Pagoda

3219 Maiko (apprentice Geisha)

3220 Waterside

2008. Tourism. Kiyomizu-dera and Gion, Kyoto.

3869	3211	80y. multicoloured	1·80	1·30
3870	3212	80y. multicoloured	1·80	1·30
3871	3213	80y. multicoloured	1·80	1·30
3872	3214	80y. multicoloured	1·80	1·30
3873	3215	80y. multicoloured	1·80	1·30
3874	3216	80y. multicoloured	1·80	1·30
3875	3217	80y. multicoloured	1·80	1·30
3876	3218	80y. multicoloured	1·80	1·30
3877	3219	80y. multicoloured	1·80	1·30
3878	3220	80y. multicoloured	1·80	1·30

Nos. 3869/70, 3871/2 and 3873/4, respectively, were issued together, *se-tenant*, each pair forming a composite design.

3221 *Kanagawa*

3222 *Mishima*

3223 *Ishibe*

2008. International Correspondence Week. 53 Stations of Tokaido by Utagawa Hiroshige.

3879	3221	90y. multicoloured	2·40	1·70
3880	3222	110y. multicoloured	2·40	1·70
3881	3223	130y. multicoloured	2·40	1·70

3224 Early Map showing Japan

2008. World Heritage. Iwami Ginzan Silver Mine. Multicoloured.

3882	80y. Type 3224	1·40	90
3883	80y. Ryugenji Mabu Mine shaft	1·40	90
3884	80y. Smelting plant ruins	1·40	90
3885	80y. Dragon (shrine fresco)	1·40	90
3886	80y. Bridge and shrine	1·40	90
3887	80y. Omori Ginzan District	1·40	90
3888	80y. Silver-plated dog	1·40	90
3889	80y. Kumagai house	1·40	90
3890	80y. Payment token	1·40	90
3891	80y. Naito house	1·40	90

3234 *Tales of Genji* (detail)

2008. 60th Anniv of Local Government, Kyoto. Multicoloured.

3892	80y. Type 3234	2·20	1·60
3893	80y. Cherry blossom	2·20	1·60
3894	80y. Thatched house, Nantan	2·20	1·60
3895	80y. Pagoda	2·20	1·60
3896	80y. Amanohashidate	2·20	1·60

3238a

2008. New Year's Greetings. Multicoloured.

3896a	3238a	50y. multicoloured	85	60
3896b	3238a	50y. multicoloured	85	60

3239 Ox

2008. New Year's Greetings. Multicoloured.

3897	50y. Type 3239	85	60
3898	80y. Figure seated on Ox	1·40	90

3242 Figure seated on Ox

2008. New Year Lottery Stamps. Multicoloured.

3899	50y.+3y. Ox	1·00	70
3900	80y.+3y. Type 3234	1·60	1·10

Each stamp carries a lottery number.

3243 Train

2008. Hometowns. Multicoloured.

3901	80y. Type 3243	1·40	90
3902	80y. Snow-covered farm	1·40	90
3903	80y. Seaside station	1·40	90
3904	80y. Bridge and waterwheel	1·40	90
3905	80y. Horse pulling timber	1·40	90
3906	80y. Mail delivery	1·40	90
3907	80y. Families in snow	1·40	90
3908	80y. Family on path	1·40	90
3909	80y. Hillside houses	1·40	90
3910	80y. Snow-covered building	1·40	90

3253/4 Yukichi Fukuzawa and Arms

3255/6 Campus Buildings

3257/8 Rugby and Baseball

3259/60 Stained Glass Window

3261/2 Stained Glass Window

2008. 150th Anniv of Keio University.

3911	3253	80y. multicoloured	2·20	1·60
3912	3254	80y. multicoloured	2·20	1·60
3913	3255	80y. multicoloured	2·20	1·60
3914	3256	80y. multicoloured	2·20	1·60
3915	3257	80y. multicoloured	2·20	1·60
3916	3258	80y. multicoloured	2·20	1·60
3917	3259	80y. multicoloured	2·20	1·60

3918	**3260**	80y. multicoloured	2·20	1·60
3919	**3261**	80y. multicoloured	2·20	1·60
3920	**3262**	80y. multicoloured	2·20	1·60

Nos. 3911/12, 3913/14, 3915/16, respectively, were issued together, *se-tenant*, each pair forming a composite design.

Nos. 3917/18 and 3919/20, were issued together, setenant pairs, each pair forming a composite design and the block of four forming a design of the stained glass window.

3263 Ox

3264 Ox

3265 Ox

3266 Ox

3267 Ox

3268 Ox

3269 Ox

3270 Ox

3271 Ox

3272 Ox

2008. Greetings Stamps. Eto Calligraphy. Year of the Ox.

3921	**3263**	80y. multicoloured	2·20	1·60
3922	**3264**	80y. multicoloured	2·20	1·60
3923	**3265**	80y. multicoloured	2·20	1·60
3924	**3266**	80y. multicoloured	2·20	1·60
3925	**3267**	80y. multicoloured	2·20	1·60
3926	**3268**	80y. multicoloured	2·20	1·60
3927	**3269**	80y. multicoloured	2·20	1·60
3928	**3270**	80y. multicoloured	2·20	1·60
3929	**3271**	80y. multicoloured	2·20	1·60
3930	**3272**	80y. multicoloured	2·20	1·60

3273/4 Blast Furnace, Chimney and Conveyor Belt

2008. 150th Anniv of Iron and Steel Industry. Multicoloured.

3931	80y. Type **3273**		2·20	1·60
3932	80y. Type **3274**		2·20	1·60
3933	80y. Aira		2·20	1·60
3934	80y. Aira (different)		2·20	1·60
3935	80y. Stylized furnace		2·20	1·60
3936	80y. Processing plant		2·20	1·60

3279 Santa

2008. Greetings Stamps. Multicoloured. Self-adhesive.

3937	50y. Type **3279**		1·40	90
3938	50y. Stylized Bell (Hoshiyama Rika)		1·40	90

3939	50y. Two Kittens (Kuroi Ken)	1·40	90
3940	50y. Bears and Parcel (Moe Nagata)	1·40	90
3941	50y. Chick (Arai Sonoko)	1·40	90
3942	80y. Two Kittens (Kuroi Ken)	1·80	1·30
3943	80y. Child as Santa (Moe Nagata)	1·80	1·30
3944	80y. Bouquet (Arai Sonoko)	1·80	1·30
3945	80y. Santa	1·80	1·30
3946	80y. Fruit and Flowers (Arai Sonoko)	1·80	1·30

3289 Silver Token

2008. Tourism. Okinawa. Multicoloured.

3947	80y. Type **3289**	1·40	90
3948	80y. Coast line (28×34 mm)	1·40	90
3949	80y. Pagoda (28×34 mm)	1·40	90
3950	80y. Bridge, Tsuwano(28×34 mm)	1·40	90
3951	80y. Dotaku (ritual bell) (28×34 mm)	1·40	90

3294/5 Shurijo Castle

3296/7 Ryukyu Dancers

3298 Mamoru Rei Gate

3299 Water Clock

3300 Parkland

3301 Kaneshiro

3302/3 Statue and Monorail

2009. Tourism Okinawa (1st issue).

3952	**3294**	80y. multicoloured	1·40	90
3953	**3295**	80y. multicoloured	1·40	90
3954	**3296**	80y. multicoloured	1·40	90
3955	**3297**	80y. multicoloured	1·40	90
3956	**3298**	80y. multicoloured	1·40	90
3957	**3299**	80y. multicoloured	1·40	90
3958	**3300**	80y. multicoloured	1·40	90
3959	**3301**	80y. multicoloured	1·40	90
3960	**3302**	80y. multicoloured	1·40	90
3961	**3303**	80y. multicoloured	1·40	90

Nos. 3952/3, 3954/5 and 3960/1, respectively, were printed, *se-tenant*, each pair forming a composite design.

3304/5 Statue and Flower

3306/7 Churaumi Aquarium

3308/9 Churaumi Aquarium

3310 Steps and Blossom, Nakizin Castle

3311 Okinawa Rail (*Gallirallus okinawae*)

3312 Cliffs

3313 Mangroves

2009. Tourism Okinawa (2nd issue).

3962	**3304**	80y. multicoloured	1·40	90
3963	**3305**	80y. multicoloured	1·40	90
3964	**3306**	80y. multicoloured	1·40	90
3965	**3307**	80y. multicoloured	1·40	90
3966	**3308**	80y. multicoloured	1·40	90
3967	**3309**	80y. multicoloured	1·40	90
3968	**3310**	80y. multicoloured	1·40	90
3969	**3311**	80y. multicoloured	1·40	90
3970	**3312**	80y. multicoloured	1·40	90
3971	**3313**	80y. multicoloured	1·40	90

3314/15 GeGeGe no Kitaro and Medama-oyaji

3316/17 Kitaro

3318/19 Villains

3320/1 Kitaro and Neko Musume

3322/3 Kitaro and Yokai

2009. Heroes and Heroines of Animation (9th issue). GeGeGe no Kitaro.

3972	**3314**	80y. multicoloured	1·40	90

3973	**3315**	80y. multicoloured	1·40	90
3974	**3316**	80y. multicoloured	1·40	90
3975	**3317**	80y. multicoloured	1·40	90
3976	**3318**	80y. multicoloured	1·40	90
3977	**3319**	80y. multicoloured	1·40	90
3978	**3320**	80y. multicoloured	1·40	90
3979	**3321**	80y. multicoloured	1·40	90
3980	**3322**	80y. multicoloured	1·40	90
3981	**3323**	80y. multicoloured	1·40	90

Nos. 3972/3, 3974/5, 3976/7, 3978/9 and 3980/1, respectively, were printed *se-tenant*, each pair forming a composite design.

3324 Hillside Houses and Cultivation

2009. Hometowns. Multicoloured.

3982	80y. Type **3324**		1·40	90
3983	80y. Planting rice		1·40	90
3984	80y. House and pennants		1·40	90
3985	80y. Rape Flowers and Cloche		1·40	90
3986	80y. Crops and family		1·40	90
3987	80y. Watermill		1·40	90
3988	80y. Women and barns		1·40	90
3989	80y. School children, conversation and train		1·40	90
3990	80y. Older woman and children		1·40	90
3991	80y. Post Office		1·40	90

3334 Temple

3335 Statue

3336 Statue, Kofukuji Temple

3337 Nara Museum

3338/9 Kasuga Shrine

3340 Deer

3341 Building

3342/3 Lake and Blossom

2009. Tourism. Nara.

3992	**3334**	80y. multicoloured	1·40	90
3993	**3335**	80y. multicoloured	1·40	90
3994	**3336**	80y. multicoloured	1·40	90
3995	**3337**	80y. multicoloured	1·40	90
3996	**3338**	80y. multicoloured	1·40	90
3997	**3339**	80y. multicoloured	1·40	90
3998	**3340**	80y. multicoloured	1·40	90
3999	**3341**	80y. multicoloured	1·40	90
4000	**3342**	80y. multicoloured	1·40	90
4001	**3343**	80y. multicoloured	1·40	90

Nos. 39996/7 and 4000/1, respectively, were printed *se-tenant*, each pair forming a composite designs.

3344

3345

3346

3347

3348

3349

3350

3351

3352

3353

3354

3355

3356

3357

3358

3359

3360

3361

3362

3363

2009. 50th Anniv of Comics for Boys (1st issue). Weekly Shonen Sunday (4002/11). Weekly Shonen Magazine (4012/21).

4002	3344	80y. multicoloured	1·80	1·20
4003	3345	80y. multicoloured	1·80	1·20
4004	3346	80y. multicoloured	1·80	1·20
4005	3347	80y. multicoloured	1·80	1·20
4006	3348	80y. multicoloured	1·80	1·20
4007	3349	80y. multicoloured	1·80	1·20
4008	3350	80y. multicoloured	1·80	1·20
4009	3351	80y. multicoloured	1·80	1·20
4010	3352	80y. multicoloured	1·80	1·20
4011	3353	80y. multicoloured	1·80	1·20
4012	3354	80y. multicoloured	1·80	1·20
4013	3355	80y. multicoloured	1·80	1·20
4014	3356	80y. multicoloured	1·80	1·20
4015	3357	80y. multicoloured	1·80	1·20
4016	3358	80y. multicoloured	1·80	1·20
4017	3359	80y. multicoloured	1·80	1·20
4018	3360	80y. multicoloured	1·80	1·20
4019	3361	80y. multicoloured	1·80	1·20
4020	3362	80y. multicoloured	1·80	1·20
4021	3363	80y. multicoloured	1·80	1·20

3364 Fan

3365 Bonbonieru

2009. 50th Wedding Anniv of Emperor Akihito and Empress Michiko.

4022	3364	80y. multicoloured	1·80	1·20
4023	3365	80y. multicoloured	1·80	1·20
MS4024	135×112 mm. 80y.×2, Type 3364; Type 3365		3·25	3·25

3366/7 Conan, Young Detectives and Dr. Agasa

3368/9 Shinich Kudo and Ayumi Yoshida

3370/1 Conan and Gin

3372/3 Conan and Ayumi Yoshida

3374/5 Kaito Kid and Conan

2009. Heroes and Heroines of Animation (10th issue). Detective Conan.

4025	3366	80y. multicoloured	1·70	1·10
4026	3367	80y. multicoloured	1·70	1·10
4027	3368	80y. multicoloured	1·70	1·10
4028	3369	80y. multicoloured	1·70	1·10
4029	3370	80y. multicoloured	1·70	1·10
4030	3371	80y. multicoloured	1·70	1·10
4031	3372	80y. multicoloured	1·70	1·10
4032	3373	80y. multicoloured	1·70	1·10
4033	3374	80y. multicoloured	1·70	1·10
4034	3375	80y. multicoloured	1·70	1·10

3376 Peonies (pink and red)   **3377** Peonies (grey, blue and pink)

3378/9 Peonies (pale pink)

3380/1 Peonies (single white, central pink)

2009. Stamp Week.

4035	3376	80y. multicoloured	1·70	1·10
4036	3377	80y. multicoloured	1·70	1·10
4037	3378	80y. multicoloured	1·70	1·10
4038	3379	80y. multicoloured	1·70	1·10
4039	3380	80y. multicoloured	1·70	1·10
4040	3381	80y. multicoloured	1·70	1·10

Nos. 4037/8 and 4039/40 were printed, *se-tenant*, each pair forming a composite design.

3382 Henry Dunant (founder) and Nobel Peace Prize Certificate

2009. 150th Anniv of Henry Dunant's Experience at Battle of Solferino (Austro–Sardinian War) (which led to start of Red Cross movement). Multicoloured.

4041	80y. Type 3382	1·80	1·20
4042	80y. Early Red Cross poster	1·80	1·20

3384 Kamikochi

2009. Tourism. Nagano. Multicoloured.

4043	80y. Type 3384	4·00	2·50
4044	80y. Rape field (28×34 mm)	4·00	2·50
4045	80y. Pagoda (28×34 mm)	4·00	2·50
4046	80y. Pagodas and azaleas (28×34 mm)	4·00	2·50
4047	80y. Statue (28×34 mm)	4·00	2·50

3389 Emblem

2009. Inauguration of Lay Judge Trials. Multicoloured.

4048	80y. Type 3389	4·25	2·50
4049	80y. Birds on scales	4·25	2·50

3391   3392

3393   3394

3395   3396

3397   3398

3399   3400

3401   3402

3403   3404

3405   3406

3407   3408

3409   3410

2009. 50th Anniv of Comics for Boys (2nd issue). Weekly Shonen Sunday (4050/9). Weekly Shonen Magazine (4060/9). .

4050	3391	80y. multicoloured	1·80	1·20
4051	3392	80y. multicoloured	1·80	1·20
4052	3393	80y. multicoloured	1·80	1·20
4053	3394	80y. multicoloured	1·80	1·20
4054	3395	80y. multicoloured	1·80	1·20
4055	3396	80y. multicoloured	1·80	1·20
4056	3397	80y. multicoloured	1·80	1·20
4057	3398	80y. multicoloured	1·80	1·20
4058	3399	80y. multicoloured	1·80	1·20
4059	3400	80y. multicoloured	1·80	1·20
4060	3401	80y. multicoloured	1·80	1·20
4061	3402	80y. multicoloured	1·80	1·20
4062	3403	80y. multicoloured	1·80	1·20
4063	3404	80y. multicoloured	1·80	1·20
4064	3405	80y. multicoloured	1·80	1·20
4065	3406	80y. multicoloured	1·80	1·20
4066	3407	80y. multicoloured	1·80	1·20
4067	3408	80y. multicoloured	1·80	1·20
4068	3409	80y. multicoloured	1·80	1·20
4069	3410	80y. multicoloured	1·80	1·20

3411/12 *Early View of Nagasaki Harbour*

3413/14 *Modern Nagasaki Harbour at Night*

3415/16 *Stylised Boats (early and modern)*

3421/2 *Early Yokohama Harbour*

3423/4 *Modern Yokohama by Night*

3429/30 *Early Hakodate Harbour*

3431/2 *Modern Hakodate by Night*

2009. 150th Anniv of Opening of Japan Ports to Foreign Visitors. Multicoloured.

4070	80y. Type **3411**	1·80	1·20
4071	80y. Type **3412**	1·80	1·20
4072	80y. Type **3413**	1·80	1·20
4073	80y. Type **3414**	1·80	1·20

4074	80y. Type **3415**	1·80	1·20
4075	80y. Type **3416**	1·80	1·20
4076	80y. Nagasaki at night	1·80	1·20
4077	80y. Oura Cathedral	1·80	1·20
4078	80y. Megami Bridge	1·80	1·20
4079	80y. Clover Park and Nagasaki Port	1·80	1·20
4080	80y. Type **3421**	1·80	1·20
4081	80y. Type **3422**	1·80	1·20
4082	80y. Type **3423**	1·80	1·20
4083	80y. Type **3424**	1·80	1·20
4084	80y. Yokonhama Bay Bridge	1·80	1·20
4085	80y. Memorial Hall	1·80	1·20
4086	80y. *Nippon Maru*(sail ship)	1·80	1·20
4087	80y. Passenger ship terminal	1·80	1·20
4088	80y. Type **3429**	1·80	1·20
4089	80y. Type **3430**	1·80	1·20
4090	80y. Type **3431**	1·80	1·20
4091	80y. Type **3432**	1·80	1·20
4092	80y. Hachiman-zaka Slope and Hakodate	1·80	1·20
4093	80y. Orthodox Church, Hakodate	1·80	1·20
4094	80y. Old Pier	1·80	1·20
4095	80y. Hakodate Park and Port	1·80	1·20

3437 *Flowering Cherry (Edohigan)*

3438 *Zelkova serrata (Keyaki)*

3439 *Red Pine*

3440 *Japanese Bird Cherry*

3441 *Magnolia kobus (Kita Kobushi)*

3442 *Camellia (Yukibata Tsubaki)*

3443 *Horse Chestnut (Buckeye)*

3444 *Japanese Flowering Dogwood (Yamaboushi)*

3445/6 *Narcissae*

2009. 60th National Planting Festival. Re-afforestation Programme.

4096	3437	50y. multicoloured	1·10	95
4097	3438	50y. multicoloured	1·10	95
4098	3439	50y. multicoloured	1·10	95
4099	3440	50y. multicoloured	1·10	95
4100	3441	50y. multicoloured	1·10	95
4101	3442	50y. multicoloured	1·10	95
4102	3443	50y. multicoloured	1·10	95
4103	3444	50y. multicoloured	1·10	95
4104	3445	50y. multicoloured	1·10	95
4105	3446	50y. multicoloured	1·10	95

3447 *Flowers in the Rain, Gunma*

2009. Hometowns. Multicoloured.

4106	80y. Type **3447**	1·80	1·20
4107	80y. Potato flowers, Hokkaido	1·80	1·20
4108	80y. Family amongst alpine flowers, Nagano	1·80	1·20
4109	80y. Terraced gardens, Yamaguchi	1·80	1·20
4110	80y. Mother, child and woman working in gardens, Hyogo	1·80	1·20
4111	80y. House, woman and child on Precipitous Path, Miyazaki	1·80	1·20
4112	80y. Rural post office, Okinawa	1·80	1·20
4113	80y. Lotus flowers and house, Ishikawa	1·80	1·20
4114	80y. Women picking flowers, Chiba	1·80	1·20
4115	80y. Peach orchard, Yamanashi	1·80	1·20

3457 *Polar Bears*

2009. International Polar Year. Preserve Polar Regions and Glaciers. Sheet 80×120 mm containing T **3457** and similar vert designs. Multicoloured. Self-adhesive.

MS4116	80y.×4, Type **3457**; Seal; Arctic fox; Penguin	7·25	7·25

3458 *Crested Ibis, Sado-ga-shima Island*

2009. Tourism. Niigata. Multicoloured.

4117	80y. Type **3458**	1·80	1·20
4118	80y. Cherry blossom, Takada (28×34 mm)	1·80	1·20
4119	80y. Fireworks, Nagaoka (28×34 mm)	1·80	1·20
4120	80y. Newt pond (28×34 mm)	1·80	1·20
4121	80y. Snow festival, Tokamachi (28×34 mm)	1·80	1·20

3463 *Statue, Kongobuji Temple*

2009

4122	3463	300y. multicoloured	7·25	7·25

No. 4122 was for use on recorded delivery letters.

3464 *Ono No Komachi*

3465 *Junii letaks*

3466 *Minstrel Jakuren Hoshi*

3467 *Sakanoue no Korenori*

3468 *Daini no Sanmi*

3469 *Blossom Tree*

3470 *Ono No Komachi*

3471 *Branches*

3472 *Junii letaka*

3473 *Green Twigs*

3474 *Minstrel Jakuren Hoshi*

3475 *Dead Trees*

3476 *Sakanoue no Korenori*

3477 *Leaves*

3478 *Daini no Sanmi*

2009. Letter Writing Day.

4123	3464	50y. multicoloured	1·80	1·20
4124	3465	50y. multicoloured	1·80	1·20
4125	3466	50y. multicoloured	1·80	1·20
4126	3467	50y. multicoloured	1·80	1·20
4127	3468	50y. multicoloured	1·80	1·20
4128	3469	80y. multicoloured (28×38 mm)	1·80	1·20
4129	3470	80y. multicoloured (28×38 mm)	1·80	1·20
4130	3471	80y. multicoloured (28×38 mm)	1·80	1·20
4131	3472	80y. multicoloured (28×38 mm)	1·80	1·20
4132	3473	80y. multicoloured (28×38 mm)	1·80	1·20
4133	3474	80y. multicoloured (28×38 mm)	1·80	1·20
4134	3475	80y. multicoloured (28×38 mm)	1·80	1·20
4135	3476	80y. multicoloured (28×38 mm)	1·80	1·20
4136	3477	80y. multicoloured (28×38 mm)	1·80	1·20
4137	3478	80y. multicoloured (28×38 mm)	1·80	1·20

3478a *Hello Kitty holding Envelope*

3478b *Hello Kitty finds Dear Daniel*

3478C *Hello Kitty and Dear Daniel Notice each Other*

3478d *Hello Kitty and Dear Daniel exchange a Letter*

3478e *Hello Kitty and Dear Daniel Together*

3478g *Hello Kitty entrusts a letter to a bird*

3478h Hello Kitty lost in Thought

3478i Hello Kitty Dear Daniel Together, after receiving Letter

3478j Hello Kitty and Envelope

3478k Hello Kitty and Envelope

2009. Greetings Stamps. Hello Kitty and Dear Daniel

4137a	**3478a**	50y. multicoloured	1·80	1·20
4137b	**3478b**	50y. multicoloured	1·80	1·20
4137c	**3478c**	50y. multicoloured	1·80	1·20
4137d	**3478d**	50y. multicoloured	1·80	1·20
4137e	**3478e**	50y. multicoloured	1·80	1·20
4137f	**3478f**	80y. multicoloured	2·75	1·90
4137g	**3478g**	80y. multicoloured	2·75	1·90
4137h	**3478h**	80y. multicoloured	2·75	1·90
4137i	**3478i**	80y. multicoloured	2·75	1·90
4137j	**3478j**	80y. multicoloured	2·75	1·90
4137k	**3478k**	80y. multicoloured	2·75	1·90

3479 *Suwa Bluff, Nippori* (Utagawa Hiroshige)

3480 *Pensive Love* (Kitagawa Utamaro-ga)

3481 *Otani Tokuji as yakko Sodesuke* (Toshusai Sharaku)

3482 *Kumano Junisha Shrine* (Utagawa Hiroshige)

3483 *Moon Promontory* (Utagawa Hiroshige)

3484 *Woman reading Letter* (Kitagawa Utamaro-ga)

3485 *Nakajima Wadaemon as Bodara Chozaemon and Nakamura Konozo as funayado Kanagawa no Gon* (Toshusai Sharaku)

3486 *Pagoda, Zojo Temple, Akabane* (Utagawa Hiroshige)

3487 *Clear Weather after Snowfall at Japan Bridge* (Utagawa Hiroshige)

3488 *Kamekichi of Sodegaura* (Kitagawa Utamaro-ga)

2009. Edo Famous Places and Ukiyo-e Paintings

4138	**3479**	80y. multicoloured	1·80	1·20
4139	**3480**	80y. multicoloured	1·80	1·20
4140	**3481**	80y. multicoloured	1·80	1·20
4141	**3482**	80y. multicoloured	1·80	1·20
4142	**3483**	80y. multicoloured	1·80	1·20
4143	**3484**	80y. multicoloured	1·80	1·20
4144	**3485**	80y. multicoloured	1·80	1·20
4145	**3486**	80y. multicoloured	1·80	1·20
4146	**3487**	80y. multicoloured	1·80	1·20
4147	**3488**	80y. multicoloured	1·80	1·20

3493/3494 Asuka Village, Takaichi District

3495/3496 Tachibana-dera Temple

3497 Stone Fountains, Asuka Historical Museum, Sekinjinzo

3498 Stone Age burial Mound

3499/3500 Tanzan Shrine

3501/3502 Founding of Tonomine (illustrated scroll)

2009. Tourism. Nara.

4152	**3493**	80y. multicoloured	1·80	1·20
4153	**3494**	80y. multicoloured	1·80	1·20
4154	**3495**	80y. multicoloured	1·80	1·20
4155	**3496**	80y. multicoloured	1·80	1·20
4156	**3497**	80y. multicoloured	1·80	1·20
4157	**3498**	80y. multicoloured	1·80	1·20
4158	**3499**	80y. multicoloured	1·80	1·20
4159	**3500**	80y. multicoloured	1·80	1·20
4160	**3501**	80y. multicoloured	1·80	1·20
4161	**3502**	80y. multicoloured	1·80	1·20

Nos. 4148/51 and Types **3489/92** are vacant.

Nos. 4152/3, 4154/5, 4158/9 and 4160/1, respectively, were printed, *se-tenant*, each pair forming a composite design.

3503 Lanterns and Script (Masoka Shiki)

2009. Haiku (poetry) in Matsuyama. Multicoloured.

4162	50y. Type **3503**		1·10	75
4163	50y. Rooftops and script (Masoka Shiki)		1·10	75
4164	50y. Mountain and script (Kyoshi Takahama)		1·10	75
4165	50y. Building facade and script (Natsumi Soseki)		1·10	75
4166	50y. Cherry blossom and script (Kawahigashi Hekigoto)		1·10	75

3508 *Popii*

3509 *Miru*

3510 *Rabu*

3511 *Bibian*

3512 *Koto*

3513 *Ramu*

3514 *Momo*   **3515** *Moko*   **3516** *Momonatsu*

3517 *Sakura*

2009. 60th Anniv of Be Kind to Animals Week. Drawings of Winning Photographs in Anniversary Competition

4167	**3508**	50y.+5y. multicoloured	1·10	75
4168	**3509**	50y.+5y. multicoloured	1·10	75
4169	**3510**	50y.+5y. multicoloured	1·10	75
4170	**3511**	50y.+5y. multicoloured		
4171	**3512**	50y.+5y. multicoloured	1·10	75
4172	**3513**	50y.+5y. multicoloured	1·10	75
4173	**3514**	50y.+5y. multicoloured		
4174	**3515**	50y.+5y. multicoloured	1·10	75
4175	**3516**	50y.+5y. multicoloured	1·10	75
4176	**3517**	50y.+5y. multicoloured	1·10	75

3518 Stadium

2009. 64th National Sports Festival. Multicoloured.

4177	50y. Type **3518**		1·10	75
4178	50y. Basketball		1·10	75
4179	50y. Boxing		1·10	75

No. 4180 and Type **3521** are left for stamp not yet received.

3522 Procession, Nagasaki

2009. Hometowns. Multicoloured.

4181	80y. Type **3522**		1·80	1·20
4182	80y. Weeding and harvesting, Satsuma		1·80	1·20
4183	80y. Carp streamers, Iwakura		1·80	1·20
4184	80y. Procession through snow, Waga-gun		1·80	1·20
4185	80y. Deer dance, Ehime		1·80	1·20
4186	80y. Crowd, Naniwa-ku		1·80	1·20
4187	80y. Dancers and family, Akumi District		1·80	1·20
4188	80y. Procession, Wakayama		1·80	1·20
4189	80y. Women floating fFlowers in river, Tottori		1·80	1·20
4190	80y. Eating outside, Tano-gun		1·80	1·20

3532 *Fujisawa*

3533 *Okitsu*

3534 *Chiryu*

2009. International Correspondence Week. 53 Stations of Tokaido by Utagawa Hiroshige.

4191	**3532**	90y. multicoloured	1·80	1·20
4192	**3533**	110y. multicoloured	2·00	1·30
4193	**3534**	130y. multicoloured	2·50	1·70

3535 *Frege Bardach*

3536 *Autumn*

3537/8 Kunsthistorisches Museum, Vienna and Empress Elizabeth of Austria

3539/40 Merck Monastery

3541/2 Mozart and Salzburg

3543/4 Hallstat

2009. Austria–Japan Year.

4194	**3535**	80y. multicoloured	1·80	1·20
4195	**3536**	80y. multicoloured	1·80	1·20
4196	**3537**	80y. multicoloured	1·80	1·20
4197	**3538**	80y. multicoloured	1·80	1·20
4198	**3539**	80y. multicoloured	1·80	1·20
4199	**3540**	80y. multicoloured	1·80	1·20
4200	**3541**	80y. multicoloured	1·80	1·20
4201	**3542**	80y. multicoloured	1·80	1·20
4202	**3543**	80y. multicoloured	1·80	1·20
4203	**3544**	80y. multicoloured	1·80	1·20

Nos. 4196/7, 4198/9, 4200/1 and 4202/3 were printed, *se-tenant*, each pair forming a composite design.

3545 Decorated Canteen

3548/9 Hungarian Parliament Building

3553/4 Porcelain Statue and Vase

2009. Hungary–Japan Exchange Year. Multicoloured.

4204		80y. Type **3545**		
4205		80y. Mount Fuji	1·80	1·20
4206		80y. Plumware pot	1·80	1·20
4207		80y. Type **3548**	1·80	1·20
4208		80y. Type **3549**	1·80	1·20
4209		80y. Macho embroidery	1·80	1·20
4210	**3551**	80y. Elizabeth Bridge	1·80	1·20
4211	**3552**	80y. Crane and bamboo embroidery	1·80	1·20
4212	**3553**	80y. Type **3553**	1·80	1·20
4213	**3553**	80y. Type **3554**	1·80	1·20

Nos. 4207/8 and 4212/13 were printed, *se-tenant*, each pair forming a composite design.

3555/6 Naruto Uzumaki and Sasuke Uchiha

3557/8 Sakura Haruno and Kakashi Hatake

3559/60 Cy and Shikamaru Nara

3561/2 Deidara and Madara Uchiha

3563/4 Jiraiya and Hokage 4

2009. Heroes and Heroines of Animation (11th issue). Naruto.

4214	**3555**	80y. multicoloured	1·80	1·20
4215	**3556**	80y. multicoloured	1·80	1·20
4216	**3557**	80y. multicoloured	1·80	1·20
4217	**3558**	80y. multicoloured	1·80	1·20
4218	**3559**	80y. multicoloured	1·80	1·20
4219	**3560**	80y. multicoloured	1·80	1·20
4220	**3561**	80y. multicoloured	1·80	1·20
4221	**3562**	80y. multicoloured	1·80	1·20
4222	**3563**	80y. multicoloured	1·80	1·20
4223	**3564**	80y. multicoloured	1·80	1·20

3565 H-II Rocket and Mount Tsukuba

2009. Tourism. Ibaraki. Multicoloured.

4224	80y. Type **3565**	1·80	1·20
4225	80y. Fukuroda waterfall	1·80	1·20
4226	80y. Tokugawa Mitsukuni	1·80	1·20
4227	80y. Fishing trawl on Lake Kasumigaura	1·80	1·20
4228	80y. Fireworks	1·80	1·20

3570 Orange Tiger, Shizuoka

2009. New Year's Greetings. Multicoloured.

4229	50y. Type **3570**	1·10	75
4230	80y. Yellow tiger, Kaga	1·80	1·20

3573 Yellow Tiger, Kaga

2009. New Year Lottery Stamps. Multicoloured.

4231	50y.+3y. Orange tiger, Shizuoka	1·10	75
4232	80y.+3y. Type **3573**	1·80	1·20

Each stamp carries a lottery number.

3574 Phoenix

3575 Green Kirin

3576 Blue Kirin

2009. 20th (2010) Anniv of Enthronement of Emperor Akihito.

4233	**3574**	80y. multicoloured	1·80	1·20
4234	**3575**	80y. multicoloured	1·80	1·20
4235	**3576**	80y. multicoloured	1·80	1·20
MS4236	135×112 mm. 80y.×2 Nos. 4234/5		5·50	5·50

3577 Tiger (cursive)

3578 Tiger (clerical script)

3579 Tiger (Western Zhou period)

3580 Tiger

3581 Tiger (Kana hirigana)

3582 Tiger (hieroglyph)

3583 Tiger (Zhou dynasty)

3584 Tiger (Geng cursive)

3585 Tiger

3586 Tiger

2009. Greetings Stamps. Calligraphy. Year of the Tiger.

4237	**3577**	80y. multicoloured	1·80	1·20
4238	**3578**	80y. multicoloured	1·80	1·20
4239	**3579**	80y. multicoloured	1·80	1·20
4240	**3580**	80y. multicoloured	1·80	1·20
4241	**3581**	80y. multicoloured	1·80	1·20
4242	**3582**	80y. multicoloured	1·80	1·20
4243	**3583**	80y. multicoloured	1·80	1·20
4244	**3584**	80y. multicoloured	1·80	1·20
4245	**3585**	80y. multicoloured	1·80	1·20
4246	**3586**	80y. multicoloured		

3587 Girl with Apple (As Finland No. 1982) (Minna Immonen)

2009. Winter Greetings Stamps. Winter. Multicoloured. Self-adhesive.

4247	50y. Type **3587**	1·10	75
4248	50y. Snowman (Masami Koide) (26×35 mm)	1·10	75
4249	50y. Angel carrying toys (Moe Nagata) (26×35 mm)	1·10	75
4250	50y. Wreath surrounding apple (Arai Sonoko) (26×35 mm)	1·10	75
4251	50y. Sad and happy (Reich Karoly (children's book illustrator)) (35×26 mm)	1·10	75
4252	50y. Wreath (As Finland Type **852**) (Minna Immonen) (26×35 mm)	1·10	75
4253	80y. Santa playing fiddle (Masami Koide) (26×35 mm)	1·10	75
4254	80y. Lamplight (Arai Sonoko) (26×35 mm)	1·10	75
4255	80y. Angel (Moe Nagata) (26×35 mm)	1·10	75
4256	80y. Decorated fir twig (Reich Karoly) (26×35 mm)	1·10	75

3597/98 Keroro Gunso and Fuyuki Hinata

3599/60 Natsumi Hinata and Corporal Giroro

3603/04 Mutsumi Houjou and Sergeant Major Kululu

3605/06 Lance Corporal Dororo and Koyuki Azumaya

3601/02 Private Tamama and Momoka Nishizawa

2010. Heroes and Heroines of Animation (12th series). Keroro Gunso.

4257	**3597**	80y. multicoloured	1·80	1·20
4258	**3598**	80y. multicoloured	1·80	1·20
4259	**3599**	80y. multicoloured	1·80	1·20
4260	**3600**	80y. multicoloured	1·80	1·20
4261	**3601**	80y. multicoloured	1·80	1·20
4262	**3602**	80y. multicoloured	1·80	1·20
4263	**3603**	80y. multicoloured	1·80	1·20
4264	**3604**	80y. multicoloured	1·80	1·20
4265	**3605**	80y. multicoloured	1·80	1·20
4266	**3606**	80y. multicoloured	1·80	1·20

3607 Fairy with Watering Can

3608 Fairy, Bird and Letter

3609 Fairies carrying Basket of Flowers

3610 Fairy riding Bluebird carrying Envelope

3611 Flower Fairy playing Violin

3613 Girl playing Flute

3612 Bouquet

Bouquet and Large Butterfly

3615 Treble Clef of Flowers

3616 Rabbit and Flowers enclosed in Heart

2010. Greetings Stamps. Spring

4267	3607	50y. multicoloured	1·80	1·20
4268	3608	50y. multicoloured	1·80	1·20
4269	3609	50y. multicoloured	1·80	1·20
4270	3610	50y. multicoloured	1·80	1·20
4271	3611	50y. multicoloured	1·80	1·20
4272	3612	80y. multicoloured	1·80	1·20
4273	3613	80y. multicoloured	1·80	1·20
4274	3614	80y. multicoloured	1·80	1·20
4275	3615	80y. multicoloured	1·80	1·20
4276	3616	80y. multicoloured	1·80	1·20

3617/18 3617-3618

3619 Sendai Castl

3621/22 Sendai Castle

3623 Tanabata Festival

3624 Zuihho Hall

3625/3626 Rinnoji in Snow

2010. Tourism. Sendai, Miyagi

4277	3617	80y. multicoloured	1·80	1·20
4278	3618	80y. multicoloured	1·80	1·20
4279	3619	80y. multicoloured	1·80	1·20
4280	3620	80y. multicoloured	1·80	1·20
4281	3621	80y. multicoloured	1·80	1·20
4282	3622	80y. multicoloured	1·80	1·20
4283	3623	80y. multicoloured	1·80	1·20
4284	3624	80y. multicoloured	1·80	1·20
4285	3625	80y. multicoloured	1·80	1·20
4286	3626	80y. multicoloured	1·80	1·20

Nos. 4277/8, 4281/2 and 4285/6, respectively, were printed, *se-tenant*, each pair forming a composite design.

3627 Daigokuden (reconstructed building), Heijokyu Palace (8th-century)

3628 Hase-dera Temple

3629 Lakeside Pavilion at Night

3630 Murouji Temple

3631 Cherry Blossom

2010. Tourism. Nara

4287	3627	80y. multicoloured	1·80	1·20
4288	3628	80y. multicoloured	1·80	1·20
4289	3629	80y. multicoloured	1·80	1·20
4290	3630	80y. multicoloured	1·80	1·20
4291	3631	80y. multicoloured	1·80	1·20

3632/33 Riverside, Kurashiki

3634 Ohara Museum of Art Building

3635 Painting

3636-37 Seto Ohashi Bridge

3638/39 Kotohira-gu

3640/41 Ritsurin Park

2010. Tourism. Seto Inland Sea (1st series)

4292	3632	80y. multicoloured	1·80	1·20
4293	3633	80y. multicoloured	1·80	1·20
4295	3635	80y. multicoloured	1·80	1·20
4296	3636	80y. multicoloured	1·80	
4297	3637	multicoloured	1·80	1·20
4298	3638	80y. multicoloured	1·80	1·20
4299	3638	80y. multicoloured	1·80	1·20
4300	3640	80y. multicoloured	1·80	1·20
4301	3641	80y. multicoloured	1·80	1·20
44294	3634	80y. multicoloured	1·80	1·20

Nos. 4292/3, 4296/7, 4298/9 and 4300/1, respectively, were printed, *se-tenant*, each pair forming a composite design.

3642 Snoopy reading Letter

3643 Peppermint Patty

3644 Snoopy and Woodstock

3645 Sally

3646 Woodstock reading

3647 Snoopy and Woodstock

3648 Snoopy giving Woodstock Envelope

3649 Charlie Brown writing Letter

2010. Greetings Stamps. Snoopy

4302	3642	80y. multicoloured	1·80	1·20
4303	3643	80y multicoloured	1·80	1·20
4304	3644	80y. multicoloured	1·80	1·20
4305	3645	80y. multicoloured	1·80	1·20
4306	3646	80y. multicoloured	1·80	1·20
4307	3647	80y. multicoloured	1·80	1·20
4308	3648	80y. multicoloured	1·80	1·20
4309	3649	80y. multicoloured	1·80	1·20

3650/51 La Republica (V. Pochini) and First Tower (Guaita)

3652/53 Apparizione di San Marino al suo popolo (E. Retrosi) (mural)

3654 Liberty (S. Galletti)

3655 San Marino Basilica

3656 Second Tower (Cesta)

3657 Belfry

3658 Sante Maria Maddalena (F. Menzocchi)

3659 San Marino

2010. San Marino

4310	3650	80y multicoloured	1·80	1·20
4311	3651	80y. multicoloured	1·80	1·20
4312	3652	80y. multicoloured	1·80	1·20
4313	3653	80y. multicoloured	1·80	1·20
4314	3654	80y. multicoloured	1·80	1·20
4315	3655	80y. multicoloured	1·80	1·20
4316	3656	80y. multicoloured	1·80	1·20
4317	3657	80y. multicoloured	1·80	1·20
4318	3658	80y. multicoloured	1·80	1·20
4319	3659	80y. multicoloured	1·80	1·20

Nos. 4310/11 and 4312/13, respectively, were printed, *se-tenant*, each pair forming a composite design.

3660 Suwa Taisha Kamiyashiro Motomiya

3661 Suwa Taisha Kamiyashiro Miyamae

3662 Kamiyashiro

3663 Ri Ki Nagamochi

3664 Onbashira

3665 Suwa Taisha Shimosha Akimiya Kaguraden

3666

2010. Suwa Taisha Shrine Complex

4320	3660	50y. multicoloured	1·10	
4321	3661	50y. multicoloured	75	75
4322	3662	50y. multicoloured	1·10	75
4323	3663	50y. multicoloured	1·10	75
4324	3664	50y. multicoloured	1·10	75
4325	3665	50y. multicoloured	1·10	75
4326	3665	50y. multicoloured	1·10	75

3667 Tiger (*Ryu-ko-zu Byoubu*)

3668 Peony (*Kacho-zu*)

3669 Bullfinches and Peonies (*Kacho-zu*)

3670 Tiger (*Tora*) (Wang Yun Fung)

2010. Philately Week

4327	3667	80y. multicoloured	1·80	1·20
4328	3668	80y. multicoloured	1·80	1·20
4329	3669	80y. multicoloured	1·80	1·20
4330	3670	80y. multicoloured	1·80	1·20

3671 Heijo Palace

3672 Inner Gate

3673 Standing Buddha

3674 Seated Guardian Deity

3675 Gate Guardian

3676 Buddha

3677 Multi-armed Deity

3678 Bodhisattva

3679 Warrior

3680 Guardian Deity

2010. 1300th Anniv of Nara Heijo-kyo Capital and Heijo Palace

4331		80y. multicoloured	2·10	1·50
4332	3672	80y. multicoloured	2·10	1·50
4333	3673	80y. multicoloured	2·10	1·50
4334	3674	80y. multicoloured	2·10	1·50
4335	3675	80y. multicoloured	2·10	1·50
4336	3676	80y. multicoloured	2·10	1·50
4337	3677	80y. multicoloured	2·10	1·50
4338	3678	80y. multicoloured	2·10	1·50
4339	3679	80y. multicoloured	2·10	1·50
4340	3680	80y. multicoloured	2·10	1·50

3681 Hello Kitty and Dragon

3682 Wearing Nihon Buyo Costume

3683 Wearing Tai Chi Cuan Costume

3684 With Origami Bird

3685 With Butterflies

3686 Wearing Traditional Dress with Cherry Blossom

3687 With Peonies

3688 With Pudong Area Skyline

3689 Wearing Chinese Dress and Peony

3690 In Yuyuan Garden

3691 With Tiger

3692 Sakamoto Ryoma (imperial loyalist) (statue) and Katsurahama Beach

2010. Greetings Stamps. Hello Kitty

4341	3681	50y. multicoloured	1·10	75
4342	3682	50y. multicoloured	1·10	75
4343	3683	50y. multicoloured	1·10	75
4344	3684	50y. multicoloured	1·10	75
4345	3685	50y. multicoloured	1·10	75
4346	3686	50y. multicoloured	1·10	75
4347	3687	80y. multicoloured	2·00	1·70
4348	3688	80y. multicoloured	2·00	1·70
4349	3689	80y. multicoloured	2·00	1·70
4350	3690	80y. multicoloured	2·00	1·70
4351	3691	80y. multicoloured	2·00	1·70

3692 Sakamoto Ryoma (imperial loyalist) (statue) and Katsurahama Beach

3693 Noradokei Turret Clock (Meiji Period)

3694 Harimaya-bashi (bridge) and Tram

3695 Niyodogawakami-no-koinobori (paper streamers)

3696 Ashizuri-misaki (Cape Ashizuri)

2010. Tourism. Kochi

4352	3692	80y. multicoloured	1·10	75
4353	3693	80y. multicoloured	1·10	75
4354	3694	80y. multicoloured	1·10	75
4355	3695	80y. multicoloured	1·10	75
4356	3696	80y. multicoloured	1·10	75

3697 Uruguay, 1930

2010. World Cup Football Championships, South Africa (1st issue). Multicoloured.

4357	80y. Type **3697**	2·10	1·50
4358	80y. Sweden, 1958	2·10	1·50
4359	80y. Italy, 1990	2·10	1·50
4360	80y. Jules Rimet trophy	2·10	1·50
4361	80y. Italy, 1934	2·10	1·50
4362	80y. Chile, 1962	2·10	1·50
4363	80y. USA, 1994	2·10	1·50
4364	80y. Hand of stars holding trophy	2·10	1·50
4365	80y. France, 1938	2·10	1·50
4366	80y. Mexico, 1970	2·10	1·50
4367	80y. France, 1998	2·10	1·50
4368	80y. Brazil, 1950	2·10	1·50
4369	80y. Argentina, 1978	2·10	1·50
4370	80y. South Korea and Japan, 2002	2·10	1·50
4371	80y. Switzerland, 1954	2·10	1·50
4372	80y. Mexico, 1986	2·10	1·50
4373	80y. Germany, 2006	2·10	1·50

3697a Football

3698 FIFA World Cup Trophy

3699 Official Poster, 2010

3700 Official Emblem, 2010

3701 Japanese National Team Emblem

2010. World Cup Football Championships, South Africa (2nd issue)

4374	3697a	80y. multicoloured	2·10	1·50
4375	3698	80y. multicoloured	2·10	1·50
4376	3699	80y. multicoloured	2·10	1·50
4377	3700	80y. multicoloured	2·10	1·50
4378	3701	80y. multicoloured	2·10	1·50

3702-3703 Cattle and Barn

3704-3705 Barn and Woman feeding Cranes in Snow

3706-3707 Barns, Cultivated Field and Tractor

3708-3709 Farm House, Barns, Children and Cattle

3710 Boats, Snow-covered Sheds and Children with Sledge

3711 Trawler and Father with Children

2010. Hometowns

4379	3702	80y. multicoloured	2·10	1·50
4380	3703	80y. multicoloured	2·10	1·50
4381	3704	80y. multicoloured	2·10	1·50
4382	3705	80y. multicoloured	2·10	1·50
4383	3706	80y. multicoloured	2·10	1·50
4384	3707	80y. multicoloured	2·10	1·50
4385	3708	80y. multicoloured	2·10	1·50
4386	3709	80y. multicoloured	2·10	1·50
4387	3710	80y. multicoloured	2·10	1·50
4388	3711	80y. multicoloured	2·10	1·50

Nos. 4379/80, 4381/2, 4383/4 and 4385/6, respectively, were printed, se-tenant, forming a composite design

3712 APEC Emblem and Flowers

2010. APEC Summit, Japan

MS4389 80y.×10, Type **3712**	21·00	21·00

No. **MS**4389 forms a composite design

3713 Academy Emblem

3714 First Award Ceremony Photos and Newspaper Articles

3715 First Awards Ceremony Venue

3716 Former Academy Hall

3717 Naganaki-dori (rooster)

2010. Centenary of Japan Academy Prize

4390	3713	80y. multicoloured	2·10	1·50
4391	3714	80y. multicoloured	2·10	1·50
4392	3715	80y. multicoloured	2·10	1·50
4393	3716	80y. multicoloured	2·10	1·50
4394	3717	80y. multicoloured	2·10	1·50

3718-3719 Edward Elric and Alphonse Elric

3720-3721 Riza Hawkeye and Roy Mustang

3722-3723 Xiao Mei and May Chang

3724-3725 Lin Yao and Lan Fan

3726-3727 Winry Rockbell and Den (Edward Elric)

2010. Heroes and Heroines of Animation (13th series). Fullmetal Alchemist

4395	3718	80y. multicoloured	2·10	1·50
4396	3719	80y. multicoloured	2·10	1·50
4397	3720	80y. multicoloured	2·10	1·50
4398	3721	80y. multicoloured	2·10	1·50
4399	3722	80y. multicoloured	2·10	1·50
4400	3723	80y. multicoloured	2·10	1·50
4401	3724	80y. multicoloured	2·10	1·50
4402	3725	80y. multicoloured	2·10	1·50
4403	3726	80y. multicoloured	2·10	1·50
4404	3727	80y. multicoloured	2·10	1·50

3728 Cormorant Fishing on the Nagara River

3729 Gifu Castle and Mount Kinka

3730 Yokokura Temple

3731 Mino-washi Akari (art festival)

3732 Magome-juku

2010. Tourism

4405	3728	80y. multicoloured	2·10	1·50
4406	3729	80y. multicoloured	2·10	1·50
4407	3730	80y. multicoloured	2·10	1·50
4408	3731	80y. multicoloured	2·10	1·50
4409	3732	80y. multicoloured	2·10	1·50

3733 National Diet Building and the United States Capitol

2010. 50th Anniv of Japan–US Mutual Cooperation and Security Treaty. Multicoloured.

4410	80y. Type **3733**		2·10	1·50
4411	80y. President Eisenhower and Prime Minister Kishi Nobu-suke signing treaty		2·10	1·50

3734-3735 Fireworks

3736-3737 Fireworks

3738-3739 Fireworks

3740-3741 Fireworks

3742-3743 Fireworks

2010. Festivals. Omagari Fireworks, Daisen, Akita

4412	3734	50y. multicoloured	1·30	90
4413	3735	50y. multicoloured	1·30	90
4414		50y. multicoloured	1·30	90
4415	3737	50y. multicoloured	1·30	90
4416	3738	50y. multicoloured	1·30	90
4417	3739	50y. multicoloured	1·30	90
4418	3740	50y. multicoloured	1·30	90
4419	3741	50y. multicoloured	1·30	90
4420	3742	50y. multicoloured	1·30	90
4421	3743	50y. multicoloured	1·30	90

3744-3745 Ama-kakeru-siroi-hashi (white bridge)

3746-3747 Jyoudo Temple

3748 Mt. Shirataki and Gohyakurakan (statues of disciples of Buddha)

3749 Koujou Temple and Three-storied Pagoda

3750 Oyamazumi Shrine

3751 Omishima Bridge

3752-3753 Imabari Castle

2010. Tourism. Seto Inland Sea (2nd series)

4422	3744	80y. multicoloured	2·10	1·50
4423	3745	80y. multicoloured	2·10	1·50
4424	3746	80y. multicoloured	2·10	1·50
4425	3747	80y. multicoloured	2·10	1·50
4426	3748	80y. multicoloured	2·10	1·50
4427	3749	80y. multicoloured	2·10	1·50
4428	3750	80y. multicoloured	2·10	1·50
4429	3751	80y. multicoloured	2·10	1·50
4430	3752	80y. multicoloured	2·10	1·50
4431	3753	80y. multicoloured	2·10	1·50

Nos. 4422/3, 4424/5 and 4430/1, respectively, were printed, *se-tenant*, each pair forming a composite design

3754 Koko Tenno

3755 Ise

3756 Sakino-daisojo Gyoson

3757 Yushi Naisinnoke-no-Ki

3758 Sutokuin

3759-3760 Violets and Koko Tenno

3761-3762 Lake Edge and Ise

3763/64 Blossom Trees and Sakino-daisojo Gyoson

3765/66 Waves and Yushi Naisinnoke-no-K

3767/68 Waterfall and Sutokuin

2010. Letter Writing Day

4432	3754	50y. multicoloured	1·80	1·20
4433	3777	50y. multicoloured	1·80	1·20
4434	3756	50y. multicoloured	1·80	1·20
4435	3757	50y. multicoloured	1·80	1·20
4436	3758	50y. multicoloured	1·80	1·20
4437	3759	80y. multicoloured	1·80	1·20
4438	3760	80y. multicoloured	1·80	1·20
4439	3761	80y. multicoloured	1·80	1·20
4440	3762	80y. multicoloured	1·80	1·20
4441	3763	80y. multicoloured	1·80	1·20
4442	3764	80y. multicoloured	1·80	1·20
4443	3765	80y. multicoloured	1·80	1·20
4444	3766	80y. multicoloured	1·80	1·20
4445	3767	80y. multicoloured	1·80	1·20
4446	3768	80y. multicoloured	1·80	1·20

3769 Suruga Street Scene (Utagawa Hiroshige)

3770 Fujyo Ninsou Jyuppon, Fumi Yomu Onna (Kitagawa Utamaro)

3771 Dyers' Quarter in Kanda (Utagawa Hiroshige)

3772 Sandai Sawamura Sojyuro no Ogishi Kurando (Toshusai Sharaku)

3773 Asakusa Rice Fields during the Cock Festival (Utagawa Hiroshige)

3774 Nishikiori Utamarogata Shinmoyou, Shiro Uchikake (Kitagawa Utamaro)

3775 Takinogawa (Utagawa Hiroshige)

3777 Uenoyamashita (Utagawa Hiroshige)

3778 Giyaman (Kitagawa Utamaro)

2010. Edo Famous Places and Ukiyo-e Paintings

4447	3769	80y. multicoloured	1·80	1·20
4448	3770	80y. multicoloured	1·80	1·20
4449	3771	80y. multicoloured	1·80	1·20
4450	3772	80y. multicoloured	1·80	1·20
4451	3773	80y. multicoloured	1·80	1·20
4452	3774	80y. multicoloured	1·80	1·20
4453	3775	80y. multicoloured	1·80	1·20
4454	3776	80y. multicoloured	1·80	1·20
4455	3777	80y. multicoloured	1·80	1·20
4456	3778	80y. multicoloured	1·80	1·20

3779 Tyranosaurus and Tojinbo Cliffs

3780 Narcissi, Eichen

3781 Azaleas and Lake, Mikata

3782 Plum Blossom and Asakura Clan Ruins

3783 Tanner Crab,
Eichen

2010. Tourism

4457	**3779**	80y. multicoloured	1·80	1·20
4458	**3780**	80y. multicoloured	1·80	1·20
4459	**3781**	80y. multicoloured	1·80	1·20
4460	**3782**	80y. multicoloured	1·80	1·20
4461	**3783**	80y. multicoloured	1·80	1·20

3784 Henri Farman III
Biplane

3786 Koken Long-Range
Prototype Plane
(Koken-ki)

3786 Kawasaki Asuka

3787 Boeing 747-400

3788 Mitsubishi Regional
Jet (MRJ)

3789 Hans Grade
Monoplane

3790 NAMC YS-11

3791 Sukhoi T-4

3792 ShinMaywa US-2

3793 JADC High Speed
Transport Program
(HSTP)

2010. Centenary of Aviation in Japan

4462	**3784**	80y. multicoloured	2·20	1·70
4463	**3785**	80y. multicoloured	2·20	1·70
4464	**3786**	80y. multicoloured	2·20	1·70
4465	**3787**	80y. multicoloured	2·20	1·70
4466	**3788**	80y. multicoloured	2·20	1·70
4467	**3789**	80y. multicoloured	2·20	1·70
4468	**3790**	80y. multicoloured	2·20	1·70
4469	**3791**	80y. multicoloured	2·20	1·70
4470	**3792**	80y. multicoloured	2·20	1·70
4471	**3793**	80y. multicoloured	2·20	1·70

3794/95 Sakura Family

3796/97 Maruko and Grandpa

3798/99 Father, Maruko and Sakiko

3800/01 Mother, Maruko and Grandma

3802/03 Hamaji, Butaro, Maruko and
Tama-chan

2010. Heros and Heroines of Animation (14th series).
Chibi Maruko-chan

4472	**3794**	80y. multicoloured	2·20	1·70
4473	**3795**	80y. multicoloured	2·20	1·70
4474	**3796**	80y. multicoloured	2·20	1·70
4475	**3797**	80y. multicoloured	2·20	1·70
4476	**3798**	80y. multicoloured	2·20	1·70
4477	**3799**	80y. multicoloured	2·20	1·70
4478	**3800**	80y. multicoloured	2·20	1·70
4479	**3801**	80y. multicoloured	2·20	1·70
4480	**3802**	80y. multicoloured	2·20	1·70
4481	**3803**	80y. multicoloured	2·20	1·70

3804/05 Akashi Kaikyo Bridge and Sun
Yat-sen Memorial Hall

3806/07 Fields of Flowers

3808/09 Awaji ningyo joruri (puppet
theatre), Awaij

3810/3811 Onaruto Bridge

3812 Whirling
Waves, Naruto

3813 Esaki
Lighthouse

2010. Tourism. Seto Inland Sea (3rd series)

4482	**3804**	80y. multicoloured	2·20	1·70
4483	**3805**	80y. multicoloured	2·20	1·70
4484	**3806**	80y. multicoloured	2·20	1·70
4485	**3807**	80y. multicoloured	2·20	1·70
4486	**3808**	80y. multicoloured	2·20	1·70
4487	**3809**	80y. multicoloured	2·20	1·70
4488	**3810**	80y. multicoloured	2·20	1·70
4489	**3811**	80y. multicoloured	2·20	1·70
4490	**3812**	80y. multicoloured	2·20	1·70
4491	**3813**	80y. multicoloured	2·20	1·70

Nos. 4482/3, 4484/5, 4486/7, 4488/9 and 4490/1, respectively, were printed, se-tenant, each pair forming a
composite design.

3814 Kinshachi, Iris
laevigata and Atsumi
Peninsula

3815 Otus scops
(Scops owl)

3816 Ginkgo
biloba

3817 Seto-yaki

3818 Cerasu
xsubhirtella

2010. 60th Anniv of Local Government, Aichi

4492	**3814**	80y. multicoloured	2·20	1·70
4493	**3815**	80y. multicoloured	2·20	1·70
4494	**3816**	80y. multicoloured	2·20	1·70
4495	**3817**	80y. multicoloured	2·20	1·70
4496	**3818**	80y. multicoloured	2·20	1·70

3819 Michitose (detail)
(Ito Shinsui)

3820 Nozaki-mura
(detail) (Kaburaki
Kiyokata)

3821 Botan-yuki (detail)
(Uemura Shouen)

2010. International Correspondence Week

4484	**3819**	90y. multicoloured	2·50	1·90
4493	**3820**	110y. multicoloured	3·00	2·20
4495	**3821**	130y. multicoloured	3·75	3·00

3822 Lake Mashu
in Frost

3823 Spotted
Seal (Phoca
largha)

3824 Mount
Tsurugi and
Tateyama
Mountain Range

3825 Japanese
Serow (Capricornis
crispus)

3826 Mountain
Village

3827 Japanese
Tree Frog (Hyla
japonica)

3828 Shimanto
River

3829 Kingfisher
(Alcedo athis)

3830
Tamatorizaki

3831 Amphiprion
ocellaris
(clownfish)

2010. Conference of Parties to Convention on Biological
Diversity, Nagoya

4500	**3822**	80y. multicoloured	2·20	1·70
4501	**3823**	80y. multicoloured	2·20	1·70
4502	**3824**	80y. multicoloured	2·20	1·70
4503	**3825**	80y. multicoloured	2·20	1·70
4504	**3826**	80y. multicoloured	2·20	1·70
4505	**3827**	80y. multicoloured	2·20	1·70
4506	**3828**	80y. multicoloured	2·20	1·70
4507	**3829**	80y. multicoloured	2·20	1·70
4508	**3830**	80y. multicoloured	2·20	1·70
4509	**3831**	80y. multicoloured	2·20	1·70

3832/33 Nanban Byobu (detail) (Kano
Naizen)

3834 Belem Tower
(World Heritage
Site)

3835 St. Vincent,
Patron Saint of
Lisbon (statue)

3836 Jeronimos
Monastery (World
Heritage Site)

3837 Historic Centre
of Evora (World
Heritage Site)

3839 Batalha
Monastery (World
Heritage Site)

3838 Historic Centre
of Oporto (World
Heritage Site)

3840 Azulejo
(decorative painted
tilework)

3841 Portuguese
Traditional Puppet

2010. 150th Anniv of Japan-Portugal Diplomatic
Relations

4510	**3832**	80y. multicoloured	2·20	1·70
4511	**3833**	80y. multicoloured	2·20	1·70
4512	**3834**	80y. multicoloured	2·20	1·70
4513	**3835**	80y. multicoloured	2·20	1·70
4514	**3836**	80y. multicoloured	2·20	1·70
4515	**3837**	80y. multicoloured	2·20	1·70

4516	3838	80y. multicoloured	2·20	1·70
4517	3839	80y. multicoloured	2·20	1·70
4518	3840	80y. multicoloured	2·20	1·70
4519	3841	80y. multicoloured	2·20	1·70

3842 Peace Statue, Nagasaki and UNI Global Union Emblem

3843/3844 People wearing Early Costumes

3845 Congress Emblem

2010. UNI Global Union World Congress

4521	3842	80y. multicoloured	2·20	1·70
4522	3843	80y. multicoloured	2·20	1·70
4523	3844	80y. multicoloured	2·20	1·70
4524	3845	80y. multicoloured	2·20	1·70

Nos. 4505/6 were printed, se-tenant, in horizontal pairs within the sheet, each pair forming a composite design.

3846 Surprised Santa (Koide Masaki)

3847 Christmas Tree of Poinsettias (Arai Sonoko)

3848 Silent Night (Kuroi Ken)

3849 Heart-shaped Wreath (Arai Sonoko)

3850 Reindeer and Aurora Borealis (Sasaki Goro)

3851 Santa (Tommi Vallisto)

3852 Decorated Tree (Tommi Vallisto)

3853 Santa's Sleigh flying over Finnish Landscape (Tommi Vallisto)

3854 Wreath (Tommi Vallisto)

3855 Santa's Reindeer (Tommi Vallisto)

3856 Starry Night (Nagata Moe)

3857 Snowman juggling (Koide Masaki)

3858 Choristers (Nakamaru Hitomi)

3859 Box containing Heart-shaped Rose (Arai Sonoko)

3860 Cakes (Hoshiyama Ayaka)

2010. Greetings Stamps. Winter

4525	3846	50y. multicoloured	1·30	95
4526	3847	50y. multicoloured	1·30	95
4527	3848	50y. multicoloured	1·30	95
4528	3849	50y. multicoloured	1·30	95
4529	3850	50y. multicoloured	1·30	95
4530	3851	80y. multicoloured	2·20	1·70
4531	3852	80y. multicoloured	2·20	1·70
4532	3853	80y. multicoloured	2·20	1·70
4533	3854	80y. multicoloured	2·20	1·70
4534	3855	80y. multicoloured	2·20	1·70
4535	3856	90y. multicoloured	2·40	1·90
4536	3857	90y. multicoloured	2·40	1·90
4537	3858	90y. multicoloured	2·40	1·90
4538	3859	90y. multicoloured	2·40	1·90
4539	3860	90y. multicoloured	2·40	1·90

3861 Rabbit (Kubifuri-shofuku-usagi (folk toy of Nishiaizu)

3862 Rabbit (Kousagi-Dorei (earthenware bells) (folk toy of Tamba City)

2010. New Year's Greetings

4540	3861	50y. multicoloured	1·30	95
4541	3862	80y. multicoloured	2·20	1·70

3863 Rabbit (Kubifuri-shofuku-usagi (folk toy of Nishiaizu)

3864 Rabbit (Kousagi-Dorei (earthenware bells) (folk toy of Tamba City)

2010. New Year Lottery Stamps

4542	3863	50y.+3y. multicoloured	1·40	1·00
4543	3864	80y.+3y. multicoloured	2·30	1·80

3865 Nebuta, Neputa and Apple

3866 Hirosaki Castle and Cherry Blossom

3867 Sansha Taisai Festival

3868 Lake Towada

3869 Horse and Shiriyazaki Lighthouse

2010. 60th Anniv of Local Government, Aomori

4544	3865	80y. multicoloured	2·20	1·70
4545	3866	80y. multicoloured	2·20	1·70
4546	3867	80y. multicoloured	2·20	1·70
4547	3868	80y. multicoloured	2·20	1·70
4548	3869	80y. multicoloured	2·20	1·70

3870 Kinbun Style (Seki Masato)

3871 Kaisho Style of Six Dynasties (Inamura Undo)

3872 Oracle Bone Script (Kataoka Shigekazu)

3873 Oracle Bone Script (Sekiguchi Shunpo)

3874 Reisho Style (Nakagawa Yusei)

3875 Seal Script (Momose Daibu)

3876 Setsumon Style (Terai Bokudo)

3877 Hiragana (Nakano Hokumei)

3878 Gyosho Style (Koyama Yasuko)

3879 Expressing Strength (Onchi Shunyo)

2010. Greetings Stamps. Eto Calligraphy. Year of the Rabbit

4549	3870	80y. multicoloured	2·20	1·70
4550	3871	80y. multicoloured	2·20	1·70
4551	3872	80y. multicoloured	2·20	1·70
4552	3873	80y. multicoloured	2·20	1·70
4553	3874	80y. multicoloured	2·20	1·70

4554	3875	80y. multicoloured	2·20	1·70
4555	3876	80y. multicoloured	2·20	1·70
4556	3877	80y. multicoloured	2·20	1·70
4557	3878	80y. multicoloured	2·20	1·70
4558	3879	80y. multicoloured	2·20	1·70

3880/81 Temporary Building, National Diet Building and Stained Glass

2010. 120th Anniv of Diet

4559	3880	80y. multicoloured	2·20	1·70
4560	3881	80y. multicoloured	2·20	1·70

3882/83 Farm and Paulownia Tree

3884/85 Bus and Mother carrying Child

3886 House, Woman, Children and Coastline

3887 Snow-covered Houses

3888/89 Single Car Train and Station in Snow Storm

3890 Children, Garden and House on Hillside

3891 Women making Kokeshi Dolls

2010. Hometowns. Tohku

4561	3882	80y. multicoloured	2·20	1·70
4562	3883	80y. multicoloured	2·20	1·70
4563	3884	80y. multicoloured	2·20	1·70
4564	3885	80y. multicoloured	2·20	1·70
4565	3886	80y. multicoloured	2·20	1·70
4566	3887	80y. multicoloured	2·20	1·70
4567	3888	80y. multicoloured	2·20	1·70
4568	3889	80y. multicoloured	2·20	1·70
4569	3890	80y. multicoloured	2·20	1·70
4570	3891	80y. multicoloured	2·20	1·70

3892 Okuma Shigenobu

3893 Yoshinogari Ruins

3894 Yutoku Inari Shrine

3895 Saga International Balloon Festival

3896 Karatsu Kunchi (festival)

2011. 60th Anniv of Local Government, Saga

4571	**3892**	80y. multicoloured	2·20	1·70
4572	**3893**	80y. multicoloured	2·20	1·70
4573	**3894**	80y. multicoloured	2·20	1·70
4574	**3895**	80y. multicoloured	2·20	1·70
4575	**3896**	80y. multicoloured	2·20	1·70

3897 Mighty Atom

3898 Doraemon

3899 Pikachu (Pokemon)

3900 Hello Kitty

3901 Rabbit riding Deer (Choju-jinbutsu-giga)

3902 Mighty Atom

3903 Doraemon

3904 Pikachu (Pokemon)

3905 Hello Kitty

3906 Rabbit riding Deer (Choju-jinbutsu-giga)

2011. Phila Nippon '11 International Stamp Exhibition (1st issue)

4576	**3897**	80y. multicoloured	2·20	1·70
4577	**3898**	80y. multicoloured	2·20	1·70
4578	**3899**	80y. multicoloured	2·20	1·70
4579	**3900**	80y. multicoloured	2·20	1·70
4580	**3901**	80y. multicoloured	2·20	1·70
4581	**3902**	80y. multicoloured	2·20	1·70
4582	**3903**	80y. multicoloured	2·20	1·70
4583	**3904**	80y. multicoloured	2·20	1·70
4584	**3905**	80y. multicoloured	2·20	1·70
4585	**3906**	80y. multicoloured	2·20	1·70

3907 Regensburg (World Heritage Site)

3908 Brandenburg Gate (Berlin)

3909 Frauenkirche (Dresden)

3910/11 Schewerin Castle

3912 Yakushiji Temple (World Heritage Site)

3913/14 Bamberg (World Heritage Site)

3915 Neuschwanstein Castle (Fussen)

3916 Zollverein Coal Mine Industrial Complex (Essen) (World Heritage Site)

2011. 150th Anniv of Japan-Germany Diplomatic Relations

4586	**3907**	80y. multicoloured	2·20	1·70
4587	**3908**	80y. multicoloured	2·20	1·70
4588	**3909**	80y. multicoloured	2·20	1·70
4589	**3910**	80y. multicoloured	2·20	1·70
4590	**3911**	80y. multicoloured	2·20	1·70
4591	**3912**	80y. multicoloured	2·20	1·70
4592	**3913**	80y. multicoloured	2·20	1·70
4593	**3914**	80y. multicoloured	2·20	1·70
4594	**3915**	80y. multicoloured	2·20	1·70
4595	**3916**	80y. multicoloured	2·20	1·70

Nos. 4589/90 and 4592/3 were printed, *se-tenant* in horizontal pairs, within sheetlets of ten stamps, each pair forming a composite design.

3917 Sapporo Snow Festival

3918 Penguins

3920 Otaru Snow Light Path

3922 Hakodate Orthodox Church

3923-3924 Shiretoko Five Lakes and Shiretoko Mountain Range

3925 *Grus Japonensis* (red-crowned crane)

3926 Drift Ice

2011. Tourism. Hokkaido

4596	**3917**	80y. multicoloured	2·20	1·70
4597	**3918**	80y. multicoloured	2·20	1·70
4598	**3919**	80y. multicoloured	2·20	1·70
4599	**3920**	80y. multicoloured	2·20	1·70
4600	**3921**	80y. multicoloured	2·20	1·70
4601	**3922**	80y. multicoloured	2·20	1·70
4602	**3923**	80y. multicoloured	2·20	1·70
4603	**3924**	80y. multicoloured	2·20	1·70
4604	**3925**	80y. multicoloured	2·20	1·70
4605	**3926**	80y. multicoloured	2·20	1·70

Nos. 4598/9 and 4602/3, respectively, were printed, *se-tenant*, in horizontal pairs, each pair forming a composite design.

3927 Crocus and Fawn

3928 Lily and the Blue Bird of Happiness

3929 Flowers and Butterfly

3930 Blue Roses and Swans

3931 Strawberries and Rabbits

3932 Boy Fairy and Flowers flowing from Hat

3933 Daffodils and Fairy

3934 Fairy riding Bird, delivering Mail

3935 Rainbow and Fairy delivering Bouquet

3936 Fairy writing amidst Flowers

2011. Greetings Stamps. Spring

4606	**3927**	50y. multicoloured	1·30	95
4607	**3928**	50y. multicoloured	1·30	95
4608	**3929**	50y. multicoloured	1·30	95
4609	**3930**	50y. multicoloured	1·30	95
4610	**3931**	50y. multicoloured	1·30	95
4611	**3932**	80y. multicoloured	2·20	1·70
4612	**3933**	80y. multicoloured	2·20	1·70
4613	**3934**	80y. multicoloured	2·20	1·70
4614	**3935**	80y. multicoloured	2·20	1·70
4615	**3936**	80y. multicoloured	2·20	1·70

3937-3938 Workers tending Plants

3939-3940 Farmhouse, Barns and Vegetable Plot

3942 Springtime

3943 Cultivating Wheat

3944 Trees and House

3945 Street Scene

3946 Western-style House

2011. Hometowns. Kanto

4616	**3937**	80y. multicoloured	2·20	1·70
4617	**3938**	80y. multicoloured	2·20	1·70
4618	**3939**	80y. multicoloured	2·20	1·70
4619	**3940**	80y. multicoloured	2·20	1·70
4620	**3941**	80y. multicoloured	2·20	1·70
4621	**3942**	80y. multicoloured	2·20	1·70
4622	**3943**	80y. multicoloured	2·20	1·70
4623	**3944**	80y. multicoloured	2·20	1·70
4624	**3945**	80y. multicoloured	2·20	1·70
4625	**3946**	80y. multicoloured	2·20	1·70

Nos. 4616/17, 4618/19 and 4620/1, respectively, were printed, *se-tenant*, in horizontal pairs, each pair forming a composite design.

3947 Peter Rabbit (*The Tale of Peter Rabbit*)

3948 Mouse (*Tailor of Gloucester*)

3949 Peter Rabbit

3950 Benjamin Bunny (*The Tale of Benjamin Bunny*)

3951 Pigling-Bland
(*The Tale of
Pigling-Bland*)

3952 Old Brown
and Squirrel
Nutkin (*The Tale of
Squirrel Nutkin*)

3953 Mrs.
Tiggy-Winkle (*The
Tale of Mrs
Tiggy-Winkle*)

3954 Jemima
Puddle-Duck (*The
Tale of Jemima
Puddle-Duck*)

3955 Squirrel
Nutkin

3956 Tom Kitten
(*The Tale of Tom
Kitten*)

2011. Greetings Stamps. Stories by Beatrix Potter

4626	**3947**	50y. multicoloured	1·30	95
4627	**3948**	50y. multicoloured	1·30	95
4628	**3949**	50y. multicoloured	1·30	95
4629	**3950**	50y. multicoloured	1·30	95
4630	**3951**	50y. multicoloured	1·30	95
4631	**3952**	50y. multicoloured	1·30	95
4632	**3953**	50y. multicoloured	1·30	95
4633	**3954**	50y. multicoloured	1·30	95
4634	**3955**	50y. multicoloured	1·30	95
4635	**3956**	50y. multicoloured	1·30	95

3957 Peter's
Family under Fir
Tree

3958 His Mother
and Sisters

3959 Peter Rabbit

3960 Mother
dressing Peter

3961 Mrs. Rabbit
Going Out

3962 Peter with
Heartburn after
too much Food

3963 Peter
sneaking into Field

3964 Peter Eating
Radish

3965 Peter seeing
Mr. McGregor

3966 Peter Being
Chased by Mr.
McGregor

2011. Greetings Stamps. *The Tale of Peter Rabbit*

4636	**3957**	80y. multicoloured	2·20	1·70
4637	**3958**	80y. multicoloured	2·20	1·70

4638	**3959**	80y. multicoloured	2·20	1·70
4639	**3960**	80y. multicoloured	2·20	1·70
4640	**3961**	80y. multicoloured	2·20	1·70
4641	**3962**	80y. multicoloured	2·20	1·70
4642	**3963**	80y. multicoloured	2·20	1·70
4643	**3964**	80y. multicoloured	2·20	1·70
4644	**3965**	80y. multicoloured	2·20	1·70
4645	**3966**	80y. multicoloured	2·20	1·70

3967-3968 Luffy and Chopper

3969-3970 Sanji and Zoro

3971-3972 Robin and Nami

3973-3974 Usopp, Brook and Franky

3975-3976

2011. Heros and Heroines of Animation (15th series).
One Piece

4646	**3967**	80y. multicoloured	2·20	1·70
4647	**3968**	80y. multicoloured	2·20	1·70
4648	**3969**	80y. multicoloured	2·20	1·70
4649	**3970**	80y. multicoloured	2·20	1·70
4650	**3971**	80y. multicoloured	2·20	1·70
4651	**3972**	80y. multicoloured	2·20	1·70
4652	**3973**	80y. multicoloured	2·20	1·70
4653	**3974**	80y. multicoloured	2·20	1·70
4654	**3975**	80y. multicoloured	2·20	1·70
4655	**3976**	80y. multicoloured	2·20	1·70

3977 Emblem
and Flowers

3978 Emblem
and Flowers

2011. 50th Anniv of Administrative Counseling System

4656	**3977**	80y. multicoloured	2·20	1·70
4657	**3978**	80y. multicoloured	2·20	1·70

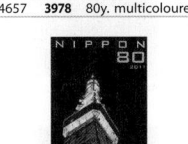
3979 Tokyo
Tower and
Chidejika
(mascot)

3980 Tokyo Sky
Tree and
Chidejika

2011. Digital Television Broadcasting

4658	**3979**	80y. multicoloured	2·20	1·70
4659	**3980**	80y. multicoloured	2·20	1·70

3981 *Post Man,
Otokichi* (Toyohara
Kunichika)

3982 *Kaika
Osanahaya Gakumon*
(Baido Kunimasa)

3983 *Tokyo Kaika
Meisho: Yokkaichi Post
Office* (Sandai
Hiroshige)

2011. Philately Week

4660	**3981**	80y. multicoloured	2·20	1·70
4661	**3982**	80y. multicoloured	2·20	1·70
4662	**3983**	80y. multicoloured	2·20	1·70

3984 Mt. Aso

3985 Kumamoto
Castle

3986 Kikuchi
Castle

3987 Sailboat

3988
Unzen-Amakusa
National Park and
Five Bridges of
Amakusa

2011. 60th Anniv of Local Government, Kumamoto

4663	**3984**	80y. multicoloured	2·20	1·70
4664	**3985**	80y. multicoloured	2·20	1·70
4665	**3986**	80y. multicoloured	2·20	1·70
4666	**3987**	80y. multicoloured	2·20	1·70
4667	**3988**	80y. multicoloured	2·20	1·70

3989 *Phoca
largha* (spotted
seal)

3990 Wheat Field

3991-3992 Lavender Fields

3993 William S.
Clark,
Hitsujigaoka
Observation Hill

3994 Cattle,
Naitai Highland
Stock Farm

3995-3996 and Mt. Rishiri

3997-3998 Higashimokoto-shibazakura
Park

2011. Tourism. Hokkaido. Summer Scenes

4668	**3989**	80y. multicoloured	2·20	1·70
4669	**3990**	80y. multicoloured	2·20	1·70
4670	**3991**	80y. multicoloured	2·20	1·70
4671	**3992**	80y. multicoloured	2·20	1·70
4672	**3993**	80y. multicoloured	2·20	1·70
4673	**3994**	80y. multicoloured	2·20	1·70
4674	**3995**	80y. multicoloured	2·20	1·70
4675	**3996**	80y. multicoloured	2·20	1·70
4676	**3997**	80y. multicoloured	2·20	1·70
4677	**3998**	80y. multicoloured	2·20	1·70

Nos. 4670/, 4674/5 and 4676/7, respectively, were
printed, *se-tenant*, in horizontal pairs, each pair forming a
composite design.

3999-4000 Antoinette and Oscar

4001-4002 Andre and Oscar

4003-4004 Fersen and Antoinette

4005-4006 Fersen and Oscar

4007-4008 Rosalie and Jeanne

2011. Heroes and Heroines of Animation (16th series).
Berusaiyu no Bara

4678	**3999**	80y. multicoloured	2·20	1·70
4679	**4000**	80y. multicoloured	2·20	1·70
4680	**4001**	80y. multicoloured	2·20	1·70
4681	**4002**	80y. multicoloured	2·20	1·70
4682	**4003**	80y. multicoloured	2·20	1·70
4683	**4004**	80y. multicoloured	2·20	1·70
4684	**4005**	80y. multicoloured	2·20	1·70
4685	**4006**	80y. multicoloured	2·20	1·70

4686	4007	80y. multicoloured	2·20	1·70
4687	4008	80y. multicoloured	2·20	1·70

4009 Tateyama Mountain Range and Ocean

4010 Kurobe Dam

4011 Rock Ptarmigan (*Lagopus mutus*)

4012 Zuiryuji Temple

4013 Gassho-style House, Gokayama

2011. 60th Anniv of Local Government, Toyama

4688	4009	80y. multicoloured	2·20	1·70
4689	4010	80y. multicoloured	2·20	1·70
4690	4011	80y. multicoloured	2·20	1·70
4691	4012	80y. multicoloured	2·20	1·70
4692	4013	80y. multicoloured	2·20	1·70

4014 Flower of Hearts

4015 Orange Bouquet

4016 Flower of Hearts and Bluebird

4017 White Bouquet

4018 Bluebird carrying Heart

2011. Higashi Nihon Earthquake

4693	4014	80y. +20y. multicoloured	2·75	2·10
4694	4015	80y. +20y. multicoloured	2·75	2·10
4695	4016	80y. +20y. multicoloured	2·75	2·10
4696	4017	80y. +20y. multicoloured	2·75	2·10
4697	4018	80y. +20y. multicoloured	2·75	2·10

4019 Hello Kitty wearing Yoshinoyama

4020 Hello Kitty wearing Kinkakuji

4021 Dear Daniel wearing Kurumabiki

4022 Hello Kitty wearing Hanagasa

4023 Hello Kitty wearing Fujimusume

4024 Hello Kitty and Dear Daniel wearing Kagamijishi

4025 Hello Kitty wearing Kinkakuji

4026 Hello Kitty and Dear Daniel wearing Yoshinoyama

4027 Hello Kitty wearing Fujimusume

4028 Hello Kitty wearing Shiokumi

4029 Dear Daniel wearing Kurumabiki

4030 Hello Kitty and Dear Daniel wearing Kagamijhi

4031 Hello Kitty wearing Kinkakuji

4032 Hello Kitty and Dear Daniel wearing Yoshinoyama

4033 Hello Kitty wearing Fujimusume

2011. Greetings Stamps. Summer. Hello Kitty and Dear Daniel wearing Kabuki Dance Costumes

4698	4019	50y. multicoloured	1·80	1·20
4699	4020	50y. multicoloured	1·80	1·20
4700	4021	50y. multicoloured	1·80	1·20
4701	4022	50y. multicoloured	1·80	1·20
4702	4023	50y. multicoloured	1·80	1·20
4703	4024	80y. multicoloured	2·20	1·70
4704	4025	80y. multicoloured	2·20	1·70
4705	4026	80y. multicoloured	2·20	1·70
4706	4027	80y. multicoloured	2·20	1·70
4707	4028	80y. multicoloured	2·20	1·70

4708	4029	80y. multicoloured	2·20	1·70
4709	4030	80y. multicoloured	2·20	1·70
4710	4031	80y. multicoloured	2·20	1·70
4711	4032	80y. multicoloured	2·20	1·70
4712	4033	80y. multicoloured	2·20	1·70

4034 Snowflake and Ice Crystals on Map of Antarctica

4035 Adélie Penguin

4036 Chinstrap Penguin

4037 Gentoo Penguin

4038 Emperor Penguin

4039 Macaroni Penguin

2011. 50th Anniv of Antarctic Treaty

4713	4034	80y. multicoloured	2·20	1·70
4714	4035	80y. multicoloured	2·20	1·70
4715	4036	80y. multicoloured	2·20	1·70
4716	4037	80y. multicoloured	2·20	1·70
4717	4038	80y. multicoloured	2·20	1·70
4718	4039	80y. multicoloured	2·20	1·70

4040 Libra

4041 Scorpio

4042 Sagittarius

4043 Lyra

4044 Aquila

4045 Cygnus

4046 Hercules

4047 Ophiuchus and Serpens

4048 Delphinus

4049 Hook

2011. Constellations (1st series)

4719	4041	80y. multicoloured	2·20	1·70
4720	4042	80y. multicoloured	2·20	1·70
4721	4043	80y. multicoloured	2·20	1·70

4722	4044	80y. multicoloured	2·20	1·70
4723	4040	80y. multicoloured	2·20	1·70
4724	4045	80y. multicoloured	2·20	1·70
4725	4046	80y. multicoloured	2·20	1·70
4726	4047	80y. multicoloured	2·20	1·70
4727	4048	80y. multicoloured	2·20	1·70
4728	4049	80y. multicoloured	2·20	1·70

4050 Kano Jigaro (founder)

4051 Japanese Athletes, Olympic Games, Tokyo, 1964

4052 Japanese Athletes in Parade, Olympic Games, Stockholm, 1912

4053 Skiers, Winter Olympic Games, Sapporo, 1972

4054 Competitors, National Sports Festival, 1946

4055 Japanese Athletes, Winter Olympic Games, Nagano, 1998

4057 Japan Sports Masters' Emblem

4058 Junior Sports Club Association Athletes

4059 Japanese Athletes, Olympic Games, Beijing, 2008

2011. Centenary of Japanese Sports Association (originally Japan Amateur Athletics Association) and Japan Olympic Committee. Multicoloured.

4729	4050	80y. multicoloured	2·20	1·70
4730	4051	80y. multicoloured	2·20	1·70
4731	4052	80y. multicoloured	2·20	1·70
4732	4053	80y. multicoloured	2·20	1·70
4733	4054	80y. multicoloured	2·20	1·70
4734	4055	80y. multicoloured	2·20	1·70
4735	4056	80y. multicoloured	2·20	1·70
4736	4057	80y. multicoloured	2·20	1·70
4737	4058	80y. multicoloured	2·20	1·70
4738	4059	80y. multicoloured	1·30	95

4060 Rosa rugosa (Hokkaido)

2011. Prefecture Flowers. Multicoloured.

4739	50y. Type **4060**	1·80	95
4740	50y. *Malus pumila* (Aomori)	1·30	95
4741	50y. Paulownia tree (Iwate)	1·30	95
4742	50y. Japanese clover (Miyagi)	1·30	95
4743	50y. *Petasites japonicus* (Akita)	1·30	95
4744	50y. *Carthamus tinctorius* (Yamagata)	1·30	95

4745	50y. Rhododendron (white with pink tinge) (Fukushima)	1·30	95
4746	50y. Rose (Ibaraki)	1·30	95
4747	50y. Rhododendron pentaphyllum (white bell-like) (Tochigi)	1·30	95
4748	50y. Japanese azalea (orange) (Gunma)	1·30	95
4749	50y. Primula sieboldi (Saitama)	1·30	95
4750	50y. Rape flowers (Chiba)	1·30	95
4751	50y. Prunus×yedoensis (Tokyo)	1·30	95
4752	50y. Lilium auratum (Kanagawa)	1·30	95
4753	50y. Red and yellow tulips (Niigata)	1·30	95
4754	50y. White tulips (Toyama)	1·30	95
4755	50y. Fritillaria (Ishikawa)	1·30	95
4756	50y. Narcissus (Fukui)	1·30	95
4757	50y. Cherry blossom (Yamanashi)	1·30	95
4758	50y. Gentiana scabra (Nagano)	1·30	95
4759	50y. Milk vetch (Gifu)	1·30	95
4760	50y. Azalea (pink) (Shizuoka)	1·30	95
4761	50y. Iris laevigata (blue) (Aichi)	1·30	95
4762	50y. Japanese iris (pink) (Mie)	1·30	95
4763	50y. Rhododendron (pink) (Shiga)	1·30	95
4764	50y. Cerasus spachiana (large single cherry) (Kyoto)	1·30	95
4765	50y. Ume and primula (pink) flowers (Osaka)	1·30	95
4766	50y. Chrysanthemum japonense (Hyogo)	1·30	95
4767	50y. Prunus verecunda (cluster of white flowers) (Nara)	1·30	95
4768	50y. Prunus mume (large single white flowers) (Wakayama)	1·30	95
4769	50y. Nijisseiki pear blossom (Tottori)	1·30	95
4770	50y. Peony (Shimane)	1·30	95
4771	50y. Peach blossom (pink) (Okayama)	1·30	1·20
4772	50y. Japanese maple leaves (Hiroshima)	1·30	95
4773	50y. Citrus natsudaidai (two large and two smaller white flowers) (Yamaguchi)	1·30	95
4774	50y. Citrus sudachi (four flowers and larger obvate leaves) (Tokushima)	1·30	95
4775	50y. Olive blossom (Kagawa)	1·30	95
4776	50y. Satsuma mandarin (Ehime)	1·30	95
4778	50y. Japanese bayberry (Kochi)	1·30	95
4779	50y. Prunus mume (pink) (Fukuoka)	1·30	95
4780	50y. Camphor laurel blossom (Saga)	1·30	95
4781	50y. Azalea (small pink flowers) (Nagasaki)	1·30	95
4782	50y. Gentian (purple) (Kumamoto)	1·30	95
4783	50y. Ume blossom (larger single pink) (Oita)	1·30	95
4784	50y. Crinum (Miyazaki)	1·30	95
4785	50y. Rhododendron kiusianum (Kagoshima)	1·30	95
4786	50y. Indian coral bean (Okinawa)	1·30	95

4061a Rosa rugosa (Hokkaido)

2011. Prefecture Flowers. Multicoloured.

4789	80y. Type **4061a**	2·20	1·70
4790	80y. Malus pumila (Aomori)	2·20	1·70
4791	80y. Paulownia tree (Iwate)	2·20	1·70
4792	80y. Japanese clover (Miyagi)	2·20	1·70
4793	80y. Petasites japonicus (Akita)	2·20	1·70
4794	80y. Carthamus tinctorius (Yamagata)	2·20	1·70
4795	80y. Rhododendron (white with pink tinge) (Fukushima)	2·20	1·70
4796	80y. Rose (Ibaraki)	2·20	1·70
4797	80y. Rhododendron pentaphyllum (white bell-like) (Tochigi)	2·20	1·70
4798	80y. Japanese azalea (orange) (Gunma)	2·20	1·70
4799	80y. Primula sieboldi (Saitama)	2·20	1·70
4800	80y. Rape flowers (Chiba)	2·20	1·70
4801	80y. Prunus×yedoensis (Tokyo)	2·20	1·70
4802	80y. Lilium auratum (Kanagawa)	2·20	1·70
4803	80y. Red and yellow tulips (Niigata)	2·20	1·70
4804	80y. White tulips (Toyama)	2·20	1·70
4805	80y. Fritillaria (Ishikawa)	2·20	1·70
4806	80y. Narcissus (Fukui)	2·20	1·70
4807	80y. Cherry blossom (Yamanashi)	2·20	1·70
4808	80y. Gentiana scabra (Nagano)	2·20	1·70
4809	80y. Milk vetch (Gifu)	2·20	1·70
4810	80y. Azalea (pink) (Shizuoka)	2·20	1·70
4811	80y. Iris laevigata (blue) (Aichi)	2·20	1·70
4812	80y. Japanese iris (pink) (Mie)	2·20	1·70
4813	80y. Rhododendron (pink) (Shiga)	2·20	1·70
4814	80y. Cerasus spachiana (large single cherry) (Kyoto)	2·20	1·70
4815	80y. Ume and primula (pink) flowers (Osaka)	2·20	1·70
4816	80y. Chrysanthemum japonense (Hyogo)	2·20	1·70
4817	80y. Prunus verecunda (cluster of white flowers) (Nara)	2·20	1·70
4818	80y. Prunus mume (large single white flowers) (Wakayama)	2·20	1·70
4819	80y. Nijisseiki pear blossom (Tottori)	2·20	1·70
4820	80y. Peony (Shimane)	2·20	1·70
4821	80y. Peach blossom (pink) (Okayama)	2·20	1·70
4822	80y. Japanese maple leaves (Hiroshima)	2·20	1·70
4823	80y. Citrus natsudaidai (two large and two smaller white flowers) (Yamaguchi)	2·20	1·70
4824	80y. Citrus sudachi (four flowers and larger obvate leaves) (Tokushima)	2·20	1·70
4825	80y. Olive blossom (Kagawa)	2·20	1·70
4826	80y. Satsuma mandarin (Ehime)	2·20	1·70
4827	80y. Japanese bayberry (Kochi)	2·20	1·70
4828	80y. Prunus mume (pink) (Fukuoka)	2·20	1·70
4829	80y. Camphor laurel blossom (Saga)	2·20	1·70
4830	80y. Azalea (small pink flowers) (Nagasaki)	2·20	1·70
4831	80y. Gentian (purple) (Kumamoto)	2·20	1·70
4832	80y. Ume blossom (larger single pink) (Oita)	2·20	1·70
4833	80y. Crinum (Miyazaki)	2·20	1·70
4834	80y. Rhododendron kiusianum (Kagoshima)	2·20	1·70
4835	80y. Indian coral bean (Okinawa)	2·20	1·70

4062 Sanka-haku-u

4063 Bishu-fujimigahara

4064 Tokaido-hodogaya

4065 Koshu-Mishima-goe

4066 Koshu-Misaka-Suimen

4067 Gaifu-Kaisei

4068 Sumidagawa-Sekiya-no-sato

4069 Kazusa-no-kaiji

4070 Toto-asakusa-hongannji

4071 Bushu-Senju

2011. Phila Nippon '11 International Stamp Exhibition (2nd issue). Paintings by Katsushika Hokusai

4836	4062	80y. multicoloured	2·20	1·70
4837	4063	80y. multicoloured	2·20	1·70
4838	4064	80y. multicoloured	2·20	1·70
4839	4065	80y. multicoloured	2·20	1·70
4840	4066	80y. multicoloured	2·20	1·70
4841	4067	80y. multicoloured	2·20	1·70
4842	4068	80y. multicoloured	2·20	1·70
4843	4069	80y. multicoloured	2·20	1·70
4844	4070	80y. multicoloured	2·20	1·70
4845	4071	80y. multicoloured	2·20	1·70

4072 Mighty Atom

4073 Draemon

4074 Pikachu

4075 Hello Kitty

4076 Rabbit riding Deer (Choju-jinbutsu-giga) (detail) and Sanka-haku-u by Katsushika Hokusai

4077 Mighty Atom

4078 Doraemon

4079 Pikachu

4080 Hello Kitty

4081 Rabbit riding Deer (Choju-jinbutsu-giga)

2011. Phila Nippon '11 International Stamp Exhibition (3rd issue)

4846	4072	80y. multicoloured	2·20	1·70
4847	4073	80y. multicoloured	2·20	1·70
4848	4074	80y. multicoloured	2·20	1·70
4849	4075	80y. multicoloured	2·20	1·70
4850	4076	80y. multicoloured	2·20	1·70
4851	4077	80y. multicoloured	2·20	1·70
4852	4078	80y. multicoloured	2·20	1·70
4853	4079	80y. multicoloured	2·20	1·70
4854	4080	80y. multicoloured	2·20	1·70
4855	4081	80y. multicoloured	2·20	1·70

4082 Meisho Edo Hyakkei (Utagawa Hiroshige)

4083 Gobijin Aikyo Kurabe. Kisegawa of Matsuba-ya (Kitagawa Utamaro)

4084 Meisho Edo Hyakkei. Shichu Han-ei Tanabata Matsuri (Utagawa Hiroshige)

4085 Ichikawa Komazo III as Shiga Daishichi (Toshusai Sharaku)

4086 Meisho Edo Hyakkei. Kamata no Baien (Utagawa Hiroshige)

4087 Toji San Bijin (Kitagawa Utamaro)

4088 Meisho Edo Hyakkei. Sujikai Uchi Yatsu-Koji (Utagawa Hiroshige)

4089 Segawa Tomisaburo II as Oogishi's wife Yadorigi (Toshusai Sharaku)

4090 Meisho Edo Hyakkei. Meguro Jiji-ga Chaya (Utagawa Hiroshige)

4091 Komyo Bijin Rokkasen. Hanaougi of Ougiya (Kitagawa Utamaro)

2011. Edo Famous Places and Ukiyo-e Paintings

4856	4082	80y. multicoloured	2·20	1·70
4857	4083	80y. multicoloured	2·20	1·70
4858	4084	80y. multicoloured	2·20	1·70
4859	4085	80y. multicoloured	2·20	1·70
4860	4086	80y. multicoloured	2·20	1·70
4861	4087	80y. multicoloured	2·20	1·70
4862	4088	80y. multicoloured	2·20	1·70
4863	4089	80y. multicoloured	2·20	1·70
4864	4090	80y. multicoloured	2·20	1·70
4865	4091	80y. multicoloured	2·20	1·70

4092 Warrior

4093 Warrior

4094-4095 Float and Haneto Dancers

4096-4097 Float and Musicians

2011. Festivals. Aomori Nebuta Matsuri, Aomori

4866	4092	80y. multicoloured	2·20	1·70
4867	4093	80y. multicoloured	2·20	1·70
4868	4094	80y. multicoloured	2·20	1·70
4869	4095	80y. multicoloured	2·20	1·70
4870	4096	80y. multicoloured	2·20	1·70
4871	4097	80y. multicoloured	2·20	1·70

4098 Tottori Sand Dunes and Sanin Coast

4099 Nijisseiki Pear

4100 Traditional Dance, Kirin-jishi

4101 Mitokusan Sanbutsu-ji Temple, Nageiredo

4102 Mt. Daisen

2011. 60th Anniv of Local Government, Tottori

4872	4098	80y. multicoloured	2·20	1·70
4873	4099	80y. multicoloured	2·20	1·70
4874	4100	80y. multicoloured	2·20	1·70
4875	4101	80y. multicoloured	2·20	1·70
4876	4102	80y. multicoloured	2·20	1·70

4103 Leopard Cat **4104** Saunders' Gull

4105 *Cypripedium marcanthum* (orchid) **4106** Green Sea Turtle

4107 *Shijimiaeoides divinus barine* (butterfly)

2011. Co-exist with Nature

4877	4103	80y. multicoloured	2·20	1·70
4878	4104	80y. multicoloured	2·20	1·70
4879	4105	80y. multicoloured	2·20	1·70
4880	4106	80y. multicoloured	2·20	1·70
4881	4107	80y. multicoloured	2·20	1·70

4108-4109 Old Air Traffic Control Tower/New Air Traffic Control Tower

4110 Tokyo International Airport Floor Plan and Aircraft **4111** New Air Traffic Control Tower and Aircraft

2011. 80th Anniv of Tokyo International Airport

4882	4108	80y. multicoloured	2·20	1·70
4883	4109	80y. multicoloured	2·20	1·70
4884	4110	80y. multicoloured	2·20	1·70
4885	4111	80y. multicoloured	2·20	1·70

4112 *Platycodon grandiflorus* **4113** *Dianthus superbus* **4114** *Osmanthus fragrans*

4115 *Cosmos* **4116** *Lespedeza* **4117** *Platycodon grandiflorus*

4118 *Dianthus superbus* **4119** *Osmanthus fragrans* **4120** *Cosmos*

4121 *Lespedeza*

2011. Seasonal Flowers

4886	4112	50y. multicoloured	1·30	95
4887	4113	50y. multicoloured	1·30	95
4888	4114	50y. multicoloured	1·30	95
4889	4115	50y. multicoloured	1·30	95
4890	4116	50y. multicoloured	1·30	95
4891	4117	80y. multicoloured	2·20	1·70
4892	4118	80y. multicoloured	2·20	1·70
4893	4119	80y. multicoloured	2·20	1·70
4894	4120	80y. multicoloured	2·20	1·70
4895	4121	80y. multicoloured	2·20	1·70

4122 Green Marsh, Kamikawa District **4123** Lake Mashu in Autumn

4124 Former Hokkaido Government Office Building **4125** Clock Tower

4126-4127 Lake Touya in Autumn

4128 Hagoromo Waterfall **4129** Glasswort (*Salicornia europaea*) by Lake Notoro

4130 Japanese Sable (*Martes zibellina brachyuran*) **4131** Flying Squirrel (*Pteromys volans orii*)

2011. Tourism. Hokkaido. Autumn and Winter Scenes

4896	4122	80y. multicoloured	2·20	1·70
4897	4123	80y. multicoloured	2·20	1·70
4898	4124	80y. multicoloured	2·20	1·70
4899	4125	80y. multicoloured	2·20	1·70
4900	4126	80y. multicoloured	2·20	1·70
4901	4127	80y. multicoloured	2·20	1·70
4902	4128	80y. multicoloured	2·20	1·70
4903	4129	80y. multicoloured	2·20	1·70
4904	4130	80y. multicoloured	2·20	1·70
4905	4131	80y. multicoloured	2·20	1·70

Nos. 4900/1 were printed, *se-tenant*, in horizontal pairs, each pair forming a composite design.

4132 Fujisan, Yamanashi **4133** Bandaisan, Fukushima

4134 Hakusan, Ishikawa **4135** Hieizan, Kyoto

4136 Ishizuchisan, Ehime **4137** Iwatesan, Iwate

4138 Tanigawadake, Gunma **4139** Akaishidake, Shizuoka

4140 Hiruzen, Okayama **4141** Asosan, Kumamoto

2011. Mountains (1st series)

4906	4132	80y. multicoloured	2·20	1·70
4907	4133	80y. multicoloured	2·20	1·70
4908	4134	80y. multicoloured	2·20	1·70
4909	4135	80y. multicoloured	2·20	1·70
4910	4136	80y. multicoloured	2·20	1·70
4911	4137	80y. multicoloured	2·20	1·70
4912	4138	80y. multicoloured	2·20	1·70
4913	4139	80y. multicoloured	2·20	1·70
4914	4140	80y. multicoloured	2·20	1·70
4915	4141	80y. multicoloured	2·20	1·70

4142 Female Athlete's Finishing Pose **4143**

2011. World Artistic Gymnastics Championships, Tokyo, 2011

4916	4142	80y. dark magenta and gold	2·20	1·70
4917	4143	80y. royal blue and gold	2·20	1·70

4144 Little Grebe on Lake Biwa, Ukimido **4145** Blossom and Boats on River, Omihachiman

4146 Boat on Lake **4147** Ishiyama-dera Temple

4148 Hikone Castle

2011. 60th Anniv of Local Government, Shiga

4918	4144	80y. multicoloured	2·20	1·70
4919	4145	80y. multicoloured	2·20	1·70
4920	4146	80y. multicoloured	2·20	1·70
4921	4147	80y. multicoloured	2·20	1·70
4922	4148	80y. multicoloured	2·20	1·70

4149 *Tsuzumi No Ne* (Uemura Shouen)

4150 *Gakuya* (detail) (Ito Shinsui)

4151 *Takekurabe-no-Midori* (detail) (Kaburaki Kiyokata)

2011. International Correspondence Week

4923	4149	90y. multicoloured	2·50	1·90
4924	4150	110y. multicoloured	3·00	2·20
4925	4151	130y. multicoloured	3·75	3·00

4152 Yoyogi National Gymnasium **4153** Yoyogi Park

4154-4155 Omotesando Illumination

4156 Omotesando **4157** Meiji Memorial Picture Gallery

4158-4159 Ginkgo Trees in Meiji Jingu Gaien Park

4160 Nezu Museum **4161** Kakitsubata-zu byobu (Ogata Korin) (Nezu Museum)

2011. Tourism. Tokyo. Omotesando

4926	4152	80y. multicoloured	2·20	1·70
4927	4153	80y. multicoloured	2·20	1·70
4928	4154	80y. multicoloured	2·20	1·70
4929	4155	80y. multicoloured	2·20	1·70
4930	4156	80y. multicoloured	2·20	1·70
4931	4157	80y. multicoloured	2·20	1·70
4932	4158	80y. multicoloured	2·20	1·70

4933	4159	80y. multicoloured	2·20	1·70
4934	4160	80y. multicoloured	2·20	1·70
4935	4161	80y. multicoloured	2·20	1·70

Nos. 4928/9 and 4932/3, respectively, were printed, *se-tenant*, each pair forming a composite design.

4162 Main Hall   4163 Recital Hall

4164 Ballet Shoes (Swan Lake)   4165 Opera Glasses (La Traviata)

4166 Keyboard   4167 Violin

2011. 50th Anniv of Tokyo Bunka Kaikan

4936	4162	80y. multicoloured	2·20	1·70
4937	4163	80y. multicoloured	2·20	1·70
4938	4164	80y. multicoloured	2·20	1·70
4939	4165	80y. multicoloured	2·20	1·70
4940	4166	80y. multicoloured	2·20	1·70
4941	4167	80y. multicoloured	2·20	1·70

4168 Christmas Wreath and Puppy (Iriyama Satoshi)   4169 Christmas Trees and Children (Sasanuma Kaori)

4170 Christmas Tree (Nakamaru Hitomi)   4171 Santa Claus Ready to go (Kuroi Ken)

4172 Christmas Wreath and Kitten (Iriyama Satoshi)   4173 Children decorating Tree

4174 Children and Decorated Tree   4175 Children in Bed and Santa Claus

4176 Santa Claus delivering Presents   4177 Children opening Presents

4178 *Nandina domestica* and Puppy (Kuroi Ken)   4179 Flowers in Vase (Arai Sonoko)

4180 Winter Hat (Tagashira Yoshitaka)   4181 Girl with Bouquet (Sasanuma Kaori)

4182 Children at Window

2011. Greetings Stamps. Winter

4942	4168	50y. multicoloured	1·30	95
4943	4169	50y. multicoloured	1·30	95
4944	4170	50y. multicoloured	1·30	95
4945	4171	50y. multicoloured	1·30	95
4946	4172	50y. multicoloured	1·30	95
4947	4173	80y. multicoloured	2·20	1·70
4948	4174	80y. multicoloured	2·20	1·70
4949	4175	80y. multicoloured	2·20	1·70
4950	4176	80y. multicoloured	2·20	1·70
4951	4177	80y. multicoloured	2·20	1·70
4952	4178	90y. multicoloured	2·20	1·70
4953	4179	90y. multicoloured	2·20	1·70
4954	4180	90y. multicoloured	2·20	1·70
4955	4181	90y. multicoloured	2·20	1·70
4956	4182	90y. multicoloured	2·20	1·70

4183 Dragon (Sagami-dorei (earthenware bell))   4184 Dragon (Tosa washi ganpi-hariko)

2011. New Year's Greetings

4957	4183	50y. multicoloured	1·80	95
4958	4184	80y. multicoloured	2·20	1·70

4185 Dragon (Sagami-dorei (earthenware bell))   4186 Dragon (Tosa washi ganpi-hariko)

2011. New Year Lottery Stamps

4959	4185	50y. +3y. multicoloured	1·90	1·00
4960	4186	80y. +3y. multicoloured	2·30	1·80

4187 Lotus, Chusonji Konjikido and Motsuji Jodo Garden   4188 Rock-Breaking Cherry Tree (Ishiwarizakura)

4189 Hayachine Kagura (masked dances)   4190 Jodogahama Beach

4191 Urushi Trees (*Toxicodendron verniciifluum*), Joboji

2011. 60th Anniv of Local Government, Iwate

4961	4187	80y. multicoloured	2·20	1·70
4962	4188	80y. multicoloured	2·20	1·70
4963	4189	80y. multicoloured	2·20	1·70
4964	4190	80y. multicoloured	2·20	1·70
4965	4191	80y. multicoloured	2·20	1·70

4192 Gyosho Style (Aoyagi Shiro)   4193 Kinbun Style (Saito Zuisen)

4194 Kinbun Style (Muroi Gensho)   4195 Sosho Style (Ohno Shoun)

4196 Kana (Iijima Harumi)   4197 Reisho Style (Ishitobi Hakko)

4198 Reisho Style (Dairaku Kasetsu)   4199 Setsumon Style of Six kingdoms (Kakishita Bokkan)

4200 Kinbun Style (seal) (Seki Masato)   4201 Kana (Yonemoto Ikko)

2011. Greetings Stamps. Eto Calligraphy. Year of the Dragon (Tatsu)

4966	4192	80y. multicoloured	2·20	1·70
4967	4193	80y. multicoloured	2·20	1·70
4968	4194	80y. multicoloured	2·20	1·70
4969	4195	80y. multicoloured	2·20	1·70
4970	4196	80y. multicoloured	2·20	1·70
4971	4197	80y. multicoloured	2·20	1·70
4972	4198	80y. multicoloured	2·20	1·70
4973	4199	80y. multicoloured	2·20	1·70
4974	4200	80y. multicoloured	2·20	1·70
4975	4201	80y. multicoloured	2·20	1·70

4202-4203 Hens, Tomatoes, Fruit Trees and Fish

2011. 50th Festival of Agriculture, Forestry and Fisheries

4976	4202	80y. multicoloured	2·20	1·70
4977	4203	80y. multicoloured	2·20	1·70

Nos. 4976/7 were printed, *se-tenant*, in pairs forming a composite design.

4204-4205 House and Children on Excursion

4206-4207 Children flying Kites

4208-4209 Houses by River and Motorcyclist

4210-4211 Koi Carp in Pond and Gardening (springtime

4212 Mt Fuji   4213 Shovelling Snow

2011. Hometowns. Koshinetsu

4978	4204	80y. multicoloured	2·20	1·70
4979	4205	80y. multicoloured	2·20	1·70
4980	4206	80y. multicoloured	2·20	1·70
4981	4207	80y. multicoloured	2·20	1·70
4982	4208	80y. multicoloured	2·20	1·70
4983	4209	80y. multicoloured	2·20	1·70
4984	4210	80y. multicoloured	2·20	1·70
4985	4211	80y. multicoloured	2·20	1·70
4986	4212	80y. multicoloured	2·20	1·70
4987	4213	80y. multicoloured	2·20	1·70

Nos. 4978/9, 4980/1, 4982/3 and 4984/5, respectively, were printed, *se-tenant*, in horizontal pairs, each pair forming a composite design.

4214 Shirase Nobu (army officer) and Namahage (Japanese ritual)   4215 Kabuki Theatre Building

4216 Cherry Blossom, Samurai Residence, Kakunodate

4217 Autumn Leaves, Tatsuko (statue) and Lake Tazawa

4218 Kamakura Snow Festival, Yokote

2012. 60th Anniv of Local Government, Akita

4988	4214	80y. multicoloured	2·20	1·70
4989	4215	80y. multicoloured	2·20	1·70
4990	4216	80y. multicoloured	2·20	1·70
4991	4217	80y. multicoloured	2·20	1·70
4992	4218	80y. multicoloured	2·20	1·70

4219-4220 Vegeta and Son Goku

4221-4222 Son Gohan and Piccolo

4223-4224 Trunks and Vegeta

4225-4226 Son Goku and Piccolo

4227-4228 Son Gohan (blonde) and Son Goku (blonde)

2012. Heroes and Heroines of Animation (17th series). Dragon Ball Z Kai

4993	4219	80y. multicoloured	2·20	1·70
4994	4220	80y. multicoloured	2·20	1·70
4995	4221	80y. multicoloured	2·20	1·70
4996	4222	80y. multicoloured	2·20	1·70
4997	4223	80y. multicoloured	2·20	1·70
4998	4224	80y. multicoloured	2·20	1·70
4999	4225	80y. multicoloured	2·20	1·70
5000	4226	80y. multicoloured	2·20	1·70
5001	4227	80y. multicoloured	2·20	1·70
5002	4228	80y. multicoloured	2·20	1·70

4229 Bluebird carrying Boy (Tagashira Yoshitaka)

4230 Girl carrying Boxes (Nakamaru Hitomi)

4231 Bear and Rabbit (Sasanuma Kaori)

4232 Bouquet and Swan (Arai Sonoko)

4233 Cherry Blossom and Fairies (Matsuda Hiroko)

4234 Kitten in Box of Flowers (Iriyama Satoshi)

4235 Puppy and Petals (Kuroi Ken)

4236 Cherry blossom Bouquet (Nakamaru Hitomi)

4236 Basket of Flowers and Bluebirds (Arai Sonoko)

4238 Letter Box and Girl holding Envelope (Nakamaru Hitomi)

2012. Greetings Stamps. Spring

5003	4229	50y. multicoloured	1·30	95
5004	4230	50y. multicoloured	1·30	95
5005	4231	50y. multicoloured	1·30	95
5006	4232	50y. multicoloured	1·30	95
5007	4233	50y. multicoloured	1·30	95
5008	4234	80y. multicoloured	2·20	1·70
5009	4235	80y. multicoloured	2·20	1·70
5010	4236	80y. multicoloured	2·20	1·70
5011	4237	80y. multicoloured	2·20	1·70
5012	4238	80y. multicoloured	2·20	1·70

4239 Violets   **4240** Rose   **4241** *Benthamidia florida* (Flowering dogwood (pink))

4242 Muscari   **4243** Poppy   **4244** Violets

4245 Roses   **4246** *Benthamidia florida* (Flowering dogwood (white))   **4247** Muscari

4248 Poppies

2013. Seasonal Flowers

5013	4239	50y. multicoloured	1·80	95
5014	4240	50y. multicoloured	1·80	95
5015	4241	50y. multicoloured	1·80	95
5016	4242	50y. multicoloured	1·80	95
5017	4243	50y. multicoloured	1·80	95
5018	4244	80y. multicoloured	2·20	1·70
5019	4245	80y. multicoloured	2·20	1·70
5020	4246	80y. multicoloured	2·20	1·70
5021	4247	80y. multicoloured	2·20	1·70
5022	4248	80y. multicoloured	2·20	1·70

4249 Mickey and Minnie   **4250** Mickey

4251 Minnie   **4252** Mickey

4253 Minnie   **4254** Mickey

4255 Minnie and Mickey   **4256** Mickey and Minnie

4257 Mickey and Minnie   **4258** Mickey and Minnie

4259 Mickey   **4260** Minnie

4261 Pluto, Daisy Duck, Mickey, Minnie, Goofy and Donald Duck   **4262** Minnie and Daisy

4263 Daisy   **4264** Donald

4265 Mickey and Pluto   **4266** Mickey

4267 Goofy, Mickey and Donald   **4268** Minnie, Pluto and Mickey

2012. Greetings Stamps. Mickey and Minnie Mouse (cartoon characters created by Walt Disney)

5023	4249	50y. multicoloured	1·80	95
5024	4250	50y. multicoloured	1·80	95
5025	4251	50y. multicoloured	1·80	95
5026	4252	50y. multicoloured	1·80	95
5027	4253	50y. multicoloured	1·80	95
5028	4254	50y. multicoloured	1·80	95
5029	4255	50y. multicoloured	1·80	95
5030	4256	50y. multicoloured	1·80	95
5031	4257	50y. multicoloured	1·80	95
5032	4258	50y. multicoloured	1·80	95
5033	4259	80y. multicoloured	2·20	1·70
5034	4260	80y. multicoloured	2·20	1·70
5035	4261	80y. multicoloured	2·20	1·70
5036	4262	80y. multicoloured	2·20	1·70
5037	4263	80y. multicoloured	2·20	1·70
5038	4264	80y. multicoloured	2·20	1·70
5039	4265	80y. multicoloured	2·20	1·70
5040	4266	80y. multicoloured	2·20	1·70
5041	4267	80y. multicoloured	2·20	1·70
5042	4268	80y. multicoloured	2·20	1·70

4269 Washington Monument and Cherry Blossom   **4270** Jefferson Memorial and Cherry Blossom

4271 *Cerasus lannesiana* (Ichiyo)   **4272** *Prunus x yedoensis* (Somei Yoshino)

4273 *Prunus lannesiana* (Shirayuki)   **4274** *Prunus lannesiana* (Kanzan)

4275 *Prunus serrulata* (Gyoiko)

2012. Centenary of Gift of Cherry Blossom Trees to USA

5043	4269	80y. multicoloured	2·20	1·70
5044	4270	80y. multicoloured	2·20	1·70
5045	4271	80y. multicoloured	2·20	1·70
5046	4272	80y. multicoloured	2·20	1·70
5047	4273	80y. multicoloured	2·20	1·70
5048	4274	80y. multicoloured	2·20	1·70
5049	4275	80y. multicoloured	2·20	1·70

4276 Shuri Castle and Kumiodri   **4277** Shuri Castle and Shureimon

4278 Ryukyu Bingata

 4279 Ryukyuan Dance

 4280 Erythrina variegate

2012. 60th Anniv of Local Government, Okinawa

5050	4276	80y. multicoloured	2·20	1·70
5051	4277	80y. multicoloured	2·20	1·70
5052	4278	80y. multicoloured	2·20	1·70
5053	4279	80y. multicoloured	2·20	1·70
5054	4280	80y. multicoloured	2·20	1·70

 4281 Magaki ni Souka-zu Fusuma (room partition with painting of *Chrysanthemum morifolium*) (detail)

 4282 Ryuko-zu Byobu (folding screen with painting of dragon and tiger) by Kano Sanraku (detail)

 4283 Shunka Kacho-zu Byobu (folding screens with painting of flowers and birds) by Kano Einou

2012. Philately Week

5055	4281	80y. multicoloured	1·60	1·30
5056	4282	80y. multicoloured	1·60	1·30
5057	4283	80y. multicoloured	1·60	1·30

 4284 Giant Panda Ri Ri (Ueno Zoological Gardens)

 4285 Giant Panda Shin Shin (Ueno Zoological Gardens)

 4286/4287 Shinobazu Pond (Ueno-onshi-koen Park)

 4288 Kaminari-mon (Senso-ji Temple, Asakusa)

 4289 Senso-ji Temple (Asakusa)

 4290/4291 Sumida River

 4292 Sumida Park

 4293 Sumida River Fireworks Festival

2012. Tourism. Tokyo. Ueno, Asakusa and Sumida River

5058	4284	80y. multicoloured	2·20	1·70
5059	4285	80y. multicoloured	2·20	1·70
5060	4286	80y. multicoloured	2·20	1·70
5061	4287	80y. multicoloured	2·20	1·70
5062	4288	80y. multicoloured	2·20	1·70
5063	4289	80y. multicoloured	2·20	1·70
5064	4290	80y. multicoloured	2·20	1·70
5065	4291	80y. multicoloured	2·20	1·70
5066	4292	80y. multicoloured	2·20	1·70
5067	4293	80y. multicoloured	2·20	1·70

 4294 *Viburnum dilatatum*

 4295 *Tricyrtis ishiiana*

 4296 *Phedimus sikokianus* (Himekirinso)

 4297 *Calypso bulbosa*

 4298 *Stigmatodactylus sikokianus*

2012. 150th Birth Anniv of Tomitaro Makino (botanist)

5068	4294	80y. multicoloured	2·20	1·70
5069	4295	80y. multicoloured	2·20	1·70
5070	4296	80y. multicoloured	2·20	1·70
5071	4297	80y. multicoloured	2·20	1·70
5072	4298	80y. multicoloured	2·20	1·70

 4299 Shurijo Castle

 4300 Shurijo Castle

 4301 *Momordica charantia*

 4302 *Mangifera indica*

 4303 Orchids

 4304 Orchids

4305 Okinawa Churaumi Aquarium

4306 Okinawa Churaumi Aquarium

 4307 Okinawa Urban Monorail and Ikema Ohashi Bridge

4308 Okinawa Urban Monorail and Ikema Ohashi Bridge

2012. 40th Anniv of Okinawa Reversion to Japan

5073	4299	80y. multicoloured	2·20	1·70
5074	4300	80y. multicoloured	2·20	1·70
5075	4301	80y. multicoloured	2·20	1·70
5076	4302	80y. multicoloured	2·20	1·70
5077	4303	80y. multicoloured	2·20	1·70
5078	4304	80y. multicoloured	2·20	1·70
5079	4305	80y. multicoloured	2·20	1·70
5080	4306	80y. multicoloured	2·20	1·70
5081	4307	80y. multicoloured	2·20	1·70
5082	4308	80y. multicoloured	2·20	1·70

 4309 Ikebana

 4310 Ikebana

 4311 Ikebana

 4312 Ikebana

 4313 Ikebana

 4314 Ikebana

 4315 Ikebana

 4316 Ikebana

4317 Ikebana

4318 Ikebana

2012. 550 Years of Ikebana (flower arranging)

5083	4309	80y. multicoloured	2·20	1·70
5084	4310	80y. multicoloured	2·20	1·70
5085	4311	80y. multicoloured	2·20	1·70
5086	4312	80y. multicoloured	2·20	1·70
5087	4313	80y. multicoloured	2·20	1·70

5088	4314	80y. multicoloured	2·20	1·70
5089	4315	80y. multicoloured	2·20	1·70
5090	4316	80y. multicoloured	2·20	1·70
5091	4317	80y. multicoloured	2·20	1·70
5092	4318	80y. multicoloured	2·20	1·70

4319/4320 *Serving Girl at a Spa* by Tsuchida Bakusen (image scaled to 34% of original size)

 4321 *Girl* by Mimani Kunzo

 4322 *Portrait of San'yutei Encho* by Kaburaki Kiyokata

 4323 *Road Cut through a Hill* by Ryusei Kishida

 4324 *Mother and Child* by Uemura Shoen

 4325 *Reading by the Window* by Ota Kijiro

 4326 *Peonies at a Back Garden after Rain* by Tokuoka Shinsen

 4327 *Seated Woman* by Yasui Sotaro

 4328 *Study of Fallen Blossoms* by Fukuda Heihachiro

2012. 60th Anniv of National Museum of Modern Art, Tokyo and 50th Anniv of National Museum of Modern Art, Kyoto

5093	4319	80y. multicoloured	2·20	1·70
5094	4320	80y. multicoloured	2·20	1·70
5095	4321	80y. multicoloured	2·20	1·70
5096	4322	80y. multicoloured	2·20	1·70
5097	4323	80y. multicoloured	2·20	1·70
5098	4324	80y. multicoloured	2·20	1·70
5099	4325	80y. multicoloured	2·20	1·70
5100	4326	80y. multicoloured	2·20	1·70
5101	4327	80y. multicoloured	2·20	1·70
5102	4328	80y. multicoloured	2·20	1·70

 4329 Wisteria

 4330 Lily-of-the-Valley

 4331 Blue Hydrangea

 4332 Sunflower

 4333 Pink Ipomoea

 4334 Wisteria

4335 Lily-of-the-Valley   **4336** Pink Hydrangea   **4337** Sunflowers

4338 Blue Ipomoea

2012. Seasonal Flowers

5103	4329	50y. multicoloured	1·80	95
5104	4330	50y. multicoloured	1·80	95
5105	4331	50y. multicoloured	1·80	95
5106	4332	50y. multicoloured	1·80	95
5107	4333	50y. multicoloured	1·80	95
5108	4334	80y. multicoloured	2·20	1·70
5109	4335	80y. multicoloured	2·20	1·70
5110	4336	80y. multicoloured	2·20	1·70
5111	4337	80y. multicoloured	2·20	1·70
5112	4338	80y. multicoloured	2·20	1·70

4439-4340 Boats and Fireworks

2012. Festivals. Tenjin Matsuri, Osaka

5113	4339	50y. multicoloured	1·30	95
5114	4340	50y. multicoloured	1·30	95

4341 Soldier   **4342** Soldier and Child

2012. 20th Anniv of Japan's Contribution to UN Peace Keeping Operations

5115	4341	80y. multicoloured	2·20	1·70
5116	4342	80y. multicoloured	2·20	1·70

4343 *Apalopteron familiare* (Bonin White-eye)   **4344** *Melastoma tetramerum*

4345 Heart Rock on Chichijima   **4346** *Boninosuccinea ogasawarae* (Snail)

4347 Ogi Ike   **4348** *Mandarina luhuana* Fossils

4349 *Schima mertensiana*   **4350** Forests on Chichijima

4351 *Tursiops aduncus* (Indo-Pacific Bottlenose Dolphin)   **4352** *Pandanus boninensis*

2012. World Heritage. Ogasawara Islands

5117	4343	80y. multicoloured	2·20	1·70
5118	4344	80y. multicoloured	2·20	1·70
5119	4345	80y. multicoloured	2·20	1·70
5120	4346	80y. multicoloured	2·20	1·70
5121	4347	80y. multicoloured	2·20	1·70
5122	4348	80y. multicoloured	2·20	1·70
5123	4349	80y. multicoloured	2·20	1·70
5124	4350	80y. multicoloured	2·20	1·70
5125	4351	80y. multicoloured	2·20	1·70
5126	4352	80y. multicoloured	2·20	1·70

4353 Hello Kitty and Dear Daniel   **4354** Hello Kitty and Fireworks

4355 Hello Kitty and Morning Glory Flowers   **4356** Hello Kitty and Platycodon Flowers   **4357** Hello Kitty and Sunflowers

4359 Hello Kitty and Dear Daniel and Fireworks   **4360** Hello Kitty and Stall selling Masks

4361 Dear Daniel   **4362** Hello Kitty and Stall selling Toffee Apples

4363 Hello Kitty and Dear Daniel holding Fireworks   **4364** Hello Kitty and Dear Daniel on Veranda

2012. Greetings Stamps. Summer. Hello Kitty

5127	4353	50y. multicoloured	1·30	95
5128	4354	50y. multicoloured	1·30	95
5129	4355	50y. multicoloured	1·30	95
5130	4356	50y. multicoloured	1·30	95
5131	4357	50y. multicoloured	1·30	95
5132	4358	80y. multicoloured	2·20	1·70
5133	4359	80y. multicoloured	2·20	1·70
5134	4360	80y. multicoloured	2·20	1·70
5135	4361	80y. multicoloured	2·20	1·70
5136	4362	80y. multicoloured	2·20	1·70
5137	4363	80y. multicoloured	2·20	1·70
5138	4364	80y. multicoloured	2·20	1·70

4365 Chuson-ji Konjikido   **4366** Chuson-ji Gilded Floral Wreath Ornaments

4367 Kyozo Hall   **4368** Motsuji Festival, Gokusui No En

4369-4370 Motsuji Garden

4371-4372 Kanjizaio-in Ato

4373 Muryo-Koin Temple Site   **4374** *Nelumbo nucifer* (Lotus)

2012. World Heritage. Hiraizumi. Temples, Gardens and Archaeological Sites Representing the Buddhist Pure Land

5139	4365	80y. multicoloured	2·20	1·70
5140	4366	80y. multicoloured	2·20	1·70
5141	4367	80y. multicoloured	2·20	1·70
5142	4368	80y. multicoloured	2·20	1·70
5143	4369	80y. multicoloured	2·20	1·70
5144	4370	80y. multicoloured	2·20	1·70
5145	4371	80y. multicoloured	2·20	1·70
5146	4372	80y. multicoloured	2·20	1·70
5147	4373	80y. multicoloured	2·20	1·70
5148	4374	80y. multicoloured	2·20	1·70

4375 *Erythronium japonicum*   **4376** Basara-Daisho

2012. Flora and Buddhist Deity

5149	4375	350y. multicoloured (As Type **1613** but redrawn)	9·00	8·00
5150	4376	500y. multicoloured (As Type **691** but redrawn)	13·75	13·00

4377 Girl seated by River   **4378** Street Vendors of Summer Festival at Night

4379 Children dragging Stick along Fence   **4380** Children and Animals in Fog

4381 Sunset   **4382** Children and White Clouds over Beach

4383 Children playing on Beached Boats   **4384** Children watching Waves from Clifftop

4385 Boat, Children and Crabs   **4386** Cricket, Cello, Bottle and Girl

2012. Seasonal Memories

5151	4377	80y. multicoloured	2·20	1·70
5152	4378	80y. multicoloured	2·20	1·70
5153	4379	80y. multicoloured	2·20	1·70
5154	4380	80y. multicoloured	2·20	1·70
5155	4381	80y. multicoloured	2·20	1·70
5156	4382	80y. multicoloured	2·20	1·70
5157	4383	80y. multicoloured	2·20	1·70
5158	4384	80y. multicoloured	2·20	1·70
5159	4385	80y. multicoloured	2·20	1·70
5160	4386	80y. multicoloured	2·20	1·70

4387 Capricorn   **4389** Pisces

4390 Cassiopeia   **4391** Pegasus

4392 Andromeda   **4393** Perseus

4394 Cepheus   **4395** Cetus

4396 Ikarboshi

4388 Aquarius

2012. Constellations (2nd series)

5161	**4387**	80y. multicoloured	2·20	1·70
5162	**4388**	80y. multicoloured	2·20	1·70
5163	**4389**	80y. multicoloured	2·20	1·70
5164	**4390**	80y. multicoloured	2·20	1·70
5165	**4391**	80y. multicoloured	2·20	1·70
5166	**4392**	80y. multicoloured	2·20	1·70
5167	**4393**	80y. multicoloured	2·20	1·70
5168	**4394**	80y. multicoloured	2·20	1·70
5169	**4395**	80y. multicoloured	2·20	1·70
5170	**4396**	80y. multicoloured	2·20	1·70

4397 Tsurugaoka Hachimangu and Yabusame

4398 Yokohama Minato Mirai 21

4399 Jogashima Lighthouse

4400 Tanzawa Mountains and Lake Miyagase

4401 Lake Ashi-no-ko, Hakone

2011. 60th Anniv of Local Government, Kumamoto

5171	**4397**	80y. multicoloured	2·20	1·70
5172	**4398**	80y. multicoloured	2·20	1·70
5173	**4399**	80y. multicoloured	2·20	1·70
5174	**4400**	80y. multicoloured	2·20	1·70
5175	**4401**	80y. multicoloured	2·20	1·70

4402 Princess Konohanasakuya

4403 Prince Yamatotakeru

4404 Susanoo (Storm god)

4405 Princess Inata

2012. 1300th Anniv of *The Kojiki, Records of Ancient Matters* (Japan's oldest chronicle)

5176	**4402**	80y. multicoloured	2·20	1·70
5177	**4403**	80y. multicoloured	2·20	1·70
5178	**4404**	80y. multicoloured	2·20	1·70
5179	**4405**	80y. multicoloured	2·20	1·70

4406 Inpumon In no Taifu

4407 Fujiwara no Toshiyuki Ason

4408 Shune-hoshi

4409 Kokamon In no Betto

4410 Sone no Yoshitada

4411 Inpumon In no Taifu

4412 Inpumon In no Taifu

4413 Fujiwara no Toshiyuki Ason

4414 Fujiwara no Toshiyuki Ason

4415 Shune-hoshi

4416 Shune-hoshi

4417 Kokamon In no Betto

4418 Kokamon In no Betto

4419 Sone no Yoshitada

4420 Sone no Yoshitada

2012. Letter Writing Day

5180	**4406**	50y. multicoloured	1·30	95
5181	**4407**	50y. multicoloured	1·30	95
5182	**4408**	50y. multicoloured	1·30	95
5183	**4409**	50y. multicoloured	1·30	95
5184	**4410**	50y. multicoloured	1·30	95
5185	**4411**	80y. multicoloured	2·20	1·70
5186	**4412**	80y. multicoloured	2·20	1·70
5187	**4413**	80y. multicoloured	2·20	1·70
5188	**4414**	80y. multicoloured	2·20	1·70
5189	**4415**	80y. multicoloured	2·20	1·70
5190	**4416**	80y. multicoloured	2·20	1·70
5191	**4417**	80y. multicoloured	2·20	1·70
5192	**4418**	80y. multicoloured	2·20	1·70
5193	**4419**	80y. multicoloured	2·20	1·70
5194	**4420**	80y. multicoloured	2·20	1·70

4420a *Ogiya Hanaogi Yosoyuki* (Chokosai Eisho)

4421 *Rokujyu Yoshu Meisho zu e / Yamashiro, Arashi-yama Togetsukyo* (Ando Hiroshige)

4422 *Tosei Onna Fuzoku tsuu / Hokkoku no keisei* (Kitagawa Utamaro)

4423 *Rokujyu Yoshu Meisho zu e / Suo, Iwakuni Kintaikyo* (Ando Hiroshige)

4424 *Furyu Setsugekka / Tsuki* (Kikukawa Eizan)

4425 *Rokujyu Yoshu Meisho zu e / Shinano, Sarashina Tagoto no tsuki Kyodaisan* (Ando Hiroshige)

4426 *Ogiya Uchi Hanaogi, Yoshino Tatsuta* (Kitagawa Utamaro)

4428 *Furyu Mutamagawa / Chofu no Tamagawa* (Kikukawa Eizan)

4429 *Rokujyu Yoshu Meisho zu e / Kai Saruhashi* (Ando Hiroshige)

4427 *Rokujyu Yoshu Meisho zu e / Awa, Naruto no Fuuha* (Ando Hiroshige)

2012. Edo Famous Places and Ukiyo-e Paintings

5195	**4420**	80y. multicoloured	2·20	1·70
5196	**4421**	80y. multicoloured	2·20	1·70
5197	**4422**	80y. multicoloured	2·20	1·70
5198	**4423**	80y. multicoloured	2·20	1·70
5199	**4424**	80y. multicoloured	2·20	1·70
5200	**4425**	80y. multicoloured	2·20	1·70
5201	**4426**	80y. multicoloured	2·20	1·70
5202	**4427**	80y. multicoloured	2·20	1·70
5203	**4428**	80y. multicoloured	2·20	1·70
5204	**4429**	80y. multicoloured	2·20	1·70

4430 Miyazaki Prefectural Office Building and the Takachiho Yokagura (Shinto theatrical dance)

4431 Pagoda, Koibitono-oka

4432 Saitobaru Burial Mounds

4433 Ebino-kogen Highlands

4434 Sakamoto-Tanada (terraced rice fields)

2012. 60th Anniv of Local Government, Miyazaki

5205	**4430**	80y. multicoloured	2·20	1·70
5206	**4431**	80y. multicoloured	2·20	1·70
5207	**4432**	80y. multicoloured	2·20	1·70
5208	**4433**	80y. multicoloured	2·20	1·70
5209	**4434**	80y. multicoloured	2·20	1·70

4435 *Sorex minutissimus* (Lesser Pygmy Shrew)

4436 *Aquila chrysaetos* (Golden Eagle)

4437 *Paeonia obovata*

4438 *Oryzias latipes* (Japanese Rice Fish)

4439 *Tachypleus tridentatus* (Horseshoe Crab species)

2012. Co-exist with Nature. Endangered Species

5210	**4435**	80y. multicoloured	2·20	1·70
5211	**4436**	80y. multicoloured	2·20	1·70
5212	**4437**	80y. multicoloured	2·20	1·70
5213	**4438**	80y. multicoloured	2·20	1·70
5214	**4439**	80y. multicoloured	2·20	1·70

4440 Cherry Blossom and *Paeonia suffruticosa*

2012. 40th Anniv of Normalization of Japan - China Diplomatic Relations

5215	**4440**	80y. multicoloured	2·20	1·70

4441 Urakami Cathedral

4442 The Peace Statue

4443-4444 Meganebashi

4445 Nagasaki Lantern Festival

4446 Soufukuji Temple

4447-4448 Glover Garden

4449 Nagasaki Kunchi Festival

4450 4450 Nagasaki Tall Ships Festival

2012. Tourism. Nagasaki

5216	**4441**	80y. multicoloured	2·20	1·70
5217	**4442**	80y. multicoloured	2·20	1·70
5218	**4443**	80y. multicoloured	2·20	1·70
5219	**4444**	80y. multicoloured	2·20	1·70
5220	**4445**	80y. multicoloured	2·20	1·70
5221	**4446**	80y. multicoloured	2·20	1·70
5222	**4447**	80y. multicoloured	2·20	1·70
5223	**4448**	80y. multicoloured	2·20	1·70
5224	**4449**	80y. multicoloured	2·20	1·70
5225	**4450**	80y. multicoloured	2·20	1·70

4451 Poskuma (post bear)

4452 Poskuma with Card

4453 Bear with Gift

4454 Bear with Gift

4455 Bear with Card

4456 Bear with Card

4457 Bear with Gift

4458 Bear with Gift

4459 Bear with Card

4460 Bear with Gift

4461 Bear with Gift

4462 Bear with Gift

4463 Bear with Card

4464 Two Bears

4465 Small Bear whispering to Larger Bear

4466 Larger Bear and Small Bear

4467 White Bear

4468 Bear with Card

4469 Bear with Flower

4470 Poskuma with Gifts

2012. Greetings Stamps. Winter. Teddie Bears

5226	**4451**	50y. multicoloured	1·30	95
5227	**4452**	50y. multicoloured	1·30	95
5228	**4453**	50y. multicoloured	1·30	95
5229	**4454**	50y. multicoloured	1·30	95
5230	**4455**	50y. multicoloured	1·30	95
5231	**4456**	50y. multicoloured	1·30	95
5232	**4457**	50y. multicoloured	1·30	95
5233	**4458**	50y. multicoloured	1·30	95
5234	**4459**	50y. multicoloured	1·30	95
5235	**4460**	50y. multicoloured	1·30	95
5236	**4461**	80y. multicoloured	2·20	1·70
5237	**4462**	80y. multicoloured	2·20	1·70
5238	**4463**	80y. multicoloured	2·20	1·70
5239	**4464**	80y. multicoloured	2·20	1·70
5240	**4465**	80y. multicoloured	2·20	1·70
5241	**4466**	80y. multicoloured	2·20	1·70
5242	**4467**	80y. multicoloured	2·20	1·70
5243	**4468**	80y. multicoloured	2·20	1·70
5244	**4469**	80y. multicoloured	2·20	1·70
5245	**4470**	80y. multicoloured	2·20	1·70

4471 Orfevre

4472 Apapane

4473 Deep Impact

4474 Still in Love

4475 Narita Brian

4476 Mejiro I' Amone

4477 Symboli Rudolf

4478 Mr. C.B.

4479 Shinzan

4480 Saint Light

2012. 150th Anniv of Horse Racing in Japan

5246	**4471**	80y. multicoloured	2·20	1·70
5247	**4472**	80y. multicoloured	2·20	1·70
5248	**4473**	80y. multicoloured	2·20	1·70
5249	**4474**	80y. multicoloured	2·20	1·70
5250	**4475**	80y. multicoloured	2·20	1·70
5251	**4476**	80y. multicoloured	2·20	1·70
5252	**4477**	80y. multicoloured	2·20	1·70
5253	**4478**	80y. multicoloured	2·20	1·70
5254	**4479**	80y. multicoloured	2·20	1·70
5255	**4480**	80y. multicoloured	2·20	1·70

4481 Hatsugochi (detail) (Kaburaki Kiyokata)

4482 Shunpo (detail) (Uemura Shouen)

4483 Hubuki (detail) (Ito Shinsui)

2012. International Correspondence Week

5256	**4481**	90y. multicoloured	2·50	1·90
5257	**4482**	110y. multicoloured	3·00	2·20
5258	**4483**	130y. multicoloured	3·50	2·50

4484 Wado Kaichin

4485 Tempo Tsuho and Kanei Tsuho

4486 Imported Chinese Copper Coins

4487 Moneychanger's Balance

4488 Hirumokin, Sekishugin, Yuzurihakin (Tokugawa Shogonate)

4489 Yamada Hagaki (early paper money)

4490 Keicho Oban

4491 'Money Tree' of Coins

4492 Keicho Chogin, Keicho Mameitagin

4493 20yen, 50sen and 2sen Coins

2012. Annual Meetings IMF and World Bank Group, 2012, Tokyo

5259	**4484**	80y. multicoloured	2·20	1·70
5260	**4485**	80y. multicoloured	2·20	1·70
5261	**4486**	80y. multicoloured	2·20	1·70
5262	**4487**	80y. multicoloured	2·20	1·70
5263	**4488**	80y. multicoloured	2·20	1·70
5264	**4489**	80y. multicoloured	2·20	1·70
5265	**4490**	80y. multicoloured	2·20	1·70
5266	**4491**	80y. multicoloured	2·20	1·70
5267	**4492**	80y. multicoloured	2·20	1·70
5268	**4493**	80y. multicoloured	2·20	1·70

4494 Yomeimon Gate, Toshogu Shrine

4495 Ashikaga Gakko

4496 'Kibuna' (Crucian Carp folk toys)

4497 SL Mooka Steam Engine

4498 Nasu Kogen

2012. 60th Anniv of Local Government, Tochigi

5269	**4494**	80y. multicoloured	2·20	1·70
5270	**4495**	80y. multicoloured	2·20	1·70
5271	**4496**	80y. multicoloured	2·20	1·70
5272	**4497**	80y. multicoloured	2·20	1·70
5273	**4498**	80y. multicoloured	2·20	1·70

4499-4500 Raskal, Stirling and Alice

4501-4502 Raskal and Stirling

4503-4504 Racoon Babies and Raskal

4505-4506 Raskal and Stirling drinking

4507-4508 Stirling taking Raskal in Canoe to Release Him back to the Wild

2012. Heroes and Heroines of Animation (18th series). Araiguma Rasukaru (Raskal the Raccoon)

5274	**4499**	80y. multicoloured	2·20	1·70
5275	**4500**	80y. multicoloured	2·20	1·70
5276	**4501**	80y. multicoloured	2·20	1·70
5277	**4502**	80y. multicoloured	2·20	1·70
5278	**4503**	80y. multicoloured	2·20	1·70
5279	**4504**	80y. multicoloured	2·20	1·70
5280	**4505**	80y. multicoloured	2·20	1·70
5281	**4506**	80y. multicoloured	2·20	1·70
5282	**4507**	80y. multicoloured	2·20	1·70
5283	**4508**	80y. multicoloured	2·20	1·70

4059 Hakata Ningyo (Fukuoka)

4510 Ogatsusuzuri (Miyagi)

4511 Kijoka Bashofu (Okinawa)

4512 Obori Somayaki (Fukushima)

4513 Tsugaru-nuri (Aomori)

4514 Kyo Sensu (Kyoto)

4515 Kaga Yuzen (Ishikawa)

4516 Kutani-yaki (Ishikawa)

4517 Nanbu-tekki (Iwate)

4518 Tsuboya-yaki (Okinawa)

2012. Traditional Crafts

5284	**4509**	80y. multicoloured	2·20	1·70
5285	**4510**	80y. multicoloured	2·20	1·70
5286	**4511**	80y. multicoloured	2·20	1·70
5287	**4512**	80y. multicoloured	2·20	1·70
5288	**4513**	80y. multicoloured	2·20	1·70
5289	**4514**	80y. multicoloured	2·20	1·70
5290	**4515**	80y. multicoloured	2·20	1·70
5291	**4516**	80y. multicoloured	2·20	1·70
5292	**4517**	80y. multicoloured	2·20	1·70
5293	**4518**	80y. multicoloured	2·20	1·70

4519 Santas and Parcel making Tree (Nakamaru hitomi)

4520 Kitten in Stocking (Iriyama satoshi)

4521 Wreath containing Children and Kitten (Sasanuma kaori)

4522 Puppy in Stocking (Iriyama satoshi)

4523 White Tree with Cardinal (Fukube Koichi)

4524 Santa and Reindeer on Roof

4525 Children at Window

4526 Children carolling

4527 Girls making Wreath and hanging Stockings

4528 Children decorating Tree

4529 Envelope and Cat on Roof (Tagashira Yoshitaka)

4530 Bird delivering Envelope to Angel (Sasanuma kaori)

4531 Squirrel and Girl posting Letter (Tagashira Yoshitaka)

4532 Flowers (Arai Sonoko)

4533 Children wearing Nightwear, Candles and Letter (Arai Sonoko)

2012. Greetings Stamps. Winter

5294	**4519**	50y. multicoloured	1·30	95
5295	**4520**	50y. multicoloured	1·30	95
5296	**4521**	50y. multicoloured	1·30	95
5297	**4522**	50y. multicoloured	1·30	95
5298	**4523**	50y. multicoloured	1·30	95
5299	**4524**	50y. multicoloured	2·20	1·70
5300	**4525**	80y. multicoloured	2·20	1·70
5301	**4526**	80y. multicoloured	2·20	1·70
5302	**4527**	80y. multicoloured	2·20	1·70
5303	**4528**	80y. multicoloured	2·20	1·70
5304	**4529**	90y. multicoloured	2·20	1·70
5305	**4530**	90y. multicoloured	2·20	1·70
5306	**4531**	90y. multicoloured	2·20	1·70
5307	**4532**	90y. multicoloured	2·20	1·70
5308	**4533**	90y. multicoloured	2·20	1·70

4534 Snake (earthenware bell)

4535 Snake (Mojigaseki doll)

2012. New Year's Greetings

5309	**4534**	50y. multicoloured	1·30	95
5310	**4535**	80y. multicoloured	2·20	1·70

4536 Snake (earthenware bell)

4537 Snake (Mojigaseki doll)

2012. New Year Lottery Stamps

5311	**4536**	50y.+3y. multicoloured	1·60	1·60
5312	**4537**	80y.+3y. multicoloured	2·50	2·50

4538 Futabayama Sadaji (sumo wrestler) and Usa-jingu Shrine

4539 *Prunus mume* and Japanese White-eye (*Zosterops japonicus*)

4540 Fukiji Temple

4541 Hita Gion Festival

4542 'Marriage Rocks', Bungo Futamigaura

2012. 60th Anniv of Local Government, Oita

5313	**4538**	80y. multicoloured	2·20	1·70
5314	**4539**	80y. multicoloured	2·20	1·70
5315	**4540**	80y. multicoloured	2·20	1·70
5316	**4541**	80y. multicoloured	2·20	1·70
5317	**4542**	80y. multicoloured	2·20	1·70

4543 Winnie the Pooh

4544 Piglet

4545 Alice in Wonderland

4546 Donald Duck

4547 Daisy Duck

4548 Cinderella

4549 Dumbo

4550 Marie

4551 Goofy

4552 Two Puppies from *One Hundred and One Dalmatians*

4553 Tinkerbell

4554 Mickey

4555 Minnie

4556 Bambi

4557 Pinocchio

4558 Snow White

4559 Pluto

4560 Ariel

4561 Stitch

4562 Three Little Pigs

2012. Greetings Stamps. Disney Characters

5318	**4543**	50y. multicoloured	1·30	95
5319	**4544**	50y. multicoloured	1·30	95
5320	**4545**	50y. multicoloured	1·30	95
5321	**4546**	50y. multicoloured	1·30	95
5322	**4547**	50y. multicoloured	1·30	95
5323	**4548**	50y. multicoloured	1·30	95
5324	**4549**	50y. multicoloured	1·30	95
5325	**4550**	50y. multicoloured	1·30	95
5326	**4551**	50y. multicoloured	1·30	95
5327	**4552**	50y. multicoloured	1·30	95
5328	**4553**	80y. multicoloured	2·20	1·70
5329	**4554**	80y. multicoloured	2·20	1·70
5330	**4555**	80y. multicoloured	2·20	1·70
5331	**4556**	80y. multicoloured	2·20	1·70
5332	**4557**	80y. multicoloured	2·20	1·70
5333	**4558**	80y. multicoloured	2·20	1·70
5334	**4559**	80y. multicoloured	2·20	1·70
5335	**4560**	80y. multicoloured	2·20	1·70
5336	**4561**	80y. multicoloured	2·20	1·70
5337	**4562**	80y. multicoloured	2·20	1·70

4563 Gyosho Style (Nagamori Soukyu)

4564 Reisho Style (Ohi Kintei)

4565 Qing Dynasty Seal (Yanagi Hekisen)

4566 Reisho Style (Kohara Doujyou)

4567 Kana (Shimoya Yoko)

4568 Kaisho Style (Kaibara Shiken)

4569 Sosho Style (Ishihara Tairyu)

4570 Gyosho Style (Yamanaka Suikoku)

4571 Small Seal (Seki Masato) **4572** Kinbun Style (Oyama Hourai)

2012. Greetings Stamps. Eto Calligraphy. Year of the Snake (Mi)

5338	4563	80y. multicoloured	2·20	1·70
5339	4564	80y. multicoloured	2·20	1·70
5340	4565	80y. multicoloured	2·20	1·70
5341	4566	80y. multicoloured	2·20	1·70
5342	4567	80y. multicoloured	2·20	1·70
5343	4568	80y. multicoloured	2·20	1·70
5344	4569	80y. multicoloured	2·20	1·70
5345	4570	80y. multicoloured	2·20	1·70
5346	4571	80y. multicoloured	2·20	1·70
5347	4572	80y. multicoloured	2·20	1·70

4573 Camellia japonica **4574** Prunus mume **4575** Adonis ramosa

4576 Cyclamen persicum **4577** Helleborus **4578** Camellia japonica

4579 Prunus mume **4580** Adonis ramosa **4581** Cyclamen persicum

4582 Helleborus

2012. Seasonal Flowers

5348	4573	50y. multicoloured	1·30	95
5349	4574	50y. multicoloured	1·30	95
5350	4575	50y. multicoloured	1·30	95
5351	4576	50y. multicoloured	1·30	95
5352	4577	50y. multicoloured	1·30	95
5353	4578	80y. multicoloured	2·20	1·70
5354	4579	80y. multicoloured	2·20	1·70
5355	4580	80y. multicoloured	2·20	1·70
5356	4581	80y. multicoloured	2·20	1·70
5357	4582	80y. multicoloured	2·20	1·70

4583 Ciconia boyciana (Oriental Stork) and Himeji-jo **4584** Meriken Park

4585 Shinkoro Tower in Izushi **4586** Shinmaiko Beach

4587 Daffodils, Nada Kuroiwa Suisenkyo

2013. 60th Anniv of Local Government, Hyogo

5358	4583	80y. multicoloured	2·20	1·70
5359	4584	80y. multicoloured	2·20	1·70
5360	4585	80y. multicoloured	2·20	1·70
5361	4586	80y. multicoloured	2·20	1·70
5362	4587	80y. multicoloured	2·20	1·70

4588-4589 Yuki-chan and Heidi

4590-4591 Alm-Onji and Heidi

4592-4593 Josef and Heidi

4594-4595 Heidi, Peter and White Rabbits

4596-4597 Heidi and Clara

2013. Heroes and Heroines of Animation (19th series). Heidi, Girl of the Alps

5363	4588	80y. multicoloured	2·20	1·70
5364	4589	80y. multicoloured	2·20	1·70
5365	4590	80y. multicoloured	2·20	1·70
5366	4591	80y. multicoloured	2·20	1·70
5367	4592	80y. multicoloured	2·20	1·70
5368	4593	80y. multicoloured	2·20	1·70
5369	4594	80y. multicoloured	2·20	1·70
5370	4595	80y. multicoloured	2·20	1·70
5371	4596	80y. multicoloured	2·20	1·70
5372	4597	80y. multicoloured	2·20	1·70

4598 Birds delivering Envelope **4599** Strawberry Wreath

4600 Cherry Blossom Wreath containing Children and Kitten **4601** Animals and Tulips

4602 Spring Cleaning **4603** Girl clasping Envelope

4604 Pink Bouquet **4605** Blue Bouquet **4606** Yellow and Orange Bouquet

4607 Poskuma (post teddy)

2013. Greetings Stamps. Spring

5373	4598	50y. multicoloured	1·30	95
5374	4599	50y. multicoloured	1·30	95
5375	4600	50y. multicoloured	1·30	95
5376	4601	50y. multicoloured	1·30	95
5377	4602	50y. multicoloured	1·30	95
5378	4603	80y. multicoloured	2·20	1·70
5379	4604	80y. multicoloured	2·20	1·70
5380	4605	80y. multicoloured	2·20	1·70
5381	4606	80y. multicoloured	2·20	1·70
5382	4607	80y. multicoloured	2·20	1·70

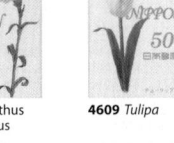

4608 Dianthus caryophyllus **4609** Tulipa

4610 Prunus cerasus **4611** Gerbera

4612 Myosotis scorpioides **4613** Dianthus caryophyllus

4614 Tulipa **4615** Prunus cerasus **4616** Gerbera

4617 Myosotis scorpioides

2013. Seasonal Flowers

5383	4608	50y. multicoloured	1·30	95
5384	4609	50y. multicoloured	1·30	95
5385	4610	50y. multicoloured	1·30	95
5386	4611	50y. multicoloured	1·30	95
5387	4612	50y. multicoloured	1·30	95
5388	4613	80y. multicoloured	2·20	1·70
5389	4614	80y. multicoloured	2·20	1·70
5390	4615	80y. multicoloured	2·20	1·70
5391	4616	80y. multicoloured	2·20	1·70
5392	4617	80y. multicoloured	2·20	1·70

4618 Fujisan, Shizuoka **4619** Tsukubasan, Ibaraki

4620 Kasagatake,Gifu **4621** Ibukiyama, Shiga

4622 Iinoyama, Kagawa **4623** Zaorenpo, Miyagi

4624 Gassan, Yamagata **4625** Ryoukamisan, Saitama

4626 Nijyozan, Osaka **4627** Kujyurenzan, Oita

2013. Mountains (2nd series)

5393	4618	80y. multicoloured	2·20	1·70
5394	4619	80y. multicoloured	2·20	1·70
5395	4620	80y. multicoloured	2·20	1·70
5396	4621	80y. multicoloured	2·20	1·70
5397	4622	80y. multicoloured	2·20	1·70
5398	4623	80y. multicoloured	2·20	1·70
5399	4624	80y. multicoloured	2·20	1·70
5400	4625	80y. multicoloured	2·20	1·70
5401	4626	80y. multicoloured	2·20	1·70
5402	4627	80y. multicoloured	2·20	1·70

4628 Winnie the Pooh and Piglet **4629** Winnie the Pooh **4630** Winnie the Pooh

4631 Tigger **4632** Winnie the Pooh **4633** Tigger

4634 Piglet **4635** Eyore **4636** Winnie the Pooh

4637 Winnie the Pooh **4638** Winnie the Pooh and Eyore

4639 Winnie the Pooh **4640** Winnie the Pooh and Piglet **4641** Tigger

4642 Winnie the Pooh and Tigger

4643 Winnie the Pooh and Hunny Pot

4644 Eyore

4645 Winnie the Pooh

4646 Winnie the Pooh, Piglet, Tigger and Eyore

4647 Winnie the Pooh and Piglet

2013. Greetings Stamps. Winnie the Pooh (from books by A.A.Milne and E.H.Shepard (cartoon created by Walt Disney))

5403	4628	50y. multicoloured	1·30	95
5404	4629	50y. multicoloured	1·30	95
5405	4630	50y. multicoloured	1·30	95
5406	4631	50y. multicoloured	1·30	95
5407	4632	50y. multicoloured	1·30	95
5408	4633	50y. multicoloured	1·30	95
5409	4634	50y. multicoloured	1·30	95
5410	4635	50y. multicoloured	1·30	95
5411	4636	50y. multicoloured	1·30	95
5412	4637	50y. multicoloured	1·30	95
5413	4638	80y. multicoloured	2·20	1·70
5414	4639	80y. multicoloured	2·20	1·70
5415	4640	80y. multicoloured	2·20	1·70
5416	4641	80y. multicoloured	2·20	1·70
5417	4642	80y. multicoloured	2·20	1·70
5418	4643	80y. multicoloured	2·20	1·70
5419	4644	80y. multicoloured	2·20	1·70
5420	4645	80y. multicoloured	2·20	1·70
5421	4646	80y. multicoloured	2·20	1·70
5422	4647	80y. multicoloured	2·20	1·70

4648 Grand Canyon National Park, USA

4649 Memphis and its Necropolis. Pyramid Fields from Giza to Dahshur, Egypt

4650 Mont-Saint-Michel, France

4651 Machu Picchu, Peru

4652 Angkor Wat, Cambodia

2013. Overseas World Heritage

5423	4648	80y. multicoloured	2·20	1·70
5424	4649	80y. multicoloured	2·20	1·70
5425	4650	80y. multicoloured	2·20	1·70
5426	4651	80y. multicoloured	2·20	1·70
5427	4652	80y. multicoloured	2·20	1·70

4653 Shidare-zakura and Iwaki-san

4654 Somei-yoshino and Hirosaki Castle

2013. Festivals. Hirosaki Sakura-matsur, Aomori

5428	4653	50y. multicoloured	1·30	95
5429	4654	50y. multicoloured	1·30	95

4655 Children, Girl and Cherry Blossom

4656 Children and Flowers

4657 Children and Cherry Blossom

4658 Girl holding Greenery

4659 Flower Fairy

4660 Children, Horsetails and Daffodils

4661 Boy and Cat amongst Tulips

4662 Tulips, Boy playing Recorder and Girl reading

4663 Girls playing with Dolls

4664 Girls playing with Dolls

2013. Seasonal Memories

5430	4655	80y. multicoloured	2·20	1·70
5431	4656	80y. multicoloured	2·20	1·70
5432	4657	80y. multicoloured	2·20	1·70
5433	4658	80y. multicoloured	2·20	1·70
5434	4659	80y. multicoloured	2·20	1·70
5435	4660	80y. multicoloured	2·20	1·70
5436	4661	80y. multicoloured	2·20	1·70
5437	4662	80y. multicoloured	2·20	1·70
5438	4663	80y. multicoloured	2·20	1·70
5439	4664	80y. multicoloured	2·20	1·70

4665 Lagopus muta (Rock Ptarmigan)

4666 Great Snow Wall

4667 Shomyo-daki

4668 Gentiana thunbergii forma

4669 Midagahara Plateau

4670 Midagahara Plateau

4671 Murodou-daira

4672 Mustela ermine (Stoat)

4673 Geum pentapetalum

4674 Daikanbo - Tateyama Cablecar

2013. Tourism. Toyama. Tateyama Kurobe Area

5440	4665	80y. multicoloured	2·20	1·70
5441	4666	80y. multicoloured	2·20	1·70
5442	4667	80y. multicoloured	2·20	1·70
5443	4668	80y. multicoloured	2·20	1·70
5444	4669	80y. multicoloured	2·20	1·70
5445	4670	80y. multicoloured	2·20	1·70
5446	4671	80y. multicoloured	2·20	1·70
5447	4672	80y. multicoloured	2·20	1·70
5448	4673	80y. multicoloured	2·20	1·70
5449	4674	80y. multicoloured	2·20	1·70

4675 One Crane   **4676** Two Cranes   **4677** Blossom

4678 Peacock with Wings Spread

4679 Peacock with Head Lowered

4680 Branch over Stream and Blossom

4681 Peacock on Rock   **4682** Peahen   **4683** Stream

4684 Two Mandarin Ducks

2013. Philately Week

5450	4675	80y. multicoloured	2·20	1·70
5451	4676	80y. multicoloured	2·20	1·70
5452	4677	80y. multicoloured	2·20	1·70
5453	4678	80y. multicoloured	2·20	1·70
5454	4679	80y. multicoloured	2·20	1·70
5455	4680	80y. multicoloured	2·20	1·70
5456	4681	80y. multicoloured	2·20	1·70
5457	4682	80y. multicoloured	2·20	1·70
5458	4683	80y. multicoloured	2·20	1·70
5459	4684	80y. multicoloured	2·20	1·70

4685 Lilium japonicum

4686 Hemerocallidaceae

4687 Syringa vulgaris

4688 Clematis

4689 Lysichitum camtschatcense

4690 Lilium japonicum

4691 Hemerocallidaceae

4692 Syringa vulgaris

4693 Clematis

4694 Lysichitum camtschatcense

2013. Seasonal Flowers

5460	4685	50y. multicoloured	1·30	95
5461	4686	50y. multicoloured	1·30	95
5462	4687	50y. multicoloured	1·30	95
5463	4688	50y. multicoloured	1·30	95
5464	4689	50y. multicoloured	1·30	95
5465	4690	80y. multicoloured	2·20	1·70
5466	4691	80y. multicoloured	2·20	1·70
5467	4692	80y. multicoloured	2·20	1·70
5468	4693	80y. multicoloured	2·20	1·70
5469	4694	80y. multicoloured	2·20	1·70

MILITARY FRANK STAMPS

軍事

(M 36)

1910. No. 139 optd with Type **M36**.

M156b	28	3s. red	£275	65·00

1913. No. 298 optd with Type **M36**.

M185e	36	3s. red	40·00	25·00

1921. No. 37 of Japanese Post Offices in China optd with Type **M36**.

M202	3s. red	£9500	£4500

PREFECTURE STAMPS

Prefecture stamps were often issued both as perforated stamps within sheets with an outer margin, and as panes of ten with three margins imperforate and a selvage at one end. Single stamps from these panes will have one side or two adjacent sides imperforate, depending on position.

In several cases stamps were issued by more than one Prefecture on the same day, for the convenience of collectors, these are listed under each Prefecture for which they were issued.

AICHI

1 Fish and Nagoya Castle

1989
1	1	62y. multicoloured	1·50	80

1990. Flowers.
2		62y. As Type **1456** of Japan	1·20	80

2 Owl and Mount Horaiji

1992
3	2	62y. multicoloured	1·50	90

3 Horse-shaped Float

1996. Nagoya Festival. Multicoloured.
4		80y. Type **3**	2·10	1·40
5		80y. Two floats	2·10	1·40

4 Satou Ichiei (painting by Fujii Tokio)

1999. Birth Centenary of Satou Ichiei (poet). Multicoloured.
6		80y. Type **4**	2·10	1·40
7		80y. *Beautiful Yamato* (painting by Munakata Shikou)	2·10	1·40

5 Willow and Frog

2000
8	5	80y. multicoloured	2·75	1·90

6 Roadway, Oohashi Bridge

2001. Automobile City. Multicoloured.
9		50y. Type **6**	1·60	1·10
10		50y. Tokyo stadium	1·60	1·10

7 Roses

2007. Flowers. Multicoloured.
11		50y. Type **7**	1·60	1·10
12		50y. Chrysanthemums	1·60	1·10
13		50y. Orchids	1·60	1·10
14		50y. Cyclamen	1·60	1·10

8 Iris

2007. Flowers and Scenery of Tokai. Multicoloured.
15		80y. Type **8**	2·50	1·70
16		80y. Gassho-zukuri houses and vetch flowers	2·50	1·70
17		80y. Lily and Nagoya Castle	2·50	1·70
18		80y. Iris and Couple rock	2·50	1·70
19		80y. Azalea and coastline, Jogasaki	2·50	1·70

Nos. 15-19 were also issued by Gifu, Mie and Shizuoka on 2 April 2007.

9-10 *Fuji* (Antarctic research ship) and Hibiscus

2007. Nagoya Port. Multicoloured.
20		80y. Type **9**	2·50	1·70
21		80y. Type **10**	2·50	1·70
22		80y. Dolphin and azalea	2·50	1·70
23		80y. Two dolphins and azaleas	2·50	1·70
24		80y. Meiko Triton bridge and double chrysanthemum	2·50	1·70
25		80y. Meiko Triton bridge and single chrysanthemum	2·50	1·70
26		80y. Pink flowers and fireworks	2·50	1·70
27		80y. Sailing ship and fireworks	2·50	1·70
28		80y. Azaleas and port, left	2·50	1·70
29		80y. Azaleas and port, right	2·50	1·70

Nos. 20-1, 22-3, 24-5, 26-7 and 28-9 were issued together, *se-tenant*, each pair forming a composite design.

11 Iris laevigata (kakitsubata)   **12** Iris laevigata (kakitsubata)

2010. Prefectural Flowers. Multicoloured.
30		50y. Peony (Shimane)	1·70	1·20
31		50y. *Citrus sudachi* (Tokushima)	1·70	1·20
32		50y. Unzen azalea (Nagasaki)	1·70	1·20
33		50y. Type **11** (Aichi)	1·70	1·20
34		50y. Camphor flowers (Saga)	1·70	1·20
35		80y. Peonies (Shimane)	2·60	1·80
36		80y. *Citrus sudachi* (Tokushima)	2·60	1·80
37		80y. Unzen azalea (Nagasaki)	2·60	1·80
38		80y. Type **12** (Aichi)	2·60	1·80
39		80y. Camphor flowers (Saga)	2·60	1·80

Stamps of the same design were issued by Nagasaki, Tokushima, Saga and Shimane on 8 March 2010.

AKITA

1990. Flowers.
1		62y. As Type **1438** of Japan	1·20	80

1 Fireworks

1990. Omagari Firework Festival.
2	1	62y. multicoloured	1·30	80

2 Coastline, Nyudo-zaki

1993
3	2	41y. multicoloured	1·20	70

---

3 Kanto Festival

1997
4	3	80y. multicoloured	2·10	1·40

4 Snow-covered Samurai Houses, Kakunodate

1999
5	4	80y. multicoloured	2·20	1·50

5 Trees and River

2000. Cherry Trees. Multicoloured.
6		80y. Type **5**	2·50	1·70
7		80y. Tree, central, Iwate	2·50	1·70
8		80y. Group of trees, Fukishima	2·50	1·70
9		80y. Tree, left, Miyagi	2·50	1·70
10		80y. Cherry blossom, Aomori	2·50	1·70
11		80y. Group of trees with spreading branches, Yamagata	2·50	1·70

Nos. 6-11 were also issued by Yamagata, Iwate, Miyagi, Aomori and Fukushima.

6 Kujuku Island

2000
12	6	80y. multicoloured	2·75	1·80

7 Igloo with Dog and Children

2001. Kamakura Igloo.
13	7	80y. multicoloured	2·50	1·70

8 Butterbur Flower

2004. Prefectural Flowers. Multicoloured.
14		50y. Type **8**	1·60	1·10
15		50y. Paulownia (Iwate)	1·60	1·10
16		50y. Japanese bush clover (Miyagi)	1·60	1·10
17		50y. Apple blossom (Aomori)	1·60	1·10
18		50y. Safflower (Yamagata)	1·60	1·10
19		50y. Alpine rose (*Rhododendron ferrugineum*) (Fukushima)	1·60	1·10

Nos. 14-19 were also issued by Yamagata, Iwate, Miyagi, Aomori and Fukushima.

9 Kanto Festival

2004. 400th Anniv of Akita City. Multicoloured.
20		50y. Type **9**	1·60	1·10
21		50y. Namahage (new year's eve demon costume)	1·60	1·10

Nos. 20-1 were issued together, *se-tenant*, forming a composite design.

---

10 Kanto Matsuri (Akita)

2006. Festivals of Tohuku. Multicoloured.
22		80y. Type **10**	2·10	1·40
23		80y. Nebuta Matsuri (Aomori)	2·10	1·40
24		80y. Hanagasa Matsuri (Yamagata)	2·10	1·40
25		80y. Sendai Tanabata Matsuri (Miyagi)	2·10	1·40

Nos. 22-5 were also issued by Aomori, Yamagata, and Miyagi.

11 Oga Penisula and Pinks

2007. North Eastern Scenery. Multicoloured.
26		80y. Type **11**	2·50	1·70
27		80y. Oirase stream	2·50	1·70
28		80y. Hirosaki Castle	2·50	1·70
29		80y. Chusonji Temple	2·50	1·70
30		80y. Rocks and lily (sukashiyuri)	2·50	1·70
31		80y. Matsushima island and rape flowers	2·50	1·70
32		80y. Dicentra and water filled crater	2·50	1·70
33		80y. Lily (nikkoukisuge) and mountain	2·50	1·70
34		80y. Skunk cabbage flowers, Oze National Park	2·50	1·70
35		80y. Safflower	2·50	1·70

Nos. 26-35 were also issued by Aomori, Fukushima, Iwate, Miyagi and Yamagata on 2 July 2007.

12 Rugby Players

2007. National Sports Festival.
36	12	50y. multicoloured	1·60	1·10

13-14 Flower Meadows

2008. National Re-afforestation Campaign. Multicoloured.
37		50y. Type **13**	1·60	1·10
38		50y. Type **14**	1·60	1·10
39		50y. Pink flower, left	1·60	1·10
40		50y. Pink flowers, right	1·60	1·10
41		50y. Maples in Autumn, left	1·60	1·10
42		50y. Maples, right	1·60	1·10
43		50y. Woods in Autumn, left	1·60	1·10
44		50y. Woods, right	1·60	1·10
45		50y. Flowers and rocks	1·60	1·10
46		50y. Waterfall	1·60	1·10

Nos. 37-8, 39-40, 41-2, 43-4 and 45-6 were issued together, *se-tenant*, each pair forming a composite design.

15 Fuki (*Petasites japonicus*)

2008. Prefectural Flowers. Multicoloured.
47		50y. Narcissus (Fukui)	1·60	1·10
48		50y. Pink plum blossom (Wakayama)	1·60	1·10
49		50y. Type **15**	1·60	1·10
50		50y. White plum blossom (Fukuoka)	1·60	1·10
51		50y. Weeping cherry blossom (Kyoto)	1·60	1·10
52		80y. Narcissus (Fukui)	2·50	1·70
53		80y. White plum blossom (Wakayama)	2·50	1·70
54		80y. Fuki (*Petasites japonicus*) (Akita)	2·50	1·70

55		80y. Pink plum blossom (Fukuoka)	2·50	1·70
56		80y. Weeping cherry blossom (Kyoto)	2·50	1·70

AOMORI

1 Apples

1990

1	1	62y. multicoloured	1·30	60

1990

2		62y. As Type **1435** of Japan	1·20	80

2 Rapids, Oirase

1993

3	2	62y. multicoloured	1·50	1·00

3 Nebuta Festival

1996

4	3	80y. multicoloured	2·10	1·40

1998

5	1	80y. multicoloured	2·10	1·40

4 Shirakami Mountains

1999

6	4	80y. multicoloured	2·10	1·40

5 Cherry Blossom

2000. Cherry Trees. Multicoloured.

7	80y. Type **5**	2·50	1·70
8	80y. Tree, central, Iwate	2·50	1·70
9	80y. Group of trees, Fukishima	2·50	1·70
10	80y. Tree, left, Miyagi	2·50	1·70
11	80y. Trees and river, Akita	2·50	1·75
12	80y. Group of trees with spreading branches, Yamagata	2·50	1·70

Nos. 7-12 were also issued by Yamagata, Iwate, Miyagi, Akita and Fukushima.

6 Mount Iwaki and Apples

2002

13	6	80y. multicoloured	2·20	1·50

7 Speed Skater and Ski Jumper

2003. Winter Asian Games, Aomori.

14	7	50y. multicoloured	1·60	1·10

8 Apple Blossom (Aomori)

2004. Prefecture Flowers. Multicoloured.

15	50y. Type **8**	1·60	1·10
16	50y. Paulownia (Iwate)	1·60	1·10
17	50y. Japanese bush clover (Miyagi)	1·60	1·10
18	50y. Butterbur flower (Akita)	1·60	1·10
19	50y. Safflower (Yamagata)	1·60	1·10
20	50y. Alpine rose (*Rhododendron ferrugineum*) (Fukushima)	1·60	1·10

Nos. 15-20 were also issued by Yamagata, Iwate, Miyagi, Akita and Fukushima.

9 Apples (Aomori)

2005. Fruits of Tohoku. Multicoloured.

21	50y. Type **9**	1·60	1·10
22	50y. Apple (Iwate)	1·60	1·10
23	50y. Cherry (Yamagata)	1·60	1·10
24	50y. Peach (Fukushima)	1·60	1·10

Nos. 21-4 were also issued by Yamagata, Iwate and Fukushima.

10 Nebuta Matsuri (Aomori)

2006. Festivals of Tohoku. Multicoloured.

25	80y. Type **10**	2·20	1·50
26	80y. Kanto Matsuri (Akita)	2·20	1·50
27	80y. Hanagasa Matsuri (Yamagata)	2·20	1·50
28	80y. Sendai Tanabata Matsuri (Miyagi)	2·20	1·50

Nos. 25-8 were also issued by Akita, Yamagata, and Miyagi.

11 Oirase Stream

2007. North Eastern Scenery. Multicoloured.

29	80y. Type **11**	2·50	1·70
30	80y. Hirosaki Castle	2·50	1·70
31	80y. Chusonji Temple	2·50	1·70
32	80y. Rocks and lily (sukashiyuri)	2·50	1·70
33	80y. Matsushima island and rape flowers	2·50	1·70
34	80y. Dicentra and water filled crater	2·50	1·70
35	80y. Oga penisula and pinks	2·50	1·70
36	80y. Lily (nikkoukisuge) and mountain	2·50	1·70
37	80y. Skunk cabbage flowers, Oze National Park	2·50	1·70
38	80y. Safflower	2·50	1·70

Nos. 29-38 were also issued by Akita, Fukushima, Iwate, Miyagi and Yamagata on 2 July 2007.

12 *Malus pumila*   **13 *Malus pumila***

2011. Prefectural Flowers. Multicoloured.

39	50y. *Rosa* (Ibaraki)	1·80	1·20
40	50y. Type **12**	1·80	1·20
41	50y. *Primula sieboldii* (Saitama)	1·80	1·20
42	50y. *Citrus natsudaidai* (Yamaguchi)	1·80	1·20
43	50y. *Rhododendron kiusianum* (Kagoshima)	1·80	1·20
44	80y. *Rosa* (Ibaraki)	2·75	1·90
45	80y. Type **13**	2·75	1·90
46	80y. *Primula sieboldii* (Saitama)	2·75	1·90
47	80y. *Citrus natsudaidai* (Yamaguchi)	2·75	1·90
48	80y. *Rhododendron kiusianum* (Kagoshima)	2·75	1·90

Stamps of the same design were issued by Ibaraki, Kagoshima, Saitama and Yamaguchi on 8 February 2011.

CHIBA

1 Raccoons

1989

1	1	62y. multicoloured	1·30	60

1990

2		62y. As Type **1445** of Japan	1·20	80

2 Woods in Autumn

1993

3	2	41y. multicoloured	1·30	90

3 Cows

1995. Holstein Show.

4	3	80y. multicoloured	1·80	1·20

4 Tunnel Entrance

1997. Tokyo-Wan Aqualine. Multicoloured.

5	80y. Type **4**	1·80	1·20
6	80y. Tunnel entrance (different)	1·80	1·20

Nos. 5-6 were also issued by Kanagawa.

5 Ooga Lotus Blossom

1999

7	5	80y. multicoloured	2·10	1·40

6 Flowers, Trees and Children floating on Bubbles

2003. National Afforestation Campaign.

8	6	50y. multicoloured	1·60	1·10

7 Rose and Mount Tsukubasan

2004. Flowers of Kanto (1st issue). Multicoloured.

9	50y. Type **7**	1·60	1·10
10	50y. Yoshi azalea and Lake Chuzenjiko	1·60	1·10
11	50y. Japanese azalea and Mt. Akagisan	1·60	1·10
12	50y. Primrose and Tajimagahara native primrose field	1·60	1·10
13	50y. Rape blossom and Nojima-zaki lighthouse	1·60	1·10

Nos. 9-13 were also issued by Tochigi, Saitama, Gunma and Ibaraki.
See also Nos. 14-18.

8 Sunflowers at Hana-hotaru (Chiba)

2005. Flowers of Kanto (2nd issue). Multicoloured.

14	50y. Type **8**	1·60	1·10
15	50y. Nikko-kisuge (Nikko day lily) and Kirifuri Heights (Tochigi)	1·60	1·10
16	50y. Azaleas, Tsutsujigaoka Park (Gunma)	1·60	1·10
17	50y. Bush clover, Kairakuen garden (Ibaraki)	1·60	1·10
18	50y. Allspice flowers and Mt. Bukousan (Saitama)	1·60	1·10

Nos. 14-18 were also issued by Gunma, Saitama, Tochigi and Ibaraki.

9 Loquat and Byobugaura

2006. Fruits of Kanto. Multicoloured.

19	80y. Type **9**	2·75	1·80
20	80y. Ume and Fukuroda Waterfall (Ibaraki)	2·75	1·80
21	80y. Apple and Oze (Gunma)	2·75	1·80
22	80y. Japanese pear and Nagatoro (Saitama)	2·75	1·80
23	80y. Strawberry and Kegon Waterfall (Tochigi)	2·75	1·80

Stamps of the same design were issued by Gunma, Ibaraki, Saitama and Tochigi on 1 September 2006.

10 Rape Flowers   **11 Rape Flowers**

2009. Prefectural Flowers. Multicoloured.

24a	50y. Peach blossom (Okayama)	1·70	1·30
25	50y. Type **10** (Chiba)	1·70	1·30
26	50y. Plum blossom and primula (Osaka)	1·70	1·30
27	50y. Bayberry (Kochi)	1·70	1·30
28	50y. Ume blossom (*Prunus mume* var. bungo) (Oita)	1·70	1·30
29	80y. Peach blossom (Okayama) (different)	2·75	1·70
30	80y. Type **11** (Chiba)	2·75	1·70
31	80y. Plum blossom and primula (Osaka) (different)	2·75	1·70
32	80y. Bayberry (Kochi) (different)	2·75	1·70
33	80y. Ume blossom (*Prunus mume* var. bungo) (Oita) (different)	2·75	1·70

Stamps of the same design were issued by Kochi, Oita, Okayama and Osaka on 1 Dec 2009.

12 Chiba Stadium

2010. 65th National Athletic Meet. Multicoloured.

34	50y. Type **12**	1·80	1·20
35	50y. Hammer throw	1·80	1·20
36	50y. Show jumping	1·80	1·20
37	50y. Mountaineering	1·80	1·20
38	50y. Pole vault	1·80	1·20

EHIME

1 Building Facade

1989. Dogo Spa.
| 1 | 1 | 62y. multicoloured | 1·30 | 90 |

1990
| 2 | | 62y. As Type **1471** of Japan | 2·40 | 1·60 |

2 Kurushima Strait

1992
| 3 | 2 | 62y. multicoloured | 2·50 | 1·70 |

3 Nishiumi Marine Park

1996
| 4 | 3 | 80y. multicoloured | 1·60 | 1·10 |

1999. Dogo Spa.
| 5 | 1 | 80y. multicoloured | 2·10 | 1·40 |

4 Pagoda and Bridge

1999. Shimanami Highway and Bridges. Multicoloured.
6	80y. Type **4**	1·80	1·20
7	80y. Islands	1·80	1·20
8	80y. Single span bridge	1·80	1·20
9	80y. Bridge pier at right	1·80	1·20
10	80y. Roadway and pier	1·80	1·20
11	80y. Ships	1·80	1·20
12	80y. Suspension wires and bridge	1·80	1·20
13	80y. Aerial view of bridge	1·80	1·20
14	80y. Suspension bridge from below	1·80	1·20
15	80y. Semi-circular bridge	1·80	1·20

Nos. 6-15 were also issued by Hiroshima.

5 Uwajima Castle

2000
| 16 | 5 | 80y. multicoloured | 2·50 | 1·70 |

6 Masaoka Shiki and Matsuyama Castle

2001. Death Centenary (2002) of Masaoka Shiki (haiku poet). Multicoloured.
| 17 | 50y. Type **6** | 1·60 | 1·10 |
| 18 | 50y. *Bocchasn* locomotive and Dogo Spa | 1·60 | 1·10 |

7 Mikan (mandarin oranges) and Sata-misaki Promontory (Ehime)

2002. Multicoloured.
| 19 | 50y. Type **7** | 1·50 | 1·00 |

20	50y. Sudachi (sour citrus fruit) and Mt. Tsurugisan (Tokushima)	1·50	1·00
21	50y. Yamamomo (bayberry) and Tengu highland (Kochi)	1·50	1·00
22	50y. Olive and Shodoshima island (Kagawa)	1·50	1·00

Nos. 19-22 were also issued by Tokushima, Kochi and Kagawa.

8 Zizouji Temple

2005. Cultural Heritage. Shizuoka Temples. Multicoloured.
23	80y. Type **8**	2·50	1·70
24	80y. Seated Buddha, Anrakuji Temple	2·50	1·70
25	80y. Inscribed belfry gateway, Jurakuji Temple	2·50	1·70
26	80y. Double roofed gateway, Kumadaniji Temple	2·50	1·70
27	80y. Pagoda, Yakuoji Temple	2·50	1·70
28	80y. Statues, ramp, lanterns and pagoda, Hotsumisakiji Temple	2·50	1·70
29	80y. Gateway and long steep steps, Shinjouji Temple	2·50	1·70
30	80y. Path, gateway, steps and main temple, Kongochoji Temple	2·50	1·70
31	80y. Buddha seated on peacock, Ryukoji Temple	2·50	1·70
32	80y. Bell and autumn colour, Butsumokuji Temple	2·50	1·70
33	80y. Dragon, Meisekiji Temple	2·50	1·70
34	80y. Steps and many roofed buildings, Daihouji Temple	2·50	1·70
35	80y. Carved decorative gable, Kokubunji Temple	2·50	1·70
36	80y. Leafless tree and snow-covered building, Yokomineji Temple	2·50	1·70
37	80y. Buddha, Kouonji Temple	2·50	1·70
38	80y. Courtyard and building, Houjuji Temple	2·50	1·70
39	80y. Inscribed pillars and gateway, Douryuji Temple	2·50	1·70
40	80y. Wall mounted statues, Goushouji Temple	2·50	1·70
41	80y. Eagle surmounting gateway, Tennouji Temple	2·50	1·70
42	80y. Courtyard with stone lined path and building, Kokubunji Temple	2·50	1·70

Nos. 23-42 were also issued by Tokushima, Kochi and Kagawa.

9 Hourinji Temple

2006. Cultural Heritage. Shizuoka Temples. Multicoloured.
43	80y. Type **9**	2·50	1·70
44	80y. Kirihata-ji (statue), Kirihata Temple	2·50	1·70
45	80y. Cherry blossom and building, Fujiidera Temple	2·50	1·70
46	80y. Snow-covered pagoda and temple, Shozanji Temple	2·50	1·70
47	80y. Wide path, inscribed pillar and gateway, Konomineji Temple	2·50	1·70
48	80y. Decorative carved roof boss and bell, Dainichiji Temple	2·50	1·70
49	80y. Cherry blossom and grass edged path, Kokubunji Temple	2·50	1·70
50	80y. Cherry blossom and statue, Zenrakuji Temple	2·50	1·70
51	80y. Cliff face and temple building, Iwayaji Temple	2·50	1·70
52	80y. Decorated footprints, Joururiji Temple	2·50	1·70
53	80y. Spot-lighted statues, Yasakaji Temple	2·50	1·70
54	80y. Lantern, tree, path, gateway and inscribed pillar, Sairinji Temple	2·50	1·70
55	80y. Temple buildings through hole in rock, Kichijoji Temple	2·50	1·70
56	80y. Cherry blossom and roofs, Maegamiji Temple	2·50	1·70
57	80y. Carving with dragon and phoenix, Sankakuji Temple	2·50	1·70
58	80y. Snow-covered roofs and trees, Unbenji Temple	2·50	1·70

59	80y. Wide path, pilgrim and gateway, Shiromineji Temple	2·50	1·70
60	80y. Row of statues, Negoroji Temple	2·50	1·70
61	80y. Lantern, courtyard and building, Ichinomiyaji Temple	2·50	1·70
62	80y. Animal statues and building, Yashimaji Temple	2·50	1·70

Nos. 43-62 were also issued by Tokushima, Kochi and Kagawa.

10 Statue

2008. Cultural Heritage. Temples. Ehime Multicoloured.
63	80y. Type **10**	2·50	1·70
64	80y. Gateway	2·50	1·70
65	80y. Square, shrub and main hall	2·50	1·70
66	80y. Trees, temple roof and hill	2·50	1·70
67	80y. Bell tower gate	2·50	1·70
68	80y. Bamboo temple	2·50	1·70
69	80y. Statues, pathway and temple	2·50	1·70
70	80y. Paved path and entrance	2·50	1·70
71	80y. Buddha	2·50	1·70
72	80y. Decorated ceiling and bell	2·50	1·70
73	80y. Temple lit from below	2·50	1·70
74	80y. Paved path, steps and temple	2·50	1·70
75	80y. Guardian statue	2·50	1·70
76	80y. Gateway	2·50	1·70
77	80y. Carved ceiling and bell	2·50	1·70
78	80y. Pagoda and temple at night	2·50	1·70
79	80y. Temple and mountains	2·50	1·70
80	80y. Pilgrims entering gateway	2·50	1·70
81	80y. Pilgrims and temple	2·50	1·70
82	80y. Temple, banners and mountains	2·50	1·70
83	80y. Well	2·50	1·70
84	80y. Kobo Daishi (statue)	2·50	1·70
85	80y. Buddha	2·50	1·70
86	80y. Three roofed pagoda	2·50	1·70
87	80y. Pilgrims, steps and gateway	2·50	1·70
88	80y. Demon	2·50	1·70
90	80y. Rock statues	2·50	1·70
91	80y. Bodhisattva	2·50	1·70
92	80y. Cave and temple at night	2·50	1·70
93	80y. Kobo Daishi (painting)	2·50	1·70

Nos. 63-93 were also issued by Tokushima, Kagawa and Kochi on 1 August 2007.

11 Satsuma

2011. Prefectural Flowers. Multicoloured.
94	50y. Azalea (Shizuoka)	1·80	1·20
95	50y. Type **11**	1·80	1·20
96	80y. Azalea (Shizuoka)	2·75	1·90
97	80y. Type **11**	2·75	1·90

Stamps of the same design were issued by Shizuoka on 2 May 2011.

FUKUI

1990. Flowers.
| 1 | | 62y. As Type **1453** of Japan | 1·20 | 80 |

1 Girl wearing Glasses

1991
| 2 | 1 | 62y. multicoloured | 1·50 | 90 |

2 Beach and Trees, Kehi-no-matsubara

1994
| 3 | 2 | 50y. multicoloured | 1·50 | 1·00 |

3 Murasaki Shikibu (novelist and poet)

1996
| 4 | 3 | 80y. multicoloured | 2·10 | 1·40 |

4 Dinosaur

1999. Dinosaurs. Multicoloured.
| 5 | 80y. Type **4** | 1·50 | 1·00 |
| 6 | 80y. Raptors | 2·10 | 1·40 |

Nos. 5-6 were issued together, *se-tenant*, forming a composite design.

5 Zuwai (snow) Crab

1999. Multicoloured.. Multicoloured..
| 7 | 80y. Type **5** | 2·10 | 1·40 |
| 8 | 80y. Cliffs, Tojinbo | 2·10 | 1·40 |

6 Narcissi Blooms

2001. Narcissi. Multicoloured.
| 9 | 50y. Type **6** | 1·60 | 1·10 |
| 10 | 80y. Flowers and cliffs | 2·50 | 1·70 |

7 Tulip

2005. Flowers of Hokuriku. Multicoloured.
11	50y. Type **7**	1·60	1·10
12	50y. Hydrangea	1·60	1·10
13	50y. Rhododendron	1·60	1·10
14	50y. Lily	1·60	1·10

Nos. 11-14 were also issued by Toyama and Ishikawa.

8 'Love, Love'

2006. Maruoka Castle. Multicoloured.
15	80y. Type **8**	2·10	1·40
16	80y. Castle roof, pink sky and hills	2·10	1·40
17	80y. Castle roof, blue sky and clouds	2·10	1·40
18	80y. Castle roof, orange sky and sun	2·10	1·40
19	80y. Castle roof, blue sky and moon	2·10	1·40

9 Narcissus

2008. Prefectural Flowers. Multicoloured.
20	50y. Type **9**	1·60	1·10
21	50y. Pink plum blossom (Wakayama)	1·60	1·10
22	50y. Fuki (*Petasites japonicus*) (Akita)	1·60	1·10

23		50y. White plum blossom (Fukuoka)	1·60	1·10
24		50y. Weeping cherry blossom (Kyoto)	1·60	1·10
25		80y. Narcissus (Fukui)	2·50	1·70
26		80y. White plum blossom (Wakayama)	2·50	1·70
27		80y. Fuki (*Petasites japonicus*) (Akita)	2·50	1·70
28		80y. Pink plum blossom (Fukuoka)	2·50	1·70
29		80y. Weeping cherry blossom (Kyoto)	2·50	1·70

FUKUOKA

1990

1		62y. As Type **1473** of Japan	1·20	80

1 Hurdler

1990. 45th National Athletics Meet.

2	**1**	62y. multicoloured	1·20	80

2 Songbird and Lake

1992. Afforestation. Photo.

3	**2**	41y. multicoloured	90	60

3 Kurodabushi

1992

4	**3**	62y. multicoloured	1·20	80

4 Fort and Map

1997. Multicoloured

5		80y. Type **4**	1·80	1·20
6		80y. Early railway and map	1·80	1·20
7		80y. Interchange and map	1·80	1·20
8		80y. Building and map	1·80	1·20

Nos. 5-8 were issued together, *se-tenant*, forming a composite design.
Nos. 5-8 were also issued by Nagasaki and Saga.

5 Hakata Gion Festival

1999

9	**5**	80y. multicoloured	2·10	1·40

6 Hakata Doll

2000

10	**6**	80y. multicoloured	2·75	1·90

7 Ooe Kouwaka-mai Dance

2001

11	**7**	80y. multicoloured	2·40	1·60

8 Kitakyushu Expo-Festival

2001

12	**8**	80y. multicoloured	2·20	1·60

9 Ume Blossom and Dazaifu-Tenmangu

2005. Flowers and Scenery of Kyushu (1st series). Multicoloured.

13		50y. Type **9**	1·60	1·10
14		50y. Sakura (cherry blossoms) and Kanmon bridge (Fukuoka)	1·60	1·10
15		50y. Kusunohana (camphor blossoms) and Ariake Sea (Saga)	1·60	1·10
16		50y. Unzen-Tsutsuji (azaleas) and Mt. Fugendake (Nagasaki)	1·60	1·10
17		50y. Tulips and Huis Ten Bosch (Nagasaki)	1·60	1·10
18		50y. Rindou (gentians) and Mt. Aso (Kumamoto)	1·60	1·10
19		50y. Ume blossoms and Mt. Takasaki (Ooita)	1·60	1·10
20		50y. Hamayu (crinums) and Nichinan beach (Miyazaki)	1·60	1·10
21		50y. Miyama-Kirishima (azaleas) and Kirishima mountains (Kagoshima)	1·60	1·10
22		50y. Hibiscus and Adan (screw-pine) (Kagoshima)	1·60	1·10

See also Nos. 23/32.
Nos. 13/22 were also issued by Saga, Nagasaki, Kumamoto, Oita, Miyazaki and Kagoshima.

10 Daffodils and Shrine (Fukuoka) Nokonoshima Island (Fukuoka)

2006. Flowers and Scenery of Kyushu (2nd series). Multicoloured.

23		80y. Type **10**	2·40	1·60
24		80y. Chinese bellflowers and Hiraodai (Fukuoka)	2·40	1·60
25		80y. Hydrangeas and Mikaeri-notaki fall (Saga)	2·40	1·60
26		80y. Cosmos and Kujukushima islands (Nagasaki)	2·40	1·60
27		80y. Camellias and the five bridges of Amakusa (Kumamoto)	2·40	1·60
28		80y. Purple flowers and Mt. Aso (Kumamoto)	2·40	1·60
29		80y. Primroses and Mt. Yufudake (Oita)	2·40	1·60
30		80y. Lavender and Kujurenzan (Oita)	2·40	1·60
31		80y. Poppies and Mt. Hinamoridake (Miyazaki)	2·40	1·60
32		80y. Field of yellow flowers and Mt. Kaimondake (Kagoshima)	2·40	1·60

Nos. 23/32 were also issued by Saga, Nagasaki, Kumamoto, Oita, Miyazaki and Kagoshima.

11-12 Procession

2008. Tanabata Festival. Multicoloured.

33		50y. Type **11**	1·60	1·10
34		50y. Type **12**	1·60	1·10
35		50y. Lanterns, left	1·60	1·10
36		50y. Lanterns, right	1·60	1·10
37		50y. Procession and roofs, left	1·60	1·10
38		50y. Procession and roofs, right	1·60	1·10
39		50y. Dancers, left	1·60	1·10
40		50y. Dancers, right	1·60	1·10
41		50y. Drummers, left	1·60	1·10
42		50y. Drummers, right	1·60	1·10

Nos. 33-4, 35-6, 37-8, 39-40 and 41-2 were issued together, *se-tenant*, each pair forming a composite design.
Nos. 78-87 were also issued by Tokushima, Okinawa, Miyagi and Tokyo on 1 August 2008.

13 White Plum Blossom

2008. Prefectural Flowers. Multicoloured.

43		50y. Narcissus (Fukui)	1·60	1·10
44		50y. Pink plum blossom (Wakayama)	1·60	1·10
45		50y. Fuki (*Petasites japonicus*) (Akita)	1·60	1·10
46		50y. Type **13**	1·60	1·10
47		50y. Weeping cherry blossom (Kyoto)	1·60	1·10
48		80y. Narcissus (Fukui)	2·50	1·70
49		80y. White plum blossom (Wakayama)	2·50	1·70
50		80y. Fuki (*Petasites japonicus*) (Akita)	2·50	1·70
51		80y. Pink plum blossom (Fukuoka)	2·50	1·70
52		80y. Weeping cherry blossom (Kyoto)	2·50	1·70

14

2011. Festivals. Hakata Dontaku. Multicoloured.

53		50y. Type **14**	1·80	1·20
54		50y. Musician and children (Torimon)	1·80	1·20
55		50y. Hakata Matsubayashi (traditional musical costume parade) (left)	1·80	1·20
56		50y. Hakata Matsubayashi (traditional musical costume parade) (right)	1·80	1·20

FUKUSHIMA

1990. Flowers.

1		62y. As Type **1440** of Japan	1·20	80

1 Peaches

1990

2	**1**	62y. multicoloured	1·20	80

2 Peony

1996. Peonies of Sukagawa.

3	**2**	80y. multicoloured	1·80	1·20

3 Streamers

1999. Summer Festivals. Multicoloured.

4		80y. Type **3**	2·10	1·40
5		80y. Festival goers and banners	2·10	1·40

Nos. 4-5 were issued together, *se-tenant*, forming a composite design.
Nos. 4-5 were also issued by Miyagi.

4 Kiku-ningyo (chrysanthemum petal doll)

1999

6	**4**	80y. multicoloured	2·10	1·40

5 Group of Trees

2000. Cherry Trees. Multicoloured.

7		80y. Type **5**	2·50	1·70
8		80y. Tree, central, Iwate	2·50	1·70
9		80y. Group of trees, Yamagata (different)	2·50	1·70
10		80y. Tree, left, Miyagi	2·50	1·70
11		80y. Cherry blossom, Aomori	2·50	1·70
12		80y. Trees and river, Akita	2·50	1·70

Nos. 7-12 were also issued by Yamagata, Iwate, Miyagi, Akita and Aomori.

6 Festival Goers

2000. Hata Festival, Kohata.

13	**6**	80y. multicoloured	2·75	1·80

7 Mount. Bandaisan and Dream Flying Machine

2001. Fukushima Expo.

14	**7**	80y. multicoloured	2·40	1·60

8 Boardwalk through Marshland, Ozegahara

2002. Oze. Multicoloured.

15		50y. Type **8**	1·50	1·00
16		50y. Day lilies, Ohe-shitsugen	1·50	1·00

9 Tsurugajo Castle and Persimmons

2003

17	**9**	80y. multicoloured	1·40	1·60

10 Alpine Rose
(*Rhododendron
ferrugineum*)
(Fukushima)

2004. Prefectural Flowers. Multicoloured.

18	50y. Type **10**		1·60	1·10
19	50y. Paulownia (Iwate)		1·60	1·10
20	50y. Japanese bush clover (Miyagi)		1·60	1·10
21	50y. Butterbur flower (Akita)		1·60	1·10
22	50y. Safflower (Yamagata)		1·60	1·10
23	50y. Apple blossom (Aomori)		1·60	1·10

Nos. 18-23 were also issued by Yamagata, Iwate, Miyagi, Aomori and Akita.

11 Peach
(Fukushima)

2005. Fruits of Tohoku. Multicoloured.

24	50y. Type **11**		1·60	1·10
25	50y. Apple (Iwate)		1·60	1·10
26	50y. Cherry (Yamagata)		1·60	1·10
27	50y. Apples (Aomori)		1·60	1·10

Nos. 24-7 were also issued by Aomori, Iwate and Fukushima.

12 Skunk
Cabbage
Flowers, Oze
National Park

2007. North Eastern Scenery. Multicoloured.

28	80y. Type **12**		2·50	1·70
29	80y. Oirase stream		2·50	1·70
30	80y. Hirosaki Castle		2·50	1·70
31	80y. Chusonji Temple		2·50	1·70
32	80y. Rocks and lily (sukashiyuri)		2·50	1·70
33	80y. Matsushima island and rape flowers		2·50	1·70
34	80y. Dicentra and water filled crater		2·50	1·70
35	80y. Oga penisula and pinks		2·50	1·70
36	80y. Lily (nikkoukisuge) and mountain		2·50	1·70
37	80y. Safflower		2·50	1·70

Nos. 28-37 were also issued by Akita, Aomori, Iwate, Miyagi and Yamagata on 2 July 2007.

13 Nemotoshakunage
(*Rhododendron
brachycarpum*)

2008. Flowers. Multicoloured.

38	50y. Type **13**		1·60	1·10
39	50y. Lily		1·60	1·10
40	50y. Sweet briar		1·60	1·10
41	50y. Safflower		1·60	1·10
42	50y. Gentian		1·60	1·10
43	80y. Lily (25×35 mm)		2·50	1·70
44	80y. Sweet briar (25×35 mm)		2·50	1·70
45	80y. Rhodedendron (25×35 mm)		2·50	1·70
46	80y. Safflower (25×35 mm)		2·50	1·70
47	80y. Gentian (25×35 mm)		2·50	1·70

Nos. 38-47 were also issued by Hokkaido, Kanagawa, Nagano and Yamagata on 1 July 2008.

GIFU

1990. Flowers.

1	62y. As Type **1454** of Japan		1·50	1·00

1 Bridge at Spring
Festival

1990. Takayama. Multicoloured.

2	62y. Type **1**		1·50	60
3	62y. Ptarmigans		1·50	60
4	62y. Lantern and procession		1·50	60
5	62y. Houses in snow		1·50	60

2 Flowers

1995

6	**2**	80y. multicoloured	1·90	1·30

3 Bridge at Spring
Festival (As Type
1)

1995. Hida. Multicoloured.

7	80y. Type **3**		1·80	60
8	80y. Ptarmigans (As No. 3)		1·80	60
9	80y. Lantern and procession (As No. 4)		1·80	60
10	80y. Houses in snow (As No. 5)		1·80	60

Nos. 7-10 differ from Nos. 2-5 both in the face value and an inscription 'Beautiful Hida' situated along the lower edge of the stamps.

4
Okaisho-Daiko
(ritual drum)

1998

11	**4**	80y. multicoloured	2·10	1·40

5 Ancient Cherry
Tree

1999

12	**5**	80y. multicoloured	2·10	1·40

6
Tanigumi-Odori
Folk Dance

2001. Tradition and Nature of Ibi. Multicoloured.

13	50y. Type **6**		1·60	1·10
14	50y. Persimmons, Fuyugaki		1·60	1·10

7 Gujou-odori
Dance

2002

15	**7**	50y. multicoloured	1·80	1·20

8 Cormorant
Fishing

2003. Cormorant Fishing on Nagaragawa River and Gifu Castle. Multicoloured.

16	50y. Type **8**		1·60	1·10

17	50y. Gifu Castle1		60	1·10

Nos. 16-17 were issued together, *se-tenant*, forming a composite design.

9 Milk Vetch,
Mount
Norikuradake
and Gifucho
Butterflies

2006. National Afforestation Campaign.

18	**9**	50y. multicoloured	1·60	1·10

10
Gassho-zukuri
Houses and
Vetch Flowers

2007. Flowers and Scenery of Tokai. Multicoloured.

19	80y. Type **10**		2·50	1·70
20	80y. Iris		2·50	1·70
21	80y. Lily and Nagoya Castle		2·50	1·70
22	80y. Iris and Couple Rock		2·50	1·70
23	80y. Azalea and coastline, Jogasaki		2·50	1·70

Nos. 19-23 were also issued by Aichi, Mie and Shizuoka on 2 April 2007.

11 Women
dancing

2009. Gujo Odori Dance Festival. Multicoloured.

24	50y. Type **11**		1·70	1·30
25	50y. Men dancing		1·70	1·30

Nos. 24-5 were printed se-tenant, each pair forming a composite design.

12 Float, Spring
Festival

2009. Takayama Spring and Autumn Festivals. Multicoloured.

26	50y. Type **12**		1·70	1·30
27	50y. Float at night, Autumn Festival		1·70	1·30

13 Milk Vetch   **14** Milk Vetch

2010. Prefectural Flowers. Multicoloured.

28	50y. Tulips (Toyama)		1·70	1·20
29	50y. Type **13** (Gifu)		1·70	1·20
30	50y. Fuji Zakura Satsuki azalea (Yamanashi)		1·70	1·20
31	50y. Indian coral bean flower (Okinawa)		1·70	1·20
32	50y. Pear blossom (Tottori)		1·70	1·20
33	80y. Tulips (Toyama)		2·00	1·40
34	80y. Type **14** (Gifu)		2·00	1·40
35	80y Fuji Zakura Satsuki azalea (Yamanashi)		2·00	1·40
36	80y. Indian coral bean flower (Okinawa)		2·00	1·40
37	80y. Pear blossom (Tottori)		2·00	1·40

Stamps of the same design were issued by Yamanashi, Okinawa, Tottori and Toyama on 1 February 2010.

GUNMA

1990. Flowers.

1	62y. As Type **1443** of Japan		1·20	80

1 Tortoise and
the Hare

1991

2	**1**	62y. multicoloured	1·50	90

2 Waterfall

1994

3	**2**	80y. multicoloured	1·90	1·10

3 River, Tree
and Mountain,
Oze

1998. Multicoloured.

4	80y. Type **3**		2·10	1·40
5	80y. Trees in autumn		2·10	1·40

4 Flints

1999

6	**4**	80y. multicoloured	2·10	1·40

5 Railway
Bridge

2000. Railways. Multicoloured.

7	50y. Type **5**		1·60	1·10
8	50y. Railway buildings		1·60	1·10

6 Azuma
Rhododendron
and Tanigawa
Mountain

2002. Mount Tanigawadake. Multicoloured.

9	50y. Type **6**		2·20	1·50
10	50y. Ichi-no kurasawa in autumn		2·20	1·50

7 Yoshi Azalea
and Lake
Chuzenjiko

2004. Flowers of Kanto (1st issue). Multicoloured.

11	50y. Type **7**		1·60	1·10
12	50y. Rose and Mount Tsukubasan		1·60	1·10
13	50y. Japanese azalea and Mt. Akagisan		1·60	1·10
14	50y. Primrose and Tajimagahara native primrose field		1·60	1·10

| 15 | | 50y. Rape blossom and Nojima-zaki lighthouse | 1·60 | 1·10 |

Nos. 11-15 were also issued by Tochigi, Saitama, Gunma and Ibaraki.
See also Nos. 16-20.

8 Azaleas, Tsutsujigaoka Park (Gunma)

2005. Flowers of Kanto (2nd issue). Multicoloured.

16	50y. Type **8**	1·60	1·10
17	50y. Nikko-kisuge (Nikko day lily) and Kirifuri Heights (Tochigi)	1·60	1·10
18	50y. Sunflowers at Hana-hotaru (Chiba)	1·60	1·10
19	50y. Bush clover, Kairakuen garden (Ibaraki)	1·60	1·10
20	50y. Allspice flowers and Mt. Bukousan (Saitama)	1·60	1·10

Nos. 16-20 were also issued by Tochigi, Saitama, Chiba and Ibaraki.
Nos. 21-5 and Type **9** have been left for 'Fruits of Kanto', issued on 1 September 2006, not yet received.

9 Apple and Oze

2006. Fruits of Kanto. Multicoloured.

21	880y. Loquat and Byobugaura	1·90	1·20
22	80y. Ume and Fukuroda Waterfall (Ibaraki)	1·90	1·20
23	80y Type **9**	1·90	1·20
24	80y. Japanese pear and Nagatoro (Saitama)	1·90	1·20
25	80y. Strawberry and Kegon Waterfall (Tochigi)	1·90	1·20

Stamps of the same design were issued by Chiba, Ibaraki, Saitama and Tochigi on 1 September 2006.

10 Azalea   **11** Azalea

2010. Prefectural Flowers. Multicoloured.

26	50y. Japanese Iris (Mie)	1·60	1·10
27	50y. Olive (Kagawa)	1·60	1·10
28	50y. Type **10**	1·60	1·10
29	50y. Foxglove tree (Iwate)	1·60	1·10
30	50y. Crinum (Miyazaki)	1·60	1·10
31	80y. Japanese Iris (Mie)	1·90	1·20
32	80y. Olive (Kagawa)	1·90	1·20
33	80y. Type **11**	1·90	1·20
34	80y. Foxglove tree (Iwate)	1·90	1·20
35	80y. Crinum (Miyazaki)	1·90	1·20

Stamps of the same design were issued by Iwate, Kagawa, Mie and Miyazaki on 30 April 2010.

HIROSHIMA

1 Junk and Islands

1989. Setonikai. Multicoloured.

| 1 | 62y. Type **1** | 1·30 | 1·60 |
| 2 | 62y. Islands and building | 1·30 | 1·60 |

Nos. 1-2 were issued together, se-tenant, forming a composite design.

2 Drummer

1990

| 3 | 62y. As Type **1467** of Japan | 1·20 | 80 |

1993. Hana-taue.

| 4 | **2** | 62y. multicoloured | 1·50 | 80 |

3 Gateway in Water

1998. Inland Sea. Multicoloured.

| 5 | 80y. Type **3** | 2·10 | 1·40 |
| 6 | 80y. Roadway and bridge | 2·10 | 1·40 |

Nos. 5-6 were issued together, se-tenant, forming a composite design.

4 Ibara Railway

1999

| 7 | **4** | 80y. multicoloured | 2·10 | 1·40 |

No. 7 was also issued by Okayama.

5 Islands

1999. Shimanami Highway and Bridges. Multicoloured.

8	80y. Type **5**	1·80	1·20
9	80y. Pagoda and Bridge	1·80	1·20
10	80y. Single span bridge	1·80	1·20
11	80y. Bridge pier at right	1·80	1·20
12	80y. Roadway and pier	1·80	1·20
13	80y. Ships	1·80	1·20
14	80y. Suspension wires and bridge	1·80	1·20
15	80y. Aerial view of bridge	1·80	1·20
16	80y. Suspension bridge from below	1·80	1·20
17	80y. Semi-circular bridge	1·80	1·20

Nos. 8-17 were also issued by Ehime.

6 Momiji (maple leaves) and Itsukushima Shrine Gate

2000. Multicoloured.

18	50y. Type **6**	1·50	1·00
19	50y. Nijisseikinashi (Japanese pear tree) and Tottori dune	1·50	1·00
20	50y. Botan (peonies) and Izumo-taisha Shrine	1·50	1·00
21	50y. Momonohana (peach blossoms) and traditional houses in Kurashiki	1·50	1·00
22	50y. Natsumikan (summer-orange blossoms) and the sea	1·50	1·00

Nos. 18-22 were also issued by Tottori, Shimane, Okayama and Yamaguchi.

7 Nukui Dam

2002. Northern Hiroshima. Multicoloured.

| 23 | 80y. Type **7** | 2·20 | 1·50 |
| 24 | 80y. On-bashi Bridge | 2·20 | 1·50 |

8 Cenotaph for Atomic Bomb Victims (Memorial Monument for Hiroshima)

2005. Peace Memorial Park. Multicoloured.

| 25 | 50y. Type **8** | 1·60 | 1·10 |
| 26 | 50y. Peace Memorial Museum | 1·60 | 1·10 |

9 Maple Leaves and Miyajima Shrine (Hiroshima)

2006. Flowers of Chugoku. Multicoloured.

27	50y. Type **9**	1·60	1·10
28	50y. Tree peonies and Hinomi-saki Lighthouse (Shimane)	1·60	1·10
29	50y. Peach blossoms and Seto-oohashi bridge (Okayama)	1·60	1·10
30	50y. Pear blossom and Yumiga-hama beach (Tottori)	1·60	1·10
31	50y. Chinese citron blossom and Oomijima island (Yamaguchi)	1·60	1·10

Nos. 27-31 were also issued by Tottori, Shimane, Okayama and Yamaguchi.

10 Ducks swimming

2007. Birds. Multicoloured.

32	80y. Type **10**	2·50	1·70
33	80y. Swans	2·50	1·70
34	80y. Pheasants	2·50	1·70
35	80y. Mandarin ducks	2·50	1·70
36	80y. Cranes	2·50	1·70

Nos. 32-36 were also issued by Okayama, Shimane, Tottori and Yamaguchi on 1 May 2007.

11 Maple   **12** Maple

2009. Prefectural Flowers. Multicoloured.

36	50y. Gentian (Kumamoto)	1·70	1·30
37	50y. Wild chrysanthemum (Hyogo)	1·70	1·30
38	50y. Bush clover blossom (Miyagi)	1·70	1·30
39	50y. Fritillary (*Fritillaria camschatcensis*) (Ishikawa)	1·70	1·30
40	50y. Type **11** (Hiroshima)	1·70	1·30
41	80y. Gentian (Kumamoto) (different)	2·75	1·70
42	80y. Wild chrysanthemum (Hyogo) (different)	2·75	1·70
43	80y. Bush clover blossom (Miyagi) (different)	2·75	1·70
44	80y. Fritillary (*Fritillaria camschatcensis*) (Ishikawa) (different)	2·75	1·70
45	80y. Type **12** (Hiroshima)	2·75	1·70

Stamps of the same design were issued by Hyogo, Ishikawa, Kumamoto and Miyagi on 1 July 2009.

HOKKAIDO

1 Building Facade

1989. Prefectural Government.

| 1 | **1** | 62y. multicoloured | 1·50 | 80 |

2 Runner

1989. 44th National Athletic Meet.

| 2 | **2** | 62y. multicoloured | 1·30 | 60 |

3 Ice Hockey Players

1990. Second Asian Winter Games.

| 3 | **3** | 62y. multicoloured | 1·20 | 85 |

1990. Flowers.

| 4 | 62y. As Type **1434** of Japan | 3·75 | 2·50 |

4 Cranes

1990

| 5 | **4** | 62y. multicoloured | 1·50 | 80 |

5 Lily of the Valley

1991. Flora. Multicoloured.

6	62y. Type **5**	1·20	80
7	62y. Pink lilac	1·20	80
8	62y. Lilies	1·20	80
9	62y. Rowan berries in snow	1·20	80

6 Foxes

1992

| 10 | **6** | 62y. multicoloured | 1·50 | 70 |

7 Largha Seals

1993

| 11 | **7** | 62y. multicoloured | 1·30 | 90 |

8 Stag, Ezo-shika

1994

| 12 | **8** | 50y. multicoloured | 1·50 | 70 |

9 Chipmunks, Ezoshimarisu

1995

| 13 | **9** | 80y. multicoloured | 1·90 | 1·30 |

10 Lady's
Slipper Orchid

1995
| 14 | **10** | 80y. multicoloured | 1·90 | 1·30 |

11 Kurione (sea angel)

1996
| 15 | **11** | 80y. multicoloured | 1·80 | 1·20 |

12 Roses

1996
| 16 | **12** | 80y. multicoloured | 2·10 | 1·40 |

13 Flowers

1997. Ezo-murasakitsutsuji.
| 17 | **13** | 80y. multicoloured | 2·10 | 1·40 |

14 Stoat

1997. Hokkaido Ermine.
| 18 | **14** | 50y. multicoloured | 1·30 | 90 |

15 Snow-covered Berries

1998. Flora. Multicoloured.
| 19 | | 80y. Type **15** | 1·80 | 1·20 |
| 20 | | 80y. Pink blossom | 1·80 | 1·20 |

16 Ice-flows

1999. Land of Snow (1st series). Multicoloured.
21		50y. Type **16**	1·20	80
22		50y. Cranes	1·20	80
23		80y. Snowflake	1·20	80
24		80y. Snowman	1·20	80

See also Nos. 42-5.

1999. Flora. Multicoloured.
25		80y. Lily (As Type **5**)	2·10	1·40
26		80y. Pink lilac (As No. **7**)	2·10	1·40
27		80y. Lilies (As No. **8**)	2·10	1·40
28		80y. Rowan berries in snow (As No. **9**)	2·10	1·40

17 Lavender Field

1999. Northern Paradise (1st series). Multicoloured.
| 29 | | 50y. Type **17** | 1·60 | 1·10 |
| 30 | | 80y. Cornfield | 2·40 | 1·60 |

See also Nos. 46-9.

1999. Fauna. Multicoloured.
| 31 | | 80y. Foxes (As Type **6**) | 2·10 | 1·40 |
| 32 | | 80y. Largha seals (As Type **7**) | 2·10 | 1·40 |

18 Eagle

1999. Birds. Multicoloured.
33		50y. Type **18**	1·30	90
34		50y. Puffin	1·30	90
35		50y. Owl	1·30	90
36		50y. Crane	1·30	90

19 Sweet Corn

1999. Vegetables and Children. Multicoloured.
37		50y. Type **19**	1·50	1·00
38		50y. Potatoes	1·50	1·00
39		50y. Asparagus	1·50	1·00
40		50y. Squash	1·50	1·00

20 Sleigh

1999. Santa Claus.
| 41 | **20** | 80y. multicoloured | 2·20 | 1·50 |

21 Nusamai Bridge

2000. Land of Snow (2nd series). Multicoloured.
42		80y. Type **21**	2·40	1·60
43		80y. Otaru canal	2·40	1·60
44		80y. Sapporo clock tower	2·40	1·60
45		80y. Orthodox Church, Hakodate	2·40	1·60

22 Potato Field and Barn

2000. Northern Paradise (2nd series). Multicoloured.
46		50y. Type **22**	1·60	1·10
47		50y. Barn and potato field	1·60	1·10
48		80y.+20y. Houses and hay field	3·25	2·20
49		80y.+20y. Hay field and barns	3·25	2·20

Nos. 48/9, each carry a premium for the aid of victims of the eruption of Mt. Usu and were on sale at all Japanese Post Offices.

23 Sable

2001. Ezo Sable.
| 50 | **23** | 80y. multicoloured | 2·40 | 1·60 |

24 Orchid

2001. Flowers of Hokkaido (1st series). Multicoloured.
| 51 | | 50y. Type **24** | 1·50 | 1·00 |
| 52 | | 50y. *Papaver fauriei* | 1·50 | 1·00 |

See also Nos. 63-6.

25 Poplar Avenue

2001. Northern Landscape. Multicoloured.
| 53 | | 80y. Type **25** | 2·40 | 1·60 |
| 54 | | 80y. Statue of Dr. William Clark (founder of Sapporo Agricultural College), Hitsuji-gaoka Hill | 2·40 | 1·60 |

26 Ezo Flying Squirrels

2002
| 55 | **26** | 80y. multicoloured | 2·20 | 1·50 |

27 Tulip Field and Windmill

2002. Colouring the North. Multicoloured.
| 56 | | 80y. Type **27** | 2·20 | 1·50 |
| 57 | | 80y. Sunflowers and field showing name of 'Hokuryu' (town) | 2·20 | 1·50 |

28 Ainu Design

2003. Cultural and Natural Heritage. Multicoloured.
| 58 | | 80y. Type **28** | 2·40 | 1·60 |
| 59 | | 80y. Lake Mashuko | 2·40 | 1·60 |

29 Kiritappu Wetland

2004. Cultural and Natural Heritage. Multicoloured.
| 60 | | 80y. Type **29** | 2·50 | 1·70 |
| 61 | | 80y. Wakka Primeval Garden | 2·50 | 1·70 |

30 Sea Ice, *Garinko-go 2* (ice-breaker) and Steller's Sea Eagle

2004
| 62 | **30** | 80y. multicoloured | 2·50 | 1·70 |

31 Sweetbrier

2005. Flowers of Hokkaido (2nd series). Multicoloured.
63		50y. Type **31**	1·60	1·10
64		50y. Lavender	1·60	1·10
65		50y. Yellow flowers	1·60	1·10
66		50y. Lily of the valley	1·60	1·10

32 Sweetbrier and former Shana Post Office

2005. Northern Hokkaido. Multicoloured.
67		80y. Type **32**	2·50	1·70
68		80y. Sea otter	2·50	1·70
69		80y. Cherry blossom	2·50	1·70
70		80y. Tufted puffin	2·50	1·70

Nos. 67-70 were issued together, se-tenant, forming a composite background design.

33 Fox

2005. Animals of Northern Hokkaido. Multicoloured.
71		50y. Type **33**	1·60	1·10
72		50y. Bear and cub	1·60	1·10
73		50y. Squirrel	1·60	1·10
74		50y. Owl	1·60	1·10

34 Cranes

2007. Fauna. Multicoloured.
75		80y. Type **34**	2·50	1·70
76		80y. Rabbits (ezoyukiusagi)	2·50	1·70
77		80y. Flying squirrels (ezo-momonga)	2·50	1·70
78		80y. Yezo deer	2·50	1·70
79		80y. Harbour seals	2·50	1·70

35 Sweet Briar Flowers

2007. National Re-Afforestation Programme.
| 80 | **35** | 50y. multicoloured | 1·60 | 1·10 |

36 Sweet Briar

2008. Flowers. Multicoloured.
81		50y. Type **36**	1·60	1·10
82		50y. Lily	1·60	1·10
83		50y. Nemotoshakunage (*Rhododendron brachycarpum*)	1·60	1·10
84		50y. Safflower	1·60	1·10
85		50y. Gentian	1·60	1·10
86		80y. Lily (25×35 mm)	2·50	1·70
87		80y. Sweet briar (25×35 mm)	2·50	1·70
88		80y. Rhodedendron (25×35 mm)	2·50	1·70
89		80y. Safflower (25×35 mm)	2·50	1·70
90		80y. Gentian (25×35 mm)	2·50	1·70

Nos. 81-90 were also issued by Fukushima, Kanagawa, Nagano and Yamagata on 1 July 2008.

HYOGO

1990. Flowers.

| 1 | | 62y. As Type **1461** of Japan | 1·20 | 80 |

1 Weathervane, Kobe

1991

| 2 | **1** | 62y. multicoloured | 1·50 | 90 |

2 Stork and Tower, Shinkoro

1994

| 3 | **2** | 50y. multicoloured | 1·50 | 1·00 |

3 Bridge

1998. Kobe-Awaji-Naruto Expressway. Multicoloured.

| 4 | | 80y. Type **3** | 2·10 | 1·40 |
| 5 | | 80y. Bridge (different) | 2·10 | 1·40 |

Nos. 4-5 were also issued by Tokushima.

4 Kobe Luminarie (light festival)

1998. (1st series).

| 6 | **4** | 80y. multicoloured | 2·10 | 1·40 |

See also Nos. 14-15.

5 Child as Bee and Flower

2000. Multicoloured.

| 7 | | 50y. Type **5** | 1·50 | 1·00 |
| 8 | | 80y. Child as fairy and flowers (26×36 mm) | 2·40 | 1·60 |

6 Pandas

2001. Multicoloured.

| 9 | | 50y. Type **6** | 2·10 | 1·40 |
| 10 | | 80y. Night scene, Kobe | 2·40 | 1·60 |

7 Takarazuka Revue

2001. Takarazuka. Multicoloured.

| 11 | | 80y. Type **7** | 2·40 | 1·60 |
| 12 | | 80y. Violets | 2·40 | 1·60 |

---

8 Fairy riding Stork

2005. Re-introduction of the Oriental White Stork.

| 13 | **8** | 80y. multicoloured | 2·50 | 1·70 |

9 Frontone (arched facade)

2005. Kobe Luminarie (2nd series). Multicoloured.

| 14 | | 50y. Type **9** | 1·60 | 1·10 |
| 15 | | 50y. Spalliera (wide facade) | 1·60 | 1·10 |

10 Nozigiku (wild chrysanthemums) (Hyogo)

2006. Flowers of Kinki. Multicoloured.

16		50y. Yae-zakura (double cherry blossoms) (Nara)	1·60	1·10
17		50y. Type **10**	1·60	1·10
18		50y. Shakunage (rhododendron) (Shiga)	1·60	1·10
19		50y. Ume blossoms (Wakayama)	1·60	1·10
20		50y. Sakuraso (primrose) (Osaka)	1·60	1·10
21		50y. Shidare-zakura (weeping cherry) (Kyoto)	1·60	1·10

Nos. 16-21 were also issued by Osaka, Nara, Shiga, Wakayama and Kyoto.

12 Himeji Castle

2007. Castles in Kinki Region. Multicoloured.

23		50y. Type **12**	1·60	1·10
24		50y. Koriyama	1·60	1·10
25		50y. Hikone	1·60	1·10
26		50y. Osaka	1·60	1·10
27		50y. Wakayama	1·60	1·10

No. 22 and Type **11** have been left for 'National Athletics Meet', issued on 1 September 2006, not yet received.

Nos. 23-7 were also issued by Nara, Osaka, Shiga and Wakayama on 1 June 2007.

13 Wild Chrysanthemum   **14** Wild Chrysanthemum

2009. Prefectural Flowers. Multicoloured.

28		50y. Gentian (Kumamoto)	1·70	1·30
29		50y. Type **13** (Hyogo)	1·70	1·30
30		50y. Bush clover blossom (Miyagi)	1·70	1·30
31		50y. Fritillary (*Fritillaria camschatcensis*) (Ishikawa)	1·70	1·30
32		50y. Maple (Hiroshima)	1·70	1·30
33		80y. Gentian (Kumamoto) (different)	2·75	1·70
34		80y. Type **14** (Hyogo)	2·75	1·70
35		80y. Bush clover blossom (Miyagi) (different)	2·75	1·70
36		80y. Fritillary (*Fritillaria camschatcensis*) (Ishikawa) (different)	2·75	1·70
37		80y. Maple (Hiroshima) (different)	2·75	1·70

Stamps of the same design were issued by Hiroshima, Ishikawa, Kumamoto and Miyagi on 1 July 2009..

IBARAKI

1990. Flowers.

| 1 | | 62y. As Type **1441** of Japan | 1·20 | 80 |

1 Young Crows

1990

| 2 | **1** | 62y. multicoloured | 1·50 | 80 |

2 Fukuroda-no-taki Waterfall

1993

| 3 | **2** | 62y. multicoloured | 1·50 | 1·00 |

3 Yacht, Lake Kasumigaura

1997

| 4 | **3** | 80y. multicoloured | 2·10 | 1·40 |

4 Koubuntei Pavilion and Ume Blossoms (Spring)

2001. Kairakuen Garden. Multicoloured.

5		50y. Type **4**	1·50	1·00
6		50y. Chumon Gate (summer)	1·50	1·00
7		50y. Togyokusen spring (autumn)	1·50	1·00
8		50y. Lake and Koubuntei pavilion (winter)	1·50	1·00

5 Mount Tsukuba, Itako (blind shaman)

2003

| 9 | **5** | 80y. multicoloured | 2·40 | 1·60 |

6 Japanese Azalea and Mount and Iris Flowers Akagisan

2004. Flowers of Kanto (1st issue). Multicoloured.

10		50y. Type **6**	1·60	1·10
11		50y. Yoshi azalea and Lake Chuzenjiko	1·60	1·10
12		50y. Rose and Mount Tsuku-basan	1·60	1·10
13		50y. Primrose and Tajimagahara native primrose field	1·60	1·10
14		50y. Rape blossom and Nojima-zaki lighthouse	1·60	1·10

Nos. 10-14 were also issued by Tochigi, Saitama, Chiba and Gunma.

See also Nos. 16-20.

---

7 Iris Flowers, Mount Tsukuba and Lake Kasumigaura

2005. National Afforestation Campaign.

| 15 | **7** | 50y. multicoloured | 1·60 | 1·10 |

8 Bush Clover, Kairakuen Garden (Ibaraki)

2005. Flowers of Kanto (2nd issue). Multicoloured.

16		50y. Type **8**	1·60	1·10
17		50y. Nikko-kisuge (Nikko day lily) and Kirifuri Heights (Tochigi)	1·60	1·10
18		50y. Sunflowers at Hana-hotaru (Chiba)	1·60	1·10
19		50y. Azaleas, Tsutsujigaoka Park (Gunma)	1·60	1·10
20		50y. Allspice flowers and Mt. Bukousan (Saitama)	1·60	1·10

Nos. 16-20 were also issued by Tochigi, Saitama, Chiba and Gunma.

9 Ume and Fukuroda Waterfall

2006. Fruits of Kanto. Multicoloured.

21		80y. Loquat and Byobugaura	2·40	1·60
22		80y. Type **9**	2·40	1·60
23		80y. Apple and Oze (Gunma)	2·40	1·60
24		80y. Japanese pear and Nagatoro (Saitama)	2·40	1·60
25		80y. Strawberry and Kegon Waterfall (Tochigi)	2·40	1·60

10 Rosa   **11** Rosa

2011. Prefectural Flowers. Multicoloured.

26		50y. Type **10**	1·80	1·20
27		50y. *Malus pumila* (Aomori)	1·80	1·20
28		50y. *Primula sieboldii* (Saitama)	1·80	1·20
29		50y. *Citrus natsudaidai* (Yamaguchi)	1·80	1·20
30		50y. *Rhododendron kiusianum* (Kagoshima)	1·80	.1·20
31		80y. Type **11**	2·75	1·90
32		80y. *Malus pumila* (Aomori)	2·75	1·90
33		80y. *Primula sieboldii* (Saitama)	2·75	1·90
34		80y. *Citrus natsudaidai* (Yamaguchi)	2·75	1·90
35		80y. *Rhododendron kiusianum* (Kagoshima)	2·75	1·90

Stamps of the same design were issued by Aomori, Kagoshima, Saitama and Yamaguchi on 8 February 2011.

ISHIKAWA

1 Bell Tower

1989. Kenroku-en.

| 1 | **1** | 62y. multicoloured | 1·30 | 60 |

1990

| 2 | | 62y. As Type **1452** of Japan | 1·20 | 80 |

2 Child in Pearl Shell

1991. 46th National Athletic Meet.
3 **2** 41y. multicoloured 1·50 70

3 Bridge, Nanao-wan

1993
4 **3** 62y. multicoloured 1·50 1·00

4 Kanazawa-jo Castle

1995
5 **4** 80y. multicoloured 1·90 1·30

5 Mount Hakusan

1998
6 **5** 50y. multicoloured 1·30 90

6 Cherry Tree and Kaiseki Pagoda

1999. Kenrokuen Garden. Multicoloured.
7 80y. Type **6** 2·10 1·40
8 80y. Fountain 2·10 1·40
9 80y. Kinjo Reitaku well 2·10 1·40
10 80y. Snow-covered Kotoji Stone Lantern 2·10 1·40

7 Festival Goers and Banners

1999. Noto Kiriko Festival.
11 **7** 80y. multicoloured 2·10 1·40

8 Samurai Warrior and Kaga Gold Lacquer Designs

2001
12 **8** 80y. multicoloured 2·40 1·60

9 *Adenophora triphylla var. hakusanensis*

2002. Alpine Flora of Mount Hakusan. Multicoloured.
13 50y. Type **9** 1·60 1·10

---

14 50y. *Fritillaria camtschatcensis* and Mt. Betsusan 1·60 1·10
15 50y. *Geranium yesoense var. nipponicum* and Mt. Gozengamine 1·60 1·10
16 50y. *Anemone narcissiflora* and Mt. Gozengamine 1·60 1·10

10 Fukada Kyuya and Mount Hakusan and Mount Betsusan

2003. Birth Centenary of Fukada Kyuya (mountaineer and writer).
17 **10** 80y. multicoloured 2·40 1·60

11 Morning Glory Flowers and Script

2003. 300th Birth Anniv of Chiyojo (haiku poet). Multicoloured.
18 50y. Type **11** 2·40 1·60
19 50y. Chiyojo 2·40 1·60

Nos. 18-19 were issued together, *se-tenant*, forming a composite design.

12 Hydrangea

2005. Flowers of Hokuriku. Multicoloured.
20 50y. Type **12** 1·60 1·10
21 50y. Tulip 1·60 1·10
22 50y. Rhododendron 1·60 1·10
23 50y. Lily 1·60 1·10

Nos. 20-3 were also issued by Toyama and Fukui.

13 Fritillary (*Fritillaria camschatcensis*)   **14** Fritillary (*Fritillaria camschatcensis*)

2009. Prefectural Flowers. Multicoloured.
24 50y. Gentian (Kumamoto) 1·70 1·30
25 50y. Wild chrysanthemum (Hyogo) 1·70 1·30
26 50y. Bush clover blossom (Miyagi) 1·70 1·30
27 50y. Type **13** (Ishikawa) 1·70 1·30
28 50y. Maple (Hiroshima) 1·70 1·30
29 80y. Gentian (Kumamoto) (different) 2·75 1·70
30 80y. Wild chrysanthemum (Hyogo) (different) 2·75 1·70
31 80y. Bush clover blossom (Miyagi) (different) 2·75 1·70
32 80y. Type **14** (Ishikawa) 2·75 1·70
33 80y. Maple (Hiroshima) (different) 2·75 1·70

Stamps of the same design were issued by Hyogo, Hiroshima, Kumamoto and Miyagi on 1 July 2009.

IWATE

1990
1 62y. As Type **1436** of Japan 1·20 80

1 Iwate Mountain

1991
2 **1** 62y. multicoloured 1·30 90

---

2 Coastline, Rikuchu

1992
3 **2** 62y. multicoloured 1·50 90

3 Caravan and Mount Iwate

1998
4 **3** 80y. multicoloured 2·10 1·40

4 Gentian

1999
5 **4** 80y. multicoloured 1·80 1·20

5 Cherry Tree

2000. Cherry Trees. Multicoloured.
6 80y. Type **5** 2·50 1·70
7 80y. Group of trees with spreading branches, Yamagata 2·50 1·70
8 80y. Group of trees, Fukishima 2·50 1·70
9 80y. Tree, left, Miyagi 2·50 1·70
10 80y. Cherry blossom, Aomori 2·50 1·70
11 80y. Trees and river, Akitan 2·50 1·70

Nos. 6-11 were also by Yamagata, Aomori, Miyagi, Akita and Fukishima.

6 Chusonji Temple

2000
12 **6** 80y. multicoloured 2·75 1·90

7 Paulownia (Iwate)

2004. Prefectural Flowers. Multicoloured.
13 50y. Type **7** 1·60 1·10
14 50y. Apple blossom (Aomori) 1·60 1·10
15 50y. Japanese bush clover (Miyagi) 1·60 1·10
16 50y. Butterbur flower (Akita) 1·60 1·10
17 50y. Safflower (Yamagata) 1·60 1·10
18 50y. Alpine rose (*Rhododendron ferrugineum*) (Fukushima) 1·60 1·10

Nos. 13-18 were also issued by Yamagata, Aomori, Miyagi, Akita and Fukushima.

8 Apple (Iwate)

2005. Fruits of Tohoku. Multicoloured.
19 50y. Type **8** 1·60 1·10
20 50y. Apples (Aomori) 1·60 1·10
21 50y. Cherry (Yamagata) 1·60 1·10
22 50y. Peach (Fukushima) 1·60 1·10

Nos. 19-22 were also issued by Yamagata, Iwate and Fukushima.

9 Chusonji Temple

2007. North Eastern Scenery. Multicoloured.
23 80y. Type **9** 2·50 1·70
24 80y. Oirase stream 2·50 1·70
25 80y. Hirosaki Castle 2·50 1·70
26 80y. Rocks and lily (sukashiyuri) 2·50 1·70
27 80y. Matsushima island and rape flowers 2·50 1·70
28 80y. Dicentra and water filled crater 2·50 1·70
29 80y. Oga penisula and pinks 2·50 1·70
30 80y. Lily (nikkoukisuge) and mountain 2·50 1·70
31 80y. Skunk cabbage flowers, Oze National Park 2·50 1·70
32 80y. Safflower 2·50 1·70

Nos. 23-32 were also issued by Akita, Aomori, Fukushima, Miyagi and Yamagata on 2 July 2007.

10 Foxglove Tree   **11** Foxglove Tree

2010. Prefectural Flowers. Multicoloured.
33 50y. Japanese Iris (Mie) 1·70 1·20
34 50y. Olive (Kagawa) 1·70 1·20
35 50y. Azalea (Gunma) 1·70 1·20
36 50y. Type **10** 1·70 1·20
37 50y. Crinum (Miyazaki) 1·70 1·20

Stamps of the same design were issued by Gunma, Kagawa, Mie and Miyazaki on 30 April 2010.

KAGAWA

1990
1 62y. As Type **1470** of Japan 4·75 3·25

1 Archer on Horseback

1991. Yashima.
2 **1** 62y. multicoloured 1·20 80

2 Peace Statues

1993
3 **2** 62y. multicoloured 1·50 1·00

3 Marugame Castle

1997
4 **3** 80y. multicoloured 2·10 1·40

4 Seto-Ohashi Bridges

1998
5 **4** 80y. multicoloured 2·10 1·40

5 Ritsurin Park

1999

| 6 | 5 | 80y. multicoloured | 2·10 | 1·40 |

6 Olive and Shodoshima Island (Kagawa)

2002. Multicoloured.

7	50y. Type **6**	1·50	1·00
8	50y. Sudachi (sour citrus fruit) and Mt. Tsurugisan (Tokushima)	1·50	1·00
9	50y. Yamamomo (bayberry) and Tengu highland (Kochi)	1·50	1·00
10	50y. Mikan (mandarin oranges) and Sata-misaki Promontory (Ehime)	1·50	1·00

Nos. 7-10 were also issued by Ehime, Kochi and Tokushima.

7 Kompira-Ohshibai Theatre and Mount Zouzusan

2003. Former Kompira-Ohshibai Theatre.

| 11 | 7 | 80y. multicoloured | 2·40 | 1·60 |

2005. Cultural Heritage. Shizuoka Temples. Multicoloured.

12	80y. As Type **8** of Ehime	2·50	1·70
13	80y. Seated Buddha, Anrakuji Temple	2·50	1·70
14	80y. Inscribed belfry gateway, Jurakuji Temple	2·50	1·70
15	80y. Double roofed gateway, Kumadaniji Temple	2·50	1·70
16	80y. Pagoda, Yakuoji Temple	2·50	1·70
17	80y. Statues, ramp, lanterns and pagoda, Hotsumisakiji Temple	2·50	1·70
18	80y. Gateway and long steep steps, Shinjouji Temple	2·50	1·70
19	80y. Path, gateway, steps and main temple, Kongochoji Temple	2·50	1·70
20	80y. Buddha seated on peacock, Ryukoji Temple	2·50	1·70
21	80y. Bell and autumn colour, Butsumokuji Temple	2·50	1·70
22	80y. Dragon, Meisekiji Temple	2·50	1·70
23	80y. Steps and many roofed buildings, Daihouji Temple	2·50	1·70
24	80y. Carved decorative gable, Kokubunji Temple	2·50	1·70
25	80y. Leafless tree and snow-covered building, Yokomineji Temple	2·50	1·70
26	80y. Buddha, Kouonji Temple	2·50	1·70
27	80y. Courtyard and building, Houjuji Temple	2·50	1·70
28	80y. Inscribed pillars and gateway, Douryuji Temple	2·50	1·70
29	80y. Wall mounted statues, Goushouji Temple	2·50	1·70
30	80y. Eagle surmounting gateway, Tennouji Temple	2·50	1·70
31	80y. Courtyard with stone lined path and building, Kokubunji Temple	2·50	1·70

Nos. 12-31 were also issued by Ehime, Kochi and Tokushima.

2006. Cultural Heritage. Temples. Multicoloured.

32	80y. As Type **9** of Ehime	2·50	1·70
33	80y. Kirihata-ji (statue), Kirihata Temple	2·50	1·70
34	80y. Cherry blossom and building, Fujiidera Temple	2·50	1·70
35	80y. Snow-covered pagoda and temple, Shozanji Temple	2·50	1·70
36	80y. Wide path, inscribed pillar and gateway, Konomineji Temple	2·50	1·70
37	80y. Decorative carved roof boss and bell, Dainichiji Temple	2·50	1·70
38	80y. Cherry blossom and grass edged path, Kokubunji Temple	2·50	1·70
39	80y. Cherry blossom and statue, Zenrakuji Temple	2·50	1·70
40	80y. Cliff face and temple building, Iwayaji Temple	2·50	1·70
41	80y. Decorated footprints, Joururiji Temple	2·50	1·70
42	80y. Spot-lighted statues, Yasakaji Temple	2·50	1·70
43	80y. Lantern, tree, path, gateway and inscribed pillar, Sairinji Temple	2·50	1·70
44	80y. Temple buildings through hole in rock, Kichijoji Temple	2·50	1·70
45	80y. Cherry blossom and roofs, Maegamiji Temple	2·50	1·70
46	80y. Carving with dragon and phoenix, Sankakuji Temple	2·50	1·70
47	80y. Snow-covered roofs and trees, Unbenji Temple	2·50	1·70
48	80y. Wide path, pilgrim and gateway, Shiromineji Temple	2·50	1·70
49	80y. Row of statues, Negoroji Temple	2·50	1·70
50	80y. Lantern, courtyard and building, Ichinomiyaji Temple	2·50	1·70
51	80y. Animal statues and building, Yashimaji Temple	2·50	1·70

Nos. 32-51 were also issued by Tokushima, Kochi and Ehime.

2007. Cultural Heritage. Temples. As T 10 of Ehime Multicoloured.

52	80y. Type **10**	2·50	1·70
53	80y. Gateway	2·50	1·70
54	80y. Square, shrub and main hall	2·50	1·70
55	80y. Trees, temple roof and hill	2·50	1·70
56	80y. Bell tower gate	2·50	1·70
57	80y. Bamboo temple	2·50	1·70
58	80y. Statues, pathway and temple	2·50	1·70
59	80y. Paved path and entrance	2·50	1·70
60	80y. Buddha	2·50	1·70
61	80y. Decorated ceiling and bell	2·50	1·70
62	80y. Temple lit from below	2·50	1·70
63	80y. Paved path, steps and temple	2·50	1·70
64	80y. Guardian statue	2·50	1·70
65	80y. Gateway	2·50	1·70
66	80y. Carved ceiling and bell	2·50	1·70
67	80y. Pagoda and temple at night	2·50	1·70
68	80y. Temple and mountains	2·50	1·70
69	80y. Pilgrims entering gateway	2·50	1·70
70	80y. Pilgrims and temple	2·50	1·70
71	80y. Temple, banners and mountains	2·50	1·70
72	80y. Well	2·50	1·70
73	80y. Kobo Daishi (statue)	2·50	1·70
74	80y. Buddha	2·50	1·70
75	80y. Three roofed pagoda	2·50	1·70
76	80y. Pilgrims, steps and gateway	2·50	1·70
77	80y. Demon	2·50	1·70
78	80y. Rock statues	2·50	1·70
79	80y. Bodhisattva	2·50	1·70
80	80y. Cave and temple at night	2·50	1·70
81	80y. Kobo Daishi (painting)	2·50	1·70

Nos. 52-81 were also issued by Ehime, Tokushima and Kochi on 1 August 2007.

8 Olive   **9** Olive

2010. Prefectural Flowers. Multicoloured.

82	50y. Japanese Iris (Mie)	1·60	1·10
83	50y. Type **8**	1·60	1·10
84	50y. Azalea (Gunma)	1·60	1·10
85	50y. Foxglove tree (Iwate)	1·60	1·10
86	50y. Crinum (Miyazaki)	1·60	1·10
87	80y. Japanese Iris (Mie)	2·50	1·80
88	80y. Type **9**	2·50	1·80
89	80y. Azalea (Gunma)	2·50	1·80
90	80y. Foxglove tree (Iwate)	2·50	1·80
91	80y. Crinum (Miyazaki)	2·50	1·80

Stamps of the same design were issued by Iwate, Gunma, Mie and Miyazaki on 30 April 2010

KAGOSHIMA

1990. Flowers.

| 1 | 62y. As Type **1479** of Japan | 1·20 | 80 |

1 Mount Sakurajima

1990

| 2 | 1 | 62y. multicoloured | 1·30 | 80 |

2 Festival Goers, Ohara

1993

| 3 | 2 | 41y. multicoloured | 1·30 | 90 |

3 Satsuma Ware Bowl

1998. 400th Satsuma-Yaki Festival. Multicoloured.

| 4 | 80y. Type **3** | 2·10 | 1·40 |
| 5 | 80y. Vase | 2·10 | 1·40 |

4 Cycle Ball and Sunset Bridge, Kaseda (for bicycles only)

2001

| 6 | 4 | 80y. multicoloured | 2·50 | 1·70 |

5 Tsubame (800 Series Shinkansen)

2004. Inauguration of Kyushu-Shinkansen Line–Tsubame (high-speed rail line).

| 7 | 5 | 50y. multicoloured | 1·60 | 1·10 |

6 Miyama-Kirishima (azaleas) and Kirishima and Mount Sakurajima mountains (Kagoshima)

2005. Flowers and Scenery of Kyushu (1st series). Multicoloured.

8	50y. Ume Blossom and Dazaifu-Tenmangu Shrine (Fukuoka)	1·60	1·10
9	50y. Sakura (cherry blossoms) and Kanmon bridge (Fukuoka)	1·60	1·10
10	50y. Kusunohana (camphor blossoms) and Ariake Sea (Saga)	1·60	1·10
11	50y. Unzen-Tsutsuji (azaleas) and Mt. Fugendake (Nagasaki)	1·60	1·10
12	50y. Tulips and Huis Ten Bosch (Nagasaki)	1·60	1·10
13	50y. Rindou (gentians) and Mt. Aso (Kumamoto)	1·60	1·10
14	50y. Ume blossoms and Mt. Takasaki (Ooita)	1·60	1·10
15	50y. Hamayu (crinums) and Nichinan beach (Miyazaki)	1·60	1·10
16	50y. Type **6**	1·60	1·10
17	50y. Hibiscus and Adan (screw-pine) (Kagoshima)	1·60	1·10

Nos. 8-17 were also issued by Fukuoka, Nagasaki, Saga, Miyazaki, Kumamoto and Oita.

7 Field of yellow flowers and Mt. Kaimondake (Kagoshima)

2006. Flowers and Scenery of Kyushu (2nd series). Multicoloured.

18	80y. Daffodils and Nokon-oshima Island (Fukuoka)	2·50	1·70
19	80y. Chinese bellflowers and Hiraodai (Fukuoka)	2·50	1·70
20	80y. Hydrangeas and Mikaeri-notaki fall (Saga)	2·50	1·70
21	80y. Cosmos and Kujukushima islands (Nagasaki)	2·50	1·70
22	80y. Camellias and the five bridges of Amakusa (Kumamoto)	2·50	1·70
23	80y. Purple flowers and Mt. Aso (Kumamoto)	2·50	1·70
24	80y. Primroses and Mt. Yufudake (Oita)	2·50	1·70
25	80y. Lavender and Kujurenzan (Oita)	2·50	1·70
26	80y. Poppies and Mt. Hinamori-dake (Miyazaki)	2·50	1·70
27	80y. Type **7**	2·50	1·70

Nos. 18-27 were also issued by Fukuoka, Nagasaki, Saga, Kumamoto, Oita and Miyazaki.

8 *Rhododendron kiusianum*   **9** *Rhododendron kiusianum*

2011. Prefectural Flowers. Multicoloured.

28	50y. *Rosa* (Ibaraki)	1·80	1·20
29	50y. *Malus pumila* (Aomori)	1·80	1·20
30	50y. *Primula sieboldii* (Saitama)	1·80	1·20
31	50y. *Citrus natsudaidai* (Yamaguchi)	1·80	1·20
32	50y. Type **10**	1·80	1·20
33	80y. *Rosa* (Ibaraki)	2·75	1·90
34	80y. *Malus pumila* (Aomori)	2·75	1·90
35	80y. *Primula sieboldii* (Saitama)	2·75	1·90
36	80y. *Citrus natsudaidai* (Yamaguchi)	2·75	1·90
37	80y. Type **11**	2·75	1·90

Stamps of the same design were issued by Aomori, Ibaraki, Saitama and Yamaguchi on 8 February 2011.

KANAGAWA

1 Doll

1989

| 1 | 1 | 62y. multicoloured | | |

1990. Flowers.

| 2 | 62y. As Type **1447** of Japan | 1·30 | 90 |

2 Shasui Waterfall (Shasui-no-taki)

1992

| 3 | 2 | 62y. multicoloured | 1·20 | 80 |

3 Flowers,
Sengokubara
Marsh

1996

4	3	80y. multicoloured	2·10	1·40

4 Tunnel
Entrance

1997. Tokyo-Wan Aqualine. Multicoloured.

5		80y. Type **4**	1·80	1·20
6		80y. Tunnel entrance (different)	1·80	1·20

Nos. 5-6 were also issued by Chiba.

5 Minamoto no
Yoritomo

1999

7	**5**	80y. multicoloured	2·10	1·40

6 Decorated
Bamboo
Banners

2000. Hiratsuka Tanabata Festival. Multicoloured.

8		50y. Type **6**	1·50	1·00
9		50y. Father and child	1·50	1·00

7 Castle and
Chrysanthemums

2000. Odwara Castle. Multicoloured.

10		50y. Type **7**	1·80	1·20
11		50y. Blossom, gate and castle	1·80	1·20

8 Ship in Dock

2002. Yokohama, Port Town. Multicoloured.

12		50y. Type **8**	1·50	1·00
13		50y. Port, ship and woman in Victorian dress	1·50	1·00

9 Rose and
Buildings at
Night, 21 Area

2004. Tourism. Multicoloured.

14		50y. Type **9**	1·60	1·10
15		50y. Lily, Kanagawa Prefectural Government, Yokohama Customs, and Yokohama Memorial Museum buildings	1·60	1·10
16		50y. Wisterias and Enoshima Island	1·60	1·10
17		50y. Hydrangea and Lake Ashinoko, Hakone	1·60	1·10

10 Azaleas,
Eboshi-iwa and
Minato-Mirai
Mount Fuji

2004. Flowers. Multicoloured.

18		80y. Type **10**	2·10	1·40
19		80y. Daffodils and avenue of pines, Sakawagawa river	2·10	1·40
20		80y. Pinks and Tanzawa mountains	2·10	1·40
21		80y. Balloon flowers and Mt. Fuji	2·10	1·40

11 Lily

2008. Flowers. Multicoloured.

22		50y. Type **11**	1·60	1·10
23		50y. Sweet briar	1·60	1·10
24		50y. Nemotoshakunage (*Rhododendron brachycarpum*)	1·60	1·10
25		50y. Safflower	1·60	1·10
26		50y. Gentian	1·60	1·10
27		80y. Lily (25×35 mm)	2·50	1·70
28		80y. Sweet briar (25×35 mm)	2·50	1·70
29		80y. Rhodedendron (25×35 mm)	2·50	1·70
30		80y. Safflower (25×35 mm)	2·50	1·70
31		80y. Gentian (25×35 mm)	2·50	1·70

Nos. 22-31 were also issued by Fukushima, Hokkaido, Nagano and Yamagata on 1 July 2008.

12 Standard
Bearers and
Dancers

2008. Hokone Procession Festival. Multicoloured.

31a		50y. Type **11**	1·70	1·30
31b		50y. Three men	1·70	1·30

Nos. 32-3 were printed *se-tenant*, each pair forming a composite design..

2010. National Afforestation Campaign. Multicoloured.

32		50y. Type **12**	1·80	1·30
33		50y. Sugi (*Cryptomeria japonica*)	1·80	1·30
34		50y. Sawtooth oak	1·80	1·30
35		50y. Japanese maple	1·80	1·30
36		50y. *Lilium auratum*	1·80	1·30
37		50y. Bamboo-leaf oak	1·80	1·30
38		50y. *Castanopsis sieboldii*	1·80	1·30
39		50y. Gingko	1·80	1·30
40		50y. Japanese beech	1·80	1·30
41		50y. Japanese gentian	1·80	1·30

KOCHI

1990

1		62y. As Type **1472** of Japan	1·90	1·30

1 Man and
Child riding on
Whale

1991

2	**1**	62y. multicoloured	1·80	80

2 Lighthouse

1995

3	**2**	80y. multicoloured	1·90	1·30

3 Cliff-top
Teahouse and
Gateway,
Katsura Beach

1999. Sakamoto Ryoma (warrior and naval pioneer). Multicoloured.

4		80y. Type **3**	2·20	1·50
5		80y. Whale tail, telescope and Sakamoto Ryoma	2·20	1·50

4 Kochi Castle

2001. Kochi Castle and Sunday Market. Multicoloured.

6		80y. Type **4**	2·40	1·60
7		80y. Sunday market	2·40	1·60

5 Yamamomo
(bayberry) and
Tengu Highland
(Kochi)

2002. Multicoloured.

8		50y. Type **5**	1·50	1·00
9		50y. Sudachi (sour citrus fruit) and Mt. Tsurugisan (Tokushima)	1·50	1·00
10		50y. Mikan (mandarin oranges) and Sata-misaki Promontory (Ehime)	1·50	1·00
11		50y. Olive and Shodoshima island (Kagawa)	1·50	1·00

Nos. 8-11 were also issued by Ehime, Tokushima and Kagawa.

6 Runners

2002. 57th National Athletic Meet.

12	**6**	50y. multicoloured	1·60	1·10

2005. Cultural Heritage. Shizuoka Temples. Multicoloured.

13		80y. As Type **8** of Ehime	2·50	1·70
14		80y. Seated Buddha, Anrakuji Temple	2·50	1·70
15		80y. Inscribed belfry gateway, Jurakuji Temple	2·50	1·70
16		80y. Double roofed gateway, Kumadaniji Temple	2·50	1·70
17		80y. Pagoda, Yakuoji Temple	2·50	1·70
18		80y. Statues, ramp, lanterns and pagoda, Hotsumisakiji Temple	2·50	1·70
19		80y. Gateway and long steep steps, Shinjouji Temple	2·50	1·70
20		80y. Path, gateway, steps and main temple, Kongochoji Temple	2·50	1·70
21		80y. Buddha seated on peacock, Ryukoji Temple	2·50	1·70
22		80y. Bell and autumn colour, Butsumokuji Temple	2·50	1·70
23		80y. Dragon, Meisekiji Temple	2·50	1·70
24		80y. Steps and many roofed buildings, Daihouji Temple	2·50	1·70
25		80y. Carved decorative gable, Kokubunji Temple	2·50	1·70
26		80y. Leafless tree and snow-covered building, Yokomineji Temple	2·50	1·70
27		80y. Buddha, Kouonji Temple	2·50	1·70
28		80y. Courtyard and building, Houjuji Temple	2·50	1·70
29		80y. Inscribed pillars and gateway, Douryuji Temple	2·50	1·70
30		80y. Wall mounted statues, Goushouji Temple	2·50	1·70
31		80y. Eagle surmounting gateway, Tennouji Temple	2·50	1·70
32		80y. Courtyard with stone lined path and building, Kokubunji Temple	2·50	1·70

Nos. 13-32 were also issued by Ehime, Tokushima and Kagawa.

2006. Cultural Heritage. Temples. Multicoloured.

33		80y. As Type **9** of Ehime	2·50	1·70
34		80y. Kirihata-ji (statue), Kirihata Temple	2·50	1·70
35		80y. Cherry blossom and building, Fujiidera Temple2	50	1·70
36		80y. Snow-covered pagoda and temple, Shozanji Temple	2·50	1·70
37		80y. Wide path, inscribed pillar and gateway, Konomineji Temple	2·50	1·70
38		80y. Decorative carved roof boss and bell, Dainichiji Temple	2·50	1·70
39		80y. Cherry blossom and grass edged path, Kokubunji Temple	2·50	1·70
40		80y. Cherry blossom and statue, Zenrakuji Temple	2·50	1·70
41		80y. Cliff face and temple building, Iwayaji Temple	2·50	1·70
42		80y. Decorated footprints, Joururiji Temple	2·50	1·70
43		80y. Spot-lighted statues, Yasakaji Temple	2·50	1·70
44		80y. Lantern, tree, gateway and inscribed pillar, Sairinji Temple	2·50	1·70
45		80y. Temple buildings through hole in rock, Kichijoji Temple	2·50	1·70
46		80y. Cherry blossom and roofs, Maegamiji Temple	2·50	1·70
47		80y. Carving with dragon and phoenix, Sankakuji Temple	2·50	1·70
48		80y. Snow-covered roofs and trees, Unbenji Temple	2·50	1·70
49		80y. Wide path, pilgrim and gateway, Shiromineji Temple	2·50	1·70
50		80y. Row of statues, Negoroji Temple	2·50	1·70
51		80y. Lantern, courtyard and building, Ichinomiyaji Temple	2·50	1·70
52		80y. Animal statues and building, Yashimaji Temple	2·50	1·70

Nos. 33-52 were also issued by Tokushima, Ehimei and Kagawa.

2007. Cultural Heritage. Temples. As T **10** of Ehime. Multicoloured.

53		80y. Type **10**	2·50	1·70
54		80y. Gateway	2·50	1·70
55		80y. Square, shrub and main hall	2·50	1·70
56		80y. Trees, temple roof and hill	2·50	1·70
57		80y. Bell tower gate	2·50	1·70
58		80y. Bamboo temple	2·50	1·70
59		80y. Statues, pathway and temple	2·50	1·70
60		80y. Paved path and entrance	2·50	1·70
61		80y. Buddha	2·50	1·70
62		80y. Decorated ceiling and bell	2·50	1·70
63		80y. Temple lit from below	2·50	1·70
64		80y. Paved path, steps and temple	2·50	1·70
65		80y. Guardian statue	2·50	1·70
66		80y. Gateway	2·50	1·70
67		80y. Carved ceiling and bell	2·50	1·70
68		80y. Pagoda and temple at night	2·50	1·70
69		80y. Temple and mountains	2·50	1·70
70		80y. Pilgrims entering gateway	2·50	1·70
71		80y. Pilgrims and temple	2·50	1·70
72		80y. Temple, banners and mountains	2·50	1·70
73		80y. Well	2·50	1·70
74		80y. Kobo Daishi (statue)	2·50	1·70
75		80y. Buddha	2·50	1·70
76		80y. Three roofed pagoda	2·50	1·70
77		80y. Pilgrims, steps and gateway	2·50	1·70
78		80y. Demon	2·50	1·70
79		80y. Rock statues	2·50	1·70
80		80y. Bodhisattva	2·50	1·70
81		80y. Cave and temple at night	2·50	1·70
82		80y. Kobo Daishi (painting)	2·50	1·70

Nos. 53-82 were also issued by Ehime, Kagawa and Tokushima on 1 August 2007.

7 Bayberry   **8** Bayberry

2009. Prefectural Flowers. Multicoloured.

83		50y. Peach blossom (Okayama)	1·70	1·30
84		50y. Rape flowers (Chiba)	1·70	1·30
85		50y. Plum blossom and primula (Osaka)	1·70	1·30
86		50y. Type **7** (Kochi)	1·70	1·30
87		50y. Ume blossom (*Prunus mume* var. bungo) (Oita)	1·70	1·30
88		80y. Peach blossom (Okayama) (different)	2·75	1·70

89	80y. Rape flowers (Chiba) (different)	2·75	1·70
90	80y. Plum blossom and primula (Osaka) (different)	2·75	1·70
91	80y. Type 8 (Kochi)	2·75	1·70
92	80y. Ume blossom (*Prunus mume* var. bungo) (Oita) (different)	2·75	1·70

Stamps of the same design were issued by Chiba, Oita, Okayama and Osaka on 1 Dec 2009..

KUMAMOTO

1 Kumamoto Castle

1989

1	1	62y. multicoloured	1·30	60

1990. Flowers.

2		62y. As Type **1476** of Japan	1·20	80

2 Aqueduct discharging Water, Tsujun-kyo

1991

3	2	62y. multicoloured	1·50	90

3 Boy

1996. Ushibuka-haiya Festival.

4	3	80y. multicoloured	1·80	1·20

4 Globe and Ball

1997. World Men's Handball Championship.

5	4	50y. multicoloured	2·10	1·40

5 Traditional Fishing Boat

1999

6	5	80y. multicoloured	2·10	1·40

6 Yachiyoza Theatre

2002

7	6	80y. multicoloured	2·20	1·50

7 Rindou (gentians) and Mt. Aso (Kumamoto)

8 Camellias and Five Bridges of Amakusa (Kumamoto)

2005. Flowers and Scenery of Kyushu (1st series). Multicoloured.

8	50y. Ume Blossom and Dazaifu-Tenmangu Shrine (Fukuoka)	1·60	1·10
9	50y. Sakura (cherry blossoms) and Kanmon bridge (Fukuoka)	1·60	1·10
10	50y. Kusunohana (camphor blossoms) and Ariake Sea (Saga)	1·60	1·10
11	50y. Unzen-Tsutsuji (azaleas) and Mt. Fugendake (Nagasaki)	1·60	1·10
12	50y. Tulips and Huis Ten Bosch (Nagasaki)	1·60	1·10
13	50y. Type **7**	1·60	1·10
14	50y. Ume blossoms and Mt. Takasaki (Ooita)	1·60	1·10
15	50y. Hamayu (crinums) and Nichinan beach (Miyazaki)	1·60	1·10
16	50y. Miyama-Kirishima (azaleas) and Kirishima mountains (Kagoshima)	1·60	1·10
17	50y. Hibiscus and Adan (screw-pine) (Kagoshima)	1·60	1·10

Nos. 8-17 were also issued by Fukuoka, Nagasaki, Saga, Miyazaki, Oita and Kagoshima.

2006. Flowers and Scenery of Kyushu (2nd series). Multicoloured.

18	80y. Daffodils and Nokon-oshima Island (Fukuoka)	2·20	1·50
19	80y. Chinese bellflowers and Hiraodai (Fukuoka)	2·20	1·50
20	80y. Hydrangeas and Mikaeri-notaki fall (Saga)	2·20	1·50
21	80y. Cosmos and Kujukushima islands (Nagasaki)	2·20	1·50
22	80y. Type **8**	2·20	1·50
23	80y. Purple flowers and Mt. Aso (Kumamoto)	2·20	1·50
24	80y. Primroses and Mt. Yu-fudake (Oita)	2·20	1·50
25	80y. Lavender and Kujurenzan (Oita)	2·20	1·50
26	80y. Poppies and Mt. Hinamori-dake (Miyazaki)	2·20	1·50
27	80y. Field of yellow flowers and Mt. Kaimondake (Kagoshima)	2·20	1·50

Nos. 18-27 were also issued by Fukuoka, Nagasaki, Saga, Oita, Miyazaki and Kagoshima
Nos. 20/5 are vacant

9 Tower and Cherry Blossom

2007. 400th Anniv of Kumamoto Castle. Multicoloured.

28	80y. Type **9**	2·50	1·70
29	80y. Castle and lawn	2·50	1·70
30	80y. Castle in autumn	2·50	1·70
31	80y. Castle in snow	2·50	1·70
32	80y. Roof tops	2·50	1·70

10 Gentian   **11** Gentian

2009. Prefectural Flowers. Multicoloured.

32	50y. Type **10** (Kumamoto)	1·70	1·30
33	50y. Wild chrysanthemum (Hyogo)	1·70	1·30
34	50y. Bush clover blossom (Miyagi)	1·70	1·30
35	50y. Fritillary (*Fritillaria camschatcensis*) (Ishikawa)	1·70	1·30
36	50y. Maple (Hiroshima)	1·70	1·30
37	80y. Type **11** (Kumamoto)	2·75	1·70
38	80y. Wild chrysanthemum (Hyogo) (different)	2·75	1·70
39	80y. Bush clover blossom (Miyagi) (different)	2·75	1·70
40	80y. Fritillary (*Fritillaria camschatcensis*) (Ishikawa) (different)	2·75	1·70
41	80y. Maple (Hiroshima) (different)	2·75	1·70

Stamps of the same design were issued by Hyogo, Ishikawa, Hiroshima and Miyagi on 1 July 2009.

KYOTO

1990. Flowers.

1		62y. As Type **1459** of Japan	3·00	2·00

1 Maiko (apprentice geisha)

1990

2	1	62y. multicoloured	1·20	80

2 Ushiwaka-maru (Aikido master)

1995

3	2	80y. multicoloured	1·90	1·30

3 Kyoto University

1997

4	3	80y. multicoloured	2·10	1·40

4 Hiyoshi Dam

1998

5	4	80y. multicoloured	2·10	1·40

5 Amanohashidate Sand Bar

1999

6	5	80y. multicoloured	2·10	1·40

6 Cherry Blossoms, Maruyama Park (spring)

2000. Four Seasons. Multicoloured.

7	80y. Type **6**	2·75	1·90
8	80y. Kamogawa river (summer)	2·75	1·90
9	80y. Togetsukyo bridge, Arashi-yama (autumn)	2·75	1·90
10	80y. Cedar forest, Kitayama (winter)	2·75	1·90

7 Carriage decorated with Japanese Wisteria

2003. Traditional Events in Kyoto. Multicoloured.

11	50y. Type **7**	1·60	1·10
12	50y. Gion-masturi (festival float)	1·60	1·10
13	50y. Okuribi (fire to send off spirits at Mt. Nyoig)	1·60	1·10
14	50y. Jidai-matsuri (royal carriage)	1·60	1·10

8 Shidare-zakura (weeping cherry) Aoi-matsuri Festival (Kyoto)

2006. Flowers of Kinki. Multicoloured.

15	50y. Type **8**	1·60	1·10
16	50y. Sakuraso (primrose) (Osaka)	1·60	1·10
17	50y. Yae-zakura (double cherry blossoms) (Nara)	1·60	1·10
18	50y. Nozigiku (wild chrysanthemums) (Hyogo)	1·60	1·10
19	50y. Shakunage (rhododendron) (Shiga)	1·60	1·10
20	50y. Ume blossoms (Wakayama)	1·60	1·10

Nos. 15-20 were also issued by Osaka, Nara, Shiga, Wakayama and Hyogo.

9 Weeping Cherry Blossom

2008. Prefectural Flowers. Multicoloured.

21	50y. Narcissus (Fukui)	1·60	1·10
22	50y. Pink plum blossom (Wakayama)	1·60	1·10
23	50y. Fuki (*Petasites japonicus*) (Akita)	1·60	1·10
24	50y. White plum blossom (Fukuoka)	1·60	1·10
25	50y. Type **9**	1·60	1·10
26	80y. Narcissus (Fukui)	2·50	1·70
27	80y. White plum blossom (Wakayama)	2·50	1·70
28	80y. Fuki (*Petasites japonicus*) (Akita)	2·50	1·70
29	80y. Pink plum blossom (Fukuoka)	2·50	1·70
30	80y. Weeping cherry blossom (Kyoto)	2·50	1·70

MIE

1990. Flowers.

1		62y. As Type **1457** of Japan	1·20	80

1 Ninja

1991

2	1	62y. multicoloured	1·50	90

2 Meoto-iwa (wedded rocks) and Plovers, Futami-ga-ura

1994

3	2	80y. multicoloured	1·90	1·30

3 Hamayu (crinum) Blossom

1996. Multicoloured.

4	80y. Type **3**	1·80	1·20
5	80y. Ama divers	1·80	1·20

4 Trees and Mountains

1999. Kumano Old Path. Multicoloured.

6	80y. Type **4**	2·10	1·40
7	80y. Trees and shoreline	2·10	1·40
8	80y. Pathway	2·10	1·40
9	80y. Scree	2·10	1·40

5 Free Fall

2000. World Parachuting Championships. Multicoloured.

10	80y. Type **5**	2·75	1·90
11	80y. Parachutist	2·75	1·90

Nos. 10-11 were issued together, se-tenant, forming a composite design.

6 Matsuo Basho (haiku poet) and Iga-ueno Castle

2002. Iga-Ueno. Multicoloured.

12	80y. Type **6**	2·20	1·50
13	80y. Iga-Ueno castle and Haisei-den hall	2·20	1·50

Nos. 12-13 were issued together, *se-tenant*, forming a composite design.

7 Ozu Yasujiro and Mitchell Camera

2003. Birth Centenary of Ozu Yasujiro (film director).

14	**7**	80y. multicoloured	2·20	1·50

8 Iris and Couple Rock

2007. Flowers and Scenry of Tokai. Multicoloured.

15	80y. Type **8**	2·50	1·70
16	80y. Iris	2·50	1·70
17	80y. Gasshó-zukuri houses and vetch flowers	2·50	1·70
18	80y. Lily and Nagoya Castle	2·50	1·70
19	80y. Azalea and coastline, Jogasaki	2·50	1·70

Nos. 15-19 were also issued by Aichi, Gifu and Shizuoka on 2 April 2007.

Nos. 20/5 are vacant.

9 Japanese Iris **10**

2010. Prefectural Flowers. Multicoloured.

26	50y. Type **9**	1·60	1·10
27	50y. Olive (Kagawa)	1·60	1·10
28	50y. Azalea (Gunma)	1·60	1·10
29	50y. Foxglove tree (Iwate)	1·60	1·10
30	0y. Crinum (Miyazaki)	1·60	1·10
31	80y. Type **10**	2·50	1·70
32	80y. Olive (Kagawa)	2·50	1·70
33	80y. Azalea (Gunma)	2·50	1·70
34	80y. Foxglove tree (Iwate)	2·50	1·70
35	80y. Crinum (Miyazaki)	2·50	1·70

Stamps of the same design were issued by Iwate, Kagawa, Gunma and Miyazaki on 30 April 2010.

MIYAGI

1990. Flowers.

1	62y. As Type **1437** of Japan	1·20	80

1 Swans

1990

2	**1**	62y. multicoloured	1·50	80

2 Coastline, Matsushima

1994

3	**2**	80y. multicoloured	1·30	80

3 Zalkova (Japanese elm) Trees

1995

4	**3**	50y. multicoloured	1·30	80

4 Festival Goers and Banners

1999. Summer Festivals. Multicoloured.

5	80y. Type **4**	2·10	1·40
6	80y. Streamers	2·10	1·40

Nos. 5-6 were issued together, se-tenant, forming a composite design.
Nos. 5/6 were also issued by Fukishima.

5 Cherry Tree

2000. Cherry Trees. Multicoloured.

7	80y. Type **5**	2·50	1·70
8	80y. Group of trees with spreading branches, Yamagata	2·50	1·70
9	80y. Group of trees, Fukishima	2·50	1·70
10	80y. Tree, central, Iwate	2·50	1·70
11	80y. Cherry blossom, Aomori	2·50	1·70
12	80y. Trees and river, Akita	2·50	1·70

Nos. 7-12 were also issued by Yamagata, Iwate, Aomori, Akita and Fukishima.

6 Float and Festival Dancers

2001. 400th Anniv of Sendai.

13	**6**	80y. multicoloured	2·50	1·70

7 Volleyball Players and Bush Clover

2001. 56th National Athletic Meet.

14	**7**	50y. multicoloured	2·10	1·40

8 Japanese Bush Clover (Miyagi)

2004. Prefectural Flowers. Multicoloured.

15	50y. Type **8**	1·60	1·10
16	50y. Apple blossom (Aomori)	1·60	1·10
17	50y. Paulownia (Iwate)	1·60	1·10
18	50y. Butterbur flower (Akita)	1·60	1·10
19	50y. Safflower (Yamagata)	1·60	1·10
20	50y. Alpine rose (*Rhododendron ferrugineum*) (Fukushima)	1·60	1·10

Nos. 15-20 were also issued by Yamagata, Aomori, Miyagi, Iwate and Fukishima.

8 Sendai Tanabata Matsuri (Miyagi)

2006. Festivals of Tohuku. Multicoloured.

21	80y. Type **9**	2·50	1·70
22	80y. Kanto Matsuri (Akita)	2·50	1·70
23	80y. Hanagasa Matsuri (Yamagata)	2·50	1·70
24	80y. Nebuta Matsuri (Aomori)	2·50	1·70

Nos. 21-4 were also issued by Akita, Aomori, and Yamagata.

10 Matsushima Island and Rape Flowers

2007. North Eastern Scenery. Multicoloured.

25	80y. Type **10**	2·50	1·70
26	80y. Oirase stream	2·50	1·70
27	80y. Hirosaki Castle	2·50	1·70
28	80y. Chusonji Temple	2·50	1·70
29	80y. Rocks and lily (sukashiyuri)	2·50	1·70
30	80y. Dicentra and water filled crater	2·50	1·70
31	80y. Oga penisula and pinks	2·50	1·70
32	80y. Lily (nikkoukisuge) and mountain	2·50	1·70
33	80y. Skunk cabbage flowers, Oze National Park	2·50	1·70
34	80y. Safflower	2·50	1·70

Nos. 25-34 were also issued by Akita, Aomori, Fukushima, Iwate and Yamaguchi on 2 July 2007.

11-12 Lanterns

2008. Tanabata Festival. Multicoloured.

35	50y. Type **11**	1·60	1·10
36	50y. Type **12**	1·60	1·10
37	50y. Procession and roofs, left	1·60	1·10
38	50y. Procession and roofs, right	1·60	1·10
39	50y. Dancers, left	1·60	1·10
40	50y. Dancers, right	1·60	1·10
41	50y. Procession, left	1·60	1·10
42	50y. Procession, right	1·60	1·10
43	50y. Drummers, left	1·60	1·10
44	50y. Drummers, right	1·60	1·10

Nos. 35-6, 37-8, 39-40, 41-2 and 43-4 were issued together, *se-tenant*, each pair forming a composite design.
Nos. 35-44 were also issued by Tokushima, Okinawa, Tokyo and Fukuoka on 1 August 2008.

13 Bush Clover Blossom **14** Bush Clover Blossom

2009. Prefectural Flowers. Multicoloured.

44	50y. Gentian (Kumamoto)	1·70	1·30

45	50y. Wild chrysanthemum (Hyogo)	1·70	1·30
46	50y. Type **13** (Miyagi)	1·70	1·30
47	50y. Fritillaria (*Fritillaria camschatcensis*) (Ishikawa)	1·70	1·30
48	50y. Maple (Hiroshima)	1·70	1·30
49	80y. Gentian (Kumamoto) (different)	2·75	1·70
50	80y. Wild chrysanthemum (Hyogo) (different)	2·75	1·70
51	80y. Type **14** (Miyagi)	2·75	1·70
52	80y. Fritillary (*Fritillaria camschatcensis*) (Ishikawa) (different)	2·75	1·70
53	80y. Maple (Hiroshima) (different)	2·75	1·70

Stamps of the same design were issued by Hyogo, Ishikawa, Kumamoto and Hiroshima on 1 July 2009.

MIYAZAKI

1990. Flowers.

1	62y. As Type **1478** of Japan	1·20	80

1 Horses and Coastline, Toi-misaki

1991

2	**1**	62y. multicoloured	2·10	1·40

2 Drummer

1996. Shimozuru Usudaiko Odori.

3	**2**	80y. multicoloured	2·10	1·40

3 Nichinan Taihei Dance

1999. Obi Town. Multicoloured.

4	80y. Type **3**	2·10	1·40
5	80y. Building and statue	2·10	1·40

4 Sekino'o-taki Waterfall

2000. Landscapes. Multicoloured.

6	80y. Type **4**	2·75	1·80
7	80y. Kirishima volcano	2·75	1·80

Nos. 6-7 were issued together, se-tenant, forming a composite design.

5 Noh Theatre

2003. Nobeoka–City of Noh. Multicoloured.

8	80y. Type **5**	2·40	1·60
9	80y. Tenkaichi Takigi-Noh (traditional dance)	2·40	1·60

6 Flowering Tree and Mountains

2004. National Afforestation Campaign.

10	**6**	50y. multicoloured	1·60	1·10

7 Hamayu (crinums) and Nichinan Beach (Miyazaki)

2005. Flowers and Scenery of Kyushu (1st series). Multicoloured.

11	50y. Type **7**	1·60	1·10
12	50y. Sakura (cherry blossoms) and Kanmon bridge (Fukuoka)	1·60	1·10
13	50y. Kusunohana (camphor blossoms) and Ariake Sea (Saga)	1·60	1·10
14	50y. Unzen-Tsutsuji (azaleas) and Mt. Fugendake (Nagasaki)	1·60	1·10
15	50y. Tulips and Huis Ten Bosch (Nagasaki)	1·60	1·10
16	50y. Rindou (gentians) and Mt. Aso (Kumamoto)	1·60	1·10
17	50y. Ume blossoms and Mt. Takasaki (Ooita)	1·60	1·10
18	50y. Ume blossom and Dazaifu-Tenmangu Shrine (Fukuoka)	1·60	1·10
19	50y. Miyama-Kirishima (azaleas) and Kirishima mountains (Kagoshima)	1·60	1·10
20	50y. Hibiscus and Adan (screw-pine) (Kagoshima)	1·60	1·10

Nos. 11-20 were also issued by Fukuoka, Nagasaki, Saga, Oita, Kumamoto and Kagoshima.

8 Poppies and Mt. Hinamoridake (Miyazaki)

2006. Flowers and Scenery of Kyushu (2nd series). Multicoloured.

21	80y. Daffodils and Nokon-oshima Island (Fukuoka)	2·40	1·60
22	80y. Chinese bellflowers and Hiraodai (Fukuoka)	2·40	1·60
23	80y. Hydrangeas and Mikaeri-notaki fall (Saga)	2·40	1·60
24	80y. Cosmos and Kujukushima islands (Nagasaki)	2·40	1·60
25	80y. Camellias and the five bridges of Amakusa (Ku-mamoto)	2·40	1·60
26	80y. Purple flowers and Mt. Aso (Kumamoto)	2·40	1·60
27	80y. Primroses and Mt. Yu-fudake (Oita)	2·40	1·60
28	80y. Lavender and Kujurenzan (Oita)	2·40	1·60
29	80y. Type **8**	2·40	1·60
30	80y. Field of yellow flowers and Mt. Kaimondake (Kagoshima)	2·40	1·60

Nos. 21-30 were also issued by Fukuoka, Nagasaki, Saga, Kumamoto, Oita and Kagoshima.

9 Crinum   **10** Crinum

2010. Prefectural Flowers. Multicoloured.

31	50y. Japanese Iris (Mie)	1·70	1·20
32	50y. Olive (Kagawa)	1·70	1·20
33	50y. Azalea (Gunma)	1·70	1·20
34	50y. Foxglove tree (Iwate)	1·70	1·20
35	50y. Type **9**	1·70	1·20
36	80y. Japanese Iris (Mie)	2·50	1·70
37	80y. Olive (Kagawa)	2·50	1·70
38	80y. Azalea (Gunma)	2·50	1·70
39	80y. Foxglove tree (Iwate)	2·50	1·70
40	80y. Type **10**	2·50	1·70

Stamps of the same design were issued by Iwate, Ka-gawa, Mie and Gunma on 30 April 2010.

NAGANO

1 Monkeys

1989

1	**1**	62y. multicoloured	1·50	80

1990. Flowers.

2		62y. As Type **1449** of Japan	3·75	2·50

2 Tsumago Inn

1990. Inns.

3	**2**	62y. ochre and brown	1·50	80
4	-	62y. yellow and brown	1·50	80

DESIGNS: No. 3 Type **2**; No. 4 Magome.

3 Matsumoto-jo Castle

1993

5	**3**	62y. multicoloured	1·50	1·00

4 Building, Kashiwabara

1994

6	**4**	80y. multicoloured	1·90	1·10

5 Conductor and Orchestra

1996. Saito Kinen Festival.

7	**5**	80y. multicoloured	2·10	1·40

6 Campanula Flowers

1996. Rindo.

8	**6**	80y. multicoloured	2·10	1·40

7 Jomon's Venus

1998

9	**7**	80y. multicoloured	2·10	1·40

8 Horse Rider

1998. Puppetry Festival. Multicoloured.

10	50y. Type **8**	1·30	90
11	50y. Bird and man	1·30	90

Nos. 10-11 were issued together, *se-tenant*, forming a composite design.

9 Kiso Observatory, Tokyo University

1999

12	**9**	80y. multicoloured	2·10	1·40

10 Matsumoto Castle

1999

13	**10**	80y. multicoloured	2·10	1·40

1999. Inns. As T **2**.

14	62y. ochre and brown	2·10	1·40
15	62y. yellow and brown	2·10	1·40

DESIGNS: No. 14 Tsumago (As Type **2**); No. 15 Magome (As No. **4**).

1999

16	**1**	80y. multicoloured	2·10	1·40

11 Cherry Blossom

2000

17	**11**	80y. multicoloured	2·40	1·60

12 Azumino

2000

18	**12**	80y. multicoloured	2·40	1·60

13 Fishing and Score

2000. Shinano-no-kuni (prefecture song). Multicoloured.

19	50y. Type **13**	1·60	1·10
20	50y. Autumnal trees, bridge and score	1·60	1·10

14 Zenkoji Temple

2001. Nagano Homeland. Multicoloured.

21	50y. Type **14**	2·50	1·70
22	50y. Mt. Iizunayama and apple blossoms	2·50	1·70

Nos. 21-2 were issued together, *se-tenant*, forming a composite design.

15 Dog's Tooth Violet Hakuba Mountains (Chushin area)

16 Apple Blossom

2005. Flora. Multicoloured.

27	50y. Type **16**	1·60	1·10
28	50y. Renge-tsutsuji (renge azalea)	1·60	1·10
29	50y. Suzuran (lily of the valley)	1·60	1·10
30	50y. Rindou (gentian)	1·60	1·10

17 Mountains of Echigo

2006. Nature of Shin'etsu. Multicoloured.

31	80y. Type **17**	2·10	1·40
32	80y. Sankayou (*Diphylleia cymosa*)	2·10	1·40
33	80y. Mt. Asamayama	2·10	1·40
34	80y. Sakurasou (*Primula sieboldii*)	2·10	1·40

Nos. 31-4 were also issued by Niigata.

18 Gentian

2008. Flowers. Multicoloured.

35	50y. Type **18**	1·60	1·10
36	50y. Lily	1·60	1·10
37	50y. Sweet briar	1·60	1·10
38	50y. Nemotoshakunage (*Rhodo-dendron brachycarpum*)	1·60	1·10
39	50y. Safflower	1·60	1·10
40	80y. Lily (25×35 mm)	2·50	1·70
41	80y. Sweet briar (25×35 mm)	2·50	1·70
42	80y. Rhodedendron (25×35 mm)	2·50	1·70
43	80y. Safflower (25×35 mm)	2·50	1·70
44	80y. Gentian (25×35 mm)	2·50	1·70

Nos. 35-44 were also issued by Fukushima, Hokkaido, Kanagawa and Yamagata on 1 July 2008.

NAGASAKI

1990. Flowers.

1	62y. As Type **1475** of Japan	1·20	80

1 Ship and Gateway

1990. Journey Expo.

2	**1**	62y. multicoloured	1·20	80

2 Dragon Dance, Kunci Festival

1994

3	**2**	62y. multicoloured	1·90	1·30

1997. Fukuoka. Multicoloured.

4	80y. Fukuoka Type **4**	1·80	1·20
5	80y. Early rail way and map	1·80	1·20
6	80y. Interchange and map	1·80	1·20
7	80y. Building and map	1·80	1·20

Nos. 4-7 were issued together, se-tenant, forming a composite design.

Nos. 4-7 were also issued by Saga and Fukuoka.

2003. Flora. Multicoloured.

23	50y. Type **15**	1·60	1·10
24	50y. Skunk cabbage and Okususobana-shizen'en (Hokushin area)	1·60	1·10
25	50y. Lilies and Mt. Kirigamine (Nanshin area)	1·60	1·10
26	50y. Cosmos and Cosmos highway (Toshin area)	1·60	1·10

3 Mount Heisei Shinzan

1998
| 8 | 3 | 80y. multicoloured | 2·10 | 1·40 |

4 Dejima (artificial island)

1999
| 9 | 4 | 80y. multicoloured | 2·10 | 1·40 |

5 Former Alt House and Part of Former Ringer House

2002. Glover Garden (home of Thomas Blake Glover (industrialist)). Multicoloured.
| 10 | 5 | 50y. Type **5** | 1·50 | 1·00 |
| 11 | | 50y. Part of former Ringer House and former Glover House | 1·50 | 1·00 |

Nos. 10-11 were issued together, *se-tenant*, forming a composite design.

6 Tulips and Huis Ten Bosch (Nagasaki)

2005. Flowers and Scenery of Kyushu. Multicoloured.
12	6	50y. Type **6**	1·60	1·10
13		50y. Sakura (cherry blossoms) and Kanmon bridge (Fukuoka)	1·60	1·10
14		50y. Kusunohana (camphor blossoms) and Ariake Sea (Saga)	1·60	1·10
15		50y. Unzen-Tsutsuji (azaleas) and Mt. Fugendake (Nagasaki)	1·60	1·10
16		50y. Ume Blossom and Dazaifu-Tenmangu Shrine (Fukuoka)	1·60	1·10
17		5y. Rindou (gentians) and Mt. Aso (Kumamoto)	1·60	1·10
18		50y. Ume blossoms and Mt. Takasaki (Ooita)	1·60	1·10
19		50y. Hamayu (crinums) and Nichinan beach (Miyazaki)	1·60	1·10
20		50y. Miyaki-Kirishima (azaleas) and Kirishima mountains (Kagoshima)	1·60	1·10
21		50y. Hibiscus and Adan (screw-pine) (Kagoshima)	1·60	1·10

Nos. 12-21 were also issued by Fukuoka, Saga, Kumamoto, Oita, Miyazaki and Kagoshima.

7 Cosmos and Kujukushima islands (Nagasaki)

2006. Flowers and Scenery of Kyushu (2nd series). Multicoloured.
22		80y. Daffodils and Nokon-oshima Island (Fukuoka)	2·10	1·40
23		80y. Chinese bellflowers and Hiraodai (Fukuoka)	2·10	1·40
24		80y. Hydrangeas and Mikaeri-notaki fall (Saga)	2·10	1·40
25		80y. Type **7**	2·10	1·40
26		80y. Camellias and the five bridges of Amakusa (Kumamoto)	2·10	1·40
27		80y. Purple flowers and Mt. Aso (Kumamoto)	2·10	1·40
28		80y. Primroses and Mt. Yufudake (Oita)	2·10	1·40
29		80y. Lavender and Kujuurenzan (Oita)	2·10	1·40

| 30 | | 80y. Poppies and Mt. Hinamori-dake (Miyazaki) | 2·10 | 1·40 |
| 31 | | 80y. Field of yellow flowers and Mt. Kaimondake (Kagoshima) | 2·10 | 1·40 |

Nos. 22-31 were also issued by Fukuoka, Miyasaki, Saga, Kumamoto, Oita and Kagoshima.

9 Unzen Azalea **10** Unzen Azalea

2010. Prefectural Flowers. Multicoloured.
32		50y. Peony (Shimane)	1·70	1·20
33		50y. *Citrus sudachi* (Tokushima)	1·70	1·20
34		50y. Type **9** (Nagasaki)	1·70	1·20
35		50y. *Iris laevigata* (Aichi)	1·70	1·20
36		50y. *Iris laevigata* (Aichi)	1·70	1·20
37		80y. Peonies (Shimane)	2·20	1·50
38		80y. *Citrus sudachi* (Tokushima)	2·20	1·50
39		880y. Type **10** (Nagasaki)	2·20	1·50
40		80y. *Iris laevigata* (Aichi)	2·20	1·50
41		880y. Camphor flowers (Saga)	2·20	1·50

Stamps of the same design were issued by Aichi, Tokushima, Saga and Shimane on 8 March 2010.

NARA

1990. Flowers.
| 1 | | 62y. As Type **1462** of Japan | 3·00 | 2·00 |

1 Mountain, Temple and Building

1991. Yoshino. Multicoloured.
| 2 | | 62y. Type **1** | 1·50 | 1·00 |
| 3 | | 62y. Blossom | 1·50 | 1·00 |

1995. Yoshino. Multicoloured.
| 4 | | 80y. Mountain, temple and building (As Type **1**) | 1·80 | 80 |
| 5 | | 80y. Blossom (As No. 3) | 1·80 | 80 |

2 Grass burning, Mount Wakakusa

1996
| 6 | **2** | 50y. multicoloured | 1·30 | 80 |

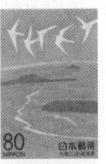

3 Birds and Landscape

1999. Asuka. Multicoloured.
| 7 | | 80y. Type **3** | 2·10 | 1·40 |
| 8 | | 80y. Kofun (megalithic tomb) | 2·10 | 1·40 |

4 Murouji's Five-Storied Pagoda and Rhododendrons

2004. National Heritage.
| 9 | **4** | 80y. multicoloured | 2·50 | 1·70 |

5 Yae-zakura (double cherry blossoms) (Nara)

2006. Flowers of Kinki. Multicoloured.
10		50y. Type **5**	1·30	80
11		50y. Nozigiku (wild chrysanthemums) (Hyogo)	1·30	80
12		50y. Shakunage (rhododendron) (Shiga)	1·30	80
13		50y. Ume blossoms (Wakayama)	1·30	80
14		50y. Sakuraso (primrose) (Osaka)	1·30	80
15		50y. Shidare-zakura (weeping cherry) (Kyoto)	1·30	80

Nos. 10-15 were also issued by Osaka, Hyogo, Shiga, Wakayama and Kyoto.

6 Koriyama Castle

2007. Castles in Kinki Region. Multicoloured.
16		50y. Type **6**	1·60	1·10
17		50y. Hikone	1·60	1·10
18		50y. Himeji	1·60	1·10
19		50y. Osaka	1·60	1·10
20		50y. Wakayama	1·60	1·10

Nos. 16-20 were also issued by Hyogo, Osaka, Shiga and Wakayama on 1 June 2007.

7 Yaezakura Cherry Blossom

2009. Prefectural Flowers. Multicoloured.
21		50y. Somei Yoshino cherry blossom (Tokyo)	1·60	1·10
22		50y. Yashio tsutsuji (*Rhododendron albrechtii*) (Tochigi)	1·60	1·10
23		50y. Tulips (Niigata)	1·60	1·10
24		50y. Rhododendron (*Rhododendron japonicum*) (Shiga)	1·60	1·10
25		50y. Type **7** (Nara)	1·60	1·10
26		80y. Somei Yoshino cherry blossom (Tokyo)	2·50	1·70
27		80y. Yashio tsutsuji (*Rhododendron albrechtii*) (Tochigi)	2·50	1·70
28		80y. Tulips (Niigata)	2·50	1·70
29		80y. Rhododendron (*Rhododendron japonicum*) (Shiga)	2·50	1·70
30		80y. Yaezakura cherry blossom (Nara)	2·50	1·70

Stamps of the same design were issued by Tokyo, Niigata, Shiga, and Tochigi on 2 February 2009.

NIIGATA

1 Prefecture Hall

1989
| 1 | **1** | 62y. multicoloured | 1·30 | 70 |

1990. Flowers.
| 2 | | 62y. As Type **1450** of Japan | 1·20 | 80 |

2 Koi Carp

1991
| 3 | **2** | 62y. multicoloured | 1·80 | 70 |

3 Gogo-an (Ryokon's hermit hut)

1992
| 4 | **3** | 41y. multicoloured | 1·20 | 80 |

4 Soma Gyofu (poet)

1995
| 5 | **4** | 80y. multicoloured | 1·90 | 1·30 |

5 Hanayome

1997. Seto no Hanayome (The Inland Sea Bride).
| 6 | **5** | 50y. multicoloured | 1·30 | 90 |

6 Snow-covered Buildings

1999. Snow Festival.
| 7 | **6** | 80y. multicoloured | 2·10 | 1·40 |

7 Kites

1999. Kite Battle, Shirone. Multicoloured.
| 8 | | 80y. Type **7** | 2·10 | 1·40 |
| 9 | | 80y. Kites (different) | 2·10 | 1·40 |

Nos. 8-9 were issued together, se-tenant, forming a composite design.

8 Two Ibis

1999. Toki (ibis (prefecture official bird)). Multicoloured.
| 10 | | 80y. Type **8** | 2·10 | 1·40 |
| 11 | | 80y. Ibis in flight | 2·10 | 1·40 |

9 Cherry Blossoms, Takada Castle at Night

2001
| 12 | **9** | 80y. multicoloured | 2·40 | 1·60 |

10 Fireworks

2001. Grand Firework Festival, Nagaoka. Multicoloured.
| 13 | | 50y. Type **10** | 1·50 | 1·00 |
| 14 | | 50y. Fireworks (different) | 1·50 | 1·00 |

Nos. 13-14 were issued together, se-tenant, forming a composite design.

11 Camellias and Kamoyama Kouen Park (Chu'etsu area)

2002. Flowers of Echigo. Multicoloured.
15   50y. Type **11**   1·50   1·00
16   50y. Daylily and Oonogame (Sado area)   1·50   1·00
17   50y. Iris and Ijimino Kouen Park (Ka'etsu area)   1·50   1·00
18   50y. *Shortia soldanelloides* and Mt. Myoukousan (Joetsu area)   1·50   1·00

2006. Nature of Shin'etsu. Nagano. Multicoloured.
19   80y. As Type **17** of Nagano   2·10   1·40
20   80y. Sankayou (*Diphylleia cymosa*)   2·10   1·40
21   80y. Mt. Asamayama   2·10   1·20
22   80y. Sakurasou (*Primula sieboldii*)   2·10   1·40

Nos. 9-22 were also issued by Nagano.

12 Tulips

2007. Flora. Multicoloured.
23   80y. Type **12**   2·50   1·70
24   80y. Rice   2·50   1·70
25   80y. Pear 'Le Lectier'   2·50   1·70
26   80y. Primula   2·50   1·70
27   80y. Iris   2·50   1·70

13 Tulips (Niigata)

2009. Prefectural Flowers. Multicoloured.
28   50y. Somei Yoshino cherry blossom (Tokyo)   1·60   1·10
29   50y. Yashio tsutsuji (*Rhododendron albrechtii*) (Tochigi)   1·60   1·10
30   50y. Type **13**   1·60   1·10
31   50y. Rhododendron (*Rhododendron japonicum*) (Shiga)   1·60   1·10
32   50y. Yaezakura Cherry Blossom (Nara)   1·60   1·10
33   80y. Somei Yoshino cherry blossom (Tokyo)   2·50   1·70
34   80y. Yashio tsutsuji (*Rhododendron albrechtii*) (Tochigi)   2·50   1·70
35   80y. Tulips (Niigata)   2·50   1·70
36   80y. Rhododendron (*Rhododendron japonicum*) (Shiga)   2·50   1·70
37   80y. Yaezakura cherry blossom (Nara)   2·50   1·70

Stamps of the same design were issued by Nara, Tokyo, Shiga, and Tochigi on 2 February 2009.

OITA

1 Monkey

1989
1   **1**   62y. multicoloured   1·50   80

1990
2   62y. As Type **1477** of Japan   1·50   80

2 Tsurusaki Dancers

1992
3   **2**   62y. multicoloured   1·20   80

3 Gion Festival, Hita

1998
4   **3**   50y. multicoloured   1·30   90

4 Cliffs

1999. Blue Tunnels. Multicoloured.
5   80y. Type **4**   2·10   1·40
6   80y. Tunnel   2·10   1·40

5 International Wheelchair Marathon

2000
7   **5**   80y. multicoloured   2·75   1·90

6 Ume Blossoms and Mount Takasaki (Ooita)

2005. Flowers and Scenery of Kyushu. Multicoloured.
8   50y. Type **6**   1·60   1·10
9   50y. Sakura (cherry blossoms) and Kanmon bridge (Fukuoka)   1·60   1·10
10   50y. Kusunohana (camphor blossoms) and Ariake Sea (Saga)   1·60   1·10
11   50y. Unzen-Tsutsuji (azaleas) and Mt. Fugendake (Nagasaki)   1·60   1·10
12   50y. Tulips and Huis Ten Bosch (Nagasaki)   1·60   1·10
13   50y. Rindou (gentians) and Mt. Aso (Kumamoto)   1·60   1·10
14   50y. Ume blossom and Dazaifu-Tenmangu Shrine (Fukuoka)   1·60   1·10
15   50y. Hamayu (crinums) and Nichinan beach (Miyazaki)   1·60   1·10
16   50y. Miyama-Kirishima (azaleas) and Kirishima mountains (Kagoshima)   1·60   1·10
17   50y. Hibiscus and Adan (screw-pine) (Kagoshima)   1·60   1·10

Nos. 8-17 were also issued by Fukuoka, Nagasaki, Saga, Miyazaki, Kumamoto and Kagoshima.

7 Primroses and Mt. Yufudake (Oita)

2006. Flowers and Scenery of Kyushu (2nd series). Multicoloured.
18   80y. Daffodils and Nokon-oshima Island (Fukuoka)   2·10   1·40
19   80y. Chinese bellflowers and Hiraodai (Fukuoka)   2·10   1·40
20   80y. Hydrangeas and Mikaeri-notaki fall (Saga)   2·10   1·40
21   80y. Cosmos and Kujukushima islands (Nagasaki)   2·10   1·40
22   80y. Camellias and the five bridges of Amakusa (Kumamoto)   2·10   1·40
23   80y. Purple flowers and Mt. Aso (Kumamoto)   2·10   1·40
24   80y. Type **7**   2·10   1·40
25   80y. Lavender and Kujurenzan (Oita)   2·10   1·40

26   80y. Poppies and Mt. Hinamori-dake (Miyazaki)   2·10   1·40
27   80y. Field of yellow flowers and Mt. Kaimondake (Kagoshima)   2·10   1·40

Nos. 18-27 were also issued by Fukuoka, Nagasaki, Saga, Kumamoto, Miyazaki and Kagoshima.

8 Oita Sports Stadium

2008. 63rd National Sports Meet. Multicoloured.
28   50y. Type **8**   1·60   1·10
29   50y. Fencing   1·60   1·10
30   50y. Athletics
31   50y. Canoeing   1·60   1·10

9 Ume blossom (*Prunus mume* var. bungo)   **10** Ume blossom (*Prunus mume* var. bungo)

2009. Prefectural Flowers. Multicoloured.
32   50y. Peach blossom (Okayama)   1·70   1·30
33   50y. Rape flowers (Chiba)   1·70   1·30
34   50y. Plum blossom and primula (Osaka)   1·70   1·30
35   50y. Bayberry (Kochi)   1·70   1·30
36   50y. Type **9** (Oita)   1·70   1·30
37   80y. Peach blossom (Okayama) (different)   2·75   1·70
38   80y. Rape flowers (Chiba) (different)   2·75   1·70
39   80y. Plum blossom and primula (Osaka) (different)   2·75   1·70
40   80y. Bayberry (Kochi) (different)   2·75   1·70
41   80y. Type **10** (Oita)   2·75   1·70

Stamps of the same design were issued by Chiba, Kochi, Okayama and Osaka on 1 Dec 2009.

OKAYAMA

1990. Flowers.
1   62y. As Type **1466** of Japan   1·20   80

1 Pot with Lid

1991. Bizen Ware. Multicoloured.
2   62y. Type **1**   1·20   80
3   62y. Red glazed pot   1·20   80

2 Calligrapher

1995. Niimi-no-sho Festival.
3a   **2**   80y. multicoloured   2·10   1·40

3 Castle

1997. 400th Anniv of Okayama Castle.
4   **3**   80y. multicoloured   2·10   1·40

1999
5   80y. As Type **4** of Hiroshima   2·10   1·40

No. 5 was also issued by Hiroshima.

4 Kurashiki District

1999
6   **4**   80y. multicoloured   2·10   1·40

5 Cranes and Ume Blossom

2000. 300th Anniv of Korakuen Garden. Multicoloured.
7   80y. Type **5**   2·40   1·60
8   80y. Kayou-no-ike pond   2·40   1·60
9   80y. Yuishinzan mound   2·40   1·60
10   80y. Cranes flying over frozen stream   2·40   1·60

6 Momonohana (peach blossoms) and Traditional Houses, Kurashiki

2000. Multicoloured..
11   50y. Type **6**   1·50   1·00
12   50y. Natsumikan (summer-orange blossoms) and sea   1·50   1·00
13   50y. Nijisseikinashi (Japanese pear tree) and Tottori dune   1·50   1·00
14   50y. Botan (peonies) and Izumo-taisha Shrine   1·50   1·00
15   50y. Momiji (maple leaves) and Itsukushima Shrine Gate   1·50   1·00

Nos. 11-15 were also issued by Yamaguchi, Shimane, Tottori and Hiroshima.

7 Cherry Blossom, Hiikawa River

2002. Multicoloured.
16   50y. Type **7**   1·50   1·00
17   50y. Pagoda, Bicchu-Kokubunji Temple   1·50   1·00

Nos. 16-17 were also issued by Shimane.

8 Main Hall, Kibitsu-jinja Shrine and Southern Zuijin Gate

2003. Kibitsu Shrine.
18   **8**   80y. multicoloured   2·40   1·60

9 Runner and Momotaro Stadium

2005. 60th National Athletic Meet.
19   **9**   50y. multicoloured   1·60   1·10

10 Peach
Blossoms and
Seto-oohashi
Bridge
(Okayama)

2006. Flowers of Chugoku. Multicoloured.

20		50y. Type **10**	1·50	1·00
21		50y. Tree peonies and Hinomi-saki Lighthouse (Shimane)	1·50	1·00
22		50y. Pear blossom and Yumiga-hama beach (Tottori)	1·50	1·00
23		50y. Maple leaves and Miyajima shrine (Hiroshima)	1·50	1·00
24		50y. Chinese citron blossom and Oomijima island (Yamaguchi)	1·50	1·00

Nos. 20-4 were also issued by Tottori, Shimane, Hiroshima, and Yamaguchi.

11 Pheasants

2007. Birds. Multicoloured.

25		80y. Type **11**	2·50	1·70
26		80y. Mandarin ducks	2·50	1·70
27		80y. Swans	2·50	1·70
28		80y. Ducks swimming	2·50	1·70
29		80y. Cranes	2·50	1·70

Nos. 25-9 were also issued by Hiroshima, Shimane, Tottori and Yamaguchi on 1 May 2007.

12 Peach
Blossom   **13** Peach
Blossom

2009. Prefectural Flowers. Multicoloured.

30		50y. Type **12** (Okayama)	1·70	1·10
31		50y. Rape flowers (Chiba)	1·70	1·10
32		50y. Plum blossom and primula (Osaka)	1·70	1·10
33		50y. Bayberry (Kochi)	1·70	1·10
34		50y. Ume blossom (*Prunus mume* var. bungo) (Oita)	1·70	1·10
35		80y. Type **13** (Okayama)	2·75	1·70
36		80y. Rape flowers (Chiba) (different)	2·75	1·70
37		80y. Plum blossom and primula (Osaka) (different)	2·75	1·70
38		80y. Bayberry (Kochi) (different)	2·75	1·70
39		80y. Ume blossom (*Prunus mume* var. bungo) (Oita) (different)	2·75	1·70

Stamps of the same design were issued by Chiba, Kochi, Oita and Osaka on 1 Dec 2009.

OKINAWA

1 Temple,
Shurei-no-mon

1989

1	**1**	62y. multicoloured	1·30	80

1990. Flowers.

2		62y. As Type **1480** of Japan	1·30	80

2 Ryukyu Dancer

1990

3	**2**	62y. multicoloured	1·20	80

3 Black Pearls

1991

4	**3**	41y. multicoloured	1·50	70

4 Boat Race

1992. Naha Ha-ree.

5	**4**	62y. multicoloured	1·20	80

5 Tug of War

1994

6	**5**	50y. multicoloured	1·20	80

6 Eisa
Drummers

1995

7	**6**	80y. multicoloured	1·90	1·30

7 Temple and Dragon

1996. Shurijo.

8	**7**	80y. multicoloured	2·10	1·40

8 Pineapples

1997. Fruit. Multicoloured.

9		50y. Type **8**	1·30	90
10		50y. Mangoes	1·30	90

9 Shanshin
(three stringed
instrument)

1998

11	**9**	80y. multicoloured	2·10	1·40

3 Ryukyu Island
5 sen Stamp
(Type **1**)

1998. 50th Anniv of Okinawa Stamps. Multicoloured.

12		80y. Type **10**	2·10	1·40
13		80y. Ryukyu Island 5c. stamp (Type **218**)	2·10	1·40

11 Woman

1999. 125th Anniv of Post. Multicoloured.

14		80y. Type **11**	2·10	1·40
15		80y. Masks	2·10	1·40

12 Ryukyu
Dancers

1999

16	**12**	80y. multicoloured	2·10	1·40

13 Boat, Fishers
and Iejima
Tatchu Rock

1999

17	**13**	80y. multicoloured	2·10	1·40

14 Royal Family
Country Villa
and Bridge

1999. Shikina-en Gardens. Multicoloured.

18		50y. Type **14**	1·50	1·00
19		50y. Tea house and bridge	1·50	1·00

Nos. 18-19 were issued together, *se-tenant*, forming a composite design.

15 Abaca Cloth
(Tamanaha Yukou)

2000

20	**15**	50y. multicoloured	1·80	1·20

16 Bankoku
Shinryokan
Conference
Centre

2000

21	**16**	80y. multicoloured	2·75	1·80

17 Memorial
and Flowers

2001

22	**17**	80y. multicoloured	2·40	1·60

18 Taiwan
Cherry and
Iejima Island

2002. Flowers. Multicoloured.

23		50y. Type **18**	1·50	1·00
24		50y. Hibiscus and Kaichu-douro highway	1·50	1·00
25		50y. Bougainvillea and traditional house, Tsuboya	1·50	1·00
26		50y. Lilies and Higashi-hennazaki	1·50	1·00
27		50y. Seishika flowers and Seishika bridge	1·50	1·00

19 Monorail,
Shurijo Castle,
and Coral Tree
Flowers

2003. Okinawa Urban Monorail. Multicoloured.

28		50y. Type **19**	1·60	1·10
29		50y. Monorail, Naha Airport, and hibiscus	1·60	1·10

20 Dancer and
Theatre Building

2005. Ryukyuan Dance and National Theatre Okinawa.

30	**20**	50y. multicoloured	1·60	1·10

21 Goya (bitter
melon)

2005

31	**21**	50y. multicoloured	1·60	1·10

22 Whale Shark

2007. Sea Fauna. Multicoloured.

32		80y. Type **22**	2·50	1·70
33		80y. Angelfish	2·50	1·70
34		80y. Clownfish	2·50	1·70
35		80y. Blue damselfish	2·50	1·70
36		80y. Manta ray	2·50	1·70

Nos. 32-6 were issued together, *se-tenant*, each strip forming a composite design.

23-24 Drummers, left

2008. Tanabata Festival. Multicoloured.

37		50y. Type **23**	1·60	1·10
38		50y. Type **24**	1·60	1·10
39		50y. Lanterns, left	1·60	1·10
40		50y. Lanterns, right	1·60	1·10
41		50y. Procession and roofs, left	1·60	1·10
42		50y. Procession and roofs, right	1·60	1·10
43		50y. Dancers, left	1·60	1·10
44		50y. Dancers, right	1·60	1·10
45		50y. Procession, left	1·60	1·10
46		50y. Procession, right	1·60	1·10

Nos. 37-8, 39-40, 41-2, 43-4 and 45-6 were issued together, *se-tenant*, each pair forming a composite design.

Nos. 37-46 were also issued by Tokushima, Tokyo, Miyagi and Fukuoka on 1 August 2008.

25 Indian Coral Bean Flower   **26** Indian Coral Bean Flower

2010. Prefectural Flowers. Multicoloured.

47	50y. Tulips (Toyama)		1·30	90
48	50y. Milk vetch (Gifu)		1·30	90
49	50y. Fuji Zakura Satsuki azalea (Yamanashi)		1·30	90
50	50y. Type **25** (Okinawa)		1·30	90
51	Pear blossom (Tottori)		1·30	90
52	80y. Tulips (Toyama)		2·00	
53	80y. Milk vetch (Gifu)		2·00	1·40
54	80y Fuji Zakura Satsuki azalea (Yamanashi)		2·00	1·40
55	80y. Type **26** (Okinawa)		2·00	1·40
56	80y. Pear blossom (Tottori)		2·00	1·40

Stamps of the same design were issued by Gifu, Yamanshi, Tottori and Toyama on 1 February 2010.

OSAKA

1 Faces

1989. Bunraku.

1	**1**	62y. multicoloured	1·30	70

1990

2		62y. As Type **1460** of Japan	1·20	80

2 Symbols of Business

1992. Business Park.

3	**2**	41y. multicoloured	1·00	50

3 Danjiri Festival

1995

4	**3**	80y. multicoloured	1·90	1·30

4 Gymnast

1999

5	**4**	80y. multicoloured	2·10	1·40

5 Performers and Puppets

2000. World Performing Arts Festival.

6	**5**	80y. multicoloured	2·75	1·80

6 Thunder God playing Table Tennis

2001. Sports. Multicoloured.

7	50y. Type **6**	1·50	1·00
8	50y. Wind God playing table tennis	1·50	1·00
9	50y. Bowling	1·50	1·00
10	50y. Taekwondo	1·50	1·00

7 Namdaemun, Seoul and Doton-bori, Osaka

2001. 14th General Assembly of World Trade Organization. Multicoloured.

11	80y. Type **7**	2·40	1·60
12	80y. Bunraku actors, Japan and Nong-ak drummers, Korea	2·40	1·60

8 Osaka Dome and Lion (part of railing, Naniwabashi bridge)

2002. 85th Lions Clubs International Convention.

13	**8**	80y. multicoloured	2·20	1·50

9 Scouts and Osaka Castle

2002. 23rd Asia-Pacific Scout Jamboree.

14	**9**	80y. multicoloured	1·80	1·20

10 Rotary Emblem and Irises

2004. Rotary International Convention, Osaka.

15	**10**	80y. multicoloured	2·50	1·70

11 Sakuraso (primrose) (Osaka)

2006. Flowers of Kinki. Multicoloured.

16	50y. Type **11**	1·50	1·00
17	50y. Shidare-zakura (weeping cherry) (Kyoto)	1·50	1·00
18	50y. Yae-zakura (double cherry blossoms) (Nara)	1·50	1·00
19	50y. Nozigiku (wild chrysanthemums) (Hyogo)	1·50	1·00
20	50y. Shakunage (rhododendron) (Shiga)	1·50	1·00
21	50y. Ume blossoms (Wakayama)	1·50	1·00

Nos. 16-21 were also issued by Hyogo, Nara, Shiga, Wakayama and Kyoto.

12 Osaka Castle

2007. Castles in Kinki Region. Multicoloured.

22	50y. Type **12**	1·60	1·10
23	50y. Koriyama	1·60	1·10
24	50y. Hikone	1·60	1·10
25	50y. Himeji	1·60	1·10
26	50y. Wakayama	1·60	1·10

Nos. 22-6 were also issued by Hyogo, Nara, Shiga and Wakayama on 1 June 2007.

13 Plum Blossom and Primula   **14** Plum Blossom and Primula

2009. Prefectural Flowers. Multicoloured.

27	50y. Peach blossom (Okayama)	1·70	1·30
28	50y. Rape flowers (Chiba)	1·70	1·30
29	50y. Type **13** (Osaka)	1·70	1·30
30	50y. Bayberry (Kochi)	1·70	1·30
31	50y. Ume blossom (*Prunus mume* var. bungo) (Oita)	1·70	1·30
32	80y. Peach blossom (Okayama) (different)	2·75	1·70
33	80y. Rape flowers (Chiba) (different)	2·75	1·70
34	80y. Type **14** (Osaka)	2·75	1·70
35	80y. Bayberry (Kochi) (different)	2·75	1·70
36	80y. Ume blossom (*Prunus mume* var. bungo) (Oita) (different)	2·75	1·70

Stamps of the same design were issued by Chiba, Kochi, Oita and Okayama on 1 Dec 2009.

SAGA

1990

1		62y. As Type **1474** of Japan	1·20	80

1 Yoshinogari Historical Park

1991

2	**1**	62y. multicoloured	1·20	80

2 Karatsu-Kunchi

1995

3	**2**	80y. multicoloured	1·90	1·30

3 Vase

1996. World Ceramic Exhibition.

4	**3**	80y. multicoloured	1·80	1·20

1997. Multicoloured.

5	80y. As Type **4** of Fukuoka	1·80	1·20
6	80y. Early rail way and map	1·80	1·20
7	80y. Interchange and map	1·80	1·20
8	80y. Building and map	1·80	1·20

Nos. 5-8 were issued together, *se-tenant*, forming a composite design.
Nos. 5-8 were also issued by Nagasaki and Fukuoka.

4 Yoshinogari Historical Park

1999

9	**4**	80y. multicoloured	2·20	1·50

5 Child in Air Balloon

2000. International Balloon Festival.

10	**5**	80y. multicoloured	2·75	1·90

6 Iroe Komainu (lion dog) and 'Sometsuke Arita Sarayama-shokunin-zukushi-ezu oozara' (blue and white ceramic ware depicting ceramic workers)

2003. Imari-Arita Ceramics.

11	**6**	80y. multicoloured	2·40	1·60

7 Kusunohana (camphor blossoms) and Ariake Sea (Saga)

2005. Multicoloured.

12	50y. Type **7**	1·60	1·10
13	50y. Sakura (cherry blossoms) and Kanmon bridge (Fukuoka)	1·60	1·10
14	50y. Ume Blossom and Dazaifu-Tenmangu Shrine (Fukuoka)	1·60	1·10
15	50y. Unzen-Tsutsuji (azaleas) and Mt. Fugendake (Nagasaki)	1·60	1·10
16	50y. Tulips and Huis Ten Bosch (Nagasaki)	1·60	1·10
17	50y. Rindou (gentians) and Mt. Aso (Kumamoto)	1·60	1·10
18	50y. Ume blossoms and Mt. Takasaki (Ooita)	1·60	1·10
19	50y. Hamayu (crinums) and Nichinan beach (Miyazaki)	1·60	1·10
20	50y. Miyama-Kirishima (azaleas) and Kirishima mountains (Kagoshima)	1·60	1·10
21	50y. Hibiscus and Adan (screw-pine) (Kagoshima)	1·60	1·10

Nos. 12-21 were also issued by Fukuoka, Nagasaki, Kumamoto, Oita, Miyazaki and Kagoshima.

8 Hydrangeas and Mikaerinotaki Falls (Saga)

2006. Flowers and Scenery of Kyushu (2nd series). Multicoloured.

22	80y. Daffodils and Nokonoshima Island (Fukuoka)	2·40	1·60
23	80y. Chinese bellflowers and Hiraodai (Fukuoka)	2·40	1·60
24	80y. Type **8**	2·40	1·60
25	80y. Cosmos and Kujukushima islands (Nagasaki)	2·40	1·60
26	80y. Camellias and the five bridges of Amakusa (Kumamoto)	2·40	1·60
27	80y. Purple flowers and Mt. Aso (Kumamoto)	2·40	1·60
28	80y. Primroses and Mt. Yufudake (Oita)	2·40	1·60
29	80y. Lavender and Kujurenzan (Oita)	2·40	1·60
30	80y. Poppies and Mt. Hinamoridake (Miyazaki)	2·40	1·60
31	80y. Field of yellow flowers and Mt. Kaimondake (Kagoshima)	2·40	1·60

Nos. 22-31 were also issued by Fukuoka, Nagasaki, Kumamoto, Oita, Miyazaki and Kagoshima.

10 Camphor Flowers   **11** Camphor Flowers

2010. Prefectural Flowers. Multicoloured.

32	50y. Peony (Shimane)		1·70	1·20
33	50y. *Citrus sudachi* (Tokushima)		1·70	1·20
34	Unzen azalea (Nagasaki)		1·70	1·20
35	50y. *Iris laevigata* (Aichi)		1·70	1·20
36	50y. Type **10** (Saga)		1·70	1·20
37	80y. Peonies (Shimane)		2·40	1·60
38	80y. *Citrus sudachi* (Tokushima)		2·40	1·60
39	80y. Unzen azalea (Nagasaki)		2·40	1·60
40	80y. *Iris laevigata* (Aichi)		2·40	1·60
41	80y. Type **11** (Saga)		2·40	1·60

Stamps of the same design were issued by Aichi, Nagasaki, Tokushima and Shimane on 8 March 2010.

SAITAMA

1990

1		62y. As Type **1444** of Japan	1·20	80

1 Stylized Children

1990. Toryanse (children's song).

2	**1**	62y. multicoloured	1·20	80

2 Kuroyama-san-taki Waterfalls

1995

3	**2**	80y. multicoloured	1·90	1·30

3 Hozoji Pond

1997

4	**3**	50y. multicoloured	1·80	1·20

4 Collared Doves and Walkers

1997. Walking Festival.

5	**4**	80y. multicoloured	2·10	1·40

5 Dove and Buildings

2000. New Urban Centre. Multicoloured.

6		50y. Type **5**	1·50	1·00
7		50y. Buildings and flowers	1·50	1·00

Nos. 6-7 were issued together, *se-tenant*, forming a composite design.

---

6 Yatai and Fireworks

2000. Night Festival, Chichibu. Multicoloured.

8		80y. Type **6**	2·75	1·90
9		80y. Kasahoko	2·75	1·90

7 Bonsai Tree

2002

10	**7**	80y. multicoloured	2·20	1·50

8 Primrose and Tajimagahara Primrose Field

2004. Flowers of Kanto (1st issue). Multicoloured.

11		50y. Type **8**	1·60	1·10
12		50y. Yoshi azalea and Lake Chuzenjiko	1·60	1·10
13		50y. Japanese azalea and Mt. Akagisan	1·60	1·10
14		50y. Rose and Mount Tsuku-basan	1·60	1·10
15		50y. Rape blossom and Nojima-zaki lighthouse	1·60	1·10

See also Nos. 17-21.
Nos. 11-15 were also issued by Tochigi, Chiba, Gunma and Ibaraki.

9 Gymnast

2004. National Athletic Meet.

16	**9**	50y. multicoloured	1·60	1·10

10 Allspice Flowers and Mount Bukousan (Saitama)

2005. Flowers of Kanto (2nd issue). Multicoloured.

17		50y. Type **10**	1·60	1·10
18		50y. Nikko-kisuge (Nikko day lily) and Kirifuri Heights (Tochigi)	1·60	1·10
19		50y. Sunflowers at Hana-hotaru (Chiba)	1·60	1·10
20		50y. Bush clover, Kairakuen garden (Ibaraki)	1·60	1·10
21		50y. Azaleas, Tsutsujigaoka Park (Gunma)	1·60	1·10

Nos. 17-21 were also issued by Gunma, Tochigi, Chiba and Ibaraki.

11 Japanese Pear and Nagatoro

2006. Fruits of Kanto. Multicoloured.

22		80y. Loquat and Byobugaura	2·30	1·60
23		80y. Ume and Fukuroda Waterfall (Ibaraki)	2·30	1·60
24		80y. Apple and Oze (Gunma)	2·30	1·60
25		80y. Type **11**	2·30	1·60
26		80y. Strawberry and Kegon Waterfall (Tochigi)	2·30	1·60

Stamps of the same design were issued by Gunma, Ibaraki, Chiba and Tochigi on 1 September 2006.

12 *Primula sieboldii*   **13** *Primula sieboldii*

2011. Prefectural Flowers. Multicoloured.

27		50y. *Rosa* (Ibaraki)	1·80	1·20
28		50y. *Malus pumila* (Aomori)	1·80	1·20
29		50y. Type **12**	1·80	1·20
30		50y. *Citrus natsudaidai* (Yamaguchi)	1·80	1·20
31		50y. *Rhododendron kiusianum* (Kagoshima)	1·80	1·20
32		80y. *Rosa* (Ibaraki)	2·75	1·90
33		80y. *Malus pumila* (Aomori)	2·75	1·90
34		80y. Type **13**	2·75	1·90
35		80y. *Citrus natsudaidai* (Yamaguchi)	2·75	1·90
36		80y. *Rhododendron kiusianum* (Kagoshima)	2·75	1·90

Stamps of the same design were issued by Aomori, Ibaraki, Kagoshima and Yamaguchi on 8 February 2011.

SHIGA

1 Figurine

1989. Shigaraki Ware.

1	**1**	62y. multicoloured	1·30	60

1990. Flowers.

2		62y. As Type **1458** of Japan	3·00	2·00

2 Yachts, Lake Biwa

1993

3	**2**	62y. multicoloured	1·50	1·00

3 Temmple

1996. Mount Hiei.

4	**3**	80y. multicoloured	2·10	1·40

4 Trout and Rhododendron

2001. Ninth International Conference on the Conservation and Management of Lakes.

5	**4**	50y. multicoloured	1·60	1·10

5 Shakunage (rhododendron) (Shiga)

2006. Flowers of Kinki. Multicoloured.

6		50y. Yae-zakura (double cherry blossoms) (Nara)	1·60	1·10
7		50y. Nozigiku (wild chrysanthemums) (Hyogo)	1·60	1·10
8		50y. Type **5**	1·60	1·10
9		50y. Ume blossoms (Wakayama)	1·60	1·10
10		50y. Sakuraso (primrose) (Osaka)	1·60	1·10
11		50y. Shidare-zakura (weeping cherry) (Kyoto)	1·50	1·10

Nos. 6-11 were also issued by Osaka, Hyogo, Nara, Wakayama and Kyoto.

6 Hikone Castle

2007. Castles in Kinki Region. Multicoloured. Photo.

12		50y. Type **6**	1·60	1·10
13		50y. Koriyama	1·60	1·10
14		50y. Himeji	1·60	1·10
15		50y. Osaka	1·60	1·10
16		50y. Wakayama	1·60	1·10

Nos. 12-16 were also issued by Hyogo, Nara, Osaka and Wakayama on 1 June 2007.

SHIMANE

1990. Flowers.

1		62y. As Type **1465** of Japan	1·20	80

1 Yasukibushi Dancer

1990

2	**1**	62y. multicoloured	1·20	80

2 Izumo-no-Okuni (dancer and founder Kubuki theatre)

1994

3	**2**	80y. multicoloured	1·90	1·10

3 Railway Bridge, Tsuwano

1999. Multicoloured.

4		80y. Type **3**	2·10	1·40
5		80y. Street, Hagi	2·10	1·40

Nos. 4-5 were also issued by Yamaguchi.

4 Botan (peonies) and Izumo-taisha Shrine

2000. Multicoloured.

6		50y. Type **4**	1·50	1·00
7		50y. Natsumikan (summer-orange blossoms) and sea	1·50	1·00
8		50y. Nijisseikinashi (Japanese pear tree) and Tottori dune	1·50	1·00
9		50y. Momonohana (peach blossoms) and traditional houses in Kurashiki	1·50	1·00
10		50y. Momiji (maple leaves) and Itsukushima Shrine Gate	1·50	1·00

Nos. 6-10 were also issued by Yamaguchi, Shimane, Okayama and Hiroshima.

5 Matsue Castle and Cherry Blossoms

2001. Matsue Castle and Tea Ceremony Culture. Multicoloured.

11		80y. Type **5**	2·40	1·60

12	80y. Meimei-an teahouse and camellias	2·40	1·60

6 Pagoda, Bicchu-Kokubunji Temple

2002. Multicoloured.

| 13 | 50y. Type **6** | 1·50 | 1·00 |
| 14 | 50y. Cherry Blossom, Hiikawa River | 1·50 | 1·00 |

Nos. 13-14 were also issued by Okayama.

7 Tree Peonies and Hinomisaki Lighthouse (Shimane)

2006. Flowers of Chugoku. Multicoloured.

15	50y. Type **7**	1·50	1·00
16	50y. Pear blossom and Yumigahama Beach (Tottori)	1·50	1·00
17	50y. Peach blossoms and Seto-oohashi bridge (Okayama)	1·50	1·00
18	50y. Maple leaves and Miyajima shrine (Hiroshima)	1·50	1·00
19	50y. Chinese citron blossom and Oomijima island (Yamaguchi)	1·50	1·00

Nos. 15-19 were also issued by Tottori, Okayama, Hiroshima and Yamaguchi.

8 Swans

2007. Birds. Multicoloured.

20	80y. Type **8**	2·50	1·70
21	80y. Mandarin ducks	2·50	1·70
22	80y. Pheasants	2·50	1·70
23	80y. Ducks swimming	2·50	1·70
24	80y. Cranes	2·50	1·70

Nos. 20-24 were also issued by Hiroshima, Okayama, Tottori and Yamaguchi on 1 May 2007.

9 Peonies   **10** Peony

2010. Prefectural Flowers. Multicoloured.

25	50y. Type **9** (Shimane)	1·60	1·10
26	50y. *Citrus sudachi* (Tokushima)	1·60	1·10
27	50y. Unzen azalea (Nagasaki)	1·60	1·10
28	50y. *Iris laevigata* (Aichi)	1·60	1·10
29	50y. Camphor flowers (Saga)	1·60	1·10
30	80y. Type **10** (Shimane)	2·60	1·80
31	80y. *Citrus sudachi* (Tokushima)	2·60	1·80
32	80y. Unzen azalea (Nagasaki)	2·60	1·80
33	80y. *Iris laevigata* (Aichi)	2·60	1·80
34	80y. Camphor flowers (Saga)	2·60	1·80

Stamps of the same design were issued by Aichi, Nagasaki, Saga and Tokushima on 8 March 2010.

SHIZUOKA

1990. Flowers.

| 1 | 62y. As Type **1455** of Japan | 3·00 | 2·00 |

1 Tea Gatherer

1990

| 2 | **1** | 62y. multicoloured | 1·20 | 50 |

2 Magpie and Mount Fuji

1993

| 3 | **2** | 41y. multicoloured | 1·30 | 90 |

3 Tea Pickers

1997

| 4 | **3** | 50y. multicoloured | 1·30 | 90 |

4 Cattle and Mount Fuji

1997. Mount Fuji. Multicoloured.

| 5 | 80y. Type **4** | 2·10 | 1·40 |
| 6 | 80y. Mount Fuji at dusk | 2·10 | 1·40 |

5 Softball Players

1998

| 7 | **5** | 80y. multicoloured | 2·10 | 1·40 |

6 Shimizu Port

1999

| 8 | **6** | 80y. multicoloured | 2·10 | 1·40 |

7 Atami-baien Ume Orchard

2000. Izu. Multicoloured.

| 9 | 50y. Type **7** | 1·80 | 1·20 |
| 10 | 50y. Kawazu-nanadaru waterfalls and statues | 1·80 | 1·20 |

8 Palace Festival Float

2001. Hamamatsu Festival. Multicoloured.

| 11 | 80y. Type **8** | 2·50 | 1·70 |
| 12 | 80y. Kite match | 2·50 | 1·70 |

9 Football Players, Mount Fuji and Azaleas

2003. National Athletic Meet.

| 13 | **9** | 50y. multicoloured | 1·60 | 1·10 |

10 Gerbera

2004. Flora. Multicoloured.

14	80y. Type **10**	2·50	1·70
15	80y. Carnations	2·50	1·70
16	80y. Roses	2·50	1·70
17	80y. Prairie gentian	2·50	1·70

11 Ryozenji Temple

2004. Cultural Heritage. Temples (1st series). Multicoloured.

18	80y. Type **11**	2·50	1·70
19	80y. Bells encircling tree, Gokurakuji Temple	2·50	1·70
20	80y. Courtyard, Konsenji Temple	2·50	1·70
21	80y. Row of statues, Dainichiji Temple	2·50	1·70
22	80y. Roofs, statue and pagoda, Tatsueji Temple	2·50	1·70
23	80y. Veranda and pagoda, Kakurinji Temple	2·50	1·70
24	80y. Trees at night, Tairyuji Temple	2·50	1·70
25	80y. Shrine and steps, Byoudouji Temple	2·50	1·70
26	80y. Decorated panels, Iwamotoji Temple	2·50	1·70
27	80y. Stone turtle, Kongoufukuji Temple	2·50	1·70
28	80y. Plants, stone lantern and monks, Enkouji Temple	2·50	1·70
29	80y. Steps and gateway, Kanjizaiji Temple	2·50	1·70
30	80y. Interior, Nankoubou Temple	2·50	1·70
31	80y. Pebbles and roofs, Taizanji Temple	2·50	1·70
32	80y. Autumn leaves and statue, Eifukuji Temple	2·50	1·70
33	80y. God (Bishamon)(statue), Sennyuji Temple	2·50	1·70
34	80y. Trees, bell and pathway, Shusshakaji Temple	2·50	1·70
35	80y. Wide path, tree, steps and gateway, Kouyamaji Temple	2·50	1·70
36	80y. Metal staff, Zentsuji Temple	2·50	1·70
37	80y. Courtyard, Kouzouji Temple	2·50	1·70

12 Silvereye Butterfly and Kawazu Cherry Blossoms

2006. Cherry Blossom. Multicoloured.

| 38 | 50y. Type **12** | 1·60 | 1·10 |
| 39 | 50y. Blossom | 1·60 | 1·10 |

13 Azalea and Coastline, Jogasaki

2007. Flowers and Scenery of Tokai. Multicoloured.

40	80y. Type **13**	2·50	1·70
41	80y. Iris	2·50	1·70
42	80y. Gassho-zukuri houses and vetch flowers	2·50	1·70
43	80y. Lily and Nagoya Castle	2·50	1·70
44	80y. Iris and Couple Rock	2·50	1·70

Nos. 40-4 were also issued by Aichi, Gifu and Mie on 2 April 2007.

13 Azalea

2011. Prefectural Flowers. Multicoloured.

45	50y. Type **14**	1·80	1·20
46	50y. Satsuma (Ehime)	1·80	1·20
47	80y. Type **13**	2·75	1·90
48	80y. Satsuma (Ehime)	2·75	1·90

Stamps of the same design were issued by Ehime on 2 May 2011.

TOCHIGI

1990. Flowers.

| 1 | 62y. As Type **1442** of Japan | 1·20 | 80 |

1 Walkers in Countryside

1991

| 2 | **1** | 62y. multicoloured | 1·20 | 80 |

2 Kirifuri-no-taki Waterfall

1995

| 3 | **2** | 50y. multicoloured | 1·30 | 80 |

3 Mountain and Lake

1999. Lake Chuzenji. Multicoloured.

| 4 | 80y. Type **3** | 2·10 | 1·40 |
| 5 | 80y. Autumn leaves and lake | 2·10 | 1·40 |

4 Ashikaga School

2001. Ashikaga School. Multicoloured.

| 6 | 50y. Type **4** | 2·10 | 1·40 |
| 7 | 80y. Gate, Ashikaga School | 2·10 | 1·40 |

5 Rape Blossom and Nojimazaki Lighthouse

2004. Flowers of Kanto (1st issue). Multicoloured.

8	50y. Type **5**	1·60	1·10
9	50y. Yoshi azalea and Lake Chuzenjiko	1·60	1·10
10	50y. Japanese azalea and Mt. Akagisan	1·60	1·10
11	50y. Primrose and Tajimagahara native primrose field	1·60	1·10
12	50y. Rose and Mount Tsukubasan	1·60	1·10

See also Nos. 13-17.

Nos. 8-12 were also issued by Tochigi, Saitama, Gunma and Ibaraki.

6 Nikko-kisuge
(Nikko day lily)
and Kirifuri
Heights
(Tochigi)

2005. Flowers of Kanto (2nd issue). Multicoloured.
13	50y. Type **6**		1·60	1·10
14	50y. Azaleas, Tsutsujigaoka Park (Gunma)		1·60	1·10
15	50y. Sunflowers at Hana-hotaru (Chiba)		1·60	1·10
16	50y. Bush clover, Kairakuen garden (Ibaraki)		1·60	1·10
17	50y. Allspice flowers and Mt. Bukousan (Saitama)		1·60	1·10

Nos. 13-17 were also issued by Gunma, Saitama, Chiba and Ibaraki.

7 Strawberry
and Kegon
Waterfall

2006. Fruits of Kanto. Multicoloured.
18	80y Loquat and Byobugaura		2·60	1·80
19	80y. Ume and Fukuroda Waterfall (Ibaraki)		2·60	1·80
20	80y. Apple and Oze (Gunma)		2·60	1·80
21	80y. Japanese pear and Nagatoro (Saitama)		2·60	1·80
22	80y. Type **7**		2·60	1·80

Stamps of the same design were issued by Gunma, Ibaraki, Saitama and Chiba on 1 September 2006.

8 Yashio
tsutsuji
(Rhododendron
albrechtii)

2009. Prefectural Flowers. Multicoloured.
23	50y. Somei Yoshino cherry blossom (Tokyo)		1·60	1·10
24	50y. Type **8** (Tochigi)		1·60	1·10
25	50y. Tulips (Niigata)		1·60	1·10
26	50y. Rhododendron (Rhododendron japonicum) (Shiga)		1·60	1·10
27	50y. Yaezakura cherry blossom (Nara)		1·60	1·10
28	80y. Somei Yoshino cherry blossom (Tokyo)		2·50	1·70
29	80y. Yashio tsutsuji (Rhododendron albrechtii) (Tochigi)		2·50	1·70
30	80y. Tulips (Niigata)		2·50	1·70
31	80y. Rhododendron (Rhododendron japonicum) (Shiga)		2·50	1·70
32	80y. Yaezakura cherry blossom (Nara)		2·50	1·70

Stamps of the same design were issued by Nara, Niigata, Shiga, and Tokyo on 2 February 2009.

TOKUSHIMA

1990
1	62y. As Type **1469** of Japan		1·50	1·00

1 Puppet (head
and shoulders)

1991
2	**1**	62y. multicoloured		1·30	70

2 Awa-odori
Dancers

1994
3	**2**	50y. multicoloured		1·50	1·00

4 Awa-odori
Dancers

1998. Kobe-Awaji-Naruto Expressway. Multicoloured.
4	80y. Type **3**		2·10	1·10
5	80y. Bridge (different)		2·10	1·40

Nos. 4-5 were also issued by Hyogo.

3 Bridge

2000
6	**4**	80y. multicoloured			

5 Sudachi (sour
citrus fruit) and
Mt. Tsurugisan
(Tokushima)

2002. Multicoloured.
7	50y. Type **5**		1·50	1·00
8	50y. Mikan (mandarin oranges) and Sata-misaki Promontory (Ehime)		1·50	1·00
9	50y. Yamamomo (bayberry) and Tengu highland (Kochi)		1·50	1·00
10	50y. Olive and Shodoshima island (Kagawa)		1·50	1·00

Nos. 7-10 were also issued by Ehime, Kochi and Kagawa.

2005. Cultural Heritage. Shizuoka Temples. Multicoloured.
11	80y. As Type **8** of Ehime		2·50	1·70
12	80y. Seated Buddha, Anrakuji Temple		2·50	1·70
13	80y. Inscribed belfry gateway, Jurakuji Temple		2·50	1·70
14	80y. Double roofed gateway, Kumadaniji Temple		2·50	1·70
15	80y. Pagoda, Yakuoji Temple		2·50	1·70
16	80y. Statues, ramp, lanterns and pagoda, Hotsumisakiji Temple		2·50	1·70
17	80y. Gateway and long steep steps, Shinjouji Temple		2·50	1·70
18	80y. Path, gateway, steps and main temple, Kongochoji Temple		2·50	1·70
19	80y. Buddha seated on peacock, Ryukoji Temple		2·50	1·70
20	80y. Bell and autumn colour, Butsumokuji Temple		2·50	1·70
21	80y. Dragon, Meisekiji Temple		2·50	1·70
22	80y. Steps and many roofed buildings, Daihouji Temple		2·50	1·70
23	80y. Carved decorative gable, Kokubunji Temple		2·50	1·70
24	80y. Leafless tree and snow-covered building, Yokomineji Temple		2·50	1·70
25	80y. Buddha, Kouonji Temple		2·50	1·70
26	80y. Courtyard and building, Houjuji Temple		2·50	1·70
27	80y. Inscribed pillars and gateway, Douryuji Temple		2·50	1·70
28	80y. Wall mounted statues, Goushouji Temple		2·50	1·70
29	80y. Eagle surmounting gateway, Tennouji Temple		2·50	1·70
30	80y. Courtyard with stone lined path and building, Kokubunji Temple		2·50	1·70

Nos. 11-30 were also issued by Ehime, Kochi and Kagawa.

2006. Cultural Heritage. Temples. Multicoloured.
31	80y. As Type **9** of Ehime		2·50	1·70
32	80y. Kirihata-ji (statue), Kirihata Temple		2·50	1·70
33	80y. Cherry blossom and building, Fujiidera Temple		2·50	1·70
34	80y. Snow-covered pagoda and temple, Shozanji Temple		2·50	1·70
35	80y. Wide path, inscribed pillar and gateway, Konomineji Temple		2·50	1·70
36	80y. Decorative carved roof boss and bell, Dainichiji Temple		2·50	1·70
37	80y. Cherry blossom and grass edged path, Kokubunji Temple		2·50	1·70
38	80y. Cherry blossom and statue, Zenrakuji Temple		2·50	1·70
39	80y. Cliff face and temple building, Iwayaji Temple		2·50	1·70
40	80y. Decorated footprints, Joururiji Temple		2·50	1·70
41	80y. Spot-lighted statues, Yasakaji Temple		2·50	1·70
42	80y. Lantern, tree, path, gateway and inscribed pillar, Sairinji Temple		2·50	1·70
43	80y. Temple buildings through hole in rock, Kichijoji Temple		2·50	1·70
44	80y. Cherry blossom and roofs, Maegamiji Temple		2·50	1·70
45	80y. Carving with dragon and phoenix, Sankakuji Temple		2·50	1·70
46	80y. Snow-covered roofs and trees, Unbenji Temple		2·50	1·70
47	80y. Wide path, pilgrim and gateway, Shiromineji Temple		2·50	1·70
48	80y. Row of statues, Negoroji Temple		2·50	1·70
49	80y. Lantern, courtyard and building, Ichinomiyaji Temple		2·50	1·70
50	80y. Animal statues and building, Yashimaji Temple		2·50	1·70

Nos. 31-50 were also issued by Ehime, Kochi and Kagawa.

2007. Cultural Heritage. Temples. As T 10 of Ehime. Multicoloured.
51	80y. Type **10**		2·50	1·70
52	80y. Gateway		2·50	1·70
53	80y. Square, shrub and main hall		2·50	1·70
54	80y. Trees, temple roof and hill		2·50	1·70
55	80y. Bell tower gate		2·50	1·70
56	80y. Bamboo temple		2·50	1·70
57	80y. Statues, pathway and temple		2·50	1·70
58	80y. Paved path and entrance		2·50	1·70
59	80y. Buddha		2·50	1·70
60	80y. Decorated ceiling and bell		2·50	1·70
61	80y. Temple lit from below		2·50	1·70
62	80y. Paved path, steps and temple		2·50	1·70
63	80y. Guardian statue		2·50	1·70
64	80y. Gateway		2·50	1·70
65	80y. Carved ceiling and bell		2·50	1·70
66	80y. Pagoda and temple at night		2·50	1·70
67	80y. Temple and mountains		2·50	1·70
68	80y. Pilgrims entering gateway		2·50	1·70
69	80y. Pilgrims and temple		2·50	1·70
70	80y. Temple, banners and mountains		2·50	1·70
71	80y. Well		2·50	1·70
72	80y. Kobo Daishi (statue)		2·50	1·70
73	80y. Buddha		2·50	1·70
74	80y. Three roofed pagoda		2·50	1·70
75	80y. Pilgrims, steps and gateway		2·50	1·70
76	80y. Demon		2·50	1·70
77	80y. Rock statues		2·50	1·70
78	80y. Bodhisattva		2·50	1·70
79	80y. Cave and temple at night		2·50	1·70
80	80y. Kobo Daishi (painting)		2·50	1·70

Nos. 51-80 were also issued by Ehime, Kagawa and Kochi on 1 August 2007.

6-7 Dancers, left

2008. Tanabata Festival. Multicoloured.
81	50y. Type **6**		1·60	1·50
82	50y. Type **7**		1·60	1·50
83	50y. Lanterns, left		1·60	1·50
84	50y. Lanterns, right		1·60	1·50
85	50y. Procession and roofs, left		1·60	1·50
86	50y. Procession and roofs, right		1·60	1·50
87	50y. Procession, left		1·60	1·50
88	50y. Procession, right		1·60	1·50
89	50y. Drummers, left		1·60	1·50
90	50y. Drummers, right		1·60	1·50

Nos. 81-2, 83-4, 85-6, 87-8 and 89-90 were issued together, se-tenant, each pair forming a composite design.

Nos. 81-90 were also issued by Tokyo, Okinawa, Miyagi and Fukuoka on 1 August 2008.

8 Citrus sudachi   9 Citrus sudachi

2010. Prefectural Flowers. Multicoloured.
91	50y. Peony (Shimane)		1·60	1·10
92	50y. Type **8** (Tokushima)		1·60	1·10
93	50y. Unzen azalea (Nagasaki)		1·60	1·10
94	50y. Iris laevigata (Aichi)		1·60	1·10
95	50y. Camphor flowers (Saga)		1·60	1·10
96	80y. Peonies (Shimane)		2·60	1·80
97	80y. Type **9** (Tokushima)		2·60	1·80
98	880y. Unzen azalea (Nagasaki)		2·60	1·80
99	80y. Iris laevigata (Aichi)		2·60	1·80
100	80y. Camphor flowers (Saga)		2·60	1·80

Stamps of the same design were issued by Aichi, Nagasaki, Saga and Shimane on 8 March 2010.

TOKYO

1 Station Building   2 Shin-Tokyo Post Office

1989. Tokyo Station.
1	**1**	62y. multicoloured		1·30	70

1990
2		62y. As Type **1448** of Japan		1·20	80

2 Shin-Tokyo Post Office

1990
3	**2**	62y. multicoloured		1·50	80

3 Fringed Orchids

1991
4	**3**	41y. multicoloured		1·30	80

1993
5	**4**	62y. multicoloured		1·50	1·00

4 Blossom and Forest,
Mount Takao-san

5 Rainbow Bridge

1994
6	**5**	50y. multicoloured		1·90	1·30

1995
7	**6**	50y. multicoloured		1·20	70

6 Akamon

7 Kaminarimon
Gate

1996
8	**7**	80y. multicoloured		2·10	1·40

8   **9**   **10**

11   **12**

1997. Places of Interest.

9	**8**	80y. multicoloured	1·80	1·20
10	**9**	80y. multicoloured	1·80	1·20
11	**10**	80y. multicoloured	1·80	1·20
12	**11**	80y. multicoloured	1·80	1·20
13	**12**	80y. multicoloured	1·80	1·20

13 Gateway

1998. Business Show.

14	**13**	80y. multicoloured	1·80	1·20

14 Tama Monorail

1998

15	**14**	80y. multicoloured	2·10	1·40

15 Orchid

1999. . Multicoloured..

16	80y. Type **15**	2·10	1·40
17	80y. Pink orchid	2·10	1·40

16 Fireworks and Bridge

1999. Sumidagawa River Firework Display. Multicoloured.

18	80y. Type **16**	2·10	1·40
19	80y. Fireworks and bridge (different)	2·10	1·40
20	80y. Pink morning glory blossom	2·10	1·40

Nos. 18-19 were issued together, *se-tenant*, forming a composite design.

17 Whales

2000. Tourism. Multicoloured.

21	50y. Type **17**	1·50	1·00
22	50y. Mother and child	1·50	1·00
23	50y. Sanja-matsuri festival	1·50	1·00
24	50y. Family and gingko trees	1·50	1·00
25	50y. Odaiba-kaihin park at night	1·50	1·00

18 Cosmos Flowers

2000. Seasonal Splendours (1st series). Multicoloured.

26	50y. Type **18**	1·50	1·00
27	50y. Roses	1·50	1·00
28	50y. Bird of Paradise flowers	1·50	1·00
29	50y. Camellias	1·50	1·00
30	50y. Freesias	1·50	1·00

See also Nos. 34-8, 43-6, 47-50, 51-4 and 55-8.

19 Children and Ducks

2000

31	**19**	80y. multicoloured	2·75	1·90

20 Shinjuku, New Centre of Tokyo

2000. Greetings from Tokyo. Multicoloured.

32	80y.+20y. Type **20**	3·50	2·40
33	80y.+20y. Tokyo at night	3·50	2·40

The premium was for the victims of eruptions and earthquakes.

21 Cherry Blossom

2001. Seasonal Splendours (2nd series). Multicoloured.

34	50y. Type **21**	1·60	1·10
35	50y. Hydrangea	1·60	1·10
36	50y. Salvia	1·60	1·10
37	50y. Chrysanthemums	1·60	1·10
38	50y. Camellias	1·60	1·10

22 Okuma Auditorium and Clock Tower

2001

39	**22**	80y. multicoloured	2·50	1·70

23 Tokyo Millenario (festival of lights)

2001

40	**23**	80y. multicoloured	2·40	1·60

24 Morning Glory Fair

2002. Fairs and Markets. Multicoloured.

41	80y. Type **24**	2·20	1·50
42	80y. Hozuki (ground cherry) fair	2·50	1·50

25 Azaleas

2002. Seasonal Splendours (3rd series). Multicoloured.

43	50y. Type **25**	1·50	1·00
44	50y. Lily	1·50	1·00
45	50y. Crape myrtle	1·50	1·00
46	50y. *Gingko biloba* (maidenhair tree)	1·50	1·00

26 Ume Blossom

2003. Seasonal Splendours (4th series). Multicoloured.

47	50y. Type **26**	1·60	1·10
48	50y. Wisteria	1·60	1·10
49	50y. Irises	1·60	1·10
50	50y. Tea blossom	1·60	1·10

27 Magnolia Blossom

2004. Seasonal Splendours (5th series). Multicoloured.

51	50y. Type **27**	1·60	1·10
52	50y. Azalea	1·60	1·10
53	50y. *Anemone flaccida*	1·60	1·10
54	50y. Bush clover	1·60	1·10

28 Ebine Orchid

2005. Seasonal Splendours (6th series). Multicoloured.

55	50y. Type **28**	1·60	1·10
56	50y. Crinum	1·60	1·10
57	50y. Kerria blossom	1·60	1·10
58	50y. Azalea	1·60	1·10

29 Cherry Blossom

2006. Seasonal Splendours (7th series). Multicoloured.

59	80y. Type **29**	2·50	1·70
60	80y. Roses and Asasaka Palace	2·50	1·70
61	80y. Cosmos, Shouwas Kinen Park	2·50	1·70
62	80y. Apricot blossom and Yushima Tenjin Shrine	2·50	1·70

30 Tokyo Tower and Winter Sweet

2007. Tourism. Multicoloured.

63	80y. Type **30**	2·50	1·70
64	80y. Bridge	2·50	1·70
65	80y. Jingu gardens and osmanthus flower	2·50	1·70
66	80y. Lake and gentians	2·50	1·70
67	80y. Bridge with lamps, Nihonbashi	2·50	1·70

31 *Nihonbashi and Edobashi Bridges* ((*100 Famous Views of Edo*)) (Hiroshige Utagawa)

2007. Ukiyoe Festival 2007. Multicoloured.

68	80y. Type **31**	2·50	1·70
69	80y. *Takashima Ohisa* (Utamaro Kitagawa)	2·50	1·70
70	80y. *Ichikawa Yaozo III as Tanabe Bunzo* (Toshusai Sharaku)	2·50	1·70
71	80y. *Iris Garden at Horikiri* (*100 Famous Views of Edo*) (Utagawa Hiroshige)	2·50	1·70
72	80y. *Asakusa Kinriyuzan* (*100 Famous Views of Edo*) (Utagawa Hiroshige)	2·50	1·70
73	80y. *Sugatami Shichinin Kesho* (Kitagawa Utamaro)	2·50	1·70
74	80y. *Arashi Ryuzou II as Ishibe Kinkichi* (Toshusai Sharaku)	2·50	1·70
75	80y. *Suidobashi Surugadai* (*100 Famous Views of Edo*) (Utagawa Hiroshige)	2·50	1·70
76	80y. *The Moon Pine at Ueno* (*100 Famous Views of Edo*) (Utagawa Hiroshige)	2·50	1·70
77	80y. *Courtesan Hanaogi of the Ogiya* (Kitagawa Utamaro)	2·50	1·70

32-33 Procession and Roofs

2008. Tanabata Festival. Multicoloured.

78	50y. Type **32**	1·60	1·50
79	50y. Type **33**	1·60	1·50
80	50y. Lanterns, left	1·60	1·50
81	50y. Lanterns, right	1·60	1·50
82	50y. Dancers, left	1·60	1·50
83	50y. Dancers, right	1·60	1·50
84	50y. Procession, left	1·60	1·50
85	50y. Procession, right	1·60	1·50
86	50y. Drummers, left	1·60	1·50
87	50y. Drummers, right	1·60	1·50

Nos. 78-9, 80-1, 82-3, 84-5 and 86-7 were issued together, *se-tenant*, each pair forming a composite design.

Nos. 78-87 were also issued by Tokushima, Okinawa, Miyagi and Fukuoka on 1 August 2008.

34 Somei Yoshino Cherry Blossom

2009. Prefectural Flowers. Multicoloured.

88	50y. Type **34** (Tokyo)	1·60	1·50
89	50y. Yashio tsutsuji (*Rhododendron albrechtii*) (Tochigi)	1·60	1·50
90	50y. Tulips (Niigata)		
91	50y. Rhododendron (*Rhododendron japonicum*) (Shiga)	1·60	1·50
92	50y. Yaezakura cherry blossom (Nara)	1·60	1·50
93	80y. Somei Yoshino cherry blossom (Tokyo)	2·50	1·70
94	80y. Yashio tsutsuji (*Rhododendron albrechtii*) (Tochigi)	2·50	1·70
95	80y. Tulips (Niigata)	2·50	1·70
96	80y. Rhododendron (*Rhododendron japonicum*) (Shiga)	2·50	1·70
97	80y. Yaezakura cherry blossom (Nara)	2·50	1·70

Stamps of the same design were issued by Nara, Niigata, Shiga, and Tochigi on 2 February 2009.

35 Shrine carried through Water

2009. Fukagawa Hachiman Festival. Multicoloured.

98	50y. Type **35**	1·70	1·30

99		50y. Shrine, water throwing and temple	1·70	1·30

Nos.98-9 were printed, se-tenant, each pair forming a composite design.

TOTTORI

1990

1		62y. As Type **1464** of Japan	1·20	80

1 Fruit

1991

2	**1**	62y. multicoloured	1·20	80

2 Shanshan Festival

1996

3	**2**	80y. multicoloured	2·10	1·40

3 Ship

1997. Tottori Expo.

4	**3**	80y. multicoloured	2·10	1·40

4 Nijisseikinashi (Japanese pear tree) and Dune

2000. Multicoloured.

5		50y. Type **4**	1·50	1·00
6		50y. Natsumikan (summer-orange blossoms) and sea	1·50	1·00
7		50y. Botan (peonies) and Izumo-taisha Shrine	1·50	1·00
8		50y. Momonohana (peach blossoms) and traditional houses in Kurashiki	1·50	1·00
9		50y. Momiji (maple leaves) and Itsukushima Shrine Gate	1·50	1·00

Nos. 5-9 were also issued by Yamaguchi, Shimane, Okayama and Hiroshima.

5 Uradome Coast and Snow Crab

2001. Homeland Tottori. Multicoloured.

10		50y. Type **5**	1·60	1·10
11		50y. Dunes	1·60	1·10
12		50y. Paper Hina dolls in river	1·60	1·10
13		50y. Mt. Daisen	1·60	1·10
14		80y. Nageiredo Hall	2·75	1·80
15		80y. Mukibanda Palaeolithic site	2·75	1·80

6 Flower Dome, Flowers and Mount Daisen

2004. Hana-Kairou Flower Park.

16	**6**	80y. multicoloured	2·50	1·70

7 Pear Blossom and Yumigahama Beach (Tottori)

2006. Flowers of Chugoku. Multicoloured.

17		50y. Type **7**	1·60	1·10
18		50y. Tree peonies and Hinomi-saki Lighthouse (Shimane)	1·60	1·10
19		50y. Peach blossoms and Seto-oohashi bridge (Okayama)	1·60	1·10
20		50y. Maple leaves and Miyajima shrine (Hiroshima)	1·60	1·10
21		50y. Chinese citron blossom and Oomijima island (Yamaguchi)	1·60	1·10

Nos. 17-21 were also issued by Shimane, Okayama, Hiroshima, and Yamaguchi.

8 Mandarin Ducks

2007. Birds. Multicoloured.

22		80y. Type **8**	2·50	1·70
23		80y. Swans	2·50	1·70
24		80y. Pheasants	2·50	1·70
25		80y. Ducks swimming	2·50	1·70
26		80y. Cranes	2·50	1·70

Nos. 22-6 were also issued by Hiroshima, Okayama, Shimane and Yamaguchi on 1 May 2007.

9 Fuji Zakura Satsuki Azalea   **10** Fuji Zakura Satsuki Azalea

2010. Prefectural Flowers. Multicoloured.

27		50y. Tulips (Toyama)	1·70	1·20
28		50y. Milk vetch (Gifu)	1·70	1·20
29		50y. Fuji Zakura Satsuki azalea (Yamanashi)	1·70	1·20
30		50y. Indian coral bean flower (Okinawa)	1·70	1·20
31		50y. Type **9** (Tottori)	1·70	1·20
32		80y. Tulips (Toyama)	2·60	1·80
33		80y. Milk vetch (Gifu)	2·60	1·80
34		80y. Fuji Zakura Satsuki azalea (Yamanashi)	2·60	1·80
35		80y. Indian coral bean flower (Okinawa)	2·60	1·80
36		80y. Type **10** (Tottori)	2·60	1·80

Stamps of the same design were issued by Gifu, Okinawa, Yamanashi and Toyama on 1 February 2010.

TOYAMA

1 Waterfall

1990. Shomyo-no-taki.

1	**1**	62y. multicoloured	1·20	80

1990. Flowers.

2		62y. As Type **1451** of Japan	1·20	80

2 Mount Tateyama

1992

3	**2**	62y. multicoloured	1·50	90

3 Bridge and Waterfall, Kurobe-kyokoku

1994

4	**3**	80y. multicoloured	1·90	1·10

4 Woman Dancer

1997. Owara Kaze no Bon. Multicoloured.

5		80y. Type **4**	1·80	1·20
6		80y. Male dancer	1·80	1·20

Nos. 5-6 were issued together, se-tenant, forming a composite design.

5 Firefly Squids

1999

7	**5**	80y. multicoloured	2·10	1·40

6 Dancer

1999

8	**6**	80y. multicoloured	2·10	1·40

7 Tateyama Mountain Range and Tulip Field

2000. Multicoloured.

9		50y. Type **7**	1·50	1·00
10		80y. Tulips	2·50	1·70

8 Badminton Player

2000. 55th National Athletic Meet.

11	**8**	50y. multicoloured	1·80	1·20

9 Sanmon Gate, Zuiryuji Temple

2004. Zuiryuji Temple.

12	**9**	80y. multicoloured	2·50	1·70

10 Child Dancers

2004. Owara Dance, Bon Festival of Wind II. Multicoloured.

13		50y. Type **10**	1·60	1·10

14		50y. Women dancers	1·60	1·10
15		50y. Men dancers	1·60	1·10
16		50y. Musicians	1·60	1·10

Nos. 13-16 were issued together, se-tenant, forming a composite design.

11 Rhododendron

2005. Flowers of Hokuriku. Multicoloured.

17		50y. Type **11**	1·60	1·10
18		50y. Hydrangea	1·60	1·10
19		50y. Tulip	1·60	1·10
20		50y. Lily	1·60	1·10

Nos. 17-20 were also issued by Ishikawa and Fukui.

12 Bon Dancers

2007. Owara Kaze no Bon. Multicoloured.

21		80y. Type**12**	2·50	1·70
22		80y. Dancers and screen	2·50	1·70
23		80y. Child performers	2·50	1·70
24		80y. Dancers woman at left	2·50	1·70
25		80y. Dancers and moon	2·50	1·70

13 Tulips   **14** Tulips

2010. Prefectural Flowers. Multicoloured.

26		50y. Type **13** (Toyama)	1·70	1·20
27		50y. Milk vetch (Gifu)	1·70	1·20
28		50y. Fuji Zakura Satsuki azalea (Yamanashi)	1·70	1·20
29		50y. Indian coral bean flower (Okinawa)	1·70	1·20
30		80y. Pear blossom (Tottori)	1·70	1·20
31		80y. Type **14** (Toyama)	1·70	1·20
32		80y. Milk vetch (Gifu)	2·60	1·80
33		80y. Fuji Zakura Satsuki azalea (Yamanashi)	2·60	1·80
34		80y. Indian coral bean flower (Okinawa)	2·60	1·80
35		80y. Pear blossom (Tottori)	2·60	1·80

Stamps of the same design were issued by Gifu, Okinawa, Tottori and Yamanashi on 1 February 2010.

WAKAYAMA

1990. Flowers.

1		62y. As Type **1463** of Japan	1·50	1·00

1 Kumano Path

1990

2	**1**	62y. multicoloured	1·20	80

2 Yachts, Waka-no-ura

1994

3	**2**	80y. multicoloured	1·90	1·20

1998

4		80y. multicoloured	2·10	1·40

3 Waterfall

1999. Southern Kii Penisula. Multicoloured.

5	80y. Type **3**	2·10	1·40
6	80y. Island at sunset	2·10	1·40

Nos. 5-6 were issued together, se-tenant, forming a composite design.

4 Mount Koya

1999. Koyasan Temples. Multicoloured.

7	80y. Type **4**	2·10	1·40
8	80y. Statue	2·10	1·40

5 Azaleas, Wakayama Marina City, and Wakaura Bay

2002

9	**5**	80y. multicoloured	2·20	1·50

6 Shakunage (rhododendron) (Shiga)

2006. Flowers of Kinki. Multicoloured.

10	50y. Yae-zakura (double cherry blossoms) (Nara)	1·60	1·10
11	50y. Nozigiku (wild chrysanthemums) (Hyogo)	1·60	1·10
12	50y. Type **6**	1·60	1·10
13	50y. Ume blossoms (Wakayama)	1·60	1·10
14	50y. Sakuraso (primrose) (Osaka)	1·60	1·10
15	50y. Shidare-zakura (weeping cherry) (Kyoto)	1·60	1·10

Nos. 10-15 were also issued by Osaka, Nara, Shiga, Hyogo and Kyoto.

7 Wakayama Castle

2007. Castles in Kinki Region. Multicoloured.

16	50y. Type **7**	1·60	1·50
17	50y. Koriyama	1·60	1·50
18	50y. Hikone	1·60	1·50
19	50y. Himeji	1·60	1·50
20	50y. Osaka	1·60	1·50

Nos. 16-20 were also issued by Hyogo, Nara, Osaka and Shiga on 1 June 2007.

8 Pink Plum Blossom

2008. Prefectural Flowers. Multicoloured.

21	50y. Narcissus (Fukui)	1·60	1·50
22	50y. Type **8**	1·60	1·50
23	50y. Fuki (Petasites japonicus) (Akita)	1·60	1·50
24	50y. White plum blossom (Fukuoka)	1·60	1·50
25	50y. Weeping cherry blossom (Kyoto)	1·60	1·50
26	80y. Narcissus (Fukui)	2·50	1·70

27	80y. White plum blossom (Wakayama)	2·50	1·70
28	80y. Fuki (Petasites japonicus) (Akita)	2·50	1·70
29	80y. Pink plum blossom (Fukuoka)	2·50	1·70
30	80y. Weeping cherry blossom (Kyoto)	2·50	1·70

9 Chamaecyparis obtusa

2011. National Afforestation Campaign and International Year of Forests. Multicoloured.

31	50y. Type **9**	1·80	1·20
32	50y. Prunus jamasakura	1·80	1·20
33	50y. Persea thunbergii	1·80	1·20
34	50y. Sciadopitys verticillata	1·80	1·20
35	50y. Prunus mume	1·80	1·20
36	50y. Quercus gilva	1·80	1·20
37	50y. Nageia nagi	1·80	1·20
38	50y. Michelia compressa	1·80	1·20
39	50y. Pseudotsuga japonica	1·80	1·20
40	50y. International Year of Forests Emblem	1·80	1·20

YAMAGATA

1 Cherries

1989

1	**1**	62y. multicoloured	1·50	80

1990. Flowers.

2	62y. As Type **1439** of Japan	1·20	80

2 Trees in Autumn, Yama-dera

1995

3	**2**	80y. multicoloured	1·90	1·00

3 Dancers, Hanagasa Festival

1998

4	**3**	50y. multicoloured	1·30	90

1999

5	**1**	80y. multicoloured	2·10	1·40

4 Group of Trees

2000. Cherry Trees. Multicoloured.

6	80y. Type **4**	2·50	1·70
7	80y. Tree, central, Iwate	2·50	1·70
8	80y. Group of trees, Fukishima	2·50	1·70
9	80y. Tree, left, Miyagi	2·50	1·70
10	80y. Cherry blossom, Aomori	2·50	1·70
11	80y. Trees and river, Akita	2·50	1·70

Nos. 6-11 were also issued by Aomori, Iwate, Miyagi, Akita and Fukush.

5 Safflowers, Mogamigawa River, and Mount Gassan

2002. National Afforestation Campaign.

12	**5**	50y. multicoloured	1·60	1·10

6 Safflower (Yamagata)

2004. Prefectural Flowers. Multicoloured.

13	50y. Type **6**	1·60	1·10
14	50y. Apple blossom (Aomori)	1·60	1·10
15	50y. Paulownia (Iwate)	1·60	1·10
16	50y. Butterbur flower (Akita)	1·60	1·10
17	50y. Japanese bush clover (Miyagi)	1·60	1·10
18	50y. Alpine rose (Rhododendron ferrugineum) (Fukushima)	1·60	1·10

Nos. 13-18 were also issued by Yamagata, Aomori, Miyagi, Iwate and Fukushima.

7 Cherry (Yamagata)

2005. Fruits of Tohoku. Multicoloured.

19	50y. Type **7**	1·60	1·10
20	50y. Apple (Iwate)	1·60	1·10
21	50y. Apples (Aomori)	1·60	1·10
22	50y. Peach (Fukushima)	1·60	1·10

Nos. 19-22 were also issued by Aomori, Iwate and Fukushima.

8 Hanagasa Matsuri (Yamagata)

2006. Festivals of Tohoku. Multicoloured.

25	80y. Type **8**	2·50	1·70
26	80y. Kanto Matsuri (Akita)	2·50	1·70
27	80y. Nebuta Matsuri (Aomori)	2·50	1·70
28	80y. Sendai Tanabata Matsuri (Miyagi)	2·50	1·70

Nos. 25-8 were also issued by Akita, Aomori, and Miyagi.

9 Dicentra and Water Filled Crater

2007. North Eastern Scenery. Multicoloured.

29	80y. Type **9**	2·50	1·70
30	80y. Oirase stream	2·50	1·70
31	80y. Hirosaki Castle	2·50	1·70
32	80y. Chusonji Temple	2·50	1·70
33	80y. Rocks and lily (sukashiyuri)	2·50	1·70
34	80y. Matsushima island and rape flowers	2·50	1·70
35	80y. Oga penisula and pinks	2·50	1·70
36	80y. Lily (nikkoukisuge) and mountain	2·50	1·70
37	80y. Skunk Cabbage Flowers, Oze National Park	2·50	1·70
38	80y. Safflower	2·50	1·70

Nos. 29-38 were also issued by Akita, Aomori, Fukushima, Iwate and Miyagi on 2 July 2007.

10 Safflower

2008. Flowers. Multicoloured.

39	50y. Type **10**	1·60	1·70
40	50y. Lily	1·60	1·10
41	50y. Sweet briar	1·60	1·10
42	50y. Nemotoshakunage (Rhododendron brachycarpum)	1·60	1·10
43	50y. Gentian	1·60	1·10
44	80y. Lily (25×35 mm)	2·50	1·70
45	80y. Sweet briar (25×35 mm)	2·50	1·70
46	80y. Rhododendron (25×35 mm)	2·50	1·70
47	80y. Safflower (25×35 mm)	2·50	1·70
48	80y. Gentian (25×35 mm)	2·50	1·70

Nos. 39-48 were also issued by Fukushima, Hokkaido, Kanagawa and Nagano on 1 July 2008.

YAMAGUCHI

1 Bird-shaped Lanterns

1989

1	**1**	62y. multicoloured	1·30	70

1990

2	62y. As Type **1468** of Japan	1·20	80

2 Lanterns

1992. Lantern Festival.

3	**2**	62y. multicoloured	1·20	80

3 Street, Hagi

1999. Multicoloured.

4	80y. Type **3**	2·10	1·40
5	80y. Railway bridge, Tsuwano	2·10	1·40

Nos. 4-5 were also issued by Shimane.

4 Natsumikan (summer-orange blossoms) and Sea

2000. Multicoloured.

6	50y. Type **4**	1·50	1·00
7	50y. Nijisseikinashi (Japanese pear tree) and Tottori dune	1·50	1·00
8	50y. Botan (peonies) and Izumo-taisha Shrine	1·50	1·00
9	50y. Momonohana (peach blossoms) and traditional houses in Kurashiki	1·50	1·00
10	50y. Momiji (maple leaves) and Itsukushima Shrine Gate	1·50	1·00

Nos. 6-10 were also issued by Tottori, Shimane, Okayama and Hiroshima.

5 Kintaikyo Bridge

2000

11	**5**	80y. multicoloured	2·75	1·90

6 Aji Wild Ducks

2001. Japan EXPO, Yamaguchi. Multicoloured.

12	50y. Type **6**	1·60	1·10
13	80y. Yamaguchi Kirara band and EXPO site	2·50	1·70

7 Kaikyo-Messe Tower, Shimonoseki and Blue Whale

2002. International Whaling Commission.

| 14 | **7** | 80y. multicoloured | 2·20 | 1·50 |

8 Kaneko Misuzu

2003. Birth Centenary of Kaneko Misuzu (poet). Multicoloured.

| 15 | | 80y. Type **8** | 2·40 | 1·60 |
| 16 | | 80y. Tairyo | 2·40 | 1·60 |

Nos. 15-16 were issued together, *se-tenant*, forming a composite design.

9 Lord Mouri Takachika's Procession

2003. 400th Anniv of Hagi City. Multicoloured.

| 17 | | 80y. Type **9** | 2·50 | 1·70 |
| 18 | | 80y. Lord Mouri Takachika's procession (different) | 2·50 | 1·70 |

Nos. 17-18 were issued together, se-tenant, forming a composite design.

10 Chinese Citron Blossom and Oomijima Island (Yamaguchi)

2006. Flowers of Chugoku. Multicoloured.

19		50y. Type **10**	1·60	1·10
20		50y. Tree peonies and Hinomi-saki Lighthouse (Shimane)	1·60	1·10
21		50y. Peach blossoms and Seto-oohashi bridge (Okayama)	1·60	1·10
22		50y. Maple leaves and Miyajima shrine (Hiroshima)	1·60	1·10
23		50y. Pear blossom and Yumiga-hama Beach (Tottori)	1·60	1·10

Nos. 19-23 were also issued by Tottori, Shimane, Okayama and Hiroshima.

11 Cranes

2007. Birds. Multicoloured.

24		80y. Type **8**	2·50	1·70
25		80y. Mandarin ducks	2·50	1·70
26		80y. Swans	2·50	1·70
27		80y. Pheasants	2·50	1·70
28		80y. Ducks swimming	2·50	1·70

Nos. 22-28 were also issued by Hiroshima, Okayama, Shimane, Tottori on 1 May 2007.

12 *Citrus natsudaidai*   **12** *Citrus natsudaidai*

2011. Prefectural Flowers. Multicoloured.

| 29 | | 50y. *Rosa* (Ibaraki) | 1·80 | 1·20 |

30		50y. *Malus pumila* (Aomori)	1·80	1·20
31		50y. *Primula sieboldii* (Saitama)	1·80	1·20
32		50y. Type **12**	1·80	1·20
33		50y. *Rhododendron kiusianum* (Kagoshima)	1·80	1·20
34		80y. *Rosa* (Ibaraki)	2·75	1·90
35		80y. *Malus pumila* (Aomori)	2·75	1·90
36		80y. *Primula sieboldii* (Saitama)	2·75	1·90
37		80y. Type **13**	2·75	1·90
38		80y. *Rhododendron kiusianum* (Kagoshima)	2·75	1·90

Stamps of the same design were issued by Aomori, Ibaraki, Kagoshima and Saitama on 8 February 2011.

14

2011. 66th National Athletic Meet. Multicoloured.

39		50y. Type **14**	1·80	1·20
40		50y. Wrestling	1·80	1·20
41		50y. Rock climbing	1·80	1·20
42		50y. Handball in Net	1·80	1·20
43		50y. Bat, baseball and pitch	1·80	1·20

YAMANASHI

1990

| 1 | | 62y. As Type **1446** of Japan | 1·20 | 80 |

1 Bride

1991

| 2 | **1** | 62y. multicoloured | 1·20 | 80 |

2 Waterfall

1996. Shosenkyo Gorge.

| 3 | **2** | 50y. multicoloured | 1·30 | 90 |

3 Leaves, Lake and Mountain

1999. Five Lakes, Fuji. Multicoloured.

4		80y. Type **3**	2·10	1·40
5		80y. Cherry blossom, lake and mountain	2·10	1·40
6		80y. Flower, lake, forest and mountain	2·10	1·40
7		80y. Shoreline, lake, jetty forest and mountain	2·10	1·40
8		80y. Trees, lake, hills and mountain	2·10	1·40

4 Symbols of Yamanashi, Mount Fuji and Jewellry

2001

| 9 | **4** | 80y. multicoloured | 2·40 | 1·60 |

5 Butterfly and Mount Mizugakisan, Azuma-Shakunage

2001. National Reforestation Campaign.

| 10 | **5** | 50y. multicoloured | 1·60 | 1·10 |

---

6 Peach Blossom and Shirane-sanzan Mountains (Kyoto area)

2001. Yamanashi Scenery. Multicoloured.

11		50y. Type **6**	1·50	1·00
12		50y. Iris and Mt. Kitadake (Kyochu area)	1·50	1·00
13		50y. Horses and Mt. Yatsuga-take (Kyohoku area)	1·50	1·00
14		50y. Snow-covered houses and Oshino-hakkai ponds (Gunn-nai area)	1·50	1·00
15		50y. Cherry blossom, Minobu (Kyonan area)	1·50	1·00

7 Sunflower and Mount Yatsugatake

2005. Flowers of Yamanashi. Multicoloured.

16		80y. Type **7**	2·50	1·70
17		80y. Gentian and Mt. Kitadake, Southern Japanese Alps	2·50	1·70
18		80y. Evening primrose and Mt. Fuji	2·50	1·70
19		80y. Lady's slipper and Mt. Fuji	2·50	1·70

8 Cherry Tree

2007. Yamanashi Scenery. Multicoloured.

20		80y. Type **8**	2·50	1·70
21		80y. Grapes and vineyard	2·50	1·70
22		80y. Azalea	2·50	1·70
23		80y. Lavender and Mt Fuji	2·50	1·70
24		80y. Peaches and blossom	2·50	1·70

9 Pear Blossom   **10** Pear Blossom

2010. Prefectural Flowers. Multicoloured.

25		50y. Tulips (Toyama)	1·60	1·10
26		50y. Milk vetch (Gifu)	1·60	1·10
27		50y. Type **9** (Yamanashi)	1·60	1·10
28		50y. Indian coral bean flower (Okinawa)	1·60	1·10
29		50y. Pear blossom (Tottori)	1·60	1·10
30		80y. Tulips (Toyama)	2·60	1·80
31		80y. Milk vetch (Gifu)	2·60	1·80
32		80y. Type **10** (Yamanashi)	2·60	1·80
33		80y. Indian coral bean flower (Okinawa)	2·60	1·80
34		80y. Pear blossom (Tottori)	2·60	1·80

Stamps of the same design were issued by Gifu, Okinawa, Tottori and Toyama on 1 February 2010.

JAPANESE TAIWAN (FORMOSA)

From 1895 to 1945 Taiwan was part of the Japanese Empire, using the stamps of Japan. During 1945 American naval and air forces disrupted communications between Taiwan and Japan. The following were issued when supplies of Japanese stamps ran short.

1 Numeral and Chrysanthemum

1945. Imperf.

J1	**1**	3s. red	60·00	75·00
J2	**1**	5s. green	65·00	65·00
J3	**1**	10s. blue	80·00	75·00

JAPANESE OCCUPATION OF CHINA

Japanese troops occupied Canton in 1938 and by 1945 had overrun much of Kwangtung province. Unoverprinted stamps of China were used until the following stamps were issued.

100 cents = 1 dollar.

I. KWANGTUNG

1 "Special for Kwangtung"

1942. Stamps of China optd with T **1**.

1	-	1c. orange (411)	2·00	2·50
2	77	1c. orange	3·00	3·75
3	58	2c. green	7·50	7·00
4	72	3c. red	3·00	3·00
5	77	5c. green	2·50	3·75
7	72	8c. olive	2·75	3·00
8	77	8c. green	3·00	4·25
9	72	10c. green	3·00	3·25
11	77	10c. emerald	3·25	3·25
12	72	16c. brown	5·00	5·25
13	72	17c. green	3·25	3·25
14	-	20c. blue (519)	3·25	3·75
15	72	30c. red	4·00	3·00
16	77	30c. red	3·25	3·25
17	72	50c. blue	4·00	7·50
18	77	50c. blue	3·25	3·75
19	72	$1 sepia and brown	9·00	10·00
20	72	$2 brown and blue	12·00	12·00
21	72	$5 green and red	12·00	12·00
22	72	$10 violet and green	22·00	20·00
23	72	$20 blue and purple	14·00	12·00

(2)

1942. Stamps of China optd with T **2**. (a) On 1938 issue.

24		2c. green	60	65
25		3c. red	60	85
26		5c. green	60	95
28		8c. green	70	90
29		10c. green	90	1·10
30		16c. brown	1·10	1·10
31		25c. blue	1·10	2·50
32		30c. red	1·00	2·20
33		50c. blue	2·00	2·50
35		$1 brown and red	8·00	11·00
37		$2 brown and blue	10·00	12·00
39		$5 green and red	13·00	23·00
40		$10 violet and green	17·00	25·00
42		$20 blue and purple	20·00	25·00

(b) On 1941 issue.

44	77	2c. blue	1·00	1·00
45	77	5c. green	1·00	1·00
46	77	8c. orange	1·00	1·00
47	77	8c. green	1·00	1·00
48	77	10c. green	1·00	1·00
49	77	17c. green	1·25	1·25
50	77	25c. purple	1·50	1·50
51	77	30c. red	1·50	1·50
52	77	50c. blue	1·75	1·50
53	77	$1 black and brown	7·00	10·00
54	77	$2 black and blue	7·00	8·50
55	77	$5 black and red	7·00	8·00
56	77	$10 black and green	13·00	15·00
57	77	$20 black and purple	20·00	20·00

(3)

1945. Canton provisionals. Surch as T **3**.

| 58 | 72 | $200 on 10c. green (No. 29) | £160 | £110 |
| 59 | 72 | $400 on 8c. olive (No. 28) | £160 | £100 |

(4)

1945. Swatow provisional. No. 508 of China surch with T **4**.

| 60 | | $400 on 1c. orange | £1300 | £800 |

POSTAGE DUE STAMPS

(D 3)

1945. Postage Due stamp of China surch with Type **D3**.

D58	**D62**	$100 on $2 orange	£1000	£1100

II. MENGKIANG (INNER MONGOLIA)

The autonomous area of Mengkiang ("the Mongolian Borderlands"), consisting of Suiyuan, South Chahar and North Shansi, was established by the Japanese in November, 1937.

For the first issue in 1941 see the note at the beginning of III North China.

(3)

1942. Stamps of China optd "**Mengkiang**" and surch half original value at T **3**.

86	-	½c. on 1c. orange (411)	25	45
69	**72**	1c. on 2c. green	2·25	1·20
93	**58**	1c. on 2c. green	10·00	12·00
87	**60**	2c. on 4c. lilac	6·00	4·50
94	**58**	2c. on 4c. green	50	65
72	**72**	4c. on 8c. green	65	65
73	**72**	5c. on 10c. green	1·00	65
99	-	5c. on 10c. purple (515)	6·50	8·25
95	**72**	8c. on 16c. brown	1·60	2·30
68	**58**	10c. on 20c. blue	48·00	45·00
88	-	10c. on 20c. blue (519)	8·00	6·50
100	-	10c. on 20c. red (418)	6·00	6·00
75	**72**	15c. on 30c. red	7·00	6·50
101	-	15c. on 30c. purple (542)	2·25	3·25
102	-	20c. on 40c. orange (524)	14·00	15·00
77	**72**	25c. on 50c. blue	10·00	9·00
103	-	25c. on 50c. green (525)	2·00	45·00
96	**72**	50c. on $1 sepia and brown	15·00	15·00
82	**72**	$1 on $2 brown and blue	20·00	18·00
98	**72**	$5 on $10 violet and green	£100	£110
84	**72**	$10 on $20 blue and purple	£110	£110

4 Dragon Pillar, Peking

1943. Fifth Anniv of Establishment of Mengkiang Post and Telegraph Service.

104	**4**	4c. orange	2·00	5·00
105	**4**	8c. blue	2·00	5·00

5 Miners

1943. Second Anniv of War in East Asia.

106	**5**	4c. green	1·75	5·00
107	**5**	8c. red	1·75	5·00

6 Stylized Horse   **7** Prince Yun

1943. First Anniv of Federation of Autonomous Governments of Mongolian Provinces.

108	**6**	3c. red	1·50	5·00
109	**7**	8c. red	1·25	5·00

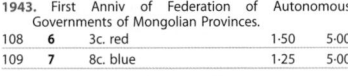

8 Blast Furnace

1944. Productivity Campaign.

110	**8**	8c. brown	1·50	4·00

1945. Stamps of China optd "**Mengkiang**" as top characters in T **3**.

117	-	1c. orange (411)	1·25	2·00
111	**58**	2c. green	18·00	13·00

112	**58**	4c. green	65·00	30·00
113	**58**	5c. green	18·00	15·00
118	-	8c. orange (514)	80	90
119	-	10c. purple (515)	30	40
120	-	20c. red (418)	2·25	2·40
121	-	30c. red (542)	40	1·25
122	-	40c. orange (524)	45	45
123	-	50c. green (525)	13·00	14·00
114	**72**	$1 sepia and brown	6·50	6·50
115	**72**	$2 brown and blue	22·00	22·00
116	**72**	$5 green and red	75·00	75·00

(10)

1945. Stamps of China optd "**Mengkiang**" (as T **3** of North China) and surch as T **10**.

124B	**60**	10c. on ½c. sepia	4·25	4·00
126B	-	10c. on 1c. orange (411)	1·00	1·10
130B	**72**	50c. on 2c. olive	1·00	1·50
135	**58**	50c. on 2c. olive	3·00	2·75
131B	**60**	50c. on 4c. lilac	80	1·00
136	**58**	50c. on 4c. green	5·00	4·00
132B	**72**	50c. on 5c. olive	70	1·40
137	**58**	50c. on 5c. green	40	40
138	-	$1 on 8c. orange (514)	30	1·70

III. NORTH CHINA

The Japanese conquered North China in 1937 and formed a puppet Government in Peking.

Type **2** of Meng Kiang and **B** to **J** are the six "district" overprints comprising North China (including Mengkiang) and a detailed list of the overprints on the stamps of China is given in the Stanley Gibbons' Catalogue, Part 17 (China).

In 1942 stamps of China overprinted with Types **B** to **J** were further overprinted with Type **1** (to commemorate the Fall of Singapore) or with Type **2** (to commemorate the tenth Anniversary of Manchukuo). These stamps are also listed in the Stanley Gibbons' Catalogue Part 17 (China).

(3)   **2x** (2 of Meng Kiang "Mengkiang")   **B** (B. "Honan")

D (D. "Hopeh")   **E** (E. "Shansi")

H (H. "Shantung")   **J** (J. "Supeh")

(1)   (2)

1942. Stamps of China optd "**Hwa Pei**" (= North China) and surch half original value at T **3**.

111	-	½c. on 1c. orange (No. 411)	25	20
88	**72**	1c. on 2c. olive	40	25
114	-	1c. on 2c. blue (No. 509)	2·50	2·00
128	**58**	2c. on 4c. green	3·25	25
116	**60**	2c. on 4c. lilac	1·00	1·00
129	**58**	2c. on 4c. green	1·25	20
91	**72**	4c. on 8c. olive	50	45
134	-	4c. on 8c. orange (No. 514)	65	25
92	**72**	5c. on 10c. green	50	40
120	-	5c. on 10c. pur (515)	5·00	5·00
130	**72**	8c. on 16c. olive	75	25
122	-	10c. on 20c. blue (No. 519)	5·00	1·10
135	-	10c. on 20c. lake (No. 418)	2·00	1·80
96	**72**	10c. on 30c. red	2·25	1·00
136	-	15c. on 30c. purple (No. 542)	75	65
137	-	20c. on 40c. orge (No. 542)	2·75	25
98	**72**	25c. on 50c. blue	2·50	1·40
138	-	25c. on 50c. grn (No. 525)	2·50	1·50
131	**72**	50c. on $1 brown and red	5·00	5·00
132	**72**	$1 on $2 brown and blue	12·00	6·00
133	**72**	$5 on $10 violet and green	40·00	40·00
109	**72**	$10 on $20 blue and purple	85·00	85·00

(4)

1943. Return to China of Foreign Concessions. Optd with T **4**.

139	**58**	2c. on 4c. green (No. 129)	1·00	2·25
140	**72**	4c. on 8c. olive (No. 91)	2·00	2·25
141	**72**	8c. on 16c. olive (No. 130)	2·50	2·50

(5)

1943. Fifth Anniv of Directorate-General of Posts for North China. Optd with T **5**.

142	**58**	2c. on 4c. green (No. 129)	1·00	2·00
143	**72**	4c. on 8c. olive (No. 91)	1·25	2·00
144	**72**	8c. on 16c. olive (No. 130)	1·50	1·50

1943. Stamps of China optd "**Hwa Pei**" as top characters in T **3**.

164	-	1c. orange (No. 411)	25	30
153	**58**	2c. olive	25	45
154	**58**	4c. green	25	1·50
155	**58**	5c. green	50	60
156	**72**	9c. olive	35	50
145	-	10c. green	50	60
165	-	10c. purple (No. 515)	30	1·00
157	**72**	16c. olive	25	45
158	**72**	18c. olive	40	50
166	-	20c. lake (No. 418)	40	50
167	-	30c. red (as No. 542)	35	35
168	-	40c. orange (No. 524)	35	60
169	-	50c. green (No. 525)	1·50	1·25
159	**72**	$1 brown and red	10·00	1·25
160	**72**	$2 brown and blue	3·50	1·25
161	**72**	$5 green and red	8·50	8·50
162	**72**	$10 violet and green	18·00	15·00
163	**72**	$20 blue and purple	15·00	18·00

(6)

1944. First Anniv of Declaration of War on Allies by Japanese-controlled Nanking Govt. Optd with T **6**.

170	**58**	4c. green (No. 154)	2·50	3·25
171	**72**	10c. green (No. 149)	3·25	3·25

(7)

1944. Fourth Anniv of North China Political Council. Optd with T **7**.

172	-	9c. olive (No. 156)	5·00	6·00
173	-	18c. olive (No. 158)	6·50	7·00
174	-	50c. green (No. 169)	12·00	11·00
175	**72**	$1 brown and red (No. 159)	10·00	12·00

(8)

1944. Stamps of Japanese Occupation of Shanghai and Nanking optd "**Hwa Pei**" and surch as T **8**.

176	**5**	9c. on 50c. orange	4·00	5·00
177	**5**	18c. on $1 green	5·00	6·00
178	**6**	36c. on $2 blue	5·00	6·00
179	**6**	90c. on $5 red	7·00	7·00

(9)

1944. Sixth Anniv of Directorate-General of Posts for North China. Optd with T **9**.

180	**72**	9c. olive (No. 156)	7·50	8·00
181	**72**	18c. olive (No. 158)	8·00	9·00
182	-	50c. green (No. 169)	9·00	10·00
183	-	$1 brown and red (No. 159)	12·00	12·00

(10)

1944. Death of Wang Ching-wei. Optd with T **10**.

184	-	20c. lake (No. 166)	12·00	13·00
185	-	50c. green (No. 169)	14·00	15·00
186	**72**	$1 brown and red (No. 159)	18·00	20·00
187	**72**	$2 brown and blue (No. 160)	22·00	22·00

(11)

1945. Second Anniv of Declaration of War on Allies by Nanking Govt. Optd with T **11**.

188	-	20c. lake (No. 166)	8·00	10·00
189	-	50c. green (No. 169)	20·00	20·00
190	**72**	$1 brown and red (No. 159)	12·00	12·00
191	**72**	$2 brown and blue (No. 160)	13·00	13·00

(12)

1945. Stamps of Japanese Occupation of Shanghai and Nanking surch as T **12**.

192	**7**	50c. on $3 orange	4·00	5·50
193	**7**	$1 on $6 blue	4·00	5·50

13 Dragon Pillar   **14** Long Bridge   **15** Imperial City Tower

16 Marble Boat, Summer Palace

1945. Fifth Anniv of Establishment of North China Political Council. Views of Peking.

194	**13**	$1 yellow	3·00	3·25
195	**14**	$2 blue	3·00	3·00
196	**15**	$5 red	2·75	2·75
197	**16**	$10 green	3·25	3·25

17

1945. Optd "**Hwa Pei**" as top characters in T **3**.

198	**17**	$1 brown	80	40
199	**17**	$2 blue	2·00	50
200	**17**	$5 red	3·00	2·50
201	**17**	$10 green	3·25	1·00
202	**17**	$20 purple	3·75	1·75
203	**17**	$50 brown	48·00	55·00

18 Wutai Mountain, Shansi   **19** Kaifeng Iron Pagoda, Honan   **20** International Bridge, Tientsin

21 Taishan Mountain, Shantung   **22** G.P.O., Peking

1945. Seventh Anniv of Directorate-General of Posts for North China.

204	**18**	$5 green	1·00	2·00
205	**19**	$10 brown	1·50	1·80
206	**20**	$20 purple	1·75	2·00
207	**21**	$30 grey	2·25	2·25
208	**22**	$50 brown	3·25	3·25

IV. NANKING AND SHANGHAI

The Japanese captured Shanghai and Nanking in 1937 and Hankow in 1938. During the same year Nanking was made the seat of Japanese-controlled administration for the Yangtse Basin. The stamps listed below were used in parts of Anhwei, Southern Kiangsu, Chekiang, Hupeh, Kiangsi, Hunan and Fukien.

N.B. With the exception of Nos. 114 to 119 the following are all surcharged on stamps of China.

20

(1)

1941. Air. Surch as T **1**.

1	**61**	10s. on 50c. brown	65	5·00
2	**61**	18s. on 90c. olive	65	5·00
4	**61**	20s. on $1 green	90	5·00
5	**61**	25s. on 90c. olive	50	4·00
6	**61**	35s. on $2 brown	55	3·75
7	**61**	60s. on 35s. on $2 brn (No. 6)	30	5·00

(2)

1943. Return to China of Shanghai Concessions. Surch as T 2.

8	72	25c. on 5c. green	2·00	2·50
9	77	50c. on 8c. orange	2·00	2·50
10	72	$1 on 16c. olive	2·00	2·50
11	77	$2 on 50c. blue	2·00	2·50

1943. As No. 422 but colour changed. Issued at Shanghai.

12	72	15c. brown	35·00	55·00

(3)   (4)

1943. Stamps of China and No. 12 above surch as T 3 (cent values) or T 4 (dollar values). (a) On T 58.

13	58	$6 on 5c. green	1·25	3·50
14	58	$20 on 15c. red	2·00	3·50
15	58	$500 on 15c. green	2·00	3·25
17	58	$1000 on 20c. blue	4·50	5·50
18	58	$1000 on 25c. blue	4·50	5·50

(b) On Martyrs issue (as T 60).

88	60	$7.50 on ½c. sepia	1·50	5·00
89	-	$15 on 1c. orange	30	1·50
91	-	$30 on 2c. blue	1·60	3·25
93	-	$200 on 1c. orange	30	1·75
94	-	$200 on 8c. orange	1·25	2·00

(c) On T 72.

19	72	25c. on 5c. green	4·25	8·00
20	72	30c. on 2c. green	1·50	3·50
21	72	50c. on 3c. red	25	30
22	72	50c. on 5c. green	25	25
23	72	50c. on 8c. green	1·00	1·50
24	72	$1 on 8c. green	25	20
26	72	$1 on 15c. brown	50	90
27	72	$1.30 on 16c. brown	25	1·25
28	72	$1.50 on 3c. red	25	40
54	72	$1.70 on 30c. red	1·25	4·00
55	72	$2 on 5c. green	1·00	2·00
30	72	$2 on 10c. green	25	30
56	72	$2 on $1 sepia and brown	5·00	6·00
59	72	$3 on 8c. green	50	75
31	72	$3 on 15c. brown	25	30
32	72	$4 on 16c. brown	65	25
33	72	$5 on 15c. brown	25	35
61	72	$6 on 5c. green	45	1·25
62	72	$6 on 8c. green	35	1·75
38	72	$6 on 10c. green	25	1·00
39	72	$10 on 10c. green	25	30
40	72	$10 on 16c. brown	65	25
41	72	$20 on 3c. red	25	65
42	72	$20 on 15c. red	2·25	5·00
43	72	$20 on 15c. brown	40	40
64	72	$20 on $2 brown and blue	2·40	2·75
65	72	$50 on 30c. red	1·40	1·90
66	72	$50 on 50c. blue	1·40	2·50
67	72	$50 on $5 green and red	1·50	3·00
68	72	$50 on $20 blue and purple	5·00	8·50
45	72	$100 on 3c. red	50	40
83	72	$100 on $10 violet and green	75	2·00
84	72	$200 on $20 blue and purple	75	1·50
46	72	$500 on 8c. green	5·00	8·00
47	72	$500 on 10c. green	5·50	8·00
48	72	$500 on 15c. red	7·00	7·00
49	72	$500 on 15c. brown	6·50	7·50
50	72	$500 on 15c. brown	5·00	7·00
51	72	$1000 on 25c. blue	6·50	9·00
86	72	$1000 on 30c. red	4·50	6·50
75	72	$1000 on 50c. blue	5·00	7·00
76	72	$1000 on $2 brown and blue	9·00	15·00
77	72	$2000 on $5 green and red	9·00	10·00
87a	72	$5000 on $10 violet & green	30·00	45·00

(d) On T 77.

95	77	5c. on ½c. sepia	30	2·00
96	77	10c. on 1c. orange	30	1·25
97	77	20c. on 1c. orange	30	1·00
98	77	40c. on 5c. green	30	1·00
99	77	$5 on 5c. green	30	35
100	77	$10 on 10c. green	30	35
101	77	$50 on ½c. sepia	30	35
102	77	$50 on 1c. orange	35	60
103	77	$50 on 17c. olive	45	1·00
104	77	$200 on 5c. green	1·00	1·25
105	77	$200 on 8c. green	1·25	1·50
106	77	$200 on 8c. orange	1·10	1·75
107	77	$500 on $5 black and red	2·25	3·50
108	77	$1000 on 1c. orange	2·00	3·00
109	77	$1000 on 25c. purple	2·25	3·00
110	77	$1000 on 30c. red	2·50	5·00
111	77	$1000 on $2 black and blue	3·50	4·00
112	77	$1000 on $10 black & green	4·00	5·00
113	77	$2000 on $5 black and red	4·50	5·00

5 Wheat and Cotton Flower   6 Purple Mountain, Nanking

1944. Fourth Anniv of Establishment of Chinese Puppet Government at Nanking.

114	5	50c. orange	75	2·00
115	5	$1 green	75	2·00
116	6	$2 blue	75	1·90
117	6	$5 red	75	1·25

7 Map of Shanghai and Foreign Concessions

1944. First Anniv of Return to China of Shanghai Foreign Concessions.

118	7	$3 orange	90	2·00
119	7	$6 blue	90	2·00

1945. Fifth Anniv of Establishment of Chinese Puppet Government at Nanking. Surch as T 4.

124	5	$15 on 50c. orange	75	2·00
125	5	$30 on $1 green	75	2·00
126	6	$60 on $2 blue	75	2·00
127	6	$200 on $5 red	75	2·00

(9)

1945. Air Raid Precautions Propaganda. Air stamps surch as T 9.

128	61	$150 on 15c. green	1·00	3·00
129	61	$250 on 25c. orange	1·00	3·00
130	61	$600 on 60c. blue	1·00	3·00
131	61	$1000 on $1 green	1·00	3·00

POSTAGE DUE STAMPS

(D 8)

1945. Postage Due stamps surch as Type D8.

D120	D62	$1 on 2c. orange	1·00	4·25
D121	D62	$2 on 5c. orange	1·00	4·00
D122	D62	$5 on 10c. orange	1·00	3·25
D123	D62	$10 on 20c. orange	1·00	3·50

Pt. 4

JAPANESE OCCUPATION OF NETHERLANDS INDIES

The Japanese occupied the Netherlands Indies from March 1942 to 1945.

100 sen (cents) = 1 rupee (gulden).

I. JAVA

1 Eastern Asia

1943. First Anniv of Japanese Occupation of Java.

1	1	2s. brown	5·50	4·75
2	-	3½s. red	5·50	4·75
3	-	5s. green	7·75	4·75
4	-	10s. blue	7·75	1·50

DESIGNS: 3½s. Farmer ploughing ricefield; 5s. Mt. Soemer; 10s. Bantam Bay.

2 Native soldier

1943. Savings Campaign.

5	2	3½c. red	45·00	13·50
6	2	10c. blue	65·00	7·75

3 Wayang puppet   5 Bird of Vishnu and Mt. Soemer

1943. Designs with rectangular panel of characters as at foot of T 3 and T 5.

7	-	3½c. red	4·00	2·50
8	3	5c. green	4·00	2·50
9	-	10c. blue	4·00	2·50
10	-	20c. olive	4·00	2·50
11	-	40c. purple	4·50	2·50
12	5	60c. orange	5·50	4·50
13	-	80c. brown	10·50	5·50
14	-	1r. violet	28·00	6·75

DESIGNS—As Type 3: 3½c. Native head; 10c. Boroboudur Temple; 20c. Map of Java; 40c. Seated dancer and Temple. As Type 5: 80c. Ploughing with oxen; 1r. Terraced ricefields.

II. SUMATRA

6 Lake Toba

1943. Designs with rectangular panel characters as at foot of T 6.

15	-	1c. olive	2·75	2·00
16	-	2c. green	2·75	2·00
17	-	3c. blue	2·75	2·00
18	-	3½c. red	5·00	2·00
19	-	4c. blue	3·50	2·00
20	-	5c. orange	2·75	1·50
21	-	10c. blue	6·75	1·50
22	-	20c. brown	3·50	1·50
23	6	30c. purple	4·00	2·75
24	6	40c. brown	4·50	3·00
25	-	50c. bistre	11·00	4·50
26	-	1r. violet	55·00	7·25

DESIGNS: 1c. to 3c. Batak house; 3½c. to 5c. Minangkabau house; 10c., 20c. Ploughing with oxen; 50c., 1r. Carabao Canyon (20×28 mm).

(7)

1944. Various stamps optd with T 7. (a) On Netherlands Indies stamps of 1933.

37A	46	1c. violet	90	2·00
38A	46	2c. purple	90	2·00
39A	46	2½c. bistre	90	2·00
40A	46	3c. green	36·00	50·00
27A	46	3½c. grey	1·10	4·00
50B	67	10c. red	1·30	2·10
42B	47	15c. blue	2·50	7·75
43B	47	20c. purple	1·20	2·00
44B	47	25c. green	2·50	4·00
45A	47	30c. blue	27·00	36·00
46B	47	35c. violet	2·50	4·00
47B	47	40c. green	4·50	4·50
34A	47	42½c. yellow	55·00	75·00
35A	47	50c. blue	26·00	36·00
48A	47	2g. green	£750	£850
36A	47	2g.50 purple	£450	£600
49B	47	5g. bistre	25·00	65·00

(b) On Nos. 429/44 of Netherlands Indies.

28A	-	10c. red	12·50	18·00
52B	-	15c. blue	2·50	3·75
53B	-	17½c. orange	2·20	3·75
43A	-	20c. mauve	20·00	36·00
44A	-	25c. green	5·50	8·25
56B	-	30c. brown	1·70	3·25
57A	-	35c. purple	27·00	14·50
58B	-	40c. green	2·50	5·25
59B	-	50c. red	4·00	4·50
60B	-	60c. blue	3·75	5·50
61B	-	80c. red	4·50	6·25
62B	-	1g. violet	5·50	7·75
63B	-	2g. green	4·75	7·25
64A	-	5g. brown	£300	£475
65A	-	10g. green	47·00	75·00
66A	68	25g. orange	£550	£650

(c) On Nos. 463/6 of Netherlands Indies.

66	-	3c. green	1·10	2·75
67	71	4c. green	1·10	2·75
68	-	5c. blue	1·10	2·75
69	-	7½c. violet	1·10	2·75

(d) On Nos. 506 and 509 of Netherlands.

70	94	5c. green	13·50	17·00
71	94	12½c. blue	6·75	14·50

III. JAPANESE NAVAL CONTROL AREA

(9)

1942. Various stamps optd with T 9. (a) On Netherlands Indies stamps of 1933.

89	46	1c. violet	5·50	21·00
90	46	2c. purple	1·10	4·75
91	46	2½c. bistre	1·10	4·75
92	46	3c. green	1·00	4·75
83	46	4c. green	33·00	55·00
84	46	5c. blue	13·50	20·00
95	47	10c. red	65·00	85·00
96	47	15c. blue	12·50	19·00
97	47	20c. purple	1·30	4·75
98	47	25c. green	5·50	11·00
86	47	30c. blue	55·00	55·00
100	47	35c. violet	1·30	5·00
101	47	40c. green	1·30	5·00
88	47	50c. blue	75·00	£100
102	47	80c. red	£275	£400
103	47	1g. violet		
104	47	2g. green		
105	47	5g. bistre		

(b) On Nos. 270 and 360 of Netherlands Indies.

107	-	5c. green	1·30	4·75
106	48	30c. blue	£300	£450

(c) On Nos. 429/44 of Netherlands Indies.

108	-	10c. red	4·00	5·25
110	-	15c. blue	4·25	20·00
111	-	17½c. orange	1·50	5·50
112	-	20c. mauve	28·00	44·00
113	-	25c. green	37·00	55·00
114	-	30c. brown	5·25	13·50
115	-	35c. purple	60·00	75·00
116	-	40c. green	25·00	35·00
117	-	50c. red	13·00	14·50
118	-	60c. blue	6·25	11·00
119	-	80c. red	10·50	19·00
120	-	1g. violet	7·25	14·50
121	-	2g. green	55·00	90·00
122	-	5g. brown		
123	68	25g. orange		

(d) On Nos. 462/6 of Netherlands Indies.

124	-	2½c. purple	6·25	10·00
125	-	3c. green	2·75	5·00
126	71	4c. green	4·00	4·75
127	-	5c. blue	8·00	19·00
128	-	7½c. violet	1·10	5·25

(e) On Nos. 506 and 509 of Netherlands.

129	94	5c. green		
130	94	12½c. blue		

1943. Air. Nos. 89 and 91 surch.

148	46	"f. 2" on 1c. violet	17·00	27·00
151	46	"f. 8.50" on 2½c. bistre	55·00	90·00

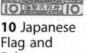
10 Japanese Flag and Palms   11 Mt. Fuji, Flag and Bird

1943

152	10	2c. brown	1·10	55·00
153	10	3c. green	1·10	55·00
154	10	3½c. orange	2·00	55·00
155	10	5c. blue	1·10	27·00
156	10	10c. red	1·10	27·00
157	10	15c. blue	1·20	27·00
158	10	20c. violet	1·20	27·00

159	11	25c. orange	4·50	27·00
160	11	30c. blue	5·25	31·00
161	11	50c. purple	11·00	33·00
162	11	1g. purple	55·00	45·00

POSTAGE DUE STAMPS

1942. Netherlands Indies Postage Due stamps of 1913 and 1937 optd with T **9**.

D142	1c. orange		9·00	18·00
D132	2½c. orange		2·00	4·75
D133	3½c. orange		4·50	9·25
D134	5c. orange		2·50	4·75
D135	7½c. orange		2·50	4·75
D136	10c. orange		1·90	4·75
D144	15c. orange		2·50	4·50
D137	20c. orange		2·50	4·75
D138	20c. on 37½c. orange		65·00	£100
D139	25c. orange		2·00	4·75
D140	30c. orange		5·00	11·00
D146	40c. orange		2·30	5·25
D147	1g. blue		7·25	13·50

Pt. 22

JAPANESE OCCUPATION OF PHILIPPINES

100 centavos or sentimos = 1 peso.

1942. Stamps of Philippines optd with bars or surch also.

J1	104	2c. green	25	45
J4a	–	5c. on 6c. brn (No. 526)	25	85
J2	–	12c. black (No. 529)	2·75	2·75
J3	–	16c. blue (No. 530)	6·75	6·25
J5	–	16c. on 30c. red (No. 505)	1·40	1·80
J6	–	50c. on 1p. black and orange (No. 534)	5·50	5·25
J7	–	1p. on 4p. black and blue (No. 508)	£100	£110

1942. No. 460 of Philippines surch **CONGRATULATIONS FALL OF BATAAN AND CORREGIDOR 1942 2**.

J8	2c. on 4c. green		5·75	5·75

J 4 Agricultural Produce

1942. Red Cross Fund.

J9	J4	2c.+1c. violet	5·75	2·75
J10	J4	5c.+1c. green	5·75	2·75
J11	J4	16c.+2c. orange	£190	80·00

1942. First Anniv of "Greater East Asia War". No. 460 of Philippines surch with native characters, **12-8-1942** and **5**.

J12	5c. on 4c. green		2·30	2·30

1943. First Anniv of Philippine Executive Commission. Nos. 566 and 569 of Philippines surch with native characters, **1-23-43** and value.

J13	105	2c. on 8c. red	1·40	1·80
J14	105	5c. on 1p. sepia	1·80	2·30

J 7 Nipa Hut   J 9 Mt. Mayon and Mt. Fuji

1943

J15	J7	1c. orange	80	80
J16	–	2c. green	80	80
J17	J7	4c. green	80	80
J18	J9	5c. brown	80	1·40
J19	–	6c. red	80	1·00
J20	J9	10c. blue	80	1·00
J21	–	12c. blue	1·40	1·70
J22	–	16c. brown	80	80
J23	J7	20c. purple	1·50	1·70
J24	J9	21c. violet	1·00	1·40
J25	–	25c. brown	1·10	80
J26	J9	1p. red	9·00	2·75
J27	–	2p. purple	23·00	6·75
J28	–	5p. olive	32·00	11·00

DESIGNS—VERT: 2, 6, 25c. Rice planter; 12, 16c., 2, 5p. Morro vinta (sailing canoe).

J 11 Map of Manila Bay

1943. First Anniv of Fall of Bataan and Corregidor.

J29	J11	2c. red	1·90	1·90
J30	J11	5c. green	1·90	1·90

1943. 350th Anniv of Printing in the Philippines. No. 531 of Philippines surch **Limbagan 1593–1943** and value.

J31	12c. on 20c. bistre		1·90	1·90

J 13 Filipino Girl

J 14

1943. Japanese Declaration of the "Independence of the Philippines". Imperf or perf. (a).

J32B	J13	5c. blue	1·90	1·90
J33B	J13	12c. orange	1·90	1·90
J34B	J13	17c. red	1·90	1·90

(b) Miniature sheet, 127×177 mm containing Nos. J32/4.

MSJ35	(sold at 2p.50)	£110	28·00

1943. Luzon Flood Relief. Surch **BAHA 1943 +** and premium.

J36	–	12c.+21c. blue (No. J21)	90	1·90
J37	J7	20c.+36c. purple	90	1·90
J38	J9	21c.+40c. violet	90	1·90

J 17 Rev. Jose Burgos

J 19 (image scaled to 49% of original size)

1944. National Heroes. Imperf or perf. (a).

J39B	–	5c. blue (Rizal)	2·75	1·50
J40B	J17	12c. red	2·75	1·50
J41B	–	17c. orange (Mabini)	2·75	1·50

(b) Miniature sheet 101×143 mm containing Nos. J39/41. Without gum.

MSJ42	(sold at 1p.)	4·50	7·50

1944. Second Anniv of Fall of Bataan and Corregidor. Nos. 567/8 of Philippines surch **REPUBLIKA NG PILIPINAS 5-7-44** and value.

J43	105	5c. on 20c. blue	2·50	3·50
J44	105	12c. on 60c. green	3·50	4·50

J 24 Jose P. Laurel

1945. First Anniv of Republican Government. Imperf.

J45	J24	5s. brown	90	2·75
J46	J24	7s. green	90	2·75
J47	J24	20s. blue	90	2·75

POSTAGE DUE STAMPS

1942. Postage Due stamp of Philippines surch **3 CVOS. 3** and bar.

JD9	D51	3c. on 4c. red	28·00	23·00

OFFICIAL STAMPS

1943. Stamps of Philippines optd variously with bars, (K.P.) and Japanese characters or surch also.

JO29	104	2c. green (No. 563)	90	2·00
JO30	–	5c. on 6c. brown (No. 526)	1·90	2·30
JO32	–	16c. on 30c. red (No. 505)	5·75	8·00

1944. No. 526 of Philippines surch **5 REPUBLIKA NG PILIPINAS (K.P.)** and four bars.

JO45	5c. on 6c. brown		1·90	2·30

1944. Official stamp of Philippines (No. 531 optd **O.B.**), further optd **Pilipinas REPUBLIKA K.P.** and bars.

JO46	20c. bistre		4·00	5·75

1944. Air stamp of Philippines optd **REPUBLIKA NG PILIPINAS (K.P.)** and two bars.

JO47	105	1p. sepia	9·75	11·50

Pt. 17

JAPANESE POST OFFICES IN CHINA

Post Offices at Shanghai and other Treaty Ports operated between 1876 and 1922.

10 rin = 1 sen; 100 sen = 1 yen.

邦 支
(1)

1900. Stamps of Japan, 1899, optd with T **1**.

1	28	5r. grey	10·50	9·75
2	28	½s. grey	8·00	4·00
3	28	1s. brown	9·25	3·25
4	28	1½s. blue	24·00	9·25
5	28	1½s. violet	14·00	4·25
6	28	2s. green	13·00	3·00
7	28	3s. purple	17·00	2·75
8	28	3s. red	9·75	2·30
9	28	4s. red	17·00	5·00
10	28	5s. yellow	33·00	5·00
11	29	6s. red	48·00	38·00
12	29	8s. green	27·00	32·00
13	29	10s. blue	25·00	2·30
14	29	15s. purple	48·00	4·00
15	29	20s. orange	44·00	3·00
16	30	25s. green	90·00	18·00
17	30	50s. brown	95·00	4·50
18	31	1y. red	£160	6·00
19	32	5y. green	£1000	£150
20	32	10y. violet	£1700	£275

1900. Imperial Wedding issue of Japan optd with T **1**.

21	33	3s. red	£100	70·00

1913. Stamps of Japan, 1913, optd with T **1**.

33	36	½s. brown	8·25	3·75
34	36	1s. orange	8·00	3·75
35	36	1½s. blue	9·25	3·25
36	36	2s. green	10·00	3·00
37	36	3s. red	7·75	2·20
38	37	4s. red	31·00	15·00
39	37	5s. violet	37·00	6·50
40	37	6s. brown	70·00	55·00
41	37	8s. grey	95·00	85·00
42	37	10s. blue	35·00	3·75
43	37	20s. red	95·00	11·50
44	37	25s. olive	£120	17·00
45	38	30s. brown	£180	£100
46	38	50s. brown	£250	£100
47	38	1y. green and brown	£350	28·00
48	38	5y. green	£3500	£1300
49	38	10y. violet	£8500	£3500

Pt. 18

JAPANESE POST OFFICE IN KOREA

10 rin = 1 sen; 100 sen = 1 yen.

計 朝
(1)

1900. Stamps of Japan, 1899, optd with T **1**.

1	28	5r. grey	18·00	15·00
2	28	1s. brown	22·00	10·50
3a	28	1½s. blue	£300	£180
4	28	2s. green	32·00	21·00
5	28	3s. purple	21·00	8·00
6	28	4s. red	£100	50·00
7	28	5s. yellow	90·00	33·00
8	29	8s. green	£350	£225
9	29	10s. blue	44·00	7·50
10	29	15s. purple	£110	10·50
11	29	20s. orange	£110	8·00
12	30	25s. green	£325	80·00
13	30	50s. brown	£200	27·00
14	31	1y. red	£550	16·00

1900. Wedding of Prince Imperial. No. 152 of Japan optd with T **1**.

15	33	3s. red	£130	41·00

Pt. 1

JASDAN

A state of India. Now uses Indian Stamps.

12 pies = 1 anna; 16 annas = 1 rupee.

1 Sun

1942

4	1	1a. green	25·00	£275

Index

Stanley Gibbons Goes Mobile

Scan the QR code below to get your **FREE APPS** from Stanley Gibbons

The Stanley Gibbons and Gibbons Stamp Monthly Apps are available now for Apple devices and are completely free to download, giving you the platform to buy 'virtual' editions of our catalogues and the UK's bestselling stamp magazine.

Find out more by visiting **www.stanleygibbons.com/app** or by scanning the QR code with your mobile device.

Est 1856
STANLEY GIBBONS

Stanley Gibbons Limited
7 Parkside, Christchurch Road, Ringwood, Hants, BH24 3SH
+44 (0)1425 472 363
www.stanleygibbons.com

Stanley Gibbons

Commonwealth Department

LOOKING FOR THAT ELUSIVE STAMP?

Send a copy of your wants list or call: Andrew Mansi on 020 7557 4455 email amansi@stanleygibbons.com
or Brian Lucas on 020 7557 4418 email blucas@stanleygibbons.com

Est 1856

Stanley Gibbons Limited
399 Strand, London, WC2R 0LX
+44 (0)20 7836 8444
www.stanleygibbons.com

Britannia Albums

The perfect solution for housing stamps from any country

From Afghanistan to Zimbabwe...

Whichever country you collect, the Britannia range of albums contains something suitable for you. The binders are made from the best quality vinyl and come with polypropylene pockets, complete with 160gsm white acid free paper used are top quality products.

Each A4 (210mm x 297mm) page is specifically designed, having a space for each stamp with the date, title, and value of the stamp shown. These albums are compiled using the Scott (rather than SG) numbering system. Binders are available in blue or maroon.

There are over 900 volumes available including single countries, states, used abroad and omnibus issues. If you are looking for something in particular or would like a full list of Britannia albums, please contact us on the details at the bottom of the page and we will do all we can to help.

Please note: Delivery of these items will take a minimum of 21 days and are only printed to order. If you are unsure about the content of these albums, please contact us prior to ordering.

For a list of Britannia albums, visit **www.stanleygibbons.com/britannia**

Est 1856
STANLEY GIBBONS

Stanley Gibbons Limited
7 Parkside, Christchurch Road, Ringwood, Hants, BH24 3SH
+44 (0)1425 472 363
www.stanleygibbons.com